TALMUD BAVLI
תלמוד בבלי

THE SCHOTTENSTEIN DAF YOMI EDITION

תלמוד בבלי

TALMUD BAVLI

מהדורת דף היומי

The ArtScroll Series®

THE HORN EDITION OF SEDER MOED

מסכת שבת

TRACTATE SHABBOS

תלמוד בבלי

מהדורת דף היומי

BAVLI

THE HORN EDITION OF SEDER MOED

מסכת שבת

TRACTATE SHABBOS

VOLUME II

Elucidated by

Rabbi Eliyahu Baruch Shulman (chapters 3,4)

Rabbi Shlomo Fox-Ashrei (chapter 5)

Rabbi Yosaif Asher Weiss (chapter 6)

Rabbi Abba Zvi Naiman (chapter 7)

under the General Editorship of

Rabbi Yisroel Simcha Schorr

in collaboration with a team of Torah Scholars

R' Hersh Goldwurm זצ"ל
General Editor
תש"נ-תשנ"ג / 1990-1993

The Schottenstein Daf Yomi Edition

TALMUD

THE GEMARA: THE CLASSIC VILNA EDITION,
WITH AN ANNOTATED, INTERPRETIVE ELUCIDATION,
AS AN AID TO TALMUD STUDY

The Hebrew folios are reproduced from
the newly typeset and enhanced
Oz Vehadar Edition of the Classic Vilna Talmud

Published by
Mesorah Publications, ltd

We gratefully acknowledge the outstanding
Torah scholars who contributed to this volume:

Rabbi Yisroel Simcha Schorr, Rabbi Chaim Malinowitz,
Rabbi Yitzchok Meir Schorr and **Rabbi Mordechai Marcus**
who reviewed and commented on the manuscript,
Rabbis Yosef Davis, Eliezer Herzka, Nesanel Kasnett, Zev Meisels,
Avrohom Neuberger, Moshe Rosenblum, Feivel Wahl, and **Yosaif Asher Weiss**
who edited, and assisted in the production of this volume.
Rabbi Yehezkel Danziger, Editorial Director

FULL-SIZE EDITION
First Impression . . . June, 1996
DAF YOMI EDITION
First Impression . . . January, 2003
Second Impression . . . March, 2005

Published and Distributed by
MESORAH PUBLICATIONS, Ltd.
4401 Second Avenue
Brooklyn, New York 11232

Distributed in Europe by
LEHMANNS
Unit E, Viking Industrial Park
Rolling Mill Road
Jarrow, Tyne & Wear NE32 3DP
England

Distributed in Israel by
SIFRIATI / A. GITLER — BOOKS
6 Hayarkon Street
Bnei Brak 51127

Distributed in Australia & New Zealand by
GOLDS WORLD OF JUDAICA
3-13 William Street
Balaclava, Melbourne 3183
Victoria Australia

Distributed in South Africa by
KOLLEL BOOKSHOP
Shop 8A Norwood Hypermarket
Norwood 2196, Johannesburg, South Africa

THE ARTSCROLL SERIES® / SCHOTTENSTEIN DAF YOMI EDITION
TALMUD BAVLI / TRACTATE SHABBOS VOL. II

ISBN: 1-57819-608-6

Typography by CompuScribe at ArtScroll Studios, Ltd.
Custom bound by **Sefercraft, Inc.,** Brooklyn, N.Y.

A PROJECT OF THE

Mesorah Heritage Foundation

Dedication of the FULL-SIZE EDITION

This volume is lovingly dedicated by

David and Bonnie Anfang **Chaim and Ruthie Anfang**
Rachel, Julie and Elliot **Ariella Hope**

In loving memory of

Leib Anfang ע"ה — ר' אריה ליב ב"ר דוד אביגדור ע"ה
Barbara Anfang ע"ה — בשה לאה בת ר' אלימלך דוב ע"ה

. . . וְגִבּוֹר כָּאֲרִי לַעֲשׂוֹת רְצוֹן אָבִיךָ שֶׁבַּשָּׁמַיִם
. . . and strong as a lion to do the will of your Father in heaven.

After surviving the horrors of the Holocaust, they emigrated to Israel, where he fought in the 1956 Sinai Campaign. Thereafter, Mr. and Mrs. Anfang came to the United States with their two young sons — and the family Torah Scroll that never left them throughout their terrible ordeals. They were dedicated to one another, and to their children and grandchildren. Their joint commitment to Torah life, family, the Jewish community and Eretz Yisrael will always remain with us as their legacy.

. . . אַשְׁרֶיךָ בָּעוֹלָם הַזֶּה וְטוֹב לָךְ בָּעוֹלָם הַבָּא
You are praiseworthy in this world and it will be good for you in the World to Come.

Mimi and Steven Rosenbaum, Stacey and Danny
Joseph Prawer **Alan and Louisa Prawer**

In loving memory of

Pinkus Prawer ע"ה — ר' פנחס ב"ר יוסף ברוך הלוי ע"ה
Genia Prawer ע"ה — גילה בת אשר יונה ע"ה

. . . הוֹלֵךְ תָּמִים וּפֹעֵל צֶדֶק, וְדֹבֵר אֱמֶת בִּלְבָבוֹ
. . . One who walks in perfect innocence, and does what is right, and speaks the truth from his heart.

In spite of the horrors of the Holocaust, their belief in Hashem and the Torah enabled them to survive. By transmitting this belief to their children and grandchildren, they perpetutated and strengthened the resolve to perform mitzvos and maintain the ideals of Torah Judaism.

and

Sarah Cukierman ע"ה — שרה בת שמעון ליב ע"ה

an extended family friend, herself a survivor, has allowed us to participate in this endeavor on her behalf.

Rabbi Eliyahu and Yehudit Fishman
Rivka and Zvi Silberstein and Leah **Akiva Yitzchak Fishman**
Rabbi Yechiel Meir and Chagit Fishman **Rabbi Yosef and Aliza Fishman**
Talia Chana, Ariel Yishai and Daniel

In loving memory of

ר' יוסף ב"ר טוביה ע"ה רודע רבקה בת ר' הירש מאיר ע"ה
Yosef and Rude Rivka Fishman ע"ה

and their children **Yechiel Meir, Leah and Chanah הי"ד**
who perished in the Holocaust

Dedication of the
DAF YOMI EDITION

This volume is dedicated
in loving memory of our dear parents

Joseph and Bess Wasserman ז"ל

יוסף בן דוב בער ע"ה   **בילא בת יעקב ע"ה**

ט' טבת תש"מ   י"ב סיון תשמ"ב

Sascha and Regina (Czaczkes) Charles ז"ל

שמריהו בן משה ע"ה   **רבקה בת הרב יוסף הכהן ע"ה**

י"ח אלול תשל"ב   ט"ו תמוז תשכ"ז

They were our inspiration in life
and their memory continues to light our way —
their *mesiras nefesh* for family,
community and Jewish children;
their endless quest for learning,
and their love of Klal Yisrael were the bridge
from a rich past to an unfolding future.

Stanley and Ellen Wasserman
and our children and grandchildren:

Alan and Svetlana Wasserman
Sasha, Jesse, Talya, Jacob, and Bella

Mark and Anne Wasserman
Joseph, Bailey, Erin, Rebeccah, and Jordyn

Neil and Yael Wasserman
Yeshayahu, Shiri, Yonatan, and Ruth

Stuart and Rivka Berger
David, Gabrielle, and Jack

The publishers pay tribute to
the memory of the unforgettable

Jerome Schottenstein ז״ל

whose wisdom, warmth, vision, and generosity wrote new chapters
of Jewish life and learning in America and around the world.
Generations from now, he will be remembered as the one
whose enlightened support made the Talmud accessible
to English-speaking Jews everywhere;

Geraldine Schottenstein תחי׳

who wears her mantle with unusual grace
and firm adherence to the values with which she set
the strong foundation of her family.
She sets a powerful and principled example
for her children and grandchildren.
We are grateful for her support and that of her children:

Jay and Jeanie Schottenstein,
Ann and Ari Deshe,
Susan and Jon Diamond,
and **Lori Schottenstein,**

friends from the start,
as staunch supporters who have been instrumental
in the ten years of the Talmud's success.
They bring energy, devotion, magnanimity, and graciousness
to a host of vital causes
in their native Columbus and throughout the world.

THE SCHOTTENSTEIN DAF YOMI EDITION

TALMUD BAVLI

This edition — in a convenient new size
to serve the growing number of people
who are making the Talmud an indispensable part of their lives —
is dedicated by

Jay and Jeanie Schottenstein

and their children

Joseph Aaron, Jonathan Richard, and Jeffrey Adam

They dedicate it in honor of their cherished loved ones
who have left indelible marks on their own lives
and the lives of countless others,
as models of inspiration, generosity, integrity,
and devotion to the noblest causes of Jewish life.

They are:
his parents

Jerome ע״ה and Geraldine Schottenstein

her parents

Leonard and Heddy Rabe

and their uncle and aunt

Saul and Sonia Schottenstein

Jay and Jeanie Schottenstein

have a perspective that transcends time and community.
Their names have become synonymous with
imaginative and effective initiatives
to bring Torah study and Jewish tradition to the masses of our people.

Through their magnanimous support of the various editions of

The Schottenstein Talmud

— this Daf Yomi Edition, the Hebrew Edition,
and the original full-size English Edition —
they spread Torah study around the globe and across generations.
Few people have ever had such a positive impact on Jewish life.
Myriads yet unborn will be indebted to them
for their vision and generosity.

PATRONS OF THE TALMUD • DAF YOMI EDITION

With generosity, vision, and devotion to the perpetuation of Torah study,
the following patrons have dedicated individual volumes
of the Daf Yomi Edition of the Talmud

BERACHOS I: In memory of
Jerome Schottenstein ע״ה
יעקב מאיר חיים בן אפרים אליעזר הכהן ע״ה

BERACHOS II: **Zvi and Betty Ryzman**
and their children
Mickey and Shelly Fenig, Aliza, Yissachar David, and Batsheva
Elie and Adina Ryzman, Leora and Yonatan Zev
Avi and Rafi
In memory of
Hagaon Harav Meir Shapiro זצ״ל, the unforgettable Rav of Lublin,
and in honor of
Hagaon Harav Yisrael Meir Lau שליט״א, Chief Rabbi of Israel

SHABBOS I: **Dr. Paul and Esther Rosenstock** **Jake and Dr. Helaine Harman**
Mrs. Faigy Harman
and their children and grandchildren
Nechama Mordechai Binyamin **Michelle Marc**
Yonina and Dov Wisnicki, Avi and Leora
Shira and Shlomie Rosenberg
in memory of our father, husband, and grandfather
מרדכי ב״ר אברהם ע״ה — Mordechai (Mottel) Harman

SHABBOS II: **Stanley and Ellen Wasserman**
and their children
Alan and Svetlana Wasserman **Mark and Anne Wasserman**
Neil and Yael Wasserman **Stuart and Rivka Berger**
and families
In loving memory of
יוסף בן דוב בער ע״ה בילא בת יעקב ע״ה — Joseph and Bess Wasserman ע״ה, and
שמריהו בן משה ע״ה רבקה בת הרב יוסף הכהן ע״ה — Sascha and Regina (Czaczkes) Charles ע״ה

SHABBOS III: **Stanley and Ellen Wasserman**
and their children
Alan and Svetlana Wasserman **Mark and Anne Wasserman**
Neil and Yael Wasserman **Stuart and Rivka Berger**
and families
in loving memory of
יוסף בן דוב בער ע״ה בילא בת יעקב ע״ה — Joseph and Bess Wasserman ע״ה, and
שמריהו בן משה ע״ה רבקה בת הרב יוסף הכהן ע״ה — Sascha and Regina (Czaczkes) Charles ע״ה

SHABBOS IV: **Malkie and Nachum Silberman**
Leonard and Cassia Friedlander
Elkie Friedlander
in honor of their mother
Gussie Friedlander שתחי׳ לאוי״ט
in memory of their father
ר׳ סיני ב״ר אריה לייב ז״ל — Sidney Friedlander ז״ל
and in memory of their grandparents
ר׳ יוסף דוד ב״ר משה ז״ל וזיסל בת ר׳ ישעיהו ע״ה — Joseph and Jennie Trattner ז״ל

ERUVIN: [two volumes] **Jerome and Geraldine Schottenstein** **Saul and Sonia Schottenstein**
Jay and Jeanie Schottenstein **Ann and Ari Deshe**
Susan and Jon Diamond **Lori Schottenstein**
in memory of
אפרים אליעזר בן יהושע הכהן ע״ה — Ephraim Schottenstein ע״ה
חנה בת צבי הירש ע״ה — Anna Schottenstein ע״ה

PATRONS OF THE TALMUD ❖ DAF YOMI EDITION

PESACHIM I: **Tommy and Judy Rosenthal**

Yitzchok and Tamar Dani and Michali Michal

in memory of his father

ר׳ יצחק ב״ר יעקב קאפיל ז״ל — Yitzchok Rosenthal

and יבלח״ט in honor of their parents עמו״ש

Magda Rosenthal שתחי׳

and her children שיחי׳

Moshe Yaakov and Beila Jakabovits שיחי׳

and their children שיחי׳

PESACHIM II: **Yisroel and Rochi Zlotowitz**

Gitty, Aaron and Sori

in memory of their beloved grandparents and great grandparents

הרב אהרן ב״ר מאיר יעקב זצ״ל והרבנית פרומא בת ר׳ חיים צבי ע״ה — Zlotowitz

ר׳ חיים חייקל ב״ר שמואל ז״ל וחיה בת הרב ישראל יהודה ע״ה — Schulman

הרב משה יהודה ב״ר יצחק צבי ז״ל ושרה בת הרב שבתי ע״ה — Maybloom

החבר שלום בן שבתי ז״ל וגיטל בת החבר פינחס צבי ע״ה — Goldman

PESACHIM III: **Lorraine and Mordy Sohn Ann and Pinky Sohn**

in memory of

ר׳ צבי ב״ר אלעזר ע״ה — Dr. Harry Sohn ע״ה

מרת הענדיל דבורה ב״ר אברהם שלמה ע״ה — Dora F. Sohn ע״ה

ר׳ יחזקאל ב״ר אליקים חנוך הלוי ע״ה — Harold Levine ע״ה

רבקה הענא בת שמעון הלוי ע״ה — Ruth Levine ע״ה

רייזל ב״ר שמשון ע״ה — Rosalie Sohn ע״ה

BEITZAH: **Eric and Joyce Austein**

and their children

Ilana and Avi Lyons Michael

Jonathan and Ilana Miriam Adam and Sara Eytan

in honor of their parents and grandparents שיחי׳

Morris and Susi Austein

Leo and Shirley Schachter

ROSH HASHANAH: **Steve and Genie Savitsky**

and their children and families

Julie and Shabsi Schreier Avi and Cheryl Savitsky Penina and Zvi Wiener Estie Savitsky

In honor of their mothers and grandmothers

Mrs. Hilda Savitsky שתחי׳ Mrs. Amelia Seif שתחי׳

And in honor of their grandparents

Mrs. Faye Raitzik שתחי׳ Max and Edith Grunfeld שתחי׳

לעילוי נשמות — And in loving memory of their grandparents

ר׳ שבתי בן ר׳ מיכאל הלוי ע״ה — Shabsi Raitzik ע״ה

ר׳ אשר זעליג בן ר׳ יהושע הלוי ע״ה רבקה בת ר׳ משה נתן ע״ה — Sigmund and Regina Schreier ע״ה

ר׳ ישראל יצחק בן ר׳ אלימלך הכהן ע״ה גולדה בת ר׳ דוד לייב ע״ה — Irving and Goldie Stein ע״ה

ר׳ שמואל סנדר בן ר׳ אליעזר ליפא ע״ה ריזל זלדה בת ר׳ שלום קלמן ע״ה — Sam and Rose Gottlieb ע״ה

ר׳ צבי הירש בן ר׳ נחום ע״ה חיה שרה גאלדא בת ר׳ יוסף ע״ה — Harry and Goldie Wiener ע״ה

And in loving memory of Cheryl Savitsky's father

ר׳ שמעון פייביש בן ר׳ ישראל יצחק הכהן ע״ה — Dr. Steven F. Stein ע״ה

YOMA I: **Mrs. Ann Makovsky**

Shmulie and Daryle Spero and children

Reuven and Dvora Makovsky and children

Leslie and Linda Spero and children

in memory of

משה דוד בן אברהם אשר ז״ל — Morris Makovsky ז״ל

אברהם אשר בן משה דוד ז״ל ופרומא דבורה בת אלחנן דוב ע״ה — Abraham Osher and Fanny Makovsky ז״ל

גמליאל בן שלמה ז״ל ורבקה בת אברהם חיים ע״ה — Meyer and Riva Nissen ז״ל

PATRONS OF THE TALMUD • DAF YOMI EDITION

YOMA II: **Trudy and David Justin**
and their children
Daniel, Brandel, Nina, Adam and Ayala Justin
in honor of their parents and grandparents
Malka Karp תחי׳
Kitty and Zoltan Justin שיחיו
and in loving memory of
Hersh Karp ז״ל — צבי בן דוב ז״ל

SUCCAH II: **Reuven and Ruth Fasman and Family**
Rudolph and Esther Lowy and Family
Allan and Ettie Lowy and Family
in memory of their parents
Marcus Lowy ז״ל — מרדכי אריה בן ר׳ רפאל הלוי ז״ל
Mina Lowy ע״ה — מינדל בת ר׳ שלמה זלמן ע״ה

TAANIS: **The Bernstein Family**
David and Jean
Matthew Peter
Scott and Andrea Samara Jonah
in memory of
Anna and Harry Bernstein ע״ה
Sarah and Joseph Furman ע״ה

MEGILLAH: In memory of
Jerome Schottenstein ע״ה
יעקב מאיר חיים בן אפרים אליעזר הכהן ע״ה

MOED KATAN: In honor of our beloved parents
Jochanan and Barbara Klein שיחי׳ לאוי״ט (Sao Paulo, Brazil)
by their children
Leon and Olga Klein Allen and Sylvia Klein Daniel and Esther Ollech and Families

CHAGIGAH: **Benzi and Esther Dunner**
in memory of their grandparents
Reb Uri Cohen ז״ל — החבר ר׳ אורי יהודה ז״ל ב״ר אברהם אריה הכהן הי״ד
נפ׳ באמשטורדם כג כסלו תשס״א
Mrs. Rivka Cohen ע״ה — מרת רבקה ע״ה בת ר׳ יצחק הי״ד
נפ׳ באמשטורדם יב מרחשון תשס״א
Reb Moshe Stempel הי״ד — הרה״צ ר׳ משה ב״ר שרגא פייבעל הי״ד
נהרג על קדה״ש ד׳ מנחם אב תש״ב

YEVAMOS I: **Phillip and Ruth Wojdyslawski and Family**
In memory of his beloved parents
Abraham Michel and Ora Wojdyslawski ע״ה
ר׳ אברהם מיכאל ב״ר פינחס ע״ה
אורה בת ר׳ צבי הירש ע״ה

YEVAMOS II: **Phillip and Ruth Wojdyslawski and Family**
In memory of her beloved mother
Chaya (Cytryn) Valt ע״ה
חיה צירל בת ר׳ שלמה זלמן ע״ה

YEVAMOS III: **Phillip and Ruth Wojdyslawski and Family**
In honor of
Benjamin C. Fishoff לאוי״ט
To the public he is a leader with vision and dedication.
To us he has always been a role model, a father,
and a constant inspiration.

KESUBOS I: **The Fishoff Families**
in memory of their beloved mother
מינדל בת ר׳ ישראל ע״ה – Mrs. Marilyn Fishoff ע״ה
נפ׳ כד תשרי תשמ״ט
and in memory of their dear grandparents
ר׳ דוב ב״ר מנחם אשר ע״ה מרת מירל בת ר׳ מנחם מענדל ע״ה – Fishoff
ר׳ ישראל ב״ר אברהם ע״ה מרת חיה זיסא בת ר׳ שרגא פייוועל ע״ה – Neider

KESUBOS II: **Moise Hendeles Hayim and Miriam Hendeles Jerry and Cecille Cohen**
and their families
in memory of their beloved father and grandfather
אליעזר ב״ר משה ז״ל – Lazare Hendeles ז״ל
נפ׳ כ׳ ניסן ד׳ חוה״מ פסח תשס״א
and in honor of their loving mother and grandmother
Mrs. Moselle Hendeles שתחי׳

KESUBOS III: **Brenda and Isaac Gozdzik**
Tova Chava Tzeryl Leah
in memory of their beloved parents and grandparents
שרגא פייוועל בן משה הענדעלעס ז״ל – Fred Hendeles ז״ל
נפ׳ ה׳ אלול תשס״ג
ביילע בת אליהו הלוי פערשלייסער ע״ה – Betty Hendeles ע״ה
נפ׳ כ״ו בניסן תשנ״ט

NEDARIM I: **Fradie Rapp**
Raizy, Menachem, Shimshon, Bashie, Tzvi
in memory of their beloved husband and father
הרב ישראל בן יעקב ז״ל – David Rapp ז״ל
נפ׳ כ׳ מרחשון תשס״ד

NEDARIM II: In memory of
Laurence A. Tisch
לייבל בן אברהם ע״ה

NAZIR I: **Andrew and Nancy Neff**
Abigail, Esther, Barnet and Philip
in honor of our parents and grandparents
Alan and Joyce Neff
Sidney and Lucy Rabin

NAZIR II: **Andrew and Nancy Neff**
Abigail, Esther, Barnet and Philip
in honor of our brothers and sisters
Garth and Valerie Heald
Lauren Neff
Douglas and Vivian Rabin
Andrew and Liat Rabin

SOTAH: **Motty and Malka Klein and Family**
In memory of
ר׳ ישעי׳ נפתלי הירץ ב״ר אהרן ז״ל – Norman Newman

GITTIN I: **Mrs. Kate Tannenbaum**
Elliot and Debra Tannenbaum Edward and Linda Zizmor
and Families
in memory of beloved husband, father and grandfather
ר׳ נפתלי ב״ר יהודה אריה ע״ה – Fred Tannenbaum ע״ה
נפטר ח׳ ניסן תשנ״ב

PATRONS OF THE TALMUD ✦ DAF YOMI EDITION

GITTIN II: **Mrs. Kate Tannenbaum**
Elliot and Debra Tannenbaum **Edward and Linda Zizmor**
and Families
in memory of beloved husband, father and grandfather
ר׳ נפתלי ב״ר יהודה אריה ע״ה — Fred Tannenbaum ע״ה
נפטר ח׳ ניסן תשנ״ב

KIDDUSHIN I: **Ellis A. and Altoon Safdeye**
in memory of their beloved parents
המנוח יהודה אצלאן ומרת צלחה ויקטוריא ע״ה — Aslan and Victoria Safdeye ע״ה
המנוח יהודה ומרת מרגלית ע״ה — Judah and Margie Sultan ע״ה
and in memory of his brother יוסף ע״ה — Joseph Safdeye ע״ה

KIDDUSHIN II: **Malcolm and Joy Lyons**
in loving memory of her father
זיסל בן אברהם דוד ז״ל — Cecil Jacobs ז״ל
and in honour of their parents שיחי׳
Leo and Eve Lyons
Mona Jacobs

BAVA KAMMA I: **Yitzchok and Shoshana Ganger**
in honor of their children and grandchildren
Aviva and Moshe Sigler
Aliza Saul Chani
Ilana and Menachem Ostreicher
Dov Ber Miriam Binyomin Paltiel
Dovid and Penina Ganger
Yosef Yaakov Gavriel Moshe Ettie
Daniella
and in memory of their fathers
ר׳ יוסף יעקב ב״ר יצחק ישעיהו ע״ה — Joseph Ganger ע״ה
נפטר טז כסלו תשנ״ו
הרב אריה ליב ב״ר מתתיהו ע״ה — Rabbi Aria Leib Newman ע״ה
נפטר כח ניסן תשס״ד

BAVA KAMMA II: **The Magid Families** (Sao Paulo, Brazil)
לעילוי נשמת — in memory of their dear husband and father
ר׳ אברהם יהודה אביר בן ר׳ יהושע ז״ל — R' Abir Magid ז״ל
נלב״ע כ״ו אדר תשמ״ב
ולעילוי נשמות — and in memory of
ר׳ יהושע ב״ר צבי חיים ז״ל וזוגתו מרת שרה פייגא בת ר׳ יששכר דוב ע״ה
ר׳ יעקב ישראל ב״ר מרדכי ז״ל וזוגתו מרת אסתר פרומה בת ר׳ חיים ע״ה

BAVA KAMMA III: **Robert and Malka Friedlander** (Sao Paulo, Brazil)
Debby, David and Daniel
in memory of their fathers and grandfathers
הרב ישראל יעקב ב״ר יצחק מאיר ז״ל — Rabbi Israel Jacob Weisberger ז״ל
הרב נפתלי צבי נח ב״ר יהודה לייביש ז״ל — Rabbi Bela Friedlander ז״ל

BAVA METZIA I: **Drs. Robert and Susan Schulman** **Howard and Tzila Schulman**
Fred and Cindy Schulman
in honor of our beloved parents
Molly Schulman
Stanley and Ruth Beck
Mrs. Sylvia Kuhr
Naftali and Berta Rendel

BAVA METZIA II: **Suzy and Yussie Ostreicher and Ricki** **Ilana and Menachem Ostreicher**
Miriam and Dovid Ostreicher **Shayna and Yitzchok Steg**
in honor of our parents and grandparents
Michael and Rose Pollack
Hershi and Helly Ostreicher

BAVA METZIA III: **Stephanie and George Saks**
in memory of
The Gluck Family
זאב בן דוד צבי ע״ה ואסתר בת אשר זעליג ע״ה – Zev and Esther Gluck ע״ה
ליבא, אשר זעליג, דוד צבי, שמואל, מנשה, יחזקאל שרגא ע״ה –
Lee, George, David H., Samuel C., Emanuel M., Henry ע״ה, and
in memory of their parents and grandparents
פייוועל בן אליה ע״ה ומלכה בת אברהם ע״ה – Philip and Mildred Pines ע״ה
יעקב יצחק בן זאב ע״ה ומיימי בת זאב ע״ה – Dr. Jack I. and Mrs. Mae Saks ע״ה
זאב בן חיים דוד ע״ה וחיה ביילע בת יצחק יעקב ע״ה – Wolf and Chaye Beilah Saks ע״ה
and in memory of
יחיאל בן משה ע״ה – Elie Neustadter ע״ה

BAVA BASRA I: **Nachum and Malkie Silberman**
in memory of his parents
ר׳ צבי ב״ר זאב הלוי ז״ל דבורה אסתר בת ר׳ ישראל ע״ה – Silberman
his paternal grandparents and their children who perished על קידוש השם in the Holocaust
ר׳ זאב ב״ר משה הלוי ז״ל הי״ד גיטל בת ר׳ אפרים אלימלך הכהן ע״ה הי״ד – Silberman
ובנותיהם רחל, לאה, ומרים ע״ה הי״ד
and his maternal grandparents
ר׳ ישראל ב״ר לוי משה ז״ל שיינדל רחל בת ר׳ יעקב ע״ה – Weitman

BAVA BASRA II: **Roger and Caroline Markfield**
and their children
Eric and **Maxine**
in memory of his parents
מרדכי ב״ר נתנאל ואודל בת ר׳ מאיר דוד ז״ל – Max and Eileen Markfield ז״ל
and his sister
זיסל ע״ה – Lynn Herzel ע״ה

BAVA BASRA III: **Jaime and Marilyn Sohacheski**
in honor of their children
Jasmine and David Brafman and their baby **Shlomo Zalman**
Melisa and her chatan Jonathan Beck
Lindsay and Bennett

SANHEDRIN I: **Martin and Rivka Rapaport**
and their children
Mordechai Ezriel Yehuda Aryeh Miriam Dreizel Shimshon
Leah Penina Eliyahu Meir Bracha
in memory of
ר׳ יהודה אריה ב״ר מרדכי הכהן ז״ל – Leo Rapaport ז״ל

SANHEDRIN II: **Martin and Rivka Rapaport**
and their children
Mordechai Ezriel Yehuda Aryeh Miriam Dreizel Shimshon
Leah Penina Eliyahu Meir Bracha
in memory of
ר׳ ישראל דוב ב״ר מרדכי ז״ל – Albert Berger ז״ל
חנה גיטל בת ר׳ עזריאל ע״ה – Chana Gittel Berger ע״ה

SANHEDRIN III: **Marvin and Roz Samuels**
in memory of
ר׳ צבי יוסף ב״ר יצחק ז״ל – Joseph Samuels ז״ל
רחל בת ר׳ זכריה מנחם ע״ה – Rose Samuels ע״ה
of Scranton, PA
בנימין נח ב״ר ישראל הלוי ז״ל – Norman Newman ז״ל
אלטא ביילא ראשקה בת נחמן הלוי ע״ה – Ruth Newman ע״ה

PATRONS OF THE TALMUD ◆ DAF YOMI EDITION

SHEVUOS: **Michael and Danielle Gross** (Herzlia and London)
in loving memory of their fathers
Paul Gross — פסח בן צבי הלוי ע"ה
David Beissah — דוד בן נתן ע"ה

MAKKOS: **The Tepper Families**
Beth and Yisroel Rabinowitz **Jay and Sari Tepper**
Hope and Moshe Abramson **Neil and Leah Tepper**
and children
in honor of their parents
David and Joan Tepper
and in memory of their grandparents
Tepper — ר' מנחם מענדל ב"ר יעקב ז"ל ומרת מינדל בת ר' אריה ליב ע"ה
Gralla — ר' ראובן ב"ר נחמיה ז"ל ומרת עטיל בת ר' ישראל נתן נטע ע"ה

AVODAH ZARAH I: **The Kuhl Family**
in memory of
Dr. Julius Kuhl יחיאל ב"ר יצחק אייזיק ע"ה
Mrs. Yvonne Kuhl פרומט בת ר' שמואל הלוי ע"ה
Sydney Kuhl שמואל ב"ר יחיאל ע"ה

AVODAH ZARAH II: In memory of
Jerome Schottenstein ע"ה
יעקב מאיר חיים בן אפרים אליעזר הכהן ע"ה

HORAYOS-EDUYOS: **Woli and Chaja Stern** (Sao Paulo, Brazil)
in honor of their children
Jacques and Ariane Stern Jaime and Ariela Landau Michäel and Annete Kierszenbaum

ZEVACHIM I: **Robin and Warren Shimoff**
in memory of his parents
Irving Shimoff ז"ל — ישראל דוב ב"ר אהרן יעקב ז"ל
Lynn Shimoff ע"ה — חיה רבקה לאה בת ר' אליעזר יהודה ע"ה
and in honor of their children שיחיו יבלח"ט
Lael Atara Alexander Ariana

ZEVACHIM II: **Abbie Spetner**
Ari and Chaya **Sara and Dovi Nussbaum** **Chanoch** **Moshe**
Rivkah Dinah **Moshe Yosef**
in honor of their father and grandfather
Kenneth Spetner שיחיי לאוי"ט
and in memory of their mother and grandmother
Rita Spetner ע"ה — רבקה דינה בת ר' משה יעקב ע"ה
נפ' ד' ניסן תשס"ב

ZEVACHIM III: **Yaakov and Yona Spinner**
Dovi **Elisheva** **Yitzy** **Shiri** **Leora**
in memory of their father and grandfather
Ephraim Spinner ז"ל — אפרים יצחק ב"ר אברהם ז"ל
נפ' י"ז שבט תשנ"ז
and in memory of their grandparents and great-grandparents
משה יודה בן דוד ע"ה רחל בת חיים דוד יהודה הכהן ע"ה
אברהם בן יוסף משה ע"ה צירל בת אברהם אליהו ע"ה
משה שלמה בן יעקב ע"ה רבקה בת משה ע"ה

MENACHOS I: **Terumah Foundation**

MENACHOS II: **Terumah Foundation**

MENACHOS III: **Terumah Foundation**

CHULLIN I: **Rabbi Heshie and Rookie Billet**

in honor of their mothers Mrs. Pearl Billet and Mrs. Phyllis Katz

their children Daniel and Hadassa Jacobson David Billet

Avraham and Chana Billet Moshe Billet Shira Billet Nava Billet

their grandchildren Tehila, Aharon, and Yehuda Jacobson

and in memory of their fathers

ר׳ אהרן ב״ר יצחק הכהן כ״ץ ז״ל — Arthur Katz ז״ל

ר׳ יהודה יעקב ב״ר אברהם ז״ל — Jack Billet ז״ל

their daughter מרים רות ע״ה — Miriam Rus ע״ה

their granddaughter אליענה שרה ע״ה — Eliana Sara ע״ה

CHULLIN II: **Elly and Brochie Kleinman**

and their children **Deenie and Yitzy Schuss** **Yossie and Blimi Kleinman**

Aliza and Lavey Freedman and families

לעילוי נשמות their fathers

ר׳ אברהם אייזיק ב״ר אלכסנדר ז״ל — Avrohom Kleinman ז״ל

ר׳ מנחם דוד ב״ר מרדכי שמואל ז״ל — Mendel Indig ז״ל

his grandparents שנהרגו על קידוש השם

ומרת סימא לאה בת ר׳ אברהם ע״ה – הי״ד ר׳ אלכסנדר ב״ר צבי אריה ז״ל — Kleinman (Weiss)

ומרת יוטא ברכה בת ר׳ אברהם ע״ה – הי״ד הרב אלימלך ב״ר ישראל ז״ל — Fischman

her grandparents

ומרת פרידה בת ר׳ מרדכי אריה ע״ה ר׳ מרדכי שמואל ב״ר יוסף יעקב ז״ל שנהרג על קדה״ש הי״ד — Indig

ומרת חיה בת ר׳ יעקב ע״ה ר׳ יעקב ב״ר שאול ז״ל — Solomon

and יבלח״ט in honor of their mothers

Mrs. Ethel Kleinman שתחי׳ Mrs. Rose Indig שתחי׳

CHULLIN III: **Members of the International Board of Governors of the Mesorah Heritage Foundation**

as a source of merit for all our brethren wherever they are

CHULLIN IV: **Terumah Foundation**

BECHOROS I: **Jeff and Leslie Gould** **Jody and Sheldon Hirst**

Rachel Jacob **Marci Tracy**

in memory of their father

ראובן בן יוסף ע״ה — Rubin Gould ע״ה

BECHOROS II: **Hilda and Yitz Applbaum**

in honor of their children

Aaron Jacob Ariel Tsvi Miriam Gabriella Zahava

and in memory of their deceased parents

אהרן ב״ר יהודה לייב ז״ל ומרים בת ר׳ מנחם מענדל ע״ה — Aaron and Miriam Goetz ע״ה

טובה גיטל בת ר׳ אברהם יהושע העשיל ע״ה — Tova Gertrude Applbaum ע״ה

ARACHIN: **The Brown Family**

in memory of

בעריש דוב בן מרדכי אליהו ז״ל וטובא בת אברהם ע״ה — Bernard and Tillie Tublin ז״ל

אברהם בן בעריש דוב ז״ל ומייטא בת ישראל ע״ה — Abraham and Mae Tublin ז״ל

נחום בן אברהם ז״ל — Neil Tublin ז״ל

Harry and Molly Brown ז״ל

Beatrice Geller ע״ה

Sophie Noble Scherr ע״ה

PATRONS OF THE TALMUD • DAF YOMI EDITION

TEMURAH: **Dr. Thomas and Anne Kohn** and their children
Dennis and Chayie Kohn **Yitzy and Dina Gunsburg** **Yaakov and Aviva Eisenberger**

Dr. Allan and Susan Seidenfeld and their children
Mordechai and Shaindy **Aaron and Dassi** **Dov and Chanala**
Yosef and Ahuva **Ahuva Libe** **Eliezer Chaim Yitzchok**
in honour of Eugene and Eva Kohn
in memory of (נפ׳ כ״ה אדר ב׳ תשס״ג) מינדל בת חיים ע״ה — Vera Rubinstein ע״ה
in honour of Daniel Rubinstein
in memory of (נפ׳ כ״ה מרחשון תש״ס) חיה מירל בת אברהם ע״ה — Margit Seidenfeld ע״ה
in honour of Salomon Seidenfeld

KEREISOS: לעילוי נשמת
מיסד ורוח החיים של רעיון הדף יומי
הגאון הרב ר׳ מאיר ב״ר יעקב שמשון שפירא זצ״ל
נפ׳ ז׳ חשון תרצ״ד
In memory of
Rabbi Meir Shapiro זצ״ל, the Lubliner Rav
whose revolutionary Daf Yomi initiative grows day by day.

ME'ILAH, TAMID, MIDDOS, KINNIM: **Steven and Renée Adelsberg**
Sarita and Rubin Gober **David** **Sammy** **Avi**
in loving memory of
שמואל שמעלקא ב״ר גדליה ז״ל — Samuel Adelsberg ז״ל
and יבלח״ט in honor of
Helen Adelsberg Weinberg שתחי׳
and
Chaim and Rose Fraiman שיחי׳

NIDDAH I: In memory of
Joseph and Eva Hurwitz ע״ה
יוסף ב״ר מרדכי הלוי וחוה פיגא ב״ר אליעזר הלוי ע״ה
and
Lorraine Hurwitz Greenblott — לאה בילא חיה בת ר׳ יוסף ע״ה
by
Marc and Rachel Hurwitz,
Elisheva Ruchama, Michal, and Nechama Leah;
Martin and Geraldine Schottenstein Hoffman,
Jay and Jeanie Schottenstein, Ann and Ari Deshe,
Susan and Jon Diamond, and Lori Schottenstein;
and Pam and Neil Lazaroff, Frank Millman, and Dawn and Avi Petel

NIDDAH II: In memory of
Jerome Schottenstein ע״ה
יעקב מאיר חיים בן אפרים אליעזר הכהן ע״ה

The Schottenstein Edition of the Talmud

They never surrendered the principles of Judaism or the love of Torah that they had absorbed in Lithuania.

This pioneering elucidation of the entire Talmud was named **THE SCHOTTENSTEIN EDITION** in memory of **EPHRAIM AND ANNA SCHOTTENSTEIN** ז"ל, of Columbus, Ohio. Mr. and Mrs. Schottenstein came to the United States as children, but they never surrendered the principles of Judaism or the love of Torah that they had absorbed in their native Lithuania. Tenacious was their devotion to the Sabbath, kashruth, and halachah; their support of needy Jews in a private, sensitive manner; their generosity to Torah institutions; and their refusal to speak ill of others.

This noble and historic gesture of dedication was made by their sons and daughters-in-law **JEROME** ז"ל **AND GERALDINE SCHOTTENSTEIN** and **SAUL AND SONIA SCHOTTENSTEIN.**

Jerome left numerous memorials of accomplishment and generosity, but surely the Schottenstein Edition of the Talmud – spanning centuries – will be the most enduring.

With the untimely passing of JEROME SCHOTTENSTEIN ז"ל, it became our sad privilege to rededicate THE SCHOTTENSTEIN EDITION to his memory, in addition to that of his parents.

Jerome Schottenstein ז"ל was a dear friend and inspirational patron. He saw the world through the lens of eternity, and devoted his mind, heart and resources to the task of assuring that the Torah would never be forgotten by its people. He left numerous memorials of accomplishment and generosity, but surely the **SCHOTTENSTEIN EDITION OF THE TALMUD** – spanning centuries – will be the most enduring.

The Schottensteins are worthy heirs to the traditions and principles of Jerome and his parents. Gracious and generous, kind and caring, they have opened their hearts to countless causes and people.

The Schottensteins are worthy heirs to the traditions and principles of Jerome and his parents. Gracious and generous, kind and caring, they have opened their hearts to countless causes and people. Quietly and considerately, they elevate the dignity and self-respect of those they help; they make their beneficiaries feel like benefactors; they imbue institutions with a new sense of mission to be worthy of the trust placed in them.

THE MESORAH HERITAGE FOUNDATION is proud and grateful to be joined with the Schottenstein family as partners in this monumental endeavor.

We pray that this great undertaking will be a source of merit for the continued health and success of the entire Schottenstein family, including the children and grandchildren:

JAY and JEANIE SCHOTTENSTEIN and their children, Joseph Aaron, Jonathan Richard, and Jeffrey Adam; **ANN and ARI DESHE** and their children, Elie Michael, David Scott, Dara Lauren, and Daniel Matthew; **SUSAN and JON DIAMOND** and their children, Jillian Leigh, Joshua Louis, and Jacob Meyer; and **LORI SCHOTTENSTEIN.**

The Schottensteins will be remembered with gratitude for as long as English-speaking Jews are nourished by the eternity of the Talmud's wisdom, for, thanks to them, millions of Jews over the generations will become closer to their heritage.

A Jew can accomplish nothing more meaningful or lasting in his sojourn on earth.

THE SCHOTTENSTEIN EDITION

TALMUD BAVLI

is reverently dedicated to the memory of
the patron of this Talmud
and of countless other noble causes in Jewish life

יעקב מאיר חיים בן אפרים אליעזר הכהן ע״ה

נפטר ה׳ אדר ב׳ תשנ״ב

Jerome Schottenstein ע״ה

and to the memory of his parents

אפרים אליעזר בן יהושע הכהן ע״ה — **חנה בת צבי הירש ע״ה**

נפטר ב׳ אייר תשט״ז — נפטרה ט״ו מנחם אב תשט״ו

Ephraim and Anna Schottenstein ע״ה

by

Geraldine Schottenstein

Saul and Sonia Schottenstein

and

Jay and Jeanie Schottenstein
and their children
Joseph Aaron, Jonathan Richard, Jeffrey Adam

Ann and Ari Deshe
and their children
Elie Michael, David Scott, Dara Lauren, Daniel Matthew

Susan and Jon Diamond
and their children
Jillian Leigh, Joshua Louis, Jacob Meyer

and

Lori Schottenstein

PATRONS OF THE SEDARIM

Recognizing the need for the holy legacy of the Talmud
to be available to its heirs in their own language,
these generous and visionary patrons have each dedicated
one of the six Sedarim/Orders of the Talmud.

THE FORMAN EDITION OF SEDER ZERAIM

is lovingly dedicated by

Mr. and Mrs. Sam Forman, Brett and Wendy

in memory of their beloved parents and grandparents

Mr. and Mrs. George Forman ע״ה **Dr. and Mrs. Morey Chapman ע״ה**

THE HORN EDITION OF SEDER MOED

is lovingly dedicated to the memory of

ר׳ משה מניס ב״ר יעקב יצחק ע״ה — Moishe Horn ע״ה

נפטר ב׳ מנחם אב תשנ״ד

by his wife **Malkie**

his parents **Jacob ע״ה and Genia Horn שתחי׳**

and her children

Shimmie and Alissa
Ari Shana Michal Tali

Devorah and Dov Elias
Moishe Ariella Eli Chaviva

Shandi and Sruli Glaser
Ruthi Jack

THE ELLIS A. SAFDEYE EDITION OF SEDER NASHIM

is reverently dedicated to the memory of

המנוח יהודה אצלאן ומרת צלחה ויקטוריא ע״ה

Aslan and Victoria Safdeye ע״ה

and

המנוח יהודה ומרת מרגלית ע״ה

Judah and Margie Sultan ע״ה

by their children

Ellis A. and Altoon Safdeye

and grandchildren

Alan Judah and Rachel Safdeye **Joseph and Rochelle Safdeye**
Ezra and Victoria Esses **Michael and Bobbi Safdeye**

PATRONS OF THE SEDARIM

THE DAVIDOWITZ FAMILY
RENOV STAHLER ROSENWALD PERLYSKY EDITION OF SEDER NEZIKIN

is lovingly dedicated to

Rozi and Morty Davis-Davidowitz

builders of this dynasty

by their children and grandchildren

Esti and Ushi Stahler

Jamie, Danny, Duvi, Lisi, Avi, Eli, Malka and Loni

Rivki and Lindsay Rosenwald

Doni, Joshy, Demi, Davey and Tamar Rina

Ruki and Kal Renov

Tova, Tani, Eli, Ari, Yoni, Yael, Emi and Benji

Laya and Dov Perlysky

Ayala Malka, Tova Batsheva, Naftali Yonatan, Atara Yael, Eitan Moshe, Shira Avital and Akiva Yair

and is lovingly dedicated to the memory of our grandparents

Emily and Nathan Selengut ע״ה

נפתלי ב״ר יעקב ע״ה ומלכה בת ר׳ אלתר חיים ע״ה

THE SCHWARTZ EDITION OF SEDER KODASHIM

is lovingly dedicated by

Avrohom Yeshaya and Sally Schwartz

and their children

Ari, Moshe, Dani, and Dovi

in memory of their beloved parents and grandparents

Isaac and Rebecca Jarnicki ז״ל — ר׳ יצחק ב״ר אשר ז״ל וחיה רבקה בת הרב בצלאל הירש ז״ל

נפ׳ יג׳ תמוז תשנ״ז נפ׳ ג׳ אדר תשס״ד

and their beloved grandmother

Mrs. Pearl Septytor ע״ה — פערל בת ר׳ מרדכי ע״ה

and in honor of יבלח״ט their parents and grandparents

Rabbi and Mrs. Gedalia Dov Schwartz שליט״א

and in memory of our grandparents

Rabbi Eliezer and Pesha Chaya Poupko ז״ל **Abraham Schwartz ז״ל**

Betzalel Hersh and Hendel Berliner ז״ל **Asher and Gittel Jarnicki ז״ל**

PATRONS OF THE TALMUD ❖ FULL-SIZE EDITION

With generosity, vision, and devotion to the perpetuation of Torah study, the following patrons have dedicated individual volumes of the Talmud

Reference/ Introduction: **George and Vita Kolber**
In loving memory of
Joseph and Frieda Hirschfeld **ע"ה**

BERACHOS I: In memory of
Jerome Schottenstein ע"ה
יעקב מאיר חיים בן אפרים אליעזר הכהן ע"ה

BERACHOS II: **Zvi and Betty Ryzman**
in honor of their children שיחיי
Mickey and Shelly Fenig — Aliza, Yissachar David, Batsheva and Aharon Yakov
Elie and Adina Ryzman — Leora and Yonatan Zev
Avi Rafi

Malcolm and Joy Lyons
in honour of their parents שיחיי
Eve Lyons
Cecil and Mona Jacobs
and in memory of his father
Leopold Lyons ע"ה — יהודה בן גרשון ע"ה נפ' כ"ב שבט תשס"ג

SHABBOS I: **Nachshon and Bruria Minucha [Nuchi] Draiman and Family**
in memory of
הר"ר יהודה ליב מנדלקורן זצ"ל בן הר"ר צבי הי"ו
Rabbi Yehuda Leib Mandelcorn זצ"ל — נפטר כ' תמוז, תשנ"ג

SHABBOS II: **David and Bonnie Anfang** — **Rachel, Julie and Elliot**
Chaim and Ruthie Anfang — **Ariella Hope** **Michael Brett**
In loving memory of
Leib Anfang ע"ה — ר' אריה ליב ב"ר דוד אביגדור ע"ה
Barbara Anfang ע"ה — בשה לאה בת ר' אלימלך דוב ע"ה

Mimi and Steven Rosenbaum — **Stacey and Danny**
Joseph and Sharon Prawer — **Dena, Dovid, Alana, Naomi**
Alan and Louisa Prawer — **Ruben Pinchas**
In loving memory of
Pinkus and Genia Prawer ע"ה, and — ר' פנחס ב"ר יוסף ברוך הלוי ע"ה גילה בת אשר יונה ע"ה
Sarah Cukierman ע"ה — שרה בת שמעון ליב ע"ה

A Hebrew edition of the Talmud Bavli is now in progress.
The Hebrew edition is dedicated by

Jay and Jeanie Schottenstein

and their children

Joseph Aaron, Jonathan Richard, and Jeffrey Adam

— in honor of their cherished loved ones who have left indelible marks on their own lives and the lives of countless others, as models of inspiration, generosity, integrity, and devotion to the noblest causes in Jewish life:
his parents **JEROME ז"ל AND GERALDINE SCHOTTENSTEIN**,
her parents **LEONARD AND HEDDY RABE**
and **SAUL AND SONIA SCHOTTENSTEIN**

JAY AND JEANIE SCHOTTENSTEIN
have a perspective that transcends time and community.
Through their dedication of these editions of the Talmud, they spread Torah study around the globe and across generations.
Multitudes yet unborn will be indebted to them for their vision and generosity.

PATRONS OF THE TALMUD ✧ FULL-SIZE EDITION

SHABBOS II: [continued]
Rabbi Eliyahu and Yehudit Fishman
Rivka and Zvi Silberstein and Leah **Akiva Yitzchak Fishman**
Rabbi Yechiel Meir and Chagit Fishman **Rabbi Yosef and Aliza Fishman**
Talia Chanah, Ariel Yishai and Daniel
In loving memory of
Yosef and Rude Rivka Fishman ע״ה — ר׳ יוסף ב״ר טוביה ע״ה רודע רבקה בת ר׳ הירש מאיר ע״ה
and their children Yechiel Meir, Leah and Chanah הי״ד who perished in the Holocaust

SHABBOS III:
Stanley and Ellen Wasserman
and their children
Alan and Svetlana Wasserman **Mark and Anne Wasserman**
Neil and Yael Wasserman **Stuart and Rivka Berger**
and families
In loving memory of
Joseph and Bess Wasserman ע״ה, and — יוסף בן דוב בער ע״ה בילא בת יעקב ע״ה
Sascha and Regina (Czaczkes) Charles ע״ה — שמריהו בן משה ע״ה רבקה בת הרב יוסף הכהן ע״ה

SHABBOS IV:
לעילוי נשמות
הורינו היקרים **ר׳ לוי ב״ר יהודה הלוי ע״ה וצירל בת ר׳ מרדכי ע״ה לוינגר**
זקנינו היקרים **ר׳ יהודה ב״ר אליעזר צבי הלוי ע״ה וטלצא בת פרומט ע״ה לוינגר**
ר׳ מרדכי ב״ר שמואל ע״ה ומלכה בת ר׳ נתן ע״ה אדלר
אחינו **שמואל הלוי ע״ה יהודה הלוי ע״ה יהונתן הלוי הי״ד**
אחותנו **לאה בת ר׳ לוי סג״ל ע״ה ובעלה ר׳ טוביה ע״ה**
גיסינו **ר׳ מיכאל ב״ר ברוך שמואל ע״ה שוויצר ר׳ שמואל ב״ר יעקב ע״ה מיכל**
ולעילוי נשמות דודינו ודודותינו ויוצאי חלוציהם שנפטרו ושנהרגו על קידוש השם הי״ד
Dedicated by **Louis and Morris Lowinger**
Teri Schweitzer **Kato Michel** **Margit Baldinger** **Eva Lowinger**

ERUVIN: [two volumes]
Jerome and Geraldine Schottenstein **Saul and Sonia Schottenstein**
Jay and Jeanie Schottenstein **Ann and Ari Deshe**
Susan and Jon Diamond **Lori Schottenstein**
in memory of
Ephraim Schottenstein ע״ה — אפרים אליעזר בן יהושע הכהן ע״ה
Anna Schottenstein ע״ה — חנה בת צבי הירש ע״ה

PESACHIM I:
Vera and Soli Spira and Family
in memory of
Baruch Spira ע״ה — ברוך בן חיים ע״ה
Bella Spira ע״ה — בילה בת נתן שלום ע״ה
Shmuel Lebovits ע״ה — שמואל בן אברהם ע״ה
and their respective families הי״ד who perished in the Holocaust
and in honor of
Caroline Lebovits תחי׳ — שפרה בת משה

The Edmond J. Safra Edition of the Talmud Bavli in French,
adapted from the Schottenstein Edition, is now in progress.

The Edmond J. Safra Edition
is dedicated by
Lily Safra
in memory of her beloved husband
Edmond J. Safra ע״ה רפאל אדמון עזרא בן אסתר ע״ה

His desire is in the Torah of HASHEM*, and in His Torah he meditates day and night.*
He shall be like a tree deeply rooted alongside brooks of water;
that yields its fruit in due season, and whose leaf never withers,
*and everything that he does will succeed (*Psalms 1:2-3).

PESACHIM II: **Vera and Soli Spira and Family**
in memory of an uncle who was like a father
and a cousin who was like a brother
ישראל בן נתן שלום ע״ה – Israel Stern ע״ה
נתן שלום בן ישראל ע״ה – Noussi Stern ע״ה

PESACHIM III: **Lorraine and Mordy Sohn** **Ann and Pinky Sohn**
in memory of
ר׳ צבי ב״ר אלעזר ע״ה – Dr. Harry Sohn ע״ה
מרת הענדיל דבורה ב״ר אברהם שלמה ע״ה – Dora F. Sohn ע״ה
ר׳ יחזקאל ב״ר אליקים חנוך הלוי ע״ה – Harold Levine ע״ה
רבקה הענא בת שמעון הלוי ע״ה – Ruth Levine ע״ה
רייזל ב״ר שמשון ע״ה – Rosalie Sohn ע״ה

SHEKALIM: In loving memory of
Mr. Maurice Lowinger ז״ל
ר׳ מאיר משה ב״ר בן ציון הלוי ז״ל
נפ׳ כ״ז אדר תשס״א

YOMA I: **A. Joseph and Rochelle Stern**
Moshe Dov, Zev, Shani, Esty, and Shaye
in honor of their parents and grandparents
Eli and Frieda Stern שיחיו
Frida Weiss שתחי׳
and in memory of
ר׳ ישעי׳ בן ר׳ ישראל שמואל ווייס ז״ל

YOMA II: **A. Leibish and Edith Elbogen and Family**
לזכר נשמות
מוה״ר אהרן בן מוה״ר יעקב קאפל עלבוגן ז״ל
וזו׳ אלטע חנה חיה מלכה בת מוה״ר חיים יצחק מאיר ע״ה
אחותי פערל עם בעלה ושבע בנים ובנות
ושלשה אחי: חיים יצחק מאיר, משה יוסף, יעקב קאפל הי״ד
בני אהרן עלבוגן שנהרגו עקד״ה
מוה״ר נתן פייטל בן מוה״ר אברהם וואלד ז״ל
וזו׳ ברכה בת מוה״ר דוד יהודה הי״ד שנאספה עקד״ה באוישוויץ

SUCCAH I: **Howard and Roslyn Zuckerman** **Steven and Shellie Zuckerman**
Leo and Rochelle Goldberg
in memory of their parents
ר׳ פסח יהודה ב״ר יצחק אייזיק ע״ה וחוה בת ר׳ יהודה לייב ע״ה – Philip and Evelyn Zuckerman ע״ה

in honor of their children
Yisroel and Shoshana Pesi Zuckerman שיחי׳
Pesach Yehudah and Asher Anshel שיחי׳
Michael (Ezra) and Lauren Zuckerman שיחי׳
Adrianne & Shawn Meller, Elliot, & Joshua Goldberg שיחי׳

in honor of their children
Glenn and Heidi, Jamie Elle, Benjamin,
Brett and Robin, Brandon Noah, Ross and T.J. שיחי׳
and in honor of their parents
Marilyn and Aaron Feinerman שיחי׳

in memory of
ר׳ ישראל צבי ב״ר ברוך ע״ה ושיינדל בת ר׳ ישראל ע״ה – Israel and Shaindel Ray ע״ה
and in memory of Mrs. Rose Ray (Glass) ע״ה

Arthur and Randi Luxenberg
in honor of their parents
Irwin and Joan Luxenberg שיחי׳ Bernard and Evelyn Beeber שיחי׳
their children Elizabeth Jewel and Jacqueline Paige שיחי׳
in memory of his grandparents
ר׳ אברהם בן אהרן מרדכי ז״ל ורחל בת ר׳ משה ע״ה – Abraham and Rose Luxenberg ע״ה
ישעיהו צבי בן הרב טוביה ז״ל ושרה צירל בת ר׳ יעקב ע״ה – Jesse and Celia Aronson ע״ה

PATRONS OF THE TALMUD ❖ FULL-SIZE EDITION

SUCCAH II: **Thomas and Lea Schottenstein** **William and Amy Schottenstein**
in memory of
אריה ליב בן אפרים אליעזר הכהן ע״ה — Leon Schottenstein ע״ה
מאיר אבנר בן דוד הלוי ע״ה — Meir Avner Levy ע״ה
and in honor of
Mrs. Jean S. Schottenstein שתחי׳ Bertram and Corinne Natelson שיחי׳
Mrs. Flory Levy שתחי׳

BEITZAH: **Paul and Suzanne Peyser** **Irwin and Bea Peyser**
in memory of
דוד בן פינחס ע״ה פריידע רייזעל בת יהושע ע״ה — David and Rose Peyser ע״ה

ROSH HASHANAH: **Steve and Genie Savitsky** **David and Roslyn Savitsky**
In memory of
יואל בן אברהם ע״ה — Jerry J. Savitsky ע״ה
ישראל בן מנחם מאנעס ע״ה — Irving Tennenbaum ע״ה
שמואל בן יצחק ע״ה — George Hillelsohn ע״ה
רחל בת דוד הלוי ע״ה — Ruth Hillelsohn ע״ה
אהרן בן יהודה אריה ע״ה — Aaron Seif ע״ה

TAANIS: **David and Jean Bernstein, and Scott**
Matthew Bernstein
Albert and Gail Nassi, **Jessica and Garrett**
in memory of
Mr. and Mrs. Harry Bernstein ע״ה Mr. and Mrs. Joseph Furman ע״ה
Mr. Samuel Nassi ע״ה

MEGILLAH: Special Commemorative Edition published in conjunction
with the *Sh'loshim* of the patron of this edition of the Talmud
Jerome Schottenstein ע״ה
יעקב מאיר חיים בן אפרים אליעזר הכהן ע״ה

MOED KATAN: **Solomon T. and Leah Scharf**
and their children
David and Tzipi Diamond **Alexander and Naomi Scharf**
Joseph Scharf **Dovid and Chani Scharf**
לזכרון עולם
ר׳ אליהו בן משה יעקב ע״ה — R' Eliyahu Scharf ע״ה
שרה בת אלכסנדר זיסקינד ע״ה — Sara Scharf ע״ה
ר׳ יוסף בן צבי הירש ע״ה — R' Joseph Felder ע״ה

CHAGIGAH: **The Alvin E. Schottenstein Family**
In memory of
חיים אברהם יונה בן אפרים אליעזר הכהן ע״ה — Alvin E. Schottenstein ע״ה
יצחק אייזיק בן עקיבא הכהן ע״ה — Irving Altman ע״ה

YEVAMOS I: **Phillip and Ruth Wojdyslawski and Family**
In memory of his beloved parents
Abraham Michel and Ora Wojdyslawski ע״ה
ר׳ אברהם מיכאל ב״ר פינחס ע״ה
אורה בת ר׳ צבי הירש ע״ה

YEVAMOS II: **Phillip and Ruth Wojdyslawski and Family**
In memory of her beloved mother
Chaya (Cytryn) Valt ע״ה
חיה צירל בת ר׳ שלמה זלמן ע״ה

PATRONS OF THE TALMUD ❖ FULL-SIZE EDITION

YEVAMOS III: **Phillip and Ruth Wojdyslawski and Family**
In honor of
Benjamin C. Fishoff לאוי"ט
To the public he is a leader with vision and dedication.
To us he has always been a role model, a father,
and a constant inspiration.

KESUBOS I: **The Fishoff Families**
in memory of their beloved mother
מינדל בת ר' ישראל ע"ה – Mrs. Marilyn Fishoff ע"ה
נפ' כד תשרי תשמ"ט
and in memory of their dear grandparents
Fishoff – ר' דוב ב"ר מנחם אשר ע"ה מרת מירל בת ר' מנחם מענדל ע"ה
Neider – ר' ישראל ב"ר אברהם ע"ה מרת חיה זיסא בת ר' שרגא פייוועל ע"ה

KESUBOS II **Arthur A. and Carla Rand**
in memory of their parents
ר' ישראל ב"ר צבי Rand ומרת ליבא מלכה ב"ר יהודה Marcus ע"ה
ר' שלמה ב"ר מרדכי יהודה Ratzersdorfer ומרת חוה ב"ר חיים Finkelstein ע"ה
and in honor of their children
ר' אריה יהושע ב"ר אליהו דוב ומרת ליבא מלכה שיחי' – Lydia M. and Lionel S. Zuckier
ר' יואל אשר ב"ר חיים שלמה ומרת גנענדל חנה שיחי' – Gigi A. and Joel A. Baum
ר' ישראל יהודה ומרת צפורה געלא ב"ר יצחק חיים שיחי' – Jay J. and Cyndi G. Finkel-Rand
and grandchildren
דניאל יעקב, נפתלי צבי, חוה, בנימין, צפורה מרים, רחל, בתשבע Baum שיחי'
שלמה יצחק, שירה חיה, צבי, שפרה לאה, בן ציון Zuckier שיחי'
אליהו אריה לייב, יעקב שלמה, צבי, חסיה ליבא, מתתיהו דוד Rand שיחי'

KESUBOS III **ישימך אלהים כשרה רבקה רחל ולאה**
May God make you like Sarah, Rebecca, Rachel and Leah

NEDARIM I: **Mrs. Goldy Golombeck**
Hyman P. and Elaine Golombeck **Blanche B. Lerer**
Moishe Zvi and Sara Leifer **Avrohom Chaim and Renee Fruchthandler**
In memory of
ר' משה יוסף ב"ר חיים פנחס ע"ה – Morris J. Golombeck ע"ה
and by Moishe Zvi and Sara Leifer in memory of
הרב ברוך יוסף ב"ר משה צבי ע"ה – האשה הצנועה מרים יוטא בת ר' לוי יצחק ע"ה
Mr. and Mrs. Baruch Leifer ע"ה

NEDARIM II: **The Rothstein Family**
In loving memory of
וועלוועל ב"ר יוסף ע"ה – Warren Rothstein ע"ה
David and Esther Rothstein ע"ה Max and Gussie Gottlieb ע"ה
and in honor of
Howard and Beatrice Rothstein

NAZIR I: **Albert and Gail Nassi**
Garrett A. Nassi
Jessica Lea Nassi
in memory of
Samuel Nassi ע"ה
Albert and Leona Nassi ע"ה
Benjamin and Adell Eisenberg ע"ה
Arthur and Sarah Dector ע"ה

Daniel and Susan Kane
Jessica, Adam and Stacey
in memory of
Abraham and Rose Kanofsky ע"ה
Benjamin and Sophie Gornstein ע"ה
Elie and Irma Darsa ע"ה
Mack and Naomi Mann ע"ה

NAZIR II: **Alan and Myrna Cohen, Alison and Matthew**
in memory of
Harry and Kate Cohen ע"ה Harry and Pauline Katkin ע"ה

PATRONS OF THE TALMUD • FULL-SIZE EDITION

SOTAH: **Motty and Malka Klein**
for the merit of their children שיחי׳
Esther and Chaim Baruch Fogel   Dovid and Chavie   Binyomin Zvi
Elana Leah   Moshe Yosef   Yaakov Eliyahu
In honor of his mother שתחי׳
Mrs. Suri Klein לאוי״ט
In memory of his father
ר׳ יהודה ב״ר דוד חלוי ז״ל נפ׳ כ״ז אדר ב׳ תשס״ג – Yidel Klein
In memory of her parents
ר׳ אשר אנשיל ב״ר משה יוסף ז״ל נפ׳ ג׳ שבט תשנ״ט – Anchel Gross
שרה בת ר׳ חיים אליהו ע״ה נפ׳ כ״ד סיון תשס״א – Suri Gross
And in memory of their grandparents who perished על קידוש השם in the Holocaust
ר׳ דוד ב״ר יעקב הלוי ע״ה ופערל בת ר׳ צבי ע״ה הי״ד – Klein
ר׳ מרדכי ב״ר דוד הלוי ע״ה ולאה בת ר׳ יעקב הלוי ע״ה הי״ד – Klein
ר׳ משה יוסף ב״ר בנימין צבי ע״ה ומלכה בת ר׳ יחיאל מיכל ע״ה הי״ד – Gross
ר׳ חיים אליהו ב״ר מרדכי ע״ה ויוטא בת ר׳ שלמה אליעזר ע״ה הי״ד – Gartenberg

GITTIN I: **Mrs. Kate Tannenbaum**
Elliot and Debra Tannenbaum   Edward and Linda Zizmor
and Families
commemorating the first *yahrzeit* of beloved husband, father and grandfather
ר׳ נפתלי ב״ר יהודה אריה ע״ה – Fred Tannenbaum ע״ה
נפטר ח׳ ניסן תשנ״ב

GITTIN II: **Richard and Bonnie Golding**
in honor of   Julian and Frances Golding   Lawrence Cohen and Helen Lee Cohen
and in memory of   Vivian Cohen ע״ה
Irving and Ethel Tromberg   Clarence and Jean Permut
in memory of
Benjamin and Sara Tromberg ע״ה   Harry and Lena Brown ע״ה
Molly and Julius Permut ע״ה   Lizzie and Meyer Moscovitz ע״ה

KIDDUSHIN I: **Ellis A. and Altoon Safdeye**
in memory of their beloved parents
המנוח יהודה אצלאן ומרת צלחה ויקטוריא ע״ה – Aslan and Victoria Safdeye ע״ה
המנוח יהודה ומרת מרגלית ע״ה – Judah and Margie Sultan ע״ה
and in memory of his brother יוסף ע״ה – Joseph Safdeye ע״ה

KIDDUSHIN II: **Mr. and Mrs. Ben Heller**
in memory of his father
יואל נתן ב״ר חיים הלוי ע״ה – Joseph Heller ע״ה
and in honor of his mother
צפורה שתחי׳ לאוי״ט בת ר׳ בנימין ע״ה – Fanya Gottesfeld-Heller שתחי׳

BAVA KAMMA I: **Yitzchok and Shoshana Ganger**
and Children
in memory of
ר׳ יצחק ישעיהו ב״ר שלמה זלמן ע״ה–רויזא גיטל בת ר׳ משה ע״ה – Ganger
מיכאל ב״ר אברהם מרדכי ע״ה–מרים יוכבד בת ר׳ בנימין ע״ה – Ferber
ר׳ משה דוד ב״ר יצחק זעליג מקוצק ע״ה–פיגא בת ר׳ אברהם מרדכי ע״ה – Morgenstern
ר׳ מתתיהו ב״ר שמואל דוב ע״ה–אסתר מלכה בת ר׳ אריה ליב ע״ה – Newman

BAVA KAMMA II: **William and Esther Bein, and**
Joseph Hillel, Abraham Chaim Zev, and Bella Leah
In memory of parents and grandparents
מנחם מענדל ב״ר שמואל יצחק הכהן ע״ה – Edward (Mendus) Bein ע״ה
לאה בת חיים זאב הכהן ע״ה – Ilus Hartstein Bein ע״ה
מרדכי בן יוסף ע״ה – Mordochej Szer ע״ה
בילה בת אברהם ע״ה – Baila Silber Szer ע״ה
שמואל יצחק הכהן ושרה ביין ע״ה – חיים זאב הכהן ושרה הרטשטיין ע״ה
יוסף ויענטה שער ע״ה – אברהם ואסתר זילבר ע״ה

PATRONS OF THE TALMUD ✧ FULL-SIZE EDITION

BAVA KAMMA III: **Dedicated to Klal Yisrael,**
and particularly to the Six Million.
הקב״ה שוכן בתוך בני ישראל והוא חד עם כנסת ישראל
"The Holy One Blessed is He dwells among the children of Israel;
He and the congregation of Israel are one."
— *Tzidkas Hatzaddik* 179

BAVA METZIA I: **Drs. Robert and Susan Schulman**
Howard and Tzila Schulman   Fred and Cindy Schulman
and Families
in memory of
מיכאל בן צבי הירש ע״ה ומלכה בת ר׳ יוסף ע״ה — Milton and Molly Schulman ע״ה

BAVA METZIA II: **Donald E. and Eydie R. Garlikov, and Jennifer**
in memory of beloved son and brother
צבי שלמה בן דן ע״ה — Kenneth Scott Garlikov ע״ה
and in memory of parents and grandparents
עזריאל וועלוויל ב״ר אנשיל ע״ה   טשארנא בת ר׳ אריה לייב ע״ה
Irve W. and Cecelia (Kiki) Garlikov ע״ה
and in honor of parents and grandparents, brother and uncle
מרדכי ואסתר פריידל ריטטער — Marcus and Elfrieda Ritter
נפתלי חיים ריטטער — Dr. Nathaniel Ritter

BAVA METZIA III: **The David H. Gluck Foundation**
in memory of
The Gluck Family
זאב בן דוד צבי ע״ה   ואסתר בת אשר זעליג ע״ה — Zev and Esther Gluck ע״ה
ליבא, אשר זעליג, דוד צבי, שמואל, מנשה, יחזקאל שרגא ע״ה —
Lee, George, David H., Samuel C., Emanuel M., Henry ע״ה, and
יעקב יצחק בן זאב ע״ה   ומיימי בת זאב ע״ה — Dr. Jack I. and Mrs. Mae Saks ע״ה
and in memory of
זאב בן חיים דוד   וחיה ביילע בת יצחק יעקב ע״ה — Wolf and Chaye Beilah Saks ע״ה
יחיאל בן משה ע״ה — Elie Neustadter ע״ה

BAVA BASRA I: In memory of
מנחם מענדל בן אלימלך יהושע העשל ע״ה
חיה בת יהושע הכהן ע״ה

BAVA BASRA II: **Paul and Beth Guez and Family**
in memory of
Felix (Mazal) Guez ע״ה

BAVA BASRA III: **Irving and Frances Schottenstein**
in honor of their beloved parents
מאיר בן יהושע הכהן ע״ה   ליבא בת הרב יצחק משה ע״ה — Meyer and Libbie Schottenstein
טוביה ע״ה   ויבדל״ח שיינדל תחי׳ — Tobias ע״ה and Jennie Polster תחי׳
Melvin ע״ה and Lenore תחי׳ Schottenstein
in honor of their beloved parents
אברהם יוסף בן יהושע הכהן ע״ה   ויבדל״ח בליה זילפה בת יצחק תחי׳
Abe J. ע״ה and Bessie (Stone) תחי׳ Schottenstein
יצחק ע״ה   ויבדל״ח שרה תחי׳ — Isadore J. ע״ה and Sophie תחי׳ Green

PATRONS OF THE TALMUD ✦ FULL-SIZE EDITION

SANHEDRIN I: **Mortimer and Barbara Klaus** **Lester and Esther Klaus**
Arthur and Vivian Klaus
in memory of their beloved parents
ר׳ שמשון ב״ר יעקב ע״ה באשא בת ר׳ מרדכי נתן ע״ה
Samuel and Bessie Klaus ע״ה
and in memory of their sister
רייזל בת ר׳ שמשון ע״ה — **Rosalie Klaus Sohn**

SANHEDRIN II: Dedicated by a fellowship of people who revere the Talmud, its sanctity and wisdom, who foster its study, and who join in helping bring its treasures to future generations, the world over.

SANHEDRIN III: **Joseph and Adina Russak**
Dr. Leonard and Bobbee Feiner
Larry and Rochelle Russak
in memory of
צבי הירש ורחל רוסק ע״ה — Mr. and Mrs. Harry Russak ע״ה
אליעזר ובריינדל דייטש ע״ה — Mr. and Mrs. Eliezer Deutsch ע״ה
יעקב ורבקה לאה פיינר ע״ה — Mr. and Mrs. Jacob Feiner ע״ה

MAKKOS: **Mr. and Mrs. Marcos Katz**
in honor of הרב אפרים לייבוש בן הרב מרדכי דוד הכהן כ״ץ שליט״א
Rabbi Ephraim Leibush Katz שליט״א

SHEVUOS: Dedicated by
Michael and Danielle Gross
(London)

AVODAH ZARAH I: **The Kuhl Family**
in memory of
יחיאל ב״ר יצחק אייזיק ע״ה Dr. Julius Kuhl ע״ה
פרומט בת ר׳ שמואל הלוי ע״ה Mrs. Yvonne Kuhl ע״ה
שמואל ב״ר יחיאל ע״ה Sydney Kuhl ע״ה

AVODAH ZARAH II: In memory of
Jerome Schottenstein ע״ה
יעקב מאיר חיים בן אפרים אליעזר הכהן ע״ה

HORAYOS-EDUYOS: **Woli and Chaja Stern** (Sao Paulo, Brazil)
in memory of his parents
ר׳ צבי בן ר׳ חיים הלוי ומרת מרים ז״ל – Stern
מרת דאכא בת ר׳ פרץ ומרת ברכה ע״ה – Tager
and in memory of her parents
ר׳ דוד אריה בן ר׳ יעקב ומרת שיינדל ז״ל – Brenner
מרת איטלה בת ר׳ חיים ומרת מדל ע״ה – Stern
and in memory of their mechutanim
ר׳ ישראל מרדכי ב״ר צבי יוסף סג״ל ז״ל – Landau
ר׳ יששכר טוביה ב״ר יוסף ז״ל – Weitman
ר׳ שמואל עקיבא ב״ר שלמה צבי ז״ל – Kierszenbaum
and in memory of their sister-in-law
מרת זלטה פסל בת ר׳ אברהם יעקב ומרת חנה גיטל ע״ה – Stern
and in honor of their children
Jacques and Ariane Stern   Jaime and Ariela Landau   Michäel and Annete Kierszenbaum

ZEVACHIM I: **Mr. and Mrs. Samson Bitensky**

ZEVACHIM II: **Victor Posner**

PATRONS OF THE TALMUD ❖ FULL-SIZE EDITION

ZEVACHIM III: **Friends of Value City Department Stores**
In memory of
יעקב מאיר חיים בן אפרים אליעזר הכהן ע״ה — Jerome Schottenstein ע״ה

MENACHOS I: **Terumah Foundation**

MENACHOS II: **Terumah Foundation**

MENACHOS III: **Terumah Foundation**

CHULLIN I: **The Kassin Family**
in memory of
הרב יעקב שאול קצין זצ״ל — Rabbi Dr. Jacob Saul Kassin זצ״ל
The late Chief Rabbi of the Syrian-Sephardic Community
and in honor of
הרב שאול יעקב קצין שליט״א — Rabbi Saul Jacob Kassin שליט״א
Chief Rabbi of the Syrian-Sephardic Community

CHULLIN II: **Marty Silverman**
in memory of
Joseph and Fannie Silverman ע״ה and Dorothy Silverman ע״ה

CHULLIN III: **Harold and Ann Platt**
in memory of their beloved parents
אליעזר ושרה פיגא ע״ה — Eliezer and Sarah Feiga (Olshak) Platkowski ע״ה of Malkinia, Poland
ברוך ולאה ע״ה — Baruch and Laura Bienstock ע״ה of Lwow, Poland
and in memory of their entire families who perished in the Holocaust

CHULLIN IV: **Terumah Foundation**

BECHOROS I: **Howard Tzvi and Chaya Friedman**
Gabrielle Aryeh Yerachmiel Alexander and Daniella
in memory of their father and grandfather
הרב ירחמיאל ברוך בן הרה״ח ר׳ אלעזר ז״ל — Yerachmiel Friedman ז״ל

BECHOROS II: **Howard and Chaya Balter**
Perri Naftali Aryeh Akiva
in memory of his mother and their grandmother
רחל בת ר׳ חיים ע״ה, נפ׳ ז׳ שבט תשנ״ט — **Ruth Balter** ע״ה
and in honor of their parents and grandparents שיחי׳
David Balter
Noah and Shirley Schall
and in beloved memory of their grandparents and great grandparents
ר׳ שלמה ב״ר דוד זאב ז״ל   אדי בת ר׳ זאב ע״ה — Balter
ר׳ חיים ב״ר לייב ז״ל   פערל בת ר׳ ביינישׁ ע״ה — Lelling
ר׳ דוב בער ב״ר אליעזר ז״ל   ליבה בת ר׳ ישראל ע״ה — Zabrowsky
ר׳ נפתלי ב״ר יעקב שלמה ז״ל   שרה בת ר׳ רפאל ע״ה — Schall

ARACHIN: **Chanoch and Hadassah Weisz and Family**
in memory of his father:
לעי״נ אביו ר׳ צבי ב״ר שמחה הלוי ע״ה, נפ׳ כ״ז מנחם אב תשמ״ה — Weisz
his maternal grandfather:
לעי״נ ר׳ שלמה ב״ר יצחק ע״ה, נפ׳ ה׳ סיון תש״א — Grunwald
his maternal grandmother and their children who perished in the Holocaust:
לעי״נ מרת גנדל בת ר׳ חנוך העניך ע״ה, שנהרגה עקה״ש כ״ז סיון תש״ד הי״ד — Grunwald
ולעי״נ בניהם משה ב״ר שלמה, יעקב ב״ר שלמה, יצחק ב״ר שלמה, בנימין ב״ר שלמה,
שנהרגו עקה״ש כ״ז סיון תש״ד הי״ד

and in memory of her grandparents:
לעי״נ ר׳ חייא בן חכם ר׳ רפאל ע״ה, נפ׳ כ״ד מנחם אב תשל״ה — Aryeh
וזוגתו מרת מלכה בת ר׳ אליהו ע״ה, נפ׳ י״ח טבת תשל״ד

PATRONS OF THE TALMUD • FULL-SIZE EDITION

TEMURAH: **Dr. and Mrs. Walter Silver**
Shlomo, Chani, and Avi Cohen
Sheri, Terri, Jennifer and Michelle Kraut
Evan and Alison Silver
in memory of our parents, and great grandparents
Harry Silver ע״ה — צבי יצחק ב״ר שמואל ע״ה
Sarah Silver ע״ה — שרה פיגא בת מענדל ע״ה
Morris Bienenfeld ע״ה — אברהם משה בן הרב שלמה זאלי ע״ה
Gertrude Bienenfeld ע״ה — גוטקה טובה בת אברהם דוד ע״ה

KEREISOS: **Mouky and Charlotte Landau** (Antwerp)
in honor of their children
Natalie and Chemi Friedman **Yanky and Miriam Landau**
Steve and Nechama Landau
and in beloved memory of their parents
Chaim Yaakov Landau ז״ל — חיים יעקב ב״ר יהושע ז״ל
Esther Landau ע״ה — אסתר בת ר׳ יעקב קאפל הכהן ע״ה
Benzion Gottlob ז״ל — בן ציון ב״ר יצחק צבי ז״ל
Cila Herskovic ע״ה — צילה בת ר׳ שמואל יהודה לייב ע״ה
and in beloved memory of our partner
מורנו הרב ר׳ יוסף יצחק בן מורנו ורבנו הרה״ג ר׳ מרדכי רוטנברג זצ״ל אבדק״ק אנטווערפן

ME'ILAH, TAMID, MIDDOS, KINNIM: **Steven and Renée Adelsberg**
Sarita and Rubin Gober **David** **Sammy** **Avi**
in loving memory of
Samuel Adelsberg ז״ל — שמואל שמעלקא ב״ר גדליה ז״ל
and in honor of
Helen Adelsberg Weinberg שתחי׳
and
Chaim and Rose Fraiman שיחי׳

NIDDAH I: In memory of
Joseph and Eva Hurwitz ע״ה
יוסף ב״ר מרדכי הלוי וחוה פיגא ב״ר אליעזר הלוי ע״ה
and
Lorraine Hurwitz Greenblott — לאה בילא חיה בת ר׳ יוסף ע״ה
by
Marc and Rachel Hurwitz,
Elisheva Ruchama, Michal, and Nechama Leah;
Martin and Geraldine Schottenstein Hoffman,
Jay and Jeanie Schottenstein, Ann and Ari Deshe,
Susan and Jon Diamond, and Lori Schottenstein;
and Pam and Neil Lazaroff, Frank Millman, and Dawn Petel

NIDDAH II: In memory of
Jerome Schottenstein ע״ה
יעקב מאיר חיים בן אפרים אליעזר הכהן ע״ה

*Guardians of the Talmud**

A society of visionary people who recognize the primacy of the Jewish people's commitment to intellect, ethics, integrity, law, and religion — and pursue it by presenting the treasures of the eternal Talmud in the language of today . . . for the generations of tomorrow.

❦ ❦ ❦

David and Jean Bernstein
Matthew Bernstein
Scott and Andrea Bernstein

in memory of
Mr. and Mrs. Harry Bernstein ע״ה
Mr. and Mrs. Joseph Furman ע״ה

❦ ❦ ❦

The publishers pay tribute to the memory of a couple that embodied Torah knowledge and service to our people

הרב יצחק בן ר׳ שמואל ז״ל – Rabbi Yitzchok Filler ז״ל

נפטר ל״ג בעומר תש״ל

הרבנית דבורה בת ר׳ אברהם בצלאל ע״ה – Mrs. Dorothy Filler ע״ה

נפטרה כ״א מרחשון תשס״ג

and the memory of a man of integrity and sensitivity

ר׳ יוסף בן הרב יהודה אריה ז״ל – George May ז״ל

נפטר כ״ז שבט תש״ס

תנצב״ה

We also honor a matriarch and role model

Mrs. Sylvia May תחי׳

❦ ❦ ❦

Stephen L. and Terri Geifman and children
Leonard and Linda Comess and children
Alan and Cherie Weiss and children

in loving memory of
משה מרדכי בן יחיאל מיכאל ז״ל – Morris M. Geifman

and in honor of
Geraldine G. Geifman

❦ ❦ ❦

Elliot and Debbie Gibber
Daniel and Amy Gibber and family, Jacob and Jennifer Gibber and family,
Marc, Michael, Mindy, and David

in memory of our parents and grandparents
אלימלך חיים בן ירמיה הלוי ז״ל – Charles Goldner ז״ל

נפ׳ כ׳ חשון תשס״ב

who completed Shas many times
מינדל בת משולם ע״ה – Kate Ettlinger Goldner ע״ה

נפ׳ כ״א תמוז תשכ״ח

*In formation

Guardians of the Talmud*

A society of visionary people who recognize the primacy of the Jewish people's commitment to intellect, ethics, integrity, law, and religion — and pursue it by presenting the treasures of the eternal Talmud in the language of today . . . for the generations of tomorrow.

Milton and Rita Kramer

in honor of their 50th wedding anniversary and Milton's 80th birthday (April 1999),
in honor of the marriage of Ellen to George Gross (September 18, 2000),
and in honor of their children and grandchildren

Daniel and Gina Kramer and Children **Jonathan and Marian Kramer and Children**
Ellen K. and George Gross and their Children

and in everlasting memory of their beloved parents and grandparents
Hyman S. and Fannie D. Kramer ע״ה — חיים שניאור זלמן הלוי (חזק) ופייגע דינה ע״ה
Adolph H. and Sadie A. Gross ע״ה — חיים אלטער ושרה חנה ע״ה
Morris L. and Rachel E. Kramer ע״ה — משה אליעזר הלוי ורחל עלקא ע״ה
Barney and Dvorah Cohen ע״ה — דוב בער הכהן ודבורה ע״ה
Herman M. and Leah Gross ע״ה — משולם צבי ולאה ע״ה
Peisach and Hannah Neustadter ע״ה — פסח אלכסנדר וחנה ע״ה

Helene and Moshe Talansky **Ida Bobrowsky** **Irene and Kalman Talansky** **Shoshana Silbert**

in honor of
Rebecca Talansky's 100th birthday עמו״ש
and in memory of
Rabbi David Talansky ז״ל — הרב דוד בן הרב אברהם חיים ז״ל
Blanche Moshel ע״ה — בלומא בת ר׳ שלמה הלוי ע״ה
Abraham R. Talansky ז״ל — ר׳ אברהם חיים בן הרב דוד ז״ל
Rabbi Jacob Bobrowsky ז״ל — הרב יעקב בן ר׳ אברהם ז״ל
Tema Bobrowsky ע״ה — תמר בת הרב יעקב ע״ה
Rebecca and Morris Weisinger ז״ל — ר׳ משה בן ר׳ לייב ז״ל – בריינה בת ר׳ זלמן ע״ה
Rabbi Avraham Silbert ז״ל — הרב אברהם בן ר׳ נחמיה ז״ל
Ruth and Marek Stromer ז״ל — ר׳ מרדכי בן ר׳ שאול ז״ל – שפרה רייזל בת ר׳ צבי ע״ה
Rose and Aaron Lerer ז״ל — ר׳ אהרון בן ר׳ שלמה אריה ז״ל – רחל בת ר׳ יהושע אהרון ע״ה

Thomas R. and Janet F. Ketteler

in memory of his mentor

Jerome Schottenstein ע״ה

Alan and Myrna Cohen

in honor of
their children
Alison and Matthew

*In formation

Guardians of the Talmud*

A society of visionary people who recognize the primacy of the Jewish people's commitment to intellect, ethics, integrity, law, and religion — and pursue it by presenting the treasures of the eternal Talmud in the language of today . . . for the generations of tomorrow.

Rona and Edward Jutkowitz

In honor of our family's continuing commitment to Torah learning and Klal Yisrael.
We dedicate this volume to our daughters, **Rebecca and Mollie,**
who are the light of our lives and our blessings, and always fill our hearts with nachas;
and to their zeide, **Mr. Herman Jutkowitz,** who is a constant source of guidance and inspiration;

and in memory of our beloved parents
Martin W. and Ruth Trencher ז״ל — משה בן מאניס ז״ל ורחל בת אברהם הכהן ע״ה
Bernice Jutkowitz ע״ה — ברכה בת שניאור זלמן ע״ה

May our daughters have the honor to teach the value of Torah to their own children,
and may Torah be the guiding light for all of Klal Yisrael.

לעילוי נשמת

Franky Ehrenberg — הבחור מרדכי גדליהו ז״ל בן משה ואסתר שיחי׳

June 22, 2003 / נפ׳ כ״ג סיון תשס״ג

With a life of Torah study and service to Klal Yisrael ahead of him,
our beloved son, brother, and uncle was plucked from this life at only twenty-three.

כי מרדכי . . . דרש טוב לעמו ודבר שלום לכל זרעו

Dr. Martin and Esther Ehrenberg
Scott Leon **Dr. Judy and Hillel Olshin**
Yonatan Eliezer **Sara Elisheva** **Shmuel Abba**

Richard Bookstaber and Janice Horowitz

In memory of his son

May his memory be a blessing
to all those whose lives he touched.

Michael and Patricia Schiff
Sophia, Juliette and Stefan

in memory and appreciation of
Jerome Schottenstein ז״ל

and in honor of beloved parents and grandparents
Shirlie and Milton Levitin **Solange and Joseph Fretas** **Judy and Robert Schiff**

and Torah scholars
Rabbi Mordechai Schiff ז״ל and **Rabbi Ephraim Schiff ז״ל**

May we all bring honor to Hashem

*In formation

The Written Word is Forever

Community Guardians of the Talmud

A community is more than a collection of individuals. It is a new entity that is a living expression of support of Torah and dedication to the heritage of Klal Yisrael.

In honor of

Rabbi Reuven Fink and the *maggidei shiur* of **Young Israel of New Rochelle**

Dr. Joey and Lisa Bernstein
in memory of
שרה אלטע בת אברהם ע״ה
Mrs. Sondra Goldman ע״ה

Meyer and Ellen Koplow
in honor of their children
Tovah and Michael Koplow,
Jonathan, and Aliza

Stanley and Sheri Raskas
in memory of his parents
ראובן ב״ר חיים שבתי לייב ע״ה וחנה בת הרב טוביה ע״ה
Ralph and Annette Raskas ז״ל

Stanley and Ellen Wasserman
in memory of
חיה פיגא בת שמריהו — Viola Charles ע״ה
רות גולדה בת שמריהו — Ruth Schreiber ע״ה
לאה בת יוסף — Lee Salzberg ע״ה

Stanley and Vivian Bernstein and children
in honor of their parents and grandparents
Jules and Adele Bernstein
Andrew and Renee Weiss

Dr. Ronald and Susan Moskovich
in honor of their children
Adam Moshe, Leah Rivka, and David
״עשה תורתך קבע״

Drs. Arthur and Rochelle Turetsky
in honor of their children and grandson
Avi and Melissa, Jonathan and Nili, Yehuda
Shmuel Chaim

Gerald and Judith Ziering
in memory of
יחיאל מיכל בן אפרים פישל ז״ל וזלטא בת נחמן ע״ה
Jesse and Laurette Ziering ז״ל

Aaron and Carol Greenwald
in honor of their children and grandchildren
Ira and Jamie Gurvitch and children
Shlomo and Tobi Greenwald and children

Karen and Michael Raskas
and Family

Mark and Anne Wasserman
in honor of their children
Joseph, Bailey, Erin, Rebeccah
and Jordyn

Daf Yomi shiur
in honor of their wives

Lakewood Links
in honor of
Rabbi Abish Zelishovsky

The Community of Great Neck, New York

YOUNG ISRAEL OF GREAT NECK
Rabbi Yaacov Lerner
Rabbi Eric Goldstein
Dr. Leeber Cohen
Professor Lawrence Schiffman

GREAT NECK SYNAGOGUE
Rabbi Ephraim R. Wolf ז״ל
Rabbi Dale Polakoff
Rabbi Shalom Axelrod
Rabbi Yoel Aryeh
Rabbi Yossi Singer

In Memoriam
Rabbi Ephraim R. Wolf ז״ל,
a pioneer of *harbotzas Torah,* a *kiruv* visionary, and a gifted spiritual leader. His legacy is the flourishing Torah community of Great Neck, New York.

The Community of Columbus, Ohio

In memory of **Jerome Schottenstein** Of Blessed Memory
and in honor of **Geraldine Schottenstein and Family**

Jay And Jeanie Schottenstein
Joseph, Jonathan, Jeffrey
Ann And Ari Deshe
Elie, David, Dara, Daniel
Susie And Jon Diamond
Jillian, Joshua, Jacob
Lori Schottenstein
Saul And Sonia Schottenstein

Sarah and Edward Arndt & Family
Irwin and Beverly Bain
Daniela & Yoram Benary
Liron & Alexandra, Oron, Doreen
Deborah & Michael Broidy
Michelle & Daniel
Families of Columbus Kollel
Naomi & Reuven Dessler
Sylvia & Murray Ebner & Family

Tod and Cherie Friedman
Rachel, Ross & Kara
Jim & Angie Gesler
Gerald & Karon Greenfield
Ben & Tracy Kraner & Family
Mike, Heidi, Brian, Deena & Leah Levey
Helene & Michael Lehv
Gary Narin
Ira & Laura Nutis & Family

Lea & Thomas Schottenstein & Family
Jeff & Amy Swanson
Jon
Marcy, Mark, Sam, & Adam Ungar
Drs. Philip & Julia Weinerman
Michael & Channa Weisz & Family
Dr. Daniel & Chaya Wuensch & Family
Main Street Synagogue
Howard Zack, Rabbi

The Written Word is Forever

*The Talmud Associates**

A fellowship of benefactors dedicated to
the dissemination of the Talmud

Audrey and Sargent Aborn and Family

Dr. Mark and Dr. Barbara Bell,
Bentzion Yosef and Mordechai Yehudah

The Belz Family

Richard Bookstaber and Janice Horowitz
In memory of his son

Michael and Bettina Bradfield
Gabrielle and Matthew
(London)

Nachi and Zippi Brown,
Jessica, Daniella, Shachar and Mindy
in honor of their parents and grandparents

Columbus Jewish Foundation

Milton Cooper and Family

Dr. and Mrs. David Diamond

Nahum and Feige Hinde Dicker and Family

Sophia, Alberto and Rose Djmal

Dr. Richard Dubin

Kenneth and Cochava Dubin

Dr. Martin and Esther Ehrenberg

David and Simone Eshaghian

Louis, Reuben and Larry Feder and Family

Rabbi Judah and Ruth Feinerman

In honor of
Mr. and Mrs. Yehoshua Chaim Fischman
by their children

Mayer and Ruthy Friedman
Ari, Yitzy, Suri, Dovi

Dr. Michael and Susan Friedman
לזכות בניהם, כלתם, ונכדם; בנותיהם, וחתניהם שיחי׳

Yeshaya and Perel Friedman

Julius Frishman

David and Sally Frenkel
לזכות בניהם וכלתם היקרים שיחיו:
דניאל שמואל ומאשה שושנה, אורי גבריאל, רונית פרימיט

The Furmanovich Family

Sander and Tracy Gerber
לזכות בניהם היקרים יעקב עקיבא, אסתר פערל, טליה גולדה,
חנה טובה, ורותי רבקה שיחי׳ שיתעלו בתורה ויראת שמים

Leon and Agi Goldenberg
in honor of the marriage of their children
Mendy and Estie Blau

Robert and Rita Gluck
לרפו״ש טויבא רחל בת פריידא שתחי׳

Shari and Jay Gold and Family

Dr. Martin and Shera Goldman and Family

Esther Henzel

Hirtz, Adler and Zupnick Families

Hashi and Miriam Herzka

Norman and Sandy Nissel Horowitz

Mrs. Farokh Imanuel, Kamram Imanuel
Dr. Mehran and Sepideh Imanuel
Eli and Fariba Maghen

David and Trudy Justin and Family
in honor of their parents
Zoltan and Kitty Justin

Nosson Shmuel and Ann Kahn and Family
ולזכות בניהם היקרים שיחיו:
חיים דוד, צבי מנחם, אברהם יצחק, ומשפחתם
ולכבוד אמו מרת גיטל שתחי׳ לאויוש״ט

David J. and Dora Kleinbart

In honor of
Mr. and Mrs. Label Kutoff
by their children

The Landowne Family

Ezriel and Miriam Langer

Mr. and Mrs. Chaim Leibel

Yehuda and Rasie Levi

Donald Light

Rudolph and Esther Lowy

Raphael and Blimie Manela
לזכות בניהם היקרים שיחיו:
מתתיהו, ישראל, ישעיהו, חיים משה, ושמעון

Howard and Debra Margolin and Family

Mendy and Phyllis Mendlowitz

*In formation

The Talmud Associates*

A fellowship of benefactors dedicated to
the dissemination of the Talmud

Robby and Judy Neuman and Family
לזכות בניהם היקרים שיחיו:
אברהם לייב, שרה מאטיל, מרדכי שרגא, זיסל,
שמואל שמעלקא, רחל ברכה, ישראל זכריהו ומנשה ברוך

RoAnna and Moshe Pascher
לזכות בניהם היקרים שיחיו:
נח צבי, דוד ישראל

Naftali Binyomin and Zypora Perlman
In honor of
Mr. and Mrs. Yosef Perlman עמו"ש

Kenneth Ephraim and Julie Pinczower
לרפו"ש ישראל חיים בן פייגלא שיחי'

Dr. Douglas and Vivian Rabin

Michael G. Reiff

Ingeborg and Ira Leon Rennert

Alan Jay and Hindy Rosenberg

Aviva and Oscar Rosenberg

John and Sue Rossler Family

Mr. and Mrs. David Rubin and Family

Dinah Rubinoff and Family

Ms. Ruth Russ

Mr. and Mrs. Alexander Scharf

Avi and Michou Schnur

Rubin and Marta Schron

Rivie and Leba Schwebel and Family

Shlomo Segev (Smouha)

Bernard and Chaya Shafran
לזכות בניהם היקרים שיחיו:
דבורה, יעקב חיים, דוד זאב, אסתר מנוחה

Jeffrey and Catherine Shachat
in honor of Rabbeim Howard Zack and Judah Dardik

Steven J. Shaer

Joel and Malka Shafran
לזכות בניהם היקרים שיחיו:
אשר נחמן, טובה חיה, תמר פעסיל, שרה חוה

Robin and Warren Shimoff

Nathan B. and Malka Silberman

The Soclof Family

Dr. Edward L. and Judith Steinberg

Avrohom Chaim and Elisa Taub
Hadassah, Yaakov Yehuda Aryeh, Shifra, Faige,
Devorah Raizel, and Golda Leah

Max Taub
and his son Yitzchak

Jay and Sari Tepper

Walter and Adele Wasser

Melvin, Armond and Larry Waxman

William and Noémie Wealcatch

The Wegbreit Family

Robert and Rachel Weinstein and Family

Dr. Zelig and Evelyn (Gutwein) Weinstein
Yaakov, Daniella, Aliza and Zev

Erwin and Myra Weiss

Morry and Judy Weiss

Shlomo and Esther Werdiger

Leslie M. and Shira Westreich

Willie and Blimie Wiesner

The Yad Velvel Foundation

Moshe and Venezia Zakheim

Dr. Harry and Holly Zinn

Mrs. Edith Zukor and Family

*In formation

In Memoriam — לזכרון עולם

Dedicated by the Talmud Associates
to those who forged eternal links

❖

Abraham — שמחה בן ר׳ יהודה לייב הכהן ע״ה
דוד חי ב״ר שלום הכהן ע״ה וחנה בת ר׳ עזרא ע״ה
אהרן בן חיים זאב ע״ה גאלדע בת ר׳ דוד ע״ה
Ashkenazy — ר׳ שלמה ב״ר יצחק זצ״ל ורעיתו עלי׳ מינדעל בת ר׳ יעקב ע״ה
Sarah T. Belz — שרה בת אהרן צבי הלוי ע״ה
Ben-Ari — אליעזר בן מרדכי ע״ה ושרה בת ר׳ אברהם ע״ה
Ben-Ari — מרדכי בן אליעזר ע״ה
Berber — משה ורחל
Bernath — מנשה ב״ר שמואל שמעלקא ע״ה Meizner — מרדכי חיים ב״ר זבולן יצחק חייא ע״ה
Biegeleisen — שמעון דוד ז״ל ב״ר יעקב שלמה שיחיי׳ לאוי״ט
Blitz — דוב מאיר ב״ר דוד הכהן ע״ה
Freddy Bradfield — יעקב בן צבי ע״ה
אהרן ב״ר דוד הכהן ז״ל
Cooperberg — שימה רייזל בת ר׳ אהרן שלמה ע״ה
Cooperberg — אברהם אשר בן ר׳ מאיר ע״ה
Cumsky — דוב בער בן אברהם יששכר ע״ה ופעשא מאטלא בת יוסף ע״ה
צבי טעביל בן ישראל ע״ה וליבע בת דוד ע״ה
Diamant — אשר ב״ר יהושע מרדכי הכהן ע״ה
Diamant — שרה בת ר׳ אריה ע״ה
Diamant — ר׳ דוב ב״ר משה ע״ה ורייזל בת ר׳ אברהם ע״ה
Diamond — דר. ר׳ יצחק ב״ר ברוך בענדיט ע״ה
Dicker — מרדכי צבי ב״ר יעקב ע״ה
Dicker — קיילא בת ר׳ משה ע״ה
Djmal — טופיק טוביה בן משה ושושנה ע״ה
Paul and Jeannette Dubin ע״ה
Mollie Dubinsky ע״ה
Abram B. Efroymson ע״ה
Sylvia Spira Efroymson ע״ה
Ehrenberg — אברהם בן עמנואל ע״ה ויוכבד בת ר׳ אלימלך ע״ה
Einhorn — משה בן ברוך ז״ל ורבקה נעכא בת חיים צבי ע״ה
Eshaghian — אברהם בן דוד ע״ה
Esrig — דוד בן שלמה ע״ה וחיה אייגא בת שלום ע״ה
Feder — מלכה בת ירחמיאל הכהן ע״ה
Feiden — ישראל בן אהרן ע״ה
Feinerman — אליעזר בן יוסף ע״ה ולאה בת ישראל יצחק ע״ה
יוסף בן צבי יחזקאל ע״ה ושרה בת ר׳ משה ע״ה
Freier — ישעיה צבי ב״ר חיים אלכסנדר יוסף ע״ה
Freier — שיינדל בת ר׳ משה הלוי ע״ה
Freilich — הרב יצחק דוב ב״ר אברהם יעקב ז״ל
Frenkel — גרשון בן יחיאל דוד ע״ה Rottenstreich — דוד בן עקיבא ע״ה
Friedman — ר׳ אהרן ב״ר יעקב מאיר ע״ה
Friedman — ר׳ אברהם ב״ר אלטר יצחק אייזיק ע״ה
Frishman — מרים בת ר׳ יוסף מרדכי ע״ה
Frishman — יצחק אריה ב״ר יהודה ע״ה ומרים לאה בת ר׳ יצחק ע״ה
Furmanovich — לע״נ שרה הניה בת פסח הלוי ע״ה
Furmanovich — לע״נ גדליה דב בן אברהם יואל ז״ל
Goldman — אמו, שפרה בת ר׳ קלונימוס קלמן ע״ה
Gugenheim — החבר אפרים בן רפאל ע״ה
Gugenheim — בריינדל בת החבר נתן הכהן ע״ה
Hanz — חיים בן מרדכי הי״ד
Henzel — אברהם בן ר׳ מנחם זאב ע״ה
Hirtz — אליעזר בן ישעיה ז״ל ולאה בת יוסף הלוי ע״ה
Horowitz — שלמה יהודה ב״ר זלמן יוסף הלוי ז״ל ומרים בת אברהם הכהן ע״ה
Imanuel — מרדכי בן רחמים ז״ל
Kahn — ר׳ ישראל אריה ב״ר שמואל הכהן ז״ל
Katzef — פרומה באדענה בת אלחנן ע״ה
Kleinbart — משה ב״ר אריה לייב ע״ה
Kleinbart — בתיה בת ר׳ משה אברהם ע״ה
Kriegel — רויזא מינצא בת הרב ישראל יהודה ע״ה
Kulefsky — הילד יהודה לייב ע״ה בן נתן נטע לאוי״ט
Langer — משה בן יצחק הי״ד
Landowne — שלמה בן יוסף ע״ה
Lasry — שאול ב״ר אברהם ע״ה וזהרה אסתר בת משה ע״ה
Lazar — אליעזר שאול בן זאב מאיר ע״ה
Lefkovich — ר׳ זאב וועלוול ב״ר יצחק אייזיק ע״ה
Lemberger — יצחק בן אריה ע״ה
Leibel — יחזקאל שרגא ב״ר חיים ע״ה
Leibel — רויזא בת ר׳ אברהם משה ע״ה
Levi — הרב חיים מאיר בן ר׳ מנחם ע״ה
Levi — שושנה טייבא רייזל בת ר׳ יחזקאל גרשון ע״ה
Light — משה גבריאל בן אברהם אליהו ז״ל וחנה בת נתן ע״ה
Lowy — מרדכי אריה ב״ר רפאל הלוי ז״ל ומינדל בת ר׳ שלמה זלמן ע״ה
May — ר׳ יוסף בן הרב יהודה אריה ע״ה
Miller — אלטער משה יוסף ב״ר צבי אריה ז״ל
Moskowitz — אליעזר ב״ר אברהם ברוך ז״ל וזהבה בת ר׳ משה ע״ה
Neuman — יצחק אייזיק ב״ר אהרן ע״ה
Nissel — שלמה מאיר בן הרב חיים לייב עזדיאל ז״ל
Paneth — אלטע חיה שרה ע״ה בת ר׳ פנחס שיחיי׳ לאוי״ט
Parnes — אריה לייבש בן יוסף יצחק ועטיא בת אשר ראובן ע״ה
Parnes — הרב אברהם זאב ב״ר ישכר ע״ה
Parsons — משה זלמן בן אהרן דוב ע״ה
Perlowitz — הרב משה ב״ר אליעזר הלל ע״ה
Pinczower — אפרים ב״ר ישראל חיים ופייגלא בת ר׳ יעקב ע״ה
Rabin — ישראל בן נחום ע״ה
Reiff — לוי יצחק ב״ר עזריאל ז״ל ויהודית בת ר׳ יצחק אייזיק ע״ה
Rennert — שרה בת יצחק יעקב ע״ה
Rennert — יונה מנחם בן אהרן ע״ה

In Memoriam — לזכרון עולם

Dedicated by the Talmud Associates
to those who forged eternal links

❖

Soclof — חיה ברכה בת צבי הירש הלוי ע״ה
Smouha — הרב אליהו בן מאיר הלוי ע״ה
Steir — משה בן מיכאל ע״ה
Steinberg — יצחק גדליה בן יהודה לייב ע״ה
Steinberg — מלכה בת מאיר לוי ע״ה
Stern — ר׳ חיים מאיר ב״ר שמחה ז״ל ובינה בת ר׳ יוסף מרדכי ע״ה
Tabak — שיינא רחל בת יוסף מרדכי ע״ה
Taub — ר׳ יעקב ב״ר יהודה אריה ע״ה נפ׳ ד׳ מנחם אב תשל״ט
Taub — אליעזר יוסף בן מענדל ע״ה
Taub — מענדל בן אליעזר יוסף חיה בת הירש ע״ה
Wealcatch — חיים דוב ב״ר זאב ואסתר בת ר׳ יוסף אייזיק ע״ה
Weiss — צבי בן יואל ע״ה
Weiss — גיטל בת ישראל ע״ה
Werdiger — ר׳ שלמה אלימלך ב״ר ישראל יצחק ע״ה
Westreich — הרב יהושע בן הרב יוסף יאסקא ז״ל
Leo Werter ע״ה
Wiesner — הרב שמעיה בן הרב זאב ע״ה
Wiesner — שרה לאה בת ר׳ צבי אריה ע״ה
Zakheim-Brecher — בתיה רחל ע״ה בת ר׳ משה יוסף שיחי׳ לאוי״ט
Zalstain — שמעון בן מרדכי יוסף הלוי ע״ה
Zimmer — ר׳ אברהם יעקב בן אהרן אליעזר ע״ה
הרב אהרן ב״ר מאיר יעקב ע״ה
הרבנית פרומא בת ר׳ חיים צבי ע״ה
Zinn — צבי יהודה בן שמעון ע״ה
Zinn — דבורה בת יחיאל מרדכי ע״ה
Leslie Zukor — ר׳ יצחק חיים ב״ר יוסף ע״ה
Zlatow — ר׳ שמואל דוד ב״ר מאיר יעקב ז״ל
הרב אהרן ב״ר מאיר יעקב זצ״ל
הרבנית פרומא בת ר׳ חיים צבי ע״ה
צבי יהודה ז״ל בן אברהם יצחק לאוי״ט
חיים מאיר בן שמחה ז״ל ובינה בת יוסף מרדכי הכהן ע״ה
אליעזר ב״ר אברהם ברוך ז״ל וגולדה זהבה בת משה הלוי ע״ה

Rosenberg — חיים נחמן ב״ר דוד ולאה בת יוסף ע״ה
Sam and Leah Rosenbloom ע״ה
Roth — ר׳ צבי יהודה ז״ל ב״ר אברהם יצחק שיחי׳ לאוי״ט
Roth — משה ב״ר יעקב הכהן ע״ה Weisner — יצחק ב״ר זאב ע״ה
In memory of the Sanz-Klausenburger Rebbe זצוק״ל
כ״ק אדמו״ר אבדק״ק צאנז-קלויזענבורג זי״ע
מרן הרהגה״צ ר׳ יקותיאל יהודה בהרהגה״צ ר׳ צבי זצוק״ל
נלב״ע ש״ק פ׳ חקת, ט׳ תמוז תשנ״ד
William Shachat ע״ה and Israel Ira Shachat ע״ה
Scharf — אליהו ב״ר משה יעקב ושרה בת אלכסנדר זיסקינד ע״ה
Scherman — ר׳ אברהם דוב ב״ר שמואל נטע ע״ה
Scherman — ליבא בת ר׳ זאב וואלף ע״ה
Schnur — אברהם יצחק בן אהרן הי״ד וחנה בת חיים יעקב ע״ה
Schoenbrun — שרגא פייבל ב״ר יעקב הכהן ומאטל אסתר בת מרדכי הלוי ע״ה
Schron — אליעזר דוב בן חיים משה ע״ה
Schron — חוה בת שמעון ע״ה
Schulman — חיים חייקל בן ר׳ שמואל ע״ה
Schulman — חיה בת הרב ישראל יהודה ע״ה
Schwebel — אברהם זכריה מנחם בן יוסף ומחלה בת ישראל מרדכי ע״ה
Scherman — חיים שמואל ב״ר אברהם דוב ע״ה
Scherman — הילד אברהם דוב ע״ה ב״ר זאב יוסף שיחי׳
Rose Schwartz — רייזל בת הרה״ג ר׳ אברהם יצחק ע״ה
Shafran — ר׳ יהושע ב״ר אברהם ע״ה
Shayovich — משה יעקב ב״ר נחום ועטיא פייגא בת מרדכי ע״ה
Shimoff — ר׳ ישראל דוב ב״ר אהרן יעקב ז״ל
Shimoff — חיה רבקה לאה בת ר׳ אליעזר יהודה ע״ה
Shubow — יוסף שלום בן משה ע״ה
Silberman — ר׳ צבי ב״ר זאב הלוי ע״ה
Silberman — דבורה אסתר בת ישראל ע״ה
Silbermintz — יהושע ב״ר יוסף שמריהו ע״ה
Singer — צבי בן ר׳ חיים ע״ה
Singer — הינדי בת ר׳ שלמה ע״ה
Soclof — אברהם אבא ב״ר שמריהו ע״ה

פטרוני התלמוד

We express our appreciation to the distinguished patrons
who have dedicated volumes in the

HEBREW ELUCIDATION OF THE SCHOTTENSTEIN EDITION OF THE TALMUD

מהדורת שוטנשטין

תלמוד בבלי

Dedicated by

JAY AND JEANIE SCHOTTENSTEIN

and their children

Joseph Aaron, Jonathan Richard, and Jeffrey Adam

SEDER ZERA'IM: **Mrs. Margot Guez and Family**
Paul Vivianne Michelle Hubert Monique Gerard Aline Yves

SEDER NASHIM: **Ellis A. and Altoon Safdeye and Family**

SEDER NEZIKIN: **Yisrael and Gittie Ury and Family** (Los Angeles)

BERACHOS I:	**Jay and Jeanie Schottenstein** (Columbus, Ohio)
BERACHOS II:	**Zvi and Betty Ryzman** (Los Angeles)
SHABBOS I:	**Moshe and Hessie Neiman** (New York)
SHABBOS II:	**David and Elky Retter and Family** (New York)
SHABBOS III:	**Mendy and Itta Klein** (Cleveland)
SHABBOS IV:	**Mayer and Shavy Gross** (New York)
ERUVIN I:	**The Schottenstein Family** (Columbus, Ohio)
ERUVIN II:	**The Schottenstein Family** (Columbus, Ohio)
PESACHIM I:	**Serge and Nina Muller** (Antwerp)
PESACHIM III:	**Morris and Devora Smith** (New York / Jerusalem)
YOMA I:	**Peretz and Frieda Friedberg** (Toronto)
YOMA II:	**Avi Klein and Family** (New York)
SUCCAH I:	**The Pruwer Family** (Jerusalem)
SUCCAH II:	**The Pruwer Family** (Jerusalem)
BEITZAH:	**Chaim and Chava Fink** (Tel Aviv)
ROSH HASHANAH:	**Avi and Meira Schnur** (Savyon)
TAANIS:	**Mendy and Itta Klein** (Cleveland)
MEGILLAH:	**In memory of Jerome Schottenstein ז״ל**
MOED KATTAN:	**Yisroel and Shoshana Lefkowitz** (New York)
CHAGIGAH:	**Steven and Hadassah Weisz** (New York)
YEVAMOS I:	**Phillip and Ruth Wojdyslawski** (Sao Paulo, Brazil)
YEVAMOS II:	**Phillip and Ruth Wojdyslawski** (Sao Paulo, Brazil)
YEVAMOS III:	**Phillip and Ruth Wojdyslawski** (Sao Paulo, Brazil)
KESUBOS I:	**Ben Fishoff and Family** (New York)
KESUBOS II:	**Jacob and Esther Gold** (New York)
KESUBOS III:	**David and Roslyn Lowy** (Forest Hills)
NEDARIM I:	**Soli and Vera Spira** (New York / Jerusalem)
NAZIR:	**Shlomo and Esther Ben Arosh** (Jerusalem)
SOTAH:	**Motty and Malka Klein** (New York)

פטרוני התלמוד

GITTIN I:	**Mrs. Kate Tannenbaum;** **Elliot and Debra Tannenbaum; Edward and Linda Zizmor**
KIDDUSHIN I:	**Ellis A. and Altoon Safdeye** (New York)
KIDDUSHIN II:	**Jacqui and Patty Oltuski** (Savyon)
BAVA KAMMA I:	**Lloyd and Hadassah Keilson** (New York)
BAVA KAMMA II:	**Faivel and Roiza Weinreich** (New York)
BAVA METZIA I:	**Joseph and Rachel Leah Neumann** (Monsey)
BAVA METZIA II:	**Shlomo and Tirzah Eisenberg** (Bnei Brak)
BAVA METZIA III:	**A. George and Stephanie Saks** (New York)
SANHEDRIN I:	**Martin and Rivka Rapaport** (Jerusalem)
SANHEDRIN III:	In honor of **Joseph and Anita Wolf** (Tel Aviv)
MAKKOS:	**Hirsch and Raquel Wolf** (New York)
SHEVUOS:	**Jacques and Miriam Monderer** (Antwerp)
HORAYOS-EDUYOS:	**Woli and Chaja Stern** (Sao Paulo, Brazil)
ZEVACHIM I:	**Mr. and Mrs. Eli Kaufman** (Petach Tikva)
ZEVACHIM II:	**Mr. and Mrs. Eli Kaufman** (Petach Tikva)
CHULLIN I:	**The Pluczenik Families** (Antwerp)
CHULLIN II:	**Avrohom David and Chaya Baila Klein** (Monsey)
CHULLIN III:	**Avrohom David and Chaya Baila Klein** (Monsey)
CHULLIN IV:	**The Frankel Family** (New York)
BECHOROS II:	**Howard and Chaya Balter** (New York)
ARACHIN:	**Mr. and Mrs. Eli Kaufman** (Petach Tikva)
NIDDAH I:	**Daniel and Margaret, Allan and Brocha, and David and Elky Retter and Families**

ACKNOWLEDGMENTS

We are grateful to the distinguished *roshei hayeshivah* and rabbinic leaders שליט״א in Israel and the United States whose guidance and encouragement have been indispensable to the success of this Talmud, from its inception. Their letters of approbation appear earlier in this volume.

A huge investment of time and resources was required to make this edition of the Talmud a reality. Only through the generous support of many people is it possible not only to undertake and sustain such a huge and ambitious undertaking, but to keep the price of the volumes within reach of the average family and student. We are grateful to them all.

The Trustees and Governors of the MESORAH HERITAGE FOUNDATION saw the need to support the scholarship and production of this and other outstanding works of Torah literature. Their names are listed on an earlier page.

JAY SCHOTTENSTEIN is chairman of the Board of Governors and has enlisted many others in support of this monumental project. In addition, he and his wife JEANIE have dedicated the HEBREW ELUCIDATION OF THE SCHOTTENSTEIN EDITION OF THE TALMUD and the DAF YOMI EDITION OF THE TALMUD in honor of their parents. But those are only formal identifications. The Schottensteins are deeply involved in a host of causes and their generosity is beyond description. Most recently they have undertaken sponsorship of the SCHOTTENSTEIN INTERLINEAR SERIES, which is bringing a new and innovative dimension of understanding to tefillah. Nevertheless, this Talmud is their *liebling*. They surpass every commitment to assure its continuity and it has justly become synonymous with their name.

HAGAON RAV DAVID FEINSTEIN שליט״א has been a guide, mentor, and friend since the first day of the ArtScroll Series. We are honored that, though complex halachic matters come to the Rosh Yeshivah from across the world, he regards our work as an important contribution to *harbatzas haTorah* and that he has graciously consented to be a trustee of the Foundation.

In addition, we are grateful to:

LAURENCE A. TISCH, JAMES S. TISCH and THOMAS J. TISCH, who have been more than gracious on numerous occasions; JOEL L. FLEISHMAN, Founding Trustee of the Foundation, whose sage advice and active intervention was a turning point in our work; ELLIS A. SAFDEYE, the dedicator of the SAFDEYE EDITION OF SEDER NASHIM, a legendary supporter of worthy causes and a warm, treasured friend; BENJAMIN C. FISHOFF, patron of several volumes of the Talmud, and a sensitive, visionary friend who has brought many people under the banner of this project; ZVI RYZMAN, patron of the HEBREW RYZMAN EDITION OF THE MISHNAH and of tractates in this Talmud edition, a dynamic and imaginative force for Torah life and scholarship, and a loyal, devoted friend; SOLI SPIRA, patron of Talmud volumes, who is respected on three continents for his learning and magnanimity; RABBI MEYER H. MAY, a man who devotes his considerable acumen and prestige to the service of Torah. He has been a proven and invaluable friend at many junctures; ABRAHAM BIDERMAN, a Trustee, whose achievement for Torah and community, here and abroad, are astounding; JUDAH SEPTIMUS, a Trustee, whose acumen and resources are devoted to numerous Torah causes; and RABBI SHLOMO GERTZULIN, whose competence and vision are invaluable assets to Klal Yisrael.

Loyal friends who have been instrumental in the success of our work and to whom we owe a debt of gratitude are, in alphabetical order:

Our very dear friends: RABBI RAPAHEL B. BUTLER, founder of the Afikim Foundation, a laboratory to create innovative Torah programs; RABBI ALAN CINER, whose warmth and erudition will draw Jews closer to Judaism in his new position in Palm Beach, Florida. RABBIS BUTLER and CINER were instrumental in moving this edition of the Talmud from dream to reality in its formative stage; REUVEN DESSLER, a good friend and respected leader who adds luster to a distinguished family lineage; ABRAHAM FRUCHTHANDLER, who has placed support for Torah institutions on a new plateau; LOUIS GLICK, who sponsored the ArtScroll Mishnah Series with the *Yad Avraham* commentary; SHIMMIE HORN, patron of the HORN EDITION OF SEDER MOED, a self-effacing gentleman to whom support of Torah is a priority; DAVID RUBIN, dedicator of the RUBIN EDITION OF THE PROPHETS, whose visionary generosity is a vital force in his community and beyond; SHLOMO SEGEV of Bank Leumi, who has been a responsible and effective friend; HESHE SEIF, patron of the SEIF EDITION TRANSLITERATED PRAYER BOOKS, who has added our work to his long list of important causes; NATHAN SILBERMAN, who makes his skills and judgment available in too many ways to mention; A. JOSEPH STERN, patron of the SEFARD ARTSCROLL MACHZORIM and of tractates in this Talmud edition, whose warmth and concern for people and causes are justly legendary; ELLIOT TANNENBAUM, a warm and gracious patron of several volumes, whose example has motivated many others; STEVEN WEISZ, whose infectious zeal for our work has brought many others under its banner; and HIRSCH WOLF, a valued friend from our very beginning, and an energetic, effective leader in many causes.

We are grateful, as well, to many other friends who have come forward when their help was needed most: DR. YISRAEL BLUMENFRUCHT, YERUCHAM LAX, YEHUDAH LEVI, RABBI ARTHUR SCHICK, FRED SCHULMAN, and MENDY YARMISH.

We thank RABBI YEHOSHUA LEIFER, head of KOLLEL OZ VEHADAR, for permission to reproduce the folios from their new edition of the classic Vilna Talmud. Newly typeset and with many additions and enhancements, it establishes a new standard in Talmud publishing.

We conclude with gratitude to *Hashem Yisbarach* for His infinite blessings and for the privilege of being the vehicle to disseminate His word. May this work continue so that all who thirst for His word may find what they seek in the refreshing words of the Torah.

Rabbi Nosson Scherman / Rabbi Meir Zlotowitz

Shevat 5763
January, 2003

מסכת שבת

TRACTATE SHABBOS

Chapter Three

Introduction

This chapter deals with two major topics: The first half discusses laws related to the *melachah* of בִּשּׁוּל, *cooking,* and the second half, beginning with the Mishnah on 42b, addresses the laws of *muktzeh.* We will introduce here the general principles pertinent to each of these subjects.

I. בִּשּׁוּל — *Cooking*

Cooking is a general classification that covers all conventional methods of using heat to alter the quality of an item, such as baking, roasting and frying. Indeed, in the Mishnah which lists the thirty-nine categories of *melachah* (below, 73a), this *melachah* is listed as *baking.* We will learn in this chapter that the prohibition of cooking applies even when a source of heat other than fire itself is utilized. This includes, for example, immersing an uncooked item in a pot of hot water that is no longer on the fire.

☙ Related Rabbinical Restrictions

Our chapter discusses numerous Rabbinical restrictions related to cooking, several of which warrant some introductory explanation.

A. שְׁהִיָּה — Leaving food on a fire

Since cooking is forbidden on the Sabbath, one must cook any food he intends to eat on the Sabbath before the advent of the holy day. This being the case, one who wishes to eat hot food on the Sabbath must resort to one of two devices. He must either allow the food to remain over a fire [שְׁהִיָּה, *shehiyah*], or he must wrap it while it is still hot in some insulating material [הַטְמָנָה, *hatmanah* (literally: hiding)] to preserve its heat. These acts are permitted under Biblical law. However, each of them opens up a certain possibility of a person forgetfully violating Biblical law.

Wood coal fires, if left unattended, form a crust of ash as they burn. This crust diminishes the level of heat radiated by the burning coals. Therefore, if one wishes to maintain the heat level of the fire, he must stoke the coals from time to time. The Rabbis, recognizing that people have a tendency to stoke their fires unthinkingly — an act prohibited as a form of the *melachah* of הַבְעָרָה, *kindling* — restricted the conditions under which a person may leave his pot over a fire (*shehiyah*) to those which make it unlikely for him to stoke the fire unthinkingly.[1]

B. חֲזָרָה — Returning food to a fire

Under the Biblical law of *cooking,* if a fully cooked food item was removed from the fire, one is permitted to return it [חֲזָרָה, *chazarah*] to the fire on the Sabbath.[2] However, the Rabbis restricted this activity, due to the concern described above in connection with *shehiyah,* and due to the additional concern that placing food upon a fire — even if it had previously been there — gives the *appearance* of cooking and might lead an unlearned observer to think that cooking is permitted.[3]

C. The dispute between Chananyah and the Sages

The first Mishnah of our chapter restricts placing food on a coal-burning stove to a case where the coals were shoveled away or fully covered with a layer of ash. However, it is a matter of Tannaic dispute whether the restriction of this Mishnah pertains to *shehiyah* or *chazarah.* According to Chananyah, once a food has been cooked until it is minimally edible (see 36b note 7), there are no restrictions on *shehiyah;* only *chazarah* is restricted. According to the Sages, even *shehiyah* is restricted. The focus of the Gemara's opening discussion is determining which view our Mishnah reflects. It is noteworthy that later authorities, down to and even within the *Shulchan Aruch,* are in dispute as to which opinion the halachah follows (see 37a note 16).

NOTES

1. Additional concerns led the Rabbis to restrict the conditions under which a person may insulate food (*hatmanah*). The rules of *hatmanah* are discussed in Chapter Four, and the concerns which led the Rabbis to impose those rules are described in the introduction to that chapter.

2. With respect to dry foods, this pertains even if the food has cooled off. With respect to liquids, however, it pertains only while the liquid is warm (see *Orach Chaim* 318:4, *Rama* 318:15 and *Mishnah Berurah* 318:24).

3. The concern that one might stoke the fire is even more pronounced in regard to *chazarah* than in regard to *shehiyah,* since the food is likely to cool while it is off the fire and upon returning it one might be inclined to stoke the fire to ensure that it is strong enough to reheat the food (*Sefer HaYashar* §237; see *Shulchan Aruch HaRav* §253 footnote 8 and *Ohr Same'ach, Hil. Shabbos,* introduction to ch. 3).

II. מוּקְצֶה — *Muktzeh*

The term מוּקְצֶה, *muktzeh,* literally means: set aside [from use]. It refers to a class of objects which, in the normal course of events, do not stand to be used on the Sabbath or Yom Tov. Such objects are deemed not to have been "prepared" for Sabbath use.

A. The *Muktzeh* Prohibition[4]

1. Consuming *Muktzeh*

It is prohibited to consume *muktzeh* items on the Sabbath. This prohibition is rooted in the Torah's admonition (*Exodus* 16:5): וְהָיָה בַּיּוֹם הַשִּׁשִּׁי וְהֵכִינוּ אֵת אֲשֶׁר־יָבִיאוּ, *On the sixth day they shall "prepare" what they bring,* which implies that the Sabbath food must be prepared in advance of the Sabbath. A *muktzeh* object, being "set aside" from use, is not considered מוּכָן, *prepared.*[5]

2. Moving *Muktzeh*

In addition to the prohibition against consuming *muktzeh,* there is a restriction against moving a *muktzeh* object from its place.[6] This aspect of the prohibition is clearly of Rabbinical origin.[7]

3. The dispute between R' Yehudah and R' Shimon

Although the basic restrictions of *muktzeh* are undisputed, there are differences of opinion about the extent of these restrictions. In particular, R' Yehudah and R' Shimon disagree on this matter. R' Yehudah is more stringent in the application of the *muktzeh* restrictions, whereas R' Shimon is lenient in regard to many aspects of *muktzeh* and considers fewer categories of objects "unprepared" for Sabbath use. A significant portion of this chapter (44a-46b) is devoted to defining the parameters of the dispute between these Tannaim.[8]

4. מגו דְאִיתְקְצַאי לְבֵין הַשְּׁמָשׁוֹת אִיתְקְצַאי לְכוּלֵי יוֹמָא — *Since it was muktzeh during bein hashemashos, it remains muktzeh for the entire day*

This principle states that since everything must be "prepared" for use before the Sabbath, if something was set aside throughout *bein hashemashos* (twilight) [at the onset of the Sabbath], it remains *muktzeh* for the duration of the day — even if the reason for which it was set aside no longer pertains. (See below, section B (2), for an example.) This principle is espoused by R' Yehudah. R' Shimon does not automatically consider something *muktzeh* for the entire day simply because it was unavailable for use during *bein hashemashos.*[9]

B. The Categories of *Muktzeh*

Essentially, *muktzeh* is any item that was not "prepared" [מוּכָן] for use before the Sabbath. This preparation, however, need not be active. Any object which in the normal course of events stands to be used is considered "prepared," and consequently may be consumed or moved about on the Sabbath. Only objects which, for one reason or another, do not stand to be used, are deemed *muktzeh.*

Several factors may cause an object to be deemed *muktzeh.* As mentioned above, R' Yehudah and R' Shimon disagree concerning the scope of the *muktzeh* restrictions. Their dispute finds expression in determining which factors are significant enough to make us consider an object "set aside." The following categories of *muktzeh* are discussed in this chapter; some are agreed upon unanimously whereas others are subject to dispute.[10]

NOTES

4. This section of the introduction is taken from *Chasam Sofer's* introduction to his *Mahadura Tinyana* on *Beitzah.*

5. Although the prohibition on consuming *muktzeh* is *based* on this verse, *Rambam* (*Hil. Yom Tov* 1:17) describes it as a Rabbinical ordinance. [A different Biblical law is derived from this verse in Tractate *Beitzah,* 2b.] However, *Rashi* to *Beitzah* (2b ד״ה לטעמיה and 26b ד״ה ואי דלא) indicates that the prohibition on consuming *muktzeh* is Biblical in nature.

Rashba (above, 29b) includes the *use* of *muktzeh* [הִשְׁתַּמְּשׁוּת וַהֲנָאָה בְּיָדַיִם] as part of the prohibition against consuming it. See *Magen Avraham* 501:12 and *Chidushei R' Akiva Eiger* to *Orach Chaim* 325:4; cf. *Magen Avraham* 325:9, 328:41, 507:3; see also *Beis HaLevi* 1:12 and *Kehillos Yaakov, Beitzah* §4. [Note that although the prohibition is based on a verse dealing with the Sabbath meals, *muktzeh* is not restricted to food items.]

6. For laws concerning *touching* a *muktzeh* object, see *Rema* to *Orach Chaim* 308:3 with *Mishnah Berurah.*

7. *Rambam* (*Hil. Shabbos* 24:12,13) gives three reasons for this Rabbinical enactment:

(a) The prophet (*Isaiah* 58:13) admonished . . . *restrain, because of the Sabbath, your feet . . . from seeking your personal needs* [i.e. those forbidden on the Sabbath] *or discussing the forbidden* [i.e. not to walk or talk on the Sabbath in the same manner as we do on the weekdays]. If so, we ought surely to refrain from moving about articles on the Sabbath in the manner we move them about on weekdays. This serves as a precaution that we not regard the Sabbath the same as a weekday and come to [spend our day] lifting and rearranging articles from one part of the house to another . . . or to put stones out of the way. Being at leisure and at home, one might look for something with which to occupy himself and as a result not rest at all.

(b) If it were permitted to handle utensils normally used for doing *melachos,* one might forget himself and inadvertently perform a *melachah* on the Sabbath.

(c) People who have no trade or craft . . . who do not work all week . . . would not be discerned as resting on the Sabbath. Therefore, the Rabbis added the prohibition of *muktzeh.*

Raavad (ibid.) explains that the laws of *muktzeh* were promulgated for the purpose of preventing people from inadvertently carrying from domain to domain on the Sabbath. Originally, this decree included *all* utensils. Later, it was modified to permit handling utensils used for permissible work (see below, 123b).

8. In general, R' Shimon recognizes as *muktzeh* only items that one consciously set aside from use, whereas R' Yehudah includes even those that one merely did not expect to use. See *Afikei Yam* II:19 for a comprehensive analysis of R' Shimon's view.

9. R' Shimon concedes, however, that if during *bein hashemashos* a person consciously abandoned hope of using an object for the *entire* Sabbath, it does remain *muktzeh* even if it becomes available later (see Gemara, 46b).

10. Much of the following material is taken from the introductions of *Beis Yosef* and *Mishnah Berurah* to *Orach Chaim* 308.

1. מוּקְצֶה מֵחֲמַת גופו — *muktzeh because of its intrinsic properties*

This refers to anything that is neither a utensil nor a food edible for humans or animals. It includes such things as stones, money, sand, building materials, a corpse and anything else not fit for use on the Sabbath. All agree that articles in this category are *muktzeh.*[11]

2. מוּקְצֶה מֵחֲמַת אִיסוּר — *muktzeh by dint of a prohibition*

This includes items that one was unable to use at the onset of the Sabbath without violating a prohibition. One example is the oil in a burning lamp, which cannot be removed from the lamp due to the prohibition of כִּיבּוּי, *extinguishing* (see 44a note 10). According to R' Yehudah, items in this category are *muktzeh* even after the underlying prohibition ceases to be applicable (e.g. the lamp went out). R' Shimon, however, disagrees.

3. מוּקְצֶה מֵחֲמַת מִיאוּס — *muktzeh by dint of repugnance*

This category consists of items that do not stand to be used on the Sabbath due to their repugnance. For example, a clay lamp cannot be used for its primary function of lighting, since that is prohibited on the Sabbath, and it is not commonly used for any other purpose (e.g. storing trinkets) since it cannot be cleansed of its oily deposits. R' Yehudah considers such an object *muktzeh,* but R' Shimon does not.

4. נוֹלָד — *nolad* [literally: just born]

Nolad is any object that first achieves its useful state on this Sabbath. Since it was not in a usable state prior to the Sabbath, it cannot be said to have been "prepared" before the day began. According to R' Yehudah, it is *muktzeh.* R' Shimon's view concerning this category is debated by Amoraim (see *Rosh,* end of *Beitzah*).

5. בָּסִיס לְדָבָר הָאָסוּר — *a base to a muktzeh object*

This group comprises all otherwise non-*muktzeh* articles upon which a *muktzeh* item rests, e.g. a barrel with a stone on it, or a bed upon which money is lying.[12] R' Yehudah and R' Shimon agree in principle that items in this category are *muktzeh,* but due to their dispute concerning other categories they disagree as to when an object is considered a base to *muktzeh.*

6. מוּקְצֶה לְמִצְוָתוֹ — *set aside for its mitzvah*

This refers to items that have been designated for use in a *mitzvah* of the day. Such items as the oil of the Sabbath lights and the wood and ornaments of a succah fall into this classification. All recognize items in this group as *muktzeh.* [However, this category of *muktzeh* differs significantly from the others (see 45a note 15).]

There are also several additional categories of *muktzeh,* which are not discussed in this chapter. These are:

7. מְחֻבָּר וּמְחֻסַּר צֵידָה — *attached [to the ground] or uncaptured*

This refers to any growing item, such as a fruit, vegetable, or tree, that had not been cut as of twilight. Should it become detached from its connection to the ground during the Sabbath or Yom Tov, it remains *muktzeh* for the rest of the day. Also included in this category is any animal that had not been trapped before the day began. This rule is relevant primarily to Yom Tov, when animals may be slaughtered and their meat cooked, but when they may not be trapped.[13]

8. מוּקְצֶה מֵחֲמַת חֶסְרוֹן כִּיס — *muktzeh for fear of monetary loss*

This category includes any utensil whose general use the owner objects to, out of concern that it will become damaged; for example, a barber's razor. Though the owner certainly uses this utensil for its primary function, that function is prohibited on the Sabbath. Since these blades must be kept perfectly sharp, the owner objects to their being used for any secondary, permissible function (e.g. as a table knife) for fear of damaging the cutting edge. Another example of this category is the special knife used to slaughter animals. This, however, is *muktzeh* only for the Sabbath, but not for Yom Tov when slaughtering is permitted.[14]

9. כְּלִי שֶׁמְּלַאכְתּוֹ לְאִסוּר — *a utensil used primarily for work prohibited on the Sabbath*

This includes any utensil (such as a hammer) whose primary use (building) is forbidden on the Sabbath, but which is also occasionally used for permissible activities, such as cracking nuts. Since the items in this category are not easily damaged, the owner does not object to their being used for these secondary purposes. The *muktzeh* restriction is therefore somewhat relaxed for the items of this category. They may be moved about and used in certain instances. Chapter Seventeen of our tractate focuses on these rules and we will leave our elaboration for the introduction to that chapter.[15]

NOTES

11. See *Kehillos Yaakov, Beitzah* §4, for a discussion of why there is no dispute concerning this category.

12. In order for an item to become a *base to muktzeh,* the *muktzeh* object must have been placed on it intentionally. According to *Rashi* (below, 51a ד״ה הרי זה נוטל ומחזיר), it suffices for the *muktzeh* item to have been placed on it with intent that it remain there until past the onset of the Sabbath. According to *Tosafos* (51a ד״ה או; cf. *Tosafos* to *Beitzah* 2a ד״ה ובית הלל), the *muktzeh* item must have been placed on the base with intent that it remain there for the entire Sabbath. Both views are represented in *Shulchan Aruch, Orach Chaim* 309:4. See *Mishnah Berurah* there §21 and *Chidushei R' Akiva Eiger* to 125b.

If the *muktzeh* item was not on the base at the onset of the Sabbath, but was placed there during the Sabbath (e.g. by a non-Jew), *Magen Avraham* (265:2) rules that the base does not become a *base to muktzeh* at all. *R' Akiva Eiger* (ad loc.), however, disputes this point. See 43a note 20. See also *Rosh Yosef* to 47a.

13. This category of *muktzeh* is discussed in the third chapter of *Beitzah.*

14. This type of *muktzeh* is discussed below, in Chapter Seventeen.

15. However, a utensil that has no permissible function at all on the Sabbath is considered intrinsically *muktzeh* and may not be moved at all (see *Pri Megadim — Eishel Avraham* 308:12 and *Avnei Nezer, Orach Chaim* §55; see also *Shulchan Aruch HaRav* 308:2 and Gemara, end of 46a). [According to *Tehillah LeDavid* 308:8, this point is the subject of disagreement between *Baal HaMaor* and *Rashba* below, 154b.]

מסורת הש"ס

א) לעיל כ., ב) [דף לד:], ג) [דף עא:], ד) [וע"ע תוס' ב"מ קג. ד"ה המקבל].

עין משפט נר מצוה

א א ב ג מיי' פ"ג מהל' שבת הלכה ד ה סמג לאוין סה טוש"ע א"ח סי' רנג סעיף א:

גמרא

למאי נפקא מינה לגיטי נשים:

הדרן עלך במה מדליקין

כירה [א]שהסיקוה בקש ובגבבא נותנים עליה תבשיל בגפת ובעצים לא יתן עד שיגרוף או עד שיתן את האפר בית שמאי אומרים חמין אבל לא תבשיל ובית הלל אומרים חמין ותבשיל בית שמאי אומרים נוטלין אבל לא מחזירין ובית הלל אומרים אף מחזירין: **גמ'** איבעיא להו האי לא יתן לא יחזיר הוא אבל לשהות משהין אף על פי שאינו גרוף ואינו קטום ומני חנניה היא דתניא [א] חנניה אומר [ב]כל שהוא כמאכל בן דרוסאי מותר לשהותו על גבי כירה אע"פ שאינו גרוף ואינו קטום או דילמא [ג]לשהות תנן ואי גרוף וקטום אין אי לא לא וכל שכן להחזיר ת"ש מדקתני תרי בבי במתני' ב"ש אומרים חמין אבל לא תבשיל ובית הלל אומרים חמין ותבשיל ב"ש אומרים נוטלין אבל לא מחזירין וב"ה אומרים אף מחזירין אי אמרת בשלמא לשהות תנן הכי קתני כירה שהסיקוה בקש ובגבבא משהין עליה תבשיל בגפת ובעצים לא ישהא עד שיגרוף או עד שיתן אפר ומה הן משהין בית שמאי אומרים חמין אבל לא תבשיל וב"ה אומרים חמין ותבשיל וכי היכי דפליגי בלשהות פליגי נמי בלהחזיר שבית שמאי אומרים נוטלין אבל לא מחזירין ובית הלל אומרים אף מחזירין אלא אי אמרת להחזיר תנן הכי קתני כירה שהסיקוה בקש ובגבבא מחזירין עליה תבשיל בגפת ובעצים לא יחזיר עד שיגרוף או עד שיתן אפר ומה הן מחזירין בית שמאי אומרים חמין אבל לא תבשיל ובית הלל אומרים חמין ותבשיל בית שמאי אומרים נוטלין אבל לא מחזירין ובית הלל אומרים אף מחזירין הא [א] תו למה לי
לעולם

רש"י

לגיטי נשים. דקיימא לן בני בבל בקיאין שצריך לכתוב גט לשמה והמביא גט משם אין צריך לומר בפני נכתב ובפני נחתם ובני שאר ארצות אין בקיאין וצריך ועכשיו בני בורסיף היא בבל ובבל של עכשיו היא בורסיף והן עמי הארץ כדאמרינן בעלמא (סנהדרין דף קט.) בור שאפי שנטלו מימיו ואני אומר נפקא מינה לגיטי נשים לענין שינה שמו ושמה ושם עירו ועירה פסול וצריך לכתוב שם של עכשיו:

הדרן עלך במה מדליקין

כירה. עשויה כעין קדירה ונותנין קדירה לתוכה: קש. זנבות השבולין: **גבבא.** הנגבב מן השדה אישטובל"א: **גפת.** פסולת של שומשמין שהוציא שומנן: **עד שיגרוף.** הגחלים משום דמוסיף הבל וטעמא פרישנא בפרק דלעיל [ג] שמא יחתה בגחלים: **או עד שיתן אפר.** על גבי גחלים לכסותם ולכננס: **בית שמאי אומרים.** נותנין עליה חמין אחר שגרפה דלא צריכי לבשולי דליכא למגזר שמא יחתה: **אבל לא תבשיל.** דניחא ליה בישוליה ואתי לאחתויי א"נ נתקיימה מחשבתו ומיחזי כמבשל (א): **לא מחזירין.** בשבת דמיחזי כמבשל: **אף מחזירין.** הואיל וגרוף: **גמ'** קטום. היינו נתן אפר על הגחלים דאפר מתרגמינן קיטמא: **תרי בבי.** בית שמאי אומרים חמין וכו' ותו תנא בבא אחריתי נוטלין ולא מחזירין: **ומה הן משהין.** בגרוף וקטום: **פליגי נמי בלהחזיר.** את המותר לשהות כגון חמין לבית שמאי וחמין ותבשיל לב"ה: **אלא אי אמרת להחזיר תנן הכי קתני.** כלומר ע"כ הכי מפרשא: **ב"ש אומרים נוטלין ולא מחזירין.** ע"כ אתבשיל קיימי דהא שרו בחמין: **הא תו למה לי.** הא תנא ליה רישא אבל לא תבשיל:
לעולם

תוספות

נפקא מינה לגיטי נשים. מה שפי' בקונטרס לענין שינה שם עירו ושם עירה אין נראה לרשב"א דבבל הוא שם מדינה ולא שם העיר כדאמר בפרק עשרה יוחסין (קדושין דף עא.) כל הארצות עיסה לארץ ישראל וארץ ישראל עיסה לבבל וקאמר נמי התם [ג] עד היכן היא בבל ולא אשכחן שום דוכתא עיר ששמה בבל אלא מדינה היא ואין כותבין שם מדינה בגט:

הדרן עלך במה מדליקין

כירה שהסיקוה בקש ובגבבא. נראה לר"י דקש היינו זנבות השבולים שנשאר בשדה הנקרא אשטובל"א בלעז ותבן הוא הנקצר עם השבולת דהכי משמע לקמן בפרק שואל (לקמן דף קנ:) דקאמר בשלמא קש משכחת לה במחובר אלא תבן היכי משכחת לה ומסיק בתבנא סריא והא דאמר בריש המקבל (בבא מציעא דף קג.) גבי מקום שנהגו לקצור אינו רשאי לעקור משום דאמר ניחא לי דתיתבן ארעאי הוה ליה למימר דתיתקש דהנשאר בקרקע נקרא קש כדפירש רש"י אלא משום דתיתבן משמע טפי לשון זיבול נקט ליה [ד]: **לא** יתן עד שיגרוף. פירש בקונטרס משום תוספת הבל ואין נראה לר"י דאפילו גרופה וקטומה היא מוספת הבל יותר מכמה דברים השנויין בבמה טומנין ועוד דחנניה שרי להשהות אף כשאינה גרופה ולא אסרו מוסיף הבל אלא דוקא בהטמנה אבל להשהות שרי וכשאינה גרופה אסרי רבנן דחנניה משום דילמא אתי לאחתויי:

חמין ותבשיל. נראה לר"י דסתם חמין ותבשיל היינו אפי' לא בשיל כל צרכו אלא כמאכל בן דרוסאי דהא כי מוקי מתניתין להחזיר תנן הוי מתניתין כחנניה דשרי חמין ותבשיל להשהות על גבי כירה אפילו בשאינה גרופה אפילו לא בשיל כל צרכו ולא כרבנן ואמאי ודילמא מתניתין אפילו כרבנן ומתני' בחמין ותבשיל שנתבשלו כל צרכן דמודו רבנן דמשהין ע"ג כירה שאינה גרופה וקטומה אלא ודאי משום דסתם חמין ותבשיל כמאכל בן דרוסאי נמי משמע ומיהו סתם חמין ותבשיל הוי נמי בשיל כל צרכו כדמוכח בסוף שמעתין (דף לח.) גבי קשיא דרבי מאיר אדרבי מאיר אע"פ שיש לדחות ושם אפרש בע"ה ואפילו אי סתם חמין ותבשיל לא הוה בשיל כל צרכו צריך לומר הא דאסרי בית שמאי להחזיר היינו אפילו חמין שהוחמו כל צרכן וכן לבית הלל באינה גרופה מדקאמר בגמרא (דף לח:) ואף רבי אושעיא סבר מחזירין אפילו בשבת דאמר רבי אושעיא פעם אחת כו' והעלנו לו קומקומוס של חמין ומזגנו לו את הכוס והחזרנוהו למקומו ואי לא אסיר בהוחמו כל צרכן מנא ליה דמחזירין אפילו בשבת דילמא הוחם כל צורכו הוה ואם תאמר ואם סתם חמין ותבשיל הוי בין בשיל כל צרכו בין לא בשיל אם כן סברי בית שמאי מצטמק ויפה לו אסור כיון דאסיר תבשיל שבישל כל צרכו ואם כן היכי שרי חמין שלא הוחמו כל צרכן והא יפה לו הוא ואור"י דודאי תבשיל אסרי בית שמאי משום דלעולם יפה לו אע"ג דנתבשל כל צרכו אבל חמין שאין יפה להם אלא עד כדי צרכן אבל מכאן ואילך רע להן כדמוכח לקמן לא אסרי בית שמאי דליכא למיגזר שמא יחתה דבלא חיתוי יוחמו כל צרכן: **וב"ה** אומרים אף מחזירין. אפילו בשבת מחזירין [ב] כדאמר בגמרא ולשון נוטלין נמי משמע דבשבת מיירי דבחול לא הוה צריך למיתני נוטלין ולמאן דאסר להחזיר אסר אפילו בחול לבית הלל כשאינה גרופה ולבית שמאי אפי' בגרופה מדקאמר בגמרא לדברי האומר מחזירין מחזירין אפילו בשבת משמע דעיקר פלוגתא הוי בחול ועוד מדקדק ר"ת מדקאמר לא יתן עד שיגרוף ואי לא יתן לא יחזיר בשבת הוא איך יגרוף או יקטום בשבת [°] והוה ליה למימר אלא אם כן גרף וקטם אלא בחול נמי אסור להחזיר וא"ת מה שיעור הוא נותן לאסור בע"ש דהיכא דסלקו בהשכמה פשיטא דשרי להחזיר ואומר ר"י דמשעה שלא יוכלו להרתיחו מבעוד יום אסור להחזיר ומיהו בשבת אפילו רותח אסור להחזיר למאן דאסר דאי לאו הכי מנא ליה דרבי אושעיא סבר מחזירין אפילו בשבת דילמא קומקמוס של חמין רותח הוה ועוד אומר ר"י דמצינו למימר דבערב שבת נמי אסור להחזיר אפילו רותח משעה שאם היה קר לא היה יכול להרתיח מבע"י וקשה לרשב"א היכי שרי להחזיר קדרה על גבי כירה בשבת והא אמר בפרק המביא כדי יין (ביצה דף לג: ושם) דבילים וקדרה וחביתא ופוריא מלמטה למעלה אסור משום אהל ואור"י דכי אסרו חכמים אהל עראי ה"מ כשעושה הדפנות תחלה ואח"כ הכיסוי אבל הכא שדופני הכירה כבר עשויות מאליהן לא אחמור רבנן לאסור ליתן קדרה על גבה ומיהו הא דאמר בהמוצא תפילין (עירובין דף קב.) גבי דיכרי דרב הונא דאמר ליה כרוך בודיא ושייר בה טפח למחר מוסיף על אוהל עראי הוא משמע דבלא שיור אסור אע"ג דהדפנות כבר עשויות אור"י התם משום דדמי אהל טפי אסור אפי' בלא עשיית דפנות אבל קדרה דלא דמי אהל כולי האי לא אסרו חכמים בלא עשיית דפנות:
לעולם

גליון הש"ס

תוס' ד"ה וב"ה אומרים וכו' והל"ל אא"כ גרף. לענ"ד הא מצינו כזה במו"ק דף ד ע"ב עד שיעמיק כו' כגון שהעמיק:

הגהות הב"ח

(א) רש"י ד"ה אבל לא תבשיל וכו' כמבשל הס"ד ואח"כ מ"ה אבל לא:

רבינו חננאל

פ"ג **כירה** שהסיקוה בקש ובגבבא וכו'. **כירה** זו היא מקום שפיתת ב' קדרות. **איבעיא** להו הא דתנינן לא יתן עד שיגרוף. או עד שיתן האפר על גבי גחלים נתינה זו בע"ש וקמ"ל דאסור לשהות ע"ג כירה אא"כ גרופה וקטומה או דילמא נתינה זו החזרת הקדירה היא בשבת וקמ"ל דאסור להחזיר אלא ע"ג כירה קטומה או גרופה אבל לשהות מותר. ומתני' מני חנניה היא דתניא כל שהוא כמאכל בן דרוסאי מותר לשהותו על גבי כירה אע"פ שאינה גרופה ולא קטומה.

רב נסים גאון

נפקא מינה לגיטי נשים. כלומר בדאלך א) המביא גט מבבל או מבורסיף אין צריך לומר בפני נכתב ובפני נחתם לדבריהם שאמרו במסכת גיטין בפר' א' (דף ו) בבל רב אמר כארץ ישראל לגיטין מכי אתא רב לבבל ובפרק עשרה יוחסין (דף עב) היכא חביל ימא אמר רב פפא סבא משמיה דרב זו פרת בורסיף ובבראשית דר' אושעיא (פרשה לח) חד תלמיד ר' יוחנן הוה יתיב קדמוי הוה מסבר ליה ולא סבר אמר ליה מה דין לית את סבר אמר ליה דאנא גלי מן אתראי אמר ליה מן הדין אתר את אמר ליה מן בורסיף אמר ליה לא תאמר כן אלא בולסיף שנאמר (בראשית יא) כי שם בלל ה' שפת כל הארץ ובגמרא דכל ישראל יש להן חלק (סנהדרין דף קט) אמרו אמר רב יוסף בבל בורסיף סימן רע לתורה מאי בורסיף אמר רב אסי בור ספת ואדוננו האיי ז"ל אמר בבל בורסיף ובורסיף בבל כוונת דבר זה לאותה ששנינו במשנה שינה שמו ושמה שם עירו ושם עירה פסול הרי נודע כי בבל ובורסיף עיר אחת הן והגט כשר:
סליק פרק במה מדליקין

הגהות על רנ"ג
א) פירושו בזה:

תוספות ישנים

א) ולא רצה לומר דתנא רישא דאפילו בחול אין מחזירין לב"ש כדמשמע עד שיגרוף וסיפא קתני דאפילו בשבת מחזירין לב"ה כדמשמע נוטלין. דבלאו תרי בבא סברא הוא דבתרוייהו פליגי דהא אי להשהות תנן ליכא אלא חד בבא בהחזרה. ומהר"מ אומר דאי משום ב"ה תני סיפא לא ה"ל למיתני דברי בית שמאי:

ב) ומיהו רש"י פי' בגמרא מחזירין אפילו בשבת למחרת דנראה דאין דעתו להחזיר ובטלה הטמנה אבל בלילה אין נראה כן:

ליקוטי רש"י

לגיטי נשים. דקיימא לן (גיטין ב.) המביא גט מחוצה לארץ צריך שיאמר בפני נכתב ובפני נחתם אי משום דאין מצויין לקיימו ואי משום דאין בקיאין לשמה והמביא מארץ ישראל אינו צריך לפי שבקיאין לשמה ועולי רגלים מצויין להכיר חתימת עדים לקיימו ואמרינן התם (גיטין ו.) בבל כארץ ישראל לגיטין לפי שהן בני תורה ובקיאין לשמה ובני ישיבה מצויין לילך וללמוד משם תורה מכל מקומות ובורסיף סמוך לבבל ואינן בני תורה כדאמרינן (סנהדרין קט.) מאי בורסיף בור שאפו את מימיו ולא נשתייר בו כלום והמביא משם צריך שיאמר אבל עכשיו נתחלף שמם הלכך המביא מבבל צריך שיאמר ומבורסיף אין צריך [סוכה לד:].

כירה. יש בה שפיתת שתי קדירות [לקמן לח: עיין מו"ק י. ובב"ח שם, נדה כו. ובתוס' שם: ד"ה בפלוגתא]. פתוחה מתנור ואין מבעירין בתוכה אש גדול [ב"ק סא.]. כלי חרס ששופתים קדירה על חללה ואין עושין בתוכה היסק גדול כמו שעושין בתנור [ב"ב כ: וע"ש בתוי"ט פ"ב מ"ב]. **קש.** זנבות שבולין אשטריי"ס [לעיל לה.]. **גפת.** פסולת של בית הבד של שמן שהוא כנוס יחד וחם מאד [לקמן מז:]. פסולת זיתים שנתעצרו בבית הבד [ב"ב יז.]. **עד שיגרוף.** מן הגחלים במגריפה שקורין וודיל"י. **שיתן את האפר.** מפזרים אפר מלמעלה כדי להפיג חומו שלא יוסיף הבל בשבת [לעיל כ.]. **חמין.** מים חמים למזוג בהן יין לשתות [שם לה:]. **בן דרוסאי.** לסטים היה ומבשל בישולו שליש [שם כ.]. לסטים היה ואוכל כל דבר המבושל קצת [ע"ז לח.]. **מותר להשהותו.** לא חיישי' אם מתבשל והולך בשבת [לעיל שם].

Chapter Three

Mishnah The Mishnah outlines the circumstances in which one may place food on a *kirah*-type stove:[1] כִּירָה שֶׁהִסִּיקוּהָ בְּקַשׁ וּבִגְבָבָא – Concerning **a *kirah* that was heated with straw or with stubble,** נוֹתְנִים עָלֶיהָ תַּבְשִׁיל – **one may place a cooked food upon it.**[2] בְּגֶפֶת וּבְעֵצִים – If it was heated **with marc**[3] **or with wood,** לֹא יִתֵּן – **one may not place** a cooked food upon it עַד שֶׁיִּגְרוֹף – **until he has shoveled away** the coals, אוֹ עַד שֶׁיִּתֵּן אֶת הָאֵפֶר – **or until he has put ash** over them.[4]

The Mishnah cites a dispute concerning what may be placed on a *kirah* whose coals were shoveled or covered with ash:

בֵּית שַׁמַּאי אוֹמְרִים – **Beis Shammai say:** חַמִּין אֲבָל לֹא תַבְשִׁיל – We may place **hot water but not cooked food** on the *kirah.* וּבֵית הִלֵּל אוֹמְרִים – **But Beis Hillel say:** חַמִּין וְתַבְשִׁיל – We may place both **hot water and cooked food** on it.[5]

NOTES

1. A *kirah* is a rectangular stove that is open on top and is large enough to accommodate two pots. The pots may be placed inside the *kirah,* either directly on the coals or suspended above them, or on the rim or cover of the *kirah* (*Rashi* here and 37a ד״ה מהו לסמוך and ד״ה גבה, and Gemara 38b; see also *Baal HaMaor* and *Tur Orach Chaim* 253 with *Beis Yosef* and *Bach*). A *kirah* is distinguished from a *tanur* [תַּנּוּר], which is a trapezoidal oven, and a *kupach* [כּוּפָּח], which is a cubical stove that accommodates only one pot. These produce more intense heat than a *kirah* and are subject to different rules, which are set forth in the next Mishnah, on 38b.

Most modern ovens have their openings on the side and do not retain heat as well as the *tanur* or *kupach;* thus, they are most comparable to the *kirah.* It is therefore these laws which apply to them (*Rama, Orach Chaim* 253:1; see also *Ran* to 38b). Similarly, the tops of our gas ranges and electric stoves are governed by the rules of a *kirah* (*Igros Moshe, Orach Chaim* vol. I §93; vol. IV §74 *bishul* 26).

The Mishnah sets forth various restrictions on placing cooked food on a *kirah.* As we shall see, the Gemara offers two very different interpretations of the Mishnah, based on a dispute between Chananyah and the Sages. According to one interpretation, these restrictions pertain to *leaving* a pot of cooked food on the *kirah* before the Sabbath so that it will continue to stew on the Sabbath, i.e. *shehiyah.* According to the other interpretation, leaving cooked food on a *kirah* before the Sabbath is generally permitted. Rather, the Mishnah's restrictions pertain to *returning* to the *kirah,* on the Sabbath, a pot of cooked food that had been left there before the Sabbath and was later removed; i.e. *chazarah* (*returning* the pot to the fire).

2. Straw is the upper part of the grain stalk, which is harvested together with the grain. Stubble is the lower part of the stalk, which remains attached to the ground after the harvest (see *Rashi* here and below, 140a ד״ה תבן; cf. *Tosafos* ד״ה כירה; see *Rosh Yosef*). If either straw or stubble was used as the fuel for the flame of a *kirah,* we may place a pot of cooked food on the *kirah.* This means either that we may place it there on Friday in order that it remain there and stay hot on the Sabbath, or that we may replace it on the *kirah* on the Sabbath itself (see Gemara).

A straw- or stubble-fueled *kirah* is not hot enough to raise the temperature of the food and advance the cooking process. Rather, it suffices merely to keep the food hot (*Rashba,* explaining *Rashi;* cf. *Rambam, Hil. Shabbos* 3:4). In this circumstance, placing cooked food on the *kirah* is permitted, as will be explained in note 4.

[The expression *cooked food* in our context does not necessarily denote food that has already been completely cooked; rather, it means a type of food whose preparation requires cooking. See Gemara.]

3. Marc is the pulp that remains after fruits have been pressed. In our Mishnah, it refers to olive and sesame pulp. After the oil has been extracted, the residue can be used for fuel (*Rav;* see *Rashi;* Gemara, 47b; *Chidushei R' Akiva Eiger* to *Orach Chaim* 253:1; *Mishnah Berurah* 253:3).

4. Before the Sabbath (see *Tosafos* ד״ה וב״ה). When an oven is heated with marc or wood, the embers remaining after the fire has gone out radiate enough heat to raise the temperature of the food and cook it further. Unless the coals are shoveled away or covered with ash to reduce their heat, it is forbidden to place any cooked food in or on top of the oven. The reason is, as the Gemara explained above (top of 34b), that we are concerned that someone might stoke the embers on the Sabbath in order to make the food cook better. This concern does not apply to a straw- or stubble-fueled *kirah,* which is incapable of cooking once the fire has gone out (*Rashi,* as explained by *Rosh Yosef;* see *Beur Halachah* 253:1 ד״ה ליתן עליה).

Covering the coals with ash means spreading ash over all the coals to cool them, so that the *kirah* is no longer hot enough to cook (see *Rashi* here and to 20a ד״ה קטום). Shoveling, according to most commentators, means removing all the coals from the *kirah* (*Ramban* et al.; see *Mishnah Berurah* 253:13 with *Shaar HaTziyun* and see *Rashi* to 20a ד״ה גרוף; cf. *Baal HaMaor, Rav, Rosh Yosef*).

The Rishonim almost unanimously object to *Rashi's* explanation that our Mishnah restricts placing food in a marc- or wood-fueled *kirah* because the coals will heat the food and cook it further. They contend that even if the coals are shoveled away or covered with ash the *kirah* remains hot enough to cook the food. Furthermore, the Gemara above (top of 34b) which *Rashi* cited as the basis for his explanation does not deal with placing a pot of food on a *kirah* (i.e. *shehiyah* or *chazarah*), but with wrapping a heated pot in a material that insulates it (i.e. *hatmanah*). It is concerning *hatmanah* that we differentiate between materials that merely keep food warm and materials that heat it further. We forbid insulating in materials that supply heat out of concern that one might insulate a pot in hot ash containing glowing embers, which he might stoke. With regard to placing food on a *kirah,* however, we need be concerned not with whether the *kirah* is hot enough to cook the food but simply with whether it contains coals that a person might unthinkingly stoke. Thus, it is permitted to leave food on a straw- or stubble-fueled *kirah* because straw and stubble leave behind little or no coals, but it is forbidden to leave food on a marc- or wood-fueled *kirah* (unless the Mishnah's guidelines are followed) because marc and wood leave behind coals that one might forgetfully stoke. The purpose of shoveling the coals away or covering them with ash is to demonstrate that one is not interested in cooking the food, but merely in keeping it warm. This allays the concern that one might stoke them (see *Tosafos* ד״ה לא יתן; *Rambam, Hil. Shabbos* 3:4 et al.). For defenses of *Rashi's* opinion, see *Pnei Yehoshua* and *Rosh Yosef.*

5. Beis Shammai maintain that only hot water that is fully cooked and merely requires being kept warm may be left on a *kirah* that was shoveled or banked (i.e. covered with ash), since in this case there is no reason for anyone to stoke the coals. In the case of food, however, which improves through stewing on the *kirah* even after it is fully cooked, one might come to stoke the coals even if they were shoveled or banked. [Although "shoveling" means removing all the coals, the concern exists that some embers might be left behind and the person might stoke them (*Rav;* cf. *Ran*).] Alternatively, Beis Shammai prohibit placing cooked food on a *kirah* because this presents the appearance of cooking on the Sabbath. Beis Hillel, however, hold that once an appropriate measure to reduce the heat has been taken, there is no concern for stoking even if a cooked food is left on the *kirah,* and there is also no concern for the appearance of cooking (*Rashi,* as explained by *Rashba* and *Rosh Yosef;* see *Pnei Yehoshua*).

[Others explain that Beis Shammai allow leaving even water that is partially cooked on a shoveled or banked *kirah.* Since water heats up easily, and once fully heated does not improve by stewing, there is never a concern for stoking if the *kirah* was shoveled or banked (*Tosafos*).]

למאי נפקא מינה לגיטי נשים:

הדרן עלך במה מדליקין

כירה [א]שהסיקוה בקש ובגבבא נותנים עליה תבשיל בגפת ובעצים לא יתן עד שיגרוף או עד שיתן את האפר בית שמאי אומרים חמין אבל לא תבשיל ובית הלל אומרים חמין ותבשיל בית שמאי אומרים נוטלין אבל לא מחזירין ובית הלל אומרים אף מחזירין: **גמ'** איבעיא להו האי לא יתן לא יחזיר הוא אבל לשהות משהין אף על פי שאינו גרוף ואינו קטום ומני חנניה היא דתניא [א]חנניה אומר [ב]כל שהוא כמאכל בן דרוסאי מותר לשהותו על גבי כירה אע"פ שאינו גרוף ואינו קטום או דילמא [ג]לשהות תנן ואי גרוף וקטום אין אי לא לא וכל שכן להחזיר ת"ש מדקתני תרי בבי במתני' ב"ש אומרים חמין אבל לא תבשיל ובית הלל אומרים חמין ותבשיל ב"ש אומרים נוטלין אבל לא מחזירין וב"ה אומרים אף מחזירין אי אמרת בשלמא לשהות תנן הכי קתני כירה שהסיקוה בקש ובגבבא משהין עליה תבשיל בגפת ובעצים לא ישהא עד שיגרוף או עד שיתן אפר ומה הן משהין בית שמאי אומרים חמין אבל לא תבשיל וב"ה אומרים חמין ותבשיל וכי היכי דפליגי בלשהות פליגי נמי בלהחזיר שבית שמאי אומרים נוטלין אבל לא מחזירין ובית הלל אומרים אף מחזירין אלא אי אמרת להחזיר תנן הכי קתני כירה שהסיקוה בקש ובגבבא מחזירין עליה תבשיל בגפת ובעצים לא יחזיר עד שיגרוף או עד שיתן אפר ומה הן מחזירין בית שמאי אומרים חמין אבל לא תבשיל ובית הלל אומרים חמין ותבשיל בית שמאי אומרים נוטלין אבל לא מחזירין ובית הלל אומרים אף מחזירין הא א) תו למה לי

לעולם

רש"י

לגיטי נשים. דקיימא לן בני בבל בקיאין שצריך לכתוב גט לשמה והמביא גט משם אין צריך לומר בפני נכתב ובפני נחתם ובני שאר ארצות אין בקיאין וצריך ועכשיו בני בורסיף היא בבל ובבל של עכשיו היא בורסיף והן עמי הארץ כדאמרינן בעלמא (סנהדרין דף קט.) בור שאפי שנטלו מימיו ואני אומר נפקא מינה לגיטי נשים לענין שינה שמו ושמה ושם עירו ועירה פסול וצריך לכתוב שם של עכשיו:

הדרן עלך במה מדליקין

כירה. עשויה כעין קדירה ונותנין קדירה לתוכה: **קש.** זנבות השבולין: **גבבא.** הנגבב מן השדה אישטובל"א: **גפת.** פסולת של שומשמין שהוציא שומנן: **עד שיגרוף.** הגחלים משום דמוסיף הבל וטעמא פרישנא בפרק דלעיל [ג] שמא יחתה בגחלים: **או עד שיתן אפר.** על גבי גחלים לכסותם ולכננס: **בית שמאי אומרים.** נותנין עליה חמין אחר שגרפה דלא צריכי לבשולי דליכא למגזר שמא יחתה: **אבל לא תבשיל.** דניחא ליה בישוליה ואתי לאחתויי א"נ נתקיימה מחשבתו ומיחזי כמבשל (א): **לא מחזירין.** בשבת דמיחזי כמבשל: **אף מחזירין.** הואיל וגרוף: **גמ' קטום.** היינו נתן אפר על הגחלים דאפר מתרגמינן קיטמא: **תרי בבי.** בית שמאי אומרים חמין וכו' ותו תנא בבא אחריתי נוטלין ולא מחזירין: **ומה הן משהין.** בגרוף וקטום: **פליגי נמי בלהחזיר.** את המותר לשהות כגון חמין לבית שמאי וחמין ותבשיל לב"ה: **אלא אי אמרת להחזיר תנן הכי קתני.** כלומר ע"כ הכי מפרשא: **ב"ש אומרים נוטלין ולא מחזירין.** ע"כ אתבשיל קיימי דהא שרו בחמין: **הא תו למה לי.** הא תנא ליה רישא אבל לא תבשיל:

לעולם

תוספות

נפקא מינה לגיטי נשים. מה שפי' בקונטרס לענין שינה שם עירו ושם עירה אין נראה לרשב"א דבבל הוא שם מדינה ולא שם העיר כדאמר בפרק עשרה יוחסין (קדושין דף עא.) כל הארצות עיסה לארץ ישראל וארץ ישראל עיסה לבבל וקאמר נמי התם [ג] עד היכן היא בבל ולא אשכחן שום דוכתא עיר ששמה בבל אלא מדינה היא ואין כותבין שם מדינה בגט:

הדרן עלך במה מדליקין

כירה שהסיקוה בקש ובגבבא. נראה לר"י דקש היינו זנבות השבולים שנשאר בשדה הנקרא אשטובל"א בלעז ותבן הוא הנקצר עם השבולת דהכי משמע לקמן בפרק שואל (לקמן דף קנ:) דקאמר בשלמא קש משכחת לה במחובר אלא תבן היכי משכחת לה ומסיק בתבנא סריא והא דאמר בריש המקבל (בבא מציעא דף קג.) גבי מקום שנהגו לקצור אינו רשאי לעקור משום דאמר ניחא לי דתיתבן ארעאי הוה ליה למימר דתיתקש דהנשאר בקרקע נקרא קש כדפירש רש"י אלא משום דתיתבן משמע טפי לשון זיבול נקט ליה [ד]: **לא** יתן עד שיגרוף. פירש בקונטרס משום תוספת הבל ואין נראה לר"י דאפילו גרופה וקטומה היא מוספת הבל יותר מכמה דברים השנויין בבמה טומנין ועוד דחנניה שרי להשהות אף כשאינה גרופה ולא אסרו מוסיף הבל אלא דוקא בהטמנה אבל להשהות שרי וכשאינה גרופה אסרי רבנן דחנניה משום דילמא אתי לאחתויי:

חמין ותבשיל. נראה לר"י דסתם חמין ותבשיל היינו אפי' לא בשיל כל צרכו אלא כמאכל בן דרוסאי דהא כי מוקי מתניתין להחזיר תנן הוי מתניתין כחנניה דשרי חמין ותבשיל להשהות על גבי כירה אפילו בשאינה גרופה אפילו לא בשיל כל צרכו ולא כרבנן ואמאי ודילמא מתניתין אפילו כרבנן ומתני' בחמין ותבשיל שנתבשלו כל צרכן דמודו רבנן דמשהין ע"ג כירה שאינה גרופה וקטומה אלא ודאי משום דסתם חמין ותבשיל כמאכל בן דרוסאי נמי משמע ומיהו סתם חמין ותבשיל הוי נמי בשיל כל צרכו כדמוכח בסוף שמעתין (דף לח.) גבי קשיא דרבי מאיר אדרבי מאיר אע"פ שיש לדחות ושם אפרש בע"ה ואפילו אי סתם חמין ותבשיל לא הוה בשיל כל צרכו צריך לומר הא דאסרי בית שמאי להחזיר היינו אפילו חמין שהוחמו כל צרכן וכן לבית הלל באינה גרופה מדקאמר בגמרא (דף לח:) ואף רבי אושעיא סבר מחזירין אפילו בשבת דאמר רבי אושעיא פעם אחת כו' והעלנו לו קומקומוס של חמין ומזגנו לו את הכוס והחזרנוהו למקומו ואי לא אסיר בהוחמו כל צרכן מנא ליה דמחזירין אפילו בשבת דילמא הוחם כל צורכו הוה ואם תאמר ואם סתם חמין ותבשיל הוי בין בשיל כל צרכו בין לא בשיל אם כן סברי בית שמאי מצטמק ויפה לו אסור כיון דאסיר תבשיל שבישל כל צרכו ואם כן היכי שרי חמין שלא הוחמו כל צרכן והא יפה לו הוא ואור"י דודאי תבשיל אסרי בית שמאי משום דלעולם יפה לו אע"ג דנתבשל כל צרכו אבל חמין שאין יפה להם אלא עד כדי צרכן אבל מכאן ואילך רע להן כדמוכח לקמן לא אסרי בית שמאי דליכא למיגזר שמא יחתה דבלא חיתוי יוחמו כל צרכן: **וב"ה** אומרים אף מחזירין. אפילו בשבת מחזירין [ב] כדאמר בגמרא ולשון נוטלין נמי משמע דבשבת מיירי דבחול לא הוה צריך למיתני נוטלין ולמאן דאסר להחזיר אסר אפילו בחול לבית הלל כשאינה גרופה ולבית שמאי אפי' בגרופה מדקאמר בגמרא לדברי האומר מחזירין מחזירין אפילו בשבת משמע דעיקר פלוגתא הוי בחול ועוד מדקדק ר"ת מדקאמר לא יתן עד שיגרוף ואי לא יתן לא יחזיר בשבת הוא איך יגרוף או יקטום בשבת ° והוה ליה למימר אלא אם כן גרף וקטם אלא בחול נמי אסור להחזיר וא"ת מה שיעור הוא נותן לאסור בע"ש דהיכא דסלקו בהשכמה פשיטא דשרי להחזיר ואומר ר"י דמשעה שלא יוכלו להרתיחו מבעוד יום אסור להחזיר ומיהו בשבת אפילו רותח אסור להחזיר למאן דאסר דאי לאו הכי מנא ליה דרבי אושעיא סבר מחזירין אפילו בשבת דילמא קומקמוס של חמין רותח הוה ועוד אומר ר"י דמלינו למימר דבערב שבת נמי אסור להחזיר אפילו רותח משעה שאם היה קר לא היה יכול להרתיח מבע"י וקשה לרשב"א היכי שרי להחזיר קדרה על גבי כירה בשבת והא אמר בפרק המביא כדי יין (ביצה דף לג: ושם) דבילים וקדרה וחביתא ופוריא מלמטה למעלה אסור משום אהל ואור"י דכי אסרו חכמים אהל עראי ה"מ כשעושה הדפנות תחלה ואח"כ הכיסוי אבל הכא שדופני הכירה כבר עשויות מאליהן לא אחמור רבנן לאסור ליתן קדרה על גבה ומיהו הא דאמר בהמוצא תפילין (עירובין דף קב.) גבי דיכרי דרב הונא דאמר ליה כרוך בודיא ושייר בה טפח למחר מוסיף על אוהל עראי הוא משמע דבלא שיור אסור אע"ג דהדפנות כבר עשויות אור"י התם משום דדמי אהל טפי אסור אפי' בלא עשיית דפנות אבל קדרה דלא דמי אהל כולי האי לא אסרו חכמים בלא עשיית דפנות:

לעולם

עין משפט נר מצוה

א א ב ג מיי' פ"ג מהל' שבת הלכה ד ה סמג לאוין סה טוש"ע א"ח סי' רנג סעיף א:

גליון הש"ס

תוס' ד"ה וב"ה אומרים וכו' והל"ל **אא"כ גרף.** לענ"ד הא מלינו כזה במו"ק דף ד ע"ב עד שיעמיק כו' כגון שהעמיק:

הגהות הב"ח

(א) רש"י ד"ה אבל לא תבשיל וכו' כמבשל הס"ד ואח"כ מ"ה אבל לא:

רבינו חננאל

פ"ג **כירה** שהסיקוה בקש ובגבבא וכו'. **כירה** זו היא מקום שפיתת ב' קדרות. **איבעיא** להו הא דתנינן לא יתן עד שיגרוף. או עד שיתן האפר על גבי גחלים נתינה זו בע"ש וקמ"ל דאסור לשהות ע"ג כירה אא"כ גרופה וקטומה או דילמא נתינה זו החזרת הקדירה היא בשבת וקמ"ל דאסור להחזיר אלא ע"ג כירה קטומה או גרופה אבל לשהות מותר. ומתני' מני חנניה היא דתניא כל שהוא כמאכל בן דרוסאי מותר לשהותו על גבי כירה אע"פ שאינה גרופה ולא קטומה.

רב נסים גאון

נפקא מינה לגיטי נשים. כלומר בדאלך א) המביא גט מבבל או מבורסיף אין צריך לומר בפני נכתב ובפני נחתם לדבריהם שאמרו במסכת גיטין בפר' א' (דף ו) בבל רב אמר כארץ ישראל לגיטין מכי אתא רב לבבל ובפרק עשרה יוחסין (דף עב) היכא חביל ימא אמר רב פפא סבא משמיה דרב זו פרת בורסיף ובבראשית דר' אושעיא (פרשה לח) חד תלמיד ר' יוחנן הוה יתיב קדמוי הוה מסבר ליה ולא סבר אמר ליה מה דין לית את סבר אמר ליה דאנא גלי מן אתראי אמר ליה מן הדין אתר את אמר ליה מן בורסיף אמר ליה לא תאמר כן אלא בולסיף שנאמר (בראשית יא) כי שם בלל ה' שפת כל הארץ ובגמרא דכל ישראל יש להן חלק (סנהדרין דף קט) אמרו אמר רב יוסף בבל בורסיף סימן רע לתורה מאי בורסיף אמר רב אסי בור ספת ואדוננו האיי ז"ל אמר בבל בורסיף ובורסיף בבל כוונת דבר זה לאותה ששנינו במשנה שינה שמו ושמה שם עירו ושם עירה פסול הרי נודע כי בבל ובורסיף עיר אחת הן והגט כשר:

סליק פרק במה מדליקין

הגהות על רנ"ג

א) פירושו בזה:

מסורת הש"ס

א) לעיל כ., ב) [דף לד:], ג) [דף עא:], ד) [וע"ע תוס' ב"מ קג. ד"ה המקבל].

תוספות ישנים

א) ולא רצה לומר דתנא רישא דאפילו בחול אין מחזירין לב"ש כדמשמע עד שיגרוף וסיפא קתני דאפילו בשבת מחזירין לב"ה כדמשמע נוטלין. דבלאו תרי בבא סברא הוא דבתרווייהו פליגי דהא אי להשהות תנן ליכא אלא חד בבא בהחזרה. ומהר"מ אומר דאי משום ב"ה תני סיפא לא ה"ל למיתני דברי בית שמאי:

ב) ומיהו רש"י פי' בגמרא מחזירין אפילו בשבת למחרת דנראה דאין דעתו להחזיר ובטלה הטמנה אבל בלילה אין נראה כן:

ליקוטי רש"י

לגיטי נשים. דקיימא לן (גיטין ב.) המביא גט ממדינת הים צריך שיאמר בפני נכתב ובפני נחתם אי משום דאין מצויין לקיימו ואי משום דאין בקיאין לשמה והמביא מארץ ישראל אינו צריך לפי שבקיאין לשמה ועולי רגלים מצויין להכיר חתימת עדים לקיימו ואמרינן התם (גיטין ו.) בבל כארץ ישראל לגיטין לפי שהן בני תורה ובקיאין לשמה ובני ישיבה מצויין לילך וללמוד משם תורה מכל מקומות ובורסיף סמוך לבבל ואינן בני תורה כדאמרינן (סנהדרין קט.) מאי בורסיף בור שפו את מימיו ולא נשתייר בו כלום והמביא משם צריך שיאמר אבל עכשיו נתחלף שמם הלכך המביא מבבל צריך שיאמר ומבורסיף אין צריך [סוכה לד:].

כירה. יש בה שפיתת שתי קדירות [לקמן לח: עיין מו"ק י. ובב"ח שם, נדה כו. ובתוס' שם: ד"ה בפלוגתא]. פחותה מתנור ואין מבעירין בתוכה אש גדול [ב"ק סא:]. כלי חרס ששופתים קדירה על חללה ואין עושין בתוכה היסק גדול כמו שעושין בתנור [ב"ב כ: וע"ש בתוי"ט פ"ב מ"ב]. **קש.** זנבות שבולין אשטרי"ם [לעיל לה.]. **גפת.** פסולת של בית הבד של שמן שהוא כנוס יחד וחם מאד [לקמן מז:]. פסולת זיתים שנתעצרו בבית הבד [ב"ב יז.]. **עד שיגרוף.** מן הגחלים במגריפה שקורין ווידיל"י. **שיתן את האפר.** מפזרים אפר מלמעלה כדי להפיג חומו שלא יוסיף הבל בשבת [לעיל כ.]. **חמין.** מים חמים למזוג בהן יין לשתות [שם לה:]. **בן דרוסאי.** לסטים היה ומבשל בישולו שליש [שם כ.]. לסטים היה ואוכל כל דבר המבושל קצת [ע"ז לח.]. **מותר להשהותו.** לא חיישי' אם מתבשל והולך בשבת [לעיל שם].

Another related dispute:
בֵּית שַׁמַּאי אוֹמְרִים – **Beis Shammai say:** נוֹטְלִין אֲבָל לֹא מַחֲזִירִין – **We may remove** something from the *kirah* on the Sabbath **but not return** it to the *kirah.* וּבֵית הִלֵּל אוֹמְרִים – **But Beis Hillel say:** אַף מַחֲזִירִין – **We may even return** it.[6]

Gemara The Gemara discusses two possible interpretations of the Mishnah's statement that one may not place food on a *kirah* that was heated with marc or wood unless the coals were shoveled away or covered with ash:

אִיבַּעְיָא לְהוּ – **They inquired:** הַאי לֹא יִתֵּן לֹא יַחֲזִיר הוּא – **Is the** meaning of **this** phrase, **"one may not place,"** that **one may not *return*** food to this *kirah* on the Sabbath, אֲבָל לְשַׁהוֹת – **but** as for **leaving** food on it before the Sabbath, מַשְׁהִין אַף עַל פִּי שֶׁאֵינוֹ גָּרוּף וְאֵינוֹ קָטוּם – **one may leave** food on it **even if [the *kirah*] was neither shoveled nor banked with ash?** וּמַנִּי – **And** according to this interpretation, **whose** view does the Mishnah reflect? חֲנַנְיָה הִיא – **It is** the view of **Chananyah.** דְּתַנְיָא – **For it was taught in a Baraisa:** חֲנַנְיָה אוֹמֵר – CHANANYAH SAYS: כֹּל שֶׁהוּא כְּמַאֲכַל בֶּן דְּרוֹסַאי – If ANY food has been cooked to the point THAT it IS AS THE FOOD OF BEN DERUSAI,[7] מוּתָּר לְשַׁהוֹתוֹ עַל גַּבֵּי כִּירָה – IT IS PERMITTED TO LEAVE IT ON A *KIRAH* before the Sabbath, אַף עַל פִּי שֶׁאֵינוֹ גָּרוּף וְאֵינוֹ קָטוּם – EVEN THOUGH [THE *KIRAH*] IS NEITHER SHOVELED NOR BANKED.[8] אוֹ דִּילְמָא לְשַׁהוֹת תְּנַן – **Or perhaps** it is in reference to **leaving** food on the *kirah* before the Sabbath that **the Mishnah stated** its ruling, וְאִי גָּרוּף וְקָטוּם אִין – **and** it means to teach that **if [the *kirah*] is shoveled or banked** one may **indeed** leave food on it, אִי לֹא לֹא – but **if not** one may **not** even leave food on it before the Sabbath, וְכָל שֶׁכֵּן לְהַחֲזִיר – **and certainly,** it is prohibited **to return** food to such a *kirah* on the Sabbath.[9] – ? –

The Gemara attempts to resolve the inquiry:

תָּא שְׁמַע – **Come, learn** a proof from the Mishnah itself, מִדְּקָתָנֵי תְּרֵי בָּבֵי בְּמַתְנִיתִין – **for** after introducing the requirement to shovel or bank a *kirah* that was heated with marc or wood, **the Mishnah states** the following **two clauses:** בֵּית שַׁמַּאי אוֹמְרִים – (a) BEIS SHAMMAI SAY: חַמִּין אֲבָל לֹא תַּבְשִׁיל – We may place HOT WATER BUT NOT COOKED FOOD on the *kirah.* וּבֵית הִלֵּל אוֹמְרִים חַמִּין וְתַבְשִׁיל – BUT BEIS HILLEL SAY: We may place both HOT WATER AND COOKED FOOD on it. בֵּית שַׁמַּאי אוֹמְרִים נוֹטְלִין אֲבָל לֹא מַחֲזִירִין – (b) BEIS SHAMMAI SAY: WE MAY REMOVE something from the *kirah* BUT NOT RETURN it. וּבֵית הִלֵּל אוֹמְרִים אַף מַחֲזִירִין – BUT BEIS HILLEL SAY: WE MAY EVEN RETURN it.[10] אִי אָמְרַת בִּשְׁלָמָא לְשַׁהוֹת תְּנַן – **All is well if you say** that in its introductory clause **the Mishnah refers to leaving** food on the *kirah* before the Sabbath, הָכִי קָתָנֵי – for accordingly, **this is what the Mishnah** means to **state** in each of its clauses: כִּירָה שֶׁהִסִּיקוּהָ בְּקַשׁ וּבִגְבָבָא – **If a *kirah* was heated with straw or with stubble,** מַשְׁהִין עָלֶיהָ תַּבְשִׁיל – **one may leave cooked food on it** before the Sabbath. בְּגֶפֶת וּבְעֵצִים – If it was heated **with marc or with wood,** לֹא יַשְׁהֶא – **one may not leave** cooked food on it, עַד שֶׁיִּגְרוֹף – **until he has shoveled away** the coals, אוֹ עַד שֶׁיִּתֵּן אֵפֶר – **or until he has put ash** over them. The second clause goes on to explain: וּמָה הֵן מַשְׁהִין – **And what** types of food **may be left** on the *kirah* after the coals have been shoveled away or covered with ash? בֵּית שַׁמַּאי אוֹמְרִים חַמִּין אֲבָל לֹא תַּבְשִׁיל – **Beis Shammai say: Hot water but not cooked food.** וּבֵית הִלֵּל אוֹמְרִים חַמִּין וְתַבְשִׁיל – **But Beis Hillel say:** Both **hot water and cooked food.** The third clause then states: וְכִי הֵיכִי דִּפְלִיגֵי בְּלַשְׁהוֹת – **And just as they** (Beis Shammai and Beis Hillel) **disagree concerning leaving** cooked food on such a *kirah* before the Sabbath, פְּלִיגֵי נַמֵּי בְּלְהַחֲזִיר – **so too they disagree concerning returning** to a *kirah* on the Sabbath the items that one was permitted to leave there and he removed.[11] שֶׁבֵּית שַׁמַּאי אוֹמְרִים נוֹטְלִין אֲבָל לֹא מַחֲזִירִין – **For Beis Shammai say: We may remove** something from the *kirah* on the Sabbath **but not return** it, וּבֵית הִלֵּל אוֹמְרִים אַף מַחֲזִירִין – **but Beis Hillel say: We may even return** it. Thus, if the restriction of the introductory clause pertains to leaving food on the *kirah* before the Sabbath, all three clauses of the Mishnah are understandable. אֶלָּא אִי אָמְרַת לְהַחֲזִיר תְּנַן – **But if you will say** that in its introductory clause **the Mishnah is referring to returning** food to the *kirah* on the Sabbath, הָכִי קָתָנֵי – then perforce, **this is what** the three clauses of **the Mishnah** mean to **state:** כִּירָה שֶׁהִסִּיקוּהָ בְּקַשׁ וּבִגְבָבָא – **If a *kirah* was heated with straw or with stubble,** מַחֲזִירִין עָלֶיהָ תַּבְשִׁיל – **one may return to it a cooked food** that had been left there before the Sabbath and was removed. בְּגֶפֶת וּבְעֵצִים – If it was heated **with marc or with wood,** לֹא יַחֲזִיר – **one may not**

NOTES

6. In addition to their previous narrow interpretation of the Mishnah's rule, Beis Shammai hold that it applies only to *leaving* the hot water on the fire before the Sabbath (i.e. *shehiyah*). Once removed, however, the hot water may not be *returned* to the *kirah* on the Sabbath (i.e. *chazarah*) because that gives the appearance of cooking on the Sabbath. [It is not actual cooking because the water is still hot at the time one replaces it on the *kirah* (see *Beur Halachah* 253:2 ד״ה ודוקא שהתבשיל; see also *Tosafos* ד״ה חמין and *Ritva, MHK* ed.) Beis Hillel, however, hold that once the *kirah* has been shoveled or banked, not only may one leave both hot water and cooked food on it before the Sabbath, he may even, if he removed them on the Sabbath, replace them (*Rashi; Rav;* see *Tosafos*).

7. Ben Derusai was a notorious bandit who, due to the uncertainties of his profession, allowed his food to cook only one-third (*Rashi* to 20a ד״ה בן דרוסאי) or one-half (*Rambam* and *Raavad, Hil. Shabbos* 9:5) its normal time. This is considered the minimum amount needed to make food edible.

8. According to Chananyah, *shehiyah* is permissible over a *kirah* even without shoveling its coals away or banking them with ash, so long as the food is already cooked as much as the food of Ben Derusai. Once the food is minimally edible, we need not be concerned that someone might stoke the coals to make it cook better (see *Rashi* to 20a ד״ה קטום).

Perhaps our Mishnah follows Chananyah's opinion, and if so, we must interpret the phrase "one may not place [food on the *kirah*]" as meaning that one may not *return* food to the *kirah* if he removed it from there on the Sabbath. It is permitted, however, to place food on the *kirah* before the Sabbath even if it was not shoveled or banked, as long as the food is minimally cooked. Thus, the Mishnah's restriction pertains not to *shehiyah,* but to *chazarah.*

9. If we interpret it literally, the Mishnah disagrees with Chananyah's opinion and rules that even *shehiyah* is prohibited if the coals are exposed. Certainly, *chazarah* is also prohibited. This is the opinion held by the Tannaim R' Yehudah and R' Meir, whose views (which differ from each other in certain respects) are set forth in a Baraisa that is cited below, on 37a.

In short, the Gemara is inquiring whether the Mishnah's restriction pertains only to *chazarah,* in accordance with Chananyah's view that *shehiyah* is permitted, or it pertains to *shehiyah* as well, and follows the view of the Sages who disagree with Chananyah. [The basis for interpreting our Mishnah less than literally and having it accord with Chananyah's opinion is that a Mishnah above (19b; see Gemara 20a) follows Chananyah's opinion, and it therefore seems reasonable that our Mishnah also does and that the halachah follows his opinion (see *Rashi* to 37b ד״ה ורב ששת; see also *Rosh* and *Rosh Yosef*).]

10. The Gemara will proceed to demonstrate that if the Mishnah's introductory statement refers to *chazarah,* the latter two clauses, which the Gemara has just quoted, are needlessly repetitive.

11. I.e. hot water, according to Beis Shammai, and both hot water and cooked food, according to Beis Hillel (*Rashi*).

למאי נפקא מינה לגיטי נשים:

הדרן עלך במה מדליקין

כירה א שהסיקוה בקש ובגבבא נותנים עליה תבשיל בגפת ובעצים לא יתן עד שיגרוף או עד שיתן את האפר בית שמאי אומרים חמין אבל לא תבשיל ובית הלל אומרים חמין ותבשיל בית שמאי אומרים נוטלין אבל לא מחזירין ובית הלל אומרים אף מחזירין: **גמ'** איבעיא להו האי לא יתן לא יחזיר הוא אבל לשהות משהין אף על פי שאינו גרוף ואינו קטום ומני חנניה היא דתניא (א) חנניה אומר ב כל שהוא כמאכל בן דרוסאי מותר לשהותו על גבי כירה אע"פ שאינו גרוף ואינו קטום או דילמא ג לשהות תנן ואי גרוף וקטום אין אי לא לא וכל שכן להחזיר ת"ש מדקתני תרי בבי במתני' ב"ש אומרים חמין אבל לא תבשיל ובית הלל אומרים חמין ותבשיל ב"ש אומרים נוטלין אבל לא מחזירין וב"ה אומרים אף מחזירין אי אמרת בשלמא לשהות תנן הכי קתני כירה שהסיקוה בקש ובגבבא משהין עליה תבשיל בגפת ובעצים לא ישהא עד שיגרוף או עד שיתן אפר ומה הן משהין בית שמאי אומרים חמין אבל לא תבשיל וב"ה אומרים חמין ותבשיל וכי היכי דפליגי בלשהות פליגי נמי בלהחזיר שבית שמאי אומרים נוטלין אבל לא מחזירין ובית הלל אומרים אף מחזירין אלא אי אמרת להחזיר תנן הכי קתני כירה שהסיקוה בקש ובגבבא מחזירין עליה תבשיל בגפת ובעצים לא יחזיר עד שיגרוף או עד שיתן אפר ומה הן מחזירין בית שמאי אומרים חמין אבל לא תבשיל ובית הלל אומרים חמין ותבשיל בית שמאי אומרים נוטלין אבל לא מחזירין ובית הלל אומרים אף מחזירין הא א) תו למה לי

לעולם

רש"י

לגיטי נשים. דקיימא לן בני בבל בקיאין שצריך לכתוב גט לשמה והמביא גט משם אין צריך לומר בפני נכתב ובפני נחתם ובני שאר ארצות אין בקיאין וצריך ועכשיו בני בורסיף היא בבל ובבל של עכשיו היא בורסיף והן עמי הארץ כדאמרינן בעלמא (סנהדרין דף קט.) בור שאפי שנטלו מימיו ואני אומר נפקא מינה לגיטי נשים לענין שינה שמו ושמה ושם עירו ועירה פסול וצריך לכתוב שם של עכשיו:

הדרן עלך במה מדליקין

כירה. עשויה כעין קדירה ונותנין קדירה לתוכה: **קש.** זנבות השבולין: **גבבא.** הנגבב מן השדה אישטובל"א: **גפת.** פסולת של שומשמין שהוציא שומנן: **עד שיגרוף.** הגחלים משום דמוסיף הבל וטעמא פרישנא בפרק דלעיל ג) שמא יחתה בגחלים: **או עד שיתן אפר.** על גבי גחלים לכסותם ולכנסם: **בית שמאי אומרים.** נותנין עליה חמין אחר שגרפה דלא צריכי לבשולי דליכא למגזר שמא יחתה: **אבל לא תבשיל.** דניחא ליה בישוליה ואתי לאחתויי א"נ נתקיימה מחשבתו ומיחזי כמבשל (א): **לא מחזירין.** בשבת דמיחזי כמבשל: **אף מחזירין.** הואיל וגרוף: **גמ' קטום.** היינו נתן אפר על הגחלים דאפר מתרגמינן קיטמא: **תרי בבי.** בית שמאי אומרים חמין וכו' ותו תנא בבא אחריתי נוטלין ולא מחזירין: **ומה הן משהין.** בגרוף וקטום: **פליגי נמי בלהחזיר.** את המותר לשהות כגון חמין לבית שמאי וחמין ותבשיל לב"ה: **אלא אי אמרת להחזיר תנן הכי קתני.** כלומר ע"כ הכי מפרשא: **ב"ש אומרים נוטלין ולא מחזירין.** ע"כ אתבשיל קיימי דהא שרו בחמין: **הא תו למה לי.** הא תנא ליה רישא אבל לא תבשיל:

לעולם

תוספות

נפקא מינה לגיטי נשים. מה שפי' בקונטרס לענין שינה שם עירו ושם עירה אין נראה לרשב"א דבבל הוא שם מדינה ולא שם העיר כדאמר בפרק עשרה יוחסין (קדושין דף עא.) כל הארצות עיסה לארץ ישראל וארץ ישראל עיסה לבבל וקאמר נמי התם ג) עד היכן היא בבל ולא אשכחן שום דוכתא עיר ששמה בבל אלא מדינה היא ואין כותבין שם מדינה בגט:

הדרן עלך במה מדליקין

כירה שהסיקוה בקש ובגבבא. נראה לר"י דקש היינו זנבות השבולים שנשאר בשדה הנקרא אשטובל"א בלעז ותבן הוא הנקצר עם השבולת דהכי משמע לקמן בפרק שואל (לקמן דף קנ:) דקאמר בשלמא קש משכחת לה במחובר אלא תבן היכי משכחת לה ומסיק בתבנא סריא והא דאמר בריש המקבל (בבא מציעא דף קג.) גבי מקום שנהגו לקצור אינו רשאי לעקור משום דאמר ניחא לי דתיתבן ארעאי הוה ליה למימר דתיתקש דהנשאר בקרקע נקרא קש כדפירש רש"י אלא משום דתיתבן משמע טפי לשון זיבול נקט ליה ד): **לא** יתן עד שיגרוף. פירש בקונטרס משום תוספת הבל ואין נראה לר"י דאפילו גרופה וקטומה היא מוספת הבל יותר מכמה דברים השנויין בבמה טומנין ועוד דחנניה שרי להשהות אף כשאינה גרופה ולא אסרו מוסיף הבל אלא דוקא בהטמנה אבל להשהות שרי וכשאינה גרופה אסרי רבנן דחנניה משום דילמא אתי לאחתויי:

חמין ותבשיל. נראה לר"י דסתם חמין ותבשיל היינו אפי' לא בשיל כל צרכו אלא כמאכל בן דרוסאי דהא כי מוקי מתניתין להחזיר תנן הוי מתניתין כחנניה דשרי חמין ותבשיל להשהות על גבי כירה אפילו בשאינה גרופה אפילו לא בשיל כל צרכו ולא כרבנן ואמאי ודילמא מתניתין אפילו כרבנן ומתני' בחמין ותבשיל שנתבשלו כל צרכן דמודו רבנן דמשהין ע"ג כירה שאינה גרופה וקטומה אלא ודאי משום דסתם חמין ותבשיל כמאכל בן דרוסאי נמי משמע ומיהו סתם חמין ותבשיל הוי נמי בשיל כל צרכו כדמוכח בסוף שמעתין (דף לח.) גבי קשיא דרבי מאיר אדרבי מאיר אע"פ שיש לדחות ושם אפרש בע"ה ואפילו אי סתם חמין ותבשיל לא הוה בשיל כל צרכו צריך לומר הא דאסרי בית שמאי להחזיר היינו אפילו חמין שהוחמו כל צרכן וכן לבית הלל בשאינה גרופה מדקאמר בגמרא (דף לח:) ואף רבי אושעיא סבר מחזירין אפילו בשבת דאמר רבי אושעיא פעם אחת כו' והעלנו לו קומקומוס של חמין ומזגנו לו את הכוס והחזרנוהו למקומו ואי לא אסיר בהוחמו כל צורכו הוה ואם תאמר ואם סתם חמין ותבשיל הוי בין בשיל כל צרכו בין לא בשיל אם כן סברי בית שמאי מצטמק ויפה לו אסור כיון דאסיר תבשיל שבישל כל צרכו ואם כן היכי שרי חמין שלא הוחמו כל צרכן והא יפה לו הוא ואור"י דודאי תבשיל אסרי בית שמאי משום דלעולם יפה לו אע"ג דנתבשל כל צרכו אבל חמין שאין יפה להם אלא עד כדי צרכן אבל מכאן ואילך רע להן כדמוכח לקמן לא אסרי בית שמאי דליכא למיגזר שמא יחתה דבלא חיתוי יוחמו כל צרכן: **וב"ה** אומרים אף מחזירין. אפילו בשבת מחזירין ב) כדאמר בגמרא ולשון נוטלין נמי משמע דבשבת מיירי דבחול לא הוה צריך למיתני נוטלין ולמאן דאסר להחזיר אסר אפילו בחול לבית הלל כשאינה גרופה ולבית שמאי אפי' בגרופה מדקאמר בגמרא לדברי האומר מחזירין מחזירין אפילו בשבת משמע דעיקר פלוגתא הוי בחול ועוד מדקדק ר"ת מדקאמר לא יתן עד שיגרוף ואי לא יתן לא יחזיר בשבת הוא איך יגרוף או יקטום בשבת ° והוה ליה למימר אלא אם כן גרף וקטם אלא בחול נמי אסור להחזיר וא"ת מה שיעור הוא נותן לאסור בע"ש דהיכא דסלקו בהשכמה פשיטא דשרי להחזיר ואומר ר"י דמשעה שלא יוכלו להרתיחו מבעוד יום אסור להחזיר ומיהו בשבת אפילו רותח אסור להחזיר למאן דאסר דאי לאו הכי מנא ליה דרבי אושעיא סבר מחזירין אפילו בשבת דילמא קומקמוס של חמין רותח הוה ועוד אומר ר"י דמצינו למימר דבערב שבת נמי אסור להחזיר אפילו רותח משעה שאם היה קר לא היה יכול להרתיח מבע"י וקשה לרשב"א היכי שרי להחזיר קדרה על גבי כירה בשבת והא אמר בפרק המביא כדי יין (ביצה דף לג: ושם) דבילים וקדרה וחביתא ופוריא מלמטה למעלה אסור משום אהל ואור"י דכי אסרו חכמים אהל עראי ה"מ כשעושה הדפנות תחלה ואח"כ הכיסוי אבל הכא שדופני הכירה כבר עשויות מאליהן לא אחמור רבנן לאסור ליתן קדרה על גבה ומיהו הא דאמר בהמוצא תפילין (עירובין דף קב.) גבי דיכרי דרב הונא דאמר ליה כרוך בודיא ושייר בה טפח למחר מוסיף על אוהל עראי הוא משמע דבלא שיור אסור אע"ג דהדפנות כבר עשויות ואור"י התם משום דדמי אהל טפי אסור אפי' בלא עשיית דפנות אבל קדרה דלא דמי אהל כולי האי לא אסרו חכמים בלא עשיית דפנות:

לעולם

מסורת הש"ס

א) לעיל כ., ב) [דף לד:], ג) [דף עא:], ד) [וע"ע תוס' ב"מ קג. ד"ה המקבל].

תוספות ישנים

א) ולא רצה לומר דתנא רישא דאפילו בחול אין מחזירין לב"ש כדמשמע עד שיגרוף וסיפא קתני דאפילו בשבת מחזירין לב"ה כדמשמע נוטלין. דבלאו תרי בבא סברא הוא דבתרווייהו פליגי דהא אי להשהות תנן ליכא אלא חד בבא בהחזרה. ומהר"מ אומר דאי משום ב"ה תני סיפא לא ה"ל למיתני דברי בית שמאי:

ב) ומיהו רש"י פי' בגמרא מחזירין אפילו בשבת למחרת דנראה דאין דעתו להחזיר ובטלה הטמנה אבל בלילה אין נראה כן:

ליקוטי רש"י

לגיטי נשים. דקיימא לן (גיטין ב.) המביא גט ממדינת הים צריך שיאמר בפני נכתב ובפני נחתם אי משום דאין מצויין לקיימו ואי משום דאין בקיאין לשמה והמביא מארץ ישראל אינו צריך לפי שבקיאין לשמה ועולי רגלים מצויין להכיר חתימת עדים לקיימו ואמרינן התם (גיטין ו.) בבל כארץ ישראל לגיטין לפי שהן בני תורה ובקיאין לשמה ובני ישיבה מצויין לילך וללמוד משם תורה מכל מקומות ובורסיף סמוך לבבל ואינן בני תורה כדאמרינן (סנהדרין קט.) מאי בורסיף בור ששפו את מימיו ולא נשתייר בו כלום והמביא משם צריך שיאמר אבל עכשיו נתחלף שמם הלכך המביא מבבל צריך שיאמר ומבורסיף אין צריך [סוכה לד:].

כירה. יש בה שפיתת שתי קדירות [לקמן לח: עיין מו"ק י. ובב"ח שם, נדה כו. ובתוס' שם: ד"ה בפלוגתא]. פתוחה מתנור ואין מבעירין בתוכה אש גדול [ב"ק סא:]. כלי חרס ששופתים קדירה על חללה ואין עושין בתוכה היסק גדול כמו שעושין בתנור [ב"ב כ: וע"ש בתוי"ט פ"ב מ"ב]. **קש.** זנבות שבולין אשטריי"ם [לעיל לה.]. **גפת.** פסולת של בית הבד של שמן שהוא כנוס יחד וחם מאד [לקמן מז:]. פסולת זיתים שנתעצרו בבית הבד [ב"ב יז.]. **עד שיגרוף.** מן הגחלים במגריפה שקורין וודיל"י. **שיתן את האפר.** מפזרים אפר מלמעלה כדי להפיג חומו שלא יוסיף הבל בשבת [לעיל כ.]. **חמין.** מים חמים למזוג בהן יין לשתות [שם לה:]. **בן דרוסאי.** לסטים היה ומבשל בישולו שליש [שם כ.]. לסטים היה ואוכל כל דבר המבושל קצת [ע"ז לח.]. **מותר להשהותו.** לא חיישי' אם מתבשל והולך בשבת [לעיל שם].

עין משפט נר מצוה

א א ב ג מיי' פ"ג מהל' שבת הלכה ד ה סמג לאוין סה טוש"ע א"ח סי' רנג סעיף א:

גליון הש"ס

תוס' ד"ה וב"ה **אומרים** וכו' והל"ל **אא"כ** גרף. לענ"ד הא מצינו כזה במו"ק דף ד ע"ב עד שיעמיק כו' כגון שהעמיק:

הגהות הב"ח

(א) רש"י ד"ה אבל לא תבשיל וכו' כמבשל הס"ד ואח"כ מ"ה אבל לא:

רבינו חננאל

פ"ג כירה שהסיקוה בקש ובגבבא וכו'. **כירה** זו היא מקום שפיתת ב' קדרות. **איבעיא** להו הא דתנינן לא יתן עד שיגרוף. או עד שיתן האפר על גבי גחלים נתינה זו בע"ש וקמ"ל דאסור לשהות ע"ג כירה אא"כ גרופה וקטומה או דילמא נתינה זו החזרת הקדירה היא בשבת וקמ"ל דאסור להחזיר אלא ע"ג כירה קטומה או גרופה אבל לשהות מותר. ומתני' מני חנניה היא דתניא כל שהוא כמאכל בן דרוסאי מותר לשהותו על גבי כירה אע"פ שאינה גרופה ולא קטומה.

רב נסים גאון

נפקא מינה לגיטי נשים. כלומר בדאלך א) המביא גט מבבל או מבורסיף אין צריך לומר בפני נכתב ובפני נחתם לדבריהם שאמרו במסכת גיטין בפר' א' (דף ו) בבל רב אמר כארץ ישראל לגיטין מכי אתא רב לבבל ובפרק עשרה יוחסין (דף עב) היכא חביל ימא אמר רב פפא סבא משמיה דרב זו פרת בורסיף ובבראשית דר' אושעיא (פרשה לח) חד תלמיד ר' יוחנן הוה יתיב קדמוי הוה מסבר ליה ולא סבר אמר ליה מה דין לית את סבר אמר ליה דאנא גלי מן אתראי אמר ליה מן הדין אתר את אמר ליה מן בורסיף אמר ליה לא תאמר כן אלא בולסיף שנאמר (בראשית יא) כי שם בלל ה' שפת כל הארץ ובגמרא דכל ישראל יש להן חלק (סנהדרין דף קט) אמרו אמר רב יוסף בבל בורסיף סימן רע לתורה מאי בורסיף אמר רב אסי בור ספת ואדוננו האיי ז"ל אמר בבל בורסיף ובורסיף בבל כוונת דבר זה לאותה ששנינו במשנה שינה שמו ושמה שם עירו ושם עירה פסול הרי נודע כי בבל ובורסיף עיר אחת הן והגט כשר:

סליק פרק במה מדליקין

הגהות על רנ"ג

א) פירושו בזה:

return anything to it, עַד שֶׁיִּגְרוֹף – **unless he has shoveled away** the coals, אוֹ עַד שֶׁיִּתֵּן אֵפֶר – **or unless he has put ash** over them. The second clause goes on to explain: וּמָה הֵן מַחֲזִירִין – **And what** types of food **may one return** to the *kirah* on the Sabbath, if its coals have been shoveled away or covered with ash? בֵּית שַׁמַּאי אוֹמְרִים חַמִּין אֲבָל לֹא תַּבְשִׁיל – **Beis Shammai say: Hot water but not cooked food** וּבֵית הִלֵּל אוֹמְרִים חַמִּין וְתַבְשִׁיל – **But Beis Hillel say:** Both **hot water and cooked food.** Now, the third clause states: בֵּית שַׁמַּאי אוֹמְרִים נוֹטְלִין אֲבָל לֹא מַחֲזִירִין – **Beis Shammai say: We may remove** something from the *kirah* on the Sabbath **but not return** it, וּבֵית הִלֵּל אוֹמְרִים אַף מַחֲזִירִין – **but Beis Hillel say: We may even return** it. In this clause, Beis Shammai must mean only to forbid returning cooked food to the *kirah,* in accordance with their opinion in the previous clause,[12] and Beis Hillel must mean to permit returning even cooked food in accordance with their previous opinion. הָא תו לָמָּה לִי – Now, **why is this additional** clause **necessary?** It is nothing more than a repetition of the previous one! Obviously then, the only viable explanation is that the introductory clause of the Mishnah refers to leaving food on the *kirah* before the Sabbath, as explained above, and since it requires shoveling away or covering the coals even in that case, it does not accord with the view of Chananyah!

NOTES

12. [In the previous clause, Beis Shammai permitted the returning of hot water to a *kirah* if its coals were shoveled away or covered with ash; thus, in the clause, when Beis Shammai *forbid* returning something to the *kirah,* they cannot be referring to hot water, but only to cooked food.]

The Gemara rejects the proof:

לְעוֹלָם אֵימָא לָךְ לְהַחֲזִיר תְּנַן – **Actually, I can tell you** that the introductory clause of **the Mishnah refers to returning** food to the *kirah,* and as for the seeming redundancy of the last clause, I will say that וְחַסּוֹרֵי מִיחַסְּרָא וְהָכִי קָתָנֵי – it is as if **[the Mishnah text] is deficient, and** this is how it **should read:** כִּירָה שֶׁהִסִּיקוּהָ בְּקַשׁ וּבְגְבָבָא – **If a *kirah* was heated with straw or with stubble,** מַחֲזִירִין עָלֶיהָ תַּבְשִׁיל – **one may *return* to it cooked food** that had been left there before the Sabbath and was removed. בְּגֶפֶת וּבְעֵצִים – If it was heated **with marc or with wood,** לֹא יַחֲזִיר – **one may not return** anything to it, עַד שֶׁיִּגְרוֹף – **unless he has shoveled away** the coals, אוֹ עַד שֶׁיִּתֵּן אֶת הָאֵפֶר – **or unless he has put ash** over them. This implies the following unspoken clause: אֲבָל לִשְׁהוֹת – **But as for leaving** food on a *kirah* before the Sabbath, מַשְׁהִין אַף עַל פִּי שֶׁאֵינוֹ גָּרוּף וְאֵינוֹ קָטוּם – **one may leave** food on it, **even if it was neither shoveled nor banked with ash.** The Mishnah's second explicit clause then clarifies the *unspoken* clause: וּמָה הֵן מַשְׁהִין – **And what** type of food **may be left** before the Sabbath on a *kirah* that was neither shoveled nor banked? בֵּית שַׁמַּאי אוֹמְרִים חַמִּין אֲבָל לֹא תַּבְשִׁיל – **Beis Shammai say: Hot water but not cooked food.** וּבֵית הִלֵּל אוֹמְרִים חַמִּין וְתַבְשִׁיל – **But Beis Hillel say:** Both **hot water and cooked food.** The third clause goes back and clarifies the explicit introductory clause, as follows: וְהַךְ חֲזָרָה דְּאָמְרִי לָךְ לָאו דִּבְרֵי הַכֹּל הִיא – **And this** rule concerning **returning that I told you** previously (i.e. that returning food to the Sabbath is permitted if the *kirah* was shoveled or banked) **is not unanimous,** אֶלָּא מַחֲלוֹקֶת בֵּית שַׁמַּאי וּבֵית הִלֵּל – **but** is, **rather,** the subject of **a dispute between Beis Shammai and Beis Hillel.** שֶׁבֵּית שַׁמַּאי אוֹמְרִים נוֹטְלִין וְלֹא מַחֲזִירִין – **For Beis Shammai say: We may remove** something from a *kirah* on the Sabbath **but not return** it, וּבֵית הִלֵּל אוֹמְרִים אַף מַחֲזִירִין – **whereas Beis Hillel say: We may even return** it.[1]

Having concluded that the wording of the Mishnah lends itself to interpretation in accordance with Chananyah's opinion as well as in dispute of his opinion, the Gemara seeks to prove on the basis of an external source that the correct interpretation is the one that follows Chananyah's opinion:

תָּא שְׁמַע – **Come, learn** a proof from the following Amoraic qualification of the Mishnah's ruling: דְּאָמַר רַבִּי חֶלְבּוֹ אָמַר רַב חָמָא בַּר גּוּרְיָא אָמַר רַב – **For R' Chelbo said in the name of Rav Chama bar Gurya who said in the name of Rav:** לֹא שָׁנוּ אֶלָּא עַל גַּבָּהּ – **They taught** this lenient ruling **only** regarding placing food **on top of [the *kirah*],**[2] which is only moderately hot, אֲבָל לְתוֹכָהּ אָסוּר – **but it is forbidden** to place food **inside [the *kirah*],** which is extremely hot.

The Gemara reasons:

אִי אָמְרַת בִּשְׁלָמָא לְהַחֲזִיר תְּנַן – **This fits well if you say that** the introductory clause of **the Mishnah refers to returning** food to the *kirah* and the Mishnah contains an unspoken clause permitting leaving food before the Sabbath on an unshoveled and unbanked *kirah.* We can say that R' Chelbo meant to qualify this unspoken lenient ruling, הַיְינוּ דְּשָׁנֵי בֵּין תּוֹכָהּ לְעַל גַּבָּהּ – and **this accounts for the distinction** that he draws **between** placing food **inside [the *kirah*] and on top of it.**[3] אֶלָּא אִי אָמְרַת לִשְׁהוֹת תְּנַן – **But if you will say** that the introductory clause of **the Mishnah refers to leaving** food on the *kirah* before the Sabbath and restricts even this to a case in which the *kirah* was shoveled or banked, and perforce R' Chelbo came to qualify this ruling, מַה לִּי תּוֹכָהּ מַה לִּי עַל גַּבָּהּ – **what is the difference whether** the food is placed **inside [the *kirah*] or on top of it?**[4] Clearly, R' Chelbo understood the introductory clause as referring to *returning* food on the *kirah* on the Sabbath, and interpreted it in accordance with Chananyah's opinion!

The Gemara rejects the proof:

מִי סָבְרַת רַבִּי חֶלְבּוֹ אַרֵישָׁא קָאֵי – **Do you think** that **R' Chelbo addressed** his qualification to **the introductory clause of the Mishnah,** which deals with leaving food on a shoveled or banked *kirah* before the Sabbath? אַסֵּיפָא קָאֵי – No! **He addressed** it to **the latter clause,** which states: וּבֵית הִלֵּל אוֹמְרִים אַף מַחֲזִירִין – BUT BEIS HILLEL SAY: WE MAY EVEN RETURN it. וְאָמַר רַבִּי חֶלְבּוֹ אָמַר רַב חָמָא בַּר גּוּרְיָא אָמַר רַב – **And** concerning this segment of the Mishnah, which deals explicitly with returning food to the *kirah,* **R' Chelbo said in the name of Rav Chama bar Gurya who said in the name of Rav:** לֹא שָׁנוּ אֶלָּא עַל גַּבָּהּ אֲבָל תּוֹכָהּ אָסוּר – **They taught** this **only** regarding returning the food **to top of [the *kirah*], but it is forbidden** to return it **inside [the kirah].**[5]

Having rejected the proof that the Mishnah follows Chananyah's opinion, the Gemara now attempts to prove that it does *not* follow Chananyah's opinion:

תָּא שְׁמַע – **Come, learn** a proof from the following Baraisa: שְׁתֵּי כִּירוֹת הַמִּתְאִימוֹת – Regarding TWIN *KIRAHS* that are built side by side and joined by a common wall, אַחַת גְּרוּפָה וּקְטוּמָה וְאַחַת שֶׁאֵינָהּ גְּרוּפָה וְאֵינָהּ קְטוּמָה – ONE of which was SHOVELED OR BANKED AND the other ONE of which was NEITHER SHOVELED NOR BANKED, מַשְׁהִין עַל גַּבֵּי גְּרוּפָה וּקְטוּמָה – the rule is that ONE MAY

NOTES

1. [Thus, the Mishnah can successfully be interpreted in accordance with Chananyah's opinion.] It emerges that there are two possible interpretations of our Mishnah, resulting in two different sets of rules regarding *shehiyah* and *chazarah.* To summarize:

According to Chananyah, once something has been cooked like the food of Ben Derusai, *shehiyah* is permitted even on a *kirah* [fueled with wood and marc] that has not been shoveled or banked. Only *chazarah* is subject to the requirement that the *kirah* be shoveled or banked (see *R' Akiva Eiger* to *Orach Chaim* 253:1 ד״ה ולא הגיע למאכל ב״ד). [Beis Shammai, however, limit the permissibility of *shehiyah* to hot water and dispute the permissibility of *chazarah* altogether.]

According to the Sages who disagree with Chananyah, even *shehiyah* is permitted only if the *kirah* has been shoveled or banked. [Beis Shammai permit it only for hot water and forbid *chazarah* altogether, but Beis Hillel permit *shehiyah* on the shoveled or banked *kirah* even for cooked foods and permit even *chazarah.*]

2. I.e. on the rim or upon the cover of the *kirah* (*Rashi* below ד״ה גבה; see note 17).

3. If R' Chelbo is addressing the unspoken ruling that permits *shehiyah* on an unbanked *kirah,* his qualification of the ruling is very understandable. For although there is no prohibition of *shehiyah,* it is forbidden to place a pot of food *inside* the *kirah* among the coals, since by inserting it among the coals one would in effect be insulating it with the coals (*hatmanah*). Insulating with coals is categorically forbidden, even before the Sabbath (*Rashi;* see top of 34b and see *Mishnah Berurah* 253:46,49 and 257:45; cf. *Tosafos, Rashba;* see *Pnei Yehoshua* and *Chidushei R' Elazar Moshe Horowitz* to *Tosafos*).

4. If the Mishnah permits only *shehiyah* on a shoveled or banked *kirah,* R' Chelbo's qualification must be coming to restrict this to placing food on top of the *kirah* but not inside it. However, this qualification is untenable with respect to a shoveled *kirah,* for if the coals were shoveled away and the food is being left there before the Sabbath, what should be the difference between leaving it on top of the *kirah* and inside it? (*Rashi*).

5. Placing food in the hot interior of the *kirah* is the normal manner of cooking, and one who does this on the Sabbath gives the appearance of cooking. It is therefore prohibited even if the food was initially in the *kirah* and he is merely replacing it there (*Ritva MHK* ed., *Chidushei HaRan, Mishnah Berurah* 253:58; see *Rashi* to 36b ד״ה לא מחזירין and *Shaar HaTziyun* 253:37). [This applies only if the *kirah* is so hot that the hand recoils from food kept in it (יד סולדת בו) (*Mishnah Berurah* 253:67 with *Shaar HaTziyun* §59).]

לעולם אימא לך להחזיר תנן וחסורי מיחסרא והכי קתני כירה שהסיקוה בקש ובגבבא מחזירין עליה תבשיל בגפת ובעצים לא יחזיר עד שיגרוף או עד שיתן את האפר אבל לשהות משהין אע"פ שאינו גרוף ואינו קטום ומה הן משהין בית שמאי אומרים חמין אבל לא תבשיל ובית הלל אומרים חמין ותבשיל והך חזרה דאמרי לך לאו דברי הכל היא אלא מחלוקת בית שמאי ובית הלל שבית שמאי אומרים נוטלין ולא מחזירין ובית הלל אומרים אף מחזירין ת"ש דאמר ר' חלבו א"ר חמא בר גוריא אמר רב לא שנו אלא על גבה אבל לתוכה אסור אי אמרת בשלמא להחזיר תנן היינו דשני בין תוכה לעל גבה אלא אי אמרת לשהות תנן מה לי תוכה מה לי על גבה מי סברת ר' חלבו ארישא קאי אסיפא קאי ובית הלל אומרים אף מחזירין ואמר ר' חלבו אמר רב חמא בר גוריא אמר רב לא שנו אלא על גבה אבל תוכה אסור (א) תא שמע (ב) ב' כירות המתאימות אחת גרופה וקטומה ואחת שאינה גרופה ואינה קטומה משהין על גבי גרופה וקטומה ואין משהין על שאינה גרופה ואינה קטומה ומה הן משהין בית שמאי אומרים ולא כלום ובית הלל אומרים חמין אבל לא תבשיל עקר דברי הכל לא יחזיר דברי רבי מאיר רבי יהודה אומר בית שמאי אומרים חמין אבל לא תבשיל ובית הלל אומרים חמין ותבשיל בית שמאי אומרים נוטלין אבל לא מחזירין ובית הלל אומרים אף מחזירין אי אמרת בשלמא לשהות תנן מתני' מני רבי יהודה היא אלא אי אמרת להחזיר תנן מתניתין מני לא רבי יהודה ולא ר' מאיר אי רבי מאיר קשיא לב"ש בחדא ולבית הלל בתרתי אי רבי יהודה קשיא גרופה וקטומה לעולם אימא לך להחזיר תנן ותנא דידן סבר לה כרבי יהודה בחדא ופליג עליה בחדא סבר לה כרבי יהודה בחדא בחמין ותבשיל ונוטלין ומחזירין ופליג עליה בחדא דאילו תנא דידן סבר לשהות ואף על פי שאינו גרוף וקטום ורבי יהודה סבר בלשהות נמי גרוף וקטום איבעיא להו מהו לסמוך בה תוכה וגבה אסור אבל לסמוך בה שפיר דמי או דילמא לא שנא תא שמע שתי כירות המתאימות אחת גרופה וקטומה ואחת שאינה גרופה וקטומה משהין על גבי גרופה וקטומה ואף על גב דקא סליק ליה הבלא מאידך דילמא שאני התם דכיון דמידליא שליט בה אוירא תא שמע דאמר רב ספרא אמר רב חייא קטמה ונתלבתה סומכין לה ומקיימין עליה ונוטלין ממנה ומחזירין לה שמע מינה לסמוך נמי קטמה אין לא קטמה לא ולטעמיך נוטלין ממנה דקתני קטמה אין לא קטמה לא אלא תנא נוטלין משום מחזירין הכא נמי תנא סומכין משום מקיימין הכי השתא התם נוטלין ומחזירין בחד מקום הוא תנא נוטלין משום מחזירין אלא הכא סומכין בחד מקום הוא ומקיימין בחד מקום הוא מאי הוי עלה ת"ש (ג) כירה שהסיקוה בגפת ובעצים סומכין לה ואין מקיימין אא"כ גרופה וקטומה (ד) גחלים שעממו או שנתן עליה נעורת של פשתן דקה הרי היא כקטומה אמר ר' יצחק בר נחמני א"ר אושעיא קטמה והובערה משהין עליה חמין שהוחמו כל צורכן ותבשיל שבישל כל צורכו שמע

רש"י

לעולם אימא לך להחזיר תנן. ואילו לשהות אע"פ שאינו גרוף שרי: והך חזרה דאמרי לך. לא יחזיר עד שיגרוף דמי גרוף מיהא שרי: לאו דברי הכל היא. ולבית שמאי לא סבירא להו: לא שנו. שריותא דמתני' אלא על גבה דלא נפיש הבלא כולי האי אבל תוכה אסור: אי אמרת בשלמא להחזיר תנן. אבל לשהות משהין אפילו בשאין גרופה כדמתסקינן ליה חסורי ורבי חלבו אשריותא דלשהות על שאינה גרופה קאי: היינו דשני בין תוכה לעל גבה. דכי משהי לתוכה דשאינה גרופה טמטין ממש ברמץ: אלא אי אמרת לשהות תנן. דאפילו לשהות בעי גרופה כיון דגרופה ומבעוד יום הוא טותנו לתוכה מה לי תוכה מה לי על גבה: ארישא. עד שיגרוף: אסיפא קאי. דאיירי בחזרה אבל רישא לשהות הוא ובין תוכה ובין גבה שרי: שתי כירות המתאימות. מחוברות יחד וקיר של חרס מפסקת ביניהם: משהין על גבי גרופה וקטומה. דלא חיישינן משום דסליק לה הבלא מאידך: ומה הן משהין. על הגרופה: לא יחזיר. בשבת: אא"ב. רישא דמתניתין לשהות קאמר דבעי גרופה ולשהות פליגי בחמין ותבשיל ובגרוף וסיפא פליגי בחזרה מתני' ר' יהודה היא: אלא אי אמרת להחזיר תנן דבעי גרופה אבל לשהות לא בעי גרופה ופלוגתא דחמין ותבשיל כשאינו גרוף דקמסקרת ומתרצת לה: קשיא לב"ש בחדא. דקאמרי ב"ש במתני' משהין חמין אף בשאינו גרוף והכא קאמר רבי מאיר לב"ש דאפילו גרוף ולא כלום וכ"ש כשאינו גרוף. והא כולה חדא פירכא היא דבית שמאי לא שני להו בין גרוף לשאינו גרוף: ולב"ה בתרתי. דבמתניתין שרי בית הלל להשהות חמין ותבשיל אף בשאינו גרוף והכא קתני דבגרוף חמין אין תבשיל לא ובשאינה גרוף אין משהין כלל ולענין חזרה בגרוף תנן במתניתין לב"ה מחזירין והכא קתני עקר דברי הכל לא יחזיר: ואי ר' יהודה. דאמר נמי כי מתניתין מ"מ גרופה וקטומה קשיא דמתניתין תרלת דפלוגתא קמייתא בשאינו גרוף ושרו ב"ש חמין ובית הלל חמין ותבשיל והכא קתני אין משהין על גבי שאינה גרופה ואינה קטומה כלל ופלוגתא דלשהות בגרופה וקטומה: בחמין ותבשיל ונוטלים ומחזירין. דמוקי פלוגתא דב"ש וב"ה בשהיית חמין ותבשיל דבית שמאי שרו חמין ותבשיל לא וב"ה חמין ותבשיל ולא כר' מאיר דאמר לב"ש לא כלום: מהו לסמוך. קדרה אצל דופן הכירה בלא גרופה שהכירה מטלטלת היא ומושיבים אותה על גבי קרקע: גבה. עובי שפתה או כסוי שעל חללה: דמדלי. הקדרה על גבי הכירה: ונתלבתה. חזרה והובערה: התם נוטלין ומחזירין בחד מקום. ולא שייך למתני מחזירין עד דתני נוטלין: נעורת. ארשט"ש: שהוחמו כל צרכן. דליכא למיחש לחיתויי: מצטמק

תוספות

לעולם אימא לך להחזיר תנן וחסורי מיחסרא כו'. משום דקיי"ל כחנניה כמו שמפרש בע"ב דחיק לאוקמא מתני' כוותיה: אא"ב להחזיר תנן היינו דשני בין תוכה לעל גבה. פי' בקונטרס משום דאי להחזיר תנן (א) א"כ לשהות משהין אפילו באינה גרופה להכי שני בין תוכה דהוי מטמין ממש ברמץ לעל גבה וקשה להר"ח דלחנניה אפילו תוכה משהין אפי' באינה גרופה דהא תנן (לעיל דף יט:) ולא תרדה על גבי גחלים אלא עד שיקרמו פניה הא קרמו פניה שרי אע"ג דמרדה בתוכה היא ובלאו הכי אור"י דבכנס דחק רש"י לפרש כן דאיכא למימר שפיר היינו דשני בין תוכה לעל גבה מהא דשרי להחזיר בגרופה והשתא דוקא לא ניחא ליה לחלק אבל בהחזרה ניחא ליה שפיר לחלק כדמוכח במאי דמשני מי סברת ארישא קאי אסיפא קאי כו' קשה לר"י (ב) היכי בעי למימר אליבא דרב דמתניתין להחזיר תנן אם כן אתיא מתניתין כחנניה ורב דלא כחנניה דהא חנניה שרי במצטמק ויפה לו דהא דתנן (שם) אין צולין בשר ובצים אלא כדי שיצולו מבעוד יום אתיא כחנניה וצילה אמרינן לקמן דמצטמק ויפה לו הוא ורב אסר לקמן (ג) דמצטמק ויפה לו וי"ל דבלאו הכי לא סבר לה רב כשום תנא דהא ר"מ ור' יהודה אסרי באינה גרופה אפילו במצטמק ורע לו ורב שרי במצטמק ורע לו אפילו באינה גרופה דבגרופה לא אשכחן שום אמורא דאסר אפילו יפה לו ועוד דרב קאי אמילתיה דרבי יוחנן דאיירי באינה גרופה וכן רבי יוחנן דשרי לקמן חמין ותבשיל שבישל כל צרכו באינה גרופה אבל לא בישל כל צרכו אסור לא אשכחן תנא דסבר הכי: מהו לסמוך. באינה גרופה קבעי ואי מתניתין לשהות תנן קא בעי להשהות ולהחזיר ואי להחזיר תנן ושרי לשהות אפי' תוכה וגבה בעי להחזיר ולהשהות היכא שאינו מבושל כמאכל בן דרוסאי: תא שמע כירה שהסיקוה כו'. ומסיק דשרי לסמוך ומכל מקום אין ללמוד מכאן לסמוך אצל האש דשאני הכא דדופני כירה מפסיקין בינו ולאש:

שמע

מסורת הש"ס

א) תוספתא פרק ג, ב) תוספתא [פרק ג], ג) לג ע"א.

תוספות ישנים

א) ואפשר דרב מוקי מתני' בלהחזיר אבל להשהות אפילו אינה גרופה שרי מצטמק ורע לו. ולרבי יוחנן אפי' מצטמק ויפה לו:

הגהות הב"ח

(א) תוס' ד"ה אא"ב וכו' דאי להחזיר תנן אבל לשהות:

גליון הש"ס

תוס' ד"ה לעולם וכו' משום דקיי"ל כחנניה. עיין זה בתוספות מגילה דף יט ע"ב ד"ה ודילמא:

ליקוטי רש"י

נעורת. דק דק שנוערין מן הפשתן וקורין ארישט"ש [לקמן מט.]. שברי גבעולין הננערין מן הפשתים כשמנפצין אותו [חולין נא:].

עין משפט נר מצוה

ב א מיי' פ"ג מהל' שבת הלכה י סמג לאוין סה טוש"ע א"ח סי' רנג סעיף ב:
ג ב שם סעיף א בהג"ה:
ד ג מיי' שם הלכה ז טוש"ע שם סעיף א:
ה ד מיי' שם הלכה ז:

רבינו חננאל

ושקלינן וטרינן ותריצנן כירה שהסיקוה בגפת או בעצים אסור להחזיר אבל לשהות משהין בה אע"פ שאינה גרופה ולא קטומה בין תבשיל בין חמין כחנניה: ואע"ג דעמדה אמרינן תוב תא שמע ב' כירות המתאימות אחת גרופה וקטומה ואחת שאינה גרופה ולא קטומה כו' לר' מאיר אליבא דבית הלל משהין ע"ג גרופה וקטומה חמין אבל לא תבשיל ולב"ש לא כלום לר' יהודה אליבא דב"ש משהין חמין אבל לא תבשיל. וב"ה חמין ותבשיל ב"ש אומרים נוטלין חמין אבל לא (תבשיל) מחזירין. וב"ה [אומרים] נוטלין אף מחזירין בשלמא אי אמרת מתני' לשהות [נמי בעינן] ע"ג גרופה וקטומה מתני' ר' יהודה היא. אלא אי אמרת להחזיר היא אבל לשהות בש"א משהין חמין ובה"א חמין ותבשיל אף על פי שאינה גרופה ולא קטומה. מני מתני' אי ר' מאיר קשיא לב"ש (בהו) [בחדא] במתני' דקתני בש"א חמין אבל לא תבשיל. ורבי מאיר קתני לבית שמאי ולא כלום. ולבית הלל בתרתי דר' מאיר קתני לב"ה משהין חמין אבל לא תבשיל. ומתני' קתני לב"ה חמין ותבשיל. ותוב דרבי מאיר קתני דברי הכל לא יחזיר ומתני' קתני לב"ה אף מחזירין. אי לרבי יהודה קשיא גרופה וקטומה דכי קתני משהין לב"ש חמין לב"ה חמין ותבשיל בגרופה וקטומה קתני ומתני' אע"פ שאינה גרופה וקטומה. ושנינן לעולם אימא לך להחזיר תנן. ותנא דידן סבר לה כרבי יהודה בחדא ופליג עליה בחדא ופשוטה היא ועמדה [הסוגיא] דמתני' להחזיר תנן. עכשיו יש מי שאומר כיון דלא איפשיטא בהדיא להחזיר אשנויי לא סמכינן [ומוקמין] מתני' לשהות. ויש מי שאומר הלכה להחזיר תנן ומסייעא ליה הא דא"ר יוחנן כירה שהסיקוה בגפת ובעצים משהין עליה חמין שלא הוחמו כל צרכן ותבשיל שלא בישל כל צרכו עקר לא יחזיר וקסבר מתני' להחזיר תנן כו'. ועוד מדאמר רבא תרוייהו תנגהי ואמרינן מכדי תרוייהו תנגהי ר' יוחנן מאי אתא לאשמעינן ואמר דיוקא דמתני' קמ"ל ש"מ דרבי יוחנן סבר דוקא דמתני' להחזיר הוא א) ושיהוי זה אינה הטמנה אלא כגון כסא של ברזל והקדירה יושבת עליה והיא תלויה (או) באבנים [או] כיוצא בה. אבל הטמנה ע"ג גחלים דברי הכל אסור. דקי"ל הטמנה בדבר המוסיף אסור ואפילו מבעוד יום: איבעיא להו מהו לסמוך לה. תוכה וגבה אסור. אבל לסמוך שרי או דילמא לא

חשק שלמה על רבינו חננאל א) עי' בבעל המאור:

LEAVE food items, before the Sabbath, ON TOP OF THE ONE THAT WAS SHOVELED OR BANKED וְאֵין מַשְׁהִין עַל שֶׁאֵינָהּ גְּרוּפָה וְאֵינָהּ קְטוּמָה – BUT ONE MAY NOT LEAVE food items ON TOP OF THE ONE THAT WAS NOT SHOVELED OR BANKED.[6] וּמָה הֵן מַשְׁהִין – AND WHAT items MAY ONE LEAVE on the *kirah* that was shoveled or banked? בֵּית שַׁמַּאי אוֹמְרִים וְלֹא כְלוּם – BEIS SHAMMAI SAY: NOTHING AT ALL.[7] וּבֵית הִלֵּל אוֹמְרִים חַמִּין אֲבָל לֹא תַבְשִׁיל – BUT BEIS HILLEL SAY: HOT WATER BUT NOT COOKED FOOD. עָקַר דִּבְרֵי הַכֹּל לֹא יַחֲזִיר – If ONE REMOVED something that had been left on the fire before the Sabbath, ALL (i.e. Beis Shammai and Beis Hillel) AGREE that HE CANNOT RETURN IT to the Sabbath. דִּבְרֵי רַבִּי מֵאִיר – These are THE WORDS OF R' MEIR.[8] רַבִּי יְהוּדָה אוֹמֵר – R' YEHUDAH SAYS: בֵּית שַׁמַּאי אוֹמְרִים חַמִּין אֲבָל לֹא תַבְשִׁיל – BEIS SHAMMAI SAY that before the Sabbath one may leave HOT WATER BUT NOT COOKED FOOD on the shoveled or banked *kirah;* וּבֵית הִלֵּל אוֹמְרִים חַמִּין וְתַבְשִׁיל – AND BEIS HILLEL SAY: One may leave both HOT WATER AND COOKED FOOD on the *kirah.* בֵּית שַׁמַּאי אוֹמְרִים נוֹטְלִין אֲבָל לֹא מַחֲזִירִין – Furthermore, BEIS SHAMMAI SAY that WE MAY REMOVE something from the *kirah* on the Sabbath BUT NOT RETURN it, וּבֵית הִלֵּל אוֹמְרִים אַף מַחֲזִירִין – AND BEIS HILLEL SAY that WE MAY EVEN RETURN it.[9]

The Gemara proceeds to compare our Mishnah with this Baraisa:

אִי אָמְרַת בִּשְׁלָמָא לִשְׁהוֹת תְּנַן – **All is well if you say that the Mishnah refers to leaving** food on the *kirah* before the Sabbath, for accordingly we can say: מַתְנִיתִין מַנִּי רַבִּי יְהוּדָה הִיא – **Whose** view **is the Mishnah** reflective of? – **It is** the view of **R' Yehudah.**[10] אֶלָּא אִי אָמְרַת לְהַחֲזִיר תְּנַן – **But if you will say that the Mishnah refers to returning** food to the *kirah* on the Sabbath, מַתְנִיתִין מַנִּי – **whose** view **is the Mishnah** reflective of? לֹא רַבִּי יְהוּדָה וְלֹא רַבִּי מֵאִיר – It is **neither** the view of **R' Yehudah nor** the view of **R' Meir!** אִי רַבִּי מֵאִיר – For **if** it is supposed to reflect the view of **R' Meir,** קַשְׁיָא לְבֵית שַׁמַּאי בַּחֲדָא וּלְבֵית הִלֵּל בִּתְרְתֵּי – **it contradicts** his version of **Beis Shammai's** opinion **on one count and** his version of **Beis Hillel's** opinion **on two counts;**[11] אִי רַבִּי יְהוּדָה – and **if** it is supposed to reflect the view of **R' Yehudah,** קַשְׁיָא גְּרוּפָה וּקְטוּמָה – **it contradicts** his view **regarding** whether the *kirah* must be **shoveled or banked** in order to allow leaving food on it before the Sabbath![12] Thus, if the Mishnah refers to returning food to the *kirah,* in accordance with Chananyah's opinion, it cannot be reconciled with this Baraisa. Perforce, it refers to leaving food on the *kirah* and does not accord with Chananyah's opinion![13]

The Gemara rejects the proof:

לְעוֹלָם אֵימָא לָךְ לְהַחֲזִיר תְּנַן – **Actually, I can tell you** that **the Mishnah refers to returning** food to the *kirah* on the Sabbath, וְתַנָּא דִידָן סָבַר לָהּ כְּרַבִּי יְהוּדָה בַּחֲדָא וּפָלֵיג עֲלֵיהּ בַּחֲדָא – **and our Tanna**[14] **agrees with R' Yehudah in one** respect **and disagrees with him in one** respect. סָבַר לָהּ כְּרַבִּי יְהוּדָה בַּחֲדָא – **He agrees with R' Yehudah in one** respect – בְּחַמִּין וְתַבְשִׁיל וְנוֹטְלִין וּמַחֲזִירִין – regarding the issues of **hot water and cooked food, and removing and returning** items on a *kirah* on the Sabbath.[15] וּפָלֵיג עֲלֵיהּ בַּחֲדָא – **And he disagrees with [R' Yehudah] in one** respect – דְּאִילּוּ תַּנָּא דִידָן סָבַר לִשְׁהוֹת וְאַף עַל פִּי שֶׁאֵינוֹ גָרוּף וְקָטוּם – **for whereas our Tanna holds** that it is permitted **to leave** food on a *kirah* **even if it was not shoveled or banked,** and requires shoveling or banking only for returning food to the *kirah,* in accordance with Chananyah's opinion, וְרַבִּי יְהוּדָה סָבַר בִּלְשְׁהוֹת נַמִּי – **R' Yehudah holds that in regard to leaving** food on the *kirah* **too,** גָּרוּף וְקָטוּם אֵין אִי לֹא לֹא – if **it was shoveled or banked,** leaving food on it is **indeed** permissible, but **if not,** it is **not** permissible.[16]

NOTES

6. One may leave food on the shoveled or banked *kirah* even though the exposed fire in its sister-*kirah* contributes heat to it, and we need not be concerned that one might forgetfully stoke the fire of the sister-*kirah* (*Rashi*). [Note, however, that the Baraisa requires shoveling or banking the first *kirah* even for *shehiyah,* in opposition to Chananyah's opinion.]

7. I.e. Beis Shammai disagree with the previous ruling and forbid leaving anything on the *kirah.* It is unclear whether Beis Shammai forbid *shehiyah* categorically or only in this case, because of the open coals in the sister-*kirah.* However, *Rashi* below (ד״ה קשיא לב״ש בחדא) implies that they forbid it categorically (see also *Rashash* to *Tosafos* ד״ה אא״ב; cf. *Rosh Yosef*).

8. R' Meir's version of the views of Beis Shammai and Beis Hillel differs radically from our Mishnah's version (see below).

9. This matches our Mishnah's version of the opinions of Beis Shammai and Beis Hillel.

10. If the Mishnah means to require shoveling or banking the *kirah* even for *shehiyah* (in opposition to Chananyah's view), its presentation of the views of Beis Shammai and Beis Hillel is identical with R' Yehudah's presentation: Beis Shammai permit *shehiyah* on a shoveled or banked *kirah* only for hot water whereas Beis Hillel permit it even for cooked foods; Beis Shammai prohibit *chazarah* altogether whereas Beis Hillel permit it (*Rashi;* see note 1).

11. If the Mishnah is dealing with replacing food on the *kirah* and follows Chananyah's opinion, it must be interpreted as saying: (a) that *chazarah* requires shoveling or banking, but *shehiyah* is permitted even over uncovered coals; (b) that Beis Shammai and Beis Hillel dispute whether *shehiyah* over uncovered coals is permitted only for hot water or even for cooked foods; (c) that Beis Shammai further dispute the permissibility of *chazarah* altogether (see note 1).

This version of Beis Shammai's opinion is at odds with R' Meir's version insofar as according to the Mishnah Beis Shammai permit the *shehiyah* of hot water even over uncovered coals whereas according to R' Meir they forbid all *shehiyah,* even on a *kirah* that was shoveled or banked.

The Mishnah's version of Beis Hillel's opinion is at odds with R' Meir's version on two counts, i.e. regarding both *shehiyah* and *chazarah.* Firstly, the Mishnah cites Beis Hillel as permitting *shehiyah* even over open coals for both hot water and cooked foods, whereas R' Meir cites them as allowing it only if the *kirah* was shoveled or banked, and even then only for hot water. Secondly, the Mishnah cites Beis Hillel as permitting *chazarah,* whereas according to R' Meir they forbid it (*Rashi*).

12. The respective opinions of Beis Shammai and Beis Hillel cited by the Mishnah match those cited by R' Yehudah. However, if we interpret the Mishnah as following Chananyah's opinion, the dispute whether *shehiyah* is permitted only for hot water or even for cooked foods pertains to *shehiyah* over open coals, whereas according to R' Yehudah it pertains to *shehiyah* over a *kirah* that was shoveled or banked and all agree that *shehiyah* over open coals is categorically forbidden (*Rashi*).

13. Thus, the Mishnah means to categorically forbid *shehiyah* over open coals and accords precisely with R' Yehudah's presentation of the views.

14. I.e. the Tanna who authored our Mishnah.

15. I.e. his version of the respective opinions stated by Beis Shammai and Beis Hillel matches R' Yehudah's version: Beis Shammai permit *shehiyah* for hot water but not for cooked foods whereas Beis Hillel permit it even for cooked foods; Beis Shammai forbid *chazarah* whereas Beis Hillel permit it.

16. Thus, according to the Mishnah, the dispute concerning hot water and cooked food pertains to an unshoveled and unbanked *kirah,* in accordance with Chananyah's opinion that *shehiyah* over such a *kirah* is permitted. According to R' Yehudah, however, the dispute pertains to a shoveled or banked *kirah; shehiyah* over open coals is categorically forbidden, in opposition to Chananyah's opinion.

The Gemara has thus failed to resolve the question of whether our Mishnah follows Chananyah's opinion or not, but has consistently demonstrated that either interpretation is tenable. *Rashi* (37b ד״ה ורב ששת), *Tosafos* (ד״ה לעולם here and to 37b ד״ה אמר רב ששת) and others rule that the halachah follows Chananyah's opinion (see 37b note 12). Thus, *shehiyah* is permitted even on an unshoveled and unbanked

לעולם אימא לך להחזיר תנן וחסורי מיחסרא והכי קתני כירה שהסיקוה בקש ובגבבא מחזירין עליה תבשיל בגפת ובעצים לא יחזיר עד שיגרוף או עד שיתן את האפר אבל לשהות משהין אע"פ שאינו גרוף ואינו קטום ומה הן משהין בית שמאי אומרים חמין אבל לא תבשיל ובית הלל אומרים חמין ותבשיל והך חזרה דאמרי לך לאו דברי הכל היא אלא מחלוקת בית שמאי ובית הלל שבית שמאי אומרים נוטלין ולא מחזירין ובית הלל אומרים אף מחזירין ת"ש דאמר ר' חלבו א"ר חמא בר גוריא אמר רב לא שנו אלא על גבה אבל לתוכה אסור אי אמרת בשלמא להחזיר תנן היינו דשני בין תוכה לעל גבה אלא אי אמרת לשהות תנן מה לי תוכה מה לי על גבה מי סברת ר' חלבו ארישא קאי אסיפא [א]קאי ובית הלל אומרים אף מחזירין ואמר ר' חלבו אמר רב חמא בר גוריא אמר רב לא שנו אלא על גבה אבל תוכה אסור (א) תא שמע [ב]ב' כירות המתאימות אחת גרופה וקטומה ואחת שאינה גרופה ואינה קטומה משהין על גבי גרופה וקטומה ואין משהין על שאינה גרופה ואינה קטומה ומה הן משהין בית שמאי אומרים ולא כלום ובית הלל אומרים חמין אבל לא תבשיל עקר דברי הכל לא יחזיר דברי רבי מאיר רבי יהודה אומר בית שמאי אומרים חמין אבל לא תבשיל ובית הלל אומרים חמין ותבשיל בית שמאי אומרים נוטלין אבל לא מחזירין ובית הלל אומרים אף מחזירין אי אמרת בשלמא לשהות תנן מתני' מני רבי יהודה היא אלא אי אמרת להחזיר תנן מתניתין מני לא רבי יהודה ולא ר' מאיר אי רבי מאיר קשיא לב"ש בחדא ולבית הלל בתרתי אי רבי יהודה קשיא גרופה וקטומה לעולם אימא לך להחזיר תנן ותנא דידן סבר לה כרבי יהודה בחדא ופליג עליה בחדא סבר לה כרבי יהודה בחדא בחמין ותבשיל ונוטלין ומחזירין ופליג עליה בחדא דאילו תנא דידן סבר לשהות ואף על פי שאינו גרוף וקטום ורבי יהודה סבר בלשהות נמי גרוף וקטום אין אי לא לא איבעיא להו מהו לסמוך בה תוכה וגבה אסור אבל לסמוך בה שפיר דמי או דילמא לא שנא תא שמע שתי כירות המתאימות אחת גרופה וקטומה ואחת שאינה גרופה וקטומה משהין על גבי גרופה וקטומה ואף על גב דקא סליק ליה הבלא מאידך דילמא שאני התם דכיון דמידליא שליט בה אוירא תא שמע דאמר רב ספרא אמר רב חייא קטמה ונתלבתה סומכין לה ומקיימין עליה ונוטלין ממנה ומחזירין לה שמע מינה לסמוך נמי קטמה אין לא קטמה לא ולטעמיך נוטלין ממנה דקתני קטמה אין לא קטמה לא אלא תנא נוטלין משום מחזירין הכא נמי תנא סומכין משום מקיימין הכי השתא התם נוטלין ומחזירין בחד מקום הוא תנא נוטלין משום מחזירין אלא הכא סומכין בחד מקום הוא ומקיימין בחד מקום הוא מאי הוי עלה ת"ש (ב) [ג]כירה שהסיקוה בגפת ובעצים סומכין לה ואין מקיימין אא"כ גרופה וקטומה [ד]גחלים שעממו או שנתן עליה נעורת של פשתן דקה הרי היא כקטומה אמר ר' יצחק בר נחמני א"ר אושעיא קטמה והובערה משהין עליה חמין שהוחמו כל צורכן ותבשיל שבישל כל צורכו

שמע

רש"י

לעולם אימא לך להחזיר תנן. ואילו לשהות אע"פ שאינו גרוף שרי: והך חזרה דאמרי לך. לא יחזיר עד שיגרוף דכי גרוף מיהא שרי: לאו דברי הכל היא. ולבית שמאי לא סבירא להו: לא שנו. שריותא דמתני' אלא על גבה דלא נפיש הבלא כולי האי אבל תוכה אסור: אי אמרת בשלמא להחזיר תנן. אבל לשהות משהין אפילו בשאין גרופה כדמחסרינן ליה חסורי ורבי חלבו אשריותא דלשהות על שאינה גרופה קאי: היינו דשני בין תוכה לעל גבה. דכי משהי לתוכה דשאינה גרופה מטמין ממש ברמץ: אלא אי אמרת לשהות תנן. דאפילו לשהות בעי גרופה כיון דגרופה ומבעוד יום הוא טותנו לתוכה מה לי תוכה מה לי על גבה: ארישא. עד שיגרוף: אסיפא קאי. דאיירי בחזרה אבל רישא לשהות הוא ובין תוכה ובין גבה שרי: שתי כירות המתאימות. מחוברות יחד וקיר של חרס מפסקת ביניהם: משהין על גבי גרופה וקטומה. דלא חיישינן משום דסליק לה הבלא מאידך: ומה הן משהין. על הגרופה: לא יחזיר. בשבת: אא"ב. רישא דמתניתין לשהות קאמר דבעי גרופה ובלשהות פליגי בחמין ובתבשיל ובגרוף וסיפא פליגי בחזרה מתני' ר' יהודה היא. אלא אי אמרת להחזיר תנן דבעי גרופה אבל לשהות לא בעי גרופה ופלוגתא דחמין ותבשיל כשאינו גרוף כדקמחסרת ומתרצת לה: קשיא לב"ש בחדא. דקאמרי ב"ש במתני' משהין חמין אף בשאינו גרוף והכא קאמר רבי מאיר לב"ש דאפילו גרוף ולא כלום וכ"ש כשאינו גרוף. והא כולה חדא פירכא היא דבית שמאי לא שני להו בין גרוף לשאינו גרוף: ולב"ה בתרתי. דבמתניתין שרי בית הלל להשהות חמין ותבשיל אף בשאינו גרוף והכא קתני דבגרוף חמין אין תבשיל לא ובשאינה גרוף אין משהין כלל ולענין חזרה בגרוף תנן במתניתין לב"ה מחזירין והכא קתני עקר דברי הכל לא יחזיר: ואי ר' יהודה. דאמר נמי כי מתניתין מ"מ גרופה וקטומה קשיא דמתניתין תרלת דפלוגתא קמייתא בשאינו גרוף ושרו ב"ש חמין ובית הלל חמין ותבשיל והכא קתני אין משהין על גבי שאינה גרופה ואינה קטומה כלל ופלוגתא דלשהות בגרופה וקטומה: בחמין ותבשיל ונוטלים ומחזירין. דמוקי פלוגתא דב"ש וב"ה בשהיית חמין ותבשיל דבית שמאי שרו חמין ותבשיל לא וב"ה חמין ותבשיל ולא כר' מאיר דאמר לב"ש לא כלום: מהו לסמוך. קדרה אצל דופן הכירה בלא גרופה שהכירה מטלטלת היא ומושיבים אותה על גבי קרקע: גבה. עובי שפתה או כסוי שעל חללה: דמדליא. הקדרה על גבי הכירה: ונתלבתה. חזרה והובערה: התם נוטלין ומחזירין בחד מקום. ולא שייך למתני מחזירין עד דתני נוטלין: נעורת. אריסט"ש: שהוחמו כל צרכן. דליכא למיחש לחיתוי:

תוספות

לעולם אימא לך להחזיר תנן וחסורי מיחסרא כו'. ° משום דקיי"ל כחנניה כמו שאפרש בע"ה דחיק לאוקמא מתני' כוותיה: אא"ב להחזיר תנן היינו דשני בין תוכה לעל גבה. פי' בקונטרס משום דאי להחזיר תנן (א) א"כ לשהות משהין אפילו באינה גרופה להכי שני בין תוכה דהוי מטמין ממש ברמץ לעל גבה וקשה להר"ח דלחנניה אפילו תוכה משהין אפי' באינה גרופה דהא תנן (לעיל דף יט:) ולא חררה על גבי גחלים אלא עד שיקרמו פניה הא קרמו פניה שרי אע"ג דחררה בתוכה היא ובלאו הכי אור"י דבחנם דחק רש"י לפרש כן דאיכא למימר שפיר היינו דשני לן בין תוכה לעל גבה מהא דשרי להחזיר בגרופה ובהשהאה דוקא לא ניחא ליה לחלק אבל בהחזרה ניחא ליה שפיר לחלק כדמוכח במאי דמשני מי סברת ארישא קאי אסיפא קאי כו' קשה לר"י א) היכי בעי למימר אליבא דרב דמתניתין להחזיר תנן אם כן אתיא מתניתין כחנניה ורב דלא כחנניה דהא חנניה שרי במצטמק ויפה לו דהא דתנן (שם) אין צולין בשר ובילה אלא כדי שיצולו מבעוד יום אתיא כחנניה ובילה אמרינן לקמן דמצטמק ויפה לו הוא ורב אסר לקמן [ג] דמצטמק ויפה לו וי"ל דבלאו הכי לא סבר לה רב כשום תנא דהא ר"מ ור' יהודה אסרי באינה גרופה אפילו במצטמק ורע לו ורב שרי במצטמק ורע לו אפילו באינה גרופה דבגרופה לא אשכחן שום אמורא דאסר אפילו יפה לו ועוד דרב קאי אמילתיה דרבי יוחנן דאיירי באינה גרופה וכן רבי יוחנן דשרי לקמן חמין ותבשיל שבישל כל צרכו באינה גרופה אבל לא בישל כל צרכו אסור לא אשכחן תנא דסבר הכי:

מהו לסמוך. באינה גרופה קבעי ואי מתניתין להשהות תנן קא בעי להשהות ולהחזיר ואי להחזיר תנן ושרי להשהות אפי' תוכה וגבה בעי להחזיר ולהשהות היכא שאינו מבושל כמאכל בן דרוסאי:

תא שמע כירה שהסיקוה כו'. ומסיק דשרי לסמוך ומכל מקום אין ללמוד מכאן לסמוך אלא האש דשאני הכא דדופני כירה מפסיקין בינו ולאש:

מסורת הש"ס

א) תוספתא פרק ג, ב) תוספתא [פרק ג], ג) לח ע"א.

תוספות ישנים

א) ולפסר דרב מוקי מתני' בלהחזיר אבל להשהות אפילו אינה גרופה שרי מצטמק ורע לו. ולרבי יוחנן אפי' מצטמק ויפה לו:

הגהות הב"ח

(א) תוס' ד"ה אא"ב וכו' דאי להחזיר תנן אבל לשהות:

גליון הש"ס

תוס' ד"ה לעולם וכו' משום דקיי"ל כחנניה. כעין זה בתוספות מגילה דף יט ע"ב ד"ה ודילמא:

ליקוטי רש"י

נעורת. דק דק שנוערין מן הפשתן וקורין אריסט"ש [לקמן מט.]. שברי גבעולין הננערין מן הפשתים כשמנפצין אותו [חולין נא:].

עין משפט נר מצוה

ב א מיי' פ"ג מהל' שבת הלכה י סמג לאוין סה טוש"ע א"ח סי' רנג סעיף ג:

ג ב שם סעיף א בהג"ה:

ד ג מיי' שם הלכה ז טוש"ע שם סעיף א:

ה ד מיי' שם הלכה ד:

רבינו חננאל

ושקלינן וטרינן ותריצנן כירה שהסיקוה בגפת או בעצים אסור להחזיר אבל לשהות משהין בה אע"פ שאינה גרופה ולא קטומה בין תבשיל בין חמין כחנניה: ואע"ג דעמדה אמרינן תוב תא שמע ב' כירות המתאימות אחת גרופה וקטומה ואחת שאינה גרופה ולא קטומה כו' לר' מאיר אליבא דבית הלל משהין ע"ג גרופה וקטומה חמין אבל לא תבשיל ולב"ש לא כלום לר' יהודה אליבא דב"ש משהין חמין אבל לא תבשיל. וב"ה חמין ותבשיל ב"ש אומרים נוטלין חמין אבל לא (תבשיל) מחזירין. וב"ה [אומרים] נוטלין אף מחזירין בשלמא אי אמרת מתני' לשהות [נמי בעינן] ע"ג גרופה וקטומה מתני' ר' יהודה היא. אלא אי אמרת להחזיר היא אבל לשהות בש"א משהין חמין ובה"א חמין ותבשיל אף על פי שאינה גרופה ולא קטומה. מני מתני' אי ר' מאיר קשיא לב"ש (בהו) [בחדא] במתני' דקתני בש"א חמין אבל לא תבשיל. ורבי מאיר קתני לבית שמאי ולא כלום. ולבית הלל בתרתי דר' מאיר קתני לב"ה משהין חמין אבל לא תבשיל. ומתני' קתני לב"ה חמין ותבשיל. ותוב דרבי מאיר קתני דברי הכל לא יחזיר ומתני' קתני לב"ה אף מחזירין. אי לרבי יהודה קשיא גרופה וקטומה דכי קתני משהין לב"ש חמין לב"ה חמין ותבשיל בגרופה וקטומה קתני ומתני' אע"פ שאינה גרופה וקטומה. ושנינן לעולם אימא לך להחזיר תנן. ותנא דידן סבר לה כרבי יהודה בחדא ופליג עליה בחדא ופשוטה היא ועמדה [הסוגיא] דמתני' להחזיר תנן. עכשיו יש מי שאומר כיון דלא איפשיטא בהדיא להחזיר אשנויי לא סמכינן [ומוקמי] מתני' לשהות. ויש מי שאומר הלכה להחזיר תנן ומסייעא ליה הא דא"ר יוחנן כירה שהסיקוה בגפת ובעצים משהין עליה חמין שלא הוחמו כל צרכן ותבשיל שלא בישל כל צרכו עקר לא יחזיר וקסבר מתני' להחזיר תנן כו'. ועוד מדאמר רבא תרוייהו תננהי ואמרינן מכדי תרוייהו תננהי ר' יוחנן מאי אתא לאשמעינן ואמר דיוקא דמתני' קמ"ל ש"מ דרבי יוחנן סבר דוקא דמתני' להחזיר הוא א) ושיהוי זה אינה הטמנה אלא כגון כסא של ברזל והקדירה יושבת עליה והיא תלויה (או) באבנים [או] כיוצא בה. אבל הטמנה ע"ג גחלים דברי הכל אסור. דקי"ל הטמנה בדבר המוסיף אסור ואפילו מבעוד יום: **איבעיא להו** מהו לסמוך לה. תוכה וגבה אסור. אבל לסמוך שרי או דילמא לא

מצטמק

חשק שלמה על רבינו חננאל א) עי' בבעל המאור:

The Gemara turns to a new issue:

אִיבַּעְיָא לְהוּ – They inquired: **מַהוּ לִסְמוֹךְ בָּהּ – What is** the law with respect to **placing** a pot of food **alongside** the exterior wall of **[a *kirah*]** that was not shoveled or banked? **תּוֹכָהּ וְגַבָּהּ אָסוּר –** Do we say that only placing a pot **inside [the *kirah*] or on top of it is forbidden,** **אֲבָל לִסְמוֹךְ בָּהּ שַׁפִּיר דָּמֵי – but placing** a pot **alongside it is acceptable?** **אוֹ דִּילְמָא לֹא שְׁנָא – Or perhaps, there is no difference** between placing a pot on top of it, and alongside it.[17] – ? –

A resolution is proposed:

תָּא שְׁמַע – Come, learn a proof from the Baraisa that was cited above, which states: **שְׁתֵּי כִּירוֹת הַמַּתְאִימוֹת** – Regarding TWIN *KIRAHS* that are built side by side and are joined by a common wall, **אַחַת גְּרוּפָה וּקְטוּמָה וְאַחַת שֶׁאֵינָהּ גְּרוּפָה וּקְטוּמָה –** ONE of which was SHOVELED OR BANKED AND the other ONE of which was NEITHER SHOVELED NOR BANKED, **מַשְׁהִין עַל גַּבֵּי גְּרוּפָה וּקְטוּמָה –** the rule is that ONE MAY LEAVE food ON TOP OF THE ONE THAT WAS SHOVELED OR BANKED etc. **וְאַף עַל גַּב דְּקָא סָלִיק לֵיהּ הַבְלָא מֵאִידָךְ –** The Baraisa permits this **even though heat enters [this *kirah*] from the other one** that was not shoveled or banked. Thus, it is permitted to place a pot next to an unshoveled and unbanked *kirah,* even though it benefits from the heat of the *kirah*![18]

The Gemara rejects the proof:

דִּילְמָא שָׁאנִי הָתָם – Perhaps it is different there, in the Baraisa's case, **דְּכֵיוָן דְּמִידַּלְיָא שָׁלִיט בָּהּ אֲוִירָא – for since [the pot] is elevated** on top of the *kirah* that was shoveled or banked **it is ventilated,** and little heat reaches it from the adjoining *kirah.*[19] Our inquiry, however, concerns placing a pot of food on the ground next to the wall of the *kirah,* where it benefits significantly from the *kirah's* heat.

The Gemara offers another resolution:

תָּא שְׁמַע – Come, learn a proof: **דְּאָמַר רַב סַפְרָא אָמַר רַב חִיָּיא – For Rav Safra said in the name of Rav Chiya:** **קְטָמָהּ וְנִתְלַבְּתָה** – If **one banked [a *kirah*] and it** subsequently **flared up** again, **סוֹמְכִין לָהּ וּמְקַיְּימִין עָלֶיהָ – one may** nevertheless **place** a pot of food **alongside [the *kirah*]** before the Sabbath **and keep** food **on top of it,** **וְנוֹטְלִין מִמֶּנָּה וּמַחֲזִירִין לָהּ –** and **remove** food **from it and replace** it **there** on the Sabbath.[20] The Gemara reasons: **שְׁמַע מִינָּהּ לִסְמוֹךְ נַמִּי –** We may **learn from this** ruling that **even in regard to placing** food **alongside [the *kirah*],** **קְטָמָהּ אִין לֹא קְטָמָהּ לֹא –** the rule is that if **one banked [the *kirah*]** it is **indeed** permitted, but if **he did not bank [the *kirah*]** it is **not** permitted![21]

The Gemara objects to this inference:

וּלְטַעְמֵיךְ – But according to your reasoning, **נוֹטְלִין מִמֶּנָּה דְּקָתָנֵי –** should we also infer from **that which [Rav Chiya] stated, "One may remove** food **from it,"** **קְטָמָהּ אִין לֹא קְטָמָהּ לֹא –** that only if **one banked [the *kirah*]** is he **indeed** permitted to remove food from it, but if **he did not bank it** he may **not** remove food from it? Why, this is certainly not correct![22]

NOTES

kirah, once something has been cooked like the food of Ben Derusai; it is only *chazarah* that requires shoveling or banking. However, *Rif, Rambam* (*Hil. Shabbos* 3:4) and others rule that the halachah does not follow Chananyah's opinion. Thus, even *shehiyah* is permitted only if a *kirah* is shoveled or banked. *Beis Yosef* (*Orach Chaim* 253:1) seems to favor the stringent opinion of *Rif* and *Rambam,* but *Rama* states that it is customary to follow the lenient opinion (see *Beur Halachah* to 253:1 ד״ה ונהגו להקל). [All agree, however, that it is permissible to leave a piece of raw meat on an unbanked *kirah* right before the Sabbath. Since it cannot cook in time for the evening meal and will certainly cook in time for the morning meal, the concern that one might stoke the coals does not apply. In fact, if one throws a piece of raw meat into a pot of cooked food, thereby demonstrating that he does not intend to use it until the morning, he may leave the entire pot on the unbanked *kirah* right before the Sabbath (Gemara above, 18b; *Orach Chaim* 253:1).]

As mentioned above (36b note 1), our present-day ovens and ranges are similar to the Talmudic *kirah* and are governed by its rules. The custom to cover the flame by placing a *blech* (Yiddish for tin), i.e. a sheet of metal, over the burners is designed to permit *shehiyah* (according to *Beis Yosef*) or *chazarah* (according to *Rama*), for this practice is considered analogous to banking the coals of a *kirah* with ash (see *Mishnah Berurah* 253:81; cf. *Chazon Ish* 37:9,11).

The following chart sets forth the various Tannaic opinions.

		SHEHIYAH	CHAZARAH
R' MEIR	BEIS SHAMMAI	categorically prohibited	prohibited
	BEIS HILLEL	permitted only for water on shoveled/banked *kirah*	
R' YEHUDAH (and Mishnah, if it does not follow Chananyah)	BEIS SHAMMAI	permitted only for water on shoveled/banked *kirah*	prohibited
	BEIS HILLEL	permitted even for food on shoveled/banked *kirah*	permitted on shoveled/banked *kirah*
The Mishnah, if it follows Chananyah	BEIS SHAMMAI	permitted for water on unshoveled/unbanked *kirah*	prohibited
	BEIS HILLEL	permitted even for food on unshoveled/unbanked *kirah*	permitted on shoveled/banked *kirah*

17. The top of the *kirah,* on which it is forbidden to place a pot, includes the rim of its walls as well as the top of its cover (*Rashi*). Although the cover of the *kirah* conceals the coals, it is forbidden to place the pot on top of it because this is the usual way of cooking. Only shoveling or banking the coals with ash, which reduces the amount of heat they generate and *demonstrates* a disinterest in stoking them, serves to permit placing a pot in the usual cooking position (see *Beur Halachah* to 253:1 ד״ה ליתן עליה and *Chazon Ish* 37:9). However, perhaps it is permitted to place a pot outside a *kirah* next to its wall even though the wall is hot, since the outside of the *kirah* is not as hot as its top and is not usually used for cooking (see *Chazon Ish* ibid.). If this is permitted, it will be permitted even in circumstances in which the wall is so hot that the hand recoils from food left there (*Mishnah Berurah* 253:17).

According to Chananyah's opinion, that once something has been cooked like the food of Ben Derusai it may be left on top of an unbanked *kirah,* it is obviously permissible to leave the food against the exterior wall of an unbanked *kirah* before the Sabbath. However, the Gemara's inquiry is relevant to food that has begun to cook but has not yet reached the state of the food of Ben Derusai. It is also relevant to *chazarah,* i.e. the permissibility of replacing against the wall of the *kirah* something that was taken from there on the Sabbath. According to those who dispute Chananyah's opinion, however, the inquiry is relevant even to the *shehiyah* of food that has been cooked like the food of Ben Derusai (*Tosafos;* cf. *Rif;* see also *Mishnah Berurah* 253:15 with *Beur Halachah*).

18. Although it was demonstrated above that this Baraisa disagrees with Chananyah as to whether food may be left on top of the unbanked *kirah* (see note 6), we may nevertheless learn from it that placing food next to a *kirah* is not like placing food on top of it. Presumably, Chananyah agrees with this, since the issue at hand does not hinge upon his dispute with the Sages (*Baal HaMaor, Rosh;* cf. *Milchamos Hashem*).

19. The Baraisa permits specifically leaving food on *top* of the *kirah* that was shoveled or banked.

20. In short, Rav Chiya rules that despite the resurgence of the fire, the *kirah* is treated in all respects like one that was banked.

21. Since Rav Chiya found it necessary to state that it is permitted to place food alongside the *kirah* even though its flame sprung back to life, he must hold that if the *kirah* had not been banked at all it would be forbidden to place food there.

[Note that Rav Chiya's ruling further implies that shoveling or banking is required for *shehiyah,* in contradiction to Chananyah's opinion. Nevertheless, we may infer from Rav Chiya's statement that placing food alongside the wall of a *kirah* is tantamount to placing it on top, for Chananyah and the Sages do not disagree concerning this point. See above, note 18.]

22. There is never any restriction on removing food from the top of a *kirah* on the Sabbath (see *Rama, Orach Chaim* 253:1 with *Magen Avraham* §18).

לעולם אימא לך להחזיר תנן וחסורי מיחסרא והכי קתני כירה שהסיקוה בקש ובגבבא מחזירין עליה תבשיל בגפת ובעצים לא יחזיר עד שיגרוף או עד שיתן את האפר אבל לשהות משהין אע"פ שאינו גרוף ואינו קטום ומה הן משהין בית שמאי אומרים חמין אבל לא תבשיל ובית הלל אומרים חמין ותבשיל והך חזרה דאמרי לך לאו דברי הכל היא אלא מחלוקת בית שמאי ובית הלל שבית שמאי אומרים נוטלין ולא מחזירין ובית הלל אומרים אף מחזירין ת"ש דאמר ר' חלבו א"ר חמא בר גוריא אמר רב לא שנו אלא על גבה אבל לתוכה אסור אי אמרת בשלמא להחזיר תנן היינו דשני בין תוכה לעל גבה אלא אי אמרת לשהות תנן מה לי תוכה מה לי על גבה מי סברת ר' חלבו ארישא קאי אסיפא [א]קאי ובית הלל אומרים אף מחזירין ואמר ר' חלבו אמר רב חמא בר גוריא אמר רב לא שנו אלא על גבה אבל תוכה אסור [א] תא שמע [ב]ב' כירות המתאימות אחת גרופה וקטומה ואחת שאינה גרופה ואינה קטומה משהין על גבי גרופה וקטומה ואין משהין על שאינה גרופה ואינה קטומה ומה הן משהין בית שמאי אומרים ולא כלום ובית הלל אומרים חמין אבל לא תבשיל עקר דברי הכל לא יחזיר דברי רבי מאיר רבי יהודה אומר בית שמאי אומרים חמין אבל לא תבשיל ובית הלל אומרים חמין ותבשיל בית שמאי אומרים נוטלין אבל לא מחזירין ובית הלל אומרים אף מחזירין אי אמרת בשלמא לשהות תנן מתני' מני רבי יהודה היא אלא אי אמרת להחזיר תנן מתניתין מני לא רבי יהודה ולא ר' מאיר אי רבי מאיר קשיא לב"ש בחדא ולבית הלל בתרתי אי רבי יהודה קשיא גרופה וקטומה לעולם אימא לך להחזיר תנן ותנא דידן סבר לה כרבי יהודה בחדא ופליג עליה בחדא סבר לה כרבי יהודה בחדא בחמין ותבשיל ונוטלין ומחזירין ופליג עליה בחדא דאילו תנא דידן סבר לשהות ואף על פי שאינו גרוף וקטום ורבי יהודה סבר בלשהות נמי גרוף וקטום **איבעיא להו** מהו לסמוך בה תוכה וגבה אסור אבל לסמוך בה שפיר דמי או דילמא לא שנא תא שמע שתי כירות המתאימות אחת גרופה וקטומה ואחת שאינה גרופה וקטומה משהין על גבי גרופה וקטומה ואף על גב דקא סליק ליה הבלא מאידך דילמא שאני התם דכיון דמידליא שליט בה אוירא תא שמע דאמר רב ספרא אמר רב חייא קטמה ונתלבתה סומכין לה ומקיימין עליה ונוטלין ממנה ומחזירין לה שמע מינה לסמוך נמי קטמה אין לא קטמה לא ולטעמיך נוטלין ממנה דקתני קטמה אין לא קטמה לא אלא תנא נוטלין משום מחזירין הכא נמי תנא סומכין משום מקיימין הכי השתא התם נוטלין ומחזירין בחד מקום הוא תנא נוטלין משום מחזירין אלא הכא סומכין בחד מקום הוא ומקיימין בחד מקום הוא מאי הוי עלה ת"ש [ג] [ג]כירה שהסיקוה בגפת ובעצים סומכין לה ואין מקיימין אא"כ גרופה וקטומה [ד]גחלים שעממו או שנתן עליה נעורת של פשתן דקה הרי היא כקטומה אמר ר' יצחק בר נחמני א"ר אושעיא קטמה והובערה משהין עליה חמין שהוחמו כל צורכן ותבשיל שבישל כל צורכו

שמע

לעולם אימא לך להחזיר תנן. ואילו לשהות אע"פ שאינו גרוף שרי: והך חזרה דאמרי לך. לא יחזיר עד שיגרוף דכי גרוף מיהא שרי: לאו דברי הכל היא. ולבית שמאי לא סבירא להו: לא שנו. שריותא דמתני' אלא על גבה דלא נפיש הבלא כולי האי אבל תוכה אסור: **אי אמרת בשלמא** להחזיר תנן. אבל לשהות משהין אפילו בשאין גרופה כדמתסרינן ליה חסורי ורבי חלבו אשריותא דלשהות על שאינה גרופה קאי: היינו דשני בין תוכה לעל גבה. דכי משהי לתוכה דשאינה גרופה מטמין ממש ברמץ: **אלא אי אמרת** לשהות תנן. דאפילו לשהות בעי גרופה כיון דגרופה ומבעוד יום הוא נותנו לתוכה מה לי תוכה מה לי על גבה: **ארישא**. עד שיגרוף: **אסיפא** קאי. דאיירי בחזרה אבל רישא לשהות הוא ובין תוכה ובין גבה שרי: שתי כירות המתאימות. מחוברות יחד וקיר של חרס מפסקת ביניהם: משהין על גבי גרופה וקטומה. דלא חיישינן משום דסליק לה הבלא מאידך: ומה הן משהין. על הגרופה: **לא יחזיר**. בשבת: **אא"ב**. רישא דמתניתין לשהות קאמר דבעי גרופה ובלשהות פליגי בחמין ובתבשיל ובגרוף וסיפא פליגי בחזרה מתני' ר' יהודה היא. אלא אי אמרת להחזיר תנן דבעי גרופה אבל לשהות לא בעי גרופה ופלוגתא דחמין ותבשיל כשאינו גרוף כדקמחסרת ומתרלת לה: **קשיא לב"ש בחדא**. דקאמרי ב"ש במתני' משהין חמין אף בשאינו גרוף והכא קאמר רבי מאיר לב"ש דאפילו גרוף ולא כלום וכ"ש כשאינו גרוף. והא כולה חדא פירכא היא דבית שמאי לא שני להו בין גרוף לשאינו גרוף: **ולב"ה בתרתי**. דבמתניתין שרי בית הלל להשהות חמין ותבשיל אף בשאינו גרוף והכא קתני דבגרוף חמין אין תבשיל לא ובשאינה גרוף אין משהין כלל ולענין חזרה בגרוף תנן במתניתין לב"ה מחזירין והכא קתני עקר דברי הכל לא יחזיר: **ואי ר' יהודה**. דאמר נמי כי מתניתין מ"מ גרופה וקטומה קשיא דמתניתין תרלת דפלוגתא קמייתא בשאינו גרוף ושרו ב"ש חמין ובית הלל חמין ותבשיל והכא קתני אין משהין על גבי שאינה גרופה ואינה קטומה כלל ופלוגתא דלשהות בגרופה וקטומה: **בחמין ותבשיל ונוטלים ומחזירין**. דמוקי פלוגתא דב"ש וב"ה בשהיית חמין ותבשיל דבית שמאי שרו חמין ותבשיל לא וב"ה חמין ותבשיל ולא כר' מאיר דאמר לב"ש לא כלום: מהו לסמוך. קדרה אצל דופן הכירה בלא גרופה שהכירה מטלטלת היא ומושיבים אותה על גבי קרקע: גבה. עובי שפתה או כסוי שעל חללה: דמדלי. הקדרה על גבי הכירה: ונתלבתה. חזרה והובערה: התם נוטלין ומחזירין בחד מקום. ולא שייך למתני מחזירין עד דתני נוטלין: נעורת. ארישט"ש: שהוחמו כל צרכן. דליכא למיחש לחיתוי:

מצטמק

לעולם אימא לך להחזיר תנן וחסורי מיחסרא כו'. [°] משום דקיי"ל כחנניה כמו שאפרש בע"ה דחיק לאוקמא מתני' כוותיה: **אא"ב** להחזיר תנן היינו דשני בין תוכה לעל גבה. פי' בקונטרס משום דאי להחזיר תנן (א) א"כ לשהות משהין אפילו באינה גרופה להכי שני בין תוכה דהוי מטמין ממש ברמץ לעל גבה וקשה להר"ח דלחנניה אפילו תוכה משהין אפי' באינה גרופה דהא תנן (לעיל דף יט:) ולא חררה על גבי גחלים אלא עד שיקרמו פניה הא קרמו פניה שרי אע"ג דחררה בתוכה היא ובלאו הכי אור"י דבחנם דחק רש"י לפרש כן דאיכא למימר שפיר היינו דשני לן בין תוכה לעל גבה מהא דשרי להחזיר בגרופה ובהשהאה דוקא לא ניחא ליה לחלק אבל בהחזרה ניחא ליה שפיר לחלק כדמוכח במאי דמשני מי סברת ארישא קאי אסיפא קאי כו' קשה לר"י א) היכי בעי למימר אליבא דרב דמתניתין להחזיר תנן אם כן אתיא מתניתין כחנניה ורב דלא כחנניה דהא חנניה שרי במצטמק ויפה לו דהא דתנן (שם) אין צולין בשר ובילה אלא כדי שיצולו מבעוד יום אתיא כחנניה ובילה אמרינן לקמן דמצטמק ויפה לו הוא ורב אסר לקמן [ג] דמצטמק ויפה לו וי"ל דבלאו הכי לא סבר לה רב כשום תנא דהא ר"מ ור' יהודה אסרי באינה גרופה אפילו במצטמק ורע לו ורב שרי במצטמק ורע לו אפילו באינה גרופה דבגרופה לא אשכחן שום אמורא דאסר אפילו יפה לו ועוד דרב קאי אמילתיה דרבי יוחנן דאיירי באינה גרופה וכן רבי יוחנן דשרי לקמן חמין ותבשיל שבישל כל צרכו באינה גרופה אבל לא בישל כל צרכו אסור לא אשכחן תנא דסבר הכי:

מהו לסמוך. באינה גרופה קבעי ואי מתניתין להשהות תנן קא בעי להשהות ולהחזיר ואי להחזיר תנן ושרי להשהות אפי' תוכה וגבה בעי להחזיר ולהשהות היכא שאינו מבושל כמאכל בן דרוסאי:

תא שמע כירה שהסיקוה כו'. ומסיק דשרי לסמוך ומכל מקום אין ללמוד מכאן לסמוך אלא האש דשאני הכא דדופני כירה מפסיקין בינו ולאש:

שמע

מסורת הש"ם

א) תוספתא פרק ג, ב) תוספתא [פרק ג], ג) לח ע"א.

תוספות ישנים

א) ואפשר דרב מוקי מתני' בלהחזיר אבל להשהות אפילו אינה גרופה שרי מצטמק ורע לו. ולרבי יוחנן אפי' מצטמק ויפה לו:

הגהות הב"ח

(א) תוס' ד"ה אא"ב וכו' דאי להחזיר תנן אבל לשהות:

גליון הש"ס

תוס' ד"ה לעולם וכו' משום דקיי"ל כחנניה. כעין זה בתוספות מגילה דף יט ע"ב ד"ה ודילמא:

ליקוטי רש"י

נעורת. דק דק שנוערין מן הפשתן וקורין ארישט"ש [לקמן מט.]. שברי גבעולין הנוערין מן הפשתים כשמנפצין אותו [חולין נא:].

עין משפט נר מצוה

ב א מיי' פ"ג מהל' שבת הלכה י' סמג לאוין סה טוש"ע א"ח סי' רנג סעיף ב:
ג ב שם סעיף א בהג"ה:
ד ג מיי' שם הלכה ז טוש"ע שם סעיף א:
ה ד מיי' שם הלכה ד:

רבינו חננאל

ושקלינן וטרינן ותריצנן כירה שהסיקוה בגפת או בעצים אסור להחזיר אבל לשהות משהין בה אע"פ שאינה גרופה ולא קטומה בין תבשיל בין חמין כחנניה: ואע"ג דעמדה אמרינן תוב תא שמע ב' כירות המתאימות אחת גרופה וקטומה ואחת שאינה גרופה ולא קטומה כו' לר' מאיר אליבא דבית הלל משהין ע"ג גרופה וקטומה חמין אבל לא תבשיל ולב"ש לא כלום לר' יהודה אליבא דב"ש משהין חמין אבל לא תבשיל. וב"ה חמין ותבשיל ב"ש אומרים נוטלין חמין אבל לא (תבשיל) מחזירין. וב"ה [אומרים] נוטלין אף מחזירין בשלמא אי אמרת מתני' לשהות [נמי בעינן] ע"ג גרופה וקטומה מתני' ר' יהודה היא. אלא אי אמרת להחזיר היא אבל לשהות בש"א משהין חמין ובה"א חמין ותבשיל אף על פי שאינה גרופה ולא קטומה. מני מתני' אי ר' מאיר קשיא לב"ש (בהו) [בחדא] במתני' דקתני בש"א חמין אבל לא תבשיל. ורבי מאיר קתני לבית שמאי ולא כלום. ולבית הלל בתרתי דר' מאיר קתני לב"ה משהין חמין אבל לא תבשיל. ומתני' קתני לב"ה חמין ותבשיל. ותוב דרבי מאיר קתני דברי הכל לא יחזיר ומתני' קתני לב"ה אף מחזירין. אי לרבי יהודה קשיא גרופה וקטומה דכי קתני משהין לב"ש חמין לב"ה חמין ותבשיל בגרופה וקטומה קתני ומתני' אע"פ שאינה גרופה וקטומה. ושנינן לעולם אימא לך להחזיר תנן. ותנא דידן סבר לה כרבי יהודה בחדא ופליג עליה בחדא ופשוטה היא ועמדה [הסוגיא] דמתני' להחזיר תנן. עכשיו יש מי שאומר כיון דלא איפשיטא בהדיא להחזיר אשנויי לא סמכינן [ומוקמי'] מתני' לשהות. ויש מי שאומר הלכה להחזיר תנן ומסייעא ליה הא דא"ר יוחנן כירה שהסיקוה בגפת ובעצים משהין עליה חמין שלא הוחמו כל צרכן ותבשיל שלא בישל כל צרכו עקר לא יחזיר וקסבר מתני' להחזיר תנן כו'. ועוד מדאמר רבא תרוייהו תנגהי ואמרינן מכדי תרוייהו תנגהי ר' יוחנן מאי אתא לאשמעינן ואמר דיוקא דמתני' קמ"ל ש"מ דרבי יוחנן סבר דוקא דמתני' להחזיר הוא א) ושיהוי זה אינה הטמנה אלא כגון כסא של ברזל והקדירה יושבת עליה והיא תלויה (או) באבנים [או] כיוצא בה. אבל הטמנה ע"ג גחלים דברי הכל אסור. דקי"ל הטמנה בדבר המוסיף אסור ואפילו מבעוד יום: **איבעיא להו** מהו לסמוך לה. תוכה וגבה אסור. אבל לסמוך שרי או דילמא לא

חשק שלמה על רבינו חננאל א) עי' בבעל המאור:

אֶלָּא תָּנָא נוֹטְלִין מִשּׁוּם מַחֲזִירִין – **Rather,** it is obvious that **[Rav Chiya] stated** that **one can remove** food only **by way of** introducing the statement that **one can** then **return** it. הָכָא נַמִּי תָּנָא סוֹמְכִין מִשּׁוּם מְקַיְּימִין – **Here, too,** in his former clause, **[Rav Chiya] stated** that **one can place** food **alongside** a *kirah* that was shoveled or banked only **by way of** introducing the statement that **one may** even **keep** food on top of it. He did not mean to imply that one may place food alongside the *kirah* only if it was shoveled or banked.

The Gemara counters:

הָכִי הַשְׁתָּא – **Now,** is **this a comparison?** הָתָם נוֹטְלִין וּמַחֲזִירִין בְּחַד מָקוֹם הוּא – **There,** in regard to removing food from the *kirah* and replacing it, **removing and returning are** done **in one place;** one cannot return food to the top of the *kirah* without first removing it from there. תָּנָא נוֹטְלִין מִשּׁוּם מַחֲזִירִין – **[Rav Chiya]** therefore properly **stated** that **one may remove** food from the *kirah* **by way of** introducing the statement that **one may return** it there. אֶלָּא הָכָא – **But here,** in regard to placing food alongside the *kirah* and keeping it on top, סוֹמְכִין בְּחַד מָקוֹם הוּא וּמְקַיְּימִין בְּחַד מָקוֹם הוּא – **placing** food **alongside** it **is** done **in one place, and keeping** it on top **is** done **in another place.** There was no need for Rav Chiya to state as an introduction that one may place food alongside the *kirah.* It is therefore proper to infer from this statement that one may *not* place food alongside the *kirah* unless it was shoveled or banked.

The Gemara nevertheless considers this inference insufficient to resolve the inquiry and states:

מַאי הָוֵי עֲלָהּ – **What was the result of [the inquiry]?** תָּא שְׁמַע – **Come, learn** a conclusive proof from the following Baraisa: כִּירָה שֶׁהִסִּיקוּהָ בְּגֶפֶת וּבְעֵצִים – Concerning A *KIRAH* THAT WAS HEATED WITH MARC OR WITH WOOD, סוֹמְכִין לָהּ – ONE MAY PLACE food ALONGSIDE IT וְאֵין מְקַיְּימִין אֶלָּא אִם כֵּן גְּרוּפָה וּקְטוּמָה – BUT ONE MAY NOT KEEP food on top of it UNLESS IT WAS SHOVELED OR BANKED. גֶּחָלִים שֶׁעָמְמוּ אוֹ שֶׁנָּתַן עָלֶיהָ נְעוֹרֶת שֶׁל פִּשְׁתָּן דַּקָּה – IF THE COALS DIED DOWN OR ONE PLACED FINE CHAFF OF FLAX ON THEM, הֲרֵי הִיא כִּקְטוּמָה – IT IS AS THOUGH [THE *KIRAH*] WAS BANKED with ash. This Baraisa teaches explicitly that it is permitted to place food alongside (but not on top of) a *kirah* even if it was neither shoveled nor banked.[23]

The Gemara turns to another related topic:[24]

אָמַר רַבִּי יִצְחָק בַּר נַחְמָנִי אָמַר רַבִּי אוֹשַׁעְיָא – **R' Yitzchak bar Nachmani said in the name of R' Oshaya:** קְטָמָהּ וְהוּבְעֲרָה – If **one banked [a *kirah*] and it flared up** again, מַשְׁהִין עָלֶיהָ חַמִּין שֶׁהוּחַמּוּ כָּל צוֹרְכָּן וְתַבְשִׁיל שֶׁבִּישֵּׁל כָּל צוֹרְכּוֹ – **he may leave on it** before the Sabbath **hot water that was fully heated and cooked food that was fully cooked.**[25]

NOTES

23. *Tosafos* point out that we should not infer from here that it is permissible to place food next to an open fire. It is only where the wall of the *kirah* separates the food from the fire that placing food there is permitted. See *Rama* 253:2 and 318:15 with *Mishnah Berurah* 318:94, and see 40b note 4.

24. The topic of the upcoming discussion is the following: We have learned that the Sages dispute Chananyah's opinion and forbid *shehiyah* over open coals even if an item has been cooked like the food of Ben Derusai. Nevertheless, even the Sages permit *shehiyah* once a food has been fully cooked and will not benefit from additional stewing, since there is no reason to be concerned that one might stoke the coals. We must clarify, however, whether the Sages permit *shehiyah* in regard to fully cooked foods that become more tasty as they stew on the fire and condense by losing moisture [מִצְטַמֵּק וְיָפֶה לוֹ]. (An example of such a food would be a stew, such as the Ashkenazic Sabbath delicacy known as *cholent.*) Does the concern for stoking extend even to a case in which the food is perfectly edible and would merely become more tasty?

25. R' Oshaya follows the opinion of the Sages that partially cooked food may not be left on an unbanked *kirah,* and he further holds that when the fire flares up the earlier banking is negated. He therefore rules that in this case fully cooked foods may be left on the *kirah* but uncooked foods may not be left there (*Rosh Yosef*).

לעולם אימא לך להחזיר תנן וחסורי מיחסרא והכי קתני כירה שהסיקוה בקש ובגבבא מחזירין עליה תבשיל בגפת ובעצים לא יחזיר עד שיגרוף או עד שיתן את האפר אבל לשהות משהין אע"פ שאינו גרוף ואינו קטום ומה הן משהין בית שמאי אומרים חמין אבל לא תבשיל ובית הלל אומרים חמין ותבשיל והך חזרה דאמרי לך לאו דברי הכל היא אלא מחלוקת בית שמאי ובית הלל שבית שמאי אומרים נוטלין ולא מחזירין ובית הלל אומרים אף מחזירין ת"ש דאמר ר' חלבו א"ר חמא בר גוריא אמר רב לא שנו אלא על גבה אבל לתוכה אסור אי אמרת בשלמא להחזיר תנן היינו דשני בין תוכה לעל גבה אלא אי אמרת לשהות תנן מה לי תוכה מה לי על גבה מי סברת ר' חלבו ארישא קאי אסיפא [א]קאי ובית הלל אומרים אף מחזירין ואמר ר' חלבו אמר רב חמא בר גוריא אמר רב לא שנו אלא על גבה אבל תוכה אסור א) תא שמע [ב]ב' כירות המתאימות אחת גרופה וקטומה ואחת שאינה גרופה ואינה קטומה משהין על גבי גרופה וקטומה ואין משהין על שאינה גרופה ואינה קטומה ומה הן משהין בית שמאי אומרים ולא כלום ובית הלל אומרים חמין אבל לא תבשיל עקר דברי הכל לא יחזיר דברי רבי מאיר רבי יהודה אומר בית שמאי אומרים חמין אבל לא תבשיל ובית הלל אומרים חמין ותבשיל בית שמאי אומרים נוטלין אבל לא מחזירין ובית הלל אומרים אף מחזירין אי אמרת בשלמא לשהות תנן מתני' מני רבי יהודה היא אלא אי אמרת להחזיר תנן מתניתין מני לא רבי יהודה ולא ר' מאיר אי רבי מאיר קשיא לב"ש בחדא ולבית הלל בתרתי אי רבי יהודה קשיא גרופה וקטומה לעולם אימא לך להחזיר תנן ותנא דידן סבר לה כרבי יהודה בחדא ופליג עליה בחדא סבר לה כרבי יהודה בחדא בחמין ותבשיל ונוטלין ומחזירין ופליג עליה בחדא דאילו תנא דידן סבר לשהות ואף על פי שאינו גרוף וקטום ורבי יהודה סבר בלשהות נמי גרוף וקטום אין אי לא לא איבעיא להו מהו לסמוך בה תוכה וגבה אסור אבל לסמוך בה שפיר דמי או דילמא לא שנא תא שמע שתי כירות המתאימות אחת גרופה וקטומה ואחת שאינה גרופה וקטומה משהין על גבי גרופה וקטומה ואף על גב דקא סליק ליה הבלא מאידך דילמא שאני התם דכיון דמידליא שליט בה אוירא תא שמע דאמר רב ספרא אמר רב חייא קטמה ונתלבתה סומכין לה ומקיימין עליה ונוטלין ממנה ומחזירין לה שמע מינה לסמוך נמי קטמה אין לא קטמה לא ולטעמיך נוטלין ממנה דקתני קטמה אין לא קטמה לא אלא תנא נוטלין משום מחזירין הכא נמי תנא סומכין משום מקיימין הכי השתא התם נוטלין ומחזירין בחד מקום הוא תנא נוטלין משום מחזירין אלא הכא סומכין בחד מקום הוא ומקיימין בחד מקום הוא מאי הוי עלה ת"ש ג) [ג]כירה שהסיקוה בגפת ובעצים סומכין לה ואין מקיימין אא"כ גרופה וקטומה [ד]גחלים שעממו או שנתן עליה נעורת של פשתן דקה הרי היא כקטומה אמר ר' יצחק בר נחמני א"ר אושעיא קטמה והובערה משהין עליה חמין שהוחמו כל צורכן ותבשיל שבישל כל צורכו

שמע

רש"י

לעולם אימא לך להחזיר תנן. ואילו לשהות אע"פ שאינו גרוף שרי: **והך חזרה דאמרי לך.** לא יחזיר עד שיגרוף דכי גרוף מיהא שרי: **לאו דברי הכל היא.** ולבית שמאי לא סבירא להו: **לא שנו.** שריותא דמתני' אלא על גבה דלא נפיש הבלא כולי האי אבל תוכה אסור: **אי אמרת בשלמא להחזיר תנן.** אבל לשהות משהין אפילו בשאין גרופה כדמחסרינן ליה חסורי ורבי חלבו אשריותא דלשהות על שאינה גרופה קאי: **היינו דשני בין תוכה לעל גבה.** דכי משהי לתוכה דשאינה גרופה מטמין ממש ברמץ: **אלא אי אמרת לשהות תנן.** דאפילו לשהות בעי גרופה כיון דגרופה ומבעוד יום הוא נותנו לתוכה מה לי תוכה מה לי על גבה: **ארישא.** עד שיגרוף: **אסיפא קאי.** דאיירי בחזרה אבל רישא לשהות הוא ובין תוכה ובין גבה שרי: **שתי כירות המתאימות.** מחוברות יחד וקיר של חרס מפסקת ביניהם: **משהין על גבי גרופה וקטומה.** דלא חיישינן משום דסליק לה הבלא מאידך: **ומה הן משהין.** על הגרופה: **לא יחזיר.** בשבת: **אא"ב.** רישא דמתניתין לשהות קאמר דבעי גרופה ובלשהות פליגי בחמין ובתבשיל ובגרוף וסיפא פליגי בחזרה מתני' ר' יהודה היא. אלא אי אמרת להחזיר תנן דבעי גרופה אבל לשהות לא בעי גרופה ופלוגתא דחמין ותבשיל כשאינו גרוף כדקמחסרת ומתרצת לה: **קשיא לב"ש בחדא.** דקאמרי ב"ש במתני' משהין חמין אף בשאינו גרוף והכא קאמר רבי מאיר לב"ש דאפילו גרוף ולא כלום וכ"ש כשאינו גרוף. והא כולה חדא פירכא היא דבית שמאי לא שני להו בין גרוף לשאינו גרוף: **ולב"ה בתרתי.** דבמתניתין שרי בית הלל להשהות חמין ותבשיל אף בשאינו גרוף והכא קתני דבגרוף חמין אין תבשיל לא ובשאינה גרוף אין משהין כלל ולענין חזרה בגרוף תנן במתניתין לב"ה מחזירין והכא קתני עקר דברי הכל לא יחזיר: **ואי ר' יהודה.** דאמר נמי כי מתניתין מ"מ גרופה וקטומה קשיא דמתניתין תרלת דפלוגתא קמייתא בשאינו גרוף ושרו ב"ש חמין ובית הלל חמין ותבשיל והכא קתני אין משהין על גבי שאינה גרופה ואינה קטומה כלל ופלוגתא דלשהות בגרופה וקטומה: **בחמין ותבשיל ונוטלים ומחזירין.** דמוקי פלוגתא דב"ש וב"ה בשהיית חמין ותבשיל דבית שמאי שרו חמין ותבשיל לא וב"ה חמין ותבשיל ולא כר' מאיר דאמר לב"ש לא כלום: **מהו לסמוך.** קדרה אצל דופן הכירה בלא גרופה שהכירה מטלטלת היא ומושיבים אותה על גבי קרקע: **גבה.** עובי שפתה או כסוי שעל חללה: **דמדלי.** הקדרה על גבי הכירה: **ונתלבתה.** חזרה והובערה: **התם** נוטלין ומחזירין בחד מקום. ולא שייך למתני מחזירין עד דתני נוטלין: **נעורת.** ארישט"ש: **שהוחמו כל צרכן.** דליכא למיחש לחיתויי:

מצטמק

תוספות

לעולם אימא לך להחזיר תנן וחסורי מיחסרא כו'. ° משום דקיי"ל כחנניה כמו שאפרש בע"ה דחיק לאוקמא מתני' כוותיה: **אא"ב להחזיר תנן היינו דשני בין תוכה לעל גבה.** פי' בקונטרס משום דאי להחזיר תנן (א) א"כ לשהות משהין אפילו באינה גרופה להכי שני בין תוכה דהוי מטמין ממש ברמץ לעל גבה וקשה להר"ח דלחנניה אפילו תוכה משהין אפי' באינה גרופה דהא תנן (לעיל דף יט:) ולא חררה על גבי גחלים אלא עד שיקרמו פניה הא קרמו פניה שרי אע"ג דחררה בתוכה היא ובלאו הכי אור"י דבחנם דחק רש"י לפרש כן דאיכא למימר שפיר היינו דשני לן בין תוכה לעל גבה מהא דשרי להחזיר בגרופה ובהשהאה דוקא לא ניחא ליה לחלק אבל בהחזרה ניחא ליה שפיר לחלק כדמוכח במאי דמשני מי סברת ארישא קאי אסיפא קאי כו' קשה לר"י א) היכי בעי למימר אליבא דרב דמתניתין להחזיר תנן אם כן אתיא מתניתין כחנניה ורב דלא כחנניה דהא חנניה שרי במצטמק ויפה לו דהא דתנן (שם) אין צולין בשר ובילה אלא כדי שיצולו מבעוד יום אתיא כחנניה ובילה אמרינן לקמן דמצטמק ויפה לו הוא ורב אסר לקמן ג) דמצטמק ויפה לו וי"ל דבלאו הכי לא סבר לה רב כשום תנא דהא ר"מ ור' יהודה אסרי באינה גרופה אפילו במצטמק ורע לו ורב שרי במצטמק ורע לו אפילו באינה גרופה דבגרופה לא אשכחן שום אמורא דאסר אפילו יפה לו ועוד דרב קאי אמילתיה דרבי יוחנן דאיירי באינה גרופה וכן רבי יוחנן דשרי לקמן חמין ותבשיל שבישל כל צרכו באינה גרופה אבל לא בישל כל צרכו אסור לא אשכחן תנא דסבר הכי:

מהו לסמוך. באינה גרופה קבעי ואי מתניתין להשהות תנן קא בעי להשהות ולהחזיר ואי להחזיר תנן ושרי להשהות אפי' תוכה וגבה בעי להחזיר ולהשהות היכא שאינו מבושל כמאכל בן דרוסאי:

תא שמע כירה שהסיקוה כו'. ומסיק דשרי לסמוך ומכל מקום אין ללמוד מכאן לסמוך אצל האש דשאני הכא דדופני כירה מפסיקין בינו ולאש:

שמע

רבינו חננאל

ושקלינן וטרינן ותריצנן כירה שהסיקוה בגפת או בעצים אסור להחזיר אבל לשהות משהין בה אע"פ שאיזה גרופה ולא קטומה בין תבשיל בין חמין כחנניה: ואע"ג דעמדה אמרינן תוב תא שמע ב' כירות המתאימות אחת גרופה וקטומה ואחת שאינה גרופה ולא קטומה כו' לר' מאיר אליבא דבית הלל משהין ע"ג גרופה וקטומה חמין אבל לא תבשיל ולב"ש לא כלום לר' יהודה אליבא דב"ש משהין חמין אבל לא תבשיל. וב"ה חמין ותבשיל ב"ש אומרים נוטלין חמין אבל לא (תבשיל) מחזירין. וב"ה [אומרים] נוטלין אף מחזירין בשלמא אי אמרת מתני' לשהות [נמי בעינן] ע"ג גרופה וקטומה מתני' ר' יהודה היא. אלא אי אמרת להחזיר היא אבל לשהות בש"א משהין חמין ובה"א חמין ותבשיל אף על פי שאינה גרופה ולא קטומה. מני מתני' אי ר' מאיר קשיא לב"ש (בהו) [בחדא] במתני' דקתני בש"א חמין אבל לא תבשיל. ורבי מאיר קתני לבית שמאי ולא כלום. ולבית הלל בתרתי דר' מאיר קתני לב"ה משהין חמין אבל לא תבשיל. ומתני' קתני לב"ה חמין ותבשיל. ותוב דרבי מאיר קתני דברי הכל לא יחזיר ומתני' קתני לב"ה אף מחזירין. אי לרבי יהודה קשיא גרופה וקטומה דכי קתני משהין לב"ש חמין לב"ה חמין ותבשיל בגרופה וקטומה קתני ומתני' אע"פ שאינה גרופה וקטומה. ושנינן לעולם אימא לך להחזיר תנן. ותנא דידן סבר לה כרבי יהודה בחדא ופליג עליה בחדא ופשוטה היא ועמדה [הסוגיא] דמתני' להחזיר תנן. עכשיו יש מי שאומר כיון דלא איפשיטא בהדיא להחזיר אשנויי לא סמכינן [ומוקמי] מתני' לשהות. ויש מי שאומר הלכה להחזיר תנן ומסייעא ליה הא דא"ר יוחנן כירה שהסיקוה בגפת ובעצים משהין עליה חמין שלא הוחמו כל צרכן ותבשיל שלא בישל כל צרכו עקר לא יחזיר וקסבר מתני' להחזיר תנן כו'. ועוד מדאמר רבא תרוייהו תנגהי ואמרינן מכדי תרוייהו תנגהי ר' יוחנן מאי אתא לאשמעינן ואמר דיוקא דמתני' קמ"ל ש"מ דרבי יוחנן סבר דוקא דמתני' להחזיר הוא א) ושיהוי זה אינה הטמנה אלא כגון כסא של ברזל והקדירה יושבת עליה והיא תלויה (או) באבנים [או] כיוצא בה. אבל הטמנה ע"ג גחלים דברי הכל אסור. דקי"ל הטמנה בדבר המוסיף אסור ואפילו מבעוד יום: **איבעיא להו** מהו לסמוך לה. תוכה וגבה אסור. אבל לסמוך שרי או דילמא לא

חשק שלמה על רבינו חננאל א) עי' בבעל המאור:

עין משפט נר מצוה

ב א מיי' פ"ג מהל' שבת הלכה י' סמג לאוין סה טוש"ע א"ח סי' רנג סעיף ב:
ג ב שם סעיף א בהג"ה:
ד ג מיי' שם הלכה ז טוש"ע שם סעיף א:
ה ד מיי' שם הלכה ד:

מסורת הש"ס

א) תוספתא פרק ג, ב) תוספתא [פרק ג], ג) לא ע"א.

תוספות ישנים

א) ואפשר דרב מוקי מתני' בלהחזיר אבל להשהות אפילו אינה גרופה שרי מצטמק ורע לו. ולרבי יוחנן אפי' מצטמק ויפה לו:

הגהות הב"ח

(א) תוס' ד"ה אא"ב וכו' דאי להחזיר תנן אבל לשהות:

גליון הש"ס

תוס' ד"ה לעולם וכו' משום דקיי"ל כחנניה. כעין זה בתוספות מגילה דף יט ע"ב ד"ה ודילמא:

ליקוטי רש"י

נעורת. דק דק שנוערין מן הפשתן וקורין ארישט"ש [לקמן מט.]. שברי גבעולין הננערין מן הפשתים כשמנפצין אותו [חולין נא:].

עין משפט
נר מצוה

ו א ב (מיי' פ"ג מהל' שבת הל' ד') סמג לאוין סה טוש"ע א"ח סימן רנג סעיף א:

מסורת הש"ס

א) לעיל יט:, ב) [ביצה כט: חולין קי.].

שמע מינה מצטמק ויפה לו מותר שאני הכא דקטמה אי הכי מאי למימרא הובערה איצטריכא ליה מהו דתימא כיון דהובערה הדרא לה למילתא קמייתא קמשמע לן אמר רבה בר בר חנה אמר רבי יוחנן קטמה והובערה משהין עליה חמין שהוחמו כל צורכן ותבשיל שבישל כל צורכו ואפי' גחלים של רותם ש"מ מצטמק ויפה לו מותר שאני הכא דקטמה אי הכי מאי למימרא הובערה אצטריכא ליה היינו הך גחלים של רותם אצטריכא ליה אמר רב ששת אמר ר' יוחנן כירה שהסיקוה בגפת ובעצים משהין עליה חמין שלא הוחמו כל צורכן ותבשיל שלא בישל כל צורכו עקר לא יחזיר עד שיגרוף או עד שיתן אפר קסבר מתניתין להחזיר תנן אבל לשהות משהין אע"פ שאינו גרוף ואינו קטום אמר רבא תרווייהו תנגהי לשהות תנינא א) אין נותנין את הפת בתוך התנור עם חשיכה ולא חררה על גבי גחלים אלא כדי שיקרמו פניה הא קרמו פניה שרי להחזיר נמי תנינא בית הלל אומרים אף מחזירין ועד כאן לא קשרו בית הלל אלא בגרופה וקטומה אבל בשאינה גרופה וקטומה לא ורב ששת נמי דיוקא דמתני' קמ"ל אמר רב שמואל בר יהודה אמר רבי יוחנן א כירה שהסיקוה בגפת ובעצים משהין (א) עליה תבשיל שבישל כל צורכו וחמין שהוחמו כל צורכן ואפי' מצטמק ויפה לו אמר ליה ההוא מדרבנן לרב שמואל בר יהודה הא רב ושמואל דאמרי תרווייהו מצטמק ויפה לו אסור אמר ליה אטו לית אנא ידע דאמר רב יוסף אמר רב יהודה אמר שמואל מצטמק ויפה לו אסור כי קאמינא לך לרבי יוחנן קאמינא אמר ליה רב עוקבא ממישן לרב אשי אתון דמקרביתו לרב ושמואל עבידו כרב ושמואל אנן נעביד כרבי יוחנן אמר ליה אביי לרב יוסף מהו לשהות אמר ליה הא רב יהודה משהו ליה ואכיל א"ל בר מיניה דרב יהודה דכיון דמסוכן הוא אפילו בשבת נמי שרי למעבד ליה לי ולך מאי אמר ליה בסורא משהו דהא רב נחמן בר יצחק ג) מרי דעובדא הוה ומשהו ליה ואכיל אמר רב אשי קאימנא קמיה דרב הונא ושהין ליה כסא דהרסנא ואכל ולא ידענא אי משום דקסבר מצטמק ויפה לו מותר אי משום דכיון דאית ביה מיחא מצטמק ורע לו הוא אמר רב א) נחמן ב מצטמק ויפה לו אסור מצטמק ורע לו מותר כללא דמלתא כל דאית ביה מיחא מצטמק ורע לו לבר מתבשיל דליפתא דאף על גב דאית ביה מיחא מצטמק ויפה לו הוא והני מילי דאית ביה בשרא אבל לית ביה בשרא מצטמק ורע לו הוא וכי אית ביה בשרא נמי לא אמרן אלא דלא קבעי לה לאורחין אבל קבעי לה לאורחין מצטמק ורע לו לפדא דייסא ותמרי מצטמק ורע להן בעו מיניה מרבי חייא בר אבא

שבח

מצטמק. מתמעט וכויץ רטריי"ט לשון שדים צומקין (הושע ט) כמו שאתה אומר בלשון צוי נצטוה ובלשון צדק נצטדק וכן כל תיבה שראש יסודה צד"י כשהיא מתפעלת נותן ט' אחר צד"י: מותר. להשהותן בכירה דאי לא במצטמק ויפה לו קאמר מאי אתא לאשמעינן אלא ע"כ במצטמק ויפה לו קאמר ואפילו הכי לא גזרו משום חיתוי הואיל ונתבשל כל צרכו ותנא חמין לאשמעינן דבעינן שהוחמו כל צרכן מבעוד יום: שאני הכא דקטמה. וגלי דעתיה דלא ניחא ליה בצמוקי: גחלים של רותם. חמין יותר משאר גחלים ואינם ממהרין לכבות כדאמרינן בהמוכר את הספינה (ב"ב דף עד:): משהין עליה. ואע"פ שלא קטמה ואמוראי נינהו אליבא דר' יוחנן: מתניתין. דקתני עד שיגרוף: להחזיר תנן. דלא שרו בית הלל להחזיר עד שיגרוף ופירוקא דמתניתין כדאמרינן לעיל חסורי מיחסרא הלכך עקר לא יחזיר הואיל ואינה גרופה: תרווייהו תנגהי. בין לשהות בשאינה גרופה תנינא בהדיא סתם משנה דמותר ועקר לא יחזיר נמי תנינא ולמה ליה לרבי יוחנן לאשמעינן: הא קרמו פניה שרי. והיינו לא בישל כל צרכו ותנור לאו גרוף וקטום הוא ואי נמי גרוף בתנור לא מהניא גריפה כדתנן במתניתין וכ"ש פת דאדעתא לבשולי יהביה בגויה: ועד כאן לא שרו כו'. דמתניתין אלאחר שיגרוף קאי דקתני לא יתן עד שיגרוף ובין למאן דאמר לא ישהה ובין למ"ד לא יחזיר מ"מ חזרה דסיפא אגרוף וקטום מהדר: ורב ששת נמי דיוקא דמתני' קמ"ל. משום דלא מתני לה בהדיא הא קרמו שרי. ואנן דמשהינן קדירה על גבי כירה שאינה גרופה אחנניה סמכינן הואיל ותנן סתם מתניתין כוותיה כדאמר הא קרמו שרי ואע"ג דלא בישל כל צרכו ואמר רב ששת משמיה דרבי יוחנן כוותיה דמתניתין דפרקין משום חזרה הוא דבעי גרופה אבל לשהות לא. וכל הני אמוראי דאסרי סברי מתניתין לשהות תנן: מהו לשהות. בשאינה גרופה: מסוכן הוא. רגיל לאוחזו בולמוס וצריך לאכול מאכל מתוק וטוב: מרי דעובדא. מדקדק במעשיו: מיחא. קמח: כסא דהרסנא. דגים המבושלים בשמן בקמח: דאית ביה בשרא. מצטמק ויפה לו שהשומן הבשר משבר כח הלפת כדאמר בברכות (דף מד:): לאורחין. צריך חתיכות חשובות לשום לפניהם ואין דרך כבוד בתבשיל המצטמק שאין הבשר ניכר בו: לפדא. מאכל שעושה מתאנים: תמרי. מאכל תמרים:

שבח

שמע מינה מצטמק ויפה לו מותר. פירש בקונטרס דאי האי תבשיל במצטמק ורע לו מאי אתא לאשמעינן וקשה לר"י הא איצטריך לאפוקי מדרבי מאיר ורבי יהודה דאסרי בשאינה גרופה אפילו חמין דמצטמק ורע להם ועוד קשה כיון דהשתא ס"ד דמשום דהובערה הדרא למילתא קמייתא כי משני שאני הכא דקטמה מאי פריך מאי למימרא הא איצטריך טובא לאפוקי ממאי דס"ד מעיקרא ונראה לר"י דהשתא ס"ד דלא חשיבא קטומה כלל משום דהובערה ואשמעינן דהדרא למילתא קמייתא דאי חשיבא קטומה אמאי נקט בישל כל צרכו אפי' לא בישל כל צרכו שרי דאפילו רבי מאיר דמחמיר מכולהו תנאי שרי בחמין שלא הוחמו כל צרכן כדפירשנו לעיל דסתם חמין ותבשיל הוי שלא הוחמו כל צורכן ופריך שמע מינה מצטמק ויפה לו מותר דהא סתם תבשיל אמר לקמן דמצטמק ויפה לו הוא ומשני שאני הכא דקטמה פירוש וחשיבא לגמרי קטומה וה"ה אפילו לא בישל כל צרכו שרי והא דנקט בישל כל צרכו לאשמעינן דאי לאו קטומה אפילו בישל כל צרכו אסור משום דמצטמק ויפה לו הוא ופריך אי הכי מאי למימרא אף על גב דאשמעינן דאי לא קטמה אסור מ"מ מדנקט למילתיה בלשון היתר משמע דהתירא אתי לאורויי לן ואף על גב דאשמעינן דלא הדרא למילתא קמייתא נראה לו דהא לא איצטריך לאשמעינן דסברא הוא דלא הדרא למילתא קמייתא ואף על גב דמעיקרא הוה בעי למימר דהדרא למילתא קמייתא לאו משום דסברא הוא לומר כן אלא משום דנקט במלתיה בישל כל צרכו היה ר"ל כן כדפרישית ומשני דמכל מקום אצטריך דמהו דתימא כו' ועוד יש לומר שאני הכא דקטמה דלאו לגמרי מהניא קטימה אלא דוקא משום דבישל כל צרכו אבל לא בישל כל צרכו אסור משום דהובערה והשתא אתי שפיר הא דנקט הכא קטמה והובערה ולעיל נקט ונתלבתה דנתלבתה הוי פחות מהובערה והויא לגמרי כקטומה ופריך א"ה מאי למימרא דהא בלאו מילתיה מסברא ה"א דלא הדרא למלתא קמייתא כמו בנתלבתה ושרי ואפי' לא בישל כל צרכו ובלשון איסור ה"ל לאשמעינן ולא בלשון היתר ומשני הובערה איצטריך ליה ואי לאו מילתיה לא היה פשוט היתר אלא הוה ס"ד למימרא דהדרא למילתא קמייתא:

אמר רב ששת אמר ר' יוחנן כירה שהסיקוה בגפת ובעצים משהין עליה תבשיל שלא בישל כל צרכו כו'. פסק ר"ח דהלכה כרב ששת אמר ר' יוחנן דרבא דאמר תרווייהו תנגהי סבירא ליה כוותיה וכן פסק רש"י דסתם מתניתין דפרק קמא (דף יט:) כחנניה ומותר להשהות אפי' באינה גרופה אבל להחזיר ודאי אסור אא"כ גרוף וקטום ואפי' ב) בישל כל צרכו כדפי' לעיל: **דיוקא** דמתני' קמ"ל. פי' רש"י דקמ"ל דקרמו פניה שפיר דמי ואין נראה דדיוק פשוט הוא דהא כיון דתנא עד שיקרמו פניה ממילא שמעינן דקרמו פניה שרי ונראה לפרש דדיוקא דמתניתין דכירה אתא לאשמעי' דלהחזיר תנן וחסורי מחסרא והכי קתני: **מהו** להשהות. באינה גרופה ולא בישל כל צרכו קבעי או במצטמק ויפה לו:

שבח

רבינו חננאל

לא שנא ופשטנא מהא דתניא כירה שהסיקוה בגפת ובעצים סומכין ואין מקיימין עליה אלא אם כן גרופה וקטומה עממו הגחלים או שנתן לתוכה נעורת של פשתן דקה הרי כקטומה (דבי) [אמר רב] (שמעון) [שמואל] בר יהודה א"ר יוחנן כירה שהסיקוה בגפת ובעצים משהין עליה חמין שהוחמו כל צרכן ותבשיל שבישל כל צרכו ודוקא כירה שהיא שפיתת ב' קדרות אבל אם אין בה אלא שפיתת קדרה אחת אסור ואפי' מצטמק ויפה לו מותר ואע"ג דרב ושמואל פליגי הא קי"ל דרבי יוחנן לגבי רב ושמואל הלכתא כר' יוחנן ומה שאמר רב (עקיבא) [עוקבא] ממישן לרב אשי אתון דמקרביתון לרב ושמואל עבידו כרב ושמואל לאו משום דהלכתא כוותיהו אלא לעולם הלכתא כר' יוחנן דשרי אבל אתון דנהיגתון איסורא כרב ושמואל הוו להו דברים המותרין ואחרים נהגו בהן איסור אי אתה רשאי להתירן בפניהם והא דאמר רב יהודה מסוכן בשבת שרי למיעבד ליה פשוטה הוא: **הא דאמר** רב נחמן בר יצחק מצטמק ויפה לו אסור מצטמק ורע לו מותר. כללא דמילתא כל דאית ליה מיחא מצטמק ורע לו הוא בר מתבשילא דליפתא דאע"ג דאית ליה מיחא מצטמק ויפה לו הוא כו'. האי כללא (לגברי) [לגבי] רב ושמואל אמרה ולית הלכתא אלא כר' יוחנן דהא סייעיה ר' עקיבא ממישן לרב אשי. **לפדא** דייסא ותמרי מצטמק ורע לו מותר

תוספות ישנים

א) לספרים דגרסי הכא רנב"י ז"ל דאליבא דרב ושמואל קאמר דהא איהו גופיה משהי ליה ואכיל: ב) תימה אמאי אסור להחזיר מ"ש מדאמר לקמן [דף מ:] נותן אדם קיתון של מים כנגד המדורה שתפיג צינתן. ושמן איכא מאן דשרי אפילו יד סולדת בו ואם כן אמאי אסור תבשיל שבישל כל צרכו להחזיר הא לא שייך ביה בישול. ולעיל [דף לד.] נמי דאסור להטמין משחשיכה אפילו באין מוסיף הבל גזרה שמא ירתיח הא לא שייך ביה בישול. וי"ל דודאי בשמן לא שייך בישול אבל בתבשיל אפילו במבושל מבעוד יום שייך בישול. והא דשרינן קיתון של מים היינו ליתן במקום שאפי' תהיה שם כל היום לא תהיה יד סולדת בו:

הגהות הב"ח

(א) גמ' אמר רב שמואל בר יהודה א"ר יוחנן כירה וכו' משהין עליה חמין שהוחמו כל צורכן ותבשיל שבישל כל צורכו ואפי' מצטמק:

ליקוטי רש"י

רותם. שאין גחליו כבים מהרה [רשב"ם ב"ב עד:]. גחלי רתמים. כל הגחלים כבו מבחוץ כבו מבפנים ואלו כבו מבחוץ ולא מבפנים [תהלים קכ, ד]. חררה. עוגת רצפים (מ"א יט) פוגאצ"ה בלע"ז [לעיל יט:]. עוגה שאופין על פני הגחלים [סוטה לה.]. יקרמו. כמו קרום קרוסטי"ן בלע"ז [לעיל שם]. **מרי דעובדא.** זהיר במעשים טובים [חולין קי.]. **כסא דהרסנא.** דגים קטנים מטוגנים בשמן קרביהן ובקמח [לקמן קיח:]. דגים קטנים מטוגנין בקמח בשומן שלהן [סוכה מד:]. קערה של מאכל דגים מטוגנין בשמן בסולת [רשב"ם ב"ב ס:]. טיגן במורייס שומן דגים עם קמח [ע"ז לח.]. **לפדא.** שם תבשיל של תאנים [ר"ן נדרים נ:]. **דייסא.** טרייס בלע"ז [תענית כד:]. מאכל של חטים מבושלים [ר"ן נדרים מט:].

The Gemara analyzes R' Oshaya's ruling:

שְׁמַע מִינָּהּ מִצְטַמֵּק וְיָפֶה לו מוּתָּר – Shall we **learn from this** that even if the food is of a type that **improves as it condenses** it **is permitted** to leave it on an unbanked *kirah*?[1]

The Gemara rejects this conclusion:

שָׁאנִי הָכָא דִּקְטָמָהּ – **Here,** in R' Oshaya's case, the situation **is different** than the usual case of an unbanked *kirah,* **because [the person]** originally **banked it.** Therefore, even though it flared up again, he may leave on it fully cooked food that improves as it condenses.[2]

The Gemara counters:

אִי הָכִי – **If so,** that R' Oshaya's ruling pertains specifically to the case in which the coals were initially banked, מַאי לְמֵימְרָא – **what is** his purpose **in stating** it? It is obvious.[3] – ? –

The Gemara answers:

הוּבְעֲרָה אִיצְטְרִיכָא לֵיהּ – **He needed** to inform us that this is permitted even though the fire in **[the *kirah*] flared up** again. מַהוּ דְּתֵימָא כֵּיוָן דְּהוּבְעֲרָה הַדְרָא לָהּ לְמִילְתָא קַמַּיְיתָא – For **you might have said that once it flared up [the *kirah*] reverts to its original status** as an unbanked one and it would be therefore forbidden to leave on it food that improves as it condenses. קָמַשְׁמַע לָן – **[R' Oshaya]** therefore **informs us** that this is not the case. Since the *kirah* was previously banked, it is permissible to leave on it fully cooked food that improves as it condenses, even though the fire flared up.[4]

The Gemara cites a similar ruling:

אָמַר רַבָּה בַּר בַּר חָנָה אָמַר רַבִּי יוֹחָנָן – **Rabbah bar bar Chanah said in the name of R' Yochanan:** קְטָמָהּ וְהוּבְעֲרָה – **If one banked [a *kirah*] and it** subsequently **flared up** again, מַשְׁהִין עָלֶיהָ חַמִּין שֶׁהוּחַמּוּ כָּל צוֹרְכָּן וְתַבְשִׁיל שֶׁבִּישֵּׁל כָּל צוֹרְכּוֹ – **we may leave on it** before the Sabbath **hot water that was fully heated and cooked food that was fully cooked,** וַאֲפִילּוּ גֶּחָלִים שֶׁל רוֹתֶם – **even** if the *kirah* was fueled with **coals of *rosem*** wood.[5]

The Gemara analyzes R' Yochanan's ruling as it did R' Oshaya's ruling:

שְׁמַע מִינָּהּ מִצְטַמֵּק וְיָפֶה לו מוּתָּר – Shall we **learn from this** that even if the food is of a type that **improves as it condenses** it **is permitted** to leave it on an unbanked *kirah*?

The Gemara responds:

שָׁאנִי הָכָא דִּקְטָמָהּ – No! **Here** in R' Yochanan's case the situation **is different** than the usual case of an unbanked *kirah,* **because [the person]** originally **banked it.**

The Gemara asks:

אִי הָכִי מַאי לְמֵימְרָא – **If so, what is** the purpose **in stating** that one may leave on it fully cooked food that improves as it condenses?

The Gemara answers:

הוּבְעֲרָה אִצְטְרִיכָא לֵיהּ – **[R' Yochanan] needed** to inform us that this is permitted even though the fire in **[the *kirah*] flared up** again.

The Gemara wonders:

הַיְינוּ הָךְ – But **this is** the same as **that** previous teaching of R' Oshaya! What did R' Yochanan add?

The Gemara answers:

גֶּחָלִים שֶׁל רוֹתֶם אִצְטְרִיכָא לֵיהּ – **He needed** to inform us that this holds true even regarding a *kirah* that was heated with **coals of *rosem*** wood.

According to the previous citation, R' Yochanan forbids leaving even fully cooked food on a *kirah* that was never banked, if the food improves as it condenses. Thus, he clearly follows the opinion of the Sages who disagree with Chananyah. The Gemara now cites a different version of R' Yochanan's opinion:

אָמַר רַב שֵׁשֶׁת אָמַר רַבִּי יוֹחָנָן – **Rav Sheishess said in the name of R' Yochanan:** כִּירָה שֶׁהִסִּיקוּהָ בְּגֶפֶת וּבְעֵצִים – Concerning **a *kirah* that was heated with marc or with wood** and was not shoveled or banked, מַשְׁהִין עָלֶיהָ חַמִּין שֶׁלֹּא הוּחַמּוּ כָּל צוֹרְכָּן וְתַבְשִׁיל שֶׁלֹּא בִּישֵּׁל כָּל צוֹרְכּוֹ – **we may leave on it** before the Sabbath **hot water that was *not* fully heated and cooked food that was *not* fully cooked.**[6] עָקַר לֹא יַחֲזִיר עַד שֶׁיִּגְרוֹף אוֹ עַד שֶׁיִּתֵּן אֵפֶר – **If one removed** something from the *kirah,* **he may not return** it **unless he has shoveled** away the coals **or placed ash** over them.

The Gemara explains this view:

קָסָבַר מַתְנִיתִין לְהַחֲזִיר תְּנַן – **[R' Yochanan, as cited by Rav Sheishess] holds** that **our Mishnah,** when it requires that a *kirah* be shoveled or banked, **refers to returning** food to the *kirah* on the Sabbath, אֲבָל לִשְׁהוֹת – **but as for leaving** food on

NOTES

1. Presumably, R' Oshaya was referring to fully cooked foods that improve as they dry out and condense, for if he was referring to foods that do not improve he should merely have mentioned hot water (which does not improve, but merely evaporates). Since he also mentioned cooked food, R' Oshaya obviously meant to inform us that one may leave a cooked item on the *kirah* even though the stewing is beneficial for it, and we are unconcerned that one might stoke the coals, since the food is already fully cooked and edible. With his additional statement that one may leave hot water that is fully heated on the *kirah* (which seems obvious, since even cooked foods that improve by stewing may be left on it), R' Oshaya meant to inform us that even though hot water cooks rather easily it must be fully heated before it can be left on the *kirah.* At any rate, since R' Oshaya holds that when the coals flare up the earlier banking is negated and he nevertheless allows leaving any fully cooked food on the *kirah,* we may presumably learn from his ruling that cooked food which improves as it condenses may be left on an unbanked *kirah,* even according to the opinion of the Sages who disagree with Chananyah (*Rashi,* as explained by *Rosh Yosef;* see also *Pnei Yehoshua*).

2. By banking the coals, the person demonstrated that he does not want the food to continue to be heated and dry out (even though this might improve its flavor) but merely to remain warm while moist. Thus, even though the coals flared up again, we need not be concerned that he might stoke them, since he would seemingly prefer that the flame be banked. If a *kirah* was not banked, however, it is possibly forbidden (according to the Sages) to leave on it even a fully cooked food that improves as it condenses, since one might come to stoke the coals.

Note, however, that R' Oshaya permits leaving on the banked and reignited *kirah* only food that is fully cooked and improves as it condenses, but not even partially uncooked food. Since the coals flared up again and the food is not fully cooked, the previous banking does not allay our concern that the person might forgetfully stoke the coals, since he certainly needs them to cook the food further (*Rashi,* as explained by *Rosh Yosef* and *Pnei Yehoshua*).

3. Obviously, a fully cooked food may be left to stew on the *kirah* once the person demonstrated that he does not really want it to be heated continually and dry out (see *Pnei Yehoshua*).

4. We have explained this passage in accordance with *Rashi's* approach, as clarified primarily by *Rosh Yosef* and similarly by *Pnei Yehoshua. Tosafos* have various objections to *Rashi's* approach and therefore offer alternative ones; however, their objections are alleviated by the clarifications of *Rosh Yosef* and *Pnei Yehoshua.*

5. Coals of *rosem* (which some equate with the broom plant) are especially hot and difficult to extinguish (*Rashi*). Unlike other coals, *rosem* coals retain a live fire deep inside even when they appear extinguished on the outside (*Rashi* to *Psalms* 120:4). [Thus, they have a tendency to flare up. R' Yochanan nevertheless permits leaving cooked food on this *kirah* since the person indicated his discontent with the live fire.]

6. Provided the water was heated and the food was cooked as much as the food of Ben Derusai (see *Hagahos R' Elazar Moshe Horowitz* and *Igros Moshe, Orach Chaim* vol. IV §74 – *bishul* 24).

שמע מינה מצטמק ויפה לו מותר שאני הכא דקטמה אי הכי מאי למימרא הובערה איצטריכא ליה מהו דתימא כיון דהובערה הדרא לה למילתא קמייתא קמשמע לן אמר רבה בר בר חנה אמר רבי יוחנן קטמה והובערה משהין עליה חמין שהוחמו כל צורכן ותבשיל שבישל כל צורכו ואפי' גחלים של רותם ש"מ מצטמק ויפה לו מותר שאני הכא דקטמה אי הכי מאי למימרא הובערה אצטריכא ליה היינו הך גחלים של רותם אצטריכא ליה אמר רב ששת אמר ר' יוחנן כירה שהסיקוה בגפת ובעצים משהין עליה חמין שלא הוחמו כל צורכן ותבשיל שלא בישל כל צורכו עקר לא יחזיר עד שיגרוף או עד שיתן אפר קסבר מתניתין להחזיר תנן אבל לשהות משהין אע"פ שאינו גרוף ואינו קטום אמר רבא תרווייהו תנגהי לשהות תנינא [א] אין נותנין את הפת בתוך התנור עם חשיכה ולא חררה על גבי גחלים אלא כדי שיקרמו פניה הא קרמו פניה שרי להחזיר נמי תנינא בית הלל אומרים אף מחזירין ועד כאן לא קשרו בית הלל אלא בגרופה וקטומה אבל בשאינה גרופה וקטומה לא ורב ששת נמי דיוקא דמתני' קמ"ל אמר רב שמואל בר יהודה אמר רבי יוחנן [א] כירה שהסיקוה בגפת ובעצים משהין (א) עליה תבשיל שבישל כל צורכו וחמין שהוחמו כל צורכן ואפי' מצטמק ויפה לו אמר ליה ההוא מדרבנן לרב שמואל בר יהודה הא רב ושמואל דאמרי תרווייהו מצטמק ויפה לו אסור אמר ליה אטו לית אנא ידע דאמר רב יוסף אמר רב יהודה אמר שמואל מצטמק ויפה לו אסור כי קאמינא לך לרבי יוחנן קאמינא אמר ליה רב עוקבא ממישן לרב אשי אתון דמקרביתו לרב ושמואל עבידו כרב ושמואל אנן נעביד כרבי יוחנן אמר ליה אביי לרב יוסף מהו לשהות אמר ליה הא רב יהודה משהו ליה ואכיל א"ל בר מיניה דרב יהודה דכיון דמסוכן הוא אפילו בשבת נמי שרי למעבד ליה לי ולך מאי אמר ליה בסורא משהו דהא רב נחמן בר יצחק [ג] מרי דעובדא הוה ומשהו ליה ואכיל אמר רב אשי קאימנא קמיה דרב הונא ושהין ליה כסא דהרסנא ואכל ולא ידענא אי משום דקסבר מצטמק ויפה לו מותר אי משום דכיון דאית ביה מיחא מצטמק ורע לו הוא אמר רב [א] נחמן [ב] מצטמק ויפה לו אסור מצטמק ורע לו מותר כללא דמלתא כל דאית ביה מיחא מצטמק ורע לו לבר מתבשיל דליפתא דאף על גב דאית ביה מיחא מצטמק ויפה לו הוא והני מילי דאית ביה בשרא אבל לית ביה בשרא מצטמק ורע לו הוא וכי אית ביה בשרא נמי לא אמרן אלא דלא קבעי לה לאורחין אבל קבעי לה לאורחין מצטמק ורע לו לפדא דייסא ותמרי מצטמק ורע להן בעו מיניה מרבי חייא בר אבא

שכח

מצטמק. מתמעט וכויץ רטיי"ט לשון שדים צומקין (הושע ט) כמו שאתה אומר בלשון צוי נצטוה ובלשון צדק נצטדק וכן כל תיבה שראש יסודה צד"י כשהיא מתפעלת נותן ט' אחר צד"י: מותר. להשהותן בכירה דאי לא במצטמק ויפה לו קאמר מאי אתא לאשמעינן אלא ע"כ במצטמק ויפה לו קאמר ואפילו הכי לא גזרו משום חיתוי הואיל ונתבשל כל צרכו ותנא חמין לאשמעינן דבעינן שהוחמו כל צרכן מבעוד יום: שאני הכא דקטמה. וגלי דעתיה דלא ניחא ליה בצמוקי: גחלים של רותם. חמין יותר משאר גחלים ואינם ממהרין לכבות כדאמרינן בהמוכר את הספינה (ב"ב דף עד:): משהין עליה. ואע"פ שלא קטמה ואמוראי נינהו אליבא דר' יוחנן: מתניתין. דקתני עד שיגרוף: להחזיר תנן. דלא שרו בית הלל להחזיר עד שיגרוף ופירוקא דמתניתין כדאמרינן לעיל חסורי מיחסרא הלכך עקר לא יחזיר הואיל ואינה גרופה: תרווייהו תנגהי. בין לשהות בשאינה גרופה תנינא בהדיא סתם משנה דמותר ועקר לא יחזיר נמי תנינא ולמה ליה לרבי יוחנן לאשמעינן: הא קרמו פניה שרי. והיינו לא בישל כל צרכו ותנור לאו גרוף וקטום הוא ואי נמי גרוף בתנור לא מהניא גריפה כדתנן במתניתין וכ"ש פת דאדעתא לבשולי יהביה בגוויה: ועד כאן לא שרו כו'. דמתניתין אלאחר שיגרוף קאי דקתני לא יתן עד שיגרוף ובין למאן דאמר לא ישהה ובין למ"ד לא יחזיר מ"מ חזרה דסיפא אגרוף וקטום מהדר: ורב ששת נמי דיוקא דמתני' קמ"ל. משום דלא מתני לה בהדיא הא קרמו שרי. ואנן דמשהינן קדירה על גבי כירה שאינה גרופה אדחנניה סמכינן הואיל ותנן סתם מתניתין כוותיה כדאמר הא קרמו שרי ואע"ג דלא בישל כל צרכו ואמר רב ששת משמיה דרבי יוחנן כוותיה דמתניתין דפרקין משום חזרה הוא דבעי גרופה אבל לשהות לא. וכל הני אמוראי דאסרי סברי מתניתין לשהות תנן: מהו לשהות. בשאינה גרופה: מסוכן הוא. רגיל לאוחזו בולמוס וצריך לאכול מאכל מתוק וטוב: מרי דעובדא. מדקדק במעשיו: מיחא. קמח: כסא דהרסנא. דגים המבושלים בשמן בקמח: דאית ביה בשרא. מצטמק ויפה לו ששומן הבשר משבר כח הלפת כדאמר בברכות (דף מד:): לאורחין. צריך חתיכות חשובות לשום לפניהם ואין דרך כבוד בתבשיל המצטמק שאין הבשר ניכר בו: לפדא. מאכל שעושה מתאנים: תמרי. מאכל תמרים:

שכח

שמע מינה מצטמק ויפה לו מותר. פירש בקונטרס דאי האי תבשיל במצטמק ורע לו מאי אתא לאשמעינן וקשה לר"י הא איצטריך לאפוקי מדרבי מאיר ורבי יהודה דאסרי בשאינה גרופה אפילו חמין דמצטמק ורע להם ועוד קשה כיון דהשתא ס"ד דמשום דהובערה הדרא למילתא קמייתא כי משני שאני הכא דקטמה מאי פריך מאי למימרא הא איצטריך טובא לאפוקי ממאי דס"ד מעיקרא ונראה לר"י דהשתא ס"ד דלא חשיבא קטומה כלל משום דהובערה ואשמעינן דהדרא למילתא קמייתא דאי חשיבא קטומה אמאי נקט בישל כל צרכו אפי' לא בישל כל צרכו שרי דאפילו רבי מאיר דמחמיר מכולהו תנאי שרי בחמין שלא הוחמו כל צרכן כדפירשנו לעיל דסתם חמין ותבשיל הוי שלא הוחמו כל צורכן ופריך שמע מינה מצטמק ויפה לו מותר דהא סתם תבשיל אמר לקמן דמצטמק ויפה לו הוא ומשני שאני הכא דקטמה פירוש וחשיבא לגמרי קטומה וה"ה אפילו לא בישל כל צרכו שרי והא דנקט בישל כל צרכו לאשמעינן דאי לאו קטומה אפילו בישל כל צרכו אסור משום דמצטמק ויפה לו הוא ופריך אי הכי מאי למימרא אף על גב דאשמעינן דאי לא קטמה אסור מ"מ מדנקט למילתיה בלשון היתר משמע דהתירא אתי לאורויי לן ואף על גב דאשמעינן דלא הדרא למילתא קמייתא נראה לו דהא לא איצטריך לאשמעינן דסברא הוא דלא הדרא למילתא קמייתא ואף על גב דמעיקרא הוה בעי למימר דהדרא למילתא קמייתא לאו משום דסברא הוא לומר כן אלא משום דנקט במלתיה בישל כל צרכו היה ר"ל כן כדפרישית ומשני דמכל מקום אצטריך דמהו דתימא כו' ועוד יש לומר שאני הכא דקטמה דלאו לגמרי מהניא קטימה אלא דוקא משום דבישל כל צרכו אבל לא בישל כל צרכו אסור משום דהובערה והשתא אתי שפיר הא דנקט הכא קטמה והובערה ולעיל נקט ונתלבתה דנתלבתה הוי פחות מהובערה והויא לגמרי כקטומה ופריך א"ה מאי למימרא דהא בלאו מילתיה מסברא ה"א דלא הדרא למלתא קמייתא כמו בנתלבתה ושרי ואפי' לא בישל כל צרכו ובלשון איסור ה"ל לאשמעינן ולא בלשון היתר ומשני הובערה איצטריך ליה ואי לאו מילתיה לא היה פשוט היתר אלא הוה ס"ד למימרא דהדרא למילתא קמייתא:

אמר רב ששת אמר ר' יוחנן כירה שהסיקוה בגפת ובעצים משהין עליה תבשיל שלא בישל כל צרכו כו'. פסק ר"ח דהלכה כרב ששת אמר ר' יוחנן דרבא דאמר תרווייהו תנגהי סבירא ליה כוותיה וכן פסק רש"י דסתם מתניתין דפרק קמא (דף יט:) כחנניה ומותר להשהות אפי' באינה גרופה אבל להחזיר ודאי אסור אא"כ גרוף וקטום ואפי' ב) בישל כל צרכו כדפי' לעיל: דיוקא דמתני' קמ"ל. פי' רש"י דקמ"ל דקרמו פניה שפיר דמי ואין נראה דדיוק פשוט הוא דהא כיון דתנא עד שיקרמו פניה ממילא שמעינן דקרמו פניה שרי ונראה לפרש דדיוקא דמתניתין דכירה אתא לאשמעי' דלהחזיר תנן ולשהות מחסרא והכי קתני: מהו להשהות. באינה גרופה ולא בישל כל צרכו קבעי או במצטמק ויפה לו:

שכח

עין משפט נר מצוה

ו א ב (מיי' פ"ג מהל' שבת הל' ד') סמג לאוין סה טוש"ע א"ח סימן רנג סעיף א:

רבינו חננאל

לא שנא ופשטנא מהא דתניא כירה שהסיקוה בגפת ובעצים סומכין ואין מקיימין עליה אלא אם כן גרופה וקטומה עממו הגחלים או שנתן לתוכה נעורת של פשתן דקה הרי כקטומה (דבי) [אמר רב] (שמעון) [שמואל] בר יהודה א"ר יוחנן כירה שהסיקוה בגפת ובעצים משהין עליה חמין שהוחמו כל צרכן ותבשיל שבישל כל צרכו ודוקא כירה שהיא שפיתת ב' קדרות אבל אם אין בה אלא שפיתת קדרה אחת אסור ואפי' מצטמק ויפה לו מותר ואע"ג דרב ושמואל פליגי הא קי"ל דרבי יוחנן לגבי רב ושמואל הלכתא כר' יוחנן ומה שאמר רב (עקיבא) [עוקבא] ממישן לרב אשי אתון דמקרביתון לרב ושמואל עבידו כרב ושמואל לאו משום דהלכתא כוותיהו אלא לעולם הלכתא כר' יוחנן דשרי אבל אתון דנהיגתון איסורא כרב ושמואל הוו להו דברים המותרין ואחרים נהגו בהן איסור אי אתה רשאי להתירן בפניהם והא דאמר רב יהודה מסוכן בשבת שרי למיעבד ליה פשוטה הוא: **הא דאמר** רב נחמן בר יצחק מצטמק ויפה לו אסור מצטמק ורע לו מותר. כללא דמילתא כל דאית ליה מיחא מצטמק ורע לו הוא בר מתבשילא דליפתא דאע"ג דאית ליה מיחא מצטמק ויפה לו הוא כו'. האי כללא (לגברי) [לגבי] רב ושמואל אמרה ולית הלכתא אלא כר' יוחנן דהא סייעיה ר' עקיבא ממישן לרב אשי. **לפדא** דייסא ותמרי מצטמק ורע לו מותר

מסורת הש"ס

א) לעיל יט:, ב) [ביצה כט: חולין קי.].

תוספות ישנים

א) לספרים דגרסי הכא רנב"י ז"ל דאליבא דרב ושמואל קאמר דהא איהו גופיה משהי ליה ואכיל: ב) תימה אמאי אסור להחזיר מ"ש מדאמר לקמן [דף מ:] נותן אדם קיתון של מים כנגד המדורה שתפיג צינתן. ושמן איכא מאן דשרי אפילו יד סולדת בו ואם כן אמאי אסור תבשיל שבישל כל צרכו להחזיר הא לא שייך ביה בישול. ולעיל [דף לד.] נמי דאסור להטמין משחשיכה אפילו באין מוסיף הבל גזרה שמא ירתיח הא לא שייך ביה בישול. וי"ל דודאי בשמן לא שייך בישול אבל בתבשיל אפילו במבושל מבעוד יום שייך בישול. והא דשרינן קיתון של מים היינו ליתן במקום שאפי' תהיה שם כל היום לא תהיה יד סולדת בו:

הגהות הב"ח

(א) גמ' אמר רב שמואל בר יהודה א"ר יוחנן כירה וכו' משהין עליה חמין שהוחמו כל צורכן ותבשיל שבישל כל צורכו ואפי' מצטמק:

ליקוטי רש"י

רותם. שאין גחליו כבים מהרה [רשב"ם ב"ב עד:]. גחלי רתמים. כל הגחלים כבו מבחוץ כבו מבפנים ואלו כבו מבחוץ ולא מבפנים [תהלים קכ, ד]. **חררה.** עוגת רצפים (מ"א יט) פוגאצ"ה בלע"ז [לעיל יט:]. עוגה שאופין על פני הגחלים [סוטה לה.]. **יקרמו.** כמו קרום קרוסטי"ן בלע"ז [לעיל שם]. **מרי דעובדא.** זהיר במעשים טובים [חולין קי.]. **כסא דהרסנא.** דגים קטנים מטוגנים בשמן קרביהן ובקמח [לקמן קיח:]. דגים קטנים מטוגנין בקמח בשומן שלהן [סוכה מד:]. קערה של מאכל דגים מטוגנין בשמן בסולת [רשב"ם ב"ב ס:]. טיגן במוריים שומן דגים עם קמח [ע"ז לח.]. **לפדא.** שם תבשיל של תאנים [ר"ן נדרים נ:]. **דייסא.** טריי"ש בלע"ז [תענית כד:]. מאכל של חטים מבושלים [ר"ן נדרים מט:].

it before the Sabbath, מַשְׁהִין אַף עַל פִּי שֶׁאֵינוֹ גָרוּף וְאֵינוֹ קָטוּם – **we may leave** food on it **even though [the *kirah*] was neither shoveled nor banked,** in accordance with Chananyah's opinion.

The Gemara cites a comment concerning the ruling just cited: אָמַר רָבָא – **Rava said:** תַּרְוַיְיהוּ תְּנֵנְהִי – **We** already **learned both** aspects of Rav Sheishess' ruling[7] **in a Mishnah!** לִשְׁהוֹת תְּנֵינָא – That **leaving** food on an unshoveled and unbanked *kirah* is permissible, **we learned in** the following **Mishnah:**[8] אֵין נוֹתְנִין אֶת הַפַּת בְּתוֹךְ הַתַּנּוּר עִם חֲשֵׁיכָה – WE MAY NOT PLACE BREAD IN THE OVEN CLOSE TO NIGHTFALL on Friday,[9] וְלֹא חֲרָרָה עַל גַּבֵּי גֶחָלִים – NOR A BISCUIT UPON COALS, אֶלָּא כְּדֵי שֶׁיִּקְרְמוּ פָנֶיהָ – UNLESS there is SUFFICIENT time FOR ITS SURFACE TO CRUST while it is yet day. הָא קָרְמוּ פָּנֶיהָ שָׁרֵי – This implies: **But** once **its surface** merely **crusted, it is permissible** to leave it in the oven or upon the coals, even though they were not banked. Thus, this Mishnah teaches the rule that we may leave partially cooked food on an unbanked *kirah* before the Sabbath, in accordance with Chananyah's opinion.[10] לְהַחֲזִיר נַמִּי תְּנֵינָא – And that **returning** food to the *kirah* on the Sabbath is permissible only if it was shoveled or banked, **we learned in** our **Mishnah,** which states: בֵּית הִלֵּל אוֹמְרִים אַף מַחֲזִירִין – BEIS HILLEL SAY: WE MAY EVEN RETURN it; וְעַד כָּאן לֹא קָשָׁרוּ בֵּית הִלֵּל אֶלָּא בִּגְרוּפָה וּקְטוּמָה – **and so far Beis Hillel allow** this **only in** the case of **[a *kirah*] that was shoveled or banked,** as is clear from the introductory clause of the Mishnah; אֲבָל בְּשֶׁאֵינָהּ גְּרוּפָה וּקְטוּמָה לֹא – **but in** the case of **[a *kirah*] that was neither shoveled nor banked – not!** Thus, our Mishnah teaches the rule that returning food to a *kirah* requires that the *kirah* be shoveled or banked.[11] Since both aspects of R' Sheishess' ruling may be inferred from the Mishnah, why was it necessary for R' Sheishess to state it at all?

The Gemara answers:

וְרַב שֵׁשֶׁת נַמִּי דִּיוּקָא דְּמַתְנִיתִין קָמַשְׁמַע לָן – **Rav Sheishess too** merely wanted to **inform us of the inference** that is contained **in the Mishnah.**[12]

The Gemara cites another opinion concerning these issues: אָמַר רַב שְׁמוּאֵל בַּר יְהוּדָה אָמַר רַבִּי יוֹחָנָן – **Rav Shmuel bar Yehudah said in the name of R' Yochanan:** כִּירָה שֶׁהִסִּיקוּהָ בְּגֶפֶת וּבְעֵצִים – Concerning **a *kirah* that was heated with marc or with wood,** מַשְׁהִין עָלֶיהָ תַּבְשִׁיל שֶׁבִּישֵּׁל כָּל צוֹרְכּוֹ וְחַמִּין שֶׁהוּחַמּוּ כָּל צוֹרְכָּן – **one may leave on it** before the Sabbath **cooked food that was fully cooked and hot water that was fully heated,** וַאֲפִילּוּ מִצְטַמֵּק וְיָפֶה לוֹ – **even** if the food is of a type that **improves as it condenses.**[13]

A discussion is cited concerning Rav Shmuel bar Yehudah's ruling:

אָמַר לֵיהּ הַהוּא מִדְּרַבָּנַן לְרַב שְׁמוּאֵל בַּר יְהוּדָה – **A certain rabbi said to Rav Shmuel bar Yehudah:** הָא רַב וּשְׁמוּאֵל דְּאָמְרֵי תַּרְוַיְיהוּ – **But Rav and Shmuel both stated** מִצְטַמֵּק וְיָפֶה לוֹ אָסוּר – that if a food **improves as it condenses** it **is forbidden** to leave it on an unbanked *kirah*. This contradicts your ruling! אָמַר לֵיהּ – **[Rav Shmuel bar Yehudah] replied:** אַטּוּ לֵית אֲנָא יָדַע – **Do I not know** that? דְּאָמַר רַב יוֹסֵף אָמַר רַב יְהוּדָה אָמַר שְׁמוּאֵל – Certainly I do, **for Rav Yosef has said in the name of Rav Yehudah who said in the name of Shmuel:** מִצְטַמֵּק וְיָפֶה לוֹ אָסוּר – If a food **improves as it condenses** it **is forbidden** to leave it on an unbanked *kirah*. כִּי קָאָמֵינָא לָךְ לְרַבִּי יוֹחָנָן קָאָמֵינָא – However, **when I said to you** that it is permitted to leave such a food on an unbanked *kirah,* **I was stating** the law **according to R' Yochanan.**

The Gemara cites a later ruling concerning this topic: אָמַר לֵיהּ רַב עוּקְבָא מִמֵּישָׁן לְרַב אַשִׁי – **Rav Ukva of Meishan said to Rav Ashi:** אַתּוּן דִּמְקָרְבִיתוּ לְרַב וּשְׁמוּאֵל – **You, who live** in Babylonia **near** the area in which **Rav and Shmuel** resided, עֲבִידוּ כְּרַב וּשְׁמוּאֵל – **should act in accordance with** the opinion of **Rav and Shmuel,** and refrain from leaving food that improves as it condenses on an unbanked *kirah*. אֲנַן נַעֲבֵיד כְּרַבִּי יוֹחָנָן – **We,** however, who live elsewhere, **will act in accordance with** the lenient opinion of **R' Yochanan.**[14]

A related discussion is cited:

אָמַר לֵיהּ אַבַּיֵּי לְרַב יוֹסֵף – **Abaye said to Rav Yosef:** מַהוּ לִשְׁהוֹת

NOTES

7. I.e. that *shehiyah* is permissible even if the *kirah* was neither shoveled nor banked (in accordance with Chananyah's opinion) and that *chazarah* is permissible only if it was shoveled or banked (*Rashi*).

8. Above, 19b.

9. Literally: with the dark (see 19b note 30).

10. A loaf that has formed a crust is not yet fully baked, but is similar to a food that has been cooked like that of Ben Derusai (see above, 20a). Yet the Mishnah permits leaving it inside an oven before the Sabbath, even though one who leaves it there clearly wants it to continue to bake. Now, the Mishnah is referring to a *tanur*-style oven, which is intensely hot (see 36b note 1). Even if the *tanur*-oven was shoveled or banked, it is equivalent to an unshoveled and unbanked *kirah,* for a Mishnah below (38b) teaches that shoveling or banking is of no avail in the case of a *tanur*-oven. Since the Mishnah permits leaving crusted bread in the *tanur*-oven, we learn that it is permitted to leave food that has cooked like that of Ben Derusai on an unbanked *kirah,* in accordance with Chananyah's opinion (*Rashi*). [And since our Mishnah also bears interpretation in accordance with Chananyah's opinion, it seems reasonable to interpret it in that fashion, in accordance with this earlier Mishnah (see *Baal HaMaor; Rosh Yosef* to 36b).]

11. Whether we interpret the beginning of our Mishnah as referring to *shehiyah* or to *chazarah* (i.e. whether in accordance with the Sages or with Chananyah), it is clearly dealing with a *kirah* that was shoveled or banked, and it is only upon such a *kirah* that Beis Hillel permit *chazarah* in the Mishnah's latter segment (*Rashi*).

12. Since the Mishnah above (19b) does not state explicitly that if the bread formed a crust it may be left in the *tanur*-oven, Rav Sheishess deemed it proper to teach us that we should draw this inference from it (*Rashi*). [*Tosafos* (ד״ה דיוקא) point out that this inference is obvious (see *Hagahos R' Elazar Moshe Horowitz*) and explain, rather, that Rav Sheishess meant to inform us that the proper way to interpret *our* Mishnah is in accordance with Chananyah's opinion.]

Rashi and *Tosafos* (ד״ה אמר רב ששת) comment that the halachah follows Chananyah's opinion, since Rav Sheishess concurs with it and Rava considered it so obvious that there was no need for Rav Sheishess to mention it. Cf. *Rif* and *Rambam* cited above, 37a note 16. See also *Milchamos Hashem* and *Rosh* for a discussion of how the Amoraim who follow the Sages' opinion (i.e. R' Oshaya and Rabbah bar bar Chanah in the name of R' Yochanan) account for the Mishnah on 19b.

13. According to Rav Shmuel bar Yehudah, R' Yochanan follows the opinion of the Sages who forbid leaving food that is not fully cooked on an unbanked *kirah*. However, he rules leniently regarding fully cooked food that improves as it condenses. This version of R' Yochanan's opinion differs from both the version of Rabbah bar bar Chanah [according to which food that improves as it condenses may not be left on an unbanked *kirah* except where it had previously been banked and flared up again] and from the version of Rav Sheishess [according to which even foods that are not fully cooked may be left on the *kirah*] (see *Tosafos* to 37a, end of ד״ה אא״ב; cf. *Rav Hai Gaon* cited by *Rashba;* see *Rosh Yosef*).

14. Rav Ukva held that the halachah follows the opinion of R' Yochanan as quoted by Rav Shmuel bar Yehudah, i.e. that it is permitted to leave food that improves as it condenses on an unbanked *kirah*. However, he maintained that residents of Babylonia, who had adopted the stringent practice of their mentors Rav and Shmuel, could not abandon that practice, because the adoption of a stringent halachic practice is similar to a vow and one must always abide by it (*Rashba;* see *Ritva MHK* ed.; see also *Yevamos* 14a, *Nedarim* 15a and *Ran, Nedarim* 81b ד״ה משום).

שמע מינה מצטמק ויפה לו מותר שאני הכא דקטמה אי הכי מאי למימרא הובערה איצטריכא ליה מהו דתימא כיון דהובערה הדרא לה למילתא קמייתא קמשמע לן אמר רבה בר בר חנה אמר רבי יוחנן קטמה והובערה משהין עליה חמין שהוחמו כל צורכן ותבשיל שבישל כל צורכו ואפי' גחלים של רותם ש"מ מצטמק ויפה לו מותר שאני הכא דקטמה אי הכי מאי למימרא הובערה אצטריכא ליה היינו הך גחלים של רותם אצטריכא ליה אמר רב ששת אמר ר' יוחנן כירה שהסיקוה בגפת ובעצים משהין עליה חמין שלא הוחמו כל צורכן ותבשיל שלא בישל כל צורכו עקר לא יחזיר עד שיגרוף או עד שיתן אפר קסבר מתניתין להחזיר תנן אבל לשהות משהין אע"פ שאינו גרוף ואינו קטום אמר רבא תרווייהו תנגהי לשהות תנינא [א] אין נותנין את הפת בתוך התנור עם חשיכה ולא חררה על גבי גחלים אלא כדי שיקרמו פניה הא קרמו פניה שרי להחזיר נמי תנינא בית הלל אומרים אף מחזירין ועד כאן לא קשרו בית הלל אלא בגרופה וקטומה אבל בשאינה גרופה וקטומה לא ורב ששת נמי דיוקא דמתני' קמ"ל אמר רב שמואל בר יהודה אמר רבי יוחנן [א] כירה שהסיקוה בגפת ובעצים משהין (א) עליה תבשיל שבישל כל צורכו וחמין שהוחמו כל צורכן ואפי' מצטמק ויפה לו אמר ליה ההוא מדרבנן לרב שמואל בר יהודה הא רב ושמואל דאמרי תרווייהו מצטמק ויפה לו אסור אמר ליה אטו לית אנא ידע דאמר רב יוסף אמר רב יהודה אמר שמואל מצטמק ויפה לו אסור כי קאמינא לך לרבי יוחנן קאמינא אמר ליה רב עוקבא ממישן לרב אשי אתון דמקרביתו לרב ושמואל עבידו כרב ושמואל אנן נעביד כרבי יוחנן אמר ליה אביי לרב יוסף מהו לשהות אמר ליה הא רב יהודה משהו ליה ואכיל א"ל בר מיניה דרב יהודה דכיון דמסוכן הוא אפילו בשבת נמי שרי למעבד ליה לי ולך מאי אמר ליה בסורא משהו דהא רב נחמן בר יצחק [ג] מרי דעובדא הוה ומשהו ליה ואכיל אמר רב אשי קאימנא קמיה דרב הונא ושהין ליה כסא דהרסנא ואכל ולא ידענא אי משום דקסבר מצטמק ויפה לו מותר אי משום דכיון דאית ביה מיחא מצטמק ורע לו הוא אמר רב (א) נחמן [ב] מצטמק ויפה לו אסור מצטמק ורע לו מותר כללא דמלתא כל דאית ביה מיחא מצטמק ורע לו לבר מתבשיל דליפתא דאף על גב דאית ביה מיחא מצטמק ויפה לו הוא והני מילי דאית ביה בשרא אבל לית ביה בשרא מצטמק ורע לו הוא וכי אית ביה בשרא נמי לא אמרן אלא דלא קבעי לה לאורחין אבל קבעי לה לאורחין מצטמק ורע לו לפדא דייסא ותמרי מצטמק ורע להן בעו מיניה מרבי חייא בר אבא

שכח

רש"י

מצטמק. מתמעט וכוין רטיי"ט לשון שדים צומקין (הושע ט) כמו שאתה אומר בלשון צווי נצטוה ובלשון צדק נצטדק וכן כל תיבה שראש יסודה צד"י כשהיא מתפעלת נותן ט' אחר צד"י: מותר. להשהותן בכירה דאי לא במצטמק ויפה לו קאמר מאי אתא לאשמעינן אלא ע"כ במצטמק ויפה לו קאמר ואפילו הכי לא גזרו משום חיתוי הואיל ונתבשל כל צרכו ותנא חמין לאשמעינן דבעינן שהוחמו כל צרכן מבעוד יום: שאני הכא דקטמה. וגלי דעתיה דלא ניחא ליה בצמוקי: גחלים של רותם. חמין יותר משאר גחלים ואינם ממהרין לכבות כדאמרינן בהמוכר את הספינה (ב"ב דף עד:): משהין עליה. ואע"פ שלא קטמה ואמוראי נינהו אליבא דר' יוחנן: מתניתין. דקתני עד שיגרוף: להחזיר תנן. דלא שרו בית הלל להחזיר עד שיגרוף ופירוקא דמתניתין כדאמרינן לעיל חסורי מיחסרא הלכך עקר לא יחזיר הואיל ואינה גרופה: תרווייהו תנגהי. בין לשהות בשאינה גרופה תנינא בהדיא סתם משנה דמותר ועקר לא יחזיר נמי תנינא ולמה ליה לרבי יוחנן לאשמעינן: הא קרמו פניה שרי. והיינו לא בישל כל צרכו ותנור לאו גרוף וקטום הוא ואי נמי גרוף בתנור לא מהניא גריפה כדתנן במתניתין וכ"ש פת דאדעתא לבשולי יהביה בגוויה: ועד כאן לא שרו כו'. דמתניתין אלאחר שיגרוף קאי דקתני לא יתן עד שיגרוף ובין למאן דאמר לא ישהה ובין למ"ד לא יחזיר מ"מ חזרה דסיפא אגרוף וקטום מהדר: ורב ששת נמי דיוקא דמתני' קמ"ל. משום דלא מתני לה בהדיא הא קרמו שרי. ואנן דמשהינן קדירה על גבי כירה שאינה גרופה אחנניה סמכינן הואיל ותנן סתם מתניתין כוותיה כדאמר הא קרמו שרי ואע"ג דלא בישל כל צרכו ואמר רב ששת משמיה דרבי יוחנן כוותיה דמתניתין דפרקין משום חזרה הוא דבעי גרופה אבל לשהות לא. וכל הני אמוראי דאסרי סברי מתניתין לשהות תנן: מהו לשהות. בשאינה גרופה: מסוכן הוא. רגיל לאוחזו בולמוס וצריך לאכול מאכל מתוק וטוב: מרי דעובדא. מדקדק במעשיו: מיחא. קמח: כסא דהרסנא. דגים המבושלים בשמן בקמח: דאית ביה בשרא. מצטמק ויפה לו שהשומן הבשר משבר כח הלפת כדאמר בברכות (דף מד:): לאורחין. צריך חתיכות חשובות לשום לפניהם ואין דרך כבוד בתבשיל המצטמק שאין הבשר ניכר בו: לפדא. מאכל שעושה מתאנים: תמרי. מאכל תמרים:

שכח

תוספות

שמע מינה מצטמק ויפה לו מותר. פירש בקונטרס דאי האי תבשיל במצטמק ורע לו מאי אתא לאשמעינן וקשה לר"י הא איצטריך לאפוקי מדרבי מאיר ורבי יהודה דאסרי בשאינה גרופה אפילו חמין דמצטמק ורע להם ועוד קשה כיון דהשתא ס"ד דמשום דהובערה הדרא למילתא קמייתא כי משני שאני הכא דקטמה מאי פריך מאי למימרא הא איצטריך טובא לאפוקי ממאי דס"ד מעיקרא ונראה לר"י דהשתא ס"ד דלא חשיבא קטומה כלל משום דהובערה ואשמעינן דהדרא למילתא קמייתא דאי חשיבא קטומה אמאי נקט בישל כל צרכו אפי' לא בישל כל צרכו שרי דאפילו רבי מאיר דמחמיר מכולהו תנאי שרי בחמין שלא הוחמו כל צרכן כדפירשנו לעיל דסתם חמין ותבשיל הוי שלא הוחמו כל צורכן ופריך שמע מינה מצטמק ויפה לו מותר דהא סתם תבשיל אמר לקמן דמצטמק ויפה לו הוא ומשני שאני הכא דקטמה פירוש וחשיבא לגמרי קטומה וה"ה אפילו לא בישל כל צרכו שרי והא דנקט בישל כל צרכו לאשמעינן דאי לאו קטומה אפילו בישל כל צרכו אסור משום דמצטמק ויפה לו הוא ופריך אי הכי מאי למימרא אף על גב דאשמעינן דאי לא קטמה אסור מ"מ מדנקט למילתיה בלשון היתר משמע דהתירא אתי לאורויי לן ואף על גב דאשמעינן דלא הדרא למילתא קמייתא נראה לו דהא לא איצטריך לאשמעינן דסברא הוא דלא הדרא למילתא קמייתא ואף על גב דמעיקרא הוה בעי למימר דהדרא למילתא קמייתא לאו משום דסברא הוא לומר כן אלא משום דנקט במלתיה בישל כל צרכו היה ר"ל כן כדפרישית ומשני דמכל מקום אצטריך דמהו דתימא כו' ועוד יש לומר שאני הכא דקטמה דלאו לגמרי מהניא קטימה אלא דוקא משום דבישל כל צרכו אבל לא בישל כל צרכו אסור משום דהובערה והשתא אתי שפיר הא דנקט הכא קטמה והובערה ולעיל נקט ונתלבתה דנתלבתה הוי פחות מהובערה והויא לגמרי כקטומה ופריך א"ה מאי למימרא דהא בלאו מילתיה מסברא ה"א דלא הדרא למלתא קמייתא כמו בנתלבתה ושרי ואפי' לא בישל כל צרכו ובלשון איסור ה"ל לאשמעינן ולא בלשון היתר ומשני הובערה איצטריך ליה ואי לאו מילתיה לא היה פשוט היתר אלא הוה ס"ד למימרא דהדרא למילתא קמייתא:

אמר רב ששת אמר ר' יוחנן כירה שהסיקוה בגפת ובעצים משהין עליה תבשיל שלא בישל כל צרכו כו'. פסק ר"ת דהלכה כרב ששת אמר ר' יוחנן דרבא דאמר תרווייהו תנגהי סבירא ליה כוותיה וכן פסק רש"י דסתם מתניתין דפרק קמא (דף יט:) כחנניה ומותר להשהות אפי' באינה גרופה אבל להחזיר ודאי אסור אא"כ גרוף וקטום ואפי' ב) בישל כל צרכו כדפי' לעיל: דיוקא דמתני' קמ"ל. פי' רש"י דקמ"ל דקרמו פניה שפיר דמי ואין נראה דדיוק פשוט הוא דהא כיון דתנא עד שיקרמו פניה ממילא שמעינן דקרמו פניה שרי ונראה לפרש דדיוקא דמתניתין דכירה אתא לאשמעי' דלהחזיר תנן וחסורי מחסרא והכי קתני: מהו להשהות. באינה גרופה ולא בישל כל צרכו קבעי או במצטמק ויפה לו:

שכח

עין משפט נר מצוה

ו א ב (מיי' פ"ג מהל' שבת הל' ד') סמג לאוין סה טוש"ע א"ח סימן רנג סעיף א:

רבינו חננאל

לא שנא ופשטנא מהא דתניא כירה שהסיקוה בגפת ובעצים סומכין ואין מקיימין עליה אלא אם כן גרופה וקטומה עממו הגחלים או שנתן לתוכה נעורת של פשתן דקה הרי כקטומה (דבי) [אמר רב] (שמעון) [שמואל] בר יהודה א"ר יוחנן כירה שהסיקוה בגפת ובעצים משהין עליה חמין שהוחמו כל צרכן ותבשיל שבישל כל צרכו ודוקא כירה שהיא שפיתת ב' קדרות אבל אם אין בה אלא שפיתת קדרה אחת אסור ואפי' מצטמק ויפה לו מותר ואע"ג דרב ושמואל פליגי הא קי"ל דרבי יוחנן לגבי רב ושמואל הלכתא כר' יוחנן ומה שאמר רב (עקיבא) [עוקבא] ממישן לרב אשי אתון דמקרביתון לרב ושמואל עבידו כרב ושמואל לאו משום דהלכתא כוותייהו אלא לעולם הלכתא כר' יוחנן דשרי אבל אתון דנהיגתון איסורא כרב ושמואל הוו להו דברים המותרין ואחרים נהגו בהן איסור אי אתה רשאי להתירן בפניהם והא דאמר רב יהודה מסוכן בשבת שרי למיעבד ליה פשוטה הוא: **הא דאמר** רב נחמן בר יצחק מצטמק ויפה לו אסור מצטמק ורע לו מותר. כללא דמילתא כל דאית ליה מיחא מצטמק ורע לו הוא בר מתבשילא דליפתא דאע"ג דאית ליה מיחא מצטמק ויפה לו הוא כו'. האי כללא (לגברי) [לגבי] רב ושמואל אמרה ולית הלכתא אלא כר' יוחנן דהא סייעיה ר' עקיבא ממישן לרב אשי. **לפדא** דייסא ותמרי מצטמק ורע לו מותר

מסורת הש"ס

א) לעיל יט:, ב) [ביצה כט: חולין קי.].

תוספות ישנים

א) לספרים דגרסי הכא רנב"י נ"ל דאליבא דרב ושמואל קאמר דהא איהו גופיה משהי ליה ואכיל: ב) תימה אמאי אסור להחזיר מ"ש מדאמר לקמן [דף מ:] נותן אדם קיתון של מים כנגד המדורה שתפיג צינתן. ושמן איכא מאן דשרי אפילו יד סולדת בו ואם כן אמאי אסור תבשיל שבישל כל צרכו להחזיר הא לא שייך ביה בישול. ולעיל [דף לד.] נמי דאסור להטמין משחשיכה אפילו באין מוסיף הבל גזרה שמא ירתיח הא לא שייך ביה בישול. וי"ל דודאי בשמן לא שייך בישול אבל בתבשיל אפילו במבושל מבעוד יום שייך בישול. והא דשרינן קיתון של מים היינו ליתן במקום שאפי' תהיה שם כל היום לא תהיה יד סולדת בו:

הגהות הב"ח

(א) גמ' אמר רב שמואל בר יהודה א"ר יוחנן כירה וכו' משהין עליה חמין שהוחמו כל צורכן ותבשיל שבישל כל צורכו ואפי' מצטמק:

ליקוטי רש"י

רותם. שאין גחליו כבים מהרה [רשב"ם ב"ב עד:]. גחלי רתמים. כל הגחלים כבו מבחוץ כבו מבפנים ואלו כבו מבחוץ ולא מבפנים [תהלים קכ, ד]. חררה. עוגת רצפים (מ"א יט) פוגאצ"ה בלע"ז [לעיל יט:]. עוגה שאופין על פני הגחלים [סוטה לה.]. יקרמו. כמו קרום קרוסטי"ן בלע"ז [לעיל שם]. מרי דעובדא. זהיר במעשים טובים [חולין קי.]. כסא דהרסנא. דגים קטנים מטוגנים בשמן קרביהן ובקמח [לקמן קיח:]. דגים קטנים מטוגנין בקמח בשומן שלהן [סוכה מד:]. קערה של מאכל דגים מטוגנין בשמן בסולת [רשב"ם ב"ב ס:]. טיגן במורייס שומן דגים עם קמח [ע"ז לח.]. לפדא. שם תבשיל של תאנים [ר"ן נדרים נ:]. דייסא. טרייס בלע"ז [תענית כד:]. מאכל של חטים מבושלים [ר"ן נדרים מט:].

– **What is** the law **concerning leaving** food on an unbanked *kirah* before the Sabbath?[15] אֲמַר לֵיהּ – **Rav Yosef replied:** הָא רַב יְהוּדָה מַשְׁהוּ לֵיהּ וְאָכִיל – **Why, they** reguarly **leave** food on an unbanked *kirah* **for Rav Yehudah and he eats it.** Clearly, it is permissible. אֲמַר לֵיהּ – **[Abaye] said to him:** בַּר מִינֵּיהּ דְּרַב יְהוּדָה – **Ignore** that practice of **Rav Yehudah!** It does not prove anything, דְּכֵיוָן דִּמְסוּכָּן הוּא אֲפִילּוּ בְּשַׁבָּת נַמִּי שָׁרֵי לְמֶעֱבַד לֵיהּ – **because since [Rav Yehudah] is dangerously ill, it is permitted to do** this (i.e. cook food) **for him even on the Sabbath** itself![16] לִי וְלָךְ מַאי – My question is: **What about for** people like **me and you?** Is it permissible to leave food on an unbanked *kirah*? אֲמַר לֵיהּ – **[Rav Yosef] replied:** בְּסוּרָא מַשְׁהוּ – **In Sura they used to leave** food on an unbanked *kirah,* דְּהָא רַב נַחְמָן בַּר יִצְחָק מָרֵי דְעוּבְדָא הֲוָה – **for Rav Nachman bar Yitzchak,** who came from Sura, **was meticulous in his actions,**[17] וּמַשְׁהוּ לֵיהּ וְאָכִיל – **yet they would leave** food on an unbanked *kirah* **for him and he would eat it.**[18]

A related episode is cited:

אָמַר רַב אַשִׁי – **Rav Ashi said:** קָאֵימְנָא קַמֵּיהּ דְּרַב הוּנָא – **I was standing before Rav Huna** one Sabbath וְשָׁהִין לֵיהּ כַּסָּא דְהַרְסָנָא וְאָכַל – **and** I saw that **they had left fish hash** on an unbanked *kirah* **for him and he ate it.**[19] וְלָא יָדַעְנָא אִי מִשּׁוּם דְּקָסָבַר מִצְטַמֵּק וְיָפֶה לוֹ מוּתָּר – **But I do not know if** he considered this permissible **because he held** that even if a food **improves as it condenses** it **is permitted** to leave it on an unbanked *kirah,* אִי מִשּׁוּם דְּכֵיוָן דְּאִית בֵּיהּ מִיחָא מִצְטַמֵּק וְרַע לוֹ הוּא – **or** it was **because since [fish hash] contains flour** he held that **it deteriorates as it condenses.**[20]

The Gemara cites a ruling concerning our topic:

אָמַר רַב נַחְמָן – **Rav Nachman said:** מִצְטַמֵּק וְיָפֶה לוֹ אָסוּר – If a food **improves as it condenses** it **is forbidden** to leave it on an unbanked *kirah,* מִצְטַמֵּק וְרַע לוֹ מוּתָּר – but if it **deteriorates as it condenses** it **is permitted** to leave it on an unbanked *kirah.* כְּלָלָא דְמִלְּתָא – And **this is the general rule** to determine whether a food improves or deteriorates as it condenses: כֹּל דְּאִית בֵּיהּ מִיחָא מִצְטַמֵּק וְרַע לוֹ – **Anything that contains flour deteriorates as it condenses,** לְבַר מִתַּבְשִׁיל דְּלִיפְתָּא – **except for a dish of turnips,** דְּאַף עַל גַּב דְּאִית בֵּיהּ מִיחָא מִצְטַמֵּק וְיָפֶה לוֹ – **which improves as it condenses even if it contains flour.** וְהָנֵי מִילֵּי דְּאִית בֵּיהּ בִּשְׂרָא – **However, this applies only if [the turnip dish]** also **contains meat,**[21] אֲבָל לֵית בֵּיהּ בִּשְׂרָא מִצְטַמֵּק וְרַע לוֹ הוּא – **but if it does not contain meat it deteriorates as it condenses.**[22] וְכִי אִית בֵּיהּ בִּשְׂרָא נַמִּי – **And even if it contains meat,** לֹא אֲמָרָן אֶלָּא דְּלָא קָבָעֵי לָהּ לְאוֹרְחִין – **we stated** that it is deemed to improve as it condenses **only concerning** a case in which **one does not need it for** serving to **guests,** אֲבָל קָבָעֵי לָהּ לְאוֹרְחִין מִצְטַמֵּק וְרַע לוֹ – **but if he needs it for** serving to **guests, it** is deemed to **deteriorate as it condenses,** since it is preferable to serve guests portions containing large, uncondensed pieces of meat.[23] לַפְדָּא דְּיַיסָא וְתַמְרֵי מִצְטַמֵּק וְרַע לְהֶן – **Dishes of figs,** of **cereal and** of **dates deteriorate as they condense.**[24]

The Gemara turns to another aspect of these laws:

בָּעוּ מִינֵּיהּ מֵרַבִּי חִיָּיא בַּר אַבָּא – **They inquired of R' Chiya bar Abba:**

NOTES

15. Abaye's inquiry is somewhat vague. *Tosafos* state that Abaye may be referring either to food that is not fully cooked (in which case his inquiry is whether the halachah follows Chananyah or the Sages) or to fully cooked food that improves as it condenses (in which case he certainly holds like the Sages but is inquiring whether the halachah follows Rav and Shmuel or R' Yochanan). See *Ritva MHK* ed.

16. [Rav Yehudah was already very aged in Abaye's youth (see *Seder HaDoros,* years 4060, 4099).] He suffered from dangerous seizures and always had to eat nutritious and well-heated food to sustain himself (*Rashi*). Thus, it would even be permissible to actually cook for him on the Sabbath if no preheated food was available (see *Ritva MHK* ed.).

There is another version of the text which reads דְּכֵיוָן דִּמְצוּנָּן הוּא וכו׳, *because since he has chills* it is permitted to do this for him even on the Sabbath. According to this reading, Rav Yehudah was not dangerously ill but suffered from chills, and the Gemara means that due to his illness it would even be permitted to have a *non-Jew* warm food for him on the Sabbath (*Ritva MHK* ed.; see also *Chidushei HaRan*).

17. Literally: a master of deeds.

18. See *Ritva* (*MHK* ed.).

19. The hash was made of fish mixed with flour and cooked in its oil (*Rashi*; see *Rashbam* to *Bava Basra* 60b ד״ה כסא).

20. [And as noted above (37a note 24), all agree that a fully cooked food which deteriorates as it condenses may be left on an unbanked *kirah.*]

21. As the dish stews and condenses, the fat of the meat is absorbed by the turnip and tempers its sharpness (*Rashi;* see *Berachos* 44b).

22. This is so even if the dish does not contain flour (see *Beur Halachah* 253:1 ד״ה והוא מיצטמיק).

23. See *Dibros Moshe* 34:8.

24. According to *Rashi* and *Tosafos,* who rule that the halachah follows Chananyah, the discussion concerning foods that improve or deteriorate as they condense is irrelevant on a practical level, since *shehiyah* on an unbanked *kirah* is permissible even if something is only cooked like the food of Ben Derusai. As for *chazarah,* it is forbidden on an unbanked *kirah* even if the food deteriorates as it condenses (due to the appearance of cooking on the Sabbath). Rav Nachman's ruling is relevant only to those who follow the opinion of the Sages, such as residents of Babylonia (*Rashba* to 38a, *Ran, Rosh;* see also *Tosafos* ד״ה אמר רב ששת; cf. *Baal HaMaor*). According to *Rif* and *Rambam,* it is relevant to all people, since the halachah follows the opinion of the Sages.

שָׁכַח קְדֵירָה עַל גַּבֵּי כִּירָה וּבִשְּׁלָה בְּשַׁבָּת מַהוּ – **If one forgot a pot** of uncooked food **on an** unbanked ***kirah*** before the Sabbath **and it cooked on the Sabbath, what is [the law]?** May he eat the food after it has cooked?[1] אִישְׁתִּיק וְלֹא אָמַר לְהוּ וְלֹא מִידֵי – **[R' Chiya bar Abba] was** initially **silent and did not reply at all.** לְמָחָר נְפַק דְּרַשׁ לְהוּ – **The next day he went out and lectured to them** as follows: הַמְבַשֵּׁל בְּשַׁבָּת בְּשׁוֹגֵג יֹאכַל בְּמֵזִיד לֹא יֹאכַל – The Mishnah states:[2] IF ONE COOKED food ON THE SABBATH INADVERTENTLY HE MAY EAT it, and if he cooked it INTENTIONALLY HE MAY NOT EAT it;[3] וְלֹא שְׁנָא – **but there is no** such **distinction** regarding food left on an unbanked *kirah* before the Sabbath. It is subject to the same rule whether it was left there inadvertently or intentionally.

R' Chiya bar Abba failed to specify whether the food is permitted or forbidden for consumption in both cases. The Gemara cites two interpretations of his ruling:

מַאי וְלֹא שְׁנָא – **What is** the meaning of the statement **"but there is no** such **distinction** regarding food left on an unbanked *kirah* before the Sabbath"? Does it mean that the food is permitted whether it was left there inadvertently or intentionally, or that it is forbidden in both instances? רַבָּה וְרַב יוֹסֵף דְּאָמְרֵי תַּרְוַיְיהוּ לְהֶיתֵּרָא – **Rabbah and Rav Yosef both say** that R' Chiya bar Abba meant to rule **permissibly** regarding both instances, and the reason this case is treated more leniently than that of cooking on the Sabbath is as follows: מְבַשֵּׁל הוּא דְּקָא עָבִיד מַעֲשֶׂה – **It is** only regarding **one who cooks** and **who** thus **does a forbidden act** on the Sabbath that we say that בְּמֵזִיד לֹא יֹאכַל – if he cooked **intentionally he may not eat** the food. אֲבָל הַאי דְּלֹא קָא עָבִיד מַעֲשֶׂה – **But** in regard to **this one,** who merely left food on an unbanked *kirah* before the Sabbath and **who did not do a forbidden act** on the Sabbath,[4] בְּמֵזִיד נַמִּי יֹאכַל – the rule is that **even** if he left it on the flame **intentionally he may eat** it. רַב נַחְמָן בַּר יִצְחָק אָמַר לְאִיסּוּרָא – **Rav Nachman bar Yitzchak said** that R' Chiya bar Abba meant to rule **prohibitively** regarding both instances of food left on the unbanked *kirah* before the Sabbath, and the reason this case is treated more stringently than that of cooking on the Sabbath is as follows: מְבַשֵּׁל הוּא דְּלֹא אָתֵי לְאִיעֲרוּמֵי – **It is** only regarding **one who cooks** on the Sabbath in violation of Biblical law, and **who will not come to engage in deceit** and cook intentionally while claiming that he did so inadvertently, בְּשׁוֹגֵג יֹאכַל – that we rule that if he cooked **inadvertently he may eat** the food.[5] אֲבָל הַאי דְּאָתֵי לְאִיעֲרוּמֵי – **But** concerning **this one,** who left food on an unbanked *kirah* before the Sabbath in violation of Rabbinical law and **who may come to engage in deceit** and leave it there intentionally while claiming that he did so inadvertently, בְּשׁוֹגֵג נַמִּי לֹא יֹאכַל – the rule is that **even** if he left it on the flame **inadvertently he may not eat** it.[6]

The Gemara challenges the interpretation of Rabbah and Rav Yosef:

מֵיתִיבֵי – **They challenged** Rabbah and Rav Yosef on the basis of the following Baraisa: שָׁכַח קְדֵירָה עַל גַּבֵּי כִּירָה – IF ONE FORGOT A POT of uncooked food ON AN unbanked *KIRAH* before the Sabbath וּבִישְּׁלָה בְּשַׁבָּת – AND IT COOKED ON THE SABBATH – בְּשׁוֹגֵג יֹאכַל – if this happened INADVERTENTLY[7] HE MAY EAT it, בְּמֵזִיד לֹא יֹאכַל – but if he left it there INTENTIONALLY HE MAY NOT EAT it. בַּמֶּה דְּבָרִים אֲמוּרִים – REGARDING WHAT type of food WAS THIS STATED? בְּחַמִּין שֶׁלֹּא הוּחַמּוּ כָּל צוֹרְכָּן וְתַבְשִׁיל שֶׁלֹּא בִּישֵּׁל כָּל צוֹרְכּוֹ – REGARDING HOT WATER THAT WAS NOT FULLY HEATED AND COOKED FOOD THAT WAS NOT FULLY COOKED at the onset of the Sabbath. אֲבָל חַמִּין שֶׁהוּחַמּוּ כָּל צוֹרְכָּן וְתַבְשִׁיל שֶׁבִּישֵּׁל כָּל צוֹרְכּוֹ – BUT regarding HOT WATER THAT WAS FULLY HEATED AND COOKED FOOD THAT WAS FULLY COOKED at the onset of the Sabbath, the rule is that בֵּין בְּשׁוֹגֵג בֵּין בְּמֵזִיד יֹאכַל – WHETHER one left it on the unbanked *kirah* INADVERTENTLY OR INTENTIONALLY HE MAY EAT it. דִּבְרֵי רַבִּי מֵאִיר – These are THE WORDS OF R' MEIR.[8] רַבִּי יְהוּדָה אוֹמֵר – R' YEHUDAH SAYS: חַמִּין שֶׁהוּחַמּוּ כָּל צוֹרְכָּן מוּתָּרִין – HOT WATER THAT WAS FULLY HEATED at the onset of the Sabbath and was left on the unbanked *kirah* IS PERMITTED for consumption, מִפְּנֵי שֶׁמִּצְטַמֵּק וְרַע לוֹ – BECAUSE [HOT WATER] DETERIORATES AS IT CONDENSES,[9] וְתַבְשִׁיל שֶׁבִּישֵּׁל כָּל צוֹרְכּוֹ אָסוּר – BUT COOKED FOOD THAT WAS FULLY COOKED at the onset of the Sabbath and was left on an unbanked *kirah* IS often FORBIDDEN for consumption, מִפְּנֵי שֶׁמִּצְטַמֵּק וְיָפֶה לוֹ – BECAUSE in many cases IT IMPROVES AS IT CONDENSES, וְכָל הַמִּצְטַמֵּק וְיָפֶה לוֹ – AND the rule is that ANY food THAT IMPROVES AS IT CONDENSES, כְּגוֹן כְּרוּב וּפוֹלִים וּבָשָׂר טָרוּף – SUCH AS CABBAGE, BEANS OR MINCED MEAT,[10] אָסוּר – IS FORBIDDEN if it was left to condense on an unbanked *kirah,*[11] וְכָל הַמִּצְטַמֵּק וְרַע לוֹ מוּתָּר – BUT ANY food THAT DETERIORATES AS IT CONDENSES IS PERMITTED even if it was left on an unbanked *kirah.*

The Gemara develops its challenge:

קָתָנֵי מִיהָא תַּבְשִׁיל שֶׁלֹּא בִּישֵּׁל כָּל צוֹרְכּוֹ – **In any event, the Baraisa** teaches that a **cooked food that was not fully cooked** may be eaten if it was left on the *kirah* inadvertently but not if it was left there intentionally. Yet R' Chiya bar Abba ruled that no such distinction is to be made! בִּשְׁלָמָא לְרַב נַחְמָן בַּר יִצְחָק לֹא קַשְׁיָא – **All is well according to** the interpretation of **Rav Nachman bar**

NOTES

1. The inquiry pertains to the opinion of the Sages, who forbid leaving the food on the *kirah* in the first place (*Rashi*). Others explain that it is also pertinent to the opinion of Chananyah, in the case of food that had been cooked less than the food of Ben Derusai at the onset of the Sabbath (*Tosafos, Rashba;* see *Rosh Yosef* and *Pnei Yehoshua* for clarification of why *Rashi* limits the pertinence of the inquiry to the Sages' opinion).

2. *Terumos* 2:3.

3. It is a matter of Tannaic dispute whether the one who cooked intentionally is prohibited from eating it only until after the Sabbath or forever, and whether the one who cooked unwittingly is permitted to eat it immediately or only after the Sabbath. It is also disputed whether other people are allowed to eat it (see *Chullin* 15a; see also *Orach Chaim* 318:1 with *Mishnah Berurah* §7).

4. But rather, sinned by failing to take action and remove the pot from the *kirah* when the Sabbath began (*Pnei Yehoshua, Rosh Yosef*).

5. People are unlikely to willfully desecrate the Sabbath by violating a Biblical prohibition. Therefore, we need not be concerned that by allowing one who cooked inadvertently to eat the food he might come to cook intentionally and rely on a claim of unwittingness to eat what he cooked (*Rashi*).

6. People do not take Rabbinical decrees as seriously as Biblical law. Thus, to ensure that people do not leave food on unbanked *kirahs* willfully and eat it by feigning error, the Rabbis were constrained to forbid even the consumption of food that was left on the unbanked *kirah* unwittingly (*Rashi*).

7. That is, the person actually forgot it, as the Baraisa just stated (*Rashi*).

8. R' Meir forbids consumption of the food only if it actually became cooked unlawfully on the Sabbath, but not if it had been fully cooked beforehand and was merely left to stew on an unbanked *kirah.* The Gemara will clarify R' Meir's opinion below.

9. I.e. as it remains on the *kirah* it evaporates, which is considered deterioration.

10. As opposed to whole pieces of meat that one intends to serve to guests (see *Rashi*).

11. According to R' Yehudah, even if the food did not actually cook on the Sabbath, but merely became more savory by stewing on the unbanked *kirah,* it is forbidden for consumption.

שכח קדירה על גבי כירה ובשלה בשבת מהו אישתיק ולא א"ל ולא מידי למחר נפק דרש להו [א] המבשל [א]בשבת [ב] בשוגג יאכל במזיד לא יאכל ולא שנא מאי ול"ש רבה ורב יוסף דאמרי תרווייהו להיתירא מבשל הוא דקא עביד מעשה במזיד לא יאכל אבל האי דלא קא עביד מעשה במזיד נמי יאכל רב נחמן בר יצחק אמר [ב]לאיסורא מבשל הוא דלא אתי לאיערומי בשוגג יאכל אבל האי דאתי לאיערומי בשוגג נמי לא יאכל מיתיבי [ג] שכח קדירה על גבי כירה ובישלה בשבת בשוגג יאכל במזיד לא יאכל בד"א בחמין שלא הוחמו כל צורכן ותבשיל שלא בישל כל צורכו אבל חמין שהוחמו כל צורכן ותבשיל שבישל כל צורכו בין בשוגג בין במזיד יאכל דברי ר"מ ר' יהודה אומר חמין שהוחמו כל צורכן מותרין מפני שמצטמק ורע לו ותבשיל שבישל כל צורכו אסור מפני שמצטמק ויפה לו וכל המצטמק ויפה לו כגון כרוב ופולים ובשר [ד] טרוף אסור וכל המצטמק ורע לו מותר קתני מיהא תבשיל שלא בישל כל צורכו בשלמא לרב נחמן בר יצחק לא קשיא כאן קודם גזרה כאן לאחר גזרה אלא רבה ורב יוסף דאמרי להיתירא אי קודם גזרה קשיא מזיד אי לאחר גזרה קשיא נמי שוגג קשיא מאי גזירתא דאמר רב יהודה בר שמואל א"ר אבא אמר רב כהנא אמר רב בתחילה היו אומרים המבשל בשבת בשוגג יאכל במזיד לא יאכל וה"ה לשוכח משרבו משהין במזיד ואומרים שכחים אנו חזרו וקנסו על השוכח קשיא דר' מאיר אדר' מאיר קשיא דר' יהודה אדר' יהודה דר' מאיר אדר"מ לא קשיא הא לכתחילה הא דיעבד דר' יהודה אדר' יהודה נמי לא קשיא כאן בגרופה וקטומה כאן בשאינה גרופה וקטומה איבעיא להו עבר ושהה מאי מי קנסוהו רבנן או לא ת"ש דאמר שמואל בר נתן א"ר חנינא כשהלך רבי יוסי לציפורי מצא חמין שנשתהו על גבי כירה ולא אסר להן ביצים מצומקות שנשתהו על גבי כירה ואסר להן מאי לאו לאותו שבת לא [ג]לשבת הבאה מכלל דביצים מצומקות מצטמקות ויפה להן נינהו אין דאמר רב חמא בר חנינא פעם אחת נתארחתי אני ורבי למקום אחד והביאו לפנינו ביצים מצומקות כעוזרדין ואכלנו מהן הרבה: ב"ה אומרים אף מחזירין: אמר רב ששת לדברי האומר

מחזירין

רש"י

שכח קדרה. אליבא מאן דאסר: המבשל בשבת. משנה היא: ולא שנא. אבל האי דשכח קדרה לא שנא בין שוגג למזיד והכי דרש להו סתמא ולא פירש אי אשוגג מדמה לה ומותר לאוכלה אי אמזיד מדמה לה ואסור: במזיד נמי. אם השהה על גבי כירה מבעוד יום יאכל: דלא אתי לאיערומי. ולעשות מזיד ולומר שוגג הייתי דלא נחשדו ישראל על השבתות: דאתי לאיערומי. דאיסור דרבנן הוא וקילא ליה ואתי לשהויי מזיד ויאמר שכחתי: מיתיבי שכח קדרה כו' בשוגג. כגון האי דשכח יאכל בשבת: במזיד. דלא שכח אלא הניח לא יאכל: ובשר טרוף. דגלי דעתיה דלא לאורחים קבעי לה: וכל המצטמק ויפה לו. כלומר וכן כל שאר המצטמק ויפה להם אסור לאוכלן אם השהן מזיד: קתני מיהת. בשלא בישל כל צרכו דיש חילוק בין שוגג למזיד במשהה קשיא בין לרבה ורב יוסף דשרו מזיד בין לרב נחמן דאסר שוגג: בשלמא לרב נחמן. מצי לתרוצי כי תניא ההיא דשוגג יאכל לפני גזירה דאמרינן לקמן דגזרו על השוכחין וכי איתמר דר' חייא בר אבא דתריצנא אליביה דשוגג אסור לאחר גזירה: אלא דרבה ורב יוסף. דאמרי אליבא דר' חייא בר אבא להתירא אף במזיד: אי קודם גזירה. אתמר דר' חייא: קשיא מיהא מזיד. דהכא תניא במזיד לא יאכל: ואי לאחר גזירה קשיא נמי שוגג. דאפי' שוגג ה"ל למיסר דאילו מתני' קודם גזירה נשנית: המבשל בשבת. בידים דאיכא חיובא דאורייתא: וה"ה לשוכח. דהמשהה נמי מבעוד יום אם שכח בשוגג יאכל ואם במזיד השהה לא יאכל כאילו בשלה בידים בשבת: קשיא דר' מאיר אדר' מאיר. דתנן לעיל בריש פירקין לר' מאיר אליבא דב"ה חמין אבל לא תבשיל והכא שרי חמין ותבשיל שבישל כל צרכו: וקשיא דר' יהודה אדר' יהודה. דהתם א"ר יהודה חמין ותבשיל והכא אסר תבשיל שבישל כל צרכו: הא לכתחלה. משנה קמייתא לשהות לכתחלה קמיירי והך בהשהה כבר קאמר דמותר לאוכלה: כאן בגרופה וקטומה. ההיא דלעיל איירי בגרופה וקטומה כדקתני בה משהין על גבי גרופה וקטומה ואין משהין על שאינה גרופה ומה הן משהין על הגרופה שהתרנו לשהות ר"מ אומר כו' הלכך אפי' לכתחלה שרי ר' יהודה והכא כשאינה גרופה הלכך דיעבד אסר: עבר ושהה במזיד מאי. מותר לאוכלה או לא: חמין לא אסר. דמצטמק ורע לו: ביצים אסר. דמצטמק ויפה לו: מאי לאו לאותו שבת. אסרן עליהן באכילה: לא לשבת הבאה. אסר להן עכשיו שלא לעשות כן לשבת הבאה אבל באכילה שרו: מכלל דביצים מצומקות כו'. בעיא היא: והביאו לפניו. בחול: כעוזרדין. שנצטמקו עד שנעשו דקות כעוזרדין קורמ"ש בלע"ז ומדאמר ואכלנו הרבה מכלל דיפה להן:

מחזירין

תוספות

שכח קדרה על גבי כירה ובישלה בשבת מהו. אע"ג דקיי"ל כחנניה הכא בעי בדלא בשיל כמאכל בן דרוסאי דמודה ביה חנניה אי נמי בעי אפי' בקידרא חייתא והא דשרינן בפ"ק (דף יח: ושם) קידרא חייתא היינו דוקא בתנור שחומו רב דלא איתוי יתבשל עד למחר אבל כירה דשליט בה אוירא אסור דאיכא למיחש שמא יחתה:

אבל האי דלא קעביד מעשה במזיד נמי יאכל. תימה דהא אמר בפ"ק (שם) לא תמלא אשה קדרה עססיות כו' ואם נתנה למוצאי שבת אסורין בכדי שיעשו וי"ל דבלאו הכי פריך שפיר מברייתא דמייתי:

בשלמא לרב נחמן בר יצחק כאן קודם גזירה כו'. תימה לר"י [א] לימא תרווייהו קודם גזירה והא דשרי בברייתא שוגג היינו בבשיל כמאכל בן דרוסאי ורב נחמן איירי בדלא בשיל כמאכל בן דרוסאי כדפי' ותירץ ר"ת דבישלה בשבת משמע שלא היתה קודם לכן כלל מבושלת. ולא בעי למימר נמי דרב נחמן סבר כר' יהודה דאסר תבשיל אפי' בישל כל צרכו וכ"ש לא בישל משום דדילמא ר' יהודה לא איירי אלא במזיד אבל בשוגג מודה לר"מ דשרי אפי' לא בישל כל צרכו:

קשיא דר' מאיר אדר' מאיר. כאן משמע דסתם חמין ותבשיל הוי נמי מבושל כל צרכו דאי לאו הכי לא הוה פריך מידי ורשב"א אומר דאפי' אי סתם חמין ותבשיל הוי בלא בשיל כל צרכו פריך שפיר דהא באינה גרופה משמע בברייתא דלעיל דאין משהין כלל אפי' בישל כל צרכו דאי הוה שרי בישל כל צרכו ה"ל לפרש מה הן משהין באינה גרופה כדמפרש אגרופה והכא שרי ר"מ בישל כל צרכו אפי' באינה גרופה מ"מ נראה דסתם חמין ותבשיל הוי נמי בבשיל כל צרכו מדפשיטא ליה לתלמודא דמאן דאסר להחזיר אסר אפי' בישל כל צרכו כדמוכח גבי ואף ר' אושעיא סבר כו':

הא לכתחלה הא דיעבד. לא סגי בהאי שינויא דהא לעיל שרי ר' מאיר סתם חמין דהויא אפי' לא הוחמו כל צורכן אפי' לכתחלה והכא אסר חמין שלא הוחמו כל צורכן אפי' דיעבד אלא צריך לשנויי כדמשני אקשיא דר' יהודה אדר' יהודה הא בגרופה וקטומה הא בשאינה גרופה ואדרבי יהודה נמי צריך לשנויא (דהכא) דהא לכתחלה הא דיעבד דהא בשאינה גרופה אסר לעיל אפי' חמין שנתבשל כל צרכו והכא שרי אלא דאיכא לשנויי הא לכתחלה הא דיעבד:

עבר ושהה מאי. בדלא בשיל כמאכל בן דרוסאי ליכא לאוקמי דהא כבר פשט לעיל לאיסורא כרב נחמן בר יצחק ונראה לר"י דמבעיא ליה בבשיל ובשוגג ואליבא דר' יהודה אע"ג דאין הלכה כר' יהודה אי אסר מצטמק ויפה לו דוקא במזיד או דילמא אפי' בשוגג ומייתי ראיה ממעשה דר' יוסי דאסר ומשמע ליה דאפי' בשוגג היה מדקאמר ונשתהו ולא קאמר ושיהו ומיהו לשון עבר ושהה משמע במזיד כמו עברה ולשה דפסחים (דף מג.) ואומר רשב"א דקודם גזירה בעו דאחר גזירה פשיטא דאסור בשוגג כמו מזיד:

לא לשבת הבאה. כולה סוגיא בשאינה גרופה דבגרופה ליכא שום אמורא דאסר כדפרישית לעיל והיינו כרב דאסר לעיל מצטמק ויפה לו:

אפי'

עין משפט נר מצוה

ז א מיי' פ"ג מהל' שבת הלכה ד ופ"ו הל' כג סמג לאוין סה טור וש"ע א"ח סימן שיח סעיף א:

ח ב ג מיי' פ"ג מהל' שבת הלכה ט סמג לאוין סה טוש"ע א"ח סימן רנג סעיף א:

רבינו חננאל

הא דבעו מר' חייא בר אבא שכח קדירה ע"ג כירה ובישלה בשבת ודרש להו המבשל בשבת בשוגג יאכל במזיד לא יאכל ולא שנא כלומר במבשל יש להפריש בין שוגג למזיד אבל בשוכח השוגג והמזיד שוין: רבה ורב יוסף אמרי שוכח בין שוגג ובין מזיד מותר לא קנסו רבנן אפילו במזיד רב נחמן בר יצחק אמר שניהן אסורין וקי"ל כוותיה ואותבינא עליה שכח קדירה על גבי כירה ובישלה בשבת בשוגג יאכל במזיד לא יאכל כו'. ועלתה לרבה ורב יוסף בקושיא ואקשינן הכא א"ר מאיר חמין שהוחמו כל צרכן ותבשיל שבישל כל צרכו בין בשוגג בין במזיד מותר ובתחלת הפרק אמר ומה הן משהין בש"א ולא כלום ובה"א חמין אבל לא תבשיל [ושנינן התם] לכתחילה דרבי יהודה אדרבי יהודה לא קשיא הא דקתני רבי יהודה הכא תבשיל שבישל כל צרכו אסור כירה שאינה גרופה ולא קטומה ולפיכך אסור והאי דקתני התם משהין ע"ג כירה לב"ה חמין ותבשיל בגרופה וקטומה וכיון שנתקשה רבה ורב יוסף נתקיימו דברי רב נחמן בר יצחק וקי"ל כוותיה כל השוכח קדירה ובישלה קודם גזירה הוה שרי ובתר גזירה קנסו רבנן אפילו שוגג ומאי גזירה דבתחלה היו אומרים המבשל בשבת בשוגג יאכל במזיד לא יאכל וה"ה לשוכח ומשרבו משהי קדירה במזיד ואומרים שוכחים אנן גזרו אף על השוכח. וכיון דסלקי דמצטמק ויפה לו אסור איבעיא לן עבר ושהה מאי ואתינן למפשטא מהא דתניא דאסיר רבי יוסי בצפורי ביצים מצומקים שנשתהו על גבי כירה (שמא) [ש"מ] עבר ושהה קנסו רבנן ודחינן לא אסר להו לעשות

רב נסים גאון

פרק כירה אמר רבי חנינא כשהלך רבי יוסי לציפורי. הדבר שגרם לו לילך לציפורי הוא שמפורש בבמה מדליקין (דף לג) יוסי ששתק יגלה לציפורי:

מסורת הש"ס

א) תוספתא פ"ג ב"ק עא. חולין טו. גיטין נג: ביצה יז: [תרומות פ"ב מ"ג כתובות לד., ב) [עי' תוספות ע"ז סו: ד"ה אמר רבא], ג) תוספתא פ"ג, ד) [פי' שמחתכין אותו חתיכות קטנות ומרסקין אותו עד שנטרף במקפה או בטיסני שכל זמן שמצטמק יוצא שמנו ומתערב עם הבישול ערוך ערך טרף ג].

תוספות ישנים

א) ושמא לתלמודא לא נראה לחלק כיון דר"מ אוסר אפילו תבשיל:

ליקוטי רש"י

בשוגג יאכל. הוא עצמו וכו ביום ואין צריך להמתין עד הערב בכדי שיעשו דהא דאמרינן בעלמא לערב בכדי שיעשו לית ליה לר"מ אלא היכא דעבד ישראל איסורא ובמזיד דאיכא חיובא דלא נמטייה הנאה מאיסורא אבל בשוגג לא. במזיד. דאיכא איסורא. לא יאכל. בו ביום עד שתחשך ובכדי שיעשו והוא הדין לאחרים נמי דאסור למיכליה בו ביום דטעמא משום דלא נמטייה הנאה מאיסורא הוא וכי שהי לאורתא בכדי שיעשו לא מטי לו הנאה מיניה ואיידי דתנא רישא בדידיה דאשמעינן רבותא להתירא תנא נמי סיפא בדידיה [חולין טו. וכעי"ז ב"ק עא.]. הוא לעולם אבל אחרים ישראלים אוכלים [כתובות לד. ע"ש בפנ"י]. מצומקות. צלויות הרבה לשון מצטמק ויפה לו דשבת [חולין ו.].

Yitzchak that R' Chiya bar Abba meant to prohibit consumption of the food in both instances – **there is no difficulty,** for we can explain that כָּאן קוֹדֶם גְּזֵרָה כָּאן לְאַחַר גְּזֵרָה – **here,** in the Baraisa which distinguishes between food left on an unbanked *kirah* inadvertently and food left there intentionally, we are dealing with the period **prior to the decree;** whereas **here,** in R' Chiya bar Abba's ruling that the food is prohibited in both instances, we are dealing with the period **after the decree.**[12] אֶלָּא רַבָּה וְרַב יוֹסֵף דְּאָמְרֵי לְהֶיתֵּירָא – **But** according to **Rabbah and Rav Yosef who said** that R' Chiya bar Abba meant to rule **permissibly** regarding both instances of food left on an unbanked *kirah,* his ruling is difficult no matter when he stated it. אִי קוֹדֶם גְּזֵרָה קַשְׁיָא מֵזִיד – For **if** he stated it **prior to the decree,** his ruling regarding food left on the unbanked *kirah* **intentionally is difficult,** since he permits consumption of the food and the Baraisa forbids it. אִי לְאַחַר גְּזֵרָה קַשְׁיָא נַמִּי שׁוֹגֵג – And **if** he stated it **after the decree, even** his ruling regarding food left on the unbanked *kirah* **inadvertently is difficult,** since he permits its consumption and after the decree it is certainly forbidden. – ? –

The Gemara concludes:

קַשְׁיָא – This is indeed **a difficulty.**[13]

The Gemara explains the circumstances that led to the enactment of the previously mentioned decree:

מַאי גְּזֵירְתָא – **What was** the basis for **this decree?** It was the following: דְּאָמַר רַב יְהוּדָה בַּר שְׁמוּאֵל אָמַר רַבִּי אַבָּא אָמַר רַב כַּהֲנָא אָמַר רַב – **For Rav Yehudah bar Shmuel said in the name of R' Abba who said in the name of Rav Kahana who said in the name of Rav:** בַּתְּחִילָּה הָיוּ אוֹמְרִים – **At first they used to say** that הַמְבַשֵּׁל בְּשַׁבָּת בְּשׁוֹגֵג יֹאכַל בְּמֵזִיד לֹא יֹאכַל – **one who cooks on the Sabbath inadvertently may eat** the food and one who cooks **intentionally may not eat it,** וְהוּא הַדִּין לְשׁוֹכֵחַ – **and the same rule** applies **to one who forgets** food on an unbanked *kirah* before the Sabbath.[14] מִשֶּׁרַבּוּ מַשְׁהִין בְּמֵזִיד וְאוֹמְרִים שְׁכֵחִים אָנוּ – But **when there was a proliferation of [people] who would leave** food on unbanked *kirahs* **intentionally and claim, "We forgot** to remove it before the Sabbath," חָזְרוּ וְקָנְסוּ עַל הַשּׁוֹכֵחַ – **[the Rabbis] revised** the law **and penalized** even **one who forgets** food on an unbanked *kirah,* and forbade him to consume it.

The Gemara analyzes the views of R' Meir and R' Yehudah in the Baraisa just cited and contrasts them with the views of the same Tannaim cited in another Baraisa above (37a):

קַשְׁיָא דְּרַבִּי מֵאִיר אַדְּרַבִּי מֵאִיר – **R' Meir's** rulings **are contradictory** קַשְׁיָא דְּרַבִּי יְהוּדָה אַדְּרַבִּי יְהוּדָה – and **R' Yehudah's** rulings **are contradictory!** In this Baraisa, R' Meir permits the consumption of both food and hot water that was fully cooked at the onset of the Sabbath and was left on an unbanked *kirah,* whereas earlier he ruled that only hot water may be left on an unbanked *kirah,* but not cooked food. Furthermore, in this Baraisa, R' Yehudah ruled that even fully cooked food that is left on a *kirah* is forbidden for consumption if it improves as it condenses, whereas earlier he ruled that it is permitted to leave fully cooked food on a *kirah.* – ? –

The Gemara resolves the difficulties:

דְּרַבִּי מֵאִיר אַדְּרַבִּי מֵאִיר לֹא קַשְׁיָא – **R' Meir's** rulings **are not contradictory.** הָא לְכַתְּחִילָּה הָא דִּיעֲבַד – **This** ruling in the earlier Baraisa refers to the procedure that is to be followed **initially,** whereas **this** ruling in our Baraisa refers to the law **after the fact.** R' Meir holds that initially, one should not leave cooked food on an unbanked *kirah.* However, if one did leave it there, R' Meir permits its consumption after the fact. דְּרַבִּי יְהוּדָה אַדְּרַבִּי יְהוּדָה נַמִּי לֹא קַשְׁיָא – **R' Yehudah's** rulings **are also not contradictory.** כָּאן בִּגְרוּפָה וּקְטוּמָה כָּאן בְּשֶׁאֵינָהּ גְּרוּפָה וּקְטוּמָה – **Here,** in the earlier Baraisa, R' Yehudah is dealing **with [a *kirah*] that was shoveled or banked,** whereas **here,** in our Baraisa, he is dealing **with [a *kirah*] that was not shoveled or banked.** When the *kirah* was shoveled or banked, R' Yehudah permits leaving fully cooked food on it, even if it improves as it condenses, but when the *kirah* was not shoveled or banked he forbids this and even forbids consumption of the food after the fact if it improves as it condenses.[15]

The Gemara cites a related inquiry:

אִיבַּעְיָא לְהוּ – **They inquired:** עָבַר וְשָׁהָה מַאי – If **[a person] violated** the law **and left** a pot on an unbanked *kirah,* **what** is the law? מִי קְנָסוּהוּ רַבָּנַן אוֹ לֹא – **Did the Rabbis penalize him** and forbid consumption of the food, **or not?**[16]

NOTES

12. As we will see below, originally the consumption of food left on an unbanked *kirah* was prohibited only if it was left there intentionally, but when the Rabbis saw that some people left food there intentionally and claimed that they had done so unwittingly, they decreed that even food left there unwittingly is prohibited. Thus, we may say that the Baraisa was taught before the decree and R' Chiya bar Abba issued his ruling after the decree (*Rashi*).

13. [R' Chiya bar Abba lived after the decree was enacted, for the Gemara will shortly state that it had already been in force in the days of Rav. Thus, according to the interpretation of Rabbah and Rav Yosef, R' Chiya bar Abba must have been unaware of the decree (*Ritva, MHK* ed.).] Due to this difficulty, it is obvious that Rav Nachman bar Yitzchak's interpretation is correct and R' Chiya bar Abba meant to *prohibit* consumption of the food left on the unbanked *kirah* whether it was left there intentionally or inadvertently (*Ritva,* ibid.; see also *Tosafos* ד״ה עבר ושהה).

14. I.e. if one left food on an unbanked *kirah* inadvertently he may eat it, but if he left it there intentionally he may not eat it (*Rashi*).

15. Note that in the earlier Baraisa, R' Yehudah forbade even leaving hot water – which deteriorates as it condenses – on an unbanked *kirah.* His ruling in our Baraisa permitting hot water means only that its consumption is permitted after the fact. The Gemara leaves this unsaid, relying on having mentioned in its resolution of R' Meir's opinion that here we are dealing with consumption of the product after the fact (see *Tosafos* ד״ה הא לכתחלה and *Chidushei R' Elazar Moshe Horowitz* for further discussion of the Gemara's answers).

16. The inquiry pertains to a case in which the person deliberately left the pot on the *kirah* (*Rashi*), as implied by the expression עָבַר, if *a person violated* the law (*Tosafos*). However, this is perplexing, for the Baraisa cited above stated clearly that this issue is a matter of dispute between R' Meir and R' Yehudah. According to R' Meir, food that was not fully cooked before the Sabbath is forbidden for consumption and food that was fully cooked is permitted. According to R' Yehudah, even fully cooked food that improves as it condenses is forbidden. What, then, is the point of the current inquiry?

Ritva (*MHK* ed.) explains that we are dealing with a case in which a person intentionally left on an unbanked *kirah* a fully cooked food that improves as it condenses, but then removed it on the Sabbath before enough time elapsed for it to condense and improve. The question is thus the following: When the Rabbis penalized a person who left this type of food on an unbanked *kirah,* did they penalize him only if the food actually condensed and improved, or did they penalize him for merely committing the forbidden act of leaving the food there, even if it did not actually improve? (see there; see also *Rosh* and *Chidushei R' Elazar Moshe Horowitz; cf. Maharsha, Pnei Yehoshua*).

For an alternative explanation of the inquiry, which is supported by a variant version of the text, see *Tosafos, Rashba, Ran, Rambam, Hil. Shabbos* 3:9 with *Maggid Mishneh,* and *Orach Chaim* 253:1 with *Mishneh Berurah* §30; see also *Baal HaMaor* and *Milchamos Hashem.*

שכח קדירה על גבי כירה ובשלה בשבת
מהו אישתיק ולא א"ל ולא מידי למחר נפק
דרש להו [א] המבשל [א] בשבת [ב] בשוגג יאכל
במזיד לא יאכל ולא שנא מאי ול"ש רבה
ורב יוסף דאמרי תרווייהו להיתירא מבשל
הוא דקא עביד מעשה במזיד לא יאכל אבל
האי דלא קא עביד מעשה במזיד נמי יאכל
רב נחמן בר יצחק אמר [ב] לאיסורא מבשל
הוא דלא אתי לאיערומי בשוגג יאכל אבל
האי דאתי לאיערומי בשוגג נמי לא יאכל
מיתיבי [ג] שכח קדירה על גבי כירה ובישלה
בשבת בשוגג יאכל במזיד לא יאכל בד"א
בחמין שלא הוחמו כל צורכן ותבשיל שלא
בישל כל צורכו אבל חמין שהוחמו כל
צורכן ותבשיל שבישל כל צורכו בין בשוגג
בין במזיד יאכל דברי ר"מ ר' יהודה אומר
חמין שהוחמו כל צורכן מותרין מפני
שמצטמק ורע לו ותבשיל שבישל כל צורכו
אסור מפני שמצטמק ויפה לו וכל המצטמק
ויפה לו כגון כרוב ופולים ובשר [ד] טרוף אסור
וכל המצטמק ורע לו מותר קתני מיהא
תבשיל שלא בישל כל צורכו בשלמא לרב
נחמן בר יצחק לא קשיא כאן קודם גזרה
כאן לאחר גזרה אלא רבה ורב יוסף דאמרי
להיתירא אי קודם גזרה קשיא מזיד אי
לאחר גזרה קשיא נמי שוגג קשיא מאי
גזירתא דאמר רב יהודה בר שמואל א"ר
אבא אמר רב כהנא אמר רב בתחילה היו
אומרים המבשל בשבת בשוגג יאכל במזיד
לא יאכל וה"ה לשוכח משרבו משהין במזיד
ואומרים שכחים אנו חזרו וקנסו על השוכח
קשיא דר' מאיר אדר' מאיר קשיא דר'
יהודה אדר' יהודה דר' מאיר אדר"מ לא
קשיא הא לכתחילה הא דיעבד דר' יהודה
אדר' יהודה נמי לא קשיא כאן בגרופה
וקטומה כאן בשאינה גרופה וקטומה
איבעיא להו עבר ושהה מאי מי קנסוהו
רבנן או לא ת"ש דאמר שמואל בר נתן א"ר
חנינא כשהלך רבי יוסי לציפורי מצא חמין
שנשתהו על גבי כירה ולא אסר להן ביצים
מצומקות שנשתהו על גבי כירה ואסר להן
מאי לאו לאותו שבת לא [ג] לשבת הבאה
מכלל דביצים מצומקות מצטמקות ויפה להן
נינהו אין דאמר רב חמא בר חנינא פעם
אחת נתארחתי אני ורבי למקום אחד
והביאו לפנינו ביצים מצומקות כעוזרדין
ואכלנו מהן הרבה: ב"ה אומרים אף
מחזירין: אמר רב ששת לדברי האומר
מחזירין

שכח קדרה. אליבא מאן דאסר: המבשל בשבת. משנה היא: ולא שנא. אבל האי דשכח קדרה לא שנא בין שוגג למזיד והכי דרש להו סתמא ולא פירש אי אשוגג מדמה לה ומותר לאוכלה אי אמזיד מדמה לה ואסור: במזיד נמי. אם השהה על גבי כירה מבעוד יום יאכל: דלא אתי לאיערומי. ולעשות מזיד ולומר שוגג הייתי דלא נחשדו ישראל על השבתות: דאתי לאיערומי. דאיסור דרבנן הוא וקילא ליה ואתי לשהויי מזיד ויאמר שכחתי: מיתיבי שכח קדרה כו' בשוגג. כגון האי דשכח יאכל בשבת: במזיד. דלא שכח אלא הניח לא יאכל: ובשר טרוף. דגלי דעתיה דלא לאורחים קבעי לה: וכל המצטמק ויפה לו. כלומר וכן כל שאר המצטמק ויפה להם אסור לאוכלן אם השהן מזיד: קתני מיהת. בשלא בישל כל צרכו דיש חילוק בין שוגג למזיד במשהה קשיא בין לרבה ורב יוסף דשרו מזיד בין לרב נחמן דאסר שוגג: בשלמא לרב נחמן. מצי לתרוצי כי תניא ההיא דשוגג יאכל לפני גזירה דאמרינן לקמן דגזרו על השוכחין וכי איתמר דר' חייא בר אבא דתריצנא אליביה דשוגג אסור לאחר גזירה: אלא דרבה ורב יוסף. דאמרי אליבא דר' חייא בר אבא להתירא אף במזיד: אי קודם גזירה. אתמר דר' חייא: קשיא מיהא מזיד. דהכא תניא במזיד לא יאכל: ואי לאחר גזירה קשיא נמי שוגג. דאפי' שוגג ה"ל למיסר דאילו מתני' קודם גזירה נשנית: המבשל בשבת. בידים דאיכא חיובא דאורייתא: וה"ה לשוכח. דהמשהה נמי מבעוד יום אם שכח בשוגג יאכל ואם במזיד השהה לא יאכל כאילו בשלה בידים בשבת: קשיא דר' מאיר אדר' מאיר. דתנן לעיל בריש פירקין לר' מאיר אליבא דב"ה חמין אבל לא תבשיל והכא שרי חמין ותבשיל שבישל כל צרכו: וקשיא דר' יהודה אדר' יהודה. דהתם א"ר יהודה חמין ותבשיל והכא אסר תבשיל שבישל כל צרכו: הא לכתחלה. משנה קמייתא לשהות לכתחלה קמיירי והך בהשהה כבר קאמר דמותר לאוכלה: כאן בגרופה וקטומה. ההיא דלעיל איירי בגרופה וקטומה כדקתני בה משהין על גבי גרופה וקטומה ואין משהין על שאינה גרופה ומה הן משהין על הגרופה שהתרנו לשהות ר"מ אומר כו' הלכך אפי' לכתחלה שרי ר' יהודה והכא כשאינה גרופה הלכך דיעבד אסר: עבר ושהה במזיד מאי. מותר לאוכלה או לא: חמין לא אסר. דמצטמק ורע לו: ביצים אסר. דמצטמק ויפה לו: מאי לאו לאותו שבת. אסרן עליהן באכילה: לא לשבת הבאה. אסר להן עכשיו שלא לעשות כן לשבת הבאה אבל באכילה שרו: מכלל דביצים מצומקות כו'. בעיא היא: והביאו לפניו. בחול: כעוזרדין. שנצטמקו עד שנעשו דקות כעוזרדין קורמ"ש בלע"ז ומדאמר ואכלנו הרבה מכלל דיפה להן: מחזירין

שכח קדרה על גבי כירה ובישלה בשבת מהו. אע"ג דקיי"ל כחנניה הכא בעי בדלא בשיל כמאכל בן דרוסאי דמודה ביה חנניה אי נמי בעי אפי' בקידרא חייתא והא דשרינן בפ"ק (דף יח: ושם) קידרא חייתא היינו דוקא בתנור שסומו רב דבלא איתוי יתבשל עד למחר אבל כירה דשליט בה אוירא אסור דאיכא למיחש שמא יחתה:

אבל האי דלא קעביד מעשה במזיד נמי יאכל. תימה דהא אמר בפ"ק (שם) לא תמלא אשה קדרה עססיות כו' ואם נתנה למוצאי שבת אסורין בכדי שיעשו וי"ל דבלאו הכי פריך שפיר מברייתא דמייתי:

בשלמא לרב נחמן בר יצחק כאן קודם גזירה כו'. תימה לר"י [א] לימא תרווייהו קודם גזירה והא דשרי בברייתא שוגג היינו בבשיל כמאכל בן דרוסאי ורב נחמן איירי בדלא בשיל כמאכל בן דרוסאי כדפי' ותירץ ר"ת דבישלה בשבת משמע שלא היתה קודם לכן כלל מבושלת. ולא בעי למימר נמי דרב נחמן סבר כר' יהודה דאסר תבשיל אפי' בישל כל צרכו וכ"ש לא בישל משום דדילמא ר' יהודה לא איירי אלא במזיד אבל בשוגג מודה לר"מ דשרי אפי' לא בישל כל צרכו:

קשיא דר' מאיר אדר' מאיר. כאן משמע דסתם חמין ותבשיל הוי נמי מבושל כל צרכו דאי לאו הכי לא הוה פריך מידי ורשב"א אומר דאפי' אי סתם חמין ותבשיל הוי בלא בשיל כל צרכו פריך שפיר דהא באינה גרופה משמע בברייתא דלעיל דאין משהין כלל אפי' בישל כל צרכו דאי הוה שרי בישל כל צרכו ה"ל לפרש מה הן משהין באינה גרופה כדמפרש אגרופה והכא שרי ר"מ בישל כל צרכו אפי' באינה גרופה מ"מ נראה דסתם חמין ותבשיל הוי נמי בבשיל כל צרכו מדפשיטא ליה לתלמודא דמאן דאסר להחזיר אסר אפי' בישל כל צרכו כדמוכח גבי ואף ר' אושעיא סבר כו':

הא לכתחלה הא דיעבד. לא סגי בהאי שינויא דהא לעיל שרי ר' מאיר סתם חמין דהויא אפי' לא הוחמו כל צורכן אפי' לכתחלה והכא אסר חמין שלא הוחמו כל צורכן אפי' דיעבד אלא צריך לשנויי כדמשני אקשיא דר' יהודה אדר' יהודה הא בגרופה וקטומה הא בשאינה גרופה ואדרבי יהודה נמי צריך לשנויא (דהכא) דהא לכתחלה הא דיעבד דהא בשאינה גרופה אסר לעיל אפי' חמין שנתבשל כל צרכו והכא שרי אלא דאיכא לשנויי הא לכתחלה הא דיעבד:

עבר ושהה מאי. בדלא בשיל כמאכל בן דרוסאי ליכא לאוקמי דהא כבר פשט לעיל לאיסורא כרב נחמן בר יצחק ונראה לר"י דמבעיא ליה בבשיל ובשוגג ואליבא דר' יהודה אע"ג דאין הלכה כר' יהודה אי אסר מצטמק ויפה לו דוקא במזיד או דילמא אפי' בשוגג ומייתי ראיה ממעשה דר' יוסי דאסר ומשמע ליה דאפי' בשוגג היה מדקאמר ונשתהו ולא קאמר ושיהו ומיהו לשון עבר ושהה משמע במזיד כמו עברה ולשה דפסחים (דף מג.) ואומר רשב"א דקודם גזירה בעו דאחר גזירה פשיטא דאסור בשוגג כמו מזיד:

לא לשבת הבאה. כולה סוגיא בשאינה גרופה דבגרופה ליכא שום אמורא דאסר כדפרישית לעיל והיינו כרב דאסר לעיל מצטמק ויפה לו: אפי'

עין משפט
נר מצוה

ז א מיי' פ"ג מהל' שבת הלכה ד ופ"ו הל' כג סמג לאוין סה טור וש"ע א"ח סימן שיח סעיף א:

ח ב ג מיי' פ"ג מהל' שבת הלכה ט סמג לאוין סה טוש"ע א"ח סימן רנג סעיף א:

רבינו חננאל

הא דבעו מר' חייא בר אבא שכח קדירה ע"ג כירה ובישלה בשבת ודרש להו המבשל בשבת בשוגג יאכל במזיד לא יאכל ולא שנא כלומר במבשל יש להפריש בין שוגג למזיד אבל בשוכח השוגג והמזיד שוין: רבה ורב יוסף אמרי שוכח בין שוגג ובין מזיד מותר לא קנסו רבנן אפילו במזיד רב נחמן בר יצחק אמר שניהן אסורין וקי"ל כוותיה ואותבינא עליה שכח קדירה על גבי כירה ובישלה בשבת בשוגג יאכל במזיד לא יאכל כו'. ועלתה לרבה ורב יוסף בקושיא ואקשינן הכא א"ר מאיר חמין שהוחמו כל צרכן ותבשיל שבישל כל צרכו בין בשוגג בין במזיד מותר ובתחלת הפרק אמר ומה הן משהין בש"א ולא כלום ובה"א חמין אבל לא תבשיל [ושנינן התם] לכתחילה דרבי יהודה אדרבי יהודה לא קשיא הא דקתני רבי יהודה הכא תבשיל שבישל כל צרכו אסור כירה שאינה גרופה ולא קטומה ולפיכך אסור והאי דקתני התם משהין ע"ג כירה לב"ה חמין ותבשיל בגרופה וקטומה וכיון שנתקשה רבה ורב יוסף נתקיימו דברי רב נחמן בר יצחק וקי"ל כוותיה כל השוכח קדירה ובישלה קודם גזירה הוה שרי ובתר גזירה קנסו רבנן אפילו שוגג ומאי גזירה דבתחלה היו אומרים המבשל בשבת בשוגג יאכל במזיד לא יאכל וה"ה לשוכח ומשרבו משהי קדירה במזיד ואומרים שוכחים אנן גזרו אף על השוכח. וכיון דסלקי דמצטמק ויפה לו אסור איבעיא לן עבר ושהה מאי ואתינן למפשטא מהא דתניא דאסיר רבי יוסי בצפורי ביצים מצומקים שנשתהו על גבי כירה (שמא) [ש"מ] עבר ושהה קנסו רבנן ודחינן לא אסר להו לעשות

רב נסים גאון

פרק כירה אמר רבי חנינא כשהלך רבי יוסי לציפורי. הדבר שגרם לו לילך לציפורי הוא שמפורש בבמה מדליקין (דף לג:) יוסי ששתק יגלה לציפורי:

מסורת הש"ם

א) תוספתא פ"ג ב"ק עא. חולין טו. גיטין נג: בילה יז: [תרומות פ"ב מ"ג כתובות לד.], ב) [עי' תוספות ע"ז סו: ד"ה אמר רבא], ג) תוספתא פ"ג, ד) [פי' שמחתכין אותו חתיכות קטנות ומרסקין אותו עד שנטרף במקפה או בטיסני שכל זמן שמצטמק יוצא שמנו ומתערב עם הבישול ערוך ערך טרף ג].

תוספות ישנים

א) ושמא לתלמודא לא נראה לחלק כיון דר"מ אוסר אפילו תבשיל:

ליקוטי רש"י

בשוגג יאכל. הוא עצמו ובו ביום ואין צריך להמתין עד הערב בכדי שיעשו דהא דאמרינן בעלמא לערב בכדי שיעשו לית ליה לר"מ אלא היכא דעבד ישראל איסורא ובמזיד דאיכא חיובא דלא נמטייה הנאה מאיסורא אבל בשוגג לא. במזיד. דאיכא איסורא. לא יאכל. בו ביום עד שתחשך ובכדי שיעשו והוא הדין לאחרים נמי דאסור למיכליה בו ביום דטעמא משום דלא נמטייה הנאה מאיסורא הוא וכי שהי לאורתא בכדי שיעשו לא מטי לו הנאה מיניה ולאידי דתנא רישא בדידיה דאשמעינן רבותא להתירא תנא נמי סיפא בדידיה [חולין טו. ובעי"ז ב"ק עא.]. הוא לעולם אבל אחרים ישראלים אוכלים [כתובות לד. ע"ש בפנ"י]. מצומקות. לגוות הרבה לשון מצטמק ויפה לו לשבת [חולין ו.].

The Gemara attempts to resolve this issue:
תָּא שְׁמַע – Come, learn a proof: **דְּאָמַר שְׁמוּאֵל בַּר נָתָן אָמַר רַבִּי חֲנִינָא – For Shmuel bar Nassan said in the name of R' Chanina: כְּשֶׁהָלַךְ רַבִּי יוֹסֵי לְצִיפּוֹרִי – When R' Yose went to Tzippori מָצָא חַמִּין שֶׁנִּשְׁתַּהוּ עַל גַּבֵּי כִּירָה – he discovered hot water that had been left on an** unbanked ***kirah*** **וְלֹא אָסַר לָהֶן – and he did not prohibit** it **to them, בֵּיצִים מְצוּמָּקוֹת שֶׁנִּשְׁתַּהוּ עַל גַּבֵּי כִּירָה** – but he also discovered **shriveled eggs that had been left on an** unbanked ***kirah*** **וְאָסַר לָהֶן – and he did prohibit** that **to them.**[17]

The Gemara reasons:
מַאי לַאו לְאוֹתוֹ שַׁבָּת – Does this **not** mean that he issued the prohibition **for that** very **Sabbath,** i.e. he prohibited the consumption of the shriveled eggs? Accordingly, we learn from here that food left on an unbanked *kirah* is prohibited for consumption![18]

The Gemara rejects the proof:
לֹא לְשַׁבָּת הַבָּאָה – No! It means that R' Yose prohibited them to repeat this practice **on the following Sabbath.** He did not, however, prohibit consumption of the eggs that he discovered on the unbanked *kirah.*[19]

The Gemara digresses slightly to analyze the episode involving R' Yose:
מִכְּלָל דְּבֵיצִים מְצוּמָּקוֹת מִצְטַמְּקוֹת וְיָפֶה לָהֶן נִינְהוּ – This implies that shriveled eggs are a food that **improve as they condense** and shrivel even further. Is this indeed so?

The Gemara replies:
אִין – Yes! דְּאָמַר רַב חָמָא בַּר חֲנִינָא – For Rav Chama bar Chanina said: פַּעַם אַחַת נִתְאָרַחְתִּי אֲנִי וְרַבִּי לְמָקוֹם אֶחָד – Rebbi and I once lodged in the same place, וְהֵבִיאוּ לְפָנֵינוּ בֵּיצִים מְצוּמָּקוֹת כְּעוּזְרְדִין – and they served us eggs that had shriveled until they were as small **as sorb-apples, וְאָכַלְנוּ מֵהֶן הַרְבֵּה – and we ate many of them.**[20]

The Mishnah stated:
בֵּית הִלֵּל אוֹמְרִים אַף מַחֲזִירִין – BEIS HILLEL SAY: WE MAY EVEN RETURN it.

The Gemara clarifies Beis Hillel's ruling:
אָמַר רַב שֵׁשֶׁת – Rav Sheishess said: לְדִבְרֵי הָאוֹמֵר –

NOTES

17. Hot water deteriorates as it condenses (for it evaporates) whereas shriveled eggs improve in flavor as they condense and shrivel even further. Therefore, R' Yose did not prohibit the hot water but did prohibit the shriveled eggs (*Rashi*).

18. The proof is based on the presumption that the eggs did not really condense on the Sabbath since they were already shriveled beforehand (*Rosh, Chidushei R' Elazar Moshe Horowitz*).

19. We are thus left with the conclusion that food left on a *kirah* illegally is not prohibited for consumption unless it actually improved. This reflects *Rashi's* understanding of the inquiry. Cf. the sources cited in note 16.

20. This incident occurred on a weekday (*Ritva, MHK* ed.). Since Rav Chama stated that he and Rebbi ate many of the tiny eggs, it is obvious that they were quite tasty. This demonstrates that shriveled eggs continue to improve as they continue to condense (*Rashi*).

שכח קדירה על גבי כירה ובשלה בשבת מהו אישתיק ולא א"ל ולא מידי למחר נפק דרש להו [א] המבשל [א] בשבת [ג] בשוגג יאכל במזיד לא יאכל ולא שנא מאי ול"ש רבה ורב יוסף דאמרי תרווייהו להיתירא מבשל הוא דקא עביד מעשה במזיד לא יאכל אבל האי דלא קא עביד מעשה במזיד נמי יאכל רב נחמן בר יצחק אמר [ב] לאיסורא מבשל הוא דלא אתי לאיערומי בשוגג יאכל אבל האי דאתי לאיערומי בשוגג נמי לא יאכל מיתיבי [ג] שכח קדירה על גבי כירה ובישלה בשבת בשוגג יאכל במזיד לא יאכל בד"א בחמין שלא הוחמו כל צורכן ותבשיל שלא בישל כל צורכו אבל חמין שהוחמו כל צורכן ותבשיל שבישל כל צורכו בין בשוגג בין במזיד יאכל דברי ר"מ ר' יהודה אומר חמין שהוחמו כל צורכן מותרין מפני שמצטמק ורע לו ותבשיל שבישל כל צורכו אסור מפני שמצטמק ויפה לו וכל המצטמק ויפה לו כגון כרוב ופולים ובשר [ד] טרוף אסור וכל המצטמק ורע לו מותר קתני מיהא תבשיל שלא בישל כל צורכו בשלמא לרב נחמן בר יצחק לא קשיא כאן קודם גזרה כאן לאחר גזרה אלא רבה ורב יוסף דאמרי להיתירא אי קודם גזרה קשיא מזיד אי לאחר גזרה קשיא נמי שוגג קשיא מאי גזירתא דאמר רב יהודה בר שמואל א"ר אבא אמר רב כהנא אמר רב בתחילה היו אומרים המבשל בשבת בשוגג יאכל במזיד לא יאכל וה"ה לשוכח משרבו משהין במזיד ואומרים שכחים אנו חזרו וקנסו על השוכח קשיא דר' מאיר אדר' מאיר קשיא דר' יהודה אדר' יהודה דר' מאיר אדר"מ לא קשיא הא לכתחילה הא דיעבד דר' יהודה אדר' יהודה נמי לא קשיא כאן בגרופה וקטומה כאן בשאינה גרופה וקטומה איבעיא להו עבר ושהה מאי מי קנסוהו רבנן או לא ת"ש דאמר שמואל בר נתן א"ר חנינא כשהלך רבי יוסי לציפורי מצא חמין שנשתהו על גבי כירה ולא אסר להן ביצים מצומקות שנשתהו על גבי כירה ואסר להן מאי לאו לאותו שבת לא [ג] לשבת הבאה מכלל דביצים מצומקות מצטמקות ויפה להן נינהו אין דאמר רב חמא בר חנינא פעם אחת נתארחתי אני ורבי למקום אחד והביאו לפנינו ביצים מצומקות כעוזרדין ואכלנו מהן הרבה: ב"ה אומרים אף מחזירין: אמר רב ששת לדברי האומר מחזירין

מחזירין

רש"י

שכח קדרה. אליבא מאן דאסר: המבשל בשבת. משנה היא: ולא שנא. אבל האי דשכח קדרה לא שנא בין שוגג למזיד והכי דרש להו סתמא ולא פירש אי אשוגג מדמה לה ומותר לאוכלה אי אמזיד מדמה לה ואסור: במזיד נמי. אם השהה על גבי כירה מבעוד יום יאכל: דלא אתי לאיערומי. ולעשות מזיד ולומר שוגג הייתי דלא נחשדו ישראל על השבתות: דאתי לאיערומי. דאיסור דרבנן הוא וקילא ליה ואתי לשהויי מזיד ויאמר שכחתי: מיתיבי שכח קדרה כו' בשוגג. כגון האי דשכח יאכל בשבת: במזיד. דלא שכח אלא הניח לא יאכל: ובשר טרוף. דגלי דעתיה דלא לאורחים קבעי לה: וכל המצטמק ויפה לו. כלומר וכן כל שאר המצטמק ויפה להם אסור לאוכלן אם השהן מזיד: קתני מיהת. בשלא בישל כל צרכו דיש חילוק בין שוגג למזיד במשהה קשיא בין לרבה ורב יוסף דשרו מזיד בין לרב נחמן דאסר שוגג: בשלמא לרב נחמן. מצי לתרולי כי תניא ההיא דשוגג יאכל לפני גזירה דאמרינן לקמן דגזרו על השוכחין וכי איתמר דר' חייא בר אבא דתרילנא אליביה דשוגג אסור לאחר גזירה: אלא לרבה ורב יוסף. דאמרי אליבא דר' חייא בר אבא להתירא אף במזיד: אי קודם גזירה. אתמר דר' חייא: קשיא מיהא מזיד. דהכא תניא במזיד לא יאכל: ואי לאחר גזירה קשיא נמי שוגג. דאפי' שוגג ה"ל למיסר דאילו מתני' קודם גזירה נשנית: המבשל בשבת. בידים דאיכא חיובא דאורייתא: וה"ה לשוכח. דהמשהה נמי מבעוד יום אם שכח בשוגג יאכל ואם במזיד השהה לא יאכל כאילו בשלה בידים בשבת: קשיא דר' מאיר אדר' מאיר. דתנן לעיל בריש פירקין לר' מאיר אליבא דב"ה חמין אבל לא תבשיל והכא שרי חמין ותבשיל שבישל כל צרכו: וקשיא דר' יהודה אדר' יהודה. דהתם א"ר יהודה חמין ותבשיל והכא אסר תבשיל שבישל כל צרכו: הא לכתחלה. משנה קמייתא לשהות לכתחלה קמיירי והך בהשהה כבר קאמר דמותר לאוכלה: כאן בגרופה וקטומה. ההיא דלעיל איירי בגרופה וקטומה כדקתני בה משהין על גבי גרופה וקטומה ואין משהין על שאינה גרופה ומה הן משהין על הגרופה שהתרנו לשהות ר"מ אומר כו' הלכך אפי' לכתחלה שרי ר' יהודה והכא כשאינה גרופה הלכך דיעבד אסר: עבר ושהה במזיד מאי. מותר לאוכלה או לא: חמין לא אסר. דמצטמק ורע לו: ביצים אסר. דמצטמק ויפה לו: מאי לאו לאותו שבת. אסרן עליהן באכילה: לא לשבת הבאה. אסר להן עכשיו שלא לעשות כן לשבת הבאה אבל באכילה שרו: מכלל דביצים מצומקות כו'. בעיא היא: והביאו לפניו. בחול: כעוזרדין. שנצטמקו עד שנעשו דקות כעוזרדין קורמ"ש בלע"ז ומדאמר ואכלנו הרבה מכלל דיפה להן: מחזירין

תוספות

שכח קדרה על גבי כירה ובישלה בשבת מהו. אע"ג דקיי"ל כחנניה הכא בעי בדלא בשיל כמאכל בן דרוסאי דמודה ביה חנניה אי נמי בעי אפי' בקידרא חייתא והא דשרינן בפ"ק (דף יח: ושם) קידרא חייתא היינו דוקא בתנור שחומו רב דלא איתוי יתבשל עד למחר אבל כירה דשליט בה אוירא אסור דאיכא למיחש שמא יחתה: **אבל** האי דלא קעביד מעשה במזיד נמי יאכל. תימה דהא אמר בפ"ק (שם) לא תמלא אשה קדרה עססיות כו' ואם נתנה למוצאי שבת אסורין בכדי שיעשו וי"ל דבלאו הכי פריך שפיר מברייתא דמייתי: **בשלמא** לרב נחמן בר יצחק כאן קודם גזירה כו'. תימה לר"י [א] לימא תרווייהו קודם גזירה והא דשרי בברייתא שוגג היינו בבשיל כמאכל בן דרוסאי ורב נחמן איירי בדלא בשיל כמאכל בן דרוסאי כדפי' ותירץ ר"ת דבישלה בשבת משמע שלא היתה קודם לכן כלל מבושלת. ולא בעי למימר נמי דרב נחמן סבר כר' יהודה דאסר תבשיל אפי' בישל כל צרכו וכ"ש לא בישל משום דדילמא ר' יהודה לא איירי אלא במזיד אבל בשוגג מודה לר"מ דשרי אפי' לא בישל כל צרכו: **קשיא** דר' מאיר אדר' מאיר. כאן משמע דסתם חמין ותבשיל הוי נמי מבושל כל צרכו דאי לאו הכי לא הוה פריך מידי ורשב"א אומר דאפי' אי סתם חמין ותבשיל הוי בלא בשיל כל צרכו פריך שפיר דהא באינה גרופה משמע בברייתא דלעיל דאין משהין כלל אפי' בישל כל צרכו דאי הוה שרי בישל כל צרכו ה"ל לפרש מה הן משהין באינה גרופה כדמפרש אגרופה והכא שרי ר"מ בישל כל צרכו אפי' באינה גרופה מ"מ נראה דסתם חמין ותבשיל הוי נמי בבשיל כל צרכו מדפשיטא ליה לתלמודא דמאן דאסר להחזיר אסר אפי' בישל כל צרכו כדמוכח גבי ואף ר' אושעיא סבר כו': **הא** לכתחלה הא דיעבד. לא סגי בהאי שינויא דהא לעיל שרי ר' מאיר סתם חמין דהויא אפי' לא הוחמו כל צורכן אפי' לכתחלה והכא אסר חמין שלא הוחמו כל צורכן אפי' דיעבד אלא צריך לשנויי כדמשני אקשיא דר' יהודה אדר' יהודה הא בגרופה וקטומה הא בשאינה גרופה ואדרבי יהודה נמי צריך לשנויא (דהכא) דהא לכתחלה הא דיעבד דהא בשאינה גרופה אסר לעיל אפי' חמין שנתבשל כל צרכו והכא שרי אלא דאיכא לשנויי הא לכתחלה הא דיעבד: **עבר** ושהה מאי. בדלא בשיל כמאכל בן דרוסאי ליכא לאוקמי דהא כבר פשט לעיל לאיסורא כרב נחמן בר יצחק ונראה לר"י דמבעיא ליה בבשיל ובשוגג ואליבא דר' יהודה אע"ג דאין הלכה כר' יהודה אי אסר מצטמק ויפה לו דוקא במזיד או דילמא אפי' בשוגג ומייתי ראיה ממעשה דר' יוסי דאסר ומשמע ליה דאפי' בשוגג היה מדקאמר ונשתהו ולא קאמר ושיהו ומיהו לשון עבר ושהה משמע במזיד כמו עברה ולשה דפסחים (דף מג.) ואומר רשב"א דקודם גזירה בעו דאחר גזירה פשיטא דאסור בשוגג כמו מזיד: **לא** לשבת הבאה. כולה סוגיא בשאינה גרופה דבגרופה ליכא שום אמורא דאסר כדפרישית לעיל והיינו כרב דאסר לעיל מצטמק ויפה לו:

אפי'

מסורת הש"ס

א) תוספתא פ"ג ב"ק עא. חולין טו. גיטין נג: בילה יח: [תרומות פ"ב מ"ג] כתובות לד., ב) [עי' תוספות ע"ז סו: ד"ה אמר רבא], ג) תוספתא פ"ג, ד) [פי' שמחתכין אותו חתיכות קטנות ומרסקין אותו עד שנטרף במקפה או בעיסוי שכל זמן שמצטמק יוצא שמנו ומתערב עם הבישול ערוך ערך טרף ג].

תוספות ישנים

א) ושמא לתלמודא לא נראה לחלק דיון דר"ח אוסר אפילו תבשיל:

ליקוטי רש"י

בשוגג יאכל. הוא עצמו ובו ביום ואין צריך להמתין עד הערב בכדי שיעשו דהא דאמרינן בעלמא לערב בכדי שיעשו לית ליה לר"מ אלא היכא דעבד ישראל איסורא ובמזיד דאיכא חיובא דלא נמטייה הנאה מאיסורא אבל בשוגג לא. במזיד. דאיכא איסורא. לא יאכל. בו ביום עד שתחשך ובכדי שיעשו והוא הדין לאחרים נמי דאסור למיכליה בו ביום דטעמא משום דלא נמטייה הנאה מאיסורא הוא וכי שהי לאורתא בכדי שיעשו לא מטי לו הנאה מיניה ואיידי דתנא רישא בדידיה דאשמעינן רבותא להתירא תנא נמי סיפא בדידיה [חולין טו. וכעי"ז ב"ק עא.]. הוא לעולם אבל אחרים ישראלים אוכלים [כתובות לד. ע"ש בפנ"י]. מצומקות. צלויות הרבה לשון מצטמק ויפה לו דשבת [חולין ו.].

עין משפט נר מצוה

ז א מיי' פ"ג מהל' שבת הלכה ד ופ"ו הל' כג סמג לאוין סה טור וש"ע א"ח סימן שיח סעיף א:

ח ב ג מיי' פ"ג מהל' שבת הלכה ט סמג לאוין סה טוש"ע א"ח סימן רנג סעיף א:

רבינו חננאל

הא דבעו מר' חייא בר אבא שכח קדירה ע"ג כירה ובישלה בשבת ודרש להו המבשל בשבת בשוגג יאכל במזיד לא יאכל ולא שנא כלומר במבשל יש להפריש בין שוגג למזיד אבל בשוכח השוגג והמזיד שוין: רבה ורב יוסף אמרי שוכח בין שוגג ובין מזיד מותר לא קנסו רבנן אפילו במזיד רב נחמן בר יצחק אמר שניהן אסורין וקי"ל כוותיה ואותבינא עליה שכח קדירה על גבי כירה ובישלה בשבת בשוגג יאכל במזיד לא יאכל כו'. ועלתה לרבה ורב יוסף בקושיא ואקשינן הכא א"ר מאיר חמין שהוחמו כל צרכן ותבשיל שבישל כל צרכו בין בשוגג בין במזיד מותר ובתחלת הפרק אמר ומה הן משהין בש"א ולא כלום ובה"א חמין אבל לא תבשיל [ושנינן התם] לכתחילה דרבי יהודה אדרבי יהודה לא קשיא הא דקתני רבי יהודה הכא תבשיל שבישל כל צרכו אסור כירה שאינה גרופה ולא קטומה ולפיכך אסור והאי דקתני התם משהין ע"ג כירה לב"ה חמין ותבשיל בגרופה וקטומה וכיון שנתקשה רבה ורב יוסף נתקיימו דברי רב נחמן בר יצחק וקי"ל כוותיה כל השוכח קדירה ובישלה קודם גזירה הוה שרי ובתר גזירה קנסו רבנן אפילו שוגג ומאי גזירה דבתחלה היו אומרים המבשל בשבת בשוגג יאכל במזיד לא יאכל וה"ה לשוכח ומשרבו משהי קדירה במזיד ואומרים שוכחים אנן גזרו אף על השוכח. וכיון דסלקי דמצטמק ויפה לו אסור איבעיא לן עבר ושהה מאי ואתינן למפשטא מהא דתניא דאסיר רבי יוסי בצפורי ביצים מצומקים שנשתהו על גבי כירה (שמא) [ש"מ] עבר ושהה קנסו רבנן ודחינן לא אסר להו לעשות

רב נסים גאון

פרק כירה אמר רבי חנינא כשהלך רבי יוסי לציפורי. הדבר שגרם לו לילך לציפורי הוא שמפורש בבמה מדליקין (דף לג) יוסי ששתק יגלה לציפורי:

עין משפט נר מצוה

ט א ב ג ד ה ו ז מיי' פ"ג מהל' שבת הלכה ה ז י סמג לאוין סה טוש"ע א"ח סימן רנג סעיף ב:
י ח מיי' פט"ז מהל' כלים הלכה יג:
יא ט י מיי' פ"ט מהל' שבת הל' ב ג טוש"ע א"ח סי' שיח סעיף ג:
יב כ מיי' פכ"ב מהל' שבת הלכה ג סמג שם טוש"ע א"ח סימן שכו סעיף ג וסימן רנז סעיף א וסעיף ו:
[יב] כ [מיי' פ"ט מהל' שבת הלכה ב]:

תוספות ישנים

א) ואי מתני' להשהות תנן בתנור נמי אסור להשהות. אע"ג דקידרא חייתא לעיל שרי ההוא כחנניא ומתני' אי להשהות תנן אתיא דלא כחנניא:
ב) ולפ"ז צריך למגרס בתר הכי ואצ"ל ע"ג ואצ"ל בתוכה. ואי גרסי' סומכין גרסי' ונותנין אפילו ע"ג ואפילו בתוכה:
ג) והא דחשיב לה כחמין שהוחמו בשבת משמע טפי כפי' ראשון:

רבינו חננאל

כן אלא לשבת הבאה וכן סוגיא דשמעתא: פיס' בה"א אף מחזירין אוקימנא הא דקתני מחזירין בשבת הוא ואפי' כמה פעמים ודוקא בכירה גרופה וקטומה והני מילי שלא הניחם ע"ג קרקע כלל אלא מחזיקם בידו ודעתו עליהם להחזירם הוא ששנינו אף מחזירין אבל אם הניחם ע"ג קרקע אע"פ שהיה בדעתו להחזירם לכירה אסור ואסיקנא לשמעתא בתרי לשני. וקי"ל כל כי האי גוונא בדאורייתא עבדינן לחומרא. ושבת איסורא דאורייתא היא: תלאם במקל או הניחם ע"ג המטה או הניחם בכרעי המטה או פינם ממיחם למיחם הני כולהו איבעא ולא אפשיטו ועלו בתיקו. וקי"ל כל תיקו דאיסורא לחומרא: מתני' תנור שהסיקו בקש ובגבבא כו' אוקמא אביי לא יסמוך. תניא כוותיה תנור שהסיקו בקש ובגבבא אין סומכין לו ואין צ"ל על גביו. ואין צ"ל שהסיקו בגפת או בעצים. כופח שהסיקוה בקש ובגבבא הרי הוא ככירה. בגפת ובעצים הרי הוא כתנור ואסור. ואע"פ שהוא גרוף וקטום. ואסיק' כופח מקום שפיתת קדירה אחת. כירה מקום שפיתת ב' קדירות. ודייקינן לה מהא דתנן כירה שנחלקה לארכה טהור לרחבה טמא פי' עדיין תורת כלי עליה דהא יכול לשפות קדירה אחת. כופח בין לארכה בין לרחבה טהורה. והאי כופח נפיש הבליה מדכירה וזוטר הבליה מדתנור וקי"ל מתני' בתנור של נחתומין. משמש בלא יחפור (ב"ב כ:) אבל תנור [דידן] ככירה של נחתומין היא: פיס' אין נותנין ביצה בצד המיחם בשביל שתתגלגל גלגל

תוספות

אפילו בשבת. פירש בקונטרס בשבת ביום המחרת ולפ"ז ה"ל למינקט אפי' ביום השבת ולמאי דפרישית דעיקר פלוגתייהו בחול אתי שפיר: **פינה** ממיחם למיחם מהו. וא"ת דבפרק במה טומנין (לקמן דף נא.) תניא וכן היה רשב"ג אומר לא אסרו אלא באותו מיחם אבל פינה ממיחם למיחם מותר אלמא במיחם אחר שרי טפי והכא משמע איפכא ואור"ת דהכא גבי השהה ע"ג כירה כשהוא באותו מיחם שהוא חם לא אתי לחתויי אבל במיחם אחר שהוא קר אתי לחתויי אבל גבי הטמנה שרי טפי כשהוא קר דבחיתוי מועט לא יועיל: **ורשב"א** מפרש בשם ר"י דהתם בהטמנה דהוי לצורך מחר ליכא למיחש לחיתויי דבלא חיתוי יתחמם הרבה אבל הכא דבעי לה בלילה איכא למיחש לחיתויי ומיהו קצת משמע התם דמיירי במטמין בלילה (ת"י):

תנור שהסיקוהו בקש ובגבבא לא יתן כו'. אי להחזיר תנן הכא נמי האי לא יתן לא יחזיר אבל להשהות משהה אפילו בתנור שאינו גרוף וקטום כדמשמע בפ"ק (דף יח:) ° דשרינן קידרא חייתא ובשיל כמאכל בן דרוסאי אפילו באינו גרוף וקטום ומשמע התם דבתנור איירי דקאי אהא דקתני התם לעיל לא תמלא אשה קדרה א) עססיות כו':

אילימא בשאינה גרופה. האי לישנא לאו דוקא דאביי סבר דלא מיתוקמה בגרופה דבגרופה לא מסתבר ליה שיהא חילוק בין גפת ועצים לקש וגבבא דאי הוה מצי אביי לאוקמה בגרופה כדמוקי לה רב אדא לא הוה מצי למפשט מידי ורב אדא דמוקי לה בגרופה סבר דיש לעולם יותר חום כשהסיקוה בגפת ובעצים אע"ג דגרופה מבקש ובגבבא:

תניא כוותיה דאביי כו'. יש דגרסי בסיפא כופח שהסיקוהו בגפת ובעצים ב) אין סומכין לה דאי גרס סומכין לה לא אתא כוותיה דאביי דאית ליה דבכופח נמי אין סומכין כדאמרינן לעיל וי"ל דאי גרסינן סומכין איכא לאוקמה בגרופה ונקט גפת ועצים לרבותא דאפילו הכי סומכין לה:

לא יטמיננה בחול. אע"ג דאמר בלא יחפור (ב"ב דף יט. ושם) דחול דקריר מקרר דחמים מחים והכא בילה היא קרה הכא מיירי בחול שהוחם בחמה דומיא דאבק דרכים:

מעשה והביאו סילון של צונן לתוך אמה של חמין כו'. מבעוד יום הביאוהו כדפירש בקונטרס ואין שום איסור כלל בהבאה כדתניא בפרק קמא (דף יח.) פותקין מים לגינה ומתמלאת והולכת כל השבת כולה ואסרו ברחיצה גזירה שמא יערבם בשבת ולערבם בשבת אסור משום תולדות האור וחשיבא כחדא גזירה ג) ואם היינו מפרשים דבסילון היו בו נקבים וכשהיו רותחים בשבת היו פותחים הנקבים ומתערבין הצוננין בחמין הוה אתי שפיר טפי דהשתא ליכא אלא חדא גזירה אטו חמי האור אך בגמרא מדמי לה להטמנה מבעוד יום ויליף מינה לאסור להטמין

גמרא

א מחזירין אפילו בשבת ואף ר' אושעיא סבר אף מחזירין אפי' בשבת דא"ר אושעיא פעם אחת היינו עומדים לעילא מר' חייא רבה והעלנו לו קומקמום של חמין מדיוטא התחתונה לדיוטא העליונה ומזגנו לו את הכוס והחזרנוהו למקומו ולא אמר לנו דבר א"ר זריקא א"ר אבא א"ר תדאי לא שנו אלא שעודן בידו אבל הניחן ע"ג קרקע אסור א"ר אמי ר' תדאי א) דעבד לגרמיה הוא דעבד אלא הכי א"ר חייא א"ר יוחנן אפילו הניחה על גבי קרקע מותר פליגי בה רב דימי ורב שמואל בר יהודה ותרוייהו משמיה דרבי אלעזר אמרי חד אמר ב עודן בידו מותר ע"ג קרקע אסור וחד אמר הניחן על גבי קרקע נמי מותר אמר חזקיה משמיה דאביי הא דאמרת עודן בידו מותר לא אמרן אלא ג שדעתו להחזיר אבל אין דעתו להחזיר אסור מכלל דעל גבי קרקע אע"פ שדעתו להחזיר אסור איכא דאמרי אמר חזקיה משמיה דאביי הא דאמרת על גבי קרקע אסור לא אמרן אלא שאין דעתו להחזיר אבל דעתו להחזיר מותר מכלל שבעודן בידו אע"פ שאין דעתו להחזיר מותר בעי ר' ירמיה תלאן במקל מהו הניחן על גבי מטה מהו בעי רב אשי פינן ממיחם למיחם מהו תיקו:

מתני' ד תנור שהסיקוהו בקש ובגבבא לא יתן בין מתוכו בין מעל גביו כופח שהסיקוהו בקש ובגבבא ה"ז ככיריים בגפת ובעצים הרי הוא כתנור:

גמ' תנור שהסיקוהו סבר רב יוסף למימר תוכו תוכו ממש על גביו על גביו ממש אבל לסמוך שפיר דמי איתיביה אביי כופח שהסיקוהו בקש ובגבבא הרי הוא ככיריים בגפת ובעצים הרי הוא כתנור ואסור הא ככירה שרי במאי עסקינן אילימא על גביו ובמאי אילימא כשאינו גרוף וקטום אלא כירה כי אינה גרופה וקטומה על גביו מי שרי אלא לאו לסמוך וקתני הרי הוא כתנור ואסיר אמר רב אדא בר אהבה הכא בכופח גרוף וקטום ותנור גרופה וקטומה עסקינן הרי הוא כתנור ה דאע"ג דגרוף וקטום על גביו אסור דאי ככירה כי גרופה וקטומה שפיר דמי: תניא כוותיה דאביי ו תנור שהסיקוהו בקש ובגבבא אין סומכין לו ואין צריך לומר על גביו ואין צריך לומר לתוכו ואין צריך לומר בגפת ובעצים כופח שהסיקוהו בקש ובגבבא סומכין לו [א] ואין נותנין על גביו בגפת ובעצים אין סומכין לו אמר ליה רב אחא בריה דרבא לרב אשי האי כופח היכי דמי אי ככירה דמי אפילו בגפת ובעצים נמי אי כתנור דמי אפילו בקש ובגבבא נמי לא אמר ליה נפיש הבליה מדכירה וזוטר הבליה מדתנור היכי דמי כופח היכי דמי כירה א"ר יוסי בר חנינא ז כופח מקום שפיתת קדרה אחת כירה מקום שפיתת שתי קדרות אמר אביי ואיתימא רבי ירמיה אף אנן נמי תנינא ט) כירה ח שנחלקה לאורכה טהורה לרחבה טמאה כופח בין לאורכו בין לרוחבו טהור:

מתני' ט אין נותנין ביצה בצד המיחם בשביל שתתגלגל ולא יפקיענה בסודרין ור' יוסי מתיר י ולא יטמיננה בחול ובאבק דרכים בשביל שתצלה מעשה שעשו אנשי טבריא כ והביאו סילון של צונן לתוך אמה של חמין אמרו להם חכמים אם בשבת כחמין שהוחמו בשבת ואסורין ברחיצה ובשתיה אם ביום טוב כחמין שהוחמו ביום טוב ואסורין ברחיצה ומותרין בשתיה:

גמ' איבעיא להו גלגל מאי אמר רב יוסף [ל] גלגל חייב חטאת אמר מר בריה דרבינא אף אנן נמי תנינא כל

רש"י

מחזירין **אפילו בשבת**. ביום המחרת ולא תימא פלוגתייהו משחשכה והתם הוא דשרו משום דמוכחא מילתא דאדעתא דאהדורי לצורך מחר שקיל ליה אבל ביום לא מוכח דשקיל ליה אדעתא דאהדורי ובטלה לה הטמנה וה"ל כמטמין לכתחלה: **קומקמוס**. יורה קטנה: **דיוטא**. עלייה: **למקומו**. לכירה: **אבל הניח על גבי קרקע** אסור. להחזיר דבטלי לה הטמנה דאתמול והוי כמטמין לכתחלה: **לגרמיה**. יחיד הוא בדבר ואין הלכה כמותו: **תלאן במקל מהו**. כעודן בידו דמי או כהניחן ע"ג קרקע דמי: **פינן ממיחם למיחם מהו**. מי הוי כמטמין לכתחלה ואסור להחזירן לכירה או לא: **מיחם**. קומקמוס שמחמם בו חמין: **מתני' תנור**. מתוך שקצר למעלה ורחב למטה נקלט חומו לתוכו טפי מכירה: **כופח**. בגמרא מפרש לה עשוי חלל ככירה אבל ארכו כרחבו ואין בו אלא שיעור שפיתת קדירה אחת וכירה יש בה שפיתת שתי קדירות: **גמ' על גביו**. על שפתו: **אבל לסמוך**. אצל דופנו: **הא ככירה שרי**. כלומר מדקתני הרי הוא כתנור מכלל דאי הוה מדמי ליה לכירה הוה שרי ושמעינן מינה דכירה שהוסק בגפת ובעצים שרי: **ובמאי קאי**. קס"ד בשאינה גרופה ואי על גבה מי שרי: **תניא כוותיה דאביי**. דאסור לסמוך אתנור: **אפי' בגפת ועצים**. לשתרי בגרופה וקטומה: **שנחלקה לאורכה**. הרי בטלו שתי שפיתותיה שנחלקת רחבה לשתים הלכך טהרה מטומאתה שהרי ניתצה: **נחלקה לרחבה**. נמלאו שתי השפיתות קיימות זו לבדה וזו לבדה: **כופח בין לאורכה בין לרחבה** טהורה. שהרי ארכה כרחבה וכולה מקום שפיתה אחת: **מתני' אין נותנין ביצה בצד המיחם**. קומקמוס של נחשת: **בשביל שתתגלגל**. שתצלה קלת עד שתהא מגולגלת: **ולא יפקיענה בסודרין**. לא ישברנה על סודר שהוחם בחמה כדי שתצלה מחומו של סודר: **בחול ובאבק דרכים**. שהוחמו מכח חמה. ובגמרא מפרש אמאי לא פליג רבי יוסי בהא: **והביאו סילון**. מבעוד יום: **של צונן**. כדי לחממן דהמים נמשכין ובאין כל השבת: **לתוך אמה**. של חמי טבריא: **אם בשבת**. אותן שבאו בשבת: ה"ג כחמין שהוחמו:

מסורת הש"ס

א) [ברכות מח. וש"נ], ב) כלים פ"ז מ"ג.

גליון הש"ס

תוס' ד"ה תנור כו' **דשרינן קידרא חייתא ובשיל כמאכל בן דרוסאי**. ק"ל הא שם לא מכר מן מאב"ד אלא סתם ובשיל שפיר דמי אלא דתוס' כתבו שם דהיינו כמאב"ד דהא קיימא לן כחנניא וא"כ איך עשו כאן הוכחה מזה דלמא באמת תנור סמיך דכמאב"ד אסור ודאמרי' ובשיל ש"ד היינו כפשוטו ובשיל לגמרי. גם אמאי לא הוכיחו כפשוטו דהא קתני ולא חררה על גבי גחלים אלא כדי שיקרמו פניה חררה היינו בתנור כמ"ש תוס' לעיל דף לו ע"א ד"ה אא"כ וכו' אף על גב דחררה בתוכה היא. והיינו ע"כ משום דחררה אופין בתנור. עכ"פ ראייתם מפ"ק תמוה מאד:

הגהות הגר"א

[א] גמ' סומכין לו ואין נותנין. נ"ב צ"ל סומכין לו ונותנין כו':

ליקוטי רש"י

לעילא מר' חייא רבה. לפניו וכן לשון הש"ס והמקרא שרפים עומדים ממעל לו (ישעיה ו) ועל שם שיראים להתקרב לפניו עומדין מרחוק [לעיל ל. ע"ש בב"ח]. **דיוטא**. היא עלייה העליונה שעל גג הבית [רשב"ם ב"ב קמח.]. **לגרמיה הוא דעבד**. אין אדם מודה לו [ברכות מח.]. **לדעתיה** [מ"ק כה:]. **תנור**. תנור וכירים כלים המטלטלין הם והם של חרס ויש להן תוך ושופת את הקדרה על נקב החלל ושניהם פיהם למעלה [ויקרא יא, לה]. תנור כלי חרס הוא שרוף ככבשן כשאר קדירות ופיו למעלה והגא לקובעו בארץ עושה בנין טיט ואבנים שיהיו לו לבסים ומושיבין אותו עליו שלא ילטננו שוליו מחמת קרקע [ב"ב יז.]. וכל תנור שבמשנה קטן הוא ומקום שפיתת ב' קדירות ופיו למעלה [ע"ז לה: עיין מו"ק י. ובב"ח שם, נדה כו. ובתוס' שם: ד"ה בפלוגתא]. **שפיתת קדרה**. כשמושיבין הסיר על גבי כירה קרי לה שפיתה [סוטה יא:]. קדירה כשמניחין אותה אצל האור על גבי כירה קרי שפיתה לשון שפות הסיר (יחזקאל כד) [ע"ז יב.]. שפות הסיר ע"פ הכירה במקום מושבה היא קרויה שפיתה בלשון המשנה מקום שפיתת שתי קדירות ועוד שניהו אחד שופת את הקדירה ואחד נותן לתוכה מים ואחד נותן לתוכה תבלין למדנו שהשפיתה היא הושבתה על פי הכירה עד שלא יתנו לתוכה כלום [יחזקאל כד, ג]. ומנחם פתר כל לשון שפיתה לשון שימה [תהלים כב, טז]. **בשביל שתתגלגל**. מגולגלת. גלויה רכה [עירובין מא.]. **לתוך אמה של חמין**. חמי טבריא מעינות רותחין [פסחים מא.].

מַחֲזִירִין – **According to the opinion of the one who said** that **one may return** food to a *kirah*, i.e. Beis Hillel, אֲפִילּוּ בְּשַׁבָּת – one may do this **even on the Sabbath** day.[1]

The Gemara cites a concurring view:

וְאַף רַבִּי אוֹשַׁעְיָא סָבַר אַף מַחֲזִירִין אֲפִילּוּ בְּשַׁבָּת – **And R' Oshaya also holds** that Beis Hillel's ruling that **one may even return** food to a shoveled or banked *kirah* applies **even on the Sabbath** day, דְּאָמַר רַבִּי אוֹשַׁעְיָא – **for R' Oshaya said:** פַּעַם אַחַת הָיִינוּ עוֹמְדִים לְעֵילָא מֵרַבִּי חִיָּיא רַבָּה – **We were once standing before**[2] **R' Chiya the Great,** וְהֶעֱלֵנוּ לוֹ קוּמְקְמוּס שֶׁל חַמִּין מִדְּיוֹטָא הַתַּחְתּוֹנָה לִדְיוֹטָא הָעֶלְיוֹנָה – **and we brought up a kettle of hot water for him from the lower floor** of the house **to the upper floor,** וּמָזַגְנוּ לוֹ אֶת הַכּוֹס – **diluted a cup** of wine **for him** with hot water[3] וְהֶחֱזַרְנוּהוּ לִמְקוֹמוֹ – **and** then **returned [the kettle] to its place** on the *kirah* on the lower floor, וְלֹא אָמַר לָנוּ דָּבָר – **and he did not tell us anything** in objection to what we had done. R' Oshaya's statement demonstrates that it is permissible to return food to a *kirah* even on the Sabbath day.[4]

The Gemara qualifies Beis Hillel's ruling that it is permitted to return food to the *kirah*:

אָמַר רַבִּי זְרִיקָא אָמַר רַבִּי אַבָּא אָמַר רַבִּי תַּדַּאי – **R' Zerika said in the name of R' Abba who said in the name of R' Taddai:** לֹא שָׁנוּ אֶלָּא שֶׁעוֹדָן בְּיָדוֹ – **They taught** that one may return food to a shoveled or banked *kirah* **only** concerning a case **where [the pot] is still in his hand,** i.e. one never let go of it from the time he removed it from the *kirah*. אֲבָל הִנִּיחָן עַל גַּבֵּי קַרְקַע אָסוּר – **But if he placed it on the ground, it is forbidden** to lift it and return it to the *kirah*.[5]

This ruling is disputed:

אָמַר רַבִּי אַמִּי – **R' Ami said:** רַבִּי תַּדַּאי דְּעָבַד לְגַרְמֵיהּ הוּא דְּעָבַד – **R' Taddai spoke**[6] **for himself** alone; the halachah does not follow him. אֶלָּא הָכִי אָמַר רַבִּי חִיָּיא אָמַר רַבִּי יוֹחָנָן – **Rather, this is what R' Chiya said in the name of R' Yochanan:** אֲפִילּוּ הִנִּיחָהּ עַל גַּבֵּי קַרְקַע מוּתָּר – **Even if one placed [the pot] on the ground, it is permissible** to return it to the *kirah*.[7]

The Gemara quotes a similar disagreement between other Amoraim:

פְּלִיגֵי בָּהּ רַב דִּימִי וְרַב שְׁמוּאֵל בַּר יְהוּדָה – **Rav Dimi and Rav Shmuel bar Yehudah disagreed concerning this** same issue, וְתַרְוַיְיהוּ מִשְּׁמֵיהּ דְּרַבִּי אֶלְעָזָר אָמְרֵי – **both of them stating** their view **in the name of R' Elazar.** חַד אָמַר עוֹדָן בְּיָדוֹ מוּתָּר עַל גַּבֵּי קַרְקַע אָסוּר – **One** of them **said** that **if [the pot] is still in his hand it is permissible** to return it to the *kirah*, but if he placed it **on the ground it is forbidden** to return it to the *kirah*. וְחַד אָמַר הִנִּיחָן עַל גַּבֵּי קַרְקַע נַמִּי מוּתָּר – **And the other one said** that if **he placed it on the ground it is also permissible** to return it to the *kirah*.

The Gemara discusses another possible qualification to the permissibility of replacing food on a *kirah*:

אָמַר חִזְקִיָּה מִשְּׁמֵיהּ דְּאַבַּיֵּי – **Chizkiyah said in the name of Abaye:** הָא דְּאָמַרְתְּ עוֹדָן בְּיָדוֹ מוּתָּר – **That which you stated** that **if [the pot] is still in his hand it is permissible** to return it to the *kirah*, לֹא אֲמָרָן אֶלָּא שֶׁדַּעְתּוֹ לְהַחֲזִיר – **was stated only** concerning a case **where he intended,** when he removed the pot from the *kirah*, **to return** it there. אֲבָל אֵין דַּעְתּוֹ לְהַחֲזִיר אָסוּר – **But if he did not** originally **intend to return** it, **it is forbidden** to return it.[8]

The Gemara comments:

מִכְּלָל דְּעַל גַּבֵּי קַרְקַע אַף – **This implies that** if one placed the pot **on the ground,** אַף עַל פִּי שֶׁדַּעְתּוֹ לְהַחֲזִיר אָסוּר – then **even if he** originally **intended to return** it to the *kirah* **it is forbidden** to return it.

Another version of the previous teachings:

אִיכָּא דְּאָמְרֵי – **There are those who cite** Chizkiyah's teaching as follows: אָמַר חִזְקִיָּה מִשְּׁמֵיהּ דְּאַבַּיֵּי – **Chizkiyah said in the name of Abaye:** הָא דְּאָמַרְתְּ עַל גַּבֵּי קַרְקַע אָסוּר – **That which you stated,** that if he placed the pot **on the ground it is forbidden** to return it to the *kirah*, לֹא אֲמָרָן אֶלָּא שֶׁאֵין דַּעְתּוֹ לְהַחֲזִיר – **was stated only** concerning a case **where he did not** originally **intend to return** it there. אֲבָל דַּעְתּוֹ לְהַחֲזִיר מוּתָּר – **But if he** originally **intended to return it** to the *kirah*,

NOTES

1. Not only do Beis Hillel permit returning it to the *kirah* in a case where it was taken off on Friday night, when it is clear that the person removed it with the intention of replacing it (so that he would have food for the next day's meal), they even permit returning it when it was taken off during the Sabbath day, when the intent to replace it is not apparent.

[Beis Hillel permit only *returning* food on the *kirah*, not placing it there initially on the Sabbath, even if it is fully cooked. Their reason is that placing new food on a *kirah* appears like cooking (*Mishnah Berurah* 253:55; see *Shulchan Aruch HaRav* 253:23 with footnote 8). Accordingly,] one might have thought that even if food was left on the *kirah* Friday and was removed on the Sabbath it is permitted to return it only if the person demonstrably intended from the outset to return it, e.g. he removed it Friday night. In that situation, his replacing is considered a permissible extension of the original *shehiyah*. However, if the person did not obviously intend to return it (e.g. he removed it on the Sabbath morning), we might have thought that by removing it from the *kirah* he terminated the original *shehiyah* and is now deemed to be placing food on the *kirah* initially, which is prohibited. Rav Sheishess therefore informs us that even though this intent is not obvious, the *shehiyah* is not terminated and the food may be returned on the *kirah* (*Rashi;* cf. *Tosafos* here and 36b ד״ה וב״ה אומרים; *Ramban; Rashba*). The Gemara will discuss below whether the person may return the pot even if he truly did not intend to do so.

Note that food may be returned to the *kirah* only while it is yet warm. If it has cooled off, the original *shehiyah* is deemed to have terminated and it is forbidden to replace the food on the *kirah* (see *Shulchan Aruch* and *Rama, Orach Chaim* 253:2 with *Mishnah Berurah* §54 and 68).

[*Rashi* uses the term *hatmanah* (insulating) here instead of *shehiyah* (leaving food on the *kirah*). This accords with his view that *hatmanah* and *shehiyah* are synonymous. However, most Rishonim differentiate between these categories, as pointed out above, 36b note 4.]

2. The translation follows *Rashi* to 30a ד״ה לעילא and to 88a ד״ה עליה.

3. In earlier times, all wine needed dilution with water before it could be drunk. The dilution was often performed with hot water (see above, 11b).

4. Although R' Oshaya did not say whether the incident occurred on Friday night or the Sabbath day, we learn from it that he permits *chazarah* even on the Sabbath day. For when he took the kettle to a different floor and poured a cup of hot water for R' Chiya, it certainly did not appear as if he intended to replace it on the *kirah*. Since he nevertheless replaced it, we learn that *chazarah* is permitted even on the Sabbath day, when the intent to return it is not evident (*Rashba*).

5. If one placed the pot on the ground after removing it from the *kirah*, he terminated the original *shehiyah*. Replacing it on the *kirah* now would be tantamount to placing food on the *kirah* initially on the Sabbath (*Rashi;* see *Mishnah Berurah* 253:55).

6. Literally: acted (see *Rashash*).

7. [According to R' Yochanan, placing the pot on the ground does not automatically terminate the original *shehiyah*. However, we will see below that this ruling may not pertain in all circumstances.]

8. Removing the pot from the *kirah* without intent to replace it terminates the original *shehiyah*. It is therefore forbidden to return the pot to the *kirah* even if it was in the person's hand throughout. One must have the intent, when removing the pot, to replace it before it cools off in order for his act to be considered "returning" rather than placing something new on the *kirah* (*Mishnah Berurah* 253:56). [The intent need not be obvious, as explained in note 1, but it must be present.]

מחזירין אפילו בשבת ואף ר' אושעיא סבר אף מחזירין אפי' בשבת דא"ר אושעיא פעם אחת היינו עומדים לעילא מר' חייא רבה והעלנו לו קומקמוס של חמין מדיוטא התחתונה לדיוטא העליונה ומזגנו לו את הכוס והחזרנוהו למקומו ולא אמר לנו דבר א"ר זריקא א"ר אבא א"ר תדאי לא שנו אלא שעודן בידו אבל הניחן ע"ג קרקע אסור א"ר אמי ר' תדאי דעבד לגרמיה הוא דעבד אלא הכי א"ר חייא א"ר יוחנן אפילו הניחה על גבי קרקע מותר פליגי בה רב דימי ורב שמואל בר יהודה ותרוייהו משמיה דרבי אלעזר אמרי חד אמר עודן בידו מותר ע"ג קרקע אסור וחד אמר הניחן על גבי קרקע נמי מותר אמר חזקיה משמיה דאביי הא דאמרת עודן בידו מותר לא אמרן אלא שדעתו להחזיר אבל אין דעתו להחזיר אסור מכלל דעל גבי קרקע אע"פ שדעתו להחזיר אסור איכא דאמרי אמר חזקיה משמיה דאביי הא דאמרת על גבי קרקע אסור לא אמרן אלא שאין דעתו להחזיר אבל דעתו להחזיר מותר מכלל שבעודן בידו אע"פ שאין דעתו להחזיר מותר בעי ר' ירמיה תלאן במקל מהו הניחן על גבי מטה מהו בעי רב אשי פינן ממיחם למיחם מהו תיקו: **מתני'** תנור שהסיקוהו בקש ובגבבא לא יתן בין מתוכו בין מעל גביו כופח שהסיקוהו בקש ובגבבא הרי זה ככיריים בגפת ובעצים הרי הוא כתנור: **גמ'** תנור שהסיקוהו סבר רב יוסף למימר תוכו תוכו ממש על גביו על גביו ממש אבל לסמוך שפיר דמי איתיביה אביי כופח שהסיקוהו בקש ובגבבא הרי הוא ככיריים בגפת ובעצים הרי הוא כתנור ואסור הא ככירה שרי במאי עסקינן אילימא על גביו ובמאי אילימא כשאינו גרוף וקטום אלא כירה כי אינה גרופה וקטומה על גביו מי שרי אלא לאו לסמוך וקתני הרי הוא כתנור ואסיר אמר רב אדא בר אהבה הכא בכופח גרוף וקטום ותנור גרופה וקטומה עסקינן הרי הוא כתנור דאע"ג דגרוף וקטום על גביו אסור דאי ככירה כי גרופה וקטומה שפיר דמי: תניא כוותיה דאביי תנור שהסיקוהו בקש ובגבבא אין סומכין לו ואין צריך לומר על גביו ואין צריך לומר לתוכו ואין צריך לומר בגפת ובעצים כופח שהסיקוהו בקש ובגבבא סומכין לו [א] ואין נותנין על גביו בגפת ובעצים אין סומכין לו אמר ליה רב אחא בריה דרבא לרב אשי האי כופח היכי דמי אי ככירה דמי אפילו בגפת ובעצים נמי אי כתנור דמי אפילו בקש ובגבבא נמי לא אמר ליה נפיש הבליה מדכירה וזוטר הבליה מדתנור היכי דמי כופח היכי דמי כירה א"ר יוסי בר חנינא כופח מקום שפיתת קדרה אחת כירה מקום שפיתת שתי קדרות אמר אביי ואיתימא רבי ירמיה אף אנן נמי תנינא כירה שנחלקה לאורכה טהורה לרחבה טמאה כופח בין לאורכו בין לרוחבו טהור: **מתני'** אין נותנין ביצה בצד המיחם בשביל שתתגלגל ולא יפקיענה בסודרין ור' יוסי מתיר ולא יטמינה בחול ובאבק דרכים בשביל שתצלה מעשה שעשו אנשי טבריא והביאו סילון של צונן לתוך אמה של חמין אמרו להם חכמים אם בשבת כחמין שהוחמו בשבת ואסורין ברחיצה ובשתיה אם ביום טוב כחמין שהוחמו ביום טוב ואסורין ברחיצה ומותרין בשתיה: **גמ'** איבעיא להו גלגל מאי אמר רב יוסף גלגל חייב חטאת אמר מר בריה דרבינא אף אנן נמי תנינא כל

מחזירין אפילו בשבת. ביום המחרת ולא תימא פלוגתייהו משתחשכה והתם הוא דשרו משום דמוכחא מילתא דלהעדתא להחזירו לצורך מחר שקיל ליה אבל ביום לא מוכח דשקיל ליה אדעתא להחזיר ובטלה לה הטמנה וה"ל כמטמין לכתחלה: **קומקמוס.** יורה קטנה: **דיוטא.** עלייה: **למקומו.** לכירה: **אבל הניחו על גבי קרקע אסור.** להחזיר דבטלה לה הטמנה דאתמול והוי כמטמין לכתחלה: **לגרמיה.** יחיד הוא בדבר ואין הלכה כמותו: **תלאן במקל מהו.** כעודן בידו דמי או כהניחן ע"ג קרקע דמי: **פינן ממיחם למיחם מהו.** מי הוי כמטמין לכתחלה ואסור להחזירן לכירה או לא: **מיחם.** קומקמוס שמחמם בו חמין: **מתני' תנור.** מתוך שקצר למעלה ורחב למטה נקלט חומו לתוכו טפי מכירה: **כופח.** בגמרא מפרש לה עשוי חלל ככירה אבל ארכו כרחבו ואין בו אלא שיעור שפיתת קדירה אחת וכירה יש בה שפיתת שתי קדירות: **גמ' על גביו.** על שפתו: **אבל לסמוך.** אצל דופנו: **הא ככירה שרי.** כלומר מדקתני הרי הוא כתנור מכלל דאי הוה מדמי ליה לכירה הוה שרי ושמעינן מינה דכירה שהוסק בגפת ובעצים שרי: **ובמאי קאי.** קס"ד בשאינה גרופה ואי על גבה מי שרי: **תניא כוותיה דאביי.** דאסור לסמוך אתנור: **אפי' בגפת ועצים.** לשתרי בגרופה וקטומה: **שנחלקה לאורכה.** הרי בטלו שתי שפיתותיה שנחלקת רחבה לשתים הלכך טהרה מטומאתה שהרי ניתצה: **נחלקה לרחבה.** נמצאו שתי השפיתות קיימות זו לבדה וזו לבדה: **כופח בין לאורכה בין לרחבה טהורה.** שהרי ארכה כרחבה וכולה מקום שפיתה אחת: **מתני' אין נותנין ביצה בצד המיחם.** קומקמוס של נחשת: **בשביל שתתגלגל.** שתצלה קצת עד שתהא מגולגלת: **ולא יפקיענה בסודרין.** לא ישברנה על סודר שהוחם בחמה כדי שתצלה מחומו של סודר: **בחול ובאבק דרכים.** שהוחמו מכח חמה. ובגמרא מפרש אמאי לא פליג רבי יוסי בהא: **והביאו סילון.** מבעוד יום של צונן. כדי לחממן דהחמים נמשכין ובאין כל השבת: **לתוך אמה.** של חמי טבריא: **אם בשבת.** אותן שבאו בשבת: ה"ג כחמין שהוחמו:

אפילו בשבת. פירש בקונטרס בשבת ביום המחרת ולפ"ז ה"ל למינקט אפי' ביום השבת ולמאי דפרישית דעיקר פלוגתייהו בחול אתי שפיר. **פינה** ממיחם למיחם מהו. וא"ת דבפרק במה טומנין (לקמן דף נא.) תניא וכן היה רשב"ג אומר לא אסרו אלא בלותו מיחם אבל פינה ממיחם למיחם מותר אלמא במיחם אחר שרי טפי והכא משמע איפכא ואור"ת דהכא גבי השהאה ע"ג כירה כשהוא בלותו מיחם שהוא חם לא אתי לחתויי אבל במיחם אחר שהוא קר אתי לחתויי אבל גבי הטמנה שרי טפי כשהוא קר דבחיתוי מועט לא יועיל:

ורשב"א מפרש בשם ר"ת דהתם בהטמנה דהוי לצורך מחר ליכא למיחש לחיתוי דבלילה מיתוי יתחממו הרבה אבל הכא דבעי לה בלילה איכא למיחש לחיתוי ומיהו קצת משמע התם דמיירי בטמנין בלילה (מ"י):

תנור שהסיקוהו בקש ובגבבא לא יתן כו'. אי להחזיר תנן הכא נמי האי לא יתן לא יחזיר אבל להשהות משהה אפילו בתנור שאינו גרוף וקטום כדמשמע בפ"ק (דף יח:) דשרינן קידרא חייתא ובשיל כמאכל בן דרוסאי אפילו באינו גרוף וקטום ומשמע התם דבתנור איירי דקאי אהא דקתני התם לעיל לא תמלא אשה קדרה א) עססיות כו':

אילימא בשאינה גרופה. האי ליסנא לאו דוקא דלאביי סבר דלא מיתוקמה בגרופה דבגרופה לא מסתבר ליה שיהא חילוק בין גפת ועצים לקש וגבבא דאי הוה מצי אביי לאוקמה בגרופה כדמוקי לה רב אדא לא הוה מצי למפשט מידי ורב אדא דמוקי לה בגרופה סבר דיש לעולם יותר חום כשהסיקוה בגפת ובעצים אע"ג דגרופה מבקש וגבבא:

תניא כוותיה דאביי כו'. יש דגרסי בכיפה כופח שהסיקוהו בגפת ובעצים ב) אין סומכין לה דאי גרס סומכין לה לא אתא כוותיה דאביי דאית ליה דבכופח נמי אין סומכין כדאמרינן לעיל וי"ל דאי גרסינן סומכין איכא לאוקמה בגרופה וקטום גפת ועצים לרבותא דאפילו הכי סומכין לה:

לא יטמינה בחול. אע"ג דאמר בלא יחפור (ב"ב דף יט. ושם) לחול דקריר מקרר דממיס מחים והכא בילה היא קרה הכא מיירי בחול שהוחם בחמה דומיא דאבק דרכים:

מעשה והביאו סילון של צונן לתוך אמה של חמין כו'. מבעוד יום הביאוהו כדפירש בקונטרס ואין שום איסור כלל בהבאה כדתניא בפרק קמא (דף יח.) פותקין מים לגינה ומתמלאת והולכת כל השבת כולה ואסרו ברחיצה גזירה שמא יערבם בשבת ולערבם בשבת אסור משום תולדות האור והשיאה כחדא גזירה ג) ולא היינו מפרשים דבסילון היו בו נקבים וכשהיו רוצים בשבת היו פותחים הנקבים ומתערבין הצוננין בחמין הוה אתי שפיר דהשתא ליכא אלא חדא גזירה אטו חמי האור אך בגמרא מדמי לה להטמנה מבעוד יום ויליף מינה לאסור להטמין

עין משפט נר מצוה

מ א ב ג ד ה ו ז מיי' פ"ג מהל' שבת הלכה ה ז סמג לאוין סה טוש"ע א"ח סימן רנג סעיף ב:
י ח מיי' פט"ו מהל' כלים הלכה יג:
יא ט י מיי' פ"ט מהל' שבת הל' ג ג טוש"ע א"ח סי' שיח סעיף ג:
יב כ מיי' פכ"ב מהל' שבת הלכה ג סמג שם טוש"ע א"ח סימן שכ סעיף ג וסימן רמ סעיף א וסעיף ו:
[יב] ל [מיי' פ"י מהל' שבת הלכה כב]:

תוספות ישנים

א) ולי מתני' להשהות תנן בתנור נמי אסור להשהות. אע"ג דקדירה כמנינה ולא שרי אלא כחנניה ומתני' אי להשהות תנן אתיא דלא כחנניה:
ב) ולפ"ז צריך למגרס בתר הכי ואי"ל כחוזה. ואי גרסי' סומכין גרסי' ונותנין אפילו ע"ג ואפילו בחוזה:
ג) והא דהשיב לה כחמין שהוחמו בשבת משמע טפי כפי' ראשון:

רבינו חננאל

כן אלא לשבת הבאה וכן סוגיא דשמעתא: פיס' בה"א אף מחזירין אוקימנא הא דקתני כמה פעמים ודוקא בכירה גרופה וקטומה והני מילי שלא הניחם ע"ג קרקע כלל אלא מחזיק בידו ודעתו עליהם להחזירם הוא ששנינו אף מחזירין אע"פ שהיה בדעתו להחזירם לכירה אסור ואסיקנא לשמעתא בתרי לשני. וקי"ל אי הני גוונא בדאורייתא עבדינן לחומרא. שבות איסורא דאורייתא היא: תלאם במקל או הניחם ע"ג המטה או הניחם בכרעי המטה או פינם ממיחם למיחם כולהו לא איפשיטו ועלו בתיקו. וקי"ל כל תיקו דאיסורא לחומרא: מתני' תנור שהסיקו בקש ובגבבא כו' אוקמא אביי לא יסמוך. תניא כוותיה תנור שהסיקו בקש ובגבבא אין סומכין לו ואין צ"ל על גביו. ואין צ"ל שהסיקו בגפת או בעצים. כופח שהסיקו בקש ובגבבא הרי הוא ככירה. בגפת ובעצים הרי הוא כתנור ואסור. ואע"פ שהוא גרוף וקטום. ואסיק כופח מקום שפיתת קדירה אחת. כירה מקום שפיתת ב' קדירות. ודייקינן לה מהא דתנן כירה שנחלקה לארכה טהור לרחבה טמא פי' עדיין תורת כלי עליה דהא יכול לשפות קדירה אחת. כופח בין לרחבה בין לארכה טהור. והאי כופח נפיש הבליה מדכירה וזוטר הבליה מדתנור וקי"ל כמתני' דתנור של נחתומין. מפורש בלא יחפור (ב"ב כ:) אבל תנור [דידן] ככירה של נחתומין היא: פיס' אין נותנין ביצה בצד המיחם בשביל שתתגלגל גלגל

מסורת הש"ס

א) [ברכות מח. וש"נ], ב) כלים פ"ז מ"ג.

גליון הש"ס

תוס' ד"ה תנור כו' דשרינן קידרא חייתא ובשיל כמאכל בן דרוסאי. ק"ל הא שם לא נזכר מן מאכ"ד אלא קמס ובשיל שפיר דמי אלא דתוס' כתבו שם דהיינו כמאכ"ד הלא קיימא לן כחנניא וא"כ איך עשו כאן הוכחה מזה דלמא באמת תנור חמיר לכמאכ"ד אסור ודאמרי' ובשיל ש"ד היינו כפשוטו ובשיל לגמרי. גם קמא לא הוכיחו כפשוטו דהא קתני ולא מרכה עד גבי גחלים אלא כדי שיקרמו פניה מרכה היינו תנור כמ"ש תוס' לעיל דף לו ע"א ד"ה אלא"ב וכו' על כל גג דמרכה כתנור היא. והיינו ע"כ משום דמרכה אופין בתנור. עכ"פ ראייתם מפ"ק תמוה מאוד:

הגהות הגר"א

[א] גמ' סומכין לו ואין נותנין. נ"ב נ"ל סומכין לו ונותנין כו':

ליקוטי רש"י

לעילא מר' חייא רבה. לפניו וכן לשון הש"ס והמקרא שרפים עומדים ממעל לו (ישעיה ו) ועל שם שיראים להתקרב לפניו עומדין מרחוק [לעיל ל. ע"ש בב"ח]. דיוטא. היא עלייה העליונה שעל גג הבית [רשב"ם ב"ב קמח.]. לגרמיה הוא דעבד. אין אדם מודה לו [ברכות מח.]. לדעתיה [מ"ק כה:]. תנור. תנור וכירים כלים המטלטלין הם והם של חרס ויש להן תוך ושופת את הקדרה על נקב החלל ושניהם פיהם למעלה [ויקרא יא, לה]. תנור כלי חרס הוא שרוף בכבשן כשאר קדירות ופיו למעלה והבא לקובעו בארץ עושה בנין טיט ואבנים שיהיו לו לבסיס ומושיבין אותו עליו שלא יתטנפו שוליו מחמת קרקע [ב"ב יז.]. וכל תנור שבמשנה קטן הוא ומקום שפיתת ב' קדירות ופיו למעלה [ע"ז לה: עיין מו"ק י. ובב"ח שם, נדה כו. ובתוס' שם: ד"ה בפלוגתא]. שפיתת קדרה. כשמושיבין הסיר על גבי כירה קרי לה שפיתה [סוטה יא:]. קדירה כשמניחין אותה אצל האור על גבי כירה קרי שפיתה לשון שפות הסיר (יחזקאל כד) [ע"ז יב.]. שפות הסיר ע"פ הכירה במקום מושבה היא קרויה שפיתה בלשון המשנה מקום שפיתת שתי קדירות ועוד שנינו אחד שופת את הקדירה ואחד נותן לתוכה מים ואחד נותן לתוכה תבלין למדנו שהשפיתה היא הושבתה על פי הכירה עד שלא יתנו לתוכה כלום [יחזקאל כד, ג]. ומנחם פתר כל לשון שפיתה לשון שימה [תהלים כב, טז]. בשביל שתתגלגל. מגולגלת. צלויה רכה [עירובין מא.]. לתוך אמה של חמין. חמי טבריא מעינות רותחין [פסחים מא.].

it is permissible to return it even though he placed it on the ground.

The Gemara comments:

מִכְּלָל שֶׁבְּעוֹדָן בְּיָדוֹ – This implies that if [the pot] is still in his hand, אַף עַל פִּי שֶׁאֵין דַּעְתּוֹ לְהַחֲזִיר מוּתָּר **– even if he did not** originally **intend to return it, it is permissible** to return it to the *kirah.*[9]

The Gemara inquires about some cases that are intermediate between holding onto the pot and placing it on the ground:

בָּעֵי רַבִּי יִרְמְיָה **– R' Yirmiyah inquired:** תְּלָאָן בְּמַקֵּל מַהוּ **– If he hung [the pot] on a peg, what is [the law]?** הִנִּיחָן עַל גַּבֵּי מִטָּה מַהוּ **– If he put it down on a bed, what is [the law]?** Are these the equivalent of placing the pot on the ground, or of holding it in one's hand?[10]

Another inquiry:

בָּעֵי רַב אַשִׁי **– Rav Ashi inquired:** פִּינָּן מְמֵיחַם לְמֵיחַם מַהוּ **– If one transferred [hot water]** that he had removed from the *kirah* **from one kettle to another, what is [the law]?** May he return the water to the *kirah* in the new kettle, or is this tantamount to placing something new on the *kirah* on the Sabbath?[11]

The Gemara offers no resolution to the inquiries, but concludes:

תֵּיקוּ **– Let them stand.**

Mishnah

Having discussed the laws pertaining to leaving and returning food on a *kirah,* the Mishnah turns its attention to other types of heating utensils:

תַּנּוּר שֶׁהִסִּיקוּהוּ בְּקַשׁ וּבִגְבָבָא – Concerning **a** ***tanur*****-oven that was heated with straw or with stubble,** לֹא יִתֵּן בֵּין
מִתּוֹכוֹ בֵּין מֵעַל גַּבָּיו **– one may not place** food **either inside it or on top of it.**[12] כּוּפָּח שֶׁהִסִּיקוּהוּ בְּקַשׁ וּבִגְבָבָא הֲרֵי זֶה
כְּכִירַיִים **– A** ***kupach*** **that was heated with straw or with stubble** is treated **like a** ***kirah.*** בְּגֶפֶת וּבְעֵצִים הֲרֵי הוּא
כְּתַנּוּר – If it was heated **with marc or with wood, it is** treated **like a** ***tanur.***[13]

Gemara

The Gemara quotes the opening segment of the Mishnah and a possible interpretation of it:

תַּנּוּר שֶׁהִסִּיקוּהוּ – Concerning A *TANUR* THAT WAS HEATED ... one may not place food either inside it or on top of it. סָבַר רַב יוֹסֵף לְמֵימַר תּוֹכוֹ תּוֹכוֹ מַמָּשׁ **– Rav Yosef was inclined to say** that the term **"inside it"** refers **literally** to placing food **inside [the** ***tanur*****]** עַל גַּבָּיו עַל גַּבָּיו מַמָּשׁ – and the term **"on top of it"** refers **literally** to placing food **on the top of [the** ***tanur*****],** i.e. its rim, and the Mishnah forbids placing food only in these areas, אֲבָל לִסְמוֹךְ שַׁפִּיר דָּמֵי **– but placing** food **alongside** the *tanur* **is acceptable.**[14]

This interpretation is challenged:

אֵיתִיבֵיהּ אַבַּיֵי **– Abaye challenged [Rav Yosef]** on the basis of the latter segment of the Mishnah, which states: כּוּפָּח שֶׁהִסִּיקוּהוּ בְּקַשׁ וּבִגְבָבָא הֲרֵי הוּא כְּכִירַיִים – A *KUPACH* THAT WAS HEATED WITH STRAW OR WITH STUBBLE IS treated LIKE A *KIRAH.* בְּגֶפֶת וּבְעֵצִים הֲרֵי הוּא כְּתַנּוּר – If it was heated WITH MARC OR WITH WOOD IT IS treated LIKE A *TANUR* – וְאָסוּר **– which means that it is forbidden** to place food on the *kupach* that was heated with marc or wood. הָא כְּכִירָה שָׁרֵי – This implies that **if, however,** the *kupach* that was heated with marc or wood would be treated **like a** ***kirah*** that was likewise fueled, **it would be permissible** to place food on it. Thus, the Mishnah is dealing with a placement of food that is permissible in the case of a *kirah* but not in the case of a *tanur* or *kupach.* בְּמַאי עַסְקִינַן – Now, **with what** case **are we dealing,** i.e. in what part of the *kupach* is the food being placed? אִילֵימָא עַל גַּבָּיו **– If you will say** we are dealing with a case in which the food is being placed **on top of [the** ***kupach*****],** I will further ask: וּבְמַאי **– And with what** type of *kupach* are we dealing? אִילֵימָא כְּשֶׁאֵינוֹ גָּרוּף וְקָטוּם **– If you will say** that it is **one that was not shoveled or banked,** I will ask: אֶלָּא כִּירָה כִּי אֵינָהּ גְּרוּפָה וּקְטוּמָה עַל גַּבָּיו מִי שָׁרֵי **– But** concerning **a** ***kirah*** **that is not shoveled or banked, is it permissible** to place food **on top of it?** Certainly not![15] אֶלָּא לָאו לִסְמוֹךְ **–Rather,** is it **not** obvious that we are dealing with **placing** the food **alongside** the *kupach,* which would be permissible in the case of a *kirah*? וְקָתָנֵי הֲרֵי הוּא כְּתַנּוּר וְאָסִיר – **And** it is concerning placing food alongside that **the Mishnah states that [the** ***kupach*****] is** treated **like a** ***tanur*** **and it is forbidden** to place the food there. Thus, the Mishnah implies that it is forbidden to place food alongside a

NOTES

9. Thus, if one held the pot in his hand throughout, *or* he originally intended to return it to the *kirah,* he may return it. According to the previous version of Chizkiyah's teaching, it is permitted to return the pot only if one held it in his hand *and* intended from the outset to return it.

It is a matter of considerable discussion among the Rishonim which version of Chizkiyah's teaching the halachah follows. See *Rashba, Ran, Rosh* and *Beis Yosef, Orach Chaim* 253. For a synopsis of the views, see *Orach Chaim* 253:2 with *Mishnah Berurah* §56 and *Beur Halachah* ד״ה ודעתו להחזירה and ד״ה ולא הניחה.

10. [If we follow the first version of Chizkiyah's previous teaching, the inquiries pertain to a case in which the person intended all along to return the pot to the *kirah.* If we follow the second version, they pertain to a case in which he did *not* originally intend to return it.]

11. The inquiry pertains to a case in which the person did not put the kettle containing the water on the ground and/or he intended from the outset to return the water to the *kirah.*

12. A *tanur* is a trapezoidal oven that has a relatively small opening on top. Its shape causes it to retain far more heat than a *kirah* (*Rashi*). Therefore, it is treated more stringently and even if it was heated with straw or stubble one may not place food on top of it or inside it. [Although straw and stubble do not create coals when burned, we are concerned that they might have left behind some sparks which the person might forgetfully stoke (*Tiferes Yisrael*).] Furthermore, the prohibition against placing food on the *tanur* pertains even if it was shoveled or banked (*Rashi* above, 37b ד״ה הא קרמו; see *Rashba* to Gemara below ד״ה הא דדייק and *Mishnah Berurah* 253:22).

As was the case with the previous Mishnah, our Mishnah may be referring either to leaving something on the *tanur* before the Sabbath (*shehiyah*) or returning something that was taken off it during the Sabbath (*chazarah*). If the previous Mishnah means to forbid *shehiyah* on an unbanked *kirah,* in opposition to Chananyah's opinion, our Mishnah should be understood as prohibiting *shehiyah* on a *tanur.* If the previous Mishnah means to prohibit only *chazarah,* in accordance with Chananyah's opinion, our Mishnah should be understood as prohibiting only *chazarah* on a *tanur; shehiyah,* however, is permitted (*Tosafos*; cf. *Baal HaMaor* to 18b).

13. A *kupach* is built like a *kirah* (i.e. its top is the same width as its bottom), but is square rather than rectangular and can contain only one pot instead of two pots. Thus, it is somewhat hotter than a *kirah* but not as hot as a *tanur* (*Rashi, Rav*). The Mishnah therefore rules that if it was heated with straw or stubble it is treated leniently and one may place food on it, and if it was heated with marc or wood it is treated stringently and one may not place food on it. The Gemara discusses whether this pertains even if the coals were shoveled away or banked.

14. Just as placing food alongside an unbanked *kirah* is permissible, as we concluded above (37a).

15. The previous Mishnah taught that it is forbidden to place food on top of an unshoveled and unbanked *kirah.* Yet it is clear from our Mishnah that the prohibited situation with which we are dealing would be permissible in the case of a *kirah.* Clearly, we are not dealing with placing food on *top* of the unbanked *kupach* or *kirah.*

מחזירין אפילו בשבת ואף ר' אושעיא סבר אף מחזירין אפי' בשבת דא"ר אושעיא פעם אחת היינו עומדים לעילא מר' חייא רבה והעלנו לו קומקמום של חמין מדיוטא התחתונה לדיוטא העליונה ומזגנו לו את הכוס והחזרנוהו למקומו ולא אמר לנו דבר א"ר זריקא א"ר אבא א"ר תדאי לא שנו אלא שעודן בידו אבל הניחן ע"ג קרקע אסור א"ר אמי ר' תדאי א) דעבד לגרמיה הוא דעבד אלא הכי א"ר חייא א"ר יוחנן אפילו הניחה על גבי קרקע מותר פליגי בה רב דימי ורב שמואל בר יהודה ותרוייהו משמיה דרבי אלעזר אמרי חד אמר עודן בידו מותר ע"ג קרקע אסור וחד אמר הניחן על גבי קרקע נמי מותר אמר חזקיה משמיה דאביי הא דאמרת עודן בידו מותר לא אמרן אלא שדעתו להחזיר אבל אין דעתו להחזיר אסור מכלל דעל גבי קרקע אע"פ שדעתו להחזיר אסור איכא דאמרי אמר חזקיה משמיה דאביי הא דאמרת על גבי קרקע אסור לא אמרן אלא שאין דעתו להחזיר אבל דעתו להחזיר מותר מכלל שבעודן בידו אע"פ שאין דעתו להחזיר מותר בעי ר' ירמיה תלאן במקל מהו הניחן על גבי מטה מהו בעי רב אשי פינן ממיחם למיחם מהו תיקו: מתני' תנור שהסיקוהו בקש ובגבבא לא יתן בין מתוכו בין מעל גביו כופח שהסיקוהו בקש ובגבבא ה"ז ככיריים בגפת ובעצים הרי הוא כתנור: גמ' תנור שהסיקוהו סבר רב יוסף למימר תוכו תוכו ממש על גביו על גביו ממש אבל לסמוך שפיר דמי איתיביה אביי כופח שהסיקוהו בקש ובגבבא הרי הוא ככיריים בגפת ובעצים הרי הוא כתנור ואסור הא ככירה שרי במאי עסקינן אילימא על גביו ובמאי אילימא כשאינו גרוף וקטום אלא כירה כי אינה גרופה וקטומה על גביו מי שרי אלא לאו לסמוך וקתני הרי הוא כתנור ואסיר אמר רב אדא בר אהבה הכא בכופח גרוף וקטום ותנור גרופה וקטומה עסקינן הרי הוא כתנור דאע"ג דגרוף וקטום על גביו אסור דאי ככירה כי גרופה וקטומה שפיר דמי: תניא כוותיה דאביי תנור שהסיקוהו בקש ובגבבא אין סומכין לו ואין צריך לומר על גביו ואין צריך לומר לתוכו ואין צריך לומר בגפת ובעצים כופח שהסיקוהו בקש ובגבבא סומכין לו [א] ואין נותנין על גביו בגפת ובעצים אין סומכין לו אמר ליה רב אחא בריה דרבא לרב אשי האי כופח היכי דמי אי ככירה דמי אפילו בגפת ובעצים נמי אי כתנור דמי אפילו בקש ובגבבא נמי לא אמר ליה נפיש הבליה מדכירה וזוטר הבליה מדתנור היכי דמי כופח היכי דמי כירה א"ר יוסי בר חנינא כופח מקום שפיתת קדרה אחת כירה מקום שפיתת שתי קדרות אמר אביי ואיתימא רבי ירמיה אף אנן נמי תנינא ב) כירה שנחלקה לאורכה טהורה לרחבה טמאה כופח בין לאורכו בין לרוחבו טהור: מתני' אין נותנין ביצה בצד המיחם בשביל שתתגלגל ולא יפקיענה בסודרין ור' יוסי מתיר ולא יטמינה בחול ובאבק דרכים בשביל שתצלה מעשה שעשו אנשי טבריא והביאו סילון של צונן לתוך אמה של חמין אמרו להם חכמים אם בשבת כחמין שהוחמו בשבת ואסורין ברחיצה ובשתיה אם ביום טוב כחמין שהוחמו ביום טוב ואסורין ברחיצה ומותרין בשתיה: גמ' איבעיא להו גלגל מאי אמר רב יוסף גלגל חייב חטאת אמר מר בריה דרבינא אף אנן נמי תנינא כל

רש"י

מחזירין אפילו בשבת. ביום המחרת ולא תימא פלוגתייהו משחשכה והתם הוא דשרו משום דמוכחא מילתא דאדעתא דאהדורי לצורך מחר שקיל ליה אבל ביום לא מוכח דשקיל ליה אדעתא דאהדורי ובטלה לה הטמנה וה"ל כמטמין לכתחלה: קומקמום. יורה קטנה: דיוטא. עלייה: למקומו. לכירה: אבל הניח על גבי קרקע אסור. להחזיר דבטלי לה הטמנה דאתמול והוי כמטמין לכתחלה: לגרמיה. יחיד הוא בדבר ואין הלכה כמותו: תלאן במקל מהו. כעודן בידו דמי או כהניחן ע"ג קרקע דמי: פינן ממיחם למיחם מהו. מי הוי כמטמין לכתחלה ואסור להחזירן לכירה או לא: מיחם. קומקמום שמחמם בו חמין: מתני' תנור. מתוך שקצר למעלה ורחב למטה נקלט חומו לתוכו טפי מכירה: כופח. בגמרא מפרש לה עשוי חלל ככירה אבל ארכו כרחבו ואין בו אלא שיעור שפיתת קדירה אחת וכירה יש בה שפיתת שתי קדירות: גמ' על גביו. על שפתו: אבל לסמוך. אצל דופנו: הא ככירה שרי. כלומר מדקתני הרי הוא כתנור מכלל דאי הוה מדמי ליה לכירה הוה שרי ושמעינן מינה דכירה שהוסק בגפת ובעצים שרי: ובמאי קאי. קס"ד בשאינה גרופה ואי על גבה מי שרי: תניא כוותיה דאביי. דאסור לסמוך אתנור: אפי' בגפת ועצים. לשתרי בגרופה וקטומה: שנחלקה לאורכה. הרי בטלו שתי שפיתותיה שנחלקת רחבה לשתים הלכך טהרה מטומאתה שהרי ניתלה: נחלקה לרחבה. נמצאו שתי השפיתות קיימות זו לבדה וזו לבדה: כופח בין לאורכה בין לרחבה טהורה. שהרי ארכה כרחבה וכולה מקום שפיתה אחת: מתני' אין נותנין ביצה בצד המיחם. קומקמום של נחשת: בשביל שתתגלגל. שתצלה קצת עד שתהא מגולגלת: ולא יפקיענה בסודרין. לא ישברנה על סודר שהוחם בחמה כדי שתצלה מחומו של סודר: בחול ובאבק דרכים. שהוחמו מכח חמה. ובגמרא מפרש אמאי לא פליג רבי יוסי בהא: והביאו סילון. מבעוד יום: של צונן. כדי לחממן דהמים נמשכין ובאין כל השבת: לתוך אמה. של חמי טבריא: אם בשבת. אותן שבאו בשבת: ה"ג כחמין שהוחמו:

תוספות

אפילו בשבת. פירש בקונטרס בשבת ביום המחרת ולפ"ז ה"ל למינקט אפי' ביום השבת ולמאי דפרישית דעיקר פלוגתייהו בחול אתי שפיר: פינה ממיחם למיחם מהו. וא"ת דבפרק במה טומנין (לקמן דף נא.) תניא וכן היה רשב"ג אומר לא אסרו אלא באותו מיחם אבל פינה ממיחם למיחם מותר אלמא במיחם אחר שרי טפי והכא משמע איפכא ואור"ת דהכא גבי השהה ע"ג כירה כשהוא באותו מיחם שהוא חם לא אתי לחתויי אבל במיחם אחר שהוא קר אתי לחתויי אבל גבי הטמנה שרי טפי כשהוא קר דבחיתוי מועט לא יועיל:

ורשב"א מפרש בשם ר"י דהתם בהטמנה דהוי לצורך מחר ליכא למיחש לחיתויי דבלא חיתוי יתחמם הרבה אבל הכא דבעי לה בלילה איכא למיחש לחיתויי ומיהו קצת משמע התם דמיירי במטמין בלילה (ת"י):

תנור שהסיקוהו בקש ובגבבא לא יתן כו'. אי להחזיר תנן הכא נמי האי לא יתן לא יחזיר אבל להשהות משהה אפילו בתנור שאינו גרוף וקטום כדמשמע בפ"ק (דף יח:) ° דשרינן קידרא חייתא ובשיל כמאכל בן דרוסאי אפילו באינו גרוף וקטום ומשמע התם דבתנור איירי דקאי אהא דקתני התם לעיל לא תמלא אשה קדרה א) עססיות כו':

אילימא בשאינה גרופה. האי לישנא לאו דוקא דאביי סבר דלא מיתוקמה בגרופה דבגרופה לא מסתבר ליה שיהא חילוק בין גפת ועצים לקש וגבבא דאי הוה מצי אביי לאוקמה בגרופה כדמוקי לה רב אדא לא הוה מצי למפשט מידי ורב אדא דמוקי לה בגרופה סבר דיש לעולם יותר חום כשהסיקוה בגפת ובעצים אע"ג דגרופה מבקש וגבבא:

תניא כוותיה דאביי כו'. יש דגרסי בסיפא כופח שהסיקוהו בגפת ובעצים ב) אין סומכין לה דאי גרס סומכין לה לא אתא כוותיה דאביי דאית ליה דבכופח נמי אין סומכין כדאמרינן לעיל וי"ל דאי גרסינן סומכין איכא לאוקמה בגרופה ונקט גפת ועצים לרבותא דאפילו הכי סומכין לה:

לא יטמינה בחול. אע"ג דאמר בלא יחפור (ב"ב דף יט. ושם) דחול דקריר מקרר דחמים מחים והכא בילה היא קרה הכא מיירי בחול שהוחם בחמה דומיא דאבק דרכים:

מעשה והביאו סילון של צונן לתוך אמה של חמין כו'. מבעוד יום הביאוהו כדפירש בקונטרס ואין שום איסור כלל בהבאה כדתניא בפרק קמא (דף יח.) פותקין מים לגינה ומתמלאת והולכת כל השבת כולה ואסרו ברחיצה גזירה שמא יערבם בשבת ולערבם בשבת אסור משום תולדות האור ושיבא כחדא גזירה ג) ואם היינו מפרשים דבסילון היו בו נקבים וכשהיו רוחצים בשבת היו פותחים הנקבים ומתערבין הצוננין בחמין הוה אתי שפיר טפי דהשתא ליכא אלא חדא גזירה אטו חמי האור אך בגמרא מדמי לה להטמנה מבעוד יום וילף מינה לאסור להטמין

עין משפט נר מצוה

ט א ב ג ד ה ו ז מיי' פ"ג מהל' שבת הלכה ה ז י סמג לאוין סה טוש"ע א"ח סימן רנג סעיף ב:

י ח מיי' פט"ז מהל' כלים הלכה יג:

יא ט י מיי' פ"ט מהל' שבת הל' ב ג טוש"ע א"ח סי' שיח סעיף ג:

יב כ מיי' פכ"ב מהל' שבת הלכה ג סמג שם טוש"ע א"ח סימן שכו סעיף ג וסימן רמו סעיף א וסעיף ו:

[יב] כ [מיי' פ"ט מהל' שבת הלכה ב]:

תוספות ישנים

א) ואי מתני' להשהות תנן בתנור נמי אסור להשהות. אע"ג דקידרא חייתא לעיל שרי ההוא כחנניא ומתני' אי להשהות תנן אתיא דלא כחנניא:

ב) ולפ"ז צריך למגרס בתר הכי ואצ"ל ע"ג ואצ"ל בתוכה. ואי גרסי' סומכין גרסי' ונותנין אפילו ע"ג ואפילו בתוכה:

ג) והא דחשיב לה כחמין שהוחמו בשבת משמע טפי כפי' ראשון:

רבינו חננאל

כן אלא לשבת הבאה וכן סוגיא דשמעתא: פיס' בה"א אף מחזירין אוקימנא הא דקתני מחזירין בשבת הוא ואפי' כמה פעמים ודוקא בכירה גרופה וקטומה והני מילי שלא הניחם ע"ג קרקע כלל אלא מחזיקם בידו ודעתו עליהם להחזירם הוא ששנינו אף מחזירין אבל אם הניחם ע"ג קרקע אע"פ שהיה בדעתו להחזירם לכירה אסור ואסיקנא לשמעתא בתרי לשני. וקי"ל כל כי האי גוונא בדאורייתא עבדינן לחומרא. ושבת איסורא דאורייתא היא: תלאם במקל או הניחם ע"ג המטה או הניחם בכרעי המטה או פינם ממיחם למיחם הני כולהו איבעא ולא אפשיטו ועלו בתיקו. וקי"ל כל תיקו דאיסורא לחומרא: מתני' תנור שהסיקו בקש ובגבבא כו' אוקמא אביי לא יסמוך. תניא כוותיה תנור שהסיקו בקש ובגבבא אין סומכין לו ואין צ"ל על גביו. ואין צ"ל שהסיקו בגפת או בעצים. כופח שהסיקוה בקש ובגבבא הרי הוא ככירה. בגפת ובעצים הרי הוא כתנור ואסור. ואע"פ שהוא גרוף וקטום. ואסיק' כופח מקום שפיתת קדירה אחת. כירה מקום שפיתת ב' קדירות. ודייקינן לה מהא דתנן כירה שנחלקה לארכה טהור לרחבה טמא פי' עדיין תורת כלי עליה דהא יכול לשפות קדירה אחת. כופח בין לארכה בין לרחבה טהורה. והאי כופח נפיש הבליה מדכירה וזוטר הבליה מדתנור וקי"ל מתני' בתנור של נחתומין. מפורש בלא יחפור (ב"ב כ:) אבל תנור [דידן] ככירה של נחתומין היא: פיס' אין נותנין ביצה בצד המיחם בשביל שתתגלגל גלגל

מסורת הש"ס

א) [ברכות מח. וש"נ], ב) כלים פ"ז מ"ג.

גליון הש"ס

תוס' ד"ה תנור כו' דשרינן קידרא חייתא ובשיל כמאכל בן דרוסאי. ק"ל הא שם לא נזכר מן מאב"ד אלא סתם ובשיל שפיר דמי אלא דתוס' כתבו שם דהיינו כמאב"ד דהא קיימא לן כחנניא וא"כ איך עשו כאן הוכחה מזה דלמא באמת תנור חמיר דכמאב"ד אסור ודאמרי' ובשיל ש"ד היינו כפשוטו ובשיל לגמרי. גם אמאי לא הוכיחו כפשוטו דהא קתני ולא חררה על גבי גחלים אלא כדי שיקרמו פניה חררה היינו בתנור כמ"ש תוס' לעיל דף לז ע"א ד"ה אא"כ וכו' אף על גב דחררה בתוכה היא. והיינו ע"כ משום דחררה אופין בתנור. עכ"פ ראייתם מפ"ק תמוה מאד:

הגהות הגר"א

[א] גמ' סומכין לו ואין נותנין. נ"ב נ"ל סומכין לו ונותנין כו':

ליקוטי רש"י

לעילא מר' חייא רבה. לפניו וכן לשון הש"ס והמקרא שרפים עומדים ממעל לו (ישעיה ו) ועל שם שיראים להתקרב לפניו עומדין מרחוק [לעיל ל. ע"ש בב"ח]. דיוטא. היא עלייה העליונה שעל גג הבית [רשב"ם ב"ב קמח.]. לגרמיה הוא דעבד. אין אדם מודה לו [ברכות מח.]. לדעתיה [מ"ק כה:]. תנור. תנור וכירים כלים המטלטלין הם והם של חרס ויש להן תוך ושופת את הקדרה על נקב החלל ושניהם פיהם למעלה [ויקרא יא, לה]. תנור כלי חרס הוא שרוף בכבשן כשאר קדירות ופיו למעלה והכא לקובעו בארץ עושה בנין טיט ואבנים שיהיו לו לבסים ומושיבין אותו עליו שלא יטלטלנו שוליו מחמת קרקע [ב"ב יז.]. וכל תנור שבמשנה קטן הוא ומקום שפיתת ב' קדירות ופיו למעלה [ע"ז לה: עיין מו"ק י. ובב"ח שם, נדה כו. ובתוס' שם: ד"ה בפלוגתא]. שפיתת קדרה. כשמושיבין הסיר על גבי כירה קרי לה שפיתה [סוטה יא:]. קדירה כשמניחין אותה אצל האור על גבי כירה קרי שפיתה לשון שפות הסיר (יחזקאל כד) [ע"ז יב.]. שפות הסיר ע"פ הכירה במקום מושבה היא קרויה שפיתה כלשון המשנה מקום שפיתת שתי קדירות ועוד שניהם אחד שופת את הקדירה ואחד נותן לתוכה מים ואחד נותן לתוכה תבלין למדנו שהשפיתה היא הושבתה על פי הכירה עד שלא יתנו לתוכה כלום [יחזקאל כד, ג]. ומנחם פתר כל לשון שפיתה לשון שימה [תהלים כב, טז]. בשביל שתתגלגל. מגולגלת. צלויה רכה [עירובין מא.]. לתוך אמה של חמין. חמי טבריא מעינות רותחין [פסחים מא.].

tanur.[16] – ? –

Abaye's challenge is rebuffed:

אָמַר רַב אַדָּא בַּר אַהֲבָה – **Rav Adda bar Ahavah said:** הָכָא בְּכוּפָּח גָּרוּף וְקָטוּם וְתַנּוּר גְּרוּפָה וּקְטוּמָה עַסְקִינַן – **Here,** in the Mishnah, **we are** in fact **dealing with a *kupach* that was shoveled or banked and** with **a *tanur* that was shoveled or banked,** and we are dealing with placing food on *top* of it, and this is what the Mishnah means: הֲרֵי הוּא כְּתַנּוּר – If a *kupach* was heated with marc or with wood **it is treated like a *tanur*** דְּאַף עַל גַּב דְּגָרוּף וְקָטוּם עַל גַּבָּיו אָסוּר – in **that even though it was shoveled or banked it is forbidden** to place food **on top of it,** דְּאִי כְּכִירָה כִּי גְּרוּפָה וּקְטוּמָה שַׁפִּיר דָּמֵי – **whereas if** the *kupach* had been treated **like a *kirah,* once it was shoveled or banked it would be acceptable** to place food on top of it.[17]

The Gemara adduces support for Abaye's view that it is forbidden to place food alongside a *tanur*:

תַּנְיָא כְּוָותֵיהּ דְּאַבַּיֵי – **A Baraisa was taught in accordance with** the view of **Abaye:** תַּנּוּר שֶׁהִסִּיקוּהוּ בְּקַשׁ וּבִגְבָבָא – Concerning **A *TANUR* THAT WAS HEATED WITH STRAW OR WITH STUBBLE** – אֵין סוֹמְכִין לוֹ – **WE MAY NOT PLACE** food **ALONGSIDE IT,** וְאֵין צָרִיךְ לוֹמַר עַל גַּבָּיו – **AND IT GOES WITHOUT SAYING** that we may not place food **ON TOP OF IT,** וְאֵין צָרִיךְ לוֹמַר לְתוֹכוֹ – **AND IT GOES WITHOUT SAYING** that we may not place food **INSIDE IT;** וְאֵין צָרִיךְ לוֹמַר בְּגֶפֶת וּבְעֵצִים – **AND IT GOES WITHOUT SAYING** that we may not place food alongside, on top of or inside it if it was heated **WITH MARC OR WITH WOOD.** כּוּפָּח שֶׁהִסִּיקוּהוּ בְּקַשׁ וּבִגְבָבָא – Concerning **A *KUPACH* THAT WAS HEATED WITH STRAW OR WITH STUBBLE** – (ואין) [ו]נוֹתְנִין עַל סוֹמְכִין לוֹ – **WE MAY PLACE** food **ALONGSIDE IT,** גַּבָּיו – **AND WE MAY PLACE** food **ON TOP OF IT.**[18] בְּגֶפֶת וּבְעֵצִים – If it was heated **WITH MARC OR WITH WOOD,** אֵין סוֹמְכִין לוֹ – **WE MAY NOT** even **PLACE** food **ALONGSIDE IT.**[19]

The Gemara analyzes the status of a *kupach:*

אָמַר לֵיהּ רַב אַחָא בְּרֵיהּ דְּרָבָא לְרַב אַשִׁי – **Rav Acha the son of Rava said to Rav Ashi:** הַאי כּוּפָּח הֵיכִי דָּמֵי – **What is** the nature of **a *kupach*?** אִי כְּכִירָה דָּמֵי אֲפִילּוּ בְּגֶפֶת וּבְעֵצִים נַמִּי – **If it is like a *kirah,*** then **even** if it is heated **with marc or with wood** one should **also** be allowed to place food on top of it as long as it was shoveled or banked.[20] אִי כְּתַנּוּר דָּמֵי אֲפִילּוּ בְּקַשׁ וּבִגְבָבָא נַמִּי לֹא – **And if it is like a *tanur,*** then **even** if it is fueled **with straw or with stubble** one **should also not** be allowed to place food on it!? אָמַר לֵיהּ – **[Rav Ashi] replied:** נְפִישׁ הַבְלֵיהּ מִדְּכִירָה וְזוּטַר הַבְלֵיהּ מִדְּתַנּוּר – **It is hotter than a *kirah* but not as hot as a *tanur.*** Its status is therefore somewhere between that of a *kirah* and that of a *tanur*: When fueled with straw or with stubble it is treated like a *kirah,* but when fueled with marc or with wood it is treated like a *tanur.*[21]

The Gemara explains how a *kupach* is distinguished from a *kirah* in its physical appearance:

הֵיכִי דָּמֵי כּוּפָּח הֵיכִי דָּמֵי כִּירָה – **What is a *kupach* like and what is a *kirah* like?** אָמַר רַבִּי יוֹסֵי בַּר חֲנִינָא – **R' Yose bar Chanina said:** כּוּפָּח מְקוֹם שְׁפִיתַת קְדֵרָה אַחַת – **A *kupach*** is square and **has room for the placement of one pot,** כִּירָה מְקוֹם שְׁפִיתַת שְׁתֵּי קְדֵרוֹת – whereas **a *kirah*** is rectangular and **has room for the placement of two pots.**

The Gemara corroborates these definitions:

אָמַר אַבַּיֵי וְאִיתֵּימָא רַבִּי יִרְמְיָה – **Abaye said, or perhaps** it was **R' Yirmiyah** who said: אַף אֲנַן נַמִּי תְּנֵינָא – **We learned likewise in the following Mishnah:**[22] כִּירָה שֶׁנֶּחְלְקָה לְאׇרְכָּהּ טְהוֹרָה – **A *KIRAH* THAT** had been *tamei* and **WAS SPLIT LENGTHWISE BECOMES *TAHOR,*** for since it can no longer accommodate a pot it is not considered a utensil. לְרׇחְבָּהּ טְמֵאָה – But if it was split **WIDTHWISE IT IS** still ***TAMEI,*** since each half can still accommodate a single pot.[23] כּוּפָּח בֵּין לְאׇרְכּוֹ בֵּין לְרׇחְבּוֹ טָהוֹר – Concerning **A *KUPACH,* WHETHER** it is split **LENGTHWISE OR WIDTHWISE IT IS *TAHOR,*** since either way it cannot accommodate a pot.[24] We learn from this Mishnah that a *kirah* that is intact can accommodate two pots whereas a *kupach* that is intact can accommodate only one pot.

NOTES

16. Abaye presumes that the Mishnah must be dealing with an unshoveled and unbanked *kupach* because he reasons that once a *kupach* was shoveled or banked it is no longer intensely hot and does not warrant being treated like a *tanur,* even though it was initially heated with marc or wood. The wording of Abaye's challenge – "If you will say [we are dealing with] a *kupach* that was not shoveled or banked" – is a bit loose, since Abaye holds that we must be dealing with such a *kupach* (*Tosafos* ד״ה אילימא).

17. Rav Adda bar Ahavah holds that a *kupach* that was heated with marc or wood remains hotter than a similarly heated *kirah* even after the *kupach* is shoveled or banked. Therefore, it is treated like a *tanur* and placing food on top of it is always forbidden. Placing food alongside the *kupach* or *tanur* is not necessarily the subject of the Mishnah's discussion and may in fact be permissible, as Rav Yosef presumed above.

Note that according to those who hold that the halachah follows Chananyah's opinion (see 37a note 16), our discussion is relevant to *replacing* food on top of or alongside a *kupach* or *tanur.* Leaving food there before the Sabbath is permitted in all circumstances, as long as it has been cooked like the food of Ben Derusai (*Rashba*).

18. Our emendation of the text follows *Hagahos HaGra.* It is indisputably correct, since the Mishnah stated that a *kupach* that was heated with straw or stubble is treated like a *kirah,* which means that one may place food on top of it even if it was not shoveled or banked.

19. According to Abaye, this pertains only if the coals were not shoveled away or banked (*Tosafos* ד״ה תניא כוותיה; see note 16).

20. *Rashi.* Rav Acha presumes that the Mishnah means to equate a marc- or wood-fueled *kupach* with a *tanur* even if the coals were shoveled or banked, as Rav Adda bar Ahavah presumed above. He questions why it is treated more stringently than a *kirah* in this respect yet equal to a *kirah* in another respect, which he goes on to mention (*Rosh;* see following note).

21. Thus, even if the coals are shoveled away or banked, it is forbidden to place food on it – just like a *tanur* (*Rosh*).

Note that this Gemara follows Rav Adda bar Ahavah's interpretation of the Mishnah as equating the marc- or wood-fueled *kupach* with a *tanur* even if it was shoveled or banked. Although a Baraisa was cited above in support of Abaye's view, it supported Abaye only insofar as forbidding the placement of food alongside a *kupach.* It offered no indication, however, whether the *kupach* to which it refers was shoveled or banked. Our Gemara considers it more reasonable to equate the marc- or wood-fueled *kupach* with the *tanur* entirely, and to forbid placing food on top, inside and alongside it even if it was shoveled or banked. Thus, the halachah follows Abaye in the regard that it is forbidden to place food alongside a marc- or wood-fueled *kupach* or a *tanur,* for the Baraisa stated this explicitly. But the halachah follows Rav Adda bar Ahavah in the regard that a marc- or wood-fueled *kupach* is treated like a *tanur* even if it was shoveled or banked (*Rosh, Rashba, Ran, Mishnah Berurah* 253:27).

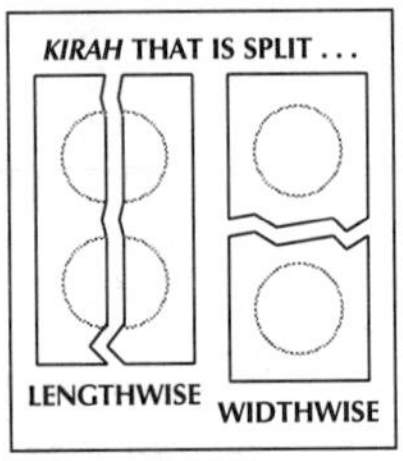

22. *Keilim* 7:3.

23. Any vessel that was *tamei* and then broke so that it no longer serves a semblance of its original function becomes *tahor* (see *Leviticus* 11:33-35; *Rambam, Hil. Keilim* 6:1). Since a *kirah* is rectangular and is designed to accommodate two pots, it becomes *tahor* only if it breaks lengthwise, so that each half cannot be used for cooking. If it breaks widthwise, however, each half can still accommodate one pot, and since it still serves a semblance of its original function it remains *tamei* (*Rashi*). See diagram (left).

24. Since the *kupach* is square, a split in either direction renders it useless (*Rashi*). See diagram (right).

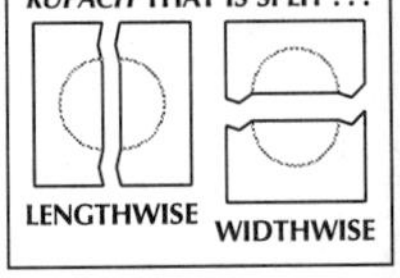

מחזירין אפילו בשבת ואף ר' אושעיא סבר אף מחזירין אפי' בשבת דא"ר אושעיא פעם אחת היינו עומדים לעילא מר' חייא רבה והעלנו לו קומקמום של חמין מדיוטא התחתונה לדיוטא העליונה ומזגנו לו את הכוס והחזרנוהו למקומו ולא אמר לנו דבר א"ר זריקא א"ר אבא א"ר תדאי לא שנו אלא שעודן בידו אבל הניחן ע"ג קרקע אסור א"ר אמי ר' תדאי [א] דעבד לגרמיה הוא דעבד אלא הכי א"ר חייא א"ר יוחנן אפילו הניחה על גבי קרקע מותר פליגי בה רב דימי ורב שמואל בר יהודה ותרוייהו משמיה דרבי אלעזר אמרי חד אמר [ב] עודן בידו מותר ע"ג קרקע אסור וחד אמר הניחן על גבי קרקע נמי מותר אמר חזקיה משמיה דאביי הא דאמרת עודן בידו מותר לא אמרן אלא [ג] שדעתו להחזיר אבל אין דעתו להחזיר אסור מכלל דעל גבי קרקע אע"פ שדעתו להחזיר אסור איכא דאמרי אמר חזקיה משמיה דאביי הא דאמרת על גבי קרקע אסור לא אמרן אלא שאין דעתו להחזיר אבל דעתו להחזיר מותר מכלל שבעודן בידו אע"פ שאין דעתו להחזיר מותר בעי ר' ירמיה תלאן במקל מהו הניחן על גבי מטה מהו בעי רב אשי פינן ממיחם למיחם מהו תיקו: **מתני'** [ד] תנור שהסיקוהו בקש ובגבבא לא יתן בין מתוכו בין מעל גביו כופח שהסיקוהו בקש ובגבבא ה"ז ככיריים בגפת ובעצים הרי הוא כתנור: **גמ'** תנור שהסיקוהו סבר רב יוסף למימר תוכו תוכו ממש על גביו על גביו ממש אבל לסמוך שפיר דמי איתיביה אביי כופח שהסיקוהו בקש ובגבבא הרי הוא ככיריים בגפת ובעצים הרי הוא כתנור ואסור הא כבירה שרי במאי עסקינן אילימא על גביו ובמאי אילימא כשאינו גרוף וקטום אלא כירה כי אינה גרופה וקטומה על גביו מי שרי אלא לאו לסמוך וקתני הרי הוא כתנור ואסיר אמר רב אדא בר אהבה הכא בכופח גרוף וקטום ותנור גרופה וקטומה עסקינן הרי הוא כתנור [ה] דאע"ג דגרוף וקטום על גביו אסור דאי ככירה כי גרופה וקטומה שפיר דמי: תניא כוותיה דאביי [ו] תנור שהסיקוהו בקש ובגבבא אין סומכין לו ואין צריך לומר על גביו ואין צריך לומר לתוכו ואין צריך לומר בגפת ובעצים כופח שהסיקוהו בקש ובגבבא סומכין לו [א] ואין נותנין על גביו בגפת ובעצים אין סומכין לו אמר ליה רב אחא בריה דרבא לרב אשי האי כופח היכי דמי אי ככירה דמי אפילו בגפת ובעצים נמי אי כתנור דמי אפילו בקש ובגבבא נמי לא אמר ליה נפיש הבליה מדכירה וזוטר הבליה מדתנור היכי דמי כופח היכי דמי כירה א"ר יוסי בר חנינא [ז] כופח מקום שפיתת קדרה אחת כירה מקום שפיתת שתי קדרות אמר אביי ואיתימא רבי ירמיה אף אנן נמי תנינא [ג] כירה [ח] שנחלקה לאורכה טהורה לרחבה טמאה כופח בין לאורכו בין לרוחבו טהור: **מתני'** [ט] אין נותנין ביצה בצד המיחם בשביל שתתגלגל ולא יפקיענה בסודרין ור' יוסי מתיר [י] ולא יטמינה בחול ובאבק דרכים בשביל שתצלה מעשה שעשו אנשי טבריא [כ] והביאו סילון של צונן לתוך אמה של חמין אמרו להם חכמים אם בשבת כחמין שהוחמו בשבת ואסורין ברחיצה ובשתיה אם ביום טוב כחמין שהוחמו ביום טוב ואסורין ברחיצה ומותרין בשתיה: **גמ'** איבעיא להו גלגל מאי אמר רב יוסף [ב] גלגל חייב חטאת אמר מר בריה דרבינא אף אנן נמי תנינא כל

מחזירין אפילו בשבת. ביום המחרת ולא תימא פלוגתייהו משחשכה והתם הוא דשרו משום דמוכחא מילתא דאדעתא דאהדורי לצורך מחר שקיל ליה אבל ביום לא מוכח דשקיל ליה אדעתא דאהדורי ובטלה לה הטמנה וה"ל כמטמין לכתחלה: קומקמום. יורה קטנה: דיוטא. עלייה: למקומו. לכירה: אבל הניח על גבי קרקע אסור. להחזיר דבטלי לה הטמנה דאתמול והוי כמטמין לכתחלה: לגרמיה. יחיד הוא בדבר ואין הלכה כמותו: תלאן במקל מהו. כעודן בידו דמי או כהניחן ע"ג קרקע דמי: פינן ממיחם למיחם מהו. מי הוי כמטמין לכתחלה ואסור להחזירן לכירה או לא: מיחם. קומקמום שמחמם בו חמין: **מתני'** תנור. מתוך שקצר למעלה ורחב למטה נקלט חומו לתוכו טפי מכירה: כופח. בגמרא מפרש לה עשוי חלל ככירה אבל ארכו כרחבו ואין בו אלא שיעור שפיתת קדירה אחת וכירה יש בה שפיתת שתי קדירות: **גמ'** על גביו. על שפתו: אבל לסמוך. אצל דופנו: הא ככירה שרי. כלומר מדקתני הרי הוא כתנור מכלל דאי הוה מדמי ליה לכירה הוה שרי ושמעינן מינה דכירה שהוסק בגפת ובעצים שרי: ובמאי קאי. קס"ד בשאינה גרופה ואי על גבה מי שרי: תניא כוותיה דאביי. דאסור לסמוך אתנור: אפי' בגפת ועצים. לשתרי בגרופה וקטומה: שנחלקה לאורכה. הרי בטלו שתי שפיתותיה שנחלקת רחבה לשתים הלכך טהרה מטומאתה שהרי ניתצה: נחלקה לרחבה. נמצאו שתי השפיתות קיימות זו לבדה וזו לבדה: כופח בין לאורכה בין לרחבה טהורה. שהרי ארכה כרחבה וכולה מקום שפיתה אחת: **מתני'** אין נותנין ביצה בצד המיחם. קומקמום של נחשת: בשביל שתתגלגל. שתצלה קצת עד שתהא מגולגלת: ולא יפקיענה בסודרין. לא ישברנה על סודר שהוחם בחמה כדי שתצלה מחומו של סודר: בחול ובאבק דרכים. שהוחמו מכח חמה. ובגמרא מפרש אמאי לא פליג רבי יוסי בהא: והביאו סילון. מבעוד יום: של צונן. כדי לחממן דהמים נמשכין ובאין כל השבת: לתוך אמה. של חמי טבריא: אם בשבת. אותן שבאו בשבת: ה"ג כחמין שהוחמו:

אפילו בשבת. פירש בקונטרס בשבת ביום המחרת ולפ"ז ה"ל למינקט אפי' ביום השבת ולמאי דפרישית דעיקר פלוגתייהו בחול אתי שפיר: **פינה** ממיחם למיחם מהו. וא"ת דבפרק במה טומנין (לקמן דף נא.) תניא וכן היה רשב"ג אומר לא אסרו אלא באותו מיחם אבל פינה ממיחם למיחם מותר אלמא במיחם אחר שרי טפי והכא משמע איפכא ואור"ת דהכא גבי השהה ע"ג כירה כשהוא באותו מיחם שהוא חם לא אתי לחתויי אבל במיחם אחר שהוא קר אתי לחתויי אבל גבי הטמנה שרי טפי כשהוא קר דחיתוי מועט לא יועיל:

ורשב"א מפרש בשם ר"י דהתם בהטמנה דהוי לצורך מחר ליכא למיחש לחיתויי דבלא חיתוי יתחמם הרבה אבל הכא דבעי לה בלילה איכא למיחש לחיתויי ומיהו קצת משמע התם דמיירי במטמין בלילה (ת"י):

תנור שהסיקוהו בקש ובגבבא לא יתן כו'. אי להחזיר תנן הכא נמי האי לא יתן לא יחזיר אבל להשהות משהה אפילו בתנור שאינו גרוף וקטום כדמשמע בפ"ק (דף יח:) [ט] דשרינן קידרא חייתא ובשיל כמאכל בן דרוסאי אפילו באינו גרוף וקטום ומשמע התם דבתנור איירי דקאי אהא דקתני התם לעיל לא תמלא אשה קדרה [א] עססיות כו':

אילימא בשאינה גרופה. האי לישנא לאו דוקא דאביי סבר דלא מיתוקמה בגרופה דבגרופה לא מסתבר ליה שיהא חילוק בין גפת ועצים לקש וגבבא דאי הוה מצי אביי לאוקמה בגרופה כדמוקי לה רב אדא לא הוה מצי למפשט מידי ורב אדא דמוקי לה בגרופה סבר דיש לעולם יותר חום כשהסיקוה בגפת ובעצים אע"ג דגרופה מבקש וגבבא:

תניא כוותיה דאביי כו'. יש דגרסי בסיפא כופח שהסיקוהו בגפת ובעצים [ב] אין סומכין לה דאי גרס סומכין לה לא אתא כוותיה דאביי דאית ליה דבכופח נמי אין סומכין כדאמרינן לעיל וי"ל דאי גרסינן סומכין איכא לאוקמה בגרופה ונקט גפת ועצים לרבותא דאפילו הכי סומכין לה:

לא יטמיננה בחול. אע"ג דאמר בלא יחפור (ב"ב דף יט. ושם) דחול דקריר מקרר דחמים מחים והכא בילה היא קרה הכא מיירי בחול שהוחם בחמה דומיא דאבק דרכים:

מעשה והביאו סילון של צונן לתוך אמה של חמין כו'. מבעוד יום הביאוהו כדפירש בקונטרס ואין שום איסור כלל בהבאה כדתניא בפרק קמא (דף יח.) פותקין מים לגינה ומתמלאת והולכת כל השבת כולה ואסרו ברחיצה גזירה שמא יערבם בשבת ולערבם בשבת אסור משום תולדות האור ושיבא כחדא גזירה [ג] ולא הייתו מפרשים דבסילון היו בו נקבים וכשהיו רוצים בשבת היו פותחים הנקבים ומתערבין הצוננין בחמין הוה אתי שפיר טפי דהשתא ליכא אלא חדא גזירה אטו חמי האור אך בגמרא מדמי לה להטמנה מבעוד יום ויליף מינה לאסור להטמין

תוספות ישנים

א) ואי מתני' להשהות תנן בתנור נמי אסור להשהות. אע"ג דקידרא חייתא לעיל שרי ההוא כחנניא ומתני' אי להשהות תנן אתיא דלא כחנניא: ב) ולפ"ז צריך למגרס בתר הכי ואל"ל ע"ג ואל"ל בתוכה. ואי גרסי' סומכין גרסי' ונותנין אפילו ע"ג ואפילו בתוכה: ג) והא דחשיב לה כחמין שהוחמו בשבת משמע טפי כפי' ראשון:

רבינו חננאל

כן אלא לשבת הבאה וכן סוגיא דשמעתא: **פיס' בה"א** אף מחזירין אוקימנא הא דקתני מחזירין בשבת הוא ואפי' כמה פעמים ודוקא בכירה גרופה וקטומה והני מילי שלא הניחם ע"ג קרקע כלל אלא מחזיקם בידו ודעתו עליהם להחזירם הוא ששנינו אף מחזירין אבל אם הניחם ע"ג קרקע אע"פ שהיה בדעתו להחזירם לכירה אסור ואסיקנא לשמעתא בתרי לשני. וקי"ל כל כי האי גוונא בדאורייתא עבדינן לחומרא. ושבת איסורא דאורייתא היא: תלאם במקל או הניחם ע"ג המטה או הניחם בכרעי המטה או פינם ממיחם למיחם הני כולהו איבעא ולא אפשיטו ועלו בתיקו. וקי"ל כל תיקו דאיסורא לחומרא: **מתני'** תנור שהסיקו בקש ובגבבא כו' אוקמא אביי לא יסמוך. תניא כוותיה תנור שהסיקו בקש ובגבבא אין סומכין לו ואין צ"ל על גביו. ואין צ"ל שהסיקו בגפת או בעצים. כופח שהסיקוה בקש ובגבבא הרי הוא ככירה. בגפת ובעצים הרי הוא כתנור ואסור. ואע"פ שהוא גרוף וקטום. ואסיק' כופח מקום שפיתת קדירה אחת. כירה מקום שפיתת ב' קדירות. ודייקינן לה מהא דתנן כירה שנחלקה לארכה טהור לרחבה טמא פי' עדיין תורת כלי עליה דהא יכול לשפות קדירה אחת. כופח בין לארכה בין לרחבה טהורה. והאי כופח נפיש הבליה מדכירה וזוטר הבליה מדתנור וקי"ל מתני' בתנור של נחתומין. מפורש בלא יחפור (ב"ב כ:) אבל תנור [דידן] ככירה של נחתומין היא: **פיס'** אין נותנין ביצה בצד המיחם בשביל שתתגלגל גלגל

גליון הש"ס

תוס' ד"ה תנור כו' דשרינן קידרא חייתא ובשיל כמאכל בן דרוסאי. ק"ל הא שם לא נזכר מן מאב"ד אלא קמס ובשיל שפיר דמי אלא דתוס' כתבו שם דהיינו כמאב"ד דהא קיימא לן כחנניא וא"כ איך עשו כאן הוכחה מזה דלמא באמת תנור חמיר דכמאב"ד אסור ודאמרי' ובשיל ש"ד היינו כפשוטו ובשיל לגמרי. גם אמאי לא הוכיחו כפשוטו דהא קתני ולא חררה על גבי גחלים אלא כדי שיקרמו פניה חררה היינו בתנור כמ"ש תוס' לעיל דף לז ע"א ד"ה אא"כ וכו' אף על גב דחררה בתוכה היא. והיינו ע"כ משום דחררה אופין בתנור. עכ"פ ראייתם מפ"ק תמוה מאד:

הגהות הגר"א

[א] גמ' סומכין לו ואין נותנין. נ"ב צ"ל סומכין לו ונותנין כו':

ליקוטי רש"י

לעילא מר' חייא רבה. לפניו וכן לשון הש"ס והמקרא שרפים עומדים ממעל לו (ישעיה ו) ועל שם שיראים להתקרב לפניו עומדין מרחוק [לעיל ל. ע"ש בב"ח]. דיוטא. היא עלייה העליונה שעל גג הבית [רשב"ם ב"ב קמח.]. לגרמיה הוא דעבד. אין אדם מודה לו [ברכות מח.]. לדעתיה [מ"ק כה:]. תנור. תנור וכירים כלים המטלטלין הם והם של חרס ויש להן תוך ושופת את הקדרה על נקב החלל וסניהם פיהם למעלה [ויקרא יא, לה]. תנור כלי חרס הוא שרוף בכבשן כשאר קדירות ופיו למעלה והכא לקובעו בארץ עושה בנין טיט ואבנים שיהיו לו לבסים ומושיבין אותו עליו שלא יטנטנו שוליו מתחת קרקע [ב"ב יז.]. וכל תנור שבמשנה קטן הוא ומקום שפיתת ב' קדירות ופיו למעלה [ע"ז לה: עיין מו"ק י. ובב"ח שם, נדה כו. ובתוס' שם: ד"ה בפלוגתא]. שפיתת קדרה. כשמושיבין הסיר על גבי כירה קרי לה שפיתה [סוטה יא:]. קדירה כשמניחין אותה אצל האור על גבי כירה קרי שפיתה לשון שפות הסיר (יחזקאל כד) [ע"ז יב.]. שפות הסיר ע"פ הכירה במקום מושבה היא קרויה שפיתה בלשון המשנה מקום שפיתת שתי קדירות ועוד שניו אחד שופת את הקדירה ואחד נותן לתוכה מים ואחד נותן לתוכה תבלין למדנו שהשפיתה היא הושבתה על פי הכירה עד שלא יתנו לתוכה כלום [יחזקאל כד, ג]. ומנחם פתר כל לשון שפיתה לשון שימה [תהלים כב, טז]. בשביל שתתגלגל. מגולגלת. צלויה רכה [עירובין מא.]. לתוך אמה של חמין. חמי טבריא מעיינות רותחין [פסחים מא.].

Mishnah The Mishnah discusses cooking on the Sabbath by means of unconventional sources of heat: **אֵין נוֹתְנִין בֵּיצָה בְּצַד הַמֵּיחַם בִּשְׁבִיל שֶׁתִּתְגַּלְגֵּל – We may not place an egg beside a** hot **kettle** on the Sabbath **in order that it be slightly roasted,**[25] **וְלֹא יַפְקִיעֶנָּה בְּסוּדָרִין – nor may one break it open** and fry it **upon** hot **scarves** that had baked in the sun, **וְרַבִּי יוֹסֵי מַתִּיר – but R' Yose permits** this;[26] **וְלֹא יַטְמִינֶנָּה בְּחוֹל וּבַאֲבַק דְּרָכִים בִּשְׁבִיל שֶׁתִּצָּלֶה – nor may one bury it in sand or in dust of the roads** that have baked in the sun **in order that it be roasted.**[27] **מַעֲשֶׂה שֶׁעָשׂוּ אַנְשֵׁי טְבֶרְיָא – There was an incident in which the people of Tiberias went ahead וְהֵבִיאוּ סִילוֹן שֶׁל צוֹנֵן לְתוֹךְ אַמָּה שֶׁל חַמִּין – and ran a pipe of cold water into a canal of hot** spring **water** before the Sabbath, so that cold water would be heated automatically on the Sabbath.[28] **אָמְרוּ לָהֶם חֲכָמִים – The Sages said to them: אִם בְּשַׁבָּת – If** water flowed through the pipe **on the Sabbath, כְּחַמִּין שֶׁהוּחַמּוּ בְּשַׁבָּת – it is like hot water that was heated** manually **on the Sabbath, וַאֲסוּרִין בִּרְחִיצָה וּבִשְׁתִיָּה – and is forbidden for** both **bathing and drinking.**[29] **אִם בְּיוֹם טוֹב – If** water would flow through it **on a festival, כְּחַמִּין שֶׁהוּחַמּוּ בְּיוֹם טוֹב –** it would be **like hot water that was heated** manually **on a festival, וַאֲסוּרִין בִּרְחִיצָה וּמוּתָּרִין בִּשְׁתִיָּה – and** would be **forbidden for bathing but permitted for drinking.**[30]

Gemara The Gemara cites an inquiry concerning the Mishnah's first ruling:

אִיבַּעְיָא לְהוּ – They inquired: גִּלְגֵּל מַאי – What if one did roast an egg **slightly** by the heat of a kettle? Did he thereby transgress the Biblical prohibition of cooking?[31]

The inquiry is resolved:

אָמַר רַב יוֹסֵף – Rav Yosef said: גִּלְגֵּל חַיָּיב חַטָּאת – If one roasted it **slightly he is liable to a *chatas* offering,** for he has transgressed a Biblical prohibition.[32]

A support is brought for Rav Yosef's ruling:

אָמַר מַר בְּרֵיהּ דְּרָבִינָא – Mar the son of Ravina said: אַף אֲנַן נַמִּי תְּנֵינָא – We learned likewise in the following **Mishnah:**[33]

NOTES

25. Literally: in order that it should roll. A raw egg does not roll freely. As the egg begins to harden by cooking or roasting, it rolls more readily (see *Rashi* and *Chachmas Manoach*; see *Mussaf HeAruch* s.v. גלגל 1). The Mishnah refers to a slight degree of roasting that is sufficient only to make the egg roll, because the wall of a kettle is not hot enough to roast an egg fully (*Ritva, MHK* ed.; see *Rashash*).

The point of the Mishnah is to teach that even after the kettle has been removed from the fire, it is forbidden to use its heat to roast an egg slightly (*Rosh Yosef*). Cooking with a source of heat that is *derived* from a fire is tantamount to cooking with fire itself (see Gemara and *Rambam, Hil. Shabbos* 9:2).

26. Although the heat of the scarves is derived not from fire, but from the sun, the Tanna Kamma nevertheless prohibits using its heat for cooking. R' Yose, however, permits cooking with heat that is derived from the sun. The Gemara (39a) explains the basis of this dispute.

27. R' Yose concedes that although the heat of the sand or dust is derived from the sun it is forbidden to cook with them. The Gemara (39a) explains his reasoning (*Rashi*).

28. The city of Tiberias is noted for its thermal springs. However, some Tiberians found the spring waters putrid and wanted to bathe in fresh water on the Sabbath. To make hot water available for this purpose, they ran a pipe of fresh water through a canal of hot spring water, so that the fresh water would be heated while passing through it. The pipe emptied into an adjacent pool in which they bathed. Since they ran the pipe through the canal and opened the tap before the Sabbath, and did nothing on the Sabbath itself, they considered this permissible even though cold water flowing through the pipe was thereby heated on the Sabbath (*Rashi,* as understood by *Pnei Yehoshua; Tosafos; Ran;* see also *Beis Meir* to *Orach Chaim* 326:3).

Ran quotes another version of *Rashi* (which is preserved in *Rashi* to the *Rif*), according to which the Tiberians bathed in the spring waters but found them too hot. They therefore ran a pipe of fresh water *into* a canal of spring water so that the waters would mix and reach the proper temperature. According to this explanation as well, the Tiberians considered this permissible even though the fresh water was thereby heated on the Sabbath, because they set their system in place before the Sabbath and it worked automatically on the Sabbath. *Tosafos* (ד״ה מעשה) also seem to understand *Rashi* in accordance with this version. However, our version, as well as several of *Rashi's* comments to the Gemara, conform more readily to the first explanation, which *Tosafos* and *Ran* themselves prefer. We have therefore followed that explanation in elucidating the Mishnah and Gemara.

29. As we learned above (38a), it is forbidden to make use of anything that was cooked on the Sabbath. Although the Tiberian heating system was set up before the Sabbath and the water ran into it automatically on the Sabbath so that no desecration of the Sabbath occurred, the Sages nevertheless forbade use of the water, like water that was heated manually, for reasons that will be explained in the Gemara (39a-b).

30. It is permitted to cook food or liquids on Yom Tov for the purpose of consuming them that day (see below, 39b, note 8). Thus, it would certainly be permitted to drink water heated automatically in the Tiberian manner. It is forbidden, however, to bathe in water that was heated on Yom Tov (see 39b). The Sages declared that this prohibition applies even if the water was heated automatically, like that of the Tiberian bath (*Milchamos Hashem, Pnei Yehoshua* to 39b).

[The expression "There was an incident" generally signifies the introduction of a precedent in support of a previously stated ruling. The Gemara (39a) will discuss which of the previous rulings is supported by this precedent.]

31. I.e. is slightly roasting the egg "until it can roll" considered sufficient to be a violation of the Biblical prohibition of cooking, or is it only prohibited Rabbinically? (*Chasam Sofer,* based on *Rashi* to 39a; see also *Chidushei HaRan, Eglei Tal, Ofeh* 37:6 and *Chazon Ish* 52:19).

[Others explain the inquiry as follows: Is cooking with a derivative of fire included in the *melachah* of cooking under Biblical law like cooking with fire itself, or is it only prohibited Rabbinically? (*Ran*).]

32. Since an egg is somewhat edible even while raw, even a very slight degree of roasting – "until it can roll" – is sufficient to make it be considered cooked under Biblical law (*Chasam Sofer, Eglei Tal* and *Chazon Ish* ibid.; cf. *Rosh Yosef* to Mishnah).

[According to the other explanation of the inquiry, Rav Yosef means to say that cooking with a derivative of fire is a violation of Biblical law (*Ran*).]

33. Below, 145b.

כֹּל שֶׁבָּא בְּחַמִּין מִלִּפְנֵי הַשַּׁבָּת – ANYTHING THAT WAS PLACED IN HOT WATER BEFORE THE SABBATH שׁוֹרִין אוֹתוֹ בְּחַמִּין בְּשַׁבָּת – MAY BE SOAKED IN HOT WATER ON THE SABBATH,[1] וְכֹל שֶׁלֹּא בָא בְּחַמִּין מִלִּפְנֵי הַשַּׁבָּת – AND ANYTHING THAT WAS NOT PLACED IN HOT WATER BEFORE THE SABBATH מְדִיחִין אוֹתוֹ בְּחַמִּין בְּשַׁבָּת – MAY BE RINSED WITH HOT WATER ON THE SABBATH,[2] חוּץ מִן הַמָּלִיחַ יָשָׁן וְקוֹלְיָיס הָאִיסְפָּנִין – EXCEPT FOR AN OLD SALTED FISH OR A SPANISH MACKEREL,[3] which may not even be rinsed with hot water on the Sabbath, שֶׁהֲדָחָתָן זוֹ הִיא גְּמַר מְלַאכְתָּן – BECAUSE THEIR RINSING with hot water COMPLETES THEIR PREPARATION. By stating that the rinsing *completes* their preparation, the Mishnah implies that once rinsed they are considered cooked under Biblical law.[4] שְׁמַע מִינָּהּ – **Learn from this** that slightly roasting an egg against the side of a kettle is also considered an act of cooking under Biblical law.[5]

The Mishnah stated:

וְלֹא יְפַקִּיעֶנָּה בְּסוּדָרִין – NOR MAY ONE BREAK IT OPEN and fry it UPON hot SCARVES that had baked in the sun, but R' Yose permits this.

The Gemara compares our Mishnah with a different Mishnah:

וְהָא דִּתְנַן – **Now,** concerning **that which we learned in** the following **Mishnah:**[6] נוֹתְנִין תַּבְשִׁיל לְתוֹךְ הַבּוֹר בִּשְׁבִיל שֶׁיְּהֵא שָׁמוּר – WE MAY PLACE A COOKED DISH IN A PIT IN ORDER THAT IT BE PRESERVED, וְאֶת הַמַּיִם הַיָּפִים בָּרָעִים בִּשְׁבִיל שֶׁיִּצֹּנוּ – GOOD WATER IN STALE WATER IN ORDER THAT IT COOL OFF,[7] וְאֶת הַצּוֹנֵן בַּחַמָּה בִּשְׁבִיל שֶׁיֵּחַמּוּ – AND COLD WATER IN THE SUN IN ORDER THAT IT BE HEATED, לֵימָא רַבִּי יוֹסֵי הִיא וְלֹא רַבָּנָן – **shall we say that this** Mishnah, which permits cooking with the heat of the sun, **is** in accord with the opinion of **R' Yose and not** the opinion of **the Rabbis?**

The Gemara answers:

אָמַר רַב נַחְמָן – **Rav Nachman said:** בַּחַמָּה דְּכוּלֵּי עָלְמָא לֹא פְּלִיגֵי דִּשְׁרֵי – Concerning cooking **in the sun** itself, **all agree that it is permissible.**[8] בְּתוֹלְדוֹת הָאוּר – Concerning cooking **with derivatives of fire** (e.g. the heat of a kettle or scarves that were heated on a fire), כּוּלֵּי עָלְמָא לֹא פְּלִיגֵי דְּאָסִיר – **all agree that it is forbidden,** for this is tantamount to cooking with fire itself! כִּי פְּלִיגֵי – **In** regard to **what** issue **do they** (R' Yose and the Sages) **disagree?** בְּתוֹלְדוֹת הַחַמָּה – It is in regard to cooking **with derivatives of** the heat of **the sun,** such as hot scarves that had baked in the sun. מַר סָבַר גָּזְרִינַן תּוֹלְדוֹת הַחַמָּה אַטּוּ תּוֹלְדוֹת הָאוּר – One **master,** i.e. the Rabbis, **holds** that **we decree** that one may not cook with **derivatives of the sun because of** the possibility that these might be confused with **derivatives of fire.**[9] וּמַר סָבַר לֹא גָּזְרִינַן – **But the** other **master,** i.e. R' Yose, **holds** that **we do not decree** this, and therefore, cooking with derivatives of the sun is permitted. Since all agree that it is permitted to cook with the heat of the sun itself, the ruling of the cited Mishnah is a unanimous one.[10]

The Mishnah stated further:

וְלֹא יְטַמְּנֶנָּה בַּחוֹל – NOR MAY ONE BURY IT IN SAND or in the dust of the roads in order that it be roasted.

The Gemara asks:

וְלִיפְלוֹג נַמִּי רַבִּי יוֹסֵי בְּהָא – It would seem that **R' Yose should dispute** the opinion of the Rabbis **in regard to this** case **as well!** Since the sand or dust in which the egg is buried is heated by the sun, R' Yose ought to permit cooking in it. Why does he not dispute this ruling as he did the previous one?[11] The Gemara presents two opinions as to why R' Yose concedes that burying food in hot sand is forbidden:

רַבָּה אָמַר – **Rabbah said:** גְּזֵרָה שֶׁמָּא יַטְמִין בְּרֶמֶץ – R' Yose concedes here due to **a decree** that was enacted out of concern that **perhaps one will insulate** food **with hot ash.**[12]

NOTES

1. I.e. any salty item that requires soaking in hot water in order to be fit for consumption, but was sufficiently soaked before the Sabbath, may be returned to a container of hot water (that is not on a fire) on the Sabbath for further soaking. Since it was prepared for consumption before the Sabbath, the further soaking is not considered an act of perfecting food [i.e. cooking] (*Rashi;* see *Beur Halachah* 318:4 ד״ה והדחתן).

2. Rinsing is permissible since this itself cannot prepare the salty food for consumption; soaking, however, is prohibited (*Rashi*; cf. *Rashi* to 145b; see *Tosafos* and *Rosh Yosef*).

3. An old salted fish is a salted fish from last year, and a Spanish mackerel is a tender type of salted fish whose salting allows it to be eaten without cooking. Both of these fish merely require rinsing with hot water to be fit for consumption (*Rashi* to 145b). [Our translation of קוֹלְיָיס הָאִיסְפָּנִין as *Spanish mackerel* follows *Rashi* here and *Aruch* ע׳ אספנן. See *Beur Halachah* ibid. for a discussion of this point as well as an application of the rule stated here to common-day herring.]

4. Since rinsing with hot water is all these fish need to be fit for consumption, this is considered their "cooking" (*Rashi* to *Beitzah* 16b and below, 145b; see *Eglei Tal, Ofeh* §37 and *Beur Halachah* 318:4 ד״ה חוץ).

5. The Mishnah implies that merely rinsing salted fish with hot water falls under the Biblical category of cooking because this itself makes it fit for consumption. It follows that slightly roasting an egg against the wall of a kettle is also a violation of Biblical law and carries *chatas* liability, since the slight degree of roasting is sufficient to make it fit for consumption (*Rashi*, as understood by *Chasam Sofer; Chidushei Ha-Ran; Eglei Tal* ibid.).

[According to the explanation of *Ran* cited above (38b notes 31-32), the Gemara means that just as rinsing salty fish with hot water, whose heat is merely a derivative of fire, is a violation of Biblical law, so too roasting an egg against the wall of a kettle that was heated on a fire is a violation of Biblical law (*Ran;* see also *Rashba* and *Ritva*, *MHK* ed.).]

6. Below, 146b.

7. I.e. we may place a cooked dish in a cool, dry pit to prevent its spoilage due to heat, and we may place a container of drinking water in a pool of stale water to cool it or protect it from heat (*Rashi* to 146b). The Gemara on 146b explains the necessity for these seemingly obvious rulings.

8. The normal method of cooking is to use the heat of a fire. Cooking with the heat of the sun is unusual and is therefore not included in the Biblical prohibition of cooking. Furthermore, the Sages saw no reason to prohibit this type of cooking, since nobody will confuse cooking in the sun with cooking on a fire (*Rashi*).

9. Since one cannot tell the difference between scarves (or other items) that were heated by the sun and those that were heated by fire, if we allow cooking on those heated by the sun an observer might think that they were heated by fire and might thus come to cook on derivatives of the heat of fire, in violation of Biblical law (*Rashi;* see note 11).

10. The halachah follows the opinion of the Rabbis that it is forbidden to cook with derivatives of the sun (*Orach Chaim* 318:3; see *Igros Moshe, Orach Chaim* vol. III §52).

11. The Gemara does not question the Mishnah's ruling that it is forbidden to roast an egg in sand, but asks only why R' Yose concurs with this particular ruling. Now, the reason given above for the Rabbis' opinion (viz. that scarves heated in the sun might be confused for scarves heated by fire) does not apply to the case of hot sand, since sand is never heated by fire. Nevertheless, it is presumable that the decree against cooking with heat derived from the sun was a blanket decree that extends even to cases in which there is no direct concern for confusion. The Gemara therefore accepts that roasting in hot sand is prohibited according to the Rabbis, and questions only why R' Yose does not maintain his previous position (*Chidushei R' Elazar Moshe Horowitz;* see also *Rashba, Pnei Yehoshua*, *Rosh Yosef* and *Rashi* below ד״ה לתוך אמה של חמין).

12. One who sees a person burying an egg in sand to cook it might think that since cooking through encasement in this hot medium is permitted it is also permitted to cook by encasing a pot of food in hot ash (*Rashi*). In fact, cooking in hot ash is forbidden Biblically, since its heat is derived from fire. Thus, although we do not ordinarily forbid cooking with derivatives of the sun, according to R' Yose, in this case we forbid it due to the resemblance of this act to a typical act of cooking that is prohibited Biblically (see *Ran* and *Pnei Yehoshua;* see also *Rashash* and note 14).

כל [א] שבא בחמין מלפני השבת שורין אותו בחמין בשבת וכל שלא בא בחמין מלפני השבת מדיחין אותו בחמין בשבת חוץ מן המליח ישן וקוליים האיספנין שהדחתן זו היא גמר מלאכתן ש"מ: ולא יפקיענה בסודרין: והא דתנן [ב] נותנין תבשיל לתוך הבור בשביל שיהא שמור ואת המים היפים ברעים בשביל שיצננו ואת הצונן בחמה בשביל שיחמו לימא רבי יוסי היא ולא רבנן אמר רב נחמן [א] בחמה דכ"ע לא פליגי דשרי בתולדות האור כ"ע לא פליגי דאסיר כי פליגי בתולדות החמה מר סבר גזרינן [ב] תולדות החמה אטו תולדות האור ומר סבר לא גזרינן: ולא יטמיננה בחול: וליפלוג נמי ר' יוסי בהא רבה אמר גזרה שמא יטמין ברמץ רב יוסף אמר מפני שמזיז עפר ממקומו מאי איכא בינייהו עפר תיחוח מיתיבי רשב"ג אומר מגלגלין ביצה על גבי גג רותח ואין מגלגלין ביצה על גבי סיד רותח בשלמא למאן דאמר גזרה שמא יטמין ברמץ ליכא למיגזר אלא למאן דאמר מפני שמזיז עפר ממקומו ליגזר סתם גג לית ביה עפר ת"ש מעשה שעשו אנשי טבריא והביאו סילון של צונן לתוך אמה של חמין וכו' בשלמא למאן דאמר גזרה שמא יטמין ברמץ היינו דדמיא להטמנה אלא למאן דאמר מפני שמזיז עפר ממקומו מאי איכא למימר מי סברת מעשה טבריא אסיפא קאי ארישא קאי לא יפקיענה בסודרין ור' יוסי מתיר והכי קאמרי ליה רבנן לר' יוסי הא מעשה דאנשי טבריא דתולדות חמה הוא ואסרי להו רבנן אמר להו ההוא תולדות אור הוא • דחלפי אפיתחא דגיהנם אמר רב חסדא

ממעשה

רש"י

גמ' כל שבא בחמין. כל מלוח שבא בחמין מע"ש שורין ושורין אותו בחמין בשבת ואין בו משום תיקון שהרי נתקן כבר: **מדיחין.** שאין זה גמר מלאכתו אבל לא שורין: **חוץ מדג מלוח ישן או קוליים האיספנין.** דג שקורין טוניי"א: **שהדחתו זהו גמר מלאכתו.** מדקרי ליה גמר מלאכתו ש"מ זהו בישולו וחייב: **והא דתנן.** בפרק חבית נותנין כו' המים לונן: **בחמה.** בשמש: **דשרי.** דאין דרך בישולו בכך וחמה באור לא מיחלפא דליגזר הא אטו הא: **בתולדות האור.** כגון אם הוחם הסודר הזה באור מתחילה: **דאסיר.** דהוי בישול: **תולדות חמה.** שהוחם הסודר בחמה: **אטו תולדות האור.** דמאן דחזי סבר דתולדות האור נינהו: **שמא יטמין ברמץ.** דמאן דחזי סבר מכדי האי לבשולי והאי לבשולי ותרווייהו דרך הטמנה מה לי רמץ מה לי חול ומשום הכי מודה ר' יוסי: **שמא יזיז עפר.** שמא לא יהא שם חול עקור לכל הצורך ואתי לאזוזי עפר הדבוק והוי חופר גומא: **עפר תיחוח.** כלומר תיחוח בעומק דליכא למיחש למזיז: **גג רותח.** שרתחו חמה: **ואין מגלגלין בסיד רותח.** דהוא תולדות האור: **ליכא למיגזר.** בגג רותח דהא לא מטמין ליה: **אלא.** לשמא יזיז עפר ויכסנו בו ליגזר: **לתוך אמה של חמין.** וחמי טבריא לאו תולדות האור נינהו ואפ"ה אסרו להו ומודה בהא ר' יוסי: **דדמיא להטמנה.** שמטמין מים במים: **מי סברת מעשה** (א) **אסיפא קאי.** לסייעתא דחול ואבק ולאורויי דתולדות חמה כי האי גוונא אסירי לדברי הכל: **ארישא קאי.** אפלוגתא ורבנן הוא דאמרי לה אבל לר' יוסי כה"ג לא מיתסר אלא משום דהני תולדות האור נינהו: **והא מעשה.** דחמי טבריא דתולדות חמה נינהו ודמי לאפקעתא דסודרין דליכא למגזר לשמא יזיז ואסרי להו:

בטלה

תוספות

להטמין מבעוד יום בדבר המוסיף הבל גזירה שמא יטמין ברמץ א) ושמא יחתה ולר"י נראה דמה שהיו מתערבין צונן בחמין לא הוה דמי להטמנה וליכא למילף מינה דאיכא למימר דאסרי להו מפני שמבשל המים צוננין ונראה לו דסילון לא היה מתערב בחמין כי היה מוקף מחילות מכל צד והיו מתחממין המים צוננים שבסילון מחמת חמי טבריא ולא היו רוצלות בחמי טבריא עצמן לפי שריחן רע והשתא דמיא להטמנה שמים צוננין היו נטמנין בתוך החמין להתחמם:

כל שבא בחמין מלפני השבת. פירוש שנתבשל לגמרי כדמפרש לקמן בפרק חבית (דף קמה:) כגון תרנגולת דרבי אבא שורין אותו בחמין אפילו בכלי ראשון וכל שלא בא כו' מדיחין אותו לפירוש רשב"א דמפרש דעירוי ככלי שני אתי שפיר הכא דאין שורין אותו בכלי ראשון אבל מדיחין אותו מכלי ראשון דרך עירוי אבל לפר"ת דמפרש דעירוי הוי ככלי ראשון ע"כ מדיחין אותו מכלי שני קאמר וא"כ מאי איריא מדיחין אפילו שורין נמי ואומר ר"י דאפילו בכלי שני אין שורין דהואיל דהמים חמין מיחזי כמבשל ואע"ג דתנן לקמן (דף מב:) אבל נותן לתוך הקערה או לתוך התמחוי היינו דוקא תבלין שהן עשוין למתק את הקדירה ולא מיחזי כמבשל א"נ ה"ה שורין אותו כיון דאיירי בכלי שני והא דנקט מדיחין לאשמעינן דאפילו הדחה הויא גמר מלאכה במליח הישן וקוליים האיספנין:

שמא יטמין ברמץ. אבל הפקעת סודרין לא גזרו אטו שמא יטמין ברמץ דסודרין לא דמו לרמץ ואטו סודרין שנתחממו באור לא בעי ר' יוסי למיגזר דאין דרך לחממן כל כך שלא יהיו נשרפין:

מפני שמזיז עפר ממקומו. פי' בקונטרס מתוך שלא יהיה לו חול עקור כל הצורך לכסות אתי לאזוזי עפר הדבוק והוי חופר גומא וקשה לריב"א דהא ליכא איסורא דאורייתא בחופר גומא ואינו צריך אלא לעפרה לרבי שמעון דאמר מלאכה שאינה צריכה לגופה פטור עליה וצריך לומר לפי פירוש הקונטרס גזירה שמא יחפור הגומא לטמון הבילה בתוכה ור"ת ב) הקשה לפירוש הקונטרס דמאי דמשני בסמוך סתם גג לית ביה עפר אדרבה הא סתם גג יש בו מעזיבה וכיון דגזרינן שמא יחפור לגזור שמא יחפור במעזיבה ויכסה ועוד שמצא בספרים ישנים מפני שמזיז עפר ממקומו ולפירוש הקונטרס צריך לגרוס שמא יזיז ומפרש ר"ת שמזיז עפר שהוא מוקצה ממקומו כשתוחב הבילה בתוך העפר וסבר רב יוסף דטלטול מן הצד שמיה טלטול ואיכא בינייהו עפר תיחוח היינו שהוא תיחוח כל כך כשמניח הבילה מידו ליפול נטמנת מעצמה בתוך העפר ואינו מזיז עפר ממקומו בידים והשתא אתי שפיר דסתם גג לית ביה עפר כל כך שיוכל להטמין בתוכו דלחפירת מעזיבה לא חיישינן ולפירוש זה הוה מצי למימר איכא בינייהו עפר מוכן ובלאו הכי איכא בינייהו טובא כגון גג דאית ביה עפר שמא יטמין ליכא למימר ושמא יזיז איכא וכגון מעשה דאנשי טבריא דשייך יטמין ולא שייך יזיז אבל קשה לרשב"א דקאמר בסמוך אלא למ"ד שמא יזיז עפר לגזור ולהאי פירוש לא שייך למימר לגזור אלא הוה ליה למימר ליתסר ויש ליישב דמשום דכל איסורי דרבנן הם גזירה אטו דאורייתא נקט האי לישנא ועוד פירש רבינו תם בספר הישר שמזיז עפר ממקומו והוי חופר שהוא תולדה דחורש אפילו בעפר תיחוח כגון חול ואבק דרכים כדמוכח בבילה (דף ח. ושם) דקאמר והא קעביד כתישה בעפר תיחוח והא קעביד גומא אלמא בעפר תיחוח שייך נמי גומא והא דקאמר הכא איכא בינייהו עפר תיחוח היינו כל כך תיחוח כשמניח בילה עליו נשקעת מאליה דבההוא ודאי לא שייך חורש וקשה לפי' דלמאי פליג רבה אדרב יוסף ולא חייש למה שמזיז עפר מדקאמר אלא למאן דאמר שמזיז כו' משמע דלרבה ניחא ויש לומר דרבה סבר דלא שייך גומא אלא כשנוטל בידו מן העפר ונשאר מקום מן הגומא אבל בנעילת בילה לא שייכא גומא לפי שאינה ניכרת:

איכא בינייהו עפר תיחוח. פירש בקונטרס דבעפר תיחוח לא שייכא גומא והא דמשמע בבילה (שם) דבעפר תיחוח נמי שייך גומא צריך לומר לפי' דהתם איירי שיש מעט עפר תיחוח וסביבו קרקע קשה דכשמסיר עפר תיחוח תשאר הגומא קיימת אבל הכא כשיש עפר תיחוח הרבה כשיעשה גומא אינה מתקיימת כי דופני הגומא יפלו ולא יוכלו להתקיים לפי שאין הקרקע קשה:

ואין מגלגלין ביצה על גבי סיד רותח. קשה אדמפליג בין תולדות חמה לתולדות האור לפלוג בתולדות חמה גופייהו בין גג רותח לחול ואבק דרכים וגג דלית ביה עפר ולמ"ד דשמא יטמין ברמץ אתי שפיר דמפליג בין גג רותח לסיד רותח שלא כדרך הטמנה אבל בתולדות חמה גופייהו לא מצי למיפלג אלא בין דרך הטמנה לשלא כדרך הטמנה דבחול נמי אם אינו מטמינו בו אלא מגלגלו על גביו שרי:

אלא למ"ד שמא יזיז וכו'. וא"ת לרב יוסף אטו מי לית ליה גזירה שמא יטמין ברמץ והא מהאי טעמא אסרינן להטמין בדבר המוסיף הבל ויש לומר דמבעוד יום איכא למיגזר שמא יטמין ברמץ ושמא יחתה אבל הכא לא שייך למיגזר דאטו אי שרינן לבשל בחמי חמה ניחוש דילמא אתי לבשל בחמי אור בשבת וא"ת הא אסרינן משחשיכה להטמין אף כשאין מוסיף הבל גזירה שמא ירתיח ויש לומר דהני מילי בדבר המבושל איכא למיחש שמא ירתיח אבל בישול גמור כי הכא לא טעו אינשי אטו תולדות חמה:

ממעשה

מסורת הש"ס

א) לקמן קמה:, ב) שם קמו ע"ב.

תוספות ישנים

א) וביו"ט נמי אסרי שמא יחתה דאף ביו"ט אסור לחתות לצורך רחילה: ב) ואין נראה כ"כ קושיא דלא חיישינן שמא יחפור במעזיב' אלא בחול דוקא חיישינן ובשאין לו כל הצורך וחסר לו מעט:

הגהות הב"ח

(א) רש"י ד"ה מי סברת מעשה טבריא אסיפא:

גליון הש"ס

גמרא **דחלפי אפיתחא דגיהנם.** עיין חולין דף ח ע"א תוס' ד"ה בחמי טבריא:

ליקוטי רש"י

כל שבא בחמין. כלומר שנתבשל. **שורין אותו בחמין.** כדי שיהא נמוח. **וכל שלא בא בחמין.** כגון בשר יבש שאוכלין אותו חי על ידי הדחק. **מדיחין אותו.** ולא אמרינן זהו בישוליה אבל לא שורין. **חוץ מן המליח ישן.** דג מליח של שנה שעברה. **וקוליים האיספנין.** שם דג שאוכלין אותו מחמת מלחו על ידי הדחה בחמין והנך אפילו הדחה נמי לא שזהו גמר מלאכתן והוי בשול [לקמן קמה:]. דג מליח הוא ורך ונאכל כמו שהוא חי אלא שנותנין עליו חמין וזה בשולו כדתנן במסכת שבת שהדחתו זו היא גמר מלאכתו [ביצה טז:]. **לתוך הבור.** שאין בו מים. **שיהא שמור.** שלא יסריח מחמת החום. **ואת המים היפים ברעים.** כלי מלא מים יפים לתוך מקוה מים רעים להשתמר [שילטננו] ולא יחמו [לקמן קמו:]. **רמץ.** אפר המעורב בגחלים [לעיל לד:]. אפר חם וכך שמו בלשון ערבי [חולין ח.]. גחלים ואפר בוערים [נדה מט:].

עין משפט נר מצוה

יג א ב מיי' פ"ט מהל' שבת הלכה ג ופכ"ב הלכה ט סמג לאוין סה טוש"ע א"ח סימן שיח סעיף ג:

רבינו חננאל

גלגל מאי. אמר רב יוסף גלגל חייב חטאת כענין מליח ישן וקוליס האיספנין שהדחתן היא גמר מלאכתן: **ולא** יפקיענה בסודרין. ור' יוסי מתיר. ואוקמה רב נחמן [בחמה כ"ע לא פליגי דשרי] בתולדות האור כולי עלמא לא פליגי [דאסור] כי פליגי בתולדות חמה ת"ק סבר גזרינן תולדות חמה אטו תולדות אור. ור' יוסי סבר לא גזרינן ואמרו ליה רבנן לרבי יוסי והא מעשה שעשו אנשי טבריא תולדות חמה הוא ואסרי להו רבנן לאנשי טבריא [אע"ג דדחי ר' יוסי ואמר תולדות אור הן

רַב יוֹסֵף אָמַר – **Rav Yosef said:** מִפְּנֵי שֶׁמֵּזִיז עָפָר מִמְּקוֹמוֹ – R' Yose concedes **because** when burying food in sand **one moves earth from its place.**[13]

The Gemara points out a ramification of this disagreement between Rabbah and Rav Yosef:

מַאי בֵּינַיְיהוּ – **What is** the practical difference **between them?** אִיכָּא בֵּינַיְיהוּ עָפָר תִּיחוּחַ – **There is** a practical difference **between them** in regard to burying an egg in hot **loose earth.** According to Rabbah even this is forbidden, but according to Rav Yosef it is permitted.[14]

Rav Yosef's opinion is challenged:

מֵיתִיבֵי – **They challenged** Rav Yosef on the basis of the following Baraisa: רַבָּן שִׁמְעוֹן בֶּן גַּמְלִיאֵל אוֹמֵר – RABBAN SHIMON BEN GAMLIEL SAYS: מְגַלְגְּלִין בֵּיצָה עַל גַּבֵּי גַג רוֹתֵחַ – ONE MAY ROAST AN EGG SLIGHTLY ON A HOT ROOF that has baked in the sun, וְאֵין מְגַלְגְּלִין בֵּיצָה עַל גַּבֵּי סִיד רוֹתֵחַ – BUT ONE MAY NOT ROAST AN EGG SLIGHTLY ON HOT LIME that was heated by fire.[15] בִּשְׁלָמָא לְמַאן דְּאָמַר גְּזֵרָה שֶׁמָּא יַטְמִין בְּרֶמֶץ – **This is understandable according to the one** (Rabbah) **who says** that burying food in hot sand is prohibited due to **a decree** that was enacted out of concern that **perhaps one will insulate** food **with hot ash;** לֵיכָּא לְמִיגְזַר – **there is no basis for applying** this **decree** to the case of roasting an egg on a hot roof, since there is not enough sand there in which to bury the egg and one merely places it on the surface of the roof. אֶלָּא לְמַאן דְּאָמַר מִפְּנֵי שֶׁמֵּזִיז עָפָר מִמְּקוֹמוֹ – **But according to the one** (Rav Yosef) **who says** that roasting in hot sand is prohibited **because** in doing so **one moves earth from its place,** לִיגְזוֹר – **[Rabban Shimon ben Gamliel] should apply the decree** even to the case of roasting on a hot roof, since there may be some earth on the roof which the person might move around in order to cover the egg. – ? –

The Gemara answers:

סְתָם גַּג לֵית בֵּיהּ עָפָר – **A typical roof does not have** loose **earth on it** and this concern therefore does not apply.

The Gemara again challenges Rav Yosef's opinion:

תָּא שְׁמַע – **Come, learn** a challenge to Rav Yosef from our Mishnah, which states: מַעֲשֶׂה שֶׁעָשׂוּ אַנְשֵׁי טְבֶרְיָא – THERE WAS AN INCIDENT IN WHICH THE PEOPLE OF TIBERIAS WENT AHEAD וְהֵבִיאוּ סִילוֹן שֶׁל צוֹנֵן לְתוֹךְ אַמָּה שֶׁל חַמִּין וכו׳ – AND RAN A PIPE OF COLD WATER INTO A CANAL OF HOT spring WATER etc. [The Sages said to them: If water flowed through the pipe on the Sabbath it is like hot water that was heated manually on the Sabbath and is forbidden for both bathing and drinking.] Now, the hot springs of Tiberias do not derive their heat from a fire, yet the Sages forbade the use of water heated by the springs, and R' Yose concurred with their ruling.[16] בִּשְׁלָמָא לְמַאן דְּאָמַר גְּזֵרָה שֶׁמָּא יַטְמִין בְּרֶמֶץ – **This is understandable according to the one** (Rabbah) **who says** that according to R' Yose burying food in hot sand is prohibited due to **a decree** that was enacted out of concern that **perhaps one will insulate** food **with hot ash;** הַיְינוּ דְּדָמְיָא לְהַטְמָנָה – **that** explains **why this** case of the Tiberian pipe **is analogous to** the case of **burying** an egg in hot sand.[17] אֶלָּא לְמַאן דְּאָמַר מִפְּנֵי שֶׁמֵּזִיז עָפָר מִמְּקוֹמוֹ – **But according to the one** (Rav Yosef) **who says that** R' Yose forbids burying an egg in sand **because** in doing so **one moves earth from its place,** מַאי אִיכָּא לְמֵימַר – **what is**

NOTES

13. In order to submerge the egg one must push aside some sand, which is *muktzeh*. Rav Yosef holds that it is forbidden to move a *muktzeh* item even indirectly [e.g. by pushing the dirt with the egg] and even for the benefit of a non-*muktzeh* item [e.g. the egg] (*Rabbeinu Tam* cited by *Tosafos;* see *Orach Chaim* 311:8 and 44a note 2). This explanation follows our version of the text.

Rashi explains Rav Yosef as saying that a person burying an egg *might* move some dirt and dig a hole for the egg, which, depending on the circumstances, is a violation of the Biblical prohibition of חורש, *plowing* (see below, 73b). This explanation follows a different version of the text, which reads שֶׁמָּא יָזִיז עָפָר – *lest one move dirt* (see *Tosafos;* see also *Rashi* below ד״ה אלא).

14. Even in the case of loose earth, the concern exists that burying an egg in it might lead one to cook by encasing food in hot ash. Thus, according to Rabbah, the prohibition extends to this case. However, the concern for moving *muktzeh* earth or that one might dig a hole does not pertain when the earth is loose and the egg can sink right into it when dropped (*Tosafos* ד״ה מפני שמזיז). [This pertains when the earth has been loosened to a significant depth, so that there is no concern at all that one might dig a hole (*Rashi;* see *Tosafos* ד״ה איכא בינייהו and *Rashba;* cf. *Rav Hai Gaon* cited by *Rashba* and *Ran*).]

We must at this point address a fundamental question. A Mishnah below (47b) teaches that it is forbidden to insulate food even before the Sabbath in any material that tends to increase its heat. This is a decree that was instituted lest one encase food in hot ash that contains glowing embers which he might be inclined to stoke on the Sabbath (see above, 34b). Furthermore, it is forbidden to insulate food *on* the Sabbath even in a material that merely preserves heat (see 34a). [These decrees constitute the prohibition of *hatmanah,* as explained in the Introduction to Chapter 4.] On the basis of these decrees, which R' Yose presumably does not contest, it should certainly be prohibited to bury an egg in hot sand on the Sabbath. Why then must the Gemara resort to other explanations for R' Yose's concession that burying an egg in hot sand is prohibited? The answer is that the Mishnah's rule against insulating in a material that adds heat pertains only to a material that is naturally hot and thus adds heat to the food continually. Sand that has baked in the sun is not included since it cools off with the passage of time (*Pnei Yehoshua;* see also *Rashba* and *Mishnah Berurah* 318:19). As for the decree against insulating on the Sabbath in a material that preserves heat, that pertains only to insulating *cooked* foods in order that they remain hot, not to insulating raw foods (see *Tosafos* ד״ה אלא). Thus, if not for the reasons provided here, it should be permissible, according to R' Yose, to bury a raw egg in hot sand in order to roast it.

We have followed *Pnei Yehoshua's* understanding of *Rashi,* according to which Rabbah and Rav Yosef are both stating new reasons for the prohibition of burying an egg in hot sand or the dust of the roads. Others explain that only Rav Yosef is stating a new reason. They understand Rabbah as merely stating that the general decree against insulating in a material that adds heat applies to hot sand as well. Indeed, Rabbah's words, גְּזֵרָה שֶׁמָּא יַטְמִין בְּרֶמֶץ, *a decree [that was enacted out of concern that] perhaps one will insulate [food] with hot ash,* are nearly identical with the words used above (34b) to describe the reason for the general prohibition (see *Tosafos* ד״ה אלא with *Maharsha, Rashba* and *Ritva MHK* ed.).

15. Rabban Shimon ben Gamliel permits roasting an egg on a hot roof because he concurs with R' Yose's opinion in our Mishnah that it is permissible to cook with heat that is derived from the sun. Accordingly, the Gemara uses Rabban Shimon ben Gamliel's ruling as a basis for determining R' Yose's reasoning (*Rashba, Ritva MHK* ed.).

16. As mentioned in the notes to the Mishnah, the phrase *There was an incident* commonly introduces a supporting precedent. In our case, the Mishnah apparently cites this incident in support of its previous anonymous ruling forbidding the burial of an egg in hot sand – a ruling with which R' Yose concurs. Clearly, the reason for prohibiting the burial of an egg in sand extends to the case of the Tiberian water pipe (see *Rashi, Rashba* and *Ritva MHK* ed.).

17. Since the pipe of cold water was enveloped by the hot water in the canal, it is fitting that the Mishnah cites this incident as proof that there was a decree issued against heating a cold item by enveloping it in a hot material (*Rashi*). [Note that although Rabbah stated his reasoning only to explain R' Yose's opinion, the Rabbis also concur with the reasoning that the concern for insulation with hot ash is a basis for prohibiting enveloping food in any hot material. That is why the Tiberian incident is cited unanimously in support of the prohibition against burying an egg in hot sand (*Rashba,* 39b).] See note 14.

כל [א] שבא בחמין מלפני השבת שורין אותו בחמין בשבת וכל שלא בא בחמין מלפני השבת מדיחין אותו בחמין בשבת חוץ מן המליח ישן וקוליים האיספנין שהדחתן זו היא גמר מלאכתן ש"מ: ולא יפקיענה בסודרין: והא דתנן [ב] נותנין תבשיל לתוך הבור בשביל שיהא שמור ואת המים היפים ברעים בשביל שיצננו ואת הצונן בחמה בשביל שיחמו לימא רבי יוסי היא ולא רבנן אמר רב נחמן [א]בחמה דכ"ע לא פליגי דשרי בתולדות האור כ"ע לא פליגי דאסיר כי פליגי בתולדות החמה מר סבר גזרינן [ג]תולדות החמה אטו תולדות האור ומר סבר לא גזרינן: ולא יטמיננה בחול: וליפלוג נמי ר' יוסי בהא רבה אמר גזרה שמא יטמין ברמץ רב יוסף אמר מפני שמזיז עפר ממקומו מאי בינייהו איכא בינייהו עפר תיחוח מיתיבי רשב"ג אומר מגלגלין ביצה על גבי גג רותח ואין מגלגלין ביצה על גבי סיד רותח בשלמא למאן דאמר גזרה שמא יטמין ברמץ ליכא למיגזר אלא למאן דאמר מפני שמזיז עפר ממקומו ליגזר סתם גג לית ביה עפר ת"ש מעשה שעשו אנשי טבריא והביאו סילון של צונן לתוך אמה של חמין וכו' בשלמא למאן דאמר גזרה שמא יטמין ברמץ היינו דדמיא להטמנה אלא למאן דאמר מפני שמזיז עפר ממקומו מאי איכא למימר מי סברת מעשה טבריא אסיפא קאי ארישא קאי לא יפקיענה בסודרין ור' יוסי מתיר והכי קאמרי ליה רבנן לר' יוסי הא מעשה דאנשי טבריא דתולדות חמה הוא ואסרי להו רבנן אמר להו ההוא תולדות אור הוא ° דחלפי אפיתחא דגיהנם אמר רב חסדא

ממעשה

רש"י

גמ' כל שבא בחמין. כל מלוח שבא בחמין מע"ש שורין אותו בחמין בשבת ואין בו משום תיקון שהרי נתקן כבר: מדיחין. שאין זה גמר מלאכתו אבל לא שורין: חוץ מדג מלוח ישן או קוליים האיספנין. דג שקורין טוניי"א: שהדחתו זהו גמר מלאכתו. מדקרי ליה גמר מלאכתו ש"מ זהו בישולו וחייב: והא דתנן. בפרק חבית נותנין כו' המים לונן: בחמה. בשמש: דשרי. דאין דרך בישולו בכך וחמה באור לא מיחלפא דליגזר הא אטו הא: בתולדות האור. כגון אם הוחם הסודר הזה באור מתחילה: דאסיר. דהוי בישול: תולדות חמה. שהוחם הסודר בחמה: אטו תולדות האור. דמאן דחזי סבר דתולדות האור נינהו: שמא יטמין ברמץ. דמאן דחזי סבר מכדי האי לבשולי והאי לבשולי ותרוייהו דרך הטמנה מה לי רמץ מה לי חול ומשום הכי מודה ר' יוסי: שמא יזיז עפר. שמא לא יהא שם חול עקור לכל הצורך ואתי לאזוזי עפר הדבוק והוי חופר גומא: עפר תיחוח. כלומר תיחוח בעומק דליכא למיחש למזיז: גג רותח. שרתחו חמה: ואין מגלגלין בסיד רותח. דהוא תולדות האור: ליכא למיגזר. בגג רותח דהא לא מטמין ליה: אלא. לשמא יזיז עפר ויכסנו בו ליגזר: לתוך אמה של חמין. וחמי טבריא לאו תולדות האור נינהו ואפ"ה אסרו להו ומודה בהא ר' יוסי: דדמיא להטמנה. שמטמינין מים במים: מי סברת מעשה (א) אסיפא קאי. לסייעתא דחול ואבק ולאורויי דתולדות חמה כי האי גוונא אסירי לדברי הכל: ארישא קאי. אפלוגתא ורבנן הוא דאמרי לה אבל לר' יוסי כה"ג לא מיתסר אלא משום דהני תולדות האור נינהו: והא מעשה. דחמי טבריא דתולדות חמה נינהו ודמי לאפקעתא דסודרין דליכא למגזר לשמא יזיז ואסרי להו:

בטלה

תוספות

להטמין מבעוד יום בדבר המוסיף הבל גזירה שמא יטמין ברמץ א) ושמא יחתה ולר"י נראה דמה שהיו מתערבין צונן בחמין לא הוה דמי להטמנה וליכא למילף מינה דאיכא למימר דאסרי להו מפני שמבשל המים צוננין ונראה לו דסילון לא היה מתערב בחמין כי היה מוקף מחילות מכל צד והיו מתחממין המים צוננים שבסילון מחמת חמי טבריא ולא היו רוצלות בחמי טבריא עצמן לפי שריחן רע והשתא דמיא להטמנה שמים צוננין היו נטמנין בתוך החמין להתחמם:

כל שבא בחמין מלפני השבת. פירוש שנתבשל לגמרי כדמפרש לקמן בפרק חבית (דף קמה:) כגון תרנגולת דרבי אבא שורין אותו בחמין אפילו בכלי ראשון וכל שלא בא כו' מדיחין אותו לפירוש רשב"א דמפרש דעירוי ככלי שני אתי שפיר הכא דאין שורין אותו בכלי ראשון אבל מדיחין אותו מכלי ראשון דרך עירוי אבל לפר"ת דמפרש דעירוי הוי ככלי ראשון ע"כ מדיחין אותו מכלי שני קאמר וא"כ מאי איריא מדיחין אפילו שורין נמי ואומר ר"י דאפילו בכלי שני אין שורין דהואיל דהמים חמין מיחזי כמבשל ואע"ג דתנן לקמן (דף מב:) אבל נותן לתוך הקערה או לתוך התמחוי היינו דוקא תבלין שהן עשויין למתק את הקדירה ולא מיחזי כמבשל א"נ ה"ה שורין אותו כיון דאיירי בכלי שני והא דנקט מדיחין לאשמעינן דאפילו הדחה הויא גמר מלאכה במליח הישן וקוליים האיספנין: **שמא** יטמין ברמץ. אבל הפקעת סודרין לא גזרו אטו שמא יטמין ברמץ דסודרין לא דמו לרמץ ואטו סודרין שנתחממו באור לא בעי ר' יוסי למיגזר דאין דרך לחממן כל כך שלא יהיו נשרפין: **מפני** שמזיז עפר ממקומו. פי' בקונטרס מתוך שלא יהיה לו חול עקור כל הצורך לכסות אתי לאזוזי עפר הדבוק והוי חופר גומא וקשה לריב"א דהא ליכא איסורא דאורייתא בחופר גומא ואינו צריך אלא לעפרה לרבי שמעון דאמר מלאכה שאינה צריכה לגופה פטור עליה וצריך לומר לפי פירוש הקונטרס גזירה שמא יחפור הגומא לטמון הבילה בתוכה ור"ת ב) הקשה לפירוש הקונטרס דמאי דמשני בסמוך סתם גג לית ביה עפר אדרבה הא סתם גג יש בו מעזיבה וכיון דגזרינן שמא יחפור לגזור שמא יחפור במעזיבה ויכסה ועוד שמצא בספרים ישנים מפני שמזיז עפר ממקומו ולפירוש הקונטרס צריך לגרוס שמא יזיז ומפרש ר"ת שמזיז עפר שהוא מוקצה ממקומו כשתוחב הבילה בתוך העפר וסבר רב יוסף דטלטול מן הצד שמיה טלטול ואיכא בינייהו עפר תיחוח היינו שהוא תיחוח כל כך כשמניח הבילה מידו ליפול נטמנת מעצמה בתוך העפר ואינו מזיז עפר ממקומו בידים והשתא אתי שפיר דסתם גג לית ביה עפר כל כך שיוכל להטמין בתוכו דלחפירת מעזיבה לא חיישינן ולפירוש זה הוה מצי למימר איכא בינייהו עפר מוכן ובלאו הכי איכא בינייהו טובא כגון גג דאית ביה עפר שמא יטמין ליכא למימר ושמא יזיז איכא וכגון מעשה דאנשי טבריא דשייך יטמין ולא שייך יזיז אבל קשה לרשב"א דקאמר בסמוך אלא למ"ד שמא יזיז עפר לגזור ולהאי פירוש לא שייך למימר לגזור אלא הוה ליה למימר ליתסר ויש ליישב דמשום דכל איסורי דרבנן הם גזירה אטו דאורייתא נקט האי לישנא ועוד פירש רבינו תם בספר הישר שמזיז עפר ממקומו והוי חופר שהוא תולדה דחורש אפילו בעפר תיחוח כגון חול ואבק דרכים כדמוכח בבילה (דף ח. ושם) דקאמר והא קעביד כתישה בעפר תיחוח והא קעביד גומא אלמא בעפר תיחוח שייך נמי גומא והא דקאמר הכא איכא בינייהו עפר תיחוח היינו כל כך תיחוח כשמניח בילה עליו נשקעת מאליה דבההוא ודאי לא שייך חורש וקשה לפי' דלמאי פליג רבה אדרב יוסף ולא חייש למה שמזיז עפר מדקאמר אלא למאן דאמר שמזיז כו' משמע דלרבה ניחא ויש לומר דרבה סבר דלא שייך גומא אלא כשנוטל בידו מן העפר ונשאר מקום מן הגומא אבל בנעילת בילה לא שייכא גומא לפי שאינה ניכרת:

איכא בינייהו עפר תיחוח. פירש בקונטרס דבעפר תיחוח לא שייכא גומא והא דמשמע בבילה (שם) דבעפר תיחוח נמי שייך גומא צריך לומר לפי' דהתם איירי שיש מעט עפר תיחוח וסביבו קרקע קשה דכשמסיר עפר תיחוח תשאר הגומא קיימת אבל הכא כשיש עפר תיחוח הרבה כשיעשה גומא אינה מתקיימת כי דופני הגומא יפלו ולא יוכלו להתקיים לפי שאין הקרקע קשה: **ואין** מגלגלין ביצה על גבי סיד רותח. קשה אדמפליג בין תולדות חמה לתולדות האור לפלוג בתולדות חמה גופייהו בין גג רותח לחול ואבק דרכים וגג דלית ביה עפר ולמ"ד דשמא יטמין ברמץ אתי שפיר דמפליג בין גג רותח לסיד רותח שלא כדרך הטמנה אבל בתולדות חמה גופייהו לא מצי למיפלג אלא בין דרך הטמנה לשלא כדרך הטמנה דבחול נמי אם אינו מטמינו בו אלא מגלגלו על גביו שרי: **אלא** למ"ד שמא יזיז וכו'. וא"ת לרב יוסף אטו מי לית ליה גזירה שמא יטמין ברמץ והא מהאי טעמא אסרינן להטמין בדבר המוסיף הבל ויש לומר דמבעוד יום איכא למיגזר שמא יטמין ברמץ ושמא יחתה אבל הכא לא שייך למיגזר דאטו אי שרינן לבשל בחמי חמה ניחוש דילמא אתי לבשל בחמי אור בשבת וא"ת הא אסרינן משחשיכה להטמין אף כשאין מוסיף הבל גזירה שמא ירתיח ויש לומר דהני מילי בדבר המבושל איכא למיחש שמא ירתיח אבל בישול גמור כי הכא לא טעו אינשי אטו תולדות חמה:

ממעשה

מסורת הש"ס

א) לקמן קמה:, ב) שם קמו ע"ב.

תוספות ישנים

א) וביו"ט נמי אסרי שמא יחתה דאף ביו"ט אסור לחתות לצורך רמילה:
ב) ואין נראה כ"כ קושיא דלא חיישינן שמא יחפור במעזיב' אלא בחול דוקא חיישינן ובשאין לו כל הצורך וחסר לו מעט:

הגהות הב"ח

(א) רש"י ד"ה מי סברת מעשה טבריא אסיפא:

גליון הש"ס

גמרא דחלפי אפיתחא דגיהנם. עיין חולין דף ח ע"א תוס' ד"ה בחמי טבריא:

ליקוטי רש"י

כל שבא בחמין. כלומר שנתבשל. שורין אותו בחמין. כדי שיהא נמוח. וכל שלא בא בחמין. כגון בשר יבש שאוכלין אותו חי על ידי הדחק. מדיחין אותו. ולא אמרינן זהו בישוליה אבל לא שורין. חוץ מן המליח ישן. דג מליח של שנה שעברה. וקוליים האיספנין. שם דג שאוכלין אותו מחמת מלחו על ידי הדחה בחמין והנך אפילו הדחה נמי לא שזהו גמר מלאכתן והוי בשול [לקמן קמה:]. דג מליח הוא ורך ונאכל כמו שהוא חי אלא שנותנין עליו חמין וזה בשולו כדתנן במסכת שבת שהדחתו זו היא גמר מלאכתו [ביצה טז:]. לתוך הבור. שאין בו מים. שיהא שמור. שלא יסריח מחמת החום. ואת המים היפים ברעים. כלי מלא מים יפים לתוך מקוה מים רעים להשתמר [שיצטננו] ולא יחמו [לקמן קמו:]. רמץ. אפר המעורב בגחלים [לעיל לד:]. אפר חם וכך שמו בלשון ערבי [חולין ח.]. גחלים ואפר בוערים [נדה מט:].

עין משפט נר מצוה

יג א ב מיי' פ"ט מהל' שבת הלכה ג ופכ"ב הלכה ט סמג לאוין סה טוש"ע א"ח סימן שיח סעיף ג:

רבינו חננאל

גלגל מאי. אמר רב יוסף גלגל חייב חטאת כענין מליח ישן וקוליס האיספנין שהדחתן היא גמר מלאכתן: ולא יפקיענה בסודרין. ור' יוסי מתיר. ואוקמה רב נחמן [בחמה כ"ע לא פליגי דשרי] בתולדות האור כולי עלמא לא פליגי [דאסור] כי פליגי בתולדות חמה ת"ק סבר גזרינן תולדות חמה אטו תולדות אור. ור' יוסי סבר לא גזרינן ואמרו ליה רבנן לרבי יוסי והא מעשה שעשו אנשי טבריא תולדות חמה הוא ואסרי להו רבנן לאנשי טבריא [אע"ג דדחי ר' יוסי ואמר תולדות אור הן

there to say? What connection can there be between the burial of an egg in sand and the incident involving the Tiberian water pipe?[18]

The Gemara responds on Rav Yosef's behalf:

מִי סָבְרַת מַעֲשֶׂה טְבֶרְיָא אַסֵּיפָא קָאֵי – **Do you think** that **the Tiberian incident is** mentioned in the Mishnah **in connection with the last clause,** which deals with burying an egg in hot sand, and that the reason the Sages prohibited use of the pipe is the same as the reason for the prohibition against burying an egg in hot sand? אַרֵישָׁא קָאֵי – No! **It is** mentioned **in connection with the earlier clause,** which states: לֹא יַפְקִיעֶנָּה בְּסוּדָרִין וְרַבִּי יוֹסֵי מַתִּיר – NOR MAY ONE BREAK [AN EGG] OPEN UPON HOT SCARVES that had baked in the sun, BUT R' YOSE PERMITS this. The incident of the Tiberian water pipe is cited by the Rabbis in support of their view that it is forbidden to cook with heat that is derived from the sun, וְהָכִי קָאָמְרֵי לֵיהּ רַבָּנָן לְרַבִּי יוֹסֵי – **and this is what the Rabbis** meant to **say to R' Yose:** הָא מַעֲשֶׂה דְאַנְשֵׁי טְבֶרְיָא דְתוֹלְדוֹת חַמָּה הוּא – **Behold, the incident of the Tiberians, which involved** heating cold water with a source of heat that is **a derivative of the sun,** i.e. the heat of the hot springs,[19] וְאָסְרֵי לְהוּ רַבָּנָן – **and the Rabbis** of that time **forbade them** to use the water![20] אָמַר לְהוּ – **[R' Yose],** however, **retorted:**[21] הַהוּא תּוֹלְדוֹת אוּר הוּא – **That** heat of the Tiberian hot springs **is** actually **a derivative of fire,** דְחָלְפֵי אַפִּיתְחָא דְגֵיהִנֹּם – **since** the waters are heated by fire when **they pass by the gates of Gehinnom.**[22]

The Gemara cites a related observation:

אָמַר רַב חִסְדָּא – **Rav Chisda said:**

NOTES

18. Obviously, the issue of displacing earth is completely irrelevant to the case of the Tiberian water pipe (*Rashi* ד״ה והא מעשה).

19. Spring waters in general are warmed by dint of the sun's heat penetrating the earth (see *Rashi* to *Pesachim* 42a ד״ה שלנו and *Mishnah Berurah* 455:2). The Tanna Kamma apparently holds that this pertains to hot springs as well. See, however, *Tosafos, Chullin* 8a ד״ה בחמי טבריא.

20. Since the Rabbis forbade them to use even water that was heated automatically by this derivative of the sun, they obviously held that cooking with heat that is derived from the sun is prohibited! (see *Rashi*). [The reason the Rabbis banned the automatic heating system was their concern that it might lead people to heat water manually in the hot springs (see *Tosafos,* 38b-39a ד״ה מעשה).]

21. This reply is not quoted in the Mishnah, but since we are now explaining that the incident was cited by the Rabbis in support of their ruling which R' Yose disputes, we must explain how R' Yose will refute the support. Presumably, he would say as follows (see *Ritva MHK* ed.).

22. This is the interpretation of the Mishnah according to Rav Yosef's view. According to Rabbah, however, the true interpretation is the one presumed above – that the incident was cited in support of the unanimous ruling prohibiting the encasement of food in a hot material such as sand.

To summarize the discussion to this point:

(a) Cooking with fire or heat derived from fire is prohibited Biblically.

(b) Cooking through exposure to the rays of the sun is permissible.

(c) Cooking with heat that is derived from the sun is the subject of a dispute. The Rabbis (as represented by the Tanna Kamma of our Mishnah) forbid it categorically, due to the concern for confusion between this and heat derived from fire. R' Yose, however, permits it.

(d) R' Yose concedes that it is forbidden to encase food in hot sand. According to Rabbah, this is a decree that was enacted out of concern that one might insulate food with hot ash. Thus, the prohibition applies not only to sand, but to enveloping food in *any* hot material, such as hot spring water. According to Rav Yosef, however, encasing food in hot sand is prohibited because of the displacement of sand [i.e. moving *muktzeh* (*Tosafos*) or the concern for digging a hole (*Rashi*)]. Thus, the prohibition is limited to cases involving sand or dust.

גמרא

כל א) שבא בחמין מלפני השבת שורין אותו בחמין בשבת וכל שלא בא בחמין מלפני השבת מדיחין אותו בחמין בשבת חוץ מן המליח ישן וקוליים האיספנין שהדחתן זו היא גמר מלאכתן ש"מ: ולא יפקיענה בסודרין: והא דתנן ג) נותנין תבשיל לתוך הבור בשביל שיהא שמור ואת המים היפים ברעים בשביל שיצננו ואת הצונן בחמה בשביל שיחמו לימא רבי יוסי היא ולא רבנן אמר רב נחמן אבחמה דכ"ע לא פליגי דשרי בתולדות האור כ"ע לא פליגי דאסיר כי פליגי בתולדות החמה מר סבר גזרינן בתולדות החמה אטו תולדות האור ומר סבר לא גזרינן: ולא יטמיננה בחול: וליפלוג נמי ר' יוסי בהא רבה אמר גזרה שמא יטמין ברמץ רב יוסף אמר מפני שמזיז עפר ממקומו מאי בינייהו איכא בינייהו עפר תיחוח מיתיבי רשב"ג אומר מגלגלין ביצה על גבי גג רותח ואין מגלגלין ביצה על גבי סיד רותח בשלמא למאן דאמר גזרה שמא יטמין ברמץ ליכא למיגזר אלא למאן דאמר מפני שמזיז עפר ממקומו ליגזר סתם גג לית ביה עפר ת"ש מעשה שעשו אנשי טבריא והביאו סילון של צונן לתוך אמה של חמין וכו' בשלמא למאן דאמר גזרה שמא יטמין ברמץ היינו דדמיא להטמנה אלא למאן דאמר מפני שמזיז עפר ממקומו מאי איכא למימר מי סברת מעשה טבריא אסיפא קאי ארישא קאי לא יפקיענה בסודרין ור' יוסי מתיר והכי קאמרי ליה רבנן לר' יוסי הא מעשה דאנשי טבריא דתולדות חמה הוא ואסרי להו רבנן אמר להו ההוא תולדות אור הוא ° דחלפי אפיתחא דגיהנם אמר רב חסדא ממעשה

רש"י

גמ' כל שבא בחמין. כל מלוח שבא בחמין מע"ש חוזרין ושורין אותו בחמין בשבת ואין בו משום תיקון שהרי נתקן כבר: מדיחין. שאין זה גמר מלאכתו אבל לא שורין: חוץ מדג מלוח ישן או קוליים האיספנין. דג שקורין טונינ"א: שהדחתו זהו גמר מלאכתו. מדקרי ליה גמר מלאכתו ש"מ זהו בישולו וחייב: והא דתנן. בפרק חבית נותנין כו' המים לונן: בחמה. בשמש: דשרי. דאין דרך בישולו בכך וחמה באור לא מיחלפא דליגזר הא אטו הא: בתולדות האור. כגון אם הוחם הסודר הזה באור מתחילה: דאסיר. דהוי בישול: תולדות חמה. שהוחם הסודר בחמה: אטו תולדות האור. דמאן דחזי סבר דתולדות האור נינהו: שמא יטמין ברמץ. דמאן דחזי סבר מכדי האי לבשולי והאי לבשולי ותרוייהו דרך הטמנה מה לי רמץ מה לי חול ומשום הכי מודה ר' יוסי: שמא יזיז עפר. שמא לא יהא שם חול עקור לכל הצורך ואתי לאזוזי עפר הדבוק והוי חופר גומא: עפר תיחוח. כלומר תיחוח בעומק דליכא למיחש למזיז: גג רותח. שרתחו חמה: ואין מגלגלין בסיד רותח. דהוא תולדות האור: ליכא למיגזר. בגג רותח דהא לא מטמין ליה: אלא. לשמא יזיז עפר ויכסנו בו ליגזר: לתוך אמה של חמין. וחמי טבריא לאו תולדות האור נינהו ואפ"ה אסרו להו ומודה בהא ר' יוסי: דדמיא להטמנה. שמטמין מים במים: מי סברת מעשה (א) אסיפא קאי. לסייעתא דחול ואבק ולאורויי דתולדות חמה כי האי גוונא אסירי לדברי הכל: ארישא קאי. אפלוגתא ורבנן הוא דאמרי לה אבל לר' יוסי כה"ג לא מיתסר אלא משום דהני תולדות האור נינהו: והא מעשה. דחמי טבריא דתולדות חמה נינהו ודמי לאפקעתא דסודרין דליכא למגזר לשמא יזיז ואסרי להו:

בטלה

תוספות

להטמין מבעוד יום בדבר המוסיף הבל גזירה שמא יטמין ברמץ: א) ושמא יחתה ולר"י נראה דמה שהיו מתערבין לונן בחמין לא הוה דמי להטמנה וליכא למילף מינה דאיכא למימר דאסרי להו מפני שמבשל המים לוננין ונראה לו דסילון לא היה מתערב בחמין כי היה מוקף מחילות מכל לד והיו מתחממין המים לוננים שבסילון מחמת חמי טבריא ולא היו רוחלות בחמי טבריא עלמן לפי שריחן רע והשתא דמיא להטמנה שמים לוננין היו נטמנין בתוך החמין להתחמם:

כל שבא בחמין מלפני השבת. פירוש שנתבשל לגמרי כדמפרש לקמן בפרק חבית (דף קמה:) כגון תרנגולת דרבי אבא שורין אותו בחמין אפילו בכלי ראשון וכל שלא בא כו' מדיחין אותו לפירוש רשב"א דמפרש דעירוי ככלי שני אתי שפיר הכא דאין שורין אותו בכלי ראשון אבל מדיחין אותו מכלי ראשון דרך עירוי אבל לפר"ת דמפרש דעירוי הוי ככלי ראשון ע"כ מדיחין אותו מכלי שני קאמר וא"כ מאי איריא מדיחין אפילו שורין נמי ואומר ר"י דאפילו בכלי שני אין שורין דהואיל דהמים חמין מיחזי כמבשל ואע"ג דתנן לקמן (דף מב:) אבל נותן לתוך הקערה או לתוך התמחוי היינו דוקא תבלין שהן עשויין למתק את הקדירה ולא מיחזי כמבשל א"נ ה"ה שורין אותו כיון דאיירי בכלי שני והא דנקט מדיחין לאשמעינן דאפילו הדחה הויא גמר מלאכה במליח הישן וקוליים האיספנין:

שמא יטמין ברמץ. אבל הפקעת סודרין לא גזרו אטו שמא יטמין ברמץ דסודרין לא דמו לרמץ ואטו סודרין שנתחממו באור לא בעי ר' יוסי למיגזר דאין דרך לחממן כל כך שלא יהיו נשרפין:

מפני שמזיז עפר ממקומו. פי' בקונטרס מתוך שלא יהיה לו חול עקור כל הצורך לכסות אתי לאזוזי עפר הדבוק והוי חופר גומא וקשה לריב"א דהא ליכא איסורא דאורייתא בחופר גומא ואינו צריך אלא לעפרה לרבי שמעון דאמר מלאכה שאינה צריכה לגופה פטור עליה וצריך לומר לפי פירוש הקונטרס גזירה שמא יחפור הגומא לטמון הבילה בתוכה ור"ת ב) הקשה לפירוש הקונטרס דמאי דמשני בסמוך סתם גג לית ביה עפר אדרבה הא סתם גג יש בו מעזיבה וכיון דגזרינן שמא יחפור לגזור שמא יחפור במעזיבה ויכסה ועוד שמלא בספרים ישנים מפני שמזיז עפר ממקומו ולפירוש הקונטרס צריך לגרוס שמא יזיז ומפרש ר"ת שמזיז עפר שהוא מוקלה ממקומו כשתוחב הבילה בתוך העפר וסבר רב יוסף דטלטול מן הלד שמיה טלטול ואיכא בינייהו עפר תיחוח היינו שהוא תיחוח כל כך כשמניח הבילה מידו ליפול נטמנת מעלמה בתוך העפר ואינו מזיז עפר ממקומו בידים והשתא אתי שפיר דסתם גג לית ביה עפר כל כך שיוכל להטמין בתוכו דלחפירת מעזיבה לא חיישינן ולפירוש זה הוה מלי למימר איכא בינייהו עפר מוכן ובלאו הכי איכא בינייהו טובא כגון גג דאית ביה עפר שמא יטמין ליכא למימר ושמא יזיז איכא וכגון מעשה דאנשי טבריא דשייך יטמין ולא שייך יזיז אבל קשה לרשב"א דקאמר בסמוך אלא למ"ד שמא יזיז עפר לגזור ולהאי פירוש לא שייך למימר לגזור אלא הוה ליה למימר ליתסר ויש ליישב דמשום דכל איסורי דרבנן הם גזירה אטו דאורייתא נקט האי לישנא ועוד פירש רבינו תם בספר הישר שמזיז עפר ממקומו והוי חופר שהוא תולדה דחורש אפילו בעפר תיחוח כגון חול ואבק דרכים כדמוכח בבילה (דף ח. ושם) דקאמר והא קעביד כתישה בעפר תיחוח והא קעביד גומא אלמא בעפר תיחוח שייך נמי גומא והא דקאמר הכא איכא בינייהו עפר תיחוח היינו כל כך תיחוח כשמניח בילה עליו נשקעת מאליה דבההוא ודאי לא שייך חורש וקשה לפי' דלמאי פליג רבה אדרב יוסף ולא חייש למה שמזיז עפר מדקאמר אלא למאן דאמר שמזיז כו' משמע דלרבה ניחא ויש לומר דרבה סבר דלא שייך גומא אלא כשנוטל בידו מן העפר ונשאר מקום מן הגומא אבל בנעילת בילה לא שייכא גומא לפי שאינה ניכרת:

איכא בינייהו עפר תיחוח. פירש בקונטרס דבעפר תיחוח לא שייכא גומא והא דמשמע בבילה (שם) דבעפר תיחוח נמי שייך גומא צריך לומר לפי' דהתם איירי שיש מעט עפר תיחוח וסביבו קרקע קשה דכשמסיר עפר תיחוח תשאר הגומא קיימת אבל הכא כשיש עפר תיחוח הרבה כשיעשה גומא אינה מתקיימת כי דופני הגומא יפלו ולא יוכלו להתקיים לפי שאין הקרקע קשה:

ואין מגלגלין ביצה על גבי סיד רותח. קשה אדמפליג בין תולדות חמה לתולדות האור לפלוג בתולדות חמה גופייהו בין גג רותח לחול ואבק דרכים וגג דאית ביה עפר ולמ"ד דשמא יטמין ברמץ אתי שפיר דמפליג בין גג רותח לסיד רותח שלא כדרך הטמנה אבל בתולדות חמה גופייהו לא מלי למיפלג אלא בין דרך הטמנה לשלא כדרך הטמנה דבחול נמי אם אינו מטמינו בו אלא מגלגלו על גביו שרי:

אלא למ"ד שמא יזיז וכו'. וא"ת לרב יוסף אטו מי לית ליה גזירה שמא יטמין ברמץ והא מהאי טעמא אסרינן להטמין בדבר המוסיף הבל ויש לומר דמבעוד יום איכא למיגזר שמא יטמין ברמץ ושמא יחתה אבל הכא לא שייך למיגזר דאטו אי שרינן לבשל בחמי חמה ניחוש דילמא אתי לבשל בחמי אור בשבת וא"ת הא אסרינן משחשיכה להטמין אף כשאין מוסיף הבל גזירה שמא ירתיח ויש לומר דהני מילי בדבר המבושל איכא למיחש שמא ירתיח אבל בישול גמור כי הכא לא טעו אינשי אטו תולדות חמה:

ממעשה

מסורת הש"ס

א) לקמן קמה:, ג) שם קמו ע"ב.

תוספות ישנים

א) וביו"ט נמי אסרי שמא יחתה דאף ביו"ט אסור לחתות לצורך רחילה:

ב) ואין נראה כ"כ קושיא דלא חיישינן שמא יחפור במעזיב' אלא בחול דוקא חיישינן וכשאין לו כל הצורך וחסר לו מעט:

הגהות הב"ח

(א) רש"י ד"ה מי סברת מעשה טבריא אסיפא:

גליון הש"ס

גמרא דחלפי אפיתחא דגיהנם. עיין חולין דף ח ע"א תוס' ד"ה בחמי טבריא:

ליקוטי רש"י

כל שבא בחמין. כלומר שנתבשל. שורין אותו בחמין. כדי שיהא נמוח. וכל שלא בא בחמין. כגון בשר יבש שאוכלין אותו חי על ידי הדחק. מדיחין אותו. ולא אמרינן זהו בישוליה אבל לא שורין. חוץ מן המליח ישן. דג מליח של שנה שעברה. וקוליים האיספנין. שם דג שאוכלין אותו מחמת מלחו על ידי הדחה בחמין והנך אפילו הדחה נמי לא שזהו גמר מלאכתן והוי בשול [לקמן קמה:]. דג מליח הוא ורך ונאכל כמו שהוא חי אלא שנותנין עליו חמין וזה בשולו כדתנן במסכת שבת שהדחתו זו היא גמר מלאכתו [ביצה טז:]. לתוך הבור. שאין בו מים. שיהא שמור. שלא יסריח מחמת החום. ואת המים היפים ברעים. כלי מלא מים יפים לתוך מקוה מים רעים להשתמר [שיצטננו] ולא יחמו [לקמן קמו:]. רמץ. אפר המעורב בגחלים [לעיל לד:]. אפר חם וכן שמו בלשון ערבי [חולין ח.]. גחלים ואפר בוערים [נדה מט:].

עין משפט נר מצוה

יג א ב מיי' פ"ט מהל' שבת הלכה ג ופכ"ב הלכה ט סמג לאוין סה טוש"ע א"ח סימן שיח סעיף ג:

רבינו חננאל

גלגל מאי. אמר רב יוסף גלגל חייב חטאת כענין מליח ישן וקוליס האיספנין שהדחתן היא גמר מלאכתן: ולא יפקיענה בסודרין. ור' יוסי מתיר. ואוקמה רב נחמן [בחמה כ"ע לא פליגי דשרי] בתולדות האור כולי עלמא לא פליגי [דאסור] כי פליגי בתולדות חמה ת"ק סבר גזרינן תולדות חמה אטו תולדות אור. ור' יוסי סבר לא גזרינן ואמרו ליה רבנן לרבי יוסי והא מעשה שעשו אנשי טבריא תולדות חמה הוא ואסרי להו רבנן לאנשי טבריא [אע"ג דדחי ר' יוסי ואמר תולדות אור הן

ממעשה שעשו אנשי טבריא ואסרי להו רבנן בטלה א) הטמנה בדבר המוסיף הבל ואפילו מבעוד יום אמר עולא הלכה כאנשי טבריא א"ל רב נחמן כבר תברינהו אנשי טבריא לסילונייהו: מעשה שעשו אנשי טבריא: מאי רחיצה אילימא רחיצת כל גופו אלא חמין שהוחמו בשבת הוא דאסורין הא חמין שהוחמו מע"ש מותרין והתניא [א] ב) חמין שהוחמו מע"ש למחר רוחץ בהן פניו ידיו ורגליו אבל לא כל גופו אלא פניו ידיו ורגליו אימא סיפא א ביו"ט כחמין שהוחמו בי"ט ואסורין ברחיצה ומותרין בשתיה לימא תנן סתמא כבית שמאי דתנן ג) בית שמאי אומרים לא יחם אדם חמין לרגליו אא"כ ראויין לשתיה וב"ה ב מתירין א"ר איקא בר חנניא להשתטף בהן כל גופו עסקינן והאי תנא הוא דתניא ג) לא ג ישתטף אדם כל גופו בין בחמין ובין בצונן דברי ר"מ ר"ש מתיר ר' יהודה אומר בחמין אסור בצונן מותר אמר רב חסדא מחלוקת בכלי אבל בקרקע דברי הכל מותר והא מעשה דאנשי טבריא בקרקע הוה ואסרי להו רבנן אלא אי איתמר ◦ הכי איתמר ד מחלוקת בקרקע אבל בכלי דברי הכל אסור אמר רבה בר בר חנה אמר רבי יוחנן הלכה כרבי יהודה א"ל רב יוסף ד) בפירוש שמיע לך או מכללא שמיע לך מאי כללא דאמר רב תנחום א"ר יוחנן א"ר ינאי אמר ה) (רב) כל מקום שאתה מוצא שנים חלוקין ואחד מכריע הלכה כדברי המכריע חוץ ו) מקולי מטלניות שאף על פי שרבי אליעזר מחמיר ורבי יהושע מיקל ור' עקיבא מכריע אין הלכה כדברי המכריע חדא דרבי עקיבא תלמיד הוא ועוד הא

הדר

רש"י

בטלה הטמנה. נאסרה הטמנה בדבר המוסיף הבל דהא מבע"י נתנו שם הסילון ומפני שהצוננין מתחממין בכך ואע"ג דממילא אסור: לסילונייהו. לסילונין שלהן שחזרו בהן: ראוין לשתיה. דמחים להו לשתייה ואי בעי רוחץ בהן פניו: להשתטף. שנותן על גופו ומשתטף: והאי תנא. ר' שמעון היא דמתיר להשתטף כל גופו בשבת בחמין שהוחמו מע"ש והיינו דקאמר כחמין שהוחמו בשבת אסור (א) הא שהוחמו מאתמול שרי ואי בי"ט כחמין שהוחמו בי"ט ואסור ברחיצה דאפי' בית הלל לא שרי להחם בי"ט אלא לפניו ידיו ורגליו אבל לשיטוף כל גופו לא: לא ישתטף. בשבת: בין בחמין. ואפי' הוחמו בחול: בכלי. דהרואה אומר היום הוחמו ומוכחא מילתא דתולדות האור נינהו ואתי להחם בשבת כגון נותן צונן בחמין: אבל בקרקע. כגון אמבטאות של מרחצאות והן חמי האור: מותר. דבטלי להו מתורת חמין: והא מעשה דאנשי טבריא כו'. אלמא במילתייהו קיימי:

הדר

תוספות

ממעשה שעשו אנשי טבריא ואסרו להם בטלה הטמנה מבע"י בדבר המוסיף הבל. וא"ת מה צריך למילף ממעשה דאנשי טבריא הא מתני' היא דאין טומנין בדבר המוסיף הבל בפרק במה טומנין (לקמן ד' מז: ושם) ומבע"י איירי דמשחשיכה אפי' בדבר שאינו מוסיף הבל אסור כדאמרינן בפ"ב (לעיל דף לד.) ואור"י דמתניתין דלקמן איכא לאוקמא בבין השמשות אבל מבעוד יום ה"א דשרי וא"ת והא קתני טומנין בגיזי צמר ואין מטלטלין אותן ואי בין השמשות איך טומנין בהן והא אסור לטלטלן וי"ל דהוה מוקמינן כרבי דאמר (לעיל ד' מ:) כל דבר שהוא משום שבות לא גזרו עליו בין השמשות וא"ת אי כרבי אתיא אי מבעוד יום שרי להטמין ביה"ש נמי שרי דכל דבר שהוא משום שבות כו' וי"ל דה"א בהטמנה החמירו וה"ר שמואל מוורדין מפרש ממעשה אנשי טבריא בטלה הטמנה דאסור אפי' לאכול כדקתני ואסורין בשתיה וה"ר יונה מפרש ◦ בטלה אפי' בקדירה חייתא והיינו דקאמר בטלה משמע לגמרי מכל דבר: **אלא** פניו ידיו ורגליו כו'. הכל היה יכול לדקדק מסיפא דקתני בי"ט כחמין שהוחמו בי"ט אילימא רחיצת כל גופו הא הוחמו מעי"ט שרי והא לקמן אסר רחיצה בי"ט דקאמר למחר נכנס ומזיע אבל רוחץ לא ודוקא שטיפה שרי בבית החילון אלא דרך הש"ס ז) מה שיכול לדקדק מרישא מדקדק ומיהו קשה לרשב"א דמגופה דמתניתין הוי מצי למידק בלא הך ברייתא דמייתי מדקתני ואסורין בשתיה כ"ש פניו ידיו ורגליו דאסירי: **אלא** אם כן ראויין לשתיה. נראה לר"י ◦ דווקא שמחמם אותם לצורך שתיה אבל לצורך רחיצה אע"ג דראוין לשתיה אסרי ב"ש ◦ דהא לית להו מתוך (ביצה ד' יב. ושם) ובפ"ב דביצה (ד' כא: ושם) אסרי ב"ש מדורה להתחמם כנגדה ואע"ג דראויה היא לבשל ולאפות ועוד אומר ר"י דמהכא נמי יש לדקדק דלא שרו ב"ש לצורך רחיצה משום דראוין לשתיה א"כ לא אתיא מתני' אפי' כב"ש דקתני ואסורין ברחיצה ומותרין בשתיה ומדקתני ומותרין בשתיה מכלל דראוין לשתיה ואפ"ה קתני דאסורין ברחיצה אלא ודאי לא שרו ב"ש אלא כשעושה לצורך שתיה ונראה לר"י דיכול לחמם אפי' ביותר מכדי שתיה כדאמר בפרק הדר (עירובין ד' סח.) ◦ נשיילה לאימיה אי צריכה נחיימו אגב אימיה ודוקא בכדי שיעור לרגליו אבל לצורך כל גופו לא והיינו טעמא שהבלנים חשודים לפעמים שיחממו עיקרן לרחיצה:

וב"ה מתירין. משמע דוקא לרגליו אבל לצורך כל גופו לא וכן משמע בכולה שמעתין דמחמירין בחמין שהוחמו בשבת וגזרו על הזיעה ביו"ט כמו בשבת כדאמר בבילה בהמביא ולקמן (דף מ. ושם) א"כ משמע שאסור לעשות הבערה משום רחיצה שאם לא כן לא היו גוזרים על הזיעה ותימה דמ"ש הבערה דרחיצה מהבערה דזיעה דשרי מדאורייתא כדמוכח התם ואומר ר"י בשם ריב"א דרחיצה אינה אלא לתענוג ואסורה כמו מוגמר דאסור בפ"ק דכתובות (ד' ז. ושם) משום דאין שוה לכל נפש וכן משמע בירושלמי דהיינו טעמא דרחיצה אבל זיעה שוה היא לכל נפש דאינה תענוג אלא לבריאות והא דתניא לקמן (ד' מ.) מרחץ שפקקו נקביו מעי"ט למחר נכנס ומזיע ה"ה אפי' הוחם בו ביום אלא נקט מעי"ט דאפ"ה דוקא מזיע אבל רוחץ לא:

בין בחמין בין בצונן. נראה לר"י דהיינו אפי' חמין שהוחמו מע"ש דהא אוסר אפי' צונן ומסתמא בהנך חמין אסיר ר' יהודה ועוד דמסתמא לא מיירי בדעבדי איסורא והאי תנא הוא דקאמר היינו ר"ש ועוד אומר ר"י דיש להוכיח דבחמין שהוחמו מע"ש פליגי דאמר בפרק חבית (לקמן ד' קמו. ושם) מה חמי טבריא חמין אף מי מערה חמין הרוחץ דיעבד אין לכתחילה לא מכלל דלהשתטף אפי' לכתחילה מני ר"ש היא דתניא לא ישתטף כו' ואי בשהוחמו בשבת פליגי אבל מערב שבת שרי ר' יהודה אמאי צריך לאוקמה כר"ש לוקמה כר' יהודה ובהוחמו מע"ש דהא דומיא דחמי טבריא קתני: **והא** מעשה דאנשי טבריא בקרקע הוה ואסרי להו. הקשה ה"ר אליעזר ממי"ץ מאי פריך התם הוחמו בשבת כדקתני כחמין שהוחמו בשבת משמע דבהוחמו מע"ש שרי והכא ג) בהוחמו מע"ש פליגי כדפרישית ומפרש הר"ר יוסף דס"ל להש"ס מדמחמיר ר"מ כ"כ דאוסר אפי' צונן מחמיר נמי לאסור ע"ש אטו שבת ולהכי פריך והא מעשה דאנשי טבריא בקרקע הוה ואסרי להו בהוחמו בשבת ורב חסדא קאמר אבל בקרקע ד"ה מותר אפי' בהוחמו בשבת דהא לר"מ אי הוה אוסר להו בהוחמו בשבת בהוחמו מע"ש נמי הוה אוסר וקשה דר"מ אוסר להשתטף בצונן אפי' בקרקע כדמסיק דבקרקע פליגי ובפרק שמונה שרצים (לקמן דף קט. ושם) משמע דשרי דקאמר התם רוחצין במי גרר ובמי חמתן ובמי עסיא ובמי טבריא אבל לא בים הגדול ורמינהו רוחצין במי טבריא ובים הגדול כו' ומוקים בתרייתא כר' מאיר וי"ל דבקרקע דהכא דאסר היינו דומיא דכלי דדמי לרוחץ בחמין והתם בנהר התירו שנראה כמיקר בנהר ואפי' בחמי טבריא לא דמי לאדם רוחץ בחמין:

אמר רבה בר בר חנה ח) הלכה כר' יהודה. אע"ג דר' יוחנן אית ליה הלכה כסתם משנה הכא משום דר' יהודה מכריע הוא אין הלכה כסתם וקשה דבפרק קמא דפסחים (דף יג. ודף כא. ושם) פריך ונימא מר הלכה כר' מאיר דסתם לן תנא כוותיה אע"ג דסבר דרבן גמליאל מכריע הוא דפריך בתר הכי ונימא מר הלכה כרבן גמליאל דהוה ליה מכריע וי"ל דסתם דהכא גריע מההוא סתם דהכא סתם במתני' ומחלוקת בברייתא והלכה כמכריע ומיהו אי לאו הכרעה הוה הלכה כסתם מתני' אע"ג דמחלוקת בברייתא: (לעיל) **הא** חמין שהוחמו מבעוד יום מותרים והתניא חמין שהוחמו כו'. תימה לוקי ההיא ברייתא דאסרה בכלי משום דהרואה אומר היום הוחמו ומתניתין בקרקע כמשמעה כדמפליג בסמוך בין כלי לקרקע וי"ל דדוקא בשיטוף דקיל איכא לפלוגי אבל ברחיצה דחמירא לא מסתברא לפלוגי בהכי:

דילמא

עין משפט נר מצוה

יד א ב מיי' פ"א מהל' יו"ט הלכה טז סמג לאוין עה טוש"ע או"ח סימן תקיא סעיף ג:
טו ג ד מיי' פכ"ב מהל' שבת הלכה ג סמג לאוין סה טוש"ע או"ח סימן שכו סעיף א:

רבינו חננאל

קי"ל כת"ק אמר רב חסדא מדאסרו להו רבנן] שמע מיניה דבטלה הטמנה בדבר המוסיף ואפילו מבעוד יום. אסיקנא דכופח מקום שפיתת קדירה אחת הוא. ואם הוסק בגפת או בעצים הרי הוא כתנור ואסור לסמוך בו. וכ"ש בתוכו או על גבו. וכן לשהות בו אע"פ שהוא גרוף וקטום אסור. נמצא האסור שני פנים. צונן שלא הוחמו כל עיקר. ותבשיל שהתחיל להתבשל ולא הגיע למאכל בן דרוסאי. ומותר שני פנים. חמין שהוחמו ולא בשלו כל עיקר ושבשלו כמאכל בן דרוסאי. ואפילו [לא] בשלו כל צרכן מותר. ומאי דקשי ליה [זיקא] מסקנא כלישנא בתראה דרב אשי דבין דגדיא ובין [דברחא] בין שריק ובין שלא שריק שרי. ולא יטמינה בחול ובאבק דרכים בשביל שתצלה דברי הכל אסור: **מעשה** שעשו אנשי טבריא הביאו סילון של צונן כו' אין הלכה כאנשי טבריא דהא תברינהו לסילונייהו אוקימנא הא דתנן אסור ברחיצה להשתטף בהן כל גופו ור' שמעון הוא דשרי בחמין שהוחמו מע"ש להשתטף דתניא אסור להשתטף בין בחמין בין בצונן דברי רבי מאיר ורבי שמעון מתיר רבי יהודה אומר בחמין אסור בצונן מותר. אמר רבה בר בר חנה אמר רבי יוחנן הלכה כר' יהודה: **הא** דקאמר שמואל חמין שהוחמו מע"ש אינו רוחץ בהן בשבת אלא פניו ידיו ורגליו תניא כוותיה וקי"ל כוותיה דשמואל בהא: **א"ל** לרבה בר בר חנה בפירוש שמיע לך מיניה דר' יוחנן דהלכתא כר' יהודה דבצונן מותר להשתטף אבל בחמין אסור. או מכללא. מאי כללא דא"ר יוחנן א"ר ינאי כל מקום ששנים חולקין ואחד מכריע הלכה כדברי המכריע חוץ מקולי מטליות שפירשנום בפרק של מעלה. והוא זה ששנינו בכלים בפרק כ"ח פחות משלשה על שלשה שהתקינה לפקק בה את המרחץ כו'. אף על פי שרבי אליעזר מחמיר ורבי יהושע מיקל ורבי עקיבא מכריע שאין הלכה כרבי עקיבא. חדא דתלמיד הוא ואין תלמיד מכריע על רבו.

רב נסים גאון

חדא דר' עקיבא לגבי רבי אליעזר ורבי יהושע תלמיד הוא. פירוש שלו

מסורת הש"ס

א) [לקמן מ.], ב) ביצה כא:, ג) לקמן קמו: ע"ש תוספתא פ"ד, ד) [ברכות ט. וש"נ], ה) [צ"ל רבי], ו) [לעיל כט.], ז) [וכ"כ תוספות עירובין טו. ד"ה אימא וכתובות נא. ד"ה מני ודף פט. ד"ה ש"מ וב"ב ס. ד"ה הא ועי' תוס' לקמן מו: ד"ה כבתה ותוס' ברכות מב. ד"ה הסבו ותוספות ב"מ יג: ד"ה הא מבני וע"ע רש"י ב"מ כג: ד"ה הא של ב"ב], ח) [אמר ר' יוחנן הלכה כו'].

תוספות ישנים

א) הא דלא מייתי בעבר ושהה מהכא דאסור דשאני הטמנה דיש להחמיר:
ב) ואם תאמר ולימא דמתני' קודם גזירה וי"ל דמסתמא אחר גזירה דגזירה קדמוני' היתה:
ג) ומהר"מ מפרש דחמין שהוחמו מע"ש היינו שנסתלקו מעל האור מבע"י. ושהוחמו בשבת היינו נמי שהוחמו מבע"י כל צורכן אך מתחממים והולכין גם בשבת דומיא דאנשי טבריא. ובהנהו פליגי ר"מ ור"י ור"ש. וצונן קרי שהיו חמין כבר ונצטננו. אבל בנסתלקו מבע"י אפילו ר"מ מודה דשרי להשתטף ולא לרחוץ. והאי תנא הוא ר"מ ור"י דאסרי חמין שמתחממין והולכין גם בשבת. והשתא פריך שפיר והא מעשה דאנשי טבריא בקרקע הוי. ויתיישב נמי ההיא דפ' שמנה שרצים דשרי ר"מ לרחוץ בקרקע. וכן בפרק חבית דמוקי כר"ש:

הגהות הב"ח

(א) רש"י ד"ה והאי תנא וכו' שהוחמו בשבת אסור ברחיצה הא שהוחמו:

גליון הש"ס

גמ' הכי איתמר מחלוקת בקרקע. עי' מ"ק דף יט ע"ב תוס' ד"ה שאסור ול"ע: תוס' ד"ה ממעשה וכו' בטלה אפילו בקדירה חייתא. עי' לקמן דף מז ע"ב תוס' ד"ה במה טומנין: ד"ה אא"כ וכו' נראה לר"י דוקא שמחמם. עי' לקמן דף עו ע"א תוס' ד"ה הואיל וראוין: בא"ד דהא לית להו מתוך. דבריהם צ"ע דלענין מתוך מה הפרש בין ראויים או אינן ראויים. ולאיתי כרשב"א שהוסיף ומאן דלית ליה מתוך לית ליה הואיל. ויסוד זה נסתר מפירכת הגמ' פסחים דף מו ע"ב וכמ"ש התוס' שם ד"ה אהבערה לא ליחייב ולע"ג. ובתשובה וגם בדרשות הארכתי בזה בעהש"י: בא"ד כדאמרינן פרק הדר נשייליה. ק"ל למאי הוצרכו לראיה זו דאפשר לצורך מילה עדיף. הא להדיא איתא ברייתא ערוכה בבילה ממלא נחתום חבית מים אע"פ שא"צ אלא לקיתון אחד:

ליקוטי רש"י

לא יחם אדם חמין. לרחוץ רגליו אוכל נפש התיר הכתוב ולא להבעיר אור בשביל רחיצה [ביצה כא:]. ר"ש מתיר. להשתטף שופכן על גופו דלאו דרך רחיצה היא שרי לכתחילה אפילו בחמין [לקמן קמו: עיי"ש]. בפירוש שמיע לך. מיניה. או מכללא. דשמעת מיניה מילתא דדייקת מיניה. מאי כללא. מאיזה כלל היה לו לומר [יבמות ס:]. הלכה כדברי המכריע. כשזה אומר כך וזה אומר כך וזה אומר דעת שלישית אפילו אמצעית היא ביניהם אין זה הכרע כגון (פסחים כ:) חבית של תרומה שנתגלגלה ב"ש אומר תשפך הכל וב"ה אומרים תעשה זילוף א"ר ישמעאל בר' יוסי אני אכריע בשדה תשפך הכל בבית תעשה זילוף אמרו לו אין הכרעה שלישית מכרעת והיכי הויא הכרעה כגון ההיא דקולי מטלניות דבמה מדליקין (שבת כט.) ר' אליעזר אומר בין מן המוכן בין שלא מן המוכן טמא ר' יהושע אומר בין מן המוכן בין שלא מן המוכן טהור ר"ע אומר מן המוכן טמא שלא מן המוכן טהור א"ר יוחנן עלה כל מקום שאתה מוצא שנים חולקים ואחד מכריע כו' אלמא כה"ג קרי הכרעה היכא דגלו (מאי) דעתייהו דשייך לפלוגי בין מוכן לשאינו מוכן אפ"ה לא פלגינן ואתא ר"ע ונתן חילוק בדבר הוי הכרעה שהכריע במוכן כר' אליעזר ונמצאו שנים מטמאים במוכן ור' יהושע יחיד מטהר ובשאינו מוכן כר' יהושע והוו שנים מטהרים בשאינו מוכן אבל גבי חבית דלא גלו דעתייהו ב"ש וב"ה דנהוי שייך חילוק בין בית לשדה שלא אמרו כך ב"ש אומר בין בבית בין בשדה תשפך הכל וב"ה אומר בין בבית בין בשדה תעשה זילוף וכא שלישי וחלק בין שדה לבית התם אין זה הכרע לדבריהם אלא דעת שלישית דהכרע לשון כף מאזנים הוי בשנים חולקין וכא שלישי ומכריע המשקל כאחד מהן או בכל הדבר או במקצת כדברי זה ומקצת כדברי זה [חולין קלז. וכעי"ז ב"ק קטז.]. הכרעה שהיא במקצת כדברי זה ומקצת כדברי זה אינה הכרעה עד שתהא כולה כדברי א' מהן דהכרעה לשון שיקול ששוקל דברי שנים יותר מאחד [נזיר נג.]. מקולי מטלניות. מטלניות הקלות בעיניו דומיא דממוקמות לפקוק מרחץ דמידי דלא חשיב הוא [לעיל כט.].

מִמַּעֲשֶׂה שֶׁעָשׂוּ אַנְשֵׁי טְבֶרְיָא וְאָסְרִי לְהוּ רַבָּנָן – **On the basis of that which the Tiberians did, and** the fact that **the Rabbis forbade them** to use the heated water, בָּטְלָה הַטְמָנָה בְּדָבָר הַמּוֹסִיף הֶבֶל – we learn that **it is prohibited**[1] **to insulate** food **with a material that increases** its heat, וַאֲפִילוּ מִבְּעוֹד יוֹם – **even when it is still daylight** on Friday afternoon.[2]

The Gemara records a dispute regarding the final disposition of the Tiberian incident:

אָמַר עוּלָּא – **Ulla said:** הֲלָכָה כְּאַנְשֵׁי טְבֶרְיָא – **The halachah** actually **follows the Tiberians,** and not the Sages who forbade the use of their water pipe.[3] אָמַר לֵיהּ רַב נַחְמָן – **Rav Nachman said to him:** כְּבָר תַּבְרִינְהוּ אַנְשֵׁי טְבֶרְיָא לְסִילוֹנַיְיהוּ – **The Tiberians** themselves **already destroyed their pipe** because they retracted their opinion and conceded that the halachah follows the Sages.

The Mishnah stated:

מַעֲשֶׂה שֶׁעָשׂוּ אַנְשֵׁי טְבֶרְיָא – THERE WAS AN INCIDENT IN WHICH THE PEOPLE OF TIBERIAS WENT AHEAD etc. The Sages said to them: If water flowed through the pipe on the Sabbath, it is like hot water that was heated manually on the Sabbath and is forbidden for both bathing and drinking etc.

The Gemara analyzes the comment of the Sages:

מַאי רְחִיצָה – To **what** type of **bathing** did the Sages refer, when they stated that the water may not be used for it? אִילֵימָא רְחִיצַת כָּל גּוּפוֹ – **If you should say** that they referred to **bathing one's entire body,** I will ask: אֶלָּא חַמִּין שֶׁהוּחַמּוּ בְּשַׁבָּת הוּא דַּאֲסוּרִין – **Now,** their statement implies that **it is** only the use of **hot water that was heated on the Sabbath that is forbidden,** הָא חַמִּין שֶׁהוּחַמּוּ מֵעֶרֶב שַׁבָּת מוּתָּרִין – **but** the use of **hot water that was heated before the Sabbath is permitted.** Accordingly, can they have been referring to bathing the entire body? וְהָתַנְיָא – **But it was taught in a Baraisa:** חַמִּין שֶׁהוּחַמּוּ מֵעֶרֶב שַׁבָּת – Concerning HOT WATER THAT WAS HEATED BEFORE THE SABBATH, לְמָחָר רוֹחֵץ בָּהֶן פָּנָיו יָדָיו וְרַגְלָיו – ON THE FOLLOWING DAY, i.e. the Sabbath, ONE MAY WASH HIS FACE, HANDS AND FEET WITH THEM, אֲבָל לֹא כָּל גּוּפוֹ – BUT NOT HIS ENTIRE BODY.[4] Since it is forbidden to bathe the entire body even with water heated before the Sabbath, the Sages could not have been referring to bathing the entire body! אֶלָּא פָּנָיו יָדָיו וְרַגְלָיו – **Rather,** perhaps you will say that they referred to washing **one's face, hands and feet,** which is permitted with water that was heated before the Sabbath and is forbidden only with water that was heated on the Sabbath.[5] אֵימָא סֵיפָא – But **consider the latter clause** of the Sages' statement: בְּיוֹם טוֹב כְּחַמִּין שֶׁהוּחַמּוּ בְּיוֹם טוֹב – If water would flow through the pipe ON A FESTIVAL, it would be LIKE HOT WATER THAT WAS HEATED manually ON A FESTIVAL וַאֲסוּרִין בִּרְחִיצָה וּמוּתָּרִין בִּשְׁתִיָּה – AND would be FORBIDDEN FOR BATHING BUT PERMITTED FOR DRINKING. Now, if the Mishnah is dealing with washing the face, hands and feet, the latter clause implies that this is forbidden with water that was heated on a festival. But this is true only according to Beis Shammai and is disputed by Beis Hillel, as we shall soon see. לֵימָא תְּנַן סְתָמָא כְּבֵית שַׁמַּאי – **Shall we say that our Mishnah has taught** an **anonymous** ruling **in accordance with** the opinion of **Beis Shammai?**[6] דִּתְנַן – **For we learned in a Mishnah:**[7] בֵּית שַׁמַּאי אוֹמְרִים – BEIS SHAMMAI SAY: לֹא יָחֵם אָדָם חַמִּין לְרַגְלָיו אֶלָּא אִם כֵּן רְאוּיִין לִשְׁתִיָּה – A PERSON MAY NOT WARM UP HOT WATER FOR HIS FEET on a festival UNLESS IT IS FIT FOR DRINKING, וּבֵית הִלֵּל מַתִּירִין – BUT BEIS HILLEL PERMIT it.[8] If you interpret our Mishnah as dealing with

NOTES

1. Literally: it has ceased [to be permitted].

2. The Tiberians ran the pipe through the hot springs before the Sabbath. Nevertheless, since the cold water became heated on the Sabbath – albeit automatically – the Rabbis forbade its use. Since even something that was heated automatically on the Sabbath [through envelopment in a hot material] is forbidden, we learn that it is forbidden to insulate food before the Sabbath in any material that will automatically add heat to it on the Sabbath (*Rashi; see Tosafos* above, 38b-39a ד״ה מעשה). [This is the prohibition of *hatmanah.*]

Tosafos ask: Why is it necessary to infer this rule from the Tiberian incident? It is taught explicitly in the first Mishnah of the following chapter (below, 47b)! One answer offered by *Tosafos* is that the Mishnah below only prohibits the act of insulating in a heat-intensifying material. The Tiberian incident teaches that any food so insulated is prohibited for consumption until after the Sabbath. See *Tosafos* and *Rashba* for additional answers; see also *Pnei Yehoshua* and *R' Akiva Eiger.* [For a discussion of how Rav Chisda's observation relates to the previous dispute between Rabbah and Rav Yosef, see *Rashba* and *Pnei Yehoshua.*]

3. Ulla holds that the Tiberian incident was cited by the Tanna Kamma of our Mishnah in support of his ruling prohibiting cooking with derivatives of the sun. Furthermore, he holds that R' Yose, who permits cooking with derivatives of the sun, disagrees even with the ruling of the earlier Sages against the Tiberian pipe. R' Yose does not hold that the Tiberian hot springs are heated by the fires of Gehinnom, but agrees that they are in fact heated by the sun. Since he permits cooking with derivatives of the sun, he holds that the Tiberians were justified in using the hot springs to heat cold water! As for the prohibition of *hatmanah*, R' Yose holds that it too does not apply to derivatives of the sun. According to Ulla, R' Yose's opinion is the prevailing one (*Milchamos Hashem, Rashba, Ritva MHK* ed.; see there, as well as *Ran* and *Pnei Yehoshua,* for alternative explanations).

4. This prohibition is a Rabbinical decree instituted in response to the practice of bathhouse attendants to heat up water on the Sabbath and claim that it had been heated before the Sabbath (Gemara, end of 40a). It is known as גְּזֵרַת מֶרְחֲצָאוֹת, *the bathhouse injunction,* or גְּזֵרַת הַבַּלָּנִין, *the bath attendants' injunction*.

5. Even after the bathhouse injunction, it is permitted to wash the face, hands and feet with water that was heated before the Sabbath. However, it is prohibited to do so with water heated on the Sabbath itself – even if no Sabbath desecration was involved – because such water is treated more stringently (see 40b notes 2 and 3 and *Beur HaGra, Orach Chaim* 326:5). [It is further prohibited to wash on the Sabbath with water heated illegally, due to the prohibition against deriving benefit from prohibited *melachah* (*Ramban* et al.).]

6. The final clause of the Mishnah, containing the incident of the Tiberian pipe, is stated anonymously. [This follows Rabbah's interpretation of the Mishnah, as explained above, 39a note 16.] Now, there is a rule that the halachah always follows anonymous Mishnahs (see below, 46a). Accordingly, how can we interpret the Mishnah in a fashion that accords with the opinion of Beis Shammai and not Beis Hillel, when we know that the halachah must follow Beis Hillel? (see *Yevamos* 14a).

7. *Beitzah* 21b.

8. In general, any *melachah* that is forbidden on the Sabbath is forbidden on Yom Tov as well, except for certain *melachos* that are necessary for the preparation of food. Beis Shammai therefore rule that one may not heat up water on Yom Tov specifically to wash his feet. He may heat it only for drinking, but may then use some of it for washing his feet (*Rashi;* see *Tosafos* ד״ה אלא אם כן, *Tosafos* to *Beitzah* 21b ד״ה לא יחם, *Pnei Yehoshua* and *Rosh Yosef*). Beis Hillel, however, hold that any *melachah* that is normally required in the preparation of food is permitted even when no food preparation is involved. Since cooking is requisite to the preparation of food, Beis Hillel permit it even for non-food purposes. They therefore permit heating water on Yom Tov even specifically to wash one's feet (*Ran* to *Beitzah* 21b).

[Beis Hillel permit heating the water only in order to wash one's feet (or hands and face – see *Mishnah Berurah* 511:9). They agree, however, that water may not be heated to wash one's entire body because no *melachah* may be performed on Yom Tov to fulfill a need that is not common to most people [אֵינוֹ שָׁוֶה לְכָל נֶפֶשׁ] and bathing the entire body in hot water was not considered a universal necessity (*Tosafos* ד״ה וב״ה מתירין). Others maintain that bathing the entire body is forbidden only under the bathhouse injunction (*Ramban*). See *Rashba* and *Beur Halachah* to *Orach Chaim* 511:2 for a discussion about heating water to wash other parts of the body.]

ממעשה שעשו אנשי טבריא ואסרי להו רבנן בטלה א) הטמנה בדבר המוסיף הבל ואפילו מבעוד יום אמר עולא הלכה כאנשי טבריא א"ל רב נחמן כבר תברינהו אנשי טבריא לסילונייהו: מעשה שעשו אנשי טבריא: מאי רחיצה אילימא רחיצת כל גופו אלא חמין שהוחמו בשבת הוא דאסורין הא חמין שהוחמו מע"ש מותרין והתניא [א] ב) חמין שהוחמו מע"ש למחר רוחץ בהן פניו ידיו ורגליו אבל לא כל גופו אלא פניו ידיו ורגליו אימא סיפא *בי"ט כחמין שהוחמו בי"ט ואסורין ברחיצה ומותרין בשתיה לימא תנן סתמא כבית שמאי דתנן ג) בית שמאי אומרים לא יחם אדם חמין לרגליו אא"כ ראויין לשתיה וב"ה [ב] מתירין א"ר איקא בר חנניא להשתטף בהן כל גופו עסקינן והאי תנא הוא דתניא ג) לא [ג] ישתטף אדם כל גופו בין בחמין ובין בצונן דברי ר"מ ר"ש מתיר ר' יהודה אומר בחמין אסור בצונן מותר אמר רב חסדא מחלוקת בכלי אבל בקרקע דברי הכל מותר והא מעשה דאנשי טבריא בקרקע הוה ואסרי להו רבנן אלא אי איתמר ° הכי איתמר ד) מחלוקת בקרקע אבל בכלי דברי הכל אסור אמר רבה בר בר חנה אמר רבי יוחנן הלכה כרבי יהודה א"ל רב יוסף ד) בפירוש שמיע לך או מכללא שמיע לך מאי כללא דאמר רב תנחום א"ר יוחנן א"ר ינאי אמר ה) (רב) כל מקום שאתה מוצא שנים חלוקין ואחד מכריע הלכה כדברי המכריע חוץ ו) מקולי מטלניות שאף על פי שרבי אליעזר מחמיר ורבי יהושע מיקל ור' עקיבא מכריע אין הלכה כדברי המכריע חדא דרבי עקיבא תלמיד הוא ועוד הא

הדר

רש"י

בטלה הטמנה. נאסרה הטמנה בדבר המוסיף הבל דהא מבע"י נתנו שם הסילון ומפני שהצוננין מתחממין בכך ואע"ג דממילא אסור: לסילונייהו. לסילונין שלהן שחזרו בהן: ראויין לשתיה. דמחים להו לשתייה ואי בעי רוחץ בהן פניו: להשתטף. שנותן על גופו ומשתטף: והאי תנא. ר' שמעון היא דמתיר להשתטף כל גופו בשבת בחמין שהוחמו מע"ש והיינו דקאמר כחמין שהוחמו בשבת אסור (א) הא שהוחמו מאתמול שרי ואי בי"ט כחמין שהוחמו בי"ט ואסור ברחיצה דאפי' בית הלל לא שרי להחם בי"ט אלא לפניו ידיו ורגליו אבל לשיטוף כל גופו לא: לא ישתטף. בשבת: בין בחמין. ואפי' הוחמו בחול: בכלי. דהרואה אומר היום הוחמו ומוכחא מילתא דתולדות האור נינהו ואתי להחם בשבת כגון נותן צונן בחמין: אבל בקרקע. כגון אמבטאות של מרחצאות והן חמי האור: מותר. דבטלי להו מתורת חמין: והא מעשה דאנשי טבריא כו'. אלמא במילתייהו קיימי:

תוספות

ממעשה שעשו אנשי טבריא ואסרו להם בטלה הטמנה מבע"י בדבר המוסיף הבל. וא"ת מה צריך למילף ממעשה דאנשי טבריא הא מתני' היא דאין טומנין בדבר המוסיף הבל בפרק במה טומנין (לקמן ד' מז: ושם) ומבע"י איירי דמשחשיכה אפי' בדבר שאינו מוסיף הבל אסור כדאמרינן בפ"ב (לעיל דף לד.) ואור"י דמתניתין דלקמן איכא לאוקמא בבין השמשות אבל מבעוד יום ה"א דשרי וא"ת והא קתני טומנין בגיזי צמר ואין מטלטלין אותן ואי בין השמשות אין טומנין בהן והא אסור לטלטלן וי"ל דהוה מוקמינן כרבי דאמר (לעיל ד' מ:) כל דבר שהוא משום שבות לא גזרו עליו בין השמשות וא"ת אי כרבי אתיא אי מבעוד יום שרי להטמין ביה"ש נמי שרי דכל דבר שהוא משום שבות כו' וי"ל דה"א בהטמנה החמירו וה"ר שמואל מוורדין מפרש ממעשה אנשי טבריא בטלה הטמנה לאסור אפי' לאכול כדקתני ואסורין בשתיה וה"ר יונה מפרש ° בטלה אפי' בקדירה חייתא והיינו דקאמר בטלה משמע לגמרי מכל דבר: אלא פניו ידיו ורגליו כו'. הכל היה יכול לדקדק מסיפא דקתני בי"ט כחמין שהוחמו בי"ט אילימא רחיצת כל גופו הא הוחמו מעי"ט שרי והא לקמן אסר רחיצה בי"ט דקאמר למחר נכנס ומזיע אבל רוחץ לא ודוקא שטיפה שרי בבית החיצון אלא דרך הש"ס ז) מה שיכול לדקדק מרישא מדקדק ומיהו קשה לרשב"א דמגופה דמתניתין הוי מצי למידק בלא הך ברייתא דמייתי מדקתני ואסורין בשתיה כ"ש פניו ידיו ורגליו דאסירי: אלא אם כן ראויין לשתיה. נראה לר"י ° דווקא שמחמם אותם לצורך שתיה אבל לצורך רחיצה אע"ג דראויין לשתיה אסרי ב"ש ° דהא לית להו מתוך (ביצה ד' יב. ושם) ובפ"ב דביצה (ד' כא: ושם) אסרי ב"ש מדורה להתחמם כנגדה ואע"ג דראויה היא לבשל ולאפות ועוד אומר ר"י דמהכא נמי יש לדקדק דאי שרו ב"ש לצורך רחיצה משום דראויין לשתיה א"כ לא אתיא מתני' אפי' כב"ש דקתני ואסורין ברחיצה ומותרין בשתיה ומדקתני ומותרין בשתיה מכלל דראויין לשתיה ואפ"ה קתני דאסורין ברחיצה אלא ודאי לא שרו ב"ש אלא כשעושה לצורך שתיה ונראה לר"י דיכול לחמם אפי' ביותר מכדי שתיה כדאמר בפרק הדר (עירובין ד' סח.) ° נשיילה לאימיה אי צריכה נחימו אגב אימיה ודוקא בכדי שיעור לרגליו אבל לצורך כל גופו לא והיינו טעמא שהבלנים חשודים לפעמים שיחממו עיקרן לרחיצה:

וב"ה מתירין. משמע דוקא לרגליו אבל לצורך כל גופו לא וכן משמע בכולה שמעתין דמחמירין בחמין שהוחמו בי"ט כחמין שהוחמו בשבת וגזרו על הזיעה ביו"ט כמו בשבת כדאמר בבילה בהמביא ולקמן (דף מ. ושם) א"כ משמע שאסור לעשות הבערה משום רחיצה שאם לא כן לא היו גוזרים על הזיעה ותימה דמ"מ הבערה דרחיצה מהבערה דזיעה דשרי מדאורייתא כדמוכח התם ואומר ר"י בשם ריב"א דרחיצה אינה אלא לתענוג ואסורה כמו מוגמר דאסור בפ"ק דכתובות (ד' ז. ושם) משום דאין שוה לכל נפש וכן משמע בירושלמי דהיינו טעמא דרחיצה אבל זיעה שוה היא לכל נפש דאינה תענוג אלא לבריאות והא דתניא לקמן (ד' מ.) מרחץ שפקקו נקביו מעי"ט למחר נכנס ומזיע ה"ה אפי' הוחם בו ביום אלא נקט מעי"ט דאפ"ה דוקא מזיע אבל רוחץ לא:

בין בחמין בין בצונן. נראה לר"י דהיינו אפי' חמין שהוחמו מע"ש דהא אוסר אפי' צונן ומסתמא בהנך חמין אסיר ר' יהודה ועוד דמסתמא לא איירי בדעבדי איסורא והאי תנא הוא דקאמר היינו ר"ש ועוד אומר ר"י דיש להוכיח דבחמין שהוחמו מע"ש פליגי דאמר בפרק חבית (לקמן ד' קמו. ושם) מה חמי טבריא חמין דיעבד אין לכתחילה לא מכלל דלהשתטף אפי' לכתחילה מני ר"ש היא דתניא לא ישתטף כו' ואי בשהוחמו בשבת פליגי אבל מערב שבת שרי ר' יהודה אמאי צריך לאוקמה כר"ש לוקמה כר' יהודה ובהוחמו מע"ש דהא דומיא דחמי טבריא קתני: והא מעשה דאנשי טבריא בקרקע הוה ואסרי להו. הקשה ה"ר אליעזר ממי"ץ מאי פריך התם הוחמו בשבת כדקתני כחמין שהוחמו בשבת משמע דבהוחמו מע"ש שרי והכא ג) בהוחמו מע"ש פליגי כדפרישית ומפרש הר"ר יוסף דס"ל להש"ס מדמחמיר ר"מ כ"כ דאוסר אפי' צונן מחמיר נמי לאסור ע"ש אטו שבת ולהכי פריך והא מעשה דאנשי טבריא בקרקע הוה ואסרי להו בהוחמו בשבת ורב חסדא קאמר אבל בקרקע ד"ה מותר אפי' בהוחמו בשבת דהא לר"מ אי הוה אוסר להו בהוחמו בשבת בהוחמו מע"ש נמי הוה אוסר וקשה דר"מ אוסר להשתטף בצונן אפי' בקרקע כדמסיק דבקרקע פליגי ובפרק שמונה שרצים (לקמן דף קט. ושם) משמע דשרי דקאמר התם רוחצין במי גרר ובמי חמתן ובמי עסיא ובמי טבריא אבל לא בים הגדול ורמינהו רוחצין במי טבריא ובים הגדול כו' ומוקים בתרייתא כר' מאיר וי"ל דבקרקע דהכא לאסר היינו דומיא דכלי דדמי לרוחץ בחמין והתם בנהר התירו שנראה כמיקר בנהר ואפי' בחמי טבריא לא דמי לאדם רוחץ בחמין:

אמר רבה בר בר חנה ח) הלכה כר' יהודה. אע"ג דר' יוחנן אית ליה הלכה כסתם משנה הכא משום דר' יהודה מכריע הוא אין הלכה כסתם וקשה דבפרק קמא דפסחים (דף יג. ודף כא. ושם) פריך ונימא מר הלכה כר' מאיר דסתם לן תנא כוותיה אע"ג דסבר דרבן גמליאל מכריע הוא דפריך בתר הכי ונימא מר הלכה כרבן גמליאל דהוה ליה מכריע וי"ל דסתם דהכא גריע מההוא סתם דהכא סתם במתני' ומחלוקת בברייתא והלכה כמכריע ומיהו אי לאו הכרעה הוה הלכה כסתם מתני' אע"ג דמחלוקת בברייתא: הא (לעיל) חמין שהוחמו מבעוד יום מותרים והתניא חמין שהוחמו כו'. תימה לוקי ההיא ברייתא דאסרה בכלי משום דהרואה אומר היום הוחמו ומתניתין בקרקע כמשמעה כדמפליג בסמוך בין כלי לקרקע וי"ל דדוקא בשיטוף דקיל איכא לפלוגי אבל ברחיצה דחמירא לא מסתברא לפלוגי בהכי:

דילמא

עין משפט נר מצוה

יד א ב מיי' פ"א מהל' יו"ט הלכה טז סמג לאוין עה טוש"ע או"ח סימן תקיא סעיף ג:

טו ג ד מיי' פכ"ב מהל' שבת הלכה ג סמג לאוין סה טוש"ע או"ח סימן שכו סעיף א:

רבינו חננאל

קי"ל כת"ק אמר רב חסדא מדאסרו להו [רבנן] שמע מיניה דבטלה הטמנה בדבר המוסיף ואפילו מבעוד יום. אסיקנא דכופח מקום שפיתת קדירה אחת הוא. ואם הוסק בגפת או בעצים הרי הוא כתנור ואסור לסמוך בו. וכ"ש בתוכו או על גבו. וכן לשהות בו אע"פ שהוא גרוף וקטום אסור. נמצא האסור שני פנים. צונן שלא הוחמו כל עיקר. ותבשיל שהתחיל להתבשל ולא הגיע למאכל בן דרוסאי. ומותר שני פנים. חמין שהוחמו ולא בשלו כל עיקר ושבשלו כמאכל בן דרוסאי. ואפילו [לא] בשלו כל צרכן מותר. ומאי דקשי ליה [זיקא] מסקנא כלישנא בתראה דרב אשי דבין דגדיא ובין [דברחא] בין שריק ובין שלא שריק שרי. ולא יטמיננה בחול ובאבק דרכים בשביל שתצלה דברי הכל אסור: מעשה שעשו אנשי טבריא הביאו סילון של צונן כו' אין הלכה כאנשי טבריא דהא תברינהו לסילונייהו אוקימנא הא דתנן אסור ברחיצה להשתטף בהן כל גופו ור' שמעון הוא דשרי בחמין שהוחמו מע"ש להשתטף דתניא אסור להשתטף בין בחמין בין בצונן דברי רבי מאיר ורבי שמעון מתיר רבי יהודה אומר בחמין אסור בצונן מותר. אמר רבה בר בר חנה אמר רבי יוחנן הלכה כר' יהודה: הא דקאמר שמואל חמין שהוחמו מע"ש אינו רוחץ בהן בשבת אלא פניו ידיו ורגליו תניא כוותיה וקי"ל כוותיה דשמואל בהא: א"ל לרבה בר בר חנה בפירוש שמיע לך מיניה דר' יוחנן דהלכתא כר' יהודה דבצונן מותר להשתטף אבל בחמין אסור. או מכללא. מאי כללא דא"ר יוחנן א"ר ינאי כל מקום ששנים חולקין ואחד מכריע הלכה כדברי המכריע חוץ מקולי מטליות שפירשנום בפרק של מעלה. והוא זה ששנינו בכלים בפרק כ"ח פחות משלשה על שלשה שהתקינה לפקק בה את המרחץ כו'. אף על פי שרבי אליעזר מחמיר ורבי יהושע מיקל ורבי עקיבא מכריע שאין הלכה כרבי עקיבא. חדא דתלמיד הוא ואין תלמיד מכריע על רבו.

רב נסים גאון

חדא דר' עקיבא לגבי רבי אליעזר ורבי יהושע תלמיד הוא. פירוש שלו

מסורת הש"ס

א) [לקמן מ.], ב) ביצה כא:, ג) לקמן קמו: ע"ש תוספתא פ"ד, ד) [ברכות ס. וש"נ], ה) [נ"ל רבי], ו) [לעיל כט.], ז) [וכ"כ תוספות עירובין סח. ד"ה אימא וכתובות נא. ד"ה מני ודף פט. ד"ה ש"מ וב"ב מ. ד"ה הא ועי' תוס' לקמן מו: ד"ה כבתה ותוס' ברכות מב. ד"ה הסבו ותוספות ב"מ יג: ד"ה הא מבני וע"ע רש"י ב"מ כג: ד"ה הא של ב"ב], ח) [אמר ר' יוחנן הלכה סו'].

תוספות ישנים

א) הא דלא מייתי בעבר ושהה מהכא דאסור דשאני הטמנה דיש להחמיר:

ב) ואם תאמר ולימא דמתני' קודם גזירה וי"ל דמסתמא אחר גזירה דגזירה קדמוני' היתה:

ג) ומהר"מ מפרש דחמין שהוחמו מע"ש היינו שנסתלקו מעל האור מבע"י. ושהוחמו בשבת היינו נמי שהוחמו מבע"י כל צורכן אך מתחממים והולכין גם בשבת דומיא דאנשי טבריא. ובהנהו פליגי ר"מ ור"י ור"ש. ולוננין קרי שהיו חמין כבר ולנטננו. אבל בנסתלקו מבע"י אפילו ר"מ מודה דשרי להשתטף ולא לרחוץ. והאי תנא הוא ר"מ ור"י דאסרי חמין שמתחממין והולכין גם בשבת. והשתא פריך שפיר והא מעשה דאנשי טבריא בקרקע הוי. ויתיישב נמי ההיא דפ' שמנה שרצים דשרי ר"מ לרחוץ בקרקע. וכן בפרק חבית דמוקי כר"ש:

הגהות הב"ח

(א) רש"י ד"ה והאי תנא וכו' שהוחמו בשבת אסור ברחילה הא שהוחמו:

גליון הש"ס

גמ' הכי איתמר מחלוקת בקרקע. עי' מ"ק דף יט ע"ב תוס' ד"ה שאסור ול"ע: תוס' ד"ה ממעשה וכו' בטלה אפילו בקדירה חייתא. עי' לקמן דף מז ע"ב תוס' ד"ה במה טומנין: ד"ה אא"כ וכו' נראה לר"י דוקא שמחמם. עי' לקמן דף עו ע"א תוס' ד"ה הואיל וראוין: בא"ד דהא לית להו מתוך. דבריהם צ"ע לענין מתוך מה הפרש בין ראויים או אינן ראויים. וראיתי ברשב"א שהוסיף ומאן דלית ליה מתוך לית ליה הואיל. ויסוד זה נסתר מפירכת הגמ' פסחים דף מז ע"ב וכמ"ש התוס' שם ד"ה אהבערה לא ליחייב ולע"ג. ובתשובה וגם בדרשות הארכתי בזה בעהש"י: בא"ד כדאמרינן פרק הדר נשייליה. ק"ל למאי הוצרכו לראיה זו דאפשר לצורך מילה עדיף. הא להדיא איתא ברייתא ערוכה בבילה ממלא נחתום חבית מים אע"פ שא"צ אלא לקיתון אחד:

ליקוטי רש"י

לא יחם אדם חמין. לרחוץ רגליו אוכל נפש התיר הכתוב ולא להבעיר אור בשביל רחילה [ביצה כא:]. ר"ש מתיר. להשתטף שופכן על גופו דלאו דרך רחיצה היא שרי לכתחילה אפילו בחמין [לקמן קמז: עיי"ש]. בפירוש שמיע לך. מיניה. או מכללא. דשמעת מיניה מילתא דדייקת מיניה. מאי כללא. מאיזה כלל היה לו לומר [יבמות ס:]. הלכה כדברי המכריע. כשזה אומר כך וזה אומר כך וזה אומר דעת שלישית אפילו אמצעית היא ביניהם אין זה הכרע כגון (פסחים כ:) חבית של תרומה שנתגלתה ב"ש אומר תשפך הכל וב"ה אומרים תעשה זילוף א"ר ישמעאל בר' יוסי אני אכריע בשדה תשפך הכל בבית תעשה זילוף אמרו לו אין הכרעה שלישית מכרעת והיכי הויא הכרעה כגון ההיא דקולי מטלניות דבמה מדליקין (שבת כט.) ר' אליעזר אומר בין מן המוכן בין שלא מן המוכן טמא ר' יהושע אומר בין מן המוכן בין שלא מן המוכן טהור ר"ע אומר מן המוכן טמא שלא מן המוכן טהור א"ר יוחנן עלה כל מקום שאתה מוצא שנים חולקים ואחד מכריע כו' אלמא כה"ג קרי הכרעה היכא דגלו (מאי) דעתייהו דשייך לפלוגי בין מוכן לשאינו מוכן אפ"ה לא פלגינן ואתא ר"ע ונתן חילוק בדבר הוי הכרעה שהכריע במוכן כר' אליעזר ונמצאו שנים מטמאים במוכן ור' יהושע יחיד מטהר ובשאינו מוכן כר' יהושע והוו שנים מטהרים בשאינו מוכן אבל גבי חבית דלא גלו דעתייהו ב"ש וב"ה דנהוי שייך חילוק בין בית לשדה שלא אמרו כך ב"ש אומר בין בבית בין בשדה תשפך הכל וב"ה אומר בין בבית בין בשדה תעשה זילוף ובא שלישי וחלק בין שדה לבית התם אין זה הכרע לדבריהם אלא דעת שלישית דהכרע לשון כף מאזנים הוי בשנים חולקין ובא שלישי ומכריע המשקל כאחד מהן או בכל הדבר או במקצתו כזה ובמקצתו כזה [חולין קלז. וכעי"ז ב"ק קטז.]. הכרעה שהיא במקצת כדברי זה ומקצת כדברי זה אינה הכרעה עד שתהא כולה כדברי א' מהן דהכרעה לשון שיכול שוקל דברי שנים יותר מאחד [נזיר נג.]. מקולי מטלניות. מטלניות הקלות בעיניו דומיא דמתוקנות לפקוק מרחץ דמידי דלא חשיב הוא [לעיל כט.].

washing the hands, face and feet, it must follow the opinion of Beis Shammai, and this cannot be correct. What type of bathing, then, are we dealing with?

The Gemara resolves the difficulty:

אָמַר רַב אִיקָא בַּר חֲנַנְיָא – **Rav Ika bar Chananya said:** לְהִשְׁתַּטֵּף בְּהֶן כָּל גּוּפוֹ עַסְקִינַן – **We are dealing with rinsing one's entire body** (i.e. showering) rather than with bathing, and our Mishnah holds that the prohibition against bathing in hot water that was heated before the Sabbath does not extend to rinsing the entire body.[9] וְהַאי תַּנָּא הוּא – **And [the Mishnah] is** reflective of the view of **the following Tanna** (i.e. R' Shimon). דְּתַנְיָא – **For it was taught in a Baraisa:** לֹא יִשְׁתַּטֵּף אָדָם כָּל גּוּפוֹ בֵּין בְּחַמִּין וּבֵין בְּצוֹנֵן – ONE MAY NOT RINSE HIS ENTIRE BODY WITH EITHER HOT WATER OR COLD WATER on the Sabbath. דִּבְרֵי רַבִּי מֵאִיר – These are THE WORDS OF R' MEIR.[10] רַבִּי שִׁמְעוֹן מַתִּיר – R' SHIMON, however, PERMITS rinsing the entire body with either hot water that was heated before the Sabbath or cold water.[11] רַבִּי יְהוּדָה אוֹמֵר – R' YEHUDAH SAYS: בְּחַמִּין אָסוּר – Rinsing the entire body WITH HOT WATER IS FORBIDDEN, even if the water was heated before the Sabbath, בְּצוֹנֵן מוּתָּר – but rinsing it WITH COLD WATER IS PERMITTED.[12] Our Mishnah reflects the view of R' Shimon.

Having cited the Tannaic dispute concerning rinsing with hot water, the Gemara clarifies it:

אָמַר רַב חִסְדָּא – **Rav Chisda said:** מַחְלוֹקֶת בִּכְלִי – **The dispute** between R' Shimon and R' Yehudah concerning rinsing with hot water **pertains** to water that is **in a vessel,** אֲבָל בְּקַרְקַע דִּבְרֵי הַכֹּל מוּתָּר – **but** as for water that is **in the ground, all agree** that **it is permissible** to rinse with it.[13]

The Gemara argues:

וְהָא מַעֲשֶׂה דְּאַנְשֵׁי טְבֶרְיָא בְּקַרְקַע הֲוָה – **But the incident of the Tiberians** involved water that was **in the ground,** וְאַסְרֵי לְהוּ רַבָּנַן – **yet the Rabbis forbade them** to rinse with it, as we concluded above.[14] – ? –

Conceding the point, the Gemara revises its report of Rav Chisda's teaching:

אֶלָּא אִי אִיתְּמַר הָכִי אִיתְּמַר – **Rather, if** anything **was stated** by Rav Chisda **this is what was stated:** מַחְלוֹקֶת בְּקַרְקַע – **The dispute pertains** to rinsing with water that is **in the ground,** אֲבָל בִּכְלִי דִּבְרֵי הַכֹּל אָסוּר – **but** as for water that is **in a vessel, all agree that it is prohibited** to rinse with it.[15]

The Gemara records a halachic ruling:

אָמַר רַבָּה בַּר בַּר חָנָה אָמַר רַבִּי יוֹחָנָן – **Rabbah bar bar Chanah said in the name of R' Yochanan:** הֲלָכָה כְּרַבִּי יְהוּדָה – **The halachah follows R' Yehudah.**[16]

A question is raised concerning how Rabbah bar bar Chanah received this ruling from R' Yochanan:

אָמַר לֵיהּ רַב יוֹסֵף – **Rav Yosef said to [Rabbah bar bar Chanah]:**

NOTES

9. The Sages therefore told the Tiberians that water which flowed through the pipe on the Sabbath is like water that was heated manually on the Sabbath, and is thus forbidden even for *rinsing* and drinking. If water would flow through the pipe on Yom Tov it would be like water that was heated on Yom Tov and would be permitted for drinking but forbidden for rinsing, since even Beis Hillel forbid heating water on Yom Tov for the purpose of rinsing the entire body. The implication is that water heated *before* the Sabbath or Yom Tov may be used for rinsing on the Sabbath or Yom Tov, which is indeed true, according to one Tannaic opinion which follows (*Rashi*). [The term "rinsing" refers to both pouring water over the body from a vessel and standing under a shower.]

10. R' Meir holds that due to the similarity between rinsing the entire body and bathing, the bathhouse injunction was applied even to rinsing. As an added stringency, it was extended even to rinsing with cold water (see *Tosafos* ד״ה והא and *Pnei Yehoshua* to *Rashi* ד״ה בכלי). Others explain that the bathhouse injunction was extended even to rinsing with cold water because it was common for people who bathed in hot water to rinse afterwards with cold water, and one who observed a person rinsing might assume that he had previously bathed in hot water (*Milchamos Hashem, Rashba*). Since R' Meir forbids even showering in cold water, his reference to hot water obviously includes water that was heated before the Sabbath (see *Rashi* and *Tosafos*).

11. R' Shimon holds that the bathhouse injunction does not extend to rinsing with either hot water that was heated before the Sabbath or cold water. He concedes, however, that it is forbidden to rinse with water that was heated on the Sabbath [since such water is treated more stringently]. This is the opinion of the Tanna of our Mishnah, who cited the Sages as forbidding bathing (i.e. rinsing) with the Tiberian water because it was like water that had been heated manually on the Sabbath (*Rashba;* see also *Rashi* ד״ה והאי תנא and *Tosafos* ד״ה בין בחמין).

12. R' Yehudah extends the injunction to rinsing with water heated before the Sabbath, but not to rinsing with cold water (see following notes).

13. According to R' Yehudah, the reason the bathhouse injunction was extended to *rinsing* with water heated before the Sabbath is the concern that someone might think the water was heated on the Sabbath and might himself come to heat water on the Sabbath. Although everyone knows that it is forbidden to cook on the Sabbath, an uninformed person might think that some cold water was mixed with the hot water on the Sabbath, as was commonly done with bath water (see 42a note 14). That person might think that it is permitted to heat cold water by mixing it with hot water. [Actually, pouring a little cold water into a pot of hot water, even after the pot has been removed from the fire, is considered a genuine act of cooking the cold water (see 40b note 16).] R' Yehudah holds that due to this concern the Rabbis forbade rinsing with hot water on the Sabbath.

However, Rav Chisda says, the Rabbis issued this prohibition only in regard to water that is in a vessel. Since the water was obviously heated on a fire, there is the concern that a person might think it is permitted to heat cold water with a derivative of fire; for example, by mixing it with hot water in a pot. If the water is in the ground – e.g. in an in-ground bathtub – it is permitted to rinse with it even according to R' Yehudah. In this case, the above concern does not apply, since in-ground water is often taken from hotsprings rather than heated on a fire. Thus, even if the water was originally heated on a fire, it is less likely that its use for rinsing will lead someone to think that it is permitted to add cold water to water that was heated on a fire (see *Rashi, Ramban* and *Pnei Yehoshua*).

14. [The pipe of fresh water that the Tiberians ran through the canal of hot water eventually emptied into an in-ground pool in which they bathed. Nevertheless, the Sages forbade them to use it for bathing or rinsing.] Evidently, hot water that is in an in-ground pool or tub is subject to the prohibition against rinsing, no less than that which is in a vessel (*Rashi*; see *Pnei Yehoshua*).

[One might ask: The Mishnah implies that the water was prohibited for rinsing only because it was heated on the Sabbath. The dispute between R' Shimon and R' Yehudah, however, pertains specifically to water that was heated *before* the Sabbath; all agree that water heated on the Sabbath may not be used for rinsing, whether it was stored in a vessel or in the ground. What then does the incident of the Tiberians prove? See *Tosafos* ד״ה והא מעשה, *Ramban* et al., who deal with this difficulty.]

15. I.e. R' Yehudah holds that the bathhouse injunction applies to rinsing with any hot water heated before the Sabbath, whether it is in a vessel or in the ground. [However, he does not extend the injunction to forbid rinsing with *cold* water, as R' Meir does.] R' Shimon, on the other hand, holds that the injunction does not apply to rinsing with water heated before the Sabbath, when the water is in the ground. Nevertheless, he concedes that it is forbidden to rinse with hot water that is in a vessel, due to the concern described above in note 13 (see *Ramban* et al.).

16. Thus, it is prohibited to bathe or rinse the entire body (or the majority of the body) on the Sabbath with hot water, even if it was heated before the Sabbath (*Orach Chaim* 326:1). It is customary to refrain from bathing at all, even in cold water (*Mishnah Berurah* 326:21; see there and *Magen Avraham* 326:8 for the reasons). Concerning showering with cold water, see *Igros Moshe, Orach Chaim* vol. IV §75. Concerning bathing on Yom Tov, see *Orach Chaim* 511:2.

ממעשה שעשו אנשי טבריא ואסרי להו רבנן בטלה א) הטמנה בדבר המוסיף הבל ואפילו מבעוד יום אמר עולא הלכה כאנשי טבריא א"ל רב נחמן כבר תברינהו אנשי טבריא לסילונייהו: מעשה שעשו אנשי טבריא: מאי רחיצה אילימא רחיצת כל גופו אלא חמין שהוחמו בשבת הוא דאסורין הא חמין שהוחמו מע"ש מותרין והתניא א ב) חמין שהוחמו מע"ש למחר רוחץ בהן פניו ידיו ורגליו אבל לא כל גופו אלא פניו ידיו ורגליו אימא סיפא א בי"ט כחמין שהוחמו בי"ט ואסורין ברחיצה ומותרין בשתיה לימא תנן סתמא כבית שמאי דתנן ב בית שמאי אומרים לא יחם אדם חמין לרגליו אא"כ ראויין לשתיה ובה"ה ב מתירין א"ר איקא בר חנניא להשתטף בהן כל גופו עסקינן והאי תנא הוא דתניא ג לא ג ישתטף אדם כל גופו בין בחמין ובין בצונן דברי ר"מ ר"ש מתיר ר' יהודה אומר בחמין אסור בצונן מותר אמר רב חסדא מחלוקת בכלי אבל בקרקע דברי הכל מותר והא מעשה דאנשי טבריא בקרקע הוה ואסרי להו רבנן אלא אי איתמר ° הכי איתמר ד מחלוקת בקרקע אבל בכלי דברי הכל אסור אמר רבה בר בר חנה אמר רבי יוחנן הלכה כרבי יהודה א"ל רב יוסף ד בפירוש שמיע לך או מכללא שמיע לך מאי כללא דאמר רב תנחום א"ר יוחנן א"ר ינאי אמר ה (רב) כל מקום שאתה מוצא שנים חלוקין ואחד מכריע הלכה כדברי המכריע חוץ ו מקולי מטלניות שאף על פי שרבי אליעזר מחמיר ורבי יהושע מיקל ור' עקיבא מכריע אין הלכה כדברי המכריע חדא דרבי עקיבא תלמיד הוא ועוד הא

הדר

רש"י

בטלה הטמנה. נאסרה הטמנה בדבר המוסיף הבל דהא מבע"י נתנו שם הסילון ומפני שהצוננין מתחממין בכך ואע"ג דממילא אסור: לסילונייהו. לסילונין שלהן שחזרו בהן: ראויין לשתיה. דמחים להו לשתייה ואי בעי רוחץ בהן פניו: להשתטף. שנותן על גופו ומשתטף: והאי תנא. ר' שמעון היא דמתיר להשתטף כל גופו בשבת בחמין שהוחמו מע"ש והיינו דקאמר כחמין שהוחמו בשבת אסור (א) הא שהוחמו מאתמול שרי ואי בי"ט כחמין שהוחמו בי"ט ואסור ברחיצה דאפי' בית הלל לא שרי להחם בי"ט אלא לפניו ידיו ורגליו אבל לשיטוף כל גופו לא: לא ישתטף. בשבת: בין בחמין. ואפי' הוחמו בחול: בכלי. דהרואה אומר היום הוחמו ומוכחא מילתא דתולדות האור נינהו ואתי להחם בשבת כגון נותן צונן בחמין: אבל בקרקע. כגון אמבטאות של מרחצאות והן חמי האור: מותר. דבטלי להו מתורת חמין: והא מעשה דאנשי טבריא כו'. אלמא במילתייהו קיימי:

הדר

תוספות

ממעשה שעשו אנשי טבריא ואסרו להם בטלה הטמנה מבע"י בדבר המוסיף הבל. וא"ת מה צריך למילף ממעשה דאנשי טבריא הא מתני' היא דאין טומנין בדבר המוסיף הבל בפרק במה טומנין (לקמן ד' מז: ושם) ומבע"י איירי דמשחשיכה אפי' בדבר שאינו מוסיף הבל אסור כדאמרינן בפ"ב (לעיל דף לד.) ואור"י דמתניתין דלקמן איכא לאוקמא בבין השמשות אבל מבעוד יום ה"א דשרי וא"ת והא קתני טומנין בגיזי צמר ואין מטלטלין אותן ואי בין השמשות איך טומנין בהן והא אסור לטלטלן וי"ל דהוה מוקמינן כרבי דאמר (לעיל ד' ח:) כל דבר שהוא משום שבות לא גזרו עליו בין השמשות וא"ת אי כרבי אתיא אי מבעוד יום שרי להטמין ביה"ש נמי שרי דכל דבר שהוא משום שבות כו' וי"ל דה"א בהטמנה החמירו וה"ר שמואל מוורדין מפרש ממעשה אנשי טבריא בטלה הטמנה דאסור אפי' לאכול כדקתני ואסורין בשתיה וה"ר יונה מפרש ° בטלה אפי' בקדירה חייתא והיינו דקאמר בטלה משמע לגמרי מכל דבר: אלא פניו ידיו ורגליו כו'. הכל היה יכול לדקדק מסיפא דקתני בי"ט כחמין שהוחמו בי"ט אילימא רחיצת כל גופו הא הוחמו מעי"ט שרי והא לקמן אסר רחיצה בי"ט דקאמר למחר נכנס ומזיע אבל רוחץ לא ודוקא שטיפה שרי בבית החיצון אלא דרך הש"ס ז) מה שיכול לדקדק מרישא מדקדק ומיהו קשה לרשב"א דמגופה דמתניתין הוי מצי למידק בלא הך ברייתא דמייתי מדקתני ואסורין בשתיה כ"ש פניו ידיו ורגליו דאסירי: אלא אם כן ראויין לשתיה. נראה לר"י ° דווקא שמחמם אותם לצורך שתיה אבל לצורך רחיצה אע"ג דראויין לשתיה אסרי ב"ש ° דהא לית להו מתוך (ביצה ד' יב. ושם) ובפ"ב דביצה (ד' כא: ושם) אסרי ב"ש מדורה להתחמם כנגדה ואע"ג דראויה היא לבשל ולאפות ועוד אומר ר"י דמהכא נמי יש לדקדק דאי שרו ב"ש לצורך רחיצה משום דראויין לשתיה א"כ לא אתיא מתני' אפי' כב"ש דקתני ואסורין ברחיצה ומותרין בשתיה ומדקתני ומותרין בשתיה מכלל דראויין לשתיה ואפ"ה קתני דאסורין ברחיצה אלא ודאי לא שרו ב"ש אלא כשעושה לצורך שתיה ונראה לר"י דיכול לחמם אפי' ביותר מכדי שתיה כדאמר בפרק הדר (עירובין ד' סח.) ° נשיילה לאימיה אי צריכה נחימו אגב אימיה ודוקא בכדי שיעור לרגליו אבל לצורך כל גופו לא והיינו טעמא שהבלנים חשודים לפעמים שיחממו עיקרן לרחיצה:

וב"ה מתירין. משמע דוקא לרגליו אבל לצורך כל גופו לא וכן משמע בכולה שמעתין דמחמירין בחמין שהוחמו בשבת וגזרו על הזיעה ביו"ט כמו בשבת כדאמר בביצה בהמביא ולקמן (דף מ. ושם) א"כ משמע שאסור לעשות הבערה משום רחיצה שאם לא כן לא היו גוזרים על הזיעה ותימה דמ"מ הבערה דרחיצה מהבערה דזיעה דשרי מדאורייתא כדמוכח התם ואומר ר"י בשם ריב"א דרחיצה אינה אלא לתענוג ואסורה כמו מוגמר דאסור בפ"ק דכתובות (ד' ז. ושם) משום דאין שוה לכל נפש וכן משמע בירושלמי דהיינו טעמא דרחיצה אבל זיעה שוה היא לכל נפש דאינה תענוג אלא לבריאות והא דתניא לקמן (ד' מ.) מרחץ שפקקו נקביו מעי"ט למחר נכנס ומזיע ה"ה אפי' הוחם בו ביום אלא נקט מעי"ט דאפ"ה דוקא מזיע אבל רוחץ לא:

בין בחמין בין בצונן. נראה לר"י דהיינו אפי' חמין שהוחמו מע"ש דהא אוסר אפי' צונן ומסתמא בהנך חמין אסיר ר' יהודה ועוד דמסתמא לא מיירי בדעבדי איסורא והאי תנא הוא דקאמר היינו ר"ש ועוד אומר ר"י דיש להוכיח דבחמין שהוחמו מע"ש פליגי דאמר בפרק חבית (לקמן ד' קמז. ושם) מה חמי טבריא חמין אף מי מערה חמין הרוחץ דיעבד אין לכתחילה לא מכלל דלהשתטף אפי' לכתחילה מני ר"ש היא דתניא לא ישתטף כו' ואי בשהוחמו בשבת פליגי אבל מערב שבת שרי ר' יהודה אמאי צריך לאוקמה כר"ש לוקמה כר' יהודה ובהוחמו מע"ש דהא דומיא דחמי טבריא קתני: והא מעשה דאנשי טבריא בקרקע הוה ואסרי להו. הקשה ה"ר אליעזר ממי"ץ מאי פריך התם הוחמו בשבת כדקתני כחמין שהוחמו בשבת משמע דבהוחמו מע"ש שרי והכא ג) בהוחמו מע"ש פליגי כדפרישית ומפרש הר"ר יוסף דס"ל להש"ס מדמחמיר ר"מ כ"כ דאוסר אפי' צונן מחמיר נמי לאסור ע"ש אטו שבת ולהכי פריך והא מעשה דאנשי טבריא בקרקע הוה ואסרי להו בהוחמו בשבת ורב חסדא קאמר אבל בקרקע ד"ה מותר אפי' בהוחמו בשבת דהא לר"מ אי הוה אוסר להו בהוחמו בשבת בהוחמו מע"ש נמי הוה אוסר וקשה דר"מ אוסר להשתטף בצונן אפי' בקרקע כדמסיק דבקרקע פליגי ובפרק שמונה שרצים (לקמן דף קט. ושם) משמע דשרי דקאמר התם רוחצין במי גרר ובמי חמתן ובמי עסיא ובמי טבריא אבל לא בים הגדול ורמינהו רוחצין במי טבריא ובים הגדול כו' ומוקים בתרייתא כר' מאיר וי"ל דבקרקע דהכא לאסר היינו דומיא דכלי דדמי לרוחץ בחמין והתם בנהר התירו שנראה כמיקר בנהר ואפי' בחמי טבריא לא דמי לאדם רוחץ בחמין:

אמר רבה בר בר חנה ח) הלכה כר' יהודה. אע"ג דר' יוחנן אית ליה הלכה כסתם משנה הכא משום דר' יהודה מכריע הוא אין הלכה כסתם וקשה דבפרק קמא דפסחים (דף יג. ודף כא. ושם) פריך ונימא מר הלכה כר' מאיר דסתם לן תנא כוותיה אע"ג דסבר דרבן גמליאל מכריע הוא דפריך בתר הכי ונימא מר הלכה כרבן גמליאל דהוה ליה מכריע וי"ל דסתם דהכא גריע מההוא סתם דהכא סתם במתני' ומחלוקת בברייתא והלכה כמכריע ומיהו אי לאו הכרעה הוה הלכה כסתם מתני' אע"ג דמחלוקת בברייתא: (לעיל) הא חמין שהוחמו מבעוד יום מותרים והתניא חמין שהוחמו כו'. תימה לוקי ההיא ברייתא דאסרה בכלי משום דהרואה אומר היום הוחמו ומתניתין בקרקע כמשמעה כדמפליג בסמוך בין כלי לקרקע וי"ל דדוקא בשיטוף דקיל איכא לפלוגי אבל ברחיצה דחמירא לא מסתברא לפלוגי בהכי:

דילמא

יד א ב מיי' פ"א מהל' יו"ט הלכה טז סמג לאוין עה טוש"ע או"ח סימן תקיא סעיף ג:
טו ג ד מיי' פכ"ב מהל' שבת הלכה ג סמג לאוין סה טוש"ע או"ח סימן שכו סעיף א:

רבינו חננאל

קי"ל כת"ק אמר רב חסדא מדאסרו להו רבנן] שמע מיניה דבטלה הטמנה בדבר המוסיף ואפילו מבעוד יום. אסיקנא דכופח מקום שפיתת קדירה אחת הוא. ואם הוסק בגפת או בעצים הרי הוא כתנור ואסור לסמוך בו. וכ"ש בתוכו או על גבו. וכן לשהות בו אע"פ שהוא גרוף וקטום אסור. נמצא האסור שני פנים. צונן שלא הוחמו כל עיקר. ותבשיל שהתחיל להתבשל ולא הגיע למאכל בן דרוסאי. ומותר שני פנים. חמין שהוחמו ולא בשלו כל עיקר ושבשלו כמאכל בן דרוסאי. ואפילו [לא] בשלו כל צרכן מותר. ומאי דקשי ליה [זיקא] מסקנא כלישנא בתראה דרב אשי דבין דגדיא ובין [דברחא] בין שריק ובין שלא שריק שרי. ולא יטמיננה בחול ובאבק דרכים בשביל שתצלה דברי הכל אסור: מעשה שעשו אנשי טבריא הביאו סילון של צונן כו' אין הלכה כאנשי טבריא דהא תברינהו לסילונייהו אוקימנא הא דתנן אסור ברחיצה להשתטף בהן כל גופו ור' שמעון הוא דשרי בחמין שהוחמו מע"ש להשתטף דתניא אסור להשתטף בין בחמין בין בצונן דברי רבי מאיר ורבי שמעון מתיר רבי יהודה אומר בחמין אסור בצונן מותר. אמר רבה בר בר חנה אמר רבי יוחנן הלכה כר' יהודה: הא דקאמר שמואל חמין שהוחמו מע"ש אינו רוחץ בהן בשבת אלא פניו ידיו ורגליו תניא כוותיה וקי"ל כוותיה דשמואל בהא: א"ל לרבה בר בר חנה בפירוש שמיע לך מיניה דר' יוחנן דהלכתא כר' יהודה דבצונן מותר להשתטף אבל בחמין אסור. או מכללא. מאי כללא דא"ר יוחנן א"ר ינאי כל מקום ששנים חולקין ואחד מכריע הלכה כדברי המכריע חוץ מקולי מטליות שפירשנום בפרק של מעלה. והוא זה ששנינו בכלים בפרק כ"ח פחות משלשה על שלשה שהתקינה לפקק בה את המרחץ כו'. אף על פי שרבי אליעזר מחמיר ורבי יהושע מיקל ורבי עקיבא מכריע שאין הלכה כרבי עקיבא. חדא דתלמיד הוא ואין תלמיד מכריע על רבו.

רב נסים גאון

חדא דר' עקיבא לגבי רבי אליעזר ורבי יהושע תלמיד הוא. פירוש שלו

מסורת הש"ס

א) [לקמן מ.], ב) ביצה כא:, ג) לקמן קמו: ע"ש תוספתא פ"ד, ד) [ברכות ט. וש"נ], ה) [נ"ל רבי], ו) [לעיל כט.], ז) [וכ"כ תוספות עירובין כח. ד"ה אימא ובכתובות נא. ד"ה מני ודף פט. ד"ה ש"מ וב"ב מ. ד"ה הא ועי' תוס' לקמן מו: ד"ה כבתה ותוס' ברכות מג. ד"ה הסבו ותוספות ב"מ יג: ד"ה הא מבני וע"ע רש"י ב"מ כג: ד"ה הא של ב"ב], ח) [אמר ר' יוחנן הלכה כו'].

תוספות ישנים

א) הא דלא מייתי בעבר ושהה מהכא דאסור דשאני הטמנה דיש להחמיר:
ב) ואם תאמר ולימא דמתני' קודם גזירה וי"ל דמסתמא אחר גזירה דגזירה קדמוני' היתה:
ג) ומהר"מ מפרש דחמין שהוחמו מע"ש היינו שנסתלקו מעל האור מבע"י. ושהוחמו בשבת היינו נמי שהוחמו מבע"י כל צורכן אך מתחממים והולכין גם בשבת דומיא דאנשי טבריא. ובהנהו פליגי ר"מ ור"י ור"ש. ולצונן קרי שהיו חמין כבר ונצטננו. אבל בנסתלקו מבע"י אפילו ר"מ מודה דשרי להשתטף ולא לרחוץ. והאי תנא הוא ר"מ ור"י דאסרי חמין שמתחממין והולכין גם בשבת. והשתא פריך שפיר והא מעשה דאנשי טבריא בקרקע הוי. ויתיישב נמי ההיא דפ' שמנה שרצים דשרי ר"מ לרחוץ בקרקע. וכן בפרק חבית דמוקי כר"ש:

הגהות הב"ח

(א) רש"י ד"ה והאי תנא וכו' שהוחמו בשבת אסור ברחילה הא שהוחמו:

גליון הש"ס

גמ' הכי איתמר מחלוקת בקרקע. עי' מ"ק דף יט ע"ב תוס' ד"ה שאסור וצ"ע: תוס' ד"ה ממעשה וכו' בטלה אפילו בקדירה חייתא. עי' לקמן דף מז ע"ב תוס' ד"ה במה טומנין: ד"ה אא"כ וכו' נראה לר"י דוקא שמחמם. עי' לקמן דף עו ע"א תוס' ד"ה הואיל וראוין: בא"ד דהא לית להו מתוך. דבריהם צ"ע דלענין מתוך מה הפרש בין ראויים או אינן ראויים. וראיתי ברשב"א שהוסיף ומאן דלית ליה מתוך לית ליה הואיל. ויסוד זה נסתר מפירכת הגמ' פסחים דף מז ע"ב וכמ"ש התוס' שם ד"ה אהבערה לא ליחייב ולע"ג. ובתשובה וגם בדרשות הארכתי בזה בעהש"י: בא"ד כדאמרינן פרק הדר נשיילה. ק"ל למאי הוצרכו לראיה זו דאפשר לצורך מילה עדיף. הא להדיא איתא ברייתא ערוכה בבילה ממלא נחתום חבית מים אע"פ שא"צ אלא לקיתון אחד:

ליקוטי רש"י

לא יחם אדם חמין. לרחוץ רגליו אוכל נפש התיר הכתוב ולא להבעיר אור בשביל רחילה [ביצה כא:]. ר"ש מתיר. להשתטף שופכן על גופו דלאו דרך רחילה היא שרי לכתחילה אפילו בחמין [לקמן קמז: עיי"ש]. בפירוש שמיע לך. מיניה. או מכללא. דשמעת מיניה מילתא דדייקת מיניה. מאי כללא. מאיזה כלל היה לו לומר [יבמות ס:]. הלכה כדברי המכריע. כשזה אומר כך וזה אומר כך וזה אומר דעת שלישית אפילו אמצעית היא ביניהם אין זה הכרע כגון (פסחים כ:) חבית של תרומה שנתגלתה ב"ש אומר תשפך הכל וב"ה אומרים תעשה זילוף א"ר ישמעאל בר' יוסי אני אכריע בשדה תשפך הכל בבית תעשה זילוף אמרו לו אין הכרעה שלישית מכרעת והיכי הויא הכרעה כגון ההיא דקולי מטלניות דבמה מדליקין (שבת כט.) ר' אליעזר אומר בין מן המוכן בין שלא מן המוכן טמא ר' יהושע אומר בין מן המוכן בין שלא מן המוכן טהור ר"ע אומר מן המוכן טמא שלא מן המוכן טהור א"ר יוחנן עלה כל מקום שאתה מוצא שנים חולקים ואחד מכריע כו' אלמא כה"ג קרי הכרעה היכא דגלו (מאי) דעתייהו דשייך לפלוגי בין מוכן לשאינו מוכן אפ"ה לא פלגינן ואתא ר"ע ונתן חילוק בדבר הוי הכרעה שהכריע במוכן כר' אליעזר ונמצאו שנים מטמאים במוכן ור' יהושע יחיד מטהר ובשאינו מוכן כר' יהושע והוו שנים מטהרים בשאינו מוכן אבל גבי חבית דלא גלו דעתייהו ב"ש וב"ה דנהוי שייך חילוק בין בית לשדה שלא אמרו כך ב"ש אומר בין בבית בין בשדה וב"ה אומר בין בבית בין בשדה תעשה זילוף ובא שלישי וחלק בין שדה לבית התם אין זה הכרע לדבריהם אלא דעת שלישית דהכרע לשון כף מאזנים הוי בשנים חולקין ובא שלישי ומכריע המשקל כאחד מהן או בכל הדבר או בחציו כזה ובחציו כזה [חולין קלז. וכעי"ז ב"ק קטז.]. הכרעה שהיא במקצת כדברי זה ומקצת כדברי זה אינה הכרעה עד שתהא כולה כדברי א' מהן דהכרעה לשון שיקול ששוקל דברי שנים יותר מאחד [נזיר נג.]. מקולי מטלניות. מטלניות הקלות בעיניו דומיא דמתוקנות לפקוק מרחץ דמידי דלא חשיב הוא [לעיל כט.].

בְּפֵירוּשׁ שְׁמִיעַ לָךְ אוֹ מִכְּלָלָא שְׁמִיעַ לָךְ – **Did you hear this explicitly from R' Yochanan, or did you learn it through inference** from something else that he said?[17]

The Gemara elaborates on Rav Yosef's conjecture:

מַאי כְּלָלָא – To **what inference** was Rav Yosef referring? Which statement of R' Yochanan might have been construed as indicating that the halachah follows R' Yehudah? דְּאָמַר רַב תַּנְחוּם אָמַר רַבִּי יוֹחָנָן אָמַר רַבִּי יַנַּאי אָמַר (רַב) [רַבִּי] – It is the following: **For Rav Tanchum said in the name of R' Yochanan, who said in the name of R' Yannai, who said in the name of Rebbi:**[18] כָּל מָקוֹם שֶׁאַתָּה מוֹצֵא שְׁנַיִם חֲלוּקִין וְאֶחָד מַכְרִיעַ – **Wherever you encounter two** Tannaim **who disagree and** a third **one who mediates** between them, הֲלָכָה כְּדִבְרֵי הַמַּכְרִיעַ – **the halachah follows the opinion of the mediator,** חוּץ מִקּוּלֵּי מַטְלָנִיּוֹת – **except for** the case of the dispute concerning **rags that were** designated for an **insignificant** use,[19] שֶׁאַף עַל פִּי שֶׁרַבִּי אֱלִיעֶזֶר מַחְמִיר וְרַבִּי יְהוֹשֻׁעַ מֵיקֵל וְרַבִּי עֲקִיבָא מַכְרִיעַ – **where although R' Eliezer rules stringently and R' Yehoshua rules leniently, and R' Akiva mediates** between them, אֵין הֲלָכָה כְּדִבְרֵי הַמַּכְרִיעַ – **the halachah does not follow the opinion of the mediator** for two reasons: חֲדָא דְּרַבִּי עֲקִיבָא תַּלְמִיד הוּא – **Firstly, because R' Akiva was a student** of R' Eliezer and R' Yehoshua, and the view of a student does not outweigh the view of his teacher, even when the student is a mediator. וְעוֹד – **And furthermore,** הָא –

NOTES

17. As the Gemara will explain, Rav Yosef suspected that Rabbah bar bar Chanah had merely inferred this from a statement of R' Yochanan and that his inference might have been erroneous.

18. The emendation of the text to read *Rebbi* (rather than *Rav*) follows *Mesoras HaShas* and is based on the fact that R' Yannai was a disciple of Rebbi and a *teacher* of Rav (see *Yevamos* 93a with *Rashi* ד״ה רב הונא כרב; see also *Rambam, Introduction* to *Mishneh Torah;* cf. *Raavad* ad loc.).

19. This dispute appeared above (29a,b), and concerns the circumstances in which such a rag is susceptible to *tumah.* It was explained there, beginning with note 27.

הָדַר בֵּיהּ רַבִּי עֲקִיבָא לְגַבֵּיהּ דְּרַבִּי יְהוֹשֻׁעַ – why, R' Akiva retracted his opinion in favor of R' Yehoshua's.[1] Perhaps this statement of R' Yochanan led Rabbah bar bar Chanah to conclude that, concerning our case, R' Yochanan would hold that the halachah follows R' Yehudah, whose position is that of a mediator.[2]

The Gemara asks:

וְאִי מִכְּלָלָא מַאי – And what if Rabbah bar bar Chanah did learn it through inference? Is the inference not valid?

The Gemara answers:

דִּילְמָא הָנֵי מִילֵּי בְּמַתְנִיתִין – It is not valid, for perhaps this principle that the halachah follows the opinion of a mediator applies only to a mediating view that is recorded in a Mishnah, like the one concerning rags that are designated for an insignificant use, אֲבָל בְּבָרַיְיתָא לָא – but not to one that is recorded in a Baraisa, such as R' Yehudah's.[3] Thus, if Rabbah bar bar Chanah did not hear R' Yochanan state explicitly that the halachah follows R' Yehudah, but merely inferred this from the previous statement, the validity of the inference is questionable.

The Gemara records Rabbah bar bar Chanah's reply to Rav Yosef:

אֲמַר לֵיהּ – He said to him: אֲנָא בְּפֵירוּשׁ שְׁמִיעַ לִי – I heard this explicitly from R' Yochanan.

Having concluded that it is forbidden to bathe or rinse one's entire body on the Sabbath with hot water, even if it was heated before the Sabbath, the Gemara cites an Amoraic discussion concerning the details of this prohibition:

אִתְּמַר – It was stated: חַמִּין שֶׁהוּחַמּוּ מֵעֶרֶב שַׁבָּת – Concerning hot water that was heated before the Sabbath: רַב אָמַר – Rav said: לְמָחָר רוֹחֵץ בָּהֶן כָּל גּוּפוֹ אֵבֶר אֵבֶר – On the following day, i.e. the Sabbath, one may wash his entire body with it, one limb at a time.[4] וּשְׁמוּאֵל אָמַר – But Shmuel said: לֹא הִתִּירוּ לִרְחוֹץ אֶלָּא פָּנָיו יָדָיו וְרַגְלָיו – They permitted washing only one's face, hands and feet with the hot water. Bathing the entire body, even one limb at a time, is forbidden.

Rav's view is challenged:

מֵיתִיבִי – They challenged Rav on the basis of the following Baraisa: חַמִּין שֶׁהוּחַמּוּ מֵעֶרֶב שַׁבָּת – Concerning HOT WATER THAT WAS HEATED BEFORE THE SABBATH: לְמָחָר רוֹחֵץ בָּהֶן פָּנָיו יָדָיו וְרַגְלָיו אֲבָל לֹא כָּל גּוּפוֹ – ON THE FOLLOWING DAY, ONE MAY WASH HIS FACE, HANDS AND FEET WITH THEM, BUT NOT HIS ENTIRE BODY.[5] תְּיוּבְתָּא דְּרַב – This seems to constitute a refutation of Rav, who allows washing the entire body one limb at a time. – ? –

The Gemara deflects the challenge:

אָמַר לָךְ רַב – Rav can tell you that the Baraisa means only לֹא כָּל גּוּפוֹ בְּבַת אַחַת – that one should not wash his entire body at once, אֶלָּא אֵבֶר אֵבֶר – but rather, should wash it one limb at a time.

The Gemara counters:

וְהָא פָּנָיו יָדָיו וְרַגְלָיו קָתָנֵי – But the Baraisa states that one may wash HIS FACE, HANDS AND FEET, thus implying that washing the entire body is forbidden, even one limb at a time! – ? –

The Gemara answers:

כְּעֵין פָּנָיו יָדָיו וְרַגְלָיו – The Baraisa may mean that one may wash his entire body in the same manner as one washes his face, hands and feet, i.e. one limb at a time.

The Gemara cites another challenge to Rav:

תָּא שְׁמַע – Come, learn a refutation of Rav's view from the following Baraisa: לֹא הִתִּירוּ לִרְחוֹץ בְּחַמִּין שֶׁהוּחַמּוּ מֵעֶרֶב שַׁבָּת – THEY DID NOT PERMIT WASHING on the Sabbath WITH HOT WATER THAT WAS HEATED BEFORE THE SABBATH אֶלָּא פָּנָיו יָדָיו וְרַגְלָיו – EXCEPT FOR ONE'S FACE, HANDS AND FEET. Apparently, washing the entire body is forbidden, even one limb at a time.

The Gemara rejects this challenge as well:

הָכָא נַמִּי – Here too, כְּעֵין פָּנָיו יָדָיו וְרַגְלָיו – the Baraisa means that one may wash his entire body in the same manner as one washes his face, hands and feet, i.e. one limb at a time.

The Gemara adduces clear support for Shmuel's view:

תַּנְיָא כְּוָותֵיהּ דִּשְׁמוּאֵל – A Baraisa was taught in accordance with the opinion of Shmuel: חַמִּין שֶׁהוּחַמּוּ מֵעֶרֶב שַׁבָּת – Concerning HOT WATER THAT WAS HEATED BEFORE THE SABBATH: לְמָחָר רוֹחֵץ בָּהֶן פָּנָיו יָדָיו וְרַגְלָיו – ON THE FOLLOWING DAY, ONE MAY WASH HIS FACE, HANDS AND FEET WITH THEM, אֲבָל לֹא כָּל גּוּפוֹ אֵבֶר אֵבֶר – BUT NOT HIS ENTIRE BODY, even ONE LIMB AT A TIME; וְאֵין צָרִיךְ לוֹמַר חַמִּין שֶׁהוּחַמּוּ בְּיוֹם טוֹב – AND IT GOES WITHOUT SAYING that the same prohibition applies to HOT WATER THAT WAS HEATED ON A FESTIVAL.[6] This Baraisa explicitly refutes Rav's view.

The Gemara cites a different version of Rav's view and the refutation that followed it:

רַבָּה מַתְנֵי לָהּ לְהָא שְׁמַעְתָּא דְּרַב בְּהַאי לִישָּׁנָא – Rabbah taught this discourse of Rav in this manner: חַמִּין שֶׁהוּחַמּוּ מֵעֶרֶב שַׁבָּת – Concerning hot water that was heated before the Sabbath: לְמָחָר אָמַר רַב רוֹחֵץ בָּהֶן כָּל גּוּפוֹ – Rav said that on the following day, one may bathe his entire body in it וּמְשַׁיֵּיר אֵבֶר אֶחָד – but must leave one limb unbathed.[7]

The Gemara comments:

אֵיתִיבֵיהּ כָּל הָנֵי תְּיוּבָתָא – According to Rabbah's version as well, they challenged [Rav] with all those challenges cited above in the first version, תְּיוּבְתָּא – and, indeed, those Baraisas constitute a refutation of Rav's opinion.[8]

NOTES

1. As stated above, 29b.

2. The basis for following the opinion of the mediator is that since he agrees with each Tanna concerning one facet of the discussion, his opinion combines with that of the Tanna with whom he agrees to form a majority view concerning that facet. This outweighs the opinion of the single Tanna with whom the mediator disagrees. Hence, the mediator is called the מַכְרִיעַ, which means, literally, *the outweigher*.

In our case, R' Yehudah agrees with R' Meir that it is forbidden to rinse with hot water, and with R' Shimon that it is permissible to rinse with cold water, thus outweighing the opposing view in each case (*Rashi*).

3. Since R' Shimon's view was recorded in the Mishnah (as the Gemara explained above) and R' Yehudah's mediating view was merely recorded in a Baraisa, perhaps the halachah does not follow the mediator (*Rashi*, as understood by *R' Elazar Moshe Horowitz;* see *Tosafos* ד״ה דילמא).

4. According to Rav, the injunction against bathing on the Sabbath with hot water that was heated before the Sabbath pertains only to bathing the entire body at once; washing one limb at a time, however, is permitted.

5. This Baraisa was cited above, 39b. See notes 4 and 5 there.

6. I.e. it is forbidden on Yom Tov to wash one's entire body, even one limb at a time, with water that was heated on Yom Tov. See 39b note 8.

7. I.e. one is permitted even to bathe his entire body at once, provided he leaves one limb unbathed (*Rashi*).

8. Even the first two challenges, which were deflected above, constitute refutations according to this version. We cannot deflect those challenges by interpreting the Baraisa as meaning that one may wash his entire body in the manner in which he washes his face, hands and feet, i.e. one limb at a time, since according to this version Rav permits bathing the entire body *at once*, provided he leaves one limb unbathed (*Rashi*).

ᵃ הדר ביה ר"ע לגביה דרבי יהושע ᵇ ואי מכללא מאי דילמא ה"מ במתניתין אבל בברייתא לא א"ל אנא בפירוש שמיע לי אתמר חמין שהוחמו מע"ש רב אמר למחר רוחץ בהן כל גופו אבר אבר ושמואל אמר לא התירו לרחוץ אלא פניו ידיו ורגליו מיתיבי חמין שהוחמו מע"ש למחר רוחץ בהן פניו ידיו ורגליו אבל לא כל גופו תיובתא דרב אמר לך רב לא כל גופו בבת אחת אלא אבר אבר והא פניו ידיו ורגליו קתני כעין פניו ידיו ורגליו תא שמע לא התירו לרחוץ בחמין שהוחמו מע"ש אלא פניו ידיו ורגליו ה"נ כעין פניו ידיו ורגליו תניא כוותיה דשמואל ᶜ א חמין שהוחמו מע"ש למחר רוחץ בהן פניו ידיו ורגליו אבל לא כל גופו אבר אבר ואצ"ל חמין שהוחמו בי"ט רבה מתני לה להא שמעתא דרב בהאי לישנא חמין שהוחמו מע"ש למחר אמר רב רוחץ בהן כל גופו ומשייר אבר אחד איתיביה כל הני תיובתא תיובתא א"ל רב יוסף לאביי רבה מי קא עביד כשמעתיה דרב א"ל לא ידענא מאי תיבעי ליה פשיטא דלא עביד דהא איתותב (ᵈ דילמא) לא שמיעא ליה ואי לא שמיעא ליה ודאי עביד ᵉ דאמר אביי כל מילי דמר עביד כרב בר מהני תלת דעביד כשמואל ᶠ מטילין מבגד לבגד ומדליקין מנר לנר והלכה כר"ש בגרירה כחומרי דרב עביד כקולי דרב לא עביד ᵍ ת"ר ב מרחץ שפקקו נקביו מע"ש למוצ"ש רוחץ בו מיד פקקו נקביו ג מעי"ט למחר נכנס ומזיע ויוצא ומשתטף בבית החיצון אמר רב יהודה מעשה במרחץ של בני ברק שפקקו נקביו מעי"ט למחר נכנס ראב"ע ור"ע והזיעו בו ויצאו ונשתטפו בבית החיצון אלא שחמין שלו מחופין בנסרים כשבא הדבר לפני חכמים אמרו אף על פי שאין חמין שלו מחופין בנסרין ומשרבו עוברי עבירה התחילו לאסור אמבטיאות של כרכין מטייל בהן ואינו חושש מאי עוברי עבירה דא"ר שמעון בן פזי אמר ריב"ל משום בר קפרא בתחלה היו רוחצין בחמין שהוחמו מע"ש התחילו הבלנים להחם בשבת ואומרים מערב שבת הוחמו אסרו את החמין והתירו את הזיעה ועדיין היו רוחצין בחמין ואומרים מזיעין אנחנו אסרו להן את הזיעה והתירו חמי טבריה ועדיין היו רוחצין בחמי האור ואומרים בחמי טבריה רחצנו אסרו להן חמי טבריה והתירו להן את הצונן ראו שאין הדבר עומד להן ᵈ התירו להן חמי טבריה ᵉ וזיעה במקומה עומדת אמר רבא האי מאן דעבר אדרבנן שרי למיקרי ליה עבריינא כמאן
כי

רש"י

הדר ביה רבי עקיבא. כדאמרינן בפירקין דלעיל (דף כט:) לשון מכריע מכביד מטה כף מאזנים ומכריע את שכנגדו כגון הכא בחמין אסור השתא הוה ליה ר' שמעון דמתיר בחמין יחיד במקום שנים נמצא ר' יהודה מכביד את כף המשקולת שהרי ר' יהודה עם רבי מאיר שוים לאיסור ובצונן מותר הוי ליה ר' מאיר בצונן יחיד במקום שנים נמצא ר' יהודה מכביד את כף המשקולת: ה"מ. דא"ר יוחנן הלכה כדברי המכריע במכריע במשנה כי ההיא דמטלניות: כעין פניו. כלומר כל אבר בפני עצמו: רוחץ בהן כל גופו. ביחד אלא שמשייר אבר אחד: איתיביה כל הני. וליכא לשנויי כעין פניו ידיו ורגליו דהא כל גופו יחד קאמר חוץ מאבר אחד: א"ל רב יוסף לאביי. משום דגדל אביי בבית רבה בר נחמני שהיה ראש קודם לרב יוסף ומת היה שואלו רב יוסף איך היה רואהו נוהג: מי עביד כשמעתי' דרב. בהא מילתא דרחיצה: מאי תבעי ליה. שיטה דהש"ם פרכא ליה: לא שמיע ליה. ᶠ לרבה הא תיובתא משום הכי מספקא ליה לרב יוסף ברבה דדילמא עביד כרב: ואי לא שמיעא ליה. אמאי מספקא ליה לרב יוסף: הא ודאי עביד. רבה בכל מילי כרב: כחומרי דרב הוה עביד. בר מהני תלת חומרי אבל כקולי דרב איכא דלא עביד והא קולא היא ודילמא לא עביד: שפקקו נקביו. שלא יצא חמימותו: רוחץ בו מיד. ואין צריך להמתין בכדי שיעשה ל"א שפקקו נקביו אותן נקבים שמרחץ מתחמם על ידיהן שאור ניסקת מבחוץ מתחתיו ᵍ לר"ה ועיקר רוחץ בו מיד שהרי לא נתחמם בשבת אבל בשבת לא שהרי גזרו על הרחיצה: ומשתטף בבית החיצון. שלפני המרחץ ולא בתוך המרחץ שלא יאמרו רוחץ הוא כדאמרן דאסרו את הרחיצה אבל הזיעה התירו והיאך היא זיעה עומד או יושב בבית המרחץ ואינו נותן מים עליו והוא מתחמם ומזיע: מחופין בנסרים. ולא היו צריכין לחוש שמא נתחממו בשבת מחומו של מרחץ: התחילו לאסור. את הזיעה: אמבטאות. בתי מרחץ גדולים: מטייל בהן. מהלך בתוכן לפי דרכו ולא להזיע: ואינו חושש. שמא יאמרו מזיע הוא ואע"ג דאסרו את הזיעה: מאי עוברי עבירה. דקאמר לעיל שאסרו זיעה על ידיהן: אסרו להן את החמין. לגמרי: ועדיין היו רוחצין בחמין. שהוחמו מבע"י: שאין הדבר עומד. שלא היו ציבור יכולין לקבל מתוך שאסרו להם את הכל: במקומה עומדת. לאיסור:

תוספות

דילמא ה"מ במתני' אבל בברייתא לא. ° אע"ג דלא קאמר במשנתינו ʸ הכא משמע דאין הלכה כמותו משום דקתם מתני' דלא כוותיה ᵖ: הלכה כדברי המכריע. הכרעה כגון קולי מטלניות שר"א ור"י הזכירו בפירוש בדבריהם מוכן ושאינו מוכן דהיינו תלאו במגוד והניחו אחורי הדלת שגילו בדבריהם שיש סברא לחלק ביניהם אלא שנראה להם דסוף סוף אין לחלק ביניהם לכך הוי ר' עקיבא שמחלק ביניהם מכריע וכן ר' יהודה הוי מכריע דר' שמעון ור"מ הזכירו בדבריהם חמין וצונן והכרעה שלישית דלא הויא הכרעה הוי כי ההיא דפ"ק דפסחים (דף כא.) חבית של יין של תרומה שנטמאה ב"ש אומרים תשפך ˡ הכל וב"ה אומר תיעשה זילוף אמר ר' ישמעאל בר' יוסי אני אכריע בשדה תשפך ᵐ הכל ובבית תעשה זילוף אמרו לו אין הכרעה שלישית מכרעת משום דלא הזכירו ב"ש וב"ה בדבריהם בית ושדה ולא גילו שיש סברא לחלק בין בית לשדה חשיב לה הכרעה שלישית ולא כפירוש הקונטרס דפירש התם דטעמייהו דב"ש לא משום תקל' אלא מטעם אחר כמו משום ריחא אלא משום דלא הזכירו בדבריהם בית ושדה כדפי' וה"ה דהוה מצי למימר ליה דאין הכרעת תלמיד הכרעה כדאמר הכא אלא רבותא אמרו דאפי' לא היה תלמיד אינה הכרעה והא דתנן בברכות (דף מג:) ב"ש אומרים מברך על השמן ואח"כ מברך על ההדס וב"ה אומרים מברך על ההדס ואח"כ על השמן א"ר גמליאל אני אכריע שמן זכינו לריחו וזכינו לסיכתו הדס לריחו זכינו לסיכתו לא זכינו וא"ר יוחנן הלכה כדברי המכריע פר"ת התם דהויא כהכרעה שבכל הש"ס ולא נהירא דלא הויא הכרעה אלא כדפי' והתם אינו אלא מפרש טעמא דבית שמאי ור"ח פי' אין הכרע' שלישית מכרעת היינו הכרע' דור שלישי כמו ר' ישמעאל בר' יוסי שהיה דור שלישי לב"ש וב"ה ולאו דוקא דור שלישי אלא ה"ה שני ובכל מקום נקט הכרעה שלישית משום ברייתא דפסחים ʸ:

למוצאי שבת רוחץ מיד. דוקא לרחוץ אבל להזיע נכנס אפי' בשבת ומזיע כמו בי"ט כדאמר בסמוך דאפי' בשבת הוי זיעה שריא עד הגזירה ולאחר גזירה אפילו בי"ט אסרו דאיום טוב קתני משרבו עוברי עבירה התחילו לאסור והוה מצי לערובינהו וליתנינהו מרחץ שפקקו נקביו מערב שבת או מערב יום טוב למחר נכנס ומזיע ולמוצאי שבת ויום טוב רוחץ מיד אלא אי עריב ותני להו הוה אמינא דדוקא בשבת אסרו הזיעה ולא ביום טוב דעובדא דמייתי בשבת הוה להכי מפליג להו השתא משרבו עוברי עבירה קאי איום טוב אבל לא אשבת דזיעה לא הוחכרה גבי שבת: אלא שחמין שלו מחופין בנסרים. פי' בקונטרס שלא היו צריכין לחוש שהוחמו בשבת מחום המרחץ משמע שסובר שנשתטפו בחמין שהוחמו מע"ש ולעיל אסר רבי יהודה גופיה ושמא יחלק בין שבת ליום טוב ומיהו בתוספתא גרסינן ונשתטפו בצונן אלא שחמין שלו מחופים ולא יסברו העולם שרחצו בחמין:
מפני

עין משפט נר מצוה

טז א מיי' פכ"ב מהלכות שבת הלכה ב סמג לאוין סה טוש"ע או"ח סימן שכו סעיף א:
יז ב שם סעיף יא:
יח ג מיי' פ"א מהלכות י"ט הלכה טז סמג לאוין עה טור שו"ע או"ח סימן תקיא סעיף ב:
יט ד מיי' פכ"ב מהלכות שבת הלכה ב סמג לאוין סה טוש"ע או"ח סימן שכו סעיף א:
כ ה מיי' שם טוש"ע שם סעיף יב:

רבינו חננאל

הדר ביה ר"ע לגבי דר' יהושע. ואסיקנא דאי מכללא מאי הוי ר' יהודה מכריע הוא והלכתא כדברי המכריע ובין [בפי' ובין] מכללא חדא הוא. ואמרינן דילמא הני מילי אם תהיה מחלוקתם במשנה אבל חלוקתם בברייתא לא. אמר ליה בפירוש שמיעא לי. והא דאמר אביי כל מילי דמר עביד כרב בר מהני תלת. אסיקנ' רבה כחומרי דרב הוה עביד. כקולי דרב לא הוה עביד: ת"ר מרחץ שפקקו. פי' פקקו סתמו נקביו מע"ש למוצאי שבת רוחץ בה מיד. פקקו נקביו מערב יום טוב למחר נכנס ומזיע ויוצא ומשתטף בבית החיצון. וכן עשו ר' אלעזר בן עזריה ור"ע במרחץ של בני ברק. משרבו עוברי עבירה התחילו לאסור שהיו מחמין בשבת ואומרים מע"ש החמנו. אסרו להן חמין והתירו הזיעה כו'. ואסיקנא אסרו להן אפילו חמין שהוחמו מע"ש ואפילו חמי טבריא וכ"ש חמי האור. ואפילו זיעה אסרו להן

רב נסים גאון

תמצאנו בנדרים בפרק הנודר מן המבושל (דף נ) ר' עקיבא אקדשא ליה ברתיה דבר כלבא שבוע כו' אמרה ליה זיל הוי בבי רב אזל הוה י"ב שנין קמיה רבי אליעזר ורבי יהושע ובהרבה מקומות תמצאנו כשהוא מדבר עם אחד מהן אומר ר' תרשני לומר לפניך דבר אחד ממה שלימדתני תגד דאלך (פירושו, תמצא זה) בר"ה (כה) בשעה ששיגר רבן גמליאל לר' יהושע גוזר אני עליך שתבוא אצלי במקלך כו' דתניא הלך ר"ע לר' יהושע מיצר א"ל ר"ע ר' תרשני לומר לפניך דבר אחד שלימדתני ובסנהדרין (פ' ד' מיתות דף סח) ר"ע אומר משום ר' יהושע שנים מלקטין קישואין כו' ובתלמוד אמרו גמרה מר' אליעזר ולא סברה הדר גמרה מר' יהושע ואסברה ניהליה. ועוד הא הדר ביה רבי עקיבא לגבי ר' יהושע מפורש זה בפרק במה מדליקין (דף כט):

מסורת הש"ס

א) [לעיל כט:], ב) [ברכות יב. וש"נ], ג) [לעיל לט:], ד) [רש"ל מ"ז], ה) לעיל כב. פסחים קא. מנחות מא:, ו) בכל המקומות איתא מתירין, ז) תוספתא שבת פ"ד, ח) מאן דגרס בגמ' דילמא גרס הכא לא שמיע ליה לרב יוסף, ט) תיבת לר"ה רמז לרבינו יהודה הלוי, י) [עי' ברכות יט. במשנתינו קאמרינן והא ברייתא היא], כ) [ועי' תוס' מנחות לה: ד"ה מי קאמר וכו' מילתו באופן אחר], ל) שם איתא הכל, מ) הכל, נ) [ועי' יתר אריכות בתוס' ב"ק קטו. ד"ה הכרעה].

גליון הש"ס

תוס' ד"ה דילמא ה"מ במתניתין וכו' אע"ג דלא קאמר במשנתנו. עי' משנה למלך ריש הלכות בית הבחירה:

ליקוטי רש"י

ואי מכללא מאי. מאי גריעותא איכא הא שפיר מצי למשמע מכללא [ברכות יב.]. מה לנו אי איתמר מכלל אי בפירוש הא מהא כללא שפיר שמעינן ומה יש לנו לגמגם בכלל זה [חולין צד.]. כל מילי דמר. רבה בר נחמני. בר מהני תלת. ומשום דהילכתא כרב באיסורי בכוליה הש"ס בר מהני תלת נקטינהו גבי הדדי. מטילין. ציצית מטלית ישן לטלית חדש ובמנחות מפרש טעמא דמאן דאסר [לעיל כב.]. מתירין ציצית של טלית זו ונותנין אותם לטלית אחרת. ומדליקין. מנר חנוכה לנר אחרת של חנוכה וא"צ להדליק בנר אחרת שאינה של חנוכה [רשב"ם פסחים קא.]. והלכה כרבי שמעון בגרירה. דאמר דבר שאין מתכוין מותר ואף על גב דקעביד חריץ והוי תולדה דחורש או בונה [לעיל שם]. גורר אדם מטה כסא וספסל כו' דדבר שאין מתכוין מותר והני ג' מילי פלוגתא דרב ושמואל בבמה מדליקין (שבת כב.) וכולהו עביד רבה כשמואל דמיקל [רשב"ם פסחים שם]. כחומרי דרב עביד. בר מהני תלת דעביד לקולא כשמואל [רש"י שם]. בקולי דרב לא עביד. ואע"ג דתניא (עירובין ו:) העושה כחומרי ב"ש כקוליהון וכחומריהון כו' הא קי"ל ה"מ היכא דסתרן אהדדי כגון כמה חסרון בשדרה כו' ואמר שמואל וכן לטריפה דחומרא דהתם קולא הוא הכא וקולא דהתם חומרא הוא הכא [רשב"ם שם]. בלנים. בלן. שומר בית המרחץ ומשמש בבית המרחץ ונוטל מכל אחד שכרו [מו"ק יא:].

The Gemara cites a discussion concerning Rabbah's practice regarding bathing on the Sabbath:

רַבָּה מִי קָא – אָמַר לֵיהּ רַב יוֹסֵף לְאַבָּיֵי – **Rav Yosef said to Abaye:** עָבִיד כִּשְׁמַעְתֵּיהּ דְּרַב – **Did Rabbah follow Rav's teaching in practice?**[9] אָמַר לֵיהּ לֹא יָדַעְנָא – **[Abaye] replied: I do not know.**

The Gemara expresses puzzlement at Rav Yosef's question:

מַאי תִּיבְּעֵי לֵיהּ – **What was his question?** פְּשִׁיטָא דְּלֹא עָבִיד דְּהָא אִיתּוֹתַב – **Obviously, [Rabbah] could not have followed** Rav's teaching **in practice, since it was refuted.** – ? –

The Gemara answers:

(דילמא) לֹא שְׁמִיעָא לֵיהּ – **[Rabbah] did not hear** the refutations. Thus, perhaps he followed Rav's opinion.[10]

The Gemara counters:

וְאִי לֹא שְׁמִיעָא לֵיהּ וַדַּאי עָבִיד – **But if [Rabbah] did not hear** the refutations, **he certainly followed** Rav's ruling **in practice,** דְּאָמַר אַבָּיֵי – **for Abaye said:** כָּל מִילֵּי דְּמַר עָבִיד כְּרַב – In **all of master's** (i.e. Rabbah's) **affairs, he acted in accordance with Rav** – בַּר מֵהָנֵי תְּלָת דְּעָבִיד כִּשְׁמוּאֵל – **with the exception of these three** cases, **where he acted in accordance with Shmuel:** מַטִּילִין מִבֶּגֶד לְבֶגֶד – He conceded that **we may attach** *tzitzis* taken **from an** old **garment to a** new **garment,**[11] וּמַדְלִיקִין מִנֵּר לְנֵר – **and** that **we may kindle from** one Chanukah **light to** another Chanukah **light,**[12] וְהִלְכְתָא כְּרַבִּי שִׁמְעוֹן בִּגְרִירָה – **and** that **the halachah follows R' Shimon in the matter of dragging** heavy furniture on the Sabbath where it may create a furrow in the ground.[13] Since as a rule Rabbah followed the opinions of Rav, why did Rav Yosef need to inquire about Rabbah's practice in regard to bathing on the Sabbath?

The Gemara answers:

בְּחוּמְרֵי דְּרַב עָבִיד – Abaye meant only that **[Rabbah] acted in accordance with** all of **Rav's stringent rulings,** except for the three cases he cited in which Rabbah followed Shmuel's lenient opinion. בְּקוּלֵּי דְּרַב לֹא עָבִיד – But **[Rabbah] did not** necessarily **act in accordance with** all of **Rav's lenient rulings.** Since Rav's opinion concerning bathing on the Sabbath represented a leniency, Rav Yosef needed to inquire whether Rabbah followed it.[14]

The Gemara cites a Baraisa which discusses the origin of the injunction against bathing in hot water on the Sabbath:

תָּנוּ רַבָּנָן – **The Rabbis taught in a Baraisa:** מֶרְחָץ שֶׁפָּקְקוּ נְקָבָיו מֵעֶרֶב שַׁבָּת – Concerning A BATHHOUSE that was heated and WHOSE VENTS WERE CLOSED BEFORE THE SABBATH:[15] לְמוֹצָאֵי שַׁבָּת רוֹחֵץ בּוֹ מִיָּד – UPON THE CONCLUSION OF THE SABBATH, ONE MAY BATHE IN IT IMMEDIATELY, but one may not bathe in it on the Sabbath itself.[16] פָּקְקוּ נְקָבָיו מֵעֶרֶב יוֹם טוֹב – Similarly, concerning a bathhouse that was heated and WHOSE VENTS WERE CLOSED BEFORE A FESTIVAL, לְמָחָר נִכְנָס וּמֵזִיעַ – ON THE NEXT DAY, i.e. the festival, ONE MAY ENTER the bathhouse AND STEAM-BATHE, וְיוֹצֵא וּמִשְׁתַּטֵּף בַּבַּיִת הַחִיצוֹן – but he must THEN EXIT AND RINSE IN THE OUTER CHAMBER of the bathhouse.[17] אָמַר רַב יְהוּדָה – R' YEHUDAH SAID: מַעֲשֶׂה בְּמֶרְחָץ שֶׁל בְּנֵי בְרַק – THERE WAS AN INCIDENT IN THE BATHHOUSE OF BNEI BRAK, שֶׁפָּקְקוּ נְקָבָיו מֵעֶרֶב יוֹם טוֹב – which had been heated and WHOSE VENTS HAD BEEN CLOSED BEFORE A FESTIVAL, לְמָחָר נִכְנַס רַבִּי אֶלְעָזָר בֶּן עֲזַרְיָה וְרַבִּי עֲקִיבָא וְהֵזִיעוּ בּוֹ – and ON THE FOLLOWING DAY, R' ELAZAR BEN AZARYAH AND R' AKIVA ENTERED the bathhouse AND STEAM-BATHED IN IT, וְיָצְאוּ וְנִשְׁתַּטְּפוּ בַּבַּיִת הַחִיצוֹן – AND THEY then EXITED AND RINSED IN THE OUTER CHAMBER. אֶלָּא שֶׁחַמִּין שֶׁלּוֹ מְחוּפִּין בִּנְסָרִים – HOWEVER, ITS tub of HOT WATER HAD BEEN COVERED WITH BOARDS.[18] כְּשֶׁבָּא הַדָּבָר לִפְנֵי חֲכָמִים אָמְרוּ – WHEN THE MATTER WAS BROUGHT TO the attention of THE SAGES, THEY

NOTES

9. Abaye was orphaned at birth (see *Kiddushin* 31b) and was raised in Rabbah's home. Since Rabbah had been head of the academy before Rav Yosef (see *Horayos* 14a) and had passed away, Rav Yosef sought to ascertain Rabbah's personal practice by inquiring of Abaye, who had presumably observed it (*Rashi*).

10. The Gemara commented above that the refutations also pertain to Rabbah's version of Rav's opinion, but Rav Yosef knew that Rabbah himself had not heard the refutations. He therefore inquired as to Rabbah's practice (*Rashi,* as explained by *Maharsha;* cf. *Maharshal, Melo HaRo'im*). Although Rav Yosef, who had heard the refutations, could certainly not follow Rav's opinion in this case, he was interested in determining whether Rabbah was accustomed to following Rav's opinions, as the Gemara goes on to explain. [Note that the word דילמא does not appear in *Rashi's* version of the text, as explained by *Maharsha;* see also *Mesoras HaShas.*]

11. And it is not considered disrespectful to the first garment if one does so (see *Aruch HaShulchan* 15:1 and *Tosafos* above, 22a ד"ה רב).

12. The novelty of this ruling was explained above (end of 22a).

13. There is a Tannaic dispute (below, 41b; *Beitzah* 23b) as to whether one may perform a permitted act on the Sabbath when it is possible that he will incidentally perform a forbidden *melachah* as well [דָּבָר שֶׁאֵין מִתְכַּוֵּן]. For example, may one drag a heavy bench across an unpaved courtyard when he might thereby create a furrow in the ground – an action that would qualify as a *toladah* of *plowing.* R' Shimon allows the person to perform the permitted act (e.g. dragging the bench) so long as he does not intend to do the forbidden labor (e.g. creating the furrow). R' Yehudah prohibits the performance of the permitted act in such a case. Abaye informs us that Rabbah concurred with Shmuel's acceptance of R' Shimon's opinion as law (*Rashi* to 22a).

14. In any event, regardless of Rabbah's practice, the Gemara has already refuted Rav's view. The halachah therefore follows Shmuel, who said that it is forbidden to bathe the entire body on the Sabbath with water that was heated before the Sabbath, even one limb at a time and even if one leaves an entire limb unbathed. Washing the face, hands and feet, however, is permitted.

Regarding bathing a portion of one's body on the Sabbath, i.e. more than the face, hands and feet but the minority of the entire body, see *Orach Chaim* 326:1.

15. Ancient bathhouses were heated by fires burning in the basement, which generated heat that was channeled into the bathhouses through vents in the floor. If the vents were closed before the Sabbath, the bathhouses were not heated further on the Sabbath (second and preferred explanation of *Rashi;* see also *Orach Chaim* 326:11 with *Mishnah Berurah* §31).

16. Since the baths were not heated on the Sabbath [and were not even heated indirectly, through the heat of the bathhouse], one need not wait until such time Saturday night by which it would have been possible to heat them after the Sabbath [בִּכְדֵי שֶׁיֵּעָשׂוּ], but may bathe in them the moment the Sabbath has ended. However, one may not bathe in them on the Sabbath itself, since bathing on the Sabbath is prohibited even in water that was heated before the Sabbath (*Rashi*). [If the vents were left open on the Sabbath, one may not use the baths until enough time elapsed after the Sabbath to heat them legally. This is a special decree that was enacted out of concern that people might leave fires burning under the bathhouses and mistakenly rake the coals on the Sabbath (*Ran; Orach Chaim* 326:11).]

17. Initially, when the Sages prohibited bathing in hot water on the Sabbath or Yom Tov, they did not prohibit steam-bathing. Nevertheless, they decreed that after steam-bathing one should not rinse his body in the inner chamber of the bathhouse, i.e. the bathing room, lest people think that he had bathed. Rather, one should exit to the outer room in order to rinse (*Rashi*). [The rule stated here pertains to the Sabbath as well as Yom Tov. For an explanation of why the Baraisa mentions it specifically concerning Yom Tov, see *Tosafos* ד"ה למוצאי שבת and *Ramban.*]

18. Thus, R' Elazar ben Azaryah and R' Akiva knew with certainty that the water had not been warmed on the festival by the heat sustained in the bathhouse from its pre-festival heating (*Rashi*).

The implication is that R' Elazar ben Azaryah and R' Akiva rinsed with hot water from the tub on Yom Tov. However, this presents a difficulty, since R' Yehudah, who cited this incident, ruled above (39b)

א) הדר ביה ר"ע לגביה דרבי יהושע ב) ואי מכללא מאי דילמא ה"מ במתניתין אבל בברייתא לא א"ל אנא בפירוש שמיע לי אתמר חמין שהוחמו מע"ש רב אמר למחר רוחץ בהן כל גופו אבר אבר ושמואל אמר לא התירו לרחוץ אלא פניו ידיו ורגליו מיתיבי חמין שהוחמו מע"ש למחר רוחץ בהן פניו ידיו ורגליו אבל לא כל גופו תיובתא דרב אמר לך רב לא כל גופו בבת אחת אלא אבר אבר והא פניו ידיו ורגליו קתני כעין פניו ידיו ורגליו תא שמע לא התירו לרחוץ בחמין שהוחמו מע"ש אלא פניו ידיו ורגליו ה"נ כעין פניו ידיו ורגליו תניא כוותיה דשמואל ג) א חמין שהוחמו מע"ש למחר רוחץ בהן פניו ידיו ורגליו אבל לא כל גופו אבר אבר ואצ"ל חמין שהוחמו בי"ט רבה מתני לה להא שמעתא דרב בהאי לישנא חמין שהוחמו מע"ש למחר אמר רב רוחץ בהן כל גופו ומשייר אבר אחד איתיביה כל הני תיובתא תיובתא א"ל רב יוסף לאביי רבה מי קא עביד כשמעתיה דרב א"ל לא ידענא מאי תיבעי ליה פשיטא דלא עביד דהא איתותב (ד) דילמא) לא שמיעא ליה ואי לא שמיעא ליה ודאי עביד ה) דאמר אביי כל מילי דמר עביד כרב בר מהני תלת דעביד כשמואל ו) מטילין מבגד לבגד ומדליקין מנר לנר והלכה כר"ש בגרירה כחומרי דרב עביד כקולי דרב לא עביד ז) ת"ר ב מרחץ שפקקו נקביו מע"ש למוצ"ש רוחץ בו מיד פקקו נקביו ג מעי"ט למחר נכנס ומזיע ויוצא ומשתטף בבית החיצון אמר רב יהודה מעשה במרחץ של בני ברק שפקקו נקביו מעי"ט למחר נכנס ראב"ע ור"ע והזיעו בו ויצאו ונשתטפו בבית החיצון אלא שחמין שלו מחופין בנסרים כשבא הדבר לפני חכמים אמרו אף על פי שאין חמין שלו מחופין בנסרין ומשרבו עוברי עבירה התחילו לאסור אמבטיאות של כרכין מטייל בהן ואינו חושש מאי עוברי עבירה דא"ר שמעון בן פזי אמר ריב"ל משום בר קפרא בתחלה היו רוחצין בחמין שהוחמו מע"ש התחילו הבלנים להחם בשבת ואומרים מערב שבת הוחמו אסרו את החמין והתירו את הזיעה ועדיין היו רוחצין בחמין ואומרים מזיעין אנחנו אסרו להן את הזיעה והתירו חמי טבריה ועדיין היו רוחצין בחמי האור ואומרים בחמי טבריה רחצנו אסרו להן חמי טבריה והתירו להן את הצונן ראו שאין הדבר עומד להן ד התירו להן חמי טבריה ה וזיעה במקומה עומדת אמר רבא האי מאן דעבר אדרבנן שרי למיקרי ליה עבריינא כמאן

כי

הדר ביה רבי עקיבא. כדאמרינן בפירקין דלעיל (דף כט:) לשון מכריע מכביד מטה כף מאזנים ומכריע את שכנגדו כגון הכא בחמין אסור השתא הוה ליה ר' שמעון דמתיר בחמין יחיד במקום שנים נמצא ר' יהודה מכביד את כף המשקולת שהרי ר' יהודה עם רבי מאיר שוים לאיסור ובצונן מותר הוי ליה ר' מאיר בצונן יחיד במקום שנים נמצא ר' יהודה מכביד את כף המשקולת: ה"מ. דא"ר יוחנן הלכה כדברי המכריע במשנה כי ההיא דמטלניות: כעין פניו. כלומר כל אבר בפני עצמו: רוחץ בהן כל גופו. ביחד אלא שמשייר אבר אחד: איתיביה כל הני. וליכא לשנויי כעין פניו ידיו ורגליו דהא כל גופו יחד קאמר חוץ מאבר אחד: א"ל רב יוסף לאביי. משום דגדל אביי בבית רבה בר נחמני שהיה ראש קודם לרב יוסף ומת היה שואלו רב יוסף איך היה רואהו נוהג: מי עביד כשמעתי' דרב. בהא מילתא דרחילה: מאי תבעי ליה. שיטה דהש"ס פרכא ליה: לא שמיע ליה. ח) לרבה הא תיובתא משום הכי מספקא ליה לרב יוסף ברבה דדילמא עביד כרב: ואי לא שמיעא ליה. אמאי מספקא ליה לרב יוסף: הא ודאי עביד. רבה בכל מילי כרב: כחומרי דרב הוה עביד. בר מהני תלת חומרי אבל כקולי דרב איכא דלא עביד והא קולא היא ודילמא לא עביד: שפקקו נקביו. שלא יצא חמימותו: רוחץ בו מיד. ואין צריך להמתין בכדי שיעשה ל"א שפקקו נקביו אותן נקבים שמרחץ מתחמם על ידיהן שאור ניסקת מבחוץ מתחתיו ט) לוי"ה ועיקר רוחץ בו מיד שהרי לא נתחמם בשבת אבל בשבת לא שהרי גזרו על הרחילה: ומשתטף בבית החיצון. שלפני המרחץ ולא בתוך המרחץ שלא יאמרו רוחץ הוא כדאמרן דאסרו את הרחילה אבל הזיעה התירו והיאך היא זיעה עומד או יושב בבית המרחץ ואינו נותן מים עליו והוא מתחמם ומזיע: מחופין בנסרים. ולא היו צריכין לחוש שמא נתחממו בשבת מחומו של מרחץ: התחילו לאסור. את הזיעה: אמבטאות. בתי מרחץ גדולים: מטייל בהן. מהלך בתוכן לפי דרכו ולא להזיע: ואינו חושש. שמא יאמרו מזיע הוא ואע"ג דאסרו את הזיעה: מאי עוברי עבירה. דקאמר לעיל שאסרו זיעה על ידיהן: אסרו להן את החמין. לגמרי: ועדיין היו רוחצין בחמין. שהוחמו מבע"י: שאין הדבר עומד. שלא היו ציבור יכולין לקבל מתוך שאסרו להם את הכל: במקומה עומדת. לאיסור:

דילמא ה"מ במתני' אבל בברייתא לא. ° אע"ג דלא קאמר במשנתינו י) הכא משמע דאין הלכה כמותו משום דסתם מתני' דלא כוותיה כ): הלכה כדברי המכריע. הכרעה כגון קולי מטלניות שר"א ור"י הזכירו בפירוש בדבריהם מוכן ושאינו מוכן דהיינו תלאו במגוד והניחו אחורי הדלת שגילו בדבריהם שיש סברא לחלק ביניהם אלא שנראה להם דסוף סוף אין לחלק ביניהם לכך הוי ר' עקיבא שמחלק ביניהם מכריע וכן ר' יהודה הוי מכריע דר' שמעון ור"מ הזכירו בדבריהם חמין וצונן והכרעה שלישית דלא הויא הכרעה הוי כי ההיא דפ"ק דפסחים (דף כא.) חבית של יין של תרומה שנטמאה ב"ש אומרים תשפך ל) הכל וב"ה אומר תיעשה זילוף אמר ר' ישמעאל בר' יוסי אני אכריע בשדה תשפך מ) הכל ובבית תעשה זילוף אמרו לו אין הכרעה שלישית מכרעת משום דלא הזכירו ב"ש וב"ה בדבריהם בית ושדה ולא גילו שיש סברא לחלק בין בית לשדה חשיב לה הכרעה שלישית ולא כפירוש הקונטרס דפירש התם דטעמייהו דב"ש לא משום תקל' אלא מטעם אחר כמו משום ריחא אלא משום דלא הזכירו בדבריהם בית ושדה כדפי' וה"ה דהוה מצי למימר ליה דאין הכרעת תלמיד הכרעה כדאמר הכא אלא רבותא אמרו דאפי' לא היה תלמיד אינה הכרעה והא דתנן בברכות (דף מג:) ב"ש אומרים מברך על השמן ואח"כ מברך על ההדס וב"ה אומרים מברך על ההדס ואח"כ על השמן א"ר גמליאל אני אכריע שמן זכינו לריחו וזכינו לסיכתו הדס לריחו זכינו לסיכתו לא זכינו וא"ר יוחנן הלכה כדברי המכריע פר"ת התם דהויא כהכרעה שבכל הש"ס ולא נהירא דלא הויא הכרעה אלא כדפי' והתם אינו אלא מפרש טעמא דבית שמאי ור"ח פי' אין הכרע' שלישית מכרעת היינו הכרע' דור שלישי כמו ר' ישמעאל בר' יוסי שהיה דור שלישי לב"ש וב"ה ולאו דוקא דור שלישי אלא ה"ה שני ובכל מקום נקט הכרעה שלישית משום ברייתא דפסחים נ):

למוצאי שבת רוחץ מיד. דוקא לרחוץ אבל להזיע נכנס אפי' בשבת ומזיע כמו בי"ט כדאמר בסמוך דאפי' בשבת הוי זיעה שריא עד הגזירה ולאחר גזירה אפילו בי"ט אסרו דאיום טוב קתני משרבו עוברי עבירה התחילו לאסור והוה מצי לערובינהו וליתנינהו מרחץ שפקקו נקביו מערב שבת או מערב יום טוב למחר נכנס ומזיע ולמוצאי שבת ויום טוב רוחץ מיד אלא אי עריב ותני להו הוה אמינא דדוקא בשבת אסרו הזיעה ולא ביום טוב דעובדא דמייתי בשבת הוה להכי מפליג להו השתא משרבו עוברי עבירה קאי איום טוב אבל לא אשבת דזיעה לא הוזכרה גבי שבת: אלא שחמין שלו מחופין בנסרים. פי' בקונטרס שלא היו צריכין לחוש שהוחמו בשבת מחום המרחץ משמע שסובר שנשתטפו בחמין שהוחמו מע"ש ולעיל אסר רבי יהודה גופיה ושמא יחלק בין שבת ליום טוב ומיהו בתוספתא גרסינן ונשתטפו בצונן אלא שחמין שלו מחופים ולא יסברו העולם שרחצו בחמין:

מפני

עין משפט נר מצוה

טז א מיי' פכ"ב מהלכות שבת הלכה ב סמג לאוין סה טוש"ע או"ח סימן שכו סעיף א:
יז ב שם סעיף יא:
יח ג מיי' פ"א מהלכות י"ט הלכה טז סמג לאוין עה טור שו"ע או"ח סימן תקיא סעיף ב:
יט ד מיי' פכ"ב מהלכות שבת הלכה ב סמג לאוין סה טוש"ע או"ח סימן שכו סעיף א:
כ ה מיי' שם טוש"ע שם סעיף יב:

רבינו חננאל

הדר ביה ר"ע לגבי דר' יהושע. ואסיקנא דאי מכללא מאי הוי ר' יהודה מכריע הוא והלכתא כדברי המכריע ובין [בפי' ובין] מכללא חדא הוא. ואמרינן דילמא הני מילי אם תהיה מחלוקתם במשנה אבל חלוקתם בברייתא לא. אמר ליה בפירוש שמיעא לי. והא דאמר אביי כל מילי דמר עביד כרב בר מהני תלת. אסיקנ' רבה כחומרי דרב הוה עביד. כקולי דרב לא הוה עביד: ת"ר מרחץ שפקקו. פי' פקקו סתמו נקביו מע"ש למוצאי שבת רוחץ בה מיד. פקקו נקביו מערב יום טוב למחר נכנס ומזיע ויוצא ומשתטף בבית החיצון. וכן עשו ר' אלעזר בן עזריה ור"ע במרחץ של בני ברק. משרבו עוברי עבירה התחילו לאסור שהיו מחמין בשבת ואומרים מע"ש החמנו. אסרו להן חמין והתירו הזיעה כו'. ואסיקנא אסרו להן אפילו חמין שהוחמו מע"ש ואפילו חמי טבריא וכ"ש חמי האור. ואפילו זיעה אסרו להן

רב נסים גאון

תמצאנו בנדרים בפרק הנודר מן המבושל (דף ג) ר' עקיבא אקדשא ליה ברתיה דבר כלבא שבוע כו' אמרה ליה זיל הוי בבי רב אזל הוה י"ב שנין קמיה רבי אליעזר ורבי יהושע ובהרבה מקומות תמצאנו כשהוא מדבר עם אחד מהן אומר ר' תרשני לומר לפניך דבר אחד ממה שלימדתני תגד דאלך (פירושו, תמצא זה) בר"ה (כה) בשעה ששיגר רבן גמליאל לר' יהושע גוזר אני עליך שתבוא אצלי במקלך כו' דתניא הלך ר"ע לר' יהושע מיצר א"ל ר"ע ר' תרשני לומר לפניך דבר אחד שלימדתני ובסנהדרין (פ' ד' מיתות דף סז) ר"ע אומר משום ר' יהושע שנים מלקטין קישואין כו' ובתלמוד אמרו גמרה מר' אליעזר ולא סברה הדר גמרה מר' יהושע ואסברה ניהליה. ועוד הא הדר ביה רבי עקיבא לגבי ר' יהושע מפורש זה בפרק במה מדליקין (דף כט):

מסורת הש"ס

א) [לעיל כט:], ב) [ברכות יב. וש"נ], ג) [לעיל לט:], ד) [רש"ל מ"ז], ה) לעיל כב. פסחים קא. מנחות מא:, ו) בכל המקומות איתא מתירין, ז) תוספתא שבת פ"ד, ח) מאן דגרס בגמ' דילמא גרס הכא לא שמיע ליה לרב יוסף, ט) תיבת לוי"ה רמז לרבינו יהודה הלוי, י) [עי' ברכות יט. במשנתינו קאמרינן והא ברייי' היא], כ) [ועי' תוס' מנחות לא: ד"ה מי קאמר וכו' תירצו באופן אחר], ל) שם איתא הכל, מ) הכל, נ) [ועי' יתר אריכות בתוס' ב"ק קטו. ד"ה הכרעה].

גליון הש"ס

תוס' ד"ה דילמא ה"מ במתניתין וכו' אע"ג דלא קאמר במשנתנו. עי' משנה למלך ריש הלכות בית הבחירה:

ליקוטי רש"י

ואי מכללא מאי. מאי גריעותא איכא הא שפיר מצי למשמע מכללא [ברכות יב.]. מה לנו אי איתמר מכלל אי בפירוש הא מהא כללא שפיר שמעינן ומה יש לנו לגמגם בכלל זה [חולין צד.]. כל מילי דמר. רבה בר נחמני. בר מהני תלת. ומשום דהילכתא כרב באיסורי בכוליה הש"ס בר מהני תלת נקטינהו גבי הדדי. מטילין. ציצית מטלית ישן לטלית חדש ובמנחות מפרש טעמא דמאן דאסר [לעיל כב.]. מתירין ציצית של טלית זו ונותנין אותם לטלית אחרת. ומדליקין. מנר חנוכה לנר אחרת של חנוכה וא"צ להדליק בנר אחרת שאינה של חנוכה [רשב"ם פסחים קא.]. והלכה כרבי שמעון בגרירה. דאמר דבר שאין מתכוין מותר ואף על גב דקעביד חריץ והוי תולדה דחורש או בונה [לעיל שם]. גורר אדם מטה כסא וספסל כו' דדבר שאין מתכוין מותר והני ג' מילי פלוגתא דרב ושמואל בבמה מדליקין (שבת כב.) וכולהו עביד רבה כשמואל דמיקל [רשב"ם פסחים שם]. כחומרי דרב עביד. בר מהני תלת דעביד לקולא כשמואל [רש"י שם]. כקולי דרב לא עביד. ואע"ג דתניא (עירובין ו:) העושה כחומרי ב"ש כקוליהון וכחומריהון כו' הא קי"ל ה"מ היכא דסתרן אהדדי כגון כמה חסרון בשדרה כו' ואמר שמואל וכן לטריפה דחומרא דהתם קולא הוא הכא וקולא דהתם חומרא הוא הכא [רשב"ם שם]. בלנים. בלן. שומר בית המרחץ ומשמשן בבית המרחץ ונוטל מכל אחד שכרו [מו"ק יא:].

SAID: אַף עַל פִּי שֶׁאֵין חַמִּין שֶׁלּוֹ מְחוּפִּין בִּנְסָרִין – It is permitted to rinse in the outer chamber EVEN IF ITS tub of HOT WATER WAS NOT COVERED WITH BOARDS.

The Baraisa continues:

וּמִשֶּׁרַבּוּ עוֹבְרֵי עֲבֵירָה – BUT AS SINNERS PROLIFERATED,[19] הִתְחִילוּ לֶאֱסוֹר – [THE SAGES] BEGAN TO FORBID steam-bathing. אַמְבַּטְיָאוֹת שֶׁל כְּרַכִּין – Nevertheless, concerning THE public BATHS OF LARGE CITIES, מְטַיֵּיל בָּהֶן וְאֵינוֹ חוֹשֵׁשׁ – ONE MAY STROLL THROUGH THEM WITHOUT CONCERN that people will suspect him of steam-bathing.[20]

The Gemara elaborates on the Baraisa:

מַאי עוֹבְרֵי עֲבֵירָה – **What** does the expression, "as **sinners** proliferated" mean? דְּאָמַר רַבִּי שִׁמְעוֹן בֶּן פַּזִּי אָמַר רַבִּי יְהוֹשֻׁעַ בֶּן לֵוִי מִשּׁוּם בַּר קַפָּרָא – It is **as R' Shimon ben Pazzi said in the name of R' Yehoshua ben Levi, who said in the name of Bar Kappara:** בַּתְּחִלָּה הָיוּ רוֹחֲצִין בְּחַמִּין שֶׁהוּחַמּוּ מֵעֶרֶב שַׁבָּת – **Originally,**[21] **[people] would bathe** on the Sabbath **in hot water that had been heated before the Sabbath.** הִתְחִילוּ הַבַּלָּנִים לְהָחֵם בַּשַּׁבָּת וְאוֹמְרִים מֵעֶרֶב שַׁבָּת הוּחַמּוּ – However, **the bathhouse attendants began heating** the baths **on the Sabbath and saying that they were heated before the Sabbath.**[22] אָסְרוּ אֶת הַחַמִּין – Thereupon, **[the Sages] forbade** bathing in any **hot water** on the Sabbath, וְהִתִּירוּ אֶת הַזֵּיעָה – **but they** still **allowed steam-bathing.**[23] וַעֲדַיִין הָיוּ רוֹחֲצִין בְּחַמִּין – **However, [people] would still bathe** in the bathhouses on the Sabbath in water heated before the Sabbath, in violation of the Sages' injunction, וְאוֹמְרִים מְזִיעִין אֲנַחְנוּ – **and** when apprehended, **would say: "We were** merely **steam-bathing!"**[24] אָסְרוּ לָהֶן אֶת הַזֵּיעָה – Thereupon, **[the Sages] forbade them** even **to steam-bathe** on the Sabbath, וְהִתִּירוּ חַמֵּי טְבֶרְיָא – **but they** still **allowed** bathing in the waters of **the Tiberian hot-springs.** וַעֲדַיִין הָיוּ רוֹחֲצִין בְּחַמֵּי הָאוּר – **However, [people]** in the Tiberias area **would still bathe in water that was heated by fire** before the Sabbath, וְאוֹמְרִים בְּחַמֵּי טְבֶרְיָא רָחַצְנוּ – **and** when apprehended, **would say: "We** actually **bathed in** waters of **the Tiberian hot-springs!"** אָסְרוּ לָהֶן חַמֵּי טְבֶרְיָא – Thereupon, **[the Sages] forbade them** to bathe in waters of **the Tiberian hot-springs** וְהִתִּירוּ לָהֶן אֶת הַצּוֹנֵן – **and allowed them** only to bathe in **cold water.** רָאוּ שֶׁאֵין הַדָּבָר עוֹמֵד לָהֶן – However, when **[the Sages] saw that this** broad injunction **could not be sustained,**[25] הִתִּירוּ לָהֶן חַמֵּי טְבֶרְיָא – **they** once again **allowed them** to bathe in the waters of **the Tiberian hot-springs.** וְזֵיעָה בִּמְקוֹמָהּ עוֹמֶדֶת – **However,** the injunction against **steam-bathing remained in place.**[26]

The Gemara cites a tangential rule that is supported by the previous Tannaic statement:

אָמַר רָבָא – **Rava said:** הַאי מַאן דְּעָבַר אַדְּרַבָּנָן – **Anyone who violates** even **a Rabbinical [prohibition]** intentionally – שָׁרֵי לְמִיקְרֵי לֵיהּ עֲבַרְיָינָא – **it is permitted to call him *a sinner.***[27]

The Gemara comments:

כְּמַאן – **With whom** does this accord?

NOTES

that it is forbidden to rinse with hot water! *Tosafos* explain that perhaps *Rashi* holds that the prohibition against rinsing with water heated before the holy day pertains only on the Sabbath but not on Yom Tov, provided one leaves the inner chamber of the bathhouse. This opinion is in fact held by *Rif* (*Beitzah* ch. 2, fol. 11a) and *Rambam* (*Hil. Yom Tov* 1:16; see *Ran* here and *Orach Chaim* 511:2; see also *Pnei Yehoshua*). However, *Maharsha* points out that *Rashi* himself indicates that this incident occurred on the Sabbath, not on Yom Tov [in accordance with a variant version of the Gemara text (*Ritva, MHK* ed.)]. *Beur HaGra* (to *Orach Chaim* ibid.), however, emends *Rashi's* commentary to accord with our version of the text, which states that the incident occurred on Yom Tov.

Tosafos themselves cite *Tosefta* (4:2) which states that R' Elazar ben Azaryah and R' Akiva rinsed with *cold* water. Accordingly, *Tosafos* explain that the Tannaim ascertained that the tub of hot water was covered in order that people not suspect that they had rinsed with the hot water on Yom Tov.

19. The Gemara will explain this expression.

20. The municipal baths of Talmudic times were large and airy structures, and one who walked through them would not necessarily perspire (see Gemara, top of 40b). Even after the Sages forbade steam-bathing, they permitted strolling through such a bathhouse on the Sabbath without intent to steam-bathe, and did not require people to refrain out of concern that others would suspect them of steam-bathing (*Rashi*).

21. I.e. before the Sages forbade bathing in hot water on the Sabbath.

22. *Yerushalmi*, cited by *Rashba*, states that they did not actually violate the Biblical prohibition against cooking on the Sabbath. Rather, they would prepare fires with plenty of fuel under the bathhouses before the Sabbath and would leave the bathhouse vents open, so that the baths would be heated automatically on the Sabbath, in violation of the Rabbinical prohibition against this. Cf. *Pnei Yehoshua*.

23. It was during this period that the episode involving R' Elazar ben Azaryah and R' Akiva took place.

24. This is the proliferation of sinners mentioned in the Baraisa (*Rashi* to 40b ד״ה כי האי תנא).

25. The masses were unable to abide by the ruling forbidding all bathing in hot water (*Rashi*) and the Sages are enjoined from instituting decrees that cannot be endured by the majority of the populace (*Avodah Zarah* 36a).

26. Thus, the final form of the injunction forbids bathing (or rinsing) the entire body in artificially heated hot water, as well as steam-bathing, but does not forbid bathing in the waters of natural hot springs. However, as mentioned above (39b note 16), it is customary not to bathe even in cold water on the Sabbath. Furthermore, bathing in naturally hot water is permitted only if the water is contained in an in-ground pool or tub, but not if it is in a portable vessel (*Orach Chaim* 326:1; see 39b note 13).

It is questionable whether the prohibition against steam-bathing extends to steam generated by hot-spring water (see *Orach Chaim* 326:2).

27. It is permitted to disparage him in this fashion in order to discourage people from emulating him (*Meiri*; see *Chofetz Chaim, Hil. Lashon Hora Klal* §4, and *Be'er Mayim Chaim* §7).

א) הדר ביה ר"ע לגביה דרבי יהושע ב) ואי מכללא מאי דילמא ה"מ במתניתין אבל בברייתא לא א"ל אנא בפירוש שמיע לי אתמר חמין שהוחמו מע"ש רב אמר למחר רוחץ בהן כל גופו אבר אבר ושמואל אמר לא התירו לרחוץ אלא פניו ידיו ורגליו מיתיבי חמין שהוחמו מע"ש למחר רוחץ בהן פניו ידיו ורגליו אבל לא כל גופו תיובתא דרב אמר לך רב לא כל גופו בבת אחת אלא אבר אבר והא פניו ידיו ורגליו קתני כעין פניו ידיו ורגליו תא שמע לא התירו לרחוץ בחמין שהוחמו מע"ש אלא פניו ידיו ורגליו ה"נ כעין פניו ידיו ורגליו תניא כוותיה דשמואל ג) א חמין שהוחמו מע"ש למחר רוחץ בהן פניו ידיו ורגליו אבל לא כל גופו אבר אבר ואצ"ל חמין שהוחמו בי"ט רבה מתני לה להא שמעתא דרב בהאי לישנא חמין שהוחמו מע"ש למחר אמר רב רוחץ בהן כל גופו ומשייר אבר אחד איתיביה כל הני תיובתא תיובתא א"ל רב יוסף לאביי רבה מי קא עביד כשמעתיה דרב א"ל לא ידענא מאי תיבעי ליה פשיטא דלא עביד דהא איתותב (ד) דילמא) לא שמיעא ליה ואי לא שמיעא ליה ודאי עביד ה) דאמר אביי כל מילי דמר עביד כרב בר מהני תלת דעביד כשמואל ו) מטילין מבגד לבגד ומדליקין מנר לנר והלכה כר"ש בגרירה בחומרי דרב עביד בקולי דרב לא עביד ז) ת"ר ב מרחץ שפקקו נקביו מע"ש למוצ"ש רוחץ בו מיד פקקו נקביו ג מעי"ט למחר נכנס ומזיע ויוצא ומשתטף בבית החיצון אמר רב יהודה מעשה במרחץ של בני ברק שפקקו נקביו מעי"ט למחר נכנס ראב"ע ור"ע והזיעו בו ויצאו ונשתטפו בבית החיצון אלא שחמין שלו מחופין בנסרים כשבא הדבר לפני חכמים אמרו אף על פי שאין חמין שלו מחופין בנסרין ומשרבו עוברי עבירה התחילו לאסור אמבטיאות של כרכין מטייל בהן ואינו חושש מאי עוברי עבירה דא"ר שמעון בן פזי אמר ריב"ל משום בר קפרא בתחלה היו רוחצין בחמין שהוחמו מע"ש התחילו הבלנים להחם בשבת ואומרים מערב שבת הוחמו אסרו את החמין והתירו את הזיעה ועדיין היו רוחצין בחמין ואומרים מזיעין אנחנו אסרו להן את הזיעה והתירו חמי טבריה ועדיין היו רוחצין בחמי האור ואומרים בחמי טבריה רחצנו אסרו להן חמי טבריה והתירו להן את הצונן ראו שאין הדבר עומד להן ד התירו להן חמי טבריה ה וזיעה במקומה עומדת אמר רבא האי מאן דעבר אדרבנן שרי למיקרי ליה עבריינא כמאן

כי

רש"י

הדר ביה רבי עקיבא. כדאמרינן בפירקין לעיל (דף כט:) לשון מכריע מכביד מטה כף מאזנים ומכריע את שכנגדו כגון הכא בחמין אסור השתא הוה ליה ר' שמעון דמתיר בחמין יחיד במקום שנים נמצא ר' יהודה מכביד את כף המשקולת שהרי ר' יהודה עם רבי מאיר שוים לאיסור ובצונן מותר הוי ליה ר' מאיר בצונן יחיד במקום שנים נמצא ר' יהודה מכביד את כף המשקולת: ה"מ. דא"ר יוחנן הלכה כדברי המכריע במכריע במשנה כי ההיא דמטלניות: כעין פניו. כלומר כל אבר בפני עצמו: רוחץ בהן כל גופו. ביחד אלא שמשייר אבר אחד: איתיביה כל הני. וליכא לשנויי כעין פניו ידיו ורגליו דהא כל גופו יחד קאמר חוץ מאבר אחד: א"ל רב יוסף לאביי. משום דגדל אביי בבית רבה בר נחמני שהיה רבו קודם לרב יוסף ומת היה שואלו רב יוסף איך היה רואהו נוהג: מי עביד כשמעתי' דרב. בהא מילתא דרחיצה: מאי תבעי ליה. שיטה דהש"ס פרכא ליה: לא שמיע ליה. ח) לרבה הא תיובתא משום הכי מספקא ליה לרב יוסף ברבה דדילמא עביד כרב: ואי לא שמיעא ליה. אמאי מספקא ליה לרב יוסף: הא ודאי עביד. רבה בכל מילי כרב: בחומרי דרב הוה עביד. בר מהני תלת חומרי אבל בקולי דרב איכא דלא עביד והא קולא היא ודילמא לא עביד: שפקקו נקביו. שלא יצא חמימותו: רוחץ בו מיד. ואין צריך להמתין בכדי שיעשה ל"א שפקקו נקביו אותן נקבים שמרחץ מתחמם על ידיהן שאור ניסקת מבחוץ מתחתיו ט) לר"ה ועיקר רוחץ בו מיד שהרי לא נתחמם בשבת אבל בשבת לא שהרי גזרו על הרחיצה: ומשתטף בבית החיצון. שלפני המרחץ ולא בתוך המרחץ שלא יאמרו רוחץ הוא כדאמרן דאסרו את הרחיצה אבל הזיעה התירו והילך היא זיעה עומד או יושב בבית המרחץ ואינו נותן מים עליו והוא מתחמם ומזיע: מחופין בנסרים. ולא היו צריכין לחוש שמא נתחממו בשבת מחומו של מרחץ: התחילו לאסור. את הזיעה: אמבטאות. בתי מרחץ גדולים: מטייל בהן. מהלך בתוכן לפי דרכו ולא להזיע: ואינו חושש. שמא יאמרו מזיע הוא ואע"ג דאסרו את הזיעה: מאי עוברי עבירה. דקאמר לעיל שאסרו זיעה על ידיהן: אסרו להן את החמין. לגמרי: ועדיין היו רוחצין בחמין. שהוחמו מבע"י: שאין הדבר עומד. שלא היו ציבור יכולין לקבל מתוך שאסרו להם את הכל: במקומה עומדת. לאיסור:

כי

תוספות

דילמא ה"מ במתני' אבל בברייתא לא. ° אע"ג דלא קאמר במשנתינו י) הכא משמע דאין הלכה כמותו משום דסתם מתני' דלא כוותיה כ): הלכה כדברי המכריע. הכרעה כגון קולי מטלניות שר"א ור"י הזכירו בפירוש בדבריהם מוכן ושאינו מוכן דהיינו תלאו במגוד והניחו אחורי הדלת שגילו בדבריהם שיש סברא לחלק ביניהם אלא שנראה להם דסוף סוף אין לחלק ביניהם לכך הוי ר' עקיבא שמחלק ביניהם מכריע וכן ר' יהודה הוי מכריע דר' שמעון ור"מ הזכירו בדבריהם חמין וצונן והכרעה שלישית דלא הויא הכרעה הוי כי ההיא דפ"ק דפסחים (דף כא.) חבית של יין של תרומה שנטמאה ב"ש אומרים תשפך ל) הכל וב"ה אומר תיעשה זילוף אמר ר' ישמעאל בר' יוסי אני אכריע בשדה תשפך מ) הכל ובבית תעשה זילוף אמרו לו אין הכרעה שלישית מכרעת משום דלא הזכירו ב"ש וב"ה בדבריהם בית ושדה ולא גילו שיש סברא לחלק בין בית לשדה חשיב לה הכרעה שלישית ולא כפירוש הקונטרס דפירש התם דטעמייהו דב"ש לא משום תקל' אלא מטעם אחר כמו משום ריחא אלא משום דלא הזכירו בדבריהם בית ושדה כדפי' וה"ה דהוה מצי למימר ליה דאין הכרעת תלמיד הכרעה כדאמר הכא אלא רבותא אמרו דאפי' לא היה תלמיד אינה הכרעה והא דתנן בברכות (דף מג:) ב"ש אומרים מברך על השמן ואח"כ מברך על ההדס וב"ה אומרים מברך על ההדס ואח"כ על השמן א"ר גמליאל אני אכריע שמן זכינו לריחו חכינו לסיכתו הדס לריחו זכינו לסיכתו לא זכינו וא"ר יוחנן הלכה כדברי המכריע פר"ת התם דהויא כהכרעה שבכל הש"ס ולא נהירא דלא הויא הכרעה אלא כדפי' והתם אינו אלא מפרש טעמא דבית שמאי ור"ח פי' אין הכרע' שלישית מכרעת היינו הכרע' דור שלישי כמו ר' ישמעאל בר' יוסי שהיה דור שלישי לב"ש וב"ה ולאו דוקא דור שלישי אלא ה"ה שני ובכל מקום נקט הכרעה שלישית משום ברייתא דפסחים נ):

למוצאי שבת רוחץ מיד. דוקא לרחוץ אבל להזיע נכנס אפי' בשבת ומזיע כמו בי"ט כדאמר בסמוך דאפי' בשבת הוי זיעה שריא עד הגזירה ולאחר גזירה אפילו בי"ט אסרו דאיום טוב קתני משרבו עוברי עבירה התחילו לאסור והוה מצי לערובינהו וליתנינהו מרחץ שפקקו נקביו מערב שבת או מערב יום טוב למחר נכנס ומזיע ולמוצאי שבת ויום טוב רוחץ מיד אלא אי עריב ותני להו הוה אמינא דדוקא בשבת אסרו זיעה ולא ביום טוב דעובדא דמייתי בשבת הוה להכי מפליג להו השתא משרבו עוברי עבירה קאי איום טוב אבל לא אשבת דזיעה לא הוחכרה גבי שבת: **אלא** שחמין שלו מחופין בנסרים. פי' בקונטרס שלא היו צריכין לחוש שהוחמו בשבת מחום המרחץ משמע שסובר שנשתטפו בחמין שהוחמו מע"ש ולעיל אסר רבי יהודה גופיה ושמא יחלק בין שבת ליום טוב ומיהו בתוספתא גרסינן ונשתטפו בצונן אלא שחמין שלו מחופים ולא יסברו העולם שרחצו בחמין:

מפני

עין משפט נר מצוה

טז א מיי' פכ"ב מהלכות שבת הלכה ב סמג לאוין סה טוש"ע או"ח סימן שכו סעיף א:

יז ב שם סעיף יא:

יח ג מיי' פ"א מהלכות י"ט הלכה טז סמג לאוין עה טור שו"ע או"ח סימן תקיא סעיף ב:

יט ד מיי' פכ"ב מהלכות שבת הלכה ב סמג לאוין סה טוש"ע או"ח סימן שכו סעיף א:

כ ה מיי' שם טוש"ע שם סעיף יב:

רבינו חננאל

הדר ביה ר"ע לגבי דר' יהושע. ואסיקנא דאי מכללא מאי הוי ר' יהודה מכריע הוא והלכתא כדברי המכריע ובין [בפי' ובין] מכללא חדא הוא. ואמרינן דילמא הני מילי אם תהיה מחלוקתם במשנה אבל חלוקתם בברייתא לא. אמר ליה בפירוש שמיעא לי. והא דאמר אביי כל מילי דמר עביד כרב בר מהני תלת. אסיקנ' רבה כחומרי דרב הוה עביד. כקולי דרב לא הוה עביד: ת"ר מרחץ שפקקו. פי' פקקו סתמו נקביו מע"ש למוצאי שבת רוחץ בה מיד. פקקו נקביו מערב יום טוב למחר נכנס ומזיע ויוצא ומשתטף בבית החיצן. וכן עשו ר' אלעזר בן עזריה ור"ע במרחץ של בני ברק. משרבו עוברי עבירה התחילו לאסור שהיו מחמין בשבת ואומרים מע"ש החמנו. אסרו להן חמין והתירו הזיעה כו'. ואסיקנא אסרו להן אפילו חמין שהוחמו מע"ש ואפילו חמי טבריא וכ"ש חמי האור. ואפילו זיעה אסרו להן

רב נסים גאון

תמצאנו בנדרים בפרק הנודר מן המבושל (דף נ) ר' עקיבא אקדשא ליה ברתיה דבר כלבא שבוע כו' אמרה ליה זיל הוי בבי רב אזל הוה י"ב שנין קמיה רבי אליעזר ורבי יהושע ובהרבה מקומות תמצאנו כשהוא מדבר עם אחד מהן אומר ר' תרשני לומר לפניך דבר אחד ממה שלימדתני תגד דאלך (פירושו, תמצא זה) בר"ה (כה) בשעה ששיגר רבן גמליאל לר' יהושע גוזר אני עליך שתבוא אצלי במקלך כו' דתניא הלך ר"ע לר' יהושע מיצר א"ל ר"ע ר' תרשני לומר לפניך דבר אחד שלימדתני ובסנהדרין (פ' ד' מיתות דף סז) ר"ע אומר משום ר' יהושע שנים מלקטין קישואין כו' ובתלמוד אמרו גמרה מר' אליעזר ולא סברה הדר גמרה מר' יהושע ואסברה ניהליה. ועוד הא הדר ביה רבי עקיבא לגבי ר' יהושע מפורש זה בפרק במה מדליקין (דף כט):

מסורת הש"ס

א) [לעיל כט:], ב) [ברכות יב. וש"נ], ג) [לעיל לט:], ד) [רש"ל מ"ו], ה) לעיל כב. פסחים קא. מנחות מא:, ו) בכל המקומות ליתא מתירין, ז) תוספתא שבת פ"ד, ח) מאן דגרס בגמ' דילמא גרס הכא לא שמיע ליה לרב יוסף, ט) תיבת לר"ה רמז לרבינו יהודה הלוי, י) [עי' ברכות יט. במשנתינו קאמרינן והא ברי' היא], כ) [ועי' תוס' מנחות לא: ד"ה מי קאמר וכו' תירצו באופן אחר], ל) שם ליתא הכל, מ) הכל, נ) [ועי' יתר אריכות בתוס' ב"ק קטו. ד"ה הכרעה].

גליון הש"ס

תוס' ד"ה דילמא ה"מ במתניתין וכו' אע"ג דלא קאמר במשנתנו. עי' משנה למלך ריש הלכות בית הבחירה:

ליקוטי רש"י

ואי מכללא מאי. מאי גריעותא איכא הא שפיר מצי למשמע מכללא [ברכות יב.]. מה לנו אי איתמר מכלל אי בפירוש הא מהא כללא שפיר שמעינן ומה יש לנו לגמגם בכלל זה [חולין צד.]. כל מילי דמר. רבה בר נחמני. בר מהני תלת. ומשום דהילכתא כרב באיסורי בכוליה הש"ס בר מהני תלת נקטינהו גבי הדדי. מטילין. ציצית מטלית ישן לטלית חדש ובמנחות מפרש טעמא דמאן דאסר [לעיל כב.]. מתירין ציצית של טלית זו ועושין אותם לטלית אחרת. ומדליקין. מנר חנוכה לנר אחרת של חנוכה וא"צ להדליק בנר אחרת שאינה של חנוכה [רשב"ם פסחים קא.]. והלכה כרבי שמעון בגרירה. דאמר דבר שאין מתכוין מותר ואף על גב דקעביד חריץ והוי תולדה דחורש או בונה [לעיל שם]. גורר אדם מטה כסא וספסל כו' דדבר שאין מתכוין מותר והני ג' מילי פלוגתא דרב ושמואל בבמה מדליקין (שבת כב.) וכולהו עביד רבה כשמואל למיקל [רשב"ם פסחים שם]. כחומרי דרב עביד. בר מהני תלת דעביד לקולא כשמואל [רש"י שם]. בקולי דרב לא עביד. ואע"ג דמניא (עירובין ו:) העושה כחומרי ב"ש כקוליהון וכחומריהון כו' הא קי"ל ה"מ היכא דסתרן אהדדי כגון כמה חסרון בשדרה כו' ואמר שמואל וכן לטריפה דחומרא דהתם קולא הוא הכא וקולא דהתם חומרא הוא הכא [רשב"ם שם]. בלנים. בלן. שומר בית המרחץ ומשמשן בבית המרחץ ונוטל מכל אחד שכרו [מו"ק יא:].

עין משפט
נר מצוה

כא א מיי' פכ"ב מהל' שבת הלכה ג סמג לאוין סה טוש"ע או"ח סימן שכו סעיף ד:
כב ב מיי' שם הלכה ד טוש"ע שם סעיף ו:
כג ג ד מיי' וסמג שם טוש"ע או"ח סימן שיח סעיף יד:
כד ה ו מיי' פכ"ב שם הלכה ה ו טור שו"ע שם סעיף יג וטוש"ע יו"ד סימן קה סעיף ב:
כה ז ח ט מיי' פ"ג מהלכות ק"ש הלכה ד ה טוש"ע או"ח סימן פה סעיף ב:
כו י מיי' פכ"א מהלכות שבת הלכה ג טוש"ע או"ח סימן שלז סעיף ג:
כז כ מיי' פ"ט מהלכות שבת הלכה ג:
כח ל מ מיי' פכ"ג מהל' שבת הלכה ה טור שו"ע או"ח סימן שלט סעיף ב:

מפני שמפשיר מים שעליו. בכולה שמעתא ובמתניתין גבי מיחם שפינהו משמע דלהפשיר מים לצורך שתייה מותר דהפשירן לא זהו בישולן. והכא דאסורין מפרש ריב"א דדומה כרוחץ במים חמין ויבא להחם חמין לרחוץ גופו:

ובלבד שלא יביא קומקומוס כו'. פירוש כל זמן שהאלונטית שם שמא יפלו המים על האלונטית ואתי לידי סחיטה אי נמי לא יביא משום רפואה וגזרו אטו שחיקת סממנים טפי מבאלונטית דלא מיחזי כרפואה כ"כ:

ושמע מינה כלי שני אינו מבשל. תימה מאי שנא כלי שני מכלי ראשון דאי יד סולדת אפי' כלי שני נמי ואי אין יד סולדת אפילו כלי ראשון נמי אינו מבשל ויש לומר לפי שכלי ראשון מתוך שעמד על האור דופנותיו חמין ומחזיק חומו זמן מרובה ולכך נתנו בו שיעור דכל זמן א) שהיד סולדת בו אסור אבל כלי שני אף על גב דיד סולדת בו מותר שאין דופנותיו חמין והולך ומתקרר: **וכי** תימא בלשון חול קאמר ליה. ואע"ג דאסור להרהר נימא דאין אסור להרהר אלא בלשון קדש והוא הרהר בלשון חול:

פשיטא

כי האי תנא אמבטיאות של כרכים מטייל בהן ואינו חושש אמר רבא דוקא כרכין אבל דכפרים לא מ"ט כיון דזוטרין נפיש הבליהו ת"ר [א] מתחמם אדם כנגד המדורה ויוצא ומשתטף בצונן ובלבד שלא ישתטף בצונן ויתחמם כנגד המדורה מפני שמפשיר מים שעליו א) ת"ר [ב] מיחם אדם אלונטית ומניחה על בני מעים בשבת ובלבד שלא יביא קומקומוס של מים חמין ויניחנו על בני מעים בשבת ודבר זה אפי' בחול אסור מפני הסכנה ב) ת"ר [ג] מביא אדם קיתון מים ומניחו כנגד המדורה לא בשביל שיחמו אלא בשביל שתפיג צינתן ר' יהודה אומר מביאה אשה פך של שמן ומניחתו כנגד המדורה לא בשביל שיבשל אלא בשביל שיפשר רשב"ג אומר אשה סכה ידה שמן ומחממתה כנגד המדורה וסכה לבנה קטן ואינה חוששת איבעיא להו שמן מה הוא לתנא קמא רבה ורב יוסף דאמרי תרוייהו להתירא רב נחמן בר יצחק אמר לאיסורא רבה ורב יוסף דאמרי תרוייהו להתירא שמן אע"פ שהיד סולדת בו מותר קסבר ת"ק שמן אין בו משום בשול ואתא רבי יהודה למימר שמן יש בו משום בשול והפשרו לא זה הוא בשולו ואתא ר' שמעון בן גמליאל למימר שמן יש בו משום בשול והפשרו זהו בשולו רב נחמן בר יצחק אמר לאיסורא שמן אע"פ שאין היד סולדת בו אסור קסבר שמן יש בו משום בשול והפשרו זהו בשולו ואתא ר' יהודה למימר הפשרו לא זהו בשולו ואתא רשב"ג למימר שמן יש בו משום בשול והפשרו זהו בשולו רשב"ג היינו ת"ק איכא בינייהו כלאחר יד א"ר יהודה אמר שמואל [ד] אחד שמן ואחד מים יד סולדת בו אסור אין יד סולדת בו מותר והיכי דמי יד סולדת בו אמר רחבא כל שכריסו של תינוק נכוית א"ר יצחק בר אבדימי פעם אחת נכנסתי אחר רבי לבית המרחץ ובקשתי להניח לו פך של שמן באמבטי [ה] ואמר לי טול בכלי שני ותן שמע מינה תלת שמע מינה שמן יש בו משום בשול וש"מ [ו] כלי שני אינו מבשל וש"מ הפשרו זהו בשולו היכי עביד הכי והאמר רבה בר בר חנה א"ר יוחנן ג) [ז] בכל מקום מותר להרהר חוץ מבית המרחץ ובית הכסא וכ"ת בלשון חול א"ל והאמר אביי [ח] דברים של חול מותר לאומרן בלשון קודש של קודש אסור לאומרן בלשון חול [ט] אפרושי מאיסורא שאני תדע דאמר ד) רב יהודה אמר שמואל מעשה ה) בתלמידו של ר' מאיר שנכנס אחריו לבית המרחץ [י] ובקש להדיח קרקע ואמר לו אין מדיחין לסוך לו קרקע אמר לו אין סכין אלמא אפרושי מאיסורא שאני הכא נמי לאפרושי מאיסורא שאני אמר רבינא שמע מינה המבשל בחמי טבריה בשבת חייב דהא מעשה דר' לאחר גזירה הוה ואמר ליה טול בכלי שני ותן איני ו) והאמר רב חסדא [כ] המבשל בחמי טבריה בשבת פטור מאי חייב נמי דקאמר ז) מכת מרדות א"ר זירא אנא חזיתיה לר' אבהו דשט באמבטי ולא ידענא אי עקר אי לא עקר פשיטא דלא עקר דתניא [ל] לא ישוט אדם בבריכה מלאה מים ואפי' עומדת בחצר [מ] לא קשיא הא

דלית

כי האי תנא. דאמר לעיל משהתחילו עוברי עבירה התחילו לאסור הזיעה והרי לא נאסרה אלא ע"י הרוחצין בחמין מאתמול ואומרים מזיעין אנחנו ואין כאן אלא עבירת דבריהם שאסרו את החמין: **נפיש** הבלייהו. ומזיע: **מפשיר.** מחמם לשון פושרין: **מיחם אדם.** מחמם: **אלונטית.** טיול"א ונראה לי בגד שמסתפגין בו דבבל דוכתא קרי ליה אלונטית: **על גבי מעיים.** כשהוא חש במעיו מחממין לו כלי או בגד ומניחו שם ומועיל: **ובלבד שלא יביא קומקומוס כו'.** שמא ישפכו עליו ונמצא רוחץ בשבת בחמין: **מפני סכנה.** פעמים שהן רותחין: **לא שיחמו.** לא שיניחם שם עד שיחמו: **אלא שתפיג צינתן.** במקלתן שתפיג שתתחלף כמו וריחו לא נמר (ירמיה מח) מתרגמין וריחיה לא פג: **לא בשביל שיבשל.** שלא תניחנו שם כדי בישול שתהא היד סולדת בו: **סכה ידה.** אבל להפשירו בפך כדרך שעושה בחול לא ופליג אדרב יהודה: **להתירא.** מאי דאסר רבי יהודה בשמן בישול שרי ת"ק ומים דוקא נקט ולא שיחמו דיש בהן בישול אבל שמן אע"פ שהיד סולדת דהיינו בישול דר' יהודה שרי לת"ק: **סולדת.** נמשכת לאחוריה מדאגה שלא תכוה וזהו לשון ואסלדה בחילה (איוב ו) ואדאג ברעדה ואמשך מתלונתי מדאגת יום הדין אם הייתי יודע שמיתתי קרובה ולא יחמול: **שמן יש בו משום בישול.** הלכך לא כדי שיבשל אלא כדי שיפשר שרי דהפשרו אין זה בישולו: **ואתא רבי שמעון** למימר דהפשירו זהו בישולו. הלכך כדעבדין בחול לא ליעביד אלא כלאחר יד על ידי שינוי: **לאיסורא.** אמרה תנא קמא לשמן דמיא הוא דשרי להפשיר אבל שמן הפשרו זהו בישולו: **איכא בינייהו כלאחר יד.** דלתנא קמא אפי' ע"י שינוי אסור: **והיכי דמי.** סלוד יש שסולד מרתיחה מועטת ויש שאינו סולד: **נכנסתי.** בשבת ובחמי טבריא הוה שלא נאסרו כדאמר לעיל התירו להם חמי טבריא: **באמבטי.** כגון בריכה עשויה בקרקע שהמים נכנסים שם ונאספין: **ובקשתי להניח שם פך שמן.** להפשיר לסוך הימנו קודם הרחילה: **טול.** מן המים: **בכלי שני.** שילטנגו מעט דכלי שני אינו מבשל ואח"כ תן הפך לתוך אותו כלי שני דהך אמבטי שהחמין נמשכין לה מן המעיין חשיב לה ככלי ראשון שנרתחו בו שאע"פ שהעבירו מעל האור מבשל כדתנן לקמן (ד' מג.) האילפס והקדירה שהעבירן מרותחין לא יתן לתוכן תבלין: **וש"מ הפשרו.** במקום הראוי לבישול: **זהו בישולו.** דהא להפשיר בעלמא הוא דקבעי ואסר ליה: **והיכי עביד הכי.** להורות הוראה שהוא דבר תורה בבית המרחץ: **להרהר.** בדברי תורה: **דברים של קדש.** דברי תורה: **אסור לאומרן.** במקום הטנופת ואפי' בלשון חול: **אין מדיחין.** דלמא אתי לאשויי גומות: **דהא מעשה דרבי אחר גזירה הוה.** שגזרו על הזיעה ועל כרחין בחמי טבריא הוא דהוי ורבי יהושע (א) דאמר לעיל בימי רבי הוה אלמא בימי רבי כבר נגזרה: **וקאמר ליה טול בכלי שני.** אבל ראשון לא אלמא יש בהן משום בישול: **מרדות.** רדוי: **שט.** לף: **דשט באמבטי.** בשבת: **ולא ידענא אי עקר.** רגליו מן הארץ דקסבר כי תנן אין שטין על פני המים במשילין פירות ח) בנהר גדול תנן דאיכא למגזר שמא יעשה חבית של שייטין כדאמרינן התם אבל באמבטי לא: **אי לא עקר.** רגליו: **לא ישוט.** דאע"ג דליכא למיגזר אסור: **ואפילו עומדת בחצר.** דליכא למיגזר שמא יתיז מים ברגליו חוץ לארבע אמות: **הא.** דאסיר:

דלית

רבינו חננאל

להן אלא צונן בלבד. ראו שאין הדבר עומד חזרו והתירו להן חמי טבריא בלבד. וזיעה במקומה עומדת באיסור אמר רבא מאן דעבר על דברי חכמי' שרי למיקריי' עבריינא. כי האי תנא דתנא משרבו עוברי עבירה: **תנא** אמבטאות של כרכין מטייל בהן ואינו חושש. והני מילי דכרכין אבל דכפרין כיון דזוטרן נפיש הבליהון: **ת"ר** מתחמם אדם כנגד המדורה ויוצא (ומשתטף בצונן) [ובלבד שלא ישתטף בצונן] ויתחמם כנגד המדורה מפני שנפשרו המים שעליו: **ת"ר** מיחם אדם אלונטית ומניחה ע"ג מעיו בשבת ובלבד (ישתטף בצונן ויתחמם כנגד המדורה מפני שתפשר המים) שלא יביא קומקומוס של חמין ויניחנו על גבי מעיו בשבת. ודבר זה אפילו בחול [אסור] מפני הסכנה שלא יכוה: **ת"ר** מניח אדם קיתון של מים כנגד המדורה לא שיחמו אלא כדי שתפוג צינתן. ר' יהודה אמר מנחת אשה פך שמן כנגד המדורה לא שיתבשל אלא כדי שתפשר. רשבג"א אשה סכה ידה שמן כנגד המדורה. וסכה לבנה קטן ואינה חוששת: **איבעיא** להו שמן מה לי בו אמר ת"ק. ואסיק' אמר רב אמר שמואל אחד שמן ואחד מים אם נתחמם כשעור שהיד סולדת בו אסור אין היד סולדת בו מותר. ושיעור שהיד סולדת בו. פי' (פירוש') [בירושל'] שהיד א) שולטת בו סולדת היא שולטת והוא כל שכריסו של תינוק נכוית הימנו. הא מעשה דר' שבקשו לו פך של שמן באמבטי ואמר להן טלו בכלי שני ותנו. שמעינן מינה תלת. ש"מ שמן יש בו משום בישול. ולפיכך בכלי ראשון אסור. שנמצא מבשל שמן בשבת. וש"מ מדשרי בכלי שני דכלי שני אינו מבשל. וש"מ הפשרו לא זהו בישולו: **אמר** רבינא ש"מ המבשל בחמי טבריא הואיל וגזרו רבנן עלייהו חייבין מכת מרדות מדרבנן. ואקשינן דר' היאך מורה הוראה במרחץ ואמר טלו בכלי שני כלומר זהו מותר וזהו אסור. והא"ר יוחנן כל מקום מותר להרהר חוץ מבית המרחץ ובית הכסא. ולא דאקשינן מדברי ר' יוחנן לר' דר' יוחנן לגבי דר' תלמיד קטן הוא. (ולא) [אלא] הא דר' יוחנן דברי הכל קבלה הוא

חשק שלמה על רבינו חננאל א) ט"ס יש כאן ולשון הירושלמי הובא בר"ש:

מסורת הש"ס

א) תוספתא שבת פ"ד, ב) [תוספתא שם], ג) ברכות כד: (לעיל י.) לקמן קנ. זבחים קב: ע"ז מד: קדושין לג., ד) [לקמן קנא:], ה) [עי' תוס' לקמן קמז: ד"ה דתניא], ו) פסחים מא., ז) [יבמות נב. כתובות מה: נזיר כג. נח: חולין קמא:], ח) [דף לו:].

תוספות ישנים

א) והכא באמבטי במקום שרגא להניח הפך היתה יד סולדת בו. והא דלא א"ל תן במקום שאין היד סולדת דהיינו במקום שרחק ודאי לא היה היד סולדת. ושמא שם לא הי' יכול להפשיר. א"נ פעמים החמירו בכלי ראשון אף אם אין היד סולדת בו. וכן החמירו חכמים אפי' בכלי שני לקמן (מג.) גבי ספל ה"ה כאמבטי:

הגהות הב"ח

(א) רש"י ד"ה דהא מעשה וכו' ור' יהושע בן לוי דאמר:

ליקוטי רש"י

מדורה. היסק גדול [ביצה כא:]. **אלונטית.** בגד שמסתפגין בו כשיוצאין מבית המרחץ [עירובין פז:]. אלונטיות. סדינין שמקנחין בהן [לקמן קמז.]. **קומקומוס.** קומקמוסין סירות קטנות של מתכת [ע"ז מג:]. יורה קטנה [לעיל לח:]. **יד סולדת.** לשון ירא ודואג שהיד סולדת בהן מלכוות ברותחין [איוב ו, י עיי"ש]. נכוית [חולין קה:]. **אסור לאומרן בלשון חול.** שאע"פ שאינה בלשון הקדש לא נפקי מקדושתייהו [ע"ז מד:]. **להדיח.** במים [לקמן קנא.]. **אין סכין.** משום אשויי גומות ואף על גב דמרחץ רצפת אבנים הוא וליכא למיחש לאשויי גומות מיחלף מיהא בקרקע אחר [שם:]. **המבשל בחמי טבריה.** מעיינות רותחין. **בשבת פטור.** דלאו תולדות אש היא הלכך לאו בישול הוא דליהוי חייב משום אב מלאכה [פסחים מא.]. **מכת מרדות.** רידוי בתוכחה שלא ירגיל בזה ואין לה קצבה אלא עד שיקבל עליו [חולין קמא:].

כִּי הַאי תַּנָּא – It is **with this** previous **Tanna,** who referred to those who violated the Rabbinical injunction against bathing in hot water on the Sabbath as "sinners."

The Gemara cites a segment of the previous Tannaic statement and clarifies it:

אַמְבַּטְיָאוֹת שֶׁל כְּרַכִּים מְטַיֵּיל בָּהֶן וְאֵינוֹ חוֹשֵׁשׁ – Concerning **THE** public **BATHS OF LARGE CITIES, ONE MAY STROLL THROUGH THEM WITHOUT CONCERN** that people will suspect him of steam-bathing. אָמַר רָבָא – **Rava said:** דַּוְקָא כְּרַכִּין אֲבָל דִּכְפָרִים לֹא – This pertains **specifically** to bathhouses of **large cities, but** one may **not** stroll through the bathhouses **of small towns.** מַאי טַעְמָא – **What is the reason?** כֵּיוָן דְּזוּטְרִין נָפִישׁ הַבְלַיְיהוּ – **Since [the bathhouses of small towns] are small, they are very steamy,** and merely strolling through them is tantamount to steam-bathing.[1]

The Gemara introduces another prohibition related to bathing on the Sabbath:

תָּנוּ רַבָּנַן – **The Rabbis taught in a Baraisa:** מִתְחַמֵּם אָדָם כְּנֶגֶד הַמְּדוּרָה וְיוֹצֵא וּמִשְׁתַּטֵּף בְּצוֹנֵן – **ONE MAY WARM HIMSELF IN FRONT OF A FIRE AND THEN GO OUT AND RINSE WITH COLD WATER,** וּבִלְבַד שֶׁלֹּא יִשְׁתַּטֵּף בְּצוֹנֵן וְיִתְחַמֵּם כְּנֶגֶד הַמְּדוּרָה – **SO LONG AS HE DOES NOT** do the opposite and first **RINSE HIMSELF WITH COLD WATER AND** then **WARM HIMSELF** while still wet **IN FRONT OF A FIRE.** מִפְּנֵי שֶׁמַּפְשִׁיר מַיִם שֶׁעָלָיו – This is forbidden **BECAUSE HE** thereby **WARMS THE WATER THAT IS ON HIM.**[2]

A related ruling:

תָּנוּ רַבָּנַן – **The Rabbis taught in a** Baraisa: מֵיחַם אָדָם אֲלוּנְטִית וּמַנִּיחָהּ עַל בְּנֵי מֵעַיִם בְּשַׁבָּת – **ONE MAY HEAT A TOWEL AND PLACE IT ON** his **STOMACH ON THE SABBATH** as a remedy for stomachache, וּבִלְבַד שֶׁלֹּא יָבִיא קוּמְקוּמוֹס שֶׁל מַיִם חַמִּין וְיַנִּיחֶנּוּ עַל בְּנֵי מֵעַיִם בְּשַׁבָּת – **SO LONG AS HE DOES NOT BRING A KETTLE OF HOT WATER AND PLACE IT ON** his **STOMACH ON THE SABBATH.**[3] וְדָבָר זֶה אֲפִילּוּ בְּחוֹל אָסוּר מִפְּנֵי הַסַּכָּנָה – **AND THIS PRACTICE IS FORBIDDEN EVEN ON A WEEKDAY BECAUSE OF THE DANGER** involved, for the water in the kettle may be scalding hot and might injure him.

Having discussed the prohibition of warming one's wet body in front of a fire, the Gemara discusses the issue of warming other substances in front of a fire:

תָּנוּ רַבָּנַן – **The Rabbis taught in a Baraisa:** מֵבִיא אָדָם קִיתוֹן מַיִם וּמַנִּיחוֹ כְּנֶגֶד הַמְּדוּרָה – **ONE MAY BRING A PITCHER OF WATER AND PLACE IT IN FRONT OF A FIRE,** לֹא בִּשְׁבִיל שֶׁיֵּחַמּוּ אֶלָּא בִּשְׁבִיל שֶׁתָּפִיג צִינָּתָן – **NOT IN ORDER FOR IT TO BE HEATED, BUT** merely **IN ORDER FOR ITS CHILL TO GO OFF.**[4] רַבִּי יְהוּדָה אוֹמֵר – **R' YEHUDAH SAYS:** מְבִיאָה אִשָּׁה פַּךְ שֶׁל שֶׁמֶן וּמַנִּיחַתּוֹ כְּנֶגֶד הַמְּדוּרָה – **A WOMAN MAY BRING A FLASK OF OIL AND PLACE IT IN FRONT OF A FIRE,** לֹא בִּשְׁבִיל שֶׁיִּבָשֵׁל אֶלָּא בִּשְׁבִיל שֶׁיִּפָּשֵׁר – **NOT IN ORDER FOR IT TO BE COOKED BUT** merely **IN ORDER FOR IT TO BE WARMED** slightly.[5] רַבָּן שִׁמְעוֹן בֶּן גַּמְלִיאֵל אוֹמֵר – **RABBAN SHIMON BEN GAMLIEL SAYS:** אִשָּׁה סָכָה יָדָהּ שֶׁמֶן וּמְחַמַּמְתָּהּ כְּנֶגֶד הַמְּדוּרָה – **A WOMAN MAY ANOINT HER HAND WITH OIL AND WARM IT IN FRONT OF A FIRE,** וְסָכָה לִבְנָהּ קָטָן – and then **ANOINT HER SMALL SON** with the warmed oil; וְאֵינָהּ חוֹשֶׁשֶׁת – **AND** she **NEED NOT BE CONCERNED** for the possibility of desecrating the Sabbath.[6]

NOTES

1. *Beis Yosef, Orach Chaim* 326, based on *Rashi* here and 40a ד״ה מטייל בהן; cf. *Rambam, Hil. Shabbos* 22:2, as understood by *Beis Yosef* ibid.; see *Mishnah Berurah* 326:35-36.

2. Although the water is merely warmed and not heated enough to be considered cooked (see note 4), so that no violation of the *melachah* of *cooking* is involved, this is nonetheless forbidden. The reason is that once the water on the person's body is warmed by the fire he is, in effect, washing his body with warm water, which is prohibited Rabbinically lest one heat up water for this purpose on the Sabbath (*Tosafos* ד״ה מפני, *Rambam, Hil. Shabbos* 22:3; cf. *Rabbeinu Tam* cited by *Rashba*).

As we learned above, the prohibition against bathing on the Sabbath with water that was heated before the Sabbath applies only to bathing the entire body. However, water that was heated on the Sabbath itself is treated more stringently; it is forbidden to bathe even part of the body on the Sabbath with such water. Accordingly, it would seem that in the case at hand, since the water is being warmed on the Sabbath itself, the prohibition should apply even if only part of the body is wet. Indeed, this is the opinion of *Rosh,* who states that even one who washes his hands should not warm them in front of a fire while they are wet (see *Beis Yosef, Orach Chaim* 326 and *Beur Halachah* to 326:5). However, *Rambam* (*Hil. Shabbos* 22:3) states that warming oneself in front of a fire is prohibited only after rinsing the entire body. His reasoning is that since the water is merely warmed and not cooked, it is treated like water that was heated before the Sabbath (*Beur HaGra* to *Orach Chaim* 326:4; cf. *Magen Avraham* §5; see *Shaar HaTziyun* §8).

3. For the hot water may spill on him, causing him to transgress the injunction against bathing in hot water (*Rashi*).

[Even if the kettle were to spill it seems unlikely that the water would drench the person's entire body. Perforce, *Rashi* understands the Baraisa as dealing with a kettle of water that was warmed on the Sabbath in a legal fashion, and *Rashi* concurs with the opinion of *Rosh* that it is forbidden to wash even a portion of one's body with such water on the Sabbath (*Shaar HaTziyun* 326:9; see also *Beis Yosef* ibid. and *Beis Meir* 326:4).]

Others explain that placing a kettle of warm water on the stomach is prohibited under the general prohibition of practicing medical remedies on the Sabbath in cases of minor illness – a prohibition that was enacted due to the concern that one might grind herbs to make medicine. Placing a warm towel on the stomach is, however, permitted because that is not an obvious medical practice (*Tosafos;* see there for yet another explanation). [According to this explanation, it is prohibited to place even a closed hot-water bottle on the stomach, whereas according to *Rashi's* explanation this would be permitted (*Mishnah Berurah* 326:19).]

4. I.e. one may leave the water in front of the fire only long enough to take its chill off, but not long enough for it to become hot (*Rashi; Rambam, Hil. Shabbos* 22:4 as explained by *Maggid Mishneh; Ramban;* see *Pnei Yehoshua*). [*Hot* in the context of our Gemara means heated to a degree that one's hand recoils when he touches it (*yad soledes bo*). With respect to liquids, this is the temperature at which the Biblical prohibition against cooking on the Sabbath sets in (see below).]

Others explain that one may place the water only near enough to the fire to get warm, but not so near that it could possibly get hot if left there (*Tosafos* below, 48a ד״ה מאי שנא; *Rashba; Rosh; Orach Chaim* 318:14). [Even according to *Rashi's* explanation, it is permissible only to warm the water in *front* of a fire. It is certainly prohibited to warm water on *top* of a fire on the Sabbath, due to the similarity of that act to cooking (*Rashba;* cf. *Ramban*).]

5. Cooking the oil means heating it until the hand recoils from it (*Rashi*). Thus, R' Yehudah's ruling concerning oil is essentially the same as the Tanna Kamma's ruling concerning water. The Gemara will shortly explain the difference between their views. [The terms *heated* and *cooked* employed by the Baraisa have the same meaning, but *heated* is used in connection with water since the only noticeable change effected in water through exposure to fire is that it becomes hot. Similarly, the terms *taking the chill off* and *warming* mean the same thing except that the former is used in counterpoint to *heating* and the latter in counterpoint to *cooking* (*Ritva, MHK* ed.; see *Eglei Tal, Ofeh* 19:13ff; cf. *Rabbeinu Baruch* cited by *Ritva, Pnei Yehoshua*).]

6. Rabban Shimon ben Gamliel disagrees with R' Yehudah and does not allow warming oil in the usual manner of placing the flask in front of a fire. He allows warming it only by means of the unusual expedient of anointing oneself with it and standing in front of a fire (*Rashi*). The Gemara will explain his rationale.

[The statement "and need not be concerned" etc. reflects the point that although warming the oil in the usual fashion is prohibited, there is no basis for prohibiting warming it in this unusual fashion. See note 11.]

כי האי תנא אמבטיאות של כרכים מטייל בהן ואינו חושש אמר רבא דוקא כרכין אבל דכפרים לא מ"ט כיון דזוטרין נפיש הבליהו ת"ר א מתחמם אדם כנגד המדורה ויוצא ומשתטף בצונן ובלבד שלא ישתטף בצונן ויתחמם כנגד המדורה מפני שמפשיר מים שעליו א) ת"ר ב מיחם אדם אלונטית ומניחה על בני מעים בשבת ובלבד שלא יביא קומקומוס של מים חמין ויניחנו על בני מעים בשבת ודבר זה אפי' בחול אסור מפני הסכנה ב) ת"ר ג מביא אדם קיתון מים ומניחו כנגד המדורה לא בשביל שיחמו אלא בשביל שתפיג צינתן ר' יהודה אומר מביאה אשה פך של שמן ומניחתו כנגד המדורה לא בשביל שיבשל אלא בשביל שיפשר רשב"ג אומר אשה סכה ידה שמן ומחממתה כנגד המדורה וסכה לבנה קטן ואינה חוששת איבעיא להו שמן מה הוא לתנא קמא רבה ורב יוסף דאמרי תרוייהו להתירא רב נחמן בר יצחק אמר לאיסורא רבה ורב יוסף דאמרי תרוייהו להתירא שמן אע"פ שהיד סולדת בו מותר קסבר ת"ק שמן אין בו משום בשול ואתא רבי יהודה למימר שמן יש בו משום בשול והפשרו לא זה הוא בשולו ואתא ר' שמעון בן גמליאל למימר שמן יש בו משום בשול והפשרו זהו בשולו רב נחמן בר יצחק אמר לאיסורא שמן אע"פ שאין היד סולדת בו אסור קסבר שמן יש בו משום בשול והפשרו זהו בשולו ואתא ר' יהודה למימר הפשרו לא זהו בשולו ואתא רשב"ג למימר שמן יש בו משום בשול והפשרו זהו בשולו רשב"ג היינו ת"ק איכא בינייהו כלאחר יד א"ר יהודה אמר שמואל ד אחד שמן ואחד מים יד סולדת בו אסור אין יד סולדת בו מותר והיכי דמי יד סולדת בו אמר רחבא כל שכריסו של תינוק נכוית א"ר יצחק בר אבדימי פעם אחת נכנסתי אחר רבי לבית המרחץ ובקשתי להניח לו פך של שמן באמבטי ה ואמר לי טול בכלי שני ותן שמע מינה תלת שמע מינה שמן יש בו משום בשול וש"מ ו כלי שני אינו מבשל וש"מ הפשרו זהו בשולו והיכי עביד הכי והאמר רבה בר בר חנה א"ר יוחנן ג) ז בכל מקום מותר להרהר חוץ מבית המרחץ ובית הכסא וכ"ת בלשון חול א"ל והאמר אביי ח דברים של חול מותר לאומרן בלשון קודש של קודש אסור לאומרן בלשון חול ט אפרושי מאיסורא שאני תדע דאמר ד) רב יהודה אמר שמואל מעשה ה) בתלמידו של ר' מאיר שנכנס אחריו לבית המרחץ י ובקש להדיח קרקע ואמר לו אין מדיחין לסוך לו קרקע אמר לו אין סכין אלמא אפרושי מאיסורא שאני הכא נמי לאפרושי מאיסורא שאני אמר רבינא שמע מינה המבשל בחמי טבריה בשבת חייב דהא מעשה דר' לאחר גזירה הוה ואמר ליה טול בכלי שני ותן איני ו) והאמר רב חסדא כ המבשל בחמי טבריה בשבת פטור מאי חייב נמי דקאמר ז) מכת מרדות א"ר זירא אנא חזיתיה לר' אבהו דשט באמבטי ולא ידענא אי עקר אי לא עקר פשיטא דלא עקר דתניא ל לא ישוט אדם בבריכה מלאה מים ואפי' עומדת בחצר מ לא קשיא הא דלית

דלית

רש"י

כי האי תנא. דאמר לעיל משהתחילו עוברי עבירה התחילו לאסור הזיעה והרי לא נאסרה אלא ע"י הרוחצין בחמין מאתמול ואומרים מזיעין אנחנו ואין כאן אלא עבירת דבריהם שאסרו את החמין: **נפיש הבליהו.** ומזיע: **מפשיר.** מחמם לשון פושרין: **מיחם אדם.** מחמם: **אלונטית.** טיול"א ונראה לי בגד שמסתפגין בו דבכל דוכתא קרי ליה אלונטית: **על גבי מעיים.** כשהוא חש במעיו מחממין לו כלי או בגד ומניחו שם ומועיל: **ובלבד שלא יביא קומקומוס כו'.** שמא ישפכו עליו ונמצא רוחץ בשבת בחמין: **מפני סכנה.** פעמים שהן רותחין: **לא שיחמו.** לא שיניחם שם עד שיחמו: **אלא שתפיג צינתן.** במקצתן שתפיג שתתחלף כמו וריחו לא נמר (ירמיה מח) מתרגמינן וריחיה לא פג: **לא בשביל שיבשל.** שלא תניחנו שם כדי בישול שתהא היד סולדת בו: **סכה ידה.** אבל להפשירו בפך כדרך שעושה בחול לא ופליג אדרב יהודה: **להתירא.** מאי דאסר רבי יהודה בשמן בישול שרי ת"ק ומים דוקא נקט ולא שיחמו דיש בהן בישול אבל שמן אע"פ שהיד סולדת דהיינו בישול דר' יהודה שרי לת"ק: **סולדת.** נמשכת לאחוריה מדאגה שלא תכוה וזהו לשון ואסלדה בחילה (איוב ו) ולדאג ברעדה ואמשך מתלונתי מדאגת יום הדין אם הייתי יודע שמיתתי קרובה ולא יחמול: **שמן יש בו משום בישול.** הלכך לא כדי שיבשל אלא כדי שיפשר שרי דהפשרו אין זה בישולו: **ואתא רבי שמעון למימר דהפשירו זהו בישולו.** הלכך כדעבדין בחול לא ליעביד אלא כלאחר יד על ידי שינוי: **לאיסורא.** אמרה תנא קמא לשמן דמיא הוא דשרי להפשיר אבל שמן הפשרו זהו בישולו: **איכא בינייהו כלאחר יד.** דלתנא קמא אפי' ע"י שינוי אסור: **והיכי דמי.** סלוד יש שסולד מרתיחה מועטת ויש שאינו סולד: **נכנסתי.** בשבת ובחמי טבריא הוה שלא נאסרו כדאמר לעיל התירו להם חמי טבריא: **באמבטי.** כגון בריכה עשויה בקרקע שהמים נכנסים שם ונאספין: **ובקשתי להניח שם פך שמן.** להפשיר לסוך הימנו קודם הרחילה: **טול.** מן המים: **בכלי שני.** שילטנו מעט דכלי שני אינו מבשל ואח"כ תן הפך לתוך אותו כלי שני דהך אמבטי שהחמין נמשכין לה מן המעיין חשיב לה ככלי ראשון שנרתחו בו שאע"פ שהעבירו מעל האור מבשל כדתנן לקמן (ד' מג.) האילפס והקדירה שהעבירן מרותחין לא יתן לתוכן תבלין: **וש"מ הפשרו.** במקום הראוי לבישול: **זהו בישולו.** דהא להפשיר בעלמא הוא דקבעי ואסר ליה: **והיכי עביד הכי.** להורות הוראה שהוא דבר תורה בבית המרחץ: **להרהר.** בדברי תורה: **דברים של קדש.** דברי תורה: **אסור לאומרן.** במקום הטנופת ואפי' בלשון חול: **אין מדיחין.** דלמא אתי לאשויי גומות: **דהא מעשה דרבי אחר גזירה הוה.** שגזרו על הזיעה ועל כרחין בחמי טבריא הוא דהוי ורבי יהושע (א) דאמר לעיל בימי רבי הוה אלמא בימי רבי כבר נגזרה: **וקאמר ליה טול בכלי שני.** אבל ראשון לא אלמא יש בהן משום בישול: **מרדות.** רדוי: **שט.** לף: **דשט באמבטי.** בשבת: **ולא ידענא אי עקר.** רגליו מן הארץ דקסבר כי תנן אין שטין על פני המים במשילין פירות (ביצה לו.) בנהר גדול תנן דאיכא למגזר שמא יעשה חבית של שייטין כדאמרינן התם אבל באמבטי לא: **אי לא עקר.** רגליו: **לא ישוט.** דאע"ג דליכא למיגזר אסור: **ואפילו עומדת בחצר.** דליכא למיגזר שמא יתיז מים ברגליו חוץ לארבע אמות: **הא.** דאסיר: דלית

תוספות

מפני שמפשיר מים שעליו. בכולה שמעתא ובמתניתין גבי מיחם שפינהו משמע דלהפשיר מים לצורך שתייה מותר דהפשירן לא זהו בישולן. והכא דאסורין מפרש ריב"א דדומה כרוחץ במים חמין ויבא להחם חמין לרחוץ גופו:

ובלבד שלא יביא קומקומוס כו'. פירוש כל זמן שהאלונטית שם שמא יפלו המים על האלונטית ואתי לידי סחיטה אי נמי לא יביא משום רפואה וגזרו אטו שחיקת סממנים טפי מבאלונטית דלא מיחזי כרפואה כ"כ:

ושמע מינה כלי שני אינו מבשל. תימה מאי שנא כלי שני מכלי ראשון דאי יד סולדת אפי' כלי שני נמי ואי אין יד סולדת אפילו כלי ראשון נמי אינו מבשל ויש לומר לפי שכלי ראשון מתוך שעמד על האור דופנותיו חמין ומחזיק חומו זמן מרובה ולכך נתנו בו שיעור דכל זמן א) שהיד סולדת בו אסור אבל כלי שני אף על גב דיד סולדת בו מותר שאין דופנותיו חמין והולך ומתקרר: **וכי** תימא בלשון חול קאמר ליה. ואע"ג דאסור להרהר נימא דאין אסור להרהר אלא בלשון קדש והוא הרהר בלשון חול: פשיטא

כא א מיי' פכ"ב מהל' שבת הלכה ג סמג לאוין סה טוש"ע או"ח סימן שכו סעיף ד:

כב ב מיי' שם הלכה ד טוש"ע שם סעיף ו:

כג ג ד מיי' וסמג שם טוש"ע או"ח סימן שיח סעיף יד:

כד ה ו מיי' פכ"ב שם הלכה ה ו טור שו"ע שם סעיף יג וטוש"ע יו"ד סימן קה סעיף ב:

כה ז ח ט מיי' פ"ג מהלכות ק"ש הלכה ד ה טוש"ע או"ח סימן פה סעיף ב:

כו י מיי' פכ"א מהלכות שבת הלכה ג טוש"ע או"ח סימן שלו סעיף ג:

כז כ מיי' פ"ט מהלכות שבת הלכה ג:

כח ל מ מיי' פכ"ג מהל' שבת הלכה ה טור שו"ע או"ח סימן שלט סעיף ב:

רבינו חננאל

להן אלא צונן בלבד. ראו שאין הדבר עומד חזרו והתירו להן חמי טבריא בלבד. וזיעה במקומה עומדת באיסור אמר רבא מאן דעבר על דברי חכמי' שרי למיקריי' עבריינא. כי האי תנא דתנא משרבו עוברי עבירה: **תנא** אמבטאות של כרכין מטייל בהן ואינו חושש. והני מילי דכרכין אבל דכפרין כיון דזוטרן נפיש הבליהון: **ת"ר** מתחמם אדם כנגד המדורה ויוצא (ומשתטף בצונן) [ובלבד שלא ישתטף בצונן] ויתחמם כנגד המדורה מפני שנפשרו המים שעליו: **ת"ר** מיחם אדם אלונטית ומניחה ע"ג מעיו בשבת ובלבד (ישתטף בצונן ויתחמם כנגד המדורה מפני שתפשר המים) שלא יביא קומקומוס של חמין ויניחנו על גבי מעיו בשבת. ודבר זה אפילו בחול [אסור] מפני הסכנה שלא יכוה: **ת"ר** מניח אדם קיתון של מים כנגד המדורה לא שיחמו אלא כדי שתפוג צינתן. ר' יהודה אמר מנחת אשה פך שמן כנגד המדורה לא שיתבשל אלא כדי שתפשר. רשבג"א אשה סכה ידה שמן כנגד המדורה. וסכה לבנה קטן ואינה חוששת: **איבעיא** להו שמן מה לי בו אמר ת"ק. ואסיק' אמר רב אמר שמואל אחד שמן ואחד מים אם נתחמם כשעור שהיד סולדת בו אסור אין היד סולדת בו מותר. ושיעור שהיד סולדת בו. פי' (פירוש') [בירושל'] שהיד א) שולטת בו סולדת היא שולטת והוא כל שכריסו של תינוק נכוית הימנו. הא מעשה דר' שבקשו לו פך של שמן באמבטי ואמר להן טלו בכלי שני ותנו. שמעינן מינה תלת. ש"מ שמן יש בו משום בישול. ולפיכך בכלי ראשון אסור. שנמצא מבשל שמן בשבת. וש"מ מדשרי בכלי שני דכלי שני אינו מבשל. וש"מ הפשרו לא זהו בישולו: אמר רבינא ש"מ המבשל בחמי טבריא הואיל וגזרו רבנן עלייהו חייבין מכת מרדות מדרבנן. ואקשינן דר' היאך מורה הוראה במרחץ ואמר טלו בכלי שני כלומר זהו מותר וזהו אסור. והא"ר יוחנן כל מקום מותר להרהר חוץ מבית המרחץ ובית הכסא. ולא דאקשינן מדברי ר' יוחנן לר' דר' יוחנן לגבי דר' תלמיד קטן הוא. (ולא) [אלא] הא דר' יוחנן דברי הכל קבלה הוא

חשק שלמה על רבינו חננאל א) ע"ס יש כאן ולשון הירושלמי הובא ברא"ש:

א) תוספתא שבת פ"ד, ב) [תוספתא שם], ג) ברכות כד: (לעיל י.) לקמן קנ. זבחים קב: ע"ז מד: קדושין לג., ד) [לקמן קנא:], ה) [עי' תוס' לקמן קמז: ד"ה דמניא], ו) פסחים מא., ז) [יבמות נב. כתובות מה: נזיר כג. נח: חולין קמא:], ח) [דף לו:].

תוספות ישנים

א) והכא באמבטי במקום שרגלה להניח הפך היתה יד סולדת בו. והא דלא א"ל תן במקום שאין היד סולדת דהיינו במקום שרחץ ודאי לא היה היד סולדת. ושמא שם לא הי' יכול להפשיר. א"נ פעמים החמירו בכלי ראשון אף אם אין היד סולדת בו. וכן החמירו חכמים אפי' בכלי שני לקמן (מב.) גבי ספל ה"ה כאמבטי:

הגהות הב"ח

(א) רש"י ד"ה דהא מעשה וכו' ור' יהושע בן לוי דאמר:

ליקוטי רש"י

מדורה. היסק גדול [ביצה כא:]. **אלונטית.** בגד שמסתפגין בו כשיוצאין מבית המרחץ [עירובין פז:]. **אלונטיות.** סדינין שמקנחין בהן [לקמן קמז.]. **קומקומוס.** קומקמוסין סירות קטנות של מתכת [ע"ז מג:]. יורה קטנה [לעיל לח:]. **יד סולדת.** לשון ירא ודואג שהיד סולדת בהן מלכוות ברותחין [איוב ו, י עיי"ש]. נכוית [חולין קה:]. **אסור לאומרן בלשון חול.** שאע"פ שאינה בלשון הקדש לא נפקי מקדושתייהו [ע"ז מד:]. **להדיח.** במים [לקמן קנא.]. **אין סכין.** משום אשויי גומות ואף על גב דמרחץ רצפת אבנים הוא וליכא למיחש לאשויי גומות מיחלף מיהא בקרקע אחר [שם:]. **המבשל בחמי טבריה.** מעיינות רותחין. **בשבת פטור.** דלאו תולדות אש היא הלכך לאו בישול הוא דליהוי חייב משום אב מלאכה [פסחים מא.]. **מכת מרדות.** רידוי בתוכחה שלא ירגיל בזה ואין לה קצבה אלא עד שיקבל עליו [חולין קמא:].

The Gemara analyzes the Baraisa:

אִיבַּעְיָא לְהוּ – **They inquired:** שֶׁמֶן מַה הוּא לְתַנָּא קַמָּא – **What is** the law concerning **oil according to the Tanna Kamma?**[7]

Two opinions in this matter are cited:

רַבָּה וְרַב יוֹסֵף דְּאָמְרֵי תַּרְוַיְיהוּ לְהֶתֵּירָא – **Rabbah and Rav Yosef both said** that the Tanna Kamma is more **permissive** in regard to oil than in regard to water. That is, he permits even placing oil in front of a fire to heat it. רַב נַחְמָן בַּר יִצְחָק אָמַר לְאִיסּוּרָא – **Rav Nachman bar Yitzchak said** that the Tanna Kamma is more **prohibitive** in regard to oil than in regard to water. That is, he forbids even placing oil in front of a fire to take its chill off.

The Gemara proceeds to explain the Tanna Kamma's opinion as well as the remainder of the Baraisa according to each of these views:

רַבָּה וְרַב יוֹסֵף דְּאָמְרֵי תַּרְוַיְיהוּ לְהֶתֵּירָא – **Rabbah and Rav Yosef both said** that the Tanna Kamma is more **permissive** in regard to oil than in regard to water, and holds that whereas water may not be placed in front of a fire for heating until the hand recoils from it, שֶׁמֶן אַף עַל פִּי שֶׁהַיָּד סוֹלֶדֶת בּוֹ מוּתָּר – in the case of **oil, even** leaving it in front of the fire to the point **that the hand recoils from it is permissible.** קָסָבַר תַּנָּא קַמָּא שֶׁמֶן אֵין בּוֹ מִשּׁוּם בִּשּׁוּל – The reason is that **the Tanna Kamma holds** that, unlike water, **oil is not subject to cooking.**[8] וְאָתָא רַבִּי יְהוּדָה לְמֵימַר – According to this interpretation of the Tanna Kamma's opinion, **R' Yehudah comes to say** that שֶׁמֶן יֵשׁ בּוֹ מִשּׁוּם בִּשּׁוּל – **oil *is* subject to cooking,** וְהֶפְשֵׁרוֹ לֹא זֶה הוּא בִּשּׁוּלוֹ – **and** like water, merely **warming it is not** the act of **cooking it.**[9] Therefore, R' Yehudah extends the Tanna Kamma's rule to oil and states that one may warm a flask of oil in front of a fire but must not heat it there. וְאָתָא רַבָּן שִׁמְעוֹן בֶּן גַּמְלִיאֵל לְמֵימַר – **Rabban Shimon ben Gamliel then comes to say** that indeed שֶׁמֶן יֵשׁ בּוֹ מִשּׁוּם בִּשּׁוּל – **oil is subject to cooking,** וְהֶפְשֵׁרוֹ זֶהוּ בִּשּׁוּלוֹ – **but,** unlike water, **warming it *is*** the act of **cooking it.**[10] Therefore, R' Shimon ben Gamliel does not allow placing a flask of oil in front of a fire even to warm it.[11]

The Gemara now elaborates the view of Rav Nachman bar Yitzchak:

רַב נַחְמָן בַּר יִצְחָק אָמַר לְאִיסּוּרָא – **Rav Nachman bar Yitzchak said** that the Tanna Kamma is more **prohibitive** in regard to oil than in regard to water, and holds that whereas water may be placed in front of a fire to take the chill off, so long as it is not heated to the degree that the hand recoils from it, שֶׁמֶן אַף עַל פִּי שֶׁאֵין הַיָּד סוֹלֶדֶת בּוֹ אָסוּר – in the case of **oil, even** merely warming it to a degree **that the hand does not recoil from it is forbidden.** קָסָבַר שֶׁמֶן יֵשׁ בּוֹ מִשּׁוּם בִּשּׁוּל וְהֶפְשֵׁרוֹ זֶהוּ בִּשּׁוּלוֹ – The reason is that **[the Tanna Kamma] holds** that **oil is subject to cooking, and** furthermore, **warming it is** the act of **cooking it.** וְאָתָא רַבִּי יְהוּדָה לְמֵימַר הֶפְשֵׁרוֹ לֹא זֶהוּ בִּשּׁוּלוֹ – According to this explanation of the Tanna Kamma's opinion, **R' Yehudah comes to say** that **warming oil is *not*** the act of **cooking it** and it is therefore permitted to place a flask of oil in front of a fire to warm it, albeit not to make it hot. וְאָתָא רַבָּן שִׁמְעוֹן בֶּן גַּמְלִיאֵל לְמֵימַר – **And Rabban Shimon ben Gamliel comes to say** that שֶׁמֶן יֵשׁ בּוֹ מִשּׁוּם בִּשּׁוּל וְהֶפְשֵׁרוֹ זֶהוּ בִּשּׁוּלוֹ – **oil *is* subject to cooking and warming it *is*** the act of **cooking it.** Accordingly, it is forbidden even to warm a flask of oil in front of a fire.

The Gemara asks:

רַבָּן שִׁמְעוֹן בֶּן גַּמְלִיאֵל הַיְינוּ תַּנָּא קַמָּא – According to the latter interpretation, the opinion of **Rabban Shimon ben Gamliel is the same as** that of **the Tanna Kamma!** Why, then, are they cited as two separate opinions in the Baraisa?

The Gemara answers:

אִיכָּא בֵּינַיְיהוּ כִּלְאַחַר יָד – **There is** a difference of opinion **between them** regarding the permissibility of warming the oil **in an unusual manner.**[12] Rabban Shimon ben Gamliel allows warming oil by anointing oneself with it and standing in front of a fire, whereas the Tanna Kamma who makes no such suggestion forbids even this.

The Gemara cites an Amoraic ruling concerning the issues discussed in the Baraisa:

אָמַר רַב יְהוּדָה אָמַר שְׁמוּאֵל – **Rav Yehudah said in the name of Shmuel:** אֶחָד שֶׁמֶן וְאֶחָד מַיִם – **Both** in regard to **oil and** in regard to **water** the rule is as follows: יָד סוֹלֶדֶת בּוֹ אָסוּר – Heating it up to the degree that **the hand recoils from it is prohibited,** אֵין יָד סוֹלֶדֶת בּוֹ מוּתָּר – but merely warming it up to a degree that **the hand does not recoil from it is permissible.**[13] וְהֵיכִי דָּמֵי יָד סוֹלֶדֶת בּוֹ – **And what is** considered the degree of heat **from which the hand recoils?** אָמַר רַחֲבָא – **Rachva said:** כֹּל שֶׁכְּרֵיסוֹ שֶׁל תִּינוֹק נִכְוֵית – **Anything that** is so hot that **an infant's** tender **belly would be scalded** by it.[14]

A related incident is cited:

אָמַר רַבִּי יִצְחָק בַּר אַבְדִּימִי – **R' Yitzchak bar Avdimi said:** פַּעַם אַחַת נִכְנַסְתִּי אַחַר רַבִּי לְבֵית הַמֶּרְחָץ – **On one occasion I followed Rebbi into a** Tiberian **bathhouse** on the Sabbath,[15] וּבִקַּשְׁתִּי לְהַנִּיחַ לוֹ פַּךְ שֶׁל שֶׁמֶן בְּאַמְבַּטִי – **and I wished to place a flask of oil in a** hot **bathtub** in order to warm it up. וְאָמַר לִי טוֹל בִּכְלִי שֵׁנִי וְתֵן – **[Rebbi] said to me: Take** some water **in a**

NOTES

7. The Tanna Kamma allowed placing a flask of water in front of a fire to take its chill off but not to heat it, and was silent regarding oil. How are we to interpret his silence? Does he forbid placing oil in front of a fire even to take its chill off or does he permit placing it there even until it is hot?

8. The prohibition against cooking does not pertain to items that are unchanged in form, taste or function by cooking. The Tanna Kamma holds that cooking does not bring about any substantive change in oil and the prohibition therefore does not apply to it. Water, however, is subject to this prohibition, since cooked water is fit for different uses than cold water (*Maggid Mishneh, Hil. Shabbos* 9:3 as explained by *Eglei Tal, Ofeh* §19; *Igros Moshe, Orach Chaim* vol. II §85; see *Rashi*).

9. Rather, it is considered cooked only when heated to the point that the hand recoils from it (*Rashi*).

10. Since oil is often warmed as a final prelude to anointing with it, warming it is similar to putting the finishing touch on a Spanish mackerel by pouring hot water over it, which is prohibited under the *melachah* of *cooking,* as explained above, 39a (*Pnei Yehoshua;* see following note).

11. He does, however, permit anointing oneself with oil and then standing in front of a fire, since this is not the usual method of warming oil (*Rashi*). It seems strange that Rabban Shimon ben Gamliel would permit cooking simply because one is doing it in an unusual fashion. Perforce, he does not consider the warming of oil to be an act of cooking under Biblical law. Rather, it was the Rabbis who considered this somewhat similar to putting the finishing touch on a Spanish mackerel and therefore forbade warming oil on the Sabbath. However, they did not apply their decree to warming it in an unusual fashion (*Pnei Yehoshua;* see also *Rosh Yosef* ד״ה ש״מ תלת).

12. Literally: as if with the back of the hand.

13. This accords with the view of R' Yehudah in the Baraisa. As stated in note 4, *Rosh* and *Shulchan Aruch* understand this to mean that it is permissible to warm water or oil only at a distance from the fire, where it cannot possibly become so hot that the hand recoils from it.

14. Since some adults have a greater tolerance for heat than others and their hand would not recoil readily, Rachva offers a more universal definition of the prohibited temperature (*Rashi*).

15. Since the bathhouse was supplied by the Tiberian hot-springs, it did not fall under the injunction against bathing, as the Gemara concluded above (*Rashi;* see note 26).

כי האי תנא אמבטיאות של כרכים מטייל בהן ואינו חושש אמר רבא דוקא כרכין אבל דכפרים לא מ"ט כיון דזוטרין נפיש הבלייהו ת"ר א מתחמם אדם כנגד המדורה ויוצא ומשתטף בצונן ובלבד שלא ישתטף בצונן ויתחמם כנגד המדורה מפני שמפשיר מים שעליו א) ת"ר ב מיחם אדם אלונטית ומניחה על בני מעים בשבת ובלבד שלא יביא קומקומוס של מים חמין ויניחנו על בני מעים בשבת ודבר זה אפי' בחול אסור מפני הסכנה ב) ת"ר ג מביא אדם קיתון מים ומניחו כנגד המדורה לא בשביל שיחמו אלא בשביל שתפיג צינתן ר' יהודה אומר מביאה אשה פך של שמן ומניחתו כנגד המדורה לא בשביל שיבשל אלא בשביל שיפשר רשב"ג אומר אשה סכה ידה שמן ומחממתה כנגד המדורה וסכה לבנה קטן ואינה חוששת איבעיא להו שמן מה הוא לתנא קמא רבה ורב יוסף דאמרי תרוייהו להתירא רב נחמן בר יצחק אמר לאיסורא רבה ורב יוסף דאמרי תרוייהו להתירא שמן אע"פ שהיד סולדת בו מותר קסבר ת"ק שמן אין בו משום בשול ואתא רבי יהודה למימר שמן יש בו משום בשול והפשרו לא זה הוא בשולו ואתא ר' שמעון בן גמליאל למימר שמן יש בו משום בשול והפשרו זהו בשולו רב נחמן בר יצחק אמר לאיסורא שמן אע"פ שאין היד סולדת בו אסור קסבר שמן יש בו משום בשול והפשרו זהו בשולו ואתא ר' יהודה למימר הפשרו לא זהו בשולו ואתא רשב"ג למימר שמן יש בו משום בשול והפשרו זהו בשולו רשב"ג היינו ת"ק איכא בינייהו כלאחר יד א"ר יהודה אמר שמואל ד אחד שמן ואחד מים יד סולדת בו אסור אין יד סולדת בו מותר והיכי דמי יד סולדת בו אמר רחבא כל שכריסו של תינוק נכוית א"ר יצחק בר אבדימי פעם אחת נכנסתי אחר רבי לבית המרחץ ובקשתי להניח לו פך של שמן באמבטי ה ואמר לי טול בכלי שני ותן שמע מינה תלת שמע מינה שמן יש בו משום בשול וש"מ ו כלי שני אינו מבשל וש"מ הפשרו זהו בשולו היכי עביד הכי והאמר רבה בר בר חנה א"ר יוחנן ג) ז בכל מקום מותר להרהר חוץ מבית המרחץ ובית הכסא וכ"ת בלשון חול א"ל והאמר אביי ח דברים של חול מותר לאומרן בלשון קודש של קודש אסור לאומרן בלשון חול ט אפרושי מאיסורא שאני תדע דאמר ד) רב יהודה אמר שמואל מעשה ה) בתלמידו של ר' מאיר שנכנס אחריו לבית המרחץ י ובקש להדיח קרקע ואמר לו אין מדיחין לסוך לו קרקע אמר לו אין סכין אלמא אפרושי מאיסורא שאני הכא נמי לאפרושי מאיסורא שאני אמר רבינא שמע מינה המבשל בחמי טבריא בשבת חייב דהא מעשה דר' לאחר גזירה הוה ואמר ליה טול בכלי שני ותן איני ו) והאמר רב חסדא כ המבשל בחמי טבריא בשבת פטור מאי חייב נמי דקאמר ז) מכת מרדות א"ר זירא אנא חזיתיה לר' אבהו דשט באמבטי ולא ידענא אי עקר אי לא עקר פשיטא דלא עקר דתניא ל לא ישוט אדם בבריכה מלאה מים ואפי' עומדת בחצר מ לא קשיא הא

דלית

רש"י

כי האי תנא. דאמר לעיל משהתחילו עוברי עבירה התחילו לאסור הזיעה והרי לא נאסרה אלא ע"י הרוחצין בחמין מאתמול ואומרים מזיעין אנחנו ואין כאן אלא עבירת דבריהם שאסרו את החמין: **נפיש הבלייהו.** ומזיע: **מפשיר.** מחמם לשון פושרין: **מיחם אדם.** מחמם: **אלונטית.** טיול"א ונראה לי בגד שמסתפגין בו דבכל דוכתא קרי ליה אלונטית: **על גבי מעיים.** כשהוא חש במעיו מחממין לו כלי או בגד ומניחו שם ומועיל: **ובלבד שלא יביא קומקומוס כו'.** שמא ישפכו עליו ונמצא רוחץ בשבת בחמין: **מפני סכנה.** פעמים שהן רותחין: **לא שיחמו.** לא שיניחם שם עד שיחמו: **אלא שתפיג צינתן.** במקצתן שתפיג שתתחלף כמו וריחו לא נמר (ירמיה מח) מתרגמין וריחיה לא פג: **לא בשביל שיבשל.** שלא תניחנו שם כדי בישול שתהא היד סולדת בו: **סכה ידה.** אבל להפשירו בפך כדרך שעושה בחול לא ופליג אדרב יהודה: **להתירא.** מאי דאסר רבי יהודה בשמן בישול שרי ת"ק ומים דוקא נקט ולא שיחמו דיש בהן בישול אבל שמן אע"פ שהיד סולדת דהיינו בישול דר' יהודה שרי לת"ק: **סולדת.** נמשכת לאחוריה מדאגה שלא תכוה והוא לשון ואסלדה בחילה (איוב ו) ודאג ברעדה ואמשך מתלונתי מדאגת יום הדין אם הייתי יודע שמיתתי קרובה ולא יחמול: **שמן יש בו משום בישול.** הלכך לא כדי שיבשל אלא כדי שיפשר שרי דהפשרו אין זה בישולו: **ואתא רבי שמעון למימר דהפשירו זהו בישולו.** הלכך כדעבדין בחול לא ליעביד אלא כלאחר יד על ידי שינוי: **לאיסורא.** אמרה תנא קמא לשמן דמיא הוא דשרי להפשיר אבל שמן הפשרו זהו בישולו: **איכא בינייהו כלאחר יד.** דלתנא קמא אפי' ע"י שינוי אסור: **והיכי דמי.** סלוד יש שסולד מרתיחה מועטת ויש שאינו סולד: **נכנסתי.** בשבת ובחמי טבריא הוה שלא נאסרו כדאמר לעיל התירו להם חמי טבריא: **באמבטי.** כגון בריכה עשויה בקרקע שהמים נכנסים שם ונאספין: **ובקשתי להניח שם פך שמן.** להפשיר לסוך הימנו קודם הרחיצה: **טול.** מן המים: **בכלי שני.** שילטנו מעט דכלי שני אינו מבשל ואח"כ תן הפך לתוך אותו כלי שני דהך אמבטי שהחמין נמשכין לה מן המעיין חשיב לה ככלי ראשון שנרתחו בו שאע"פ שהעבירו מעל האור מבשל כדתנן לקמן (ד' מב.) האילפס והקדירה שהעבירן מרותחין לא יתן לתוכן תבלין: **וש"מ הפשרו.** במקום הראוי לבישול: **זהו בישולו.** דהא להפשיר בעלמא הוא דקבעי ואסר ליה: **והיכי עביד הכי.** להורות הוראה שהוא דבר תורה בבית המרחץ: **להרהר.** בדברי תורה: **דברים של קדש.** דברי תורה: **אסור לאומרן.** במקום הטנופת ואפי' בלשון חול: **אין מדיחין.** דלמא אתי לאשויי גומות: **דהא מעשה דרבי אחר גזירה הוה.** שגזרו על הזיעה ועל כרחין בחמי טבריא הוא דהוי ורבי יהושע (א) דאמר לעיל בימי רבי הוה אלמא בימי רבי כבר נגזרה: **וקאמר ליה טול בכלי שני.** אבל ראשון לא אלמא יש בהן משום בישול: **מרדות.** רדוי: **שט.** לף: **דשט באמבטי.** בשבת: **ולא ידענא אי עקר.** רגליו מן הארץ דקסבר כי תנן אין שטין על פני המים במשילין פירות (ביצה לו:) בנהר גדול תנן דאיכא למגזר שמא יעשה חבית של שייטין כדאמרינן התם אבל באמבטי לא: **אי לא עקר.** רגליו: **לא ישוט.** דאע"ג דליכא למיגזר אסור: **ואפילו עומדת בחצר.** דליכא למיגזר שמא יתיז מים ברגליו חוץ לארבע אמות: **הא.** דאסיר:

דלית

תוספות

מפני שמפשיר מים שעליו. בכולה שמעתא ובמתניתין גבי מיחס שפינהו משמע להפשיר מים לצורך שתייה מותר דהפשירן לא זהו בישולן. והכא דאסורין מפרש ריב"א דדומה כרוחץ במים חמין ויבא להחם חמין לרחוץ גופו:

ובלבד שלא יביא קומקומוס כו'. פירוש כל זמן שהאלונטית שם שמא יפלו המים על האלונטית ואתי לידי סחיטה אי נמי לא יביא משום רפואה וגזרו אטו שחיקת סממנים טפי מבאלונטית דלא מיחזי כרפואה כ"כ:

ושמע מינה כלי שני אינו מבשל. תימה מאי שנא כלי שני מכלי ראשון דאי יד סולדת אפי' כלי שני נמי ואי אין יד סולדת אפילו כלי ראשון נמי אינו מבשל ויש לומר לפי שכלי ראשון מתוך שעמד על האור דופנותיו חמין ומחזיק חומו זמן מרובה ולכך נתנו בו שיעור דכל זמן א) שהיד סולדת בו אסור אבל כלי שני אף על גב דיד סולדת בו מותר שאין דופנותיו חמין והולך ומתקרר: **וכי** תימא בלשון חול קאמר ליה. ואע"ג דאסור להרהר נימא דאין אסור להרהר אלא בלשון קדש והוא הרהר בלשון חול:

פשיטא

עין משפט נר מצוה

כא א מיי' פכ"ב מהל' שבת הלכה ג סמג לאוין סה טוש"ע או"ח סימן שכו סעיף ד:

כב ב מיי' שם הלכה ד טוש"ע שם סעיף ו:

כג ג ד מיי' וסמג שם טוש"ע או"ח סימן שיח סעיף יד:

כד ה ו מיי' פכ"ב שם הלכה ה ו טור שו"ע שם סעיף יג וטוש"ע יו"ד סימן קה סעיף ב:

כה ז ח ט מיי' פ"ג מהלכות ק"ש הלכה ד ה טוש"ע או"ח סימן פה סעיף ב:

כו י מיי' פכ"א מהלכות שבת הלכה ג טוש"ע או"ח סימן שלז סעיף ג:

כז כ מיי' פ"ט מהלכות שבת הלכה ג:

כח ל מ מיי' פכ"ג מהל' שבת הלכה ה טור שו"ע או"ח סימן שלט סעיף ב:

רבינו חננאל

להן אלא צונן בלבד. ראו שאין הדבר עומד חזרו והתירו להן חמי טבריא בלבד. וזיעה במקומה עומדת באיסור אמר רבא מאן דעבר על דברי חכמי' שרי למיקריי' עבריינא. כי האי תנא דתנא משרבו עוברי עבירה: **תנא** אמבטאות של כרכין מטייל בהן ואינו חושש. והני מילי דכרכין אבל דכפרין כיון דזוטרן נפיש הבליהון: **ת"ר** מתחמם אדם כנגד המדורה ויוצא (ומשתטף בצונן) [ובלבד שלא ישתטף בצונן] ויתחמם כנגד המדורה מפני שנפשרו המים שעליו: **ת"ר** מיחם אדם אלונטית ומניחה ע"ג מעיו בשבת ובלבד (ישתטף בצונן ויתחמם כנגד המדורה מפני שתפשר המים) שלא יביא קומקומוס של חמין ויניחנו על גבי מעיו בשבת. ודבר זה אפילו בחול [אסור] מפני הסכנה שלא יכוה: **ת"ר** מניח אדם קיתון של מים כנגד המדורה לא שיחמו אלא כדי שתפוג צינתן. ר' יהודה אמר מנחת אשה פך שמן כנגד המדורה לא שיתבשל אלא כדי שתפשר. רשבג"א אשה סכה ידה שמן כנגד המדורה. וסכה לבנה קטן ואינה חוששת: **איבעיא** להו שמן מה לי בו אמר ת"ק. ואסיק' אמר רב אמר שמואל אחד שמן ואחד מים אם נתחמם כשעור שהיד סולדת בו אסור אין היד סולדת בו מותר. ושיעור שהיד סולדת בו. פי' (פירוש') [בירושל'] שהיד א) שולטת בו סולדת היא שולטת והוא כל שכריסו של תינוק נכוית הימנו. הא מעשה דר' שבקשו לו פך של שמן באמבטי ואמר להן טלו בכלי שני ותנו. שמעינן מינה תלת. ש"מ שמן יש בו משום בישול. ולפיכך בכלי ראשון אסור. שנמצא מבשל שמן בשבת. וש"מ מדשרי בכלי שני דכלי שני אינו מבשל. וש"מ הפשרו לא זהו בישולו: **אמר** רבינא ש"מ המבשל בחמי טבריא הואיל וגזרו רבנן עלייהו חייבין מכת מרדות מדרבנן. ואקשינן דר' היאך מורה הוראה במרחץ ואמר טלו בכלי שני כלומר זהו מותר וזהו אסור. והא"ר יוחנן כל מקום מותר להרהר חוץ מבית המרחץ ובית הכסא. ולא דאקשינן מדברי ר' יוחנן לר' דר' יוחנן לגבי דר' תלמיד קטן הוא. (ולא) [אלא] הא דר' יוחנן דברי הכל קבלה הוא

מסורת הש"ס

א) תוספתא שבת פ"ד, ב) [תוספתא שם], ג) ברכות כד: (לעיל י.) לקמן קנ. זבחים קב: ע"ז מד: קדושין לג., ד) [לקמן קנא:], ה) [עי' תוס' לקמן קמז: ד"ה דתניא], ו) פסחים מא., ז) [יבמות נב. כתובות מה: נזיר כג. נח: חולין קמא:], ח) [דף לו:].

תוספות ישנים

א) והכא באמבטי במקום שרצה להניח הפך היתה יד סולדת בו. והא דלא א"ל תן במקום שאין היד סולדת דהיינו במקום שרחץ ודאי לא היה היד סולדת. ושמא שם לא הי' יכול להפשיר. א"נ פעמים החמירו בכלי ראשון אף אם אין היד סולדת בו. וכן החמירו חכמים אפי' בכלי שני לקמן (מג.) גבי ספל ה"ה כאמבטי:

הגהות הב"ח

(א) רש"י ד"ה דהא מעשה וכו' ור' יהושע בן לוי דאמר:

ליקוטי רש"י

מדורה. היסק גדול [ביצה כא:]. **אלונטית.** בגד שמסתפגין בו כשיוצאין מבית המרחץ [עירובין פז:]. **אלונטיות.** סדינין שמקנחין בהן [לקמן קמז.]. **קומקומוס.** קומקמוסין סירות קטנות של מתכת [ע"ז מג:]. יורה קטנה [לעיל לח:]. **יד סולדת.** לשון ירא ודואג שהיד סולדת בהן מלכוות ברותחין [איוב ו, י עיי"ש]. נכוית [חולין קה:]. **אסור לאומרן בלשון חול.** שאע"פ שאינה בלשון הקדש לא נפקי מקדושתייהו [ע"ז מד:]. **להדיח.** במים [לקמן קנא.]. **אין סכין.** משום אשויי גומות ואף על גב דמרחץ רצפת אבנים הוא וליכא למיחש לאשויי גומות מיחלף מיהא בקרקע אחר [שם:]. **המבשל בחמי טבריה.** מעינות רותחין. **בשבת פטור.** דלאו תולדות אש היא הלכך לאו בישול הוא דליהוי חייב משום אב מלאכה [פסחים מא.]. **מכת מרדות.** רידוי בתוכחה שלא ירגיל בזה ואין לה קצבה אלא עד שיקבל עליו [חולין קמא:].

חשק שלמה על רבינו חננאל א) ע"ס יש כאן ולשון הירושלמי הובא ברא"ש:

secondary vessel and place the flask into that vessel to warm it.[16]

The Gemara comments on this episode:

שְׁמַע מִינָּהּ תְּלָת – We **learn three** things **from this.** שְׁמַע מִינָּהּ שֶׁמֶן יֵשׁ בּוֹ מִשּׁוּם בִּשּׁוּל – Firstly, we **learn from it** that **oil is subject to cooking.** וּשְׁמַע מִינָּהּ כְּלִי שֵׁנִי אֵינוֹ מְבַשֵּׁל – Secondly, we **learn from it** that **a secondary vessel is not capable of cooking.** וּשְׁמַע מִינָּהּ הֶפְשֵׁרוֹ זֶהוּ בִּשּׁוּלוֹ – **And** finally, we **learn from it** that **warming [oil] is** the act of **cooking it.**[17]

The Gemara digresses to question how Rebbi could have made the previous remark inside the bathhouse:

הֵיכִי עָבִיד הָכִי – **How could he have done this?** וְהָאָמַר רַבָּה בַּר בַּר חָנָה אָמַר רַבִּי יוֹחָנָן – **But Rabbah bar bar Chanah said in the name of R' Yochanan:** בְּכָל מָקוֹם מוּתָּר לְהַרְהֵר חוּץ מִבֵּית הַמֶּרְחָץ וּבֵית הַכִּסֵּא – **It is permitted to think** about Torah matters **in every place except a bathhouse and a lavatory!** וְכִי תֵּימָא בִּלְשׁוֹן חוֹל אָמַר לֵיהּ – **And if you will say that [Rebbi] said it to [Rav Yitzchak bar Avdimi] in a secular language** rather than in the holy tongue, and that this is a mitigating factor,[18] וְהָאָמַר אַבָּיֵי – **but Abaye said:** דְּבָרִים שֶׁל חוֹל מוּתָּר לְאוֹמְרָן בִּלְשׁוֹן קוֹדֶשׁ – **Secular matters may be spoken** in an unclean environment, even **in the holy tongue,** שֶׁל קוֹדֶשׁ אָסוּר לְאוֹמְרָן בִּלְשׁוֹן חוֹל – but **sacred [matters] may not be spoken** in an unclean environment, even **in a secular language. – ? –**

The Gemara answers:

אַפְרוּשֵׁי מֵאִיסּוּרָא שָׁאנֵי – **Preventing a transgression is different.** It is permitted to speak about Torah matters in an unclean environment in order to prevent someone from committing a transgression, as Rebbi did.[19]

The Gemara corroborates this distinction:

תֵּדַע – **You may know** this distinction to be true from the following account: דְּאָמַר רַב יְהוּדָה אָמַר שְׁמוּאֵל – **For Rav Yehudah said in the name of Shmuel:** מַעֲשֶׂה בְּתַלְמִידוֹ שֶׁל רַבִּי מֵאִיר – **There was an incident involving a student of R' Meir,** שֶׁנִּכְנַס אַחֲרָיו לְבֵית הַמֶּרְחָץ וּבִקֵּשׁ לְהָדִיחַ קַרְקַע – **who followed [R' Meir] into a bathhouse and wanted to wash** the **floor** of the bathing pool for him,[20] וְאָמַר לוֹ אֵין מְדִיחִין – **and [R' Meir] said to him: One may not wash** a floor on the Sabbath.[21] לָסוּךְ לוֹ קַרְקַע – The student then wanted **to smear** the **floor** with fragrant oil,[22] אָמַר לוֹ אֵין סָכִין – whereupon **[R' Meir] said to him: One may not smear** a floor on the Sabbath.[23] Now, how could R' Meir have stated these halachic rulings in a bathhouse? אַלְמָא אַפְרוּשֵׁי מֵאִיסּוּרָא שָׁאנֵי – **Evidently, preventing a transgression is different** from an ordinary case and is permissible. הָכָא נַמִּי לְאַפְרוּשֵׁי מֵאִיסּוּרָא שָׁאנֵי – **Here too,** concerning the incident involving Rebbi and R' Yitzchak bar Avdimi, we are correct in saying that **preventing a transgression is different.**[24]

The Gemara had learned three things from Rebbi's remark to R' Yitzchak bar Avdimi. It now cites a further lesson that may be gleaned from that remark:

אָמַר רָבִינָא – **Ravina said:** שְׁמַע מִינָּהּ הַמְבַשֵּׁל בְּחַמֵּי טְבֶרְיָא בְּשַׁבָּת חַיָּיב – We may further **learn from [Rebbi's remark]** that **one who cooks with** the heat of **the Tiberian hot-springs on the Sabbath is liable** for Sabbath desecration.[25] דְּהָא מַעֲשֶׂה דְּרַבִּי לְאַחַר גְּזֵירָה הֲוָה – **For the incident involving Rebbi occurred**

NOTES

16. The tubs in this bathhouse were in-ground pools (similar to modern-day *mikvehs*) into which water flowed directly from the hot springs. Since the water in the tub was attached to its source in the ground, it was analogous to cooked water that is in the original vessel in which it was heated. As we will learn in a Mishnah below (42a), hot water that is in its primary vessel [כְּלִי רִאשׁוֹן] is considered capable of cooking. That is, when water is heated in a vessel, even after the vessel is removed from the fire the hot water inside it has the capacity to cook something that is immersed in it or upon which it is poured. Rebbi considered the hot-spring water in the bathtub to be in its "primary vessel," since it was connected to its source in the ground. He therefore instructed Rav Yitzchak bar Avdimi to transfer the water to a second vessel, where it would cool off somewhat and would no longer be considered capable of cooking (*Rashi* as explained by *Terumas HaDeshen* §181).

The capacity of hot water in a primary vessel to cook exists only while the water is so hot that the hand recoils from it, as the water in the bathtub was. Once transferred to a second vessel, however, the water is deemed incapable of cooking even while the hand recoils from it, because the cold walls of the vessel cause it to cool rapidly (*Tosafos* ד״ה ושמע מינה). [See *Taz, Yoreh Deah* 92:30, for a discussion of whether the vessel that was dipped into the tub to take water qualified as the secondary vessel even though its walls were immersed in the hot water, or it was necessary to transfer the hot water to another vessel whose walls were cold.]

17. I.e. [although we concluded above that warming oil in front of a fire is not like cooking it] warming it in a place that is fit for cooking (viz. a first vessel) is forbidden Rabbinically, just like actually cooking it is forbidden Biblically. We learn this for Rav Yitzchak bar Avdimi merely wanted to *warm* the oil in the hot pool and Rebbi nevertheless instructed him to do it in a secondary vessel (*Rashi* as explained by *Ritva MHK* ed., *Maharam* and *Rosh Yosef;* cf. *Rashba* and *Rosh* §11 with *Korban Nesanel* §60, who cite a variant version of the text).

18. Although it is forbidden even to think about Torah matters in an unclean environment, perhaps Rebbi gathered his thoughts in a secular language as well (*Tosafos;* see *Rashash;* cf. *Sfas Emes*).

19. One might ask: Why was this matter in doubt? Is it not obvious that the prevention of a transgression is warranted even inside a bathhouse? The answer is that the Gemara initially held that Rebbi should have stopped Rav Yitzchak bar Avdimi by saying, "I do not want the oil to be warmed in the tub," rather than saying, "Take some water in a secondary vessel and place the oil in it," which is laden with halachic content (for we derived three laws from it). The Gemara now concludes that, when preventing a transgression, it is permissible even to employ halachic terminology (*Rashba*).

20. [The bathhouse had in-ground pools for bathing.] The student emptied the water of a pool and wanted to wash its floor before refilling it with clean water (*Meiri*).

21. This is a Rabbinical injunction, enacted out of concern that one might fill in depressions in a dirt floor while washing it [which would be a violation of the *melachah* of בּוֹנֶה, *building*] (*Rashi*). The injunction, however, applies not only to dirt floors, but to tile or wooden floors as well (*Orach Chaim* 337:3).

22. It was common to do this in order to disguise unpleasant odors (*Meiri*).

23. Again, because of the concern that while doing so one might smooth out depressions in the floor (*Rashi* below, 151b ד״ה קרקע בקרקע מיחלף).

24. R' Meir went even further than Rebbi, for he stated explicit halachic rulings – "One may not wash," "One may not smear" – whereas Rebbi merely employed a statement containing halachic implications. We learn from this latter incident that, when preventing a transgression, it is permitted even to state the halachah explicitly in an unclean environment. The reason is that it is important to teach the listener that his intended act is forbidden and not merely undesirable (*Ritva MHK* ed.; see also *Maharam* and *Chidushei R' Elazar Moshe Horowitz;* cf. *Maharshal, Maharsha*).

25. Ravina seems to be saying that the person is liable to a *chatas* offering if he did this inadvertently, or to the death penalty if he did it willfully, for he has transgressed the Biblical prohibition of cooking. The Gemara stated earlier (38b-39a) that under Biblical law one is liable for cooking only with the heat of fire or its derivative, and the Gemara there (end of 39a) further described a difference of opinion as to whether the heat of the Tiberian hot-springs is derived from fire. According to the simple meaning of Ravina's words, he means to conclude on the basis of Rebbi's remark that the halachah follows the opinion that the heat of the Tiberian hot-springs is derived from fire (see *Ritva, MHK* ed. to 39a ד״ה ומהדרינן מי סברת and *Sfas Emes*). Ravina goes on to explain the basis for this conclusion.

עין משפט נר מצוה

כא א מיי׳ פכ״ב מהל׳ שבת הלכה ג סמג לאוין סה טוש״ע או״ח סימן שכו סעיף ד:
כב ב מיי׳ שם הלכה ד טוש״ע שם סעיף ו:
כג ג ד מיי׳ וסמג שם טוש״ע או״ח סימן שיח סעיף יד:
כד ה ו מיי׳ פכ״ב שם הלכה ה ו טור שו״ע שם סעיף יג וטוש״ע יו״ד סימן קה סעיף ב:
כה ז ח ט מיי׳ פ״ג מהלכות ק״ש הלכה ד ה טוש״ע או״ח סימן פה סעיף ב:
כו י מיי׳ פכ״א מהלכות שבת הלכה ג טוש״ע או״ח סימן שלז סעיף ג:
כז כ מיי׳ פ״ט מהלכות שבת הלכה ג:
כח ל מ מיי׳ פכ״ג מהל׳ שבת הלכה ה טור שו״ע או״ח סימן שלט סעיף ב:

כי האי תנא אמבטיאות של כרכים מטייל בהן ואינו חושש אמר רבא דוקא כרכין אבל דכפרים לא מ״ט כיון דזוטרין נפיש הבלייהו ת״ר [א]מתחמם אדם כנגד המדורה ויוצא ומשתטף בצונן ובלבד שלא ישתטף בצונן ויתחמם כנגד המדורה מפני שמפשיר מים שעליו (א) ת״ר [ב]מיחם אדם אלונטית ומניחה על בני מעים בשבת ובלבד שלא יביא קומקומוס של מים חמין ויניחנו על בני מעים בשבת ודבר זה אפי׳ בחול אסור מפני הסכנה (ב) ת״ר [ג]מביא אדם קיתון מים ומניחו כנגד המדורה לא בשביל שיחמו אלא בשביל שתפיג צינתן ר׳ יהודה אומר מביאה אשה פך של שמן ומניחתו כנגד המדורה לא בשביל שיבשל אלא בשביל שיפשר רשב״ג אומר אשה סכה ידה שמן ומחממתה כנגד המדורה וסכה לבנה קטן ואינה חוששת איבעיא להו שמן מה הוא לתנא קמא רבה ורב יוסף דאמרי תרוייהו להתירא רב נחמן בר יצחק אמר לאיסורא רבה ורב יוסף דאמרי תרוייהו להתירא שמן אע״פ שהיד סולדת בו מותר קסבר ת״ק שמן אין בו משום בשול ואתא רבי יהודה למימר שמן יש בו משום בשול והפשרו לא זה הוא בשולו ואתא ר׳ שמעון בן גמליאל למימר שמן יש בו משום בשול והפשרו זהו בשולו רב נחמן בר יצחק אמר לאיסורא שמן אע״פ שאין היד סולדת בו אסור קסבר שמן יש בו משום בשול והפשרו זהו בשולו ואתא ר׳ יהודה למימר הפשרו לא זהו בשולו ואתא רשב״ג למימר שמן יש בו משום בשול והפשרו זהו בשולו רשב״ג היינו ת״ק איכא בינייהו כלאחר יד א״ר יהודה אמר שמואל [ד]אחד שמן ואחד מים יד סולדת בו אסור אין יד סולדת בו מותר והיכי דמי יד סולדת בו אמר רחבא כל שכריסו של תינוק נכוית א״ר יצחק בר אבדימי פעם אחת נכנסתי אחר רבי לבית המרחץ ובקשתי להניח לו פך של שמן באמבטי [ה]ואמר לי טול בכלי שני ותן שמע מינה תלת שמע מינה שמן יש בו משום בשול וש״מ [ו]כלי שני אינו מבשל וש״מ הפשרו זהו בשולו היכי עביד הכי והאמר רבה בר בר חנה א״ר יוחנן (ג) [ז]בכל מקום מותר להרהר חוץ מבית המרחץ ובית הכסא וכ״ת בלשון חול א״ל והאמר אביי [ח]דברים של חול מותר לאומרן בלשון קודש של קודש אסור לאומרן בלשון חול [ט]אפרושי מאיסורא שאני תדע דאמר (ד) רב יהודה אמר שמואל מעשה (ה) בתלמידו של ר׳ מאיר שנכנס אחריו לבית המרחץ [י]ובקש להדיח קרקע ואמר לו אין מדיחין לסוך לו קרקע אמר לו אין סכין אלמא אפרושי מאיסורא שאני הכא נמי לאפרושי מאיסורא שאני אמר רבינא שמע מינה המבשל בחמי טבריה בשבת חייב דהא מעשה דר׳ לאחר גזירה הוה ואמר ליה טול בכלי שני ותן איני (ו) והאמר רב חסדא [כ]המבשל בחמי טבריה בשבת פטור מאי חייב נמי דקאמר (ז) מכת מרדות א״ר זירא אנא חזיתיה לר׳ אבהו דשט באמבטי ולא ידענא אי עקר אי לא עקר פשיטא דלא עקר דתניא [ל]לא ישוט אדם בבריכה מלאה מים ואפי׳ עומדת בחצר [מ]לא קשיא הא
דלית

רש״י

כי האי תנא. דאמר לעיל משהתחילו עוברי עבירה התחילו לאסור הזיעה והרי לא נאסרה אלא ע״י הרוחצין בחמין מאתמול ואומרים מזיעין אנחנו ואין כאן אלא עבירת דבריהם שאסרו את החמין: נפיש הבלייהו. ומזיע: מפשיר. מחמם לשון פושרין: מיחם אדם. מחמם: אלונטית. טיול״א ונראה לי בגד שמסתפגין בו דבכל דוכתא קרי ליה אלונטית: על גבי מעיים. כשהוא חש במעיו מחממין לו כלי או בגד ומניחו שם ומועיל: ובלבד שלא יביא קומקומוס כו׳. שמא ישפכו עליו ונמצא רוחץ בשבת בחמין: מפני סכנה. פעמים שהן רותחין: לא שיחמו. לא שיניחם שם עד שיחמו: אלא שתפיג צינתן. במקצתן שתפיג שתתחלף כמו וריחו לא נמר (ירמיה מח) מתרגמינן וריחיה לא פג: לא בשביל שיבשל. שלא תניחנו שם כדי בישול שתהא היד סולדת בו: סכה ידה. אבל להפשירו בפך כדרך שעושה בחול לא ופליג אדרב יהודה: להתירא. מאי דאסר רבי יהודה בשמן בישול שרי ת״ק ומים דוקא נקט ולא שיחמו דיש בהן בישול אבל שמן אע״פ שהיד סולדת דהיינו בישול דר׳ יהודה שרי לת״ק: סולדת. נמשכת לאחוריה מדאגה שלא תכוה וחהו לשון ואסלדה בחילה (איוב ו) ואדאג ברעדה ואמשך מתלונתי מדאגת יום הדין אם הייתי יודע שמיתתי קרובה ולא יחמול: שמן יש בו משום בישול. הלכך לא כדי שיבשל אלא כדי שיפשר שרי דהפשרו אין זה בישולו: ואתא רבי שמעון למימר דהפשירו זהו בישולו. הלכך כדעבדין בחול לא ליעביד אלא כלאחר יד על ידי שינוי: לאיסורא. אמרה תנא קמא לשמן דמיא הוא דשרי להפשיר אבל שמן הפשרו זהו בישולו: איכא בינייהו כלאחר יד. דלתנא קמא אפי׳ ע״י שינוי אסור: והיכי דמי. סלוד יש שסולד מרתיחה מועטת ויש שאינו סולד: נכנסתי. בשבת ובחמי טבריא הוה שלא נאסרו כדאמר לעיל התירו להם חמי טבריא: באמבטי. כגון בריכה עשויה בקרקע שהמים נכנסים שם ואספין: ובקשתי להניח שם פך שמן. להפשיר לסוך הימנו קודם הרחילה: טול. מן המים: בכלי שני. שילטננו מעט דכלי שני אינו מבשל ואח״כ תן הפך לתוך אותו כלי שני דהך אמבטי שהחמין נמשכין לה מן המעיין חשיב לה ככלי ראשון שנרתחו בו שאע״פ שהעבירו מעל האור מבשל כדתנן לקמן (ד׳ מב.) האילפס והקדירה שהעבירן מרותחין לא יתן לתוכן תבלין: וש״מ הפשרו. במקום הראוי לבישול: זהו בישולו. דהא להפשיר בעלמא הוא דקבעי ואסר ליה: והיכי עביד הכי. להורות הוראה שהוא דבר תורה בבית המרחץ: להרהר. בדברי תורה: דברים של קדש. דברי תורה: אסור לאומרן. במקום הטנופת ואפי׳ בלשון חול: אין מדיחין. דלמא אתי לאשויי גומות: דהא מעשה דרבי אחר גזירה הוה. שגזרו על הזיעה ועל כרחין בחמי טבריא הוא דהוי ורבי יהושע (א) דאמר לעיל בימי רבי הוה אלמא בימי רבי כבר נגזרה: וקאמר ליה טול בכלי שני. אבל ראשון לא אלמא יש בהן משום בישול: מרדות. רדוי: שט. לף: דשט באמבטי. בשבת: ולא ידענא אי עקר. רגליו מן הארץ דקסבר כי תנן אין שטין על פני המים במשילין פירות (ח) בנהר גדול תנן דאיכא למגזר שמא יעשה חבית של שייטין כדאמרינן התם אבל באמבטי לא: אי לא עקר. רגליו: לא ישוט. דאע״ג דליכא למיגזר אסור: ואפילו עומדת בחצר. דליכא למיגזר שמא יתיז מים ברגליו חוץ לארבע אמות: הא. דאסיר:
דלית

תוספות

מפני שמפשיר מים שעליו. בכולה שמעתא ובמתניתין גבי מיחם שפינהו משמע דלהפשיר מים לצורך שתייה מותר דהפשירן לא זהו בישולן. והכא דאסורין מפרש ריב״א דדומה כרוחץ במים חמין ויבא להחם חמין לרחוץ גופו:

ובלבד שלא יביא קומקומוס כו׳. פירוש כל זמן שהאלונטית שם שמא יפלו המים על האלונטית ואתי לידי סחיטה אי נמי לא יביא משום רפואה וגזרו אטו שחיקת סממנים טפי מבאלונטית דלא מיחזי כרפואה כ״כ:

ושמע מינה כלי שני אינו מבשל. תימה מאי שנא כלי שני מכלי ראשון דאי יד סולדת אפי׳ כלי שני נמי ואי אין יד סולדת אפילו כלי ראשון נמי אינו מבשל ויש לומר לפי שכלי ראשון מתוך שעמד על האור דופנותיו חמין ומחזיק חומו זמן מרובה ולכך נתנו בו שיעור דכל זמן א) שהיד סולדת בו אסור אבל כלי שני אף על גב דיד סולדת בו מותר שאין דופנותיו חמין והולך ומתקרר: וכי תימא בלשון חול קאמר ליה. ואע״ג דאסור להרהר נימא דאין אסור להרהר אלא בלשון קדש והוא הרהר בלשון חול:
פשיטא

מסורת הש״ס

א) תוספתא שבת פ״ד, ב) [תוספתא שם], ג) ברכות כד: (לעיל י.) לקמן קנ. זבחים קב: ע״ז מד: קדושין לג., ד) [לקמן קנא:], ה) [עי׳ תוס׳ לקמן קמז: ד״ה דמניא], ו) פסחים מא., ז) [יבמות נב. כתובות מה: נזיר כג. נח: חולין קמא:], ח) [דף לו:].

תוספות ישנים

א) והכא באמבטי במקום שרגלו להניח הפך היתה יד סולדת בו. והא דלא א״ל תן במקום שאין היד סולדת דהיינו במקום שרחץ ודאי לא היה היד סולדת. ושמא שם לא הי׳ יכול להפשיר. א״נ פעמים החמירו בכלי ראשון אף אם אין היד סולדת בו. וכן החמירו חכמים אפי׳ בכלי שני לקמן (מב.) גבי ספל ה״ה כאמבטי:

הגהות הב״ח

(א) רש״י ד״ה דהא מעשה וכו׳ ור׳ יהושע בן לוי דאמר:

ליקוטי רש״י

מדורה. היסק גדול [ביצה כא:]. אלונטית. בגד שמסתפגין בו כשיוצאין מבית המרחץ [עירובין פז:]. אלונטיות. סדינין שמקנחין בהן [לקמן קמז.]. קומקומוס. קומקמוסין סירות קטנות של מתכת [ע״ז מג:]. יורה קטנה [לעיל לח:]. יד סולדת. לשון ירא ודואג שהיד סולדת בהן מלכוות ברותחין [איוב ו, י עיי״ש]. נכוית [חולין קה:]. אסור לאומרן בלשון חול. שאע״פ שאינה בלשון הקדש לא נפקי מקדושתייהו [ע״ז מד:]. להדיח. במים [לקמן קנא.]. אין סכין. משום אשויי גומות ואף על גב דמרחץ רצפת אבנים הוא וליכא למיחש לאשויי גומות מיחלף מיהא בקרקע אחר [שם:]. המבשל בחמי טבריה. מעיינות רותחין. בשבת פטור. דלאו תולדות אש היא הלכך לאו בישול הוא דליהוי חייב משום אב מלאכה [פסחים מא.]. מכת מרדות. רידוי במוכחה שלא ירגיל בזה ואין לה קצבה אלא עד שיקבל עליו [חולין קמא:].

רבינו חננאל

להן אלא צונן בלבד. ראו שאין הדבר עומד חזרו והתירו להן חמי טבריא בלבד. וזיעה במקומה עומדת באיסור אמר רבא מאן דעבר על דברי חכמי׳ שרי למיקריי׳ עבריינא. כי האי תנא דתנא משרבו עוברי עבירה: תנא אמבטאות של כרכין מטייל בהן ואינו חושש. והני מילי דכרכין אבל דכפרין כיון דזוטרן נפיש הבליהון: ת״ר מתחמם אדם כנגד המדורה ויוצא (ומשתטף בצונן) [ובלבד שלא ישתטף בצונן] ויתחמם כנגד המדורה מפני שנפשרו המים שעליו: ת״ר מיחם אדם אלונטית ומניחה ע״ג מעיו בשבת ובלבד (ישתטף בצונן ויתחמם כנגד המדורה מפני שתפשר המים) שלא יביא קומקומוס של חמין ויניחנו על גבי מעיו בשבת. ודבר זה אפילו בחול [אסור] מפני הסכנה שלא יכוה: ת״ר מניח אדם קיתון של מים כנגד המדורה לא שיחמו אלא כדי שתפוג צינתן. ר׳ יהודה אמר מנחת אשה פך שמן כנגד המדורה לא שיתבשל אלא כדי שתפשר. רשבג״א אשה סכה ידה שמן כנגד המדורה. וסכה לבנה קטן ואינה חוששת: איבעיא להו שמן מה לי בו אמר ת״ק. ואסיק׳ אמר רב אמר שמואל אחד שמן ואחד מים אם נתחמם כשעור שהיד סולדת בו אסור אין היד סולדת בו מותר. ושיעור שהיד סולדת בו. פי׳ (פירוש׳) [בירושל׳] שהיד א) שולטת בו סולדת היא שולטת והוא כל שכריסו של תינוק נכוית הימנו. הא מעשה דר׳ שבקשו לו פך של שמן באמבטי ואמר להן טלו בכלי שני ותנו. שמעינן מינה תלת. ש״מ שמן יש בו משום בישול. ולפיכך בכלי ראשון אסור. שנמצא מבשל שמן בשבת. וש״מ מדשרי בכלי שני דכלי שני אינו מבשל. וש״מ הפשרו לא זהו בישולו: אמר רבינא ש״מ המבשל בחמי טבריא הואיל וגזרו רבנן עלייהו חייבין מכת מרדות מדרבנן. ואקשינן דר׳ היאך מורה הוראה במרחץ ואמר טלו בכלי שני כלומר זהו מותר וזהו אסור. והא״ר יוחנן כל מקום מותר להרהר חוץ מבית המרחץ ובית הכסא. ולא דאקשינן מדברי ר׳ יוחנן לר׳ דר׳ יוחנן לגבי דר׳ תלמיד קטן הוא. (ולא) [אלא] הא דר׳ יוחנן דברי הכל קבלה הוא

חשק שלמה על רבינו חננאל א) ע״ש יש כאן ולשון הירושלמי הובא ברא״ש:

after the enactment of **the decree** against steam-bathing on the Sabbath, and thus, the bathhouse that he entered must have been supplied by the Tiberian hot-springs, to which the decree does not apply.[26] וְאָמַר לֵיהּ טוֹל בִּכְלִי שֵׁנִי וְתֵן – **Yet he said to [R' Yitzchak bar Avdimi]: "Take** some water from the pool **in a secondary vessel and place** the flask into that vessel to warm it," but would not allow him to warm it in the bath itself. Clearly, Rebbi held that the prohibition against cooking extends to using the heat of the Tiberian hot-springs!

The Gemara questions Ravina's conclusion:

אִינִי – **Is this** indeed **so?** וְהָאָמַר רַב חִסְדָּא – **But Rav Chisda said:** הַמְבַשֵּׁל בְּחַמֵּי טְבֶרְיָא בְּשַׁבָּת פָּטוּר – The law is that **one who cooks with** the heat of **the Tiberian hot-springs on the Sabbath is not liable,** since this is not prohibited under Biblical law.[27] – ? –

The Gemara answers by clarifying Ravina's statement:

מַאי חַיָּיב נַמִּי דְּקָאָמַר – **What is in fact** the meaning of **[Ravina's] expression "he is liable"?** מַכַּת מַרְדּוּת – It means that the person is liable to **lashes for rebelliousness,** since by cooking in the hot springs he violates a Rabbinical injunction.[28]

Having discussed above the injunction against bathing in hot water on the Sabbath, the Gemara cites an incident concerning a similar law – the injunction against swimming on the Sabbath:[29]

אָמַר רַבִּי זֵירָא – **R' Zeira said:** אֲנָא חֲזִיתֵיהּ לְרַבִּי אַבָּהוּ דְּשָׁט בְּאַמְבַּטֵי – **I** once **observed R' Abahu** apparently **floating in an** in-ground **bathtub** on the Sabbath,[30] וְלֹא יָדַעְנָא אִי עָקַר – **but I do not know if he lifted** his feet off the ground and actually floated, אִי לֹא עָקַר – **or he did not lift** his feet off the ground and did not really float at all.[31]

The Gemara expresses surprise at R' Zeira's uncertainty:

פְּשִׁיטָא דְּלֹא עָקַר – But it should be **obvious that he did not lift** his feet off the ground! דְּתַנְיָא – **For it was taught in a Baraisa:** לֹא יָשׁוּט אָדָם בִּבְרֵיכָה מְלֵאָה מַיִם – ONE MAY NOT SWIM IN A POOL FULL OF WATER, וַאֲפִילּוּ עוֹמֶדֶת בֶּחָצֵר – EVEN IF IT IS SITUATED IN AN enclosed YARD.[32] Why was R' Zeira in doubt about this?

The Gemara answers:

לֹא קַשְׁיָא – There is **no difficulty.** הָא – **This [ruling]** of the Baraisa, which forbids swimming in a pool,

NOTES

26. It is evident that the decrees against bathing and steam-bathing had been enacted in Rebbi's times from the fact that R' Yehoshua ben Levi, who was Rebbi's contemporary, was quoted above (40a) as describing this injunction (*Rashi*). Although it is evident from another Gemara (*Berachos* 27b) that the decree against steam-bathing had not yet been enacted during the earlier part of Rebbi's life, it is clear that the incident cited here occurred in Rebbi's old age, for R' Yitzchak bar Avdimi was one of his very last disciples (*Chidushei R' Elazar Moshe Horowitz, Sfas Emes; cf. Baal HaMaor; Rashba; Ritva, MHK* ed.; see *Rashash*). [According to the view that *steam-bathing* is prohibited even in a sauna supplied by hot-spring water (see 40a note 26), we must say that Rebbi entered the bathhouse to *bathe* in the spring water, which is permissible (see *Rashi* above ד״ה ובקשתי and *Pnei Yehoshua*).]

27. Because the hot springs are heated by the sun (*Rosh Yosef*). It is, however, forbidden by Rabbinical injunction to cook in the hot-spring water as with any other source of heat that is derived from the sun (see 39a).

28. מַכַּת מַרְדּוּת, *lashes for rebelliousness,* is the term used to describe Rabbinically authorized lashes.

29. The Mishnah in Tractate *Beitzah* (36b) states that the Rabbis forbade swimming (or floating) in water on the Sabbath or Yom Tov. The Gemara there explains that this injunction was enacted out of concern that one might make a swimmer's tube, i.e. a life preserver [which would be a violation of the *melachah* of מְתַקֵּן מָנָא, *completing a utensil,* and possibly other *melachos,* depending on the method of constructing the tube (see *Rashi* below, 74b ד״ה חייב י״א)]. The following Gemara discusses whether it is prohibited under this injunction to swim or float only in large bodies of water such as a river or lake, where one would normally use a life preserver, or even to swim or float in a small pool or in-ground tub. It is clear, however, that the injunction does not pertain to swimming or floating in vessels, such as portable bathtubs (see *Ran* and *Orach Chaim* 339:2).

30. Presumably, the tub was filled with either cold water or hot-spring water so that the injunction against bathing in hot water on the Sabbath did not apply.

31. Thus, I was unable to determine whether R' Abahu considered it permissible to float in a small pool or tub (*Rashi*).

32. If the pool is situated in an open area, one may certainly not swim in it, lest he splash some water out of the pool (which is a רְשׁוּת הַיָּחִיד, *a private domain,* by virtue of its walls) into the open area, violating the prohibition against transferring something from a private domain to a public domain on the Sabbath. The Baraisa teaches that even if the pool is situated in an enclosed yard, so that no such concern exists, it is nevertheless forbidden to swim in it, because of the injunction against swimming on the Sabbath (*Rashi*).

דְּלֵית לֵיהּ גִּידוּדֵי – refers to a case **where [the pool] does not have an embankment,** הָא – whereas **this [incident],** in which R' Zeira entertained the thought that R' Abahu was floating in an in-ground tub, דְּאִית לֵיהּ גִּידוּדֵי – involved a case **where [the tub] had an embankment.**[1]

Having cited an incident in which R' Zeira was in doubt concerning a practice of R' Abahu, the Gemara cites another, unrelated instance in which this occurred:

וְאָמַר רַבִּי זֵירָא – **And R' Zeira** also **said:** אֲנָא חֲזִיתֵיהּ לְרַבִּי אַבָּהוּ שֶׁהִנִּיחַ יָדָיו כְּנֶגֶד פָּנָיו שֶׁל מַטָּה – **I observed R' Abahu,** when bathing in a river, **place his hand over his "lower face,"**[2] וְלָא יָדַעְנָא אִי נָגַע אִי לָא נָגַע – **but I do not know whether he touched** the male member **or not.**

The Gemara expresses surprise at R' Zeira's uncertainty:

פְּשִׁיטָא דְּלָא נָגַע – But it should be **obvious that he did not touch** it! דְּתַנְיָא – **For it was taught in a Baraisa:** רַבִּי אֱלִיעֶזֶר אוֹמֵר – R' ELIEZER SAYS: כָּל הָאוֹחֵז בָּאַמָּה וּמַשְׁתִּין כְּאִילּוּ מֵבִיא מַבּוּל לָעוֹלָם – WHOEVER HOLDS HIS MALE MEMBER WHILE URINATING IS considered AS IF HE IS BRINGING A FLOOD ONTO THE WORLD.[3] Obviously, then, R' Abahu did not touch his member. – ? –

The Gemara answers:

אָמַר אַבָּיֵי – **Abaye said:** עֲשָׂאוּהָ כְּבוֹלֶשֶׁת – [R' Abahu's case] is **treated** by the same principle **as** that governing the case of **a troop of marauding soldiers.** דִּתְנַן – **For we learned in a Mishnah:**[4] בּוֹלֶשֶׁת שֶׁנִּכְנְסָה לָעִיר – If A TROOP OF MARAUDING SOLDIERS ENTERED A CITY and entered a Jew's home, בִּשְׁעַת שָׁלוֹם – if it was IN PEACETIME, חָבִיּוֹת פְּתוּחוֹת אֲסוּרוֹת סְתוּמוֹת מוּתָּרוֹת – the OPEN BARRELS of wine in the home ARE PROHIBITED while the SEALED ONES ARE PERMITTED, בִּשְׁעַת מִלְחָמָה אֵלּוּ וָאֵלּוּ מוּתָּרוֹת – but if it was IN WARTIME, BOTH ARE PERMITTED לְפִי שֶׁאֵין פְּנַאי לְנַסֵּךְ – BECAUSE THERE IS NO TIME TO POUR LIBATIONS during war.[5] אַלְמָא כֵּיוָן דִּבְעִיתֵי לָא מְנַסְּכֵי – **Thus,** we see that during war **since they are frightened** and distracted **they do not pour** their customary **libations.** הָכָא נַמִּי – **Here too** in a case such as that of R' Abahu, where someone is bathing in a river, כֵּיוָן דִּבְעִית לָא אָתֵי לְהִרְהוּרֵי – **since he is frightened** and distracted **he will not come to think** improper thoughts.[6] R' Zeira therefore entertained the possibility that R' Abahu touched the male member while covering his lower face.[7]

The Gemara asks:

וְהָכָא מַאי בִּיעֲתוּתָא – **And here,** in the case of bathing, **what fear** is there?

The Gemara answers:

בִּיעֲתוּתָא דְּנַהֲרָא – The **fear of** drowning in **the river.**

The Gemara questions R' Abahu's behavior from a different perspective:

אִינִי – **Is it so** that R' Abahu covered his lower face while bathing? וְהָאָמַר רַבִּי אַבָּא אָמַר רַב הוּנָא אָמַר רַב – **But R' Abba said in the name of Rav Huna, who said in the name of Rav:** כָּל הַמֵּנִיחַ יָדָיו כְּנֶגֶד פָּנָיו שֶׁל מַטָּה – **Whoever places his hand over his lower face** כְּאִילּוּ כּוֹפֵר בִּבְרִיתוֹ שֶׁל אַבְרָהָם אָבִינוּ – **is** considered **as if he has denied the covenant of our father Abraham,** since he appears to be ashamed of his circumcision. – ? –

The Gemara answers:

לָא קַשְׁיָא – There is **no difficulty.** הָא כִּי נָחֵית – **This** behavior, i.e. leaving the lower face exposed, is appropriate **when one goes down** into the river and his back is to the public, הָא כִּי סָלִיק – whereas **this** behavior, i.e. covering the lower face, is appropriate **when one comes up** from the river and is facing the public.[8] כִּי הָא דְּרָבָא שָׁחֵי – **As** we see from the fact **that** whereas **Rava would bend over** when walking to and from the river, to conceal his private parts, רַבִּי זֵירָא זָקִיף – and **R' Zeira would stand straight,** so as not to appear ashamed of his circumcision, רַבָּנָן דְּבֵי רַב אַשִׁי – **the rabbis of Rav Ashi's academy** forged a compromise: כִּי קָא נָחֲתֵי זָקְפֵי – When going down into the river **they would stand straight,** כִּי קָא סָלְקֵי שָׁחֵי – but **when coming up** from the river **they would bend over.**[9]

The Gemara cites another incident which teaches some lessons about bathing:

רַבִּי זֵירָא הֲוָה קָא מִשְׁתַּמֵּיט מִדְּרַב יְהוּדָה – **R' Zeira was avoiding** meeting **Rav Yehudah,** דְּבָעֵי לְמִיסַּק לְאַרְעָא דְּיִשְׂרָאֵל – **because he wanted to go up to** live in **the Land of Israel** and he knew that Rav Yehudah would not approve, דְּאָמַר רַב יְהוּדָה – **for Rav Yehudah said:** כָּל הָעוֹלֶה מִבָּבֶל לְאֶרֶץ יִשְׂרָאֵל עוֹבֵר בַּעֲשֵׂה – **One who goes up from Babylonia to the Land of Israel violates a positive commandment,** שֶׁנֶּאֱמַר ,,בָּבֶלָה יוּבָאוּ וְשָׁמָּה יִהְיוּ" – **for**

NOTES

1. A pool that has no rim or embankment is similar to a lake. Therefore, the injunction against swimming – which was enacted out of concern that one might make a life preserver and applies primarily to swimming in natural bodies of water – was extended to pools that have no embankment. However, a pool that has a rim or embankment is more similar to a portable tub, in which it is certainly permitted to swim since there is no concern that one might make a life preserver. Since R' Zeira saw R' Abahu apparently floating in an in-ground tub that had a rim, it occurred to him that R' Abahu might have lifted his feet and floating there is indeed permitted (*Rashi's* preferred explanation, *Ran;* cf. *Rif, Milchamos Hashem;* see *Beur Halachah* to 339:2).

As mentioned previously (39b note 16), nowadays it is customary not to bathe or swim at all on the Sabbath.

2. I.e. he covered his private parts with his hand, out of modesty (*Rashi*).

3. Touching the male member can arouse a person and ultimately lead to a seminal emission. Emitting semen in vain was the grave sin of the Generation of the Flood and led to their destruction, as Scripture states (*Genesis* 6:12): כִּי־הִשְׁחִית כָּל־בָּשָׂר אֶת־דַּרְכּוֹ עַל־הָאָרֶץ, *for all flesh has perverted its way upon the earth* (*Rashi;* see *Sanhedrin* 108b and *Orach Chaim* 3:14).

4. *Avodah Zarah* 70b.

5. The Sages prohibited the wine of a Jew that was left in the charge of an idolater, out of concern for the possibility that the idolater used it to pour a libation for his idol (*Avodah Zarah* 69a). In the case at hand, during peacetime, i.e. when the troop is not at war but is simply plundering, the open barrels of wine in the house are prohibited because of their exposure to the marauding soldiers. The sealed barrels, however, are permitted, because they were obviously not used for libations. [Since the soldiers are not afraid to be caught plundering, if they had opened the barrels they would not have bothered resealing them.] In wartime, even the open barrels are permitted because the soldiers are too preoccupied with the concerns of war to perform libations (see *Rashi*).

6. I.e. touching the male member will not cause him to become aroused.

7. [R' Zeira was apparently in doubt whether this case is analogous to that of the troop of marauding soldiers. He therefore said that although he saw R' Abahu place his hand over his lower face, he did not know whether R' Abahu actually touched the member, and he was unable to resolve his doubt.]

8. When one's back is to the public, covering the lower face is not required out of modesty and thus appears like an expression of disdain for the circumcision. When facing the public, covering the lower face is an appropriate expression of modesty (*Rashi*).

9. Rava and the Rabbis of Rav Ashi's academy bent over, rather than cover the lower face with the hand, because they did not accept Abaye's analogy to the case of marauding soldiers and wanted to avoid the possibility of touching the member (*R' Elazar Moshe Horowitz*). Furthermore, Rava would bend over out of modesty even while walking towards the river because he did not consider this an expression of disdain for the circumcision like covering it with the hand (*Rashash*). However, the Rabbis of Rav Ashi's academy acted in accordance with the compromise described above, standing tall when walking towards the river and bending over when returning.

דלית ליה גידודי הא דאית ליה גידודי: וא"ר זירא אנא חזיתיה לר' אבהו שהניח ידיו כנגד פניו של מטה ולא ידענא אי נגע אי לא נגע פשיטא דלא נגע דתניא (א) ר' אליעזר אומר א כל האוחז באמה ומשתין כאילו מביא מבול לעולם אמר אביי עשאוה כבולשת דתנן (ב) בולשת שנכנסה לעיר בשעת שלום חביות פתוחות אסורות סתומות מותרות בשעת מלחמה אלו ואלו מותרות לפי שאין פנאי לנסך אלמא כיון דבעיתי לא מנסכי ה"נ כיון דבעית לא אתי להרהורי והכא מאי ביעתותא ביעתותא דנהרא איני והאמר ר' אבא אמר רב הונא אמר רב כל המניח ידיו כנגד פניו של מטה כאילו כופר בבריתו של אברהם אבינו לא קשיא הא כי נחית הא כי סליק כי הא דרבא שחי ר' זירא זקיף רבנן דבי רב אשי כי קא נחתי זקפי כי קא סלקי שחי (ג) ר' זירא הוה קא משתמיט מדרב יהודה דבעי למיסק לארעא דישראל דאמר רב יהודה ב כל העולה מבבל לא"י עובר בעשה שנאמר (א) בבלה יובאו ושמה יהיו אמר איזיל ואשמע מיניה מילתא ואיתי ואיסק אזל אשכחיה דקאי בי באני וקאמר ליה לשמעיה הביאו לי נתר הביאו לי מסרק פתחו פומייכו ואפיקו הבלא ואשתו ממיא דבי באני אמר אילמלא (ד) (לא) באתי אלא לשמוע דבר זה דיי בשלמא הביאו נתר הביאו מסרק קמ"ל דברים של חול מותר לאומרם בלשון קדש פתחו פומייכו ואפיקו הבלא נמי כדשמואל דאמר שמואל הבלא מפיק הבלא אלא אשתו מיא דבי באני מאי מעליותא דתניא ג אכל ולא שתה אכילתו דם וזהו תחילת חולי מעיים (ה) אכל ולא הלך ד' אמות אכילתו מרקבת וזהו תחילת ריח רע הנצרך (ו) לנקביו ואכל דומה לתנור שהסיקוהו ע"ג אפרו וזהו תחילת ריח זוהמא רחץ בחמין ולא שתה מהן דומה לתנור שהסיקוהו מבחוץ ולא הסיקוהו מבפנים רחץ בחמין ולא נשתטף בצונן דומה לברזל שהכניסוהו לאור ולא הכניסוהו לצונן רחץ ולא סך דומה למים ע"ג חבית:

מתני' מוליאר הגרוף שותין הימנו בשבת אנטיכי אע"פ שגרופה אין שותין הימנה:

גמ' היכי דמי מוליאר הגרוף תנא מים מבפנים וגחלים מבחוץ אנטיכי רבה אמר בי כירי רב נחמן בר יצחק אמר בי דודי מאן דאמר בי דודי כ"ש בי כירי ומאן דאמר בי כירי אבל בי דודי לא תניא כוותיה דרב נחמן אנטיכי אע"פ שגרופה וקטומה אין שותין הימנה מפני שנחושתה מחממתה:

מתני' המיחם שפינהו לא יתן לתוכו צונן בשביל שיחמו אבל נותן הוא לתוכו או לתוך הכוס כדי להפשירן:

גמ' מאי קאמר אמר רב אדא בר מתנא הכי קאמר ד המיחם שפינה ממנו מים חמין לא יתן לתוכו מים מועטים כדי שיחמו אבל נותן לתוכו מים מרובים כדי להפשירן והלא

רש"י

דלית ליה גידודי. שאין שפתה גבוהה שיהיו המים עמוקים אצל שפתה כמו באמצע דכיון שאין עמוקים שם כי מטי סמוך לשפתה נועץ רגליו בקרקע וחופר וממחה העפר לתוך המים ודמי למגבל ולי נראה דאית ליה גידודי שרי דלא דמי לנהר אלא לכלי דלית ליה גידודי דמיא לנהר ואסור: שהניח ידיו. כשהיה רוחץ משום לניעות: אי נגע. באמה: כאילו מביא מבול לעולם. שמתחמם ובא לידי קרי וזה קלקולו של דור המבול מוציאים שכבת זרע לבטלה דכתיב כי השחית כל בשר וגו' (בראשית ו): כבולשת. עשאוה להא דר' אבהו בולשת חיילות גיים הבא לעיר על שם שמחפשין ובולשים את העיר קרי לה בולשת: בשעת שלום. כגון שהוא של אותה מלכות: כאילו כופר. דנראה שהוא בוש בדבר: כי נחית. לנהר פניו כלפי הנהר ואין כאן משום לניעות אסור לכסותו: כי סליק. ופניו כלפי העם מותר משום לניעות: ר' זירא זקיף. דסייש לדרב שלא יראה ככופר: משתמיט. היה ירא לראות לו משום דהוה בעי רבי זירא למיסק לארעא דישראל ורב יהודה לא סבירא ליה וירא פן יגזור עליו מלילך: בבלה יובאו ושמה יהיו עד יום פקדי וגו'. ור' זירא אמר לך האי קרא בכלי שרת כתיב כדאמרינן בשני דייני גזירות (כתובות קיא.): הביאו לי נתר. לחוף את ראשי וקאמר להו בלשון הקודש: פתחו פומייכו. ויכנס הבל בית המרחץ לתוך הגוף ויוציא הבל של זיעה: ואשתו. מן מים חמין ואפי' לא הוחמו אלא לרחילה: מותר לאומרן. בבית המרחץ ואפי' בלשון קודש: הבלא. דמרחץ הנכנס דרך הפה: מפיק הבלא. דזיעה: ולא הלך ד' אמות. קודם שישן: מרקבת. אינה מתעכלת לעשות זבל: ריח רע. ריח הפה: ריח זוהמא. כל גופו מזוהם בזיעה תמיד: ולא הסיקוהו מבפנים. שאינו מטיב לכלום: ולא הכניסוהו לצונן. שהן מחזקין את הברזל: למים ע"ג חבית. על שוליו ולדדיו שאינם נכנסים לתוכו: מתני' מוליאר הגרוף. מן הגחלים מבע"י: שותין. ממימיו בשבת ואע"פ שהוחמו קצת מחמת הכלי לפי שאינו מוסיף הבל אלא משמר ומקיים חום שלהם שלא יצטננו בגמרא מפרש מוליאר מים מבפנים וגחלים מבחוץ כלי שיש בו בית קיבול קטן אצל דופנו מבחוץ מחובר לו ונותן שם גחלים והמים בקיבולו הגדול ורבותינו מפרשים מוליאר שני שולים ואנטיכי בי דודי מחילה בינתיים ולי נראה להפך דאם כן ה"ל למיתני מים מלמעלה וגחלים מלמטה ועוד דנחשתה דתני באנטיכי לשון שולים הן והן אומרים לשון נחושת ושאני נחשת מחרס: אנטיכי. מפרש בגמרא: גמ' בי כירי. אצל יש בכירה אצל חלליה שהגחלים בו ומים נתונים בחללה השני ואע"ג דדמי למוליאר מיהו כירה דופנה עב והאור תדיר בתוכה כל ימות החול ודופנה חם מאד ומוסיף הבל במים אע"פ שגרופה מן הגחלים: בי דודי. יורה גדולה עושין לה שתי שולים ונותנין גחלים בין שניהם והמים על העליונים: וכל שכן. דבי כירי אסור דכירה שמתוך שהאור תדיר בו ודופנו עב מרתיח: אבל בי דודי לא. שהרי הוא כמוליאר: שנחושתה. נחושת שלה אלמא ביורה של נחשת קאי ונחשת משמר רתיחתו ואני אומר נחושתה לשון שולים כדכתיב (יחזקאל טז) יען השפך נחשתך ולשון של המשנה נחשתו של תנור במסכת כלים (פ"ח מ"ג) ושאני אנטיכי ממוליאר דמתוך שהשולים מכוסים חומם משתמר ואע"ג שגרפו גחליהם: מתני' המיחם. קומקמוס של חמין: שפינהו. כולה מתניתין מפרש בגמרא: גמ' מאי קאמר. מאי פינהו ומאי לא יתן והדר אמר אבל נותן: והלא

תוספות

פשיטא דלא נגע דתניא ר' אליעזר אומר כו'. ואע"ג דרבנן פליגי עליה ושרו בפרק כל היד (נדה יג. ושם) לא שרי אלא משום ממזרות שלא יראה ככרות שפכה ויוציאו לעז על בניו שהן ממזרים (ז): **רחץ** ולא סך. ול"ג מעיקרא דהא בכולי הש"ס רחילה קודם סיכה כדאמר בפ"ק דקידושין (דף כב:) רחצו סכו וקרא כתיב ורחצת וסכת (רות ג) מיהו קרא איכא לאוקמי בסיכה שהיתה מתקשטת עצמה לריח טוב לכן לא היתה סכה בתחלה שעל ידי רחילה היתה מעברת הסיכה מעליה:

מוליאר הגרוף שותין ממנו בשבת. פי' בקונטרס לפי שאין מוסיף הבל אלא משמר ומקיים חום שלהן ואנטיכי אפי' גרופה אין שותין הימנה לפי שמוספת הבל ואין נראה דלא שייך למיגזר במוסיף הבל אלא בהטמנה גזירה שמא יטמין ברמץ ועוד דדוחק לומר דמתני' איירי כשעשה האיסור ועוד דאנטיכי אוסר בכל ענין לשתות הימנו אפילו בהשאה ואי להחזיר תנן משהין אפילו באינו גרוף ועוד אי משום תוספת הבל אסרה ליה מתני' בשתיה תקשה לרבה ורב יוסף דשרו לעיל (דף לח.) בשכח קדרה ע"ג כירה ובשלה בשבת אע"ג דלא נתבשלה כמאכל בן דרוסאי ואפי' במזיד ונראה כפי' ה"ר פורת מוליאר הגרוף שותין הימנו בשבת שמוזגין המים חמין ביין לפי שהמים אינן כ"כ חמין במוליאר שיתבשל היין מן המים שמוזגין לתוכו אבל אנטיכי אע"פ שגרופה אין שותין הימנה לפי שאנטיכי יש בה הבל יותר ומתבשל היין מן המים בשעת מזיגה וכ"מ בירושלמי:

מסורת הש"ס

א) נדה יג. מג., ב) ע"ז ע: כתובות ס. [נדה יג.], ג) כתובות קי. ברכות כד:, ד) [עי' תוספות מגילה כח. ד"ה אלמלא], ה) [עי' ב"מ קיג:], ו) [לקמן דף פב. ע"ש], ז) [וע"ע תוספות יומא ל. ד"ה מלוה].

תורה אור השלם

א) בָּבֶלָה יוּבָאוּ וְשָׁמָּה יִהְיוּ עַד יוֹם פָּקְדִי אֹתָם נְאֻם יְיָ וְהַעֲלִיתִים וַהֲשִׁבֹתִים אֶל הַמָּקוֹם הַזֶּה: [ירמיה כז, כב]

ליקוטי רש"י

כאילו מביא מבול. שעבירה זו היתה בידם דכתיב (בראשית ו) כי השחית כל בשר ואמרו ברותחין קלקלו [נדה יג.]. שמחמם את אבריו ומביא לידי קרי וזהו קלקול דור המבול שנאמר (בראשית ו) כי השחית כל בשר [שם מג.]. **בולשת.** חיל המלך [לקמן קמה:]. חיל על שם שמחפשין ומותרין קרי להו בולשת כדמתרגמינן ויחפש ובלש [ע"ז ע:]. בולשת חיל שמחפשין ובחוזין כדמתרגמינן (בראשית לא) ויחפש ובלש [נדה יג.]. חיל על שם שמחפשים כל המטמונים [כתובות כז.]. **משתמיט.** לא היה נראה אליו לפי שהיה כו' חפץ לעלות לארץ ישראל ורב יהודה אוסר לו לפיכך לא היה נכנס לבית המדרש [ברכות כד:]. **דבעי למיסק.** ורב יהודה מוחה בידו להכי הוה משתמיט מיניה [כתובות קי:]. **נתר.** קרקע הוא או אבן כעין שקורין קרי"א בלע"ז [תענית יג.]. מין אדמה הוא וקורין לה ניתרא [סנהדרין מט:]. מין כיבוס הוא שמעביר את הגיעול [זבחים פח.]. **ואשתו ממיא דבי באני.** דקיימא לן הרוחץ בחמין ולא שתה מהן דומה לו כמבשלת שבת [גיטין סט:]. **ריח רע.** ריח הפה שהוא מרקב מעיים ויוצא ריח קל פיו. **ריח זוהמא.** כל גופו מסריח זיעה מקרסת שהריח נבלעה בבשרו ומגבליו ועכשיו זוהו כו לזיעה מזוהמת [לקמן פב.]. **ולא הכניסוהו לצונן.** כשכלי מתכות חם ועומן לצונן מחזקים את הכלי וזו היא גמר מלאכה הצורפין שרתיחת האור מפשפשתו וקרוב להשבר והמים מצרפין פעפעויו שולדרי"ר בלע"ז [לקמן ע"ב].

עין משפט נר מצוה

כט א מיי' פכ"א מהל' איסורי ביאה הלכה כג טוש"ע או"ח סימן ג סעיף יד וטוש"ע אה"ע סימן כג סעיף ד:
ל ב מיי' פ"ה מהלכות מלכים הלכה יב:
לא ג מיי' פ"ד מהלכות דעות הלכה ב:
לב ד מיי' פכ"ב מהל' שבת הלכה א ופכ"ב הלכה ו סמג לאוין סה טוש"ע או"ח סימן שיח סעיף יב:

רבינו חננאל

הוא ומשום דשמעיה מר' יוחנן הוכיח בעל השמועה. ושנינן לאפרושי מאיסורי שרי כמעשה דתלמידו של ר' מאיר: **תניא** לא ישוט אדם בבריכה מליאה מים ואפילו עומדת בחצר א"ר זירא חזיתיה לר' אבהו שהניח ידיו כנגד פניו של מטה וכו' פי' ר' אבהו היה יורד בנהר לטבול ואפילו (לא) נגע לא חיישינן (לה) [והא] דתניא ר' אליעזר אומר כל האוחז באמה ומשתין מביא מבול לעולם כלומ' מתחמם ומוציא ש"ז ונמצא משחית זרעו על הארץ. הני מילי היכא דלא מיבעית אבל היכא דמיבעית כגון ר' אבהו דהוה מבעית מעליית הנהר אין לו פנאי להתחמם כמו שאין פנאי לבלשת לנסך. הלכך אפילו נגע לא חיישינן ליה והני מילי דשרי להניח ידיו כנגד פניו של מטה כשעולה מן הנהר אבל כשיורד בנהר לא כרב דאמר כל המניח ידיו כנגד פניו של מטה כאילו כופר בבריתו של אברהם אבינו וכרבנן דבי רב אשי דכי נחתי זקפו כי סלקי שחו: **אמר** רב יהודה כל העולה מבבל לא"י עובר בעשה שנאמר בבלה יובאו ושמה [יהיו] עד יום פקדי אותם נאם ה'. והלך ר' אבא ומצא לר' יהודה במרחץ והי' אומר לשמשיו בלה"ק הביאו לי נתר הביאו לי מסרק פתחו פומייכו והסיקו הבלא ואשתו מיא דבי באני למדנו ממנו כי דברים של חול מותר לאומרן במרחץ בלה"ק. אמר אילו לא [באתי] אלא לשמוע דבר זה דיי: **מתני'** מולייר תנא מים מבחוץ וגחלים מבפנים והוא של חרס ואם גרף גחלים שרי: **אנטיכי** א"ר נחמן בי דודי ושל נחושת היא ותניא כרב נחמן אנטיכי אע"פ שגרופה אין שותין הימנה בשבת מפני שנחושתה מחממתה: **ירושלמי** מולייר שאינו גרוף אסור מפני שהגחלים נוגעות בגופו ר' חנניא בר הלל אמר מפני שהרוח נכנסת לתוכו והגחלים בוערות. ר' יוסי בר אבין א' מפני שעשו פרקין פרקין ומתיירא שמא נתאכל דיבוקו ומוסיף מים. אנטיכי בשם ר' יוחנן אמרי מפני שמתחממת מכתליה: **פיסקא** מיחם שפינהו לא יתן לתוכו צונן

it is stated: *They shall be brought to Babylonia and there shall they remain.* [10] אָמַר – However, before departing, **[R' Zeira] said:** אֵיזִיל וְאֶשְׁמַע מִינֵּיהּ מִילְּתָא – **Let me go and learn one** last **thing from [Rav Yehudah]** וְאֵיתֵי וְאֵיסַּק – **and I will** then **return** home **and** leave to **go up** to the Land of Israel. אֲזַל אַשְׁכְּחֵיהּ דְּקָאֵי בֵּי בָּאנֵי – **He went and found [Rav Yehudah] standing in a bathhouse** וְקָאָמַר לֵיהּ לְשַׁמָּעֵיהּ – **and saying to his attendants:** הָבִיאוּ לִי נֶתֶר הָבִיאוּ לִי מַסְרֵק – **"Bring me *niter*; bring me a comb;** [11] פִּתְחוּ פּוּמַיְיכוּ וְאַפִּיקוּ הַבְלָא – **open your mouths** and inhale steam **so that you will** sweat and **discharge heat;** וְאִשְׁתּוּ מִמַּיָּא דְּבֵי בָאנֵי – **and drink of the water of the bathhouse."** [12] אָמַר – **[R' Zeira] said:** אִילְמָלֵא (לֹא) בָּאתִי אֶלָּא לִשְׁמוֹעַ דָּבָר זֶה דַּיִּי – **Had I come only to hear this statement it would have been sufficient for me,** because of the many lessons that I gleaned from it.

The Gemara analyzes Rav Yehudah's words, bringing to light the lessons they contain:

בִּשְׁלָמָא הָבִיאוּ נֶתֶר הָבִיאוּ מַסְרֵק קָמַשְׁמַע לָן – **It is understandable** that the statement, **"Bring** me **soap; bring** me **a comb,"** since it was spoken in the holy tongue, **teaches us** that דְּבָרִים שֶׁל חוֹל מוּתָּר לְאוֹמְרָם בִּלְשׁוֹן קֹדֶשׁ – **secular matters may be spoken** in a bathhouse even **in the holy tongue.** [13] פִּתְחוּ פּוּמַיְיכוּ וְאַפִּיקוּ הַבְלָא נַמִּי כִּדִשְׁמוּאֵל – Furthermore, the statement, **"Open your mouths** and inhale steam **so that you will** sweat and **discharge heat,"** also teaches a lesson **in accordance with** that **of Shmuel.** דְּאָמַר שְׁמוּאֵל הַבְלָא מַפִּיק הַבְלָא – **For Shmuel said: Heat drives out heat,** i.e. inhaling the hot steam of the bathhouse helps the body sweat out its own heat. אֶלָּא אִשְׁתּוּ מַיָּא דְּבֵי בָאנֵי – **But** as for the statement, **"Drink of the water of the bathhouse,"** מַאי מַעַלְיוּתָא – **what is the benefit** in that?

The Gemara replies:

דְּתַנְיָא – It is as **we learned in a Baraisa:** אָכַל וְלֹא שָׁתָה אֲכִילָתוֹ דָּם – If ONE ATE AND DID NOT DRINK, HIS EATING IS tantamount to shedding his own BLOOD, וְזֶהוּ תְּחִילַּת חוֹלִי מֵעַיִים – AND THIS IS THE BEGINNING OF INTESTINAL AILMENTS. אָכַל וְלֹא הָלַךְ אַרְבַּע אַמּוֹת אֲכִילָתוֹ מַרְקֶבֶת – If ONE ATE AND DID NOT afterwards WALK at least FOUR *AMOS*, HIS FOOD ROTS inside him, וְזֶהוּ תְּחִילַּת רֵיחַ רַע – AND THIS IS THE BEGINNING OF BAD BREATH. הַנִּצְרָךְ לִנְקָבָיו וְאָכַל – ONE WHO NEEDED TO RELIEVE HIMSELF AND ATE without doing so דּוֹמֶה לְתַנּוּר שֶׁהֱסִיקוּהוּ עַל גַּבֵּי אֶפְרוֹ – IS ANALOGOUS TO AN OVEN THAT WAS HEATED OVER ITS old ASHES, וְזֶהוּ תְּחִילַּת רֵיחַ זוּהֲמָא – AND THIS IS THE BEGINNING OF PERSPIRATIONAL ODOR. [14] רָחַץ בְּחַמִּין וְלֹא שָׁתָה מֵהֶן – If ONE BATHED IN HOT WATER AND DID NOT DRINK [HOT WATER], דּוֹמֶה לְתַנּוּר שֶׁהֱסִיקוּהוּ מִבַּחוּץ וְלֹא הֱסִיקוּהוּ מִבִּפְנִים – HE IS ANALOGOUS TO AN OVEN THAT WAS HEATED ON THE OUTSIDE BUT WAS NOT HEATED ON THE INSIDE. [15] רָחַץ בְּחַמִּין וְלֹא נִשְׁתַּטֵּף בְּצוֹנֵן – If ONE BATHED IN HOT WATER AND DID NOT RINSE HIMSELF afterwards WITH COLD WATER, דּוֹמֶה לְבַרְזֶל שֶׁהִכְנִיסוּהוּ לָאוּר וְלֹא הִכְנִיסוּהוּ לְצוֹנֵן – HE IS ANALOGOUS TO IRON THAT WAS PUT IN THE FIRE BUT WAS NOT afterwards PUT INTO COLD WATER to be strengthened. רָחַץ וְלֹא סָךְ – If ONE BATHED AND DID NOT ANOINT himself WITH OIL, [16] דּוֹמֶה לְמַיִם עַל גַּבֵּי חָבִית – [HIS BATHING] IS ANALOGOUS TO pouring WATER ON THE OUTSIDE OF A BARREL; the water does not penetrate and does no good. We learn from this Baraisa that it is beneficial to drink hot water after bathing in hot water, as Rav Yehudah advised.

Mishnah מוּלְיָאר הַגָּרוּף – Concerning a ***miliarium*** [17] **that was shoveled** clear of its coals before the Sabbath, שׁוֹתִין הֵימֶנּוּ בְּשַׁבָּת – **we may drink from it on the Sabbath.** [18] אַנְטִיכִי – Concerning **an *antichi,*** [19] אַף עַל פִּי שֶׁגְּרוּפָה – **even if it was shoveled** clear of its coals before the Sabbath, אֵין שׁוֹתִין הֵימֶנָּה – **we may not drink from it** on the Sabbath. [20]

NOTES

10. *Jeremiah* 27:22. The verse concludes: *until the day that I take heed of them, says Hashem; then will I bring them up and restore them to this place.* Rav Yehudah understood this verse as containing a commandment to remain in the Diaspora until the ultimate redemption (*Lechem Mishneh* to *Hil. Melachim* 5:12, explaining *Rashi* to *Kesubos* 111a; cf. *Rambam, Hil. Melachim* 5:12). R' Zeira, however, understood this prophecy as referring not to the Jewish people but to the Temple vessels, which are mentioned in the preceding verse, and as predicting that the vessels would remain in Babylonia for some time. He avoided meeting Rav Yehudah because he was afraid that Rav Yehudah (who was his teacher) would forbid him to move to Eretz Yisrael (*Rashi;* see *Kesubos* ibid. with *Maharit*; see also *Avnei Nezer, Yoreh Deah* §454).

11. [נֶתֶר, *niter*, is a type of earth that was used as a cleanser (see *Jeremiah* 2:22 and *Rashi* there; see also above, 16a note 3).] Rav Yehudah said this in the holy tongue (*Rashi*) and then switched to Aramaic.

12. I.e. [when you are bathing in heated water] drink some hot water, even if the only water available is that which was heated for the baths (*Rashi;* see *Hagahos Yaavetz*).

13. After making this statement in the holy tongue (apparently to teach that secular matters may be spoken in the holy tongue) Rav Yehudah switched to Aramaic because the rest of his statements contained health-related information which he wanted to convey even to the unlearned people in the bathhouse (*R' Elazar Moshe Horowitz*).

14. It causes his entire body to perspire constantly (*Rashi*).

15. Just as it is useless to fire an oven from the outside and not the inside, so too there is no therapeutic benefit to the body from bathing unless one also drinks hot water (*Rashi*). This was the lesson contained in Rav Yehudah's final remark.

16. Before bathing (see *Rashi* above, 40b ד״ה ובקשתי). Alternatively: after bathing (*Tosafos* ד״ה רחץ ולא סך). See *Shabbos Shel Mi.*

17. A *miliarium* is a vessel used for heating water. It consists of a large bowl for water that is surrounded by a narrow receptacle for coals (*Rashi;* see notes 20 and 21). [*Miliarium* is a Greek word.]

18. Once its coals are removed, the *miliarium's* purpose is only to retain heat, not to increase it. Although it might initially make the water slightly warmer, its walls gradually cool and over a longer period merely keep the water warm. We may therefore keep water in it on the Sabbath and drink from it (*Rashi,* as explained by *Rosh Yosef*). If, however, the coals were not removed from the *miliarium,* it adds heat to the water and one is forbidden to keep water in it and to drink from it. See note 20.

19. The Gemara will explain what type of vessel this is.

20. An *antichi* continues to add heat to the water, even after its coals are removed (*Rashi*). Accordingly, one may not keep water immersed in it over the Sabbath, nor drink from water that was kept in it.

The following issue must be addressed here: The Gemara above (36b) recorded a dispute between Chananyah and the Sages about whether it is permitted to leave food before the Sabbath (*shehiyah*) on a *kirah* that was not shoveled or banked. Although such a *kirah* adds heat to the food, Chananyah permits leaving food on it. *Rashi* (37b ד״ה ורב ששת), *Tosafos* (ibid. ד״ה אמר) and numerous other Rishonim rule that the halachah follows Chananyah (see 37a note 16). Accordingly, why should it be forbidden to leave water in an *antichi* or in a *miliarium* whose coals were not removed? The *antichi* and *miliarium* should be treated no more stringently in this regard than a *kirah*! Due to this difficulty (as well as other difficulties) *Tosafos, Rashba* and *Ran* suggest completely different interpretations of our Mishnah.

In defense of *Rashi's* interpretation, several explanations have been offered. One possibility is that we are dealing with water that was not heated like the food of Ben Derusai before the Sabbath. Even Chananyah agrees that in such a case it is prohibited to leave the water on a *kirah* that adds heat (see above, 36b). Another explanation is that since the water is contained within the *miliarium* and surrounded by coals, rather than being placed in a pot on top of them, it is governed by the rules of *hatmanah* (insulating) rather than the rules of *shehiyah.* Even Chananyah concedes that *hatmanah* in a medium that adds heat is forbidden (see *Tos. Yom Tov, Maginei Shlomo, Rosh Yosef;* see also *Rashba* and *Ritva MHK* ed.).

דלית ליה גידודי הא דאית ליה גידודי: וא"ר זירא אנא חזיתיה לר' אבהו שהניח ידיו כנגד פניו של מטה ולא ידענא אי נגע אי לא נגע פשיטא דלא נגע דתניא [א] ר' אליעזר אומר [א] כל האוחז באמה ומשתין כאילו מביא מבול לעולם אמר אביי עשאוה כבולשת דתנן [ב] בולשת שנכנסה לעיר בשעת שלום חביות פתוחות אסורות סתומות מותרות בשעת מלחמה אלו ואלו מותרות לפי שאין פנאי לנסך אלמא כיון דבעיתי לא מנסכי ה"נ כיון דבעית לא אתי להרהורי והכא מאי ביעתותא ביעתותא דנהרא איני והאמר ר' אבא אמר רב הונא אמר רב כל המניח ידיו כנגד פניו של מטה כאילו כופר בבריתו של אברהם אבינו לא קשיא הא כי נחית הא כי סליק כי הא דרבא שחי ר' זירא זקיף רבנן דבי רב אשי כי קא נחתי זקפי כי קא סלקי שחי [ג] ר' זירא הוה קא משתמיט מדרב יהודה דבעי למיסק לארעא דישראל דאמר רב יהודה [ב] כל העולה מבבל לא"י עובר בעשה שנאמר [א] בבלה יובאו ושמה יהיו אמר איזיל ואשמע מיניה מילתא ואיתי ואיסק אזל אשכחיה דקאי בי באני וקאמר ליה לשמעיה הביאו לי נתר הביאו לי מסרק פתחו פומייכו ואפיקו הבלא ואשתו ממיא דבי באני אמר אילמלא [ד] (לא) באתי אלא לשמוע דבר זה דיי בשלמא הביאו נתר הביאו מסרק קמ"ל דברים של חול מותר לאומרם בלשון קדש פתחו פומייכו ואפיקו הבלא נמי כדשמואל דאמר שמואל הבלא מפיק הבלא אלא אשתו מיא דבי באני מאי מעליותא דתניא [ג] אכל ולא שתה אכילתו דם וזהו תחילת חולי מעיים [ה] אכל ולא הלך ד' אמות אכילתו מרקבת וזהו תחילת ריח רע הנצרך [ו] לנקביו ואכל דומה לתנור שהסיקוהו ע"ג אפרו וזהו תחילת ריח זוהמא רחץ בחמין ולא שתה מהן דומה לתנור שהסיקוהו מבחוץ ולא הסיקוהו מבפנים רחץ בחמין ולא נשתטף בצונן דומה לברזל שהכניסוהו לאור ולא הכניסוהו לצונן רחץ ולא סך דומה למים ע"ג חבית: **מתני'** מוליאר הגרוף שותין הימנו בשבת אנטיכי אע"פ שגרופה אין שותין הימנה: **גמ'** היכי דמי מוליאר הגרוף תנא מים מבפנים וגחלים מבחוץ אנטיכי רבה אמר בי כירי רב נחמן בר יצחק אמר בי דודי מאן דאמר בי דודי כ"ש בי כירי ומאן דאמר בי כירי אבל בי דודי לא תניא כוותיה דרב נחמן אנטיכי אע"פ שגרופה וקטומה אין שותין הימנה מפני שנחושתה מחממתה: **מתני'** המיחם שפינהו לא יתן לתוכו צונן בשביל שיחמו אבל נותן הוא לתוכו או לתוך הכוס כדי להפשירן: **גמ'** מאי קאמר אמר רב אדא בר מתנא הכי קאמר [ד] המיחם שפינה ממנו מים חמין לא יתן לתוכו מים מועטים כדי שיחמו אבל נותן לתוכו מים מרובים כדי להפשירן והלא

רש"י

דלית ליה גידודי. שאין שפתה גבוהה שיהיו המים עמוקים אלא שפתה כמו באמצע דכיון שאין עמוקים שם כי מטי סמוך לשפתה נועץ רגליו בקרקע וחופר וממחה העפר לתוך המים ודמי למגבל ולי נראה דאית ליה גידודי שרי דלא דמי לנהר אלא לכלי דלית ליה גידודי דמיא לנהר ואסור: שהניח ידיו. כשהיה רוחץ משום צניעות: אי נגע. באמה: כאילו מביא מבול לעולם. שמתחמם ובא לידי קרי וזה קלקולו של דור המבול מוציאים שכבת זרע לבטלה דכתיב כי השחית כל בשר וגו' (בראשית ו): כבולשת. עשאוה להא דר' אבוה בולשת חיילות גייס הבא לעיר על שם שמחפשין ובולשים את העיר קרי לה בולשת: בשעת שלום. כגון שהוא של אותה מלכות: כאילו כופר. דנראה שהוא בוש בדבר: כי נחית. לנהר פניו כלפי הנהר ואין כאן משום צניעות אסור לכסותו: כי סליק. ופניו כלפי העם מותר משום צניעות: ר' זירא זקיף. דחייש לדרב שלא יראה ככופר: משתמיט. היה ירא לראות לו משום דהוה בעי רבי זירא למיסק לארעא דישראל ורב יהודה לא סבירא ליה וירא פן יגזור עליו מלילך: בבלה יובאו ושמה יהיו עד יום פקדי וגו'. ור' זירא אמר לך האי קרא בכלי שרת כתיב כדאמרינן בשני דייני גזירות (כתובות קיא.): הביאו לי נתר. לחוף את ראשי וקאמר להו בלשון הקודש: פתחו פומייכו. ויכנס הבל בית המרחץ לתוך הגוף ויוציא הבל של זיעה: ואשתו. מן מים חמין ואפי' לא הוחמו אלא לרחיצה: מותר לאומרן. בבית המרחץ ואפי' בלשון קודש: הבלא. דמרחץ הנכנס דרך הפה: מפיק הבלא. דזיעה: ולא הלך ד' אמות. קודם שישן: מרקבת. אינה מתעכלת לעשות זבל: ריח רע. ריח הפה: ריח זוהמא. כל גופו מזוהם בזיעה תמיד: ולא הסיקוהו מבפנים. שאינו מטיב לכלום: ולא הכניסוהו לצונן. שהן מחזקין את הברזל: למים ע"ג חבית. על שוליו ולדדיו שאינם נכנסים לתוכו: **מתני'** מוליאר הגרוף. מן הגחלים מבע"י: שותין. ממימיו בשבת ואע"פ שהוחמו קצת מחמת הכלי לפי שאינו מוסיף הבל אלא משמר ומקיים חום שלהם שלא יצטננו בגמרא מפרש מוליאר מים מבפנים וגחלים מבחוץ כלי שיש בו בית קיבול קטן אצל דופנו מבחוץ מחובר לו ונותן שם גחלים והמים בקיבולו הגדול ורבותינו מפרשים מוליאר שני שולים ואנטיכי בי דודי מחילה בינתיים ולי נראה להפך דאם כן ה"ל למיתני מים מלמעלה וגחלים מלמטה ועוד דנחשתה דתני באנטיכי לשון שולים הן והן אומרים לשון נחושת ושאני נחשת מחרם: אנטיכי. מפרש בגמרא: **גמ'** בי כירי. חלל יש בכירה אצל חלליה שהגחלים בו ומים נתונים בחללה השני ואע"ג דדמי למוליאר מיהו כירה דופנה עב והאור תדיר בתוכה כל ימות החול ודופנה חם מאד ומוסיף הבל במים אע"פ שגרופה מן הגחלים: בי דודי. יורה גדולה עושין לה שתי שוליים ונותנין גחלים בין שניהם והמים על העליונים: וכל שכן. דבי כירי אסור כדפרישית שמתוך שהאור תדיר בו ודופנו עב מרתיח: אבל בי דודי לא. שהרי הוא כמוליאר: שנחושתה. נחושת שלה אלמא ביורה של נחשת קאי ונחשת משמר רתיחתו ואני אומר נחושתה לשון שולים כדכתיב (יחזקאל טז) יען השפך נחשתך ולשון של המשנה נחשתו של תנור במסכת כלים (פ"ח מ"ג) ושאני אנטיכי ממוליאר דמתוך שהשולים מכוסים חומם משתמר ואע"ג שגרפו גחליהם: **מתני'** המיחם. קומקמום של חמין: שפינהו. כולה מתניתין מפרש בגמרא: **גמ'** מאי קאמר. מאי פינהו ומאי לא יתן והדר אמר אבל נותן: והלא

תוספות

פשיטא דלא נגע דתניא ר' אליעזר אומר כו'. ואע"ג דרבנן פליגי עליה ושרו בפרק כל היד (נדה יג. ושם) לא שרי אלא משום ממזרות שלא יראה ככרות שפכה ויוציאו לעז על בניו שהן ממזרים [ז]: **רחיץ** ולא סך. ול"ג מעיקרא דהא בכולי הש"ס רחילה קודם סיכה כדאמר בפ"ק דקידושין (דף כב:) רחצו סכו וקרא כתיב ורחצת וסכת (רות ג) מיהו קרא איכא לאוקמי בסיכה שהיתה מתקשטת עצמה לריח טוב לכן לא היתה סכה בתחלה שעל ידי רחיצה היתה מעברת הסיכה מעליה:

מוליאר הגרוף שותין ממנו בשבת. פי' בקונטרס לפי שאין מוסיף הבל אלא משמר ומקיים חום שלהן ואנטיכי אפי' גרופה אין שותין הימנה לפי שמוספת הבל ואין נראה דלא שייך למיגזר במוסיף הבל אלא בהטמנה גזירה שמא יטמין ברמץ ועוד דדוחק לומר דמתני' איירי כשעשה האיסור ועוד דאנטיכי אוסר בכל ענין לשתות הימנו אפילו בהשהאה ואי להחזיר תנן משהין אפילו באינו גרוף ועוד אי משום תוספת הבל אסרה ליה מתני' בשתיה תקשה לרבה ורב יוסף דשרו לעיל (דף לח.) בשכח קדרה ע"ג כירה ובשלה בשבת אע"ג דלא נתבשלה כמאכל בן דרוסאי ואפי' במזיד ונראה כפי' ה"ר פורת מוליאר הגרוף שותין הימנו בשבת שמחוגין המים חמין ביין לפי שהמים אינן כ"כ חמין במוליאר שיתבשל היין מן המים שמחוגין לתוכו אבל אנטיכי אע"פ שגרופה אין שותין הימנה לפי שאנטיכי יש בה הבל יותר ומתבשל היין מן המים בשעת מזיגה וכ"מ בירושלמי:

מסורת הש"ס

א) נדה יג. מג., ב) ע"ז ע: כתובות מ. [נדה יג.], ג) כתובות קי. ברכות כד:, ד) [עי' תוספות מגילה כח. ד"ה אלמלא], ה) [עי' ב"מ קיג:], ו) [לקמן דף פב. ע"ש], ז) [וע"ע תוספות יומא ל. ד"ה מלהי].

תורה אור השלם

א) בָּבֶלָה יוּבָאוּ וְשָׁמָּה יִהְיוּ עַד יוֹם פָּקְדִי אֹתָם נְאֻם יְיָ וְהַעֲלִיתִים וַהֲשִׁבֹתִים אֶל הַמָּקוֹם הַזֶּה: [ירמיה כז, כב]

ליקוטי רש"י

כאילו מביא מבול. שעבירה זו היתה בידם דכתיב (בראשית ו) כי השחית כל בשר ואמרו ברותחין קלקלו [נדה יג.]. שמחמם את אבריו ומביא לידי קרי חהו קלקול דור המבול שנאמר (בראשית ו) כי השחית כל בשר [שם מג.]. **בולשת.** חיל המלך [לקמן קמה:]. חיל על שם שמחפשין ומתרגמין קרי להו בולשת כדמתרגמינן ויחפש ובלש [ע"ז ע:]. בולשת חיל שמחפשין ובוחין כדמתרגמינן (בראשית לא) ויחפש ובלש [נדה יג.]. חיל על שם שמחפשים כל המטמונים [כתובות כז.]. **משתמיט.** לא היה נראה אליו לפי שהיה כו' חפץ לעלות לארץ ישראל ורב יהודה אוסר לו לפיכך לא היה נכנס לבית המדרש [ברכות כד:]. **דבעי למיסק.** ורב יהודה מוחה בידו להכי הוה משתמיט מיניה [כתובות קי:]. **נתר.** קרקע הוא או אבן כעין שקורין קרי"א בלע"ז [תענית יג.]. מין אדמה הוא וקורין לה גיתרא [סנהדרין מט:]. מין כיבוס הוא שמעביר את הגיעול [זבחים פח.]. **ואשתו ממיא דבי באני.** דקיימא לן הרוחץ בחמין שותה מהם והם רפואה לו במסכת שבת [גיטין סט:]. **ריח רע.** ריח הפה שהזבל מרקב במעיים ויוצא ריח דרך פיו. **ריח זוהמא.** כל גופו מסריח בזיעה מסרחת שהריח נבלע בבשרו ובאבריו והוה בו לזיעה מזוהמת [לקמן סב.]. **ולא הכניסוהו לצונן.** כשלוי מתכות חם ונותן לתוכו צונן מחזקים את הכלי וזו היא גמר מלאכת הצורפין שרתיחת האור מפעפעתו וקרוב להשבר והמים מצרפין פעפועיו שולדי"ר בלע"ז [לקמן ע"ב].

עין משפט נר מצוה

כט א מיי' פכ"א מהל' איסורי ביאה הלכה כג טוש"ע או"ח סימן ג סעיף יד וטוש"ע אה"ע סימן כג סעיף ד:
ל ב מיי' פ"ה מהלכות מלכים הלכה יב:
לא ג מיי' פ"ד מהלכות דעות הלכה ב:
לב ד מיי' פכ"ב מהל' שבת הלכה ה ופכ"ג הלכה ו סמג לאוין סה טוש"ע או"ח סימן שיח סעיף יב:

רבינו חננאל

הוא ומשום דשמעיה מר' יוחנן הוכיח בעל השמועה. ושנינן לאפרושי מאיסורי שרי כמעשה דתלמידו של ר' מאיר: **תניא** לא ישוט אדם בבריכה מליאה מים ואפילו עומדת בחצר א"ר זירא חזיתיה לר' אבהו שהניח ידיו כנגד פניו של מטה וכו' פי' ר' אבהו היה יורד בנהר לטבול ואפילו (לא) נגע לא חיישינן (לה) [והא] דתניא ר' אליעזר אומר כל האוחז באמה ומשתין מביא מבול לעולם כלומ' מתחמם ומוציא ש"ז ונמצא משחית זרעו על הארץ. הני מילי היכא דלא מיבעית אבל היכא דמיבעית כגון ר' אבהו דההוה מבעית מעליית הנהר אין לו פנאי להתחמם כמו שאין פנאי לבלשת לנסך. הלכך אפילו נגע לא חיישינן ליה והני מילי דשרי להניח ידיו כנגד פניו של מטה כשעולה מן הנהר אבל כשיורד בנהר לא כרב דאמר כל המניח ידיו כנגד פניו של מטה כאילו כופר בבריתו של אברהם אבינו וכרבנן דבי רב אשי דכי נחתי זקפו כי סלקי שחו: **אמר** רב יהודה כל העולה מבבל לא"י עובר בעשה שנאמר בבלה יובאו ושמה [יהיו] עד יום פקדי אותם נאם ה'. והלך ר' אבא ומצא לר' יהודה במרחץ והי' אומר לשמשיו בלה"ק הביאו לי נתר הביאו לי מסרק פתחו פומייכו והסיקו הבלא ואשתו מיא דבי באני למדנו ממנו כי דברים של חול מותר לאומרן במרחץ בלה"ק. אמר אילו לא [באתי] אלא לשמוע דבר זה דיי: **מתני'** מוליד תנא מים מבחוץ וגחלים מבפנים והוא של חרס ואם גרוף גחלים שרי: **אנטיכי** א"ר נחמן בי דודי ושל נחושת היא ותניא כרב נחמן אנטיכי אע"פ שגרופה אין שותין הימנה בשבת מפני שנחושתה מחממתה: **ירושלמי** מוליאר שאינו גרוף אסור מפני שהגחלים נוגעות בגופו ר' חנניא בר הלל אמר מפני שהרוח נכנסת לתוכו והגחלים בוערות. ר' יוסי בר אבין א' מפני שעשו פרקין פרקין ומתירא שמא נתאכל דיבוקו ומוסיף מים. אנטיכי בשם ר' יוחנן אמרי מפני שמחממת מכחליה: **פיסקא** מיחם שפינהו לא יתן לתוכו צונן

Gemara The Gemara defines the vessels mentioned in the Mishnah:

הֵיכִי דָּמֵי מוּלְיָאר הַגָּרוּף – **What is the case of a *miliarium* that was shoveled** clear of its coals? תָּנָא מַיִם מִבִּפְנִים וְגֶחָלִים מִבַּחוּץ – **It was taught in a Baraisa:** A *miliarium* is a vessel that contains **WATER ON THE INSIDE AND COALS ON THE OUTSIDE.**[21]

אַנְטִיכִי – What is the ***antichi*?** רַבָּה אָמַר – **Rabbah said:** בֵּי כִּירֵי – It is **a compartmental *kirah*.**[22] רַב נַחְמָן בַּר יִצְחָק אָמַר – **Rav Nachman bar Yitzchak said:** בֵּי דוּדֵי – It is **a two-tier pot.**[23]

The Gemara compares these two views:

מַאן דְּאָמַר בֵּי דוּדֵי – According to **the one who said** that an *antichi* is **a two-tier pot,** כָּל שֶׁכֵּן בֵּי כִּירֵי – the prohibition mentioned in regard to the *antichi* **certainly** applies also to **a compartmental *kirah*,** which is even hotter. וּמַאן דְּאָמַר בֵּי כִּירֵי – **But** according to **the one who said** that an *antichi* is **a compartmental *kirah*,** the prohibition is restricted to this utensil, אֲבָל בֵּי דוּדֵי לֹא – **but** it does **not** extend to **a two-tier pot.**[24]

The Gemara adduces support for the view of Rav Nachman bar Yitzchak:

תַּנְיָא כְּוָותֵיהּ דְּרַב נַחְמָן – **A Baraisa was taught in accordance with** the view of **Rav Nachman:** אַנְטִיכִי אַף עַל פִּי שֶׁגְּרוּפָה וּקְטוּמָה אֵין שׁוֹתִין הֵימֶנָּה – Concerning **AN *ANTICHI,* EVEN IF IT WAS SHOVELED OR BANKED, WE MAY NOT DRINK FROM IT,** מִפְּנֵי שֶׁנְּחוֹשְׁתָּהּ מְחַמַּמְתָּהּ – **BECAUSE ITS BOTTOM HEATS IT.**[25] The Baraisa indicates that an *antichi* is heated from its bottom, which corroborates Rav Nachman bar Yitzchak's definition.

Mishnah The Mishnah discusses heating liquid by pouring it into a hot vessel that was removed from a fire: הַמֵּיחַם שֶׁפִּינָּהוּ – Concerning **a kettle that was cleared,**[26] לֹא יִתֵּן לְתוֹכוֹ צוֹנֵן בִּשְׁבִיל שֶׁיֵּחַמּוּ – **one may not put cold water into it in order that it be heated,** אֲבָל נוֹתֵן הוּא לְתוֹכוֹ אוֹ לְתוֹךְ הַכּוֹס כְּדֵי לְהַפְשִׁירָן – **but he may put** cold water **into [the kettle] or into a cup** of hot water **so as to warm it.**[27]

Gemara The Gemara seeks to clarify the Mishnah's rulings:

מַאי קָאָמַר – **What does [the Mishnah]** mean **to say?** I.e. what is the meaning of the expression *a kettle that was cleared,* and how do we distinguish between heating and warming water in it?[28] אָמַר רַב אַדָּא בַּר מַתְנָא – **Rav Adda bar Masna said:** הָכִי קָאָמַר – **This is what [the Mishnah]** means **to say:** הַמֵּיחַם שֶׁפִּינָּה מִמֶּנּוּ מַיִם חַמִּין – Concerning **a kettle from which the hot water was cleared,** לֹא יִתֵּן לְתוֹכָן מַיִם מוּעָטִים כְּדֵי שֶׁיֵּחַמּוּ – **one may not put a small quantity of** cold **water into it in order to heat [the water].** אֲבָל נוֹתֵן לְתוֹכוֹ מַיִם מְרוּבִּים כְּדֵי לְהַפְשִׁירָן – **However, one may put a large quantity of** cold **water into it in order to warm [the water].**[29]

NOTES

21. This is *Rashi's* version of the text. *Rabbeinu Chananel* and *Rambam* (*Commentary to Mishnah*) have the reading מַיִם מִבַּחוּץ וְגֶחָלִים מִבִּפְנִים, *water on the outside* (i.e. in the outer receptacle) *and coals on the inside.* See *Rashi* to the Mishnah, who cites yet another explanation in the name of his teachers.

22. I.e. a *kirah-*stove with a compartment for water adjacent to the compartment containing the coals. Although the construction of the *antichi* is similar to that of a *miliarium* (which also has two compartments for water and coals) it is forbidden to leave water in the *antichi* even if the coals were shoveled out. This is because, in contrast to a *miliarium,* the compartments of the *antichi* are divided by a thick wall and coal is burned in it all week long. Thus, the dividing wall becomes very hot and retains its heat, causing it to add heat to the water even after the coals are removed (*Rashi*).

23. I.e. a double-bottomed pot, which contains coals in the lower compartment and water in the upper one. Since the lower compartment is covered, the heat remains trapped in it even after the coals have been cleared away, and it therefore continues to heat the water (*Rashi*).

24. The two-tier pot whose coals were removed is not as hot as the compartmental *kirah.* Therefore, it is treated like a *miliarium* and one is permitted to leave water inside it once he has removed its coals (*Rashi*).

In summary, there are three grades of hot-water receptacles. From coolest to hottest these are: a *miliarium,* a two-tier pot and a compartmental *kirah.* The Mishnah states clearly that it is permitted to keep water in a *miliarium* over the Sabbath, once one removes the coals. It is certainly forbidden to keep water in a compartmental *kirah* over the Sabbath, even after the coals are removed. Rabbah and Rav Nachman bar Yitzchak differ in regard to a two-tier pot. According to Rav Nachman bar Yitzchak, this is the *antichi* of the Mishnah and may not be used even if the coals are removed. According to Rabbah, it is like a *miliarium* and may be used once the coals are removed; the *antichi* of the Mishnah is a compartmental *kirah.*

25. I.e. its double bottom retains heat even after the coals are removed or covered with ash, and it continues to add heat to the water in the upper compartment (see *Rashi*).

26. The Gemara discusses the precise meaning of this expression. However, the reference is certainly to a kettle that had been heated on a fire and was removed from it.

27. As mentioned above (40b note 16), a vessel that was heated on a fire (כְּלִי רִאשׁוֹן, *a primary vessel*) is considered capable of cooking something that is added to it as long as it is so hot that the hand recoils from it. A vessel to which hot food or liquid was transferred from a primary vessel (כְּלִי שֵׁנִי, *a secondary vessel*) is generally not deemed capable of cooking. [The basis for this distinction has been explained above. For further study, see *Orach Chaim* 318:9; *Chayei Adam, Hil. Shabbos* 20:3-5; *Shevisas HaShabbos,* introduction to *Hil. Bishul*; and *Chazon Ish, Orach Chaim* 52:18-19.]

Our Mishnah teaches that one may not add water to a kettle that was removed from the fire in order to heat it, for since the kettle is a primary vessel, this is considered an act of cooking. However, one may add water to a kettle in order to merely warm it. The Gemara will clarify this.

The Mishnah further teaches that one may add cold water to a *cup* of hot water, i.e. a secondary vessel, in order to warm it. It would seem that this does not mean to preclude adding water in order to heat it, for since a secondary vessel is incapable of "cooking," there should be no restriction against adding water to a secondary vessel. Rather, the Mishnah must mean that *any* water added to a secondary vessel is deemed to be merely "warmed" and not "heated," i.e. cooked. [However, this matter is the subject of a dispute that is cited below, 42a] (*Ritva MHK* ed.; *Ramban, Rashba, Ran* to 42a; cf. *Rav;* see also *Tos. R' Akiva Eiger* and 42a note 18).

28. Since the Mishnah refers to a single kettle that is at a specific temperature, the water that is poured in will be either heated or warmed. Yet the Mishnah implies that both are possible and one may not heat the water but may warm it. To what type of kettle does the Mishnah refer and what, precisely, does it mean? (see *Rashi* and *Ritva MHK* ed.; cf. *Pnei Yehoshua, Rosh Yosef*).

29. I.e. one may pour water in only if it is of a quantity that will not become heated but will merely be warmed before cooling the walls of the kettle (*Ritva MHK* ed.; see also *Pnei Yehoshua,* and *Rama, Orach Chaim* 318:12, and see 41b note 4). The definition of *heated* is that the hand recoils from it.

דלית ליה גידודי הא דאית ליה גידודי: וא"ר זירא אנא חזיתיה לר' אבהו שהניח ידיו כנגד פניו של מטה ולא ידענא אי נגע אי לא נגע פשיטא דלא נגע דתניא [א] ר' אליעזר אומר [א] כל האוחז באמה ומשתין כאילו מביא מבול לעולם אמר אביי עשאוה כבולשת דתנן [ב] בולשת שנכנסה לעיר בשעת שלום חביות פתוחות אסורות סתומות מותרות בשעת מלחמה אלו ואלו מותרות לפי שאין פנאי לנסך אלמא כיון דבעיתי לא מנסכי ה"נ כיון דבעית לא אתי להרהורי והכא מאי ביעתותא ביעתותא דנהרא איני והאמר ר' אבא אמר רב הונא אמר רב כל המניח ידיו כנגד פניו של מטה כאילו כופר בבריתו של אברהם אבינו לא קשיא הא כי נחית הא כי סליק כי הא דרבא שחי ר' זירא זקיף רבנן דבי רב אשי כי קא נחתי זקפי כי קא סלקי שחי [ג] ר' זירא הוה קא משתמיט מדרב יהודה דבעי למיסק לארעא דישראל דאמר רב יהודה [ב] כל העולה מבבל לא"י עובר בעשה שנאמר [א] בבלה יובאו ושמה יהיו אמר איזיל ואשמע מיניה מילתא ואיתי ואיסק אזל אשכחיה דקאי בי באני וקאמר ליה לשמעיה הביאו לי נתר הביאו לי מסרק פתחו פומייכו ואפיקו הבלא ואשתו ממיא דבי באני אמר אילמלא [ד] (לא) באתי אלא לשמוע דבר זה דיי בשלמא הביאו נתר הביאו מסרק קמ"ל דברים של חול מותר לאומרם בלשון קדש פתחו פומייכו ואפיקו הבלא נמי כדשמואל דאמר שמואל הבלא מפיק הבלא אלא אשתו מיא דבי באני מאי מעליותא דתניא [ג] אכל ולא שתה אכילתו דם וזהו תחילת חולי מעיים [ה] אכל ולא הלך ד' אמות אכילתו מרקבת וזהו תחילת ריח רע הנצרך [ו] לנקביו ואכל דומה לתנור שהסיקוהו ע"ג אפרו וזהו תחילת ריח זוהמא רחץ בחמין ולא שתה מהן דומה לתנור שהסיקוהו מבחוץ ולא הסיקוהו מבפנים רחץ בחמין ולא נשתטף בצונן דומה לברזל שהכניסוהו לאור ולא הכניסוהו לצונן רחץ ולא סך דומה למים ע"ג חבית: **מתני'** מוליאר הגרוף שותין הימנו בשבת אנטיכי אע"פ שגרופה אין שותין הימנה: **גמ'** היכי דמי מוליאר הגרוף תנא מים מבפנים וגחלים מבחוץ אנטיכי רבה אמר בי כירי רב נחמן בר יצחק אמר בי דודי מאן דאמר בי דודי כ"ש בי כירי ומאן דאמר בי כירי אבל בי דודי לא תניא כוותיה דרב נחמן אנטיכי אע"פ שגרופה וקטומה אין שותין הימנה מפני שנחושתה מחממתה: **מתני'** המיחם שפינהו לא יתן לתוכו צונן בשביל שיחמו אבל נותן הוא לתוכו או לתוך הכוס כדי להפשירן: **גמ'** מאי קאמר אמר רב אדא בר מתנא הכי קאמר [ד] המיחם שפינה ממנו מים חמין לא יתן לתוכו מים מועטים כדי שיחמו אבל נותן לתוכו מים מרובים כדי להפשירן והלא

רש"י

דלית ליה גידודי. שאין שפתה גבוהה שיהיו המים עמוקים אצל שפתה כמו באמצע דכיון שאין עמוקים שם כי מטי סמוך לשפתה נועץ רגליו בקרקע וחופר וממחה העפר לתוך המים ודמי למגבל ולי נראה דאית ליה גידודי שרי דלא דמי לנהר אלא לכלי דלית ליה גידודי דמיא לנהר ואסור: שהניח ידיו. כשהיה רוחץ משום צניעות: אי נגע. באמה: כאילו מביא מבול לעולם. שמתחמם ובא לידי קרי וזה קלקולו של דור המבול מוציאים שכבת זרע לבטלה דכתיב כי השחית כל בשר וגו' (בראשית ו): כבולשת. עשאוה להא דר' אבוה בולשת חיילות גייס הבא לעיר על שם שמחפשין ובולשים את העיר קרי לה בולשת: בשעת שלום. כגון שהוא של אותה מלכות: כאילו כופר. דנראה שהוא בוש בדבר: כי נחית. לנהר פניו כלפי הנהר ואין כאן משום צניעות אסור לכסותו: כי סליק. ופניו כלפי העם מותר משום צניעות: ר' זירא זקיף. דחייש לדרב שלא יראה ככופר: משתמיט. היה ירא לראות לו משום דהוה בעי רבי זירא למיסק לארעא דישראל ורב יהודה לא סבירא ליה וירא פן יגזור עליו מלילך: בבלה יובאו ושמה יהיו עד יום פקדי וגו'. ור' זירא אמר לך האי קרא בכלי שרת כתיב כדאמרינן בשני דייני גזירות (כתובות קי.): הביאו לי נתר. לחוף את ראשי וקאמר להו בלשון הקודש: פתחו פומייכו. ויכנס הבל בית המרחץ לתוך הגוף ויוציא הבל של זיעה: ואשתו. מן מים חמין ואפי' לא הוחמו אלא לרחילה: מותר לאומרן. בבית המרחץ ואפי' בלשון קודש: הבלא. דמרחץ הנכנס דרך הפה: מפיק הבלא. דזיעה: ולא הלך ד' אמות. קודם שישן: מרקבת. אינה מתעכלת לעשות זבל: ריח רע. ריח הפה: ריח זוהמא. כל גופו מזוהם בזיעה תמיד: ולא הסיקוהו מבפנים. שאינו מטיב לכלום: ולא הכניסוהו לצונן. שהן מחזקין את הברזל: למים ע"ג חבית. על שוליו ולדדיו שאינם נכנסים לתוכו: **מתני'** מוליאר הגרוף. מן הגחלים מבע"י: שותין. ממימיו בשבת ואע"פ שהוחמו קצת מחמת הכלי לפי שאינו מוסיף הבל אלא משמר ומקיים חום שלהם שלא יצטננו בגמרא מפרש מוליאר מים מבפנים וגחלים מבחוץ כלי שיש בו בית קיבול קטן אצל דופנו מבחוץ מחובר לו ונותן שם גחלים והמים בקיבולו הגדול ורבותינו מפרשים מוליאר שני שולים ואנטיכי בי דודי מחילה בינתיים ולי נראה להפך דאם כן ה"ל למיתני מים מלמעלה וגחלים מלמטה ועוד דנחשתה דתני באנטיכי לשון שולים הן והן אומרים לשון נחושת ואני נחשת מתרם: אנטיכי. מפרש בגמרא: **גמ'** בי כירי. אלל יש בכירה אלל חלליה שהגחלים בו ומים נתונים בחללה השני ואע"ג דדמי למוליאר מיהו כירה דופנה עב והאור תדיר בתוכה כל ימות החול ודופנה חם מאד ומוסיף הבל במים אע"פ שגרופה מן הגחלים: בי דודי. יורה גדולה עושין לה שתי שוליים ונותנין גחלים בין שניהם והמים על העליונים: וכל שכן. דבי כירי אסור כדפרישית שמתוך שהאור תדיר בו ודופנו עב מרתיח: אבל בי דודי לא. שהרי הוא כמוליאר: שנחושתה. נחושת שלה אלמא ביורה של נחשת קאי ונחשת משמע רתיחתו ואני אומר נחושתה לשון שולים כדכתיב (יחזקאל טז) יען השפך נחשתך ולשון של המשנה נחשתו של תנור במסכת כלים (פ"ח מ"ג) ושאני אנטיכי ממוליאר דמתוך שהשולים מכוסים חומם משתמר ואע"ג שגרפו גחליהם: **מתני'** המיחם. קומקמום של חמין: שפינהו. כולה מתניתין מפרש בגמרא: **גמ'** מאי קאמר. מאי פינהו ומאי לא יתן והדר אמר אבל נותן: והלא

תוספות

פשיטא דלא נגע דתניא ר' אליעזר אומר כו'. ואע"ג דרבנן פליגי עליה ושרו בפרק כל היד (נדה יג. ושם) לא שרי אלא משום ממזרות שלא יראה ככרות שפכה ויוציאו לעז על בניו שהן ממזרים [ז]: **רחץ** ולא סך. ול"ג מעיקרא דהא בכולי הש"ס רחילה קודם סיכה כדאמר בפ"ק דקידושין (דף כב:) רחצו סכו וקרא כתיב ורחצת וסכת (רות ג) מיהו קרא איכא לאוקמי בסיכה שהיתה מתקשטת עצמה בריח טוב לכן לא היתה סכה בתחלה שעל ידי רחילה היתה מעברת הסיכה מעליה:

מוליאר הגרוף שותין ממנו בשבת. פי' בקונטרס לפי שאין מוסיף הבל אלא משמר ומקיים חום שלהן ואנטיכי אפי' גרופה אין שותין הימנה לפי שמוספת הבל ואין נראה דלא שייך למיגזר במוסיף הבל אלא בהטמנה גזירה שמא יטמין ברמץ ועוד דדוחק לומר דמתני' איירי כשעשה האיסור ועוד דאנטיכי אוסר בכל ענין לשתות הימנו אפילו בהשהאה ואי להחזיר תנן משהין אפילו באינו גרוף ועוד אי משום תוספת הבל אסרה ליה מתני' בשתיה תקשה לרבה ורב יוסף דשרו לעיל (דף לח.) בשכח קדרה ע"ג כירה ובשלה בשבת אע"ג דלא נתבשלה כמאכל בן דרוסאי ואפי' במזיד ונראה כפי' ה"ר פורת מוליאר הגרוף שותין הימנו בשבת שמוזגין המים חמין ביין לפי שהמים אינן כ"כ חמין במוליאר שיתבשל היין מן המים שמוזגין לתוכו אבל אנטיכי אע"פ שגרופה אין שותין הימנה לפי שאנטיכי יש בה הבל יותר ומתבשל היין מן המים בשעת מזיגה וכ"מ בירושלמי:

עין משפט נר מצוה

כט א מיי' פכ"א מהל' איסורי ביאה הלכה כג טוש"ע או"ח סימן ג סעיף יד וטוש"ע אה"ע סימן כג סעיף ד:
ל ב מיי' פ"ה מהלכות מלכים הלכה יב:
לא ג מיי' פ"ד מהלכות דעות הלכה ב:
לב ד מיי' פכ"ב מהל' שבת הלכה א ופכ"ב הלכה ו סמג לאוין סה טוש"ע או"ח סימן שיח סעיף יב:

רבינו חננאל

הוא ומשום דשמעיה מר' יוחנן הוכיח בעל השמועה. ושנינן לאפרושי מאיסורי שרי כמעשה דתלמידו של ר' מאיר: **תניא** לא ישוט אדם בבריכה מליאה מים ואפילו עומדת בחצר א"ר זירא חזיתיה לר' אבהו שהניח ידיו כנגד פניו של מטה וכו' פי' ר' אבהו היה יורד בנהר לטבול ואפילו (לא) נגע לא חיישינן (לה) [והא] דתניא ר' אליעזר אומר כל האוחז באמה ומשתין מביא מבול לעולם כלומ' מתחמם ומוציא ש"ז ונמצא משחית זרעו על הארץ. הני מילי היכא דלא מיבעית אבל היכא דמיבעית כגון ר' אבהו דהוה מבעית מעליית הנהר אין לו פנאי להתחמם כמו שאין פנאי לבלשת לנסך. הלכך אפילו נגע לא חיישינן ליה והני מילי דשרי להניח ידיו כנגד פניו של מטה כשעולה מן הנהר אבל כשיורד בנהר לא כרב דאמר כל המניח ידיו כנגד פניו של מטה כאילו כופר בבריתו של אברהם אבינו וכרבנן דבי רב אשי דכי נחתי זקפו כי סלקי שחו: **אמר** רב יהודה כל העולה מבבל לא"י עובר בעשה שנאמר בבלה יובאו ושמה [יהיו] עד יום פקדי אותם נאם ה'. והלך ר' אבא ומצא לר' יהודה במרחץ והי' אומר לשמשיו בלה"ק הביאו לי נתר הביאו לי מסרק פתחו פומייכו והסיקו הבלא ואשתו מיא דבי באני למדנו ממנו כי דברים של חול מותר לאומרן במרחץ בלה"ק. אמר אילו לא [באתי] אלא לשמוע דבר זה דיי: **מתני'** מולייר תנא מים מבחוץ וגחלים מבפנים והוא של חרס ואם גרף גחלים שרי: **אנטיכי** א"ר נחמן בי דודי ושל נחושת היא ותניא כרב נחמן אנטיכי אע"פ שגרופה אין שותין הימנה בשבת מפני שנחושתה מחממתה: **ירושלמי** מולייר שאינו גרוף אסור מפני שהגחלים נוגעות בגופו ר' חנניא בר הלל אמר מפני שהרוח נכנסת לתוכו והגחלים בוערות. ר' יוסי בר אבין א' מפני שעשו פרקין פרקין ומתיירא שמא נתאכל דיבוקו ומוסיף מים. אנטיכי בשם ר' יוחנן אמרי מפני שמתחממת מכתליה: **פיסקא** מיחם שפינהו לא יתן לתוכו צונן

מסורת הש"ס

א) נדה יג. מג., ב) ע"ז ע:, כתובות ס. [נדה יג.], ג) כתובות קי. ברכות כד:, ד) [עי' תוספות מגילה כח. ד"ה אלמלא], ה) [עי' ב"מ קיג:], ו) [לקמן דף פב. ע"ש], ז) [וע"ע תוספות יומא ל. ד"ה מלוה].

תורה אור השלם

א) בָּבֶלָה יוּבָאוּ וְשָׁמָּה יִהְיוּ עַד יוֹם פָּקְדִי אֹתָם נְאֻם יְיָ וְהַעֲלִיתִים וַהֲשִׁבֹתִים אֶל הַמָּקוֹם הַזֶּה: [ירמיה כז, כב]

ליקוטי רש"י

כאילו מביא מבול. שעבירה זו היתה בידם דכתיב (בראשית ו) כי השחית כל בשר ואמרו ברותחין קלקלו [נדה יג.]. שמחמם את אבריו ומביא לידי קרי וזהו קלקול דור המבול שנאמר (בראשית ו) כי השחית כל בשר [שם מג.]. בולשת. חיל המלך [לקמן קמה:]. חיל על שם שמחפשין ותופרין קרי להו בולשת כדמתרגמינן ויחפש ובלש [ע"ז ע:]. בולשת חיל שמחפשין ובוזזין כדמתרגמינן (בראשית לא) ויחפש ובלש [נדה יג.]. חיל על שם שמחפשים כל המטמונים [כתובות כז.]. משתמיט. לא היה נראה אליו לפי שהיה ר' חפץ לעלות לארץ ישראל ורב יהודה אוסר לו לפיכך לא היה נכנס לבית המדרש [ברכות כד:]. דבעי למיסק. ורב יהודה מוחה בידו להכי הוה משתמיט מיניה [כתובות קי:]. נתר. קרקע הוא או אבן כעין שקורין קרי"א בלע"ז [תענית יג.]. מין אדמה הוא וקורין לה גיתרא [סנהדרין מט:]. מין כיבוס הוא שמעביר את הגיעול [זבחים פח.]. ואשתו ממיא דבי באני. דקיימא לן הרוחץ בחמין שותה מהם והם רפואה לו במסכת שבת [גיטין סט:]. ריח רע. ריח הפה שהזבל מרקב במעיים ויוצא ריח דרך פיו. ריח זוהמא. כל גופו מסריח בזיעה מסרחת שהריח נבלע בבשרו ובאבריו והוה בו לזיעה מזוהמת [לקמן פב.]. ולא הכניסוהו לצונן. כשכלי מתכות חם ונותן לתוכו צונן מחזקים את הכלי וזו היא גמר מלאכת הצורפין שרתיחת האור מפעפעתו וקרוב להשבר והמים מצרפין פעפועיו שולדי"ר בלע"ז [לקמן ע"ב].

והלא מצרף ר' שמעון היא דאמר [א] דבר שאין מתכוין מותר מתקיף לה אביי מידי מיחם שפינה ממנו מים קתני מיחם שפינהו קתני אלא אמר אביי הכי קאמר המיחם שפינהו ויש בו מים חמין לא יתן לתוכו מים מועטין בשביל שיחומו אבל נותן לתוכו מים מרובים כדי להפשירן ומיחם שפינה ממנו מים לא יתן לתוכו מים א) כל עיקר מפני שמצרף ור' יהודה היא דאמר דבר שאין מתכוין אסור אמר רב ל"ש אלא להפשיר אבל לצרף אסור ושמואל אמר אפי' לצרף נמי מותר לצרף לכתחילה מי שרי אלא אי איתמר הכי איתמר אמר רב לא שנו אלא שיעור להפשיר אבל שיעור לצרף אסור ושמואל אמר אפי' שיעור לצרף מותר

רש"י

והלא מצרף. כשכלי מתכות חם ונותן לתוכו צונן מחזקים את הכלי וזו היא גמר מלאכת הצורפין שרתיחת האור מפעפעתו וקרוב להשבר והמים מצרפין פעפועיו שולדי"ר בלע"ז: שפינהו. משמע שפינהו לעצמו מעל האור: אבל לצרף. שפינהו ממנו החמין: הכי איתמר לא שנו. דפינהו שרי לתת לתוכו צונן: אלא שיעור להפשיר. ולא לצרף כגון שלא מלאהו כולו ורב משמע ליה פינהו כרב אדא שפינה ממנו חמין: אפילו שיעור לצרף. שמלאהו כולו:

מותר

תוספות

והלא מצרף. וליכא לשנויי בשלא הגיע לצירוף כדמשני בפרק אמר להם הממונה (יומא דף לד: ושם) דסתם מיחם הגיע לצירוף הוא:

מידי מיחם שפינה הימנו מים קתני המיחם שפינהו קתני. תימה והכתיב ופנו את הבית (ויקרא יד) ואנכי פניתי הבית (בראשית כד) סולו פנו דרך (ישעיה נז) וכן בש"ס [ב] פנו מקום לבר ליואי שאינו מפנה אלא מה שבתוכם וי"ל כיון דבכמה מקומות הוזכר פינוי על הדבר המפנין כגון [ג] המפנה חפציו מזוית לזוית [ד] מפנין ד' וה' קופות [ה] פנו כלים (מבית) הטומאה [ו] (תבן) ועתיד לפנותו לא הוה ליה למנקט פינהו אלא פנה ממנו מים כיון דאיכא למיטעי:

מיחם שפינה ממנו מים לא יתן לתוכו מים כל עיקר מפני שמצרף ורבי יהודה היא. אבל לר"ש שרי אע"פ שמצרף כיון דאינו מבשל כגון שיש בו מים הרבה שאין המיחם מספיק לבשל רוב המים שבתוכו כדאשכחן בפרק אמר להם הממונה (יומא דף לד: ושם) שאין מבשל ומצרף דקאמר רבי יהודה מביאין עששיות של ברזל ומטילין לתוך המים שתפיג צינתן ואם היה מבשל היה אסור ואפ"ה פריך והלא מצרף ואע"ג דאביי סבר כר"ש דהא אמר לעיל [ז] כל מילי דמר עביד כרב לבר מהני תלת דעביד כשמואל וחד מינייהו הלכה כר"ש בגרירה ומסתמא אביי כרבה רביה סבירא ליה מ"מ מוקי מתניתין כרבי יהודה משום דקשיא ליה מידי מיחם שפינה ממנו מים קתני ורב אדא לא חייש לקושיית אביי ומוקי לה כהלכתא כר"ש ול"ג לעיל אמר רב אדא בר מתנא אמר רב דרב סבר [ח] כר' יהודה בגרירה ועוד דבהדיא מוקי בסמוך מתני' כר' יהודה ונ"ל דלא הוי פסיק רישיה שיכול להיות שלא יצרף דבפסיק רישיה מודה ר"ש והא דפריך והלא מצרף ה"ק והלא שמא מצרף קשה דהכא משמע דבצירוף אסר ר' יהודה נמי דבר שאין מתכוין ובפרק אמר להם הממונה גרים רש"י ה"מ לאורייתא אבל הכא צירוף דרבנן ול"ג אין שבות במקדש ומפרש דדוקא בדבר שהוא מן התורה אית ליה לר' יהודה דבר שאין מתכוין אסור אבל בצירוף שהוא דרבנן לא ומיהו בלאו הכי קשה לפי' דהא ר' יהודה אסר בגרירה במתניתין דביצה דפרק י"ט (דף כג:) דתנן ואינה נגררת אלא ע"ג כלים דמשמע אבל ע"ג קרקע לא ומוקמינא כר' יהודה דאסר באין מתכוין אע"ג דבגרירה ליכא איסורא דאורייתא אפי' במתכוין כדמשמע בסוף פירקין דהוי חורש כלאחר יד ועוד דשמעתא דהתם קשה דמשני אביי אפי' תימא כשהגיע לצירוף דבר שאינו מתכוין מותר ופריך ומי אמר אביי הכי והתניא ימול בשר ערלתו אפי' במקום בהרת יקוץ דברי רבי אושעיא והוינן בה קרא ל"ל ואמר אביי לא נצרכה אלא לר' יהודה דאמר דבר שאין מתכוין אסור והשתא אמאי לא מייתי ההיא דביצה דהיא משנה שלמה דאסר ר' יהודה דבר שאין מתכוין ומייתי מילתיה דאביי ועוד מוחק הספר דגרס ואין שבות במקדש לכך נראה לפרש התם אביי אמר אפילו כו' דבר שאין מתכוין מותר פי' מותר לר' יהודה ולא אסר [ט] ליה ר' יהודה דבר שאין מתכוין אלא מדרבנן ופריך מימול בשר ערלתו דמוקי אביי דאיצטריך לר' יהודה קרא א"כ ש"מ דאסר ר' יהודה אין מתכוין מן התורה ומשני וה"ג ה"מ בכל התורה כולה פי' בכל התורה כולה חוץ משבת אסור מן התורה אבל צירוף דגבי שבת לא אסור אין מתכוין אלא מדרבנן דכיון דאין מתכוין לא הויא מלאכת מחשבת ושרי דאין שבות במקדש והשתא א"ש הכא וסוגיא דהתם וקשה דבפרק ספק אכל (כריתות דף כ: [ט] ושם) א"ר אשי כגון שנתכוין לכבות העליונות והובערו התחתונות מחלוקת ת"ק סבר לה כר"י דאמר דבר שאין מתכוין אסור ולכך קאמר דחייב חטאת ומאן דפטר כר"ש דאמר דבר שאין מתכוין מותר אלמא משמע דדבר שאין מתכוין אסור לר"י אפי' בשבת מן התורה וי"ל דהתם הוי פסיק רישיה שאי אפשר כלל לכבות העליונות אם לא יובערו התחתונות וחשיב מלאכת מחשבת ואע"ג דהוי פסיק רישיה פטר ר"ש משום דהויא מלאכה שאינה צריכה לגופה דאינו צריך להבערת התחתונות והא דנקט לישנא מתכוין ושאין מתכוין ולא נקט ת"ק כר"י דאמר מלאכה שאינה צריכה כו' משום רבותא דר"י נקט דלא תימא דלא מחייב ר"י מלאכה שאינה צריכה לגופה אלא במקום שמתכוין לעשות המלאכה כגון מכבה גחלת של עץ שלא יוזקו רבים שמתכוין לכיבוי אבל התם שאינו מתכוין להבעיר התחתונות לא קמ"ל כיון דהוי פסיק רישיה חייב ובההיא דהחותה גחלים להתחמם והובערו מאליהן נקט הא ר"י דאמר מלאכה שאינה צריכה לגופה חייב הא ר"ש כו' אע"ג דאין כוונתו להבעיר מדפטר ר"ש דאי כוונתו להבעיר הויא צריכה לגופה מ"מ כיון דניחא ליה בהך הבערה לא קרינן ביה שאינו מתכוין ולהכי לא נקט לישנא דאין מתכוין אבל בנתכוין לכבות העליונות לא ניחא ליה בהבערת התחתונות כלל שהרי בא לכבות שייך לישנא דאין מתכוין אע"ג דהוי פסיק רישיה ור"ש שרי בחותה גחלים להתחמם אע"ג דבפרק הבונה (לקמן קג. ושם) משמע דהתולש לאכילה או לבהמה בארעא דידיה חייב חטאת בכל שהוא אע"ג דאין מתכוין ליפות הקרקע לא דמי לכל מלאכה שאינה צריכה לגופה כגון חותה להתחמם דהתם אע"פ שאין מתכוין ליפות אנן סהדי דניחא ליה אבל בחותה אינו נהנה בהבערה זו דבלא הבערה זו יתחמם וכיון שאינו נהנה (א) בברור לא נתכוון להבעיר והויא מלאכה שאינה צריכה לו [י]:

לא שנו אלא להפשיר. מתוך פי' הקונט' משמע דמפרש הסוגיא כן לא שנו אלא בדבר שאין שייך צירוף אלא פישור כגון מיחם שפינהו אבל לצרף פי' בדבר ששייך צירוף כגון מיחם שפינה ממנו מים אסור ושמואל אמר אף לצרף כלומר אף בדבר ששייך צירוף מותר ומשמע אפי' במתכוין ולהכי פריך ולצרף לכתחילה מי שרי אלא אי איתמר הכי איתמר לא שנו דפינה ממנו מים שרי לתת לתוכו צונן אלא שיעור להפשיר ולא לצרף כגון שלא מלאהו כולו דליכא צירוף עד שימלאנו על כל גדותיו ורב מפרש פינהו כרב אדא והא דפריך לעיל והא מצרף משום דמשמע ליה הא דקאמר אבל נותן לתוכו מים מרובין שיש שיעור לצרף מדקאמר מרובים אבל כשפינהו והמים בתוכו א"א להיות צירוף ודוחק ור"י מפרש בענין אחר דפינהו נמי איכא צירוף כשמילאהו ובפינה ממנו מים כל שהוא יש בו שיעור לצרף מדפריך לעיל והלא מצרף ולא משני שאין בו שיעור לצרף ועוד מדקאמר אביי אבל מיחם שפינה ממנו מים אסור מפני שמצרף משמע דהתם פשיטא ליה שמצרף ולא שייך לפלוגי ביה דבכל שהוא הוא מצרף וה"פ לא שנו אלא להפשיר פי' שמתכוין להפשיר השתא סבירא ליה דמיירי רב אפי' בשיעור לצרף אבל לצרף שמתכוין לצרף אסור כר"ש ומפרש פינהו שפינה ממנו מים כרב אדא אי נמי פינהו עם המים כאביי ומיירי כשיש בו שיעור לצרף כגון שממלאו כולו מים צוננין דאע"ג דהמים חמין שבתוכו לא נסתלקו יש שיעור לצרף ומחלק בין אין מתכוין למתכוין כר"ש ולא כאביי דמוקי לה באין בו שיעור לצרף וכר' יהודה וכי פריך אליבא דשמואל ולצרף לכתחילה מי שרי ה"ה דהוה מצי למיפרך אליבא דרב כיון דסבר דהלכה כרבי יהודה דהיינו בגרירה בדבר שאינו מתכוין מאי דוחקיה לאוקמי מתני' כשיש בו שיעור לצרף וכר"ש לוקמה כשאין בו שיעור לצרף כאביי וכרבי יהודה דסבירא ליה כוותיה אלא אדשמואל קפריך דעדיפא ליה אלא אי איתמר הכי איתמר השתא מפרש מתניתין כאביי לגמרי שפינהו עם המים וה"פ לא שנו אלא שיעור להפשיר שאינו ממלא המיחם על כל גדותיו אבל שיעור לצרף אע"פ שאינו מתכוין אלא להפשיר אסור כרבי יהודה דסבר כוותיה אבל פינה ממנו מים לעולם אסור דבכל ענין יש שיעור לצרף כדפי' וכי קאמר אביי אבל מיחם שפינה ממנו מים כו' ה"ה דמצי למימר בד"א בשיעור להפשיר אבל שיעור לצרף אסור אלא ניחא ליה למינקט האי לישנא משום דמלשון פינהו דייק דאתיא כר' יהודה ושמואל אומר אף שיעור לצרף מותר כר"ש וא"ת מדקאמר שמואל אף שיעור לצרף אם כן מוקי מתני' כאביי דדייק שפינהו דלרב אדא דמפרש שפינה ממנו מים לעולם יש שיעור לצרף ומאי אף שיעור לצרף דקאמר שמואל וכיון דמפרש כאביי אם כן נידוק דווקא פינהו הא פינה ממנו אסור כר"י וי"ל דשמואל קאי אמילתיה דרב וקאמר אף שיעור לצרף שרי דאנא סבירא לי כר"ש מוקמי' מתני' כוותיה דרב אדא כשפינה ממנו מים ויש לעולם שיעור לצרף:

לא שנו אלא להפשיר. פ"ה דרב משמע ליה מתני' פינהו כרב אדא שפינה ממנו המים ושיעור להפשיר כשלא מלאהו ושיעור לצרף כשמילאהו וקשה כי פריך לעיל והלא מצרף לימא כשלא מילאהו ועוד מדקאמר אביי אבל מיחם שפינה ממנו מים לא יתן לתוכו כל עיקר מפני שהוא מצרף משמע בכל ענין הוא מצרף אפי' לא מילאהו וי"ל דמשמע ליה פינהו כאביי וקאמר לא שנו אלא שיעור להפשיר שלא נתן בו מים כ"כ שיצטננו החמין אבל נתן בו מים כ"כ שיצטננו החמין אסור ואע"פ שאינו מתכוין לצרף מיתסר (תו"י בשם מהר"ם ממירזבורג):

אפילו

רבינו חננאל

אוקמא מיחם שפינהו מע"ג הכירה ויש בו מים חמין לא יתן לתוכו מים מועטין בשביל שיחמו אבל נותן לתוכו מים מרובין כדי לפשר. פינה ממנה החמין לא יתן לתוכו מים כל עיקר מפני (הוא) שמצרף. ור' יהודה הוא דאמר דבר שאין מתכוון אסור אמר רב לא שנו אלא מים מועטין שיעור להפשיר אבל מים מרובין שיעור לצרף אסור. פי' צירוף הכלי בעת שיתחמם נעשה כגחלת וכשמביאו בשעת גמר מלאכתו בצונן מחזקתו ולוטש פניו ונמצא לו כמו צירוף רב אמר שיעור לצרף אסור ושמואל אמר אפילו שיעור לצרף נמי מותר א) ואוקמה שמואל כר"ש ורב אדא בר מתנה כר' שמעון ודאביי נמי בבא דרישא (נמי) קאי כשמואל וסוגינא כשמואל אליבא דר"ש [ור' אדא] ואקשינן

חשק שלמה על רבינו חננאל

א) מן ואוקמה עד קאי כשמואל הובא גם ברמב"ן במלחמת בשם ר"ח:

רב נסים גאון

ר"ש היא דאמר דבר שאינו מתכוין מותר וזה העיקר בפרק במה מדליקין (דף כט) דתניא ר"ש אומר גורר אדם מטה כסא וספסל ובלבד שלא יתכוין לעשות חריץ. ור' יהודה דאמר דבר שאין מתכוין אסור עיקר דברי ר' יהודה במשנה במס' יו"ט בפ' יום טוב שחל להיות ערב שבת (דף כג) דתנן ר' יהודה אומר אין מקרדין ביו"ט מפני שהוא עושה חבורה ובגמ' גרסי ר' יהודה סבר דבר שאין מתכוין אסור ובמס' בכורות בפ' כל פסולי המוקדשין (דף לג) שנינו בכור שאחזו דם אפילו מת אין מקיזין לו את הדם דברי ר' יהודה כו' ר' שמעון אומר יקיז אע"פ שהוא עושה מום הרי מיכן תדע שר' יהודה סבר דבר שאין מתכוין אסור ור"ש [סבר] דבר שאין מתכוין מותר:

מסורת הש"ס

א) [לעיל כט: ביצה כג: כתובות ה: פסחים כה: נזיר מב. לקמן ג. כריתות כ:], ב) [כתובות עז:], ג) [ערובין כ:], ד) [לקמן קכו:], ה) [פנו כלים מפני הטומאה ברכות כח:], ו) [עפר ועתיד לפנותו עירובין עט.], ז) דף כב., ח) [לעיל כב.], ט) [ע"ש], י) [וע"ע תוספות בסמוך ד"ה ל"ש ותוס' לקמן מב. ד"ה אפי' ותוס' לקמן קג. ד"ה לא צריכא ותוס' לקמן קיא. ד"ה האי ותוספות יומא לד: ד"ה ה"מ ותוספות סוכה לג: ד"ה מודה ותוספות כתובות ה: ד"ה את"ל ועוד שם ו. ד"ה האי ותוס' כריתות כ: ד"ה סבירא].

תוספות ישנים

א) לסברת התוס' אליבא דרש"י דאינו מצרף אלא כשהוא מלא ממש צריך למחוק תיבות כל עיקר:

הגהות הב"ח

(א) תום' סוף ד"ה מיחם וכו' וכיון שאינו נהנה. נ"ב ע"ל פ' כלל גדול דף עה בד"ה טפי ניחא:

גליון הש"ס

תום' ד"ה מיחם שפינה וכו' ליה ר"י דבר שאינו מתכוין אלא מדרבנן. וכ"כ רש"י לקמן קכא ע"ב ד"ה לפי תומו. ועיין לקמן דף לה ע"א תוס' ד"ה המכבד:

ליקוטי רש"י

והלא מצרף. הנותן ברזל מן האש למים מצרפו מחזקו ומקשהו [יומא לד:]. מצרף בלשון חכמים מחזק ומקשה כלי חרס וכלי מתכות בדבר המחזקן בין (ביד) [במים] בין באור [ביצה לב.]. ר' שמעון היא כו'. פלוגתא דרבי יהודה ורבי שמעון במסכת שבת (כב.) בגרירת מטה כסא וספסל ובמסכת ביצה (כג:) [פסחים כה:].

The Gemara accepts that a large quantity of cold water will not be cooked in the kettle, but points out that pouring it in may violate a different prohibition:

וְהָלֹא מְצָרֵף – But by pouring a large quantity of cold water into a hot, empty kettle, **one is hardening** the steel of the kettle, which is forbidden on the Sabbath.[1] – ? –

The Gemara answers:

רַבִּי שִׁמְעוֹן הִיא – [The Mishnah] is reflective of the view of **R' Shimon, דְּאָמַר דָּבָר שֶׁאֵין מִתְכַּוֵּין מוּתָּר – who said** that **something that is unintended is permitted,** and in this case one does not intend to harden the steel.[2]

Rav Adda bar Masna's interpretation of the Mishnah is challenged:

מַתְקִיף לָהּ אַבָּיֵי – Abaye objected to this: מִידִי מֵיחַם שֶׁפִּינָה מִמֶּנּוּ מַיִם קָתָנֵי – Does [the Mishnah] state: ***a kettle from which the water was cleared?*** **מֵיחַם שֶׁפִּינָּהוּ קָתָנֵי** – No! **It states: A KETTLE THAT WAS CLEARED,** implying that the kettle itself was cleared, not that the water was cleared from it.[3] – ? –

Abaye offers his own interpretation of the Mishnah:

אֶלָּא אָמַר אַבָּיֵי – Rather, said Abaye: הָכִי קָאָמַר – This is what [the Mishnah] means to **say: הַמֵּיחַם שֶׁפִּינָּהוּ וְיֵשׁ בּוֹ מַיִם חַמִּין –** Concerning **a kettle that was cleared** from the fire **and** which still **contains hot water, לֹא יִתֵּן לְתוֹכוֹ מַיִם מוּעָטִין בִּשְׁבִיל שֶׁיָּחוֹמּוּ – one may not put a small quantity of** cold **water into it in order to heat it, אֲבָל נוֹתֵן לְתוֹכוֹ מַיִם מְרוּבִּים כְּדֵי לְהַפְשִׁירָן – but one may put a large quantity of** cold **water into it in order to** merely **warm it.**[4] **וּמֵיחַם שֶׁפִּינָּה מִמֶּנּוּ מַיִם – And** this implies that in the case of **a kettle from which** the hot **water** ***was*** **cleared, לֹא יִתֵּן לְתוֹכוֹ מַיִם כָּל עִיקָּר – one may not put** cold **water into it at all,** even a large quantity that will merely be warmed, **מִפְּנֵי שֶׁמְּצָרֵף – because** by doing so **he hardens** the steel of the kettle.[5] **וְרַבִּי יְהוּדָה הִיא – And** according to this interpretation, **[the Mishnah] is** reflective of the view of **R' Yehudah, דְּאָמַר דָּבָר שֶׁאֵין מִתְכַּוֵּין אָסוּר – who said** that **something that is unintended is prohibited.**[6] Thus, although the person does not intend to harden the steel, he is prohibited from filling the kettle with cold water.

The Gemara cites a related dispute:

אָמַר רַב – Rav said: לֹא שָׁנוּ אֶלָּא לְהַפְשִׁיר – They taught that it is permissible to add a large quantity of cold water to a hot kettle **only** in order **to warm** the water, **אֲבָל לְצָרֵף אָסוּר – but hardening** the kettle **is forbidden.** Accordingly, the Mishnah must be dealing with a kettle that still contains hot water and will not be hardened when the cold water is added.[7] **וּשְׁמוּאֵל אָמַר – But Shmuel said: אֲפִילּוּ לְצָרֵף נַמִי מוּתָּר – It is permissible even to harden** the kettle. Accordingly, the Mishnah refers even to an empty kettle.[8]

The Gemara questions Shmuel's view:

לְצָרֵף לְכַתְּחִילָּה מִי שָׁרֵי – But is it permissible to initially set out to **harden** the kettle?[9]

Due to this difficulty, the Gemara revises the statements of Rav and Shmuel:

אֶלָּא אִי אִיתְּמַר הָכִי אִיתְּמַר – Rather, if anything **was stated** by Rav and Shmuel **this is what was stated: אָמַר רַב – Rav said: לֹא שָׁנוּ אֶלָּא שִׁיעוּר לְהַפְשִׁיר – They taught** that it is permissible to add cold water to a hot kettle **only** concerning **a measure** of water that is great enough **to be warmed, אֲבָל שִׁיעוּר לְצָרֵף אָסוּר –**

NOTES

1. Steel is hardened by heating it and then quenching it with cold water. It forbidden to do this to a steel utensil on the Sabbath, as it is a form of the *melachah* of מַכֶּה בְּפַטִּישׁ, *striking the final blow,* i.e. putting the finishing touch on an otherwise complete utensil. In our case, since the kettle was heated on the fire, it likely became so hot that its metal softened somewhat and by pouring in a large quantity of cold water one will harden it. How can this be permitted? (see *Rashi, Tosafos* here ד״ה והלא מצרף and to *Yoma* 34b ד״ה הני מילי; cf. *Rambam, Hil. Shabbos,* 12:2).

2. When a person performs a permissible act and as a result a second, forbidden act also takes place, this second act is classified as דָּבָר שֶׁאֵין מִתְכַּוֵּין, *something that is unintended.* The person was *aware* that the prohibited act might occur but he did not *intend* for it to occur. According to R' Shimon, one is not required to refrain from the permissible act even though he knows that the forbidden act may result, provided he does not intend for it. [R' Shimon's view in this regard is disputed by R' Yehudah (see above, 40a note 13).] In our case, then, according to R' Shimon, one may pour a large quantity of cold water into a heated kettle if his intention is merely to warm the water, even though he might thereby be hardening the steel.

It is important to note, however, that R' Shimon does not permit the performance of the permissible act if the forbidden consequence is inevitable [פְּסִיק רֵישֵׁיהּ]. In our case, it is not inevitable that the kettle will be hardened, for several reasons. Firstly, the kettle may have been fully hardened before this heating. Secondly, it may not have been heated sufficiently this time for it to be hardened by the cold water (*Milchamos Hashem, Rashba, Ritva MHK* ed., *Ran;* see also *Beur Halachah* 316:3 ד״ה ולכן; cf. *Maggid Mishneh, Hil. Shabbos* 12:2).

3. Although the expression שֶׁפִּינָּהוּ, *that was cleared,* can also mean that it was cleared of something it had contained, it is usually used in the sense of clearing an item from its previous location. Therefore, if the Mishnah had meant that the kettle was cleared of its water, it would have been more specific (*Tosafos* ד״ה מידי; see *Pnei Yehoshua* and *Chidushei R' Elazar Moshe Horowitz*).

4. I.e. one may pour in a quantity of water that is so great that the resulting mixture will not be so hot that the hand recoils from it (*Mishnah Berurah* 318:84). [One should not pour the cold water in small increments that might be cooked immediately, but should pour all of it at once (*Chayei Adam* cited by *Mishnah Berurah* ibid. §83; see *Pnei Yehoshua* to end of 41a).]

5. By focusing on a case in which the kettle was removed from the flame but the hot water was *not* removed from it, the Mishnah implies that if the hot water would be removed a different rule would apply. Now, the Mishnah certainly does not mean that it is permissible to add a small quantity of water to a hot kettle that is empty, since the water will thereby be cooked. Perforce, the Mishnah means to forbid even adding a large quantity of water to the hot, empty kettle, because the steel is likely to be hardened, and the Mishnah forbids this even though the person does not intend to harden the steel (see *Tosafos* ד״ה מיחם and *Ritva MHK* ed.). Abaye goes on to explain the basis for this ruling.

6. I.e. one must refrain from a permissible act if he knows that it might result in the accomplishment of a prohibited *melachah* (see 40a note 13; for further clarification, see our General Introduction to Tractate *Shabbos,* printed in vol. I). [Note that *Rashi* states below (ד״ה אלא and ד״ה אפילו) that a kettle will not be hardened unless it is filled to the brim with cold water (see note 10). This creates a degree of difficulty with explaining Abaye's statement here: לֹא יִתֵּן לְתוֹכוֹ מַיִם כָּל עִיקָּר, *one may not pour* cold *water into it* ***at all.*** *Tos. Yeshanim* propose deleting the words *at all* from the text. However, it is possible that Abaye merely employs this expression to contrast this case with that of a kettle containing hot water, to which it is permitted to add a large quantity of cold water.]

7. Rav's view corresponds to that of Abaye in the preceding Gemara.

8. Shmuel's view corresponds to that of Rav Adda bar Masna above.

9. Shmuel's wording implies that it is permissible even to harden the kettle deliberately (see *Tosafos* ד״ה לא שנו). But this is untenable, as even R' Shimon would permit filling the kettle with water only when one's primary intent is to warm the water and the hardening of the kettle is merely an unintended result (as explained in note 2).

והלא מצרף ר' שמעון היא דאמר [א] דבר שאין מתכוין מותר מתקיף לה אביי מידי מיחם שפינה ממנו מים קתני מיחם שפינהו קתני אלא אמר אביי הכי קאמר המיחם שפינהו ויש בו מים חמין לא יתן לתוכו מים מועטין בשביל שיחומו אבל נותן לתוכו מים מרובים כדי להפשירן ומיחם שפינה ממנו מים לא יתן לתוכו מים א) כל עיקר מפני שמצרף ור' יהודה היא דאמר דבר שאין מתכוין אסור אמר רב ל"ש אלא להפשיר אבל לצרף אסור ושמואל אמר אפי' לצרף נמי מותר לצרף לכתחילה מי שרי אלא אי איתמר הכי איתמר אמר רב לא שנו אלא שיעור להפשיר אבל שיעור לצרף אסור ושמואל אמר אפי' שיעור לצרף מותר

רש"י

והלא מצרף. כשכלי מתכות חם ונותן לתוכו צונן מחזקים את הכלי וזו היא גמר מלאכת הצורפין שרתיחת האור מפעפעתו וקרוב להשבר והמים מצרפין פעפועיו שולדי"ר בלע"ז: **שפינהו.** משמע שפינהו לעצמו מעל האור: **אבל לצרף.** שפינהו ממנו החמין: **הכי איתמר לא שנו.** דפינהו שרי לתת לתוכו צונן: **אלא שיעור להפשיר.** ולא לצרף כגון שלא מלאהו כולו ורב משמע ליה פינהו כרב אדא שפינה ממנו חמין: **אפילו שיעור לצרף.** שמלאהו כולו: מותר

תוספות

והלא מצרף. וליכא לשנויי בשלא הגיע לצירוף כדמשני בפרק אמר להם הממונה (יומא דף לד: ושם) דסתם מיחם הגיע לצירוף הוא: **מידי** מיחם שפינה הימנו מים קתני המיחם שפינהו קתני. תימה והכתיב ופנו את הבית (ויקרא יד) ואנכי פניתי הבית (בראשית כד) סולו פנו דרך (ישעיה מ) וכן בש"ס [ב] פנו מקום לבר ליואי שאינו מפנה אלא מה שבתוכם וי"ל כיון דבכמה מקומות החכר פינוי על הדבר המפנין כגון [ג] המפנה חפציו מזוית לזוית [ד] מפנין ד' וה' קופות [ה] פנו כלים (מבית) הטומאה [ו] (תנן) ועתיד לפנותו לא הוה ליה למנקט פינהו אלא פנה ממנו מים כיון דאיכא למיטעי: **מיחם** שפינה ממנו מים לא יתן לתוכו מים כל עיקר מפני שמצרף ורבי יהודה היא. אבל לר"ש שרי אע"פ שמצרף כיון דאינו מבשל כגון שיש בו מים הרבה שאין המיחם מספיק לבשל רוב המים שבתוכו כדאשכחן בפרק אמר להם הממונה (יומא דף לד: ושם) שאין מבשל ומצרף דקאמר רבי יהודה מביאין עששיות של ברזל ומטילין לתוך המים שתפיג צינתן ואם היה מבשל היה אסור ואפ"ה פריך והלא מצרף ואע"ג דאביי סבר כר"ש דהא אמר לעיל [ז] כל מילי דמר עביד כרב לבר מהני תלת דעביד כשמואל וחד מינייהו הלכה כר"ש בגרירה ומסתמא אביי כרביה סבירא ליה מ"מ מוקי מתניתין כרבי יהודה משום דקשיא ליה מידי מיחם שפינה ממנו מים קתני ורב אדא לא חייש לקושיית אביי ומוקי לה כהלכתא כר"ש ול"ג לעיל אמר רב אדא בר מתנא אמר רב דרב סבר [ח] כר' יהודה בגרירה ועוד דבהדיא מוקי בסמוך מתני' כר' יהודה וצ"ל דלא הוי פסיק רישיה שיכול להיות שלא יצרף דבפסיק רישיה מודה ר"ש והא דפריך והלא מצרף ה"ק והלא שמא מצרף קשה דהכא משמע דבצירוף אסר ר' יהודה נמי דבר שאין מתכוין ובפרק אמר להם הממונה גרים רש"י ה"מ דאורייתא אבל הכא צירוף דרבנן ול"ג אין שבות במקדש ומפרש דדוקא בדבר שהוא מן התורה אית ליה לר' יהודה דבר שאין מתכוין אסור אבל בצירוף שהוא דרבנן לא ומיהו בלאו הכי קשה לפי' דהא ר' יהודה אסר בגרירה במתניתין דבילה דפרק י"ט (דף כג:) דתנן ואינה נגררת אלא ע"ג כלים דמשמע אבל ע"ג קרקע לא ומוקמינא כר' יהודה דאסר באין מתכוין אע"ג דבגרירה ליכא איסורא דאורייתא אפי' במתכוין כדמשמע בסוף פירקין דהוי חורש כלאחר יד ועוד דשמעתא דהתם קשה דמשני אביי אפי' תימא כשהגיע לצירוף דבר שאינו מתכוין מותר ופריך ומי אמר אביי הכי והתניא ימול בשר ערלתו אפי' במקום בהרת יקוץ דברי רבי אושעיא והוינן בה קרא ל"ל ואמר אביי לא נצרכה אלא לר' יהודה דאמר דבר שאין מתכוין אסור והשתא אמאי לא מייתי ההיא דבילה דהיא משנה שלמה דאסר ר' יהודה דבר שאין מתכוין ומייתי מילתיה דאביי ועוד מותק הספר דגרס ואין שבות במקדש לכך נראה לפרש התם אביי אמר אפילו כו' דבר שאין מתכוין מותר פי' מותר לר' יהודה ולא אסר ° ליה ר' יהודה דבר שאין מתכוין אלא מדרבנן ופריך מימול בשר ערלתו דמוקי אביי דאיצטריך לר' יהודה קרא א"כ ש"מ דאסר ר' יהודה אין מתכוין מן התורה ומשני וה"ג ה"מ בכל התורה כולה פי' בכל התורה כולה חוץ משבת אסור מן התורה אבל צירוף דגבי שבת לא אסור אין מתכוין אלא מדרבנן דכיון דאין מתכוין לא הויא מלאכת מחשבת ושרי דאין שבות במקדש והשתא א"ש הכא וסוגיא דהתם וקשה דבפרק ספק אכל (כריתות דף כ: [ט] ושם) א"ר אשי כגון שנתכוין לכבות העליונות והובערו התחתונות מאליהן ת"ק סבר לה כר"י דאמר דבר שאין מתכוין אסור ולכך קאמר דחייב חטאת ומאן דפטר כר"ש דאמר דבר שאין מתכוין מותר אלמא משמע דדבר שאין מתכוין אסור לר"י אפי' בשבת מן התורה וי"ל דהתם הוי פסיק רישיה שאי אפשר כלל לכבות העליונות אם לא יובערו התחתונות וחשיב מלאכת מחשבת ואע"ג דהוי פסיק רישיה פטר ר"ש משום דהויא מלאכה שאינה צריכה לגופה דאינו צריך להבערת התחתונות והא דנקט לישנא מתכוין ושאין מתכוין ולא נקט ת"ק כר"י דאמר מלאכה שאינה צריכה כו' משום רבותא דר"י נקט דלא תימא דלא מחייב ר"י מלאכה שאינה צריכה לגופה אלא במקום שמתכוין לעשות המלאכה כגון מכבה גחלת של עץ שלא יזוקו רבים שמתכוין לכיבוי אבל התם שאינו מתכוין להבעיר התחתונות לא קמ"ל כיון דהוי פסיק רישיה חייב וההיא דהחותה גחלים להתחמם והובערו מאליהן נקט הא ר"י דאמר מלאכה שאינה צריכה לגופה חייב הא ר"ש כו' אע"ג דאין כוונתו להבעיר מדפטר ר"ש דאי כוונתו להבעיר הויא צריכה לגופה מ"מ כיון דניחא ליה בהך הבערה לא קרינן ביה שאינו מתכוין ולהכי לא נקט לישנא דאין מתכוין אבל בנתכוין לכבות העליונות לא ניחא ליה בהבערת התחתונות כלל שהרי בא לכבות שייך לישנא דאין מתכוין אע"ג דהוי פסיק רישיה ור"ש שרי בחותה גחלים להתחמם אע"ג דבפרק הבונה (לקמן קג. ושם) משמע דהתולש לאכילה או לבהמה בארעא דידיה חייב חטאת בכל שהוא אע"ג דאין מתכוין ליפות הקרקע לא דמי לכל מלאכה שאינה צריכה לגופה כגון חותה להתחמם דהתם אע"פ שאין מתכוין ליפות אנן סהדי דניחא ליה אבל בחותה אינו נהנה בהבערה זו דבלא הבערה זו יתחמם וכיון שאינו נהנה (א) בברור לא נתכוון להבעיר והויא מלאכה שאינה צריכה לו [י]: **לא שנו אלא להפשיר.** מתוך פי' הקונט' משמע דמפרש הסוגיא כן לא שנו אלא בדבר שאין שייך צירוף אלא פישור כגון מיחם שפינו ממנו מים אסור ושמואל אמר אף לצרף כלומר אף בדבר ששייך צירוף מותר ומשמע אפי' במתכוין ולהכי פריך ולצרף לכתחילה מי שרי אלא אי איתמר הכי איתמר לא שנו דפינה ממנו מים שרי לתת לתוכו צונן אלא שיעור להפשיר ולא לצרף כגון שלא מלאהו כולו דליכא צירוף עד שימלאנו על כל גדותיו ורב מפרש פינהו כרב אדא והא דפריך לעיל והא מצרף משום דמשמע ליה הא דקאמר אבל נותן לתוכו מים מרובין שיש שיעור לצרף מדקאמר מרובים אבל כשפינהו והמים בתוכו א"א להיות צירוף ודוחק ור"י מפרש בענין אחר דפינהו נמי איכא צירוף כשמילאהו ובפינה ממנו מים כל שהוא יש בו שיעור לצרף מדפריך לעיל והלא מצרף ולא משני שאין בו שיעור לצרף ועוד מדקאמר אביי אבל מיחם שפינה ממנו מים אסור מפני שמצרף משמע דהתם פשיטא ליה שמצרף ולא שייך לפלוגי ביה דבכל שהוא הוא מצרף וה"פ לא שנו אלא להפשיר פי' שמתכוין להפשיר השתא סבירא ליה דמיירי רב אפי' בשיעור לצרף אבל לצרף שמתכוין לצרף אסור כר"ש ומפרש פינהו שפינה ממנו מים כרב אדא אי נמי פינהו עם המים כאביי ומיירי כשיש בו שיעור לצרף כגון שממלאו כולו מים צוננין דאע"ג דהמים חמין שבתוכו לא נסתלקו יש שיעור לצרף ומחלק בין אין מתכוין למתכוין כר"ש ולא כאביי דמוקי לה באין בו שיעור לצרף וכר' יהודה וכי פריך אליבא דשמואל ולצרף לכתחילה מי שרי ה"ה דהוה מצי למיפרך אליבא דרב כיון דסבר דהלכה כרבי יהודה בגרירה דהיינו בדבר שאינו מתכוין מאי דוחקיה לאוקמי מתני' כשיש בו שיעור לצרף וכר"ש לוקמה כשאין בו שיעור לצרף כאביי וכרבי יהודה דסבירא ליה כוותיה אלא אדשמואל קפריך דעדיפא ליה אלא אי איתמר הכי איתמר השתא מפרש מתניתין כאביי לגמרי שפינהו עם המים וה"פ לא שנו אלא שיעור להפשיר שאינו ממלא המיחם על כל גדותיו אבל שיעור לצרף אע"פ שאינו מתכוין אלא להפשיר אסור כרבי יהודה דסבר כוותיה אבל פינה ממנו מים לעולם אסור דבכל ענין יש שיעור לצרף כדפי' וכי קאמר אביי אבל מיחם שפינה ממנו מים כו' ה"ה דמצי למימר בד"א בשיעור להפשיר אבל שיעור לצרף אסור אלא ניחא ליה למינקט האי לישנא משום דמלשון פינהו דייק דאתיא כר' יהודה שמואל אומר אף שיעור לצרף מותר כר"ש וא"ת מדקאמר שמואל אף שיעור לצרף אם כן מוקי מתני' כאביי דדייק שפינהו דלרב אדא דמפרש שפינה ממנו מים לעולם יש שיעור לצרף ומאי אף שיעור לצרף דקאמר שמואל וכיון דמפרש כאביי אם כן נידוק דווקא פינהו הא פינה ממנו אסור כר"י וי"ל דשמואל קאי אמילתיה דרב וקאמר אף שיעור לצרף שרי דאנא סבירא לי כר"ש מוקמי' מתני' כוותיה דרב אדא כשפינה ממנו מים ויש לעולם שיעור לצרף:

לא שנו אלא להפשיר. פ"ה דרב משמע ליה מתני' פינהו כרב אדא שפינה ממנו המים ושיעור להפשיר כשלא מלאהו ושיעור לצרף כשמילאהו וקשה כי פריך לעיל והלא מצרף לימא כשלא מילאהו ועוד מדקאמר אביי אבל מיחם שפינה ממנו מים לא יתן לתוכו כל עיקר מפני שהוא מצרף משמע בכל ענין הוא מצרף אפי' לא מילאהו וי"ל דמשמע ליה פינהו כאביי וקאמר לא שנו אלא שיעור להפשיר שלא נתן בו מים כ"כ שיצטנו החמין אבל נתן בו מים כ"כ שיצטנו החמין אסור ואע"פ שאינו מתכוין לצרף מיתסר (תו"י בשם מהר"ש משירבורג):

אפילו

רבינו חננאל

אוקמא מיחם שפינהו מע"ג הכירה ויש בו מים חמין לא יתן לתוכו מים מועטין בשביל שיחמו אבל נותן לתוכו מים מרובין כדי לפשר. פינה ממנה החמין לא יתן לתוכו מים כל עיקר מפני (הוא) שמצרף. ור' יהודה הוא דאמר דבר שאין מתכוון אסור אמר רב לא שנו אלא מים מועטין שיעור להפשיר אבל מים מרובין שיעור לצרף אסור. פי' צירוף הכלי בעת שיתחמם נעשה כגחלת וכשמביאו בשעת גמר מלאכתו בצונן מחזקתו ולוטש פניו ונמצא לו כמו צירוף רב אמר שיעור לצרף אסור ושמואל אמר אפילו שיעור לצרף נמי מותר א) ואוקמה שמואל כר"ש ורב אדא בר מתנה כר' שמעון ודאביי נמי בבא דרישא (נמי) קאי כשמואל וסוגינא כשמואל אליבא דר"ש [ור' אדא] ואקשינן

חשק שלמה על רבינו חננאל

א) מן ואוקמה עד קאי כשמואל הובא גם ברמב"ן במלחמת בשם ר"ח:

רב נסים גאון

ר"ש היא דאמר דבר שאינו מתכוין מותר וזה העיקר בפרק במה מדליקין (דף כט) דתניא ר"ש אומר גורר אדם מטה כסא וספסל ובלבד שלא יתכוין לעשות חריץ. ור' יהודה דאמר דבר שאין מתכוין אסור עיקר דברי ר' יהודה במשנה במס' יו"ט בפ' יום טוב שחל להיות ערב שבת (דף כג) דתנן ר' יהודה אומר אין מקרדין ביו"ט מפני שהוא עושה חבורה ובגמ' גרסי ר' יהודה סבר דבר שאין מתכוין אסור ובמס' בכורות בפ' כל פסולי המוקדשין (דף לג) שנינו בכור שאחזו דם אפילו מת אין מקיזין לו את הדם דברי ר' יהודה כו' ר' שמעון אומר יקיז אע"פ שהוא עושה מום הרי מיכן תדע שר' יהודה סבר דבר שאין מתכוין אסור ור"ש [סבר] דבר שאין מתכוין מותר:

מסורת הש"ס

א) [לעיל כט: בילה כג: כתובות ה: פסחים כה: מיר מב. לקמן ג. כריתות כ:], ב) [כתובות עז:], ג) [ערובין כ:], ד) [לקמן קכו:], ה) [פנו כלים מפני הטומאה ברכות כח:], ו) [עפר ועתיד לפנותו עירובין עט.], ז) דף כב., ח) [לעיל כב.], ט) [ע"ש], י) [וע"ע תוספות בסמוך ד"ה ל"ש ותוס' לקמן מב. ד"ה אפי' ותוס' לקמן קג. ד"ה לא צריכא ותוס' לקמן קיא. ד"ה האי ותוספות יומא לד: ד"ה ה"מ ותוספות סוכה לג: ד"ה מודה ותוספות כתובות ה: ד"ה אמ"ל ועוד שם ו. ד"ה האי ותוס' כריתות כ: ד"ה סבירא].

תוספות ישנים

א) לסברת התוס' אליבא דרש"י דאינו מצרף אלא כשהוא מלא ממש צריך למחוק תיבות כל עיקר:

הגהות הב"ח

(א) תוס' סוף ד"ה מיחם וכו' וכיון שאינו נהנה. נ"ב ע"ל פ' כלל גדול דף עה בד"ה טפי ניחא:

גליון הש"ס

תוס' ד"ה מיחם שפינה וכו' ליה ר"י דבר שאינו מתכוין אלא מדרבנן. וכ"כ רש"י לקמן קכא ע"ב ד"ה לפי תומו. ועיין לקמן דף נה ע"א תוס' ד"ה המכבד:

ליקוטי רש"י

והלא מצרף. הנותן ברזל מן האש למים מצרפו מחזקו ומקשהו [יומא לד:]. מצרף בלשון חכמים מחזק ומקשה כלי חרס וכלי מתכות בדבר המחזקן בין (ביד) [במים] בין באור [ביצה לב.]. **ר' שמעון היא כו'.** פלוגתא דרבי יהודה ורבי שמעון במסכת שבת (כב.) בגרירת מטה כסא וספסל ובמסכת בילה (כג:) [פסחים כה:].

but adding **a measure** that is great enough **to harden** the kettle **is forbidden.**[10] **וּשְׁמוּאֵל אָמַר** – **But Shmuel said:** **אֲפִילוּ שִׁיעוּר לְצָרֵף** – Even adding **a measure** of cold water that is great enough **to harden** the kettle[11]

NOTES

10. A kettle will not be hardened unless it is filled to the brim with cold water. [The reason is that only the metal near the rim becomes hot enough to be softened by the fire. The lower part of the kettle, which contains the water, is prevented by the water from being heated intensely and therefore does not need hardening (*Pnei Yehoshua*).] Now, Rav understands the Mishnah as dealing with an empty kettle, for he agrees with Rav Adda bar Masna's view that this is the implication of the expression, *a kettle that was cleared.* However, Rav holds that something that is unintended is forbidden, in accordance with the view of R' Yehudah. Therefore, Rav interprets the Mishnah as meaning that it is permissible to add a measure of water that is so great that it will merely be warmed but not heated; however, it is forbidden to fill the kettle to the brim, since it might thereby be hardened (*Rashi,* as elaborated by *Tosafos* ד״ה לא שנו; cf. *Tosafos*).

11. I.e. filling it to the brim (*Rashi*).

מוּתָּר – **is permissible,** provided it is not the person's intent to harden it.

The Gemara questions this version of Shmuel's statement:

לְמֵימְרָא דִשְׁמוּאֵל כְּרַבִּי שִׁמְעוֹן סְבִירָא לֵיהּ – Is this **to say that Shmuel concurs with** the opinion of **R' Shimon** that something that is unintended is permitted? וְהָאָמַר שְׁמוּאֵל – **But Shmuel said:** מְכַבִּין גַּחֶלֶת שֶׁל מַתֶּכֶת בִּרְשׁוּת הָרַבִּים – **One may extinguish a piece of burning metal** that is lying **in the public domain** בִּשְׁבִיל שֶׁלֹּא יִזּוֹקוּ בָּהּ רַבִּים – **so that the public not be harmed by it,** אֲבָל לֹא גַּחֶלֶת שֶׁל עֵץ – **but not a piece of burning wood.**[1] וְאִי סַלְקָא דַעְתָּךְ סָבַר לָהּ כְּרַבִּי שִׁמְעוֹן – **Now, if you should think that [Shmuel] concurs with R' Shimon,** אֲפִילּוּ שֶׁל עֵץ נַמִּי – he should permit extinguishing **even** a burning piece **of wood as well.**[2] – ? –

The Gemara resolves the difficulty:

בְּדָבָר שֶׁאֵין מִתְכַּוֵּין – **With regard to** the issue of **something that is unintended,** סָבַר לָהּ כְּרַבִּי שִׁמְעוֹן – **[Shmuel] concurs with R' Shimon** that such an act is permissible. בִּמְלָאכָה שֶׁאֵינָהּ צְרִיכָה לְגוּפָהּ – **With regard to** the issue of **a labor not needed for its defined purpose,** however, סָבַר לָהּ כְּרַבִּי יְהוּדָה – **he concurs with R' Yehudah** that such an act is prohibited Biblically. Therefore, Shmuel prohibits extinguishing a burning piece of wood that is in the public domain but permits filling a hot kettle with enough water to harden it.[3]

Having seen that Shmuel waives the Rabbinical prohibition against extinguishing a piece of burning metal for the sake of public safety, the Gemara draws a conclusion:

אָמַר רָבִינָא – **Ravina said:** הִלְכָּךְ קוֹץ בִּרְשׁוּת הָרַבִּים – **Therefore,** if there is **a thorn in a public domain,** מוֹלִיכוֹ פָּחוֹת פָּחוֹת מֵאַרְבַּע אַמּוֹת – **one may move it less than four** ***amos*** **at a time** to the side of the thoroughfare.[4] וּבְכַרְמְלִית אֲפִילּוּ טוּבָא – **And** if the thorn is **in a** ***karmelis,***[5] one may move it **even many** *amos* at a time.[6]

The Mishnah stated:

אֲבָל נוֹתֵן כוּ׳ – BUT HE MAY PUT **etc.** [cold water into the kettle or into a cup in order to warm it].

The Gemara details the conditions for mixing hot and cold water on the Sabbath:

תָּנוּ רַבָּנָן – **The Rabbis taught in a Baraisa:** נוֹתֵן אָדָם חַמִּין לְתוֹךְ הַצּוֹנֵן – ONE MAY PUT HOT WATER INTO COLD WATER, וְלֹא הַצּוֹנֵן לְתוֹךְ הַחַמִּין – BUT NOT COLD WATER INTO HOT WATER. דִּבְרֵי בֵּית שַׁמַּאי – THESE ARE THE WORDS OF BEIS SHAMMAI.[7]

NOTES

1. The Biblical prohibition of extinguishing a fire applies only to a piece of wood [which actually burns], not to a piece of metal [which merely glows]. Although extinguishing a glowing piece of metal is nevertheless forbidden by Rabbinical decree, the Rabbis did not extend their prohibition to a case in which there is a potential for damage to the public. Extinguishing a burning piece of wood, however, being a Biblical prohibition, is forbidden in all cases (*Rashi;* cf. *Rashba, Ran;* see *Rashi* below, 134a ד״ה בגחלת).

2. The Gemara alludes here to another dispute between R' Shimon and R' Yehudah regarding the purpose for which a forbidden labor must be performed on the Sabbath in order for the performer to be liable. R' Shimon maintains that a *melachah* is prohibited Biblically only if it is done to achieve the creative purpose inherent in the *melachah* itself. A *melachah* performed only in reaction to an undesirable condition – either to prevent it or rectify it – is not one for which the performer is liable (although it is still prohibited Rabbinically). Such a *melachah* is termed מְלָאכָה שֶׁאֵינָהּ צְרִיכָה לְגוּפָהּ, *a labor not needed for its defined purpose.* For example, one who carries boards from the domain they are in to the domain in which they are needed is performing a *melachah* that contributes towards a creative design, namely, the erection of a building. Hence, he has violated the Biblical prohibition against *melachah* and is liable to punishment. One who carries a corpse out of his house, however, is not contributing towards any creative design, since he does not need the corpse in the place he deposits it; he is merely ridding his house of it. R' Shimon therefore maintains that he is not subject to punishment for carrying the corpse out (see *Rashi;* cf. *Tosafos* to 94a ד״ה רבי שמעון; see also General Introduction to Tractate *Shabbos*). R' Yehudah, on the other hand, draws no such distinction. In his view one is liable even for a *melachah* performed not for its own sake.

This same dispute manifests itself in regard to the *melachah* of כִּבּוּי, *extinguishing.* One who extinguishes a flame in order to prevent damage is not involved in a creative process but is, rather, preventing a loss. R' Shimon therefore does not consider this act to be prohibited Biblically. Only one who extinguishes a flame to produce charcoal or to prepare a wick for relighting readily is engaged in achieving a creative purpose through extinguishing (*Rashi*).

Since Shmuel forbids extinguishing a burning piece of wood even to eliminate a public menace, he obviously considers this act to be a Biblical prohibition. Thus, it is clear that Shmuel does not agree with R' Shimon. How, then, can the Gemara suggest that Shmuel concurs with R' Shimon?

3. The Gemara answers that the issues of דָּבָר שֶׁאֵינוֹ מִתְכַּוֵּן, *something that is unintended,* and מְלָאכָה שֶׁאֵינָהּ צְרִיכָה לְגוּפָהּ, *a labor that is not needed for its defined purpose,* are not interdependent. In the former case, the person's intention is not at all for the prohibited act; he is endeavoring to perform a permitted act, and the prohibited act, if it occurs at all, will emerge only as an outgrowth. In the latter case, the person intends to perform the forbidden act; the saving grace is only that his intention is to eliminate a nuisance rather than achieve a creative goal. Hence, while Shmuel may side with the stringent opinion of R' Yehudah in regard to a labor not needed for its defined purpose, he may still agree with the lenient opinion of R' Shimon insofar as something that is unintended.

Indeed, this distinction seems so obvious that *Tosafos* wonder why the Gemara ever equated the issues in the first place. See *Tosafos, Rashba, Ritva MHK* ed. and *Pnei Yehoshua* for some possible resolutions.

4. The Biblical prohibition against carrying an object in a public domain on the Sabbath is violated only by moving it four *amos* at once, without pausing to rest. Moving something by increments of less than four *amos* is only prohibited Rabbinically. Ravina reasons that the Rabbis waived their prohibition in the interests of public safety, as they did in the case of a burning piece of metal (*Rashi;* see also *Mishnah Berurah* 308:77).

5. [I.e. a thoroughfare that does not meet the specifications of a public domain. A public domain (רְשׁוּת הָרַבִּים) is a highway, city street or square, or an open road leading to any of the aforementioned. These streets must measure at least sixteen cubits wide, not be roofed, pass through the city entirely and be frequented by many people. On the Biblical level, the prohibition against carrying four *amos* on the Sabbath applies only to such a public domain. However, the Rabbis extended this prohibition to a *karmelis,* which is the technical term for a type of area that in certain respects resembles a public domain and in others a private one (see Introduction to Chapter One). A public thoroughfare that does not meet the specifications just mentioned is considered a *karmelis.*]

6. Since the prohibition against carrying in a *karmelis* is Rabbinical, it is waived in the interests of public safety, and one may therefore remove a thorn from a *karmelis* without resorting to carrying it in increments of less than four *amos.*

7. Beis Shammai permit pouring hot water even from a primary vessel [כְּלִי רִאשׁוֹן] into cold water, but they forbid pouring cold water into hot water even when the hot water is in a secondary vessel [כְּלִי שֵׁנִי] (*Tosafos;* see below).

Beis Shammai's reasoning is that when something hot is poured into something cold or vice versa, *the lower one dominates* [תַּתָּאָה גָּבַר]. I.e. if the cold substance is in the lower vessel and the hot substance is poured into it, the cold substance will cool off the hot one before the hot one is able to cook it. And if the hot substance is in the lower vessel and the cold one is poured into it, the hot one will cook the cold one before the cold one cools it off. Thus, although Beis Shammai permit pouring hot water into cold water, they forbid pouring cold water into hot water (see *Rashi;* cf. *Tosafos, Rashba, Ritva MHK* ed.; see also *Pnei Yehoshua* and *Beur HaGra* to *Orach Chaim* 318:12; see *Pesachim* 76a for a related application of this principle).

[Under Biblical law, it would be permitted to pour cold water into hot water when the hot water is in the secondary vessel, since a secondary vessel is not deemed capable of cooking even when it is the lower one. However, Beis Shammai forbid this Rabbinically, out of concern that a secondary vessel might be confused with a primary vessel (*Tosafos, Rashba, Ran*).]

מותר למימרא דשמואל כרבי שמעון סבירא ליה א) והאמר שמואל א מכבין גחלת של מתכת ברה"ר בשביל שלא יוזקו בה רבים ב אבל לא גחלת של עץ ואי ס"ד סבר לה כרבי שמעון אפילו של עץ נמי ב) בדבר שאין מתכוין סבר לה כרבי שמעון במלאכה שאינה צריכה לגופה סבר לה כרבי יהודה אמר רבינא ג הלכך ג) קוץ ברשות הרבים מוליכו פחות פחות מד' אמות ובכרמלית אפילו טובא: אבל נותן כו': ת"ר נותן אדם חמין לתוך הצונן ולא הצונן לתוך החמין דברי בית שמאי ובית הלל אומרים ד בין חמין לתוך הצונן ובין צונן לתוך החמין מותר בד"א בכוס אבל באמבטי חמין לתוך הצונן ולא צונן לתוך החמין ורבי שמעון בן מנסיא אוסר אמר רב נחמן הלכה כר"ש בן מנסיא סבר רב יוסף למימר ספל הרי הוא כאמבטי א"ל אביי תני ר' חייא ספל אינו כאמבטי ולמאי דסליק אדעתא מעיקרא דספל הרי הוא כאמבטי ואמר רב נחמן הלכה כרבי שמעון בן מנסיא אלא בשבת רחיצה בחמין ליכא מי סברת רבי שמעון אסיפא קאי ארישא קאי ובית הלל מתירין בין חמין לתוך צונן ובין צונן לתוך החמין ורבי שמעון בן מנסיא אוסר צונן לתוך חמין לימא רבי שמעון בן מנסיא דאמר כב"ש הכי קאמר ד) לא נחלקו ב"ש וב"ה בדבר זה אמר רב הונא בריה דרב יהושע חזינא ליה לרבא דלא קפיד ה) אמנא מדתני רבי חייא נותן אדם קיתון של מים לתוך ספל של מים בין חמין לתוך צונן ובין צונן לתוך חמין אמר ליה רב הונא לרב אשי דילמא שאני התם דמיפסק כלי אמר ליה מערה איתמר ה מערה אדם קיתון של מים לתוך ספל של מים בין חמין לתוך צונן בין צונן לתוך חמין: מתני' ו) האילפס והקדרה שהעבירן מרותחין לא יתן לתוכן תבלין אבל

רש"י

מותר. שאין מתכוין לכך: גחלת של מתכת. שמשליכין לתוך פסולת של ברזל דלא שייך כבוי בהכי מדאורייתא ומדרבנן אסורה והיכא דאיכא נזקא לרבים לא גזרו על השבות: אבל לא של עץ. דאיסורא דאורייתא היא וחייב סקילה: אפילו של עץ נמי. דהא לרבי שמעון מלאכה שאינה צריכה לגופה פטור עליה וכל כיבוי אינו צריך לגופו חוץ מעושי פחמין או מהבהבי פתילה: הלכך. כיון דאמרת לא גזרו שבות דכיבוי מתכת במקום נזקא דרבים: קוץ ברשות הרבים מוליכו פחות פחות מד' אמות. עד שיסלקנו לצידי רשות הרבים דאיסורא דרבנן הוא: ובכרמלית. דטלטול דידיה דרבנן: אפילו טובא. יעבירנו בעקירה אחת: חמין לתוך צונן. דקסבר תתאה גבר ואין החמין מרתיחין את הצונן אלא מפשירין: ולא צונן לתוך חמין. שהתחתונים מרתיחים את העליונים דתתאה גבר: בכוס. דלשתיה קבעי להו ולא ניחא ליה שיחמו הרבה ועוד דכלי שני הוא: אוסר. אפילו חמין לתוך צונן: ספל הרי הוא כאמבטי. ואף על גב דכלי שני הוא הואיל ולאו לשתיה אלא לרחיצה אמירי דניחא ליה שיחמו הרבה וגזרינן: אלא בשבת רחיצה בחמין ליכא. בתמיה דהא לרבי שמעון אפילו חמין לתוך צונן אסור לא משכחת חמין שהוחמו ואפילו מע"ש שלא יהיו צריכין להפיג רתיחתן ואם כן לא ירחוץ אפילו פניו ידיו ורגליו בחמין: מי סברת ר' שמעון אסיפא קאי. דלא שרי ת"ק אלא חמין לתוך צונן ואתא איהו ואסר אף חמין לתוך צונן: ארישא קאי. לשתיה וצונן לתוך חמין דקשרו ב"ה קאסר: מתני' שהעבירן. מן האור: מרותחין. בין השמשות: לא יתן לתוכן תבלין. משתחשך דכלי ראשון כל זמן שרותח מבשל:

אבל

תוספות

אפילו של עץ נמי. ואם תאמר ומאי ס"ד דמקשה וכי משום דסבר שמואל כרבי שמעון באין מתכוין יסבור כמותו במלאכה שאינו צריך לגופה וי"ל דס"ד דמקשה דודאי הא בהא תליא משום דסבר רבי יהודה דמלאכה שאינו צריך לגופה חייב עליה היכא דמתכוין בשאין מתכוין נמי החמירו חכמים אבל לרבי שמעון דפטור עליה מן התורה אף במתכוין לא חש לאסור מדרבנן כשאין מתכוין כיון דמתכוין עצמו ליכא אלא איסורא דרבנן ומיהו לפי האמת לאו הא בהא תליא דשמואל אע"ג דבמלאכה שאינה צריכה לגופה סבר כרבי יהודה דחייב [מתיר] באין מתכוין ולרבי יהודה נמי אסור אין מתכוין אפילו בגרירה דמתכוין עצמו לא אסיר אלא מדרבנן כדאמרי' לקמן ובשילהי כל התדיר (זבחים דף נא: ושם") דאמר שמואל המתנדב יין מביאו ומזלפו ע"ג האשים ופריך והא קא מכבה ומשני דסבר דבר שאין מתכוין מותר ופריך כי הכא דאמר שמואל מכבין גחלת של מתכת אבל לא של עץ והשתא אומר רשב"א דפריך מכ"ש דכיון דסבר שמואל דמלאכה שאינה צריכה לגופה חייב א"כ סבירא ליה נמי בשבת דבר שאין מתכוין אסור דסבר המקשה דהתם דהא בהא תליא כמו מקשה דהכא וכיון דבשבת אסור אין מתכוין כ"ש בעלמא אך הקשה דמשמע דאי הוי סבר שמואל מלאכה שאינה צריכה לו פטור עליה הוה אתי שפיר ואמאי והא מלאכה שאינה צריכה לגופה בשאר איסורים דלאו שבת חייב עליה וכיון דסבירא ליה דהא בהא תליא א"כ אמאי קאמר התם דבר שאין מתכוין מותר: נותן אדם חמין לתוך צונן. א) אפי' בכלי ראשון דחמין לתוך צונן אינו מבשל כמו שאפרש ולא צונן לתוך חמין אפילו בכלי שני דגזרי ב"ש כלי שני אטו כלי ראשון וב"ה דפליגי ושרו צונן לתוך חמין היינו דוקא בכלי שני כדקתני בד"א בכוס משמע דבכלי ראשון מודו ב"ה ולא משום דסברה הך ברייתא דתתאה גבר כדפירש בקונטרס דאם כן יקשה מהכא למ"ד ח) עילאה גבר ולמאן דאמר תתאה גבר נמי הא מבשל כדי קליפה כמו שאפרש לקמן בע"ה אלא נראה כמו שאומר ר"ת דחמין לתוך צונן משמע שהצוננין של מטה מרובים שדרך ליתן המועט במרובה ולכך אין מבשלים החמין המועטים כלל לפי שמתערבין בצוננין המרובין ומתבטל חמימותן ולא צונן לתוך חמין שהחמין של מטה מרובין ומתערבין בהן הצוננין המועטין ומתבשלין: אבל באמבטי כו'. נראה דהאי אמבטי איירי כגון שהוא כלי שני ולא הוי כההוא אמבטי דלעיל ט) דקאמר בקשתי להניח פך באמבטי מדקאמר ספל אינו כאמבטי והאי ספל ע"כ כלי שני דאי כלי ראשון אמאי אינו כאמבטי ודכוותיה אמבטי הוי כלי שני ועוד דאי באמבטי שהוא כלי ראשון איירי לא הוה ליה למינקט אמבטי אלא מיחם שהוא לשתיה דומיא דכוס ומדנקט אמבטי משמע דבכלי שני איירי ואתא לפלוגי בכלי שני בין כוס שהוא לשתיה לאמבטי לפי שחמין הרבה ואיכא למיגזר דהרואה אותן חמין כל כך סבור דכלי ראשון הוא ובמתני' דנקט במיחם שהוא ראשון לא יתן לתוכו מים הוה מצי למימר באמבטי שהוא שני לא יתן לתוכו מים אלא דמתני' איירי בשתיה ומפליג בין מיחם לכוס: מי סברת ר"ש בן מנסיא אסיפא קאי ארישא קאי. היינו דוקא למאי דס"ד לרב יוסף מעיקרא אבל למאי דמסקי' דספל אינו כאמבטי קאי אסיפא בכוס וסבר שפיר ר"ש בן מנסיא כב"ה דאפילו צונן לתוך חמין מותר ואתיא מתני' דשריא לתוך הכוס אליבא דהלכתא דהלכה כר"ש בן מנסיא וא"ת למאי דסלקא דעתך דארישא קאי ואסר בכוס צונן לתוך חמין מאי קמ"ל רב יוסף דספל הרי הוא כאמבטי כוס נמי הרי הוא כאמבטי לר"ש בן מנסיא דהלכתא כוותיה וי"ל דרב יוסף לב"ה אתא לאשמעינן דשרו בכוס: נותן אדם קיתון של מים. וא"ת ואמאי לא מייתי ברייתא דלעיל דספל אינו כאמבטי ואמאי איצטריך נמי רבי חייא למיתני תרוייהו וי"ל דהשתא קמ"ל בין חמין לתוך צונן בין צונן לתוך חמין דההיא דספל אינו כאמבטי ה"א דקאי אר"ש בן מנסיא דאסר באמבטי אפי' חמין לתוך צונן ועליה קאמר דספל אינו כאמבטי ושרי חמין לתוך צונן אבל צונן לתוך חמין ה"א דאסור ואפשר דההיא דלעיל היינו הך דהכא אלא שקילרה ונקט לישנא דרב יוסף דמייתי עלה: שאני התם דמפסיק כלי. וא"ת דאמר לעיל (דף מ:) טול בכלי שני ותן אבל בכלי ראשון לא אע"ג דמפסיק מנא וי"ל דהתם בכלי ראשון והכא דבכלי שני שאני:

אבל

מסורת הש"ס

א) זבחים לא:, ב) [שם לב.], ג) [ביצה כח:], ד) [לקמן קלה. יבמות כח. ב"ק לב. סוכה טו.], ה) [בהרא"ש ליתא ועי' ברב אלפס], ו) פסחים מ:, ז) [ושם לב.], ח) [פסחים עו.], ט) [דף מ:].

תוספות ישנים

א) עוד טכל לומר דחמין לתוך צונן דוקא בכ"ש שרי ב"ש אבל בכלי ראשון אסור אטו צונן לתוך חמין:

ליקוטי רש"י

גחלת של מתכת. לא שייך בה כיבוי דאינו נעשה פחם [לקמן קלד.]. לאו בת כיבוי [היא] ואיסורא דרבנן הוא דאיכא ובמקום היזק רבים לא גזור רבנן [זבחים צא:]. אבל לא גחלת של עץ. גחלת אקרי פחם שאינו בוער כדאמרינן (ברכות נג:) גחלים עוממות מפי רבי [סנהדרין ק:]. דבת כיבוי הוא ואיסורא דאורייתא הוא ואי כר"ש לא משכחת כיבוי [מן התורה] אלא במתכוין לעשות פחמין בכיבויו וצריך להם דאר"ש מלאכה שאינה צריכה לגופה פטור עליה וכיבוי [זה] לאו צורך גופו הוא שיהא צריך לו דהלואי שלא בא עליו ודמי למוציא את המת לקברו מעל פניו דפטר עליה ר"ש במסכת שבת בפרק המצניע (צד.) [זבחים צב.]. בגחלת של עץ אסור דשייך בה כיבוי לפי שעושה פחם [לקמן שם]. מוליכו פחות פחות מד' אמות. עד שמסלקנה לצדי רה"ר כדי שלא תזיק [ביצה כח:]. מעל האור מרותחין ערב שבת עם שקיעה. לא יתן לתוכן תבלין. דכלי ראשון מבשל ונמצא מבשל תבלין בשבת [פסחים מ:].

עין משפט נר מצוה

לג א ב מיי' פ"א מהל' שבת הלכה ז ופי"ב הלכה ב טוש"ע או"ח סי' שלד סעיף כז:

לד ג מיי' שם פ"א הל' ז טוש"ע או"ח סי' שח סעיף יח:

לה ד ה מיי' פכ"ב מהל' שבת הלכה ו טוש"ע או"ח סימן שיח סעיף יב:

לו ו מיי' שם טור שו"ע שם סעיף ט:

רבינו חננאל

למימרא דשמואל כר' שמעון (ורב אדא) והאמר שמואל מכבין גחלת של מתכת ברה"ר בשביל שלא יוזקו בה רבים אבל גחלת של עץ לא ואילו ר"ש סבר אפילו של עץ מותר לפי שאין מתכוין לכבות אלא כדי שלא יוזק וכי האי גוונא פטר ר' שמעון ואסיק' לעולם כר' יהוד' סבירא לי' דאמר מלאכה שאינה צריכה לגופה חייב עליה א) מיהו דבר שיש בו היזק לרבים כגון צידת נחש וכבוי גחלת של מתכת בזמן שהיא חמה והיא שחורה והרואה אותה דומה שהיא צוננת לפי שאין בה אדמומית כגחלת לוחשת ונמצאו בני אדם ניזוקין בו לפיכך מותר אבל הגחלת של עץ אם תסיר אדמומיתה נכבת כבר ואינה מזקת ואם אדמומיתה בה כל הרואה אותה מתרחק ממנה ומכל פנים אין אדם ניזוק שהשחורה כבר כבתה והאדומה מתרחקין ממנה לפיכך המכבה אותה חייב ולפיכך היה שמואל אוסר בגחלת של עץ. (ומדוקיה) אמר רבינא קרץ ברה"ר מוליכו פחות פחות מד' אמות ואע"ג דרב ושמואל הלכה כרב באיסורי בהא קיי"ל כשמואל דאמר במלאכה שאינה צריכה לגופה סבר לה כר' יהודה בדבר שאין מתכוין סבר לה כר"ש ומדרב אחא ורבינא שמע מינייהו דהלכתא כר' שמעון: פיסקא אבל נותן הוא לתוכו או לתוך הכוס כדי להפשירן. ת"ר לא יתן אדם חמין לתוך צונן [ולא צונן] לתוך חמין וב"ה מתירין כו'. ואוקימנא להא דר"ש בן מנסיא שאוסר כלומר לא נחלקו ב"ש וב"ה אלא אפילו ב"ה אוסרין ואע"ג דאמר רב נחמן הלכתא כר' שמעון בן מנסיא כיון דאמר רב הונא חזינא לרבא דלא קפיד זימנין עביד כמר וזמנין עביד כמר מדתני ר' חייא דתני ר' חייא נותן אדם קיתון של מים לתוך ספל כו' ורב אשי מתרץ לה לרב הונא ואמר ליה מערה תניא כלומר מערה אדם קיתון של מים לתוך ספל של מים בין חמין לתוך צונן בין צונן לתוך חמין קיי"ל כוותייהו דאינון בתראי ומעשה רב ולא

דמו ספל לאמבטי וכוס למיחם דאוקימנא ליה שאסור לתת בתוכו צונן מועטין בהיות חמין בו כדי שיחמו אלא מרובין כדי להפשיר כי המיחם הוא עצמו מיחם אבל ספל ואמבטי וכוס מתחממין בכלי אחד ומערין בתוך

חשק שלמה על רבינו חננאל א) עי' ביאור דברי רבינו ז"ל בחדושי הרשב"א ז"ל ד"ה גחלת של מתכות ע"ש היטב:

וּבֵית הִלֵּל אוֹמְרִים – BUT BEIS HILLEL SAY: בֵּין חַמִּין לְתוֹךְ הַצּוֹנֵן וּבֵין צוֹנֵן לְתוֹךְ הַחַמִּין מוּתָּר – BOTH putting HOT WATER INTO COLD WATER AND COLD WATER INTO HOT WATER ARE PERMISSIBLE. בַּמֶּה דְּבָרִים אֲמוּרִים – REGARDING WHAT case WAS THIS STATED? בְּכוֹס – REGARDING the case of pouring into A CUP.[8] אֲבָל בְּאַמְבָּטִי – BUT WITH REGARD TO pouring into A BATHTUB, the rule is that חַמִּין לְתוֹךְ הַצּוֹנֵן וְלֹא צוֹנֵן לְתוֹךְ הַחַמִּין – it is permissible to pour HOT WATER INTO COLD WATER BUT NOT COLD WATER INTO HOT WATER.[9] וְרַבִּי שִׁמְעוֹן בֶּן מְנַסְיָא אוֹסֵר – BUT R' SHIMON BEN MENASYA FORBIDS it.[10]

A halachic ruling is cited:

אָמַר רַב נַחְמָן – Rav Nachman said: הֲלָכָה כְּרַבִּי שִׁמְעוֹן בֶּן מְנַסְיָא – **The halachah follows R' Shimon ben Menasya.**

The Baraisa outlined the laws governing a cup and a bathtub. The Gemara now considers the case of a washbasin:[11]

סָבַר רַב יוֹסֵף לְמֵימַר סֵפֶל הֲרֵי הוּא כְּאַמְבָּטִי – **Rav Yosef was inclined to say a washbasin is** treated **like a bathtub.**[12] אָמַר לֵיהּ אַבַּיֵי – However, **Abaye said to him:** תָּנֵי רַבִּי חִיָּיא – **R' Chiya has taught a Baraisa** which states: סֵפֶל אֵינוֹ כְּאַמְבָּטִי – A WASHBASIN IS NOT LIKE A BATHTUB.[13]

The Gemara questions how Rav Yosef could ever have considered the first possibility:

וּלְמַאי דִּסְלִיק אַדַּעְתָּא מֵעִיקָּרָא דְּסֵפֶל הֲרֵי הוּא כְּאַמְבָּטִי – **Now, according to [Rav Yosef's] original inclination that a washbasin is like a bathtub,** וְאָמַר רַב נַחְמָן הֲלָכָה כְּרַבִּי שִׁמְעוֹן בֶּן מְנַסְיָא – **and** taking into account the fact that **Rav Nachman said** that **the halachah follows R' Shimon ben Menasya,** who apparently forbids even pouring hot bath water into a tub of cold water, consider the following difficulty: אֶלָּא בְּשַׁבָּת רְחִיצָה בְּחַמִּין לֵיכָּא – **Is there no** possibility of **washing with hot water on the Sabbath?**[14]

The Gemara resolves the difficulty:

מִי סָבְרַת רַבִּי שִׁמְעוֹן אַסֵּיפָא קָאֵי – **Do you think** that **R' Shimon ben Menasya was referring to the latter clause** of the Baraisa and that he meant to forbid pouring hot water into cold water?[15] אַרֵישָׁא קָאֵי – No! **He was** actually **referring to the first clause** of the Baraisa, וּבֵית הִלֵּל מַתִּירִין בֵּין חַמִּין לְתוֹךְ צוֹנֵן וּבֵין צוֹנֵן לְתוֹךְ הַחַמִּין – which states that **Beis Hillel permit** pouring **both hot water into** a cup of **cold water and cold water into** a cup of **hot water.** In reference to this ruling, the Baraisa concludes: וְרַבִּי שִׁמְעוֹן בֶּן מְנַסְיָא אוֹסֵר צוֹנֵן לְתוֹךְ חַמִּין – **But R' Shimon ben Menasya forbids** pouring **cold water into** a cup of **hot water.** With respect to pouring hot water into a tub of cold water, however, R' Shimon ben Menasya agrees that it is permitted.[16]

The Gemara objects to this interpretation of R' Shimon ben Menasya's statement:

לֵימָא רַבִּי שִׁמְעוֹן בֶּן מְנַסְיָא דְּאָמַר כְּבֵית שַׁמַּאי – **Shall we say,** then, **that R' Shimon ben Menasya stated** his opinion **in accordance with Beis Shammai** against Beis Hillel?[17]

The Gemara defends the interpretation:

הָכִי קָאָמַר – **This is what [R' Shimon ben Menasya]** means to **say:** לֹא נֶחְלְקוּ בֵּית שַׁמַּאי וּבֵית הִלֵּל בְּדָבָר זֶה – **Beis Shammai and Beis Hillel never disagreed on this issue,** for even Beis Hillel forbid pouring cold water into a cup of hot water.[18]

The Gemara continues its discussion of this issue:

אָמַר רַב הוּנָא בְּרֵיהּ דְּרַב יְהוֹשֻׁעַ – **Rav Huna the son of Rav**

NOTES

8. Since water in a cup is intended for drinking, one does not want it to be intensely hot. [Thus, he will add enough cold water to ensure that the resulting mixture is not scalding, and the cold water will not be cooked.] Furthermore, the cup is a secondary vessel [and is thus incapable of cooking on the Biblical level]. Therefore, Beis Hillel permit pouring cold water into it (*Rashi;* see *Rambam, Hil. Shabbos* 22:5,6).

9. This pertains to pouring cold water into a bathtub that is a primary vessel, viz. either one in which the water was heated or one that is fed directly by a hot spring (see 40b note 16). It is forbidden to add cold water because the hot water in the tub is capable of cooking on the Biblical level and the person is likely to add only a small amount of cold water, since one ordinarily wants a bath to remain very hot (see *Ran, Pnei Yehoshua* and *Rashi* below ד״ה ספל; cf. *Tosafos, Rashba*).

It is permissible, however, to pour hot water, even that which was heated in a bathtub, into a tub of cold water. Since the rule is that the lower one dominates, even very hot water will not cook the cold water that is already in the tub (see *Ran* and *Tur Orach Chaim* 318 with *Beis Yosef*). [For a discussion of whether this applies even when there is far more hot water than cold water, see *Tosafos* ד״ה נותן and see *Beur Halachah* to 318:11-12 ד״ה אבל נותן, ד״ה שבזה האמבטי וד״ה והוא.]

10. It is unclear what R' Shimon ben Menasya means to forbid. The Gemara below will initially understand him as coming to forbid pouring hot water into a cold bathtub.

11. As explained earlier, hot water in a cup is treated more leniently than hot water in a bathtub for two reasons: Firstly, because the cup is a secondary vessel; and secondly, because water mixed for drinking is generally brought to a lower temperature than water intended for bathing. The Gemara now considers the case of hot water in a washbasin. Like a cup, a washbasin is a secondary vessel; however, the water in it is intended for bathing and is maintained at a high temperature (see *Rashi* ד״ה ספל הרי הוא כאמבטי).

12. Although the washbasin is a secondary vessel and is not capable of cooking, the Rabbis forbade adding cold water to it because one normally maintains water in a washbasin at a very high temperature [and it is thus similar to a bathtub] (*Rashi*).

13. [I.e. the Rabbis issued no decree against adding cold water to a washbasin.]

14. We know that it is permissible to wash one's face, hands and feet on the Sabbath with hot water that was heated before the Sabbath, for a Baraisa stated so above (39b). Now, any water that was heated for bathing — even that which was heated before the Sabbath and left on a banked *kirah* — must be diluted with cold water before anyone can wash with it. According to R' Shimon ben Menasya, whose opinion is accepted halachically by Rav Nachman, it is forbidden to perform this dilution in a bathtub. If a washbasin is treated like a bathtub, there is no permissible way to perform the dilution at all (unless one does it by tiny increments, in a cup). It thus emerges that according to Rav Yosef's original inclination it is *impossible* on a practical basis to wash with warm water on the Sabbath! (*Rashi*). Why, then, does the Baraisa state that it is permitted?

15. The Gemara, in posing its question, assumed that when the Baraisa concluded, *but R' Shimon ben Menasya forbids it,* it meant that he forbids that which Beis Hillel permitted in the immediately preceding clause, i.e. pouring hot water into a cold bath (*Rashi*). The Gemara now suggests a different interpretation.

16. R' Shimon ben Menasya agrees with the rule that the lower one dominates and thus permits pouring hot bath water into a cold tub or basin. It would thus be possible to wash one's face, hands and feet on the Sabbath even if we would treat a basin like a tub. R' Shimon simply disagrees with Beis Hillel's sanction of adding cold water to a hot cup, for he holds that since the lower one dominates we cannot add cold water even to a secondary vessel (see *Rashi*).

17. [According to the proposed interpretation, R' Shimon ben Menasya concurs fully with Beis Shammai, which is highly unlikely. Furthermore, Rav Nachman stated above that the halachah follows R' Shimon ben Menasya! Obviously, the interpretation is incorrect.]

18. That is, R' Shimon ben Menasya disputes the Baraisa's initial assertion that Beis Hillel permit adding cold water to a cup of hot water. [Note that this bears directly on the meaning of our Mishnah (on 41a), which permits pouring cold water into a hot cup so as to warm it. If we interpret the Mishnah in accordance with R' Shimon ben Menasya, it means that one may *not* pour a small quantity of cold water into the cup in order to heat it, but may only pour in a large quantity so as to merely warm it. However, if we interpret it in accordance with the first version of Beis Hillel's opinion, it means that one may add cold water to a cup unconditionally because any water added to a cup is deemed to be "warmed" and not "heated" (see 41a note 27).]

גמרא

מותר למימרא דשמואל כרבי שמעון סבירא ליה [א] והאמר שמואל [א]מכבין גחלת של מתכת ברה"ר בשביל שלא יוזקו בה רבים [ב]אבל לא גחלת של עץ ואי ס"ד סבר לה כרבי שמעון אפילו של עץ נמי [ג] בדבר שאין מתכוין סבר לה כרבי שמעון במלאכה שאינה צריכה לגופה סבר לה כרבי יהודה אמר רבינא [ג]הלכך [ג]קוץ ברשות הרבים מוליכו פחות מד' אמות ובכרמלית אפילו טובא: אבל נותן כו': ת"ר נותן אדם חמין לתוך הצונן ולא הצונן לתוך החמין דברי בית שמאי ובית הלל אומרים [ד]בין חמין לתוך הצונן ובין צונן לתוך החמין מותר בד"א בכוס אבל באמבטי חמין לתוך הצונן ולא צונן לתוך החמין ורבי שמעון בן מנסיא אוסר אמר רב נחמן הלכה כר"ש בן מנסיא סבר רב יוסף למימר ספל הרי הוא כאמבטי א"ל אביי תני ר' חייא ספל אינו כאמבטי ולמאי דסליק אדעתא מעיקרא דספל הרי הוא כאמבטי ואמר רב נחמן הלכה כרבי שמעון בן מנסיא אלא בשבת רחיצה בחמין ליכא מי סברת רבי שמעון אסיפא קאי ארישא קאי ובית הלל מתירין בין חמין לתוך צונן ובין צונן לתוך החמין ורבי שמעון בן מנסיא אוסר צונן לתוך חמין לימא רבי שמעון בן מנסיא דאמר כב"ש הכי קאמר [ד] לא נחלקו ב"ש וב"ה בדבר זה אמר רב הונא בריה דרב יהושע חזינא ליה לרבא דלא קפיד [ה] אמנא מדתני רבי חייא נותן אדם קיתון של מים לתוך ספל של מים בין חמין לתוך צונן ובין צונן לתוך חמין אמר ליה רב הונא לרב אשי דילמא שאני התם דמיפסק כלי אמר ליה מערה איתמר [ה]מערה אדם קיתון של מים לתוך ספל של מים בין חמין לתוך צונן בין צונן לתוך חמין:

מתני'

מתני' [י][ו]האילפס והקדרה שהעבירן מרותחין לא יתן לתוכן תבלין אבל

רש"י

מותר. שאין מתכוין לכך: גחלת של מתכת. שמשליכין לחוץ פסולת של ברזל דלא שייך כבוי בהכי מדאורייתא ומדרבנן אסורה והיכא דאיכא נזקא לרבים לא גזרו על השבות: אבל לא של עץ. דאיסורא דאורייתא היא וחייב סקילה: אפילו של עץ נמי. דהא לרבי שמעון מלאכה שאינה צריכה לגופה פטור עליה וכל כיבוי אינו צריך לגופו חוץ מעושי פחמין או מהבהבי פתילה: הלכך. כיון דאמרת לא גזרו שבות דכיבוי מתכת במקום נזקא דרבים: קוץ ברשות הרבים מוליכו פחות פחות מד' אמות. עד שיסלקנו לצידי רשות הרבים דאיסורא דרבנן הוא: ובכרמלית. דטלטול דידיה דרבנן: אפילו טובא. יעבירנו בעקירה אחת: חמין לתוך צונן. דקסבר תתאה גבר ואין החמין מרתיחין את הצונן אלא מפשירין: ולא צונן לתוך חמין. שהתחתונים מרתיחים את העליונים דתתאה גבר: בכוס. דלשתיה קבעי להו ולא ניחא ליה שיחומו הרבה ועוד דכלי שני הוא: אוסר. אפילו חמין לתוך צונן: ספל הרי הוא כאמבטי. ואף על גב דכלי שני הוא הואיל ולאו לשתיה אלא לרחיצה אסירי דניחא ליה שיחמו הרבה וגזרינן: אלא בשבת רחיצה בחמין ליכא. בתמיה דהא לרבי שמעון אפילו חמין לתוך צונן אסור לא משכחת חמין שהוחמו ואפילו מע"ש שלא יהיו צריכין להפיג רתיחתן ואם כן לא ירחוץ אפילו פניו ידיו ורגליו בחמין: מי סברת ר' שמעון אסיפא קאי. דלא שרי ת"ק אלא חמין לתוך צונן ואתא איהו ואסר אף חמין לתוך צונן: ארישא קאי. לשתיה וצונן לתוך חמין דקשרו ב"ה קאסר: מתני' שהעבירן. מן האור: מרותחין. בין השמשות: לא יתן לתוכן תבלין. משתחשך דכלי ראשון כל זמן שרותח מבשל:

אבל

תוספות

אפילו של עץ נמי. ואם תאמר ומאי ס"ד דמקשה וכי משום דסבר שמואל כרבי שמעון באין מתכוין יסבור כמותו במלאכה שאינו צריך לגופה וי"ל דס"ד דמקשה דודאי הא בהא תליא משום דסבר רבי יהודה דמלאכה שאינו צריך לגופה חייב עליה היכא דמתכוין בשאין מתכוין נמי החמירו חכמים אבל לרבי שמעון דפטור עליה מן התורה אף במתכוין לא חש לאסור מדרבנן כשאין מתכוין כיון דמתכוין עצמו ליכא אלא איסורא דרבנן ומיהו לפי האמת לאו הא בהא תליא דשמואל אע"ג דבמלאכה שאינה צריכה לגופה סבר כרבי יהודה דחייב [מתיר] באין מתכוין ולרבי יהודה נמי אסור אין מתכוין אפילו בגרירה דמתכוין עצמו לא אסיר אלא מדרבנן כדאמרי' לקמן ובשילהי כל התדיר (זבחים דף צא: ושם[ו]) דאמר שמואל המתנדב יין מביאו ומזלפו ע"ג האשים ופריך והא קא מכבה ומשני דסבר דבר שאין מתכוין מותר ופריך כי הכא דאמר שמואל מכבין גחלת של מתכת אבל לא של עץ והשתא אומר רשב"א דפריך מכ"ש דכיון דסבר שמואל דמלאכה שאינה צריכה לגופה חייב א"כ סבירא ליה נמי בשבת דבר שאין מתכוין אסור דסבר המקשה דהתם דהא בהא תליא כמו מקשה דהכא וכיון דבשבת אסור אין מתכוין כ"ש בעלמא אך הקשה דמשמע דאי הוי סבר שמואל מלאכה שאינה צריכה לו פטור עליה הוה אתי שפיר ואמאי והא מלאכה שאינה צריכה לגופה בשאר איסורים דלאו שבת חייב עליה וכיון דסבירא ליה דהא בהא תליא א"כ אמאי קאמר התם דבר שאין מתכוין מותר:

נותן אדם חמין לתוך צונן. א) אפי' בכלי ראשון דחמין לתוך צונן אינו מבשל כמו שאפרש ולא צונן לתוך חמין אפילו בכלי שני דגזרי ב"ש כלי שני אטו כלי ראשון וב"ה דפליגי ושרו צונן לתוך חמין היינו דוקא בכלי שני כדקתני בד"א בכוס משמע דבכלי ראשון מודו ב"ה ולא משום דסברה הך ברייתא דתתאה גבר כדפירש בקונטרס דאם כן יקשה מהכא למ"ד [ח] עילאה גבר ולמאן דאמר תתאה גבר נמי הא מבשל כדי קליפה כמו שאפרש לקמן בע"ה אלא נראה כמו שאומר ר"ת דחמין לתוך צונן משמע שהצוננין של מטה מרובים שדרך ליתן המועט במרובה ולכך אין מבשלים החמין המועטים כלל לפי שמתערבין בצוננין המרובין ומתבטל חמימותן ולא צונן לתוך חמין שהחמין של מטה מרובין ומתערבין בהן הצוננין המועטין ומתבשלין: **אבל** באמבטי כו'. נראה דהאי אמבטי איירי כגון שהוא כלי שני ולא הוי כההוא אמבטי דלעיל [ט] דקאמר בקשתי להניח פך באמבטי מדקאמר ספל אינו כאמבטי והאי ספל ע"כ כלי שני דאי כלי ראשון אמאי אינו כאמבטי ודכוותיה אמבטי הוי כלי שני ועוד דאי באמבטי שהוא כלי ראשון איירי לא הוה ליה למינקט אמבטי אלא מיחם שהוא לשתיה דומיא דכוס ומדנקט אמבטי משמע דבכלי שני איירי ואתא לפלוגי בכלי שני בין כוס שהוא לשתיה לאמבטי לפי שחמין הרבה ואיכא למיגזר דהרואה אותן חמין כל כך סבור דכלי ראשון הוא ובמתני' דנקט במיחם שהוא ראשון לא יתן לתוכו מים הוה מצי למימר באמבטי שהוא שני לא יתן לתוכו מים אלא דמתני' איירי בשתיה ומפליג בין מיחם לכוס: **מי** סברת ר"ש בן מנסיא אסיפא קאי ארישא קאי. היינו דוקא למאי דס"ד לרב יוסף מעיקרא אבל למאי דמסקי' דספל אינו כאמבטי קאי אסיפא בכוס וסבר שפיר ר"ש בן מנסיא כב"ה דאפילו צונן לתוך חמין מותר ואתיא מתני' דשריא לתוך הכוס אליבא דהלכתא דהלכה כר"ש בן מנסיא וא"ת למאי דסלקא דעתך דארישא קאי ואסר בכוס צונן לתוך חמין מאי קמ"ל רב יוסף דספל הרי הוא כאמבטי כוס נמי הרי הוא כאמבטי לר"ש בן מנסיא דהלכתא כוותיה וי"ל דרב יוסף לב"ה אתא לאשמעינן דשרו בכוס: **נותן** אדם קיתון של מים. וא"ת ואמאי לא מייתי ברייתא דלעיל דספל אינו כאמבטי ואמאי איצטריך נמי רבי חייא למיתני תרווייהו וי"ל דהשתא קמ"ל בין חמין לתוך צונן בין צונן לתוך חמין דההיא דספל אינו כאמבטי ה"א דקאי אר"ש בן מנסיא דאסר באמבטי אפי' חמין לתוך צונן ועליה קאמר דספל אינו כאמבטי ושרי חמין לתוך צונן אבל צונן לתוך חמין ה"א דאסור ואפשר ההיא דלעיל היינו הך דהכא אלא שקיצרה ונקט לישנא דרב יוסף דמייתי עלה: **שאני** התם דמפסיק כלי. וא"ת דאמר לעיל (דף מ:) טול בכלי שני ותן אבל בכלי ראשון לא אע"ג דמפסיק מנא וי"ל דהתם בכלי ראשון והכא דבכלי שני שאני:

אבל

מסורת הש"ס

א) זבחים לא., ב) [שם לב.], ג) [ביצה כח:], ד) [לקמן קלה. יבמות כח. ב"ק לד. סוכה טו.], ה) [בהרא"ש ליתא ועי' ברב אלפס], ו) פסחים מ:, ז) [ושם לב.], ח) [פסחים עו.], ט) [דף מ:].

תוספות ישנים

א) עוד נוכל לומר דחמין לתוך צונן דוקא בכ"ש שרי ב"ש אבל בכלי ראשון אסור אטו צונן לתוך חמין:

ליקוטי רש"י

גחלת של מתכת. לא שייך בה כיבוי דאינו נעשה פחם [לקמן קלד.]. לאו בת כיבוי [היא] ואיסורא דרבנן הוא דאיכא ובמקום היזק רבים לא גזור רבנן [זבחים צא:]. **אבל לא** גחלת של עץ. גחלת אקרי פחם שאינו בוער כדאמרינן (ברכות נג:) גחלים עוממות מפי רבי [סנהדרין ק:]. דבת כיבוי הוא ואיסורא דאורייתא הוא ואי כר"ש לא משכחת כיבוי [מן התורה] אלא במתכוין לעשות פחמין בכיבויו וצריך להם דאר"ש מלאכה שאינה צריכה לגופה פטור עליה וכיבוי [זה] לאו צורך גופו הוא שיהא צריך לו דהלואי שלא בא עליו ודמי למוציא את המת לסלקו מעל פניו דפטר עליה ר"ש במסכת שבת בפרק המצניע (לד.) [זבחים צב.]. בגחלת של עץ אסור דשייך בה כיבוי לפי שעושה פחם [לקמן שם]. מוליכו פחות פחות מד' אמות. עד שמסלקנו לצדי רה"ר כדי שלא מזיק [ביצה כח:]. שהעבירן. מעל האור מרותחין ערב שבת עם חשיכה. לא יתן לתוכן תבלין. דכלי ראשון מבשל ונמצא מבשל תבלין בשבת [פסחים מ:].

עין משפט נר מצוה

לג א ב מיי' פ"א מהל' שבת הלכה ז ופי"ב הלכה ב טוש"ע או"ח סי' שלד סעיף כז:
לד ג מיי' שם פ"א הל' ז טוש"ע או"ח סי' שח סעיף יח:
לה ד ה מיי' פכ"ב מהל' שבת הלכה ו טוש"ע או"ח סימן שיח סעיף יג:
לו ו מיי' שם טור שו"ע שם סעיף ט:

רבינו חננאל

למימרא דשמואל כר' שמעון (ורב אדא) והאמר שמואל מכבין גחלת של מתכת ברה"ר בשביל שלא יוזקו בה רבים אבל גחלת של עץ לא ואילו ר"ש סבר אפילו של עץ מותר לפי שאין מתכוון לכבות אלא כדי שלא יוזק וכי האי גוונא פטר ר' שמעון ואסיק' לעולם כר' יהוד' סבירא לי' דאמר מלאכה שאינה צריכה לגופה חייב עליה א) מיהו דבר שיש בו היזק לרבים כגון צידת נחש וכבוי גחלת של מתכת בזמן שהיא חמה והיא שחורה והרואה אותה דומה שהיא צוננת לפי שאין בה אדמומית כגחלת לוחשת ונמצאו בני אדם ניזוקין בו לפיכך מותר אבל הגחלת של עץ אם תסיר אדמומיתה נכבת כבר ואינה מזקת ואם אדמומיתה בה כל הרואה אותה מתרחק ממנה ומכל פנים אין אדם ניזוק שהשחורה כבר כבתה והאדומה מתרחקין ממנה לפיכך המכבה אותה חייב ולפיכך היה שמואל אוסר בגחלת של עץ. (ומדוקיה) אמר רבינא קוץ ברה"ר מוליכו פחות פחות מד' אמות ואע"ג דרב ושמואל הלכה כרב באיסורי בהא קיי"ל כשמואל דאמר במלאכה שאינה צריכה לגופה סבר לה כר' יהודה בדבר שאין מתכוין סבר לה כר"ש ומדרב אחא ורבינא שמע מינייהו דהלכתא כר' שמעון: **פיסקא** אבל נותן הוא לתוכו או לתוך הכוס כדי להפשירן. ת"ר לא יתן אדם חמין לתוך צונן [ולא צונן] לתוך חמין וב"ה מתירין כו'. ואוקימנא להא דר"ש בן מנסיא שאוסר כלומר לא נחלקו ב"ש וב"ה אלא אפילו ב"ה אוסרין ואע"ג דאמר רב נחמן הלכתא כר' שמעון בן מנסיא כיון דאמר רב הונא חזינא לרבא דלא קפיד זימנין עביד כמר וזמנין עביד כמר מדתני ר' חייא דתני ר' חייא נותן אדם קיתון של מים לתוך ספל כו' ורב אשי מתרץ לה לרב הונא ואמר ליה מערה תניא כלומר מערה אדם קיתון של מים לתוך ספל של מים בין חמין לתוך צונן בין צונן לתוך חמין קיי"ל כוותיהו דאינון בתראי ומעשה רב ולא דמו ספל לאמבטי וכוס למיחם דאוקימנא ליה שאסור לתת בתוכו צונן מועטין בהיות חמין בו כדי שיחמו אלא מרובין כדי להפשיר כי המיחם הוא עצמו מייחם אבל ספל ואמבטי וכוס מתחממין בכלי אחד ומערין בתוך

חשק שלמה על רבינו חננאל א) עי' ביאור דברי רבינו ז"ל בחידושי הרשב"א ז"ל ד"ה גחלת של מתכות ע"ש היטב:

Yehoshua said: חֲזֵינָא לֵיהּ לְרָבָא דְּלֹא קָפֵיד אַמָּנָא – **I observed Rava having no reservations about** pouring cold water into **a** secondary **vessel,** such as a cup or washbasin that contained hot water.[19] מִדְּתָנֵי רַבִּי חִיָּיא – Rava **based** his opinion **on the** following **Baraisa taught by R' Chiya:** נוֹתֵן אָדָם קִיתוֹן שֶׁל מַיִם לְתוֹךְ סֵפֶל שֶׁל מַיִם – ONE MAY PUT A FLASK OF WATER INTO A WASHBASIN OF WATER, בֵּין חַמִּין לְתוֹךְ צוֹנֵן וּבֵין צוֹנֵן לְתוֹךְ חַמִּין – WHETHER HOT WATER INTO COLD WATER OR COLD WATER INTO HOT WATER. The Baraisa clearly permits introducing cold water into a washbasin of hot water.

An objection is raised:

אָמַר לֵיהּ רַב הוּנָא לְרַב אַשִׁי – **Rav Huna said to Rav Ashi:** דִּילְמָא שָׁאנֵי הָתָם דְּמִיפְסַק כְּלִי – **Perhaps there,** in the case discussed by the Baraisa, **it is different** than in Rava's case, **for** the walls of **the vessel,** i.e. the flask, **separate** the cold water in the flask from the hot water in the washbasin. How do we know that one may actually *pour* cold water into a basin of hot water?

Rav Ashi replies:

אָמַר לֵיהּ – **He said to [Rav Huna]:** מְעָרֶה אִיתְּמַר – **What was** actually **stated** in the Baraisa **is:** ***one may pour,*** not *one may put.* Thus, the correct reading is as follows: מְעָרֶה אָדָם קִיתוֹן שֶׁל מַיִם לְתוֹךְ סֵפֶל שֶׁל מַיִם – ONE MAY POUR A FLASK OF WATER INTO A WASHBASIN OF WATER, בֵּין חַמִּין לְתוֹךְ צוֹנֵן בֵּין צוֹנֵן לְתוֹךְ חַמִּין – WHETHER HOT WATER INTO COLD WATER OR COLD WATER INTO HOT WATER. This version explicitly supports Rava's practice.[20]

Mishnah הָאִילְפָּס וְהַקְּדֵרָה שֶׁהֶעֱבִירָן מְרוּתָּחִין – Concerning **a frying pan**[21] **or a pot that were removed** from the fire **while boiling,**[22] לֹא יִתֵּן לְתוֹכָן תְּבָלִין – **one may not add spices to them,**[23]

NOTES

19. [See *Rashi* printed alongside *Rif.*] Rava held that the halachah follows the opinion of Beis Hillel as originally cited by the Baraisa. He rejected Rav Nachman's assertion that the halachah follows R' Shimon ben Menasya (*Rif;* cf. *Tosafos* ד״ה מי סברת; see *Rosh*).

20. To summarize:

(a) Pouring cold water into a hot bathtub (a primary vessel) is forbidden according to all opinions, since the lower one – i.e. the hot water in the tub – dominates.

(b) Pouring hot water into a cold bath is permissible, based on the principle that the lower one dominates.

(c) Pouring hot water into a cup of cold water is permissible, based on the same principle.

(d) Pouring cold water into a cup of hot water (a secondary vessel) is a matter of dispute. Beis Shammai forbid it but Beis Hillel permit it, and R' Shimon ben Menasya holds that even Beis Hillel forbid it. The halachah is that it is permissible, in accordance with Rava's practice (*Orach Chaim* 318:12).

(e) A washbasin is treated like a cup, not like a bathtub.

This summary follows *Rashi's* explanation of the preceding passage. *Tosafos* and other Rishonim have alternative explanations.

21. The translation is based on *Rambam, Hil. Chametz U'Matzah* 6:6 and *Hil. Bikkurim* 6:12 (see *Radvaz* there). See also *Rashi* to *Beitzah* 32a ד״ה אלפסין חרניות and *Rav* to *Eduyos* 2:5.

22. In this context, *boiling* means that they are so hot that the hand recoils from them; see following note.

23. The frying pan or pot is a primary vessel, which retains its ability to cook something else as long as it remains hot enough that the hand recoils from it (*Rashi*). [*Rashi* states that the Mishnah refers to pots which were removed during *bein hashemashos* (which is when boiling pots are ordinarily removed from an open fire – see *Magen Avraham* 253:18 and *Shevisas HaShabbos, Hil. Bishul* p. 44b), and that one may not add spices to them after nightfall. *Rashi* seems to imply that during *bein hashemashos* it is permissible to add spices to the pot. It is not clear, however, why this should be the case. *Tos. R' Akiva Eiger* (below, 22:2) explains as follows: Later in the Mishnah, R' Yehudah permits adding spices even to a primary vessel that has been removed from the fire (see Gemara). [This pertains specifically to spices; R' Yehudah agrees that other foods become cooked in a primary vessel (*Tosafos,* 42b ד״ה לכל).] It is therefore likely that the Tanna Kamma prohibits adding spices only as a Rabbinic enactment and not Biblically, for it is unusual to find a dispute where the participants disagree to such extremes. Where a Rabbinic enactment is involved, we permit it *bein hashemashos,* for the purpose of a mitzvah, such as preparing the Sabbath meal (see above, 34a). Cf. *Rosh Yosef* to 42b.

מותר למימרא דשמואל כרבי שמעון סבירא ליה [א] והאמר שמואל [א]מכבין גחלת של מתכת ברה"ר בשביל שלא יוזקו בה רבים [ב]אבל לא גחלת של עץ ואי ס"ד סבר לה כרבי שמעון אפילו של עץ נמי [ב] בדבר שאין מתכוין סבר לה כרבי שמעון במלאכה שאינה צריכה לגופה סבר לה כרבי יהודה אמר רבינא [ג]הלכך [ג] קוץ ברשות הרבים מוליכו פחות פחות מד' אמות ובכרמלית אפילו טובא: אבל נותן כו': ת"ר נותן אדם חמין לתוך הצונן ולא הצונן לתוך החמין דברי בית שמאי ובית הלל אומרים [ד]בין חמין לתוך הצונן ובין צונן לתוך החמין מותר בד"א בכוס אבל באמבטי חמין לתוך הצונן ולא צונן לתוך החמין ורבי שמעון בן מנסיא אוסר אמר רב נחמן הלכה כר"ש בן מנסיא סבר רב יוסף למימר ספל הרי הוא כאמבטי א"ל אביי תני ר' חייא ספל אינו כאמבטי ולמאי דסליק אדעתא מעיקרא דספל הרי הוא כאמבטי ואמר רב נחמן הלכה כרבי שמעון בן מנסיא אלא בשבת רחיצה בחמין ליכא מי סברת רבי שמעון אסיפא קאי ארישא קאי ובית הלל מתירין בין חמין לתוך צונן ובין צונן לתוך החמין ורבי שמעון בן מנסיא אוסר צונן לתוך חמין לימא רבי שמעון בן מנסיא דאמר כב"ש הכי קאמר [ד] לא נחלקו ב"ש וב"ה בדבר זה אמר רב הונא בריה דרב יהושע חזינא ליה לרבא דלא קפיד [ה] אמנא מדתני רבי חייא נותן אדם קיתון של מים לתוך ספל של מים בין חמין לתוך צונן ובין צונן לתוך חמין אמר ליה רב הונא לרב אשי דילמא שאני התם דמיפסק כלי אמר ליה מערה איתמר [ה]מערה אדם קיתון של מים לתוך ספל של מים בין חמין לתוך צונן בין צונן לתוך חמין: **מתני'** [ו] [ו]האילפס והקדרה שהעבירן מרותחין לא יתן לתוכן תבלין אבל

רש"י

מותר. שאין מתכוין לכך: **גחלת של מתכת.** שמשליכין לחוץ פסולת של ברזל דלא שייך כבוי בהכי מדאורייתא ומדרבנן אסורה והיכא דאיכא נזקא לרבים לא גזרו על השבות: **אבל לא של עץ.** דאיסורא דאורייתא היא וחייב סקילה: **אפילו של עץ נמי.** דהא לרבי שמעון מלאכה שאינה צריכה לגופה פטור עליה וכל כיבוי אינו צריך לגופו חוץ מעושי פחמין או מהבהבי פתילה: **הלכך.** כיון דאמרת לא גזרו שבות דכיבוי מתכת במקום נזקא דרבים: **קוץ ברשות הרבים מוליכו פחות מד' אמות.** עד שיסלקנו לצידי רשות הרבים דאיסורא דרבנן הוא: **ובכרמלית.** דטלטול דידיה דרבנן: **אפילו טובא.** יעבירנו בעקירה אחת: **חמין לתוך צונן.** דקסבר תתאה גבר ואין החמין מרתיחין את הצונן אלא מפשירין: **ולא צונן לתוך חמין.** שהתחתונים מרתיחים את העליונים דתתאה גבר: **בכוס.** דלשתיה קבעי להו ולא ניחא ליה שיחומו הרבה ועוד דכלי שני הוא: **אוסר.** אפילו חמין לתוך צונן: **ספל הרי הוא כאמבטי.** ואף על גב דכלי שני הוא הואיל ולאו לשתיה אלא לרחיצה אסירי דניחא ליה שיחמו הרבה וגזרינן: **אלא בשבת רחיצה בחמין ליכא.** בתמיה דהא לרבי שמעון אפילו חמין לתוך צונן אסור לא משכחת חמין שהוחמו ואפילו מע"ש שלא יהיו צריכין להפיג רתיחתן ואם כן לא ירחוץ אפילו פניו ידיו ורגליו בחמין: **מי סברת ר' שמעון אסיפא קאי.** דלא שרי ת"ק אלא חמין לתוך צונן ואתא איהו ואסר אף חמין לתוך צונן: **ארישא קאי.** לשתיה וצונן לתוך חמין דקשרו ב"ה קאסר: **מתני'** שהעבירן. מן האור: מרותחין. בין השמשות: **לא יתן לתוכן תבלין.** משתחשך דכלי ראשון כל זמן שרותח מבשל:

אבל

תוספות

אפילו של עץ נמי. ואם תאמר ומאי ס"ד דמקשה וכי משום דסבר שמואל כרבי שמעון באין מתכוין יסבור כמותו במלאכה שאינו צריך לגופה וי"ל דס"ד דמקשה דודאי הא בהא תליא משום דסבר רבי יהודה דמלאכה שאינו צריך לגופה חייב עליה היכא דמתכוין בשאין מתכוין נמי החמירו חכמים אבל לרבי שמעון דפטור עליה מן התורה אף במתכוין לא חש לאסור מדרבנן כשאין מתכוין כיון דמתכוין עצמו ליכא אלא איסורא דרבנן ומיהו לפי האמת לאו הא בהא תליא דשמואל אע"ג דבמלאכה שאינה צריכה לגופה סבר כרבי יהודה דחייב [מתיר] באין מתכוין ולרבי יהודה נמי אסור אין מתכוין אפילו בגרירה דמתכוין עצמו לא אסיר אלא מדרבנן כדאמרי' לקמן ובשילהי כל התדיר (זבחים דף צא: ושם[ז]) דאמר שמואל המתנדב יין מביאו ומזלפו ע"ג האשים ופריך והא קא מכבה ומשני דסבר דבר שאין מתכוין מותר ופריך כי הכא דאמר שמואל מכבין גחלת של מתכת אבל לא של עץ והשתא אומר רשב"א דפריך מכ"ש דכיון דסבר שמואל דמלאכה שאינה צריכה לגופה חייב א"כ סבירא ליה נמי בשבת דבר שאין מתכוין אסור דסבר המקשה דהתם דהא בהא תליא כמו מקשה דהכא וכיון דבשבת אסור אין מתכוין כ"ש בעלמא אך הקשה דמשמע דאי הוי סבר שמואל מלאכה שאינה צריכה לו פטור עליה הוה אתי שפיר ואמאי והא מלאכה שאינה צריכה לגופה בשאר איסורים דלאו שבת חייב עליה וכיון דסבירא ליה דהא בהא תליא א"כ אמאי קאמר התם דבר שאין מתכוין מותר:

נותן אדם חמין לתוך צונן. [א] אפי' בכלי ראשון דחמין לתוך צונן אינו מבשל כמו שאפרש ולא צונן לתוך חמין אפילו בכלי שני דגזרי ב"ש כלי שני אטו כלי ראשון וב"ה דפליגי ושרו צונן לתוך חמין היינו דוקא בכלי שני כדקתני בד"א בכוס משמע דבכלי ראשון מודו ב"ה ולא משום דסברה הך ברייתא דתתאה גבר כדפירש בקונטרס דאם כן יקשה מהכא למ"ד [ח] עילאה גבר ולמאן דאמר תתאה גבר נמי הא מבשל כדי קליפה כמו שאפרש לקמן בע"ה אלא נראה כמו שאומר ר"ת דחמין לתוך צונן משמע שהצוננין של מטה מרובים שדרך ליתן המועט במרובה ולכך אין מבשלים החמין המועטים כלל לפי שמתערבין בצוננין המרובין ומתבטל חמימותן ולא צונן לתוך חמין שהחמין של מטה מרובין ומתערבין בהן הצוננין המועטין ומתבשלין: **אבל** באמבטי כו'. נראה דהאי אמבטי איירי כגון שהוא כלי שני ולא הוי כההוא אמבטי דלעיל [ט] דקאמר בקשתי להניח פך באמבטי מדקאמר ספל אינו כאמבטי והאי ספל ע"כ כלי שני דאי כלי ראשון אמאי אינו כאמבטי ודכוותיה אמבטי הוי כלי שני ועוד דאי באמבטי שהוא כלי ראשון איירי לא הוה ליה למינקט אמבטי אלא מיחם שהוא לשתיה דומיא דכוס ומדנקט אמבטי משמע דבכלי שני איירי ואתא לפלוגי בכלי שני בין כוס שהוא לשתיה לאמבטי לפי שחמין הרבה ואיכא למיגזר דהרואה אותן חמין כל כך סבור דכלי ראשון הוא ובמתני' דנקט במיחם שהוא ראשון לא יתן לתוכו מים הוה מצי למימר באמבטי שהוא שני לא יתן לתוכו מים אלא דמתני' מיירי בשתיה ומפליג בין מיחם לכוס: **מי** סברת ר"ש בן מנסיא אסיפא קאי ארישא קאי. היינו דוקא למאי דס"ד לרב יוסף מעיקרא אבל למאי דמסקי' דספל אינו כאמבטי קאי אסיפא בכוס וסבר שפיר ר"ש בן מנסיא כב"ה דאפילו צונן לתוך חמין מותר ואתיא מתני' דשריא לתוך הכוס אליבא דהלכתא דהלכה כר"ש בן מנסיא וא"ת למאי דסלקא דעתך דארישא קאי ואסר בכוס צונן לתוך חמין מאי קמ"ל רב יוסף דספל הרי הוא כאמבטי כוס נמי הרי הוא כאמבטי לר"ש בן מנסיא דהלכתא כוותיה וי"ל דרב יוסף לב"ה אתא לאשמעינן דשרו בכוס: **נותן** אדם קיתון של מים. וא"ת ואמאי לא מייתי ברייתא דלעיל דספל אינו כאמבטי ומאי איצטריך נמי רבי חייא למיתני תרוייהו וי"ל דהשתא קמ"ל בין חמין לתוך צונן בין צונן לתוך חמין דהויא דספל אינו כאמבטי ה"א דקאי אר"ש בן מנסיא דאסר באמבטי אפי' חמין לתוך צונן ועליה קאמר דספל אינו כאמבטי ושרי חמין לתוך צונן אבל צונן לתוך חמין ה"א דאסור ואפשר דהיא דלעיל היינו הך דהכא אלא שקיצרה ונקט לישנא דרב יוסף דמייתי עלה: **שאני** התם דמפסיק כלי. וא"ת דאמר לעיל (דף מ:) טול בכלי שני ותן אבל בכלי ראשון לא אע"ג דמפסיק מנא וי"ל דהתם בכלי ראשון והכא דבכלי שני שאני:

אבל

עין משפט נר מצוה

לג א ב מיי' פ"א מהל' שבת הלכה ז ופי"ב הלכה ג טוש"ע או"ח סי' שלד סעיף כז:

לד ג מיי' שם פ"א הל' ז טוש"ע או"ח סי' שח סעיף יח:

לה ד ה מיי' פכ"ב מהל' שבת הלכה ו טוש"ע או"ח סימן שיח סעיף יב:

לו ו מיי' שם טור שו"ע שם סעיף ט:

רבינו חננאל

למימרא דשמואל כר' שמעון (ורב אדא) והאמר שמואל מכבין גחלת של מתכת ברה"ר בשביל שלא יוזקו בה רבים אבל גחלת של עץ לא ואילו ר"ש סבר אפילו של עץ מותר לפי שאין מתכוון לכבות אלא כדי שלא יוזק וכי האי גוונא פטר ר' שמעון ואסיק' לעולם כר' יהוד' סבירא לי' דאמר מלאכה שאינה צריכה לגופה חייב עליה [א] מיהו דבר שיש בו היזק לרבים כגון צידת נחש וכבוי גחלת של מתכת בזמן שהיא חמה והיא שחורה והרואה אותה דומה שהיא צוננת לפי שאין בה אדמומית כגחלת לוחשת ונמצאו בני אדם ניזוקין בו לפיכך מותר אבל הגחלת של עץ אם תסיר אדמומיתה נכבת כבר ואינה מזקת ואם אדמומיתה בה כל הרואה אותה מתרחק ממנה ומכל פנים אין אדם ניזוק שהשחורה כבר כבתה והאדומה מתרחקין ממנה לפיכך המכבה אותה חייב ולפיכך היה שמואל אוסר בגחלת של עץ. (ומדוקיה) אמר רבינא קוץ ברה"ר מוליכו פחות פחות מד' אמות ואע"ג דרב ושמואל הלכה כרב באיסורי בהא קיי"ל כשמואל דאמר במלאכה שאינה צריכה לגופה סבר לה כר' יהודה בדבר שאין מתכוין סבר לה כר"ש ומדרב אחא ורבינא שמע מינייהו דהלכתא כר' שמעון: **פיסקא** אבל נותן הוא לתוכו או לתוך הכוס כדי להפשירן. ת"ר לא יתן אדם חמין לתוך צונן [ולא צונן] לתוך חמין וב"ה מתירין כו'. ואוקימנא להא דר"ש בן מנסיא שאוסר כלומר לא נחלקו ב"ש וב"ה אלא אפילו ב"ה אוסרין ואע"ג דאמר רב נחמן הלכתא כר' שמעון בן מנסיא כיון דאמר רב הונא חזינא לרבא דלא קפיד זימנין עביד כמר וזמנין עביד כמר מדתני ר' חייא דתני ר' חייא נותן אדם קיתון של מים לתוך ספל כו' ורב אשי מתרץ לה לרב הונא ואמר ליה מערה תניא כלומר מערה אדם קיתון של מים לתוך ספל של מים בין חמין לתוך צונן בין צונן לתוך חמין קיי"ל כוותייהו דאינון בתראי ומעשה רב ולא דמו ספל לאמבטי וכוס למיחם דאוקימנא ליה שאסור לתת בתוכו צונן מועטין בהיות חמין בו כדי שיחמו אלא מרובין כדי להפשיר כי המיחם הוא עצמו מייחם אבל ספל ואמבטי וכוס מתחממין בכלי אחד ומערין בתוך

מסורת הש"ס

א) זבחים לא:, ב) [שם לב.], ג) [ביצה כח:], ד) [לקמן קלה. יבמות כח. ב"ק לד. סוכה טו.], ה) [בהרא"ש ליתא ועי' ברב אלפס], ו) פסחים מ:, ז) [ושם לב.], ח) [פסחים עו.], ט) [דף מ:].

תוספות ישנים

א) עוד טכל לומר דחמין לתוך צונן דוקא בכ"ש שרי ב"ש אבל בכלי ראשון אסור אטו צונן לתוך חמין:

ליקוטי רש"י

גחלת של מתכת. לא שייך בה כיבוי דאינו נעשה פחם [לקמן קלד.]. לאו בת כיבוי [היא] ואיסורא דרבנן הוא דאיכא ובמקום היזק רבים לא גזור רבנן [זבחים צא:]. **אבל לא גחלת של עץ.** גחלת אקרי פחם שאינו בוער כדאמרינן (ברכות נג:) גחלים עוממות מפי רבי [סנהדרין ק:]. דבת כיבוי הוא ואיסורא דאורייתא הוא ואי כר"ש לא משכחת כיבוי [מן התורה] אלא במתכוין לעשות פחמין בכיבויו וצריך להם דאר"ש מלאכה שאינה צריכה לגופה פטור עליה וכיבוי [זה] לאו צורך גופו הוא שיהא צריך לו דהלואי שלא בא עליו ודמי למוציא את המת לסלקו מעל פניו דפטר עליה ר"ש במסכת שבת בפרק המצניע (לג.) [זבחים צב.]. בגחלת של עץ אסור דשייך בה כיבוי לפי שעושה פחם [לקמן שם]. **מוליכו פחות פחות מד' אמות.** עד שמסלקנה לצדי רה"ר כדי שלא מזיק [ביצה כח:]. **שהעבירן.** מעל האור מרותחין ערב שבת עם חשיכה. **לא יתן לתוכן תבלין.** דכלי ראשון מבשל ונמצא מבשל תבלין בשבת [פסחים מ:].

חשק שלמה על רבינו חננאל א) עי' ביאור דברי רבינו ז"ל בחידושי הרשב"א ז"ל ד"ה גחלת של מתכות ע"ש היטב:

אבל נותן הוא לתוך הקערה או לתוך התמחוי רבי יהודה אומר ה) לכל הוא נותן חוץ מדבר שיש בו חומץ וציר: **גמ'** איבעיא להו רבי יהודה ארישא קאי ולקולא או דילמא אסיפא קאי ולחומרא ת"ש דתניא רבי יהודה אומר לכל אילפסין הוא נותן לכל הקדירות רותחות הוא נותן חוץ מדבר שיש בו חומץ וציר סבר רב יוסף למימר מלח הרי הוא כתבלין דבכלי ראשון בשלה ובכלי שני לא בשלה א"ל אביי תני רבי חייא מלח אינה כתבלין דבכלי שני נמי בשלה ופליגא דרב נחמן דאמר רב נחמן צריכא מילחא בישולא כבשרא דתורא ואיכא דאמרי סבר רב יוסף למימר מלח הרי הוא כתבלין דבכלי ראשון בשלה בכלי שני לא בשלה א"ל אביי תני ר' חייא א מלח אינה כתבלין דבכלי ראשון נמי לא בשלה והיינו דאמר רב נחמן צריכא מילחא בישולא כבישרא דתורא: **מתני'** ב אין נותנין כלי תחת הנר לקבל בו את השמן ואם נתנוה מבעוד יום מותר ואין ניאותין ממנו לפי שאינו מן המוכן: **גמ'** אמר רב חסדא ג אע"פ שאמרו אין נותנין כלי תחת תרנגולת לקבל ביצתה אבל כופה עליה כלי שלא תשבר אמר רבה מ"ט דרב חסדא קסבר תרנגולת עשויה להטיל ביצתה באשפה ואינה עשויה להטיל ביצתה במקום מדרון והצלה מצויה התירו והצלה שאינה מצויה לא התירו איתיבי' אביי והצלה שאינה מצויה לא התירו והתניא ג) נשברה לו חבית של טבל בראש גגו מביא כלי ומניח תחתיה בגולפי חדתי דשכיחי דפקעי איתיביה ד) נותנין כלי תחת הנר לקבל ניצוצות נמי שכיחי איתיביה

רש"י

אבל נותן הוא לתוך הקערה. דכלי שני אינו מבשל: תמחוי. כעין קערה גדולה שמערה כל האילפס לתוכה ומשם מערה לקערות: ר' יהודה אומר לכל וכו'. בגמ' מפרש אהי קאי אכלי ראשון או אכלי שני: חוץ מדבר שיש בו חומץ או ציר. שהן מבשלין את התבלין כשהן רותחין: ציר. הנוטף מן הדגים כשכובשים אותן במכבש: גמ' ארישא קאי. אאילפס דקא אסר ת"ק וקאמר ר' יהודה לכל אילפסין הוא נותן דכלי ראשון לא מבשל: או דילמא אסיפא קאי. אקערה ותמחוי דקא שרי ת"ק וקא אמר ליה רבי יהודה בכל קערות ותמחוין מודינא לך חוץ מדבר שיש בו חומץ ואפילו כלי שני נמי לא: דבכלי ראשון נמי לא בשלה. ומותר ליתן ואפילו בכלי ראשון משהעבירו מן האור: מתני' אין נותנין. בשבת: כלי תחת הנר. לקבל בו שמן המטפטף משום דשמן מוקצה הוא וקסבר אין כלי ניטל בשבת אלא לצורך דבר הניטל אי נמי קסבר אסור לבטל כלי מהיכנו להושיב כלי במקום שלא יוכל עוד ליטלו ד) (משום) דהוי כקובע לו מקום ומחברו בטיט ודמי למלאכה וכלי זה משיפול בו השמן המוקצה יהא אסור לטלטלו: מותר. להניחה שם: ואין ניאותין. נהנין: גמ' אע"פ שאמרו אין נותנין כלי תחת תרנגולת לקבל ביצתה. כשהיא מטילתה במקום מדרון שמא תתגלגל ותשבר ומדיוקא דמתניתין שמעינן לה דדמי לנותן כלי תחת הנר לקבל בו שמן: אבל כופה עליה כלי. ולא תימא אין כלי ניטל אלא לצורך דבר הניטל: באשפה. ויש לחוש שמא תשבר ברגלי אדם וכופה עליה כלי: והצלה מצויה התירו. לטלטל כלי לצרכה ואף על פי שהבילה דבר שאינו ניטל בשבת: שאינה מצויה. כגון מדרון וטיפטוף דשמן דמתני': נשברה לו חבית של טבל גרסינן: מביא כלי. ואף על גב דטבל דבר שאינו ניטל הוא וחבית לא שכיחא דפקעה: גולפי. חביות: נותנין כלי. מתניתין היא ומותיב ליה מינה: ניצוצות. שלהבת הנוטפת מן הנר כדי שלא ידלק מה שתחתיה ואע"ג דניצוצות לא מיטלטלי ולא שכיחי: איתיביה

תוספות

אבל נותן הוא לתוך הקערה כו'. מהכא ליכא למידק דעירוי ככלי שני מדקתני לא יתן לתוכה תבלין ולא אשמעינן רבותא אפילו שלא יערה על הקערה שתבלין בתוכה דאדרבה דוק מסיפא דקתני אבל נותן הוא לתוך הקערה ולא קתני מערה על הקערה שתבלין בתוכה ורבינו שמואל מביא ראיה דעירוי ככלי שני מהא דקי"ל תתאה גבר ולר"י נראה דעירוי ככלי ראשון ומביא ראיה דבזבחים בפרק דם חטאת (דף צה: ושם) ת"ר אשר תבושל בו אין לי אלא שבישל בו עירה לתוכו רותח מניין תלמוד לומר [אשר תבושל] בו ישבר אלמא דעירוי חשיב מבשל ובירושלמי בפרק כירה בעי מהו ליתן תבלין מלמטה ולערות עליהן מלמעלה ר' יונה אמר אסור דעירוי ככלי ראשון חיליה דר' יונה מן הדא אחד שבישל בו ואחד שעירה לתוכו רותח ודחי ר' יוסי תמן כלי חרס בולע תבלין אינו מתבשל השיב רבי יוסי בר בון והתניא מניין שבכלי נחשת כן תלמוד לומר ואם בכלי נחשת בשלה אית לן למימר כלי נחשת בלע בתמיה פי' ע"י עירוי אם אינו מבשל לא בלע אלמא דמסיק דעירוי ככלי ראשון ונראה דעירוי לא הוי ככלי ראשון ולא ככלי שני אלא מבשל כדי קליפה דהא קי"ל כשמואל דאמר תתאה גבר דתניא כוותיה בכילד צולין (פסחים עו.) ומ"מ מבשל כדי קליפה דאמר התם תניא כוותיה דשמואל חם לתוך צונן או צונן לתוך צונן מדיח ופריך חם לתוך צונן אדמיקר ליה בלע אלא אימא חם לתוך צונן קולף צונן לתוך צונן מדיח וכן משמע בשילהי מסכת ע"ז (דף עו.) דאמר מר ה) עוקבא זבן יורה מעכו"ם אהדר ליה גדנפא ומסיק כבולעו כך פולטו מה בולעו בניצוצות אף פולטו בניצוצות ואי עירוי ככלי ראשון ° מאי איריא משום דבלע בניצוצות אפילו בלע בליעה גמורה פלט בניצוצות שהוא עירוי אלא ודאי לא מבשל אלא כדי קליפה ואם עירו רותחים על התרנגולת צריכה קליפה וכלי שתשמישו ע"י עירוי כגון קערות יכול להגעילן ע"י עירוי דכבולעו כך פולטו אבל כלי שנתבשל בו איסור לא סגי להגעילו על ידי עירוי והא דאמר בפרק בתרא דע"ז (דף עד:) דרש רבא נעוה ארתחיה דהתם מסתמא ע"י עירוי שאני התם דאותה נעוה לא בלעה ע"י רותח א) ו):

לכל קדרות רותחות הוא נותן. נראה דדוקא בתבלין פליג אבל בשאר דברים מודה דכלי ראשון מבשל אף כשהעבירו מעל האור: **והיינו** דר"נ. נראה דאף לפי' הקונטרס שפי' ז) דבכל מקום דאיכא לישני דפליגי בשל תורה הלך אחר המחמיר ובשל סופרים הלך אחר המיקל ולר"ת בשל סופרים הלך אחר אחרון וכן לריב"א שפירש שבכל מקום איכא דאמרי טפל לגבי לשון ראשון שהוא עיקר הכא הלכה כלישנא בתרא דללישנא קמא פליג ברייתא דרבי חייא אדרב נחמן וללישנא בתרא היינו דרב נחמן ומתוך כך פסק רבינו שמואל שמותר לתת מלח בתבשיל בשבת אפילו בכלי ראשון שהעבירו מן האור והמחמיר כלישנא קמא שלא ליתן מלח בקערה כל זמן שהיד סולדת בו תבא עליו ברכה: **ואם** נתנוהו מבעוד יום מותר. הלשון דחוק דהוה ליה למימר אבל מבעוד יום נותנין: **ואין** נאותין ממנו לפי שאינו מן המוכן. איכא לאוקמה כר"ש ח) דמתיר מותר השמן שבנר ואין ניאותין דקתני הכא היינו כל זמן שדולק ° דמוקצה מחמת מצוה מודה ר"ש כדאמר בגמ' לקמן (דף מה.) אין מוקצה לר"ש אלא שמן שבנר בשעה שהוא דולק הואיל והוקצה למצותו הוקצה לאיסורו ולא שבנר ממש קאמר דההיא אסור בלאו הכי משום מכבה כדאמר בביצה פ"ב (דף כב. ושם) המסתפק ממנו חייב משום מכבה אלא כלומר שמן המטפטף מן הנר והטלטול דנר עצמו אין לאסור מטעם דהוקצה למצותו ולא אסור לטלטלו אלא משום דנעשה בסיס לדבר האסור כדאמרינן בסוף פירקין (דף מז.) הנח לנר שמן ופתילה הואיל ונעשה בסיס לדבר האסור אבל מטעם דהוקצה למצותו לא היה אסור לטלטלו שאין ביטול מצוה במה שמטלטלו: **אע"פ** שאמרו חכמים אין נותנין כו'. אין נותנין כלי תחת הנר לקבל בו את השמן ה"ל למימר דתנן במתניתין וכלי לקבל ביצה לא שמעינן אלא מדיוקא דמתני' אלא משום דבעי למימר אבל כופה עליה כלי נקט ביצה: **הצלה** שאינה מצויה לא התירו. פי' בקונטרס לדבר שאינו ניטל וגרס בההוא דפריך אביי מינה בסמוך נשברה לו חבית של טבל בראש גגו דטבל אינו ניטל וקשה לריב"א דאי גרס בה טבל אמאי פריך לרב יוסף מברייתא אחרת מהך דהכא הוה ליה לאקשויי ועוד דבפרק כל כתבי (לקמן דף קיז: ושם) משמע בהדיא דלא גרסי' בברייתא דהכא טבל דלא בשל טבל איירי דקתני סיפא נזדמנו לו אורחין מביא כלי אחר כו' ונראה לו לפרש דהצלה שאינה מצויה לא התירו לטרוח בכל דבר אפילו בדבר המיטל משום טירחא: **שאינה** מצויה לא התירו. והא דאין נותנין כלי תחת הנר לקבל שמן חשיב הצלה שאינה מצויה לפי שרגילים לעולם לתת כלי תחת הנר מבעוד יום וניצוצות אע"ג דקאמר בסמוך דשכיחי לא שכיחי כולי האי שיחושו לתת שם כלי מבעוד יום ולהכי חשיב לה הצלה מצויה: דמבטל

עין משפט נר מצוה

לז א מיי' פכ"ב מהל' שבת הלכה ו טוש"ע או"ח סימן שיח סעיף ט:
לח ב מיי' פכ"ה מהלכות שבת הלכה כג ופ"ה הלכה יג סמג לאוין סה טור שו"ע או"ח סימן רסה סעיף ג:
לט ג מיי' פכ"ה שם סמג שם טור ושו"ע או"ח סימן שי סעיף ו וסימן שכב סעיף א וסי' תקיג סעיף ד:

רבינו חננאל

בתוך חללו לפיכך מותר שנמצאו כלי שני וקיי"ל כלי שני מותר: ר' יהודה אומר לכל הוא נותן כו' אסיק' ר' יהודה ארישא דקתני האלפס והקדירה שהעבירן מרותחין לא יתן בתוכן תבלין התם פליג ומקיל הוא דתניא ר"י אומר לכל אלפסין רותחין [הוא נותן] לכל קדרות רותחין הוא נותן חוץ מדבר שיש בו חומץ וציר. מלח כתבלין הוא אי לא ואסיק' כדתני ר' חייא מלח אינו כתבלין דכלי ראשון נמי לא בשלה והיינו דרב נחמן דאמר צריכה מילחא בשולי כבשרא דתורא ש"מ כי נותן מלח בתבשיל בשבת ואפילו בכלי ראשון אינו בישול: מתניתין אין נותנין כלי תחת הנר לקבל בו את השמן כו' אמר רב חסדא אע"פ שאמרו אין נותנין נר תחת התרנגולת כו' כלומר אפילו אם עומדת במקום מדרון ורואין כיון שתלד תפול הביצה במקום מדרון ותשבר לא התירו לו להטיל תחתיה כלי לקבלה לביצה כדי שלא תשבר שזה לילד התרנגולת במקום מדרון דבר שאינו מצוי הוא ומשום אחת שנזדמנה לה כך לא חיישינן לה. אבל כיון שדרך רוב התרנגולת להטיל ביציהן לאשפה התירו לכפות על אותה ביצה כלי בשביל שלא תשבר וזהו פירוש הצלה מצויה התירו הצלה שאינה מצויה לא התירו ואקשינן והצלה שאינה מצויה לא התירו והא חבית שנשברה בראש גגו כו' ושנינן בגולפי חדתי פי' קנקנים חדשים שהן מצוין להפקיע. וניצוצות תחת הנר נמי מילתא דשכיחא היא ובבתי גחיני כלומר בתים נמוכים להיאחז בהן דליקה מילתא דשכיחא היא וכן כולם. פירק רבא לדבריו דהצלה מצויה התירו הצלה שאינה מצויה לא התירו אליבא דרב חסדא. רב יוסף אמר מ"ט דרב חסדא משום דאי שרית ליה לקבל הביצה בכלי במקום מדרון כבר ביטל אותו הכלי היום שאסור לטלטלו והביצה בתוכו. כשם שאסור לטלטל הביצה. אבל כפיית הכלי על הביצה אינו ביטול שאם הצרך הכלי מותר לו לטלטלו שהרי אין בכלי כלום ולא מבטל כלי מהיכנו. איתיביה אביי (טלטל) [חבית של טבל] כו' והא טבל אסור לטלטלו ושני ליה טבל מוכן הוא שאם עבר ותיקנו מתוקן הוא. ושני בניצוצות. ניצוצות אין

מסורת הש"ס

א) [כהאי גוונא במעשרות פ"א מ"ו], ב) לקמן קיז: ע"ש, ג) לקמן מג. מז:, ד) [נ"ל משם], ה) יש ספרים שגורסין כאן במוס' רב עקיבא כמו שהביא הגאון מהרי"ף בע"ז שם בהגהותיו. ואולי יגלה גירסת מר עוקבא מסוגיא דב"מ ע. ההוא דולא דבי מר עוקבא כמו שהעיר בסה"ד, ו) [וע' תוספות זבחים צה: ד"ה עירה כו'], ז) [עי' תוס' ע"ז ז. ד"ה בשל תורה], ח) [לקמן מד.].

תוספות ישנים

א) א"נ ארתחי' שיעשה האש למטה והיא של חרס. דכפ' כל שעה איכא למ"ד זה וזה לפטור המעסה והחלוטה ומוגלשין ואיירי בשים למלוס כשיעור חלה. ולהכי בין תתאה גבר בין עילאה גבר מבשל כדי קליפה ובצר ליה משיעור חלה:

גליון הש"ס

תוס' ד"ה אבל וכו'. מאי איריא משום דבלע בניצוצות. ק"ל לטעמיך אף אם עירוי לא הוי ככ"ר היינו בעירוי על צונן אבל הכא דהעירוי על גופה הכלי שהוא חם אף אם היה העירוי מצונן לחם היה חם דמתאי גבר מכ"ש בעירוי מכ"ר על כ"ר. וה' יאיר עיני: שם ד"ה ואין נאותין וכו' דבמוקצה מחמת מצוה מודה ר"ש. וכיון דאינו ראוי לאכלו ממש באותה שעה הוי מוקצה בעצמותו כדין כל מאכל שאינו חזי לכלום. עי' מג"א ריש סימן תקט"ו. ורק בטלטול הנר בשעה שהוא דולק להאיר זהו מדינא מותר אלולי טעמא דבסיס ולק"מ קושית המהרש"א:

ליקוטי רש"י

לכל הוא נותן. לכל מיני מאכל הוא נותן תבלין בכלי שני חוץ מדבר שיש בו חומץ וציר שהחומץ מבשלן [פסחים מ:]. ציר. ציר מזיעה חיבום של דגים כשכובשין אותן במכבש כדאמרינן במועד קטן (יא.) ונעשה חזק כחומץ ומטבל בו [ע"ז לא:]. גולפי. כלי חרס [ע"ז לב.].

אֲבָל נוֹתֵן הוּא לְתוֹךְ הַקְּעָרָה אוֹ לְתוֹךְ הַתַּמְחוּי – **but one may add** spices to hot food **in a bowl or in a tureen.**[1] רַבִּי יְהוּדָה אוֹמֵר – **R' Yehudah says:** לַכֹּל הוּא נוֹתֵן – **One may add** spices **to anything,** חוּץ מִדָּבָר שֶׁיֵּשׁ בּוֹ חוֹמֶץ וְצִיר – **except something containing vinegar or fish brine.**[2]

Gemara The Gemara seeks to clarify R' Yehudah's position: רַבִּי יְהוּדָה אַרֵישָׁא – אִיבַּעְיָא לְהוּ – **They inquired:** קָאֵי וּלְקוּלָּא – Did **R' Yehudah address the first clause** of the Mishnah, which deals with a pot, **and** mean to rule **leniently** that it is permissible to introduce spices even into a primary vessel that is not on the fire if it does not contain vinegar or brine? אוֹ דִּילְמָא אַסֵּיפָא קָאֵי וּלְחוּמְרָא – **Or, perhaps, he addressed the latter clause** of the Mishnah, which deals with a bowl and tureen, and he meant to rule **stringently**, that it is prohibited to introduce spices even to a secondary vessel if it contains vinegar or brine. – ? –

The Gemara resolves the inquiry:

תָּא שְׁמַע – **Come, learn** a proof, דְּתַנְיָא – **for it was taught in a Baraisa:** רַבִּי יְהוּדָה אוֹמֵר – R' YEHUDAH SAYS: לְכָל אִילְפָּסִין הוּא נוֹתֵן – ONE MAY ADD spices TO ANY FRYING PAN, לְכָל הַקְּדֵירוֹת רוֹתְחוֹת הוּא נוֹתֵן – and ONE MAY ADD spices TO ANY BOILING POT, חוּץ מִדָּבָר שֶׁיֵּשׁ בּוֹ חוֹמֶץ וְצִיר – EXCEPT SOMETHING CONTAINING VINEGAR OR FISH BRINE. In this Baraisa, R' Yehudah explicitly permits introducing spices to primary vessels that do not contain vinegar or fish brine.[3]

Having clarified R' Yehudah's position, the Gemara enters a discussion that pertains to the opinion of the Tanna Kamma, who forbids adding spices to a primary vessel but permits adding them to a secondary vessel regardless of the presence of vinegar or brine:[4] סָבַר רַב יוֹסֵף לְמֵימַר מֶלַח הֲרֵי הוּא כְּתַבְלִין – **Rav Yosef was inclined to say** that **salt is similiar to spices,** דְּבִכְלִי רִאשׁוֹן בָּשְׁלָה – **in that it can become cooked in a primary vessel,** וּבִכְלִי שֵׁנִי לֹא בָּשְׁלָה – **but will not become cooked in a secondary vessel.**[5] אָמַר לֵיהּ אַבַּיֵּי – However, **Abaye said to him:** תָּנֵי רַבִּי חִיָּיא – **R' Chiya has taught a Baraisa** which states: מֶלַח אֵינָהּ כְּתַבְלִין – SALT IS NOT SIMILIAR TO SPICES, דְּבִכְלִי שֵׁנִי נַמִּי בָּשְׁלָה – FOR IT CAN BECOME COOKED EVEN IN A SECONDARY VESSEL.[6] וּפְלִיגָא דְּרַב נַחְמָן – **But Rav Nachman's** opinion in this regard **differs** from both of the previous views. דְּאָמַר רַב נַחְמָן – **For Rav Nachman said:** צְרִיכָא מִילְחָא בִּישׁוּלָא כְּבִשְׂרָא דְּתוֹרָא – **Salt needs** as intense a **cooking as the meat of an ox,** i.e. it does not cook even in a primary vessel that has been removed from the fire, but only on the fire.[7]

Another version of this discussion:

וְאִיכָּא דְּאָמְרִי – **And there are those who say** that the previous discussion proceeded as follows: סָבַר רַב יוֹסֵף לְמֵימַר מֶלַח הֲרֵי הוּא כְּתַבְלִין – **Rav Yosef was inclined to say** that **salt is similiar to spices,** דְּבִכְלִי רִאשׁוֹן בָּשְׁלָה בִּכְלִי שֵׁנִי לֹא בָּשְׁלָה – **in that it can become cooked in a primary vessel but will not become cooked in a secondary vessel.** אָמַר לֵיהּ אַבַּיֵּי – However, **Abaye said to him:** תָּנֵי רַבִּי חִיָּיא – **R' Chiya has taught a Baraisa** which states: מֶלַח אֵינָהּ כְּתַבְלִין – SALT IS NOT SIMILIAR TO SPICES, דְּבִכְלִי רִאשׁוֹן נַמִּי לֹא בָּשְׁלָה – FOR IT WILL NOT BECOME COOKED EVEN IN A *PRIMARY* VESSEL. וְהַיְינוּ דְּאָמַר רַב נַחְמָן – **And this is** the same as **that which Rav Nachman said:** צְרִיכָא מִילְחָא בִּישׁוּלָא כְּבִשְׂרָא דְּתוֹרָא – **Salt needs** as intense a **cooking as the meat of an ox.**[8]

Mishnah For the remainder of the chapter, the Mishnah shifts its focus to the subject of *muktzeh*:[9] אֵין נוֹתְנִין כְּלִי תַּחַת הַנֵּר לְקַבֵּל בּוֹ אֶת הַשֶּׁמֶן – **We may not place a vessel under a lamp to catch the**

NOTES

1. Spices may be added to a bowl or tureen into which the contents of a pot have been transferred. The bowl or tureen is a secondary vessel and is not capable of cooking the spices (*Rashi*). This ruling applies only where the secondary vessel contains liquids. If, however, there is hot, solid food in the secondary vessel, many authorities rule that we may not add spices to it as long as the food is still hot enough that the hand recoils from it. Solid food does not lose its heat as rapidly as does liquid and may remain capable of cooking even after being transferred to a secondary vessel (*Mishnah Berurah* 318:65).

2. These acidic substances enable the hot water to cook more readily. The Gemara will discuss whether R' Yehudah is referring to a primary vessel or a secondary vessel (*Rashi*).

[The Mishnah has discussed adding spices to a primary vessel, which is forbidden, and to a secondary vessel, which is permitted. There is, however, another case that is not mentioned here. This is the case in which spices are placed into an empty bowl and liquid from a primary vessel is poured on top of them (עירוי). In degree of severity, this case ranks below adding spices to a primary vessel, but ranks above adding them to a secondary vessel, since the hot liquid does not blend with the spices but strikes them before coming to rest in the secondary vessel. The Rishonim are divided regarding the permissibility of this act; however, the halachah follows the opinion that it is forbidden. See *Tosafos, Rosh* et al. for lengthy discussions of this topic, and *Orach Chaim* 318:10 for the halachic ruling. See also *HaAruch MiShach, Yoreh Deah* 105.]

3. R' Yehudah's opinion pertains specifically to spices [which do not cook as readily as other foods] (*Tosafos*). Furthermore, it pertains only to a pot that has been removed from the fire. A pot that is on the fire is obviously capable of cooking anything (*Ran*).

4. The halachah follows the Tanna Kamma (*Orach Chaim* 318:9).

5. Accordingly, it would be forbidden to add salt to a primary vessel, but permissible to add it to a secondary vessel.

6. According to this Baraisa, it is forbidden to add salt even to a secondary vessel (so long as the liquid in it is so hot that the hand recoils from it).

7. According to Rav Nachman, one can add salt even to a primary vessel, so long as it is not on a fire (*Rashi;* see *Aruch HaShulchan* 318:39; see also *Ramban* to *Avodah Zarah* 74b and *Mishbetzos Zahav* to *Yoreh Deah* 68 ד"ה הדין הב').

8. *Shulchan Aruch* (*Orach Chaim* 318:9) rules that salt cooks only on an actual fire, in accordance with Rav Nachman's view and the final version of R' Chiya's view. However, *Rama* (ad loc.) writes that it is preferable to take into account the view that salt cooks even in a secondary vessel; accordingly, one should not add salt even to a secondary vessel (see *Tosafos* ד"ה והיינו דר"נ). [This discussion pertains to salt that is mined from the ground and is uncooked. Salt that is produced by boiling sea water or that is refined by boiling is not subject to this stricture, since it has already been cooked. Nevertheless, one should not add it to a vessel that is on a fire or to a primary vessel that has been removed from the fire (*Mishnah Berurah* 318:71).]

Our Mishnah and Gemara have focused on spices and salt, and have taught that these may certainly be added to liquid in a secondary vessel. We also learned above that it is permitted to warm water (see 42a) or oil (see 40b) by placing it in a secondary vessel. There are, however, certain foods that cook readily (e.g. eggs – see 38b note 32) and which may therefore not be placed even in liquid in a secondary vessel, so long as the hand recoils from it (see *Chazon Ish* 52:19). Since we do not know with certainty which foods cook readily and which do not, it is customary not to add any uncooked food to a secondary vessel when the hand recoils from it. The only exceptions to this rule are spices, water and oil, which are known not to cook in a secondary vessel (*Orach Chaim* 318:5 with *Mishnah Berurah* §42,45; see also §47). Once the hot liquid is transferred to a *third* vessel, it is treated less stringently (see *Mishnah Berurah* ibid. §47; *Chazon Ish* ibid.; *Aruch HaShulchan* 318:28; *Igros Moshe, Orach Chaim* vol. IV §74 – *bishul* §4,15; and *Shemiras Shabbos KeHilchasah* 1:57).

9. See Chapter Introduction for a discussion of this topic. For an explanation of why these laws appear in this chapter, see *Tiferes Yisrael*. See also *Tosafos* above, 2a ד"ה יציאות השבת.

אבל נותן הוא לתוך הקערה או לתוך התמחוי רבי יהודה אומר א) לכל הוא נותן חוץ מדבר שיש בו חומץ וציר: **גמ'** איבעיא להו רבי יהודה ארישא קאי ולקולא או דילמא אסיפא קאי ולחומרא ת"ש דתניא רבי יהודה אומר לכל אילפסין הוא נותן לכל הקדירות רותחות הוא נותן חוץ מדבר שיש בו חומץ וציר סבר רב יוסף למימר מלח הרי הוא כתבלין דבכלי ראשון בשלה ובכלי שני לא בשלה א"ל אביי תני רבי חייא מלח אינה כתבלין דבכלי שני נמי בשלה ופליגא דרב נחמן דאמר רב נחמן צריכא מילחא בישולא כבשרא דתורא ואיכא דאמרי סבר רב יוסף למימר מלח הרי הוא כתבלין דבכלי ראשון בשלה בכלי שני לא בשלה א"ל אביי תני ר' חייא א מלח אינה כתבלין דבכלי ראשון נמי לא בשלה והיינו דאמר רב נחמן צריכא מילחא בישולא כבישרא דתורא: **מתני'** ב אין נותנין כלי תחת הנר לקבל בו את השמן ואם נתנוה מבעוד יום מותר ואין ניאותין ממנו לפי שאינו מן המוכן: **גמ'** אמר רב חסדא ג אע"פ שאמרו אין נותנין כלי תחת תרנגולת לקבל ביצתה אבל כופה עליה כלי שלא תשבר אמר רבה מ"ט דרב חסדא קסבר תרנגולת עשויה להטיל ביצתה באשפה ואינה עשויה להטיל ביצתה במקום מדרון והצלה מצויה התירו והצלה שאינה מצויה לא התירו איתיבי' אביי והצלה שאינה מצויה לא התירו והתניא ד) נשברה לו חבית של טבל בראש גגו מביא כלי ומניח תחתיה בגולפי חדתי דשכיחי דפקעי איתיביה ג) נותנין כלי תחת הנר לקבל ניצוצות נמי שכיחי איתיביה

רש"י

אבל נותן הוא לתוך הקערה. דכלי שני אינו מבשל: תמחוי. כעין קערה גדולה שמערה כל האילפס לתוכה ומשם מערה לקערות: ר' יהודה אומר לכל וכו'. בגמ' מפרש אהי קאי אכלי ראשון או אכלי שני: חוץ מדבר שיש בו חומץ או ציר. שהן מבשלין את התבלין כשהן רותחין: ציר. הנוטף מן הדגים כשכובשים אותן במכבש: **גמ'** ארישא קאי. אאילפס דקא אסר ת"ק וקאמר ר' יהודה לכל אילפסין הוא נותן דכלי ראשון לא מבשל: או דילמא אסיפא קאי. אקערה ותמחוי דקא שרי ת"ק וקא אמר ליה רבי יהודה בכל קערות ותמחויין מודינא לך חוץ מדבר שיש בו חומץ ואפילו כלי שני נמי לא: דבכלי ראשון נמי לא בשלה. ומותר ליתן ואפילו בכלי ראשון משהעבירו מן האור: **מתני'** אין נותנין. בשבת: כלי תחת הנר. לקבל בו שמן המטפטף משום דשמן מוקצה הוא וקסבר אין כלי ניטל בשבת אלא לצורך דבר הניטל אי נמי קסבר אסור לבטל כלי מהיכנו להושיב כלי במקום שלא יוכל עוד ליטלו ד) (משום) דהוי כקובע לו מקום ומחברו בטיט ודמי למלאכה וכלי זה משיפול בו השמן המוקצה יהא אסור לטלטלו: מותר. להניחה שם: ואין ניאותין. נהנין: **גמ'** אע"פ שאמרו אין נותנין כלי תחת תרנגולת לקבל ביצתה. כשהיא מטילתה במקום מדרון שמא תתגלגל ותשבר ומדיוקא דמתניתין שמעינן לה דדמי לנותן כלי תחת הנר לקבל בו שמן: אבל כופה עליה כלי. ולא תימא אין כלי ניטל אלא לצורך דבר הניטל: באשפה. ויש לחוש שמא תשבר ברגלי אדם וכופה עליה כלי: והצלה מצויה התירו. לטלטל כלי לצרכה ואף על פי שהבילה דבר שאינו ניטל בשבת: שאינה מצויה. כגון מדרון וטיפטוף דשמן דמתני': נשברה לו חבית של טבל גרסינן: מביא כלי. ואף על גב דטבל דבר שאינו ניטל הוא וחבית לא שכיחא דפקעה: גולפי. חביות: נותנין כלי. מתניתין היא ומותיב ליה מינה: ניצוצות. שלהבת הנוטפת מן הנר כדי שלא ידלק מה שתחתיה ואע"ג דניצוצות לא מיטלטלי ולא שכיחי: איתיביה

תוספות

אבל נותן הוא לתוך הקערה כו'. מהכא ליכא למידק דעירוי ככלי שני מדקתני לא יתן לתוכה תבלין ולא אשמעינן רבותא אפילו שלא יערה על הקערה שתבלין בתוכה דאדרבה דוק מסיפא דקתני אבל נותן הוא לתוך הקערה ולא קתני מערה על הקערה שתבלין בתוכה ורבינו שמואל מביא ראיה דעירוי ככלי שני מהא דקי"ל תתאה גבר ולר"י נראה דעירוי ככלי ראשון ומביא ראיה דבזבחים בפרק דם חטאת (דף צה: ושם) ת"ר אשר תבושל בו אין לי אלא שבישל בו עירה לתוכו רותח מניין תלמוד לומר [אשר תבושל] בו ישבר אלמא דעירוי חשיב מבשל ובירושלמי בפרק כירה בעי מהו ליתן תבלין מלמטה ולערות עליהן מלמעלה ר' יונה אמר אסור דעירוי ככלי ראשון חיליה דר' יונה מן הדא אחד שבישל בו ואחד שעירה לתוכו רותח ודחי ר' יוסי תמן כלי חרס בולע תבלין אינו מתבשל השיב רבי יוסי בר בון והתניא מניין שבכלי נחשת כן תלמוד לומר ואם בכלי נחשת בשלה אית לן למימר כלי נחשת בלע בתמיה פי' ע"י עירוי אם אינו מבשל לא בלע אלמא דמסיק דעירוי ככלי ראשון ונראה דעירוי לא הוי ככלי ראשון ולא ככלי שני אלא מבשל כדי קליפה דהא קי"ל כשמואל דאמר תתאה גבר דתניא כוותיה בכילד צולין (פסחים עו.) ומ"מ מבשל כדי קליפה דאמר התם תניא כוותיה דשמואל חם לתוך צונן או צונן לתוך צונן מדיח ופריך חם לתוך צונן אדמיקר ליה בלע אלא אימא חם לתוך צונן קולף צונן לתוך צונן מדיח וכן משמע בשילהי מסכת ע"ז (דף עו.) דאמר מר ה) עוקבא זבן יורה מעכו"ם אהדר ליה גדנפא ומסיק כבולעו כך פולטו מה בולעו בניצוצות אף פולטו בניצוצות ואי עירוי ככלי ראשון ° מאי איריא משום דבלע בניצוצות אפילו בלע בליעה גמורה פלט בניצוצות שהוא עירוי אלא ודאי לא מבשל אלא כדי קליפה ואם עירו רותחים על התרנגולת צריכה קליפה וכלי שתשמישו ע"י עירוי כגון קערות יכול להגעילן ע"י עירוי דכבולעו כך פולטו אבל כלי שנתבשל בו איסור לא סגי להגעילו על ידי עירוי והא דאמר בפרק בתרא דע"ז (דף עד:) דרש רבא נעוה ארתחיה דהתם מסתמא ע"י עירוי שאי התם לאותה נעוה לא בלעה ע"י רותח א) ו):

לכל קדרות רותחות הוא נותן. נראה דדוקא בתבלין פליג אבל בשאר דברים מודה דכלי ראשון מבשל אף כשהעבירו מעל האור: **והיינו** דר"נ. נראה דאף לפי' הקונטרס שפי' ז) דבכל מקום דאיכא לישני דפליגי בשל תורה הלך אחר המחמיר ובשל סופרים הלך אחר המיקל וכן לריב"א שפירש שבכל מקום איכא דאמרי טפל לגבי לשון ראשון שהוא עיקר הכא הלכה כלישנא בתרא דללישנא קמא פליג ברייתא דרבי חייא אדרב נחמן וללישנא בתרא היינו דרב נחמן ומתוך כך פסק רבינו שמואל שמותר לתת מלח בתבשיל בשבת אפילו בכלי ראשון שהעבירו מן האור והמחמיר כלישנא קמא שלא ליתן מלח בקערה כל זמן שהיד סולדת בו תבא עליו ברכה: **ואם** נתנוהו מבעוד יום מותר. **ואין** נאותין ממנו לפי שאינו מן המוכן. איכא לאוקמה כר"ש ח) דמתיר מותר הלשון דחוק דהוה ליה למימר אבל מבעוד יום נותנין: השמן שבנר ואין ניאותין דקתני הכא היינו כל זמן שדולק ° דבמוקצה מחמת מצוה מודה ר"ש כדאמר בגמ' לקמן (דף מה.) אין מוקצה לר"ש אלא שמן שבנר בשעה שהוא דולק הואיל והוקצה למצותו הוקצה לאיסורו ולא שבנר ממש קאמר דההיא אסור בלאו הכי משום מכבה כדאמר בביצה פ"ב (דף כב. ושם) המסתפק ממנו חייב משום מכבה אלא כלומר שמן המטפטף מן הנר והטלטול דנר עצמו אין לאסור מטעם דהוקצה למצותו ולא אסור לטלטלו אלא משום דנעשה בסיס לדבר האסור כדאמרינן בסוף פירקין (דף מז.) הנח לנר שמן ופתילה הואיל ונעשה בסיס לדבר האסור אבל מטעם דהוקצה למצותו לא היה אסור לטלטלו שאין ביטול מצוה במה שמטלטלו:

אע"פ שאמרו חכמים אין נותנין כו'. אין נותנין כלי תחת הנר לקבל בו את השמן ה"ל למימר דתנן במתניתין וכלי לקבל בילה לא שמעינן אלא מדיוקא דמתני' אלא משום דבעי למימר אבל כופה עליה כלי נקט בילה: **הצלה** שאינה מצויה לא התירו. פי' בקונטרס לדבר שאינו ניטל וגרס בההוא דפריך אביי מינה בסמוך נשברה לו חבית של טבל בראש גגו דטבל אינו ניטל וקשה לריב"א דאי גרס בה טבל אמאי פריך לרב יוסף מברייתא אחרת מהך דהכא הוה ליה לאקשויי ועוד דבפרק כל כתבי (לקמן דף קיז: ושם) משמע בהדיא דלא גרסי' בברייתא דהכא טבל דלא בשל טבל איירי דקתני סיפא נזדמנו לו אורחין מביא כלי אחר כו' ונראה לו לפרש דהצלה שאינה מצויה לא התירו לטרוח בכל דבר אפילו בדבר הניטל משום טירחא:

שאינה מצויה לא התירו. והא דאין נותנין כלי תחת הנר לקבל שמן חשיב הצלה שאינה מצויה לפי שרגילים לעולם לתת כלי תחת הנר מבעוד יום וניצוצות אע"ג דקאמר בסמוך דשכיחי לא שכיחי כולי האי שיחושו לתת שם כלי מבעוד יום ולהכי חשיב לה הצלה מצויה:

דמבטל

עין משפט נר מצוה

לז א מיי' פכ"ב מהל' שבת הלכה ו טוש"ע או"ח סימן שיח סעיף ט:
לח ב מיי' פכ"ה מהלכות שבת הלכה כג ופ"ה הלכה יג סמג לאוין סה טור שו"ע או"ח סימן רסה סעיף ג:
לט ג מיי' פכ"ה שם סמג שם טור ושו"ע או"ח סימן שי סעיף ו וסימן שכב סעיף א וסי' תקיג סעיף ד:

רבינו חננאל

בתוך חללו לפיכך מותר שנמצאו כלי שני וקיי"ל כלי שני מותר: ר' יהודה אומר לכל הוא נותן כו' אסיק' ר' יהודה ארישא דקתני האלפס והקדירה שהעבירן מרותחין לא יתן בתוכן תבלין התם פליג ומקיל הוא דתניא ר"י אומר לכל אלפסין רותחין [הוא נותן] לכל קדרות רותחין הוא נותן חוץ מדבר שיש בו חומץ וציר. מלח כתבלין הוא אי לא ואסיק' כדתני ר' חייא מלח אינו כתבלין דבכלי ראשון נמי לא בשלה והיינו דרב נחמן דאמר צריכה מילחא בשולי כבשרא דתורא ש"מ כי נותן מלח בתבשיל בשבת ואפילו בכלי ראשון אינו בישול: מתניתין אין נותנין כלי תחת הנר לקבל בו את השמן כו' אמר רב חסדא אע"פ שאמרו אין נותנין נר תחת התרנגולת כו' כלומר אפילו אם עומדת במקום מדרון ורואין כיון שתלד תפול הביצה במקום מדרון ותשבר לא התירו לו להטיל תחתיה כלי לקבלה לביצה כדי שלא תשבר שזה לילד התרנגולת במקום מדרון דבר שאינו מצוי הוא ומשום אחת שנזדמנה לה כך לא חיישינן לה. אבל כיון שדרך רוב התרנגולת להטיל ביציהן לאשפה התירו לכפות על אותה ביצה כלי בשביל שלא תשבר וזהו פירוש הצלה מצויה התירו הצלה שאינה מצויה לא התירו ואקשינן והצלה שאינה מצויה לא התירו והא חבית שנשברה בראש גגו כו' ושנינן בגולפי חדתי פי' קנקנים חדשים שהן מצוין להפקיע. וניצוצות תחת הנר נמי מילתא דשכיחא היא ובבתי גחיני כלומר בתים נמוכים להיאחז בהן דליקה מילתא דשכיחא היא וכן כולם. פירק רבא לדבריו דהצלה מצויה התירו הצלה שאינה מצויה לא התירו אליבא דרב חסדא. רב יוסף אמר מ"ט דרב חסדא משום דאי שרית ליה לקבל הביצה בכלי במקום מדרון כבר ביטל אותו הכלי היום שאסור לטלטלו והביצה בתוכו. כשם שאסור לטלטל הביצה. אבל כפיית הכלי על הביצה אינו ביטול שאם הוצרך הכלי מותר לו לטלטלו שהרי אין בכלי כלום ולא מבטל כלי מהיכנו. איתיביה אביי (טלטל) [חבית של טבל] כו' והא טבל אסור לטלטלו ושני ליה טבל מוכן הוא שאם עבר ותיקנו מתוקן הוא. ושני בניצוצות. ניצוצות אין

מסורת הש"ס

א) [כהאי גוונא במעשרות פ"א מ"ז], ב) לקמן קיח: ע"ש, ג) לקמן מג. מז:, ד) [נ"ל משם], ה) יש ספרים שגורסין כאן בתוס' רב עקיבא כמו שהביא הגאון מהרי"ף בע"ז שם בהגהותיו. ואולי יצאה גירסת מר עוקבא מסוגיא דב"מ ע. ההוא דודא דבני מר עוקבא כמו שהעיר בסה"ד, ו) [וע' תוספות זבחים צה: ד"ה עירה כו'], ז) [עי' תוס' ע"ז ז. ד"ה בשל תורה], ח) [לקמן מד.].

תוספות ישנים

א) א"נ ארתחי' שיעשה האש למטה והיא של חרס. דבפ' כל שעה איכא למ"ד זה וזה לפטור המעסה והחלוטה ומוגלגין ואיירי בשיש למלוס כשיעור חלה. ולהכי בין תתאה גבר בין עילאה גבר מבשל כדי קליפה ובלר ליה משיעור חלה:

גליון הש"ס

תוס' ד"ה אבל וכו'. מאי איריא משום דבלע בניצוצות. ק"ל דלטעמיך אף אם עירוי לא הוי ככ"ר היינו בעירוי על צונן אבל הכא דהעירוי על גובה הכלי שהוא חם אף אם היה העירוי מצונן לחם היה חם דמתאי גבר מכ"ש בעירוי מכ"ר על כ"ר. וה' יאיר עיני: שם ד"ה ואין נאותין וכו' דבמוקצה מחמת מצוה מודה ר"ש. וכיון דאינו ראוי לאכלו ממש באותה שעה הוי מוקצה בעצמותו כדין כל מאכל שאינו חזי לכלום. עי' מג"א ריש סימן תקט"ו. ורק בטלטול הנר בשעה שהוא דולק להאיר זהו מדינא מותר אלולי טעמא דבסיס ולק"מ קושית המהרש"א:

ליקוטי רש"י

לכל הוא נותן. לכל מיני מאכל הוא נותן תבלין בכלי שני חוץ מדבר שיש בו חומץ וציר שהחומץ מבשלן [פסחים מ:]. ציר. ציר מזיעה חיבות של דגים כשכובשין אותן במכבש כדאמרינן במועד קטן (יא.) ונעשה חזק כחומץ ומטבל בו [ע"ז לא:]. גולפי. כלי חרס [ע"ז לב.].

dripping **oil in it,**[10] וְאִם נְתָנוּהָ מִבְּעוֹד יוֹם מוּתָּר – **but if one places it while it is yet day it is permitted.**[11] וְאֵין נֵיאוֹתִין מִמֶּנּוּ – **And we may not benefit from [the oil],** לְפִי שֶׁאֵינוֹ מִן הַמּוּכָן – **since it is not something prepared** for Sabbath use.[12]

Gemara The Gemara quotes an Amoraic ruling that bears on our Mishnah:

אָמַר רַב חִסְדָּא – **Rav Chisda said:** אַף עַל פִּי שֶׁאָמְרוּ אֵין נוֹתְנִין כְּלִי תַּחַת תַּרְנְגוֹלֶת לְקַבֵּל בֵּיצָתָהּ – **Although they said** that **one may not place a vessel under a hen in order to receive her egg** and prevent it from rolling off an incline, אֲבָל כּוֹפֶה עָלֶיהָ כְּלִי שֶׁלֹּא תִּשָּׁבֵר – **one may nevertheless invert a vessel over [a newly laid egg] so that it should not break.**[13]

The Gemara analyzes Rav Chisda's ruling:

אָמַר רַבָּה – **Rabbah said:** מַאי טַעְמָא דְּרַב חִסְדָּא – **What is Rav's Chisda's reasoning?** קָסָבַר תַּרְנְגוֹלֶת עֲשׂוּיָה לְהַטִּיל בֵּיצָתָהּ בָּאַשְׁפָּה – **He holds** that **a hen is likely to lay its egg in a trash heap** or similiar place, where it is in danger of being crushed, וְאֵינָהּ עֲשׂוּיָה לְהַטִּיל בֵּיצָתָהּ בִּמְקוֹם מִדְרוֹן – **but it is unlikely to lay its egg on an incline** where it would roll off and break. וְהַצָּלָה מְצוּיָה הִתִּירוּ – **And [the Rabbis] allowed** taking **precautions that are** needed to prevent **commonplace** losses, even where doing so involves moving a non-*muktzeh* item for the sake of a *muktzeh* item, וְהַצָּלָה שֶׁאֵינָהּ מְצוּיָה לֹא הִתִּירוּ – **but they did not allow** taking **precautions that are** needed to prevent **uncommon** losses, when doing so involves moving a non-*muktzeh* item for the sake of a *muktzeh* item.[14]

According to Rabbah's explanation of Rav Chisda's teaching, it is prohibited to move a non-*muktzeh* item for the sake of a *muktzeh* item, except to prevent a commonplace loss. Abaye initiates a series of challenges to this view:

אֵיתִיבֵיהּ אַבָּיֵי – **Abaye challenged [Rabbah]:** וְהַצָּלָה שֶׁאֵינָהּ מְצוּיָה לֹא הִתִּירוּ – **Did they not allow** taking **precautions that are** needed to prevent **uncommon** losses, even when doing so involves moving a non-*muktzeh* item for the sake of a *muktzeh* one? וְהָתַנְיָא – **But it was taught in a Baraisa:** נִשְׁבְּרָה לוֹ חָבִית שֶׁל טֶבֶל בְּרֹאשׁ גַּגּוֹ – IF A BARREL OF *TEVEL*[15] BROKE ON ONE'S ROOFTOP, מֵבִיא כְּלִי וּמַנִּיחַ תַּחְתֶּיהָ – HE MAY BRING A VESSEL AND PLACE IT UNDERNEATH [THE BROKEN BARREL] in order to save its contents. Now, *tevel* is *muktzeh* and the breakage of a barrel is an uncommon occurrence, yet the Baraisa permits moving a vessel for the sake of saving the *tevel*. – ? –

NOTES

10. I.e. on the Sabbath we may not place a vessel near the base of a lighted lamp in order to catch oil that drips from the lamp. The Gemara will advance two possible reasons for this prohibition:

(a) The Tanna of our Mishnah holds that it is forbidden to move a non-*muktzeh* object for the use of an object that may itself not be moved (i.e. *muktzeh*). Now, the oil in the lamp is *muktzeh* for various reasons. Firstly, it was set aside for the mitzvah of kindling the Sabbath lamps (see 45a). Secondly, since it is generally prohibited to remove oil from the lamp on the Sabbath due to the *melachah* of כִּבּוּי, *extinguishing,* the oil is *muktzeh by dint of a prohibition* (see 44a note 10 and *Ramban* to 45a). Finally, the oil is a *base for muktzeh,* since the flame, which is *muktzeh,* rests on the wick which in turn rests on the oil (see 47a). Even the oil that drips out while the lamp is burning is *muktzeh,* since the mitzvah for which it was set aside is still in effect (see *Tosafos* ד״ה ואין ניאותין, *Pnei Yehoshua* to 43a בד״ה בעודן עליו and *Rashash*). Accordingly, it is forbidden to move a non-*muktzeh* vessel on the Sabbath for the sake of catching it (*Rashi*).

(b) When the oil drips into the vessel, the vessel will be effectively immobilized, since one will be forbidden to move it due to the *muktzeh* oil it contains. Immobilizing it in this fashion is called בִּטּוּל כְּלִי מֵהֵיכָנוֹ, *nullification of the preparedness of the utensil,* i.e. nullifying its non-*muktzeh* state and making it unavailable for movement and use. The Rabbis considered this similar to cementing a utensil in place [which is a violation of the *melachah* of בּוֹנֶה, *building*] and they therefore prohibited it (*Rashi;* see also *Rashi* to 43a ד״ה מפני שמבטל כלי מהיכנו, cited in note 8 there). [*Tosafos* (43a ד״ה דמבטל) point out that *Rashi* elsewhere (128b ד״ה והא קמבטל, 154b ד״ה והא מבטל) compares immobilizing a utensil to the *melachah* of סוֹתֵר, *destroying,* rather than *building.* For a resolution of this apparent contradiction, see *Pnei Yehoshua* to *Tosafos* (loc. cit.) and *Chasam Sofer's* introduction to *Beitzah* ד״ה בימי. [A collection of *Chasam Sofer's* novellae concerning *muktzeh* are printed as an introduction to his novellae to *Beitzah.*] See also *Mishbetzos Zahav* 265:1 and *Toras Rafael, Hil. Shabbos* §19.

11. If someone placed the vessel under the lamp before the Sabbath he is permitted to leave it there (*Rashi*).

[This implication is that even on Friday it is preferable that one not place a vessel there because we are fearful that he may inadvertently move the vessel about on the Sabbath after the oil has begun to drip into it. This consideration is, however, not sufficient for us to require him to remove it (*Tos. Yom Tov*).

Tosafos and *Tur* (*Orach Chaim* 265) reject this conclusion and permit placing the vessel under the lamp on Friday without reservation. *Tosafos* admit that according to their opinion, the Mishnah should have read אֲבָל מִבְּעוֹד יוֹם נוֹתְנִים, *but when it is yet day we may place it,* which would imply that one may go ahead and do so initially. See *Gur Aryeh, Pnei Yehoshua* and *Korban Nesanel* for possible resolutions of this difficulty.]

12. That which was not prepared for Sabbath use is *muktzeh* (see Chapter Introduction). Both the oil in the lamp and that which drips out are *muktzeh.* Removing oil from the lamp is also generally prohibited under the *melachah* of כִּבּוּי, *extinguishing* (see *Tosafos* ד״ה ואין with *Rashash*). Since the oil is *muktzeh,* it is forbidden not only to benefit from it but even to move it (*Gilyon HaShas*; *Chasam Sofer,* Introduction to *Beitzah;* cf. *Maharsha*).

13. An egg that is laid on the Sabbath is *muktzeh,* since it is in the category of *nolad,* i.e. just born (see Chapter Introduction). Thus, placing a vessel under a hen to catch the egg that it lays is analogous to placing a vessel under a lamp in order to catch any dripping oil, which our Mishnah forbids. Rav Chisda states that although it is forbidden to receive the egg in a vessel, once the egg is laid it is permissible to cover it with a vessel, even though the egg is *muktzeh.* We do not forbid moving the vessel for the use of the *muktzeh* egg (*Rashi*). The Gemara proceeds to explain why, then, it is forbidden to receive the egg in a vessel.

14. Rabbah holds that the reason our Mishnah forbids placing a vessel under a lamp to catch the dripping oil is that it is forbidden to move a non-*muktzeh* item (the vessel) for the use of an item that may not itself be moved (the oil). For this same reason Rav Chisda forbade placing a non-*muktzeh* vessel under a hen to receive its *muktzeh* egg. Accordingly, it ought to be prohibited to cover a newly laid egg with a vessel, since this too involves moving the vessel for the sake of the *muktzeh* egg. The reason this is permitted is that since the need to prevent newly laid eggs from being crushed underfoot on the Sabbath (when, being *muktzeh,* they cannot be picked up and collected) is commonplace, the Rabbis relaxed the prohibition against moving a non-*muktzeh* item for the sake of a *muktzeh* item for this case. By contrast, the likelihood that a hen will lay its egg on an incline is remote and the Rabbis did not feel a need to relax their prohibition for the rare case in which this does occur (see *Rashi;* cf. *Tosafos* ד״ה הצלה.)

In our Mishnah's case, the Rabbis did not relax their prohibition because it is uncommon for enough oil to drip from a lamp to be worth saving (*Rashi,* as explained by *Ritva MHK* ed.). Others explain that even though oil commonly drips from a lamp, people are aware of this situation in advance and generally put a vessel underneath their lamp before the Sabbath (see end of note 11). The situation of someone forgetting to do so is considered a remote occurrence (*Tosafos* ד״ה שאינה מצויה; see *Rashba*).

15. [*Tevel* is produce grown in Eretz Yisrael that has not had *terumah* and other tithes separated from it and is therefore unfit for consumption. Since it is prohibited Rabbinically to separate *terumah* on the Sabbath, the produce is unsuitable for use on the Sabbath and therefore may not be moved.] The Baraisa is dealing with liquid *tevel,* e.g. wine or oil (see *Rashi* and Gemara below, 117b; cf. *Tosafos* ד״ה הצלה).

אבל נותן הוא לתוך הקערה או לתוך התמחוי רבי יהודה אומר [א] לכל הוא נותן חוץ מדבר שיש בו חומץ וציר: **גמ'** איבעיא להו רבי יהודה ארישא קאי ולקולא או דילמא אסיפא קאי ולחומרא ת"ש דתניא רבי יהודה אומר לכל אילפסין הוא נותן לכל הקדירות רותחות הוא נותן חוץ מדבר שיש בו חומץ וציר סבר רב יוסף למימר מלח הרי הוא כתבלין דבכלי ראשון בשלה ובכלי שני לא בשלה א"ל אביי תני רבי חייא מלח אינה כתבלין דבכלי שני נמי בשלה ופליגא דרב נחמן דאמר רב נחמן צריכא מילחא בישולא כבשרא דתורא ואיכא דאמרי סבר רב יוסף למימר מלח הרי הוא כתבלין דבכלי ראשון בשלה בכלי שני לא בשלה א"ל אביי תני ר' חייא [א] מלח אינה כתבלין דבכלי ראשון נמי לא בשלה והיינו דאמר רב נחמן צריכא מילחא בישולא כבישרא דתורא: **מתני'** [ב] אין נותנין כלי תחת הנר לקבל בו את השמן ואם נתנוה מבעוד יום מותר ואין ניאותין ממנו לפי שאינו מן המוכן: **גמ'** אמר רב חסדא [ג] אע"פ שאמרו אין נותנין כלי תחת תרנגולת לקבל ביצתה אבל כופה עליה כלי שלא תשבר אמר רבה מ"ט דרב חסדא קסבר תרנגולת עשויה להטיל ביצתה באשפה ואינה עשויה להטיל ביצתה במקום מדרון והצלה מצויה התירו והצלה שאינה מצויה לא התירו איתיבי' אביי והצלה שאינה מצויה לא התירו והתניא [ד] נשברה לו חבית של טבל בראש גגו מביא כלי ומניח תחתיה בגולפי חדתי דשכיחי דפקעי איתיביה [ה] נותנין כלי תחת הנר לקבל ניצוצות נמי שכיחי איתיביה

רש"י

אבל נותן הוא לתוך הקערה. דכלי שני אינו מבשל: תמחוי. כעין קערה גדולה שמערה כל האילפס לתוכה ומשם מערה לקערות: ר' יהודה אומר לכל וכו'. בגמ' מפרש אהי קאי אכלי ראשון או אכלי שני: חוץ מדבר שיש בו חומץ או ציר. שהן מבשלין את התבלין כשהן רותחין: ציר. הנוטף מן הדגים כשכובשים אותן במכבש: גמ' ארישא קאי. אאילפס דקא אסר ת"ק וקאמר ר' יהודה לכל אילפסין הוא נותן דכלי ראשון לא מבשל: או דילמא אסיפא קאי. אקערה ותמחוי דקא שרי ת"ק וקא אמר ליה רבי יהודה בכל קערות ותמחויין מודינא לך חוץ מדבר שיש בו חומץ ואפילו כלי שני נמי לא: דבכלי ראשון נמי לא בשלה. ומותר ליתן ואפילו בכלי ראשון משהעבירו מן האור: מתני' אין נותנין. בשבת: כלי תחת הנר. לקבל בו שמן המטפטף משום דשמן מוקצה הוא וקסבר אין כלי ניטל בשבת אלא לצורך דבר הניטל אי נמי קסבר אסור לבטל כלי מהיכנו להושיב כלי במקום שלא יוכל עוד ליטלו [ד] (משום) דהוי כקובע לו מקום ומחברו בטיט ודמי למלאכה וכלי זה משיפול בו השמן המוקצה יהא אסור לטלטלו: מותר. להניחה שם: ואין ניאותין. נהנין: גמ' אע"פ שאמרו אין נותנין כלי תחת תרנגולת לקבל ביצתה. כשהיא מטילתה במקום מדרון שמא תתגלגל ותשבר ומדיוקא דמתניתין שמעינן לה דדמי לנותן כלי תחת הנר לקבל בו שמן: אבל כופה עליה כלי. ולא תימא אין כלי ניטל אלא לצורך דבר הניטל: באשפה. ויש לחוש שמא תשבר ברגלי אדם וכופה עליה כלי: והצלה מצויה התירו. לטלטל כלי לצרכה ואף על פי שהבילה דבר שאינו ניטל בשבת: שאינה מצויה. כגון מדרון וטיפטוף דשמן דמתני': נשברה לו חבית של טבל גרסינן: מביא כלי. ואף על גג דטבל דבר שאינו ניטל הוא וחבית לא שכיחא דפקעה: גולפי. חביות: נותנין כלי. מתניתין היא ומותיב ליה מינה: ניצוצות. שלהבת הנוטפת מן הנר כדי שלא ידלק מה שתחתיה ואע"ג דניצוצות לא מיטלטלי ולא שכיחי: איתיביה

תוספות

אבל נותן הוא לתוך הקערה כו'. מהכא ליכא למידק דעירוי ככלי שני מדקתני לא יתן לתוכה תבלין ולא אשמעינן רבותא אפילו שלא יערה על הקערה שתבלין בתוכה לאדרבה דוק מסיפא דקתני אבל נותן הוא לתוך הקערה ולא קתני מערה על הקערה שתבלין בתוכה ורבינו שמואל מביא ראיה דעירוי ככלי שני מהא דקי"ל תתאה גבר ולר"י נראה דעירוי ככלי ראשון ומביא ראיה דבזבחים בפרק דם חטאת (דף צה: ושם) ת"ר אשר תבושל בו אין לי אלא שבישל בו עירה לתוכו רותח מניין תלמוד לומר [אשר תבושל] בו ישבר אלמא דעירוי חשיב מבשל ובירושלמי בפרק כירה בעי מהו ליתן תבלין מלמטה ולערות עליהן מלמעלה ר' יונה אמר אסור דעירוי ככלי ראשון חיליה דר' יונה מן הדא אחד שבישל בו ואחד שעירה לתוכו רותח ודחי ר' יוסי תמן כלי חרס בולע תבלין אינו מתבשל השיב רבי יוסי בר בון והתניא מניין שבכלי נחשת כן תלמוד לומר ואם בכלי נחשת בשלה אית לן למימר כלי נחשת בלע בתמיה פי' ע"י עירוי אם אינו מבשל לא בלע אלמא דמסיק דעירוי ככלי ראשון ונראה דעירוי לא הוי ככלי ראשון ולא ככלי שני אלא מבשל כדי קליפה דהא קי"ל כשמואל דאמר תתאה גבר דתניא כוותיה בכילד צולין (פסחים עו.) ומ"מ מבשל כדי קליפה דאמר התם תניא כוותיה דשמואל חם לתוך צונן או צונן לתוך צונן מדיח ופריך חם לתוך צונן אדמיקר ליה בלע אלא אימא חם לתוך צונן קולף צונן לתוך צונן מדיח וכן משמע בשילהי מסכת ע"ז (דף עו.) דאמר מר [ה] עוקבא זבן יורה מעכו"ם אהדר ליה גדנפא ומסיק כבולעו כך פולטו מה בולעו בניצוצות אף פולטו בניצוצות ואי עירוי ככלי ראשון [ט] מאי איריא משום דבלע בניצוצות אפילו בלע בליעה גמורה פלט בניצוצות שהוא עירוי אלא ודאי לא מבשל אלא כדי קליפה ואם עירו רותחים על התרנגולת צריכה קליפה וכלי שתשמישו ע"י עירוי כגון קערות יכול להגעילן ע"י עירוי דכבולעו כך פולטו אבל כלי שנתבשל בו איסור לא סגי להגעילו על ידי עירוי והא דאמר בפרק בתרא דע"ז (דף עד:) דרש רבא נעוה ארתחיה דהתם מסתמא ע"י עירוי שאני התם דאותה נעוה לא בלעה ע"י רותח [ו]:

לכל קדרות רותחות הוא נותן. נראה דדוקא בתבלין פליג אבל בשאר דברים מודה דכלי ראשון מבשל אף כשהעבירו מעל האור: **והיינו** דר"נ. נראה דאף לפי' הקונטרס שפי' [ז] דבכל מקום דאיכא לישני דפליגי בשל תורה הלך אחר המחמיר ובשל סופרים הלך אחר אחרון ולר"ת בשל סופרים הלך אחר המיקל וכן לריב"א שפירש שבכל מקום איכא דאמרי טפל לגבי לשון ראשון שהוא עיקר הכא הלכה כלישנא בתרא דללישנא קמא פליג ברייתא דרבי חייא אדרב נחמן וללישנא בתרא היינו דרב נחמן ומתוך כך פסק רבינו שמואל שמותר לתת מלח בתבשיל בשבת אפילו בכלי ראשון שהעבירו מן האור והמחמיר כלישנא קמא שלא ליתן מלח בקערה כל זמן שהיד סולדת בו תבא עליו ברכה: **ואם** נתנוהו מבעוד יום מותר. **ואין** נאותין ממנו לפי שאינו מן המוכן. איכא לאוקמה כר"ש [ח] דמתיר מותר הלשון דחוק דהוה ליה למימר אבל מבעוד יום נותנין: השמן שבנר ואין ניאותין דקתני הכא היינו כל זמן שדולק [ט] דמוקצה מחמת מצוה מודה ר"ש כדאמר בגמ' לקמן (דף מה.) אין מוקצה לר"ש אלא שמן שבנר בשעה שהוא דולק הואיל והוקצה למצותו הוקצה לאיסורו ולא שבנר ממש קאמר דההיא אסור בלאו הכי משום מכבה כדאמר בביצה פ"ב (דף כב. ושם) המסתפק ממנו חייב משום מכבה אלא כלומר שמן המטפטף מן הנר והטלטול דנר עצמו אין לאסור מטעם דהוקצה למצותו ולא אסור לטלטלו אלא משום דנעשה בסיס לדבר האסור כדאמרינן בסוף פירקין (דף מז.) הנח לנר שמן ופתילה הואיל ונעשה בסיס לדבר האסור אבל מטעם דהוקצה למצותו לא היה אסור לטלטלו שאין ביטול מצוה במה שמטלטלו: **אע"פ** שאמרו חכמים אין נותנין כו'. אין נותנין כלי תחת הנר לקבל בו את השמן ה"ל למימר דתנן במתניתין וכלי לקבל ביצה לא שמעינן אלא מדיוקא דמתני' אלא משום דבעי למימר אבל כופה עליה כלי נקט ביצה: **הצלה** שאינה מצויה לא התירו. פי' בקונטרס לדבר שאינו ניטל וגרס בההוא דפריך אביי מינה בסמוך נשברה לו חבית של טבל בראש גגו דטבל אינו ניטל וקשה לריב"א דאי גרס בה טבל אמאי פריך לרב יוסף מברייתא אחרת מהך דהכא הוה ליה לאקשויי ועוד דבפרק כל כתבי (לקמן דף קיז: ושם) משמע בהדיא דלא גרסי' בברייתא דהכא טבל דלא בשל טבל מיירי דקתני סיפא נזדמנו לו אורחין מביא כלי אחר כו' ונראה לו לפרש דהצלה שאינה מצויה לא התירו לטרוח בכל דבר אפילו בדבר הניטל משום טירחא: **שאינה** מצויה לא התירו. והא דאין נותנין כלי תחת הנר לקבל שמן חשיב הצלה שאינה מצויה לפי שרגילים לעולם לתת כלי תחת הנר מבעוד יום וניצוצות אע"ג דקאמר בסמוך דשכיחי לא שכיחי כולי האי שיחושו לתת שם כלי מבעוד יום ולהכי חשיב לה הצלה מצויה:

דמבטל

עין משפט נר מצוה

לז א מיי' פכ"ב מהל' שבת הלכה ו טוש"ע או"ח סימן שיח סעיף ט:
לח ב מיי' פכ"ה מהלכות שבת הלכה כג ופ"ה הלכה יג סמג לאוין סה טור שו"ע או"ח סימן רסה סעיף ג:
לט ג מיי' פכ"ה שם סמג שם טור ושו"ע או"ח סימן שי סעיף ו וסימן שכב סעיף א וסי' תקיג סעיף ד:

רבינו חננאל

בתוך חללו לפיכך מותר שנמצאו כלי שני וקיי"ל כלי שני מותר: **ר' יהודה** אומר לכל הוא נותן כו' אסיק' ר' יהודה ארישא דקתני האלפס והקדירה שהעבירן מרותחין לא יתן בתוכן תבלין התם פליג ומקיל הוא דתניא ר"י אומר לכל אלפסין רותחין [הוא נותן] לכל קדרות רותחין הוא נותן חוץ מדבר שיש בו חומץ וציר. מלח כתבלין הוא אי לא ואסיק' כדתני ר' חייא מלח אינו כתבלין דכלי ראשון נמי לא בשלה והיינו דרב נחמן דאמר צריכה מילחא בשולי כבשרא דתורא ש"מ כי נותן מלח בתבשיל בשבת ואפילו בכלי ראשון אינו בישול: **מתניתין** אין נותנין כלי תחת הנר לקבל בו את השמן כו' אמר רב חסדא אע"פ שאמרו אין נותנין נר תחת התרנגולת כו' כלומר אפילו אם עומדת במקום מדרון ורואין כיון שתלד תפול הביצה במקום מדרון ותשבר לא התירו לו להטיל תחתיה כלי לקבלה לביצה כדי שלא תשבר שזה לילד התרנגולת במקום מדרון דבר שאינו מצוי הוא ומשום אחת שנזדמנה לה כך לא חיישינן לה. אבל כיון שדרך רוב התרנגולת להטיל ביציהן לאשפה התירו לכפות על אותה ביצה כלי בשביל שלא תשבר וזהו פירוש הצלה מצויה התירו הצלה שאינה מצויה לא התירו ואקשינן והצלה שאינה מצויה לא התירו והא חבית שנשברה בראש גגו כו' ושנינן בגולפי חדתי פי' קנקנים חדשים שהן מצוין להפקיע. וניצוצות תחת הנר נמי מילתא דשכיחא היא ובבתי גחיני כלומר בתים נמוכים להיאחז בהן דליקה מילתא דשכיחא היא וכן כולם. פירק רבא לדבריו דהצלה מצויה התירו הצלה שאינה מצויה לא התירו אליבא דרב חסדא. רב יוסף אמר מ"ט דרב חסדא משום דאי שרית ליה לקבל הביצה בכלי במקום מדרון כבר ביטל אותו הכלי היום שאסור לטלטלו והביצה בתוכו. כשם שאסור לטלטל הביצה. אבל כפיית הכלי על הביצה אינו ביטול שאם הוצרך הכלי מותר לו לטלטלו שהרי אין בכלי כלום ולא מבטל כלי מהיכנו. איתיביה אביי (טלטל) [חבית של טבל] כו' והא טבל אסור לטלטלו ושני ליה טבל מוכן הוא שאם עבר ותיקנו מתוקן הוא. ושני בניצוצות. ניצוצות אין

מסורת הש"ס

א) [כהאי גוונא במעשרות פ"א מ"ו], ב) לקמן קיז:, ע"ש, ג) לקמן מג. מז:, ד) [צ"ל משם], ה) יש ספרים שגורסין כאן בתוס' רב עקיבא כמו שהביא הגאון מהרי"ף בע"ז שם בהגהותיו. ואולי יצאה גירסת מר עוקבא מסוגיא דב"מ ע. ההוא דודא דבני מר עוקבא כמו שהעיר בסה"ד, ו) [וע' תוספות זבחים צה: ד"ה עירה כו'], ז) [עי' תוס' ע"ז ז. ד"ה בשל תורה], ח) [לקמן מד.].

תוספות ישנים

א) א"נ ארתחי' שיעשה האש למטה והיא של חרס. דבפ' כל שעה איכא למ"ד זה וזה לפטור המעסה והחלוטה ומוגלשין ואיירי בשיש במלוא כשיעור חלה. ולהכי בין תתאה גבר בין עילאה גבר מבשל כדי קליפה ובצר ליה משיעור חלה:

גליון הש"ס

תוס' ד"ה אבל וכו'. מאי איריא משום דבלע בניצוצות. ק"ל לטעמיך אף אם עירוי לא הוי ככ"ר היינו בעירוי על צונן אבל הכא דהעירוי על גופה הכלי שהוא חם אף אם היה העירוי מצונן לחם היה חם דתתאי גבר מכ"ש בעירוי מכ"ר על כ"ר. וה' יאיר עיני: שם ד"ה ואין נאותין וכו' דבמוקצה מחמת מצוה מודה ר"ש. וכיון דאינו ראוי לאכלו ממש באותה שעה הוי מוקצה בעצמותו כדין כל מאכל שאינו חזי לכלום. עי' מג"א ריש סימן תקט"ו. ורק בטלטול הנר בשעה שהוא דולק להאיר וזהו מדינא מותר אלולי טעמא דבסיס ולק"מ קושית המהרש"א:

ליקוטי רש"י

לכל הוא נותן. לכל מיני מאכל הוא נותן תבלין בכלי שני חוץ מדבר שיש בו חומץ וציר שהחומץ מבשלן [פסחים מ:]. ציר. ציר מזיעה וזיבות של דגים כשכובשין אותן במכבש כדאמרינן במועד קטן (יא.) ונעשה חזק כחומץ ומטבל בו [ע"ז לא:]. גולפי. כלי חרס [ע"ז לב.].

Rabbah replies:
בְּגוּלְפֵי חַדְתֵי דִשְׁכִיחֵי דְפָקְעֵי – The Baraisa is dealing **with** the case of **new earthenware kegs, which frequently burst.** Thus, it represents a commonplace loss.

Abaye's next challenge:
אֵיתִיבֵיהּ – **He challenged [Rabbah]** on the basis of the following Mishnah:[16] **נוֹתְנִין כְּלִי תַּחַת הַנֵּר לְקַבֵּל נִיצוֹצוֹת** – WE MAY PLACE A VESSEL UNDER A LAMP TO CATCH falling SPARKS. Now, sparks are intrinsically *muktzeh* and are not commonly produced by a lamp, yet the Mishnah permits moving a vessel to catch them. – ? –

Rabbah responds:
נִיצוֹצוֹת נַמִּי שְׁכִיחֵי – **Sparks, too, are commonplace.**[17]

NOTES

16. Below, 47b.

17. I.e. the incidence of a lamp producing sparks is more commonplace than the occurrence of a hen laying an egg on an incline. However, it is not so commonplace that most people take precautions against it before the Sabbath (*Tosafos* ד״ה שאינה מצויה).

Abaye's next challenge:

אִיתִיבֵיהּ – **He challenged [Rabbah]** on the basis of the following Mishnah:[1] כּוֹפִין קְעָרָה עַל הַנֵּר שֶׁלֹּא יֶאֱחוֹ בַּקּוֹרָה – WE MAY INVERT A BOWL OVER A LAMP IN ORDER THAT IT NOT SET FIRE TO AN overhead BEAM.[2] Now, the beam is *muktzeh* and it is not common for a beam to be in danger of catching fire from a lamp, yet the Mishnah permits moving a bowl for the sake of protecting the beam.[3] – ? –

Rabbah answers:

בְּבָתֵּי גְחִינֵי דִּשְׁכִיחַ בְּהוּ דְּלֵיקָה – That Mishnah is dealing **with houses that have low ceilings, in which fires are commonplace** due to the proximity of the lamps to the ceilings.

The next challenge:

וְכֵן קוֹרָה שֶׁנִּשְׁבְּרָה – Come, learn a refutation from the following Mishnah:[4] AND SO TOO with regard to A BEAM THAT BROKE on the Sabbath – סוֹמְכִין אוֹתָהּ בְּסַפְסָל וּבַאֲרוּכּוֹת הַמִּטָּה – WE MAY SUPPORT IT WITH A BENCH OR WITH THE SIDEBOARDS OF A BED etc.[5] Now, the breakage of a beam is not a common occurrence, yet the Mishnah permits moving a bench or bed to support the broken beam, even though it is *muktzeh*. – ? –

Rabbah responds:

בִּכְשׁוּרֵי חַדְתֵּי דַּעֲבִידֵי דְּפָקְעֵי – That Mishnah is dealing **with new** and untried **beams, which often break** when a roof is first laid on them.

The next challenge:

נוֹתְנִין כְּלִי תַּחַת הַדֶּלֶף בְּשַׁבָּת – Come, learn a refutation from the following Mishnah:[6] WE MAY PUT A VESSEL UNDER LEAKING RAINWATER ON THE SABBATH. Now, leaks are uncommon and the leaking water is generally *muktzeh,* since it is not suitable for use,[7] yet the Mishnah permits moving a vessel for the sake of catching it. – ? –

Rabbah replies:

בְּבָתֵּי חַדְתֵּי דִּשְׁכִיחֵי דְּדָלְפֵי – That Mishnah is dealing **with new houses, which commonly leak.**

Having concluded the discussion of Rabbah's interpretation of Rav Chisda's ruling, the Gemara cites another interpretation:

רַב יוֹסֵף אָמַר – **Rav Yosef said:** הַיְינוּ טַעְמָא דְּרַב חִסְדָּא – **The following is the reasoning of Rav Chisda,** who forbade placing a utensil under a hen to receive its egg: מִשּׁוּם דְּקָא מְבַטֵּל כְּלִי מֵהֵיכָנוֹ – It is **because** by doing so **one is nullifying the preparedness of the utensil,** since it will be forbidden to move the utensil once the *muktzeh* egg falls into it.[8]

Abaye initiates a series of challenges to Rav Yosef's view:

אִיתִיבֵיהּ אַבָּיֵי – **Abaye challenged [Rav Yosef]** on the basis of the following Baraisa: חָבִית שֶׁל טֶבֶל שֶׁנִּשְׁבְּרָה – IF A BARREL OF *TEVEL* BROKE, מֵבִיא כְּלִי אַחֵר וּמַנִּיחַ תַּחְתֶּיהָ – ONE MAY BRING ANOTHER VESSEL AND PLACE IT UNDER [THE BROKEN BARREL] in order to salvage its contents. Now, *tevel* is *muktzeh,*[9] yet the Baraisa allows receiving it in a non-*muktzeh* vessel, even though this will nullify the preparedness of the vessel. – ? –

Rav Yosef responds:

אָמַר לֵיהּ – **He said to [Abaye]:** טֶבֶל מוּכָן הוּא אֵצֶל שַׁבָּת – ***Tevel* is considered prepared for Sabbath use,** שֶׁאִם עָבַר וְתִקְּנוֹ מְתוּקָּן – **for if someone transgressed and perfected it** by separating *terumah,* **it is perfected.**[10] Since the *tevel* is considered prepared for use, receiving it in a vessel does not nullify the vessel's preparedness.

The next challenge:

נוֹתְנִין כְּלִי תַּחַת הַנֵּר לְקַבֵּל נִיצוֹצוֹת – Come, learn a refutation from the following Mishnah:[11] WE MAY PLACE A VESSEL UNDER A LAMP TO CATCH falling SPARKS. Now, the sparks are *muktzeh,* yet the Mishnah permits catching them in a non-*muktzeh* vessel, even though this nullifies the preparedness of the vessel. – ? –

The challenge is rebuffed:

אָמַר רַב הוּנָא בְּרֵיהּ דְּרַב יְהוֹשֻׁעַ – **Rav Huna the son of Rav Yehoshua said:** נִיצוֹצוֹת אֵין בָּהֶן מַמָּשׁ – **Sparks have no substance.** Thus, it is permissible to move the vessel even after the sparks fall in.[12]

The next challenge:

וְכֵן קוֹרָה שֶׁנִּשְׁבְּרָה – Come, learn a refutation from the following Mishnah:[13] AND SO TOO regarding A BEAM THAT BROKE on the Sabbath – סוֹמְכִין אוֹתָהּ בְּסַפְסָל אוֹ בַּאֲרוּכּוֹת הַמִּטָּה – WE MAY SUPPORT IT WITH A BENCH OR WITH THE SIDEBOARDS OF A BED etc. Now, once one wedges a bench under a sagging beam, he can no

NOTES

1. Below, 121a.

2. Provided we do not extinguish the lamp (*Rashi* to 121a). That is, we must leave a gap between the bowl and lamp so as not to cut off its oxygen supply (*Mishnah Berurah* 277:24).

The rule stated here pertains specifically to an earthenware bowl (*Rashi*). It is forbidden to use a metal bowl because if the metal becomes red-hot one will have violated the *melachah* of הַבְעָרָה, *kindling* (*Mishnah Berurah* 277:22). [Of course, in a situation where there is a danger of a life-threatening fire breaking out, even a metal bowl may be used (ibid.).]

3. *Rashi* to 121a. The beam is intrinsically *muktzeh* [מוּקְצֶה מֵחֲמַת גּוּפוֹ], since it is not a utensil but a building material (see *Mishnah Berurah* 308:74).

4. Below, 151b.

5. *Rashi* specifies that this Mishnah is dealing with a beam that broke on the Sabbath [for supporting the beam is only permitted when the danger (of the house collapsing) could not have been removed before the Sabbath]. [The Mishnah there concludes that we may use the bench or bed not to lift the beam (as this would constitute *building* – *Rav* ad loc.) but merely to support it so it will not fall further. The Mishnah cites this as a parallel to a similar law it stated earlier.]

6. *Beitzah* 35b.

7. Presumably, the water that leaks through a roof is too dirty to drink. Since it is useless, it is intrinsically *muktzeh.*

8. Thus, he is taking a utensil that had been in a state of preparedness for Sabbath use and making it *muktzeh* (*Rashi;* see 42b note 10, *Rosh Yosef* and *Mishbetzos Zahav* 265:1). I.e. he is turning it into a *base for muktzeh* (*Maharsha* to *Tosafos* ד״ה בעודן עליו, *Beis Yosef* and *R' Akiva Eiger, Orach Chaim* 265; cf. *Magen Avraham* 265:2; see note 20).

Rav Chisda permits, however, placing a utensil *over* the newly laid egg, since this does not nullify the preparedness of the utensil. Although the non-*muktzeh* utensil is being moved for the sake of the *muktzeh* egg, this is acceptable, according to Rav Yosef. He holds that it is permitted to move a non-*muktzeh* item for the sake of a *muktzeh* item, even without the dispensation for preventing a commonplace loss (*Pnei Yehoshua*).

9. See 42b note 15.

10. Since the prohibition against separating *terumah* on the Sabbath is merely of Rabbinical origin, and under Biblical law the produce can be perfected for consumption on the Sabbath, if someone comes along and separates *terumah* the produce will become permitted for consumption and will not be deemed *muktzeh* on the basis of the earlier prohibition. The existence of a Rabbinical prohibition at the onset of the Sabbath does not render something *muktzeh* for the entire Sabbath. Thus, although the produce is *muktzeh* while it is *tevel,* since it can become permitted on the Sabbath, receiving it in a utensil is not considered a nullification of the utensil's preparedness (*Rashi* here and *Beitzah* 34b ד״ה הא קמ״ל; see also *Rashi, Beitzah* 31b ד״ה נוטל ממקום הפחת and *Tosafos* there ד״ה ונפחת; cf. *Tosafos* to 128a ד״ה אבל, *Rashba, Ritva MHK* ed.; see *Tosafos* here ד״ה טבל and see note 18).

11. Below, 47b.

12. *Rashi* as emended by *Magen Avraham* 265:6; see *Rashi* to 47b ד״ה אין בהן ממש and *Pri Megadim, Eishel Avraham* 256:6.

13. Below, 151b; see note 5 above.

איתיביה כופין קערה על הנר שלא יאחז בקורה בבתי גחיני דשכיח בהו דליקה וכן קורה שנשברה סומכין אותה בספסל ובארוכות המטה בכשורי חדתי דעבידי דפקעי נותנין כלי תחת הדלף בשבת בבתי חדתי דשכיחי דדלפי רב יוסף אמר היינו טעמא דרב חסדא משום דקא מבטל כלי מהיכנו איתיביה אביי חבית של טבל שנשברה מביא כלי אחר ומניח תחתיה א"ל טבל מוכן הוא אצל שבת שאם עבר ותקנו מתוקן נותנין כלי תחת הנר לקבל ניצוצות א"ר הונא בריה דרב יהושע ניצוצות אין בהן ממש וכן קורה שנשברה סומכין אותה בספסל או בארוכות המטה דרפי דאי בעי שקיל ליה נותנין כלי תחת הדלף בשבת בדלף הראוי כופין את הסל לפני האפרוחין שיעלו וירדו קסבר מותר לטלטלו והתניא אסור לטלטלו בעודן עליו והתניא אע"פ שאין עודן עליו אסור א"ר אבהו בעודן עליו כל בין השמשות מיגו דאיתקצאי לבין השמשות איתקצאי לכולי יומא א"ר יצחק כשם שאין נותנין כלי תחת תרנגולת לקבל ביצתה כך אין כופין עליה כלי בשביל שלא תשבר קסבר אין כלי ניטל אלא לדבר הניטל בשבת מיתיבי כל הני תיובתא ושני בצריך למקומו תא שמע אחת ביצה שנולדה בשבת ואחת ביצה שנולדה ביום טוב אין מטלטלין לא לכסות בה את הכלי ולסמוך בה כרעי המטה אבל כופה עליה כלי בשביל שלא תשבר הכא נמי בצריך למקומו ת"ש פורסין מחצלות על גבי אבנים בשבת באבנים מקורזלות דחזיין לבית הכסא ת"ש פורסין מחצלות על גבי לבנים בשבת דאישתיור מבנינא דחזיין למיזגא עליהו ת"ש פורסין מחצלת על גבי כוורת דבורים בשבת בחמה מפני החמה ובגשמים מפני הגשמים ובלבד שלא יתכוין לצוד הכא במאי עסקינן דאיכא דבש א"ל רב עוקבא ממישן לרב אשי תינח בימות החמה דאיכא

איתיביה כופין קערה. של חרס על גבי הנר כו': גחיני. נמוכין: וכן קורה שנשברה כו'. משנה היא לקמן: שנשברה. בשבת: ארוכות המטה. לימונ"ש: בספסל. דכלי הוא ומותר לטלטלו: בכשורי חדתי. שלא נבדקו עדיין וכשמכביד משא הבית עליהן שהיו טחין על גגותיהן בטיט שכיחי דפקעי: תחת הדלף. לקבלו: טעמא דרב חסדא. דאין נותנין כלי תחת התרנגולת: מפני שמבטל כלי מהיכנו. שהיה מוכן מתחלה לטלטלו ועכשיו עושהו מוקצה: מוכן הוא. שאין בו מוקצה אלא איסורו ואם בא אחד ועבר על דברי חכמים שאסרו לתרום בשבת ותיקנו מתוקן ומותר לטלטלו ולאוכלו הלכך לאו מבטל כלי מהיכנו חשיב ליה: אין בהן ממש. ומותר ליטלן אחר שנפלו לתוכו: וכן קורה כו'. קס"ד שמהדקו שם ואינו יכול שוב ליטלו: הראוי. לשתיה כל אלו משניות הן: כל בין השמשות. אבל נתנו שם משחשיכה מותר ליטלו אם אין האפרוחים עליו: בצריך למקומו. להשתמש במקום הכלי ומתוך שיכול ליטלו לצורך מקומו מוליכו למקום שירצה: לכסות בה את הכלי. לסתום פי צלוחית: על גבי אבנים. מפני הגשמים שלא ימחו או לא יקבלו טיט מאחר שרויות במים: מקורזלות. ראשן חד וראויות לקינוח דהוי דבר הניטל: למיזגא. להשען שכל הסבתן כך היתה יושב קצת ונשען קצת על שמאלו: דאיכא

דמבטל כלי מהיכנו. בפרק בתרא פירש בקונטרס דאסור משום דמתחזי כסותר וכאן פירש דחשיב כאלו מחברו שם בטיט: **טבל** מוכן הוא אצל שבת. אף על פי שאסור לטלטלו כדתנן בפרק מפנין (לקמן קכו:) מ"מ לא חשיב מבטל כלי מהיכנו כיון דאם עבר ותיקנו מתוקן ק' לרשב"א דתנן במסכת תרומות בפ"ב (משנה ג) ומייתי לה בהניזקין (גיטין נד.) המעשר בשבת בשוגג יאכל במזיד לא יאכל ולישנא דקאמר הכא אם עבר ותיקנו משמע במזיד מדלא קאמר ° שאם שגג ותיקנו ונראה דנקט עבר כגון דלית ליה פירי אחריני דאמר בביצה בפרק י"ט (דף יז:) דאפילו במזיד יאכל עוד הקשה דבפרק בתרא (דף קנד:) תניא היתה בהמתו טעונה טבל ועששית מתיר את החבלים והשקים נופלים ואע"פ שמשתברין משמע דאסור להניח תחתיהן כרים וכסתות אלמא טבל לאו מוכן הוא ואור"י דאף על פי שמשתברין לא קאי אטבל אלא אעששית ועוד הקשה כי היכי דאמר דאם עבר ותיקנו מתוקן ה"נ כשמניח כלי תחת תרנגולת לקבל ביצתה נימא שאם עבר והסיר הביצה מותר הכלי לטלטל ואם כן ביטלת תורת ביטול כלי מהיכנו ולאו פירכא היא דהא כמו שהכלי עם הביצה אין לה היתר אבל טבל יש לו היתר על ידי תיקון ועוד הקשה היכא דאית ליה פירי אחריני בשוגג אמאי יאכל נימא מגו דאיתקצאי לבין השמשות איתקצאי לכולי יומא ועוד מ"ש דהכא אמר דאם עבר ותיקנו מתוקן ובביצה בפ' אין לדין (דף כו: ושם) גבי בכור לר"ש דאמר אין רואין מומין בי"ט אמר שאם עבר וביקרו אינו מבוקר ואדא בר אוכמי דאמר בשוגג מבוקר אמרינן התם דליתא דמשבש ותני (א): **כופין** את הסל. לעיל לא מצי פריך מינה דהכלה מגויה היא: **בעודן** עליו. אבל אחר שירדו מותר לטלטלו נראה לר"י דקסבר דאין מוקצה לחצי שבת דלמ"ד בפ' אין לדין (ביצה כו: ושם) דיש מוקצה אסור לטלטלו אף אחר שירדו וקשה לרשב"א למ"ד יש מוקצה לחצי שבת אמאי כופין את הסל לפני האפרוחים והא מבטל כלי מהיכנו וקי"ל דאסור לבטלו דבסוף פירקין פריך סתמא דהש"ס והא קא מבטל כלי מהיכנו וכן בפ' מפנין (לקמן קכח:) ובפ' בתרא (דף קנד:) פריך אליבא דרב הונא אע"ג דלא מצינו שהיה סובר כן משמע דלכ"ע אסור לבטל כלי מהיכנו וכן אפרש בסמוך וי"ל דלמ"ד יש מוקצה לחצי שבת הך דכופין את הסל מוקי כר"ש דלדידיה ודאי שרי לטלטל הסל כשירדו דאפי' מיגו דאיתקצאי לבין השמשות איתקצאי לכולי יומא לית ליה דהא מתיר להסתפק מן הנר שכבה ° א"נ הא דיש מוקצה לחצי שבת היינו לאכילה ולא לטלטול וא"ת רב יוסף דמפרש מתני' משום דאסור לבטל כלי מהיכנו לא אתיא מתני' כר"ש דלדידיה לא מבטל כלי מהיכנו כיון דשרי לאחר שכבה כי היכי דלא חשבינן הכא כפיית הסל ביטול כלי משום דשרי אחר שירדו וי"ל דלא דמי דהכא ודאי לא חשיב ביטול כלי כי מיד כשבאו על הסל בידו להפריחם ולהבריחם משם: **בעודן** עליו כל בין השמשות. תימה הא כיון דבידו להפריחם למטה הוי גמרו בידי אדם ולית לן למימר מיגו דאיתקצאי לבין השמשות כדמוכח בפ' אין לדין (ביצה כו:) דפריך ר' זירא למ"ד יש מוקצה לחצי שבת והא פולין ועדשים דמבשלים בי"ט למעיקרא חזו לכוס כי שדינהו בקדרה חייתא (א) אידחו להו גמר בישולייהו אישתרו להו א"ל אביי ולטעמיך תקשי לך קדירות דעלמא דהא קדירות דשבתא בין השמשות רותחות הן ולאורתא קא אכלינן מינייהו אלא גמרו בידי אדם לא קמבעיא ליה כי קא מיבעיא ליה גמרו בידי שמים וי"ל דשאני קדירות אם הוה צריך להו בין השמשות היה מקררן וכן פולין ועדשים רצונו שיתבשלו בלא שום דיחוי אבל הכא רצונו היה שיעלו האפרוחין על הסל שלכך כפאו והרי שעה אחת הקצה אותו לצרכן ומיגו דאיתקצאי לבין השמשות איתקצאי לכולי יומא: **ושני** ליה בצריך למקומו. ההיא דנותנין כלי תחת הדלף איכא נמי לשנויי בדלף הראוי כדשני לעיל ובפרק משילין (ביצה לו. ושם) משני ליה הכי לרבי יצחק תימה לר"י מ"ש דגבי שמן תנא אין נותנין וגבי ניצוצות נותנין בתרוייהו הוה מצי למתני נותנין בצריך למקומו או בתרוייהו אין נותנין באין צריך למקומו ונראה לר"י דמעיקרא אשמעינן דאין כלי ניטל אלא לדבר הניטל בשבת וגבי ניצוצות דבתר הכי אשמעינן דבצריך למקומו שרי אי נמי ר' יצחק אית ליה נמי דאסור לבטל כלי מהיכנו ולהכי גבי שמן אין נותנין אפילו בצריך למקומו ולרב הונא נפרש בסמוך דאית ליה נמי תרוייהו אין כלי ניטל אלא לדבר הניטל ואסור לבטל כלי מהיכנו ואם נאמר דלרב יוסף לא אתיא מתניתין כר"ש דכיון דלדידיה מותר לאחר שכבה לא חשיב ביטול כלי אם כן מצינן למימר דאפילו רבה אית ליה דאסור לבטל כלי מהיכנו ואיצטריך למימר דהכלה שאינה מגויה לא התירו כדי לאוקמה מתניתין כר"ש וא"ת מאי צריך בכל הני משניות לאשמעינן דבצריך למקומו שרי ויש לומר דלגבי ניצוצות איצטריך לאשמעינן דלא תימא אפילו בצריך למקומו אסור משום דילמא אתי לכבויי וכן ההיא דכופין קערה שלא תאחוז כו' וההיא דקורה שנשברה נראה לרשב"א דאיצטריך לאשמעינן דלא חיישינן שמא יעלה את הקורה דאסור להעלות כדתנן בפ' שואל (לקמן קנא:) וכן קורה שנשברה סומכין אותה כו' לא שתעלה אלא שלא תוסיף: **כופה** עליה כלי שלא תשבר כו'. כל הנהו דמייתי ידע המקשה דמצי לשנויי בצריך למקומו אלא שרוצה לידע אם יש לתרץ בענין אחר: **דאייתור** מבניינא. כדאמר לקמן בפ' כל הכלים (דף קכד:) הני לבני דאייתרי מבניינא שרי לטלטולינהו:

דחשיב

עין משפט נר מצוה

מ א מיי' פכ"ה מהלכות שבת הלכה כג סמג לאוין סה טור שו"ע או"ח סימן שי סעיף ו:

מא ב מיי' שם הל' כה:

מב ג מיי' שם טוש"ע או"ח סימן שיג סעיף ז:

מג ד מיי' שם הלכה כד טוש"ע או"ח סימן שלח סעיף ח וסימן תקכא סעיף ג:

מד ה ו מיי' שם הלכה כה סמג שם טוש"ע או"ח סימן שח סעיף לט:

מה ז מיי' וסמג שם טוש"ע או"ח סימן שט"ז סעיף ד:

רבינו חננאל

בהם ממש והכלי שמקבל בו הניצוצות לא מיבטיל ומותר להשתמש בה. וספסל שסמוך בה הקורה רפויה היא שיכול ליטלה ולהשתמש בה. והכלי שמקבל בו הדלף בדלף הראוי לשתיה שהמים מותרים וכ"ש הכלי. וכן הסל שכופין שיעלו וירדו בו האפרוחים אוקמה בעודן האפרוחים עומדין על הסל [או שהיו עומדין על הסל] בין השמשות אסור לטלטל אותו הסל שנעשה מוקצה ואם לאו מותר. ור' יצחק חולק על רב חסדא ואומר אפי' כלי לכוף עליה בשביל שלא תישבר ביצה בשבת אסור. קסבר אין כלי ניטל [אלא] לדבר הניטל בשבת. ואותיבנא עליה כל הני תיובתא. ומשני בצריך למקומו. ת"ש אחת ביצה [שנולדה] בשבת ואחת ביצה שנולדה ביו"ט אין מטלטלין אותה לא לכסות בה את הכלי ולא לסמוך בה כרעי המטה. אבל כופה עליה כלי כו' ומשני הכא נמי בצריך לאותו מקום. פי' לאותו מקום של כלי ולא למקום הביצה.

רב נסים גאון

באבנים מקורזלות של בית הכסא. תמצא פירושו בפרק המוציא יין (דף פא) זונין על לבי מדרשא אמר להו רבותיי שיעור אבנים מקורזלות בכמה אמרו לו כזית וכאגוז וכביצה תנו רבנן בשבת ג' אבנים מקורזלות מותר להכניסן לבית הכסא כו': **בליבני** דאייתור מבניינא דחזיין למיזגא עלייהו עיקרם בפרק כל הכלים ניטלין בשבת (דף קכד) אמר רב נחמן הני ליבני דאשתיור מבניינא שרי לטלטולינהו בשבתא משום דחזו למיזגא עלייהו ובמס' יום טוב (דף לא) בפרק המביא כדי יין ממקום למקום. אמר ליה לא נצרכה אלא לאותן ב' חלות מנהג הוא בעת חתיכת הדבש מן הכוורת להניח ב' חלות לעסק הדבורים ותישתכח עיקר דיליה בבבא [בתרא] בפרק המוכר את הספינה (דף פ) חלות דבש מניח שתי חלות חיצונות:

מסורת הש"ס

א) לקמן קז. קכא., ב) נ"א ת"ש, ג) לקמן קכא., ד) נ"א ת"ש, ה) ביצה לה., ו) [לקמן מז: קכח: קכד:], ז) [תוספתא פ"ד], ח) [ביצה לד: לה.], ט) נ"א ת"ש, י) לעיל מב: לקמן מז., כ) נ"א ת"ש, ל) נ"א ת"ש, מ) לקמן קכח., נ) נ"א ת"ש, ס) [תוספ' פט"ז], ע) [תוספתא שם], פ) [ביצה לו.], צ) ביצה ג., ק) [שם לו. כל הסוגיא ע"ש כמה שינויים], ר) שם לו., ש) [דף קנד: וכ"כ רש"י לקמן קכח: ד"ה והא], ת) [דף מז:].

תוספות ישנים

א) וזה אין להקשות דלר"ש אמאי חשיב במתניתין ביטול כלי מהיכנו הא עבר וכיבה מותר השמן כמו גבי טבל שאם עבר כו'. וי"ל שאני דכיבוי איסורא דאורייתא ולא אמר ביה שאם עבר כו':

הגהות הב"ח

(א) תום' ד"ה בעודן וכו' כי שדינהו בקדר' אידחו כצ"ל ותיבת חייתא נמחק:

גליון הש"ס

תום' ד"ה טבל מוכן וכו'. שאם שגג. עי' לעיל לח ע"א תוס' ד"ה עבר. ובפסחים דף מב ע"א ברש"י ד"ה היכא דאתמר. וברא"ש שם: תום' ד"ה בעודן עליו וכו'. א"נ הא דיש מוקצה. עיין לקמן דף מד ע"ב תוס' ד"ה יש עליה מעות:

ליקוטי רש"י

כופין. לכתחילה ולא שיכבה את הנר ואשמעינן דכלי ניטל להצלת דבר שאינו ניטל בשבת [לקמן קז.]. **על הנר.** ובלבד שלא יכבה ואף על פי שנוטל כלי להצלת קורה שאינה ניטלת בשבת [שם קכא.]. **ארוכות.** אשפונד"ש [עירובין טו:]. **כשורי.** קורות [לקמן סז.]. **דלף.** גשמים הנוטפים מן הגג. **תחת הדלף.** לקבלו בתוכו מפני טנוף הבית [ביצה לה:]. הרי שהכלי ניטל לקבל בו מוקצה כי האי דלא חזי למידי [שם לו.]. **משום דקא מבטל כלי מהיכנו.** אסור לבטל כלי מהיכנו להושיב כלי במקום שלא יוכל עוד ליטלו [משם] דהוי כקובע לו מקום ומחברו בטיט ודמי למלאכה [לעיל מב:]. דמשהניחם תחתיה אין יכול לטלטלן דדומה לסותר בנין מדרבנן [לקמן קכח:]. כשמניחן תחת דבר שאין ניטל מבטלן מהיכנן דשוב לא יטלם משם ודמי לסותר [שם קנד: ועי' כאן בתוס']. **טבל מוכן הוא.** שאם בא אדם אחד ועבר ותקנו מתוקן, ומותר לאכול ולא אמרינן לא מהניא ליה הזמנה כל זמן שלא נתקן דהא מוקצה מחמת אסור טבל הוא ואסחיה מדעתיה קמשמע לן כיון דהגבהת תרומה ומעשר מדאורייתא בשבת שרי אין זה מוקצה מחמת איסור [ביצה לד:]. **נותנין כלי תחת הנר לקבל ניצוצות.** והא קא מבטל כלי מהיכנו דלא יוכל ליטלו משם כל היום דנעשה בסיס לניצוצות לימא תהוי תיובתיה דרב חסדא דאמר. **אין בהן ממש.** משכנו ומותר ליטלן [לקמן מז:]. **בדלף הראוי.** שהן צלולין וראוין לבהמה. **אלא לדבר הניטל.** לצורך דבר הניטל. מידי דלאו בר טלטול אין כלי ניטל לצורכו [ביצה לו.]. **לסמוך בה.** זוקפה כנגד חודה וסומך בה. **אבל כופה עליה כו'.** ואף על גב דהיא אינה ניטלת מטלטלין את הכלי לצורכה. **בצריך למקומו.** של כלי [שם ג:]. **על גבי אבנים.** שנגוזין לבנין וכשהן מתלחלחין צריך לחזור ולנגבן שאין מקבלות את הטיט יפה והבנין שוהה ליבש. **לבית הכסא.** לקנח [שם לו.]. **מבנינא.** שנשתיירו לו לאחר שגמר בנינו שרי לטלטולינהו דמעתה לאו לבנין קיימי אלא למזגא עלייהו ותורת כלי עליהן [שם לא:]. שהשלים בניינו ויתותר ומהשתא לא קיימי לבנין אלא לישב עליהם ותורת כלי עליהם [לקמן קכד:].

longer move it and its preparedness is thus nullified.[14] Nevertheless, the Mishnah permits this. – ? –

Rav Yosef responds:

דְּרָפֵי דְּאִי בָּעֵי שָׁקִיל לֵיהּ – The Mishnah means that one may place the bench under the beam **loosely, so that if he wishes he may remove it.** Thus, its preparedness is not nullified when it is placed there.

The next challenge:

נוֹתְנִין כְּלִי תַּחַת הַדֶּלֶף בְּשַׁבָּת – Come, learn a refutation from the following Mishnah:[15] WE MAY PUT A VESSEL UNDER LEAKING RAINWATER ON THE SABBATH. Now, leaking water is generally *muktzeh,* yet the Mishnah permits receiving it in a non-*muktzeh* vessel. – ? –

Rav Yosef answers:

בְּדֶלֶף הָרָאוּי – That Mishnah is dealing **with leaking water that is suitable** for drinking and is therefore not *muktzeh.*[16]

The next challenge:

כּוֹפִין אֶת הַסַּל לִפְנֵי הָאֶפְרוֹחִין שֶׁיַּעֲלוּ וְיֵרְדוּ – Come, learn a refutation from the following Baraisa: ONE MAY INVERT A BASKET IN FRONT OF YOUNG BIRDS SO THAT THEY MAY CLIMB UP to AND DOWN from their nest. Now, since the birds are *muktzeh*, allowing them to climb on the basket nullifies its preparedness, yet the Baraisa permits this.[17] – ? –

Rav Yosef replies:

קָסָבַר מוּתָּר לְטַלְטְלוֹ – **[The Tanna of this Baraisa] holds** that **it is permitted to move [the basket]** after the birds climb off it. Thus, inverting it on their behalf does not nullify its preparedness.[18]

The Gemara objects:

וְהָתַנְיָא אָסוּר לְטַלְטְלוֹ – **But it was taught in** that selfsame **Baraisa:**[19] And IT IS FORBIDDEN TO MOVE [THE BASKET]. – ? –

The Gemara answers:

בְּעוֹדָן עָלָיו – That pertains only **while [the birds] are on it,** but once the birds climb off it, one is permitted to move it.

The Gemara persists:

וְהָתַנְיָא – **But it was taught in a Baraisa:** **אַף עַל פִּי שֶׁאֵין עוֹדָן עָלָיו אָסוּר** – EVEN IF [THE BIRDS] ARE NO LONGER ON [THE BASKET] IT IS FORBIDDEN to move it. – ? –

The Gemara answers:

אָמַר רַבִּי אַבָּהוּ – **R' Abahu said:** **בְּעוֹדָן עָלָיו כָּל בֵּין הַשְּׁמָשׁוֹת** – That Baraisa refers to a case **where [the birds] were on [the basket] throughout *bein hashemashos*** at the onset of the Sabbath. In that case, it is prohibited to move the basket even after the birds climb off, **מִיגּוֹ דְּאִיתְקְצַאי לְבֵין הַשְּׁמָשׁוֹת אִיתְקְצַאי לְכוּלֵּי יוֹמָא** – for **since it was *muktzeh* during *bein hashemashos* it is *muktzeh* for the entire day.**[20]

Having concluded its discussion of Rabbah's and Rav Yosef's respective explanations of Rav Chisda's ruling, the Gemara proceeds to cite the opinion of an Amora who differs with Rav Chisda:[21]

אָמַר רַבִּי יִצְחָק – **R' Yitzchak said:** **כְּשֵׁם שֶׁאֵין נוֹתְנִין כְּלִי תַּחַת תַּרְנְגוֹלֶת לְקַבֵּל בֵּיצָתָהּ** – **Just as we may not place a vessel under a hen to receive her egg,** **כָּךְ אֵין כּוֹפִין עָלֶיהָ כְּלִי בִּשְׁבִיל שֶׁלֹּא תִּשָּׁבֵר** – **so too we may not invert a vessel over [a newly laid egg] so that it should not break.**

The Gemara explains R' Yitzchak's reasoning:

קָסָבַר אֵין כְּלִי נִיטָּל אֶלָּא לְדָבָר הַנִּיטָּל בְּשַׁבָּת – **He holds** that a non-*muktzeh* **utensil may be moved only for** the use of **an item**

NOTES

14. *Rashi.* [This act is not forbidden under the prohibition of *muktzeh*; rather, it is the act of nullifying the utensil from its state of usefulness that is prohibited. See further in *Mishnah Berurah* 370:8, and *Dibros Moshe* 34:33.]

15. *Beitzah* 35b.

16. [Rabbah too could have said this answer above, when he was challenged on the basis of this Mishnah, but chose instead to respond in a manner that matched his responses to the other challenges posed to him (*Ritva MHK* ed.).]

17. Living creatures are intrinsically *muktzeh,* since they are not fit for consumption while alive (*Mishnah Berurah* 308:146; see also *Tosafos* to 45b ד״ה הכא במאי עסקינן; cf. *Tosafos, Chullin* 14a ד״ה אם).

Since the birds are *muktzeh,* the basket cannot be moved while the birds are on it. By inverting it on behalf of the birds, one is designating it for a *muktzeh* function for the remainder of the day, thus nullifying its preparedness. How are we permitted to do this on the Sabbath? (*Ritva MHK* ed.; see following note).

[Note that Abaye did not cite this Baraisa as a challenge to Rabbah, who stated above that a non-*muktzeh* item may be moved for the sake of a *muktzeh* item only to prevent a commonplace loss. This is because the situation of young birds being lost due to their inability to climb into or out of their roost is a commonplace one, which warrants moving a non-*muktzeh* basket. However, the Baraisa does represent a challenge to Rav Yosef, who maintains that it is forbidden to nullify the preparedness of a non-*muktzeh* item, since Rav Yosef grants no dispensation for the prevention of monetary loss (*Tosafos* ד״ה כופין; see also *Tosafos* to 43b ד״ה כבר תירגמה and *Baal HaMaor* below, 154b).]

18. The basket is not considered *designated* for a *muktzeh* function simply because it was inverted on behalf of the birds. And although it will be forbidden to move the basket while the birds are on it (see note 20), placing it in their path does not nullify its preparedness since they will not remain on it the entire Sabbath but will climb off (*Ritva MHK* ed.; see *Aruch HaShulchan* 308:65).

[The implication is that the preparedness of a utensil is not considered nullified unless it is immobilized for the duration of the Sabbath. Indeed, this is the opinion of *Baal HaMaor* and *Chidushei Ramban* below, 154b, and is implicit in *Rashi* cited in note 10 and *Rashi* to 47b ד״ה והא קא מבטל and 154b ד״ה והא מבטל כלי and ד״ה מטנפי. Accordingly, one might ask: Why is it prohibited to place a vessel under a hen to catch its egg or under a lamp to catch the oil? Since one can spill the egg or oil out and then use the vessel, he has not nullified its preparedness! The answer is that presumably one will not want to forfeit the egg or oil but intends to leave it in the vessel until the end of the Sabbath, when he will be able to move it to a safe location (*Baal HaMaor* and *Ramban* ibid.). However, others maintain that even the temporary immobilization of a utensil due to *muktzeh* is considered a nullification of its preparedness. They offer another interpretation of our Gemara. See *Tosafos* ד״ה בעודן עליו, and *Rashba* and *Ran* to 154b. See also *Magen Avraham* 265:2 with *Pri Megadim* and *Mishnah Berurah* §5, and *Mishnah Berurah* 308:147.]

19. See *Tosefta* 16:1.

20. It is a general principle of *muktzeh* that an object that was *muktzeh* during *bein hashemashos* (twilight) at the onset of the Sabbath remains *muktzeh* throughout the Sabbath even if the underlying reason for its *muktzeh* status was removed. (This will be discussed more fully below, 44a-45a.) Therefore, if one allowed birds to climb onto a basket prior to the onset of the Sabbath and they remained there throughout *bein hashemashos,* the basket is rendered a *base to muktzeh* (see Chapter Introduction) and remains *muktzeh* for the entire Sabbath, even after the birds climb off it. [The principle that something which was *muktzeh* during *bein hashemashos* remains *muktzeh* for the entire day is actually a matter of Tannaic dispute (see 44a note 3). R' Abahu means to answer that the Baraisa follows the opinion of the Tanna who accepts this principle, i.e. R' Yehudah (*Ritva MHK* ed.; see also *Tosafos,* first ד״ה בעודן עליו; cf. *Tosafos* to 156b, first ד״ה והא).]

By contrast, when one inverts the basket for the birds on the Sabbath itself, it is not rendered *muktzeh* for the entire Sabbath and may be moved once the birds climb off (see *Rashi* and *Tosafos* ד״ה בעודן עליו). It is considered a *base to muktzeh* as long as the birds are on it, but reverts to its non-*muktzeh* state when they climb off. Only that which was *muktzeh* during *bein hashemashos* remains *muktzeh* after the underlying cause has been removed (*Maharsha* to *Tosafos* ד״ה בעודן עליו, *Beis Yosef* and *R' Akiva Eiger, Orach Chaim* 265; see note 8; cf. *Magen Avraham* 265:2, *Shulchan Aruch HaRav* 308:78; see also *Ritva MHK* ed. and note 12 to the chapter introduction).

21. Rav Chisda ruled that although one may not place a vessel under a hen to receive her egg, one may invert a vessel over the egg to prevent

איתיביה כופין קערה על הנר שלא יאחז בקורה בבתי גחיני דשכיח בהו דליקה וכן קורה שנשברה סומכין אותה בספסל ובארוכות המטה בכשורי חדתי דעבידי דפקעי נותנין כלי תחת הדלף בשבת בבתי חדתי דשכיחי דדלפי רב יוסף אמר היינו טעמא דרב חסדא משום דקא מבטל כלי מהיכנו איתיביה אביי חבית של טבל שנשברה מביא כלי אחר ומניח תחתיה א"ל טבל מוכן הוא אצל שבת שאם עבר ותקנו מתוקן נותנין כלי תחת הנר לקבל ניצוצות א"ר הונא בריה דרב יהושע ניצוצות אין בהן ממש וכן קורה שנשברה סומכין אותה בספסל או בארוכות המטה דרפי דאי בעי שקיל ליה נותנין כלי תחת הדלף בשבת בדלף הראוי כופין את הסל לפני האפרוחין שיעלו וירדו קסבר מותר לטלטלו והתניא אסור לטלטלו בעודן עליו והתניא אע"פ שאין עודן עליו אסור א"ר אבהו בעודן עליו כל בין השמשות מיגו דאיתקצאי לבין השמשות איתקצאי לכולי יומא א"ר יצחק כשם שאין נותנין כלי תחת תרנגולת לקבל ביצתה כך אין כופין עליה כלי בשביל שלא תשבר קסבר אין כלי ניטל אלא לדבר הניטל בשבת מיתיבי כל הני תיובתא ושני בצריך למקומו תא שמע אחת ביצה שנולדה בשבת ואחת ביצה שנולדה ביום טוב אין מטלטלין לא לכסות בה את הכלי ולסמוך בה כרעי המטה אבל כופה עליה כלי בשביל שלא תשבר הכא נמי בצריך למקומו ת"ש פורסין מחצלות על גבי אבנים בשבת באבנים מקורזלות דחזיין לבית הכסא ת"ש פורסין מחצלות על גבי לבנים בשבת דאישתיור מבנינא דחזיין למיזגא עלייהו ת"ש פורסין מחצלת על גבי כוורת דבורים בשבת בחמה מפני החמה ובגשמים מפני הגשמים ובלבד שלא יתכוון לצוד הכא במאי עסקינן דאיכא דבש א"ל רב עוקבא ממישן לרב אשי תינח בימות החמה

דאיכא

רש"י

איתיביה כופין קערה. של חרס על גבי הנר כו': **גחיני.** נמוכין: **וכן קורה שנשברה כו'.** משנה היא לקמן: **שנשברה.** בשבת: **ארוכות המטה.** לימונ"ש: **בספסל.** דכלי הוא ומותר לטלטלו: **בכשורי חדתי.** שלא נבדקו עדיין וכשמכביד משא הבית עליהן שהיו טחין על גגותיהן בטיט שכיחי דפקעי: **תחת הדלף.** לקבלו: **טעמא דרב חסדא.** דאין נותנין כלי תחת התרנגולת: **מפני שמבטל כלי מהיכנו.** שהיה מוכן מתחלה לטלטלו ועכשיו עושהו מוקצה: **מוכן הוא.** שאין בו מוקצה אלא איסורו ואם בא אחד ועבר על דברי חכמים שאסרו לתרום בשבת ותיקנו מתוקן ומותר לטלטלו ולאוכלו הלכך לאו מבטל כלי מהיכנו חשיב ליה: **אין בהן ממש.** ומותר ליטלן אחר שנפלו לתוכו: **וכן קורה כו'.** קס"ד שמהדקו שם ואינו יכול שוב ליטלו: **הראוי.** לשתיה כל אלו משניות הן: **כל בין השמשות.** אבל נתנו שם משחשיכה מותר ליטלו אם אין האפרוחים עליו: **בצריך למקומו.** להשתמש במקום הכלי ומתוך שיכול ליטלו לצורך מקומו מוליכו למקום שירצה: **לכסות בה את הכלי.** לסתום פי צלוחית: **על גבי אבנים.** מפני הגשמים שלא ימחו או לא יקבלו טיט מאחר ששרויות במים: **מקורזלות.** ראשן חד וראויות לקינוח דהוי דבר הניטל: **למיזגא.** להשען שכל הסבתן כך היתה יושב קצת ונשען קצת על שמאלו:

דאיכא

תוספות

דמבטל כלי מהיכנו. בפרק בתרא פירש בקונטרס דאסור משום דמתחזי כסותר וכאן פירש דחשיב כאלו מחברו שם בטיט: **טבל** מוכן הוא אצל שבת. אף על פי שאסור לטלטלו כדתנן בפרק מפנין (לקמן קכו:) מ"מ לא חשיב מבטל כלי מהיכנו כיון דאם עבר ותיקנו מתוקן ק' לרשב"א דתנן במסכת תרומות בפ"ב (משנה ג) ומייתי לה בהניזקין (גיטין נג.) המעשר בשבת בשוגג יאכל במזיד לא יאכל ולישנא דקאמר הכא אם עבר ותיקנו משמע במזיד מדלא קאמר שאם שגג ותיקנו ונראה דנקט עבר כגון דלית ליה פירי אחריני דאמר בביצה בפרק י"ט (דף יז:) דאפילו במזיד יאכל עוד הקשה דבפרק בתרא (דף קנד:) תניא היתה בהמתו טעונה טבל ועששית מתיר את החבלים והשקים נופלים ואע"פ שמשתברין משמע דאסור להניח תחתיהן כרים וכסתות אלמא טבל לאו מוכן הוא ואור"י דאף על פי שמשתברין לא קאי אטבל אלא אעששית ועוד הקשה כי היכי דאמר דאם עבר ותיקנו מתוקן ה"נ כשמניח כלי תחת תרנגולת לקבל ביצתה נימא שאם עבר והסיר הביצה מותר הכלי לטלטל ואם כן ביטלת תורת ביטול כלי מהיכנו ולאו פירכא היא דהא כמו שהכלי עם הביצה אין לה היתר אבל טבל יש לו היתר על ידי תיקון ועוד הקשה היכא דאית ליה פירי אחריני בשוגג אמאי יאכל נימא מגו דאיתקצאי לבין השמשות איתקצאי לכולי יומא ועוד מ"ש דהכא אמר דאם עבר ותיקנו מתוקן ובביצה בפ' אין צדין (דף כו: ושם) גבי בכור לר"ש דאמר אין רואין מומין בי"ט אמר שאם עבר וביקרו אינו מבוקר ואדא בר אוכמי דאמר בשוגג מבוקר אמרינן התם דליתא דמשבש ותני (א): **כופין** את הסל. לעיל לא מצי פריך מינה דהכלה מגויה היא: **בעודן** עליו. אבל אחר שירדו מותר לטלטלו נראה לר"י דקסבר דאין מוקצה לחצי שבת דלמ"ד בפ' אין צדין (ביצה כו: ושם) דיש מוקצה אסור לטלטלו אף אחר שירדו וקשה לרשב"א למ"ד יש מוקצה לחצי שבת אמאי כופין את הסל לפני האפרוחים והא מבטל כלי מהיכנו וקי"ל דאסור לבטלו דבסוף פירקין פריך סתמא דהש"ס והא קא מבטל כלי מהיכנו וכן בפ' מפנין (לקמן קכח:) ובפ' בתרא (דף קנד:) פריך אליבא דרב הונא אע"ג דלא מצינו שהיה סובר כן משמע דלכ"ע אסור לבטל כלי מהיכנו וכן אפרש בסמוך וי"ל דלמ"ד יש מוקצה לחצי שבת הך דכופין את הסל מוקי כר"ש דלדידיה ודאי שרי לטלטל הסל כשירדו דאפי' מיגו דאיתקצאי לבין השמשות איתקצאי לכולי יומא לית ליה דהא מתיר להסתפק מן הנר שכבה א"נ הא דיש מוקצה לחצי שבת היינו לאכילה ולא לטלטול וא"ת רב יוסף דמפרש מתני' משום דאסור לבטל כלי מהיכנו לא אתיא מתני' כר"ש דלדידיה לא מבטל כלי מהיכנו כיון דשרי לאחר שכבה כי היכי דלא חשבינן הכא כפיית הסל ביטול כלי משום דשרי אחר שירדו וי"ל דלא דמי דהכא ודאי לא חשיב ביטול כלי כי מיד כשבאו על הסל בידו להפריחם ולהבריחם משם: **בעודן** עליו כל בין השמשות. תימה הא כיון דבידו להפריחם למטה הוי גמרו בידי אדם ולית לן למימר מיגו דאיתקצאי לבין השמשות כדמוכח בפ' אין צדין (ביצה כו:) דפריך ר' זירא למ"ד יש מוקצה לחצי שבת והא פולין ועדשים דמבשלים בי"ט דמעיקרא חזו לכוס כי שדינהו בקדרה הייתא (א) אידחו להו גמר בישולייהו איטתרו להו א"ל אביי ולטעמיך תקשי לך קדירות דעלמא דהא קדירות דשבתא בין השמשות רותחות הן ולאורתא קא אכלינן מינייהו אלא גמרו בידי אדם לא קמבעיא ליה כי קא מיבעיא ליה גמרו בידי שמים וי"ל דשאני קדירות אם הוה צריך להו בין השמשות היה מקררן וכן פולין ועדשים רצונו שיתבשלו בלא שום דיחוי אבל הכא רצונו היה שיעלו האפרוחין על הסל שלכך כפאו והרי שעה אחת הקצה אותו לצרכן ומיגו דאיתקצאי לבין השמשות איתקצאי לכולי יומא: **ושני** ליה בצריך למקומו. ההיא דנותנין כלי תחת הדלף איכא נמי לשנויי בדלף הראוי כדשני לעיל ובפרק משילין (ביצה לו. ושם) משני ליה הכי לרבי יצחק תימה לר"י מ"ש דגבי שמן תנא אין נותנין וגבי ניצוצות נותנין בתרוייהו הוה מצי למתני נותנין בצריך למקומו או בתרוייהו אין נותנין באין צריך למקומו ונראה לר"י דמעיקרא אשמעינן דאין כלי ניטל אלא לדבר הניטל בשבת וגבי ניצוצות דבתר הכי אשמעינן דבצריך למקומו שרי אי נמי ר' יצחק אית ליה נמי דאסור לבטל כלי מהיכנו ולהכי גבי שמן אין נותנין אפילו בצריך למקומו ולרב הונא נפרש בסמוך דאית ליה נמי תרוייהו אין כלי ניטל אלא לדבר הניטל ואסור לבטל כלי מהיכנו ואם נאמר דלרב יוסף לא אתיא מתניתין כר"ש דכיון דלדידיה מותר לאחר שכבה לא חשיב ביטול כלי אם כן מצינן למימר דאפילו רבה אית ליה דאסור לבטל כלי מהיכנו ואיצטריך למימר דהכלה שאינה מגויה לא התירו כדי לאוקמה מתניתין כר"ש וא"ת מאי צריך בכל הני משניות לאשמעינן דבצריך למקומו שרי ויש לומר דלגבי ניצוצות איצטריך לאשמעינן דלא תימא אפילו בצריך למקומו אסור משום דילמא אתי לכבויי וכן ההיא דכופין קערה שלא תאחז כו' וההיא דקורה שנשברה נראה לרשב"א דאיצטריך לאשמעינן דלא חיישינן שמא יעלה את הקורה דאסור להעלות כדתנן בפ' שואל (לקמן קנא:) וכן קורה שנשברה סומכין אותה כו' לא שתעלה אלא שלא תוסיף: **כופה** עליה כלי שלא תשבר כו'. כל הנהו דמייתי ידע המקשה דמצי לשנויי בצריך למקומו אלא שרוצה לידע אם יש לתרץ בענין אחר: **דאייתור** מבניינא. כדאמר לקמן בפ' כל הכלים (דף קכד:) הני לבני דאייתרי מבניינא שרי לטלטולינהו:

דחשיב

עין משפט נר מצוה

מ א מיי' פכ"ה מהלכות שבת הלכה כג סמג לאוין סה טור שו"ע או"ח סימן שי סעיף ו:
מא ב מיי' שם הל' כה:
מב ג מיי' שם טוש"ע או"ח סימן שיג סעיף ז:
מג ד מיי' שם הלכה כד טוש"ע או"ח סימן שלא סעיף ח וסימן תקכא סעיף ג:
מד ה ו מיי' שם הלכה כה סמג שם טוש"ע או"ח סימן שח סעיף לט:
מה ז מיי' וסמג שם טוש"ע או"ח סימן שט"ז סעיף ד:

רבינו חננאל

בהם ממש והכלי שמקבל בו הניצוצות לא מיבטיל ומותר להשתמש בה. וספסל שסמוך בה הקורה רפויה היא שיכול ליטלה ולהשתמש בה. והכלי שמקבל בו הדלף בדלף הראוי לשתיה שהמים מותרים וכ"ש הכלי. וכן הסל שכופין שיעלו וירדו בו האפרוחים אוקמה בעודן האפרוחים עומדין על הסל [או שהיו עומדין על הסל] בין השמשות אסור לטלטל אותו הסל שנעשה מוקצה ואם לאו מותר. ור' יצחק חולק על רב חסדא ואומר אפי' כלי לכוף עליה בשביל שלא תישבר ביצה בשבת אסור. קסבר אין כלי ניטל [אלא] לדבר הניטל בשבת. ואותיבנא עליה כל הני תיובתא. ומשני בצריך למקומו. ת"ש אחת ביצה [שנולדה] בשבת ואחת ביצה שנולדה ביו"ט אין מטלטלין אותה לא לכסות בה את הכלי ולא לסמוך בה כרעי המטה. אבל כופה עליה כלי כו' ומשני הכא נמי בצריך לאותו מקום. פי' לאותו מקום של כלי ולא למקום הביצה.

רב נסים גאון

באבנים מקורזלות של בית הכסא. תמצא פירושו בפרק המוציא יין (דף פא) זונין על לבי מדרשא אמר להו רבותיי שיעור אבנים מקורזלות בכמה אמרו לו כזית וכאגוז וכביצה תנו רבנן בשבת ג' אבנים מקורזלות מותר להכניסן לבית הכסא כו': **בליבני** דאייתור מבניינא דחזיין למיזגא עלייהו עיקרם בפרק כל הכלים ניטלין בשבת (דף קכד) אמר רב נחמן הני ליבני דאשתיור מבניינא שרי לטלטולינהו בשבתא משום דחזו למיזגא עלייהו ובמס' יום טוב (דף לא) בפרק המביא כדי יין ממקום למקום. אמר ליה לא נצרכה אלא לאותן ב' חלות מנהג הוא בעת חתיכת הדבש מן הכוורת להניח ב' חלות לעסק הדבורים ותישתכח עיקר דיליה בבבא [בתרא] בפרק המוכר את הספינה (דף פ) חלות דבש מניח שתי חלות חיצונות:

מסורת הש"ס

א) לקמן קז. קכא., ב) ג"א ת"ש, ג) לקמן קנא:, ד) ג"א ת"ש, ה) ביצה לה., ו) [לקמן מז: קכח: קכד:], ז) [תוספתא פ"ד], ח) [ביצה לד: לה.], ט) ג"א ת"ש, י) לעיל מב: לקמן מז., כ) ג"א ת"ש, ל) ג"א ת"ש, מ) לקמן קכח:, נ) ג"א ת"ש, ס) [תוספ' פט"ו], ע) [תוספתא שם], פ) [ביצה לו.], צ) ביצה ג:, ק) [שם לו. כל הסוגיא ע"ש כמה שינויים], ר) שם לו., ש) [דף קנד: וכ"כ רש"י לקמן קכח: ד"ה והא], ת) [דף מז:].

תוספות ישנים

א) וזה אין להקשות דלר"ש אמאי חשיב במתניתין ביטול כלי מהיכנו הא עבר וכיבה מותר השמן כמו גבי טבל שאם עבר כו'. וי"ל שאני התם דכיבוי איסורא דאורייתא ולא אמר ביה שאם עבר כו':

הגהות הב"ח

(א) תום' ד"ה בעודן וכו' כי שדינהו בקדר' אידחו כצ"ל ותיבת הייתא נמחק:

גליון הש"ס

תום' ד"ה טבל מוכן וכו'. **שאם שגג.** עי' לעיל לח ע"א תוס' ד"ה עבר. ובפסחים דף מב ע"א ברש"י ד"ה היכא דאמר. וברא"ש שם: תום' ד"ה בעודן עליו וכו'. **א"נ הא דיש** מוקצה. עיין לקמן דף מד ע"ב תוס' ד"ה יש עליה מעות:

ליקוטי רש"י

כופין. לכתחילה ולא שיכבה את הנר ואשמעינן דכלי ניטל להצלת דבר שאינו ניטל בשבת [לקמן קז.]. **על הנר.** ובלבד שלא יכבה ואף על פי שנוטל כלי להצלת קורה שאינה ניטלת בשבת [שם קכא.]. **ארוכות.** אשפונד"ש [עירובין טו:]. **כשורי.** קורות [לקמן סז.]. **דלף.** גשמים הנוטפים מן הגג. **תחת הדלף.** לקבלו בתוכו מפני טנוף הבית [ביצה לה:]. הרי שהכלי ניטל לקבל בו מוקצה כי האי דלא חזי למידי [שם לו.]. **משום דקא מבטל כלי מהיכנו.** אסור לבטל כלי מהיכנו להושיב כלי במקום שלא יוכל עוד ליטלו [משם] דהוי כקובע לו מקום ומחברו בטיט ודמי למלאכה [לעיל מב:]. דמשהניחם תחתיה אין יכול לטלטלן דדומה לסותר בנין מדרבנן [לקמן קכח:]. כשמניחן תחת דבר שאין ניטל מבטלן מהיכנן דשוב לא יטלם משם ודמי לסותר [שם קנד: ועי' כאן בתוס']. **טבל מוכן הוא.** שאם בא אדם אחד ועבר ותקנו מתוקן, ומותר לאכול ולא אמרינן לא מהניא ליה הזמנה כל זמן שלא נתקן דהא מוקצה מחמת אסור טבל הוא ואסמיה מדעתיה קמשמע לן כיון דהגבהת תרומה ומעשר מדאורייתא בשבת שרי אין זה מוקצה מחמת איסור [ביצה לד:]. **נותנין כלי תחת הנר לקבל ניצוצות.** והא קא מבטל כלי מהיכנו דלא יוכל ליטלו משם כל היום דנעשה בסיס לניצוצות לימא תהוי תיובתיה דרב חסדא דאסר. **אין בהן ממש.** משכנו ומותר ליטלן [לקמן מז:]. **בדלף הראוי.** שהן ללולין ולאוין לבהמה. **אלא לדבר הניטל.** לצורך דבר הניטל. מידי דלאו בר טלטול אין כלי ניטל לצורכו [ביצה לו.]. **לסמוך בה.** זוקפה כנגד מודה וסומך בה. **אבל כופה עליה כו'.** ואף על גב דהיא אינה ניטלת מטלטלין את הכלי לצורכה. **בצריך למקומו.** של כלי [שם ג:]. **על גבי אבנים.** שנגובין לבנין וכשהן מתלחלחין צריך לחזור ולנגבן שאינן מקבלות את הטיט יפה והבנין שוהה ליבש. **לבית הכסא.** לקנח [שם לו.]. **דאישתיור מבנינא.** שנשתיירו לו לאחר שגמר בניינו שרי לטלטלינהו דמעתה לאו לבנין קיימי אלא למזגא עלייהו ותורת כלי עליהן [שם לא:]. שהשלים בניינו ונימותר ומהשתא לא קיימי לבנין אלא ליתב עליהם ותורת כלי עליהם [לקמן קכד:].

that may be moved on the Sabbath. It is forbidden, however, to move a non-*muktzeh* item for the use of a *muktzeh* item. Since the egg is *muktzeh,* one may not move a vessel in order to protect it.[22]

R' Yitzchak is exposed to all the challenges that Abaye marshalled against Rabbah and Rav Yosef:

מֵיתִיבֵי כָּל הָנֵי תְּיוּבָתָא – **They challenged [R' Yitzchak] with all of those challenges** that were brought to bear against Rabbah and Rav Yosef, i.e. the numerous Mishnahs and Baraisos that permit moving a non-*muktzeh* item for the use of a *muktzeh* item,[23] וְשַׁנֵּי בְּצָרִיךְ לִמְקוֹמוֹ – **and he answered** that all of those teachings deal with cases **where [the person] needed the place occupied by [the non-*muktzeh* item]** for some other use and thus had to move it anyway. The Mishnahs and Baraisos teach that once he is handling the non-*muktzeh* item, he is permitted to deposit it wherever he pleases, even in a location where it will benefit a *muktzeh* item.[24] It is forbidden, however, to initially move a non-*muktzeh* item for the sake of a *muktzeh* item.

The Gemara further challenges R' Yitzchak's principle:

תָּא שְׁמַע – **Come, learn** a refutation of this view from the following Baraisa: אַחַת בֵּיצָה שֶׁנּוֹלְדָה בְּשַׁבָּת וְאַחַת בֵּיצָה שֶׁנּוֹלְדָה בְּיוֹם טוֹב – Concerning BOTH AN EGG THAT WAS LAID ON THE SABBATH AND AN EGG THAT WAS LAID ON A FESTIVAL – אֵין מְטַלְטְלִין – WE MAY NOT MOVE it, לֹא לְכַסּוֹת בָּהּ אֶת הַכְּלִי – NEITHER TO COVER the mouth of A UTENSIL WITH IT, וְלִסְמוֹךְ בָּהּ כַּרְעֵי הַמִּטָּה – NOR TO SUPPORT THE LEGS OF A BED WITH IT.[25] אֲבָל כּוֹפֶה עָלֶיהָ כְּלִי בִּשְׁבִיל שֶׁלֹּא תִּשָּׁבֵר – HOWEVER, ONE MAY INVERT A VESSEL OVER [THE EGG] SO THAT IT SHOULD NOT BREAK. This Baraisa seems to permit moving a non-*muktzeh* vessel for the sake of protecting a *muktzeh* egg. – ? –

The Gemara rejects the challenge:

הָכָא נַמִּי בְּצָרִיךְ לִמְקוֹמוֹ – **Here too,** we may say that the Mishnah refers to a case **where one needs the place occupied by [the vessel]** for some other purpose. Since he has a legitimate need to move the vessel, he is permitted to place it over the egg.[26]

Another challenge:

תָּא שְׁמַע – **Come, learn** a refutation from the following Baraisa: פּוֹרְסִין מַחְצָלוֹת עַל גַּבֵּי אֲבָנִים בְּשַׁבָּת – WE MAY SPREAD MATS OVER STONES ON THE SABBATH to protect them from the elements.[27] The Baraisa permits moving the mats for the benefit of the stones even though they are intrinsically *muktzeh.* – ? –

The Gemara rejects the challenge:

בַּאֲבָנִים מְקוּרְזָלוֹת – The Baraisa is dealing **with pointed stones,** דַּחֲזִיין לְבֵית הַכִּסֵּא – **which are suitable for** use in **the outhouse.**[28]

Another challenge:

תָּא שְׁמַע – **Come, learn** a refutation from the following Baraisa: פּוֹרְסִין מַחְצָלוֹת עַל גַּבֵּי לְבֵנִים בְּשַׁבָּת – WE MAY SPREAD MATS OVER BRICKS ON THE SABBATH to protect them from the elements. The Baraisa permits moving the mats for the benefit of the bricks even though they are *muktzeh.*[29] – ? –

The Gemara rejects the challenge:

דְּאִישְׁתְּיוּר מִבִּנְיָנָא – The Baraisa is dealing with **bricks that were left over from construction,** דַּחֲזִיין לְמִיזְגָּא עֲלַיְיהוּ – **which are suitable to recline upon.**[30]

The next challenge:

תָּא שְׁמַע – **Come, learn** a refutation from the following Baraisa: פּוֹרְסִין מַחְצֶלֶת עַל גַּבֵּי כַּוֶּורֶת דְּבוֹרִים בְּשַׁבָּת – WE MAY SPREAD A MAT OVER A BEEHIVE ON THE SABBATH, בַּחַמָּה מִפְּנֵי הַחַמָּה – IN THE SUN, to protect the hive FROM THE SUN, וּבַגְּשָׁמִים מִפְּנֵי הַגְּשָׁמִים – AND IN THE RAIN, to protect it FROM THE RAIN, וּבִלְבַד שֶׁלֹּא יִתְכַּוֵּין לָצוּד – PROVIDED THAT ONE DOES NOT INTEND TO TRAP the bees. A beehive is *muktzeh,*[31] yet the Baraisa permits moving a mat to protect it. – ? –

The challenge is rejected:

הָכָא בְּמַאי עַסְקִינַן – **What are we dealing with here?** דְּאִיכָּא דְּבַשׁ – It is with a case **where there is honey** in the hive. Since the honey is not *muktzeh,* the mat may be spread to protect it.

The Gemara objects to this explanation:

אָמַר לֵיהּ רַב עוּקְבָא מִמֵּישָׁן לְרַב אַשִׁי – **Rav Ukva of Meishan said to Rav Ashi:** תִּינַח בִּימוֹת הַחַמָּה – **This** answer **is fine for the summer,**

NOTES

its being crushed. The following Amora differs.

22. According to Rabbah's explanation of Rav Chisda's ruling, Rav Chisda also agrees to this principle, but maintains that the Rabbis granted a dispensation for the prevention of a commonplace loss, such as the crushing of a newly laid egg (see 42b note 14). R' Yitzchak allows no such dispensation.

23. These are: the Baraisa that permits placing a vessel under a broken barrel of *tevel* to salvage it; the Mishnah that permits placing a vessel under a lamp to catch the falling sparks; the Mishnah that permits placing a bowl over a lamp to prevent an overhead beam from catching fire; the Mishnah that permits supporting a sagging beam with a bench or the sideboards of a bed; the Mishnah that permits placing a vessel under leaking rainwater; and the Baraisa that permits inverting a basket on behalf of young birds.

Rabbah had responded to most of these challenges by explaining that those teachings deal with situations involving commonplace losses, in which case the Rabbis waived the prohibition against moving a non-*muktzeh* item for the sake of a *muktzeh* item. This solution, however, is not available to R' Yitzchak, who allows no such dispensation. Rav Yosef's resolutions are also of no avail to R' Yitzchak, because they addressed only the issue of nullifying a utensil's availability, not that of moving a utensil for the use of *muktzeh.* [The only exception is the interpretation of the Mishnah concerning a leak as dealing with potable water (*Tosafos* ד״ה ושני ליה).] Thus, a new resolution is required of R' Yitzchak.

24. *Rashi;* see also *Rashba* to *Beitzah* 3b and *Orach Chaim* 308:3 with *Mishnah Berurah* §13. See *Tosafos,* end of ד״ה ושני ליה, for a discussion of why so many Mishnahs and Baraisos are needed to teach this principle.

25. An egg when stood lengthwise is structurally capable of supporting a heavier object (see *Rashi* to *Beitzah* 3b). However, since the egg that was laid on the Sabbath or Yom Tov is *muktzeh* (see 42b note 13) it may not be used for any purpose (*Rashba* above, 29b; see *Beis HaLevi* I:12 and *Kehillos Yaakov, Beitzah* §4 ד״ה ובעיקר).

26. The one who brought the challenge to bear knew that it could be deflected in this fashion, but sought to ascertain whether any other answer could be given. The same holds true concerning all the challenges that follow, which are indeed rejected through novel explanations (*Tosafos* ד״ה כופה).

27. I.e. we may cover stones that are designated for construction to protect them from disintegrating in the rain or becoming waterlogged and unsuitable for having mortar adhere to them (*Rashi*).

28. [In Talmudic times stones were used in lieu of toilet paper.] For the sake of human dignity, the Sages granted a dispensation from the *muktzeh* laws to allow one to handle stones that have a sharp edge, which are suitable for this use (*Rashi* to *Succah* 36b; cf. *Aruch* cited by *Maharshal;* see also below, 81a). Since these pointed stones may be moved on the Sabbath (for this purpose – see *Orach Chaim* 312:1), carrying a mat to cover them falls under the category of moving a utensil for the sake of something that may itself be moved on the Sabbath (*Rashi*).

29. Bricks that are earmarked as raw material for construction are not considered utensils at all and are thus intrinsically *muktzeh* (*Mishnah Berurah* 308:74).

30. I.e. to sit upon. In ancient times, people would not sit upright while eating, but would recline slightly (*Rashi*). Since the leftover bricks are no longer designated for construction they stand to be used as seats and are therefore classified as non-*muktzeh* utensils (*Rashi* to 124b ד״ה דאייתור).

31. [The beehive is a *base to muktzeh,* since it always contains bees.]

איתיביה [א] כופין קערה על הנר שלא יאחז בקורה בבתי גחיני דשכיח בהו דליקה [ב][ג] וכן קורה שנשברה סומכין אותה בספסל ובארוכות המטה בכשורי חדתי דעבידי דפקעי [ד][ה] נותנין כלי תחת הדלף בשבת בבתי חדתי דשכיחי דדלפי רב יוסף אמר היינו טעמא דרב חסדא [א] משום [ו] דקא מבטל כלי מהיכנו איתיביה אביי [ז][ב] חבית של טבל שנשברה מביא כלי אחר ומניח תחתיה א"ל [ח] טבל מוכן הוא אצל שבת שאם עבר ותקנו מתוקן [ט][י] נותנין כלי תחת הנר לקבל ניצוצות א"ר הונא בריה דרב יהושע ניצוצות אין בהן ממש [כ][ג] וכן קורה שנשברה סומכין אותה בספסל או בארוכות המטה דרפי דאי בעי שקיל ליה [ל][מ] נותנין כלי [ד] תחת הדלף בשבת בדלף הראוי [נ][ס] כופין [ה] את הסל לפני האפרוחין שיעלו וירדו קסבר מותר לטלטלו והתניא [ע] אסור לטלטלו [ו] בעודן עליו והתניא אע"פ שאין עודן עליו אסור א"ר אבהו בעודן עליו כל בין השמשות מיגו דאיתקצאי לבין השמשות איתקצאי לכולי יומא א"ר יצחק כשם שאין נותנין כלי תחת תרנגולת לקבל ביצתה כך אין כופין עליה כלי בשביל שלא תשבר [פ] קסבר אין כלי ניטל אלא לדבר הניטל בשבת מיתיבי כל הני תיובתא ושני בצריך למקומו תא שמע [צ] אחת ביצה שנולדה בשבת ואחת ביצה שנולדה ביום טוב אין מטלטלין לא לכסות בה את הכלי ולסמוך בה כרעי המטה אבל כופה עליה כלי בשביל שלא תשבר הכא נמי בצריך למקומו [ק] ת"ש פורסין מחצלות על גבי אבנים בשבת באבנים מקורזלות דחזיין לבית הכסא ת"ש [ר] פורסין מחצלות על גבי לבנים בשבת דאישתיור מבנינא דחזיין למיזגא עלייהו ת"ש [ז] פורסין מחצלת על גבי כוורת דבורים בשבת בחמה מפני החמה ובגשמים מפני הגשמים ובלבד שלא יתכוין לצוד הכא במאי עסקינן דאיכא דבש א"ל רב עוקבא ממישן לרב אשי תינח בימות החמה

דאיכא

רש"י

איתיביה כופין קערה. של חרס על גבי הנר כו': גחיני. נמוכין: וכן קורה שנשברה כו'. משנה היא לקמן: שנשברה. בשבת: ארוכות המטה. לימוני"ש: בספסל. דכלי הוא ומותר לטלטלו: בכשורי חדתי. שלא נבדקו עדיין וכשמכביד משא הבית עליהן שהיו טחין על גגותיהן בטיט שכיחי דפקעי: תחת הדלף. לקבלו: טעמא דרב חסדא. דאין נותנין כלי תחת התרנגולת: מפני שמבטל כלי מהיכנו. שהיה מוכן מתחלה לטלטלו ועכשיו עושהו מוקצה: מוכן הוא. שאין בו מוקצה אלא איסורו ואם בא אחד ועבר על דברי חכמים שאסרו לתרום בשבת ותיקנו מתוקן ומותר לטלטלו ולאוכלו הלכך לאו מבטל כלי מהיכנו חשיב ליה: אין בהן ממש. ומותר ליטלן אחר שנפלו לתוכו: וכן קורה כו'. קס"ד שמהדקו שם ואינו יכול שוב ליטלו: הראוי. לשתיה כל אלו משניות הן: כל בין השמשות. אבל נתנו שם משחשיכה מותר ליטלו אם אין האפרוחים עליו: בצריך למקומו. להשתמש במקום הכלי ומתוך שיכול ליטלו לצורך מקומו מוליכו למקום שירצה: לכסות בה את הכלי. לסתום פי צלוחית: על גבי אבנים. מפני הגשמים שלא ימחו או לא יקבלו סיד מאחר שסרויות במים: מקורזלות. ראשן חד וראויות לקינוח דהוי דבר הניטל: למיזגא. להשען שכל הסבתן כך היתה יושב קצת ונשען קצת על שמאלו:

דאיכא

תוספות

דמבטל כלי מהיכנו. בפרק בתרא [ש] פירש בקונטרס דאסור משום דמתחזי כסותר וכאן פירש דחשיב כאלו מחברו בטיט: טבל מוכן הוא אצל שבת. אף על פי שאסור לטלטלו כדתנן בפרק מפנין (לקמן קכו:) מ"מ לא חשיב מבטל כלי מהיכנו כיון דאם עבר ותיקנו מתוקן ק' לרשב"א דתנן במסכת תרומות בפ"ב (משנה ג) ומייתי לה בהניזקין (גיטין נד.) המעשר בשבת בשוגג יאכל במזיד לא יאכל ולישנא דקאמר הכא אם עבר ותיקנו משמע במזיד מדלא קאמר ° שאם שגג ותיקנו ונראה דנקט עבר כגון דלית ליה פירי אחריני דאמר בביצה בפרק י"ט (דף יז:) דאפילו במזיד יאכל עוד הקשה דבפרק בתרא (דף קנד:) תניא היתה בהמתו טעונה טבל ועששית מתיר את החבלים והשקים נופלים ואע"פ שמשתברין משמע דאסור להניח תחתיהן כרים וכסתות אלמא טבל לאו מוכן הוא ואור"י דאף על פי שמשתברין לא קאי אטבל אלא אעששית ועוד הקשה כי היכי דאמר דאם עבר ותיקנו מתוקן ה"נ כשמניח כלי תחת תרנגולת לקבל ביצתה נימא שאם עבר והסיר הביצה מותר הכלי לטלטל ואם כן ביטלת תורת ביטול כלי מהיכנו ולאו פירכא היא דהא כמו שהכלי עם הביצה אין לה היתר אבל טבל יש לו היתר על ידי תיקון ועוד הקשה היכא דאית ליה פירי אחריני בשוגג אמאי יאכל נימא מגו דאיתקצאי לבין השמשות איתקצאי לכולי יומא ועוד מ"ש דהכא אמר דאם עבר ותיקנו מתוקן ובביצה בפ' אין צדין (דף כו: ושם) גבי בכור לר"ש דאמר אין רואין מומין בי"ט אמר שאם עבר וביקרו אינו מבוקר ואדא בר אוכמי דאמר בשוגג מבוקר אמרינן התם דליתא דמשבש ותניא): כופין את הסל. לעיל לא מצי פריך מינה דהגלה מגויה היא: בעודן עליו. אבל אחר שירדו מותר לטלטלו נראה לר"י דקסבר דאין מוקצה לחצי שבת דלמ"ד בפ' אין צדין (ביצה כו: ושם) דיש מוקצה אסור לטלטלו אף אחר שירדו וקשה לרשב"א למ"ד יש מוקצה לחצי שבת אמאי כופין את הסל לפני האפרוחים והא מבטל כלי מהיכנו וקי"ל דאסור לבטלו דבסוף פירקין [ת] פריך סתמא דהש"ס והא קא מבטל כלי מהיכנו וכן בפ' מפנין (לקמן קכח:) ובפ' בתרא (דף קנד:) פריך אליבא דרב הונא אע"ג דלא מצינו שהיה סובר כן משמע דלכ"ע אסור לבטל כלי מהיכנו וכן אפרש בסמוך וי"ל דלמ"ד יש מוקצה לחצי שבת הך דכופין את הסל מוקי כר"ש דלדידיה ודאי שרי לטלטל הסל כשירדו דאפי' מיגו דאיתקצאי לבין השמשות איתקצאי לכולי יומא לית ליה דהא מתיר להסתפק מן הנר שכבה ° א"נ הא דיש מוקצה לחצי שבת היינו לאכילה ולא לטלטול וא"ת רב יוסף דמפרש מתני' משום דאסור לבטל כלי מהיכנו לא אתיא מתני' כר"ש דלדידיה לא מבטל כלי מהיכנו כיון דשרי לאחר שכבה כי היכי דלא חשבינן הכא כפיית הסל ביטול כלי משום דשרי אחר שירדו וי"ל דלא דמי דהכא ודאי לא חשיב ביטול כלי כי מיד כשבאו על הסל בידו להפריחם ולהבריחם משם: בעודן עליו כל בין השמשות. תימה הא כיון דבידו להפריחם למטה הוי גמרו בידי אדם ולית לן למימר מיגו דאיתקצאי לבין השמשות כדמוכח בפ' אין צדין (ביצה כו:) דפריך ר' זירא למ"ד יש מוקצה לחצי שבת והא פולין ועדשים דמבשלים בי"ט דמעיקרא חזו לכוס כי שדינהו בקדרה הייתא (א) אידחו להו גמר בישולייהו אישתרו להו א"ל אביי ולטעמיך תקשי לך קדירות דעלמא דהא קדירות דשבתא בין השמשות רותחות הן ולאורתא קא אכלינן מינייהו אלא גמרו בידי אדם לא קמבעיא ליה כי קא מיבעיא ליה גמרו בידי שמים וי"ל דשאני קדירות אם הוה צריך להו בין השמשות היה מקררן וכן פולין ועדשים רצונו שיתבשלו בלא שום דיחוי אבל הכא רצונו היה שיעלו האפרוחין על הסל שלכך כפאו והרי שעה אחת הקלה אותו לצרכן ומיגו דאיתקצאי לבין השמשות איתקצאי לכולי יומא: ושני ליה בצריך למקומו. ההיא דנותנין כלי תחת הדלף איכא נמי לשנויי בדלף הראוי כדשני לעיל ובפרק משילין (ביצה לו. ושם) משני ליה הכי לרבי יצחק תימה לר"י מ"ש דגבי שמן תנא אין נותנין וגבי ניצוצות נותנין בתרוייהו הוה מצי למתני נותנין בצריך למקומו או בתרוייהו אין נותנין באין צריך למקומו ונראה לר"י דמעיקרא אשמעינן דאין כלי ניטל אלא לדבר הניטל בשבת וגבי ניצוצות דבתר הכי אשמעינן דבצריך למקומו שרי אי נמי ר' יצחק אית ליה נמי דאסור לבטל כלי מהיכנו ולהכי גבי שמן אין נותנין אפילו בצריך למקומו ולרב הונא נפרש בסמוך דאית ליה נמי תרוייהו אין כלי ניטל אלא לדבר הניטל ואסור לבטל כלי מהיכנו ואם נאמר דלרב יוסף לא אתיא מתניתין כר"ש דכיון דלדידיה מותר לאחר שכבה לא חשיב ביטול כלי אם כן מצינן למימר דאפילו רבה אית ליה דאסור לבטל כלי מהיכנו ואיצטריך למימר דהגלה שאינה מגויה לא התירו כדי לאוקמה מתניתין כר"ש וא"ת מאי צריך בכל הני משניות לאשמעינן דבצריך למקומו שרי ויש לומר דלגבי ניצוצות איצטריך לאשמעינן דלא תימא אפילו בצריך למקומו אסור משום דילמא אתי לכבויי וכן ההיא דכופין קערה שלא תאחוז כו' וההיא דקורה שנשברה נראה לרשב"א דאיצטריך לאשמעינן דלא חיישינן שמא יעלה את הקורה דאסור להעלות כדתנן בפ' שואל (לקמן קנא:) וכן קורה שנשברה סומכין אותה כו' לא שתעלה אלא שלא תוסיף: כופה עליה כלי שלא תשבר כו'. כל הנהו דמייתי ידע המקשה דמצי לשנויי בצריך למקומו אלא שרוצה לידע אם יש לתרץ בענין אחר: דאייתור מבניינא. כדאמר לקמן בפ' כל הכלים (דף קכד:) הני לבני דאייתרי מבניינא שרי לטלטולינהו:

דחשיב

עין משפט נר מצוה

מ א מיי' פכ"ה מהלכות שבת הלכה כג סמג לאוין סה טור שו"ע או"ח סימן שי סעיף ו:
מא ב מיי' שם הל' כה:
מב ג מיי' שם טוש"ע או"ח סימן שיג סעיף ז:
מג ד מיי' שם הלכה כד טוש"ע או"ח סימן שלח סעיף ח וסימן תקכא סעיף ג:
מד ה ו מיי' שם הלכה כה סמג שם טוש"ע או"ח סימן שח סעיף לט:
מה ז מיי' וסמג שם טוש"ע או"ח סימן שט"ז סעיף ד:

רבינו חננאל

בהם ממש והכלי שמקבל בו הניצוצות לא מיבטיל ומותר להשתמש בה. וספסל שסמוך בה הקורה רפויה היא שיכול ליטלה ולהשתמש בה. והכלי שמקבל בו הדלף בדלף הראוי לשתיה שהמים מותרים וכ"ש הכלי. וכן הסל שכופין שיעלו וירדו בו האפרוחים אוקמה בעודן האפרוחים עומדין על הסל [או שהיו עומדין על הסל] בין השמשות אסור לטלטל אותו הסל שנעשה מוקצה ואם לאו מותר. ור' יצחק חולק על רב חסדא ואומר אפי' כלי לכוף עליה בשביל שלא תישבר ביצה בשבת אסור. קסבר אין כלי ניטל [אלא] לדבר הניטל בשבת. ואותיבנא עליה כל הני תיובתא. ומשני בצריך למקומו. ת"ש אחת ביצה [שנולדה] בשבת ואחת ביצה שנולדה ביו"ט אין מטלטלין אותה לא לכסות בה את הכלי ולא לסמוך בה כרעי המטה. אבל כופה עליה כלי כו' ומשני הכא נמי בצריך לאותו מקום. פי' לאותו מקום של כלי ולא למקום הביצה.

רב נסים גאון

באבנים מקורזלות של בית הכסא. תמצא פירושו בפרק המוציא יין (דף פא) זונין על לבי מדרשא אמר להו רבותיי שיעור אבנים מקורזלות בכמה אמרו לו כזית וכאגוז וכביצה תנו רבנן בשבת ג' אבנים מקורזלות מותר להכניסן לבית הכסא כו': **בליבני** דאייתור מביניינא דחזיין למיזגא עלייהו עיקרם בפרק כל הכלים ניטלין בשבת (דף קכד) אמר רב נחמן הני ליבני דאשתיור מבניינא שרי לטלטולינהו בשבתא משום דחזו למיזגא עלייהו ובמס' יום טוב (דף לא) בפרק המביא כדי יין ממקום למקום. אמר ליה לא נצרכה אלא לאותן ב' חלות מנהג הוא בעת חתיכת הדבש מן הכוורת להניח ב' חלות לעסק הדבורים ותישתכח עיקר דיליה בבבא [בתרא] בפרק המוכר את הספינה (דף פ) חלות דבש מניח שתי חלות חיצונות:

מסורת הש"ס

א) לקמן קז. קכא., ב) כ"א ת"ש, ג) לקמן קנא:, ד) כ"א ת"ש, ה) ביצה לה:, ו) [לקמן מז: קכח: קנד:], ז) [תוספתא פ"ד], ח) [ביצה לד: לה.], ט) כ"א ת"ש, י) לעיל מב: לקמן מז:, כ) כ"א ת"ש, ל) כ"א ת"ש, מ) לקמן קכח:, נ) כ"א ת"ש, ס) [תוספ' פט"ז], ע) [תוספתא שם], פ) [ביצה לו.], צ) ביצה ג:, ק) [שם לו. כל הסוגיא ע"ש כמה שינויים], ר) שם לו:, ש) [דף קנד: וכ"כ רש"י לקמן קכח: ד"ה והא], ת) [דף מז:].

תוספות ישנים

א) וזה אין להקשות דלר"ש אמאי חשיב במתניתין ביטל כלי מהיכנו הא עבר וכיבה מותר השמן כמו גבי טבל שאם עבר כו'. וי"ל שאני הכא דכיבוי איסורא דאורייתא ולא אמר ביה שאם עבר כו':

הגהות הב"ח

(א) תום' ד"ה בעודן וכו' כי שדינהו בקדר' אידחו כצ"ל ותיבת הייתא נמחק:

גליון הש"ס

תוס' ד"ה טבל מוכן וכו'. שאם שגג. עי' לעיל לח ע"א תוס' ד"ה עבר. ובפסחים דף מב ע"א ברש"י ד"ה היכא דאמר. וברא"ש שם: תוס' ד"ה בעודן עליו וכו'. א"נ הא דיש מוקצה. עיין לקמן דף מד ע"ב תוס' ד"ה יש עליה מעות:

ליקוטי רש"י

כופין. לכתחילה ולא שיכבה את הנר ואשמעינן דכלי ניטל להצלת דבר שאינו ניטל בשבת [לקמן קז.]. על הנר. ובלבד שלא יכבה ואף על פי שנוטל כלי להצלת קורה שאינה ניטלת בשבת [שם קכא.]. ארוכות. אשפונד"ש [עירובין טו:]. כשורי. קורות [לקמן סז.]. דלף. גשמים הנוטפים מן הגג. תחת הדלף. לקבלו בתוכו מפני טנוף הבית [ביצה לה:]. הרי שהכלי ניטל לקבל בו מוקצה כי האי דלא חזי למידי [שם לו.]. משום דקא מבטל כלי מהיכנו. אסור לבטל כלי מהיכנו להושיב כלי במקום שלא יוכל עוד ליטלו [משם] דהוי קובע לו מקום ומחברו בטיט ודמי למלאכה [לעיל מב:]. דמשהכניסם תחתיה אין יכול לטלטלן דדומה לסותר בנין מדרבנן [לקמן קכח:]. כשמניחן תחת דבר שאין ניטל מבטלן מהיכנן דשוב לא יטלם משם ודמי לסותר [שם קנד: ועי' כאן בתוס']. טבל מוכן הוא. שאם בא אדם אחד ועבר ותקנו מתוקן, ומותר לאכול ולא אמרינן לא מהניא ליה הזמנה כל זמן שלא נתקן דהא מוקצה מחמת אסור טבל הוא ואסחיה מדעתיה קמשמע לן כיון דהגבהת תרומה ומעשר מדאורייתא בשבת שרי אין זה מוקצה מחמת איסור [ביצה לד:]. נותנין כלי תחת הנר לקבל ניצוצות. והא קא מבטל כלי מהיכנו דלא יוכל ליטלו משם כל היום דנעשה בסיס לניצוצות לימא תהוי תיובתיה דרב חסדא לאסר. אין בהן ממש. משכנו ומותר ליטלן [לקמן מז:]. בדלף הראוי. שהן צלולין וראוין לבהמה. אלא לדבר הניטל. לצורך דבר הניטל. מידי דלאו בר טלטול אין כלי ניטל לצורכו [ביצה לו.]. לסמוך בה. זוקפה כנגד חודה וסומך בה. אבל כופה עליה כו'. ואף על גב דהיא אינה ניטלת מטלטלין את הכלי לצורכה. בצריך למקומו. של כלי [שם ג:]. על גבי אבנים. שנגודין לבנין וכשהן מתלחלחין צריך לחזור ולנגבן שאין מקבלות את הטיט יפה והבנין שוהה ליבש. לבית הכסא. לקנח [שם לו.]. דאישתיור מבנינא. שנשתיירו לו לאחר שגמר בניינו שרי לטלטלינהו דמעתה לאו לבנין קיימי אלא למזגא עלייהו ותורת כלי עליהן [שם לא:]. שהשלים בניינו וניתותר ומהשתא לא קיימי לבנין אלא לישב עליהם ותורת כלי עליהם [לקמן קכד:].

עין משפט נר מצוה

מו א מיי' פכ"ה מהלכ' שבת הלכה כ ופכ"ו הלכה כב סמג לאוין סה טוש"ע או"ח סימן שיא סעיף ו:

מז ב ג מיי' שם פכ"ה הלכה כא טור ש"ע או"ח שם סעיף ח:

מסורת הש"ס

א) [לעיל ל: לקמן קמב:], ב) [לקמן קכב. קמא.], ג) [תוספתא פי"ד] יומא דף פה., ד) יומא שם, ה) מה"ר שכאל הגיה והלא משמע דלעג"ג ללשון כו', ו) נ"י דהכא.

דאיכא דבש בימות הגשמים דליכא דבש מאי איכא למימר לא נצרכא אלא לאותן שתי חלות והא מוקצות נינהו דחשיב עלייהו הא לא חשיב עלייהו מאי אסור אי הכי הא דתני ובלבד שלא יתכוין לצוד לפלוג ולתני בדידה בד"א כשחישב עליהן אבל לא חישב עליהן אסור הא קמ"ל אע"פ שחישב עליהן ובלבד שלא יתכוין לצוד מני אי ר"ש א) לית לי' מוקצה אי ר' יהודה כי לא מתכוין מאי הוי הא דבר שאין מתכוין אסור לעולם ר' יהודה מאי ובלבד שלא יתכוין לצוד שלא יעשנה כמצודה דלישבוק להו רווחא כי היכי דלא ליתצדו ממילא רב אשי אמר מי קתני בימות החמה ובימות הגשמים בחמה מפני החמה ובגשמים מפני הגשמים קתני ביומי ניסן וביומי תשרי דאיכא חמה (ואיכא צינה) ואיכא גשמים ואיכא דבש אמר להו רב ששת פוקו ואמרו ליה לר' יצחק כבר תרגמא רב הונא לשמעתיך בבבל דא"ר הונא עושין מחיצה למת בשביל חי ואין עושין מחיצה למת בשביל מת מאי היא דא"ר שמואל בר יהודה וכן תנא שילא מרי א) מת המוטל בחמה באים שני בני אדם ויושבין בצדו חם להם מלמטה זה מביא מטה ויושב עליה וזה מביא מטה ויושב עליה חם להם מלמעלה מביאים מחצלת ופורסין עליהן זה זוקף מטתו ונשמט והולך לו וזה זוקף מטתו ונשמט והולך לו ונמצאת מחיצה עשויה מאליה איתמר מת המוטל בחמה רב יהודה אמר שמואל ב) הופכו ממטה למטה רב חנינא בר שלמיא משמיה דרב אמר ה) מניח עליו ככר או תינוק ומטלטלו היכא דאיכא ככר או תינוק כולי עלמא לא פליגי דשרי ° כי פליגי דלית ליה מ"ס ו) טלטול מן הצד שמיה טלטול ומ"ס לא שמיה טלטול לימא כתנאי ג) אין מצילין את המת מפני הדליקה אמר ר' יהודה בן לקיש שמעתי שמצילין את המת מפני הדליקה היכי דמי אי דאיכא ככר או תינוק מ"ט דתנא קמא אי דליכא מ"ט דר' יהודה בן לקיש אלא לאו בטלטול מן הצד פליגי דמר סבר טלטול מן הצד שמיה טלטול ומ"ס לא שמיה טלטול לא ג) דכ"ע טלטול מן הצד שמיה טלטול והיינו טעמא דר' יהודה בן לקיש ז) דמתוך שאדם בהול על מתו

אי

רש"י

דאיכא דבש. דבר הניטל: שתי חלות. כל הכוורת עושין אותה הדבורים חלות חלות של לפיחים של דבש ושעוה וכשרודים אותן מניחין בה שתים שיתפרנסו מהן הדבורים כל ימות הגשמים כדתנן בהמוכר את הספינה (ב"ב פ.) הלוקח חלות כוורתו של חבירו מניח שתי חלות דסתמא לא מכוין: מוקצות נינהו. לדבורים הדר הוה ליה דבר שאינו ניטל ואפ"ה מטלטלין מחצלת להצלתן: דחשיב עלייהו. מאתמול לאכילה: ומני. היא שהצרכת לתרוצה כשחישב וקתני לדבר שאין מתכוין מותר כר"ש: אי ר"ש. אמר ° למה לי לאוקמיה בשחישב: שלא יעשנו כמצודה. שלא יכסנה כולה אלא דנשבוק רווחא שיוכלו לצאת כי היכי דלא ליתצדו בהאי כיסוי ממילא ואע"ג דלא מיכוין למיצד אסור: רב אשי אמר. לעולם דאיכא דבש טובא ודקשיא לך ימות הגשמים מי קתני בה ימות הגשמים: לשמעתיך. דאין כלי ניטל אלא לדבר הניטל: מת המוטל בחמה. ויש לחוש שמא ימהר להסריח: ויושבין בצדו. ע"ג הקרקע כדי שיצטערו מחום הקרקע ויצטרכו להביא מטות לישב עליהן והמטות יהיו למחילה כדמסיים ואזיל: חם להם למטה. מן הקרקע שרתחו חמה: ופורסין. על ראשן לצל: זה זוקף מטתו. שתהא המחצלת מונחת עליה וכן זה נמצאת מחילה עשויה מאליה ולכשירצו נשמטין והולכין להם ודוקא נקט חם להם מלמטה ברישא שיביאו המטות לישיבה ברישא והדר מחצלת לפרוס עליהן לצל ואוחזין אותה בידיהן עד לאחר שעה שיזקפום וישמטום דהוה ליה כי ההוא דאמרינן (עירובין דף קב.) האי מדורתא מלמעלה למטה שרי אבל לאתויי מעיקרא מטות לצורך האהל לא דהוה ליה מלמטה למעלה כדרך בנין וקי"ל אין עושין אהל עראי בתחילה בשבת: הופכו ממטה למטה. עד שמגיע לצל: מן הצד. כלאחר יד: אי דליכא. והאי מצילין דקאמר ר' יהודה בן לקיש דמטלטל ליה להדיא הוא: מאי טעמא דר' יהודה. אלא לאו מן הצד הוא דקשרי:

תוספות

דחשיב עלייהו. וא"ת והא אסור לרודים כדתניא בסוף פרק המצניע (לקמן צה. ושם) הרודה חלות דבש בשוגג חייב חטאת דברי ר"א ולרבנן שבות מיהא איכא והוי דבר שאינו ניטל וי"ל דמיירי ברדויות ומונחות שם בכוורת אי נמי רגילות שיש דבש צף ע"ג חלות ואותו אינו צריך רדייה:

שלא יעשנו כעין מצודה. וא"ת מאי קמ"ל פשיטא דאי עביד כעין מצודה דאסור ה) והא לא משמע מברייתא דאע"ג דאינו מתכוין אסור וי"ל דאמר בפ' משילין (ביצה לו: ושם) דקמ"ל דס"ד במינו ניצוד אסור שאין במינו ניצוד מותר:

רב אשי אמר כו'. מסתמא רב אשי השיב מיד כן לרב עוקבא כששאלו אלא שסידר הש"ס תירוץ שלו תחילה ורשב"א אומר דשניהם השיב רב אשי דבמסכת ביצה גרס א"ל לא נצרכה אלא לאותן שתי חלות ובשינויא דהכא גרס ואב"א מי קתני בימות החמה כו':

כבר תירגמ' רב הונא לשמעתיך. בפרק בתרא (דף קנד:) משמע דאית ליה נמי לרב הונא דאסור לבטל כלי מהיכנו דפריך אמילתיה דקאמר התם רב הונא היתה בהמתו טעונה כלי זכוכית מביא כרים וכסתות ומניח תחתיהן והא קמבטל כלי מהיכנו ומשני בשליפי זוטרי וא"ת אכתי תקשה ליה התם דהא רב הונא סבר הכא דאין כלי ניטל אלא לדבר הניטל וי"ל דמיירי בצריך למקומו וא"ת וכי פריך ליה התם מההיא דהיתה בהמתו טעונה טבל ועששית לימא דמיירי באין צריך למקומו וי"ל דהוה מצי לשנויי הכי דה"נ הוה מצי לשנויי בשליפי רברבי ור"י מתרץ דאיסור דאין כלי ניטל אלא לדבר הניטל שרי ב) היכא דאיכא הפסד מרובה וכן משמע דקאמר התם מהו דתימא כי היכי דלהפסד מרובה חששו כו' משמע חששו והתירו לטלטל אף לדבר שאינו ניטל דמה חששו ג) להתיר אם לא זה האיסור:

חם להם מלמטה. תימה בלא שום חום מאי איסור איכא שיביאו כל אחד מטה לישב עליה ותו אמאי מייתי ברישא מטה והדר מחצלת ימתינו עד שיחם להם גם מלמעלה ויביאו מטות ומחצלות יחד ונראה דאחמור רבנן למיעבד היכרא שהוא לצורך חי כל כמה דאיפשר למיעבד:

ופורסין עליהן זה זוקף כו'. דוקא בכה"ג כמו שפי' רש"י אבל ממטה למעלה אסור משום אהל כדאמרי' בהמביא כדי יין (ביצה לג: ושם) אמר רב יהודה מדורתא מלמעלה למטה שרי מלמטה למעלה אסור וכן ביעתא וכן קידרא וכן חביתא ופוריא דהא דאמרי' בהמוצא תפילין (עירובין קב.) גבי דיכרי דרב הונא אתא לקמיה דרב א"ל זיל כרוך בודיא ושייר בה טפח למחר פשטוה מוסיף על אהל עראי הוא ושפיר דמי אבל בלא שיור אסור היינו משום שהמחילות התחתונות היו כבר עשויות ואם היה פורש עליהן היה עושה אהל כדרך לעשות אהל ואע"ג דרב הונא אית ליה הכא דאין כלי ניטל אלא לדבר הניטל ° מה שהיה מוסיף למחר לא חשיב טלטול או שמא היו מושיבין שם אדם א"נ משום הפסד מרובה שרי כדפירש לעיל:

זה זוקף מטתו. תימה לר"י ו) דרבא לא שרי אלא בשביל חי ובפ' מי שהוציאוהו (שם מד. ושם) תניא זוקף את המטה פורס עליה סדין שלא תפול החמה על המת ועל האוכלין והתם מוקי לה במחילה רביעית שסוכה כשירה בלאו הכי ולא הוי אלא תוספת אהל אבל מ"מ (אין) ניטל הכלי בשביל מת ויש לומר דהתם נמי לא שרי אלא בענין שאומר כאן שעושה בשביל חי אי נמי שיש אוכלין עם המת:

ונשמט והולך לו. ואין צריך לישאר שם תחת האהל כדי שיהא נראה שנעשה בשביל חי כיון דבשעת עשייה היה נראה שעושה בשביל חי:

דכ"ע טלטול מן הצד שמיה טלטול. נראה לר"י דכן הלכה מדלא קאמר דכ"ע לא שמיה טלטול וכגון דליכא ככר ותינוק ואין לו אלא מטה אחת וטעם דרבי יהודה בן לקיש מתוך שאדם בהול כו'. אלא משום דהלכתא דשמיה טלטול נקט הכי וקשה לר"י דבריש כל הכלים (לקמן קכג.) פסיק רב נחמן כר' אלעזר בן תדאי דקסבר לא שמיה טלטול וע"ק דרב אדרב דהכא סבר שמיה טלטול ובסוף פ' תולין (שם קמא.) אמרי בי רב טלטול מן הצד לא שמיה טלטול ° ובדוכתא אחריתי פריך מדרב אאמרי בי רב ובפרק השואל (ב"מ קב:) ובפרק בית כור (ב"ב קה:) מגריך מילתיה דרב ודאמרי בי רב ועוד אמאי אסר

רב

רבינו חננאל

וכיון שמותר לפנותו מאותו מקום ולטלטלו מטלטלו למקום הביצה (כו') וכופהו על הביצה וכן כולם א) ולא יתכן לישב ע"ג הביצה כדי שלא יטנפו בגדיו. לפיכך כופה עליה [כלי] וישב עליו. וכל התיובתות פשוטות הן. ושנינו על הכוורת באותן ב' חלות ששנינו בפ' המוכר את הספינה בענין המוכר חלת דבש כוורתו לחבירו שחייב הקונה להניח לו שתי חלות דבש כדי שיהו מזון לדבורים שלא יברחו. ולפיכך אמרנו אותן ב' חלות מוקצות ממאכל אדם הן (לא השאילו) דשאולין לדבורים. ושנינן כגון (שחייב) [שחשב] עליהן בפירוש למאכל אדם. ואקשינן אי הכי אדתני ומזהיר בפריסת ע"ג הכוורת ובלבד שלא יתכוין לצוד. ליפלוג עליה כו'. ואסיקנא לעולם ר' יהודה [היא] והאי דקתני ובלבד שלא יתכוין לצוד. שלא ישלשל המחצלת וידחקנה בכותלי הכוורת שנמצא הדבורין כסתומין בכוורת אלא ירויח כמעט המחצלת מן הנקב של כוורת שהוא פתח לצאת ולכנוס בו הדבורים כו'. אמר רב ששת כבר תירגם רב הונא לשמעתיה דר' יצחק בבבל דאמר עושין מחיצה למת בשביל החי ואין עושין מחיצה למת בשביל המת כיצד מת מוטל בחמה באין ב' בני אדם ויושבין בצידו. חם להם מלמטה [זה] מביא מטה ויושב עליה וזה מביא מטה ויושב עליה כו'. איתמר מת המוטל בחמה רב יהודה אמר שמואל הופכו ממטה למטה. ומשמיה דרב אמרו מניח עליו ככר או תינוק ומטלטלו. ואסקינן בשיש ככר או תינוק כ"ע לא פליגי שמניח עליו ככר או תינוק ומטלטלו (וכ"ע) [כי פליגי היכא] דל"ל [מ"ס] טלטול מן הצד שמיה טלטול. [ומ"ס] לא שמיה טלטול. ואתינן ואוקמינן בתנאי. אין מצילין [את המת] מפני הדליקה. אמר ר' יהודה בן לקיש שמעתי שמצילין את המת מפני הדליקה. ואמרינן כ"ע טלטול מן הצד שמיה טלטול. היינו טעמא דר' יהודה בן לקיש מתוך שאדם בהול על מת [אי לא] שרית ליה לטלטולי אתי לכבויי ולמעבד איסורא דאורייי' א"ר יהודה בר שילא א"ר אסי א"ר יוחנן הלכה כר' יהודה בן לקיש במת: ואין נאותין ממנו לפי שאינו מן המוכן: ת"ר מותר השמן שבנר ושבקערה אסור להסתפק ממנו. ור"ש מתיר (מטלטלין נר חדש אבל לא ישן) אע"ג דקי"ל דהלכתא כר' שמעון בכולה שבת בהא לית הלכתא כוותיה. דתנא דידן קתני דברי ר' יהודה סתמא במתניתין [מטלטלין נר חדש אבל לא ישן]. ובברייתא מפרש

חשק שלמה על רבינו חננאל א) ע"ש כאן ופי' אמר הוא נצרך למקום הבילה ליכא:

תוספות ישנים

א) ומשמע ליה שיש שם חלות הרבה דלא הוי מוקצה מחמת מיאוס כיון: ב) ולעיל מייתי מינה ר"ה לשנויי דברי משום הפסד אלא למשני שיהיה הדבר לכולהו כלריך למקומו: ג) ומיהו דוחק הרשב"א דמשמע להתיר טורח (דהמלאכה) [דהא רבנן] דמפרש טעמא משום הלכה שאינה מלויה וליה ליה דניטל כלי דלא ניטל (אלא) [הלא] מיקני ליה ברייתא דאמר בפ' בתרא דף קנד: לדהניה מתמת כרים וכסתות אלא ודאי משום טורח:

גליון הש"ס

גמ' כי פליגי דלית ליה. ק"ל אמאי לא הוי המטה עלמה כמקום ככר או תינוק. ועי' מג"א סי' שם ס"ק כ"ה ובתוספת שבת. ומזה לא העירו כלום ועש"ג: רש"י ד"ה אי ר"ש למה לי לאוקמיה בשחישב. משמע דמכ"מ לריכים לשיעור דליכא ב' חלות דמ"ל לר"ש אף כל דליכא לדינא אפילו לר"ש דמיקל במוקצה. ועיין בביצה כ' בתוס' ד"ה דלר"ש ל"ל לאוקמי דליכא ב' חלות משום דמ"ש לר"ש שם (דלר"ש ליכא לדינא דר"י). ולדברי רש"י כאן שהכריח כמכתב דר"י הוא רק לר"י ולכך עלה שכ"ב רש"י: תוס' ד"ה ופורסין וכו' מה שהיה מוסיף למחר. עי' לקמן דף נג ע"ב תוס' ד"ה מהו ליתן: שם ד"ה דכ"ע וכו' ובדוכתא אחריתי. עי' בכורות דף מ ע"ב:

ליקוטי רש"י

חלות. הכוורת לאחר שעשאה פירות ויאלו הנחילין לוקחין את הדבש והן עושין חלות לבד זה משעוה ודבש מעורב יחד [רשב"ם ב"ב פ.]. לאותן שתי חלות. של לפיחים מניחין בכוורת כשרודין אותה ומהן פרנסה לדבורים כל ימות הגשמים אותן שתי חלות מותר לכסות כל דבש הכוורת עשו עליות עליות של חלות. דחשיב עלייהו. לאדם. אי הכי הא דתני ובלבד שלא יתכוין לצוד. משמע דלא ימלא לחלק את דבריו ולאסור עד שלכן מאיסור טלטול לאיסור צידה. לפלוג ולתני בדידה. באיסור טלטול גופיה יכול לחלק את דבריו ולמצוא לך איסור לדבר בדלא חשב עלייהו לא יטלטל המחצלת לכרכס. הא קמ"ל אף על פי שחישב עליהן כו'. אף בשחשב לא ללמדך שיש בו איסור במתכוין לצוד ואף על גב דעיקר להלכה מפני הגשמים מכוון. לעולם ר' יהודה. כלומר מדהוה לך לפרושי ארישא הא מני ר' שמעון דלית ליה מוקצה והדרא לשנויי דחיקי למימר משום שתי החלות כרבי יהודה בעית לאוקמא משום דרבי יצחק דמותבינן ליה הנך תיובתא אית ליה מוקצה כר' יהודה [ביצה לו. עיין בהג"ש כאן]. רב אשי אמר. לעולם כדשנינן מעיקרא דליכא דבש למאכל אדם ודקשיא לך בימות הגשמים מי איכא דבש לא קשיא דמי קתני ימות החמה וימות הגשמים [שם:]. מן הצד. שאינו אוחזו ממש בידו [לקמן קכג.]. שמצילין את המת. לחצר המעורבת דליכא איסור אלא טלטול [יומא פה.].

דְּאִיכָּא דְּבַשׁ – when there is honey in the hive; it may then be covered to protect the honey. **בִּימוֹת הַגְּשָׁמִים דְּלֵיכָּא דְּבַשׁ מַאי אִיכָּא לְמֵימַר – But in the winter, when there is no honey** in the hive, **what is there to say?** Why may a mat be moved then to protect the hive?[1]

The Gemara answers:

לֹא נִצְרְכָא אֶלָּא לְאוֹתָן שְׁתֵּי חַלּוֹת – This is applicable only because of the two honeycombs that are left in the hive during the winter to sustain the bees.[2] Since that honey is edible, a mat may be moved to protect it.

The Gemara objects:

וְהָא מוּקְצוֹת נִינְהוּ – But [these two honeycombs] themselves **are** ***muktzeh,*** since they are left in the hive for the bees' use. Why may the mat be moved to protect them?

The Gemara responds:

דְּחָשִׁיב עֲלַיְיהוּ – This Baraisa is dealing with a case where [the person] planned before the Sabbath **to** use **[the two honeycombs]** for human consumption. They are therefore not *muktzeh* and the mat may be moved to protect them.

The Gemara questions this interpretation of the Baraisa:

הָא לֹא חָשִׁיב עֲלַיְיהוּ מַאי – But if he did not plan to use **them, what** is the law? **אָסוּר – Is it prohibited? אִי הָכִי – If so, הָא דְּתָנֵי וּבִלְבַד שֶׁלֹּא יִתְכַּוֵּין לָצוּד – when the Baraisa teaches** the qualification: **PROVIDED THAT ONE DOES NOT INTEND TO TRAP** the bees, **לִפְלוֹג וְלִתְנֵי בְּדִידָהּ – it should** rather **draw a distinction regarding** the law of *muktzeh* **itself,** and say: **בַּמֶּה דְּבָרִים אֲמוּרִים – When is it said** that one may cover the beehive **כְּשֶׁחִישֵּׁב עֲלֵיהֶן – when he planned to** use **[the combs], אֲבָל לֹא חִישֵּׁב עֲלֵיהֶן אָסוּר – but** if **he did not plan to** use **them, it is prohibited!** Why did the Baraisa state instead an extraneous qualification to its first ruling?[3]

The Gemara answers:

הָא קָא מַשְׁמַע לָן – [The Baraisa] is teaching us אַף עַל פִּי שֶׁחִישֵּׁב עֲלֵיהֶן – that even if he planned to use **[the combs], וּבִלְבַד שֶׁלֹּא יִתְכַּוֵּין לָצוּד –** he may cover the hive only **provided he does not intend to trap** the bees.[4]

The Gemara asserted that the Baraisa's leniency in allowing a beehive to be covered with a mat even during the winter refers to a case in which the owner planned to use the two honeycombs. The Gemara now questions whether this interpretation is compatible with the other clauses of the Baraisa:

מַנִּי – Who is the author of this Baraisa? **אִי רַבִּי שִׁמְעוֹן – If** it is **R' Shimon,** it is unnecessary for the owner to make this plan, **לֵית לֵיהּ מוּקְצֶה – since [R' Shimon] does not accept** a broad application of ***muktzeh.***[5] **אִי רַבִּי יְהוּדָה –** And **if** the author of the Baraisa is **R' Yehudah,** who does accept a broad application of *muktzeh,* **כִּי לֹא מִתְכַּוֵּין מַאי הָוֵי –** of **what** benefit **is it if [the person] does not intend** to trap the bees? **הָא דָּבָר שֶׁאֵין מִתְכַּוֵּין אָסוּר – Why,** R' Yehudah holds that even **something that is unintended is forbidden!**[6] Accordingly, it should be forbidden to cover the hive even if one does not intend to trap the bees. – ? –

The Gemara answers:

לְעוֹלָם רַבִּי יְהוּדָה – Actually, the author of the Baraisa is **R' Yehudah. מַאי וּבִלְבַד שֶׁלֹּא יִתְכַּוֵּין לָצוּד –** And **what** is the meaning of the Baraisa's qualification: **PROVIDED THAT ONE DOES NOT INTEND TO TRAP** the bees? **שֶׁלֹּא יַעֲשֶׂנָּה כְּמְצוּדָה –** It means **that he must not make [the mat]** function **like a trap** by covering the entire hive. **דְּלִישְׁבוֹק לְהוּ רְווֹחָא – That** is, **he should leave [the bees] room** to escape, **כִּי הֵיכִי דְּלָא לִיתְצְדוּ מִמֵּילָא – so that they should not be trapped unintentionally.**[7]

Rav Ashi offers a different solution to Rav Ukva's original difficulty:[8]

NOTES

1. The Gemara assumes that the Baraisa's references to בַּחַמָּה, *in the sun,* and בַּגְּשָׁמִים, *in the rain,* refer to the sunny season (summer) and the rainy season (winter).

2. A hive has many layers of honeycombs. When the honey is removed for human consumption, two combs are left inside the hive to provide sustenance for the bees during the winter months (*Rashi;* see *Bava Basra* 80a; see also *Tosafos* ד״ה דחשיב).

3. Since the Baraisa did not qualify its lenient ruling regarding *muktzeh* with a stringency based on the law of *muktzeh* itself, but chose instead a qualifying stringency based on the laws of צָד, *trapping,* it is apparent that no stringency could be found which derived from the law of *muktzeh.* But if R' Yitzchak's interpretation of the Baraisa is correct and the leniency in the first section is due to the person's intention to use the honey, the Baraisa could have taught a stringency arising out of the *muktzeh* law: If the person did not intend to use the honey the entire hive is *muktzeh,* and he may not cover it (*Rashi* to *Beitzah* 36a).

4. The Baraisa wants to teach that even in the case where the person intended to use the honey there is place for a qualifying stringency, viz. if he intended to trap the bees in the hive (*Rashi* to *Beitzah* 36a).

5. Although the basic prohibition of *muktzeh* is not disputed, Tannaim (in particular, R' Shimon and R' Yehudah) disagree sharply on the extent of these restrictions. R' Shimon is more lenient, and so is described as holding אֵין מוּקְצֶה, *there is no [broad application of] muktzeh.* R' Yehudah is more stringent; his opinion is cited as יֵשׁ מוּקְצֶה, *there is [a broad application of] muktzeh.*

This dispute finds expression in many areas of the laws of *muktzeh.* It stems from a disagreement over how to interpret the basic rule that whatever was set aside from being used on the Sabbath is *muktzeh.* According to R' Yehudah, this includes any object that in the normal course of events does not stand to be used on the Sabbath. Since the owner did not intend or expect to use the object, it lacks "preparation" for Sabbath use and is *muktzeh.* R' Shimon, on the other hand, holds that the mere fact that an object does not stand to be used is not a consideration. Rather, as long as something is fit for use, it is not rendered *muktzeh* unless the owner consciously sets it aside from being used (*Chasam Sofer's* introduction to *Beitzah – Mahadura Tinyana; Afikei Yam* vol. II §19; *Kehillos Yaakov, Beitzah* §4; see *Rashi* to *Beitzah* 2a ד״ה קא סלקא דעתין and 26b ד״ה ואי דלא אחזו). [The Gemara below, beginning on 44a, deals at length with the delineation of R' Shimon's view.]

The preceding interpretation of the Baraisa, which considers the two honeycombs left in the hive over the winter to be *muktzeh* unless the owner *planned* before the Sabbath to eat them, reflects the view of R' Yehudah. [In his view, since the honeycombs were left in the hive for the use of the bees rather than humans, they are *muktzeh* unless the owner planned to use them. But according to R' Shimon, even if the owner did not *plan* to use them they are not *muktzeh,* since he did not *reject* them from use.] Thus, the interpretation presumes that the Baraisa follows not the view of R' Shimon, but the view of R' Yehudah who accepts a broad application of *muktzeh* (*Rashi;* see *Rashi* to *Beitzah* 36a ד״ה במאי אוקימתא, with elucidation of *Gilyon HaShas* here, for a different explanation of the Gemara's question).

6. I.e. it is forbidden to do any act that may unintentionally result in the performance of a prohibited *melachah;* see 40a note 13 and 41b note 2. In our case, the permissible act of covering the beehive to protect it may result in the trapping of bees (see following note).

7. Covering the entire hive, however, is prohibited according to R' Yehudah even if one does not intend to trap the bees, since they may thereby be trapped (*Rashi*). [Actually, even according to R' Shimon one may not cover the entire hive, since doing so would *inevitably* trap the bees and R' Shimon concedes that when the unintended consequence is inevitable [פְּסִיק רֵישֵׁיהּ] the act is forbidden. However, according to R' Shimon it is sufficient to leave a tiny window so that the trapping of the bees is not inevitable, whereas according to R' Yehudah one must leave a large space through which the bees can definitely escape (*Ritva MHK* ed.; *Tosafos* to *Beitzah* 36b). See *Beitzah* 36b for further elaboration of the Gemara's answer. See also *Tosafos* here ד״ה שלא יעשנו.]

8. [I.e. the question of how may one move the mat for the sake of covering the hive in the winter, when there is no honey in it.] Note that

דאיכא דבש בימות הגשמים דליכא דבש מאי איכא למימר לא נצרכא אלא לאותן שתי חלות והא מוקצות נינהו דחשיב עלייהו הא לא חשיב עלייהו מאי אסור אי הכי הא דתני ובלבד שלא יתכוין לצוד לפלוג ולתני בדידה בד"א כשחישב עליהן אבל לא חישב עליהן אסור הא קמ"ל אע"פ שחישב עליהן ובלבד שלא יתכוין לצוד מני אי ר"ש א) לית לי' מוקצה אי ר' יהודה כי לא מתכוין מאי הוי הא דבר שאין מתכוין אסור לעולם ר' יהודה מאי ובלבד שלא יתכוין לצוד שלא יעשנה כמצודה דלישבוק להו רווחא כי היכי דלא ליתצדו ממילא רב אשי אמר מי קתני בימות החמה ובימות הגשמים בחמה מפני החמה ובגשמים מפני הגשמים קתני ביומי ניסן וביומי תשרי דאיכא חמה (ואיכא צינה) ואיכא גשמים ואיכא דבש אמר להו רב ששת פוקו ואמרו ליה לר' יצחק כבר תרגמא רב הונא לשמעתיך בבבל דא"ר הונא עושין מחיצה למת בשביל חי ואין עושין מחיצה למת בשביל מת מאי היא דא"ר שמואל בר יהודה וכן תנא שילא מרי א מת המוטל בחמה באים שני בני אדם ויושבין בצדו חם להם מלמטה זה מביא מטה ויושב עליה וזה מביא מטה ויושב עליה חם להם מלמעלה מביאים מחצלת ופורסין עליהן זה זוקף מטתו ונשמט והולך לו וזה זוקף מטתו ונשמט והולך לו ונמצאת מחיצה עשויה מאליה איתמר מת המוטל בחמה רב יהודה אמר שמואל ב הופכו ממטה למטה רב חנינא בר שלמיא משמיה דרב אמר א) מניח עליו ככר או תינוק ומטלטלו היכא דאיכא ככר או תינוק כולי עלמא לא פליגי דשרי ° כי פליגי דלית ליה מ"ס ג) טלטול מן הצד שמיה טלטול ומ"ס לא שמיה טלטול לימא כתנאי ג) אין מצילין את המת מפני הדליקה אמר ר' יהודה בן לקיש שמעתי שמצילין את המת מפני הדליקה היכי דמי אי דאיכא ככר או תינוק מ"ט דתנא קמא אי דליכא מ"ט דר' יהודה בן לקיש אלא לאו בטלטול מן הצד פליגי דמר סבר טלטול מן הצד שמיה טלטול ומ"ס לא שמיה טלטול לא ג דכ"ע טלטול מן הצד שמיה טלטול והיינו טעמא דר' יהודה בן לקיש ד) דמתוך שאדם בהול על מתו אי

רש"י

דאיכא דבש. דבר הניטל: **שתי חלות.** כל הכוורת עושין אותה הדבורים חלות חלות של לפיחית דבש ושעוה וכשרודים אותן מניחין בה שתים שיתפרנסו מהן הדבורים כל ימות הגשמים כדתנן בהמוכר את הספינה (ב"ב פ.) הלוקח חלות כוורתו של חבירו מניח שתי חלות דסתמא לא מכרן: **מוקצות נינהו.** לדבורים הדר הוה ליה דבר שאינו ניטל ואפ"ה מטלטלין מחצלת להצלתן: **דחשיב עלייהו.** מאתמול לאכילה: **ומני.** היא שהצרכת לתרוצה כשחישב וקתני לדבר שאין מתכוין מותר כר"ש: **אי ר"ש.** אמר ° למה לי לאוקמיה בשחישב: **שלא יעשנו כמצודה.** שלא יכסנה כולה אלא דנשבוק רווחא שיוכלו לצאת כי היכי דלא ליתצדו בהאי כיסוי ממילא ואע"ג דלא מיכוין למיצד אסור: **רב אשי אמר.** לעולם דאיכא דבש טובא ודקשיא לך ימות הגשמים מי קתני בה ימות הגשמים: **לשמעתיך.** דאין כלי ניטל אלא לדבר הניטל: **מת המוטל בחמה.** ויש לחוש שמא ימהר להסריח: **ויושבין בצדו.** ע"ג הקרקע כדי שיצטערו מחום הקרקע ויצטרכו להביא מטות לישב עליהן והמטות יהיו למחיצה כדמסיים ואזיל: **חם להם למטה.** מן הקרקע שרתחו חמה: **ופורסין.** על ראשן נגל: **זה זוקף מטתו.** שתהא המחצלת מונחת עליה וכן זה נמצאת מחילה עשויה מאליה ולכשירצו נשמטין והולכין להם ודוקא נקט חם להם מלמטה ברישא שיביאו המטות לישיבה ברישא והדר מחצלת לפרוש עליהן נגל ואוחזין אותה בידיהן עד לאחר שעה שזוקפום ושמטום דהוה ליה כי ההוא דאמרינן (עירובין דף קב.) האי מדורתא מלמעלה למטה שרי אבל לאתויי מעיקרא מטות לצורך האהל לא דהוה ליה מלמטה למעלה כדרך בנין וקי"ל אין עושין אהל עראי בתחילה בשבת: **הופכו ממטה למטה.** עד שמגיע לצל: **מן הצד.** כלאחר יד: **אי דליכא.** והאי מצילין דקאמר ר' יהודה בן לקיש דמטלטל ליה להדיא הוא: **מאי טעמא דר' יהודה.** אלא לאו מן הצד הוא דקשרי:

תוספות

דחשיב עלייהו. וא"ת והא אסור לרדותם כדתניא בסוף פרק המצניע (לקמן צה. ושם) הרודה חלות דבש בשוגג חייב חטאת דברי ר"א ולרבנן שבות מיהא איכא והוי דבר שאינו ניטל וי"ל דמיירי ברדויות ומונחות שם בכוורת אי נמי רגילות שיש דבש אף ע"ג חלות ואותו אינו צריך רדייה:

שלא יעשנו כעין מצודה. וא"ת מאי קמ"ל פשיטא דאי עביד כעין מצודה דאסור ה) והא לא משמע מברייתא דאע"ג דאינו מתכוין אסור וי"ל דאמר בפ' משילין (ביצה לו: ושם) דקמ"ל דס"ד במינו ניצוד אסור שאין במינו ניצוד מותר: **רב** אשי אמר כו'. מסתמא רב אשי השיב מיד כן לרב עוקבא כששאלו אלא שסידר הש"ס תירוץ שלו תחילה ורשב"א אומר דשניהם השיב רב אשי דבמסכת ביצה גרס א"ל לא נצרכה אלא לאותן שתי חלות ובשינויא דהכא גרס ואב"א מי קתני בימות החמה כו':

כבר תירגמי' רב הונא לשמעתיך. בפרק בתרא (דף קנד:) משמע דאית ליה נמי לרב הונא דאסור לבטל כלי מהיכנו דפריך אמילתיה דקאמר התם רב הונא היתה בהמתו טעונה כלי זכוכית מביא כרים וכסתות ומניח תחתיהן והא קמבטל כלי מהיכנו ומשני בשליפי זוטרי וא"ת אכתי תקשה ליה התם דהא רב הונא סבר הכא דאין כלי ניטל אלא לדבר הניטל וי"ל דמיירי בצריך למקומו וא"ת וכי פריך ליה התם מההיא דהיתה בהמתו טעונה טבל ועששית לימא דמיירי באין צריך למקומו וי"ל דהוה מצי לשנויי הכי דה"נ הוה מצי לשנויי בשליפי רברבי ור"י מתרץ דאיסור דאין כלי ניטל אלא לדבר הניטל שרי ב) היכא דאיכא הפסד מרובה וכן משמע דקאמר התם מהו דתימא כי היכי דלהפסד מרובה חששו כו' משמע חששו והתירו לטלטל אף לדבר שאינו ניטל דמה חששו ג) להתיר אם לא זה האיסור:

חם להם מלמטה. תימה בלא שום חום מאי איסור איכא שיביאו כל אחד מטה לישב עליה ותו אמאי מייתי ברישא מטה והדר מחצלת ימתינו עד שיחם להם גם מלמעלה ויביאו מטות ומחצלות יחד ונראה דאחמור רבנן למיעבד היכרא שהוא לצורך חי כל כמה דאיפשר למיעבד: **ופורסין** עליהן זה זוקף כו'. דוקא בכה"ג כמו שפי' רש"י אבל ממטה למעלה אסור משום אהל כדאמרי' בהמביא כדי יין (ביצה לב: ושם) אמר רב יהודה מדורתא מלמעלה למטה שרי מלמטה למעלה אסור וכן ביעתא וכן קידרא וכן חביתא ופוריא דהא דאמרי' בהמוצא תפילין (עירובין קב.) גבי ליכרי דרב הונא אתא לקמיה דרב א"ל זיל כרוך בודיא ושייר בה טפח למחר פשטוה מוסיף על אהל עראי הוא ושפיר דמי אבל בלא שיור אסור היינו משום שהמחילות התחתונות היו כבר עשויות ואם היה פורש עליהן היה עושה אהל כדרך לעשות אהל ואע"ג דרב הונא אית ליה הכא דאין כלי ניטל אלא לדבר הניטל ° מה שהיה מוסיף למחר לא חשיב טלטול או שמא היו מושיבין שם אדם א"נ משום הפסד מרובה שרי כדפירש לעיל: **זה** זוקף מטתו. תימה לר"י ו) דרבא לא שרי אלא בשביל חי ובפ' מי שהוציאוהו (שם מד. ושם) תניא זוקף את המטה פורס עליה סדין שלא תפול החמה על המת ועל האוכלין והתם מוקי לה במחילה רביעית שסוכה כשירה בלאו הכי ולא הוי אלא תוספת אהל אבל מ"מ (אין) ניטל הכלי בשביל מת ויש לומר דהתם נמי לא שרי אלא בענין שאומר כאן שעושה בשביל חי אי נמי שיש אוכלין עם המת: **ונשמט** והולך לו. ואין צריך לישאר שם תחת האהל כדי שיהא נראה שנעשה בשביל חי כיון דבשעת עשייה היה נראה שעושה בשביל חי: **דכ"ע** טלטול מן הצד שמיה טלטול. נראה לר"י דכן הלכה מדלא קאמר דכ"ע לא שמיה טלטול וכגון דליכא ככר ותינוק ואין לו אלא מטה אחת וטעם דרבי יהודה בן לקיש מתוך שאדם בהול כו'. אלא משום דהלכתא דשמיה טלטול נקט הכי וקשה לר"י דבריש כל הכלים (לקמן קכג.) פסיק רב נחמן כר' אלעזר בן תדאי דקסבר לא שמיה טלטול וע"ק דרב אדרב דהכא סבר שמיה טלטול ובסוף פ' תולין (שם קמא.) אמרי בי רב טלטול מן הצד לא שמיה טלטול ° ובדוכתא אחריתי פריך מדרב אאמרי בי רב ובפרק השואל (ב"מ קב:) ובפרק בית כור (ב"ב קה:) מגריך מילתיה דרב ודאמרי בי רב ועוד אמאי אסר רב

הגהות: **על פי שחישב עליהן כו'.** אף בשחשב בא ללמדך שיש בד איסור במתכוין לצוד ואף על גב דעיקר להצלה מפני הגשמים מכוון. **לעולם ר' יהודה.** כלומר מדהוה לך לתרוצי ארישא הא מני ר' שמעון דלית ליה מוקצה ומהדרו אשנויי דסיקי למימר משום שתי החלות כרבי יהודה בעית לאוקמא משום דרבי יצחק דמותבינן ליה הנך מיותבתא אינו ליה מוקצה כר' יהודה [ביצה לו. עיין בגה"ש כאן]. **רב אשי אמר.** לעולם כדשנינן מעיקרא דליכא דבש למאכל אדם ודקשיא לך בימות הגשמים מי איכא דבש לא קשיא דמי קתני ימות החמה וימות הגשמים [שם:]. **מן הצד.** שאינו אוחזו ממש בידו [לקמן קכג.]. **שמצילין את המת.** לחצר המעורבת דליכא איסור אלא טלטול [יומא פה.].

(מטלטלין נר חדש אבל לא ישן) אע"ג דקיי"ל דהלכתא כר' שמעון בכולה שבת בהא לית הלכתא כוותיה. דתנא דידן קתני דברי ר' יהודה סתמא במתניתין [מטלטלין נר חדש אבל לא ישן]. ובברייתא מפרש ממנו. ור"ש מתיר

חשק שלמה על רבינו חננאל א) ע"ס כאן ופי' אמר הוא נצריך למקום הביצה ליסב:

עין משפט נר מצוה

מו א מיי' פכ"ה מהלכו' שבת הלכה ו ופכ"ו הלכה כב סמג לאוין סה טוש"ע או"ח סימן שיא סעיף ו:

מז ב ג מיי' שם פכ"ו הלכה כא טור שו"ע או"ח שם סעיף א:

רבינו חננאל

וכיון שמותר לפנותו מאותו מקום ולטלטלו מטלטלו למקום הביצה (כו') וכופהו על הביצה וכן כלים א) ולא יתכן לישב ע"ג הביצה כדי שלא יטנפו בגדיו. לפיכך כופה עליה [כלי] וישב עליו. וכל התיובתות פשוטות הן. ושנינו על הכוורת באותן ב' חלות ששנינו בפ' המוכר את הספינה בענין המוכר חלת דבש כוורתו לחבירו שחייב הקונה להניח לו שתי חלות דבש כדי שיהו מזון לדבורים שלא יברחו. ולפיכך אמרנו אותן ב' חלות מוקצות ממאכל אדם הן (לא השאילו) דשאולין לדבורים. ושנינו כגון (שחייב) [שחשב] עליהן בפירוש למאכל אדם. ואקשינן אי הכי אדתני ומזהיר בפריסת ע"ג הכוורת ובלבד שלא יתכוין לצוד. ליפלוג עליה כו'. ואסיקנא לעולם ר' יהודה [היא] והאי דקתני ובלבד שלא יתכוין לצוד. שלא ישלשל המחצלת וידחקנה בכותלי הכוורת שנמצא הדבורין כסתומין בכוורת אלא ירחיב כמעט המחצלת מן הנקב של כוורת שהוא פתח לצאת ולכנוס בו הדבורים כו'. אמר רב ששת כבר תירגם רב הונא לשמעתיה דר' יצחק בבבל דאמר עושין מחיצה למת בשביל החי ואין עושין מחיצה למת בשביל המת כיצד מת מוטל בחמה באין ב' בני אדם ויושבין בצידו. חם להם מלמטה [זה] מביא מטה ויושב עליה וזה מביא מטה ויושב עליה כו'. איתמר מת המוטל בחמה רב יהודה אמר שמואל הופכו ממטה למטה. ומשמיה דרב אמרו מניח עליו ככר או תינוק ומטלטלו. ואסקינן בשיש ככר או תינוק כ"ע לא פליגי שמניח עליו ככר או תינוק ומטלטלו (וכ"ע) [כי פליגי היכא] דל"ל מ"ס] טלטול מן הצד שמיה טלטול. [ומ"ס לא שמיה טלטול]. ואתינן ואוקמינן בתנאי. אין מצילין [את המת] מפני הדליקה. אמר ר' יהודה בן לקיש שמעתי שמצילין את המת מפני הדליקה. ואמרינן כ"ע טלטול מן הצד שמיה טלטול. היינו טעמא דר' יהודה בן לקיש מתוך שאדם בהול על מת [אי לאו] שרית ליה לטלטולי אתי לכבויי ולמעבד איסורא דאורייתא. א"ר יהודה בר שילא א"ר אסי א"ר יוחנן הלכה כר' יהודה בן לקיש במת: ואין נאותין ממנו לפי שאינו מן המוכן: ת"ר מותר השמן שבנר ושבקערה אסור להסתפק ממנו. ור"ש מתיר

מסורת הש"ס

א) [לעיל ל: לקמן קמב:], ב) [לקמן קכג. קמא.], ג) [תוספתא פי"ד] יומא דף פה., ד) יומא שם, ה) מה"ר שכנא הגיה הכא משמע דאע"ג דאינו כו', ו) נ"ל דהכא.

תוספות ישנים

א) ומשמע ליה שיש שם חלות הרבה דלא הוי מוקצה מחמת חסרון כיס: ב) ולעיל מייתי ה"מ לשנויי דשרי משום הפסד אלא דמשני שיעול חדא לכולהו בצריך למקומו: ג) ומיהו דוחק הרשב"א דמשמע להתיר טורח (דהמלאכה) [דהא רבה] דמפרש טעמא משום הללה שאינה מגיה ולית ליה דיטול כלי ולא טעמא דאין כלי ניטל (אלא) [הלא] מיקשי ליה ברייתא דאסר בפ' בתרא דף קנד: להביא מתחיו כרים וכסתות אלא ודאי משום טורח:

גליון הש"ס

גמ' כי פליגי דלית ליה. ק"ל אמאי לא הוי המטה עלמה במקום ככר או תינוק. ועי' מג"א סי' שם ס"ק כ"א ובתוספת שבת. ומזה לא העירו כלום ועע"ג: רש"י ד"ה אי ר"ש למה לי לאוקמיה בשחישב. משמע דמכ"מ לריכים לשינויא דאיכא ב' חלות דס"ל לרש"י שם דלר"ש ליכא לדינא דרי"ן היינו אפילו לר"ש דמיקל במוקצה. ואולם רש"י בביצה ל' באמת דפירכת הש"ס דלר"ש ל"ל כלל לתרץ דאיכא ב' חלות מבואר דס"ל לרש"י שם (דלר"ש ליכא לדינא דרי"ן). ולדברי רש"י אלו כוונת הרז"ה פ' מי שהמשיך שכתב דרי"ן הוא רק לר"י וכתב עלה שכ"כ רש"י: תוס' ד"ה ופורסין וכו' מה שהיה מוסיף למחר. עי' לקמן דף נג ע"א תוס' ד"ה מהו ליתן: שם ד"ה דכו"ע וכו' ובדוכתא אחריתי. עי' בכורות דף כו ע"ב:

ליקוטי רש"י

חלות. הכוורת לאחר שעשתה פירות ויצאו הנחילין לוקחין את הדבש והוא עשוי חלות חלות או עשרים זה בצד זה משעוה ודבש מעורב יחד [רשב"ם ב"ב פ.]. **לאותן שתי חלות.** של לפיחית מניחין בכוורת כשרודין אותה ומהן פרנסה לדבורים כל ימות הגשמים אותן שתי חלות מותר לכסות כל דבש הכוורת עשוי עליוס עליהן של חלות. **דחשיב עלייהו.** לאדם. **אי הכי הא דתני ובלבד שלא יתכוין לצוד.** משמע דלא יתמלא לחלק את דבריו ולאסור על שדלג מלאסור לפלוג ולתני בדידה. באיסור טלטול גופיה יכול לחלק את דבריו ולמצוא לו איסור לדבר בדלא חשב עלייהו לא יטלטל המחצלה לכסם. **הא קמ"ל** אף

מִי קָתָנֵי בִּימוֹת הַחַמָּה וּבִימוֹת – רַב אַשִׁי אָמַר – **Rav Ashi said:** הַגְּשָׁמִים – **Does the Baraisa teach** that the hive may be covered **"in the summer and in the winter,"** as you understood it to mean? No! בַּחַמָּה מִפְּנֵי הַחַמָּה וּבַגְּשָׁמִים מִפְּנֵי הַגְּשָׁמִים קָתָנֵי – It teaches that one may cover it IN THE SUN, to protect FROM THE SUN, AND IN THE RAIN, to protect FROM THE RAIN. בְּיוֹמֵי נִיסָן וּבְיוֹמֵי תִּשְׁרֵי דְּאִיכָּא חַמָּה (ואיכא צינה) וְאִיכָּא גְּשָׁמִים – This refers **to the days of Nissan and Tishrei, when there are sunny** days **and rainy** days,[9] וְאִיכָּא דְּבַשׁ – **and there is honey** in the hive. The beehive may therefore be covered since this honey is certainly not *muktzeh.* In the winter, however, the Baraisa would prohibit spreading a mat over the *muktzeh* beehive, in accordance with R' Yitzchak's ruling that one may not move a non-*muktzeh* item for the sake of a *muktzeh* one.

The Gemara cites support for R' Yitzchak's opinion:

פּוּקוּ – אָמַר לְהוּ רַב שֵׁשֶׁת – **Rav Sheishess said to [his students]:** – וְאִמְרוּ לֵיהּ לְרַבִּי יִצְחָק – **Go out and tell R' Yitzchak:** כְּבָר תַּרְגְּמָא רַב הוּנָא לִשְׁמַעְתֵּיךְ בְּבָבֶל – **Rav Huna has already elaborated your** very **teaching in Babylonia.**[10] דְּאָמַר רַב הוּנָא – **For Rav Huna said:** עוֹשִׂין מְחִיצָה לְמֵת בִּשְׁבִיל חַי – **We may erect an awning**[11] **for** the sake of protecting **a corpse** from the sun if we erect it also **on behalf of a living person;** וְאֵין עוֹשִׂין מְחִיצָה לְמֵת בִּשְׁבִיל מֵת – **but we may not erect an awning for** the sake of protecting **a corpse** if we erect it solely **on behalf of the corpse.**[12]

The Gemara elucidates Rav Huna's ruling:

מַאי הִיא – **What is** the meaning of **this** teaching? דְּאָמַר רַב שְׁמוּאֵל בַּר יְהוּדָה וְכֵן תָּנָא שִׁילָא מָרִי – It is as **Rav Shmuel bar Yehudah said, and so too, Shela Mari taught a Baraisa** which states: מֵת הַמּוּטָּל בַּחַמָּה – If **a corpse is lying in the sun** and is in danger of putrefying, בָּאִים שְׁנֵי בְנֵי אָדָם וְיוֹשְׁבִין בְּצִדּוֹ – **two people come and sit next to [the corpse]** on the hot ground, one on each side of the corpse. חַם לָהֶם מִלְּמַטָּה – When **they feel hot on bottom,** זֶה מֵבִיא מִטָּה וְיוֹשֵׁב עָלֶיהָ וְזֶה מֵבִיא מִטָּה וְיוֹשֵׁב עָלֶיהָ – **this one brings a bed and sits upon it and that one brings a bed and sits upon it.** חַם לָהֶם מִלְמַעְלָה – When **they feel hot on top,** מְבִיאִים מַחְצֶלֶת וּפוֹרְסִין עֲלֵיהֶן – **they bring a mat and spread it over their heads** and over the corpse that is between them. זֶה זוֹקֵף מִטָּתוֹ וְנִשְׁמָט וְהוֹלֵךְ לוֹ – **This one** then **raises his bed upright** to support one end of the mat **and slips away,** וְזֶה זוֹקֵף מִטָּתוֹ וְנִשְׁמָט וְהוֹלֵךְ לוֹ – **and that one raises his bed upright** to support the other end of the mat **and slips away;** וְנִמְצֵאת מְחִיצָה עֲשׂוּיָה מֵאֵלֶיהָ – **and** in this manner, **it emerges that the awning** protecting the corpse **was,** so to speak, **made automatically.**[13]

The Gemara digresses to discuss permissible methods of removing a corpse from the sun on the Sabbath:

אִיתְּמַר – **It was stated:** מֵת הַמּוּטָּל בַּחַמָּה – If **a corpse is lying** on a bed **in the sun** and one wishes to transfer it to the shade, רַב יְהוּדָה אָמַר שְׁמוּאֵל – **Rav Yehudah said in the name of Shmuel:** הוֹפְכוֹ מִמִּטָּה לְמִטָּה – **One should roll [the corpse] over from bed to bed** until it reaches the shade.[14] רַב חֲנִינָא בַּר שְׁלָמְיָא מִשְּׁמֵיהּ דְּרַב אָמַר – But **Rav Chanina bar Shelamya said in the name of Rav:** מֵנִיחַ עָלָיו כִּכָּר אוֹ תִּינוֹק וּמְטַלְטְלוֹ – **One should place a loaf of bread or an infant on [the corpse] and** then **move [the corpse].**[15]

NOTES

although Rav Ukva posed his question to Rav Ashi, the Gemara presented a different answer before recording Rav Ashi's own response. The reason is that when Rav Ashi redacted the Gemara he gave precedence to the alternative answer (*Tosafos* ד״ה רב אשי, *Tos. HaRosh;* see there for an alternative explanation, which is based on a variant reading of the parallel Gemara, *Beitzah* 36a-b).

9. I.e. during the spring (Nissan) and fall (Tishrei) seasons, which are partially sunny and partially rainy. Thus, the terms גְּשָׁמִים, *rain,* and חַמָּה, *sun,* do not refer to the rainy and sunny *seasons* (i.e. winter and summer). Rather, they refer to the rainy and sunny days in the spring and fall seasons. [The parenthesized portion of the text does not appear in the parallel Gemara in *Beitzah* and seems superfluous (*Rashash*).]

10. [R' Yitzchak flourished in Eretz Yisrael; Rav Huna, in Babylonia.]

11. Literally: barrier, wall.

12. [A corpse is intrinsically *muktzeh,* since it may not be used for any purpose.] Rav Huna teaches that if on the Sabbath a corpse is lying in the sun, where it is in danger of putrefying, one may set up an awning to shade it only if the awning will also protect a living person. This accords with R' Yitzchak's opinion that a non-*muktzeh* item (i.e. the awning) may not be moved for the benefit of a *muktzeh* item (i.e. the corpse). Thus Rav Huna expounded in Babylonia the very same principle that R' Yitzchak expounded in Eretz Yisrael (*Rashi;* see also *Tosafos* ד״ה כבר תרגמה; cf. *Raavad* cited by *Rashba, Chidushei R' Elazar Moshe Horowitz*). The Gemara goes on to clarify what Rav Huna meant by "on behalf of a living person."

13. The elaborate procedure described here is designed to avoid two halachic difficulties. The first of these is R' Yitzchak's prohibition against moving a non-*muktzeh* item for the sake of a *muktzeh* item. Because of this prohibition, it is forbidden to carry the mat and the beds for the sake of the corpse; they must be put in place for the sake of living people who then absent themselves and leave the awning in place for the corpse. [Since this is really a stratagem for creating the awning on behalf of the corpse, the Rabbis required the people to initially sit on the hot ground, so that when they ultimately bring the beds it will be evident that they did not do this solely for the benefit of the corpse. However, once this has been established and the awning is built, the people need not remain under it but may slip away (*Tosafos*).]

A second consideration is the prohibition against constructing a tent-like structure on the Sabbath. Such construction is deemed a form of the *melachah* of בּוֹנֶה, *building.* However, when the structure is a temporary one, such as the awning described here, building it is merely prohibited Rabbinically. The Rabbinical prohibition against building a temporary structure applies only to building in the normal manner, viz. first the walls and then the ceiling. If the ceiling is held up first and the walls are then propped up underneath it the Rabbis allowed its construction (see *Eruvin* 101a and *Beitzah* 32b). Therefore, Rav Shmuel bar Yehudah states that the two people should initially bring the beds to sit upon, then spread the mat over their heads manually and only then raise their beds upright to support it. Since the awning is in place before the supporting walls, when the walls are raised the structure is "made automatically" (*Rashi, Tosafos;* see *Mishnah Berurah* 311:20; for a discussion of this issue, see *Beis Meir* to *Orach Chaim* 315).

[It emerges from our Gemara that Rav Huna's ruling is grounded in R' Yitzchak's principle that it is forbidden to move a non-*muktzeh* item for the sake of a *muktzeh* item. It is worth noting, however, that *Rambam* (*Hil. Shabbos* 26:22) records Rav Huna's ruling despite the fact that he does not accept R' Yitzchak's principle as halachah. For a resolution of this difficulty, see *Kesef Mishneh* ad loc.; cf. *Ramban* below, 154b; see also *Rashba* and *Ritva MHK* ed.]

14. Since the corpse is *muktzeh* one cannot lift the bed and carry it away (see *Ran MHK* ed.). Rather, Shmuel recommends that one place a second bed next to the bed upon which the corpse lies and roll the corpse from the first bed onto the second one. This procedure should be repeated until the corpse has reached the shade. The basis for permitting this is that one is not moving the corpse in the usual manner (*Rashi*). [See *Ran,* who infers from *Rashi* that one may roll the corpse manually, so long as he does not lift it. *Ran* himself contends that it is permitted only to tilt the bed so that the corpse rolls off automatically.]

15. It is permitted to move the corpse while the bread or infant is on it because the corpse is considered ancillary to the non-*muktzeh* bread or infant, and thus, one is primarily moving the bread or infant (*Ritva MHK* ed.; *Chasam Sofer* to 142b). [A loaf of bread or an infant are given merely as examples (presumably because they are lightweight and usually available). Any other non-*muktzeh* item will do equally well. One may also place the non-*muktzeh* item on the bed next to the corpse and move the bed (*Mishnah Berurah* 311:1-2).]

This is a special dispensation granted for the sake of preserving the dignity of the corpse; it is not normally permitted to move a *muktzeh* item simply because there is a non-*muktzeh* item resting upon it or with

דאיכא דבש בימות הגשמים דליכא דבש מאי איכא למימר לא נצרכא אלא לאותן שתי חלות והא מוקצות נינהו דחשיב עלייהו הא לא חשיב עלייהו מאי אסור אי הכי הא דתני ובלבד שלא יתכוין לצוד לפלוג ולתני בדידה בד"א כשחישב עליהן אבל לא חישב עליהן אסור הא קמ"ל אע"פ שחישב עליהן ובלבד שלא יתכוין לצוד מני אי ר"ש א) לית לי' מוקצה אי ר' יהודה כי לא מתכוין מאי הוי הא דבר שאין מתכוין אסור לעולם ר' יהודה מאי ובלבד שלא יתכוין לצוד שלא יעשנה כמצודה דלישבוק להו רווחא כי היכי דלא ליתצדו ממילא רב אשי אמר מי קתני בימות החמה ובימות הגשמים בחמה מפני החמה ובגשמים מפני הגשמים קתני ביומי ניסן וביומי תשרי דאיכא חמה (ואיכא צינה) ואיכא גשמים ואיכא דבש אמר להו רב ששת פוקו ואמרו ליה לר' יצחק כבר תרגמא רב הונא לשמעתיך בבבל דא"ר הונא עושין מחיצה למת בשביל חי ואין עושין מחיצה למת בשביל מת מאי היא דא"ר שמואל בר יהודה וכן תנא שילא מרי א מת המוטל בחמה באים שני בני אדם ויושבין בצדו חם להם מלמטה זה מביא מטה ויושב עליה וזה מביא מטה ויושב עליה חם להם מלמעלה מביאים מחצלת ופורסין עליהן זה זוקף מטתו ונשמט והולך לו וזה זוקף מטתו ונשמט והולך לו ונמצאת מחיצה עשויה מאליה איתמר מת המוטל בחמה רב יהודה אמר שמואל ב הופכו ממטה למטה רב חנינא בר שלמיא משמיה דרב אמר א) מניח עליו ככר או תינוק ומטלטלו היכא דאיכא ככר או תינוק כולי עלמא לא פליגי דשרי ° כי פליגי דלית ליה מ"ס ג) טלטול מן הצד שמיה טלטול ומ"ס לא שמיה טלטול לימא כתנאי ג אין מצילין את המת מפני הדליקה אמר ר' יהודה בן לקיש שמעתי שמצילין את המת מפני הדליקה היכי דמי אי דאיכא ככר או תינוק מ"ט דתנא קמא אי דליכא מ"ט דר' יהודה בן לקיש אלא לאו בטלטול מן הצד פליגי דמר סבר טלטול מן הצד שמיה טלטול ומ"ס לא שמיה טלטול לא ג דכ"ע טלטול מן הצד שמיה טלטול והיינו טעמא דר' יהודה בן לקיש ד) דמתוך שאדם בהול על מתו אי

דאיכא דבש. דבר הניטל: **שתי חלות.** כל הכוורת עושין אותה הדבורים חלות חלות של לפיחית דבש ושעוה וכשרודים אותן מניחין בה שתים שיתפרנסו מהן הדבורים כל ימות הגשמים כדתנן בהמוכר את הספינה (ב"ב פ.) הלוקח חלות כוורתו של חבירו מניח שתי חלות דסתמא לא מכרן: **מוקצות נינהו.** לדבורים הדר הוה ליה דבר שאינו ניטל ואפ"ה מטלטלין מחצלת להצלתן: **דחשיב עלייהו.** מאתמול לאכילה: **ומני.** היא שהצרכת לתרולה כשחישב וקתני לדבר שאין מתכוין מותר כר"ש: **אי ר"ש.** אמר ° למה לי לאוקמיה בשחישב: **שלא יעשנו כמצודה.** שלא יכסנה כולה אלא דנשבוק רווחא שיוכלו לצאת כי היכי דלא ליתצדו בהאי כיסוי ממילא ואע"ג דלא מיכוין למיצד אסור: **רב אשי אמר.** לעולם דאיכא דבש טובא ודקשיא לך ימות הגשמים מי קתני בה ימות הגשמים: **לשמעתיך.** דאין כלי ניטל אלא לדבר הניטל: **מת המוטל בחמה.** ויש לחוש שמא ימהר להסריח: **ויושבין בצדו.** ע"ג הקרקע כדי שילטערו מחום הקרקע וילטרכו להביא מטות לישב עליהן והמטות יהיו למחילה כדמסיים ואזיל: **חם להם למטה.** מן הקרקע שרתחו חמה: **ופורסין.** על ראשן נגל: **זה זוקף מטתו.** שתהא המחצלת מונחת עליה וכן זה נמצאת מחילה עשויה מאליה ולכשירצו נשמטין והולכין להם ודוקא נקט חם להם מלמטה ברישא שיביאו המטות לישיבה ברישא והדר מחצלת לפרוש עליהן נגל ואוחזין אותה בידיהן עד לאחר שעה שיזקפום וישמטום דהוה ליה כי ההוא דאמרינן (עירובין דף קא.) האי מדורתא מלמעלה למטה שרי אבל לאתויי מעיקרא מטות לצורך האהל לא דהוה ליה מלמטה למעלה כדרך בנין וקי"ל אין עושין אהל עראי בתחילה בשבת: **הופכו ממטה למטה.** עד שמגיע נגל: **מן הצד.** כלאחר יד: **אי דליכא.** והאי מצילין דקאמר ר' יהודה בן לקיש דמטלטל ליה להדיא הוא: **מאי טעמא דר' יהודה.** אלא לאו מן הצד הוא דקשרי: אי

דחשיב עלייהו. וא"ת והא אסור לרדותם כדתניא בסוף פרק המצניע (לקמן צה. ושם) הרודה חלות דבש בשוגג חייב חטאת דברי ר"א ולרבנן שבות מיהא איכא והוי דבר שאינו ניטל וי"ל דמיירי ברדויות ומונחות שם בכוורת אי נמי רגילות שיש דבש לף ע"ג חלות ואותו אינו צריך רדייה: **שלא** יעשנו כעין מצודה. וא"ת מאי קמ"ל פשיטא דאי עביד כעין מצודה דאסור ה) והא לא משמע מברייתא דאע"ג דאינו מתכוין אסור וי"ל דאמר בפ' משילין (ביצה לו: ושם) דקמ"ל דס"ד במינו ניצוד אסור שאין במינו ניצוד מותר: **רב** אשי אמר כו'. מסתמא רב אשי השיב מיד כן לרב עוקבא כששאלו אלא שסידר הש"ס תירוץ שלו תחילה ורשב"א אומר דשניהם השיב רב אשי דבמסכת ביצה גרס א"ל לא נצרכה אלא לאותן שתי חלות ובשינויא דהכא גרס ואב"א מי קתני בימות החמה כו': **כבר** תירגמ' רב הונא לשמעתיך. בפרק בתרא (דף קכד:) משמע דאית ליה נמי לרב הונא דאסור לבטל כלי מהיכנו דפריך אמילתיה דקאמר התם רב הונא היתה בהמתו טעונה כלי זכוכית מביא כרים וכסתות ומניח תחתיהן והא קמבטל כלי מהיכנו ומשני בשליפי זוטרי וא"ת אכתי תקשה ליה התם דהא רב הונא סבר הכא דאין כלי ניטל אלא לדבר הניטל וי"ל דמיירי בצריך למקומו וא"ת וכי פריך ליה התם מהיא דהיתה בהמתו טעונה טבל ועששית לימא דמיירי באין צריך למקומו וי"ל דהוה מצי לשנויי הכי דה"נ הוה מצי לשנויי בשליפי רברבי ור"י מתרץ דאיסור דאין כלי ניטל אלא לדבר הניטל שרי ב) היכא דאיכא הפסד מרובה וכן משמע דקאמר התם מהו דתימא כי היכי דלהפסד מרובה חששו כו' משמע חששו והתירו לטלטל אף לדבר שאינו ניטל דמה חששו ג) להתיר אם לא זה האיסור: **חם** להם מלמטה. תימה בלא שום חום מאי איסור איכא שיביאו כל אחד מטה לישב עליה ותו אמאי מייתי ברישא מטה והדר מחצלת ימתינו עד שיחם להם גם מלמעלה ויביאו מטות ומחצלות יחד ונראה דאחמור רבנן למיעבד היכרא שהוא לצורך חי כל כמה דאיפשר למיעבד: **ופורסין** עליהן זה זוקף כו'. דוקא בכה"ג כמו שפי' רש"י אבל ממטה למעלה אסור משום אהל כדאמרי' בהמביא כדי יין (ביצה לב: ושם) אמר רב יהודה מדורתא מלמעלה למטה שרי מלמטה למעלה אסור וכן ביעתא וכן קידרא וכן חביתא ופוריא דהא דאמרי' בהמוצא תפילין (עירובין קב.) גבי דיכרי דרב הונא אתא לקמיה דרב א"ל זיל כרוך בודיא ושייר בה טפח למחר פשטוה מוסיף על אהל עראי הוא ושפיר דמי אבל בלא שיור אסור היינו משום שהמחילות התחתונות היו כבר עשויות ואם היה פורש עליהן היה עושה אהל כדרך לעשות אהל ואע"ג דרב הונא אית ליה הכא דאין כלי ניטל אלא לדבר הניטל ° מה שהיה מוסיף למחר לא חשיב טלטול או שמא היו מושיבין שם אדם א"נ משום הפסד מרובה שרי כדפירש לעיל: **זה** זוקף מטתו. תימה לר"י ו) דרבא לא שרי אלא בשביל חי ובפ' מי שהוציאוהו (שם מד. ושם) תניא זוקף את המטה פורש עליה סדין שלא תפול החמה על המת ועל האוכלין והתם מוקי לה במחילה רביעית שסוכה כשירה בלאו הכי ולא הוי אלא תוספת אהל אבל מ"מ (אין) ניטל הכלי בשביל מת ויש לומר דהתם נמי לא שרי אלא בענין שאומר כאן שעושה בשביל חי אי נמי שיש אוכלין עם המת: **ונשמט** והולך לו. ואין צריך לישאר שם תחת האהל כדי שיהא נראה שנעשה בשביל חי כיון דבשעת עשייה היה נראה שעושה בשביל חי: **דכ"ע** טלטול מן הצד שמיה טלטול. נראה לר"י דכן הלכה מדלא קאמר דכ"ע לא שמיה טלטול וכגון דליכא ככר ותינוק ואין לו אלא מטה אחת וטעם דרבי יהודה בן לקיש מתוך שאדם בהול כו'. אלא משום דהלכתא דשמיה טלטול נקט הכי וקשה לר"י דבריש כל הכלים (לקמן קכג.) פסיק רב נחמן כר' אלעזר בן תדאי דקסבר לא שמיה טלטול וע"ק דרב אדרב דהכא סבר שמיה טלטול ובסוף פ' תולין (שם קמא.) אמרי בי רב טלטול מן הצד לא שמיה טלטול ° ובדוכתא אחריתי פריך מדרב אאמרי בי רב ובפרק השואל (ב"מ קב:) ובפרק בית כור (ב"ב קה:) מצריך מילתיה דרב ודאמרי בי רב ועוד אמאי אסר רב

עין משפט נר מצוה

מז א מיי' פכ"ה מהלכו' שבת הלכה ו ופכ"ו הלכה כב סמג לאוין סה טוש"ע או"ח סימן שיא סעיף ו:

מז ב ג מיי' שם פכ"ו הלכה כא טור שו"ע או"ח שם סעיף א:

רבינו חננאל

וכיון שמותר לפנותו מאותו מקום ולטלטלו מטלטלו למקום הביצה (כו') וכופהו על הביצה וכן כולם א) ולא יתכן לישב ע"ג הביצה כדי שלא יטנפו בגדיו. לפיכך כופה עליה [כלי] וישב עליו. וכל התיובתות פשוטות הן. ושנינו על הכוורת באותן ב' חלות ששנינו בפ' המוכר את הספינה בענין המוכר חלת דבש כוורתו לחבירו שחייב הקונה להניח לו שתי חלות דבש כדי שיהו מזון לדבורים שלא יברחו. ולפיכך אמרנו אותן ב' חלות מוקצות ממאכל אדם הן (לא השאילו) דשאולין לדבורים. ושנינן כגון (שחייב) [שחשב] עליהן בפירוש למאכל אדם. ואקשינן אי הכי אדתני ומזהיר בפריסת ע"ג הכוורת ובלבד שלא יתכוין לצוד. ליפלוג עליה כו'. ואסיקנא לעולם ר' יהודה [היא] והאי דקתני ובלבד שלא יתכוין לצוד. שלא ישלשל המחצלת וידחקנה בכותלי הכוורת שנמצא הדבורין כסתומין בכוורת אלא ירויח כמעט המחצלת מן הנקב של כוורת שהוא פתח לצאת ולכנוס בו הדבורים כו'. אמר רב ששת כבר תירגם רב הונא לשמעתיה דר' יצחק בבבל דאמר עושין מחיצה למת בשביל החי ואין עושין מחיצה למת בשביל המת כיצד מת מוטל בחמה באין ב' בני אדם ויושבין בצידו. חם להם מלמטה [זה] מביא מטה ויושב עליה וזה מביא מטה ויושב עליה כו'. איתמר מת המוטל בחמה רב יהודה אמר שמואל הופכו ממטה למטה. ומשמיה דרב אמרו מניח עליו ככר או תינוק ומטלטלו. ואסקינן בשיש ככר או תינוק כ"ע לא פליגי שמניח עליו ככר או תינוק ומטלטלו (וכ"ע) [כי פליגי היכא דל"ל מ"ס] טלטול מן הצד שמיה טלטול. [ומ"ס לא שמיה טלטול]. ואתינן ואוקמינן בתנאי. אין מצילין [את המת] מפני הדליקה. אמר ר' יהודה בן לקיש שמעתי שמצילין את המת מפני הדליקה. ואמרינן כ"ע טלטול מן הצד שמיה טלטול. היינו טעמא דר' יהודה בן לקיש מתוך שאדם בהול על מת [אי לא] שרית ליה לטלטולי אתי לכבויי ולמעבד איסורא דאוריי'. א"ר יהודה בר שילא א"ר אסי א"ר יוחנן הלכה כר' יהודה בן לקיש במת: ואין נאותין ממנו לפי שאינו מן המוכן: **ת"ר** מותר השמן שבנר ושבקערה אסור להסתפק ממנו. ור"ש מתיר (מטלטלין נר חדש אבל לא ישן) אע"ג דקיי"ל דהלכתא כר' שמעון בכולה שבת בהא לית הלכתא כוותיה. דתנא דידן קתני דברי ר' יהודה סתמא במתניתין [מטלטלין נר חדש אבל לא ישן]. ובברייתא מפרש

חשק שלמה על רבינו חננאל א) ט"ס כאן ופי' אמר הוא בצריך למקום הבילה ליטב:

מסורת הש"ס

א) [לעיל ל: לקמן קמג:], ב) [לקמן קכג. קמא.], ג) [תוספתא פי"ד] יומא דף פה., ד) יומא שם, ה) מה"ר שכנא הגיה והלא משמע דאע"ג דאינו כו', ו) נ"ל דהכא.

תוספות ישנים

א) ומשמע ליה שיש שם חלות הרבה דלא הוי מוקצה מחמת חסרון כיס: ב) ולעיל מייה ה"מ לשנויי דשרי משום הפסד אלא דמשני שינויא חדא לכולהו בצריך למקומו: ג) ומיהו דוחק הרשב"א דחששו להתיר טורח (דהמלאכה) [דהא רבה] דמפרש טעמא משום הצלה שאינה מצויה ולית ליה דביטול כלי ולא טעמא דאין כלי ניטל (אלא) [הלא] תיקשי ליה ברייתא דאסר' בפ' בתרא דף קכד: להביא תחתיו כרים וכסתות אלא ודאי משום טורח:

גליון הש"ס

גמ' כי פליגי דלית ליה. ק"ל אמאי לא הוי המטה עלמה במקום ככר או תינוק. ועי' מג"א סי' שח ס"ק כ"א ובתוספת שבת. ומזה לא העירו כלום ולע"ג: רש"י ד"ה **אי ר"ש למה לי לאוקמיה בשחישב.** משמע דמכ"מ נריכים לשינויא דאיכא ב' חלות דס"ל לרש"י שם דלר"ש ליכא לדינא דרי"ן היינו אפילו לר"ש דמיקל במוקצה. ואולם רש"י בבילה כ' באמת דפירכת הש"ס דלר"ש ל"ל כלל לתרץ דאיכא ב' חלות מבואר דס"ל לרש"י שם (דלר"ש ליכא לדינא דרי"ן). ולדברי רש"י אלו כוונת הרז"ה פ' מי שהחשיך שכתב דרי"ן הוא רק לר"י וכתב עלה שכ"כ רש"י: תוס' ד"ה ופורסין וכו' מה שהיה מוסיף למחר. עי' לקמן דף נג ע"א תוס' ד"ה מהו ליתן: שם ד"ה דכו"ע וכו' ובדוכתא אחריתי. עי' בכורות דף כו ע"ב:

ליקוטי רש"י

חלות. הכוורת לאחר שעשתה פירות ויצאו הנחילין לוקחין את הדבש והוא עשוי חלות חלות ויש בו י' חלות או עשרים זה בלד זה משעוה ודבש מעורב יחד [רשב"ם ב"ב פ.]. **לאותן שתי חלות.** של לפיחית מניחין בכוורת כשרודין אותה ומהן פרנסה לדבורים כל ימות הגשמים אותן שתי חלות מותר לכסות כל דבש הכוורת עשוי עליות עליות של חלות. **דחשיב עלייהו.** לאדם. **אי הכי הא דתני ובלבד שלא יתכוין לצוד.** משמע דלא ימלא לחלק את דבריו ולאסור עד שדלג מאיסור טלטול לאיסור לידה. **לפלוג ולתני בדידה.** באיסור טלטול גופיה יכול לחלק את דבריו ולמצוא לד איסור לדבר בדלא חשב עלייהו לא יטלטל המחצלת לנרכס. **הא קמ"ל אף על פי שחושב עליהן כו'.** אף כשחשב בא ללמדך שיש לך איסור במתכוין לצוד ואף על גב דעיקר להצלה מפני הגשמים מכוון. **לעולם ר' יהודה.** כלומר מדהוה לך לתרוצי אריש' הא מני ר' שמעון דלית ליה מוקצה ומהדרת אשנויי דחיקי למימר משום שתי החלות כרבי יהודה בעית לאוקמא משום דרבי יצחק דמותבינן ליה הנך תיובתא אית ליה מוקצה כר' יהודה [ביצה לו. עיין בגה"ש כאן]. **רב אשי אמר.** לעולם כדשנינן מעיקרא דאיכא דבש למאכל אדם ודקשיא לך בימות הגשמים מי איכא דבש לא קשיא דמי קתני ימות החמה וימות הגשמים [שם:]. **מן הצד.** שאינו אוחז ממש בידו [לקמן קכג.]. **שמצילין את המת.** לחצר המעורבת דליכא איסור אלא טלטול [יומא פה.].

The Gemara analyzes the opinions of Rav and Shmuel:
הֵיכָא דְּאִיכָּא כִּכָּר אוֹ תִּינוֹק – **Where there is a loaf of bread or an infant** available, כּוּלֵּי עָלְמָא לֹא פְּלִיגֵי דְּשָׁרֵי – **all agree that it is permitted** to move the corpse by first placing the bread or infant upon it. כִּי פְּלִיגֵי – **Where do they disagree?** דְּלֵית לֵיהּ – It is concerning a case **where one does not have** a loaf of bread or an infant available.[16] מַר סָבַר טִלְטוּל מִן הַצַּד שְׁמֵיהּ טִלְטוּל – One **master** (Rav) **holds that moving** something **indirectly**[17] **is deemed moving** it with respect to the prohibition against moving *muktzeh*. Accordingly, he does not permit rolling the corpse from bed to bed, since that involves moving the corpse indirectly. וּמַר סָבַר לֹא שְׁמֵיהּ טִלְטוּל – **But** the other **master** (Shmuel) **holds** that **[moving indirectly] is not deemed moving** with respect to *muktzeh*. He therefore allows rolling the corpse from bed to bed.

The Gemara suggests that this same issue may already have been disputed by Tannaim:
לֵימָא כְּתַנָּאֵי – **Shall we say** that this issue is **a matter of Tannaic dispute?** For it was taught in a Baraisa: אֵין מַצִּילִין אֶת הַמֵּת מִפְּנֵי הַדְּלֵיקָה – WE MAY NOT SAVE A CORPSE FROM A FIRE by moving it. אָמַר רַבִּי יְהוּדָה בֶּן לָקִישׁ – R' YEHUDAH BEN LAKISH SAID: שָׁמַעְתִּי שֶׁמַּצִּילִין אֶת הַמֵּת מִפְּנֵי הַדְּלֵיקָה – I HEARD a tradition THAT WE MAY SAVE A CORPSE FROM A FIRE by moving it. הֵיכִי דָּמֵי – Now, **what is the case** with which this Baraisa is dealing? אִי דְּאִיכָּא כִּכָּר אוֹ תִּינוֹק – **If there is a loaf of bread or an infant** available to place upon the corpse, מַאי טַעְמָא דְּתַנָּא קַמָּא – **what is the reasoning of the Tanna Kamma,** who forbids moving the corpse?[18] אִי דְּלֵיכָּא – **If,** on the other hand, **there is no** loaf of bread or infant available, מַאי טַעְמָא דְּרַבִּי יְהוּדָה בֶּן לָקִישׁ – **what is the reasoning of R' Yehudah ben Lakish,** who permits moving the corpse?[19] אֶלָּא לָאו בְּטִלְטוּל מִן הַצַּד פְּלִיגֵי – **Rather,** is it **not** presumable that we are dealing with a case in which no bread or infant is available and **they disagree concerning** the issue of **moving** the corpse **indirectly?** דְּמַר סָבַר טִלְטוּל מִן הַצַּד שְׁמֵיהּ טִלְטוּל – Their dispute is **that** one **master** (the Tanna Kamma) **holds** that **moving indirectly is deemed moving** with respect to *muktzeh* and he therefore forbids moving the corpse, even indirectly; וּמַר סָבַר לֹא שְׁמֵיהּ טִלְטוּל – **whereas** the other **master** (R' Yehudah ben Lakish) **holds** that moving indirectly **is not deemed moving** with respect to *muktzeh* and he therefore permits moving the corpse indirectly, by rolling it from one bed to another as Shmuel prescribed above. It emerges that the issue of moving *muktzeh* indirectly, which Rav and Shmuel debated, was previously debated by the Tannaim of this Baraisa. – ? –

The Gemara responds:
לֹא דְּכוּלֵּי עָלְמָא טִלְטוּל מִן הַצַּד שְׁמֵיהּ טִלְטוּל – **No!** In fact, all the Tannaim of this Baraisa **agree that moving indirectly is deemed** moving with respect to *muktzeh,* and it would normally be forbidden to move a corpse even indirectly.[20] וְהַיְינוּ טַעְמָא דְּרַבִּי יְהוּדָה בֶּן לָקִישׁ – **And the reasoning of R' Yehudah ben Lakish,** who permits moving the corpse in order to save it from a fire, **is** דְּמִתּוֹךְ שֶׁאָדָם בָּהוּל עַל מֵתוֹ – **that since a person is** likely to be **extremely distressed about** the possibility of losing **his** relative's **corpse** to a fire,

NOTES

it (see below, 142b with *Rashi* ד״ה אלא למת). For further discussion of this matter, see *Gilyon HaShas, Rashash* and *Chazon Ish* 47:23.

16. I.e. there is no non-*muktzeh* item readily available (*Tosafos* cited by *Ritva MHK* ed.; cf. *Ramban* cited there; see *Rosh Yosef*).

17. Literally: from the side.

18. [As we stated earlier, the expedient of placing a loaf of bread or an infant on a corpse is accepted universally.]

19. Can it be that he permits moving the corpse directly? (*Rashi*).

20. I.e. it would be forbidden to roll a corpse from bed to bed simply to remove it from a sunny area or for a similar purpose (*Rashi,* 44a).

אִי לָא שָׁרֵית לֵיהּ אָתֵי לְכַבּוּיֵי – **if you do not permit him** to move it when it is in danger of being burned **he may come to extinguish** the fire in order to save it. The Rabbis therefore granted a special dispensation for this case, allowing him to move the corpse.[1]

The Gemara records a final ruling concerning moving a corpse away from a fire:

אָמַר רַבִּי יְהוּדָה בֶּן שִׁילָא אָמַר רַבִּי אַסִּי אָמַר רַבִּי יוֹחָנָן – **R' Yehudah ben Shela said in the name of R' Assi who said in the name of R' Yochanan:** הֲלָכָה כְּרַבִּי יְהוּדָה בֶּן לָקִישׁ בְּמֵת – **The halachah follows R' Yehudah ben Lakish regarding a corpse.**[2]

The Gemara turns its attention to the final segment of our Mishnah, which states:

אֵין נֵיאוֹתִין הֵימֶנּוּ לְפִי שֶׁאֵינוֹ מִן הַמּוּכָן – AND WE MAY NOT BENEFIT FROM [THE OIL] SINCE IT WAS NOT PREPARED for Sabbath use.

The Mishnah does not state whether this prohibition attaches to the oil only while the flame is burning, or even after it goes out. The Gemara cites a Baraisa which addresses this point:

תָּנוּ רַבָּנַן – **The Rabbis taught in a Baraisa:** מוֹתַר הַשֶּׁמֶן שֶׁבַּנֵּר וְשֶׁבַּקְּעָרָה אָסוּר – THE LEFTOVER OIL IN A LAMP OR IN A BOWL IS PROHIBITED, even after the flame goes out; וְרַבִּי שִׁמְעוֹן מַתִּיר – BUT R' SHIMON PERMITS it.[3]

Mishnah מְטַלְטְלִין נֵר חָדָשׁ אֲבָל לֹא יָשָׁן – **We may move a new lamp, but not an old one.**[4] רַבִּי שִׁמְעוֹן אוֹמֵר – **R' Shimon says:** כָּל הַנֵּרוֹת מְטַלְטְלִין – **All lamps may be moved,** חוּץ מִן הַנֵּר הַדּוֹלֵק בְּשַׁבָּת – **except for a lamp that is** actually **burning on the Sabbath.**[5]

Gemara The Gemara cites a Baraisa in which various Tannaic views about the *muktzeh* status of a lamp are presented:

תָּנוּ רַבָּנַן – **The Rabbis taught in a Baraisa:** מְטַלְטְלִין נֵר חָדָשׁ אֲבָל לֹא יָשָׁן – WE MAY MOVE A NEW LAMP, BUT NOT AN OLD ONE. דִּבְרֵי רַבִּי יְהוּדָה – These are THE WORDS OF R' YEHUDAH.[6] רַבִּי מֵאִיר אוֹמֵר – R' MEIR SAYS: כָּל הַנֵּרוֹת מְטַלְטְלִין – ALL LAMPS MAY BE MOVED, חוּץ מִן הַנֵּר שֶׁהִדְלִיקוּ בּוֹ בְּשַׁבָּת – EXCEPT FOR A LAMP IN WHICH a flame HAD BEEN LIT FOR THE SABBATH.[7] רַבִּי שִׁמְעוֹן אוֹמֵר – R' SHIMON SAYS: חוּץ מִן הַנֵּר הַדּוֹלֵק בְּשַׁבָּת – All lamps may be moved EXCEPT FOR A LAMP THAT IS still BURNING ON THE SABBATH. כָּבְתָה מוּתָּר לְטַלְטְלָהּ – ONCE IT HAS GONE OUT, however, IT IS PERMITTED TO MOVE IT.[8] אֲבָל כּוֹס וּקְעָרָה וַעֲשָׁשִׁית – BUT with respect to A CUP, A BOWL AND A BEAKER that were

NOTES

1. To preclude the possibility of someone violating the Biblical *melachah* of כִּיבּוּי, *extinguishing*, out of extreme distress, the Rabbis relaxed their prohibition of moving *muktzeh* for this case [see next note] (*Tosafos, Rosh;* see *Ran* and *Ritva MHK* ed.; see also *Mishnah Berurah* 278:3). Barring this exception, however, one may not move a corpse even indirectly. Furthermore, there are severe limitations on which items a person may save from a fire (see below, 117b and *Orach Chaim* 334).

2. I.e. it is permitted to move a corpse away from a fire. On the basis of R' Yehudah ben Lakish's reasoning (that a dispensation was necessary for this case of extreme distress), it is permitted even to move a corpse *directly* when there is no other way to save it from a fire (*Rosh, Ran,* based on *Rashi* to 43b ד״ה אי דליכא and *Rambam, Hil. Shabbos* 26:21; cf. *Rabbeinu Yonah* cited by *Rosh* and *Ran;* see *Orach Chaim* 311:1).

Regarding the broader issue of whether the indirect moving of *muktzeh* is forbidden on the Sabbath, most Rishonim conclude that the halachah follows Rav's view that it is generally forbidden. Nevertheless, many Rishonim distinguish between a case in which one's primary objective is to move the *muktzeh* item but he uses an indirect method to do so, and a case in which one's primary motive is to move a non-*muktzeh* item, but must thereby indirectly move a *muktzeh* item that is resting on it. In the latter case the halachah is more permissive; so long as one does not move the *muktzeh* directly it is permitted to move the non-*muktzeh* item (see *Tosafos, Rif, Rosh* et al. and *Orach Chaim* 311:8).

3. As explained earlier (43b note 5), R' Yehudah and R' Shimon disagree regarding the scope of *muktzeh*. One of their areas of disagreement concerns the principle of מִיגּוֹ דְּאִתְקַצַּאי לְבֵין הַשְּׁמָשׁוֹת אִתְקַצַּאי לְכוּלֵּי יוֹמָא, *since it was muktzeh during bein hashemashos (twilight) it remains muktzeh for the entire day.* This principle is accepted by R' Yehudah, who holds that if an item was *muktzeh* for the duration of *bein hashemashos* at the onset of the Sabbath it can no longer be considered "prepared" for Sabbath use and therefore remains *muktzeh* for the entire Sabbath, even if the underlying reason for its being *muktzeh* no longer exists. R' Shimon, on the other hand, does not accept that an item designated as *muktzeh* during *bein hashemashos* automatically retains that designation for the entire day. Rather, he holds that if it was anticipated that the item would become available for use during the Sabbath, its *muktzeh* status is lifted when it becomes available.

In the case at hand, R' Yehudah holds that since the oil was *muktzeh* at the onset of the Sabbath – due to the fact that the lamp was burning (as explained above, 42b note 10) – it remains *muktzeh* throughout the Sabbath, even after the flame has gone out. R' Yehudah's view is reflected in the statement of the Tanna Kamma of the Baraisa. R' Shimon, however, holds that the oil is *muktzeh* only as long as the flame burns. Once it is extinguished, the leftover oil – both that which remains in the lamp and that which has dripped into the bowl below – becomes permitted (see *Rashi* below ד״ה בזוטא and *Beitzah* 30b with *Rashi* ד״ה אדם יושב ומצפה; see also *Afikei Yam* II:19).

4. I.e. we may handle on the Sabbath an earthenware oil-lamp that has never been used, for it has not yet become grimy and is still usable for other purposes, e.g. for storing small items. An earthenware lamp that has been used, however, would not commonly be used for other purposes, since it has become grimy, and therefore falls into the category of מוּקְצֶה מֵחֲמַת מִיאוּס, *muktzeh by dint of repugnance* (*Rashi* here and *Chullin* 14b; see *Beur Halachah* to 279:6). [Although the vessel is certainly usable as a lamp, this is a use which is prohibited on the Sabbath. Since due to its repugnance it is not fit for any permissible use on the Sabbath, the lamp is deemed completely *muktzeh* (*Pnei Yehoshua*).]

5. R' Shimon does not recognize the category of *muktzeh by dint of repugnance* and therefore permits handling even a used lamp. However, he forbids moving the lamp while the flame is burning lest one inadvertently extinguish the flame (see *Rashi* to beginning of Gemara; see also *Tosafos* to 42b ד״ה ואין ניאותין).

[*Rashi's* explanation that R' Shimon forbids moving a lit lamp out of concern that one might extinguish the flame is taken from the Gemara below, 46b. However, the Gemara there rejects this explanation on the grounds that even if one would inadvertently extinguish the flame this would merely be an unintended consequence of his act and, as we learned earlier (41b; see note 2 there), R' Shimon permits the performance of something that is unintended (דָּבָר שֶׁאֵין מִתְכַּוֵּין). Rather, the Gemara (47a) concludes that according to R' Shimon the reason it is forbidden to move the lamp while the flame is still burning is that the lamp, including the oil and the wick, serves as a base to the flame and, thus, is a *base to muktzeh.* For explanations of why *Rashi* here chose to follow the rejected view, see *Rosh Yosef* ד״ה וראב״ש and *Chasam Sofer.*]

6. R' Yehudah's view is that of the Tanna Kamma of our Mishnah: A used lamp is *muktzeh by dint of repugnance,* whereas a new and unused one is not.

7. [And which was burning during *bein hashemashos.*] This lamp is *muktzeh by dint of a prohibition* (see previous note). R' Meir recognizes the category of *muktzeh by dint of a prohibition,* but rejects the concept of *muktzeh by dint of repugnance.* Therefore, R' Meir rules that a used lamp is not *muktzeh,* despite its repugnance, so long as it was not burning at the onset of the Sabbath. But a lamp that was burning at the onset of Sabbath became *muktzeh* by dint of the prohibition and remains *muktzeh* for the entire Sabbath, even after it is no longer burning (*Rashi*).

8. R' Shimon holds that it is prohibited to move the lamp only while the flame is burning, lest one extinguish the flame. Once the flame goes out

אי לא שרית ליה אתי לכבויי א"ר יהודה בן שילא א"ר אסי א"ר יוחנן [א] הלכה כר' יהודה בן לקיש במת: אין ניאותין הימנו לפי שאינו מן המוכן: תנו רבנן [א] [ב] מותר השמן שבנר ושבקערה אסור ורבי שמעון מתיר:

מתני' [ג] מטלטלין נר חדש אבל לא ישן רבי שמעון אומר כל הנרות מטלטלין חוץ מן הנר הדולק בשבת:

גמ' [ג] ת"ר מטלטלין נר חדש אבל לא ישן דברי רבי יהודה ר"מ אומר [ג] כל הנרות מטלטלין חוץ מן הנר שהדליקו בו [ד] בשבת ר' שמעון אומר חוץ מן הנר הדולק בשבת כבתה מותר לטלטלה אבל כוס וקערה ועששית לא יזיזם ממקומם ור' אליעזר בר' שמעון אומר מסתפק מן הנר הכבה ומן השמן המטפטף ואפי' בשעה שהנר דולק אמר אביי רבי אליעזר ברבי שמעון סבר לה כאבוה בחדא ופליג עליה בחדא סבר לה כאבוה בחדא דלית ליה מוקצה ופליג עליה בחדא דאילו אבוה סבר כבה אין לא כבה לא ואיהו סבר אע"ג דלא כבה אבל כוס וקערה ועששית לא יזיזם ממקומם מאי שנא הני אמר עולא סיפא אתאן לר' יהודה מתקיף לה מר זוטרא אי הכי מאי אבל אלא אמר מר זוטרא לעולם רבי שמעון וכי קשרי רבי שמעון בנר זוטא דדעתיה עלויה אבל הני דנפישי לא והתניא מותר השמן שבנר ושבקערה אסור ורבי שמעון מתיר התם קערה דומיא דנר הכא קערה דומיא דכוס א"ר זירא פמוט שהדליקו בו בשבת לדברי המתיר אסור לדברי האוסר מותר למימרא דרבי יהודה מוקצה מחמת מיאוס אית ליה מוקצה מחמת איסור לית ליה והתניא [ה] ר' יהודה אומר כל הנרות של מתכת מטלטלין חוץ מן הנר שהדליקו בו [ו] בשבת אלא אי איתמר הכי איתמר א"ר זירא פמוט שהדליקו עליו בשבת ד"ה אסור לא הדליקו עליו ד"ה מותר: אמר [ז] רב יהודה א"ר מטה שיחדה למעות אסור לטלטלה מיתיבי' רב נחמן בר יצחק מטלטלין נר חדש אבל לא ישן ומה

רש"י

אי לא שרית ליה וכו'. אבל במוטל לחמה לא שרי: **מתני'** **מטלטלין נר חדש.** שאינו מאוס וחזי לאשתמושי (א) להדיא שלא דלק בו נר מעולם: **אבל לא ישן.** דמוקצה מחמת מיאוס הוא: **גמ'** **חוץ מן הנר שהדליקו.** ואף על גב שכבה אסור דאית ליה לרבי מאיר מוקצה מחמת איסור ולית ליה מוקצה מחמת מיאוס: [ט] **חוץ מן הנר הדולק בשבת.** בעוד שהוא דולק אסור שמא יכבה הנר: **עששית.** כוס גדול של זכוכית שקורין לנפ"א: **לא יזיזם ממקומן.** ואפי' כבה הנר ולקמן מפרש טעמא: **מן הנר הכבה.** דכיון דכבה והולך לא מחייב תו משום מכבה: **כבה אין לא כבה לא.** דלא שמעינן ליה לרבי שמעון דשרי במתני' אלא מותר שמן שבנר ושבקערה דמשמע לאחר שכבה: **מאי אבל.** מדקאמר אבל מכלל דבנר מותר: **בזוטא.** דדעתי' עליה מבע"י סבר שיכלה השמן מהר ואשתמש בנר לכשיכבה: **אבל הני.** לא אסיק אדעתיה שיכבו כל היום: **ור' שמעון מתיר.** וקערה נפישא קשיא קערה אקערה: **דומיא דנר.** קתני לה זוטרא: **פמוט.** מנורה של מתכת ואינה מאוסה: **לדברי המתיר.** ר' מאיר המתיר בנר ישן: **אוסר.** בהאי דמוקצה מחמת איסור כדקתני לעיל חוץ מן הנר שהדליקו בו בשבת: **לדברי האוסר.** רבי יהודה האוסר בנר ישן של חרס התם הוא דמאיס אבל הכא שרי ולית ליה מוקצה מחמת איסור: **נר של מתכת.** לא מאיס כגון של נחשת דלא בלע: **שיחדה למעות.** מיתסרא בהזמנה בעלמא ואע"פ שלא הניח עליה מעולם: **מטלטלין נר חדש.** והא רבי יהודה קאמר לה דאית ליה מוקצה אלמא לא מיתסר בהזמנה מדקאמר אבל לא ישן ולא קתני אבל לא המיוחד לכך:

הניח

תוספות

רב הכא טלטול מן הצד הא תנן בפ' נוטל (לקמן קמב:) מעות שע"ג הכר מנער את הכר והן נופלות ואבן שעל פי החבית מטה על צדה וכו' ומוקי לה רב התם בשוכח אבל במניח נעשה בסים לדבר האסור והכא (ב) (חשיב) בשוכח מדשרי שמואל וכל דבר שדעתו ליטלו בשבת ולא להניחו כל השבת ° אפילו מניח חשיב כשוכח כי ההיא דמנער את הכיסוי והם נופלות אע"פ שבמתכוין כיסה בדבר שאינו ניטל ואפי' רבנן דרבי אלעזר בן תדאי שרו בכי האי גוונא דהכא דהא שרו פגה שהטמינה בתבן וחררה שהטמינה בגחלים אם מגולה מקצתה ובמכוסה כולה פליגי דרבי אלעזר שרי אפי' מכוסה כולה דתוחב בכוש או בכרכר ואומר ר"י דיש לחלק ° דהכא עיקר הטלטול לצורך מת ולא דמי לכל הנהו שעושה עיקר הטלטול לצורך כר וחבית ולא לצורך מעות ואבן א) ולהכי לא מייתי הכא פלוגתא דר' אלעזר בן תדאי ורבנן וע"ק לר"י דאפי' בטלטול דמת שיש לאסור יותר משאר טלטול מן הצד כדפי' שרי שמואל ובסוף במה טומנין (לקמן דף נ:) אמר שמואל האי סכינא דביני אורבי דלה ושלפה והדר דלה שרי ואי לא אסיר ופירש בקונט' לקמן דאסור משום טלטול מן הצד וכן קשה דרב הונא אמר התם האי סליקוסתא דלה ושלפה והדר דלה שרי ואי לאו אסור א"כ אסר טלטול מן הצד ובסוף תולין אמרי בי רב טלטול מן הצד לא שמיה טלטול ואמרי בי רב היינו רב הונא כמו שמפרש ר"ת בספ"ק דסנהדרין [ט] (דף ח: וכס) ונראה לר"י דרב הונא ושמואל לא אסרי התם משום טלטול מן הצד אלא משום שמסיר עפר ומרחיב הגומא ואיירי דאיירי לעיל מיניה בגומא נקטה ומותיב מהטומן לפת וצנונות דהתם לפת וצנונות לאו דלה ושלפה ולהכי חשיב הש"ם תיובתא ור"ה ושמואל ° הוו ידעי לה דמתני' היא בסדר זרעים אלא דדחקי לאוקמה בדלה ושלפה והש"ס לא ניחא ליה לאוקמה הכי ועומדת בתיובתא:

[י] **מתוך** שאדם בהול על מתו אי לא שרית לי' אתי לכבויי. ואע"ג דגבי ממון אמרינן [כ] איפכא אי שרית ליה אתי לכבויי היינו משום שאין מצטער על ממונו כמו על מתו ואי שרית ליה מתוך שיהא טרוד להציל ישכח שהיום שבת ויבא לכבות בשוגג אבל על מתו מצטער ביותר ואי לא שרית ליה אתי לכבויי במזיד:

שבנר ושבקערה **אסור** ור' שמעון מתיר. ואחר השבת מותר אפי' לר' יהודה וה"נ תניא לקמן גבי נויי סוכה אסור להסתפק מהן עד מוצאי י"ט האחרון אבל בתר הכי שרי וקשה לר"י דמ"ש מנר חנוכה דתניא [ל] כבה ליל ראשון מוסיף עליו בליל ב' ומדליק בו כבה ליל ח' עושה לו מדורה בפני עצמו מפני שהוקצה למצותו ואומר ר"י דנר חנוכה עיקרו לא להנאתו בא אלא לפרסומי ניסא ומשום חביבותא דנס אינו מצפה שיכבה אלא מקצה לגמרי למצוה אבל נר שבת להנאתו בא יושב ומצפה שיכבה ולכך מותר וא"ת ומ"ש נר שכבה דאסור לטלטל לר' יהודה מסוכה רעועה דעלמא דמהני בה תנאי כדאמר לקמן בשמעתין ואם התנה עליה הכל לפי תנאו ומוקי לה במסכת ביצה (דף ל:) בסוכה דעלמא ורעועה דאתמול דעתיה עילויה שתפול ונר נמי דעתיה עילויה שיכבה ואמאי אין מועיל תנאי להסתפק ממותר השמן ולר"ש נמי יועיל תנאי להסתפק מן השמן המטפטף בשעה שהנר דולק וי"ל דהתם סוכה דעלמא היתה עשויה מזמן גדול ועתה ביה"ש אינו בודל ממנה ויושב ומצפה מתי תפול אבל נר עיקר הקצאתו הוא ביה"ש ודחייה בידי' לצורך שבת ואמיר טפי ולא מהני ביה תנאי ב):

לדברי המתיר אסור. פי' בקונטרס לדברי ר' מאיר וא"ת מאי קמ"ל הא בהדיא קאסר ר' מאיר נר שהדליקו בה באותו שבת וי"ל דה"א ה"מ בנר של חרס דאית ביה תרתי מוקצה מחמת מיאוס ומחמת איסור קמ"ל דאפי' בשל מתכת דלא מאיס ולית ביה אלא מוקצה מחמת איסור אסר ר' מאיר ואין נראה לר"ת דלפי זה הא דמסיק דברי הכל אסור לא הוי אלא ר' מאיר ור' יהודה דקאי עלייהו ולא ר"ש ומפרש וכן פר"ח לדברי המתיר היינו ר' שמעון אסר כאן בפמוט דהא פמוט גדול הוא ככוס וקערה ועששית כמו פמוטות של בית ר' דשילהי כל כתבי (לקמן קכא:) לדברי האוסר היינו ר' מאיר ור' יהודה דאסרי בנר חרס שהדליקו בו באותו שבת וה"מ בנר של חרס דאיכא תרתי מוקצה מחמת מיאוס ומחמת איסור אבל בנר מתכת שרו ומסיק דאפי' בשל מתכת אסר ר' מאיר וה"נ אמרי' בפ"ק דחולין (דף טו.) ע"כ לא שרי רבי מאיר אלא במבשל דראוי לכוס אבל בשוחט לא ג):

מטה שיחדה למעות אסור לטלטלה. נראה דאפי' לצורך גופה או לצורך מקומה אסור דכיון שיחדה למעות שוב אין עושין ממנה שום תשמיש ° והויא כחצוצרות דאסור לטלטלה לרבי יהודה אפילו לצורך גופה ומקומה ולרבי שמעון לא אסור שום מוקצה לצורך גופו ומקומו אלא מוקצה מחמת חסרון כיס:

ומה

מסורת הש"ס

א) [לקמן מו: ביצה ל:], ב) חולין יד:, ג) תוספתא שבת פ"ד, ד) י"ג באותה שבת, ה) חולין טו., ו) בכ"י באותה שבת, ז) [לפמ"ש תוס' יבמות קמ: ד"ה אמר וכו' מוכח דהי' גרסת' הכא רב הונא ע"ש], ח) [דבור זה שייך לעיל במשנה], ט) בתוד"ה אלא, י) שייך לעמוד הקודם, כ) [לקמן קיז:], ל) [בש"ס לא נמצא מקומו אלא בשאלתות פ' וישלח הביאו הרא"ש פרק במה מדליקין רס"ט ובטור וב"י סימן תרעו].

תוספות ישנים

א) וא"ש דהכא שרי טפי ככר או תינוק מטלטול מן הצד. ובפ' נוטל (דף קמב:) אמר לא אמרו ככר או תינוק אלא למת בלבד ואמרינן לכ"ע ע"י ככר או תינוק שאר דברים שלא במת אע"ג דשרי טלטול מן הצד למת:

ב) ורשב"א מפ' דהכא חמיר טפי לפי שהוא בסיס לדבר האסור:

ג) ורשב"א מפרש דאפילו למאי דס"ד אמי ההיא דחולין שפיר דבמוקצה מחמת איסור דהתם אפי' ר"ש מוד'. אף על גב דשרי בנתגלגלה בשבת התם אינו מעלה על לבו שישחטנה שום אדם בשבת והוי כמו דיש במינו במחובר דפרש"י דבילה [דף כד:] דאפילו ר"ש אסר כגרוגרות וצימוקין מדלא לקמן מאתמול אקצינהו:

הגהות הב"ח

(א) רש"י ד"ה מטלטלין וכו' לאשתמושי ביה להדיא: (ב) תוס' ד"ה דכ"ע טלטול וכו' אבל במניח נעשה בסים לדבר האסור והכא חשיב כשכח מדשרי שמואל דאפילו מניח דבר שדעתו ליטלו בשבת ולא להניחו כל השבת חשוב כשכח כי ההיא דמנער:

גליון הש"ס

תוס' ד"ה דכ"ע כו' **אפילו מניח חשיב כשוכח כי ההיא דמנער.** עי' לקמן דף נא ע"א תוס' ד"ה או שמן: **באו"ד דהכא עיקר.** עי' לעיל דף לט ע"א תוס' ד"ה מפני שמזיז: **באו"ד הוו ידעי לה דמתני' היא.** עי' מנחות דף ט ע"א תוס' ד"ה חסר הלוג. ומו"ק דף ה ע"א תוס' ד"ה לאתויי: תוס' ד"ה מטה שיחדה כו' **והויא כחצוצרות.** לעיל דף לו ע"א:

ליקוטי רש"י

מותר השמן שבנר ושבקערה. נר קרויז"ל מותר השמן שנותן בנר או בקערה שמן המיתן להדלקת הנר של שבת וכבה המותר יש בה משום מוקצה ואסור. **ורבי שמעון מתיר.** אדם יושב ומצפה אימתי תכבה נרו שיודע שסופה לכבות הלכך בין השמשות דעתיה על המותר [ביצה ל:]. **נר חדש.** שלא הדליקו בו מעולם נר של חרס וכשהוא חדש חזי למרמי ביה פירי. **אבל לא ישן.** דמוקצה הוא מחמת מיאוס שהדעת קצה בו [חולין יד:]. **חוץ מן הנר שהדליקו בו בשבת.** שהיה נר דולק בו בין השמשות דמוקצה מחמת איסור שאסור לכבות הנר נאסר גם הוא לטלטל וכיון שהוקצה לבין השמשות הוקצה לכל היום [שם טו.]. **עששית.** כלי גדול של זכוכית בלעז לנטרנ"א [לעיל כג.]. **פמוט.** מנורה קטנה [מנחות כח.]. **כל הנרות של מתכת מטלטלין.** דשל מתכות לא מאיסי אפילו ישנים כגון של נחושת וכיוצא בהן [חולין שם].

עין משפט נר מצוה

מח א מיי' פכ"ו מהל' שבת הלכה כא סמג לאוין סה טוש"ע או"ח סימן שיא סעיף א:

מט ב מיי' פ"ה מהל' שבת הלכה יב ופרק כו הלכה יד סמג לאוין סה טוש"ע או"ח סימן רסה סעיף ג וסימן רעט סעיף א:

נ ג מיי' פכ"ה מהלכות שבת הלכה י יא טוש"ע או"ח סימן רעט סעיף א:

רבינו חננאל

דברי ר' יהודה מטלטלין נר חדש אבל לא ישן. ר' מאיר [אומר] כל הנרות מטלטלין חוץ מן הנר שהדליקו בה באותה שבת. נמצא ר' מאיר ור' יהודה שניהן אוסרין בנר שהדליקו בו באותה שבת. ור"ש מתיר ואין הלכתא כוותיה. דהוא יחיד במקום רבים ואע"פ דא"ר יוחנן אנו אין לנו אלא בנר כר' שמעון [לר' שמעון] אמרו וליה [לר'] יוחנן לא סבירא ליה טעמא דר"ש. ואפילו ר"ש לא שרי לטלטולי בשבת בנר שכבה אלא בנר קטן דכיון דהוא נר קטן ושמנו מעט דעתו עליו מאתמול לכשיכבה יטלטלנו ואינו מוקצה. אבל נר גדול כגון כוס וקערה ועששית שיתכן שידליקו היום כולו לא אמרינן דחשיב עלייהו מאתמול לכשיכבו יטלטלם. אלא אמרינן ודאי כיון דגדולים הן נתייאשו מלטלטלן ומוקצין הן. לפיכך קתני סיפא אבל כוס וקערה ועששית לא יזיזם ממקומן וכן כיוצא בהן. פעמים שיש קערה ועששית קטנה דומיא דנר קטן ודינם כדין נר קטן ופעמים שיש נר גדול דומיא דקערה ועששית ודינו כדינם. והא דא"ר אלעזר [בר"ש] מסתפק אדם מנר הכבה ומשמן המטפטף אע"פ שהנר דולק א) א"ר זירא פמוט שהדליקו עליו לדברי המתיר בנר אסר בפמוט. כלומר לר' שמעון דמתיר בנר קטן בפמוט שהוא גדול אוסר. ולדברי ר' מאיר ור' יהודה שאוסרין בנר של חרש מפני שהוא מטונף. והוא צאו כלי. ולפיכך הוקצהו מאתמול בפמוט שהוא של מתכת ואינו מטונף מתיר: **ירושל'** נר מאוס. פמוט אינו מאוס. תני נר המונח על הדלת פותח ונועל בשבת ובלבד שלא יתכוין לכבות. רב ושמואל פותרין לה בשוכח ומקללין למאן דעבד כן [יכרת] ה' לאיש אשר יעשנה וגו'. ואקשי' ולר' יהודה מוקצה מחמת מיאוס אית ליה מוקצה מחמת איסור שהדליקו בה באותה שבת לא. והתניא ר' יהודה אומר כל הנרות של מתכת מטלטלין חוץ מן הנר שהדליקו בה באותה שבת. ואסיקנ' הכי לדברי

חשק שלמה על רבינו חננאל

א) עי' ברשב"א וברמב"ן:

רב נסים גאון

אמר ר' זירא פמוט שהדליקו עליו באותה שבת לדברי המתיר אוסר לדברי האוסר מתיר פמוט מין מנורה ויש לה קנה אחד ובמנחות בפרק הקומץ את המנחה (דף כח) כשאמרו על דרך קושיא ואימא נמי באה

filled with oil and used as lamps, לֹא יְזִיזֵם מִמְּקוֹמָם – **ONE MAY NOT MOVE THEM FROM THEIR PLACE,** even after they are extinguished.[9] וְרַבִּי אֱלִיעֶזֶר בְּרַבִּי שִׁמְעוֹן אוֹמֵר – **BUT R' ELIEZER**[10] **THE SON OF R' SHIMON SAYS:** מִסְתַּפֵּק מִן הַנֵּר הַכָּבֶה – **ONE MAY TAKE** oil directly **FROM A LAMP THAT IS GOING OUT,** וּמִן הַשֶּׁמֶן הַמְטַפְטֵף וַאֲפִילוּ בְּשָׁעָה שֶׁהַנֵּר דוֹלֵק – **OR OIL THAT IS DRIPPING** from the lamp **EVEN WHILE THE LAMP IS BURNING.**[11]

The Gemara analyzes the view of R' Eliezer the son of R' Shimon:

אָמַר אַבַּיֵי – **Abaye said:** רַבִּי אֱלִיעֶזֶר בְּרַבִּי שִׁמְעוֹן סָבַר לָהּ כַּאֲבוּהַ בַּחֲדָא וּפָלִיג עֲלֵיהּ בַּחֲדָא – **R' Eliezer the son of R' Shimon concurs with his father in one** point **and differs with him in one** point. סָבַר לָהּ כַּאֲבוּהַ בַּחֲדָא – **He concurs with his father in one** point דְּלֵית לֵיהּ מוּקְצֶה – in **that he,** too, **does not accept** a broad application of ***muktzeh.***[12] וּפָלִיג עֲלֵיהּ בַּחֲדָא – **And he differs with him in one** point דְּאִילּוּ אֲבוּהַ סָבַר כָּבָה אִין לֹא כָּבָה לֹא – in **that his father,** R' Shimon, **holds that** after **[the flame] went out** the lamp and the oil are **indeed** permitted for use, but if **[the flame] has not** yet **gone out** they are **not** permitted; וְאִיהוּ סָבַר אַף עַל גַּב דְּלֹא כָּבָה – **whereas he holds that** the lamp and the oil are permitted for use **even if [the flame] has not** yet **gone out.**[13]

The Gemara cites a segment of the Baraisa and analyzes it:

אֲבָל כּוֹס וּקְעָרָה וַעֲשָׁשִׁית לֹא יְזִיזֵם מִמְּקוֹמָם – **BUT** with respect to **A CUP, A BOWL AND A BEAKER** that were filled with oil and used as lamps, **ONE MAY NOT MOVE THEM FROM THEIR PLACE,** even after they are extinguished. מַאי שְׁנָא הָנֵי – **What is the difference** between **these** and ordinary lamps, which R' Shimon permits moving after they are extinguished?[14]

The Gemara answers

אָמַר עוּלָּא – **Ulla said:** סֵיפָא אֲתָאן לְרַבִּי יְהוּדָה – In this **last clause we have arrived** once again **at** the view of **R' Yehudah** who ruled earlier in the Baraisa that it is forbidden to move any used lamp. R' Shimon, however, permits moving even a cup, bowl and beaker, once the flame has been extinguished.[15]

Ulla's explanation is rejected:

מַתְקִיף לָהּ מַר זוּטְרָא – **Mar Zutra objected to this:** אִי הָכִי מַאי אֲבָל – **If** it is **so,** that the Baraisa does not mean to differentiate between these and ordinary lamps, **what is** the meaning of the introductory word ***But*** with which the Baraisa prefaces this clause?

Mar Zutra therefore advances another explanation:

אֶלָּא אָמַר מַר זוּטְרָא – **Rather, Mar Zutra said:** לְעוֹלָם רַבִּי שִׁמְעוֹן – **Actually,** this clause is part of the statement of **R' Shimon,** וְכִי קָשָׁרֵי רַבִּי שִׁמְעוֹן – **and when does R' Shimon permit** using the lamp and the oil once the flame has gone out? בְּנֵר זוּטָא דְּדַעְתֵּיהּ עִלָּוֵיהּ – It is **in** the case of an ordinary, **small lamp, concerning which one has intent** from the outset to use it after it has gone out, since he expects it to go out sometime during the Sabbath. אֲבָל הָנֵי דִּנְפִישֵׁי לֹא – **But** in regard to **these,** viz. oil-filled cups, bowls and beakers, **which are large** and are expected to burn until the end of the Sabbath, R' Shimon does **not** permit using them if they go out. He concedes that they are *muktzeh* since the owner abandoned hope of using them at all on the Sabbath.[16]

The Gemara challenges Mar Zutra's explanation:

וְהָתַנְיָא – **But it was taught in a Baraisa** cited above: מוֹתַר הַשֶּׁמֶן שֶׁבַּנֵּר וְשֶׁבַּקְּעָרָה אָסוּר – **THE LEFTOVER OIL IN A LAMP OR IN A BOWL IS PROHIBITED,** even after the flame goes out; וְרַבִּי שִׁמְעוֹן מַתִּיר – **BUT R' SHIMON PERMITS** it. Here, R' Shimon permits even the oil that is in a *bowl,* once the flame goes out. – ? –

The Gemara answers:

הָתָם קְעָרָה דּוּמְיָא דְּנֵר – **There,** in that Baraisa, where the bowl is mentioned together with a lamp, the reference is to **a bowl that is similar to a lamp,** i.e. a small bowl that holds little oil. הָכָא קְעָרָה דּוּמְיָא דְּכוֹס – **Here** in our Baraisa, however, where the bowl is mentioned together with a cup, the reference is to **a bowl that**

NOTES

the lamp may be moved and the oil may be used (*Rashi*). R' Shimon does not consider the lamp *muktzeh* on the basis of the prohibition that was in effect during *bein hashemashos,* and he also rejects the concept of *muktzeh by dint of repugnance.*

9. The Gemara will explain below why these are different than an ordinary lamp.

10. It would seem that the correct reading should be *R' Elazar,* as is cited by *Rabbeinu Chananel.*

11. Removing oil from a lamp that is burning brightly is a violation of the *melachah* of *extinguishing* (*Beitzah* 22a). The reason is that by removing oil one reduces the brightness of the flame, which shines brighter when it has more oil to draw from (*Tosafos* ad loc.; cf. *Rosh* ad loc.). R' Eliezer the son of R' Shimon rules, however, that once a flame is sputtering this is not a factor and one may remove some oil (*Rashi,* as explained by *Rosh Yosef;* see also *Maharam* and *Pnei Yehoshua;* cf. *Ritva MHK* ed., *Chidushei HaRan*).

This ruling is based on the additional consideration that the oil is not considered *muktzeh.* For the same reason, R' Eliezer the son of R' Shimon holds that one may take oil that is dripping from a lamp even while the lamp is burning. The Gemara goes on to clarify his view.

12. See note 8 above and 43b note 5.

13. R' Shimon, in the Baraisa cited (above, before the Mishnah), permitted only using the *leftover* oil in a lamp or bowl, i.e. only the oil remaining after the flame has been extinguished. He concedes that while the lamp is burning even the oil in the bowl is *muktzeh* [because it has been set aside for a mitzvah, and he recognizes this category of *muktzeh* (see below, 45a). However, he disputes the principle that something that is *muktzeh* during *bein hashemashos* remains *muktzeh* for the entire day, and therefore, he permits usage of the lamp and oil after the flame is extinguished] (*Rashi; Tosafos* to 42b ד״ה ואין נאותין; see *Maharsha*).

R' Eliezer, on the other hand, permits taking oil even while the flame is burning (provided one does not thereby extinguish the flame) because he does not consider it *muktzeh* at all. Thus, he rules even more leniently than his father (see *Ritva MHK* ed., *Chidushei HaRan, Maharam* and *Rosh Yosef*).

14. The Gemara understands the clause concerning a cup, bowl and beaker to be part of R' Shimon's statement.

15. Thus, the clause concerning a cup, bowl and beaker is not part of R' Shimon's statement, but a separate statement that reflects R' Yehudah's view. Apparently, it comes to teach that according to R' Yehudah even a glass vessel, which does not become repugnant through use, is *muktzeh* if a flame was burning in it at the onset of the Sabbath. I.e. it is *muktzeh by a dint of a prohibition* (see *Pnei Yehoshua* and *Rosh Yosef*).

16. R' Shimon distinguishes between a case in which one anticipated during *bein hashemashos* that the item would become available for permissible use and a case where one did not. Thus, with respect to a small lamp, since one can anticipate that the flame will go out some time during the Sabbath, the lamp is *muktzeh* only until such time as it actually goes out; beyond that point it is considered prepared for Sabbath use. But in the case of a large cup or bowl filled with oil, which might easily burn through the entire Sabbath, one does not anticipate that the flame will go out at all until after the Sabbath. Consequently, they are *muktzeh* for the entire Sabbath even if the flame happens to go out earlier (*Rashi* here and *Beitzah* 30b ד״ה אדם יושב ומצפה; see also *Ritva MHK* ed. and *Chidushei HaRan*).

Note that in the case of a small lamp, R' Shimon permits even the use of any leftover oil. Although the person could not have anticipated that there would be oil left over, his intent to use the lamp when it goes out covers any remnant oil as well. In the case of a large lamp, however, a person totally abandons hope of using it (*Ramban, Rashba*; cf. *Rashash*). [For an enlightening explanation of why Ulla understood R' Shimon's position differently, see *Afikei Yam* II:19.]

אי לא שרית ליה אתי לכבויי א"ר יהודה בן שילא א"ר אסי א"ר יוחנן [א] הלכה כר' יהודה בן לקיש במת: אין ניאותין הימנו לפי שאינו מן המוכן: תנו רבנן (א) [ב] מותר השמן שבנר ושבקערה אסור ורבי שמעון מתיר:

מתני' (ב) מטלטלין נר חדש אבל לא ישן רבי שמעון אומר כל הנרות מטלטלין חוץ מן הנר הדולק בשבת: **גמ'** (ג) ת"ר מטלטלין נר חדש אבל לא ישן דברי רבי יהודה ר"מ אומר [ג] כל הנרות מטלטלין חוץ מן הנר שהדליקו בו (ד) בשבת ר' שמעון אומר חוץ מן הנר הדולק בשבת כבתה מותר לטלטלה אבל כוס וקערה ועששית לא יזיז ממקומם ור' אליעזר בר' שמעון אומר מסתפק מן הנר הכבה ומן השמן המטפטף ואפי' בשעה שהנר דולק אמר אביי רבי אליעזר ברבי שמעון סבר לה כאבוה בחדא ופליג עליה בחדא סבר לה כאבוה בחדא דלית ליה מוקצה ופליג עליה בחדא דאילו אבוה סבר כבה אין לא כבה לא ואיהו סבר אע"ג דלא כבה אבל כוס וקערה ועששית לא יזיז ממקומם מאי שנא הני אמר עולא סיפא אתאן לר' יהודה מתקיף לה מר זוטרא אי הכי מאי אבל אלא אמר מר זוטרא לעולם רבי שמעון וכי קשרי רבי שמעון בנר זוטא דדעתיה עלויה אבל הני דנפישי לא והתניא מותר השמן שבנר ושבקערה אסור ורבי שמעון מתיר התם קערה דומיא דנר הכא קערה דומיא דכוס א"ר זירא פמוט שהדליקו בו בשבת לדברי המתיר אסור לדברי האוסר מותר למימרא דרבי יהודה מוקצה מחמת מיאוס אית ליה מוקצה מחמת איסור לית ליה והתניא (ה) ר' יהודה אומר כל הנרות של מתכת מטלטלין חוץ מן הנר שהדליקו בו (ו) בשבת אלא אי איתמר הכי איתמר א"ר זירא פמוט שהדליקו עליו בשבת ד"ה אסור לא הדליקו עליו ד"ה מותר: אמר (ז) רב יהודה א"ר מטה שיחדה למעות אסור לטלטלה מיתיבי' רב נחמן בר יצחק מטלטלין נר חדש אבל לא ישן ומה

רש"י

אי לא שרית ליה וכו'. אבל במוטל לחמה לא שרי: **מתני' מטלטלין נר חדש.** שאינו מאוס וחזי לאישתמושי (א) להדיא שלא דלק בו נר מעולם: **אבל לא ישן.** דמוקצה מחמת מיאוס הוא: **גמ' חוץ מן הנר שהדליקו.** ואף על גב שכבה אסור דאית ליה לרבי מאיר מוקצה מחמת איסור ולית ליה מוקצה מחמת מיאוס: (ח) **חוץ מן הנר הדולק בשבת.** בעוד שהוא דולק אסור שמא יכבה הנר: **עששית.** כוס גדול של זכוכית שקורין לנפ"א: **לא יזיז ממקומן.** ואפי' כבה הנר ולקמן מפרש טעמא: **מן הנר הכבה.** דכיון דכבה והולך לא מחייב תו משום מכבה: **כבה אין לא כבה לא.** דלא שמעינן ליה לרבי שמעון דשרי במתני' אלא מותר שמן שבנר ושבקערה דמשמע לאחר שכבה: **מאי אבל.** מדקאמר אבל מכלל דבנר מותר: **בזוטא.** דדעתי' עליה מבע"י סבר שיכלה השמן מהר ואשתמש בנר לכשיכבה: **אבל הני.** לא אסיק אדעתיה שיכבו כל היום: **ור' שמעון מתיר.** וקערה נפישא קשיא קערה אקערה: **דומיא דנר.** קתני לה לזוטרא: **פמוט.** מנורה של מתכת ואינה מאוסה: **לדברי המתיר.** ר' מאיר המתיר בנר ישן: **אוסר.** בהאי דמוקצה מחמת איסור כדקתני לעיל חוץ מן הנר שהדליקו בו בשבת: **לדברי האוסר.** רבי יהודה האוסר בנר ישן של חרס התם הוא דמאיס אבל הכא שרי ולית ליה מוקצה מחמת איסור: **נר של מתכת.** לא מאיס כגון של נחשת דלא בלע: **שיחדה למעות.** מיתסרא בהזמנה בעלמא ואע"פ שלא הניח עליה מעולם: **מטלטלין נר חדש.** והא רבי יהודה קאמר לה דאית ליה מוקצה אלמא לא מיתסר בהזמנה מדקאמר אבל לא ישן ולא קתני אבל לא המיוחד לכך: הניח

תוספות

רב הכא טלטול מן הצד הא תנן בפ' נוטל (לקמן קמב:) מעות שע"ג הכר מנער את הכר והן נופלות ואבן שעל פי החבית מטה על צדה וכו' ומוקי לה רב התם בשוכח אבל במניח נעשה בסיס לדבר האסור והכא (ב) (חשיב) בשוכח מדשרי שמואל וכל דבר שדעתו ליטלו בשבת ולא להניחו כל השבת ° אפילו מניח חשיב כשוכח כי ההיא דמנער את הכיסוי והם נופלות אע"פ שבמתכוין כיסה בדבר שאינו ניטל ואפי' רבנן דרבי אלעזר בן תדאי שרו בכי האי גוונא דהכא דהא שרו פגה שהטמינה בתבן וחררה שהטמינה בגחלים אם מגולה מקצתה ובמכוסה כולה פליגי דרבי אלעזר שרי אפי' מכוסה כולה דתוחב בכוש או בכרכר ואומר ר"י דיש לחלק ° דהכא עיקר הטלטול לצורך מת ולא דמי לכל הנהו שעושה עיקר הטלטול לצורך כר וחבית ולא לצורך מעות ואבן א) ולהכי לא מייתי הכא פלוגתא דר' אלעזר בן תדאי ורבנן וע"ק לר"י דאפי' בטלטול דמת שיש לאסור יותר משאר טלטול מן הצד כדפי' שרי שמואל ובסוף במה טומנין (לקמן דף נ:) אמר שמואל האי סכינא דביני אורבי דלה ושלפה והדר דלה שרי ואי לא אסיר ופירש בקונט' לקמן דאסור משום טלטול מן הצד וכן קשה דרב הונא אמר התם האי סליקוסתא דלה ושלפה והדר דלה שרי ואי לאו אסור א"כ אסר טלטול מן הצד ובסוף חולין אמרי בי רב טלטול מן הצד לא שמיה טלטול ואמרי בי רב היינו רב הונא כמו שמפרש ר"ת בספ"ק דסנהדרין (ט) (דף יח: ושם) ונראה לר"י דרב הונא ושמואל לא אסרי התם משום טלטול מן הצד אלא משום שמסיר עפר ומרחיב הגומא ואיידי דאיירי לעיל מיניה בגומא נקטה ומותיב מהטומן לפת וצנונות דסתם לפת וצנונות לאו דלה ושלפה ולהכי חשיב הש"ס תיובתא ור"ה ושמואל ° הוו ידעי לה דמתני' היא בסדר זרעים אלא דדחקי לאוקמה בדלה ושלפה והש"ס לא ניחא ליה לאוקמה הכי ועומדת בתיובתא:

(ט) **מתוך** שאדם בהול על מתו אי לא שרית לי' אתי לכבויי. ואע"ג דגבי ממון אמרינן (כ) איפכא אי שרית ליה אתי לכבויי היינו משום שאין מצטער על ממונו כמו על מתו ואי שרית ליה מתוך שיהא טרוד להציל ישכח שהיום שבת ויבא לכבות בשוגג אבל על מתו מצטער ביותר ואי לא שרית ליה אתי לכבויי במזיד:

שבנר ושבקערה אסור ור' שמעון מתיר. ואחר השבת מותר אפי' לר' יהודה וה"נ תניא לקמן גבי נויי סוכה אסור להסתפק מהן עד מוצאי י"ט האחרון אבל בתר הכי שרי וקשה לר"י דמ"ש מנר חנוכה דתניא (ל) כבה ליל ראשון מוסיף עליו בליל ב' ומדליק בו כבה ליל ח' עושה לו מדורה בפני עצמו מפני שהוקצה למצותו ואומר ר"י דנר חנוכה עיקרו לא להנאתו בא אלא לפרסומי ניסא ומשום חביבותא דנס אינו מצפה שיכבה אלא מקצה לגמרי למצוה אבל נר שבת להנאתו בא יושב ומצפה שיכבה ולכך מותר וא"ת ומ"ש נר שכבה דאסור לטלטל לר' יהודה מסוכה רעועה דעלמא דמהני בה תנאי כדאמר לקמן בשמעתין ואם התנה עליה הכל לפי תנאו ומוקי לה במסכת ביצה (דף ל:) בסוכה דעלמא ורעועה דאתמול דעתיה עלויה שתפול ונר נמי דעתיה עלויה שיכבה ואמאי אין מועיל תנאי להסתפק ממותר השמן ולר"ש נמי יועיל תנאי להסתפק מן השמן המטפטף בשעה שהנר דולק וי"ל דהתם סוכה דעלמא היתה עשויה מזמן גדול ועתה ביה"ש אינו בודל ממנה ויושב ומצפה מתי תפול אבל נר עיקר הקצאתו הוא ביה"ש ודחייה בידי' לצורך שבת ותמיר טפי ולא מהני ביה תנאי ב): **לדברי** המתיר אסור. פי' בקונטרס לדברי ר' מאיר וא"ת מאי קמ"ל הא בהדיא קאסר ר' מאיר נר שהדליקו בה באותו שבת וי"ל דה"א ה"מ בנר של חרס דאית ביה תרתי מוקצה מחמת מיאוס ומחמת איסור קמ"ל דאפי' בשל מתכת דלא מאיס ולית ביה אלא מוקצה מחמת איסור אסר ר' מאיר ואין נראה לר"ת דלפי זה הא דמסיק דברי הכל אסור לא הוי אלא ר' מאיר ור' יהודה דקאי עלייהו ולא ר"ש ומפרש וכן פר"ח לדברי המתיר היינו ר' שמעון אסר כאן בפמוט דהא פמוט גדול הוא ככוס וקערה ועששית כמו פמוטות של בית ר' דשילהי כל כתבי (לקמן קכא:) לדברי האוסר היינו ר' מאיר ור' יהודה דאסרי בנר חרס שהדליקו בו באותו שבת וה"מ בנר של חרס דאיכא תרתי מוקצה מחמת מיאוס ומחמת איסור אבל בנר מתכת שרו ומסיק דאפי' בשל מתכת אסר ר' מאיר וה"נ אמרי' בפ"ק דחולין (דף טו.) ע"כ לא שרי רבי מאיר אלא במבשל דראוי לכוס אבל בשוחט לא ג): **מטה** שיחדה למעות אסור לטלטלה. נראה דאפי' לצורך גופה או לצורך מקומה אסור דכיון שיחדה למעות שוב אין עושין ממנה שום תשמיש ° והויא כחצוצרות דאסור לטלטלה לרבי יהודה אפילו לצורך גופה ומקומה ולרבי שמעון לא אסור שום מוקצה לצורך גופו ומקומו אלא מוקצה מחמת חסרון כיס:

ומה

עין משפט נר מצוה

מח א מיי' פכ"ו מהל' שבת הלכה כא סמג לאוין סה טוש"ע או"ח סימן שיא סעיף א:

מט ב מיי' פ"ה מהל' שבת הלכה יב ופרק כו הלכה יד סמג לאוין סה טוש"ע או"ח סימן רסה סעיף ג וסימן רעט סעיף א:

נ ג מיי' פכ"ה מהלכות שבת הלכה י יא טוש"ע או"ח סימן רעט סעיף א:

רבינו חננאל

דברי ר' יהודה מטלטלין נר חדש אבל לא ישן. ר' מאיר [אומר] כל הנרות מטלטלין חוץ מן הנר שהדליקו בה באותה שבת. נמצא ר' מאיר ור' יהודה שניהן אוסרין בנר שהדליקו בו באותה שבת. ור"ש מתיר ואין הלכתא כוותיה. דהוא יחיד במקום רבים ואע"פ דא"ר יוחנן אנו אין לנו אלא בנר כר' שמעון [לר' שמעון] אמרו וליה [לר'] יוחנן לא סבירא ליה טעמא דר"ש. ואפילו ר"ש לא שרי לטלטולי בשבת בנר שכבה אלא בנר קטן דכיון דהוא נר קטן ושמנו מעט דעתו עליו מאתמול לכשיכבה יטלטלנו ואינו מוקצה. אבל נר גדול כגון כוס וקערה ועששית שיתכן שידליקו היום כולו לא אמרינן דחשיב עלייהו מאתמול לכשיכבו יטלטלם. אלא אמרינן ודאי כיון דגדולים הן נתייאשו מלטלטלן ומוקצין הן. לפיכך קתני סיפא אבל כוס וקערה ועששית לא יזיזם ממקומן וכן כיוצא בהן. פעמים שיש קערה ועששית קטנה דומיא דנר קטן ודינם כדין נר קטן ופעמים שיש נר גדול דומיא דקערה ועששית ודינו כדינם. והא דא"ר אלעזר [בר"ש] מסתפק אדם מנר הכבה ומשמן המטפטף אע"פ שהנר דולק א) א"ר זירא פמוט שהדליקו עליו לדברי המתיר בנר אסר בפמוט. כלומר לר' שמעון דמתיר בנר קטן בפמוט שהוא גדול אוסר. ולדברי ר' מאיר ור' יהודה שאוסרין בנר של חרש מפני שהוא מטונף. והוא צאו כלי. ולפיכך הוקצהו מאתמול בפמוט שהוא של מתכת ואינו מטונף מתיר: **ירושל'** נר מאוס. פמוט אינו מאוס. תני נר המונח על הדלת פותח ונועל בשבת ובלבד שלא יתכוין לכבות. רב ושמואל פותרין לה בשוכח ומקללין למאן דעבד כן [יכרת] ה' לאיש אשר יעשנה וגו'. ואקשי' ולר' יהודה מוקצה מחמת מיאוס אית ליה מוקצה מחמת איסור שהדליקו בה באותה שבת לא. והתניא ר' יהודה אומר כל הנרות של מתכת מטלטלין חוץ מן הנר שהדליקו בה באותה שבת. ואסיקנ' הכי לדברי

חשק שלמה על רבינו חננאל

א) עי' נכשב"א ונרמב"ן:

מסורת הש"ס

א) [לקמן מו: ביצה ל:], ב) חולין יד:, ג) תוספתא שבת פ"ד, ד) י"ג באותה שבת, ה) חולין טו., ו) בכ"י באותה שבת, ז) [לפמ"ש תוס' יבמות קח: ד"ה אמר וכו' מוכח דהי' גרסת' הכא רב הונא ע"ש], ח) [דבור זה שייך לעיל במשנה], ט) בתוד"ה אלא, י) שייך לעמוד הקודם, כ) [לקמן קיז:], ל) [בש"ס לא נמצא מקומו אלא בשאלתות פ' וישלח הביאו הרא"ש פרק במה מדליקין רס"ט ובטור וב"י סימן תרעז].

תוספות ישנים

א) וא"ש דהכא שרי טפי ככר או תינוק מטלטול מן הצד. ובפ' נוטל (דף קמב:) אמר לא אמרו ככר או תינוק אלא למת בלבד ואסרינן לכ"ע ע"י ככר או תינוק שאר דברים שלא במת אע"ג דשרי טלטול מן הצד למת:

ב) ורשב"א מפ' דהכא אמיר טפי לפי שהוא בסיס לדבר האסור:

ג) ורשב"א מפרש דאפילו למאי דס"ד אתי ההיא דחולין שפיר דבמוקצה מחמת איסור דהתם אפי' ר"ש מוד'. אף על גב דשרי בנתנבלה בשבת התם אינו מעלה על לבו שישחטנה שום אדם בשבת והוי כמו דיש במינו במחובר דפרש"י דבילה [דף כד:] דאפילו ר"ש אסר כגרוגרות וצימוקין מדלא לקטן מאתמול אקצינהו:

הגהות הב"ח

(א) רש"י ד"ה מטלטלין וכו' לאישתמושי ביה להדיא: (ב) תוס' ד"ה דכ"ע טלטול וכו' אבל במניח נעשה בסיס לדבר האסור והכא חשיב כשכח מדשרי שמואל דאפילו מניח דבר שדעתו ליטלו בשבת ולא להניחו כל השבת חשוב כשכח כי ההיא דמנער:

גליון הש"ס

תוס' ד"ה דכ"ע כו' **אפילו מניח חשיב כשוכח כי ההיא דמנער.** עי' לקמן דף נא ע"א תוס' ד"ה או שטמן: **בא"ד דהכא עיקר.** עי' לעיל דף לט ע"א תוס' ד"ה מפני שמזיז: **בא"ד הוו ידעי לה דמתני' היא.** עי' מנחות דף ט ע"א תוס' ד"ה חסר הלוג. ומו"ק דף ה ע"א תוס' ד"ה לאפוקי: תוס' ד"ה מטה שיחדה כו' והויא כחצוצרות. לעיל דף לו ע"א:

ליקוטי רש"י

מותר השמן שבנר ושבקערה. נר קרוויי"ל מותר השמן שנותן בנר או בקערה שמן הניתן להדלקת הנר של שבת וכבה המותר יש בה משום מוקצה ואסור. **ורבי שמעון מתיר.** אדם יושב ומצפה אימתי תכבה נרו שיודע שסופה לכבות הלכך בין השמשות דעתיה על המותר [ביצה ל:]. **נר חדש.** שלא הדליקו בו מעולם נר של חרס וכשהוא חדש חזי למרמי ביה פירי. **אבל לא ישן.** דמוקצה הוא מחמת מיאוס שהדעת קצה בו [חולין יד:]. **חוץ מן הנר שהדליקו בו בשבת.** שהיה נר דולק בו בין השמשות דמוקצה מחמת איסור שאסור לכבות הנר נאסר גם הוא לטלטל וכיון שהוקצה לבין השמשות הוקצה לכל היום [שם טו.]. **עששית.** כלי גדול של זכוכית בלעז לנטרנ"א [לעיל כג.]. **פמוט.** מנורה קטנה [מנחות כח.]. **כל הנרות של מתכת מטלטלין.** דשל מתכות לא מאיסי אפילו ישנים כגון של נחושת וכיוצא בהן [חולין שם].

רב נסים גאון

אמר ר' זירא פמוט שהדליקו עליו באותה שבת לדברי המתיר אוסר לדברי האוסר מתיר פמוט מין מנורה ויש לה קנה אחד ובמנחות בפרק הקומץ את המנחה (דף כח) כשאמרו על דרך קושיא ואימא נמי באה

is similar to a cup, i.e. a large bowl that holds a great deal of oil.[17]

In the previous Baraisa, R' Yehudah forbade moving a used lamp, thus indicating that he subscribes to the concept of *muktzeh by dint of repugnance,* whereas R' Meir says that the lamp may be moved, thus indicating that he rejects this concept.[18] The Gemara now discusses the views of R' Yehudah and R' Meir concerning *muktzeh by dint of a prohibition*:

אָמַר רַבִּי זֵירָא – R' Zeira said: פָּמוּט שֶׁהִדְלִיקוּ בּוֹ בְּשַׁבָּת – Concerning **a** metal **candlestick upon which** a flame **had been lit for the Sabbath: לְדִבְרֵי הַמַּתִּיר אָסוּר – According to the opinion of the one who permits** moving a used lamp (R' Meir), **it is forbidden** to move the metal candlestick,[19] **לְדִבְרֵי הָאוֹסֵר מוּתָּר – and according to the opinion of the one who forbids** moving a used lamp (R' Yehudah), **it is permitted** to move the metal candlestick.[20]

The Gemara questions R' Zeira's assertion:

לְמֵימְרָא דְּרַבִּי יְהוּדָה מוּקְצֶה מֵחֲמַת מִיאוּס אִית לֵיהּ – Does this mean **to say that R' Yehudah accepts** the concept of ***muktzeh by dint of repugnance*** **מוּקְצֶה מֵחֲמַת אִיסוּר לֵית לֵיהּ** – but **does not accept** the concept of ***muktzeh by dint of a prohibition?*** **וְהָתַנְיָא – But it was taught in a Baraisa: רַבִּי יְהוּדָה אוֹמֵר – R' YEHUDAH SAYS: כָּל הַנֵּרוֹת שֶׁל מַתֶּכֶת מְטַלְטְלִין – ALL METAL LAMPS MAY BE MOVED** on the Sabbath,[21] **חוּץ מִן הַנֵּר שֶׁהִדְלִיקוּ בּוֹ בְּשַׁבָּת – EXCEPT FOR A LAMP IN WHICH** a flame **HAD BEEN LIT FOR THE SABBATH.** Thus, R' Yehudah accepts *muktzeh by dint of a prohibition.* – ? –

Conceding the point, the Gemara revises its account of R' Zeira's teaching:

אֶלָּא אִי אִיתְּמַר הָכִי אִיתְּמַר – Rather, if anything was stated by R' Zeira, **this is what was stated: אָמַר רַבִּי זֵירָא – R' Zeira said: פָּמוּט שֶׁהִדְלִיקוּ עָלָיו בְּשַׁבָּת** – Concerning **a** metal **candlestick upon which** a flame **had been lit for the Sabbath, דִּבְרֵי הַכֹּל אָסוּר – all** (i.e. R' Meir and R' Yehudah) **agree** that **it is forbidden** to move it even after the flame goes out. **לֹא הִדְלִיקוּ עָלָיו** – But if a flame **had not been lit upon it** for the Sabbath, **דִּבְרֵי הַכֹּל מוּתָּר – all agree** that **it is permitted** to move it, even if it is a used candlestick.[22]

The Gemara introduces a new ruling:

אָמַר רַב יְהוּדָה אָמַר רַב – Rav Yehudah said in the name of Rav: מִטָּה שֶׁיִּחֲדָהּ לְמָעוֹת אָסוּר לְטַלְטְלָהּ – A bed that someone verbally **designated** to be used **for** the storage of **money may not be moved** on the Sabbath.[23]

Rav Yehudah's ruling is challenged:

מֵיתִיבֵיהּ רַב נַחְמָן בַּר יִצְחָק – Rav Nachman bar Yitzchak challenged this on the basis of our Mishnah, which states: **מְטַלְטְלִין נֵר חָדָשׁ אֲבָל לֹא יָשָׁן – WE MAY MOVE A NEW LAMP, BUT NOT AN OLD ONE.** This implies that only an old lamp that has actually been used is *muktzeh*, but a lamp that has never been used is not *muktzeh* even though it has been designated for use.[24] Accordingly, the following argument may be made:

NOTES

17. A large bowl remains *muktzeh* even if the flame should unexpectedly go out, but a small bowl is not *muktzeh*, according to R' Shimon, and may be moved when the flame goes out.

18. See notes 6 and 7 above.

19. Since at the onset of the Sabbath the candlestick contained a burning flame, it is *muktzeh by dint of a prohibition* (as explained in note 7), and R' Meir holds that it may therefore not be moved. Thus, although R' Meir rejects the category of *muktzeh by dint of repugnance,* he recognizes the category of *muktzeh by dint of a prohibition.* This accords with R' Meir's explicit statement in the Baraisa that it is permitted to move any lamp except one that had been lit for the Sabbath (*Rashi*). For a discussion of why R' Zeira found it necessary to make this point, see *Tosafos.* Cf. *Rabbeinu Tam* cited by *Tosafos, Ramban* et al.

20. In contrast to earthenware lamps, metal candlesticks do not become foul with use [even when oil is burned in them]. Thus, they are never *muktzeh* by dint of repugnance. R' Zeira informs us that even if the candlestick supported a burning flame at the onset of the Sabbath, R' Yehudah permits handling it after the flame goes out because he does not subscribe to the concept of *muktzeh by dint of a prohibition.* Thus, R' Yehudah's position is exactly the reverse of R' Meir's – he accepts *muktzeh by dint of repugnance* but rejects *muktzeh by dint of a prohibition* (*Rashi*).

21. I.e. even used ones. The Baraisa is dealing with lamps made of non-absorbent metals, such as copper, which do not become repugnant with use (*Rashi*; see *Rashash*). [Lamps made of other metals, however, are not like metal candlesticks, but are like earthenware lamps, and become repugnant with use (*Rosh Yosef*).]

22. R' Yehudah and R' Meir agree that if it had been lit at the onset of the Sabbath it is *muktzeh by dint of a prohibition,* for both of them recognize this category of *muktzeh.* They also agree that if it had not been lit it is not *muktzeh.* Even R' Yehudah, who subscribes to the category of *muktzeh by dint of repugnance,* concedes that the candlestick is not *muktzeh* since a used metal candlestick is not repugnant.

23. Once designated for the storage of money, which is intrinsically *muktzeh,* the bed no longer serves a permissible function. Even if money was never placed on the bed, the mere verbal designation for that purpose causes it to be considered *muktzeh*. This follows the opinion of R' Yehudah, who applies *muktzeh* broadly (*Rashi*).

[*Rashi* (to 44b ד״ה הניח עליה מעות, see also *Rashi* to 35b ד״ה חצוצרות and to 45b ד״ה אלא לתרנגולין, and *Pnei Yehoshua* to 45b; cf. *Keren Orah*) implies that the bed is merely like a utensil that is used primarily for a prohibited function (כְּלִי שֶׁמְּלַאכְתּוֹ לְאִיסּוּר) which may be moved in limited circumstances (see also *Beis Yosef* and *Rama, Orach Chaim* 310:7). However, this explanation is rejected by *Tosafos* (here ד״ה מטה, 35b ד״ה והתניא and 36a ד״ה הוא ר׳ יהודה), who state that since the bed is designated *exclusively* for the storage of money it is completely *muktzeh* (see also *Magen Avraham* 310:5, *Mishnah Berurah* 310:25,27 and above, 36a note 4).]

24. The Mishnah does not say, "But not one that has been designated for use." It says, "But not an *old* one." Since the Mishnah reflects R' Yehudah's opinion (see note 6), we learn from it that the mere designation for the *muktzeh* function does not make a lamp *muktzeh* (*Rashi;* cf. *Tosafos*, 44b ד״ה ומה נר, *Ramban* et al.).

אי לא שרית ליה אתי לכבויי א"ר יהודה בן שילא א"ר אסי א"ר יוחנן א הלכה כר' יהודה בן לקיש במת: אין ניאותין הימנו לפי שאינו מן המוכן: תנו רבנן א) ב מותר השמן שבנר ושבקערה אסור ורבי שמעון מתיר:

מתני' ב) מטלטלין נר חדש אבל לא ישן רבי שמעון אומר כל הנרות מטלטלין חוץ מן הנר הדולק בשבת:

גמ' ג) ת"ר מטלטלין נר חדש אבל לא ישן דברי רבי יהודה ר"מ אומר ג כל הנרות מטלטלין חוץ מן הנר שהדליקו בו ד) בשבת ר' שמעון אומר חוץ מן הנר הדולק בשבת כבתה מותר לטלטלה אבל כוס וקערה ועששית לא יזיזם ממקומם ור' אליעזר בר' שמעון אומר מסתפק מן הנר הכבה ומן השמן המטפטף ואפי' בשעה שהנר דולק אמר אביי רבי אליעזר ברבי שמעון סבר לה כאבוה בחדא ופליג עליה בחדא סבר לה כאבוה בחדא דלית ליה מוקצה ופליג עליה בחדא דאילו אבוה סבר כבה אין לא כבה לא ואיהו סבר אע"ג דלא כבה אבל כוס וקערה ועששית לא יזיזם ממקומם מאי שנא הני אמר עולא סיפא אתאן לר' יהודה מתקיף לה מר זוטרא אי הכי מאי אבל אלא אמר מר זוטרא לעולם רבי שמעון וכי קשרי רבי שמעון בנר זוטא דדעתיה עלויה אבל הני דנפישי לא והתניא מותר השמן שבנר ושבקערה אסור ורבי שמעון מתיר התם קערה דומיא דנר הכא קערה דומיא דכוס א"ר זירא פמוט שהדליקו בו בשבת לדברי המתיר אסור לדברי האוסר מותר למימרא דרבי יהודה מוקצה מחמת מיאוס אית ליה מוקצה מחמת איסור לית ליה והתניא ה) ר' יהודה אומר כל הנרות של מתכת מטלטלין חוץ מן הנר שהדליקו בו ו) בשבת אלא אי איתמר הכי איתמר א"ר זירא פמוט שהדליקו עליו בשבת ד"ה אסור לא הדליקו עליו ד"ה מותר: אמר ז) רב יהודה א"ר מטה שיחדה למעות אסור לטלטלה מיתיבי' רב נחמן בר יצחק מטלטלין נר חדש אבל לא ישן ומה

רש"י

אי לא שרית ליה וכו'. אבל במוטל לחמה לא שרי: **מתני' מטלטלין נר חדש.** שאינו מאוס וחזי לאישתמושי (א) להדיא שלא דלק בו נר מעולם: **אבל לא ישן.** דמוקצה מחמת מיאוס הוא: **גמ' חוץ מן הנר שהדליקו.** ואף על גב שכבה אסור דאית ליה לרבי מאיר מוקצה מחמת איסור ולית ליה מוקצה מחמת מיאוס: ח) **חוץ מן הנר הדולק בשבת.** בעוד שהוא דולק אסור שמא יכבה הנר: **עששית.** כוס גדול של זכוכית שקורין לנפ"א: **לא יזיזם ממקומן.** ואפי' כבה הנר ולקמן מפרש טעמא: **מן הנר הכבה.** דכיון דכבה והולך לא מחייב תו משום מכבה: **כבה אין לא כבה לא.** דלא שמעינן ליה לרבי שמעון דשרי במתני' אלא מותר שמן שבנר ושבקערה דמשמע לאחר שכבה: **מאי אבל.** מדקאמר אבל מכלל דבנר מותר: **בזוטא.** דדעתי' עליה מבע"י סבר שיכלה השמן מהר ואשתמש בנר לכשיכבה: **אבל הני.** לא אסיק אדעתיה שיכבו כל היום: **ור' שמעון מתיר.** וקערה נפישא קשיא קערה אקערה: **דומיא דנר.** קתני לה דזוטרא: **פמוט.** מנורה של מתכת ואינה מאוסה: **לדברי המתיר.** ר' מאיר המתיר בנר ישן: **אוסר.** בהאי דמוקצה מחמת איסור כדקתני לעיל חוץ מן הנר שהדליקו בו בשבת: **לדברי האוסר.** רבי יהודה האוסר בנר ישן של חרס התם הוא דמאיס אבל הכא שרי ולית ליה מוקצה מחמת איסור: **נר של מתכת.** לא מאיס כגון של נחשת דלא בלע: **שיחדה למעות.** מיתסרא בהזמנה בעלמא ואע"פ שלא הניח עליה מעולם: **מטלטלין נר חדש.** והא רבי יהודה קאמר לה דאית ליה מוקצה אלמא לא מיתסר בהזמנה מדקאמר אבל לא ישן ולא קתני אבל לא המיוחד לכך:

הניח

תוספות

רב הכא טלטול מן הצד הא תנן בפ' נוטל (לקמן קמב:) מעות שע"ג הכר מנער את הכר והן נופלות ואבן שעל פי החבית מטה על צדה וכו' ומוקי לה רב התם בשוכח אבל במניח נעשה בסיס לדבר האסור והכא (ג) (חשיב) בשוכח מדשרי שמואל וכל דבר שדעתו ליטלו בשבת ולא להניחו כל השבת • אפילו מניח חשיב כשוכח כי ההיא דמנער את הכיסוי והם נופלות אע"פ שבמתכוין כיסה בדבר שאינו ניטל ואפי' רבנן דרבי אלעזר בן תדאי שרו בכי האי גוונא דהכא דהא שרו פגה שהטמינה בתבן וחררה שהטמינה בגחלים אם מגולה מקצתה ובמכוסה כולה פליגי דרבי אלעזר שרי אפי' מכוסה כולה דתוחב בכוש או בכרכר ואומר ר"י דיש לחלק • דהכא עיקר הטלטול לצורך מת ולא דמי לכל הנהו שעושה עיקר הטלטול לצורך כר וחבית ולא לצורך מעות ואבן א) ולהכי לא מייתי הכא פלוגתא דר' אלעזר בן תדאי ורבנן וע"ק לר"י דאפי' בטלטול דמת שיש לאסור יותר משאר טלטול מן הצד כדפי' שרי שמואל ובסוף במה טומנין (לקמן דף נ:) אמר שמואל האי סכינא דביני אורבי דלה ושלפה והדר דלה שרי ואי לא אסיר ופירש בקונט' לקמן דאסור משום טלטול מן הצד וכן קשה דרב הונא אמר התם האי סליקוסתא דלה ושלפה והדר דלה שרי ואי לאו אסור א"כ אסר טלטול מן הצד ובסוף חולין אמרי בי רב טלטול מן הצד לא שמיה טלטול ואמרי בי רב היינו רב הונא כמו שמפרש ר"ת בספ"ק דסנהדרין ט) (דף יז: ושם) ונראה לר"י דרב הונא ושמואל לא אסרי התם משום טלטול מן הצד אלא משום שמסיר עפר ומרחיב הגומא ואיידי דאיירי לעיל מיניה בגומא נקטה ומותיב מהטומן לפת וצנונות דסתם לפת וצנונות לאו דלה ושלפה ולהכי חשיב הש"ס תיובתא ור"ה ושמואל • הוו ידעי לה דמתני' היא בסדר זרעים אלא דדחקי לאוקמה בדלה ושלפה והש"ס לא ניחא ליה לאוקמה הכי ועומדת בתיובתא:

י) **מתוך** שאדם בהול על מתו אי לא שרית לי' אתי לכבויי. ואע"ג דגבי ממון אמרינן י) איפכא אי שרית ליה אתי לכבויי היינו משום שאין מצטער על ממונו כמו על מתו ואי שרית ליה מתוך שיהא טרוד להציל ישכח שהיום שבת ויבא לכבות בשוגג אבל על מתו מצטער ביותר ואי לא שרית ליה אתי לכבויי במזיד:

שבנר ושבקערה אסור ור' שמעון מתיר. ואחר השבת מותר אפי' לר' יהודה וה"נ תניא לקמן גבי נוי סוכה אסור להסתפק מהן עד מוצאי י"ט האחרון אבל בתר הכי שרי וקשה לר"י דמ"ש מנר חנוכה דתניא כ) כבה ליל ראשון מוסיף עליו בליל ב' ומדליק בו כבה ליל ח' עושה לו מדורה בפני עצמו מפני שהוקצה למצותו ואומר ר"י דנר חנוכה עיקרו לא להנאתו בא אלא לפרסומי ניסא ומשום חביבותא דנס אינו מצפה שיכבה אלא מקצה לגמרי למצוה אבל נר שבת להנאתו בא יושב ומצפה שיכבה ולכך מותר וא"ת ומ"ש נר שכבה דאסור לטלטל לר' יהודה מסוכה רעועה דעלמא דמהני בה תנאי כדאמר לקמן בשמעתין ואם התנה עליה הכל לפי תנאו ומוקי לה במסכת ביצה (דף ל:) בסוכה דעלמא ורעועה דאתמול דעתיה עלויה שתפול ונר נמי דעתיה עלויה שיכבה ואמאי אין מועיל תנאי להסתפק ממותר השמן ולר"ש נמי יועיל תנאי להסתפק מן השמן המטפטף בשעה שהנר דולק וי"ל דהתם סוכה דעלמא היתה עשויה מזמן גדול ועתה ביה"ש אינו בודל ממנה ויושב ומצפה מתי תפול אבל נר עיקר הקצאתו הוא ביה"ש ודחייה בידי' לצורך שבת וחמיר טפי ולא מהני ביה תנאי ב): **לדברי** המתיר אסור. פי' בקונטרס לדברי ר' מאיר וא"ת מאי קמ"ל הא בהדיא קאסר ר' מאיר נר שהדליקו בה באותו שבת וי"ל דה"א ה"מ בנר של חרס דאית ביה תרתי מוקצה מחמת מיאוס ומחמת איסור קמ"ל דאפי' בשל מתכת דלא מאיס ולית ביה אלא מוקצה מחמת איסור אסר ר' מאיר ואין נראה לר"ת דלפי זה הא דמסיק דברי הכל אסור לא הוי אלא ר' מאיר ור' יהודה דקאי עלייהו ולא ר"ש ומפרש וכן פר"ח לדברי המתיר היינו ר' שמעון אסר כאן בפמוט דהא פמוט גדול הוא ככוס וקערה ועששית כמו פמוטות של בית ר' דשילהי כל כתבי (לקמן קכא:) לדברי האוסר היינו ר' מאיר ור' יהודה דאסרי בנר חרס שהדליקו בו באותו שבת וה"מ בנר של חרס דאיכא תרתי מוקצה מחמת מיאוס ומחמת איסור אבל בנר מתכת שרו ומסיק דאפי' בשל מתכת אסר ר' מאיר וה"נ אמרי' בפ"ק דחולין (דף טו.) ע"כ לא שרי רבי מאיר אלא במבשל דראוי לכוס אבל בשוחט לא ג): **מטה** שיחדה למעות אסור לטלטלה. נראה דאפי' לצורך גופה או לצורך מקומה אסור דכיון שיחדה למעות שוב אין עושין ממנה שום תשמיש • והויא כחצוצרות דאסור לטלטלה לרבי יהודה אפילו לצורך גופה ומקומה ולרבי שמעון לא אסור שום מוקצה לצורך גופו ומקומו אלא מוקצה מחמת חסרון כיס:

ומה

עין משפט נר מצוה

מח א מיי' פכ"ו מהל' שבת הלכה כא סמג לאוין סה טוש"ע או"ח סימן שיא סעיף א:

מט ב מיי' פ"ה מהל' שבת הלכה יג ופרק כו הלכה יד סמג לאוין סה טוש"ע או"ח סימן רסה סעיף ג וסימן רעט סעיף א:

נ ג מיי' פכ"ה מהלכות שבת הלכה י יא טוש"ע או"ח סימן רעט סעיף א:

רבינו חננאל

דברי ר' יהודה מטלטלין נר חדש אבל לא ישן. ר' מאיר [אומר] כל הנרות מטלטלין חוץ מן הנר שהדליקו בה באותה שבת. נמצא ר' מאיר ור' יהודה שניהן אוסרין בנר שהדליקו בו באותה שבת. ור"ש מתיר ואין הלכתא כוותיה. דהוא יחיד במקום רבים ואע"פ דא"ר יוחנן אנו אין לנו אלא בנר כר' שמעון [לר' שמעון] אמרו וליה [לר'] יוחנן לא סבירא ליה טעמא דר"ש. ואפילו ר"ש לא שרי לטלטולי בשבת בנר שכבה אלא בנר קטן דכיון דהוא נר קטן ושמנו מעט דעתו עליו מאתמול לכשיכבה יטלטלנו ואינו מוקצה. אבל נר גדול כגון כוס וקערה ועששית שיתכן שידליקו היום כולו לא אמרינן דחשיב עלייהו מאתמול לכשיכבו יטלטלם. אלא אמרינן ודאי כיון דגדולים הן נתייאשו מלטלטלן ומוקצין הן. לפיכך קתני סיפא אבל כוס וקערה ועששית לא יזיזם ממקומן וכן כיוצא בהן. פעמים שיש קערה ועששית קטנה דומיא דנר קטן ודינם כדין נר קטן ופעמים שיש נר גדול דומיא דקערה ועששית ודינו כדינם. והא דא"ר אלעזר [בר"ש] מסתפק אדם מנר הכבה ומשמן המטפטף אע"פ שהנר דולק א) א"ר זירא פמוט שהדליקו עליו לדברי המתיר בנר אסר בפמוט. כלומר לר' שמעון דמתיר בנר קטן בפמוט שהוא גדול אוסר. ולדברי ר' מאיר ור' יהודה שאוסרין בנר של חרש מפני שהוא מטונף. והוא צאו כלי. ולפיכך הוקצהו מאתמול בפמוט שהוא של מתכת ואינו מטונף מתיר: ירושל' נר מאוס. פמוט אינו מאוס. תני נר המונח על הדלת פותח ונועל בשבת ובלבד שלא יתכוין לכבות. רב ושמואל פותרין לה בשוכח ומקללין למאן דעבד כן [יכרת] ה' לאיש אשר יעשנה וגו'. ואקשי' ולר' יהודה מוקצה מחמת מיאוס אית ליה מוקצה מחמת איסור שהדליקו בה באותה שבת לא. והתניא ר' יהודה אומר כל הנרות של מתכת מטלטלין חוץ מן הנר שהדליקו בה באותה שבת. ואסיקנ' הכי לדברי

חשק שלמה על רבינו חננאל

א) עי' ברשב"א וברמב"ן:

מסורת הש"ס

א) [לקמן מו: ביצה ל:], ב) חולין יד:, ג) תוספתא שבת פ"ד, ד) י"ג באותה שבת, ה) חולין טו., ו) נכ"י באותה שבת, ז) [לקמן מו: תוס' יבמות קמ: ד"ה אמר וכו' מוכח דהי' גרסא' הכא רב הונא ע"ש], ח) [דבור זה שייך לעיל במשנה], ט) כתו' ד"ה אלא, י) שייך לעמוד הקודם, כ) [לקמן קח:], ל) [בס"א לא נמצא מקומו אלא בשאלתות פ' ויצלח הביאו הרא"ש פרק במה מדליקין רס"ט ובטור וב"י סימן תרעז].

תוספות ישנים

א) וא"ת דהכא שרי טפי ככר או תינוק מטלטול מן הצד. ובפ' נוטל (דף קמב:) אמר לא אמרו ככר או תינוק אלא למת בלבד ואפרינן לכ"ע ע"י ככר או תינוק שאר דברים שלא במת אע"ג דשרי טלטול מן הצד למת: ב) ורשב"א מפ' דהכא אמיר טפי לפי שהוא בסיס לדבר האסור: ג) ורשב"א מפרש דאפילו למאי דס"ד אמי הסיא דחולין שפיר דבמוקצה מחמת איסור הכא אפי' ר"ש מודה. אף על גב דשרי בנכנלה בשבת התם אינו מעלה על לבו שיתכבה שום אדם בשבת והוי כמו דיש במינו כמוכבר דפרש"י דבילה [דף כד:] דאפילו ר"ש אסר כגרוגרות וצימוקין מדלא לקמן מאתמול אקלינהו:

הגהות הב"ח

(א) רש"י ד"ה מטלטלין וכו' לאישתמושי ביה להדיא: (ב) תוס' ד"ה דכ"ע טלטול וכו' אבל במניח נעשה בסיס לדבר האסור והכא חשיב כשכח מדשרי שמואל דאפילו מניח כל דבר שדעתו ליטלו בשבת ולא להניחו כל השבת חשוב כשכח כי הסיא דמנער:

גליון הש"ס

תוס' ד"ה דכ"ע כו' אפילו מניח חשיב כשוכח כי ההיא דמנער. עי' לקמן דף נא ע"א תוס' ד"ה או שמן: באד"ה דהכא עיקר. עי' לעיל דף לט ע"א תוס' ד"ה מפני שמזיז: באד"ה הוו ידעי לה דמתני' היא. עי' מנחות דף ט ע"א תוס' ד"ה אסר הלוג. ומו"ק דף ה ע"א תוס' ד"ה לאפוקי: תוס' ד"ה מטה שיחדה כו' והויא כחצוצרות. לעיל דף לו ע"א:

ליקוטי רש"י

מותר השמן שבנר ושבקערה. נר קרויזי"ל מותר השמן שנותן בנר או בקערה שמן הכינו להדלקת הנר של שבת וכבה המותר יש בה משום מוקצה ואסור. **ורבי שמעון מתיר.** אדם יושב ומצפה אימתי תכבה נרו שיודע שסופה לכבות הלכך בין השמשות דעתיה על המותר [ביצה ל:]. **נר חדש.** שלא הדליקו בו מעולם נר של חרס וכשהוא חדש חזי למרמי ביה פירי. **אבל לא ישן.** דמוקצה הוא מחמת מיאוס שהדעת קצה בו [חולין יד:]. **חוץ מן הנר שהדליקו בו בשבת.** שהיה נר דולק בו בין השמשות דמוקצה מחמת איסור שאסור לכבות הנר נאסר גם הוא לטלטל וכיון שהוקצה לבין השמשות הוקצה לכל היום [שם טו.]. **עששית.** כלי גדול של זכוכית בלעז לנטרנ"א [לעיל כג.]. **פמוט.** מנורה קטנה [מנחות כח.]. **כל הנרות של מתכת מטלטלין.** דשל מתכות לא מאיסי אפילו ישנים כגון של נחושת וכיוצא בהן [חולין שם].

רב נסים גאון

אמר ר' זירא פמוט שהדליקו עליו באותה שבת לדברי המתיר אוסר לדברי האוסר מתיר פמוט מין מנורה ויש לה קנה אחד ובמנחות בפרק הקומץ את המנחה (דף כח) כשאמרו על דרך קושיא ואימא נמי באה

ומה נר דלהכי עבידא כי לא הדליק בה שרי לטלטולה מטה דלאו להכי עבידא לא כ"ש אלא אי איתמר הכי איתמר אמר רב יהודה אמר רב [א]מטה שיחדה למעות הניח עליה מעות אסור לטלטלה לא הניח עליה מעות מותר לטלטלה לא יחדה למעות יש עליה מעות אסור לטלטלה אין עליה מעות מותר לטלטלה והוא שלא היו עליה בין השמשות אמר עולא מתיב ר' [א]אליעזר [ג]מוכני שלה ◦ בזמן שהיא נשמטת אין חיבור לה ואין נמדדת עמה ואין מצלת עמה באהל המת ואין גוררין אותה בשבת בזמן שיש עליה מעות הא אין עליה מעות שריא אף על גב דהוו עליה ביה"ש ההיא ר' שמעון היא דלית ליה מוקצה ורב כרבי יהודה סבירא ליה

הכי

הניח עליה מעות. אפילו בחול הרי הוקצה לאיסור ואסור לטלטלה ואפילו נסתלקו המעות מבעוד יום ולא דמי לנר של מתכת דשרי רבי יהודה דהתם בלא יחדו: לא יחדה למעות. אין עליה מעות בשבת: מותר לטלטלה. ואע"ג דהניח עליה מעות בחול: והוא. שנסתלקו מבעוד יום שלא היו עליה כל בין השמשות אבל היו עליה כל בין השמשות איתקצי לכולי יומא: מוכני שלה. גבי שידה תנן במסכת כלים והיא עגלה של עץ מוקפת מחילות למרכב אנשים ונשים. מוכני אופן: בזמן שהיא נשמטת. כעין אופני עגלה שלנו שאדם יכול לסלקו מן העגלה: אינו חיבור לה. דחשובה היא כלי לעצמה דאי שידה בת קבולי טומאה היא כגון שאינה מחזקת מ' סאה בלח ונטמאה השידה לא נטמא המוכני ואי לאו בת קבולי טומאה היא ונגעה טומאה במוכני המוכני טמאה לעצמה דלא חשיבה משידה והיא מטלטלה מלאה וריקנית דיש לה בית קיבול: ואינה נמדדת עמה. לענין טומאה כדפרישית דכלי עץ המחזיק מ' סאה בלח שהן כוריים ביבש טהור כדאמרי' בבמה מדליקין (דף לה.) דכלי עץ איתקש לשק שיהא מיטלטל מלא וריקן וזו אינו מיטלטל מלא ותנן במסכת כלים [ג] ומייתינן בגמ' דמנחות [ז] השידה ב"ה אומרים נמדדת מבחוץ דרואין אותה כאילו היא עומדת בתוך כלי גדול ואם מחזיק אותו כלי מ' סאה טהורה השידה ואע"פ שהיא אינה מחזקת מ' סאה דקסבר אף עוביה נמדד עמה והמוכני אינו נמדד עמה להשלים דרואין כאילו ניטל המוכני ואח"כ תנתן השידה לתוך הכלי: ואינה מצלת עמה באהל המת. דאם השידה מחזקת מ' [סאה] דאינה מקבלת טומאה מצלת באהל המת והוי אהל לעצמה ולא שנכנסה לבית שהמת בו דא"כ אין כאן הצלה שהרי הגג מאהיל על הטהרות מלמעלה אלא כגון שנכנסה לבית הקברות כדאמרינן בעירובין [ח] ר' יהודה אומר אף בבה"ק מפני שיכול לחוץ בשידה תיבה ומגדל בפ' בכל מערבין [ט] דקסבר אהל זרוק כלומר אהל המיטלטל שמיה אהל ומפסיק (א) כלפי הטומאה והמוכני אם הוא גבוה מדופני השידה וכלים [בולטים] מלמעלה מדופני השידה וגובה המוכני מגין עליהם אינו מצילן דמוכני כלי הוא לעצמו ומקבל טומאה ואינו חוצץ בפני הטומאה ורבותי דוחקין ומפרשין אותה באהל המת ממש ובשל חרס המוקפת צמיד פתיל והרבה תשובות יש חדא דנמדדת לא שייך בשל חרס דלא איתקש לשק ובין מיטלטל ובין אינו מיטלטל טמא ועוד אם המוכני מוקף צמיד פתיל יציל בפני עצמו כלים שבתוכו ועוד בפירוש נשנית במסכת כלים בהלכות כלי עץ והלכות כלי חרס נשנו לבדן והלכות כלי עץ נשנו לבדן: ההיא ר' שמעון היא. ומיהו מעות לא חזו מידי ומודה רבי שמעון דעודן עליו אסור:

מניחין

ומה נר דלהכי עבידא כו'. פי' בקונטרס דדייק מדקתני אבל לא ישן משמע דוקא ישן אבל חדש אפילו יחדו וקשה לר"י דלמאי דמסיק נמי מטה שיחדה והניח עליה מעות כו' תקשה ליה מנר של מתכת דשרי ר' יהודה אפילו יחדו לעיל מדקתני חוץ מן הנר שהדליקו בה באותה שבת אבל לא הדליקו בה באותה שבת אע"פ שיחדה והדליקו בה בחול שרי ונראה לר"י דלא דייק כלל מדקתני אבל לא ישן אלא דוקא בנר של חרס הוא דקאמ' דלהכי עבידא שתחלת עשייתה היא להדלקה והוי כמו יחוד שמיד שמדליקין בה פעם אחת נמאסת ואין ראויה לתשמיש אחר ולכך תחלת עשייתה אינה אלא להדלקה אע"פ שראויה לתשמיש אחר בין עשייה להדלקה מ"מ אין עושין אותה לכך שאין זה אלא זמן מועט אבל בנר מתכת אין עשייתה להדלקה לבד דראויה כל שעה לתשמיש אחר: לא הניח עליה מעות מותר לטלטלה. ואצוצרות דאסר ר' יהודה לעיל (דף לו.) נראה לר"י דאסר אפי' לא תקע בה דחצוצרות לא חזיא אלא לתקיעה ואין לחלק בין תקע ללא תקע אבל מטה ונר חזי לתשמיש אחרינא: יש עליה מעות אסור לטלטלה. ע"כ במניח איירי א) דבשבת תנן פרק נוטל (לקמן קמב:) מנער הכר והן נופלות ובמניח בשבת איירי דבהניח מבעוד יום והיו עליה בין השמשות אפילו אין עליה מעות אסור לטלטלה כדקאמר בסיפא דמילתיה וקשה דאיך יכול להיות שמניח לדעת בשבת וי"ל כגון שהניח נכרי או תינוק לדעת ישראל וא"ת אמאי לא מוכח מהכא בפ' אין לדין (ביצה כו:) דאין מוקצה לחצי שבת וי"ל דאיכא לאוקמא כגון שהניחם לדעת ישראל כדי להסירם אחר שעה והוו כגמרו בידי אדם ולמאי דפרישית לעיל דהא דיש מוקצה לחצי שבת היינו באיסור אכילה ולא בטלטול א"ש: מוכני שלה. פי' בקונטרס דגבי שידה תנן לה במסכת כלים (פי"ח מ"א) והיא עשויה למרכבת אנשים ונשים ב) ואין נראה לר"י דאי חזיא למדרס לא שייך בה מדידה דלא איתקש לשק ולא בעינן מיטלטל מלא וריקן כדמוכח בפרק אלו מומין (בכורות לח. ושם) דפריך ושאין לו תוך בכלי שטף מקבל טומאה הוא והא דומיא דשק בעינן ומשני בהנך דחזו למדרסות לכך נראה דאינה עשויה אלא לכלים והא דאמר לקמן בפרק רבי עקיבא (דף פד. ושם) שלש תיבות הן תיבה שפתחה מלדה טמאה מדרס מלמעלה טמאה מת פי' אבל מדרס לא לפי שאומרים עמוד ונעשה מלאכתנו והבאה במדה טהורה מכלום פי' שיש לה מ' סאה אור"י דצריך לומר דלא קאי אפתחה מלדה דכיון דחזיא למדרס אפילו באה במדה טמאה כדפי'[ז]: ואין מצלת עמה באהל המת. פי' בקונט' בבית הקברות (ב) שהכלים על דופני השידה וקשה דמי יביא טומא' על הכלים ומפרש ריב"א דמיירי שפיר דקיימא השידה באהל המת ומוקפת צמיד פתיל ואע"ג דכלי עץ אינו מציל בצמיד פתיל היכא דמקבל ארבעים סאה מציל כיון דלא מקבל טומאה כדתנן במסכת כלים ואלו מצילין בצמיד פתיל כלי גללים כו' וכלי עץ הטהורים ואין צ"ל דמוכני יש לו בית קיבול אלא פשוטי כלי עץ הוא ויש נקב בשידה בגלה והכלים בתוך השידה והמוכני חופפת שם וממעטת אותו נקב עד שאין נשאר פותח טפח וקאמר כיון דנשמטת אינו ממעט דדוקא כי מבטלו שם ממעט בחלון כדמוכח בלא יחפור (ב"ב כ: ושם) דפריך אהא דקתני דכלי חרס ממעט בחלון הא קחזי ליה פי' ולא מבטל התם והיכי ממעט ומשני דמטונף ומיירי שאינו סותם כל הנקב דאם סותם כל הנקב אפי' אינו מבטלו שם סותם כדאמר בפ' בתרא (דף קנז.) בימי אבא שאול בן בטנית פקקו את המאור בטפיח והתם לא בטלוהו שאם ביטלוהו בשבת היה חייב משום בונה דהא מוסיפים על הבנין אלא ודאי בלא ביטול איירי ואפ"ה סותם ובכלי עץ אמרינן נמי בפ' בתרא דמגילה (דף כו:) ההיא בי כנישתא דרומאי דהות פתיחה להההוא אדרונא דהוו מחתי בה מיתי בעו כהני למיזל לצלויי התם אמרו ליה לרבא אמר להו זילו דלו תיבותא ואותבוהו אבבא דה"ל כלי עץ העשוי לנחת ומסתמא לא היו מבטלין אותו שם שהרי ס"ת מניחין בתוכו ומיהו תבן וגרוגרות אין להם דין כלים דאפי' סותמין כל החלון צריכין ביטול כדמוכח בפרק לא יחפור (ב"ב יט:) ולר"ת אין נראה לפרש דמוכני הוי אופן דאין דרך להניח מעות על האופן דקתני ואין גוררין אותה בשבת בזמן שיש עליה מעות ומפרש דמוכני היינו כן של שידה כמו את הכיור ואת כנו (שמות ל) וכמו מכונות במלכים (א ז) פי' בסים שהשידה מונחת עליו ויש בשידה נקב מתחתיה כנגד המוכני והיא בבה"ק והטומאה נכנסת דרך נקב בשידה ואין המוכני מצלת כיון שהיא נשמטת ואין מבטלין אותה שם ומיירי נמי שאין סותמת כל הנקב אלא ממעטת אותו מפותח טפח כדפי' לעיל וצ"ל דמיירי שאין הטומאה כנגד הנקב דכשהטומאה נגד הנקב אפילו אין בו פותח טפח בוקעת ועולה כדאמר בפ"ק דסוכה (דף יח. ושם) ארובה בבית ואין בה פותח טפח טומאה כנגד ארובה כל הבית טהור לפי שבוקעת ועולה וכן במסכת אהלות [ח] ומייתי לה בהעור והרוטב (חולין קכה:) חבילי המטה וסריגי חלונות כו' פירסן על המת באויר הנוגע כנגד הנקב טמא שלא כנגד הנקב טהור והתם אין בנקבים פותח טפח דקתני רישא דמפסיק בין בית לעלייה: אין גוררין אותה בשבת בזמן שיש עליה מעות. מפרש ר"י דכשהיא נשמטת היא כלי בפני עצמה אבל כשאינה נשמטת מותר לגוררה אע"פ שיש עליה מעות דכיון שאינס ע"ג השידה שהיא עיקר הכלי שרי: הא אין עליה מעות שריא אע"ג דהוו עליה כל בין השמשות. קשה לרשב"א דמאי פריך לוקמא בשבת ולהכי אין עליה מעות אע"ג דהוו עליה כל בין השמשות שריא כדאמר בפרק נוטל (לקמן קמב:) ובזמן שיש עליה מעות אסור לגוררה אפי' בשבת שהוא טלטול גמור וקמ"ל דבאינה נשמטת שרי לגוררה טלטול גמור ומתרץ דע"כ במניח איירי דהא אין גוררין אותה משמע אפי' לצורך מקומה ואי בשבת הא אמרי' בפרק נוטל (ג"ז שם) לא שנו אלא לצורך גופו אבל לצורך מקומו מטלטלו ועודן עליו [ט] ומיהו מטה שיחדה והניח עליה מעות ◦ איכא למימר דמודה ר"ש דמקפיד עליה מיחד לה מקום כדאמרי' בריש כל הכלים (שם קכג. ושם) הכל מודים אפי' ר"ש והא דפריך לעיל מנר היינו משום שאין לחלק בין מטה לשאר דברים אלא כשהניח עליה מעות ולפ"ז לא קשה לעיל אפי' הקונטרס שפי' דדייק מדקתני אבל לא ישן):

הכי

עין משפט נר מצוה

נא א מיי' פכ"ה מהל' שבת הלכה י טוש"ע או"ח סימן שי סעיף ז:

רבינו חננאל

הכל פמוט שהוא מנורה שאין לה אלא קנה אחד ואין על ראשה אלא כף אחת הדליקו עליו באותה שבת דברי הכל (אחד) [אסור]. לא הדליקו עליו דברי הכל מותר. הא דאמר רב מטה שייחדה למעות והניח עליה מעות א) והיו עליה המעות כל בין השמשות. אע"פ שנטלו המעות עכשיו ואינם במטה אסור לטלטלה. אסיקנא דרב כר' יהודה אמרה לשמעתיה. מתיב ר' אליעזר הא דתנן בכלים פ' י"ח מוכני שלה בזמן שהיא נשמטת אינה חבור ואינה נמדלת עמה ואינה נצלת באהל המת. פי' (כאן) [כן] של שידה בזמן שהיא נשמטת אינה כמו השידה ואינה נשלפת עמה ולא נצלת עמה מפני שהשידה כלי וזו אינה כלי ב) מכללא לפיכך אמרו אין גוררין

חשק שלמה על רבינו חננאל

א) ע"ס כאן: ב) ע"ס כאן ועי' ברמב"ן וברשב"א.

רב נסים גאון

זהב באה קנים אינה באה זהב אינה באה קנים השיבו ההוא פמוט מיתקרי והפמוט שהזכיר ר' זירא בשמועה זו נחשת היא וחדש ואינו נמאס ואם הדליקו עליו נר באותו שבת הרי הוא מוקצה מחמת איסור ולפי שהוא מנוקה מלכלוך לא הוי מוקצה מחמת מיאוס ועל דעת ר' מאיר שהיה מתיר טלטול הפמוט אם לא הדליקו עליו באותה שבת זה הפמוט אע"פ שהוא כחדש שאינו נמאס אסור לטלטלו לפי שנהיה מוקצה מחמת איסורו מפני הנר שהדליקו עליו באותו יום ועל דעת ר' יהודה שהיה אוסר טלטול נר [נר ישן] (חדש) [של חרש] הרי הפמוט מותר לטלטלו לפי שנראה נר חדש ואינו מאוס ולפיכך באה הקושיא מידי למימרא דר' יהודה מוקצה מחמת מיאוס אית ליה מוקצה מחמת איסורו לית ליה והתניא ובגמ' דבני מערב' גרסי מעשה היה וטילטלו פמוט מתחת הנר בשבת מה אנן קיימין אי כר' מאיר אפילו פמוט יהא אסור כמו שאמר כל הנרות מטלטלין חוץ מן הנר שהדליקו בה באותה שבת וזה הפמוט הדליקו בו באותה שבת והרי הוא לר' מאיר אסור ואי כר"ש אפילו נר עצמו יהא מותר וכל שכן הפמוט שיהא מותר ואין אנו צריכים להודיענו זה ההיתר בפמוט על דעת ר' שמעון שהיה סובר נר עצמו מותר לטלטלו וכ"ש פמוט מתחתיו אלא כן אנן כר' יהודה דר' יהודה אומר נר מאוס פמוט אינו מאוס וזה סיוע הפירוש שפירשנו אבל בארתי זה הטעם כי ראיתי מי שפירש אותו בטעם אחר וסבר שר' שמעון

שהוא

מסורת הש"ס

א) צ"ל אלעזר, ב) [לקמן מו.] כלים פי"ח מ"ב, ג) פי"א מ"א, ד) [דף לא.], ה) [דף ל.], ו) [שם], ז) [ועי' תוס' מנחות לא. ד"ה שידה], ח) [הוא בתוספתא דאהלות פ"ט], ט) רש"ל מ"ז ומהרש"א כתב שזהו שייך לסוף דיבור שאח"ז ועי' מהר"ם.

תוספות ישנים

א) ובסוכה [דף מג:] דקאמר גבי מורביות וכו' ע"ש משמע דדוקא ע"י ע"ה אבל ת"ח לא היו עושין אף על גב דבייתוסין לא הניחו לדעתם לא חשיב כשבת. א"נ לא היו יכולין לנערם בלא טלטול קצת אע"ג דקאמר ושמטום:

ב) ורשב"א פירש במשניות דכיון דאין נכנסין לה אלא באקראי בעלמא לא הוי בכך מיוחד למדרס שהרי ספינה עשויה לישב בה בני אדם ואפ"ה כשמחזקת מ' סאה טהורה:

הגהות הב"ח

(א) רש"י ד"ה ואינה מצלת וכו' ומפסיק בפני הטומאה: (ב) תוס' ד"ה ואין מצלת וכו' בבית הקברות והכלים מעל דופני השידה:

גליון הש"ס

גמ' בזמן שהיא נשמטת. עי' לקמן דף מח ע"ב תוס' ד"ה דבר תורה: תוס' ד"ה הא אין וכו'. איכא למימר דמודה ר"ש. עי' לעיל ד' לו ע"א תוס' ד"ה הא ר' יהודה:

וּמָה נֵר דִּלְהָכִי עֲבִידָא – **If even** in regard to **a lamp, which was made for this very purpose** of being used for lighting, **כִּי לֹא הִדְלִיק בָּהּ שָׁרֵי לְטַלְטוּלָהּ** – the rule is that **as long as one did not** actually **light in it, it is permitted to move it** for it is not yet *muktzeh*, **מִטָּה דְּלָאו לְהָכִי עֲבִידָא** – then in the case of **a bed, which was not made for this purpose** of storing money, but was merely designated verbally, **לֹא כָּל שֶׁכֵּן** – **is it not certain** that it is permitted to move it as long as one did not actually store money on it?

Conceding the point, the Gemara revises its account of Rav Yehudah's ruling:

אֶלָּא אִי אִיתְּמַר הָכִי אִיתְּמַר – **Rather, if** anything **was stated, this is what was stated: אָמַר רַב יְהוּדָה אָמַר רַב** – **Rav Yehudah said in the name of Rav: מִטָּה שֶׁיִּחֲדָהּ לְמָעוֹת** – Concerning **a bed that someone** verbally **designated** to be used **for** the storage of **money: הִנִּיחַ עָלֶיהָ מָעוֹת אָסוּר לְטַלְטְלָהּ** – If **he** actually **placed money on it,** even on a weekday, **it is** subsequently **forbidden to move it** on the Sabbath, **לֹא הִנִּיחַ עָלֶיהָ מָעוֹת מוּתָּר לְטַלְטְלָהּ** – but **if he did not** ever **place money on it, it is permitted to move it** on the Sabbath.[1] **לֹא יִחֲדָהּ לְמָעוֹת** – If, on the other hand, **he did not designate it** verbally **for** the storage of **money, יֵשׁ עָלֶיהָ מָעוֹת אָסוּר לְטַלְטְלָהּ** – then if **there is money** lying **on [the bed]** on the Sabbath, **it is forbidden to move it, אֵין עָלֶיהָ מָעוֹת מוּתָּר לְטַלְטְלָהּ** – but if **there is no money** lying **on [the bed] it is permitted to move it,** even if money was once placed on it.[2] **וְהוּא שֶׁלֹּא הָיוּ עָלֶיהָ בֵּין הַשְּׁמָשׁוֹת** – **However, this is** true only **if there was no [money] on [the bed] during *bein hashemashos*** at the onset of the Sabbath.[3]

From the last proviso in Rav's ruling it emerges that a bed which served as a base to *muktzeh* at the onset of the Sabbath remains *muktzeh* for the entire Sabbath. The Gemara proceeds to challenge this:

אָמַר עוּלָּא – **Ulla said: מָתִיב רַבִּי אֱלִ(י)עֶזֶר** – **R' Elazar challenged** this on the basis of the following Mishnah, which deals principally with laws of *tumah* pertaining to a wooden coach:[4] **מוּכְנִי שֶׁלָּהּ** – Concerning ITS WHEEL:[5] **בִּזְמַן שֶׁהִיא נִשְׁמֶטֶת** – WHEN IT IS REMOVABLE, **אֵין חִיבּוּר לָהּ** – IT IS NOT considered ATTACHED TO [THE COACH],[6] **וְאֵין נִמְדֶּדֶת עִמָּהּ** – NOR IS IT MEASURED TOGETHER WITH [THE COACH] when determining the volume of the coach,[7] **וְאֵין מַצֶּלֶת עִמָּהּ בְּאֹהֶל הַמֵּת** – NOR DOES IT combine WITH [THE COACH] to PROTECT the contents of the coach from contracting *tumah* WHEN PASSING OVER A CORPSE,[8] **וְאֵין גּוֹרְרִין אוֹתָהּ בְּשַׁבָּת בִּזְמַן שֶׁיֵּשׁ עָלֶיהָ מָעוֹת** – NOR MAY WE DRAG IT ON THE SABBATH WHEN THERE IS MONEY ON IT.[9] **הָא אֵין עָלֶיהָ מָעוֹת שַׁרְיָא** – This implies: **But if there is no money on [the wheel] it is permitted** to drag it, **אַף עַל גַּב דַּהֲווֹ עָלֶיהָ בֵּין הַשְּׁמָשׁוֹת** – **even if there was money on it during *bein hashemashos*** at the onset of the Sabbath. We do not say that since there was money on it during *bein hashemashos* it became *muktzeh* and remains that way throughout the Sabbath.

The Gemara resolves the difficulty:

הַהִיא רַבִּי שִׁמְעוֹן הִיא דְּלֵית לֵיהּ מוּקְצֶה – **That** Mishnah **is** reflective of the view of **R' Shimon, who does not accept** a broad application of ***muktzeh,***[10] **וְרַב כְּרַבִּי יְהוּדָה סְבִירָא**

NOTES

1. The mere verbal designation is insufficient to make the bed *muktzeh*. Only if one followed the verbal designation by actually using the bed for its newly designated purpose does it become *muktzeh*. If he did place money on the bed, it is *muktzeh* on the basis of his designation and usage, and may not be moved even if he removed the money before the Sabbath (see *Rashi*).

2. Merely storing money on the bed without verbally designating the bed for this usage does not change its status to *muktzeh*. Thus, as long as there is no money on the bed during the Sabbath it may be moved. R' Yehudah's ruling in the previously cited Baraisa – that it is permitted to move a used metal lamp that was not lit for this Sabbath – reflects this rule, and refers to a metal vessel that has not been designated verbally as a lamp but had merely been used for this purpose (*Rashi;* see *Tosafos* ד״ה ומה נר and ד״ה הא אין עליה מעות).

3. If there was money on the bed during *bein hashemashos*, it would have been *a base to muktzeh* at that time and we would apply the principle that since it is *muktzeh* during *bein hashemashos* it remains *muktzeh* for the entire day (*Rashi*).

4. *Keilim* 18:2.

5. The translation follows *Rashi*. Cf. *Rabbeinu Tam*, cited by *Tosafos* ד״ה ואין, who interprets מוּכְנִי as *the base; Rambam, Hil. Keilim* 3:5 (and *Commentary to Mishnah, Keilim* 18:2, Kafich ed.) renders it *a drawer*. See also *Raavad* ad loc.

6. The coach and its removable wheel are considered separate utensils and thus, if the coach becomes *tamei* the wheel does not automatically become *tamei* with it. [The fact that the wheel is touching the coach is irrelevant since utensils do not convey *tumah* to other utensils that they touch.] Likewise, if the coach is too large to be susceptible to *tumah* (see following note), the wheel itself is susceptible to *tumah*, since it is considered a separate utensil. [Since wooden utensils do not contract *tumah* unless they have a receptacle,] we are perforce dealing with a wheel that has a hollow, which serves as a receptacle (*Rashi;* cf. *Tosafos* ד״ה ואין).

7. In general, wooden vessels can contract *tumah* only if they are small enough to be considered portable even when full (see below, 83b, and *Sifra* to *Leviticus* 11:32, where this is derived through Biblical exegesis). If their liquid volume is forty *se'ah* or greater, they are considered too large to be portable when full and therefore do not contract *tumah* (see *Keilim* 15:1 for several exceptions to this rule). In this context, the walls of a vessel are included in the measure of its volume, i.e. if the vessel including its walls *displaces* a volume of forty *se'ah*, it will not contract *tumah* (see *Keilim* 18:1). The Mishnah teaches that when the wheel of a coach is removable it is not measured together with the coach to determine whether the coach has a volume of forty *se'ah* (*Rashi*).

8. Normally, a person or vessel that passes over a corpse or a grave becomes *tamei,* unless there is a barrier (a "tent") that interposes between the person or vessel and the corpse or grave, and does not allow the *tumah* to pass through. If the coach is of a large measure so that it is not susceptible to *tumah,* when it passes through a graveyard its floor constitutes a barrier between the graves and the coach's contents, and protects them from contracting *tumah*. However, if some of the contents protrude from the sides of the coach above the wheel, they do become *tamei* by passing over the graves. Since the wheel is not considered part of the coach, it itself contracts *tumah* from graves and cannot constitute a barrier between the *tumah* and the objects above it (*Rashi,* as cited by *Ritva MHK* ed.; *Rav* to *Keilim* 18:2; see *Rambam* and *Raavad, Hil. Tumas Meis* 12:2, and *Tos. Yom Tov, Oholos* 6:1 ד״ה אפילו כלי גללים). [The explanation that appears in our version of *Rashi* is difficult to understand – see *Tosafos* ד״ה ואין with *Maharsha*.]

9. If money was placed on the wheel, we may not drag the coach and wheel, since the wheel is a base to *muktzeh*. This pertains specifically to a removable wheel, which is considered a separate utensil from the coach. If the wheel is attached permanently, it is considered ancillary to the coach, and since the body of the coach is not serving as a base to *muktzeh* it is permissible to move the wheel along with it (*Tosafos* ד״ה אין גוררין; see *Rama, Orach Chaim* 310:7 with *Mishnah Berurah* §29-31 for a very relevant application of this rule).

10. [Thus, he disputes the principle that since something was *muktzeh* during *bein hashemashos* it automatically remains *muktzeh* for the entire day (see following note).] Nevertheless, even according to R' Shimon's narrow application, money is *muktzeh* since it has no practical function at all, and a wheel upon which money was placed may not be moved *while the money is on it* (*Rashi*).

ומה נר דלהכי עבידא כי לא הדליק בה שרי לטלטולה מטה דלאו להכי עבידא לא כ"ש אלא אי איתמר הכי איתמר אמר רב יהודה אמר רב [א]מטה שיחדה למעות הניח עליה מעות אסור לטלטלה לא הניח עליה מעות מותר לטלטלה לא יחדה למעות יש עליה מעות אסור לטלטלה אין עליה מעות מותר לטלטלה והוא שלא היו עליה בין השמשות אמר עולא מתיב ר' [א]אליעזר [ג]מוכני שלה ° בזמן שהיא נשמטת אין חיבור לה ואין נמדדת עמה ואין מצלת עמה באהל המת ואין גוררין אותה בשבת בזמן שיש עליה מעות הא אין עליה מעות שריא אף על גב דהוו עליה ביה"ש ההיא ר' שמעון היא דלית ליה מוקצה ורב כרבי יהודה סבירא ליה הכי

הניח עליה מעות. אפילו בחול הרי הוקצה לאיסור ואסור לטלטלה ואפילו נסתלקו המעות מבעוד יום ולא דמי לנר של מתכת דשרי רבי יהודה דהתם בלא יחדו: לא יחדה למעות. אין עליה מעות בשבת: מותר לטלטלה. ואע"ג דהניח עליה מעות בחול: והוא. שנסתלקו מבעוד יום שלא היו עליה כל בין השמשות אבל היו עליה כל בין השמשות איתקצי לכולי יומא: מוכני שלה. גבי שידה תנן במסכת כלים והיא עגלה של עץ מוקפת מחילות למרכב אנשים ונשים. מוכני אופן: בזמן שהיא נשמטת. כעין אופני עגלה שלנו שאדם יכול לסלקו מן העגלה: אינו חיבור לה. דחשובה היא כלי לעצמה דאי שידה בת קבולי טומאה היא כגון שאינה מחזקת מ' סאה בלח ונטמאה השידה לא נטמא המוכני ואי לאו בת קבולי טומאה היא ונגעה טומאה במוכני המוכני טמאה לעצמה דלא חשיבה משידה והיא מטלטלה מלאה וריקנית דיש לה בית קיבול: ואינה נמדדת עמה. לענין טומאה כדפרישית דכלי עץ המחזיק מ' סאה בלח שהן כוריים ביבש טהור כדאמרי' בבמה מדליקין (דף לה.) דכלי עץ איתקש לשק שיהא מיטלטל מלא וריקן וזו אינו מיטלטל מלא ותנן במסכת כלים [ג] ומייתינן בגמ' דמנחות [ד] השידה ב"ה אומרים נמדדת מבחוץ דרואין אותה כאילו היא עומדת בתוך כלי גדול ואם מחזיק אותו כלי מ' סאה טהורה השידה ואע"פ שהיא אינה מחזקת מ' סאה דקסבר אף עוביה נמדד עמה והמוכני אינו נמדד עמה להשלים דרואין כאילו ניטל המוכני ואח"כ תנתן השידה לתוך הכלי: ואינה מצלת עמה באהל המת. דאם השידה מחזקת מ' [סאה] דאינה מקבלת טומאה מגלת באהל המת והוי אהל לעצמה ולא שנכנסה לבית שהמת בו דא"כ אין כאן הצלה שהרי הגג מאהיל על הטהרות מלמעלה אלא כגון שנכנסה לבית הקברות כדאמרינן בעירובין [ה] ר' יהודה אומר אף בבה"ק מפני שיכול לחוץ בשידה תיבה ומגדל בפ' בכל מערבין [ו] דקסבר אהל זרוק כלומר אהל המיטלטל שמיה אהל ומפסיק (א) כלפי הטומאה והמוכני אם הוא גבוה מדופני השידה וכלים [בולטים] מלמעלה מדופני השידה וגובה המוכני מגין עליהם אינו מצילן דמוכני כלי הוא לעצמו ומקבל טומאה ואינו חוצץ בפני הטומאה ורבותי דוחקין ומפרשין אותה באהל המת ממש ובשל חרס המוקפת צמיד פתיל והרבה תשובות יש חדא דנמדדת לא שייך בשל חרס דלא איתקש לשק ובין מיטלטל ובין אינו מיטלטל טמא ועוד אם המוכני מוקף צמיד פתיל יציל בפני עצמו כלים שבתוכו ועוד בפירוש נשנית במסכת כלים בהלכות כלי עץ והלכות כלי חרס נשנו לבדן והלכות כלי עץ נשנו לבדן: ההיא ר' שמעון היא. ומיהו מעות לא חזו מידי ומודה רבי שמעון דעודן עליו אסור: מניחין

ומה נר דלהכי עבידא כו'. פי' בקונטרס דדייק מדקתני אבל לא ישן משמע דוקא ישן אבל חדש אפילו יחדו וקשה לר"י דלמאי דמסיק נמי מטה שיחדה והניח עליה מעות כו' תקשה ליה מנר של מתכת דשרי ר' יהודה אפילו יחדו לעיל מדקתני חוץ מן הנר שהדליקו בה באותה שבת אבל לא הדליקו בה באותה שבת אע"פ שיחדה והדליקו בה בחול שרי ונראה לר"י דלא דייק כלל מדקתני אבל לא ישן אלא דוקא בנר של חרס הוא דקאמ' דלהכי עבידא שתחלת עשייתה היא להדלקה והוי כמו יחוד שמיד שמדליקין בה פעם אחת נמאסת ואין ראויה לתשמיש אחר ולכך תחלת עשייתה אינה אלא להדלקה אע"פ שראויה לתשמיש אחר בין עשייה להדלקה מ"מ אין עושין אותה לכך שאין זה אלא זמן מועט אבל בנר מתכת אין עשייתה להדלקה לבד דראויה כל שעה לתשמיש אחר: לא הניח עליה מעות מותר לטלטלה. ואצולרות דאסר ר' יהודה לעיל (דף לו.) נראה לר"י דאסר אפי' לא תקע בה דאצולרות לא חזיא אלא לתקיעה ואין לחלק בין תקע ללא תקע אבל מטה ונר חזי לתשמיש אחרינא: יש עליה מעות אסור לטלטלה. ע"כ במניח איירי א) דבשבת תנן פרק נוטל (לקמן קמב:) מנער הכר והן נופלות ובמניח בשבת איירי דבהניח מבעוד יום והיו עליה בין השמשות אפילו אין עליה מעות אסור לטלטלה כדקאמר בסיפא דמילתיה וקשה דאיך יכול להיות שמניח לדעת בשבת וי"ל כגון שהניח נכרי או תינוק לדעת ישראל וא"ת אמאי לא מוכח מהכא בפ' אין לדין (ביצה כו:) דאין מוקצה לחצי שבת וי"ל דאיכא לאוקמא כגון שהניחם לדעת ישראל כדי להסירם אחר שעה והוו כגמרו בידי אדם ולמאי דפרישית לעיל דהא דיש מוקצה לחצי שבת היינו באיסור אכילה ולא בטלטול א"ש: מוכני שלה. פי' בקונטרס דגבי שידה תנן לה במסכת כלים (פי"ח מ"א) והיא עשויה למרכבת אנשים ונשים ב) ואין נראה לר"י דאי חזיא למדרס לא שייך בה מדידה דלא איתקש לשק ולא בעינן מיטלטל מלא וריקן כדמוכח בפרק אלו מומין (בכורות לח. ושם) דפריך ושאין לו תוך בכלי שטף מקבל טומאה הוא והא דומיא דשק בעינן ומשני בהנך דחזו למדרסות לכך נראה דאינה עשויה אלא לכלים והא דאמר לקמן בפרק רבי עקיבא (דף פד. ושם) שלש תיבות הן תיבה שפתחה מלדה טמאה מדרס מלמעלה טמאה מת פי' אבל מדרס לא לפי שאומרים עמוד ונעשה מלאכתנו והבאה במדה טהורה מכלום פי' שיש לה מ' סאה אור"י דצריך לומר דלא קאי אפתחה מלדה דכיון דחזיא למדרס אפילו באה במדה טמאה כדפי' [ז]: ואין מצלת עמה באהל המת. פי' בקונט' בבית הקברות (ב) שהכלים על דופני השידה וקשה דמי יביא טומא' על הכלים ומפרש ריב"א דמיירי שפיר דקיימא השידה באהל המת ומוקפת צמיד פתיל ואע"ג דכלי עץ אינו מגיל בצמיד פתיל היכא דמקבל ארבעים סאה מגיל כיון דלא מקבל טומאה כדתנן במסכת כלים ואלו מגילין בצמיד פתיל כלי גללים כו' וכלי עץ הטהורים ואין צ"ל דמוכני יש לו בית קיבול אלא פשוטי כלי עץ הוא ויש נקב בשידה בלדה והכלים בתוך השידה והמוכני חופפת שם וממעטת אותו נקב עד שאין נשאר פותח טפח וקאמר כיון דנשמטת אינו ממעט דדוקא כי מבטלו שם ממעט בחלון כדמוכח בלא יחפור (ב"ב כ: ושם) דפריך אהא דקתני דכלי חרס ממעט בחלון הא קחזי ליה פי' ולא מבטל התם והיכי ממעט ומשני דמטונף ומיירי שאינו סותם כל הנקב דאם סותם כל הנקב אפי' אינו מבטלו שם סותם כדאמר בפ' בתרא (דף קנז.) בימי אבא שאול בן בטנית פקקו את המאור בטפיח והתם לא בטלוהו שאם ביטלוהו בשבת היה חייב משום בונה דהא מוסיפים על הבנין אלא ודאי בלא ביטול איירי ואפ"ה סותם ובכלי עץ אמרינן נמי בפ' בתרא דמגילה (דף כו:) ההיא בי כנישתא דרומאי דהות פתיחה לההוא אדרונא דהוו מחתי בה מיתי בעו כהני למיזל לצלויי התם אמרו ליה לרבא אמר להו זילו דלו תיבותא ואותבוהו אבבא דה"ל כלי עץ העשוי לנחת ומסתמא לא היו מבטלין אותו שם שהרי ס"ת מניחין בתוכו ומיהו תבן וגרוגרות אין להם דין כלים דאפי' סותמין כל החלון צריכין ביטול כדמוכח בפרק לא יחפור (ב"ב יט:) ולר"ת אין נראה לפרש דמוכני הוי אופן דאין דרך להניח מעות על האופן דקתני ואין גוררין אותה בשבת בזמן שיש עליה מעות ומפרש דמוכני היינו כן של שידה כמו את הכיור ואת כנו (שמות ל) וכמו מכונות במלכים (א ז) פי' בסים שהשידה מונחת עליו ויש בשידה נקב מתחתיה כנגד המוכני והיא בבה"ק והטומאה נכנסת דרך נקב בשידה ואין המוכני מגלת כיון שהיא נשמטת ואין מבטלין אותה שם ומיירי נמי שאין סותמת כל הנקב אלא ממעטת אותו מפותח טפח כדפי' לעיל וצ"ל דמיירי שאין הטומאה כנגד הנקב דכשהטומאה נגד הנקב אפילו אין בו פותח טפח בוקעת ועולה כדאמר בפ"ק דסוכה (דף יח. ושם) ארובה בבית ואין בה פותח טפח טומאה כנגד ארובה כל הבית טהור לפי שבוקעת ועולה וכן במסכת אהלות [ח] ומייתי לה בהעור והרוטב (חולין קכה:) חבילי המטה וסריגי חלונות כו' פירסן על המת באויר הנוגע כנגד הנקב טמא שלא כנגד הנקב טהור והתם אין בנקבים פותח טפח דקתני רישא דמפסיק בין בית לעלייה: אין גוררין אותה בשבת בזמן שיש עליה מעות. מפרש ר"י דכשהיא נשמטת היא כלי בפני עצמה אבל כשאינה נשמטת מותר לגוררה אע"פ שיש עליה מעות דכיון שאינס ע"ג השידה שהיא עיקר הכלי שרי: הא אין עליה מעות שריא אע"ג דהוו עליה כל בין השמשות. קשה לרשב"א דמאי פריך לוקמא בשבת ולהכי אין עליה מעות אע"ג דהוו עליה כל בין השמשות שריא כדאמר בפרק נוטל (לקמן קמב:) ובזמן שיש עליה מעות אסור לגוררה אפי' בשבת שהוא טלטול גמור וקמ"ל דבאינה נשמטת שרי לגוררה טלטול גמור ומתרץ דע"כ במניח איירי דהא אין גוררין אותה משמע אפי' לצורך מקומה ואי בשבת הא אמרי' בפרק נוטל (ג"ז שם) לא שנו אלא לצורך גופו אבל לצורך מקומו מטלטלו ועודן עליו ([ט]) ומיהו מטה שיחדה והניח עליה מעות ° איכא למימר דמודה ר"ש דמקפיד עליה מיחד לה מקום כדאמרי' בריש כל הכלים (שם קכג. ושם) הכל מודים כיון דקפיד עליה מיחד לה מקום ופר"ת דהכל מודים אפי' ר"ש והא דפריך לעיל מנר היינו משום שאין לחלק בין מטה לשאר דברים אלא כשהניח עליה מעות ולפ"ז לא קשה לעיל אפי' הקונטרס שפי' דדייק מדקתני אבל לא ישן): הכי

עין משפט נר מצוה

נא א מיי' פכ"ה מהל' שבת הלכה י טוש"ע או"ח סימן שי סעיף ז:

רבינו חננאל

הכל פמוט שהוא מנורה שאין לה אלא קנה אחד ואין על ראשה אלא כף אחת הדליקו עליו באותה שבת דברי הכל (אחד) [אסור]. לא הדליקו עליו דברי הכל מותר. הא דאמר רב מטה שייחדה למעות והניח עליה מעות א) והיו עליה המעות כל בין השמשות. אע"פ שנטלו המעות עכשיו ואינם במטה אסור לטלטלה. אסיקנא דרב כר' יהודה אמרה לשמעתיה. מתיב ר' אליעזר הא דתנן בכלים פ' י"ח מוכני שלה בזמן שהיא נשמטת אינה חבור ואינה נמדלת עמה ואינה נצלת באהל המת. פי' (כאן) [כן] של שידה בזמן שהיא נשמטת אינה כמו השידה ואינה נשלפת עמה ולא נצלת עמה מפני שהשידה כלי וזו אינה כלי ב) מכללא לפיכך אמרו אין גוררין

חשק שלמה על רבינו חננאל

א) ע"ם כאן: ב) ע"ם כאן ועי' ברמב"ן וברשב"א.

רב נסים גאון

זהב באה קנים אינה באה זהב אינה באה קנים השיבו ההוא פמוט מיתקרי והפמוט שהזכיר ר' זירא בשמועה זו נחשת היא וחדש ואינו נמאס ואם הדליקו עליו נר באותו שבת הרי הוא מוקצה מחמת איסור ולפי שהוא מנוקה מלכלוך לא הוי מוקצה מחמת מיאוס ועל דעת ר' מאיר שהיה מתיר טלטול הפמוט אם לא הדליקו עליו באותה שבת זה הפמוט אע"פ שהוא כחדש שאינו נמאס אסור לטלטלו לפי שנהיה מוקצה מחמת איסורו מפני הנר שהדליקו עליו באותו יום ועל דעת ר' יהודה שהיה אוסר טלטול נר [נר ישן] (חדש) [של חרש] הרי הפמוט מותר לטלטלו לפי שנראה נר חדש ואינו מאוס ולפיכך באה הקושיא מידי למימרא דר' יהודה מוקצה מחמת מיאוס אית ליה מוקצה מחמת איסורו לית ליה והתניא ובגמ' דבני מערב' גרסי מעשה היה וטילטלו פמוט מתחת הנר בשבת מה אנן קיימין אי כר' מאיר אפילו פמוט יהא אסור כמו שאמר כל הנרות מטלטלין חוץ מן הנר שהדליקו בה באותה שבת וזה הפמוט הדליקו בו באותה שבת והרי הוא לר' מאיר אסור ואי כר"ש אפילו נר עצמו יהא מותר וכל שכן הפמוט שיהא מותר ואין אנו צריכים להודיענו זה ההיתר בפמוט על דעת ר' שמעון שהיה סובר נר עצמו מותר לטלטלו וכ"ש פמוט מתחתיו אלא כן אנן כר' יהודה דר' יהודה אומר נר מאוס פמוט אינו מאוס וזה סיוע הפירוש שפירשנו אבל בארתי זה הטעם כי ראיתי מי שפירש אותו בטעם אחר וסבר שר' שמעון שהוא

מסורת הש"ס

א) נ"ל אלעזר, ב) [לקמן מו.] כלים פי"ח מ"ב, ג) פי"א מ"א, ד) [דף לא.], ה) [דף ל.], ו) [שם], ז) [ועי' תוס' מנחות לא. ד"ה שידה], ח) [הוא בתוספתא דאהלות פ"ט], ט) רש"ל מ"ז ומהרש"א כתב שזהו שייך לסוף דיבור שאח"ז ועי' מהר"מ.

תוספות ישנים

א) ובסוכה [דף מג:] דקאמר גבי מורביות וכו' ע"ס משמע דדוקא ע"י ע"ה אבל ת"ח לא היו עושין אף על גב דייחוסין לא הניחו לדעתם לא חשיב כשבת. א"נ לא היו יכולין לנערם בלא טלטול קצת אע"ג דקאמר ושמטוס:

ב) ורשב"א פירש במשניות דכיון דאין נכנסין לה אלא באקראי בעלמא לא הוי בכך מיוחד למדרס שהרי ספינה עשויה לישב בה בני אדם ואפ"ה כשמחזקת מ' סאה טהורה:

הגהות הב"ח

(א) רש"י ד"ה ואינה מגלת וכו' ומפסיק בפני הטומאה: (ב) תום' ד"ה ואין מגלת וכו' בבית הקברות והכלים מעל דופני השידה:

גליון הש"ס

גמ' בזמן שהיא נשמטת. עי' לקמן דף מח ע"ב תוס' ד"ה דבר תורה: תוס' ד"ה הא אין וכו'. איכא למימר דמודה ר"ש. עי' לעיל ד' לו ע"א תוס' ד"ה הא ר' יהודה:

לֵיהּ – **whereas Rav concurs with R' Yehudah** who accepts a broad application of *muktzeh*. Accordingly, Rav holds that a bed which served as a base to *muktzeh* at the onset of the Sabbath remains *muktzeh* for the entire day.[11]

NOTES

11. According to R' Yehudah's broad application, anything that was *muktzeh* during *bein hashemashos* remains *muktzeh* for the entire day.

Note that although R' Shimon concedes that a *muktzeh* item that one abandoned hope of using – such as a large lamp – is *muktzeh* for the entire Sabbath, he holds that in our case the bed is not *muktzeh*. It is only in the case of a large lamp, where the person deliberately poured in enough oil to last the entire Sabbath, that we presume he abandoned hope of using the lamp for another purpose. However, a person does not totally abandon hope of using a bed that has money on it – even though he is not allowed to remove the money on the Sabbath – since there is always a possibility that a child or a gentile will remove it. Thus, if the money is in fact removed, the bed remains *muktzeh* only according to R' Yehudah, who follows the principle that since it was *muktzeh* during *bein hashemashos* it remains *muktzeh* for the entire day (*Ramban* to 45a, *Rashba*, *Ritva MHK* ed.; cf. *Chazon Ish* 41:4).

The Gemara finds support for this answer:

הָכִי נַמִּי מִסְתַּבְּרָא דְּרַב כְּרַבִּי יְהוּדָה סְבִירָא לֵיהּ – **In fact, it seems reasonable** to conclude **that Rav concurs with R' Yehudah,** דְּאָמַר רַב – **for Rav said:** מַנִּיחִין נֵר עַל גַּבֵּי דֶּקֶל בְּשַׁבָּת – **We may place a** burning **lamp on a palm tree for the Sabbath,** וְאֵין מַנִּיחִין נֵר עַל גַּבֵּי דֶּקֶל בְּיוֹם טוֹב – **but we may not place a** burning **lamp on a palm tree for a festival.**[1] אִי אָמְרַת בִּשְׁלָמָא דְּרַב כְּרַבִּי יְהוּדָה סְבִירָא לֵיהּ – **This fits well if you say that Rav concurs with R' Yehudah,** that something that is *muktzeh* during *bein hashemashos* remains *muktzeh* for the entire day, הַיְינוּ דְּשַׁנֵּי בֵּין שַׁבָּת לְיוֹם טוֹב – for **that** explains **why [Rav] distinguishes between the Sabbath and a festival.** אֶלָּא אִי אָמְרַת כְּרַבִּי שִׁמְעוֹן סְבִירָא לֵיהּ – **But if you will say** that **[Rav] concurs with R' Shimon,** that something that is *muktzeh* during *bein hashemashos* does not necessarily remain *muktzeh* the entire day, מָה לִי שַׁבָּת וּמָה לִי יוֹם טוֹב – **what is the difference between the Sabbath and a festival?**[2] Clearly, then, Rav concurs with R' Yehudah, as we stated above.[3]

The Gemara asks:

וְרַב כְּרַבִּי יְהוּדָה סְבִירָא לֵיהּ – **But does Rav** really **concur with R' Yehudah?** וְהָא בָּעוּ מִינֵּיהּ דְּרַב – **Why, they inquired of Rav:** מַהוּ לְטַלְטוּלֵי שְׁרָגָא דַּחֲנוּכְּתָא מִקַּמֵּי חַבָּרֵי בְּשַׁבְּתָא – **What is** the law with respect to **moving a Chanukah menorah away from** where it may be seen by **the Chabarin on the Sabbath,** after the flames have gone out?[4] וַאֲמַר לְהוּ שַׁפִּיר דָּמֵי – **And [Rav] replied: It is proper** to do so. Evidently, Rav does not consider the menorah *muktzeh* after the flames go out. Thus, he does not concur with R' Yehudah. – ? –

The Gemara resolves the difficulty:

שְׁעַת הַדְּחָק שָׁאנִי – **A time of emergency is different.** Ordinarily, however, Rav does forbid handling a lamp that has been extinguished on the Sabbath. דְּהָא אָמְרוּ לֵיהּ רַב כָּהֲנָא וְרַב אַשִׁי לְרַב – **For Rav Kahana and Rav Ashi said to Rav,** when he permitted moving the Chanukah menorah: הָכִי הִלְכְתָא – **Is this** really **the law?** Do you not consider the lamp *muktzeh* even after the flame goes out, in accordance with R' Yehudah's view? אָמַר לְהוּ – **And he replied:** כְּדַי הוּא רַבִּי שִׁמְעוֹן לִסְמוֹךְ עָלָיו בִּשְׁעַת הַדְּחָק – **R' Shimon is** sufficiently **worthy to be relied upon** as an authority **in a time of emergency.** Rav's response implies that he ordinarily follows the view of R' Yehudah.[5]

We have seen that R' Shimon has a narrow definition of *muktzeh,* according to which it is permitted to move or use items that are inherently fit for use – even if, at the onset of the Sabbath, they did not stand to be used.[6] The Gemara now considers R' Shimon's position concerning a related case:

בְּעָא מִינֵּיהּ רֵישׁ לָקִישׁ מֵרַבִּי יוֹחָנָן – **Reish Lakish inquired of R' Yochanan:** חִטִּים שֶׁזְּרָעָן בַּקַּרְקַע וּבֵיצִים שֶׁתַּחַת תַּרְנְגוֹלֶת מַהוּ – **What is** R' Shimon's opinion concerning **wheat that one planted in the ground,**[7] **and eggs that were** placed **under a hen** to incubate? כִּי לֵית לֵיהּ לְרַבִּי שִׁמְעוֹן מוּקְצֶה – Shall we say that **when does R' Shimon not apply** the law of ***muktzeh*** to a useful item – הֵיכָא דְּלָא דַּחְיֵיהּ בְּיָדַיִם – **it is** only regarding a situation **where one has not actively**[8] **set it aside** from being used, הֵיכָא דְּדַחְיֵיהּ בְּיָדַיִם אִית לֵיהּ מוּקְצֶה – but in a situation **where one actively set it aside, [R' Shimon] applies** the law of ***muktzeh*** to it?[9] אוֹ דִּילְמָא לָא שְׁנָא – **Or perhaps, there is no difference** between items that were actively set aside and those that were passively unintended for use, and R' Shimon does not apply the law of *muktzeh* to any useful item.[10] – ? –

R' Yochanan responds:

אָמַר לֵיהּ – **He said to [Reish Lakish]:** אֵין מוּקְצֶה לְרַבִּי שִׁמְעוֹן – **Nothing** that is useful **is *muktzeh* according to R' Shimon** on the basis of having been set aside, אֶלָּא שֶׁמֶן שֶׁבַּנֵּר בְּשָׁעָה שֶׁהוּא דוֹלֵק – **except oil in a lamp while it is burning,** which is *muktzeh* הוֹאִיל וְהוּקְצָה לְמִצְוָתוֹ – **since it was set aside for the**

NOTES

1. It is prohibited by Rabbinical decree to ascend or make use of a tree on the Sabbath or festival, lest one forgetfully tear a branch off it in violation of the *melachah* of קוֹצֵר, *reaping* (see *Beitzah* 36b). Nevertheless, Rav teaches that we may leave a burning lamp on a tree before the Sabbath. There is no concern that one might remove the lamp from the tree on the Sabbath in violation of the said decree, for since the burning lamp was *muktzeh* during *bein hashemashos* it will remain *muktzeh* the entire Sabbath, even after it goes out, and nobody will remove it. On Yom Tov, however, when a burning oil lamp is not *muktzeh* at all, we may not leave it on a tree beforehand, since one might be tempted to remove it from the tree during Yom Tov in violation of the decree (*Rashi;* see *Rama, Orach Chaim* 336:1; cf. *Rosh* below, 5:2; see *Chasam Sofer,* introduction to *Beitzah*).

2. It ought to be forbidden to leave a burning lamp on a tree on the Sabbath as well as on Yom Tov, since even on the Sabbath the lamp will no longer be *muktzeh* when the flame goes out and one might then be tempted to remove it from the tree (*Rashi*).

3. [Thus, we are correct in saying that Rav's view – that if a bed had money on it during *bein hashemashos* it may not be moved the entire Shabbos – follows R' Yehudah's opinion.]

It seems somewhat superfluous for the Gemara to prove that Rav concurs with R' Yehudah, as Rav's *initial* ruling above (that if a bed was designated and once used for storing money it becomes *muktzeh*) is itself based on R' Yehudah's broad definition of *muktzeh.* R' Shimon would not consider the bed *muktzeh,* since it is fit for permissible functions. Why, then, was it necessary to bring additional proof that in the latter part of his ruling Rav concurs with R' Yehudah? *Tosafos* answer that the Gemara needed to prove that Rav concurs with R' Yehudah even concerning the principle that since something is *muktzeh* during *bein hashemashos* it remains *muktzeh* for the entire day. Cf. *Tosafos* to 44b ד״ה הא, as explained by *Maharsha; Ramban, Rashba.*

4. The Chabarin were a violent people who for a time ruled Babylonia together with the Persians (see *Rashi* here and to *Kiddushin* 72a ד״ה חברין; cf. *Tosafos* to Gittin 17a ד״ה הא), and who forbade the kindling of Chanukah lights. Others explain that Chanukah coincided with a festival on which they would not allow lights to be kindled anywhere except at their temples (*Rashi*).

Nevertheless, if there were no Chabarin in the vicinity at the time for lighting, people would sometimes light their menorahs at the doors of their courtyards as should optimally be done (see above, 21b) and would bring them in after the lights went out, so that any passing Chabarin would not realize that their decree had been violated. They inquired of Rav whether it would be permitted to move the menorah on the Sabbath after the lights went out (see *Rashi;* see *Tosafos* with *Maharsha;* see also *Tosafos* above, 21b ד״ה ובשעת הסכנה).

5. The danger posed by the Chabarin was not life-threatening. If it had been, there would have been no question that the prohibition of moving *muktzeh* is set aside on account of the emergency. Rather, the danger was merely one of physical or monetary harm, and Rav ruled that in the face of this threat the opinion of R' Shimon is sufficiently worthy to be relied upon. Thus, if someone left his menorah outside on a Sabbath, he could move it inside when it went out (*Ritva MHK* ed.; see also *Rosh Yosef* and *R' Akiva Eiger*).

6. For example, the two honeycombs that are left in a beehive over the winter – see 43b note 5.

7. [On Friday], but which did not yet take root (*Rashi*). If the wheat took root, it would be forbidden to remove it from the ground even if it is not *muktzeh,* as this would be a violation of the *melachah* of *reaping* (*Ritva MHK* ed.; see there where it is explained why there is no prohibition of *plowing* or moving the earth [which is *muktzeh*] in this case).

8. Literally: with his hands.

9. Thus, R' Shimon concedes that since the person rejected the grain from future use by planting it, or rejected the egg from use until it hatches by placing it under the hen, it is *muktzeh* and may not be removed on the Sabbath.

10. [We know, however, that R' Shimon concedes that items which are intrinsically unfit for use (e.g. stones) are *muktzeh* (see Gemara below).]

מסורת הש"ס

א) [כריתות יט: עירובין מו. גיטין עו. נדה ו. ע"ז], ב) צ"ל והוקצה [תוס' ישנים], ג) לעיל כב. ביצה ל: סוכה י, [תוספתא סוכה פ"א], ד) ביצה ל:, ה) ביצה כו:, ו) [ביצה מ.]

הגהות הב"ח

(א) רש"י ד"ה היה אוכל וכו' רבותא אשמעי' אע"פ דהוה:

גליון הש"ס

תוס' ד"ה אלא שמן וכו'. נר הדולק לטלטל כדפי'. לעיל דף מב ע"ב תוס' ד"ה ולאו נאותין:

ליקוטי רש"י

חברי. פרסיים רשעים ומבזין ואינם מכירים כבודם של ישראל [יבמות סג:]. פרסאי [גיטין יז.]. אומה הסמוכה לפרסיים ומשמשים הם וטורפסים הם יותר מפרסיים [קידושין עב.]. בשעת הדחק. אבל שלא בשעת הדחק לא [ברכות ט.]. [illegible]

עין משפט נר מצוה

נב א מיי' פ"ה מהלכות שבת הלכה יח ופ"ד מהלכות י"ט הלכה ה סמג לאוין סה טור שו"ע או"ח סימן רעז סעיף ד וסימן תקי"ד סעיף ו:

נג ב מיי' פכ"ו מהלכות שבת הלכה יד סמג לאוין סה טוש"ע או"ח סימן שי סעיף ב:

הכי נמי מיסתברא

הכי נמי מיסתברא דרב כר' יהודה סבירא ליה דאמר רב [א]מניחין נר על גבי דקל בשבת ואין מניחין נר ע"ג דקל בי"ט אי אמרת בשלמא דרב כרבי יהודה סבירא ליה היינו דשני בין שבת לי"ט אלא אי אמרת כרבי שמעון סבירא ליה מה לי שבת ומה לי י"ט ורב כרבי יהודה ס"ל והא בעו מיניה דרב מהו לטלטולי שרגא דחנוכתא מקמי חברי בשבתא ואמר להו שפיר דמי שעת הדחק שאני דהא א"ל רב כהנא ורב אשי לרב הכי הלכתא אמר להו [ה]כדי הוא ר' שמעון לסמוך עליו בשעת הדחק בעא מיניה ריש לקיש מר' יוחנן חטים שזרען בקרקע וביצים שתחת תרנגולת מהו כי לית ליה לר' שמעון מוקצה היכא דלא דחייה בידים היכא דדחייה בידים אית ליה מוקצה או דילמא [ב]לא שנא א"ל אין מוקצה לרבי שמעון אלא שמן שבנר בשעה שהוא דולק הואיל והוקצה למצותו [ג]הוקצה לאיסורו ולית ליה הוקצה למצותו [ג]והתניא סיככה כהלכתה ועיטרה בקרמים ובסדינין המצויירין ותלה בה אגוזין אפרסקין שקדים ורמונין ואפרכלי של ענבים ועטרות של שבולין יינות שמנים וסלתות אסור להסתפק מהן עד מוצאי י"ט האחרון ואם התנה עליהן הכל לפי תנאו וממאי דר' שמעון היא דתני [ד]ר' חייא בר יוסף קמיה דר' יוחנן אין נוטלין עצים מן הסוכה בי"ט אלא מן הסמוך לה ור' שמעון מתיר ושוין בסוכת החג בחג שהיא אסורה ואם התנה עליה הכל לפי תנאו כעין שמן שבנר קאמרינן הואיל והוקצה למצותו הוקצה לאיסורו איתמר נמי א"ר חייא בר אבא א"ר יוחנן אין מוקצה לרבי שמעון אלא כעין שמן שבנר בשעה שהוא דולק הואיל והוקצה למצותו הוקצה לאיסורו אמר רב יהודה אמר שמואל אין מוקצה לר' שמעון אלא גרוגרות וצימוקים בלבד ומידי אחרינא לא והתניא [ה]היה אוכל בתאנים והותיר והעלן לגג לעשות מהן גרוגרות בענבים והותיר והעלן לגג לעשות מהן צימוקין לא יאכל עד שיזמין וכן אתה אומר באפרסקין וחבושין ובשאר כל מיני פירות מני אילימא רבי יהודה ומה היכא דלא דחייה בידים אית ליה מוקצה היכא דדחייה בידים לא כל שכן אלא לאו ר' שמעון היא לעולם רבי יהודה ואוכל אצטריכא ליה סד"א כיון דקאכיל ואזיל לא ליבעי הזמנה קמ"ל כיון דהעלן לגג אסוחי אסחי לדעתיה מינייהו [ו]בעא מיניה רבי שמעון בר רבי מרבי

פצעילי

רש"י

מניחין נר. מבעוד יום: ע"ג דקל. וידלק שם בשבת דליכא למיחש לכשיכבה ליטלה מיניה ונמצא משתמש במחובר דכיון דאקצייה לדבר האסור בין השמשות איתקצי לכולי יומא: ואין מניחין כו' בי"ט. דשקיל ומנח ליה ומשתמש באילן: מה לי שבת כו'. בשבת נמי שקיל ליה לכשיכבה: שרגא דחנוכתא. אחר שכבה: מקמי חברי. שלא יראוהו בתגר כדאמרינן בפרקין לעיל (דף כא:) דנותנו בטפח הסמוך לרשות הרבים וידעו שהדליקו בו נר והם גזרו שלא להדליק אי נמי ביום חגם אין מניחין לדלוק אור אלא בבית ע"ז: חברי. שם אומה שהיתה עם פרסיים: הכי הילכתא. בתמיה: בשעת הדחק. סכנה אלמא שלא בשעת הדחק אסור: שזורען בקרקע. ועדיין לא השרישו מהו ללקוט ולאכול: אין מוקצה לר' שמעון בדבר הראוי. אלא בשמן שבנר בשעה שהוא דולק כדתניא לעיל: הואיל והוקצה למצותו. לשבת: הוקצה לאיסורו. איסור כיבוי: והוקצה למצותו לית ליה. בתמיה דקס"ד שמן שבנר דוקא קאמר דאיכא תרתי מוקצה למצוה ומוקצה של שעת דליקתו משום איסור כיבוי אבל מוקצה למצוה גרידא לא אסר ואפילו בשעת המצוה: והתניא סיככה. לסוכה כו': קרמים. בגדי צבעונים שקורין אובריי"א: אפרסקין. פירסיק"י בלע"ז: יינות שמנים. בכלי זכוכית: עד מוצאי י"ט האחרון. והכא מוקצה למצוה איכא מוקצה דאיסור ליכא דאי משום סתירת אהל כי מטא חולו של מועד לסתרי דומיא דנר שכבה: והא ממאי דר' שמעון היא. דמותיבנא לך מיניה: דתני ר' חייא כו' אין נוטלין עצים. בפסח ועצרת מסוכה העשויה לנוי ואפילו נפלו משום מוקצה דאיתקצאי מחמת סתירת אהל בי"ט: אלא מן הסמוך לה. אם סמך חבילות עצים אצל דופנה ליכא איסור מוקצה דדעתיה עילויה מאתמול למישקלינהו למחר דלא סתר בהו אהלא ומהן דתני ר' חייא בר יוסף הוי מצי לאותבי ברישא אלא ניחא ליה לאותבי ממתניתא דר' חייא ור' אושעיא כדאמרינן בעלמא (חולין דף קמא.) כל מתניתא דלא מיתניא בי ר' חייא כו': ור' שמעון מתיר. אם נפלה דלית ליה מוקצה והכי מוקמינן ליה במסכת ביצה: ושוין בסוכת החג בחג. שהוקצה למצותה למצותה כל שבעה אלמא כל שעת מצותה נוהג מוקצה שלה ואע"ג דליכא איסור סתירה: כעין שמן קאמינא. ולא משום איסור אלא משום מצוה דהואיל דהוקצה למצותו דשבת הוקצה לכל זמן איסור דליקתו ולא יותר דאין מצותו אלא בשעת דליקתו ומשכבה אין בו מצוה אבל בסוכת החג מצותה כל שבעה והקצאתה כל זמן מצותה: אלא גרוגרות וצמוקין. גרוגרות תאנים שמעלה לגג ליבשן ומשנשתהו שם מעט אין ראוים לאכילה עד שיתייבשו וכן צימוקים דענבים: היה אוכל בתאנים. רבותא אשמעי' (א) דהוה אכיל ואזיל מכיון דאסקינהו אסח דעתיה ואקצן: חבושין. קוייני"ן: וכן אתה אומר כו'. ואע"ג דהני חזו כל שעתא ואפי' נשתהו לא נתקלקלו מיהו הואיל ואסקינהו אסירי: אי נימא ר"י. למה לי הנך דנקט דדחינהו בידים אפי' הכניסן נמי לאוצר בעו הזמנה:

פלעילי

תוספות

הכי נמי מסתברא דרב כר' יהודה ס"ל. בכמה מקומות אשכחן דרב סבר כר' יהודה דאסר מטה שייחדה למעות והניח עליה מעות ואילו לר' שמעון שרי דהא שרי מנורות אפי' תקע בה כמה זימני ודכרכי דוחי (לעיל דף יט:) אלא דבעי לאוכוחי דסבר כר' יהודה במיגו דאיתקצאי בין השמשות כו': מקמי חברי בשבתא. שביום חג שלהם לא היו מניחין נר אלא בבית ע"ז ומאי דקמבעיא ליה בנר חנוכה טפי מבנר שבת משום דלצורך אכילה היו מניחים להם ואע"ג דבשעת הסכנה אמרינן בבמה מדליקין (לעיל דף כא:) דמניחה על שולחנו ודיו הכא מיירי אם יארע שלא הניחה על שולחנו א"נ אומר ר"י דשעת הסכנה דלעיל לאו סכנת חברים קאמר אלא סכנת גזירה שגזרו שלא להדליק נר חנוכה: היכא דדחייה בידים אית ליה. ואף על גב דנר שכבה שרי ר' שמעון אף על גב דדחייה בידים דהתם שאני כיון שכבר פסק דיחוי שלה אבל הכא לעולם הן דחויין כל זמן שמונחין שם: אלא שמן שבנר. לאו דווקא שבנר דההוא אסור משום מכבה כדאמר בפ"ב דביצה (דף כב.) המסתפק ממנו חייב משום מכבה אלא המטפטף מנר ומשום דמוקצה למצותו לא אסור [°]נר הדולק לטלטל כדפרישית לעיל אלא כדאמר בסוף פירקין משום דהוי בסיס לדבר האסור תימה לר"י דאמאי נקט שמן שבנר טפי ה"ל למינקט אין מוקצה לר' שמעון אלא גרוגרות וצימוקין דדמו טפי לחיטין שזרען דלא איתקצאי לא מחמת מצוה ולא מחמת איסור וליכא למימר דסבר ר' יוחנן דלר' שמעון אין מוקצה בגרוגרות וצימוקין דהא רבי קאמר בסמוך דאית ליה לרבי שמעון מוקצה בגרוגרות וצימוקין ומסתמא לא פליג: עד מוצאי י"ט האחרון של חג. הקשה ר"ת ביום טוב האחרון דלא אסר אלא מטעם מיגו דאיתקצאי בין השמשות מחמת יום שעבר והא רבי שמעון שרי מותר השמן שבנר אף על גב דהוקצה בין השמשות למצותו משום יום הבא ונראה לר"י דבמה שאוסרת הברייתא יום טוב האחרון לא אתיא כר' שמעון: ולא מן הסמוך לה. בפרק המביא כדי יין (ביצה ל: ושם) גרס במשנה אלא מן הסמוך לה ופריך בגמ' והא קסתר אוהלא ומשני מאי מן הסמוך לה סמוך לדפנות והשתא אי גרס בברייתא דהכא אלא מן הסמוך לה הוי בסמוך לדפנות ואי גרס ולא מן הסמוך לה מיירי במה שעל הסכך וטעמא משום דסתר אוהלא כדאמר התם: ואם התנה הכל לפי תנאו. בריש המביא (ג"ז שם) פריך עלה והא קא סתר אוהלא ומוקי לה בסוכה נפולה וברעועה דמאתמול דעתיה עלה: אלא בגרוגרות וצימוקין. בירושלמי מפ' שמסריחין בינתיים כיון שמתקלקלין כל כך אין דעתו לקחתם עד שיתקנו היטב: וכן אתה אומר באפרסקין. אף על פי שאין מתקלקלין כל כך מקצה אותם מדעתו: היכא דלא דחייה בידים אית ליה מוקצה. כגון הא דתנן בפרק מפנין (לקמן קכו:) ולא את האוצר ותנן נמי בפרק בתרא (דף קנז:) רבי יהודה אומר אם לא היתה נבלה מע"ש אסורה כו':

ואוכל איצטריכא ליה. מדנקט אוכל במוקצה דדחייה בידים נראה דאזיל ואכיל שרי ליה לר"י במוקצה דלא דחייה בידים כגון גבי אוצר:

לדבריו

רבינו חננאל

אותה בשבת. בזמן שיש עליה מעות. פי' מוכני כן. מלשון את הכיור ואת כנו. נמדלת מלשון שילוף. כדתנן המידל בגפנים. וגרסינן במשקין (מ"ק ג) מאי מדלי שלופי. נמצלת מלשון צל. קתני מיהת אין גוררין אותה בשבת בזמן שיש עליה מעות הא אין עליה מעות שרי. ואע"ג דהוו עליה בין השמשות. ושנינן משנה זו לר' שמעון היא. ורב דאמר כרבי יהודה. דהא רב הוא דאמר מניחין נר ע"ג דקל בשבת [ואין מניחין נר ע"ג דקל ביום טוב]. מכלל דרב כר' יהודה סבר ליה דאמר הנר שהדליקו בו בשבת אין מטלטלין אותו. אבל ביו"ט שמטלטלין אותו ונמצא משתמש במחובר לקרקע אסור. (ואין מניחין נר ע"ג דקל ביו"ט) ואוקימנא אליבא דר' יהודה דשני ליה בין שבת ליו"ט. אבל ר' שמעון לא שני ליה בטלטול הנר בין שבת ליו"ט. איני דרב כר' יהודה עביד ליה. והא רב התיר לטלטל נר מפני חבארי בשבת. ושנינן הא אמר רב בהא כדאי הוא ר"ש לסמוך עליו בשעת הדחק מכלל דרב סבר לית הלכתא כר' שמעון. והא דא"ר יוחנן אין מוקצה לר"ש אלא מידי דאיתקצאי לאיסורא כגון שמן שבנר בשעה שדולק או כגון עיטורי סוכה וכיוצא בהן הואיל והוקצו למצוה פשוטה היא

ואם התנה עליה. אסוכה דעלמא קאי ואריש' דברייתא קא מהדר דאיפלגו בה תנא קמא ורבי שמעון דקתני אין נוטלין עצים מן הסוכה ואוקימנא בשנפלה ומשום מוקצה וקאמר אם התנה עליה מבעוד יום שאם תפול מחר יסיקנה הכל לפי תנאו [ביצה [illegible] הרש"א]. אלא גרוגרות וצימוקים. שמעלה אותן על מנת ליבשן ומקצה אותן לכך ומשמתחילין ליבש [illegible] שייבשו לגמרי. ענבים יבשין קרוין צמוקים ותאנים שנתיבשו קרוין גרוגרות [שם כו:]. שכן ממעלה לאויין [illegible] בידים להעלותן ליבשן ושוב אינן ראויין עד שייבשו [שם מ:]. היה אוכל בתאנים והותיר. רבותא נקט דלא תימא כיון דאוכל והולך לא ליבעי הזמנה [שם כו:].

רב נסים גאון

שהוא מתיר בנר אוסר בפמוט ולדבריהם בתלמוד ארץ ישראל או כר' שמעון אפילו נר עצמו והא מותר נתבאר כבר שר' שמעון מתיר הנר עצמו וכ"ש הפמוט: מהו לטלטולי שרגא דחנוכה מקמי חבארא בשבתא. שמענו כי בימי החברים פרסיי היו חברים מחזרין בכל בתי ישראל ומכבין את הנרות ולוקחין מכל בית נר והיה צער גדול לישראל מזה המעשה מפני שהיו מוליכין את נרותיהם לע"ז ואשכחנן בפרק ב' (גיטין דף טז) רבה בר בר חנה חלש על ר' יהודה ורבנן לשיולי ביה בעו מיניה שנים שהביאו גט ממדינת הים צריכים שיאמרו בפנינו נכתב בפנינו נחתם או אין צריכין אמר להו אין צריכין מה אילו אמרו בפנינו גירשה מי לא מהימני אדהכי אתא ההוא חברא שקלא לשרגא מקמייהו אמר רחמנא או בטולך או בטולא דבר עשו למימרא דרומאי מעלו מפרסאי והא תני ר' חייא מאי דכתיב (איוב כח) אלהים הבין דרכה והוא ידע את מקומה ידע הקב"ה בישראל שאין יכולים לקבל גזירות של עשו הרשע לפיכך הגלה אותם לבבל ובמס' יבמות [illegible] על יבמתו (דף סג) אמרו מאי דכתיב בגוי נבל אכעיסם ר' יוחנן אמר אלו חברים אמרו ליה לר' יוחנן אתו חבארי לבבל (שאג) [שגא] תנפל [א"ל] מקבלי שוחדא תריץ ויתיב גזרו על שלש מפני שלש על בשר מפני המתנות [illegible] טבילה קא מחטטי שכבי מפני ששמחים ביום אידם ובשאלתות דרב אחא מן שבחא כך פי' בפרשת [illegible] ובמלכות פרסיים היו חברים שבהן מחזרין על בתי ישראל ומכבין את הנרות וחותין את הגחלים ומול[illegible] שלהן שהיא ע"ז ולא היו עחבים לא אש ולא גחלים שילינו בלילה חוץ מע"ז שלהן שהיא בית נורא: כדי הוא ר' שמעון [illegible] בן יוחי לסמוך עליו בשעת הדחק. הוא ר' שמעון שאמר הנר שכבתה מותר לטלטלה דלית ליה מוקצ[illegible]

במשנה ובברייתא הוא ר"ש בן יוחאי וכל ר' יהודה סתם הוא ר' יהודה בר' אלעאי ובמס' מנחות בפרק הקומץ (דף יח) אמרו מפני שר' יהודה בנו של ר' אלעאי ור' אילעאי תלמידו של ר' אליעזר שנה לך משנת ר' אליעזר:

mitzvah of kindling the Sabbath lights וְהוּקְצָה לְאִיסּוּרוֹ – and **was set aside for** the duration of **its prohibition.**[11]

Understanding this to mean that R' Shimon recognizes something as *muktzeh* only when it was set aside on account of the two factors of a mitzvah and a prohibition, the Gemara asks:

וְלֵית לֵיהּ הוּקְצָה לְמִצְוָתוֹ – **Does [R' Shimon] not recognize** as *muktzeh* something that was merely **set aside for a mitzvah** but was not set aside on account of a prohibition? וְהָתַנְיָא – **But it was taught in a Baraisa:** סִיכְּכָהּ כְּהִלְכָתָהּ – IF ONE COVERED A SUCCAH IN ACCORDANCE WITH ITS LAW,[12] וְעִיטְּרָהּ בְּקְרָמִין וּבְסְדִינִין הַמְצוּיָּירִין – AND HE DECORATED IT WITH COLORED CLOTH AND EMBROIDERED LINENS וְתָלָה בָּהּ אֱגוֹזִין אֲפַרְסְקִין שְׁקֵדִים וְרִמּוֹנִין – AND HUNG IN IT NUTS, PEACHES, ALMONDS, POMEGRANATES, וְאַפַּרְכְּלֵי שֶׁל עֲנָבִים וַעֲטָרוֹת שֶׁל שִׁבּוֹלִין – CLUSTERS OF GRAPES, WREATHS OF GRAIN, יֵינוֹת שְׁמָנִים וּסְלָתוֹת – or glass bottles of WINE, OIL AND FINE FLOUR – אָסוּר לְהִסְתַּפֵּק מֵהֶן – HE IS PROHIBITED TO USE THEM עַד מוֹצָאֵי יוֹם טוֹב הָאַחֲרוֹן – UNTIL THE NIGHT FOLLOWING THE LAST DAY OF THE FESTIVAL.[13] וְאִם הִתְנָה עֲלֵיהֶן – BUT IF HE MADE A STIPULATION ABOUT THEM, הַכֹּל לְפִי תְּנָאוֹ – EVERYTHING FOLLOWS HIS STIPULATION.[14] In absence of a stipulation, however, he is prohibited to use them because they are *muktzeh*. Since the only basis for considering them *muktzeh* is that they were designated for the mitzvah of succah, it is obvious that designation for a mitzvah is itself sufficient to make something *muktzeh*![15]

וּמִמַּאי דְּרַבִּי שִׁמְעוֹן הִיא – **And on what** basis do we say **that [this Baraisa] is** expressing the view of **R' Shimon?**[16] דְּתָנֵי רַבִּי חִיָּיא בַּר יוֹסֵף קַמֵּיהּ דְּרַבִּי יוֹחָנָן – It is **because R' Chiya bar Yosef taught** the following **Baraisa before R' Yochanan:** אֵין נוֹטְלִין עֵצִים מִן הַסּוּכָּה בְּיוֹם טוֹב – WE MAY NOT DETACH WOOD FROM A HUT ON A FESTIVAL, אֶלָּא מִן הַסָּמוּךְ לָהּ – EXCEPT FROM WHAT ADJOINS IT.[17] וְרַבִּי שִׁמְעוֹן מַתִּיר – BUT R' SHIMON PERMITS it.[18]

NOTES

11. Apparently, R' Yochanan means that the only case of *muktzeh* that R' Shimon recognizes (when an item is intrinsically useful) is one in which the two factors of *muktzeh by dint of a mitzvah* and *muktzeh by dint of a prohibition* coexist. In the case of oil used for the Sabbath lights both of these factors are present, since it is a mitzvah to let the Sabbath lights burn and it is further prohibited to remove oil due to the *melachah* of *extinguishing* (see 44a note 7; see also note 5 there). R' Shimon therefore concedes that the oil is *muktzeh* while the light is burning, as he stated in a Baraisa above (44a). However, in any situation where these dual factors are not present, the mere fact that a person set something aside (e.g. by planting seeds or putting an egg under a hen) will not make it *muktzeh,* according to R' Shimon (*Rashi*). [According to *Tos. Yeshanim,* the Gemara text reads explicitly: הואיל וְהוּקְצָה לְמִצְוָתוֹ וְהוּקְצָה לְאִיסּוּרוֹ, *since it was set aside for its mitzvah* ***and*** *was set aside for its prohibition.*]

[Note that it is unnecessary to prohibit taking oil from a burning lamp on the basis of *muktzeh,* since this is prohibited under the *melachah* of *extinguishing*. What is prohibited under the law of *muktzeh* is the use of oil that drips out of the lamp. Since the oil was set aside for a mitzvah and was additionally put out of mind due to the prohibition of *extinguishing,* it is *muktzeh* for as long as the lamp burns. Afterwards, its *muktzeh* status is lifted, since it was put out of mind only for as long as the lamp burns and R' Shimon rejects the notion that since it was *muktzeh* during *bein hashemashos* it remains *muktzeh* for the entire day (*Tosafos* ד״ה אלא שמן שבנר; see also *Ramban*).]

12. I.e. according to the legal requirements of סְכָךְ, *s'chach,* the covering (roof) of a succah, as described in Tractate *Succah*.

13. I.e. until the beginning of the weekday (see *Tosafos* to *Beitzah* 30b ד״ה עד). The decorations are *muktzeh* by virtue of having been designated for the mitzvah of succah (see note 15).

14. I.e. if he made an appropriate stipulation before the onset of the festival, he can prevent the decorations from becoming *muktzeh*. The Gemara in Tractate *Beitzah* (30b) explains the stipulation as being a declaration by the owner that he does not relinquish his right to remove the items from the succah. This declaration prevents them from becoming designated for the mitzvah of succah.

15. The concept of *muktzeh by dint of a prohibition* does not apply here. The prohibition of סוֹתֵר, *demolishing,* is not a factor, for this prohibition – and the *muktzeh* status that it confers – apply only on the holy days of the festival, not on the intermediate days (*chol hamoed*). Since the Baraisa prohibits use of the decorations the *entire* festival including *chol hamoed,* it is obvious that they are prohibited for personal use purely on the basis of having been designated for the mitzvah for the duration of the festival. Thus, the designation for a mitzvah is itself sufficient grounds to prohibit use of an item for a mundane purpose (*Rashi*).

[*R' Akiva Eiger* wonders why *Rashi* had to resort to the fact that the state of *muktzeh* exists on *chol hamoed* as proof that it is not based on the prohibition of *demolishing*. This is readily known from the fact that the Baraisa explicitly lists items such as bottles of wine, which are not part of the succah structure and whose removal does not constitute *demolishing*! (See also *Rashash*.) Possibly, *Rashi* holds that, on the holy days, since a person "sets aside" the walls of the succah due to the prohibition of *demolishing,* he also sets aside the decorations that are ancillary to the structure. Thus, the decorations would be *muktzeh* by dint of the prohibition even though, strictly speaking, the prohibition of *demolishing* does not apply to them (see *Rashi* to *Beitzah* 30b ד״ה הכל לפי תנאו and ד״ה אביי ורבא and *Ramban* here).]

Note that *muktzeh* due to designation for a mitzvah differs in concept from the standard *muktzeh* of the Sabbath, and shares only its name. The latter is based on the concept that, in order to be permitted for use on the Sabbath (or Yom Tov), an object must be in a state of preparedness (מוּכָן) prior to the holy day (*Rashi* to *Beitzah* 26b ד״ה ואי דלא אחזו). If it is not in a state of preparedness during *bein hashemashos,* it becomes *muktzeh* at that point and, once *muktzeh,* may not be used *or even moved* on the holy day. The *muktzeh* status of a succah and its decorations on *chol hamoed,* however, is based on a different concept. An object that has been set aside for the performance of a mitzvah may not be used (even on a *weekday*) for any purpose other than that mitzvah. The object may be moved on the weekday, provided that moving it does not interfere with the mitzvah (see *Tosafos* to 42b ד״ה ואין נאותין with *Gilyon HaShas*). The restriction against using the object for a different purpose remains in force throughout the time frame in which the mitzvah is to be done. Thus, the designation of the succah decorations for the mitzvah precludes their removal even on *chol hamoed* (see *Beitzah* 30b and *Succah* 46b; see also *Ramban, Ritva MHK* ed., *Tosafos* above, 22a ד״ה סוכה with *Maharsha* and *Karnei Re'eim,* and 22a note 15). [On the Sabbath and the holy days of a festival, the fact that something was set aside for a mitzvah can give it the additional *muktzeh* status associated with the holy days, and can engender a prohibition against moving it (see *Gilyon HaShas* ibid., and *Mishnas R' Aharon, Kuntres Maseches Shabbos* §9).]

On the basis of the Baraisa just cited, we learn that something which was set aside for a mitzvah is prohibited for personal use even if there is no additional *muktzeh* factor present. Accordingly, the oil dripping from a Sabbath light should be prohibited for use while the light is burning on the mere basis of having been set aside for the mitzvah, even without the additional factor of *muktzeh by dint of a prohibition.*

16. We must prove this, for otherwise we cannot present it as a challenge to R' Yochanan, who was discussing R' Shimon's opinion (*Rashi;* cf. *Pnei Yehoshua, Chidushei R' Elazar Moshe Horowitz*).

17. This refers to a person sitting in a hut to enjoy its shade on the festivals of Pesach or Shavuos. Detaching wood from the structure would be a violation of the *melachah* of *demolishing*. Even if the hut collapses the wood remains *muktzeh* because it was part of the structure at the onset of the festival and was prohibited for removal at that time. Since it was *muktzeh* by dint of the prohibition during *bein hashemashos,* it remains *muktzeh* for the entire day. However, the pieces of wood that stand around the walls of the structure and are not an integral part of the hut may be removed. Since they are not woven into the fabric of the walls, removing them would not be a violation of the *melachah* of *demolishing*. By extension, they are not *muktzeh* (*Rashi*).

18. R' Shimon is obviously not referring to a case in which the hut is still standing, since taking wood from a standing hut would involve the *melachah* of *demolishing*. Rather, R' Shimon refers to a case in which the hut has collapsed and the only possible reason for prohibiting use of the wood is that it is deemed *muktzeh*. In R' Shimon's view, it is not *muktzeh* and may be used (*Rashi*).

[The Gemara in *Beitzah* (30b) adds that R' Shimon refers specifically

הכי נמי מיסתברא דרב כר' יהודה סבירא ליה דאמר רב א מניחין נר על גבי דקל בשבת ואין מניחין נר ע"ג דקל בי"ט אי אמרת בשלמא דרב כרבי יהודה סבירא ליה היינו דשני בין שבת לי"ט אלא אי אמרת כרבי שמעון סבירא ליה מה לי שבת ומה לי י"ט ורב כרבי יהודה ס"ל והא בעו מיניה דרב מהו לטלטולי שרגא דחנוכתא מקמי חברי בשבתא ואמר להו שפיר דמי שעת הדחק שאני דהא א"ל רב כהנא ורב אשי לרב הכי הלכתא אמר להו א) כדי הוא ר' שמעון לסמוך עליו בשעת הדחק בעא מיניה ריש לקיש מר' יוחנן חטים שזרען בקרקע וביצים שתחת תרנגולת מהו כי לית ליה לר' שמעון מוקצה היכא דלא דחייה בידים היכא דדחייה בידים אית ליה מוקצה או דילמא ב לא שנא א"ל אין מוקצה לרבי שמעון אלא שמן שבנר בשעה שהוא דולק הואיל והוקצה למצותו ג) הוקצה לאיסורו ולית ליה הוקצה למצותו ג) והתניא סיככה כהלכתה ועיטרה בקרמים ובסדינין המצויירין ותלה בה אגוזין אפרסקין שקדים ורמונין ואפרכלי של ענבים ועטרות של שבולין יינות שמנים וסלתות אסור להסתפק מהן עד מוצאי י"ט האחרון ואם התנה עליהן הכל לפי תנאו וממאי דר' שמעון היא דתני ד) ר' חייא בר יוסף קמיה דר' יוחנן אין נוטלין עצים מן הסוכה בי"ט אלא מן הסמוך לה ור' שמעון מתיר ושוין בסוכת החג בחג שהיא אסורה ואם התנה עליה הכל לפי תנאו כעין שמן שבנר קאמרינן הואיל והוקצה למצותו הוקצה לאיסורו איתמר נמי א"ר חייא בר אבא א"ר יוחנן אין מוקצה לרבי שמעון אלא כעין שמן שבנר בשעה שהוא דולק הואיל והוקצה למצותו הוקצה לאיסורו אמר רב יהודה אמר שמואל אין מוקצה לר' שמעון אלא גרוגרות וצימוקים בלבד ומידי אחרינא לא והתניא ה) היה אוכל בתאנים והותיר והעלן לגג לעשות מהן גרוגרות בענבים והותיר והעלן לגג לעשות מהן צימוקין לא יאכל עד שיזמין וכן אתה אומר באפרסקין וחבושין ובשאר כל מיני פירות מני אילימא רבי יהודה ומה היכא דלא דחייה בידים אית ליה מוקצה היכא דדחייה בידים לא כל שכן אלא לאו ר' שמעון היא לעולם רבי יהודה ואוכל אצטריכא ליה סד"א כיון דקאכיל ואזיל לא ליבעי הזמנה קמ"ל כיון דהעלן לגג אסוחי אסחי לדעתיה מינייהו ו) בעא מיניה רבי שמעון בר רבי מרבי

פצעילי

מניחין נר. מבעוד יום: ע"ג דקל. וידלק שם בשבת דליכא למיחש לכשיכבה לישקליה מיניה ונמצא משתמש במחובר דכיון דאקצייה לדבר האסור בין השמשות איתקצי לכולי יומא: ואין מניחין כו' בי"ט. דשקיל ומנח ליה ומשתמש באילן: מה לי שבת כו'. בשבת נמי שקיל ליה לכשיכבה: שרגא דחנוכתא. אחר שכבה: מקמי חברי. שלא יראוהו בחצר כדאמרינן בפרקין דלעיל (דף כא:) דנותנו בטפח הסמוך לרשות הרבים וידעו שהדליקו בו נר והם גזרו שלא להדליק אי נמי ביום חגם אין מניחין לדלוק אור אלא בבית ע"ז: חברי. שם אומה שהיתה עם פרסיים: הכי הילכתא. בתמיה: בשעת הדחק. סכנה אלמא שלא בשעת הדחק אסור: שזרען בקרקע. ועדיין לא השרישו מהו ללקוט ולאכול: אין מוקצה לר' שמעון בדבר הראוי. אלא בשמן שבנר בשעה שהוא דולק כדתניא לעיל: הואיל והוקצה למצותו. לשבת: הוקצה לאיסורו. איסור כיבוי: והוקצה למצותו לית ליה. בתמיה דקס"ד שמן שבנר דוקא קאמר דאיכא תרתי מוקצה למצוה ומוקצה של שעת דליקתו משום איסור כיבוי אבל מוקצה למצוה גרידא לא אסר ואפילו בשעת המצוה: והתניא סיככה. לסוכה כו': קרמים. בגדי צבעונים שקורין אובריי"א: אפרסקין. פירסיק"י בלע"ז: יינות שמנים. בכלי זכוכית: עד מוצאי י"ט האחרון. והכא מוקצה למצוה איכא מוקצה לאיסור ליכא דאי משום סתירת אהל כי מטא חולו של מועד לסתרי דומיא דנר שכבה: והא ממאי דר' שמעון היא. דמותיבנא לך מיניה: דתני ר' חייא כו' אין נוטלין עצים. בפסח ועצרת מסוכה העשויה לנוי ואפילו נפלו משום מוקצה דאיתקצאי מחמת סתירת אהל בי"ט: אלא מן הסמוך לה. אם סמך חבילות עצים אצל דופנה ליכא איסור מוקצה דדעתיה עילויה מאתמול למישקלינהו למחר דלא סתר בהו אהלא ומהך דתני ר' חייא בר יוסף הוי מצי לאותבי ברישא אלא ניחא ליה לאותבי ממתניתא דר' חייא ור' אושעיא כדאמרינן בעלמא (חולין דף קמא.) כל מתניתא דלא מיתניא בי ר' חייא כו': ור' שמעון מתיר. אם נפלה דלית ליה מוקצה והכי מוקמינן ליה במסכת ביצה: ושוין בסוכת החג בחג. שהוקצה למצותה דמצותה כל שבעה אלמא כל שעת מצותה נוהג מוקצה שלה ואע"ג דליכא איסור סתירה: כעין שמן קאמינא. ולא משום איסור אלא משום מצוה דהואיל דהוקצה למצותו דשבת הוקצה לכל זמן איסור דליקתו ולא יותר דאין מצותו אלא בשעת דליקתו ומסכה אין בו מצוה אבל בסוכת החג מצותה כל שבעה והקצאתה כל זמן מצותה: אלא גרוגרות וצמוקין. גרוגרות תאנים שמעלה לגג ליבשן ומשנשתהו שם מעט אין ראוים לאכילה עד שיתייבשו וכן צימוקים לענבים: היה אוכל בתאנים. רבותא אשמעי' (א) דהוה אכיל ואזיל מכיון דאסקינהו אסח דעתיה ואקצן: חבושין. קויי"ן: וכן אתה אומר כו'. ואע"ג דהני חזי כל שעתא ואפי' נשתהו לא נתקלקלו מיהו הואיל ואקצינהו אסירי: אי נימא ר"י. למה לי הנך דנקט דדחינהו בידים אפי' הכניסן נמי לאוצר בעו הזמנה:

פלעילי

הכי נמי מסתברא דרב כר' יהודה ס"ל. בכמה מקומות אשכחן דרב סבר כר' יהודה דאסר מטה שייחדה למעות והניח עליה מעות ואילו לר' שמעון שרי דהא שרי אנוגרות אפי' תקע בה כמה זימני ודכרכי לחוי (לעיל דף יט:) אלא דבעי לאוכוחי דסבר כר' יהודה במיגו דאיתקצאי בין השמשות כו': מקמי חברי בשבתא. שביום חג שלהם לא היו מניחין נר אלא בבית ע"ז ומאי דקמבעיא ליה בנר חנוכה טפי מבנר שבת משום דלצורך אכילה היו מניחים להם ואע"ג דבשעת הסכנה אמרינן בבמה מדליקין (לעיל דף כא:) דמניחה על שולחנו ודיו הכא מיירי אם יארע שלא הניחה על שולחנו א"נ אומר ר"י דשעת הסכנה דלעיל לאו סכנת חברים קאמר אלא סכנת גזירה שגזרו שלא להדליק נר חנוכה: היכא דדחייה בידים אית ליה. ואף על גב דנר שכבה שרי ר' שמעון אף על גב דדחייה בידים התם שאני כיון שכבה פסק ליחוי שלה אבל הכא לעולם הן דחוין כל זמן שמונחין שם: אלא שמן שבנר. לאו דווקא שבנר דההוא אסור משום מכבה כדאמר בפ"ב דביצה (דף כב.) המסתפק ממנו חייב משום מכבה אלא המטפטף מנר ומשום דמוקצה למצותו לא אסור ° נר הדולק לטלטל כדפרישית לעיל אלא כדאמר בסוף פירקין משום דהוי בסיס לדבר האסור תימה לר"י דמאי נקט שמן שבנר טפי ה"ל למינקט אין מוקצה לר' שמעון אלא גרוגרות וצימוקין דדמו טפי לחיטין שזרען דלא איתקצאי לא מחמת מצוה ולא מחמת איסור וליכא למימר דסבר ר' יוחנן דלר' שמעון אין מוקצה בגרוגרות וצימוקין דהא רבי קאמר בסמוך דאית ליה לרבי שמעון מוקצה בגרוגרות וצימוקין ומסתמא לא פליג: עד מוצאי י"ט האחרון של חג. הקשה ר"ת ביום טוב האחרון דלא אסר אלא מטעם מיגו דאיתקצאי בין השמשות מחמת יום שעבר והא רבי שמעון שרי מותר השמן שבנר אף על גב דהוקצה בין השמשות למצותו משום יום הבא ונראה לר"י דבמה שאוסרת הברייתא יום טוב האחרון לא אתיא כר' שמעון: ולא מן הסמוך לה. בפרק המביא כדי יין (ביצה ל: ושם) גרס במשנה אלא מן הסמוך לה ופריך בגמ' והא קסתר אוהלא ומשני מאי מן הסמוך לה סמוך לדפנות והשתא אי גרס בברייתא דהכא אלא מן הסמוך לה הוי בסמוך לדפנות ואי גרס ולא מן הסמוך לה מיירי במה שעל הסכך וטעמא משום דסתר אוהלא כדאמר התם: ואם התנה הכל לפי תנאו. בריש המביא (ג"ז שם) פריך עלה והא קא סתר אוהלא ומוקי לה בסוכה נפולה וברעועה דמאתמול דעתיה עלה: אלא בגרוגרות וצימוקין. בירושלמי מפ' שמסריחין בינתיים כיון שמתקלקלין כל כך אין דעתו לקחתם עד שיתקנו היטב: וכן אתה אומר באפרסקין. אף על פי שאין מתקלקלין כל כך מקצה אותם מדעתו: היכא דלא דחייה בידים אית ליה מוקצה. כגון הא דתנן בפרק מפנין (לקמן קכו:) ולא את האוצר ותנן נמי בפרק בתרא (דף קנו:) רבי יהודה אומר אם לא היתה נבלה מע"ש אסורה כו': ואוכל איצטריכא ליה. מדנקט אוכל במוקצה דדחייה בידים נראה דאזיל ואכיל שרי ליה לר"י במוקצה דלא דחייה בידים כגון גבי אוצר:

לדבריו

מסורת הש"ס

א) [ברכות ט. עירובין מו.] גיטין יט. נדה ו. ט:, ב) נ"ל והוקצה [תוס' ישנים], ג) לעיל כב. ביצה ל: סוכה י. [תוספתא סוכה פ"א], ד) ביצה ל:, ה) ביצה כו:, ו) [ביצה מ.].

הגהות הב"ח

(א) רש"י ד"ה היה אוכל וכו' רבותא אשמעי' אע"פ דהוה:

גליון הש"ס

תוס' ד"ה אלא שמן וכו'. נר הדולק לטלטל כדפי'. לעיל דף מב ע"ב תוס' ד"ה ואין נאותין:

ליקוטי רש"י

חברי. פרסיים רשעים ומבזין ואינם מכירים כבודם של ישראל [יבמות סג:]. פרסאי [גיטין יז. ועיי"ש בתוס']. אומה הסמוכה לפרסיים ומשמשיהם הם וטרפנים הם יותר מפרסיים [קידושין עב.]. בשעת הדחק. אבל שלא בשעת הדחק לא [ברכות ט.]. ועטרה. יפה בסדינין ובקרמין המצויירין [ביצה ל:]. בקרמים. פארה ביריעות של צבעים שקורין אובריי"ן [לעיל כב.]. מעשה אורג כגון בגדי צבעונין שקורין אובריי"ן [סוכה י.]. ובסדינין. לבנים של פשתן [ביצה שם]. המצויירין. שצורתן בולטת כגון מעשה רוקם או מעשה אורג שקורין גלינסק"ש. יינות שמנים. טומנין בכוסות של זכוכית לנוי [סוכה שם]. ואם התנה עליהן. מבעוד יום איני בודל מהם מהיות כותי חכומי בהם ליטלן כל שהות אורך של בין השמשות של ערב יום טוב הלכך בשעת ביאת היום שהיתה קדושה צריכה לחול עליהם לא חלה לפיכך לא הוקצה [ביצה שם]. וכגון דאמר איני בודל מהם כל בין השמשות של יום טוב הראשון דלא חל קדושה עלייהו והכי מוקים לה במסכת ביצה בהמביא (ל:) ותנאה אחרינא לא מהני בהו [סוכה שם: ובעי"ז לעיל שם]. אין נוטלין עצים מן הסוכה. שנפלה ביו"ט דליכא סתירת אהל וטעמא דתנא קמא משום מוקצה דהא בין השמשות היתה קיימת ומוקצה היא מחמת איסור סתירה אבל הסמוך לה לאו מוקצה הוא דלית ביה משום סתירה. אלא מן הסמוך לה. קנים המוקפים סביבות לדפנות כיון שלא נארגו עם הדופן לא בטלי לגבי דופן ואינו דומה לסמוך לסכך שהסכך אינו ארוג לפיכך הכל שוה העליון כתחתון סכך הוא. ורבי שמעון מתיר. בסוכה רעועה דמסיק אדעתיה דנפלה ולמחר נפלה הלכך לרבי שמעון מוקצה ליכא דאמרינן דעתיה מאתמול עלויה ולתנא קמא לא אמרינן דעתיה עלויה בשום מידי דלא חזי בין השמשות. שהיא אסורה. אפילו בחוש"מ. ואם התנה עליה. אסוכה דעלמא קאי ואריש' דברייתא קא מהדר דאיפלגו בה תנא קמא ורבי שמעון דקתני אין נוטלין עצים מן הסוכה ואוקימנא בשנפלה ומשום מוקצה וקאמר אם התנה עליה מבעוד יום שאם תפול מחר יסיקנה הכל לפי תנאו [ביצה שם ועי' כאן בתוס' ובמהרש"א]. אלא גרוגרות וצימוקים. שמעלה אותן על מנת ליבשן ומקצה אותן לכך ומשמתחילין ליבש אין ראוין לאכילה עד שייבשו לגמרי. ענבים יבשין קרוין צמוקים ותאנין שנתייבשו קרוין גרוגרות [שם כו:]. שהן מתחלה ראוין לאכילה והוא דחה אותן בידים להעלותן ליבשן ושוב אינן ראוין עד שייבשו [שם מ:]. היה אוכל בתאנים והותיר. רבותא נקט דלא תימא כיון דאוכל והולך לא ליבעי הזמנה [שם כו:].

עין משפט נר מצוה

נב א מיי' פ"ה מהלכות שבת הלכה יח ופ"ד מהלכות י"ט הלכה ה סמג לאוין סה טור שו"ע או"ח סימן רעז סעיף ד וסימן תקי"ד סעיף ו:

נג ב מיי' פכ"ו מהלכות שבת הלכה יד סמג לאוין סה טוש"ע או"ח סימן שי סעיף ב:

רבינו חננאל

אותה בשבת. בזמן שיש עליה מעות. פי' מוכני כן. מלשון את הכיור ואת כנו. נמדלת מלשון שילוף. כדתנן המידל בגפנים. וגרסינן במשקין (מ"ק ג) מאי מדלי שלופי. נמצלת מלשון צל. קתני מיהת אין גוררין אותה בשבת בזמן שיש עליה מעות הא אין עליה מעות שרי. ואע"ג דהוו עליה בין השמשות. ושנינן משנה זו לר' שמעון היא. ורב דאמר כרבי יהודה. דהא רב הוא דאמר מניחין נר ע"ג דקל בשבת [ואין מניחין נר ע"ג דקל ביום טוב]. מכלל דרב כר' יהודה סבר ליה דאמר הנר שהדליקו בו בשבת אין מטלטלין אותו. אבל ביו"ט שמטלטלין אותו תמצא משתמש במחובר לקרקע אסור. (ואין מניחין נר ע"ג דקל ביו"ט) ואוקימנא אליבא דר' יהודה דשני ליה בין שבת ליו"ט. אבל ר' שמעון לא שני ליה בטלטול הנר בין שבת ליו"ט. איני דרב כר' יהודה עביד ליה. והא רב התיר לטלטל נר מפני חבארי בשבת. ושנינן הא אמר רב בהא כדאי הוא ר"ש לסמוך עליו בשעת הדחק מכלל דרב סבר לית הלכתא כר' שמעון. והא דא"ר יוחנן אין מוקצה לר"ש אלא מידי דאיתקצאי לאיסורא כגון שמן שבנר בשעה שדולק או כגון עיטורי סוכה וכיוצא בהן הואיל והוקצו למצוה פשוטה היא

רב נסים גאון

שהוא מתיר בנר אוסר בפמוט ולדבריהם בתלמוד ארץ ישראל או כר' שמעון אפילו נר עצמו יהא מותר נתבאר כבר שר' שמעון מתיר הנר עצמו וכ"ש הפמוט: מהו לטלטולי שרגא דחנוכה מיקמי חבארא בשבתא. שמענו כי בימי החברים פרסיי' היו חברים מחזרין בכל בתי ישראל ומכבין את הנרות ולוקחין מכל בית נר והיה צער גדול לישר' מזה המעשה מפני שהיו מוליכין את נרותיהם לע"ז ואשכחן בפרק ב' (דגיטין דף טז) רבה בר בר חנה חלש על ר' יהודה ורבנן לשוילי ביה בעו מיניה שנים שהביאו גט ממדינת הים צריכים שיאמרו בפנינו נכתב בפנינו נחתם או אין צריכין אמר להו אין צריכין ומה אילו אמרו בפנינו גירשה מי לא מהימני אדהכי אתא ההוא חברא שקלא לשרגא מיקמייהו אמרי רחמנא או בטולך או בטולא דבר עשו למימרא דרומאי מעלו מפרסאי והא תני ר' חייא מאי דכתיב (איוב כח) אלהים הבין דרכה והוא ידע את מקומה ידע הקב"ה בישראל שאין יכולים לקבל גזירות של עשו הרשע לפיכך הגלה אותם לבבל ובמס' יבמות בפרק הבא על יבמתו (דף סג) אמרו מאי דכתיב בגוי נבל אכעיסם ר' יוחנן אמר אלו חברים אמרו ליה לר' יוחנן אתו חבארי לבבל (שאג) [שגא] ונפל [א"ל] מקבלי שוחדא תריץ ויתיב גזרו על שלש מפני שלש על בשר מפני המתנות על מרחצאות מפני טבילה קא מחטטי שכבי מפני ששמחים ביום אידם ובשאלתות דרב אחא מן שבחא כך פי' בפרשת וארא אל אברהם ובמלכות פרסיים היו חברים שבהן מחזרין על בתי ישראל ומכבין את הנרות וחותין את הגחלים ומוליכין אותן לבית האור שלהן שהיא ע"ז ולא היו עוזבים לא אש ולא גחלים שילינו בלילה חוץ מע"ז שלהן שהיא בית נורא: כדי הוא ר' שמעון בן יוחי לסמוך עליו בשעת הדחק. הוא ר' שמעון שאמר הנר שכבתה מותר לטלטלה דלית ליה מוקצה וכל ר' שמעון סתם במשנה ובברייתא הוא ר"ש בן יוחאי וכל ר' יהודה סתם הוא ר' יהודה בר' אלעאי ובמס' מנחות בפרק הקומץ (דף יח) אמרו מפני שר' יהודה בנו של ר' אלעאי ור' אילעאי תלמידו של ר' אליעזר שנה לך משנת ר' אליעזר:

וְשָׁוִין בְּסוּכַּת הֶחָג בֶּחָג שֶׁהִיא אֲסוּרָה – AND ALL AGREE ABOUT THE SUCCAH DURING THE SUCCOS festival THAT [ITS WOOD] IS PROHIBITED.[19] וְאִם הִתְנָה עָלֶיהָ – BUT IF HE MADE A STIPULATION ABOUT IT before the festival, הַכֹּל לְפִי תְּנָאוֹ – EVERYTHING FOLLOWS HIS STIPULATION.[20] We see from this Baraisa that R' Shimon concedes that the wood of a succah is *muktzeh* simply on the basis of having been set aside for a mitzvah.[21]

The Gemara resolves the difficulty by clarifying R' Yochanan's statement:

כְּעֵין שֶׁמֶן שֶׁבַּנֵּר קָאַמְרִינַן – **We** (i.e. R' Yochanan) meant to **say** that nothing useful is *muktzeh* according to R' Shimon except that which is ***similar*** **to the oil in a** Sabbath **lamp** while it is burning, in the respect that it is currently being used for a mitzvah. However, when the mitzvah has ended it is no longer *muktzeh,* הוֹאִיל וְהוּקְצָה לְמִצְוָתוֹ – for **since it was set aside for its mitzvah** הוּקְצָה לְאִיסּוּרוֹ – **it is set aside** only **for** the duration of **the prohibition of** terminating **[the mitzvah],** e.g. for as long as the lamp burns.[22]

The Gemara corroborates this interpretation:

אִיתְּמַר נַמִּי – **It was similarly stated:** אָמַר ר׳ חִיָּיא בַּר אַבָּא אָמַר ר׳ יוֹחָנָן – **R' Chiya bar Abba said in the name of R' Yochanan:** אֵין מוּקְצֶה לְרַבִּי שִׁמְעוֹן – **Nothing** useful **is** ***muktzeh,*** **according to R' Shimon,** on the basis of having been set aside, אֶלָּא כְּעֵין שֶׁמֶן שֶׁבַּנֵּר בְּשָׁעָה שֶׁהוּא דוֹלֵק – **except** that which is **similar to the oil in a** Sabbath **lamp while it is burning,** הוֹאִיל וְהוּקְצָה לְמִצְוָתוֹ הוּקְצָה לְאִיסּוּרוֹ – for **since it was set aside for its mitzvah it was set aside** only **for** the duration of **the prohibition of** terminating **[the mitzvah].**

Having established that R' Shimon does not consider any useful item *muktzeh* on the basis of having been set aside, except that which was set aside for a mitzvah, the Gemara turns to another type of item that R' Shimon concedes is *muktzeh*:

אָמַר רַב יְהוּדָה אָמַר שְׁמוּאֵל – **Rav Yehudah said in the name of Shmuel:** אֵין מוּקְצֶה לְרַבִּי שִׁמְעוֹן – **There is no** food that is ***muktzeh,*** **according to R' Shimon,** on the basis of having been set aside, אֶלָּא גְּרוֹגְרוֹת וְצִימּוּקִין בִּלְבַד – **except for dried figs and raisins** that were set out to dry before the advent of the Sabbath and have not yet dried out completely. R' Shimon concedes that these are *muktzeh,* since they are unfit for consumption.[23]

The Gemara asks:

וּמִידֵי אַחֲרִינָא לָא – **But** are **other things not** rendered *muktzeh* by being set aside, according to R' Shimon? וְהָתַנְיָא – **Why, it was taught in a Baraisa:** הָיָה אוֹכֵל בִּתְאֵנִים וְהוֹתִיר – If SOMEONE WAS EATING FIGS AND LEFT OVER some, וְהֶעֱלָן לַגַּג לַעֲשׂוֹת מֵהֶן גְּרוֹגְרוֹת – AND HE TOOK THEM UP TO THE ROOF TO MAKE DRIED FIGS OUT OF THEM, בַּעֲנָבִים וְהוֹתִיר – or if he was eating GRAPES AND LEFT OVER some, וְהֶעֱלָן לַגַּג לַעֲשׂוֹת מֵהֶן צִימּוּקִין – AND HE TOOK THEM UP TO THE ROOF TO MAKE RAISINS OUT OF THEM – לֹא יֹאכַל עַד שֶׁיְּזַמֵּין – HE MAY NOT EAT them UNLESS HE DESIGNATES THEM for use before the Sabbath.[24] וְכֵן אַתָּה אוֹמֵר בַּאֲפַרְסְקִין וְחַבּוּשִׁין – AND SO DO YOU FIND the same ruling REGARDING PEACHES, QUINCES וּבִשְׁאָר כָּל מִינֵי פֵּירוֹת – AND ALL OTHER TYPES OF FRUITS. The Baraisa states that *all* fruits are rendered *muktzeh* by being put out to dry, not only figs and grapes![25] מַנִּי – Now consider: **Who** could be the author of this Baraisa? אִילֵימָא רַבִּי יְהוּדָה – **If you will say** that it is **R' Yehudah,** that is impossible: וּמַה הֵיכָא דְּלֹא דַחְיֵיהּ בְּיָדַיִם אִית לֵיהּ מוּקְצֶה – For **if even** in a case **where one did not actively set something aside** but merely failed to prepare it for Sabbath use **[R' Yehudah] considers it**

NOTES

to a case in which the hut was rickety and in imminent danger of collapse at the onset of the festival. Accordingly, the owner anticipated that it would collapse and its wood would become available. In such a case, R' Shimon does not consider the wood to be *muktzeh* once the hut has collapsed, just as he does not consider the leftover oil in a small lamp to be *muktzeh* once the flame has gone out. But where the hut was sturdy and its fall was unanticipated, R' Shimon agrees that if it should unexpectedly collapse its wood remains *muktzeh,* just as he agrees that in the case of a large lamp the oil remains *muktzeh* even if the flame goes out unexpectedly, as the Gemara explained earlier (44a; see note 16 there).]

19. I.e. it is prohibited to take wood from a collapsed succah, even during *chol hamoed,* when *muktzeh* by dint of the prohibition of *demolishing* is not applicable, because the wood of the succah was set aside for a mitzvah. Thus, we see that even according to R' Shimon designation for a mitzvah is itself a basis for considering something *muktzeh* (*Rashi* here and *Beitzah* 30b).

20. This clause refers only to a *hut* that collapsed. The Tanna Kamma agrees that if a person who anticipated its collapse stipulated that he intended to use the wood, it does not become *muktzeh.* [This stipulation is ineffective with regard to the wood of a succah on the Succos festival] (see *Beitzah* 30b and *Rashi* there ד״ה סיפה and ד״ה אביי ורבא; see also *Maharsha* to *Tosafos* ד״ה ואם התנה).

21. The Gemara could have challenged R' Yochanan directly on the basis of this second Baraisa. The reason it initially cited the first Baraisa (which does not explicitly attribute its opinion to R' Shimon) is that only the first Baraisa was taught by R' Chiya and R' Oshaya, whose Baraisos are considered authoritative. It therefore relies on this second Baraisa merely to prove that the first Baraisa is attributable to R' Shimon (*Rashi;* see *Chullin* 141a-b).

22. Thus, R' Yochanan means that the designation for a mitzvah is itself sufficient to make something *muktzeh,* even according to R' Shimon. However, an item so designated does not remain *muktzeh* after the mitzvah has been completed [because R' Shimon rejects the concept that since it was *muktzeh* during *bein hashemashos* it remains *muktzeh* for the entire day]. In the case of the Sabbath lights, the mitzvah extends for as long as they burn, and R' Shimon therefore forbids use of the dripping oil throughout that period, but no longer. In the case of succah, though, the mitzvah extends all seven days of the festival and R' Shimon therefore agrees that the wood and decorations are forbidden for another use throughout the festival (*Rashi;* cf. *Ritva MHK* ed., *Chidushei HaRan, Pnei Yehoshua*).

23. In earlier times, fresh figs and grapes would be put out to dry on rooftops to become dried figs and raisins. Once they began to bake in the sun, these figs and grapes would become unfit for consumption until they dried out properly. Since, the fruits are unfit for consumption, R' Shimon concedes that they are *muktzeh* (*Rashi;* see also *Tosafos* ד״ה אלא). Thus, if someone wants to eat them before they have completely dried out, he may not, for they are *muktzeh* (see *Rashi* to 45b ד״ה פצעילי תמרה and *Tosafos* here). [*Ran* states that even if they finished drying out on the Sabbath, they remain *muktzeh* for the entire day. However, according to R' Shimon, this pertains only if one did not anticipate that they would finish drying out on the Sabbath (see *Beitzah* 26b, *Haamek She'eilah* 47:7 and *Afikei Yam* II:21).]

[Note that R' Shimon concedes that many other things are *muktzeh.* The Gemara here refers only to foods, teaching that even foods that were actively set aside are not *muktzeh,* according to R' Shimon, except for partially dried figs and raisins (see *Rambam, Hil. Shabbos* 26:14 and *Orach Chaim* 310:2 with *Beur HaGra*).]

24. [I.e. if he explicitly states his intention to eat the drying fruit before it is fully ready, it is not rendered *muktzeh.*] The Gemara in *Beitzah* (26b) limits the effectiveness of such a designation to a case where the drying figs or raisins were marginally fit to be eaten at the time that he made the designation. The designation is worthless if the fruit is totally unfit for consumption.

The Baraisa teaches that even if a person was already eating from the figs and grapes, once he takes them up to the roof to dry they become *muktzeh* without explicit designation (*Rashi*).

25. Although other fruits do not initially become spoiled when left out in the sun as figs and grapes do, the Baraisa teaches that they become *muktzeh* on the mere basis of having been set out to dry, since the person actively rejected them from current use (*Rashi;* see *Tosafos*).

הכי נמי מיסתברא דרב כר' יהודה סבירא ליה דאמר רב א מניחין נר על גבי דקל בשבת ואין מניחין נר ע"ג דקל בי"ט אי אמרת בשלמא דרב כרבי יהודה סבירא ליה היינו דשני בין שבת לי"ט אלא אי אמרת כרבי שמעון סבירא ליה מה לי שבת ומה לי י"ט ורב כרבי יהודה ס"ל והא בעו מיניה דרב מהו לטלטולי שרגא דחנוכתא מקמי חברי בשבתא ואמר להו שפיר דמי שעת הדחק שאני דהא א"ל רב כהנא ורב אשי לרב הכי הלכתא אמר להו א) כדי הוא ר' שמעון לסמוך עליו בשעת הדחק בעא מיניה ריש לקיש מר' יוחנן חטים שזרען בקרקע וביצים שתחת תרנגולת מהו כי לית ליה לר' שמעון מוקצה היכא דלא דחייה בידים היכא דדחייה בידים אית ליה מוקצה או דילמא ב לא שנא א"ל אין מוקצה לרבי שמעון אלא שמן שבנר בשעה שהוא דולק הואיל והוקצה למצותו ג) הוקצה לאיסורו ולית ליה הוקצה למצותו ג) והתניא סיככה כהלכתה ועיטרה בקרמים ובסדינין המצויירין ותלה בה אגוזין אפרסקין שקדים ורמונין ואפרכלי של ענבים ועטרות של שבולין יינות שמנים וסלתות אסור להסתפק מהן עד מוצאי י"ט האחרון ואם התנה עליהן הכל לפי תנאו וממאי דר' שמעון היא דתני ד) ר' חייא בר יוסף קמיה דר' יוחנן אין נוטלין עצים מן הסוכה בי"ט אלא מן הסמוך לה ור' שמעון מתיר ושוין בסוכת החג בחג שהיא אסורה ואם התנה עליה הכל לפי תנאו כעין שמן שבנר קאמרינן הואיל והוקצה למצותו הוקצה לאיסורו איתמר נמי א"ר חייא בר אבא א"ר יוחנן אין מוקצה לרבי שמעון אלא כעין שמן שבנר בשעה שהוא דולק הואיל והוקצה למצותו הוקצה לאיסורו אמר רב יהודה אמר שמואל אין מוקצה לר' שמעון אלא גרוגרות וצימוקים בלבד ומידי אחרינא לא והתניא ה) היה אוכל בתאנים והותיר והעלן לגג לעשות מהן גרוגרות בענבים והותיר והעלן לגג לעשות מהן צימוקין לא יאכל עד שיזמין וכן אתה אומר באפרסקין וחבושין ובשאר כל מיני פירות מני אילימא רבי יהודה ומה היכא דלא דחייה בידים אית ליה מוקצה היכא דדחייה בידים לא כל שכן אלא לאו ר' שמעון היא לעולם רבי יהודה ואוכל אצטריכא ליה סד"א כיון דקאכיל ואזיל לא ליבעי הזמנה קמ"ל כיון דהעלן לגג אסוחי אסחי לדעתיה מינייהו ו) בעא מיניה רבי שמעון בר רבי מרבי פצעילי

רש"י

מניחין נר. מבעוד יום: ע"ג דקל. וידלק שם בשבת דליכא למיחש לכשיכבה ליסקליה מיניה ונמלא משתמש במחובר דכיון דאקלייה לדבר האסור בין השמשות איתקלי לכולי יומא: ואין מניחין כו' בי"ט. דשקיל ומנח ליה ומשתמש באילן: מה לי שבת כו'. בשבת נמי שקיל ליה לכשיכבה: שרגא דחנוכתא. אחר שכבה: מקמי חברי. שלא יראוהו בנר כדאמרינן בפרקין דלעיל (דף כב:) דנותנו בטפח הסמוך לרשות הרבים וידעו שהדליקו בו נר והם גזרו שלא להדליק אי נמי ביום חגם אין מניחין לדלוק אור אלא בבית ע"ז: חברי. שם אומה שהיתה עם פרסיים: הכי הילכתא. בתמיה: בשעת הדחק. סכנה אלמא שלא בשעת הדחק אסור: שזרען בקרקע. ועדיין לא השרישו מהו ללקוט ולאכול: אין מוקצה לר' שמעון בדבר הראוי. אלא בשמן שבנר בשעה שהוא דולק כדתניא לעיל: הואיל והוקצה למצותו. לשבת: הוקצה לאיסורו. איסור כיבוי: והוקצה למצותו לית ליה. בתמיה דקס"ד שמן שבנר דוקא קאמר דאיכא תרתי מוקצה למצוה ומוקצה של שעת דליקתו משום איסור כיבוי אבל מוקצה למצוה גרידא לא אסר ואפילו בשעת המצוה: והתניא סיככה. לסוכה כו': קרמים. בגדי לבעונים שקורין אובריי"ש: אפרסקין. פירסיק"ש בלע"ז: יינות שמנים. בכלי זכוכית: עד מוצאי י"ט האחרון. והכא מוקצה למצוה איכא מוקצה דאיסור ליכא דאי משום סתירת אהל כי מטא חולו של מועד לשתרי דומיא דנר שכבה: והא ממאי דר' שמעון היא. למותיבנא לך מיניה: דתני ר' חייא כו' אין נוטלין עצים. בפסח ועצרת מסוכה העשויה לצל ואפילו נפלו משום מוקצה דאיתקצאי מחמת סתירת אהל בי"ט: אלא מן הסמוך לה. אם סמך חבילות עצים אצל דופנה ליכא איסור מוקצה דדעתיה עילויה מאתמול למישקלינהו למחר דלא סתר בהו אהלא ומהך דתני ר' חייא בר יוסף הוי מצי לאותבי ברישא אלא ניחא ליה לאותבי ממתניתא דר' חייא ור' אושעיא כדאמרינן בעלמא (חולין דף קמא.) כל מתניתא דלא מיתניא בי ר' חייא כו': ור' שמעון מתיר. אם נפלה דלית ליה מוקצה והכי מוקמינן ליה במסכת ביצה: ושוין בסוכת החג בחג. שהוקצה למצותה דמצותה כל שבעה אלמא כל שעת מצותה נוהג מוקצה שלה ואע"ג דליכא איסור סתירה: כעין שמן קאמינא. ולא משום איסור אלא משום מצוה דהואיל דהוקצה למצותו לשבת הוקצה לכל זמן איסור דליקתו ולא יותר דאין מצותו אלא בשעת דליקתו ומשכבה אין בו מצוה אבל בסוכת החג מצותה כל שבעה והקצאתה כל זמן מצותה: אלא גרוגרות וצמוקין. גרוגרות תאנים שמעלה לגג ליבשן ומשנשתהו שם מעט אין ראוים לאכילה עד שיתייבשו וכן צימוקים דענבים: היה אוכל בתאנים. רבותא אשמעי' (א) דהוה אכיל ואזיל מכיון דאסקינהו אסח דעתיה ואקצן: חבושין. קוינ"ץ: וכן אתה אומר כו'. ואע"ג דהני חזי כל שעתא ואפי' נשתהו לא נתקלקלו מיהו הואיל ואקלינהו אסירי: אי נימא ר"י. למה לי הנך דנקט דדחינהו בידים אפי' הכניסן נמי לאוצר בעו הזמנה: פצעילי

תוספות

הכי נמי מסתברא דרב כר' יהודה ס"ל. בכמה מקומות אשכחן דרב סבר כר' יהודה דאסר מטה שייחדה למעות והניח עליה מעות ואילו לר' שמעון שרי דהא שרי אנוגרות אפי' תקע בה כמה זימני ודכרכי דזוזי (לעיל דף יט:) אלא דבעי לאוכוחי דסבר כר' יהודה במיגו דאיתקצאי בין השמשות כו': מקמי חברי בשבתא. שביום חג שלהם לא היו מניחין נר אלא בבית ע"ז ומאי דקמבעיא ליה בנר חנוכה טפי מבנר שבת משום דלצורך אכילה היו מניחים להם ואע"ג דבשעת הסכנה אמרינן בבמה מדליקין (לעיל דף כא:) דמניחה על שולחנו ודיו הכא מיירי אם יארע שלא הניחה על שולחנו א"נ אומר ר"י דשעת הסכנה דלעיל לאו סכנת חברים קאמר אלא סכנת גזירה שגזרו שלא להדליק נר חנוכה: היכא דדחייה בידים אית ליה. ואף על גב דנר שכבה שרי ר' שמעון אף על גב דדחייה בידים להתם שאני כיון שכבר פסק דיחוי שלה אבל הכא לעולם הן דחוין כל זמן שמונחין שם: אלא שמן שבנר. לאו דווקא שבנר דההוא אסור משום מכבה כדאמר בפ"ב דביצה (דף כב.) המסתפק ממנו חייב משום מכבה אלא המטפטף מנר ומשום דמוקצה למצותו לא אסור ° נר הדולק לטלטל כדפרישית לעיל אלא כדאמר בסוף פירקין משום דהוי בסיס לדבר האסור תימה לר"י דאמאי נקט שמן שבנר טפי ה"ל למינקט אין מוקצה לר' שמעון אלא גרוגרות וצימוקין דדמו טפי לחיטין שזרען דלא איתקצאי לא מחמת מצוה ולא מחמת איסור וליכא למימר דסבר ר' יוחנן דלר' שמעון אין מוקצה בגרוגרות וצימוקין דהא רבי קאמר בסמוך דאית ליה לרבי שמעון מוקצה בגרוגרות וצימוקין ומסתמא לא פליג: עד מוצאי י"ט האחרון של חג. הקשה ר"ת ביום טוב האחרון דלא אסר אלא מטעם מיגו דאיתקצאי בין השמשות מחמת יום שעבר והא רבי שמעון שרי מותר השמן שבנר אף על גב דהוקצה בין השמשות למצותו משום יום הבא ונראה לר"י דבמה שאוסרת הברייתא יום טוב האחרון לא אתיא כר' שמעון: ולא מן הסמוך לה. בפרק המביא כדי יין (ביצה ל: ושם) גרס במשנה אלא מן הסמוך לה ופריך בגמ' והא קסתר אוהלא ומשני מאי מן הסמוך לה סמוך לדפנות והשתא אי גרס בברייתא דהכא אלא מן הסמוך לה הוי בסמוך לדפנות ואי גרס ולא מן הסמוך לה מיירי במה שעל הסכך וטעמא משום דסתר אוהלא כדאמר התם: ואם התנה הכל לפי תנאו. בריש המביא (ג"ז שם) פריך עלה והא קא סתר אוהלא ומוקי לה בסוכה נפולה וברעועה דמאתמול דעתיה עלה: אלא בגרוגרות וצימוקין. בירושלמי מפ' שמסריחין בינתיים כיון שמתקלקלין כל כך אין דעתו לקחתם עד שיתקנו היטב: וכן אתה אומר באפרסקין. אף על פי שאין מתקלקלין כל כך מקצה אותם מדעתו: היכא דלא דחייה בידים אית ליה מוקצה. כגון הא דתנן בפרק מפנין (לקמן קכו:) ולא את האוצר ותנן נמי בפרק בתרא (דף קנו:) רבי יהודה אומר אם לא היתה נבלה מע"ש אסורה כו':

ואוכל איצטריכא ליה. מדנקט אוכל במוקצה דדחייה בידים נראה דאזיל ואכיל שרי ליה לר"י במוקצה דלא דחייה בידים כגון גבי אוצר: לדבריו

עין משפט נר מצוה

נב א מיי' פ"ה מהלכות שבת הלכה יח ופ"ד מהלכות י"ט הלכה ה סמג לאוין סה טור שו"ע או"ח סימן רעז סעיף ד וסימן תקי"ד סעיף ו:

נג ב מיי' פכ"ו מהלכות שבת הלכה יד סמג לאוין סה טוש"ע או"ח סימן שי סעיף ב:

רבינו חננאל

אותה בשבת. בזמן שיש עליה מעות. פי' מוכני כן. מלשון את הכיור ואת כנו. נמדלת מלשון שילוף. כדתנן המדיל בגפנים. וגרסינן במשקין (מ"ק ג) מאי מדלי שלופי. נמצלת מלשון צל. קתני מיהת אין גוררין אותה בשבת בזמן שיש עליה מעות הא אין עליה מעות שרי. ואע"ג דהוו עליה בין השמשות. ושנינן משנה זו לר' שמעון היא. ורב דאמר כרבי יהודה. דהא רב הוא דאמר מניחין נר ע"ג דקל בשבת [ואין מניחין נר ע"ג דקל ביום טוב]. מכלל דרב כר' יהודה סבר ליה דאמר הנר שהדליקו בו בשבת אין מטלטלין אותו. אבל ביו"ט שמטלטלין אותו ונמצא משתמש במחובר לקרקע אסור. (ואין מניחין נר ע"ג דקל ביו"ט) ואוקימנא אליבא דר' יהודה דשני ליה בין שבת ליו"ט. אבל ר' שמעון לא שני ליה בטלטול הנר בין שבת ליו"ט. איני דרב כר' יהודה עביד ליה. והא רב התיר לטלטל נר מפני חבארי בשבת. ושנינן הא אמר רב בהא כדאי הוא ר"ש לסמוך עליו בשעת הדחק מכלל דרב סבר לית הלכתא כר' שמעון. והא דא"ר יוחנן אין מוקצה לר"ש אלא מידי דאיתקצאי לאיסורא כגון שמן שבנר בשעה שדולק או כגון עיטורי סוכה וכיוצא בהן הואיל והוקצו למצוה פשוטה היא

רב נסים גאון

שהוא מתיר בנר אוסר בפמוט ולדבריהם בתלמוד ארץ ישראל או כר' שמעון אפילו נר עצמו יהא מותר נתבאר כבר שר' שמעון מתיר הנר עצמו וכ"ש הפמוט: מהו לטלטולי שרגא דחנוכה מיקמי חבארא בשבתא. שמענו כי בימי החברים פרסי' היו חברים מחזרין בכל בתי ישראל ומכבין את הנרות ולוקחין מכל בית נר והיה צער גדול לישר' מזה המעשה מפני שהיו מוליכין את נרותיהם לע"ז ואשכחנן בפרק ב' (דגיטין דף טז) רבה בר בר חנה חלש על ר' יהודה ורבנן לשיולי ביה בעו מיניה שנים שהביאו גט ממדינת הים צריכים שיאמרו בפנינו נכתב בפנינו נחתם או אין צריכין אמר להו אין צריכין ומה אילו אמרו בפנינו גירשה מי לא מהימני אדהכי אתא ההוא חברא שקלא לשרגא מיקמייהו אמרי רחמנא או בטולך או בטולא דבר עשו למימרא דרומאי מעלו מפרסאי והא תני ר' חייא מאי דכתיב (איוב כח) אלהים הבין דרכה והוא ידע את מקומה ידע הקב"ה בישראל שאין יכולים לקבל גזירות של עשו הרשע לפיכך הגלה אותם לבבל ובמס' יבמות בפרק הבא על יבמתו (דף סג) אמרו מאי דכתיב בגוי נבל אכעיסם ר' יוחנן אמר אלו חברים אמרו ליה לר' יוחנן אתו חבארי לבבל (שאג) [שגא] ונפל [א"ל] מקבלי שוחדא תריץ ויתיב גזרו על שלש מפני שלש על בשר מפני המתנות על מרחצאות מפני טבילה קא מחטטי שכבי מפני ששמחים ביום אידם ובשאלתות דרב אחא מן שבחא כך פי' בפרשת וארא אל אברהם ובמלכות פרסיים היו חברים שבהן מחזרין על בתי ישראל ומכבין את הנרות וחותין את הגחלים ומוליכין אותן לבית האור שלהן שהיא ע"ז ולא היו עובים לא אש ולא גחלים שילינו בלילה חוץ מע"ז שלהן שהיא בית נורא: כדי הוא ר' שמעון בן יוחי לסמוך עליו בשעת הדחק. הוא ר' שמעון שאמר הנר שכבתה מותר לטלטלה דלית ליה מוקצה וכל ר' שמעון סתם במשנה ובברייתא הוא ר"ש בן יוחאי וכל ר' יהודה סתם הוא ר' יהודה בר' אלעאי ובמס' מנחות בפרק הקומץ (דף יח) אמרו מפני שר' יהודה בנו של ר' אלעאי ור' אילעאי תלמידו של ר' אליעזר שנה לך משנת ר' אליעזר:

מסורת הש"ס

א) [ברכות ע. עירובין מו.] גיטין יט. נדה ו. ט:, ב) ל"ל והוקצה [תוס' ישנים], ג) לעיל כב. ביצה ל: סוכה י. [תוספתא סוכה פ"א], ד) ביצה ל:, ה) ביצה כו:, ו) [ביצה מ.].

הגהות הב"ח

(א) רש"י ד"ה היה אוכל וכו' רבותא אשמעי' אע"פ דהוה:

גליון הש"ס

תוס' ד"ה אלא שמן וכו'. נר הדולק לטלטל כדפי'. לעיל דף מב ע"ב תוס' ד"ה ואין נאותין:

ליקוטי רש"י

חברי. פרסיים רשעים ומבזין ואינם מכירים כבודם של ישראל [יבמות סג:]. פרסאי [גיטין יז. ועיי"ש בתוס']. אומה הסמוכה לפרסיים ומשמשים הם וטורפים הם יותר מפרסיים [קידושין עב.]. בשעת הדחק. אבל שלא בשעת הדחק לא [ברכות ט.]. ועטרה. יפה בסדינין ובקרמין המצויירין [ביצה ל:]. בקרמים. אלה בירעיות של צבעים שקורין אובריי"ן [לעיל כב.]. מעשה אורג כגון בגדי צבעונין שקורין אובריי"ן [סוכה י.]. ובסדינין. לבנים של פשתן [ביצה שם]. המצויירין. שאורגן בולטת כגון מעשה רוקם או מעשה אורג שקורין גליגשק"ש. יינות שמנים. נותנין בכוסות של זכוכית לנוי [סוכה שם]. ואם התנה עליהן. מבעוד יום לאיני בודל מהם מהיות כוסי חכוסי בהם ליטלן כל שהות אורך של בין השמשות של ערב יום טוב הלכך בשעת ביאת היום שהיא קדושה לריכה לחול עליהם לא חלה לפיכך לא הוקצה [ביצה שם]. וכגון דאמר איני בודל מהם כל בין השמשות של יום טוב הראשון דלא אל קדושה עליהו והכי מוקים לה במסכת ביצה בהמביא (ל:) ותנאה אחרינא לא מהני בהו [סוכה שם; וכעיי"ז לעיל שם]. אין נוטלין עצים מן הסוכה. שנפלה ביו"ט דליכא סתירת אהל וטעמא דמנא משום מוקצה דהא בין השמשות היתה קיימת ומוקצה היא מחמת איסור סתירה אבל הסמוך לה לאו מוקצה הוא דלית ביה משום סתירה. אלא מן הסמוך לה. קנים המוקפים סביבות לדפנות כיון שלא נאגדו עם הדופן לא בטלי לגבי דופן ואינו דומה לסמוך לסכך שהסכך אינו ארוג לפיכך הכל שוה העליון כתחתון סכך הוא. ורבי שמעון מתיר. בסוכה רעועה דמסיק אדעתיה דנפלה ולמחר נפלה הלכך לרבי שמעון מוקצה ליכא דאמרינן דעתיה מאתמול עלויה ולתנא קמא לא אמרינן דעתיה עלויה בשום מידי דלא חזי בין השמשות. שהיא אסורה. אפילו במוע"מ. ואם התנה עליה. אסוכה דעלמא קאי ואריישא דברייתא קא מהדר דאיפלגו בה תנא קמא ורבי שמעון דקתני אין נוטלין עצים מן הסוכה ואוקימנא בשנפלה ומשום מוקצה וקאמר אם התנה עליה מבעוד יום שאם תפול מחר יסיקנה הכל לפי תנאו [ביצה שם ועי' כאן בתוס' ובמהרש"א]. אלא גרוגרות וצימוקים. שמעלה אותן על מנת ליבשן ומקצה אותן לכך ומשמתחילין ליבש אין ראוין לאכילה עד שייבשו לגמרי. ענבים יבשין קרוין צמוקים ותאנין שנתייבשו קרוין גרוגרות [שם כו:]. שהן מתחלה ראויין לאכילה והוא דחה אותן בידים להעלותן ליבשן ובשוב אינן ראויין עד שייבשו [שם מ.]. היה אוכל בתאנים והותיר. רבותא נקט דלא תימא כיון דאוכל והולך לא ליבעי הזמנה [שם כו:].

muktzeh,[26] הֵיכָא דְּדַחְיֵיהּ בְּיָדַיִם לֹא כָּל שֶׁכֵּן – in a case **where one actively set something aside is it not obvious** that it is *muktzeh*? Certainly it is! Thus, if the Baraisa was expressing the view of R' Yehudah, it would not have needed to refer to the specific case of fruits that were set out to dry. **אֶלָּא לָאו רַבִּי שִׁמְעוֹן הִיא – Rather,** is it **not** clear that **[the Baraisa] is** expressing the view of **R' Shimon,** and it teaches that according to R' Shimon *all* fruits are rendered *muktzeh* by being put out to dry, not only raisins and grapes?

The Gemara deflects the challenge:

לְעוֹלָם רַבִּי יְהוּדָה – Actually, the Baraisa is expressing the view of **R' Yehudah, וְאוֹכֵל אִצְטְרִיכָא לֵיהּ – and he found it necessary** to teach that the fruits are *muktzeh* even though the person **had been eating** them and then decided to put the remainder out to dry. **סָלְקָא דַעְתָּךְ אָמִינָא** – For **it might have occurred to you to say** that **כֵּיוָן דְּקָאָכִיל וְאָזִיל – since he is occupied in eating** some of **the fruit** and is implicitly demonstrating his intention to eat all of it, **לֹא לִיבָּעֵי הַזְמָנָה – he should not have to** explicitly **prepare** the remainder of the fruit for Sabbath use, and even that which he puts out to dry should not be rendered *muktzeh.* **קָמַשְׁמַע לָן** – **[R' Yehudah]** therefore **informs us** that **כֵּיוָן דְּהֶעֱלָן לַגַּג – since [the person] brought them up on the roof** to dry, **אַסּוּחֵי אַסְחֵי לְדַעְתֵּיהּ מִינַּיְיהוּ – he has taken his mind off them** and does not plan to use them on the Sabbath. Consequently, they are *muktzeh* even though he was previously eating them.[27]

Having established that according to R' Shimon even an item that was actively set aside is not *muktzeh* if it was fit for use at the onset of the Sabbath, the Gemara considers the opposite case: an item that was unfit for use at the onset of the Sabbath but was never actively set aside:

בְּעָא מִינֵּיהּ רַבִּי שִׁמְעוֹן בַּר רַבִּי מֵרַבִּי – R' Shimon bar Rebbi inquired of Rebbi:

NOTES

26. This applies, for example, to items that were in storage at the onset of the Sabbath. Although not actively rejected from Sabbath use, such items are *muktzeh* according to R' Yehudah, since one did not expect to use them on the Sabbath. It is permitted to use them only if one "prepares" them beforehand by stipulating his intention to use them (*Rashi*).

27. In conclusion: According to R' Shimon, simply rejecting an item from Sabbath use does not render it *muktzeh* unless the item itself is unfit for use at the onset of the Sabbath, as in the case of drying figs and raisins. According to R' Yehudah, rejecting an item, or even failing to prepare it for the Sabbath, is itself sufficient cause for the item to be considered *muktzeh.* The Baraisa which rules that even other types of fruit are rendered *muktzeh* when put out to dry reflects the view of R' Yehudah.

מסורת הש"ס

א) [ברכות ט. עירובין מו.] גיטין יט. נדה ו. ט:, ב) ל"ל והוקצה [תוס' ישנים], ג) לעיל כב. ביצה ל: סוכה י. [תוספתא סוכה פ"א], ד) ביצה ל:, ה) ביצה כו:, ו) [ביצה מ.].

הגהות הב"ח

(א) רש"י ד"ה היה אוכל וכו' רבותא אשמעי' אע"פ דהוה:

גליון הש"ס

תוס' ד"ה אלא שמן וכו'. נר הדולק לטלטל כדפי'. לעיל דף מב ע"ב תוס' ד"ה ואין נאותין:

ליקוטי רש"י

חברי. פרסיים רשעים ומבזין ואינם מכירים כבודם של ישראל [יבמות סג:]. פרסאי [גיטין יז. ועיי"ש בתוס']. אומה הסמוכה לפרסיים ומשמישים הם וערפנים הם יותר מפרסיים [קידושין עב.]. בשעת הדחק. אבל שלא בשעת הדחק לא [ברכות ט.]. ועטרה. יפה כסדינין ובקרמין המצויירין [ביצה ל:]. בקרמים. פארה ביריעות של צבעים שקורין אובריי"ן [לעיל כב.]. מעשה אורג כגון בגדי צבעונין שקורין אובריי"ן [סוכה י.]. ובסדינין. לבנים של פשתן [ביצה שם]. המצויירין. שאורגן בולטת כגון מעשה רוקם או מעשה אורג שקורין גלינסק"ש. יינות שמנים. נותנין בכוסות של זכוכית לנוי [סוכה שם]. ואם התנה עליהן. מבעוד יום איני בודל מהם מהיות כוחי חכותי בהם ליטלן כל שהום אורך של בין השמשות של ערב יום טוב הלכך בשעת ביאת היום שהיתה קדושה צריכה לחול עליהם לא חלה [illegible]

הכי נמי מיסתברא דרב כר' יהודה סבירא ליה דאמר רב [א]מניחין נר על גבי דקל בשבת ואין מניחין נר ע"ג דקל בי"ט אי אמרת בשלמא דרב כרבי יהודה סבירא ליה היינו דשני בין שבת לי"ט אלא אי אמרת כרבי שמעון סבירא ליה מה לי שבת ומה לי י"ט ורב כרבי יהודה ס"ל והא בעו מיניה דרב מהו לטלטולי שרגא דחנוכתא מקמי חברי בשבתא ואמר להו שפיר דמי שעת הדחק שאני דהא א"ל רב כהנא ורב אשי לרב הכי הלכתא אמר להו [א]כדי הוא ר' שמעון לסמוך עליו בשעת הדחק בעא מיניה ריש לקיש מר' יוחנן חטים שזרען בקרקע וביצים שתחת תרנגולת מהו כי לית ליה לר' שמעון מוקצה היכא דלא דחייה בידים היכא דדחייה בידים אית ליה מוקצה או דילמא [ב]לא שנא א"ל אין מוקצה לרבי שמעון אלא שמן שבנר בשעה שהוא דולק הואיל והוקצה למצותו [ג]הוקצה לאיסורו ולית ליה הוקצה למצותו [ג]והתניא סיככה כהלכתה ועיטרה בקרמים ובסדינין המצויירין ותלה בה אגוזין אפרסקין שקדים ורמונין ואפרכלי של ענבים ועטרות של שבולין יינות שמנים וסלתות אסור להסתפק מהן עד מוצאי י"ט האחרון ואם התנה עליהן הכל לפי תנאו וממאי דר' שמעון היא דתני [ד]ר' חייא בר יוסף קמיה דר' יוחנן אין נוטלין עצים מן הסוכה בי"ט אלא מן הסמוך לה ור' שמעון מתיר ושוין בסוכת החג בחג שהיא אסורה ואם התנה עליה הכל לפי תנאו כעין שמן שבנר קאמרינן הואיל והוקצה למצותו הוקצה לאיסורו איתמר נמי א"ר חייא בר אבא א"ר יוחנן אין מוקצה לרבי שמעון אלא כעין שמן שבנר בשעה שהוא דולק הואיל והוקצה למצותו הוקצה לאיסורו אמר רב יהודה אמר שמואל אין מוקצה לר' שמעון אלא גרוגרות וצימוקים בלבד ומידי אחרינא לא והתניא [ה]היה אוכל בתאנים והותיר והעלן לגג לעשות מהן גרוגרות בענבים והותיר והעלן לגג לעשות מהן צימוקין לא יאכל עד שיזמין וכן אתה אומר באפרסקין וחבושין ובשאר כל מיני פירות מני אילימא רבי יהודה ומה היכא דלא דחייה בידים אית ליה מוקצה היכא דדחייה בידים לא כל שכן אלא לאו ר' שמעון היא לעולם רבי יהודה ואוכל אצטריכא ליה סד"א כיון דקאכיל ואזיל לא ליבעי הזמנה קמ"ל כיון דהעלן לגג אסוחי אסחי לדעתיה מינייהו [ו]בעא מיניה רבי שמעון בר רבי מרבי פצעילי

רש"י

מניחין נר. מבעוד יום: ע"ג דקל. וידלק שם בשבת דליכא למיחש לכשיכבה לישקליה מיניה ונמלא משתמש במחובר דכיון דאקצייה לדבר האסור בין השמשות איתקצי לכולי יומא: ואין מניחין כו' בי"ט. דשקיל ומנח ליה ומשתמש באילן: מה לי שבת כו'. בשבת נמי שקיל ליה לכשיכבה: שרגא דחנוכתא. אחר שכבה: מקמי חברי. שלא יראוהו בנר כדאמרינן בפרקין דלעיל (דף כג:) דנותנו בטפח הסמוך לרשות הרבים וידעו שהדליקו בו נר והם גזרו שלא להדליק אי נמי ביום חגם אין מניחין לדלוק אור אלא בבית ע"ז: חברי. שם אומה שהיתה עם פרסיים: הכי הילכתא. בתמיה: בשעת הדחק. סכנה אלמא שלא בשעת הדחק אסור: שזרען בקרקע. ועדיין לא השרישו מהו ללקוט ולאכול: אין מוקצה לר' שמעון בדבר הראוי. אלא בשמן שבנר בשעה שהוא דולק כדתניא לעיל: הואיל והוקצה למצותו. לשבת: הוקצה לאיסורו. איסור כיבוי: והוקצה למצותו לית ליה. בתמיה דקס"ד שמן שבנר דוקא קאמר דאיכא תרתי מוקצה למצוה ומוקצה של שעת דליקתו משום איסור כיבוי אבל מוקצה למצוה גרידא לא אסר ואפילו בשעת המצוה: והתניא סיככה. לסוכה כו': קרמים. בגדי צבועים שקורין אובריי"א: אפרסקין. פירסיק"י בלע"ז: יינות שמנים. בכלי זכוכית: עד מוצאי י"ט האחרון. והכא מוקצה למצוה איכא מוקצה לאיסור ליכא דאי משום סתירת אהל כי מטא חולו של מועד לשתרי דומיא דנר שכבה: והא ממאי דר' שמעון היא. דמותיבנא לך מיניה: דתני ר' חייא כו' אין נוטלין עצים. בפסח ועצרת מסוכה העשויה לצל ואפילו נפלו משום מוקצה דאיתקצאי מחמת סתירת אהל בי"ט: אלא מן הסמוך לה. אם סמך חבילות עצים אצל דופנה ליכא איסור מוקצה דדעתיה עילויה מאתמול למישקלינהו למחר דלא סתר בהו אהלא ומהך דתני ר' חייא בר יוסף הוי מצי לאותבי ברישא אלא ניחא ליה לאותבי ממתניתא דר' חייא ור' אושעיא כדאמרינן בעלמא (חולין דף קמא.) כל מתניתא דלא מיתניא בי ר' חייא כו': ור' שמעון מתיר. אם נפלה דלית ליה מוקצה והכי מוקמינן ליה במסכת ביצה: ושוין בסוכת החג בחג. שהוקצה למצותה דמצותה כל שבעה אלמא כל שעת מצותה נוהג מוקצה שלה ואע"ג דליכא איסור סתירה: כעין שמן קאמינא. ולא משום איסור אלא משום מצוה דהואיל דהוקצה למצותו דשבת הוקצה לכל זמן איסור דליקתו ולא יותר דאין מצותו אלא בשעת דליקתו ומשכבה אין בו מצוה אבל בסוכת החג מצותה כל שבעה והקצאתה כל זמן מצותה: אלא גרוגרות וצמוקין. גרוגרות תאנים שמעלה לגג ליבשן ומשנשתהו שם מעט אין ראוים לאכילה עד שיתייבשו וכן צימוקים דענבים: היה אוכל בתאנים. רבותא אשמעי' (א) דהוה אכיל ואזיל מכיון דאסקינהו אסח דעתיה ואקצן: חבושין. קויי"ן: וכן אתה אומר כו'. ואע"ג דהני חזי כל שעתא ואפי' נשתהו לא נתקלקלו מיהו הואיל ואסקינהו אסירי: אי נימא ר"י. למה לי הנך דנקט דדחינהו בידים אפי' הכניסן נמי לאוצר בעו הזמנה: פצעילי

תוספות

הכי נמי מסתברא דרב כר' יהודה ס"ל. בכמה מקומות אשכחן דרב סבר כר' יהודה דאסר מטה שייחדה למעות והניח עליה מעות ואילו לר' שמעון שרי דהא שרי אגוזרות אפי' תקע בה כמה זימני ודכרכי לחוי (לעיל דף יט:) אלא דבעי לאוכוחי דסבר כר' יהודה במיגו דאיתקצאי בין השמשות כו': מקמי חברי בשבתא. שביום חג שלהם לא היו מניחין נר אלא בבית ע"ז ומאי דקמבעיא ליה בנר חנוכה טפי מבנר שבת משום דלצורך אכילה היו מניחים להם ואע"ג דבשעת הסכנה אמרינן בבמה מדליקין (לעיל דף כא:) דמניחה על שולחנו ודיו הכא מיירי אם יארע שלא הניחה על שולחנו א"נ אומר ר"י דשעת הסכנה דלעיל לאו סכנת חברים קאמר אלא סכנת גזירה שגזרו שלא להדליק נר חנוכה: היכא דדחייה בידים אית ליה. ואף על גב דנר שכבה שרי ר' שמעון אף על גב דדחייה בידים דהתם שאני כיון שכבר פסק דיחוי שלה אבל הכא לעולם הן דחוין כל זמן שמונחין שם: אלא שמן שבנר. לאו דווקא שבנר דההוא אסור משום מכבה כדאמר בפ"ב דביצה (דף כב.) המסתפק ממנו חייב משום מכבה אלא המטפטף מנר ומשום דמוקצה למצותו לא אסור ° נר הדולק לטלטל כדפרישית לעיל אלא כדאמר בסוף פירקין משום דהוי בסיס לדבר האסור תימה לר"י דמאי נקט שמן שבנר טפי ה"ל למינקט אין מוקצה לר' שמעון אלא גרוגרות וצימוקין דדמו טפי לחיטין שזרען דלא איתקצאי לא מחמת מצוה ולא מחמת איסור וליכא למימר דסבר ר' יוחנן דלר' שמעון אין מוקצה בגרוגרות וצימוקין דהא רבי קאמר בסמוך דאית ליה לרבי שמעון מוקצה בגרוגרות וצימוקין ומסתמא לא פליג: עד מוצאי י"ט האחרון של חג. הקשה ר"ת ביום טוב האחרון דלא אסר אלא מטעם מיגו דאיתקצאי בין השמשות מחמת יום שעבר והא רבי שמעון שרי מותר השמן שבנר אף על גב דהוקצה בין השמשות למצותו משום יום הבא ונראה לר"י דבמה שאוסרת הברייתא יום טוב האחרון לא אתיא כר' שמעון: ולא מן הסמוך לה. בפרק המביא כדי יין (ביצה ל: ושם) גרס במשנה אלא מן הסמוך לה ופריך בגמ' והא קסתר אוהלא ומשני מאי מן הסמוך לה סמוך לדפנות והשתא אי גרס בברייתא דהכא אלא מן הסמוך לה הוי בסמוך לדפנות ואי גרס ולא מן הסמוך לה מיירי במה שעל הסכך וטעמא משום דסתר אוהלא כדאמר התם: ואם התנה הכל לפי תנאו. בריש המביא (ג"ז שם) פריך עלה והא קא סתר אוהלא ומוקי לה בסוכה נפולה וברעועה דמאתמול דעתיה עלה: אלא בגרוגרות וצימוקין. בירושלמי מפ' שמסריחין בינתיים כיון שמתקלקלין כל כך אין דעתו לקחתם עד שיתקנו היטב: וכן אתה אומר באפרסקין. אף על פי שאין מתקלקלין כל כך מקצה אותם מדעתו: היכא דלא דחייה בידים אית ליה מוקצה. כגון הא דתנן בפרק מפנין (לקמן קכו:) ולא את האוצר ותנן נמי בפרק בתרא (דף קנז:) רבי יהודה אומר אם לא היתה נבלה מע"ש אסורה כו': ואוכל איצטריכא ליה. מדנקט אוכל במוקצה דדחייה בידים נראה דאזיל ואכיל שרי ליה לר"י במוקצה דלא דחייה בידים כגון גבי אוצר: לדבריו

עין משפט נר מצוה

נב א מיי' פ"ה מהלכות שבת הלכה יח ופ"ד מהלכות י"ט הלכה ה סמג לאוין סה טור שו"ע או"ח סימן רעז סעיף ד וסימן תקי"ד סעיף ו:

נג ב מיי' פכ"ו מהלכות שבת הלכה יד סמג לאוין סה טוש"ע או"ח סימן שי סעיף ב:

רבינו חננאל

אותה בשבת. בזמן שיש עליה מעות. פי' מוכני כן. מלשון את הכיור ואת כנו. נמדלת מלשון שילוף. כדתנן המידל בגפנים. וגרסינן במשקין (מ"ק ג) מאי מדלי שלופי. נמצלת מלשון צל. קתני מיהת אין גורדין אותה בשבת בזמן שיש עליה מעות הא אין עליה מעות שרי. ואע"ג דהוו עליה בין השמשות. ושנינן משנה זו לר' שמעון היא. ורב דאמר כרבי יהודה. דהא רב הוא דאמר מניחין נר ע"ג דקל בשבת [ואין מניחין נר ע"ג דקל ביום טוב]. מכלל דרב כר' יהודה סבר ליה דאמר הנר שהדליקו בו בשבת אין מטלטלין אותו. אבל ביו"ט שמטלטלין אותו ונמצא משתמש במחובר לקרקע אסור. (ואין מניחין נר ע"ג דקל ביו"ט) ואוקימנא אליבא דר' יהודה דשני ליה בין שבת ליו"ט. אבל ר' שמעון לא שני ליה בטלטול הנר בין שבת ליו"ט. איני דרב כר' יהודה עביד ליה. והא רב התיר לטלטל נר מפני חבארי בשבת. ושנינן הא אמר רב בהא כדאי הוא ר"ש לסמוך עליו בשעת הדחק מכלל דרב סבר לית הלכתא כר' שמעון. והא דא"ר יוחנן אין מוקצה לר"ש אלא מידי דאיתקצאי לאיסורא כגון שמן שבנר בשעה שדולק או כגון עיטורי סוכה וכיוצא בהן הואיל והוקצו למצוה פשוטה היא

רב נסים גאון

שהוא מתיר בנר אוסר בפמוט ולדבריהם בתלמוד ארץ ישראל או כר' שמעון אפילו נר עצמו יהא מותר נתבאר כבר שר' שמעון מתיר הנר עצמו וכ"ש הפמוט: מהו לטלטולי שרגא דחנוכה מיקמי חבארא בשבתא. שמענו כי בימי החברים פרסיי' היו חברים מחזרין בכל בתי ישראל ומכבין את הנרות ולוקחין מכל בית נר והיה צער גדול לישר' מזה המעשה מפני שהיו מוליכין את נרותיהם לע"ז ואשכחנן בפרק ב' (דגיטין דף טז) רבה בר בר חנה חלש על ר' יהודה ורבנן לשיולי ביה בעו מיניה שנים שהביאו גט ממדינת הים צריכים שיאמרו בפנינו נכתב בפנינו נחתם או אין צריכין אמר להו אין צריכין ומה אילו אמרו בפנינו גירשה מי לא מהימני אדהכי אתא ההוא חברא שקלא לשרגא מקמייהו אמרי רחמנא או בטולך או בטולא דבר עשו למימרא דרומאי מעלו מפרסאי והא תני ר' חייא מאי דכתיב (איוב כח) אלהים הבין דרכה והוא ידע את מקומה ידע הקב"ה בישראל שאין יכולים לקבל גזירות של עשו הרשע לפיכך הגלה אותם לבבל ובמס' יבמות בפרק הבא על יבמתו (דף סג) אמרו מאי דכתיב בגוי נבל אכעיסם ר' יוחנן אמר אלו חברים אמרו ליה לר' יוחנן אתו חבארי לבבל (שאג) [שגא] תפל [א"ל] מקבלי שוחדא תריץ ויתיב גזרו על שלש מפני שלש על בשר מפני המתנות על מרחצאות מפני טבילה קא מחטטי שכבי מפני ששמחים ביום אידם ובשאלתות דרב אחא מן שבחא כך פי' בפרשת וארא אל אברהם ובמלכות פרסיים היו חברים שבהן מחזרין על בתי ישראל ומכבין את הנרות וחותין את הגחלים ומוליכין אותן לבית האור שלהן שהיא ע"ז ולא היו עובים לא אש ולא גחלים שילינו בלילה חוץ מע"ז שלהן שהיא בית נורא: כדי הוא ר' שמעון בן יוחי לסמוך עליו בשעת הדחק. הוא ר' שמעון שאמר הנר שכבתה מותר לטלטלה דלית ליה מוקצה וכל ר' שמעון סתם במשנה ובברייתא הוא ר"ש בן יוחאי וכל ר' יהודה סתם הוא ר' יהודה בר' אלעאי ובמס' מנחות בפרק הקומץ (דף יח) אמרו מפני שר' יהודה בנו של ר' אלעאי ור' אילעאי תלמידו של ר' אליעזר שנה לך משנת ר' אליעזר:

ליקוטי רש"י (המשך): סוכה דעלמא קאי ואריש דברייתא קא מהדר דאיפלגו בה תנא קמא ורבי שמעון דקתני אין נוטלין עצים ... נפלה ומשום מוקצה וקאמר אם התנה עליה מבעוד יום שאם תפול מחר יסיקנה הכל לפי תנאו [ביצה ... ש"א]. אלא גרוגרות וצימוקים. שמעלה אותן על מנת ליבשן ומקצה אותן לכך ומשמסלקן ליבש ... יבשו לגמרי. ענבים יבשין קרוין צמוקים ותאנים שנתייבשו קרוין גרוגרות [שם כו:]. שכן מסלקה ראויין בידים להעלותן ליבשן ושוב אינן ראויין עד שייבשו [שם מ:]. היה אוכל בתאנים והותיר. רבותא נקט דלא תימא כיון דאוכל והולך לא ליבעי הזמנה [שם כו:].

עין משפט
נר מצוה

נד א מיי' פכ"ו מהל' שבת הלכה יד סמג לאוין סה טוש"ע או"ח סימן שי סעיף ב:
נה ב ג מיי' פ"ב מהל' יו"ט הלכה ב סמג לאוין עה טור שו"ע או"ח סימן תצז סעיף ב וסימן תקל סעיף ג:

פצעילי [ה] תמרה לרבי שמעון מהו א"ל [א] אין מוקצה לר"ש אלא גרוגרות וצימוקין בלבד ורבי לית ליה מוקצה והתנן [ו] [ב] אין משקין ושוחטין את המדבריות אבל משקין ושוחטין את הבייתות ותניא [ג] [ג] אלו הן מדבריות כל שיוצאות בפסח ונכנסות ברביעה בייתות כל שיוצאות ורועות חוץ לתחום ובאות ולנות בתוך התחום ר' אומר אלו ואלו בייתות הן ואלו הן מדבריות כל שרועות באפר ואין נכנסות לישוב לא בימות החמה ולא בימות הגשמים איבעית אימא הני נמי כגרוגרות וצימוקין דמיין ואי בעית אימא לדבריו דר"ש קאמר ליה וליה לא סבירא ליה ואיבעית אימא לדבריהם דרבנן קאמר להו לדידי לית לי מוקצה כלל לדידכו אודו לי מיהת דהיכא דיוצאות בפסח ונכנסות ברביעה דבייתות נינהו ורבנן אמרו ליה לא מדבריות נינהו אמר רבה בר בר חנה אמר ר' יוחנן אמרו הלכה כרבי שמעון ומי א"ר יוחנן הכי והא בעא מיניה ההוא סבא קרויא ואמרי לה סרויא מר' יוחנן קינה של תרנגולת מהו לטלטולי בשבת אמר ליה כלום עשוי אלא לתרנגולין הכא במאי עסקינן דאית ביה אפרוח מת הניחא למר בר אמימר משמיה [ד] (דרב) [ה] דאמר מודה היה ר' שמעון בבעלי חיים שמתו שאסורין אלא למר בריה דרב יוסף משמיה דרבא דאמר חלוק היה רבי שמעון [אפי'] בבעלי חיים שמתו שהן מותרין מאי איכא למימר הכא במאי עסקינן בדאית ביה ביצה והאמר [ו] רב נחמן מאן דאית ליה מוקצה אית ליה נולד דלית ליה מוקצה לית ליה נולד דאית ביה ביצת אפרוח כי אתא רב יצחק בר' יוסף א"ר יוחנן הלכה כר' יהודה ור' יהושע בן לוי אמר הלכה כרבי שמעון אמר רב יוסף היינו דאמר רבה בר בר חנה א"ר יוחנן אמרו הלכה כרבי שמעון אמרו וליה לא סבירא ליה א"ל אביי לרב יוסף ואת לא תסברא דר' יוחנן כר' יהודה הא ר' אבא ורבי אסי איקלעו לבי ר' אבא דמן חיפא ונפל מנרתא על גלימיה דר' אסי ולא טילטלה מאי טעמא לאו משום דרבי אסי תלמידיה דר' יוחנן הוה ור' יוחנן כרבי יהודה ס"ל דאית ליה מוקצה א"ל מנרתא קאמרת מנרתא שאני דא"ר אחא בר חנינא א"ר אסי הורה ריש לקיש בצידן מנורה הניטלת בידו אחת מותר לטלטלה בשתי ידיו אסור לטלטלה ור' יוחנן אמר אנו אין לנו אלא בנר כרבי שמעון אבל מנורה בין ניטלה בידו אחת בין ניטלה בשתי ידיו אסור לטלטלה וטעמא מאי רבה ורב יוסף דאמרי תרווייהו הואיל ואדם קובע לה מקום אמר ליה אביי לרב יוסף והרי כילת חתנים דאדם קובע לו מקום ואמר שמואל משום רבי חייא [י] כילת חתנים מותר

לדברין דר' שמעון קאמר ליה וליה לא סבירא ליה. משמע דמספקא ליה אי ר' סבר לה כר' שמעון ותימה אמאי לא מוכח מהיא דלקמן דסבר כר"ש דאמר פעם אחת הלך ר' כו' והורה במנורה כר"ש בנר וכן מברייתא דמייתי באין לדין [ט] בכור תם שנפל לבור ר' יהודה הנשיא אומר ירד מי שבקי במומין ויראה אם יש בו מום יעלה וישחוט כו' ומיהו במאי דמתיר לראות במומין לא אתי כר"ש אלא במאי דלית ליה מוקצה ומיהו רש"י לא גרים בכור תם אלא בכור שנפל לבור והשתא מלי אתי כר' יהודה ויראה אם היה בו מום זה מעי"ט [ט]: הכא במאי עסקינן דאית ביה אפרוח מת. פירש הר"ר יוסף דלא נקט אפרוח חי משום דחי חזי לשתק בו תינוק כשבוכה ואין נראה דהא בההיא דכופין את הסל לפני האפרוחין (לעיל דף מג.) משמע דאסור לטלטל ועוד אי מחיים שרי אמאי קאמר בסמוך דמודה ר"ש בבעלי חיים שמתו שאסורין אלא ודאי בעלי חיים [ג] מוקצין הם כגרוגרות וצימוקין ומקצה אותם גם מכלבים ולא דמי לבשר תפל שמותר לר"ש מדפריך בפרק מפנין (לקמן קכח.) על רב הונא דשרי והא תלמיד דרב הוה ורב כר' יהודה סבירא ליה אבל לר' שמעון משמע דשרי משום דאינו מקצהו מכלבים כמו בעלי חיים:
דאית ביה ביצה. דאסור משום נולד ל"ע דר' יוחנן גופיה [י] מפרש טעמא דבילה משום משקין שזבו ואפשר דמשום הכי לא הוה אסר ר"ש לטלטלה אלא לאכילה:
דאית ביה ביצת אפרוח. נראה לר"י דאסור לר' שמעון משום דכיון דאית ביה אפרוח הוי [ד] כמו גרוגרות וצימוקין וקא מיבעיא ליה לסבא קירויא אי שרי לטלטולי על ידי שינער משם הבילה אי חשיב כמו מניח או כשכח והשיב לו רבי יוחנן כלום עשוי אלא לתרנגולין ואין זה כשכח אלא כמניח ואסור:
אמר ליה מנרתא שאני. וא"ת אמאי לא מוכח מהא דא"ר יוחנן בפ' לולב וערבה (סוכה מו:) דסוכה אפי' בשמיני אסורה אלמא אית ליה מיגו דאיתקצאי כו' כר' יהודה ותירץ ר"י דנר אינו מוקצה למצותו מטלטול שאין ביטול מצוה בטלטול ולא דמי לסוכה דאיתקצאי ביה"ש מחמת מצוה ולהכי אינו יכול להוכיח מסוכה אנר: לעיל לאו משום דר' אסי תלמידו דר' יוחנן כו'. וא"ת דילמא ר' אסי כרב רביה סבירא ליה כדאמר לעיל גבי שרגא דחנוכה אמרו ליה רב כהנא ורב אסי לרב הילכתא הכי ונראה דרב אסי דלעיל לאו היינו ר' אסי דהכא דההוא דלעיל חבירו של רב כהנא והכא ר' אסי חבירו של ר' אמי [כ]: אין לנו אלא בנר כר' שמעון. פי' במוקצה מחמת מיאוס דהיינו נר ישן שלא הדליקו בה באותה שבת ולעיל דפסיק כרבי יהודה היינו בהדליקו בה באותה שבת דהוי מוקצה מחמת איסור והא דפסיק בפרק בתרא [ל] כר"ש בנבלה לפני הכלבים אף על גב דנבלה מוקצה מחמת איסור היא כדפר"ת (לעיל יט: ד"ה ושמואל) התם [מ] לא דחייה בידים אבל הכא דדחייה בידים סבר כר' יהודה ולפי זה לא קיימי ר' יוחנן וריב"ל דפסקי כר' שמעון אחדא ברייתא דר' יוחנן קאי אברייתא דכל הנרות של מתכת מטלטלין כו' אבל במאי דקאמר ר' יהודה בברייתא דלעיל מטלטלין נר חדש אבל לא ישן לא סבר רבי יוחנן כוותיה וריב"ל אברייתא דמטלטלין נר חדש קאי דבההיא ברייתא שרי רבי

פצעילי תמרה. א) תמרים הנלקטים קודם בישולן וכונסין אותם בסלים שעושין מלולבין והן מתבשלות מאליהן מהו לאכול מהן קודם בישולן מי מודה בהן דמוקצות הן כגרוגרות וצימוקין או לא: אלא בגרוגרות וצימוקין. דאיכא תרתי דדחינהו בידים ולא חזו: ור' לית ליה מוקצה. דקס"ד מדבעי מיניה אליבא דרבי שמעון אלמא הוה שמיע ליה מאבוה דכרבי שמעון סבירא ליה: משקין. דרך להשקות בהמה לפני שחיטה שתהא נוחה להפשיט: המדבריות. הברייתות: ברביעה. במרחשון: ואלו מדבריות כל שרועות באפר. והני מיהא אסירי אלמא אית ליה מוקצה: איבעית אימא הני. מדבריות נמי כגרוגרות דמי דדחינהו בידים ויש טורח לילך ולהביאם: ואיבעית אימא. ההיא דפצעילי תמרה לדבריו דרבי שמעון קאמר ולר' לא ס"ל: ה"ג אמר רבה בר בר חנה א"ר יוחנן אמרו הלכה כר' שמעון: אמרו. בני הישיבה: סרוייא קרוייא. על שם מקומו: כלום עשוי. לשום תשמיש: אלא לתרנגולין. הלכך ה"ל מלאכתו לאיסור ואסור אלמא אית ליה מוקצה: דאית ביה אפרוח מת. דלא חזי למיכל ולכלבים נמי לא חזי ואף על גב דא"ר שמעון מחתכין את הנבלה לפני הכלבים הני מילי במסוכנת אבל בריאה לא דלא הוה דעתיה מאתמול לכלבים והאי אפרוח שמת בשבת נמי לא הוה דעתיה מאתמול לכלבים: הניחא למר כו' דאמר מודה היה ר"ש. דאע"ג דאמר מחתכין הנבלה לפני הכלבים ה"מ במסוכנת דדעתיה עליה מאתמול לכלבים אבל מודה הוא בבעלי חיים כלומר בבריאים שמתו שאסורין שפיר קתרלת דלרבי שמעון גופיה לא חזי לכלבים: מאי איכא למימר. הא חזי לכלבים: דאית בה ביצה. שנולדה היום ומודה ר' שמעון בנולד: והא אמר רב נחמן כו'. בשמעתא קמייתא דבילה: דאית בה ביצת אפרוח. וכלב לא אכיל לה משום ב) קליפה: וליה לא סבירא ליה. לר' יוחנן לא סבירא דתיהוי הלכה כר' שמעון והיינו דרב יצחק: ואת לא תסברא. ומקמי דשמעת ליה לדרב יצחק לא הוה ידעת דר' יוחנן כר' יהודה: בשתי ידים אסור לטלטלה. כדמפרש טעמא לקמיה דלאו לטלטולי עבידא דאדם קובע לה מקום: ור' יוחנן אמר אנו אין לנו. שום היתר בהלכות טלטול נרות: אלא בנר. ישן כרבי שמעון דמתיר אבל מנורה כו' הלכך אי לאו מדרב יצחק לא הוה ידענא ליה אבל השתא ידענא דכר' יהודה סבירא ליה בכולהו בר ממוקצה מחמת מיאוס דנר ישן:

רבינו חננאל

וכן הא דאמר ליה [ר'] לר' שמעון בריה אין מוקצה לר' שמעון אלא גרוגרות וצמוקין בלבד פשוטה היא: אמר רבה בר בר חנה א"ר יוחנן אמרו הלכה כר"ש איני והא בעא מיניה ההוא סבא קרוייה קינה של תרנגולין מהו לטלטלה בשבת ואמר ליה אסור כלום עשוי אלא לתרנגולים מכלל דר' יוחנן כר' יהודה סבירא ליה דאית ליה מוקצה. ושנינן בדאית ליה בהאי קינה אפרוח מת ומשום הכי אסורה לטלטלה. הניחא למ"ד בעלי חיים שמתו בשבת דברי הכל אסור לטלטלן בשבת הא אפילו לר' שמעון ואלא למ"ד ר"ש מתיר בבעלי חיים שמתו שמותר לטלטלן אע"ג דאית בהאי קינה אפרוח שמת בשבת ר"ש מתיר אמאי קא אסר ר' יוחנן והא איהו הלכתא כר' שמעון סבירא ליה. ואסיקנא בדאית בהאי קינה ביצה שיש בה אפרוח דלדברי הכל אסורה. ואעפ"כ לא נתברר כי ר' יוחנן כר' שמעון סבירא ליה. וכי אתא רב יצחק בר' יוסף א"ר יוחנן הלכתא כר' יהודה וריב"ל אמר הלכה כר"ש. אמר רב יוסף היינו דאמר רבה בר בר חנה א"ר יוחנן אמרו הלכה כר"ש וליה לא סבירא ליה. ודייק נמי אביי מדר' אסי נפלה מנרתא על גלימיה [בבי] ר' אבא ולא טלטלה. ואמר (משמיה) [משום] דר' אסי תלמיד דר' יוחנן הוא. ור' יוחנן במוקצה סבר לה כר' יהודה. ודחינן להא דאביי. ואמרינן לא אפילו תימא ר' יוחנן כר' שמעון מנרתא שני

מסורת הש"ס

א) בילה מ., ב) שם. [לקמן קמ.], ג) [בילה שם], ד) [נ"ל דרבא], ה) בילה מ:, ו) שם ב., ז) עירובין קב. לקמן קלח., ח) [בילה דף כו.], ט) [וע"ע תוספות בילה כו. ד"ה ת"ר], י) [בילה ג.], כ) [ועי' תוספות חולין יט. ד"ה אמר רב הונא], ל) [דף קנו:], מ) התוס' המתחיל ולפ"ז וכו' הנרשם בס"א נמלא בדף מו ע"א כי שם מקומו.

תוספות ישנים

א) אין נראה לר"י פירוש זה דל"ד לגרוגרות ולימוקין דלא דחיה בידים. ונ"ל כפירוש הערוך שפירש פלעילי תמרה לשון מפלע שמפלעין תמרים כדי להתבשל ולהתייבש ובשעת הפליעה מתקלקלת מראיתה ואחר זמן משתבחות ודמי לגרוגרות ולימוקין אך שגרוגרות ולימוקין מתקלקלות יותר מהם:
ב) קשה דאפשר להסיר הקליפה ויאכלנה הכלב:
ג) והא דלא בעי באפרוח חי אם מותר לטלטל הקינה משום דאפשר להפריחו:
ד) א"נ הוי מוקלה מחמת חסרון כיס:

ליקוטי רש"י

פצעילי תמרה. תמרים שאין מתבשלות באילן לעולם וגודרין אותן מהאילן ועושין להן מוקלות הן כלי כפות תמרים וכונסין אותן לתוכן ומתבשלות [ביצה מ.]. מהו. לאכול מהן ביום טוב. אלא גרוגרות וצימוקין. שהן מתחלה ראויין לאכילה והוא דחה אותן בידים להעלותן ליבשן ושוב אינן ראויין עד שייבשו אבל אלו לא דחה אותן בידים ואיכא דאכיל מנייהו. ורבי לית ליה מוקצה. הכי קא סלקא דעתיה מדפריש ליה מילתיה דרבי שמעון אלמא כר' שמעון סבירא ליה [שם:]. אין משקין ושוחטין. משום מוקצה. משקין. משום סרכא דמשכא שתהא נוחה להפשיטה שהוא נדבק יותר מדאי בבשר [שם.]. אורחא דמילתא נקט משום סירכא דמשכא שתהא נוחה להפשיט [לקמן קנז.]. ונכנסות. לישוב [ביצה שם]. איבעית אימא הני. מדבריות שאין נכנסות לישוב כלל כגרוגרות ולמוקין דמיין שמקצה אותן מאלנו בידים. ואי בעית אימא. אין מוקצה לרבי שמעון קאמר ליה אבל לדידי יש מוקצה. ואיבעית אימא. מתני' לדבריהם דרבנן דאית להו מוקצה קאמר להו [שם:]. בבעלי חיים. בהמה בריאה בין השמשות. שמתו. ביום טוב. שאסורין. וכי שריא במסוכנת בין השמשות דדעתיה עלויה להאכילה לכלבים [שם כז:]. הכא במאי עסקינן בדאית ביה ביצה. דקא סלקא דעתין דאפילו לרבי שמעון דשרי במוקצה בנולד אסיר דאילו במוקצה סבירא ליה לא מקצי איניש מדעתיה מידי דחזי ליה אבל נולד לא הוה ידע דנהוי דעתיה עלויה [שם ב.]. כילת חתנים. לא דמיא לשאר כילות שאר כילות פרוסות על גבי קינוף שהיא לארבע רגלים ויש לה גג דהוי אהל ושל חתנים על גבי נקליטין שאינם אלא שנים באמצעית המטה וקנה נתון עליהם והבגד נתון עליו ונופל לכאן ולכאן ואין לה גג טפח הלכך לאו אהל הוא [לקמן קלח:]. לאו אהל הוא מפני שאין לה גג למעלה רוחב טפח מפני שהיא נתונה בשיפוע והיא יריעה שפורסין סביב למטה לישן [עירובין קב.].

פַּצְעִילֵי תְּמָרָה לְרַבִּי שִׁמְעוֹן מַהוּ – **What is** the law concerning eating **unripe dates** on the Sabbath or festival **according to R' Shimon?**[1] אָמַר לֵיהּ – **[Rebbi] replied:** אֵין מוּקְצֶה לְרַבִּי שִׁמְעוֹן – **There is no** food that is ***muktzeh*** **according to R' Shimon,** אֶלָּא גְּרוֹגְרוֹת וְצִימּוּקִין בִּלְבַד – **except dried figs and raisins** that were set out to dry before the advent of the Sabbath and have not yet dried out completely.[2]

The Gemara presumes that since R' Shimon bar Rebbi posed to his father, Rebbi, an inquiry that is based on R' Shimon's opinion, he must have known that Rebbi agrees with it. The Gemara therefore asks:

וְרַבִּי לֵית לֵיהּ מוּקְצֶה – **But does Rebbi not subscribe to** a broad application of ***muktzeh?*** וְהָתְנַן – **Why, we learned in a Mishnah:**[3] אֵין מַשְׁקִין וְשׁוֹחֲטִין אֶת הַמִּדְבָּרִיּוֹת – WE MAY NOT WATER AND SLAUGHTER RANGE ANIMALS on a festival,[4] אֲבָל מַשְׁקִין וְשׁוֹחֲטִין אֶת הַבַּיְיתוֹת – BUT WE MAY WATER AND SLAUGHTER DOMESTIC ANIMALS. וְתַנְיָא – **And** the following elaboration of this law **was taught in a Baraisa:** אֵלּוּ הֵן מִדְבָּרִיּוֹת – THESE ARE THE RANGE ANIMALS: כָּל שֶׁיּוֹצְאוֹת בַּפֶּסַח וְנִכְנָסוֹת בָּרְבִיעָה – ANY animals THAT GO OUT DURING the PESACH season[5] and graze in the pasture AND then RETURN to a settlement DURING THE first RAINS.[6] בַּיְיתוֹת – And these are DOMESTIC ANIMALS: כָּל שֶׁיּוֹצְאוֹת וְרוֹעוֹת חוּץ לַתְּחוּם וּבָאוֹת וְלָנוֹת בְּתוֹךְ הַתְּחוּם – ANY animals THAT GO OUT AND PASTURE BEYOND THE *TECHUM* of a settled area BUT COME BACK TO SPEND THE NIGHT WITHIN THE *TECHUM* of a settled area.[7] רַבִּי אוֹמֵר – REBBI SAYS: אֵלּוּ וָאֵלּוּ בַּיְיתוֹת הֵן – BOTH OF THESE ARE DOMESTIC ANIMALS. וְאֵלּוּ הֵן מִדְבָּרִיּוֹת – RATHER, THESE ARE RANGE ANIMALS: כָּל שֶׁרוֹעוֹת בָּאֲפָר – ANY animals THAT go out and GRAZE IN THE PASTURE וְאֵין נִכְנָסוֹת לַיִּשּׁוּב – AND DO NOT RETURN TO A SETTLEMENT לֹא בִימוֹת הַחַמָּה וְלֹא בִימוֹת הַגְּשָׁמִים – EITHER IN THE SUMMER OR IN THE WINTER. Now, range animals are *muktzeh* only according to R' Yehudah. Since Rebbi provides a definition for range animals, he evidently follows R' Yehudah's view regarding *muktzeh* and not R' Shimon's view. – ? –

The Gemara presents three possible answers:

אִיבָּעֵית אֵימָא – **If you prefer, say:** הָנֵי נַמִּי כִּגְרוֹגְרוֹת וְצִימּוּקִין דָּמְיָין – **These** (the range animals) **are analogous to dried figs and raisins.**[8] Therefore, even R' Shimon agrees that they are *muktzeh.* וְאִי בָּעֵית אֵימָא – **And if you prefer, say:** לְדִבְרָיו דְּרַבִּי שִׁמְעוֹן קָאָמַר לֵיהּ – **[R' Shimon bar Rebbi] posed this** inquiry **to [Rebbi]** to clarify **the opinion of R' Shimon** and Rebbi responded in kind, וְלֵיהּ לָא סְבִירָא לֵיהּ – **but [Rebbi] himself does not subscribe to this** view. Rather, he concurs with R' Yehudah's broad application of *muktzeh.* וְאִיבָּעֵית אֵימָא – **And if you prefer, say:** לְדִבְרֵיהֶם דְּרַבָּנַן קָאָמַר לְהוּ – In the cited Baraisa, **[Rebbi] said** his definition of range animals **according to the opinion of the Rabbis,** i.e. the Tanna Kamma. He meant as follows: לְדִידִי לֵית לִי מוּקְצֶה כְּלָל – **As for me, I do not apply *muktzeh* at all,** except in the case of dried figs and raisins. Hence, I maintain that range animals are not *muktzeh.* לְדִידְכוּ – But even **according to you,** who apply *muktzeh* broadly, אוֹדוּ לִי מִיהַת – you should **at least concede to me** דְּהֵיכָא דְּיוֹצְאוֹת בַּפֶּסַח וְנִכְנָסוֹת בָּרְבִיעָה – **that if [animals] go out** and graze in the pasture **during the Pesach season and** then **return during the** first **rains** דְּבַיְיתוֹת נִינְהוּ – **they are domestic animals,** and are therefore not *muktzeh.* וְרַבָּנַן אָמְרוּ לֵיהּ – **But the Rabbis replied:** לֹא מִדְבָּרִיּוֹת נִינְהוּ – **No! They are** considered **range animals** and are therefore *muktzeh.*

The Gemara begins a lengthy discussion about whether R' Yochanan concurs with R' Yehudah or R' Shimon concerning *muktzeh:*

אָמַר רַבָּה בַּר בַּר חָנָה אָמַר רַבִּי יוֹחָנָן – **Rabbah bar bar Chanah said in the name of R' Yochanan:** אָמְרוּ הֲלָכָה כְּרַבִּי שִׁמְעוֹן – **They said** that **the halachah follows R' Shimon** concerning *muktzeh.*[9]

The Gemara asks:

וּמִי אָמַר ר׳ יוֹחָנָן הָכִי – **Did R' Yochanan** really **say this?** וְהָא בְּעָא מִינֵּיהּ הַהוּא סָבָא קְרוּיָא וְאָמְרִי לָהּ סְרוּיָא מֵר׳ יוֹחָנָן – **But a certain Keruyan elder – and some say** it was **a Seruyan**[10] elder **– inquired of R' Yochanan:** קִינָּה שֶׁל תַּרְנְגֹלֶת מַהוּ לְטַלְטוּלֵי בְּשַׁבָּת – **What is** the law with regard to **moving a** portable **chicken coop on the Sabbath?** אָמַר לֵיהּ כְּלוּם עָשׂוּי אֶלָּא לְתַרְנְגוֹלִין – And **[R' Yochanan] replied: Is it made for any** purpose **other than** to house **chickens?** Since it is obviously not, it is *muktzeh.*[11] R' Yochanan's response implies that he concurs with R' Yehudah. – ? –

NOTES

1. פַּצְעִילֵי תְּמָרָה refers to a species of dates which do not ripen on the tree. Therefore, baskets are made from palm leaves for the purpose of storing these dates until they ripen. Although the dates are not yet fit to be eaten, they were not actively rejected from Sabbath use. R' Shimon bar Rebbi therefore inquired whether R' Shimon treats them like partially dried figs and raisins, which are also unfit for consumption, and forbids eating them while they are ripening (see *Rashi* here and *Beitzah* 40a; see also *Tosafos, Beitzah* 40a ד״ה פצעילי תמרה, *Rosh Yosef* and *Dibros Moshe*).

2. In that case two factors are present: The one who put the figs and raisins out to dry has actively rejected them *and* they are unfit for consumption when they begin to dry (*Rashi*). By contrast, unripe dates were never rejected from Sabbath use. Therefore R' Shimon does not consider them *muktzeh.* See *Rashi* to *Beitzah* 40b.

3. *Beitzah* 40a.

4. Range animals are those which pasture freely and are not seen for an extended period of time. Since they are not always accessible to their owner at the onset of Yom Tov, they cannot be considered prepared for Yom Tov use and are therefore *muktzeh* according to R' Yehudah, whose view this Mishnah follows. The Mishnah therefore teaches that we may not slaughter them on Yom Tov. The prohibition on watering is a reference to the practice of watering animals before their slaughter to facilitate their skinning (*Rashi;* cf. *Shulchan Aruch Orach Chaim* 497:2 with *Beur HaGra* and *Mishnah Berurah*; see *Maharatz Chayes*).

5. I.e. at the end of the winter.

6. The rainy season begins during the month of Cheshvan (*Rashi* to *Beitzah* ibid.; see *Taanis* 6a).

7. The *techum* is the two thousand-*amah* boundary beyond which it is prohibited to walk on the Sabbath or Yom Tov. Even animals that pasture beyond the *techum* are considered prepared for Yom Tov use if they return to spend the nights within the *techum.*

8. Range animals as defined by Rebbi, i.e. those which do not return to a settled area even during the winter, are analogous to dried figs and raisins, since by driving them away the owner actively rejected them from festival use, and furthermore, there is considerable bother involved in retrieving them (*Rashi* here and *Beitzah* 40b). [Presumably, the element of bother corresponds to the inherent unfitness of the drying figs and raisins. Thus, the two factors that render drying figs and raisins *muktzeh* are present as well in the case of these range animals.]

9. "They" is a reference to the members of the academy (*Rashi*). Since R' Yochanan repeated their opinion it would seem that he concurs with it.

10. The elder was described by the area from which he hailed (*Rashi*).

11. A chicken, like any other live animal, is intrinsically *muktzeh* on the Sabbath (*Tosafos* ד״ה הכא במאי עסקינן). Since the coop is designated for the use of chickens [and may not be moved while it contains them], it is designated for a forbidden function and may not be moved according to R' Yehudah (*Rashi*; see 44a note 23). This is analogous to a bed that was designated and used for storing money, which on the basis of its designation is *muktzeh* according to R' Yehudah, as the Gemara concluded above, 44b (see *Pnei Yehoshua* and *Avnei Nezer*, *Orach Chaim* §55).

[The coop is not, however, a *base to muktzeh* because of the live chicks in it, since the chickens come and go, and can easily be shooed off it (*Tos. Yeshanim, Ritva MHK* ed.; see also *Pnei Yehoshua*).]

פצעילי [א] תמרה לרבי שמעון מהו א"ל [א] אין מוקצה לר"ש אלא גרוגרות וצימוקין בלבד ורבי לית ליה מוקצה והתנן [ב] [ב] אין משקין ושוחטין את המדבריות אבל משקין ושוחטין את הבייתות ותניא [ג] [ג] אלו הן מדבריות כל שיוצאות בפסח ונכנסות ברביעה בייתות כל שיוצאות ורועות חוץ לתחום ובאות ולנות בתוך התחום ר' אומר אלו ואלו בייתות הן ואלו הן מדבריות כל שרועות באפר ואין נכנסות לישוב לא בימות החמה ולא בימות הגשמים איבעית אימא הני נמי כגרוגרות וצימוקין דמיין ואי בעית אימא לדבריו דר"ש קאמר ליה וליה לא סבירא ליה ואיבעית אימא לדבריהם דרבנן קאמר להו לדידי לית לי מוקצה כלל לדידכו אודו לי מיהת דהיכא דיוצאות בפסח ונכנסות ברביעה דבייתות נינהו ורבנן אמרו ליה לא מדבריות נינהו אמר רבה בר בר חנה אמר ר' יוחנן אמרו הלכה כרבי שמעון ומי א"ר יוחנן הכי והא בעא מיניה ההוא סבא קרויא ואמרי לה סרויא מר' יוחנן קינה של תרנגולת מהו לטלטולי בשבת אמר ליה כלום עשוי אלא לתרנגולין הכא במאי עסקינן דאית ביה אפרוח מת הניחא למר בר אמימר משמיה [ד] (דרב) [ה] דאמר מודה היה ר' שמעון בבעלי חיים שמתו שאסורין אלא למר בריה דרב יוסף משמיה דרבא דאמר חלוק היה רבי שמעון [אפי'] בבעלי חיים שמתו שהן מותרין מאי איכא למימר הכא במאי עסקינן בדאית ביה ביצה והאמר [ו] רב נחמן מאן דאית ליה מוקצה אית ליה נולד דלית ליה מוקצה לית ליה נולד דאית ביה ביצת אפרוח כי אתא רב יצחק בר' יוסף א"ר יוחנן הלכה כר' יהודה ור' יהושע בן לוי אמר הלכה כרבי שמעון אמר רב יוסף היינו דאמר רבה בר בר חנה א"ר יוחנן אמרו הלכה כרבי שמעון אמרו וליה לא סבירא ליה א"ל אביי לרב יוסף ואת לא תסברא דר' יוחנן כר' יהודה הא ר' אבא ורבי אסי איקלעו לבי ר' אבא דמן חיפא ונפל מנרתא על גלימיה דר' אסי ולא טילטלה מאי טעמא לאו משום דרבי אסי תלמידיה דר' יוחנן הוה ור' יוחנן כרבי יהודה ס"ל דאית ליה מוקצה א"ל מנרתא קאמרת מנרתא שאני דא"ר אחא בר חנינא א"ר אסי הורה ריש לקיש בצידן מנורה הניטלת בידו אחת מותר לטלטלה בשתי ידיו אסור לטלטלה ור' יוחנן אמר אנו אין לנו אלא בנר כרבי שמעון אבל מנורה בין ניטלה בידו אחת בין ניטלה בשתי ידיו אסור לטלטלה וטעמא מאי רבה ורב יוסף דאמרי תרווייהו הואיל ואדם קובע לה מקום אמר ליה אביי לרב יוסף והרי כילת חתנים דאדם קובע לו מקום ואמר שמואל משום רבי חייא [ז] כילת חתנים
מותר

פצעילי תמרה. א) תמרים הנלקטים קודם בישולן וכונסין אותם בסלים שעושין מלולבין והן מתבשלות מאליהן מהו לאכול מהן קודם בישולן מי מודה בהן דמוקצות הן כגרוגרות וצימוקין או לא: **אלא בגרוגרות וצימוקין.** דאיכא תרתי דדחינהו בידים ולא חזו: **ור' לית ליה מוקצה.** דקס"ד מדבעי מיניה אליבא דרבי שמעון אלמא הוה שמיע ליה מאבוה דכרבי שמעון סבירא ליה: **משקין.** דרך להשקות בהמה לפני שחיטה שתהא נוחה להפשיט: **המדבריות.** הברייתות: **ברביעה.** במרחשון: **ואלו מדבריות כל שרועות באפר.** והני מיהא אסירי אלמא אית ליה מוקצה: **איבעית אימא הני.** מדבריות נמי כגרוגרות דמי דדחינהו בידים ויש טורח לילך ולהביאם: **ואיבעית אימא.** ההיא דפצעילי תמרה לדבריו דרבי שמעון קאמר ולר' לא ס"ל: ה"ג אמר רבה בר בר חנה א"ר יוחנן אמרו הלכה כר' שמעון: **אמרו.** בני הישיבה: **סרוייא קרוייא.** על שם מקומו: **כלום עשוי.** לשום תשמיש: **אלא לתרנגולין.** הלכך ה"ל מלאכתו לאיסור ואסור אלמא אית ליה מוקצה: **דאית ביה אפרוח מת.** דלא חזי למיכל ולכלבים נמי לא חזי ואף על גב דא"ר שמעון מחתכין את הנבלה לפני הכלבים הני מילי במסוכנת אבל בריאה לא דלא הוה דעתיה מאתמול לכלבים והאי אפרוח שמת בשבת נמי לא הוה דעתיה מאתמול לכלבים: **הניחא למר** כו' **דאמר מודה היה ר"ש.** דאע"ג דאמר מחתכין הנבלה לפני הכלבים ה"מ במסוכנת דדעתיה עליה מאתמול לכלבים אבל מודה הוא בבעלי חיים כלומר בבריאים שמתו שאסורין שפיר קתרצת לרבי שמעון גופיה לא חזי לכלבים: **מאי איכא למימר.** הא חזי לכלבים: **דאית בה ביצה.** שנולדה היום ומודה ר' שמעון בנולד: **והא אמר רב נחמן כו'.** בשמעתא קמייתא דביצה: **דאית בה ביצת אפרוח.** וכלב לא אכיל לה משום ב) קליפה: **וליה לא סבירא ליה.** לר' יוחנן לא סבירא דתיהוי הלכה כר' שמעון והיינו דרב יצחק: **ואת לא תסברא.** ומקמי דשמעת ליה לדרב יצחק לא הוה ידעת דר' יוחנן כר' יהודה: **בשתי ידים אסור לטלטלה.** כדמפרש טעמא לקמיה דלאו לטלטולי עבידא דאדם קובע לה מקום: **ור' יוחנן אמר אנו אין לנו.** שום היתר בהלכות טלטול נרות: **אלא בנר.** ישן כרבי שמעון דמתיר אבל מנורה כו' הלכך אי לאו מדרב יצחק לא הוה ידענא ליה אבל השתא ידענא דכר' יהודה סבירא ליה בכולהו בר ממוקצה מחמת מיאוס דנר ישן:
מותר

לדבריו דר' שמעון קאמר ליה וליה לא סבירא ליה. משמע דמספקא ליה אי ר' סבר לה כר' שמעון ותימה אמאי לא מוכח מהכא דלקמן דסבר כר"ש דאמר פעם אחת הלך ר' כו' והורה במנורה כר"ש בנר וכן מברייתא דמייתי באין לדין [ס] בכור תם שנפל לבור ר' יהודה הנשיא אומר ירד מי שבקי במומין ויראה אם יש בו מום יעלה וישחוט כו' ומיהו במאי דמתיר לראות במומין לא אתי כר"ש אלא במאי דלית ליה מוקצה ומיהו רש"י לא גריס בכור תם אלא בכור שנפל לבור והשתא מצי אתי כר' יהודה ויראה אם היה בו מום זה מעי"ט [ט]: **הכא** במאי עסקינן דאית ביה אפרוח מת. פירש הר"ר יוסף דלא נקט אפרוח חי משום דחזי לשתק בו תינוק כשבוכה ואין נראה דהא בההיא דכופין את הסל לפני האפרוחין (לעיל דף מג.) משמע דאסור לטלטל ועוד אי מחיים שרי אמאי קאמר בסמוך דמודה ר"ש בבעלי חיים שמתו שאסורין אלא ודאי בעלי חיים ג) מוקצין הם כגרוגרות וצימוקין ומקצה אותם גם מכלבים ולא דמי לבשר תפל שמותר לר"ש מדפריך בפרק מפנין (לקמן קכח.) על רב הונא דשרי והא תלמיד דרב הוה ורב כר' יהודה סבירא ליה אבל לר' שמעון משמע דשרי משום דאינו מקצהו מכלבים כמו בעלי חיים:

דאית ביה ביצה. דאסור משום נולד צ"ע דר' יוחנן גופיה [י] מפרש טעמא דביצה משום משקין שזבו ואפשר דמשום הכי לא הוה אסר ר"ש לטלטלה אלא לאכילה:

דאית ביה ביצת אפרוח. נראה לר"י דאסור לר' שמעון משום דכיון דאית ביה אפרוח הוי ד) כמו גרוגרות וצימוקין וקא מיבעיא ליה לסבא קירויא אי שרי לטלטולי על ידי שינער משם הביצה אי חשיב כמו מניח או כשכח והשיב לו רבי יוחנן כלום עשוי אלא לתרנגולין ואין זה כשכח אלא כמניח ואסור:

אמר ליה מנרתא שאני. וא"ת אמאי לא מוכח מהא דא"ר יוחנן בפ' לולב וערבה (סוכה מו:) דסוכה אפי' בשמיני אסורה אלמא אית ליה מיגו דאיתקצאי כו' כר' יהודה ותירץ ר"י דנר אינו מוקצה למצותו מטלטול שאין ביטול מצוה בטלטול ולא דמי לסוכה דאיתקצאי ביה"ש מחמת מצוה ולהכי אינו יכול להוכיח מסוכה לנר: (לעיל) **לאו** משום דר' אסי תלמידו דר' יוחנן כו'. וא"ת דילמא ר' אסי כרב רביה סבירא ליה כדאמר לעיל גבי שרגא דחנוכה אמרו ליה רב כהנא ורב אסי לרב הילכתא הכי ונראה דרב אסי דלעיל לאו היינו ר' אסי דהכא דההוא דלעיל חבירו של רב כהנא והכא ר' אסי חבירו של ר' אמי [כ]: **אין** לנו אלא בנר כר' שמעון. פי' במוקצה מחמת מיאוס דהיינו נר ישן שלא הדליקו בה באותה שבת ולעיל דפסיק כרבי יהודה היינו בהדליקו בה באותה שבת דהוי מוקצה מחמת איסור והא דפסיק בפרק בתרא [ל] כר"ש בנבלה לפני הכלבים אף על גב דנבלה מוקצה מחמת איסור היא כדפר"ת (לעיל יט: ד"ה ושמואל) התם [מ] לא דחייה בידים אבל הכא דדחייה בידים סבר כר' יהודה ולפי זה לא קיימי ר' יוחנן וריב"ל דפסקי כר' שמעון אחדא ברייתא דר' יוחנן קאי אברייתא דכל הנרות של מתכת מטלטלין כו' אבל במאי דקאמר ר' יהודה בברייתא דלעיל מטלטלין נר חדש אבל לא ישן לא סבר רבי יוחנן כוותיה וריב"ל אברייתא דמטלטלין נר חדש קאי דבההיא ברייתא שרי
רבי

עין משפט נר מצוה

נד א מיי' פכ"ו מהל' שבת הלכה יד סמג לאוין סה טוש"ע או"ח סימן שי סעיף ב:

נה ב ג מיי' פ"ב מהל' יו"ט הלכה ב סמג לאוין עה טור שו"ע או"ח סימן תצז סעיף ב וסימן תצח סעיף ג:

רבינו חננאל

וכן הא דאמר ליה [ר'] לר' שמעון בריה אין מוקצה לר' שמעון אלא גרוגרות וצמוקין בלבד פשוטה היא: **אמר** רבה בר בר חנה א"ר יוחנן אמרו הלכה כר"ש איני והא בעא מיניה ההוא סבא קרוייה קינה של תרנגולין מהו לטלטלה בשבת ואמר ליה אסור כלום עשוי אלא לתרנגולים מכלל דר' יוחנן כר' יהודה סבירא ליה דאית ליה מוקצה. ושנינן בדאית ליה בהאי קינה אפרוח מת ומשום הכי אסורה לטלטלה. הניחא למ"ד בעלי חיים שמתו בשבת דברי הכל אסור לטלטלן בשבת הא אפילו לר' שמעון ואלא למ"ד ר"ש מתיר בבעלי חיים שמתו שמותר לטלטלן אע"ג דאית בהאי קינה אפרוח שמת בשבת ר"ש מתיר אמאי קא אסר ר' יוחנן והא איהו הלכתא כר' שמעון סבירא ליה. ואסיקנא בדאית בהאי קינה ביצה שיש בה אפרוח דלדברי הכל אסורה. ואעפ"כ לא נתברר כי ר' יוחנן כר' שמעון סבירא ליה. וכי אתא רב יצחק בר' יוסף א"ר יוחנן הלכתא כר' יהודה וריב"ל אמר הלכה כר"ש. אמר רב יוסף היינו דאמר רבה בר בר חנה א"ר יוחנן אמרו הלכה כר"ש וליה לא סבירא ליה. ודייק נמי אביי מדר' אסי נפלה מנרתא על גלימיה [בבין] ר' אבא ולא טלטלה. ואמר (משמיה) [משום] דר' אסי תלמיד דר' יוחנן הוא. ור' יוחנן במוקצה סבר לה כר' יהודה. ודחינן להא דאביי. ואמרינן לא אפילו תימא ר' יוחנן כר' שמעון מנרתא שני

מסורת הש"ס

א) ביצה מ., ב) שם. [לקמן קנו.], ג) [ביצה שם], ד) [צ"ל דרבא], ה) ביצה מ:, ו) שם ב., ז) עירובין קב. לקמן קלח:, ח) [ביצה דף כו.], ט) [וע"ע תוספות ביצה כו. ד"ה ת"ר], י) [ביצה ג.], כ) [וע' תוספות חולין יט. ד"ה אמר רב הונא], ל) [דף קנו:], מ) התוס' המתחיל ולפ"ז וכו' הנרשם בס"א נמצא בדף מו ע"א כי שם מקומו.

תוספות ישנים

א) אין נראה לר"י פירוש זה דל"ד לגרוגרות וצימוקין דלא דחיה בידים. ונ"ל כפירוש הערוך שפירש פצעילי תמרה לשון מפצע שמפצעין תמרים כדי להתבשל ולהתייבש ובשעת הפציעה מתקלקלת מראיתה ואחר זמן משתבחות ודמי לגרוגרות וצימוקין אך שגרוגרות וצימוקין מתקלקלות יותר מהם:

ב) קשה דאפשר להסיר הקליפה ויאכלנה הכלב:

ג) והא דלא בעי באפרוח חי אם מותר לטלטל הקינה משום דאפשר להפריחו:

ד) א"נ הוי מוקצה מחמת חסרון כיס:

ליקוטי רש"י

פצעילי תמרה. תמרים שאין מתבשלות באילן לעולם וגודרין אותן מהאילן ועושין להן חותלות הן כלי כפות תמרים וכונסין אותן לתוכן ומתבשלות [ביצה מ.]. **מהו.** לאכול מהן ביום טוב. **אלא גרוגרות וצימוקין.** שהן מתחלה ראויין לאכילה והוא דחה אותן בידים להעלותן ליבשן ושוב אינן ראויין עד שייבשו אבל אלו לא דחה אותן בידים ואיכא דאכיל מנייהו. **ורבי לית ליה מוקצה.** הכי קא סלקא דעתיה מדפריש ליה מילתיה דרבי שמעון אלמא כר' שמעון סבירא ליה [שם:]. **אין משקין ושוחטין.** משום מוקצה. **משקין.** משום סרכא דמשכא שתהא נוחה להפשיטה שהוא נדבק יותר מדאי בבשר [שם.]. אורחא דמילתא נקט משום סירכא דמשכא שתהא נוחה להפשיט [לקמן קנו.]. **ונכנסות.** לישוב [ביצה שם]. **איבעית אימא הני.** מדבריות שאין נכנסות לישוב כלל כגרוגרות וצמוקין דמיין שמקצה אותן מאכלו בידים. **ואי בעית אימא.** אין מוקצה לרבי שמעון קאמר ליה אבל לדידי יש מוקצה. **ואיבעית אימא.** מתני' לדבריהם דרבנן דאית להו מוקצה קאמר להו [שם:]. **בבעלי חיים.** בהמה בריאה בין השמשות. **שמתו.** ביום טוב. **שאסורין.** וכי שריא במסוכנת בין השמשות דדעתיה עלויה להאכילה לכלבים [שם כז:]. **הכא במאי עסקינן בדאית ביה ביצה.** דקא סלקא דעתין דאפילו לרבי שמעון דשרי במוקצה בנולד אסיר דאילו במוקצה סבירא ליה לא מקצי איניש מדעתיה מידי דחזי ליה אבל נולד לא הוה ידע דנהוי דעתיה עלויה [שם ב.]. **כילת חתנים.** לא דמיא לשאר כילות שאר כילות פרוסות על גבי קינוף שהיא לארבע רגלים ויש לה גג דהוי אהל ושל חתנים על גבי נקליטין שאינם אלא שנים באמצעית המטה וקנה נתון עליהם והבגד נתון עליו ונופל לכאן ולכאן ואין לה גג טפח הלכך לאו אהל הוא [לקמן קלח:]. לאו אהל הוא מפני שאין לה גג למעלה רוחב טפח מפני שהיא נתונה בשיפוע והיא יריעה שפורסין סביב למטה לישן [עירובין קב.].

The Gemara resolves the contradiction:

הָכָא בְּמַאי עַסְקִינַן – Here, in the case of the chicken coop, **what are we dealing with?** דְּאִית בֵּיהּ אֶפְרוֹחַ מֵת – It is with a case **where there is in [the coop] a chick that died** on the Sabbath. Since the coop is now a base to the dead chick, even R' Shimon would agree that it is *muktzeh.*[12]

This resolution assumes that a dead chick is indeed *muktzeh,* even according to R' Shimon. The Gemara points out that this is not universally accepted:

הָנִיחָא לְמַר בַּר אֲמֵימַר מִשְּׁמֵיהּ (דרב) [דְּרָבָא] דְּאָמַר – **This** answer **is fine according to Mar bar Ameimar in the name of Rava, who said** מוֹדֶה הָיָה ר' שִׁמְעוֹן בְּבַעֲלֵי חַיִּים שֶׁמֵּתוּ שֶׁאֲסוּרִין – that **R' Shimon concedes** to R' Yehudah **that** healthy **animals which died** on the Sabbath **are prohibited.**[13] אֶלָּא לְמַר בְּרֵיהּ דְּרַב יוֹסֵף מִשְּׁמֵיהּ דְּרָבָא דְּאָמַר – **But according to Mar the son of Rav Yosef in the name of Rava, who said** חָלוּק הָיָה רַבִּי שִׁמְעוֹן [אֲפִילּוּ] בְּבַעֲלֵי חַיִּים שֶׁמֵּתוּ שֶׁהֵן מוּתָּרִין – that **R' Shimon disagreed** with R' Yehudah **even in regard to** healthy **animals that died** on the Sabbath, holding **that they are permitted,**[14] מַאי אִיכָּא לְמֵימַר – **what is there to say?** Since a chick that died on the Sabbath is not *muktzeh,* how shall we resolve R' Yochanan's statement that a chicken coop is *muktzeh*?

The Gemara offers a different solution:

הָכָא בְּמַאי עַסְקִינַן – **What are we dealing with here,** in the case of the chicken coop? בִּדְאִית בֵּיהּ בֵּיצָה – It is with a case **where there is a** newly laid **egg in it.** Since the egg was laid on the Sabbath it qualifies as *nolad,*[15] which is *muktzeh* even according to R' Shimon. Consequently, the coop is a base to *muktzeh.*

The Gemara points out that this answer, too, is not valid according to all views:

וְהָאָמַר רַב נַחְמָן – **But Rav Nachman said** that מַאן דְּאִית לֵיהּ מוּקְצֶה אִית לֵיהּ נוֹלָד – **the [Tanna] who subscribes to** a broad application of *muktzeh,* i.e. R' Yehudah, **subscribes to** the prohibition of ***nolad,*** דְּלֵית לֵיהּ מוּקְצֶה לֵית לֵיהּ נוֹלָד – **but the one who does not subscribe to** a broad application of ***muktzeh,*** i.e. R' Shimon, **does not subscribe to** the prohibition of ***nolad.***[16] According to Rav Nachman's interpretation of R' Shimon's opinion, why should a chicken coop be *muktzeh*?

The Gemara offers a different solution:

דְּאִית בֵּיהּ בֵּיצַת אֶפְרוֹחַ – We are dealing with a case **where there is in [the coop] an** unhatched **egg containing a chick.** Such an egg is certainly *muktzeh,* and consequently, the coop is a base to *muktzeh.*[17]

The previous discussion was based on the presumption that R' Yochanan concurs with R' Shimon, in accordance with the halachic ruling that R' Yochanan cited. A further teaching, however, sheds new light on R' Yochanan's view:

כִּי אֲתָא רַב יִצְחָק בְּר' יוֹסֵף – **When Rav Yitzchak the son of R' Yosef arrived** from Eretz Yisrael, אָמַר רַבִּי יוֹחָנָן הֲלָכָה כְּר' יְהוּדָה – **he said in the name of Rav Yochanan** that **the halachah follows R' Yehudah;** and he added: וְר' יְהוֹשֻׁעַ בֶּן לֵוִי אָמַר הֲלָכָה כְּרַבִּי שִׁמְעוֹן – **But R' Yehoshua ben Levi said** that **the halachah follows R' Shimon.** אָמַר רַב יוֹסֵף – Upon hearing this, **Rav Yosef said:** הַיְינוּ דְּאָמַר רַבָּה בַּר בַּר חָנָה אָמַר רַבִּי יוֹחָנָן – **This is what Rabbah bar bar Chanah** must have meant when he **said in the name of R' Yochanan:** אָמְרוּ הֲלָכָה כְּרַבִּי שִׁמְעוֹן – ***They said*** that **the halachah follows R' Shimon.** אָמְרוּ וְלֵיהּ לֹא סְבִירָא לֵיהּ – He meant that **they,** i.e. R' Yehoshua ben Levi and R' Yochanan's other colleagues, **said** that the halachah follows R' Shimon; **but [R' Yochanan]** himself **does not concur.**[18]

Abaye expresses surprise that Rav Yosef failed to reach this conclusion before hearing Rav Yitzchak's report:

אָמַר לֵיהּ אַבַּיֵי לְרַב יוֹסֵף – **Abaye said to Rav Yosef:** וְאַתְּ לֹא תִּסְבְּרָא דְּר' יוֹחָנָן כְּר' יְהוּדָה – **Did you not realize** all along **that R' Yochanan concurs with R' Yehudah?** הָא ר' אַבָּא וְר' אַסִּי אִיקְלְעוּ לְבֵי ר' אַבָּא דְּמִן חֵיפָא – **But** there was an incident in which **R' Abba and R' Assi once arrived at the home of R' Abba of Haifa** for the Sabbath, וְנָפַל מְנַרְתָּא עַל גְּלִימֵיהּ דְּר' אַסִּי – **and a**

NOTES

12. For even R' Shimon agrees that dead animals are *muktzeh* when they are unfit for consumption [and the dead chick was not ritually slaughtered]. Now, if the chick had died before the Sabbath, R' Shimon would not consider it *muktzeh*, since it would be fit for feeding dogs. However, when it was healthy before the Sabbath and died unexpectedly on the Sabbath, R' Shimon concedes that it is *muktzeh* because the owner did not plan before the Sabbath to use it for dogs (*Rashi*).

[According to this explanation, the inquiry posed by the elder was whether the coop qualifies as a *base to muktzeh* when it contains a dead chick. When R' Yochanan retorted, "Is it made for any purpose other than the use of chickens," he meant the following: Since a coop is made for chickens and it is common for young chicks to die, the coop must be considered a *base to muktzeh* when it contains a dead chick. Had it not been made for chickens, it would not become a *base to muktzeh*, since an item attains this designation only when *muktzeh* is intentionally left on it (see *Rosh* and *Pnei Yehoshua*).]

13. I.e. although R' Shimon rules in a Mishnah (below, 156b) that it is permitted to cut up the carcass of an animal that died on the Sabbath and feed it to dogs, that ruling is limited to the case of an animal that was deathly ill at the onset of the Sabbath. Since the owner was aware that it might die on the Sabbath and that the carcass would then be used for his dogs, it is considered prepared for Sabbath use (like a small lamp and a rickety succah). If a healthy animal died on the Sabbath, however, R' Shimon concedes that it may not be cut up for dogs, since it was not prepared for this use at the onset of the Sabbath (like a large lamp and a sturdy succah). According to this understanding of R' Shimon's opinion, a healthy chick that died unexpectedly on the Sabbath is indeed *muktzeh* and the previous answer is correct (*Rashi; see Beur HaGra* to *Orach Chaim* 324:7).

14. According to Mar the son of Rav Yosef, R' Shimon permits even the carcasses of healthy animals that died unexpectedly on the Sabbath to be used as dog food. The difference between this and a large lamp that unexpectedly went out, or a sturdy succah that unexpectedly collapsed, lies in the fact that in those cases the oil and the succah were actively rejected from Sabbath use when the lamp was lit and the succah erected, whereas here, the healthy animal was never actively rejected from being used for dog food upon its death (see *Tosafos* below ד״ה אין לנו and *Milchamos Hashem* to *Beitzah* 24b; see also *Afikei Yam* II:19; see, however, *Chasam Sofer* to 46a ד״ה והנלפע״ד).

15. I.e. something newly formed on the Sabbath and thus not "prepared" in advance for Sabbath use. See Chapter Introduction.

16. Numerous Amoraim disagree with Rav Nachman on this point, for they hold that since the object first came into existence on the Sabbath, R' Shimon concedes that the owner cannot be considered to have "prepared" it before the Sabbath. Rav Nachman, however, holds that since it was anticipated that the egg would be laid on the Sabbath, R' Shimon considers it "prepared" (see *Rosh,* at the conclusion of Tractate *Beitzah*, at length; see also *Rashi* and *Tosafos* to *Beitzah* 2a ד״ה קא סלקא דעתין).

17. An unhatched egg containing a chick is certainly *muktzeh* because it is utterly unfit for use. Humans would not eat the chicken embryo (*Ritva MHK* ed.) and dogs cannot eat it because of its shell (*Rashi;* cf. *Tos. Yeshanim*; see *Rashi* to *Beitzah* 6a ד״ה לכלבים). Due to its utter uselessness, it is intrinsically *muktzeh*, like a stone (see *Pnei Yehoshua* to *Beitzah* 6b; cf. *Tosafos* ד״ה דאית ביה ביצת אפרוח).

[According to this explanation as well, the elder inquired whether the coop qualified as a *base to muktzeh*, and R' Yochanan replied that, since it is made for the use of chickens and they commonly lay eggs, it is as though the unhatched egg was placed there intentionally (*Tosafos* ibid.).]

18. [Thus, R' Yochanan's ruling above that a chicken coop is *muktzeh* pertains even to a coop that does not contain an unhatched embryo, in accordance with R' Yehudah's opinion.]

פצעילי א) תמרה לרבי שמעון מהו א"ל אאין מוקצה לר"ש אלא גרוגרות וצימוקין בלבד ורבי לית ליה מוקצה והתנן ב) באין משקין ושוחטין את המדבריות אבל משקין ושוחטין את הבייתות ותניא ג) גאלו הן מדבריות כל שיוצאות בפסח ונכנסות ברביעה בייתות כל שיוצאות ורועות חוץ לתחום ובאות ולנות בתוך התחום ר' אומר אלו ואלו בייתות הן ואלו הן מדבריות כל שרועות באפר ואין נכנסות לישוב לא בימות החמה ולא בימות הגשמים איבעית אימא הני נמי כגרוגרות וצימוקין דמיין ואי בעית אימא לדבריו דר"ש קאמר ליה וליה לא סבירא ליה ואיבעית אימא לדבריהם דרבנן קאמר להו לדידי לית לי מוקצה כלל לדידכו אודו לי מיהת דהיכא דיוצאות בפסח ונכנסות ברביעה דבייתות נינהו ורבנן אמרו ליה לא מדבריות נינהו אמר רבה בר בר חנה אמר ר' יוחנן אמרו הלכה כרבי שמעון ומי א"ר יוחנן הכי והא בעא מיניה ההוא סבא קרויא ואמרי לה סרויא מר' יוחנן קינה של תרנגולת מהו לטלטולי בשבת אמר ליה כלום עשוי אלא לתרנגולין הכא במאי עסקינן דאית ביה אפרוח מת הניחא למר בר אמימר משמיה ד) (דרב) ה) דאמר מודה היה ר' שמעון בבעלי חיים שמתו שאסורין אלא למר בריה דרב יוסף משמיה דרבא דאמר חלוק היה רבי שמעון [אפי'] בבעלי חיים שמתו שהן מותרין מאי איכא למימר הכא במאי עסקינן בדאית ביה ביצה והאמר ו) רב נחמן מאן דאית ליה מוקצה אית ליה נולד דלית ליה מוקצה לית ליה נולד דאית ביה ביצת אפרוח כי אתא רב יצחק בר' יוסף א"ר יוחנן הלכה כר' יהודה ור' יהושע בן לוי אמר הלכה כרבי שמעון אמר רב יוסף היינו דאמר רבה בר בר חנה א"ר יוחנן אמרו הלכה כרבי שמעון אמרו וליה לא סבירא ליה א"ל אביי לרב יוסף ואת לא תסברא דר' יוחנן כר' יהודה הא ר' אבא ורבי אסי איקלעו לבי ר' אבא דמן חיפא ונפל מנרתא על גלימיה דר' אסי ולא טילטלה מאי טעמא לאו משום דרבי אסי תלמידיה דר' יוחנן הוה ור' יוחנן כרבי יהודה ס"ל דאית ליה מוקצה א"ל מנרתא קאמרת מנרתא שאני דא"ר אחא בר חנינא א"ר אסי הורה ריש לקיש בצידן מנורה הניטלת בידו אחת מותר לטלטלה בשתי ידיו אסור לטלטלה ור' יוחנן אמר אנו אין לנו אלא בנר כרבי שמעון אבל מנורה בין ניטלה בידו אחת בין ניטלה בשתי ידיו אסור לטלטלה וטעמא מאי רבה ורב יוסף דאמרי תרווייהו הואיל ואדם קובע לה מקום אמר ליה אביי לרב יוסף והרי כילת חתנים דאדם קובע לו מקום ואמר שמואל משום רבי חייא ז) כילת חתנים מותר

רש"י

פצעילי תמרה. א) תמרים הנלקטים קודם בישולן וכונסין אותם בסלים שעושין מלולבין והן מתבשלות מאליהן מהו לאכול מהן קודם בישולן מי מודה בהן דמוקצות הן כגרוגרות וצימוקין או לא: אלא בגרוגרות וצימוקין. דאיכא תרתי דדחינהו בידים ולא חזו: ור' לית ליה מוקצה. דקס"ד מדבעי מיניה אליבא דרבי שמעון אלמא הוה שמיע ליה מאבוה דכרבי שמעון סבירא ליה: משקין. דרך להשקות בהמה לפני שחיטה שתהא נוחה להפשיט: המדבריות. הברייתות: ברביעה. במרחשון: ואלו מדבריות כל שרועות באפר. והני מיהא אסירי אלמא אית ליה מוקצה: איבעית אימא הני. מדבריות נמי כגרוגרות דמי דדחינהו בידים ויש טורח לילך ולהביאם: ואיבעית אימא. ההיא דפצעילי תמרה לדבריו דרבי שמעון קאמר ולר' לא ס"ל: ה"ג אמר רבה בר בר חנה א"ר יוחנן אמרו הלכה כר' שמעון: אמרו. בני הישיבה: סרוייא קרוייא. על שם מקומו: כלום עשוי. לשום תשמיש: אלא לתרנגולין. הלכך ה"ל מלאכתו לאיסור ואסור אלמא אית ליה מוקצה: דאית ביה אפרוח מת. דלא חזי למיכל ולכלבים נמי לא חזי ואף על גב דא"ר שמעון מחתכין את הנבלה לפני הכלבים הני מילי במסוכנת אבל בריאה לא דלא הוה דעתיה מאתמול לכלבים והאי אפרוח שמת בשבת נמי לא הוה דעתיה מאתמול לכלבים: הניחא למר כו' דאמר מודה היה ר"ש. דאע"ג דאמר מחתכין הנבלה לפני הכלבים ה"מ במסוכנת דדעתיה עליה מאתמול לכלבים אבל מודה הוא בבעלי חיים כלומר בבריאים שמתו שאסורין שפיר קתרצת לרבי שמעון גופיה לא חזי לכלבים: מאי איכא למימר. הא חזי לכלבים: דאית בה ביצה. שנולדה היום ומודה ר' שמעון בנולד: והא אמר רב נחמן כו'. בשמעתא קמייתא דביצה: דאית בה ביצת אפרוח. וכלב לא אכיל לה משום ב) קליפה: וליה לא סבירא ליה. לר' יוחנן לא סבירא דתיהוי הלכה כר' שמעון והיינו דרב יצחק: ואת לא תסברא. ומקמי דשמעת ליה לדרב יצחק לא הוה ידעת דר' יוחנן כר' יהודה: בשתי ידים אסור לטלטלה. כדמפרש טעמא לקמיה דלאו לטלטולי עבידא דאדם קובע לה מקום: ור' יוחנן אמר אנו אין לנו. שום היתר בהלכות טלטול נרות: אלא בנר. ישן כרבי שמעון דמתיר אבל מנורה כו' הלכך אי לאו מדרב יצחק לא הוה ידענא ליה אבל השתא ידענא דכר' יהודה סבירא ליה בכולהו בר ממוקצה מחמת מיאוס דנר ישן: מותר

תוספות

לדבריו דר' שמעון קאמר ליה וליה לא סבירא ליה. משמע דמספקא ליה אי ר' סבר לה כר' שמעון ותימה אמאי לא מוכח מההיא דלקמן דסבר כר"ש דאמר פעם אחת הלך ר' כו' והורה במנורה כר"ש בנר וכן מברייתא דמייתי באין לדין ח) בכור תם שנפל לבור ר' יהודה הנשיא אומר ירד מי שבקי במומין ויראה אם יש בו מום יעלה וישחוט כו' ומיהו במאי דמתיר לראות במומין לא אתי כר"ש אלא במאי דלית ליה מוקצה ומיהו רש"י לא גרים בכור תם אלא בכור שנפל לבור והשתא מצי אתי כר' יהודה ויראה אם היה בו מום זה מעי"ט ט): **הכא** במאי עסקינן דאית ביה אפרוח מת. פירש הר"ר יוסף דלא נקט אפרוח חי משום דחי חזי לשתק בו תינוק כשבוכה ואין נראה דהא בההיא דכופין את הסל לפני האפרוחין (לעיל דף מג.) משמע דאסור לטלטל ועוד אי מחיים שרי אמאי קאמר בסמוך דמודה ר"ש בבעלי חיים שמתו שאסורין אלא ודאי בעלי חיים ג) מוקצין הם כגרוגרות וצימוקין ומקצה אותם גם מכלבים ולא דמי לבשר תפל שמותר לר"ש מדפריך בפרק מפנין (לקמן קכח.) על רב הונא דשרי והא תלמיד דרב הוה ורב כר' יהודה סבירא ליה אבל לר' שמעון משמע דשרי משום דאינו מקצהו מכלבים כמו בעלי חיים:

דאית ביה ביצה. דאסור משום נולד ל"ע דר' יוחנן גופיה י) מפרש טעמא דביצה משום משקין שזבו ואפשר דמשום הכי לא הוה אסר ר"ש לטלטלה אלא לאכילה:

דאית ביה ביצת אפרוח. נראה לר"י דאסור לר' שמעון משום דכיון דאית ביה אפרוח הוי ד) כמו גרוגרות וצימוקין וקא מיבעיא ליה לסבא קירויא אי שרי לטלטולי על ידי שינער משם הביצה אי חשיב כמו מניח או כשכח והשיב לו רבי יוחנן כלום עשוי אלא לתרנגולין ואין זה כשכח אלא כמניח ואסור:

אמר ליה מנרתא שאני. וא"ת אמאי לא מוכח מהא דא"ר יוחנן בפ' לולב וערבה (סוכה מו:) דסוכה אפי' בשמיני אסורה אלמא אית ליה מיגו דאיתקצאי כו' כר' יהודה ותירץ ר"י דנר אינו מוקצה למצותו מטלטול שאין ביטול מצוה בטלטול ולא דמי לסוכה דאיתקצאי ביה"ש מחמת מצוה ולהכי אינו יכול להוכיח מסוכה אנר: **לאו** משום דר' אסי תלמידו דר' יוחנן כו'. וא"ת דילמא ר' אסי כרב רביה סבירא ליה כדאמר לעיל גבי שרגא דחנוכה אמרו ליה רב כהנא ורב אסי לרב הילכתא הכי ונראה דרב אסי דלעיל לאו היינו ר' אסי דהכא דההוא דלעיל חבירו של רב כהנא והכא ר' אסי חבירו של ר' אמי כ): **אין** לנו אלא בנר כר' שמעון. פי' במוקצה מחמת מיאוס דהיינו נר ישן שלא הדליקו בה באותה שבת ולעיל דפסיק כרבי יהודה היינו בהדליקו בה באותה שבת דהוי מוקצה מחמת איסור והא דפסיק בפרק בתרא ל) כר"ש בנבלה לפני הכלבים אף על גב דנבלה מוקצה מחמת איסור היא כדפר"ת (לעיל יט: ד"ה ושמואל) התם מ) לא דחייה בידים אבל הכא דדחייה בידים סבר כר' יהודה ולפי זה לא קיימי ר' יוחנן וריב"ל דפסקי כר' שמעון אחדא ברייתא דר' יוחנן קאי אברייתא דכל הנרות של מתכת מטלטלין כו' אבל במאי דקאמר ר' יהודה בברייתא דלעיל מטלטלין נר חדש אבל לא ישן לא סבר רבי יוחנן כוותיה וריב"ל אברייתא דמטלטלין נר חדש קאי דבההיא ברייתא שרי רבי

מסורת הש"ס

א) ביצה מ., ב) שם. [לקמן קנו.], ג) [ביצה שם], ד) [נ"ל דרבא], ה) ביצה מ:, ו) שם ב., ז) עירובין קב. לקמן קלח:, ח) [ביצה דף כו.], ט) [וע"ע תוספות ביצה כו. ד"ה מ"ר], י) [ביצה ג.], כ) [ועי' תוספות חולין יט. ד"ה אמר רב הונא], ל) [דף קנו:], מ) התוס' המתחיל ולפ"ז וכו' הנרשם בס"א נמצא בדף מו ע"א כי שם מקומו.

תוספות ישנים

א) אין נראה לר"י פירוש זה דל"ד לגרוגרות וצימוקין דלא דחיה בידים. ונ"ל כפירוש הערוך שפירש פצעילי תמרה לשון מפצע שמפצעין תמרים כדי להתבשל ולהתייבש ובשעת הפציעה מתקלקלת מראיתה ואחר זמן משתבחות ודמי לגרוגרות וצימוקין אך שגרוגרות וצימוקין מתקלקלות יותר מהם:

ב) קשה דאפשר להסיר הקליפה ויאכלנה הכלב:

ג) והא דלא בעי באפרוח חי אם מותר לטלטל הקינה משום דאפשר להפריחו:

ד) א"נ הוי מוקצה מחמת חסרון כיס:

ליקוטי רש"י

פצעילי תמרה. תמרים שאין מתבשלות באילן לעולם וגודרין אותן מהאילן ועושין להן חותלות הן כלי כפות תמרים וכונסין אותן לתוכן ומתבשלות [ביצה מ.]. מהו. לאכול מהן ביום טוב. אלא גרוגרות וצימוקין. שהן מתחלה ראויין לאכילה והוא דחה אותן בידים להעלותן ליבשן ושוב אינן ראויין עד שייבשו אבל אלו לא דחה אותן בידים ואיכא דאכיל מנייהו. ורבי לית ליה מוקצה. הכי קא סלקא דעתיה מדפריש ליה מילתיה דרבי שמעון אלמא כר' שמעון סבירא ליה [שם:]. אין משקין ושוחטין. משום מוקצה. משקין. משום סרכא דמשכא שתהא נוחה להפשיט שהוא נדבק יותר מדאי בבשר [שם.]. אורחא דמילתא נקט משום סירכא דמשכא שתהא נוחה להפשיט [לקמן קנו.]. ונכנסות. לישוב [ביצה שם]. איבעית אימא הני. מדבריות שאין נכנסות לישוב כלל כגרוגרות וצמוקין דמיין שמקצה אותן מאכלו בידים. ואי בעית אימא. אין מוקצה לרבי שמעון קאמר ליה אבל לדידי יש מוקצה. ואיבעית אימא. מתני' לדבריהם דרבנן דאית להו מוקצה קאמר להו [שם:]. בבעלי חיים. בהמה בריאה בין השמשות. שמתו. ביום טוב. שאסורין. וכי שריא במסוכנת בין השמשות דדעתיה עלויה להאכילה לכלבים [שם כז:]. הכא במאי עסקינן בדאית ביה ביצה. דקא סלקא דעתין דאפילו לרבי שמעון דשרי במוקצה בנולד אסיר דאילו במוקצה סבירא ליה לא מקצי איניש מדעתיה מידי דחזי ליה אבל נולד לא הוה ידע דנהוי דעתיה עליה [שם ב.]. כילת חתנים. לא דמיא לשאר כילות שאר כילות פרוסות על גבי קינוף שהיא לארבע רגליו ויש לה גג דהוי אהל ושל חתנים על גבי נקליטין שאינם אלא שנים באמצעית המטה וקנה נתון עליהם והבגד נתון עליו ונופל לכאן ולכאן ואין לה גג טפח הלכך לאו אהל הוא [לקמן קלח:]. לאו אהל הוא מפני שאין לה גג למעלה רוחב טפח מפני שהיא נתונה בשיפוע והיא יריעה שפורסין סביב למטה לישן [עירובין קב.].

עין משפט נר מצוה

נד א מיי' פכ"ו מהל' שבת הלכה יד סמג לאוין סה טוש"ע או"ח סימן שי סעיף ב:

נה ב ג מיי' פ"ב מהל' יו"ט הלכה ב סמג לאוין עה טור שו"ע או"ח סימן תצז סעיף ב וסימן תקג סעיף ג:

רבינו חננאל

וכן הא דאמר ליה [ר'] לר' שמעון בריה אין מוקצה לר' שמעון אלא גרוגרות וצמוקין בלבד פשוטה היא: אמר רבה בר בר חנה א"ר יוחנן אמרו הלכה כר"ש איני והא בעא מיניה ההוא סבא קרוייה קינה של תרנגולין מהו לטלטלה בשבת ואמר ליה אסור כלום עשוי אלא לתרנגולים מכלל דר' יוחנן כר' יהודה סבירא ליה דאית ליה מוקצה. ושנינן בדאית ליה בהאי קינה אפרוח מת ומשום הכי אסורה לטלטלה. הניחא למ"ד בעלי חיים שמתו בשבת דברי הכל אסור לטלטלן בשבת הא אפילו לר' שמעון ואלא למ"ד ר"ש מתיר בבעלי חיים שמתו שמותר לטלטלן אע"ג דאית בהאי קינה אפרוח שמת בשבת ר"ש מתיר אמאי קא אסר ר' יוחנן והא איהו הלכתא כר' שמעון סבירא ליה. ואסיקנא בדאית בהאי קינה ביצה שיש בה אפרוח דלדברי הכל אסורה. ואעפ"כ לא נתברר כי ר' יוחנן כר' שמעון סבירא ליה. וכי אתא רב יצחק בר' יוסף א"ר יוחנן הלכתא כר' יהודה וריב"ל אמר הלכה כר"ש. אמר רב יוסף היינו דאמר רבה בר בר חנה א"ר יוחנן אמרו הלכה כר"ש וליה לא סבירא ליה. ודייק נמי אביי מדר' אסי נפלה מנרתא על גלימיה [בבי] ר' אבא ולא טלטלה. ואמר (משמיה) [משום] דר' אסי תלמיד דר' יוחנן הוא. ור' יוחנן במוקצה סבר לה כר' יהודה. ודחינן להא דאביי. ואמרינן לא אפילו תימא ר' יוחנן כר' שמעון מנרתא שני

candelabra fell on R' Assi's cloak, וְלֹא טִילְטְלָהּ **– and he did not move it,** since he considered it *muktzeh.*[19] מַאי טַעְמָא – **What is the reason** that he considered it *muktzeh*? לַאו מִשּׁוּם דְּרַבִּי אַסִּי תַּלְמִידֵיהּ דְּר׳ יוֹחָנָן הֲוָה – **Is it not because R' Assi was a student of R' Yochanan,** וְרַבִּי יוֹחָנָן כְּרַבִּי יְהוּדָה סְבִירָא לֵיהּ דְּאִית לֵיהּ מוּקְצֶה – **and R' Yochanan concurs with R' Yehudah, who subscribes to** a broad application of ***muktzeh*** and considers a lamp *muktzeh* even after it has gone out?[20] Thus, it was evident even before Rav Yitzchak's report that R' Yochanan concurs with R' Yehudah. – ? –

Rav Yosef responds:

אָמַר לֵיהּ – **He said to [Abaye]:** מְנַרְתָּא קָאָמְרַת – **You are citing** an incident involving **a candelabra** as proof?! מְנַרְתָּא שָׁאנֵי – **A candelabra is different** than a lamp and is *muktzeh* even according to R' Shimon. דְּאָמַר רַבִּי אַחָא בַּר חֲנִינָא אָמַר רַבִּי אַסִּי – **For R' Acha bar Chanina said in the name of R' Assi:** הוֹרָה רֵישׁ לָקִישׁ בְּצִידָן – **Reish Lakish ruled,** while **in Sidon:** מְנוֹרָה הַנִּיטֶּלֶת בְּיָדוֹ אַחַת מוּתָּר לְטַלְטְלָהּ – A lightweight **candelabra that can be moved with one hand may be moved** on the Sabbath, בִּשְׁתֵּי יָדָיו אָסוּר לְטַלְטְלָהּ – whereas a heavy one that can be moved only **with two hands may not be moved** on the Sabbath.[21] וְר׳ יוֹחָנָן אָמַר – **But R' Yochanan said:** אָנוּ אֵין לָנוּ אֶלָּא בְּנֵר כְּרַבִּי שִׁמְעוֹן – **We have no** allowance for moving any lighting implement on the Sabbath, **except for a** used **lamp, in accordance with** the view of **R' Shimon.**[22] אֲבָל מְנוֹרָה – **But** as for **a candelabra,** בֵּין נִיטְּלָה בְּיָדוֹ אַחַת בֵּין נִיטְּלָה בִּשְׁתֵּי יָדָיו אָסוּר לְטַלְטְלָהּ – **whether it can be moved with one hand or** must be **moved with two hands, it may not be moved** on the Sabbath. While Reish Lakish and R' Yochanan dispute the status of lightweight candelabras, they both agree that heavy candelabras are *muktzeh* even according to R' Shimon. Thus, R' Assi's reluctance to move the fallen candelabra does not indicate that he and his teacher R' Yochanan follow R' Yehudah's opinion. I was therefore unaware that R' Yochanan does follow it until I heard Rav Yitzchak's report.

The Gemara now seeks to ascertain the reason for the special status of candelabras:

וְטַעְמָא מַאי – **And what is the reason** that it is particularly forbidden to move a candelabra? רַבָּה וְרַב יוֹסֵף דְּאָמְרֵי תַּרְוַיְיהוּ – **Rabbah and Rav Yosef both said:** הוֹאִיל וְאָדָם קוֹבֵעַ לָהּ מָקוֹם – It is **because a person designates a place for it.**[23]

Abaye challenges this explanation:

אָמַר לֵיהּ אַבַּיֵי לְרַב יוֹסֵף – **Abaye said to Rav Yosef:** וַהֲרֵי כִּילַּת חֲתָנִים – **But consider** the case of **the canopy of a bridal bed,**[24] דְּאָדָם קוֹבֵעַ לוֹ מָקוֹם – **for which a person designates a place,** וְאָמַר שְׁמוּאֵל מִשּׁוּם רַבִּי חִיָּיא – **yet Shmuel said in the name of R' Chiya:** כִּילַּת חֲתָנִים – **The canopy of a bridal bed**

NOTES

19. I.e. he did not move it with his hands. Presumably, he shook it off his cloak, since it is permitted to move *muktzeh* indirectly for the use of a non-*muktzeh* item (*Ritva MHK* ed.; see 44a note 2).

20. [Abaye presumed that R' Assi considered the candelabra *muktzeh* because it had been burning at the onset of the Sabbath. Thus, it was *muktzeh* only according to R' Yehudah but not according to R' Shimon (see 44a note 3).]

21. The reason will be explained shortly.

22. I.e. the only case in which I permit moving a lamp on the Sabbath is that of a used lamp that had not been lit at the onset of the Sabbath. Since the only reason to consider it *muktzeh* is its repugnance, I permit moving it, for I concur with R' Shimon in rejecting *muktzeh by dint of repugnance*. However, I concur with R' Yehudah regarding all other categories of *muktzeh*. Hence, I forbid moving a lamp that had been lit at the onset of the Sabbath, since it is *muktzeh by dint of a prohibition* (*Rashi*; see *Ran* to *Beitzah* 28b [fol. 15b of *Rif*] ד״ה ומכאן). [This was also the meaning of Rav Yitzchak's previously cited report that R' Yochanan concurs with R' Yehudah (*Ritva MHK* ed.; cf. *Tosafos*).]

23. I.e. a candelabra is not meant to be moved, but is set down in a specific location with the intent that it remain there. This intent renders it *muktzeh* (*Rashi;* cf. *Tosafos* to 35a ד״ה ואפילו; see *Chazon Ish* 43:17). [R' Yochanan and Reish Lakish disagree whether this pertains to all candelabras or only to very heavy ones.]

24. A bridal bed has two vertical poles – one attached to the middle of each end of the bed – and a third pole that extends across the top of the two vertical poles. A canopy is formed by draping a curtain over this framework (*Rashi* to 46a). See diagram.

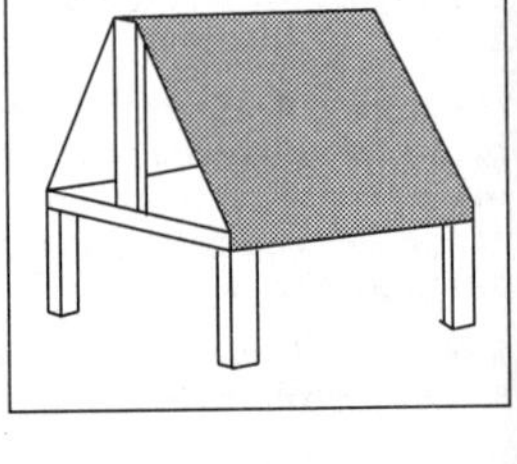

מוּתָּר לִנְטוֹתָהּ וּמוּתָּר לְפָרְקָהּ בְּשַׁבָּת – **may be spread open and may be taken down on the Sabbath.**[1] Thus, even something for which one designates a place is not *muktzeh.*

Having refuted Rav Yosef's explanation of why candelabras are particularly forbidden, Abaye provides an explanation of his own: אֶלָּא אָמַר אַבַּיֵי – **Rather, said Abaye:** בְּשֶׁל חוּלְיוֹת – Reish Lakish and R' Yochanan were dealing **with [a candelabra]** composed **of sections** that might come apart if it fell. The Rabbis forbade moving such a candelabra out of concern that it might fall and break, and one might then come to reassemble it.[2]

The Gemara challenges this explanation:

אִי הָכִי מַאי טַעְמָא דְּרַבִּי שִׁמְעוֹן בֶּן לָקִישׁ דְּשָׁרֵי – **If so, what is the reasoning of R' Shimon ben Lakish who permits** moving lightweight candelabras? The concern just mentioned applies to light ones as well as heavy ones. – ? –

The Gemara concedes the point and therefore revises Abaye's explanation:

מַאי חוּלְיוֹת – **What is** the meaning of a candelabra composed of **sections?** כְּעֵין חוּלְיוֹת – It means a candelabra that **appears as** if it has **sections,** דְּאִית בָּהּ חִידְקֵי – i.e. a solid candelabra **that has grooves** which create the appearance that it is composed of separate parts. Since an observer might mistake a grooved candelabra for a sectional one, the Rabbis forbade moving even grooved candelabras. It is concerning this additional aspect of the prohibition that R' Yochanan and Reish Lakish disagree.

The Gemara summarizes the laws pertaining to candelabras, in the process clarifying the disputed point:

הִלְכָּךְ חוּלְיוֹת בֵּין גְּדוֹלָה בֵּין קְטַנָּה אֲסוּרָה לְטַלְטְלָהּ – **Therefore,** if a candelabra is actually made up of **sections, whether it is large or small,** i.e. it must be moved with two hands or can be moved with one hand, **it is forbidden to move it.** גְּדוֹלָה נַמִּי דְּאִית בָּהּ חִידְקֵי – **A large [candelabra] that has grooves, as well,** may not be moved, גְּזֵירָה אַטּוּ גְּדוֹלָה דְּחוּלְיוֹת – due to **a decree** that the Rabbis enacted **because of** the concern that this would be confused with **a large [candelabra]** composed **of sections,** which it resembles.[3] כִּי פְּלִיגֵי – **Where do they** (R' Yochanan and Reish Lakish) **disagree?** בִּקְטַנָּה דְּאִית בָּהּ חִידְקֵי – It is **in** regard to **a small [candelabra] that has grooves.** מָר סָבַר גָּזְרִינַן – One **master** (R' Yochanan) **holds** that **[the Rabbis] decreed** that even this candelabra may not be moved, וּמָר סָבַר לֹא גָּזְרִינַן – **whereas** the other **master** (Reish Lakish) **holds** that **[the Rabbis] did not decree** that this type of candelabra may not be moved.[4]

The Gemara returns to its original topic, now challenging R' Yitzchak's report that R' Yochanan ruled in accordance with R' Yehudah:

וּמִי אָמַר רַבִּי יוֹחָנָן הָכִי – **Did R' Yochanan** really **say this?** וְהָאָמַר רַבִּי יוֹחָנָן – **But R' Yochanan** himself **said** הֲלָכָה כִּסְתָם מִשְׁנָה – that **the halachah** always **follows an anonymous Mishnah!** וּתְנַן – **And we learned in a Mishnah,** which deals primarily with laws of *tumah* pertaining to a wooden coach:[5] מוּכְנִי שֶׁלָּהּ – Concerning ITS WHEEL, בִּזְמַן שֶׁהִיא נִשְׁמֶטֶת – WHEN IT IS REMOVABLE, אֵין חִיבּוּר לָהּ – it IS NOT considered ATTACHED TO [THE COACH], וְאֵין נִמְדֶּדֶת עִמָּהּ – NOR IS IT MEASURED TOGETHER WITH [THE COACH] when determining the volume of the coach, וְאֵין מַצֶּלֶת עִמָּהּ בְּאֹהֶל הַמֵּת – NOR DOES IT combine WITH [THE COACH] to PROTECT the contents of the coach from contracting *tumah* WHEN PASSING OVER A CORPSE, וְאֵין גּוֹרְרִין אוֹתָהּ בְּשַׁבָּת בִּזְמַן שֶׁיֵּשׁ עָלֶיהָ מָעוֹת – NOR MAY WE DRAG IT ON THE SABBATH WHEN THERE IS MONEY ON IT. הָא אֵין עָלֶיהָ מָעוֹת שָׁרְיָא – This implies: **But if there is no money on [the wheel] it is permitted** to drag it, וְאַף עַל גַּב דַּהֲווּ עָלֶיהָ בֵּין הַשְּׁמָשׁוֹת – **even if there was [money] on it during** ***bein hashemashos*** at the onset of the Sabbath. This anonymous Mishnah follows the view of R' Shimon, for it rejects the principle that since it was *muktzeh* during *bein hashemashos* it remains *muktzeh* for the entire day. How can you say that R' Yochanan concurs with R' Yehudah?[6]

The Gemara answers:

אָמַר רַבִּי זֵירָא – **R' Zeira said:** תְּהֵא מִשְׁנָתֵינוּ שֶׁלֹּא הָיוּ עָלֶיהָ מָעוֹת כָּל בֵּין הַשְּׁמָשׁוֹת – **Let** the implication of our **Mishnah be** interpreted as dealing with a case **where there was no money on [the wheel] throughout** ***bein hashemashos*** at the onset of the Sabbath, שֶׁלֹּא לִשְׁבּוֹר דְּבָרָיו שֶׁל רַבִּי יוֹחָנָן – **in order not to break the words of R' Yochanan,** i.e. in order to avoid a contradiction between R' Yochanan's rulings.[7]

The Gemara cites another halachic ruling regarding *muktzeh*:

אָמַר רַבִּי יְהוֹשֻׁעַ בֶּן לֵוִי – **R' Yehoshua ben Levi said:** פַּעַם אַחַת הָלַךְ רַבִּי לְדְיוֹסְקַפְּרָא – **Rebbi once traveled to Deiospera** וְהוֹרָה בִּמְנוֹרָה כְּרַבִּי שִׁמְעוֹן בְּנֵר – **and,** while there, **he ruled in regard to a candelabra as R' Shimon** did **in regard to a lamp.**

R' Yehoshua ben Levi's account is ambiguous, which leads to the following discussion:

אִיבַּעְיָא לְהוּ – **They inquired:** הוֹרָה בִּמְנוֹרָה כְּרַבִּי שִׁמְעוֹן בְּנֵר לְהֶיתֵּרָא – Does R' Yehoshua ben Levi mean that Rebbi issued a single ruling and **ruled** permissibly **regarding** moving **a candelabra** ***just as*** **R' Shimon** ruled **permissibly regarding** moving a used **lamp?** אוֹ דִילְמָא – **Or perhaps,** he meant that Rebbi issued two separate rulings, one concerning a grooved candelabra and the other concerning a used lamp, הוֹרָה בִּמְנוֹרָה לְאִיסּוּרָא – **and he ruled prohibitively** regarding moving **a** grooved **candelabra** וּכְרַבִּי שִׁמְעוֹן בְּנֵר לְהֶיתֵּרָא – ***and,*** **in accordance with** the opinion

NOTES

1. Shmuel teaches that since this canopy is not horizontal, but slanting, and is less than a *tefach* wide at its peak, it is not the type of "tent" whose erection and demolition are prohibited on the Sabbath (*Rashi;* see 43b note 13). At any rate, we learn from Shmuel's ruling that the canopy is not *muktzeh,* even though one designates a place for it. Perforce, one does not mean to set it aside from Sabbath use (see *Tosafos* ד״ה והא).

2. By reassembling the candelabra, one would be crafting a utensil (*Rashi*) which is a violation of the *melachah* of מַכֶּה בְּפַטִּישׁ, *striking the final hammer blow,* i.e. putting the finishing touch on a utensil (*Rashi* to 47a ד״ה חייב חטאת; see *Beur HaGra* to *Orach Chaim* 314:1 and 47a note 22).

3. Since large candelabras are often made of separable sections, the Rabbis forbade moving any large, grooved candelabra, as it might be confused with a sectional one. Even Reish Lakish concedes this point, and he therefore states that a candelabra which is so heavy that it must be moved with two hands may not be moved on the Sabbath (*Rashi*).

4. Since small candelabras are usually made of one piece, people who see someone moving a grooved one are unlikely to think that it is a sectional one. Reish Lakish therefore rules that a grooved candelabra which is small enough to be moved with one hand may be moved on the Sabbath. R' Yochanan, however, holds that the Rabbis issued a blanket decree against moving any grooved or sectional candelabra (see *Rashi* and *Ritva MHK* ed.).

5. *Keilim* 18:2. This Mishnah was cited above, 44b, and was explained in notes 5-9 there.

6. Since R' Yochanan holds that a lamp which was burning *bein hashemashos* remains *muktzeh* for the entire day (see 45b note 22), he should also hold that a wheel which was a base to *muktzeh* during *bein hashemashos* remains *muktzeh* for the entire day (see *Rashba*).

7. Thus, the final clause of the Mishnah means as follows: Nor may we drag it on the Sabbath when there was money on it *throughout bein hashemashos.* This teaches that even if the money was removed during the Sabbath we may not drag the coach, for since it was *muktzeh* throughout *bein hashemashos* it remains *muktzeh* for the entire day. Thus, the Mishnah follows the view of R' Yehudah and not R' Shimon (*Rashi*).

מותר לנטותה ומותר לפרקה בשבת אלא אמר אביי בשל חוליות אי הכי מ"ט דר"ש בן לקיש דשרי מאי חוליות כעין חוליות דאית בה חידקי הלכך [א]חוליות בין גדולה בין קטנה אסורה לטלטלה גדולה נמי דאית בה חידקי גזירה אטו גדולה דחוליות כי פליגי בקטנה דאית בה חידקי [ב]מר סבר גזרינן ומר סבר לא גזרינן ומי א"ר יוחנן הכי והאמר ר' יוחנן [א]הלכה כסתם משנה ותנן [ג]מוכני שלה בזמן שהיא נשמטת אין חיבור לה ואין נמדדת עמה ואין מצלת עמה באהל המת ואין גוררין אותה בשבת בזמן שיש עליה מעות הא אין עליה מעות שריא ואע"ג דהוו עליה ביה"ש א"ר זירא תהא משנתינו שלא היו עליה מעות כל ביה"ש שלא לשבור דבריו של ר' יוחנן א"ר יהושע בן לוי פעם אחת הלך רבי לדיוספרא והורה במנורה כר' שמעון בנר איבעיא להו הורה במנורה כר' שמעון בנר להיתרא או דילמא הורה במנורה לאיסורא וכר' שמעון בנר להיתרא תיקו רב מלכיא איקלע לבי רבי שמלאי וטילטל שרגא ואיקפד ר' שמלאי ר' יוסי גלילאה איקלע לאתריה דר' יוסי ברבי חנינא טילטל שרגא ואיקפד ר' יוסי בר' חנינא [ג]ר' אבהו כי איקלע לאתריה דר' יהושע בן לוי הוה מטלטל שרגא כי איקלע לאתריה דר' יוחנן [ד]לא הוה מטלטל שרגא מה נפשך אי כרבי יהודה סבירא ליה ליעבד כרבי יהודה אי כר' שמעון סבירא ליה ליעבד כר' שמעון לעולם כר' שמעון ס"ל ומשום כבודו דר' יוחנן הוא דלא הוה עביד [ה]א"ר יהודה שרגא דמשחא שרי לטלטולה דנפטא אסור לטלטולה רבה ורב יוסף דאמרי תרוייהו דנפטא נמי שרי לטלטולה [ה](דהואיל וחזי לכסות ביה מנא) רב אויא איקלע לבי רבא הוה מאיסן בי כרעיה בטינא אתיבי אפוריא קמיה דרבא איקפד רבא בעא לצעוריה א"ל מ"ט רבה ורב יוסף דאמרי תרווייהו שרגא דנפטא נמי שרי לטלטוליה א"ל הואיל וחזיא לכסויי בה מנא אלא מעתה כל צרורות שבחצר מטלטלין הואיל וחזיא לכסויי בהו מנא א"ל הא איכא תורת כלי עליה הני ליכא תורת כלי עליה מי לא תניא

השירים

השירים

רש"י

מותר לנטותה. דסתם כילת חתנים אין לה גג טפח שנקליטין יוצאין לשני ראשי המטה באמצעה אחד לכאן ואחד לכאן ונותן כלונס' מזה לזה ומשליך האהל עליה והוא שופע לכאן ולכאן וכיון שאינו רחב טפח אינו אהל ואין בו לא בנין ולא סתירה: בשל חוליות. במנורה של פרקים שמא תפול ותתפרק ויחזירנה ונמצא עושה כלי: חידקי. חיתוכין סביב לה קרונ"ש ודומה לפרקים ומאן דחזי סבר של פרקים הוא: גדולה. הואיל ודרכה לעשותה של חוליות כי אית ביה חידקי סברי דחוליות הן ואסור אפילו לריש לקיש כדאמר לעיל ניטלת בשתי ידים אסור לטלטלה: כי פליגי בקטנה דאית בה חידקי. דכולי עלמא ידעי דלאו חוליות נינהו: גזרינן. אטו חוליות: ומי אמר רבי יוחנן הכי. הלכה כר' יהודה: תהא משנתינו. דמוכני דקתני הא אין עליה מעות שריא כגון שלא היו עליה בין השמשות והכי תידוק מינה טעמא דיש עליה מעות כשקדש היום הא אין עליה כשקדש היום שריא: לדיוספרא. מקום: איבעיא להו. חדא הוראה הואי והכי קאמר הורה במנורה להיתרא כדרך שהיה ר' שמעון מתיר בנר ישן או דילמא שתי הוראות הוו הורה במנורה לאיסור כדאמרן בדאית חידקי וגזרינן אטו חוליות וכר"ש הורה בנר להיתר: וטלטל שרגא. נר שכבה: לעולם כרבי שמעון סבירא ליה. דאי סבירא ליה דאסור לא הוה מטלטל ליה לכבוד ר' יהושע בן לוי דליעבד איסורא: שרגא דמשחא. שדלק נר של שמן: שרי לטלטולה. אחר שכבה כר' שמעון דלא מאיס: אבל בנפטא. דמסרח אפילו רבי שמעון מודה דלא חזי אלא למלאכתו: איקפד רבא. משום טינוף המטה: ובעא לצעוריה. בשאלות:

השירים

תוספות

רבי שמעון נר שהדליקו באותה שבת והא דלא פסיק רבי יוחנן כרבי מאיר דהא סבר לגמרי כוותיה דשרי מוקצה מחמת מיאוס ואסר מוקצה מחמת איסור נקט רבי יהודה משום דבכל מקום הוזכר גבי מוקצה ועוד דלא מצינו דאית ליה לרבי מאיר מוקצה מחמת איסור גרידא אלא בנר ישן דאיכא תרתי מחמת מיאוס ומחמת איסור אך לפי זה קשה לרשב"א דמשמע דנקט במנורה אין לנו כרבי שמעון אבל רבי שמעון מיהא שרי במנורה ולמאי דמפרש טעמא דמנורה משום דאדם קובע לו מקום היכי שרי רבי שמעון הא אמרי' בריש כל הכלים (לקמן דף קכג.) הכל מודים בסיכי וזירי ומזורי כיון דקפיד עלייהו מיחד להו מקום ונראה לפרש דרבי יוחנן פסק כרבי יהודה במוקצה מחמת מיאום וכ"ש במוקצה מחמת איסור [א] כדמוכח בפרק בתרא (דף קנז.) דקאמר בכולי שבת הלכה כרבי שמעון בר ממוקצה מחמת מיאום וחד אמר במוקצה מחמת מיאום נמי הלכה כרבי שמעון בר ממוקצה מחמת איסור דהיינו שהדליקו בה באותה שבת והא דקאמר אנו אין לנו אלא בנר כרבי שמעון לאו משום דסבר כוותיה בנר אלא כלומר אין לנו שיתיר אפי' רבי שמעון דמיקל אלא בנר אבל במנורה אסר והשתא קיימי תרוייהו אחד ברייתא ולא מצי נמי למינקט רבי מאיר:

והא כילת חתנים דאדם קובע לה מקום. פי' רשב"א דאדם קובע לה מקום כמו למנורה ואפ"ה שרי שמואל אלא ודאי לא חשיב קביעות שלה ושל מנורה קביעות אלא היכא דקבע מקום לגמרי כדאמר בפ' כל הכלים (לקמן קכג. ושם):

דחוליות בין גדולה בין קטנה אסורה. קשה לר"י דבפ"ב דביצה (דף כא:) תנן ג' דברים ר"ג מחמיר כב"ש ותשיב אין זוקפין את המנורה ומשמע דב"ה שרי ומפרש התם בגמרא [י] הכא במנורה של חוליות עסקינן משום דמיחזי כבונה דב"ש סברי יש בנין בכלים ויש סתירה בכלים וב"ה סברי אין בנין כו' אלמא שרי ב"ה מנורה של חוליות להחזיר ומאן דשרי בסוף פירקא להחזיר מטה של חוליות ברפוי איכא לאוקמא ה"נ ברפוי אבל למאן דאסר קשה ותירץ ר"י דהתם מיירי כגון שהחוליות מחוברין יחד ואינם מתפרקין ופעמים מטין אותן ופעמים זוקפין אותן [י]: **הורה** במנורה להיתרא וכר"ש בנר נמי להיתרא או דילמא במנורה הורה לאיסורא וכר"ש בנר להיתרא. וא"ת אמאי לא קאמר נמי או דילמא הורה במנורה להיתרא כרבי שמעון בנר וכרבי שמעון בנר לא סבירא ליה דכה"ג איתא באלו טריפות (חולין דף ט: ושם) הורו בטרפחת כרבי בזפק איבעיא להו הורו בטרפחת לאיסורא וכרבי בזפק להיתרא או דילמא הורו בטרפחת להיתרא כרבי בזפק וכרבי בזפק לא סבירא להו וי"ל דהכא לא שייך למיתלי מנורה בנר כדתלי טרפחת בזפק דהכא אין טעם אחד לשניהם דנר משום מוקצה ומנורה משום בנין ועוד דלא בעי למימר דר' לא סבר בנר כר"ש משום דריב"ל פסיק לעיל כר"ש ואם תאמר ובההיא דאלו טריפות אמאי לא קאמר נמי תרוייהו להיתרא כדאמר הכא או דילמא הורו בטרפחת להיתרא וכר' בזפק נמי להיתרא ומיהו בלאו הכי מגיהין שם הספרים ול"ג הורו בטרפחת לאיסורא דהא כ"ע שרו לה דתניא התם [ס] היא האם היא טרפחת היא שלחופית וביטל האם [ע] הוה עובדא והאכילה רבי טרפון לכלבים ואמר הלכה חמורך טרפון ואמר ליה רבי עקיבא טועה בדבר משנה אתה וגרס התם הורו בטרפחת להיתרא וכרבי בזפק להיתרא כו' ורש"י פי' הורה במנורה להיתרא כר"ש בנר וחדא הוראה הוי ואין נראה דאין לתלות מנורה בנר ועוד דאכתי הוי ליה למיבעיא או דילמא תרוייהו להיתרא: **דנפטא** אסור לטלטלה. פי' בקונט' אפילו לר"ש וכן משמע דהא שרגא דמשחא דשרי לטלטולה היינו לר' שמעון ועוד מדפריך רבא בסמוך לרבה ורב יוסף מ"ש מצרורות שבחצר ואי שרי ר' שמעון דנפטא תיקש' ליה לכ"ע אליבא דרבי שמעון לכך פי' בקונט' דהכא אליבא דר' שמעון קאי ואע"ג דרב אית ליה מוקצה [כ] גבי מטה שיחדה למעות [ס] ורבה נמי אית ליה כדאמר אביי [פ] כל מילי דמר עביד כרב ורב יוסף נמי משמע דאית ליה מוקצה בפ' נוטל (לקמן קמב:) דקאמר כמה חריפא שמעתתא דדרדקי איסור דאמור בשבת לכתחילה מי אמור הכא אליבא דר"ש קאמר וליה לא ס"ל ומיהו נראה לפרש דהכא מיירי נמי אליבא דרבי יהודה ולא מיירי בהדליקו בו באותה שבת וה"ק שרגא דמשחא של מתכת שרי לטלטולה ואפילו לרבי יהודה כדתניא לעיל (ד' מד.) כל הנרות של מתכת מטלטלין דנפטא אסור אפי' לרבי שמעון דמאיס טפי מנר ישן ורבה ורב יוסף שרו אפי' לרבי יהודה דלא מאיס אלא שריחו רע וחזי לכסויי ביה מנא אבל נר ישן מקצה ליה לגמרי משום דמאיס ואפילו מכיסוי מנא: [ועי' תוס' מנחות מח: ד"ה כל מילי]:

ואמר

עין משפט נר מצוה

נו א ב מיי' פכ"ו מהל' שבת הלכה יא טוש"ע או"ח סי' רעט סעיף ז:

רבינו חננאל

שני דא"ר יוחנן אנו אין לנו כר"ש אלא בנר. אבל מנורה בין ניטלת בידו אחת בין ניטלת בב' ידים אסור לטלטלה וטעמא מאי ואוקמה רחבה במנורה דאית בה חידקי חידקי שהן כעין חוליו' שנראה המעמידה או המטלטלה כבונה. הילכך דחוליות בין גדולה בין קטנה אסורה. לית בה חוליות ואית בה חידקי חידקי גדולה אסורה דמיחלפא בגדול' של חוליות. כי פליגי במנורה קטנה דאית בה חידקי חידקי. ר' יוחנן סבר גזרינן קטנה דאית בה חידקי אטו גדולה דאית בה חידקי. וריש לקיש סבר לא גזרינן. איני דגזר ר' יוחנן והא איהו דאמר הלכה כסתם משנה. ותנן סתמא בכלים פ' י"ח במוכני של שידה ואין גוררין אותה בשבת בזמן שיש עליה מעות. ודייקינן מינה. הא אין עליה מעות שריא. ואע"ג דהוו עליה כל בין השמשות ולא גזרינן כשאין עליה מעות אטו כשיש עליה מעות. וא"ר זירא תהא משנתנו בשלא היו עליה מעות כל בין השמשות (גזרי') שלא לשבור דברי ר' יוחנן. כלומר לא תקשי לך דר' יוחנן אדר' יוחנן. והא דהורה ר' (זירא ספרא) [בדיוספרא] עלתה בתיקו. ועבדינן בה לחומרא ומוקמינן לה הורה ר' במנורה לאיסורא וכר' שמעון בנר להיתרא: ר' אבהו מטלטל שרגא כר"ש. ובאתריה דר' יוחנן לא הוה מטלטל ליה משום כבודו דר' יוחנן (רב) [אמר רב יהודה] שרגא דמשחא שרי לטלטלה. אבל שרגא דנפטא (הוה) אסיר ורבה ורב יוסף שרו אפילו שרגא דנפטא. ואסיקנ' משום דחזו לכסויי בהו מני דנפטא. ואם תאמר אי הכי כל צרורות שבחצר יטלטלו הואיל וחזו לכסויי בהו מנא דנפטא. שני

מסורת הש"ם

א) [לקמן פא: קיב: קמז: קמח: קנו: עירובין לג. ביצה לז: תענית יח. יבמות טז: מב: גיטין פא: ב"ק כט: לג. סט. לד: ב"מ לג. סנהדרין לד: שבועות ג: מנחות נב: חולין לא: מג. נדה ג. ט:], ב) [לעיל מד: כלים פי"ח מ"ב], ג) יבמות יד. ע"ש, ד) [עי' תוספות יבמות יד. ד"ה לא הוה], ה) רש"ל מוחק זה, ו) [דף כב.], ז) [ועי' תוספות ביצה כב. ד"ה וב"ה], ח) [חולין נה:], ט) [סנהדרין לג.], י) [לעיל מד:], כ) [לעיל כב.].

תוספות ישנים

א) ולפי זה חמור מוקצה מחמת מיאוס ממוקצה מחמת איסור לר' יוחנן דלא דמייה בידים כמו נבילה דפסק כר"ש. ורב סבר איפכא דקאמר בפ"ק דחולין [דף טו.] ע"כ לא שרי ר"מ כו' אבל שוחט דאין ראוי לכום לא. ור"מ לית ליה בפרקין [לעיל מד.] מוקצה מחמת מיאוס להכי אמר בפרק בתרא דרב סבר כר"י מדכרכי דוזי אסור דהוי מוקצה מחמת מיאוס כדפי' ר"ת בפ"ק מוכח מכ"ש דלדידיה מחמת איסור חמיר טפי:

גליון הש"ס

גמ' אמר ר' יהודה שרגא דמשחא. עי' לקמן דף קכב ע"ב תוס' ד"ה רמת: תוס' ד"ה דנפטא וכו' ורבה נמי אית ליה. עי' מנחות דף מח ע"ב תוס' ד"ה כל מילי. ובעירובין דף לג ע"ב תוס' ד"ה לא תימא:

ליקוטי רש"י

הלכה כסתם משנה. רבי הוא סדר המשנה וכשראה דברי חכם וישרו בעיניו שנאן סתם ולא הזכיר שם אומרו עליהן כדי שלא יהו שנויה מפי יחיד ונראין כאילו נשנו מפי המרובים ויעשו כמותן [ביצה ב:]. מוכני שלה. גבי שידה תנן במסכת כלים והיא עגלה של עץ מוקפת מחיצות למרכב אנשים ונשים. מוכני. אופן. בזמן שהיא נשמטת. כעין אופני עגלה שלנו שאדם יכול לסלקו מן העגלה. אין חיבור לה. דחשובה היא כלי לעצמה דאי שידה בת קבולי טומאה היא כגון שאינה מחזקת ארבעים סאה בלח ונטמאה השידה לא נטמא המוכני ואי לאו בת קבולי טומאה היא ונגעה טומאה במוכני המוכני טמאה לעצמה דלא חשיבה משידה והיא מטלטלה מלאה וריקנית דיש לה בית קיבול. ואין נמדדת עמה. לענין טומאה כדפרישית דכלי עץ המחזיק ארבעים סאה בלח שהן כוריים ביבש טהור כדאמרינן בבמה מדליקין (שבת לה.) דכלי עץ איתקש לשק שיהא מיטלטל מלא וריקן וזו אינו מיטלטל מלא ותנן במסכת כלים ומייתינן בגמרא דמנחות (לא.) בית הלל אומרים נמדדת מבחוץ דרואין אותה כאילו היא עומדת בתוך כלי גדול ואם מחזיק אותו כלי ארבעים סאה טהורה השידה ואף על פי שהיא אינה מחזקת ארבעים סאה דקסבר אף עוביה נמדד עמה והמוכני אינו נמדד עמה להשלים דרואין כאילו ניטל המוכני ואחר כך מתנן השידה לתוך הכלי. ואין מצלת עמה באהל המת. דאם השידה מחזקת ארבעים [סאה] דאינה מקבלת טומאה מצלת באהל המת והוי אהל לעצמה ולא שנכנסה לבית שהמת בו דאם כן אין כאן הצלה שהרי הגג מאהיל על הטהרות מלמעלה אלא כגון שנכנסה לבית הקברות כדאמרינן בעירובין (ל.) ר' יהודה אומר אף בבית הקברות מפני שיכול לחוץ בשידה תיבה ומגדל בפרק בכל מערבין (שם) דקסבר אהל זרוק כלומר אהל המיטלטל שמיה אהל ומפסיק [בפני] הטומאה והמוכני אם הוא גבוה מדופני השידה וכלים [בולטים] מלמעלה מדופני השידה וגובה המוכני מגין עליהם אינו מצילן דמוכני כלי הוא לעצמו ומקבל טומאה ואינו חוצץ בפני הטומאה ורבותי דוחקין ומפרשין אותה באהל המת ממש ובשל חרס המוקפת צמיד פתיל והרבה תשובות יש חדא דנמדדת לא שייך בשל חרס דלא איתקש לשק ובין מיטלטל ובין אינו מיטלטל טמא ועוד אם המוכני מוקף צמיד פתיל יציל בפני עצמו כלים שבתוכו ועוד בפירוש נשנית במסכת כלים בהלכות כלי עץ והלכות כלי חרס נשנו לבדן והלכות כלי עץ נשנו לבדן [לעיל מד:]. שרגא. נר של חרס קרויו"ל בלע"ז [ביצה כב.]. מטלטל שרגא. נר שהדליקו בו בשבת וכבה דקסבר לה כרבי יהושע כר"ש דלית ליה מוקצה ור' יוחנן סבר לה כר' יהודה דאית ליה מוקצה אפי' שלא מחמת איסור [יבמות יד.]. דנפטא. נפט מין שמן שריחו רע כדאמרינן בסדר יומא (לט.) בא למדוד נפט אומרים לו מדוד לעצמך שאין אדם רוצה לסייעו [לעיל כד:].

of **R' Shimon,** ruled **permissibly regarding** moving **a lamp?**[8]

The Gemara does not resolve the inquiry, but concludes: תֵּיקוּ – **Let it stand.**

The Gemara continues its halachic discussion regarding *muktzeh*:

רַב מַלְכִּיָּא אִיקְלַע לְבֵי רַבִּי שִׂמְלַאי – **Rav Malkiya** once **visited the home of R' Simlai** וְטִילְטֵל שְׁרָגָא – **and,** while there, he **moved a lamp** that had been lit at the onset of the Sabbath and had since gone out, וְאִיקְפַּד רַבִּי שִׂמְלַאי – **and R' Simlai objected.** We thus see that Rav Malkiya concurred with R' Shimon, whereas R' Simlai concurred with R' Yehudah.

Another related incident:

רַבִּי יוֹסֵי גְּלִילָאָה אִיקְלַע לְאַתְרֵיהּ דְּרַבִּי יוֹסֵי בְּרַבִּי חֲנִינָא – **R' Yose the Galilean**[9] once **visited the locale of R' Yose the son of R' Chanina** טִילְטֵל שְׁרָגָא – and, while there, **he moved a lamp** that had been gone out on the Sabbath, וְאִיקְפַּד רַבִּי יוֹסֵי בְּרַבִּי חֲנִינָא – **and R' Yose the son of R' Chanina objected.** We see that these two Amoraim, too, disagreed about this issue.

Above (45b), R' Yitzchak reported that R' Yochanan concurs with R' Yehudah whereas R' Yehoshua ben Levi concurs with R' Shimon. The Gemara now describes the practice of R' Abahu, who was a disciple of both R' Yochanan and R' Yehoshua ben Levi:[10] ר׳ אַבָּהוּ – **R' Abahu,** כִּי אִיקְלַע לְאַתְרֵיהּ דְּרַבִּי יְהוֹשֻׁעַ בֶּן לֵוִי הֲוָה מְטַלְטֵל שְׁרָגָא – **when visiting the locale of R' Yehoshua ben Levi, would move a lamp** that had gone out on the Sabbath, כִּי אִיקְלַע לְאַתְרֵיהּ דְּרַבִּי יוֹחָנָן לֹא הֲוָה מְטַלְטֵל שְׁרָגָא – but **when visiting the locale of R' Yochanan, would not move** such **a lamp.**

The Gemara questions R' Abahu's behavior:

מַה נַּפְשָׁךְ – **Whatever possibility you consider** is difficult: אִי כְּרַבִּי יְהוּדָה סְבִירָא לֵיהּ – **If he concurred with R' Yehudah** לֶיעֱבַד כְּרַבִּי יְהוּדָה – **he should have** consistently **acted in accordance with** the opinion of **R' Yehudah,** אִי כְּרַבִּי שִׁמְעוֹן סְבִירָא לֵיהּ – **and if** he **concurs with R' Shimon** לֶיעֱבַד כְּרַבִּי שִׁמְעוֹן – **he should have** consistently **acted in accordance with** the opinion of **R' Shimon.** – ? –

The Gemara explains:

לְעוֹלָם כְּרַבִּי שִׁמְעוֹן סְבִירָא לֵיהּ – **Actually, [R' Abahu]** himself **concurs with R' Shimon** and with R' Yehoshua ben Levi, that it is permissible to move such a lamp. וּמִשּׁוּם כְּבוֹדוֹ דְּרַבִּי יוֹחָנָן הוּא דְּלֹא הֲוָה עָבִיד – **And it was out of deference to R' Yochanan that he would not act** in accordance with this view when in R' Yochanan's jurisdiction.[11]

We learned above (44a) that R' Yehudah considers a used lamp *muktzeh by dint of repugnance,* whereas R' Shimon disputes this. The Gemara again turns its attention to this issue:

אָמַר רַב יְהוּדָה – **Rav Yehudah said:** שְׁרָגָא דְּמִשְׁחָא שָׁרֵי לְטַלְטוּלָהּ – **An oil lamp may be moved** on the Sabbath, דְּנַפְטָא אָסוּר לְטַלְטוּלָהּ – but **a naphtha**[12] **[lamp] may not be moved.**[13] רַבָּה וְרַב יוֹסֵף דְּאָמְרֵי תַּרְוַיְיהוּ – However, **Rabbah and Rav Yosef both said:** דְּנַפְטָא נַמִּי שָׁרֵי לְטַלְטוּלָהּ (דהואיל וחזי לכסות ביה מנא) – **Even a naphtha [lamp] may be moved.**[14]

The Gemara recounts an episode which sheds light on the view of Rabbah and Rav Yosef:

רַב אַוְיָא אִיקְלַע לְבֵי רָבָא – **Rav Avya** once **visited Rava's home,** הֲוָה מְאִיסָן בֵּי כַּרְעֵיהּ בְּטִינָא – **and his shoes were sullied with mud.** אַתְיבֵי אַפּוּרְיָא קַמֵּיהּ דְּרָבָא – Nevertheless, **he put them** up **on a bed in front of Rava.** אִיקְפַּד רָבָא בְּעָא לְצַעוּרֵיהּ – **Rava objected and sought to unsettle [Rav Avya]** by challenging him with questions. אָמַר לֵיהּ – **He said to him:** מַאי טַעְמָא רַבָּה וְרַב יוֹסֵף דְּאָמְרֵי תַּרְוַיְיהוּ – **What is the reasoning** of **Rabbah and Rav Yosef who both said** שְׁרָגָא דְּנַפְטָא נַמִּי שָׁרֵי לְטַלְטוּלֵיהּ – that even **a naphtha lamp may be moved** on the Sabbath? אָמַר לֵיהּ – **[Rav Avya] replied:** הוֹאִיל וְחַזְיָא לְכַסּוּיֵי בָּהּ מָנָא – It is **because [the lamp] is fit** to be used on the Sabbath **to cover a vessel.**[15] אֶלָּא מֵעַתָּה – Rava countered: **But now,** if this is correct, כָּל צְרוֹרוֹת שֶׁבֶּחָצֵר מְטַלְטְלִין – **we should** be permitted to **move all the stones that are** scattered **in a courtyard,** הוֹאִיל וְחַזְיָא לְכַסּוּיֵי בְּהוּ מָנָא – **since they are fit** to be used **to cover a vessel.** אָמַר לֵיהּ – **[Rav Avya] replied:** הָא אִיכָּא תּוֹרַת כְּלִי עָלֶיהָ – **This,** i.e. a naphtha lamp, **has the status of a utensil,** הָנֵי לֵיכָּא תּוֹרַת כְּלִי עָלֶיהָ – whereas **those,** i.e. stones, **do not have the status of utensils.**[16]

Rav Avya corroborates his view:

מִי לֹא תַּנְיָא – **Was it not taught in a Baraisa:**

NOTES

8. *Rashi. Tosafos,* however, contend that the first proposal seems implausible, for the issues of a grooved candelabra and a used lamp are entirely unrelated! *Tosafos* therefore explain the inquiry differently. See also *Maharsha.* However, see *Pnei Yehoshua* and *Hagahos R' Elazar Moshe Horowitz* for resolutions of *Rashi's* approach.

9. [This is not the Tanna, R' Yose HaGlili, but an Amora with a similar name.]

10. See *Yerushalmi, Bava Basra* 6:1.

11. We cannot say that the opposite is true, for if he had held that the halachah follows R' Yehudah he would not have violated the halachah and moved a lamp out of deference to R' Yehoshua ben Levi when in his locale (*Rashi*). As it was, when in R' Yochanan's locale, he merely refrained from what he considered the permissible act of moving a lamp.

12. Naphtha is a foul-smelling fuel [that is a derivative of pitch] (*Rashi* here and above, 24b).

13. Rav Yehudah (the Amora) concurs with R' Shimon and therefore rules that an oil lamp may be moved – after it has gone out – in accordance with R' Shimon's ruling in the Mishnah (44a). Its repugnance does not make it *muktzeh.* However, Rav Yehudah teaches, even R' Shimon concedes that a naphtha lamp is *muktzeh* and may not be moved. Such a lamp is so repugnant that it *cannot* be used to hold anything other than fuel for lighting. And since it has absolutely no permissible function on the Sabbath, R' Shimon concedes that it is *muktzeh* (*Rashi, Ramban, Rosh;* see *Pri Megadim – Eishel Avraham* 308:12, *Shulchan Aruch HaRav* 308:85, *Avnei Nezer, Orach Chaim* §55 and *Tehillah LeDavid* 308:8 [cited in the Chapter Introduction, note 15]).

14. According to R' Shimon (see *Rashi;* cf. *Tosafos*). The Gemara will clarify the reasoning of Rabbah and Rav Yosef. [The parenthesized words are deleted by *Maharshal;* see Gemara below.]

15. I.e. although nothing can be placed *inside* the lamp due to its repugnance, it can be used to cover another vessel, and since it has this permissible function it is not *muktzeh,* according to R' Shimon (*Ramban*).

16. Rav Avya replied that something which has the status of a utensil and will be usable for its proper function after the Sabbath does not become *muktzeh* (according to R' Shimon) unless it is utterly useless on the Sabbath. Since a naphtha lamp can be used on the Sabbath at least for the far-fetched function of covering a vessel, it is not *muktzeh* and may be moved. [Obviously, since its primary function is one that is forbidden on the Sabbath, it is subject to the restrictions pertaining to כְּלִי שֶׁמְּלַאכְתּוֹ לְאִסּוּר, *a utensil used primarily for a prohibited function.*] By contrast, something that does not have the status of a utensil, such as a stone, is intrinsically *muktzeh.* The fact that it is fit for some type of function does not alter its intrinsic status (*Ramban;* see also *Avnei Nezer* ibid. and *Kehillos Yaakov, Beitzah* §4).

Chasam Sofer and *Chazon Yechezkel* illuminate this discussion as follows: The Gemara below (124b) cites Rava as ruling that since shards are fit to be used to cover vessels, they are not *muktzeh* and may be used to scrape the mud off one's shoes. Rav Avya, however, had deliberately placed his muddy shoes on Rava's bed, to demonstrate his disagreement with Rava's ruling. Rava therefore sought an opening to ask Rav Avya: Since you agree with my reasoning that something which is fit to be used for covering a utensil is not *muktzeh,* why did you not take a shard from the courtyard and wipe the mud off your shoes before entering my home? However, Rav Avya foiled this attempt. Rava's reasoning is clarified on 124b.

כירה פרק שלישי שבת מו.

מותר לנטותה ומותר לפרקה בשבת אלא אמר אביי בשל חוליות אי הכי מ"ט דר"ש בן לקיש דשרי מאי חוליות כעין חוליות דאית בה חידקי הלכך [א] חוליות בין גדולה בין קטנה אסורה לטלטלה גדולה נמי דאית בה חידקי גזירה אטו גדולה דחוליות כי פליגי בקטנה דאית בה חידקי [ב] מר סבר גזרינן ומר סבר לא גזרינן ומי א"ר יוחנן הכי והאמר ר' יוחנן א) הלכה כסתם משנה ותנן ב) מוכני שלה בזמן שהיא נשמטת אין חיבור לה ואין נמדדת עמה ואין מצלת עמה באהל המת ואין גוררין אותה בשבת בזמן שיש עליה מעות הא אין עליה מעות שריא ואע"ג דהוו עליה ביה"ש א"ר זירא תהא משנתינו שלא היו עליה מעות כל ביה"ש שלא לשבור דבריו של ר' יוחנן א"ר יהושע בן לוי פעם אחת הלך רבי לדיוספרא והורה במנורה כר' שמעון בנר איבעיא להו הורה במנורה כר' שמעון בנר להיתרא או דילמא הורה במנורה לאיסורא וכר' שמעון בנר להיתרא תיקו רב מלכיא איקלע לבי רבי שמלאי וטילטל שרגא ואיקפד ר' שמלאי ר' יוסי גלילאה איקלע לאתריה דר' יוסי ברבי חנינא טילטל שרגא ואיקפד ר' יוסי בר' חנינא ג) ר' אבהו כי איקלע לאתריה דר' יהושע בן לוי הוה מטלטל שרגא כי איקלע לאתריה דר' יוחנן ד) לא הוה מטלטל שרגא מה נפשך אי כרבי יהודה סבירא ליה ליעבד כרבי יהודה אי כר' שמעון סבירא ליה ליעבד כר' שמעון לעולם כר' שמעון ס"ל ומשום כבודו דר' יוחנן הוא דלא הוה עביד ° א"ר יהודה שרגא דמשחא שרי לטלטולה דנפטא אסור לטלטולה רבה ורב יוסף דאמרי תרוייהו דנפטא נמי שרי לטלטולה ה) (דהואיל וחזי לכסות ביה מנא) רב אויא איקלע לבי רבא הוה מאיסן בי כרעיה בטינא אתיבי אפוריא קמיה דרבא איקפד רבא בעא לצעוריה א"ל מ"ט רבה ורב יוסף דאמרי תרוייהו שרגא דנפטא נמי שרי לטלטוליה א"ל הואיל וחזיא לכסויי בה מנא אלא מעתה כל צרורות שבחצר מטלטלין הואיל וחזיא לכסויי בהו מנא א"ל הא איכא תורת כלי עליה הני ליכא תורת כלי עליה מי לא תניא

השירים

רש"י

מותר לנטותה. דפעמים כילת חתנים אין לה גג טפח שנקליטין יוצאין לשני ראשי המטה באמצעה אחד לכאן ואחד לכאן ונותן כלונס' מזה לזה ומשליך האהל עליה והוא שופע לכאן ולכאן וכיון שאינו רחב טפח אינו אהל ואין בו לא בנין ולא סתירה: בשל חוליות. במנורה של פרקים שמא תפול ותתפרק ויחזירנה ונמצא עושה כלי: חידקי. חיתוכין סביב לה קרונ"ש ודומה לפרקים ומאן דחזי סבר של פרקים הוא: גדולה. הואיל ודרכה לעשותה של חוליות כי אית ביה חידקי סברי דחוליות הן ואסור אפילו לר"ש לקיש כדאמר לעיל ניטלת בשתי ידים אסור לטלטלה: כי פליגי בקטנה דאית בה חידקי. דכולי עלמא ידעי דלאו חוליות נינהו: גזרינן. אטו חוליות: ומי אמר רבי יוחנן הכי. הלכה כר' יהודה: תהא משנתינו. דמוכני דקתני הא אין עליה מעות שריא כגון שלא היו עליה בין השמשות והכי תידוק מינה טעמא דיש עליה מעות כשקדש היום הא אין עליה כשקדש היום שריא: לדיוספרא. מקום: איבעיא להו. חדא הוראה הואי והכי קאמר הורה במנורה להיתרא כדרך שהיה ר' שמעון מתיר בנר ישן או דילמא שתי הוראות הוו הורה במנורה לאיסור כדאמרן בדאית חידקי וגזרינן אטו חוליות וכר"ש הורה בנר להיתר: וטלטל שרגא. נר שכבה: לעולם כרבי שמעון סבירא ליה. דאי סבירא ליה דאסור לא הוה מטלטל ליה לכבוד ר' יהושע בן לוי דליעבד איסורא: שרגא דמשחא. שדלק נר של שמן: שרי לטלטולה. אחר שכבה כר' שמעון דלא מאיס: אבל בנפטא. דמסרח אפילו רבי שמעון מודה דלא חזי אלא למלאכתו: איקפד רבא. משום טינוף המטה: ובעא לצעוריה. בשאלות:

השירים

תוספות

רבי שמעון נר שהדליקו באותה שבת והא דלא פסיק רבי יוחנן כרבי מאיר דהא סבר לגמרי כוותיה דשרי מוקצה מחמת מיאוס ואסר מוקצה מחמת איסור נקט רבי יהודה משום דבכל מקום הוזכר גבי מוקצה ועוד דלא מלינו דאית ליה לרבי מאיר מוקצה מחמת איסור גרידא אלא בנר ישן דאיכא תרתי מחמת מיאוס ומחמת איסור אך לפי זה קשה לרשב"א דמשמע דנקט במנורה אין לנו כרבי שמעון אבל רבי שמעון מיהא שרי במנורה ולמאי דמפרש טעמא דמנורה משום דאדם קובע לו מקום היכי שרי רבי שמעון הא אמרי' בריש כל הכלים (לקמן דף קכג.) הכל מודים בסיכי וזירי ומזורי כיון דקפיד עלייהו מיחד להו מקום ונראה לפרש דרבי יוחנן פסק כרבי יהודה במוקצה מחמת מיאוס וכ"ש במוקצה מחמת איסור א) כדמוכח בפרק בתרא (דף קנז.) דקאמר בכולי שבת הלכה כרבי שמעון בר ממוקצה מחמת מיאוס וחד אמר במוקצה מחמת מיאוס נמי הלכה כרבי שמעון בר ממוקצה מחמת איסור דהיינו שהדליקו בה באותה שבת והא דקאמר אנו אין לנו אלא בנר כרבי שמעון לאו משום דסבר כוותיה בנר אלא כלומר אין לנו שיתיר אפי' רבי שמעון דמיקל אלא בנר אבל במנורה אסר והשתא קיימי תרוייהו אחד ברייתא ולא מצי נמי למינקט רבי מאיר:

והא כילת חתנים דאדם קובע לה מקום. פי' רשב"א דאדם קובע לה מקום כמו למנורה ואפ"ה שרי שמואל אלא ודאי לא חשיב קביעות שלה ושל מנורה קביעות אלא היכא דקבע מקום לגמרי כדאמר בפ' כל הכלים (לקמן קכג. ושם):

דחוליות בין גדולה בין קטנה אסורה. קשה לר"י דבפ"ב דביצה (דף כב:) תנן ג' דברים ר"ג מחמיר כב"ש וחשיב אין זוקפין את המנורה ומשמע דב"ה שרי ומפרש התם בגמרא י) הכא במנורה של חוליות עסקינן משום דמיחזי כבונה דב"ש סברי יש בנין בכלים ויש סתירה בכלים וב"ה סברי אין בנין כו' אלמא שרי ב"ה מנורה של חוליות להחזיר ומאן דשרי בסוף פירקא להחזיר מטה של חוליות ברפוי איכא לאוקמא ה"נ ברפוי אבל למאן דאסר קשה ותירץ ר"י דהתם איירי כגון שהחוליות מחוברין יחד ואינם מתפרקין ופעמים מטין אותן ופעמים זוקפין אותן י):

הורה במנורה להיתרא וכר"ש בנר נמי להיתרא או דילמא במנורה הורה לאיסורא וכר"ש בנר להיתרא. וא"ת אמאי לא קאמר נמי או דילמא הורה במנורה להיתרא כרבי שמעון בנר וכרבי שמעון בנר לא סבירא ליה דכה"ג איתא באלו טריפות (חולין דף נו: ושם) הורו בטרפחת כרבי בזפק איבעיא להו הורו בטרפחת לאיסורא וכרבי בזפק להיתרא או דילמא הורו בטרפחת להיתרא כרבי בזפק וכרבי בזפק לא סבירא להו וי"ל דהכא לא שייך למיתלי מנורה בנר כדתלי טרפחת בזפק דהכא אין טעם אחד לשניהם דנר משום מוקצה ומנורה משום בנין ועוד דלא בעי למימר דר' לא סבר בנר כר"ש משום דריב"ל פסיק לעיל כר"ש ואם תאמר ובההיא דאלו טריפות אמאי לא קאמר נמי תרוייהו להיתרא כדאמר הכא או דילמא הורו בטרפחת להיתרא וכר' בזפק נמי להיתרא ומיהו בלאו הכי מגיהין שם הספרים ול"ג הורו בטרפחת לאיסורא דהא כ"ע שרו לה דתניא התם ח) היא האם היא טרפחת היא שלחופית ובניטל האם ט) הוה עובדא והאכילה רבי טרפון לכלבים ואמר הלכה חמורך טרפון ואמר ליה רבי עקיבא טועה בדבר משנה אתה וגרס התם הורו בטרפחת להיתרא וכרבי בזפק להיתרא כו' ורש"י פי' הורה במנורה להיתרא כר"ש בנר וחדא הוראה הוי ואין נראה דאין לתלות מנורה בנר ועוד דאכתי הוי ליה למיבעיא או דילמא תרוייהו להיתרא:

דנפטא אסור לטלטלה. פי' בקונט' אפילו לר"ש וכן משמע דהא שרגא דמשחא דשרי לטלטולה היינו לר' שמעון ועוד מדפריך רבא בסמוך לרבה ורב יוסף מ"ש מצרורות שבחצר ואי שרי ר' שמעון דנפטא תיקשי' ליה לכ"ע אליבא דרבי שמעון לכך פי' בקונט' דהכא אליבא דר' שמעון קאי ואע"ג דרב אית ליה מוקצה י) גבי מטה שיחדה למעות ° ורבה נמי אית ליה כדאמר אביי כ) כל מילי דמר עביד כרב ורב יוסף נמי משמע דאית ליה מוקצה בפ' נוטל (לקמן קמב:) דקאמר כמה חריפא שמעתתא דרדקי אימור דאמור בשבת לכתחילה מי אמור הכא אליבא דר"ש קאמר וליה לא ס"ל ומיהו נראה לפרש דהכא איירי נמי אליבא דרבי יהודה ולא איירי בהדליקו בו באותה שבת וה"ק שרגא דמשחא של מתכת שרי לטלטולה ואפילו לרבי יהודה כדתניא לעיל (ד' מד.) כל הנרות של מתכת מטלטלין דנפטא אסור אפי' לרבי שמעון דמאיס טפי מנר ישן ורבה ורב יוסף שרו אפי' לרבי יהודה דלא מאיס אלא שריחו רע וחזי לכסויי ביה מנא אבל נר ישן מקצה ליה לגמרי משום דמאיס ואפילו מכיסוי מנא: [ועי' תוס' מנחות מא: ד"ה כל מילי]:

ואמר

מסורת הש"ס

א) [לקמן פא: קיב: קמז: קמח: קנו: עירובין לב. ביצה לז: תענית יח. יבמות טז: מב: גיטין פא: ב"ק כט: לב. סט. לד: ב"מ לג. סנהדרין לד: שבועות ג: מנחות נב: חולין לא: מג. נדה ג. ע:], ב) [לעיל מד:], כלים פי"ח מ"ב], ג) יבמות יז. ע"ש, ד) [עי' תוספות יבמות יז. ד"ה לא הוה], ה) רש"ל מוחק זה, ו) [דף כב.], ז) [ועי' תוספות ביצה כב. ד"ה וב"ה], ח) [חולין נה:], ט) [סנהדרין לג.], י) [לעיל מד:], כ) [לעיל כב.]

תוספות ישנים

א) ולפי זה חמור מוקצה מחמת מיאוס ממוקצה מחמת איסור לר' יוחנן דלא דמייה בידים כמו נבילה דפסק כר"ש. ורב סבר איפכא דקאמר בפ"ק דחולין [דף טו.] ע"כ לא שרי ר"מ כו' אבל שוחט דאין ראוי לכום לא. ור"מ לית ליה בפרקין [לעיל מד.] מוקצה מחמת מיאוס להכי אמר בפרק בתרא דרב סבר כר"י מדכרכי דזוזי אסור דהוי מוקצה מחמת מיאוס כדפי' ר"ת בפ"ק מוכח מכ"ש דלדידיה מחמת איסור חמיר טפי:

גליון הש"ס

גמ' **אמר ר' יהודה שרגא דמשחא.** עי' לקמן דף קכב ע"ב תוס' ד"ה רחם: תוס' ד"ה **דנפטא וכו' ורבה נמי אית ליה.** עי' מנחות דף מא ע"ב תוס' ד"ה כל מילי. ובעירובין דף לג ע"ב תוס' ד"ה לא תימא:

ליקוטי רש"י

הלכה כסתם משנה. רבי הוא סדר המשנה וכשראה דברי חכם ונראו בעיניו שנאן סתם ולא הזכיר שם אומרו עליהן כדי שלא יהו שנויה מפי יחיד ונראין כאלו נשנו מפי המרובים ועשו הלכה כמותן [ביצה ב:]. מוכני שלה. גבי שידה תנן במסכת כלים והיא עגלה של עץ מוקפת מחיצות למרכב אנשים ונשים. מוכני. אופן. בזמן שהיא נשמטת. כמין אופני עגלה שלנו שאדם יכול לסלקן מן העגלה. אין חיבור לה. [illegible]

עין משפט נר מצוה

נו א ב מיי' פכ"ו מהל' שבת הלכה יא טוש"ע או"ח סי' רעט סעיף ז:

רבינו חננאל

שני דא"ר יוחנן אנו אין לנו כר"ש אלא בנר. אבל מנורה בין ניטלת בידו אחת בין ניטלת בב' ידים אסור לטלטלה וטעמא מאי ואוקמה רחבה במנורה דאית בה חידקי חידקי שהן כעין חוליו' שנראה המעמידה או המטלטלה כבונה. הילכך דחוליות בין גדולה בין קטנה אסורה. לית בה חוליות ואית בה חידקי חידקי גדולה אסורה דמיחלפא בגדול' של חוליות. כי פליגי במנורה קטנה דאית בה חידקי חידקי. ר' יוחנן סבר גזרינן קטנה דאית בה חידקי אטו גדולה דאית בה חידקי. וריש לקיש סבר לא גזרינן. איני דגזר ר' יוחנן והא איהו דאמר הלכה כסתם משנה. ותנן סתמא בכלים פ' י"ח במוכני של שידה ואין גוררין אותה בשבת בזמן שיש עליה מעות. ודייקינן מינה. הא אין עליה מעות שריא. ואע"ג דהוו עליה כל בין השמשות ולא גזרינן כשאין עליה מעות אטו כשיש עליה מעות. וא"ר זירא תהא משנתנו בשלא היו עליה מעות כל בין השמשות (גזורי') שלא לשבור דברי ר' יוחנן. כלומר לא תקשי לך דר' יוחנן אדר' יוחנן. והא דהורה ר' (זירא ספרא) [בדיוספרא] עלתה בתיקו. ועבדינן בה לחומרא ומוקמינן לה הורה ר' במנורה לאיסורא וכר' שמעון בנר להיתרא: ר' אבהו מטלטל שרגא כר"ש. ובאתריה דר' יוחנן לא הוה מטלטל ליה משום כבודו דר' יוחנן (רב) [אמר רב יהודה] שרגא דמשחא שרי לטלטלה. אבל שרגא דנפטא (הוה) אסיר ורבה ורב יוסף שרו אפילו שרגא דנפטא. ואסיקנ' משום דחזו לכסויי בהו מני דנפטא. ואם תאמר אי הכי כל צרורות שבחצר יטלטלו הואיל וחזו לכסויי בהו מנא דנפטא. שני

הגהות

בגמרא למנחות (לא.) בית הלל אומרים נמדדת מבחוץ דרואין אותה כאלו היא עומדת בתוך כלי גדול ואם מחזיק אותו כלי ארבעים סאה טהורה השידה ואף על פי שהיא אינה מחזקת ארבעים סאה דקסבר אף עוביה נמדד עמה והמוכני אינו נמדד עמה להשלים כאלו ניטל המוכני ואחר כך תנתן השידה לתוך הכלי. ואין מצלת עמה באהל המת. [illegible]

יומא (עט.) בא למדוד נפש אומרים לו מדוד לעצמך שאין אדם רואה לחבירו [לעיל כד:]

א) [א] השירים והנזמים והטבעות הרי הן ככל הכלים הנטלים בחצר ° ואמר עולא מה טעם הואיל ואיכא תורת כלי עליה הכא נמי הואיל ואיכא תורת כלי עליה א"ר נחמן בר יצחק בריך רחמנא דלא כסיפיה רבא לרב אויא רמי ליה אביי לרבה תניא [ב] מותר השמן שבנר ושבקערה אסור ורבי שמעון מתיר אלמא לר' שמעון לית ליה מוקצה ורמינהו [ג] רבי שמעון אומר כל שאין מומו ניכר מעי"ט אין זה מן המוכן הכי השתא התם אדם יושב ומצפה אימתי תכבה נרו הכא אדם יושב ומצפה מתי יפול בו מום מימר אמר מי יימר דנפיל ביה מומא ואת"ל דנפיל ביה מומא מי יימר דנפיל ביה מום קבוע ואם תמצי לומר דנפל ביה מום קבוע מי יימר דמזדקק ליה חכם מתיב רמי בר חמא [ד] מפירין נדרים בשבת [ונשאלין לנדרים שהן] לצורך השבת ואמאי לימא מי יימר דמיזדקק לה בעל התם כדרב פנחס משמיה דרבא [ה] דאמר רב פנחס משמיה דרבא כל הנודרת על דעת בעלה היא נודרת ת"ש [ו] נשאלין לנדרים של צורך השבת בשבת ואמאי לימא מי יימר דמזדקק ליה חכם התם אי לא מיזדקק ליה חכם סגיא ליה בג' הדיוטות הכא מי יימר דמיזדקק ליה חכם רמי ליה אביי לרב יוסף מי אמר ר' שמעון כבתה מותר לטלטלה כבתה אין לא כבתה לא מאי טעמא דילמא בהדי דנקיט לה כבתה הא שמעינן ליה לר' שמעון דאמר דבר שאין מתכוין מותר דתניא [ז] ר' שמעון אומר גורר אדם כסא מטה וספסל ובלבד שלא יתכוין לעשות חריץ כל היכא דכי מיכוין איכא איסורא דאורייתא כי לא מיכוין גזר ר"ש מדרבנן כל היכא דכי מיכוין איכא איסורא דרבנן כי לא מיכוין שרי ר"ש לכתחילה מתיב רבא [ח] מוכרי כסות מוכרין כדרכן ובלבד שלא יתכוין בחמה מפני החמה ובגשמים מפני הגשמים והצנועין מפשילין במקל לאחוריהן והא הכא דכי מיכוין איסורא דאורייתא איכא כי לא מיכוין שרי רבי שמעון לכתחילה אלא אמר רבא
הנח

השירים. אצעדות: הרי הן ככל הכלים. אע"פ שאסור לצאת בהן לרה"ר כדאמרי' בפרק במה אשה יוצאה (לקמן נט:) גזירה דילמא שלפא ומחויא מיהו תורת כלי עליהן ומותר לטלטלן שלא כדרך מלבוש: מומו ניכר. גבי בכור קאי: מי יימר דמזדקק ליה חכם. שימצא חכם שיזקק לו ביו"ט לראות אם מום קבוע הוא או לא: מפירין נדרים. בעל לאשתו: ונשאלין לנדרים. לחכם להתירן: שהן לצורך שבת. כגון נדר שלא יאכל היום: ואמאי. מותרת לאכול ואפי' שרי לה בעל ליתסר לה משום מוקצה דהא אסחה דעתה ואמרה מי יימר דמזדקק לה בעל: על דעת בעלה. ע"מ אם ירצה הבעל וסמכה עליה דמזדקק לה ביום שמעו: הכא מי יימר כו'. והדיוטות לא מצו למישרייה לבכור אלא במום הידוע לכל כגון מחוסר אבר: איסורא דאורייתא. כיבוי אב מלאכה הוא חריץ ליכא איסור דאורייתא דחופר כלאחר יד הוא דחופר דאמר לקמן תולדה דחורש וחייב ה"מ חופר כדרכו במרא וקרדום: מוכרין כדרכן. ואפי' של כלאים לובשו להראותו בשוק: ובלבד שלא יתכוין. להנאת חימום והא ר"ש היא מדאזיל בתר כוונה:
לדבר

ואמר עולא מה טעם. להכי איצטריך לפרושי האי טעמא משום דמשמע ליה דסבר האי תנא כמאן דאסר לקמן להתקשט בהן בחצר מדקתני הרי הן ככל הכלים הניטלין בחצר פירוש ככל הכלים שמלאכתן לאיסור דשרי לצורך גופן ומקומן ולהכי מפרש עולא דאיכא תורת כלי עליה וקשה לר"י דאמר בפ' מי שהפך (מ"ק יב: ושם) ר' יהודה נשיאה נפק בחומרתא דמדושא [עי' פי' רש"י שם] שמע ר' אמי ואיקפיד אמר רב יוסף מ"ט איקפיד והתניא השירים והנזמים כו' ומאי פריך מינה אדרבה מינה משמע דאסור לצאת בהן כדפי' והתם קאמר נפק דמשמע דרך מלבוש ונראה לר"י דחומרתא דמדושא היינו טבעת של עץ כמו שמפרשים רבותיו של רש"י ולא של אלמוג כמו שהוא מפרש דאלמוגין מפרש בראש השנה (דף כג.) כסיתא והכא קאמר דמדושא אלא של עץ אחר הוא ששמו מדושא ואין שם תכשיט עליו וכשיוצאים בו דרך מלבוש לא הוי קישוט אלא טלטול בעלמא ולהכי ידע רב יוסף דר' אמי לא איקפד אלא משום טלטול והשתא מייתי שפיר מהך ברייתא דשרי לטלטל לצורך גופו או לצורך מקומו כשאר כלי' שמלאכתן לאיסור דניטלין לצורך גופו או לצורך מקומו ונפק לחצר קאמר אבל לרה"ר אסור כדאמרי' בפ' הדר (עירובין סט. ושם) ההוא גברא דנפיק בחומרתא דמדושא חזייה לר' יהודה נשיאה כסייה אמר כגון זה מבטל רשות לר' יהודה: **והתנן** ר"ש אומר כל שאין מומו ניכר מעי"ט אין זה מן המוכן. קשה לר"י מאי קא פריך הא ע"כ טעמא דר"ש לאו משום מוקצה אלא משום דסבר דאין רואין מומין ביו"ט דהא ר' יהודה דאית ליה טפי מוקצה שרי התם בריש אין צדין (ביצה כה: ושם) בכור שנפל לבור יורד מומחה ויראה אם יש בו מום יעלה וישחוט ואם לאו לא ישחוט וי"ל דדייק מדלא קתני ר"ש אוסר לפי שאין רואין מומין בי"ט דהוה משמע לכתחילה אסור אבל בדיעבד מבוקר ומדקתני אין זה מן המוכן משמע דהוי מוקצה ואפי' בקרו אינו מבוקר והכי פליגי דר' יהודה סבר רואין מומין בי"ט הלכך לא הוי מוקצה דמיירי בנפל בו מום מעי"ט כדמוקי לה התם ור"ש סבר אין רואין ולכך אפי' ביקרו אינו מבוקר משום מוקצה וא"ת דבבילה משמע דאביי סבר כאדא בר אוכמי דאמר לר"ש היכא דנפל בו מום מעי"ט אם בקרו מבוקר דאמר אביי התם כוותיה דרבה בר רב הונא מסתברא מדקתני תלת בבי בברייתא [ט](ומוקמא ההיא ברייתא כאדא בר אוכמי) וע"כ הא דשני ליה בין נפל בו מום קבוע מעי"ט לנפל בו מום בי"ט משום דנפל בו בי"ט [ב] איכא תלתא מי יימר כדקאמר בסמוך ונפל בו מעי"ט ליכא אלא חד מי יימר דמיזדקיק ליה חכם מאי קשיא מנר שכבה דליכא כל הני מי יימר וי"ל דחזר בו אביי ולית ליה [י](דאדא בר אוכמי) משמע מתני' דרב אושעיא דאדא בר אוכמי משבש ותני דמתני' דהתם נמי דיקא כרב אושעיא כדמפרש התם: **מי** יימר דנפיל ביה מומא. נראה דכל הני מי יימר דקאמר רבה לאו דווקא דהא ר"ש אסר אפי' בנפל בו מום קבוע מעי"ט דהשתא ליכא אלא חד מי יימר דמיזדקיק ליה חכם דהא קאי אר' יהודה דלא שרי אלא כשהיה בו מום קבוע מעי"ט דהא פריך אהא דקאמר ר' יהודה ואם לאו לא ישחוט פשיטא ומשני לא צריכא דנפל ביה מאתמול מום עובר והשתא הוה ליה מום קבוע מהו דתימא כיון דדעתיה עילויה נשחטיה קמ"ל א"כ הא דקאמר אם יש בו מום יעלה וישחוט היינו ע"כ מום קבוע מעי"ט ואפי' לאדא בר אוכמי דשרי ר"ש בדיעבד בחד מי יימר מ"מ בנפל בו מום עובר מעי"ט דאיכא תרתי מי יימר לכאורה משמע התם דאסר לכך נראה דלאו דוקא הן דאפי' בחד מי יימר סגי וכן מוכחא מאתקפתא דרמי בר חמא דפריך מחד מי יימר: **מי** יימר דמיזדקיק לה בעל. ואע"ג דפירות שנדרה מהם אינם מוקצין לענין טלטול ° דהא חזו לשאר בני אדם מ"מ אית לן למימר מיגו דאיתקצאי בין השמשות מאכילתם איתקצאי לכולי יומא אי נמי מיירי בפירות שלה ואסרתן לכל אדם: **מי** יימר דמיזדקיק לה בעל. תימה מי דמי התם ודאי לא מיזדקיק ליה חכם דאין רואין מומין בי"ט אבל הכא דאין לך איסור בדבר מיזדקק לה בעל ולית לן למימר מי יימר דהא לר' יהודה דקסבר רואין מומין בי"ט לא אמרי' מי יימר [ג] וי"ל דבעל נמי לא ניחא להזדקק דזימנין דשרי נדרים שנדרה לדבר מצוה: **התם** אי לא מיזדקיק ליה חכם סגי ליה בג' הדיוטות אבל הכא כו'. ואע"ג דבפ"ק דחולין (דף יח:) אמר רב יהודה אמר ר' ירמיה ספק משמיה דרב ספק משמיה דשמואל ג' מתירין את הבכור במקום שאין מומחה היינו דוקא במומין מובהקין כגון ניסמת עינו נקטעה ידו נשברה רגלו כדאמרינן בשילהי כל פסולי המוקדשין (בכורות לו:) וה"נ דהוה מצי למימר מי יימר דמזדקקי ליה ג' הדיוטות דודאי לא מיזדקקי ליה משום דאין רואין מומין בי"ט והא דנקט דמיזדקק ליה חכם משום דחכם שרי בכל מומין:

ולפ"ז א"ש גבי טבל דאמר אם עבר ותיקנו מתוקן דדוקא חכם אמר הכא לא מיזדקיק אבל בג' הדיוטות לא אמר מי יימר ומיהו לפי מ"ש בפנים ה"נ המ"ל כו' לא א"ש טבל כדפי' לעיל ולהכי נקט חכם משום דלמתיר בכל מומין ועיקר טעמא משום דהכא איכא איסורא והתם ליכא והא דנקט התם אם לא מיזדקיק ליה חכם סגיא בג' הדיוטות אע"ג דשרי חשיב מוקצה אי לא סגיא ליה בג' הדיוטות [ת"י]:

כבתה אין לא כבתה לא. כן דרך הש"ס דאע"ג דהוה מצי לאתויי רישא דקתני בהדיא חוץ מן הנר הדולק בשבת מייתי סיפא ודייק מינה [כ]: **דכל** היכא דקמכוין איכא איסורא דאורייתא. וא"ת דהכא בכיבוי ליכא איסורא דאורייתא לר"ש דמלאכה שאינה צריכה לגופה היא וי"ל דה"ק דכי מיכוין איכא איסורא דאורייתא כגון בפתילה וצריך להבהבה ° אע"פ שזה התירוץ דחוק הוא הא בלאו הכי פריך ליה שפיר הרב פור"ת:
הנח

רבינו חננאל

שני צרורר' הואיל ואינה תורת כלי עליהן כמו (ש"מ עולה) [שא' עולא] בשירים ונזמים וטבעות הואיל [תורת] כלי עליהן: **תנא** מותר שמן שבנר ושבקערה אסור להסתפק ממנו. ור"ש מתיר. אלמא לר"ש לית ליה מוקצה. איני והא לענין בכור שנפל בו מום ביו"ט אמר ר"ש אין זה מן המוכן. ושנינן שני זה מזה. אדם מצפה מתי תכבה נרו ויסתפק מן השמן ומכין ליה. אבל לגבי מום ליכא למימר הכי. דאמר מי יימר דנפיל ביה מומא. ואי נפל מי יימר דמזדקיק ליה חכם ומותבינן מהא דתנן מפירין נדרים בשבת א) לצורך השבת ושנינן כל הנודרת על דעת בעלה היא נודרת ומבתחלה כך נדרה בחזקת שיפר לה בעלה והא [דתנן] נשאלין נדרים לצורך השבת נימא מי יימר דמיזדקיק ליה חכם. ושנינן שני התם דסגיא בג' הדיוטות: **רמי** אביי ומי אמר ר' שמעון כבה הנר מותר לטלטלו. מכלל דאי לא כבה חייש. דילמא כי מטלטל ליה שמא יכבה והא איהו דאמר גורר אדם מטה כסא וספסל ובלבד שלא יתכוין לעשות חריץ הנה דאע"ג דנעשה חריץ כיון דבלא כוונה נעשה לא חייש ר' שמעון. ושני כל היכא דכי מכוין אתי למנגע באיסורא דאורייתא כגון כביית הנר וכיוצא בו חייש ר"ש וגזר מדרבנן. וכל היכא דכי מכוין איסורא [דרבנן] היא. כי לא מכוין שרי ר"ש לכתחלה איני והא מוכרי כסות כו' וכלאים איסורא דאורייתא היא. וכי לא מיכוין שרי ר"ש לכתחלה. ומשני רבא

חשק שלמה על רבינו חננאל

א) עי' בתלופי גרסאות:

רב נסים גאון

התם אי לא מזדקק ליה חכם סגיא בג' הדיוטות. משתכח עיקר דילה במסכתא דנדרים בפרק נערה מאורסה (דף עח) אהרן ובניו וכל ישראל בפרשת נדרים למאי הילכתא אמר רב אחא בר יעקב להכשיר ג' הדיוטות וכותיה גרסי' בפרק יש נוחלין (בבא בתרא דף קכ):

מסורת הש"ס

א) מו"ק יב., ב) [לעיל מד.] ביצה ל:, ג) ביצה כו., ד) לקמן קמ. נדרים עז., ה) יבמות כט: גיטין פג: נדרים עג: נדה מו., ו) לקמן קמ. נדרים עז:, ז) [תוספתא ביצה פ"ב] [לעיל כב. כט: ביצה כג: פסחים קא. מנחות מא:], ח) כלאים פ"ט מ"ה לעיל כט: פסחים כו., ט) רש"ל מ"ז, י) רש"ל מ"ז, כ) [עי' תוס' לעיל לט: ד"ה אלא פניו וע' הר"מ].

תוספות ישנים

א) הא דלא מייתי מתניתין דכל הכלים נוטל אדם קורנס לפצוע בו אגוזים. משום דהתם נמי מיוחד להיתר לפצוע בו אגוזים. אבל השירים כו' אין עושין כ"א ללבוש וכיון דאסור להתקשט בהן ה"ל לאסרן לטלטל אפ"ה כיון דאיכא תורת כלי עליה שרי והכא נמי ל"ש:

ב) וליכא למימר דאע"ג דנפל מום מעי"ט איכא ג' מי יימר דהבעלים לא היו יודעים כלל שהיה בו מום. לא היא דהתם מפ' כל שאין מומו ניכר לחכם משמע אבל בעלים יודעים. ולאדא בר אוכמי צ"ל דאע"ג דר"ש איירי דנפל ביה מום מעי"ט מדקאי על ר"י מ"מ מיירי נמי בנפל בו מום בי"ט או מום עובר מעי"ט מדקתני אין זה מן המוכן דמשמע אפילו ביקרו אינו מבוקר:

ג) והר"ס מירץ דהכא בנדרים דדמיא בידים הי' לנו לאסור כי התם דלא דמיא בידים:

גליון הש"ס

גמ' ואמר עולא. עי' לקמן דף נט ע"ב תוס' ד"ה מאן דרכה: תוס' ד"ה מי יימר דמזדקק לה בעל ואע"ג וכו' דהא חזי לשאר ב"א. עי' לקמן דף קמו ע"ב תוס' ד"ה כיון דתניא: שם ד"ה דכל היכא וכו' אע"פ שזה התירוץ דחוק. עי' בבכורות דף כה ע"א תוס' ד"ה דהוי ליה:

ליקוטי רש"י

השירים. צמידין [ע"ז מג:]. אצעדה מתרגמינן שירין (במדבר לא) [קידושין מח.]. נושקי"א בלעז [מו"ק יב:]. **מותר השמן שבנר ושבקערה.** נר קרויי"ל מותר השמן שנותן בנר או בקערה שמן הניתן להדלקת הנר של שבת וכבה המותר יש בה משום מוקצה ואסור. **אדם יושב ומצפה אימתי תכבה נרו.** שיודע שסופה לכבות הלכך בין השמשות דעתיה על המותר. **הכא אדם יושב ומצפה וכו'.** בתמיה ומי נביא הוא [ביצה ל:]. **מפירין נדרים בשבת.** בעל לאשתו ואב לבתו. שהן לצורך השבת. כגון שנדרה מאכילה או מתכשיטין [נדרים עז.]. **כל הנודרת על דעת בעלה היא נודרת.** נהי דהפרה דבעל גזרת הכתוב היא מיהו מש"ה זכתה תורה לבעל בהפרת נדריה משום דעל דעת בעלה היא נודרת [ר"ן שם עג:]. על דעת בעלה על מנת שאם ירצה ואם לאו לא יהא נדר [גיטין פג:]. **לא כבתה לא.** בעוד שהוא דולק אסור שמא יכבה הנר [לעיל מד.]. **גורר אדם כסא מטה וספסל.** ואף על גב דקעביד חריץ והוי תולדה דחורש או בונה [שם כב.]. **מוכרין כדרכן.** כסות של כלאים לובשו בשוק כדי להראותו למוכרו דלא אסרה תורה אלא לבישה שהיא להתחמם כדרך כל הלובשים והעלאה דומיא דלבישה נמי דמיתהני בה [שם כט:]. מעוטפין בכסות כלאים דאין מתכוין להנאת לבישה. **והצנועין.** פרושים שמתרחקין מן הכיעור ומן הדומה לו [פסחים כו:]. כשרים שמרחיקין עצמן מכל לזות שפתים [לעיל שם].

הַשִּׁירִים וְהַנְּזָמִים וְהַטַּבָּעוֹת – BRACELETS, NOSE RINGS AND RINGS הֲרֵי הֵן כְּכָל הַכֵּלִים הַנִּטָּלִים בֶּחָצֵר – ARE LIKE ALL other UTENSILS THAT MAY BE MOVED IN A COURTYARD?[1] וְאָמַר עוּלָּא – And Ulla said: מַה טַּעַם – What is the reason that these items are not considered *muktzeh*? הוֹאִיל וְאִיכָּא תּוֹרַת כְּלִי עֲלֵיהּ – It is because they have the status of utensils.[2] הָכָא נַמִי הוֹאִיל וְאִיכָּא תּוֹרַת כְּלִי עֲלֵיהּ – Rav Avya concludes: Here too, in the case of a naphtha lamp, it is not *muktzeh* because it has the status of a utensil.

The Gemara comments:

אָמַר רַב נַחְמָן בַּר יִצְחָק – Rav Nachman bar Yitzchak said: בְּרִיךְ רַחֲמָנָא דְּלָא כַּסְפֵיהּ רָבָא לְרַב אַוְיָא – Blessed is the Merciful One, Who saw to it that Rava did not embarrass Rav Avya.

The Gemara notes an apparent contradiction in R' Shimon's teachings:

רָמֵי לֵיהּ אַבַּיֵי לְרַבָּה – Abaye posed the following contradiction to Rabbah: תַּנְיָא – It was taught in a Baraisa: מוֹתַר הַשֶּׁמֶן שֶׁבַּנֵּר וְשֶׁבַּקְּעָרָה אָסוּר – THE LEFTOVER OIL IN A LAMP OR IN A BOWL IS PROHIBITED, even after the flame goes out; וְרַבִּי שִׁמְעוֹן מַתִּיר – BUT R' SHIMON PERMITS it.[3] אַלְמָא לְרַבִּי שִׁמְעוֹן לֵית לֵיהּ מוּקְצֶה – Evidently, R' Shimon does not accept a broad application of *muktzeh*. וּרְמִינְהוּ – But contrast this with [the following Mishnah] and note the contradiction: רַבִּי שִׁמְעוֹן אוֹמֵר – R' SHIMON SAYS: כֹּל שֶׁאֵין מוּמוֹ נִיכָּר מֵעֶרֶב יוֹם טוֹב – IN EVERY CASE WHERE ITS BLEMISH WAS NOT RECOGNIZED, i.e. detected WHILE IT WAS STILL THE DAY PRIOR TO THE FESTIVAL, אֵין זֶה מִן הַמּוּכָן – [A *BECHOR*] IS NOT CONSIDERED PREPARED and may not be slaughtered on the festival.[4] – ? –

Rabbah resolves the contradiction:

הָכִי הַשְׁתָּא – Is this a comparison? הָתָם אָדָם יוֹשֵׁב וּמְצַפֶּה אֵימָתַי תִּכְבֶּה נֵרוֹ – There, in the case of oil in a lamp, a person waits and anticipates the moment when his lamp will go out and he will be able to use the oil. Therefore, R' Shimon holds that although it was not available for use during *bein hashemashos* it is not *muktzeh* and becomes permitted when the anticipated moment arrives.[5] הָכָא אָדָם יוֹשֵׁב וּמְצַפֶּה מָתַי יִפּוֹל בּוֹ מוּם – Here, however, can we say that a person waits and anticipates the moment when [his *bechor*] will develop a blemish and become permitted for consumption? Certainly not! מֵימַר אָמַר מִי יֵימַר דְּנָפִיל בֵּיהּ מוּמָא – If it does not have a blemish before the festival, he says to himself: "Who is to say that it will develop a blemish? וְאִם תִּמְצֵי לוֹמַר דְּנָפִיל בֵּיהּ מוּמָא מִי יֵימַר דְּנָפִיל בֵּיהּ מוּם קָבוּעַ – And even if you assume that it will develop a blemish, who is to say that it will develop a *permanent* blemish? וְאִם תִּמְצֵי לוֹמַר דְּנָפִיל בֵּיהּ מוּם קָבוּעַ מִי יֵימַר דְּמִיזְדַּקֵק לֵיהּ חָכָם – And even if you assume that it will develop a permanent blemish, who is to say that an expert will get involved with examining it on the festival?" Since the owner does not anticipate that the animal will become available on Yom Tov, it remains *muktzeh*, even according to R' Shimon.[6]

Rabbah's explanation is challenged:

מָתִיב רָמֵי בַּר חָמָא – Rami bar Chama challenged this on the basis of the following Mishnah:[7] מְפִירִין נְדָרִים בְּשַׁבָּת – WE MAY ANNUL VOWS ON THE SABBATH,[8] וְנִשְׁאָלִין לִנְדָרִים שֶׁהֵן לְצוֹרֶךְ הַשַּׁבָּת – AND WE MAY SEEK RELEASE FROM VOWS for things THAT ARE NECESSARY FOR THE SABBATH.[9] Thus, if a woman vowed not

NOTES

1. We will learn in Chapter Six that the Rabbis forbade women to go out wearing certain articles of clothing and jewelry on the Sabbath. They instituted this rule upon noticing that women occasionally took these items off in the street to show their friends and then continued walking, thus violating the prohibition against carrying something four *amos* in the public domain (*Rashi* to 57a ד״ה במה). There is an opinion (see Gemara, 64b) that the Rabbis forbade wearing these articles even in an enclosed courtyard, so as to prevent people from unwittingly going out to the public domain while wearing them. This Baraisa follows that opinion and rules that although the articles may not be worn they are not *muktzeh* and may be moved about in a courtyard (see *Rashi* here and to 64b ד״ה אסור לצאת לחצר, *Tosafos* here ד״ה ואמר עולא and *Ritva MHK* ed.; see also 57a note 8).

2. I.e. although they cannot be used for their primary function and have hardly any other use, they can be put to some sort of secondary use on the Sabbath. Therefore they do not lose their status as non-*muktzeh* utensils (*Ritva MHK* ed.).

3. This Baraisa was cited above (44a), and was elucidated there in note 3. The relevant point is that R' Shimon rejects the view that something which was set aside on account of a prohibition during *bein hashemashos* remains *muktzeh* for the entire Sabbath.

4. *Beitzah* 26a. The Torah states that a *bechor* (i.e. the firstborn male offspring of a cow, sheep, or goat) becomes sanctified at birth and must be given to a Kohen (see *Exodus* 13:12). The Kohen then brings it to the Temple, where it is offered as a sacrifice (*Numbers* 18:17-18). The *bechor* may not be slaughtered outside the Temple unless it is afflicted with a permanent *blemish* (מום) that disqualifies it from being offered in the Temple (see *Deuteronomy* 15:21-22). In case of a permanent blemish, the *bechor* is the Kohen's ordinary property, to be slaughtered and eaten outside of the Temple.

When a *bechor* is suspected of having a blemish, the law stipulates that only an expert (מוּמְחֶה) who is specifically ordained to judge these matters may determine whether it is considered a permanent blemish that would render a *bechor* invalid for a sacrifice and permit its slaughter outside of the Temple.

The laws of *bechor* apply even in our time when there is no Temple. Although a *bechor* cannot be offered nowadays, it is nevertheless possesses the sanctity of a sacrifice and subject to the attendant laws prohibiting its slaughter unless pronounced permanently blemished by an expert. Since an unblemished *bechor* cannot be slaughtered, it is *muktzeh* even on Yom Tov, when slaughtering is normally permitted. R' Shimon rules that even if a *bechor* developed a blemish but the blemish was not seen by a qualified expert before Yom Tov, the *bechor* is *muktzeh*. This ruling is based on R' Shimon's view that it is prohibited for an expert to pass judgment on a *bechor* on Yom Tov (because this is similar to adjudicating a lawsuit, which is prohibited Rabbinically – see *Beitzah* 36b). Thus, even if an expert should examine the *bechor* illegally on Yom Tov and pronounce it blemished, it remains forbidden for the rest of the day, since it was not "prepared" before Yom Tov. But this seems to contradict R' Shimon's ruling in the previous Baraisa, which rejects the application of *muktzeh* on account of a prohibition that was in effect during *bein hashemashos* (see *Tosafos* ד״ה והתנן and *Ritva MHK* ed.; see also *Pnei Yehoshua*).

5. Indeed, the Gemara above (44a) explained that R' Shimon referred specifically to oil in a small bowl, or a lamp, in which case a person anticipates that the light will go out.

6. Even if the *bechor* developed a permanent blemish before Yom Tov, it is *muktzeh* on the basis of the single point that who is to say an expert will be willing to examine it illegally on Yom Tov (*Tosafos* ד״ה מי יימר דנפל ביה מומא, *Ritva MHK* ed.; see *Pnei Yehoshua*). [Although R' Shimon does not usually consider something *muktzeh* unless its owner actively set it aside like drying figs and raisins (see 45b note 2), he concedes that a *bechor* is *muktzeh*, because its potential permissibility hinges on the willingness of another person (i.e. an expert) to get involved, and that is something that the owner cannot anticipate at all (*Ritva MHK* ed.; cf. *Milchamos Hashem* to *Beitzah* 24b; see note 10).]

7. Below, 157a.

8. I.e. on the Sabbath, a husband may exercise his right to annul his wife's vow [and a father may exercise his right to annul his minor daughter's vow] (*Rashi;* see *Numbers* 30:2-17).

9. I.e. we may apply to a Sage to release us from a vow by finding a basis for declaring it erroneous, but only if the release is necessary for the Sabbath itself, e.g. one vowed not to eat on the Sabbath (*Rashi*). [See *Ran* to 157a for the reason for this limitation, and see the Gemara there for a discussion of whether this limitation applies also to a husband or father annulling vows. See also *Maharam, Pnei Yehoshua* and *R' Akiva Eiger.*]

[א] [א] השירים והנזמים והטבעות הרי הן ככל הכלים הנטלים בחצר ° ואמר עולא מה טעם הואיל ואיכא תורת כלי עליה הכא נמי הואיל ואיכא תורת כלי עליה א"ר נחמן בר יצחק בריך רחמנא דלא כסיפיה רבא לרב אויא רמי ליה אביי לרבה תניא [ב] מותר השמן שבנר ושבקערה אסור ורבי שמעון מתיר אלמא לר' שמעון לית ליה מוקצה ורמינהו [ג] רבי שמעון אומר כל שאין מומו ניכר מעי"ט אין זה מן המוכן הכי השתא התם אדם יושב ומצפה אימתי תכבה נרו הכא אדם יושב ומצפה מתי יפול בו מום מימר אמר מי יימר דנפיל ביה מומא ואת"ל דנפיל ביה מומא מי יימר דנפיל ביה מום קבוע ואם תמצי לומר דנפל ביה מום קבוע מי יימר דמזדקק ליה חכם מתיב רמי בר חמא [ד] מפירין נדרים בשבת [ונשאלין לנדרים שהן] לצורך השבת ואמאי לימא מי יימר דמיזדקק לה בעל התם כדרב פנחס משמיה דרבא [ה] דאמר רב פנחס משמיה דרבא כל הנודרת על דעת בעלה היא נודרת ת"ש [ו] נשאלין לנדרים של צורך השבת בשבת ואמאי לימא מי יימר דמזדקק ליה חכם התם אי לא מיזדקק ליה חכם סגיא ליה בג' הדיוטות הכא מי יימר דמיזדקק ליה חכם רמי ליה אביי לרבה יוסף מי אמר ר' שמעון כבתה מותר לטלטלה כבתה אין לא כבתה לא מאי טעמא דילמא בהדי דנקיט לה כבתה הא שמעינן ליה לר' שמעון דאמר דבר שאין מתכוין מותר דתניא [ז] ר' שמעון אומר גורר אדם כסא מטה וספסל ובלבד שלא יתכוין לעשות חריץ כל היכא דכי מיכוין איכא איסורא דאורייתא כי לא מיכוין גזר ר"ש מדרבנן כל היכא דכי מיכוין איכא איסורא דרבנן כי לא מיכוין שרי ר"ש לכתחילה מתיב רבא [ח] מוכרי כסות מוכרין כדרכן ובלבד שלא יתכוין בחמה מפני החמה ובגשמים מפני הגשמים והצנועין מפשילין במקל לאחוריהן והא הכא דכי מיכוין איסורא דאורייתא איכא כי לא מיכוין שרי רבי שמעון לכתחילה אלא אמר רבא
הנח

רש"י

השירים. אצעדות: הרי הן ככל הכלים. אע"פ שאסור לצאת בהן לרה"ר כדאמרי' בפרק במה אשה יוצאה (לקמן נט:) גזירה דילמא שלפא ומחויא מיהו תורת כלי עליהן ומותר לטלטלן שלא כדרך מלבוש: מומו ניכר. גבי בכור קאי: מי יימר דמזדקק ליה חכם. שימצא חכם שיזקק לו ביו"ט לראות אם מום קבוע הוא או לא: מפירין נדרים. בעל לאשתו: ונשאלין לנדרים. לחכם להתירן: שהן לצורך שבת. כגון נדר שלא יאכל היום: ואמאי. מותרת לאכול ואפי' שרי לה בעל ליתסר לה משום מוקצה דהא אסחה דעתה ואמרה מי יימר דמזדקק לה בעל: על דעת בעלה. ע"מ אם ירצה הבעל וסמכה עליה דמזדקק לה ביום שמעו: הכא מי יימר כו'. והדיוטות לא מצו למישרייה לבכור אלא במום הידוע לכל כגון מחוסר אבר: איסורא דאורייתא. כיבוי אב מלאכה הוא חריץ ליכא איסור דאורייתא דחופר כלאחר יד הוא דחופר דאמר לקמן תולדה דחורש וחייב ה"מ חופר כדרכו במרא וקרדום: מוכרין כדרכן. ואפי' של כלאים לובשו להראותו בשוק: ובלבד שלא יתכוין. להנאת חימום והא ר"ש היא מדאזיל בתר כוונה:
לדבר

תוספות

ואמר עולא מה טעם. להכי איצטריך לפרושי האי טעמא משום דמשמע ליה דסבר האי תנא כמאן דאסר לקמן להתקשט בהן בחצר מדקתני הרי הן ככל הכלים הניטלין בחצר פירוש ככל הכלים שמלאכתן לאיסור דשרי לצורך גופן ומקומן ולהכי מפרש עולא דאיכא תורת כלי עליה וקשה לר"י דאמר בפ' מי שהפך (מ"ק יב: ושם) ר' יהודה נשיאה נפק בחומרתא דמדושא [עי' פי' רש"י שם] שמע ר' אמי ואיקפיד אמר רב יוסף מ"ט איקפיד והתניא השירים והנזמים כו' ומאי פריך מינה אדרבה מינה משמע דאסור לצאת בהן כדפי' והתם קאמר נפק דמשמע דרך מלבוש ונראה לר"י דחומרתא דמדושא היינו טבעת של עץ כמו שמפרשים רבותיו של רש"י ולא של אלמוג כמו שהוא מפרש דאלמוגין מפרש בראש השנה (דף כג.) כסיתא והכא קאמר דמדושא אלא של עץ אחר הוא ששמו מדושא ואין שם תכשיט עליו וכשיוצאים בו דרך מלבוש לא הוי קישוט אלא טלטול בעלמא ולהכי ידע רב יוסף דר' אמי לא איקפד אלא משום טלטול והשתא מייתי שפיר מהך ברייתא דשרי לטלטל לצורך גופו או לצורך מקומו כשאר כלי' שמלאכתן לאיסור דניטלין לצורך גופו או לצורך מקומו ונפק לחצר קאמר אבל לרה"ר אסור כדאמרי' בפ' הדר (עירובין סט. ושם) ההוא גברא דנפיק בחומרתא דמדושא חזייה לר' יהודה נשיאה כסייה אמר כגון זה מבטל רשות לר' יהודה: והתנן ר"ש אומר כל שאין מומו ניכר מעי"ט אין זה מן המוכן. קשה לר"י מאי קא פריך הא ע"כ טעמא דר"ש לאו משום מוקצה אלא משום דסבר דאין רואין מומין ביו"ט דהא ר' יהודה דאית ליה מוקצה שרי התם בריש אין צדין (ביצה כה: ושם) בכור שנפל לבור ירד מומחה ויראה אם יש בו מום יעלה וישחוט ואם לאו לא ישחוט וי"ל דדייק מדלא קתני ר"ש אוסר לפי שאין רואין מומין בי"ט דהוה משמע לכתחילה אסור אבל בדיעבד מבוקר ומדקתני אין זה מן המוכן משמע דהוי מוקצה ואפי' בקרו אינו מבוקר והכי פליגי דר' יהודה סבר רואין מומין בי"ט הלכך לא הוי מוקצה דמיירי בנפל בו מום מעי"ט כדמוקי לה התם ור"ש סבר אין רואין ולכך אפי' ביקרו אינו מבוקר משום מוקצה וא"ת דבביצה משמע דאביי סבר כאדא בר אוכמי דאמר לר"ש היכא דנפל בו מום מעי"ט אם בקרו מבוקר דאמר אביי התם כוותיה דרבה בר רב הונא מסתברא מדקתני תלת בבי בברייתא [ט] (ומוקמא ההיא ברייתא כאדא בר אוכמי) וע"כ הא דשני ליה בין נפל בו מום קבוע מעי"ט לנפל בו מום בי"ט משום דבנפל בו בי"ט [ב] איכא תלתא מי יימר כדקאמר בסמוך ובנפל בו מעי"ט ליכא אלא חד מי יימר דמיזדקק ליה חכם מאי קשיא מנר שכבה דליכא כל הני מי יימר וי"ל דחזר בו אביי ולית ליה [י] (דאדא בר אוכמי) משמע מתני' דרב אושעיא דאדא בר אוכמי משבש ותני דמתני' דהתם נמי דיקא כרב אושעיא כדמפרש התם: מי יימר דנפל ביה מומא. נראה דכל הני מי יימר דקאמר רבה לאו דווקא דהא ר"ש אסר אפי' בנפל בו מום קבוע מעי"ט דהשתא ליכא אלא חד מי יימר דמיזדקק ליה חכם דהא קאי אר' יהודה דלא שרי אלא כשהיה בו מום קבוע מעי"ט דהא פריך אהא דקאמר ר' יהודה ואם לאו לא ישחוט פשיטא ומשני לא צריכא דנפל ביה מאתמול מום עובר והשתא הוה ליה מום קבוע מהו דתימא כיון דלדעתיה עילויה נשחטיה קמ"ל א"כ הא דקאמר אם יש בו מום יעלה וישחוט היינו ע"כ מום קבוע מעי"ט ואפי' לאדא בר אוכמי דשרי ר"ש בדיעבד בחד מי יימר מ"מ בנפל בו מום עובר מעי"ט דאיכא תרתי מי יימר לכאורה משמע התם דאסר לכך נראה דלאו דוקא הן דאפי' בחד מי יימר סגי וכן מוכחא מאתקפתא דרמי בר חמא דפריך מחד מי יימר: מי יימר דמיזדקק לה בעל. ואע"ג דפירות שנדרה מהם אינם מוקצין לענין טלטול ° דהא חזו לשאר בני אדם מ"מ אית לן למימר מיגו דאיתקצאי בין השמשות מאכילתה איתקצאי לכולי יומא אי נמי איירי בפירות שלה ואסרתן לכל אדם: מי יימר דמיזדקק לה בעל. תימה מי דמי התם ודאי לא מיזדקק ליה חכם אבל הכא דאין לך איסור בדבר מיזדקק לה בעל ולית לן למימר מי יימר דהא לר' יהודה דקסבר רואין מומין בי"ט לא אמרי' מי יימר [ג] וי"ל דבעל נמי לא ניחא להזדקק דזימנין דשרי נדרים שנדרה לדבר מצוה: התם אי לא מיזדקק ליה חכם סגי ליה בג' הדיוטות אבל הכא כו'. ואע"ג דבפ"ק דחולין (דף יח:) אמר רב יהודה אמר ר' ירמיה ספק משמיה דרב ספק משמיה דשמואל ג' מתירין את הבכור במקום שאין מומחה היינו דוקא במומין מובהקין כגון ניסמת עינו נקטעה ידו נשברה רגלו כדאמרינן בשילהי כל פסולי המוקדשין (בכורות לו:) וה"נ דהוה מצי למימר מי יימר דמזדקקי ליה ג' הדיוטות דודאי לא מיזדקקי ליה משום דאין רואין מומין בי"ט והא דנקט דמיזדקק ליה חכם משום דחכם שרי בכל מומין: ולפ"ז א"ש גבי טבל דאמר אם עבר ותיקנו מתוקן דדוקא חכם אמר הכא לא מיזדקק אבל בג' הדיוטות לא אמר מי יימר ומיהו לפי מ"ש בפנים ה"נ המ"ל כו' לא א"ש טבל כדפי' לעיל ולהכי נקט חכם משום דמתיר בכל מומין ועיקר טעמא משום דהכא איכא איסורא והתם ליכא והא דנקט התם אם לא מיזדקק ליה חכם סגיא בג' הדיוטות אע"ג דשרי חשיב מוקצה אי לא סגיא ליה בג' הדיוטות [ת"י]: כבתה אין לא כבתה לא. כן דרך הש"ס דאע"ג דהוה מצי לאתויי רישא דקתני בהדיא חוץ מן הנר הדולק בשבת מייתי סיפא ודייק מינה [כ]: דכל היכא דקמכוין איכא איסורא דאורייתא. וא"ת דהכא בכיבוי ליכא איסורא דאורייתא לר"ש דמלאכה שאינה צריכה לגופה היא וי"ל דה"ק דכי מיכוין איכא איסורא דאורייתא כגון בפתילה וצריך להבהבה ° אע"פ שזה התירוץ דחוק הוא בלאו הכי פריך ליה שפיר הרב פור"ת:
הנח

רבינו חננאל

שני צרורי' הואיל ואינה תורת כלי עליהן כמו (שי"מ עולה) [שא' עולא] בשירים ונזמים וטבעות הואיל [תורת] כלי עליהן: תנא מותר שמן שבנר ושבקערה אסור להסתפק ממנו. ור"ש מתיר. אלמא לר"ש לית ליה מוקצה. ושני הא לענין בכור שנפל בו מום ביו"ט אמר ר"ש אין זה מן המוכן. ושנינן שני זה מזה. אדם מצפה מתי תכבה נרו ויסתפק מן השמן ומכין ליה. אבל לגבי מום ליכא למימר הכי. דאמר מי יימר דנפיל ביה מומא. ואי נפל מי יימר דמזדקק ליה חכם ומותבינן מהא דתנן מפירין נדרים בשבת א) לצורך השבת ושנינן כל הנודרת על דעת בעלה היא נודרת ומבתחלה כך נדרה בחזקת שיפר לה בעלה והא [דתנן] נשאלין נדרים לצורך השבת נימא מי יימר דמיזדקק ליה חכם. ושנינן שני התם דסגיא בג' הדיוטות: רמי אביי מי אמר ר' שמעון כבה הנר מותר לטלטלו. מכלל דאי לא כבה חייש. דילמא אי מטלטל ליה שמא יכבה והא איהו דאמר גורר אדם מטה כסא וספסל ובלבד שלא יתכוין לעשות חריץ הנה דאע"ג דנעשה חריץ כיון דבלא כוונה נעשה לא חייש ר' שמעון. ושני כל היכא דכי מכוין אתי למגע באיסורא דאורייתא כגון כביית הנר וכיוצא בו חייש ר"ש וגזר מדרבנן. וכל היכא דכי מכוין איסורא [דרבנן] היא. כי לא מכוין שרי ר"ש לכתחלה איני והא מוכרי כסות כו' וכלאים איסורא דאורייתא היא. וכי לא מיכוין שרי ר"ש לכתחלה. ומשני רבא

חשק שלמה על רבינו חננאל

א) עי' בחלופי גרסאות:

רב נסים גאון

התם אי לא מזדקק ליה חכם סגיא בג' הדיוטות. משתכח עיקר דילה במסכתא דנדרים בפרק נערה מאורסה (דף עח) אהרן ובניו וכל ישראל בפרשת נדרים למאי הילכתא אמר רב אחא בר יעקב להכשיר ג' הדיוטות וכותיה גרסי' בפרק יש נוחלין (בבא בתרא דף קכ):

מסורת הש"ס

א) מו"ק יב:, ב) [לעיל מד.] ביצה ל:, ג) ביצה כו., ד) לקמן קמ. נדרים עו., ה) יבמות כט: גיטין סג: נדרים עג: נדה מו:, ו) לקמן קמ. נדרים עז:, ז) [תוספתא ביצה פ"ב] [לעיל כב. כט: ביצה כג: פסחים קא. מנחות מא:], ח) כלאים פ"ט מ"ה לעיל כט: פסחים כו:, ט) רש"ל מ"ז, י) רש"ל מ"ז, כ) [עי' תוס' לעיל לט: ד"ה אלא פניו וע' הר"מ].

תוספות ישנים

א) הא דלא מייתי מתניתין דכל הכלים נוטל אדם קורנס לפצוע בו אגוזים. משום דהתם נמי מיוחד להיתר לפצוע בו אגוזים. אבל השירים כו' אין עושין כ"א ללבוש וכיון דאסור להתקשט בהן ה"ל לאסרן לטלטל אפ"ה כיון דאיכא תורת כלי עליה שרי והכא נמי ל"ש:

ב) וליכא למימר דאע"ג דנפל מום מעי"ט איכא ג' מי יימר דהבעלים לא היו יודעים כלל שהיה בו מום. לא היא דהתם מפ' כל שאין מומו ניכר לחכם משמע אבל בעלים יודעים. ולאדא בר אוכמי צ"ל דאע"ג דר"ש איירי דנפל ביה מום מעי"ט מדקאי על ר"י מ"מ איירי נמי בנפל בו מום בי"ט או מום עובר מעי"ט מדקתני אין זה מן המוכן דמשמע אפילו ביקרו אינו מבוקר:

ג) והר"ס תירץ דהכא בנדרים דדמיא בידים הי' לנו לאסור כי התם דלא דמיא בידים:

גליון הש"ס

גמ' ואמר עולא. עי' לקמן דף נט ע"ב תוס' ד"ה מאן דרכה: תוס' ד"ה מי יימר דמזדקק לה בעל ואע"ג וכו' דהא חזו לשאר ב"א. עי' לקמן דף קמ ע"ב תוס' ד"ה כיון דמצי: שם ד"ה דכל היכא וכו' אע"פ שזה התירוץ דחוק. עי' בבכורות דף כה ע"א תוס' ד"ה דהוי ליה:

ליקוטי רש"י

השירים. צמידין [ע"ז מג:]. אצעדה מתרגמינן שירין (במדבר לא) [קידושין מח.]. נושקי"א בלעז [מו"ק יב:]. מותר השמן שבנר ושבקערה. נר קרויזי"ל מותר השמן שנותן בנר או בקערה שמן הניתן להדלקת הנר של שבת וכבה המותר יש בה משום מוקצה ואסור. אדם יושב ומצפה אימתי תכבה נרו. שיודע שסופה לכבות הלכך בין השמשות דעתיה על המותר. הכא אדם יושב ומצפה וכו'. בתמיה וכי נביא הוא [ביצה ל:]. מפירין נדרים בשבת. בעל לאשתו ואב לבתו. שהן לצורך השבת. כגון שנדרה מאכילה או מתכשיטין [נדרים עז.]. כל הנודרת על דעת בעלה היא נודרת. נכי הפרה דבעל גורם הכתוב היא מיהו מש"ה זכתה תורה לבעל בהפרת נדריה משום דעל דעת בעלה היא נודרת [ר"ן שם עג:]. על דעת בעלה על מנת שאם ירצה ואם לאו לא יהא נדר [גיטין סג:]. לא כבתה לא. בעוד שהוא דולק אסור שמא יכבה הנר [לעיל מד.]. גורר אדם כסא מטה וספסל. ואף על גב דקעביד חריץ והוי תולדה דחורש או בונה [שם כב.]. מוכרין כדרכן. כסות של כלאים לובשו בשוק כדי להראותו למוכרו דלא אסרה תורה אלא לבישה שהיא להתחמם כדרך כל הלובשים והעלאה דומיא דלבישה נמי דמיתהני בה [שם כט:]. מעוטפין בכסות כלאים דאין מתכוין להנאת לבישה. והצנועין. פרושים שמתרחקין מן הכיעור ומן הדומה לו [פסחים כו:]. כשרים שמרחיקין עצמן מכל לזות שפתים [לעיל שם].

to eat a certain food on the Sabbath, her husband may annul the vow and she may then eat it. וְאַמַּאי – **But why?** לֵימָא מִי יֵימַר דְּמִיזְדַּקֵּק לָהּ בַּעַל – **We should say** that at the onset of the Sabbath there exists the doubt of **who is to say that the husband will get involved with** annulling **[the vow]?** Since the woman cannot anticipate that the vow will be annulled, the item embraced by it should remain *muktzeh* for her even after the annulment.[10] – ? –

The Gemara rejects the challenge:

הָתָם כִּדְרַב פִּנְחָס מִשְּׁמֵיהּ דְּרָבָא – **There, it is as Rav Pinchas said in the name of Rava.** דְּאָמַר רַב פִּנְחָס מִשְּׁמֵיהּ דְּרָבָא – **For Rav Pinchas said in the name of Rava:** כֹּל הַנּוֹדֶרֶת – **Any woman who vows,** עַל דַּעַת בַּעְלָהּ הִיא נוֹדֶרֶת – **vows subject to the consent of her husband.** Since she bases her vow on her husband's consent, she anticipates that he will get involved with annulling it when he hears about it.[11]

Although this solution resolves the difficulty posed by the first clause of the Mishnah, there remains a difficulty with the second clause, as the Gemara proceeds to point out:

תָּא שְׁמַע – **Come, learn** a refutation from the next clause of this Mishnah, which teaches that נִשְׁאָלִין לִנְדָרִים שֶׁל צוֹרֶךְ הַשַּׁבָּת בְּשַׁבָּת – **we may seek release from vows on the Sabbath** for things **that are necessary for the Sabbath.** Thus, if one vowed not to eat a certain food, he can petition a sage to release him from his vow and may then eat it. וְאַמַּאי – **But why?** לֵימָא מִי יֵימַר דְּמִיזְדַּקֵּק לֵיהּ חָכָם – **We should say** that at the onset of the Sabbath there exists the doubt of **who is to say that a sage will get involved with** releasing **[the vow],** and the item should therefore be *muktzeh.* – ? –

The Gemara answers:

הָתָם אִי לֹא מִיזְדַּקֵּק לֵיהּ חָכָם סַגְיָא לֵיהּ בִּשְׁלֹשָׁה הֶדְיוֹטוֹת – **There, even if a sage does not get involved with it, three laymen are sufficient to** release **him** from the vow. Since one can always find three laymen, he anticipates that he may be released from the vow on the Sabbath, and the item is therefore not *muktzeh.* הָכָא מִי יֵימַר דְּמִיזְדַּקֵּק לֵיהּ חָכָם – **Here,** however, in the case of *bechor,* which can be declared blemished *only* by a qualified expert, **who is to say that an expert will** be willing to **get involved with** examining **[the *bechor*]?** Thus, one cannot anticipate that the *bechor* will become permitted on the festival.

The Gemara revisits R' Shimon's earlier ruling (on 44a) that it is permitted to move a lamp on the Sabbath after it has gone out:

רָמֵי לֵיהּ אַבַּיֵי לְרַב יוֹסֵף – **Abaye posed** the following **contradiction to Rav Yosef:** מִי אָמַר רַבִּי שִׁמְעוֹן ,,כָּבְתָה מוּתָּר לְטַלְטְלָהּ" – **Did R' Shimon say: "Once [a lamp] has gone out it is permitted to move it,"** implying that כָּבְתָה אִין לֹא כָּבְתָה לֹא – only after **it has gone out** is it **indeed** permitted to move it, but if **it has not** yet **gone out,** it is **not** permitted to move it? מַאי טַעְמָא – **And what is** presumably **the reason** for the prohibition of moving it while it is burning? דִּילְמָא בַּהֲדֵי דְּנָקִיט לָהּ כָּבְתָה – It is the concern that **perhaps while one carries it, it will be extinguished,** and he will have unintentionally committed the prohibited act of extinguishing a flame.[12] הָא שְׁמָעִינַן לֵיהּ לְרַבִּי שִׁמְעוֹן דְּאָמַר – **But we have learned that R' Shimon says** that דָּבָר שֶׁאֵין מִתְכַּוֵּין מוּתָּר – **something that is unintended is permitted!**[13] דְּתַנְיָא – **For it was taught in a Baraisa:** רַבִּי שִׁמְעוֹן אוֹמֵר – **R' SHIMON SAYS:** גּוֹרֵר אָדָם כִּסֵּא מִטָּה וְסַפְסָל – **A PERSON MAY DRAG A CHAIR, BED OR BENCH** across the ground on the Sabbath, וּבִלְבַד שֶׁלֹּא יִתְכַּוֵּין לַעֲשׂוֹת חָרִיץ – **SO LONG AS HE DOES NOT INTEND TO MAKE A FURROW.** Since R' Shimon holds that something that is unintended is permitted, he should permit moving a burning lamp, so long as one does not intend to extinguish it. – ? –

Rav Yosef responds:

כָּל הֵיכָא דְּכִי מִיכַּוֵּין אִיכָּא אִיסוּרָא דְּאוֹרָיְיתָא – **Wherever** circumstances are such that **if one would intend** for the forbidden act **there would be a Biblical prohibition** against it, such as the case of extinguishing a lamp by moving it, כִּי לֹא מִיכַּוֵּין גָּזַר רַבִּי שִׁמְעוֹן מִדְּרַבָּנָן – even **when one does not intend** for it **R' Shimon decrees** that the act which may lead to it is prohibited **Rabbinically.** כָּל הֵיכָא דְּכִי מִיכַּוֵּין אִיכָּא אִיסוּרָא דְּרַבָּנָן – But **wherever** circumstances are such that even **if one would intend** for the forbidden act **there would be** only **a Rabbinical prohibition** against it, such as the case of digging a furrow by dragging a bench, כִּי לֹא מִיכַּוֵּין שָׁרֵי רַבִּי שִׁמְעוֹן לְכַתְּחִילָּה – **when one does not intend** for it **R' Shimon permits outright** the act which may lead to it.[14]

Rav Yosef's resolution is challenged:

מָתִיב רָבָא – **Rava challenged** this on the basis of the following

NOTES

10. Although others are allowed to eat the food, the woman herself should not be allowed to eat it since she could not have anticipated its availability and it is thus *muktzeh* for her. [She would be allowed to move the food, since it is fit for consumption by others and is thus not subject to the prohibition against moving *muktzeh*. However, since it was not "prepared" for her consumption, she should be barred from eating it under the prohibition of consuming *muktzeh*] (see *Rashi, Tosafos* in [ד״ה מי יימר דמיזדקיק לה בעל [א and *Rashba;* see also *Tosafos* to 127b ד״ה כיון דחזיא and Chapter Introduction; cf. *Ramban* to 47a ד״ה קרטין).

[The Rishonim point out a dissimilarity between this case and that of *bechor.* It is understandable that one cannot anticipate that his *bechor* will be pronounced blemished on Yom Tov, since it is *prohibited* for an expert to pass judgment on a *bechor's* blemish on Yom Tov. But perhaps a woman does anticipate that her husband will do the *permitted* act of annulling her vow on the Sabbath!? *Ritva* (*MHK* ed.) answers that the pertinent point is that since it is not within her power to make the food available to herself, nor can she expect this to occur through natural means, she abandons hope of using it. Any item that can become available only through the intervention of another person who is not under one's control is not considered "prepared" for Sabbath use, even according to R' Shimon. Thus, the basis for prohibiting its consumption is not the fact that it was *muktzeh* during *bein hashemashos,* but the fact that the owner abandoned all hope of using it, thus rendering it *muktzeh* for the entire Sabbath (see also *Rashi* ד״ה ואמאי; cf. *Tosafos* in [ד״ה מי יימר דמיזדקיק לה בעל [ב).]

11. *Rashi.* I.e. she relies upon the reasonable possibility that he will choose to annul her vow, and thus, she does not abandon hope of eating the food (*Dibros Moshe* 34:45).

12. [Abaye presumes that since R' Shimon follows a narrow definition of *muktzeh,* his only possible basis for prohibiting movement of the burning lamp is the concern that it might thereby be extinguished.]

Although we concluded above (45a) that R' Shimon recognizes the concept of *muktzeh by dint of a mitzvah,* he would not prohibit moving the lit Sabbath lamp on that basis, since moving it does not detract from the mitzvah. He relies on that concept only to prohibit taking oil from the lamp (*Tosafos* to 42b ד״ה ואין ניאותין). See *Tosafos* ד״ה כבתה, *Rosh Yosef, R' Akiva Eiger* and *Chidushei R' Elazar Moshe Horowitz.*

13. I.e. it is permitted to engage in a permissible act notwithstanding the possibility that he will incidentally perform a prohibited act (see 41b note 2).

14. Since *extinguishing* is a Biblically prohibited *melachah* [and shaking a lamp is a normal way of extinguishing it], R' Shimon forbids moving a burning lamp even if one does not intend to extinguish it. By contrast, digging furrows by dragging a bench across the ground is an unusual method of digging and therefore does not fall under the Biblical prohibition. Only digging in the normal manner with a shovel or spade is prohibited Biblically (*Rashi;* see *Tosafos* ד״ה דכל היכא and General Introduction to this tractate). Since dragging a bench with intent to dig would be prohibited only Rabbinically, R' Shimon permits dragging it when one does not intend to dig. See *Tosafos* to *Pesachim* 25b ד״ה לא אפשר.

א) [א] השירים והנזמים והטבעות הרי הן ככל הכלים הנטלים בחצר • ואמר עולא מה טעם הואיל ואיכא תורת כלי עליה הכא נמי הואיל ואיכא תורת כלי עליה א"ר נחמן בר יצחק בריך רחמנא דלא כסיפיה רבא לרב אויא רמי ליה אביי לרבה תניא ב) מותר השמן שבנר ושבקערה אסור ורבי שמעון מתיר אלמא לר' שמעון לית ליה מוקצה ורמינהו ג) רבי שמעון אומר כל שאין מומו ניכר מעי"ט אין זה מן המוכן הכי השתא התם אדם יושב ומצפה אימתי תכבה נרו הכא אדם יושב ומצפה מתי יפול בו מום מימר אמר מי יימר דנפיל ביה מומא ואת"ל דנפיל ביה מומא מי יימר דנפיל ביה מום קבוע ואם תמצי לומר דנפל ביה מום קבוע מי יימר דמזדקק ליה חכם מתיב רמי בר חמא ד) מפירין נדרים בשבת [ונשאלין לנדרים שהן] לצורך השבת ואמאי לימא מי יימר דמיזדקק לה בעל התם כדרב פנחס משמיה דרבא ה) דאמר רב פנחס משמיה דרבא כל הנודרת על דעת בעלה היא נודרת ת"ש ו) נשאלין לנדרים של צורך השבת בשבת ואמאי לימא מי יימר דמזדקק ליה חכם התם אי לא מיזדקק ליה חכם סגיא ליה בג' הדיוטות הכא מי יימר דמיזדקק ליה חכם רמי ליה אביי לרב יוסף מי אמר ר' שמעון כבתה מותר לטלטלה כבתה אין לא כבתה לא מאי טעמא דילמא בהדי דנקיט לה כבתה הא שמעינן ליה לר' שמעון דאמר דבר שאין מתכוין מותר דתניא ז) ר' שמעון אומר גורר אדם כסא מטה וספסל ובלבד שלא יתכוון לעשות חריץ כל היכא דכי מיכוון איכא איסורא דאורייתא כי לא מיכוון גזר ר"ש מדרבנן כל היכא דכי מיכוון איכא איסורא דרבנן כי לא מיכוון שרי ר"ש לכתחילה מתיב רבא ח) מוכרי כסות מוכרין כדרכן ובלבד שלא יתכוין בחמה מפני החמה ובגשמים מפני הגשמים והצנועין מפשילין במקל לאחוריהן והא הכא דכי מיכוון איסורא דאורייתא איכא כי לא מיכוון שרי רבי שמעון לכתחילה אלא אמר רבא
הנח

רש"י

השירים. אצעדות: הרי הן ככל הכלים. אע"פ שאסור לצאת בהן לרה"ר כדאמרי' בפרק במה אשה יוצאה (לקמן נט:) גזירה דילמא שלפא ומחויא מיהו תורת כלי עליהן ומותר לטלטלן שלא כדרך מלבוש: מומו ניכר. גבי בכור קאי: מי יימר דמזדקק ליה חכם. שימצא חכם שיזקק לו ביו"ט לראות אם מום קבוע הוא או לא: מפירין נדרים. בעל לאשתו: ונשאלין לנדרים. לחכם להתירן: שהן לצורך שבת. כגון נדר שלא יאכל היום: ואמאי. מותרת לאכול ואפי' שרי לה בעל ליתסר לה משום מוקצה דהא אסחה דעתה ואמרה מי יימר דמזדקק לה בעל: על דעת בעלה. ע"מ אם ירצה הבעל וסמכה עליה דמזדקק לה ביום שמעו: הכא מי יימר כו'. והדיוטות לא מצו למישרייה לבכור אלא במום הידוע לכל כגון מחוסר אבר: איסורא דאורייתא. כיבוי אב מלאכה הוא חריץ ליכא איסור דאורייתא דחופר כלאחר יד הוא דחופר דאמר לקמן תולדה דחורש וחייב ה"מ חופר כדרכו במרא וקרדום: מוכרין כדרכן. ואפי' של כלאים לובשו להראותו בשוק: ובלבד שלא יתכוין. להנאת חימום והא ר"ש היא מדאזיל בתר כוונה:
לדבר

תוספות

ואמר עולא מה טעם. להכי אצטריך לפרושי האי טעמא משום דמשמע ליה דסבר האי תנא כמאן דאסר לקמן להתקשט בהן בחצר מדקתני הרי הן ככל הכלים הניטלין בחצר פירוש ככל הכלים שמלאכתן לאיסור דשרי לצורך גופן ומקומן ולהכי מפרש עולא דאיכא תורת כלי עליה וקשה לר"י דאמר בפ' מי שהפך (מ"ק יב: ושם) ר' יהודה נשיאה נפק בחומרתא דמדושא [עי' פי' רש"י שם] שמע ר' אמי ואיקפיד אמר רב יוסף מ"ט איקפיד והתניא השירים והנזמים כו' ומאי פריך מינה אדרבה מינה משמע דאסור לצאת בהן כדפי' והתם קאמר נפק דמשמע דרך מלבוש ונראה לר"י דחומרתא דמדושא היינו טבעת של עץ כמו שמפרשים רבותיו של רש"י ולא של אלמוג כמו שהוא מפרש דאלמוגין מפרש בראש השנה (דף כג.) כסיתא והכא קאמר דמדושא אלא של עץ אחר הוא ששמו מדושא ואין שם תכשיט עליו וכשיוצאים בו דרך מלבוש לא הוי קישוט אלא טלטול בעלמא ולהכי ידע רב יוסף דר' אמי לא איקפד אלא משום טלטול והשתא מייתי שפיר מהך ברייתא דשרי לטלטל לצורך גופו או לצורך מקומו כשאר כלי' שמלאכתן לאיסור דניטלין לצורך גופו או לצורך מקומו ונפק לחצר קאמר אבל לרה"ר אסור כדאמרי' בפ' הדר (עירובין סט. ושם) ההוא גברא דנפיק בחומרתא דמדושא חזייה לר' יהודה נשיאה כסייה אמר כגון זה מבטל רשות לר' יהודה: והתנן ר"ש אומר כל שאין מומו ניכר מעי"ט אין זה מן המוכן. קשה לר"י מאי קא פריך הא ע"כ טעמא דר"ש לאו משום מוקצה אלא משום דסבר דאין רואין מומין ביו"ט דהא ר' יהודה דאית ליה טפי מוקצה שרי התם בריש אין צדין (ביצה כה: ושם) בכור שנפל לבור יורד מומחה ורואה אם יש בו מום יעלה וישחוט ואם לאו לא ישחוט וי"ל דדייק מדלא קתני ר"ש אוסר לפי שאין רואין מומין בי"ט דהוה משמע לכתחילה אסור אבל בדיעבד מבוקר ומדקתני אין זה מן המוכן משמע דהוי מוקצה ואפי' בקרו אינו מבוקר ובהכי פליגי דר' יהודה סבר רואין מומין בי"ט הלכך לא הוי מוקצה דמיירי בנפל בו מום מעי"ט כדמוקי לה התם ור"ש סבר אין רואין ולכך אפי' ביקרו אינו מבוקר משום מוקצה ואת"ל דבבילה משמע דאביי סבר כאדא בר אוכמי דאמר לר"ש היכא דנפל בו מום מעי"ט אם בקרו מבוקר דאמר אביי התם כוותיה דרבה בר רב הונא מסתברא מדקתני תלת בבי בברייתא ט) (ומוקמא ההיא ברייתא כאדא בר אוכמי) וע"כ הא דשני ליה בין נפל בו מום קבוע מעי"ט לנפל בו מום בי"ט משום דבי"ט ב) איכא תלתא מי יימר כדקאמר בסמוך ונפל בו מעי"ט ליכא אלא חד מי יימר דמיזדקק ליה חכם מאי קשיא מנר שכבה דליכא כל הני מי יימר וי"ל דחזר בו אביי ולית ליה י) (דאדא בר אוכמי) משמע מתני' דרב אושעיא דאדא בר אוכמי משבש ותני דמתני' דהתם נמי דיקא כרב אושעיא כדמפרש התם: מי יימר דנפל ביה מומא. נראה דכל הני מי יימר דקאמר רבה לאו דווקא דהא ר"ש אסר אפי' בנפל בו מום קבוע מעי"ט דהשתא ליכא אלא חד מי יימר דמיזדקק ליה חכם דהא קאי אר' יהודה דלא שרי אלא כשהיה בו מום קבוע מעי"ט דהא פריך אהא דקאמר ר' יהודה ואם לאו לא ישחוט פשיטא ומשני לא צריכא דנפל ביה מאתמול מום עובר והשתא הוה ליה מום קבוע מהו דתימא כיון דדעתיה עילויה נשחטיה קמ"ל א"כ הא דקאמר אם יש בו מום יעלה וישחוט היינו ע"כ מום קבוע מעי"ט ואפי' לאדא בר אוכמי דשרי ר"ש בדיעבד בחד מי יימר מ"מ בנפל בו מום עובר מעי"ט דאיכא תרתי מי יימר לכאורה משמע התם דאסר לכך נראה דלאו דוקא הן דאפי' בחד מי יימר סגי וכן מוכחא מאתקפתא דרמי בר חמא דפריך מחד מי יימר: מי יימר דמיזדקק לה בעל. ואע"ג דפירות שנדרה מהם אינם מוקצין לענין טלטול • דהא חזו לשאר בני אדם מ"מ אית לן למימר מיגו דאיתקצאי בין השמשות מאכילתם איתקצאי לכולי יומא אי נמי מיירי בפירות שלה ואסרתן לכל אדם: מי יימר דמיזדקק לה בעל. תימה מי דמי התם ודאי לא מיזדקק ליה חכם דאין רואין מומין בי"ט אבל הכא דאין לך איסור בדבר מיזדקק לה בעל ולית לן למימר מי יימר דהא לר' יהודה דקסבר רואין מומין בי"ט לא אמרי' מי יימר ג) וי"ל דבעל נמי לא ניחא להזדקק דזימנין דשרי נדרים שנדרה לדבר מצוה: התם אי לא מיזדקק ליה חכם סגי ליה בג' הדיוטות אבל הכא כו'. ואע"ג דבפ"ק דחולין (דף יח:) אמר רב יהודה אמר ר' ירמיה ספק משמיה דרב ספק משמיה דשמואל ג' מתירין את הבכור במקום שאין מומחה היינו דוקא במומין מובהקין כגון ניסמת עינו נקטעה ידו נשברה רגלו כדאמרינן בשילהי כל פסולי המוקדשין (בכורות לו:) וה"נ דהוה מצי למימר מי יימר דמזדקקי ליה ג' הדיוטות דודאי לא מיזדקקי ליה משום דאין רואין מומין בי"ט והא דנקט דמיזדקק ליה חכם משום דחכם שרי בכל מומין:

ולפ"ז א"ש גבי טבל דאמר אם עבר ותיקנו מתוקן דדוקא חכם אמר הכא לא מיזדקק אבל בג' הדיוטות לא אמר מי יימר ומיהו לפי מ"ש בפנים ה"נ המ"ל כו' לא א"ש טבל כדפי' לעיל ולהכי נקט חכם משום דמתיר בכל מומין ועיקר טעמא משום דהכא איכא איסורא והתם ליכא והא דנקט התם אם לא מיזדקק ליה חכם סגיא בג' הדיוטות אע"ג דשרי חשיב מוקצה אי לא סגיא ליה בג' הדיוטות [ת"י]:

כבתה אין לא כבתה לא. כן דרך הש"ס דאע"ג דהוה מצי לאתויי רישא דקתני בהדיא חוץ מן הנר הדולק בשבת מייתי סיפא ודייק מינה כ): דכל היכא דקמכוין איכא איסורא דאורייתא. וא"ת דהכא בכיבוי ליכא איסורא דאורייתא לר"ש דמלאכה שאינה צריכה לגופה היא וי"ל דה"ק דכי מיכוין איכא איסורא דאורייתא כגון בפתילה וצריך להבהבה • אע"פ שזה התירוץ דחוק הוא הא בלאו הכי פריך ליה שפיר הרב פור"ת:
הנח

רבינו חננאל

שני צרורו' הואיל ואינה תורת כלי עליהן כמו (ש"מ עולה) [שא' עולא] בשירים ונזמים וטבעות הואיל [תורת] כלי עליהן: **תנא** מותר שמן שבנר ושבקערה אסור להסתפק ממנו. ור"ש מתיר. אלמא לר"ש לית ליה מוקצה. איני והא לענין בכור שנפל בו מום ביו"ט אמר ר"ש אין זה מן המוכן. ושנינן שני זה מזה. אדם מצפה מתי תכבה נרו ויסתפק מן השמן ומכין ליה. אבל לגבי מום ליכא למימר הכי. דאמר מי יימר דנפיל ביה מומא. ואי נפל מי יימר דמזדקיק ליה חכם ומותבינן מהא דתנן מפירין נדרים בשבת א) לצורך השבת ושנינן כל הנודרת על דעת בעלה היא נודרת ומבתחלה כך נדרה בחזקת שיפר לה בעלה והא [דתנן] נשאלין נדרים לצורך השבת נימא מי יימר דמיזדקיק ליה חכם. ושנינן שני התם דסגיא בג' הדיוטות: **רמי** אביי ומי אמר ר' שמעון כבה הנר מותר לטלטלו. מכלל דאי לא כבה חייש. דילמא כי מטלטל ליה שמא יכבה והא איהו דאמר גורר אדם מטה כסא וספסל ובלבד שלא יתכוין לעשות חריץ הנה דאע"ג דנעשה חריץ כיון דבלא כוונה נעשה לא חייש ר' שמעון. ושני כל היכא דכי מכוין אתי למנגע באיסורא דאורייתא כגון כביית הנר וכיוצא בו חייש ר"ש וגזר מדרבנן. וכל היכא דכי מכוין איסורא [דרבנן] היא. כי לא מכוין שרי ר"ש לכתחלה איני והא מוכרי כסות כו' וכלאים איסורא דאורייתא היא. וכי לא מיכוין שרי ר"ש לכתחלה. ומשני רבא

חשק שלמה על רבינו חננאל

א) עי' בתוספי גרסאות:

רב נסים גאון

התם אי לא מזדקק ליה חכם סגיא בג' הדיוטות. משתכח עיקר דילה במסכתא דנדרים בפרק נערה מאורסה (דף עח) אהרן ובניו וכל ישראל בפרשת נדרים למאי הילכתא אמר רב אחא בר יעקב להכשיר ג' הדיוטות וכותיה גרסי' בפרק יש נוחלין (בבא בתרא דף קכ):

מסורת הש"ס

א) מו"ק יב:, ב) [לעיל מד.] ביצה ל:, ג) ביצה כו:, ד) לקמן קמ. נדרים עז:, ה) יבמות כט: גיטין פג: נדרים עג: נדה מו:, ו) לקמן קמ. נדרים עז:, ז) [תוספתא ביצה פ"ב] [לעיל כב. כט: ביצה כג: פסחים קא. מנחות מא:], ח) כלאים פ"ט מ"ה לעיל כט: פסחים כו:, ט) רש"ל מ"ז, י) רש"ל מ"ז, כ) [עי' תוס' לעיל לט: ד"ה אלא פניו וע' הר"מ].

תוספות ישנים

א) הא דלא מייתי מתניתין דכל הכלים נוטל אדם קורנס לפצוע בו אגוזים. משום דהתם נמי מיוחד להיתר לפצוע בו אגוזים. אבל השירים כו' אין עושין כ"א ללבוש וכיון דאסור להתקשט בהן ה"ל לאסרן לטלטל אפ"ה כיון דאיכא תורת כלי עליה שרי והכא נמי ל"ש:

ב) וליכא למימר דאע"ג דנפל מום מעי"ט איכא ג' מי יימר דהבעלים לא היו יודעים כלל שהיה בו מום. לא היא דהתם מפ' כל שאין מומו ניכר לחכם משמע אבל בעלים יודעים. ולאדא בר אוכמי צ"ל דאע"ג דר"ש איירי דנפל ביה מום מעי"ט מדקאי על ר"י מ"מ מיירי נמי בנפל בו מום בי"ט או מום עובר מעי"ט מדקתני אין זה מן המוכן דמשמע אפילו ביקרו אינו מבוקר:

ג) והר"ס תירץ דהכא בנדרים דדמיא בידים הי' לנו לאסור כי התם דלא דמיא בידים:

גליון הש"ס

גמ' ואמר עולא. עי' לקמן דף נט ע"ב תוס' ד"ה מאן דרכה: תוס' ד"ה מי יימר דמזדקק לה בעל ואע"ג וכו' דהא חזי לשאר ב"א. עי' לקמן דף קמ ע"ב תוס' ד"ה כיון דתניא: שם ד"ה דכל היכא וכו' אע"פ שזה התירוץ דחוק. עי' בבכורות דף כה ע"א תוס' ד"ה דהוי ליה:

ליקוטי רש"י

השירים. לצמידין [ע"ז מג:]. אצעדה מתרגמינן שירין (במדבר לא) [קידושין מח.]. נוסקי"א בלעז [מו"ק יב:]. **מותר השמן שבנר ושבקערה.** נר קרוזיי"ל מותר השמן שנותן בנר או בקערה שמן הניתן להדלקת הנר של שבת וכבה המותר יש בה משום מוקצה ואסור. **אדם יושב ומצפה אימתי תכבה נרו.** שיודע שסופה לכבות הלכך בין השמשות דעתיה על המותר. **הכא אדם יושב ומצפה וכו'.** בתמיה וכי נביא הוא [ביצה ל:]. **מפירין נדרים בשבת.** בעל לאשתו ואב לבתו. **שהן לצורך השבת.** כגון שנדרה מאכילה או מתכשיטין [נדרים עז.]. **כל הנודרת על דעת בעלה היא נודרת.** נהי דהפרה דבעל גזרת הכתוב היא מיהו מש"ה זכתה תורה לבעל בהפרת נדריה משום דעל דעת בעלה היא נודרת [ר"ן שם עג:]. **על דעת בעלה.** על מנת שאם ירצה ואם לאו לא יהא נדר [גיטין פג:]. **לא כבתה לא.** בעוד שהוא דולק אסור שמא יכבה הנר [לעיל מד.]. **גורר אדם כסא מטה וספסל.** ואף על גב דקעביד חריץ והוי תולדה דחורש או בונה [שם כב.]. **מוכרין כדרכן.** כסות של כלאים לובשו בשוק כדי להראותו למוכרו דלא אסרה תורה אלא לבישה שהיא להתחמם כדרך כל הלובשים והעלאה דומיא דלבישה נמי דמיתהני בה [שם כט:]. מעוטפין בכסות כלאים דאין מתכוין להנאת לבישה. **והצנועין.** פרושים שמתרחקין מן הכיעור ומן הדומה לו [פסחים כו:]. כשרים שמרחקין עצמן מכל לזות שפתים [לעיל שם].

Mishnah:[15] מוֹכְרֵי כְסוּת מוֹכְרִין כְּדַרְכָּן – GARMENT SELLERS MAY SELL IN THEIR USUAL MANNER[16] וּבִלְבַד שֶׁלֹּא יִתְכַּוֵּין בַּחַמָּה מִפְּנֵי הַחַמָּה – SO LONG AS THEY DO NOT INTEND IN THE SUMMER[17] to protect themselves FROM THE SUN, וּבַגְּשָׁמִים מִפְּנֵי הַגְּשָׁמִים – AND IN THE WINTER[18] to protect themselves FROM THE RAIN and cold.[19] וְהַצְּנוּעִין מַפְשִׁילִין בְּמַקֵּל לַאֲחוֹרֵיהֶן – AND THE DISCREET ONES[20] HANG them ON A STICK BEHIND THEM. וְהָא הָכָא דְּכִי מִיכַּוֵּין אִיסוּרָא דְּאוֹרַיְיתָא אִיכָּא – Now here, if [the salesman] would intend to derive benefit from the garment there would be a Biblical prohibition against wearing it, כִּי לֹא מִיכַּוֵּין שָׁרֵי רַבִּי שִׁמְעוֹן לְכַתְּחִילָּה – yet when he does not intend to derive benefit, R' Shimon, whose view this Mishnah reflects, permits him to wear the garment outright. Clearly R' Shimon permits that which is unintended even when an intentional performance of the same act would involve a Biblical prohibition. – ? –

Having refuted Rav Yosef's thesis, Rava offers a different explanation of why R' Shimon prohibits moving a lamp while it is still burning even though one has no intention of extinguishing it: אֶלָּא אָמַר רָבָא – Rather, Rava said:

NOTES

15. *Kilayim* 9:5.

16. Garment sellers are allowed to wear their *shaatnez*-containing merchandise in order to model it for customers, for the Torah prohibits the wearing of *shaatnez* (*Deuteronomy* 22:11) only when the garment is worn for the usual purpose of providing physical benefit to the wearer. The garment seller, however, does not don *shaatnez* apparel for his own pleasure (*Rashi* here and above, 29b). [*Ritva MHK* ed. (above, 29b) disputes *Rashi's* interpretation of the Mishnah, arguing that in the winter it is inevitable (פְּסִיק רֵישָׁא) that the seller will be warmed by the *shaatnez* garment (cf. *Tosafos* ד״ה ובלבד; see also *Ran* to *Chullin,* fol. 32a of *Rif*). *Ritva* therefore understands the Mishnah as permitting the seller only to drape the *shaatnez* garment over his shoulder, in which case such enjoyment is not inevitable. See also *Ramban* below, 111a, and *Kesef Mishneh, Hil. Kilayim* 10:18.]

17. Literally: sun.

18. Literally: rain.

19. This Mishnah follows the opinion of R' Shimon, who holds that – with respect to any prohibition in the Torah – something that is unintended is permitted (*Rashi*).

20. Those who eschew even the permissible wearing of *shaatnez* so as to distance themselves from becoming potential objects of slander (*Rashi* to 29b).

הַנַּח לְנֵר שֶׁמֶן וּפְתִילָה – **Leave** the issue of **a lamp** and its **oil and wick aside;** these may not be moved while the lamp is burning, הואיל (ד)[ו]נַעֲשָׂה בָּסִיס לְדָבָר הָאָסוּר – **because they serve as a base to something that** it **is forbidden** to move, viz. the flame.[1]

Having mentioned the concept of a *base to muktzeh,* the Gemara cites a related discussion:

אָמַר רַבִּי זֵירָא אָמַר רַבִּי אַסִּי אָמַר רַבִּי יוֹחָנָן אָמַר רַבִּי חֲנִינָא אָמַר רַבִּי רוּמָנוּס – **R' Zeira said in the name of R' Assi, who said in the name of R' Yochanan, who said in the name of R' Chanina, who said in the name of R' Rumnus:** לִי הִתִּיר רַבִּי לְטַלְטֵל מַחְתָּה בְּאֶפְרָהּ – **Rebbi permitted me to move a censer along with its** leftover **ashes.**[2] אָמַר לֵיהּ ר׳ זֵירָא לְר׳ אַסִּי – **R' Zeira,** when he heard this teaching, **said to R' Assi:** מִי אָמַר ר׳ יוֹחָנָן הָכִי – **Did R' Yochanan say this?** וְהָתְנַן – **But we learned in a Mishnah:**[3] נוֹטֵל אָדָם בְּנוֹ וְהָאֶבֶן בְּיָדוֹ – A MAN MAY TAKE HIS SON in his arms WHEN THERE IS A STONE IN HIS HAND,[4] אוֹ כַּלְכָּלָה וְהָאֶבֶן בְּתוֹכָהּ – OR A BASKET WHEN THERE IS A STONE INSIDE IT. וְאָמַר רַבָּה בַּר בַּר חָנָה אָמַר רַבִּי יוֹחָנָן – **And Rabbah bar bar Chanah said in the name of R' Yochanan:** בְּכַלְכָּלָה מְלֵאָה פֵּירוֹת עָסְקִינַן – In this Mishnah, **we are dealing** specifically **with a basket** that is **filled with fruit** and is thus not considered a base to the *muktzeh* stone.[5] טַעְמָא דְאִית בָּהּ פֵּירֵי – R' Yochanan has thus taught that **the reason** the basket may be moved **is that it contains fruit,** הָא לֵית בָּהּ פֵּירֵי לֹא – **but** if it **would not contain fruit** it could **not** be moved, for it would be a *base to muktzeh.* How then could R' Yochanan have stated that Rebbi permitted moving a censer that is filled with *muktzeh* ashes?[6]

The Gemara records R' Assi's reaction:

אִישְׁתּוֹמֵם כְּשָׁעָה חֲדָא – **He was confounded for a moment,**[7] וְאָמַר – **and** then **said:** הָכָא נַמִּי דְאִית בֵּיהּ קַרְטִין – **Here too,** we are dealing with a case **where [the censer] contains** some leftover **granules** of unburned incense and is thus not considered a *base to muktzeh.*[8]

R' Assi's explanation is rejected:

אָמַר אַבַּיֵי – **Abaye said:** קַרְטִין בֵּי רַבִּי מִי חֲשִׁיבֵי – **Were** leftover incense **granules of any significance in Rebbi's house?** Certainly not! Thus, the censer should have been considered *a base to muktzeh* even if it contained some granules.[9] וְכִי תֵּימָא חֲזוּ לַעֲנִיִּים – **And if you should say** that since **[the granules] are fit for** the use of **poor people** their presence in the censer is a mitigating factor even in the house of a wealthy person like Rebbi, I will counter: וְהַתַנְיָא – **But it was taught in a Baraisa:** בִּגְדֵי עֲנִיִּים לַעֲנִיִּים – CLOTHING FIT FOR POOR PEOPLE is classified as clothing FOR POOR PEOPLE and is susceptible to *tumah* when in their possession; בִּגְדֵי עֲשִׁירִים לַעֲשִׁירִים – CLOTHING FIT FOR WEALTHY PEOPLE is classified as clothing FOR WEALTHY PEOPLE and is susceptible to *tumah* when in their possession.[10] This implies: אֲבָל דַּעֲנִיִּים לַעֲשִׁירִים לֹא – **But** clothing fit **for poor people** is **not** classified as clothing **for wealthy people** and is not susceptible to *tumah* when in their possession. It follows that a censer containing leftover granules that are fit only for poor people is *muktzeh* when in the possession of a wealthy person.[11] – ? –

Having rejected R' Assi's reasoning, Abaye offers his own explanation of why Rebbi permitted R' Rumnus to move the censer:

אֶלָּא אָמַר אַבַּיֵי – **Rather, Abaye said:** מִידֵי דַהֲוָה אַגְּרָף שֶׁל רְעִי – It is **because [a censer filled with ashes] is analogous to a vessel** used **for excrement,** and it is permitted to remove such a vessel from one's house due to the discomfort it engenders.[12]

NOTES

1. A burning flame may not be touched on the Sabbath, because touching it involves a prohibition [of *extinguishing*]. Since the flame cannot exist without a wick, oil and lamp, they are considered a base to it and may also not be moved while the flame is burning, even according to R' Shimon (see *Ritva MHK* ed. and *Pnei Yehoshua* to *Rashi* ד״ה א״ר רומנוס; cf. *Chazon Ish* 41:16 and *Dibros Moshe* 34:47).

2. [A censer is a vessel used for burning incense.] Since it is a utensil that is used primarily for a prohibited function [כְּלִי שֶׁמְּלַאכְתּוֹ לְאִסּוּר], it may be moved only if it is needed for a permitted act or if its location is needed for another object (*Ritva MHK* ed.; see below, 122b). Now, R' Rumnus apparently referred to a censer containing ashes that were *muktzeh,* viz. ashes that had not been expected to be used on the Sabbath. Such ashes may not be moved for any purpose. [The ashes are fit to be used to cover wastes, and are therefore *muktzeh* only according to R' Yehudah (*Rashi,* as explained by *Maharsha;* see *Dibros Moshe* 34:48).] R' Rumnus taught that in a case where it was necessary to move the censer Rebbi permitted him to move also the ashes that were upon it (*Rashi;* see *Ramban, Rashba* and *Pnei Yehoshua*).

3. Below, 141b.

4. This is permitted even though by lifting the child he is indirectly moving the *muktzeh* stone. The Gemara below, 141b, limits the application of this ruling to a case where the child longs for his father to pick him up and might become ill if he is ignored. The Sages relaxed the prohibition against moving *muktzeh* indirectly for this case of possible minor illness (see *Rashi* to 141b ד״ה בתינוק).

5. Since the non-*muktzeh* fruits are more valuable than the *muktzeh* stone, the basket is not considered a *base to muktzeh* (see *Ramban*). [The Gemara below (142a) states that even in this case it is permitted to lift the basket with the stone inside (thus moving the stone indirectly) only if it is not feasible to tilt the basket and make the stone fall out.]

6. R' Yochanan teaches that when a non-*muktzeh* utensil contains only *muktzeh* it becomes a subordinate base to the *muktzeh* and loses its intrinsic non-*muktzeh* status. [Thus, it may not even be tilted to remove the *muktzeh* item.] Now, ashes of burnt incense that one did not expect to use are *muktzeh,* according to R' Yehudah. It follows that, according to R' Yehudah, when a censer contains only ashes, it is considered a *base to muktzeh* and may not be moved. Since we learned above (45b; see note 22 there) that R' Yochanan concurs with R' Yehudah, he should prohibit moving a censer that is filled with ashes (*Rashi* as explained by *Maharsha;* see also *Pnei Yehoshua* and *Melo HaRo'im*).

7. This expression is borrowed from *Daniel* 4:16.

8. The granules of incense are not *muktzeh,* since their fragrance is pleasurable. Thus, the censer containing incense granules and ashes is analogous to a basket containing fruit and a stone (*Rashi*). [Since the granules are more valuable than the ashes, the censer is not considered a *base to muktzeh.*]

9. Since Rebbi was the *Nasi* and was extremely wealthy, no significance was accorded in his home to the leftover granules of incense that remained in a censer (*Rashi*). Thus, the granules themselves were *muktzeh* (*Ritva MHK* ed.; see *Chidushei HaRan* and *Chazon Ish* 43:19; cf. *Magen Avraham* 310:9 with *Pri Megadim;* see *Dibros Moshe* 34:51).

10. Poor people will use even a small scrap of cloth that measures at least three fingerbreadths by three fingerbreadths. They will also use fabric woven of coarse fibers. Wealthy people, by contrast, will use only fine cloth that measures at least three handbreadths by three handbreadths. A piece of cloth that is fit for the use of poor people is susceptible to *tumah* only when in the possession of a poor person. However, a piece that is fit for the use of wealthy people is susceptible to *tumah* when in the possession of a wealthy person — and certainly when in the possession of a poor person (*Rashi;* cf. *Tosafos;* see *Dibros Moshe* 34:50).

11. Just as the fact that poor people value a small scrap of cloth is irrelevant when the scrap is in the possession of a wealthy person, so too the fact that they value leftover incense granules is irrelevant when the granules are in the possession of a wealthy person (see *Rashi*).

12. A special dispensation from the *muktzeh* law was granted for removing items such as a commode from one's presence, to alleviate discomfort (see *Beitzah* 36b). Rebbi was disturbed by the sight of the leftover ashes and took advantage of this dispensation to allow R' Rumnus to remove the censer from his presence (*Rashi*).

הנח לנר שמן ופתילה הואיל (א) דנעשה בסיס לדבר האסור א"ר זירא א"ר אסי א"ר יוחנן אמר ר' חנינא אמר רבי רומנוס לי התיר רבי לטלטל מחתה באפרה א"ל רבי זירא לרבי אסי מי אמר רבי יוחנן הכי והתנן א) נוטל אדם בנו והאבן בידו או כלכלה והאבן בתוכה ואמר רבה בר בר חנה א"ר יוחנן בכלכלה מלאה פירות עסקינן טעמא דאית בה פירי הא לית בה פירי לא ב) א) אישתומם כשעה חדא ואמר הכא נמי דאית בה קרטין אמר אביי קרטין בי רבי מי חשיבי וכי תימא חזו לעניים והתניא ג) בגדי עניים לעניים בגדי עשירים לעשירים ד) אבל דעניים לעשירים לא אלא אמר אביי מידי דהוה אגרף של ריעי אמר רבא שתי תשובות בדבר חדא גרף של ריעי מאים והאי לא מאים ועוד גרף של ריעי מיגלי והאי מיכסי אלא אמר רבא כי הוינן בי רב נחמן א) הוה ה) מטלטלינן כנונא אגב קיטמא ואע"ג דאיכא עליה שברי עצים מיתיבי ושוין שאם יש בה שברי פתילה שאסור לטלטל ו) אמר אביי ב) בגלילא שנו לוי בר שמואל אשכחינהו לרבי אבא ולרב הונא בר חייא דהוו קיימי אפיתחא דבי רב הונא אמר להו מהו להחזיר מטה של טרסיים בשבת אמרו ליה ג) שפיר דמי אתא לקמיה דרב יהודה אמר הא רב ושמואל דאמרי תרוייהו המחזיר מטה של טרסיים בשבת חייב חטאת מיתיבי ז) המחזיר קנה מנורה בשבת חייב חטאת קנה סיידין לא יחזיר ואם החזיר פטור אבל אסור רבי סימאי אומר ה) קרן עגולה חייב קרן פשוטה פטור אינהו דאמור כי האי תנא דתניא מלבנות המטה וכרעות המטה ולווחים של סקיבס ד) לא יחזיר ואם החזיר פטור אבל

רשב"ג

רש"י

לדבר האסור. לשלהבת דכי האי מוקצה מודה ר"ש שהכלי טפל לשלהבת בעודה בו ולאו משום דחייש לכבייה: בסים. מושב את כנו מתרגמינן בסיסיה: א"ר רומנוס לי התיר רבי לטלטל מחתה. של לבונה באפרה קס"ד באפרה עם אפרה קאמר שהאפר מוקצה ולא היו צריכין לו ואשמעינן דאגב מחתה דאיכא תורת כלי עליה טלטלה עם אפרה: נוטל אדם. הכלכלה בשבת והאבן בתוכה: הא ליכא פרי לא. דכלי נעשה בסים לאבן וטפלה לו ובטל תורת כלי דידיה והכי נמי נעשית מחתה בסים לאפר ורבי יוחנן שמעי' ליה לעיל דכר' יהודה סבירא ליה: דאית ביה קרטין. שנשתיירו מן האור ולבונה דחזיא להריח ואגב לבונה מטלטל למחתה עם אפרה דומיא דכלכלה מלאה פירות והאבן בתוכה: קרטין. של שיור לבונה: בי רבי. דנשיא ועשיר הוה מי חשיבי: בגדי עניים. שלש על שלש או שחוטן עבה הוו בגדים לעניים לענין טומאה: בגדי עשירים. שלשה על שלשה הוו בגדים לעשירים וכל שכן לעניים אבל בגדי עניים לעשירים לא הוה בגד גבייהו ולא מקבלי טומאה הכא נמי בי רבי (ג) בטלי קרטין: אלא אמר אביי. הא דשרי ליה לטלטל מחתה באפרה משום דאפרה מאיס עליה לראותו והוי כגרף של רעי דתניא במסכת ביצה (דף לו:) מותר להוציאו לאשפה שבחצר: גרף. כלי חרס המוכן לכך: מיכסי. כל מחתות מכוסות הן ויש בהן נקבים להוציא הריח: כנונא. כלי נחשת שמביאין בו האור לפני שרים להתחמם: אגב קטמיה. שהיו צריכין לאפרו לכסות רוק או צואה וא"ת מה צד איסור יש כאן היינו רבותא דאע"ג דאיכא עליה שברי עצים והא דר' רומנוס נמי האי מחתה באפרה דקאמר מחתה בשביל אפרה שהיה צריך לו ודעתייהו עליה מאתמול ורבותא אשמעינן (כיון) אע"ג דאיכא עליה שברי עצים דהוי ככלכלה של פירות והאבן בתוכה: ושוין. ר' יהודה ור"ש שנחלקו בנר ישן: בגלילא שנו. שחשובות להן שברי פתילה שאין בגדים של פשתן מצויין להם הלכך לא בטלי ונעשה נר בסים להן: טרסיים. צורפי נחשת או גרדיים והולכין מעיר לעיר למלאכתן ונושאין עמהן מטות של פרקים: חייב חטאת. הוא תחלתו וגמרו ונמצא עושה כלי וחייב משום מכה בפטיש אב לכל גומרי מלאכה ולא משום בנין דאין בנין בכלים: קנה מנורה. שיוצאין ממנה קנים לנרות הרבה ונוטלין הימנה ובשעת הצורך מחזירין אותו: קנה של סיידין. הטחין ומלבנין הבית בסיד יש להן קנים של פרקים ונותן מטלית בראשה ושורין בסיד המחוי וטח את הבית וכשהוא טח מלמטה אי אפשר לו אלא בקנה קצר וכשהוא הולך ומגביה מוסיף קנה על קנה ומאריכו: פטור. שאין זה גמרו שהרי צריך לחזור ולפרקו תמיד: קרן עגולה וקרן פשוטה. שניהם מין כלי זמר והוא עשוי נקבים נקבים ככברה ומכנים בהן חלילים ומוציאין קולות הרבה קרן עגולה מעשה אומן הוא וצריך לתקוע בנקבים בחוזק והויא מלאכה ובקרן פשוט מכניסו בריוח ודרכן לפרקם תמיד ופטור קתני מיהת בקני מנורה דחייב והוא הדין למטה של טרסיים: אינהו. רבי אבא ורב הונא בר חייא: דאמור כי האי תנא. כרבי שמעון דמתיר לכתחלה: מלבנות המטה. כעין רגלים קטנים ויש להן בית קיבול ומכנים לתוכן ראשי כרעי המטה שלא ירקבו בארץ: לווחים של סקיבס. עץ קטן כמין דף שתוקעין בקשת שקורין אבלשטר"א שעליו מושך החץ:

יתקע

תוספות

הנח לנר שמן ופתילה הואיל ונעשה בסיס לדבר האסור. איצטריך למימר בשמן דנעשה בסיס לדבר האסור דאי לאו הכי לא היה הנר אסור לטלטל דהוי בסיס לדבר האסור ולדבר המותר ושרי כדאמר בסמוך כי הוינן בי רב נחמן הוה מטלטלינן כנונא אגב קיטמא אע"ג דאיכא עליה שברי עצים ואם תאמר פתילה אמאי קאמר דהויא בסיס לדבר האסור היא עצמה הויא דבר האסור כדאמר לקמן ושוין שאם יש בה שברי פתילות שאסור לטלטלה וי"ל דשברי פתילה הוי שברי כלים ודמי לצרורות אבל פתילה שלימה שהיא כלי הוה שרי אי לאו דנעשה בסיס לדבר האסור:

לי התיר רבי לטלטל מחתה באפרה. השתא ס"ד דאפר מחתה מוקצה הוא: ואמר רבה ב"ב חנה א"ר יוחנן כו'. תימה אמאי לא פריך בלאו מילתיה דרבי יוחנן ממתני' דפ' נוטל (לקמן דף קמב:) דתנן מעות שע"ג הכר מנער את הכר והן נופלות וכן אבן שעל פי החבית מטה על צדה והיא נופלת אבל טלטול גמור אסור ואור"י דה"א דשאני מעות דחשיבי ולא בטלי ואבן שע"פ החבית ה"א דמיירי שהוא מתוקן לסתום פי החבית והחבית צריכה לה ולכך לא בטלה:

בגדי עניים לעניים. אומר ר"ת דדוקא בטומאת מדרס דבייחוד תליא מלתא אבל בשאר טומאות לא תליא מלתא בייחוד דאפי' היה מוטל באשפה מרדינן ח) מוהבגד דשלש על שלש מיטמא בין לעניים בין לעשירים דקרא לא מפליג מידי ומייתי ר"ת ראיה דתנן במסכת כלים (פרק כ"ז מ"ב) דבגד מטמא משום שלשה על שלשה למדרס משום שלש על שלש לטמא מת וע"כ בעשירים מיירי דבפכ"ח תנן התם בגדי עניים אע"פ שאין בהם שלשה על שלשה טמאין מדרס וא"ת הכא דפריך מברייתא אמאי לא פריך ממתני' דפכ"ח דכלים שהבאתי ואור"י דאי ממתני' ה"א דבגדי עניים היינו כעין שק שעיקרו עשוי לעניים ואפי' ביד עשירים אינו צריך שלשה על שלשה אבל שאר בגדים בעי שלשה על שלשה שאינו עומד אלא לעשירים להכי מייתי ברייתא דלא שייך לפרשה הכי:

הוה מטלטלינן כנונא אגב קיטמא. פי' כנונא מחתה והיינו מחתה באפרה דלעיל פי' אגב אפרה שהוסק מע"ש דמוכן הוא דחזי לכסות בה רוק או צואה וקשה דמשמע דוקא אגב קיטמא שרי הא לאו הכי נעשה בסיס לדבר האסור ואילו בפ"ב דביצה (כא: ושם) אמר גבי אין מזמנין נכרי בשבת משום שיורי כוסות פריך וניטלטלינהו אגב כסא מי לא אמר רבא כי הוינן בי רב נחמן הוה מטלטלינן כנונא אגב קיטמא אף על גב דאיכא עליה שברי עצים ומאי פריך שאני כנונא דאגב קטמא מטלטל לה אבל בכוס ליכא אלא דבר האסור ואור"י דשיורי כוסות לא חשיבי למיהוי כוס בטל לגבייהו אף על גב שאין היתר עמהן בכוס טפי גרעי משברי עצים שעם הקיטמא בכונא:

אע"ג דאיכא עליה שברי עצים. נראה לרבינו תם דשברי עצים חשיבי טפי מאבן שבכלכלה דאם לא כן מאי קמ"ל ואדמקשי ליה מברייתא דשוין כו' ליסייעיה ממתני' דכלכלה והאבן בתוכה אלא שברי עצים חשיבי טפי ויש לדמות שברי עצים לגבי אפר כשברי פתילה לגבי שמן:

בגלילא שנו. פי' בקונט' שחשובות להן שברי פתילה שאין בגדי פשתן מצויין להם ואין נראה לר"ת דהא אמרי' בשילהי ב"ק (דף קיח:) לוקחין מן הנשים כלי צמר ביהודה וכלי פשתן בגליל משמע שמצוי פשתן הרבה שם ומפרש ר"ת בגלילא שנו שהיה להם רוב שמן ולהכי לא בטלי שברי פתילה אגב שמן וכן משמע בפ"ק דסנהדרין (דף יא:) גבי טול איגרת וכתוב לאחנא בני גלילאה עילאה ותתאה כו' דזמן ביעורא מטא לאפרושא מעשרא ממעטני זיתא ואמר בנזיר בפרק בית שמאי (דף לא:) בגלילא שנו דחמרא עדיף ממשחא ויין היה מצוי להם הרבה כדאמר בהמוציא יין (לקמן עז.) גבי מים כדי לשוף בהן את הקילור וקאמר בגלילא שנו א) דרפואת מים שכיח טפי משתיה שהיה להן רוב יין והיו שותין הכל יין ואפילו הכי חמרא עדיף להו ממישחא כי השמן היה להם בזול יותר ורש"י פי' נמי בהמוציא (שם) שמחמת עניותא היו עושין רפואה מן המים ואין עושין מן היין רק שתייה ולפיכך היתה רפואת מים שכיחא ואין נראה דכיון שלא היה להם יין לשיפות הקילור א"כ שכיחא שתיית מים טובא ואמרי' בעלמא ט) אף ערב יוה"כ בגליל שהיו מרדים בסעודה משמע שעשירים היו [וע"ע תוספות חגיגה כה: ד"ה בגלילא]:

עין משפט נר מצוה

נז א ב מיי' פכ"ו מהל' שבת הלכה יג טור שו"ע או"ח סימן שי סעיף ח:

נח ג ד מיי' פכ"ב מהל' שבת הלכה כו כח סמג לאוין סה טור שו"ע או"ח סימן שיג סעיף ו:

רבינו חננאל

הנח לנר ופתילה ושמן דלא גזר ר"ש אלא הואיל ונעשה כל אחד בסיס לדבר האסור. ופשוטה היא: אמר רבא כי היינו בי רב נחמן היינו מטלטלי כנונא אגב קיטומה אף על גב דאיכא עליה שברי עצים. מיתיבי ושוין שאם יש בה שברי פתילה שאסור לטלטלה. ופריק אביי בגלילא שנו. פירוש בגליל שנו שדרכם להדליק בשברי פתילות. וכיון שדרכם להדליק בשברי פתילות נעשו מוקצות בשבת לפיכך אסור לטלטל אפילו הנרות שיש בהן שברי פתילות. אבל שברי עצים דכנונא לא חשיבי ובטלי: לוי בר שמואל בעא מר' אבא ומרב הונא בר חייא מהו להחזי' מטה של (פרסיים) [טרסיים] בשבת אמרו ליה שרי. אמר להו רב יהודה רב ושמואל דאמרי תרווייהו המחזיר מטה של (פרסיים) [טרסיים] בשבת חייב חטאת. מיתיבי המחזיר קנה מנורה בשבת חייב חטאת קנה של ציירין לא יחזיר ואם החזיר פטור אבל אסור. ר' סימאי א' קרן [עגולה חייב קרן] פשוטה פטור. קתני מיהת המחזיר קנה מנורה בשבת חייב חטאת. קשיא לר' אבא ולרב הונא דשרי. ושניג' אינהו דאמור כי האי תנא דתניא אם היה רפוי מותר. דתניא מלבנות המטה וכרעי המטה [ולווחין] של סקיבס לא יחזיר. ואם החזיר פטור אבל

רב נסים גאון

אלא אמר אביי מידי דהוה אגרף של רעי. משתכח במס' יום טוב בפרק משילין פירות (דף לו) אמר שמואל גרף של רעי ועביט מימי רגלים מותר להוציאו לאשפה ובפרק נוטל אדם את בנו (דף קמג) אמרו הני גרעיני דתמרי כול' רב הונא בריה דרב יהושע עביד להו גרף של רעי וכן אמימר עביד להו גרף של רעי: אמר אביי בגלילא שנו. כבר טרחו בזה השינוי ששינה אביי הרבה מן החכמים ולא שמעתי מהם כלום ולא מצאתי בו לאחד מן הגאונים פירוש אבל טרחתי על שינויו ומצאתי במס' נזירות בפ' בית שמאי אומרים הקדש טעות הקדש (דף לא) והא שמן עדיף מיין אי משום הא לא קשיא בגלילא שנו דחמרא עדיף ממשחא זה מודיע שהשמן היה אצלם מצוי הרבה וכי מה שהושם בנר ויש בו שברי פתילה אין לו חשיבות אצלם ואינן משתמשין בו לצרכם והרי הוא כדין המוקצה שאסור לטלטלו ולכך שנו חכמים כי בגליל אסור לטלטל נר שיש בו שברי פתילה לפי שהשמן הנותר בנר לא חשיב להו וכבר זה הפירוש הודענו באלו הימים לתלמידנו ופירשנו להם בזה הענין ואפשר להיאמר בו פירוש אחר

שאנשי גליל לפי שלא היו מקפידין על לשונם ולא דייקי לישנא ולא גמיר מחד רבה ולא גלו מסכתא למסכתא כמו שהוא מפורש במסכת עירובין בפרק כיצד מעברין (דף נג) ולא היה תלמודם מקויים בידם אסרו עליהם החכמים טלטול נר שיש בתוכו שברי פתילה א) עלי דרך האיסורים ואל תחבט ואל תסייג ויקרי דאלך איצא קולהום פי עדה (מוצאע) [מואצע] מן אל תלמוד מתל הדא אל קול עלי טריק אל תנקין להם

חשק שלמה על רב נסים גאון א) פירוש בערבי על דרך האיסורים והגדר והסייג ונמצא סיוע לזה במקומות הרבה מהתלמוד משל זה המאמר על דרך הגירעון להם נזכר מזה מה שנמצא בספר' מומר בקודש:

מסורת הש"ס

א) לקמן קמא:, ב) [מו"ק ג: קידושין לט: סוכה מד. חולין כא.], ג) [עירובין כט:], ד) [עי' תוספות לקמן קמ: ד"ה כיון וכו'], ה) ביצה דף כא: ע"ש, ו) [לקמן עח.], ז) [תוספ' פי"ג], ח) [לעיל כו:], ט) [חולין פג.].

תוספות ישנים

א) ורבינו מאיר פי' כי מרוב שתיית יין הי' להם חכלילי עינים ושכיחי רפואת מים טובא:

הגהות הב"ח

(א) גמ' ופתילה הואיל ונעשה בסיס: (ג) רש"י ד"ה בגדי עשירים וכו' ה"נ בי רבי לא חשיבי קרטין ובטלי הס"ד:

גליון הש"ס

גמ' קרן עגולה חייב. עי' כלים פי"א מ"ז:

תורה אור השלם

א) אֱדַיִן דָּנִיֵּאל דִּי שְׁמֵהּ בֵּלְטְשַׁאצַּר אֶשְׁתּוֹמַם כְּשָׁעָה חֲדָה וְרַעְיֹנֹהִי יְבַהֲלֻנֵּהּ עָנֵה מַלְכָּא וְאָמַר בֵּלְטְשַׁאצַּר חֶלְמָא וּפִשְׁרֵא אַל יְבַהֲלָךְ עָנֵה בֵלְטְשַׁאצַּר וְאָמַר מָרִי חֶלְמָא לְשָׂנְאָךְ וּפִשְׁרֵהּ לְעָרָךְ: [דניאל ד, טו]

ליקוטי רש"י

בסים. [כדמתרגמינן כנו בסיסיה (שמות ל) מקום מושבו [פסחים פג.]. והאבן בידו. כתלר ולא אמרינן דמטלטל לאבן [לקמן קמא:]. מלאה פירות. דעיקר נעשית בסים לפירות הלכך אבן מיטלטלא אגב כלי ופירות שהוא מותר [שם קמב.]. אישתומם. שתק והיה מחשב מה יענה [חולין כא.]. לשון משומם כאדם נבהל ונאלם ובעל מחשבות כמו (איוב יח, כ) על יומו נשמו אחרונים (ירמיה ב, יב) שומו שמים (דניאל ד, טו) אשתומם כשעה חדא [בראשית כד, כא]. שומם ל' אלם ומשותק כמו אשתומם כשעה חדא (דניאל ג) ואשב שם שבעת ימים משמים בתוכם כמו אלם (יחזקאל ג) [דניאל ח, יג]. בגדי עניים. שלש על שלש מקבלין טומאה לעניים. בגדי עשירים. שלשה על שלשה מקבלין טומאה אף לעשירים [עירובין כט:]. מידי דהוה אגרף של ריעי. שמותר לטלטלו ולפנותו לאשפה מחמת מאוס כדאמרינן בפרק במה (ביצה לו:) [ביצה כא:]. גרף. גרף ועביט כלי חרס הן אלא של רעי קרוי גרף ושל מימי רגלים קרוי עביט [שם לו:]. כנונא. כלי שמשימים בו הגחלים. אגב קיטמא. שהיו צריכין לאפרו והוכן מערב שבת לכסות רוק או צואה. ואף על גב דאיכא עליה שברי עצים. דלא חזו מטלטל להו עם כנונא [שם כא:].

Abaye's explanation too is rejected:

אָמַר רָבָא – **Rava said:** שְׁתֵּי תְּשׁוּבוֹת בַּדָּבָר – **There are two rejoinders to this** analogy: חֲדָא גְּרָף שֶׁל רְעִי מָאִיס וְהַאי לֹא מָאִיס – **Firstly, a vessel** used **for excrement is repugnant whereas this** censer **is not repugnant.** וְעוֹד – **And furthermore,** גְּרָף שֶׁל רְעִי מִיגַּלֵּי וְהַאי מִיכַּסֵּי – **a vessel** used **for excrement is open whereas this** censer **is covered.**[13] Thus, there is no basis for extending to a censer the dispensation granted for removing a vessel used for excrement from one's house. – ? –

Rava therefore offers his own explanation:

אֶלָּא אָמַר רָבָא – **Rather, Rava said:** כִּי הֲוֵינַן בֵּי רַב נַחְמָן – **When we were** students **at the house of Rav Nachman,** הֲוָה מְטַלְטְלִינַן כָּנוּנָא אַגַּב קִיטְמָא – **we would move a brazier because of** our need for its non-*muktzeh* **ashes,** וְאַף עַל גַּב דְּאִיכָּא עֲלֵיהּ שִׁבְרֵי עֵצִים – **even when there were broken pieces of wood on it** which were *muktzeh*.[14] When Rebbi permitted R' Rumnus to move a censer filled with ashes, it was in a similar situation, where the ashes were not *muktzeh*,[15] and Rebbi's innovation was that it was permitted to move it for the use of the ashes even though there were *muktzeh* pieces of wood on it.

Rava's explanation is challenged:

מֵיתִיבֵי – **They challenged this** on the basis of the following Baraisa, which focuses on the dispute between R' Yehudah and R' Shimon concerning the status of a used lamp:[16] וְשָׁוִין – BUT THEY (R' Yehudah and R' Shimon) AGREE שֶׁאִם יֵשׁ בָּהּ שִׁבְרֵי פְּתִילָה – THAT IF [THE LAMP] CONTAINS REMNANTS OF A WICK שֶׁאָסוּר לְטַלְטֵל – IT IS FORBIDDEN TO MOVE the lamp, because it is a base to the *muktzeh* remnants in it. The Baraisa considers the lamp a *base to muktzeh* even though it also contains oil, which is presumably more valuable than the wick remnants.[17] – ? –

The challenge is deflected:

אָמַר אַבָּיֵי – **Abaye said:** בְּגָלִילָא שָׁנוּ – **They taught this** Baraisa **in the Galilee,** where flax for the manufacture of wicks was scarce. The Galileans therefore valued the wick remnants no less than the leftover oil.[18]

Having concluded its discussion of *muktzeh,* the Gemara returns to a topic it touched upon earlier (46a) – that of reassembling utensils on the Sabbath:[19]

לֵוִי בַּר שְׁמוּאֵל אַשְׁכְּחִינְהוּ לְרַבִּי אַבָּא וּלְרַב הוּנָא בַּר חִיָּיא – **Levi bar Shmuel met R' Abba and Rav Huna bar Chiya** דַּהֲווּ קָיְימֵי אַפִּיתְחָא דְּבֵי רַב הוּנָא – **as they were standing at Rav Huna's doorstep,** אָמַר לְהוּ – **and said to them:** מַהוּ לְהַחֲזִיר מִטָּה שֶׁל טַרְסִיִּים בְּשַׁבָּת – **What is** the law concerning **reassembling a coppersmith's bed**[20] **on the Sabbath?**[21] אָמְרוּ לֵיהּ – **They replied:** שַׁפִּיר דָּמֵי – **It is permitted.** אֲתָא לְקַמֵּיהּ דְּרַב יְהוּדָה – **[Levi bar Shmuel]** later **came before Rav Yehudah** and told him this ruling, אָמַר – whereupon **[Rav Yehudah] said:** הָא רַב וּשְׁמוּאֵל דְּאָמְרֵי תַּרְוַיְיהוּ – **Why, Rav and Shmuel both said** הַמַּחֲזִיר מִטָּה שֶׁל טַרְסִיִּים בְּשַׁבָּת חַיָּיב חַטָּאת – that **one who reassembles a coppersmith's bed on the Sabbath is liable to a** ***chatas*** **offering!**[22]

The Gemara challenges the permissive view of R' Abba and Rav Huna bar Chiya:

מֵיתִיבֵי – **They challenged** this on the basis of the following Baraisa: הַמַּחֲזִיר קְנֵה מְנוֹרָה בְּשַׁבָּת חַיָּיב חַטָּאת – ONE WHO REAFFIXES A BRANCH OF A CANDELABRA ON THE SABBATH IS LIABLE TO A *CHATAS* OFFERING.[23] קְנֵה סַיָּידִין לֹא יַחֲזִיר – As for A PLASTERER'S POLE,[24] ONE SHOULD NOT REASSEMBLE it (i.e. add sections to it) on the Sabbath, וְאִם הֶחֱזִיר – BUT IF ONE DID REASSEMBLE it פָּטוּר אֲבָל אָסוּר – HE IS EXEMPT from liability, THOUGH HE IS FORBIDDEN by Rabbinical decree to do so.[25] רַבִּי סִימַאי אוֹמֵר – R' SIMAI SAID: קֶרֶן עֲגוּלָּה חַיָּיב – If one assembles A ROUND HORN HE IS LIABLE, קֶרֶן פְּשׁוּטָה פָּטוּר – but if

NOTES

13. The censer has a perforated cover through which the fragrance escapes (*Rashi*). Since the ashes are covered, they do not engender discomfort.

14. [A brazier is a pan in which coals are burned for heat.] Rava stated that when they needed the ashes that were in the brazier for covering dirt, they would move the brazier even though it also contained broken pieces of wood, which were *muktzeh*. [The ashes were not *muktzeh* because their need had been anticipated (see *Rashba* and next note).] The rationale for moving the brazier was that the ashes, being fit for covering dirt, were more valuable than the chips of wood, and thus, the brazier was not considered a *base to muktzeh* but was like a basket containing fruit and a stone. [Although ashes are not comparable to fruit, they are nevertheless more significant than useless chips of wood] (*Rashi* as understood by *Beis Meir, Orach Chaim* 310:8; see also *Ramban, Rashba, Ritva MHK* ed. and *Mishnah Berurah* 310:33).

15. Because their use had been anticipated before the Sabbath (*Rashi*).

16. See 44a with notes 4 and 5.

17. The used oil is not as valuable as fruit, but is more useful than the wick remnants. Thus, this case is analogous to that of a brazier or censer containing useful ashes and worthless chips of wood, which Rava does not consider a *base to muktzeh*. However, the Baraisa does consider the land a *base to muktzeh*. Evidently, a vessel containing *muktzeh* is considered a *base to muktzeh* unless it also contains a non-*muktzeh* item that is far more valuable than the *muktzeh* – as in the case of a basket containing fruit and a stone (see *Ramban, Rashba, Ritva MHK* ed.; cf. *Tosafos* ד״ה אע״ג).

18. *Rashi,* as explained by *Beis Meir* ibid.; cf. *Tosafos* ד״ה בגלילא שנו.

19. *Pnei Yehoshua*.

20. Alternatively: *a weaver's bed.* Both translations are offered by *Rashi*. See *Tosafos, Avodah Zarah* 17b ד״ה רבן של תרסיים, who demonstrate that the word טַרְסִיִּים has both meanings.

21. Itinerant coppersmiths (or weavers) would take with them a type of portable bed that came apart in sections on their travels (*Rashi*). It was not assembled with screws or nails, but was simply fitted together loosely (see below). Levi bar Shmuel inquired whether there was any prohibition involved in assembling it on the Sabbath.

22. According to Rav and Shmuel, one who reassembles the bed has violated the *melachah* of מַכֶּה בְּפַטִּישׁ, *striking the final hammer blow*. This *melachah* encompasses any act that completes the formation of a utensil. It applies in our case, since the one who assembles the bed has begun and completed its construction with one act. However, he has not violated the *melachah* of בּוֹנֶה, *building*, since that *melachah* does not pertain to utensils [but only to fixed objects] (*Rashi;* see below, 102b and *Beur HaGra* to *Orach Chaim* 314:1).

The preceding reflects *Rashi's* view. *Ramban* (*Milchamos Hashem* below, 102b), however, maintains that merely reassembling a collapsible bed, without nailing it together, is not sufficiently final an act to fall under the heading of *striking the final blow*. In his view, Rav and Shmuel hold the person liable for violating the *melachah* of *building* (which does not require the element of finality). Although the Gemara in *Beitzah* (22a) and elsewhere states explicitly that utensils are excluded from the *melachah* of *building*, *Ramban* maintains that Rav and Shmuel do not accept this exclusion. See *Ramban's* detailed discussion of our Gemara. [For yet other views see *Tosafos*, 47b ד״ה רבן, 74b ד״ה חביתא and 102b ד״ה האי; *Rashba* and *Ritva MHK* ed. here; *Chidushei HaRamban* and *Rashba* below, 102b. For a far-ranging discussion of this and related issues see *Toras Refael, Hil. Shabbos* §19.]

23. The Baraisa refers to a candelabra that has removable branches, which can be removed and used as individual lamps and then returned to the main body of the candelabra (*Rashi*). If someone reaffixes one of the branches on the Sabbath, he has violated the *melachah* of *striking the final blow* (according to *Rashi*).

24. This is a long pole made up of sections, on top of which sits a brush or rag to apply plaster. By adding or subtracting sections, the plasterer can adjust the pole's length to his convenience (*Rashi*).

25. He has not violated the Biblical prohibition of *striking the final blow*, for since he constantly needs to adjust the pole to various lengths, there is nothing final about assembling it to its full extension (*Rashi*).

הנח לנר שמן ופתילה הואיל (א) דנעשה בסיס לדבר האסור א"ר זירא א"ר אסי א"ר יוחנן אמר ר' חנינא אמר רבי רומנוס לי התיר רבי לטלטל מחתה באפרה א"ל רבי זירא לרבי אסי מי אמר רבי יוחנן הכי והתנן נוטל אדם בנו והאבן בידו או כלכלה והאבן בתוכה ואמר רבה בר בר חנה א"ר יוחנן בכלכלה מלאה פירות עסקינן טעמא דאית בה פירי הא לית בה פירי לא אישתומם כשעה חדא ואמר הכא נמי דאית בה קרטין אמר אביי קרטין בי רבי מי חשיבי וכי תימא חזו לעניים והתניא בגדי עניים לעניים בגדי עשירים לעשירים אבל דעניים לעשירים לא אלא אמר אביי מידי דהוה אגרף של ריעי אמר רבא שתי תשובות בדבר חדא גרף של ריעי מאים והאי לא מאים ועוד גרף של ריעי מיגלי והאי מיכסי אלא אמר רבא כי הוינן בי רב נחמן הוה מטלטלינן כנונא אגב קיטמא ואע"ג דאיכא עליה שברי עצים מיתיבי ושוין שאם יש בה שברי פתילה שאסור לטלטל אמר אביי בגלילא שנו לוי בר שמואל אשכחינהו לרבי אבא ולרב הונא בר חייא דהוו קיימי אפיתחא דבי רב הונא אמר להו מהו להחזיר מטה של טרסיים בשבת אמרו ליה שפיר דמי אתא לקמיה דרב יהודה אמר הא רב ושמואל דאמרי תרוייהו המחזיר מטה של טרסיים בשבת חייב חטאת מיתיבי המחזיר קנה מנורה בשבת חייב חטאת קנה סיידין לא יחזיר ואם החזיר פטור אבל אסור רבי סימאי אומר קרן עגולה חייב קרן פשוטה פטור אינהו דאמור כי האי תנא דתניא מלבנות המטה וכרעות המטה ולווחים של סקיבס לא יחזיר ואם החזיר פטור אבל

רש"י

לדבר האסור. לשלהבת דבכי האי מוקצה מודה ר"ש שהכלי טפל לשלהבת בעודה בו ולאו משום דחייש לכבייה: בסיס. מושב את כנו מתרגמינן בסיסיה: א"ר רומנוס לי התיר רבי לטלטל מחתה. של לבונה באפרה קס"ד באפרה עם אפרה קאמר שהאפר מוקצה ולא היו צריכין לו ואשמעינן דאגב מחתה דאיכא תורת כלי עליה טלטלה עם אפרה: נוטל אדם. הכלכלה בשבת והאבן בתוכה: הא ליכא פרי לא. דכלי נעשה בסיס לאבן וטפלה לו ובטל תורת כלי דידיה והכי נמי נעשית מחתה בסיס לאפר ורבי יוחנן שמעי' ליה לעיל דכדר' יהודה סבירא ליה: דאית ביה קרטין. שנשתיירו מן האור ולבונה דחזיא להריח ואגב לבונה מטלטל למחתה עם אפרה דומיא דכלכלה מלאה פירות והאבן בתוכה: קרטין. של שיור לבונה: בי רבי. דנשיא ועשיר הוה מי חשיבי: בגדי עניים. שלש על שלש או שחותך עבה הוו בגדים לעניים לענין טומאה: בגדי עשירים. שלשה על שלשה הוו בגדים לעשירים וכל שכן לעניים אבל בגדי עניים לעשירים לא הוה בגד גבייהו ולא מקבלי טומאה הכא נמי בי רבי (ב) בטלי קרטין: אלא אמר אביי. הא דשרי ליה לטלטל מחתה באפרה משום דאפרה מאיס עליה לראותו והוי כגרף של רעי דתניא במסכת ביצה (דף לו:) מותר להוציאו לאשפה שבחצר: גרף. כלי חרס המוכן לכך: מיכסי. כל מחתות מכוסות הן ויש בהן נקבים להוציא הריח: כנונא. כלי נחשת שמביאין בו האור לפני שרים להתחמם: אגב קטמיה. שהיו צריכין לאפרו לכסות רוק או צואה וא"ת מה בד איסור יש כאן היינו רבותא דאע"ג דאיכא עליה שברי עצים והא דר' רומנוס נמי האי מחתה באפרה דקאמר מחתה בשביל אפרה שהיה צריך לו ודעתייהו עליה מאתמול ורבותא אשמעינן (כיון) אע"ג דאיכא עליה שברי עצים דהוי ככלכלה של פירות והאבן בתוכה: ושוין. ר' יהודה ור"ש שנחלקו בנר ישן: בגלילא שנו. שחשובות להן שברי פתילה שאין בגדים של פשתן מצויין להם הלכך לא בטלי ונעשה נר בסיס להן: טרסיים. צורפי נחשת או גרדיים והולכין מעיר לעיר למלאכתן ונושאין עמהן מטות של פרקים: חייב חטאת. הוא תחלתו וגמרו ונמצא עושה כלי וחייב משום מכה בפטיש אב לכל גומרי מלאכה ולא משום בנין דאין בנין בכלים: קנה מנורה. שיוצאין ממנה קנים לנרות הרבה ונוטלין הימנה ובשעת הצורך מחזירין אותו: קנה של סיידין. הטחין ומלבנין הבית בסיד יש להן קנים של פרקים ונותן מטלית בראשה ושורין בסיד המחוי וטח את הבית וכשהוא טח מלמטה אי אפשר לו אלא בקנה קצר וכשהוא הולך ומגביה מוסיף קנה על קנה ומאריכו: פטור. שאין זה גמרו שהרי צריך לחזור ולפרקו תמיד: קרן עגולה וקרן פשוטה. שניהם מין כלי זמר והוא עשוי נקבים נקבים ככברה ומכניס בהן חלילים ומוציאין קולות הרבה קרן עגולה מעשה אומן הוא וצריך לתקוע בנקבים בחוזק והויא מלאכה ובקרן פשוט מכניסו בריוח ודרכן לפרקס תמיד ופטור קתני מיהת בקני מנורה דחייב והוא הדין למטה של טרסיים: אינהו. רבי אבא ורב הונא בר חייא: דאמור כי האי תנא. כרבי שמעון דמתיר לכתחלה: מלבנות המטה. כעין רגלים קטנים ויש להן בית קיבול ומכנים לתוכן ראשי כרעי המטה שלא ירקבו בארץ: לווחים של סקיבס. עץ קטן כמין דף שתוקעין בקשת שקורין אבלשטר"א שעליו מושך החץ:

יתקע

תוספות

הנח לנר שמן ופתילה הואיל ונעשה בסיס לדבר האסור. אילטריך למימר בשמן דנעשה בסיס לדבר האסור דאי לאו הכי לא היה הנר אסור לטלטל דהוי בסיס לדבר האסור ולדבר המותר ושרי כדאמר בסמוך כי הוינן בי רב נחמן הוה מטלטלינן כנונא אגב קיטמא אע"ג דאיכא עליה שברי עצים ואם תאמר פתילה אמאי קאמר דהויא בסיס לדבר האסור היא עצמה הויא דבר האסור כדאמר לקמן ושוין שאם יש בה שברי פתילות שאסור לטלטלה וי"ל דשברי פתילה הוי שברי כלים ודמי לצרורות אבל פתילה שלימה שהיא כלי הוה שרי אי לאו דנעשה בסיס לדבר האסור:

לי התיר רבי לטלטל מחתה באפרה. השתא ס"ד דאפר מחתה מוקצה הוא:

ואמר רבה ב"ב חנה א"ר יוחנן כו'. תימה אמאי לא פריך בלאו מילתיה דרבי יוחנן ממתני' דפ' נוטל (לקמן דף קמב:) דתנן מעות שע"ג הכר מנער את הכר והן נופלות וכן אבן שעל פי החבית מטה על לדה והיא נופלת אבל טלטול גמור אסור ואור"י דה"א דשאני מעות דחשיבי ולא בטלי ואבן שע"פ החבית ה"א דמיירי שהוא מתוקן לסתום פי החבית והחבית צריכה לה ולכך לא בטלה:

בגדי עניים לעניים. אומר ר"ת דדוקא בטומאת מדרס דבייחוד תליא מלתא אבל בשאר טומאות לא תליא מלתא בייחוד דאפי' היה מוטל באשפה מרבינן ח) מוהבגד דשלש על שלש מיטמא בין לעניים בין לעשירים דבקרא לא מפליג מידי ומייתי ר"ת ראיה דתנן במסכת כלים (פרק כ"ז מ"ג) דבגד מטמא משום שלשה על שלשה למדרס משום שלש על שלש לטמא מת וע"כ בעשירים מיירי דבפכ"ח תנן התם בגדי עניים אע"פ שאין בהם שלשה על שלשה טמאין מדרס וא"ת הכא דפריך מברייתא אמאי לא פריך ממתני' דפכ"ח דכלים שהבאתי ואור"י דאי ממתני' ה"א דבגדי עניים היינו כעין שק שעיקרו עשוי לעניים ואפי' ביד עשירים אינו צריך שלשה על שלשה אבל שאר בגדים בעי שלשה על שלשה שאינו עומד אלא לעשירים להכי מייתי ברייתא דלא שייך לפרשה הכי:

הוה מטלטלינן כנונא אגב קיטמא. פי' כונא מחתה והיינו מחתה באפרה דלעיל פי' אגב אפרה שהוסק מע"ש דמוכן הוא דחזי לכסות בה רוק או צואה וקשה דמשמע דוקא אגב קיטמא שרי הא לאו הכי נעשה בסיס לדבר האסור ואילו בפ"ב דבילה (כא: ושם) אמר גבי אין מזמנין נכרי בשבת משום שיורי כוסות פריך וניטלטלינהו אגב כסא מי לא אמר רבא כי הוינן בי רב נחמן הוה מטלטלינן כונא אגב קיטמא אף על גב דאיכא עליה שברי עצים ומאי פריך שאני כונא דאגב קטמא מטלטל לה אבל בכוס ליכא אלא דבר האסור ואור"י דשיורי כוסות לא חשיבי למיהוי כוס בטל לגבייהו אף על גב שאין היתר עמהן בכוס טפי גרעי משברי עצים שעם הקיטמא בכונא:

אע"ג דאיכא עליה שברי עצים. נראה לרבינו תם דשברי עצים חשיבי טפי מאבן שבכלכלה דאם לא כן מאי קמ"ל ולדמקשי ליה מברייתא דשוין כו' ליסייעיה ממתני' דכלכלה והאבן בתוכה אלא שברי עצים חשיבי טפי ויש לדמות שברי עצים לגבי אפר כשברי פתילה לגבי שמן:

בגלילא שנו. פי' בקונט' שחשובות להן שברי פתילה שאין בגדי פשתן מצויין להם ואין נראה לר"ת דהא אמרי' בשילהי ב"ק (דף קיט:) לוקחין מן הנשים כלי צמר ביהודה וכלי פשתן בגליל משמע שמצוי פשתן הרבה שם ומפרש ר"ת בגלילא שנו שהיה להם רוב שמן ולהכי לא בטלי שברי פתילה אגב שמן וכן משמע בפ"ק דסנהדרין (דף יא:) גדי טול איגרת וכתוב לאחנא בני גלילאה עילאה ותתאה כו' דזמן ביעורא מטא לאפרושא מעשרא ממעטני זיתא ואמר בנזיר בפרק בית שמאי (דף לא:) בגלילא שנו דחמרא עדיף ממשחא ויין היה מצוי להם הרבה כדאמר בהמוציא יין (לקמן עז.) גבי מים כדי לשוף בהן את הקילור וקאמר בגלילא שנו א) דרפואת מים שכיח טפי משתיה שהיה להן רוב יין והיו שותין הכל יין ואפילו הכי חמרא עדיף להו ממשחא כי השמן היה להם בזול יותר ורש"י פי' נמי בהמוציא (שם) שמחמת עניותא היו עושין רפואה מן המים ואין עושין מן היין רק שתייה ולפיכך היתה רפואת מים שכיחה ואין נראה דכיון שלא היה להם יין לשיפות הקילור א"כ שכיחה שתיית מים טובא ולמאי דמשמע בעלמא ב) לא ערב יוה"כ בגליל שהיו מרבים בסעודה משמע שעשירים היו [וע"ע תוספות חגיגה כה: ד"ה בגליל]:

רשב"ג

עין משפט נר מצוה

נז א ב מיי' פכ"ו מהל' שבת הלכה יג טור שו"ע או"ח סימן שי סעיף ח:
נח ג ד מיי' פכ"ב מהל' שבת הלכה כו כח סמג לאוין סה טור שו"ע או"ח סימן שיג סעיף ו:

רבינו חננאל

הנח לנר ופתילה ושמן דלא גזר ר"ש אלא הואיל ונעשה כל אחד בסיס לדבר האסור. ופשוטה היא: אמר רבא כי היינו בי רב נחמן היינו מטלטלי כנונא אגב קיטומה אף על גב דאיכא עליה שברי עצים. מיתיבי ושוין שאם יש בה שברי פתילה שאסור לטלטלה. ופריק אביי בגלילא שנו. פירוש בגליל שנו שדרכם להדליק בשברי פתילות. וכיון שדרכם להדליק בשברי פתילות נעשו מוקצות בשבת לפיכך אסור לטלטל אפילו הנרות שיש בהן שברי פתילות. אבל שברי עצים דכנונא לא חשיבי ובטלי: לוי בר שמואל בעא מר' אבא ומרב הונא בר חייא מהו להחזי' מטה של (פרסיים) [טרסיים] בשבת אמרו ליה שרי. אמר להו רב יהודה רב ושמואל דאמרי תרווייהו המחזיר מטה של (פרסיים) [טרסיים] בשבת חייב חטאת. מיתיבי המחזיר קנה מנורה בשבת חייב חטאת קנה של ציירין לא יחזיר ואם החזיר פטור אבל אסור. ר' סימאי א' קרן [עגולה חייב קרן] פשוטה פטור. קתני מיהת המחזיר קנה מנורה בשבת חייב חטאת. קשיא לר' אבא ולרב הונא דשרי. ושני' אינהו דאמור כי האי תנא אם היה רפוי מותר. דתניא מלבנות המטה וכרעי המטה (ולוחין) [ולווחין] של סקיבס לא יחזיר. ואם החזיר פטור אבל

רב נסים גאון

אלא אמר אביי מידי דהוה אגרף של רעי. משתכח במס' יום טוב בפרק משילין פירות (דף לו) אמר שמואל גרף של רעי ועביט מימי רגלים מותר להוציאו לאשפה ובפרק נוטל אדם את בנו (דף קמב) אמרו הני גרעיני דתמרי כול' רב הונא בר חייא דרב יהושע עביד להו גרף של רעי וכן אמימר עביד להו גרף של רעי: אמר אביי בגלילא שנו. כבר טרחנו בזה השינוי ששינה אביי הרבה מן החכמים ולא שמעתי מהם בזה כלום ולא מצאתי בו לאחד מן הגאונים פירוש אבל טרחתי על שינויו ומצאתי במס' נזירות בפ' בית שמאי אומרים הקדש טעות הקדש (דף לא) והא שמן עדיף מיין ויש בו הא לא קשיא בגלילא שנו דחמרא עדיף ממשחא וזה מודיע שהשמן היה אצלם מצוי הרבה וכי מפני שהושם בנר ויש בו שברי פתילה אין לו חשיבות אצלם ואינן משתמשים בו לצרכם והרי הוא כדין המוקצה שאסור לטלטלו ולכך שנו חכמים כי בגליל אסור לטלטל נר שיש בו שברי פתילה לפי שהשמן הנותר בנר לא חשיב להו וזה הפירוש הדענו באלו הימים לתלמידנו ופירשנו להם בזה הענין ואפשר להיאמר בו פירוש אחר והוא שאנשי גליל לפי שלא היו מקפידין על לשונם ולא דייקי לישנא ולא גמיר מחד רבה ולא גלו מסכתא למסכתא כמו שהוא מפורש במסכת עירובין בפרק כיצד מעברין (דף נג) ולא היה התלמוד מקוים בידם אסרו עליהם החכמים טלטול נר שיש בתוכו שברי פתילה א) עלי דרך האיסורים ולא חשבו ולא חשיב ויקיר דאלך איצא קולהום פי עדה (מוצאצ) [מואצע] מן אל תלמוד מתל הדא אל קול עלי טריק אל תנקין להם

חשק שלמה על רב נסים גאון א) פירוש בערבי על דרך האיסורים והגדר והסייג ונמצא קולא זו במקומות הרבה מהתלמוד משל זה המאמר על דרך הגינוי להם שלא יבואו לזה מוסר מזה לגבי אומר בקודש:

מסורת הש"ס

א) לקמן קמא., ב) [מו"ק ג. קידושין לג: סוכה מד. חולין כא.], ג) [עירובין כט:], ד) [עי' תוספות לקמן קמ: ד"ה כיון וכו'], ה) ביצה דף כא: ע"ש, ו) [לקמן עח.], ז) [תוספ' פי"ג], ח) [לעיל כו:], ט) [חולין פב.]

תוספות ישנים

א) ורבינו מאיר פי' כי מרוב שתיית יין הי' להם מכלולי עינים ושכיחי רפואות מים טובא:

הגהות הב"ח

(א) גמ' ופתילה הואיל ונעשה בסיס: (ב) רש"י ד"ה בגדי עשירים וכו' ה"נ בי רבי לא חשיבי קרטין ובטלי הס"ד:

גליון הש"ס

גמ' קרן עגולה חייב. עי' כלים פי"א מ"ז:

תורה אור השלם

א) אֱדַיִן דָּנִיֵּאל דִּי שְׁמֵהּ בֵּלְטְשַׁאצַּר אֶשְׁתּוֹמַם כְּשָׁעָה חֲדָה וְרַעְיֹנֹהִי יְבַהֲלֻנֵּהּ עָנֵה מַלְכָּא וְאָמַר בֵּלְטְשַׁאצַּר חֶלְמָא וּפִשְׁרֵא אַל יְבַהֲלָךְ עָנֵה בֵלְטְשַׁאצַּר וְאָמַר מָרִי חֶלְמָא לְשָׂנְאָךְ וּפִשְׁרֵהּ לְעָרָךְ: [דניאל ד, טז]

ליקוטי רש"י

בסיס. [כמתרגמינן כנו בסיסיה (שמות ל) מקום מושבו (פסחים פג.]. והאבן בידו. בתלוי ולא אמרינן דמטלטל לאבן (לקמן קמא.). מלאה פירות. דעיקר עשיית בסיס לפירות הלכך אבן מיטלטלת אגב כלי ופירות שהוא מותר [שם קמב.]. אישתומם. שתק והיה מחשב מה יענה [חולין כא.]. לשון משומם כאדם נבהל ותמה ולא מחשבות כמו (איוב יח, כ) על יומו נשמו אחרונים (ירמיה ב, יב) שומו שמים [דניאל ד, טז] ואשב שם שבעת ימים משמים בתוכם (יחזקאל ג) כמו אלם [דניאל ח, כז]. בגדי עניים. שלש על שלש מקבלין טומאה לעניים. בגדי עשירים. שלשה על שלשה מקבלין טומאה אף לעשירים [עירובין כט:]. מידי דהוה אגרף של ריעי. שמותר לטלטלו ולהוציאו לאשפה מחמת מאוס כדאמרינן בפרק בתרא (ביצה לו:). גרף. כלי חרס הן שגרף ועביט כלי חרס הן אלא של רעי קרוי גרף ושל מימי רגלים קרוי עביט (שם לו:) [ביצה כא.]. כנונא. כלי שמשימים בו הגחלים. אגב קיטמא. שהיו צריכין אפרו לכסות רוק או צואה. ואף על גב דאיכא עליה שברי עצים. דלא חזו מטלטל להו עם כנונא [שם כא:].

one assembles A STRAIGHT HORN HE IS EXEMPT from liability.[26] Now, since the Baraisa teaches that one is liable for reaffixing the branch of a candelabra, which is analogous in its degree of permanence to the reassembly of a coppersmith's bed, we learn that one who reassembles the coppersmith's bed is liable. – ? –

The Gemara concedes that this Baraisa cannot be reconciled with the view of R' Abba and Rav Huna bar Chiya, but nevertheless defends their ruling:

אִינְהוּ דְּאָמוּר כִּי הַאי תַּנָּא – **They stated** their ruling **in accordance with the following Tanna:** דְּתַנְיָא – **For it was taught in a Baraisa:** מַלְבְּנוֹת הַמִּטָּה וְכַרְעוֹת הַמִּטָּה וּלְוָוחִים שֶׁל סְקִיבָּס – Concerning BED SOCKETS,[27] BED LEGS,[28] AND CROSSBOW NUTS,[29] לֹא יַחֲזִיר – ONE SHOULD NOT REATTACH them on the Sabbath, וְאִם הֶחֱזִיר – BUT IF ONE DID REATTACH them פָּטוּר – HE IS EXEMPT from liability,

NOTES

26. A round horn and a straight horn are musical wind instruments consisting of perforated bases, into which pipes of varying pitch are inserted (cf. *Rav* to *Keilim* 11:7). The pipes of a round horn are inserted tightly and must be inserted by a technician; doing so is therefore a true act of completing a utensil and is a violation of *striking the final blow.* The pipes of a straight horn are inserted loosely and are made to be inserted and removed constantly; inserting them is, therefore, merely a violation of Rabbinical law (*Rashi*).

27. In earlier times, when houses had dirt floors, the [wooden] legs of beds would be inserted in sockets which rested on the ground and protected the legs from moisture (*Rashi*). [These sockets were part of the bed assembly.]

28. I.e. the legs of the bed itself, which can be detached from the frame and reattached.

29. The nut is a notched piece of wood that attaches to a crossbow and serves to guide the arrow (see *Rashi*).

גמרא

הנח לנר שמן ופתילה הואיל (א) דנעשה בסיס לדבר האסור א"ר זירא א"ר אסי א"ר יוחנן אמר ר' חנינא אמר רבי רומנוס לי התיר רבי לטלטל מחתה באפרה א"ל רבי זירא לרבי אסי מי אמר רבי יוחנן הכי והתנן א) נוטל אדם בנו והאבן בידו או כלכלה והאבן בתוכה ואמר רבה בר בר חנה א"ר יוחנן בכלכלה מלאה פירות עסקינן טעמא דאית בה פירי הא לית בה פירי לא ג) א) אישתומם כשעה חדא ואמר הכא נמי דאית בה קרטין אמר אביי קרטין בי רבי מי חשיבי וכי תימא חזו לעניים והתניא ג) בגדי עניים לעניים בגדי עשירים לעשירים ד) אבל דעניים לעשירים לא אלא אמר אביי מידי דהוה אגרף של ריעי אמר רבא שתי תשובות בדבר חדא גרף של ריעי מאים והאי לא מאים ועוד גרף של ריעי מיגלי והאי מיכסי אלא אמר רבא כי הוינן בי רב נחמן א) הוה ה) מטלטלינן כנונא אגב קיטמא ואע"ג דאיכא עליה שברי עצים מיתיבי ושוין שאם יש בה שברי פתילה שאסור לטלטל ו) אמר אביי ב) בגלילא שנו לוי בר שמואל אשכחינהו לרבי אבא ולרב הונא בר חייא דהוו קיימי אפיתחא דבי רב הונא אמר להו מהו להחזיר מטה של טרסיים בשבת אמרו ליה ג) שפיר דמי אתא לקמיה דרב יהודה אמר הא רב ושמואל דאמרי תרוייהו המחזיר מטה של טרסיים בשבת חייב חטאת מיתיבי ז) המחזיר קנה מנורה בשבת חייב חטאת קנה סיידין לא יחזיר ואם החזיר פטור אבל אסור רבי סימאי אומר ח) קרן עגולה חייב קרן פשוטה פטור אינהו דאמור כי האי תנא דתניא מלבנות המטה וכרעות המטה ולווחים של סקיבס ד) לא יחזיר ואם החזיר פטור אבל

רש"י

לדבר האסור. לשלהבת דכי האי מוקצה מודה ר"ש שהכלי טפל לשלהבת בעודה בו ולאו משום דחייש לכבייה: בסיס. מושב את כנו מתרגמינן בסיסיה: א"ר רומנוס לי התיר רבי לטלטל מחתה. של לבונה באפרה קס"ד באפרה עם אפרה קאמר שהאפר מוקצה ולא היו צריכין לו ואשמעינן דאגב מחתה דאיכא תורת כלי עליה טלטלה עם אפרה: נוטל אדם. הכלכלה בשבת והאבן בתוכה: הא ליכא פרי לא. דכלי נעשה בסיס לאבן וטפלה לו ובטל תורת כלי דידיה והכי נמי נעשית מחתה בסיס לאפר ורבי יוחנן שמעי' ליה לעיל דכדר' יהודה סבירא ליה: דאית ביה קרטין. שנשתיירו מן האור ולבונה דחזיא להריח ואגב לבונה מטלטל למחתה עם אפרה דומיא דכלכלה מלאה פירות והאבן בתוכה: קרטין. של שיור לבונה: בי רבי. דנשיא ועשיר הוה מי חשיבי: בגדי עניים. שלש על שלש או שחוטן עבה הוו בגדים לעניים לענין טומאה: בגדי עשירים. שלשה על שלשה הוו בגדים לעשירים וכל שכן לעניים אבל בגדי עניים לעשירים לא הוה בגד גבייהו ולא מקבלי טומאה הכא נמי בי רבי (ג) בטלי קרטין: אלא אמר אביי. הא דשרי ליה לטלטל מחתה באפרה משום דאפרה מאים עליה לראותו והוי כגרף של רעי דתניא במסכת ביצה (דף לו:) מותר להוציאו לאשפה שבחצר: גרף. כלי חרס המוכן לכך: מיכסי. כל מחתות מכוסות הן ויש בהן נקבים להוציא הריח: כנונא. כלי נחשת שמציאין בו האור לפני שרים להתחמם: אגב קטמיה. שהיו צריכין לאפרו לכסות רוק או צואה וא"ת מה צד איסור יש כאן היינו רבותא דאע"ג דאיכא עליה שברי עצים והא דר' רומנוס נמי האי מחתה באפרה דקאמר מחתה בשביל אפרה שהיה צריך לו ודעתייהו עליה מאתמול ורבותא אשמעינן (כיון) אע"ג דאיכא עליה שברי עצים דהוי ככלכלה של פירות והאבן בתוכה: ושוין. ר' יהודה ור"ש שנחלקו בנר ישן: בגלילא שנו. שחשובות להן שברי פתילה שאין בגדים של פשתן מצויין להם הלכך לא בטלי ונעשה נר בסיס להן: טרסיים. צורפי נחשת או גרדיים והולכין מעיר לעיר למלאכתן ונושאין עמהן מטות של פרקים: חייב חטאת. הוא תחלתו וגמרו ונמצא עושה כלי וחייב משום מכה בפטיש אב לכל גומרי מלאכה ולא משום בנין דאין בנין בכלים: קנה מנורה. שיוצאין ממנה קנים לנרות הרבה ונוטלין הימנה ובשעת הצורך מחזירין אותו: קנה של סיידין. הטחין ומלבנין הבית בסיד יש להן קנים של פרקים ונותן מטלית בראשה ושורין בסיד המחוי וטח את הבית וכשהוא טח מלמטה אי אפשר לו אלא בקנה קצר וכשהוא הולך ומגביה מוסיף קנה על קנה ומאריכו: פטור. שאין זה גמרו שהרי צריך לחזור ולפרקו תמיד: קרן עגולה וקרן פשוטה. שניהם מין כלי זמר והוא עשוי נקבים נקבים ככברה ומכנים בהן חלילים ומוציאין קולות הרבה קרן עגולה מעשה אומן הוא וצריך לתקוע בנקבים בחוזק והויא מלאכה ובקרן פשוט מכניסו בריוח ודרכן לפרקס תמיד ופטור קתני מיהת בקני מנורה דחייב והוא הדין למטה של טרסיים: אינהו. רבי אבא ורב הונא בר חייא: דאמור כי האי תנא. כרבי שמעון דמתיר לכתחלה: מלבנות המטה. כעין רגלים קטנים ויש להן בית קיבול ומכנים לתוכן ראשי כרעי המטה שלא ירקבו בארץ: לווחים של סקיבס. עץ קטן כמין דף שתוקעין בקשת שקורין אבלשטר"א שעליו מושך החץ:

יתקע

תוספות

הנח לנר שמן ופתילה הואיל ונעשה בסיס לדבר האסור. איצטריך למימר בשמן דנעשה בסיס לדבר האסור דאי לאו הכי לא היה הנר אסור לטלטל דהוי בסיס לדבר האסור ולדבר המותר ושרי כדאמר בסמוך כי הוינן בי רב נחמן הוה מטלטלינן כונא אגב קיטמא אע"ג דאיכא עליה שברי עצים ואם תאמר פתילה אמאי קאמר דהויא בסיס לדבר האסור היא עצמה הויא דבר האסור כדאמר לקמן ושוין שאם יש בה שברי פתילות שאסור לטלטלה וי"ל דשברי פתילה הוי שברי כלים ודמי לצרורות אבל פתילה שלימה שהיא כלי הוה שרי אי לאו דנעשה בסיס לדבר האסור:

לי התיר רבי לטלטל מחתה באפרה. השתא ס"ד דאפר מחתה מוקצה הוא:

ואמר רבה ב"ב חנה א"ר יוחנן כו'. תימה אמאי לא פריך בלאו מילתיה דרבי יוחנן ממתני' דפ' נוטל (לקמן דף קמב:) דתנן מעות שע"ג הכר מנער את הכר והן נופלות וכן אבן שעל פי החבית מטה על צדה והיא נופלת אבל טלטול גמור אסור ואור"י דה"א דשאני מעות דחשיבי ולא בטלי ואבן שע"פ החבית ה"א דמיירי שהוא מתוקן לסתום פי החבית והחבית צריכה לה ולכך לא בטלה:

בגדי עניים לעניים. אומר ר"ת דדוקא בטומאת מדרס דבייחוד תליא מלתא אבל בשאר טומאות לא תליא מלתא בייחוד דאפי' היה מוטל באשפה מרבינן ח) מוהבגד דשלש על שלש מיטמא בין לעניים בין לעשירים דבקרא לא מפליג מידי ומייתי ר"ת ראיה דתנן במסכת כלים (פרק כ"ז מ"ב) דבגד מטמא משום שלשה על שלשה למדרס משום שלש על שלש לטמא מת וע"כ בעשירים מיירי דבפכ"ח תנן התם בגדי עניים אע"פ שאין בהם שלשה על שלשה טמאין מדרס וא"ת הכא דפריך מברייתא אמאי לא פריך ממתני' דפכ"ח דכלים שהבאתי ואור"י דאי ממתני' ה"א דבגדי עניים היינו כעין שק שעיקרו עשוי לעניים ואפי' ביד עשירים אינו צריך שלשה על שלשה אבל שאר בגדים בעי שלשה על שלשה שאינו עומד אלא לעשירים להכי מייתי ברייתא דלא שייך לפרשה הכי:

הוה מטלטלינן כנונא אגב קיטמא. פי' כונא מחתה והיינו מחתה באפרה דלעיל פי' אגב אפרה שהוסק מע"ש דמוכן הוא דחזי לכסות בה רוק או צואה וקשה דמשמע דוקא אגב קיטמא שרי הא לאו הכי נעשה בסיס לדבר האסור ואילו בפ"ב דביצה (כא: ושם) אמר גבי אין מזמנין נכרי בשבת משום שיורי כוסות פריך וניטלטלינהו אגב כסא מי לא אמר רבא כי הוינן בי רב נחמן הוה מטלטלינן כונא אגב קיטמא אף על גב דאיכא עליה שברי עצים ומאי פריך שאני כונא דאגב קטמא מטלטל לה אבל בכוס ליכא אלא דבר האסור ואור"י דשיורי כוסות לא חשיבי למיהוי כוס בטל לגבייהו אף על גב שאין היתר עמהן בכוס טפי גרעי משברי עצים שעם הקיטמא בכונא:

אע"ג דאיכא עליה שברי עצים. נראה לרבינו תם דשברי עצים חשיבי טפי מאבן שבכלכלה דאם לא כן מאי קמ"ל ואדמקשי ליה מברייתא דשוין כו' ליסייעיה ממתני' דכלכלה והאבן בתוכה אלא שברי עצים חשיבי טפי ויש לדמות שברי עצים לגבי אפר כשברי פתילה לגבי שמן:

בגלילא שנו. פי' בקונט' שחשובות להן שברי פתילה שאין בגדי פשתן מצויין להם ואין נראה לר"ת דהא אמרי' בשילהי ב"ק (דף קיט:) לוקחין מן הנשים כלי צמר ביהודה וכלי פשתן בגליל משמע שמצוי פשתן הרבה שם ומפרש ר"ת בגלילא שנו שהיה להם רוב שמן ולהכי לא בטלי שברי פתילה אגב שמן וכן משמע בפ"ק דסנהדרין (דף יא:) גבי טול איגרת וכתוב לאחנא בני גלילאה עילאה ותתאה כו' דזמן ביעורא מטא לאפרושא מעשרא ממעטני זיתא ואמר בנזיר בפרק בית שמאי (דף לא:) בגלילא שנו דחמרא עדיף ממשחא ויין היה מצוי להם הרבה כדאמר בהמוציא יין (לקמן עח.) גבי מים כדי לשוף בהן את הקילור וקאמר בגלילא שנו א) דרפואת מים שכיח טפי משתיה שהיה להן רוב יין והיו שותין הכל יין ואפילו הכי חמרא עדיף להו ממישחא כי השמן היה להם בזול יותר ורש"י פי' נמי בהמוציא (שם) שמחמת עניותא היו עושין רפואה מן המים ואין עושין מן היין רק שתייה ולפיכך היתה רפואת מים שכיחא ואין נראה דכיון שלא היה להם יין לשיפות הקילור א"כ שכיחא שתיית מים טובא ואמרי' בעלמא ט) אף ערב יוה"כ בגליל שהיו מרדים בסעודה משמע שעשירים היו [וע"ע תוספות חגיגה כה: ד"ה בגלילא]:

רשב"ג

עין משפט נר מצוה

נז א ב מיי' פכ"ו מהל' שבת הלכה יג טור שו"ע או"ח סימן שי סעיף ח:
נח ג ד מיי' פכ"ב מהל' שבת הלכה כו כח סמג לאוין סה טור שו"ע או"ח סימן שיג סעיף ו:

רבינו חננאל

הנח לנר ופתילה ושמן דלא גזר ר"ש אלא הואיל ונעשה כל אחד בסיס לדבר האסור. ופשוטה היא: אמר רבא כי היינו בי רב נחמן היינו מטלטלי כנונא אגב קיטומה אף על גב דאיכא עליה שברי עצים. מיתיבי ושוין שאם יש בה שברי פתילה שאסור לטלטלה. ופריק אביי בגלילא שנו. פירוש בגליל שנו שדרכם להדליק בשברי פתילות. וכיון שדרכם להדליק בשברי פתילות נעשו מוקצות בשבת לפיכך אסור לטלטל אפילו הנרות שיש בהן שברי פתילות. אבל שברי עצים דכנונא לא חשיבי ובטלי: לוי בר שמואל בעא מר' אבא ומרב הונא בר חייא מהו להחזי' מטה של (פרסיים) [טרסיים] בשבת אמרו ליה שרי. אמר להו רב יהודה רב ושמואל דאמרי תרווייהו המחזיר מטה של (פרסיים) [טרסיים] בשבת חייב חטאת. מיתיבי המחזיר קנה מנורה בשבת חייב חטאת קנה של ציירין לא יחזיר ואם החזיר פטור אבל אסור. ר' סימאי א' קרן [עגולה חייב קרן] פשוטה פטור. קתני מיהת המחזיר קנה מנורה בשבת חייב חטאת. קשיא לר' אבא ולרב הונא דשרי. ושניני' אינהו דאמור כי האי תנא דתניא אם היה רפוי מותר. דתניא מלבנות המטה וכרעי המטה [ולווחין] של סקיבס לא יחזיר. ואם החזיר פטור אבל

רב נסים גאון

אלא אמר אביי מידי דהוה אגרף של רעי. משתכח במס' יום טוב בפרק משילין פירות (דף לו) אמר שמואל גרף של רעי ועביט מימי רגלים מותר להוציאו לאשפה ובפרק נוטל אדם את בנו (דף קמג) אמרו הני גרעיני דתמרי כול' רב הונא בריה דרב יהושע עביד להו גרף של רעי וכן אמימר עביד להו גרף של רעי: אמר אביי בגלילא שנו. כבר טרחו בזה השינוי ששינה אביי הרבה מן החכמים ולא שמעתי מהם כלום ולא מצאתי בו לאחד מן הגאונים פירוש אבל טרחתי על שינויו ומצאתי במס' נזירות בפ' בית שמאי אומרים הקדש טעות הקדש (דף לא) והא שמן עדיף מיין אי משום הא לא קשיא בגלילא שנו דחמרא עדיף ממשחא זה מודיע שהשמן היה אצלם מצוי הרבה וכי מה שהושם בנר ויש בו שברי פתילה אין לו חשיבות אצלם ואינם משתמשין בו לצרכם והרי הוא כדין המוקצה שאסור לטלטלו ולכך שנו חכמים כי בגליל אסור לטלטל נר שיש בו שברי פתילה לפי שהשמן הנותר בנר לא חשיב להו וכבר זה הפירוש הודענו באלו הימים לתלמידנו ופירשנו להם בזה הענין ואפשר להיאמר בו פירוש אחר

שאנשי גליל לפי שלא היו מקפידין על לשונם ולא דייקי לישנא ולא גמיר מחד רבה ולא גלו מסכתא למסכתא כמו שהוא מפורש במסכת עירובין בפרק כיצד מעברין (דף נג) ולא היה תלמודם מקויים בידם אסרו עליהם החכמים טלטול נר שיש בתוכו שברי פתילה א) עלי דרך האיסורים ואל תחבט ואל תסייג ויקוי דאלך איצא קולהום פי עדה (מרצעא) [מואצע] מן אל תלמוד מתל הדא אל קול עלי טריק אל תנקין להם

חשק שלמה על רב נסים גאון א) פירוש בערבי על דרך האיסורים והגדר והסייג ונמצא סיוע לזה במקומות הרבה מהתלמוד משל זה המאמר על דרך הגירעון להם מסיר מזה מה שנמצא בפר' אומר בקודש:

מסורת הש"ס

א) לקמן קמא:, ב) [מו"ק ג: קידושין לט: סוכה מד. חולין כא.], ג) [עירובין כט:], ד) [עי' תוספות לקמן קמ: ד"ה כיון וכו'], ה) ביצה דף כא: ע"ש, ו) [לקמן עח.], ז) [תוספ' פי"ג], ח) [לעיל כו:], ט) [חולין פג.].

תוספות ישנים

א) ורבינו מאיר פי' כי מרוב שתיית יין הי' להם חכלילי עינים ושכיחי רפואת מים טובא:

הגהות הב"ח

(א) גמ' ופתילה הואיל ונעשה בסיס: (ב) רש"י ד"ה בגדי עשירים וכו' ה"נ בי רבי לא חשיבי קרטין ובטלי הס"ד:

גליון הש"ס

גמ' קרן עגולה חייב. עי' כלים פי"א מ"ו:

תורה אור השלם

א) אֱדַיִן דָּנִיֵּאל דִּי שְׁמֵהּ בֵּלְטְשַׁאצַּר אֶשְׁתּוֹמַם כְּשָׁעָה חֲדָה וְרַעְיֹנֹהִי יְבַהֲלֻנֵּהּ עָנֵה מַלְכָּא וְאָמַר בֵּלְטְשַׁאצַּר חֶלְמָא וּפִשְׁרֵא אַל יְבַהֲלָךְ עָנֵה בֵלְטְשַׁאצַּר וְאָמַר מָרִי חֶלְמָא לְשָׂנְאָךְ וּפִשְׁרֵהּ לְעָרָךְ: [דניאל ד, טז]

ליקוטי רש"י

בסים. [כדמתרגמינן כנו] בסיסיה (שמות ל) מקום מושבו [פסחים פג.]. והאבן בידו. בתלר ולא אמרינן דמטלטל לאבן [לקמן קמא:]. מלאה פירות. דעיקר נעשית בסיס לפירות הלכך אבן מיטלטלת אגב כלי ופירות שהוא מותר [שם קמב.]. אישתומם. שתק והיה מחשב מה יענה [חולין כא.]. לשון משומם באדם נבהל ונאלם ובעל מחשבות כמו (איוב יח, כ) על יומו נשמו אחרונים (ירמיה ב, יב) שומו שמים (דניאל ד, טו) אשתומם כשעה חדא [בראשית כד, כא]. שומם ל' אלם ומשותק כמו אשתומם כשעה חדא (דניאל ג) ואשב שם שבעת ימים משמים בתוכם כמו אלם (יחזקאל ג) [דניאל ח, יג]. בגדי עניים. שלש על שלש מקבלין טומאה לעניים. בגדי עשירים. שלשה על שלשה מקבלין טומאה אף לעשירים [עירובין כט:]. מידי דהוה אגרף של ריעי. שמותר לטלטלו ולפנותו לאשפה מחמת מאוס כדאמרינן בפרק בתרא (ביצה לו:) [ביצה כא:]. גרף. גרף ועביט כלי חרס הן אלא של רעי קרוי גרף ושל מימי רגלים קרוי עביט [שם לו:]. כנונא. כלי שמשימים בו הגחלים. אגב קיטמא. שהיינו צריכין לאפרו והוכן מערב שבת לכסות רוק או צואה. ואף על גב דאיכא עליה שברי עצים. דלא חזו מטלטל להו עם כנונא [שם כא:].

עין משפט נר מצוה

נט א מיי' פכ"ב מהל' שבת הלכה ו וסמג שם טוש"ע שם סעיף ו וסעיף ט:

ס ב מיי' שם טור שו"ע שם סעיף ו:

סא ג מיי' שם פ"ה הלכה יג סמג שם טוש"ע או"ח סימן רסה סעיף ד:

א ד ה מיי' פ"ד מהלכות שבת הלכה א טוש"ע או"ח סימן רנז סעיף ג:

רבינו חננאל

אסור. לא יתקע ואם תקע חייב חטאת רבן שמעון בן גמליאל אומר אם היה רפוי מותר המחזיר קני מנורה חייב חטאת כמשמעו מפני שמתקן כלי כבנין. קנה של ציידין דרכם לתת קנה דק דק בתוך ראש קנה עבה כדי שיהא (נכוה) [גבוה] ולא יהא נשבר וזהו פטור אבל אסור. קרן עגולה חייב פשוטה פטור. אלו הן כלי שיר. והן של חליות ויש מהן קרן עגולה וקרן פשוטה כדכתיב (דניאל ג) קל קרנא משרוקיתא. וזה שהיא עגולה היא כלי יש בו מלאכה להחזירה לפיכך חייב חטאת אבל פשוטה אין בה עסק כלום כדתנן בכלים פ' י"א. הכוש והאימא והמקל וסומפאניא וחליל של מתכת טמאין והמצופין טהורין וסמפאניא שיש בה בית קיבול כנפים בין כך ובין כך טמאה. קרן עגולה טמאה וכו' טמאין ובשעת חבורן הכל טמאה בי רב חמא הוה ליה מיטה גליתא והוו מהדרי ליה בי"ט א"ל לרב חמא מאי דעתיך בנין מן הצד הוא נהי דאיסורא דאוריי' ליכא דרבנן מיהא איכא. א"ל רב חמא אנא כרבן שמעון בן גמליאל סבירא לי אם היה רפוי מותר. נמצא רב חמא כר' אבא ורב הונא דשרו. ומסתברא מטה של טורסיים הוא כגון מטה גיליתא: **נותנין** כלי תחת הנר לקבל בו ניצוצות. והא קא מבטל כלי מהיכנו. אמר רב הונא בריה דרב יהושע ניצוצות אין בהן ממש ומותר להשתמש באותו כלי ולא יתן בתוכו מים מפני שהוא מכבה. לימא תנן סתמא כר' יוסי דאמר גרם כבוי אסור דתנן ר' יוסי אוסר לעשות מחיצה שלא תעבור הדליקה בכלי חרש חדשים מלאים מים שאין יכולין לקבל את האור והן מתבקעין ומכבין הדליק' ודחי אימור דאסר ר' יוסי בשבת. בע"ש מי אסר. וכי תימא הכא נמי כי תנן אסור בשבת אבל בע"ש שרי. והא תניא נותנין כלי תחת הנר לקבל ניצוצות בשבת ואין צורך לומר בע"ש. ולא יתן לתוכו מים בע"ש מפני שהוא מכבה ואין צריך לומר בשבת. ואוקמה רב אשי אפילו לרבנן דפליגי עליה דר' יוסי הכא אסרי מפני שמקרב כיבויו פי' כיון שנופלין הניצוצות במים מיד נכבין ובכלים עד שיתבקעו. וקי"ל דהלכתא כר"ש דאפי' במוקצה מחמת מיאוס שרי: **ואין** הלכה כר"ש במוקצה מחמת איסור כגון במנורה ופמוט שהדליקו עליהן באותה שבת וכיוצא בהן וכגון מטה שיחדה למעות ונכרי שהביא דורון לישראל דבר המחובר לקרקע וכיוצא בהן דמוקצה מחמת איסור הן. וגרסי' במי שהחשיך בדרך פליגי בה רב אחא ורבינא חד אמר בכולה שבת הלכתא כר"ש בר ממוקצה מחמת מיאוס וחד אמר אפילו במוקצה מחמת מיאוס נמי הלכתא כר"ש בר ממוקצה מחמת איסור בלבד וקי"ל דבכל התורה רב אחא לחומרא ורבינא לקולא והלכתא כרבינא לקולא בר מהני תלת אומצא כר' ואע"ג דעולא ולוי ורב אמרו הלכה כר' יהודה הא שמואל וזעירי ור' יוחנן אמרו הלכתא כר' שמעון. ורבינא דהוא בתראה פסק הלכתא כר' שמעון כדאמרן. לפיכך כל מוקצה מותר לבר ממוקצה מחמת איסור כמו שפירשנו. ומוקצה מחמת חסרון כיס מודה ר' שמעון וגרוגרות וצמוקין כדאמרן: הדרן עלך כירה

פרק רביעי במה טומנין ובמה אין טומנין כו' אין טומנין בגפת. אוקימנא בגפת של שומשין וכל שכן בגפת של זיתים דמסיק נמי הבלא אסיק' אמר רבא אנוחי כוזא דמיא אפומא דקומקומא משום דמיא צונן ומוליד חימום. ואסו

תוספות

רבן שמעון בן גמליאל אומר אם היה רפוי מותר. ולעיל נמי מיירי ברפוי ° וקשה קצת דהיכי פליגי כולי האי דמר מחייב חטאת ומר שרי אפי' לכתחלה ועוד הא אין בנין וסתירה בכלים ועוד תקשה לרב יהודה הך ברייתא דליכא תנא דמחייב חטאת ויש לומר דהכי קאמר לעיל הא רב ושמואל דאמרי תרווייהו המחזיר מטה של טרסיים בשבת חייב חטאת כשאינו רפוי ואם כן ברפוי אין סברא להתיר לכתחלה:

לימא תנן סתמא כרבי יוסי דאמר גורם לכיבוי אסור. הוה מצי למימר וליטעמיך הא רבי יוסי גופיה לא אמרה אלא בדליקה משום דאדם בהול על ממונו אי שרינא ליה אתי לכבויי והכי מפרש בכל כתבי (לקמן קכ:) אבל הכא ליכא למגזר דהא יש כלי תחת הנר ואינו בהול ובכמה מקומות בהש"ס יכול לומר וליטעמיך ואינו אומר:

מפני שמקרב את כבויו. פירוש דגזרינן ע"ש אטו שבת ובשבת יכול לבא לידי כיבוי אם יגביה הכלי בשעת נפילת הניצוצות ואם תאמר מאי שנא שריית דיו וסממנים ופריסת מצודה דשרינן בפ"ק (דף יח:) עם השמש והכא אסרינן מע"ש שלא יבא לעשות בשבת ותירץ הרב פור"ת דהתם ליכא למיחש שמא יעשה כן בשבת דהא אב מלאכה הן אבל הכא איכא למיחש דלא דמי איסור כל כך במה שמניח כלי תחת הניצוצות ואיכא למיחש שמא יבא לידי כיבוי שיתחיל ליתן המים קודם נפילת הניצוצות וקודם גמר הנתינה יפלו ומכבה בידים או שיגביה הכלי עם המים כנגד הניצוצות כדפרישית ואף על גב דבאותו כיבוי אין בו חיוב חטאת לר' שמעון דמלאכה שאינה צריכה לגופה היא החמירו אטו כיבוי דחיוב חטאת ואע"ג דהוי גזירה לגזירה קים להו לרבנן דהכא שייך למגזר טפי ורש"י דפי' דהוה מכבה ממש לאו דוקא אלא כלומר שיוכל לבא לידי כיבוי ור"ת גרים כפירוש ר"ח מפני שמקרב כיבוי דהתם הוא דשרי לעשות מחיצה מכלים שיש בתוכן מים שאינו מכבה כלום עד שיתבקעו הכלים אבל הכא אין הפסק בין מים לניצוצות ומיד נכבות כשנופלות בכלי והוי כמחיצת מים דאסירא כגון מחיצת שלג וברד וקשה לפירושו דבירושלמי מוקי מתני' כר' יוסי אבל לרבנן אפי' מחיצות של מים מותר ובפ' כל כתבי (לקמן קכ:) נמי שרו רבנן דר' יוסי בטלית שאחז בו האור מצד אחד ליתן עליו מים מצד אחר ואם כבתה כבתה ונראה דלפי הש"ס שלנו יש לחלק דבמחיצה של מים אע"ג דאין דבר מפסיק מ"מ שרי שאין האש נופלת לתוך המים להדיא כי הכא שהמים תחת הניצוצות ומקרב כיבוין טפי ועוד דאיכא למימר דהש"ס שלנו אוסר במחיצות של מים לרבנן ומשום הכי מוקי מתניתין כרבנן ופליג אירושלמי ולא דמי לטלית שאחז בו האור מצד אחד שאינו אלא שלא תתפשט האור ומה שרגילים לתת מים בזוכית שקורין לאמפ"א ונותנין עליה שמן בע"ש אין זה קרוי קירוב כיבוי דכיון שאין מתכוין לכיבוי כלל אלא להגביה את השמן לא שייך למגזר מידי שמא יעשה בשבת ושרי אפי' לר' יוסי וכ"ש לרבנן דאל"כ אפי' בלא מים אסור שהניצוצות נופלות בשמן: ועוד איכא למימר דתלמוד שלנו אסר מחיצה של מים לרבנן ומש"ה מוקי מתני' כר' יוסי ופליג אירושלמי ול"ד לטלית שאחז בו האור מצד אחד שאינו אלא שלא תתפשט האור [ת"י]:

הדרן עלך כירה

במה טומנין וכו' אין טומנין לא בגפת. פירש הר"ר יוסף בשם רבינו שמואל דמיירי בבשיל ולא בשיל ° אבל קדרא חייתא ובשיל שרינן בפ"ק (דף יח:) ואין נראה לר"ת דהא אית לן לאוקמא מתניתין בסתם קדרות שהן מבושלים בין השמשות ועוד דמסתמא איירי מתני' דומיא דמתני' דכירה דמיירי בבשיל כמאכל בן דרוסאי ונראה לר"ת שיש לחלק בין השהאה להטמנה דודאי להשהות מותר כשהוא מאכל בן דרוסאי שאין חיתוי מעט מועיל לו שהרי מגולה הוא ושליט ביה אוירא אבל הטמנה שעושין לצורך מחר והוא מוטמן יש לחוש שמא יחתה שמעט חיתוי מועיל לו ליתפס חומו וגזרו להטמין בכל דבר המוסיף הבל גזירה שמא יטמין ברמץ ויחתה:

גמרא

אבל אסור [א] ולא יתקע ואם תקע חייב חטאת רשב"ג אומר [ב] אם היה רפוי מותר בי רב חמא הוה מטה גללניתא הוה מהדרי לה ביומא טבא א"ל ההוא מדרבנן לרבא מאי דעתיך בנין מן הצד הוא נהי דאיסורא דאורייתא ליכא איסורא דרבנן מיהא איכא אמר ליה אנא כרשב"ג סבירא לי דאמר אם היה רפוי מותר: **מתני'** [א] [ג] נותנין כלי תחת הנר לקבל ניצוצות ולא יתן לתוכו מים מפני שהוא מכבה: **גמ'** והא [ג] קמבטל כלי מהיכנו אמר רב הונא בריה דרב יהושע ניצוצות אין בהן ממש: ולא יתן לתוכו מים מפני שהוא מכבה: לימא תנן סתמא כרבי יוסי [ג] דאמר גורם לכיבוי אסור ותסברא אימור דאמר ר' יוסי בשבת בערב שבת מי אמר וכי תימא הכא נמי בשבת והתניא נותנין כלי תחת הנר לקבל ניצוצות בשבת ואין צריך לומר בע"ש ולא יתן לתוכו מים מפני שהוא מכבה מע"ש ואין צריך לומר בשבת אלא אמר רב אשי אפילו תימא רבנן שאני הכא מפני שמקרב את כיבויו:

הדרן עלך כירה

במה [ה] [ד] טומנין ובמה אין טומנין אין טומנין לא בגפת ולא בזבל לא במלח ולא בסיד ולא בחול בין לחין בין יבשין ולא בתבן ולא בזגין ולא במוכין ולא בעשבין בזמן שהן לחין אבל טומנין בהן כשהן יבשין: **גמ'** איבעיא להו גפת של זיתים תנן אבל דשומשמין שפיר דמי או דילמא דשומשמין תנן וכל שכן דזיתים ת"ש דאמר ר' זירא משום חד דבי ר' ינאי קופה שטמן בה אסור להניחה על גפת של זיתים ש"מ של זיתים תנן לעולם אימא לך [ה] לענין הטמנה דשומשמין נמי אסור לענין אסוקי

רש"י

יתקע. בחוזק על ידי יתדות שקורין קוי"ש: מטה גללניתא. טירנדי"ן והוא כעין של טרסיים [ה]: מן הצד. מפני שאינה תקועה ומהדקה בחוזק קרי לה מן הצד כלומר ע"י שינוי: **גמ'** והא קא מבטל כלי מהיכנו. דלא יוכל ליטלו משם כל היום דנעשה בסיס לניצוצות ולימא תהוי תיובתיה דרב חסדא דאסר בפירקין (דף מג.): **אין בהן ממש.** משכנו ומותר ליטלן: **כרבי יוסי.** בכל כתבי הקדש דקתני עושה מחיצה בכל הכלים בין מלאין בין ריקנין כדי שלא תעבור הדליקה רבי יוסי אוסר בכלי חרס חדשים מלאים מים שאין יכולין לקבל האור והן מתבקעים ומכבין את הדליקה: **בערב שבת.** כגון זה שנותן המים מבעוד יום בכלי תחת הנר: **וכי תימא הכא נמי.** אין נותנין לתוכו מים בשבת קאמר ור' יוסי היא: **והתניא.** אפילו בע"ש אסור ואי לגרם כיבוי מדמית לה אפילו כרבי יוסי לא מיתוקמה דבע"ש לא אמר רבי יוסי: **אלא אמר רב אשי.** מתניתין אפילו לרבנן דלא דמי לגרם כיבוי דהתם כי מטי דליקה לכלים דליקה הוא דפקע להו וגרמא בעלמא הוא אבל זה שנתן המים ממש תחת הנר מכבה ממש הוא וגזירה מבעוד יום אטו משחשכה: **שמקרב את כיבויו.** זימן כיבוי להדיא והוה ליה מכבה ממש אי הוה יהיב ליה בשבת:

הדרן עלך כירה

במה טומנין. הבא לסלק קדירה מעל גבי כירה ולטומנה בדבר אחר ואמרו חכמים [י] אין טומנין בדבר המוסיף הבל אלא בדבר המעמיד הבל מי הוא המוסיף ואסור: **גפת.** פסולת של בית הבד של שמן שהוא כנוס יחד וחם מאד: **לחין.** יש בהן הבל הרבה יותר מיבשין: **זגין.** פסולת של יקב יין: **מוכין.** כל דבר רך קרוי מוכין כגון צמר גפן ותלישי צמר רך של בהמה וגרירת בגדים בלויים: **גמ' קופה שטמן בה.** שנותן בה מוכין וטומן בה קדירה: **לענין הטמנה.** לטומנו בתוכה: **אסוקי** דזיתים

ליקוטי רש"י

שהיה מוכן מתחלה לטלטלו ועכשיו עושהו מוקצה [שם מג.]. דמשהכניסם תחתיו אין יכול לטלטלן דדומה לסותר בנין מדרבנן [לקמן קכח:]. כשמניחן תחת דבר שאין ניטל מבטלן מהיכנן דשוב לא יטלם משם ודמי לסותר [שם קנד: ועי' בתוס' לעיל מג.]. **אין** בהן ממש. ומותר ליטלן אחר שנפלו לתוכו [לעיל מג.]. **גורם לכיבוי.** כי האי גוונא כשמגיע למים הוא כבה [לקמן קכ:]. במה טומנין. את החמין בשבת דאמור רבנן דאסור להטמין בדבר המוסיף הבל והתם מפרש טעמא גזירה שמא יטמין ברמץ [ב"ב יט.]. **אין** טומנין וכו'. בדבר המוסיף הבל אפילו מבעוד יום [לעיל לד.]. **מוכין.** של שחקי בגדים שהסורק מוציא מבגד הצמר בקוצים [ב"ב שם]. **גפת של זיתים.** פסולת זיתים שנתעצרו בבית הבד [שם יז.]. **דשומשמין.** פסולת של שומשמי שהוציא שומנן [לעיל לו:].

ואם תקע. בחוזקה בסכין ויתדות והוה ליה גמר מלאכה וחייב משום מכה בפטיש [לקמן קכב.]. **מטה גללניתא.** הוא שם מקום ומפרקין מטותיהן וכשאוסין וטוענין אותן עמהן וחוזרין ומחזירין אותן [שם קלח.]. **לקבל ניצוצות.** שלהבת הנוטפת מן הנר כדי שלא ידלק מה שתחתיה ואף על גב דניצוצות לא מיטלטלי ולא שכיחי [לעיל מב:]. **והא קמבטל כלי מהיכנו.** אסור לבטל כלי מהיכנו להושיב כלי במקום שלא יוכל עוד ליטלו [משם] דהוי כקובע לו מקום ומחברו בטיט ודמי למלאכה [לעיל מב:].

מסורת הש"ס

א) [לעיל דף מב: מג.], ב) [לעיל דף מג: וש"נ], ג) לקמן קכ., ד) בבא בתרא יט. [מדרש ג: מיר ב.], ה) ע' לקמן קלח. רש"י ד"ה וכסא גלין, ו) לעיל לד:.

גליון הש"ס

תוס' ד"ה רשב"ג וכו' וקשה קצת. ע' לקמן דף קלח ע"א: שם בד"ה במה טומנין וכו' אבל קידרא חייתא. ע' לעיל דף לט ע"ב תוספות ד"ה ממעשה:

רב נסים גאון

נדבר מן דאלך מא יחצרנא בפרק חומר בקודש (דף כה) אמרו אמר רב יוסף בגלילא שנו מיגו דלא מהימני אקודש לא מהימני אתרומה נמי בנדרים בפרק א) ואלו נדרים ובגליל אסורין שאין אנשי גליל מכירין את חרמי כהנים ובפרק המוציא יין (דף עח) ובפרק מקום שנהגו (דף נה) בפסחים עוד ובגמרא (ירושלמי שבת פרק כל כתבי הלכה ח) גרסי אמר עולא י"ח שנין עבד רבן יוחנן בן זכאי יתיב בהדה ערב ולא אתא קימוי אלא אילין תרתין עובדיה אמר גליל גליל שנאת את התורה סופך להעשות כמציקין וכל דין סיוע לפירושנו: **לימא** תנן סתמא כר' יוסי דאמר גרם כיבוי אסור. עיקר דיליה במשנה בפרק כל כתבי הקודש (דף קכ) דתנן ר' יוסי אוסר בכלי חרש חדשים מלאים מים שאין יכולין לקבל את האור והם מתבקעין ומכבין את הדליקה ובגמ' גרסי' ר' יוסי סבר גרם כיבוי אסור:

סליק פרק כירה

חשק שלמה על רב נסים גאון

א) נ"ל ואלו מותרין דף יח במשנה.

אֲבָל אָסוּר – THOUGH HE IS FORBIDDEN by Rabbinical decree to do so.[1] וְלֹא יִתְקַע – AND ONE SHOULD certainly NOT NAIL them in; וְאִם תָּקַע חַיָּיב חַטָּאת – AND IF ONE DID NAIL them in HE IS LIABLE TO A *CHATAS* OFFERING.[2] רַבָּן שִׁמְעוֹן בֶּן גַּמְלִיאֵל אוֹמֵר – RABBAN SHIMON BEN GAMLIEL SAYS: אִם הָיָה רָפוּי מוּתָּר – IF [THE ATTACHMENT] WAS LOOSELY FITTING IT IS PERMITTED to attach it, provided one does not nail it in.[3] R' Abba and Rav Huna bar Chiya, who permitted reassembling a coppersmith's bed, were referring to one whose parts fit together loosely, and they followed the opinion of Rabban Shimon ben Gamliel.[4]

The Gemara recounts a related episode:

בֵּי רַב חָמָא הֲוָה מִטָּה גַּלְלָנִיתָא – **In Rav Chama's home there was a sectional bed,**[5] הֲוָה מַהַדְרִי לָהּ בְּיוֹמָא טָבָא – **which they would reassemble on Yom Tov.** אָמַר לֵיהּ הַהוּא מֵרַבָּנַן לְרָבָא – **A certain rabbi said to Rava:**[6] מַאי דַּעְתָּיךְ – **What is your reason** for permitting it? בִּנְיָן מִן הַצַּד הוּא – Is it because **this is an indirect manner of assembly?**[7] נְהִי דְּאִיסּוּרָא דְּאוֹרַיְיתָא לֵיכָּא – But this is not sufficient reason to allow it, for **although there is no Biblical prohibition** against such assembly אִיסּוּרָא דְּרַבָּנָן מִיהָא אִיכָּא – **there is nevertheless a Rabbinical prohibition** against it, as the Tanna Kamma stated in the Baraisa, above. אָמַר לֵיהּ – **He replied:** אֲנָא כְּרַבָּן שִׁמְעוֹן בֶּן גַּמְלִיאֵל סְבִירָא לִי – **I concur with Rabban Shimon ben Gamliel,** דְּאָמַר אִם הָיָה רָפוּי מוּתָּר – **who said,** in that Baraisa: IF [THE ATTACHMENT] WAS LOOSELY FITTING IT IS PERMITTED.[8]

Mishnah נוֹתְנִין כְּלִי תַּחַת הַנֵּר לְקַבֵּל נִיצוֹצוֹת – **We may place a vessel under a lamp to catch** the falling **sparks,**[9] וְלֹא יִתֵּן לְתוֹכוֹ מַיִם – **but one may not place water in [the vessel],** מִפְּנֵי שֶׁהוּא מְכַבֶּה – **because he** thereby **extinguishes** the sparks.[10]

Gemara The Gemara questions the Mishnah's permit to place a utensil under a lamp on the Sabbath to catch the falling sparks:

וְהָא קָמְבַטֵּל כְּלִי מֵהֵיכָנוֹ – **But** why is this permissible? **After all,** by doing so **one is nullifying the preparedness of the utensil.**[11] – ? –

The Gemara answers:

אָמַר רַב הוּנָא בְּרֵיהּ דְּרַב יְהוֹשֻׁעַ – **Rav Huna the son of Rav Yehoshua said:** נִיצוֹצוֹת אֵין בָּהֶן מַמָּשׁ – **Sparks have no substance.**[12]

The Mishnah stated:

וְלֹא יִתֵּן לְתוֹכוֹ מַיִם מִפְּנֵי שֶׁהוּא מְכַבֶּה – BUT ONE MAY NOT PLACE WATER IN [THE VESSEL], BECAUSE HE thereby EXTINGUISHES the sparks.

The Gemara analyzes the reason for this prohibition:

לֵימָא תְּנַן סְתָמָא כְּרַבִּי יוֹסֵי – **Shall we say** that **we have learned** here **an anonymous Mishnah in accordance with** the view of **R' Yose,** דְּאָמַר גּוֹרֵם לְכִיבּוּי אָסוּר – **who said** that **indirectly causing** a fire **to be extinguished is forbidden** on the Sabbath?[13]

NOTES

1. Since these attachments are designed to be detached regularly, attaching them is not considered a violation of *striking the final blow*. Nevertheless, the Rabbis prohibited this out of concern that one might nail the attachments in, which would be a violation of Biblical law (*Ran;* see following note).

2. Nailing the pieces in does violate the *melachah* of *striking the final blow* (*Ran*).

3. Rabban Shimon ben Gamliel concedes that nailing the pieces in is a violation of Biblical law. He disagrees, however, with the Tanna Kamma's unqualified ruling that reassembly without nailing is prohibited Rabbinically. According to Rabban Shimon ben Gamliel, the Rabbinical prohibition pertains only if the pieces are fitted tightly. If they are fitted loosely, we need not be concerned that one might nail them in (*Ran;* see *Ramban* to 102b).

4. *Tosafos* ask: If the discussion above pertained to a loosely fitting bed, how could Rav and Shmuel have stated that one who assembles it is liable? Even the Tanna Kamma of this Baraisa, whose opinion is stringent, stated only that it is forbidden Rabbinically, and there is no Tanna who holds that it is forbidden Biblically! *Tosafos* answer that Rav and Shmuel were referring to a bed whose parts fit together *tightly*, and they followed the opinion of the previous Baraisa, which stated that in such a case (e.g. that of a candelabra) one who reassembles it is liable. Nevertheless, the opinion of Rav and Shmuel was cited as contradictory to that of R' Abba and Rav Huna bar Chiya, who ruled leniently regarding a bed whose parts are fitted *loosely*. The reason is that if the reassembly of a utensil with tightly fitting parts is prohibited Biblically, as Rav and Shmuel stated, the reassembly of a utensil with loosely fitting parts must be prohibited at least Rabbinically. The Gemara responded that R' Abba and Rav Huna bar Chiya follow the opinion of Rabban Shimon ben Gamliel, who holds that the reassembly of a utensil with tightly fitting parts is prohibited only Rabbinically and the reassembly of one with loosely fitting parts is permitted outright. See also *Ramban, Rashba* and *Ritva MHK* ed.

5. Similar to a coppersmith's bed (*Rashi*).

6. It seems strange that Rava should have had to answer for the actions of Rav Chama's household. *Rif,* in fact, has the reading *Rav Chama,* instead of *Rava* (cf. *Rashash*).

7. I.e. do you hold that since it is assembled loosely and without screws, this is not the usual method [of completing a utensil] and no Biblical prohibition is involved? (*Rashi*).

8. This is also the final halachah as recorded in *Shulchan Aruch, Orach Chaim* 313:6. However, *Beis Yosef* and *Rama* (ad loc.) add the proviso (based on *Milchamos Hashem* to 102b) that the sections of the utensils must actually be designed to fit together loosely; one may not reassemble a utensil that is designed to fit together tightly, even if he fits the parts together loosely.

9. Either before the Sabbath or on the Sabbath (see Gemara).

10. I.e. he causes the sparks to be extinguished on the Sabbath. The Gemara will explain the reason for this prohibition more fully.

11. See 42b note 10. Since the sparks are *muktzeh,* as they fall into the vessel it will become a *base to muktzeh,* and it will be impossible to move the vessel for the remainder of the Sabbath. Thus, the Mishnah seems to contradict the ruling of Rav Chisda (as explained by Rav Yosef above, 43a) that it is forbidden to nullify the preparedness of a utensil (*Rashi;* see 43a notes 8 and 18).

12. Once the sparks are extinguished what remains of them is so insubstantial that the utensil cannot be considered a base to them (*Rosh Yosef,* explaining *Rashi*; see the sources cited above, 43a note 12).

13. The Mishnah below (120a) states that on the Sabbath one may prevent a fire from spreading by lining up a row of vessels – either empty ones or ones containing water – in the fire's path. The Tanna Kamma of that Mishnah does not restrict this ruling. R' Yose, however, prohibits the use of new earthenware utensils that are filled with water, because the heat of the fire may burst these vessels, thereby releasing the water and quenching the fire. This fits into the category of גְּרָם כִּבּוּי, *indirectly causing a fire to be extinguished,* rather than extinguishing it by direct effort. [All agree that the causation (rather than direct performance) of a *melachah* is generally prohibited Rabbinically. However, according to the Tanna Kamma, in a case of financial loss such as the threat of a spreading fire, the Rabbis did not prohibit it. R' Yose, on the other hand, holds that causation is prohibited even in cases involving financial loss (see *Rama, Orach Chaim* 334:22; cf. *Shaar HaTziyun* 514:31).]

Now the case of our Mishnah, where one puts a container of water under the lamp to catch the falling sparks, would seem to be similar to that case. Here too, one is indirectly extinguishing the sparks in order to prevent them from causing a fire [that would result in a financial loss; see, however, *Magen Avraham, Orach Chaim* 265:2]. And since our Mishnah prohibits this, it would seem to reflect R' Yose's view (see *Rashi*).

אבל אסור [א] ולא יתקע ואם תקע חייב חטאת רשב"ג אומר [ב] אם היה רפוי מותר בי רב חמא הוה מטה גללניתא הוה מהדרי לה ביומא טבא א"ל ההוא מדרבנן לרבא מאי דעתך בנין מן הצד הוא נהי דאיסורא דאורייתא ליכא איסורא דרבנן מיהא איכא אמר ליה אנא כרשב"ג סבירא לי דאמר אם היה רפוי מותר: **מתני'** [א] [ג] נותנין כלי תחת הנר לקבל ניצוצות ולא יתן לתוכו מים מפני שהוא מכבה: **גמ'** והא [ב] קמבטל כלי מהיכנו אמר רב הונא בריה דרב יהושע ניצוצות אין בהן ממש: ולא יתן לתוכו מים מפני שהוא מכבה: לימא תנן סתמא כרבי יוסי [ג] דאמר גורם לכיבוי אסור ותסברא אימור דאמר ר' יוסי בשבת בערב שבת מי אמר וכי תימא הכא נמי בשבת והתניא נותנין כלי תחת הנר לקבל ניצוצות בשבת ואין צריך לומר בע"ש ולא יתן לתוכו מים מפני שהוא מכבה מע"ש ואין צריך לומר בשבת אלא אמר רב אשי אפילו תימא רבנן שאני הכא מפני שמקרב את כיבויו:

הדרן עלך כירה

במה [ד] [ד] טומנין ובמה אין טומנין אין טומנין לא בגפת ולא בזבל לא במלח ולא בסיד ולא בחול בין לחין בין יבשין ולא בתבן ולא בזגין ולא במוכין ולא בעשבין בזמן שהן לחין אבל טומנין בהן כשהן יבשין: **גמ'** איבעיא להו גפת של זיתים תנן אבל דשומשמין שפיר דמי או דילמא דשומשמין תנן וכל שכן דזיתים ת"ש דאמר ר' זירא משום חד דבי ר' ינאי קופה שטמן בה אסור להניחה על גפת של זיתים ש"מ של זיתים תנן לעולם אימא לך [ה] לענין הטמנה דשומשמין נמי אסור לענין אסוקי

רש"י

יתקע. בחוזק על ידי יתדות שקורין קויינ"ש: מטה גללניתא. טירנדי"ן והוא כעין של טרסיים [ה]: מן הצד. מפני שאינה תקועה ומהדקה בחוזק קרי לה מן הצד כלומר ע"י שינוי: **גמ'** והא קא מבטל כלי מהיכנו. דלא יוכל ליטלו משם כל היום דנעשה בסיס לניצוצות ולימא תהוי תיובתיה דרב חסדא דאסר בפירקין (דף מג.): אין בהן ממש. משככו ומותר ליטלן: כרבי יוסי. בכל כתבי הקדש דקתני עושה מחילה בכל הכלים בין מלאין בין ריקנין כדי שלא תעבור הדליקה רבי יוסי אוסר בכלי חרס חדשים מלאים מים שאין יכולין לקבל האור והן מתבקעים ומכבין את הדליקה: בערב שבת. כגון זה שנותן המים מבעוד יום בכלי תחת הנר: וכי תימא הכא נמי. אין נותנין לתוכו מים בשבת קאמר ור' יוסי היא: והתניא. אפילו בע"ש אסור ואי לגרם כיבוי מדמית לה אפילו כרבי יוסי לא מיתוקמה דבע"ש לא אמר רבי יוסי: אלא אמר רב אשי. מתניתין אפילו לרבנן דלא דמי לגרם כיבוי דהתם כי מטי דליקה לכלים דליקה הוא דפקע להו וגרמא בעלמא הוא אבל זה שנתן המים ממש תחת הנר מכבה ממש הוא וגזירה מבעוד יום אטו משחשכה: שמקרב את כיבויו. זימן כיבוי להדיא והוה ליה מכבה ממש אי הוה יהיב ליה בשבת:

הדרן עלך כירה

במה טומנין. הבא לסלק קדירה מעל גבי כירה ולטומנה בדבר אחר ואמרו חכמים [ו] אין טומנין בדבר המוסיף הבל אלא בדבר המעמיד הבל מי הוא המוסיף ואסור: גפת. פסולת של בית הבד של שמן שהוא כנוס יחד וחם מאד: לחין. יש בהן הבל הרבה יותר מיבשין: זגין. פסולת של יקב יין: מוכין. כל דבר רך קרוי מוכין כגון למר גפן ותלישי למר רך של בהמה וגרירת בגדים בלויים: **גמ'** קופה שטמן בה. שנותן בה מוכין וטומן בה קדירה: לענין הטמנה. לטומנו בתוכה: אסוקי דזיתים

תוספות

רבן שמעון בן גמליאל אומר אם היה רפוי מותר. ולעיל נמי מיירי ברפוי ° וקשה קצת דהיכי פליגי כולי האי דמר מחייב חטאת ומר שרי אפי' לכתחלה ועוד הא אין בנין וסתירה בכלים ועוד תקשה לרב יהודה הך ברייתא דליכא תנא דמחייב חטאת ויש לומר דהכי קאמר לעיל הא רב ושמואל דאמרי תרוייהו המחזיר מטה של טרסיים בשבת חייב חטאת כשאינו רפוי ואם כן ברפוי אין סברא להתיר לכתחלה:

לימא תנן סתמא כרבי יוסי דאמר גורם לכיבוי אסור. הוה מצי למימר וליטעמיך הא רבי יוסי גופיה לא אמרה אלא בדליקה משום דאדם בהול על ממונו אי שרינא ליה אתי לכבויי והכי מפרש בכל כתבי (לקמן קכ:) אבל הכא ליכא למגזר דהא יש כלי תחת הנר ואינו בהול ובכמה מקומות בהש"ס יכול לומר וליטעמיך ואינו אומר:

מפני שמקרב את כבויו. פירוש דגזרינן ע"ש אטו שבת ובשבת יכול לבא לידי כיבוי אם יגביה הכלי בשעת נפילת הנילוצות ואם תאמר מאי שנא שריית דיו וסממנים ופריסת מצודה דשרינן בפ"ק (דף יח:) עם השמש והכא אסרינן מע"ש שלא יבא לעשות בשבת ותירץ הרב פור"ת דהתם ליכא למיחש שמא יעשה כן בשבת דהא אב מלאכה הן אבל הכא איכא למיחש דלא דמי איסור כל כך במה שמניח כלי תחת הנילוצות ואיכא למיחש שמא יבא לידי כיבוי שיתחיל ליתן המים קודם נפילת הנילוצות וקודם גמר הנתינה יפלו ומכבה בידים או שיגביה הכלי עם המים כנגד הנילוצות כדפרישית ואף על גב דבאותו כיבוי אין בו חיוב חטאת לר' שמעון דמלאכה שאינה צריכה לגופה היא החמירו אטו כיבוי דחיוב חטאת ואע"ג דהוי גזירה לגזירה קים להו לרבנן דהכא שייך למגזר טפי ורש"י דפי' דהוה מכבה ממש לאו דוקא אלא כלומר שיוכל לבא לידי כיבוי ור"ת גרים כפירוש ר"ח מפני שמקרב כיבוי דהתם הוא דשרי לעשות מחילה מכלים שיש בתוכן מים שאינו מכבה כלום עד שיתבקעו הכלים אבל הכא אין הפסק בין מים לנילוצות ומיד נכבות כשנופלות בכלי והוי כמחילת מים דאסירא כגון מחילת שלג וברד וקשה לפירושו דירושלמי מוקי מתני' כר' יוסי אבל לרבנן אפי' מחילות של מים מותר ובפ' כל כתבי (לקמן קכ:) נמי שרו רבנן דר' יוסי בטלית שאחז בו האור מצד אחד ליתן עליו מים מצד אחר ואם כבתה כבתה ונראה דלפי הש"ס שלנו יש לחלק דבמחילה של מים אע"ג דאין דבר מפסיק מ"מ שרי שאין האש נופלת לתוך המים להדיא כי הכא שהמים תחת הנילוצות ומקרב כיבוין טפי ועוד דאיכא למימר דהש"ס שלנו אוסר במחילות של מים לרבנן ומשום הכי מוקי מתניתין כרבנן ופליג אירושלמי ולא דמי לטלית שאחז בו האור מצד אחד שאינו אלא שלא תתפשט האור ומה שרגילים לתת מים בזוכית שקורין לאמפ"א ונותנין עליה שמן בע"ש אין זה קרוי קירוב כיבוי דכיון שאין מתכוין לכיבוי כלל אלא להגביה את השמן לא שייך למגזר מידי שמא יעשה בשבת ושרי אפי' לר' יוסי וכ"ש לרבנן דאל"כ אפי' בלא מים אסור שהנילוצות נופלות בשמן:

ועוד איכא למימר דהתלמוד שלנו אסר מחילה של מים לרבנן ומש"ה מוקי מתני' כר' יוסי ופליג אירושלמי ול"ד לטלית שאחז בו האור מצד אחד שאינו אלא שלא תתפשט האור [ת"י]:

הדרן עלך כירה

במה טומנין וכו' אין טומנין לא בגפת. פירש הר"ר יוסף בשם רבינו שמואל דמיירי בבשיל ולא בשיל ° אבל קדרא חייתא ובשיל שרינן בפ"ק (דף יח:) ואין נראה לר"ת דהא אית לן לאוקמא מתניתין בסתם קדרות שהן מבושלים בין השמשות ועוד דמסתמא איירי מתני' דומיא דמתני' דכירה דמיירי בבשיל כמאכל בן דרוסאי ונראה לר"ת שיש לחלק בין השהאה להטמנה דודאי להשהות מותר כשהוא מאכל בן דרוסאי שאין חיתוי מעט מועיל לו שהרי מגולה הוא ושליט ביה אוירא אבל הטמנה שעושין לצורך מחר והוא מוטמן יש לחוש שמא יחתה שמעט חיתוי מועיל לו ליתפס חומו וגזרו להטמין בכל דבר המוסיף הבל גזירה שמא יטמין ברמץ ויחתה:

עין משפט נר מצוה

נט א מיי' פכ"ב מהל' שבת הלכה ו וסמג שם טוש"ע שם סעיף ו וסעיף ט:
ס ב מיי' שם טור שו"ע שם סעיף ו:
סא ג מיי' שם פ"ה הלכה יג סמג שם טוש"ע או"ח סימן רסה סעיף ד:
א ד ה מיי' פ"ד מהלכות שבת הלכה א טוש"ע או"ח סימן רנז סעיף ג:

רבינו חננאל

אסור. לא יתקע ואם תקע חייב חטאת רבן שמעון בן גמליאל אומר אם היה רפוי מותר המחזיר קני מנורה חייב חטאת כמשמעו מפני שמתקן כלי כבנין. קנה של ציידין דרכם לתת קנה דק דק בתוך ראש קנה עבה כדי שיהא (נכוה) [גבוה] ולא יהא נשבר וזהו פטור אבל אסור. קרן עגולה חייב פשוטה פטור. אלו הן כלי שיר. והן של חליות ויש מהן קרן עגולה וקרן פשוטה כדכתיב (דניאל ג) קל קרנא משרוקיתא. וזה שהיא עגולה היא כלי יש בו מלאכה להחזירה לפיכך חייב חטאת אבל פשוטה אין בה עסק כלום כדתנן בכלים פ' י"א. הכוש והאימא והמקל וסומפאניא וחליל של מתכת טמאין והמצופין טהורין וסמפאניא שיש בה בית קיבול כנפים בין כך ובין כך טמאה. קרן עגולה טמאה וכו' טמאין ובשעת חבורן הכל טמאה בי רב חמא הוה ליה מיטה גליתא והוו מהדרי ליה בי"ט א"ל לרב חמא מאי דעתיך בנין מן הצד הוא נהי דאיסורא דאוריי' ליכא דרבנן מיהא איכא. א"ל רב חמא אנא כרבן שמעון בן גמליאל סבירא לי אם היה רפוי מותר. נמצא רב חמא כר' אבא ורב הונא דשרו. ומסתברא מטה של טורסיים הוא כגון מטה גיליתא: **נותנין** כלי תחת הנר לקבל בו ניצוצות. והא קא מבטל כלי מהיכנו. אמר רב הונא בריה דרב יהושע ניצוצות אין בהן ממש ומותר להשתמש באותו כלי ולא יתן בתוכו מים מפני שהוא מכבה. לימא תנן סתמא כר' יוסי דאמר גרם כבוי אסור דתנן ר' יוסי אוסר לעשות מחיצה שלא תעבור הדליקה בכלי חרש חדשים מלאים מים שאין יכולין לקבל את האור והן מתבקעין ומכבין הדליק' ודחי אימור דאסר ר' יוסי בשבת. בע"ש מי אסר. וכי תימא הכא נמי כי תנן אסור בשבת אבל בע"ש שרי. והא תניא נותנין כלי תחת הנר לקבל ניצוצות בשבת ואין צורך לומר בע"ש. ולא יתן לתוכו מים בע"ש מפני שהוא מכבה ואין צריך לומר בשבת. ואוקמה רב אשי אפילו לרבנן דפליגי עליה דר' יוסי הכא אסרי מפני שמקרב כיבויו פי' כיון שנופלין הניצוצות במים מיד נכבין והכלים עד שיתבקעו. וקי"ל דהלכתא כר"ש דאפי' במוקצה מחמת מיאוס שרי: ואין הלכה כר"ש במוקצה מחמת איסור כגון במנורה ופמוט שהדליקו עליהן באותה שבת וכיוצא בהן וכגון מטה שיחדה למעות ונכרי שהביא דורון לישראל דבר המחובר לקרקע וכיוצא בהן דמוקצה מחמת איסור הן. וגרסי' במי שהחשיך בדרך פליגי בה רב אחא ורבינא חד אמר בכולה שבת הלכתא כר"ש בר ממוקצה מחמת מיאוס וחד אמר אפילו במוקצה מחמת מיאוס נמי הלכתא כר"ש בר ממוקצה מחמת איסור בלבד וקי"ל דבכל התורה רב אחא לחומרא ורבינא לקולא והלכתא כרבינא לקולא בר מהני תלת אומצא כו' ראע"ג דעולא ולוי ורב אמרו הלכה כר' יהודה הא שמואל ועירי ור' יוחנן אמרו הלכתא כר' שמעון. ורבינא דהוא בתראה פסק הלכתא כר' שמעון כדאמרן. לפיכך כל מוקצה מותר לבר ממוקצה מחמת איסור כמו שפירשנו. ומוקצה מחמת חסרון כיס מודה ר' שמעון וגרוגרות וצמוקין כדאמרן: הדרן עלך כירה

פרק רביעי במה טומנין ובמה אין טומנין כו' אין טומנין בגפת. אוקימנא בגפת של שומשין וכל שכן בגפת של זיתים דמסיק נמי הבלא אסיק' אמר רבא אנוחי כוזא דמיא אפומא דקומקומא משום דמיא צונן ומוליד חימום. ואס

מסורת הש"ס

א) [לעיל דף מג: מג.], ב) [לעיל דף מג: וש"נ], ג) לקמן קכ., ד) בבא בתרא יט. [מדרש ג: מיר ב.], ה) ע"י לקמן קלח. רש"י ד"ה וכפא גליף, ו) לעיל לד:.

גליון הש"ס

תוס' ד"ה רשב"ג וכו' וקשה קצת. ע"י לקמן דף קלח ע"א: שם בד"ה במה טומנין וכו' אבל קידרא חייתא. ע"י לעיל לג ע"ב תוספות ד"ה ממעשה:

רב נסים גאון

נדבר מן דאלך מא יחצרנא בפרק חומר בקודש (דף כה) אמרו אמר רב יוסף בגלילא שנו מיגו דלא מהימני אקודש לא מהימני אתרומה נמי בנדרים בפרק א) ואלו נדרים ובגליל אסורין שאין אנשי גליל מכירין את חרמי כהנים ובפרק המוציא יין (דף עח) ובפרק מקום שנהגו (דף נה) בפסחים עוד ובגמרא (ירושלמי שבת פרק כל כתבי הלכה ח) גרסי אמר עולא י"ח שנין עבד רבן יוחנן בן זכאי יתיב בהדה ערב ולא אתא קימוי אלא אילין תרתין עובדיה אמר גליל גליל שנאת את התורה סופך להעשות כמציקין וכל דין סיוע לפירושנו: לימא תנן סתמא כר' יוסי דאמר גרם כיבוי אסור. עיקר דיליה במשנה בפרק כל כתבי הקודש (דף קכ) דתנן ר' יוסי אוסר בכלי חרש חדשים מלאים מים שאין יכולין לקבל את האור והם מתבקעין ומכבין את הדליקה ובגמ' גרסי' ר' יוסי סבר גרם כיבוי אסור: סליק פרק כירה

חשק שלמה על רב נסים גאון

א) נ"ל ואלו מותרין דף יח במשנה.

ליקוטי רש"י

ואם תקע. במזוקה נסכין ויתדות והוה ליה גמר מלאכה וחייב משום מכה בפטיש [לקמן קכב:]. מטה גללניתא. הוא שם מקום ומפרקין מטותיהן וכשאותן ומוטנין אותן עמהן וחוזרין ומחזירין אותן [שם קלח.]. לקבל ניצוצות. שלהבת הנוטפת מן הנר כדי שלא ידלק מה שתחתיה ואף על גב דנילוצות לא מטלטלי ולא שמיי [לעיל מב:]. והא קמבטל כלי מהיכנו. אסור לבטל כלי מהיכנו להושיבו במקום שלא יוכל עוד ליטלו [משם] דהוי כקובע לו מקום ומחברו בטיט ודמי למלאכה [לעיל מב:]. שהיה מוכן מתחלה לטלטלו ועכשיו עושהו מוקצה [שם מג.]. דמשהכניסם תחתיה אין יכול לטלטלן דדומה לסותר בנין מדרבנן [לקמן קכח:]. כשמניחן תחת דבר שאין ניטל מבטלן מהיכנן דשוב לא יטלם משם ודמי לסותר [שם קנד: ועי' בתוס' לעיל מג.]. אין בהן ממש. ומותר ליטלן אחר שנפלו לתוכו [לעיל מג.]. גורם לכיבוי. כי האי גוונא כשמגיע למים הוא כבה [לקמן קכ:]. במה טומנין. את החמין בשבת דאמור רבנן לאסור להטמין בדבר המוסיף הבל והתם מפרש טעמא גזירה שמא יטמין ברמץ [ב"ב יט.]. אין טומנין וכו'. בדבר המוסיף הבל אפילו מבעוד יום [לעיל לד.]. מוכין. של שחקי בגדים שהסורק מוליא מבגד הצמר בקוליס [ב"ב שם]. גפת של זיתים. פסולת זיתים שנתעגלו בבית הבד [שם יז.]. דשומשמין. פסולת של שומשמין שהוליא שומן [לעיל לו:].

The Gemara counters:

וְתִסְבְּרָא – **But do you** really **consider this** explanation of our Mishnah **reasonable?** It is not, אֵימוּר דְּאָמַר רַבִּי יוֹסֵי – for I could **say** that **when R' Yose said** that one may not indirectly cause a fire to be extinguished, בְּשַׁבָּת – it was regarding doing so **on the Sabbath** itself. בְּעֶרֶב שַׁבָּת מִי אָמַר – **Did he** ever **say** that one may not do so **before the Sabbath?** No![14] Yet our Mishnah seems to forbid placing a bowl filled with water under a lamp even before the Sabbath.[15] וְכִי תֵּימָא הָכָא נַמִּי בְּשַׁבָּת – **And if you should say** that perhaps **here too** our Mishnah means to forbid this only **on the Sabbath,** וְהָתַנְיָא – **but it was taught** explicitly **in a Baraisa:** נוֹתְנִין כְּלִי תַּחַת הַנֵּר לְקַבֵּל נִיצוֹצוֹת – WE MAY PLACE A VESSEL UNDER A LAMP TO CATCH the falling SPARKS, בְּשַׁבָּת – even ON THE SABBATH, וְאֵין צָרִיךְ לוֹמַר בְּעֶרֶב שַׁבָּת – AND IT GOES WITHOUT SAYING that we may do this BEFORE THE SABBATH. וְלֹא יִתֵּן לְתוֹכוֹ מַיִם מִפְּנֵי שֶׁהוּא מְכַבֶּה – BUT ONE MAY NOT PLACE WATER IN [THE VESSEL] BECAUSE HE thereby EXTINGUISHES the sparks – מֵעֶרֶב שַׁבָּת – this is prohibited even BEFORE THE SABBATH, וְאֵין צָרִיךְ לוֹמַר בְּשַׁבָּת – AND IT GOES WITHOUT SAYING that it is prohibited ON THE SABBATH itself. Since the prohibition against filling the vessel with water applies even before the Sabbath, you cannot explain it by attributing it to R' Yose. – ? –

The Gemara concedes the point and therefore advances a different explanation:

אֶלָּא אָמַר רַב אַשִׁי – **Rather, Rav Ashi said:** אֲפִילּוּ תֵּימָא רַבָּנָן – **You can even say** that our Mishnah accords with the view of **the Rabbis** who differ with R' Yose. שַׁאנִי הָכָא – And this case **here is different** than the case discussed by the Rabbis and R' Yose, מִפְּנֵי שֶׁמְּקָרֵב אֶת כִּיבּוּיוֹ – **because** here **he readies the** direct **extinguishing of [the sparks].**[16]

הדרן עלך כירה

WE SHALL RETURN TO YOU, KIRAH

NOTES

14. R' Yose, in the Mishnah below, forbade only lining up the water-filled kegs on the Sabbath itself; he never expressed an objection to arranging them on Friday and leaving them in place over the Sabbath.

15. [Unlike the previous Mishnah (on 42b), which stated a dispensation concerning an act done before the Sabbath, our Mishnah states unequivocally that one may not fill the vessel with water. The implication is that the prohibition applies even before the Sabbath.]

16. Unlike setting up a fire-wall of water-filled vessels, which involves nothing more than causing the fire to burst the vessels, placing water under a lamp can easily involve extinguishing sparks directly: Should any sparks fall as he pours, or should he happen to lift the utensil at the same moment that sparks are falling towards it, he would be culpable for directly performing the *melachah* of *extinguishing*. Because of this danger, the Rabbis went so far as to forbid placing water under a lamp even on Friday, lest one come to do so on the Sabbath itself (*Rashi*, as elaborated by *Tosafos;* cf. elaboration of *Ritva MHK* ed.; for other approaches see *Tosafos* and *Rashba* here, and *Ramban* below, 120a).

Chapter Four

Introduction

This chapter deals with *hatmanah,* literally: hiding, i.e. insulating hot food by wrapping the pot with some material as a way of preserving its heat for the Sabbath. The laws of *hatmanah* may be summed up in two short rules, as follows: Before the Sabbath, one may insulate with substances that *maintain* the food's heat, but not with substances that *add heat* to the food. On the Sabbath proper, one may not insulate with *any* substance.

These two rules were enacted for separate reasons. Insulating on the Sabbath proper was prohibited for fear that should one, on coming to insulate his pot, find the food to have cooled, he may forgetfully come to reheat it. Insulating before the Sabbath with materials that add heat was prohibited lest one come to insulate the pot with hot ash mixed with live coals, which, in turn, may lead to his raking the coals on the Sabbath in order to hasten the cooking (Gemara above, 34a-b).[1]

Because many of the substances suited for insulation are *muktzeh,* a significant portion of this chapter is also devoted to the laws of *muktzeh.*

NOTES

1. As we learned in the previous chapter, this same concern – lest one come to rake the coals – lies behind the prohibition of *shehiyah,* i.e. allowing food to remain over a fire on the Sabbath. Accordingly, some Rishonim maintain that as with the prohibition of *shehiyah,* the prohibition of *hatmanah* does not apply to totally raw foods, fully cooked foods (above, 18b), and, according to the view of Chananyah on 36b, even to foods that have been cooked to the Ben Derusai stage (*Rashbam,* cited by *Tosafos* to 47b ד״ה במה; some suggest that *Rashi* agrees with this view – see *Ramban* and *Ritva MHK* ed. to the beginning of chapter 3 and *Pnei Yehoshua* to *Tosafos* ibid.; see also *Shulchan Aruch HaRav, Mahadura Basra* §259; but see *Rashi* to 34b ד״ה גזירה שמא יחתה). Most Rishonim, however, noting that none of the exclusions mentioned in regard to *shehiyah* are ever mentioned by the Gemara in regard to *hatmanah,* maintain that the Rabbis prohibited *hatmanah* in all cases, without consideration as to the state of readiness of the food (see *Tosafos* and Rishonim here; see also *Or Zarua, Hil. Erev Shabbos* §8).

A second fundamental disagreement concerns how fully the pot has to be enveloped in order for the case to qualify as *hatmanah. Rabbeinu Tam* (*Sefer HaYashar* 235) maintains that the prohibition applies only if the pot is fully covered or, at the very least, covered in its greater part. Many other Rishonim, however (*Rabbeinu Chananel* bottom of 37a, *Ramban, Rashba*), disagree and maintain that even where the pot is in contact with the heat-producing substance on only one side, the pot is considered "insulated" (see also *Shulchan Aruch HaRav* ibid. ד״ה והנכון). See *Shulchan Aruch* and *Rema,* end of *Orach Chaim* 253:1 and 257:8 regarding the final halachah.

אבל אסור א ולא יתקע ואם תקע חייב חטאת רשב"ג אומר ב אם היה רפוי מותר בי רב חמא הוה מטה גללניתא הוה מהדרי לה ביומא טבא א"ל ההוא מדרבנן לרבא מאי דעתיך בנין מן הצד הוא נהי דאיסורא דאורייתא ליכא איסורא דרבנן מיהא איכא אמר ליה אנא כרשב"ג סבירא לי דאמר אם היה רפוי מותר: **מתני'** א) ג נותנין כלי תחת הנר לקבל ניצוצות ולא יתן לתוכו מים מפני שהוא מכבה: **גמ'** והא ב) קמבטל כלי מהיכנו אמר רב הונא בריה דרב יהושע ניצוצות אין בהן ממש: ולא יתן לתוכו מים מפני שהוא מכבה: לימא תנן סתמא כרבי יוסי ג) דאמר גורם לכיבוי אסור ותסברא אימור דאמר ר' יוסי בשבת בערב שבת מי אמר וכי תימא הכא נמי בשבת והתניא נותנין כלי תחת הנר לקבל ניצוצות בשבת ואין צריך לומר בע"ש ולא יתן לתוכו מים מפני שהוא מכבה מע"ש ואין צריך לומר בשבת אלא אמר רב אשי אפילו תימא רבנן שאני הכא מפני שמקרב את כיבויו:

הדרן עלך כירה

במה ד) ד טומנין ובמה אין טומנין אין טומנין לא בגפת ולא בזבל לא במלח ולא בסיד ולא בחול בין לחין בין יבשין ולא בתבן ולא בזגין ולא במוכין ולא בעשבין בזמן שהן לחין אבל טומנין בהן כשהן יבשין: **גמ'** איבעיא להו גפת של זיתים תנן אבל דשומשמין שפיר דמי או דילמא דשומשמין תנן וכל שכן דזיתים ת"ש דאמר ר' זירא משום חד דבי ר' ינאי קופה שטמן בה אסור להניחה על גפת של זיתים ש"מ של זיתים תנן לעולם אימא לך ה לענין הטמנה דשומשמין נמי אסור לענין אסוקי

רש"י

יתקע. בחוזק על ידי יתדות שקורין קויי"ש: מטה גללניתא. טירנדי"ן והוא כעין של טרסיים ה): מן הצד. מפני שאינה תקועה ומהדקה בחוזק קרי לה מן הצד כלומר ע"י שינוי: גמ' והא קא מבטל כלי מהיכנו. דלא יוכל ליטלו משם כל היום דנעשה בסיס לניצוצות לימא תהוי תיובתיה דרב חסדא דאסר בפירקין (דף מג.): אין בהן ממש. משכנו ומותר ליטלן: כרבי יוסי. בכל כתבי הקדש דקתני עושה מחילה בכל הכלים בין מלאין בין ריקנין כדי שלא תעבור הדליקה רבי יוסי אוסר בכלי חרס חדשים מלאים מים שאין יכולין לקבל האור והן מתבקעים ומכבין את הדליקה: בערב שבת. כגון זה שנותן המים מבעוד יום בכלי תחת הנר: וכי תימא הכא נמי. אין נותנין לתוכו מים בשבת קאמר ור' יוסי היא: והתניא. אפילו בע"ש אסור ואי לגרם כיבוי מדמית לה אפילו כרבי יוסי לא מיתוקמא דבע"ש לא אמר רבי יוסי: אלא אמר רב אשי. מתניתין אפילו לרבנן דלא דמי לגרם כיבוי דהתם כי מטי דליקה לכלים דליקה הוא דפקע להו וגרמא בעלמא הוא אבל זה שנתן המים ממש תחת הנר מכבה ממש הוא וגזירה מבעוד יום אטו משחשכה: שמקרב את כיבויו. זימן כיבוי להדיא והוה ליה מכבה ממש אי הוה יהיב ליה בשבת:

הדרן עלך כירה

במה טומנין. הנא לסלק קדירה מעל גבי כירה ולטומנה בדבר אחר ואמרו חכמים ו) אין טומנין בדבר המוסיף הבל אלא בדבר המעמיד הבל מי הוא המוסיף ואסור: גפת. פסולת של בית הבד של שמן שהוא כנוס יחד וחם מאד: לחין. יש בהן הבל הרבה יותר מיבשין: זגין. פסולת של יקב יין: מוכין. כל דבר רך קרוי מוכין כגון צמר גפן ותלישי צמר רך של בהמה וגרירת בגדים בלויים: גמ' קופה שטמן בה. שנותן בה מוכין וטומן בה קדירה: לענין הטמנה. לטומנו בתוכה: אסוקי

תוספות

רבן שמעון בן גמליאל אומר אם היה רפוי מותר. ולעיל נמי מיירי ברפוי ° וקשה קצת דהיכי פליגי כולי האי דמר מחייב חטאת ומר שרי אפי' לכתחלה ועוד הא אין בנין וסתירה בכלים ועוד תקשה לרב יהודה הך ברייתא דליכא תנא דמחייב חטאת ויש לומר דהכי קאמר לעיל הא רב ושמואל דאמרי תרווייהו המחזיר מטה של טרסיים בשבת חייב חטאת כשאינו רפוי ואם כן ברפוי אין סברא להתיר לכתחלה:

לימא תנן סתמא כרבי יוסי דאמר גורם לכיבוי אסור. הוה מצי למימר וליטעמיך הא רבי יוסי גופיה לא אמרה אלא בדליקה משום דאדם בהול על ממונו אי שרינא ליה אתי לכבויי והכי מפרש בכל כתבי (לקמן קכ:) אבל הכא ליכא למגזר דהא יש כלי תחת הנר ואינו בהול ובכמה מקומות בהש"ס יכול לומר וליטעמיך ואינו אומר:

מפני שמקרב את כבויו. פירוש דגזרינן ע"ש אטו שבת ובשבת יכול לבא לידי כיבוי אם יגביה הכלי בשעת נפילת הנילוצות ואם תאמר מאי שנא שריית דיו וסממנים ופריסת מצודה דשרינן בפ"ק (דף יח:) עם השמש והכא אסרינן מע"ש שלא יבא לעשות בשבת ותירץ הרב פור"ת דהתם ליכא למיחש שמא יעשה כן בשבת דהא אב מלאכה הן אבל הכא איכא למיחש דלא דמי איסור כל כך במה שמניח כלי תחת הנילוצות ואיכא למיחש שמא יבא לידי כיבוי שיתחיל ליתן המים קודם נפילת הנילוצות וקודם גמר הנתינה יפלו ומכבה בידים או שיגביה הכלי עם המים כנגד הנילוצות כדפרישית ואף על גב דאותו כיבוי אין בו חיוב חטאת לר' שמעון דמלאכה שאינה צריכה לגופה היא החמירו אטו כיבוי דחיוב חטאת ואע"ג דהוי גזירה לגזירה קים להו לרבנן דהכא שייך למגזר טפי ורש"י דפי' דהוה מכבה ממש לאו דוקא אלא כלומר שיוכל לבא לידי כיבוי ור"ת גריס כפירוש ר"ח מפני שמקרב כיבוי דהתם הוא דשרי לעשות מחילה מכלים שיש בתוכן מים שאינו מכבה כלום עד שיתבקעו הכלים אבל הכא אין הפסק בין מים לנילוצות ומיד נכבות כשנופלות בכלי והוי כמחילת מים דאסירא כגון מחילת שלג וברד וקשה לפירושו דבירושלמי מוקי מתני' כר' יוסי אבל לרבנן אפי' מחילות של מים מותר ובפ' כל כתבי (לקמן קכ:) נמי שרו רבנן דר' יוסי בטלית שאחז בו האור מצד אחד ליתן עליו מים מצד אחר ואם כבתה כבתה ונראה דלפי הש"ס שלנו יש לחלק דבמחילה של מים אע"ג דאין דבר מפסיק מ"מ שרי שאין האש נופלת לתוך המים להדיא כי הכא שהמים תחת הנילוצות ומקרב כיבוין טפי ועוד דאיכא למימר דהש"ס שלנו אוסר במחילות של מים לרבנן ומשום הכי מוקי מתניתין כרבנן ופליג אירושלמי ולא דמי לטלית שאחז בו האור מצד אחד שאינו אלא שלא תתפשט האור ומה שרגילים לתת מים בזכוכית שקורין לאמפ"א ונותנין עליה שמן בע"ש אין זה קרוי קירוב כיבוי דכיון שאין מתכוין לכיבוי כלל אלא להגביה את השמן לא שייך למגזר מידי שמא יעשה בשבת ושרי אפי' לר' יוסי וכ"ש לרבנן דאל"כ אפי' בלא מים אסור שהנילוצות נופלות בשמן: ועוד איכא למימר דתלמוד שלנו אסר מחילה של מים לרבנן ומש"ה מוקי מתני' כר' יוסי ופליג אירושלמי ול"ד לטלית שאחז בו האור מצד אחד שאינו אלא שלא תתפשט האור [ת"י]:

הדרן עלך כירה

במה טומנין וכו' אין טומנין לא בגפת. פירש הר"ר יוסף בשם רבינו שמואל דמיירי בבשיל ולא בשיל ° אבל קדרא חייתא ובשיל שרינן בפ"ק (דף יח:) ואין נראה לר"ת דהא אית לן לאוקמא מתניתין בסתם קדרות שהן מבושלים בין השמשות ועוד דמסתמא איירי מתני' דומיא דמתני' דכירה דמיירי בבשיל כמאכל בן דרוסאי ונראה לר"ת שיש לחלק בין השהאה להטמנה דודאי להשהות מותר כשהוא מאכל בן דרוסאי שאין חיתוי מעט מועיל לו שהרי מגולה הוא ושליט ביה אוירא אבל הטמנה שעושין לצורך מחר והוא מוטמן יש לחוש שמא יחתה שמעט חיתוי מועיל לו ליתפס חומו וגזרו להטמין בכל דבר המוסיף הבל גזירה שמא יטמין ברמץ ויחתה:

דזיתים

עין משפט נר מצוה

נט א מיי' פכ"ג מהל' שבת הלכה ו וסמג שם טוש"ע שם סעיף ו וסעיף ט:
ס ב מיי' שם טור שו"ע שם סעיף ו:
סא ג מיי' שם פ"ה הלכה יג סמג שם טוש"ע או"ח סימן רסה סעיף ד:
א ד ה מיי' פ"ד מהלכות שבת הלכה א טוש"ע או"ח סימן רנז סעיף ג:

רבינו חננאל

אסור. לא יתקע ואם תקע חייב חטאת רבן שמעון בן גמליאל אומר אם היה רפוי מותר המחזיר קני מנורה חייב חטאת כמשמעו מפני שמתקן כלי כבנין. קנה של ציידין דרכם לתת קנה דק דק בתוך ראש קנה עבה כדי שיהא (נכוה) [גבוה] ולא יהא נשבר וזהו פטור אבל אסור. קרן עגולה חייב פשוטה פטור. אלו הן כלי שיר. והן של חליות ויש מהן קרן עגולה וקרן פשוטה כדכתיב (דניאל ג) קל קרנא משרוקיתא. וזה שהיא עגולה היא כלי יש בו מלאכה להחזירה לפיכך חייב חטאת אבל פשוטה אין בה עסק כלום כדתנן בכלים פ' י"א. הכוש והאימא והמקל וסומפאניא וחליל של מתכת טמאין והמצופין טהורין וסמפאניא שיש בה בית קיבול כנפים בין כך ובין כך טמאה. קרן עגולה טמאה וכו' טמאין ובשעת חבורן הכל טמאה בי רב חמא הוה ליה מיטה גליתא והוו מהדרי ליה בי"ט א"ל לרב חמא מאי דעתיך בנין מן הצד הוא נהי דאיסורא דאוריי' ליכא דרבנן מיהא איכא. א"ל רב חמא אנא כרבן שמעון בן גמליאל סבירא לי אם היה רפוי מותר. נמצא רב חמא כר' אבא ורב הונא דשרו. ומסתברא מטה של טורסיים הוא כגון מטה גיליתא: **נותנין** כלי תחת הנר לקבל בו ניצוצות. והא קא מבטל כלי מהיכנו. אמר רב הונא בריה דרב יהושע ניצוצות אין בהן ממש ומותר להשתמש באותו כלי ולא יתן בתוכו מים מפני שהוא מכבה. לימא תנן סתמא כר' יוסי דאמר גרם כבוי אסור דתנן ר' יוסי אוסר לעשות מחיצה שלא תעבור הדליקה בכלי חרש חדשים מלאים מים שאין יכולין לקבל את האור והן מתבקעין ומכבין הדליק' ודחי אימור דאסר ר' יוסי בשבת. בע"ש מי אסר. וכי תימא הכא נמי כי תנן אסור בשבת אבל בע"ש שרי. והא תניא נותנין כלי תחת הנר לקבל ניצוצות בשבת ואין צורך לומר בע"ש. ולא יתן לתוכו מים בע"ש מפני שהוא מכבה ואין צריך לומר בשבת. ואוקמה רב אשי אפילו לרבנן דפליגי עליה דר' יוסי הכא אסרי מפני שמקרב כיבויו פי' כיון שנופלין הניצוצות במים מיד נכבין ובכלים עד שיתבקעו. וקי"ל דהלכתא כר"ש דאפי' במוקצה מחמת מיאוס שרי: **ואין** הלכה כר"ש במוקצה מחמת איסור כגון במנורה ופמוט שהדליקו עליהן באותה שבת וכיוצא בהן וכגון מטה שיחדה למעות ונכרי שהביא דורון לישראל דבר המחובר לקרקע וכיוצא בהן דמוקצה מחמת איסור הן. וגרסי' במי שהחשיך בדרך פליגי בה רב אחא ורבינא חד אמר בכולה שבת הלכתא כר"ש בר ממוקצה מחמת מיאוס וחד אמר אפילו במוקצה מחמת מיאוס נמי הלכתא כר"ש בר ממוקצה מחמת איסור בלבד וקי"ל דבכל התורה רב אחא לחומרא ורבינא לקולא והלכתא כרבינא לקולא בר מהני תלת אומצא כר' ואע"ג דעולא ולוי ורב אמרו הלכה כר' יהודה הא שמואל וזעירי ור' יוחנן אמרו הלכתא כר' שמעון. ורבינא דהוא בתראה פסק הלכתא כר' שמעון כדאמרן. לפיכך כל מוקצה מותר לבד ממוקצה מחמת איסור כמו שפירשנו. ומוקצה מחמת חסרון כיס מודה ר' שמעון וגרוגרות וצמוקין כדאמרן: **הדרן עלך כירה**

פרק רביעי במה טומנין ובמה אין טומנין כו' אין טומנין בגפת. אוקימנא בגפת של שומשין וכל שכן בגפת של זיתים דמסיק נמי הבלא אסיק' אמר רבא אנוחי כוזא דמיא אפומא דקומקומא משום דמיא צונן ומוליד חימום. ואסר

מסורת הש"ס

א) [לעיל דף מג: מג.], ב) [לעיל דף מג: וש"נ], ג) לקמן קכ., ד) בבא בתרא יט. [נדרים ג: מיר ב.], ה) ע' לקמן קלח. רש"י ד"ה וכסא גלין, ו) לעיל לד:.

גליון הש"ס

תוס' ד"ה רשב"ג וכו' וקשה קצת. ע' לקמן דף קלח ע"א: שם בד"ה במה טומנין וכו' אבל קידרא חייתא. ע' לעיל דף לט ע"ב תוספות ד"ה ממעשה:

רב נסים גאון

נדבר מן דאלך מא יחצרנא בפרק חומר בקודש (דף כה) אמרו אמר רב יוסף בגלילא שנו מיגו דלא מהימני אקודש לא מהימני אתרומה נמי בנדרים בפרק א) ואלו נדרים ובגליל אסורין שאין אנשי גליל מכירין את חרמי כהנים ובפרק המוציא יין (דף עח) ובפרק מקום שנהגו (דף נה) בפסחים עוד ובגמרא (ירושלמי שבת פרק כל כתבי הלכה ח) גרסי אמר עולא י"ח שנין עבד רבן יוחנן בן זכאי יתיב בהדה ערב ולא אתא קימוי אלא אילין תרתין עובדיה אמר גליל גליל שנאת את התורה סופך להעשות כמציקין וכל דין סיוע לפירושנו: **לימא** תנן סתמא כר' יוסי דאמר גרם כיבוי אסור. עיקר דיליה במשנה בפרק כל כתבי הקודש (דף קכ) דתנן ר' יוסי אוסר בכלי חרש חדשים מלאים מים שאין יכולין לקבל את האור והם מתבקעין ומכבין את הדליקה ובגמ' גרסי' ר' יוסי סבר גרם כיבוי אסור:
סליק פרק כירה

חשק שלמה על רב נסים גאון

א) נ"ל ואלו מותרין דף יח במשנה:

ליקוטי רש"י

ואם תקע. בחוזקה בסכין ויתדות והוה ליה גמר מלאכה וחייב משום מכה בפטיש [לקמן קכב.]. **מטה גללניתא.** הוא שם מקום ומפרקין מטותיהן וכסאותן וטוענין אותן עמהן וחוזרין ומחזירין אותן [שם קלח.]. **לקבל ניצוצות.** שלהבת הנוטפת מן הנר כדי שלא ידלק מה שתחתיה ואף על גב דנילוצות לא מיטלטלי ולא שכיחי [לעיל מב:]. **והא קמבטל כלי מהיכנו.** אסור לבטל כלי מהיכנו להושיב כלי במקום שלא יוכל עוד ליטלו [משם] דהוי כקובע לו מקום ומחברו בטיט ודמי למלאכה [לעיל מב:]. שהיה מוכן מתחלה לטלטלו ועכשיו עושהו מוקלה [שם מג.]. דמשהניחם תחתיה אין יכול לטלטלן דדומה לסותר בנין מדרבנן [לקמן קכח:]. כשמניחן תחת דבר שאין ניטל מבטלן מהיכנן דשוב לא יטלם משם ודמי לסותר [שם קנד: ועי' בתוס' לעיל מג.]. **אין בהן ממש.** ומותר ליטלן אחר שנפלו לתוכו [לעיל מג.]. **גורם לכיבוי.** כי האי גוונא כשמגיע למים הוא כבה [לקמן קכ:]. **במה טומנין.** את החמין בשבת דאמור רבנן לאסור להטמין בדבר המוסיף הבל והתם מפרש טעמא גזירה שמא יטמין ברמץ [ב"ב יט.]. **אין טומנין וכו'.** בדבר המוסיף הבל אפילו מבעוד יום [לעיל לד.]. **מוכין.** של שחקי בגדים שהסורק מוציא מבגדי הצמר בקוצים [ב"ב שם]. **גפת של זיתים.** פסולת זיתים שנתעלרו בבית הבד [שם יז.]. **דשומשמין.** פס[...] שהוציא שומנן [לעיל לו:].

Chapter Four

Mishnah It is forbidden to insulate pots before the Sabbath with substances that add heat to the food. The Mishnah enumerates those substances included in this prohibition:

בַּמֶּה טוֹמְנִין וּבַמֶּה אֵין טוֹמְנִין – **With what may one insulate** hot foods **and with what may one not insulate** them? I.e. one who removes a pot from the stove on Friday and wishes to preserve its heat, what may he use to insulate the pot? אֵין טוֹמְנִין לֹא בְגֶפֶת וְלֹא בְזֶבֶל לֹא בְמֶלַח וְלֹא בְסִיד וְלֹא בְחוֹל – **One may not insulate with marc,**[1] **nor with manure, nor with salt, nor with lime, nor with sand,** בֵּין לַחִין בֵּין יְבֵשִׁין – **either wet or dry.**[2] וְלֹא בְתֶבֶן וְלֹא בְזָגִין וְלֹא בְמוֹכִין וְלֹא בַעֲשָׂבִין בִּזְמַן שֶׁהֵן לַחִין – **Nor with straw, nor with grape skins, nor with flocking,**[3] **nor with grasses, when they are moist,** אֲבָל טוֹמְנִין בָּהֶן כְּשֶׁהֵן יְבֵשִׁין – **but one may insulate with them when they are dry.**[4]

Gemara The Gemara analyzes the Mishnah's first ruling:

אִיבַּעְיָא לְהוּ גֶּפֶת שֶׁל זֵיתִים תְּנַן אֲבָל דְּשׁוּמְשְׁמִין שַׁפִּיר דָּמֵי – **They inquired:** In listing marc among the substances that add heat to food, **does the Mishnah refer to olive marc,** whose heat is relatively intense, **but** as for the marc **of sesame,** whose heat is less intense, **it is fine** to insulate food in it? אוֹ דִילְמָא דְּשׁוּמְשְׁמִין תְּנַן וְכָל שֶׁכֵּן דְּזֵיתִים – **Or, perhaps, does the Mishnah refer** even **to** the marc **of sesame, and** as for the marc **of olives** it goes without saying that **certainly** one is forbidden to insulate with it?

The Gemara seeks to resolve the issue:

תָּא שְׁמַע – **Come, learn** a proof from the following: דְּאָמַר רַבִּי זֵירָא מִשּׁוּם חַד דְּבֵי רַבִּי יַנַּאי – **For R' Zeira said in the name of one** of the members **of R' Yannai's academy:** קוּפָּה שֶׁטָּמַן בָּהּ אָסוּר לְהַנִּיחָהּ עַל גֶּפֶת שֶׁל זֵיתִים – Regarding **a box in which one insulated** hot food, **it is forbidden to place it on top of olive marc.**[5] שְׁמַע מִינָּהּ שֶׁל זֵיתִים תְּנַן – Since R' Zeira specifies "olive marc," one can **conclude from this** that only olive marc adds heat, not sesame marc; accordingly, **the Mishnah refers to** the marc **of olives.**

The Gemara rejects the proof:

לְעוֹלָם אֵימָא לָךְ לְעִנְיַן הַטְמָנָה דְּשׁוּמְשְׁמִין נַמִּי אָסוּר – **In fact I can tell you** that **in regard to** actual **insulation** the marc **of sesame is also forbidden.** לְעִנְיַן – However, **in regard to**

NOTES

1. A mass of the pulp of olives (or of sesame; see Gemara below) that remains after the oil is pressed (*Rashi*).

2. Not only may one not use these substances when they are damp and tend to increase the heat greatly, but even when dry they are not permitted, for they still tend to generate some heat (see *Rashi*).

3. I.e. tufts of unprocessed soft material such as cotton, soft wool, or shreds of worn-out clothing (*Rashi*).

4. I.e. straw, grape skins, flocking and grass cause the temperature of an item enveloped within them to rise only when they are damp, not when they are dry.

5. As explained in the introduction to this chapter, *hatmanah* is forbidden only with a substance that adds heat to the food; it is permitted to insulate hot food with a substance that does not add heat (provided that the *hatmanah* takes place before nightfall). R' Zeira teaches that where the food is placed in a box containing insulation of a type that does not add heat, and that box, in turn, is placed on top of a material that does add heat, such as olive marc, it is treated as a case of *hatmanah* with a substance that adds heat and is forbidden.

אַסּוּקֵי הַבְלָא דְּזֵיתִים מַסְּקֵי הַבְלָא דְּשׁוּמְשְׁמִין לֹא מַסְּקֵי הַבְלָא – **radiating heat upwards,** the marc **of olives radiates heat upwards** but the marc **of sesame does not radiate heat upwards.**[1]

The Gemara records an incident which relates to insulating: רַבָּה וְרַבִּי זֵירָא אִיקְלְעוּ לְבֵי רֵישׁ גָּלוּתָא – **Rabbah and R' Zeira once visited the house of the Exilarch.** חַזְיוּהַ לְהָהוּא עַבְדָּא דְּאַנַּח כּוּזָא דְּמַיָּא אַפּוּמָּא דְקוּמְקוּמָא – **They observed a certain servant placing a jug** of water **on the mouth of a kettle** in order to heat the water in the jug.[2] נַזְהֵיהּ רַבָּה – Upon seeing this **Rabbah scolded [the servant].**

R' Zeira questions Rabbah's actions:

אָמַר לֵיהּ רַבִּי זֵירָא מַאי שְׁנָא מְמֵיחַם עַל גַּבֵּי מֵיחַם – **R' Zeira said to [Rabbah]: How is [this case] different from [the case of] a kettle on top of a kettle,** which is permitted?[3]

Rabbah responds:

אָמַר לֵיהּ הָתָם אוֹקוּמֵי קָא מוֹקִים – **He answered him: There,** in the case of the Baraisa, by placing the two kettles together **one is** merely **preserving** the heat of the top kettle; הָכָא אוֹלוּדֵי קָא מוֹלִיד – but **here,** by placing the jug on top of the kettle **one is engendering** heat in the jug of cold water.[4]

The story continues:

הֲדַר חַזְיֵיהּ דִּפְרַס סְּתוּדָר אַפּוּמֵיהּ דְּכוּבָא וְאַנַּח נַטְלָא עִילָּוֵיהּ – **[Rabbah] later observed [the servant] spreading a turban over the mouth of a jug and laying a ladle on it.** נַזְהֵיהּ רַבָּה – Again **Rabbah scolded him.** אָמַר לֵיהּ רַבִּי זֵירָא אַמַּאי – **R' Zeira said to him: Why** are you scolding him now? אָמַר לֵיהּ הַשְׁתָּא חָזֵית – **He answered him: You will soon see.** לְסוֹף חַזְיֵיהּ דְּקָא מְעַצַּר לֵיהּ – **Ultimately he saw [the servant] squeezing [the turban]** in order to extract the water it had absorbed, thereby violating the Sabbath.[5] It was in anticipation of just this eventuality that Rabbah had scolded the servant.[6] אָמַר לֵיהּ מַאי שְׁנָא מִפַּרְוַנְקָא – **R' Zeira said to [Rabbah]:** Still and all, **how does this** case **differ from** using **a rag** to cover a bowl of liquid, a practice which we allow on the Sabbath, and we do not anticipate that someone will squeeze out the rag? אָמַר לֵיהּ הָתָם לֹא קָפִיד עִילָּוֵיהּ הָכָא קָפִיד עִילָּוֵיהּ – **[Rabbah] answered him: There,** in the case of a rag, **he does not care about [the rag]** and will not be tempted to squeeze it out; but **here,** in the case of a turban, **he cares about it** and is likely to squeeze it out, as indeed happened.[7]

The Mishnah states:

וְלֹא בְּתֶבֶן – NOR WITH STRAW, nor with grape skins, nor with flocking . . . when they are moist, etc.

The Gemara raises a question:

בְּעָא מִינֵּיהּ רַב אַדָּא בַּר מַתְנָה מֵאַבַּיֵי – **Rav Adda bar Masnah inquired of Abaye:** מוֹכִין שֶׁטָּמַן בָּהֶן מַהוּ לְטַלְטְלָן בְּשַׁבָּת – Regarding dry **flocking with which one insulated** food on Friday, **may one move it on the Sabbath?**[8] אָמַר לֵיהּ – **[Abaye] answered him:** וְכִי מִפְּנֵי שֶׁאֵין לוֹ קוּפָּה שֶׁל תֶּבֶן עוֹמֵד וּמַפְקִיר קוּפָּה שֶׁל מוֹכִין – **Just because one does not have a box of straw** handy to use for insulating **does he** therefore **renounce a** valuable **box of flocking?**[9]

NOTES

1. Perhaps actual *hatmanah* is forbidden even with sesame marc, despite its less intense heat; but a case such as R' Zeira's, where the pot is not in direct contact with the heat source, is forbidden only with olive marc, whose heat is intense enough to radiate upwards and heat the pot above it (*Rashi*). See *Tosafos* and *Shulchan Aruch, Orach Chaim* 257:8 for practical applications of this rule.

2. There was not sufficient heat generated by the kettle to cook the water in the jug; the servant wished merely to warm the water somewhat (*Pnei Yehoshua*).

3. The Gemara below, 51b, cites the *Tosefta* (4:14) as teaching that it is permitted to place two kettles one on top of the other [on the Sabbath] (*Rashi*) in order to preserve the heat of the top kettle. Obviously, placement on top of a hot kettle is not regarded as *hatmanah*. It ought therefore likewise be permitted to place a jug of cold water on top of a hot kettle (*Pnei Yehoshua*).

4. In the case of the *Tosefta* both kettles are hot; the placement of one kettle on top of the other serves merely to insure that the top one does not cool down (*Rashi*). Since such placement is not a true case of *hatmanah*, it is permitted. [*Shulchan Aruch HaRav (Mahadura Basra* to *Orach Chaim* 259) suggests that the reason that such placement is not considered *hatmanah* is based on the fact that insulating with a substance that adds heat was forbidden for fear that one might come to insulate with hot ash (see the Chapter Introduction). But a kettle is grossly different from hot ash. Therefore, it is not classified as insulation in regard to the prohibition against *hatmanah*.] But where the top vessel is cold, such as in the present case, and the bottom vessel engenders heat in the top vessel, the Rabbis regarded the case as *similar* to *hatmanah* and forbade it (*Maginei Shlomo* to 37b, in explanation of the case according to *Rashi;* see *Pnei Yehoshua* here). [It should be pointed out, however, that the Rabbis did not give even this case the *full* status of *hatmanah* with a substance that adds heat, to the point that such placement is forbidden even on Friday. Rather, since the bottom kettle is constantly losing heat, it is considered a substance that adds heat only insofar as placement on the Sabbath proper is concerned (see *Beis Yosef* end of *Orach Chaim* 259 and *Beur Halachah* to 257:6 ד״ה אפילו).]

An alternate explanation of the incident: The servant intended only to warm the water, not to cook it; however, the situation was such that if the water would remain on top of the kettle for a long time, it would in fact cook. R' Zeira argued that such placement was permitted, and as proof pointed to the widespread practice of placing two kettles one on top of the other on the Sabbath. Rabbah responded that the practice was only to place a *hot* kettle on top of a hot one. However, placing a *cold* kettle on top of a hot one, even with the intention of removing the cold one before the water in it cooks, is in fact forbidden, lest the person forget and leave the top one in place until the water cooks (*Tosafos; Rashi,* however, cannot subscribe to this explanation, because, as explained on 40b note 4, *Rashi* permits warming a bottle of water even in a spot where it could cook if left there for a long period). [According to this explanation, the incident bears no connection at all to the laws of *hatmanah* discussed in this chapter. See *Ran* in the name of *Rabbeinu Yonah* for yet a third explanation.]

5. [Wringing out clothes wet with water is a *toladah* of the *melachah* of *whitening* (see Gemara below, 111a-b).] See *Menachem Meishiv Nefesh*.

6. [It is unreasonable to assume that Rabbah actually stood idly by as the servant desecrated the Sabbath. *Sfas Emes* therefore suggests that the Gemara in fact means that the servant was *about* to wring out the turban; however, Rabbah prevented him from doing so.]

7. [From the incident with the servant it would appear that placing an article of clothing over a barrel is prohibited only if a utensil is then placed on top of the clothing, for the weight of the utensil is likely to cause the clothing to sag or fall into the water (see *Chidushei HaRan*). This is indeed the ruling of *Shulchan Aruch* (*Orach Chaim* 320:15). From *Rambam,* however (*Hil. Shabbos* 22:15), it would appear that the prohibition applies even if no utensil is placed on top (*Chidushei R' Akiva Eiger*).]

8. In general, flocking is *muktzeh* since it is reserved to be made into felt [an activity which is forbidden on the Sabbath] (*Rashi*). Since the flocking is earmarked as raw material for felt, it does not qualify as a utensil at all and is considered *intrinsically muktzeh* (*Shulchan Aruch HaRav* 308:3; cf. *Mishnah Berurah* 259:3).

Rav Adda bar Masnah inquired whether the fact that one used the flocking demonstrates that he is now permanently reserving it for *hatmanah* [i.e. it is no longer reserved for making felt] and it is therefore no longer *muktzeh* (*Rashi*).

9. Normally one would insulate food with some almost worthless material such as straw. Obviously, someone who uses flocking to insulate food must not have had any straw at hand for the moment. But that is no reason to assume that he means to permanently designate the valuable flocking for *hatmanah*. The flocking, therefore, continues to be *muktzeh* (see *Rashi*).

אסוקי הבלא דזיתים מסקי הבלא דשומשמין לא מסקי הבלא רבה ורבי זירא איקלעו לבי ריש גלותא חזיוה להוא עבדא דאנח כוזא דמיא אפומא דקומקומא [א] נזהיה רבה א"ל ר' זירא מאי שנא ממיחם על גבי מיחם א"ל התם אוקומי קא מוקים הכא אולודי קא מוליד הדר חזייה דפרס דסתודר אפומיה דכובא ואנח נטלא עילויה [ב] נזהיה רבה א"ל ר' זירא אמאי אמר ליה השתא חזית לסוף חזייה דקא מעצר ליה א"ל מאי שנא מפרונקא א"ל התם לא קפיד עילויה הכא קפיד עילויה: ולא בתבן: בעא מיניה רב אדא בר מתנה מאביי מוכין שטמן בהן מהו לטלטלן בשבת א"ל [ג] וכי מפני שאין לו קופה של תבן עומד ומפקיר קופה של מוכין לימא מסייע ליה [א] טומנין בגיזי צמר ובציפי צמר ובלשונות של ארגמן ובמוכין ואין מטלטלין אותן אי משום הא לא איריא הכי קאמר אם לא טמן בהן אין מטלטלין אותן אי הכי מאי למימרא מהו דתימא חזי למזגא עלייהו קמ"ל: רב חסדא [ד] שרא לאהדורי [ב] אודרא לבי סדיא בשבתא איתיביה רב חנן בר חסדא לרב חסדא מתירין בית הצואר בשבת אבל לא פותחין ואין נותנין את המוכין לא לתוך הכר ולא לתוך הכסת ביו"ט ואין צריך לומר בשבת לא קשיא הא בחדתי הא בעתיקי תניא נמי הכי אין נותנין את המוכין לא לתוך הכר ולא לתוך הכסת בי"ט ואין צריך לומר בשבת נשרו מחזירין אותן בשבת ואין צריך לומר ביום טוב אמר רב יהודה אמר רב [ג] [ה] הפותח בית הצואר בשבת חייב חטאת מתקיף לה רב כהנא

מה

אסוקי הבלא. כגון זה שהטמין בדבר אחר והניח קופה על הגפת דליכא אלא שהגפת מעלה הבל למעלה ומרתיח קדרה שבקופה: **אפומא דקומקומא.** מיחם של חמין והכוזא היתה מלאה צונן: **נזהיה.** גער בו: **מאי שנא ממיחם על גבי מיחם.** דתניא בברייתא בסוף פרקין דשרי: **התם אוקומי מוקים.** שהמיחם העליון גם בו יש מים חמין והתחתון אינו אלא מעמיד חומו שלא יפיג: **דסתודר.** סודר של ראש: **דכובא.** קנקן: **נטלא.** כלי ששואבין יין מן הכובא: **דקא עצר.** שהיה סוחטו מן המים שנבלעו בו: **מאי שנא מפרונקא.** בגד העשוי לפרוס על הגיגית שפורסין אותו בשבת: **לא קפיד עליה.** אם שרוי במים שהרי לכך עשוי ולא אתי לידי סחיטה: **מוכין.** אינן אלא לעשות מהן לבדין שקורין פלט"ר ומוקצין הן למלאכה ואסור לטלטלן ואלו שטמן בהן מי אמרינן יחדן להטמנה ואיכא תורת כלי עליהן ומותר לטלטלן בשבת או לא: **שומד ומפקיר לכך.** קופה של מוכין שדמיה יקרין אין דרך בכך ולא בטלי להטמנה: **גיזי של צמר.** כמות שנגזזו: **ציפי צמר.** לאחר שנפצוה וטמוה כמין מחללות משטיחין: **לשונות.** לאחר שצבען וסורקין אותן כעין לשונות ארוכין לטוותן: **ואין מטלטלין אותן.** קס"ד דהכי קאמר ואע"פ שטמן בהן אין מטלטלין אותן: **אם לא טמן בהן כו'.** ומילי מילי קתני ברישא אשמועינן דטומנין בהן דלא מוספי הבלא ואשמועינן סיפא דסתם מוכין מוקצות נינהו אבל הני דטמן בהן הוי כמי שיחדן לכך: **למזגא.** להיסב עליהן: **לאהדורי אודרא לבי סדיא.** להחזיר מוכין שנפלו מן הכר לתוכן: **מתירין בית הצואר.** שדרך הכובסים לקושרן: **אבל לא פותחין.** לכתחילה דהשתא עביד ליה מנא: **בחדתי.** שלא היו מעולם לתוכו אסור דהשתא עביד ליה מנא: **בעתיקי.** להחזירו לכר זה שנפלו ממנו: **הפותח בית הצואר.** של חלוק לכתחילה: **חייב חטאת.** דהשתא קמשוי ליה מנא וחייב משום מכה בפטיש והיינו גמר מלאכה:

מה

דזיתים מסקי הבלא. מכאן יש לאסור להניח גחלים תחת הקדרה אפי' יתן עליהן אפר אין להטמין קדרה עליהם שהרי הגחלים מעלין הבל למעלה כמו גפת של זיתים ויש תימה היאך אנו מטמינין על כירות שלנו שקורין אשטר"א ואע"פ שגורפין אותו הוא מוסיף הבל כמו גפת של זיתים ואומר ר"י שיש ליתן טעם לקיים המנהג דגבי גפת איכא למיחש שמא יטמין כולה בתוכה אבל בכירות שלנו לא שייך למיחש הכי ועוד יש שעושין חפירה גדולה ועושין בה בנין לבנים סביב מכל צד ולמטה ומחמין אותה היטב וגורפין אותה ומטמינין בה את הקדרה ולא דמיא למטמין בדבר המוסיף הבל דלא אסרו אלא כשמטמין ומדביק סביב הקדרה דומיא דרמץ אבל תנור או חפירה שיש אויר בין הדפנות לקדרה אין לאסור יותר מהשהאה אף על פי שכל הקדרה בתוך התנור ורבינו ברוך פי' שיש לחלק בין תוספת הבל דגפת לתוספת הבל דכירה שלנו לפי שהכירה אין חומה אלא מחמת האש ולעולם מתקרר והולך אבל הגפת מוסיף הבל מעצמו אומר רבינו שמואל דמותר לשום תפוחים אצל האש סמוך לחשכה אע"פ שלא יוכלו לצלות מבע"י דנאכלין טפי כמו שהן חיין מתבשיל שנתבשל כמאכל בן דרוסאי דשרי ואע"ג דבפ"ק (ד' יט:) תנן אין צולין בשר בצל וביצה אלא כדי שיצולו מבע"י אע"פ שפעמים אוכלים בצל חי מ"מ אינו ראוי לאכול חי כמו תפוחים ורוצה להפיג חריפותן ולמתקן בבישולו ואם הטמין תפוחים עם הקדרה אסור להחזיר כרים וכסתות על הקדרה שעמהן או להוסיף על אותן כרים אע"ג דאם אין שם תפוחים מותר להחזיר כדתנן בפירקין (ד' נא.) כסהו ונתגלה מותר לכסותו ולהוסיף נמי אמרינן בגמרא (שם.) אם בא להוסיף מוסיף כשיש עם הקדרה תפוחים אסור דאם מחזיר קודם שנתבשלו נמצא מבשל בשבת ומה שנהגו להסיר הקדרה מעל הכירה ומניחין על הקרקע עד שיגרפו הכירה שמא סבירא לן כהך לישנא דריש כירה (לעיל דף לח:) דשרי חזקיה משמיה דאביי הניחו על גבי קרקע אם דעתו להחזיר: **מאי** שנא ממיחם ע"ג מיחם. קשה לר"י דבברייתא גופה דשרי מיחם ע"ג מיחם בסוף פרקין קתני בהדיא ולא בשביל שיחמו אלא בשביל שיהו משומרין ואומר ר"י דברייתא לא שמיע ליה ולא מכח ברייתא פריך אלא ממעשים בכל יום שנותנין מיחם על גבי מיחם תימה דהיכי דמי אי יד סולדת בו היכי הוה בעי למישרי אע"פ שמבשל מי לא ידע דתולדות האור כאור דתנן (לעיל דף לח:) אין נותנין ביצה בצד המיחם ואמר אם גלגל חייב חטאת ותנן נמי (דף מא.) המיחם שפינהו לא יתן לתוכו צונן ואי להפשיר היכי מסיק דאסור והא תניא בפ' כירה (דף מ:) נותן אדם קיתון של מים כנגד המדורה לא בשביל שיחמו אלא בשביל שתפוג צינתן והיינו הפשר כדמוכח סוגיא דהתם ורב יהודה נמי קאמר התם אחד מים ואחד שמן יד סולדת בו אסור אין יד סולדת בו מותר ואין לחלק דגבי מדורה יזהר שלא יבשל כיון שהוא אצל האש אבל הכא אפילו אין יד סולדת בו אסור דשמא יבא לטעות ויניח עד שיתבשל דהא גבי מיחם שרינן לתת לתוכו מים מרובין כדי להפשירן ולא גזרינן אטו מים מועטין אע"פ שאינו אצל האש ונראה לרשב"א דהא דשרינן לתת קיתון של מים כנגד המדורה היינו ברחוק מן המדורה שלעולם לא יוכל לבא לידי בשול אבל בקרוב אסור אפי' להפשיר דילמא משתלי ואתי להניחן שם עד שיתבשל ולהכי מסיק הכא דאסור ולא בשביל שיחמו דקתני התם היינו כלומר במקום שיכול לבא לידי שיחמו והלשון דחוק קצת: **מאי** שנא מפרונקא. פר"ח דאמר רבא בפרק תולין (לקמן קלט:) האי פרונקא אפלגא דכובא שרי דלא הוי אהל ולא חיישינן שמא יסחוט: **התם** לא קפיד. פר"ת בפ"ק דכתובות (דף ו.[ד]): **וכי** מפני שאין לו קופה של תבן כו'. וא"ת מאי קבעי הא תנן במתניתין טומנין בגיזי צמר ואין מטלטלין אותן והיינו אפילו טמן דהא קתני בהדיא כיצד עושה מנער את הכיסוי והן נופלות וכי מייתי מברייתא דמסייע ליה לייתי ממתניתין דלא מצי למדחי ממתניתין כדדחי ברייתא וליכא למימר דמתני' איכא לאוקומי בשל הפקק כדמוקי לקמן רבינא ע"כ סוגיא דהכא לא סבירא כרבינא מדלא מוקי ברייתא דמייתי בשל הפקק ותירץ ר"י דגיזי צמר חשיבי טפי ממוכין ואסורים לטלטל יותר ואע"ג דרבא קאמר לקמן דאפילו גיזי צמר טמן בהן מטלטלין אין לחוש אי פליגא אאביי דהכא כיון דלא קיימא לקמן מילתיה דרבא ולמאי דמשני רבינא מילתיה דרבא ומוקי מתניתין בשל הפקק ודרבא בשאין של הפקק אומר רשב"א דה"נ מיירי במוכין של הפקק ולא פליגא דרבא אדאביי אך ק"ק דמאי משני בסמוך מהו דתימא חזי למזגא עלייהו כיון דמיירי בשל הפקק היכי ס"ד דשרי לטלטל משום דחזי למזגא עלייהו:

ה"ק אם לא טמן אין מטלטלין אותן. אמוכין קאי ולא אגיזי צמר דגיזי צמר אפי' טמן אין מטלטלין: **הא** בחדתי הא בעתיקי. אומר ר"י שאם נתקו חוטי הסרבל אם הנקב רחב ויכול להכניס בלא טורח שרי כיון דעתיקי ובלבד שיתנם בענין זה שלא יהא לחוש שמא יתקע דבענין שהוא רגילות לתקוע ולקשור נראה דאסורין להחזיר כדאסרינן בריש כל הכלים (דף קכב:) החזרת שידה תיבה ומגדל גזירה שמא יתקע:

וכי

א) ב"ב יט., ב) [גי' הערוך אודרא פי' הטלה], ג) מכות ג., ד) ד"ה האי.

ליקוטי רש"י

כוזא. כלי חרס קטן [לקמן עז:]. **מיחם.** קומקמוס שמחמם בו חמין [לעיל לח:]. של נחשת [לקמן נא:]. **כובא.** גיגית [ב"מ כה.]. **נטלא.** של זכוכית קרי נטלא [חולין קז.]. כלי קטן [ר"ן נדרים נא.]. **פרונקא.** בגד ששוטחין על גיגית יין לכסותה [לקמן קלט. וע"ע ע"ז ל.]. **ציפי צמר.** לאחר שסרקו ונפצו במסרק. **לשונות של ארגמן.** צמר צבוע ואחר כך חזרו והסליקוהו במסרק ועשוי לשונות לשונות [ב"ב יט.]. צמר סרוק ומשוך כמין לשון וצבוע ארגמן ומלויין הן [ב"מ כא.]. **ארגמן.** צמר צבוע ממין צבע ששמו ארגמן [שמות כה, ד]. **ואין מטלטלין אותם.** שהן מוקצים למלאכת בגדים [ב"ב שם]. **חזי למזגא עלייהו.** כן היתה ישיבתם שוטחין בגדים על גבי הקרקע ונסמכין ויושבין על ברכיהן כפופין כדאמרינן בפסחים (קח.) הוה זגינן אברכי דהדדי [ביצה י.]. להשען שכל הסבתן כך היתה יושב קצת ונשען קצת על שמאלו [לעיל מג.]. **אודרא.** מוכין [לקמן קמא.]. **הפותח בית הצואר.** שעשה פה לחלוק חדש. **חייב.** שתיקן כלי [מכות ג:].

ב א טוש"ע או"ח סימן שיח סעיף יח:
ג ב מיי' פכ"ב מהלכות שבת הלכה טו טור ושו"ע או"ח סימן שכ סעיף טו:
ד ג מיי' פכ"ו מהלכות שבת הלכה יג טוש"ע או"ח סימן רנט סעיף א:
ה ד מיי' פכ"ב מהלכות שבת הלכה כג טור ושו"ע או"ח סימן ש"מ סעיף ח:
ו ה מיי' פ"י מהלכות שבת הלכה י טוש"ע או"ח סימן שיז סעיף ג:

רבינו חננאל

נמי למפרס סודרא אפומא דכובא ולאנוחי נטלא אגביה דסודרא משום (דשארי) [דשיורי] הכוס מתחזין בסודרא וקפיד בשירא דסודרא וסחיט ליה ולא דמי לפרונקא שהיא מטלית קשורה בפומא דכובא כדגרסי' בפ' דר' אליעזר אומר תולין (ד' קלט.) אמר רבא האי פרונקא אפלגי דכובא שרי ולא חייש דניחזי כמו מסננת אפומא דכולא כובא אסיר דהא עביד (אבל) אהל כמסננת. ואמאי שרי רבא התם אפלגי דכובא ליחוש שמא יסחוט המטלית. ושנינו מטלית לא קפיד בשירותא מלשון (לקמן קמו:) מי שנשרו כליו בדרך שוטחן בחמה אבל לא כנגד העם סודר קפיד בשירותא הילכך האי אסור והאי שרי: פי' מוכין סמרטוטין. בגדים מקרצין כדתנן בנגעים פרק י"א בגד מוסגר שנתערב באחרים כולן טהורין קיצצו ועשאו מוכין טהור. מוכין אסיקנא כי הא דתניא אין נותנין מוכין לא לתוך הכר ולא לתוך הכסת בי"ט ואין צריך לומר בשבת נשרו מחזירין אותן בשבת [ואין צריך לומ' ביו"ט]. אמר רב הפותח בבגד בית הצואר בשבת חייב

רב נסים גאון

פ"ד **אמר** ליה ר' זירא מאי שנא ממיחם על גבי מיחם. בסוף הפרק (דף נא) בברייתא גרסי ומניחין מיחם על גבי מיחם ומאי שנא מפורנקא. עיקר דיליה בפרק ר' אליעזר אומר תולין את המשמרת ביו"ט (דף קלט) אמר רבא האי פרונקא אפלגא דפומא דכובא שרי וכו' ואיכא דאמרי מאי שנא מפרונקיה דמר לפי שר' זירא עם רבא הוה מפליג והוא בעל השמועה:

The Gemara seeks support for Abaye's ruling:

לֵימָא מְסַיַּיע לֵיהּ – Let us say that [the following Baraisa] supports him: טוֹמְנִין בְּגִיזֵּי צֶמֶר וּבְצִיפֵּי צֶמֶר וּבִלְשׁוֹנוֹת שֶׁל אַרְגָּמָן וּבְמוֹכִין – ONE MAY INSULATE WITH WOOL SHEARINGS, WITH MATS OF COMBED WOOL, WITH STRIPS OF PURPLE WOOL AND WITH FLOCKING, וְאֵין מְטַלְטְלִין אוֹתָן – BUT ONE MAY NOT MOVE THEM.[10] The Baraisa seems to state clearly that flocking, even when used for insulation, remains *muktzeh* and cannot be moved.

The Gemara rejects the proof:

אִי מִשּׁוּם הָא לָא אִירְיָא – **If** your support for Abaye's ruling is **based on this, no parallel** can be drawn. הָכִי קָאָמַר אִם לֹא טָמַן בָּהֶן אֵין מְטַלְטְלִין אוֹתָן – For when the Baraisa says that flocking cannot be moved **it means as follows: If one did not use [the flocking] for insulation, one cannot move it.** If it was used for insulation, however, the flocking is in fact not *muktzeh*.

The Gemara questions this interpretation:

אִי הָכִי מַאי לְמֵימְרָא – **If so,** that the Baraisa means that one cannot move flocking when it was *not* used for insulation, **why** does the Baraisa need to **state this** at all? It is obvious that flocking that is not being used for insulation is *muktzeh,* since it is reserved to be made into felt. – ? –

The Gemara answers:

מַהוּ דְּתֵימָא חֲזֵי לְמִזְגָּא עֲלַיְיהוּ קָמַשְׁמַע לָן – The Baraisa's ruling is not obvious: **You might have thought that [the flocking] is fit to recline on;** since it has a useful Sabbath function it is not *muktzeh.* **[The Baraisa]** therefore **informs us** that this is not so; since the flocking would not normally be used for reclining, it is *muktzeh.*

The Gemara quotes an unrelated ruling which also involves flocking:

רַב חִסְדָּא שָׁרָא לְאַהְדּוּרֵי אוּדְרָא לְבֵי סַדְיָא בְּשַׁבְּתָא – **Rav Chisda allowed returning stuffing** (i.e. flocking) **into a pillow on the Sabbath;** he did not consider this a violation of the prohibition against fashioning a utensil on the Sabbath.[11]

An objection is raised:

אֵיתִיבֵיהּ רַב חָנָן בַּר חִסְדָּא לְרַב חִסְדָּא – **Rav Chanan bar Chisda challenged Rav Chisda** from the following Baraisa: מַתִּירִין בֵּית הַצַּוָּאר בְּשַׁבָּת אֲבָל לֹא פּוֹתְחִין – ONE MAY UNTIE THE NECK OPENING of a garment ON THE SABBATH[12] BUT ONE MAY NOT OPEN it up in the first place.[13] וְאֵין נוֹתְנִין אֶת הַמּוֹכִין לֹא לְתוֹךְ הַכַּר וְלֹא לְתוֹךְ הַכֶּסֶת בְּיוֹם טוֹב וְאֵין צָרִיךְ לוֹמַר בְּשַׁבָּת – NOR MAY ONE PLACE FLOCKING INTO A MATTRESS OR INTO A PILLOW ON A FESTIVAL, AND IT GOES WITHOUT SAYING ON THE SABBATH.[14] The Baraisa states clearly that it is forbidden to put stuffing into a pillow on the Sabbath, thus contradicting Rav Chisda's ruling. – ? –

The Gemara answers on Rav Chisda's behalf:

לֹא קַשְׁיָא – **There is no difficulty** here: הָא בְּחַדְתֵי הָא בְּעַתִּיקֵי – **The one** case, viz. that of the Baraisa, **concerns new** pillows that have never before been stuffed; by placing stuffing inside them one is fashioning them into a pillow, which is forbidden. But **the other** case, viz. that of Rav Chisda, **concerns old** pillows from which the stuffing has fallen out; since the pillow has already been fashioned, merely returning the stuffing into it is not considered fashioning a utensil and is not forbidden.

The Gemara finds support for this distinction between a new and an old pillow:

תַּנְיָא נַמִּי הָכִי – **We learned likewise in the following Baraisa:** אֵין נוֹתְנִין אֶת הַמּוֹכִין לֹא לְתוֹךְ הַכַּר וְלֹא לְתוֹךְ הַכֶּסֶת בְּיוֹם טוֹב וְאֵין צָרִיךְ לוֹמַר בְּשַׁבָּת – ONE MAY NOT PLACE STUFFING INTO A MATTRESS OR INTO A PILLOW ON A FESTIVAL, AND IT GOES WITHOUT SAYING ON THE SABBATH; נָשְׁרוּ מַחֲזִירִין אוֹתָן בְּשַׁבָּת וְאֵין צָרִיךְ לוֹמַר בְּיוֹם טוֹב – but if [THE STUFFING] FELL OUT ONE MAY RETURN IT ON THE SABBATH, AND IT GOES WITHOUT SAYING ON A FESTIVAL.

The previously quoted Baraisa mentioned that it is forbidden to open up a collar for the first time on the Sabbath. The Gemara addresses this topic:

אָמַר רַב יְהוּדָה אָמַר רַב – **Rav Yehudah said in the name of Rav:** הַפּוֹתֵחַ בֵּית הַצַּוָּאר בְּשַׁבָּת חַיָּיב חַטָּאת – **One who opens up the neck opening** in a garment for the first time **on the Sabbath is liable to a *chatas* offering,** i.e. he has violated the Sabbath on the Biblical level.

This ruling is questioned:

מַתְקִיף לָהּ רַב כָּהֲנָא – **Rav Kahana challenged this:**

NOTES

10. [The flocking is *muktzeh* because it is reserved to be made into felt, and the wool because it is reserved to be made into thread (see *Rashi*).]

11. See *Rashi* ד״ה בחדתי; cf. *Rambam, Hil. Shabbos* 22:23. [Fashioning a utensil is a *toladah* of the *melachah* of מַכֶּה בְּפַטִּישׁ, *striking the final hammer blow;* see *Rambam, Hil. Shabbos,* 10:16ff.]

12. Clothing would customarily come back from the laundry with the collar tied shut (*Rashi*). Because the knot was never meant to be permanent, it was permitted to untie it on the Sabbath (*Tur, Orach Chaim* 317). [For further discussion of the circumstances under which it is permitted to untie a temporary knot on the Sabbath see below, 111b ff, and *Shulchan Aruch, Orach Chaim* 317.]

13. I.e. one may not tear a piece of fabric to open up a collar hole in order that it be used as a garment. This would violate the prohibition against fashioning a utensil, viz. a garment, on the Sabbath (see *Rashi;* cf. *Ritva* to *Makkos* 3b and *Beur Halachah,* 340:14 ד״ה ולא, who discuss why *Rashi* did not state more simply that this would violate the *melachah* of *tearing*).

14. Since this would constitute fashioning a utensil.

[The laws of the Sabbath are, in many respects, more stringent than those of the festivals. Therefore, any stringency that applies on a festival will certainly apply on the Sabbath; likewise, any leniency that applies on the Sabbath will certainly apply on a festival.]

אסוקי הבלא דזיתים מסקי הבלא דשומשמין לא מסקי הבלא רבה ורבי זירא איקלעו לבי ריש גלותא חזיוה לההוא עבדא דאנח כוזא דמיא אפומא דקומקומא [א] נזהיה רבה א"ל ר' זירא מאי שנא ממיחם על גבי מיחם א"ל התם אוקומי קא מוקים הכא אולודי קא מוליד הדר חזייה דפרס דסתודר אפומיה דכובא ואנח נטלא עילויה [ב] נזהיה רבה א"ל ר' זירא אמאי אמר ליה השתא חזית לסוף חזייה דקא מעצר ליה א"ל מאי שנא מפרונקא א"ל התם לא קפיד עילויה הכא קפיד עילויה: ולא בתבן: בעא מיניה רב אדא בר מתנה מאביי מוכין שטמן בהן מהו לטלטלן בשבת א"ל [ג] וכי מפני שאין לו קופה של תבן עומד ומפקיר קופה של מוכין לימא מסייע ליה [א] טומנין בגיזי צמר ובציפי צמר ובלשונות של ארגמן ובמוכין ואין מטלטלין אותן אי משום הא לא איריא הכי קאמר אם לא טמן בהן אין מטלטלין אותן אי הכי מאי למימרא מהו דתימא חזי למזגא עלייהו קמ"ל: רב חסדא [ד] שרא לאהדורי [ב] אודרא לבי סדיא בשבתא איתיביה רב חנן בר חסדא לרב חסדא מתירין בית הצואר בשבת אבל לא פותחין ואין נותנין את המוכין לא לתוך הכר ולא לתוך הכסת ביו"ט ואין צריך לומר בשבת לא קשיא הא בחדתי הא בעתיקי תניא נמי הכי אין נותנין את המוכין לא לתוך הכר ולא לתוך הכסת בי"ט ואין צריך לומר בשבת נשרו מחזירין אותן בשבת ואין צריך לומר ביום טוב אמר רב יהודה אמר רב [ג] [ה] הפותח בית הצואר בשבת חייב חטאת מתקיף לה רב כהנא מה

רש"י

אסוקי הבלא. כגון זה שהטמין בדבר אחר והניח קופה על הגפת דליכא אלא שהגפת מעלה הבל למעלה ומרתיח קדרה שבקופה: אפומא דקומקומא. מיחם של חמין והכוז היתה מלאה צונן: נזהיה. גער בו: מאי שנא ממיחם על גבי מיחם. דתניא בברייתא בסוף פרקין דשרי: התם אוקומי מוקים. שהמיחם העליון גם בו יש מים חמין והתחתון אינו אלא מעמיד חומו שלא יפיג: דסתודר. סודר של ראש: דכובא. קנקן: נטלא. כלי ששואבין יין מן הכובא: דקא עצר. שהיה סוחטו מן המים שנבלעו בו: מאי שנא מפרונקא. בגד העשוי לפרוס על הגיגית שפורסין אותו בשבת: לא קפיד עליה. אם שרוי במים שהרי לכך עשוי ולא אתי לידי סחיטה: מוכין. אינן אלא לעשות מהן לבדין שקורין פלט"ר ומוקצין הן למלאכה ואסור לטלטלן ואלו שטמן בהן מי אמרינן יחדן להטמנה ואיכא תורת כלי עליהן ומותר לטלטלן בשבת או לא: שומד ומפקיר לכך. קופה של מוכין שדמיה יקרין אין דרך בכך ולא בטלי להטמנה: גיזי של צמר. כמות שנגזזו: ציפי צמר. לאחר שנפצוה ושטחוה כמין מחצלות משטיחין: לשונות. לאחר שצבען וסורקין אותן כעין לשונות ארוכין לטוותן: ואין מטלטלין אותן. קס"ד דהכי קאמר ואע"פ שטמן בהן אין מטלטלין אותן: אם לא טמן בהן כו'. ומילי מילי קתני ברישא אשמועינן דטומנין בהן דלא מוספי הבלא ואשמועינן סיפא דסתם מוכין מוקצות נינהו אבל הני דטמן בהן הוי כמי שיחדן לכך: למזגא. להיסב עליהן: לאהדורי אודרא לבי סדיא. להחזיר מוכין שנפלו מן הכר לתוכן: מתירין בית הצואר. שדרך הכובסים לקושרן: אבל לא פותחין. לכתחילה דהשתא עביד ליה מנא: בחדתי. שלא היו מעולם לתוכו אסור דהשתא עביד ליה מנא: בעתיקי. להחזירו לכר זה שנפלו ממנו: הפותח בית הצואר. של חלוק לכתחילה: חייב חטאת. דהשתא קמשוי ליה מנא וחייב משום מכה בפטיש והיינו גמר מלאכה: מה

תוספות

מסקי הבלא. מכאן יש לאסור להניח גחלים תחת הקדרה אפי' יתן עליהן אפר אין להטמין קדרה עליהם שהרי הגחלים מעלין הבל למעלה כמו גפת של זיתים ויש תימה היאך אנו מטמינין על כירות שלנו שקורין אשטר"א ואע"פ שגורפין אותו הוא מוסיף הבל כמו גפת של זיתים ואומר ר"י שיש ליתן טעם לקיים המנהג דגבי גפת איכא למיחש שמא יטמין כולה בתוכה אבל בכירות שלנו לא שייך למיחש הכי ועוד יש שעושין חפירה גדולה ועושין בה בנין לבנים סביב מכל צד ולמלטה ומחמין אותה היטב וגורפין אותה ומטמינין בה את הקדרה ולא דמיא למטמין בדבר המוסיף הבל דלא אסרו אלא כשמטמין ומדביק סביב הקדרה דומיא דרמץ אבל תנור או חפירה שיש אויר בין הדפנות לקדרה אין לאסור יותר מהשהאה אף על פי שכל הקדרה בתוך התנור ורבינו ברוך פי' שיש לחלק בין תוספת הבל דגפת לתוספת הבל דכירה שלנו לפי שהכירה אין חומה אלא מחמת האש ולעולם מתקרר והולך אבל הגפת מוסיף הבל מעצמו אומר רבינו שמואל דמותר לשום תפוחים אצל האש סמוך לחשכה אע"פ שלא יוכלו לצלות מבע"י דנאכלין טפי כמו שהן חיין מתבשיל שנתבשל כמאכל בן דרוסאי דשרי ואע"ג דבפ"ק (ד' יט:) תנן אין צולין בשר בצל וביצה אלא כדי שיצולו מבע"י אע"פ שפעמים אוכלים בצל חי מ"מ אינו ראוי לאכול חי כמו תפוחים ורוצה להפיג חריפותן ולמתקן בבישולו ואם הטמין תפוחים עם הקדרה אסור להחזיר כרים וכסתות על הקדרה שעמהן או להוסיף על אותן כרים אע"ג דאם אין שם תפוחים מותר להחזיר כדתנן בפירקין (ד' נא.) כסהו ונתגלה מותר לכסותו ולהוסיף נמי אמרינן בגמרא (שם.) אם בא להוסיף מוסיף כשיש עם הקדרה תפוחים אסור דאם מחזיר קודם שנתבשלו נמצא מבשל בשבת ומה שנהגו להסיר הקדרה מעל הכירה ומניחין על הקרקע עד שיגרפו הכירה שמא סבירא לן כהך לישנא דריש כירה (לעיל דף לח:) דשרי חזקיה משמיה דאביי הניחו על גבי קרקע אם דעתו להחזיר:

מאי שנא ממיחם ע"ג מיחם. קשה לר"י דבברייתא גופה דשרי מיחם ע"ג מיחם בסוף פרקין קתני בהדיא ולא בשביל שיחמו אלא בשביל שיהו משומרין ואומר ר"י דברייתא לא שמיע ליה ולא מכח ברייתא פריך אלא ממעשים בכל יום שנותנין מיחם על גבי מיחם תימה דהיכי דמי אי יד סולדת בו היכי הוה בעי למישרי אע"פ שמבשל מי לא ידע דתולדות האור כאור דתנן (לעיל דף לט:) אין נותנין ביצה בצד המיחם ואמר אם גלגל חייב חטאת ותנן נמי (דף מא.) המיחם שפינהו לא יתן לתוכו צונן ואי להפשיר היכי מסיק דאסור והא תניא בפ' כירה (דף מ:) נותן אדם קיתון של מים כנגד המדורה לא בשביל שיחמו אלא בשביל שתפוג צינתן והיינו הפשר כדמוכח סוגיא דהתם ורב יהודה נמי קאמר התם אחד מים ואחד שמן יד סולדת בו אסור אין יד סולדת בו מותר ואין לחלק דגבי מדורה יזהר שלא יבשל כיון שהוא אצל האש אבל הכא אפילו אין יד סולדת בו אסור דשמא יבא לטעות ויניח עד שיתבשל דהא גבי מיחם שרינן לתת לתוכו מים מרובין כדי להפשירן ולא גזרינן אטו מים מועטין אע"פ שאינו אצל האש ונראה לרשב"א דהא דשרינן לתת קיתון של מים כנגד המדורה היינו ברחוק מן המדורה שלעולם לא יוכל לבא לידי בשול אבל בקרוב אסור אפי' להפשיר דילמא משתלי ואתי להניחן שם עד שיתבשל ולהכי מסיק הכא דאסור ולא בשביל שיחמו דקתני התם היינו כלומר במקום שיכול לבא לידי שיחמו והלשון דחוק קצת: מאי שנא מפרונקא. פר"ח דאמר רבא בפרק תולין (לקמן קלט:) האי פרונקא אפלגא דכובא שרי דלא הוי אהל ולא חיישינן שמא יסחוט: התם לא קפיד. פר"ת בפ"ק דכתובות (דף ו.) וכי מפני שאין לו קופה של תבן כו'. וא"ת מאי קבעי הא תנן במתניתין טומנין בגיזי צמר ואין מטלטלין אותן והיינו אפילו טמן דהא קתני בהדיא כיצד עושה מנער את הכיסוי והן נופלות וכי מייתי מברייתא דמסייע ליה לייתי ממתניתין דלא מצי למדחי ממתניתין כדדחי ברייתא וליכא למימר דמתני' איכא לאוקומי בבעל הפתק כדמוקי לקמן רבינא ע"כ סוגיא דהכא לא סבירא כרבינא מדלא מוקי ברייתא דמייתי בבעל הפתק ותירץ ר"י דגיזי צמר חשיבי טפי ממוכין ואסורים לטלטל יותר ואע"ג דרבא קאמר לקמן דאפילו גיזי צמר טמן בהן מטלטלין אין לחוש אי פליגא אאביי דהכא כיון דלא קיימא לקמן מילתיה דרבא ולמאי דמשני רבינא מילתיה דרבא ומוקי מתניתין בבעל הפתק ודרבא בשאין של הפתק אומר רשב"א דה"נ מיירי במוכין של הפתק ולא פליגא דרבא אדאביי אך ק"ק דמאי משני בסמוך מהו דתימא חזי למזגא עלייהו כיון דמיירי בשל הפתק היכי ס"ד דשרי לטלטל משום דחזי למזגא עלייהו:

ה"ק אם לא טמן אין מטלטלין אותן. אמוכין קאי ולא אגיזי צמר דגיזי צמר אפי' טמן אין מטלטלין: הא בחדתי הא בעתיקי. אומר ר"י שאם נתקו חוטי הסרבל אם הנקב רחב ויכול להכניסם בלא טורח שרי כיון דעתיקי ובלבד שיתנם בענין זה שלא יהא לחוש שמא יתקע דבענין שהוא רגילות לתקוע ולקשור נראה דאסורין להחזיר כדאסרינן בריש כל הכלים (דף קכג:) החזרת שידה תיבה ומגדל גזירה שמא יתקע:

וכי

עין משפט נר מצוה

ב א טוש"ע או"ח סימן שיח סעיף יח:
ג ב מיי' פכ"ב מהלכות שבת הלכה טו טור ושו"ע או"ח סימן שכ סעיף טו:
ד ג מיי' פכ"ו מהלכות שבת הלכה יב טוש"ע או"ח סימן רנט סעיף א:
ה ד מיי' פכ"ב מהלכות שבת הלכה כג טור ושו"ע או"ח סימן ש"מ סעיף ח:
ו ה מיי' פ"י מהלכות שבת הלכה י טוש"ע או"ח סימן שיז סעיף ג:

רבינו חננאל

נמי למפרס סודרא אפומא דכובא ולאנוחי נטלא אגביה דסודרא משום (דשארי) [דשיורי] הכוס מתחזין בסודרא וקפיד בנשירא דסודרא וסחיט ליה ולא דמי לפרונקא שהיא מטלית קשורה בפומא דכובא כדגרסי' בפ' דר' אליעזר אומר תולין (ד' קלט.) אמר רבא האי פרונקא אפלגי דכובא שרי ולא חייש דניחזי כמו מסננת אפומא דכולא כובא אסיר דהא עביד (אבל) אהל כמסננת. ואמאי שרי רבא התם אפלגי דכובא ליחוש שמא יסחוט המטלית. ושנינו מטלית לא קפיד בנשירותא מלשון (לקמן קמו:) מי שנשרו כליו בדרך שוטחן בחמה אבל לא כנגד העם סודר קפיד בנשירותא הילכך האי אסור והאי שרי: פי' מוכין סמרטוטין. בגדים מקוצצין כדתנן בנגעים פרק י"א בגד מוסגר שנתערב באחרים כולן טהורין קיצצו ועשאו מוכין טהור. מוכין אסיקנא כי הא דתניא אין נותנין מוכין לא לתוך הכר ולא לתוך הכסת בי"ט ואין צריך לומר בשבת נשרו מחזירין אותן בשבת [ואין צריך לומ' ביו"ט]. אמר רב הפותח בבגד בית הצואר בשבת חייב

רב נסים גאון

פ"ד אמר ליה ר' זירא מאי שנא ממיחם על גבי מיחם. בסוף הפרק (דף נא) בברייתא גרסי' ומניחין מיחם על גבי מיחם ומאי שנא מפורנקא. עיקר דיליה בפרק ר' אליעזר אומר תולין את המשמרת ביו"ט (דף קלט) אמר רבא האי פרונקא אפלגא דפומא דכובא שרי וכו' ואיכא דאמרי מאי שנא מפרונקיה דמר לפי שר' זירא עם רבא הוה מפליג והוא בעל השמועה:

מסורת הש"ס

א) ב"ב יט., ב) [גי' הערוך אודרא פי' הצולה], ג) מכות ג., ד) ד"ה הא.

ליקוטי רש"י

כוזא. כלי חרס קטן [לקמן עז:]. מיחם. קומקמוס שמחמם בו חמין [לעיל לח:]. של נחשת [לקמן נא:]. כובא. גיגית [ב"מ כה.]. נטלא. של זכוכית קרי נטלא [חולין קז.]. כלי קטן [ר"ן נדרים נא.]. פרונקא. בגד שטוחין על גיגית יין לכסותה [לקמן קלט. וע"ע ע"ז ל.]. ציפי צמר. לאחר שסרקו ונפצו במסרק. לשונות של ארגמן. צמר צבוע ואחר כך מוזרו והחליקוהו במסרק ועשוי לשונות לשונות [ב"ב יט.]. צמר סרוק ומשוך כמין לשון וצבוע ארגמן ומצויין הן [ב"מ כא.]. ארגמן. צמר צבוע ממין צבע ששמו ארגמן [שמות כה, ד]. ואין מטלטלין אותם. שהן מוקצים למלאכת בגדים [ב"ב שם]. חזי למזגא עלייהו. כן היתה ישיבתם שוטחין בגדים על גבי הקרקע ונסמכין ויושבין על ברכיהן כפופין כדאמרינן בפסחים (קח.) הוה זגינן אברכי דהדדי [ביצה י.]. להשען שכל הסבתן כך היתה יושב קצת ונשען קצת על שמאלו [לעיל מג.]. אודרא. מוכין [לקמן קמא.]. הפותח בית הצואר. שעשה פה לחלוק חדש. חייב. שתיקן כלי [מכות ג:].

מה בין זו למגופת חבית א"ל רבא זה חיבור וזה אינו חיבור רמי ליה ר' ירמיה לרבי זירא תנן ב) א שלל של כובסין ושלשלת של מפתחו' והבגד שהוא תפור בכלאים חיבור לטומאה עד שיתחיל להתיר אלמא שלא בשעת מלאכה נמי חיבור ורמינהו ג) מקל (א) שעשה יד לקורדום חיבור לטומאה בשעת מלאכה בשעת מלאכה אין שלא בשעת מלאכה לא א"ל התם שלא בשעת מלאכה אדם עשוי לזורקו לבין העצים הכא שלא בשעת מלאכה נמי ניחא ליה דאי מיטנפו הדר מחוור להו בסורא מתנו לה להא שמעתא משמיה דרב חסדא בפומבדיתא מתנו משמי' דרב כהנא ואמרי לה משמיה דרבא מאן תנא הא מלתא דאמור רבנן כל המחובר לו הרי הוא כמוהו א"ר יהודה אמר רב ר"מ היא דתנן ד) ג בית הפך ובית התבלין ובית הנר שבכירה מטמאין במגע ואין מטמאין באויר דברי ר' מאיר ור"ש מטהר בשלמא לר"ש קסבר לאו כבירה דמו אלא לר' מאיר אי כבירה דמו אפילו באויר נמי ליטמו אי לאו כבירה דמו אפילו במגע נמי לא ליטמו לעולם לאו כבירה דמו ורבנן הוא דגזרו בהו אי גזרו בהו באויר נמי ליטמו ° עבדו בהו רבנן היכרא כי היכי דלא אתי למשרף עליה תרומה וקדשים ה) תנו רבנן ד מספורת של פרקים ואיזמל של רהיטני חיבור לטומאה ואין חיבור להזאה מה נפשך אי חיבור הוא אפילו להזאה נמי אי לאו חיבור הוא אפילו לטומאה נמי לא אמר רבא דבר תורה בשעת מלאכה חיבור בין לטומאה בין להזאה ושלא בשעת מלאכה אינו חיבור לא לטומאה ולא להזאה וגזרו

רש"י

מה בין זו למגופת חבית. דתניא בפרק חבית שנשברה (לקמן דף קמו.) מביא אדם חבית ומתיז את ראשה בסייף ומניחה לפני האורחים: מגופה. אינה מן החבית עצמו ואע"פ שדבוקה בו אינו חשוב חיבור שהרי לינטל עומדת אבל הבגד כשנארג כולו חבור: שלל של כובסים. דרכם לשלול הבגדים זה עם זה קטנים עם הגדולים כדי שלא יאבדו י): ובגד שתפרו בכלאים. והן שתי חתיכות של בגד צמר שתפרו בחוט של פשתן דודאי סופו ליקרע ולהפרד זה מזה משום איסור כלאים וכן שלל של כובסין סופן להפרד אפ"ה חיבור לטומאה ואם נטמא זה נטמא זה: עד שיתחיל להתיר. דמעשה מוליא מיד מעשה וכיון שהתחיל להתיר גלי על ידי מעשה דלאו חד בגד הוא: שלא בשעת מלאכה. כגון שלל של כובסין שלא הוצרך לשוללו אלא משום שעת כיבוס ואפילו הכי חשיב ליה חיבור אחר כיבוס: מקל. של עצים בעלמא: שעשאו יד לקורדום. שלא קבעו לתוכו: חיבור בשעת מלאכה. ואע"פ דבאנפי נפשיה פשוטי כלי עץ לא מקבלי טומאה הכא בית יד הוא ונתרבו ידות לכל תורת כלי או האוכל בפ' העור והרוטב (חולין קיח.): לזורקו. למקל ומצניע הקורדום לבדו: ניחא להו. שיהו שלולין: דאי מיטנפי הדר מחוור להו. ע"י השלל הזה: להא שמעתין. דלקמיה מאן תנא להא כו'. כל המחובר לו כגון שלל של כובסין דאמרן לעיל חיבור ונטמא אף זה שלא נגעה בו הטומאה ואי לאו דחיבור הוא הוי טהור ואע"ג דנגע בהאי דאין כלי מקבל טומאה אלא מאב הטומאה: בית הפך ובית התבלין ובית הנר שבכירה. כירה זו מיטלטלת היא ומחוברין לה כלי חרס קטנים. בית הפך שמושיבין בתוכו שמן להפשיר: מטמאין במגע. אם נפלה טומאה באוירן או לאויר הכירה ונגעה הטומאה לשולי הכירה נטמאו גם אלו או נגעה טומאה לשוליהם של אלו נטמאת הכירה: ואין מטמאין. בטומאת הכירה כלומר בטומאת האויר שאם נפל שרץ באויר הכירה ולא נגעה הטומאה בדופניה היא טמאה דכלי חרס מטמא באויר והן טהורין שאין חיבור לה אלא לענין מגע כדמפרש טעמא לקמיה: ור' שמעון מטהר. במגע את מי שלא נגעה בו הטומאה דכל חד כלי באנפי נפשיה הוא אלמא לרבי מאיר חיבור ופליגי עליה: אפי' באויר ליטמו. מחמת כירה אם נטמאת כירה מאוירה בלא נגיעה: דגזרו בהו. דליהוו חיבור מדרבנן: עבוד בהו רבנן היכרא. דלא עבדו להו ככירה ממש ליטמא באויר כי היכי דלידעו שחיבור מדבריהם ולא לשרוף על טומאתן תרומה וקדשים: איזמל של רהיטני. פליינ"א שממחקים בה את התריסין ונותנין הברזל לתוך דפוס של עץ המתוקן לו ולאחר מלאכתו נוטלו הימנו: חיבור לטומאה. נטמא זה טמא זה: ואין חיבור להזאה. וצריך להזות על שניהם:

תוספות

וכי מה בין זה למגופת חבית. פי' בקונטרס דתניא לקמן בפרק חבית (דף קמו. ושם) רשב"ג אומר מתיזה בסייף ומניחה לפני האורחין ואין נראה לר"י דא"כ מאי משני זה חיבור וזה אינו חיבור התם נמי חיבור הוא דרשב"ג שרי להתיז אפילו גוף החבית עם המגופה כדמוכח התם דבעו מיניה מרב ששת מהו למיברז חביתא בבורטיא כו' אמר להו לפתחא קא מכוין ואסור ופריך מהא דשרי רשב"ג להתיז ראשה בסייף ומשני התם ודאי לעין יפה קא מכוין אבל הכא אי לעין יפה קא מכוין ליפתחיה מיפתח והא דאסר למיברז חביתא היינו בגוף החבית דחביתא חבית גופא משמע ועוד דמגופה שרי דתנן במתני' אין נוקבין מגופה של חבית דברי רבי יהודה וחכמים מתירין משמע דשרי רשב"ג אפי' בגוף החבית דלעין יפה קא מיכוין והכי הוה ליה לשנויי בשמעתין הכא לפתחא מכוין התם לעין יפה מכוין ופיר"ת וכי מה בין זה לנקיבת מגופת חבית דתנן בפ' חבית (גם זה שם) אין נוקבין מגופת חבית דברי ר' יהודה וחכמים מתירין וא"ת [התם] לכ"ע לא מיחייב חטאת כדאמר התם בגמ' דבר תורה כל פתח שאינו עשוי להכנים ולהוציא אינו פתח אבל הכא פתח בית הצואר עשוי הוא להכנים ולהוציא ואם כן מאי קשיא ליה ויש לומר דהכי פריך כיון דמחייבת חטאת בפותח בית הצואר משום דעשוי להכנים ולהוציא א"כ נמי גבי מגופה אם עשוי להכנים ולהוציא היה חייב חטאת הלכך השתא נמי שאינו עשוי אלא להוציא היה לאסור מדרבנן ומשני זה חיבור וזה אינו חיבור שהמגופה אינה מן החבית ואפילו אם היה עשוי נקב שבמגופה להכנים ולהוציא לא היה חייב חטאת לכך שרו רבנן: חיבור עד שיתחיל להתיר. האי חיבור היינו לטומאה ולא להזאה כדתנן במסכת פרה (פי"ב מ"ט) וא"ת ואמאי לא מייתי מתני' דמסכת פרה וי"ל משום דלא קתני בה עד שיתחיל להתיר ולא הוה מצי לאוכוחי מינה דשלא בשעת מלאכה נמי חיבור: אמר רב יהודה אמר רב רבי מאיר היא. אההיא דשלל של כובסים קאי וכן פירש בקונטרס דבההוא דמקל שמא אפי' רבי שמעון מודה דכיון שצריך הקרדום למקל הוי חיבור: עבדו רבנן היכרא כו'. וגבי שלל של כובסין איכא נמי היכרא מה שאינו חיבור להזאה והכא גבי כירה לא שייך הך היכרא דלית ביה הזאה: אי חיבור הוא אפי' להזאה נמי כו'. קשה לר"י דבשלל של כובסין נמי תקשה לן הכי אי חיבור הוא אפילו להזאה נמי אי לאו חיבור הוא לטומאה נמי לא ורבא נמי דקאמר דבר תורה בשעת מלאכה חיבור בין לטומאה בין להזאה אמאי לא קאמר דבין בשעת מלאכה בין שלא בשעת מלאכה גזרו בה רבנן טומאה כי ההיא דשלל של כובסין ותירץ ר"י דשלל של כובסין ודאי לא הוי חיבור אלא מדרבנן אפילו בשעת מלאכה שאינם צריכים זה לזה ולהכי מדמה לה לבית הפך ולבית התבלין שכל אחד הוא תשמיש בפני עצמו ולהכי אינו חיבור להזאה כיון דמדאורייתא אינו חיבור אבל מספורת של פרקים פשיטא ליה דבשעת מלאכה הוי חיבור דבר תורה כיון שמשמשין שניהם תשמיש א' ° וצריכים זה לזה בשעת מלאכה מה שאין כן בשלל של כובסים שאין תשמיש בגד זה צריך לזה כלל והא דפריך אי לאו חיבור הוא אפילו לטומאה נמי לא לאו דוקא ועיקר קושיתו הוא דאמאי אינו חיבור להזאה ורשב"א מפרש דגבי שלל של כובסין אתי ליה שפיר אע"ג דאינו חיבור להזאה משום דלא הוי חיבור מן התורה גזרו רבנן שיהא חיבור לטומאה כיון שכל בגד טמא בפני עצמו מן התורה אבל גבי מספורת פריך שפיר אי לאו חיבור הוא מדאורייתא אם כן אמאי גזרו חכמים טומאה כלל דהא כל פרק בפני עצמו טהור מדאורייתא לרבנן דתנן במס' כלים בפי"ג (מ"א) מספורת שנחלקה לשנים רבי יהודה מטמא וחכמים מטהרים אף על גב דאיכא למימר דהתם מיירי כשאינה של פרקים ולפי זה הא דאמר השחור והזוג של מספרים אף על פי שנחלקו טמאים אתי כרבי יהודה ודוחק והא דאמר דגזרו על הזאה שבשעת מלאכה משום הזאה שלא בשעת מלאכה אף על גב דשלא בשעת מלאכה טהור גמור הוא ואין צריך הזאה כלל מ"מ כשחוזרים ועושים בו מלאכה חוזר לטומאתו ישנה והחמירו חכמים בטומאה ישנה שלא תועיל לו הזאה שלא בשעת מלאכה כיון שאינו חיבור דבר תורה וגזרו על הזאה שבשעת מלאכה אטו הזאה שלא בשעת מלאכה. רשב"א: דבר תורה בשעת מלאכה חיבור. תימה מאי שנא ממוכני דאמר (לעיל דף מד:) בזמן שהיא נשמטת דאינו חיבור וצריך לחלק: ועל

עין משפט נר מצוה

ז א מיי' פי"ב מהלכות פרה הלכה ו:
ח ב מיי' פ"כ מהלכות כלים הלכה יג:
ט ג מיי' פי"ז מהלכות כלים הלכה ה:
י ד מיי' פי"ב מהלכות פרה הלכה ד:

רבינו חננאל

חטאת מפני שהוא מחובר בבגד אבל מגופת החבית שאינה מן החבית עצמה מותר לפתחה בשבת. רמי ליה (ר' יוחנן) ר' ירמי' לר"ז שלל הכובסין כו' עד המקל שעשאו יד לקורדום כו' פירוש הכובסין שוללין יריעות זו עם זו כדי שיהו נוחין לכביסה ואינה תפירה אלא שלילה מלשון (מו"ק כב:) על המתים כולן שולל לאחר שבעה ומשני ליה ר' זירא מקל שעשאו יד לקורדום כיון שמשלים מלאכתו זורק אותו מקל לבין העצים אבל שלל של כובסין אע"פ ששלמה כביסתם רוצה בשלילותן שמא יטנפו יחזור ויחוורום: מאן תנא כל המחובר לו הרי הוא כמוהו אמר רב ר"מ היא ונדחה ופשוטה היא: ת"ר מספורת של פרקין. פי' שמתפרק זה מזה וכן איזמל של רהיטי. חיבור לטומאה ואם נטמא אחד נטמא האחר ואינן חיבור להזאה. פרשה רבא דבר תורה בשעת מלאכה. כלומר בשעה שגוזז בהן חיבור הן לטומאה ולהזאה. שלא בשעת מלאכה אינן חיבור לא לטומאה ולא

רב נסים גאון

אי כבירה דמו אפילו באויר נמי ליטמו. עיקר דילה משתכח בתורת כהנים וכל כלי חרש אשר יפול מהם אל תוכו מתוכו הוא מיטמא ואינו מטמא מאחוריו כו' יכול אף הכלים יהו מיטמאין באויר כלי חרש תלמוד לומר [וכו'] אוכלין מיטמאין באויר כלי חרס ואין הכלים מיטמאין באויר כלי חרס ובפרק ב' מן מס' כלים שנינו כלי חרס וכלי נתר טומאתן שוה ומטמאין באויר [illegible] יציאות השבת (דף טז) והמשנה והתוס' מלאה מענין זה ובתלמוד בפ' ראשון מן שחיטת חולין (דף כד) שנו במשנה הטהור בכל הכלים טמא בכלי חרס ובברייתא גרסינן ת"ר אויר כלי חרס טמא וגבו טהור:

מסורת הש"ס

א) [עוקלין פרק ג מ"ו ע"ש], ב) [גי' הערוך בערך שלל תנן שלל הכובסין והבגד שהוא תפור בכלאים חיבור לטומאה וכו'], ג) כלים פ"כ מ"ג, ד) כלים פ"ה מ"ג, ה) לקמן נח: [שתי ברייתות הן בתוספתא דכלים ב"מ פ"ג], ו) וביצה ז. פירש"י בטס"א בלע"ז ע"ש.

הגהות הב"ח

(א) גמ' מקל שעשאו יד:

גליון הש"ס

גמ' עבדו בהו רבנן היכרא. לעיל דף טז ע"א. נדה דף לד ע"א: תוס' ד"ה אי חיבור וכו' וצריכים זה לזה בשעת מלאכה. עי' ביצה דף כג ע"ב תוס' ד"ה משום שלשה כלים:

ליקוטי רש"י

מה בין זה למגופת החבית. דאמרינן בפרק חבית שנשברה (שבת קמו.) דמתיז ראשה בשבת בסייף לפתוח את החבית. זה. דבית הצואר היה חיבור הלכך פתח תיקון חדש הוא וזה אבל המגופה אע"פ שהיא טוחה על פי החבית בטיט אין זה חיבור והוה לה כפתוחה ועומדת [מכות ג:]. שלל. בטס"א כמו שלל של כובסין [ביצה ז.]. שוללין. מתקבלין כמו מן השלל של גילים (ביצה ז.) [ב"ק סא.]. מספורת של פרקים. שתי סכינים שלה מתפרדין. ואיזמל של רהיטני. פליינ"ה של אומנים תריסים שנותנים האיזמל לתוך בין שני עצים העשוין לכך ולאחר מלאכתו נוטלו ומצניעו. ושלא בשעת מלאכה. הואיל ואין צריכין להיות מחוברין הוו להו כשני כלים ואין חיבור ואף על פי שמחוברין דעל כרחך שלא בשעת מלאכה דומיא דשעת מלאכה קאמר ובשעת מלאכה מחוברין הן אלמא במחוברין עסקינן וגזרו לחומרא על הטומאה דליהוי חיבור ועל הזאה דלא ליהוי חיבור ומשום הכי קתני חיבור לטומאה לעולם ואין חיבור להזאה לעולם [לקמן נח.].

מַה בֵּין זוֹ לִמְגוּפַת חָבִית – **How does this differ from a barrel lid?** We know from a Baraisa cited below (on 146a) that one may lop off the top of a sealed barrel with a sword in order to open the barrel and remove its contents. We see from this that the mere creation of an opening is not considered completing a utensil.[1] – ? –

The challenge is refuted:

אָמַר לֵיהּ רָבָא – **Rava said to [Rav Kahana]:** זֶה חִיבּוּר – **This** material, in which the shirt opening is made, **is bonded,** i.e. it is one unbroken piece of material. Therefore, opening it up is creating something new and is in the category of *completing a utensil.* וְזֶה אֵינוֹ חִיבּוּר – **But this,** the lid which seals the opening of the barrel, **is not bonded,** i.e. it is not one piece with the barrel. Therefore the barrel is considered to have had an opening even before its top was lopped off, and the opening created thereby is not in the category of *completing a utensil.*[2]

Having mentioned a distinction between attached ("bonded") and unattached items, the Gemara digresses to discuss other laws related to this point:

רָמֵי לֵיהּ רַבִּי יִרְמְיָה לְרַבִּי זֵירָא – **R' Yirmiyah posed a contradiction to R' Zeira:** תְּנַן – **We learned in a Mishnah:**[3] שְׁלַל שֶׁל כּוֹבְסִין – Regarding ARTICLES OF CLOTHING LOOSELY STITCHED TOGETHER BY LAUNDERERS,[4] וְשַׁלְשֶׁלֶת שֶׁל מַפְתְּחוֹת – AND A KEY CHAIN, וְהַבֶּגֶד שֶׁהוּא תָּפוּר בְּכִלְאַיִם – AND A GARMENT whose component pieces were SEWN together WITH *SHAATNEZ* thread (e.g. sections of woolen garments sewn together with linen thread), חִיבּוּר לְטוּמְאָה – they ARE considered JOINED, i.e. treated as a single utensil, FOR purposes of *TUMAH,* i.e. if one of the articles joined by these mediums becomes *tamei,* the other article becomes *tamei* as well, עַד שֶׁיַּתְחִיל לְהַתִּיר – UNTIL [THE PERSON] BEGINS TO SEPARATE THEM.[5] אַלְמָא שֶׁלֹּא בִּשְׁעַת מְלָאכָה נַמֵּי חִיבּוּר – Now, the laundry bundle was stitched together only in order to facilitate washing, and yet the Mishnah treats the bundle as a single unit even after the person finishes washing it. **Evidently,** once utensils are joined for the purpose of performing certain work with them, they are considered **joined even while no work** is being performed with them. וּרְמִינְהוּ – **But contrast [this Mishnah with the following Mishnah]:**[6] מַקֵּל שֶׁעֲשָׂה יָד לְקוּרְדּוֹם – Regarding A STICK WHICH ONE MADE INTO A makeshift AX HANDLE, i.e. he inserted a wooden stick into an ax head in a temporary fashion without fastening it there, חִיבּוּר לְטוּמְאָה בִּשְׁעַת מְלָאכָה – it IS considered JOINED to the ax FOR purposes of *TUMAH* WHILE WORK is being performed with the ax.[7] The implication is that בִּשְׁעַת מְלָאכָה אִין – **while work** is being performed, **yes,** the handle and ax head are considered one utensil, שֶׁלֹּא בִּשְׁעַת מְלָאכָה לֹא – but **while work is not** being performed, they are **not** considered as one. Thus, we see that an attachment is considered significant for *tumah* only while the attachment is needed. – ? –

R' Zeira responded:

אָמַר לֵיהּ – **He said to [R' Yirmiyah]:** הָתָם – **There,** in the case of the ax handle, שֶׁלֹּא בִּשְׁעַת מְלָאכָה – **while no work** is being performed, i.e. when finished using the ax, אָדָם עָשׂוּי לְזוֹרְקוֹ לְבֵין הָעֵצִים – **a person is wont to** remove the stick and **toss it among the** other **pieces of wood.**[8] הָכָא – **Here,** in the case of the garments stitched together by launderers, שֶׁלֹּא בִּשְׁעַת מְלָאכָה נַמֵּי נִיחָא לֵיהּ – even **while no work** is being performed, i.e. after the garments are laundered, **one is also pleased** that the stitches remain in place, דְּאִי מִיטַּנְּפוּ הָדַר מְחַוַּור לְהוּ – **so that if [the clothing] should become soiled** again, **he can relaunder them** without having to restitch them.

From the Mishnah regarding the garments stitched together by launderers it is evident that items that are by themselves independent of each other and that are attached only for the sake of convenience are considered as one utensil for purposes of *tumah.*[9] The Gemara focuses on this point:

בְּסוּרָא מַתְנוּ לַהּ לְהָא שְׁמַעְתָּא מִשְּׁמֵיהּ דְּרַב חִסְדָּא – **In Sura they taught the following teaching in the name of Rav Chisda,** בְּפוּמְבְּדִיתָא מַתְנוּ מִשְּׁמֵיהּ דְּרַב כָּהֲנָא – **in Pumbidesa they taught** it **in the name of Rav Kahana,** וְאָמְרֵי לַהּ מִשְּׁמֵיהּ דְּרָבָא – **and others say it in the name of Rava:** מַאן תָּנָא הָא מִלְּתָא דְּאָמוּר רַבָּנָן – **Who,** i.e. which Tanna, **taught this principle that the Rabbis say:** כֹּל הַמְחוּבָּר לוֹ הֲרֵי הוּא כָּמוֹהוּ – **Whatever is attached to [a thing],** even if not necessary for that thing's operation, **is considered like [the thing] itself?** אָמַר רַב יְהוּדָה אָמַר רַב – **Rav Yehudah said in the name of Rav:** רַבִּי מֵאִיר הִיא – **It is R' Meir.** דִּתְנַן – **For we learned in a Mishnah:**[10] הַפַּךְ וּבֵית הַתַּבְלִין וּבֵית הַנֵּר שֶׁבְּכִירָה – Regarding A FLASK RECEPTACLE AND A SPICE RECEPTACLE AND A LAMP RECEPTACLE OF A *KIRAH,*[11] מִטַּמְּאִין בְּמַגָּע – they BECOME *TAMEI* THROUGH CONTACT, i.e. if the *kirah* (its inside walls or floor) is contacted by *tumah* these receptacles likewise become *tamei,* וְאֵין מִטַּמְּאִין בָּאֲוִיר – BUT THEY DO NOT BECOME *TAMEI* THROUGH *tumah* falling into the *kirah's* AIRSPACE.[12] דִּבְרֵי רַבִּי מֵאִיר – These are THE

NOTES

1. Since the sealed barrel is not usable until it is broken open, opening it should fall under the heading of completing a utensil.

2. Although the lid was cemented to the top of the barrel, this was done with the intention of later removing the lid. Thus, it is not considered bonded with the barrel (*Rashi*). Moreover, even if one breaks the barrel open below the point where the lid is attached, so that he cuts into the barrel itself, it is nevertheless permitted. The fact that the cover is a separate piece from the body of the barrel, although they are sealed together, gives the barrel the status of a usable utensil even before it is cut open. Cutting it open, therefore, is not considered fashioning a new utensil (see *Ritva* to *Makkos* 3b, in explanation of *Rashi;* cf. *Tosafos*).

3. This "Mishnah" appears to be an amalgam of *Parah* 12:9 and *Uktzin* 2:6 (cf. *Tosafos* and *R' Akiva Eiger*).

4. It was the practice of professional laundrymen to loosely stitch together small articles of clothing so that they would not become lost in the wash (*Rashi*).

5. Even though the laundered garments are destined to be detached from each other after laundering, and the pieces of material are destined to have their connecting thread removed because of the prohibition of *shaatnez,* they are considered as one article as long as the person has not begun detaching them. Once he has begun to detach them, however [even before he finishes doing so], they are considered two articles, because the act of detaching them undoes the effect of the original joining (*Rashi*). [*Rashi* and the other Rishonim do not appear to have had "a key chain" mentioned in their texts of the Gemara here.]

6. *Keilim* 20:3.

7. As part of the metal ax, the handle can contract *tumah*; by itself it cannot. This is in accordance with the rule that wooden utensils cannot contract *tumah* unless they possess a receptacle (*Rashi*).

8. Since it is a mere piece of wood and was not crafted into a proper handle, he generally removes it immediately after use and tosses it into the wood pile.

9. It is this fact that causes the item not touched by the *tumah* to become *tamei.* If not for this fact, the item not touched by the *tumah* would remain *tahor* even if it contacted the item that did touch the *tumah,* because the law is that a utensil can become *tamei* only by contact with a primary source of *tumah* [e.g. a *sheretz*], not by contact with something that itself contracted *tumah* only by contacting a primary source [e.g. a garment that touched a *sheretz*] (*Rashi*).

10. *Keilim* 5:3.

11. The practice was to attach small receptacles to a *kirah* (a type of stove – see above, 36b note 1). These receptacles would hold flasks of oil (in order to warm them by the heat of the *kirah*), spices or lamps (*Rashi*).

12. Earthenware vessels possess the unique feature that they become *tamei* when *tumah* merely enters their interior, even if the *tumah* does

מה בין זו למגופת חבית א"ל רבא זה חיבור וזה אינו חיבור רמי ליה ר' ירמיה לרבי זירא (א) תנן (ב) א שלל של כובסין ושלשלת של מפתחו' והבגד שהוא תפור בכלאים חיבור לטומאה עד שיתחיל להתיר אלמא שלא בשעת מלאכה נמי חיבור ורמינהו (ג) מקל ב שעשה (א) יד לקורדום חיבור לטומאה בשעת מלאכה בשעת מלאכה אין שלא בשעת מלאכה לא א"ל התם שלא בשעת מלאכה אדם עשוי לזורקו לבין העצים הכא שלא בשעת מלאכה נמי ניחא ליה דאי מיטנפו הדר מחוור להו בסורא מתנו לה להא שמעתא משמיה דרב חסדא בפומבדיתא מתנו משמי' דרב כהנא ואמרי לה משמיה דרבא מאן תנא הא מלתא דאמור רבנן כל המחובר לו הרי הוא כמוהו א"ר יהודה אמר רב ר"מ היא דתנן (ד) ג בית הפך ובית התבלין ובית הנר שבכירה מטמאין במגע ואין מטמאין באויר דברי ר' מאיר ור"ש מטהר בשלמא לר"ש קסבר לאו ככירה דמו אלא לר' מאיר אי ככירה דמו אפילו באויר נמי ליטמו אי לאו ככירה דמו אפילו במגע נמי לא ליטמו לעולם לאו ככירה דמו ורבנן הוא דגזרו בהו אי גזרו בהו אפילו באויר נמי ליטמו ° עבדו בהו רבנן היכרא כי היכי דלא אתי למשרף עליה תרומה וקדשים (ה) תנו רבנן ד מספורת של פרקים ואיזמל של רהיטני חיבור לטומאה ואין חיבור להזאה מה נפשך אי חיבור הוא אפילו להזאה נמי אי לאו חיבור הוא אפילו לטומאה נמי לא אמר רבא דבר תורה בשעת מלאכה חיבור בין לטומאה בין להזאה ושלא בשעת מלאכה אינו חיבור לא לטומאה ולא להזאה

וגזרו

רש"י

מה בין זו למגופת חבית. דתניא בפרק חבית שנשברה (לקמן דף קמו.) מביא אדם חבית ומתיז את ראשה בסייף ומניחה לפני האורחים: מגופה. אינה מן החבית עצמו ואע"פ שדבוקה בו אינו חשוב חיבור שהרי לינטל עומדת אבל הבגד כשנארג כולו חבור: שלל של כובסים. דרכם לשלול הבגדים זה עם זה קטנים עם הגדולים כדי שלא יאבדו (ו): ובגד שתפרו בכלאים. והן שתי חתיכות של בגד צמר שתפרו בחוט של פשתן דודאי סופו ליקרע ולהפרד זה מזה משום איסור כלאים וכן שלל של כובסין סופן להפרד אפ"ה חיבור לטומאה ואם נטמא זה נטמא זה: עד שיתחיל להתיר. דמעשה מוליא מיד מעשה וכיון שהתחיל להתיר גלי על ידי מעשה דלאו חד בגד הוא: שלא בשעת מלאכה. כגון שלל של כובסין שלא הוצרך לשוללו אלא משום שעת כיבוס ואפילו הכי חשיב ליה חיבור אחר כיבוס: מקל. של עצים בעלמא: שעשאו יד לקורדום. שלא קבעו לתוכו: חיבור בשעת מלאכה. ואע"פ דבאנפי נפשיה פשוטי כלי עץ לא מקבלי טומאה הכא בית יד הוא ונתרבו ידות לכל תורת כלי או האוכל בפ' העור והרוטב (חולין קיח.): לזורקו. למקל ומלניע הקורדום לבדו: ניחא להו. שיהו שלולין: דאי מיטנפי הדר מחוור להו. ע"י השלל הזה: להא שמעתין. דלקמיה מאן תנא להא כו'. כל המחובר לו כגון שלל של כובסין דאמרן לעיל חיבור ונטמא אף זה שלא נגעה בו הטומאה ואי לאו דחיבור הוא הוי טהור ואע"ג דנגע בהאי דאין כלי מקבל טומאה אלא מאב הטומאה: בית הפך ובית התבלין ובית הנר שבכירה. כירה זו מיטלטלת היא ומחוברין לה כלי חרס קטנים. בית הפך שמושיבין בתוכו שמן להפשיר: מטמאין במגע. אם נפלה טומאה באוירן או לאויר הכירה ונגעה הטומאה לשולי הכירה נטמאו גם אלו או נגעה טומאה לשוליהם של אלו נטמאת הכירה: ואין מטמאין. בטומאת הכירה כלומר בטומאת האויר שאם נפל שרץ באויר הכירה ולא נגעה הטומאה בדופניה היא טמאה דכלי חרס מטמא באויר והן טהורין שאין חיבור לה אלא לענין מגע כדמפרש טעמא לקמיה: ור' שמעון מטהר. במגע את מי שלא נגעה בו הטומאה דכל חד כלי באנפי נפשיה הוא אלמא לרבי מאיר חיבור ופליגי עליה: אפי' באויר ליטמו. מחמת כירה אם נטמאת כירה מאוירה בלא נגיעה: דגזרו בהו. דליהוו חיבור מדרבנן: עבוד בהו רבנן היכרא. דלא עבדו להו ככירה ממש ליטמא באויר כי היכי דלידעו שחיבור מדבריהם ולא לשרוף על טומאתן תרומה וקדשים: איזמל של רהיטני. פליינ"א שממחקים בה את התריסין ונותנין הברזל לתוך דפוס של עץ המתוקן לו ולאחר מלאכתו נוטלו הימנו: חיבור לטומאה. נטמא זה טמא זה: ואין חיבור להזאה. וצריך להזות על שניהם:

וגזרו

תוספות

וכי מה בין זה למגופת חבית. פי' בקונטרס דתניא לקמן בפרק חבית (דף קמו. ושם) רשב"ג אומר מתיזה בסייף ומניחה לפני האורחין ואין נראה לר"י דא"כ מאי משני זה חיבור וזה אינו חיבור התם נמי חיבור הוא דרשב"ג שרי להתיז אפילו גוף החבית עם המגופה כדמוכח התם דבעו מיניה מרב ששת מהו למיברז חביתא בבורטיא כו' אמר להו לפתחא קא מכוין ואסור ופריך מהא דשרי רשב"ג להתיז ראשה בסייף ומשני התם ודאי לעין יפה קא מכוין אבל הכא אי לעין יפה קא מכוין ליפתחיה מיפתח והא דאסר למיברז חביתא היינו בגוף החבית דחביתא חבית גופא משמע ועוד דמגופה שרי דתנן במתני' אין נוקבין מגופה של חבית דברי רבי יהודה וחכמים מתירין משמע דשרי רשב"ג אפי' בגוף החבית דלעין יפה קא מיכוין והכי הוה ליה לשנויי בשמעתין הכא לפתחא מכוין התם לעין יפה מכוין ופיר"ת וכי מה בין זה לנקיבת מגופת חבית דתנן בפ' חבית (גם זה שם) אין נוקבין מגופת חבית דברי ר' יהודה וחכמים מתירין וא"ת [התם] לכ"ע לא מיחייב חטאת כדאמר התם בגמ' דבר תורה כל פתח שאינו עשוי להכניס ולהוציא אינו פתח אבל הכא פתח בית הצואר עשוי הוא להכניס ולהוציא ואם כן מאי קשיא ליה ויש לומר דהכי פריך כיון דמחייבת חטאת בפותח בית הצואר משום דעשוי להכניס ולהוציא א"כ נמי גבי מגופה אם עשוי להכניס ולהוציא היה חייב חטאת הלכך השתא נמי שאינו עשוי אלא להוציא היה לאסור מדרבנן ומשני זה חיבור וזה אינו חיבור שהמגופה אינה מן החבית ואפילו אם היה עשוי נקב שבמגופה להכניס ולהוציא לא היה חייב חטאת לכך שרו רבנן:

חיבור עד שיתחיל להתיר. הא חיבור היינו לטומאה ולא להזאה כדתנן במסכת פרה (פי"ב מ"ט) וא"ת ואמאי לא מייתי מתני' דמסכת פרה וי"ל משום דלא קתני בה עד שיתחיל להתיר ולא הוה מצי לאוכוחי מינה דשלא בשעת מלאכה נמי חיבור:

אמר רב יהודה אמר רב רבי מאיר היא. אההיא דשלל של כובסים קאי וכן פירש בקונטרס דבההוא דמקל שמא אפי' רבי שמעון מודה דכיון שצריך הקרדום למקל הוי חיבור:

עבדו רבנן היכרא כו'. וגבי שלל של כובסין איכא נמי היכרא מה שאינו חיבור להזאה והכא גבי כירה לא שייך הך היכרא דלית ביה הזאה:

אי חיבור הוא אפי' להזאה נמי כו'. קשה לר"י דבשלל של כובסין נמי תקשה לן הכי אי חיבור הוא אפילו להזאה נמי אי לאו חיבור הוא לטומאה נמי לא ורבא נמי דקאמר דבר תורה בשעת מלאכה חיבור בין לטומאה בין להזאה אמאי לא קאמר דבין בשעת מלאכה בין שלא בשעת מלאכה גזרו בה רבנן טומאה כי ההיא דשלל של כובסין ותירץ ר"י דשלל של כובסין ודאי לא הוי חיבור אלא מדרבנן אפילו בשעת מלאכה שאינם צריכים זה לזה ולהכי מדמה לה לבית הפך ולבית התבלין שכל אחד הוא תשמיש בפני עצמו ולהכי אינו חיבור להזאה כיון דמדאורייתא אינו חיבור אבל מספורת של פרקים פשיטא ליה דבשעת מלאכה הוי חיבור דבר תורה כיון שמשמשין שניהם תשמיש א' ° וצריכים זה לזה בשעת מלאכה מה שאין כן בשלל של כובסים שאין תשמיש בגד זה צריך לזה כלל והא דפריך אי לאו חיבור הוא אפילו לטומאה נמי לא לאו דוקא ועיקר קושיתו הוא דאמאי אינו חיבור להזאה ורשב"א מפרש דגבי שלל של כובסין אתי ליה שפיר אע"ג דאינו חיבור להזאה משום דלא הוי חיבור מן התורה גזרו רבנן שיהא חיבור לטומאה כיון שכל בגד טמא בפני עצמו מן התורה אבל גבי מספורת פריך שפיר אי לאו חיבור הוא מדאורייתא אם כן אמאי גזרו חכמים טומאה כלל דהא כל פרק בפני עצמו טהור מדאורייתא לרבנן דתנן במס' כלים בפי"ג (מ"א) מספורת שנחלקה לשנים רבי יהודה מטמא וחכמים מטהרים אף על גב דאיכא למימר דהתם איירי כשאינה של פרקים ולפי זה הא דאמר השחור והזוג של מספרים אף על פי שנחלקו טמאים אתי כרבי יהודה ודוחק והא דאמר דגזרו על הזאה שבשעת מלאכה משום הזאה שלא בשעת מלאכה אף על גב דשלא בשעת מלאכה טהור גמור הוא ואין צריך הזאה כלל מ"מ כשמחזירים ועושים בו מלאכה חוזר לטומאתו ישנה והחמירו חכמים בטומאה ישנה שלא תועיל לו הזאה שלא בשעת מלאכה כיון שאינו חיבור דבר תורה וגזרו על הזאה שבשעת מלאכה אטו הזאה שלא בשעת מלאכה. רשב"א:

דבר תורה בשעת מלאכה חיבור. תימה מאי שנא ממוכני דאמר (לעיל דף מד:) בזמן שהיא נשמטת דאינו חיבור וצריך לחלק:

ועל

עין משפט נר מצוה

ז א מיי' פי"ב מהלכות פרה הלכה ו:
ח ב מיי' פ"כ מהלכות כלים הלכה יג:
ט ג מיי' פי"ז מהלכות כלים הלכה ה:
י ד מיי' פי"ב מהלכות פרה הלכה ד:

רבינו חננאל

חטאת מפני שהוא מחובר בבגד אבל מגופת החבית שאינה מן החבית עצמה מותר לפתחה בשבת. רמי ליה (ר' יוחנן) ר' ירמי' לר"ז שלל הכובסין כו' עד המקל שעשאו יד לקורדום כו' פירוש הכובסין שוללין יריעות זו עם זו כדי שיהו נוחין לכביסה ואינה תפירה אלא שלילה מלשון (מו"ק כב:) על המתים כולן שולל לאחר שבעה ומשני ליה ר' זירא מקל שעשאו יד לקורדום כיון שמשלים מלאכתו זורק אותו מקל לבין העצים אבל שלל של כובסין אע"פ שמשלמה כביסתם רוצה בשלילותן שמא יטנפו יחזור ויחוורום: מאן תנא כל המחובר לו הרי הוא כמוהו אמר רב ר"מ היא ונדחה ופשוטה היא: ת"ר מספורת של פרקין. פי' שמתפרק זה מזה וכן איזמל של רהיטי. חיבור לטומאה ואם נטמא אחד נטמא האחר ואינן חיבור להזאה. פרשה רבא דבר תורה בשעת מלאכה. כלומר בשעה שגוזז בהן חיבור הן לטומאה ולהזאה. שלא בשעת מלאכה אינן חיבור לא לטומאה ולא

רב נסים גאון

אי ככירה דמו אפילו באויר נמי ליטמו. עיקר דילה משתכח בתורת כהנים וכל כלי חרש אשר יפול מהם אל תוכו מתוכו הוא מיטמא ואינו מטמא מאחוריו כו' יכול אף הכלים יהו מיטמאין באויר כלי חרש תלמוד לומר [וכו'] אוכלין מיטמאין באויר כלי חרס ואין הכלים מיטמאין באויר כלי חרס ובפרק ב' מן מס' כלים שנינו כלי חרס וכלי נתר טומאתן שוה ומטמאין באויר ותמצא בפרק יציאות השבת (דף טו) והמשנה והתוס' מליאה מענין זה ובתלמוד בפ' ראשון מן שחיטת חולין (דף כד) שנו במשנה הטהור בכל הכלים טמא בכלי חרס ובברייתא גרסינן ת"ר אויר כלי חרס טמא וגבו טהור:

מסורת הש"ס

א) [עוקצין פרק ב מ"ו ע"ש], ב) [גי' הערוך בערך שלל תנן שלל הכובסין והבגד שהוא תפור בכלאים חיבור לטומאה וכו'], ג) כלים פ"כ מ"ג, ד) כלים פ"ה מ"ג, ה) לקמן נח: [שתי ברייתות הן בתוספתא דכלים ב"מ פ"ג], ו) וביצה ז. פירש"י בטש"א בלע"ז ע"ש.

הגהות הב"ח

(א) גמ' מקל שעשאו יד:

גליון הש"ם

גמ' עבדו בהו רבנן היכרא. לעיל דף טז ע"א. נדה דף לד ע"א: תוס' ד"ה אי חיבור וכו' וצריכים זה לזה בשעת מלאכה. עי' ביצה דף כג ע"ב תוס' ד"ה משום שלשה כלים:

ליקוטי רש"י

מה בין זה למגופת החבית. דאמרינן בפרק חבית שנשברה (שבת קמו.) דמתיז ראשה בשבת בסייף לפתוח את החבית. זה. דבית הצואר היה חיבור הלכך פתח תיקון חדש הוא וזה אבל המגופה אע"פ שהיא טוחה על פי החבית בטיט אין זה חיבור והוה לה כפתוחה ועומדת [מכות ג:]. שלל. בשט"א כמו שלל של כובסין [ביצה ז.]. שוללין. מתקבלין כמו מן השלל של בילים (ביצה ז.) [ב"ק סא.]. מספורת של פרקים. שתי סכינים שלה מתפרדין. ואיזמל של רהיטני. פליינ"ה של אומנים חריסים שנותנים האיזמל לתוך בין שני עלים העשוין לכך ולאחר מלאכתו נוטלו ומלניעו. ושלא בשעת מלאכה. הואיל ואין צריכין להיות מחוברין הוו להו כשני כלים ואין חיבור ואף על פי שמחוברין דעל כרחך שלא בשעת מלאכה דומיא דשעת מלאכה קאמר ובשעת מלאכה מחוברין הן אלמא במחוברין עסקינן וגזרו לחומרא על הטומאה דליהוי חיבור ועל הזאה דלא ליהוי חיבור ומשום הכי קתני חיבור לטומאה לעולם ואין חיבור להזאה לעולם [לקמן נח:].

WORDS OF R' MEIR. וְרַבִּי שִׁמְעוֹן מְטַהֵר – BUT R' SHIMON DECLARES the receptacles *TAHOR* in all cases.

These receptacles are not necessary for the use of the *kirah* itself and are attached to it only for the sake of convenience. Yet R' Meir says that for purposes of *tumah* they are considered as one utensil with the *kirah*. Similarly, R' Meir would consider garments or keys or pieces of material that are attached to each other for convenience sake as one utensil.

The Gemara asks regarding the above Mishnah:

בִּשְׁלָמָא לְרַבִּי שִׁמְעוֹן קָסָבַר לָאו כְּכִירָה דָּמוּ – **It is well in regard to R' Shimon, for he maintains** that **[the receptacles] are not** considered **like the *kirah*** itself. אֶלָּא לְרַבִּי מֵאִיר – **But as for R' Meir,** what does he hold? אִי כְּכִירָה דָּמוּ אֲפִילוּ בָּאֲוִיר נַמֵּי לִיטַמּוּ – **If** he holds that **they are** considered **like the *kirah*** itself, then **let them contract *tumah* even through** *tumah* falling into the **airspace** of the *kirah*. אִי לָאו כְּכִירָה דָּמוּ אֲפִילוּ בְּמַגָּע נַמֵּי לֹא לִיטַמּוּ – **If,** on the other hand, he maintains that **they are not considered like the *kirah*** itself, then **they should not contract *tumah* even through** *tumah* coming into physical **contact** with the *kirah*! – ? –

The Gemara answers:

לְעוֹלָם לָאו כְּכִירָה דָּמוּ – On a Biblical level, **they are in fact not** treated **like the *kirah*** itself, וְרַבָּנָן הוּא דְּגָזְרוּ בְּהוּ – **and it was the Rabbis who decreed concerning them** that they be considered joined to the *kirah*. Accordingly, the Rabbis decreed that they be considered joined only insofar as *tumah* contracted through contact, but not insofar as *tumah* contracted through airspace.

The Gemara asks:

אִי גָּזְרוּ בְּהוּ – But **if [the Rabbis] decreed regarding [the receptacles]** that they be considered attached to the *kirah*, אֲפִילוּ בָּאֲוִיר נַמֵּי לִיטַמּוּ – **let them become *tamei* even via** the *kirah's* contracting *tumah* through **airspace!** Why did the Rabbis consider the *kirah* and its receptacles as attached for purposes of one method of contracting *tumah* but not for purposes of another method?

The Gemara answers:

עָבְדוּ בְּהוּ רַבָּנָן הֶיכֵּרָא – By not fully treating the compartments as one with the stove, **the Rabbis made a distinguishing feature in regard to them,** כִּי הֵיכִי דְּלֹא אָתֵי לְמִשְׂרַף עֲלֵיהּ תְּרוּמָה וְקָדָשִׁים – **so that one should not come to burn *terumah* and *kodashim* on account of it** [*tumah* contracted through this connection].[13]

The Gemara cites another Tannaic teaching pertaining to connection for *tumah*:

תָּנוּ רַבָּנָן – **The Rabbis taught in a Baraisa:**[14] מִסְפּוֹרֶת שֶׁל פְּרָקִים – SCISSORS MADE OF two SECTIONS, i.e. one whose blades are made to come apart when not in use, וְאִיזְמֵל שֶׁל רְהִיטְנִי – AND THE blade and handle of a CARPENTER'S PLANE, i.e. a plane whose blade is made to be removed from its wooden handle after use, חִיבּוּר לְטוּמְאָה – ARE considered ATTACHED WITH REGARD TO *TUMAH*, i.e. if one part contracts *tumah* the other part is automatically *tamei* as well, וְאֵין חִיבּוּר לְהַזָּאָה – BUT they are NOT considered ATTACHED WITH REGARD TO purification through SPRINKLING of the *parah adumah* ashes, i.e. both parts must be sprinkled on separately.

The Gemara questions the consistency of this ruling:

מַה נַּפְשָׁךְ – **Whichever way you wish** to view these utensils, the Baraisa's ruling is difficult. אִי חִיבּוּר הוּא אֲפִילוּ לְהַזָּאָה נַמֵּי – **If [their attachment] is** legally considered **an attachment,** then the parts should be considered joined **even with regard to sprinkling.** אִי לָאו חִיבּוּר הוּא אֲפִילוּ לְטוּמְאָה נַמֵּי לֹא – **If,** on the other hand, **[the attachment] is not a** legal **attachment,** then **even with regard to *tumah*** they should **not** be considered attached. – ? –

The Gemara answers:

אָמַר רָבָא – **Rava said:**[15] דְּבַר תּוֹרָה בִּשְׁעַת מְלָאכָה חִיבּוּר בֵּין לְטוּמְאָה בֵּין לְהַזָּאָה – **By Torah law, while** the scissors and plane are **in use** they are considered **attached both with regard to *tumah* and with regard to sprinkling.**[16] וְשֶׁלֹּא בִּשְׁעַת מְלָאכָה אֵינוֹ חִיבּוּר לֹא לְטוּמְאָה וְלֹא לְהַזָּאָה – **And while** they are **not in use they are not** considered **attached, neither with regard to *tumah* nor with regard to sprinkling.**

NOTES

not come in contact with the surface of the vessel. R' Meir states that if *tumah* falls into the interior of the earthenware *kirah* and touches its walls or floor, the side receptacles attached to the *kirah* also become *tamei;* likewise, if *tumah* falls into the interior of the side receptacles and touches their walls or floor, the *kirah* also becomes *tamei*. However, if the *tumah* merely falls into the *kirah's* airspace and does not touch its walls or floor, only the *kirah* is *tamei* but not the receptacles [and vice versa], because the *kirah* and receptacles are considered joined only insofar as *tumah* by contact. The Gemara will explain shortly the reason for this unusual law (*Rashi*).

13. *Terumah* and *kodashim* that are *tahor* must, by Biblical law, be guarded and may not be burned. On the other hand, when they are *tamei* they must be burned. However, when the *tumah* involved is only on the Rabbinic level, the *terumah* and *kodashim* cannot be burned because, generally, one cannot be lax regarding a Biblical law on account of a Rabbinic *tumah*. Nor can the *tumah* or *kodashim* be eaten, because they are, after all, *tamei* by Rabbinic law. Therefore they are "suspended" – neither burned nor eaten. They are left to decay, after which they can be discarded.

Thus, in our case of the receptacles attached to the stove, it is important to impress upon the minds of the populace that the *tumah* state which is conveyed to the receptacle when the *kirah* becomes *tamei* (or vice versa) is not Biblical, so that they do not erroneously burn *terumah* or *kodashim* that comes in contact with the receptacle. To this end, the Rabbis were purposely lenient in one aspect of the *tumah* conveyance and did not consider the receptacle totally connected to the *kirah*, so that people should realize that its *tumah* is only by Rabbinic law. They therefore purposely declared that where the *kirah* becomes *tamei* only by *tumah* falling into its airspace, the side receptacles remain *tahor* (*Rashi*).

[*Tosafos* explain that in regard to the garments of launderers as well the Rabbis made a distinguishing feature to indicate that the connecting is only Rabbinic – they decreed that where the garments became contaminated with corpse *tumah*, the sprinkling of the ashes of the *parah adumah* on one garment should not suffice to purify both garments. The Rabbis were not able to employ this same distinguishing feature for the stove and its appurtenances, however, because these utensils, being made of earthenware, are not subject to purification through sprinkling.]

14. [This Baraisa is cited and explained below, on 58b; see notes 31-40 there.]

15. [See *Dikdukei Soferim*, who cites a variant reading of אָמַר רַבָּה, *Rabbah said*; this reading is also found below, on 58b.]

16. [It would seem that by the same token a bundle of laundry should be considered joined on a Biblical level when in use, i.e. while being washed. *Tosafos*, however, demonstrate from the Gemara above that such items would not be considered Biblically joined. *Tosafos* answer by distinguishing between that case and the cases of this Baraisa. The various garments that make up the bundle are perfectly good utensils in their own right; they need not be bundled together in order to function as utensils. Therefore, on a Biblical level, they cannot be considered a single utensil even when being washed together. But the blades of a scissors are designed to function together; likewise, a carpenter's plane with its blade. Therefore, they are considered a single utensil while in use.]

וְגָזְרוּ רַבָּנָן עַל טוּמְאָה שֶׁלֹּא בִּשְׁעַת מְלָאכָה – But the Rabbis decreed that we should rule stringently **with respect to *tumah*** that occurred **when they are not in use** מִשּׁוּם טוּמְאָה שֶׁבִּשְׁעַת מְלָאכָה **– because of** the fear that one might incorrectly rule leniently with respect to ***tumah*** that occurred **when they are in use;** וְעַל הַזָּאָה שֶׁבִּשְׁעַת מְלָאכָה – **likewise,** they decree that we should rule stringently **with respect to sprinkling** that was performed **when they are in use** מִשּׁוּם הַזָּאָה שֶׁלֹּא בִּשְׁעַת מְלָאכָה – **because of** the fear that one might incorrectly rule leniently with respect to **sprinkling that** occurred **when they were not in use.**[1]

The Mishnah states:

בִּזְמַן שֶׁהֵן לַחִין – Not with straw . . . WHEN THEY ARE MOIST, but one may insulate with them when they are dry.

The Gemara analyzes this ruling:

אִיבַּעְיָא לְהוּ – They inquired: לַחִין מֵחֲמַת עַצְמָן – When the Mishnah says that these substances are forbidden to be used for insulation only when they are moist, does it mean when they are **moist on their own account,** i.e. with their own, natural moisture, אוֹ דִילְמָא לַחִין מֵחֲמַת דָּבָר אַחֵר – **or, perhaps,** does it mean also[2] when they are **moist because of an external factor,** even if their natural moisture is gone?

The Gemara seeks to resolve this issue:

תָּא שְׁמַע – Come, learn a proof from our Mishnah: לֹא בְתֶבֶן וְלֹא בְזָגִים וְלֹא בְמוֹכִין וְלֹא בַעֲשָׂבִים בִּזְמַן שֶׁהֵן לַחִין – NOT WITH STRAW, NOR WITH GRAPE SKINS, NOR WITH FLOCKING, NOR WITH GRASSES, WHEN THEY ARE MOIST. Consider that among these substances is flocking. אִי אָמְרַת בִּשְׁלָמָא לַחִין מֵחֲמַת דָּבָר אַחֵר שַׁפִּיר – Now **it is well if you say** that moist here means **moist because of an external factor,** for then we have no trouble understanding how flocking could be moist. אֶלָּא אִי אָמְרַת לַחִין מֵחֲמַת עַצְמָן – **But if you say** that moist here means **moist on their own,** מוֹכִין לַחִין מֵחֲמַת עַצְמָן הֵיכִי מַשְׁכַּחַת לָהּ – **how is it possible for flocking to be moist on its own;** i.e. what natural moisture does flocking have?

The Gemara rejects this proof:

מִמְּרְטָא דְּבֵינֵי אַטְמֵי – The Mishnah refers to wool **pluckings** that come **from between the thighs** of the sheep, where the wool is damp from the sweat of the animal.

The Gemara attempts another proof:

וְהָא דְּתָנֵי רַבִּי אוֹשַׁעְיָא – But consider that Baraisa which R' Oshaya taught: טוֹמְנִין בִּכְסוּת יְבֵשָׁה וּבְפֵירוֹת יְבֵשִׁין – ONE MAY INSULATE WITH DRY CLOTHING AND WITH DRY PRODUCE, אֲבָל לֹא בִּכְסוּת לַחָה וְלֹא בְּפֵירוֹת לַחִין – BUT NOT WITH MOIST CLOTHING OR WITH MOIST PRODUCE. כְּסוּת לַחָה מֵחֲמַת עַצְמָהּ הֵיכִי מַשְׁכַּחַת לָהּ – Clearly this can only mean moist because of an external factor, for **how is it possible for clothing to be moist on its own?**

The Gemara rejects this proof as well:

מִמְּרְטָא דְּבֵינֵי אַטְמֵי – It is possible where the clothing is spun **from** wool **pluckings** that come **from between the thighs** of the sheep.

The question thus remains unresolved.

Mishnah טוֹמְנִין בִּכְסוּת וּבְפֵירוֹת – **One may insulate with clothing, with produce,**[3] בְּכַנְפֵי יוֹנָה וּבִנְסֹרֶת שֶׁל חָרָשִׁים וּבִנְעוֹרֶת שֶׁל פִּשְׁתָּן דַּקָּה – **with dove's feathers,**[4] **with carpenters' sawdust, or with fine flax combings.**[5] רַבִּי יְהוּדָה אוֹסֵר בְּדַקָּה וּמַתִּיר בְּגַסָּה – **R' Yehudah prohibits** insulating **with fine** ones **but permits** insulating **with coarse** ones.

Gemara Since the Mishnah mentioned dove's feathers, the Gemara cites an unrelated teaching in which dove's feathers also figure:

אָמַר רַבִּי יַנַּאי – R' Yannai said: תְּפִילִּין צְרִיכִין גּוּף נָקִי כֶּאֱלִישָׁע בַּעַל כְּנָפַיִם – **Tefillin require** one who wears them to maintain a **clean body,** such **as** was maintained by **Elisha the Winged One.**[6]

The Gemara explains R' Yannai's teaching:

מַאי הִיא – What is it that is meant by: *a clean body*? אַבַּיֵי אָמַר שֶׁלֹּא יָפִיחַ בָּהֶן – **Abaye says:** It means that **one should not pass wind** while dressed **in them.**[7] רָבָא אָמַר שֶׁלֹּא יִישַׁן בָּהֶן – **Rava says:** It means that **one should not sleep in them.**[8]

The Gemara explains the reference to *Elisha the Winged One*:[9]

וְאַמַּאי קָרֵי לֵיהּ בַּעַל כְּנָפַיִם – And why was [Elisha] called: ***the Winged One?*** שֶׁפַּעַם אַחַת גָּזְרָה מַלְכוּת רוֹמִי הָרְשָׁעָה גְּזֵירָה עַל יִשְׂרָאֵל – **Because it once happened that the wicked Roman government passed an edict against Israel** שֶׁכָּל הַמַּנִּיחַ תְּפִילִּין יְנַקְּרוּ אֶת מוֹחוֹ – stating **that anyone who dons tefillin would**

NOTES

1. Since the distinction between when the utensil is in use and when it is not in use might not be clear to everyone (see below, 58b notes 38-39), the Rabbis legislated that these utensils always be treated stringently. In the context of *tumah,* where the stringency lies in treating them as a single utensil, they are always treated as a single utensil; in the context of sprinkling, where the stringency lies in treating them as separate utensils, they are treated as separate utensils (*Rashi*).

2. [See *Rashi* ד״ה לחין; cf. *Rambam, Hil. Shabbos* 4:1.]

3. E.g. wheat or beans (*Rashi*). [Although the immediately preceding Gemara quoted a Baraisa which distinguished between moist clothing or produce and dry clothing or produce, our Mishnah disagrees and makes no such distinction (*Tosafos* ד״ה אבל; cf. *Tos. Rid*).]

4. [כָּנָף, in Rabbinic Hebrew, can denote feathers or wings; cf. *Chullin* 56a. In Biblical Hebrew it almost always denotes wings; see *Ramban,* Commentary to *Leviticus* 1:17; but cf. *Rashi,* ad loc.]

Other feathers as well may be used for *hatmanah* (*Meiri; Rama, Orach Chaim* 257:3). Dove's (pigeon's) feathers are used as an example only because they were the most commonly used in Mishnaic times (*Mishnah Berurah* 257:22; cf. *Rashash*).

5. I.e. the splinters that fall from the flax when it is combed out.

6. The Gemara will explain this reference shortly.

7. He must feel confident that should he feel the urge to pass wind, he will be able to contain himself (*Rashi*) until he first removes his tefillin (*Tosafos*).

8. He must be able to restrain himself from falling asleep while wearing tefillin, lest while asleep he pass wind or experience a seminal emission (*Rashi; cf. Tosafos*).

Rava maintains that in saying that "tefillin require a clean body," R' Yannai could not have been referring to the ability to contain oneself from passing wind, because *anyone* is capable of this. Rather R' Yannai meant that one must be able to withhold himself from falling asleep while wearing tefillin, which is a more difficult feat (*Rashi,* as explained by *Ritva MHK* ed.; cf. *Sfas Emes'* explanation of *Rashi*). [It should be remembered that in former times tefillin were worn all day long. This is why the ability to contain oneself from passing wind or falling asleep while wearing tefillin were considered "qualifications." It is precisely because of our inability nowadays to control ourselves in these areas for long periods of time that the practice became to wear tefillin only during the relatively short period of morning prayers (*Tur, Orach Chaim* 37).]

9. Nothing in the story the Gemara is about to relate indicates that Elisha maintained a clean body while wearing tefillin. However, since a miracle was performed for Elisha on account of his tefillin, it is to be assumed that he was scrupulous in keeping all of the laws regarding tefillin, one of which is the requirement to maintain a clean body (*Tosafos*).

וגזרו רבנן על טומאה שלא בשעת מלאכה משום טומאה שבשעת מלאכה ועל הזאה שבשעת מלאכה משום הזאה שלא בשעת מלאכה: בזמן שהן לחין: איבעיא להו [א]לחין מחמת עצמן או דילמא לחין מחמת דבר אחר ת"ש לא בתבן ולא בזגים ולא במוכין ולא בעשבים בזמן שהן לחין אי אמרת בשלמא לחין מחמת דבר אחר שפיר אלא אי אמרת לחין מחמת עצמן מוכין לחין מחמת עצמן היכי משכחת לה ממרטא דביני אטמי והא דתני רבי אושעיא טומנין בכסות יבשה ובפירות יבשין אבל לא בכסות לחה ולא בפירות לחין כסות לחה מחמת עצמה היכי משכחת לה ממרטא דביני אטמי: **מתני'** [ב]טומנין בכסות ובפירות בכנפי יונה ובנסורת של חרשים ובנעורת של פשתן [א]דקה רבי יהודה אוסר בדקה ומתיר בגסה: **גמ'** [ג]א"ר ינאי [ג]תפילין צריכין גוף נקי [ג]כאלישע בעל כנפים מאי היא אביי אמר שלא יפיח בהן רבא אמר שלא יישן בהן ואמאי קרי ליה בעל כנפים שפעם אחת גזרה מלכות רומי הרשעה גזירה על ישראל שכל המניח תפילין ינקרו את מוחו והיה אלישע מניחם ויוצא לשוק ראהו קסדור אחד רץ מפניו ורץ אחריו וכיון שהגיע אצלו נטלן מראשו ואחזן בידו אמר לו מה זה בידך אמר לו כנפי יונה פשט את ידו ונמצאו כנפי יונה לפיכך קורין אותו אלישע בעל כנפים [ד]ומאי שנא כנפי יונה משאר עופות משום דאמתיל כנסת ישראל ליונה שנאמר [א]כנפי יונה נחפה בכסף וגו' מה יונה כנפיה מגינות עליה אף ישראל מצות מגינות עליהן: בנסורת של חרשין וכו': איבעיא להו רבי יהודה אנסורת של חרשין קאי או אנעורת של פשתן קאי ת"ש דתניא [ה]רבי יהודה אומר נעורת של פשתן דקה הרי הוא כזבל ש"מ אנעורת של פשתן קאי ש"מ: **מתני'** [ד]טומנין בשלחין ומטלטלין אותן בגיזי צמר ואין מטלטלין אותן כיצד הוא עושה [ה]נוטל את הכסוי והן נופלות ר"א בן עזריה אומר קופה מטה על צדה ונוטל שמא יטול ואינו יכול להחזיר וחכ"א נוטל ומחזיר: **גמ'** יתיב ר' יונתן בן עכינאי ורבי יונתן בן אלעזר ויתיב ר' חנינא בר חמא גבייהו וקא מיבעיא להו שלחין של בעה"ב תנן אבל של אומן כיון דקפיד עלייהו לא מטלטלינן להו או דילמא של אומן תנן וכ"ש של בעה"ב אמר להו ר' יונתן בן אלעזר מסתברא של בעה"ב תנן אבל של אומן קפיד עלייהו אמר להו ר' חנינא בר חמא כך אמר ר' ישמעאל בר' יוסי

אבא

רש"י

וגזרו על הטומאה שלא בשעת מלאכה. שיהא חיבור: **ועל הזאה שבשעת מלאכה.** שלא יהא חיבור הלכך חיבור לטומאה לעולם ואין חיבור להזאה כלל: **לחין מחמת עצמן.** מחממות טפי מלחין מחמת משקין שנופלין עליהן משיבשו: ה"ג מוכין לחין מחמת עצמן היכי משכחת לה: **ממרטא דביני אטמי.** מלמר הנמרט מבין ירכותיה של בהמה שהוא מלא זיעה והוא לח מעצמו להכי קרי ליה מרטא דלאו בר גיזה הוא: **מתני' נעורת.** דק דק שנוערין מן הפשתן וקורין אריסט"ש: **נסורת.** שמנסרים הנגרים מן העצים: **ובפירות.** כגון חטין וקטניות: **כנפי יונה.** נוצה: **גמ' שלא יפיח.** שיכול להעמיד עצמו בשעת הרוח: **שלא יישן בהן.** שמא יפיח או יראה קרי אבל אם יכול להזהר שלא יישן בהן כל הגופים נקיים בהפחה שיכולין להעמיד עצמן: **ינקרו את מוחו.** שהוא תחת התפילין. ינקרו לשון ניקור עינים: **קסדור.** מגיסטרא"ל שהיה ממונה על כך: **כנפי יונה.** כדמפרש לקמיה מפני שהם מצות והם מגינין לישראל והויא להם ככנפים ליונה שהיא נמשלת ליונה והמצות ככנפים: **כנפיה מגינות עליה.** מן הצנה ומכל עוף ואדם הבא עליה היא נלחמת ומכה בראש גפה מה שאין כן בשאר עופות: **הרי הוא כזבל.** דמוסיף הבל: **מתני' שלחין.** עורות כמו והפשיט תרגום וישלח: **ומטלטלין אותן.** בין שטמן בהן בין שלא טמן בהן דחזו למזגא עלייהו: **ואין מטלטלין אותן.** דמוקצות הן לטוות ולארוג: **כיצד הוא עושה.** זה שטמן בהן כילד יטול קדרתו הואיל ואסור לטלטלן שהרי היא טמונה כולה בהן: **נוטל כיסוי.** של קדרה שיש תורת כלי עליה ואף על גב שהן עליה לא איכפת לן דלא נעשית בסיס להן שאין עשוי אלא לכסות קדרה: **רבי אלעזר בן עזריה אומר קופה מטה על צדה ונוטל.** כשבא ליטול הקדרה מטה הקופה על לדה: **שמא יטול.** הקדרה ויפלו הגיזין שמכאן ומכאן לתוך גומא שישבה בהן ואם יצטרך לחזור ולהטמינה לא יוכל לטלטל גיזין לכאן ולכאן ולעשות גומא להחזירה בתוכה: **נוטל ומחזיר.** בגמרא מפרש לה: **גמ' שלחין של בעה"ב תנן.** דמותר לטלטלן שאין עומדין לימכר ולא קפיד עלייהו כי מטנפי וחזי למזגא עלייהו: **אבל של אומן.** שעומדות למוכרן קפיד עלייהו הלכך לא למזגא קיימי ואין מטלטלין אותן:

שלחא

תוספות

ועל הזאה שבשעת מלאכה משום הזאה שלא בשעת מלאכה. תימה דהא גבי מקל שעשאו יד לקורדום קאמר דהוי חיבור לטומאה משמע אבל לא להזאה ואמאי והא לא שייך למגזר התם אטו שלא בשעת מלאכה כדאמר לעיל דאדם עשוי לזורקו בין העצים וי"ל דהתם לא הוי חיבור להזאה משום דאפילו בשעת מלאכה לא הוי חיבור דבר תורה דלא חשיב כלל בית יד בשום פעם כיון שהוא עשוי לזורקו כל שעה:

אבל לא בכסות לחה כו'. נראה דרבי אושעיא פליג אמתני':

כאלישע בעל כנפים. להכי נקט אלישע דמסתמא כיון שנעשה לו נס בתפילין היה זהיר בהן והיה לו גוף נקי ומזה הטעם אין אנו יכולין ליפטר שהרי בזה אנו יכולין להזהר ואין תימה על מה שמצוה זאת רפויה בידינו שגם בימי חכמים היתה רפויה כדתניא בפרק ר' אליעזר דמילה (לקמן קל.) ר"ש בן אלעזר אומר כל מצוה שלא מסרו עצמן ישראל עליה בשעת גזירת המלכות כגון תפילין עדיין היא רפויה בידם והא דאמרינן בפ"ק דראש השנה (דף יז.) פושעי ישראל בגופן קרקפתא דלא מנח תפילין אומר ר"ת דמיירי באותן שעושין מחמת מרד ומבזין המצות ושוחקין ברצועה שבידם ובראשם כדאמר ביומא (דף לו:) פשעים אלו המרדין והא דאמר במדרש תפילין מפני מה לא החזיקו בהן מפני הרמאים אין נראה לר"י דמשום רמאין נמנעו מלעשות מצוה אלא ה"פ מפני מה לא החזיקו נאמנות באדם המניח תפילין [י]וקאמר מפני הרמאין שהיו מניחין תפילין לרמות בני אדם כדמפרש התם מעשה בתלמיד אחד שהפקיד מעותיו אצל אחד שהיה מניח תפילין כשתבע בו אמר להד"ס אמר ליה אותו תלמיד לא לך הפקדתי אלא לתפילין שעל ראשך וע"ע שם:

אביי אמר שלא יפיח בהן. שיוכל לשמור עצמו מלהפיח עד שיסיר תפילין כדפירש בקונט' אבל לא חייש שמא ישן דאע"ג דפעמים יוכל ליזהר משינה ורבא מצריך גם שיוכל להעמיד עצמו בשעה שתאחזנו השינה שלא ישן פתאום ומיהו אביי נמי מודה דאסור לישן בהן כדתניא בפרק הישן (סוכה כו. ושם) דאסור לישן בתפילין בין שינת קבע בין שינת עראי:

שלא יישן בהן. משום שלא יפיח בהן בשעת שינה או משום היסח הדעת אבל משום קרי אין לחוש כדאמר בפ' הישן (ג"ז שם:) דא"ר יוסי ילדים לעולם חולין מפני שרגילין בטומאה ופריך לימא קסבר ר' יוסי בעל קרי אסור להניח תפילין ומשני הכא בילדים ונשותיהם עמהם עסקין שמא יבאו לידי הרגל דבר אבל משום קרי לא בעי למיסר:

נטלם מראשו. ואף על גב דאמר בסנהדרין (דף עד: ושם) בשעת גזרת המלכות אפי' על מצוה קלה יהרג ואל יעבור ואפילו לשנויי ערקתא דמסאנא אסור היינו משום דבשינוי ערקתא מתנהג כעובד כוכבים ודומה שמוציא עצמו מכלל ישראל אבל הכא אינו עושה כלום אלא שאין לו תפילין בראשו שעה אחת והרבה ישראל שאין להם תפילין כמותו:

כנפיה מגינות עליה. אור"י דאמרינן במדרש [ז] כל העופות כשהן יגעין ניוחין ע"ג סלע והיונה בשעה שהיא יגעה פורחת באחת וניוחת באחת:

טומנין בשלחין ומטלטלין אותן. הא דאמר בפ"ק דביצה (דף יא.) נותנין העור לפני הדורסן להתירו סופן משום תחילתן פי' כדי שישחוט לצורך יו"ט אבל עור דמערב יו"ט משמע התם דאסור לטלטל ובפרק כל כתבי (לקמן קטז:) קאמר אם מטלטלין תיק הספר עם הספר לא נטלטל עור אגב בשר משמע דעור בלא בשר אסור פירש"י בפרק כל כתבי (ג"ז שם [ח]) דהכא מיירי בעור בהמה גסה והתם בעור בהמה דקה דלא חזי למזגא כולי האי ולפירושו האי דביצה נמי מיירי בעור בהמה דקה והא דתנן בפ' כל כתבי (דף קכ.) פורסין עור גדי על גבי התבה כו' צריך לומר לפי' דמיירי כשיחדו לישיבה ° ור"ת מפרש דהכא מיירי ביבשין דחזו למזגא עלייהו והתם בלחין:

אבא

עין משפט נר מצוה

יא א מיי' פ"ד מהלכות שבת הלכה א:

יב ב מיי' פ"ד מהלכות שבת הלכה א טוש"ע או"ח סימן רנז סעיף ג:

יג ג מיי' פ"ד מהלכות תפילין הלכה טו סמג עשין כב טוש"ע או"ח סימן לז סעיף ב ג:

יד ד מיי' פ"ד מהלכות שבת הלכה א:

טו ה מיי' פ"ד מהלכות שבת שם ופכ"ו הל' יב סמג לאוין סה טור שו"ע או"ח סימן רנט סעיף א:

רבינו חננאל

לחוזה וגזרו שאם נטמא הא' שלא בשעת מלאכה נטמא גם האחר בכל מקר' שהוא. ודוק' אם הוא (מחברן) מחובר עדיין משום טומאה שבשעת מלאכה. וגזרו נמי על הזאה שאם יזה על הא' אפילו בשעת מלאכה לא נטהר האחר אע"פ שהוא מחובר עמו משו' הזאה שלא בשעת מלאכה. פי' אם יראה שהזה בשעת מלאכה על האחד ונטהר גם האחר יטהר הוא כשיזה על האחד אפילו השני שלא בשעת מלאכה: **פי'** מירטא דביני אטמא העמר שבין הירכות של בהמה כיון שתמיד השתנתה שותת בין ירכותיה יש בו לחלוחית לעולם ואינו מתנגב לעולם ואפילו עושה מאותו צמר כסות יש בו לחלוחית: **תפלין** צריכין גוף נקי. קיי"ל כרבא דאמר שלא יישן בהן: **ר' יהודה** אוסר. אוקימנא בנעורת: **טומנין** בשלחין ומטלטלין אותן. פירוש שלחין עורות גלשין שנגזז (כצמר) [הצמר] ועדיין לא נעבדו: **אבא** שלחא פירוש

מסורת הש"ס

א) [בר"ף ובר"ש ליתא], ב) לקמן קל., ג) [עי' תוספות בבא בתרא י: ד"ה אלא], ד) [ברכות נג: ע"ש גיטין מה. סנהדרין לה. לקמן קל.], ה) [לקמן נא:], ו) [ועי' ירושלמי פרק היה קורא הלכה ד], ז) [רבה סדר לך לך פרשה לט], ח) בד"ה בתרתי פליגי.

גליון הש"ס

תוס' ד"ה טומנין בשלחין וכו' ור"ת מפרש. עי' זבחים דף לג ע"ב תוס' ד"ה מנין בקה"ד:

תורה אור השלם

א) אִם תִּשְׁכְּבוּן בֵּין שְׁפַתָּיִם כַּנְפֵי יוֹנָה נֶחְפָּה בַכֶּסֶף וְאֶבְרוֹתֶיהָ בִּירַקְרַק חָרוּץ: [תהלים סח, יד]

ליקוטי רש"י

נסורת. עצים דקים שנופלין מן החתיכה [מ"ק יב:]. שמגררין נגרים במגירה פגומה וקוצצים בה עצים והיא נסורת דקה כעפר [חולין פח:]. **ינקרו.** יקרו. פוריי"ר בלע"ז לשון יקרוה עורבי נחל (משלי ל') ולשון תנקר לא נעלה (במדבר טז). **קסדור.** ממונה [לקמן קל.]. שם פקידות הוא כגון סרדיוט והוא שוטר [יומא יא.]. **דאמתיל כנסת ישראל ליונה.** דכתיב יונתי תמתי (שיר השירים ה) [גיטין מה.]. **כנפי יונה.** פלומ"א בלע"ז. **נחפה בכסף.** בכספה ובחמדתה של תורה ומצות [תהלים סח, יד]. **מגינות עליהן.** אינה נלחמת בחרטומיה אלא בכנפיה [לקמן שם]. יונה אינה נצולת אלא בכנפיה או פורחת או נלחמת בראשי אגפיה [ברכות נג:]. **הרי הוא כזבל.** דמוסיף הבלא ואין טומנין בה אפילו מבעוד יום [לקמן נא:]. **ומטלטלין אותן.** עור בהמה גסה דחזי לאיסטמיה ולמיזגא עליה [לקמן קטז: ועי' כאן בתוס'].

have his brain (which lies beneath the spot of the head tefillin) **gouged out.** וְהָיָה אֱלִישָׁע מַנִּיחָם וְיוֹצֵא לַשּׁוּק – **Now this Elisha would don them and go out into the marketplace,** in defiance of the edict. רָאָהוּ קַסְדּוֹר אֶחָד – **An officer**[10] **saw him.** רָץ מִפָּנָיו וְרָץ אַחֲרָיו – **[Elisha] fled from him and [the officer] pursued him.** וְכֵיוָן שֶׁהִגִּיעַ אֶצְלוֹ נְטָלָן מֵרֹאשׁוֹ וַאֲחָזָן בְּיָדוֹ – **As [the officer] caught up to him, [Elisha] took [the tefillin] off his head and held them in his hand.** אָמַר לוֹ מַה זֶּה בְּיָדְךָ – **[The officer] demanded: What is that in your hand?** אָמַר לוֹ כַּנְפֵי יוֹנָה – **[Elisha] answered: Dove's wings.** פָּשַׁט אֶת יָדוֹ וְנִמְצְאוּ כַּנְפֵי יוֹנָה – **He opened his hand and,** lo, **they were found to be dove's wings.** לְפִיכָךְ קוֹרִין אוֹתוֹ אֱלִישָׁע בַּעַל כְּנָפַיִם – **Because of this** miracle **they called him: Elisha the Winged One.** וּמַאי שְׁנָא כַּנְפֵי יוֹנָה מִשְּׁאָר עוֹפוֹת – **And why wings of a dove rather than** the wings **of some other bird?** מִשּׁוּם דְּאִמְתִּיל כְּנֶסֶת יִשְׂרָאֵל לְיוֹנָה – **Because the Congregation of Israel is compared to a dove,** שֶׁנֶּאֱמַר ,,כַּנְפֵי יוֹנָה נֶחְפָּה בַכֶּסֶף וגו׳" – **as it says:**[11] ***[like] the wings of a dove covered with silver,* etc.** מַה יּוֹנָה כְּנָפֶיהָ מְגִינּוֹת עָלֶיהָ אַף יִשְׂרָאֵל מִצְוֹת מְגִינּוֹת עֲלֵיהֶן – **Just as** with **a dove, its wings protect it,**[12] **so too** with **Israel, the commandments** that it performs **protect it.**

Since the commandments are compared to the wings of a dove, it was appropriate for Elisha's tefillin to miraculously metamorphose into dove's wings.[13]

The Mishnah states:

בִּנְסוֹרֶת שֶׁל חָרָשִׁין וכו׳ – WITH CARPENTERS' SAWDUST, **etc.** or with fine flax combings. R' Yehudah prohibits insulating with fine ones but permits with coarse ones.

The Gemara analyzes R' Yehudah's statement:

אִיבַּעְיָא לְהוּ – **They inquired:** רַבִּי יְהוּדָה אַנְּסוֹרֶת שֶׁל חָרָשִׁין קָאֵי אוֹ אַנְּעוֹרֶת שֶׁל פִּשְׁתָּן קָאֵי – When he distinguished between fine ones and coarse ones, **was R' Yehudah referring to carpenters' sawdust or to flax combings?**

The Gemara answers:

תָּא שְׁמַע – **Come, learn** the answer. דְּתַנְיָא – **For it was taught in a Baraisa:** רַבִּי יְהוּדָה אוֹמֵר נְעוֹרֶת שֶׁל פִּשְׁתָּן דַּקָּה הֲרֵי הוּא כְּזֶבֶל – R' YEHUDAH SAYS: FINE FLAX COMBINGS ARE LIKE MANURE, i.e. they add heat to the food when used as insulation. שְׁמַע מִינָּהּ אַנְּעוֹרֶת שֶׁל פִּשְׁתָּן קָאֵי – **Conclude from this that [R' Yehudah] referred to flax combings.** שְׁמַע מִינָּהּ – Indeed, **conclude** so **from this.**

Mishnah טוֹמְנִין בִּשְׁלָחִין וּמְטַלְטְלִין אוֹתָן – **One may insulate with** animal **hides on Friday, and one may move them;**[14] בְּגִיזֵּי צֶמֶר וְאֵין מְטַלְטְלִין אוֹתָן – **with wool shearings, but one may not move them.**[15] כֵּיצַד הוּא עוֹשֶׂה – **What should one do** if one insulated a pot with wool shearings? By what means can he gain access to the pot without handling the shearings? נוֹטֵל אֶת הַכִּסּוּי וְהֵן נוֹפְלוֹת – **He removes the lid and they fall,** i.e. by lifting the lid he causes them to slide off by themselves.[16]

After explaining how to uncover the pot, the Mishnah proceeds to discuss the proper procedure for removing the food from the pot:

רַבִּי אֶלְעָזָר בֶּן עֲזַרְיָה אוֹמֵר – **R' Elazar ben Azaryah says:** קוּפָּה מַטֶּה עַל צִדָּהּ וְנוֹטֵל – **He tilts the** entire **box,** containing the shearings and the pot, **on its side and removes** the food by pouring out the amount he requires, leaving the rest of the food in the pot for the next meal. He should not lift the pot out of the box שֶׁמָּא יִטּוֹל וְאֵינוֹ יָכוֹל לְהַחֲזִיר – **lest he remove** the pot **and be unable to replace** it.[17] וַחֲכָמִים אוֹמְרִים נוֹטֵל וּמַחֲזִיר – **But the Sages say: He may remove and replace** it.[18]

Gemara The Mishnah's first ruling is analyzed:

יָתִיב רַבִּי יוֹנָתָן בֶּן עֲכִינַאי וְרַבִּי יוֹנָתָן בֶּן אֶלְעָזָר – **R' Yonasan ben Achinai and R' Yonasan ben Elazar were seated** together וְיָתִיב רַבִּי חֲנִינָא בַּר חָמָא גַּבַּיְיהוּ – **and R' Chanina bar Chama was seated with them,** וְקָא מִיבַּעְיָא לְהוּ – **and they raised the** following **question:** שְׁלָחִין שֶׁל בַּעַל הַבַּיִת תְּנַן – **Does the Mishnah refer** exclusively **to the hides of a** private **householder,** who does not plan on selling them and would therefore not be reluctant to use them as a rug, אֲבָל שֶׁל אוּמָּן כֵּיוָן דְּקָפִיד עֲלַיְיהוּ לֹא מְטַלְטְלִינַן לְהוּ – **but** as for the hides **of a craftsman,** who intends to fashion them into utensils and sell them, **since he is particular with them** lest they become soiled he would not be willing to use them as a rug, and, therefore, **one may not move them?**[19] אוֹ דִילְמָא שֶׁל אוּמָּן תְּנַן וְכָל שֶׁכֵּן שֶׁל בַּעַל הַבַּיִת – **Or, perhaps, does the Mishnah refer** even **to the hides of a craftsman,** deeming even these to be useful as a rug, **and all the more**

NOTES

10. In ancient Rome the prosecutor at a criminal trial was called a *quaestor.*

11. *Psalms* 68:14.

12. From the cold; also, unlike other birds, a dove uses its wings [rather than its beak] to fend off attackers (*Rashi;* cf. *Tosafos*; see also *Radak* to *Genesis* 8:7 in the name of the Geonim, for a novel interpretation of this phrase).

13. [Based on this story, some have the custom of wrapping the straps of their tefillin when putting them away after use so as to form dove's wings (*Magen Avraham, Orach Chaim* 28:4).]

[See *Tosafos* and *Rishonim* et al., who discuss why Elisha was not obligated to defy the officer even on pain of death (based on *Sanhedrin* 74a, where it is taught that one must forfeit his life rather than violate even a minor mitzvah in the face of oppressive governmental decrees designed to stamp out Torah observance); see also *Ran,* who discusses why he was allowed to put his life at risk initially.]

14. Whether or not they were used for insulating they may be moved, because they sometimes are used as a rug upon which to recline (*Rashi*). Since they have a useful purpose on the Sabbath, they are not *muktzeh.*

15. These are generally reserved to be made into thread and are deemed *muktzeh* (*Rashi*).

16. He grasps the lid by its handle, which protrudes out of the shearings (*Tiferes Yisrael*), and tilts them off. This constitutes indirect movement of *muktzeh,* which is permissible.

We learned on 47a that an item that is a base (*bosis*) for a *muktzeh* item becomes *muktzeh* itself. The question thus arises: Why is the lid, which supports the shearings, not itself considered *muktzeh*?

The answer is that the function of the lid is merely to cover the pot. It is not meant to support something on top of it. Such an item, even if if happens to be supporting a *muktzeh* item in a particular case, does not acquire the status of a base to *muktzeh* (*Rashi*; see *Sfas Emes*).

17. If he removes the pot, and the shearings on both sides fall into the cavity, he will not be permitted to move them aside when he later wishes to replace the pot with the remaining food, since the shearings are *muktzeh* (*Rashi;* cf. *Rambam, Commentary to the Mishnah.*)

18. I.e. he may replace the pot into the original cavity if it is still extant after he finishes taking out the food he needs.

The Gemara will explain the point of issue between R' Elazar ben Azaryah and the Sages.

19. As explained in note 14, hides are considered non-*muktzeh* only because one would be likely to use them as a rug. The Gemara suggests

וגזרו רבנן על טומאה שלא בשעת מלאכה משום טומאה שבשעת מלאכה ועל הזאה שבשעת מלאכה משום הזאה שלא בשעת מלאכה: בזמן שהן לחין: איבעיא להו א לחין מחמת עצמן או דילמא לחין מחמת דבר אחר ת"ש לא בתבן ולא בזגים ולא במוכין ולא בעשבים בזמן שהן לחין אי אמרת בשלמא לחין מחמת דבר אחר שפיר אלא אי אמרת לחין מחמת עצמן מוכין לחין מחמת עצמן היכי משכחת לה ממרטא דביני אטמי והא דתני רבי אושעיא טומנין בכסות יבשה ובפירות יבשין אבל לא בכסות לחה ולא בפירות לחין כסות לחה מחמת עצמה היכי משכחת לה ממרטא דביני אטמי: **מתני'** ב טומנין בכסות ובפירות בכנפי יונה ובנסורת של חרשים ובנעורת של פשתן ח) דקה רבי יהודה אוסר בדקה ומתיר בגסה: **גמ'** ג) א"ר ינאי ג תפילין צריכין גוף נקי ד) כאלישע בעל כנפים מאי היא אביי אמר שלא יפיח בהן רבא אמר שלא יישן בהן ואמאי קרי ליה בעל כנפים שפעם אחת גזרה מלכות רומי הרשעה גזירה על ישראל שכל המניח תפילין ינקרו את מוחו והיה אלישע מניחם ויוצא לשוק ראהו קסדור אחד רץ מפניו ורץ אחריו וכיון שהגיע אצלו נטלן מראשו ואחזן בידו אמר לו מה זה בידך אמר לו כנפי יונה פשט את ידו ונמצאו כנפי יונה לפיכך קורין אותו אלישע בעל כנפים ז) ומאי שנא כנפי יונה משאר עופות משום דאמתיל כנסת ישראל ליונה שנאמר א) כנפי יונה נחפה בכסף וגו' מה יונה כנפיה מגינות עליה אף ישראל מצות מגינות עליהן: בנסורת של חרשין וכו': איבעיא להו רבי יהודה אנסורת של חרשין קאי או אנעורת של פשתן קאי ת"ש דתניא ח) רבי יהודה אומר נעורת של פשתן דקה הרי הוא כזבל ש"מ אנעורת של פשתן קאי ש"מ: **מתני'** ד טומנין בשלחין ומטלטלין אותן בגיזי צמר ואין מטלטלין אותן כיצד הוא עושה ה נוטל את הכסוי והן נופלות ר"א בן עזריה אומר קופה מטה על צדה ונוטל שמא יטול ואינו יכול להחזיר וחכ"א נוטל ומחזיר: **גמ'** יתיב ר' יונתן בן עכינאי ורבי יונתן בן אלעזר ויתיב ר' חנינא בר חמא גבייהו וקא מיבעיא להו שלחין של בעה"ב תנן אבל של אומן כיון דקפיד עלייהו לא מטלטלינן להו או דילמא של אומן תנן וכ"ש של בעה"ב אמר להו ר' יונתן בן אלעזר מסתברא של בעה"ב תנן אבל של אומן קפיד עלייהו אמר להו ר' חנינא בר חמא כך אמר ר' ישמעאל בר' יוסי אבא

רש"י

וגזרו על הטומאה שלא בשעת מלאכה. שיהא חיבור: ועל הזאה שבשעת מלאכה. שלא יהא חיבור הלכך אין חיבור לטומאה לעולם ואין חיבור להזאה כלל: לחין מחמת עצמן. מחממות טפי מלחין מחמת משקין שטופלין עליהן משיבשו: ה"ג מוכין לחין מחמת עצמן היכי משכחת לה: ממרטא דביני אטמי. מצמר הנמרט מבין ירכותיה של בהמה שהוא מלא זיעה והוא לח מעצמו להכי קרי ליה מרטא דלאו בר גיזה הוא: מתני' נעורת. דק דק שנוערין מן הפשתן וקורין אריסט"ש: נסורת. שמנסרים הנגרים מן העצים: ובפירות. כגון חטין וקטניות: כנפי יונה. נוצה: גמ' שלא יפיח. שיכול להעמיד עצמו בשעת הרוח: שלא יישן בהן. שמא יפיח או יראה קרי אבל אם יכול להזהר שלא יישן בהן כל הגופים נקיים בהפחה שיכולין להעמיד עצמן: ינקרו את מוחו. שהוא תחת התפילין. ינקרו לשון ניקור עינים: קסדור. מניסטרא"ל שהיה ממונה על כך: כנפי יונה. כדמפרש לקמיה מפני שהם מצות והם מגינין לישראל והויא להם ככנפים ליונה שהיא נמשלת ליונה והמצות ככנפים: כנפיה מגינות עליה. מן הצנה ומכל עוף ואדם הבא עליה היא נלחמת ומכה בראש גפה מה שאין כן בשאר עופות: הרי הוא כזבל. דמוסיף הבל: מתני' שלחין. עורות כמו והפשיט תרגום ויְשלח: ומטלטלין אותן. בין שטמן בהן בין שלא טמן בהן דחזו למזגא עלייהו: ואין מטלטלין אותן. דמוקצות הן לטוות ולארוג: כיצד הוא עושה. זה שטמן בהן כיצד יטול קדרתו הואיל ואסור לטלטלן שהרי היא טמונה כולה בהן: נוטל כיסוי. של קדרה שיש תורת כלי עליה ואף על גב שהן עליה לא איכפת לן דלא נעשית בסיס להן שאין עשוי אלא לכסות קדרה: רבי אלעזר בן עזריה אומר קופה מטה על צדה ונוטל. כשבא ליטול הקדרה מטה הקופה על צדה: שמא יטול. הקדרה ויפלו הגיזין שמכאן ומכאן לתוך גומא שישבה בהן ואם יצטרך לחזור ולהטמינה לא יוכל לטלטל גיזין לכאן ולכאן ולעשות גומא להחזירה בתוכה: נוטל ומחזיר. בגמרא מפרש לה: גמ' שלחין של בעה"ב תנן. דמותר לטלטלן שאין עומדין לימכר ולא קפיד עלייהו כי מטנפי וחזי למזגא עלייהו: אבל של אומן. שעומדות למוכרן קפיד עלייהו הלכך לא למזגא קיימי ואין מטלטלין אותן:
שלחא

תוספות

ועל הזאה שבשעת מלאכה משום הזאה שלא בשעת מלאכה. תימה דהא גבי מקל שעשאו יד לקורדום קאמר דהוי חיבור לטומאה משמע אבל לא להזאה ואמאי והא לא שייך למגזר התם אטו שלא בשעת מלאכה כדאמר לעיל דאדם עשוי לזורקו בין העצים וי"ל דהתם לא הוי חיבור להזאה משום דאפילו בשעת מלאכה לא הוי חיבור דבר תורה דלא חשיב כלל בית יד בשום פעם כיון שהוא עשוי לזורקו כל שעה:

אבל לא בכסות לחה כו'. נראה דרבי אושעיא פליג אמתני':

כאלישע בעל כנפים. להכי נקט אלישע דמסתמא כיון שנעשה לו נס בתפילין היה זהיר בהן והיה לו גוף נקי ומזה הטעם אין אנו יכולין ליפטר שהרי בזה אנו יכולין להזהר ואין תימה על מה שמצוה זאת רפויה בידינו שגם בימי חכמים היתה רפויה כדתניא בפרק ר' אליעזר דמילה (לקמן קל.) ר"ש בן אלעזר אומר כל מצוה שלא מסרו עצמן ישראל עליה בשעת גזירת המלכות כגון תפילין עדיין היא רפויה בידם והא דאמרינן בפ"ק דר"ה (דף יז.) פושעי ישראל בגופן קרקפתא דלא מנח תפילין אומר ר"ת דמיירי באותן שעושין מחמת מרד ומבזין המצות ושוחקין ברצועה שבידם ובראשם כדאמר ביומא (דף לו:) פשעים אלו המרדין והא דאמר במדרש תפילין מפני מה לא החזיקו בהן מפני הרמאים אין נראה לר"י דמשום רמאין נמנעו מלעשות מצוה אלא ה"פ מפני מה לא החזיקו נאמנות באדם המניח תפילין ו) וקאמר מפני הרמאין שהיו מניחין תפילין לרמות בני אדם כדמפרש התם מעשה בתלמיד אחד שהפקיד מעותיו אצל אחד שהיה מניח תפילין כשתבע בו אמר להד"ס אמר ליה אותו תלמיד לא לך הפקדתי אלא לתפילין שעל ראשך וע"ע שם:

אביי אמר שלא יפיח בהן. שיוכל לשמור עצמו מלהפיח עד שיסיר תפילין כדפירש בקונט' אבל לא חייש שמא ישן דאע"ג דפעמים יוכל ליזהר משינה ורבא מצריך גם שיוכל להעמיד עצמו בשעה שתאחזנו השינה שלא ישן פתאום ומיהו אביי נמי מודה דאסור לישן בהן כדתניא בפרק הישן (סוכה כו. ושם) דאסור לישן בתפילין בין שינת קבע בין שינת עראי:

שלא יישן בהן. משום שלא יפיח בהן בשעת שינה או משום היסח הדעת אבל משום קרי אין לחוש כדאמר בפ' הישן (ג"ז שם:) דא"ר יוסי ילדים לעולם חולין מפני שרגילין בטומאה ופריך לימא קסבר ר' יוסי בעל קרי אסור להניח תפילין ומשני הכא בילדים ונשותיהם עמהם עסקינן שמא יבאו לידי הרגל דבר אבל משום קרי לא בעי למיסר:

נטלם מראשו. ואף על גב דאמר בסנהדרין (דף עד: ושם) בשעת גזרת המלכות אפי' על מצוה קלה יהרג ואל יעבור ואפילו לשנויי ערקתא דמסאנא אסור היינו משום דבשינוי ערקתא מתנהג כעובד כוכבים ודומה שמוציא עצמו מכלל ישראל אבל הכא אינו עושה כלום אלא שאין לו תפילין בראשו שעה אחת והרבה ישראל שאין להם תפילין כמותו:

כנפיה מגינות עליה. אור"י דאמרינן במדרש ז) כל העופות כשהן יגעין ניוחין ע"ג סלע והיונה בשעה שהיא יגעה פורחת באחת וניוחת באחת:

טומנין בשלחין ומטלטלין אותן. הא דאמר בפ"ק דביצה (דף יא.) נותנין העור לפני הדורסן דהתירו סופן משום תחלתן פי' כדי שישחוט לצורך יו"ט אבל עור דמערב יו"ט משמע התם דאסור לטלטל ובפרק כל כתבי (לקמן קטז:) קאמר אם מטלטלין תיק הספר עם הספר לא נטלטל עור אגב בשר משמע דעור בלא בשר אסור פירש"י בפרק כל כתבי (ג"ז שם ח) דהכא מיירי בעור בהמה גסה והתם בעור בהמה דקה דלא חזי למזגא כולי האי ולפירושו האי דביצה נמי מיירי בעור בהמה דקה והא דתנן בפ' כל כתבי (דף קכ.) פורסין עור גדי על גבי התבה כו' צריך לומר לפי' דמיירי כשיחדו לישיבה ° ור"ת מפרש דהכא מיירי ביבשין דחזי למזגא עלייהו והתם בלחין:
אבא

עין משפט נר מצוה

יא א מיי' פ"ד מהלכות שבת הלכה א:
יב ב מיי' פ"ד מהלכות שבת הלכה א טוש"ע או"ח סימן רנז סעיף ג:
יג ג מיי' פ"ד מהלכות תפילין הלכה טו סמג עשין כב טוש"ע או"ח סימן לח סעיף ב ג:
יד ד מיי' פ"ד מהלכות שבת הלכה א:
טו ה מיי' פ"ד מהלכות שבת שם ופכ"ו הל' יג סמג לאוין סה טור שו"ע או"ח סימן רנט סעיף א:

רבינו חננאל

להזאה וגזרו שאם נטמא הא' שלא בשעת מלאכה נטמא גם האחר בכל מקר' שהוא. ודוק' אם הוא (מחברן) מחובר עדיין משום טומאה שבשעת מלאכה. וגזרו נמי על הזאה שאם יזה על הא' אפילו בשעת מלאכה לא נטהר האחר אע"פ שהוא מחובר עמו משו' הזאה שלא בשעת מלאכה. פי' אם יראה שהזה בשעת מלאכה על האחד ונטהר גם האחר יטהר הוא כשיזה על האחד אפילו השני שלא בשעת מלאכה: פי' מירטא דביני אטמא העמר שבין הירכות של בהמה כיון שתמיד השתנתה שותת בין ירכותיה יש בו לחלוחית לעולם ואינו מתנגב לעולם ואפילו עושה מאותו צמר כסות יש בו לחלוחית: תפלין צריכין גוף נקי. קיי"ל כרבא דאמר שלא יישן בהן: ר' יהודה אוסר. אוקימנא בנעורת: טומנין בשלחין ומטלטלין אותן. פירוש שלחין עורות גלשין שנגזז (כצמר) [הצמר] ועדיין לא נעבדו: אבא שלחא פירש

מסורת הש"ס

א) [כרי"ף וברא"ש ליתא], ב) לקמן קל., ג) [עי' תוספות בבא בתרא י: ד"ה אלא], ד) [ברכות עג: ע"ש גיטין מה. סנהדרין לה. לקמן קל.], ה) [לקמן נא:], ו) [ועי' ירושלמי פרק היה קורא הלכה ד], ז) [רבה סדר לך לך פרשה לט], ח) בד"ה במרתי פליגי.

גליון הש"ס

תוס' ד"ה טומנין בשלחין וכו' ור"ת מפרש. עי' זבחים דף לג ע"ב תוס' ד"ה מנין בסה"ד:

תורה אור השלם

א) אִם תִּשְׁכְּבוּן בֵּין שְׁפַתָּיִם כַּנְפֵי יוֹנָה נֶחְפָּה בַכֶּסֶף וְאֶבְרוֹתֶיהָ בִּירַקְרַק חָרוּץ: [תהלים סח, יד]

ליקוטי רש"י

נסורת. עלים דקים שנופלין מן החתיכה [מ"ק יב:]. שמגררין נגרים במגירה פגומה וקוצצים בה עצים והיא מסרת נסורת דקה כעפר [חולין פח:]. ינקרו. יקרו. פוריי"ר בלע"ז לשון יקרוה עורבי נחל (משלי ל') ולשון תנקר לא נעלה (במדבר טז). קסדור. ממונה [לקמן קל.]. שם פקידות הוא כגון סרדיוט והוא שוטר [יומא יא.]. דאמתיל כנסת ישראל ליונה. דכתיב יונתי תמתי (שיר השירים ה) [גיטין מה.]. כנפי יונה. פלומ"א בלע"ז. נחפה בכסף. נכספה ומחמדה של תורה ומצות [תהלים סח, יד]. מגינות עליהן. אינה נלחמת בחרטומיה אלא בכנפיה [לקמן שם]. יונה אינה נצולת אלא בכנפיה או פורחת או נלחמת בראשי אגפיה [ברכות נג:]. הרי הוא כזבל. דמוסיף הבלא ואין טומנין בה אפילו מבעוד יום [לקמן נא:]. ומטלטלין אותן. עור בהמה גסה דחזי למישטחיה ולמיזגא עליה [לקמן קטז: ועי' כאן בתוס'].

so the hides **of a householder?**

One Amora offers his opinion:

אָמַר לְהוּ רַבִּי יוֹנָתָן בֶּן אֶלְעָזָר – R' Yonasan bar Elazar said to [his colleagues]: מִסְתַּבְּרָא שֶׁל בַּעַל הַבַּיִת תְּנַן אֲבָל שֶׁל אוּמָּן קָפִּיד עֲלַיְיהוּ – It seems logical that the Mishnah refers only **to** the hides **of a householder, but** as for those **of a craftsman, he is** indeed **particular with them** and they should be deemed *muktzeh.*

Another Amora disagrees:

אָמַר לְהוּ רַבִּי חֲנִינָא בַּר חָמָא – R' Chanina bar Chama said to them: כָּךְ אָמַר רַבִּי יִשְׁמָעֵאל בְּרַבִּי יוֹסֵי – So said R' Yishmael the son of R' Yose:

NOTES

that perhaps a leather craftsman would not be likely to allow his hides to be used as a rug, for fear of their becoming damaged and unsalable. His hides, therefore, should be deemed *muktzeh for fear of monetary loss* (see Introduction to Chapter 3).

גמרא

וגזרו רבנן על טומאה שלא בשעת מלאכה משום טומאה שבשעת מלאכה ועל הזאה שבשעת מלאכה משום הזאה שלא בשעת מלאכה: בזמן שהן לחין: איבעיא להו [א] לחין מחמת עצמן או דילמא לחין מחמת דבר אחר ת"ש לא בתבן ולא בזגים ולא במוכין ולא בעשבים בזמן שהן לחין אי אמרת בשלמא לחין מחמת דבר אחר שפיר אלא אי אמרת לחין מחמת עצמן מוכין לחין מחמת עצמן היכי משכחת לה ממרטא דביני אטמי והא דתני רבי אושעיא טומנין בכסות יבשה ובפירות יבשין אבל לא בכסות לחה ולא בפירות לחין כסות לחה מחמת עצמה היכי משכחת לה ממרטא דביני אטמי: **מתני'** [ב] טומנין בכסות ובפירות בכנפי יונה ובנסורת של חרשים ובנעורת של פשתן [ו] דקה רבי יהודה אוסר בדקה ומתיר בגסה: **גמ'** א"ר ינאי [ג] תפילין צריכין גוף נקי [ג] כאלישע בעל כנפים מאי היא אביי אמר שלא יפיח בהן רבא אמר שלא יישן בהן ואמאי קרי ליה בעל כנפים שפעם אחת גזרה מלכות רומי הרשעה גזירה על ישראל שכל המניח תפילין ינקרו את מוחו והיה אלישע מניחם ויוצא לשוק ראהו קסדור אחד רץ מפניו ורץ אחריו וכיון שהגיע אצלו נטלן מראשו ואחזן בידו אמר לו מה זה בידך אמר לו כנפי יונה פשט את ידו ונמצאו כנפי יונה לפיכך קורין אותו אלישע בעל כנפים [ז] ומאי שנא כנפי יונה משאר עופות משום דאמתיל כנסת ישראל ליונה שנאמר [א] כנפי יונה נחפה בכסף וגו' מה יונה כנפיה מגינות עליה אף ישראל מצות מגינות עליהן: בנסורת של חרשין וכו': איבעיא להו רבי יהודה אנסורת של חרשין קאי או אנעורת של פשתן קאי ת"ש דתניא [ח] רבי יהודה אומר נעורת של פשתן דקה הרי הוא כזבל ש"מ אנעורת של פשתן קאי ש"מ: **מתני'** [ד] טומנין בשלחין ומטלטלין אותן בגיזי צמר ואין מטלטלין אותן כיצד הוא עושה [ה] נוטל את הכסוי והן נופלות ר"א בן עזריה אומר קופה מטה על צדה ונוטל שמא יטול ואינו יכול להחזיר וחכ"א נוטל ומחזיר: **גמ'** יתיב ר' יונתן בן עכינאי ורבי יונתן בן אלעזר ויתיב ר' חנינא בר חמא גבייהו וקא מיבעיא להו שלחין של בעה"ב תנן אבל של אומן כיון דקפיד עלייהו לא מטלטלינן להו או דילמא של אומן תנן וכ"ש של בעה"ב אמר להו ר' יונתן בן אלעזר מסתברא של בעה"ב תנן אבל של אומן קפיד עלייהו אמר להו ר' חנינא בר חמא כך אמר ר' ישמעאל בר' יוסי אבא

רש"י

וגזרו על הטומאה שלא בשעת מלאכה. שיהא חיבור: **ועל הזאה שבשעת מלאכה.** שלא יהא חיבור הלכך חיבור לטומאה לעולם ואין חיבור להזאה כלל: **לחין מחמת עצמן.** מחממות טפי מלחין מחמת משקין שנופלין עליהן מתייבשו: ה"ג מוכין לחין מחמת עצמן היכי משכחת לה: **ממרטא דביני אטמי.** מלמר הנמרט מבין ירכותיה של בהמה שהוא מלא זיעה והוא לח מעצמו להכי קרי ליה מרטא דלאו בר גיזה הוא: **מתני' נעורת.** דק דק שנוערין מן הפשתן וקורין אריסט"ש: **נסורת.** שמנסרים הנגרים מן העצים: **ובפירות.** כגון חטין וקטניות: **כנפי יונה.** נוצה: **גמ' שלא יפיח.** שיכול להעמיד עצמו בשעת הרוח: **שלא יישן בהן.** שמא יפיח או יראה קרי אבל אם יכול להזהר שלא יישן בהן כל הגופים נקיים בהפחה שיכולין להעמיד עצמן: **ינקרו את מוחו.** שהוא תחת התפילין. ינקרו לשון ניקור עינים: **קסדור.** מנישטרא"ל שהיה ממונה על כך: **כנפי יונה.** כדמפרש לקמיה מפני שהם מצות והם מגינין לישראל והוא להם ככנפים ליונה שהיא נמשלת ליונה והמצות ככנפים: **כנפיה מגינות עליה.** מן הצנה ומכל עוף ואדם הבא עליה היא נלחמת ומכה בראש גפה מה שאין כן בשאר עופות: **הרי הוא כזבל.** דמוסיף הבל: **מתני' שלחין.** עורות כמו והפשיט תרגום וישלח: **ומטלטלין אותן.** בין שטמן בהן בין שלא טמן בהן דחזו למזגא עלייהו: **ואין מטלטלין אותן.** דמוקצות הן לטוות ולארוג: **כיצד הוא עושה.** זה שטמן בהן כילד יטול קדרתו הואיל ואסור לטלטלן שהרי היא טמונה כולה בהן: **נוטל כיסוי.** של קדרה שיש תורת כלי עליה ואף על גב שהן עליה לא איכפת לן דלא נעשית בסיס להן שאין עשוי אלא לכסות קדרה: **רבי אלעזר בן עזריה אומר קופה מטה על צדה ונוטל.** כשבא ליטול הקדרה מטה הקופה על צדה: **שמא יטול.** הקדרה ויפלו הגיזין שמכאן ומכאן לתוך גומא שישבה בהן ואם יצטרך לחזור ולהטמינה לא יוכל לטלטל גיזין לכאן ולכאן ולעשות גומא להחזירה בתוכה: **נוטל ומחזיר.** בגמרא מפרש לה: **גמ' שלחין של בעה"ב תנן.** דמותר לטלטלן שאין עומדין לימכר ולא קפיד עלייהו כי מטנפי וחזי למזגא עלייהו: **אבל של אומן.** שעומדות למוכרן קפיד עלייהו הלכך לאו למזגא קיימי ואין מטלטלין אותן:

שלחא

תוספות

ועל הזאה שבשעת מלאכה משום הזאה שלא בשעת מלאכה. תימה דהא גבי מקל שעשאו יד לקורדס קאמר דהוי חיבור לטומאה משמע אבל לא להזאה ואמאי והא לא שייך למגזר התם אטו שלא בשעת מלאכה כדאמר לעיל דאדם עשוי לזורקו בין העצים וי"ל דהתם לא הוי חיבור להזאה משום דאפילו בשעת מלאכה לא הוי חיבור דבר תורה דלא חשיב כלל בית יד בשום פעם כיון שהוא עשוי לזורקו כל שעה:

אבל לא בכסות לחה כו'. נראה דרבי אושעיא פליג אמתני':

כאלישע בעל כנפים. להכי נקט אלישע דמסתמא כיון שנעשה לו נס בתפילין היה זהיר בהן והיה לו גוף נקי ומזה הטעם אין אנו יכולין ליפטר שהרי בזה אנו יכולין להזהר ואין תימה על מה שמצוה זאת רפויה בידינו שגם בימי חכמים היתה רפויה כדתניא בפרק ר' אליעזר דמילה (לקמן קל.) ר"ש בן אלעזר אומר כל מצוה שלא מסרו עצמן ישראל עליה בשעת גזירת המלכות כגון תפילין עדיין היא רפויה בידם והא דאמרינן בפ"ק דר"ה השנה (דף יז.) פושעי ישראל בגופן קרקפתא דלא מנח תפילין אומר ר"ת דמיירי באותן שעושין מחמת מרד ומבזין המצות ושוחקין ברלועה שבידם וכראשם כדאמר ביומא (דף לו:) פשעים אלו המרדין והא דאמר במדרש תפילין מפני מה לא החזיקו בהן מפני הרמאים אין נראה לר"י דמשום רמאין נמנעו מלעשות מצוה אלא ה"פ מפני מה לא החזיקו נאמנות באדם המניח תפילין [י] וקאמר מפני הרמאין שהיו מניחין תפילין לרמות בני אדם כדמפרש התם מעשה בתלמיד אחד שהפקיד מעותיו אצל אחד שהיה מניח תפילין כשתבע בו אמר להד"ס אמר ליה אותו תלמיד לא לך הפקדתי אלא לתפילין שעל ראשך וכו' ע"ש:

אביי אמר שלא יפיח בהן. שיוכל לשמור עצמו מלהפיח עד שיסיר תפילין כדפירש בקונט' אבל לא חייש שמא ישן דאע"ג דפעמים יוכל ליזהר משינה ורבא מצריך גם שיכול להעמיד עצמו בשעה שתאחזנו השינה שלא ישן פתאום ומיהו אביי נמי מודה דאסור לישן בהן כדתניא בפרק הישן (סוכה כו. ושם) דאסור לישן בתפילין בין שינת קבע בין שינת עראי:

שלא יישן בהן. משום שלא יפיח בהן בשעת שינה או משום היסח הדעת אבל משום קרי אין לחוש כדאמר בפ' הישן (ג"ז שם:) דא"ר יוסי ילדים לעולם חולין מפני שרגילין בטומאה ופריך לימא קסבר ר' יוסי בעל קרי אסור להניח תפילין ומשני הכא בילדים ונשותיהם עמהם עסקינן שמא יבאו לידי הרגל דבר אבל משום קרי לא בעי למיסר:

נטלם מראשו. ואף על גב דאמר בסנהדרין (דף עד: ושם) בשעת גזרת המלכות אפי' על מצוה קלה יהרג ואל יעבור ואפילו לשנויי ערקתא דמסאנא אסור היינו משום דבשינוי ערקתא מתנהג כעובד כוכבים ודומה שמוליא עצמו מכלל ישראל אבל הכא אינו עושה כלום אלא שאין לו תפילין בראשו שעה אחת והרבה ישראל שאין להם תפילין כמותו:

כנפיה מגינות עליה. אור"י דאמרינן במדרש [ז] כל העופות כשהן יגעין מינוחין ע"ג סלע והיונה בשעה שהיא יגעה פורחת באחת ומינוחת באחת:

טומנין בשלחין ומטלטלין אותן. הא דאמר בפ"ק דבילה (דף יא.) נותנין העור לפני הדורסן דהתירו סופן משום תחילתן פי' כדי שיחוט לצורך יו"ט אבל עור דמערב יו"ט משמע התם דאסור לטלטל ובפרק כל כתבי (לקמן קטז:) קאמר אם מטלטלין תיק הספר עם הספר לא נטלטל עור אגב בשר משמע דעור בלא בשר אסור פירש"י בפרק כל כתבי (ג"ז שם [ס]) דהכא מיירי בעור בהמה גסה והתם בעור בהמה דקה דלא חזי למזגא כולי האי ולפירושו האי דבילה נמי מיירי בעור בהמה דקה והא דתנן בפ' כל כתבי (דף קכ.) פורסין עור גדי על גבי התבה כו' צריך לומר לפי' דמיירי כשיחדו לישיבה ° ור"ת מפרש דהכא מיירי ביבשין דחזי למזגא עלייהו והתם בלחין:

אבא

מסורת הש"ס

[א] [בכר"ף וברא"ש ליתא], [ב] לקמן קל., [ג] [עי' תוספות בבא בתרא י: ד"ה אלא], [ד] [ברכות נג: ע"ש גיטין מה. סנהדרין לה. לקמן קל.], [ה] [לקמן נא:], [ו] [ועי' ירושלמי פרק היה קורא הלכה ד], [ז] [רבה סדר לך לך פרשה לט], [ח] כד"ה במתני' פליגי.

גליון הש"ס

תוס' ד"ה טומנין בשלחין וכו' ור"ת מפרש. עי' זבחים דף לג ע"ב תוס' ד"ה מנין כסה"ד:

תורה אור השלם

א) אִם תִּשְׁכְּבוּן בֵּין שְׁפַתָּיִם כַּנְפֵי יוֹנָה נֶחְפָּה בַכֶּסֶף וְאֶבְרוֹתֶיהָ בִּירַקְרַק חָרוּץ: [תהלים סח, יד]

ליקוטי רש"י

נסורת. עלים דקים שנופלין מן החתיכה [מ"ק יב:]. שמגררין נגרים במגירה פגומה וקוללים בה עלים והיא משרת נסורת דקה כעפר [חולין פח:]. **ינקרו.** יקרו. פוריי"ר בלע"ז לשון יקרוה עורבי נחל (משלי ל') ולשון תנקר לא נעלה (במדבר טז). **קסדור.** ממונה [לקמן קל.]. שם פקידות הוא כגון סרדיוט והוא שוטר [יומא יא.]. **דאמתיל כנסת ישראל ליונה.** דכתיב יונתי תמתי (שיר השירים ה) [גיטין מה.]. **כנפי יונה.** פלומ"א בלע"ז. **נחפה בכסף.** בכספה ומחמדה של תורה ומצות [תהלים סח, יד]. **מגינות עליהן.** אינה נלחמת בחרטומיה אלא בכנפיה [לקמן שם]. יונה אינה נצולת אלא בכנפיה או בורחת או נלחמת בראשי אגפיה [ברכות נג:]. **הרי הוא כזבל.** דמוסיף הבלא ואין טומנין בה אפילו מבעוד יום [לקמן נא:]. **ומטלטלין אותן.** עור בהמה גסה דחזי למישטחיה ולמיזגא עליה [לקמן קטז: ועי' כאן בתוס'].

עין משפט נר מצוה

יא א מיי' פ"ד מהלכות שבת הלכה א:

יב ב מיי' פ"ד מהלכות שבת הלכה א טוש"ע או"ח סימן רנז סעיף ג:

יג ג מיי' פ"ד מהלכות תפילין הלכה טו סמג עשין כב טוש"ע או"ח סימן לח סעיף ב ג:

יד ד מיי' פ"ד מהלכות שבת הלכה א:

טו ה מיי' פ"ד מהלכות שבת שם ופכ"ו הל' יב סמג לאוין סה טור שו"ע או"ח סימן רנט סעיף א:

רבינו חננאל

להזאה וגזרו שאם נטמא הא' שלא בשעת מלאכה נטמא גם האחר בכל מקר' שהוא. ודוק' אם הוא (מחברן) מחובר עדיין משום טומאה שבשעת מלאכה. וגזרו נמי על הזאה שאם יזה על הא' אפילו בשעת מלאכה לא נטהר האחר אע"פ שהוא מחובר עמו משו' הזאה שלא בשעת מלאכה. פי' אם יראה שהזה בשעת מלאכה על האחד ונטהר גם האחר יטהר הוא כשיזה על האחד אפילו השני שלא בשעת מלאכה: פי' מירטא דביני אטמא העמר שבין הירכות של בהמה כיון שתמיד השתנתה שותת בין ירכותיה יש בו לחלוחית לעולם ואינו מתנגב לעולם ואפילו עושה מאותו צמר כסות יש בו לחלוחית: **תפלין** צריכין גוף נקי. קיי"ל כרבא דאמר שלא יישן בהן: ר' **יהודה** אוסר. אוקימנא בנעורת: טומנין בשלחין ומטלטלין אותן. פירוש שלחין עורות גלשין שנגזו (כצמר) [הצמר] ועדיין לא נעבדו: **אבא** שלחא פירש

אבא שלחא הוה ואמר הביאו שלחין ונשב עליהן מיתיבי נסרין של בעה"ב מטלטלין אותן ושל אומן אין מטלטלין אותן ואם חישב לתת עליהן פת לאורחין בין כך ובין כך מטלטלין שאני נסרים דקפיד עלייהו ת"ש עורות בין עבודין ובין שאין עבודין מותר לטלטלן בשבת לא אמרו עבודין אלא לענין טומאה בלבד מאי לאו לא שנא של בעל הבית ולא שנא של אומן לא של בעה"ב אבל של אומן מאי אין מטלטלין אי הכי הא דתני ולא אמרו עבודין אלא לענין טומאה בלבד לפלוג וליתני בדידה בד"א בשל בעה"ב אבל בשל אומן לא כולה בבעל הבית קמיירי כתנאי עורות של בעה"ב מטלטלין אותן ושל אומן אין מטלטלין אותן ר' יוסי אומר אחד זה ואחד זה מטלטלין אותן: הדור יתבי וקמיבעיא להו הא דתנן אבות מלאכות ארבעים חסר אחת כנגד מי אמר להו ר' חנינא בר חמא כנגד עבודות המשכן אמר להו ר' יונתן בר' אלעזר כך אמר רבי שמעון ברבי יוסי בן לקוניא כנגד מלאכה מלאכתו ומלאכת שבתורה ארבעים חסר אחת בעי רב יוסף ויבא הביתה לעשות מלאכתו ממנינא הוא או לא א"ל אביי וליתי ספר תורה ולימני מי לא אמר רבה בר בר חנה א"ר יוחנן לא זזו משם עד שהביאו ספר תורה ומנאום אמר ליה כי קא מספקא לי משום דכתיב והמלאכה היתה דים ממנינא הוא והא כמאן דאמר לעשות צרכיו נכנס או דילמא ויבא הביתה לעשות מלאכתו ממנינא הוא והאי והמלאכה היתה דים הכי קאמר דשלים ליה עבידתא תיקו תניא כמאן דאמר כנגד עבודות המשכן דתניא אין חייבין אלא על מלאכה שכיוצא בה היתה במשכן הם זרעו ואתם לא תזרעו הם קצרו ואתם לא תקצרו הם העלו את הקרשים מקרקע לעגלה ואתם לא תכניסו מרה"ר לרה"י הם הורידו את הקרשים מעגלה לקרקע ואתם לא תוציאו מרה"י לרה"ר הם הוציאו מעגלה לעגלה ואתם לא תוציאו מרה"י לרה"י מרה"י לרשות היחיד מאי קא עביד אביי ורבא דאמרי תרווייהו ואיתימא רב אדא בר אהבה מרשות היחיד לרה"י דרך רשות הרבים: בגיזי צמר ואין מטלטלין: אמר רבא לא שנו אלא שלא טמן בהן אבל טמן בהן מטלטלין אותן איתיביה ההוא מרבנן בר יומיה לרבא טומנין בגיזי צמר ואין מטלטלין אותן כיצד הוא עושה נוטל

רש"י

שלחא הוה. אומן לעבד עורות: ואמר. בחול: הביאו שלחין ונשב עליהן. אלמא לא קפיד: דקפיד עלייהו. שמא יתקלקלו: ולא אמרו עבודין. לא הוזכרו לחלק בין עבודין לשאינן עבודין: אלא לענין טומאה. דעבודין מקבלין טומאה ולא שאינן עבודין: לפלוג בדידה. בטלטול גופיה איכא לפלוגי בשל אומן בין עבודין לשאינן עבודין דעבודין קפיד עלייהו: בד"א. דעבודין מותר לטלטלן בשל בעה"ב אבל של אומן מאחר שעבדן קפיד עלייהו: כולה בבעה"ב איירי. ומהדר ליפלוגי בבעה"ב דאיירי ביה ולא אשכח לפלוגי אלא לענין טומאה ולאי שבקיה לבעה"ב דאיירי ביה ונקט אומן מפסקה למילתיה טפי מדהשתא: הדור יתבי. הנך רבנן דלעיל: כנגד עבודות המשכן. אותן המנויות שם בפרק כלל גדול היו צריכין למשכן ופרשת שבת נסמכה לפרשת מלאכת המשכן ללמוד הימנה: שבתורה. שכתובים בכל התורה והכי קאמר קרא (שמות כ) לא תעשה כל מלאכה כמנין כל מלאכה שבתורה: לא זזו משם. לא ידענא היכא איתמר ומיהו [אפשר] לענין וי"ו דגחון אתמר מדפרכינן לה נמי בקדושין גבי וי"ו דגחון ומתרלינן אינהו הוו בקיאי בחסרות ויתרות ש"מ לענין אותיות איתמר והכא ליכא לשנויי הכי: משום דכתיב והמלאכה היתה דים. ואי מנינן לתרוייהו הוו ארבעים ומדתנן אבות מלאכות ארבעים חסר אחת איכא חד דלא ממנינא ובהני תרי דאיכא למימר דלא מלאכה נינהו ולא ידענא הי מינייהו נפיק והכי קא מיבעיא ליה והמלאכה היתה דים ממנינא היא ומלאכה ממש קאמר והכי קאמר המלאכה שהיו עושין היו עושין די לא פחות מן הצורך ולא יותר מן הצורך כגון רידודי טסין לציפוי הקרשים לדי היו מרדדין אותם וכן בטווי של יריעות והאי לעשות מלאכתו הוא דמפיק ומסייע למאן דאמר במסכת סוטה לעשות צרכיו נכנס לשכב עמה אלא שנראתה לו דמות דיוקנו של אביו ואמר לו עתידין אחיך ליכתב על אבני אפוד רצונך שימחה שמך מביניהם כו' או דילמא האי לעשות מלאכתו מלאכה ממש הוא ומסייע לה לאידך: והאי והמלאכה היתה דים. לאו מלאכה היא אלא כדמשמע קרא בהבאת נדבה וכמאן דאמר שלימא ליה עבידתא מלאכת ההבאה שלא היו צריכין עוד וכל מידי דרמי עליה דאינש קרי ליה עבידתא כדאמרינן במסכת סוטה (דף לג.) בטילת עבידתא דאמר סנאה לאייתואה להיכלא ואינו אלא צבא מלחמה להחריב: הם זרעו וקצרו סמנין. לצבוע תכלת ועורות אילים וטחנו ולשו נמי סמנין לצבוע ואופה דקתני במתני' באבות מלאכות הוא בישול סמנין אלא דנקט סידורה דפת והכי מפרש בפרק כלל גדול (לקמן דף עד:): קרקע. רשות הרבים: עגלה. רשות היחיד שגבוהה י' ורחבה ד': דרך רשות הרבים. דאויר שבין העגלות רשות הרבים: אבל טמן בהן מטלטלין אותן. קס"ד השתא דמילי מילי קתני מתניתין ולאו אהנך דטמן בהן קאי: ההוא מרבנן בר יומיה. אותו היום בא לבית מדרשו תחלה: נוטל

תוספות

אבא שלחא. פר"ח ואמר הביאו לי שלחין בשבת והלכה כר' יוסי דקי"ל מעשה רב וכן נראה דאי בחול מיירי כדפי' בקונט' ולא מייתי ראיה אלא דאומן נמי לא קפיד טפי הוה ליה לאתויי דר' יוסי אבוה דשרי לקמן בהדיא של אומן: לא אמרו עבודין אלא לענין טומאה בלבד. פרש"י שאין עור מקבל טומאה עד לאחר עיבוד ואם תאמר והא אמר בזבחים בפ' דם חטאת (דף צג: ושם) מניין לרבות עור משהופשט תלמוד לומר אשר יזה עליה תכובס יכול אף עור שלא הופשט תלמוד לומר בגד מה בגד מקבל טומאה אף כל דבר המקבל טומאה משמע דעור משהופשט מקבל טומאה ויש לומר דהתם כשיחדו לישיבה והכא כשלא יחדו ואפ"ה מותר לטלטלו בשבת והא דאמר רבא בריש כל הכלים (לקמן קכג.) מדלענין טומאה לאו מנא הוא לענין שבת נמי לאו מנא הוא גבי מחט שניטל חורה או עוקצה ה"פ מדלענין טומאה לאו מנא הוא אפי' ע"י יחוד דניטל חורה או עוקצה טהורה ולא מהני בה יחוד והא דתנן במסכת כלים בפרק י"ג (משנה ה) מחט שניטל חורה או עוקצה טהורה ואם התקינה למיתוח טמאה אומר ר"י דהתם מיירי כשעשה בה שום שינוי ותיקון למיתוח אבל ביחוד בעלמא למיתוח אינה טמאה אבל היכא דהוי מנא לענין טומאה ע"י יחוד לגבי שבת הוי מנא בלא יחוד וכן משמע התם דקאמר תרגמא אביי אליבא דרבא בגלמי דזימנין דמימליך עלייהו ומשוי להו מנא להכי מותר לטלטלה אע"ג דאכתי לא אימליך עלה והיא טהורה:

ארבעים אבות מלאכות חסר אחת כנגד מי. דהרבה מלאכות יש דדמיין להדדי והוה לן למחשבינהו כולן כאחת כדפריך בפרק כלל גדול (לקמן עג:) היינו זורה היינו בורר היינו מרקד ומשום חילוק מועט שביניהם לא הוה מחלקינן להו אי לאו דקים להו דל"ט מלאכות הן כנגד שום דבר לכך בעי כנגד מי:

כנגד כל מלאכה שבתורה. לכאורה נראה דיליף נמי ממשכן שהרי לכך נסמכה פרשת שבת לפרשת משכן ועוד דאי לא יליף ממשכן א"כ היכי ידעינן לדידיה הי נינהו אבות מלאכות והי תולדות דאין סברא לומר שמדעתם בירכו מלאכות החשובות ועשאום אבות ועוד דבהדיא תנן לקמן בהזורק המושיט חייב שכך היתה עבודת הלוים אלא לפי שיש מלאכות דומות זו לזו ואנו עושין שתיהן אבות כגון מרקד ובורר לכך חלקום חכמים להשלים מנין מלאכות שבתורה הואיל וחלוקות קצת זו מזו ואי אפשר לומר כן דלא פליג מדקאמר בסמוך תניא כמ"ד כנגד עבודות המשכן משמע דפליגי ועוד למאן דלית ליה דרשא דמלאכת ומלאכה מנא ליה דחשיב זורה ובורר בשתים ועוד לקמן משמע דמטעם דכנגד עבודות המשכן גרידא אית לן לאחשובינהו בתרתי דקאמר אביי ורבא בפרק כלל גדול (לקמן עג:) כל מילתא דהואי במשכן אע"ג דאיכא דדמיא לה חשיב לה: הם העלו קרשים כו'. אפילו רבנן דפליגי אדרבי יוסי ברבי יהודה גבי נעץ קנה ברשות הרבים ובראשו טרסקל ולית להו גוד אחית מודו בעגלה שהיא רשות היחיד כיון דעגלה גופה יש אורך בזקיפה עשרה ורוחב ארבעה אע"פ שתחתיה רשות הרבים וברים כל גגות (עירובין פט.) [ד"ה במחילות] האארכתי יותר: ואתם אל תכניסו. ואפ"ה לא הויא אב כדפרישית לעיל (דף ב.) [ד"ה פשט]:

אלא

עין משפט נר מצוה

טז א מיי' פכ"ו מהלכות שבת הלכה יב סמג לאוין סה טוש"ע או"ח סימן שח סעיף כה:

יז ב שם סעיף כו:

יח ג מיי' פכ"ו מהלכות שבת שם סמג שם טור שו"ע או"ח סימן רנט סעיף א:

רבינו חננאל

פושט עורות היה וקבלנו מרבותינו דהלכתא כר' יוסי דקיי"ל מעשה רב ואמר ר' ישמעאל בר' יוסי אבא שלחא הוה ואמר הביאו שלחין ונשב עליהן. נמצא כי עשה מעשה כשמועתו דתניא עורות של בעל הבית מטלטלין אותן. של אומן אין מטלטלין אותן. ר' יוסי אומר זה וזה מטלטלין הלכך עורות של אומן הואיל וראויין לישב עליהן ואין נפסדין אינו מקפיד עליהן ומותר לטלטלן. אבל נסרין של אומן הואיל ואם ישב עליהן נפגמין הלכך קפיד עליהן ואסור לטלטלן: אמר ר' חנינה הא דתנן אבות מלאכות ארבעים חסר אחת כנגד עבודות המשכן. ותניא כוותיה אין חייבין אלא על מלאכה שכיוצא בה היתה במשכן כיצד הן זרעו וקצרו והעלו קרשים מקרקע לעגלה אתם לא תזרעו ולא תקצרו כו' הא דתנן אבות מלאכות ארבעים חסר אחת כו'. וא"ר יונתן בן אלעזר כנגד מלאכת ומלאכה שבתורה א) והן ס"א. כשתוציא ג' מלאכות הכתובין בויכולו השמים וד' שכתוב בהן ועשית ויעשה ותעשה ולרגל המלאכה וי"ג שכתב כל מלאכת עבודה הרי כ"א נשארו מ' ובכללם ששת ימים וכו' לא תעשה מלאכה. ולמה (זכה) כי בפירוש אמרו בתלמוד א"י שבא זה הכתוב להשלים ל"ט מלאכות בתורה ויש מי שמוציא מכלל אלו מ' ויבא יוסף הביתה לעשות מלאכתו. ונשארו ל"ט ויש מי שמוציא והמלאכה היתה דים ולדברי הכל נשארים ל"ט מלאכות: פיס' בגיזי צמר ואין מטלטלין אותן. וקיי"ל

חשק שלמה על רבינו חננאל

א) עי' ראב"ן סימן ש"נ שמבאר היטב דברי הר"ח כמ"ש כאן וכרמב"ן וברשב"א ע"ש:

רב נסים גאון

ולא אמרו עבודין אלא לענין טומאה בלבד. עיקר דיליה מישתכח במסכת חולין בפ' העור והרוטב (דף קכב) וכולן שעיבדן או שהילך בהן כדי עבודה טהורין ובתוספתא וכולן שעיבדן ושהילך בהן כדי עבודה טהורין משום עור: אותיביה ההוא מרבנן בר יומיה לרבא זה התלמיד אמרו עליו באותו היום נכנס לבית המדרש על כן קרו ליה בר יומיה וכיוצא בו אמרנו בשחיטת קדשים (זבחים פ"ה דף נז) היה שם תלמיד אחד שבא לשמש לבית

מסורת הש"ס

א) ב"ק ב. לקמן עג. וש"נ, ב) [ועי' תוי"ט שבת פ"ז מ"ב סד"ה אבות ועי' חידושי רמב"ן ורשב"א בשם פיר"ח], ג) קידושין ל. ע"ש, ד) סוטה לו:, ה) ס"א מספקא, ו) [דף ל.], ז) [פי' אמר רב אידי הוה דהוה קרי לי' בר בי רב דחד יומא בחגיגה ה: ערוך], ח) [דף לו.], ט) [לעיל ה. לקמן קא.].

גליון הש"ס

רש"י ד"ה לא זזו לא ידענא כו'. עיין ברכות דף כה ע"ב רש"י ד"ה מאן שמעת ליה וש"נ:

תורה אור השלם

א) וַיְהִי כְּהַיּוֹם הַזֶּה וַיָּבֹא הַבַּיְתָה לַעֲשׂוֹת מְלַאכְתּוֹ וְאֵין אִישׁ מֵאַנְשֵׁי הַבַּיִת שָׁם בַּבָּיִת: [בראשית לט, יא]

ב) וְהַמְּלָאכָה הָיְתָה דַיָּם לְכָל הַמְּלָאכָה לַעֲשׂוֹת אֹתָהּ וְהוֹתֵר: [שמות לו, ז]

ליקוטי רש"י

ויבא הביתה לעשות מלאכתו. רב ושמואל חד אמר מלאכתו ממש וחד אמר לעשות צרכיו עמה אלא שנראית לו דמות דיוקנו של אביו וכו' כדאיתא במסכת סוטה (לו:) [בראשית לט, יא]. לעשות צרכיו. תשמיש [סוטה לו:]. והאי והמלאכה היתה דים. ומלאכת ההבאה היתה דים של עושי המשכן לכל המלאכה של משכן לעשות אותה ולהותר [שמות לו, ז]. דשלים ליה עבידתא. שהיה הנדבה כדי להשלים [לקמן צו:]. הם העלו את הקרשים מקרקע לעגלה. שארבע עגלות היו לבני מררי שהיו נושאין קרשי המשכן והן הולכין שתים כאחד זו בצד זו כדאמרינן בגמרא וכשהיו פורקין את המשכן לטעון על העגלות היו מעמידין העגלות כדרך הליכתן שתים זו אצל זו סמוך למשכן ושתים זו אצל זו לפניהם דרך הליכתן לאורך רשות הרבים שהיו רוצים להלך אחר עמוד הענן ההולך לפניהם ופורקי המשכן היו מושיטין הקרשים לאותן שעל שתי העגלות הסמוכות למשכן והן מושיטין לאותן שלפניהם [שם.]

אַבָּא שַׁלְחָא הֲוָה – **Father was a** professional **tanner,** וְאָמַר הָבִיאוּ שְׁלָחִין וְנֵשֵׁב עֲלֵיהֶן – **yet he would say,**[1] **"Bring** out **hides that we may sit on them."** Thus we see that even a craftsman is not particular about using his hides.

The latter opinion is questioned:

מֵיתִיבֵי – **They challenged** this view from a Baraisa: נְסָרִין שֶׁל בַּעַל הַבַּיִת מְטַלְטְלִין אוֹתָן – Wooden **BOARDS OF A HOUSEHOLDER MAY BE MOVED** וְשֶׁל אוּמָּן אֵין מְטַלְטְלִין אוֹתָן – **BUT THOSE OF A CRAFTSMAN MAY NOT BE MOVED.** וְאִם חִישֵּׁב לָתֵת עֲלֵיהֶן פַּת לְאוֹרְחִין – **BUT IF HE INTENDED** on Friday **TO SERVE BREAD TO GUESTS ON THEM,** בֵּין כָּךְ וּבֵין כָּךְ מְטַלְטְלִין – **WHETHER THIS OR THAT,** i.e. whether the boards belong to a householder or a craftsman, **THEY MAY BE MOVED.** Thus we see that a craftsman's wares are *muktzeh.* – ? –

The Gemara answers:

שָׁאנֵי נְסָרִים דְּקָפִיד עֲלַיְיהוּ – **Boards are different, because [the craftsman] is particular with them** lest they become warped.

The Gemara attempts to resolve the foregoing Amoraic dispute concerning hides of a craftsman:

תָּא שְׁמַע – **Come, learn** a proof from a Baraisa: עוֹרוֹת בֵּין עֲבוּדִין וּבֵין שֶׁאֵין עֲבוּדִין מוּתָּר לְטַלְטְלָן בְּשַׁבָּת – **HIDES, WHETHER TANNED OR UNTANNED, MAY BE MOVED ON THE SABBATH;** לֹא אָמְרוּ עֲבוּדִין אֶלָּא לְעִנְיַן טוּמְאָה בִּלְבַד – **THEY** [the Sages] **DID NOT MENTION TANNED** as a factor **EXCEPT IN REGARD TO THE MATTER OF *TUMAH* ALONE** [i.e. that tanned hides are susceptible to *tumah* while untanned hides are not].[2] מַאי לָאו לֹא שְׁנָא שֶׁל בַּעַל הַבַּיִת וְלֹא שְׁנָא שֶׁל אוּמָּן – Now **is it not** implied by the Baraisa's ruling that hides are *never* considered *muktzeh*, **no matter** whether those **of a householder or** those **of a craftsman?**

The Gemara responds:

לֹא – **No.** שֶׁל בַּעַל הַבַּיִת – The Baraisa refers only to those **of a householder.**

The Gemara asks:

אֲבָל שֶׁל אוּמָּן מַאי – **But what of those of a craftsman** – אֵין מְטַלְטְלִין – do you assert that **they may not be moved?** אִי הָכִי הָא דְּתָנֵי וְלֹא אָמְרוּ עֲבוּדִין אֶלָּא לְעִנְיַן טוּמְאָה בִּלְבַד – **If so,** then regarding **that which the Baraisa teaches: THEY DID NOT MENTION TANNED** as a factor **EXCEPT IN REGARD TO THE MATTER OF *TUMAH* ALONE,** לִפְלוֹג וְלִיתְנֵי בְּדִידָהּ – **let [the Baraisa] distinguish and teach** the same distinction between tanned and untanned hides **in regard to [the matter of *muktzeh*] itself,** i.e. rather than present the law of *tumah* as the sole case regarding which the Sages drew a distinction between tanned and untanned hides, let the Baraisa say that such a distinction exists even in regard to *muktzeh.* The second clause of the Baraisa should read as follows: בַּמֶּה דְבָרִים אֲמוּרִים בְּשֶׁל בַּעַל הַבַּיִת – **When was this ruling stated** [that there is no difference between moving tanned or untanned hides]? It was stated **in regard to** hides **of a householder.** אֲבָל בְּשֶׁל אוּמָּן לֹא – **But in regard to** hides **of a craftsman,** this statement is **not** true. Rather, only the untanned hides of a craftsman may be moved; his tanned hides, however, may not be moved because once the craftsman has tanned them he is particular with them. – ? –

The Gemara answers:

כּוּלָּהּ בְּבַעַל הַבַּיִת קָמַיְירֵי – **The entire [Baraisa] deals** solely **with a householder.** Thus, the only distinction the Baraisa could draw was in regard to *tumah,* because it is only in regard to *tumah* that there exists a difference between a householder's tanned and untanned hides. In regard to a craftsman, however, the Baraisa would in fact agree that this distinction exists even in reference to *muktzeh.*

The Gemara concludes:

כְּתַנָּאֵי – In fact, **it** [i.e. the question of whether or not the hides of a craftsman are considered *muktzeh*] **is a matter of** dispute between **Tannaim.** For it was taught in a Baraisa: עוֹרוֹת שֶׁל בַּעַל הַבַּיִת מְטַלְטְלִין אוֹתָן – **THE HIDES OF A HOUSEHOLDER MAY BE MOVED** וְשֶׁל אוּמָּן אֵין מְטַלְטְלִין אוֹתָן – **AND THOSE OF A CRAFTSMAN MAY NOT BE MOVED.** רַבִּי יוֹסֵי אוֹמֵר – **R' YOSE SAYS:** אֶחָד זֶה וְאֶחָד זֶה מְטַלְטְלִין אוֹתָן – **BOTH THESE AND THOSE MAY BE MOVED.**

The focus of discussion between the above-mentioned Amoraim (R' Yonasan ben Achinai, R' Yonasan ben Elazar and R' Chanina bar Chama) shifts to a different topic:

הֲדוּר יָתְבֵי וְקָמִיבַּעְיָא לְהוּ – **Again they sat and pondered** the following: הָא דִּתְנַן – Regarding **that which we learned in a Mishnah:**[3] אֲבוֹת מְלָאכוֹת אַרְבָּעִים חָסֵר אַחַת – **THE PRIMARY *MELACHOS* ARE FORTY MINUS ONE,** כְּנֶגֶד מִי – **to what do they correspond?**

Two views are propounded:

אָמַר לְהוּ רַבִּי חֲנִינָא בַּר חָמָא – **R' Chanina bar Chama said to [his colleagues]:** כְּנֶגֶד עֲבוֹדוֹת הַמִּשְׁכָּן – **They correspond to the labors of the Tabernacle,** i.e. to the thirty-nine activities necessary for the construction of the Tabernacle.[4]

אָמַר לְהוּ רַבִּי יוֹנָתָן בְּרַבִּי אֶלְעָזָר – **R' Yonasan the son of R' Elazar said to them:** כָּךְ אָמַר רַבִּי שִׁמְעוֹן בְּרַבִּי יוֹסֵי בֶּן לָקוֹנְיָא – **So said R' Shimon the son of R' Yose ben Lakonya:** כְּנֶגֶד ,,מְלָאכָה" ,,מְלַאכְתּוֹ" וּ,,מְלֶאכֶת" שֶׁבַּתּוֹרָה אַרְבָּעִים חָסֵר אַחַת – **They correspond to** the mentions of **"work," "his work" and "work of"** appearing **in the Torah,** which number **forty minus one.**[5]

A question is raised concerning the latter opinion:

בָּעֵי רַב יוֹסֵף – **Rav Yosef inquired:** ,,וַיָּבֹא הַבַּיְתָה לַעֲשׂוֹת מְלַאכְתּוֹ" מִמִּנְיָנָא הוּא אוֹ לֹא – **Is** the word "his work" in the verse

NOTES

1. On the weekdays (*Rashi;* cf. *Tosafos*; see *Ritva, MHK* ed.).

2. Untanned hides do not yet possess the status of a "utensil," the basic prerequisite necessary for an item to be capable of contracting *tumah.* See *Tosafos* ד״ה לא אמרו.

3. Below, 73a. [The phrase of the Mishnah cited here introduces the list of the thirty-nine forbidden *melachos*.]

4. Thirty-nine separate acts were necessary for the construction of the Mishkan and the preparation of its components. That these acts are the forms of work prohibited on the Sabbath is indicated by the Torah's juxtaposition [in the beginning of *Exodus* ch. 35] of the prohibition to do work on the Sabbath with the section concerning the construction of the Mishkan (*Rashi*).

5. [The word *melachah, work,* is mentioned in the Torah thirty-nine times.] Thus, when God stated at Sinai (*Exodus* 20:10): *You shall not do any work,* He meant: Do not perform any of the forms of work alluded to by the number of times the word "work" is mentioned in the Torah (*Rashi*).

The commentaries point out that in actual fact there are many more than thirty-nine mentions of the word *melachah* in the Torah. We must therefore say that the Gemara does not count all of the mentions. Various explanations have been advanced as to which mentions are excluded from the Gemara's count – see *Rabbeinu Chananel* (cited by *Ramban, Rashba* and *Ritva*), *Tos. Yom Tov* 7:2, *Mareh HaPanim* to *Yerushalmi Shabbos* ch. 7, and *Yefei Einayim* here. [Interestingly, *Netzach Yisrael* (cited by *Torah Sheleimah* to *Genesis* 39 §97) points out that if the possessive form מְלֶאכֶת, *work of,* is not counted, there are indeed exactly thirty-nine mentions of the word "work." However, this explanation does not accord with our text of the Gemara, which specifically states that the word מְלָאכָה is included in the count.]

Ramban explains that even R' Yonasan, who asserts that the number thirty-nine emerges from the number of times the word *melachah* appears in the Torah, agrees that the *melachos* also correspond to the *melachos* of the Mishkan, for if this were not the case, how could the Rabbis have determined to which thirty-nine forms of work the Torah refers? Rather, R' Yonasan means that the count of the words *melachah* in the Torah teaches us to *limit* the list of forbidden *melachos* to those that appeared in the Mishkan, which numbered thirty-nine, and not to include other forms of work as well. Cf. *Tosafos.*

עין משפט נר מצוה

טז א מיי' פכ"ו מהלכות שבת הלכה יב סמג לאוין סה טוש"ע או"ח סימן שח סעיף כה:
יז ב שם סעיף כו:
יח ג מיי' פכ"ו מהלכות שבת שם סמג שם טור שו"ע או"ח סימן רנט סעיף א:

רבינו חננאל

פושט עורות היה וקבלנו מרבותינו דהלכתא כר' יוסי דקיי"ל מעשה רב ואמר ר' ישמעאל בר' יוסי אבא שלחא הוה ואמר הביאו שלחין ונשב עליהן. נמצא כי עשה מעשה כשמועתו דתניא עורות של בעל הבית מטלטלין אותן. של אומן אין מטלטלין אותן. ר' יוסי אומר זה וזה מטלטלין הלכך עורות של אומן הואיל וראויין לישב עליהן ואין נפסדין אינו מקפיד עליהן ומותר לטלטלן. אבל נסרין של אומן הואיל ואם ישב עליהן נפגמין הלכך קפיד עליהן ואסור לטלטלן: **אמר** ר' חנינה הא דתנן אבות מלאכות ארבעים חסר אחת כנגד עבודות המשכן. ותניא כוותיה אין חייבין אלא על מלאכה שכיוצא בה היתה במשכן כיצד הן זרעו וקצרו והעלו קרשים מקרקע לעגלה אתם לא תזרעו ולא תקצרו כו' הא דתנן אבות מלאכות ארבעים חסר אחת כו'. וא"ר יונתן בן אלעזר כנגד מלאכת ומלאכה שבתורה א) והן ס"א. כשתוציא ג' מלאכות הכתובין ביריכולו השמים וד' שכתוב בהן ועשית ויעשה ותעשה ולרגל המלאכה וי"ג שכתב כל מלאכת עבודה הרי כ"א נשארו מ' ובכללם ששת ימים וכו' לא תעשה מלאכה. ולמה (זכה) כי בפירוש אמרו בתלמוד א"י שבא זה הכתוב להשלים ל"ט מלאכות בתורה ויש מי שמוציא מכלל אלו מ' ויבא יוסף הביתה לעשות מלאכתו. ונשארו ל"ט ויש מי שמוציא והמלאכה היתה דים ולדברי הכל נשארים ל"ט מלאכות: **פיס'** בגיזי צמר ואין מטלטלין אותן. וקיי"ל

חשק שלמה על רבינו חננאל

א) עי' רא"ש סימן ש"ג שמבאר היטב דברי הר"ח כמ"ש כאן ורמב"ן ורשב"א ט"ס:

רב נסים גאון

ולא אמרו עבודין אלא לענין טומאה בלבד. עיקר דיליה משיחכת במסכת חולין בפ' העור והרוטב (דף קכב) וכולן שעיבדן או שהילך בהן כדי עבודה טהורין ובתוספתא וכולן שעיבדן ושהילך בהן כדי עבודה טהורין משום עור: **אותיביה** ההוא מרבנן בר יומיה לרבא זה התלמיד אמרו עליו באותו היום נכנס לבית המדרש על כן קרו ליה בר יומיה וכיוצא בו אמרנו בשחיטת קדשים (זבחים פ"ה דף נז) היה שם תלמיד אחד שבא לשמש לבית

תוספות

אבא שלחא. פר"ח ואמר הביאו לי שלחין בשבת והלכה כר' יוסי דקי"ל מעשה רב וכן נראה דאי בחול איירי כדפי' בקונט' ולא מייתי ראיה אלא דאומן נמי לא קפיד טפי הוה ליה לאתויי דר' יוסי אבוה דשרי לקמן בהדיא של אומן: **לא** אמרו עבודין אלא לענין טומאה בלבד. פרש"י שאין עור מקבל טומאה עד לאחר עיבוד ואם תאמר והא אמר בזבחים בפ' דם חטאת (דף צג: ושם) מניין לרבות עור משהופשט תלמוד לומר אשר יזה עליה תכובס יכול אף עור שלא הופשט תלמוד לומר בגד מה בגד מקבל טומאה אף כל דבר המקבל טומאה משמע דעור משהופשט מקבל טומאה ויש לומר דהתם כשיחדו לישיבה והכא כשלא יחדו ואפ"ה מותר לטלטלו בשבת והא דאמר רבא בריש כל הכלים (לקמן קכג.) מדלענין טומאה לאו מנא הוא לענין שבת נמי לאו מנא הוא גבי מחט שניטל חורה או עוקצה ה"פ מדלענין טומאה לאו מנא הוא אפי' ע"י יחוד דניטל חורה או עוקצה טהורה ולא מהני בה יחוד והא דתנן במסכת כלים בפרק י"ג (משנה ה) מחט שניטל חורה או עוקצה טהורה ואם התקינה למיתוח טמאה אומר ר"י דהתם איירי כשעשה בה שום שינוי ותיקון למיתוח אבל ביחוד בעלמא למיתוח אינה טמאה אבל היכא דהוי מנא לענין טומאה ע"י יחוד לגבי שבת הוי מנא בלא יחוד וכן משמע התם דקאמר תרגמא אביי אליבא דרבא בגלמי דזימנין דמימליך עלייהו ומשוי להו מנא להכי מותר לטלטלה אע"ג דאכתי לא אימליך עלה והיא טהורה: **ארבעים** אבות מלאכות חסר אחת כנגד מי. דהרבה מלאכות יש דדמיין להדדי והוה לן למחשבינהו כולן כאחת כדפריך בפרק כלל גדול (לקמן עג:) היינו זורה היינו בורר היינו מרקד ומשום חילוק מועט שביניהם לא הוה מחלקינן להו אי לאו דקים להו דל"ט מלאכות הן כנגד שום דבר לכך בעי כנגד מי: **כנגד** כל מלאכה שבתורה. לכאורה נראה דיליף נמי ממשכן שהרי לכך נסמכה פרשת שבת לפרשת משכן ועוד דאי לא יליף ממשכן א"כ היכי ידעינן לדידיה הי ניהו אבות מלאכות והי תולדות דאין סברא לומר שמדעתם בירכו מלאכות החשובות ועשאום אבות ועוד דבהדיא תנן לקמן בהזורק ח) המושיט חייב שכך היתה עבודת הלוים אלא לפי שיש מלאכות דומות זו לזו ואנו עושין שתיהן אבות כגון מרקד וזורר לכך חלקום חכמים להשלים מנין מלאכות שבתורה הואיל וחלוקות קצת זו מזו ואי אפשר לומר כן דלא פליג מדקאמר בסמוך תניא כמ"ד כנגד עבודות המשכן משמע דפליגי ועוד למאן דלית ליה דרשא דמלאכת ומלאכה מנא ליה דחשיב זורה וזורר בשתים ועוד לקמן משמע דמטעם דכנגד עבודות המשכן גרידא אית לן לאחשובינהו בתרתי דקאמר אביי ורבא בפרק כלל גדול (לקמן עג:) כל מילתא דהואי במשכן אע"ג דאיכא דדמיא לה חשיב לה: **הם** העלו קרשים כו'. אפילו רבנן דפליגי ארבי יוסי ברבי יהודה גבי ט) נעץ קנה ברשות הרבים ובראשו טרסקל ולית להו גוד אחית מודו בעגלה שהיא רשות היחיד כיון דעגלה גופה יש אורך בזקיפה עשרה ורוחב ארבעה אע"פ שתחתיה רשות הרבים וברים כל גגות (עירובין פט.) [ד"ה במחילות] הארכתי יותר: **ואתם** אל תכניסו. ואפ"ה לא הויא אב כדפרישית לעיל (דף ב.) [ד"ה פשט]:

אלא

גמרא

אבא שלחא הוה א) ואמר הביאו שלחין ונשב עליהן מיתיבי ב) נסרין של בעה"ב מטלטלין אותן ושל אומן אין מטלטלין אותן ואם חישב לתת עליהן פת לאורחין בין כך ובין כך מטלטלין שאני נסרים דקפיד עלייהו ת"ש עורות בין עבודין ובין שאין עבודין מותר לטלטלן בשבת לא אמרו עבודין אלא לענין טומאה בלבד מאי לאו לא שנא של בעל הבית ולא שנא של אומן לא של בעה"ב אבל של אומן מאי אין מטלטלין אי הכי הא דתני ולא אמרו עבודין אלא לענין טומאה בלבד לפלוג וליתני בדידה בד"א בשל בעה"ב אבל בשל אומן לא כולה בבעל הבית קמיירי כתנאי עורות של בעה"ב מטלטלין אותן ושל אומן אין מטלטלין אותן ר' יוסי אומר אחד זה ואחד זה מטלטלין אותן: הדור יתבי וקמיבעיא להו הא א) דתנן אבות מלאכות ארבעים חסר אחת כנגד מי אמר להו ר' חנינא בר חמא כנגד עבודות המשכן אמר להו ר' יונתן בר' אלעזר כך אמר רבי שמעון ברבי יוסי בן לקוניא כנגד ג) מלאכה מלאכתו ומלאכת שבתורה ארבעים חסר אחת בעי רב יוסף א) ויבא הביתה לעשות מלאכתו ממנינא הוא או לא א"ל אביי וליתי ספר תורה ולימני מי לא ג) אמר רבה בר בר חנה א"ר יוחנן לא זזו משם עד שהביאו ספר תורה ומנאום אמר ליה כי קא מספקא לי משום דכתיב ב) והמלאכה היתה דים ממנינא הוא והא כמאן דאמר ד) לעשות צרכיו נכנס או דילמא ויבא הביתה לעשות מלאכתו ממנינא הוא והאי והמלאכה היתה דים הכי קאמר דשלים ליה עבידתא תיקו תניא כמאן דאמר כנגד עבודות המשכן דתניא אין חייבין אלא על מלאכה שכיוצא בה היתה במשכן הם זרעו ואתם לא תזרעו הם קצרו ואתם לא תקצרו הם העלו את הקרשים מקרקע לעגלה ואתם לא תכניסו מרה"ר לרה"י הם הורידו את הקרשים מעגלה לקרקע ואתם לא תוציאו מרה"י לרה"ר הם הוציאו מעגלה לעגלה ואתם לא תוציאו מרה"י לרה"י מרה"י לרשות היחיד מאי קא עביד אביי ורבא דאמרי תרווייהו ואיתימא רב אדא בר אהבה מרשות היחיד לרה"י דרך רשות הרבים: בגיזי צמר ואין מטלטלין: אמר רבא ג) לא שנו אלא שלא טמן בהן אבל טמן בהן מטלטלין אותן איתיביה ההוא מרבנן בר יומיה לרבא טומנין בגיזי צמר ואין מטלטלין אותן כיצד הוא עושה

נוטל

רש"י

שלחא הוה. אומן לעבד עורות: ואמר. בחול: הביאו שלחין ונשב עליהן. אלמא לא קפיד: דקפיד עלייהו. שמא יתקלקלו: ולא אמרו עבודין. לא הוזכרו לחלק בין עבודין לשאינן עבודין: אלא לענין טומאה. דעבודין מקבלין טומאה ולא שאינן עבודין: לפלוג בדידה. בטלטול גופיה איכא לפלוגי בשל אומן בין עבודין לשאינן עבודין דעבודין קפיד עלייהו: בד"א. דעבודין מותר לטלטלן בשל בעה"ב אבל של אומן מאחר שעבדן קפיד עלייהו: כולה בבעה"ב איירי. ומהדר ליפלוגי בבעה"ב דאיירי ביה ולא אשכח לפלוגי אלא לענין טומאה ואי שבקיה לבעה"ב דאיירי ביה ונקט אומן ה) מפסקה למילתיה טפי מדהשתא: הדור יתבי. הנך רבנן דלעיל: כנגד עבודות המשכן. אותן המנויות שם בפרק כלל גדול היו צריכין למשכן ופרשת שבת נסמכה לפרשת מלאכת המשכן ללמוד הימנה: שבתורה. שכתובים בכל התורה והכי קאמר קרא (שמות כ) לא תעשה כל מלאכה כמנין כל מלאכה שבתורה: לא זזו משם. ° לא ידענא היכא איתמר ומיהו [אפשר] לענין וי"ו דגחון אתמר מדפרכינן לה נמי בקדושין ו) גבי וי"ו דגחון ומתרצינן אינהו הוו בקיאי בחסרות ויתרות ש"מ לענין אותיות איתמר והכא ליכא לשנויי הכי: משום דכתיב והמלאכה היתה דים. ואי מנינן לתרוייהו הוו ארבעים ומדתנן אבות מלאכות ארבעים חסר אחת איכא חד דלא ממנינא ובהני תרי דאיכא למימר דלא מלאכה נינהו ולא ידענא הי מינייהו נפיק והכי קא מיבעיא ליה והמלאכה היתה דים ממנינא היא ומלאכה ממש קאמר והכי קאמר המלאכה שהיו עושין היו עושין די לא פחות מן הצורך ולא יותר מן הצורך כגון רידודי טסין לציפוי הקרשים לדי היו מרדדין אותם וכן בטווי של יריעות והאי לעשות מלאכתו הוא דמפיק ומסייע למאן דאמר במסכת סוטה לעשות צרכיו נכנס לשכב עמה אלא שנראתה לו דמות דיוקנו של אביו ואמר לו עתידין אחיך ליכתב על אבני אפוד רצונך שימחה שמך מביניהם כו' או דילמא האי לעשות מלאכתו מלאכה ממש הוא ומסייע לה לאידך: והאי והמלאכה היתה דים. לאו מלאכה היא אלא כדמשמע קרא בהבאת נדבה וכמאן דאמר שלימא ליה עבידתא מלאכת ההבאה שלא היו צריכין עוד וכל מידי דרמי עליה דאינש קרי ליה עבידתא כדאמרינן במסכת סוטה (דף לג.) בטילת עבידתא דאמר סנאה לאייתויא להיכלא ואינו אלא צבא מלחמה להחריב: הם זרעו וקצרו סמנין. לצבוע תכלת ועורות אילים וטחנו ולשו נמי סמנין לצבוע ואופה דקתני במתני' באבות מלאכות הוא בישול סמנין אלא דנקט סידורה דפת והכי מפרש בפרק כלל גדול (לקמן דף עד:): קרקע. רשות הרבים: עגלה. רשות היחיד שגבוהה י' ורחבה ד': דרך רשות הרבים. דאויר שבין העגלות רשות הרבים: אבל טמן בהן מטלטלין אותן. קס"ד השתא דמילי מילי קתני מתניתין ולאו אהנך דטמן בהן קאי: ההוא מרבנן בר יומיה. אותו היום בא לבית מדרשו תחלה ז):

נוטל

מסורת הש"ס

א) ב"ק ב. לקמן עג. וש"נ, ב) [ועי' תוי"ט שבת פ"ז מ"ב סד"ה אבות ועי' חידושי רמב"ן ורשב"א בשם פיר"ח], ג) קידושין ל. ע"ש, ד) סוטה לו:, ה) מ"א מספקא, ו) [דף ל.], ז) [פי' אמר רב אדי הוא דהוה קרי לי' בר בי רב דחד יומא בחגיגה ה: ערוך], ח) [דף לו.], ט) [לעיל ה. לקמן קא.].

גליון הש"ס

רש"י ד"ה לא זזו לא ידענא כו'. עיין ברכות דף כה ע"ב רש"י ד"ה מאן שמעת ליה וש"נ:

תורה אור השלם

א) וַיְהִי כְּהַיּוֹם הַזֶּה וַיָּבֹא הַבַּיְתָה לַעֲשׂוֹת מְלַאכְתּוֹ וְאֵין אִישׁ מֵאַנְשֵׁי הַבַּיִת שָׁם בַּבָּיִת: [בראשית לט, יא]

ב) וְהַמְּלָאכָה הָיְתָה דַיָּם לְכָל הַמְּלָאכָה לַעֲשׂוֹת אֹתָהּ וְהוֹתֵר: [שמות לו, ז]

ליקוטי רש"י

ויבא הביתה לעשות מלאכתו. רב ושמואל חד אמר מלאכתו ממש וחד אמר לעשות צרכיו עמה אלא שנראית לו דמות דיוקנו של אביו וכו' כדאיתא במסכת סוטה (לו:) [בראשית לט, יא]. **לעשות צרכיו.** תשמיש [סוטה לו:]. **והאי והמלאכה היתה דים.** ומלאכת ההבאה היתה דים של עושי המשכן לכל המלאכה של משכן לעשות אותה והותר [שמות לו, ז]. **דשלים ליה עבידתא.** שהיה הנדבה כדי להשלים [לקמן צו:]. **הם העלו את הקרשים מקרקע לעגלה.** שארבע עגלות היו לבני מררי שהיו נושאין קרשי המשכן והן הולכין שתים כאחד זו בצד זו כדאמרינן בגמרא וכשהיו פורקין את המשכן לטעון על העגלות היו מעמידין העגלות כדרך הליכתן שתים זו אצל זו סמוך למשכן ושתים זו אצל זו לפניהם דרך הליכתן לאורך רשות הרבים שהיו רוצים להלך אחר עמוד הענן ההולך לפניהם ופורקי המשכן היו מושיטין הקרשים לאותן שעל שתי העגלות הסמוכות למשכן והן מושיטין לאותן שלפניהם [שם.].

and he entered the house to do his work[6] **included in the count, or not?** וְלֵיתֵי סֵפֶר **— Abaye said to him:** אָמַר לֵיהּ אַבַּיֵי תּוֹרָה וְלִימְנֵי **— Let us bring a Torah scroll and count,** and we shall find the answer! מִי לֹא אָמַר רַבָּה בַּר בַּר חָנָה אָמַר רַבִּי יוֹחָנָן **—** For in regard to a similar question[7] **did not Rabbah bar bar Chanah** once **say:** לֹא זָזוּ מִשָּׁם עַד שֶׁהֵבִיאוּ סֵפֶר תּוֹרָה וּמְנָאוּם **— They did not move from there until they brought a Torah scroll and counted them?** Let us do the same![8] אָמַר לֵיהּ **— [Rav Yosef] answered him:** כִּי קָא מְסַפְּקָא לִי מִשּׁוּם דִּכְתִיב **— The reason I am in doubt is because it is** also **written:** ,,וְהַמְּלָאכָה הָיְתָה דַיָּם'' **— *And the work was enough.***[9] That is, counting both verses (*and he entered the house to do his work* and *and the work was enough*) there are in fact *forty* mentions of the word "work" in the Torah. The question thus is: מִמִּנְיָנָא הוּא **— Is the word** "work" in the verse **[*and the work was enough*]** understood to mean actual work? If so, it is **included in the count.** וְהָא כְּמַאן דְּאָמַר לַעֲשׂוֹת צְרָכָיו נִכְנַס **— And** the word "work" in the verse *and he entered the house to do his work* would then not be included in the count, because **this** verse would be expounded **in accordance with the** view of **the one who says** that it was **to "perform his needs,"** i.e. to cohabit with the wife of Potiphar, that **[Joseph] entered.**[10] Accordingly, the word "work" in this verse does not refer to actual work, but is rather a euphemism for cohabitation.[11] אוֹ דִילְמָא **— Or perhaps** the word "work" in the verse ,,וַיָּבֹא הַבַּיְתָה לַעֲשׂוֹת מְלַאכְתּוֹ'' מִמִּנְיָנָא הוּא **— *and he entered the house to do his work* is included in the count,** because it refers to Joseph's actual work, i.e. his household chores, וְהַאי ,,וְהַמְּלָאכָה הָיְתָה דַיָּם'' הָכִי קָאָמַר **— and this** verse ***and the work was enough*** is *not* included in the count, for it **means as follows,** דִּשְׁלִים לֵיהּ עֲבִידְתָּא **— that the task** of bringing donations to the Tabernacle **was completed.**[12]

The Gemara concludes:

תֵּיקוּ **— Let [the question] stand** unresolved.

The Gemara cites support for one of the views cited above as to the source for the number thirty-nine:

תַּנְיָא כְּמַאן דְּאָמַר כְּנֶגֶד עֲבוֹדוֹת הַמִּשְׁכָּן **— A Baraisa was taught in accordance with the one who says** that the number thirty-nine **corresponds to the** thirty-nine **labors of the Tabernacle.** דְּתַנְיָא **— For it was taught in a Baraisa:** אֵין חַיָּיבִין אֶלָּא עַל מְלָאכָה שֶׁכַּיּוֹצֵא בָהּ הָיְתָה בַּמִּשְׁכָּן **— ONE IS NOT LIABLE EXCEPT FOR A LABOR THE LIKES OF WHICH WAS** performed **IN THE TABERNACLE.** For example, הֵם זָרְעוּ וְאַתֶּם לֹא תִּזְרְעוּ **— THEY PLANTED, AND** likewise **YOU SHALL NOT PLANT;** הֵם קָצְרוּ וְאַתֶּם לֹא תִּקְצְרוּ **— THEY REAPED, AND** likewise **YOU SHALL NOT REAP;**[13] הֵם הֶעֱלוּ אֶת הַקְּרָשִׁים מִקַּרְקַע לָעֲגָלָה **— THEY LIFTED THE** Tabernacle **BOARDS FROM THE GROUND** of the public domain **ONTO THE WAGON,** which was a private domain,[14] וְאַתֶּם לֹא תַּכְנִיסוּ מֵרְשׁוּת הָרַבִּים לִרְשׁוּת הַיָּחִיד **— AND** likewise **YOU SHALL NOT BRING** articles **IN FROM THE PUBLIC DOMAIN TO THE PRIVATE DOMAIN;** הֵם הוֹרִידוּ אֶת הַקְּרָשִׁים מֵעֲגָלָה לְקַרְקַע **— THEY LOWERED THE BOARDS FROM THE WAGON TO THE GROUND,** וְאַתֶּם לֹא תּוֹצִיאוּ מֵרְשׁוּת הַיָּחִיד לִרְשׁוּת הָרַבִּים **— AND** likewise **YOU SHALL NOT TAKE** articles **OUT FROM THE PRIVATE DOMAIN TO THE PUBLIC DOMAIN;** הֵם הוֹצִיאוּ מֵעֲגָלָה לָעֲגָלָה **— THEY TRANSFERRED** the boards **FROM WAGON TO WAGON,**[15] וְאַתֶּם לֹא תּוֹצִיאוּ מֵרְשׁוּת הַיָּחִיד לִרְשׁוּת הַיָּחִיד **— AND** likewise **YOU SHALL NOT TRANSFER** articles **FROM** one **PRIVATE DOMAIN TO** another **PRIVATE DOMAIN.**

The Gemara asks:

מֵרְשׁוּת הַיָּחִיד לִרְשׁוּת הַיָּחִיד מַאי קָא עָבִיד **— From** one **private domain to** another **private domain? What does one do** wrong by transferring in this manner?[16]

The Gemara answers:

אַבַּיֵי וְרָבָא דְּאָמְרֵי תַּרְוַיְיהוּ **— Abaye and Rava both say,** וְאִיתֵימָא רַב אַדָּא בַּר אַהֲבָה **— and others say** it was **Rav Adda bar Ahavah:** The Baraisa means: מֵרְשׁוּת הַיָּחִיד לִרְשׁוּת הַיָּחִיד דֶּרֶךְ רְשׁוּת הָרַבִּים **— From** one **private domain to** another **private domain by way of the public domain.**[17]

The Mishnah states:

בְּגִיזֵּי צֶמֶר וְאֵין מְטַלְטְלִין **—** One may insulate **WITH WOOL SHEARINGS BUT ONE MAY NOT MOVE THEM.**

This ruling is qualified:

אָמַר רָבָא **— Said Rava:** לֹא שָׁנוּ אֶלָּא שֶׁלֹּא טָמַן בָּהֶן **— They did not teach** the ruling that wool shearings may not be moved **except where one did not insulate with them.** אֲבָל טָמַן בָּהֶן מְטַלְטְלִין אוֹתָן **— But where he insulated with them, they may be moved.**[18]

NOTES

6. *Genesis* 39:11. The verse refers to Joseph, and goes on to relate how, after he entered the house, the wife of his master Potiphar attempted to seduce him.

7. [*Rashi* states that he is unsure as to exactly what question this refers.]

8. Let us simply count all the mentions of the word *melachah* in the Torah and see if this verse is included in the tally of the thirty-nine (see, however, note 5).

9. *Exodus* 36:7. The verse relates that when asked to contribute materials for the sake of the building of the Mishkan, the Jews responded so enthusiastically that soon there was enough.

10. The Gemara in *Sotah* 36b cites an opinion which interprets the verse to mean that Joseph initially entered the house intending to sin with Potiphar's wife (i.e. to "do his work"), but that he overcame his desire at the last moment (see *Rashi*).

11. However, according to this position the word "work" in the verse *and the work was enough* refers to actual work; i.e. it means that all the work necessary for the construction, such as the production of the gold plating for the boards and the weaving of the curtains, was completed (see *Rashi* and *Rashash*).

12. A task is sometimes referred to as "work." The verse means that the task that the Jews had undertaken to bring donations to the Mishkan was sufficient to supply it with all its needs. The verse does not refer to actual work, however. Thus, it is not included in the count of the thirty-nine (*Rashi*; see also *Rashi* ad loc.; cf. *Ramban* there).

[Thus Rav Yosef answered that bringing a Torah scroll would be of no use, as his uncertainty was based on how to *understand* the verses.]

13. Herbs were planted and reaped to provide the dyes necessary for coloring the various skins and wools needed in the Mishkan (*Rashi*; see *Eglai Tal, P'sichah,* 1:26, 27).

14. As part of the system employed in the Wilderness for transporting the Mishkan from place to place, two pairs of wagons were parked in the public domain in front of the Mishkan, one pair behind the other, and the boards which formed the walls of the Mishkan were loaded onto the wagons. The wagons each measured at least four by four *tefachim* and possessed walls ten *tefachim* high. This gave them the status of private domains. Hence, the Leviim passed objects from the *reshus harabim* to a *reshus hayachid (Rashi)*.

15. Leviim standing on the ground passed the boards to Leviim standing on the two wagons parked closest to the Mishkan. These Leviim, in turn, passed the boards to Leviim standing on the second set of two wagons parked in front of the first. Thus, boards were passed from one private domain to the other.

16. It is Biblically permitted to transfer from one *reshus hayachid* to another!

17. The two sets of wagons were not parked flush up against each other; rather, a strip of the public domain separated between them. Thus, we learn from the Leviim's actions that it is forbidden to pass an object from one *reshus hayachid* to another *reshus hayachid* via a *reshus harabim*. (This is the *toladah* of מושיט, *handing over,* and is discussed by the Mishnah on 96a; see *Dibros Moshe* 39:14.)

18. Rava presently understands the phrase in the Mishnah "but one may not move them" to be referring to where the wool shearings were not used for insulating a pot. However, where the shearings were used for insulation, they are no longer *muktzeh* (*Rashi*).

אבא שלחא הוה [א] ואמר הביאו שלחין ונשב עליהן מיתיבי [ב] נסרין של בעה"ב מטלטלין אותן ושל אומן אין מטלטלין אותן ואם חישב לתת עליהן פת לאורחין בין כך ובין כך מטלטלין שאני נסרים דקפיד עלייהו ת"ש עורות בין עבודין ובין שאין עבודין מותר לטלטלן בשבת לא אמרו עבודין אלא לענין טומאה בלבד מאי לאו לא שנא של בעל הבית ולא שנא של אומן לא של בעה"ב אבל של אומן מאי אין מטלטלין אי הכי הא דתני ולא אמרו עבודין אלא לענין טומאה בלבד לפלוג וליתני בדידה בד"א בשל בעה"ב אבל בשל אומן לא כולה בבעל הבית קמיירי כתנאי עורות של בעה"ב מטלטלין אותן ושל אומן אין מטלטלין אותן ר' יוסי אומר אחד זה ואחד זה מטלטלין אותן: הדור יתבי וקמיבעיא להו הא [ה] דתנן אבות מלאכות ארבעים חסר אחת כנגד מי אמר להו ר' חנינא בר חמא כנגד עבודות המשכן אמר להו ר' יונתן בר' אלעזר כך אמר רבי שמעון ברבי יוסי בן לקוניא כנגד [ג] מלאכה מלאכתו ומלאכת שבתורה ארבעים חסר אחת בעי רב יוסף [א] ויבא הביתה לעשות מלאכתו ממנינא הוא או לא א"ל אביי וליתי ספר תורה ולימני מי לא [ג] אמר רבה בר בר חנה א"ר יוחנן לא זזו משם עד שהביאו ספר תורה ומנאום אמר ליה כי קא מספקא לי משום דכתיב [ב] והמלאכה היתה דים ממנינא הוא והא כמאן דאמר [ד] לעשות צרכיו נכנס או דילמא ויבא הביתה לעשות מלאכתו ממנינא הוא והאי והמלאכה היתה דים הכי קאמר דשלים ליה עבידתא תיקו תניא כמאן דאמר כנגד עבודות המשכן דתניא אין חייבין אלא על מלאכה שכיוצא בה היתה במשכן הם זרעו ואתם לא תזרעו הם קצרו ואתם לא תקצרו הם העלו את הקרשים מקרקע לעגלה ואתם לא תכניסו מרה"ר לרה"י הם הורידו את הקרשים מעגלה לקרקע ואתם לא תוציאו מרה"י לרה"ר הם הוציאו מעגלה לעגלה ואתם לא תוציאו מרה"י לרה"י מרה"י לרשות היחיד מאי קא עביד אביי ורבא דאמרי תרווייהו ואיתימא רב אדא בר אהבה מרשות היחיד לרה"י דרך רשות הרבים: בגיזי צמר ואין מטלטלין: אמר רבא [ג] לא שנו אלא שלא טמן בהן אבל טמן בהן מטלטלין אותן איתיביה ההוא מרבנן בר יומיה לרבא טומנין בגיזי צמר ואין מטלטלין אותן כיצד הוא עושה

נוטל

רש"י

שלחא הוה. אומן לעבד עורות: ואמר. בחול: הביאו שלחין ונשב עליהן. אלמא לא קפיד: דקפיד עלייהו. שמא יתקלקלו: ולא אמרו עבודין. לא הוזכרו לחלק בין עבודין לשאינן עבודין: אלא לענין טומאה. דעבודין מקבלין טומאה ולא שאינן עבודין: לפלוג בדידה. בטלטול גופיה איכא לפלוגי בשל אומן בין עבודין לשאינן עבודין דעבודין קפיד עלייהו: בד"א. דעבודין מותר לטלטלן בשל בעה"ב אבל של אומן מאחר שעבדן קפיד עלייהו: כולה בבעה"ב איירי. ומהדר ליפלוגי בבעה"ב דאיירי ביה ולא אשכח לפלוגי אלא לענין טומאה ואי שבקיה לבעה"ב דאיירי ביה ונקט אומן [ה] מפסקה למילתיה טפי מדהשתא: הדור יתבי. הנך רבנן דלעיל: כנגד עבודות המשכן. אותן המנויות שם בפרק כלל גדול היו צריכין למשכן ופרשת שבת נסמכה לפרשת מלאכת המשכן ללמוד הימנה: שבתורה. שכתובים בכל התורה והכי קאמר קרא (שמות כ) לא תעשה כל מלאכה כמנין כל מלאכה שבתורה: לא זזו משם. ° לא ידענא היכא איתמר ומיהו [אפשר] לענין וי"ו דגחון אתמר מדפרכינן לה נמי בקדושין [ו] גבי וי"ו דגחון ומתרצינן אינהו הוו בקיאי בחסרות ויתרות ש"מ לענין אותיות איתמר והכא ליכא לשנויי הכי: משום דכתיב והמלאכה היתה דים. ואי מנין לתרוייהו הוו ארבעים ומדתנן אבות מלאכות ארבעים חסר אחת איכא חד דלא ממנינא ובהני תרי דאיכא למימר דלא מלאכה נינהו ולא ידענא הי מינייהו נפיק והכי קא מיבעיא ליה והמלאכה היתה דים ממנינא היא ומלאכה ממש קאמר והכי קאמר המלאכה שהיו עושין היו עושין די לא פחות מן הצורך ולא יותר מן הצורך כגון רידודי טסין לציפוי הקרשים לדי היו מרדדין אותם וכן בטווי של יריעות והאי לעשות מלאכתו הוא דמפיק ומסייע למאן דאמר במסכת סוטה לעשות צרכיו נכנס לשכב עמה אלא שנראתה לו דמות דיוקנו של אביו ואמר לו עתידין אחיך ליכתב על אבני אפוד רצונך שימחה שמך מביניהם כו' או דילמא האי לעשות מלאכתו מלאכה ממש הוא ומסייע לה לאידך: והאי והמלאכה היתה דים. לאו מלאכה היא אלא כדמשמע קרא בהבאת נדבה וכמאן דאמר שלימא ליה עבידתא מלאכת ההבאה שלא היו צריכין עוד וכל מידי דרמי עליה דאינש קרי ליה עבידתא כדאמרינן במסכת סוטה (דף לג.) בטילת עבידתא דאמר סנאה לאייתויא להיכלא ואינו אלא צבא מלחמה להחריב: הם זרעו וקצרו סמנין. לצבוע תכלת ועורות אילים וטחנו ולשו נמי סמנין לצבוע ואופה דקתני במתני' באבות מלאכות הוא בישול סמנין אלא דנקט סידורה דפת והכי מפרש בפרק כלל גדול (לקמן דף עד:): קרקע. רשות הרבים: עגלה. רשות היחיד שגבוהה י' ורחבה ד': דרך רשות הרבים. לאויר שבין העגלות רשות הרבים: אבל טמן בהן מטלטלין אותן. קס"ד השתא דמילי מילי קתני מתניתין ולאו אהנך דטמן בהן קאי: ההוא מרבנן בר יומיה. אותו היום בא לבית מדרשו תחלה [ז]:

נוטל

תוספות

אבא שלחא. פר"ח ואמר הביאו לי שלחין בשבת והלכה כר' יוסי דקי"ל מעשה רב וכן נראה דאי בחול איירי כדפי' בקונט' ולא מייתי ראיה אלא דאומן נמי לא קפיד טפי הוה ליה לאתויי דר' יוסי אבוה דשרי לקמן בהדיא של אומן: לא אמרו עבודין אלא לענין טומאה בלבד. פרש"י שאין עור מקבל טומאה עד לאחר עיבוד ואם תאמר והא אמר בזבחים בפ' דם חטאת (דף צג: ושם) מניין לרבות עור משהופשט תלמוד לומר אשר יזה עליה תכובס יכול אף עור שלא הופשט תלמוד לומר בגד מה בגד מקבל טומאה אף כל דבר המקבל טומאה משמע דעור משהופשט מקבל טומאה ויש לומר דהתם כשיחדו לישיבה והכא כשלא יחדו ואפ"ה מותר לטלטלו בשבת והא דאמר רבא בריש כל הכלים (לקמן קכג.) מדלענין טומאה לאו מנא הוא לענין שבת נמי לאו מנא הוא גבי מחט שניטל חורה או עוקצה ה"פ מדלענין טומאה לאו מנא הוא אפי' ע"י יחוד דניטל חורה או עוקצה טהורה ולא מהני בה יחוד והא דתנן במסכת כלים בפרק י"ג (משנה ה) מחט שניטל חורה או עוקצה טהורה ואם התקינה למיתוח טמאה אומר ר"י דהתם איירי כשעשה בה שום שינוי ותיקון למיתוח אבל ביחוד בעלמא למיתוח אינה טמאה אבל היכא דהוי מנא לענין טומאה ע"י יחוד לגבי שבת הוי מנא בלא יחוד וכן משמע התם דקאמר תרגמא אביי אליבא דרבא בגלמי דזימנין דמימליך עלייהו ומשוי להו מנא להכי מותר לטלטלה אע"ג דאכתי לא אימליך עלה והיא טהורה: ארבעים אבות מלאכות חסר אחת כנגד מי. דהרבה מלאכות יש דדמיין להדדי והוה לן למחשבינהו כולן כאחת כדפריך בפרק כלל גדול (לקמן עג:) היינו זורה היינו בורר היינו מרקד ומשום חילוק מועט שביניהם לא הוה מחלקינן להו אי לאו דקים להו דל"ט מלאכות הן כנגד שום דבר לכך בעי כנגד מי: כנגד כל מלאכה שבתורה. לכאורה נראה דיליף נמי ממשכן שהרי לכך נסמכה פרשת שבת לפרשת משכן ועוד דאי לא יליף ממשכן א"כ היכי ידעינן לדידיה הי ניניהו אבות מלאכות והי תולדות דאין סברא לומר שמדעתם בירו מלאכות החשובות ועשאום אבות ועוד דבהדיא תנן לקמן בהזורק [ח] המושיט חייב שכך היתה עבודת הלוים אלא לפי שיש מלאכות דומות זו לזו ואנו עושין שתיהן אבות כגון מרקד ובורר לכך חלקום חכמים להשלים מנין מלאכות שבתורה הואיל וחלוקות קצת זו מזו ואי אפשר לומר כן דלא פליג מדקאמר בסמוך תניא כמ"ד כנגד עבודות המשכן משמע דפליגי ועוד למאן דלית ליה דרשא דמלאכת ומלאכה מנא ליה דחשיב זורה ובורר בשתים ועוד לקמן משמע דמטעם דכנגד עבודות המשכן גרידא אית לן לאחשובינהו בתרתי דקאמר אביי ורבא בפרק כלל גדול (לקמן עג:) כל מילתא דהואי במשכן אע"ג דאיכא דדמיא לה חשיב לה: הם העלו קרשים כו'. אפילו רבנן דפליגי ארבי יוסי ברבי יהודה גבי [ט] נעץ קנה ברשות הרבים ובראשו טרסקל ולית להו גוד אסיק מודו בעגלה שהיא רשות היחיד כיון דעגלה גופה יש אורך בזקיפה עשרה ורוחב ארבעה אע"פ שתחתיה רשות הרבים ובריש כל גגות (עירובין פט.) [ד"ה במחילות] הארכתי יותר: ואתם אל תכניסו. ואפ"ה לא הויא אב כדפרישית לעיל (דף ב.) [ד"ה פשט]:

אלא

עין משפט נר מצוה

טז א מיי' פכ"ו מהלכות שבת הלכה יב סמג לאוין סה טוש"ע או"ח סימן שח סעיף כה:
יז ב שם סעיף כו:
יח ג מיי' פכ"ו מהלכות שבת שם סמג שם טור שו"ע או"ח סימן רנט סעיף א:

רבינו חננאל

פושט עורות היה וקבלנו מרבותינו דהלכתא כר' יוסי דקיי"ל מעשה רב ואמר ר' ישמעאל בר' יוסי אבא שלחא הוה ואמר הביאו שלחין ונשב עליהן. נמצא כי עשה מעשה כשמועתו דתניא עורות של בעל הבית מטלטלין אותן. של אומן אין מטלטלין אותן. ר' יוסי אומר זה וזה מטלטלין הלכך עורות של אומן הואיל וראויין לישב עליהן ואין נפסדין אינו מקפיד עליהן ומותר לטלטלן. אבל נסרין של אומן הואיל ואם ישב עליהן נפגמין הלכך קפיד עליהן ואסור לטלטלן: **אמר** ר' חנינה הא דתנן אבות מלאכות ארבעים חסר אחת כנגד עבודות המשכן. ותניא כוותיה אין חייבין אלא על מלאכה שכיוצא בה היתה במשכן כיצד הן זרעו וקצרו והעלו קרשים מקרקע לעגלה אתם לא תזרעו ולא תקצרו כו' הא דתנן אבות מלאכות ארבעים חסר אחת כו'. וא"ר יונתן בן אלעזר כנגד מלאכת ומלאכה שבתורה [א] והן ס"א. כשתוציא ג' מלאכות הכתובין בויכולו השמים וד' שכתוב בהן ועשית ויעשה ותעשה ולרגל המלאכה וי"ג שכתב כל מלאכת עבודה הרי כ"א נשארו מ' ובכללם ששת ימים וכו' לא תעשה מלאכה. ולמה (זכה) כי בפירוש אמרו בתלמוד א"י שבא זה הכתוב להשלים ל"ט מלאכות בתורה ויש מי שמוציא מכלל אלו מ' ויבא יוסף הביתה לעשות מלאכתו. ונשארו ל"ט ויש מי שמוציא והמלאכה היתה דים ולדברי הכל נשארים ל"ט מלאכות: **פיס'** בגיזי צמר ואין מטלטלין אותן. וקיי"ל

חשק שלמה על רבינו חננאל

[א] עי' ראב"ן סימן ש"נ שמבאר היטב דברי הר"ח כמ"ש כאן ורמב"ן ורשב"א ע"ש:

רב נסים גאון

ולא אמרו עבודין אלא לענין טומאה בלבד. עיקר דיליה מישתכח במסכת חולין בפ' העור והרוטב (דף קכב) וכולן שעיבדן או שהילך בהן כדי עבודה טהורין ובתוספתא וכולן שעיבדן ושהילך בהן כדי עבודה טהורין משום עור: **אותיביה** ההוא מרבנן בר יומיה לרבא זה התלמיד אמרו עליו באותו היום נכנס לבית המדרש על כן קרו ליה בר יומיה וכיוצא בו אמרנו בשחיטת קדשים (זבחים פ"ה דף נז) היה שם תלמיד אחד שבא לשמש לבית

מסורת הש"ס

א) ב"ק ב. לקמן עג. וש"נ, ב) [ועי' תוי"ט שבת פ"ז מ"ב סד"ה אבות ועי' חידושי רמב"ן ורשב"א בשם פיר"ח], ג) קידושין ל. ע"ש, ד) סוטה לו:, ה) ס"א מספקא, ו) [דף ל.], ז) [פי' אמר רב אידי הוה דהוה קרי לי' בר בי רב דחד יומא בחגיגה ה: ערוך], ח) [דף צו.], ט) [לעיל ה. לקמן קא.].

גליון הש"ס

רש"י ד"ה לא זזו לא ידענא כו'. עיין ברכות דף כה ע"ב רש"י ד"ה מאן שמעת ליה וש"נ:

תורה אור השלם

א) וַיְהִי כְּהַיּוֹם הַזֶּה וַיָּבֹא הַבַּיְתָה לַעֲשׂוֹת מְלַאכְתּוֹ וְאֵין אִישׁ מֵאַנְשֵׁי הַבַּיִת שָׁם בַּבָּיִת: [בראשית לט, יא]

ב) וְהַמְּלָאכָה הָיְתָה דַיָּם לְכָל הַמְּלָאכָה לַעֲשׂוֹת אֹתָהּ וְהוֹתֵר: [שמות לו, ז]

ליקוטי רש"י

ויבא הביתה לעשות מלאכתו. רב ושמואל חד אמר מלאכתו ממש וחד אמר לעשות צרכיו עמה אלא שנראית לו דמות דיוקנו של אביו וכו' כדאיתא במסכת סוטה (לו:) [בראשית לט, יא]. **לעשות צרכיו.** תשמיש [סוטה לו:]. **והאי והמלאכה היתה דים.** ומלאכת ההבאה היתה דים של עושי המשכן לכל המלאכה של משכן לעשות אותה ולהותר [שמות לו, ז]. **דשלים ליה עבידתא.** שהיה הנדבה כדי להשלים [לקמן צו:]. **הם העלו את הקרשים מקרקע לעגלה.** שארבע עגלות היו לבני מררי שהיו נושאין קרשי המשכן והן הולכין שתים כאחד זו בצד זו כדאמרינן בגמרא וכשהיו פורקין את המשכן לטעון על העגלות היו מעמידין העגלות כדרך הליכתן שתים זו אצל זו סמוך למשכן ושתים זו אצל זו לפניהם דרך הליכתן לאורך רשות הרבים שהיו רוצים להלך אחר עמוד הענן ההולך לפניהם ופורקי המשכן היו מושיטין הקרשים לאותן שעל שתי העגלות הסמוכות למשכן והן מושיטין לאותן שלפניהם [שם.].

Rava's ruling is questioned:

אֵיתִיבֵיהּ הַהוּא מֵרַבָּנָן בַּר יוֹמֵיהּ לְרָבָא – **A certain student of one day's standing** [one who had come to the study hall that day for the first time] **challenged** the ruling of **Rava.**[19] The Mishnah states: טוֹמְנִין בְּגִיזֵּי צֶמֶר וְאֵין מְטַלְטְלִין אוֹתָן – One may insulate WITH WOOL SHEARINGS BUT HE MAY NOT MOVE THEM. כֵּיצַד הוּא עוֹשֶׂה – WHAT SHOULD HE DO to gain access to the pot?

NOTES

19. [From the Gemara below it is evident that the Gemara here does not mean that the student actually spoke to Rava. Rather, he challenged the *ruling* of Rava (*Ritva MHK* ed., *R' Yaakov Emden;* cf. *Tosafos* to 50a ד״ה אלא).]

נוֹטֵל אֶת הַכִּיסּוּי וְהֵן נוֹפְלוֹת – HE REMOVES THE LID AND THEY FALL, i.e. they slide off by themselves. Thus, we see that even after being used for insulation, the shearings may not be moved except indirectly. – ? –

The Gemara revises Rava's ruling:

אֶלָּא אִי אִיתְּמַר הָכִי אִיתְּמַר – Rather, if [Rava's ruling] was stated at all, **this is how it was stated: אָמַר רָבָא – Rava said: לֹא שָׁנוּ אֶלָּא שֶׁלֹּא יִחֲדָן לְהַטְמָנָה – They did not teach** that wool shearings may not be moved **except if one did not** permanently **designate them for insulating, אֲבָל יִחֲדָן לְהַטְמָנָה מְטַלְטְלִין אוֹתָן – but if one** permanently **designated them for insulating, they may be moved.** According to this revised version, Rava agrees that merely using the shearings for insulation one time without permanently designating them for this purpose does not relieve them of their *muktzeh* status.

The Gemara adduces support for this revised ruling:

אִיתְּמַר נַמִּי – It was also said: כִּי אָתָא רָבִין אָמַר רַבִּי יַעֲקֹב אָמַר רַבִּי אַסִּי בֶּן שָׁאוּל אָמַר רַבִּי – When Ravin came, he stated in the name of R' Yaakov who stated in the name of R' Assi ben Shaul who stated in the name of Rebbi: לֹא שָׁנוּ אֶלָּא שֶׁלֹּא יִחֲדָן לְהַטְמָנָה – They did not teach that wool shearings may not be moved **except if one did not** permanently **designate them for insulating, אֲבָל יִחֲדָן לְהַטְמָנָה מְטַלְטְלִין אוֹתָן – but if one** permanently **designated them for insulating, they may be moved.**

Another Amora disputes this revision:

רָבִינָא אוֹמֵר – Ravina said: Actually, Rava's ruling is as cited originally, that merely using the wool shearings once relieves them of their *muktzeh* status. And as for the fact that our Mishnah indicates otherwise, Rava was not referring to our Mishnah's case.[1] **בְּשֶׁל הֶפְתֵּק שָׁנוּ** – Rather, when **they taught** in the Mishnah that wool shearings may not be moved even after having been used for insulation, they spoke only **in reference to** wool shearings **of a warehouse,** i.e. shearings that a merchant stocks on his shelves for sale. Such shearings, even if removed from the shelves, are destined to be returned there. They therefore remain *muktzeh*. Rava, on the other hand, was referring to ordinary shearings. These lose their *muktzeh* status even if used for insulation only once.[2]

The Gemara adduces support for this ruling:

תַּנְיָא נַמִּי הָכִי – It was also taught so in a Baraisa: גִּיזֵּי צֶמֶר שֶׁל הֶפְתֵּק אֵין מְטַלְטְלִין אוֹתָן – WOOL SHEARINGS OF A WAREHOUSE MAY NOT BE MOVED. וְאִם הִתְקִינָן בַּעַל הַבַּיִת לְהִשְׁתַּמֵּשׁ בָּהֶן מְטַלְטְלִין אוֹתָן – BUT IF THE HOUSEHOLDER PREPARED THEM TO USE THEM, THEY MAY BE MOVED.

The Gemara digresses to discuss how other *muktzeh* items may be released from their *muktzeh* status:

תָּנָא רַבָּה בַּר בַּר חָנָה קַמֵּיהּ דְּרַב – Rabbah bar bar Chanah taught a Baraisa before Rav: חֲרָיוֹת שֶׁל דֶּקֶל שֶׁגְּדָרָן לְעֵצִים – If one had hardened **BRANCHES OF A DATE PALM THAT ONE HARVESTED FOR** fire**WOOD**, which are *muktzeh*, **וְנִמְלַךְ עֲלֵיהֶן לִישִׁיבָה – AND HE** then **CHANGED HIS MIND REGARDING THEM** and decided to use them **FOR SITTING**, i.e. as a seat, **צָרִיךְ לִקְשֹׁר – HE MUST TIE** them into bundles before the Sabbath in order to render them non-*muktzeh*. **רַבָּן שִׁמְעוֹן בֶּן גַּמְלִיאֵל אוֹמֵר – RABBAN SHIMON BEN GAMLIEL SAYS: אֵין צָרִיךְ לִקְשֹׁר – HE NEED NOT TIE THEM.** It is sufficient if he merely intends to sit on them on the Sabbath. **הוּא תָּנֵי לָהּ וְהוּא אָמַר לָהּ – He** [Rabbah bar bar Chanah] **taught [the Baraisa] and he commented about it: הֲלָכָה כְּרַבָּן שִׁמְעוֹן בֶּן גַּמְלִיאֵל – The halachah follows Rabban Shimon ben Gamliel.**

The Gemara cites a parallel Amoraic dispute regarding this matter:

אִיתְּמַר – It was said: רַב אָמַר קוֹשֵׁר – Rav says: To release the branches from their *muktzeh* status, **he ties** them into bundles. **וּשְׁמוּאֵל אָמַר חוֹשֵׁב – And Shmuel says: He intends** to sit on them. **וְרַב אַסִּי אָמַר יוֹשֵׁב – And Rav Assi says: He sits** on them on Friday, **אַף עַל פִּי שֶׁלֹּא קִישֵׁר וְאַף עַל פִּי שֶׁלֹּא חִישֵּׁב – even though he did not tie** them **and even though he did not intend** to sit on them.[3]

The Gemara asks:

בִּשְׁלָמָא רַב הוּא דְּאָמַר כְּתַנָּא קַמָּא – It is well in regard to **Rav,** for **he rules according to the Tanna Kamma. וּשְׁמוּאֵל נַמִּי הוּא דְּאָמַר כְּרַבָּן שִׁמְעוֹן בֶּן גַּמְלִיאֵל – And Shmuel also** is understandable, for **he rules according to Rabban Shimon ben Gamliel. אֶלָּא רַב אַסִּי דְּאָמַר כְּמַאן – But Rav Assi, in accordance with whom does he rule?** None of the above Tannaim are so lenient as to permit merely sitting on the branches on Friday, without tying them or intending to sit on them tomorrow. – ? –

The Gemara answers:

הוּא דְּאָמַר כִּי הַאי תַּנָּא – [Rav Assi] stated his ruling **in accordance with the following Tanna. דְּתַנְיָא – For it was taught in a Baraisa: יוֹצְאִין בְּפָקוֹרִין וּבְצִיפָא – ONE MAY GO OUT** into the public domain on the Sabbath **WITH COMBED FLAX OR COMBED WOOL** applied to his wound, **בִּזְמַן שֶׁצְּבָעָן בְּשֶׁמֶן וּכְרָכָן בִּמְשִׁיחָה – PROVIDED THAT HE DIPPED THEM INTO OIL** before the Sabbath **AND WRAPPED THEM AROUND WITH A STRING. לֹא צְבָעָן בְּשֶׁמֶן וְלֹא כְּרָכָן בִּמְשִׁיחָה – IF HE DID NOT DIP THEM IN OIL AND DID NOT WRAP THEM AROUND WITH A STRING, אֵין יוֹצְאִין בָּהֶם – HE MAY NOT GO OUT WITH THEM.**[4] **וְאִם יָצָא בָּהֶן שָׁעָה אַחַת מִבְּעוֹד יוֹם – BUT IF HE**

NOTES

1. Although Rava was originally cited (on 49b) as making his statement in reference to our Mishnah [''*They* (the Rabbis of our Mishnah) did not teach . . .''], Ravina maintains that this is a misquote of Rava's words (see *Ritva MHK* ed.; cf. *Tosafos*).

2. [This seems to contradict Abaye's ruling on 48a that flockings remain *muktzeh* even after being used for insulation. Given that the Gemara does not point out that Rava here disputes Abaye above, we must say that Abaye was referring specifically to flockings from a warehouse (*Tosafos* to 48a ד״ה וכי). Alternatively, flockings are more valuable than wool shearings. Thus, while one who uses wool shearings for insulation even just once is apt to retain them for this purpose, one who uses flockings for insulation is likely to return them afterwards to their primary purpose of making felt (see *Rosh* §7; cf. *Ri* cited by *Tosafos* ibid.).]

3. It is not necessary for him to consciously intend to sit on them on the Sabbath. As long as he sits on them on Friday, he indicates that he wishes to use them as a seat (*Rashi*).

[It will be noted that whereas all agree that wool shearings are released from their *muktzeh* status by insulating with them or designating them for insulation, the requirement for releasing palm branches from their *muktzeh* status is the subject of a dispute: Some are more strict with the palm branches (requiring tying) and some are more lenient (requiring only sitting on them on Friday). This is because there are aspects of palm branches that militate for giving them a stricter law than wool shearings and aspects that militate for giving them a more lenient law. On the one hand, palm branches are not as suited for sitting on as wool shearings are for insulating. This should result in a stricter requirement for rendering palm branches non-*muktzeh*. On the other hand, wool shearings are more valuable for use in weaving and spinning than palm branches are as firewood. This should make it easier to render palm branches non-*muktzeh* (*Ritva MHK* ed.).]

4. [Our translation of וּכְרָכָן as ''*and* wrapped them around'' follows *Rambam* (*Shabbos* 19:16). *Tur* and *Shulchan Aruch* (308:24), however, render: ''*or* wrapped them around.'']

These bandages are worn to prevent the wearer's clothing from rubbing against the wound and irritating it. If they are dipped in oil, they achieve this goal in the optimum fashion and are considered garments. Hence, wearing them is not considered carrying. But if they are not dipped in oil, they themselves tend to rub against the wound and irritate it. Since they are not totally effective in protecting the wound, wearing them outside is considered carrying (see *Rashi* and

נוטל את הכיסוי והן נופלות אלא אי איתמר הכי איתמר אמר רבא לא שנו אלא שלא יחדן להטמנה אבל יחדן להטמנה מטלטלין אותן איתמר נמי כי אתא רבין א"ר יעקב א"ר אסי בן שאול אמר רבי לא שנו אלא שלא יחדן להטמנה אבל יחדן להטמנה מטלטלין אותן רבינא אומר [א]בשל הפתק שנו תניא נמי הכי (א) גיזי צמר של הפתק אין מטלטלין אותן ואם התקינן בעל הבית להשתמש בהן מטלטלין אותן תנא רבה בר בר חנה קמיה דרב (ג) חריות של דקל שגדרן לעצים ונמלך עליהן לישיבה צריך לקשר רשב"ג [ב]אומר אין צריך לקשר הוא תני לה והוא אמר לה הלכה כרשב"ג איתמר רב אמר קושר ושמואל אמר חושב (ג) ורב אסי אמר [ג]יושב אע"פ שלא קישר ואע"פ שלא חישב בשלמא רב הוא דאמר כת"ק ושמואל נמי הוא דאמר כרשב"ג אלא רב אסי דאמר כמאן הוא דאמר כי האי תנא דתניא (ד) [ד]יוצאין בפקורין ובציפא בזמן שצבען (ה) (בשמן) וכרכן במשיחה לא צבען (ה) (בשמן) ולא כרכן במשיחה אין יוצאין בהם ואם יצא בהן שעה אחת מבעוד יום אע"פ שלא צבע ולא כרכן במשיחה מותר לצאת בהן אמר רב אשי אף אנן נמי תנינא (ו) הקש שעל גבי המטה לא ינענעו בידו אבל מנענעו בגופו אבל אם היה (עליו) מאכל בהמה או שהיה עליו כר או סדין מבעוד יום מנענעו בידו ש"מ ומאן תנא דפליג עליה דרשב"ג רבי חנינא בן עקיבא דכי אתא רב דימי אמר זעירי א"ר חנינא פעם אחת הלך רבי חנינא בן עקיבא למקום אחד ומצא חריות של דקל שגדרום לשום עצים ואמר להם לתלמידיו צאו וחשבו כדי שנשב עליהן למחר ולא ידענא אי בית המשתה הוה אי בית האבל הוה מדקאמר אי בית המשתה הוה אי בית האבל הוה דוקא בית האבל או בית המשתה דטרידי אבל הכא קשר אין לא קשר לא (ז) אמר רב יהודה [ה]מכנים אדם מלא קופתו עפר ועושה בה כל צרכו דרש מר זוטרא משמיה דמר זוטרא רבה [ו]והוא שיחד לו קרן זוית אמרו רבנן קמיה דרב פפא כמאן כרבן שמעון בן גמליאל דאי כרבנן האמרי בעינן מעשה אמר להו רב פפא אפילו תימא רבנן עד כאן לא קאמרי רבנן דבעינן מעשה אלא מידי דבר עבידא ביה מעשה אבל מידי דלא בר מיעבדא ביה מעשה לא נימא כתנאי בכל [ז]חפין את הכלים חוץ מכלי כסף בגרתקון (ח) הא נתר וחול מותר והתניא (ט) נתר וחול אסור מאי לאו בהא קמיפלגי דמר סבר בעינן מעשה ומר סבר לא בעינן מעשה לא דכולי עלמא לא בעינן מעשה ולא קשיא (י) (הא רבי יהודה הא ר' שמעון) הא (כ) רבי יהודה דאמר דבר שאין מתכוין אסור הא ר' שמעון דאמר (ל) דבר שאין מתכוין מותר במאי אוקימתא להא דשרי כר"ש אימא סיפא אבל לא יחוף בהם שערו ואי ר"ש משרא קשרי דתנן

נזיר

רש"י

נוטל את הכיסוי. אלמא בהנך דטמן נמי קאסר לטלטולי אלא על ידי כיסוי: **יחדן להטמנה.** לעולם: **רבינא אומר.** לעולם כדקאמר רבא אם טמן בהן מותר לטלטל דכמאן דיחדן להכי דמו ורבא לאו אמתניתין קאי דמתניתין בגיזין של הפתק דודאי עתיד להחזירן משם ולא יחדן לכך: **הפתק.** מערכה גדולה שעורכין ומושיבין להקצותן לסחורה שקורין ט"ש בין של בגדים בין של צמר בין של חגבים ובשר מלוח: **חריות.** ענפים קשים כעץ משהוקשו שדראות של לולבין ונפלו עלין שלהן קרי להן חריות: **שגדרן.** כל (לקיטת) [קצילת] תמרים קרי גדירה: **צריך לקשר.** לקשרם יחד מבעוד יום להוכיח שלישיבה עומדים ואם לא קשרם יחד אסור לטלטלן למחר דלא הוי יחוד במחשבה: **ורב אסי אמר ישב.** עליהן מבעוד יום: **ואע"פ שלא חישב.** עליהן לישב למחר גלי דעתיה דלישיבה קיימי: **פקורין.** פשתן סרוק שנותנין על המכה: **בציפא.** צמר מנופץ הניתן על המכה: **בזמן שצבען בשמן.** גלי דעתיה דלמכה קיימי להניחן עליה בשבת דלאו לרפואה נינהו אלא שלא ישרטו מלבושיו את מכתו והוה ליה כמלבוש דעלמא אבל לא צבען בשמן דלאו מלבוש נינהו הוה ליה משאוי ואין יוצאין בו לר"ה: **ואם יצא בהן כו'.** היינו כרב אסי דאמר ישב אע"פ שלא קשר ולא חישב: **אף אנן נמי תנינא.** כרב אסי: **קש.** סתמיה לטינא קאי ללבנים או להסקה ומוקצה הוא ואם היה נתון על המטה ולא לשכב עליו ובא בשבת לשכב עליו והוצרך לנענעו ולשוטחו לשכיבה שלא יהא צבור וקשה: **לא ינענעו בידו.** שאסור לטלטלו: **אבל מנענעו בגופו.** כלאחר יד: **או שהיה עליו כר או סדין.** ששכב עליו מבעוד יום ואע"פ שלא יחדו לכך ולא חישב עליו דהיינו כרב אסי: **ומאן תנא.** דלעיל דאמר צריך לקשור ופליג אדרבן שמעון: **ולא ידענא.** זעירי קאמר לה: **דטרידי.** ולא יכלו לקשור מבעוד יום והתם הוא דשרי בלא קישור אבל בעלמא לא: **מכנים מלא קופתו עפר.** לכסות בו צואה ורוק ומערה העפר בביתו לארץ ונוטלו תמיד לכל צרכיו: **והוא שייחד לו קרן זוית.** דהוי כמוכן ועומד לכך אבל נתנו באמצע ביתו למדרס רגלים הרי הוא בטל לגבי קרקעית הבית ומוקצה ואסור: **כרבן שמעון.** דשרי במחשבה בעלמא שאין מעשה מוכיח שעומד לעשות צרכיו: **דבר מעביד מעשה.** שבן מעשה הוא שיכול לעשות בו מעשה הוכחה: **לימא כתנאי.** הא דרב יהודה במידי דלאו בר מעשה: **חפין.** משפשפין את הכלים בשבת לנאותן: **חוץ מכלי כסף בגרתקון.** כמין עפר שגדל בחבית של יין וקורין לו אלו"ס והוא עיקר תקון כלי כסף וגורר אותו שהכסף רך והוא ממחק שהוא אב מלאכה: **אבל נתר וחול מותר.** דלא גריר ליה לכסף: **מאי לאו.** הא דתניא אסור לאו משום דגריר ליה אלא משום מוקצה קאסר ליה ותנא דשרי כגון שהכניס מלא קופתו לכך ועירה על גבי קרקע ומאן דאסר קסבר בעינן מעשה וזה לא יכול: **לא דכולי עלמא.** במידי דלאו בר מעשה לא בעינן מעשה דאית להו הא דרב יהודה וטעמא מאן דאסר דזימנין דגריר ואף על גב דלא מיכוין לגרור אסור כרבי יהודה דאמר דבר שאין מתכוין אסור ומאן דשרי כר"ש ומיהו גרתקון אסור דודאי גריר ומודה ר"ש בפסיק רישיה ולא ימות: **לא יחוף בהן.** בנתר וחול שערו בשבת מפני שמשירו:

נזיר

תוספות

אלא אי איתמר כו'. אין גירסא זו נכונה דלכאורה משמע שלרבא עצמו היה מקשה וטפי הוי ניחא אי הוה גרס אלא אמר רבא אבל לפי זה הוה צריך לומר דרבינא לפלוגי אתא:

רבינא אומר בשל הפתק שנו. ומילתא דרבא כדקאמר מעיקרא ובשאינה של הפתק ותימה דרבא קאמר לא שנו משמע דאמתניתין קאי והא מתניתין מיירי בשל הפתק וי"ל דרישא מיירי בכל גיזי צמר בין של הפתק בין שאינם של הפתק דאין מטלטלים אותן וקאמר רבא לא שנו בהנהו שאינה של הפתק אלא שלא טמן בהן אבל טמן בהן מטלטלים אותן והא דקתני סיפא כילד הוא עושה כו' בשל הפתק קאמר ואע"פ שטמן בהן אין מטלטלין כיון שלא הזמינן:

ורב אסי אמר ישב אע"פ שלא קשר ושלא חישב. רבינו שמשון הזקן פסק כרב אסי מדקאמר בסמוך רב אשי שהוא בתרא מתני' נמי דיקא ור"ת פוסק כרב מכח קושיא כמו שמפורש בפרק כל הכלים (לקמן דף קכו. בד"ה ר"י אומר ושם):

בפקורין ובציפא. פר"ח כיפה שיש בה שער ונותנין אותה בראש הקרח ונראה שהוא שער ראשו: **אבל** לא צבען בשמן אין יוצאין בהן. לאו דוקא אין יוצאין דאפילו לטלטלם אסור לפי שאינם מוכנים אלא נקט אין יוצאין אגב רישא ובסמוך נמי דקאמר אבל יצא בהן שעה אחת מבעוד יום לאו דוקא יצא דהוא הדין ישב בהן בביתו:

ואם יצא בהן שעה אחת כו'. אע"פ (מ) שלא צבע ולא חישב היינו כרב אסי דאמר ישב אע"פ שלא חישב ולא קישר קשה לר"י רישא דקתני יוצאין בהן בזמן שצבען מאי אריא צבען אפילו חישב נמי דהא כיון דמתיר יצא אע"פ שלא צבע ולא חישב כל שכן חישב ולא צבע דלכאורה ישיבה גריעא ממחשבה וכן נמי יציאה ותירץ דהאי דקאמר צבען לא לצאת בהן בשבת אלא כדי לצאת בהן מבעוד יום ואחר כך נמלך ואפ"ה יכול לצאת בהן בשבת:

ולא ידענא אי בית האבל הוה. פי' אי משום בית האבל התיר אי משום בית המשתה:

רבי

עין משפט נר מצוה

יט א (מיי' פכ"ה מהל' שבת) סמג לאוין סה טוש"ע או"ח סימן רנט סעיף א:

כ ב ג מיי' פכ"ה מהל' שבת הלכה כא טור שו"ע או"ח סימן שח סעיף כ:

כא ד מיי' פי"ט מהל' שבת הלכה טו טור שו"ע שם סעיף כד [וסי' שא סעיף כ]:

כב ה ו מיי' פכ"ה מהל' שבת הלכה כב סמג שם טוש"ע שם סעיף לח וסימן תלא סעיף יז:

כג ז מיי' פכ"ג מהלכות שבת הלכה ז סמג שם טוש"ע או"ח סימן שכג סעיף ט:

רבינו חננאל

כרבא דאמר לא שנו אלא שלא יחדן להטמנה אבל יחדן להטמנה מטלטלין אותן דהא ר' נמי תני כוותיה. ורבינא דהוא בתראה אוקמה למשנתנו בשל הפתק א). פי' הפתק לשון יוני הוא. כגון אוצר המוטל לסחורה. כדתנן בע"ז (ל"ט:) החגבים הבאים מן הסלילה אסורין ומן ההפתק מותרין ותני' (שם מ:) חגבין והקפלוטאות הבאים מן ההפתק ומן האוצר ומן הספינה מותרין. כדתנינן גיזי צמר של הפתק אין מטלטלין אותן אם התקינן בעל הבית להשתמש בהן מותר: **חריות** של דקל שגדרן לעצים ונמלך עליהן לישיבה. אוקימנא ר' חנינא בן עקיבא אומר צריך לקשר. ר' שמעון בן גמליאל אומר אין צריך לקשר. אמר רבה בר בר חנה הלכתא כרשב"ג ואע"ג דאמר רב יקשור הא אמר שמואל יחשוב כרבה בר בר חנה. ודר' אסי נמי דאמר כי האי תנא דתני יוצאין בפיקריון ובציפא כו' פי' פאה נכרית והוא שיער שעושה בקפח והקרח נותנן בראשו ונראה כי אותו שיער שבקפח שיער ראשו הוא ואם יצא בהן שעה אחת מבעוד יום דיו והא דאמר רב אסי עדיפא מדשמואל. ונמצא רב לגבייהו יחיד ויחיד ורבים הלכה כרבים: **הא דאמר** רב יהודה מכניס אדם מלא קופתו עפר כבר פירשנו' במס' י"ט ולא (אכרע בהא מילתא) [בר מיעבדא

חשק שלמה על רבינו חננאל

א) עיין ערוך ערך פתק.

מסורת הש"ס

א) [תוספתא פרק ד], ב) לקמן קכה: קכו., ג) [עי' תוס' לקמן קכה: סד"ה ואודו], ד) [תוספתא פ"ו], ה) רש"ל מ"ז ע"ש, ו) לקמן קמא., ז) ביצה ח., ח) נ"א אבל, ט) [תוספתא ביצה פ"ד], י) ח"מ מ"ז, כ) [לעיל מא:], ל) [שם וש"נ], מ) שלא צבען ולא כרכן במשיחה והיינו כרב אסי כצ"ל.

רב נסים גאון

המדרש ור' יוסי הגלילי שמו וכבר היה רב אידי אבוה דר' יעקב בר אידי הוו קרי ליה בר בי רב דחד יומא כמו שאמרו (חגיגה דף ה) רב אידי אבוה דר' יעקב בר אידי הוה רגיל דהוה אתי תלתא ירחין באורחא והוה קאי חד יומא בבי רב והדר אזיל תלתא ירחין באורחא הוה קאי חד יומא באושפיזיה והדר אתי הוה קא קרו ליה בר בי רב דחד יומא חלש דעתיה קרי אנפשיה (איוב יב) שחוק לרעהו אהיה אמר ליה ר' יוחנן במטותא מינך לא תעניש רבנן נפק ר' יוחנן ודרש (ישעיה נח) ואותי יום יום ידרשון וכי ביום דורשין אותו ובלילה אין דורשין אותו אלא לומר לך כל העוסק בתורה אפילו יום אחד בשנה לשמה מעלה עליו הכתוב כאילו עוסק כל השנה כולה:

ליקוטי רש"י

חריות. מרוטא. ענף הדקל משנתקשה שתי שנים ושלש ויוצאין בו לולבין הרבה שנשרו עליהן ונתקשו גם הם ונעשו עץ זה פונה לכאן וזה פונה לכאן כענפי שאר אילנות [סוכה לב.]. **שגדרן לעצים.** שחתכן להיסק [לקמן קכה:]. **וכרכן במשיחה.** לונצ"י בלע"ז קושרם בחוט של משיחה [ר"ה כב:]. משיחה. חוט [גיטין עח:]. **הקש שעל גבי המטה.** וסתמא להסקה ומוקצה הוא ובא לשכב עליו ומנענעו כדי שיהא צף ורך לשכב. **לא ינענעו בידו.** דמוקצה הוא. **אבל מנענעו בגופו.** בכתפיו וטלטול מן הצד הוא דלא שמיה טלטול. **או שהיה עליו כר או סדין.** דגלי דעתיה דאקלייה לשכיבה מעתה תורת כלי עליו [לקמן קמא.]. **מכנים אדם מלא קופתו עפר.** בקתא ונותנו במקום אחד ועושה בה כל צרכיו ולא אמרינן בטלה לה לגבי קרקע הבית איידי דזוטרא. **והוא שיחד לו כו'.** ולא שטחה דמוכחא מילתא דלצרכיו קא בעי לה ובעפר תיחוח קאמר שאינו מחוסר לא חפירה ולא כתישה אלא הכנה [ביצה ח.]. **נתר.** קרקע הוא או אבן כעין שקורין קרי"א בלע"ז [תענית יג.]. מין אדמה הוא וקורין לה ניתרא [סנהדרין מט: וכעי"ז לקמן פט:].

WENT OUT WITH THEM EVEN FOR A SHORT TIME WHILE IT WAS STILL DAYTIME on Friday, אַף עַל פִּי שֶׁלֹּא צָבַע וְלֹא כְּרָכָן בִּמְשִׁיחָה – EVEN IF HE DID NOT DIP them in oil AND WRAP THEM AROUND WITH A STRING, מוּתָּר לָצֵאת בָּהֶן – HE IS PERMITTED TO GO OUT WITH THEM on the Sabbath. This agrees with Rav Assi, who maintains that sitting on the branches on Friday is sufficient to render them non-*muktzeh,* even without tying them or intending to sit on them on the Sabbath.[5]

Further support for Rav Assi is adduced:

אָמַר רַב אַשִׁי – **Rav Ashi said:** אַף אֲנַן נַמֵּי תְּנֵינָא – **We also learned so in a Mishnah:**[6] הַקַּשׁ שֶׁעַל גַּבֵּי הַמִּטָּה – Regarding STRAW THAT IS ON A BED, לֹא יְנַעְנְעוֹ בְּיָדוֹ – ONE MAY NOT MOVE IT WITH HIS HAND אֲבָל מְנַעְנְעוֹ בְּגוּפוֹ – BUT HE MAY MOVE IT WITH HIS BODY, i.e. he may shift it around with his body while lying on the bed.[7] אֲבָל אִם הָיָה (עליו) מַאֲכַל בְּהֵמָה – BUT IF [THE STRAW] WAS designated as FODDER FOR ANIMALS, which is not *muktzeh,* אוֹ שֶׁהָיָה עָלָיו כַּר אוֹ סָדִין מִבְּעוֹד יוֹם – OR IF A PILLOW OR SHEET WAS OVER IT, i.e. if the person had lain on top of the straw before the Sabbath, מְנַעְנְעוֹ בְּיָדוֹ – HE MAY even MOVE IT WITH HIS HAND. שְׁמַע מִינַּהּ – **Learn from this** that the status of *muktzeh* is removed even without consciously intending to use it on the Sabbath, as Rav Assi ruled.

The Gemara asks:

וּמַאן תַּנָּא דִּפְלִיג עֲלֵיהּ דְּרַבָּן שִׁמְעוֹן בֶּן גַּמְלִיאֵל – **And who is the Tanna who disputes Rabban Shimon ben Gamliel** and requires tying the branches?

The Gemara answers:

רַבִּי חֲנִינָא בֶּן עֲקִיבָא – **It is R' Chanina ben Akiva.** דְּכִי אֲתָא רַב דִּימִי אָמַר זְעֵירִי אָמַר רַבִּי חֲנִינָא – **For when Rav Dimi came he stated in the name of Zeiri who stated in the name of R' Chanina:** פַּעַם אַחַת הָלַךְ רַבִּי חֲנִינָא בֶּן עֲקִיבָא לְמָקוֹם אֶחָד – **Once R' Chanina ben Akiva went to a certain place** וּמָצָא חֲרָיוֹת שֶׁל דֶּקֶל שֶׁגְּדָרוּם לְשׁוּם עֵצִים – **and he found branches of a date palm that were harvested for the sake of** firewood, וְאָמַר לָהֶם לְתַלְמִידָיו – **and he said to his students:** צְאוּ וְחִשְׁבוּ כְּדֵי שֶׁנֵּשֵׁב עֲלֵיהֶן לְמָחָר – **"Go out and intend,** i.e. mentally designate the branches, **so that we may sit on them tomorrow."** וְלֹא יָדַעְנָא אִי בֵּית הַמִּשְׁתֶּה הֲוָה אִי בֵּית הָאֵבֶל הֲוָה – **But** (continued Zeiri) **I do not know whether it was at a house of feasting,** i.e. a wedding, **or at a house of mourning** that he gave this instruction.[8] מִדְּקָאָמַר אִי בֵּית הַמִּשְׁתֶּה הֲוָה אִי בֵּית הָאֵבֶל הֲוָה – Now (concludes the Gemara) **since [Zeiri] said, "I do not know whether it was at a house of feasting or at a house of mourning,"** דַּוְקָא בֵּית הָאֵבֶל אוֹ בֵּית הַמִּשְׁתֶּה דִּטְרִידֵי – it can be deduced that it is **only** at a **house of mourning or a house of feasting, where [the participants] are preoccupied** and do not have time to tie the bundles, that R' Chanina ben Akiva allowed merely intending to sit on them. אֲבָל הָכָא – **But here,** in an ordinary case, קָשַׁר אִין לֹא קָשַׁר לֹא – **where one tied** the bundles, **yes,** they may be moved on the Sabbath; if **one did not tie** them, **no,** they may not be moved.

The Gemara cites a related ruling:

אָמַר רַב יְהוּדָה – **Rav Yehudah said:** מַכְנִיס אָדָם מְלֹא קוּפָּתוֹ עָפָר וְעוֹשֶׂה בָּהּ כָּל צָרְכּוֹ – **A person may bring a basketful of earth** into his house before the Sabbath **and use it for all his needs** on the Sabbath, e.g. to cover unsightly filth or saliva on the floor of his house. דָּרַשׁ מָר זוּטְרָא מִשְּׁמֵיהּ דְּמָר זוּטְרָא רַבָּה – **Mar Zutra expounded in the name of Mar Zutra Rabbah:** וְהוּא שֶׁיִּחֵד לוֹ קֶרֶן זָוִית – **This** leniency of Rav Yehudah **applies** only **to where [the person] set aside a corner** of the house **for** the storage of **[the earth];** i.e. he piled it up in one corner and did not spread it out on the ground. However, if he scattered it over the ground of the house, where it will be trodden upon by the residents of the house, it becomes subordinate to the ground and remains *muktzeh.*[9] אָמְרוּ רַבָּנָן קַמֵּיהּ דְּרַב פָּפָּא – **The Rabbis said before Rav Pappa:** כְּמַאן כְּרַבָּן שִׁמְעוֹן בֶּן גַּמְלִיאֵל – **According to whom** was this statement of Rav Yehudah made? Surely it was made **according to Rabban Shimon ben Gamliel,** who says that only intention is required. דְּאִי כְּרַבָּנָן הָאָמְרֵי בָּעֵינַן מַעֲשֶׂה – **For if** it was made **according to the Rabbis, why, they say** that **we require an act** to be performed to the object in order to render it non-*muktzeh*![10]

אָמַר לְהוּ רַב פָּפָּא – **Rav Pappa said to [the Rabbis]:** אֲפִילּוּ תֵּימָא רַבָּנָן – **You may even say** that Rav Yehudah's statement follows **the Rabbis.** עַד כָּאן לֹא קָאָמְרֵי רַבָּנָן דִּבְעֵינַן מַעֲשֶׂה – For **thus far the Rabbis did not state that we require an act** to be performed to the object אֶלָּא מִידִי דְּבַר עֲבִידָא בֵּיהּ מַעֲשֶׂה – **except** in regard to **something that is** *capable* **of having an act performed to it,** such as palm branches, where tying them into bundles makes them more suitable for use as a seat and indicates that the person wishes to use them for this purpose. אֲבָל מִידִי דְּלָא בַּר מִיעֲבְדָא בֵּיהּ מַעֲשֶׂה לֹא – **But** regarding **something** such as earth, which is **not capable of having an act performed to it,** since there is nothing that can be done to it to make it more suited for covering filth, the Rabbis did **not** require that an action be performed. In this case, merely *intending* to use the earth on the Sabbath suffices.

The Gemara further discusses Rav Yehudah's ruling in light of Rav Pappa's explanation:

נֵימָא כְּתַנָּאֵי – **Let us say that it** [the issue of whether intention suffices in a case in which no action is feasible] **is the**

NOTES

Meiri). [The string is necessary so that the bandage should not fall off on the Sabbath (*Chidushei HaRan*).]

[Although it is forbidden to perform acts of healing on the Sabbath (unless the patient is so sick that he must repair to bed), applying the bandage in this case is permitted, since the bandage does not heal the wound but merely prevents it from becoming irritated (see *Rashi* and *Meiri*).]

5. Although the Baraisa mentions only that where the bandages were not dipped in oil one is forbidden to *go out* with them on the Sabbath, it is also true that they are considered *muktzeh* [because linen and wool strips are ordinarily destined for use in the forbidden *melachos* of weaving or spinning]. The Baraisa mentions going out only because the first part of the Baraisa discussed this point (i.e. it permitted not only handling bandages dipped in oil, but even wearing them outside). Thus, since the Baraisa states that wearing the bandage on Friday permits one to wear it outside on the Sabbath, we see that such wearing also removes the prohibition of *muktzeh (Tosafos)*.

6. Below, 141a.

7. Straw is usually used for manufacturing bricks or as kindling. It is therefore *muktzeh.* The Mishnah teaches that if the person wishes to spread the straw evenly over the bed so as to make it comfortable to lie on, he may do so only with his body since he is handling the straw in an unusual manner (כִּלְאַחַר יָד) (*Rashi*; cf. *Rashi* below, 141a).

8. That is, when R' Chanina ben Akiva told his students to intend to sit on the branches, he specified that he was telling them to do so only because of the unusual circumstance at hand. When Zeiri later reported this incident, he added that was unsure whether that circumstance was a wedding or a house of mourning (*Ramban;* see *Ritva MHK* ed.).

9. *Rashi*; cf. *Rashi* to *Beitzah* 8a ד״ה והוא שיחד; see *Dibros Moshe* 39:17. [See *Orach Chaim* 308:22, where the parameters of "setting aside" are discussed; see also *Dibros Moshe* 39:18.]

10. Bringing the earth into the house is not considered an act performed to the earth [because doing so only changes the earth's location; it does not make the earth *intrinsically* more suitable for covering filth] (*Tos. HaRosh*).

נוטל את הכיסוי והן נופלות אלא אי איתמר הכי איתמר אמר רבא לא שנו אלא שלא יחדן להטמנה אבל יחדן להטמנה מטלטלין אותן איתמר נמי כי אתא רבין א"ר יעקב א"ר אסי בן שאול אמר רבי לא שנו אלא שלא יחדן להטמנה אבל יחדן להטמנה מטלטלין אותן רבינא אומר [א]בשל הפתק שנו תניא נמי הכי [א]גיזי צמר של הפתק אין מטלטלין אותן ואם התקינן בעל הבית להשתמש בהן מטלטלין אותן תנא רבה בר בר חנה קמיה דרב [ג]חריות של דקל שגדרן לעצים ונמלך עליהן לישיבה צריך לקשר רשב"ג [ב]אומר אין צריך לקשר הוא תני לה והוא אמר לה הלכה כרשב"ג איתמר רב אמר קושר ושמואל אמר חושב [ג]ורב אסי אמר [ז]יושב אע"פ שלא קישר ואע"פ שלא חישב בשלמא רב הוא דאמר כת"ק ושמואל נמי הוא דאמר כרשב"ג אלא רב אסי דאמר כמאן הוא דאמר כי האי תנא דתניא [ד]יוצאין בפקורין ובציפא בזמן שצבען [ה](בשמן) וכרכן במשיחה לא צבען [ה](בשמן) ולא כרכן במשיחה אין יוצאין בהם ואם יצא בהן שעה אחת מבעוד יום אע"פ שלא צבע ולא כרכן במשיחה מותר לצאת בהן אמר רב אשי אף אנן נמי תנינא [ו]הקש שעל גבי המטה לא ינענעו בידו אבל מנענעו בגופו אבל אם היה (עליו) מאכל בהמה או שהיה עליו כר או סדין מבעוד יום מנענעו בידו ש"מ ומאן תנא דפליג עליה דרשב"ג רבי חנינא בן עקיבא דכי אתא רב דימי אמר זעירי א"ר חנינא פעם אחת הלך רבי חנינא בן עקיבא למקום אחד ומצא חריות של דקל שגדרום לשום עצים ואמר להם לתלמידיו צאו וחשבו כדי שנשב עליהן למחר ולא ידענא אי בית המשתה הוה אי בית האבל הוה מדקאמר אי בית המשתה הוה אי בית האבל הוה דוקא בית האבל או בית המשתה דטרידי אבל הכא קשר אין לא קשר לא [י]אמר רב יהודה [ח]מכניס אדם מלא קופתו עפר ועושה בה כל צרכו דרש מר זוטרא משמיה דמר זוטרא רבה [י]והוא שיחד לו קרן זוית אמרו רבנן קמיה דרב פפא כמאן כרבן שמעון בן גמליאל דאי כרבנן האמרי בעינן מעשה אמר להו רב פפא אפילו תימא רבנן עד כאן לא קאמרי רבנן דבעינן מעשה אלא מידי דבר עבידא ביה מעשה אבל מידי דלא בר מיעבדא ביה מעשה לא נימא כתנאי בכל [י]חפין את הכלים חוץ מכלי כסף בגרתקון [כ]הא נתר וחול מותר והתניא [ט]נתר וחול אסור מאי לאו בהא קמיפלגי דמר סבר בעינן מעשה ומר סבר לא בעינן מעשה לא דכולי עלמא לא בעינן מעשה ולא קשיא [י](הא רבי יהודה הא ר' שמעון) הא [כ]רבי יהודה דאמר דבר שאין מתכוין אסור הא ר' שמעון דאמר [ל]דבר שאין מתכוין מותר במאי אוקימתא להא דשרי כר"ש אימא סיפא אבל לא יחוף בהם שערו ואי ר"ש משרא קשרי דתנן

נזיר

נוטל את הכיסוי. אלמא בהנך דטמן נמי קאסר לטלטולי אלא על ידי כיסוי: יחדן להטמנה. לעולם: רבינא אומר. לעולם כדקאמר רבא אם טמן בהן מותר לטלטל דכמאן דיחדן להכי דמו ורבא לאו אמתניתין קאי דמתניתין בגיזין של הפתק דודאי עתיד להחזירן משם ולא יחדן לכך: הפתק. מערכה גדולה שעורכין ומושיבין להקלותן לסחורה שקורין ט"ש בין של בגדים בין של למר בין של חגבים ובשר מלוח: חריות. ענפים קשים כעץ משהוקשו שדראות של לולבין ונפלו עלין שלהן קרי להן חריות: שגדרן. כל (לקיטת) [קלילת] תמרים קרי גדירה: צריך לקשר. לקשרם יחד מבעוד יום להוכיח שלישיבה עומדים ואם לא קשרם יחד אסור לטלטלן למחר דלא הוי יחוד במחשבה: ורב אסי אמר ישב. עליהן מבעוד יום: ואע"פ שלא חישב. עליהן לישב למחר גלי דעתיה דלישיבה קיימי: פקורין. פשתן סרוק שנותנין על המכה: בציפא. למר מנופץ הניתן על המכה: בזמן שצבען בשמן. גלי דעתיה דלמכה קיימי להניחן עליה בשבת דלאו לרפואה ניניהו אלא שלא ישרטו מלבושיו את מכתו והוה ליה כמלבוש דעלמא אבל לא צבען בשמן דלאו מלבוש ניניהו הוה ליה משאוי ואין יוצאין בו לר"ה: ואם יצא בהן כו'. היינו כרב אסי דאמר ישב אע"פ שלא קשר ולא חישב: אף אנן נמי תנינא. כרב אסי: קש. סתמיה לטינא קאי ללבנים או להסקה ומוקצה הוא ואם היה נתון על המטה ולא לשכב עליו ובא בשבת לשכב עליו והוצרך לנענעו ולשוטחו לשכיבה שלא יהא צבור וקשה: לא ינענעו בידו. שאסור לטלטלו: אבל מנענעו בגופו. כלאחר יד: או שהיה עליו כר או סדין. ששכב עליו מבעוד יום ואע"פ שלא יחדו לכך ולא חישב עליו דהיינו כרב אסי: ומאן תנא. דלעיל דאמר צריך לקשור ופליג אדרבן שמעון: ולא ידענא. זעירי קאמר לה: דטרידי. ולא יכלו לקשור מבעוד יום והתם הוא דשרי בלא קישור אבל בעלמא לא: מכנים מלא קופתו עפר. לכסות בו צואה ורוק ומערה העפר בביתו לארץ ונוטלו תמיד לכל צרכיו: והוא שייחד לו קרן זוית. דהוי כמוכן ועומד לכך אבל נתנו באמצע ביתו למדרס רגלים הרי הוא בטל לגבי קרקעית הבית ומוקצה ואסור: כרבן שמעון. דשרי במחשבה בעלמא שאין מעשה מוכיח שעומד לעשות צרכיו: דבר מעביד מעשה. שבן מעשה הוא שיכול לעשות בו מעשה הוכחה: לימא כתנאי. הא דרב יהודה במידי דלאו בר מעשה: חפין. משפשפין את הכלים בשבת לנאותן: חוץ מכלי כסף בגרתקון. כמין עפר שגדל בחבית של יין וקורין לו אלו"ם והוא עיקר תקון כלי כסף וגורר אותו שהכסף רך והוא ממחק שהוא אב מלאכה: אבל נתר וחול מותר. דלא גריר ליה לכסף: מאי לאו. הא דתניא אסור לאו משום דגריר ליה אלא משום מוקצה קאסר ליה ותנא דשרי כגון שהכנים מלא קופתו לכך ועירה על גבי קרקע ומאן דאסר קסבר בעינן מעשה וזה לא יכול: לא דכולי עלמא. במידי דלאו בר מעשה לא בעינן מעשה דאית להו הא דרב יהודה וטעמא מאן דאסר דזימנין דגריר ואף על גב דלא מיכוין לגרור אסור כרבי יהודה דאמר דבר שאין מתכוין אסור ומאן דשרי כר"ש ומיהו גרתקון אסור דודאי גריר ומודה ר"ש בפסיק רישיה ולא ימות: לא יחוף בהן. בנתר וחול שערו בשבת מפני שמשירו:

נזיר

אלא אי איתמר כו'. אין גירסא זו נכונה דלכאורה משמע שלרבא עצמו היה מקשה וטפי הוי ניחא אי הוה גרס אלא אמר רבא אבל לפי זה הוה צריך לומר דרבינא לפלוגי אתא:

רבינא אומר בשל הפתק שנו. ומילתא דרבא כדקאמר מעיקרא ובשאינה של הפתק ותימה דרבא קאמר לא שנו משמע דאמתניתין קאי והא מתניתין מיירי בשל הפתק וי"ל דרישא מיירי בכל גיזי צמר בין של הפתק בין שאינם של הפתק דאין מטלטלים אותן וקאמר רבא לא שנו בהנהו שאינה של הפתק אלא שלא טמן בהן אבל טמן בהן מטלטלים אותן והא דקתני סיפא כיצד הוא עושה כו' בשל הפתק קאמר ואע"פ שטמן בהן אין מטלטלין כיון שלא הזמינן:

ורב אסי אמר ישב אע"פ שלא קשר ושלא חישב. רבינו שמשון הזקן פסק כרב אסי מדקאמר בסמוך רב אסי שהוא בתרא מתני' נמי דיקא ור"ת פוסק כרב מכח קושיא כמו שמפורש בפרק כל הכלים (לקמן דף קכו. בד"ה ר"י אומר ושם):

בפקורין ובציפא. פר"ח ליפה שיש בה שער ונותנין אותה בראש הקרח ונראה שהוא שער ראשו: אבל לא צבען בשמן אין יוצאין בהן. לאו דוקא אין יוצאין דאפילו לטלטלם אסור לפי שאינם מוכנים אלא נקט אין יוצאין אגב רישא ובסמוך נמי דקאמר אבל יצא בהן שעה אחת מבעוד יום לאו דוקא יצא דהוא הדין ישב בהן בביתו:

ואם יצא בהן שעה אחת כו'. אע"פ [מ]שלא צבע ולא חישב היינו כרב אסי דאמר ישב אע"פ שלא חישב ולא קישר קשה לר"י רישא דקתני יוצאין בהן בזמן שצבען מאי אריא צבען אפילו חישב נמי דהא כיון דמתיר יצא אע"פ שלא צבע ולא חישב כל שכן חישב ולא צבע דלכאורה ישיבה גריעא ממחשבה וכן נמי יליאה ותירץ דהאי דקאמר צבען לא ללאת בהן בשבת אלא כדי ללאת בהן מבעוד יום ואחר כך נמלך ואפ"ה יכול ללאת בהן בשבת:

ולא ידענא אי בית האבל הוה. פי' אי משום בית האבל התיר אי משום בית המשתה:

רבי

מסורת הש"ס

א) [תוספתא פרק ד], ב) לקמן קכה: קכו., ג) [עי' תוס' לקמן קכה: סד"ה ואודו], ד) [תוספתא פ"ו], ה) רש"ל מ"ז ע"ש, ו) לקמן קמא., ז) ביצה ח., ח) נ"א אבל, ט) [תוספתא ביצה פ"ד], י) ח"מ מ"ז, כ) [לעיל מא:], ל) [שם וש"נ], מ) שלא צבען ולא כרכן במשיחה והיינו כרב אסי כצ"ל.

רב נסים גאון

המדרש ור' יוסי הגלילי שמו וכבר היה רב אידי אבוה דר' יעקב בר אידי הוו קרי ליה בר בי רב דחד יומא כמו שאמרו (חגיגה דף ה) רב אידי אבוה דר' יעקב בר אידי הוה רגיל דהוה אתי תלתא ירחין באורחא והוה קאי חד יומא בבי רב והדר אזיל תלתא ירחין באורחא הוה קאי חד יומא באושפיזיה והדר אתי הוה קא קרו ליה בר בי רב דחד יומא חלש דעתיה קרי אנפשיה (איוב יב) שחוק לרעהו אהיה אמר ליה ר' יוחנן במטותא מינך לא תעניש רבנן נפק ר' יוחנן ודרש (ישעיה נח) ואותי יום יום ידרושון וכי ביום דורשין אותו ובלילה אין דורשין אותו אלא לומר לך כל העוסק בתורה אפילו יום אחד בשנה לשמה מעלה עליו הכתוב כאילו עוסק כל השנה כולה:

ליקוטי רש"י

חריות. חרותא. ענף הדקל משנתקשה שתי שנים ושלש ויואלין בו לולבין הרבה שנשרו עליהן ונתקשו גם הם ונעשו עץ זה פונה לכאן וזה פונה לכאן כענפי שאר אילנות [סוכה לב.]. שגדרן לעצים. שחתכן להיסק [לקמן קכה:]. וכרכן במשיחה. לונל"י בלע"ז קושרם בחוט של משיחה [ר"ה כב:]. משיחה. חוט [גיטין עח:]. הקש שעל גבי המטה. וסתמא להסקה ומוקצה הוא ובא לשכב עליו ומנענעו כדי שיהא לף ורך לשכב. לא ינענעו בידו. דמוקצה הוא. אבל מנענעו בגופו. בכתפיו וטלטול מן הצד הוא דלא שמיה טלטול. או שהיה עליו כר או סדין. דגלי דעתיה דאקלייה לשכיבה מעתה תורת כלי עליו [לקמן קמא.]. מכנים אדם מלא קופתו עפר. בסתם ונותנו במקום אחד ועושה בה כל צרכיו ולא אמרינן בטלה לה לגבי קרקע הבית איידי דזוטרא. והוא שיחד לו כו'. ולא שטחה דמוכחא מילתא דלצרכיו קא בעי לה ובעפר תיחוח קאמר שאינו מחוסר לא חפירה ולא כתישה אלא הכנה [ביצה ח.]. נתר. קרקע הוא או אבן כעין שקורין קרי"א בלע"ז [תענית יג.]. מין אדמה הוא וקורין לה ניתרא [סנהדרין מט: וכעי"ז לקמן פט:].

עין משפט נר מצוה

יט א (מיי' פכ"ה מהל' שבת) סמג לאוין סה טוש"ע או"ח סימן רנט סעיף א:

כ ב ג מיי' פכ"ה מהל' שבת הלכה כא טור שו"ע או"ח סימן שח סעיף כ:

כא ד מיי' פי"ט מהל' שבת הלכה טו טור שו"ע שם סעיף כד [וסי' שא סעיף כ]:

כב ה ו מיי' פכ"ה מהל' שבת הלכה כב סמג שם טוש"ע שם סעיף לח וסימן תלא סעיף יז:

כג ז מיי' פכ"ג מהלכות שבת הלכה ז סמג שם טוש"ע או"ח סימן שכג סעיף ט:

רבינו חננאל

כרבא דאמר לא שנו אלא שלא יחדן להטמנה אבל יחדן להטמנה מטלטלין אותן דהא ר' נמי תני כוותיה. ורבינא דהוא בתראה אוקמה למשנתנו בשל הפתק א). פי' הפתק לשון יוני הוא. כגון אוצר המוטל לסחורה. כדתנן בע"ז (ל"ט:) החגבים הבאים מן הסלילה אסורין ומן ההפתק מותרין ותני' (שם מ:) חגבין והקפלוטאות הבאים מן ההפתק ומן האוצר ומן הספינה מותרין. כדתנינן גידי צמר של הפתק אין מטלטלין אותן אם התקינן בעל הבית להשתמש בהן מותר: חריות של דקל שגדרן לעצים ונמלך עליהן לישיבה. אוקימנא ר' חנינא בן עקיבא אומר צריך לקשר. ר' שמעון בן גמליאל אומר אין צריך לקשר. אמר רבה בר בר חנה הלכתא כרשב"ג ואע"ג דאמר רב יקשור הא אמר שמואל יחשוב כרבה בר בר חנה. ודר' אסי נמי דאמר כי האי תנא דתני יוצאין בפיקריון ובציפא כו' פי' פאה נכרית והוא שיער שעושה בקפח והקרח נותנן בראשו ונראה כי אותו שיער שבקפח שיער ראשו הוא ואם יצא בהן שעה אחת מבעוד יום דיו והא דאמר רב אסי עדיפא מדשמואל. ונמצא רב לגבייהו יחיד ויחיד ורבים הלכה כרבים: הא דאמר רב יהודה מכניס אדם מלא קופתו עפר כבר פרשתי' במס' י"ט ולא (אכרע בהא מילתא) [בר מיעבדא

חשק שלמה על רבינו חננאל

א) עיין ערוך ערך אפתק:

subject of a dispute between **Tannaim.** For it was taught in a Baraisa: **בְּכֹּל חָפִין אֶת הַכֵּלִים** – ONE MAY RUB UTENSILS to shine them on the Sabbath WITH ANYTHING, i.e. any substance, **חוּץ מִכְּלֵי כֶסֶף בְּגַרְתְּקוֹן** – EXCEPT SILVER UTENSILS WITH TARTAR.[11] Silver is a soft metal, and applying tartar scrapes the silver smooth.[12] **הָא נֶתֶר וְחוֹל מוּתָּר** – It is **implied** by this Baraisa **that** using **niter or sand** to shine silver **is permitted,** for these agents do not smooth silver. **וְהָתַנְיָא נֶתֶר וְחוֹל אָסוּר** – **Yet it was taught in a** second **Baraisa:** NITER AND SAND ARE FORBIDDEN. **מַאי לַאו בְּהָא קָמִיפַּלְגֵי** – Now **is it not so that [these Baraisos] differ regarding the following, דְּמַר סָבַר בְּעִינַן מַעֲשֶׂה** – **that** one **master holds we require an act** to remove the *muktzeh* status of sand or niter **וּמַר סָבַר לֹא בְּעִינַן מַעֲשֶׂה** – **and** the other **master holds we do not require an act?**[13]

The Gemara responds:

לֹא – **No,** not necessarily. **דְּכוּלֵּי עָלְמָא לֹא בְּעִינַן מַעֲשֶׂה** – It may be **that all agree** that where no act is feasible, **we do not require an act, וְלֹא קַשְׁיָא** – **yet there is no difficulty. הָא רַבִּי יְהוּדָה הָא רַבִּי שִׁמְעוֹן** – **This** Baraisa **follows R' Yehudah, and that** Baraisa **follows R' Shimon.** That is, it may be that rubbing silver utensils with niter or sand might unintentionally result in the utensils being smoothed out. Accordingly, **הָא רַבִּי יְהוּדָה דְּאָמַר דָּבָר שֶׁאֵין מִתְכַּוֵּין אָסוּר** – **this** Baraisa, which forbids the use of niter and sand, **follows R' Yehudah, who maintains that an unintentional act is forbidden, הָא רַבִּי שִׁמְעוֹן דְּאָמַר דָּבָר שֶׁאֵין מִתְכַּוֵּין מוּתָּר** – **while that** Baraisa, which permits using niter or sand, **follows R' Shimon, who maintains that an unintentional act is permitted.**[14]

The Gemara asks:

בְּמַאי אוֹקִימְתָּא לְהָא דְּשָׁרֵי – **How have you established that** Baraisa – **which permits** using niter and sand – **כְּרַבִּי שִׁמְעוֹן** – **in accordance with R' Shimon? אֵימָא סֵיפָא** – **But consider the later clause** of that Baraisa: **אֲבָל לֹא יָחוֹף בָּהֶם שְׂעָרוֹ** – BUT HE MAY NOT RUB HIS HAIR WITH THEM. **וְאִי רַבִּי שִׁמְעוֹן מִשְׁרָא קָשָׁרֵי** – **And if** the Baraisa follows **R' Shimon, why, he permits** this. **דִּתְנַן** – **For we learned in a Mishnah:**[15]

NOTES

11. Tartar is the deposit that forms in barrels of wine (*Rashi;* cf. *Aruch*).

12. *Rashi;* cf. *Rambam, Hil. Shabbos* 23:7. *Smoothing* (מְמַחֵק) is an *av melachah.*

13. The Gemara presently assumes that all agree that niter and sand do not smooth out the silver. The issue is rather one of *muktzeh.* [Sand and niter (which is a type of earth; see above, 41a note 11)) are both *muktzeh;* see above, 39a.] The Baraisa that permits the use of these substances refers to where the person brought in a basketful of them and set aside a spot for their storage. This suffices to lift the *muktzeh* prohibition even according to the Rabbis, as explained by Rav Pappa above. The Baraisa which forbids using these substances, on the other hand, disputes Rav Pappa and maintains that according to the Rabbis an act must be performed to the substances to render them non-*muktzeh.* Since no such act is possible here, the items remain *muktzeh (Rashi).*

Had Rav Pappa not advanced his explanation, we could have simply said that the Baraisa which permits using the niter and sand follows Rabban Shimon ben Gamliel, who maintains that intention suffices, while the Baraisa which rules that niter and sand may not be used follows the Rabbis, who require an act. But now that Rav Pappa has explained that all agree that where no act is possible the person's intention to use the item suffices, we have no choice but to say that this point is disputed by the Baraisos (*Rosh Yosef*).

14. As explained on 41b note 2, R' Yehudah and R' Shimon dispute the permissibility of an act on the Sabbath which, although performed for a permissible purpose, may result in the performance of a *melachah.* Thus, if we assume that using niter and sand sometimes results in the utensil being smoothed out, we can say that the dispute of the Baraisos depends on the general dispute of R' Yehudah and R' Shimon regarding an unintentional act.

15. *Nazir* 42a.

נוטל את הכיסוי והן נופלות אלא אי איתמר הכי איתמר אמר רבא לא שנו אלא שלא יחדן להטמנה אבל יחדן להטמנה מטלטלין אותן איתמר נמי כי אתא רבין א"ר יעקב א"ר אסי בן שאול אמר רבי לא שנו אלא שלא יחדן להטמנה אבל יחדן להטמנה מטלטלין אותן רבינא אומר [א]בשל הפתק שנו תניא נמי הכי [א]גיזי צמר של הפתק אין מטלטלין אותן ואם התקינן בעל הבית להשתמש בהן מטלטלין אותן תנא רבה בר בר חנה קמיה דרב [ב]חריות של דקל שגדרן לעצים ונמלך עליהן לישיבה צריך לקשר רשב"ג [ב]אומר אין צריך לקשר הוא תני לה והוא אמר לה הלכה כרשב"ג איתמר רב אמר קושר ושמואל אמר חושב [ג]ורב אסי אמר [ג]יושב אע"פ שלא קישר ואע"פ שלא חישב בשלמא רב הוא דאמר כת"ק ושמואל נמי הוא דאמר כרשב"ג אלא רב אסי דאמר כמאן הוא דאמר כי האי תנא דתניא [ד]יוצאין [ד]בפקורין ובציפא בזמן שצבען [ה](בשמן) וכרכן במשיחה לא צבען [ה](בשמן) ולא כרכן במשיחה אין יוצאין בהם ואם יצא בהן שעה אחת מבעוד יום אע"פ שלא צבע ולא כרכן במשיחה מותר לצאת בהן אמר רב אשי אף אנן נמי תנינא [ו]הקש שעל גבי המטה לא ינענעו בידו אבל מנענעו בגופו אבל אם היה (עליו) מאכל בהמה או שהיה עליו כר או סדין מבעוד יום מנענעו בידו ש"מ ומאן תנא דפליג עליה דרשב"ג רבי חנינא בן עקיבא דכי אתא רב דימי אמר זעירי א"ר חנינא פעם אחת הלך רבי חנינא בן עקיבא למקום אחד ומצא חריות של דקל שגדרום לשום עצים ואמר להם לתלמידיו צאו וחשבו כדי שנשב עליהן למחר ולא ידענא אי בית המשתה הוה אי בית האבל הוה מדקאמר אי בית המשתה הוה אי בית האבל הוה דוקא בית האבל או בית המשתה דטרידי אבל הכא קשר אין לא קשר לא [ז]אמר רב יהודה [ה]מכנים אדם מלא קופתו עפר ועושה בה כל צרכו דרש מר זוטרא משמיה דמר זוטרא רבה [ו]והוא שיחד לו קרן זוית אמרו רבנן קמיה דרב פפא כמאן כרבן שמעון בן גמליאל דאי כרבנן האמרי בעינן מעשה אמר להו רב פפא אפילו תימא רבנן עד כאן לא קאמרי רבנן דבעינן מעשה אלא מידי דבר עבידא ביה מעשה אבל מידי דלא בר מיעבדא ביה מעשה לא נימא כתנאי בכל [ז]חפין את הכלים חוץ מכלי כסף בגרתקון [ח]הא נתר וחול מותר והתניא [ט]נתר וחול אסור מאי לאו בהא קמיפלגי דמר סבר בעינן מעשה ומר סבר לא בעינן מעשה לא דכולי עלמא לא בעינן מעשה ולא קשיא [י](הא רבי יהודה הא ר' שמעון) הא [כ]רבי יהודה דאמר דבר שאין מתכוין אסור הא ר' שמעון דאמר [ל]דבר שאין מתכוין מותר במאי אוקימתא להא דשרי כר"ש אימא סיפא אבל לא יחוף בהם שערו ואי ר"ש משרא קשרי דתנן נזיר

רש"י

נוטל את הכיסוי. אלמא בהנך דטמן נמי קאסר לטלטולי אלא על ידי כיסוי: **יחדן להטמנה.** לעולם: **רבינא אומר.** לעולם כדקאמר רבא אם טמן בהן מותר לטלטל דכמאן דיחדן להכי דמו ורבא לאו אמתניתין קאי דמתניתין בגיזין של הפתק דודאי עתיד להחזירן משם ולא יחדן לכך: **הפתק.** מערכה גדולה שעורכין ומושיבין להקלותן לסחורה שקורין ט"ש בין של בגדים בין של צמר בין של חגבים ובשר מלוח: **חריות.** ענפים קשים כעץ משהוקשו שדראות של לולבין ונפלו עלין שלהן קרי להן חריות: **שגדרן.** כל (לקיטת) [קצירת] תמרים קרי גדירה: **צריך לקשר.** לקשרם יחד מבעוד יום להוכיח שלישיבה עומדים ואם לא קשרם יחד אסור לטלטלן למחר דלא הוי יחוד במחשבה: **ורב אסי אמר ישב.** עליהן מבעוד יום: **ואע"פ שלא חישב.** עליהן לישב למחר גלי דעתיה דלישיבה קיימי: **פקורין.** פשתן סרוק שנותנין על המכה: **בציפא.** צמר מנופץ הניתן על המכה: **בזמן שצבען בשמן.** גלי דעתיה דלמכה קיימי להניחן עליה בשבת דלאו לרפואה נינהו אלא שלא ישרטו מלבושיו את מכתו והוה ליה כמלבוש דעלמא אבל לא צבען בשמן דלאו מלבוש נינהו הוה ליה משאוי ואין יוצאין בו לר"ה: **ואם יצא בהן כו'.** היינו כרב אסי דאמר ישב אע"פ שלא קשר ולא חישב: **אף אנן נמי תנינא.** כרב אסי: **קש.** סתמיה לטינא קאי ללבנים או להסקה ומוקצה הוא ואם היה נתון על המטה ולא לשכב עליו ובא בשבת לשכב עליו והוצרך לנענעו ולשוטחו לשכיבה שלא יהא צבור וקשה: **לא ינענעו בידו.** שאסור לטלטלו: **אבל מנענעו בגופו.** כלאחר יד: **או שהיה עליו כר או סדין.** ששכב עליו מבעוד יום ואע"פ שלא יחדו לכך ולא חישב עליו דהיינו כרב אסי: **ומאן תנא.** דלעיל דאמר צריך לקשור ופליג אדרבן שמעון: **ולא ידענא.** זעירי קאמר לה: **דטרידי.** ולא יכלו לקשור מבעוד יום והתם הוא דשרי בלא קישור אבל בעלמא לא: **מכנים מלא קופתו עפר.** לכסות בו צואה ורוק ומערה העפר בביתו לארץ ונוטלו תמיד לכל צרכיו: **והוא שייחד לו קרן זוית.** דהוי כמוכן ועומד לכך אבל נתנו באמצע ביתו למדרס רגלים הרי הוא בטל לגבי קרקעית הבית ומוקצה ואסור: **כרבן שמעון.** דשרי במחשבה בעלמא שאין מעשה מוכיח שעומד לעשות צרכיו: **דבר מעביד מעשה.** שכן מעשה הוא שיכול לעשות בו מעשה הוכחה: **לימא כתנאי.** הא דרב יהודה במידי דלאו בר מעשה: **חפין.** משפשפין את הכלים בשבת לצחצחן: **חוץ מכלי כסף בגרתקון.** כמין עפר שגדל בחבית של יין וקורין לו אלו"ס והוא עיקר תקון כלי כסף וגורר אותו שהכסף רך והוא ממחק שהוא אב מלאכה: **אבל נתר וחול מותר.** דלא גריר ליה לכסף: **מאי לאו.** הא דתניא אסור לאו משום דגריר ליה אלא משום מוקצה קאסר ליה ותנא דשרי כגון שהכניס מלא קופתו לכך ועירה על גבי קרקע ומאן דאסר קסבר בעינן מעשה וזה לא יכול: **לא דכולי עלמא.** במידי דלאו בר מעשה לא בעינן מעשה דאית להו הא דרב יהודה וטעמא מאן דאסר דזימנין דגריר ואף על גב דלא מיכוין לגרור אסור כרבי יהודה דאמר דבר שאין מתכוין אסור ומאן דשרי כר"ש ומיהו גרתקון אסור דודאי גריר ומודה ר"ש בפסיק רישיה ולא ימות: **לא יחוף בהן.** בנתר וחול שערו בשבת מפני שמשירו: נזיר

תוספות

אלא אי איתמר כו'. אין גירסא זו נכונה דלכאורה משמע שלרבא עצמו היה מקשה וטפי הוי ניחא אי הוה גרס אלא אמר רבא אבל לפי זה הוה צריך לומר דרבינא לפלוגי אתא:

רבינא אומר בשל הפתק שנו. ומילתא דרבא כדקאמר מעיקרא ובשאינה של הפתק ותימה דרבא קאמר לא שנו משמע דאמתניתין קאי והא מתניתין איירי בשל הפתק וי"ל דרישא איירי בכל גיזי צמר בין של הפתק בין שאינם של הפתק דאין מטלטלים אותן וקאמר רבא לא שנו בהנהו שאינה של הפתק אלא שלא טמן בהן אבל טמן בהן מטלטלים אותן והא דקתני סיפא כיצד הוא עושה כו' בשל הפתק קאמר ואע"פ שטמן בהן אין מטלטלין כיון שלא הזמינן:

ורב אסי אמר ישב אע"פ שלא קשר ושלא חישב. רבינו שמשון הזקן פסק כרב אסי מדקאמר בסמוך רב אשי שהוא בתרא מתני' נמי דיקא ור"ת פוסק כרב מכח קושיא כמו שמפורש בפרק כל הכלים (לקמן דף קכו. בד"ה ר"י אומר ושם):

בפקורין ובציפא. פר"ח כיפה שיש בה שער ונותנין אותה בראש הקרח ונראה שהוא שער ראשו: **אבל** לא צבען בשמן אין יוצאין בהן. לאו דוקא אין יוצאין דאפילו לטלטלם אסור לפי שאינם מוכנים אלא נקט אין יוצאין אגב רישא ובסמוך נמי דקאמר אבל יצא בהן שעה אחת מבעוד יום לאו דוקא יצא דהוא הדין ישב בהן בביתו:

ואם יצא בהן שעה אחת כו'. אע"פ [מ]שלא צבע ולא חישב היינו כרב אסי דאמר ישב אע"פ שלא חישב ולא קישר קשה לר"י רישא דקתני יוצאין בהן בזמן שצבען מאי אריא צבען אפילו חישב נמי דהא כיון דמתיר יצא אע"פ שלא צבע ולא חישב כל שכן חישב ולא צבע דלכאורה ישיבה גריעא ממחשבה וכן נמי יציאה ותירץ דהאי דקאמר צבען לא לצאת בהן בשבת אלא כדי לצאת בהן מבעוד יום ואחר כך נמלך ואפ"ה יכול לצאת בהן בשבת:

ולא ידענא אי בית האבל הוה. פי' אי משום בית האבל התיר אי משום בית המשתה:

רבי

עין משפט נר מצוה

יט א (מיי' פכ"ה מהל' שבת) סמג לאוין סה טוש"ע או"ח סימן רנט סעיף א:

כ ב ג מיי' פכ"ה מהל' שבת הלכה כא טור שו"ע או"ח סימן שח סעיף כ:

כא ד מיי' פי"ט מהל' שבת הלכה טו טור שו"ע שם סעיף כד [וסי' שא סעיף כ]:

כב ה ו מיי' פכ"ה מהל' שבת הלכה כב סמג שם טוש"ע שם סעיף לח וסימן תלא סעיף יח:

כג ז מיי' פכ"ג מהלכות שבת הלכה ז סמג שם טוש"ע או"ח סימן שכג סעיף ט:

רבינו חננאל

כרבא דאמר לא שנו אלא שלא יחדן להטמנה אבל יחדן להטמנה מטלטלין אותן דהא ר' נמי תני כוותיה. ורבינא דהוא בתראה אוקמה למשנתנו בשל הפתק א). פי' הפתק לשון יוני הוא. כגון אוצר המוטל לסחורה. כדתנן בע"ז (ל"ט:) החגבים הבאים מן הסלילה אסורין ומן ההפתק מותרין ותני' (שם מ:) חגבין והקפלוטאות הבאים מן ההפתק ומן האוצר ומן הספינה מותרין. כדתנינן גיזי צמר של הפתק אין מטלטלין אותן אם התקינן בעל הבית להשתמש בהן מותר: **חריות** של דקל שגדרן לעצים ונמלך עליהן לישיבה. אוקימנא ר' חנינא בן עקיבא אומר צריך לקשר. ר' שמעון בן גמליאל אומר אין צריך לקשר. אמר רבה בר בר חנה הלכתא כרשב"ג ואע"ג דאמר רב יקשור הא אמר שמואל יחשוב כרבה בר בר חנה. ודר' אסי נמי דאמר כי האי תנא דתני יוצאין בפיקריון ובציפא כו' פי' פאה נכרית והוא שיער שעושה בקפה והקרח נותנן בראשו ונראה כי אותו שיער שבקפה שיער ראשו הוא ואם יצא בהן שעה אחת מבעוד יום דיו והא דאמר רב אסי עדיפא מדשמואל. ונמצא רב לגבייהו יחיד ויחיד ורבים הלכה כרבים: **הא** דאמר רב יהודה מכנים אדם מלא קופתו עפר כבר פרשתי' במס' י"ט ולא (אכרע בהא מילתא) [בר מיעבדא]

חשק שלמה על רבינו חננאל

א) עיין ערוך ערך אפתק:

מסורת הש"ס

א) [תוספתא פרק ד], ב) לקמן קכה: קכו., ג) [עי' תוס' לקמן קכה: סד"ה ואזדו], ד) [תוספתא פ"ו], ה) רש"ל מ"ז עי"ש, ו) לקמן קמא., ז) ביצה ח., ח) נ"א אבל, ט) [תוספתא ביצה פ"ד], י) מ"מ מ"ז, כ) [לעיל מא:], ל) [שם וש"נ], מ) שלא צבען ולא כרכן במשיחה והיינו כרב אסי כצ"ל.

רב נסים גאון

המדרש ור' יוסי הגלילי שמו וכבר היה רב אידי אבוה דר' יעקב בר אידי הוו קרי ליה בר בי רב דחד יומא כמו שאמרו (חגיגה דף ה) רב אידי אבוה דר' יעקב בר אידי הוה רגיל דהוה אתי תלתא ירחין באורחא והוה קאי חד יומא בבי רב והדר אזיל תלתא ירחין באורחא הוה קאי חד יומא באושפיזיה והדר אתי הוה קא קרו ליה בר בי רב דחד יומא חלש דעתיה קרי אנפשיה (איוב יב) שחוק לרעהו אהיה אמר ליה ר' יוחנן במטותא מינך לא תענישא רבנן נפק ר' יוחנן ודרש (ישעיה נח) ואותי יום יום ידרושון וכי ביום דורשין אותו ובלילה אין דורשין אותו אלא לומר לך כל העוסק בתורה אפילו יום אחד בשנה לשמה מעלה עליו הכתוב כאילו עוסק כל השנה כולה:

ליקוטי רש"י

חריות. חרותא. ענף הדקל משנתקשה שתי שנים ושלש ויוצאין בו לולבין הרבה שנשרו עליהן ונתקשו גם הם ונעשו עץ זה פונה לכאן וזה פונה לכאן כענפי שאר אילנות [סוכה לב.]. **שגדרן לעצים.** שחתכן להיסק [לקמן קכה:]. **וכרכן במשיחה.** לנוי"ש בלע"ז קושרם בחוט של משיחה [ר"ה כב:]. משיחה. חוט [גיטין עח:]. **הקש שעל גבי המטה.** וסתמא להסקה ומוקצה הוא ובא לשכב עליו ומנענעו כדי שיהא רך ורך לשכב. **לא ינענעו בידו.** דמוקצה הוא. **אבל מנענעו בגופו.** בכתפיו וטלטול מן הצד הוא דלא שמיה טלטול. **או שהיה עליו כר או סדין.** דגלי דעתיה דאקצייה לשכיבה מעתה תורת כלי עליו [לקמן קמא.]. **מכנים אדם מלא קופתו עפר.** בסתם ונותנו במקום אחד ועושה בה כל צרכיו ולא אמרינן בטלה לה לגבי קרקע הבית איידי דזוטרא. **והוא שיחד לו כו'.** ולא שטחה דמוכחא מילתא דלצרכיו קא בעי לה ובעפר תיחוח קאמר שאינו מחוסר לא חפירה ולא כתישה אלא הכנה [ביצה ח.]. **נתר.** קרקע הוא או אבן כעין שקורין קרי"א בלע"ז [תענית יג.]. מין אדמה הוא וקורין לה ניתרא [סנהדרין מט: וכעי"ז לקמן פט:].

גמרא

[א] נזיר חופף [ל] ומפספס אבל לא סורק אלא הא והא ר' יהודה היא ותרי תנאי אליבא דר' יהודה האי תנא אליבא דר' יהודה סבר גריר והאי תנא אליבא דר' יהודה סבר לא גריר במאי אוקימתא כר' יהודה אימא סיפא אבל פניו ידיו ורגליו מותר הא מעבר שיער איבעית אימא בקטן ואיבעית אימא באשה ואיבעית אימא בסרים אמר רב יהודה [ב] עפר לבינתא שרי אמר רב יוסף [מ] כוספא דיסמין שרי אמר רבא עפר פלפלי שרי אמר רב ששת ברדא שרי מאי ברדא אמר רב יוסף תילתא אהלא ותילתא אסא ותילתא סיגלי אמר רב נחמיה בר יוסף [ג] כל היכא דליכא רובא אהלא שפיר דמי בעו מיניה מרב ששת מהו לפצוע זיתים בשבת אמר להו וכי בחול מי התירו קסבר משום הפסד אוכלין לימא פליגא דשמואל דאמר שמואל [ג] [ד] עושה אדם כל צורכו בפת אמרי פת לא מאיסא הני מאיסי אמימר ומר זוטרא ורב אשי הוו יתבי אייתו לקמייהו ברדא אמימר ורב אשי משו מר זוטרא לא משא אמרו ליה לא סבר לה מר להא דאמר רב ששת ברדא שרי אמר להו רב מרדכי בר מיניה דמר דאפילו בחול נמי לא ס"ל סבר לה כי הא דתניא מגרר אדם גלדי צואה וגלדי מכה שעל בשרו בשביל צערו אם בשביל ליפות אסור ואינהו כמאן סברוה כי הא דתניא [ה] רוחץ אדם פניו ידיו ורגליו בכל יום בשביל קונו משום שנאמר [א] כל פעל ה' למענהו: רבי אלעזר בן עזריה אומר קופה מטה על צדה ונוטל שמא יטול וכו': אמר רבי אבא אמר רבי חייא בר אשי [ה] (אמר רב) [ה] הכל מודים שאם נתקלקלה הגומא שאסור להחזיר תנן וחכמים אומרים נוטל ומחזיר היכי דמי אי דלא נתקלקלה הגומא [י] שפיר קא אמרי רבנן אלא לאו אף על פי דנתקלקלה הגומא לא לעולם דלא נתקלקלה והכא בחוששין קמיפלגי מר סבר חוששין שמא נתקלקלה הגומא ומר סבר [ו] אין חוששין אמר רב הונא [ז] האי סליקוסתא [י] דצה שלפה והדר דצה שריא ואי לאו אסיר אמר שמואל האי [ח] סכינא דביני אורבי דצה שלפה והדר דצה שרי ואי לאו אסיר מר זוטרא ואיתימא רב אשי אמר בגורדיתא דקני שפיר דמי אמר ליה רב מרדכי לרבא מתיב רב קטינא תיובתא [ס] הטומן לפת וצנונות תחת הגפן אם היה מקצת עליו מגולים אינו חושש לא

רש"י

נזיר. בחול ככל אדם בשבת: חופף. שערו בנתר וחול[ט]: ומפספס. מנפץ שערו דכיון דאינו מתכוין מותר ועל כרחיך ר"ש קא אמר לה אלמא נתר וחול זימנין דאינו משיר ולא דמי לפסיק רישיה ולא ימות: אבל לא סורק. במסרק דודאי משיר: אלא הא והא. הנך תרתי מתני' דלעיל דפליגי בנתר וחול ר' יהודה ומאן דאסר סבר זימנין דגריר ור' יהודה האמר דבר שאין מתכוין אסור ומאן דשרי סבר לא גריר כלל ואין כאן משום ממחק: במאי אוקימתא כר' יהודה ה"ג. ול"ג להא דתניא אסור דהא תרוייהו כר' יהודה אוקימנא להו ועוד הך סיפא דפריך אבל פניו ידיו ורגליו מותר לאו סיפא דההיא דתניא אסור הוא אלא סיפא דההיא דתניא מותר דהכי תני בה לא יחוף בהן שערו אבל פניו ידיו ורגליו מותר והא מלתא גבי הך דתני מותר פריכנא ליה לעיל: בקטן אשה וסרים. דלית להו זקן: עפר לבינתא. כתישת לבינה: שרי. לחוף פניו ואפי' מי שיש לו זקן: כוספא דיסמין. פסולת שומשמין: עפר פילפלי. שחיקת פלפלין: ברדא שרי. לרחוץ פניו: אהלא. שורש עשב ששמו אהל: אסא. הדס: סגלי. עשב שקורין ויאו"ל ויש בו שלשה עלין: כל היכא דליכא רובא אהלא שפיר דמי. ואפי' הוי טפי מתלתא אהלא ופליג אדרב יוסף דרב יוסף תלתא אהלא דווקא קאמר שהאהל עשוי ללבן ולהלהא כבורית ומשיר שיער: לפצוע זיתים. בליי"א בלע"ז על הסלע למתק מרירותו: כל צורכו. בין תשמיש בין לפרר אותה ולמחתה בתבשיל רותח: משום ליפות את עצמו אסור. משום לא ילבש גבר שמלת אשה (דברים כב): בשביל קונהו. לכבוד קונהו דכתיב (בראשית ט) כי בצלם אלהים עשה וגו' ועוד דהרואה בריות נאות אומר ברוך שככה לו בעולמו: כל פעל ה' למענהו. הכל ברא לכבודו: שאם נתקלקלה הגומא. שנפלו הגיזין למקום מושב הקדרה: שאסור להחזיר. לפי שמזיז הגיזין לכאן ולכאן: שפיר קאמרי רבנן. ומאי טעמא דר' אלעזר: חוששין. אי שרית ליה ליטול לכתחילה בקופה זקופה פעמים שנתקלקלה ואתי נמי להחזירה הלכך תקון ליה רבנן להטות קופה על לדה: סליקוסתא. עשב שהוא נאה למראה ולהריח וממלאין כד עפר לח ותוחבין אותו לתוכו ונותנו לפני שרים וכשהוא רוצה נוטלו ומריח בו ומחזירו למקומו ואי מבעוד יום דלה לתוך העפר ושלפה והדר דלה שפיר דמי ליטלה למחר ולהחזירה שהרי הורחב מקום מושבה והוחלק מבעוד יום ואינו מזיז עפר: סכינא דביני אורבי. שנועצין סכין בין שורות הלבנים שבבנין להשתמר: בגורדיתא דקני. קנים הדקלים (א) שיולאין הרבה בגזע אחד ותכופין זה בזה שפיר דמי לנעוץ בתוכן סכין לשמרו ואין חוששין שמא יגרור הקליפה וחייב משום מוחק: מתיב רב קטינא תיובתא. להנך רבנן דאמרי דאי לא דלה ושלפה אסור: הטומן לפת. להשתמר בקרקע שכן דרכו הא דנקט מקצת עליו מגולין משום ניטלין בשבת נקט לה ולאו משום מידי אחריני דאי אין מקצת עליו מגולין אין לו במה לאוחזה אא"כ מזיז העפר בידים: לא

תוספות

[י] רבי שמעון אומר נזיר חופף ומפספס כו'. ומיירי בנתר וחול דתנן בתר הכי בפ' ג' מינין (נזיר דף מב.) ר' ישמעאל אומר נזיר לא יחוף ראשו באדמה לפי שמשיר את השער: אבל לא סורק. התם מפרש טעמא משום דלהשרת נימין המדולדלות מתכוין:

במאי אוקימתא כר' יהודה אימא סיפא כו'. בשלמא אי כר"ש אתיא שפיר דאיכא למימר דשערות פניו ידיו ורגליו אינם נושרות מהר ולא הוי פסיק רישיה ושרי אבל בראשו אסור דהוי פסיק רישיה אבל השתא דאוקימתא כר' יהודה אע"ג דלא הוה פסיק רישיה הוה לן למיסר:

מהו לפצוע זיתים בשבת. פירש בקונט' להכותם על הסלע למתק מרירותן ומיבעיא ליה אי אסיר בשבת משום שווי אוכלא ותיקוני אוכלא ופריך ובחול מי התירו דאיכא הפסד אוכלין שנפסד המשקה הזב מהן:
וקשה לפ"ו דבפ' חבית גבי דיני סחיטה ה"ל למיתני ועוד מה הפסד אוכלין יש כיון שעושה לתקנם ומפרש ר"י מהו לפצוע לחוף פניו ידיו ורגליו כי ההוא דלעיל ודרך מי זיתים להעביר וללבן כדאמר במסכת ע"ז מולטן ברותחין או מולגן במי זיתים ופריך ובחול מי התירו דאיכא הפסד דנמאסין לאכילה. (ת"י)

בשביל צערו. ואם אין לו צער אחר אלא שמתבייש לילך בין בני אדם שרי דאין לך צער גדול מזה:

הכל מודים שאם נתקלקלה הגומא שאסורה להחזיר. ואפי' לר"א בן תדאי דאמר בפרק כל הכלים (לקמן קכג.) תוחב בכוש או בכרכר והן ננערות מאליהן דטלטול מן הצד לא שמיה טלטול וכן קי"ל הכא עדיף טפי מטלטול מן הצד שצריך לטלטל אילך ואילך כשרולין להטמין: אי לא נתקלקלה הגומא פשיטא. טפי הוה ליה למפרך מ"ט דמאן דאסר:

גורדיתא דקני. מין אילן כפירוש הקונטרס כדמשמע בעושין פסין (עירובין יט:) ומיירי למטה מג' דליכא איסור משתמש במחובר כדאמר בפרק כל הכלים (לקמן קכה:) ובפרק בתרא דעירובין (דף ק.):

הטומן לפת וצנונות כו'. ע"כ בשלא השרישו מיירי דבהשרישו לא היו ניטלין בשבת ואם תאמר בשלמא כלאים ושביעית איצטריך לאשמעינן דלא גזרינן כשמתכוין להטמין אטו דילמא אתי לנטועה אבל מעשר אמאי נקטיה דאפי' השרישו לא שייך מעשר כיון דליכא תוספת ואי נקטיה דשרי לעשר מן התלוש ממקום אחר עליו או לעשותו מעשר על התלוש ולא חיישי' דילמא אתי לעשר מן התלוש על המחובר או להפך א"כ הוה ליה למינקט תרומה דבכל דוכתא רגיל להזכיר תרומה על זה כדאמר (תרומות פ"א מ"ה) אין תורמין מן התלוש על המחובר [ס] פירות ערוגה זו תלושין יהיו תרומה על פירות ערוגה זו מחוברין ואומר ר"י דרגילות הוא שמתוספין מחמת ליחלוחית הקרקע כמו שאנו רואין שומין ובצלים שמתוספין אפי' כשמונחין בחלון ועל אותו תוספת קאמר דלא בעי לעשורי ודוקא נקט הטומן אבל במתכוין לנטיעה חושש משום כולן:

מקצת עליו מגולים. משום דבעי למתני וניטלין בשבת נקט מקצת עליו מגולים כדפירש בקונטרס ובערוך[ל] משמע דמשום כולהו נקט דפירש בשם רב האי גאון דגרס אם היו מקצתם מגולים שאם האמהות טמונים בקרקע והעלים מגולים הרי זו זריעה מעולה אלא דוקא מקצתן מגולים אינו חושש משום כלאים ושביעית דלאו זריעה היא ומה שהקשה והלא זריעה מעולה היא לאו פירכא היא דבלא השרישו איירי כדפרישית ולפירושו קשה דבפרק חלון (עירובין דף עז. ושם) קאמר רב יחיאל כפה ספל ממעט ופריך והא ניטלת בשבת הוא

עין משפט נר מצוה

כד א מיי' פ"ה מהלכות נזירות הלכה יד סמג לאוין מד:
כה ב ג מיי' פכ"ב מהל' שבת הלכה יג סמג לאוין סה טוש"ע או"ח סימן שכו סעיף ט:
כו ד טוש"ע או"ח סימן קנח סעיף ה:
כז ה ו מיי' פכ"א ופכ"ו מהלכות שבת [דין זה ליתא בהרמב"ם ועיין בכ"מ] סמג שם טוש"ע או"ח סימן רנט סעיף ג:
כח ז מיי' פכ"א מהל' שבת הלכה טו טור שו"ע או"ח סימן שיא סעיף ו:
כט ח טוש"ע או"ח סי' שי"ד ס"א:

גליון הש"ס

גמ' האי סליקוסתא. עי' לעיל דף מג ע"ב תוס' ד"ה דכו"ע טלטול:

תורה אור השלם

א) כָּל פָּעַל יְיָ לַמַּעֲנֵהוּ וְגַם רָשָׁע לְיוֹם רָעָה: [משלי טז, ד]

רבינו חננאל

מיעבדא ביה מעשה]: נימא כתנאי בכל חפץ את הכלים כו' מלשון אשה חופפת וסורקת כו' ברחיצת ידים דקא אמרי' אבל רוחץ פניו ידיו ורגליו הא תנא דסבר דבר השרת נימין מדולדלות. אליבא דר' יהודה מוקים להו בקטן וסרים ואשה דלית להון שיער אבל הלכה כר' שמעון דאפי' גברי בעלי שיער שרו ושרי עפר לבינתא שרי למימשא ביה ידיה. ויש מי שמפרש לבינתא מלשון (ש"ה ג) מור ולבונה וכן כוספא דיסמין. וכן בראדא דהיא תילתא אהלא. תילתא סיגלי. תילתא אסא הני כולהו לענין רחיצת ידים בהן. וקיי"ל דבכולהו הני שרי אבל רובא אהלא רב נחמיה לא הוה שרי וכן כולה (אוכלין וכ"ש בשבת) לפצוע זיתים וכיוצא בהן לרחוץ בהן ידיו בחול אסור משום הפסד אוכלין. וכ"ש בשבת שאסור. והא שאמר שמואל עושה אדם כל צורכיו בפת לית הלכתא כוותיה והאוסר ידיו לרחוץ (ברב אדא) [בברדא] סבר לה כי האי תנא דתניא מגרר אדם גילדי צואה וגילדי מכה שעל בשרו בשביל צערו. ואם לייפות עצמו אסור. והמתיר סבר לה כר' שמעון בן גמליאל דאמר רוחץ אדם פניו ידיו ורגליו בשביל כבוד קונו משום שנאמר כל פעל ה' למענהו: מתני' ר' אלעזר בן עזריה אומר קופה מטה על צדה ונוטל כו'. איסקנא הכל מודים שאם נתקלקלה הגומא שאסור להחזיר סליקוסתא שהיא אגודה של חבצלת וכיוצא בה אמר רב הונא דעצה בחול או בטיט וחלצה והריח בטיט מע"ש כדי שתהא נכנסת ויוצא בגומא מותרת (כולה) [לטלטלה] בשבת וכן אמר שמואל בסכינא דנעיצא ביני אורבי כמו שאמר בסליקוסתא. ומותבינן עליה הטומן לפת וצנונות תחת הגפן אם היו מקצתן

מסורת הש"ס

א) לקמן פא: נזיר מב., ב) [פי' פסולת שומשמין שכותשין אותו כותש על יסמין ומייבשין אותו ושוחקין אותו ורוחצין בהן ידים מזוהמות ערוך בערך כספ ועיין רש"י שקיצר בזה], ג) ברכות נ: לקמן קמג. ביצה כא:, ד) [תוספתא ברכות פ"ד ע"ש], ה) ברכות לז., ו) ס"א פשיטא, ז) [כמו דעלה אלא שמבליע העי"ן ומקלף את לשון כ"כ רש"י פ' ויצא למ"ד פל"ס], ח) לקמן קיז. עירובין עז. כלאים פרק א מ"ט [ער' תוספות מנחות מ: ד"ה חסר וכו' מה שהניחו בתימה ועיין תוס' לעיל מג: סד"ה דכו"ע טלטול וכו' ויתוס' התימה], ט) [ער' רש"י ברכות נ: ד"ה מפוספס], י) [שלא תיבות הללו ר"ש אומר לריך סיקון וה"א לומר הסגי כך הי' לפניהם שהרי להדיא אמרינן בנזיר מב. עלה הכך תנאי דתנן נזיר חופף וכו' ומופף ומפספס מני ר"ש היא דאמר דבר שאין מתכוין וכו' ע"ש], כ) [קידושין כב:], ל) [ערך לפת].

הגהות הב"ח

(א) רש"י ד"ה בגורדיתא דקני (קנים הדקלים). תא"מ ונ"ב ס"א קנים הדקלים:

ליקוטי רש"י

חופף. כמו חופף עליו כל היום (דברים לג) לשון מגהד ובלע"ז פרי"ר [נזיר מב.]. לשון שפשוף כמו נזיר חופף ומפספס [נזיר מב.]. מפליא שערו [מגילה כו:]. ומפספס. שמפריד שערותיו זו מזו אבל לא במסרק [נזיר שם]. אבל לא סורק. במסרק דודאי משיר שיער ומודה ר' שמעון בפסיק רישיה ולא ימות אלא חופף ומפספס שאינו משיר וכשמשיר דבר שאין מתכוין מותר [לקמן שם]. סיגלי. דודאים. עשב ריח טוב והלשון ישמעאל יסמין [בלע"ז ויאול"ש] [בראשית ל, יד]. ויול"ש בלע"ז [ברכות מג.]. עיקרי עשבים והוא ממיני בשמים ולאמהות של אותן עשבים קרי סגלי [סנהדרין צט:]. עושה אדם כל צורכו בפת. ומטלטל על ידי הפת ולא חיישינן לבזיון אוכלין [ביצה כא:]. משתמש בו ואין כאן משום בזיון וממחמה בתבשיל [לקמן קמג.]. כל פעל ה' למענהו. הכל עשה בשביל קילוסו כמו (תהלים קמח) ר"ל להעיד עליו כלומר פעלו מעיד עליו על גבורותיו שניה' בהגדת תהלים [משלי טז, ד]. דצה. נעלה [ע"ז עו:]. דון לשון מיקוע כדאמר דלה שלפה (שבת נ:) [יבמות קט:]. ויגב. תרגומו ודעיך לשון תמיהה ונעילה הוא בלשון ארמית והרבה יש בתלמוד (שבת נ:) דלה ושלפה (חולין לג:) דך ביה מידי, דלה כמו דעלה אלא שמקצר את לשונו [בראשית ל, לח]. ביני אורבי. בין שורות הבנין כמותל [ב"מ מב.]. בין לבינה ללבינה [ע"ז מז:]. בגורדיתא דקני. קנים מחוברים הרבה בעץ אחד סמוך לארץ ולמעלה הן מתפרשין [עירובין יט:]. הטומן. להצניע. מקצת עליו מגולים. משום שבת נקט ליה דבעי למיתני ניטלין בשבת שנוטלו ואוחזו בעלין שלהן. אינו חושש. משום כלאי הכרם [שם עז.]. לפי שאינה מושרשת [לקמן קיג.].

נָזִיר חוֹפֵף וּמְפַסְפֵּס אֲבָל לֹא סוֹרֵק – A *NAZIR* MAY RUB the hair of his head with niter and sand AND MAY SEPARATE the hairs by hand, BUT HE MAY NOT COMB them.[1] Thus, we see that using niter and sand will not inevitably remove hair.[2] – ? –

The Gemara accepts this refutation and offers a new answer: אֶלָּא הָא וְהָא רַבִּי יְהוּדָה הִיא – **Rather, both this and that,** i.e. both the Baraisa that permits rubbing utensils with niter and sand and the Baraisa that forbids doing so, **are** in accordance with **R' Yehudah,** וּתְרֵי תַּנָּאֵי אַלִּיבָּא דְּרַבִּי יְהוּדָה – **and** these **two Tannaim** differ **in accordance with** the opinion of **R' Yehudah,** i.e. they disagree as to how R' Yehudah would rule in this case. הַאי תַּנָּא אַלִּיבָּא דְּרַבִּי יְהוּדָה סָבַר גָּרִיר – **This Tanna according to R' Yehudah maintains that [niter and sand]** may **scrape** the utensil smooth. Thus, he forbids using these agents. וְהַאי תַּנָּא אַלִּיבָּא דְּרַבִּי יְהוּדָה סָבַר לֹא גָּרִיר – **And that Tanna according to R' Yehudah maintains that [niter and sand] will not scrape** the utensil. Hence, he permits their use.[3]

The Gemara asks:

בְּמַאי אוֹקִימְתָּא כְּרַבִּי יְהוּדָה – **How have you established** the Baraisos – **according to R' Yehudah?** אֵימָא סֵיפָא – But **consider the final section** of the first Baraisa:[4] אֲבָל פָּנָיו יָדָיו וְרַגְלָיו מוּתָּר – BUT washing HIS FACE, HANDS AND FEET with these agents IS PERMITTED.[5] הָא מְעַבֵּר שֵׂיעָר – **But surely [using these agents] removes hair** from the face! How can R' Yehudah permit this?[6]

The Gemara answers:

אִיבָּעֵית אֵימָא בְּקָטָן – **If you prefer, say** that the Baraisa refers **to a minor;** וְאִיבָּעֵית אֵימָא בְּאִשָּׁה – **and if you prefer, say** that it refers **to a woman;** וְאִיבָּעֵית אֵימָא בְּסָרִיס – **and if you prefer, say** that it refers **to a eunuch.** None of these have facial hair.

The Gemara discusses the use of other agents for washing on the Sabbath:

אָמַר רַב יְהוּדָה – **Rav Yehudah said:** עֲפַר לְבֵינְתָא שָׁרֵי – Using **powdered brick** to wash the face **is permitted,** even for one who has a beard.[7] אָמַר רַב יוֹסֵף – **Rav Yosef said:** כּוּסְפָּא דְּשׁוּמְשְׁמִין שָׁרֵי – **Sesame pulp is permitted.** אָמַר רָבָא – **Rava said:** עֲפַר פִּלְפְּלֵי שָׁרֵי – **Crushed pepper is permitted.** אָמַר רַב שֵׁשֶׁת – **Rav Sheishess said:** בַּרְדָּא שָׁרֵי – ***Barda* is permitted.** מַאי בַּרְדָּא – **What is *barda*?** אָמַר רַב יוֹסֵף – **Rav Yosef said:** תִּילְתָּא אַהֲלָא וְתִילְתָּא אָסָא וְתִילְתָּא סִיגְלֵי – **One-third aloes, one-third myrtle and one-third violets.** אָמַר רַב נְחֶמְיָה בַּר יוֹסֵף – **Rav Nechemyah bar Yosef said:** כָּל הֵיכָא דְּלֵיכָּא רוּבָּא אַהֲלָא שַׁפִּיר דָּמֵי – **As long as less than the majority** of the mixture **is aloes, it is permitted.**[8]

The Gemara switches to a different topic:

בְּעוֹ מִינֵּיהּ מֵרַב שֵׁשֶׁת – **They inquired of Rav Sheishess:** מַהוּ לִפְצוֹעַ זֵיתִים בְּשַׁבָּת – **May one bruise olives** on a rock **on the Sabbath** in order to sweeten them?[9] אָמַר לְהוּ – **He said to them:** וְכִי בְּחוֹל מִי הִתִּירוּ – **And is [this practice] permitted** even **during the week?**

The Gemara explains:

קָסָבַר מִשּׁוּם הֶפְסֵד אוֹכָלִין – **Rav Sheishess holds** that this is forbidden **on account of wasting food.**[10]

The Gemara suggests:

לֵימָא פְּלִיגָא דִּשְׁמוּאֵל – **Let us say** that **this** ruling of Rav Sheishess **disputes that of Shmuel,** דְּאָמַר שְׁמוּאֵל – **for Shmuel said:** עוֹשֶׂה אָדָם כָּל צוֹרְכּוֹ בְּפַת – **A person may use bread** (or any other food) **for all of his needs.** It should thus be permitted to bruise olives to sweeten them.

The Gemara responds that this is not necessarily so:

אָמְרֵי – **They said:** פַּת לֹא מְאִיסָא – **Bread is not rendered repulsive** by such usage as Shmuel permitted. הָנֵי מְאִיסֵי – **These** juices discharged by the olives, however, **are rendered repulsive.**[11]

The Gemara returns to its original topic:

אֲמֵימָר וּמָר זוּטְרָא וְרַב אַשִׁי הֲווּ יָתְבֵי – **Ameimar, Mar Zutra and Rav Ashi were sitting** together one Sabbath. אַיְיתוּ לְקַמַּיְיהוּ בַּרְדָּא – **They brought before them *barda*.** אֲמֵימָר וְרַב אַשִׁי

NOTES

1. A *nazir* is forbidden to remove hairs from his head in any manner. Although washing his hair with niter and sand or separating the hair by hand is liable to remove some hairs, these activities are permitted to a *nazir,* since any removal of hair that results is purely unintentional. This follows the view of R' Shimon, who permits performing an act that might unintentionally result in a forbidden consequence, as long as that consequence is not inevitable. Combing the hair is forbidden, however, since it is inevitable that some hair will be removed (*Rashi*).

2. For even R' Shimon, whose opinion this Baraisa follows, would prohibit their use if it was inevitable that they would remove hair.

3. According to R' Yehudah, even if it is only possible – not inevitable – that the utensil will be smoothed by using a particular agent, using that agent is forbidden. The Tanna of one Baraisa maintains that niter and sand possess the capability of smoothing. Hence he forbids their use according to R' Yehudah. The Tanna of the other Baraisa maintains that niter and sand are not capable of smoothing a utensil. Accordingly, he rules that these agents may be used even according to R' Yehudah (*Rashi*).

4. I.e. the Baraisa that permits using niter and sand (see *Rashi*).

5. This statement follows on the heels of the Baraisa's previous statement that one may not use niter and sand to wash his head. The Baraisa concludes that washing one's face, hands and feet, however, is permitted.

6. Had we explained this Baraisa as following R' Shimon, we could have said that loosening hairs is an inevitable consequence of washing the head, whereas washing the face only possibly, not inevitably, produces such a consequence. Thus, washing the head is forbidden while washing the face is permitted. But now that we have explained the Baraisa in accordance with R' Yehudah, the Baraisa should have forbidden washing even the face, although hair removal in this case is not inevitable (see *Tosafos*).

7. Since powdered brick does not necessarily remove hair, it is permitted (*Meiri*) according to R' Shimon (whom the halachah follows).

8. Rav Yosef permitted a mixture containing no more than one-third aloes. Rav Nechemyah, on the other hand, permits up to half aloes. Beyond this amount, however, even Rav Nechemyah admits that the high aloes content is sure to remove hair and is forbidden (*Rashi*).

9. Bruising olives blunts their bitter taste (*Rashi;* see *Bava Metzia* 89b). The questioners wondered whether this practice is forbidden on the Sabbath as שַׁוּוּיֵי אוֹכְלָא, *making a substance into food* [which, according to one opinion on 155a, is considered a form of מוֹלִיד, *creating something new*]. Alternatively, they considered that it was forbidden because of טִרְחָא בְּאוֹכְלָא, *excessive toil for [already edible] food* (see *Tosafos* in explanation of *Rashi,* and Gemara below, 155a; see also *Pnei Yehoshua*).

The above explanation follows *Rashi.* However, according to this approach the inquiry seems totally out of place in the midst of a discussion about depilatories. Most other Rishonim, therefore, following the Geonim, explain the Gemara to be asking whether olives may be crushed in order to use for washing one's hands [since olive pulp has the tendency to remove hair].

10. Bruising the olives causes the liquid squeezed out to go to waste (*Tosafos,* in explanation of *Rashi*).

According to the Geonic explanation cited in the previous note, R' Sheishess meant that using olives as a form of soap is considered wasting food (see *Ritva, MHK* ed.).

11. *Tosafos,* in explanation of *Rashi's* approach.

According to the Geonic explanation, the Gemara means that crushing the olives renders the *olives* repulsive.

א נזיר חופף א) ומפספס אבל לא סורק אלא הא והא ר' יהודה היא ותרי תנאי אליבא דר' יהודה האי תנא אליבא דר' יהודה סבר גריר והאי תנא אליבא דר' יהודה סבר לא גריר במאי אוקימתא כר' יהודה אימא סיפא אבל פניו ידיו ורגליו מותר הא מעבר שיער איבעית אימא בקטן ואיבעית אימא באשה ואיבעית אימא בסרים אמר רב יהודה ב עפר לבינתא שרי אמר רב יוסף ב) כוספא דיסמין שרי אמר רבא עפר פלפלי שרי אמר רב ששת ברדא שרי מאי ברדא אמר רב יוסף תילתא אהלא ותילתא אסא ותילתא סיגלי אמר רב נחמיה בר יוסף ג כל היכא דליכא רובא אהלא שפיר דמי בעו מיניה מרב ששת מהו לפצוע זיתים בשבת אמר להו וכי בחול מי התירו קסבר משום הפסד אוכלין לימא פליגא דשמואל דאמר שמואל ג) ד עושה אדם כל צורכו בפת אמרי פת לא מאיסא הני מאיסי אמימר ומר זוטרא ורב אשי הוו יתבי אייתו לקמייהו ברדא אמימר ורב אשי משו מר זוטרא לא משא אמרו ליה לא סבר לה מר להא דאמר רב ששת ברדא שרי אמר להו רב מרדכי בר מיניה דמר דאפילו בחול נמי לא ס"ל סבר לה כי הא דתניא מגרד אדם גלדי צואה וגלדי מכה שעל בשרו בשביל צערו אם בשביל ליפות אסור ואינהו כמאן סברוה כי הא דתניא ד) רוחץ אדם פניו ידיו ורגליו בכל יום בשביל קונו משום שנאמר א) כל פעל ה' למענהו: רבי אלעזר בן עזריה אומר קופה מטה על צדה ונוטל שמא יטול וכו': אמר רבי אבא אמר רבי חייא בר אשי ה) (אמר רב) ה הכל מודים שאם נתקלקלה הגומא שאסור להחזיר תנן וחכמים אומרים נוטל ומחזיר היכי דמי אי דלא נתקלקלה הגומא ו) שפיר קא אמרי רבנן אלא לאו אף על פי דנתקלקלה הגומא לא לעולם דלא נתקלקלה והכא בחוששין קמיפלגי מר סבר חוששין שמא נתקלקלה הגומא ומר סבר ו אין חוששין אמר רב הונא ז האי סליקוסתא ז) דרצה שלפה והדר דצה שריא ואי לאו אסיר אמר שמואל האי ח סכינא דביני אורבי דצה שלפה והדר דצה שרי ואי לאו אסיר מר זוטרא ואיתימא רב אשי אמר בגורדיתא דקני שפיר דמי אמר ליה רב מרדכי לרבא מתיב רב קטינא תיובתא ט) הטומן לפת וצנונות תחת הגפן אם היה מקצת עליו מגולים אינו חושש

לא

רש"י

נזיר. בחול ככל אדם בשבת: חופף. שערו בנתר וחול ט): ומפספס. מנפץ שערו דכיון דאינו מתכוון מותר ועל כרחיך ר"ש קא אמר לה אלמא נתר וחול זימנין דאינו משיר ולא דמי לפסיק רישיה ולא ימות: אבל לא סורק. במסרק דודאי משיר: אלא הא והא. הנך תרתי מתני' דלעיל דפליגי בנתר וחול ר' יהודה ומאן דאסר סבר זימנין דגריר ור' יהודה האמר דבר שאין מתכוין אסור ומאן דשרי סבר לא גריר כלל ואין כאן משום ממחק: במאי אוקימתא כר' יהודה ה"ג. ול"ג להא דתניא אסור דהא תרוייהו כר' יהודה אוקימנא להו ועוד הך סיפא דפריך אבל פניו ידיו ורגליו מותר לאו סיפא דההיא דתניא אסור הוא אלא סיפא דההיא דתניא מותר דהכי תני בה לא יחוף בהן שערו אבל פניו ידיו ורגליו מותר והא מלתא גבי הך דתני מותר פריכנא ליה לעיל: בקטן אשה וסרים. דלית להו זקן: עפר לבינתא. כתישת לבינה: שרי. לחוף פניו ואפי' מי שיש לו זקן: כוספא דיסמין. פסולת שומשמין: עפר פילפלי. שחיקת פלפלין: ברדא שרי. לרחוץ פניו: אהלא. שורש עשב ששמו אהל: אסא. הדס: סגלי. עשב שקורין ויאו"ל ויש בו שלשה עלין: כל היכא דליכא רובא אהלא שפיר דמי. ואפי' הוי טפי מתלתא אהלא ופליג אדרב יוסף דרב יוסף תלתא אהלא דווקא קאמר שהאהל עשוי ללבן ולנאה כבורית ומשיר שיער: לפצוע זיתים. בלילי"א בלע"ז על הסלע למתק מרירותו: כל צורכו. בין תשמיש בין לפרר אותה ולמחתה בתבשיל רותח: משום ליפות את עצמו אסור. משום לא ילבש גבר שמלת אשה (דברים כב): בשביל קונהו. לכבוד קונהו דכתיב (בראשית ט) כי בצלם אלהים עשה וגו' ועוד דהרואה בריות נאות אומר ברוך שככה לו בעולמו: כל פעל ה' למענהו. הכל ברא לכבודו: שאם נתקלקלה הגומא. שנפלו הגיזין למקום מושב הקדרה: שאסור להחזיר. לפי שמזיז הגיזין לכאן ולכאן: שפיר קאמרי רבנן. ומאי טעמא דר' אלעזר: חוששין. אי שרית ליה ליטול לכתחילה בקופה זקופה פעמים שנתקלקלה ואתי נמי להחזירה הלכך תקון ליה רבנן להטות קופה על לדה: סליקוסתא. עשב שהוא נאה למראה ולהריח וממלאין כד עפר לח ותוחבין אותו לתוכו ונותנו לפני שרים וכשהוא רולה נוטלו ומריח בו ומחזירו למקומו ואי מבעוד יום דלה לתוך העפר ושלפה והדר דלה שפיר דמי ליטלה למחר ולהחזירה שהרי הורחב מקום מושבה והוחלק מבעוד יום ואינו מזיז עפר: סכינא דביני אורבי. שנועצין סכין בין שורות הלבנים שבבנין להשתמר: בגורדיתא דקני. קנים הדקלים (א) שיוצאין הרבה בגזע אחד ותכופין זה בזה שפיר דמי לנעוץ בתוכן סכין לשמרו ואין חוששין שמא יגרור הקליפה וחייב משום מוחק: מתיב רב קטינא תיובתא. להנך רבנן דאמרי דאי לא דלה ושלפה אסור: הטומן לפת. להשתמר בקרקע שכן דרכו הא דנקט מקצת עליו מגולין משום ניטלין בשבת נקט לה ולאו משום מידי אחריני דאי אין מקצת עליו מגולין אין לו במה לאוחזה אא"כ מזיז העפר בידים:

לא

תוספות

רבי שמעון אומר נזיר חופף ומפספס כו'. ומיירי בנתר וחול דתנן בתר הכי בפ' ג' מינין (נזיר דף מב.) ר' ישמעאל אומר נזיר לא יחוף ראשו באדמה לפי שמשיר את השער: אבל לא סורק. התם מפרש טעמא משום דלהשרת נימין המדולדלות מתכוין:

במאי אוקימתא כר' יהודה אימא סיפא כו'. בשלמא אי כר"ש אתיא שפיר דאיכא למימר דשערות פניו ידיו ורגליו אינם נושרות מהר ולא הוי פסיק רישיה ושרי אבל בראשו אסור דהוי פסיק רישיה אבל השתא דאוקימתא כר' יהודה אע"ג דלא הוה פסיק רישיה הוה לן למיסר:

מהו לפצוע זיתים בשבת. פירש בקונט' להכותם על הסלע למתק מרירותן ומיבעיא ליה אי אסיר בשבת משום שוי אוכלא ותיקוני אוכלא ופריך ובחול מי התירו דאיכא הפסד אוכלין שנפסד המשקה הזב מהן:

וקשה לפ"ז דבפ' חבית גבי דיני סחיטה ה"ל למיתני ועוד מה הפסד אוכלין יש כיון שעושה לתקנם ומפרש ר"י מהו לפצוע לחוף פניו ידיו ורגליו כי ההוא דלעיל והכך מי זיתים להעביר וללבן כדאמר במסכת ע"ז חולטן ברותחין או מולגן במי זיתים ופריך ובחול מי התירו דאיכא הפסד דנמאסין לאכילה. (ת"י)

בשביל צערו. ואם אין לו צער אחר אלא שמתבייש לילך בין בני אדם שרי דאין לך צער גדול מזה:

הכל מודים שאם נתקלקלה הגומא שאסורה להחזיר. ואפי' לר"א בן תדאי דאמר בפרק כל הכלים (לקמן קכג.) תוחב בכוש או בכרכר והן ננערות מאליהן דטלטול מן הצד לא שמיה טלטול וכן קי"ל הכא עדיף טפי מטלטול מן הצד שצריך לטלטל אילך ואילך כשרוצין להטמין: אי לא נתקלקלה הגומא פשיטא. טפי הוה ליה למפרך מ"ט דמאן דאסר:

גורדיתא דקני. מין אילן כפירוש הקונטרס כדמשמע בעושין פסין (עירובין יט:) ומיירי למטה מג' דליכא איסור משתמש במחובר כדאמר בפרק כל הכלים (לקמן קכה:) ובפרק בתרא דעירובין (דף ק.):

הטומן לפת וצנונות כו'. ע"כ בשלא השרישו מיירי דכהשרישו לא היו ניטלין בשבת ואם תאמר בשלמא כלאים ושביעית איצטריך לאשמעינן דלא גזרינן כשמתכוין להטמין אטו דילמא אתי לנוטעה אבל מעשר אמאי נקטיה דאפי' השרישו לא שייך מעשר כיון דליכא תוספת ואי נקטיה דשרי לעשר מן התלוש ממקום אחר עליו או לעשותו מעשר על התלוש ולא חיישי' דילמא אתי לעשר מן התלוש על המחובר או להפך א"כ הוה ליה למינקט תרומה דבכל דוכתא רגיל להזכיר תרומה על זה כדאמר (תרומות פ"א מ"ה) אין תורמין מן התלוש על המחובר כ) פירות ערוגה זו תלושין יהיו תרומה על פירות ערוגה זו מחוברין ואומר ר"י דרגילות הוא שמתוספין מחמת ליחלוחית הקרקע כמו שאנו רואין שומין ובצלים שמתוספין אפי' כשמונחין בחלון ועל אותו תוספת קאמר דלא בעי לעשורי ודוקא נקט הטומן אבל במתכוין לנטיעה חושש משום כולן:

מקצת עליו מגולים. משום דבעי למתני וניטלין בשבת נקט מקצת עליו מגולים כדפירש בקונטרס ובערוך ל) משמע דמשום כולהו נקט דפירש בשם רב האי גאון דגרס אם היו מקצתם מגולים שאם האמהות טמונים בקרקע והעלים מגולים הרי זו זריעה מעולה אלא דוקא מקצתן מגולים אינו חושש משום כלאים ושביעית דלאו זריעה היא ומה שהקשה והלא זריעה מעולה היא לאו פירכא היא דבלא השרישו איירי כדפרישית ולפירושו קשה דבפרק חלון (עירובין דף עז. ושם) קאמר רב יחיאל כפה ספל ממעט ופריך והא ניטלת בשבת הוא

כד א מיי' פ"ה מהלכות נזירות הלכה יד סמג לאוין כד:

כה ב ג מיי' פכ"ב מהל' שבת הלכה יג סמג לאוין סה טוש"ע או"ח סימן שכו סעיף ט:

כו ד טוש"ע או"ח סימן קעא סעיף א:

כז ה ו מיי' פ"ד ופכ"ו מהלכות שבת [דין זה ליתא בהרמב"ם ועיין בכ"מ] סמג שם טוש"ע או"ח סימן רנט סעיף ג:

כח ז מיי' פכ"ה מהל' שבת הלכה טו טור שו"ע או"ח סימן שלו סעיף ו:

כט ח שו"ע או"ח סי' שי"ד ס"א:

גליון הש"ס

גמ' האי סליקוסתא. עי' לעיל דף מג ע"ב תוס' ד"ה דכו"ע טלטול:

תורה אור השלם

א) כֹּל פָּעַל יְיָ לַמַּעֲנֵהוּ וְגַם רָשָׁע לְיוֹם רָעָה: [משלי טז, ד]

רבינו חננאל

מיעבדא ביה מעשה]: נימא כתנאי בכל חפין את הכלים כו' מלשון אשה חופפת וסורקת כו' ברחיצת ידים דקא אמרי' אבל רוחץ פניו ידיו ורגליו הא תנא דסבר משום השרת נימין מדולדלות. אליבא דר' יהודא מוקים לה בקטן וסריס ואשה דלית להון שיער אבל הלכה כר' שמעון דאפי' גברי בעלי שיער שרו וכן עפר לבינתה שרי למימשא ביה ידיה. ויש מי שמפרש לבינתה מלשון (ש"ה ג) מור ולבונה וכן כוספא דיסמין. וכן בראדא דהיא תילתא אהלא. תילתא סיגלי. תילתא אסא הני כולהו לענין רחיצת ידים בהן. וקיי"ל דבכולהי הני שרי אבל רובא אהלא רב נחמיה לא הוה שרי וכ"ש כולה (אוכלין וכ"ש בשבת) לפצוע זיתים וכיוצא בהן לרחוץ בהן ידיו בחול אסור משום הפסד אוכלין. וכ"ש בשבת שאסור. וזה שאמר שמואל עושה אדם כל צורכיו בפת לית הלכתא כוותיה והאוסר ידיו לרחוץ (כרב אדא) [בברדא] סבר ליה כי האי תנא דתניא מגרד אדם גילדי צואה וגילדי מכה שעל בשרו בשביל צערו. ואם לייפות עצמו אסור. והמתיר סבר לה כר' שמעון בן גמליאל דאמר רוחץ אדם פניו ידיו ורגליו בשביל כבוד קונו משום שנאמר כל פעל ה' למענהו: מתני' ר' אלעזר בן עזריה אומר קופה מטה על צדה ונוטל כו'. אסיקנא הכל מודים שאם נתקלקלה הגומא שאסור להחזיר סליקוסתא שהיא אגודה של חבצלת וכיוצא בה אמר רב הונא דעצה בחול או בטיט וחלצה והריח בטיט מע"ש כדי שתהא נכנסת ויוצא בגומא מותרת (כולה) [לטלטלה] בשבת וכן אמר שמואל בסכינא דנעיצא ביני אורבי כמו שאמר בסליקוסתא. ומותבינן עליה הטומן לפת וצנונות תחת הגפן אם היו מקצתן

מסורת הש"ס

א) לקמן פא: נזיר מב., ב) [פי' פסולת שומשמין שכובשין אותו בורד של יסמין ומייבשין אותן ושוחקין אותן ורוחצין בהן ידים מזוהמות ערוך בערך כספן ועיין רש"י שקיצר בזה למאד], ג) ברכות נ: לקמן קמג. ביצה כא:, ד) [תוספתא ברכות פ"ד ע"ש], ה) ברא"ש ליתא, ו) ס"א פשיטא, ז) [כמו דעצה אלא שמבליע העי"ן ומקצר את לשונו כ"כ רש"י פ' ויצא למ"ד פל"ח], ח) לקמן קיג. עירובין עז. כלאים פרק א מ"ט [עי' תוספות מנחות ע. ד"ה חסר וכו' מה שהניחו בתימה ועיין תוס' לעיל מג: סד"ה דכו"ע טלטול וכו' ישוב התימה], ט) עי' רש"י ברכות ו. ד"ה מחופיא, י) [שלש תיבות הללו ר"ש אומר לריך תיקון וא"א לומר דהגי' כך הי' לפניהם שהרי להדיא אמרינן בנזיר מב. עלה דהך משנה דתנן נזיר חופף וכו' וחופף ומפספס מני ר"ש היא דאמר דבר שאין מתכוין וכו' ע"ש], כ) [קידושין סב:], ל) [ערך לפת].

הגהות הב"ח

(א) רש"י ד"ה בגורדיתא דקני (קנים הדקלים). תא"מ ונ"ב ס"א קנים הדוקרים:

ליקוטי רש"י

חופף. כמו חופף עליו כל היום (דברים לג) לשון מגרד ובלעז פרי"ר [נזיר מב.]. לשון שפשוף כמו נזיר חופף ומפספס (נזיר מב.) [מגילה כו.]. מחליק שערו [לקמן פא:]. ומפספס. שמפריד שערותיו זו מזו אבל לא במסרק [נזיר שם]. קרפי"ר. אבל לא סורק. במסרק דודאי משיר שיער ומודה ר' שמעון בפסיק רישיה ולא ימות אבל חופף ומפספס פעמים שאינו משיר וכשמשיר דבר שאין מתכוין מותר [לקמן שם]. סיגלי. דודאים. עשב הוא ובלשון ישמעאל יסמי"ן [בלע"ז ויאול"י] [בראשית ל, יד]. ויול"ש בלעז [ברכות מג:]. עיקרי עשבים והוא ממיני בשמים ואמהות של אותן עשבים קרי סגלי [סנהדרין צט:]. עושה אדם כל צורכו בפת. ומטלטל על ידי הפת ולא חיישינן לבזיון דאוכלין [ביצה כא:]. משתמש בו ואין כאן משום בזיון וממחהו בתבשיל [לקמן קמג.]. כל פעל ה' למענהו. הכל עשה בשביל קילוסו כמו ענו לה' בתודה (תהלים קמז) ד"א להעיד עליו כלומר פעלו מעיד עליו על גבורותיו שניה' בהגדת תהלים [משלי טז, ד]. דצה. נעצה [ע"ז עו:]. דין לשון תיקוע כדאמר דצה שלפה (שבת נ:) [יבמות קט:]. ויגז. תרגומו ודעיך לשון תחיבה ונעילה הוא בלשון ארמית והרבה יש בתלמוד (שבת נ:) דצה ושלפה (חולין לג:) דץ ביה מידי, דצה כמו דעצה אלא שמקצר את לשונו [בראשית ל, לח]. ביני אורבי. בין שורות הבנין בכותל [ב"מ מב.]. בין לבינה ללבינה [ע"ז מז:]. בגורדיתא דקני. קנים מחוברים הרבה בעץ אחד סמוך לארץ ולמעלה הן מתפרשין [עירובין יט:]. הטומן. להנטיע. מקצת עליו מגולים. משום שבת נקט ליה דבעי למיתני ניטלין בשבת שנוטלן ואוחזן בעלין שלהן. אינו חושש. משום כלאי הכרם [שם עז.]. לפי שאינה מושרשת [לקמן קיג.].

מָשׁוּ מַר זוּטְרָא לֹא מָשָׁא – **Ameimar and Rav Ashi washed** with it, but **Mar Zutra did not wash.** אָמְרוּ לֵיהּ – **They said to him:** לֹא סָבַר לָהּ מַר לְהָא דְּאָמַר רַב שֵׁשֶׁת בַּרְדָּא שְׁרִי – **Does master not hold of that which Rav Sheishess said, that *barda* is permitted?** אָמַר לְהוּ רַב מָרְדְּכַי – **Rav Mordechai,** who was also present, **said to them:** בַּר מִינֵּיהּ דְּמַר דַּאֲפִילּוּ בְּחוֹל נַמִּי לֹא סְבִירָא לֵיהּ – **Exclude the master** [Mar Zutra] from this discussion, **for even during the weekdays he does not hold it** to be permitted. סָבַר לָהּ כִּי הָא דְּתַנְיָא – **He agrees with that which was taught in a Baraisa:** מְגָרֵר אָדָם גִּלְדֵי צוֹאָה וְגִלְדֵי מַכָּה שֶׁעַל בְּשָׂרוֹ בִּשְׁבִיל צַעֲרוֹ – **A MAN MAY SCRAPE CRUSTS OF FILTH AND CRUSTS OF A WOUND** from **UPON HIS FLESH BECAUSE OF HIS DISCOMFORT,** אִם בִּשְׁבִיל לְיַפּוֹת אָסוּר – **BUT IF** done **TO BEAUTIFY HIMSELF, IT IS FORBIDDEN.**[12]

The Gemara explains the position of Ameimar and Rav Ashi: וְאִינְהוּ כְּמַאן סַבְרוּהָ – **And they, with whom do they hold?** כִּי הָא דְּתַנְיָא – They hold **in accordance with that which was taught in a Baraisa:** רוֹחֵץ אָדָם פָּנָיו יָדָיו וְרַגְלָיו בְּכָל יוֹם בִּשְׁבִיל קוֹנוֹ – **A MAN SHOULD WASH HIS FACE, HANDS AND FEET EACH DAY IN HONOR OF HIS CREATOR,** מִשּׁוּם שֶׁנֶּאֱמַר ,,כֹּל פָּעַל ה׳ לַמַּעֲנֵהוּ'' – **BECAUSE IT SAYS:**[13] ***ALL HAS HASHEM WROUGHT FOR HIS SAKE.***[14]

The Mishnah states:

רַבִּי אֶלְעָזָר בֶּן עֲזַרְיָה אוֹמֵר קוּפָּה מַטָּה עַל צִדָּהּ וְנוֹטֵל שֶׁמָּא יִטּוֹל וכו׳ – **R' ELAZAR BEN AZARYAH SAYS: HE TILTS THE BOX ON ITS SIDE AND REMOVES** the food, **LEST HE REMOVE etc.** [the pot and be unable to replace it. But the Sages say: He may remove and replace it.]

R' Elazar ben Azaryah is concerned that if the pot is removed and the shearings on the sides fall into the cavity, the person will not be able to move them aside when replacing the pot. The Sages, however, have no such concern. The Gemara discusses this dispute:

אָמַר רַבִּי אַבָּא אָמַר רַבִּי חִיָּיא בַּר אַשִׁי (אָמַר רַב) – **R' Abba said in the name of R' Chiya bar Ashi (who said in the name of Rav):** הַכֹּל מוֹדִים שֶׁאִם נִתְקַלְקְלָה הַגּוּמָּא שֶׁאָסוּר לְהַחֲזִיר – **All agree that if the cavity became disarranged,** i.e. the shearings fell into it, **that one is forbidden to return** the pot thereto, for this would necessitate moving the shearings. The dispute concerns a case in which the cavity did not become disarranged.

The Gemara questions this statement:

תְּנַן – **We learned in the Mishnah:** וַחֲכָמִים אוֹמְרִים נוֹטֵל וּמַחֲזִיר – **BUT THE SAGES SAY: HE MAY REMOVE AND RETURN** the pot. הֵיכִי דָּמֵי – Now **what is the case?** אִי דְּלֹא נִתְקַלְקְלָה הַגּוּמָּא – **If the cavity did not become disarranged,** i.e. the shearings did not fall in, שַׁפִּיר קָא אָמְרֵי רַבָּנָן – then **the Rabbis spoke correctly** when they ruled that the pot may be replaced. Why would R' Elazar argue?[15] אֶלָּא לַאו אַף עַל פִּי דְּנִתְקַלְקְלָה הַגּוּמָּא – **Rather,** are we **not** referring **even** to **where the cavity became disarranged?** Thus, we see that even in such a case the Rabbis permit the pot to be replaced. – ? –

The Gemara answers:

לֹא – **No,** your reasoning is incorrect. לְעוֹלָם דְּלֹא נִתְקַלְקְלָה – **Actually,** the Mishnah refers to **where [the cavity] did not become disarranged,** וְהָכָא בְּחוֹשְׁשִׁין קָמִיפַּלְגֵי – **and here they dispute whether we are concerned** that if we permit the person to remove the pot, the shearings on the sides will fall in. The person would then come to move the *muktzeh* shearings when attempting to replace the pot. מַר סָבַר חוֹשְׁשִׁין שֶׁמָּא נִתְקַלְקְלָה הַגּוּמָּא – One **master,** i.e. R' Elazar ben Azaryah, **holds** that **we are concerned lest the cavity become disarranged.** Thus, he forbids removing the pot. וּמַר סָבַר אֵין חוֹשְׁשִׁין – **And** the other **master,** i.e. the Rabbis, **hold** that **we are not concerned** for this possibility. They therefore permit removal of the pot. Certainly, however, if the shearings did in fact fall in, even the Rabbis forbid replacing the pot.

The Gemara discusses another law concerning *muktzeh:*

אָמַר רַב הוּנָא – **Rav Huna said:** הַאי סְלִיקוּסְתָּא – Regarding **this *slikusta*** plant,[16] דָּצָה שַׁלְפָהּ וְהָדַר דָּצָהּ שַׁרְיָא – if **one inserted it** into the earth, **withdrew it and inserted it once again** before the Sabbath, **it is permissible** on the Sabbath to remove it from the earth and replace it there. One need not worry that he will thereby move the *muktzeh* soil, because the hole in which the *slikusta* stands has already been sufficiently widened by the insertion and withdrawal on Friday to allow for removal on the Sabbath without moving the soil.[17] וְאִי לַאו אָסִיר – **But if** one did **not** perform the above procedure on Friday, **it is forbidden** to remove the *slikusta* on the Sabbath, because doing so will cause the *muktzeh* soil to move.[18]

A similar ruling by another Amora:

אָמַר שְׁמוּאֵל – **Shmuel said:** הַאי סַכִּינָא דְּבֵינֵי אוּרְבֵּי – Regarding **this knife** that is stored **between the rows of bricks** for safekeeping, דָּצָה שַׁלְפָהּ וְהָדַר דָּצָהּ שְׁרִי – if **one inserted it, withdrew it and inserted it once again** before the Sabbath, **it is permissible** on the Sabbath to withdraw and reinsert it. וְאִי לַאו אָסִיר – **But if** one did **not** perform the above procedure before the Sabbath, **it is forbidden** to remove it.[19]

Another Amoraic ruling concerning storing knives:

מַר זוּטְרָא וְאִיתֵּימָא רַב אַשִׁי אָמַר – **Mar Zutra, and others say Rav Ashi, said:** בְּגוּרְדִּיתָא דְּקָנֵי שַׁפִּיר דָּמֵי – **It is fine** to insert the knife for safekeeping **into a comb of reeds.**[20]

NOTES

12. Because of the verse (*Deuteronomy* 22:5): *A man shall not wear a feminine garment* (*Rashi*), which is construed by the Rabbis as a prohibition for a man not to groom himself as does a woman (see *Targum Onkelos* ad loc. and Gemara below, 94b).

13. *Proverbs* 16:4.

14. I.e. for His glory (*Rashi*). Keeping clean brings honor to God, for man was created in God's image. Additionally, one who sees handsome creatures is bidden to bless God (*Rashi,* from *Berachos* 58b). See also *Ritva, MHK* ed.

15. Since replacing the pot does not require moving the shearings, there seems to be no reason to forbid its replacement.

16. *Slikusta* was a beautiful and fragrant plant. It was the practice of wealthy people to fill pots with moist earth and insert these plants into it. The person would then pick up the plant, inhale its scent, and replace it into the earth (*Rashi*).

17. Since the earth is moist, the hole keeps its shape. The person can thus on the Sabbath remove and replace the *slikusta* at will, without moving the earth (see *Rashi*).

18. [Our explanation of Rav Huna's ruling (and that of Shmuel below) – that the issue is one of *muktzeh* – follows the Rishonim's understanding of *Rashi* (see *Tosafos* to 44a ד״ה רכ״ע, *Rashba, Ritva MHK* ed. here). Others suggest, however, that *Rashi* understands the issue to be one of חוֹפֵר, *excavating* (see *Maharshal* and *Pnei Yehoshua* to *Tosafos* ibid.).]

19. Since a hole was not previously formed, removing the knife will cause the loose mortar and sand that lie between the bricks to move. [According to the alternate explanation cited in the previous note, removing the knife is prohibited because by removing it one is widening the hole (קוֹדֵחַ) which is a *toladah* of בּוֹנֶה, *building* (see *Terumas HaDeshen* 64, cited by *Beis Yosef,* end of *Orach Chaim* 314).]

20. I.e. a cluster of densely packed reeds. One need not be concerned that by doing so he will scrape off the peel of a reed and become liable for מְמַחֵק, *smoothing* (*Rashi,* with emendation of *R' Yaakov Emden;* see *Dibros Moshe* 39:22 for why *Rashi* does not explain that scraping off the peel would involve the *melachah* of קוֹצֵר, *reaping).*

א נזיר חופף א) ומפספס אבל לא סורק אלא הא והא ר' יהודה היא ותרי תנאי אליבא דר' יהודה האי תנא אליבא דר' יהודה סבר גריר והאי תנא אליבא דר' יהודה סבר לא גריר במאי אוקימתא כר' יהודה אימא סיפא אבל פניו ידיו ורגליו מותר הא מעבר שיער איבעית אימא בקטן ואיבעית אימא באשה ואיבעית אימא בסרים אמר רב יהודה ב עפר לבינתא שרי אמר רב יוסף י) כוספא דיסמין שרי אמר רבא עפר פלפלי שרי אמר רב ששת ברדא שרי מאי ברדא אמר רב יוסף תילתא אהלא ותילתא אסא ותילתא סיגלי אמר רב נחמיה בר יוסף ג כל היכא דליכא רובא אהלא שפיר דמי בעו מיניה מרב ששת מהו לפצוע זיתים בשבת אמר להו וכי בחול מי התירו קסבר משום הפסד אוכלין לימא פליגא דשמואל ז) דאמר שמואל ד עושה אדם כל צורכו בפת אמרי פת לא מאיסא הני מאיסי אמימר ומר זוטרא ורב אשי הוו יתבי אייתו לקמייהו ברדא אמימר ורב אשי משו מר זוטרא לא משא אמרו ליה לא סבר לה מר להא דאמר רב ששת ברדא שרי אמר להו רב מרדכי בר מיניה דמר דאפילו בחול נמי לא ס"ל סבר לה כי הא דתניא מגרד אדם גלדי צואה וגלדי מכה שעל בשרו בשביל צערו אם בשביל ליפות אסור ואינהו כמאן סברוה כי הא דתניא ח) רוחץ אדם פניו ידיו ורגליו בכל יום בשביל קונו משום שנאמר א כל פעל ה' למענהו: רבי אלעזר בן עזריה אומר קופה מטה על צדה ונוטל שמא יטול וכו': אמר רבי אבא אמר רבי חייא בר אשי ט) (אמר רב) ה הכל מודים שאם נתקלקלה הגומא שאסור להחזיר תנן וחכמים אומרים נוטל ומחזיר היכי דמי אי דלא נתקלקלה הגומא ו שפיר קא אמרי רבנן אלא לאו אף על פי דנתקלקלה הגומא לא לעולם דלא נתקלקלה והכא בחוששין קמיפלגי מר סבר חוששין שמא נתקלקלה הגומא ומר סבר ז אין חוששין אמר רב הונא ° י האי סליקוסתא י) דרצה שלפה והדר דרצה שריא ואי לאו אסיר אמר שמואל האי ח סכינא דביני אורבי דרצה שלפה והדר דרצה שרי ואי לאו אסיר מר זוטרא ואיתימא רב אשי אמר בגורדיתא דקני שפיר דמי אמר ליה רב מרדכי לרבא מתיב רב קטינא תיובתא כ) הטומן לפת וצנונות תחת הגפן אם היה מקצת עליו מגולים אינו חושש לא

רש"י

נזיר. בחול ככל אדם בשבת: חופף. שערו בנתר וחול ט): ומפספס. מנפץ שערו דכיון דאינו מתכוין מותר ועל כרחיך ר"ש קא אמר לה אלמא נתר וחול זימנין דאינו משיר ולא דמי לפסיק רישיה ולא ימות: אבל לא סורק. במסרק דודאי משיר: אלא הא והא. הנך תרתי מתני' דלעיל דפליגי בנתר וחול ר' יהודה ומאן דאסר סבר זימנין דגריר ור' יהודה האמר דבר שאין מתכוין אסור ומאן דשרי סבר לא גריר כלל ואין כאן משום ממחק: במאי אוקימתא כר' יהודה ה"ג. ול"ג להא דתניא אסור דהא תרוייהו כר' יהודה אוקימנא להו ועוד הך סיפא דפריך אבל פניו ידיו ורגליו מותר לאו סיפא דההיא דתניא אסור הוא אלא סיפא דההיא דתניא מותר דהכי תני בה לא יחוף בהן שערו אבל פניו ידיו ורגליו מותר והא מלתא גבי הך דתני מותר פריכנא ליה לעיל: בקטן אשה וסרים. דלית להו זקן: עפר לבינתא. כתישת לבינה: שרי. לחוף פניו ואפי' מי שיש לו זקן: כוספא דיסמין. פסולת שומשמין: עפר פילפלי. שחיקת פלפלין: ברדא שרי. לרחוץ פניו: אהלא. שורש עשב ששמו אהל: אסא. הדס: סגלי. עשב שקורין ויאו"ל ויש בו שלשה עלין: כל היכא דליכא רובא אהלא שפיר דמי. ואפי' הוי טפי מתלתא אהלא ופליג אדרב יוסף דרב יוסף תלתא אהלא דווקא קאמר שהאהל עשוי ללבן ולאחא כבורית ומשיר שיער: לפצוע זיתים. בליל"א בלע"ז על הסלע למתק מרירותו: כל צורכו. בין תשמיש בין לפרר אותה ולמחתה בתבשיל רותח: משום ליפות את עצמו אסור. משום לא ילבש גבר שמלת אשה (דברים כב): בשביל קונהו. לכבוד קונהו דכתיב (בראשית ט) כי בצלם אלהים עשה וגו' ועוד דהרואה בריות נאות אומר ברוך שככה לו בעולמו: כל פעל ה' למענהו. הכל ברא לכבודו: שאם נתקלקלה הגומא. שנפלו הגיזין למקום מושב הקדרה: שאסור להחזיר. לפי שמזיז הגיזין לכאן ולכאן: שפיר קאמרי רבנן. ומאי טעמא דר' אלעזר: חוששין. אי שרית ליה ליטול לכתחילה בקופה זקופה פעמים שנתקלקלה ואתי נמי להחזירה הלכך תקון ליה רבנן להטות קופה על צדה: סליקוסתא. עשב שהוא נאה למראה ולהריח וממלאין כד עפר לח ותוחבין אותו לתוכו ונותנו לפני שרים וכשהוא רוצה נוטלו ומריח בו ומחזירו למקומו ואי מבעוד יום דצה לתוך העפר ושלפה והדר דצה שפיר דמי ליטלה למחר ולהחזירה שהרי הורחב מקום מושבה והוחלק מבעוד יום ואינו מזיז עפר: סכינא דביני אורבי. שנועצין סכין בין שורות הלבנים שבבנין להשתמר: בגורדיתא דקני. קנים הדקלים (א) שיוצאין הרבה בגזע אחד ותכופין זה בזה שפיר דמי לנעוץ בתוכן סכין לשמרו ואין חוששין שמא יגרור הקליפה וחייב משום מוחק: מתיב רב קטינא תיובתא. להנך רבנן דאמרי דאי לא דצה ושלפה אסור: הטומן לפת. להשתמר בקרקע שכן דרכו הא דנקט מקצת עליו מגולין משום ניטלין בשבת נקט לה ולאו משום מידי אחריני דאי אין מקצת עליו מגולין אין לו במה לאוחזו אא"כ מזיז העפר בידים: לא

תוספות

י) רבי שמעון אומר נזיר חופף ומפספס כו'. ומיירי בנתר וחול דתנן בתר הכי בפ' ג' מינין (נזיר דף מב.) ר' ישמעאל אומר נזיר לא יחוף ראשו באדמה לפי שמשיר את השער: אבל לא סורק. התם מפרש טעמא משום דלהשרת נימין המדולדלות מתכוין:

במאי אוקימתא כר' יהודה אימא סיפא כו'. בשלמא אי כר"ש אתיא שפיר דאיכא למימר דשערות פניו ידיו ורגליו אינם נושרות מהר ולא הוי פסיק רישיה ושרי אבל בראשו אסור דהוי פסיק רישיה אבל השתא דאוקימתא כר' יהודה אע"ג דלא הוה פסיק רישיה הוה לן למיסר:

מהו לפצוע זיתים בשבת. פירש בקונט' להכותם על הסלע למתק מרירותן ומיבעיא ליה אי אסיר בשבת משום שוי אוכלא ותיקוני אוכלא ופריך ובחול מי התירו דאיכא הפסד אוכלין שנפסד המשקה הזב מהן:

וקשה לפ"ז דבפ' חבית גבי דיני סחיטה ה"ל למיתני ועוד מה הפסד אוכלין יש כיון שעושה לתקנם ומפרש ר"י מהו לפצוע לחוף פניו ידיו ורגליו כי ההוא דלעיל ודרך מי זיתים להעביר וללבן כדאמר במסכת ע"ז מולטן ברותחין או מולגן במי זיתים ופריך ובחול מי התירו דאיכא הפסד דנמאסין לאכילה. (ת"י)

בשביל צערו. ואם אין לו צער אחר אלא שמתבייש לילך בין בני אדם שרי דאין לך צער גדול מזה:

הכל מודים שאם נתקלקלה הגומא שאסורה להחזיר. ואפי' לר"א בן תדאי דאמר בפרק כל הכלים (לקמן קכג.) תוחב בכוש או בכרכר והן ננערות מאליהן דטלטול מן הצד לא שמיה טלטול וכן קי"ל הכא עדיף טפי מטלטול מן הצד שצריך לטלטל אילך ואילך כשרוצין להטמין: אי לא נתקלקלה הגומא פשיטא. טפי הוה ליה למפרך מ"ט דמאן דאסר:

גורדיתא דקני. מין אילן כפירוש הקונטרס כדמשמע בעושין פסין (עירובין יט:) ומיירי למטה מג' דליכא איסור משתמש במחובר כדאמר בפרק כל הכלים (לקמן קכה:) ובפרק בתרא דעירובין (דף ק.):

הטומן לפת וצנונות כו'. ע"כ בשלא השרישו מיירי דבהשרישו לא היו ניטלין בשבת ואם תאמר בשלמא כלאים ושביעית איצטריך לאשמעינן דלא גזרינן כשמתכוין להטמין אטו דילמא אתי לנוטעה אבל מעשר מאי נקטיה דאפי' השרישו לא שייך מעשר כיון דליכא תוספת ואי נקטיה דשרי לעשר מן התלוש ממקום אחר עליו או לעשותו מעשר על התלוש ולא חיישי' דילמא אתי לעשר מן התלוש על המחובר או להפך א"כ הוה ליה למינקט תרומה דבכל דוכתא רגיל להזכיר תרומה על זה כדאמר (תרומות פ"א מ"ה) אין תורמין מן התלוש על המחובר ל) פירות ערוגה זו תלושין יהיו תרומה על פירות ערוגה זו מחוברין ואומר ר"י דרגילות הוא שמתוספין מחמת ליחלוחית הקרקע כמו שאנו רואין שומין ובצלים שמתוספין אפי' כשמונחין בחלון ועל אותו תוספת קאמר דלא בעי לעשורי ודוקא נקט הטומן אבל במתכוין לנטיעה חושש משום כולן:

מקצת עליו מגולים. משום דבעי למתני וניטלין בשבת נקט מקצת עליו מגולים כדפירש בקונטרס ובערוך ל) משמע דמשום כולהו נקט דפירש בשם רב האי גאון דגרס אם היו מקצתם מגולים שאם האמהות טמונים בקרקע והעלים מגולים הרי זו זריעה מעולה אלא דוקא מקצתן מגולים אינו חושש משום כלאים ושביעית דלאו זריעה היא ומה שהקשה והלא זריעה מעולה היא לאו פירכא היא דבלא השרישו איירי כדפרישית ולפירושו קשה דבפרק חלון (עירובין דף עו. ושם) קאמר רב יחיאל כפה ספל ממעט ופריך והא ניטלת בשבת הוא

עין משפט נר מצוה

כד א מיי' פ"ה מהלכות נזירות הלכה יד סמג לאוין כד:
כה ב ג מיי' פכ"ב מהל' שבת הלכה יג סמג לאוין סה טוש"ע או"ח סימן שכו סעיף ט:
כו ד טוש"ע או"ח סימן קעא סעיף א:
כז ה ו מיי' פ"ד ופכ"ו מהלכות שבת [דין זה ליתא בהרמב"ם ועיין בכ"מ] סמג שם טוש"ע או"ח סימן רנט סעיף ג:
כח ז מיי' פכ"ה מהל' שבת הלכה טו טור שו"ע או"ח סימן שלו סעיף ו:
כט ח שו"ע או"ח סי' שי"ד ס"א:

גליון הש"ס

גמ' האי סליקוסתא. עי' לעיל דף מג ע"ב תוס' ד"ה דכו"ע טלטול:

תורה אור השלם

א) כֹּל פָּעַל יְיָ לַמַּעֲנֵהוּ וְגַם רָשָׁע לְיוֹם רָעָה: [משלי טז, ד]

רבינו חננאל

מיעבדא ביה מעשה]: נימא כתנאי בכל חפין את הכלים כו' מלשון אשה חופפת וסורקת כו' ברחיצת ידים דקא אמרי' אבל רוחץ פניו ידיו ורגליו הא תנא דסבר משום השרת נימין מדולדלות. אליבא דר' יהודא מוקים לה בקטן וסריס ואשה דלית להון שיער אבל הלכה כר' שמעון דאפי' גברי בעלי שיער שרו וכן עפר לבינתה שרי למימשא ביה ידיה. ויש מי שמפרש לבינתה מלשון (ש"ה ג) מור ולבונה וכן כוספא דיסמין. וכן בראדא דהיא תילתא אהלא. תילתא סיגלי. תילתא אסא הני כולהו לענין רחיצת ידים בהן. וקיי"ל דבכולהי הני שרי אבל רובא אהלא רב נחמיה לא הוה שרי וכ"ש כולה (אוכלין וכ"ש בשבת) לפצוע זיתים וכיוצא בהן לרחוץ בהן ידיו בחול אסור משום הפסד אוכלין. וכ"ש בשבת שאסור. וזה שאמר שמואל עושה אדם כל צורכיו בפת לית הלכתא כוותיה והאוסר ידיו לרחוץ (כרב אדא) [בברדא] סבר ליה כי האי תנא דתניא מגרר אדם גילדי צואה וגילדי מכה שעל בשרו בשביל צערו. ואם לייפות עצמו אסור. והמתיר סבר לה כר' שמעון בן גמליאל דאמר רוחץ אדם פניו ידיו ורגליו בשביל כבוד קונו משום שנאמר כל פעל ה' למענהו: מתני' ר' אלעזר בן עזריה אומר קופה מטה על צדה ונוטל כו'. אסיקנא הכל מודים שאם נתקלקלה הגומא שאסור להחזיר סליקוסתא שהיא אגודה של חבצלת וכיוצא בה אמר רב הונא דעצה בחול או בטיט וחלצה והריח בטיט מע"ש כדי שתהא נכנסת ויוצא בגומא מותרת (כולה) [לטלטלה] בשבת וכן אמר שמואל בסכינא דנעיצא ביני אורבי כמו שאמר בסליקוסתא. ומותבינן עליה הטומן לפת וצנונות תחת הגפן אם היו מקצתן

מסורת הש"ס

א) לקמן פא: נזיר מב., ב) [פי' פסולת שומשמין שכותשין אותו בורד של יסמין ומייבשין אותן ושוחקין אותן ורוחצין בהן ידים מזוהמות ערוך בערך כספן ועיין רש"י שקיצר בזה למאד], ג) ברכות נ: לקמן קמג. ביצה כא., ד) [תוספתא ברכות פ"ד ע"ש], ה) ברא"ש ליתא, ו) ס"א פשיטא, ז) [כמו דעלה אלא שמבליע העי"ן ומקצר את לשונו כ"כ רש"י פי' וילא למ"ד פל"ח], ח) לקמן קיג. עירובין עז. כלאים פרק א מ"ט [עי' תוספות מנחות ט. ד"ה חסר וכו' מה שהניחו בתימה ועיין תוס' לעיל מג: סד"ה דכו"ע טלטול וכו' יתישב התימה], ט) עי' רש"י ברכות ו. ד"ה מתופיא, י) [שלש תיבות הללו ר"ש אומר לריך תיקון וא"א לומר דהגי' כך הי' לפניהם שהרי להדיא אמרינן בנזיר מב. עלה דהך משנה דתנן נזיר חופף וכו' וחופף ומפספס מני ר"ש היא דאמר דבר שאין מתכוין וכו' ע"ש], כ) [קידושין סב:], ל) [ערך לפת].

הגהות הב"ח

(א) רש"י ד"ה בגורדיתא דקני (קנים הדקלים). תא"מ ונ"ב ס"א קנים הדוקרים:

ליקוטי רש"י

חופף. כמו חופף עליו כל היום (דברים לג) לשון מגרד ובלעז פרי"ר [נזיר מב.]. לשון שפשוף כמו נזיר חופף ומפספס (נזיר מב.) [מגילה כו.]. מחליק שערו [לקמן פא:]. ומפספס. שמפריד שערותיו זו מזו אבל לא במסרק [נזיר שם]. קרפי"ר. אבל לא סורק. במסרק דודאי משיר שיער ומודה ר' שמעון בפסיק רישיה ולא ימות אבל חופף ומפספס פעמים שאינו משיר וכשמשיר דבר שאין מתכוין מותר [לקמן שם]. סיגלי. דודאים. שיגלי עשב הוא ובלשון ישמעאל יסמי"ן [בלע"ז ויאול"ש] [בראשית ל, יד]. ויול"ש בלעז [ברכות מג:]. עיקרי עשבים והוא ממיני בשמים ואמהות של אותן עשבים קרי סגלי [סנהדרין צט:]. עושה אדם כל צורכו בפת. ומטלטל על ידי הפת ולא חיישינן לבזיון דאוכלין [ביצה כא:]. משתמש בו ואין כאן משום בזיון וממחהו בתבשיל [לקמן קמג.]. כל פעל ה' למענהו. הכל עשה בשביל קילוסו כמו ענו לה' בתודה (תהלים קמז) ד"א להעיד עליו כלומר פעלו מעיד עליו על גבורותיו שניה' בהגדת תהלים [משלי טז, ד]. דצה. נעלה [ע"ז עו:]. דוך לשון תיקוע כדאמר דלה שלפה (שבת נ:) [יבמות קט:]. ויל"ג. תרגומו ודעיך לשון תחיבה ונעילה הוא בלשון ארמית והרבה יש בתלמוד (שבת נ:) דצה ושלפה (חולין נג:) דך ביה מידי, דצה כמו דעצה אלא שמקצר את לשונו [בראשית ל, לח]. ביני אורבי. בין שורות הבנין בכותל [ב"מ מב.]. בין לבינה ללבינה [ע"ז מז:]. בגורדיתא דקני. קנים מחוברים הרבה בעץ אחד סמוך לארץ ולמעלה הן מספרשין [עירובין יט:]. הטומן. להצניע. מקצת עליו מגולים. משום שבת נקט ליה דבעי למיתני ניטלין בשבת שנוטלן ואוחזן בעלין שלהן. אינו חושש. משום כלאי הכרם [שם עז.:]. לפי שאינה מושרשת [לקמן קיג.].

The rulings of Rav Huna and Shmuel, who require that the *slikusta* or knife be inserted and withdrawn before the Sabbath, are challenged:

מָתִיב **אָמַר לֵיהּ רַב מָרְדְּכַי לְרָבָא** – **Rav Mordechai said to Rava:** **רַב קְטִינָא תְּיוּבְתָּא** – **Rav Ketina presented a refutation** of these rulings from a Mishnah:[21] **הַטּוֹמֵן לֶפֶת וּצְנוֹנוֹת תַּחַת הַגֶּפֶן** – ONE WHO BURIES A TURNIP OR RADISHES in the ground UNDER A GRAPEVINE for storage, **אִם הָיָה מִקְצָת עָלָיו מְגוּלִּים** – IF SOME OF ITS LEAVES ARE EXPOSED,[22] **אֵינוֹ חוֹשֵׁשׁ** – HE NEED NOT BE CONCERNED

NOTES

21. *Kilayim* 1:9.

22. This requirement that some of the leaves be exposed is necessary only for the Sabbath ruling at the end of the Baraisa (because if none of the leaves are exposed, one would be forced to directly move the *muktzeh* earth to get at the vegetable). The other rulings, however, (regarding *kilayim, sheviis* and *maaser*) hold true even if none of the leaves are exposed (*Rashi*; cf. *Tosafos*).

וְלֹא מִשּׁוּם כִּלְאַיִם – FOR a violation of the laws of *KILAYIM*,[1] וְלֹא מִשּׁוּם שְׁבִיעִית – NOR FOR a violation of the laws of *SHEVIIS*,[2] וְלֹא מִשּׁוּם מַעֲשֵׂר – NOR FOR an obligation for the laws of *MAASER*,[3] וְנִטָּלִין בְּשַׁבָּת – AND [THE TURNIP OR RADISH] MAY BE REMOVED ON THE SABBATH by grasping its leaves. Now, removing the turnip or radish in this manner will surely move the earth in which it is embedded. Yet the Mishnah permits this. Thus we see that we are unconcerned with such indirect movement of the *muktzeh* earth. Similarly, it should be permitted to remove the *slikusta* or knife in the above cases without inserting and removing it on Friday. – ? –

The Gemara concedes:

תְּיוּבְתָּא – This is indeed **a refutation** of Rav Huna's and Shmuel's rulings.[4]

Mishnah The Mishnah continues discussing the laws of insulating with substances that do not add heat: לֹא כִסָּהוּ מִבְּעוֹד יוֹם – If **he did not cover [the pot]** with insulation **when it was yet day,** i.e. before the Sabbath, לֹא יְכַסֶּנּוּ מִשֶּׁתֶּחְשַׁךְ – **he may not cover it after dark.**[5] כִּסָּהוּ וְנִתְגַּלָּה מוּתָּר לְכַסּוֹתוֹ – If **he covered it** before dark **and it became uncovered, he may cover it** again after dark.[6]

מְמַלֵּא אֶת הַקִּיתוֹן – **One may fill a bottle** with cold water וְנוֹתֵן לְתַחַת הַכַּר אוֹ תַחַת הַכֶּסֶת – **and place it under a cushion or under a bolster.**[7]

Gemara The Gemara cites an Amoraic ruling regarding insulating on the Sabbath:

אָמַר רַב יְהוּדָה אָמַר שְׁמוּאֵל – **Rav Yehudah said in the name of Shmuel:** מוּתָּר לְהַטְמִין אֶת הַצּוֹנֵן – **It is permitted to insulate cold [food]** on the Sabbath in order to keep it cold.

The necessity for this ruling is questioned:

אָמַר רַב יוֹסֵף – **Rav Yosef said:** מַאי קָמַשְׁמַע לָן – **What is [Shmuel] teaching us** that we did not already know? תְּנֵינָא – Why, we already **learned in the Mishnah:** מְמַלֵּא אָדָם קִיתוֹן וְנוֹתֵן תַּחַת הַכַּר אוֹ תַחַת הַכֶּסֶת – ONE MAY FILL A BOTTLE of cold water AND PLACE IT UNDER A CUSHION OR UNDER A BOLSTER. – ? –

The Gemara defends Shmuel:

אָמַר לֵיהּ אַבַּיֵי – **Abaye said to [Rav Yosef]:** טוּבָא קָמַשְׁמַע לָן – **[Shmuel] is informing us of a great deal.** דְּאִי מִמַּתְנִיתִין – **For if** only **from our Mishnah,** הֲוָה אָמִינָא הָנֵי מִילֵּי דָּבָר שֶׁאֵין דַּרְכּוֹ לְהַטְמִין – **I would have said that this** permit to insulate food in order to keep it cold **applies only to an item** such as cold water, **which is not normally insulated** in order to warm it up.[8] אֲבָל דָּבָר שֶׁדַּרְכּוֹ לְהַטְמִין לֹא – **But** in the case of **an item** such as a cooked food, **which is normally insulated** in order to warm it up,[9] I might have thought that insulating it is **not** permitted even in order to keep it cool, lest one come to insulate it in order to warm it up. קָמַשְׁמַע לָן – **[Shmuel]** therefore **informs us** that this is not the case. Rather, it is always permitted to insulate cold foods on the Sabbath.

Further discussion of this topic:

אָמַר רַב הוּנָא (אמר רב) [אָמַר רַבִּי][10] – **Rav Huna said in the name of Rebbi:** אָסוּר לְהַטְמִין אֶת הַצּוֹנֵן – **It is forbidden to insulate cold [food]** on the Sabbath.

The Gemara asks:

וְהָתַנְיָא – **But we learned in a Baraisa:** רַבִּי הִתִּיר לְהַטְמִין אֶת הַצּוֹנֵן – REBBI PERMITTED INSULATING COLD [FOOD]! – ? –

The Gemara answers:

לֹא קַשְׁיָא – **There is no difficulty.** הָא מִקַּמֵּיהּ דְּלִישְׁמְעֵיהּ מֵרַבִּי יִשְׁמָעֵאל בְּרַבִּי יוֹסֵי – **The one** ruling of Rebbi was issued **before he heard [the lenient ruling] from R' Yishmael the son of R' Yose,** הָא לְבָתַר דְּלִישְׁמְעֵיהּ – whereas **the other** ruling of Rebbi was issued **after he heard [the lenient ruling]** from R' Yishmael the son of R' Yose.

The Gemara explains:

כִּי הָא דְּיָתִיב רַבִּי וְאָמַר – As recorded **in the following** account: **Rebbi was** once **sitting** and teaching, **and he said:** אָסוּר לְהַטְמִין

NOTES

1. There are several mixtures forbidden by the Torah that are called *kilayim*. Specifically, this Mishnah refers to the prohibition against planting fruits or grains in a vineyard (*kil'ei hakerem*). The Mishnah teaches that one need not be concerned that by burying these vegetables under a grapevine he has planted *kilayim*, since the vegetables have not taken root (see *Rashi*, and *Tosafos* to 50b ד״ה הטומן).

2. If it is the seventh, *shemittah* year, he need not worry that he is considered to be planting the vegetables.

3. We do not say that the already-tithed vegetables are considered subordinate to the ground, thus making their removal a new act of harvesting and necessitating a new tithing for any possible additional growth (*Rashi*). [Even vegetables that do not take root may increase in size due to ground moisture (*Tosafos* ibid.).]

4. For the movement of the *muktzeh* earth or sand particles caused by the removal of the *slikusta* or knife is deemed indirect movement, which is permitted. [See *Ben Uri*, who discussed why the prohibition of excavating (see above, 50b note 18) would not apply in this case.]

[Actually, whether or not indirect movement of *muktzeh* is permitted is the subject of a Tannaic dispute on 123a. However, even the stricter view there permits the type of indirect movement discussed by our Gemara, whereby the earth or sand is not actually lifted but is (merely moved aside or is) easily shaken off (see *Tosafos* to *Eruvin* 77b ד״ה מקצת).]

5. Covering the pot after dark for the first time would constitute *hatmanah* on the Sabbath proper, which may not be done even with materials that do not add heat to the food, lest one be tempted to reheat the food prior to the *hatmanah* (*Rashi;* see Chapter Introduction).

6. That is, even if it became uncovered *before* dark, he may cover it after dark (*Tosafos*). Alternatively, the Mishnah means that if the pot became uncovered *after* dark, it may be covered after dark (see *Shulchan Aruch, Orach Chaim* 257:4, based on *Smag* and *Smak*).

[The person may also *intentionally* uncover the pot after dark and then cover it again. The Mishnah uses the expression "it *became* uncovered," implying that only where the pot was uncovered on its own may it be covered, because, according to the first explanation cited in the previous paragraph, the Mishnah wishes to imply that if the person knowingly uncovered the pot before dark, even with the intention not to cover it until after dark, he may not cover it again (*Tosafos*). According to the second explanation cited in the previous paragraph, the Mishnah wishes to imply that if the pot became uncovered *before* dark, even on its own, it may not be covered after dark (*Beis Yosef, Orach Chaim* 257:4, *Mishnah Berurah* 257:25).]

7. I.e. even on the Sabbath, one may place it under a cushion or under a bolster that is filled with some substance that does not add heat to the food, such as felting, to keep it cold and insulated from the heat of the day (*Rashi*). Although one may not insulate warm food on the Sabbath to keep it warm, insulating cold food to keep it cold is permitted.

[The above follows *Rashi*. Most Rishonim, however (see *Ran*), explain the Gemara to mean that one may insulate cold foods even to warm them (i.e. take the chill out of them).]

8. Storing something cold under a pillow increases the temperature of that thing only slightly. One who wishes to warm up cold water is not satisfied with this slight increase (see *Rashi*).

9. For solids, the slight increase in temperature provided by storing under a pillow is sometimes sufficient (see *Rashi*).

10. Emendation follows *Mesoras HaShas* (cf. *Rashash*).

לא משום כלאים ולא משום שביעית ולא משום מעשר וניטלין בשבת תיובתא:

מתני' לא כסהו מבעוד יום לא יכסנו משתחשך א כסהו ונתגלה מותר לכסותו ממלא את הקיתון ונותן לתחת הכר או תחת הכסת: **גמ'** אמר רב יהודה אמר שמואל ב מותר להטמין את הצונן אמר רב יוסף מאי קמ"ל תנינא ממלא אדם קיתון ונותן תחת הכר או תחת הכסת אמר ליה אביי טובא קמ"ל דאי ממתני' הוה אמינא ה"מ דבר שאין דרכו להטמין אבל דבר שדרכו להטמין לא קמ"ל אמר רב הונא א) (אמר רב) אסור להטמין את הצונן והתניא רבי התיר להטמין את הצונן לא קשיא הא מקמיה (א) דלישמעיה מר' ישמעאל ברבי יוסי הא לבתר דלישמעי' ב) כי הא דיתיב רבי ואמר אסור להטמין את הצונן אמר לפניו רבי ישמעאל ברבי יוסי אבא התיר להטמין את הצונן אמר ג) כבר הורה זקן אמר רב פפא ד) בא וראה כמה מחבבין זה את זה שאילו ר' יוסי קיים היה כפוף ויושב לפני רבי דהא רבי ישמעאל ברבי יוסי דממלא מקום אבותיו הוה וכפוף ויושב לפני רבי וקאמר כבר הורה זקן אמר ליה רב נחמן לדרו עבדיה אטמין לי צונן ואייתי לי מיא דאחים קפילא ארמאה ה) שמע רבי אמי ואיקפד אמר רב יוסף מ"ט איקפד כרבוותיה עביד חדא כרב וחדא כשמואל כשמואל דאמר רב יהודה אמר שמואל מותר להטמין את הצונן כרב ו) דאמר רב שמואל בר רב יצחק אמר רב ג כל שהוא נאכל כמות שהוא חי אין בו משום בשולי נכרים: (ז) הוא) סבר ח) אדם חשוב שאני: ט) ת"ר ד אע"פ שאמרו י) אין טומנין אפילו בדבר שאינו מוסיף הבל משחשכה אם בא להוסיף מוסיף כיצד הוא עושה רשב"ג אומר נוטל את הסדינין ומניח את הגלופקרין או נוטל את הגלופקרין ומניח את הסדינין וכן היה רשב"ג אומר ה לא אסרו אלא אותו מיחם אבל פינה ממיחם למיחם מותר השתא אקורי קא מקיר לה ארתוחי קא מירתח לה כ) ו טמן וכיסה בדבר הניטל בשבת או טמן בדבר שאינו ניטל בשבת וכיסה בדבר הניטל בשבת הרי זה נוטל ומחזיר ז טמן וכיסה בדבר שאינו ניטל בשבת או שטמן בדבר הניטל בשבת וכיסה בדבר שאינו ניטל בשבת אם היה מגולה מקצתו נוטל ומחזיר ואם לאו אינו

רש"י

לא משום כלאים. דאין זו שתילה: ולא משום מעשר. דנימא בטלה לה אגב קרקע והרי הוא כלוקטה מתחלה ויהא צריך לעשר על הנוסף שמא ניתוסף: וניטלין בשבת. שאוחזו במקצת עליה המגולין ולא חייש אם העפר ניזח מאליו וה"ה לסליקוסתא: **מתני'** לא יכסנו משתחשך. הא פרישנא טעמא בפ"ב (דף לד.) מפני מה אמרו אין טומנין בדבר שאינו מוסיף הבל משחשיכה גזירה שמא ירתיח: ממלא הקיתון. של צונן: ונותן לתוך הכר. שלא יחמו בחום הקיץ והחמה כגון כר וכסת של נבדין שאינו מחמם: **גמ'** מותר להטמין את הצונן. מפני החמה שלא יחמו ולא גזרינן אטו הטמנה כדי שיחמו: אי ממתני' הוה אמינא הני מילי. כגון מים צוננין שאין דרכן להטמין תחת כר וכסת לחממן שאין מתחממין בכך הלכך ליכא למיגזר: אבל דבר שדרכו להטמין. לחמם כגון תבשיל אימא לא יטמיננו מפני החמה: התיר להטמין את הצונן. מפני החום: זקן. ר' יוסי: ממלא מקום אבותיו. גדול כאביו: היה כפוף ויושב לפני רבי. מפני כבוד הנשיאות ולא היה מורה לפניו אע"פ שגדול הימנו: כבר הורה זקן. גדלו ונשאו עליו: אטמין לי צונן. בשבת: ואייתי לי מיא דאחים קפילא ארמאה. שהחמן נחתום נכרי ובחול ולאשמועינן דאין בהן משום בשולי נכרים: כרבוותיה. כרבותיו: אדם חשוב שאני. שהרואה אותו שהוא מיקל עומד ומיקל יותר: אין טומנין את החמין משחשיכה ואפילו בדבר שאינו מוסיף הבל. וכדאמרן שמא ימצא קדרתו צוננת כשירצה להטמינה וירתיחנה בשבת אבל אם בא להוסיף כיסוי על כיסוי משחשיכה מוסיף: גלופקרא. קו"ט ויש בו הבל יותר מן הסדינין ונוטל את הגלופקרא בימות החמה אם ירא שמא יקדיח תבשילו מחמת רוב כיסוי: וכן היה רשב"ג. מיקל קולא אחריתי בהטמנה: לא אסרו. להטמין משחשיכה אלא במיחם שהוחמו בו דהתם הוא דאיכא למיגזר שמא ירתיח: אבל מפנה הוא ממיחם למיחם אחר ומטמין זהו לשון התוספתא והיינו נמי פינהו ממיחם למיחם מותר דהשתא ליכא למיגזר שמא ירתיח דהשתא אקורי קא מיקר להו במתכוין ארתוחי מרתח להו בתמיה: טמן. הקדרה בדבר הניטל מה שנתן סביבותיה הוי דבר מוכן: וכיסה. על פיה נמי דבר המוכן כגון כלי: או שטמן בדבר שאינו ניטל. וכיסה בדבר הניטל: הרי זה נוטל ומחזיר. דהואיל והכיסוי ניטל מגלה הקדרה ואוחזה אבל טמן וכיסה בדבר שאינו ניטל או אפי' טמן בדבר הניטל וכיסה בדבר שאינו ניטל אם אין מקצת פיה מגולה לא יטול דאין לו במה יאחזנה ואם תאמר יפנה סביבותיה הואיל ודבר הניטל הוא ויאחזנה בדופניה (ב) ויטנה על צדה ויפול הכיסוי כי ההיא דתנן לקמן (פרק נוטל דף קמב:) האבן שעל פי החבית מטה על צדה והיא נופלת ואם היתה בין החביות מגביהה ומטה על צדה והיא נופלת הא אוקימנא התם בשכח אבל במניח נעשה בסיס לדבר האסור והיכא דמגולה מקצתו אין זה טלטול שמגלגלו והכיסוי נופל מאליו: הרי

תוספות

הוא ואמאי ממעט ומשני דאית לה אוגנים וחבריה בארעא ופריך וכי יש לו מאי הוי והתנן הטומן לפת כו' ואי גרס מקצת מגולים מאי פריך הא לא דמי לספל שיש לו אוגנים ואומר ר"י דיש לומר דבנטיעה איכא קרקע קשה ודבוק ביותר ומדמה ליה לספל שיש לו אוגנים ואין להקשות לפירוש הערוך דמאי פריך מינה לשמואל לימא דהך משנה סבר טלטול מן הצד לא שמיה טלטול (ג) כאלעזר בן תדאי ומקצת מגולין נקט משום אחריני ולא משום שבת ושמואל סבר כרבנן דאיכא למימר דמשמע ליה דמשום שבת נמי נקט לה מדלא תנא בהדיא וניטלין בשבת אפילו מכוסין ש"מ דמכוסין אסורין כרבנן ואפ"ה מקצתן מגולין שרי:

כסהו ונתגלה מותר לכסותו. נראה לר"י דה"ה דמותר לגלותו בידים ולחזור ולכסותו כמו שמותר ליטול הקדרה ולהחזירה והא דנקט כסהו ונתגלה משום דנתגלה מבעוד יום איירי דומיא דרישא לא כסהו מבעוד יום וקאמר דמותר לכסותו משתחשך אבל אם גילהו בידים מבעוד יום כדי לכסותו משתחשך אסור לכסותו משתחשך דדמיא לתחלת הטמנה:

אילו היה ר' יוסי קיים היה כפוף כו'. פי' רבינו שלמה מחמת נשיאותו דהא ר"י היה גדול מרבי כדמוכח בפ"ב דנדה (דף יד: ושם) דאמר ליה רבי ישמעאל ברבי יוסי לר' חמא בר ביסנא כדברי רבי אומר לך או כדברי אבא אמר ליה כדברי רבי אמור לי אמר ליה זהו שאומרים עליו דאדם גדול הוא שמניח דברי הרב ושומע דברי התלמיד ור"ת מפרש דודאי מתחלה היה רבי תלמידו של רבי יוסי אבל אח"כ נתחכם רבי כדקאמ' התם ור' חמא סבר רבי ריש מתיבתא שכיחי רבנן גביה ומחדדן שמעתתיה:

כיצד הוא עושה רשב"ג אומר נוטל את הסדינין כו'. נראה לר"י ולה"ר פור"ת דל"ג כילד הוא עושה דרשב"ג פליג את"ק דלא שרי אלא להוסיף אבל להחליף אסור ורשב"ג שרי אף להחליף וכ"ש ליטול ולהחזיר אותו דבר דלא הוי כל כך תחלת הטמנה והיינו דקאמר וכן היה רשב"ג אומר כלומר שהיה מיקל קולא אחריתי גבי הטמנה:

אבל פינה ממיחם למיחם מותר. ול"ד להוא דכירה דבעי בפרק כירה (לעיל לח:) פינה ממיחם למיחם מהו דהתם רוצה בחמימותן לכך יש לאסור כשהוא צונן אבל הכא גבי הטמנה כל כמה שהוא צונן טפי שפיר דמי כדאמר לעיל רבי התיר להטמין את הצונן וא"ת ורבי לא ידע לעיל דמותר להטמין את הצונן וכי לא ידע דשמיע ליה מאבוה הכא דשרי וי"ל דהכא דוקא דמוכח מילתא שנתכוין לצנן שפינהו ממיחם למיחם אבל קיתון של מים דלא מוכח מידי יהא אסור להטמין. מתוספות רבינו יהודה (ת"י):

או שטמן בדבר הניטל וכיסה בדבר שאינו ניטל. הקשה בקונט' יפנה סביבה ויאחזנה בדופניה ויגביהנה ויטנה על צדה כדתנן בפרק נוטל (לקמן קמב:) היתה בין החביות מגביהה כו' ומתרץ דהא אוקמינן התם בשכח אבל במניח נעשה בסיס לדבר האסור וקשה דאי חשיב הכא כמניח אם כן במגולה מקצתה היאך נוטל ומחזיר מה בין זה לאבן שעל פי החבית דאסרי' במניח אפי' להטותה על צדה ועוד קשה לר"ת דהא תנן נוער את הכיסוי והן נופלות אפי' אין מגולות מקצתן ועל כן אומר ר"ת דלא חשיב כמניח ° כיון שדעתו ליטלו בשבת ובפ' נוטל (שם דף קמג.) נמי תנן בית שמאי אומרים מגביהין מעל גבי השלחן עצמות וקליפים וב"ה אומרים מסלק את הטבלא ומנערה ולא חשיב לב"ה כמניח והכא מיירי בכיסוי כעין כלי חרס שנותנים על הקדרה שהקדרה בלועה בתוכה ואי אפשר לנער הכיסוי אלא אם כן יגביהו קצת ור"י מפרש כגון שטמן הקדרה בקופה בדבר הניטל ולמעלה מן הקדרה מילא כל הקופה בדבר שאינו ניטל שאי אפשר לו להגיע לקדרה אם לא יטלטל דבר שאינו ניטל בידים [ל]: אינו

מסורת הש"ס

א) [נ"ל אמר רבין], ב) סנהדרין כד., ג) [שם ודף כט:], ד) [שם כד.], ה) [מו"ק יב:], ו) מו"ק יב: יבמות מו. ע"ז לח. נט., ז) [נ"ל והוא], ח) [לקמן קמב: ברכות יט. פסחים קי. מו"ק יא: יב. מגילה כב: כתובות נב: פו. ב"מ עג. ע"ז ח: כח. מח: חולין קלד:], ט) תוספתא פ"ד, י) [לעיל לד.], כ) [תוספתא שם כל הענין עד סוף הפרק], ל) [ועי' תוספות לקמן קכג. ד"ה האי פוגלא].

הגהות הב"ח

(א) גמ' מקמיה דשמעיה מר' ישמעאל וכו' לבתר דשמעיה כו': (ב) רש"י ד"ה או שטמן וכו' ויאחזנה בדופניה ויגביהנה ויטנה: (ג) תום' ד"ה מקצת וכו' טלטול כרבי אלעזר בן תדאי:

גליון הש"ס

תוס' ד"ה או שטמן וכו' כיון שדעתו ליטלו בשבת. עי' לעיל דף מג ע"ב תוס' ד"ה דכו"ע טלטול:

ליקוטי רש"י

ולא משום שביעית. אם שנה שביעית היא. ולא משום מעשר. לשמא נשרש וניתוסף ואם היה חושש למעשר צריך לעשר את תוספתו ליכא למיחש להכי דלא נשרש [עירובין עז:]. להיות בטילה בנטיעה זו וכשנוטלה יצטרך לחזור ולעשר [לקמן קיג.]. לא יכסנו משתחשך. גזירה שמא ימצא קדרתו שנצטננה כשירצה להטמינה, וירתיחנה תחילה, ונמצא מבשל בשבת [לעיל לד.]. אסור להטמין את הצונן. מים צונן ומתיירא שלא יוחמו אסור להטמינן בחול צונן (לצורך שבת) [בשבת]. הורה זקן. ר' יוסי דאזלינן בתריה. ממלא מקום אבותיו. חשוב כאביו [סנהדרין כד.]. כל שהוא נאכל כמות שהוא חי. ומילא שתו אינשי כמות שהן [מו"ק יב:]. אין בו משום בשולי נכרים. שגזרו חכמים בבשולי נכרים משום חתנות ועל שנאכל כמו שהוא חי לא גזרו על בשולו דכיון שנאכל כמו שהוא חי אינו בשול דלא אהני מידי [ביצה טז.]. אדם חשוב שאני. יש לו להחמיר על עצמו יותר ולא הוה ליה וכו' ולא למשתי מיא דאחים קפילא נכרי [מו"ק שם]. לפי שלמדין הימנו [כתובות פו.]. סדינין. של פשתן. גלופקרין. שקורין קו"ץ והוא של למר [ב"מ פא.].

עין משפט נר מצוה

כט א מיי' פ"ד מהל' שבת הלכה ד סמג לאוין סה טוש"ע או"ח סימן רנז סעיף ד:
ל ב מיי' שם טוש"ע שם סעיף ו:
לא ג מיי' פי"ז מהלכות מאכלות אסורות הל' יד סמג לאוין קמב טור שו"ע יו"ד סימן קיג סעיף א:
לב ד מיי' פ"ד מהלכות שבת הלכה ד סמג לאוין סה טוש"ע או"ח סימן רנז סעיף ד:
לג ה מיי' שם הלכה ה טוש"ע שם סעיף ה:
לד ו (מיי') סמג שם טוש"ע או"ח סימן רנט סעיף ד:
לה ז שם סעיף ה:

רבינו חננאל

מגולין אין חושש משום כלאים דלא ירק באילן הוא ולאו משום שביעית דלאו זריעה היא וכן משום מעשר ונטלין בשבת דלאו מחובר לקרקע אינון. ועלתה בתיובתא לשמואל. וקיי"ל כי הא מתניתא דמותבינא מינה ש"מ דסליקוסתא אע"ג דלא ארווח בגומא שרי וכ"ש סכין דנעיצה בין הנדבך ובין הקנים. רוו הלפת טומנה להתרכך כגון טמינת פגא בתבן: ממלא קיתון כו' ואסיק' מותר להטמין את הצונן אפי' בדבר שדרכו להטמין [כי] הא דאמר רב נחמן לדראי עבדיה אטמין לי את הצונן ואייתי לי חמין דאחים קפילא ארמאה. ואסי' אע"ג דקיי"ל דשרי להטמין

אֶת הַצּוֹנֵן – **It is forbidden to insulate cold [food]** on the Sabbath. אָמַר לְפָנָיו רַבִּי יִשְׁמָעֵאל בְּרַבִּי יוֹסֵי – **R' Yishmael the son of R' Yose said before [Rebbi]:** אַבָּא הִתִּיר לְהַטְמִין אֶת הַצּוֹנֵן – **Father permitted one to insulate cold [food]** on the Sabbath. אָמַר כְּבָר הוֹרָה זָקֵן – Upon hearing this **[Rebbi] declared: The elder** [R' Yose] **has already ruled** otherwise on the matter, and I bow to his opinion.

An Amora comments on this incident:

אָמַר רַב פַּפָּא – **Rav Pappa said:** בֹּא וּרְאֵה כַּמָּה מְחַבְּבִין זֶה אֶת זֶה – **Come and see how** greatly **[these Tannaim] cherished each other** (i.e. held each other in regard)! שֶׁאִילּוּ רַבִּי יוֹסֵי קַיָּים הָיָה כָּפוּף וְיוֹשֵׁב לִפְנֵי רַבִּי – **For had R' Yose** himself **been alive, he would have sat subordinately before Rebbi.**[11] We know this to be true דְּהָא רַבִּי יִשְׁמָעֵאל בְּרַבִּי יוֹסֵי דִּמְמַלֵּא מְקוֹם אֲבוֹתָיו הֲוָה – **for R' Yishmael the son of R' Yose was his father's successor** (i.e. his equal) in scholarship וְכָפוּף וְיוֹשֵׁב לִפְנֵי רַבִּי – **and he sat subordinately before Rebbi,** as the above account records. Presumably, therefore, his father would have done the same. וְקָאָמַר כְּבָר הוֹרָה זָקֵן – **Yet** when Rebbi heard of R' Yose's ruling **he** immediately withdrew his own and **said: "The elder sage has already ruled."**

Another incident relating to this same topic:

אָמַר לֵיהּ רַב נַחְמָן לְדָרוּ עַבְדֵּיהּ – **Rav Nachman said to Daru his servant:** אַטְמִין לִי צוֹנֵן – **Insulate some cold [food] for me** on the Sabbath, וְאַיְיתִי לִי מַיָּא דְּאַחִים קְפִילָא אַרְמָאָה – **and,** on a weekday, **bring me** to drink **some water that was heated by an Aramean,** i.e. a non-Jewish, **cook.** Rav Nachman intended to demonstrate two rulings: that it is permitted to insulate cold food on the Sabbath in order to keep it cold, and that water cooked by a gentile does not fall under the prohibition against foods cooked by a gentile.[12] שָׁמַע רַבִּי אַמִי וְאִיקְפַּד – **R' Ami heard** of these instructions **and objected** to them.

Rav Ami's reaction is questioned:

אָמַר רַב יוֹסֵף מַאי טַעְמָא אִיקְפַּד – **Said Rav Yosef: Why did [R' Ami] object?** כְּרַבְּוָותֵיהּ עָבִיד – After all, **[Rav Nachman] was** only **acting in accordance with** the views of **his** own **teachers;** חֲדָא כְּרַב וַחֲדָא כִּשְׁמוּאֵל – in **one** instance **in accordance with** a ruling of his teacher **Rav and** in **the other** instance **in accordance with** a ruling of his teacher **Shmuel,** as follows: כִּשְׁמוּאֵל – In instructing the servant to insulate cold food on the Sabbath, Rav Nachman was acting **in accordance with** the view of **Shmuel,** דְּאָמַר רַב יְהוּדָה אָמַר שְׁמוּאֵל – **for,** as we learned earlier, **Rav Yehudah said in the name of Shmuel:** מוּתָּר לְהַטְמִין אֶת הַצּוֹנֵן – **It is permitted to insulate cold [food]** on the Sabbath. כְּרַב – And in instructing the servant to serve him water heated by a gentile he was acting **in accordance with** the view of **Rav,** דְּאָמַר רַב שְׁמוּאֵל בַּר רַב יִצְחָק אָמַר רַב – **for Rav Shmuel bar Rav Yitzchak said in the name of Rav:** כֹּל שֶׁהוּא נֶאֱכָל כְּמוֹת שֶׁהוּא חַי – **Whatever is** normally **eaten in its raw state** אֵין בּוֹ מִשּׁוּם בִּשּׁוּלֵי נָכְרִים – **does not fall under** the prohibition against **gentile cooking,** even if that food happened to have been cooked by a gentile.[13] Why then did R' Ami object to Rav Nachman's rulings?

The Gemara answers:

[וְ]הוּא סָבַר אָדָם חָשׁוּב שָׁאנֵי – **But [R' Ami] was of the opinion that an important person** such as Rav Nachman **is different** from an ordinary Jew, and should hold himself to a stricter standard.[14]

We learned in the Mishnah that if a pot was insulated before the Sabbath with a substance that does not add heat and it later became uncovered, one may cover it again on the Sabbath. The Gemara quotes a Baraisa which has bearing on this law:

תָּנוּ רַבָּנָן – **The Rabbis taught in a Baraisa:**[15] אַף עַל פִּי שֶׁאָמְרוּ אֵין טוֹמְנִין אֲפִילּוּ בְּדָבָר שֶׁאֵינוֹ מוֹסִיף הֶבֶל מִשֶּׁחֲשֵׁכָה – ALTHOUGH [THE RABBIS] SAID THAT ONE MAY NOT INSULATE AFTER NIGHTFALL EVEN WITH A SUBSTANCE THAT DOES NOT ADD HEAT, אִם בָּא לְהוֹסִיף מוֹסִיף – nevertheless IF the pot was already insulated and ONE merely WISHES TO ADD additional insulation on top of the original insulation,[16] HE MAY ADD. כֵּיצַד הוּא עוֹשֶׂה – HOW DOES HE PROCEED? רַבָּן שִׁמְעוֹן בֶּן גַּמְלִיאֵל אוֹמֵר – RABBAN SHIMON BEN GAMLIEL SAYS: נוֹטֵל אֶת הַסְּדִינִין וּמַנִּיחַ אֶת הַגְּלוּפְקְרִין – HE REMOVES THE SHEETS from on top of the pot AND PLACES THE COATS in their stead; אוֹ נוֹטֵל אֶת הַגְּלוּפְקְרִין וּמַנִּיחַ אֶת הַסְּדִינִין – OR, conversely, HE REMOVES THE COATS from on top of the pot AND PLACES THE SHEETS in their stead.[17]

NOTES

11. Though he was greater than Rebbi in Torah knowledge, he would have submitted to Rebbi in deference to his position as *Nasi,* and would not have rendered halachic decisions in his presence (*Rashi;* cf. *Tosafos*).

12. As an impediment to social intimacy and intermarriage with gentiles, the Rabbis prohibited the eating of foods cooked by gentiles, even if cooked in a Jew's utensils and in his presence, with no possibility of contamination with non-kosher substances. The Gemara will shortly make clear why this prohibition does not apply to cooked water.

13. Thus, since water is drunk uncooked as well as cooked, it does not fall under this prohibition (but see *Eglei Tal, Ofeh* 19:11 ff).

14. Seeing a celebrated sage such as Rav Nachman relying on such leniencies, ordinary onlookers would allow themselves still greater leniencies that might go beyond what is permissible (*Rashi*).

15. *Tosefta* 4:12-15.

16. [*Rashi;* cf. *Maggid Mishneh* and *Kesef Mishneh* to *Hil. Shabbos,* 4:4.]

17. Rabban Shimon ben Gamliel teaches that not only may one add additional insulation on the Sabbath *on top of* the original insulation, one may even *remove* the original insulation and replace it with *different* insulation.

[Although we already know from the previous Mishnah (49a) that one may remove a pot from its insulation and replace it on the Sabbath and, likewise, we learned in our Mishnah that one may uncover and cover a pot on the Sabbath, one might have thought that this applies only where one is replacing the pot in its *original* insulation. But where one replaces the insulation with *new* insulation, one might have thought that this should be viewed as a completely new act of *hatmanah* on the Sabbath and, thus, should be forbidden. Rabban Shimon ben Gamliel therefore teaches that this is not the case; the new *hatmanah* is seen as a continuation of the old and, therefore, is permitted. Furthermore, Rabban Shimon ben Gamliel teaches that this is true even where the new insulating material is more effective an insulator than the old material, as where he replaces sheets with coats (*Ran;* cf. *Maggid Mishneh* ibid. and *Korban Nesanel* to *Rosh* here). Of course, the new material cannot be so effective that it actually adds heat to the food; allowing a pot to remain insulated on the Sabbath in a substance that adds heat to the food is always forbidden (see the introduction to this chapter).]

The Rishonim dispute whether Rabban Shimon ben Gamliel is taking issue with the first, anonymous Tanna of the Baraisa or is merely elaborating on his ruling. *Tosafos* understand Rabban Shimon ben Gamliel to be in dispute with the first Tanna; according to *Tosafos,* the first Tanna of the Baraisa allows only adding new insulating *on top of* the old insulation, not replacing the old insulation entirely with new. *Tosafos* delete from the Baraisa the words *How does he proceed,* which indicate that Rabban Shimon ben Gamliel is merely elaborating on the previous Tanna's view. *Rabbeinu Yonah,* however (cited by *Rosh*), understands Rabban Shimon ben Gamliel as elaborating on the view of the first Tanna; according to *Rabbeinu Yonah,* both the first Tanna and Rabban Shimon ben Gamliel agree that one may either add new insulation on top of the old insulation or replace the old insulation entirely.

לא משום כלאים ולא משום שביעית ולא משום מעשר וניטלין בשבת תיובתא:

מתני' לא כסהו מבעוד יום לא יכסנו משתחשך [א]כסהו ונתגלה מותר לכסותו ממלא את הקיתון ונותן לתחת הכר או תחת הכסת:

גמ' אמר רב יהודה אמר שמואל [ב]מותר להטמין את הצונן אמר רב יוסף מאי קמ"ל תנינא ממלא אדם קיתון ונותן תחת הכר או תחת הכסת אמר ליה אביי טובא קמ"ל דאי ממתני' הוה אמינא ה"מ דבר שאין דרכו להטמין אבל דבר שדרכו להטמין לא קמ"ל אמר רב הונא [א](אמר רב) אסור להטמין את הצונן והתניא רבי התיר להטמין את הצונן לא קשיא הא מקמיה (א) דלישמעיה מר' ישמעאל ברבי יוסי הא לבתר דלישמעי' [ב]כי הא דיתיב רבי ואמר אסור להטמין את הצונן אמר לפניו רבי ישמעאל ברבי יוסי אבא התיר להטמין את הצונן אמר [ג]כבר הורה זקן אמר רב פפא [ד]בא וראה כמה מחבבין זה את זה שאילו ר' יוסי קיים היה כפוף ויושב לפני רבי דהא רבי ישמעאל ברבי יוסי דממלא מקום אבותיו הוה וכפוף ויושב לפני רבי וקאמר כבר הורה זקן אמר ליה רב נחמן לדרו עבדיה אטמין לי צונן ואייתי לי מיא דאחים קפילא ארמאה [ה]שמע רבי אמי ואיקפד אמר רב יוסף מ"ט איקפד כרבוותיה עביד חדא כרב וחדא כשמואל כשמואל דאמר רב יהודה אמר שמואל מותר להטמין את הצונן כרב [ו]דאמר רב שמואל בר רב יצחק אמר רב [ג]כל שהוא נאכל כמות שהוא חי אין בו משום בשולי נכרים ([ז]הוא) סבר [ח]אדם חשוב שאני: [ט]ת"ר [ד]אע"פ שאמרו [י]אין טומנין אפילו בדבר שאינו מוסיף הבל משחשכה אם בא להוסיף מוסיף כיצד הוא עושה רשב"ג אומר נוטל את הסדינין ומניח את הגלופקרין או נוטל את הגלופקרין ומניח את הסדינין וכן היה רשב"ג אומר [ה]לא אסרו אלא אותו מיחם אבל פינה ממיחם למיחם מותר השתא אקורי קא מקיר לה ארתוחי קא מירתח לה [כ][ו]טמן וכיסה בדבר הניטל בשבת או טמן בדבר שאינו ניטל בשבת וכיסה בדבר הניטל בשבת הרי זה נוטל ומחזיר [ז]טמן וכיסה בדבר שאינו ניטל בשבת או שטמן בדבר הניטל בשבת וכיסה בדבר שאינו ניטל בשבת אם היה מגולה מקצתו נוטל ומחזיר ואם לאו אינו

רש"י

לא משום כלאים. דאין זו שתילה: ולא משום מעשר. דנימא בטלה לה אגב קרקע והרי הוא כלוקטה מתחלה ויהא צריך לעשר על הנוסף שמא ניתוסף: וניטלין בשבת. שאוחזה במקצת עליה המגולין ולא חייש אם העפר ניזוח מאליו וה"ה לסליקוסתא: מתני' לא יכסנו משתחשך. הא פרישנא טעמא בפ"ב (דף לד.) מפני מה אמרו אין טומנין בדבר שאינו מוסיף הבל משחשיכה גזירה שמא ירתיח: ממלא הקיתון. של צונן: ונותן לתוך הכר. שלא יחמו בחום הקיץ והחמה כגון כר וכסת של נבדין שאינו מחמם: גמ' מותר להטמין את הצונן. מפני החמה שלא יחמו ולא גזרינן אטו הטמנה כדי שיחמו: אי ממתני' הוה אמינא הני מילי. כגון מים צוננין שאין דרכן להטמין תחת כר וכסת לחממן שאין מתחממין בכך הלכך ליכא למיגזר: אבל דבר שדרכו להטמין. לחמם כגון תבשיל אימא לא יטמינו מפני החמה: התיר להטמין את הצונן. מפני החום: זקן. ר' יוסי: ממלא מקום אבותיו. גדול כאביו: היה כפוף ויושב לפני רבי. מפני כבוד הנשיאות ולא היה מורה לפניו אע"פ שגדול הימנו: כבר הורה זקן. גדלו ונשאו עליו: אטמין לי צונן. בשבת: ואייתי לי מיא דאחים קפילא ארמאה. שהחמן נחתום נכרי ובחול ולאשמועינן דאין בהן משום בשולי נכרים: כרבוותיה. כרבותיו: אדם חשוב שאני. שהרואה אותו שהוא מיקל עומד ומיקל יותר: אין טומנין את החמין משחשיכה ואפילו בדבר שאינו מוסיף הבל. וכדאמרן שמא ימצא קדרתו צוננת כשירצה להטמינה וירתיחנה בשבת אבל אם בא להוסיף כיסוי על כיסוי משחשיכה מוסיף: גלופקרא. קו"ט ויש בו הבל יותר מן הסדינין ונוטל את הגלופקרא בימות החמה אם ירא שמא יקדיח תבשילו מחמת רוב כיסוי: וכן היה רשב"ג. מיקל קולא אחריתי בהטמנה: לא אסרו. להטמין משחשיכה אלא במיחם שהוחמו בו דהתם הוא דאיכא למיגזר שמא ירתיח: אבל מפנה הוא ממיחם למיחם אחר ומטמין וזהו לשון התוספתא והיינו נמי פינהו ממיחם למיחם מותר דהשתא ליכא למיגזר שמא ירתיח דהשתא אקורי קא מיקר להו במתכוין ארתוחי מרתח להו בתמיה: טמן. הקדרה בדבר הניטל מה שנתן סביבותיה הוי דבר מוכן: וכיסה. על פיה נמי דבר המוכן כגון כלי: או שטמן בדבר שאינו ניטל. וכיסה בדבר הניטל: הרי זה נוטל ומחזיר. דהואיל והכיסוי ניטל מגלה הקדרה ואוחזה אבל טמן וכיסה בדבר שאינו ניטל או אפי' טמן בדבר הניטל וכיסה בדבר שאינו ניטל אם אין מקצת פיה מגולה לא יטול דאין לו במה יאחזנה ואם תאמר יפנה סביבותיה הואיל ודבר הניטל הוא ויאחזנה בדופניה (ב) ויטנה על צדה ויפול הכיסוי כי ההיא דתנן לקמן (פרק נוטל דף קמב:) האבן שעל פי החבית מטה על צדה והיא נופלת ואם היתה בין החביות מגביהה ומטה על צדה והיא נופלת הא אוקימנא התם בשכח אבל במניח נעשה בסיס לדבר האסור והיכא דמגולה מקצתו אין זה טלטול שמלדדו והכיסוי נופל מאליו:

הרי

תוספות

הוא ואמאי ממעט ומשני דאית לה אוגנים וחבריה בארעא ופריך וכי יש לו מאי הוי והתנן הטומן לפת כו' ואי גרם מקצת מגולים מאי פריך הא לא דמי לספל שיש לו אוגנים ואומר ר"י דיש לומר דבנטיעה איכא קרקע קשה ודבוק ביותר ומדמה ליה לספל שיש לו אוגנים ואין להקשות לפירוש הערוך דמאי פריך מינה לשמואל לימא דהך משנה סבר טלטול מן הצד לא שמיה טלטול (ג) כאלעזר בן תדאי ומקצת מגולין נקט משום אחריני ולא משום שבת ושמואל סבר כרבנן דאיכא למימר דמשמע ליה דמשום שבת נמי נקט לה מדלא תנא בהדיא וניטלין בשבת אפילו מכוסין ש"מ דמכוסין אסורין כרבנן ואפ"ה מקצתן מגולין שרי:

כסהו ונתגלה מותר לכסותו. נראה לר"י דה"ה דמותר לגלותו בידים ולחזור ולכסותו כמו שמותר ליטול הקדרה ולהחזירה והא דנקט כסהו ונתגלה משום דנתגלה מבעוד יום איירי דומיא דרישא לא כסהו מבעוד יום וקאמר דמותר לכסותו משתחשך אבל אם גילהו בידים מבעוד יום כדי לכסותו משתחשך אסור לכסותו משתחשך דדמיא לתחלת הטמנה:

אילו היה ר' יוסי קיים היה כפוף כו'. פי' רבינו שלמה מחמת נשיאותו דהא ר"י היה גדול מרבי כדמוכח בפ"ב דנדה (דף יד: ושם) דאמר ליה רבי ישמעאל ברבי יוסי לר' חמא בר ביסנא כדברי רבי אומר לך או כדברי אבא אמר ליה כדברי רבי אמור לי אמר ליה זהו שאומרים עליו דאדם גדול הוא שמניח דברי הרב ושומע דברי התלמיד ור"ת מפרש דודאי מתחלה היה רבי תלמידו של רבי יוסי אבל אח"כ נתחכם רבי כדקאמ' התם ור' חמא סבר רבי ריש מתיבתא שכיחי רבנן גביה ומחדדן שמעתתיה:

כיצד הוא עושה רשב"ג אומר נוטל את הסדינין כו'. נראה לר"י ולה"ר פור"ת דל"ג כילד הוא עושה דרשב"ג פליג את"ק דלא שרי אלא להוסיף אבל להחליף אסור ורשב"ג שרי אף להחליף וכ"ש ליטול ולהחזיר אותו דבר דלא הוי כל כך תחלת הטמנה והיינו דקאמר וכן היה רשב"ג אומר כלומר שהיה מיקל קולא אחריתי גבי הטמנה:

אבל פינה ממיחם למיחם מותר. ול"ד להואל דכירה דבעי בפרק כירה (לעיל לח:) פינה ממיחם למיחם מהו דהתם רוצה בחמימותן לכך יש לאסור כשהוא צונן אבל הכא גבי הטמנה כל כמה שהוא צונן טפי שפיר דמי כדאמר לעיל רבי התיר להטמין את הצונן וא"ת ורבי לא ידע לעיל דמותר להטמין את הצונן וכי לא ידע דשמיע ליה מאבוה הכא דשרי וי"ל דהכא דוקא דמוכח מילתא שנתכוין לצנן שפינהו ממיחם למיחם אבל קיתון של מים דלא מוכח מידי יהא אסור להטמין. מתוספות רבינו יהודה (ת"י):

או שטמן בדבר הניטל וכיסה בדבר שאינו ניטל. הקשה בקונט' יפנה סביבה ויאחזנה בדופניה ויגביהנה ויטנה על צדה כדתנן בפרק נוטל (לקמן קמב:) היתה בין החביות מגביהה כו' ומתרץ דהא אוקמינן התם בשכח אבל במניח נעשה בסיס לדבר האסור וקשה דאי חשיב הכא כמניח אם כן במגולה מקצתה היאך נוטל ומחזיר מה בין זה לאבן שעל פי החבית דאסרי' במניח אפי' להטותה על צדה ועוד קשה לר"ת דהא תנן נוער את הכיסוי והן נופלות אפי' אינן מגולות מקצתן ועל כן אומר ר"ת דלא חשיב כמניח ° כיון שדעתו ליטלו בשבת ובפ' נוטל (שם דף קמג.) נמי תנן בית שמאי אומרים מגביהין מעל גבי השלחן עצמות וקליפים וב"ה אומרים מסלק את הטבלא ומנערה ולא חשיב לב"ה כמניח והכא איירי בכיסוי כעין כלי חרס שנותנים על הקדרה שהקדרה בלועה בתוכה ואי אפשר לנער הכיסוי אלא אם כן יגביהו קצת ור"י מפרש כגון שטמן הקדרה בקופה בדבר הניטל ולמעלה מן הקדרה מילא כל הקופה בדבר שאינו ניטל שאי אפשר לו להגיע לקדרה אם לא יטלטל דבר שאינו ניטל בידים (ל):

אינו

מסורת הש"ס

א) [נ"ל אמר רבי], ב) סנהדרין כד., ג) [שם ודף כט:], ד) [שם כד.], ה) [מו"ק יב:], ו) מו"ק יב: יבמות מו. ע"ז לח. נט., ז) [נ"ל והוא], ח) [לקמן קמב: ברכות יט. פסחים קי. מו"ק יא: יב. מגילה כב: כתובות נב: פו. ב"מ עג. ע"ז ח: כח. מח: חולין קלד:], ט) תוספתא פ"ד, י) [לעיל לד.], כ) [תוספתא שם כל הענין עד סוף הפרק], ל) [ועי' תוספות לקמן קמג. ד"ה הא פוגלא].

הגהות הב"ח

(א) גמ' מקמיה דשמעיה מר' ישמעאל וכו' לבתר דשמעיה כו': (ב) רש"י ד"ה או שטמן וכו' ויאחזנה בדופניה ויגביהנה ויטנה: (ג) תוס' ד"ה מקצת וכו' טלטול כרבי אלעזר בן תדאי:

גליון הש"ס

תוס' ד"ה או שטמן וכו' כיון שדעתו ליטלו בשבת. עי' לעיל דף מג ע"ב תוס' ד"ה דכו"ע טלטול:

ליקוטי רש"י

ולא משום שביעית. אם שנה שביעית היא. ולא משום מעשר. לשמא נשרש וניתוסף ואם היה חושש למעשר צריך לעשר את תוספתו ליכא למיחש להכי דלא נשרש [עירובין עז:]. להיות בטילה בנטיעה זו וכשנוטלה יצטרך לחזור ולעשר [לקמן קיג.]. לא יכסנו משתחשך. גזירה שמא ימצא קדרתו שנצטננה כשירצה להטמינה, וירתיחנה תחילה, ונמצא מבשל בשבת [לעיל לד.]. אסור להטמין את הצונן. מים צונן ומתיירא שלא יוחמו אסור להטמין בחול צונן (לצורך שבת) [בשבת]. הורה זקן. ר' יוסי דאזלינן בתריה. ממלא מקום אבותיו. חשוב כאביו [סנהדרין כד.]. כל שהוא נאכל כמות שהוא חי. ומיא שתו אינשי כמות שהן [מו"ק יב:]. אין בו משום בשולי נכרים. שגזרו חכמים בבשולי נכרים משום חתנות ועל שנאכל כמו שהוא חי לא גזרו על בשולו דכיון שנאכל כמו שהוא חי אינו בשול דלא אהני מידי [ביצה טז.]. אדם חשוב שאני. יש לו להחמיר על עצמו יותר ולא הוה ליה וכו' ולא למשתי מיא דאחים קפילא נכרי [מו"ק שם]. לפי שלמדין הימנו [כתובות פו.]. סדינין. של פשתן. גלופקרין. שקורין קו"ץ והוא של צמר [ב"מ פא:].

עין משפט נר מצוה

כט א מיי' פ"ד מהל' שבת הלכה ד סמג לאוין סה טוש"ע או"ח סימן רנז סעיף ד:

ל ב מיי' שם טוש"ע שם סעיף ו:

לא ג מיי' פי"ז מהלכות מאכלות אסורות הל' יד סמג לאוין קמב טור שו"ע יו"ד סימן קיג סעיף א:

לב ד מיי' פ"ד מהלכות שבת הלכה ד סמג לאוין סה טוש"ע או"ח סימן רנז סעיף ד:

לג ה מיי' שם הלכה ה טוש"ע שם סעיף ה:

לד ו (מיי') סמג שם טוש"ע או"ח סימן רנט סעיף ד:

לה ז שם סעיף ה:

רבינו חננאל

מגולין אין חושש משום כלאים דלא ירק באילן הוא ולאו משום שביעית דלאו זריעה היא וכן משום מעשר ונטלין בשבת דלאו מחובר לקרקע אינון. ועלתה בתיובתא לשמואל. וקיי"ל כי הא מתניתא דמותבינא מינה ש"מ דסליקוסתא אע"ג דלא ארווח בגומא שרי וכ"ש סכין דנעיצה בין הנדבך ובין הקנים. וזו הלפת טומנה להתרכך כגון טמינת פגא בתבן: ממלא קיתון כו' ואסיק' מותר להטמין את הצונן אפי' בדבר שדרכו להטמין [כי] הא דאמר רב נחמן לדראי עבדיה אטמין לי את הצונן ואייתי לי חמין דאחים קפילא ארמאה. ואסי' אע"ג דקיי"ל דשרי להטמין

The Baraisa continues:

וְכֵן הָיָה רַבָּן שִׁמְעוֹן בֶּן גַּמְלִיאֵל אוֹמֵר – AND LIKEWISE RABBAN SHIMON BEN GAMLIEL issued another lenient ruling regarding insulating on the Sabbath, and SAID: לֹא אָסְרוּ אֶלָּא אוֹתוֹ מֵיחַם – [THE RABBIS] FORBADE insulating on the Sabbath ONLY where the food is still in THE SAME POT in which it was cooked. אֲבָל פִּינָּה מִמֵּיחַם לְמֵיחַם מוּתָּר – BUT IF ONE EMPTIED the food FROM THE POT in which it was cooked INTO ANOTHER POT, IT IS PERMITTED to insulate the second pot on the Sabbath.

The Gemara explains the rationale behind this leniency:

הַשְׁתָּא אַקּוּרֵי קָא מְקִיר לָהּ אַרְתּוּחֵי קָא מִירְתַּח לָהּ – Now if he purposely **cools [the food] down** by pouring it from pot to pot, **is he [likely] to boil it up?**[18]

The Gemara resumes its recitation of the Baraisa. As we have learned, it is permitted to remove a pot from its insulation on the Sabbath and then put it back. However, where the pot lies under a cover that is *muktzeh,* or where the insulation itself is *muktzeh,* doing so presents difficulty. The Baraisa proceeds to outline the law regarding such cases:

טָמַן וְכִיסָּה בְּדָבָר הַנִּיטָּל בְּשַׁבָּת – If HE both INSULATED the pot around its sides AND COVERED its mouth WITH SOMETHING THAT MAY BE MOVED ON THE SABBATH, i.e. with non-*muktzeh* materials,[19] אוֹ טָמַן בְּדָבָר שֶׁאֵינוֹ נִיטָּל בְּשַׁבָּת וְכִיסָּה בְּדָבָר הַנִּיטָּל בְּשַׁבָּת – OR even if HE INSULATED it WITH SOMETHING THAT MAY NOT BE MOVED ON THE SABBATH BUT COVERED it WITH SOMETHING THAT MAY BE MOVED ON THE SABBATH, הֲרֵי זֶה נוֹטֵל וּמַחֲזִיר – HE MAY REMOVE the pot AND REPLACE it.[20] טָמַן וְכִיסָּה בְּדָבָר שֶׁאֵינוֹ נִיטָּל בְּשַׁבָּת – But if HE both INSULATED the pot AND COVERED it WITH SOMETHING THAT MAY NOT BE MOVED ON THE SABBATH, אוֹ שֶׁטָּמַן בְּדָבָר הַנִּיטָּל בְּשַׁבָּת וְכִיסָּה בְּדָבָר שֶׁאֵינוֹ נִיטָּל בְּשַׁבָּת – OR even if HE INSULATED it WITH SOMETHING THAT MAY BE MOVED ON THE SABBATH BUT COVERED it WITH SOMETHING THAT MAY NOT BE MOVED ON THE SABBATH, אִם הָיָה מְגוּלֶּה מִקְצָתוֹ נוֹטֵל וּמַחֲזִיר – then the rule is as follows: IF PART OF [THE MOUTH OF THE POT] IS EXPOSED, i.e. the *muktzeh* item did not cover the entire mouth of the pot, HE MAY REMOVE the pot AND REPLACE it;[21] וְאִם לָאו – BUT IF NOT, i.e. if the entire mouth of the pot is covered by the *muktzeh* cover,

NOTES

18. As explained in the introduction to this chapter, the reason that the Rabbis forbade insulating food on the Sabbath is the fear that one might be tempted to reheat the food before insulating it. But by transferring the food from the pot that stood on the fire to a different pot, one demonstrates that he actually *wants* the food to cool down; in such a case there is little likelihood that he will come to reheat the food. Consequently, he is permitted to insulate it (*Rashi*), even if he does not intend for the food to cool (see *Mishnah Berurah* 257:29).

[This permit applies, of course, only to insulating in a substance that does not add heat; insulating in a substance that adds heat is always forbidden.]

19. That is, he placed an open pot in some insulating substance that has been earmarked for the purpose of *hatmanah* and, hence, is not *muktzeh.* The insulation encases the sides of the pot, but does not cover it. He then covers the mouth of the pot with a non-*muktzeh* utensil (*Sfas Emes,* explaining *Rashi*).

20. He can remove the cover and extract the pot [by grasping it by the rim and lifting it out]. (The fact that the sides of the pot are encased in a *muktzeh* material need not bother him, as we learned in the Mishnah above, 49a.)

21. Since he can remove the pot without moving the *muktzeh* cover. He simply tilts the pot and allows the *muktzeh* material to slide off by itself (*Rashi;* see next note).

לא משום כלאים ולא משום שביעית ולא משום מעשר וניטלין בשבת תיובתא:

מתני' לא כסהו מבעוד יום לא יכסנו משתחשך [א] כסהו ונתגלה מותר לכסותו ממלא את הקיתון ונותן לתחת הכר או תחת הכסת:

גמ' אמר רב יהודה אמר שמואל [ב] מותר להטמין את הצונן אמר רב יוסף מאי קמ"ל תנינא ממלא אדם קיתון ונותן תחת הכר או תחת הכסת אמר ליה אביי טובא קמ"ל דאי ממתני' הוה אמינא ה"מ דבר שאין דרכו להטמין אבל דבר שדרכו להטמין לא קמ"ל אמר רב הונא (א) (אמר רב) אסור להטמין את הצונן והתניא רבי התיר להטמין את הצונן לא קשיא הא מקמיה (א) דלישמעיה מר' ישמעאל ברבי יוסי הא לבתר דלישמעי' [ג] כי הא דיתיב רבי ואמר אסור להטמין את הצונן אמר לפניו רבי ישמעאל ברבי יוסי אבא התיר להטמין את הצונן אמר [ג] כבר הורה זקן אמר רב פפא [ד] בא וראה כמה מחבבין זה את זה שאילו ר' יוסי קיים היה כפוף ויושב לפני רבי דהא רבי ישמעאל ברבי יוסי דממלא מקום אבותיו הוה וכפוף ויושב לפני רבי וקאמר כבר הורה זקן אמר ליה רב נחמן לדרו עבדיה אטמין לי צונן ואייתי לי מיא דאחים קפילא ארמאה [ה] שמע רבי אמי ואיקפד אמר רב יוסף מ"ט איקפד כרבוותיה עביד חדא כרב וחדא כשמואל כשמואל דאמר רב יהודה אמר שמואל מותר להטמין את הצונן כרב [ו] דאמר רב שמואל בר רב יצחק אמר רב [ג] כל שהוא נאכל כמות שהוא חי אין בו משום בשולי נכרים ([ז] הוא) סבר [ח] אדם חשוב שאני: [ט] ת"ר [ד] אע"פ שאמרו [ח] אין טומנין אפילו בדבר שאינו מוסיף הבל משחשכה אם בא להוסיף מוסיף כיצד הוא עושה רשב"ג אומר נוטל את הסדינין ומניח את הגלופקרין או נוטל את הגלופקרין ומניח את הסדינין וכן היה רשב"ג אומר [ה] לא אסרו אלא אותו מיחם אבל פינה ממיחם למיחם מותר השתא אקורי קא מקיר לה ארתוחי קא מירתח לה [כ] [י] טמן וכיסה בדבר הניטל בשבת או טמן בדבר שאינו ניטל בשבת וכיסה בדבר הניטל בשבת הרי זה נוטל ומחזיר [ז] טמן וכיסה בדבר שאינו ניטל בשבת או שטמן בדבר הניטל בשבת וכיסה בדבר שאינו ניטל בשבת אם היה מגולה מקצתו נוטל ומחזיר ואם לאו אינו

רש"י

לא משום כלאים. דאין זו שתילה: **ולא משום מעשר.** דנימא בטלה לה אגב קרקע והרי הוא כלוקטה מתחלה ויהא צריך לעשר על הנוסף שמא ניתוסף: **וניטלין בשבת.** שאוחזה במקלת עליה המגולין ולא חייש אם העפר ניזוח מאליו וה"ה לסליקוסתא: **מתני' לא יכסנו משתחשך.** הא פרישנא טעמא בפ"ב (דף לד.) מפני מה אמרו אין טומנין בדבר שאינו מוסיף הבל משחשיכה גזירה שמא ירתיח: **ממלא הקיתון.** של צונן: **ונותן לתוך הכר.** שלא יחמו בחום הקיץ והחמה כגון כר וכסת של לבדין שאינו מחמם: **גמ' מותר להטמין את הצונן.** מפני החמה שלא יחמו ולא גזרינן אטו הטמנה כדי שיחמנו: **אי ממתני' הוה אמינא הני מילי.** כגון מים צוננין שאין דרכן להטמין תחת כר וכסת לחממן שאין מתחממין בכך הלכך ליכא למיגזר: **אבל דבר שדרכו להטמין.** לחמם כגון תבשיל אימא לא יטמינו מפני החמה: **התיר להטמין את הצונן.** מפני החום: **זקן.** ר' יוסי: **ממלא מקום אבותיו.** גדול כאביו: **היה כפוף ויושב לפני רבי.** מפני כבוד הנשיאות ולא היה מורה לפניו אע"פ שגדול הימנו: **כבר הורה זקן.** גדלו ונשאו עליו: **אטמין לי צונן.** בשבת: **ואייתי לי מיא דאחים קפילא ארמאה.** שהחמן נחתום נכרי ובחול ולאשמועינן דאין בהן משום בשולי נכרים: **כרבוותיה.** כרבותיו: **אדם חשוב שאני.** שהרואה אותו שהוא מיקל עומד ומיקל יותר: **אין טומנין את החמין משחשיכה ואפילו בדבר שאינו מוסיף הבל.** וכדאמרן שמא ימצא קדרתו צוננת כשירצה להטמינה וירתיחנה בשבת אבל אם בא להוסיף כיסוי על כיסוי משחשיכה מוסיף: **גלופקרא.** קו"ט ויש בו הבל יותר מן הסדינין ונוטל את הגלופקרא בימות החמה אם ירא שמא יקדיח תבשילו מחמת רוב כיסוי: **וכן היה רשב"ג.** מיקל קולא אחריתי בהטמנה: **לא אסרו.** להטמין משחשיכה אלא במיחם שהוחמו בו דהתם הוא דאיכא למיגזר שמא ירתיח: אבל מפנה הוא ממיחם למיחם אחר ומטמין זהו לשון התוספתא והיינו נמי פינהו ממיחם למיחם מותר דהשתא ליכא למיגזר שמא ירתיח דהשתא אקורי קא מיקר להו במתכוין ארתוחי מרתח להו בתמיה: **טמן.** הקדרה בדבר הניטל מה שנתן סביבותיה הוי דבר מוכן: **וכיסה.** על פיה נמי דבר המוכן כגון כלי: **או שטמן בדבר שאינו ניטל.** וכיסה בדבר הניטל: **הרי זה נוטל ומחזיר.** דהואיל והכיסוי ניטל מגלה הקדרה ואוחזה אבל טמן וכיסה בדבר שאינו ניטל או אפי' טמן בדבר הניטל וכיסה בדבר שאינו ניטל אם אין מקלת פיה מגולה לא יטול דאין לו במה יאחזנה ואם תאמר יפנה סביבותיה הואיל ודבר הניטל הוא ויאחזנה בדופניה (ג) ויטנה על צדה ויפול הכיסוי כי ההיא דתנן לקמן (פרק נוטל דף קמב:) האבן שעל פי החבית מטה על צדה והיא נופלת ואם היתה בין החביות מגביהה ומטה על צדה והיא נופלת הא אוקימנא התם בשכח אבל במניח נעשה בסיס לדבר האסור והיכא דמגולה מקלתו אין זה טלטול שמגלגלו והכיסוי נופל מאליו: הרי

תוספות

הוא ואמאי ממעט ומשני דאית לה אוגנים וחבריה בארעא ופריך וכי יש לו מאי הוי והתנן הטומן לפת כו' ואי גרם מקלת מגולים מאי פריך הא לא דמי לספל שיש לו אוגנים ואומר ר"י דיש לומר דבנטיעה איכא קרקע קשה ודבוק ביותר ומדמה ליה לספל שיש לו אוגנים ואין להקשות לפירוש הערוך דמאי פריך מינה לשמואל לימא דהך משנה סבר טלטול מן הצד לא שמיה טלטול (ג) כאלעזר בן תדאי ומקלת מגולין נקט משום אחריני ולא משום שבת ושמואל סבר כרבנן דאיכא למימר דמשמע ליה דמשום שבת נמי נקט לה מדלא תנא בהדיא וניטלין בשבת אפילו מכוסין ש"מ דמכוסין אסורין כרבנן ואפ"ה מקלתן מגולין שרי:

כסהו ונתגלה מותר לכסותו. נראה לר"י דה"ה דמותר לגלותו בידים ולחזור ולכסותו כמו שמותר ליטול הקדרה ולהחזירה והא דנקט כסהו ונתגלה משום דנתגלה מבעוד יום איירי דומיא דרישא לא כסהו מבעוד יום וקאמר דמותר לכסותו משתחשך אבל אם גילהו בידים מבעוד יום כדי לכסותו משתחשך אסור לכסותו משתחשך דדמיא לתחלת הטמנה:

אילו היה ר' יוסי קיים היה כפוף כו'. פי' רבינו שלמה מחמת נשיאותו דהא ר"י היה גדול מרבי כדמוכח בפ"ב דנדה (דף יד: ושם) דאמר ליה רבי ישמעאל ברבי יוסי לר' חמא בר ביסנא כדברי רבי אומר לך או כדברי אבא אמר ליה כדברי רבי אמור לי אמר ליה זהו שאומרים עליו דאדם גדול הוא שמניח דברי הרב ושומע דברי התלמיד ור"ת מפרש דודאי מתחלה היה רבי תלמידו של רבי יוסי אבל אח"כ נתחכם רבי כדקאמ' התם ור' חמא סבר רבי ריש מתיבתא שכיחי רבנן גביה ומחדדן שמעתתיה:

כיצד הוא עושה רשב"ג אומר נוטל את הסדינין כו'. נראה לר"י ולה"ר פור"ת דל"ג כיצד הוא עושה דרשב"ג פליג את"ק דלא שרי אלא להוסיף אבל להחליף אסור ורשב"ג שרי אף להחליף וכ"ש ליטול ולהחזיר אותו דבר דלא הוי כל כך תחלת הטמנה והיינו דקאמר וכן היה רשב"ג אומר כלומר שהיה מיקל קולא אחריתי גבי הטמנה:

אבל פינה ממיחם למיחם מותר. ול"ד להוא דכירה דבעי בפרק כירה (לעיל לח:) פינה ממיחם למיחם מהו דהתם רוצה בחמימותן לכך יש לאסור כשהוא צונן אבל הכא גבי הטמנה כל כמה שהוא צונן טפי שפיר דמי כדאמר לעיל רבי התיר להטמין את הצונן וא"ת ורבי לא ידע לעיל דמותר להטמין את הצונן וכי לא ידע דשמיע ליה מאבוה הכא דשרי וי"ל דהכא דוקא דמוכח מילתא שנתכוין לצנן שפינהו ממיחם למיחם אבל קיתון של מים דלא מוכח מידי יהא אסור להטמין. מתוספות רבינו יהודה (ת"י):

או שטמן בדבר הניטל וכיסה בדבר שאינו ניטל. הקשה בקונט' יפנה סביבה ויאחזנה בדופניה ויגביהנה ויטנה על צדה כדתנן בפרק נוטל (לקמן קמב:) היתה בין החביות מגביהה כו' ומתרץ דהא אוקמינן התם בשכח אבל במניח נעשה בסיס לדבר האסור וקשה דאי חשיב הכא כמניח אם כן במגולה מקלתה היאך נוטל ומחזיר מה בין זה לאבן שעל פי החבית דאסרי' במניח אפי' להטותה על צדה ועוד קשה לר"ת דהא תנן נוער את הכיסוי והן נופלות אפי' אין מגולות מקלתן ועל כן אומר ר"ת דלא חשיב כמניח ° כיון שדעתו ליטלו בשבת ובפ' נוטל (שם דף קמג.) נמי תנן בית שמאי אומרים מגביהין מעל גבי השלחן עצמות וקליפים וב"ה אומרים מסלק את הטבלא ומנערה ולא חשיב לב"ה כמניח והכא איירי בכיסוי כעין כלי חרס שנותנים על הקדרה שהקדרה בלועה בתוכה ואי אפשר לנער הכיסוי אלא אם כן יגביהו קצת ור"י מפרש כגון שטמן הקדרה בקופה בדבר הניטל ולמעלה מן הקדרה מילא כל הקופה בדבר שאינו ניטל שאי אפשר לו להגיע לקדרה אם לא יטלטל דבר שאינו ניטל בידים [ל]: אינו

עין משפט נר מצוה

כט א מיי' פ"ד מהל' שבת הלכה ד סמג לאוין סה טוש"ע או"ח סימן רנז סעיף ד:
ל ב מיי' שם טוש"ע שם סעיף ו:
לא ג מיי' פי"ז מהלכות מאכלות אסורות הל' יד סמג לאוין קמב טור שו"ע יו"ד סימן קיג סעיף א:
לב ד מיי' פ"ד מהלכות שבת הלכה ד סמג לאוין סה טוש"ע או"ח סימן רנז סעיף ד:
לג ה מיי' שם הלכה ה טוש"ע שם סעיף ה:
לד ו (מיי') סמג שם טוש"ע או"ח סימן רנט סעיף ד:
לה ז שם סעיף א:

רבינו חננאל

מגולין אין חושש משום כלאים דלא ירק באילן הוא ולאו משום שביעית דלאו זריעה היא וכן משום מעשר ונטלין בשבת דלאו מחובר לקרקע אינון. ועלתה בתיובתא לשמואל. וקיי"ל כי הא מתניתא דמותבינא מינה ש"מ דסליקוסתא אע"ג דלא ארווח בגומא שרי וכ"ש סכין דנעיצה בין הנדבך ובין הקנים. וזו הלפת טומנה להתרכך כגון טמינת פגא בתבן: **ממלא** קיתון כו' ואסיק' מותר להטמין את הצונן אפי' בדבר שדרכו להטמין [כי] הא דאמר רב נחמן לדראי עבדיה אטמין לי את הצונן ואייתי לי חמין דאחים קפילא ארמאה. ואסי' אע"ג דקיי"ל דשרי להטמין

מסורת הש"ס

א) [צ"ל אמר רבי], ב) סנהדרין כד., ג) [שם ודף כט:], ד) [שם כד.], ה) [מו"ק יב:], ו) מו"ק יב: יבמות מו. ע"ז לח. נט., ז) [צ"ל והוא], ח) [לקמן קמב: ברכות יט. פסחים קי. מו"ק יא: יב. מגילה כב: כתובות נב: פו. ב"מ עג. ע"ז ח: כח. מח: חולין קלד:], ט) תוספתא פ"ד, י) [לעיל לד.], כ) [תוספתא שם כל הענין עד סוף הפרק], ל) [ועי' תוספות לקמן קכג. ד"ה האי פוגלא].

הגהות הב"ח

(א) גמ' מקמיה דשמעיה מר' ישמעאל וכו' לבתר דשמעיה כו': (ב) רש"י ד"ה או שטמן וכו' ויאחזנה בדופניה ויגביהנה ויטנה: (ג) תום' ד"ה מקלת וכו' טלטול כרבי אלעזר בן תדאי:

גליון הש"ס

תוס' ד"ה או שטמן וכו' כיון שדעתו ליטלו בשבת. עי' לעיל דף מג ע"ב תוס' ד"ה דכו"ע טלטול:

ליקוטי רש"י

ולא משום שביעית. אם שנה שביעית היא. **ולא משום מעשר.** לשמא נשרש ויתוסף ואם היה חושש למעשר צריך לעשר את תוספתו ליכא למיחש להכי דלא נשרש [עירובין עז:]. להיות בטילה בנטיעה זו וכשנוטלה יצטרך לחזור ולעשר [לקמן קיג.]. **לא יכסנו משתחשך.** גזירה שמא ימצא קדרתו שנצטננה כשירצה להטמינה, וירתיחנה תחילה, ונמצא מבשל בשבת [לעיל לד.]. **אסור להטמין את הצונן.** מים צונן ומתיירא שלא יוחמו אסור להטמינן בחול צונן (לצורך שבת) [בשבת]. **הורה זקן.** ר' יוסי דאזלין בתריה. **ממלא מקום אבותיו.** חשוב כאביו [סנהדרין כד.]. **כל שהוא נאכל כמות שהוא חי.** ומיא שתו אינשי כמות שהן [מו"ק יב:]. **אין בו משום בשולי נכרים.** שגזרו חכמים בבשולי נכרים משום חתנות ועל שנאכל כמו שהוא חי לא גזרו על בשולו דכיון שנאכל כמו שהוא חי אינו בשול דלא אהני מידי [ביצה טז.]. **אדם חשוב שאני.** יש לו להחמיר על עצמו יותר ולא הוה ליה וכו' ולא למשתי מיא דאחים קפילא נכרי [מו"ק שם]. לפי שלמדין הימנו [כתובות פו.]. **סדינין.** של פשתן. **גלופקרין.** שקורין קו"ץ והוא של צמר [ב"מ פא:].

אינו נוטל ומחזיר (א) רבי יהודה אומר נעורת של פשתן דקה הרי היא כזבל א מניחין מיחם על גבי מיחם וקדרה על גבי קדרה (ב) אבל לא קדרה על גבי מיחם ומיחם על גבי קדרה וטח את פיה בבצק ולא בשביל שיחמו אלא בשביל שיהיו משומרים וכשם שאין טומנין את החמין כך אין טומנין את הצונן רבי התיר להטמין את הצונן (ג) ב ואין מרסקין לא את השלג ולא את הברד בשבת בשביל שיזובו מימיו אבל נותן הוא לתוך הכוס או לתוך הקערה ואינו חושש:

הדרן עלך במה טומנין

(ד) **במה** ג בהמה יוצאה ובמה אינה יוצאה יוצא הגמל (ה) באפסר ונאקה בחטם ולובדקים בפרומביא וסוס בשיר ד וכל בעלי השיר יוצאין בשיר ונמשכין בשיר (ו) ומזין עליהן (ז) וטובלין (א) במקומן: **גמ׳** מאי נאקה בחטם אמר רבה בר בר חנה (ח) נאקתא חיורתי בזוממא דפרזלא: ולובדקים בפרומביא: אמר רב הונא חמרא ה לובא (ט) בפגי דפרזלא לוי שדר זוזי לבי חוזאי למיזבן ליה חמרא לובא צרו שדרו ליה שערי למימר דניגרי דחמרא שערי אמר רב יהודה אמר שמואל מחליפין לפני רבי של זו בזו מהו נאקה באפסר לא תיבעי לך כיון דלא מינטרא ביה משאוי הוא כי תיבעי לך גמל בחטם מאי כיון דסגי ליה באפסר משאוי הוא או דילמא נטירותא יתירתא לא אמרי׳ משאוי הוא אמר לפניו ר׳ ישמעאל ברבי יוסי כך אמר אבא ו ארבע בהמות יוצאות באפסר הסוס והפרד והגמל והחמור למעוטי מאי לאו למעוטי גמל בחטם לא למעוטי נאקה באפסר במתניתא תנא לובדקים וגמל יוצאין באפסר כתנאי אין חיה יוצאה בסוגר חנניה אומר יוצאה בסוגר ובכל דבר המשתמר במאי עסקינן אילימא בחיה גדולה מי סגי לה סוגר ואלא בחיה קטנה מי לא סגי לה סוגר אלא לאו חתול איכא בינייהו תנא קמא סבר כיון דסגי לה במיתנא בעלמא משאוי הוא וחנניה סבר כל נטירותא יתירתא לא אמרינן משאוי הוא אמר רב הונא בר חייא אמר שמואל הלכה כחנניה לוי בריה דרב הונא בר חייא ורבה בר רב הונא הוו קאזלי באורחא קדמיה חמרא דלוי לחמרא דרבה בר רב הונא חלש דעתיה דרבה בר רב הונא אמר אימא ליה מילתא כי היכי דאיתותב

רש״י

הרי זה כזבל. למוסיף הבלא ואין טומנין בה אפילו מבעוד יום: מיחם. של נחשת: קדרה. משל חרס יש ספרים שכתוב בהן אבל לא מיחם על גבי קדירה ומפרשים טעמא מפני שהקדירה מרבה חמימות ומוספת הבלא למיחם אבל בתוספתא גרסינן ומיחם על גבי קדירה: וטח את פיה (ב) בבצק. הגילום מבעו״י כל הנך מניחין נמי בשבת: ולא שיחמו. שיהא העליון צונן ונתנו כדי שיחום מחומו של תחתון: אלא שיהו משומרין. שהיו שניהן חמין ונתנו על גביו של זה כדי שיהא חומו משתמר בהן: ואין מרזקין. כמו מרסקין משברין לחתיכות דקות ברד גלצ״א בלע״ז: כדי שיזובו מימיו. משום דקא מוליד בשבת ודמי למלאכה שבורא המים הללו: אבל נותן לתוך הכוס. של יין בימות החמה כדי לצנן ואע״פ שנימוח מאליו ואינו חושש:

הדרן עלך במה טומנין

במה בהמה יוצאה כו׳. לפי שאדם מצווה על שביתת בהמתו בשבת ומידי דמינטרא ביה בהמה הוי תכשיט ואורחא ולא הוי משוי ומידי דלא מינטרא ביה הוי משוי: אפסר. קבישטר״א: נאקה. דרומי״ל: בחטם. מפרש בגמרא: ולובדקים בפרומביא. מפרש בגמ׳: בשיר. כמו אצעדה סביב צוארו וטבעת קבוע בה ומכניסין בו רצועה או חבל ומושכין הבהמה: וכל בעלי השיר. כגון כלבים [של] ציידים וחיות קטנות שנותנין שיר לצוארם לנוי: יוצאין ונמשכין. מפרש בגמ׳: ומזין עליהם במקומן. כמו שהם בצואר הבהמה אם נטמאו: וטובלין במקומן. מכניסין בהמה למים להטביל את השיר: גמ׳ מאי נאקה. ומאי חטם: חיורתי. שהיא קשה להשתמר מפני שבורחת: בזוממא דפרזלא. מוזי״ל בלע״ז נוקב את חוטמו ומכניסו בתוכו והוא כמין טבעת: חמרא לובא. חמור הבא ממדינת לוב כמו הכושים והלובים דאסא בדברי הימים (ב טז): בפגי דפרזלא. פריי׳ כעין שלנו פגי כמו זה קנה חמור ובית פגי (ב״מ ד׳ ט.) קיבלניי״ל בית ראשה ולחייה: צרו שדרו ליה שערי. צרו מעותיו ושלחו לו שעורים בצרור מעותיו ולא רצו לקנות לו חמור מפני שהוא רחוק מבבל מהלך חצי שנה כדאמר בהגוזל (ב״ק ד׳ קיב:) והשיאוהו עצה לקנות חמור במקומו ויאכילנו שעורים תמיד ונמצא חמורו טוב ומשובח: ניגרי דחמרא שערי. פסיעותיו של חמור לפי שעורים שהוא אוכל: מחליפין. שאילתם נאקה באפסר וגמל בחטם מהו משוי הוא ואסור: לאו למעוטי גמל בחטם. והכי קאמר ארבע בהמות הללו משתמרים באפסר ואסורות לצאת בחטם: לא למעוטי נאקה באפסר. דהואיל ולא מינטרא ביה משאוי הוא אבל נטירותא יתירתא כגון חטם לגמל לאו משאוי הוא: יוצאין באפסר. דלובדקי נמי מינטרא ביה: ה״ג כתנאי אין חיה יוצאה בסוגר: כתנאי. נטירותא יתירתא אי משוי הוא או לא: בסוגר. קולא״ר של חבל כדמתרגמינן ויתנהו בסוגר בקולרין (יחזקאל יט): בחיה גדולה. כגון דוב: קטנה. כגון נמייה וחולדה: חתול. לא בעי נטירותא אפילו כחיה קטנה שאינו תאב לברוח כל כך: במיתנא. חבל קטן: הלכה כחנניה. ונטירותא יתירתא לאו משאוי הוא: חלשא דעתיה דרבה בר רב הונא. שהיה גדול וכסבור שעשה מדעת:

דאיתותב

תוספות

אינו נוטל ומחזיר. נראה לרשב״א דהיינו כרשב״ג דאמר בפרק נוטל כל היכא דאיכא איסורא והיתרא בהיתרא טרחינן באיסורא לא טרחינן אבל לרבנן דפליגי עליה שרו במכוסות לגמרי ליטול בידים דבר שאינו ניטל דבפרק נוטל (לקמן קמב:) מתני׳ דהיתה בין החביות מגביהה ומטה על צדה מוקי לה כרשב״ג משמע דרבנן דרשב״ג שרו לטלטל את האבן עצמו:

אין מרסקין לא את השלג ולא את הברד. מכאן יש ליזהר שלא ירחוץ ידיו בשלג וברד בשבת (י) ופעמים שמתקרשים ויש ברד מעורב בהם אין לרחוץ בהן דאי אפשר שלא ירסק הברד וכל הזהיר בו תבא עליו ברכה:

הדרן עלך במה טומנין

במה בהמה יוצאה. דאדם מוזהר על שביתת בהמתו דכתיב למען ינוח וגו׳ ומיהו לאו דלא תעשה מלאכה אתה ובהמתך ליכא אלא במחמר אחר בהמתו כדמוכח בריש מי שהחשיך (לקמן קנג.) ובריש נדרים (דף ב:) דייק בהך דהכא ובכל הני דלעיל דאיכא דוכתא דתנא ברישא הא דסליק מיניה ואיכא דוכתא דתני ברישא הא דפתח ביה:

חמרא לובא. אומר ר״ת דלובא היינו מצרים דכתיב (נחום ג) פוט ולובים היו בעזרתך ואמרינן בירושלמי גרים הבאים מלוב מהו להמתין להם שלשה דורות ומייתי עלה דהדא עלם מצראה דלווחין ליה לוב (כ):

או דילמא כל נטירותא יתירתא לאו משוי היא. וא״ת תפשוט ממתניתין דתנן ולובדקים בפרומביא אע״ג דסגי לה באפסר כדאמר בסמוך תנא לובדקים וגמל יוצאים באפסר ופרומביא עדיפא מאפסר דאמר לקמן חמור שעסקיו רעים כגון זה מהו לצאת בפרומביא בשבת אלמא משמע דעדיף מאפסר וי״ל דלא הוי נטירותא יתירתא ואורחיה נמי בהכי ולא חשיב משוי:

קדמיה חמרא דלוי. משמע שמכבדין בדרכים ובפ׳ אמר להם הממונה (יומא לז.) נמי אמרינן שלשה שהיו מהלכין בדרך הרב באמצע גדול מימינו וקטן משמאלו וכן מצינו במלאכי השרת שבאו אצל אברהם וכו׳ והקשה ר״ת דבפ׳ שלשה שאכלו (ברכות מז.) מסיק דאין מכבדין אלא בפתח הראוי למזוזה ותירץ רבינו תם דהתם כשאין הולכים בחבורה אחת אלא כל אחד הולך לצורך עצמו אבל כשהולכים בחבורה אחת מכבדים בכל מקום:

אמר

עין משפט נר מצוה

לז א מיי׳ פ״ד מהלכות שבת הלכה ו סמג לאוין סה טוש״ע או״ח סימן רנח וסימן שיח סעיף ו:

לח ב מיי׳ פכ״א מהלכות שבת הלכה יג סמג לאוין סה טוש״ע או״ח סימן שכ סעיף טו וסי׳ שיח סעיף טז:

א ג מיי׳ פ״כ מהלכות שבת הלכה ח סמג לאוין סה טוש״ע או״ח סימן שה סעיף א:

ב ד מיי׳ שם טור שו״ע שם סעיף ה:

ג ה מיי׳ שם טור שו״ע שם סעיף ג:

ד ו מיי׳ שם טור שו״ע שם סעיף א:

רבינו חננאל

את הצונן וכל הנאכל כמות שהוא חי אין בו משום בשולי נכרים. אדם חשוב לא איבעי ליה למיעבד הכי: ת״ר אע״פ שאמרו אין טומנין בדבר שאינו מוסיף [הבל] אבל אם בא להוסיף מוסיף כיצד ר״ש ב״ג אומר נוטל הסדינין ומניח [את] הגלופקרין כו׳ פשוטה היא ר׳ יהודה אומר נעורת של פשתן דקה הרי הוא כזבל ומניחין מיחם ע״ג מיחם וקדירה על גבי קדירה וקדירה ע״ג מיחם ומיחם על גבי קדירה וטח פיהן בבצק. ולא כדי שיחמו אלא כדי שישתמרו כו׳ רבי התיר להטמין את הצונן כו׳:

הדרן עלך במה טומנין

פ״ה במה בהמה יוצאה ובמה אינה יוצאה. יוצאה הגמל באפסר כו׳ ונאקה בחטם נקתא חורתי בזממא דפרזלא. לובדקים בפרומפיא. חמרא לובא בפגי דפרזלא לבדקם לובא חמור לוב. ממקום ששמו לוב כדכתיב (דניאל י״א) לובים וכושים במצעדיו. כדגרסי׳ בירושלמי גרים הבאים מלוב מהו להמתין להו ג׳ דורות וקיי״ל כר׳ יוסי דאמר ארבע בהמות יוצאות באפסר בשבת הסוס והפרד והחמור והגמל: **ירושלמי** אמר חזקיה וסמניך וכן תהיה מגפת הסוס וגו׳ למעוטי גמל בחטם שלא יצא. רב אמר הלכה כר׳ יוסי. ולית הלכתא כחנניה דתני כל נטירותא יתירתא לאו (משום) [משוי] הוא ושפיר דמי ואע״ג דאמר שמואל הילכתא כחנניה פליג רב עליה

מסורת הש״ס

א) [לעיל מט.], ב) הך אבל לא הוא טעות וצ״ל וקדירה ע״ג וכו׳ ואע״ג דרש״י גרס אבל לא הייט במיחם ע״ג קדירה אבל בקדירה ע״ג מיחם ליכא מאן דפליג עי׳ בב״י בטא״ח סימן רנח, ג) [בתוספתא פ״ד איתא מרסקין בסמ״ך וכ״א בפירש״י דהכא על נכון וכן בערוך ורי״ף ורא״ש ובב״י סי׳ שיח מרסיקין], ד) [נדרים ב: מיר ב.], ה) פי׳ רשן, ו) [עי׳ תוס׳ נג. ד״ה מזין], ז) [עי׳ תוס׳ שם ד״ה וטובלין], ח) גמלא נקיבה גדולה ערוך, ט) פי׳ רסן שבלחי, י) צ״ל ומים שמתקרשים רש״א, כ) [וע״ע תוס׳ בכורות ה: ד״ה תשעים וכו׳].

הגהות הב״ח

(א) במשנה ומזין עליהן במקומן וטובלין: (ב) רש״י ד״ה וטח את פיה בשבת בבלק:

ליקוטי רש״י

נעורת. דק דק שנוערין מן הפשתן וקורין אריסט״ש [לעיל מט.]. אפסר. קבישט״ר כלומר בית אחיזה [קידושין כז.]. ונאקה בחטם. ומתני׳, תרגם יונתן זמם והוא של ברזל ותוחבין אותו בנחירי הנאקה ומשכת בו לפי שעסקיה רעים והוא ששינו ונאקה בחוטם [מ״ב יט, כח]. זממא, מנקבין לנאקה בחוטמה ונותנין בה טבעת של רצועה וקושרין אותה ועומדת שם לעולם וכשרוצה לקושרה לבהמה קושר רצועה ארוכה באותה טבעת וקושרין בה ופעמים שמתירה [לקמן קיא:]. חמרא לובא. חמרי לובאי, חמורים גדולים ממצרים [תמיד לב.]. פרומביא. רסן [ב״ק יז:]. ניגרי. פסיעות [לקמן סו:].

אֵינוֹ נוֹטֵל וּמַחֲזִיר – then **HE MAY NOT REMOVE** the pot **AND REPLACE** it, i.e. there is no permissible way for him to remove the pot.[1]

The Baraisa continues with several other rulings concerning insulating:

רַבִּי יְהוּדָה אוֹמֵר – **R' YEHUDAH SAYS:** נְעוֹרֶת שֶׁל פִּשְׁתָּן דַּקָּה הֲרֵי הִיא כְּזֶבֶל – **FINE FLAX COMBINGS ARE LIKE MANURE,** i.e. they add heat to the food and may not be used as insulation for the Sabbath.[2] מַנִּיחִין מֵיחַם עַל גַּבֵּי מֵיחַם וּקְדֵרָה עַל גַּבֵּי קְדֵרָה – On the Sabbath **ONE MAY PLACE A KETTLE ON TOP OF A KETTLE, OR A POT ON TOP OF A POT,**[3] (אבל לא) [וּ]קְדֵרָה עַל גַּבֵּי מֵיחַם וּמֵיחַם עַל גַּבֵּי קְדֵרָה – **OR**[4] **A POT ON TOP OF A KETTLE, OR A KETTLE ON TOP OF A POT,** וְטָח אֶת פִּיהָ בְּבָצֵק – **AND SEAL [THE TOP VESSEL'S MOUTH] WITH DOUGH;**[5] וְלֹא בִּשְׁבִיל שֶׁיֵּחַמּוּ אֶלָּא בִּשְׁבִיל שֶׁיְּהוּ מְשׁוּמָּרִים – **NOT IN ORDER TO HEAT THEM UP,** i.e. he may not place a cold vessel on top of a hot one in order to heat the top vessel, **BUT RATHER SO THAT** the heat that **THEY** already possess **WILL BE MAINTAINED,** i.e. he may place a hot vessel on top of another hot vessel in order that the top vessel retain its heat.[6]

וּכְשֵׁם שֶׁאֵין טוֹמְנִין אֶת הַחַמִּין כָּךְ אֵין טוֹמְנִין אֶת הַצּוֹנֵן – **AND JUST AS ONE MAY NOT INSULATE HOT [FOOD]** on the Sabbath, **SO MAY ONE NOT INSULATE COLD [FOOD]** on the Sabbath.[7] רַבִּי הִתִּיר לְהַטְמִין אֶת הַצּוֹנֵן – **REBBI,** however, **PERMITTED INSULATING COLD [FOOD]** on the Sabbath.[8]

The Baraisa discusses a final, unrelated law:

וְאֵין מְרַסְּקִין לֹא אֶת הַשֶּׁלֶג וְלֹא אֶת הַבָּרָד בְּשַׁבָּת – **AND ONE MAY NOT CRUSH SNOW OR HAIL ON THE SABBATH** בִּשְׁבִיל שֶׁיָּזוּבוּ מֵימָיו – **IN ORDER THAT ITS WATER SHOULD FLOW OUT** and be collected.[9] אֲבָל נוֹתֵן הוּא לְתוֹךְ הַכּוֹס אוֹ לְתוֹךְ הַקְּעָרָה – **HOWEVER, HE MAY PLACE** snow or hail **INTO A CUP OR A BOWL** of liquid in order to cool the liquid, וְאֵינוֹ חוֹשֵׁשׁ – **AND HE NEED NOT BE APPREHENSIVE** that he is thereby violating any prohibition.[10]

הדרן עלך במה טומנין

WE SHALL RETURN TO YOU, BAMEH TOMNIN

NOTES

1. Since he cannot extract the pot without removing the cover, which is *muktzeh,* there is no permissible way for him to remove the pot.

Rashi raises the following difficulty: The Mishnah later (142b) states that where a stone, which is *muktzeh,* lies on top of a barrel of wine and one wishes to pick up the barrel, it is permissible to tilt the barrel and allow the stone to slide off. Since one is not handling the stone directly, this is classified as *indirect movement of muktzeh* and is permitted. Furthermore, where it is impractical to slide the stone off the barrel at that spot (e.g. where the falling stone might break other barrels), it is even permissible to pick the barrel up and remove it to somewhere else where one will be able to slide off the stone. The question thus arises: In the case in the Baraisa where only the cover was *muktzeh* but the surrounding insulation was not, why does the Baraisa forbid removing the pot; why can the person not remove the insulation from the sides of the pot and tilt the pot over, allowing the cover, which is *muktzeh,* to slide off?

Rashi resolves this difficulty by pointing out that the Gemara (ibid.) states that one may move the barrel in this manner only where the stone was *inadvertently* left on the barrel in the first place; but if the stone was *purposely* left there, the barrel becomes a *base to muktzeh* and may not be moved at all (see the introduction to Chapter 3). Likewise, says *Rashi,* since in the Baraisa's case the *muktzeh* cover was certainly left on the pot on purpose, the pot becomes a *base to muktzeh* and may not be moved.

Nevertheless, where part of the pot was exposed the Baraisa *does* allow removing the pot. *Rashi* explains that in that case one is not moving the *muktzeh* item at all; one merely tilts the pot and the cover falls down of its own accord (see end of this note). In such a case it is permitted to move the pot [despite its being a *base to muktzeh*].

[Although *Rashi* to the Mishnah on 49a (cited there in note 16) stated that *muktzeh* wool shearings do not make what is beneath them a *base to muktzeh, Rashi* there was referring to a case in which the shearings were placed on top of the *lid* of a pot. Since the lid's function is only to cover the pot, not to support something on top of itself, it does not acquire the status of a *base to muktzeh.* Here, however, the Baraisa discusses a case in which the *muktzeh* insulation was placed on *the mouth* of the pot (in lieu of a lid). Since the pot is meant to have a lid, the pot becomes a *base to muktzeh* (*Sfas Emes*).]

Rashi's explanation seems difficult: If the pot is a *base to muktzeh* then it too is *muktzeh* (see *Rashi* to 142b ד״ה נעשה חבית בסיס לדבר האסור). It should thus be forbidden to move the pot in any fashion, regardless of whether by doing so one will be moving the cover as well. In fact, other Rishonim reject *Rashi's* explanation and maintain that, for various reasons, the pot is not a *base to muktzeh* at all (see *Rosh Yosef* for a summary of these reasons).

Maginei Shlomo points out, however, that *Rashi* on 125b ד״ה לא שנו appears to be of the opinion that intentionally leaving the stone on the barrel prohibits only *lifting* the barrel to tilt off the stone. *Tilting* the barrel without lifting it, however, is permitted in all cases. If this is true, it is understandable that where part of the pot's opening is exposed, in which case tilting the pot is sufficient to slide the *muktzeh* covering off, *Rashi* permits removing the pot. Where the entire mouth of the pot is covered by the slightly dome-shaped *muktzeh* cover, however, in which case the pot would have to be lifted in order to shake off the lid, there is no way to remove the pot. See, however, *Tos. R' Akiva Eiger* to the Mishnah on 142b who proves rather conclusively that even merely tilting a *base* to *muktzeh* without lifting it is forbidden. See also *Rashi* to 142b ד״ה לא שנו wherein he appears to contradict his explanation on 125b. See *Meiri,* who resolves this difficulty; see also *Ben Uri.*

2. [Even on Friday; see above, 49a.]

3. [The difference between a kettle and a pot is that a pot is made of earthenware and is, therefore, hotter than a kettle, which is made of copper (*Rashi*).]

4. [Our texts of the Gemara read: אֲבָל לֹא קְדֵירָה וכו׳, *but not a pot,* etc., but *Rashi* notes that the correct text is as it appears in the Tosefta: וּקְדֵירָה וכו׳, *or a pot,* etc.]

5. To better preserve its heat.

The dough must be prepared before the Sabbath [since preparing dough on the Sabbath is forbidden] (*Rashi;* see *Beur Halachah* to 318:6 ד״ה ויכול).

6. See above 48a note 4. [For the halachic parameters of this ruling, see *Orach Chaim* §258 and 318:6,7.]

7. This Tanna differs with Shmuel's ruling above (51a) and forbids insulating even cold food on the Sabbath.

8. [Rebbi's ruling was quoted in the Gemara earlier (ibid.).]

9. The Rabbis forbade this because it has the appearance of creating something new. It thus appears akin to a *melachah* (*Rashi*). Alternatively, they forbade this act lest one confuse it with squeezing juice out of fruit [which is a *toladah* of the *melachah* of *threshing*] (*Ran;* for a practical difference between these two reasons, see *Magen Avraham* 320:13).

10. The Rabbis did not forbid this since he does not directly melt the snow by his own actions but merely causes it to melt on its own (*Rashi*).

Chapter Five

Introduction

The Torah forbids the owner of an animal to let it perform a forbidden labor (*melachah*) on the Sabbath.[1] As was discussed in the first chapter of this tractate, one of the forbidden labors is transferring objects either from a private domain to a public domain, or vice versa, or transporting them for a distance of four *amos* within a public domain. Consequently, one may not allow his animal to go out from its enclosure into a public domain[2] on the Sabbath while it is carrying a burden of any kind.

It is permitted, however, to let one's animal go out into a public domain wearing an article of apparel. Apparel is defined here as anything that shields the animal from the elements or otherwise serves to protect or enhance its well-being.[3] Furthermore, an animal is allowed out wearing gear that a person would need to restrain or lead it.

Under Rabbinic law, an animal may not go out wearing an object that might become dislodged and fall. The reason is that one might come to inadvertently carry it four *amos* in the public domain. The Rabbis also banned items for various other reasons.

This chapter delineates which items an animal may wear in a public domain (e.g. an article of apparel or a restraint), and which it may not (either because it is a burden or because it is Rabbinically forbidden).[4]

NOTES

1. This law is a negative commandment of the Torah (*Deuteronomy* 5:14; see also *Exodus* 20:10): לֹא־תַעֲשֶׂה כָל־מְלָאכָה אַתָּה . . . וְכָל־בְּהֶמְתֶּךָ, *You shall not do any work – you . . . and your every animal* (*Rashi* to *Avodah Zarah* 15a). [Although this is a negative commandment, the Gemara below (154a-b) concludes that one is not liable to lashes for its violation.]

Other Rishonim, however, maintain that this verse prohibits only the specific act of מְחַמֵּר – leading an animal that is carrying a burden (see Gemara below, 153b-154b). In their view, the source for the general prohibition against letting one's animal perform any labor [even without one's personal involvement] is the positive commandment (*Exodus* 23:12): וּבַיּוֹם הַשְּׁבִיעִי תִּשְׁבֹּת לְמַעַן יָנוּחַ שׁוֹרְךָ וַחֲמֹרֶךָ, *and on the seventh day you shall desist* [from work] *so that your ox will be at ease as well as your donkey* (*Tosafos* to 51b ד״ה במה; *Tos. HaRosh* ibid.; see also *Rambam, Hil. Shabbos* 20:1,2 with *Maggid Mishneh; Meiri;* see also *Sfas Emes* on *Tosafos*).

This prohibition does not entail restraining one's animal from grazing, although grazing involves the forbidden labor of קוֹצֵר, *reaping* [or from performing other labors on its own, for its own sake]. The Torah insists that one's animal "be at ease" on the Sabbath (*Exodus* ibid.). Were one to prevent it from grazing, it would not be at ease, but in pain! (*Mechilta,* cited by *Rashi* ibid. and by *Tosafos* to 122a ד״ה מעמיד; see *Ramban* to *Exodus* 20:10; see also *Pnei Yehoshua* and *Chidushei R' Moshe Kazis*).

2. See *Magen Avraham, Orach Chaim* 305:6, who discusses the law of a *karmelis* in this context; see also *Beur Halachah* to 305:11 ד״ה ופוקק זוג.

3. The Rishonim dispute whether an animal is allowed to wear an item that serves only purposes of decoration [תַּכְשִׁיט, *adornment*]. *Rashi* maintains that an adornment is permitted. *Ran* (top of folio 24b) adds that this is true only of an adornment that the animal would wear even during the week. An adornment that is not usually worn is classified as a burden. In the view of *Tosafos* (52a ד״ה או), however, an adornment is not permitted under any circumstances (see *Mishnah Berurah* 305:12).

4. The reason why this topic is recorded in this part of our tractate is that it continues the theme of preparations one must make *before* the Sabbath. Since an animal is likely to run out of its enclosure without the owner's knowledge, the owner must ensure before the Sabbath that it is not carrying or wearing any forbidden item (*Pnei Yehoshua*).

אינו נוטל ומחזיר רבי יהודה אומר נעורת של פשתן דקה הרי היא כזבל מניחין מיחם על גבי מיחם וקדרה על גבי קדרה אבל לא קדרה על גבי מיחם ומיחם על גבי קדרה וטח את פיה בבצק ולא בשביל שיחמו אלא בשביל שיהיו משומרים וכשם שאין טומנין את החמין כך אין טומנין את הצונן רבי התיר להטמין את הצונן ואין מרזקין לא את השלג ולא את הברד בשבת בשביל שיזובו מימיו אבל נותן הוא לתוך הכוס או לתוך הקערה ואינו חושש:

הדרן עלך במה טומנין

במה בהמה יוצאה ובמה אינה יוצאה יוצא הגמל באפסר ונאקה בחטם ולובדקים בפרומביא וסוס בשיר וכל בעלי השיר יוצאין בשיר ונמשכין בשיר ומזין עליהן (א) וטובלן במקומן: גמ' מאי נאקה בחטם אמר רבה בר בר חנה נאקתא חיורתי בזממא דפרזלא: ולובדקים בפרומביא: אמר רב הונא חמרא לובא בפגי דפרזלא לוי שדר זוזי לבי חוזאי למיזבן ליה חמרא לובא צרו שדרו ליה שערי למימר דניגרי דחמרא שערי אמר רב יהודה אמר שמואל מחליפין לפני רבי של זו בזו מהו נאקה באפסר לא תיבעי לך כיון דלא מינטרא ביה משאוי הוא כי תיבעי לך גמל בחטם מאי כיון דסגי ליה באפסר משאוי הוא או דילמא נטירותא יתירתא לא אמרי' משאוי הוא אמר לפניו ר' ישמעאל ברבי יוסי כך אמר אבא ארבע בהמות יוצאות באפסר הסוס והפרד והגמל והחמור למעוטי מאי לאו למעוטי גמל בחטם לא למעוטי נאקה באפסר במתניתא תנא לובדקים וגמל יוצאין באפסר כתנאי אין חיה יוצאה בסוגר חנניה אומר יוצאה בסוגר ובכל דבר המשתמר במאי עסקינן אילימא בחיה גדולה מי סגי לה סוגר ואלא בחיה קטנה מי לא סגי לה סוגר אלא לאו חתול איכא בינייהו תנא קמא סבר כיון דסגי לה במיתנא בעלמא משאוי הוא וחנניה סבר כל נטירותא יתירתא לא אמרינן משאוי הוא אמר רב הונא בר חייא אמר שמואל הלכה כחנניה לוי בריה דרב הונא בר חייא ורבה בר רב הונא הוו קאזלי באורחא קדמיה חמרא דלוי לחמרא דרבה בר רב הונא חלש דעתיה דרבה בר רב הונא אמר איהו ליה מילתא כי היכי דאיתותב

הרי זה כזבל. דמוסיף הבלא ואין טומנין בה אפילו מבעוד יום: מיחם. של נחשת: קדרה. משל חרס יש ספרים שכתוב בהן אבל לא מיחם על גבי קדירה ומפרשים טעמא מפני שהקדירה מרבה חמימות ומוספת הבלא למיחם אבל בתוספתא גרסינן ומיחם על גבי קדירה: וטח את פיה (ב) בבצק. הילוש מבעו"י כל הנך מניחין נמי בשבת: ולא שיחמו. שיהא העליון צונן ונתנו כדי שיחום מחומו של תחתון: אלא שיהו משומרין. שהיו שניהן חמין ונתנו על גביו של זה כדי שיהא חומו משתמר בהן: ואין מרזקין. כמו מרסקין משברין לחתיכות דקות ברד גלצ"א בלע"ז: כדי שיזובו מימיו. משום דקא מוליד בשבת ודמי למלאכה שבורא המים הללו: אבל נותן לתוך הכוס. של יין בימות החמה כדי לצנן ואע"פ שנימוח מאליו ואינו חושש:

הדרן עלך במה טומנין

במה בהמה יוצאה כו'. לפי שאדם מצווה על שביתת בהמתו בשבת ומידי דמינטרא ביה בהמה הוי תכשיט ואורחא ולא הוי משוי ומידי דלא מינטרא ביה הוי משוי: אפסר. קבישטר"א: נאקה. דרומי"ל: בחטם. מפרש בגמרא: ולובדקים בפרומביא. מפרש בגמ': בשיר. כמו אצעדה סביב צוארו וטבעת קבוע בה ומכניסין בו רצועה או חבל ומושכין הבהמה: וכל בעלי השיר. כגון כלבים [של] ציידים וחיות קטנות שנותנין שיר לצוארם לנוי: יוצאין ונמשכין. מפרש בגמ': ומזין עליהם במקומן. כמו שהם בצואר הבהמה אם נטמאו: וטובלן במקומן. מכניסין בהמה למים להטביל את השיר: גמ' מאי נאקה. ומאי חטם: חיורתי. שהיא קשה להשתמר מפני שבורחת: בזממא דפרזלא. מוזי"ל בלע"ז נוקב את חוטמו ומכניסו בתוכו והוא כמין טבעת: חמרא לובא. חמור הבא ממדינת לוב כמו הכושים והלובים דאסא בדברי הימים (ב טז): בפגי דפרזלא. פריי' כעין שלנו פגי כמו זה קנה חמור וזית פגי (ב"מ ד' ט.) קיבלי"ל בית ראשה ולחייה: צרו שדרו ליה שערי. צרו מעותיו ושלחו לו שעורים בצרור מעותיו ולא רצו לקנות לו חמור מפני שהוא רחוק מבבל מהלך אלי שנה כדאמר בהגחל (ב"ק ד' קיב:) והשיאוהו עצה לקנות חמור במקומו ויאכילנו שעורים תמיד ונמצא חמורו טוב ומשובח: ניגרי דחמרא שערי. פסיעותיו של חמור לפי שעורים שהוא אוכל: מחליפין. שאילתם נאקה באפסר וגמל בחטם מהו משוי הוא ואסור: לאו למעוטי גמל בחטם. והכי קאמר ארבע בהמות הללו משתמרים באפסר ואסורות לצאת בחטם: לא למעוטי נאקה באפסר. דהואיל ולא מינטרא ביה משאוי הוא אבל נטירותא יתירתא כגון חטם לגמל לאו משאוי הוא: יוצאין באפסר. דלובדקי נמי מינטרא ביה: ה"ג כתנאי: כתנאי. נטירותא יתירתא אי משוי הוא או לא: בסוגר. קולא"ר של חבל כדמתרגמינן ויתנהו בסוגר בקולרין (יחזקאל יט): בחיה גדולה. כגון דוב: קטנה. כגון נמייה וחולדה: חתול. לא בעי נטירותא אפילו כחיה קטנה שאינו תאב לברוח כל כך: במיתנא. חבל קטן: הלכה כחנניה. ונטירותא יתירתא לאו משאוי הוא: חלשא דעתיה דרבה בר רב הונא. שהיה גדול וכסבור שעשה מדעת: דאיתותב

אינו נוטל ומחזיר. נראה לרשב"א דהיינו כרשב"ג דאמר בפרק נוטל כל היכא דאיכא איסורא והיתרא בהיתרא טרחינן באיסורא לא טרחינן אבל לרבנן דפליגי עליה שרו במכוסות לגמרי ליטול בידים דבר שאינו ניטל דבפרק נוטל (לקמן קמב:) מתני' דהיתה בין החביות מגביהה ומטה על צדה מוקי לה כרשב"ג משמע דרבנן דרשב"ג שרו לטלטל את האבן עצמו:

אין מרסקין לא את השלג ולא את הברד. מכאן יש ליזהר שלא ירחוץ ידיו בשלג וברד בשבת ופעמים שמתקרשים ויש ברד מעורב בהם אין לרחוץ בהן דאי אפשר שלא ירסק הברד וכל הזהיר בו תבא עליו ברכה:

הדרן עלך במה טומנין

במה בהמה יוצאה. דאדם מוזהר על שביתת בהמתו דכתיב למען ינוח וגו' ומיהו לאו דלא תעשה מלאכה אתה ובהמתך ליכא אלא במחמר אחר בהמתו כדמוכח בריש מי שהחשיך (לקמן קנג.) ובריש נדרים (דף ג:) דייק בהך דהכא ובכל הני דלעיל דאיכא דוכתא דתנא ברישא הא דסליק מיניה ואיכא דוכתא דתני ברישא הא דפתח ביה:

חמרא לובא. אומר ר"ת דלובא היינו מצרים דכתיב (נחום ג) פוט ולובים היו בעזרתך ואמרינן בירושלמי גרים הבאים מלוב מהו להמתין להם שלשה דורות ומייתי עלה דהדא עלם מצראה דנוחין ליה לוב:

או דילמא כל נטירותא יתירתא לאו משוי היא. וא"ת תפשוט ממתניתין דתנן ולובדקים בפרומביא אע"ג דסגי לה באפסר כדאמר בסמוך תנא לובדקים וגמל יוצאים באפסר ופרומביא עדיפא מאפסר דאמר לקמן חמור שעסקיו רעים כגון זה מהו לצאת בפרומביא בשבת אלמא משמע דעדיף מאפסר וי"ל דלא הוי נטירותא יתירתא ואורחיה נמי בהכי ולא חשיב משוי:

קדמיה חמרא דלוי. משמע שמכבדין בדרכים ובפ' אמר להם הממונה (יומא מ.) נמי אמרינן שלשה שהיו מהלכין בדרך הרב באמצע גדול מימינו וקטן משמאלו וכן מצינו במלאכי השרת שבאו אצל אברהם וכו' והקשה ר"ת דבפ' שלשה שאכלו (ברכות מו.) מסיק דאין מכבדין אלא בפתח הראוי למזוזה ותירץ רבינו תם דהתם כשאין הולכים בחבורה אחת אלא כל אחד הולך לצורך עצמו אבל כשהולכים בחבורה אחת מכבדים בכל מקום: אמר

עין משפט נר מצוה

לו א מיי' פ"ד מהלכות שבת הלכה ו סמג לאוין סה טוש"ע או"ח סימן רנח וסימן שיח סעיף ו:
לז ב מיי' פכ"א מהלכות שבת הלכה יג סמג לאוין סה טוש"ע או"ח סימן שכ סעיף טו וסי' שיח סעיף טז:
א ג מיי' פ"כ מהלכות שבת הלכה ח סמג לאוין סה טוש"ע או"ח סימן שה סעיף א:
ב ד מיי' שם טור שו"ע שם סעיף ה:
ג ה מיי' שם טור שו"ע שם סעיף ג:
ד ו מיי' שם טור שו"ע שם סעיף א:

רבינו חננאל

את הצונן וכל הנאכל כמות שהוא חי אין בו משום בשולי נכרים. אדם חשוב לא איבעי ליה למיעבד הכי: ת"ר אע"פ שאמרו אין טומנין בדבר שאינו מוסיף [הבל] אבל אם בא להוסיף מוסיף כיצד ר"ש ב"ג אומר נוטל הסדינין ומניח [את] הגלופקרין כו' פשוטה היא ר' יהודה אומר נעורת של פשתן דקה הרי הוא כזבל ומניחין מיחם ע"ג מיחם וקדירה על גבי קדירה וקדירה ע"ג מיחם ומיחם על גבי קדירה וטח פיהן בבצק. ולא כדי שיחמו אלא כדי שישתמרו כו' רבי התיר להטמין את הצונן כו':
הדרן עלך
במה טומנין

פ"ה במה בהמה יוצאה ובמה אינה יוצאה. יוצאה הגמל באפסר כו' ונאקה בחטם נקתא חורתי בזממא דפרזלא. לובדקים בפרומפיא. חמרא לובא בפגי דפרזלא לבדקם לובא חמור לוב. ממקום ששמו לוב כדכתיב (דניאל י"א) לובים וכושים במצעדיו. כדגרסי' בירושלמי גרים הבאים מלוב מהו להמתין להו ג' דורות וקיי"ל כר' יוסי דאמר ארבע בהמות יוצאות באפסר בשבת הסוס והפרד והחמור והגמל: ירושלמי אמר חזקיה וסמניך וכן תהיה מגפת הסוס וגו' למעוטי גמל בחטם שלא יצא. רב אמר הלכה כר' יוסי. ולית הלכתא כחנניה דתני כל נטירותא יתירתא לאו (משום) [משוי] הוא ושפיר דמי ואע"ג דאמר שמואל הילכתא כחנניה פליג רב עליה

מסורת הש"ס

א) [לעיל מט.], ב) הך אבל לא הוא טעות וצ"ל וקדירה ע"ג וכו' ואע"ג דרש"י גרס אבל לא היינו במיחם ע"ג קדירה אבל בקדירה ע"ג מיחם ליכא מאן דפליג עי' בב"י בטא"ח סימן רנח, ג) [בתוספתא פ"ד איתא מרסקין בסמ"ך וכ"א בפירש"י דהכא על נכון וכן בערוך ורי"ף ורא"ש ובב"י סי' שיח מרסיקין], ד) [נדרים ג: מיר ג.], ה) פי' רשן, ו) [עי' תוס' נג. ד"ה מזין], ז) [עי' תוס' שם ד"ה וטובלין], ח) גמלא נקיבה גדולה ערוך, ט) פי' רשן שבלחי, י) צ"ל ומים שמתקרשים רש"א, כ) [וע"ע תוס' בכורות ה: ד"ה תשעים וכו'].

הגהות הב"ח

(א) במשנה ומזין עליהן במקומן וטובלין:
(ב) רש"י ד"ה וטח את פיה בשבת בבלק:

ליקוטי רש"י

נעורת. דק דק שנוערין מן הפשתן וקורין אריסט"ש [לעיל מט.]. אפסר. קבישט"ר כלומר בית אחיזה [קידושין כז.]. ונאקה בחטם. ומתגי, תרגם יונתן זמם והוא של ברזל ותוחבין אותו בנחירי הנאקה ומשכת בו לפי שעסקיה רעים והוא ששינו ונאקה בחוטם [מ"ב יט, כח]. וזממא, מנקבין לנאקה בחוטמה ונותנין בה טבעת של רצועה וקושרין אותה ועומדת שם לעולם וכשרוצה לקושרה לבהמה קושר רצועה ארוכה באותה טבעת וקושרין בה ופעמים שמתירה [לקמן קיא:]. חמרא לובא. חמרי לובאי, חמורים גדולים ממצרים [תמיד לב.]. פרומביא. רסן [ב"ק יז:]. ניגרי. פסיעות [לקמן סו:].

Chapter Five

Mishnah The Torah forbids the owner of an animal to let it do work on the Sabbath.[1] Accordingly, one may not allow his animal to carry a burden through a public domain, from a private to a public domain or vice versa. In this context, a "burden" includes not only an animal's load, but also its gear. However, gear that is used to control the animal is not considered a burden and the animal may go out with it on the Sabbath:[2]

בַּמֶּה בְּהֵמָה יוֹצְאָה – **With what may an animal go out** וּבַמָּה אֵינָהּ יוֹצְאָה – **and with what may it not go out?**[3] יוֹצֵא הַגָּמָל בְּאַפְסָר – **A camel may go out with a halter,**[4] וְנָאקָה בַּחֲטָם – **a female dromedary**[5]**with a** ***chatom,*** וְלוּבְדְּקִים בִּפְרוּמְבִּיָא – ***luvdekim*** **with a** ***prumbia***[6] וְסוּס בְּשֵׁיר – **and a horse with a collar.**[7] וְכָל בַּעֲלֵי הַשֵּׁיר יוֹצְאִין בְּשֵׁיר וְנִמְשָׁכִין בְּשֵׁיר – **And all animals that** normally **wear a collar**[8] **may go out with a collar and may be pulled by a collar.**[9]

The Mishnah records other laws concerning an animal's collar:[10]

וּמַזִּין עֲלֵיהֶן – **One may sprinkle** the ash water of the *parah adumah* **upon [such collars]** even while they are in their place on the animal's neck,[11] וְטוֹבְלָן בִּמְקוֹמָן – **and one may** also **immerse them** while they are **in their place** on the animal's neck.[12]

Gemara The Gemara defines some of the terms used in the Mishnah:

מַאי נָאקָה בַּחֲטָם – **What** does the Mishnah mean by: A FEMALE DROMEDARY WITH A *CHATOM?*[13] אָמַר רַבָּה בַּר בַּר חָנָה – **Rabbah bar bar Chanah said:** נָאקְתָא חִיוַּרְתֵּי בִּזְמָמָא דְּפַרְזְלָא – It means **a white female dromedary with a nose ring of iron.**[14]

The Mishnah stated:

וְלוּבְדְּקִים בִּפְרוּמְבִּיָא – **And** *LUVDEKIM* WITH A *PRUMBIA*.

The Gemara explains:

אָמַר רַב הוּנָא – **Rav Huna said:** חֲמָרָא לוּבָא בְּפַגֵּי דְּפַרְזְלָא – It means **a donkey from Luv with an iron bit.**[15]

The Gemara relates an anecdote about a Luvian donkey:

לֵוִי שַׁדַּר זוּזֵי לְבֵי חוֹזָאֵי לְמִיזְבַּן לֵיהּ חֲמָרָא לוּבָא – **Levi sent money to Bei Choza'ei**[16] for some people there **to buy him a Luvian donkey.** צָרוּ שַׁדְּרוּ לֵיהּ שַׂעֲרֵי – **They wrapped up** Levi's money and **sent** it back to **him** with some grains of **barley,** לְמֵימַר דְּנִיגְרֵי דַּחֲמָרָא שַׂעֲרֵי – **to tell** him **that the strides** (i.e. strength) **of a donkey are** commensurate with the **barley** it eats.[17]

NOTES

1. For the Biblical source, see Chapter Introduction, note 1.

2. Such an item has the same status as an adornment (*Rashi;* see *Pnei Yehoshua*), or an article of clothing (*Ritva MHK* ed.; see Chapter Introduction and note 3 there).

3. Into a public domain. [See Chapter Introduction, note 2.]

4. An אַפְסָר, *afsar* [halter], is used to lead an animal (see *Tosafos* to 52a ד״ה אמר). It consists of a length of rope whose end is tied to the animal's mouth (*Rambam, Commentary to the Mishnah*). Since it serves to control the animal, it is not deemed a burden, and thus may be worn by a camel [and certain other animals (see Gemara below)] in a public domain on the Sabbath.

5. The Gemara will explain that the reference is to a particular type of female dromedary (see *Chidushei HaRan*).

6. The terms *chatom, luvdekim* and *prumbia* are defined in the Gemara (*Rashi*).

7. A band placed around the animal's neck. To this band is affixed a ring into which one inserts a rope or strap by which the animal is led (*Rashi*).

8. I.e. all animals that typically wear collars for adornment, such as hunting dogs or other smaller animals (*Rashi;* see Chapter Introduction, note 3).

9. The Gemara below (52a) explains what the Mishnah means by "may go out ... and may be pulled" (*Rashi*). [The term "may be pulled" appears to be redundant (see 52a note 29).]

10. These laws are not related to the Sabbath. *Tosafos* (52a ד״ה וטובלין) explain why they are introduced here.

11. [Some editions of the Mishnah insert the word בִּמְקוֹמָן, *in their place,* after וּמַזִּין עֲלֵיהֶם (*Rashi, Bach* §1).]

A *parah adumah* (red cow) is a cow which is completely red and unblemished and has never done any work. Its ashes are used in the purification of utensils (or people) that have contracted *tumah* from a corpse, as follows: A *tahor* person immerses hyssop in a mixture of these ashes and water from a spring or river. He sprinkles from this mixture onto the contaminated utensils during the third and seventh days of their contamination. The utensils are then immersed in a *mikveh.* They become *tahor* at nightfall of the seventh day (see *Numbers* ch. 19).

The Mishnah teaches that one may sprinkle the ash water of the *parah adumah* on an animal's collar even while it is around the animal's neck. *Ritva* (*MHK* ed., citing *Tosafos* to 52a ד״ה ומזין) explains why it was necessary for the Mishnah to teach this point: The law is that if the water were to fall on the animal [before reaching the collar], the water remaining in the hyssop would become invalid (see Mishnah, *Parah* 12:3). This must be avoided, because the Torah requires that the water of the *parah adumah* be protected from invalidation. Therefore, one might have thought that the collar should be removed from the animal before the sprinkling so that no water accidentally falls on the animal first. The Mishnah teaches that this is not necessary, because the person sprinkling the water can be relied upon to ensure that all the water falls directly onto the collar (see also *Ritva* to *Yoma* 14a ד״ה נתכוין and *Rashi* ibid. ד״ה לא ישנה; cf. *Tos. Yom Tov* here and *Rashash* to 52a on *Tosafos*).

12. The animal is taken through a *mikveh* so that the collar will be immersed in its waters (*Rashi*). There must be open space around the collar so that the water can reach every part of it (see Gemara below, 52b).

13. We know that a נָאקָה is a female dromedary. However, there are many types of such camels. To which type does the Mishnah refer? (*Chidushei HaRan*).

The Gemara also seeks the meaning of חֲטָם, *chatom* (*Rashi*).

14. A ring inserted through a hole made in the camel's nose. [One leads the camel with a leash attached to this ring.]

A white female dromedary is harder to control than other camels, because it has a greater tendency to flee (*Rashi*). Therefore, it requires a more powerful restraint than the type of halter described in note 4.

15. A לוּבְדְּקִי, *luvdeki,* is a donkey that originates from the country of לוּב, *Luv,* which is referred to in *II Chronicles* 16:8 (*Rashi*). *Tosafos* identify *Luv* as Egypt. [לוּבְדְּקִים, *luvdekim,* is the plural form of the noun. In some versions, the Mishnah's text reads, לוּבְדְּקִים, *luvdekis* – a singular noun.]

Luvdekim are bigger and more aggressive than other donkeys [as the anecdote cited next in the Gemara illustrates] (*Rav* to *Kilayim* 8:4) Hence, the Mishnah specifies this strain of donkey as the only one requiring a bit (see note 25).

16. A city in [a remote part of] Babylonia (*Rashi, Taanis* 21b).

17. They did not want to buy [and send] him a donkey because Bei Choza'ei was a six-month [caravan] journey away from [the main part of] Babylonia. They advised Levi instead to buy a donkey in his own locale and always feed it barley. Such a donkey would be of excellent quality (*Rashi*).

אינו נוטל ומחזיר [א] רבי יהודה אומר נעורת של פשתן דקה הרי היא כזבל [א] מניחין מיחם על גבי מיחם וקדרה על גבי קדרה [ב] אבל לא קדרה על גבי מיחם ומיחם על גבי קדרה וטח את פיה בבצק ולא בשביל שיחמו אלא בשביל שיהיו משומרים וכשם שאין טומנין את החמין כך אין טומנין את הצונן רבי התיר להטמין את הצונן [ג] [ב] ואין מרסקין לא את השלג ולא את הברד בשבת בשביל שיזובו מימיו אבל נותן הוא לתוך הכוס או לתוך הקערה ואינו חושש:

הדרן עלך במה טומנין

[ד] **במה** [ג] בהמה יוצאה ובמה אינה יוצאה יוצא הגמל [ה] באפסר ונאקה בחטם ולובדקים בפרומביא וסוס בשיר [ד] וכל בעלי השיר יוצאין בשיר ונמשכין בשיר [ו] ומזין עליהן (א) [ז] וטובלן במקומן: **גמ'** מאי נאקה בחטם אמר רבה בר בר חנה [ח] נאקתא חיורתי בזממא דפרזלא: ולובדקים בפרומביא: אמר רב הונא חמרא [ה] לובא [ט] בפגי דפרזלא לוי שדר זוזי לבי חוזאי למיזבן ליה חמרא לובא צרו שדרו ליה שערי למימר דניגרי דחמרא שערי אמר רב יהודה אמר שמואל מחליפין לפני רבי של זו בזו מהו נאקה באפסר לא תיבעי לך כיון דלא מינטרא ביה משאוי הוא כי תיבעי לך גמל בחטם מאי כיון דסגי ליה באפסר משאוי הוא או דילמא נטירותא יתירתא לא אמרי' משאוי הוא אמר לפניו ר' ישמעאל ברבי יוסי כך אמר אבא [ו] ארבע בהמות יוצאות באפסר הסוס והפרד והגמל והחמור למעוטי מאי לאו למעוטי גמל בחטם לא למעוטי נאקה באפסר במתניתא תנא לובדקים וגמל יוצאין באפסר כתנאי אין חיה יוצאה בסוגר חנניה אומר יוצאה בסוגר ובכל דבר המשתמר במאי עסקינן אילימא בחיה גדולה מי סגי לה סוגר ואלא בחיה קטנה מי לא סגי לה סוגר אלא לאו חתול איכא בינייהו תנא קמא סבר כיון דסגי לה במיתנא בעלמא משאוי הוא וחנניה סבר כל נטירותא יתירתא לא אמרינן משאוי הוא אמר רב הונא בר חייא אמר שמואל הלכה כחנניה לוי בריה דרב הונא בר חייא ורבה בר רב הונא הוו קאזלי באורחא קדמיה חמרא דלוי לחמרא דרבה בר רב הונא חלש דעתיה דרבה בר רב הונא אמר אימא ליה מילתא כי היכי דאיתותב

רש"י

הרי זה כזבל. דמוסיף הבלא ואין טומנין בה אפילו מבעוד יום: מיחם. של נחשת: קדרה. משל חרס יש ספרים שכתוב בהן אבל לא מיחם על גבי קדירה ומפרשים טעמא מפני שהקדירה מרבה חמימות ומוספת הבלא למיחם אבל בתוספתא גרסינן ומיחם על גבי קדירה: וטח את פיה (ב) בבצק. הנילוש מבעו"י כל הנך מניחין נמי בשבת: ולא שיחמו. שיהא העליון לוקח ונותן כדי שיחום מחומו של תחתון: אלא שיהו משומרין. שהיו שניהן חמין ונתנו על גביו של זה כדי שיהא חומו משתמר בהן: ואין מרזקין. כמו מרסקין משברין לחתיכות דקות ברד גלל"א בלע"ז: כדי שיזובו מימיו. משום דקא מוליד בשבת ודמי למלאכה שבורא המים הללו: אבל נותן לתוך הכוס. של יין בימות החמה כדי לצנן ואע"פ שנימוח מאליו ואינו חושש:

הדרן עלך במה טומנין

במה בהמה יוצאה כו'. לפי שאדם מצווה על שביתת בהמתו בשבת ומידי דמינטרא ביה בהמה הוי תכשיט ואורחא ולא הוי משוי ומידי דלא מינטרא ביה הוי משוי: אפסר. קבישטר"א: נאקה. דרומי"ל: בחטם. מפרש בגמרא: ולובדקים בפרומביא. מפרש בגמ': בשיר. כמו אצעדה סביב צוארו וטבעת קבוע בה ומכניסין בו רצועה או חבל ומושכין הבהמה: וכל בעלי השיר. כגון כלבים [של] ציידים וחיות קטנות שנותנין שיר בצוארם לנוי: יוצאין ונמשכין. מפרש בגמ': ומזין עליהם במקומן. כמו שהם בצואר הבהמה אם נטמאו: וטובלן במקומן. מכניסין בהמה למים להטביל את השיר: **גמ'** מאי נאקה. ומאי חטם: חיורתי. שהיא קשה להשתמר מפני שבורחת: בזממא דפרזלא. מחי"ל בלע"ז נוקב את חוטמו ומכניסו בתוכו והוא כמין טבעת: חמרא לובא. חמור הבא ממדינת לוב כמו הכושים והלודים דאסא בדברי הימים (ב טז): בפגי דפרזלא. פרי' כעין שלנו פגי כמו זה קנה חמור ובית פגי (ב"מ ד ט.) קיבצי"ל בית רסנה ולחייה: צרו שדרו ליה שערי. צרו מעותיו ושלחו לו שעורים בצרור מעותיו ולא רצו לקנות לו חמור מפני שהוא רחוק מבבל מהלך חצי שנה כדאמר בהגוזל (ב"ק ד קיב:) והשיאוהו עצה לקנות חמור במקומו ויאכילנו שעורים תמיד ונמצא חמורו טוב ומשובח: ניגרי דחמרא שערי. פסיעותיו של חמור לפי שעורים שהוא אוכל: מחליפין. שאילתם נאקה באפסר וגמל בחטם מהו משוי הוא ואסור: לאו למעוטי גמל בחטם. והכי קאמר ארבע בהמות הללו משתמרים באפסר ואסורות לצאת בחטם: לא למעוטי נאקה באפסר. דהואיל ולא מינטרא ביה משאוי הוא אבל נטירותא יתירתא כגון חטם לגמל לאו משאוי הוא: יוצאין באפסר. דלובדקי נמי מינטרא ביה: ה"ג כתנאי אין חיה יוצאה בסוגר: כתנאי. נטירותא יתירתא אי משוי הוא או לא: בסוגר. קולא"ר של חבל כדמתרגמינן ויתנהו בסוגר בקולרין (יחזקאל יט): בחיה גדולה. כגון דוב: קטנה. כגון נמייה וחולדה: חתול. לא בעי נטירותא אפילו כחיה קטנה שאינו תאב לברוח כל כך: במיתנא. חבל קטן: הלכה כחנניה. ונטירותא יתירתא לאו משאוי הוא: חלשא דעתיה דרבה בר רב הונא. שהיה גדול וכסבור שעשה מדעת דאיתותב

תוספות

אינו נוטל ומחזיר. נראה לרשב"א דהיינו כרשב"ג דאמר בפרק נוטל כל היכא דאיכא איסורא והיתרא בהיתרא טרחינן באיסורא לא טרחינן אבל לרבנן דפליגי עליה שרו במכוסות לגמרי ליטול בידים דבר שאינו ניטל דבפרק נוטל (לקמן קמב:) מתני' דהיתה בין החביות מגביהה ומטה על לדה מוקי לה כרשב"ג משמע דרבנן דרשב"ג שרו לטלטל את האבן עצמו:

אין מרסקין לא את השלג ולא את הברד. מכאן יש ליזהר שלא ירחוץ ידיו בשלג וברד בשבת [י] ופעמים שמתקרשים ויש ברד מעורב בהם אין לרחוץ בהן דאי אפשר שלא ירסק הברד וכל הזהיר בו תבא עליו ברכה:

הדרן עלך במה טומנין

במה בהמה יוצאה. דאדם מוזהר על שביתת בהמתו דכתיב למען ינוח וגו' ומיהו לאו דלא תעשה מלאכה אתה ובהמתך ליכא אלא במחמר אחר בהמתו כדמוכח בריש מי שהחשיך (לקמן קנג.) ובריש נדרים (דף ג:) דייק בהן דהכא ובכל הני דלעיל דאיכא דוכתא דתנא ברישא הא דסליק מיניה ואיכא דוכתא דתני ברישא הא דפתח ביה:

חמרא לובא. אומר ר"ת דלובא היינו מצרים דכתיב (נחום ג) פוט ולובים היו בעזרתך ואמרינן בירושלמי גרים הבאים מלוב מהו להמתין להם שלשה דורות ומייתי עלה דהדא עלם מצראה דלווחין ליה לוב [כ]:

או דילמא כל נטירותא יתירתא לאו משוי היא. וא"ת תפשוט ממתניתין דתנן ולובדקים בפרומביא אע"ג דסגי לה באפסר כדאמר בסמוך תנא לובדקים וגמל יוצאים באפסר ופרומביא עדיפא מאפסר דאמר לקמן חמור שעסקיו רעים כגון זה מהו לצאת בפרומביא בשבת אלמא משמע דעדיף מאפסר וי"ל דלא הוי נטירותא יתירתא ואורחיה נמי בהכי ולא חשיב משוי:

קדמיה חמרא דלוי. משמע שמכבדין בדרכים ובפ' אמר להם הממונה (יומא מ.) נמי אמרינן שלשה שהיו מהלכין בדרך הרב באמצע גדול מימינו וקטן משמאלו וכן מצינו במלאכי השרת שבאו אצל אברהם וכו' והקשה ר"ת דבפ' שלשה שאכלו (ברכות מו.) מסיק דאין מכבדין אלא בפתח הראוי למזוזה ותירץ רבינו תם דהתם כשאין הולכים בחבורה אחת אלא כל אחד הולך לצורך עצמו אבל כשהולכים בחבורה אחת מכבדים בכל מקום:

עין משפט נר מצוה

לו א מיי' פ"ד מהלכות שבת הלכה ו סמג לאוין סה טוש"ע או"ח סימן רנח וסימן שיח סעיף ו:

לז ב מיי' פכ"א מהלכות שבת הלכה יג סמג לאוין סה טוש"ע או"ח סימן שכ סעיף טו וסי' שיח סעיף טז:

א ג מיי' פ"כ מהלכות שבת הלכה ח סמג לאוין סה טוש"ע או"ח סימן שה סעיף א:

ב ד מיי' שם טור שו"ע שם סעיף ה:

ג ה מיי' שם טור שו"ע שם סעיף ג:

ד ו מיי' שם טור שו"ע שם סעיף א:

רבינו חננאל

את הצונן וכל הנאכל כמות שהוא חי אין בו משום בשולי נכרים. אדם חשוב לא איבעי ליה למיעבד הכי: ת"ר אע"פ שאמרו אין טומנין בדבר שאינו מוסיף [הבל] אבל אם בא להוסיף מוסיף כיצד ר"ש ב"ג אומר נוטל הסדינין ומניח [את] הגלופקרין כו' פשוטה היא ר' יהודה אומר נעורת של פשתן דקה הרי הוא כזבל ומניחין מיחם ע"ג מיחם וקדירה על גבי קדירה וקדירה ע"ג מיחם ומיחם על גבי קדירה וטח פיהן בבצק. ולא כדי שיחמו אלא כדי שישתמרו כו' רבי התיר להטמין את הצונן כו':

הדרן עלך במה טומנין

פ"ה במה בהמה יוצאה ובמה אינה יוצאה. יוצאה הגמל באפסר כו' ונאקה בחטם נקתא חורתי בזממא דפרזלא. לובדקים בפרומפיא. חמרא לובא בפגי דפרזלא לבדקם לובא חמור לוב. ממקום ששמו לוב כדכתיב (דניאל י"א) לובים וכושים במצעדיו. כדגרסי' בירושלמי גרים הבאים מלוב מהו להמתין להו ג' דורות וקיי"ל כר' יוסי דאמר ארבע בהמות יוצאות באפסר בשבת הסוס הפרד והחמור והגמל: ירושלמי אמר חזקיה וסמיך וכן התהיה מגבת הסוס וגו' למעוטי גמל בחטם שלא יצא. רב אמר הלכה כחנניה. ולית הלכתא כחנניה דתני כל נטירותא יתירתא לאו (משום) [משוי] הוא ושפיר דמי ואע"ג דאמר שמואל הילכתא כחנניה פליג רב עליה

מסורת הש"ס

א) [לעיל מט.], ב) הך אבל לא הוא טעות וצ"ל וקדירה ע"ג וכו' ולע"ג דרש"י גרס אבל לא הייט במיחם ע"ג קדירה אבל בקדירה ע"ג מיחם ליכא מאן דפליג עי' בב"י בטא"ח סימן רנח, ג) [בתוספתא פ"ד איתא מרסקין בסמ"ך וכ"א בפירש"י דהכא על נכון וכן בערוך ורי"ף ורא"ש ובב"י סי' שיח מרסיקין], ד) [נדרים ג: נזיר ב.], ה) פי' רסן, ו) [עי' תוס' נב. ד"ה מזין], ז) [עי' תוס' שם ד"ה וטובלן], ח) גמלא נקיבה גדולה ערוך, ט) פי' רסן שבלחי, י) צ"ל ומים שמתקרשים רש"א, כ) [וע"ע תוס' בכורות ה: ד"ה תשעים וכו'].

הגהות הב"ח

(א) במשנה ומזין עליהן במקומן וטובלין:
(ב) רש"י ד"ה וטח את פיה בשבת בבלק:

ליקוטי רש"י

נעורת. דק דק שנוערין מן הפשתן וקורין אריסט"ש [לעיל מט.]. אפסר. קבישט"ר כלומר בית אחיזה [קידושין כז.]. ונאקה בחטם. ומתגי, תרגם יונתן זמם והוא של ברזל ותוחבין אותו בנחירי הנאקה ונמשכת בו לפי שעסקיה רעים והוא שנינו ונאקה בחוטם [מ"ב יט, כח]. זממא, מנקבין לנאקה בחוטמה ותוחבין בה טבעת של רצועה וקושרין אותה ועומדת שם לעולם וכשרוצה לקושרה לבהמה קושר רצועה ארוכה באותה טבעת וקושרין בה ופעמים שמתירה [לקמן קיא:]. חמרא לובא. חמרי לובאי, חמורים גדולים ממצרים [תמיד לב.]. פרומביא. רסן [ב"ק יז:]. ניגרי. פסיעות [לקמן סו:].

The Gemara records a dialogue between Rebbi and his students regarding our Mishnah's statement: "A camel may go out with a halter and a female dromedary with a nose ring":

אָמַר רַב יְהוּדָה אָמַר שְׁמוּאֵל – **Rav Yehudah said in the name of Shmuel:** מַחֲלִיפִין לִפְנֵי רַבִּי – **They switched** the cases **before Rebbi,** i.e. they asked Rebbi the following: שֶׁל זוֹ בְּזוֹ מַהוּ – If the restraint **of one** type of animal is put **on the other** type of animal, **what is [the law]?** That is, may a camel go out with the restraint of a female dromedary (i.e. a nose ring) and may a female dromedary go out with the restraint of a camel (i.e. a halter)?[18]

Rebbi[19] responds:

נָאקָה בְּאַפְסָר לֹא תִּיבָּעֵי לָךְ – In the case of **a female dromedary with a halter, you have no need to ask.** כֵּיוָן דְּלָא מִינַּטְרָא בֵּיהּ – **Since [a female dromedary] is not restrained by [a halter],**[20] מַשּׂאוֹי הוּא – [the halter] is considered **a burden** and is therefore prohibited. כִּי תִּיבָּעֵי לָךְ – **Rather, you should ask** only the following: גָּמָל בַּחֲטָם מַאי – In the case of an ordinary **camel with a nose ring, what** is the law? כֵּיוָן דְּסַגֵּי לֵיהּ בְּאַפְסָר – On the one hand, perhaps we say that **since a halter is sufficient for [an ordinary camel],** מַשּׂאוֹי הוּא – **[a nose ring]** is an excessive restraint and **is** therefore deemed **a burden?**[21] אוֹ דִּילְמָא נְטִירוּתָא יְתֵירְתָא לֹא אָמְרִינַן מַשּׂאוֹי הוּא – **Or perhaps we do not say that an excessive restraint is deemed a burden?**[22]

Shmuel continues his account of what took place in the presence of Rebbi:

אָמַר לְפָנָיו רַבִּי יִשְׁמָעֵאל בְּרַבִּי יוֹסֵי – **R' Yishmael the son of R' Yose said before [Rebbi]** to answer the inquiry: כָּךְ אָמַר אַבָּא – **Thus said my father:** אַרְבַּע בְּהֵמוֹת יוֹצְאוֹת בְּאַפְסָר – **"Four animals may go out with a halter** on the Sabbath: הַסּוּס וְהַפֶּרֶד וְהַגָּמָל וְהַחֲמוֹר – **The horse, mule, camel and donkey."** לְמַעוּטֵי מַאי – Now, **what** does this statement serve **to exclude?** לָאו לְמַעוּטֵי גָּמָל בַּחֲטָם – **Does it not exclude a camel with a nose ring?**[23] This proves that one may not let a camel go out with a nose ring.

Rebbi rejects the proof from R' Yose's statement:

לֹא לְמַעוּטֵי נָאקָה בְּאַפְסָר – **No!** R' Yose possibly meant **to exclude a female dromedary with a halter.**[24]

The Gemara quotes a Baraisa:

בְּמַתְנִיתָא תָּנָא – **A Tanna taught in a Baraisa:** לוּבְדְקִים וְגָמָל יוֹצְאִין בְּאַפְסָר – LUVIAN DONKEYS AND A CAMEL MAY GO OUT WITH A HALTER.[25]

The Gemara continues discussing whether an animal may go out with an excessive restraint (e.g. a camel with a nose ring):

כְּתַנָּאֵי – This issue is the same **as** that debated by **Tannaim** in the following Baraisa: אֵין חַיָּה יוֹצְאָה בְּסוּגַר – A BEAST MAY NOT GO OUT WITH A COLLAR OF ROPE. חֲנַנְיָה אוֹמֵר – But CHANANYAH SAYS: יוֹצְאָה בְּסוּגַר וּבְכָל דָּבָר הַמִּשְׁתַּמֵּר – IT MAY GO OUT WITH A COLLAR OF ROPE OR WITH ANYTHING THAT RESTRAINS it.

The Gemara analyzes this Baraisa:

בְּמַאי עַסְקִינַן – **What** type of beast **are we dealing with** here? אִילֵימָא בְּחַיָּה גְּדוֹלָה – **If one says** that the Baraisa refers to **a large beast,** such as a bear, מִי סַגֵּי לָהּ סוּגַר – **is a rope collar sufficient for it?** Certainly not![26] וְאֶלָּא בְּחַיָּה קְטַנָּה – **But,** on the

NOTES

18. A halter is not strong enough for a white female dromedary, whereas a nose ring is excessive for an ordinary camel. The students were asking whether an inadequate restraint (e.g. a halter on a white female dromedary) is a burden, and also whether an excessive restraint (e.g. a nose ring on a camel) is a burden. [No proof can be derived from the fact that our Mishnah specifies a halter in the case of a regular camel and a nose ring in the case of a female dromedary. It is possible that the Mishnah specifies these cases not for any halachic reason, but simply because they are the most typical.]

19. *Pnei Yehoshua;* cf. *Sfas Emes.*

20. A halter is totally ineffective in controlling this type of dromedary (*Rashba*), and [therefore] it is never used for that purpose (see *Ritva MHK* ed.; see also note 25).

21. A nose ring is a very powerful restraint which is never used for an ordinary camel (*Rashba*). [Since an animal does not usually wear an excessive restraint, it should be deemed a burden (see note 25).]

22. [At the present, the restraint can serve the purpose of controlling the animal. Hence, although it is unusual for the animal to wear such a restraint, it should not be classified as a burden.]

23. It is currently assumed that when R' Yose said, "Four animals may go out with a halter," he meant specifically a halter, as opposed to a nose ring. His point is that a halter suffices to control these four animals, and hence a nose ring would be forbidden (*Rashi*).

Rashba explains that R' Yose must have intended to teach more than he actually said. The purpose of his statement could not have been merely to teach that a horse, mule [or donkey] may go out with a halter, because that is obvious. [And the fact that a camel may go out with a halter has already been taught in our Mishnah.] Rather, R' Yose sought to imply that these animals may go out *only* with a halter, and not with a nose ring (see *Rashba* to 52a ד״ה אמר ליה אביי and *Ritva MHK* ed. here; see also *Chidushei HaRan*).

24. Rebbi suggests that R' Yose possibly meant: Only these four animals (for which a halter is sufficient) may go out with a halter, but other animals may not. Therefore, a white female dromedary, which cannot be controlled by a halter, may not go out with one. According to this interpretation, R' Yose does not mean to imply anything about an *excessive* restraint, e.g. a camel with a nose ring. It is possible that he would permit an excessive restraint (*Rashi*).

R' Yishmael the son of R' Yose, on the other hand, reasoned that the purpose of his father's statement must have been to prohibit an excessive restraint. It could not have been to prohibit an inadequate restraint (e.g. a dromedary with a halter), because it is *obvious* that such a restraint is forbidden, as stated in the Gemara above (see *Rashba* ibid. and *Ritva MHK* ed. here).

25. This Baraisa informs us that even a Luvian donkey is adequately protected with a halter [and hence may go out with one] (see *Rashi*).

It is not immediately clear why this Baraisa is cited here. It does not seem to be relevant to the give and take of the Gemara's discussion. *Sfas Emes* explains that the Baraisa is being used to refute Rebbi's suggested interpretation of R' Yose's statement. Rebbi suggested that R' Yose permits only these four animals (horse, mule etc.) to go out with a halter, while all other animals (e.g. a white female dromedary) may not. This Baraisa, however, rules that even a Luvian donkey, which was not listed by R' Yose, may go out with a halter. Thus, we see that R' Yose's list was not exhaustive. Since that is so, there are no grounds for asserting that he intended to exclude a white female dromedary. [This explanation given by *Sfas Emes* is compatible with *Rashi*. See *Rif* and *Rosh* (with *Maharsha* and *Maharam*) for a different approach.]

The Rishonim ask: This Baraisa indicates that a halter suffices to control a Luvian donkey, yet our Mishnah permits even a bit, which is stronger than a halter (as indicated by the Gemara on the top of 52a; see note 2 there). Why did our Gemara not cite this as proof that an excessive restraint is permitted? The Rishonim answer that although a bit is stronger than a halter, it was normal for either one to be used on a Luvian donkey. People are not necessarily meticulous in choosing a restraint for their animal, and they will use whichever restraint does the job, regardless of whether it is somewhat stronger or weaker than the ideal. Therefore, a Luvian donkey may be allowed out on the Sabbath with either a halter or a bit. The Gemara's question concerns only a restraint that is significantly excessive and would not normally be used, as in the case of a camel and a nose ring (see *Rashba,* et al.).

However, the preceding applies only to a Luvian donkey. In the case of an ordinary donkey, a bit is certainly excessive (see note 15). Hence, although an ordinary donkey may go out with a halter (as R' Yose stated), it may not go out with a bit [according to the view that forbids an excessive restraint] (*Tos. HaRosh*).

26. Consequently, there is no basis for Chananyah's permit. [Indeed, Chananyah himself says that the item must be a דָּבָר הַמִּשְׁתַּמֵּר, *something that restrains it.*]

אינו נוטל ומחזיר [א] רבי יהודה אומר נעורת של פשתן דקה הרי היא כזבל [א] מניחין מיחם על גבי מיחם וקדרה על גבי קדרה [ב] אבל לא קדרה על גבי מיחם ומיחם על גבי קדרה וטח את פיה בבצק ולא בשביל שיחמו אלא בשביל שיהיו משומרים וכשם שאין טומנין את החמין כך אין טומנין את הצונן רבי התיר להטמין את הצונן [ג] [ב] ואין מרזקין לא את השלג ולא את הברד בשבת בשביל שיזובו מימיו אבל נותן הוא לתוך הכוס או לתוך הקערה ואינו חושש:

הדרן עלך במה טומנין

[ד] **במה** [ג] בהמה יוצאה ובמה אינה יוצאה יוצא הגמל [ה] באפסר ונאקה בחטם ולובדקים בפרומביא וסוס בשיר [ד] וכל בעלי השיר יוצאין בשיר ונמשכין בשיר [ו] ומזין עליהן (א) [ז] וטובלן במקומן: **גמ'** מאי נאקה בחטם אמר רבה בר בר חנה [ח] נאקתא חיורתי בזממא דפרזלא: ולובדקים בפרומביא: אמר רב הונא חמרא [ה] לובא [ט] בפגי דפרזלא לוי שדר זוזי לבי חוזאי למיזבן ליה חמרא לובא צרו שדרו ליה שערי למימר דניגרי דחמרא שערי אמר רב יהודה אמר שמואל מחליפין לפני רבי של זו בזו מהו נאקה באפסר לא תיבעי לך כיון דלא מינטרא ביה משאוי הוא כי תיבעי לך גמל בחטם מאי כיון דסגי ליה באפסר משאוי הוא או דילמא נטירותא יתירתא לא אמרי' משאוי הוא אמר לפניו ר' ישמעאל ברבי יוסי כך אמר אבא [ו] ארבע בהמות יוצאות באפסר הסוס והפרד והגמל והחמור למעוטי מאי לאו למעוטי גמל בחטם לא למעוטי נאקה באפסר במתניתא תנא לובדקים וגמל יוצאין באפסר כתנאי אין חיה יוצאה בסוגר חנניה אומר יוצאה בסוגר ובכל דבר המשתמר במאי עסקינן אילימא בחיה גדולה מי סגי לה סוגר ואלא בחיה קטנה מי לא סגי לה סוגר אלא לאו חתול איכא בינייהו תנא קמא סבר כיון דסגי לה במיתנא בעלמא משאוי הוא וחנניה סבר כל נטירותא יתירתא לא אמרינן משאוי הוא אמר רב הונא בר חייא אמר שמואל הלכה כחנניה לוי בריה דרב הונא בר חייא ורבה בר רב הונא הוו קאזלי באורחא קדמיה חמרא דלוי לחמרא דרבה בר רב הונא חלש דעתיה דרבה בר רב הונא אמר אימא ליה מילתא כי היכי דאיתותב

רש"י

הרי זה כזבל. דמוסיף הבלא ואין טומנין בה אפילו מבעוד יום: מיחם. של נחשת: קדרה. משל חרס יש ספרים שכתוב בהן אבל לא מיחם על גבי קדירה ומפרשים טעמא מפני שהקדירה מרבה חמימות ומוספת הבלא למיחם אבל בתוספתא גרסינן ומיחם על גבי קדירה: וטח את פיה (ב) בבצק. הנילוש מבעו"י כל הנך מניחין נמי בשבת: ולא שיחמו. שיהא העליון לונן ונתנו כדי שיחום מחומו של תחתון: אלא שיהו משומרין. שהיו שניהן חמין ונתנו על גביו של זה כדי שיהא חומו משתמר בהן: ואין מרזקין. כמו מרסקין משברין לחתיכות דקות ברד גלצ"א בלע"ז: כדי שיזובו מימיו. משום דקא מוליד בשבת ודמי למלאכה שבורא המים הללו: אבל נותן לתוך הכוס. של יין בימות החמה כדי לצנן ואע"פ שנימוח מאליו ואינו חושש:

הדרן עלך במה טומנין

במה בהמה יוצאה כו'. לפי שאדם מצווה על שביתת בהמתו בשבת ומידי דמינטרא ביה בהמה הוי תכשיט ואורחא ולא הוי משוי ומידי דלא מינטרא ביה הוי משוי: אפסר. קביסטר"א: נאקה. דרומי"ל: בחטם. מפרש בגמרא: ולובדקים בפרומביא. מפרש בגמ': בשיר. כמו אצעדה סביב צוארו וטבעת קבוע בה ומכניסין בו רצועה או חבל ומושכין הבהמה: וכל בעלי השיר. כגון כלבים [של] ציידים וחיות קטנות שנותנין שיר לצוארם לנוי: יוצאין ונמשכין. מפרש בגמ': ומזין עליהם במקומן. כמו שהם בצואר הבהמה אם נטמאו: וטובלן במקומן. מכניסין בהמה למים להטביל את השיר: גמ' מאי נאקה. ומאי חטם: חיורתי. שהיא קשה להשתמר מפני שבורחת: בזממא דפרזלא. מוזי"ל בלע"ז נוקב את חוטמו ומכניסו בתוכו והוא כמין טבעת: חמרא לובא. חמור הבא ממדינת לוב כמו הכושים והלודים דאסא בדברי הימים (ב טז): בפגי דפרזלא. פריי' כעין שלנו פגי כמו זה קנה חמור ובית פגי (ב"מ ד' ט.) קיבלי"ל בית ראשה ולחייה: צרו שדרו ליה שערי. צרו מעותיו ושלחו לו שעורים בצרור מעותיו ולא רצו לקנות לו חמור מפני שהוא רחוק מבבל מהלך חצי שנה כדאמר בהגוזל (ב"ק ד' קיב:) והשיאוהו עצה לקנות חמור במקומו ויאכילנו שעורים תמיד ונמצא חמורו טוב ומשובח: ניגרי דחמרא שערי. פסיעותיו של חמור לפי שעורים שהוא אוכל: מחליפין. שאילתם נאקה באפסר וגמל בחטם מהו משוי הוא ואסור: לאו למעוטי גמל בחטם. והכי קאמר ארבע בהמות הללו משתמרים באפסר ואסורות לצאת בחטם: לא למעוטי נאקה באפסר. דהואיל ולא מינטרא ביה משאוי הוא אבל נטירותא יתירתא כגון חטם לגמל לאו משאוי הוא: יוצאין באפסר. דלובדקי נמי מינטרא ביה: ה"ג כתנאי אין חיה יוצאה בסוגר: כתנאי. נטירותא יתירתא אי משוי הוא או לא: בסוגר. קולא"ר של חבל כדמתרגמינן ויתנהו בסוגר בקולרין (יחזקאל יט): בחיה גדולה. כגון דוב: קטנה. כגון נמייה וחולדה: חתול. לא בעי נטירותא אפילו כחיה קטנה שאינו תאב לברוח כל כך: במיתנא. חבל קטן: הלכה כחנניה. ונטירותא יתירתא לאו משאוי הוא: חלשא דעתיה דרבה בר רב הונא. שהיה גדול וכסבור שעשה מדעת:

דאיתותב

תוספות

אינו נוטל ומחזיר. נראה לרשב"א דהיינו כרשב"ג דאמר בפרק נוטל כל היכא דאיכא איסורא והיתרא בהיתרא טרחינן באיסורא לא טרחינן אבל לרבנן דפליגי עליה שרו במכוסות לגמרי ליטול בידים דבר שאינו ניטל דבפרק נוטל (לקמן קמב:) מתני' דהיתה בין החביות מגביהה ומטה על צדה מוקי לה כרשב"ג משמע דרבנן דרשב"ג שרו לטלטל את האבן עצמו:

אין מרסקין לא את השלג ולא את הברד. מכאן יש ליזהר שלא ירחוץ ידיו בשלג וברד בשבת [י] ופעמים שמתקרשים ויש ברד מעורב בהם אין לרחוץ בהן דאי אפשר שלא ירסק הברד וכל הזהיר בו תבא עליו ברכה:

הדרן עלך במה טומנין

במה בהמה יוצאה. דאדם מוזהר על שביתת בהמתו דכתיב למען ינוח וגו' ומיהו לאו דלא תעשה מלאכה אתה ובהמתך ליכא אלא במחמר אחר בהמתו כדמוכח בריש מי שהחשיך (לקמן קנג.) ובריש נדרים (דף ג:) דייק בהך דהכא ובכל הני דלעיל דאיכא דוכתא דתנא ברישא הא דסליק מיניה ואיכא דוכתא דתני ברישא הא דפתח ביה:

חמרא לובא. אומר ר"ת דלובא היינו מצרים דכתיב (נחום ג) פוט ולובים היו בעזרתך ואמרינן בירושלמי גרים הבאים מלוב מהו להמתין להם שלשה דורות ומייתי עלה דהדא עלם מצראה דלווחין ליה לוב [כ]:

או דילמא כל נטירותא יתירתא לאו משוי היא. וא"ת תפשוט ממתניתין דתנן ולובדקים בפרומביא אע"ג דסגי לה באפסר כדאמר בסמוך תנא לובדקים וגמל יוצאים באפסר ופרומביא עדיפא מאפסר דאמר לקמן חמור שעסקיו רעים כגון זה מהו לצאת בפרומביא בשבת אלמא משמע דעדיף מאפסר וי"ל דלא הוי נטירותא יתירתא ואורחיה נמי בהכי ולא חשיב משוי:

קדמיה חמרא דלוי. משמע שמכבדין בדרכים ובפ' אמר להם הממונה (יומא לז.) נמי אמרינן שלשה שהיו מהלכין בדרך הרב באמצע גדול מימינו וקטן משמאלו וכן מצינו במלאכי השרת שבאו אצל אברהם וכו' והקשה ר"ת דבפ' שלשה שאכלו (ברכות מז.) מסיק דאין מכבדין אלא בפתח הראוי למזוזה ותירץ רבינו תם דהתם כשאין הולכים בחבורה אחת אלא כל אחד הולך לצורך עצמו אבל כשהולכים בחבורה אחת מכבדים בכל מקום:

אמר

עין משפט נר מצוה

לו א מיי' פ"ד מהלכות שבת הלכה ו סמג לאוין סה טוש"ע או"ח סימן רנח וסימן שיח סעיף ו:

לז ב מיי' פכ"א מהלכות שבת הלכה יג סמג לאוין סה טוש"ע או"ח סימן של סעיף טו וסי' שיח סעיף טז:

א ג מיי' פ"כ מהלכות שבת הלכה ח סמג לאוין סה טוש"ע או"ח סימן שה סעיף א:

ב ד מיי' שם טור שו"ע שם סעיף ה:

ג ה מיי' שם טור שו"ע שם סעיף ג:

ד ו מיי' שם טור שו"ע שם סעיף א:

רבינו חננאל

את הצונן וכל הנאכל כמות שהוא חי אין בו משום בשולי נכרים. אדם חשוב לא איבעי ליה למיעבד הכי: ת"ר אע"פ שאמרו אין טומנין בדבר שאינו מוסיף [הבל] אבל אם בא להוסיף מוסיף כיצד ר"ש ב"ג אומר נוטל הסדינין ומניח [את] הגלופקרין כו' פשוטה היא ר' יהודה אומר נעורת של פשתן דקה הרי הוא כזבל ומניחין מיחם ע"ג מיחם וקדירה על גבי קדירה וקדירה ע"ג מיחם ומיחם על גבי קדירה וטח פיהן בבצק. ולא כדי שיחמו אלא כדי שישתמרו כו' רבי התיר להטמין את הצונן כו':

הדרן עלך במה טומנין

פ"ה **במה בהמה יוצאה** ובמה אינה יוצאה. יוצאה הגמל באפסר כו' ונאקה בחטם נקתא חורתי בזממא דפרזלא. לובדקים בפרומפיא. חמרא לובא בפגי דפרזלא לבדקם לובא חמור לוב. ממקום ששמו לוב כדכתיב (דניאל י"א) לובים וכושים במצעדיו. כדגרסי' בירושלמי גרים הבאים מלוב מהו להמתין להו ג' דורות וקיי"ל כר' יוסי דאמר ארבע בהמות יוצאות באפסר בשבת הסוס והפרד והחמור והגמל: **ירושלמי** אמר חזקיה וסמניך וכן תהיה מגפת הסוס וגו' למעוטי גמל בחטם שלא יצא. רב אמר הלכה כר' יוסי. ולית הלכתא כחנניה דתני כל נטירותא יתירתא לאו (משום) [משוי] הוא ושפיר דמי ואע"ג דאמר שמואל הילכתא כחנניה פליג רב עליה

מסורת הש"ס

א) [לעיל מט.], ב) הך אבל לא הוא טעות וצ"ל וקדירה ע"ג וכו' ואע"ג דרש"י גרס אבל לא היינו במיחם ע"ג קדירה אבל בקדירה ע"ג מיחם ליכא מאן דפליג עי' בב"י בטא"ח סימן רנח, ג) [בתוספתא פ"ד איתא מרסקין בסמ"ך וכ"א בפירש"י דהכא על נכון וכן בערוך ורי"ף ורא"ש ובב"י סי' שיח מרסיקין], ד) [נדרים ג: נזיר ג.], ה) פי' רשן, ו) [עי' תוס' נב. ד"ה מזין], ז) [עי' תוס' שם ד"ה וטובלין], ח) גמלא נקיבה גדולה ערוך, ט) פי' רסן שבלחי, י) נ"ל ומים שמתקרשים רש"א, כ) [וע"ע תוס' בכורות ה: ד"ה תשעים וכו'].

הגהות הב"ח

(א) במשנה ומזין עליהן במקומן וטובלין: (ב) רש"י ד"ה וטח את פיה בשבת בבצק:

ליקוטי רש"י

נעורת. דק דק שנוערין מן הפשתן וקורין אריסט"ש [לעיל מט.]. אפסר. קבישט"ר כלומר בית אחיזה [קידושין כז.]. ונאקה בחטם. ומתגי, תרגם יונתן זמם והוא של ברזל ותוחבין אותו בנחירי הנאקה ונמשכת בו לפי שעסקיה רעים והוא ששנינו ונאקה בחוטם [מ"ב יט, כח]. זממא, מנקבין לנאקה בחוטמה ונותנין בה טבעת של רצועה וקושרין אותה ועומדת שם לעולם וכשרוצה לקושרה לבהמה קושר רצועה ארוכה באותה טבעת וקושרין בה ופעמים שמחירה [לקמן קיא:]. חמרא לובא. חמרי לובאי, חמורים גדולים ממצרים [תמיד לב.]. פרומביא. רסן [ב"ק יז:]. ניגרי. פסיעות [לקמן סו:].

other hand, if it refers to **a small beast,** such as a marten or weasel, **מִי לֹא סַגִּי לָהּ סוּגַר – is a rope collar not sufficient for it?**[27] **אֶלָּא לָאו חָתוּל אִיכָּא בֵּינַיְיהוּ – Rather,** the law of **a cat is surely** the point of dispute **between them,**[28] as follows: **תַּנָּא קַמָּא סָבַר כֵּיוָן דְּסַגִּי לָהּ בְּמִיתְנָא בְּעָלְמָא – The Tanna Kamma holds** that **since an ordinary cord is enough for [a cat], מַשּׂאוּי הוּא – [a rope collar]** is considered excessive and therefore **a burden. וַחֲנַנְיָה סָבַר כָּל נְטִירוּתָא יְתֵירְתָא לֹא אָמְרִינַן מַשּׂאוּי הוּא – And Chananyah holds** that **any excessive restraint is not considered a burden.**

The Gemara cites a legal decision:

אָמַר רַב הוּנָא בַּר חִיָּיא אָמַר שְׁמוּאֵל – Rav Huna bar Chiya said in the name of Shmuel: הֲלָכָה כַּחֲנַנְיָה – The law follows Chananyah.[29]

The Gemara relates an anecdote involving this law:

לֵוִי בְּרֵיהּ דְּרַב הוּנָא בַּר חִיָּיא וְרַבָּה בַּר רַב הוּנָא הֲווּ קָאָזְלֵי בְּאוֹרְחָא – Levi the son of Rav Huna bar Chiya and Rabbah bar Rav Huna were traveling along the road on donkeys. **קַדְמֵיהּ חֲמָרָא דְּלֵוִי לַחֲמָרָא דְּרַבָּה בַּר רַב הוּנָא – Levi's donkey went ahead of Rabbah bar Rav Huna's donkey. חֲלַשׁ דַּעְתֵּיהּ דְּרַבָּה בַּר רַב הוּנָא – Rabbah bar Rav Huna was disturbed.**[30] **אָמַר – [Levi] said** to himself: **אֵימָא לֵיהּ מִילְּתָא כִּי הֵיכִי – I will say something to him so**

NOTES

27. A rope collar would certainly be appropriate for such an animal. Thus, the Tanna Kamma of this Baraisa would have no reason to forbid it.

28. A cat requires even less control than a weasel or marten, because it is not as eager to run away (*Rashi*).

29. As we shall see below (52a), Shmuel's decision is not universally accepted.

30. [When traveling with one's teacher or a great scholar, one should position oneself slightly behind him and to his side (see *Yoma* 37a with *Rashi* ד״ה דמצדד and *Shulchan Aruch Yoreh Deah* 242:16). Therefore,] Rabbah bar Rav Huna, who was the senior scholar here, was disturbed because he thought that Levi had gone ahead of him deliberately (*Rashi;* see *Sfas Emes'* interpretation of *Rashi*).

דְּאִיתּוֹתַב דַּעְתֵּיהּ – **that his mind will be put at ease.**[1] אָמַר לֵיהּ – **[Levi] said to him:** חֲמוֹר שֶׁעֲסָקָיו רָעִים כְּגוֹן זֶה – "**Regarding a donkey whose behavior is untoward, such as this one,** מַהוּ לָצֵאת בִּפְרוּמְבְּיָא בְּשַׁבָּת – **what is [the law]** as to whether it may **go out with a bit on the Sabbath?"**[2] אָמַר לֵיהּ – **[Rabbah bar Rav Huna] said to [Levi]:** הָכִי אָמַר אֲבוּךְ מִשְּׁמֵיהּ דִּשְׁמוּאֵל – **"Thus said your father**[3] **in the name of Shmuel:** הֲלָכָה כַּחֲנַנְיָא – **The law follows Chananyah** [who permits even an excessive restraint]."[4]

The Gemara discusses the law of a goat:

תָּנָא דְּבֵי מְנַשְּׁיָא – **The academy of Menashiya taught the following Baraisa:** עֵז שֶׁחָקַק לָהּ בֵּין קַרְנֶיהָ יוֹצְאָה בְּאַפְסָר בְּשַׁבָּת – A GOAT [WHOSE OWNER] CARVED OUT holes BETWEEN ITS HORNS MAY GO OUT WITH A HALTER ON THE SABBATH.[5]

The Gemara raises an inquiry:

בָּעֵי רַב יוֹסֵף – **Rav Yosef asked:** תָּחַב לָהּ בִּזְקָנָהּ מַהוּ – If one **inserted [a halter] into [a goat's] beard,**[6] **what is [the law]?** כֵּיוָן דְּאִי מְנַתַּח לָהּ כָּאֵיב לָהּ – Do we say that **since, if [the goat] cuts herself loose,**[7] **[her beard] will hurt her,**[8] לֹא אַתְיָא לְנַתּוּחָהּ – **she will not come to cut herself loose?** It should therefore be permitted to let a goat go out in this manner, since there is little risk that the halter will come off. אוֹ דִּילְמָא זִימְנִין דְּרָפֵי וְנָפִיל – **Or perhaps** we say in such a case that **sometimes [the halter] will become loose and fall off** by itself, וְאָתֵי לְאַתּוּיֵי אַרְבַּע אַמּוֹת בִּרְשׁוּת הָרַבִּים – **and he will come to carry** it **four** ***amos*** **in the public domain.**[9] Accordingly, it should be forbidden to let a goat go out in this manner.

The Gemara concludes:

תֵּיקוּ – **Let it stand.** Rav Yosef's question cannot be resolved at present.

Returning to its main topic (namely, whether an excessive restraint is considered a burden), the Gemara cites a Mishnah:

תְּנַן הָתָם – **We learned** in a Mishnah **there:**[10] וְלֹא בִּרְצוּעָה שֶׁבֵּין קַרְנֶיהָ – AND a cow may NOT go out WITH A STRAP BETWEEN ITS HORNS.

The Gemara cites an Amoraic dispute regarding this Mishnah:

אָמַר (ליה) רַבִּי יִרְמְיָה בַּר אַבָּא – **R' Yirmiyah bar Abba said:** פְּלִיגֵי בָהּ רַב וּשְׁמוּאֵל – **Rav and Shmuel disagree about it.** חַד אָמַר בֵּין לְנוֹי בֵּין לְשַׁמֵּר אָסוּר – **One says** that **whether** the strap is **for decoration**[11] **or to control** the cow,[12] **it is forbidden.**[13] וְחַד אָמַר לְנוֹי אָסוּר וּלְשַׁמֵּר מוּתָּר – **And one says** that if the strap is **for decoration it is forbidden, but** if it is **to control** the cow **it is permitted.**[14]

The Gemara seeks to attribute these opinions:

אָמַר רַב יוֹסֵף – **Rav Yosef said:** תִּסְתַּיֵּים דִּשְׁמוּאֵל הוּא דְּאָמַר – **You may determine that it was Shmuel who said** that לְנוֹי אָסוּר לְשַׁמֵּר מוּתָּר – if it is **for decoration it is forbidden,** but if it is **to control** the cow, **it is permitted,** דְּאָמַר רַב הוּנָא בַּר חִיָּיא אָמַר שְׁמוּאֵל – **for Rav Huna bar Chiya said in the name of Shmuel:** הֲלָכָה כַּחֲנַנְיָא – **The law follows Chananyah,** who permits even an excessive restraint.[15]

Abaye disagrees:

אָמַר לֵיהּ אַבַּיֵי – **Abaye said to [Rav Yosef]:** אַדְּרַבָּה – **On the contrary!** תִּסְתַּיֵּים דִּשְׁמוּאֵל הוּא דְּאָמַר בֵּין לְנוֹי בֵּין לְשַׁמֵּר אָסוּר – **You may determine that it was Shmuel who said** that **whether** the strap is **for decoration or to control** the cow, **it is forbidden,** דְּאָמַר רַב יְהוּדָה אָמַר שְׁמוּאֵל – **for Rav Yehudah said in the name of Shmuel:**[16] מַחֲלִיפִין לִפְנֵי רַבִּי – "**They switched** the cases **before Rebbi,** i.e. they asked Rebbi the following: שֶׁל זוֹ בְּזוֹ מַהוּ – If the restraint **of one** type of animal is put **on the other** type of animal, **what is [the law]?** אָמַר לְפָנָיו רַבִּי יִשְׁמָעֵאל בְּרַבִּי יוֹסֵי – **And R' Yishmael the son of R' Yose said before [Rebbi]:** כָּךְ אָמַר אַבָּא – **Thus said** my **father:** אַרְבַּע בְּהֵמוֹת יוֹצְאוֹת בְּאַפְסָר – **Four animals may go out with a halter:** הַסּוּס הַפֶּרֶד וְהַגָּמָל וְהַחֲמוֹר – **The horse, mule, camel and donkey.** לָאו לְמַעוּטֵי גָּמָל בַּחֲטָם – Does this statement **not exclude a camel with a nose ring?** [I.e. a camel may not go out with a nose ring, because it is an excessive restraint.]" Since Shmuel reported this proof, he presumably agrees with it. This demonstrates that Shmuel *prohibits* an excessive restraint.[17]

NOTES

1. I want him to know that I did not go ahead on purpose (*Rashi*).

2. Would it be considered an excessive restraint or not? (*Rashi*).

In normal circumstances, a donkey may go out only with a halter, and not with a bit [unless it is a Luvian donkey] (see 51b notes 15 and 25). Levi's question was whether his donkey, which, he implied, was unusually aggressive, was subject to the same limitation (see *Ran MHK* ed. to 51b ד"ה כי תיבעי; see also *Sfas Emes*).

3. I.e. Rav Huna the son of Chiya (above, 51b).

4. Therefore it makes no difference whether or not a bit is excessive for this donkey (*Rashi; cf. Maharsha* ד"ה שם רבינא and *Pnei Yehoshua* ד"ה בגמרא רבינא). Either way, it is permitted.

[Levi surely knew this ruling, which his own father had taught. The question he asked Rabbah bar Rav Huna, which implies that an excessive restraint is forbidden, was stated only as a way of pointing out that his donkey was difficult to control.]

5. He cut holes in its horns and inserted the halter in the holes (*Rashi*).

A goat may go out with a halter only if the halter is attached to it in this manner. If the halter is just tied on, it is forbidden, because a goat's head is narrow and thus when it thrashes its head about as it is being pulled, the halter might slip off. The owner might then commit the Biblical transgression of carrying the halter four *amos* in a public domain (*Rashi*). [The Acharonim discuss why *Rashi* did not say that the reason for the prohibition is that since the halter is an inadequate restraint, it is a burden (see *Maharsha, R' Akiva Eiger* and *Sfas Emes*).]

6. I.e. he tied the goat's beard into a loop and threaded the halter through it (*Rashi*).

7. By thrashing from side to side in order to escape (*Rashi*).

8. For the halter will pull out the hairs of its beard (*Rashi*).

9. See end of note 5.

10. Below, 54b.

11. I.e. the strap is colored and braided, and serves only decorative purposes. One does not use it to hold the cow (*Rashi*).

12. I.e. one does use it to control the cow (*Rashi*).

13. One who is taking a cow from place to place need not hold onto it. Rather, he can make it go in front of him [and gently direct it when necessary]. A strap, therefore, is an excessive restraint. This Amora classifies an excessive restraint as a burden (*Rashi*).

When the strap serves only to decorate the cow it is certainly prohibited, because such a decoration is unusual (see Chapter Introduction note 3).

14. This Amora holds that an excessive restraint is *not* considered a burden (*Rashi*).

15. Since Shmuel himself ruled in accordance with Chananyah (above, 51b), he clearly holds that although a strap is an excessive restraint for a cow, it is permitted [provided that it is used for purposes of control, and not for decoration].

16. The following is excerpted from Shmuel's statement recorded on 51b. See notes 18-23 there.

17. Shmuel, therefore, must have been the one who ruled that a cow may not go out with a strap [even if it is used as a restraint].

It emerges that there are conflicting versions of Shmuel's opinion. According to Rav Huna bar Chiya (who reported that Shmuel said, "The law follows Chananyah"), Shmuel permits an excessive restraint. But according to Rav Yehudah (who reported in the name of Shmuel a proof to the effect that a camel may not go out with a nose ring), Shmuel *prohibits* an excessive restraint. Evidently, these Amoraim – Rav Huna bar Chiya and Rav Yehudah – disagree as to Shmuel's opinion

דאיתותב דעתיה א"ל חמור שעסקיו רעים כגון זה מהו לצאת בפרומביא בשבת א"ל הכי אמר אבוך משמיה דשמואל הלכה כחנניא תנא דבי מנשיא [א]עז שחקק לה בין קרניה יוצאה באפסר בשבת בעי רב יוסף תחב לה בזקנה מהו כיון דאי מנתח לה כאיב לה לא אתיא לנתוחה או דילמא [ב]זימנין דרפי ונפיל ואתי לאתויי ד"א ברה"ר תיקו [ה]תנן התם ולא ברצועה שבין קרניה אמר (ליה) ר' ירמיה בר אבא פליגי בה רב ושמואל חד אמר [ג]בין לנוי בין לשמר אסור וח"א לנוי אסור ולשמר מותר אמר רב יוסף תסתיים דשמואל הוא דאמר לנוי אסור לשמר מותר דאמר רב הונא בר חייא אמר שמואל הלכה כחנניא א"ל אביי אדרבה תסתיים דשמואל הוא דאמר בין לנוי בין לשמר אסור דאמר רב יהודה אמר שמואל מחליפין לפני רבי של זו בזו מהו אמר לפניו [ו]ר' ישמעאל בר' יוסי כך אמר אבא ד' בהמות יוצאות באפסר הסוס הפרד והגמל והחמור לאו למעוטי גמל בחטם סמי הא מקמי הא ומאי חזית דמסמית הא מקמי הא סמי הא מקמי הא [ג](דאשכחן שמואל הוא דאמר לנוי אסור לשמר מותר דאתמר) רב חייא בר אשי [ד]אמר רב בין לנוי בין לשמר אסור ורב חייא בר אבין [ה]אמר שמואל לנוי אסור לשמר מותר מיתיבי קשרה בעליה במוסרה כשרה ואי ס"ד משאוי הוא [א]אשר לא עלה עליה עול אמר רחמנא אמר אביי במוליכה מעיר לעיר רבא אמר שאני פרה דדמיה יקרין רבינא אמר [ד]במורד': הסוס בשיר וכו': מאי יוצאין ומאי נמשכין אמר רב הונא [ה]או יוצאין כרוכין או נמשכין ושמואל אמר יוצאין נמשכין ואין יוצאין כרוכין במתניתא תנא יוצאין כרוכין לימשך אמר רב יוסף חזינא להו לעיגלי דבי רב הונא יוצאין באפסריהן כרוכין בשבת כי אתא רב דימי אמר ר' חנינא מולאות של בית רבי יוצאות באפסריהן בשבת איבעיא להו כרוכין או נמשכין ת"ש כי אתא רב שמואל בר יהודה א"ר חנינא מולאות של בית רבי יוצאות באפסריהן כרוכים בשבת אמרוה רבנן קמיה דרב אסי הא דרב שמואל בר יהודה לא צריכא מדרב דימי נפקא דאי ס"ד דרב דימי נמשכין קאמר מדרב יהודה אמר שמואל נפקא דאמר רב יהודה אמר שמואל מחליפין היו לפני רבי של זו בזו מהו אמר לפניו ר' ישמעאל בר' יוסי כך אמר אבא ארבע בהמות יוצאות באפסר הסוס והפרד והגמל והחמור אמר להו רב אסי איצטריך להו דאי מדרב יהודה נפקא הוה אמינא אמר לפניו ולא קיבלה מיניה קמ"ל דרב דימי ואי דרב דימי הוה אמינא ה"מ נמשכין אבל כרוכין לא קמ"ל דרב שמואל בר (רב) יהודה: ומזין עליהן וטובלן במקומן: למימרא דבני קבולי טומאה נינהו והתנן [ו][ו]טבעת אדם טמאה [ז]וטבעת בהמה וכלים [ח]ושאר כל הטבעו' טהורות

רש"י

דאיתותב דעתיה. להודיעו שלא נתכוונתי: בפרומביא. מי הוי נטירותא יתירתא לגביה או לא: הלכה כחנניא. ולא איכפת לן אי הוי נטירותא יתירתא: יוצאה באפסר. אם תחבו בחקיקת קרן אבל בקשירה בעלמא לא דילמא שלפא מרישה מתוך שראשה דק והיא מתנתקת לכאן ולכאן כשמושכין אותה ואתי לאתויי ארבע אמות ברשות הרבים: תחב לה בזקנה. שקשר שער זקנה כמין נקב ותחב האפסר לתוכו: מנתחא. מתנתקת וקופלת אנה ואנה לברוח מידו: כאיב לה. הזקן שנתלש השער ומכאיבה: תנן התם. בסוף פרקין ולא פרה ברצועה שבין קרניה: לנוי. שצובעה וקולעה לנוי בין קרניה כמין קליעה מקרן לקרן ואינו אוחזה בה: לשמר. שאוחזה בה: אסור. דפרה מינטרא בלא אחיזה אלא מוליכה לפניו וקסבר נטירותא יתירתא משוי הוא: ולשמר מותר. קסבר נטירותא יתירתא לאו משוי הוא: ארבע בהמות. וקס"ד דהכי קאמר באפסר יוצאו' ולא בחטם אלמא נטירותא יתירתא משוי הוא: ומאי חזית. דמסמית הא דשמואל מקמיה ההיא סמי ההיא מקמי הא: דאיתמר. בהדיא דשמואל הוא דשרי וההוא דמחליפין כדאוקימנא דלא (א) למעוטיהו מחטם אלא למעוטי נאקה מאפסר דלא מינטרא ביה: קשרה בעליה. לפרה אדומה: במוסרה. אפסר: במוליכה מעיר לעיר. וסתם פרה פונה למקום מרבץ שלה וצריך לאוחזה כשמוליכה לעיר אחרת ולאו נטירותא יתירתא הוא אלא אורחא היא: שאני פרה. אדומה: דדמיה יקרים. ובעי נטירותא יתירתא משטולדה: יוצאין כרוכין. הרצועה סביב צוארן ואע"פ שאינו אוחזה לאו משוי הוא דלנוי נמי אורחייהו הוא: נמשכין. שמושכה ברצועה הקבועה בטבעת השיר: יוצאין נמשכים. דנטירותא אורחא הוא: ואין יוצאין כרוכים. דלנוי לאו אורחא הוא: כרוכין לימשך. כרוכים בריוח שיכול להכניס ידו בין הכרך לצואר או יניח מעט מן החבל שאם באת לברוח ימהר ויאחזנה: מולאות. פרדות: דאי ס"ד רב דימי נמשכין לחוד קאמר. אבל כרוכין לא ולא אתא לאשמעינן אלא דמולאות משתמרות באפסר ולא הוי משוי להו: מדרב יהודה אמר שמואל נפקא. דקס"ד דקיבלה רבי מיניה דרבי ישמעאל ברבי יוסי: טבעת אדם. שנותן באצבע לנוי: טמאה. דתכשיט הוא וממדין ילפינן דמנה בהן תכשיטין אצעדה וצמיד וגו' ואכולהו קאי תתחטאו אתם ושביכם (במדבר לא): טבעת בהמה. כגון שיר: טבעת כלים. כעין שעושין בראש ידות הכלים: ושאר כל הטבעות. כגון העשויות לדלת:
טהורות

תוספות

אמר שמואל הלכה כחנניא. פר"ח דהלכה כרב דאמר בין לנוי בין לשמר אסור מדמשני אביי ורבא ורבינא דהוו בתראי אליביה ההיא דקשרה בעליה במוסרה ועוד דקיי"ל (ו) דהלכתא כרב באיסורי הלכך אומר הרב פור"ת דכל נטירותא יתירתא אסור כגון פרה באפסר וכל נוי בהמה אסור לצאת ומיהו עגלים יוצאות באפסר כדאמר בסמוך ויוצא סוס ברסן דאורחיה בהכי או באפסר אבל בשניהם ברסן ובאפסר אסור ומותר להסיר הרסן או האפסר בראש הסוס בשבת ואין בו איסור טלטול דמוכן הוא לבהמה ואדם המנהיג סוס ברשות הרבים יזהר שלא יוציא ראש החבל מתחת ידו טפח ומה שבין ידו לסוס יגביה מן הקרקע טפח דהכי אמרינן לקמן בפרקין (ב) ומותר לכרוך חבל האפסר סביב צואר הבהמה ולצאת דהא עגלי דרב הונא ומולאות של בית רבי יוצאים כרוכין:

אדרבה תסתיים דשמואל הוא דאמר כו'. תימה לרשב"א מה ראייה מייתי מדאמר שמואל מחליפין לפני רבי כו' דלכאורה משמע דהא דקאמר לעיל לא למעוטי נאקה באפסר דכל זה מדברי שמואל:

קשרה בעליה במוסרה. הוה מצי לשנויי הא מני חנניא היא והא דמשמע בריש הכונס (ב"ק נה:) דמוסרה שמירה פחותה היא היינו דוקא בשור:

או יוצאין כרוכין. פי' בקונט' דמכוין לנוי וכן פירש במתניתין וקשה לרשב"א ולהרב פור"ת דלעיל משמע דלנוי לכ"ע אסור ותירץ הרב פור"ת דבהא פליגי דרב הונא סבר דנטירותא נמי איכא בכרוכין שאם רוצה הבהמה לברוח יתפסנה בכריכת האפסר ולא הוי משוי ושמואל סבר כרוכין לא הוי נטירותא:

במתניתא תנא כרוכין לימשך. רב הונא מתרץ כרוכים לימשך שיש חלל בין אפסר לצואר שהוא נוח לימשך כשירצה ושמואל סבר לימשך דוקא שיש חבל תלוי באפסר:

[ח] **בבאין** מנוי אדם לנוי בהמה. פירש"י ובעודו לאדם נטמא ובחנם פירש כן דאפילו אחר שיחדו לבהמה מקבל טומאה שאינו עולה מלקבל טומאה מכאן ואילך אלא בשינוי מעשה כדמוכח בפ"ק דסוכה (דף יג:) גבי קוצר לאכילה ונמלך לסיכוך ורש"י בעצמו פירש כן בריש במה אשה (לקמן נח:) ° וכופת שאור שיחדו לישיבה דאמר טהור אור"י דמיירי כשיש שינוי מעשה:

[ט] **ומזין** עליהם במקומן. אצטריך לאשמעינן במקומן דלא חיישינן שמא תפול הזאה על הבהמה ויפסלו דתנן במסכת פרה (פי"ב מ"ג) נתכוון להזות על האדם והזה על הבהמה אם יש באזוב [לא] ישנה:

וטובלין במקומן. הקשה הר"ר אליעזר אמאי לא מקשה הכא טבילה מאן דכר שמיה כדפריך בריש במה אשה (דף נז.) אמאי דתנן ולא תטבול עד שתרפס ותירץ ר"ת דהכא לא פריך משום דמתני' מיירי בדין כלים שמחלק בין כלי לכלי ואיזה מותר לצאת בו ואיזה אסור ואגב אורחיה אשמעינן שאר דיני כלים ומזין עליהם וטובלן במקומן דכן דרך התנא כי ההוא (לקמן דף סו.) דקיטע יוצא בקב שלו ואם יש בו בית קבול כתותין טמא אבל בריש במה אשה דמיירי בדיני כלים ואשמעינן דין טבילת אשה פריך שפיר טבילה מאן דכר שמיה:
והא

עין משפט נר מצוה

ה א ב מיי' פ"כ מהל' שבת הלכה יא:
ו ג מיי' שם סמג לאוין סה טוש"ע או"ח סי' שה סעיף יח:
ז ד מיי' שם ופ"א מהל' פרה אדומה הלכה ז' סמג עשין רלב טוש"ע א"ח סי' שה סעיף ד:
ח ה (מיימ' פ"כ מהל' שבת הל' ח') טור ושו"ע שם סעיף ה:
ט ו מיי' פ"ח מהל' כלים הלכה ו:
י ז שם הלכה ז:
יא ח שם הלכה ט:

רבינו חננאל

ואמר בין לנוי בין לשמר אסור. ושמואל אמר לנוי אסור לשמר מותר. ומותבנן לרב קשרה לפרה אדומה בעליה במוסרה כשרה. קשיא לרב דאמר לשמור בשבת אסור שנמצאת מוסרה בפרה (מחזי) [משוי]. והמשאוי פוסל בפרה אמאי קתני כשרה. ופריק אביי ורבא ורבינא דאיהו בתרא לעולם לשמר כמשאוי והכא בפרה מורדת ומשום הכי לא היה מוסרה משאוי עליה. אבל כולי עלמא משאוי היא כרב ומדמשני רבינא לאוקמה כרב שמע מינה הלכתא כוותיה דרב: יוצאין כרוכין. שהיו אפסריהן כרוכין על צואריהן. ואסיקנא דיוצאין כרוכין וכ"ש נמשכין. מולאות פי' פרדות של בית רבי היו יוצאות באפסריהן כרוכין בשבת. יוצאין בשיר ונמשכין בשיר ומזין עליהן וטובלין במקומן. פי' שיר כעין צמידין. כדמתרגמינן שירין. ואקשינן וכי טבעות של בהמה בני קיבולי טומאה נינהו. והתנן בכלים פ' י"ב טבעת אדם טמאה. טבעת בהמה וכלים ושאר כל

רב נסים גאון

פ"ה שאני פרה דדמיה יקרין. במס' ע"ז בפרק אין מעמידין בהמה (דף כ"ד) דברו עלה (א) פי דאלך למא קאל ר"א אומר ישראל היו משמרין אותה משעה שנוצרה הסב מאגא אל תירוץ קאלו עלי טריק אל סואל מנא ידעינן וג' אל גואב אמר רב כהנא כוס אדום מעבירין לפניה בשעה שעולה עליה זכר אי הכי אמאי דמיה יקרין הואיל ושתי שערות פוסלות בה:

חשק שלמה על רב נסים גאון

(א) כוונת הדברים כן הוא. כי דברו בזה הענין למה שאמר רבי אליעזר לפי מה שבא הסירוך אמרו מדרך שאלה מנא ידעינן ובאה התשובה אמר רב כהנא וכו':

מסורת הש"ס

(א) לקמן נד:, ב) [תוספ' פ"ה], ג) ס"א ליתא וה"ג מאי הוה עלה אתמר וכו', ד) [לקמן נד:], ה) [שם], ו) כלים פי"ב מ"א, ז) [בכורות מט:], ח) שייך לע"ב, ט) [ג' דבורים אלו שייך לעיל במשנה].

הגהות הב"ח

(א) רש"י ד"ה דאמר וכו' דלאו למעוטי גמל מחטם אלא: (ב) תוס' ד"ה אמר וכו' לקמן בפירקין. נ"ב דף נד ע"ב:

גליון הש"ס

תוס' ד"ה בבאין וכו' וכופת שאור שיחדו לישיבה דאמר טהור. חולין קכט ע"א. ועי' ב"ב יט ע"ב תוס' ד"ה תיפוק ליה:

תורה אור השלם

א) זֹאת חֻקַּת הַתּוֹרָה אֲשֶׁר צִוָּה יְיָ לֵאמֹר דַּבֵּר אֶל בְּנֵי יִשְׂרָאֵל וְיִקְחוּ אֵלֶיךָ פָרָה אֲדֻמָּה תְּמִימָה אֲשֶׁר אֵין בָּהּ מוּם אֲשֶׁר לֹא עָלָה עָלֶיהָ עֹל: [במדבר יט, ב]

ליקוטי רש"י

ולא ברצועה שבין קרניה. משאוי הוא ואינו תכשיט לה [ביצה כג.]. בין לנוי בין לשמר אסור. דכל נטירותא יתירתא אמרינן משאוי הוא [לקמן נד:].

The Gemara accepts Abaye's argument:

סַמֵּי הָא מִקַּמֵּי הָא – **Eliminate that** version of Shmuel's view **in favor of this** one.[18]

The Gemara counters:

וּמַאי חָזֵית דְּמְסַמֵּית הָא מִקַּמֵּי הָא – **But** for **what** reason **did you see** fit **to eliminate that** version **in favor of this** one? סַמֵּי הָא מִקַּמֵּי הָא – Instead, **eliminate this one in favor of that one!**[19]

דְּאַשְׁכְּחַן שְׁמוּאֵל הוּא דְּאָמַר – **For we find that** indeed **it was Shmuel who said:** לְנוֹי אָסוּר לְשַׁמֵּר מוּתָּר – If the strap is **for decoration it is forbidden,** but if it is **to control** the cow **it is permitted.** דְּאִתְּמַר – **For it was stated:** רַב חִיָּיא בַּר אַשִׁי אָמַר רַב – **Rav Chiya bar Ashi said in the name of Rav:** בֵּין לְנוֹי בֵּין לְשַׁמֵּר אָסוּר – **Whether** the strap is **for decoration or to control** the cow, **it is forbidden.** וְרַב חִיָּיא בַּר אָבִין אָמַר שְׁמוּאֵל – **And Rav Chiya bar Avin said in the name of Shmuel:** לְנוֹי אָסוּר לְשַׁמֵּר מוּתָּר – If it is **for decoration it is forbidden,** but if it is **to control** the cow **it is permitted.**[20]

The Gemara challenges Rav's view that an excessive restraint is classified as a burden:

מֵיתִיבִי – **They challenged** it from the following Baraisa: קְשָׁרָהּ בְּעָלֶיהָ בְּמוֹסֵרָה כְּשֵׁרָה – If THE OWNER [OF A *PARAH ADUMAH*][21] TIED A LEASH[22] TO IT, IT IS nevertheless VALID. וְאִי סַלְקָא דַעְתָּךְ מַשּׂאוֹי הוּא – **Now, if you should think that [an excessive restraint] is a burden,** as Rav ruled, the *parah adumah*[23] would *not* be valid, ,,אֲשֶׁר לֹא־עָלָה עָלֶיהָ עֹל'' אָמַר רַחֲמָנָא – because **the Merciful One said** in His Torah:[24] ***upon which a yoke has never gone,*** which teaches that a *parah adumah* is valid only if it never carried a burden.[25] – ? –

Three Amoraim advance solutions in defense of Rav:

אָמַר אַבַּיֵּי – **Abaye said:** בְּמוֹלִיכָהּ מֵעִיר לְעִיר – The Baraisa refers to a case **where [the owner] is leading [the *parah adumah*] from city to city.**[26]

רָבָא אָמַר – **Rava says:** שָׁאנִי פָּרָה דְּדָמֶיהָ יְקָרִין – **The** *parah adumah* **is different** from all other cows, **because it is expensive.**[27]

רָבִינָא אָמַר – **Ravina says:** בְּמוֹרֶדֶת – The Baraisa refers **to a rebellious [cow].**[28]

The Gemara quotes from the Mishnah:

הַסּוּס בְּשֵׁיר וכו' – THE HORSE may go out WITH A COLLAR etc. [and all animals that wear a collar may go out with a collar and may be pulled by a collar].

The Gemara asks:

מַאי יוֹצְאִין וּמַאי נִמְשָׁכִין – **What** is meant by **"may go out"** and **what** is meant by **"may be pulled"?**[29]

Amoraim disagree over the meaning of this clause:

אָמַר רַב הוּנָא – **Rav Huna said:** אוֹ יוֹצְאִין כְּרוּכִין אוֹ נִמְשָׁכִין – It means that these animals **may go out** either with the leash of the collar **wrapped** around their necks **or pulled** by the leash.[30]

NOTES

on this matter. Abaye decided in favor of Rav Yehudah, because Rav Yehudah had a reputation for meticulousness in reporting teachings in the name of others [see *Chullin* 18b] (*Rashba, Ritva MHK* ed., *Ran MHK* ed.).

The Rishonim raise an obvious difficulty: How could Abaye infer from Rav Yehudah's statement in the name of Shmuel that Shmuel agrees with R' Yishmael's proof [that an excessive restraint is forbidden]? After all, that very statement concluded with Rebbi's deflection of the proof: לֹא לְמַעוּטֵי נָאקָה בְּאַפְסָר, *No! It excludes a female dromedary with a halter* (see Gemara above, 51b).

In view of this problem, some commentators explain the passage on 51b differently: R' Yishmael cited only his father's teaching ("Four animals may go out with a halter" etc.). He did not spell out what he sought to prove from that teaching. Rather, it was Shmuel who concluded the proof by adding: לְמַעוּטֵי מַאי, *What does it exclude?* לָאו לְמַעוּטֵי גָּמָל בַּחֲטָם, *Does it not exclude a camel with a nose ring?* And then the Amoraim of the Gemara deflected the proof by arguing: לֹא לְמַעוּטֵי נָאקָה בְּאַפְסָר, *No! It excludes a female dromedary with a halter.* According to this version, it is clear that Shmuel prohibits a camel with a nose ring (*Ritva MHK* ed. to 51b [first opinion]; *Sfas Emes;* see *Pnei Yehoshua*).

However, the plain meaning of the Gemara on 51b seems to be that this entire discussion was between R' Yishmael and Rebbi, and it was later reported by Rav Yehudah in the name of Shmuel (*Tosafos*). The difficulty is thus reinstated: Why did Abaye assume that Shmuel agreed with R' Yishmael's proof and not with Rebbi's deflection of the proof?

Some Rishonim answer that, in Abaye's opinion, Rebbi's deflection was not intended seriously. Abaye reasoned that the proof is certainly valid (for the reasons given above, 51b notes 23 and 24) and that Rebbi deflected it only for the sake of argument (*Ritva MHK* ed. ibid. in the name of *Baal HaTerumos;* see *Rashba*).

18. That is, we must conclude that Rav Huna bar Chiya's version of Shmuel's view is mistaken in light of the evidence to the contrary cited by Rav Yehudah (see previous note).

Therefore, the Gemara holds at this point that it was Shmuel (and not Rav) who prohibited a cow from going out with a strap between its horns (even if it is used as a restraint).

19. That is, Rav Yehudah's report in the name of Shmuel of the dialogue between Rebbi and his students cannot be used as proof that Shmuel prohibits an excessive restraint (see next note).

20. Since it was reported explicitly [and not through inference] that Shmuel made this statement, the Gemara finally accepts that this is indeed Shmuel's view (see *Rashi;* see also *Mahadura Basra*).

The Gemara has concluded that Shmuel permits an excessive restraint. This conforms with Rav Huna bar Chiya's version of Shmuel's opinion ("The law follows Chananyah"). But it apparently contradicts Rav Yehudah, who reported in the name of Shmuel a proof to the effect that an excessive restraint is prohibited. [It is unlikely that Rav Yehudah erred in his reporting, because Rav Yehudah was exceptionally meticulous in these matters.] We must therefore say that Abaye erred in assuming that Shmuel agreed with the proof. In fact, Shmuel agreed with Rebbi's deflection of the proof, which Shmuel also reported [see note 17] (*Rashi*).

21. See 51b note 11. A *parah adumah* is invalidated if it performs work or if it is yoked (see note 25).

22. This refers to a halter (*Rashi*).

23. For whom a leash is an excessive restraint (see note 13).

24. *Numbers* 19:2.

25. [Or performed any other labor (see *Sotah* 46a).] Thus, the Baraisa, which rules that a leash does not disqualify a *parah adumah,* proves that an excessive restraint is not deemed a burden.

26. A cow tends to go to its regular resting place. Hence, when taking it to a different city, one must hold onto it to prevent it from turning back that way. In such a circumstance, a leash is not an excessive restraint, but normal trappings (*Rashi*).

27. A cow that met the requirements of a *parah adumah* was so rare that it was priceless (see *Kiddushin* 31a). Therefore, if a completely red calf was born to one's herd, one would guard it with extreme care. In this instance, a halter would not be considered an excessive restraint for a cow (*Rashi*).

28. When used for a cow of a particularly rebellious nature, a halter would not be deemed an excessive restraint (see *Rashba* ד״ה אמר ליה הכי).

[Regarding the question of whether there are halachic differences between these answers, see *Ritva MHK* ed., *R' Akiva Eiger* and *Shabbos Shel Mi.*]

29. [The words "may be pulled by a collar" are apparently unnecessary. The very reason why collars and other restraints are permitted is that a person needs them to pull (or otherwise control) his animals. It therefore should go without saying that one may use them for that purpose.]

30. The Mishnah adds "may be pulled by a collar" (where the collar serves as a restraint) to intimate that the preceding permit "may go out with a collar" applies even where the collar cannot serve as a restraint. Such a situation arises where the leash of the collar is wrapped around the animal's neck. The collar then serves as an adornment of the animal. Rav Huna maintains that such an adornment is typically used

דאיתותב דעתיה א"ל חמור שעסקיו רעים כגון זה מהו לצאת בפרומביא בשבת א"ל הכי אמר אבוך משמיה דשמואל הלכה כחנניא תנא דבי מנשיא [א] עז שחקק לה בין קרניה יוצאה באפסר בשבת בעי רב יוסף תחב לה בזקנה מהו כיון דאי מנתח לה כאיב לה לא אתיא לנתוחה או דילמא [ב] זימנין דרפי ונפיל ואתי לאתויי ד"א ברה"ר תיקו [א] תנן התם ולא ברצועה שבין קרניה אמר (ליה) ר' ירמיה בר אבא פליגי בה רב ושמואל חד אמר [ג] בין לנוי בין לשמר אסור וח"א לנוי אסור ולשמר מותר אמר רב יוסף תסתיים דשמואל הוא דאמר לנוי אסור לשמר מותר דאמר רב הונא בר חייא אמר שמואל הלכה כחנניא א"ל אביי אדרבה תסתיים דשמואל הוא דאמר בין לנוי בין לשמר אסור דאמר רב יהודה אמר שמואל מחליפין לפני רבי של זו בזו מהו אמר לפניו [ג] ר' ישמעאל בר' יוסי כך אמר אבא ד' בהמות יוצאות באפסר הסוס הפרד והגמל והחמור לאו למעוטי גמל בחטם סמי הא מקמי הא ומאי חזית דמסמית הא מקמי הא סמי הא מקמי הא [ג] (דאשכחן שמואל הוא דאמר לנוי אסור לשמר מותר דאתמר) רב חייא בר אשי [ד] אמר רב בין לנוי בין לשמר אסור ורב חייא בר אבין [ה] אמר שמואל לנוי אסור לשמר מותר מיתיבי קשרה בעליה במוסרה כשרה ואי ס"ד משאוי הוא [א] אשר לא עלה עליה עול אמר רחמנא אמר אביי במוליכה מעיר לעיר רבא אמר שאני פרה דדמיה יקרין רבינא אמר [ד] במורד': הסוס בשיר וכו': מאי יוצאין ומאי נמשכין אמר רב הונא [ה] או יוצאין כרוכין או נמשכין ושמואל אמר יוצאין נמשכין ואין יוצאין כרוכין במתניתא תנא יוצאין כרוכין לימשך אמר רב יוסף חזינא להו לעיגלי דבי רב הונא יוצאין באפסריהן כרוכין בשבת כי אתא רב דימי אמר ר' חנינא מולאות של בית רבי יוצאות באפסריהן בשבת איבעיא להו כרוכין או נמשכין ת"ש כי אתא רב שמואל בר יהודה א"ר חנינא מולאות של בית רבי יוצאות באפסריהן כרוכים בשבת אמרוה רבנן קמיה דרב אסי הא דרב שמואל בר יהודה לא צריכא מדרב דימי נפקא דאי ס"ד דרב דימי נמשכין קאמר מדרב יהודה אמר שמואל נפקא דאמר רב יהודה אמר שמואל מחליפין היו לפני רבי של זו בזו מהו אמר לפניו ר' ישמעאל בר' יוסי כך אמר אבא ארבע בהמות יוצאות באפסר הסוס והפרד והגמל והחמור אמר להו רב אסי איצטריך להו דאי מדרב יהודה נפקא הוה אמינא אמר לפניו ולא קיבלה מיניה קמ"ל דרב דימי ואי דרב דימי הוה אמינא ה"מ נמשכין אבל כרוכין לא קמ"ל דרב שמואל בר (רב) יהודה: ומזין עליהן וטובלן במקומן: למימרא דבני קבולי טומאה נינהו והתנן [ו] [ז] טבעת אדם טמאה [ז] וטבעת בהמה וכלים [ח] ושאר כל הטבעו' טהורות

דאיתותב דעתיה. להודיעו שלא נתכוונתי: בפרומביא. מי הוי נטירותא יתירתא לגביה או לא: הלכה כחנניא. ולא איכפת לן אי הוי נטירותא יתירתא: יוצאה באפסר. אם תחבו בחקיקת קרן אבל בקשירה בעלמא לא דילמא שלפא מרישה מתוך שראשה דק והיא מתנתקת לכאן ולכאן כשמושכין אותה ואתי לאתויי ארבע אמות ברשות הרבים: תחב לה בזקנה. שקשר שער זקנה כמין נקב ותחב האפסר לתוכו: מנתחא. מתנתקת וקופלת אנה ואנה לברוח מידו: כאיב לה. הזקן שנתלש השער ומכאיבה: תנן התם. בסוף פרקין ולא פרה ברצועה שבין קרניה: לנוי. שצובעה וקולעה לנוי בין קרניה כמין קליעה מקרן לקרן ואינו אוחזו בה: לשמר. שאוחזה בה: אסור. דפרה מינטרא בלא אחיזה אלא מוליכה לפניו וקסבר נטירותא יתירתא משוי הוא: ולשמר מותר. קסבר נטירותא יתירתא לאו משוי הוא: ארבע בהמות. וקס"ד דהכי קאמר באפסר יוצאו' ולא בחטם אלמא נטירותא יתירתא משוי הוא: ומאי חזית. דמסמית הא דשמואל מקמיה ההיא סמי ההיא מקמי הא: דאיתמר. בהדיא דשמואל הוא דשרי וההוא דמחליפין כדאוקימנא דלא (א) למעוטינהו מחטם אלא למעוטי נאקה מאפסר דלא מינטרא ביה: קשרה בעליה. לפרה אדומה: במוסרה. אפסר: במוליכה מעיר לעיר. וכתם פרה פונה למקום מרבץ שלה וצריך לאוחזה כשמוליכה לעיר אחרת ולאו נטירותא יתירתא הוא אלא אורחא היא: שאני פרה. אדומה: דדמיה יקרים. ובעי נטירותא יתירתא משנולדה: יוצאין כרוכין. הרצועה סביב צוארן ואע"פ שאינו אוחזה לאו משוי הוא דלנוי נמי אורחייהו הוא: נמשכין. שמושכה ברצועה הקבועה בטבעת השיר: יוצאין נמשכים. דנטירותא אורחא הוא: ואין יוצאין כרוכים. דלנוי לאו אורחא הוא: כרוכין לימשך. כרוכים בריוח שיכול להכניס ידו בין הכרך לצואר או יניח מעט מן החבל שאם באת לברוח ימהר ויאחזנה: מולאות. פרדות: דאי ס"ד רב דימי נמשכין לחוד קאמר. אבל כרוכין לא ולא אתא לאשמעינן אלא דמולאות משתמרות באפסר ולא הוי משוי להו: מדרב יהודה אמר שמואל נפקא. דקס"ד דקיבלה רבי מיניה דרבי ישמעאל ברבי יוסי: טבעת אדם. שנותן באצבע לנוי: טמאה. דתכשיט הוא וממדין ילפינן דמנה בהן תכשיטין אצעדה וצמיד וגו' ואכולהו קאי תתחטאו אתם ושביכם (במדבר לא): טבעת בהמה. כגון שיר: טבעת כלים. כעין שעושין בראש ידות הכלים: ושאר כל הטבעות. כגון העשויות לדלת: טהורות

אמר שמואל הלכה כחנניא. פר"ח דהלכה כרב דאמר בין לנוי בין לשמר אסור מדמשני אביי ורבא ורבינא דהוו בתראי אליביה ההיא דקשרה בעליה במוסרה ועוד דקיי"ל [ז] דהלכתא כרב באיסורי הלכך אומר הרב פור"ת דכל נטירותא יתירתא אסור כגון פרה באפסר וכל נוי בהמה אסור לצאת ומיהו עגלים יוצאות באפסר כדאמר בסמוך ויוצא סוס ברסן דאורחיה בהכי או באפסר אבל בשניהם ברסן ובאפסר אסור ומותר להשים הרסן או האפסר בראש הסוס בשבת ואין בו איסור טלטול דמוכן הוא לבהמה ואדם המנהיג סוס ברשות הרבים יזהר שלא יוציא ראש החבל מתחת ידו טפח ומה שבין ידו לסוס יגביה מן הקרקע טפח דהכי אמרינן לקמן בפרקין (ב) ומותר לכרוך חבל האפסר סביב צואר הבהמה ולצאת דהא עגלי דרב הונא ומולאות של בית רבי יוצאים כרוכין:

אדרבה תסתיים דשמואל הוא דאמר כו'. תימה לרשב"א מה ראייה מייתי מדאמר שמואל מחליפין לפני רבי כו' דלכאורה משמע דהא דקאמר לעיל לא למעוטי נאקה באפסר דכל זה מדברי שמואל:

קשרה בעליה במוסרה. הוה מצי לשנויי הא מני חנניה היא והא דמשמע בריש הכונס (ב"ק נה:) דמוסרה שמירה פחותה היא היינו דוקא בשור: **או** יוצאין כרוכין. פי' בקונט' דמכוין לנוי וכן פירש במתניתין וקשה לרשב"א ולהרב פור"ת דלעיל משמע דלנוי לכ"ע אסור ותירץ הרב פור"ת דבהא פליגי דרב הונא סבר דנטירותא נמי איכא בכרוכין שאם רוצה הבהמה לברוח יתפסנה בכריכת האפסר ולא הוי משוי ושמואל סבר כרוכין לא הוי נטירותא:

במתניתא תנא כרוכין לימשך. רב הונא מתרץ כרוכים לימשך שיש חבל בין אפסר לצואר שהוא נוח לימשך כשירצה ושמואל סבר לימשך דוקא שיש חבל תלוי באפסר: [ח] **בבאין** מנוי אדם לנוי בהמה. פירש"י ובעודו לאדם נטמא ובחנם פירש כך דאפילו אחר שיחדו לבהמה מקבל טומאה שאינו עולה מלקבל טומאה מכאן ואילך אלא בשינוי מעשה כדמוכח בפ"ק דסוכה (דף יג:) גבי קוצר לאכילה ונמלך לסיכוך ורש"י בעצמו פירש כן בריש במה אשה (לקמן נח:) [ט] וכופת שאור שיחדו לישיבה דאמר טהור אור"י דמיירי כשיש שינוי מעשה:

[ט] **ומזין** עליהם במקומן. איצטריך לאשמעינן במקומן דלא חיישינן שמא תפול הזאה על הבהמה ויפסלו דתנן במסכת פרה (פי"ב מ"ג) נתכוון להזות על האדם והזה על הבהמה אם יש באזוב [לא] ישנה:

וטובלין במקומן. הקשה הר"ר אליעזר אמאי לא מקשה הכא טבילה מאן דכר שמיה כדפריך בריש במה אשה (דף נז.) אמאי דתנן ולא תטבול עד שתרפס ותירץ ר"ת דהכא לא פריך משום דמתני' מיירי בדין כלים שמחלק בין כלי לכלי ואיזה מותר לצאת בו ואיזה אסור ואגב אורחיה אשמעינן שאר דיני כלים ומזין עליהם וטובלן במקומן דכן דרך התנא כי ההוא (לקמן דף סו.) דקיטע יוצא בקב שלו ואם יש בו בית קבול כתותין טמא אבל בריש במה אשה דמיירי בדיני כלים ואשמעינן דין טבילת אשה פריך שפיר טבילה מאן דכר שמיה:

והא

עין משפט נר מצוה

ה א ב מיי' פ"כ מהל' שבת הלכה יא:
ו ג מיי' שם סמג לאוין סה טוש"ע או"ח סי' שה סעיף יז:
ז ד מיי' שם ופ"א מהל' פרה אדומה הלכה ז' סמג עשין רלב טוש"ע א"ח סי' שה סעיף ד:
ח ה (מיימ' פ"כ מהל' שבת הל' ח') טור ושו"ע שם סעיף ה:
ט ו מיי' פ"ח מהל' כלים הלכה ו:
י ז שם הלכה ז:
יא ח שם הלכה ט:

רבינו חננאל

ואמר בין לנוי בין לשמר אסור. ושמואל אמר לנוי אסור לשמר מותר. ומותבנן לרב קשרה לפרה אדומה בעליה במוסרה כשרה. קשיא לרב דאמר לשמור בשבת אסור שנמצאת מוסרה בפרה (מחזי) [משוי]. והמשאוי פוסל בפרה אמאי קתני כשרה. ופריק אביי ורבא ורבינא דאיהו בתרא לעולם לשמר כמשאוי והכא בפרה מורדת ומשום הכי לא היה מוסרה משאוי עליה. אבל כולי עלמא משאוי היא כרב ומדמשני רבינא לאוקמה כרב שמע מינה הלכתא כוותיה דרב: **יוצאין** כרוכין. שהיו אפסריהן כרוכין על צואריהן. ואסיקנא דיוצאין כרוכין וכ"ש נמשכין. מולאות פי' פרדות של בית רבי היו יוצאות באפסריהן כרוכין בשבת. יוצאין בשיר ונמשכין בשיר ומזין עליהן וטובלין במקומן. פי' שיר כעין צמידין. כדמתרגמינן שירין. ואקשינן וכי טבעות של בהמה בני קיבולי טומאה נינהו. והתנן בכלים פ' י"ב טבעת אדם טמאה. טבעת בהמה וכלים ושאר כל

רב נסים גאון

פ"ה **שאני** פרה דדמיה יקרין. במס' ע"ז בפרק אין מעמידין בהמה (דף כ"ד) דברו עלה א) פי דאלך למא קאל ר"א אומר ישראל היו משמרין אותה משעה שנוצרה הסבב מאגא אל תירוץ קאלו עלי טריק אל סואל מנא ידעינן וג' אל גואב אמר רב כהנא כוס אדום מעבירין לפניה בשעה שעולה עליה זכר אי הכי אמאי דמיה יקרין הואיל ושתי שערות פוסלות בה:

חשק שלמה על רב נסים גאון

א) טועת הדברים כך הוא. כי דברו בזה הענין למה שאמר רבי אליעזר לפי מה שבא המירוץ אמרו בדרך שאלה מנא ידעינן ובאה התשובה אמר רב כהנא וכו':

מסורת הש"ס

א) לקמן נד:, ב) [תוספ' פ"ה], ג) ס"א איתו וה"ג מאי הוה עלה אתמר וכו', ד) [לקמן נד:], ה) [שם], ו) כלים פי"ב מ"א, ז) [בכורות מט:], ח) שייך לע"ב, ט) [ג' דבורים אלו שייך לעיל במשנה].

הגהות הב"ח

(א) רש"י ד"ה דאתמר וכו' דלאו למעוטי גמל מחטם אלא: (ב) תוס' ד"ה אמר וכו' לקמן בפירקין. נ"ב דף נד ע"ב:

גליון הש"ס

תוס' ד"ה בבאין וכו' וכופת שאור שיחדו לישיבה דאמר טהור. חולין קכט ע"א. ועי' ב"ב יט ע"ב תוס' ד"ה תיפוק ליה:

תורה אור השלם

א) זֹאת חֻקַּת הַתּוֹרָה אֲשֶׁר צִוָּה יְיָ לֵאמֹר דַּבֵּר אֶל בְּנֵי יִשְׂרָאֵל וְיִקְחוּ אֵלֶיךָ פָרָה אֲדֻמָּה תְּמִימָה אֲשֶׁר אֵין בָּהּ מוּם אֲשֶׁר לֹא עָלָה עָלֶיהָ עֹל: [במדבר יט, ב]

ליקוטי רש"י

ולא ברצועה שבין קרניה. משאוי הוא ואינו תכשיט לה [ביצה כג.]. בין לנוי בין לשמר אסור. דכל נטירותא יתירתא אמרינן משאוי הוא [לקמן נד:].

וּשְׁמוּאֵל אָמַר – **But Shmuel says:** יוֹצְאִין נִמְשָׁכִין – It means that **they may go out pulled** by the leash, וְאֵין יוֹצְאִין כְּרוּכִין – **but they may not go out** with the leash **wrapped** around their necks.[31]

The Gemara cites a Baraisa:

בְּמַתְנִיתָא תָּנָא – **A Tanna taught in a Baraisa:** יוֹצְאִין כְּרוּכִין לִימָּשֵׁךְ – THEY MAY GO OUT with the leash WRAPPED around their necks TO BE PULLED by the leash.[32]

The Gemara records the practice of Sages in this matter:

אָמַר רַב יוֹסֵף – **Rav Yosef says:** חֲזֵינָא לְהוּ לְעִיגְלֵי דְּבֵי רַב הוּנָא יוֹצְאִין בְּאַפְסָרֵיהֶן כְּרוּכִין בְּשַׁבָּת – **I saw the calves of Rav Huna's household go out with their halters wrapped** around their necks **on the Sabbath.**[33]

כִּי אֲתָא רַב דִּימִי אָמַר רַבִּי חֲנִינָא – **When Rav Dimi came** from Eretz Yisrael to Babylonia, **he said in the name of R' Chanina:** מוּלָאוֹת שֶׁל בֵּית רַבִּי יוֹצְאוֹת בְּאַפְסָרֵיהֶן בְּשַׁבָּת – **The mules of Rebbi's household go out with their halters on the Sabbath.**

The Gemara raises a question concerning Rav Dimi's report:

אִיבַּעְיָא לְהוּ – **They asked:** כְּרוּכִין אוֹ נִמְשָׁכִין – Did Rebbi's mules go out with their halters **wrapped** around their necks **or** were they **pulled** by their halters?

To answer this inquiry the Gemara cites further testimony:

תָּא שְׁמַע – **Come, hear** the following evidence: כִּי אֲתָא רַב שְׁמוּאֵל בַּר יְהוּדָה אָמַר רַבִּי חֲנִינָא – **When Rav Shmuel bar Yehudah came** from Eretz Yisrael to Babylonia, **he said in the name of R' Chanina:** מוּלָאוֹת שֶׁל בֵּית רַבִּי יוֹצְאוֹת בְּאַפְסָרֵיהֶן כְּרוּכִים בְּשַׁבָּת – **The mules of Rebbi's household go out with their halters wrapped** around their necks **on the Sabbath.**

The Gemara now questions whether this latter testimony is necessary:

אֲמַרוּהָ רַבָּנַן קַמֵּיהּ דְּרַב אַסִּי – **The rabbinic students said [Rav Shmuel bar Yehudah's statement] before Rav Assi,** and they added: הָא דְּרַב שְׁמוּאֵל בַּר יְהוּדָה לֹא צְרִיכָא – **This** testimony **of Rav Shmuel bar Yehudah is not needed,** מִדְּרַב דִּימִי נַפְקָא – because **it** (i.e. the fact that Rebbi permits halters wrapped around the animal's neck) **emerges from** the testimony **of Rav Dimi.**[34] דְּאִי סַלְקָא דַּעְתָּךְ דְּרַב דִּימִי נִמְשָׁכִין קָאָמַר – **For if it would enter your mind that Rav Dimi meant** only that Rebbi's mules could be **pulled** by their halters, he need not have said anything, מִדְּרַב יְהוּדָה אָמַר שְׁמוּאֵל נַפְקָא – because **[that point] emerges from** the testimony **of Rav Yehudah in the name of Shmuel.** דְּאָמַר רַב יְהוּדָה אָמַר שְׁמוּאֵל – **For Rav Yehudah said in the name of Shmuel:**[35] מַחֲלִיפִין הָיוּ לִפְנֵי רַבִּי – **"They switched** the cases **before Rebbi,** i.e. they asked Rebbi the following: שֶׁל זוֹ בְּזוֹ מַהוּ – If the restraint **of one** type of animal is put **on the other** type of animal, **what is [the law]?** אָמַר לְפָנָיו רַבִּי יִשְׁמָעֵאל בְּרַבִּי יוֹסֵי – **And R' Yishmael the son of R' Yose said before [Rebbi]:** כָּךְ אָמַר אַבָּא – **Thus said my father:** אַרְבַּע בְּהֵמוֹת יוֹצְאוֹת בְּאַפְסָר – **Four animals may go out with a halter** on the Sabbath: הַסּוּס וְהַפֶּרֶד וְהַגָּמָל וְהַחֲמוֹר – **The horse, mule, camel and donkey."** Since it was not reported that Rebbi said anything to the contrary, he apparently accepted this ruling. Hence, from here alone it is evident that Rebbi would allow a mule out with a halter on the Sabbath if it could be pulled by the halter.[36] Rav Dimi's statement (viz. that Rebbi's mules went out with their halters on the Sabbath) would therefore be redundant unless it means that Rebbi's mules went out even with their halters wrapped around their necks. Since this point is evident from Rav Dimi's statement, we do not need to derive it from Rav Shmuel bar Yehudah's statement.

Rav Assi rejects this reasoning:

אָמַר לְהוּ רַב אַסִּי – **Rav Assi said to them:** אִיצְטְרִיךְ לְהוּ – **They** [both the testimony of Rav Dimi and that of Rav Shmuel bar Yehudah] **are needed.** דְּאִי מִדְּרַב יְהוּדָה נַפְקָא – **For if** one were to argue that **[Rebbi's position] can be derived from** the statement of **Rav Yehudah** in the name of Shmuel (viz. that R' Yishmael the son of R' Yose said before Rebbi that a mule may go out with a halter), one could counter: הֲוָה אֲמִינָא אָמַר לְפָנָיו וְלֹא קִיבְּלָהּ מִינֵּיהּ – **I could say that [R' Yishmael] said** it **before Rebbi, but [Rebbi] did not accept it from him.** קָמַשְׁמַע לָן דְּרַב דִּימִי – The testimony **of Rav Dimi** (viz. that Rebbi's mules went out with their halters) is therefore needed to **inform us** that Rebbi did accept that a mule may go out with a halter. וְאִי דְּרַב דִּימִי – **And if** we had only the testimony **of Rav Dimi** הֲוָה אֲמִינָא הָנֵי מִילֵּי נִמְשָׁכִין אֲבָל כְּרוּכִין לֹא – **I could say that this [testimony]** means that the mules could be **pulled** by their halters, **but not** that they went out with their halters **wrapped** around their necks. קָמַשְׁמַע לָן דְּרַב שְׁמוּאֵל בַּר (רַב) יְהוּדָה – The testimony **of Rav Shmuel bar Yehudah** (viz. that Rebbi's mules went out with their halters wrapped around their necks) is therefore needed to **inform us** of this point.

NOTES

even during the week and hence is permitted on the Sabbath (*Rashi;* cf. *Tosafos*).

It emerges that where the leash is dangling somewhat or wrapped loosely around the animal, and thus *could* be used as a restraint, the animal is certainly allowed out with it. Rav Huna's point is that even where it cannot be used as a restraint (i.e. it is wrapped tightly around the animal with no part dangling), it is still permitted.

31. According to Shmuel, the terms יוֹצְאִין (may go out) and נִמְשָׁכִין (may be pulled) should be read together – יוֹצְאִין נִמְשָׁכִין, *they may go out pulled.* That is, they are allowed out wearing a collar only if its leash could be used to pull them. They may *not* go out with the leash wrapped [tightly] around their necks. In Shmuel's opinion, this is not a form of adornment typically used during the week, and consequently, it is forbidden on the Sabbath (*Rashi*).

32. The leash may be wrapped around the animal's neck. However, it must be wrapped loosely so that the owner can insert his hand between the leash and the neck [to pull the animal if necessary]. Alternatively, some part of the leash must be left hanging so that if the animal tries to run away the owner can quickly grasp it (*Rashi*).

This Baraisa supports Shmuel who rules that a collar is permitted only if it can be used to pull the animal. It contradicts Rav Huna, who permits a collar even where it is merely an adornment and cannot be used for pulling [i.e. the leash is wrapped tightly around the animal's neck and no part of it is dangling]. How can Rav Huna rule contrary to a Baraisa? *Ritva* (*MHK* ed.) gives two answers: (a) Rav Huna did not know of the Baraisa. (b) Rav Huna holds that the Baraisa is contradicted by the Mishnah, whose wording "may go out . . . and may be pulled" indicates that the animal may go out with a collar even where it cannot be pulled by it. [See *Tosafos* et al. who interpret Rav Huna's opinion in a manner that does not conflict with the Baraisa.]

33. This shows that Rav Huna implemented his lenient ruling in practice. Alternatively, it shows that he was not concerned about the Baraisa [cited above] which contradicts his ruling (see *Ritva MHK* ed.).

We learned above (note 13) that a cow does not require a restraint of any kind. A halter would therefore be an excessive restraint, which is forbidden according to Rav (Gemara above). How, then, could Rav Huna, who was a student of Rav, allow his calves to go out with a halter? The answer is that young calves, unlike a mature cow, are rebellious in nature and for them a halter would not be considered excessive (*Rashba* ד"ה אמר ליה הכי).

34. Although Rav Dimi said only that Rebbi's mules "went out with their halters," he must have meant that the halters were wrapped [tightly] around their necks, as the Gemara proceeds to prove.

35. The following is excerpted from the discussion which is recorded on 51b.

36. For this is the minimum taught by R' Yose's statement.

דאיתותב דעתיה א"ל חמור שעסקיו רעים כגון זה מהו לצאת בפרומביא בשבת א"ל הכי אמר אבוך משמיה דשמואל הלכה כחנניא תנא דבי מנשיא [א]עז שחקק לה בין קרניה יוצאה באפסר בשבת בעי רב יוסף תחב לה בזקנה מהו כיון דאי מנתח לה כאיב לה לא אתיא לנתוחה או דילמא [ב]זימנין דרפי ונפיל ואתי לאתויי ד"א ברה"ר תיקו [א]תנן התם ולא ברצועה שבין קרניה אמר (ליה) ר' ירמיה בר אבא פליגי בה רב ושמואל חד אמר [ג]בין לנוי בין לשמר אסור וח"א לנוי אסור ולשמר מותר אמר רב יוסף תסתיים דשמואל הוא דאמר לנוי אסור לשמר מותר דאמר רב הונא בר חייא אמר שמואל הלכה כחנניא א"ל אביי אדרבה תסתיים דשמואל הוא דאמר בין לנוי בין לשמר אסור דאמר רב יהודה אמר שמואל מחליפין לפני רבי של זו בזו מהו אמר לפניו [ב]ר' ישמעאל בר' יוסי כך אמר אבא ד' בהמות יוצאות באפסר הסוס הפרד והגמל והחמור לאו למעוטי גמל בחטם סמי הא מקמי הא ומאי חזית דמסמית הא מקמי הא סמי הא מקמי הא [ג](דאשכחן שמואל הוא דאמר לנוי אסור לשמר מותר דאתמר) רב חייא בר אשי [ד]אמר רב בין לנוי בין לשמר אסור ורב חייא בר אבין [ה]אמר שמואל לנוי אסור לשמר מותר מיתיבי קשרה בעליה במוסרה כשרה ואי ס"ד משאוי הוא [א]אשר לא עלה עליה עול אמר רחמנא אמר אביי במוליכה מעיר לעיר רבא אמר שאני פרה דדמיה יקרין רבינא אמר [ד]במורד': הסוס בשיר וכו': מאי יוצאין ומאי נמשכין אמר רב הונא [ה]או יוצאין כרוכין או נמשכין ושמואל אמר יוצאין נמשכין ואין יוצאין כרוכין במתניתא תנא יוצאין כרוכין לימשך אמר רב יוסף חזינא להו לעיגלי דבי רב הונא יוצאין באפסריהן כרוכין בשבת כי אתא רב דימי אמר ר' חנינא מולאות של בית רבי יוצאות באפסריהן בשבת איבעיא להו כרוכין או נמשכין ת"ש כי אתא רב שמואל בר יהודה א"ר חנינא מולאות של בית רבי יוצאות באפסריהן כרוכים בשבת אמרוה רבנן קמיה דרב אסי הא דרב שמואל בר יהודה לא צריכא מדרב דימי נפקא דאי ס"ד דרב דימי נמשכין קאמר מדרב יהודה אמר שמואל נפקא דאמר רב יהודה אמר שמואל מחליפין היו לפני רבי של זו בזו מהו אמר לפניו ר' ישמעאל בר' יוסי כך אמר אבא ארבע בהמות יוצאות באפסר הסוס והפרד והגמל והחמור אמר להו רב אסי איצטריך להו דאי מדרב יהודה נפקא הוה אמינא אמר לפניו ולא קיבלה מיניה קמ"ל דרב דימי ואי דרב דימי הוה אמינא ה"מ נמשכין אבל כרוכין לא קמ"ל דרב שמואל בר (רב) יהודה: ומזין עליהן וטובלן במקומן: למימרא דבני קבולי טומאה נינהו והתנן [ו][ו]טבעת אדם טמאה [ז]וטבעת בהמה וכלים [ח]ושאר כל הטבעו' טהורות

רש"י

דאיתותב דעתיה. להודיעו שלא נתכוונתי: בפרומביא. מי הוי נטירותא יתירתא לגביה או לא: הלכה כחנניא. ולא איכפת לן אי הוי נטירותא יתירתא: יוצאה באפסר. אם תחבו במקיקת קרן אבל בקשירה בעלמא לא דילמא שלפא מרישה מתוך שראשה דק והיא מתנתקת לכאן ולכאן כשמושכין אותה ואתי לאתויי ארבע אמות ברשות הרבים: תחב לה בזקנה. שקשר שער זקנה כמין נקב ותחב האפסר לתוכו: מנתחא. מתנתקת וקופלת אנה ואנה לברוח מידו: כאיב לה. הזקן שנתלש השער ומכאיבה: תנן התם. בסוף פרקין ולא פרה ברצועה שבין קרניה: לנוי. שצובעה וקולעה לנוי בין קרניה כמין קליעה מקרן לקרן ואינו אוחזו בה: לשמר. שאוחזו בה: אסור. דפרה מינטרא בלא אחיזה אלא מוליכה לפניו וקסבר נטירותא יתירתא משוי הוא: ולשמר מותר. קסבר נטירותא יתירתא לאו משוי הוא: ארבע בהמות. וקס"ד דהכי קאמר באפסר יוצאו' ולא בחטם אלמא נטירותא יתירתא משוי הוא: ומאי חזית. דמסמית הא דשמואל מקמיה ההיא סמי ההיא מקמי הא: דאיתמר. בהדיא דשמואל הוא דשרי וההוא דמחליפין כדאוקימנא דלא (א) למעוטינהו מחטם אלא למעוטי נאקה מאפסר דלא מינטרא ביה: קשרה בעליה. לפרה אדומה: במוסרה. אפסר: במוליכה מעיר לעיר. וסתם פרה פונה למקום מרבץ שלה וצריך לאוחזה כשמוליכה לעיר אחרת ולאו נטירותא יתירתא הוא אלא אורחא היא: שאני פרה. אדומה: דדמיה יקרים. ובעי נטירותא יתירתא משמולדה: יוצאין כרוכין. הרצועה סביב צוארן ואע"פ שאינו אוחזה לאו משוי הוא דלנוי נמי אורחייהו הוא: נמשכין. שמושכה ברצועה הקבועה בטבעת השיר: יוצאין נמשכים. דנטירותא אורחא הוא: ואין יוצאין כרוכים. דלנוי לאו אורחא הוא: כרוכין לימשך. כרוכים בריוח שיכול להכניס ידו בין הכרך לצואר או יניח מעט מן החבל שאם באת לברוח ימהר ויאחזנה: מולאות. פרדות: דאי ס"ד רב דימי נמשכין לחוד קאמר. אבל כרוכין לא ולא אתא לאשמעינן אלא דמולאות משתמרות באפסר ולא הוי משוי להו: מדרב יהודה אמר שמואל נפקא. דקס"ד דקיבלה רבי מיניה דרבי ישמעאל ברבי יוסי: טבעת אדם. שנותן באצבע לנוי: טמאה. דתכשיט הוא וממדין ילפינן דמנה בהן תכשיטין אצעדה וצמיד וגו' ולכולהו קאי תתחטאו אתם ושביכם (במדבר לא): טבעת בהמה. כגון שיר: טבעת כלים. כעין שעושין בראש ידות הכלים: ושאר כל הטבעות. כגון העשויות לדלת:

תוספות

אמר שמואל הלכה כחנניא. פר"ח דהלכה כרב דאמר בין לנוי בין לשמר אסור מדמשני אביי ורבא ורבינא דהוו בתראי אליביה ההיא דקשרה בעליה במוסרה ועוד דקיי"ל [ז]דהלכתא כרב באיסורי הלכך אומר הרב פור"ת דכל נטירותא יתירתא אסור כגון פרה באפסר ובכל נוי בהמה אסור לצאת ומיהו עגלים יוצאות באפסר כדאמר בסמוך ויוצא סוס ברסן דאורחיה בהכי או באפסר אבל בשניהם ברסן ובאפסר אסור ומותר להשים הרסן או האפסר בראש הסוס בשבת ואין בו איסור טלטול דמוכן הוא לבהמה ואדם המנהיג סוס ברשות הרבים יזהר שלא יוציא ראש החבל מתחת ידו טפח ומה שבין ידו לסוס יגביה מן הקרקע טפח דהכי אמרינן לקמן בפרקין (ב) ומותר לכרוך חבל האפסר סביב צואר הבהמה ולצאת דהא עגלי דרב הונא ומולאות של בית רבי יוצאים כרוכין:

אדרבה תסתיים דשמואל הוא דאמר כו'. תימה לרשב"א מה ראייה מייתי מדאמר שמואל מחליפין לפני רבי כו' דלכאורה משמע הא דקאמר לעיל לא למעוטי נאקה באפסר דכל זה מדברי שמואל:

קשרה בעליה במוסרה. הוה מצי לשנויי הא מני חנניא היא והא דמשמע בריש הכונס (ב"ק נה:) דמוסרה שמירה פחותה היא היינו דוקא בשור:

או יוצאין כרוכין. פי' בקונט' דמכוין לנוי וכן פירש במתניתין וקשה לרשב"א ולהרב פור"ת דלעיל משמע דלנוי לכ"ע אסור ותירץ הרב פור"ת דהא פליגי דרב הונא סבר דנטירותא נמי איכא בכרוכין שאם רוצה הבהמה לברוח יתפסנה בכריכת האפסר ולא הוי משוי ושמואל סבר כרוכין לא הוי נטירותא:

במתניתא תנא כרוכין לימשך. רב הונא מתרץ כרוכים לימשך שיש חלל בין אפסר לצואר שהוא נוח לימשך כשירצה ושמואל סבר לימשך דוקא שיש חבל תלוי באפסר:

[ח]בבאין מנוי אדם לנוי בהמה. פירש"י ובעודו לאדם נטמא ובחנם פירש כך דאפילו אחר שיחדו לבהמה מקבל טומאה שאינו עולה מלקבל טומאה מכאן ואילך אלא בשינוי מעשה כדמוכח בפ"ק דסוכה (דף יג:) גבי קולר לאכילה ונמלך לסיכוך ורש"י בעצמו פירש כן בריש במה אשה (לקמן נח:) [°]וכופת שאור שיחדו לישיבה דאמר טהור אור"י דמיירי כשיש שינוי מעשה:

[ט]ומזין עליהם במקומן. אצטריך לאשמעינן במקומן דלא חיישינן שמא תפול הזאה על הבהמה ויפסלו דתנן במסכת פרה (פי"ב מ"ג) נתכוון להזות על האדם והזה על הבהמה אם יש באזוב [לא] ישנה:

וטובלין במקומן. הקשה הר"ר אליעזר אמאי לא מקשה הכא טבילה מאן דכר שמיה כדפריך בריש במה אשה (דף נ.) אמאי דתנן ולא תטבול עד שתרפס ותירץ ר"ת דהכא לא פריך משום דמתני' מיירי בדין כלים שמחלק בין כלי לכלי ואיזה מותר לצאת בו ואיזה אסור ואגב אורחיה אשמעינן שאר דיני כלים ומזין עליהם וטובלן במקומן דכן דרך התנא כי ההוא (לקמן דף סו.) דקיטע יוצא בקב שלו ואם יש בו בית קבול כתותין טמא אבל בריש במה אשה דמיירי בדיני כלים ואשמעינן דין טבילת אשה פריך שפיר טבילה מאן דכר שמיה:

והא

מסורת הש"ס

א) לקמן נד:, ב) [תוספ' פ"ה], ג) ס"א אינו וה"ג מאי הוה עלה אתמר וכו', ד) [לקמן נד:], ה) [שם], ו) כלים פי"ב מ"א, ז) [בכורות מט:], ח) שייך לע"ב, ט) [כ' דבורים אלו שייך לעיל במשנה].

הגהות הב"ח

(א) רש"י ד"ה דאתמר וכו' דלאו למעוטי גמל מחטם אלא: (ב) תום' ד"ה אמר וכו' לקמן בפירקין. נ"ב דף נד ע"ב:

גליון הש"ס

תום' ד"ה בבאין וכו' וכופת שאור שיחדו לישיבה דאמר טהור. חולין קכט ע"א. ועי' ב"ב יט ע"ב תוס' ד"ה פיפוק ליה:

תורה אור השלם

א) זֹאת חֻקַּת הַתּוֹרָה אֲשֶׁר צִוָּה יְיָ לֵאמֹר דַּבֵּר אֶל בְּנֵי יִשְׂרָאֵל וְיִקְחוּ אֵלֶיךָ פָרָה אֲדֻמָּה תְּמִימָה אֲשֶׁר אֵין בָּהּ מוּם אֲשֶׁר לֹא עָלָה עָלֶיהָ עֹל: [במדבר יט, ב]

ליקוטי רש"י

ולא ברצועה שבין קרניה. משאוי הוא ואינו תכשיט לה [ביצה כג.]. בין לנוי בין לשמר אסור. דכל נטירותא יתירתא אמרינן משאוי הוא [לקמן נד:].

עין משפט נר מצוה

ה א ב מיי' פ"כ מהל' שבת הלכה יא:
ו ג מיי' שם סמג לאוין סה טוש"ע או"ח סי' שה סעיף יח:
ז ד מיי' שם ופ"א מהל' פרה אדומה הלכה ז' סמג עשין רלב טוש"ע א"ח סי' שה סעיף ד:
ח ה (מיימ' פ"כ מהל' שבת הל' ח') טור ושו"ע שם סעיף ה:
ט ו מיי' פ"ח מהל' כלים הלכה ו:
י ז שם הלכה ז:
יא ח שם הלכה ט:

רבינו חננאל

ואמר בין לנוי בין לשמר אסור. ושמואל אמר לנוי אסור לשמר מותר. ומותבנן לרב קשרה לפרה אדומה בעליה במוסרה כשרה. קשיא לרב דאמר לשמור בשבת אסור שנמצאת מוסרה בפרה (מחזי) [משוי]. והמשאוי פוסל בפרה אמאי קתני כשרה. ופריק אביי ורבא ורבינא דאיהו בתרא לעולם לשמר כמשאוי והכא בפרה מורדת ומשום הכי לא היה מוסרה משאוי עליה. אבל כולי עלמא משאוי היא כרב ומדמשני רבינא לאוקמה כרב שמע מינה הלכתא כוותיה דרב: יוצאין כרוכין. שהיו אפסריהן כרוכין על צואריהן. ואסיקנא דיוצאין כרוכין וכ"ש נמשכין. מולאות פי' פרדות של בית רבי היו יוצאות באפסריהן כרוכין בשבת. יוצאין בשיר ונמשכין בשיר ומזין עליהן וטובלין במקומן. פי' שיר כעין צמידין. כדמתרגמינן שירין. ואקשינן וכי טבעות של בהמה בני קיבולי טומאה נינהו. והתנן בכלים פ' י"ב טבעת אדם טמאה. טבעת בהמה וכלים ושאר כל

רב נסים גאון

פ"ה שאני פרה דדמיה יקרין. במס' ע"ז בפרק אין מעמידין בהמה (דף כ"ד) דברו עלה א) פי דאלך למא קאל ר"א אומר ישראל היו משמרין אותה משעה שנוצרה הסבב מאגא אל תירוץ קאלו עלי טריק אל סואל מנא ידעינן וג' אל גואב אמר רב כהנא כוס אדום מעבירין לפניה בשעה שעולה עליה זכר אי הכי אמאי דמיה יקרין הואיל ושתי שערות פוסלות בה:

חשק שלמה על רב נסים גאון

א) כוונת הדברים כן הוא. כי דברו בזה הענין למה שאמר רבי אליעזר לפי מה שבא הסירוץ אמרו בדרך שאלה מנא ידעינן ובאה התשובה אמר רב כהנא וכו':

The Gemara quotes the end of our Mishnah:

וּמַזִּין עֲלֵיהֶן וְטוֹבְלָן בִּמְקוֹמָן – AND ONE MAY SPRINKLE the ash-water of the *parah adumah* UPON [THE COLLARS] even while they are in their place on the animal's neck, AND one may also IMMERSE THEM while they are IN THEIR PLACE on the animal's neck.

The Gemara asks:

לְמֵימְרָא דִּבְנֵי קַבּוּלֵי טוּמְאָה נִינְהוּ – **Is this to say that [animal collars] are capable of contracting *tumah*?** וְהָתְנַן – **But we learned in a Mishnah**[37] to the contrary: טַבַּעַת אָדָם טְמֵאָה – THE RING OF A PERSON IS capable of becoming *TAMEI*,[38] וְטַבַּעַת בְּהֵמָה וְכֵלִים וּשְׁאָר כָּל הַטַּבָּעוֹת – BUT THE RING OF AN ANIMAL[39] OR OF UTENSILS[40] AND ALL OTHER types of RINGS[41]

NOTES

37. *Keilim* 12:1.

38. I.e. a ring worn on the finger as an adornment. The adornments of a person are susceptible to contracting *tumah,* as is evident from the passage about the war with Midian (*Numbers* ch. 31). It is stated there that when the soldiers returned from the battlefield, Moses told them to purify themselves and their plunder from the *tumah* of the slain corpses (ibid. vs. 19-20). This plunder included *anklets, bracelets, rings, earrings and clasps* [ibid. v. 50] (*Rashi;* see *Rashash* and *Sfas Emes*). [Thus, we see that although a human adornment is neither a garment nor any other type of כְּלִי, *utensil,* it can nevertheless contract *tumah.*]

39. E.g. a collar (*Rashi*).

40. Like those made at the end of a utensil's handle (*Rashi*).

41. E.g. a ring made for a door (*Rashi*) [for decorative purposes or as a support on which to hang things].

דאיתותב דעתיה א"ל חמור שעסקיו רעים כגון זה מהו לצאת בפרומביא בשבת א"ל הכי אמר אבוך משמיה דשמואל הלכה כחנניא תנא דבי מנשיא [א]עז שחקק לה בין קרניה יוצאה באפסר בשבת בעי רב יוסף תחב לה בזקנה מהו כיון דאי מנתח לה כאיב לה לא אתיא לנתוחה או דילמא [ב]זימנין דרפי ונפיל ואתי לאתויי ד"א ברה"ר תיקו [א)]תנן התם ולא ברצועה שבין קרניה אמר (ליה) ר' ירמיה בר אבא פליגי בה רב ושמואל חד אמר [ג]בין לנוי בין לשמר אסור וח"א לנוי אסור ולשמר מותר אמר רב יוסף תסתיים דשמואל הוא דאמר לנוי אסור לשמר מותר דאמר רב הונא בר חייא אמר שמואל הלכה כחנניא א"ל אביי אדרבה תסתיים דשמואל הוא דאמר בין לנוי בין לשמר אסור דאמר רב יהודה אמר שמואל מחליפין לפני רבי של זו בזו מהו אמר לפניו [ב)]ר' ישמעאל בר' יוסי כך אמר אבא ד' בהמות יוצאות באפסר הסוס הפרד והגמל והחמור לאו למעוטי גמל בחטם סמי הא מקמי הא ומאי חזית דמסמית הא מקמי הא סמי הא מקמי הא [ג)](דאשכחן שמואל הוא דאמר לנוי אסור לשמר מותר דאתמר) רב חייא בר אשי [ד)]אמר רב בין לנוי בין לשמר אסור ורב חייא בר אבין [ה)]אמר שמואל לנוי אסור לשמר מותר מיתיבי קשרה בעליה במוסרה כשרה ואי ס"ד משאוי הוא [א)]אשר לא עלה עליה עול אמר רחמנא אמר אביי במוליכה מעיר לעיר רבא אמר שאני פרה דדמיה יקרין רבינא אמר [ד]במורד: הסוס בשיר וכו': מאי יוצאין ומאי נמשכין אמר רב הונא [ה]או יוצאין כרוכין או נמשכין ושמואל אמר יוצאין נמשכין ואין יוצאין כרוכין במתניתא תנא יוצאין כרוכין לימשך אמר רב יוסף חזינא להו לעיגלי דבי רב הונא יוצאין באפסריהן כרוכין בשבת כי אתא רב דימי אמר ר' חנינא מולאות של בית רבי יוצאות באפסריהן בשבת איבעיא להו כרוכין או נמשכין ת"ש כי אתא רב שמואל בר יהודה א"ר חנינא מולאות של בית רבי יוצאות באפסריהן כרוכים בשבת אמרוה רבנן קמיה דרב אסי הא דרב שמואל בר יהודה לא צריכא מדרב דימי נפקא דאי ס"ד דרב דימי נמשכין קאמר מדרב יהודה אמר שמואל נפקא דאמר רב יהודה אמר שמואל מחליפין היו לפני רבי של זו בזו מהו אמר לפניו ר' ישמעאל בר' יוסי כך אמר אבא ארבע בהמות יוצאות באפסר הסוס והפרד והגמל והחמור אמר להו רב אסי איצטריך להו דאי מדרב יהודה נפקא הוה אמינא אמר לפניו ולא קיבלה מיניה קמ"ל דרב דימי ואי דרב דימי הוה אמינא ה"מ נמשכין אבל כרוכין לא קמ"ל דרב שמואל בר (רב) יהודה: ומזין עליהן וטובלן במקומן: למימרא דבני קבולי טומאה נינהו והתנן [ו)][ו]טבעת אדם טמאה [ז]וטבעת בהמה וכלים [ח]ושאר כל הטבעו'

טהורות

רש"י

דאיתותב דעתיה. להודיעו שלא נתכוונתי: בפרומביא. מי הוי נטירותא יתירתא לגביה או לא: הלכה כחנניא. ולא איכפת לן אי הוי נטירותא יתירתא: יוצאה באפסר. אם תחבו בחקיקת קרן אבל בקשירה בעלמא לא דילמא שלפא מרישה מתוך שראשה דק והיא מתנתקת לכאן ולכאן כשמושכין אותה ואתי לאתויי ארבע אמות ברשות הרבים: תחב לה בזקנה. שקשר שער זקנה כמין נקב ותחב האפסר לתוכו: מנתחא. מתנתקת וקופצת אנה ואנה לברוח מידו: כאיב לה. הזקן שנתלש השער ומכאיבה: תנן התם. בסוף פרקין ולא פרה ברצועה שבין קרניה: לנוי. שצובעה וקולעה לנוי בין קרניה כמין קליעה מקרן לקרן ואינו אוחזה בה: לשמר. שאוחזה בה: אסור. דפרה מינטרא בלא אחיזה אלא מוליכה לפניו וקסבר נטירותא יתירתא משוי הוא: ולשמר מותר. קסבר נטירותא יתירתא לאו משוי הוא: ארבע בהמות. וקס"ד דהכי קאמר באפסר יוצאו' ולא בחטם אלמא נטירותא יתירתא משוי הוא: ומאי חזית. דמסמית הא דשמואל מקמיה ההיא סמי ההיא מקמי הא: דאיתמר. בהדיא דשמואל הוא דשרי וההוא דמחליפין כדאוקימנא דלא (א) למעוטינהו מחטם אלא למעוטי נאקה מאפסר דלא מינטרא ביה: קשרה בעליה. לפרה אדומה: במוסרה. אפסר: במוליכה מעיר לעיר. וסתם פרה פונה למקום מרבץ שלה וצריך לאוחזה כשמוליכה לעיר אחרת ולאו נטירותא יתירתא הוא אלא אורחא היא: שאני פרה. אדומה: דדמיה יקרים. ובעי נטירותא יתירתא משנולדה: יוצאין כרוכין. הרצועה סביב צוארן ואע"פ שאינו אוחזה לאו משוי הוא דלנוי נמי אורחייהו הוא: נמשכין. שמושכה ברצועה הקבועה בטבעת השיר: יוצאין נמשכים. דנטירותא אורחא הוא: ואין יוצאין כרוכים. דלנוי לאו אורחא הוא: כרוכין לימשך. כרוכים בריוח שיכול להכניס ידו בין הכרך לצואר או יניח מעט מן החבל שאם באת לברוח ימהר ויאחזנה: מולאות. פרדות: דאי ס"ד רב דימי נמשכין לחוד קאמר. אבל כרוכין לא ולא אתא לאשמעינן אלא דמולאות משתמרות באפסר ולא הוי משוי להו: מדרב יהודה אמר שמואל נפקא. דקס"ד דקיבלה רבי מיניה דרבי ישמעאל ברבי יוסי: טבעת אדם. שנותן באצבע לנוי: טמאה. דתכשיט הוא וממדין ילפינן דמנה בהן תכשיטין אצעדה וצמיד וגו' ואכולהו קאי תתחטאו אתם ושביכם (במדבר לא): טבעת בהמה. כגון שיר: טבעת כלים. כעין שעושין בראש ידות הכלים: ושאר כל הטבעות. כגון העשויות לדלת:

טהורות

תוספות

אמר שמואל הלכה כחנניא. פר"ת דהלכה כרב דאמר בין לנוי בין לשמר אסור מדמשני אביי ורבא ורבינא דהוו בתראי אליביה ההיא דקשרה בעליה במוסרה ועוד דקיי"ל [ו)]דהלכתא כרב באיסורי הלכך אומר הרב פור"ת דכל נטירותא יתירתא אסור כגון פרה באפסר ובכל נוי בהמה אסור לצאת ומיהו עגלים יוצאות באפסר כדאמר בסמוך ויוצא סוס ברסן דאורחיה בהכי או באפסר אבל בשניהם ברסן ובאפסר אסור ומותר להשים הרסן או האפסר בראש הסוס בשבת ואין בו איסור טלטול דמוכן הוא לבהמה ואדם המנהיג סוס ברשות הרבים יזהר שלא יוציא ראש החבל מתחת ידו טפח ומה שבין ידו לסוס יגביה מן הקרקע טפח דהכי אמרינן לקמן בפרקין (ב) ומותר לכרוך חבל האפסר סביב צואר הבהמה ולצאת דהא עגלי דרב הונא ומולאות של בית רבי יוצאים כרוכין:

אדרבה תסתיים דשמואל הוא דאמר כו'. תימה לרשב"א מה ראייה מייתי מדאמר שמואל מחליפין לפני רבי כו' דלכאורה משמע דהא דקאמר לעיל לא למעוטי נאקה באפסר דכל זה מדברי שמואל:

קשרה בעליה במוסרה. הוה מלי לשנויי הא מני חנניא היא והא דמשמע בריש הכונס (ב"ק נה:) דמוסרה שמירה פחותה היא היינו דוקא בשור: **או** יוצאין כרוכין. פי' בקונט' דמכוין לנוי וכן פירש במתניתין וקשה לרשב"א ולהרב פור"ת דלעיל משמע דלנוי לכ"ע אסור ותירץ הרב פור"ת דבהא פליגי דרב הונא סבר דנטירותא נמי איכא בכרוכין שאם רוצה הבהמה לברוח יתפסנה בכריכת האפסר ולא הוי משוי ושמואל סבר כרוכין לא הוי נטירותא:

במתניתא תנא כרוכין לימשך. רב הונא מתרץ כרוכים לימשך שיש חבל בין אפסר לצואר שהוא נוח לימשך כשירצה ושמואל סבר לימשך דוקא שיש חבל תלוי באפסר: [ח)]**בבאין** מנוי אדם לנוי בהמה. פירש"י ובעודו לאדם נטמא ובחנם פירש כן דאפילו אחר שיחדו לבהמה מקבל טומאה שאינו עולה מלקבל טומאה מכאן ואילך אלא בשינוי מעשה כדמוכח בפ"ק דסוכה (דף יג:) גבי קוצר לאכילה ונמלך לסיכוך ורש"י בעצמו פירש כן בריש במה אשה (לקמן נח:) °וכופת שאור שיחדו לישיבה דאמר טהור אור"י דמיירי כשיש שינוי מעשה:

[ט)]**ומזין** עליהם במקומן. אצטריך לאשמעינן במקומן דלא חיישינן שמא תפול הזאה על הבהמה ויפסלו דתנן במסכת פרה (פי"ב מ"ג) נתכוון להזות על האדם והזה על הבהמה אם יש באזוב [לא] ישנה: **וטובלין** במקומן. הקשה הר"ר אליעזר אמאי לא מקשה הכא טבילה מאן דכר שמיה כדפריך בריש במה אשה (דף נז.) אמאי דתנן ולא תטבול עד שתרפס ותירץ ר"ת דהכא לא פריך משום דמתני' מיירי בדין כלים שמחלק בין כלי לכלי ואיזה מותר לצאת בו ואיזה אסור ואגב אורחיה אשמעינן שאר דיני כלים ומזין עליהם וטובלן במקומן דכן דרך התנא כי ההוא (לקמן דף סו.) דקיטע יוצא בקב שלו ואם יש בו בית קבול כתותין טמא אבל בריש במה אשה דמיירי בדיני כלים ואשמעינן דין טבילת אשה פריך שפיר טבילה מאן דכר שמיה:

והא

מסורת הש"ס

א) לקמן נד:, ב) [תוספ' פ"ה], ג) ס"א ליתא וה"ג מאי הוה עלה אתמר וכו', ד) [לקמן נד:], ה) [שם], ו) כלים פי"ב מ"א, ז) [בכורות מט:], ח) שייך לע"ב, ט) [ג' דבורים אלו שייך לעיל במשנה].

הגהות הב"ח

(א) רש"י ד"ה דאתמר וכו' דלאו למעוטי גמל מחטם אלא: (ב) תוס' ד"ה אמר וכו' לקמן בפירקין. נ"ב דף נד ע"ב:

גליון הש"ס

תוס' ד"ה בבאין וכו' וכופת שאור שיחדו לישיבה דאמר טהור. חולין קכט ע"א. ועי' ב"ב יט ע"ב תוס' ד"ה סיפוק ליה:

תורה אור השלם

א) זֹאת חֻקַּת הַתּוֹרָה אֲשֶׁר צִוָּה יְיָ לֵאמֹר דַּבֵּר אֶל בְּנֵי יִשְׂרָאֵל וְיִקְחוּ אֵלֶיךָ פָרָה אֲדֻמָּה תְּמִימָה אֲשֶׁר אֵין בָּהּ מוּם אֲשֶׁר לֹא עָלָה עָלֶיהָ עֹל: [במדבר יט, ב]

ליקוטי רש"י

ולא ברצועה שבין קרניה. משאוי הוא ואינו תכשיט לה [ביצה כג.]. בין לנוי בין לשמר אסור. דכל נטירותא יתירתא אמרינן משאוי הוא [לקמן נד:].

עין משפט נר מצוה

ה א ב מיי' פ"כ מהל' שבת הלכה יא:
ו ג מיי' שם סמג לאוין סה טוש"ע או"ח סי' שה סעיף יח:
ז ד מיי' שם ופ"א מהל' פרה אדומה הלכה ז' סמג עשין רלב טוש"ע א"ח סי' שה סעיף ד:
ח ה (מיימ' פ"כ מהל' שבת הל' ח') טור ושו"ע שם סעיף ה:
ט ו מיי' פ"ח מהל' כלים הלכה ו:
י ז שם הלכה ז:
יא ח שם הלכה ט:

רבינו חננאל

ואמר בין לנוי בין לשמר אסור. ושמואל אמר לנוי אסור לשמר מותר. ומותבנן לרב קשרה לפרה אדומה בעליה במוסרה כשרה. קשיא לרב דאמר לשמור בשבת אסור שנמצאת מוסרה בפרה (מחזי) [משוי]. והמשאוי פוסל בפרה אמאי קתני כשרה. ופריק אביי ורבא ורבינא דאיהו בתרא לעולם לשמר כמשאוי והכא בפרה מורדת ומשום הכי לא היה מוסרה משאוי עליה. אבל כולי עלמא משאוי היא כרב ומדמשני רבינא לאוקמה כרב שמע מינה הלכתא כוותיה דרב: יוצאין כרוכין. שהיו אפסריהן כרוכין על צואריהן. ואסיקנא דיוצאין כרוכין וכ"ש נמשכין. מולאות פי' פרדות של בית רבי היו יוצאות באפסריהן כרוכין בשבת. יוצאין בשיר ונמשכין בשיר ומזין עליהן וטובלין במקומן. פי' שיר כעין צמידין. כדמתרגמינן שירין. ואקשינן וכי טבעות של בהמה בני קיבולי טומאה נינהו. והתנן בכלים פ' י"ב טבעת אדם טמאה. טבעת בהמה וכלים ושאר כל

רב נסים גאון

פ"ה שאני פרה דדמיה יקרין. במס' ע"ז בפרק אין מעמידין בהמה (דף כ"ד) דברו עלה א) פי דאלך למא קאל ר"א אומר ישראל היו משמרין אותה משעה שנוצרה הסב מאגא אל תירוץ קאלו עלי טריק אל סואל מנא ידעינן וג' אל גואב אמר רב כהנא כוס אדום מעבירין לפניה בשעה שעולה עליה זכר אי הכי אמאי דמיה יקרין הואיל ושתי שערות פוסלות בה:

חשק שלמה על רב נסים גאון

א) סוגא הדברים כך הוא. כי דברו בזה הענין למה שאמר רבי אליעזר לפי מה שבא המירוץ אמרו בדרך שאלה מנא ידעינן ובאה התשובה אמר רב כהנא וכו':

טהורות א"ר יצחק (נפחא) [א]בבאין מנוי אדם לנוי בהמה ורב יוסף אמר [ב]הואיל ואדם מושך בהם את הבהמה מי לא תניא [ג]מקל של בהמה של מתכת מקבל טומאה מה טעם הואיל ואדם רודה בהן ה"נ הואיל ואדם מושך בהן: [ד]וטובלן במקומן: והאיכא חציצה א"ר אמי בשריתכן לימא ר' אמי כרב יוסף סבירא ליה דאי כר' יצחק ([א] נפחא) דאמר בבאין מנוי אדם לנוי בהמה כיון דריתכן עבד בהו מעשה ופרחה לה טומאה מינייהו דתנן [ג] כל [ה]הכלים יורדין לידי טומאתן במחשבה ואין עולין מטומאתן אלא בשינוי מעשה סבר לה כרבי יהודה דאמר מעשה לתקן לאו מעשה הוא דתניא ר' יהודה אומר לא אמר שינוי מעשה לתקן אלא לקלקל במתניתא תני במחוללין [ג] שאל תלמיד אחד מגליל העליון את ר"א שמעתי שחולקין בין טבעת לטבעת אמר לו שמא לא שמעת אלא לענין שבת דאי לענין טומאה דא ודא חדא היא ולענין טומאה דא ודא אחת היא [ד] והתנן טבעת אדם טמאה וטבעת בהמה וכלים [ה] ושאר כל הטבעות טהורות כי קאמר ליה איהו נמי דאדם קאמר ליה ודאדם דא ודא אחת היא והתניא[ה] [ו]טבעת שהתקינה לחגור בה מתניו ולקשר בה בין כתפיו טהורה ולא אמרו טמאה אלא של אצבע בלבד כי קאמר ליה איהו נמי דאצבע קאמר ליה ודאצבע דא ודא אחת היא והתנן [ו] [ז]טבעת של מתכת וחותמה של אלמוג טמאה היא של אלמוג וחותמה של מתכת טהורה כי קאמר ליה איהו נמי כולה של מתכת קאמר ליה ועוד שאל שמעתי שחולקין בין מחט למחט אמר ליה שמא לא שמעת אלא לענין שבת [ה] דאי לענין טומאה דא ודא אחת היא [ו] והתנן [ח]מחט שניטל חורה או עוקצה טהורה כי קאמר ליה [ה] בשלימה ובשלימה דא ודא אחת היא [ח] והתנן [ט]מחט שהעלתה חלודה אם מעכב את התפירה טהורה ואם לאו טמאה ואמרי דבי ר' ינאי והוא שרישומה ניכר כי קאמר ליה בשיפא קאמר לי' ובשיפא דא ודא אחת היא והתניא [ט] מחט בין נקובה בין אינה נקובה מותר לטלטלה בשבת ולא [י]אמרינן נקובה אלא לענין טומאה בלבד הא [כ]תרגמא אביי אליבא דרבא בגלמי: **מתני'** [י]חמור יוצא במרדעת בזמן שהיא קשורה בו זכרים יוצאין לבובין רחלות יוצאות שחוזות כבולות וכבונות העזים יוצאות צרורות רבי יוסי אוסר בכולן חוץ מן הרחלין הכבונות רבי יהודה אומר עזים יוצאות צרורות ליבש אבל לא לחלב:

גמ'

רש"י

טהורות. דלאו משום תכשיט מיטמאו דאין תכשיט לכלי וכלי נמי לא הוו אלא תכשיט כלי ומיהו בעודן מחוברות לכלי מיטמו עם הכלי דהוי יד לכלי דכל המחובר לו הרי הוא כמוהו: **בבאין מנוי אדם לנוי** בהמה. מתני' כגון שנעשה שיר זה לתכשיט אדם ובעודו לאדם נטמא ולאחר טומאתו נתנו לבהמה וצריך להטבילו מטומאתו ראשונה שלא יגע בטהרות: **הואיל ואדם מושך בהן** את הבהמה. חשיב ליה כלי תשמיש לאדם: **מקל של בהמה.** שרודין בו את הגמל או את האנקה [ל] אי נמי כעין שעושין להנהיג את הדוב: **של מתכת.** דאילו של עץ פשוטי כלי עץ לא מקבלי טומאה: **מאי טעם.** הרי לורך בהמה: **רודה.** מכה ומייסרה: **והאיכא חציצה.** שטבעת הקבוע בשיר קבוע בו בחוזק ואין המים נכנסין שם: **בשריתכן.** הכה בפטיש עד שנתפשט ונתרחק הנקב סביב סביב: **כרב יוסף סבירא ליה.** דאמר כשהן של בהמה נמי מקבלי טומאה הואיל ואדם מושך בהן הלכך כי ריתכן לאחר טומאה אכתי במילתייהו קיימי ולא פרחה טומאתן דאכתי חזו לבהמה: **דאי כרבי יצחק.** דאמר לא מקבלי טומאה אלא בעודן לאדם טומאה זו שקבלו בעודן לאדם כיון דריתכן ושוב אין נאים לאדם בטלי להו מתורת תכשיט וטהרו מטומאתן: **יורדין לידי טומאתן במחשבה.** מאחר שחישב עליו שיניחנו כמות שהוא עכשיו ולא יוסיף תיקון אחר הוא גמר מלאכתן ומקבל טומאה: **ואין עולין מטומאתן.** מאחר שחישב על העור לעשות שטיח ירד לידי טומאה ואם חזר וחישב עליו לרצועו' וסנדלים לא בטל מתורת כלי [מ] ולא טהר בכך עד שיתן בו אזמל דהוי שינוי מעשה הא בשינוי מעשה מיהא עולה מטומאתו: **לתקן.** וזו היא תקונו לצורך בהמה: **לאו מעשה הוא.** לבטל מתורת כלי: **במחוללין.** מתחלה נעשו חלולין רחבים שיש חלל בדדיקתן שנתן טבעת בתוך טבעת כמות שהוא רחב: **שחולקין.** יש חילוק בהלכותיהן ואיני יודע מהו חילוקן: **אלא לענין שבת.** לענין הוצאת שבת יש חילוק בין יש עליה חותם לשאין עליה חותם כדאמר לקמן בפ' במה אשה (דף נט.): **דא ודא אחת היא.** כל טבעות דין אחד להן: **שהתקינה לחגור בה מתניו.** שקבעה בראש רצועה ועשאה כמין בוקלא שעושין לסרגין של סוסים: **ולקשור בה בין כתפיו.** בתי זרועותיו ברלאי"ר"א: **טהורה.** דהדר הוא לה כטבעת כלים ולא דמיא לאדם מושך בהם שאינו משתמש בה כלום אלא מונחת ועומדת לרצועה ומיהו עם הרצועה מקבלת טומאה אבל אם היה נוטלה ומחזירה אינה מקבלת טומאה לעצמה: **כי קאמר ליה איהו נמי.** דא ודא אחת היא: **דאצבע קאמר ליה.** ולענין שבת יש חילוק: **אלמוג.** עצי אלמוגים והוא נאה: **טמאה.** דבתר טבעת אזלינן ופשוטי כלי מתכות טמאים: **היא של אלמוג טהורה.** דפשוטי כלי עץ הוא: **אלא לענין שבת.** לענין הוצאת שבת יש חילוק בין נקובה לשאינו נקובה דנקובה קתני חייב חטאת ושאינה נקובה כגון אישפינגל"א שהיא תכשיט קתני אינו חייב חטאת בפרק במה אשה (דף מ:): **חורה.** חור שלה: **עוקצה.** פונטא: **חלודה.** רואיר"ה: **והוא שרישומה.** של מחט ניכר דהוי כלי וטמאה. ל"א שרישומה של חלודה ניכר בבגד היינו עיכוב תפירה וטהורה: **בשיפא.** ניסופת בשופינא שקורין לימ"א שאין בה חלודה: **מותר לטלטלה בשבת.** בתר דהא חזיא ליטול את הקוץ ותורת כלי עליה: **ולא אמרו נקובה.** חלוקה להלכותיה אלא לענין טומאה בלבד דנקובה מקבלת טומאה ושאינה נקובה לא: **הא תרגמא אביי.** בפרק כל הכלים: **בגלמי.** שהוא גולם שנקצצה מן החוט ועומדת לינקב התם הוא דכל זמן שלא נקבה אינה מקבלת טומאה דהא לא נגמרת מלאכתה ולענין טומאה כלי מעשה כתיב (במדבר לא) שגמר כל מעשהו ומיהו לענין שבת שריא דזימנין דממליך עלה ומנח לה הכי ומשוי לה מנא לנטילת קוץ אבל מחט שנגמרה מלאכתה כגון אישפינגל"א שאינה עומדת לינקב דא ודא אחת היא לטומאה: **מתני'** מרדעת. בשטי"ל ומניחין אותו כל היום על החמור לחממו דאמרי אינשי חמרא אפילו בתקופת תמוז קריר ליה: **שהיא קשורה בו.** בגמ' מפרש: **זכרים.** אילים: **לבובים שחוזות כבולות וכבונות.** מפרש בגמרא: **צרורות.** דדיהן צרורות פעמים ליבש שמהדקן כדי שלא יחלבו עוד ויתעברו או יהו שמנות לאכול ופעמים לחלב לשמור חלבן שלא יטפטף לארץ וקושרין להם כיס בדדיהן: **ר' יוסי אוסר בכולן.** דמשוי הוא: **חוץ מן הרחלים הכבונות.** שהוא שמירת צמרן שלא יטנף והוי להו תכשיט: **יוצאות צרורות ליבש.** ר' יהודה סבירא ליה כתנא קמא דלאו משוי הוא ומיהו ליבש דמיהדק שפיר וליכא למיחש דילמא נפיל ואתי לאיתויי אבל ליחלב דלא מיהדק שפיר חיישינן:

גמרא

תוספות

והא איכא חציצה. פירש בקונטרס שטבעת תקוע בשיר בחוזק ואין המים נכנסים שם ואומר ר"י דצריך לומר שפעמים מסירים אותן ועושים מהן מלאכה בפני עצמן שאם כל שעה היו קבועים בצואר הבהמה היה הכל חשיב כלי אחד ולא הוי חציצה ור"ת פירש והא איכא חציצה לפי שהוא דבוק בצואר הבהמה:

בשריתכן. להכי לא מוקי לה במחוללין דאין דרך השיר להיות כן:

טבעת שהתקינה לחגור בה מתניו. נראה לר"י דהיינו לחגור מלבושיו שהן רחבים ואוגדם כנגד מתניו בטבעת כעין שפי' בקונטרס לקשור בה את כתפיו:

היא של אלמוג וחותמה של מתכת. וא"ת והא יש בה בית קיבול מקום מושב החותם וי"ל דאין זה בית קיבול דאמרינן בית קיבול העשוי למלאות [ס] לא שמיה בית קבול [י]:

והתניא מחט בין נקובה בין אינה נקוב'. נראה לר"י דלא פריך אליב' דאביי דאיהו הוה מפרש שאינה נקובה היינו שניטל חורה או עוקצה אלא אליב' דרבא פריך דלדידיה לא מצינן לפרש הכי כדמוכח בריש כל הכלים (לקמן קכג.) ותימה לר"י דכיון דלא ידע המקשה דמיירי בגלמי א"כ בלאו הכי תקשה ליה לרבא דפריך בריש כל הכלים (ג"ז שם):

והוא

עין משפט נר מצוה

יב א מיי' פ"ח מהל' כלים הלכה י:
יג ב ג שם הלכה ט:
יד ד מיי' פ"ג מהל' מקוואות הלכה טז:
טו ה מיי' פ"ח מהל' כלים הלכה י:
טז ו שם הלכה ט:
יז ז מיי' פ"ד מהל' כלים הלכה ו:
יח ח מיי' פי"א מהל' כלים הלכה יד:
יט ט שם הלכה טז:
כ י מיי' פ"כ מהל' שבת הלכה י סמג לאוין סה טוש"ע א"ח סי' שה סעיף ז:

רבינו חננאל

הטבעות טהורות. ואוקמה ר' יצחק נפחא בבאין מנוי אדם. כלומר טבעת אדם היתה ונעשה עתה שיר לבהמה. ואוקמה רב יוסף הואיל ואדם מושך בהן. פי' פעמים שמכניס אדם אצבעו באותו השיר ומושך בה הבהמה שנמצאת טבעת העשוי' לאצבעו של אדם. כמו מקל בהמה של מתכת טמאה מפני שמחזיקה אדם ורודה בה כו'. וטובלן במקומה והא עביד חציצה. כלומר כיון שהשירים הללו נושכין זה לזה הרי מקום הנשיכה סתום ואין המים באין בהם. ופריק ר' אמי בשריתכן. כלומר ריתכן באור והטבילן במים בעודן השירין כמו גחלים לוחשות שהמים באין אליהם מכל צד. ואמרינן האי פירוקא דר' אמי דלא כר' יצחק נפחא היא. דאי אליבא דר' יצחק נפחא טבעת של בהמה יורד לקבל טומאה. אפי' אם יחשב עליה להיות טבעת של אדם. וטבעת של אדם אינה עולה מידי טומאה להבטל מעליה תורת כלי אלא בשינוי מעשה כדתנן כל הכלים יורדין לידי טומאתן כו' ואי בשריתכן הנה עשה בהן מעשה ונסתלקה תורת כלי מעליהן. ואין צריכין לא הזאה ולא טבילה. (כי בעינן) [ושנינן] מעשה לסלק תורת כלי מעליהו מעש' לקלקל כגון שבירה וכיוצא בה. אבל ריתוך שהוא תיקון וחיזוק לכלי מתכת כי האי גוונא אינו מעשה לטהר ולא מבטל הטומאה מעל הטבעת. במתניתא תנא במחוללין. כלומר חלולין הן מלשון נבובים אלו השירין. והמים באין בהם מכל צד. ואין שם חציצה: **תנא** (תוספתא פ"ה) ומכניס חבילין לתוך ידו. ובלבד שלא יכרוך לתוך ידו. ובלבד שלא יכרוך ע"ג ידו ולא ישלשל חבלים מידו יותר מטפח: **שאל** תלמיד את ר' אלעזר שמעתי חלוקה בין טבעת לטבעת. א"ל לענין שבת בין טבעת שיש עליה חותם. לטבעת שאין עליה חותם. אבל לענין טומאה כל טבעות דינם אחד. ואסיקנא טבעת של אדם של אצבע של מתכת הכל דינם אחד לענין טומאה. וכן נמי מחט שלימה שיפא [נקובה ושאינה] נקובה הכל דינם אחד לענין טומאה. ואם היא ניטל חרירה או עוקצה או העלת חלודה ומעכבת התפירה (או נקובה) טהורה היא. ואקשינן ולענין (שבת אנה) [טומאה אינה] היא חלוקה בין מחט למחט. והתניא מחט בין נקובה בין שאינה נקובה מותר לטלטלה בשבת. [ולא אמרו כו'] ושנינן הא תרגמה אביי זו הברייתא אליבא דרבא דאמר מחט שניטל עוקצה או חרירה מדלענין טומאה לאו כלי וטהורה היא. לענין שבת נמי לאו כלי ואסור לטלטלה. מתניתא דקתני בין נקובה בין שאינה נקובה מותר לטלטלה בגלומי כלי מתכת היא. כלומר עדיין גולם הוא חוט של ברזל ועדיין הוא צריך לנקבו ולחדר לו עוקם לעשותה מחט. ועכשיו אין לה לא נקב ולא עוקם. ואמרינן זמנין דממליך עליה דהאי גולם ומשוי ליה מנא כמות שהיא. אבל מחט שניטל חרירה שלה או עוקצה לבין גרוטאות זריק לה: **[מתני'] חמור יוצא** במרדעת בזמן שהיא קשורה לו כו'. אוקמה שמואל בשקשורה לו מע"ש. וקיי"ל כוותיה. ומתניתא מסייעא ליה. נתינת מרדעת ע"ג חמור דברי הכל

מסורת הש"ס

א) ברש"י ליתא, ב) כלים פכ"ה מ"ט לקמן נח: סוכה יג: קדושין נט. [מנחות סט:], ג) תוספתא דכלים (ב"מ) פ"ב, ד) כלים פי"ב מ"א, ה) תוספתא שם, ו) לקמן נט: כלים פי"ג מ"ו, ז) לקמן קכג. כלים שם מ"ה, ח) כלים שם, ט) לקמן קכג. [תוספתא שם], י) ל"ל אמרו, כ) [לקמן פב. קטו: קכג. עירובין פח: פסחים יב: סוכה יט. כתובות קי. ב"מ כב. פ: קז. קט. בכורות נה. וע' סוכה כ': ובתוס' שם ד"ה הישן], ל) רש"ל כ' דהאי א"נ שייך אחר דיבור רודה ואינו דרש"י בא להשמיענו ענינו של מקל אבל ודאי דמה שפי' רודה מכה ומיסרה אינו אלא לפי' אחד של רש"י ולא"נ פי' של רודה שמכה בו את הבהמה, מ) לטהר בכך כצ"ל, נ) [ועי' תוס' סוכה יג: ד"ה מהו דתימא ומה שנכתב שם על הגליון ויש ליישב קלת].

רב נסים גאון

והא איכא חציצה. בראש מס' (עירובין דף ד) אמרו חציצין דאורייתא נינהו דכתיב (ויקרא טו) ורחץ במים את כל בשרו שלא יהא דבר חוצץ בין מים לבשרו ועיקר דילה במס' (סוכה דף ו) בפרק א' ובמס' מקוואות בפ' ט': **הא** תירגמא אביי בגלומי.

גליון הש"ס

גמרא ושאר כל הטבעות. עי' כלים פ"א מ"ג בר"ש ד"ה למעלה מן המשכב: **שם דאי לענין טומאה דא ודא אחת היא.** עי' לקמן ס ע"א תוס' ד"ה למאי חזיא: **שם בשלימה.** עי' לקמן ס ע"א תוס' ד"ה הואיל ואשה אוגרת: **תוס' ד"ה היא של אלמוג וכו' לא שמיה בית קבול.** עי' לעיל ד' יז ע"א תוס' ד"ה ועל שאר. סוכה דף יג ע"ב תד"ה מהו דתימא:

ליקוטי רש"י

כל הכלים יורדין לידי טומאתן במחשבה. כגון גולמי כלים דאמר בהכל שוחטין (חולין כה.) כל שעתיד לשוף לשבץ ולגרר ואמר התם דלאכתי חסרון מלאכה הוא וטהורים ואם חישב עליה שלא לשוף ושלא לשבץ הביאתו מחשבה זו לידי גמר מלאכה מכאן ולהבא [קידושין נט.]. [כגון] שחשב עליו לדבר שאין בו חסרון מלאכה כגון עור מתוקן שסתמו למנעלים עומד ואינו מקבל טומאה עד שיעשו המנעלים חישב עליו לעשותו שולחן דאינו חסר שום מלאכה דהשתא מיד ראוי לשולחן מקבל טומאה מיד [מנחות סט.]. [משחישב] עליו שזה יהא גמר מלאכתן כגון שעידו לדרגש או לדולבקי כיון שעידו מקבל טומאה ואלמלי עידו לרצועות וסנדלין אין מקבלים טומאה עד שיגמרו למלאכת הסנדלין [סוכה יד.]. **ואין עולין מטומאתן.** משקבלוה [קידושין שם]. אם נטמאו [מנחות שם]. ממחשבת תורת קבלת טומאה אין עולין במחשבה כגון עידו לשלחן ולדרגש וחישב עליו לרצועות וסנדלין אין מחשבתו מבטלתן מתורת קבלת טומאה [סוכה שם]. מתורת טומאה שירדה להן ואף על פי שעדיין לא נטמאו משנמלך עליהן אין עולין מלקבל טומאה אלא בשינוי מעשה [לקמן נח:]. **אלא בשינוי מעשה.** שיעשה בה מעשה לקלקלם שישברם או ינקבם וכן עד שלא יקבלו טומאה אין עולין מתורת קבלת טומאה שירדו במחשבה זו אלא בשינוי מעשה עד שיתחיל לשוף לשבץ ולגרר [קידושין שם]. כגון נשברו טהרו [מנחות שם]. עד שיתן בו איזמל [סוכה שם]. **אלמוג.** מין עץ הוא ובלע"ז קוראל"ו [ר"ה כג.]. אילן שגדל בים ויקר הרבה וקורין קוריי"ל [רשב"ם ב"ב פא.]. עלי אלגומים. מפרש בפסקים כתוב אחד אומר אלמוגים וכתוב אחד אומר אלגומים אלא אלגומים שמם ונקרא אלמוגים לפי שהיה ממחוגג ונכפף מתוך רכיכתו כמו כוסות שהוא נכפף מתוך חשיבתו [דה"ב ט, י]. **וחותמה.** צורה לחתום בה איגרת או כל דבר סגור [לקמן נז.]. **שניטל חורה או עוקצה טהורה.** דלענין טומאה בטל שם כלי מינה [שם קכג.]. [המשך בדף נג.]

טְהוֹרוֹת – ARE *TAHOR,* i.e. not capable of becoming *tamei.* [1]

The Gemara cites two answers:

אָמַר רַבִּי יִצְחָק (נַפָּחָא) – **R' Yitzchak (Nafcha) said:** בְּבָאִין מִנּוֹי אָדָם לְנוֹי בְּהֵמָה – Our Mishnah is speaking **about [collars] that were transferred**[2] **from** serving as **an adornment for a person to** serving as **an adornment for an animal.**[3]

וְרַב יוֹסֵף אָמַר – **But Rav Yosef says:** הוֹאִיל וְאָדָם מוֹשֵׁךְ בָּהֶם אֶת הַבְּהֵמָה – **Since a person pulls an animal with [the collar],** it is classified as the utensil of a person.[4]

Rav Yosef corroborates the theory behind his answer:

מִי לֹא תַנְיָא – **Was it not taught in a Baraisa:**[5] מַקֵּל שֶׁל בְּהֵמָה שֶׁל מַתֶּכֶת מְקַבֵּל טוּמְאָה – AN ANIMAL'S STAFF[6] OF METAL[7] CAN CONTRACT *TUMAH*? מַה טַּעַם – Now, **what is the reason** for this?[8] הוֹאִיל וְאָדָם רוֹדֶה בָּהֶן – Surely, the reason is that **since a person drives** animals **with [these staffs],**[9] they are classified as utensils of a person. הָכָא נַמִּי – **Here, too,** in the case of animal collars, the same reasoning can be applied: הוֹאִיל וְאָדָם מוֹשֵׁךְ בָּהֶן – **Since a person pulls** animals **with them,** they are classified as utensils of a person.

The Gemara quotes from our Mishnah:

וְטוֹבְלָן בִּמְקוֹמָן – AND ONE MAY IMMERSE [ANIMAL COLLARS] even while they are IN THEIR PLACE on the animal's neck.

The Gemara asks:

וְהָאִיכָּא חֲצִיצָה – **But there is an interposition** between the water and the collar, which renders the immersion invalid![10]

The Gemara answers:

אָמַר רַבִּי אַמִּי – **R' Ami said:** בְּשֶׁרִיתְּכָן – The Mishnah speaks of a case **where he hammered it out,**[11] thus removing the interposition.

The Gemara suggests that this answer conforms with only one of the two explanations given above as to how the animal collar could contract *tumah* in the first place:

לֵימָא רַבִּי אַמִּי כְּרַב יוֹסֵף סְבִירָא לֵיהּ – **Let us say** that **R' Ami agrees with Rav Yosef,** who said that an animal collar is regarded as a utensil of a person. דְּאִי כְּרַבִּי יִצְחָק (נַפָּחָא) – **For if** he agrees **with R' Yitzchak (Nafcha),** דְּאָמַר בְּבָאִין מִנּוֹי אָדָם לְנוֹי בְּהֵמָה – **who said** that the Mishnah refers **to [collars] that were transferred from the adornment of a person to the adornment of an animal,** the following difficulty would arise: כֵּיוָן דְּרִיתְּכָן עָבֵד בְּהוּ מַעֲשֶׂה – **When one hammers out [such collars], he performs an act** that makes a physical change **in them,** וּפָרְחָה לָהּ טוּמְאָה מִינַּיְיהוּ – **and** hence **the *tumah* should depart**[12] **from them** without immersion. דִּתְנַן – **For we learned in a Mishnah:**[13] כָּל הַכֵּלִים יוֹרְדִין לִידֵי טוּמְאָתָן בְּמַחֲשָׁבָה – ALL UTENSILS DESCEND [become susceptible] TO contracting *TUMAH* THROUGH THOUGHT,[14] וְאֵין עוֹלִין מִטּוּמְאָתָן אֶלָּא בְּשִׁינּוּי מַעֲשֶׂה – BUT THEY DO NOT EMERGE FROM THEIR *TUMAH* EXCEPT THROUGH A PHYSICAL CHANGE.[15] This Mishnah teaches that if a *tamei* utensil undergoes a physical change that renders it unfit for its previous use, the utensil ceases to be *tamei* and no immersion is required. Hence, if the collar discussed in our Mishnah became

NOTES

1. These rings are not utensils in their own right. They are only adornments of utensils [or animals] and as such they cannot become *tamei* (*Rashi;* see *Rashi* to 58a ד״ה אין מקבלין טומאה and *Chidushei Maharam Banet*). [The Torah taught that an adornment can contract *tumah* only in reference to the adornment of a person (see 52a note 38).]

The preceding applies only when the ring is no longer attached to the utensil. If it is attached, it is deemed part of the utensil and hence could become *tamei* together with the utensil (*Rashi;* see *Dibros Moshe* 43:3).

2. Literally: come.

3. The collar mentioned in the Mishnah was originally made as an adornment for a human being, and while still serving that purpose it became *tamei.* Afterwards it was put on an animal (*Rashi*).

Rashi specifies that the collar became *tamei* while still being used as a human adornment. This implies that once it is transferred to animal use it can no longer become *tamei. Tosafos* (printed on 52a) object that since the collar was originally made as a human ornament, merely transferring it to animal use does not remove its susceptibility to *tumah.* As stated in the Gemara below, the only way to rid an item of its susceptibility to *tumah* is to physically change it. [See *Pnei Yehoshua* for two explanations of *Rashi.*]

4. A utensil in this context is defined as any object that a person uses. Therefore, since people use an animal's collar [to pull the animal], it has the status of a utensil (*Rashi*).

5. The law that follows is also found in the Mishnah, *Keilim* 11:6 (*Rashash*).

6. A rod used to prod an animal, such as a camel. Alternatively, this is the type of rod used to tow a bear (*Rashi*).

7. The Mishnah specifies metal in contrast to wood. A utensil that lacks a hollow (such as a rod) cannot contract *tumah* if it is made of wood (*Rashi*).

8. Why should an animal's staff be susceptible to *tumah*? After all, it is used only with animals (*Rashi*).

9. A person prods the animal [with the staff in order to urge it on] (*Rashi*).

10. The ring of the collar (see 51b note 7) is so firmly attached that water cannot flow between it and the collar (*Rashi*). [The waters of the *mikveh* must reach the entire surface of the item being immersed for the immersion to be valid.]

The reference is to a ring that is sometimes removed from the collar and used separately. [Thus the collar and the ring are two distinct items.] Otherwise, there would be no need for water to flow between the ring and the collar, since together they would constitute a single utensil (*Tosafos* in explanation of *Rashi;* see *Rashba*).

11. He pounded the collar with a hammer and thereby widened the hole into which the ring was inserted (see *Rashi*).

12. Literally: fly away.

13. *Keilim* 25:9.

14. A utensil is not susceptible to *tumah* until the craftsman has fully fashioned it into its completed form. If it has not yet reached this final stage (e.g. it has not yet been engraved or sanded down), it cannot contract *tumah* (*Chullin* 25a-b). The Mishnah here teaches a qualification of this rule. Sometimes, an incomplete utensil need not actually undergo a physical improvement to become susceptible to *tumah;* it can also reach this status through the craftsman's *thought.* This can occur if the craftsman mentally decides that he does not wish to add anything more to the utensil, and that it serves his purposes to use it as is, in its unfinished state. This thought serves in place of labor to "complete" the vessel, and it then becomes susceptible to contracting *tumah* (*Rashi* here and to *Kiddushin* 59a ד״ה יורדין).

15. In this clause, the Mishnah speaks both of utensils that have already become *tamei* and of those that have merely become susceptible to contracting *tumah.* It teaches that both revert to their previous state only if they undergo a "physical change." In the case of a utensil that has already become *tamei,* the physical change must be one that renders the utensil unfit for its previous use. In the case of a utensil that has merely become susceptible to *tumah,* the "physical change" required is of a less drastic nature: For example, the craftsman must begin to work on the utensil that he previously decided was finished; he must start sanding it, or decorating it. By doing so, he demonstrates that the utensil has not, in fact, reached its final stage of completion [and therefore, it is not yet in a state that renders it susceptible to *tumah*] (*Rashi* to *Kiddushin,* end of 59a).

Rashi (here) illustrates the laws of this Mishnah with the following example: If one decides to use a piece of leather as a mat [a utensil for which it is fit in its current state], that very thought imbues the leather with the legal status of a utensil and it immediately becomes susceptible to *tumah.* However, should he then change his mind and decide to use the leather for straps or sandals, it retains its status as a utensil [although it is incomplete in terms of his present intention]. It is only when he starts cutting the leather that it loses its susceptibility to *tumah.* [If it were already *tamei,* it would become *tahor* at the point that it ceases to be fit for use as a mat.]

טהורות א"ר יצחק (נפחא) [א] בבאין מנוי אדם לנוי בהמה ורב יוסף אמר [ב] הואיל ואדם מושך בהם את הבהמה מי לא תניא [ג] מקל של בהמה של מתכת מקבל טומאה מה טעם הואיל ואדם רודה בהן ה"נ הואיל ואדם מושך בהן: [ד] וטובלן במקומן: והאיכא חציצה א"ר אמי בשריתכן לימא ר' אמי כרב יוסף סבירא ליה דאי כר' יצחק ([א] נפחא) דאמר בבאין מנוי אדם לנוי בהמה כיון דריתכן עבד בהו מעשה ופרחה לה טומאה מינייהו דתנן [ב] כל [ה] הכלים יורדין לידי טומאתן במחשבה ואין עולין מטומאתן אלא בשינוי מעשה סבר לה כרבי יהודה דאמר מעשה לתקן לאו מעשה הוא דתניא ר' יהודה אומר לא אמר שינוי מעשה לתקן אלא לקלקל במתניתא תני במחוללין [ג] שאל תלמיד אחד מגליל העליון את ר"א שמעתי שחולקין בין טבעת לטבעת אמר לו שמא לא שמעת אלא לענין שבת דאי לענין טומאה דא ודא חדא היא ולענין טומאה דא ודא אחת היא [ד] והתנן טבעת אדם טמאה וטבעת בהמה וכלים [ה] ושאר כל הטבעות טהורות כי קאמר ליה איהו נמי דאדם קאמר ליה ודאדם דא ודא אחת היא והתניא [ו] [ו] טבעת שהתקינה לחגור בה מתניו ולקשר בה בין כתפיו טהורה ולא אמרו טמאה אלא של אצבע בלבד כי קאמר ליה איהו נמי דאצבע קאמר ליה ודאצבע דא ודא אחת היא והתנן [ז] [ז] טבעת של מתכת וחותמה של אלמוג טמאה היא של אלמוג וחותמה של מתכת טהורה כי קאמר ליה איהו נמי כולה של מתכת קאמר ליה ועוד שאל שמעתי שחולקין בין מחט למחט אמר ליה שמא לא שמעת אלא לענין שבת [ח] דאי לענין טומאה דא ודא אחת היא ולענין טומאה דא ודא אחת היא [ט] והתנן [ח] מחט שניטל חורה או עוקצה טהורה כי קאמר ליה [י] בשלימה ובשלימה דא ודא אחת היא [כ] והתנן [ט] מחט שהעלתה חלודה אם מעכב את התפירה טהורה ואם לאו טמאה ואמרי דבי ר' ינאי והוא שרישומה ניכר כי קאמר ליה בשיפא קאמר לי' ובשיפא דא ודא אחת היא והתניא [ל] [י] מחט בין נקובה בין אינה נקובה מותר לטלטלה בשבת ולא [מ] אמרינן נקובה אלא לענין טומאה בלבד הא [נ] תרגמא אביי אליבא דרבא בגלמי: **מתני'** [כ] חמור יוצא במרדעת בזמן שהיא קשורה בו זכרים יוצאין לבובין רחלות יוצאות שחוזות כבולות וכבונות העזים יוצאות צרורות רבי יוסי אוסר בכולן חוץ מן הרחלין הכבונות רבי יהודה אומר עזים יוצאות צרורות ליבש אבל לא לחלב:

גמ'

רש"י

טהורות. דלאו משום תכשיט מיטמאו דאין תכשיט לכלי וכלי נמי לא הוו אלא תכשיט כלי ומיהו בעודן מחוברות לכלי מיטמו עם הכלי דהוי יד לכלי דכל המחובר לו הרי הוא כמוהו: בבאין מנוי אדם לנוי בהמה. מתני' כגון שנעשה שיר זה לתכשיט אדם ובעודו לאדם נטמא ולאחר טומאתו נתנו לבהמה וצריך להטבילו מטומאתו ראשונה שלא יגע בטהרות: הואיל ואדם מושך בהן את הבהמה. חשיב ליה כלי תשמיש לאדם: מקל של בהמה. שרודין בו את הגמל או את האנקה [ל] אי נמי כעין שעושין להנהיג את הדוב: של מתכת. דאילו של עץ פשוטי כלי עץ לא מקבלי טומאה: מאי טעם. הרי לצורך בהמה: רודה. מכה ומייסרה: והאיכא חציצה. שטבעת הקבוע בשיר קבוע בו בחוזק ואין המים נכנסין שם: בשריתכן. הכה בפטיש עד שנתפשט ונתרחק הנקב סביב סביב: כרב יוסף סבירא ליה. דאמר כשהן של בהמה נמי מקבלי טומאה הואיל ואדם מושך בהן הלכך כי ריתכן לאחר טומאה אכתי במילתייהו קיימי ולא פרחה טומאתן דאכתי חזו לבהמה: דאי כרבי יצחק. דאמר לא מקבלי טומאה אלא בעודן לאדם טומאה זו שקבלו בעודן לאדם כיון דריתכן ושוב אין נאים לאדם בטלי להו מתורת תכשיט וטהרו מטומאתן: יורדין לידי טומאתן במחשבה. מאחר שחישב עליו שיניחנו כמות שהוא עכשיו ולא יוסיף תיקון אחר הוא גמר מלאכתן ומקבל טומאה: ואין עולין מטומאתן. מאחר שחישב על העור לעשות שטיח ירד לידי טומאה ואם חזר וחישב עליו לרצוע' וסנדלים לא בטל מתורת כלי [מ] ולא טהר בכך עד שיתן בו אזמל דהוי שינוי מעשה הא בשינוי מעשה מיהא עולה מטומאתו: לתקן. וזו היא תקונו לצורך בהמה: לאו מעשה הוא. לבטל מתורת כלי: במחוללין. מתחלה נעשו חלולין רחבים שיש חלל בדביקתן שנתן טבעת בתוך טבעת כמות שהוא רחב: שחולקין. יש חילוק בהלכותיהן ואיני יודע מהו חילוקן: אלא לענין שבת. לענין הוצאת שבת יש חילוק בין יש עליה חותם לשאין עליה חותם כדאמר לקמן בפ' במה אשה (דף נט.): דא ודא אחת היא. כל טבעות דין אחד להן: שהתקינה לחגור בה מתניו. שקבעה ברצועה ועשאה כמין בוקלא שעושין לסרגין של סוסים: ולקשור בה בין כתפיו. בתי זרועותיו ברצלייר"א: טהורה. דהדר הויא לה כטבעת כלים ולא דמיא לאדם מושך בהם שאינו משתמש בה כלום אלא מונחת ועומדת ברצועה ומיהו עם הרצועה מקבלת טומאה אבל אם היה נוטלה ומחזירה אינה מקבלת טומאה לעצמה: כי קאמר ליה איהו נמי. דא ודא אחת היא: דאצבע קאמר ליה. ולענין שבת יש חילוק: אלמוג. עצי אלמוגים והוא נאה: טמאה. דבתר טבעת אזלינן ופשוטי כלי מתכות טמאים: היא של אלמוג טהורה. דפשוטי כלי עץ הוא: אלא לענין שבת. לענין הוצאת שבת יש חילוק בין נקובה לשאינו נקובה דנקובה קתני חייב חטאת ושאינה נקובה כגון איספינגל"א שהיא תכשיט קתני אינו חייב חטאת בפרק במה אשה (דף ס:): חורה. חור שלה: עוקצה. פונטא: חלודה. רוליי"ה: והוא שרישומה. של מחט ניכר דהוי כלי וטמאה. ל"א שרישומה של חלודה ניכר בבגד היינו עיכוב תפירה וטהורה: בשיפא. נישופת בשופינא שקורין לימ"א שאין בה חלודה: מותר לטלטלה בשבת. בתר דהא חזיא ליטול את הקוץ ותורת כלי עליה: ולא אמרו נקובה. חלוקה להלכותיה אלא לענין טומאה בלבד דנקובה מקבלת טומאה ושאינה נקובה לא: הא תרגמא אביי. בפרק כל הכלים: בגלמי. שהוא גולם שנקצצה מן החוט ועומדת לינקב התם הוא דכל זמן שלא נקבה אינה מקבלת טומאה דהא לא נגמרת מלאכתה ולענין טומאה כלי מעשה כתיב (במדבר לא) שגמר כל מעשהו ומיהו לענין שבת שריא דזימנין דממליך עלה ומנח לה הכי ומשוי לה מנא לנטילת קוץ אבל מחט שנגמרה מלאכתה כגון איספינגל"א שאינה עומדת לינקב דא ודא אחת היא לטומאה: מתני' מרדעת. בשטי"ל ומניחין אותו כל היום על החמור לחממו דאמרי אינשי חמרא אפילו בתקופת תמוז קריר ליה: שהיא קשורה בו. בגמ' מפרש: זכרים. אילים: לבובים שחוזות כבולות וכבונות. מפרש בגמרא: צרורות. דדיהן צרורות פעמים ליבש שמהדקן כדי שלא יחלבו עוד ויתעברו או יהו שמנות לאכול ופעמים לחלב לשמור חלבן שלא יטפטף לארץ וקושרין להם כיס בדדיהן: ר' יוסי אוסר בכולן. דמשוי הוא: חוץ מן הרחלים הכבונות. שהוא שמירת צמרן שלא יטנף והוי להו תכשיט: יוצאות צרורות ליבש. ר' יהודה סבירא ליה כתנא קמא דלאו משוי הוא ומיהו ליבש דמיהדק שפיר וליכא למיחש דילמא נפיל ואתי לאיתויי אבל ליחלב דלא מיהדק שפיר חיישינן:

גמרא

תוספות

והא איכא חציצה. פירש בקונטרס שטבעת תקוע בשיר בחוזק ואין המים נכנסים שם ואומר ר"י דצריך לומר שפעמים מסירים אותן ועושים מהן מלאכה בפני עצמן שאם כל שעה היו קבועים בצואר הבהמה היה הכל חשיב כלי אחד ולא הוי חציצה וה"ר פור"ת פירש והא איכא חציצה לפי שהוא דבוק בצואר הבהמה:

בשריתכן. להכי לא מוקי לה במחוללין דאין דרך השיר להיות כן:

טבעת שהתקינה לחגור בה מתניו. נראה לר"י דהיינו לחגור מלבושיו שהן רחבים ואוגדם כנגד מתניו בטבעת כעין שפי' בקונטרס לקשור בה את כתפיו:

היא של אלמוג וחותמה של מתכת. וא"ת והא יש בה בית קיבול מקום מושב החותם וי"ל דאין זה בית קיבול דאמרינן בית קיבול העשוי למלאות [ס] לא שמיה בית קבול [ו]:

והתניא מחט בין נקובה בין אינה נקוב'. נראה לר"י דלא פריך אליב' דאביי דאיהו הוה מפרש שאינה נקובה היינו שניטל חורה או עוקצה אלא אליב' דרבא פריך דלדידיה לא מצינן לפרש הכי כדמוכח בריש כל הכלים (לקמן קכג.) ותימה לר"י דכיון דלא ידע המקשה דמיירי בגלמי א"כ בלאו הכי תקשה ליה לרבא כדפריך בריש כל הכלים (ג"ז שם):

והוא

עין משפט
נר מצוה

יב א מיי' פ"ח מהל' כלים הלכה י:
יג ב ג שם הלכה ט:
יד ד מיי' פ"ג מהל' מקוואות הלכה טז:
טו ה מיי' פ"ח מהל' כלים הלכה י:
טז ו שם הלכה ט:
יז ז מיי' פ"ד מהל' כלים הלכה ו:
יח ח מיי' פי"א מהל' כלים הלכה יד:
יט ט שם הלכה טז:
כ י מיי' פ"כ מהל' שבת הלכה י סמג לאוין סה טוש"ע א"ח סי' שה סעיף ז:

רבינו חננאל

הטבעות טהורות. ואוקמה ר' יצחק נפחא בבאין מנוי אדם. כלומר טבעת אדם היתה ונעשה עתה שיר לבהמה. ואוקמה רב יוסף הואיל ואדם מושך בהן. פי' פעמים שמכניס אדם אצבעו באותו השיר ומושך בה הבהמה שנמצאת טבעת העשוי' לאצבעו של אדם. כמו מקל בהמה של מתכת טמאה מפני שמחזיקה אדם ורודה בה כו'. וטובלן במקומה והא עביד חציצה. כלומר כיון שהשירים הללו נושכין זה לזה הרי מקום הנשיכה סתום ואין המים באין בהם. ופריק ר' אמי בשריתכן. כלומר ריתכן באור והטבילן במים בעודן השירין כמו גחלים לוחשות שהמים באין אליהם מכל צד. ואמרינן האי פירוקא דר' אמי דלא כר' יצחק נפחא היא. דאי אליבא דר' יצחק נפחא טבעת של בהמה יורד לקבל טומאה. אפי' אם יחשב עליה להיות טבעת של אדם. וטבעת של אדם אינה עולה מידי טומאה להבטל מעליה תורת כלי אלא בשינוי מעשה כדתנן כל הכלים יורדין לידי טומאתן כו' ואי בשריתכן הנה עשה בהן מעשה ונסתלקה תורת כלי מעליהן. ואין צריכין לא הזאה ולא טבילה. (כי בעינן) [ושנינן] מעשה לסלק תורת כלי מעליהו מעש' לקלקל כגון שבירה וכיוצא בה. אבל ריתוך שהוא תיקון וחיזוק לכלי מתכת כי האי גוונא אינו מעשה לטהר ולא מבטל הטומאה מעל הטבעת. במתניתא תנא במחוללין. כלומר חלולין הן מלשון נבובים אלו השירין. והמים באין בהם מכל צד. ואין שם חציצה: **תנא** (תוספתא פ"ה) ומכניס חבילין לתוך ידו. ובלבד שלא יכרוך לתוך ידו. ובלבד שלא יכרוך ע"ג ידו ולא ישלשל חבלים מידו יותר מטפח: **שאל** תלמיד את ר' אלעזר שמעתי חלוקה בין טבעת לטבעת. א"ל לענין שבת בין טבעת שיש עליה חותם. לטבעת שאין עליה חותם. אבל לענין טומאה כל טבעות דינם אחד. ואסיקנא טבעת של אדם של אצבע של מתכת הכל דינם אחד לענין טומאה. וכן נמי מחט שלימה שיפא [נקובה ושאינה] נקובה הכל דינם אחד לענין טומאה. ואם היא ניטל חרירה או עוקצה או העלת חלודה ומעכבת התפירה (או נקובה) טהורה היא. ואקשינן ולענין (שבת אנה) [טומאה אינה] היא חלוקה בין מחט למחט. והתניא מחט בין נקובה בין שאינה נקובה מותר לטלטלה בשבת. [ולא אמרו כו'] ושנינן הא תרגמה אביי זו הברייתא אליבא דרבא דאמר מחט שניטל עוקצה או חרירה מדלענין טומאה לאו כלי הוא וטהורה היא. לענין שבת נמי לאו כלי ואסור לטלטלה. מתניתא דקתני בין נקובה בין שאינה נקובה מותר לטלטלה בגלומי כלי מתכת היא. כלומר עדיין גולם הוא חוט של ברזל ועדיין הוא צריך לנקבו ולחדד לו עוקם לעשותה מחט. ועכשיו אין לה לא נקב ולא עוקם. ואמרינן זמנין דמימליך עליה דהאי גולם ומשוי ליה מנא כמות שהיא. אבל מחט שניטל חרירה שלה או עוקצה לבין גרוטאות זריק לה: **[מתני'] חמור יוצא** במרדעת בזמן שהיא קשורה לו כו'. אוקמה שמואל בשקשורה לו מע"ש. וקיי"ל כוותיה. ומתניתא מסייעא ליה. נתינת מרדעת ע"ג חמור דברי הכל

מסורת הש"ס

א) ברש"י ליתא, ב) כלים פכ"ה מ"ט לקמן נח: סוכה יג: קדושין נט. [מנחות סט:], ג) תוספתא דכלים (ב"מ) פ"ב, ד) כלים פי"ב מ"א, ה) תוספתא שם, ו) לקמן נט: כלים פי"ג מ"ו, ז) לקמן קכג. כלים שם מ"ה, ח) כלים שם, ט) לקמן קכג. [תוספתא שם], י) צ"ל אמרו, כ) [לקמן פג. קטו: קכג. עירובין פח: פסחים יב: סוכה יט. כתובות קי. ב"מ כב. פ: קז. קטו. בכורות נה. ועי' סוכה כ': ובתוס' שם ד"ה הישן], ל) רש"ל כ' דהאי ה"נ שייך אחר דיבור רודה ואינו דרש"י בא להשמיענו ענינו של מקל אבל ודאי דמה שפי' רודה מכה ומיסרה אינו אלא לפי' אחד של רש"י ולא"נ פי' של רודה שמכה בו את הבהמה, מ) לטהר בכך כצ"ל, נ) [ועי' תוס' סוכה יב: ד"ה מהו דתימא ומה שנכתב שם על הגליון ויש ליישב קצת].

רב נסים גאון

והא איכא חציצה. בראש מס' (עירובין דף ד) אמרו חציצין דאורייתא נינהו דכתיב (ויקרא טו) ורחץ במים את כל בשרו שלא יהא דבר חוצץ בין מים לבשרו ועיקר דילה במס' (סוכה דף ו) בפרק א' ובמס' מקוואות בפ' ט': **הא** תירגמא אביי בגלומי.

גליון הש"ס

גמרא ושאר כל הטבעות. עי' כלים פ"א מ"ג בר"ש ד"ה למעלה מן המשכב: **שם דאי לענין טומאה דא ודא אחת היא.** עי' לקמן ס ע"א תוס' ד"ה למאי חזיא: **שם בשלימה.** עי' לקמן ס ע"א תוס' ד"ה הואיל ואשה אוגרת: **תוס' ד"ה היא של אלמוג וכו' לא שמיה בית קבול.** עי' לעיל ד' יז ע"א תוס' ד"ה ועל שאר. סוכה דף יב ע"ב תד"ה מהו דתימא:

ליקוטי רש"י

כל הכלים יורדין לידי טומאתן במחשבה. כגון גולמי כלים דאמר בהכל שוחטין (חולין כה.) כל שעתיד לשוף לשבן ולגרר ואמר התם דאכתי חסרון מלאכה הוא וטהורים ואם חישב עליה שלא לשוף ושלא לשבן הביאתו מחשבה זו לידי גמר מלאכה מכאן ולהבא [קידושין נט.]. [כגון] שחשב עליו לדבר שאין בו חסרון מלאכה כגון עור מתוקן סתמו למנעלים עומד ואינו מקבל טומאה עד שיעשו המנעלים חישב עליו לעשותו שולחן דאינו חסר שום מלאכה דהשתא מיד ראוי לשולחן מקבל טומאה מיד [מנחות סט.]. [משחישב] עליו שזה יהא גמר מלאכתן כגון שעידו לדרגש או לדולבקי כיון שעידו מקבל טומאה ואלמלי עידו לרצועות וסנדלין אין מקבלים טומאה עד שיגמרו למלאכת הסנדלין [סוכה יד.]. **ואין עולין מטומאתן.** משקבלוה [קידושין שם]. אם נטמאו [מנחות שם]. ממחשבת תורת קבלת טומאה אין עולין במחשבה כגון עידו לשלחן ולדרגש וחישב עליו לרצועות וסנדלין אין מחשבתו מבטלתן מתורת קבלת טומאה [סוכה שם]. מתורת טומאה שירדה להן ואף על פי שעדיין לא נטמאו משנמלך עליהן אין עולין מלקבל טומאה אלא בשינוי מעשה [לקמן נח:]. **אלא בשינוי מעשה.** שיעשה בה מעשה לקלקלם שישברם או ינקבם וכן עד שלא יקבלו טומאה אין עולין מתורת קבלת טומאה שירדו במחשבה זו אלא בשינוי מעשה עד שיתחיל לשוף לשבן ולגרר [קידושין שם]. כגון נשברו טהרו [מנחות שם]. **עד שיתן בו אזמל** [סוכה שם]. **אלמוג.** מין עץ העולה בקרקע הים ושמו קוראל"ו [ר"ה כג.]. אילן שגדל בים ויקר הרבה וקורין קוריי"ל [רשב"ם ב"ב פא.]. **עצי אלגומים.** מפרש בפסיקתא כתוב אחד אומר אלמוגים וכתוב אחד אומר אלגומים אלא אלגומים שמם ונקרא אלמוגים לפי שהיה ממוגג וכנסף מתוך רכיכתו כמו כוסות שהוא נכפף מתוך חשיבתו [דה"ב ט, י]. **וחותמה.** צורה לחתום בה איגרת או כל דבר סגור [לקמן נז.]. **שניטל חורה או עוקצה טהורה.** דלענין טומאה בטל שם כלי מינה [שם קכג.]. [המשך בדף נג.]

tamei when it was a human adornment (as R' Yitzchak Nafcha asserts) and was subsequently hammered out (as R' Ami asserts), it would no longer require immersion.[16] Our Mishnah however, implies that immersion is necessary.[17] Thus, R' Ami's explanation of the Mishnah is not compatible with that of R' Yitzchak Nafcha.[18] – ? –

The Gemara proposes a way to reconcile R' Ami's answer with that of R' Yitzchak Nafcha:

סְבַר לָהּ כְּרַבִּי יְהוּדָה דְּאָמַר – These opinions can be reconciled if **[R' Ami] agrees with R' Yehudah, who said:** מַעֲשֶׂה לְתַקֵּן לַאו מַעֲשֶׂה הוּא – **A constructive action is not** deemed **an action** that could rid an object of its *tumah*.[19] דְּתַנְיָא – **For it was taught in a Baraisa:** רַבִּי יְהוּדָה אוֹמֵר – R' YEHUDAH SAYS: לֹא אָמַר שִׁינּוּי מַעֲשֶׂה לְתַקֵּן – HE [the Tanna of the Mishnah cited above] SPOKE NOT OF A CONSTRUCTIVE PHYSICAL CHANGE, אֶלָּא לְקַלְקֵל – BUT of a DESTRUCTIVE physical change, i.e. only a destructive physical change can rid an object of its *tumah*. According to this view, since hammering out a collar is a constructive action,[20] the collar remains *tamei* and requires immersion.

The Gemara gives another solution to its original problem concerning an interposition between the *mikveh* water and the collar: בְּמַתְנִיתָא תָּנֵי – **A Tanna taught in a Baraisa:** בִּמְחוּלָּלִין – Our Mishnah is dealing WITH [COLLARS] THAT HAVE wide HOLES.[21]

The Gemara above (end of 52a) quoted a Mishnah about the *tumah* of rings. It now records a discussion that includes this Mishnah:

שָׁאַל תַּלְמִיד אֶחָד מִגָּלִיל הָעֶלְיוֹן אֶת רַבִּי אֱלִיעֶזֶר – A Baraisa[22] states: A CERTAIN STUDENT FROM THE UPPER GALILEE ASKED R' ELIEZER: שָׁמַעְתִּי שֶׁחוֹלְקִין בֵּין טַבַּעַת לְטַבַּעַת – I HEARD THAT THERE IS some legal DISTINCTION[23] BETWEEN ONE type of RING AND ANOTHER, but I do not know what that distinction is. אָמַר לוֹ – [R' ELIEZER] SAID TO HIM: שֶׁמָּא לֹא שָׁמַעְתָּ אֶלָּא לְעִנְיַן שַׁבָּת – PERHAPS YOU HEARD about such a distinction ONLY IN REGARD TO THE laws of the SABBATH.[24] דְּאִי לְעִנְיַן טוּמְאָה – FOR IN REGARD TO the laws of *TUMAH*, דָּא וְדָא חֲדָא הִיא – ONE type of ring IS THE SAME AS ANOTHER.[25]

The Gemara asks:

וּלְעִנְיַן טוּמְאָה דָּא וְדָא אַחַת הִיא – **But** is it true that **in regard to *tumah*, one** type of ring **is the same as another?** וְהָתְנַן – **Why, we have learned in a Mishnah:** טַבַּעַת אָדָם טְמֵאָה – A RING OF A PERSON IS capable of becoming *TAMEI*, וְטַבַּעַת בְּהֵמָה וְכֵלִים וּשְׁאָר כָּל הַטַּבָּעוֹת טְהוֹרוֹת – BUT A RING OF AN ANIMAL OR OF UTENSILS AND ALL OTHER types of RINGS ARE PURE, i.e. not capable of becoming *tamei*.[26] – ? –

The Gemara answers:

כִּי קָאָמַר לֵיהּ אִיהוּ נַמִּי דְּאָדָם קָאָמַר לֵיהּ – **When [R' Eliezer] told [the student]** that there is no distinction between rings, **he too was referring** only **to** the rings **of a person.**

The Gemara asks further:

וּדְאָדָם דָּא וְדָא אַחַת הִיא – **But** even regarding the rings **of a person,** is it true that **one** type **is the same as another** with respect to *tumah*? וְהָתַנְיָא – **Why, it was taught in a Baraisa:**[27] טַבַּעַת שֶׁהִתְקִינָהּ לַחְגּוֹר בָּהּ מָתְנָיו וּלְקַשֵּׁר בָּהּ בֵּין כְּתֵפָיו טְהוֹרָה – A RING THAT ONE PREPARED TO GIRD HIS LOINS[28] OR TO TIE his sleeves BETWEEN HIS SHOULDERS[29] IS PURE, i.e. not capable of becoming *tamei*.[30] וְלֹא אָמְרוּ טְמֵאָה אֶלָּא שֶׁל אֶצְבַּע בִּלְבַד – AND THEY DID NOT SAY that a ring of a person is capable of becoming *TAMEI* EXCEPT in reference to the ring OF A FINGER. Thus, we see that even rings used by people are not all the same with respect to *tumah*. – ? –

The Gemara answers:

כִּי קָאָמַר לֵיהּ אִיהוּ נַמִּי דְּאֶצְבַּע קָאָמַר לֵיהּ – **When [R' Eliezer] told [the student]** that there is no distinction between rings, **he too** was referring only to the rings **of a finger.**[31]

The Gemara asks further:

וּדְאֶצְבַּע דָּא וְדָא אַחַת הִיא – **But** even regarding the rings **of a finger,** is it true that **one** type **is the same as another** with respect to *tumah*? וְהָתְנַן – **Why, we have learned in a Mishnah:**[32] טַבַּעַת שֶׁל מַתֶּכֶת וְחוֹתָמָהּ שֶׁל אַלְמוּג טְמֵאָה – A RING OF METAL WHOSE SIGNET IS OF *ALMOG*[33] IS SUSCEPTIBLE TO *TUMAH*. הִיא שֶׁל אַלְמוּג וְחוֹתָמָהּ שֶׁל מַתֶּכֶת טְהוֹרָה – [A RING] OF

NOTES

16. Once he hammers it out, it loses its beauty. It is no longer fit for its previous use as a person's adornment, and consequently it becomes *tahor* (*Rashi;* see *Rashash*).

17. [For our Mishnah teaches that the collar's immersion is valid.]

18. It is compatible, however, with Rav Yosef's approach. Rav Yosef explained that an animal's collar is susceptible to *tumah* [even if it was never used as a human adornment] because people use it to pull the animal. That use is still viable even after the collar is hammered out (*Rashi*). Thus, the hammering would not rid the collar of its *tumah* and it would still require immersion. Since R' Ami can explain our Mishnah only in conjunction with Rav Yosef's approach, he evidently agrees with Rav Yosef's point that an animal collar is deemed a utensil for human use.

19. R' Yehudah disagrees with the view (presented in note 15) that a *tamei* object becomes *tahor* through any physical change that renders it unfit for its present use (see *Tos. R' Akiva Eiger* to *Keilim* ch. 26 §51). In R' Yehudah's opinion, if the physical change includes some element of improvement, it does not make the object *tahor*.

20. Insofar as it renders the collar fit for an animal (*Rashi;* see *Rashash* and *Dibros Moshe* end of 43:5).

21. Thus, there is a gap between the ring and the collar through which water can pass (see *Rashi* and *Ritva MHK* ed.).

Why did the Gemara not give this solution immediately? One answer given is that it is unusual for a collar to be formed in this manner (see *Tosafos* ד״ה בשריתכן; cf. *Rashba*).

22. *Tosefta Keilim,* section II ch. 2.

23. Literally: [we] differentiate.

24. Regarding the *melachah* of transferring, there is a difference between a ring with a seal and a ring without a seal (*Rashi*). E.g. if a woman wears a ring into a public domain, she is Biblically liable only if it has a seal. If it lacks a seal, she commits only a Rabbinic transgression (see Gemara below, 59b-60a and 62a).

25. I.e. as far as the laws of *tumah* are concerned, all rings have the same status (*Rashi*).

26. See above, note 1.

27. *Tosefta* loc. cit.

28. I.e. to use as the buckle of a belt (*Rashi*).

29. This is a band worn around the sleeve [near the shoulder] that serves to gather in the sleeve (see *Rashi;* see also *Tosafos* ד״ה טבעת).

30. This type of ring is not susceptible to *tumah* because it is only the ring of a utensil [the belt or garment] (see above, note 1). It cannot be compared to an animal collar, which the Gemara above classified as a utensil for human use, because people do not actively use it; rather, it is left in place, holding the belt [or garment] in position.

However, when the ring is joined to the belt or garment, it becomes a part of that utensil and thus contracts *tumah* together with it. This Baraisa refers to such a ring when it is not attached (*Rashi;* see *Ritva MHK* ed.).

31. Regarding the laws of the Sabbath, there is a difference even between one type of finger ring and another (*Rashi;* see note 24).

32. *Keilim* 13:6.

33. I.e. the "wood" of *almogim* (a type of cedar) [see *I Kings* 10:11,12], which looks exquisite (*Rashi*). Some commentators identify it as coral (*Rav* to *Keilim* ibid; *Rashi* and *Radak* to *I Kings* ibid.; see *Bava Basra* 80b-81a with *Rashbam*). [In their view, the reason why Scripture refers to coral as "wood" is possibly that a coral reef resembles a tree in appearance and also because it grows perpetually.]

טהורות א"ר יצחק (נפחא) בבאין מנוי אדם לנוי בהמה ורב יוסף אמר הואיל ואדם מושך בהם את הבהמה מי לא תניא מקל של בהמה של מתכת מקבל טומאה מה טעם הואיל ואדם רודה בהן ה"נ הואיל ואדם מושך בהן: וטובלן במקומן: והאיכא חציצה א"ר אמי בשריתכן לימא ר' אמי כרב יוסף סבירא ליה דאי כר' יצחק (נפחא) דאמר בבאין מנוי אדם לנוי בהמה כיון דריתכן עבד בהו מעשה ופרחה לה טומאה מינייהו דתנן כל הכלים יורדין לידי טומאתן במחשבה ואין עולין מטומאתן אלא בשינוי מעשה סבר לה כרבי יהודה דאמר מעשה לתקן לאו מעשה הוא דתניא ר' יהודה אומר לא אמר שינוי מעשה לתקן אלא לקלקל במתניתא תני במחוללין שאל תלמיד אחד מגליל העליון את ר"א שמעתי שחולקין בין טבעת לטבעת אמר לו שמא לא שמעת אלא לענין שבת דאי לענין טומאה דא ודא חדא היא ולענין טומאה דא ודא אחת היא והתנן טבעת אדם טמאה וטבעת בהמה וכלים ושאר כל הטבעות טהורות כי קאמר ליה איהו נמי דאדם קאמר ליה ודאדם דא ודא אחת היא והתניא טבעת שהתקינה לחגור בה מתניו ולקשר בה בין כתפיו טהורה ולא אמרו טמאה אלא של אצבע בלבד כי קאמר ליה איהו נמי דאצבע קאמר ליה ודאצבע דא ודא אחת היא והתנן טבעת של מתכת וחותמה של אלמוג טמאה היא של אלמוג וחותמה של מתכת טהורה כי קאמר ליה איהו נמי כולה של מתכת קאמר ליה ועוד שאל שמעתי שחולקין בין מחט למחט אמר ליה שמא לא שמעת אלא לענין שבת דאי לענין טומאה דא ודא אחת היא ולענין טומאה דא ודא אחת היא והתנן מחט שניטל חורה או עוקצה טהורה כי קאמר ליה בשלימה ובשלימה דא ודא אחת היא והתנן מחט שהעלתה חלודה אם מעכב את התפירה טהורה ואם לאו טמאה ואמרי דבי ר' ינאי והוא שרישומה ניכר כי קאמר ליה בשיפא קאמר לי' ובשיפא דא ודא אחת היא והתניא מחט בין נקובה בין אינה נקובה מותר לטלטלה בשבת ולא אמרינן נקובה אלא לענין טומאה בלבד הא תרגמא אביי אליבא דרבא בגלמי:

מתני' חמור יוצא במרדעת בזמן שהיא קשורה בו זכרים יוצאין לבובין רחלות יוצאות שחוזות כבולות וכבונות העזים יוצאות צרורות רבי יוסי אוסר בכולן חוץ מן הרחלין הכבונות רבי יהודה אומר עזים יוצאות צרורות ליבש אבל לא לחלב:

גמ'

תוספות

והא איכא חציצה. פירש בקונטרס שטבעת תקוע בשיר בחוזק ואין המים נכנסים שם ואומר ר"י דצריך לומר שפעמים מסירים אותן ועושים מהן מלאכה בפני עצמן שאם כל שעה היו קבועים בצואר הבהמה היה הכל חשיב כלי אחד ולא הוי חציצה וה"ר פור"ת פירש והא איכא חציצה לפי שהוא דבוק בצואר הבהמה:

בשריתכן. להכי לא מוקי לה במחוללין דאין דרך השיר להיות כן:

טבעת שהתקינה לחגור בה מתניו. נראה לר"י דהיינו לחגור מלבושיו שהן רחבים ואוגדם כנגד מתניו בטבעת כעין שפי' בקונטרס לקשור בה את כתפיו:

היא של אלמוג וחותמה של מתכת. וא"ת והא יש בה בית קיבול מקום מושב החותם וי"ל דאין זה בית קיבול דאמרינן בית קיבול העשוי למלאות לא שמיה בית קבול:

והתניא מחט בין נקובה בין אינה נקוב'. נראה לר"י דלא פריך אליב' דאביי דאיהו הוה מפרש שאינה נקובה היינו שניטל חורה או עוקצה אלא אליב' דרבא פריך דלדידיה לא מצינן לפרש הכי כדמוכח בריש כל הכלים (לקמן קכג.) ותימה לר"י דכיון דלא ידע המקשה דמיירי בגלמי א"כ בלאו הכי תקשה ליה לרבא כדפריך בריש כל הכלים (ג"ז שם):

והוא

רש"י

טהורות. דלאו משום תכשיט מיטמאו דאין תכשיט לכלי וכלי נמי לא הוו אלא תכשיט כלי ומיהו בעודן מחוברות לכלי מיטמו עם הכלי דהוי יד לכלי דכל המחובר לו הרי הוא כמוהו: **בבאין מנוי אדם לנוי בהמה.** מתני' כגון שנעשה שיר זה לתכשיט אדם ובעודו לאדם נטמא ולאחר טומאתו נתנו לבהמה וצריך להטבילו מטומאתו ראשונה שלא יגע בטהרות: **הואיל ואדם מושך בהן את הבהמה.** חשיב ליה כלי תשמיש לאדם: **מקל של בהמה.** שרודין בו את הגמל או את האנקה אי נמי כעין שעושין להנהיג את הדוב: **של מתכת.** דאילו של עץ פשוטי כלי עץ לא מקבלי טומאה: **מאי טעם.** הרי לורך בהמה: **רודה.** מכה ומייסרה: **והאיכא חציצה.** שטבעת הקבוע בשיר קבוע בו בחוזק ואין המים נכנסין שם: **בשריתכן.** הכה בפטיש עד שנתפשט ונתרחק הנקב סביב סביב: **כרב יוסף סבירא ליה.** דאמר כשהן של בהמה נמי מקבלי טומאה הואיל ואדם מושך בהן הלכך כי ריתכן לאחר טומאה אכתי במילתייהו קיימי ולא פרחה טומאתן דאכתי חזו לבהמה: **דאי כרבי יצחק.** דאמר לא מקבלי טומאה אלא בעודן לאדם טומאה זו שקבלו בעודן לאדם כיון דריתכן ושוב אין נאים לאדם בטלי להו מתורת תכשיט וטהרו מטומאתן: **יורדין לידי טומאתן במחשבה.** מאחר שחישב עליו שיניחנו כמות שהוא עכשיו ולא יוסיף תיקון אחר הוא גמר מלאכתן ומקבל טומאה: **ואין עולין מטומאתן.** מאחר שחישב על העור לעשות שטיח ירד לידי טומאה ואם חזר וחישב עליו לרצועו' וסנדלים לא בטל מתורת כלי ולא טהר בכך עד שיתן בו אזמל דהוי שינוי מעשה הא בשינוי מעשה מיהא עולה מטומאתו: **לתקן.** וזו היא תקונו לצורך בהמה: **לאו מעשה הוא.** לבטל מתורת כלי: **במחוללין.** מתחלה נעשו חלולין רחבים שיש חלל בדביקתן שנתן טבעת בתוך טבעת כמות שהוא רחב: **שחולקין.** יש חילוק בהלכותיהן ואיני יודע מהו חילוקן: **אלא לענין שבת.** לענין הוצאת שבת יש חילוק בין יש עליה חותם לשאין עליה חותם כדאמר לקמן בפ' במה אשה (דף נט.): **דא ודא אחת היא.** כל טבעות דין אחד להן: **שהתקינה לחגור בה מתניו.** שקבעה בראש רצועה ועשאה כמין בוקלא שעושין לסרגין של סוסים: **ולקשור בה בין כתפיו.** בתי זרועותיו ברצ"יר"א: **טהורה.** דהדר הויא לה כטבעת כלים ולא דמיא לאדם שמושך בהם כלום אלא מונחת ועומדת לרצועה ומיהו עם הרצועה מקבלת טומאה אבל אם היה נוטלה ומחזירה אינה מקבלת טומאה לעצמה: **כי קאמר ליה איהו נמי.** דא ודא אחת היא: **דאצבע קאמר ליה.** ולענין שבת יש חילוק: **אלמוג.** עצי אלמוגים והוא נאה: **טמאה.** דבתר טבעת אזלינן ופשוטי כלי מתכות טמאים: **היא של אלמוג טהורה.** דפשוטי כלי עץ הוא: **אלא לענין שבת.** לענין הוצאת שבת יש חילוק בין נקובה לשאינו נקובה דנקובה קתני חייב חטאת ושאינה נקובה כגון אישפינגל"א שהיא תכשיט קתני אינו חייב חטאת בפרק במה אשה (דף ס:): **חורה.** חור שלה: **עוקצה.** פונטא: **חלודה.** רואיל"ה: **והוא שרישומה.** של מחט ניכר דהוי כלי וטמאה. ל"א שרישומה של חלודה ניכר בבגד היינו עיכוב תפירה וטהורה: **בשיפא.** נישופת בשופינא שקורין לימ"א שאין בה חלודה: **מותר לטלטלה בשבת.** בתר דהא חזיא ליטול את הקוץ ותורת כלי עליה: **ולא אמרו נקובה.** חלוקה להלכותיה אלא לענין טומאה בלבד דנקובה מקבלת טומאה ושאינה נקובה לא: **הא תרגמא אביי.** בפרק כל הכלים: **בגלמי.** שהוא גולם שנקצצה מן החוט ועומדת לינקב התם הוא דכל זמן שלא נקבה אינה מקבלת טומאה דהא לא נגמרת מלאכתה ולענין טומאה כלי מעשה כתיב (במדבר לא) שגמר כל מעשהו ומיהו לענין שבת שריא דזימנין דממליך עלה ומנח לה הכי ומשוי לה מנא לנטילת קוץ אבל מחט שנגמרה מלאכתה כגון אישפינגל"א שאינה עומדת לינקב דא ודא אחת היא לטומאה: **מתני' מרדעת.** בשטי"ל ומניחין אותו כל היום על החמור לחממו דאמרי אינשי חמרא אפילו בתקופת תמוז קריר ליה: **שהיא קשורה בו.** בגמ' מפרש: **זכרים.** אילים: **לבובים שחוזות כבולות וכבונות.** מפרש בגמרא: **צרורות.** דדיהן צרורות פעמים ליבש שמהדקן כדי שלא יחלבו עוד ויתעברו או יהו שמנות לאכול ופעמים לחלב לשמור חלבן שלא יטפטף לארץ וקושרין להם כיס בדדיהן: **ר' יוסי אוסר בכולן.** דמשוי הוא: **חוץ מן הרחלים הכבונות.** שהוא שמירת צמרן שלא יטנף והוי להו תכשיט: **יוצאות צרורות ליבש.** ר' יהודה סבירא ליה כתנא קמא דלאו משוי הוא ומיהו ליבש דמיהדק שפיר וליכא למיחש דילמא נפיל ואתי לאיתויי אבל ליחלב דלא מיהדק שפיר חיישינן:

גמרא

עין משפט נר מצוה

יב א מיי' פ"ח מהל' כלים הלכה י:

יג ב ג שם הלכה ט:

יד ד מיי' פ"ג מהל' מקוואות הלכה טז:

טו ה מיי' פ"ח מהל' כלים הלכה י:

טז ו שם הלכה ט:

יז ז מיי' פ"ד מהל' כלים הלכה ו:

יח ח מיי' פי"א מהל' כלים הלכה יד:

יט ט שם הלכה טז:

כ י מיי' פ"כ מהל' שבת הלכה י סמג לאוין סה טוש"ע א"ח סי' שה סעיף ז:

רבינו חננאל

הטבעות טהורות. ואוקמה ר' יצחק נפחא בבאין מנוי אדם. כלומר טבעת אדם היתה ונעשה עתה שיר לבהמה. ואוקמה רב יוסף הואיל ואדם מושך בהן. פי' פעמים שמכניס אדם אצבעו באותו השיר ומושך בה הבהמה שנמצאת טבעת העשוי' לאצבעו של אדם. כמו מקל בהמה של מתכת טמאה מפני שמחזיקה אדם ורודה בה כו'. וטובלן במקומה והא עביד חציצה. כלומר כיון שהשירים הללו נושכין זה לזה הרי מקום הנשיכה סתום ואין המים באין בהם. ופריק ר' אמי בשריתכן. כלומר ריתכן באור והטבילן במים בעודן השירין כמו גחלים לוחשות שהמים באין אליהם מכל צד. ואמרינן האי פירוקא דר' אמי דלא כר' יצחק נפחא היא. דאי אליבא דר' יצחק נפחא טבעת של בהמה יורד לקבל טומאה. אפי' אם יחשב עליה להיות טבעת של אדם. וטבעת של אדם אינה עולה מידי טומאה להבטל מעליה תורת כלי אלא בשינוי מעשה כדתנן כל הכלים יורדין לידי טומאתן כו' ואי בשריתכן הנה עשה בהן מעשה ונסתלקה תורת כלי מעליהן. ואין צריכין לא הזאה ולא טבילה. (כי בעינן) [ושנינן] מעשה לסלק תורת כלי מעליהו מעש' לקלקל כגון שבירה וכיוצא בה. אבל ריתוך שהוא תיקון וחיזוק לכלי מתכת כי האי גוונא אינו מעשה לטהר ולא מבטל הטומאה מעל הטבעת. במתניתא תנא במחוללין. כלומר חלולין הן מלשון נבובים אלו השירין. והמים באין בהם מכל צד. ואין שם חציצה: תנא (תוספתא פ"ה) ומכניס חבילין לתוך ידו. ובלבד שלא יכרוך לתוך ידו. ובלבד שלא יכרוך ע"ג ידו ולא ישלשל חבלים מידו יתר מטפח: שאל תלמיד את ר' אלעזר שמעתי חלוקה בין טבעת לטבעת. א"ל לענין שבת בין טבעת שיש עליה חותם. לטבעת שאין עליה חותם. אבל לענין טומאה כל טבעות דינם אחד. ואסיקנא טבעת של אדם של אצבע של מתכת הכל דינם אחד לענין טומאה. וכן נמי מחט שלימה שיפא [נקובה ושאינה] נקובה הכל דינם אחד לענין טומאה. ואם היא ניטל חרירה או עוקצה או העלת חלודה ומעכבת התפירה (או נקובה) טהורה היא. ואקשינן ולענין (שבת אנה) [טומאה אינה] היא חלוקה בין מחט למחט. והתניא מחט בין נקובה בין שאינה נקובה מותר לטלטלה בשבת. [ולא אמרו כו'] ושנינן הא תרגמה אביי זו הברייתא אליבא דרבא דאמר מחט שניטל עוקצה או חרירה מדלענין טומאה לאו כלי הוא וטהורה היא. לענין שבת נמי לאו כלי ואסור לטלטלה. מתניתא דקתני בין נקובה בין שאינה נקובה מותר לטלטלה בגלומי כלי מתכת היא. כלומר עדיין גולם הוא חוט של ברזל ועדיין הוא צריך לנקבו ולחרר לו עוקם לעשותה מחט. ועכשיו אין לה לא נקב ולא עוקם. ואמרינן זמנין דמימליך עליה דהאי גולם ומשוי ליה מנא כמות שהיא. אבל מחט שניטל חרירה שלה או עוקצה לבין גרוטאות זריק לה: **[מתני'] חמור יוצא** במרדעת בזמן שהיא קשורה לו כו'. אוקמה שמואל בשקשורה לו מע"ש. וקיי"ל כוותיה. ומתניתא מסייעא ליה. נתינת מרדעת ע"ג חמור דברי הכל

מסורת הש"ס

א) ברש"י ליתא, ב) כלים פכ"ה מ"ט לקמן נח: סוכה יג: קדושין נט. [מנחות סט:], ג) תוספתא דכלים (ב"מ) פ"ב, ד) כלים פי"ב מ"א, ה) תוספתא שם, ו) לקמן נט: כלים פי"ג מ"ו, ז) לקמן קכג. כלים שם מ"ה, ח) כלים שם, ט) לקמן קכג. [תוספתא שם], י) נ"ל אמרו, כ) [לקמן פב. קטו: קכג. עירובין פח: פסחים יב: סוכה יט. כתובות קי. ב"מ כב. פ: קז. קטו. בכורות נה. וע' סוכה כ': ובתוס' שם ד"ה הישן], ל) רש"ל כ' דהאי א"נ שייך אחר דיבור רודה ואינו דרש"י בא להשמיעו ענינו של מקל אבל ודאי דמה שפי' רודה מכה ומיסרה אינו אלא לפי' אחד של רש"י ולא"נ פי' של רודה שמכה בו את הבהמה, מ) לטהר בכך כצ"ל, נ) [ועי' תוס' סוכה יב: ד"ה מהו דתימא ומה שנכתב שם על הגליון ויש ליישב קצת].

רב נסים גאון

והא איכא חציצה. בראש מס' (עירובין דף ד) אמרו חציצין דאורייתא נינהו דכתיב (ויקרא טו) ורחץ במים את כל בשרו שלא יהא דבר חוצץ בין מים לבשרו ועיקר דילה במס' (סוכה דף ו) בפרק א' ובמס' מקוואות בפ' ט': **הא** תירגמא אביי בגלומי.

גליון הש"ס

גמרא ושאר כל הטבעות. עי' כלים פ"א מ"ג בר"ש ד"ה למעלה מן המשכב: **שם דאי לענין טומאה דא ודא אחת היא.** עי' לקמן ס ע"א תוס' ד"ה למאי חזיא: **שם בשלימה.** עי' לקמן ס ע"א תוס' ד"ה הואיל ואשה אוגרת: **תוס' ד"ה היא של אלמוג וכו' לא שמיה בית קבול.** עי' לעיל ד' יז ע"א תוס' ד"ה ועל שאר. סוכה דף יב ע"ב תד"ה מהו דתימא:

ליקוטי רש"י

כל הכלים יורדין לידי טומאתן במחשבה. כגון גולמי כלים דאמר בהכל שוחטין (חולין כה.) כל שעתיד לשוף לשבץ ולגרר ואמר התם דאכתי חסרון מלאכה הוא וטהורים ואם חישב עליה שלא לשוף ושלא לשבץ הביאתו מחשבה זו לידי גמר מלאכה מכאן ולהבא [קידושין נט.]. [כגון] שחשב עליו לדבר שאין בו חסרון מלאכה כגון עור מתוקן סתמו למנעלים עומד ואינו מקבל טומאה עד שיעשו המנעלים חישב עליו לעשותו שולחן דאינו חסר שום מלאכה דהשתא מיד ראוי לשולחן מקבל טומאה מיד [מנחות סט.]. [משחישב] עליו שזה יהא גמר מלאכתן כגון שעידו לדרגש או לדולבקי כיון שעידו מקבל טומאה ואלמלי עידו לרצועות וסנדלין אין מקבלים טומאה עד שיגמרו למלאכת הסנדלין [סוכה יד.]. **ואין עולין מטומאתן.** משקבלוה [קידושין שם]. אם נטמאו [מנחות שם]. ממחשבת תורת קבלת טומאה אין עולין במחשבה כגון עידו לשלחן ולדרגש וחישב עליו לרצועות וסנדלין אין מחשבתו מבטלתן מתורת קבלת טומאה [סוכה שם]. מתורת טומאה שירדה להן ואף על פי שעדיין לא נטמאו משנמלך עליהן אין עולין מלקבל טומאה אלא בשינוי מעשה [לקמן נח:]. **אלא בשינוי מעשה.** שיעשה בה מעשה לקלקלם שישברם או ינקבם וכן עד שלא יקבלו טומאה אין עולין מתורת קבלת טומאה שירדו במחשבה זו אלא בשינוי מעשה עד שיתחיל לשוף לשבץ ולגרר [קידושין שם]. כגון נשברו טהרו [מנחות שם]. עד שיתן בו איזמל [סוכה שם]. **אלמוג.** מין עץ העולה בקרקע הים ושמו קורא"ל"ו [ר"ה כג.]. אילן שגדל בים ויקר הרבה וקורין קוריי"ל [רשב"ם ב"ב פא.]. **עצי אלגומים.** מפרש בפסיקת' כתוב אחד אומר אלמוגים וכתוב אחד אומר אלגומים אלא אלגומים שמם ונקרא אלמוגים לפי שהיה מתמוגג ונכפף מתוך רכיכתו כמו כוסות שהוא נכפף מתוך חשיבתו [דה"ב ט, י]. **וחותמה.** צורה לחתום בה איגרת או כל דבר סגור [לקמן נז.]. **שניטל חורה או עוקצה טהורה.** דלענין טומאה בטל שם כלי מינה [שם קכג.]. [המשך בדף נג.]

***ALMOG* WHOSE SIGNET IS OF METAL IS *TAHOR*,** i.e. not capable of becoming *tamei*.[34]

The Gemara answers:

כִּי קָאָמַר לֵיהּ אִיהוּ נַמִּי כּוּלָּהּ שֶׁל מַתֶּכֶת קָאָמַר לֵיהּ – **When [R' Eliezer] told [the student]** that there is no distinction between rings, **he too was referring** only **to** finger rings made **entirely of metal.**[35]

The Baraisa continues with a similar discussion regarding needles:

וְעוֹד שָׁאַל – [THE STUDENT] ASKED R' Eliezer FURTHER: שָׁמַעְתִּי שֶׁחוֹלְקִין בֵּין מַחַט לְמַחַט – I HEARD THAT THERE IS some legal DISTINCTION BETWEEN ONE type of NEEDLE[36] AND ANOTHER, but I do not know what the distinction is. אָמַר לֵיהּ – [R' ELIEZER] SAID TO HIM: שֶׁמָּא לֹא שָׁמַעְתָּ אֶלָּא לְעִנְיַן שַׁבָּת – PERHAPS YOU HEARD about such a distinction ONLY IN REGARD TO THE laws of the SABBATH.[37] דְּאִי לְעִנְיַן טוּמְאָה דָּא וְדָא אַחַת הִיא – FOR IN REGARD TO the laws of *TUMAH*, ONE type of needle IS THE SAME AS ANOTHER.

The Gemara asks:

וּלְעִנְיַן טוּמְאָה דָּא וְדָא אַחַת הִיא – **But** is it true that **in regard to** ***tumah*****, one** type of needle **is the same as another?** וְהָתְנַן – **Why, we have learned in a Mishnah:**[38] מַחַט שֶׁנִּיטַּל חוּרָהּ אוֹ עוּקְצָהּ טְהוֹרָה – A NEEDLE WHOSE EYE OR POINT HAS BEEN REMOVED IS PURE, i.e. cannot become *tamei*.[39] A complete needle, however, can become *tamei*. This shows that in regard to *tumah* as well not all needles are the same. – ? –

The Gemara answers:

כִּי קָאָמַר לֵיהּ בִּשְׁלֵימָה – **When [R' Eliezer] told [the student]** that there is no distinction between needles, he was referring **to a complete [needle].**

The Gemara asks further:

וּבִשְׁלֵימָה דָּא וְדָא אַחַת הִיא – **But** even **regarding a complete [needle],** is it true that **one** type of needle **is the same as another** with respect to *tumah*? וְהָתְנַן – **Why, we have learned in a Mishnah:**[40] מַחַט שֶׁהֶעֶלְתָה חֲלוּדָה – The law of A NEEDLE THAT HAS BECOME RUSTY is as follows: אִם מְעַכֵּב אֶת הַתְּפִירָה טְהוֹרָה – IF it is so rusty that IT OBSTRUCTS THE SEWING, IT IS *TAHOR*.[41] וְאִם לָאו טְמֵאָה – BUT IF it does NOT obstruct the sewing, IT IS *TAMEI*.

The Gemara adds parenthetically:

וְאָמְרֵי דְּבֵי רַבִּי יַנַּאי – **And** the scholars **of the academy of R' Yannai said:** וְהוּא שֶׁרִישׁוּמָהּ נִכָּר – **But this** law **applies** only **where its impression is discernible.**[42]

At any rate, we see that even among complete needles there is a difference between one needle and another with respect to *tumah*. – ? –

The Gemara answers:

כִּי קָאָמַר לֵיהּ בְּשִׁיפָא קָאָמַר לֵיהּ – **When [R' Eliezer] told [the student]** that there is no distinction between needles, **he was referring** only **to a polished [needle],** which is not rusty.

The Gemara asks further:

וּבְשִׁיפָא דָּא וְדָא אַחַת הִיא – **But** even **regarding a polished [needle],** is it true that **one** type of needle **is the same as another** with respect to *tumah*? וְהָתַנְיָא – **Why, it was taught in a Baraisa:**[43] מַחַט בֵּין נְקוּבָה בֵּין אֵינָהּ נְקוּבָה – WHETHER A NEEDLE IS PIERCED (i.e. it has an eye) OR IT IS NOT PIERCED, מוּתָּר לְטַלְטְלָהּ בְּשַׁבָּת – ONE IS PERMITTED TO MOVE IT ON THE SABBATH.[44] וְלָא אָמְרִינַן נְקוּבָה אֶלָּא לְעִנְיַן טוּמְאָה בִּלְבַד – AND WE DO NOT SAY that BEING PIERCED makes a difference EXCEPT IN REGARD TO the laws of *TUMAH*.[45] Thus, we see that even complete polished needles are not all the same with respect to *tumah*. – ? –

The Gemara answers:

הָא תַּרְגְּמָא אַבַּיֵי אַלִּיבָּא דְּרָבָא בְּגָלְמֵי – **But Abaye has explained [that Baraisa] in accordance with** the opinion **of Rava** as referring **to unfinished [needles].**[46]

Mishnah

The Mishnah continues enumerating cases in which a person may let his animal out into a public domain on the Sabbath:

חֲמוֹר יוֹצֵא בְּמַרְדַּעַת בִּזְמַן שֶׁהִיא קְשׁוּרָה בּוֹ – **A donkey may go out with a saddle cloth**[47] **when it is tied onto**

NOTES

34. The determinant is the material of the main part of the ring. Utensils or jewelry that have no hollow or indentation [such as a ring] are susceptible to *tumah* only if they are made of metal, and not if they are made of wood (see *Keilim* 2:1 and 11:1). Since *almog* is legally classified as wood [see previous note], a ring of this material cannot become *tamei* (*Rashi;* see Gemara below, 59b-60a, for a dissenting opinon).

Tosafos explain that the indentation in the ring into which the seal is fitted is disregarded, because it was made to be permanently filled. (See, however, *Tosafos* to *Sukkah* 12b ד״ה מהו; see also *Sfas Emes* and *Meromei Sadeh* here.)

35. All such rings are susceptible to *tumah.*

36. [The Hebrew word מַחַט signifies both needles and pins. For the sake of brevity, we will translate it simply as "needle."]

37. A woman who wears a needle that has an eye (a sewing needle) into a public domain on the Sabbath commits a Biblical transgression [Mishnah below, 62a]. However, a woman who wears a "needle" that does not have an eye (a decorative pin) is not Biblically liable [Mishnah, 57a; see Gemara on 60a] (*Rashi*).

38. *Keilim* 13:5.

39. [Since it is no longer fit for its previous use, even if it were actually *tamei,* it is now *tahor* (see note 15).]

40. *Keilim* ibid.

41. See note 39.

42. That is, even if the needle is usable, it is not considered a utensil [and hence susceptible to *tumah*] unless its shape is still discernible beneath the rust.

Alternatively, the Gemara is qualifying the first part of the Mishnah: A rusty needle is considered unusable only if it is so corroded that it leaves an "impression" (i.e a stain) of rust on the cloth (*Rashi*).

43. *Mesoras HaShas* refers to *Tosefta Keilim,* section II ch. 2.

44. [I.e. it is not *muktzeh* and hence may be moved within a private domain.] Since even a needle without any eye can be used to extract a thorn, it has the status of a utensil (*Rashi;* see *Orach Chaim* 308:11).

45. At this point, the Gemara apparently holds that a needle without an eye (a pin) is not classified as a utensil in regard to *tumah* (see *Meromei Sadeh*).

The Gemara could have challenged R' Eliezer with this Baraisa immediately. However, it chose first to raise objections that were based on Mishnahs, rather than on Baraisos (see *Maharsha*).

46. In the Gemara below (123a), Abaye defends an opinion of Rava by explaining our Baraisa as speaking of an unfinished needle, i.e. one in which an eye has not yet been formed. Such a "needle" is not susceptible to *tumah,* because the Torah (*Numbers* 31:51) specifies כְּלִי מַעֲשֶׂה, *a fashioned utensil,* which implies a utensil that is completely finished [for its originally intended purpose]. In regard to the laws of *muktzeh,* however, this requirement does not apply. Therefore, since a person might sometimes change his mind and decide to leave the "needle" in its current state (i.e. without an eye) and to use it for extracting thorns, it already has the status of a utensil [with respect to *muktzeh*] (*Rashi*).

The preceding applies to a piece of metal that the craftsman intended to make into a needle. If his original purpose, however, was to make it into a pin, it is complete [and hence susceptible to *tumah*] even without an eye. When R' Eliezer said that all rust-free needles are the same with respect to *tumah,* he was referring to needles and pins that are complete for their respective purposes (*Rashi*).

47. [A מַרְדַּעַת, *saddle cloth,* is placed on an animal's back underneath the saddle (see *Rashi* to *Eruvin* 16a ד״ה עביטין and to *Genesis* 31:34).] It is left on the donkey all day long to keep it warm, because donkeys chronically feel chilled even at the height of summer (*Rashi;* see *Beur HaGra* to *Orach Chaim* 305:7).

טהורות א״ר יצחק (נפחא) א בבאין מנוי אדם לנוי בהמה ורב יוסף אמר ב הואיל ואדם מושך בהם את הבהמה מי לא תניא ג מקל של בהמה של מתכת מקבל טומאה מה טעם הואיל ואדם רודה בהן ה״נ הואיל ואדם מושך בהן: ד וטובלן במקומן: והאיכא חציצה א״ר אמי בשריתכן לימא ר׳ אמי כרב יוסף סבירא ליה דאי כר׳ יצחק (א) נפחא) דאמר בבאין מנוי אדם לנוי בהמה כיון דריתכן עבד בהו מעשה ופרחה לה טומאה מינייהו דתנן ב) כל ה הכלים יורדין לידי טומאתן במחשבה ואין עולין מטומאתן אלא בשינוי מעשה סבר לה כרבי יהודה דאמר מעשה לתקן לאו מעשה הוא דתניא ר׳ יהודה אומר לא אמר שינוי מעשה לתקן אלא לקלקל במתניתא תני במחוללין ג) שאל תלמיד אחד מגליל העליון את ר״א שמעתי שחולקין בין טבעת לטבעת אמר לו שמא לא שמעת אלא לענין שבת דאי לענין טומאה דא ודא חדא היא ולענין טומאה דא ודא אחת היא ד) והתנן טבעת אדם טמאה וטבעת בהמה וכלים ה) ושאר כל הטבעות טהורות כי קאמר ליה איהו נמי דאדם קאמר ליה ודאדם דא ודא אחת היא והתניא ו) ו טבעת שהתקינה לחגור בה מתניו ולקשר בה בין כתפיו טהורה ולא אמרו טמאה אלא של אצבע בלבד כי קאמר ליה איהו נמי דאצבע קאמר ליה ודאצבע דא ודא אחת היא והתנן ז) ז טבעת של מתכת וחותמה של אלמוג טמאה היא של אלמוג וחותמה של מתכת טהורה כי קאמר ליה איהו נמי כולה של מתכת קאמר ליה ועוד שאל שמעתי שחולקין בין מחט למחט אמר ליה שמא לא שמעת אלא לענין שבת ט) דאי לענין טומאה דא ודא אחת היא ולענין טומאה דא ודא אחת היא ח) והתנן ח מחט שניטל חורה או עוקצה טהורה כי קאמר ליה י) בשלימה ובשלימה דא ודא אחת היא ט) והתנן ט מחט שהעלתה חלודה אם מעכב את התפירה טהורה ואם לאו טמאה ואמרי דבי ר׳ ינאי והוא שרישומה ניכר כי קאמר ליה בשיפא קאמר לי׳ ובשיפא דא ודא אחת היא והתניא ט) מחט בין נקובה בין אינה נקובה מותר לטלטלה בשבת ולא י) אמרינן נקובה אלא לענין טומאה בלבד הא כ) תרגמא אביי אליבא דרבא בגלמי: מתני׳ י חמור יוצא במרדעת בזמן שהיא קשורה בו זכרים יוצאין לבובין רחלות יוצאות שחוזות כבולות וכבונות העזים יוצאות צרורות רבי יוסי אוסר בכולן חוץ מן הרחלין הכבונות רבי יהודה אומר עזים יוצאות צרורות ליבש אבל לא לחלב:

גמ׳

טהורות. דלאו משום תכשיט מיטמאו דאין תכשיט לכלי וכלי נמי לא הוו אלא תכשיט כלי ומיהו בעודן מחוברות לכלי מיטמו עם הכלי דהוי יד לכלי דכל המחובר לו הרי הוא כמוהו: בבאין מנוי אדם לנוי בהמה. מתני׳ כגון שנעשה שיר זה לתכשיט אדם ובעודו לאדם נטמא ולאחר טומאתו נתנו לבהמה וצריך להטבילו מטומאתו ראשונה שלא יגע בטהרות: הואיל ואדם מושך בהן את הבהמה. חשיב ליה כלי תשמיש לאדם: מקל של בהמה. שרודין בו את הגמל או את האנקה ל) אי נמי כעין שעושין להנהיג את הדוב: של מתכת. דאילו של עץ פשוטי כלי עץ לא מקבלי טומאה: מאי טעם. הרי לורך בהמה: רודה. מכה ומייסרה: והאיכא חציצה. שטבעת הקבוע בשיר קבוע בו בחוזק ואין המים נכנסין שם: בשריתכן. הכה בפטיש עד שנתפשט ונתרחק הנקב סביב סביב: כרב יוסף סבירא ליה. דאמר כשהן של בהמה נמי מקבלי טומאה הואיל ואדם מושך בהן הלכך כי ריתכן לאחר טומאה אכתי במילתייהו קיימי ולא פרחה טומאתן דאכתי חזו לבהמה: דאי כרבי יצחק. דאמר לא מקבלי טומאה אלא בעודן לאדם טומאה זו שקבלו בעודן לאדם כיון דריתכן ושוב אין נאים לאדם בטלי להו מתורת תכשיט וטהרו מטומאתן: יורדין לידי טומאתן במחשבה. מאחר שחישב עליו שיניחנו כמות שהוא עכשיו ולא יוסיף תיקון אחר הוא גמר מלאכתן ומקבל טומאה: ואין עולין מטומאתן. מאחר שחישב על העור לעשות שטיח ירד לידי טומאה ואם חזר וחישב עליו לרצועו׳ וסנדלים לא בטל מתורת כלי מ) ולא טהר בכך עד שיתן בו אזמל דהוי שינוי מעשה הא בשינוי מעשה מיהא עולה מטומאתו: לתקן. וזו היא תקונו לצורך בהמה: לאו מעשה הוא. לבטל מתורת כלי: במחוללין. מתחלה נעשו חלולין רחבים שיש חלל בדביקתן שנתן טבעת בתוך טבעת כמות שהוא רחב: שחולקין. יש חילוק בהלכותיהן ואיני יודע מהו חילוקן: אלא לענין שבת. לענין הוצאת שבת יש חילוק בין יש עליה חותם לשאין עליה חותם כדאמר לקמן בפ׳ במה אשה (דף נט.): דא ודא אחת היא. כל טבעות דין אחד להן: שהתקינה לחגור בה מתניו. שקבעה בראש רצועה ועשאה כמין בוקלא שעושין לסרגין של סוסים: ולקשור בה בין כתפיו. בתי זרועותיו ברצלייר״א: טהורה. דהדר הויא לה כטבעת כלים ולא דמיא לאדם מושך בהם שאינו משתמש בה כלום אלא מונחת ועומדת לרצועה ומיהו עם הרצועה מקבלת טומאה אבל אם היה נוטלה ומחזירה אינה מקבלת טומאה לעצמה: כי קאמר ליה איהו נמי. דא ודא אחת היא: דאצבע קאמר ליה. ולענין שבת יש חילוק: אלמוג. עצי אלמוגים והוא נאה: טמאה. דבתר טבעת אזלינן ופשוטי כלי מתכות טמאים: היא של אלמוג טהורה. דפשוטי כלי עץ הוא: אלא לענין שבת. לענין הוצאת שבת יש חילוק בין נקובה לשאינו נקובה דנקובה קתני חייב חטאת ובשאינה נקובה כגון אישפיגל״א שהיא תכשיט קתני אינו חייב חטאת בפרק במה אשה (דף ס:): חורה. חור שלה: עוקצה. פונטא: חלודה. רואיל״ה: והוא שרישומה. של מחט ניכר דהוי כלי וטמאה. ל״א שרישומה של חלודה ניכר בבגד היינו עיכוב תפירה וטהורה: בשיפא. נישופת בשופינא שקורין לימ״א שאין בה חלודה: מותר לטלטלה בשבת. בתגר דהא חזיא ליטול את הקוץ ותורת כלי עליה: ולא אמרו נקובה. חלוקה להלכותיה אלא לענין טומאה בלבד דנקובה מקבלת טומאה ושאינה נקובה לא: הא תרגמא אביי. בפרק כל הכלים: בגלמי. שהוא גולם שנקללה מן החוט ועומדת לינקב התם הוא דלכל זמן שלא נקבה אינה מקבלת טומאה דהא לא נגמרה מלאכתה ולענין טומאה כלי מעשה כתיב (במדבר לא) שגמר כל מעשהו ומיהו לענין שבת שריא דזימנין דממליך עלה ומנח לה הכי ומשוי לה מנא לנטילת קוץ אבל מחט שנגמרה מלאכתה כגון אישפינגל״א שאינה עומדת לינקב דא ודא אחת היא לטומאה: מתני׳ מרדעת. בשטי״ל ומניחין אותו כל היום על החמור לחממו דאמרי אינשי חמרא אפילו בתקופת תמוז קריר ליה: שהיא קשורה בו. בגמ׳ מפרש: זכרים. אילים: לבובים שחוזות כבולות וכבונות. מפרש בגמרא: צרורות. דדיהן צרורות פעמים ליבש שמהדקן כדי שלא יחלבו עוד ויתעברו או יהו שמנות לאכול ופעמים לחלב לשמור חלבן שלא יטפטף לארץ וקושרין להם כיס בדדיהן: ר׳ יוסי אוסר בכולן. דמשוי הוא: חוץ מן הרחלים הכבונות. שהוא שמירת צמרן שלא יטנף והוי להו תכשיט: יוצאות צרורות ליבש. ר׳ יהודה סבירא ליה כתנא קמא דלאו משוי הוא ומיהו ליבש דמיהדק שפיר וליכא למיחש דילמא נפיל ואתי לאיתויי אבל ליחלב דלא מיהדק שפיר חיישינן:

גמרא

והא איכא חציצה. פירש בקונטרס שטבעת תקוע בשיר בחחק ואין המים נכנסים שם ואומר ר״י דצריך לומר שפעמים מסירים אותן ועושים מהן מלאכה בפני עצמן שאם כל שעה היו קבועים בצואר הבהמה היה הכל חשיב כלי אחד ולא הוי חציצה וה״ר פור״ת פירש והא איכא חציצה לפי שהוא דבוק בצואר הבהמה: בשריתכן. להכי לא מוקי לה במחוללין דאין דרך השיר להיות כן: טבעת שהתקינה לחגור בה מתניו. נראה לר״י דהיינו לחגור מלבושיו שהן רחבים ואוגדם כנגד מתניו בטבעת כעין שפי׳ בקונטרס לקשור בה את כתפיו: היא של אלמוג וחותמה של מתכת. וא״ת והא יש בה בית קיבול מקום מושב החותם וי״ל דאין זה בית קיבול דאמרינן בית קיבול העשוי למלאות ס) לא שמיה בית קבול נ): והתניא מחט בין נקובה בין אינה נקוב׳. נראה לר״י דלא פריך אליב׳ דאביי דאיהו הוה מפרש שאינה נקובה היינו שניטל חורה או עוקצה אלא אליב׳ דרבא פריך דלדידיה לא מצינן לפרש הכי כדמוכח בריש כל הכלים (לקמן קכג.) ותימה לר״י דכיון דלא ידע המקשה דמיירי בגלמי א״כ בלאו הכי תקשה ליה לרבא כדפריך בריש כל הכלים (ג״ז שם):

והוא

עין משפט נר מצוה

יב א מיי׳ פ״ח מהל׳ כלים הלכה י:
יג ב ג שם הלכה ט:
יד ד מיי׳ פ״ג מהל׳ מקוואות הלכה טו:
טו ה מיי׳ פ״ח מהל׳ כלים הלכה י:
טז ו שם הלכה ט:
יז ז מיי׳ פ״ד מהל׳ כלים הלכה ו:
יח ח מיי׳ פי״א מהל׳ כלים הלכה יד:
יט ט שם הלכה טז:
כ י מיי׳ פ״כ מהל׳ שבת הלכה י סמג לאוין סה טוש״ע א״ח סי׳ שה סעיף ז:

רבינו חננאל

הטבעות טהורות. ואוקמה ר׳ יצחק נפחא בבאין מנוי אדם. כלומר טבעת אדם היתה ונעשה עתה שיר לבהמה. ואוקמה רב יוסף הואיל ואדם מושך בהן. פי׳ פעמים שמכניס אדם אצבעו באותו השיר ומושך בה הבהמה שנמצאת טבעת העשוי׳ לאצבעו של אדם. כמו מקל בהמה של מתכת טמאה מפני שמחזיקה אדם ורודה בה כו׳. וטובלן במקומה והא עביד חציצה. כלומר כיון שהשירים הללו נושכין זה לזה הרי מקום הנשיכה סתום ואין המים באין בהם. ופריק ר׳ אמי בשריתכן. כלומר ריתכן באור והטבילן במים בעודן השירין כמו גחלים לוחשות שהמים באין אליהם מכל צד. ואמרינן האי פירוקא דר׳ אמי דלא כר׳ יצחק נפחא היא. דאי אליבא דר׳ יצחק נפחא טבעת של בהמה יורד לקבל טומאה. אפי׳ אם יחשב עליה להיות טבעת של אדם. וטבעת של אדם אינה עולה מידי טומאה להבטל מעליה תורת כלי אלא בשינוי מעשה כדתנן כל הכלים יורדין לידי טומאתן כו׳ ואי בשריתכן הנה עשה בהן מעשה ונסתלקה תורת כלי מעליהן. ואין צריכין לא הזאה ולא טבילה. (כי בעינן) [ושנינן] מעשה לסלק תורת כלי מעליהו מעש׳ לקלקל כגון שבירה וכיוצא בה. אבל ריתוך שהוא תיקון וחיזוק לכלי מתכת כי האי גוונא אינו מעשה לטהר ולא מבטל הטומאה מעל הטבעת. במתניתא תנא במחוללין. כלומר חלולין הן מלשון נבובים אלו השירין. והמים באין בהם מכל צד. ואין שם חציצה: תנא (תוספתא פ״ה) ומכניס חבילין לתוך ידו. ובלבד שלא יכרוך לתוך ידו. ובלבד שלא יכרוך ע״ג ידו ולא ישלשל חבלים מידו יתר מטפח: שאל תלמיד את ר׳ אלעזר שמעתי חלוקה בין טבעת לטבעת. א״ל לענין שבת בין טבעת שיש עליה חותם. לטבעת שאין עליה חותם. אבל לענין טומאה כל טבעות דינם אחד. ואסיקנא טבעת של אדם של אצבע של מתכת הכל דינם אחד לענין טומאה. וכן נמי מחט שלימה שיפא [נקובה ושאינה] נקובה הכל דינם אחד לענין טומאה. ואם היא ניטל חרירה או עוקצה או העלת חלודה ומעכבת התפירה (או נקובה) טהורה היא. ואקשינן ולענין (שבת אנה) [טומאה אינה] היא חלוקה בין מחט למחט. והתניא מחט בין נקובה בין שאינה נקובה מותר לטלטלה בשבת. [ולא אמרו כו׳] ושנינן הא תרגמה אביי זו הברייתא אליבא דרבא דאמר מחט שניטל עוקצה או חרירה מדלענין טומאה לאו כלי הוא וטהורה היא. לענין שבת נמי לאו כלי ואסור לטלטלה. מתניתא דקתני בין נקובה בין שאינה נקובה מותר לטלטלה בגלומי כלי מתכת היא. כלומר עדיין גולם הוא חוט של ברזל ועדיין הוא צריך לנקבו ולחרר לו עוקם לעשותה מחט. ועכשיו אין לה לא נקב ולא עוקם. ואמרינן זמנין דמימליך עליה דהאי גולם ומשוי ליה מנא כמות שהיא. אבל מחט שניטל חרירה שלה או עוקצה לבין גרוטאות זריק לה: [מתני׳] חמור יוצא במרדעת בזמן שהיא קשורה לו כו׳. אוקמה שמואל בשקשורה לו מע״ש. וקיי״ל כוותיה. ומתניתא מסייעא ליה. נתינת מרדעת ע״ג חמור דברי הכל

מסורת הש״ס

א) ברש״י ליתא, ב) כלים פכ״ה מ״ע לקמן נח:, סוכה יג: קדושין נט. [מנחות סט:], ג) תוספתא דכלים (ב״מ) פ״ב, ד) כלים פי״ב מ״א, ה) תוספתא שם, ו) לקמן נט: כלים פי״ג מ״ו, ז) לקמן קכג. כלים פי״א מ״ה, ח) כלים שם, ט) לקמן קכג. [תוספתא שם], י) נ״ל אמרו, כ) [לקמן פב. קטו: קכב. עירובין פח: פסחים יג: סוכה יג. כתובות קו: ב״מ כב. פ: קו. קט. בכורות נה. וע׳ תוס׳ בכורות כה. ד״ה השן], ל) רש״ל ד׳ דהא׳ א״י שייך אחר דיבור רודה ואינו דרש״י בא להשמיענו עניננו של מקל אבל ודאי דמה ספי׳ רודה מכה ומייסרה אינו אלא לפי שמוסב לשון ולא׳ פי׳ של רודה שמכה בו את הבהמה, מ) לטהר בכך כצ״ל, נ) [וע׳ תוס׳ סוכה יג: ד״ה מהו דתימא ומה שנכתב שם על הגליון ויש ליישב קצת].

רב נסים גאון

והא איכא חציצה. בראש מס׳ (עירובין דף ד׳) אמרו חציצין דאורייתא נינהו דכתיב (ויקרא טו) ורחץ במים את כל בשרו שלא יהא דבר חוצץ בין מים לבשרו ועיקר דילה במס׳ (סוכה דף ו׳) בפרק א׳ ובמס׳ מקואות בפ׳ ט׳: הא תירגמא אביי בגלמי.

גליון הש״ס

גמרא ושאר כל הטבעות. עי׳ כלים פי״ג מ״ג ברע״ב ד״ה למעלה מן המסכת: שם דאי לענין טומאה דא ודא אחת היא. עי׳ לקמן נ״ח ע״ב תוס׳ ד״ה למאי חזיא: שם בשלימה. עי׳ לקמן ע״א תוס׳ ד״ה הואיל ואשה מוגרת. תוס׳ ד״ה היא של אלמוג וכו׳ לא שמיה בית קבול. עי׳ לעיל ד׳ יז ע״א תוס׳ ד״ה ועל שאר. סוכה דף יג ע״ב תד״ה מהו דתימא:

ליקוטי רש״י

כל הכלים יורדין לידי טומאתן במחשבה. כגון גולמי כלים דאמר בהכל שוחטין (חולין כה.) כל שעתיד לשוף ולשבץ ולגרר ולאחר חסרון מלאכה הוא וטהורים ואם חישב עליה שלא לשוף ולשבץ הוגמרה מחשבה זו לידי גמר מלאכתן מכאן ולהבא [קידושין נט.] [כגון] שחשב עליו לדבר שאין בו חסרון מלאכה כגון עור המתוקן סתמו למנעלים עומד ולא מקבל טומאה עד שיעשו המנעלים חישב עליו לעשותו שולחן דאינו חסר שום מלאכה דהשתא מיד ראוי לשולחן מקבל טומאה מיד [מנחות סט.] [משחישב] עליו שזה יהא גמר מלאכתן כגון שעידו לדרגש או לדולבקי כיון שעידו מקבל טומאה ואלמלי עידו לרצועות וסנדלין אין מקבלים טומאה עד שיגמרו למלאכת הסנדלין [סוכה יד.]. ואין עולין מטומאתן. משקבלוה [קידושין שם]. אם נטמאו [מנחות שם]. ממחשבת תורת קבלת טומאה אין עולין במחשבה כגון עידו לשלחן ולדרגש וחישב עליו לרצועות וסנדלין אין מחשבתו מבטלתן מתורת קבלת טומאה [סוכה שם]. מתורת טומאה שירדה להן ואף על פי שעדיין לא נטמאו משנמלך עליהן אין עולין מלקבל טומאה אלא בשינוי מעשה [לקמן נח:]. אלא בשינוי מעשה. שיעשה בה מעשה לקלקלם שישברם או ינקבם וכן עד שלא יקבלו טומאה אין עולין מתורת קבלת טומאה שירדו במחשבה זו אלא בשינוי מעשה עד שיתחיל לשוף לשבץ ולגרר [קידושין שם]. כגון נשברו טהרו [מנחות שם]. עד שיתן בו אזמל [סוכה שם]. אלמוג. מין עץ העולה בקרקע הים ושמו קוראל״ו [ר״ה כג.]. אילן שגדל בים ויקר הרבה וקורין קוריי״ל [רשב״ם ב״ב פא.]. עצי אלגומים. מפרש בפסיקת׳ כתוב אחד אומר אלמוגים וכתוב אחד אומר אלגומים אלא אלגומים שמם ונקרא אלמוגים לפי שהיה מתמוגג ונכפף מתוך רכיכתו כמו כוסות שהוא נכפף מתוך חשיבתו [דה״ב ט, י]. וחותמה. צורה לחתום בה איגרת או כל דבר סגור [לקמן נז.]. שניטל חורה או עוקצה טהורה. דלענין טומאה בטל שם כלי מינה [שם קכג.]. [המשך בדף נג.]

it.[48] **זְכָרִים יוֹצְאִין לְבוּבִין – Rams may go out attached.** **רְחֵלוֹת יוֹצְאוֹת שְׁחוּזוֹת כְּבוּלוֹת וּכְבוּנוֹת – Ewes may go out held, tied or fastened.**[49] **הָעִזִּים יוֹצְאוֹת צְרוּרוֹת – Goats may go out** with their udders **tied.**[50]

A dissenting view:

רַבִּי יוֹסֵי אוֹסֵר בְּכוּלָּן חוּץ מִן הָרְחֵלִין הַכְּבוּנוֹת – R' Yose forbids all of these [cases], except for that of **the ewes that go out fastened.**[51]

Another dissenting view:

רַבִּי יְהוּדָה אוֹמֵר – R' Yehudah says: **עִזִּים יוֹצְאוֹת צְרוּרוֹת לְיַבֵּשׁ – Goats may go out** with their udders **tied for** the sake of **drying** them up, **אֲבָל לֹא לֶחָלָב – but not for** the sake of **being milked.**[52]

NOTES

48. The Gemara (below, 53a) explains this requirement (*Rashi*).

49. The Gemara (53b-54a) explains the case of attached [*levuvin*] as well as the cases of held [*shechuzos*], tied [*kevulos*] and fastened [*kevunos*] (*Rashi*). [See 54a note 14.]

50. A goat's udders are sometimes tied tightly to stop lactation – either to allow the goats to conceive or to cause them to become fatter. Sometimes a pouch is tied on to the udders to prevent the milk from dripping and being wasted (*Rashi*). [The Tanna Kamma permits a goat to go out with her udders tied in both of these cases.]

51. In all of these cases, R' Yose considers the animal to be carrying a burden (*Rashi*). The exception of fastened [*kevunos*] is explained below, 54a note 14.

52. I.e. they may go out with their udders tied tightly in order to dry up the milk. R' Yehudah agrees with the Tanna Kamma, who considers the pouch an article of attire rather than a burden. He permits this, however, only if the pouch is tied tightly in order to dry up the milk. In the case of a pouch tied on to catch the dripping milk, since the pouch is tied loosely, there is the possibility that the pouch will fall off, and the goatherd will carry it (*Rashi;* see, however, *Rashi* to 53b ד״ה ליחלב and note 36 ibid.; cf. *Tosafos* and *Rashba* ibid.).

Gemara The Gemara explains the Mishnah's opening statement, "A donkey may go out with a saddle cloth if it is tied on":

אָמַר שְׁמוּאֵל – Shmuel said: וְהוּא שֶׁקְּשׁוּרָה לוֹ מֵעֶרֶב שַׁבָּת – And it means **that the [saddle cloth] was tied on to [the donkey] since before the Sabbath.**[1]

The Gemara cites support for Shmuel's statement:

אָמַר רַב נַחְמָן – Rav Nachman said: מַתְנִיתִין נַמִּי דַּיְקָא – Our Mishnah[2] **also implies** this, **דְּקָתָנֵי – for it teaches: אֵין הַחֲמוֹר יוֹצֵא בְּמַרְדַּעַת בִּזְמַן שֶׁאֵינָהּ קְשׁוּרָה לוֹ – A DONKEY MAY NOT GO OUT WITH A SADDLE CLOTH IF IT IS NOT TIED ONTO IT. הֵיכִי דָּמֵי – What is the case** to which this part of the Mishnah refers? **אִילֵימָא שֶׁאֵינָהּ קְשׁוּרָה לוֹ כְּלָל – If you say** it means **that [the saddle cloth] is not tied onto [the donkey] at all, פְּשִׁיטָא –** it is **obvious** that the donkey may not go out with it, **דִּלְמָא נָפְלָה לֵיהּ וְאָתֵי לְאֲתוּיֵי – for perhaps [the saddle cloth] will fall off and one might come to carry** it four *amos* in the public domain. There is no need for the Mishnah to teach such an obvious prohibition. **אֶלָּא לָאו שֶׁאֵינָהּ קְשׁוּרָה לוֹ מֵעֶרֶב שַׁבָּת – Rather, it surely means that [the saddle cloth] was not tied on since before the Sabbath. מִכְּלָל דְּרֵישָׁא שֶׁקְּשׁוּרָה לוֹ מֵעֶרֶב שַׁבָּת –** Now, **this implies that the first part** of the Mishnah (which states that a donkey *may* go out with a saddle cloth if it is tied on) refers to a case **where it was tied on since before the Sabbath,** as Shmuel stated.[3] **שְׁמַע מִינָּהּ – Learn** a conclusive proof **from this.**

The Gemara cites further support for Shmuel:

תַּנְיָא נַמִּי הָכִי – This was also taught in a Baraisa: חֲמוֹר יוֹצֵא בְּמַרְדַּעַת בִּזְמַן שֶׁקְּשׁוּרָה לוֹ מֵעֶרֶב שַׁבָּת – A DONKEY MAY GO OUT WITH A SADDLE CLOTH IF IT WAS TIED ONTO IT SINCE BEFORE THE SABBATH. וְלֹא בְאוּכָּף אַף עַל פִּי שֶׁקְּשׁוּרָה לוֹ מֵעֶרֶב שַׁבָּת – HOWEVER, it may **NOT** go out **WITH A SADDLE**[4] **EVEN IF IT WAS TIED ONTO IT SINCE BEFORE THE SABBATH.**[5] **רַבָּן שִׁמְעוֹן בֶּן גַּמְלִיאֵל אוֹמֵר – RABBAN SHIMON BEN GAMLIEL SAYS: אַף בְּאוּכָּף בִּזְמַן שֶׁקְּשׁוּרָה לוֹ מֵעֶרֶב שַׁבָּת –** A donkey may go out **EVEN WITH A SADDLE IF IT WAS TIED ONTO IT SINCE BEFORE THE SABBATH,**[6] **וּבִלְבַד שֶׁלֹּא יִקְשׁוֹר לוֹ מַסְרִיכָן – PROVIDED THAT ONE DOES NOT TIE BREAST-STRAPS ONTO IT,**[7] **וּבִלְבַד שֶׁלֹּא יִפְשׁוֹל לוֹ רְצוּעָה תַּחַת זְנָבוֹ – AND PROVIDED THAT ONE DOES NOT SUSPEND A STRAP BENEATH ITS TAIL.**[8]

The Gemara discusses a different law concerning a saddle cloth:

בְּעָא מִינֵּיהּ רַב אַסִּי בַּר נָתָן מֵרַבִּי חִיָּיא בַּר רַב אַשִׁי – Rav Assi bar Nassan asked R' Chiya bar Rav Ashi: מַהוּ לִיתֵּן מַרְדַּעַת עַל גַּבֵּי חֲמוֹר בְּשַׁבָּת – What is [the law] as to whether one may **put a saddle cloth on a donkey on the Sabbath?**[9] **אָמַר לֵיהּ – [R' Chiya bar Rav Ashi] answered him: מוּתָּר – It is permitted.**[10] **אָמַר לֵיהּ – [Rav Assi bar Nassan]** then **said to him: וְכִי מַה בֵּין זֶה לְאוּכָּף – But what is** the difference **between this** [a saddle cloth] **and a saddle?**[11] **אִישְׁתִּיק – [R' Chiya bar Ashi] was**

NOTES

1. [Even if the saddle cloth is currently tied on, the donkey may not go out with it unless it was tied on before the Sabbath. The reason is as follows:] If the donkey was wearing the saddle cloth since before the Sabbath, the donkey evidently needs it to keep warm, and thus it is considered a garment. If, however, the donkey was not wearing it since before the Sabbath, we assume that it does not need it. Should the saddle cloth then be tied on during the Sabbath, it is viewed as a burden (*Rashi* to 54b ד״ה כדאמרן as explained by *Tosafos* here; see *Dibros Moshe* 43:6 for further explanation; cf. *Tosafos* with *Maharsha* and *Maharam;* see also *Shaar HaTziyun* 305:21 and *Rosh Yosef*).

Other commentators explain that one may not tie a saddle cloth on during the Sabbath, lest one lean against the animal, thus violating the Rabbinic prohibition against making use of an animal on the Sabbath. To prevent this, the Rabbis prohibited a donkey to go out with a saddle cloth that was tied on during the Sabbath (*Rashba, Rosh* et al., based on *Yerushalmi;* see *Keren Orah*). [The prohibition against *tying* is not an issue here, because the knot was tied in a permitted manner (*Ritva MHK* ed.; *Chidushei HaRan;* see *Rosh*).]

2. I.e. the continuation of our Mishnah (below, 54b).

3. The Rishonim ask: Why did the Gemara have to cite the Mishnah on 54b to prove its point? The same inference could have been made from our Mishnah, which states: "A donkey may go out with a saddle cloth if it is tied onto it." Here too one could reason: Surely the Mishnah does not need to tell us the obvious fact that the saddle cloth must presently be tied on. Therefore, the clause, "if it is tied onto it," must mean that it was tied on since the previous day! *Tosafos* answer that one could not make this inference from our Mishnah, because it could be argued that, on the contrary, our Mishnah comes to *dispel* the notion that it must presently be tied on since the previous day. It possibly serves to teach that the donkey may go out even if the saddle cloth was tied on only during the Sabbath. [Only the Mishnah on 54b ("A donkey may *not* go out with a saddle cloth when it is *not* tied on etc."), which would be superfluous were it referring to a saddle cloth that is not tied on at all, proves that the saddle cloth must have been tied on before the Sabbath (see *Maharsha, Rashash* and *Melo HaRo'im*).]

4. An אוּכָּף, *ukaf* (*saddle*), is used to carry a rider or a load (*Ran; Chidushei HaRan;* cf. *Meiri*).

5. This Tanna permits a saddle cloth because it is sometimes used to warm the donkey [and thus is considered an article of attire, provided that it was tied on before the Sabbath (see note 1)]. A saddle, however, is deemed a burden even if it was tied on before the Sabbath (*Ritva MHK* ed.).

6. Since a saddle also helps to warm the donkey [to some extent] (*Rashi*), Rabban Shimon ben Gamliel regards it as an article of attire, similar to the saddle cloth.

According to the Tanna Kamma, however, the warmth provided by a saddle is not sufficiently significant. Unlike a saddle cloth, which warms the animal's entire body, a saddle warms only the relatively small area that it covers (*Bach* to *Orach Chaim* §305 ד״ה ומ״ש ולא יצא באוכף; *Mishnah Berurah* ibid. §28).

7. [Straps attached to the saddle that extend around the donkey's breastbone at the base of its neck.] They prevent the saddle and its burden from slipping backwards when the donkey goes uphill (*Rashi* ד״ה רצועה).

A donkey may not go out with these straps attached to the saddle [even if they were tied on before the Sabbath], because they give the impression that the owner wants to load a burden onto the donkey (*Rashi*).

8. This strap, which anchors the saddle to the donkey's tail, prevents the saddle from slipping forward when the donkey goes downhill (*Rashi*). In this case, too, the reason for the prohibition is that one who uses such a strap appears to want to load the donkey (*Chidushei HaRan*).

9. This question does not concern going out into a public domain. [As stated above, if the saddle cloth was tied on during the Sabbath, the donkey may not wear it in a public domain.] Rather, the question is whether one may put a saddle cloth on a donkey inside a private domain so that it will not be cold (*Rashi*).

The Rishonim ask why Rav Assi bar Nassan thought that this might be forbidden. Some answer that it is possibly a violation of the Rabbinic prohibition against unnecessarily exerting oneself on the Sabbath (*Tosafos; Tos. HaRosh;* cf. *Tos. Yeshanim* ד״ה תולין). *Rashi's* view regarding this point is not clear. See *Dibros Moshe* (43:7), who concludes that according to *Rashi* as well the reason is unnecessary exertion (cf. *Rosh Yosef, Meromei Sadeh* and *Chelkas Binyamin*).

The Gemara is asking only whether one may *throw* the saddle cloth onto the donkey. It is certainly forbidden to *tie* it on [lest one lean on the animal] (*Chidushei HaRan;* see note 1).

10. The reason for this permit is discussed below (note 19).

11. Rav Assi bar Nassan presently quotes a Baraisa that forbids one even to remove a saddle from a donkey [and certainly to put one on] (based on *Rashi* ד״ה איתיביה; cf. *Ritva MHK* ed. and *Chidushei HaRan;* see *Sfas Emes*).

[Therefore, Rav Assi bar Nassan asks why it is permitted to put a saddle cloth on a donkey. The same type of exertion is involved in putting on either a saddle cloth or a saddle. Hence, if such exertion is deemed excessive, one should be prohibited to put even a saddle cloth on; and if it is not excessive, one should be allowed to put even a saddle on.]

גמ' אמר שמואל א והוא שקשורה לו מע"ש אמר רב נחמן מתני' נמי דיקא דקתני א) אין החמור יוצא במרדעת בזמן שאינה קשורה לו היכי דמי אילימא שאינה קשורה לו כלל פשיטא דילמא נפלה ליה ואתי לאתויי אלא לאו שאינה קשורה מע"ש מכלל דרישא שקשורה לו מע"ש ש"מ תניא נמי הכי ב) חמור יוצא במרדעת בזמן שקשורה לו מע"ש ב ולא באוכף אע"פ שקשורה לו מע"ש רבן שמעון בן גמליאל אומר אף באוכף בזמן שקשורה לו מע"ש ובלבד שלא יקשור לו מסריכן ובלבד שלא יפשול לו רצועה תחת זנבו בעא מיניה רב אסי בר נתן מר' חייא בר רב אשי מהו ליתן מרדעת על גבי חמור בשבת אמר ליה ג מותר א"ל וכי מה בין זה לאוכף אישתיק איתיביה ד אוכף שעל גבי חמור לא יטלטלנה בידו אלא מוליכה ומביאה בחצר והוא נופל מאיליו השתא ליטול אמרת לא להניח מיבעיא אמר ליה ר' זירא שבקיה כרביה סבירא ליה דאמר רב חייא בר אשי אמר רב תולין ג) טרסקל לבהמה בשבת וקל וחומר למרדעת ומה התם דמשום תענוג שרי הכא דמשום צער לא כל שכן שמואל אמר מרדעת מותר ה טרסקל אסור אזל ר' חייא בר יוסף אמרה לשמעתא דרב קמיה דשמואל א"ל אי הכי אמר אבא לא ידע במילי דשבתא ולא כלום כי סליק ר' זירא אשכחיה לר' בנימין בר יפת דיתיב וקאמר ליה משמיה דר' יוחנן נותנין מרדעת על גבי חמור בשבת א"ל ז) יישר וכן תרגמה אריוך בבבל ח) אריוך מנו שמואל והא רב נמי אמרה אלא שמעיה דהוה מסיים ביה ואין תולין טרסקל בשבת א"ל יישר וכן תרגמה אריוך בבבל דכולי עלמא מיהת מרדעת מותר מאי שנא מאוכף שאני התם דאפשר דנפיל ממילא רב פפא אמר כאן לחמה כאן לצנה לחמה אית לה צערא לצנה לית לה צערא והיינו דאמרי אינשי חמרא אפי' בתקופת תמוז קרירא לה מיתיבי ו) לא יצא הסוס בזנב שועל ולא ז) בזהורית שבין עיניו ח) לא יצא הזב בכים שלו ולא עזים בכים שבדדיהן ולא פרה בחסום שבפיה ולא סייחים בטרסקלין שבפיהם לרה"ר ולא בהמה בסנדל שברגליה ולא בקמיע אע"פ שהוא מומחה וזו חומר בבהמה מבאדם אבל יוצא הוא באגד שעל גבי המכה ט) ובקשישין שעל גבי השבר ובשליא המדולדלת בה י) ופוקקין לה זוג בצוארה ומטיילת עמו בחצר קתני מיהת ולא סייחין בטרסקלים שבפיהם לרה"ר לרה"ר הוא דלא הא בחצר שפיר דמי מאי לאו בגדולים ומשום תענוג לא י בקטנים ומשום צער דיקא נמי דקתני דומיא

רש"י

גמ' מתניתין נמי דיקא. לקמן בהאי פירקא: אף באוכף. דאיהו נמי מהני לחממה: ובלבד שלא יקשור לו מסריכן. פוטרא"ל דמיחזי כמי שרוצה להטעינו משוי: רצועה תחת זנבו. פושל"א שנותנים שם שלא תרד האוכף והמשוי על צוארה כשהיא יורדת לעמק והמסרך שלא תרד על זנבה כשהיא עולה על ההרים: מהו ליתן מרדעת. ולא לצאת לרה"ר אלא בחצר ומפני הלינה: ה"ג אמר ליה מותר א"ל וכי מה בין זה לאוכף אישתיק: איתיביה כו'. כסבור הא דאישתיק משום דלא אסגא ביה דסבר אוכף נמי שרי ואותיביה מברייתא דאסור ליטלה והשתא ליטול אמרת לא להניח מיבעי' דדמי כאילו צריך להטעינה משוי: כרביה. רב: טרסקל. סל מלא שעורים תולין לה בצוארה ופיה נתון לתוכו ואוכלת ותענוג בעלמא הוא שלא תטרח לשוח צוארה לארץ: צער. של לינה: מרדעת מותר. דלצערא היא הלכך אורחה בהכי ולאו משוי הוא: לשמעתא דרב. דשרי בטרסקל: אבא. ס) חברי כמו אברך אבא למלכא (בראשית מא): שמואל קרי אריוך על שם שהיה בקי בדינין ושופט כמלך השופט על הארץ לשון ריכא ע) מלך (ב"ב דף ד.): והא רב נמי אמרה. דכיון דשרי בטרסקל כ"ש מרדעת: מאי שנא מאוכף. שאסור ליטול וכ"ש להניחו: דנפיל ממילא. כדקתני מוליכו ומביאו לחצר והוא נופל מאליו: כאן לחמה. מרדעת צריך לחממה ומותר משום צער דלינה אבל נטילת אוכף אינו אלא שילטנן שנתחממה ע"י משאוי שנשאה מבעוד יום ואי לא שקיל ליה לא איכפת לן שהרי הוא יצטנן מאליו דאמרי אינשי וכו': בזנב שועל. שתולין לו בין עיניו שלא ישלוט בו עין: זהורית. נוי: בכים שלו. שתולין לו באמתו לקבל זוב ולבדוק מנין ראיותיו שאינו תכשיט לו: בכים שבדדיהן. לקבל חלב הנוטף אי נמי שלא ישרטו דדיהן על הקוצים שהיו דדיהן גסין: בחסום שבפיה. שחוסמין אותה שלא תרעה בשדות אחרים וכשמגיעין למקום מרעיתם נוטלין אותה הימנה: בסנדל שברגליה. שעושין לה סנדל של מתכת שלא יזיקוה האבנים: קמיע. כתב לרפואת חולי: מומחה. שריפא כבר ג' פעמים: וזה חומר בבהמה מבאדם. קס"ד השתא דאקמיע קאי דאמרינן לקמן בפרק במה אשה יוצאה (ד' סא.) שהאדם יוצא בקמיע מומחה וכל הני דקתני לא תצא הנך דלאו שמירת גופה הוא אלא משאוי וסנדל משום דדילמא מישתליף ואתי לאתויי: אגד שעל גבי המכה. ניכא למימר אתי לאתויי: קשישין שעל השבר. בהמה שנשבר בה עצם עושין לה דפין מכאן ומכאן וקושרים אותן שם והן מעמידין העצם שלא ינוד אנה ואנה עד שמתחבר: ובשליא המדולדלת בה. שיצתה מקצתה: ופוקקין לה זוג. אבל כשאינו פקוק אפי' בחצר לא תצא מפני שהעינבל שבתוכה מקשקש ומוליד קול לכך פוקק בצמר או במוכין שלא יקשקש העינבל שבתוכה: זוג. אישקלי"ט: עינבל. בטדי"ל: ומטיילת. באותו זוג בחצר אבל לא תצא בו לרה"ר כדמפרש לקמן בפרקין (דף נד:) דמיחזי כמאן דאזיל לחינגא: מאי לאו. בסייחים גדולים קאמר דצוארן ארוך ואין להם צער לשוח ולאכול מע"ג הקרקע ותולה להן טרסקל לתענוג וקשיא לשמואל: קטנים. ארכובותיהן גבוהין וצוארן קטן ויש להם צער לשוח ע"ג הקרקע ולאכול:

תוספות

והוא שקשורה לו מע"ש. רש"י פי' לקמן דבקשורה מע"ש הוי מלבוש החמור אבל באינה קשורה מע"ש הוי משאוי ועוד יש לפרש דבאינה קשורה מע"ש מיחזי כמתכוין להוצאת המרדעת וה"ר פור"ת פירש דמיחזי כאילו מתכוין להוליך הבהמה למקום רחוק:

אילימא שאינה קשורה לו כלל פשיטא. ולא בעי למפרך דמרישא שמעינן לה דקתני בזמן שהיא קשורה הא אינה קשורה לא דדרך משניות כן במסכת ע"ז (דף לה:) אלו דברים אסורין באכילה כבשים שדרכן לתת לתוכן יין כו' ובסיפא (שם דף לט:) קתני ואלו מותרים באכילה כו' וכבשים שאין דרכן לתת כו' ובפרק אלו טרפות (חולין דף מב.) קתני אלו כשרות אע"ג דאיכא מינייהו דשמעי' מרישא מ) וא"ת ונפשוט מרישא דבקשורה מערב שבת איירי מדאיצטריך למיתני בזמן שהיא קשורה דבלאו הכי הוה ידעי' דאיירי בקשורה דאי באינה קשורה פשיטא דאסור דילמא נפלה ואתי לאתויי כדקאמר הכא אילימא כו' אלא ודאי בזמן שקשורה מע"ש קאמר וי"ל דמרישא לא תפשוט דאדרבה ה"א דלהכי תנא בזמן שהיא קשורה לאשמעי' דאפי' קשורה בשבת דאי לא תנא ליה ה"א דוקא בקשורה לו מע"ש אבל בקשורה בשבת לא קמ"ל להכי דייק מסיפא:

מהו ליתן המרדעת ע"ג חמור בשבת. ואין לאסור משום דאין כלי ניטל אלא לדבר הניטל דבהמה חשיבא כדבר הניטל כיון דיכול למושכה ולהוליכה בכל מקום ורב אסי בר נתן דבעי אם אסור אין לפרש משום דמיחזי כרוצה להוליך הבהמה למקום רחוק דא"כ היכי דייק דמאן דשרי טרסקל כ"ש מרדעת. ואין לפרש נמי דבעי למיסר בחצר אטו רה"ר כדאמר גבי אשה בפ' במה אשה (לקמן דף סד:) דגבי בהמה לא גזרו כדתניא בסמוך גבי זוג ומטיילת עמו בחצר אלא נראה לר"י דטעמא משום טרחא דשבת ואע"ג דשריא קרצוף בפ"ב דביצה (דף כג.) התם יש לה צער ביותר א"נ לא שרי אלא בי"ט אבל בשבת אסור:

אוכף שע"ג החמור. וא"ת ויתיר האוכף וינער ויפול כדאמר בפ' ס) כל כתבי גבי היתה בהמתו טעונה טבל כו' וי"ל דהתם מיירי בשקין שתוכל הבהמה להתקלקל אבל מחמת האוכף לא תוכל הבהמה להתקלקל לכך לא התירו:

תולין טרסקל. וא"ת ותאסר משום דמשתמש בבע"ח כי היכי דאסור להניח נר על גבי דקל בשבת משום דמשתמש במחובר וי"ל דהתם מנענע הענפים אבל הכא אינו מנענע הבהמה בכך ורב אסי ברבי נתן דבעי למיסר פ) אפשר משום דילמא אתי להשתמש בבע"ח (ת"י):

אריוך. שם מלך כדכתיב אריוך מלך אלסר (בראשית יד) ונקט' טפי משאר מלכים לפי שמובלע בו לשון ארי:

דשמעיה דקא מסיים בה כו'. אע"ג דקיי"ל צ) כרב באיסורי היינו לגבי שמואל לחודיה אבל הכא ר' יוחנן דקי"ל כוותיה לגבי רב קאי כשמואל וברייתא דאוכף נמי קיימא כשמואל למאי דמשני כאן לחממה כאן לצנה ומתני' דאין סכין ומפרכסין לבהמה דמייתי לקמן נמי פליגא אדרב כדפירש בקונטרס:

מאי לאו בגדולים ומשום תענוג. וא"ת ומאי קושיא דילמא הכא מיירי בטרסקל שנתלה מע"ש אבל לתלות בשבת אפי' בחצר אסור ותירץ דדייק מדנקט רה"ר גבי טרסקל טפי משאר דכולהו נמי ברה"ר איירי אלא נקט רה"ר דבחצר מותר בכל ענין:

עין משפט נר מצוה

כא א ב מיי' פ"כ מהל' שבת הל' י סמג לאוין סה טוש"ע א"ח סי' שה סעיף ז:
כב ג מיי' שם הל' יג טוש"ע שם סעי' ח:
כג ד מיי' שם טוש"ע שם סעיף ט:
כד ה מיי' שם טוש"ע שם סעיף י:
כה ו מיי' שם טוש"ע שם סעיף יא:
כו ז שם סעיף י:

רבינו חננאל

מותר לדחות צער בהמה לתלות (קרצטל) [טרסקל] בפיה משום תענוג הוא. ור' יוחנן ושמואל אסרי וכן הלכה והני מילי בבהמות גדולות ומשום תענוג. אבל קטנים דמשום צערא הוא ברה"ר אסורים לצאת הסייחין (בקרצטלין) [בטרסקלין] שבפיהם אבל בחצר שרי. מסורכו פי' חגורו: תניא יוצא אדם באגד שעל גבי (בהמה) [המכה].

רב נסים גאון

ותמצא עיקר דיבור זה בפ' כל הכלים (ד' קכג) הניטלין בשבת ואני אבאר לך פירושו כי ראיתי פירוש להרבה מן החכמים מחט נקובה שנגמרה מלאכתה אם ניטל עוקצה טהורה עוקצה התנבא שלה שהוא פי המחט או חרירה הוא מקום הנקב כבר אין לה תקנה ויצאה מתורת כלי ונתיאשו הבעלים ממנה ולפיכך שנינו בה טהורה כי מעת שניטל עוקצה או חרירא אדם זורקה לבין הגרוטאות ונתיאש ממנה מלעשותה כלי וטהורה היא ואם היתה מחט שאינה נקובה ויש לה עוקץ וכבר שיפה אותה ומירקה ואע"פ שעדיין לא נקבה מפני שהיא ראויה ליטול בה את הקרץ הרי היא כתורת כלי וטמאה כמו הנקובה לפי שהנקובה ראויה לתפירה והיא ראויה להוציא בה את הקרץ וזו וזו שוין בתורת טומאה כמו שאמרו אבל לענין טומאה דא ודא אחת היא ובכדומה לו אמרו בתוספתא (דב"מ דכלים פי"א) ואם מתחילה עשאו לכן אפי' פחות מיכן טמא ובגסטרא אמרו (מס' כלים פ"ד מ"ג) אי זו היא גסטרא כל שניטלו אזניה ואמרו בתוספתא (ב"ק דכלים פ"ג) ואם מתחלה עשאה בלא אזנים נידונית כחבית ואשר אמרו בין נקובה ובין שאינה נקובה מותר לטלטלה בשבת ולא אמרו נקובה אלא לענין טומאה בלבד הוא דתירגם אביי אליבא דרבה בגלומי והוא ברזל חתוך שראויה להעשות מחט והואיל ויש לומר שאם ירצה בעלה לעשותה כלי יכול הוא לעשות כמו שאמרו דימנין דממליך עלה ומשוי לה כלי מותר לטלטלה בשבת ונחשוב אותה לענין טלטול כמו הכלים והיא כמו מחט נקובה לענין שבת אבל לענין טומאה לא והרי היא בחזקת טהורה עד שיגמור מלאכתה ותהיה כלי כמו שאמרו בתוספתא בסוף בבא קמא דכלים גולמי כלי מתכות הרי הן ככל הכלים אלא שהן טהורין: אמר

מסורת הש"ס

א) לקמן נד:, ב) [תוספ' פ"ה], ג) [גיר' הערוך קרסטל וכן איתא כרי"ף], ד) [ברכות מב: וש"נ], ה) [חולין עו:], ו) [תוספת' פ"ה], ז) [פי' לשון של זהורית שתולין לסוס משום עי' ערוך], ח) [לעיל יא:], ט) [גיר' הערוך בערך קש ובקשקשין], י) לקמן סד:, כ) עי' ברש"י חולין מה:, ל) [ובחולין עו: פרש"י על שם אריוך מלך אלסר כמ"ש תוס' כאן ובמנחות לח: פרש"י כמו גור ארי' יהודה ולהכי קרי לשמואל אריוך דקי"ל הלכתא כשמואל בדינא ובקדושין לט. לא פרש"י כלום] מ"כ טעם אחר דאריוך מלך היינו דהלכה כוותיה בדינא כמו דינא דמלכות' אלסר נוטריקון אל אסר כלומר אוך מלעניין איסור' דאין הל' כותי' אלא כרב, מ) [חולין מב. וע"ש בתוס' ד"ה ניקב ותוס' נד. ד"ה ואלו כשרות כולהו צריכי וקל"ע], נ) נ"ל במרא ד' קנד:, ס) נ"ל אפשר, ע) [בכורות מט:].

ליקוטי רש"י

חלודה. רקביבות. רדולי"א מלודה [דהויא בכלין] ברזל שאין משתמשין בו [יומא לח:]. ולא [אמרו] נקובה. להיות תורת כלי עליה יותר משאין נקובה אלא לענין טומאה [לקמן קכג.]. תרגמא אביי אליבא דרבא. במקום (אביי) ובכילו שהאה משנה זו מתורגמת לפי דבריו [סוכה יט. בסוגיין רבא]. בגלמי. גולמי מחטין העומדות לינקב דנקובה נגמרה מלאכתה ושאינה נקובה אינה נגמרה מלאכתה הלכך לענין טומאה הוא דלא הוי כלי אבל בטלטול שריא דחזי לקוץ [לקמן שם]. מרדעת. העשויה כמין כר [בראשית לא, לד]. [ע"כ שייך לד נב:].

והוא שקשורה לו מע"ש. גלי מאתמול שיהא צריכה לכך שיהא לה למלבוש [לקמן נד: ועי' כאן בתוס']. אוכף. בול"א בלע"ז [ב"ק יז:]. אבא. שמואל היה קורא לרב אבא לכבודו [ברכות מז.]. רב הכי הוה קרי ליה שמואל דרב הוה עדיף מיניה אני שמעתי אבא ואית דגרסי אבא חברי [חולין מה:]. רב [שמואל] הוי קרי ליה הכי משום כבוד [שם לח.]. כך שמו של רב אלא בכבוד קורין אותו רב בבבל הכי כמו שקורין לרבי יהודה הנשיא בארץ ישראל רבינו וכן מוכיח בשחיטת חולין (קלז:) דאמרי' מאן ריש סידרא בבבל אבא אריכא וברב מיירי שהיה רב ארוך בדורו כדאמרינן במסכת נדה (כד:) [רשב"ם פסחים קיט:]. יישר. שפיר קאמרת [חולין עה:]. אריוך. קרי שמואל על שם אריוך מלך אלסר (בראשית יד) דהלכתא כוותיה בדיני [שם עו: ועי' כאן בתוס']. לשון מלך כמו (בראשית מט) גור אריה יהודה להכי קרי לשמואל אריוך דקיימא לן (בכורות מט:) הלכה כשמואל בדיני כי היכי דדינא דמלכותא דינא [מנחות לח:]. בכים שלו. כיס שעושין לזב וקושרו לפי האמה לקבל בו את הזוב [לעיל יא:]. בקמיע. שכותבין וטוענין לרפואה [לקמן ס.]. זוג. לנוי עביד [שם נח.].

silent. Rav Assi bar Nassan thought that R' Chiya bar Rav Ashi disregarded the question because he held that it is permitted to put a saddle on as well. אֵיתִיבֵיהּ – **[Rav Assi bar Nassan]** therefore **challenged [R' Chiya bar Rav Ashi]** on the basis of the following Baraisa: אוּכָּף שֶׁעַל גַּבֵּי חֲמוֹר – A SADDLE THAT IS ON THE BACK OF A DONKEY, לֹא יְטַלְטְלֶנָּה בְּיָדוֹ – ONE MAY NOT MOVE IT (i.e. take it off the donkey) WITH ONE'S HAND,[12] אֶלָּא מוֹלִיכָהּ וּמְבִיאָהּ בֶּחָצֵר – BUT ONE MAY WALK [THE DONKEY] TO AND FRO IN A COURTYARD וְהוּא נוֹפֵל מֵאֵילָיו – AND [THE SADDLE] WILL FALL OFF BY ITSELF. הַשְׁתָּא לִיטּוֹל אָמְרַת לֹא – **Now** that **you** (i.e. the Baraisa) **say** that one is **not** allowed **to take** a saddle off a donkey, לְהַנִּיחַ מִיבַּעְיָא – **is it** even **necessary** to say that one is not allowed **to put** it on?![13] From this Baraisa it is evident that one may *not* put a saddle on a donkey.[14] – ? –

R' Zeira defends R' Chiya bar Rav Ashi:

אָמַר לֵיהּ רַבִּי זֵירָא – **R' Zeira said to [Rav Assi bar Nassan]:** שַׁבְקֵיהּ – **Leave him alone!** כְּרַבֵּיהּ סְבִירָא לֵיהּ – **He agrees with his teacher** [Rav], דְּאָמַר רַב חִיָּיא בַּר אַשִׁי אָמַר רַב – **for Rav Chiya bar Ashi said in the name of Rav:** תּוֹלִין טְרַסְקָל לִבְהֵמָה בְּשַׁבָּת – **"One may hang a feed bag on an animal on the Sabbath."**[15] וְקַל וָחוֹמֶר לְמַרְדַּעַת – **Now,** from this ruling we can derive **a *kal vachomer*** which has application **to** the case of **a saddle cloth,** as follows: וּמַה הָתָם דְּמִשּׁוּם תַּעֲנוּג שָׁרֵי – **Since that,** i.e. a feed bag, **which is** only **for** the animal's **pleasure,**[16] **is permitted,** הָכָא דְּמִשּׁוּם צַעַר לֹא כָּל שֶׁכֵּן – then **this,** i.e. a saddle cloth, **which is for** the purpose of alleviating the animal's **suffering,**[17] should be permitted **all the more so!**[18]

As previously stated, Rav permits one to put a feed bag (and certainly a saddle cloth) on a donkey on the Sabbath. The Gemara now cites a dissenting view:

שְׁמוּאֵל אָמַר – **But Shmuel says:** מַרְדַּעַת מוּתָּר טְרַסְקָל אָסוּר – **A saddle cloth is permitted; a feed bag is forbidden.**[19]

The Gemara narrates:

אֲזַל רַבִּי חִיָּיא בַּר יוֹסֵף אֲמָרָהּ לִשְׁמַעְתָּא דְּרַב קַמֵּיהּ דִּשְׁמוּאֵל – **R' Chiya bar Yosef went** and **recounted the teaching of Rav before Shmuel.**[20] אָמַר לֵיהּ – **[Shmuel] said to him:** אִי הָכִי אָמַר אַבָּא – **If that** is what **Abba**[21] **said,** לֹא יָדַע בְּמִילֵּי דְשַׁבְּתָא וְלֹא כְּלוּם – **he does not know anything at all about the laws of the Sabbath!**

The Gemara further relates:

כִּי סְלִיק רַבִּי זֵירָא – **When R' Zeira went up** from Babylonia to Eretz Yisrael, אַשְׁכְּחֵיהּ לְרַבִּי בִּנְיָמִין בַּר יֶפֶת דְּיָתִיב וְקָאָמַר לֵיהּ מִשְּׁמֵיהּ דְּרַבִּי יוֹחָנָן – **he found R' Binyamin bar Yefes sitting and saying to him in the name of R' Yochanan:** נוֹתְנִין מַרְדַּעַת עַל גַּבֵּי חֲמוֹר בְּשַׁבָּת – **"One may put a saddle cloth on a donkey on the Sabbath."** אָמַר לֵיהּ – **[R' Zeira] said to him:** יִישַׁר וְכֵן תַּרְגְּמָהּ אַרְיוֹךְ בְּבָבֶל – **"Well said! And Aryoch in Babylonia explained likewise!"**

The Gemara identifies Aryoch:

אַרְיוֹךְ מַנּוּ – **Who is "Aryoch"?** שְׁמוּאֵל – **Shmuel.**[22]

The Gemara asks:

וְהָא רַב נַמִּי אֲמָרָהּ – **But Rav also said it!**[23] Why did R' Zeira specify Shmuel?

The Gemara answers:

אֶלָּא שַׁמְעֵיהּ דַּהֲוָה מְסַיֵּים בֵּיהּ – **Rather, [R' Zeira] heard [R'**

NOTES

12. It is an unnecessary exertion (*Beis Yosef, Orach Chaim* end of 305:8; *Mishnah Berurah* ibid. §33; cf. *Meromei Sadeh*).

13. Putting a saddle on a donkey is more likely to be forbidden than taking it off, because one thereby appears as though he needs to load a burden onto the donkey (*Rashi*).

14. The Baraisa thus contradicts R' Chiya bar Rav Ashi, whose silence was construed by Rav Assi bar Nassan as meaning that it is permitted to put a saddle on a donkey.

15. A basket full of barley that is hung on the animal's neck and fits around its mouth (*Rashi*). [Rav permits one to hang such a bag on an animal inside a private domain.]

16. It increases the donkey's comfort in that it alleviates the need for the animal to bend down toward the floor to eat (*Rashi*).

17. From the cold (*Rashi*).

18. It has thus been shown that Rav permits one to put a saddle cloth on a donkey during the Sabbath. Therefore, when R' Chiya bar Rav Ashi responded to Rav Assi bar Nassan that a saddle cloth is permitted, he was only quoting the opinion of his teacher, Rav. It can now be understood why R' Chiya bar Rav Ashi was silent in the face of Rav Assi bar Nassan's objection (namely, why is a saddle different?). He disregarded the problem not because he held that a saddle is also permitted (as assumed previously), but rather because he felt that any objections to Rav's ruling are the responsibility of Rav himself. Hence, Rav Chiya bar Rav Ashi could well agree that it is *prohibited* to put a saddle on a donkey on the Sabbath, as Rav Assi bar Nassan derived from the Baraisa (see *Mahadura Basra;* cf. *Ritva MHK* ed. and *Chidushei HaRan*). [It is discussed below whether in fact putting on a saddle is permitted or prohibited, and if prohibited, why it is different from a saddle cloth.]

19. Since the purpose of a saddle cloth is to prevent suffering, its use is widespread and frequent. It is therefore a typical part of an animal's trappings, and is not considered a burden (*Rashi*). [A feed bag, on the other hand, which serves only to provide comfort, is forbidden, for it is considered an unnecessary exertion.]

[*Rashi's* use of the word "burden" in this context requires explanation. Surely the question of whether an item is defined as a burden is relevant only to the matter of wearing it in a public domain. In this context, though, the issue is whether putting the item on an animal in a private domain is an excessive exertion [see note 9] (*Rashash; Meromei Sadeh*). This problem can be solved on the basis of *Ritva* (*MHK* ed. ד״ה וכי), who writes that *removing* a saddle is a prohibited exertion *because* a saddle is not a real article of attire; the animal, for example, may not go out with it into a public domain. Thus, we see that there is some correlation between the two issues. Putting an item on an animal or removing it is more likely to be deemed an excessive exertion if that item is a burden than if it is attire. (See *Dibros Moshe* 43:7, who connects the two issues in a different manner.)

Having established that *Rashi* here means a burden with respect to the concept of excessive exertion, we can clarify the following point: In reference to the first passage on this *amud, Rashi* taught that a saddle cloth tied on *during* the Sabbath is a burden (see note 1). This apparently contradicts *Rashi* here, who writes that it is *not* a burden! However, this is in fact not a contradiction at all, because *Rashi* above was speaking of a burden in the sense of an item that may not be taken into a public domain, while here he means a burden with respect to the laws of unnecessary exertion. Since the donkey needs the saddle cloth to warm up, putting on the saddle cloth is not a burden as far as unnecessary exertion is concerned. (Cf. *Meromei Sadeh.*)]

20. He told Shmuel that Rav permits one to put a feed bag on an animal during the Sabbath (*Rashi*).

21. The word אַבָּא, which literally means father, is used in this context as a term of endearment signifying a friend. A similar usage is found in *Genesis* 41:43, where Joseph is called אַבְרֵךְ, which is rendered by Targum Onkelos as אַבָּא לְמַלְכָּא, literally: father of the king [although in fact Joseph was subordinate to the king] (*Rashi*).

Elsewhere, *Rashi* writes that Shmuel referred to Rav as אַבָּא, *father,* to show his respect (*Chullin* 38a ד״ה לאבא; ibid. 45b ד״ה אבא).

22. אַרְיוֹךְ stems from רֵיכָא, which is Aramaic for king (see *Bava Basra* 4a; see also *Rashi* to *Genesis* ibid.). Shmuel was called this because as an expert in civil law, he judged the people like a king, who serves as the supreme judge of the land (*Rashi*). Furthermore, the halachah follows Shmuel in matters of financial law, just as a king's authority invests his decisions with the force of law (*Rashi* to *Menachos* 38b).

Another explanation is that this name was derived from אַרְיוֹךְ, *Aryoch,* king of Ellasar, mentioned in *Genesis* 14:1 (*Rashi* to *Chullin* 76b ד״ה אריוך). The name Aryoch was chosen from among other names of kings, because it includes the word אֲרִי, *lion* [which is a symbol of monarchy, as in *Genesis* 49:9] (*Tosafos* here; see *Rashi* to *Menachos* ibid.; cf. *Chidushei HaRan*).

23. Since Rav permits a feed bag, he would certainly permit a saddle cloth (*Rashi,* from Gemara above).

גמ' אמר שמואל [א] והוא שקשורה לו מע"ש אמר רב נחמן מתני' נמי דיקא דקתני א) אין החמור יוצא במרדעת בזמן שאינה קשורה לו היכי דמי אילימא שאינה קשורה לו כלל פשיטא דילמא נפלה ליה ואתי לאתויי אלא לאו שאינה קשורה מע"ש מכלל דרישא שקשורה לו מע"ש ש"מ תניא נמי הכי ב) חמור יוצא במרדעת בזמן שקשורה לו מע"ש [ב] ולא באוכף אע"פ שקשורה לו מע"ש רבן שמעון בן גמליאל אומר אף באוכף בזמן שקשורה לו מע"ש ובלבד שלא יקשור לו מסריכן ובלבד שלא יפשול לו רצועה תחת זנבו בעא מיניה רב אסי בר נתן מר' חייא בר רב אשי מהו ליתן מרדעת על גבי חמור בשבת אמר ליה [ג] מותר א"ל וכי מה בין זה לאוכף אישתיק איתיביה [ד] אוכף שעל גבי חמור לא יטלטלנה בידו אלא מוליכה ומביאה בחצר והוא נופל מאליו השתא ליטול אמרת לא להניח מיבעיא אמר ליה ר' זירא שבקיה כרביה סבירא ליה דאמר רב חייא בר אשי אמר רב תולין ג) טרסקל לבהמה בשבת וקל וחומר למרדעת ומה התם דמשום תענוג שרי הכא דמשום צער לא כל שכן שמואל אמר מרדעת מותר [ה] טרסקל אסור אזל ר' חייא בר יוסף אמרה לשמעתא דרב קמיה דשמואל א"ל אי הכי אמר אבא לא ידע במילי דשבתא ולא כלום כי סליק ר' זירא אשכחיה לר' בנימין בר יפת דיתיב וקאמר ליה משמיה דר' יוחנן נותנין מרדעת על גבי חמור בשבת א"ל ד) יישר וכן תרגמה אריוך בבבל ה) אריוך מנו שמואל והא רב נמי אמרה אלא שמעיה דהוה מסיים ביה ואין תולין טרסקל בשבת א"ל יישר וכן תרגמה אריוך בבבל דכולי עלמא מיהת מרדעת מותר מאי שנא מאוכף שאני התם דאפשר דנפיל ממילא רב פפא אמר כאן לחממה כאן לצננה לחממה אית לה צערא לצננה לית לה צערא והיינו דאמרי אינשי חמרא אפי' בתקופת תמוז קרירא לה מיתיבי ו) [ו] לא יצא הסוס בזנב שועל ולא ז) בזהורית שבין עיניו ח) לא יצא הזב בכים שלו ולא עזים בכים שבדדיהן ולא פרה בחסום שבפיה ולא סייחים בטרסקלין שבפיהם לרה"ר ולא בהמה בסנדל שברגליה ולא בקמיע אע"פ שהוא מומחה וזו חומר בבהמה מבאדם אבל יוצא הוא באגד שעל גבי המכה ט) ובקשישין שעל גבי השבר ובשליא המדולדלת בה י) ופוקקין לה זוג בצוארה ומטיילת עמו בחצר קתני מיהת ולא סייחין בטרסקלים שבפיהם לרה"ר לרה"ר הוא דלא הא בחצר שפיר דמי מאי לאו בגדולים ומשום תענוג לא [ז] בקטנים ומשום צער דיקא נמי דקתני

דומיא

רש"י

גמ' מתניתין נמי דיקא. לקמן בהאי פירקא: אף באוכף. דאיהו נמי מהני לחממה: ובלבד שלא יקשור לו מסריכן. פוטרא"ל דמיחזי כמי שרוצה להטעינו משוי: רצועה תחת זנבו. פושל"א שנותנים שם שלא תרד האוכף והמשוי על צוארה כשהיא יורדת לעמק והמסרך שלא תרד על זנבה כשהיא עולה על ההרים: מהו ליתן מרדעת. ולא לצאת לרה"ר אלא בחצר ומפני הצינה: ה"ג אמר ליה מותר א"ל וכי מה בין זה לאוכף אישתיק: איתיביה כו'. כסבור הא דאישתיק משום דלא אסגא ביה דסבר אוכף נמי שרי ואותיביה מברייתא דאסור ליטלה והשתא ליטול אמרת לא להניח מיבעי' דדמי כאילו צריך להטעינה משוי: כרביה. רב: טרסקל. סל מלא שעורים תולין לה בצוארה ופיה נתון לתוכו ואוכלת ותענוג בעלמא הוא שלא תטרח לשוח צוארה לארץ: צער. של צינה: מרדעת מותר. דצערא היא הלכך אורחה בהכי ולאו משוי הוא: לשמעתא דרב. דשרי בטרסקל: אבא. כ) חברי כמו אברך אבא למלכא (בראשית מא): שמואל קרי אריוך על שם שהיה בקי בדינין ושופט כמלך השופט על הארץ לשון ריכא ל) מלך (ב"ב דף ד.): והא רב נמי אמרה. דכיון דשרי בטרסקל כ"ש מרדעת: מאי שנא מאוכף. שאסור ליטול וכ"ש להניחו: דנפיל ממילא. כדקתני מוליכו ומביאו לחצר והוא נופל מאליו: כאן לחממה. מרדעת צריך לחממה ומותר משום צער דצינה אבל נטילת אוכף אינו אלא שיצטנן שנתחממה ע"י משאוי שנשאה מבעוד יום ואי לא שקיל ליה לא איכפת לן שהרי הוא יצטנן מאליו דאמרי אינשי וכו': בזנב שועל. שתולין לו בין עיניו שלא ישלוט בו עין: זהורית. לנוי: בכים שלו. שתולין לו באמתו לקבל זוב ולבדוק מנין ראיותיו שאינו תכשיט לו: בכים שבדדיהן. לקבל חלב הנוטף אי נמי שלא ישרטו דדיהן על הקוצים שהיו דדיהן גסין: בחסום שבפיה. שחוסמין אותה שלא תרעה בשדות אחרים וכשמגיעין למקום מרעיתם נוטלין אותה הימנה: בסנדל שברגליה. שעושין לה סנדל של מתכת שלא יזיקוה האבנים: קמיע. כתב לרפואת חולי: מומחה. שריפא כבר ג' פעמים: וזה חומר בבהמה מבאדם. קס"ד השתא דאקמיע קאי דאמרינן לקמן בפרק במה אשה יוצאה (ד' סא.) שהאדם יוצא בקמיע מומחה וכל הני דקתני לא תצא הנך דלאו שמירת גופה הוא אלא משאוי וסנדל משום דדילמא מישתליף ואתי לאתויי: אגד שעל גבי המכה. ליכא למימר אתי לאתויי: קשישין שעל השבר. בהמה שנשבר בה עצם עושין לה דפין מכאן ומכאן וקושרים אותן שם והן מעמידין העצם שלא ינוד אנה ואנה עד שמתחבר: ובשליא המדולדלת בה. שיצתה מקצתה: ופוקקין לה זוג. אבל כשאינו פקוק אפי' בחצר לא תצא מפני שהעינבל שבתוכה מקשקש ומוליד קול לכך פוקק בצמר או במוכין שלא יקשקש העינבל שבתוכה: זוג. אישקלי"ט: עינבל. בטדי"ל: ומטיילת. באותו זוג בחצר אבל לא תצא בו לרה"ר כדמפרש לקמן בפרקין (דף נד:) דמיחזי כמאן דאזיל לחינגא: מאי לאו. בסייחים גדולים קאמר דצוארן ארוך ואין להם צער לשוח ולאכול מע"ג הקרקע ותולה להן טרסקל לתענוג וקשיא לשמואל: קטנים. ארכובותיהן גבוהין וצוארן קטן ויש להם צער לשוח ע"ג הקרקע ולאכול:

דומיא

תוספות

והוא שקשורה לו מע"ש. רש"י פי' לקמן דבקשורה מע"ש הוי מלבוש החמור אבל באינה קשורה מע"ש הוי משאוי ועוד יש לפרש דבאינה קשורה מע"ש מיחזי כמתכוין להוצאת המרדעת וה"ר פור"ת פירש דמיחזי כאילו מתכוין להוליך הבהמה למקום רחוק:

אילימא שאינה קשורה לו כלל פשיטא. ולא בעי למפרך דמרישא שמעינן לה דקתני בזמן שהיא קשורה הא אינה קשורה לא דדרך משניות כן במסכת ע"ז (דף לה:) אלו דברים אסורין באכילה כבשים שדרכן לתת לתוכן יין כו' ובסיפא (שם דף לט:) קתני ואלו מותרים באכילה כו' וכבשים שאין דרכן לתת כו' ובפרק אלו טרפות (חולין דף מד.) קתני אלו כשרות אע"ג דאיכא מינייהו דשמעי' מרישא מ) וא"ת ונפשוט מרישא דבקשורה מערב שבת איירי מדאיצטריך למיתני בזמן שהיא קשורה דבלאו הכי הוה ידעי' דאיירי בקשורה דאי באינה קשורה פשיטא דאסור דילמא נפלה ואתי לאתויי כדקאמר הכא אילימא כו' אלא ודאי בזמן שקשורה מע"ש קאמר וי"ל דמרישא לא תפשוט דאדרבה ה"א דלהכי תנא בזמן שהיא קשורה לאשמעי' דאפי' קשורה בשבת דאי לא תנא ליה ה"א דוקא בקשורה לו מע"ש אבל בקשורה בשבת לא קמ"ל להכי דייק מסיפא:

מהו ליתן המרדעת ע"ג חמור בשבת. ואין לאסור משום דאין כלי ניטל אלא לדבר הניטל דבהמה חשיבא כדבר הניטל כיון דיכול למושכה ולהוליכה בכל מקום ורב אסי בר נתן דבעי אם אסור אין לפרש משום דמיחזי כרוצה להוליך הבהמה למקום רחוק דא"כ היכי דייק דמאן דשרי טרסקל כ"ש מרדעת. ואין לפרש נמי דבעי למיסר בחצר אטו רה"ר כדאמר גבי אשה בפ' במה אשה (לקמן דף סד:) דגבי בהמה לא גזרו כדתניא בסמוך גבי זוג ומטיילת עמו בחצר אלא נראה לר"י דטעמא משום טרחא דשבת ואע"ג דשריא קרצוף בפ"ב דבילה (דף כג.) התם יש לה צער ביותר א"נ לא שרי אלא בי"ט אבל בשבת אסור:

אוכף שע"ג החמור. וא"ת ויתיר האוכף וינער ויפול כדאמר בפ' נ) כל כתבי גבי היתה בהמתו טעונה טבל כו' וי"ל דהתם מיירי בשקין שתוכל הבהמה להתקלקל אבל מחמת האוכף לא תוכל הבהמה להתקלקל לכך לא התירו:

תולין טרסקל. וא"ת ותאסר משום דמשתמש בבע"ח כי היכי דאסור להניח נר על גבי דקל בשבת משום דמשתמש במחובר וי"ל דהתם מנענע הענפים אבל הכא אינו מנענע הבהמה בכך ורב אסי ברבי נתן דבעי למיסר ס) אפשר משום דילמא אתי להשתמש בבע"ח (ת"י):

אריוך. שם מלך כדכתיב אריוך מלך אלסר (בראשית יד) ונקטי' טפי משאר מלכים לפי שמובלע בו לשון ארי: דשמעיה דקא מסיים בה כו'. אע"ג דקיי"ל ע) כרב באיסורי היינו לגבי שמואל לחודיה אבל הכא ר' יוחנן דקי"ל כוותיה לגבי רב קאי כשמואל וברייתא דאוכף נמי קיימא כשמואל למאי דמשני כאן לחממה כאן לצננה ומתני' דאין סכין ומפרכסין לבהמה דמייתי לקמן נמי פליגא אדרב כדפירש בקונטרס:

מאי לאו בגדולים ומשום תענוג. וא"ת ומאי קושיא דילמא הכא מיירי בטרסקל שנתלה מע"ש אבל לתלות בשבת אפי' בחצר אסור ותירץ דדייק מדנקט רה"ר גבי טרסקל טפי משאר דכולהו נמי ברה"ר איירי אלא נקט רה"ר דבחצר מותר בכל ענין:

כגון

עין משפט נר מצוה

כא א ב מיי' פ"כ מהל' שבת הל' י סמג לאוין סה טוש"ע א"ח סי' שה סעיף ז:
כב ג מיי' שם הל' יג טוש"ע שם סעי' ח:
כג ד מיי' שם טוש"ע שם סעיף ט:
כד ה מיי' שם טוש"ע שם סעיף י:
כה ו מיי' שם טוש"ע שם סעיף יא:
כו ז שם סעיף י:

רבינו חננאל

מותר לדחות צער בהמה לתלות (קרצטל) [טרסקל] בפיה משום תענוג הוא. ור' יוחנן ושמואל אסרי וכן הלכה והני מילי בבהמות גדולות ומשום תענוג. אבל קטנים דמשום צערא הוא ברה"ר אסורים לצאת הסייחין (בקרצטלין) [בטרסקלין] שבפיהם אבל בחצר שרי. מסורכו פי' חגורו: תניא יוצא אדם באגד שעל גבי (בהמה) [המכה].

רב נסים גאון

ותמצא עיקר דיבור זה בפ' כל הכלים (ד' קכג) הניטלין בשבת ואני אבאר לך פירושו כי ראיתי פירוש להרבה מן החכמים מחט נקובה שנגמרה מלאכתה אם ניטל עוקצה טהורה עוקצה התתבא שלה שהוא פי המחט או חרירה הוא מקום הנקב כבר אין לה תקנה ויצאה מתורת כלי ונתיאשו הבעלים ממנה ולפיכך שנינו בה טהורה כי מעת שניטל עוקצה או חרירא אדם זורקה לבין הגרוטאות ונתיאש ממנה מלעשותה כלי וטהורה היא ואם היתה מחט שאינה נקובה ויש לה עוקץ וכבר שיפה אותה ומירקה ואע"פ שעדיין לא נקבה מפני שהיא ראויה ליטול בה את הקוץ הרי היא כתורת כלי וטמאה כמו הנקובה לפי שהנקובה ראויה לתפירה והיא ראויה להוציא בה את הקוץ וזו וזו שוין בתורת טומאה כמו שאמרו אבל לענין טומאה דא ודא אחת היא ובכדומה לו אמרו בתוספתא (דב"מ דכלים פי"א) ואם מתחילה עשאו לכן אפי' פחות מיכן טמא ובגסטרא אמרו (מס' כלים פ"ד מ"ג) אי זו היא גסטרא כל שניטלו אזניה ואמרו בתוספתא (ב"ק דכלים פ"ג) ואם מתחלה עשאה בלא אזנים נידונית כחבית ואשר אמרו בין נקובה ובין שאינה נקובה מותר לטלטלה בשבת ולא אמרו נקובה אלא לענין טומאה בלבד הוא דתירגם אביי אליבא דרבה בגלומי והוא ברזל חתוך שראויה להעשות מחט והואיל ויש לומר שאם ירצה בעלה לעשותה כלי יכול הוא לעשות כמו שאמרו זימנין דמימליך עלה ומשוי לה כלי מותר לטלטלה בשבת ונחשוב אותה לענין טלטול כמו הכלים והיא כמו מחט נקובה לענין שבת אבל לענין טומאה לא והרי היא בחזקת טהורה עד שיגמור מלאכתה ותהיה כלי כמו שאמרו בתוספתא בסוף בבא קמא דכלים גולמי כלי מתכות הרי הן ככל הכלים אלא שהן טהורין:

אמר

מסורת הש"ס

א) לקמן נד:, ב) [תוספ' פ"ה], ג) [גיר' הערוך קרסטל וכן איתא ברי"ף], ד) [ברכות מב:], ה) [חולין עז:], ו) [תוספ' פ"ה], ז) [פי' לשון של זהורית תולין לסוס משום עין ערוך], ח) [לעיל יא:], ט) [גיר' הערוך בערך קש ובקשישין], י) לקמן סד:, [illegible]

ליקוטי רש"י

[illegible]

Binyamin bar Yefes] conclude: וְאֵין תּוֹלִין טְרַסְקָל בְּשַׁבָּת – **"But one may not hang a feed bag** on an animal **on the Sabbath."** Since regarding this point R' Binyamin followed Shmuel (and not Rav), אָמַר לֵיהּ – **[R' Zeira] said to him:** יִישַּׁר וְכֵן תִּרְגְּמָהּ אַרְיוֹךְ בְּבָבֶל – **"Well said! And Aryoch** [Shmuel] **in Babylonia explained likewise!"**

The Gemara raises a problem:

דְּכוּלֵּי עַלְמָא מִיהַת מַרְדַּעַת מוּתָּר – **At any rate, everyone**[24] **agrees that a saddle cloth is permitted.** מַאי שְׁנָא מֵאוּכָּף – **Why is it different from a saddle,** which is forbidden?[25]

The Gemara answers:

שַׁאנִי הָתָם – It is **different there,** in the case of a saddle, דְּאֶפְשָׁר דְּנָפִיל מִמֵּילָא – **for it is possible that [the saddle] will fall off by itself.**[26]

Rav Pappa gives a different answer:

רַב פָּפָּא אָמַר – **Rav Pappa says:** כָּאן לְחַמְּמָהּ – **Here,** in the case of putting on a saddle cloth, the purpose is **to warm [the donkey];** כָּאן לְצַנְּנָהּ – whereas **here,** in the case of removing a saddle, the purpose is **to cool [the donkey].** לְחַמְּמָהּ אִית לָהּ צַעֲרָא – When one's purpose is **to warm [the donkey], it is** evidently **suffering** from the cold. לְצַנְּנָהּ לֵית לָהּ צַעֲרָא – However, when one's purpose is **to cool [the donkey], it is not** really **suffering** at all. וְהַיְינוּ דְּאָמְרֵי אִינְשֵׁי – **And this is** in accord with the maxim **that people say:** חֲמָרָא אֲפִילּוּ בִתְקוּפַת תַּמּוּז קְרִירָא לָהּ – **"A donkey is cold even during the summer season."**[27]

Shmuel holds that one may put trappings on an animal in order to alleviate its suffering, but not merely to increase its comfort.[28] The Gemara challenges this position:

מֵיתִיבֵי – **They challenged** it on the basis of the following Baraisa: לֹא יֵצֵא הַסּוּס בִּזְנַב שׁוּעָל וְלֹא בְּזַהֲרוּרִית שֶׁבֵּין עֵינָיו – A HORSE MAY NOT GO OUT into a public domain on the Sabbath WITH A FOX TAIL[29] OR WITH A RED STRIP[30] BETWEEN ITS EYES. לֹא יֵצֵא הַזָּב בְּכִיס שֶׁלּוֹ – A *ZAV* MAY NOT GO OUT WITH HIS POUCH;[31] וְלֹא עִזִּים בְּכִיס שֶׁבְּדַדֵּיהֶן – AND GOATS may NOT go out WITH A POUCH ON THEIR UDDERS;[32] וְלֹא פָּרָה בַּחֲסוֹם שֶׁבְּפִיהָ – AND A COW may NOT go out WITH A MUZZLE ON ITS MOUTH;[33] וְלֹא סְיָיחִים בִּטְרַסְקָלִין

NOTES

24. Rav, Shmuel and R' Yochanan.

25. It is forbidden to remove a saddle from a donkey [Baraisa above] and certainly to put it on (*Rashi,* from Gemara above; see note 13).

[The question raised here is the same as the one posed by Rav Assi bar Nassan to R' Chiya bar Rav Ashi (see notes 11 and 14). The Gemara does not resolve this difficulty until now.]

26. As the Baraisa states above: "One may walk [the donkey] to and fro in a courtyard and [the saddle] will fall off by itself" (*Rashi*). Since it is possible to remove the saddle without handling it, one is forbidden to remove it by hand, for that would be an exertion that is truly unnecessary.

This logic obviously applies only to the removal of a saddle, and not to putting it on. Therefore, one can no longer argue that since the Baraisa prohibits a saddle's removal, it certainly prohibits its placement. It is possible that only removing a saddle is forbidden (because the saddle could fall off by itself), while putting it on is permitted. Thus, the premise of the Gemara's question (viz. why is putting on a saddle cloth permitted, but putting on a saddle is prohibited) has been eliminated. In point of fact, both activities could well be permitted (*Maharam; Menachem Meishiv Nefesh*).

According to this answer given by the Gemara, the cases can be summarized, in order of decreasing stringency, as follows:

(a) *Feed bag* – Rav and Shmuel disagree as to whether putting on a feed bag, which only increases the animal's comfort, is permitted.

(b) *Saddle* – Both agree, however, that putting on a saddle is permitted, because it alleviates *some* of the donkey's suffering (see note 6).

(c) *Saddle cloth* – Putting on a saddle cloth is certainly permitted, because it alleviates the donkey's suffering completely.

Removing a saddle is prohibited according to all (regardless of any benefit to the donkey), because one could let the saddle fall off by itself.

27. [Literally: the equinox of *Tammuz.*] The purpose of removing a saddle from a donkey on the Sabbath would be to let it cool down from the exertion of having carried a load before the Sabbath began. However, even if one does not remove it, the donkey will not really suffer, for since donkeys are chronically chilled, it will soon cool down of its own accord. On the other hand, putting a saddle cloth on a donkey [when it is cold] truly relieves it of suffering (*Rashi;* see *Beur HaGra* to *Orach Chaim* 305:8). It is understandable, therefore, that removing a saddle is prohibited, while putting on a saddle cloth is permitted.

Rav Pappa does not directly address the Gemara's original question (viz. why putting on a saddle cloth is permitted, whereas putting on a saddle is prohibited). It seems that, in Rav Pappa's view, this is not a problem at all, because the benefit of a saddle to a donkey is negligible compared to the benefit of a saddle cloth. The only issue that Rav Pappa considered worthy of discussion is why putting on a saddle cloth is permitted whereas *removing* a saddle is prohibited. After all, in both cases the animal receives a real benefit. To this Rav Pappa answers that putting on a saddle cloth relieves the donkey from pain, while removing a saddle merely gives it pleasure.

Rav Pappa would list the cases, in decreasing order of stringency, as follows:

(a) *Saddle* – Rav and Shmuel both prohibit putting a saddle on a donkey, because it gives the donkey no significant benefit.

(b) *Feed bag* – In the case of putting on a feed bag, which gives the donkey pleasure, Rav permits and Shmuel prohibits.

(c) *Saddle cloth* – Rav and Shmuel both permit putting a saddle cloth on a donkey because it alleviates the animal's suffering.

As to the issue of *removing* a saddle, Rav would rule that this is permitted because it gives the donkey pleasure. It thus emerges that Rav is contradicted by the Baraisa, which explicitly forbids removing a saddle. This is not a problem, because, as stated in several places in the Gemara, Rav has the status of a Tanna in that he has the authority to disagree with Tannaic rulings (see *Rashi* to 53b לא דגמר מכה and *Chidushei HaRan* there).

[These summaries reflect one understanding of this passage as it is explained by *Rashi.* For further discussion, see the commentaries on *Tur* and *Shulchan Aruch Orach Chaim* §305, *Chelkas Binyamin, Rosh Yosef, Meromei Sadeh, Dibros Moshe* 43:6,7 and others.]

28. As stated above, Shmuel permits a saddle cloth, which relieves a donkey of its suffering [from the cold], but he forbids a feed bag, whose purpose is only to increase the animal's comfort (see Gemara above with notes 15-19).

29. The fox tail is hung between the horse's eyes to ward off עַיִן הָרַע, *the evil eye* (*Rashi*). This and most of the items listed below may not be worn in a public domain because they are in the category of a burden (*Rashi* ד״ה וזה חומר).

30. A red strip of cloth used to decorate the horse (*Rashi*). Since most people do not decorate horses in this manner, it is considered a burden (*Rashba*).

31. A *zav* is a male who experiences a gonorrheal emission, similar (but not identical) to a seminal emission. Two emissions on the same day or on two consecutive days render him *tamei* for at least seven days. Three emissions on the same day or on two or three consecutive days also obligate him to bring a pair of bird offerings (see *Leviticus* 15:1-15). A *zav* would attach a pouch to his organ in which to collect the emissions so that he would know their number and frequency. Since this pouch is neither an article of clothing nor an adornment, a *zav* may not wear it in a public domain on the Sabbath (*Rashi;* see Gemara above, 11b-12a).

32. The pouch collects any dripping milk. Alternatively, it protects large udders from being scratched by thorns (*Rashi*). [According to the first explanation, the pouch could be a burden (see 53b note 37). But according to the second explanation, it is really an article of attire, because it serves to protect the animal. The reason why it is forbidden in that case is that it is not tied on securely and could fall off (see *Maharsha* to 53b ד״ה בד״ה ליבש).]

33. A cow is muzzled to prevent it from grazing in other people's fields. When the cow reaches its own pasture, the muzzle is removed (*Rashi*). [A muzzle is regarded as a burden.]

א והוא **גמ'** אמר שמואל והוא שקשורה לו מע"ש אמר רב נחמן מתני' נמי דיקא דקתני א) אין החמור יוצא במרדעת בזמן שאינה קשורה לו היכי דמי אילימא שאינה קשורה לו כלל פשיטא דילמא נפלה ליה ואתי לאתויי אלא לאו שאינה קשורה מע"ש מכלל דרישא שקשורה לו מע"ש ש"מ תניא נמי הכי ב) חמור יוצא במרדעת בזמן שקשורה לו מע"ש ב ולא באוכף אע"פ שקשורה לו מע"ש רבן שמעון בן גמליאל אומר אף באוכף בזמן שקשורה לו מע"ש ובלבד שלא יקשור לו מסריכן ובלבד שלא יפשול לו רצועה תחת זנבו בעא מיניה רב אסי בר נתן מר' חייא בר רב אשי מהו ליתן מרדעת על גבי חמור בשבת אמר ליה ג מותר א"ל וכי מה בין זה לאוכף אישתיק איתיביה ד אוכף שעל גבי חמור לא יטלטלנה בידו אלא מוליכה ומביאה בחצר והוא נופל מאליו השתא ליטול אמרת לא להניח מיבעיא אמר ליה ר' זירא שבקיה כרביה סבירא ליה דאמר רב חייא בר אשי אמר רב תולין ג) טרסקל לבהמה בשבת וקל וחומר למרדעת ומה התם דמשום תענוג שרי הכא דמשום צער לא כל שכן שמואל אמר מרדעת מותר ה טרסקל אסור אזל ר' חייא בר יוסף אמרה לשמעתא דרב קמיה דשמואל א"ל אי הכי אמר אבא לא ידע במילי דשבתא ולא כלום כי סליק ר' זירא אשכחיה לר' בנימין בר יפת דיתיב וקאמר ליה משמיה דר' יוחנן נותנין מרדעת על גבי חמור בשבת א"ל ד) יישר וכן תרגמה אריוך בבבל ה) אריוך מנו שמואל והא רב נמי אמרה אלא שמעיה דהוה מסיים ביה ואין תולין טרסקל בשבת א"ל יישר וכן תרגמה אריוך בבבל דכולי עלמא מיהת מרדעת מותר מאי שנא מאוכף שאני התם דאפשר דנפיל ממילא רב פפא אמר כאן לחממה כאן לצננה לחממה אית לה צערא לצננה לית לה צערא והיינו דאמרי אינשי חמרא אפי' בתקופת תמוז קרירא לה מיתיבי ו) לא יצא הסוס בזנב שועל ולא ז) בזהרורית שבין עיניו ח) לא יצא הזוב בכים שלו ולא עזים בכים שבדדיהן ולא פרה בחסום שבפיה ולא סייחים בטרסקלין שבפיהם לרה"ר ולא בהמה בסנדל שברגליה ולא בקמיע אע"פ שהוא מומחה וזו חומר בבהמה מבאדם אבל יוצא הוא באגד שעל גבי המכה ט) ובקשישין שעל גבי השבר ובשליא המדולדלת בה י) ופוקקין לה זוג בצוארה ומטיילת עמו בחצר קתני מיהת ולא סייחין בטרסקלים שבפיהם לרה"ר לרה"ר הוא דלא הא בחצר שפיר דמי מאי לאו בגדולים ומשום תענוג לא ז בקטנים ומשום צער דיקא נמי דקתני

דומיא

רש"י

גמ' מתניתין נמי דיקא. לקמן בהאי פירקא: **אף באוכף.** דלאיהו נמי מהני לחממה: **ובלבד שלא יקשור לו מסריכן.** פוטרא"ל דמיחזי כמי שרוצה להטעינו משוי: **רצועה תחת זנבו.** פושל"א שנותנים שם שלא תרד האוכף והמשוי על צוארה כשהיא יורדת לעמק והמסרכן שלא תרד על זנבה כשהיא עולה על ההרים: **מהו ליתן מרדעת.** ולא לצאת לרה"ר אלא בחצר ומפני הצינה: ה"ג אמר ליה מותר א"ל וכי מה בין זה לאוכף אישתיק: **איתיביה כו'.** כסבור הא דאישתיק משום דלא אסגא ביה דסבר אוכף נמי שרי ואותיביה מברייתא דאסור ליטלה והשתא ליטול אמרת לא להניח מיבעי' דדמי כאילו צריך להטעינה משוי: **כרביה.** רב: **טרסקל.** סל מלא שעורים תולין לה בצוארה ופיה נתון לתוכו ואוכלת ותענוג בעלמא הוא שלא תטרח לשוח צוארה לארץ: **צער.** של צינה: **מרדעת מותר.** דלצערא היא הלכך אורחה בהכי ולאו משוי הוא: **לשמעתא דרב.** דשרי בטרסקל: **אבא.** כ) חברי כמו אברך אבא למלכא (בראשית מא): **שמואל** קרי אריוך על שם שהיה בקי בדינין ושופט כמלך השופט על הארץ לשון ריכא ל) מלך (ב"ב דף ד.): **והא רב נמי אמרה.** דכיון דשרי בטרסקל כ"ש מרדעת: **מאי שנא מאוכף.** שאסור ליטול וכ"ש להניחו: **דנפיל ממילא.** כדקתני מוליכו ומביאו לחצר והוא נופל מאליו: **כאן לחממה.** מרדעת צריך לחממה ומותר משום צער דצינה אבל נטילת אוכף אינו אלא שיצטנן שנתחממה ע"י משאוי שנשאה מבעוד יום ואי לא שקיל ליה לא איכפת לן שהרי הוא יצטנן מאליו דאמרי אינשי וכו': **בזנב שועל.** שתולין לו בין עיניו שלא ישלוט בו עין: **זהרורית.** לנוי: **בכים שלו.** שתולין לו באמתו לקבל זוב ולבדוק מנין ראיותיו שאינו תכשיט לו: **בכים שבדדיהן.** לקבל חלב הנוטף אי נמי שלא ישרטו דדיהן על הקוצים שהיו דדיהן גסין: **בחסום שבפיה.** שחוסמין אותה שלא תרעה בשדות אחרים וכשמגיעין למקום מרעיתם נוטלין אותה הימנה: **בסנדל שברגליה.** שעושין לה סנדל של מתכת שלא יזיקוה האבנים: **קמיע.** כתב לרפואת חולי: **מומחה.** שריפא כבר ג' פעמים: **וזה חומר בבהמה מבאדם.** קס"ד השתא דאקמיע קאי דאמרינן לקמן בפרק במה אשה יוצאה (ד' סא.) שהאדם יוצא בקמיע מומחה וכל הני דקתני לא תצא הנך דלאו שמירת גופה הוא אלא משאוי וסנדל משום דדילמא מישתליף ואתי לאתויי: **אגד שעל גבי המכה.** ליכא למימר אתי לאתויי: **קשישין שעל השבר.** בהמה שנשבר בה עצם עושין לה דפין מכאן ומכאן וקושרים אותן שם והן מעמידין העצם שלא ינוד אנה ואנה עד שמתחבר: **ובשליא המדולדלת בה.** שילתה מקצתה: **ופוקקין לה זוג.** אבל כשאינו פקוק אפי' בחצר לא תצא מפני שהעינבל שבתוכה מקשקש ומוליד קול לכך פוקק בצמר או במוכין שלא יקשקש העינבל שבתוכה: **זוג.** אישקלי"ט: **עינבל.** בטדי"ל: **ומטיילת.** באותו זוג בחצר אבל לא תצא בו לרה"ר כדמפרש לקמן בפרקין (דף נד:) דמיחזי כמאן דאזיל לחינגא: **מאי לאו.** בסייחים גדולים קאמר דצוארן ארוך ואין להם צער לשוח ולאכול מע"ג הקרקע ותולה להן טרסקל לתענוג וקשיא לשמואל: **קטנים.** ארכובותיהן גבוהין וצוארן קטן ויש להם צער לשוח ע"ג הקרקע ולאכול:

תוספות

והוא שקשורה לו מע"ש. רש"י פי' לקמן דבקשורה מע"ש הוי מלבוש החמור אבל באינה קשורה מע"ש הוי משאוי ועוד יש לפרש דבאינה קשורה מע"ש מיחזי כמתכוין להוצאת המרדעת וה"ר פור"ת פירש דמיחזי כאילו מתכוין להוליך הבהמה למקום רחוק:

אילימא שאינה קשורה לו כלל פשיטא. ולא בעי למפרך דמרישא שמעינן לה דקתני בזמן שהיא קשורה הא אינה קשורה לא דדרך משניות כן במסכת ע"ז (דף לה:) אלו דברים אסורין באכילה כבשים שדרכן לתת לתוכן יין כו' ובסיפא (שם דף לט:) קתני ואלו מותרים באכילה כו' וכבשים שאין דרכן לתת כו' ובפרק אלו טרפות (חולין דף נד.) קתני אלו כשרות אע"ג דאיכא מינייהו דשמעי' מרישא מ) וא"ת ונפשוט מרישא דבקשורה מערב שבת איירי מדאיצטריך למיתני בזמן שהיא קשורה דבלאו הכי הוה ידעי' דאיירי בקשורה דאי באינה קשורה פשיטא דאסור דילמא נפלה ואתי לאתויי כדקאמר הכא אילימא כו' אלא ודאי בזמן שקשורה מע"ש קאמר וי"ל דמרישא לא תפשוט דאדרבה ה"א דלהכי תנא בזמן שהיא קשורה לאשמעי' דאפי' קשורה בשבת דאי לא תנא ליה ה"א דוקא בקשורה לו מע"ש אבל בקשורה בשבת לא קמ"ל להכי דייק מסיפא:

מהו ליתן המרדעת ע"ג חמור בשבת. ואין לאסור משום דאין כלי ניטל אלא לדבר הניטל דבהמה חשיבא כדבר הניטל כיון דיכול למושכה ולהוליכה בכל מקום ורב אסי בר נתן דבעי אם אסור אין לפרש משום דמיחזי כרוצה להוליך הבהמה למקום רחוק דא"כ היכי דייק דמאן דשרי טרסקל כ"ש מרדעת. ואין לפרש נמי דבעי למיסר בחצר אטו רה"ר כדאמר גבי אשה בפ' במה אשה (לקמן דף סד:) דגבי בהמה לא גזרו כדתניא בסמוך גבי זוג ומטיילת עמו בחצר אלא נראה לר"י דטעמא משום טרחא דשבת ואע"ג דשריא קרצוף בפ"ב דביצה (דף כג.) התם יש לה צער ביותר א"נ לא שרי אלא בי"ט אבל בשבת אסור:

אוכף שע"ג החמור. וא"ת ויתיר האוכף וינער ויפול כדאמר בפ' נ) כל כתבי גבי היתה בהמתו טעונה טבל כו' וי"ל דהתם מיירי בשקין שתוכל הבהמה להתקלקל אבל מחמת האוכף לא תוכל הבהמה להתקלקל לכך לא התירו:

תולין טרסקל. וא"ת ותאסר משום דמשתמש בבע"ח כי היכי דאסור להניח נר על גבי דקל בשבת משום דמשתמש במחובר וי"ל דהתם מנענע הענפים אבל הכא אינו מנענע הבהמה בכך ורב אסי ברבי נתן דבעי למיסר ס) אפשר משום דילמא אתי להשתמש בבע"ח (ת"י):

אריוך. שם מלך כדכתיב אריוך מלך אלסר (בראשית יד) ונקטי' טפי משאר מלכים לפי שמובלע בו לשון ארי: **דשמעיה** דקא מסיים בה כו'. אע"ג דקיי"ל ע) כרב באיסורי היינו לגבי שמואל לחודיה אבל הכא ר' יוחנן דקי"ל כוותיה לגבי רב קאי כשמואל ובריית' דאוכף נמי קיימא כשמואל למאי דמשני כאן לחממה כאן לצננה ומתני' דאין סכין ומפרכסין לבהמה דמייתי לקמן נמי פליגא אדרב כדפירש בקונטרס: **מאי** לאו בגדולים ומשום תענוג. וא"ת ומאי קושיא דילמא הכא מיירי בטרסקל שנתלה מע"ש אבל לתלות בשבת אפי' בחצר אסור ותירץ דדייק מדנקט רה"ר גבי טרסקל טפי משאר דכולהו נמי ברה"ר איירי אלא נקט רה"ר דבחצר מותר בכל ענין:

כגון

מסורת הש"ס

א) לקמן נד:, ב) [תוספ' פ"ה], ג) [גיר' הערוך קרסטל וכן איתא בר"ף], ד) [ברכות מב: וש"נ], ה) [חולין עו:], ו) [תוספת' פ"ה], ז) [פי' לשון של זהורית שתולין לסוס משום עין ערוך], ח) [לעיל יא:], ט) [גיר' הערוך בערך קש ובקשקשין], י) לקמן סד:, כ) עי' ברש"י חולין מה:, ל) [וכחולין עו: פרש"י על שם אריוך מלך אלסר כמ"ש תוס' כאן ובמנחות לח: פרש"י כמו גור ארי' יהודה ולהכי קרי לשמואל אריוך דקי"ל הלכתא כשמואל בדינא ובקדושין לט. לא פרש"י כלום] מ"כ טעם אחר לאריוך מלך היינו דהלכה כוותיה בדינא כמו דינא דמלכות' אלסר נוטריקון אל אסר כלומר חוץ מלענין איסור' דאין הל' כותי' אלא כרב, מ) [חולין מג. וע"ש בתוס' ד"ה ניקב ותוס' נד. ד"ה ואלו כשרות כולהו צריכי וקל"ע], נ) צ"ל בתרא ד' קנד:, ס) צ"ל אפשר, ע) [בכורות מט:].

ליקוטי רש"י

חלודה. רקביבות. רדולי"א חלודה [דהויא בכלי] ברזל שאין משתמשין בו [יומא לח:]. **ולא [אמרו] נקובה.** להיות תורת כלי עליה יותר משאין נקובה אלא לענין טומאה [לקמן קכג.]. **תרגמא אביי אליבא דרבא.** במקום (אביי) ובשבילו שתהא משנה זו מתורגמת לפי דבריו [סוכה יט. בסוגיין רבא]. **בגלמי.** גולמי מחטין העומדות לינקב דנקובה נגמרה מלאכתה ושאינה נקובה אינה נגמרה מלאכתה הלכך לענין טומאה הוא דלא הוי כלי אבל בטלטול שריא דחזי לקנח [לקמן שם]. **מרדעת.** העשויה כמין כר [בראשית לא, לד]. [ע"כ שייך לד נב:]

והוא שקשורה לו מע"ש. גלי מלתמואל דמה צריכה לכך שיהא לה למלבוש [לקמן נד: ועי' כאן בתוס']. **אוכף.** שול"א בלע"ז [ב"ק יז:]. **אבא.** שמואל היה קורא לרב אבא לכבודו [ברכות מז.]. רב הכי הוה קרי ליה שמואל דרב הוה עדיף מיניה אבל שמעתי אבא ולית דגרסי אבא מבדי [חולין מה:]. רב [שמואל] הוי קרי ליה הכי משום כבוד [שם לח.]. כך שמו של רב אלא בכבוד קורין אותו רב כמו שקורין לרבי יהודה הנשיא רבינו וכן [illegible] [illegible] בבבל [illegible] [נדה כד:] [רשב"ם פסחים קיט.]. **יישר.** שפיר עבדת [חולין עו.]. **אריוך.** קרי שמואל על שם אריוך מלך אלסר (בראשית יד) דהלכתא כוותיה בדינין [שם ועי' רש"י בראשית יד א]. לשון מלך כמו (בראשית מט) גור אריה יהודה לכך קרי ליה אריוך דקיימא לן (בכורות מט) הלכה כשמואל בדיני כי הכי דינא דמלכותא דינא [מנחות לח:]. **בכים שלו.** כיס שעושין לזב וקושרו לפני האמה לקבל בו את הזוב [לעיל יא:]. **בקמיע.** שכותבין וטוענין לרפואה [לקמן ס.]. **זוג.** נוי עביד [שם נח.].

עין משפט נר מצוה

כא א ב מיי' פ"כ מהל' שבת הל' י סמג לאוין סה טוש"ע א"ח סי' שה סעיף ז:
כב ג מיי' שם הל' יג טוש"ע שם סעי' ח:
כג ד מיי' שם טוש"ע שם סעיף ט:
כד ה מיי' שם טוש"ע שם סעיף י:
כה ו מיי' שם טוש"ע שם סעיף יא:
כו ז שם סעיף י:

רבינו חננאל

מותר לדחות צער בהמה לתלות (קרצטל) [טרסקל] בפיה משום תענוג הוא. ור' יוחנן ושמואל אסרי וכן הלכה והני מילי בבהמות גדולות ומשום תענוג. אבל קטנים דמשום צערא הוא ברה"ר אסורים לצאת הסייחין (בקרצטלין) [בטרסקלין] שבפיהם אבל בחצר שרי. מסורכו פי' חגורו: תניא יוצא אדם באגד שעל גבי (בהמה) [המכה].

רב נסים גאון

ותמצא עיקר דיבור זה בפ' כל הכלים (ד' קכג) הניטלין בשבת ואני אבאר לך פירושו כי ראיתי פירוש להרבה מן החכמים מחט נקובה שנגמרה מלאכתה אם ניטל עוקצה טהורה עוקצה התונבא שלה שהוא פי המחט או חרירה הוא מקום הנקב כבר אין לה תקנה ויצאה מתורת כלי ונתיאשו הבעלים ממנה ולפיכך שנינו בה טהורה כי מעת שניטל עוקצה או חרירא אדם זורקה לבין הגרוטאות ונתיאש ממנה מלעשותה כלי וטהורה היא ואם היתה מחט שאינה נקובה ויש לה עוקץ וכבר שיפה אותה ומירקה ואע"פ שעדיין לא נקבה מפני שהיא ראויה ליטול בה את הקוץ הרי היא כתורת כלי וטמאה כמו הנקובה לפי שהנקובה ראויה לתפירה והיא ראויה להוציא בה את הקוץ וזו שוין בתורת טומאה כמו שאמרו אבל לענין טומאה דא ודא אחת היא ובכדומה לו אמרו בתוספתא (דב"מ דכלים פי"א) ואם מתחילה עשאו לכן אפי' פחות מכן טמא ובגסטרא אמרו (מס' כלים פי"ד מ"ג) אי זו היא גסטרא כל שניטלו אזניה ואמרו בתוספתא (ב"ק דכלים פ"ג) ואם מתחלה עשאה בלא אזנים נידונית כחבית ואשר אמרו בין נקובה ובין שאינה נקובה מותר לטלטלה בשבת ולא אמרו נקובה אלא לענין טומאה בלבד הוא דתירגם אביי אליבא דרבה בגלומי והוא ברזל חתוך שראויה להעשותו מחט והואיל ויש לומר שאם ירצה בעלה לעשותו כלי יכול הוא לעשות כמו שאמרו דזימנין דממליך עלה ומשוי לה כלי מותר לטלטלה בשבת ונחשוב אותה לענין טלטול כמו הכלים והיא כמו מחט נקובה לענין שבת אבל לענין טומאה לא והרי היא בחזקת טהורה עד שיגמור מלאכתה ותהיה כלי כמו שאמרו בתוספתא בסוף בבא קמא דכלים גולמי כלי מתכת הרי הן ככל הכלים אלא שהן טהורין:

אמר

שֶׁבְּפִיהֶם לִרְשׁוּת הָרַבִּים – AND COLTS may NOT go out WITH FEED BAGS AROUND THEIR MOUTHS INTO A PUBLIC DOMAIN;[34] וְלֹא בְהֵמָה בְּסַנְדָּל שֶׁבְּרַגְלֶיהָ – AND AN ANIMAL may NOT go out WITH A SHOE ON ITS FOOT[35] וְלֹא בְקָמִיעַ אַף עַל פִּי שֶׁהוּא מוּמְחֶה – OR WITH AN AMULET[36] EVEN IF IT IS proven EFFECTIVE.[37] וְזוֹ חוֹמֶר בִּבְהֵמָה מִבְּאָדָם – AND in THIS respect the law is more STRINGENT FOR AN ANIMAL THAN FOR A PERSON.[38]

אֲבָל יוֹצֵא הוּא בְּאֶגֶד שֶׁעַל גַּבֵּי הַמַּכָּה – BUT [AN ANIMAL] MAY GO OUT WITH A BANDAGE ON A WOUND,[39] וּבְקַשְׁשִׁין שֶׁעַל גַּבֵּי הַשֶּׁבֶר – WITH SPLINTS ON A FRACTURE[40] וּבְשִׁלְיָא הַמְדוּלְדֶּלֶת בָּהּ – AND WITH A PLACENTA DANGLING OUT OF IT.[41] וּפוֹקְקִין לָהּ זוּג בְּצַוָּארָהּ – AND if ONE STOPS UP THE BELL that is AROUND ITS THROAT, וּמְטַיֶּילֶת עִמּוֹ בֶּחָצֵר – ONE MAY WALK AROUND WITH IT IN A COURTYARD.[42]

The Gemara shows how this Baraisa contradicts Shmuel's view:

קָתָנֵי מִיהַת – **At any rate, the Baraisa teaches:** וְלֹא סְיָיחִין בְּטַרְסְקָלִים שֶׁבְּפִיהֶם לִרְשׁוּת הָרַבִּים – AND COLTS may NOT go out WITH FEED BAGS AROUND THEIR MOUTHS INTO A PUBLIC DOMAIN. By specifying "into a public domain," the Baraisa implies: לִרְשׁוּת הָרַבִּים הוּא דְּלֹא – **It is** only **into a public domain that** colts may **not** go with feed bags; הָא בְּחָצֵר שַׁפִּיר דָּמֵי – **but in a courtyard this is permitted.** מַאי לָאו בִּגְדוֹלִים – Now, **surely** the Baraisa refers even **to grown [colts],** וּמִשּׁוּם תַּעֲנוּג – **and** it permits one to put feed bags on them in a courtyard **for the sake of** their **pleasure.**[43] Thus, we see that even activities which only increase an animal's comfort (rather than relieve it of actual suffering) are permitted on the Sabbath. This conforms with the opinion of Rav and contradicts the opinion of Shmuel.[44] – ? –

The Gemara answers:

לֹא בִּקְטַנִּים – **No,** the Baraisa speaks only **of young [colts],** וּמִשּׁוּם צַעַר – **and** it permits one to put feed bags on them only **for the sake of** alleviating their **suffering.**[45] Shmuel agree that exertions to relieve an animal of suffering are permitted.

The Gemara bolsters this answer:

דַּיְקָא נַמִי דְּקָתָנֵי – **This also can be inferred from** the fact that **the Baraisa teaches** the law of the fodder bag along with the law of the amulet, which implies that the case of the feed bag is

NOTES

34. [A feed bag cannot be classified as an article of attire, for it is not used to protect the animal. Rather, it is deemed a burden.]

35. A metal shoe that protects the animal's foot from being injured by rocks (*Rashi*). Since it protects the animal, it is not a burden. The reason why it is forbidden is that it might fall off the animal and one might carry it four *amos* in a public domain (*Rashi* ד״ה וזה חומר). [This prohibition does not apply to a horseshoe, which is securely nailed onto the horse's hoof and is unlikely to fall off (*Mishnah Berurah* 305:41).]

36. A charm inscribed [with supplications and special combinations of God's Names] to cure sickness (*Rashi*). It is hung around the subject's neck (*Meiri* to Mishnah 60a; see *Shiltei HaGiborim,* end of ch. 6).

37. I.e. it has already healed a sickness three times (*Rashi,* from Gemara below, 61a-b; see there for elaboration). [The Gemara (53b) explains why an effective amulet is deemed a burden for an animal.]

38. The Gemara [below, 53b] initially assumes that this statement refers to the law of an amulet, for a person is allowed to wear an effective amulet in a public domain [below, 61a-b] (*Rashi*).

39. It is classified as clothing [because it protects the body] (*Chidushei HaRan*). There are no grounds for concern that it will fall off and one might come to carry it (*Rashi; Chidushei HaRan;* see next note).

40. Boards tied onto the sides of a broken limb to hold the bone in place until it mends (*Rashi*).

Since the animal needs these splints, they are not considered a burden. Also, if they fall off, the owner is unlikely to carry them four *amos* in the public domain, because they are only inexpensive pieces of wood (*Ritva MHK* ed.; see *Rashi* below, 54b ד״ה דלא הדר). The same is true of a bandage (*Meiri*).

41. Some of the placenta had emerged (*Rashi*). [Even the section that is protruding is regarded as part of the animal's body.]

42. If the bell is not stopped up, it may not be worn even in a private domain, because it will ring. [It is forbidden to create a sound on the Sabbath with an instrument designed for that purpose (see *Orach Chaim* ch. 338; see also *Magen Avraham* 305:5).] Therefore, one must stuff the bell with plugs of wool or rags to prevent it from ringing (*Rashi;* cf. *Ritva MHK* ed. and *Chidushei HaRan*).

Even if the bell is muffled, however, the animal may not wear it in a public domain. The reason is that the owner might thereby give the impression that he is taking the animal to be sold in the market (*Rashi,* from Gemara below, 54b). It was customary to hang a bell on an animal one wished to sell in order to make it look attractive (*Rashi* ibid.).

43. Grown colts have long necks and it is not difficult for them to bend over and eat from the ground. A feed bag serves only to increase their comfort (*Rashi*).

44. *Tosafos* ask: Why does the Gemara assume that the Baraisa contradicts Shmuel? Maybe it permits one to let his animal wear a feed bag in a courtyard only if it was put on *before* the Sabbath [when there is no prohibition of excessive exertion]. *Tosafos* answer by pointing out that although the entire Baraisa speaks of a public domain, it uses the words "into a public domain" only in conjunction with a feed bag. This extra phrase serves to teach that *all* prohibitions associated with a feed bag are limited to a public domain. In a courtyard, however, one is permitted even to put it on during the Sabbath.

45. Young colts have high knees and short necks, and it is painful for them to bend down to the ground to eat (*Rashi*).

גמ' אמר שמואל א) והוא שקשורה לו מע"ש אמר רב נחמן מתני' נמי דיקא דקתני א) אין החמור יוצא במרדעת בזמן שאינה קשורה לו היכי דמי אילימא שאינה קשורה לו כלל פשיטא דילמא נפלה ליה ואתי לאתויי אלא לאו שאינה קשורה מע"ש מכלל דרישא שקשורה לו מע"ש ש"מ תניא נמי הכי ב) חמור יוצא במרדעת בזמן שקשורה לו מע"ש ב) ולא באוכף אע"פ שקשורה לו מע"ש רבן שמעון בן גמליאל אומר אף באוכף בזמן שקשורה לו מע"ש ובלבד שלא יקשור לו מסריכן ובלבד שלא יפשול לו רצועה תחת זנבו בעא מיניה רב אסי בר נתן מר' חייא בר רב אשי מהו ליתן מרדעת על גבי חמור בשבת אמר ליה ג) מותר א"ל וכי מה בין זה לאוכף אישתיק איתיביה ד) אוכף שעל גבי חמור לא יטלטלנה בידו אלא מוליכה ומביאה בחצר והוא נופל מאליו השתא ליטול אמרת לא להניח מיבעיא אמר ליה ר' זירא שבקיה כרביה סבירא ליה דאמר רב חייא בר אשי אמר רב תולין ג) טרסקל לבהמה בשבת וקל וחומר למרדעת ומה התם דמשום תענוג שרי הכא דמשום צער לא כל שכן שמואל אמר מרדעת מותר ה) טרסקל אסור אזל ר' חייא בר יוסף אמרה לשמעתא דרב קמיה דשמואל א"ל אי הכי אמר אבא לא ידע במילי דשבתא ולא כלום כי סליק ר' זירא אשכחיה לר' בנימין בר יפת דיתיב וקאמר ליה משמיה דר' יוחנן נותנין מרדעת על גבי חמור בשבת א"ל ו) יישר וכן תרגמה אריוך בבבל ה) אריוך מנו שמואל והא רב נמי אמרה אלא שמעיה דהוה מסיים ביה ואין תולין טרסקל בשבת א"ל יישר וכן תרגמה אריוך בבבל דכולי עלמא מיהת מרדעת מותר מאי שנא מאוכף שאני התם דאפשר דנפיל ממילא רב פפא אמר כאן לחממה כאן לצננה לחממה אית לה צערא לצננה לית לה צערא והיינו דאמרי אינשי חמרא אפי' בתקופת תמוז קרירא לה מיתיבי ו) ז) לא יצא הסוס בזנב שועל ולא ז) בזהורית שבין עיניו ח) לא יצא הזב בכים שלו ולא עזים בכים שבדדיהן ולא פרה בחסום שבפיה ולא סייחים בטרסקלין שבפיהם לרה"ר ולא בהמה בסנדל שברגליה ולא בקמיע אע"פ שהוא מומחה וזו חומר בבהמה מבאדם אבל יוצא הוא באגד שעל גבי המכה ט) ובקשישין שעל גבי השבר ובשליא המדולדלת בה י) ופוקקין לה זוג בצוארה ומטיילת עמו בחצר קתני מיהת ולא סייחין בטרסקלים שבפיהם לרה"ר לרה"ר הוא דלא הא בחצר שפיר דמי מאי לאו בגדולים ומשום תענוג לא י) בקטנים ומשום צער דיקא נמי דקתני דומיא

רש"י

גמ' מתניתין נמי דיקא. לקמן בהאי פירקא: אף באוכף. דאיהו נמי מהני לחממה: ובלבד שלא יקשור לו מסריכן. פוטרא"ל דמיחזי כמי שרוצה להטעינו משוי: רצועה תחת זנבו. פושל"א שנותנים שם שלא תרד האוכף והמשוי על צוארה כשהיא יורדת לעמק והמסרך שלא תרד על זנבה כשהיא עולה על ההרים: מהו ליתן מרדעת. ולא לצאת לרה"ר אלא בחצר ומפני הצינה: ה"ג אמר ליה מותר א"ל וכי מה בין זה לאוכף אישתיק: איתיביה כו'. כסבור הא דאישתיק משום דלא אשגח ביה דסבר אוכף נמי שרי ואותיביה מברייתא דאסור ליטלה והשתא ליטול אמרת לא להניח מיבעי' דדמי כאילו צריך להטעינה משוי: כרביה. רב: טרסקל. סל מלא שעורים תולין לה בצוארה ופיה נתון לתוכו ואוכלת ותענוג בעלמא הוא שלא תטרח לשוח צוארה לארץ: צער. של צינה: מרדעת מותר. לעולם היא הלכך אורחה בהכי ולאו משוי הוא: לשמעתא דרב. דשרי בטורסקל: אבא. ה) תברי כמו אברך אבא למלכא (בראשית מא): שמואל קרי אריוך על שם שהיה בקי בדינין ושופט כמלך השופט על הארץ לשון ריכא ו) מלך (ב"ב דף ד.): והא רב נמי אמרה. דכיון דשרי בטרסקל כ"ש מרדעת: מאי שנא מאוכף. שאסור ליטול וכ"ש להניחו: דנפיל ממילא. כדקתני מוליכו ומביאו לחצר והוא נופל מאליו: כאן לחממה. מרדעת צריך לחממה ומותר משום צער דצינה אבל נטילת אוכף אינו אלא שיצטנן שנתחממה ע"י משאוי שנשאה מבעוד יום ואי לא שקיל ליה לא איכפת לן שהרי הוא יצטנן מאליו דאמרי אינשי וכו': בזנב שועל. שתולין לו בין עיניו שלא ישלוט בו עין: זהורית. לנוי: בכים שלו. שתולין לו באמתו לקבל זוב ולבדוק מנין ראיותיו שאינו תכשיט לו: בכים שבדדיהן. לקבל חלב הנוטף אי נמי שלא ישרטו דדיהן על הקוצים שהיו דדיהן גסין: בחסום שבפיה. שחוסמין אותה שלא תרעה בשדות אחרים וכשמגיעין למקום מרעיתם נוטלין אותה הימנה: בסנדל שברגליה. שעושין לה סנדל של מתכת שלא יזיקוה האבנים: קמיע. כתב לרפואת חולי: מומחה. שריפא כבר ג' פעמים: וזה חומר בבהמה מבאדם. קס"ד השתא דאקמיע קאי דאמרינן לקמן בפרק במה אשה יוצאה (ד' סא.) שהאדם יוצא בקמיע מומחה וכל הני דקתני לא תנא הנך דלאו שמירת גופה הוא אלא משאוי וסנדל משום דדילמא מישתליף ואתי לאתויי: אגד שעל גבי המכה. ליכא למימר אתי לאתויי: קשישין שעל השבר. בהמה שנשבר בה עצם עושין לה דפין מכאן ומכאן וקושרים אותן שם והן מעמידין העצם שלא ינוד אנה ואנה עד שמתחבר: ובשליא המדולדלת בה. שיליתה מקצתה: ופוקקין לה זוג. אבל כשאינו פקוק אפי' בחצר לא תצא מפני שהעינבל שבתוכה מקשקש ומוליד קול לכך פוקק בצמר או במוכין שלא יקשקש העינבל שבתוכה: זוג. אישקלי"ט: עינבל. בטדי"ל: ומטיילת. באותו זוג בחצר אבל לא תצא בו לרה"ר כדמפרש לקמן בפרקין (דף נד:) דמיחזי כמאן דאזיל לחינגא: מאי לאו. בסייחים גדולים קאמר דצוארן ארוך ואין להם צער לשוח ולאכול מע"ג הקרקע ותולה להן טרסקל לתענוג וקשיא לשמואל: קטנים. שצואריהן גבוהין וצוארן קטן ויש להם צער לשוח ע"ג הקרקע ולאכול:

דומיא

תוספות

והוא שקשורה לו מע"ש. רש"י פי' לקמן דבקשורה מע"ש הוי מלבוש החמור אבל באינה קשורה מע"ש הוי משאוי ועוד יש לפרש דבאינה קשורה מע"ש מיחזי כמתכוין להוצאת המרדעת וה"ר פור"ת פירש דמיחזי כאילו מתכוין להוליך הבהמה למקום רחוק:

אילימא שאינה קשורה לו כלל פשיטא. ולא בעי למפרך דמרישא שמעינן לה דקתני בזמן שהיא קשורה הא אינה קשורה לא דדרך משניות כן במסכת ע"ז (דף לה:) אלו דברים אסורין באכילה כבשים שדרכן לתת לתוכן יין כו' ובסיפא (שם דף לט:) קתני ואלו מותרים באכילה כו' וכבשים שאין דרכן לתת כו' ובפרק אלו טרפות (חולין דף נד.) קתני אלו כשרות אע"ג דאיכא מינייהו דשמעי' מרישא מ) וא"ת ונפשוט מרישא דבקשורה מערב שבת איירי מדאיצטריך למיתני בזמן שהיא קשורה דבלאו הכי הוה ידעי' דאיירי בקשורה דאי באינה קשורה פשיטא דאסור דילמא נפלה ואתי לאתויי כדקאמר הכא אילימא כו' אלא ודאי בזמן שקשורה מע"ש קאמר וי"ל דמרישא לא תפשוט דאדרבה ה"א דלהכי תנא בזמן שהיא קשורה לאשמעי' דאפי' קשורה בשבת דאי לא תנא ליה ה"א דוקא בקשורה לו מע"ש אבל בקשורה בשבת לא קמ"ל להכי דייק מסיפא:

מהו ליתן המרדעת ע"ג חמור בשבת. ואין לאסור משום דאין כלי ניטל אלא לדבר הניטל דבהמה חשיבא כדבר הניטל כיון דיכול למושכה ולהוליכה בכל מקום ורב אסי בר נתן דבעי אם אסור אין לפרש משום דמיחזי כרוצה להוליך הבהמה למקום רחוק דא"כ היכי דייק דמאן דשרי טרסקל כ"ש מרדעת. ואין לפרש נמי דבעי למיסר בחצר אטו רה"ר כדאמר גבי אשה בפ' במה אשה (לקמן דף סד:) דגבי בהמה לא גזרו כדתניא בסמוך גבי זוג ומטיילת עמו בחצר אלא נראה לר"י דטעמא משום טרחא דשבת ואע"ג דשריא קרצוף בפ"ב דביצה (דף כג.) התם יש לה צער ביותר א"נ לא שרי אלא בי"ט אבל בשבת אסור:

אוכף שע"ג החמור. וא"ת ויתיר האוכף וינער ויפול כדאמר בפ' ו) כל כתבי גבי היתה בהמתו טעונה טבל כו' וי"ל דהתם מיירי בשקין שתוכל הבהמה להתקלקל אבל מחמת האוכף לא תוכל הבהמה להתקלקל לכך לא התירו:

תולין טרסקל. וא"ת ותאסר משום דמשתמש בבע"ח כי היכי דאסור להניח נר על גבי דקל בשבת משום דמשתמש במחובר וי"ל דהתם מנענע הענפים אבל הכא אינו מנענע הבהמה בכך ורב אסי ברבי נתן דבעי למיסר פ) אפשר משום דילמא אתי להשתמש בבע"ח (ת"י):

אריוך. שם מלך כדכתיב אריוך מלך אלסר (בראשית יד) ונקט' טפי משאר מלכים לפי שמובלע בו לשון ארי:

דשמעיה דקא מסיים בה כו'. אע"ג דקיי"ל ע) כרב באיסורי היינו לגבי שמואל לחודיה אבל הכא ר' יוחנן דקיי"ל כוותיה לגבי רב קאי כשמואל וברייתא דאוכף נמי קיימא כשמואל למאי דמשני כאן לחממה כאן לצננה ומתני' דאין סכין ומפרכסין לבהמה דמייתי לקמן נמי פליגא אדרב כדפירש בקונטרס:

מאי לאו בגדולים ומשום תענוג. וא"ת ומאי קושיא דילמא הכא מיירי בטרסקל שנתלה מע"ש אבל לתלות בשבת אפי' בחצר אסור ותירץ דדייק מדנקט רה"ר גבי טרסקל טפי משאר דכולהו נמי ברה"ר איירי אלא נקט רה"ר דבחצר מותר בכל ענין:

עין משפט נר מצוה

כא א ב מיי' פ"כ מהל' שבת הל' י סמג לאוין סה טוש"ע א"ח סי' שה סעיף ז:
כב ג מיי' שם הל' יג טוש"ע שם סעי' ח:
כג ד מיי' שם טוש"ע שם סעיף ט:
כד ה מיי' שם טוש"ע שם סעיף י:
כה ו מיי' שם טוש"ע שם סעיף יא:
כו ז שם סעיף י:

רבינו חננאל

מותר לדחות צער בהמה לתלות (קרצטל) [טרסקל] בפיה משום תענוג הוא. ור' יוחנן ושמואל אסרי וכן הלכה והני מילי בבהמות גדולות ומשום תענוג. אבל קטנים דמשום צערא הוא ברה"ר אסורים לצאת הסייחין (בקרצטלין) [בטרסקלין] שבפיהם אבל בחצר שרי. מסורכו פי' חגורו: תניא יוצא אדם באגד שעל גבי (בהמה) [המכה].

רב נסים גאון

ותמצא עיקר דיבור זה בפ' כל הכלים (ד' קכג) הניטלין בשבת ואני אבאר לך פירושו כי ראיתי פירוש להרבה מן החכמים מחט נקובה שנגמרה מלאכתה אם ניטל עוקצה טהורה עוקצה התתבא שלה שהוא פי המחט או חרירה הוא מקום הנקב כבר אין לה תקנה ויצאה מתורת כלי ונתיאשו הבעלים ממנה ולפיכך שנינו בה טהורה כי מעת שניטל עוקצה או חרירא אדם זורקה לבין הגרוטאות ונתיאש ממנה מלעשותה כלי וטהורה היא ואם היתה מחט שאינה נקובה ויש לה עוקץ וכבר שיפה אותה ומירקה ואע"פ שעדיין לא נקבה מפני שהיא ראויה ליטול בה את הקוץ הרי היא כתורת כלי וטמאה כמו הנקובה לפי שהנקובה ראויה לתפירה והיא ראויה להוציא בה את הקוץ וזו וזו שוין בתורת טומאה כמו שאמרו אבל לענין טומאה דא ודא אחת היא ובכדומה לו אמרו בתוספתא (דב"מ דכלים פי"א) ואם מתחילה עשאו לכן אפי' פחות מיכן טמא ובגסטרא אמרו (מס' כלים פ"ד מ"ג) אי זו היא גסטרא כל שניטלו אזניה ואמרו בתוספתא (ב"ק דכלים פ"ג) ואם מתחלה עשאה בלא אזנים נידונית כחבית ואשר אמרו בין נקובה ובין שאינה נקובה מותר לטלטלה בשבת ולא אמרו נקובה אלא לענין טומאה בלבד הוא דתירגם אביי אליבא דרבה בגלומי והוא ברזל חתוך שראויה להעשות מחט והואיל ויש לומר שאם ירצה בעלה לעשותה כלי יכול הוא לעשות כמו שאמרו זימנין דמימליך עלה ומשוי לה כלי מותר לטלטלה בשבת ונחשוב אותה לענין טלטול כמו הכלים והיא כמו מחט נקובה לענין שבת אבל לענין טומאה לא והרי היא בחזקת טהורה עד שיגמור מלאכתה ותהיה כלי כמו שאמרו בתוספתא בסוף בבא קמא דכלים גולמי כלי מתכות הרי הן ככל הכלים אלא שהן טהורין:

אמר

מסורת הש"ס

א) לקמן נד:, ב) [תוספ' פ"ה], ג) [גיר' הערוך קרטסל וכן איתא בר"ף], ד) [ברכות מב: וש"נ], ה) [חולין עו:], ו) [תוספת' פ"ה], ז) [פי' לשון של זהורית שתולין לסוס משום עין ערוך], ח) [לעיל יא.], ט) [גיר' הערוך בערך קש ובקשקשין], י) לקמן סד:, כ) ע' ברש"י חולין מה:, ל) [ובחולין עו: פרש"י על שם אריוך מלך אלסר כמ"ש תוס' כאן ובמנחות לח: פרש"י כמו גור ארי' יהודה ולהכי קרי לשמואל אריוך דקי"ל הלכתא כשמואל בדינא ובקדושין נט. לא פרש"י כלום] מ"כ טעם אחר דאריוך מלך היינו דהלכה כוותיה בדינא כמו דינא דמלכותא' אלסר נוטריקון אל אסר כלומר מון מלענין איסור' דאין הל' כותי' אלא כרב, מ) [חולין מב. וע"ש בתוס' ד"ה ניקב ותוס' נד. ד"ה ואלו כשרות כולהו ערוכי וקצ"ע], נ) נ"ל בחרא ד' קנד:, ס) נ"ל אפשר, ע) [בכורות מט:].

ליקוטי רש"י

חלודה. רקביבות, רדולי"א תלודה [דהיא] בכלין ברזל שאין משתמשין בו [יומא לח:]. ולא [אמרו] נקובה. להיות תורת כלי עליה יותר משאין נקובה אלא לענין טומאה [לקמן קכב.]. תרגמא אביי אליבא דרבה. במקום (אביי) ובשבילו שהמה משנה זו מתורגמת לפי דבריו [סוכה יט. בסוגיין רבא]. בגלמי. גולמי מתכות העומדות ליעשות כלים לנקובה גמרה מלאכתה ושאינה נקובה אינה נגמרה מלאכתה הלכך לענין טומאה הוא דלא הוי כלי אבל בטלטול שריא דחזי לקוץ [לקמן שם]. מרדעת. העשויה כמין כר [בראשית לא, לד]. [ע"כ שייך לד נב:].

והוא שקשורה לו מע"ש. גלי מאתמול שיהא צריכה לכך שיהא לה למלבוש [לקמן נד: ועי' כאן בתוס']. אוכף. שול"א בלע"ז [ב"ק יז:]. אבא. שמואל היה קורא לרב אבא לכבודו [ברכות מז.]. רב הכי הוה קרי ליה שמואל לרב הוה עדיף מיניה אני שמעתי אבא ואית דגרסי אבא אבא תברי [חולין מה:]. רב [שמואל] הוי קרי ליה הכי משום כבוד [שם לח:]. כך שמו של רב אבא ככבוד קורין אותו רב בבבל הכי כמו שקורין לרבי יהודה הנשיא בארץ ישראל רבינו וכן מוכח בשמעתא תולין (קלו:) דאמרי' מאן ריש סידרא בבבל אבא אריכא ובכבר מיירי שהיה רב ארוך בדורו כדאמרינן במסכת נדה (כד:) [רשב"ם פסחים קיט:]. יישר. שפיר קאמרת [חולין עה:]. אריוך. קרי שמואל על שם אריוך מלך אלסר (בראשית יד) דהלכתא כוותיה בדיני [שם עו: ועי' כאן בתוס']. לשון מלך כמו (בראשית מט) גור אריה יהודה להכי קרי לשמואל אריוך דקיימא לן (בכורות מט:) הלכה כשמואל בדיני כי היכי דדינא דמלכותא דינא [מנחות לח:]. בכים שלו. כיס שעושין לזב וקושרו לפי האמה לקבל בו את הזוב [לעיל יא:]. בקמיע. שכותבין וטוענין לרפואה [לקמן ס.]. זוג. נוי עביד [שם נח.].

דומיא דקמיע ש"מ: אמר מר ולא בקמיע אע"פ שהוא מומחה והא אנן תנן [א] ולא בקמיע שאינו מומחה הא מומחה שפיר דמי ה"נ [א] שאינו מומחה והא אע"פ שהוא מומחה קתני מומחה לאדם ואינו מומחה לבהמה ומי איכא מומחה לאדם ולא הוי מומחה לבהמה אין אדם [ב] דאית ליה מזלא מסייע ליה בהמה דלית לה מזלא לא מסייע לה אי הכי מאי זה חומר בבהמה מבאדם מי סברת אקמיע קאי אסנדל קאי ת"ש [ב] סכין [ג] ומפרכסין לאדם ואין סכין ומפרכסין לבהמה מאי לאו דאיכא מכה ומשום צער לא [ג] דגמר מכה ומשום תענוג ת"ש בהמה שאחזה דם אין מעמידין אותה במים בשביל שתצטנן אדם שאחזו דם מעמידין אותו במים בשביל שיצטנן אמר עולא גזירה משום שחיקת סממנין אי הכי [ד] אדם נמי אדם נראה כמיקר א"ה בהמה נמי נראה כמיקר אין מיקר לבהמה [ה] ולבהמה מי גזרינן והתניא [ה] היתה עומדת חוץ לתחום קורא לה והיא באה ולא גזרינן דילמא אתי לאתויי ואמר רבינא כגון שהיה תחום שלה מובלע בתוך תחום שלו ר"נ בר יצחק אמר שחיקת סממנין גופה תנאי היא דתני' בהמה שאכלה כרשינין לא יריצנה בחצר בשביל שתתרפה ורבי [ו] [ד] אושעיא מתיר דרש רבא הלכה כרבי [ז] אושעיא: אמר מר לא יצא הזב בכיס שלו ולא עזים בכיס שבדדיהן והתניא יוצאות עזים בכיס שבדדיהן אמר רב יהודה לא קשיא הא דמיהדק הא דלא מיהדק רב יוסף אמר [ח] תנאי שקלת מעלמא תנאי היא דתנן העזים יוצאות צרורות רבי יוסי אוסר בכלן חוץ מן הרחילות הכבונות ר' יהודה אומר עזים יוצאות צרורות ליבש אבל לא ליחלב ואיבעית אימא הא והא ר' יהודה ולא קשיא [ה] כאן ליבש כאן ליחלב תניא אמר ר' יהודה מעשה בעזים בית אנטוכיא שהיו דדיהן גסין ועשו להן כיסין כדי שלא יסרטו דדיהן: ת"ר מעשה באחד שמתה אשתו והניחה בן לינק ולא היה לו שכר מניקה ליתן ונעשה לו נס ונפתחו לו דדין כשני דדי אשה והניק את בנו אמר רב יוסף בא וראה כמה גדול אדם זה שנעשה לו נס כזה א"ל אביי אדרבה כמה [א] גרוע אדם זה שנשתנו לו סדרי בראשית אמר רב יהודה בא וראה כמה קשים מזונותיו של אדם שנשתנו עליו סדרי בראשית אמר רב נחמן תדע דמתרחיש ניסא ולא אברו מזוני: ת"ר מעשה באדם אחד שנשא אשה גידמת ולא הכיר בה עד יום מותה אמר [ט] רב בא וראה כמה צנועה אשה זו שלא הכיר בה בעלה אמר לו רבי חייא זו דרכה בכך אלא כמה צנוע אדם זה שלא הכיר באשתו: [ו] זכרים יוצאין לבובין: מאי לבובין אמר רב הונא תותרי מאי משמע דהאי לבובין לישנא דקרובי הוא דכתיב [א] לבבתני אחותי כלה עולא אמר עור שקושרין להם כנגד לבם כדי שלא יפלו עליהן זאבים זאבים אזכרים נפלי אנקיבות לא נפלי משום דמסגו בריש עדרא ואבין בריש עדרא נפלי בסוף עדרא לא נפלי אלא משום דשמני ובנקבות ליכא שמני ותו מי ידעי בין הני להני אלא משום דזקפי חוטמייהו ומסגו כי דוו רב נחמן בר יצחק אמר עור שקושרין להן תחת זכרותן כדי שלא יעלו על הנקבות ממאי מדקתני סיפא [ז] והרחלים יוצאות שחוזות מאי שחוזות שאוחזין האליה שלהן למעלה כדי שיעלו עליהן זכרים רישא כדי שלא יעלו על הנקבות וסיפא כדי שיעלו עליהן זכרים מאי משמע דהאי שחוזות לישנא דגלויי הוא דכתיב [ב] והנה אשה לקראתו

שית

תוספות

כגון שהיה תחום שלה מובלע כו'. ומ"מ לא התירו אלא דרך קריאה אבל לילך מעבר לבהמה ולרודפה לעיר לא:

תנאי היא. רב יהודה ידע שפיר דתנאי היא אלא דניחא ליה לאוקמי תרי סתמי דברייתא אליבא דחד תנא:

כאן ליבש כאן ליחלב. פי' בקונט' ליחלב שיקבלו בכיס את החלב וקשה דהא ודאי משוי הוא ולכ"ע חייב דהויא מלאכה הצריכה לגופה ופי' ה"ר פור"ת ליחלב לשמור החלב בדדיהן שלא יזוב לארץ ושרי ת"ק דהוי כמו רחלים כבונות דחשבי' ליה מלבוש אף על פי שאינו עשוי לצורך עצמן אלא לשמור הצמר ור"י פירש דבין ליבש ובין ליחלב תרווייהו עבדי להו כדי שלא יסרטו דדיהן כדאמרינן בסמוך וליבש בזמן שאינו חפץ בחלב שרי לפי שמהדקו וליכא למיחש דילמא נפיל ואתי לאתויי אבל ליחלב שאינו רוצה שיתייבשו אינו מיהדק איכא למימר דילמא נפיל ואתי לאתויי:

שקושרין להן כנגד זכרותן כו'. ולשון לבובין הוי שלא לקרב כמו ובכל תבואתי תשרש (איוב לא) וכמוהו הרבה:

ממאי מדקתני סיפא. טפי הוי ליה לאתויי כבולות דהוי ממש כעין זה אלא משום דשחוזות הוי ברישא:

רש"י

דומיא דקמיע. משום חולי: והא אנן תנן. גבי אדם לקמן בפ' במה אשה (דף ס.): הא מומחה שפיר דמי. מאי שנא בהמה מאדם: מזליה. מלאך שלו ומליץ עליו: אי הכי. דבהמה נמי נפקא בקמיע המומחה לבהמה: מאי זה חומר. אדם נמי לא נפיק אלא בקמיע מומחה לאדם: אסנדל קאי. וזה חומר דקתני ולא בהמה בסנדל שברגליה: סכין. שמן: ומפרכסין. גלדי מכה: ומשום צער. [ואפילו] הכי לבהמה לא וקשיא בין לרב בין לשמואל דשרי במרדעת: לא דגמר מכה. שנתרפאה המכה וסיכה ופירכוס משום תענוג ולרב ודאי קשיא והיא מתניתא קמייתא דאוכף נמי קשיא ליה דנהי נמי דלדידיה ליכא צער תענוג מיהא הוא אלא רב תנא הוא ופליג: שאחזה דם. אנפודור"א: אין מעמידין כו'. אלמא אפילו צער נמי אסור: גזירה משום שחיקת סממנים. במידי דרפואה גזור רבנן דאי שרית שום רפואה אתי למישרי שחיקת סממנים והוא איסורא דאורייתא דהוי טוחן: אין מיקר לבהמה. אין דרך להקר בהמה הלכך כולי עלמא ידעי דלרפואה קמיכוין ואתי למישרי שחיקת סממנים: ומי גזרינן. במקום פסידא כי האי גוונא: חוץ לתחום. קס"ד חוץ לתחום שלו היתה עומדת בהמה: שהיה תחום שלה מובלעת בתוך תחום שלו. דחוץ לתחום דקתני חוץ לתחום שלה שהבהמה המסורה לרועה המיוחד הרי היא כרגלי הרועה וזה הקורא לה בעליה ויכול לילך כגון שהוא שבת קרוב לאותו מקום ואפילו הכי לא יביאנה ממש בידיו הואיל והיא יוצאה חוץ לתחומה אין לה אלא ד' אמות ומיהו קורא לה והיא באה דלא החזר הוא על תחום בהמתו ובלבד שלא יביאנה ממש בידיו: תנאי היא. דאיכא דלא גזר שאר רפואות אטו שחיקת סממנין: שאכלה כרשינין. הרבה ועל ידי אכילה מרובה אחזה חולי שקורין מינייזונ"א וצריכה להשתלשל ולהוציא רעי ומריצה: כדי שתתרפה. גרסינן הכא לשון ריפוי שיהיו מעיה רפויים בשילשול ומוציאה רעי: לא יריצנה. גזירה בכל רפואה אטו שחיקת סממנין: דמיהדק. דליכא למיחש דילמא נפיל ואתי לאתויי: תנאי שקלת מעלמא. אידכת כולם שאין אתה מוצא תנאים שנחלקו בכך דתוקי הנך תרתי מתניית' חדא כמר וחדא כמר: תנאי היא. במתניתין ר"מ שרי ר' יוסי אסר: ליבש. מיהדק שפיר ולענין משוי נמי לא הוי משוי דצורך גופה היא דחלבה מכחישה: ליחלב. הוי משוי שטוענת את החלב בכים: גסין. גדולין ונגררין על הקוצין ומסרטין דדיהן: שנשתנו עליו כו'. ולא זכה ליפתח לו שערי שכר: תדע. דקשין: דמרחשי ניסא. מן השמים לכמה הצלות לנפשות אדם: ולא איברו מזוני. ואין נס זה רגיל שיבראו מזונות לצדיקים בביתם שימצאו חיטין גדילין באוצרותיהן: גידמת. ידה קטועה: זו דרכה בכך. לכסות כל אשה עצמה וכ"ש זו שהיתה צריכה לכך: תותרי. קופל"א שמחברין אותם בקשר שנים שנים שלא יברחו: לבבתני. קרבתני אצלך מחמת נוי מעשיך: דרך זאבים לאחוז בהמה בלבה: אנקבות לא נפלי. בתמיה: דמסגי. מהלכין: בסוף עדרא לא נפלי. בתמיה: כי דוו. מביטין כאן וכאן לפיכך מתקנאין בהם כסבורים שרוצים להלחם בהם: אליה. זנב שלהן קושרים כלפי גבן שלא יכסה ערותן:

שית

עין משפט נר מצוה

כז א מיי' פ"כ מהל' שבת הלכה יג טוש"ע א"ח סי' שה סעי' ח בהג"ה:

כח ב ג מיי' פכ"א מהל' שבת הל' ל' סמג לאוין סה טוש"ע א"ח סי' שכח סעיף כב וסי' שלב סעיף ג:

כט ד מיי' וסמג שם טוש"ע א"ח סי' שלב סעיף ג וסעיף ד:

ל ה ו ז מיי' פ"כ מהל' שבת הל' יב סמג שם טוש"ע א"ח סי' שה סעיף ו:

רבינו חננאל

ובקשישין: תניא אדם שאחזו דם מעמידין אותו במים בשביל לרפאותו. מ"ט משום דנראה כמיקר. אבל בהמה שאחזה דם אין מעמידין אותה במים כו'. אמר עולא בהמה גזירה משום שחיקת סמנים. ושחיקת סמנים תנאי היא. דתניא בהמה שאכלה כרשינין הרבה אין מריצין אותה בחצר בשביל לרפאותה. ור' יאשיה מיקל. והלכתא כוותיה דדרש רבא הלכתא כר' יאשיה. והא דר' יאשיה מסייעא לשמואל. מעשה שנעשה נס ונפתחו שני דדין כשני דדי אשה כו' וזו שהיתה גידמת כו'. פשוטות הן: פי' תותרי. סמרטוטין של רקמה ושל משי שעושין על הבהמה ליפותה. עולא אמר עור שמעמידין להן כנגד לבן שלא יפלו עליהן זאבים. משום דמסגו כי דוו. ומסתברא כוותיה דתנן (בע"ז דף כט:) באיסורי הנאה ועורות לבובין. ות"ר (שם דף לב.) איזהו עור לבוב. כל שהוא קרוע כנגד הלב. (וקרודה) [וקדורה] כמו ארובה כו'. שחוות מלשון שית זונה:

תורה אור השלם

א) לִבַּבְתִּנִי אֲחֹתִי כַלָּה לִבַּבְתִּינִי בְּאַחַת מֵעֵינַיִךְ בְּאַחַד עֲנָק מִצַּוְּרֹנָיִךְ: [שיר השירים ד, ט]

ב) וְהִנֵּה אִשָּׁה לִקְרָאתוֹ שִׁית זוֹנָה וּנְצֻרַת לֵב: [משלי ז, י]

מסורת הש"ס

א) [לקמן ס.], ב) [ב"ק כ:], ג) [גיר' הערוך ומפרכין פי' מגרדין], ד) [ביצה יח.], ה) [לקמן קנא. ותוספתא פי"ח], ו) [נ"ל יאשיה וכ"א בר"א והרא"ש וכן העתיקו תוס' מ"ק י: ד"ה ואין], ז) [נ"ל יאשיה], ח) [עירובין לו: פסחים מה: ביצה יט. סנהדרין סא.], ט) [נ"ל רבי].

תוספות ישנים

א) ובבראשית רבה על פסוק ויהי אומן את הדסה שנפתחו למרדכי שני דדים כדדי אשה ליכא למיפרך הכי דהכי קאמר נשתנו דלא ה"ל שכר מניקה ומרדכי ה"ל שכר אך לא הי' מוצא מניקה:

גליון הש"ס

גמ' ולבהמה מי גזרינן והתניא. ק"ל דלמא משום שחיקת סממנים דאורייתא גזרי' אבל בתחומין דרבנן לא:

ליקוטי רש"י

ולא בקמיע שאינו מומחה. אבל בקמיע מומחה שרי דתכשיט הוא לחולה כאחד ממלבושיו [לקמן ס.]. גזירה משום שחיקת סממנין. דכל רפואה אסרו חכמים לעשותה בשבת היכא דליכא סכנה משום שחיקת סממנין במסכת שבת [ע"ז כח.]. דכל רפואה בשבת גזור בה רבנן משום שחיקת סממנין שהיא אב מלאכה טוחן [ביצה יח:]. וכן כל דבר רפואה שאין מלאכה אלא שבות הוא שגזרו חכמים בכל רפואות גזירה משום שחיקת סמנין [שם יא:]. כרשינין. מאכל בהמה בינ"א בלע"ז [לעיל יז:]. צרורות. דדיהן צרורות פעמים ליבש שמהדקן כדי שלא יחלבו עוד ויתעברו או יהו שמנות לאכול ופעמים לחלב לשמור חלבן שלא יטפטף לארץ וקושרין להם כיס בדדיהן. רבי יוסי אוסר בכלן. דמשוי הוא. חוץ מן הרחילות הכבונות. שהוא שמירת צמרן שלא יטנף והוי להו תכשיט. יוצאות צרורות ליבש. ר' יהודה סבירא ליה כתנא קמא דלאו משוי הוא ומיהו ליבש דמיהדק שפיר וליכא למיחש דילמא נפיל ואתי לאיתויי אבל ליחלב דלא מיהדק שפיר חיישינן [שם נב: ועי' כאן במהרש"א ובמהר"ם]. לבבתני. משכת את לבי אליך [שה"ש ד, ט]. והנה אשה. כמשמעה, ד"א אחד מן אפיקורסים [משלי ז, י].

דּוּמְיָא דְּקָמֵיעַ – **similar to** that of the **amulet.** Thus, just as the amulet serves to relieve the animal from suffering,[1] so does the feed bag.[2] שְׁמַע מִינָּהּ – **Learn** a conclusive proof **from this.**[3]

The Gemara discusses another law in this Baraisa:

אָמַר מַר – **Master said** in the Baraisa: וְלֹא בְקָמֵיעַ אַף עַל פִּי שֶׁהוּא מוּמְחֶה – AND an animal may NOT go out WITH AN AMULET EVEN IF IT IS proven EFFECTIVE.

The Gemara asks:

וְהָא אֲנַן תְּנַן – **But we have learned in a Mishnah:**[4] וְלֹא בְקָמֵיעַ שֶׁאֵינוֹ מוּמְחֶה – AND a person may NOT go out into a public domain on the Sabbath WITH AN AMULET THAT IS NOT proven EFFECTIVE. This implies: הָא מוּמְחֶה שַׁפִּיר דָּמֵי – **But** if it is proven EFFECTIVE it **is permitted!**[5] – ? –

The Gemara answers:

הָכָא נַמִּי שֶׁאֵינוֹ מוּמְחֶה – **Here too,** our Baraisa speaks of an amulet **that is not** proven **effective.**

The Gemara objects:

וְהָא אַף עַל פִּי שֶׁהוּא מוּמְחֶה קָתָנֵי – **But [the Baraisa] teaches** explicitly: EVEN IF IT IS proven EFFECTIVE!

The Gemara answers:

מוּמְחֶה לְאָדָם וְאֵינוֹ מוּמְחֶה לִבְהֵמָה – The Baraisa refers to an amulet that is proven **effective for man but not** proven **effective for animals.**[6]

The Gemara asks:

וּמִי אִיכָּא מוּמְחֶה לְאָדָם וְלֹא הָוֵי מוּמְחֶה לִבְהֵמָה – **But is there** such a thing as an amulet that is proven **effective for man and not** proven **effective for animals?**[7]

The Gemara answers:

אִין – **Yes!** אָדָם דְּאִית לֵיהּ מַזָּלָא מְסַיַּיע לֵיהּ – **A man, who has *mazal*, is assisted,**[8] בְּהֵמָה דְּלֵית לָהּ מַזָּלָא לֹא מְסַיַּיע לָהּ – whereas **an animal, which does not have *mazal*, is not assisted.** Hence, an amulet proven effective for a person is not necessarily effective for an animal.[9]

The Gemara asks:

אִי הָכִי מַאי – **If so,**[10] **what** does the Baraisa mean by: זֶה חוֹמֶר בִּבְהֵמָה מִבְּאָדָם – In THIS respect the law is more STRINGENT FOR AN ANIMAL THAN FOR A PERSON?[11]

The Gemara answers:

מִי סָבְרַת אַקָּמֵיעַ קָאֵי – **Did you think [this statement] refers to** the law of **an amulet?** אַסַּנְדָּל קָאֵי – **It refers to** the law of **a shoe!**[12]

Rav and Shmuel both agree (53a) that one may perform activities on the Sabbath for the sake of alleviating an animal's suffering. The Gemara challenges this ruling:

תָּא שְׁמַע – **Come, learn** a proof from the following Baraisa: סָכִין וּמְפַרְכְּסִין לְאָדָם – ONE MAY ANOINT a sore with oil AND SCRAPE off a scab[13] FOR A PERSON וְאֵין סָכִין וּמְפַרְכְּסִין לִבְהֵמָה – BUT ONE MAY NOT ANOINT a sore with oil OR SCRAPE off a scab FOR AN ANIMAL.[14] מַאי לָאו דְּאִיכָּא מַכָּה – **Now,** the Baraisa **surely** refers even to a case **where the wound is** still festering, וּמִשּׁוּם צַעַר – **and** hence this treatment is required **for the sake of** alleviating **suffering.** Yet the Baraisa rules that it may not be performed for an animal.[15] – ? –

The Gemara answers:

לֹא – **No!** דִּגְמַר מַכָּה – The Baraisa refers exclusively to a case **where the wound has finished** (i.e. healed), וּמִשּׁוּם תַּעֲנוּג – **and** this treatment is performed only **for the sake of** giving **pleasure.**[16]

The Gemara raises another challenge to the ruling of Rav and Shmuel:

תָּא שְׁמַע – **Come, hear** the following Baraisa: בְּהֵמָה שֶׁאֲחָזָהּ דָּם – If AN ANIMAL SUFFERS FROM A CONGESTION OF BLOOD, אֵין מַעֲמִידִין אוֹתָהּ בַּמַּיִם בִּשְׁבִיל שֶׁתִּצְטַנֵּן – ONE MAY NOT STAND IT IN WATER SO THAT IT WILL COOL OFF. אָדָם שֶׁאֲחָזוֹ דָּם – But if A PERSON SUFFERS FROM A CONGESTION OF BLOOD, מַעֲמִידִין אוֹתוֹ בַּמַּיִם בִּשְׁבִיל שֶׁיִּצְטַנֵּן – ONE MAY STAND HIM IN WATER SO THAT HE WILL COOL OFF.[17] This treatment is required to alleviate

NOTES

1. It is worn to rid the animal of sickness (*Rashi*).

2. I.e. one is allowed to hang a feed bag on an animal only where it serves to alleviate suffering (as in the case of young colts), and not where it merely increases comfort.

3. See note 16.

4. Below, 60a. [The text quoted here is slightly different (see also Gemara below, 61a).]

5. A person is allowed to go out wearing a proven amulet, whereas an animal is not. Why should the law for an animal be different [i.e. more stringent] than for a person? (*Rashi;* see *Pnei Yehoshua;* see also *Maharsha* and *Maharam*).

6. When the Baraisa says "even if it is proven," it means that the amulet has been proven effective for people. It has not, however, been proven to work for animals. Therefore, such an amulet would be considered a burden if worn by an animal.

7. *Ritva* (*MHK* ed.) asks why the Gemara assumes that any amulet proven effective for man should also be effective for animals. After all, each disease and each patient requires its own remedy! *Ritva* answers that when the Gemara says "proven," it means that the person who made the amulet has been proven (i.e. he has made effective amulets for people for three different diseases – see Gemara below, 61a). Since he has been established as reliable in making amulets, he should be reliable in making amulets for animals as well.

8. Literally: it (i.e. his *mazal*) assists him.

9. מַזָּל, *mazal,* signifies a person's angel who advocates his cause in the Heavenly Court (*Rashi*). Since only a person enjoys this assistance, an amulet is more likely to work for a person than for an animal.

Alternatively, *mazal* means intelligence (*Rashi* to *Bava Kamma* 2b [first explanation]). In accord with this definition, *Meiri* explains here that an amulet is more effective for a person because a person believes in its therapeutic benefits.

The converse is also true: An amulet that works for an animal will not necessarily work for a person, because an animal has a stronger constitution than a person (*Meiri;* see *Maharsha* and *Sfas Emes*). [The Gemara's point is that people and animals are totally different in this regard, and hence even an expert in making amulets for one category cannot be relied upon for the other (see note 7).]

10. I.e. that the Baraisa refers to an amulet not proven effective for an animal.

11. In effect, the law is the same for people as it is for animals. Each may go out only with an amulet proven effective for its respective category (see *Rashi*).

12. The Baraisa stated that an animal may not go out wearing a shoe [lest it fall off] (*Rashi*). A person, however, is allowed to wear shoes in a public domain.

13. See *Mishnah Berurah* 332:2 and *Shaar HaTziyun* there.

14. This is prohibited on account of the Rabbinic prohibition against unnecessarily exerting oneself on the Sabbath (see *Ritva MHK* ed.). [It is permitted in the case of a person, because a relatively minor activity (such as this one) that serves to alleviate a person's pain or give him pleasure does not fall under the prohibition of unnecessary exertion (based on *Ritva MHK* ed. ד"ה אי הכי).]

15. This contradicts both Rav and Shmuel, who agree that alleviating an animal's suffering is permitted (*Rashi*).

16. The Baraisa has thus been reconciled with the view of Shmuel. However, it still contradicts Rav, who permits even activities that serve merely to increase an animal's comfort. In this case, too, we are forced to invoke the rule that Rav has the authority to disagree with the Tannaim [see 53a note 27] (*Rashi;* see *Ritva MHK* ed.).

17. See note 14.

דומיא דקמיע ש"מ: אמר מר ולא בקמיע אע"פ שהוא מומחה והא אנן תנן ולא בקמיע שאינו מומחה הא מומחה שפיר דמי ה"נ שאינו מומחה והא אע"פ שהוא מומחה קתני מומחה לאדם ואינו מומחה לבהמה ומי איכא מומחה לאדם ולא הוי מומחה לבהמה אין אדם דאית ליה מזלא מסייע ליה בהמה דלית לה מזלא לא מסייע לה אי הכי מאי זה חומר בבהמה מבאדם מי סברת אקמיע קאי אסנדל קאי ת"ש סכין ומפרכסין לאדם ואין סכין ומפרכסין לבהמה מאי לאו דאיכא מכה ומשום צער לא דגמר מכה ומשום תענוג ת"ש בהמה שאחזה דם אין מעמידין אותה במים בשביל שתצטנן אדם שאחזו דם מעמידין אותו במים בשביל שיצטנן אמר עולא גזירה משום שחיקת סממנין אי הכי אדם נמי אדם נראה כמיקר א"ה בהמה נמי נראה כמיקר אין מיקר לבהמה ולבהמה מי גזרינן והתניא היתה עומדת חוץ לתחום קורא לה והיא באה ולא גזרינן דילמא אתי לאתויי ואמר רבינא כגון שהיה תחום שלה מובלע בתוך תחום שלו ר"נ בר יצחק אמר שחיקת סממנין גופה תנאי היא דתני' בהמה שאכלה כרשינין לא יריצנה בחצר בשביל שתתרפה ורבי אושעיא מתיר דרש רבא הלכה כרבי אושעיא: אמר מר לא יצא הזב בכיס שלו ולא עזים בכיס שבדדיהן והתניא יוצאות עזים בכיס שבדדיהן אמר רב יהודה לא קשיא הא דמיהדק הא דלא מיהדק רב יוסף אמר תנאי שקלת מעלמא תנאי היא דתנן העזים יוצאות צרורות רבי יוסי אוסר בכלן חוץ מן הרחילות הכבונות ר' יהודה אומר עזים יוצאות צרורות ליבש אבל לא ליחלב ואיבעית אימא הא והא ר' יהודה ולא קשיא כאן ליבש כאן ליחלב תניא אמר ר' יהודה מעשה בעזים בית אנטוכיא שהיו דדיהן גסין ועשו להן כיסין כדי שלא יסרטו דדיהן: ת"ר מעשה באחד שמתה אשתו והניחה בן לינק ולא היה לו שכר מניקה ליתן ונעשה לו נס ונפתחו לו דדין כשני דדי אשה והניק את בנו אמר רב יוסף בא וראה כמה גדול אדם זה שנעשה לו נס כזה א"ל אביי אדרבה כמה גרוע אדם זה שנשתנו לו סדרי בראשית אמר רב יהודה בא וראה כמה קשים מזונותיו של אדם שנשתנו עליו סדרי בראשית אמר רב נחמן תדע דמתרחיש ניסא ולא אברו מזוני: ת"ר מעשה באדם אחד שנשא אשה גידמת ולא הכיר בה עד יום מותה אמר רב בא וראה כמה צנועה אשה זו שלא הכיר בה בעלה אמר לו רבי חייא זו דרכה בכך אלא כמה צנוע אדם זה שלא הכיר באשתו: זכרים יוצאין לבובין: מאי לבובין אמר רב הונא תותרי מאי משמע דהאי לבובין לישנא דקרובי הוא דכתיב א) לבבתני אחותי כלה עולא אמר עור שקושרין להם כנגד לבם כדי שלא יפלו עליהן זאבים זאבים אזכרים נפלי אנקיבות לא נפלי משום דמסגו בריש עדרא וזאבין בריש עדרא נפלי בסוף עדרא לא נפלי אלא משום דשמני ובנקבות ליכא שמני ותו מי ידעי בין הני להני אלא משום דזקפי חוטמייהו ומסגו כי דוו רב נחמן בר יצחק אמר עור שקושרין להן תחת זכרותן כדי שלא יעלו על הנקבות ממאי מדקתני סיפא והרחלים יוצאות שחוזות מאי שחוזות שאוחזין האליה שלהן למעלה כדי שיעלו עליהן זכרים רישא כדי שלא יעלו על הנקבות וסיפא כדי שיעלו עליהן זכרים מאי משמע דהאי שחוזות לישנא דגלויי הוא דכתיב ב) והנה אשה לקראתו
שית

תוספות

כגון שהיה תחום שלה מובלע כו'. ומ"מ לא התירו אלא דרך קריאה אבל לילך מעבר לבהמה ולרודפה לעיר לא:

תנאי היא. רב יהודה ידע שפיר דתנאי היא אלא דניחא ליה לאוקמי תרי סתמי דברייתא אליבא דחד תנא:

כאן ליבש כאן ליחלב. פי' בקונט' ליחלב שיקבלו בכים את החלב וקשה דהא ודאי משוי הוא ולכ"ע חייב דהויא מלאכה הצריכה לגופה ופי' ה"ר פור"ת ליחלב לשמור החלב בדדיהן שלא יזוב לארץ ושרי ת"ק דהוי כמו רחלים כבונות דחשבי' ליה מלבוש אף על פי שאינו עשוי לצורך עצמן אלא לשמור הצמר ור"י פירש דבין ליבש ובין ליחלב תרווייהו עבדי להו כדי שלא יסרטו דדיהן כדאמרינן בסמוך וליבש בזמן שאינו חפץ בחלב שרי לפי שמהדקו וליכא למיחש דילמא נפיל ואתי לאתויי אבל ליחלב שאינו רוצה שיתייבשו אינו מיהדק איכא למימר דילמא נפיל ואתי לאתויי:

שקושרין להן כנגד זכרותן כו'. ולשון לבובין הוי שלא לקרב כמו ובכל תבואתי תשרש (איוב לא) וכמוהו הרבה:

ממאי מדקתני סיפא. טפי הוי ליה לאתויי כבולות דהוי ממש כעין זה אלא משום דשחוזות הוי ברישא:

רש"י

דומיא דקמיע. משום חולי: והא אנן תנן. גבי אדם לקמן בפ' במה אשה (דף ס.): הא מומחה שפיר דמי. מאי שנא בהמה מאדם: מזליה. מלאך שלו ומליץ עליו: אי הכי. דבהמה נמי נפקא בקמיע המומחה לבהמה: מאי זה חומר. אדם נמי לא נפיק אלא בקמיע מומחה לאדם: אסנדל קאי. וזה חומר דקתני ולא בהמה בסנדל שברגליה: סכין. שמן: ומפרכסין. גלדי מכה: ומשום צער. [ואפילו] הכי לבהמה לא וקשיא בין לרב בין לשמואל דשרי במרדעת: לא דגמר מכה. שנתרפאה המכה וסיכה ופירכוס משום תענוג ולרב ודאי קשיא והיא מתניתא קמייתא דאוקף נמי קשיא ליה דנהי נמי דלצינה ליכא לצער תענוג מיהא הוא אלא רב תנא הוא ופליג: שאחזה דם. אנפודור"א: אין מעמידין כו'. אלמא אפילו לצער נמי אסור: גזירה משום שחיקת סממנים. במידי דרפואה גזור רבנן דאי שרית שום רפואה אתי למישרי שחיקת סממנים והוא איסורא דאורייתא דהוי טוחן: אין מיקר לבהמה. אין דרך להקר בהמה הלכך כולי עלמא ידעי דלרפואה קמיכוין ואתי למישרי שחיקת סממנים: ומי גזרינן. במקום פסידא כי האי גוונא: חוץ לתחום. קס"ד חוץ לתחום שלו היתה עומדת בהמה: שהיה תחום שלה מובלעת בתוך תחום שלו. דחוץ לתחום דקתני חוץ לתחום שלה שהבהמה המסורה לרועה המיוחד הרי היא כרגלי הרועה וזה הקורא לה בעליה ויכול לילך כגון שהוא שבת קרוב לאותו מקום ואפילו הכי לא יביאנה ממש בידיו הואיל והיא יוצאה חוץ לתחומה אין לה אלא ד' אמות ומיהו קורא לה והיא באה דלאו החזר הוא על תחום בהמתו ובלבד שלא יביאנה ממש בידיו: תנאי היא. דאיכא דלא גזר שאר רפואות אטו שחיקת סממנין: שאכלה כרשינין. הרבה ועל ידי אכילה מרובה אחזה חולי שקורין מינייזונ"א וצריכה להשתלשל ולהוציא רעי ומריצה: כדי שתתרפה. גרסינן הכא לשון ריפוי שיהיו מעיה רפויים בשלשול ומוציאה רעי: לא יריצנה. גזירה בכל רפואה אטו שחיקת סממנין: דמיהדק. דליכא למיחש דילמא נפיל ואתי לאתויי: תנאי שקלת מעלמא. אידכת כולם שאין אתה מוצא תנאים שנחלקו בכך דתוקי הנך תרתי מתניית' חדא כמר וחדא כמר: תנאי היא. במתניתין ר"מ שרי ר' יוסי אסר: ליבש. מיהדק שפיר ולענין משוי נמי לא הוי משוי דצורך גופה היא דחלבה מכחישה: ליחלב. הוי משוי שטוענת את החלב בכים: גסין. גדולין ונגררין על הקוצין ומסרטין דדיהן: שנשתנו עליו כו'. ולא זכה ליפתח לו שערי שכר: תדע. דקשין: דמרחשי ניסא. מן השמים לכמה הצלות לנפשות אדם: ולא איברו מזוני. ואין נס זה רגיל שיבראו מזונות לצדיקים בביתם שימצאו חיטין גדלין באוצרותיהן: גידמת. ידה קטועה: זו דרכה בכך. לכסות כל אשה עצמה וכ"ש זו שהיתה צריכה לכך: תותרי. קופל"א שמחברין אותם בקשר שנים שנים שלא יברחו: לבבתני. קרבתני אצלך מחמת נוי מעשיך: דרך זאבים לאחוז בהמה בלבה: אנקבות לא נפלי. בתמיה: דמסגי. מהלכין: בסוף עדרא לא נפלי. בתמיה: כי דוו. מביטין כאן וכאן לפיכך מתקנאין בהם כסבורים שרוצים להלחם בהם: אליה. זנב שלהן קושרים כלפי גבן שלא יכסה ערותן:
שית

עין משפט נר מצוה

כז א מיי' פ"כ מהל' שבת הלכה יג טוש"ע א"ח סי' שה סעי' ח בהג"ה:
כח ב ג מיי' פכ"א מהל' שבת הל' ל' סמג לאוין סה טוש"ע א"ח סי' שכח סעיף כב וסי' שלב סעיף ג:
כט ד מיי' וסמג שם טוש"ע א"ח סי' שלב סעיף ג וסעיף ד:
ל ה ו ז מיי' פ"כ מהל' שבת הל' יג סמג שם טוש"ע א"ח סי' שה סעיף ו:

רבינו חננאל

ובקששין: **תניא** אדם שאחזו דם מעמידין אותו במים בשביל לרפאותו. מ"ט משום דנראה כמיקר. אבל בהמה שאחזה דם אין מעמידין אותה במים כו'. אמר עולא בהמה גזירה משום שחיקת סמנים. ושחיקת סמנים תנאי היא. דתניא בהמה שאכלה כרשינין הרבה אין מריצין אותה בחצר בשביל לרפאותה. ור' יאשיה מיקל. והלכתא כוותיה דדרש רבא הלכתא כר' יאשיה. והא דר' יאשיה מסייעא לשמואל. מעשה שנעשה נס ונפתחו שני דדין כשני דדי אשה כו' וזו שהיתה גידמת כו'. פשוטות הן: **פי'** תותרי. סמרטוטין של רקמה ושל משי שעושין על הבהמה ליפותה. עולא אמר עור שמעמידין להן כנגד לבן שלא יפלו עליהן זאבים. משום דמסגו כי דוו. ומסתברא כוותיה דתנן (בע"ז דף כט:) באיסורי הנאה ועורות לבובין. ות"ר (שם דף לב.) איזהו עור לבוב. כל שהוא קרוע כנגד הלב. (וקרודה) [וקדורה] כמו ארובה כו'. שחוזות מלשון שית זונה:

תורה אור השלם

א) לְבַּבְתִּנִי אֲחֹתִי כַלָּה לִבַּבְתִּינִי בְּאַחַת מֵעֵינַיִךְ בְּאַחַד עֲנָק מִצַּוְּרֹנָיִךְ: [שיר השירים ד, ט]

ב) וְהִנֵּה אִשָּׁה לִקְרָאתוֹ שִׁית זוֹנָה וּנְצֻרַת לֵב: [משלי ז, י]

מסורת הש"ס

א) [לקמן ס.], ב) [ב"ק ב:], ג) [גיר' הערוך ומפרכין פי' מגרדין], ד) [ביצה יח.], ה) [לקמן קנא. ותוספתא פי"ח], ו) [נ"ל יאשיה וכ"א בר"א והרא"ש וכן העתיקו תוס' מ"ק י: ד"ה ואין], ז) [נ"ל יאשיה], ח) [עירובין לו: פסחים מה: ביצה יט. סנהדרין סא.], ט) [נ"ל רבי].

תוספות ישנים

א) ובבראשית רבה על פסוק ויהי אומן את הדסה שנפתחו למרדכי שני דדים כדדי אשה ליכא למיפרך הכי דהכי קאמר נשתנו דלא ה"ל שכר מניקה ומרדכי ה"ל שכר אך לא הי' מוצא מניקה:

גליון הש"ס

גמ' ולבהמה מי גזרינן והתניא. ק"ל דלמא משום שחיקת סממנים דאורייתא גזרי' אבל בתחומין דרבנן לא:

ליקוטי רש"י

ולא בקמיע שאינו מומחה. אבל בקמיע מומחה שרי דתכשיט הוא לחולה כאחד ממלבושיו [לקמן ס.]. **גזירה משום שחיקת סממנין.** דכל רפואה אסרו חכמים לעשותה בשבת היכא דליכא סכנה משום שחיקת סממנין במסכת שבת [ע"ז כח.]. דכל רפואה בשבת גזור בה רבנן משום שחיקת סממנין שהיא אב מלאכה טוחן [ביצה יח:]. וכן כל דבר רפואה שאין מלאכה אלא שבות הוא שגזרו חכמים בכל רפואות גזירה משום שחיקת סמנין [שם יא:]. **כרשינין.** מאכל בהמה בינ"א בלע"ז [לעיל יז:]. **צרורות.** דדיהן צרורות פעמים ליבש שמהדקן כדי שלא יחלבו עוד ויתעברו או יהו שמנות לאכול ופעמים לחלב לשמור חלבן שלא יטפטף לארץ וקושרין להם כיס בדדיהן. **רבי יוסי אוסר בכלן.** דמשוי הוא. **חוץ מן הרחילות הכבונות.** שהוא שמירת לצמרן שלא יטנף והוי להו תכשיט. **יוצאות צרורות ליבש.** ר' יהודה סבירא ליה כתנא קמא דלאו משוי הוא ומיהו ליבש דמיהדק שפיר וליכא למיחש דילמא נפיל ואתי לאיתויי אבל ליחלב דלא מיהדק שפיר חיישינן [שם נב: ועי' כאן במהרש"א ובמהר"ם]. **לבבתני.** משכת את לבי אליך [שה"ש ד, ט]. **והנה אשה.** כמשמעה, ד"א אחד מן אפיקורסים [משלי ז, י].

suffering, and yet it is forbidden in the case of an animal. – ? –

The Gemara answers:

אָמַר עוּלָּא – **Ulla said:** גְּזֵירָה מִשּׁוּם שְׁחִיקַת סַמְמָנִין – This prohibition is **a preventive measure** that was enacted **for the sake of** preventing the **grinding** of ingredients for **medicines.**[18]

The Gemara objects:

אִי הָכִי – **If** that is **so,** אָדָם נַמִּי – one should not be allowed to stand **a person** in water **either!**[19] – ? –

The Gemara answers:

אָדָם נִרְאֶה כְּמֵיקֵר – This is permitted in the case of **a person** because he **appears to be cooling** himself **off** from the heat of the day.[20]

The Gemara objects:

אִי הָכִי – **If** that is **so,** בְּהֵמָה נַמִּי נִרְאֶה כְּמֵיקֵר – it should be permitted in the case of **an animal as well,** because **one appears to be cooling** it **off.** – ? –

The Gemara answers:

אֵין מֵיקֵר לִבְהֵמָה – **One does not cool off animals.**[21]

The Gemara raises another objection to Ulla's defense of Shmuel:

וְלִבְהֵמָה מִי גָּזְרִינַן – **But do we decree** preventive measures **in the case of animals?**[22] וְהָתַנְיָא – **Why, it was taught in a Baraisa:** הָיְתָה עוֹמֶדֶת חוּץ לַתְּחוּם – If [ONE'S ANIMAL] WAS STANDING OUTSIDE THE SABBATH BOUNDARY, קוֹרֵא לָהּ וְהִיא בָּאָה – HE MAY CALL TO IT SO THAT IT WILL COME to him.[23] וְלָא גָּזְרִינַן דִּילְמָא אָתֵי לְאַתּוּיֵי – **Now,** in this case, **we do not decree** that the owner is forbidden to call the animal **lest he come to** walk outside his Sabbath boundary and **bring** the animal back by hand! This proves that where a financial loss could result (e.g. the loss of an animal), the Sages do not apply preventive measures. The Baraisa thus contradicts Ulla's position that the Rabbinic decree against medical treatments applies even to animals.[24] – ? –

The Gemara answers:

אָמַר רָבִינָא – **Ravina said:** כְּגוֹן שֶׁהָיָה תְּחוּם שֶׁלָּהּ מוּבְלָע בְּתוֹךְ תְּחוּם שֶׁלּוֹ – The Baraisa speaks of **a case where [the animal's] Sabbath boundary overlaps**[25] **[the owner's] Sabbath boundary,** and the animal is inside the owner's boundary.[26] In such a case, there is no concern that the owner might go outside his boundary; hence, no preventive measure is necessary to prevent him from doing so.[27]

Ulla asserted that the Rabbinic prohibition against medical treatments (which was designed to prevent the grinding of medicinal ingredients) applies even in treating animals. The Gemara now notes that this is not accepted by all Tannaim:

רַב נַחְמָן בַּר יִצְחָק אָמַר – **Rav Nachman bar Yitzchak says:** שְׁחִיקַת סַמְמָנִין גּוּפָהּ תַּנָּאֵי הִיא – The Rabbinic decree to prevent **the grinding of medicines is itself a** subject of **dispute among Tannaim** with respect to treating animals: דְּתַנְיָא – **For it was taught in a Baraisa:** בְּהֵמָה שֶׁאָכְלָה כַּרְשִׁינִין – If AN ANIMAL is sick because it HAS EATEN an excess of VETCHES, לֹא יְרִיצֶנָּה בֶּחָצֵר בִּשְׁבִיל שֶׁתִּתְרַפֵּא – ONE MAY NOT MAKE IT RUN IN A COURT-

NOTES

18. The Sages prohibited any kind of medical treatment [for minor ailments] on the Sabbath. The reason is that if such treatments were allowed, someone might come to grind substances (e.g. herbs) to make medicines, which would be a violation of the Scriptural prohibition against טוֹחֵן, *grinding* (*Rashi*).

The Gemara is answering that in general it is permitted to exert oneself to obviate an animal's suffering. Medical treatments, however, are forbidden, because they could lead to a Biblical transgression. Hence, this Baraisa does not contradict the permit stated by Rav and Shmuel, which does not extend to medical treatments.

19. If this activity falls under the category of prohibited medical treatments, it should be forbidden in the case of a person as well. It is therefore difficult to understand why the Baraisa rules that one may stand a person in cold water. However, if this is not a prohibited medical treatment (but is forbidden only on account of exertion), the Baraisa's distinction between animals and people is understandable, as explained in note 14 (*Ritva MHK* ed.).

20. The Sages did not apply their ban against medical treatments to activities that are also performed by healthy people. For example, the Mishnah below (109b) permits a sick person to eat for medicinal purposes foods that healthy people would also eat. In our case, therefore, since healthy people sometimes stand in water to cool off, it is permitted for the sick as well (*Ritva MHK* ed.).

For the same reason, the preceding Baraisa permits one to anoint a wound and remove the scab. This is not prohibited as a medical treatment because healthy people also anoint and rub their skin (see *Ritva MHK* ed.; see also *Mishnah Berurah* 328:70).

21. It is not customary to put animals in water just to cool them off from the heat of the day. Hence any onlooker would know that this was being done for medical purposes and might conclude that grinding herbs [for medicines] is also permissible (*Rashi*).

22. The Gemara is questioning whether such preventive measures [i.e. decrees that prohibit a permissible activity for fear that it might lead to a forbidden activity] were applied in cases of financial loss (*Rashi;* cf. *Ritva MHK* ed.; see *Dibros Moshe* 43:9 for an explanation of the Gemara's comparison).

23. On the Sabbath a person is forbidden to go more than 2,000 *amos* from where he was residing when the Sabbath began. This limit is known as תְּחוּם שַׁבָּת, *the Sabbath boundary.* If for some reason one did go out of his Sabbath boundary, he is then restricted to a distance of four *amos* from where he is currently located.

The Gemara assumes the Baraisa to mean that the animal is outside its owner's Sabbath boundary (*Rashi*).

24. The commentators object that these two cases are not analogous. The prohibition against medical treatments was designed to prevent the grinding of herbs, which is a Biblical transgression, whereas going beyond the Sabbath boundary is only a Rabbinic transgression. The Gemara could therefore answer that the Sages did apply their decrees in cases of financial loss (as Ulla maintains), but only to prevent Biblical violations, and not to prevent Rabbinic ones (*Gilyon HaShas;* see *Mitzpeh Eisan;* see also *Dibros Moshe* ibid.). [See the approach of *Ritva MHK* ed., which avoids this problem.]

25. Literally: is swallowed within.

26. Normally, animals and utensils are limited to their owner's Sabbath boundary (Mishnah *Beitzah* 37a). [That is, they may not be taken more than 2,000 *amos* from his place of residence.] If, however, they were transferred before the Sabbath to the safekeeping of another person, they are restricted to that person's boundary. The Gemara is suggesting that our Baraisa speaks of a case in which the animal was entrusted to a shepherd, whose boundary differed from that of the owner. On the Sabbath, the animal was found outside the shepherd's boundary, but within the owner's boundary. In such a case, the owner is permitted to bring the animal towards him, since he need not go outside his boundary to do so. Although he will thereby cause the animal to go more than four *amos* outside its boundary (see note 23), he does not commit any violation, because a person is not responsible for keeping his animal within its prescribed area on the Sabbath. [This is similar to the law that one may let his animal graze on the Sabbath – see Chapter Introduction.] However, he may not pull the animal by hand; he may only call out to it so that it will come to him of its own accord (*Rashi;* see *Mishnah Berurah* 306:7 and 305:77).

In addition to the problem mentioned in note 24, there are several difficulties with *Rashi's* approach to this passage: (a) Why does the Gemara say that the animal's boundary *overlaps* the owner's boundary? Surely the main point is that the animal's current position [after it has left its boundary] is within the owner's boundary (see, however, *Rashash*). (b) Since the owner is forbidden to move the animal by hand, why did the Rabbis not forbid him to call out to it lest he come to move it by hand? [These and other problems are raised by *Hagahos R' Eliezer Moshe Horowitz.* See the approach given there and that of *Ritva MHK* ed., which avoids these difficulties.]

27. But where there are grounds for a preventive measure, it is applied even if financial loss will result, as Ulla evidently maintains.

דומיא דקמיע ש"מ: אמר מר ולא בקמיע אע"פ שהוא מומחה והא אנן תנן [א] ולא בקמיע שאינו מומחה הא מומחה שפיר דמי ה"נ [א] שאינו מומחה והא אע"פ שהוא מומחה קתני מומחה לאדם ואינו מומחה לבהמה ומי איכא מומחה לאדם ולא הוי מומחה לבהמה אין אדם [ב] דאית ליה מזלא מסייע ליה בהמה דלית לה מזלא לא מסייע לה אי הכי מאי זה חומר בבהמה מבאדם מי סברת אקמיע קאי אסנדל קאי ת"ש [ב] סכין [ג] ומפרכסין לאדם ואין סכין ומפרכסין לבהמה מאי לאו דאיכא מכה ומשום צער לא [ג] דגמר מכה ומשום תענוג ת"ש בהמה שאחזה דם אין מעמידין אותה במים בשביל שתצטנן אדם שאחזו דם מעמידין אותו במים בשביל שיצטנן אמר עולא גזירה משום שחיקת סממנין אי הכי [ד] אדם נמי אדם נראה כמיקר א"ה בהמה נמי נראה כמיקר אין מיקר לבהמה [ה] ולבהמה מי גזרינן והתניא [ו] היתה עומדת חוץ לתחום קורא לה והיא באה ולא גזרינן דילמא אתי לאתויי ואמר רבינא כגון שהיה תחום שלה מובלע בתוך תחום שלו ר"נ בר יצחק אמר שחיקת סממנין גופה תנאי היא דתני' בהמה שאכלה כרשינין לא יריצנה בחצר בשביל שתתרפה ורבי [ז] [ד] אושעיא מתיר דרש רבא הלכה כרבי [ח] אושעיא: אמר מר לא יצא הזב בכיס שלו ולא עזים בכיס שבדדיהן והתניא יוצאות עזים בכיס שבדדיהן אמר רב יהודה לא קשיא הא דמיהדק הא דלא מיהדק רב יוסף אמר [ט] תנאי שקלת מעלמא תנאי היא דתנן העזים יוצאות צרורות רבי יוסי אוסר בכלן חוץ מן הרחילות הכבונות ר' יהודה אומר עזים יוצאות צרורות ליבש אבל לא ליחלב ואיבעית אימא הא והא ר' יהודה ולא קשיא [ה] כאן ליבש כאן ליחלב תניא אמר ר' יהודה מעשה בעזים בית אנטוכיא שהיו דדיהן גסין ועשו להן כיסין כדי שלא ישרטו דדיהן: ת"ר מעשה באחד שמתה אשתו והניחה בן לינק ולא היה לו שכר מניקה ליתן ונעשה לו נס ונפתחו לו דדין כשני דדי אשה והניק את בנו אמר רב יוסף בא וראה כמה גדול אדם זה שנעשה לו נס כזה א"ל אביי אדרבה כמה [א] גרוע אדם זה שנשתנו לו סדרי בראשית אמר רב יהודה בא וראה כמה קשים מזונותיו של אדם שנשתנו עליו סדרי בראשית אמר רב נחמן תדע דמתרחיש ניסא ולא אברו מזוני: ת"ר מעשה באדם אחד שנשא אשה גידמת ולא הכיר בה עד יום מותה אמר [ט] רב בא וראה כמה צנועה אשה זו שלא הכיר בה בעלה אמר לו רבי חייא זו דרכה בכך אלא כמה צנוע אדם זה שלא הכיר באשתו: [ו] זכרים יוצאין לבובין: מאי לבובין אמר רב הונא תותרי מאי משמע דהאי לבובין לישנא דקרובי הוא דכתיב [א] לבבתני אחותי כלה עולא אמר עור שקושרין להם כנגד לבם כדי שלא יפלו עליהן זאבים זאבים אזכרים נפלי אנקיבות לא נפלי משום דמסגו בריש עדרא וזאבין בריש עדרא נפלי בסוף עדרא לא נפלי אלא משום דשמני ובנקבות ליכא שמני ותו מי ידעי בין הני להני אלא משום דזקפי חוטמייהו ומסגו כי דוו רב נחמן בר יצחק אמר עור שקושרין להן תחת זכרותן כדי שלא יעלו על הנקבות ממאי מדקתני סיפא [ז] והרחלים יוצאות שחוזות מאי שחוזות שאוחזין האליה שלהן למעלה כדי שיעלו עליהן זכרים רישא כדי שלא יעלו על הנקבות וסיפא כדי שיעלו עליהן זכרים מאי משמע דהאי שחוזות לישנא דגלויי הוא דכתיב [ב] והנה אשה לקראתו

שית

כגון שהיה תחום שלה מובלע כו'. ומ"מ לא התירו אלא דרך קריאה אבל לילך מעבר לבהמה ולרודפה לעיר לא:

תנאי היא. רב יהודה ידע שפיר דתנאי היא אלא דניחא ליה לאוקמי תרי סתמי דברייתא אליבא דחד תנא:

כאן ליבש כאן ליחלב. פי' בקונט' ליחלב שיקבלו בכיס את החלב וקשה דהא ודאי משוי הוא ולכ"ע חייב דהויא מלאכה הצריכה לגופה ופי' ה"ר פור"ת ליחלב לשמור החלב בדדיהן שלא יזוב לארץ ושרי ת"ק דהוי כמו רחלים כבונות דחשבי' ליה מלבוש אף על פי שאינו עשוי לצורך עצמן אלא לשמור הצמר ור"י פירש דבין ליבש ובין ליחלב תרווייהו עבדי להו כדי שלא ישרטו דדיהן כדאמרינן בסמוך וליבש בזמן שאינו חפץ בחלב שרי לפי שמהדקו וליכא למיחש דילמא נפיל ואתי לאתויי אבל ליחלב שאינו רוצה שיתייבשו אינו מיהדק איכא למימר דילמא נפיל ואתי לאתויי:

שקושרין להן כנגד זכרותן כו'. ולשון לבובין הוי שלא לקרב כמו ובכל תבואתי תשרש (איוב לא) וכמוהו הרבה:

ממאי מדקתני סיפא. טפי הוי ליה לאתויי כבולות דהוי ממש כעין זה אלא משום דשחוזות הוי ברישא:

עד

דומיא דקמיע. משום חולי: והא אנן תנן. גבי אדם לקמן בפ' במה אשה (דף ס.): הא מומחה שפיר דמי. מאי שנא בהמה מאדם: מזליה. מלאך שלו ומליץ עליו: אי הכי. דבהמה נמי נפקא בקמיע המומחה לבהמה: מאי זה חומר. אדם נמי לא נפיק אלא בקמיע מומחה לאדם: אסנדל קאי. חה חומר דקתני ולא בהמה בסנדל שברגליה: סכין. שמן: ומפרכסין. גלדי מכה: ומשום צער. [ואפילו] הכי לבהמה לא וקשיא בין לרב בין לשמואל דשרי במרדעת: לא דגמר מכה. שנתרפאה המכה וסיכה ופירכוס משום תענוג ולרב ודאי קשיא והיא מתניתא קמייתא דאוכף נמי קשיא ליה דנהי נמי דלצינה ליכא צער תענוג מיהא הוא אלא רב תנא הוא ופליג: שאחזה דם. אנפודור"א: אין מעמידין כו'. אלמא אפילו צער נמי אסור: גזירה משום שחיקת סממנים. במידי דרפואה גזור רבנן דאי שרית שום רפואה אתי למישרי שחיקת סממנים והוא איסורא דאורייתא דהוי טוחן: אין מיקר לבהמה. אין דרך להקר בהמה הלכך כולי עלמא ידעי דלרפואה קמיכוין ואתי למישרי שחיקת סממנים: ומי גזרינן. במקום פסידא כי האי גוונא: חוץ לתחום. קס"ד חוץ לתחום שלו היתה עומדת בהמה: שהיה תחום שלה מובלעת בתוך תחום שלו. דחוץ לתחום דקתני חוץ לתחום שלה שהבהמה המסורה לרועה המיוחד הרי היא כרגלי הרועה וזה הקורא לה בעליה ויכול לילך כגון שהוא שבת קרוב לאותו מקום ואפילו הכי לא יביאנה ממש בידיו הואיל והיא יוצאה חוץ לתחומה אין לה אלא ד' אמות ומיהו קורא לה והיא באה דלא הוזהר הוא על תחום בהמתו ובלבד שלא יביאנה ממש בידיו: תנאי היא. דאיכא דלא גזר שאר רפואות אטו שחיקת סממנין: שאכלה כרשינין. הרבה ועל ידי אכילה מרובה אחזה חולי שקורין מינייזונ"א וצריכה להשתלשל ולהוציא רעי ומריצה: כדי שתתרפה. גרסינן הכא לשון ריפוי שיהיו מיעיה רפויים בשילשול ומוליאה רעי: לא יריצנה. גזירה בכל רפואה אטו שחיקת סממנין: דמיהדק. דליכא למיחש דילמא נפיל ואתי לאתויי: תנאי שקלת מעלמא. איבדת כולם שאין אתה מוצא תנאים שנחלקו בכך דתוקי הנך תרתי מתניית' חדא כמר וחדא כמר: תנאי היא. במתניתין ר"מ שרי ר' יוסי אסר: ליבש. מיהדק שפיר ולענין משוי נמי לא הוי משוי דלורך גופה היא דחלבה מכחישה: ליחלב. הוי משוי שטוענת את החלב בכים: גסין. גדולין ונגררין על הקוצין ומסרטין דדיהן: שנשתנו עליו כו'. ולא זכה ליפתח לו שערי שכר: תדע. דקשין: דמרחשי ניסא. מן השמים לכמה הצלות לנפשות אדם: ולא איברו מזוני. ואין נס זה רגיל שיבראו מזונות לצדיקים בביתם שימצאו חיטין גדלין באוצרותיהן: גידמת. ידה קטועה: זו דרכה בכך. לכסות כל אשה עצמה וכ"ש זו שהיתה צריכה לכך: תותרי. קופל"א שמחברין אותם בקשר שנים שנים שלא יברחו: לבבתני. קרבתני אצלך מחמת נוי מעשיך: דרך זאבים לאחוז בהמה בלבה: אנקבות לא נפלי. בתמיה: דמסגי. מהלכין: בסוף עדרא לא נפלי. בתמיה: כי דוו. מביטין כאן וכאן לפיכך מתקנאין בהם כסבורים שרוצים להלחם בהם: אליה. זנב שלהן קושרים כלפי גבן שלא יכסה ערותן:

שית

עין משפט נר מצוה

כז א מיי' פ"כ מהל' שבת הלכה יג טוש"ע א"ח סי' שה סעי' ז בהג"ה:
כח ב ג מיי' פכ"א מהל' שבת הל' ל' סמג לאוין סה טוש"ע א"ח סי' שכח סעיף כב וסי' שלב סעיף ג:
כט ד מיי' וסמג שם טוש"ע א"ח סי' שלב סעיף ג וסעיף ד:
ל ה ו ז מיי' פ"כ מהל' שבת הל' יג סמג שם טוש"ע א"ח סי' שה סעיף ו:

רבינו חננאל

ובקשישין: **תניא** אדם שאחזו דם מעמידין אותו במים בשביל לרפאותו. מ"ט משום דנראה כמיקר. אבל בהמה שאחזה דם אין מעמידין אותה במים כו'. אמר עולא בהמה גזירה משום שחיקת סמנים. ושחיקת סמנים תנאי היא. דתניא בהמה שאכלה כרשינין הרבה אין מריצין אותה בחצר בשביל לרפאותה. ור' יאשיה מיקל. והלכתא כוותיה דדרש רבא הלכתא כר' יאשיה. והא דר' יאשיה מסייעא לשמואל. מעשה שנעשה נס ונפתחו שני דדין כשני דדי אשה כו' וזו שהיתה גידמת כו'. פשוטות הן: **פי'** תותרי. סמרטוטין של רקמה ושל משי שעושין על הבהמה ליפותה. עולא אמר עור שמעמידין להן כנגד לבן שלא יפלו עליהן זאבים. משום דמסגו כי דוו. ומסתברא כוותיה דתנן (בע"ז דף כט:) באיסורי הנאה ועורות לבובין. ות"ר (שם דף לב.) איזהו עור לבוב. כל שהוא קרוע כנגד הלב. (וקרודה) [וקדורה] כמו ארובה כו'. שחוזות מלשון שית זונה:

תורה אור השלם

א) לִבַּבְתִּנִי אֲחֹתִי כַלָּה לִבַּבְתִּינִי בְּאַחַת מֵעֵינַיִךְ בְּאַחַד עֲנָק מִצַּוְּרֹנָיִךְ: [שיר השירים ד, ט]

ב) וְהִנֵּה אִשָּׁה לִקְרָאתוֹ שִׁית זוֹנָה וּנְצֻרַת לֵב: [משלי ז, י]

מסורת הש"ס

א) [לקמן ס.], ב) [נ"ק כ:], ג) [גיר' הערוך ומפרכין פי' מגרדין], ד) [ביצה יח.], ה) [לקמן קנג. ותוספתא פי"ח], ו) [נ"ל **יאשיה** וכ"ה בר"ח והרא"ש וכן העתיקו תוס' מ"ק י: ד"ה ואין], ז) [נ"ל **יאשיה**], ח) [עירובין לו: פסחים מה: ביצה יט. סנהדרין סא.], ט) [נ"ל רבין].

תוספות ישנים

א) ובבראשית רבה על פסוק ויהי אומן את הדסה שנפתחו למרדכי שני דדים כדדי אשה ליכא למיפרך הכי דהכי קאמר נשתנו דלא הו"ל שכר מניקה ומרדכי הו"ל שכר אך לא הי' מוצא מניקה:

גליון הש"ס

גמ' ולבהמה מי גזרינן והתניא. ק"ל דלמא משום שחיקת סממנים דאורייתא גזרי' אבל בתחומין דרבנן לא:

ליקוטי רש"י

ולא בקמיע שאינו מומחה. אבל בקמיע מומחה שרי דמכשיט הוא לחולה כאחד ממלבושיו [לקמן ס.]. **גזירה משום שחיקת סממנין.** דכל רפואה אסרו חכמים לעשותה בשבת היכא דליכא סכנה משום שחיקת סממנין במסכת שבת [ע"ז כח.]. דכל רפואה בשבת גזור בה רבנן משום שחיקת סממנין שהיא אב מלאכה טוחן [ביצה יח:]. וכן כל דבר רפואה שאין מלאכה אלא שבות הוא שגזרו חכמים בכל רפואות גזירה משום שחיקת סמנין [שם יא:]. **כרשינין.** מאכל בהמה בינ"א בלע"ז [לעיל יז:]. **צרורות.** דדיהן צרורות פעמים ליבש שמהדקן כדי שלא יחלבו עוד ויתעברו או יהו שמנות לאכול ופעמים לחלב לשמור חלבן שלא יטפטף לארץ וקושרין להם כיס בדדיהן. **רבי יוסי אוסר בכלן.** דמשוי הוא. **חוץ מן הרחילות הכבונות.** שהוא שמירת צמרן שלא יטנף והוי להו מכשיט. **יוצאות צרורות ליבש.** ר' יהודה סבירא ליה כתנא קמא דלאו משוי הוא ומיהו ליבש דמיהדק שפיר וליכא למיחש דילמא נפיל ואתי לאיתויי אבל ליחלב דלא מיהדק שפיר מיישינן [שם נב: ועי' כאן במהרש"א ובמהר"ם]. **לבבתני.** משכת את לבי אליך [שה"ש ד, ט]. **והנה אשה.** כמשמעה, ד"א אחד מן אפיקורסים [משלי ז, י].

YARD SO THAT [ITS BOWELS] WILL BE LOOSENED.[28] וְרַבִּי אוֹשַׁעְיָא מַתִּיר – BUT R' OSHAYA[29] PERMITS this.[30]

The Gemara adds:

דָּרֵשׁ רָבָא – **Rava lectured:** הֲלָכָה כְּרַבִּי אוֹשַׁעְיָא – **The law follows R' Oshaya.**[31]

The Gemara returns to the Baraisa quoted at the end of 53a:

אָמַר מַר – **Master said** in the Baraisa: "לֹא יֵצֵא הַזָּב בְּכִיס שֶׁלּוֹ – THE *ZAV* MAY NOT GO OUT WITH HIS POUCH, וְלֹא עִזִּים בְּכִיס שֶׁבְּדַדֵּיהֶן" – AND GOATS may NOT go out WITH A POUCH ON THEIR UDDERS.

The Gemara asks:

וְהָתַנְיָא – **But it was taught in a** different **Baraisa** to the contrary: יוֹצְאוֹת עִזִּים בְּכִיס שֶׁבְּדַדֵּיהֶן – GOATS MAY GO OUT WITH A POUCH ON THEIR UDDERS! – ? –

The Gemara solves the contradiction:

אָמַר רַב יְהוּדָה – **Rav Yehudah said:** לֹא קַשְׁיָא – **There is no contradiction.** הָא דְּמִיהַדַּק – **This** second Baraisa, which permits the goats' pouch, refers to one **that is fastened securely,** הָא דְּלֹא מִיהַדַּק – whereas **this** first Baraisa, which prohibits the pouch, refers to one **that is not fastened securely.**[32]

Rav Yosef rejects this solution in favor of a different one:

רַב יוֹסֵף אָמַר – **Rav Yosef said:** תַּנָּאֵי שָׁקְלַת מֵעָלְמָא – **Have you removed** all the **Tannaim from the world!?**[33] תַּנָּאֵי הִיא – **It is a dispute between Tannaim!** That is, the two Baraisos represent the opposing views of two Tannaim. דִּתְנַן – **For we learned in our Mishnah:** הָעִזִּים יוֹצְאוֹת צְרוּרוֹת – GOATS MAY GO OUT with a pouch TIED onto their udders. רַבִּי יוֹסֵי אוֹסֵר בְּכֻלָּן חוּץ מִן הָרְחֵילוֹת הַכְּבוּנוֹת – R' YOSE FORBIDS ALL OF THESE CASES SAVE FOR that of THE EWES THAT GO OUT FASTENED.[34] רַבִּי יְהוּדָה אוֹמֵר – R' YEHUDAH SAYS: עִזִּים יוֹצְאוֹת צְרוּרוֹת לְיַבֵּשׁ – GOATS MAY GO OUT with a pouch TIED onto their udders if it is used TO DRY UP the milk, אֲבָל לֹא לֵיחָלֵב – BUT NOT if it is used TO COLLECT THE MILK.[35]

Rav Yosef suggests another solution of the contradiction between the Baraisos:

וְאִיבָּעִית אֵימָא הָא וְהָא רַבִּי יְהוּדָה – **Or, if you wish, say that** both **this** Baraisa **and that** Baraisa follow **R' Yehudah.** וְלֹא קַשְׁיָא – **And yet there is no contradiction** between them, כָּאן לְיַבֵּשׁ – because **here** [the Baraisa that permits the goats' pouch] the reference is to a pouch used **to dry up** the milk,[36] כָּאן לֵיחָלֵב – whereas **here** [the Baraisa that forbids the pouch] the reference is to a pouch used **to collect the milk.**[37]

The Gemara cites another Baraisa on this topic:

תַּנְיָא – **It was taught in a Baraisa:** אָמַר רַבִּי יְהוּדָה – R' YEHUDAH SAID: מַעֲשֶׂה בְּעִזִּים בֵּית אַנְטוֹכְיָא – IT HAPPENED WITH THE GOATS OF ANTOCHIA שֶׁהָיוּ דַּדֵּיהֶן גַּסִּין – THAT THEIR UDDERS

NOTES

28. This Tanna holds that *all* medical treatments [even those for animals] are forbidden, lest one come to grind ingredients for medicines (*Rashi*). This is the view followed by Ulla.

29. The text should read ר׳ יֹאשִׁיָּה, *R' Yoshiyah* (*Mesoras HaShas*).

30. [*Rif, Rabbeinu Chananel* and most other Rishonim have the text, ור׳ יֹאשִׁיָּה מֵיקֵל, *But R' Yoshiyah rules leniently* (see next note).] R' Yoshiyah maintains that the Rabbinic prohibition against practicing medicine on the Sabbath does not apply to treating animals. The reason is that when an animal falls sick one is not likely to become so agitated that he forgets that it is the Sabbath and grinds herbs for its cure (*Rif, Rosh;* cf. *Ritva MHK* ed.; see *Beur Halachah* 332 ד״ה ואם).

31. The Baraisa's language מֵיקֵל, *he rules leniently* (see previous note), carries a weaker connotation than the more common expression, מַתִּיר, *he rules that it is permitted.* Some Rishonim infer from here that although treating animals is permissible, we do not publicize this law [lest people take advantage of it]. Other Rishonim argue that, on the contrary, since the Gemara says דָּרֵשׁ רָבָא, *Rava lectured,* which denotes addressing a large assembly, we see that this law may be publicized (*Rashba, Meiri*).

32. According to Rav Yehudah, both Baraisos follow the Tanna Kamma of our Mishnah (52b), who rules that the pouch is not classified as a burden. However, the Tanna Kamma certainly agrees that if the pouch is not tied on securely, it is forbidden, lest it fall off and one carry it four *amos* in a public domain (*Tosafos* ד״ה תנאי as explained by *Maharam;* cf. *Maharsha*).

33. Are you unable to find Tannaim who disagree over this matter, so that you can attribute one Baraisa to one Tanna and the other Baraisa to the other Tanna? (*Rashi*).

34. See below, 54a note 10.

35. The Mishnah recorded a three-way dispute: (a) The Tanna Kamma *permits* animals to go out with a pouch tied to their udders in all circumstances [provided that it is secure]; (b) R' Yose *prohibits* this practice in all circumstances; (c) R' Yehudah permits it where the pouch is used to stop lactation, and prohibits it where the pouch is used to stop the milk from dripping onto the ground.

Rav Yosef attributes the Baraisa that permits goats to go out with a pouch to R' Meir [the anonymous Tanna of a Mishnah is usually R' Meir (see *Maharsha*)] and the Baraisa that prohibits this practice to R' Yose (*Rashi;* cf. *Chidushei HaRan*). [In view of the fact that Rav Yosef does not say otherwise, it is unlikely that he attributes either Baraisa to R' Yehudah. This is because R' Yehudah's ruling applies only in limited circumstances, whereas the Baraisos do not mention any limitations.]

Thus, Rav Yehudah [the Amora – not to be confused with R' Yehudah the Tanna] maintains that both Baraisos follow a single Tanna, viz. R' Meir (see note 32), while Rav Yosef attributes them to two dissenting Tannaim, viz. R' Meir and R' Yose. Their respective reasons are as follows:

Rav Yehudah reasoned that since both Baraisos are anonymous, it is more likely that they follow one Tanna than two dissenting Tannaim (*Tosafos*). Hence, he attributed both Baraisos to R' Meir, and explained one as referring to a pouch that is tied securely and the other as referring to a pouch that is not tied securely.

Rav Yosef, though, rejected this approach, because he reasoned that there is no need for any Baraisa to teach that a pouch is prohibited if it is not secured tightly. As the Gemara stated above (53a, in reference to a saddle cloth), it is obvious that a loosely attached item is forbidden lest it fall off (see however, *Sfas Emes* cited there). Rav Yosef therefore argued that since there are Tannaim who disagree as to whether a pouch is prohibited *even if it is attached securely,* it is surely preferable to attribute the Baraisos to them (*Ritva MHK* ed.; *Maharam;* cf. *Maharsha*).

36. In such a case, the pouch is tied on tightly. Furthermore, it is not a burden – the reason being that since it is used to stop lactation, which weakens the animal, the pouch is viewed as protecting the animal's body [and thus has the status of a garment] (*Rashi*).

37. [Literally: to be milked.] In this case, the pouch is a burden, because its purpose is to carry milk (*Rashi*).

The Gemara requires explanation. Rav Yosef argued above that the two Baraisos follow different Tannaim, and here Rav Yosef himself attributes them to the same Tanna. This difficulty can be resolved according to the approach presented in note 34. There it was explained that the main thrust of Rav Yosef's objection to Rav Yehudah's answer was not that Rav Yehudah attributed both Baraisos to one Tanna, but rather that R' Yehudah interpreted one of the Baraisos as referring to a pouch that was not fastened securely. That objection does not apply to Rav Yosef's current approach, since it interprets both Baraisos as speaking of a securely attached pouch.

It can now be understood why *Rashi* here gives a different explanation than the one he gave on the Mishnah. There *Rashi* explained that according to R' Yehudah, a pouch used for milking purposes is not a burden (see *Tosafos* here ד״ה כאן and *Rosh Yosef*), and it is forbidden only because it is not attached securely. That explanation is not viable in the context of Rav Yosef's answer, since, as explained above, Rav Yosef does not consider it acceptable to interpret either Baraisa as speaking of a pouch that is not attached securely. Therefore, *Rashi* had to give an explanation that would conform to Rav Yosef's approach – namely, that a pouch used for milking purposes is forbidden because it is a burden [and thus is forbidden even if it is attached securely] (*Maharam;* cf. *Maharsha;* see *Shabbos Shel Mi,* who agrees with *Maharam's* approach).

דומיא דקמיע ש"מ: אמר מר ולא בקמיע אע"פ שהוא מומחה והא אנן תנן [א] ולא בקמיע שאינו מומחה הא מומחה שפיר דמי ה"נ [א] שאינו מומחה והא אע"פ שהוא מומחה קתני מומחה לאדם ואינו מומחה לבהמה ומי איכא מומחה לאדם ולא הוי מומחה לבהמה אין אדם [ב] דאית ליה מזלא מסייע ליה בהמה דלית לה מזלא לא מסייע לה אי הכי מאי זה חומר בבהמה מבאדם מי סברת אקמיע קאי אסנדל קאי ת"ש [ב] סכין [ג] ומפרכסין לאדם ואין סכין ומפרכסין לבהמה מאי לאו דאיכא מכה ומשום צער לא [ג] דגמר מכה ומשום תענוג ת"ש בהמה שאחזה דם אין מעמידין אותה במים בשביל שתצטנן אדם שאחזו דם מעמידין אותו במים בשביל שיצטנן אמר עולא גזירה משום שחיקת סממנין אי הכי [ד] אדם נמי אדם נראה כמיקר א"ה בהמה נמי נראה כמיקר אין מיקר לבהמה • ולבהמה מי גזרינן והתניא [ה] היתה עומדת חוץ לתחום קורא לה והיא באה ולא גזרינן דילמא אתי לאתויי ואמר רבינא כגון שהיה תחום שלה מובלע בתוך תחום שלו ר"נ בר יצחק אמר שחיקת סממנין גופה תנאי היא דתני' בהמה שאכלה כרשינין לא ירִיצנה בחצר בשביל שתתרפה ורבי [ו] [ד] אושעיא מתיר דרש רבא הלכה כרבי [ז] אושעיא: אמר מר לא יצא הזב בכיס שלו ולא עזים בכיס שבדדיהן והתניא יוצאות עזים בכיס שבדדיהן אמר רב יהודה לא קשיא הא דמיהדק הא דלא מיהדק רב יוסף אמר [ח] תנאי שקלת מעלמא תנאי היא דתנן העזים יוצאות צרורות רבי יוסי אוסר בכלן חוץ מן הרחילות הכבונות ר' יהודה אומר עזים יוצאות צרורות ליבש אבל לא ליחלב ואיבעית אימא הא והא ר' יהודה ולא קשיא [ה] כאן ליבש כאן ליחלב תניא אמר ר' יהודה מעשה בעזים בית אנטוכיא שהיו דדיהן גסין ועשו להן כיסין כדי שלא יסרטו דדיהן: ת"ר מעשה באחד שמתה אשתו והניחה בן לינק ולא היה לו שכר מניקה ליתן ונעשה לו נס ונפתחו לו דדין כשני דדי אשה והניק את בנו אמר רב יוסף בא וראה כמה גדול אדם זה שנעשה לו נס כזה א"ל אביי אדרבה כמה [א] גרוע אדם זה שנשתנו לו סדרי בראשית אמר רב יהודה בא וראה כמה קשים מזונותיו של אדם שנשתנו עליו סדרי בראשית אמר רב נחמן תדע דמתרחיש ניסא ולא אברו מזוני: ת"ר מעשה באדם אחד שנשא אשה גידמת ולא הכיר בה עד יום מותה אמר [ט] רב בא וראה כמה צנועה אשה זו שלא הכיר בה בעלה אמר לו רבי חייא זו דרכה בכך אלא כמה צנוע אדם זה שלא הכיר באשתו: [ו] זכרים יוצאין לבובין: מאי לבובין אמר רב הונא תותרי מאי משמע דהאי לבובין לישנא דקרובי הוא דכתיב [א] לבבתני אחותי כלה עולא אמר עור שקושרין להם כנגד לבם כדי שלא יפלו עליהן זאבים זאבים אזכרים נפלי אנקיבות לא נפלי משום דמסגו בריש עדרא וזאבין בריש עדרא נפלי בסוף עדרא לא נפלי אלא משום דשמני ובנקבות ליכא שמני ותו מי ידעי בין הני להני אלא משום דזקפי חוטמייהו ומסגו כי דוו רב נחמן בר יצחק אמר עור שקושרין להן תחת זכרותן כדי שלא יעלו על הנקבות ממאי מדקתני סיפא [ז] והרחלים יוצאות שחוזות מאי שחוזות שאוחזין האליה שלהן למעלה כדי שיעלו עליהן זכרים רישא כדי שלא יעלו על הנקבות וסיפא כדי שיעלו עליהן זכרים מאי משמע דהאי שחוזות לישנא דגלויי הוא דכתיב [ב] והנה אשה לקראתו

שית

כגון שהיה תחום שלה מובלע כו'. ומ"מ לא התירו אלא דרך קריאה אבל לילך מעבר לבהמה ולרודפה לעיר לא: **תנאי** היא. רב יהודה ידע שפיר דתנאי היא אלא דניחא ליה לאוקמי תרי סתמי דברייתא אליבא דחד תנא: **כאן** ליבש כאן ליחלב. פי' בקונט' ליחלב שיקבלו בכיס את החלב וקשה דהא ודאי משוי הוא ולכ"ע חייב דהויא מלאכה הצריכה לגופה ופי' ה"ר פור"ת ליחלב לשמור החלב בדדיהן שלא יזוב לארץ ושרי ת"ק דהוי כמו רחלים כבונות דחשבי' ליה מלבוש אף על פי שאינו עשוי לצורך עצמן אלא לשמור הצמר ור"י פירש דבין ליבש ובין ליחלב תרווייהו עבדי להו כדי שלא יסרטו דדיהן כדאמרינן בסמוך וליבש בזמן שאינו חפץ בחלב שרי לפי שמהדקו וליכא למיחש דילמא נפיל ואתי לאתויי אבל ליחלב שאינו רוצה שיתייבשו אינו מיהדק איכא למימר דילמא נפיל ואתי לאתויי: **שקושרין** להן כנגד זכרותן כו'. ולשון לבובין הוי שלא לקרב כמו ובכל תבואתי תשרש (איוב לא) וכמוהו הרבה: **ממאי** מדקתני סיפא. טפי הוי ליה לאתויי כבולות דהוי ממש כעין זה אלא משום דשחוזות הוי ברישא:

עד

דומיא דקמיע. משום חולי: והא אנן תנן. גבי אדם לקמן בפ' במה אשה (דף ס.): הא מומחה שפיר דמי. מאי שנא בהמה מאדם: מזליה. מלאך שלו ומליץ עליו: אי הכי. דבהמה נמי נפקא בקמיע המומחה לבהמה: מאי זה חומר. אדם נמי לא נפיק אלא בקמיע מומחה לאדם: אסנדל קאי. וזה חומר דקתני ולא בהמה בסנדל שברגליה: סכין. שמן: ומפרכסין. גלדי מכה: ומשום צער. [ואפילו] הכי לבהמה לא וקשיא בין לרב בין לשמואל דשרי במרדעת: לא דגמר מכה. שנתרפאה המכה וסיכה ופירכוס משום תענוג ולרב ודאי קשיא וההיא מתניתא קמייתא דאוקף נמי קשיא ליה דנהי נמי דלדידה ליכא צער תענוג מיהא הוא אלא רב תנא הוא ופליג: שאחזה דם. אנפודור"א: אין מעמידין כו'. אלמא אפילו צער נמי אסור: גזירה משום שחיקת סממנים. במידי דרפואה גזור רבנן דאי שרית שום רפואה אתי למישרי שחיקת סממנים והוא איסורא דאורייתא דהוי טוחן: אין מיקר לבהמה. אין דרך להקר בהמה הלכך כולי עלמא ידעי דלרפואה קמיכוין ואתי למישרי שחיקת סממנים: ומי גזרינן. במקום פסידא כי האי גוונא: חוץ לתחום. קס"ד חוץ לתחום שלו היתה עומדת בהמה: שהיה תחום שלה מובלעת בתוך תחום שלו. דחוץ לתחום דקתני חוץ לתחום שלה שהבהמה המסורה לרועה המיוחד הרי היא כרגלי הרועה וזה הקורא לה בעליה ויכול לילך כגון שהוא שבת קרוב לאותו מקום ואפילו הכי לא יביאנה ממש בידיו הואיל והיא יוצאה חוץ לתחומה אין לה אלא ד' אמות ומיהו קורא לה והיא באה דלא החזר הוא על תחום בהמתו ובלבד שלא יביאנה ממש בידיו: תנאי היא. דאיכא דלא גזר שאר רפואות אטו שחיקת סממנין: שאכלה כרשינין. הרבה ועל ידי אכילה מרובה אחזה חולי שקורין מינייזונ"א וצריכה להשתלשל ולהוציא רעי ומרילה: כדי שתתרפה. גרסינן הכא לשון ריפוי שיהיו מיעיה רפויים בשילשול ומוציאה רעי: לא ירִיצנה. גזירה בכל רפואה אטו שחיקת סממנין: דמיהדק. דליכא למיחש דילמא נפיל ואתי לאתויי: תנאי שקלת מעלמא. איבדת כולם שאין אתה מוצא תנאים שנחלקו בכך דתוקי הנך תרתי מתניית' חדא כמר וחדא כמר: תנאי היא. במתניתין ר"מ שרי ר' יוסי אסר: ליבש. מיהדק שפיר ולענין משוי נמי לא הוי משוי דלצורך גופה היא דחלבה מכחישה: ליחלב. הוי משוי שטוענת את החלב בכיס: גסין. גדולין ונגררין על הקוצין ומסרטין דדיהן: שנשתנו עליו כו'. ולא זכה ליפתח לו שערי שכר: תדע. דקשין: דמרחשי ניסא. מן השמים לכמה הצלות לנפשות אדם: ולא איברו מזוני. ואין נס זה רגיל שיבראו מזונות לצדיקים בביתם שימצאו חיטין גדלין באוצרותיהן: גידמת. ידה קטועה: זו דרכה בכך. לכסות כל אשה עצמה וכ"ש זו שהיתה צריכה לכך: תותרי. קופל"א שמחברין אותם בקשר שנים שנים שלא יברחו: לבבתני. קרבתני אצלך מחמת נוי מעשיך: דרך זאבים לאחוז בהמה בלבה: אנקבות לא נפלי. בתמיה: דמסגי. מהלכין: בסוף עדרא לא נפלי. בתמיה: כי דוו. מביטין כאן וכאן לפיכך מתקנאין בהם כסבורים שרוצים להלחם בהם: אליה. זנב שלהן קושרים כלפי גבן שלא יכסה ערותן:

שית

עין משפט נר מצוה

כז א מיי' פ"כ מהל' שבת הלכה יג טוש"ע א"ח סי' שה סעי' ח בהג"ה:
כח ב ג מיי' פכ"א מהל' שבת הל' ל' סמג לאוין סה טוש"ע א"ח סי' שכח סעיף כב וסי' שלב סעיף ג:
כט ד מיי' וסמג שם טוש"ע א"ח סי' שלב סעיף ג וסעיף ד:
ל ה ו ז מיי' פ"כ מהל' שבת הל' יב סמג שם טוש"ע א"ח סי' שה סעיף ו:

רבינו חננאל

ובקששין: תניא אדם שאחזו דם מעמידין אותו במים בשביל לרפאותו. מ"ט משום דנראה כמיקר. אבל בהמה שאחזה דם אין מעמידין אותה במים כו'. אמר עולא בהמה גזירה משום שחיקת סמנים. ושחיקת סמנים תנאי היא. דתניא בהמה שאכלה כרשינין הרבה אין מריצין אותה בחצר בשביל לרפאותה. ור' יאשיה מיקל. והלכתא כוותיה דדרש רבא הלכתא כר' יאשיה. והא דר' יאשיה מסייעא לשמואל. מעשה שנעשה נס ונפתחו שני דדין כשני דדי אשה כו' וזו שהיתה גידמת כו'. פשוטות הן: פי' תותרי. סמרטוטין של רקמה ושל משי שעושין על הבהמה ליפותה. עולא אמר עור שמעמידין להן כנגד לבן שלא יפלו עליהן זאבים. משום דמסגו כי דוו. ומסתברא כוותיה דתנן (בע"ז דף כט:) באיסורי הנאה ועורות לבובין. ות"ר (שם דף לב.) איזהו עור לבוב. כל שהוא קרוע כנגד הלב. (וקרודה) [וקדורה] כמו ארובה כו'. שחוזות מלשון שית זונה:

תורה אור השלם

א) לִבַּבְתִּנִי אֲחֹתִי כַלָּה לִבַּבְתִּנִי בְּאַחַת מֵעֵינַיִךְ בְּאַחַד עֲנָק מִצַּוְּרֹנָיִךְ: [שיר השירים ד, ט]

ב) וְהִנֵּה אִשָּׁה לִקְרָאתוֹ שִׁית זוֹנָה וּנְצֻרַת לֵב: [משלי ז, י]

מסורת הש"ס

א) [לקמן ס.], ב) [כ"ק ג:], ג) [גיר' הערוך ומפרכין פי' מגרדין], ד) [ביצה יח.], ה) [לקמן קנג. ותוספתא פי"ח], ו) [נ"ל יאשיה וכ"א בר"א והרא"ש וכן העתיקו תוס' מ"ק י: ד"ה ואין], ז) [נ"ל יאשיה], ח) [עירובין לו: פסחים מה: ביצה יט. סנהדרין סא.], ט) [נ"ל רבי].

תוספות ישנים

א) ובבראשית רבה על פסוק ויהי אומן את הדסה שנפתחו למרדכי שני דדים כדדי אשה ליכא למיפרך הכי דהכי קאמר נשתנו דלא הו"ל שכר מניקה ומרדכי הו"ל שכר אך לא הי' מוצא מניקה:

גליון הש"ס

גמ' ולבהמה מי גזרינן והתניא. ק"ל דלמא משום שחיקת סממנים דאורייתא גזרי' אבל בתחומין דרבנן לא:

ליקוטי רש"י

ולא בקמיע שאינו מומחה. אבל בקמיע מומחה שרי דתכשיט הוא לחולה כאחד ממלבושיו [לקמן ס.]. גזירה משום שחיקת סממנין. דכל רפואה אסרו חכמים לעשותה בשבת היכא דליכא סכנה משום שחיקת סממנין במסכת שבת [ע"ז כח.]. דכל רפואה בשבת גזור בה רבנן משום שחיקת סממנין שהיא אב מלאכה טוחן [ביצה יח:]. וכן כל דבר רפואה שאין מלאכה אלא שבות הוא שגזרו חכמים בכל רפואות גזירה משום שחיקת סממנין [שם יא:]. כרשינין. מאכל בהמה בי"ה בלע"ז [לעיל יז:]. צרורות. דדיהן צרורות פעמים ליבש שמהדקן כדי שלא יחלבו עוד ויתעברו או יהו שמנות לאכול ופעמים לחלב לשמור חלבן שלא יטפטף לארץ וקושרין להם כיס בדדיהן. רבי יוסי אוסר בכלן. דמשוי הוא. חוץ מן הרחילות הכבונות. שהוא שמירת צמרן שלא יטנף והוי להו תכשיט. יוצאות צרורות ליבש. ר' יהודה סבירא ליה כתנא קמא דלאו משוי הוא ומיהו ליבש דמיהדק שפיר וליכא למיחש דילמא נפיל ואתי לאיתויי אבל ליחלב דלא מיהדק שפיר חיישינן [שם נב: ועי' כאן במהרש"א ובמהר"ם]. לבבתני. משכת את לבי אליך [שה"ש ד, ט]. והנה אשה. כמשמעה, ד"א אחד מן אפיקורסים [משלי ז, י].

WERE LARGE, וְעָשׂוּ לָהֶן כִּיסִין כְּדֵי שֶׁלֹּא יִסָּרְטוּ דַּדֵּיהֶן – AND THEY MADE POUCHES FOR THEM SO THAT THEIR UDDERS WOULD NOT BE LACERATED.[38]

Having mentioned udders of an unusual nature, the Gemara relates a story about udders of a miraculous nature:

תָּנוּ רַבָּנָן – **The Rabbis taught in a Baraisa:** מַעֲשֶׂה בְּאֶחָד שֶׁמֵּתָה אִשְׁתּוֹ – IT HAPPENED WITH A CERTAIN PERSON THAT HIS WIFE DIED וְהִנִּיחָה בֵּן לִינֹק – LEAVING A SON TO NURSE, וְלֹא הָיָה לוֹ שְׂכַר מֵנִיקָה לִיתֵּן – AND HE DID NOT HAVE enough money TO PAY THE FEE OF A WETNURSE. וְנַעֲשָׂה לוֹ נֵס – A MIRACLE WAS PERFORMED FOR HIM – וְנִפְתְּחוּ לוֹ דַּדִּין כִּשְׁנֵי דַּדֵּי אִשָּׁה – HIS BREASTS WERE OPENED LIKE THE TWO BREASTS OF A WOMAN, וְהֵינִיק אֶת בְּנוֹ – AND HE NURSED HIS SON.

The Gemara quotes a discussion regarding this incident:

אָמַר רַב יוֹסֵף – **Rav Yosef said:** בֹּא וּרְאֵה כַּמָּה גָּדוֹל אָדָם זֶה – **"Come and see how great this man was,** שֶׁנַּעֲשָׂה לוֹ נֵס כָּזֶה – **for such a miracle was performed on his behalf!"** אָמַר לוֹ אַבַּיֵי – Abaye said to [Rav Yosef]: אַדְּרַבָּה – **"On the contrary!** כַּמָּה גָּרוּעַ אָדָם זֶה – **How inferior this man was,** שֶׁנִּשְׁתַּנּוּ לוֹ סִדְרֵי בְרֵאשִׁית – **for the natural order was changed on his behalf!"**[39]

The Gemara cites another observation:

אָמַר רַב יְהוּדָה – **Rav Yehudah said:** בֹּא וּרְאֵה כַּמָּה קָשִׁים מְזוֹנוֹתָיו שֶׁל אָדָם – **Come and see how difficult** it is to provide **a person's food,** שֶׁנִּשְׁתַּנּוּ עָלָיו סִדְרֵי בְרֵאשִׁית – **for the natural order was changed on [this man's] behalf.**[40]

This observation is supported:

אָמַר רַב נַחְמָן – **Rav Nachman said:** תֵּדַע – **You may know** that this is so from the fact דְּמִתְרְחִישׁ נִיסָּא וְלָא אִבְּרוּ מְזוֹנֵי – that **miracles happen** to save people's lives, **but food is not created.**[41]

The Gemara relates another story:[42]

תָּנוּ רַבָּנָן – **The Rabbis taught** in a Baraisa: מַעֲשֶׂה בְּאָדָם אֶחָד שֶׁנָּשָׂא אִשָּׁה גִּידֶּמֶת – IT HAPPENED WITH A CERTAIN MAN THAT HE MARRIED A WOMAN WHOSE HAND HAD BEEN CUT OFF, וְלֹא הִכִּיר בָּהּ עַד יוֹם מוֹתָהּ – AND HE DID NOT PERCEIVE that HER hand was missing UNTIL THE DAY OF HER DEATH.

Amoraim discuss this incident:

אָמַר רַב – **Rav said:** בֹּא וּרְאֵה כַּמָּה צְנוּעָה אִשָּׁה זוֹ – **"Come and see how modest this woman was,** שֶׁלֹּא הִכִּיר בָּהּ בַּעְלָהּ – **for her husband did not perceive** that **her** hand was missing!" אָמַר לוֹ רַבִּי חִיָּיא – **R' Chiya said to [Rav]:** זוֹ דַּרְכָּהּ בְּכָךְ – **"That is her way!**[43] אֶלָּא כַּמָּה צָנוּעַ אָדָם זֶה – **Rather,** see **how modest this man was,** שֶׁלֹּא הִכִּיר בְּאִשְׁתּוֹ – **for he did not perceive** that **his wife** was missing a hand!"[44]

The Gemara quotes the next part of our Mishnah:

זְכָרִים יוֹצְאִין לְבוּבִין – RAMS MAY GO OUT ATTACHED [*levuvin*].

This term is defined:

אָמַר רַב הוּנָא – **Rav Huna said:** מַאי לְבוּבִין – **What is** the meaning of ***levuvin?*** תּוּתְרֵי – It means tied together in **pairs.**[45]

The Gemara states the derivation of this term:

מַאי מַשְׁמַע דְּהַאי לְבוּבִין לִישָּׁנָא דְּקֵרוּבֵי הוּא – **What indicates that this** word ***levuvin*** **denotes "closeness"?** דִּכְתִיב ,,לִבַּבְתִּנִי אֲחֹתִי כַלָּה'' – **For it is written:** ***You have captured my heart (libavtini), my sister, O bride.***[46]

Ulla gives a different explanation of *levuvin:*

עוּלָּא אָמַר – **Ulla says:** עוֹר שֶׁקּוֹשְׁרִין לָהֶם כְּנֶגֶד לִבָּם – It denotes a piece of **leather that is tied to [rams] over their hearts,**[47] כְּדֵי שֶׁלֹּא יִפְּלוּ עֲלֵיהֶן זְאֵבִים – **so that wolves will not fall upon them.**[48]

The Gemara objects:

וּזְאֵבִים אַזְּכָרִים נָפְלֵי אַנְּקֵיבוֹת לָא נָפְלֵי – **Do wolves fall** only **upon male [sheep] and not upon female [sheep]?**[49]

The Gemara answers:

מִשּׁוּם דְּמַסְגּוּ בְּרֵישׁ עֶדְרָא – The males are attacked **because they go at the head of the flock.**

The Gemara counters:

וּזְאֵבִין בְּרֵישׁ עֶדְרָא נָפְלֵי בְּסוֹף עֶדְרָא לָא נָפְלֵי – **But do wolves fall** only **upon** the sheep at **the head of the flock and not upon** those at **the end of the flock?**

The Gemara revises its explanation:

אֶלָּא מִשּׁוּם דִּשְׁמִינֵי – **Rather,** the males are attacked **because they are fat.**

The Gemara objects:

וּבִנְקֵבוֹת לֵיכָּא שְׁמֵינֵי – **But are there no fat ones among the female [sheep]?!** וְתוּ מִי יָדְעֵי בֵּין הָנֵי לְהָנֵי – **Furthermore, do**

NOTES

38. They were so large that they dragged on the thorns and were lacerated (*Rashi;* see 53a note 32).

39. He did not merit that the "gates of income" be opened for him [i.e. to earn a livelihood in the normal way] (*Rashi*).

This person certainly had some merit, for otherwise the miracle would not have been performed for him. However, he was inferior in that he was prevented from earning a living in the normal way and thus had to be sustained with a miracle. A person for whom a miracle is performed must "pay" for it with merits acquired through his good deeds. Thus, his later reward for these deeds is lessened [see above, 32a] (*Maharsha;* cf. *Maharal*).

40. *Maharal* explains that God provides food to each person *individually,* which is an act of Divine grace that transcends nature. Moreover, unlike other miracles (e.g. the splitting of the Red Sea) which involve a change in matter that already exists, the provision of food entails a more fundamental "creation." Thus, providing food is more "difficult" [i.e. deviates further from the natural order] than other miracles (see ibid. for elucidation of these concepts).

41. It is not unusual for God to save people's lives in a miraculous fashion. However, we do not find as often that God miraculously creates food for the righteous – for instance, by causing the amount of wheat in their storehouses to increase (*Rashi*).

42. [The following story is quoted here presumably because, like the previous one, it is an extraordinary incident involving a man whose wife died which also provoked contrasting comments.]

43. It is natural for any woman to cover herself, and especially this woman, who needed to do so (*Rashi*).

44. The commentators suggest explanations as to how he became aware of this deformity on the day of her death (see *Benayahu* [in *Ben Yehoyada*] and *Iyun Yaakov*).

Dibros Moshe (43:10) gives a lengthy analysis of the halachic implications of this story.

45. Rams were strapped to each other in pairs so that they would not run away (*Rashi;* cf. *Rosh*). [Ewes, which are less aggressive, were not restrained in this manner (*Chidushei Maharam Banet*).]

46. *Song of Songs* 4:9. In this verse, God addresses Israel, saying: "You have drawn Me close to you [through the attractiveness of your deeds]" (*Rashi*). The verse employs an allegory in which a husband speaks to his wife using the term of endearment "sister." The word לִבַּבְתִּנִי (from לֵב, *heart*), which means *you have captured my heart* (see *Rashi* ibid.), is related to לְבוּבִין, *levuvin.* This shows that *levuvin* signifies closeness.

47. Hence, the term לְבוּבִין, *levuvin* (which is from לֵב, *heart*).

48. Wolves seize an animal at its heart [i.e. underbelly] (*Rashi*).

A ram rears itself up on its hind legs to fight a wolf. The wolf then claws at the ram's underbelly (*Chidushei HaRan*).

49. If this is the meaning of *levuvin,* why does the Mishnah speak specifically of rams?

עין משפט
נר מצוה

כז א מיי' פ"כ מהל' שבת הלכה יג טוש"ע א"ח סי' שה סעי' יח בהג"ה:
כח ב ג מיי' פכ"א מהל' שבת הל' ל' סמג לאוין סה טוש"ע א"ח סי' שכח סעיף כב וסי' שלב סעיף ב:
כט ד מיי' וסמג שם טוש"ע א"ח סי' שלב סעיף ג וסעיף ד:
ל ה ו ז מיי' פ"כ מהל' שבת הל' יב סמג שם טוש"ע א"ח סי' שה סעיף ו:

דומיא דקמיע ש"מ: אמר מר ולא בקמיע אע"פ שהוא מומחה והא אנן תנן [א] ולא בקמיע שאינו מומחה הא מומחה שפיר דמי ה"נ א שאינו מומחה והא אע"פ שהוא מומחה קתני מומחה לאדם ואינו מומחה לבהמה ומי איכא מומחה לאדם ולא הוי מומחה לבהמה אין אדם [ב] דאית ליה מזלא מסייע ליה בהמה דלית לה מזלא לא מסייע לה אי הכי מאי זה חומר בבהמה מבאדם מי סברת אקמיע קאי אסנדל קאי ת"ש ב סכין [ג] ומפרכסין לאדם ואין סכין ומפרכסין לבהמה מאי לאו דאיכא מכה ומשום צער לא ג דגמר מכה ומשום תענוג ת"ש בהמה שאחזה דם אין מעמידין אותה במים בשביל שתצטנן אדם שאחזו דם מעמידין אותו במים בשביל שיצטנן אמר עולא גזירה משום שחיקת סממנין אי הכי [ד] אדם נמי אדם נראה כמיקר א"ה בהמה נמי נראה כמיקר אין מיקר לבהמה ° ולבהמה מי גזרינן והתניא [ה] היתה עומדת חוץ לתחום קורא לה והיא באה ולא גזרינן דילמא אתי לאתויי ואמר רבינא כגון שהיה תחום שלה מובלע בתוך תחום שלו ר"נ בר יצחק אמר שחיקת סממנין גופה תנאי היא דתני' בהמה שאכלה כרשינין לא יריצנה בחצר בשביל שתתרפה ורבי [ו] ד אושעיא מתיר דרש רבא הלכה כרבי [ז] אושעיא: אמר מר לא יצא הזב בכיס שלו ולא עזים בכיס שבדדיהן והתניא יוצאות עזים בכיס שבדדיהן אמר רב יהודה לא קשיא הא דמיהדק הא דלא מיהדק רב יוסף אמר [ח] תנאי שקלת מעלמא תנאי היא דתנן העזים יוצאות צרורות רבי יוסי אוסר בכלן חוץ מן הרחילות הכבונות ר' יהודה אומר עזים יוצאות צרורות ליבש אבל לא ליחלב ואיבעית אימא הא והא ר' יהודה ולא קשיא ה כאן ליבש כאן ליחלב תניא אמר ר' יהודה מעשה בעזים בית אנטוכיא שהיו דדיהן גסין ועשו להן כיסין כדי שלא יסרטו דדיהן: ת"ר מעשה באחד שמתה אשתו והניחה בן לינק ולא היה לו שכר מניקה ליתן ונעשה לו נס ונפתחו לו דדין כשני דדי אשה והניק את בנו אמר רב יוסף בא וראה כמה גדול אדם זה שנעשה לו נס כזה א"ל אביי אדרבה כמה [א] גרוע אדם זה שנשתנו לו סדרי בראשית אמר רב יהודה בא וראה כמה קשים מזונותיו של אדם שנשתנו עליו סדרי בראשית אמר רב נחמן תדע דמתרחיש ניסא ולא אברו מזוני: ת"ר מעשה באדם אחד שנשא אשה גידמת ולא הכיר בה עד יום מותה אמר [ט] רב בא וראה כמה צנועה אשה זו שלא הכיר בה בעלה אמר לו רבי חייא זו דרכה בכך אלא כמה צנוע אדם זה שלא הכיר באשתו: ו זכרים יוצאין לבובין: מאי לבובין אמר רב הונא תותרי מאי משמע דהאי לבובין לישנא דקרובי הוא דכתיב [א] לבבתני אחותי כלה עולא אמר עור שקושרין להם כנגד לבם כדי שלא יפלו עליהן זאבים זאבים אזכרים נפלי אנקיבות לא נפלי משום דמסגו בריש עדרא וזאבין בריש עדרא לא נפלי בסוף עדרא נפלי אלא משום דשמני ובנקבות ליכא שמני ותו מי ידעי בין הני להני אלא משום דזקפי חוטמייהו ומסגו כי דוו רב נחמן בר יצחק אמר עור שקושרין להן תחת זכרותן כדי שלא יעלו על הנקבות ממאי מדקתני סיפא ז והרחלים יוצאות שחוזות מאי שחוזות שאוחזין האליה שלהן למעלה כדי שיעלו עליהן זכרים רישא כדי שלא יעלו על הנקבות וסיפא כדי שיעלו עליהן זכרים מאי משמע דהאי שחוזות לישנא דגלויי הוא דכתיב [ב] והנה אשה לקראתו
שית

רש"י

דומיא דקמיע. משום חולי: והא אנן תנן. גבי אדם לקמן בפ' במה אשה (דף ס.): הא מומחה שפיר דמי. מאי שנא בהמה מאדם: מוליה. מלאך שלו ומליץ עליו: אי הכי. דבהמה נמי נפקא בקמיע המומחה לבהמה: מאי זה חומר. אדם נמי לא נפיק אלא בקמיע מומחה לאדם: אסנדל קאי. זה חומר דקתני ולא בהמה בסנדל שברגליה: סכין. שמן: ומפרכסין. גלדי מכה: ומשום צער. [ואפילו] הכי לבהמה לא וקשיא בין לרב בין לשמואל דשרי במרדעת: לא דגמר מכה. שנתרפאה המכה וסיכה ופירכוס משום תענוג ולרב ודאי קשיא והיא מתניתא קמייתא דאותיב נמי קשיא ליה דנהי נמי דלצינה ליכא צער תענוג מיהא הוא אלא רב תנא הוא ופליג: שאחזה דם. אנפודור"א: אין מעמידין כו'. אלמא אפילו צער נמי אסור: גזירה משום שחיקת סממנים. במידי דרפואה גזור רבנן דאי שרית שום רפואה אתי למישרי שחיקת סממנים והוא איסורא דאורייתא דהוי טוחן: אין מיקר לבהמה. אין דרך להקר בהמה הלכך כולי עלמא ידעי דלרפואה קמיכוין ואתי למישרי שחיקת סממנים: ומי גזרינן. במקום פסידא כי האי גוונא: חוץ לתחום. קס"ד חוץ לתחום שלו היתה עומדת בהמה: שהיה תחום שלה מובלעת בתוך תחום שלו. דחוץ לתחום דקתני חוץ לתחום שלה שהבהמה המסורה לרועה המיוחד הרי היא כרגלי הרועה וזה הקורא לה בעליה ויכול לילך כגון שהוא שבת קרוב לאותו מקום ואפילו הכי לא יביאנה ממש בידיו הואיל והיא יוצאה חוץ לתחומה אין לה אלא ד' אמות ומיהו קורא לה והיא באה דלא הוזהר הוא על תחום בהמתו ובלבד שלא יביאנה ממש בידיו: תנאי היא. דאיכא דלא גזר שאר רפואות אטו שחיקת סממנין: שאכלה כרשינין. הרבה ועל ידי אכילה מרובה אחזה חולי שקורין מינייזונ"א וצריכה להשתלשל ולהוציא רעי ומריצה: כדי שתתרפה. גרסינן הכא לשון ריפוי שיהיו מעיה רפויים בשילשול ומוציאה רעי: לא יריצנה. גזירה בכל רפואה אטו שחיקת סממנין: דמיהדק. דליכא למיחש דילמא נפיל ואתי לאתויי: תנאי שקלת מעלמא. איבדת כולם שאין אתה מוצא תנאים שנחלקו בכך דתוקי הנך תרתי מתניית' חדא כמר וחדא כמר: תנאי היא. במתניתין ר"מ שרי ר' יוסי אסר: ליבש. מיהדק שפיר ולענין משוי נמי לא הוי משוי דצורך גופה היא דחלבה מכחישה: ליחלב. הוי משוי שטוענת את החלב בכיס: גסין. גדולין ונגררין על הקוצין ומסרטין דדיהן: שנשתנו עליו כו'. ולא זכה ליפתח לו שערי שכר: תדע. דקשין: דמרחשי ניסא. מן השמים לכמה הצלות לנפשות אדם: ולא איברו מזוני. ואין נס זה רגיל שיבראו מזונות לצדיקים בביתם שימצאו חיטין גדלין באוצרותיהן: גידמת. ידה קטועה: זו דרכה בכך. לכסות כל אשה עצמה וכ"ש זו שהיתה צריכה לכך: תותרי. קופל"א שמחברין אותם בקשר שנים שנים שלא יברחו: לבבתני. קרבתני אצלך מחמת נוי מעשיך: דרך זאבים לאחוז בהמה בלבה: אנקבות לא נפלי. בתמיה: דמסגי. מהלכין: בסוף עדרא לא נפלי. בתמיה: כי דוו. מביטין כאן וכאן לפיכך מתקנאין בהם כסבורים שרוצים להלחם בהם: אליה. זנב שלהן קושרים כלפי גבן שלא יכסה ערותן:
שית

תוספות

כגון שהיה תחום שלה מובלע כו'. ומ"מ לא התירו אלא דרך קריאה אבל לילך מעבר לבהמה ולרודפה לעיר לא:

תנאי היא. רב יהודה ידע שפיר דתנאי היא אלא דניחא ליה לאוקמי תרי סתמי דברייתא אליבא דחד תנא:

כאן ליבש כאן ליחלב. פי' בקונט' ליחלב שיקבלו בכיס את החלב וקשה דהא ודאי משוי הוא ולכ"ע חייב דהויא מלאכה הצריכה לגופה ופי' ה"ר פור"ת ליחלב לשמור החלב בדדיהן שלא יזוב לארץ ושרי ת"ק דהוי כמו רחלים כבונות דחשבי' ליה מלבוש אף על פי שאינו עשוי לצורך עצמן אלא לשמור הצמר ור"י פירש דבין ליבש ובין ליחלב תרווייהו עבדי להו כדי שלא יסרטו דדיהן כדאמרינן בסמוך וליבש בזמן שאינו חפץ בחלב שרי לפי שמהדקו וליכא למיחש דילמא נפיל ואתי לאתויי אבל ליחלב שאינו רוצה שיתייבשו אינו מיהדק איכא למימר דילמא נפיל ואתי לאתויי:

שקושרין להן כנגד זכרותן כו'. ולשון לבובין הוי שלא לקרב כמו ובכל תבואתי תשרש (איוב לא) וכמוהו הרבה:

ממאי מדקתני סיפא. טפי הוי ליה לאתויי כבולות דהוי ממש כעין זה אלא משום דשחוזות הוי ברישא:

רבינו חננאל

ובקשישין: תניא אדם שאחזו דם מעמידין אותו במים בשביל לרפאותו. מ"ט משום דנראה כמיקר. אבל בהמה שאחזה דם אין מעמידין אותה במים כו'. אמר עולא בהמה גזירה משום שחיקת סמנים. ושחיקת סמנים תנאי היא. דתניא בהמה שאכלה כרשינין הרבה אין מריצין אותה בחצר בשביל לרפאותה. ור' יאשיה מיקל. והלכתא כוותיה דדרש רבא הלכתא כר' יאשיה. והא דר' יאשיה מסייעא לשמואל. מעשה שנעשה נס ונפתחו שני דדין כשני דדי אשה כו' וזו שהיתה גידמת כו'. פשוטות הן: פי' תותרי. סמרטוטין של רקמה ושל משי שעושין על הבהמה ליפותה. עולא אמר עור שמעמידין להן כנגד לבן שלא יפלו עליהן זאבים. משום דמסגו כי דוו. ומסתברא כוותיה דתנן (בע"ז דף כט:) באיסורי הנאה ועורות לבובין. ות"ר (שם דף לב.) איזהו עור לבוב. כל שהוא קרוע כנגד הלב. (וקרודה) [וקדורה] כמו ארובה כו'. שחוזות מלשון שית זונה:

תורה אור השלם

א) לִבַּבְתִּנִי אֲחֹתִי כַלָּה לִבַּבְתִּינִי בְּאַחַת מֵעֵינַיִךְ בְּאַחַד עֲנָק מִצַּוְּרֹנָיִךְ: [שיר השירים ד, ט]

ב) וְהִנֵּה אִשָּׁה לִקְרָאתוֹ שִׁית זוֹנָה וּנְצֻרַת לֵב: [משלי ז, י]

מסורת הש"ס

א) [לקמן ס.], ב) [כ"ק ב:], ג) [גיר' הערוך ומפרכין פי' מגרדין], ד) [ביצה יח.], ה) [לקמן קנא. ותוספתא פי"ח], ו) [נ"ל יאשיה וכ"א בר"א והרא"ש וכן העתיקו תוס' מ"ק י: ד"ה ואין], ז) [נ"ל יאשיה], ח) [עירובין לז: פסחים מה: ביצה יט. סנהדרין סא.], ט) [נ"ל רבי].

תוספות ישנים

א) ובבראשית רבה על פסוק ויהי אומן את הדסה שנפתחו למרדכי שני דדים כדדי אשה ליכא למיפרך הכי דהכי קאמר נשתנו דלא ה"ל שכר מניקה ומרדכי ה"ל שכר אך לא הי' מוצא מניקה:

גליון הש"ס

גמ' ולבהמה מי גזרינן והתניא. ק"ל דלמא משום שחיקת סממנים דאורייתא גורי' אבל בתחומין דרבנן לא:

ליקוטי רש"י

ולא בקמיע שאינו מומחה. אבל בקמיע מומחה שרי דתכשיט הוא לחולה כאחד ממלבושיו [לקמן ס.]. גזירה משום שחיקת סממנין. דכל רפואה אסרו חכמים לעשותה בשבת היכא דליכא סכנה משום שחיקת סממנין במסכת שבת [ע"ז כח.]. דכל רפואה בשבת גזור בה רבנן משום שחיקת סממנין שהיא אב מלאכה טוחן [ביצה יח:]. וכן כל דבר רפואה שאין מלאכה אלא שבות הוא שגזרו חכמים בכל רפואות גזירה משום שחיקת סמנין [שם יא:]. כרשינין. מאכל בהמה בינ"א בלע"ז [לעיל יז:]. צרורות. דדיהן צרורות פעמים ליבש שמהדקן כדי שלא יחלבו עוד ויתעברו או יהו שמנות לאכול ופעמים לחלב לשמור חלבן שלא יטפטף לארץ וקושרין להם כיס בדדיהן. רבי יוסי אוסר בכלן. דמשוי הוא. חוץ מן הרחילות הכבונות. שהוא שמירת צמרן שלא יטנף והוי להו תכשיט. יוצאות צרורות ליבש. ר' יהודה סבירא ליה כתנא קמא דלאו משוי הוא ומיהו ליבש דמיהדק שפיר וליכא למיחש דילמא נפיל ואתי לאיתויי אבל ליחלב דלא מיהדק שפיר חיישינן [שם נב: ועי' כאן במהרש"א ובמהר"ם]. לבבתני. משכת את לבי אליך [שה"ש ד, ט]. והנה אשה. כמשמעה, ד"א אחד מן אפיקורסים [משלי ז, י].

[wolves] know the difference **between these and those?**[50]

The Gemara concludes:

אֶלָּא מִשּׁוּם דְּזָקְפֵי חוֹטְמַיְיהוּ וּמַסְגוּ כִּי דָווּ – **Rather,** the male sheep are attacked **because they hold their noses up and walk while looking** from side to side.[51]

The Gemara cites a third opinion about the meaning of *levuvin:*

רַב נַחְמָן בַּר יִצְחָק אָמַר – **Rav Nachman bar Yitzchak said:** עוֹר שֶׁקּוֹשְׁרִין לָהֶן תַּחַת זַכְרוּתָן – It denotes a piece of **leather that is tied to [rams] under their genitals** כְּדֵי שֶׁלֹּא יַעֲלוּ עַל הַנְּקֵבוֹת – **so that they will not mount the females.**[52] מִמַּאי – **From what** is this definition derived? מִדְּקָתָנֵי סֵיפָא – It is derived **from that which the next part**[53] **of the Mishnah teaches:** וְהָרְחֵלִים יוֹצְאוֹת שְׁחוּזוֹת – EWES MAY GO OUT HELD [*shechuzos*]. מַאי שְׁחוּזוֹת – Now, **what is** the meaning of ***shechuzos*?** שֶׁאוֹחֲזִין הָאַלְיָה שֶׁלָּהֶן לְמַעְלָה – It means that **their tails are held upwards**[54] exposing their genitals, כְּדֵי שֶׁיַּעֲלוּ עֲלֵיהֶן זְכָרִים – **so that the males will mount them.** It is reasonable to assume that *levuvin* is related in some way to the word *shechuzos* which appears next in the Mishnah. Thus, we can say: רֵישָׁא כְּדֵי שֶׁלֹּא יַעֲלוּ עַל הַנְּקֵבוֹת – **The first term** (*levuvin*) speaks of something done **so that [the males] will not mount the females,** וְסֵיפָא כְּדֵי שֶׁיַּעֲלוּ עֲלֵיהֶן זְכָרִים – **and the next term** (*shechuzos*) speaks of something done **so that the males will mount [the females].**

The Gemara gives the derivation of the term *shechuzos:*

מַאי מַשְׁמַע דְּהַאי שְׁחוּזוֹת לִישָּׁנָא דְּגַלּוּיֵי הוּא – **What indicates that this** word ***shechuzos*** **denotes "exposure"?**[55]

The Gemara answers:

דִּכְתִיב – **For it is written:**[56] ,,וְהִנֵּה אִשָּׁה לִקְרָאתוֹ – ***And behold, a woman comes to meet him,***

NOTES

50. [When wolves want to attack the sheep at the back of the flock (which are mostly females), do they know that there are fat (male) sheep at the head of the flock?]

51. Therefore, the wolves are antagonized because they think that the rams want to attack them (*Rashi*).

52. One would not want his ewes to conceive while they are needed to suckle their young (*Chidushei HaRan*).

We learned above that *levuvin* signifies closeness. According to the present interpretation, however, it connotes the *prevention* of closeness. This word is one of several that can signify the very negation of its primary meaning. Another example is the verb שרש which can mean *to take root* and *to uproot* (*Tosafos*).

53. Literally: the end.

54. The word שְׁחוּזוֹת, *shechuzos,* is interpreted as a contraction of שֶׁאֲחוּזוֹת, *which are held* (see *Rashash*).

55. The Gemara above implied that שְׁחוּזוֹת, *shechuzos,* derives from אחז, *hold* (see previous note). It thus connotes that the ewes' tails are held in a specific position. However, it is not clear whether it means that the tails are fastened upwards, exposing the genitals, or fastened downwards, covering the genitals. Hence, the Gemara's question (*Rashash*).

56. *Proverbs* 7:10.

שִׁית זוֹנָה וּנְצֻרַת לֵב״ – ***exposed like a harlot***[1] ***and with a surrounded heart.***[2]

The Gemara quotes the next term in the Mishnah:

הָרְחֵלִים יוֹצְאוֹת כְּבוּלוֹת – EWES MAY GO OUT ... TIED [*kevulos*].

This term is defined:

מַאי כְּבוּלוֹת – **What is** the meaning of ***kevulos?*** שֶׁמְּכַבְּלִין אַלְיָה שֶׁלָּהֶן לְמַטָּה – It denotes **that [their owners] tie their tails**[3] **downward,** covering their genitals, כְּדֵי שֶׁלֹּא יַעֲלוּ עֲלֵיהֶן הַזְּכָרִים – **so that the males will not mount them.**

The Gemara asks:

מַאי מַשְׁמַע דְּהַאי כָּבוּל לִישָּׁנָא דְּלָא עָבֵיד פֵּירֵי הוּא – **What indicates that this** term ***kavul*** **denotes non-productivity?**[4]

The Gemara answers:

דִּכְתִיב – **For it is written:**[5] ,,מָה הֶעָרִים [הָאֵלֶּה] אֲשֶׁר־נָתַתָּ[ה] לִי אָחִי – ***What are these cities that you gave me, my brother?*** וַיִּקְרָא לָהֶם אֶרֶץ כָּבוּל עַד הַיּוֹם הַזֶּה״ – ***And he called them "the land of kavul" to this day.*** מַאי ,,אֶרֶץ כָּבוּל״ – **What is** meant by **"the land of *kavul*"?** אָמַר רַב הוּנָא – **Rav Huna said:** שֶׁהָיוּ בָּהּ בְּנֵי אָדָם שֶׁמְּכוּבָּלִין בְּכֶסֶף וּבְזָהָב – It means **that there were people in [that land] who were wrapped in silver and gold.**[6]

The Gemara objects to this interpretation of the verse:

אָמַר לֵיהּ רָבָא – **Rava said to [Rav Huna]:** אִי הָכִי – **If that is** what it means, הַיְינוּ דִּכְתִיב – how will you explain **that which is written** in the preceding verse: ,,(כִּי לֹא) [וְלֹא] יָשְׁרוּ בְּעֵינָיו״ – *Chirom departed from Tzor to see the cities Solomon had given him,* ***and they did not please him?*** מִפְּנֵי שֶׁמְּכוּבָּלִין בְּכֶסֶף וּבְזָהָב – Now, can you say that **because [the people of these cities] were wrapped in silver and gold,** לֹא יָשְׁרוּ בְּעֵינָיו – **[the cities] did not please him?!**

Rav Huna answers:

אָמַר לֵיהּ – **He said to [Rava]:** אֵין – **Yes!** That *is* why they did not please him! כֵּיוָן דַּעֲתִירֵי וּמְפַנְּקֵי – **Since [the inhabitants] were wealthy and fastidious,** לָא עָבְדֵי עֲבִידְתָּא – **they would not do work,** i.e. they would not be pressed into the king's service.[7]

The Gemara offers another interpretation of the phrase, "the land of *kavul*":

רַב נַחְמָן בַּר יִצְחָק אָמַר – **Rav Nachman bar Yitzchak says:** אֶרֶץ חוּמְטוֹן הָיְתָה – **It was a land of *chumton.***[8] וְאַמַּאי קָרֵי לָהּ ,,כָּבוּל״ – **And why did he call it "*kavul*"?** דְּמִשְׁתַּרְגָּא בָּהּ כַּרְעָא עַד כַּבְלָא – **Because one's foot would sink into it up to the ankle** (*kavla*). וְאָמְרֵי אִינְשֵׁי – **And people said** that אַרְעָא מְכַבְלָא דְּלָא עָבֵד פֵּירֵי – **it was an ankle-deep land that does not produce fruit.**[9]

The Gemara quotes the next term used in the Mishnah:

כְּבוּנוֹת – Ewes may go out . . . FASTENED [*kevunos*].

This term is defined:

מַאי כְּבוּנוֹת – **What is** the meaning of ***kevunos?*** שֶׁמְּכַבְּנִין אוֹתוֹ לְמֵילָת – It denotes **that [the sheep] is** protected with a covering **fastened**[10] around it so that its wool can be used **for *meilas.***[11] כִּדְתְנַן – **As we learned in a Mishnah:**[12] שְׂאֵת כְּצֶמֶר לָבָן – The color of *SE'EIS* IS LIKE WHITE WOOL.[13] And it was stated in explanation of this Mishnah: מַאי צֶמֶר לָבָן – To **what** type of **white wool** does it refer? אָמַר רַב בִּיבִי בַּר אַבָּיֵי – **Rav Bivi the son of Abaye said:** כְּצֶמֶר נָקִי בֶּן יוֹמוֹ – The Mishnah means **like the clean wool of a day-old [lamb]** שֶׁמְּכַבְּנִין אוֹתוֹ לְמֵילָת – around **which** a covering **is fastened for** the purpose of producing ***meilas.***[14]

The Mishnah stated:

וְהָעִזִּים יוֹצְאוֹת צְרוּרוֹת – AND THE GOATS MAY GO OUT with a pouch TIED onto their udders.

This case is the subject of a three-way dispute: (a) The Tanna Kamma permits the pouch in all circumstances; (b) R' Yose prohibits it in all circumstances; (c) R' Yehudah permits it where it is used to cause the milk to dry up, and prohibits it where it is used to collect any dripping milk.[15]

The Gemara discusses which view is accepted as halachah:

אִיתְּמַר – **It was stated:** רַב אָמַר – **Rav says:** הֲלָכָה כְּרַבִּי יְהוּדָה – **The law follows R' Yehudah.** וּשְׁמוּאֵל אָמַר – **But Shmuel says:** הֲלָכָה כְּרַבִּי יוֹסֵי – **The law follows R' Yose.**

NOTES

1. The word שְׁחוּזוֹת, *shechuzos,* is formed from the expression שִׁית זוֹנָה (see *Rashi*). [It thus connotes exposure.]

שִׁית literally means the private parts, as in *II Samuel* 10:4 (*Rashi* here and to *Proverbs* ibid.).

2. Thoughts of licentiousness and vice surround her heart (see *Rashi* ibid.).

3. מְכַבְּלִין, which derives from כֶּבֶל, *chain,* means *[they] tie* (*Rashi*).

4. We know that כָּבוּל, *kavul* (singular of כְּבוּלוֹת, *kevulos*), is related to מְכַבְּלִין, *[they] tie.* The Gemara here is asking how we know that the Mishnah uses this word in the sense of *tied to prevent productivity* (*Rashash* to 53b; see note 55 ibid.).

5. *I Kings* 9:13. Chirom, king of Tzor, provided precious materials and skilled craftsmen for the building of Solomon's Temple. Solomon paid Chirom by giving him twenty cities in the Galilee. The verse records Chirom's reaction to this payment (see *Malbim* ibid.).

6. Here כָּבוּל, *kavul,* is used in the sense of being tied up or wrapped (*Rashi*). [The connection between this word and non-productivity is demonstrated presently.] Cf. *Chasam Sofer.*

7. The word *kavul,* is used in reference to people who do not produce for the king. The Gemara has thus demonstrated a link between the word *kavul* and non-productivity (*Ritva MHK* ed.). [Hence, when the Mishnah says "ewes may go out . . . *kevulos,*" it means that their tails would be tied downward, preventing copulation.]

8. The earth was salty and cracked (*Rashi*), or sandy (*Rabbeinu Chananel*).

Chumton is a type of earth with a high salt content. It is used as a preservative (*Rashi* above, 31a ד״ה קב חומטון).

9. This interpretation, too, links *kavul* to non-productivity.

10. כְּבוּנוֹת, *kevunos,* is from the root כבן which means to clasp or fasten (see *Rashi* here and to *Shevuos* 6b ד״ה מכבנין).

11. When a lamb is born, its fleece is licked clean by its mother, and it is never whiter than at that moment. To preserve the whiteness, a piece of leather is bound around the lamb and clasped together with hooks, where it remains until the wool is sheared (*Rashi* ibid.). *Meilas* is the exquisitely clean wool that results from this process.

It was customary to perform this process only on the female sheep, because their wool is exceptionally white (*Meiri;* cf. *Rambam, Commentary to the Mishnah*).

12. *Negaim* 1:1.

13. *Se'eis* is one of the skin discolorations symptomatic of *tzaraas* (see *Leviticus* 13:2).

14. To summarize: The Gemara has explained the various terms in our Mishnah as follows:

"Rams may go out *levuvin,*" i.e. (a) tied in pairs, or (b) with a protective covering around the heart, or (c) with a covering on the genitals. "Ewes may go out *shechuzos,*" i.e. with their tails tied upward [exposing their genitals]; ". . *kevulos,*" i.e. with their tails tied downwards [covering their genitals]; ". . . *kevunos,*" i.e. with a covering fastened around their wool [to keep the wool clean].

In each of these cases, the Tanna Kamma rules that the item attached to the sheep is permitted, either because it serves as a restraint (as in the first definition of *levuvin*) or because it serves to protect the animal (e.g. it ensures that the ewes conceive in the proper time). R' Yose, on the other hand, classifies most of these items as a burden. He agrees, however, that the covering used in the case of *kevunos* is an adornment, because it protects the wool from becoming soiled (*Rashi* to 52b ד״ה חרץ; see *Rashash* there).

15. See 53b notes 36 and 37.

שית זונה ונצורת לב: הרחלים יוצאות כבולות: מאי כבולות [א]שמכבלין אליה שלהן למטה כדי שלא יעלו עליהן הזכרים מאי משמע דהאי כבול לישנא דלא עביד פירי הוא דכתיב [א] מה הערים [האלה] אשר נתת לי אחי ויקרא [א] (להן) ארץ כבול עד היום הזה מאי ארץ כבול א"ר הונא שהיו בה בני אדם שמכובלין בכסף ובזהב אמר ליה רבא אי הכי היינו דכתיב (ב) [ב] כי לא) ישרו בעיניו מפני שמכובלין בכסף ובזהב לא ישרו בעיניו אמר ליה אין כיון דעתירי ומפנקי לא עבדי עבידתא רב נחמן בר יצחק אמר ארץ חומטון היתה ואמאי קרי לה כבול דמשתרגא בה כרעא עד כבלא ואמרי אינשי ארעא מכבלא דלא עבד פירי: כבונות: מאי כבונות [ב]שמכבנין אותו למילת [ג] כדתנן שאת כצמר לבן [ד] מאי צמר לבן אמר רב ביבי בר אביי כצמר נקי בן יומו שמכבנין אותו למילת: והעזים יוצאות צרורות: איתמר רב אמר [ג]הלכה כר' יהודה ושמואל אמר הלכה כר' יוסי ואיכא דמתני להא שמעתא באפי נפשיה רב אמר ליבש מותר ולא לחלב ושמואל אמר אחד זה ואחד זה אסור ואיכא דמתני לה אהא עזים יוצאות צרורות ליבש אבל לא לחלב משום ר' יהודה בן בתירא אמרו כך הלכה אבל מי מפים איזו ליבש ואיזו לחלב ומתוך שאין מכירים אחד זה ואחד זה אסור אמר שמואל ואמרי לה אמר רב יהודה אמר שמואל הלכה כר' יהודה בן בתירא כי אתא רבין אמר ר"י הלכה כת"ק: **מתני'** ובמה אינה יוצאה לא יצא גמל במטולטלת לא עקוד ולא רגול וכן שאר כל הבהמות [ד]לא יקשור גמלים זה בזה וימשוך אבל מכנים חבלים לתוך ידו וימשוך ובלבד שלא יכרוך: **גמ'** תנא [ה]לא יצא הגמל במטולטלת הקשורה לו בזנבו אבל יוצא הוא במטולטלת הקשורה בזנבו ובחוטרתו אמר רבה בר רב הונא יוצא הגמל במטולטלת הקשורה לה בשילייתה: לא [ו]עקוד ולא רגול: א"ר יהודה [ה] עקוד עקידת יד ורגל כיצחק בן אברהם רגול שלא יכוף ידו על גבי זרועו ויקשור מיתיבי עקוד שתי ידים ושתי רגלים רגול שלא יכוף ידו על גבי זרועו ויקשור הוא דאמר כי האי תנא דתניא עקוד עקידת יד ורגל או שתי ידים ושתי רגלים רגול שלא יכוף ידו ע"ג זרועו ויקשור ואכתי לא דמי בשלמא רישא וסיפא ניחא מציעתא קשיא אלא הוא דאמר כי האי תנא עקוד עקידת יד ורגל כיצחק בן אברהם רגול שלא יכוף ידו על גבי זרועו ויקשור: ולא יקשור גמלים: מאי טעמא אמר רב אשי משום דמיחזי [ו] כמאן דאזיל לחינגא: אבל מכנים: אמר רב אשי לא שנו אלא לענין כלאים דמאי אילימא כלאים דאדם והתנן [ז] אדם [ז]מותר עם כולם לחרוש ולמשוך אלא כלאים דחבלים [ח] והתניא [ט] התוכף [ח]תכיפה אחת אינה חיבור לעולם כלאים דחבלים והכי קאמר ובלבד שלא יכרוך ויקשור אמר שמואל [ט]ובלבד שלא יצא [חבל] מתחת ידו טפח והא תנא דבי שמואל טפחיים אמר אביי השתא דאמר שמואל טפח ותנא דבי שמואל [י]טפחיים שמואל [י] הלכה למעשה אתא לאשמעינן

והתניא

רש"י

שית זונה. נוטריקון דשחוות: שית. בית הבשת: שכבולין. לשון כבלי ברזל קשורה: ויקרא להם. בעשרים ושתים עיר שנתן שלמה לחירס משתעי קרא: מכובלין. מעוטפין ומקושרין: עבידתא. אנגריא של מלך: חומטון. מלחה ומתבקעת: דמשתרגא בה כרעא. טובעת בה הרגל: עד כבלא. פרק התחתון שקורין קויל"ה: שמכבנין. קושרין בגד סביבו [ס]ביום שנולד שלמרו נקי ומשמר למרו שלא יטנף: למילת. לעשות מלמרו כלי מילת [ל]: מכבנין. על שעושין כמין קרסי מתכת לחבר הבגד כמו תנתן כבינתי לבתי (גיטין דף טו.) נוסק"א בלע"ז: באנפי נפשה. ולא אפלוגתא דמתני': ואיכא דמתני. להא דשמואל אהא: כך הלכה. דליבש מותר ולחלב אסור: אבל מי מפים. מי מטיל גורל ומבחין איזו ליבש ואיזו לחלב והרואה אותם צרורות ליבש אומר דלחלב הוא ואתי למישרי תרווייהו: כת"ק. דמתני' דשרי בתרווייהו: מתני' מטולטלת. י"מ פושלא שתחת זנבו וי"מ מרדעת והאחרון נראה בעיני דאי רצועה שתחת הזנב קשורה ומחוברת לסרגא ואין תפול וטעמא דמתני' משום שמא תפול ומייתי לה הוא: לא עקוד ולא רגול. מפרשינן בגמ' שעוקדים ידיהם עם רגליהם בכבלים שלא יברחו: ולא יקשור גמלים זו לזו וימשוך. האחד כדמפרש בגמרא: ובלבד שלא יכרוך. החבלים בכרך אחד ובגמרא מפרש טעמא: גמ' בזנבו ובחוטרתו. דכיון דקשורה בשניהם לא נפלה: חוטרתו. חלדרוב"א שיש לכל גמלים על גביהם: בשלייתה. דכיון דכאיב לא מנתחא לי' ול"נ מטולטלת כר קטן מלא מוכין נותנין לו תחת הזנב כדי שלא תשחית הרצועה הבשר לפי שהמשוי שעל גבה כשהגמל יורד מכביד ויורד כלפי צוארה אלא שהרצועה מעכבתו: יד ורגל. אחד מן הידים ואחד מן הרגלים כופל ביחד: יד על גב זרועו. אחד מידיו כופף כלפי מעלה וקושר כדי שלא יהו לו אלא ג' רגלים לברוח: שתי ידים. כאחד או שתי רגלים כאחד: ואכתי לא דמי. האי תנא לדרב יהודה: רישא וסיפא ניחא. כדרב יהודה אבל מציעתא דקתני או שתי ידים או שתי רגלים קשיא לדרב יהודה דלא קרי עקוד אלא יד ורגל כיצחק בן אברהם דכתיב (בראשית כב) ויעקד כפף ידיו ורגליו לאחוריו וקשר יד ורגל יחד ונפשט צוארו לאחוריו: לחינגא. לשוק למוכרם חינגא ע"ש שסובבין את השוק מחולות מחולות עגולות של בני אדם: לענין כלאים שנוי. האי שלא יכרוך דמתני' לא שייך ביה איסור שבת אלא משום כלאים אסר ליה כדמפרש ואזיל: כלאים דחבלים. שיש בהן חבלי צמר וחבלי פשתן וכי כריך להו הוו כלאים וידו מתחממת באחיזתן וקסבר [ס]דבר שאין מתכוין אסור: אי נימא כלאים דאדם. דכי כריך להן סביבות ידו נמצא קשור עם הגמלים ופעמים שהן מושכין שום דבר ונמצא אדם וגמל מנהיגין יחד: והתנן אדם מותר עם כולם. עם כל הבהמות לחרוש ולמשוך שלא אסרה תורה אלא שני מיני בהמה יחד כעין שור וחמור ומשנה זו במסכת כלאים: התוכף. בגדי צמר ופשתים: בתכיפה אחת. כגון ע"י מחט פעם אחת או שקשר קשר אחד: אינו חיבור. דכתיב (דברים כב) צמר ופשתים יחדו לא אסרה התורה אלא חבור יפה המתקיים: כריכה וקשירה. בשתי תכיפות: שלא יצא חבל. ראש החבל לא יצא מתחת ידו טפח למטה דדמי כמי שנושאה בידו ולא מתחזיא שהיא מאפסר הגמלים: שמואל. דאמר טפח לאורויי הלכה למעשה אתא לאשמעינן דהבא לימלך לפנינו אמרינן ליה טפח שלא להקל באיסורין ומיהו עד טפחיים ליכא איסור:

והתניא

תוספות

עד כבלא. מפרש ר"י עד השוק כדאמר בפ' במה אשה (לקמן דף סג:) בירית באחת כבלים בשתים שמניחין הכבלים בשוק:

רב אמר ליבש מותר כו'. וא"ת לימא מר הלכה כמר וי"ל משום [מ]דאיכא דמפכי להו לתנאי [מ]:

הלכה כר' יהודה בן בתירא. הא דנקט ר' יהודה בן בתירה ולא נקט ר' יוסי משום דבמקום שאין עושין כלל אלא כדי ליבש שרי ר' יהודה בן בתירא דלא שייך התם מי מפים ור' יוסי אוסר משום דילמא נפיל: ר"ת גרים

אמר רב הלכה כת"ק ושמואל אמר כו' וכן כי אתא רבין א"ר יוחנן הלכה כתנא קמא ואתי שפיר איכא דמתני לה לדרב ושמואל דלעיל אהא:

והתנן אדם מותר עם כולם לחרוש ולמשוך. וא"ת אפי' יהא אדם נמי אסור תקשה דמאי כלאים שייך הכא כיון שאינו מושך בעגלה ובקרון דהא בשבת איירי ואין לומר דאסור להנהיג בכלאים אפי' לא ימשוך שום דבר דאם כן יהא אסור להוליך ולהזיז ממקומו שור פסולי המוקדשין דחשיב כשני מינים כדאמרי' בפרק בתרא דמכות (דף כב.) המנהיג בשור פסולי המוקדשין לוקה גוף אחד הוא ועשאו הכתוב שני גופים וי"ל דה"ק אילימא כלאים דאדם והא דקתני ובלבד שלא יכרוך בחול קאמר כדאוקימנא לעיל (פ"ב דף כג:) ולא בשמן שריפה דאיירי ביו"ט ומיירי שמושכין שום דבר אי נמי י"ל דחשיב משיכה מה שנושאים שניהם את החבלים:

מ"ט

עין משפט נר מצוה

לא א ב ג מיי' פ"כ מהל' שבת הלכה יג סמג לאוין סה טוש"ע א"ח סי' שה סעיף ו:

לב ד מיי' שם הלכה ט טוש"ע שם סעי' טו:

לג ה מיי' שם הלכה י טוש"ע שם סעיף יג:

לד ו מיי' שם טוש"ע שם סעיף יד:

לה ז מיי' פ"ט מהל' כלאים הלכה יו"ד סמג לאוין רפ"ג טוש"ע י"ד סי' רצז סעיף טו:

לו ח מיי' פ"י מהל' כלאים הלכה כד סמג לאוין רפג טוש"ע י"ד סי' ש' סעיף ג:

לז ט מיי' פ"כ מהל' שבת הלכה ט סמג לאוין סה טוש"ע א"ח סי' ש"ה סעיף טז:

רבינו חננאל

כבולות מלשון כבלים כדכתיב ארץ כבול וגו' ופי' [דמשתקעא] כרעא בגוה כי כבלא שהיא עפרא וחול וזו היא חומטון. **כבונות.** מכבנין עור הטלה מיום לידתו עד ח' ימים וזהו צמר רך הנקרא (מילא) [מילת]. ר' יהודה אומר עזים יוצאות צרורות ליבש אבל לא לחלב כיון דאשתכח' ת"ק דברייתא כר' יהודה דמתניתין ורב אמר הלכתא כוותייהו הלכה כמותם ואפי' ר' יהודה לא חלק אלא אמר כך הלכה. לצרור דדי הבהמה לצמקן כדי שתתעבר הבהמה מותר. אבל מי מפיס כלומר מי המבחין בין קשירת דד ליבש לקשירת דד לחלב וקי"ל הלכתא כרב באיסורי וכן הלכתא ואע"פ שר' יוסי חולק: **לא יצא הגמל** במטולטלת כו' תנא [לא] יצא הגמל במטולטלת בחטרתא שתכנס בו הרוח אבל יוצא בזנבו הקשורה בחטרתו שלא תכנס בו הרוח. לא עקוד ולא רגול. אוקמה רב יהודה עקוד יד ורגל כעקידת יצחק בן אברהם. רגול שלא יכוף על זרועו ויקשור. ותניא כוותיה ולא יקשור גמלים זה בזה וימשוך: **ירושלמי** שלא יהו אומרים פלוני יוצא לעשות מלאכתו בשבת. פי' חינגא שוקי מלשון חגאיד חגיגת נכרים. אבל מכניס הוא חבלים לתוך ידו ובלבד שלא יכרוך. אתינו למימר הא דתנן ובלבד שלא יכרוך משום דנראה כאלו מושך האדם עם הבהמה ומשום כלאים. והתנן בכלאים בסוף פרק ח' אדם מותר עם כולם לחרוש ולמשוך אלא משום כלאים דחבלין חיישינן דלמא חבל אחד צמר ואחד פשתים וכיון שיכרוך עובר משום כלאים והתנן התוכף תכיפה אחת אינה חבור הנה תכיפה שהיא כגון תפידה אחת אינה חיבור וכ"ש כריכה שאינה חיבור. ושנינן מתניתין לא יכרוך ויקשור שנמצאת כריכה ותפירה כעין שתי תכיפות. אמר שמואל ובלבד שלא יהא אפסר יוצא מתחת ידו טפח ואסיק' הלכה למעשה שלא יהא אפסר יוצא מתחת ידו טפח כלומר אינו משולשל האפסר מתחת ידו כדי כריכה וכן לא יהא אפסר הניתן בראש הבהמה

וראש

מסורת הש"ס

א) [נ"ל להם], ב) [נ"ל ולא], ג) שבועות ה: נגעים פרק א מ"א, ד) [שבועות ו:], ה) [תמיד לא:], ו) [ביצה דף לג.], ז) כלאים פ"ח מ"ו [ב"ק נד:], ח) [נ"ל והתנן], ט) כלאים פרק ט מ"י [יבמות ה: מנחות לט.], י) [ביצה כט:], כ) [ברכות כד. ושם נסמן], ל) [עי' רש"י יחזקאל כז יח ד"ה וצמר צחר], מ) [ועיין תוספות מנחות ל: ד"ה ולימא].

גליון הש"ס

רש"י ד"ה שמכבנין וכו' ביום שנולד. עי' רש"י יחזקאל כז יח: שם ד"ה כלאים דחבלים וכו' דבר שאין מתכוין אסור. עי' לקמן קמ ע"א ברש"י ד"ה אבל נוטל: תוס' ד"ה רב אמר וכו' דאיכא דמפכי להו לתנאי. כעין זה מגילה לב ע"א:

תורה אור השלם

א) וַיֹּאמֶר מָה הֶעָרִים הָאֵלֶּה אֲשֶׁר נָתַתָּה לִּי אָחִי וַיִּקְרָא לָהֶם אֶרֶץ כָּבוּל עַד הַיּוֹם הַזֶּה: [מלכים א' ט, יג]

ב) וַיֵּצֵא חִירָם מִצֹּר לִרְאוֹת אֶת הֶעָרִים אֲשֶׁר נָתַן לוֹ שְׁלֹמֹה וְלֹא יָשְׁרוּ בְּעֵינָיו: [מלכים א' ט, יב]

ליקוטי רש"י

שית זונה. כמו שתותיהם (שמואל ב' י') כלומר ערות זונה. ונצורת לב. כמו עיר נצורה (ישעי' א) המוקפת כרכום וכן לבה של זו מוקפת זימת אולת [משלי ז, י]. רב נחמן בר יצחק אמר כו'. ארץ כבלים ארץ טיט שהרגל משתקע ונכבלת בה [מ"א ט, יג]. שמכבנין אותו למילת. ביום שנולד הטלה וטהרתו אמו בלחיכתה עושין כסות ומכבנין אותו סביבו בקרסים כדי שיהא צמרו נקי [יחזקאל כז, יח]. כמו (גיטין יד:) תנתן כבנתי לבתי פרמו"ל והוא [בית] נפש שקורין נושקא שמכברין בה פתיחות פי החלוק כך כשנולד הכבש והאם לוחכתו אין צמרו נקי [כאותו] יום והרוצה להגיעו למילת עושה לכבש מעטה עור ומכבנו עליו שלא יתפרד ונמצא הצמר מכוסה כל הימים [שבועות ו:]. מלבישים לבוש שלא יתלכלך צמרו [סנהדרין מד.]. מפים. לשון פיים [לקמן קמח:]. ובחוטרתו. דבשת. חטוטר' חלדרוב"א בלע"ז יש לו לגמל במקום טעינת המשא וע"ש שמתרקבת תמיד ומכין שם דבש לרפואה קרויה דבשת כדאמרינן בב"מ דבש והדבים חזי לכתישא דגמלי [ישעיה ל, ו]. עקידת יד ורגל כיצחק. ידיו ורגליו מאחוריו הידים והרגלים ביחד היא עקידה והוא לשון (בראשית ל, לט) עקודים שהיו קרסוליהם לבנים מקום שעוקדין אותן בו היה ניכר [בראשית כב, ט]. דמיחזי כמאן דאזיל לחינגא. אסרו חכמים משום מראית העין שלא יחשדוהו באיסור [לקמן סד:]. חינגא. מחול ועל שם שבני אדם סובבים והולכים בשוק כעין סובבות במחולות קרי ליה חנגא [ביצה לג.]. התוכף תכיפה אחת. תכיפה פוינ"ט שתוחב תחיבה אחת במחט ומחבר כלאים בגד צמר ובגד פשתים יחד. אינה חיבור. בפחות משתי תכיפות להכי כתיב יחדיו עד שיתחברו יחד יפה [יבמות ה:]. תנא דבי שמואל. בתוספתא שסידר שמואל מתנאים שלפניו כמו שסדרו רבי חייא ורבי אושעיא וכמו שסידר רבי את המשנה. שמואל הלכה למעשה אתי לאשמעינן. שהבא לשאול הלכה לעשות מעשה מורין לו אסור ואי חזינן איניש דעביד לא מחינן בידיה דהלכה דמותר ואין מורין כן [ביצה כט.]. הלכה למעשה. להורות על המעשה [ע"ז עד.].

The Gemara records a different version:

וְאִיכָּא דְּמַתְנֵי לְהָא שְׁמַעְתָּא בְּאַפֵּי נַפְשֵׁיהּ – And some report that this discussion between Rav and Shmuel was stated by itself (i.e. without reference to the dispute in our Mishnah), as follows: רַב אָמַר – Rav says: לְיַבֵּשׁ מוּתָּר – If the pouch is used to dry up the milk, it is permitted; וְלֹא לְחָלָב – but if it is used to collect the milk, it is prohibited.[16] וּשְׁמוּאֵל אָמַר – And Shmuel says: אֶחָד זֶה וְאֶחָד זֶה – In both this case and that case, אָסוּר – it is prohibited.[17]

The Gemara reports yet another version of Shmuel's[18] statement:

וְאִיכָּא דְּמַתְנֵי לַהּ אַהָא – And some report that it was stated in reference to this Baraisa: עִזִּים יוֹצְאוֹת צְרוּרוֹת לְיַבֵּשׁ – GOATS MAY GO OUT with a pouch TIED to their udders if it is used TO DRY UP the milk, אֲבָל לֹא לְחָלָב – BUT NOT if it is used TO COLLECT THE MILK. מִשּׁוּם רַבִּי יְהוּדָה בֶּן בְּתֵירָא אָמְרוּ – IN THE NAME OF R' YEHUDAH BEN BESEIRA THEY SAID: כָּךְ הֲלָכָה – THAT IS indeed THE LAW. אֲבָל מִי מֵפִיס – BUT WHO WILL DRAW LOTS[19] to determine אֵיזוֹ לְיַבֵּשׁ – in WHICH case the pouch is used TO DRY UP the milk, וְאֵיזוֹ לְחָלָב – AND in WHICH case it is used TO COLLECT THE MILK? וּמִתּוֹךְ שֶׁאֵין מַכִּירִים – AND SINCE [PEOPLE] CANNOT DISCERN the difference between them, אֶחָד זֶה וְאֶחָד זֶה אָסוּר – we rule that in both THIS CASE AND THAT CASE IT IS PROHIBITED.[20] אָמַר שְׁמוּאֵל – Shmuel said in reference to this Baraisa, וְאָמְרֵי לַהּ אָמַר רַב יְהוּדָה אָמַר שְׁמוּאֵל – and some say that Rav Yehudah reported it in the name of Shmuel: הֲלָכָה כְּרַבִּי יְהוּדָה בֶּן בְּתֵירָא – The law follows R' Yehudah ben Beseira.[21]

As stated above, Rav and Shmuel disagree as to whether the law follows R' Yehudah or R' Yose. The Gemara now cites a third view: כִּי אֲתָא רָבִין – When Ravin came from Eretz Yisrael to Babylonia, אָמַר רַבִּי יוֹחָנָן – he said in the name of R' Yochanan: הֲלָכָה כְּתַנָּא קַמָּא – The law follows the Tanna Kamma of our Mishnah,[22] who permits the pouch whether it is used to dry up the milk or to collect it.

Mishnah Having enumerated cases in which an animal may be allowed out on the Sabbath, the Mishnah now delineates cases in which this is forbidden:

וּבַמָּה אֵינָה יוֹצְאָה – And with what may [an animal] not go out?[23] לֹא יֵצֵא גָּמָל בִּמְטוּלְטֶלֶת – A camel may not go out with a *metulteles.*[24] לֹא עָקוּד וְלֹא רָגוּל – It may not go out bound or hobbled.[25] וְכֵן שְׁאָר כָּל הַבְּהֵמוֹת – And so is the law with all other animals.[26] לֹא יִקְשׁוֹר גְּמַלִּים זֶה בָּזֶה וְיִמְשׁוֹךְ – One may not tie camels to each other and pull one of them so that the others follow,[27] אֲבָל מַכְנִיס חֲבָלִים לְתוֹךְ יָדוֹ וְיִמְשׁוֹךְ – but he may gather their ropes into his hand and pull each one by its own rope,[28] וּבִלְבַד שֶׁלֹּא יִכְרוֹךְ – provided that he does not wind the ropes around his hand.[29]

Gemara A Baraisa qualifies our Mishnah's first ruling: תָּנָא – A Tanna taught in a Baraisa: לֹא יֵצֵא הַגָּמָל בִּמְטוּלְטֶלֶת הַקְּשׁוּרָה לוֹ בִּזְנָבוֹ – THE CAMEL MAY NOT GO OUT WITH A *METULTELES* TIED TO ITS TAIL; אֲבָל יוֹצֵא הוּא בִּמְטוּלְטֶלֶת

NOTES

16. [The opinion of R' Yehudah.]

17. [The opinion of R' Yose.] The Rishonim ask why, according to this report, Rav and Shmuel did not simply say that the law follows R' Yehudah or R' Yose. They answer that this could have been misleading, because there are versions of the Mishnah in which the opinions of R' Yose and R' Yehudah are reversed (*Tosafos* et al.).

18. The following version includes a statement by Shmuel, but not a statement by Rav (from *Rashi;* cf. *Tosafos, Rosh* et al.).

19. I.e. it is so hard to make the following determination that one might as well draw lots.

20. [Simply by looking, there is no way to tell whether the pouch is attached to dry up the milk or to collect it (see *Pnei Yehoshua*). Therefore,] someone who sees a goat in a public domain on the Sabbath with a pouch tied to its udders might assume that it is for collecting the milk when in fact it is for drying the milk up. He might then conclude that the pouch is permitted even if used to collect the milk (*Rashi*). To prevent such a mistake, R' Yehudah ben Beseira prohibits the pouch even where its purpose is to dry up the milk.

21. According to this version too, Shmuel forbids the pouch whether it is used to dry up the milk or to collect it. However, in the first version (where Shmuel rules in accordance with R' Yose) the reason is that the pouch is deemed a burden in both cases (see *Maharam* ד״ה בא״ד ור׳ יוסי). In this version, though, Shmuel agrees that where the pouch is used to dry up the milk, it is not a burden. He prohibits its use in such a case only because it might be confused with a pouch used to collect the milk. There are practical differences between these versions. For instance, in a locale where such a pouch is used *only* to dry up the milk, and hence there are no grounds for confusion, it would be permitted for that purpose according to the second version, but not according to the first version (*Tosafos* et al.; see *Sfas Emes* for another practical difference).

22. *Rashi;* cf. *Rashba,* who maintains that the reference is to the Tanna Kamma of the Baraisa.

According to *Rashi,* Ravin's statement is independent. (I.e. it is not connected to the preceding discussion about the Baraisa.) It therefore presumably refers to the Mishnah (*Maharsha*).

[See also the versions of the text according to *Tosafos, Rif* and *Rosh.*]

23. The first Mishnah of our chapter began: "With what may an animal go out, and with what may it not go out?" This Mishnah takes up the second part of that question.

24. Some maintain that a מְטוּלְטֶלֶת, *metulteles,* is a strap that anchors the animal's load to its tail and prevents the load from sliding forward when the animal goes downhill (see 53a note 8). Others hold that a *metulteles* is a saddle cloth, similar to the מַרְדַּעַת of a donkey (see *Melo HaRo'im* at length). The latter explanation is preferable, because the Gemara implies that the reason a *metulteles* is forbidden is that it might fall off and one might carry it four *amos* in the public domain (see note 22). Hence, it is unlikely to be the tail strap, which is tied securely to the saddle and cannot fall off (*Rashi*).

In *Rashi's* own opinion, a *metulteles* is a small cushion that goes between the tail and the tail strap, which prevents the strap from chafing the animal's skin (*Rashi* ד״ה בשלייתה; see *Maharshal* and *Rosh Yosef; Meiri* and *Ran* also give this definition; cf. *Rambam, Commentary to the Mishnah*).

25. "Bound" means that its legs are chained together in a particular manner (explained in the Gemara), so that it will not run away (*Rashi*). "Hobbled" means that its one lower foreleg is bent upward toward the upper foreleg and tied (Gemara below). This, too, was done to prevent the animal from running away by leaving it only three free legs (*Rashi* ד״ה יד על גב זרועו).

In these cases, the trappings (chains etc.) are forbidden because they cause pain to the animal and hence are a burden to it. Alternatively, the reason is that they might fall off and be carried four *amos* in a public domain (*Mishnah Berurah* 305:48; see *Sfas Emes*).

26. I.e. other animals, too, may not go out "bound" or "hobbled" (*Meiri;* cf. *Pnei Yehoshua*).

27. [E.g. he may not tie camels one behind the other and pull only the lead camel.] The Gemara below states the reason for this prohibition (*Rashi*).

28. [I.e. he may gather the tethers of all the camels into his hand, if he does not tie the camels together.]

29. The Gemara below explains this restriction (*Rashi*).

שית זונה ונצורת לב: הרחלים יוצאות כבולות: מאי כבולות [א]שמכבלין אליה שלהן למטה כדי שלא יעלו עליהן הזכרים מאי משמע דהאי כבול לישנא דלא עביד פירי הוא דכתיב [א] מה הערים [האלה] אשר נתת לי אחי ויקרא [א] (להן) ארץ כבול עד היום הזה מאי ארץ כבול א"ר הונא שהיו בה בני אדם שמכובלין בכסף ובזהב אמר ליה רבא אי הכי היינו דכתיב (ב) [ב] כי לא) ישרו בעיניו מפני שמכובלין בכסף ובזהב לא ישרו בעיניו אמר ליה אין כיון דעתירי ומפנקי לא עבדי עבידתא רב נחמן בר יצחק אמר ארץ חומטון היתה ואמאי קרי לה כבול דמשתרגא בה כרעא עד כבלא ואמרי אינשי ארעא מכבלא דלא עבד פירי: כבונות: מאי כבונות [ב]שמכבנין אותו למילת [ג] כדתנן שאת כצמר לבן [ד] מאי צמר לבן אמר רב ביבי בר אביי כצמר נקי בן יומו שמכבנין אותו למילת: והעזים יוצאות צרורות: איתמר רב אמר [ג]הלכה כר' יהודה ושמואל אמר הלכה כר' יוסי ואיכא דמתני להא שמעתא באפי נפשיה רב אמר ליבש מותר ולא לחלב ושמואל אמר אחד זה ואחד זה אסור ואיכא דמתני לה אהא עזים יוצאות צרורות ליבש אבל לא לחלב משום ר' יהודה בן בתירא אמרו כך הלכה אבל מי מפים איזו ליבש ואיזו לחלב ומתוך שאין מכירים אחד זה ואחד זה אסור אמר שמואל ואמרי לה אמר רב יהודה אמר שמואל הלכה כר' יהודה בן בתירא כי אתא רבין אמר ר"י הלכה כת"ק: **מתני'** ובמה אינה יוצאה לא יצא גמל במטולטלת לא עקוד ולא רגול וכן שאר כל הבהמות [ד]לא יקשור גמלים זה בזה וימשוך אבל מכניס חבלים לתוך ידו וימשוך ובלבד שלא יכרוך: **גמ'** תנא [ה]לא יצא הגמל במטולטלת הקשורה לו בזנבו אבל יוצא הוא במטולטלת הקשורה בזנבו ובחוטרתו אמר רבה בר רב הונא יוצא הגמל במטולטלת הקשורה לה בשילייתה: לא [ו]עקוד ולא רגול: א"ר יהודה [ה] עקוד עקידת יד ורגל כיצחק בן אברהם רגול שלא יכוף ידו על גבי זרועו ויקשור מיתיבי עקוד שתי ידים ושתי רגלים רגול שלא יכוף ידו על גבי זרועו ויקשור הוא דאמר כי האי תנא דתניא עקוד עקידת יד ורגל או שתי ידים ושתי רגלים רגול שלא יכוף ידו ע"ג זרועו ויקשור ואכתי לא דמי בשלמא רישא וסיפא ניחא מציעתא קשיא אלא הוא דאמר כי האי תנא עקוד עקידת יד ורגל כיצחק בן אברהם רגול שלא יכוף ידו על גבי זרועו ויקשור: ולא יקשור גמלים: מאי טעמא אמר רב אשי משום דמיחזי [ו] כמאן דאזיל לחינגא: אבל מכנים: אמר רב אשי לא שנו אלא לענין כלאים דמאי אילימא כלאים דאדם והתנן [ז] אדם [ז]מותר עם כולם לחרוש ולמשוך אלא כלאים דחבלים [ח] והתניא [ט] התוכף [ח]תכיפה אחת אינה חיבור לעולם כלאים דחבלים והכי קאמר ובלבד שלא יכרוך ויקשור אמר שמואל [ט]ובלבד שלא יצא [חבל] מתחת ידו טפח והא תנא דבי שמואל טפחיים אמר אביי השתא דאמר שמואל טפח ותנא דבי שמואל [י] טפחיים שמואל [כ] הלכה למעשה אתא לאשמעינן

והתניא

שית זונה. נוטריקון דשחוות: שית. בית הבשת: שמבוללין. לשון כבלי ברזל קשורה: ויקרא להם. בעשרים ושתים עיר שנתן שלמה לחירם משתעי קרא: מכובלין. מעוטפין ומקושרין: עבידתא. אנגריא של מלך: חומטון. מלחה ומתבקעת: דמשתרגא בה כרעא. טובעת בה הרגל: עד כבלא. פרק התחתון שקורין קויל"ה: שמכבנין. קושרין בגד סביבו ביום שנולד שצמרו נקי ומשמר צמרו שלא יטנף: למילת. לעשות מצמרו כלי מילת [ל]: מכבנין. על שעושין כמין קרסי מתכת לחבר הבגד כמו תנתן כבינתי לבתי (גיטין דף טו.) נושק"א בלע"ז: באנפי נפשה. ולא אפלוגתא דמתני': ואיכא דמתני. להא דשמואל אהא: כך הלכה. דליבש מותר ולחלב אסור: אבל מי מפים. מי מטיל גורל ומבחין איזו ליבש ואיזו לחלב והרואה אותם צרורות ליבש אומר לחלב הוא ואתי למישרי תרוויהו: כת"ק. דמתני' דשרי בתרוייהו: מתני' מטולטלת. י"מ פושלא שתחת זנבו וי"מ מרדעת והאחרון נראה בעיני דאי רצועה שתחת הזנב קשורה ומחוברת לסרגא ואיך תפול וטעמא דמתני' משום שמא תפול ומייתי לה הוא: לא עקוד ולא רגול. מפרשינן בגמ' שעוקדים ידיהם עם רגליהם בכבלים שלא יברחו: ולא יקשור גמלים זו לזו וימשוך. האחד כדמפרש בגמרא: ובלבד שלא יכרוך. החבלים בכרך אחד ובגמרא מפרש טעמא: גמ' בזנבו ובחוטרתו. דכיון דקשורה בשניהם לא נפלה: חוטרתו. חלדרוב"א שיש לכל גמלים על גביהם: בשלייתה. דכיון דכאיב לא מנתחא לי' ול"נ מטולטלת כר קטן מלא מוכין נותנין לו תחת הזנב כדי שלא תשחית הרצועה הבשר לפי שהמשוי שעל גבה כשהגמל יורד מכביד ויורד כלפי צוארה אלא שהרצועה מעכבתו: יד ורגל. אחד מן הידים ואחד מן הרגלים כובל ביחד: יד על גב זרועו. אחד מידיו כופף כלפי מעלה וקושר כדי שלא יהו לו אלא ג' רגלים לברוח: שתי ידים. כאחד או שתי רגלים כאחד: ואכתי לא דמי. האי תנא לדרב יהודה: רישא וסיפא ניחא. כדרב יהודה אבל מציעתא דקתני או שתי ידים או שתי רגלים קשיא לדרב יהודה דלא קרי עקוד אלא יד ורגל כיצחק בן אברהם דכתיב (בראשית כב) ויעקד כפף ידיו ורגליו לאחוריו וקשר יד ורגל יחד ונפשט צוארו לאחוריו: לחינגא. לשוק למוכרם חינגא ע"ש שסובבין את השוק מחולות מחולות עגולות של בני אדם: לענין כלאים שנוי. האי שלא יכרוך דמתני' לא שייך ביה איסור שבת אלא משום כלאים אסר ליה כדמפרש ואזיל: כלאים דחבלים. שיש בהן חבלי צמר וחבלי פשתן וכי כריך להו הוו כלאים וידו מתחממת באחיזתן וקסבר [ס]דבר שאין מתכוין אסור: אי נימא כלאים דאדם. דכי כריך להן סביבות ידו נמצא קשור עם הגמלים ופעמים שהן מושכין שום דבר ונמצא אדם וגמל מנהיגין יחד: והתנן אדם מותר עם כולם. עם כל הבהמות לחרוש ולמשוך שלא אסרה תורה אלא שני מיני בהמה יחד כעין שור וחמור ומשנה זו במסכת כלאים: התוכף. בגדי צמר ופשתים: בתכיפה אחת. כגון ע"י מחט פעם אחת או שקשר קשר אחד: אינו חיבור. דכתיב (דברים כב) צמר ופשתים יחדו לא אסרה התורה אלא חבור יפה המתקיים: כריכה וקשירה. בשתי תכיפות: שלא יצא חבל. ראש החבל לא יצא מתחת ידו טפח למטה דדמי כמי שנושאה בידו ולא מתחזיא שהיא מאפסר הגמלים: שמואל. דאמר טפח לאורויי הלכה למעשה אתא לאשמעינן דהבא לימלך לפנינו אמרינן ליה טפח שלא להקל באיסורין ומיהו עד טפחיים ליכא איסור:

והתניא

עד כבלא. מפרש ר"י עד השוק כדאמר בפ' במה אשה (לקמן דף סג:) בירית באחת כבלים בשתים שמניחין הכבלים בשוק:

רב אמר ליבש מותר כו'. וא"ת לימא מר הלכה כמר וי"ל משום [ס] דאיכא דמפכי להו לתנאי [מ]:

הלכה כר' יהודה בן בתירא. הא דנקט ר' יהודה בן בתירה ולא נקט ר' יוסי משום דבמקום שאין עושין כלל אלא כדי ליבש שרי ר' יהודה בן בתירא דלא שייך התם מי מפים ור' יוסי אוסר משום דילמא נפיל: ר"ת גרים

אמר רב הלכה כת"ק ושמואל אמר כו' וכן כי אתא רבין א"ר יוחנן הלכה כתנא קמא ואתי שפיר איכא דמתני לה לדרב ושמואל דלעיל אהא:

והתנן אדם מותר עם כולם לחרוש ולמשוך. וא"ת אפי' יהא אדם נמי אסור תקשה דמאי כלאים שייך הכא כיון שאינו מושך בעגלה ובקרון דהא בשבת איירי ואין לומר דאסור להנהיג בכלאים אפי' לא ימשוך שום דבר דאם כן יהא אסור להוליך ולהזיז ממקומו שור פסולי המוקדשין דחשיב כשני מינים כדאמרי' בפרק בתרא דמכות (דף כב.) המנהיג בשור פסולי המוקדשין לוקה גוף אחד הוא ועשאו הכתוב שני גופים וי"ל דה"ק אילימא כלאים דאדם והא דקתני ובלבד שלא יכרוך בחול קאמר כדאוקימנא לעיל (פ"ג דף כג:) ולא בשמן שריפה דאיירי ביו"ט ומיירי שמושכין שום דבר אי נמי י"ל דחשיב משיכה מה שנושאים שניהם את החבלים:

מ"ט

קרסוליהם לבנים מקום שעוקדין אותן בו היה ניכר [בראשית כב, ט]. דמיחזי כמאן דאזיל לחינגא. אסרו חכמים משום מראית העין שלא יחשדוהו באיסור [לקמן סד:]. חינגא. מחול ועל שם שבני אדם סובבים והולכים בשוק כעין סובבות במחולות קרי ליה חגגא [ביצה לג.]. התוכף תכיפה אחת. תכיפה פויינ"ט שתוחב תחיבה אחת במחט ומחבר כלאים בגד צמר ובגד פשתים יחד. אינה חיבור. בפחות משתי תכיפות להכי כתיב יחדיו עד שיחברם יחד יפה [יבמות ה:]. תנא דבי שמואל. בתוספתא שסידר שמואל מתנאים שלפניו כמו שסדרו רבי חייא ורבי אושעיא וכמו שסידר רבי את המשנה. שמואל הלכה למעשה אתי לאשמעינן. שהבא לשאול הלכה לעשות מעשה מורין לו אסור ואי חזינן איניש דעביד לא מחינן בידיה דהלכה דמותר ואין מורין כן [ביצה כט.]. הלכה למעשה. להורות על המעשה [ע"ז עד.].

מסורת הש"ס

א) [צ"ל להם], ב) [צ"ל ולא], ג) שבועות ה: נגעים פרק א מ"א, ד) [שבועות ו:], ה) [תמיד לא:], ו) [ביצה דף לג.], ז) כלאים פ"ח מ"ו [ב"ק נד:], ח) [צ"ל והתנן], ט) כלאים פרק ט מ"י [יבמות ה: מנחות לט.], י) [ביצה כט:], כ) [ברכות כד. ושם נסמן], ל) [עי' רש"י יחזקאל כז יח ד"ה וצמר צחר], מ) [ועיין תוספות מנחות ל: ד"ה ולימא].

גליון הש"ס

רש"י ד"ה שמכבנין וכו' ביום שנולד. עי' רש"י יחזקאל כז יח: שם ד"ה כלאים דחבלים וכו' דבר שאין מתכוין אסור. עי' לקמן קמ ע"א ברש"י ד"ה אבל נוטל: תוס' ד"ה רב אמר וכו' דאיכא דמפכי להו לתנאי. כעין זה מגילה לב ע"א:

תורה אור השלם

א) וַיֹּאמֶר מָה הֶעָרִים הָאֵלֶּה אֲשֶׁר נָתַתָּה לִּי אָחִי וַיִּקְרָא לָהֶם אֶרֶץ כָּבוּל עַד הַיּוֹם הַזֶּה: [מלכים א' ט, יג]

ב) וַיֵּצֵא חִירָם מִצֹּר לִרְאוֹת אֶת הֶעָרִים אֲשֶׁר נָתַן לוֹ שְׁלֹמֹה וְלֹא יָשְׁרוּ בְּעֵינָיו: [מלכים א' ט, יב]

ליקוטי רש"י

שית זונה. כמו שתותיהם (שמואל ב' י') כלומר ערות זונה. ונצורת לב. כמו עיר נצורה (ישעי' א) המוקפת כרכום וכן לבה של זו מוקפת זימת אולת [משלי ז, י]. רב נחמן בר יצחק אמר כו'. ארץ כבלים ארץ טיט שהרגל משתקע ונכבלת בה [מ"א ט, יג]. שמכבנין אותו למילת. ביום שנולד הטלה וטהרתו אמו בלחיכתה עושין כסות ומכבנין אותו סביבו בקרסים כדי שיהא צמרו נקי [יחזקאל כז, יח]. כמו (גיטין יד:) תנתן כבנתי לבתי פרמוי"ל והוא [בית] נפש שקורין נושקא שמחברין בה פתיחות פי החלוק כך כשנולד הכבש והאם לוחכתו אין צמרו נקי [כאותו] יום והרוצה להצניעו למילת עושה לכבש מעטה עור ומכבנו עליו שלא יתפרד ונמצא הצמר מכוסה כל הימים [שבועות ו:]. מלבישים לבוש שלא יתלכלך צמרו [סנהדרין מד.]. מפים. לשון פיים [לקמן קמח:]. ובחוטרתו. דבשת. חטוטר' אלדרוב"א בלע"ז יש לו לגמל במקום טעינת המשא וע"ש שמתרקבת תמיד וסכין שם דבש לרפואה קרויה דבשת כדאמרינן בב"מ דבש והדבים חזי לכתישא דגמלי [ישעיה ל, ו]. עקידת יד ורגל כיצחק. ידיו ורגליו מאחוריו הידים והרגלים ביחד היא עקידה והוא לשון (בראשית ל, לט) עקודים שהיו

עין משפט נר מצוה

לא א ב ג מיי' פ"כ מהל' שבת הלכה יב סמג לאוין סה טוש"ע א"ח סי' שה סעיף ו:

לב ד מיי' שם הלכה ט טוש"ע שם סעי' טו:

לג ה מיי' שם הלכה י טוש"ע שם סעיף יג:

לד ו מיי' שם טוש"ע שם סעיף יד:

לה ז מיי' פ"ט מהל' כלאים הלכה יו"ד סמג לאוין רפ"ב טוש"ע י"ד סי' רצז סעיף טו:

לו ח מיי' פ"י מהל' כלאים הלכה כד סמג לאוין רפג טוש"ע י"ד סי' ש' סעיף ב:

לז ט מיי' פ"כ מהל' שבת הלכה ט סמג לאוין סה טוש"ע א"ח סי' ש"ה סעיף טז:

רבינו חננאל

כבולות מלשון כבלים כדכתיב ארץ כבול וגו' ופי' [דמשתקעא] כרעא בגוה כי כבלא שהיא עפרא וחול וזו היא חומטון. **כבונות.** מכבנין עור הטלה מיום לידתו עד ח' ימים וזהו צמר רך הנקרא (מילא) [מילת]. ר' יהודה אומר עזים יוצאות צרורות ליבש אבל לא לחלב כיון דאשתכח' ת"ק דברייתא כר' יהודה דמתניתין ורב אמר הלכתא כוותייהו הלכה כמותם ואפי' ר' יהודה לא חלק אלא אמר כך הלכה. לצרור דדי הבהמה לצמקן כדי שתתעבר הבהמה מותר. אבל מי מפיס כלומר מי המבחין בין קשירת דד ליבש לקשירת דד לחלב וקי"ל הלכתא כרב באיסורי וכן הלכתא ואע"פ שר' יוסי חולק: **לא** יצא הגמל במטולטלת כו' תנא [לא] יצא הגמל במטולטלת בחטרתא שתכנס בו הרוח אבל יוצא בזנבו הקשורה בחטרתו שלא תכנס בו הרוח. לא עקוד ולא רגול. אוקמה רב יהודה עקוד יד ורגל כעקידת יצחק בן אברהם. רגול שלא יכוף על זרועו ויקשור. ותניא כוותיה ולא יקשור גמלים זה בזה וימשוך: **ירושלמי** שלא יהו אומרים פלוני יוצא לעשות מלאכתו בשבת. פי' חינגא שוקי מלשון חגאיד חגיגת נכרים. אבל מכניס הוא חבלים לתוך ידו ובלבד שלא יכרוך. אתינו למימר הא דתנן ובלבד שלא יכרוך משום דנראה כאלו מושך האדם עם הבהמה ומשום כלאים. והתנן בכלאים בסוף פרק ח' אדם מותר עם כולם לחרוש ולמשוך אלא משום כלאים דחבלין חיישינן דלמא חבל אחד צמר ואחד פשתים וכיון שיכרוך עובר משום כלאים והתנן התוכף תכיפה אחת אינה חבור הנה תכיפה שהיא כגון תפירה אחת אינה חיבור וכ"ש כריכה שאינה חיבור. ושנינן מתניתין לא יכרוך ויקשור שנמצאת כריכה ותפירה כעין שתי תכיפות. אמר שמואל ובלבד שלא יהא אפסר יוצא מתחת ידו טפח ואסיק' הלכה למעשה שלא יהא אפסר יוצא מתחת ידו טפח כלומר אינו משולשל האפסר מתחת ידו כדי כריכה וכן לא יהא אפסר הניתן בראש הבהמה

וראש

הַקְּשׁוּרָה בִּזְנָבוֹ וּבְחוֹטַרְתּוֹ – BUT IT MAY GO OUT WITH A *METULTELES* TIED TO both ITS TAIL AND ITS HUMP.[30]

The Gemara adds:

אָמַר רַבָּה בַּר רַב הוּנָא – **Rabbah bar Rav Huna said:** יוֹצֵא הַגָּמָל בִּמְטוּלְטֶלֶת הַקְּשׁוּרָה לָהּ בְּשִׁילְיָיתָהּ – **The camel may go out with a *metulteles* tied to its placenta.**[31]

The Mishnah continued:

לֹא עָקוּד וְלֹא רָגוּל – It may NOT go out BOUND OR HOBBLED.

These terms are defined:

אָמַר רַב יְהוּדָה – **Rav Yehudah said:** עָקוּד עֲקֵידַת יָד וָרֶגֶל – **"Bound"** means **the binding of hand and foot,** כְּיִצְחָק בֶּן אַבְרָהָם – **as Isaac the son of Abraham** was tied.[32] רָגוּל שֶׁלֹּא יָכוּף יָדוֹ עַל גַּבֵּי זְרוֹעוֹ וְיִקְשׁוֹר – When the Mishnah says **"hobbled,"** it means **that one should not bend its lower foreleg** (literally: hand) **on to its upper foreleg and tie** it there.[33]

The Gemara challenges Rav Yehudah's definition of "bound":

מֵיתִיבֵי – **They challenged** it from the following Baraisa: עָקוּד שְׁתֵּי יָדַיִם וּשְׁתֵּי רַגְלַיִם – "BOUND" means the TWO FORELEGS tied together OR the TWO HINDLEGS tied together. רָגוּל שֶׁלֹּא יָכוּף יָדוֹ עַל גַּבֵּי זְרוֹעוֹ וְיִקְשׁוֹר – The prohibition of "HOBBLED" entails THAT ONE SHOULD NOT BEND ITS LOWER FORELEG ONTO ITS UPPER FORELEG AND TIE it there.[34] – ? –

The Gemara answers that this Baraisa does not refute Rav Yehudah's view because Rav Yehudah has alternative Tannaic support:

הוּא דְּאָמַר כִּי הַאי תַּנָּא – **[Rav Yehudah] follows this Tanna,** whose view is recorded in the following Baraisa: דְּתַנְיָא – **For it was taught in a Baraisa:** עָקוּד עֲקֵידַת יָד וָרֶגֶל – "BOUND" means A FORELEG AND A HINDLEG tied together, אוֹ שְׁתֵּי יָדַיִם וּשְׁתֵּי רַגְלַיִם – OR THE TWO FORELEGS tied together OR the TWO HINDLEGS tied together. רָגוּל שֶׁלֹּא יָכוּף יָדוֹ עַל גַּבֵּי זְרוֹעוֹ וְיִקְשׁוֹר – The prohibition of "HOBBLED" entails THAT ONE SHOULD NOT BEND ITS LOWER FORELEG ONTO ITS UPPER FORELEG AND TIE it there.

The Gemara objects:

וְאַכַּתִּי לֹא דָּמֵי – **But** Rav Yehudah's position **is still not the same** as that of any Tanna! בִּשְׁלָמָא רֵישָׁא וְסֵיפָא נִיחָא – **It is all understandable** when **the first part** of this Baraisa says, "bound means a foreleg and a hindleg tied together," **and the last part** of the Baraisa says "hobbled etc.," because that is **fine** according to Rav Yehudah. מְצִיעֲתָא קַשְׁיָא – But **the middle part** of the Baraisa, which says "[bound also means] the two forelegs or the two hindlegs tied together," **is a contradiction** of Rav Yehudah's view.[35] – ? –

The Gemara answers:

אֶלָּא הוּא דְּאָמַר כִּי הַאי תַּנָּא – **Rather, [Rav Yehudah] follows *this* Tanna,** who says: עָקוּד עֲקֵידַת יָד וָרֶגֶל – "BOUND" means THE BINDING OF HAND AND FOOT, כְּיִצְחָק בֶּן אַבְרָהָם – AS ISAAC THE SON OF ABRAHAM was tied. רָגוּל שֶׁלֹּא יָכוּף יָדוֹ עַל גַּבֵּי זְרוֹעוֹ וְיִקְשׁוֹר – The prohibition of "HOBBLED" entails THAT ONE SHOULD NOT BEND ITS LOWER FORELEG ONTO ITS UPPER FORELEG AND TIE it there.

The Mishnah continued:

וְלֹא יִקְשׁוֹר גְּמַלִּים – ONE MAY NOT TIE CAMELS to each other and pull one of them.

The Gemara explains:

מַאי טַעְמָא – **What is the reason** for this prohibition? אָמַר רַב אָשֵׁי – **Rav Ashi said:** מִשּׁוּם דְּמִיחֱזֵי כְּמַאן דְּאָזֵיל לְחִינְגָּא – **Because he appears like one who is going to** sell his camels in the **market.**[36]

The Mishnah continued:

אֲבָל מַכְנִיס – BUT HE MAY GATHER their ropes into his hand and pull them all together, provided that he does not wind the ropes around his hand.

The Gemara explains why he may not wind the ropes around his hand:

אָמַר רַב אָשֵׁי – **Rav Ashi said:** לֹא שָׁנוּ אֶלָּא לְעִנְיַן כִּלְאַיִם – **They did not teach** this **except in regard to** the laws of ***kilayim.***[37]

The Gemara asks:

כִּלְאַיִם דְּמַאי – ***Kilayim* of what?** To which type of *kilayim* does Rav Ashi refer? אִילֵימָא כִּלְאַיִם דְּאָדָם – **If one says** that he means ***kilayim* of the person,** who is pulling together with the camels,[38]

NOTES

30. Since it is tied to both, it will not fall off (*Rashi*). [Evidently, a *metulteles* is not considered a burden, for otherwise it would be forbidden even if it could not fall off. See *Sfas Emes,* who ponders why a *metulteles* is not a burden in light of *Rashi's* last two definitions of this word (see note 24).]

31. [I.e. a placenta that is partially hanging out.] In this case the camel will not try to shake off the *metulteles,* because doing so would cause it pain (*Rashi*). Hence, it is unlikely to fall off.

32. One of the animal's forelegs is chained to one of its hindlegs (*Rashi*).

When Isaac was bound as a sacrifice, his hands and feet were tied together behind him, and his neck was thus stretched backwards (*Rashi* ד"ה רישא; *Meiri,* citing *Midrash*). This position would facilitate the act of slaughter, which is performed at the neck (see *Sfas Emes*). Since the verse (*Genesis* 22:9) states: וַיַּעֲקֹד אֶת יִצְחָק, *He* [Abraham] *bound Isaac,* it is evident that the root עקד signifies tying the hands and feet together.

Although Rav Yehudah cites the example of Isaac, he does not mean that an animal is tied in exactly the same way. Isaac's hands and feet were tied together tightly, whereas an animal's legs are tied sufficiently far apart that it can walk. [Another difference is that both of Isaac's hands and both of his feet were tied, while only one of the camel's forelegs is tied to only one of its hindlegs (*Maharsha*).] Rav Yehudah mentions the example of Isaac simply to show that עָקוּד, *bound,* means a foreleg tied to a hindleg, as opposed to the two forelegs tied together or the two hindlegs tied together (*Ritva MHK* ed.; see *Maharsha;* see also *Yad David;* who explains *Rashi* to *Genesis* 22:9 in accordance with our Gemara).

In fact, according to Rav Yehudah it would be permissible for an animal to go out with its two forelegs or two hindlegs tied to each other (*Meiri;* see *Mishnah Berurah* 305:48 and *Shaar HaTziyun* §44, 45; cf. *Sfas Emes*).

33. See note 25.

34. Rav Yehudah said that "bound" means a foreleg tied to a hindleg, but the Baraisa defines it as a foreleg tied to a foreleg or a hindleg to a hindleg.

35. The Baraisa gave a second definition of "bound" – namely, the two forelegs tied to each other or the two hindlegs tied to each other. It thus contradicts Rav Yehudah, who defined "bound" *only* as a foreleg tied to a hindleg [see note 32] (*Rashi*).

36. חִינְגָּא literally means *a dance.* It is used in reference to a market because the movement of people making their rounds among the vendors resembles the movement of dancers going around in a circle (*Rashi* here and to *Beitzah* 33a ד"ה חנגא).

If all the camels are tied together, it seems that they are being taken to be sold [which is Rabbinically forbidden (see *Shach Yoreh Deah* 87:6)]. One who takes his camels out for some other purpose (e.g. to drink at a river) would simply hold each one's leash in his hand (*Chidushei HaRan*).

37. The prohibition against wrapping the ropes around his hand is not related to the Sabbath. It is forbidden on account of *kilayim,* as the Gemara proceeds to explain (*Rashi*), and thus applies even during the week (see *Tosafos*).

כִּלְאַיִם, *kilayim,* denotes forbidden mixtures. There are several prohibitions that fall under this category, of which two are mentioned in this passage: (a) One may not make animals of different species pull something (e.g. a plough) together (*Deuteronomy* 22:10); (b) one may not wear a garment that contains both wool and linen [*shaatnez*] (*Leviticus* 19:19, *Deuteronomy* ibid. v. 11).

38. If he were to wrap the rope around his hand, he would in effect be tied to the animals. Then, if the animals are pulling something, it emerges that he is pulling it together with them (*Rashi;* cf. *Tosafos'* second approach).

שית זונה ונצורת לב: הרחלים יוצאות כבולות: מאי כבולות [א]שמכבלין אליה שלהן למטה כדי שלא יעלו עליהן הזכרים מאי משמע דהאי כבול לישנא דלא עביד פירי הוא דכתיב (א) מה הערים [האלה] אשר נתת לי אחי ויקרא (ה) (להן) ארץ כבול עד היום הזה מאי ארץ כבול א"ר הונא שהיו בה בני אדם שמכובלין בכסף ובזהב אמר ליה רבא אי הכי היינו דכתיב (ב) (ג) כי לא) ישרו בעיניו מפני שמכובלין בכסף ובזהב לא ישרו בעיניו אמר ליה אין כיון דעתירי ומפנקי לא עבדי עבידתא רב נחמן בר יצחק אמר ארץ חומטון היתה ואמאי קרי לה כבול דמשתרגא בה כרעא עד כבלא ואמרי אינשי ארעא מכבלא דלא עבד פירי: כבונות: מאי כבונות [ב]שמכבנין אותו למילת (ו) כדתנן שאת כצמר לבן (ד) מאי צמר לבן אמר רב ביבי בר אביי כצמר נקי בן יומו שמכבנין אותו למילת: והעזים יוצאות צרורות: איתמר רב אמר [ג]הלכה כר' יהודה ושמואל אמר הלכה כר' יוסי ואיכא דמתני להא שמעתא באפי נפשיה רב אמר ליבש מותר ולא לחלב ושמואל אמר אחד זה ואחד זה אסור ואיכא דמתני לה אהא עזים יוצאות צרורות ליבש אבל לא לחלב משום ר' יהודה בן בתירא אמרו כך הלכה אבל מי מפים איזו ליבש ואיזו לחלב ומתוך שאין מכירים אחד זה ואחד זה אסור אמר שמואל ואמרי לה אמר רב יהודה אמר שמואל הלכה כר' יהודה בן בתירא כי אתא רבין אמר ר"י הלכה כת"ק: **מתני'** ובמה אינה יוצאה לא יצא גמל במטולטלת לא עקוד ולא רגול וכן שאר כל הבהמות [ד]לא יקשור גמלים זה בזה וימשוך אבל מכניס חבלים לתוך ידו וימשוך ובלבד שלא יכרוך: **גמ'** תנא [ה]לא יצא הגמל במטולטלת הקשורה לו בזנבו אבל יוצא הוא במטולטלת הקשורה בזנבו ובחוטרתו אמר רבה בר רב הונא יוצא הגמל במטולטלת הקשורה לה בשילייתה: לא [ו]עקוד ולא רגול: א"ר יהודה (ט) עקוד עקידת יד ורגל כיצחק בן אברהם רגול שלא יכוף ידו על גבי זרועו ויקשור מיתיבי עקוד שתי ידים ושתי רגלים רגול שלא יכוף ידו על גבי זרועו ויקשור הוא דאמר כי האי תנא דתניא עקוד עקידת יד ורגל או שתי ידים ושתי רגלים רגול שלא יכוף ידו ע"ג זרועו ויקשור ואכתי לא דמי בשלמא רישא וסיפא ניחא מציעתא קשיא אלא הוא דאמר כי האי תנא עקוד עקידת יד ורגל כיצחק בן אברהם רגול שלא יכוף ידו על גבי זרועו ויקשור: ולא יקשור גמלים: מאי טעמא אמר רב אשי משום דמיחזי (י) כמאן דאזיל לחינגא: אבל מכנים: אמר רב אשי לא שנו אלא לענין כלאים דמאי אילימא כלאים דאדם והתנן (ז) אדם [ז]מותר עם כולם לחרוש ולמשוך אלא כלאים דחבלים (ח) והתניא (ט) התוכף [ח]תכיפה אחת אינה חיבור לעולם כלאים דחבלים והכי קאמר ובלבד שלא יכרוך ויקשור אמר שמואל [ט]ובלבד שלא יצא [חבל] מתחת ידו טפח והא תנא דבי שמואל טפחיים אמר אביי השתא דאמר שמואל טפח ותנא דבי שמואל (י) טפחיים שמואל (כ) הלכה למעשה אתא לאשמעינן

והתניא

רש"י

שית זונה. נוטריקון דשחוות: שית. בית הבשת: שכבולין. לשון כבלי ברזל קשורה: ויקרא להם. בעשרים ושתים עיר שנתן שלמה לחירם משתעי קרא: מכובלין. מעוטפין ומקושרין: עבידתא. אנגריא של מלך: חומטון. מלחה ומתבקעת: דמשתרגא בה כרעא. טובעת בה הרגל: עד כבלא. פרק התחתון שקורין קויל"ה: שמכבנין. קושרין בגד סביבו (ס) ביום שנולד שצמרו נקי ומשמר צמרו שלא יטנף: למילת. לעשות מצמרו כלי מילת (ל): מכבנין. על שעושין כמין קרסי מתכת לחבר הבגד כמו תנתן כבינתי לבתי (גיטין דף טו.) נושק"א בלע"ז: באנפי נפשה. ולא אפלוגתא דמתני': ואיכא דמתני. להא דשמואל אהא: כך הלכה. דליבש מותר ולחלב אסור: אבל מי מפים. מי מטיל גורל ומבחין איזו ליבש ואיזו לחלב והרואה אותם צרורות ליבש אומר דלחלב הוא ואתי למישרי תרווייהו: כת"ק. דמתני' דשרי בתרווייהו: **מתני'** מטולטלת. י"מ פוטלא שתחת זנבו וי"מ מרדעת והאחרון נראה בעיני דאי רצועה שתחת הזנב קשורה ומחוברת לסרגא ואיך תפול וטעמא דמתני' משום שמא תפול ומייתי לה הוא: לא עקוד ולא רגול. מפרשינן בגמ' שעוקדים ידיהם עם רגליהם בכבלים שלא יברחו: ולא יקשור גמלים זו לזו וימשוך. האחד כדמפרש בגמרא: ובלבד שלא יכרוך. החבלים בכרך אחד ובגמרא מפרש טעמא: **גמ'** בזנבו ובחוטרתו. דכיון דקשורה בשניהם לא נפלה: חוטרתו. חלדרוב"א שיש לכל גמלים על גביהם: בשלייתה. דכיון דכאיב לא מנחא לי' ול"נ מטולטלת כר קטן מלא מוכין נותנין לו תחת הזנב כדי שלא תשחית הרצועה הבשר לפי שהמשוי שעל גבה כשהגמל יורד מכביד ויורד כלפי צוארה אלא שהרצועה מעכבתו: יד ורגל. אחד מן הידים ואחד מן הרגלים כופל ביחד: יד על גב זרועו. אחד מידיו כופף כלפי מעלה וקושר כדי שלא יהו לו אלא ג' רגלים לברוח: שתי ידים. כאחד או שתי רגלים כאחד: ואכתי לא דמי. האי תנא לדרב יהודה: רישא וסיפא ניחא. כדרב יהודה אבל מציעתא דקתני או שתי ידים או שתי רגלים קשיא לדרב יהודה דלא קרי עקוד אלא יד ורגל כיצחק בן אברהם דכתיב (בראשית כב) ויעקד כפף ידיו ורגליו לאחוריו וקשר יד ורגל יחד ונפשט צוארו לאחוריו: לחינגא. לשוק למוכרם חינגא ע"ש שסובבין את השוק מחולות מחולות עגולות של בני אדם: לענין כלאים שנוי. האי שלא יכרוך דמתני' לא שייך ביה איסור שבת אלא משום כלאים אסר ליה כדמפרש ואזיל: כלאים דחבלים. שיש בהן חבלי צמר וחבלי פשתן וכי כריך להו הוו כלאים וידו מתחממת באחיזתן וקסבר (ע) דבר שאין מתכוין אסור: אי נימא כלאים דאדם. דכי כריך להן סביבות ידו נמצא קשור עם הגמלים ופעמים שהן מושכין שום דבר ונמצא אדם וגמל מנהיגין יחד: והתנן אדם מותר עם כולם. עם כל הבהמות לחרוש ולמשוך שלא אסרה תורה אלא שני מיני בהמה יחד כעין שור וחמור ומשנה זו במסכת כלאים: התוכף. בגדי צמר ופשתים: בתכיפה אחת. כגון ע"י מחט פעם אחת או שקשר קשר אחד: אינו חיבור. דכתיב (דברים כב) צמר ופשתים יחדו לא אסרה התורה אלא חבור יפה המתקיים: כריכה וקשירה. בשתי תכיפות: שלא יצא חבל. ראש החבל לא יצא מתחת ידו טפח למטה דדמי כמי שנושאו בידו ולא מתחזיא שהיא מאפסר הגמלים: שמואל. דאמר טפח לאורויי הלכה למעשה אתא לאשמעינן דהבא לימלך לפנינו אמרינן ליה טפח שלא להקל באיסורין ומיהו עד טפחיים ליכא איסור:

תוספות

עד כבלא. מפרש ר"י עד השוק כדאמר בפ' במה אשה (לקמן דף סג:) בירית באחת כבלים בשתים שמניחין הכבלים בשוק:

רב אמר ליבש מותר כו'. וא"ת לימא מר הלכה כמר וי"ל משום (ס) דאיכא דמפכי להו לתנאי (מ):

הלכה כר' יהודה בן בתירא. הא דנקט ר' יהודה בן בתירה ולא נקט ר' יוסי משום דבמקום שאין עושין כלל אלא כדי ליבש שרי ר' יהודה בן בתירא דלא שייך התם מי מפים ור' יוסי אוסר משום דילמא נפיל: ר"ת גרים

אמר רב הלכה כת"ק ושמואל אמר כו' וכן כי אתא רבין א"ר יוחנן הלכה כתנא קמא ואתי שפיר איכא דמתני לה לדרב ושמואל דלעיל אהא:

והתנן אדם מותר עם כולם לחרוש ולמשוך. וא"ת אפי' יהא אדם נמי אסור תקשה דמאי כלאים שייך הכא כיון שאינו מושך בעגלה ובקרון דהא בשבת איירי ואין לומר דאסור להנהיג בכלאים אפי' לא ימשוך שום דבר דאם כן יהא אסור להוליך ולהזיז ממקומו שור פסולי המוקדשין דחשיב כשני מינים כדאמרי' בפרק בתרא דמכות (דף כב.) המנהיג בשור פסולי המוקדשין לוקה גוף אחד הוא ועשאו הכתוב שני גופים וי"ל דה"ק אילימא כלאים דאדם והא דקתני ובלבד שלא יכרוך בחול קאמר כדאוקימנא לעיל (פ"ב דף כג:) ולא בשמן שריפה דאיירי ביו"ט ומיירי שמושכין שום דבר אי נמי י"ל דחשיב משיכה מה שנושאים שניהם את החבלים:

מ"ט

עין משפט נר מצוה

לא א ב ג מיי' פ"כ מהל' שבת הלכה יב סמג לאוין סה טוש"ע א"ח סי' שה סעיף ו:

לב ד מיי' שם הלכה ט טוש"ע שם סעי' טו:

לג ה מיי' שם הלכה י טוש"ע שם סעיף יג:

לד ו מיי' שם טוש"ע שם סעיף יד:

לה ז מיי' פ"ט מהל' כלאים הלכה יו"ד סמג לאוין רפ"ב טוש"ע י"ד סי' רצז סעיף טז:

לו ח מיי' פ"י מהל' כלאים הלכה כד סמג לאוין רפג טוש"ע י"ד סי' ש' סעיף ב:

לז ט מיי' פ"כ מהל' שבת הלכה ט סמג לאוין סה טוש"ע א"ח סי' ש"ה סעיף טז:

רבינו חננאל

כבולות מלשון כבלים כדכתיב ארץ כבול וגו' ופי' [דמשתקעא] כרעא בגוה כי כבלא שהיא עפרא וחול וזו היא חומטון. **כבונות.** מכבנין עור הטלה מיום לידתו עד ח' ימים וזהו צמר רך הנקרא (מילא) [מילת]. ר' יהודה אומר עזים יוצאות צרורות ליבש אבל לא לחלב כיון דאשתכח' ת"ק דברייתא כר' יהודה דמתניתין ורב אמר הלכתא כוותייהו הלכה כמותם ואפי' ר' יהודה לא חלק אלא אמר כך הלכה. לצרור דדי הבהמה לצמקן כדי שתתעבר הבהמה מותר. אבל מי מפיס כלומר מי המבחין בין קשירת דד ליבש לקשירת דד לחלב וקי"ל הלכתא כרב באיסורי וכן הלכתא ואע"פ שר' יוסי חולק: **לא** יצא הגמל במטולטלת כו' תנא [לא] יצא הגמל במטולטלת בחטרתא שתכנס בו הרוח אבל יוצא בזנבו הקשורה בחטרתו שלא תכנס בו הרוח. לא עקוד ולא רגול. אוקמה רב יהודה עקוד יד ורגל כעקידת יצחק בן אברהם. רגול שלא יכוף על זרועו ויקשור. ותניא כוותיה ולא יקשור גמלים זה בזה וימשוך: **ירושלמי** שלא יהו אומרים פלוני יוצא לעשות מלאכתו בשבת. פי' חינגא שוקי מלשון חגאיד חגיגת נכרים. אבל מכניס הוא חבלים לתוך ידו ובלבד שלא יכרוך. אתינו למימר הא דתנן ובלבד שלא יכרוך משום דנראה כאלו מושך האדם עם הבהמה ומשום כלאים. והתנן בכלאים בסוף פרק ח' אדם מותר עם כולם לחרוש ולמשוך אלא משום כלאים דחבלין חיישינן דלמא חבל אחד צמר ואחד פשתים וכיון שיכרוך עובר משום כלאים והתנן התוכף תכיפה אחת אינה חבור הנה תכיפה שהיא כגון תפירה אחת אינה חיבור וכ"ש כריכה שאינה חיבור. ושנינן מתניתין לא יכרוך ויקשור שנמצאת כריכה ותפירה כעין שתי תכיפות. אמר שמואל ובלבד שלא יהא אפסר יוצא מתחת ידו טפח ואסיק' הלכה למעשה שלא יהא אפסר יוצא מתחת ידו טפח כלומר אינו משולשל האפסר מתחת ידו כדי כריכה וכן לא יהא אפסר הניתן בראש הבהמה וראש

מסורת הש"ם

א) [נ"ל להם], ב) [נ"ל ולא], ג) שבועות ה: נגעים פרק א מ"א, ד) [שבועות ו:], ה) [תמיד לא:], ו) [ביצה דף לג.], ז) כלאים פ"ח מ"ו [ב"ק נד:], ח) [נ"ל והתנן], ט) כלאים פרק ט מ"י [יבמות ה: מנחות לט.], י) [ביצה כט:], כ) [ברכות כד. ושם נסמן], ל) [עי' רש"י יחזקאל כז יח ד"ה וצמר צחר], מ) [ועיין תוספות מנחות ל: ד"ה ולימא].

גליון הש"ס

רש"י ד"ה שמכבנין וכו' ביום שנולד. עי' רש"י יחזקאל כז יח: שם ד"ה כלאים דחבלים וכו' דבר שאין מתכוין אסור. עי' לקמן קמ ע"א ברש"י ד"ה אבל נוטל: תוס' ד"ה רב אמר וכו' דאיכא דמפכי להו לתנאי. כעין זה מגילה לב ע"א:

תורה אור השלם

א) וַיֹּאמֶר מָה הֶעָרִים הָאֵלֶּה אֲשֶׁר נָתַתָּה לִּי אָחִי וַיִּקְרָא לָהֶם אֶרֶץ כָּבוּל עַד הַיּוֹם הַזֶּה: [מלכים א' ט, יג]

ב) וַיֵּצֵא חִירָם מִצֹּר לִרְאוֹת אֶת הֶעָרִים אֲשֶׁר נָתַן לוֹ שְׁלֹמֹה וְלֹא יָשְׁרוּ בְּעֵינָיו: [מלכים א' ט, יב]

ליקוטי רש"י

שית זונה. כמו שתותיהם (שמואל ב' י') כלומר ערות זונה. ונצורת לב. כמו עיר נצורה (ישעי' א) המוקפת כרכום וכן לבה של זו מוקפת זימת אולת [משלי ז, י]. רב נחמן בר יצחק אמר כו'. ארץ כבלים ארץ טיט שהרגל משתקע ונכבלת בה [מ"א ט, יג]. שמכבנין אותו למילת. ביום שנולד הטלה וטהרתו אמו בלחיכתה עושין כסות ומכבנין אותו סביבו בקרסים כדי שיהא צמרו נקי [יחזקאל כז, יח]. כמו (גיטין יד:) תנתן כבנתי לבתי פרמוי"ל והוא [בית] נפש שקורין נושקא שמחברין בה פתיחות פי החלוק כך כשנולד הכבש והאם לוחכתו אין צמרו נקי [כאותו] יום והרוצה להצניעו למילת עושה לכבש מעטה עור ומכבנו עליו שלא יתפרד ונמצא הצמר מכוסה כל הימים [שבועות ו:]. מלבישים לבוש שלא יתלכלך צמרו [סנהדרין מד.]. מפים. לשון פיים [לקמן קמח:]. ובחוטרתו. דבשת. חטוטר' אלדרוב"א בלע"ז יש לו לגמל במקום טעינת המשא וע"ש שמתרקבת תמיד וסכין שם דבש לרפואה קרויה דבשת כדאמרינן בב"מ דבש והדביש חזי לכתישא דגמלי [ישעיה ל, ו]. עקידת יד ורגל ביצחק. ידיו ורגליו מאחוריו הידים והרגלים ביחד היא עקידה והוא לשון (בראשית ל, לט) עקודים שהיו קרסוליהם לבנים מקום שעוקדין אותן בו היה ניכר [בראשית כב, ט]. דמיחזי כמאן דאזיל לחינגא. אסרו חכמים משום מראית העין שלא יחשדוהו באיסור [לקמן סד:]. חינגא. מחול ועל שם שבני אדם סובבים והולכים בשוק כעין סובבות במחולות קרי ליה חגגא [ביצה לג.]. התוכף תכיפה אחת. תכיפה פויינ"ט שתוחב תחיבה אחת במחט וחיבר כלאים בגד צמר ובגד פשתים יחד. אינה חיבור. בפחות משתי תכיפות להכי כתיב יחדיו עד שיתחברו יחד יפה [יבמות ה:]. תנא דבי שמואל. בתוספתא שסידר שמואל מתנאים שלפניו כמו שסדרו רבי חייא ורבי אושעיא וכמו שסידר רבי את המשנה. שמואל הלכה למעשה אתי לאשמעינן. שהבא לשאול הלכה לעשות מעשה מורין לו אסור ואי חזינן איניש דעביד לא מחינן בידיה דהלכה דמותר ואין מורין כן [ביצה כט.]. הלכה למעשה. להורות על המעשה [ע"ז עד.].

is this possible? וְהָתְנַן – **But we have learned in a Mishnah:**[39] אָדָם מוּתָּר עִם כּוּלָּם לַחֲרוֹשׁ וְלִמְשׁוֹךְ – A PERSON IS PERMITTED TO PLOW OR PULL some other load TOGETHER WITH ALL OF THEM, i.e. any species of animal.[40]

The Gemara considers and rejects another possibility:

אֶלָּא כִּלְאַיִם דַּחֲבָלִים – **Rather,** perhaps you will say that Rav Ashi refers to ***kilayim* of the ropes.**[41] וְהָתַנְיָא – **But** this too cannot be, for **it was taught** in a Mishnah:[42] הַתּוֹכֵף תְּכִיפָה אַחַת אֵינָהּ חִיבּוּר – ONE WHO MAKES only ONE CONNECTION between wool and linen IS NOT considered to have created A forbidden COMBINATION.[43]

The Gemara resolves the dilemma:

לְעוֹלָם כִּלְאַיִם דַּחֲבָלִים – **Actually,** Rav Ashi refers to ***kilayim* of the ropes,** וְהָכִי קָאָמַר – **and this is what [our Mishnah] means:** וּבִלְבַד שֶׁלֹּא יִכְרוֹךְ וְיִקְשׁוֹר – He may gather ropes into his hand ... **provided that he does not wrap** them **and tie** them.[44]

The Gemara records another qualification of our Mishnah's law that one may pull camels by their leashes in a public domain on the Sabbath:

אָמַר שְׁמוּאֵל – **Shmuel said:** וּבִלְבַד שֶׁלֹּא יֵצֵא [חֶבֶל] מִתַּחַת יָדוֹ טֶפַח – This is allowed **provided that the** end of the **rope does not extend a *tefach* below his hand.**[45]

The Gemara objects:

וְהָא תָּנָא דְּבֵי שְׁמוּאֵל – **But Shmuel's** own **academy taught** the following Baraisa: טְפָחַיִים – The rope may extend TWO *TEFACHIM* below his hand. – ? –

Abaye resolves the contradiction:

אָמַר אַבַּיֵי – **Abaye said:** הַשְׁתָּא דְּאָמַר שְׁמוּאֵל טֶפַח – **Now that Shmuel said a *tefach*,** וְתָנָא דְּבֵי שְׁמוּאֵל טְפָחַיִים – **and Shmuel's academy taught two *tefachim*,** שְׁמוּאֵל הֲלָכָה לְמַעֲשֶׂה אָתָא לְאַשְׁמְעִינַן – it is evident that **Shmuel came to inform us** only **of the practical halachah.**[46]

NOTES

39. *Kilayim* 8:6.

40. The Torah states: לֹא תַחֲרֹשׁ בְּשׁוֹר וּבַחֲמֹר יַחְדָּו, *You shall not plow with an ox and a donkey together* (*Deuteronomy* 22:10). In fact, not only an ox and a donkey, but any two different species may not be worked together. The Torah specifies an ox and a donkey to teach that the prohibition applies only to mixing different kinds of animals, and not to mixing an animal with a person (*Rashi*).

41. If some ropes are of wool and some are of linen, then should he wrap them together around his hand, a "cloth" of *kilayim* would be encircling his hand and warming it [like a garment] (*Rashi*).

Although he has no intent to warm himself with the ropes, the Mishnah nevertheless forbids this act. It follows the view of R' Yehudah, who prohibits דָּבָר שֶׁאֵינוֹ מִתְכַּוֵּן, *something that is unintended* [see 40a and note 13 there] (*Rashi*).

Others maintain that our Mishnah is consistent even with the view of R' Shimon, who permits "something that is unintended." R' Shimon agrees that in a case such as this one, where the unintended outcome is inevitable [פְּסִיק רֵישֵׁיהּ וְלֹא יָמוּת], the act in question is forbidden (see *Shiltei HaGiborim* and *Shach* to *Yoreh Deah* 300:6; cf. *Meiri;* see also Gemara on 29b and *Tosafos* ibid. ד"ה ובלבד).

42. *Kilayim* 9:10. [The text should read וְהָתְנַן, which is used to introduce a Mishnah, as opposed to וְהָתַנְיָא, which is used for a Baraisa (*Mesoras HaShas*).]

43. The Torah (*Deuteronomy* 22:11) states: לֹא תִלְבַּשׁ שַׁעַטְנֵז צֶמֶר וּפִשְׁתִּים יַחְדָּו, *You shall not wear shaatnez;* [that is,] *wool and linen together.* From the word "together" it is derived that these materials are forbidden only if they are joined together in a lasting fashion, and not if the connection between them is weak [e.g. a woolen cloth is attached to a linen cloth with only one pass of the needle, or they are tied together with only one knot] (*Rashi*). Hence, in our case, where the separate ropes of wool and linen are merely wrapped together around his hand, he commits no transgression.

44. That is, he may not tie them together with *two* knots [thus creating a garment of *kilayim*], and then wrap the knotted ropes around his hand [thus benefiting from the forbidden "garment"] (*Rashi* as explained by *Shenos Eliyahu;* see, however, *Rabbeinu Chananel; Beis Yosef* and *Bach* to *Yoreh Deah* 300:1, 2; see also *Dibros Moshe* 43:13).

45. The end of the rope should not hang down a *tefach* (or more) below one's hand. Otherwise, it would look as if he is carrying the rope, and it would not be apparent that he is using it to lead the camel (*Rashi*).

46. In point of fact, the law is that up to [but not including] two *tefachim* are allowed. However, Shmuel teaches that if a rabbi is asked how far the rope is allowed to hang down, he should respond that less than one *tefach* is allowed. The purpose of this stringency is to prevent people from violating the basic prohibition (*Rashi*).

שית זונה ונצורת לב: הרחלים יוצאות כבולות: מאי כבולות א שמכבלין אליה שלהן למטה כדי שלא יעלו עליהן הזכרים מאי משמע דהאי כבול לישנא דלא עביד פירי הוא דכתיב א) מה הערים [האלה] אשר נתת לי אחי ויקרא (להן) ארץ כבול עד היום הזה מאי ארץ כבול א"ר הונא שהיו בה בני אדם שמכובלין בכסף ובזהב אמר ליה רבא אי הכי היינו דכתיב (ב) כי לא) ישרו בעיניו מפני שמכובלין בכסף ובזהב לא ישרו בעיניו אמר ליה אין כיון דעתירי ומפנקי לא עבדי עבידתא רב נחמן בר יצחק אמר ארץ חומטון היתה ואמאי קרי לה כבול דמשתרגא בה כרעא עד כבלא ואמרי אינשי ארעא מכבלא דלא עבד פירי: כבונות: מאי כבונות ב שמכבנין אותו למילת ג) כדתנן שאת כצמר לבן ד) מאי צמר לבן אמר רב ביבי בר אביי כצמר נקי בן יומו שמכבנין אותו למילת: והעזים יוצאות צרורות: איתמר רב אמר ג הלכה כר' יהודה ושמואל אמר הלכה כר' יוסי ואיכא דמתני להא שמעתא באפי נפשיה רב אמר ליבש מותר ולא לחלב ושמואל אמר אחד זה ואחד זה אסור ואיכא דמתני לה אהא עזים יוצאות צרורות ליבש אבל לא לחלב משום ר' יהודה בן בתירא אמרו כך הלכה אבל מי מפים איזו ליבש ואיזו לחלב ומתוך שאין מכירים אחד זה ואחד זה אסור אמר שמואל ואמרי לה אמר רב יהודה אמר שמואל הלכה כר' יהודה בן בתירא כי אתא רבין אמר ר"י הלכה כת"ק: מתני' ובמה אינה יוצאה לא יצא גמל במטולטלת לא עקוד ולא רגול וכן שאר כל הבהמות ד לא יקשור גמלים זה בזה וימשוך אבל מכניס חבלים לתוך ידו וימשוך ובלבד שלא יכרוך: גמ' תנא ה לא יצא הגמל במטולטלת הקשורה לו בזנבו אבל יוצא הוא במטולטלת הקשורה בזנבו ובחוטרתו אמר רבה בר רב הונא יוצא הגמל במטולטלת הקשורה לה בשלייתה: לא ו עקוד ולא רגול: א"ר יהודה ה) עקוד עקידת יד ורגל כיצחק בן אברהם רגול שלא יכוף ידו על גבי זרועו ויקשור מיתיבי עקוד שתי ידים ושתי רגלים רגול שלא יכוף ידו על גבי זרועו ויקשור הוא דאמר כי האי תנא דתניא עקוד עקידת יד ורגל או שתי ידים ושתי רגלים רגול שלא יכוף ידו ע"ג זרועו ויקשור ואכתי לא דמי בשלמא רישא וסיפא ניחא מציעתא קשיא אלא הוא דאמר כי האי תנא עקוד עקידת יד ורגל כיצחק בן אברהם רגול שלא יכוף ידו על גבי זרועו ויקשור: ולא יקשור גמלים: מאי טעמא אמר רב אשי משום דמיחזי ו) כמאן דאזיל לחינגא: אבל מכנים: אמר רב אשי לא שנו אלא לענין כלאים כלאים דמאי אילימא כלאים דאדם והתנן ז) אדם ז מותר עם כולם לחרוש ולמשוך אלא כלאים דחבלים ח) והתניא ט) התוכף ח תכיפה אחת אינה חיבור לעולם כלאים דחבלים והכי קאמר ובלבד שלא יכרוך ויקשור אמר שמואל ט ובלבד שלא יצא [חבל] מתחת ידו טפח והא תנא דבי שמואל טפחיים אמר אביי השתא דאמר שמואל טפח ותנא דבי שמואל י) טפחיים שמואל כ) הלכה למעשה אתא לאשמעינן

והתניא

שית זונה. נוטריקון דשחוות: שית. בית הבשת: שכבולין. לשון כבלי ברזל קשורה: ויקרא להם. בעשרים ושתים עיר שנתן שלמה לחירם משתעי קרא: מכובלין. מעוטפין ומקושרין: עבידתא. אנגריא של מלך: חומטון. מלחה ומתבקעת: דמשתרגא בה כרעא. טובעת בה הרגל: עד כבלא. פרק התחתון שקורין קויל"ה: שמכבנין. קושרין בגד סביבו ° ביום שנולד שצמרו נקי ומשמר צמרו שלא יטנף: למילת. לעשות מצמרו כלי מילת ל): מכבנין. על שעושין כמין קרסי מתכת לחבר הבגד כמו תנתן כבינתי לבתי (גיטין דף טו.) נושק"א בלע"ז: באנפי נפשה. ולא אפלוגתא דמתני': ואיכא דמתני. להא דשמואל אהא: כך הלכה. דליבש מותר ולחלב אסור: אבל מי מפים. מי מטיל גורל ומבחין איזו ליבש ואיזו לחלב והרואה אותם צרורות ליבש אומר דלחלב הוא ואתי למישרי תרווייהו: כת"ק. דמתני' דשרי בתרוייהו: מתני' מטולטלת. י"מ פושלא שתחת זנבו וי"מ מרדעת והאחרון נראה בעיני דאי רצועה שתחת הזנב קשורה ומחוברת לסרגא ואיך תפול וטעמא דמתני' משום שמא תפול ומייתי לה הוא: לא עקוד ולא רגול. מפרשינן בגמ' שעוקדים ידיהם עם רגליהם בכבלים שלא יברחו: ולא יקשור גמלים זו לזו וימשוך. האחד כדמפרש בגמרא: ובלבד שלא יכרוך. החבלים בכרך אחד ובגמרא מפרש טעמא: גמ' בזנבו ובחוטרתו. דכיון דקשורה בשניהם לא נפלה: חוטרתו. חלדרוב"א שיש לכל גמלים על גביהם: בשלייתה. דכיון דכאיב לא מנחא לי' ול"נ מטולטלת כר קטן מלא מוכין נותנין לו תחת הזנב כדי שלא תשחית הרצועה הבשר לפי שהמשוי שעל גבה כשהגמל יורד מכביד ויורד כלפי צוארה אלא שהרצועה מעכבתו: יד ורגל. אחד מן הידים ואחד מן הרגלים כובל ביחד: יד על גב זרועו. אחד מידיו כופף כלפי מעלה וקושר כדי שלא יהו לו אלא ג' רגלים לברוח: שתי ידים. כאחד או שתי רגלים כאחד: ואכתי לא דמי. האי תנא לדרב יהודה: רישא וסיפא ניחא. כדרב יהודה אבל מציעתא דקתני או שתי ידים או שתי רגלים קשיא לדרב יהודה דלא קרי עקוד אלא יד ורגל כיצחק בן אברהם דכתיב (בראשית כב) ויעקד כפף ידיו ורגליו לאחוריו וקשר יד ורגל יחד ונפשט צוארו לאחוריו: לחינגא. לשוק למוכרם חינגא ע"ש שסובבין את השוק מחולות מחולות עגולות של בני אדם: לענין כלאים שנוי. האי שלא יכרוך דמתני' לא שייך ביה איסור שבת אלא משום כלאים אסר ליה כדמפרש ואזיל: כלאים דחבלים. שיש בהן חבלי צמר וחבלי פשתן וכי כריך להו הוו כלאים וידו מתחממת באחיזתן וקסבר ° דבר שאין מתכוין אסור: אי נימא כלאים דאדם. דכי כריך להן סביבות ידו נמצא קשור עם הגמלים ופעמים שהן מושכין שום דבר ונמצא אדם וגמל מנהיגין יחד: והתנן אדם מותר עם כולם. עם כל הבהמות לחרוש ולמשוך שלא אסרה תורה אלא שני מיני בהמה יחד כעין שור וחמור ומשנה זו במסכת כלאים: התוכף. בגדי צמר ופשתים: בתכיפה אחת. כגון ע"י מחט פעם אחת או שקשר קשר אחד: אינו חיבור. דכתיב (דברים כב) צמר ופשתים יחדו לא אסרה התורה אלא חבור יפה המתקיים: כריכה וקשירה. בשתי תכיפות: שלא יצא חבל. ראש החבל לא יצא מתחת ידו טפח למטה דדמי כמי שנושאה בידו ולא מתחזיא שהיא מאפסר הגמלים: שמואל. דאמר טפח לאורויי הלכה למעשה אתא לאשמעינן דהבא לימלך לפנינו אמרינן ליה טפח שלא להקל באיסורין ומיהו עד טפחיים ליכא איסור:

עד כבלא. מפרש ר"י עד השוק כדאמר בפ' במה אשה (לקמן דף סג:) בירית באחת כבלים בשתים שמניחין הכבלים בשוק:

רב אמר ליבש מותר כו'. וא"ת לימא מר הלכה כמר וי"ל משום ° דאיכא דמפכי להו לתנאי מ):

הלכה כר' יהודה בן בתירא. הא דנקט ר' יהודה בן בתירה ולא נקט ר' יוסי משום דבמקום שאין עושין כלל אלא כדי ליבש שרי ר' יהודה בן בתירא דלא שייך התם מי מפים ור' יוסי אוסר משום דילמא נפיל: ר"ת גריס

אמר רב הלכה כת"ק ושמואל אמר כו' וכן כי אתא רבין א"ר יוחנן הלכה כתנא קמא ואתי שפיר איכא דמתני לה לדרב ושמואל דלעיל אהא:

והתנן אדם מותר עם כולם לחרוש ולמשוך. וא"ת אפי' יהא אדם נמי אסור תקשה דמאי כלאים שייך הכא כיון שאינו מושך בעגלה ובקרון דהא בשבת איירי ואין לומר דאסור להנהיג בכלאים אפי' לא ימשוך שום דבר דאם כן יהא אסור להוליך ולהזיז ממקומו שור פסולי המוקדשין דחשיב כשני מינים כדאמרי' בפרק בתרא דמכות (דף כב.) המנהיג בשור פסולי המוקדשין לוקה גוף אחד הוא ועשאו הכתוב שני גופים וי"ל דה"ק אילימא כלאים דאדם והא דקתני ובלבד שלא יכרוך בחול קאמר כדאוקימנא לעיל (פ"ב דף כג:) ולא בשמן שריפה דאיירי ביו"ט ומיירי שמושכין שום דבר אי נמי י"ל דחשיב משיכה מה שנושאים שניהם את החבלים:

מ"ט

מסורת הש"ס

א) [צ"ל להם], ב) [צ"ל ולא], ג) שבועות ה: נגעים פרק א מ"א, ד) [שבועות ו:], ה) [תמיד לא:], ו) [ביצה דף לג.], ז) כלאים פ"ח מ"ו [ב"ק נד:], ח) [צ"ל והתנן], ט) כלאים פרק ט מ"י [יבמות ה: מנחות לט.], י) [ביצה כט:], כ) [ברכות כד. ושם נסמן], ל) [עי' רש"י יחזקאל כז יח ד"ה וצמר צחר], מ) [ועיין תוספות מנחות לו: ד"ה ולימא].

גליון הש"ס

רש"י ד"ה שמכבנין וכו' ביום שנולד. עי' רש"י יחזקאל כז יח: שם ד"ה כלאים דחבלים וכו' דבר שאין מתכוין אסור. עי' לקמן קמ ע"א ברש"י ד"ה אבל נוטל: תוס' ד"ה רב אמר וכו' דאיכא דמפכי להו לתנאי. כעין זה מגילה לג ע"א:

תורה אור השלם

א) וַיֹּאמֶר מָה הֶעָרִים הָאֵלֶּה אֲשֶׁר נָתַתָּה לִּי אָחִי וַיִּקְרָא לָהֶם אֶרֶץ כָּבוּל עַד הַיּוֹם הַזֶּה: [מלכים א', ט, יג]

ב) וַיֵּצֵא חִירָם מִצֹּר לִרְאוֹת אֶת הֶעָרִים אֲשֶׁר נָתַן לוֹ שְׁלֹמֹה וְלֹא יָשְׁרוּ בְּעֵינָיו: [מלכים א', ט, יב]

ליקוטי רש"י

שית זונה. כמו שתותיהם (שמואל ב' י') כלומר ערות זונה. ונצורת לב. כמו עיר נצורה (ישעי' א) המוקפת כרכום וכן לבה של זו מוקפת זימת אולת [משלי ז, י]. רב נחמן בר יצחק אמר כו'. ארץ כבלים ארץ טיט שהרגל משתקע ונכבלת בה [מ"א ט, יג]. שמכבנין אותו למילת. ביום שנולד הטלה וטהרתו אמו בלחיכתה עושין כסות ומכבנין אותו סביבו בקרסים כדי שיהא צמרו נקי [יחזקאל כז, יח]. כמו (גיטין יד:) תנתן כבנתי לבתי פרמוי"ל והוא [בית] אפס שקורין נוסקא שמחברין בה פתיחות פי החלוק כך כשנולד הכבש האם לוחכתו אין צמרו נקי [כאותו] יום והרואה הגיעו למילת עושה כבש מעטה עור ומכבנו עליו שלא יתפרד ונמצא צמר מכוסה כל הימים [שבועות ו:]. מלבישים כוס שלא יתלכלך צמרו [סנהדרין מד.]. מפים. לשון פיים [לקמן קמח:]. בחוטרתו. דבשת. טוטר' חלדרוב"א בלע"ז יש לו לגמל במקום טעינת משא וע"ש שמתרקבת מיד וסכין שם דבש יפואה קרויה דבשת דאמרינן בב"מ דבש דבים חזי לכתישא דגמלי [ישעיה ל, ו]. עקידת יד ורגל כיצחק. ידיו ורגליו מאחוריו הידים והרגלים ביחד היא עקידה והוא לשון (בראשית ל, ל) עקודים שהיו רסוליהם לבנים מקום שעוקדין אותן בו היה ניכר [בראשית כב, ט]. דמיחזי כמאן דאזיל לחינגא. אסרו חכמים משום מראית העין שלא יחשדוהו באיסור [לקמן סד:]. חינגא. מחול ועל שם שבני אדם סובבים והולכים בשוק כעין סובבות במחולות קרי ליה חגא [ביצה לג.]. התוכף תכיפה אחת. תכיפה פויינ"ט שתוחב תחיבה אחת במחט ומחבר כלאים בגד צמר ובגד פשתים יחד. אינה חיבור. בפחות משתי תכיפות להכי כתיב יחדיו עד שיתחברו יחד יפה [יבמות ה:]. תנא דבי שמואל. בתוספתא שסידר שמואל מתנאים שלפניו כמו שסדרו רבי חייא ורבי אושעיא וכמו שסידר רבי את המשנה. שמואל הלכה למעשה אתי לאשמעינן. שהבא לשאול הלכה לעשות מעשה מורין לו אסור ואי חזינן דעביד לא מחינן בידיה דהלכה למותר ואין מורין כן [ביצה כח:]. הלכה למעשה. להורות על המעשה [ע"ז עב.].

עין משפט נר מצוה

לא א ב ג מיי' פ"כ מהל' שבת הלכה יג סמג לאוין סה טוש"ע א"ח סי' שה סעיף ו:

לב ד מיי' שם הלכה ט טוש"ע שם סעי' טו:

לג ה מיי' שם הלכה י טוש"ע שם סעיף יג:

לד ו מיי' שם טוש"ע שם סעיף יד:

לה ז מיי' פ"ט מהל' כלאים הלכה יו"ד סמג לאוין רפ"ב טוש"ע י"ד סי' רצז סעיף טז:

לו ח מיי' פ"י מהל' כלאים הלכה כד סמג לאוין רפג טוש"ע י"ד סי' ש' סעיף ב:

לז ט מיי' פ"כ מהל' שבת הלכה ט סמג לאוין סה טוש"ע א"ח סי' ש"ה סעיף טז:

רבינו חננאל

כבולות מלשון כבלים כדכתיב ארץ כבול וגו' ופי' [דמשתקעא] כרעא בגוה כי כבלא שהיא עפרא וחול רו היא חומטון. כבונות. מכבנין עור הטלה מיום לידתו עד ח' ימים וזהו צמר רך הנקרא (מילא) [מילת]. ר' יהודה אומר עזים יוצאות צרורות ליבש אבל לא לחלב כיון דאשתכח' ת"ק דברייתא כר' יהודה דמתניתין ורב אמר הלכתא כוותייהו הלכה כמותם ואפי' ר' יהודה לא חלק אלא אמר כך הלכה. לצרור דדי הבהמה לצמקן כדי שתתעבר הבהמה מותר. אבל מי מפיס כלומר מי המבחין בין קשירת דד ליבש לקשירת דד לחלב וקי"ל הלכתא כרב באיסורי וכן הלכתא ואע"פ שר' יוסי חולק: לא יצא הגמל במטולטלת כו' תנא [לא] יצא הגמל במטולטלת בחטרתא שתכנס בו הרוח אבל יוצא בזנבו הקשורה בחטרתו שלא תכנס בו הרוח. לא עקוד ולא רגול. אוקמה רב יהודה עקוד יד ורגל כעקידת יצחק בן אברהם. רגול שלא יכוף על זרועו ויקשור. ותניא כוותיה ולא יקשור גמלים זה בזה וימשוך: ירושלמי שלא יהו אומרים פלוני יוצא לעשות מלאכתו בשבת. פי' חינגא שוקי מלשון חגאיד חגיגת נכרים. אבל מכניס הוא חבלים לתוך ידו ובלבד שלא יכרוך. אתינו למימר הא דתנן ובלבד שלא יכרוך משום דנראה כאלו מושך האדם עם הבהמה ומשום כלאים. והתנן בכלאים בסוף פרק ח' אדם מותר עם כולם לחרוש ולמשוך אלא משום כלאים דחבלין חיישינן דלמא חבל אחד צמר ואחד פשתים וכיון שיכרוך עובר משום כלאים והתנן התוכף תכיפה אחת אינה חבור הנה תכיפה שהיא כגון תפירה אחת אינה חיבור וכ"ש כריכה שאינה חיבור. ושנינן מתניתין לא יכרוך ויקשור שנמצאת כריכה ותפירה כעין שתי תכיפות. אמר שמואל ובלבד שלא יהא אפסר יוצא מתחת ידו טפח ואסיק' הלכה למעשה שלא יהא אפסר יוצא מתחת ידו טפח כלומר אינו משולשל האפסר מתחת ידו כדי כריכה וכן לא יהא אפסר הניתן בראש הבהמה וראש

והתניא ובלבד שיגביה מן הקרקע טפח כי תניא ההיא בחבלא דביני ביני: **מתני'** (א) אין חמור יוצא במרדעת בזמן שאינה קשורה לו (ג) ולא בזוג אף על פי שהוא פקוק ולא בסולם שבצוארו ולא ברצועה שברגלו ואין התרנגולים יוצאין בחוטין ולא ברצועה שברגליהם ואין הזכרים יוצאין בעגלה שתחת האליה שלהן ואין הרחלים יוצאות חנונות ואין העגל יוצא בגימון ולא פרה בעור (ג) הקופר ולא (ד) ברצועה שבין קרניה (ה) פרתו של רבי אלעזר בן עזריה היתה יוצאה ברצועה שבין קרניה שלא ברצון חכמים: **גמ'** מאי טעמא (י) כדאמרן: ולא בזוג אע"פ שהוא פקוק: משום (י) דמיחזי כמאן דאזיל לחינגא: ולא בסולם שבצוארו: א"ר הונא בי לועא למאי עבדי ליה להיכא דאית ליה מכה דלא הדר חייך ביה: ולא ברצועה שברגלו: דעבדי ליה לגיזרא: ואין התרנגולין יוצאין בחוטין: דעבדי ליה סימנא כי היכי דלא ליחלפו: ולא ברצועה: דעבדי ליה כי היכי דלא ליתברו מאני: ואין הזכרים יוצאין בעגלה: כי היכי דלא לחמטן אלייתיה: ואין הרחלים יוצאות חנונות: יתיב רב אחא בר עולא קמיה דרב חסדא ויתיב וקאמר משעה שגוזזין אותה טומנין לה עזק בשמן ומניחין לה על פדחתה כדי שלא תצטנן אמר ליה רב חסדא א"כ עשית' מר עוקבא אלא יתיב רב פפא בר שמואל קמיה דרב (ס) חסדא ויתיב וקאמר בשעה שכורעת לילד טומנין לה שני עזקין של שמן ומניחין לה אחד על פדחתה ואחד על הרחם כדי שתתחמם א"ל רב נחמן אם כן עשיתה ילתא אלא א"ר הונא עץ אחד יש בכרכי הים וחנון שמו ומביאין קיסם ומניחין לה בחוטמה כדי שתתעטש ויפלו דרני ראשה אי הכי זכרים נמי כיון דמנגחי זכרים בהדדי ממילא נפלן שמעון נזירא אמר קיסמא דריתמא בשלמא דרב הונא היינו דקתני חנונות אלא לרבנן מאי חנונות דעבדינן להו מילתא דמרחמינן עלייהו: ואין העגל יוצא בגימון: מאי עגל בגימון א"ר הונא בר נירא אמר ר' אלעזר מאי משמע דהאי גימון לישנא דמיכף דכתיב (א) הלכוף כאגמון ראשו: ולא פרה בעור הקופר: דעבדי לה כי היכי דלא למציוה יאלי: ולא ברצועה שבין קרניה: אי (ב) לרב (דאמר) (ט) בין לנוי בין לשמר אסור אי לשמואל (דאמר) לנוי אסור לשמר מותר: פרתו של רבי אלעזר בן עזריה: (י) וחדא פרה הויא ליה והא אמר רב ואמרי לה אמר רב יהודה אמר רב תריסר אלפי עגלי הוה מעשר רבי אלעזר בן עזריה מעדריה כל שתא ושתא תנא לא שלו היתה אלא של שכינתו היתה ומתוך שלא מיחה בה נקראת על שמו (ס) רב ורבי חנינא ור' יוחנן ורב חביבא מתנו בכוליה דסדר מועד כל כי האי זוגא חלופי רבי יוחנן ומעייל רבי יונתן (ג) כל מי שאפשר למחות לאנשי ביתו ולא מיחה נתפס על אנשי ביתו באנשי עירו נתפס על אנשי עירו בכל העולם כולו נתפס על כל העולם כולו אמר רב פפא והני דבי ריש גלותא נתפסו על כולי עלמא כי הא דאמר רבי חנינא מאי דכתיב (ב) ה' במשפט יבא עם זקני עמו ושריו אם שרים חטאו זקנים

רש"י

והתניא ובלבד שיגביה מן הקרקע טפח. אבל כל כמה דבעי ניפוק מתותיה ידיה: בחבלא דביני ביני. שבין ידו לגמל בההוא קאמר כמה דבעי נהוי ובלבד שיגביהנו מן הקרקע טפח כדי שתהא נראה הבהמה נמשכה בו דאי לא לא מיתחזי נטירותא דבהמה אלא כמשאוי בעלמא שאין נראה שאוחז ראשה בידו: **מתני'** בזוג. אישקליטא: אע"פ. שחללו פקוק במוכין שאין העינבל שלו מקשקש להשמיע קול ובגמ' מפרש טעמא: סולם ורצועה וכל הנך דמתניתין מפרש בגמרא וכולהו משום דחיים עלייהו ואי נפלי אתי לאיתויי: עגלה. כגון קרון קטן שעושין לו תחת זנבו שראש זנב אותן האילים רחב כמין כר קטן ואין בו עצם אלא שומן ועב וכבד וכשנגרר לארץ נשרט ונשחת ועושים לו עגלה מתגלגלת אחריו כשהוא הולך והזנב קשור עליה: קופר. שרץ הוא שנימיו הדין כמחט וקורין לו הריצו"ן וקושרין עורו בדדי הפרה שלא יניקוה שרצים: ולא ברצועה שבין קרניה. דמשאוי הוא לה כדמפרש בגמרא: **גמ'** כדאמרן. שאינה קשורה בו מע"ש דלא גלי מאתמול שיהא צריכה לכך שיהא לה למלבוש: פקוק. סתום: לחינגא. לשוק למכור ותולין לו זוג להנאותו: בי לועא. שקושרין אצל הלחי: דלא הדר חייך לה. שלא יוכל להחזיר צוארו לצד המכה לחככה בשיניו וקושרן בצוארו וחשובים הן יותר מקשישין שעל גבי השבר ואי נפלו חיים עלייהו ומייתי להו בשגגה: לגיזרא. אנטורטלייר"ש בלע"ז בהמה שפסיעותיה קצרים ומכה רגליה זה בזה עושין לה כמין טבעת של עקלים או רצועות עבות וקושרין אותה למעלה מפרסות הרגל מקום שמנקשין זו בזו: דלא ליחלפו. בתרנגולי חבריהם: דלא ליתברו מאני. שקושרין שני רגליה יחד ברצועה קצרה שלא תוכל להרים רגליה ולהתיז: דלא ליחמטן. שלא ילקו בסלעים וטרשים בלנצי"ר בלע"ז: לאחר שגוזזין אותה טומנים לה עזק בשמן. עד שיגדל צמרה: עזק. צמר גפן או כל דבר רך: פדחתה. מצחה: עשיתה מר עוקבא. ניהגת ברחל זו חשיבותו של מר עוקבא שהיה עשיר ואב בית דין וכי דרך חשיבותה לכך: ילתא. אשתו של רב נחמן: דרני. תולעים: קיסמא דריתמא. קיסם של רותם שמניחין לה בחוטמה: בר נירא. עול קטן שמניחין (ל) לעגל בצוארו שיהיה למוד לכוף ראשו לכשיגדל: דלא למציוה יאלי. שלא ינקוה עלוקה שקורין סנגסו"ש: בין לנוי בין לשמר אסור. דכל נטירותא יתירתא אמרי' משאוי הוא: (מתנו) בכולי סדר מועד כל כי האי זוגא. ארבעתן יחד: חלופי ר' יוחנן. יש מחליפין ר' יוחנן ומעיילי ר' יונתן: נתפש. נענש על עבירות שבידן: בכל העולם כולו. בכל ישראל כגון מלך ונשיא שאפשר לו למחות שיראין מפניו ומקיימין דבריו: זקנים

תוספות

מאי טעמא דילמא נפיל ואתי לאתויי. אע"ג דאוקימנא לעיל דאיירי בקשורה הכא מפרש לפום משמעות ריהטא דמתני' ומשום שהאריך לעיל לא חש להאריך הכא ומתוך פי' הקונט' משמע דל"ג דילמא נפיל ואתי לאתויי: **משום** דמיחזי כמאן דאזיל לחינגא. אבל משוי אינו שבטל אגב אפסר ומשום דילמא נפיל נמי ליכא למיחש כדחיש גבי זוג בריש במה אשה (לקמן דף נח: ושם) דהכא מיירי באריג ואמר התם כל שהוא אריג לא גזרו: **דלא** למציוה יאלי. פירש"י שאנגשוא"ש דהיינו עלוקה ואין נראה דאין מוצצות אלא דם ועוד דהוה ליה למימר עלוקות ולא אשכחן דקרי להו יאלי בשום מקום ונראה דיאלי היינו נמי קופר דמתני' כדאמר בריש בבא בתרא (דף ד.) גבי הורדוס אהדר ליה כלילא דיאלי ונקרינהו לעיניה והאנקה מתרגמינן יאלי (ויקרא יא) והוא שקורין הירצו"ן: **הוה** מעשר ר' אלעזר בן עזריה כל שתא ושתא. הקשה ר"ת דאמר בפ' בתרא דבכורות (דף נג: ושם) דאין מעשר בהמה נוהג אחר החורבן מפני התקלה א"כ בזמן הבית הוה מעשר ומסתמא בן י"ג שנה היה כשעישר וא"כ מאי קאמר דהוה מעשר כל שתא ושתא דע"כ לא היה בשעת חורבן הבית לכל היותר כי אם בן י"ד או ט"ו שהרי רבי יוחנן בן זכאי משך נשיאותו אחר החורבן שנה או שנתים דכמה תקנות תקן אחר החורבן כדתנן (מ) משחרב בהמ"ק התקין רבי יוחנן בן זכאי ואחריו ר"ג היה נשיא שנתים או ג' קודם שמינו רבי אלעזר בן עזריה כדאמר בפרק תפלת השחר (דף כח:) אשתקד לצעריה (נ) לרבי צדוק וקודם לכן לצעריה לרבי יהושע על תקנת המועדות וכשהעמידוהו נשיא היה בן י"ח שנה כדאמר התם הרי בשעת החורבן היה בן י"ד או ט"ו לכל היותר וי"ל דקודם גזרה הוה מעשר אי נמי אפוטרופוס הוה מעשר בקטנותו (ס) והר"ר אלחנן מפרש הוה מעשר אחר חורבן בהמת ארנונא למלך (ס): **רב** ור' חנינא ור' יוחנן ורב חביבא מתני. פירוש מתני הך שמעתא דאמר בסמוך והשתא פסק הש"ס למילתיה וקאמר בכולי (ע) (הש"ס) (א) כל כה"ג זוגא מיחלפא רבי יוחנן כו' ולא קאי מתני' אחילוף כך קבל רבינו שמואל בשם רבינו שלמה ששמע מרבי אליעזר רבו: ואף

עין משפט נר מצוה

לח א ב מיי' פ"כ מהל' שבת הלכה י יא סמג לאוין סה טוש"ע א"ח סי' שה סעיף יח [ורב אלפס ב"מ עו.]:
לט ג מיי' פ"ו מהל' דיעות הלכה ז סמג עשין יא:

רבינו חננאל

וראש האפסר (בין) [ביד] המושך הבהמה אותו וביני ביני יגביהנו שלא יהא קרוב לקרקע טפח. וכן הלכה. פי' מטוטלת צפיחה. פי' דלא נחמטה שלא יעלה כעין עיפוש באליה. חנונות עץ ושמו עץ וחנון. ומניחין קיסם ממנו בחוטמו כדי שתתעטש ויפלו דרני ראשה. שמעון נזירא אומר כו'. גמון עץ קטן כמו עול. לא פרה בעור הקופר ברצועה שבין קרניה אי לרב בין כך ובין כך אסור אי לשמואל לשמר מותר לנוי אסור וזה היתה לנוי: כל מי שיש בידו ספק למחות ואינו מוחה נתפס עליו כו'. ה' במשפט יבא עם זקני עמו ושריו אם שרים חטאו זקנים מה חטאו אלא על שלא מיחו:

רב נסים גאון

אמר ליה רב נחמן אם כן עשיתה ילתא היא אשתו של רב נחמן ותגד דאלך (א) בסוף פרק שלשה שאכלו כאחת (ברכות דף נא) עולא בר רב איקלע לבי רב נחמן בריך וכו' שמעא ילתא ואיקפדה ובעשרה יוחסין (קדושין דף ע) אמר רב נחמן לרב יהודה נישדר מר שלמא לילתא:

חשק שלמה על רב נסים גאון

(א) הוראתו ותמצא זה:

גליון הש"ס

תוס' ד"ה הוה מעשר וכו' והר"ר **אלחנן** מפרש. עי' מ"ל רפ"ו מהלכות בכורות:

תורה אור השלם

א) הֲכָזֶה יִהְיֶה צוֹם אֶבְחָרֵהוּ יוֹם עַנּוֹת אָדָם נַפְשׁוֹ הֲלָכֹף כְּאַגְמֹן רֹאשׁוֹ וְשַׂק וָאֵפֶר יַצִּיעַ הֲלָזֶה תִּקְרָא צוֹם וְיוֹם רָצוֹן לַיְיָ: [ישעיה נח, ה]

ב) יְיָ בְּמִשְׁפָּט יָבוֹא עִם זִקְנֵי עַמּוֹ וְשָׂרָיו וְאַתֶּם בִּעַרְתֶּם הַכֶּרֶם גְּזֵלַת הֶעָנִי בְּבָתֵּיכֶם: [ישעיה ג, יד]

מסורת הש"ס

א) [לעיל נג.], ב) [לקמן סד:], ג) [גיר' הערוך הקופד], ד) [לעיל נג.], ה) עדיו' פ"ג מי"ב ביצה דף כג., ו) לעיל נג., ז) [לעיל ע"א וביצה לג.], ח) גירס' רש"ל רב נחמן, ט) [לעיל נג.], י) ביצה כג., כ) סוכה ד: מגילה ז., ל) בד"א שמנהיגין, מ) [ר"ה דף כט:], נ) [במעשה דרבי צדוק כצ"ל], ס) [וע' תוספות בכורות נג. ד"ה אלא וכו' שם דחו פי' זה וגם לתי' דאפוטרופוס ע"ש אבל בביצה כג. ד"ה תליסר וכו' כתבו כמו הכא וע"ע תוס' ע"ז יג. ותוס' יומא סו. ד"ה אין מקדישין], ע) [צ"ל סדר מועד].

הגהות הב"ח

(א) תוס' ד"ה רב וכו' בכולי' סדר מועד כל כי האי זוגא מיחלפא:

ליקוטי רש"י

מרדעת. העשויה כמין כר [בראשית לא, לד]. בשטי"ל ומניחין אותו כל היום על החמור לחממו דאמרי אינשי חמרא אפילו בתקופת תמוז קריר ליה [לעיל נב:]. **ולא בזוג אף על פי שהוא פקוק.** ואינו מוליד קול לא תצא בהמה בו וטעמא פרישנא בפרק במה בהמה (נד:) משום דמיחזי כאזיל לחינגא [לקמן סד:]. **הקופר.** האנקה מתרגמינן ילא (ויקרא יא) והוא שרץ שקורין הרצו"ן ושערו קשה כמחטין [ב"ב ד.]. קפוד. הרצו"ן בלע"ז [ישעיה יד, כג וע' כאן ברש"י ובתוס' ד"ה דלא]. **ברצועה שבין קרניה.** לנוי ואמור רבנן משאוי הוא ואינו תכשיט לה [ביצה כג.]. **כמאן דאזיל לחינגא.** אסרו חכמים משום מראית העין שלא יחשדוהו באיסור [לקמן שם]. **חינגא.** מחול ועל שם שבני אדם סובבים והולכים בשוק כעין סובבות במחולות קרי ליה חנגא [ביצה לג.]. ע"ש שסובבין את השוק מחולות מחולות עגולות של בני אדם [לעיל ע"א]. **ילתא** אשת רב נחמן והיא בת הנשיא ואשת אב בית דין וחשובה כדאמרי' בהעור והרוטב (חולין קכד.) דרב נחמן חתנא דבי נשיאה הוה [גיטין סז:]. **הלכון כאגמון ראשו.** הלכוף ה"א זו תמיהא כלומר שמא לכוף כאגמון ראשו אני צריך. אגמון הוא כמין מחט כפוף ולדין בו דגים וקורין לו איי"ם בלע"ז [ישעיה נח, ה]. **לנוי** שצובעה וקולעה לנוי בין קרניה כמין קליעה מקיף לקרן ואינו אוחזה בו **לשמר.** שאוחזה בו **אסור.** דפרה מינטרא בלא אחיזה אלא מוליכו לפניו וקסבר נטירותא יתירתא משוי הוא. **לשמר מותר.** קסבר נטירותא יתירתא לאו משוי הוא [לעיל נב.]. **רב ור' חנינא ור' יוחנן ורב חביבא מתנו.** להך מילתא דלקמן [סוכה ד:]. הא דאמרי' לקמן [מגילה ז.]. **בכולי דסדר מועד.** כל היכא דאמרינן האי זוגא כי הדדי בשמעתא איכא אמוראי דמחלפי ר' יוחנן ומעיילי ר' יונתן [סוכה שם]. שהוזכרה שם זוג זה של ארבע חכמים הללו, חלופי רבי יוחנן ומכניסין רבי יונתן [מגילה שם]. **ה' במשפט יבא עם זקני עמו.** שהי' להם למחות [ישעיה ג, י

The Gemara objects:

וְהָתַנְיָא – **But it was taught in a Baraisa:** וּבִלְבַד שֶׁיַּגְבִּיהַּ מִן הַקַּרְקַע טֶפַח – One may pull an animal by its leash **PROVIDED THAT HE RAISES** the leash **A *TEFACH* FROM THE GROUND.**[1] – ? –

The Gemara answers:

כִּי תַּנְיָא הַהִיא בְּחַבְלָא דְּבֵינֵי בֵּינֵי – **That [Baraisa] was taught regarding** the part of **the rope** that is **between** the person and the animal.[2]

Mishnah The Mishnah continues enumerating cases in which an animal may not be allowed out into a public domain on the Sabbath:

אֵין חֲמוֹר יוֹצֵא בְּמַרְדַּעַת בִּזְמַן שֶׁאֵינָהּ קְשׁוּרָה לוֹ – **A donkey may not go out with a saddle cloth if it is not tied onto it;** וְלֹא בְזוּג אַף עַל פִּי שֶׁהוּא פָּקוּק – **nor with a bell even if it is stopped up;**[3] וְלֹא בְסוּלָּם שֶׁבְּצַוָּארוֹ – **nor with a "ladder"**[4] **on its neck;** וְלֹא בִרְצוּעָה שֶׁבְּרַגְלוֹ – **nor with a strap on its leg.** וְאֵין הַתַּרְנְגוֹלִים יוֹצְאִין בְּחוּטִין – **Chickens may not go out with cords,** וְלֹא בִרְצוּעָה שֶׁבְּרַגְלֵיהֶם – **nor with a strap on their legs.** וְאֵין הַזְּכָרִים יוֹצְאִין בָּעֲגָלָה שֶׁתַּחַת הָאַלְיָה שֶׁלָּהֶן – **Rams may not go out with a wagonette under their tail.**[5] וְאֵין הָרְחֵלִים יוֹצְאוֹת חֲנוּנוֹת – **Ewes may not go out *chanunos*.** וְאֵין הָעֵגֶל יוֹצֵא בְגִימוֹן – **A calf may not go out with a *gimon*.** וְלֹא פָרָה בְּעוֹר הַקּוּפָּד – **A cow** may **not** go out **with a hedgehog skin** on its udders,[6] וְלֹא בִרְצוּעָה שֶׁבֵּין קַרְנֶיהָ – **nor with a strap between her horns.**[7] פָּרָתוֹ שֶׁל רַבִּי אֶלְעָזָר בֶּן עֲזַרְיָה הָיְתָה יוֹצְאָה בִרְצוּעָה שֶׁבֵּין קַרְנֶיהָ – **The cow of R' Elazar ben Azaryah used to go out with a strap between her horns,** שֶׁלֹּא בִרְצוֹן חֲכָמִים – **against the will of the Sages.**[8]

Gemara The Gemara discusses the Mishnah's first ruling:

מַאי טַעְמָא – For **what reason** may a donkey not go out with a saddle cloth when it is not tied onto it? כִּדְאָמְרָן – The reason is **as we said** above.[9]

The Mishnah continued:

וְלֹא בְזוּג אַף עַל פִּי שֶׁהוּא פָּקוּק – **AND** a donkey may **NOT** go out **WITH A BELL EVEN IF IT IS STOPPED UP.**

The Gemara gives the reason:

מִשּׁוּם דְּמֶיחֱזֵי כְּמַאן דְּאָזִיל לְחִינְגָּא – This is forbidden **because [the owner] looks like someone who is going to the market** to sell the donkey.[10]

The Mishnah continued:

וְלֹא בְסוּלָּם שֶׁבְּצַוָּארוֹ – **AND** a donkey may **NOT** go out **WITH A "LADDER" ON ITS NECK.**

The term "ladder" is defined:

אָמַר רַב הוּנָא – **Rav Huna said:** בֵּי לוֹעָא – It is **a brace** tied next **to the** animal's **cheek.**[11]

The Gemara describes its function:

לְמַאי עָבְדֵי לֵיהּ – For **what** purpose **is it made?** לְהֵיכָא דְּאִית לֵיהּ מַכָּה – It is tied on **when [the animal] has a wound,** דְּלָא הָדַר חָיֵיךְ בֵּיהּ – so **that it will not turn around and scratch it.**[12]

The Mishnah continued:

וְלֹא בִרְצוּעָה שֶׁבְּרַגְלוֹ – **AND** a donkey may **NOT** go out **WITH A STRAP ON ITS LEG.**

The Gemara explains:

דְּעָבְדֵי לֵיהּ לְגִיזְרָא – This is a strap **that they make for [the animal] to** prevent it from **injuring** itself.[13]

The Mishnah continued:

וְאֵין הַתַּרְנְגוֹלִין יוֹצְאִין בְּחוּטִין – **CHICKENS MAY NOT GO OUT WITH CORDS.**

The Gemara explains:

דְּעָבְדֵי לֵיהּ סִימָנָא כִּי הֵיכִי דְּלָא לִיחַלְּפוּ – These are cords **that are made for them as identifying marks so that they will not be** unwittingly **exchanged** for chickens belonging to others.

NOTES

1. This Baraisa implies that the end of the leash may extend beneath his hand as far as he likes [provided it is at least a *tefach* above the ground] (*Rashi*). It thus contradicts Shmuel, who ruled that it may not protrude even one or two *tefachim*.

2. The Baraisa refers not to the end of the rope, but to the part between the person's hand and the animal. This part may be of any length provided that all of it remains at least a *tefach* above the ground. The reason is that if the rope would be too close to the ground, it would not be apparent that someone is using the rope to pull the animal. Rather, the rope would appear as a burden that the animal is carrying (*Rashi;* cf. *Chidushei HaRan* and *Meiri*).

[However, if only a *short* section of the leash is dangling, it is permitted even if no one is holding onto it (see 52a note 30 and *Rashi* there ד״ה כרוכין לימשך).]

3. Even though the inside of the bell is stuffed with wool or cotton so that it cannot ring, it is nevertheless forbidden. The Gemara will state the reason (*Rashi*).

4. This term and all those that follow are explained in the Gemara. In each of these cases, the reason for the prohibition is that the item might fall off the animal. Since it has value, the owner, forgetting that it is the Sabbath, may pick it up and carry it in the public domain (*Rashi;* cf. *Rambam, Commentary to the Mishnah* [end]).

5. The end of the tail of these rams is wide, like a small cushion. Since it has no bone, and it is very thick and heavy, it drags on the earth. Consequently, it was in danger of becoming bruised and lacerated. They would, therefore, tie a miniature wagon under the tail, which the animal would pull along behind it (*Rashi*). [In his commentary to the Mishnah, *Rambam* writes that similar sheep were found in Egypt in his day.]

6. The hedgehog skin was tied over the cow's udders to prevent rodent from sucking the milk (*Rashi;* see also note 30).

7. In this case, the reason for the prohibition is that the strap is deeme a burden, as explained in the Gemara [see Gemara below and on 52a (*Rashi*).

8. R' Elazar ben Azaryah held that the strap is not a burden, but permissible adornment (*Rashi* to *Beitzah* 23a ד״ה ברצועה).

9. The Gemara above (53a) taught that a donkey may not go out with saddle cloth unless it was tied on *before* the Sabbath (*Ritva MHK* ed. The reason is that otherwise there is no evidence that it is needed as garment to keep the donkey warm (*Rashi;* see note 1 ibid.; see als *Rashash* here).

10. It was customary to hang a bell on an animal one wished to sell i order to make it look attractive (*Rashi*; see *Ritva MHK* ed. and *Chasar Sofer* ד״ה כתב).

11. This brace was in the shape of a ladder (see *Rambam, Commentar to the Mishnah*).

12. The brace prevents the animal from turning its head towards th wound and scratching it with its teeth.

We learned above (53a) that an animal is permitted to go out wit splints on a broken limb. The brace mentioned here, however, forbidden, because it is more valuable than the splints. Therefore, if th brace falls off, the owner, forgetting that it is the Sabbath, may carry (*Rashi;* see *Sfas Emes*).

13. An animal whose strides were short, causing its feet to knock again each other, would wear protective bands above its hooves (*Rashi*; *Rambam, Commentary to the Mishnah*).

והתניא ובלבד שיגביה מן הקרקע טפח כי תניא ההיא בחבלא דביני ביני: **מתני'** [א] אין [א]חמור יוצא במרדעת בזמן שאינה קשורה לו [ב] ולא בזוג אף על פי שהוא פקוק ולא בסולם שבצוארו ולא ברצועה שברגלו ואין התרנגולים יוצאין בחוטין ולא ברצועה שברגליהם ואין הזכרים יוצאין בעגלה שתחת האליה שלהן ואין הרחלים יוצאות חנונות ואין העגל יוצא בגימון ולא פרה בעור [ג] הקופר ולא [ד] ברצועה שבין קרניה [ה] פרתו של רבי אלעזר בן עזריה היתה יוצאה ברצועה שבין קרניה שלא ברצון חכמים: **גמ'** מאי טעמא [ו] כדאמרן: ולא בזוג אע"פ שהוא פקוק: משום [ז] דמיחזי כמאן דאזיל לחינגא: ולא בסולם שבצוארו: א"ר הונא בי לועא למאי עבדי ליה להיכא דאית ליה מכה דלא הדר חייך ביה: ולא ברצועה שברגלו: דעבדי ליה לגיזרא: ואין התרנגולין יוצאין בחוטין: דעבדי ליה סימנא כי היכי דלא ליחלפו: ולא ברצועה: דעבדי ליה כי היכי דלא ליתברו מאני: ואין הזכרים יוצאין בעגלה: כי היכי דלא לחמטן אלייתיה: ואין הרחלים יוצאות חנונות: יתיב רב אחא בר עולא קמיה דרב חסדא ויתיב וקאמר משעה שגוזזין אותה טומנין לה עזק בשמן ומניחין לה על פדחתה כדי שלא תצטנן אמר ליה רב חסדא א"כ עשית' מר עוקבא אלא יתיב רב פפא בר שמואל קמיה דרב [ח] חסדא ויתיב וקאמר בשעה שכורעת לילד טומנין לה שני עזקין של שמן ומניחין לה אחד על פדחתה ואחד על הרחם כדי שתתחמם א"ל רב נחמן אם כן עשיתה ילתא אלא א"ר הונא עץ אחד יש בכרכי הים וחנון שמו ומביאין קיסם ומניחין לה בחוטמה כדי שתתעטש ויפלו דרני ראשה אי הכי זכרים נמי כיון דמנגחי זכרים בהדדי ממילא נפלן שמעון נזירא אמר קיסמא דריתמא בשלמא דרב הונא היינו דקתני חנונות אלא לרבנן מאי חנונות דעבדינן להו מילתא דמרחמינן עלייהו: ואין העגל יוצא בגימון: מאי עגל בגימון א"ר הונא בר נירא אמר ר' אלעזר מאי משמע דהאי גימון לישנא דמיכף דכתיב [א] הלכוף כאגמון ראשו: ולא פרה בעור הקופר: דעבדי לה כי היכי דלא למציוה יאלי: ולא ברצועה שבין קרניה: אי [ב] לרב (דאמר) [ט] בין לנוי בין לשמר אסור אי לשמואל (דאמר) לנוי אסור לשמר מותר: פרתו של רבי אלעזר בן עזריה: [י] וחדא פרה הויא ליה והא אמר רב ואמרי לה אמר רב יהודה אמר רב תריסר אלפי עגלי הוה מעשר רבי אלעזר בן עזריה מעדריה כל שתא ושתא תנא לא שלו היתה אלא של שכינתו היתה ומתוך שלא מיחה בה נקראת על שמו [כ] רב ורבי חנינא ור' יוחנן ורב חביבא מתנו בכוליה דסדר מועד כל כי האי זוגא חלופי רבי יוחנן ומעייל רבי יונתן [ג]כל מי שאפשר למחות לאנשי ביתו ולא מיחה נתפס על אנשי ביתו באנשי עירו נתפס על אנשי עירו בכל העולם כולו נתפס על כל העולם כולו אמר רב פפא והני דבי ריש גלותא נתפסו על כולי עלמא כי הא דאמר רבי חנינא מאי דכתיב [ב] ה' במשפט יבא עם זקני עמו ושריו אם שרים חטאו זקנים

רש"י

והתניא ובלבד שיגביה מן הקרקע טפח. אבל כל כמה דבעי ניפוק מתותיה ידיה: בחבלא דביני ביני. שבין ידו לגמל בההוא קאמר כמה דבעי נהוי ובלבד שיגביהנו מן הקרקע טפח כדי שתהא נראה הבהמה נמשכה בו דאי לא לא מיתחזי נטירותא דבהמה אלא כמשאוי בעלמא שאין נראה שאוחז ראשה בידו: **מתני'** בזוג. אישקליטא: אע"פ. שחללו פקוק במוכין שאין העינבל שלו מקשקש להשמיע קול ובגמ' מפרש טעמא: סולם ורצועה וכל הנך דמתניתין מפרש בגמרא וכולהו משום דחיים עלייהו ואי נפלי אתי לאיתויי: עגלה. כגון קרון קטן שעושין לו תחת זנבו שראש זנב אותן האילים רחב כמין כר קטן ואין בו עצם אלא שומן ועב וכבד וכשנגרר לארץ נסרט ונשחת ועושים לו עגלה מתגלגלת אחריו כשהוא הולך והזנב קשור עליה: קופר. שרץ הוא שמימיו חדין כמחט וקורין לו הריצו"ן וקושרין עורו בדדי הפרה שלא יניקוה שרצים: ולא ברצועה שבין קרניה. דמשאוי הוא לה כדמפרש בגמרא: **גמ'** כדאמרן. שאינה קשורה בו מע"ש דלא גלי מאתמול שיהא צריכה לכך שיהא לה למלבוש: פקוק. סתום: לחינגא. לשוק למכור ותולין לו זוג להנאותו: בי לועא. שקושרין אצל הלחי: דלא הדר חייך לה. שלא יוכל להחזיר צוארו לצד המכה לחככה בשיניו וקושרן בצוארו ותשובים הן יותר מקשישין שעל גבי השבר ואי נפלו חיים עלייהו ומייתי להו בשגגה: לגיזרא. אנטורטליר"י בלע"ז בהמה שפסיעותיה קצרים ומכה רגליה זה בזה עושין לה כמין טבעת של עקלים או רצועות עבות וקושרין אותה למעלה מפרסות הרגל מקום שמנקשין זו בזו: דלא ליחלפו. בתרנגולי חבריהם: דלא ליתברו מאני. שקושרין שני רגליה יחד ברצועה קצרה שלא תוכל להרים רגליה ולהתיז: דלא ליחמטן. שלא ילקו בסלעים וטרשים בלניי"ר בלע"ז: לאחר שגוזזין אותה טומנים לה עזק בשמן. עד שיגדל צמרה: עזק. צמר גפן או כל דבר רך: פדחתה. מצחה: עשיתה מר עוקבא. ניהגת ברחל זו חשיבותו של מר עוקבא שהיה עשיר ואב בית דין וכי דרך חשיבותה לכך: ילתא. אשתו של רב נחמן: דרני. תולעים: קיסמא דריתמא. קיסם של רותם שמניחין לה בחוטמה: בר נירא. עול קטן שמניחין [ל] לעגל בצוארו שיהיה למוד לכוף ראשו לכשיגדל: דלא למציוה יאלי. שלא ינקוה עלוקה שקורין שנשוא"ש: בין לנוי בין לשמר אסור. דכל נטירותא יתירתא אמרי' משאוי הוא: (מתנו) בכולי סדר מועד כל כי האי זוגא. ארבעתן יחד: חלופי ר' יוחנן. יש מחליפין ר' יוחנן ומעיילי ר' יונתן: נתפש. נענש על עבירות שבידן: בכל העולם כולו. בכל ישראל כגון מלך ונשיא שאפשר לו למחות שיראין מפניו ומקיימין דבריו:

זקנים

תוספות

מאי טעמא דילמא נפיל ואתי לאתויי. אע"ג דאוקימנא לעיל דאיירי בקשורה הכא מפרש לפוס משמעות ריהטא דמתני' ומשום שהאריך לעיל לא חש להאריך הכא ומתוך פי' הקונט' משמע דל"ג דילמא נפיל ואתי לאתויי: **משום** דמיחזי כמאן דאזיל לחינגא. אבל משוי אינו שבטל אגב אפסר ומשום דילמא נפיל נמי ליכא למיחש כדמיים גבי זוג בריש במה אשה (לקמן דף נח: ושם) דהכא מיירי בארוג ואמר התם כל שהוא ארוג לא גזרו: **דלא** למציוה יאלי. פירש"י שאנשו"ש דהיינו עלוקה ואין נראה דאין מוצצות אלא דם ועוד דהוה ליה למימר עלוקות ולא אשכחן דקרי להו יאלי בשום מקום ונראה דיאלי היינו נמי קופר דמתני' כדאמר בריש בבא בתרא (דף ד.) גבי הורדוס אהדר ליה כלילא דיאלי ונקרינהו לעייניה והאנקה מתרגמינן יאלי (ויקרא יא) והוא שקורין הירצו"ן: **הוה** מעשר ר' אלעזר בן עזריה כל שתא ושתא. הקשה ר"ת דאמר בפ' בתרא דבכורות (דף נג: ושם) דאין מעשר בהמה נוהג אחר החורבן מפני התקלה א"כ בזמן הבית הוה מעשר ומסתמא בן י"ג שנה היה כשעישר וא"כ מאי קאמר דהוה מעשר כל שתא ושתא דע"כ לא היה בשעת חורבן הבית לכל היותר כי אם בן י"ד או ט"ו שהרי רבי יוחנן בן זכאי משך נשיאותו אחר החורבן שנה או שנתים דכמה תקנות תקן אחר החורבן כדתנן [מ] משחרב בהמ"ק התקין רבי יוחנן בן זכאי ואחריו ר"ג היה נשיא שנתים או ג' קודם שמינו רבי אלעזר בן עזריה כדאמר בפרק תפלת השחר (דף כח:) אשתקד לעריה [נ] לרבי צדוק וקודם לכן לעריה לרבי יהושע על תקנת המועדות וכשהעמידוהו נשיא היה בן י"ח שנה כדאמר התם הרי בשעת החורבן היה בן י"ד או ט"ו לכל היותר וי"ל דקודם גזרה הוה מעשר אי נמי אפוטרופוס הוה מעשר בקטנותו ° והר"ר אלחנן מפרש הוה מעשר אחר חורבן בהמת ארנונא למלך [ס]: **רב** ור' חנינא ור' יוחנן ורב חביבא מתני. פירוש מתני הך שמעתא דאמר בסמוך והשתא פסק הש"ס למילתיה וקאמר בכולי [ע] (הש"ס) (א) כל כה"ג זוגא מיחלפא רבי יוחנן כו' ולא קאי מתני' אחילוף כך קבל רבינו שמואל בשם רבינו שלמה ששמע מרבי אליעזר רבו:

ואף

עין משפט נר מצוה

לח א ב מיי' פ"כ מהל' שבת הלכה י יא סמג לאוין סה טוש"ע א"ח סי' שה סעיף יח [ורב אלפס ב"מ עז.]:

לט ג מיי' פ"ו מהל' דיעות הלכה ז סמג עשין יא:

רבינו חננאל

וראש האפסר (בין) [ביד] המושך הבהמה אותו וביני ביני יגביהנו שלא יהא קרוב לקרקע טפח. וכן הלכה. פי' מטוטלת צפיחה. פי' דלא נחמטה שלא יעלה כעין עיפוש באליה. חנונות עץ ושמו עץ וחנון. ומניחין קיסם ממנו בחוטמו כדי שתתעטש ויפלו דרני ראשה. שמעון נזירא אומר כו'. גמון עץ קטן כמו עול. לא פרה בעור הקופר ברצועה שבין קרניה אי לרב בין כך ובין כך אסור אי לשמואל לשמר מותר לנוי אסור וזה היתה לנוי: כל מי שיש בידו ספק למחות ואינו מוחה נתפס עליו כו'. ה' במשפט יבא עם זקני עמו ושריו אם שרים חטאו זקנים מה חטאו אלא על שלא מיחו:

רב נסים גאון

אמר ליה רב נחמן אם כן עשיתה ילתא היא אשתו של רב נחמן ותגד דאלך א) בסוף פרק שלשה שאכלו כאחת (ברכות דף נא) עולא בר רב איקלע לבי רב נחמן בריך וכו' שמעא ילתא ואיקפדה ובעשרה יוחסין (קדושין דף ע) אמר רב נחמן לרב יהודה נישדר מר שלמא לילתא:

חשק שלמה על רב נסים גאון

א) הורלאו ותמלא זה:

גליון הש"ס

תוס' ד"ה הוה מעשר וכו' והר"ר אלחנן מפרש. עי' מ"ל רפ"ו מהלכות בכורות:

תורה אור השלם

א) הֲכָזֶה יִהְיֶה צוֹם אֶבְחָרֵהוּ יוֹם עַנּוֹת אָדָם נַפְשׁוֹ הֲלָכֹף כְּאַגְמֹן רֹאשׁוֹ וְשַׂק וָאֵפֶר יַצִּיעַ הֲלָזֶה תִּקְרָא צוֹם וְיוֹם רָצוֹן לַייָ: [ישעיה נח, ה]

ב) יְיָ בְּמִשְׁפָּט יָבוֹא עִם זִקְנֵי עַמּוֹ וְשָׂרָיו וְאַתֶּם בִּעַרְתֶּם הַכֶּרֶם גְּזֵלַת הֶעָנִי בְּבָתֵּיכֶם: [ישעיה ג, יד]

מסורת הש"ס

א) [לעיל נג.], ב) [לקמן סד:], ג) [גיר' הערוך הקופד], ד) [לעיל נב.], ה) עדיו' פ"ג מי"ב ביצה דף כג., ו) לעיל נג., ז) [לעיל ע"א וביצה לג.], ח) גירס' רש"ל רב נחמן, ט) [לעיל נב.], י) ביצה כג., כ) סוכה ד: מגילה ז., ל) בד"א שמנהיגין, מ) [ר"ה דף כט:], נ) [במעשה דרבי לדוק כל"ל], ס) [וע' תוספות בכורות נג. ד"ה אלא וכו' שם דאו פי' זה וגם לפי' דאפוטרופוס ע"ש אבל ביצה כג. ד"ה תליסר וכו' כתבו כמו הכא וע"ע תוס' ע"ז יג. ותוס' יומא סו. ד"ה אין מקדישין], ע) [צ"ל סדר מועד].

הגהות הב"ח

(א) תוס' ד"ה רב וכו' בכולי' סדר מועד כל כי האי זוגא מיחלפא:

ליקוטי רש"י

מרדעת. העשויה כמין כר [בראשית לא, לד]. בשטי"ל ומניחין אותו כל היום על החמור לחממו דאמרי אינשי חמרא אפילו בתקופת תמוז קריר ליה [לעיל נב:]. ולא בזוג אף על פי שהוא פקוק. ואינו מוליד קול לא תלי בהמה בו וטעמא פרישנא בפרק במה בהמה (נג:) משום דמיחזי כאזיל לחינגא [לקמן סד:]. הקופר. האנקה מתרגמינן ילא (ויקרא יא) והוא שרץ שקורין הרצו"ן ושער קשה כמחטין [ב"ב ד.]. קפוד. הריצו"ן בלע"ז [ישעיה יד, כג ועי' כא ברש"י ובתוס' ד"ה דלא]. ברצועה שבין קרניה. לנוי ואמור רבנן משאוי הוא ואינו תכשיט לה [ביצה כג.]. כמאן דאזיל לחינגא. אסרו חכמים משום מראית העין של יחשדוהו באיסור [לקמן שם]. חינגא. מחול ... שם שבני אדם סובבים והולכים בשוק ... סובבות במחולות קרי ליה חגא [ביצה לג.]. ע"ש שסובבין את השוק מחולות מחולות עגולות של בני אדם [לעיל ע"א]. ילתא. אשת רב נחמן והיא בת הנשיא ואשת אב בית דין וחשובה כדאמרי' בהע... והרוטב (חולין קכד.) דרב נחמן חתנא דבי נשיאה הוה [גיטין סז:]. הלכוף כאגמון ראשו. הלכוף ה"א זו תמיהה כלומר שמא לכוף כאגמון ראשו אני צריך. אגמון הוא כמו מחט כפוף ולדין בו דגים וקורין לו אי"ס בלע"ז [ישעיה נח, ה]. לנוי. שלובעה וקולעה לנוי בין קרניה כמין קליעה מקרן לקרן ואינו אוחזה בה. לשמר. שאוחזה בה. אסור. דפרה מינטרא בלא אחיזה אלא מוליכה לפניו וקסבר נטירותא יתירתא משוי הוא. לשמר מותר. קסבר נטירותא יתירתא לאו משוי הוא [לעיל נב.]. רב ור' חנינא ור' יוחנן ורב חביבא מתנו. להך מילתא דלקמן [סוכה ד:]. הא דאמר לקמן [מגילה ז.]. בכולי דסדר מועד. כל היכא דאמרינן האי זוגא כי הא בשמעתא איכא אמוראי דמחלפי ר' יוחנן ומעיילי ר' יונתן [סוכה שם]. שהוזכרה שם זוג זה של ארבע חכמים הללו, חלופי רבי יוחנן ומכניסין רבי יונתן [מגילה שם]. ה' במשפט יבא עם זקני עמו. שהי' להם למחות [ישעיה ג, י

The Mishnah continued:

וְלֹא בִרְצוּעָה – AND chickens may NOT go out WITH A STRAP on their legs.

The Gemara explains:

דְּעָבְדֵי לֵיהּ כִּי הֵיכִי דְּלָא לִיתַּבְרוּ מָאנֵי – This is a strap **that they make for [a chicken] so that** it will **not** cause **vessels** to **be broken.**[14]

The Mishnah continued:

וְאֵין הַזְּכָרִים יוֹצְאִין בָּעֲגָלָה – RAMS MAY NOT GO OUT WITH A WAGONETTE under their tail.

The Gemara explains:

כִּי הֵיכִי דְּלָא לְחַמְטַן אַלְיָיתֵיהּ – The wagonette is used **so that [the ram's] tail will not be bruised** by stones and rocks.[15]

The Mishnah continued:

וְאֵין הָרְחֵלִים יוֹצְאוֹת חֲנוּנוֹת – AND EWES MAY NOT GO OUT *CHANUNOS.*

The Gemara defines *chanunos*:

יָתִיב רַב אַחָא בַּר עוּלָּא קַמֵּיהּ דְּרַב חִסְדָּא – **Rav Acha bar Ulla was** once **sitting before Rav Chisda,** וְיָתִיב וְקָאָמַר – **and he sat and said:**[16] מִשָּׁעָה שֶׁגּוֹזְזִין אוֹתָהּ – **From the time when they shear [a sheep]** until the wool grows back, טוֹמְנִין לָהּ עֶמֶק בְּשֶׁמֶן – **they immerse**[17] **a compress in oil for it** וּמַנִּיחִין לָהּ עַל פַּדַּחְתָּהּ – **and place [the compress] on its forehead** כְּדֵי שֶׁלֹּא תִּצְטַנֵּן – **so that it will not become cold.**

This explanation is rejected:

אָמַר לֵיהּ רַב חִסְדָּא – **Rav Chisda said to [Rav Acha] bar Ulla:** אִם כֵּן עֲשִׂיתָהּ מַר עוּקְבָא – **If so, you are treating [a sheep] like Mar Ukva!**[18]

The Gemara gives a different definition of *chanunos*:

אֶלָּא – **Rather,** the explanation is as follows: יָתִיב רַב פַּפָּא בַּר שְׁמוּאֵל קַמֵּיהּ דְּרַב חִסְדָּא – **Rav Pappa bar Shmuel was** once **sitting before Rav Chisda,**[19] וְיָתִיב וְקָאָמַר – **and he sat and said:** בְּשָׁעָה שֶׁכּוֹרַעַת לֵילֵד טוֹמְנִין לָהּ שְׁנֵי עֲמָקִין שֶׁל שֶׁמֶן – **When [a sheep] is crouching to give birth they immerse two compresses in oil for it,** וּמַנִּיחִין לָהּ אֶחָד עַל פַּדַּחְתָּהּ וְאֶחָד עַל הָרֶחֶם – **and they place one on its forehead and one on the womb** כְּדֵי שֶׁתִּתְחַמֵּם – **so that it will become warm.**

This explanation is also rejected:

אָמַר לוֹ רַב נַחְמָן – **Rav Nachman said to [Rav Pappa bar Shmuel]:** אִם כֵּן עֲשִׂיתָהּ יַלְתָּא – **If so, you are treating [a sheep] like Yalta!**[20]

The Gemara gives a different definition of *chanunos*:

אֶלָּא – **Rather,** the explanation is as follows: אָמַר רַב הוּנָא – **Rav Huna said:** עֵץ אֶחָד יֵשׁ בִּכְרַכֵּי הַיָּם – **There is a certain tree overseas,**[21] וְחָנוּן שְׁמוֹ – **and its name is *chanun.*** וּמְבִיאִין קֵיסָם וּמַנִּיחִין לָהּ בְּחוֹטְמָהּ – **They bring a chip** of its wood **and put it in [the sheep's] nostril** כְּדֵי שֶׁתִּתְעַטֵּשׁ וְיִפְּלוּ דַּרְנֵי רֹאשָׁהּ – **so that it will sneeze and the worms in its head will fall out.**

The Gemara asks:

אִי הָכִי זְכָרִים נַמֵּי – **If so,** this should be done for **male [sheep]** as **well!** Why does our Mishnah specify ewes?[22]

The Gemara answers:

כֵּיוָן דִּמְנַגְּחֵי זְכָרִים בַּהֲדָדֵי – **Since male [sheep] butt each other,** מִמֵּילָא נָפְלָן – **[the worms on their heads] fall out anyway.**

The Gemara gives another definition of *chanunos,* which is the same as the previous one except in regard to the type of wood used:

שִׁמְעוֹן נְזִירָא אָמַר – **Shimon Nezira said:** קִיסְמָא דְּרִיתְמָא – They put **a chip of *rosem*** wood[23] into the sheep's nostril to make it sneeze.

The Gemara asks:

בִּשְׁלָמָא דְּרַב הוּנָא הַיְינוּ דְּקָתָנֵי חֲנוּנוֹת – **According to Rav Huna, it is understandable why the Mishnah states *chanunos,*** for, in Rav Huna's opinion, it refers to *chanun* wood. אֶלָּא לְרַבָּנָן מַאי חֲנוּנוֹת – **But according to the rabbis** who proposed the three other explanations,[24] **what is** the significance of the word ***chanunos?***

The Gemara answers:

דְּעָבְדִינָן לְהוּ מִילְּתָא דִּמְרַחֲמִינַן עֲלַיְיהוּ – It signifies **something that we do for [the sheep],** i.e. warm them or remove their worms, **out of mercy for them.**[25]

The Mishnah continued:

וְאֵין הָעֵגֶל יוֹצֵא בְּגִימוֹן – A CALF MAY NOT GO OUT WITH A *GIMON.*

This term is defined:

מַאי עֵגֶל בְּגִימוֹן – **What is** the meaning of **"a calf ... with a *gimon*"?** אָמַר רַב הוּנָא – **Rav Huna said:** בַּר נִירָא – A *gimon* is **a small yoke,**[26] which is used to train the calf to bend its head.[27]

The Gemara gives the word's derivation:

אָמַר רַבִּי אֱלִיעֶזֶר – **R' Eliezer said:** מַאי מַשְׁמַע דְּהַאי גִּימוֹן לִישָּׁנָא דְּמֵיכַף – **What indicates that this** word ***gimon* denotes bending?** דִּכְתִיב – **For it is written:** ,,הֲלָכֹף כְּאַגְמֹן רֹאשׁוֹ'' – ***Is it to bend one's head like a fishhook*** (*agmon*)?[28]

NOTES

14. The two legs of the chicken were tied together with a short strap so that it could not raise its feet and scatter pebbles as it walked [which could hit vessels and break them] (*Rashi;* see *Mishnah Berurah* 305:55 and *Shaar HaTziyun* §50).

15. See above, note 5.

16. Rav Acha bar Ulla was sitting in the study hall of his teacher, Rav Chisda. When he wanted to say something, he rose out of respect for his teacher and requested the teacher's permission to speak; when he received it, he took his seat once again and began speaking. Hence, the Gemara mentions twice that "he sat" (*Mishnas Chachamim,* cited by *Margaliyos HaYam* to *Sanhedrin* 101a §6).

17. Literally: hide.

18. You are treating this sheep as if it were as important as Mar Ukva. [Mar Ukva was a wealthy man who held the position of *Av Beis Din.*] It was surely not the custom to treat sheep so well (*Rashi;* see *Meiri,* who states that even if one *does* treat a sheep this way, the compresses are still a burden). Therefore, this cannot be the meaning of *chanunos.*

19. *Maharshal* emends the text to read רַב נַחְמָן, *Rav Nachman.*

20. Yalta was Rav Nachman's wife (*Rashi*). Rav Nachman's point is similar to that made by Rav Chisda above (note 18).

21. Literally: in the cities by the sea.

22. The commentators ask why the Gemara did not raise this problem with the first explanation [viz. that *chanunos* refers to a compress applied to a sheep after it has been sheared] (see *Sfas Emes*). See *Rosh Yosef* for a possible solution.

23. See 37b note 5.

24. Rav Acha bar Ulla, Rav Pappa bar Shmuel and Shimon Nezira.

25. These Amoraim relate חֲנוּנוֹת, *chanunos,* to חַנּוּן, *chanun* [merciful] (see *Genesis* 43:29 with *Targum Onkelos* and *Numbers* 6:25 with *Targum Onkelos*).

26. Literally: son of a yoke.

27. By wearing this small yoke when it is young, a cow becomes accustomed to bend its head (*Rashi*).

28. *Isaiah* 58:5. God explains to the people that He rejected their fasting, because it was not accompanied by sincere repentance: *Is this the fast I have chosen ... to bend one's head like a fishhook* [in an outward demonstration of contrition]?

The verse uses a fishhook for its simile, because a fishhook is bent (*Rashi* ibid.; cf. *Kiddushin* 62b, and *Radak* and *Metzudos* loc. cit.).

The word גִּימוֹן, *gimon,* shares the same root as אַגְמוֹן, *fishhook*. This shows that גִּימוֹן, *gimon*, is related to bending.

והתניא ובלבד שיגביה מן הקרקע טפח כי תניא ההיא בחבלא דביני ביני: מתני' א) אין א חמור יוצא במרדעת בזמן שאינה קשורה לו ב) ולא בזוג אף על פי שהוא פקוק ולא בסולם שבצוארו ולא ברצועה שברגלו ואין התרנגולים יוצאין בחוטין ולא ברצועה שברגליהם ואין הזכרים יוצאין בעגלה שתחת האליה שלהן ואין הרחלים יוצאות חנונות ואין העגל יוצא בגימון ולא פרה בעור ג) הקופר ולא ד) ברצועה שבין קרניה ה) פרתו של רבי אלעזר בן עזריה היתה יוצאה ברצועה שבין קרניה שלא ברצון חכמים:

גמ' מאי טעמא ו) כדאמרן: ולא בזוג אע"פ שהוא פקוק: משום ז) דמיחזי כמאן דאזיל לחינגא: ולא בסולם שבצוארו: א"ר הונא בי לועא למאי עבדי ליה להיכא דאית ליה מכה דלא הדר חייך ביה: ולא ברצועה שברגלו: דעבדי ליה לגיזרא: ואין התרנגולין יוצאין בחוטין: דעבדי ליה סימנא כי היכי דלא ליחלפו: ולא ברצועה: דעבדי ליה כי היכי דלא ליתברו מאני: ואין הזכרים יוצאין בעגלה: כי היכי דלא לחמטן אלייתיה: ואין הרחלים יוצאות חנונות: יתיב רב אחא בר עולא קמיה דרב חסדא ויתיב וקאמר משעה שגוזזין אותה טומנין לה עזק בשמן ומניחין לה על פדחתה כדי שלא תצטנן אמר ליה רב חסדא א"כ עשית' מר עוקבא אלא יתיב רב פפא בר שמואל קמיה דרב ח) חסדא ויתיב וקאמר בשעה שכורעת לילד טומנין לה שני עזקין של שמן ומניחין לה אחד על פדחתה ואחד על הרחם כדי שתתחמם א"ל רב נחמן אם כן עשיתה ילתא אלא א"ר הונא עץ אחד יש בכרכי הים וחנון שמו ומביאין קיסם ומניחין לה בחוטמה כדי שתתעטש ויפלו דרני ראשה אי הכי זכרים נמי כיון דמנגחי זכרים בהדדי ממילא נפלן שמעון נזירא אמר קיסמא דריתמא בשלמא דרב הונא היינו דקתני חנונות אלא לרבנן מאי חנונות דעבדינן להו מילתא דמרחמינן עלייהו: ואין העגל יוצא בגימון: מאי עגל בגימון א"ר הונא בר נירא אמר ר' אלעזר מאי משמע דהאי גימון לישנא דמיכף דכתיב א) הלכוף כאגמון ראשו: ולא פרה בעור הקופר: דעבדי לה כי היכי דלא למציוה יאלי: ולא ברצועה שבין קרניה: אי ב לרב (דאמר) ט) בין לנוי בין לשמר אסור אי לשמואל (דאמר) לנוי אסור לשמר מותר: פרתו של רבי אלעזר בן עזריה: י) וחדא פרה הויא ליה והא אמר רב ואמרי לה אמר רב יהודה אמר רב תריסר אלפי עגלי הוה מעשר רבי אלעזר בן עזריה מעדריה כל שתא ושתא תנא לא שלו היתה אלא של שכינתו היתה ומתוך שלא מיחה בה נקראת על שמו כ) רב ורבי חנינא ור' יוחנן ורב חביבא מתנו בכוליה דסדר מועד כל כי האי זוגא חלופי רבי יוחנן ומעייל רבי יונתן ג כל מי שאפשר למחות לאנשי ביתו ולא מיחה נתפס על אנשי ביתו באנשי עירו נתפס על אנשי עירו בכל העולם כולו נתפס על כל העולם כולו אמר רב פפא והני דבי ריש גלותא נתפסו על כולי עלמא כי הא דאמר רבי חנינא מאי דכתיב ב) ה' במשפט יבא עם זקני עמו ושריו אם שרים חטאו זקנים

רש"י

והתניא ובלבד שיגביה מן הקרקע טפח. אבל כל כמה דבעי ניפוק מתותיה ידיה: בחבלא דביני ביני. שבין ידו לגמל בההוא קאמר כמה דבעי נהוי ובלבד שיגביהנו מן הקרקע טפח כדי שתהא נראה הבהמה נמשכת בו דאי לא לא מיתחזי נטירותא דבהמה אלא כמשאוי בעלמא שאין נראה שאוחז ראשה בידו: מתני' בזוג. אישקליטא: אע"פ. שחללו פקוק במוכין שאין העינבל שלו מקשקש להשמיע קול ובגמ' מפרש טעמא: סולם ורצועה וכל הנך דמתניתין מפרש בגמרא וכולהו משום דחיים עלייהו ואי נפלי אתי לאיתויי: עגלה. כגון קרון קטן שעושין לו תחת זנבו שראש זנב אותן האילים רחב כמין כר קטן ואין בו עלם אלא שומן ועב וכבד וכשנגרר לארץ נשרט ונשחת ועושים לו עגלה מתגלגלת אחריו כשהוא הולך והזנב קשור עליה: קופר. שרץ הוא שנימיו חדין כמחט וקורין לו הריצו"ן וקושרין עורו בדדי הפרה שלא יניקוה שרצים: ולא ברצועה שבין קרניה. דמשאוי הוא לה כדמפרש בגמרא: גמ' כדאמרן. שאינה קשורה בו מע"ש דלא גלי מאתמול שיהא צריכה לכך שיהא לה למלבוש: פקוק. סתום: לחינגא. לשוק למכור ותולין לו זוג להנאותו: בי לועא. שקושרין אצל הלחי: דלא הדר חייך לה. שלא יוכל להחזיר צוארו לצד המכה לחככה בשיניו וקושרן בצוארו ותשובים הן יותר מקשישין שעל גבי השבר ואי נפלו חיים עלייהו ומייתי להו בשגגה: לגיזרא. אנטורטלייר"י בלע"ז בהמה שפסיעותיה קלרים ומכה רגליה זה בזה עושין לה כמין טבעת של עקלים או רצועות עבות וקושרין אותה למעלה מפרסות הרגל מקום שמנקשין זו בזו: דלא ליחלפו. בתרנגולי חבריהם: דלא ליתברו מאני. שקושרין שני רגליה יחד ברצועה קצרה שלא תוכל להרים רגליה ולהתיז: דלא ליחמטן. שלא ילקו בסלעים וטרשים בלנייי"ר בלע"ז: לאחר שגוזזין אותה טומנים לה עזק בשמן. עד שיגדל למרה: עזק. למר גפן או כל דבר רך: פדחתה. מלחה: עשיתה מר עוקבא. ניהגת ברחל זו חשיבותו של מר עוקבא שהיה עשיר ואב בית דין וכי דרך חשיבותה לכך: ילתא. אשתו של רב נחמן: דרני. תולעים: קיסמא דריתמא. קיסם של רותם שמניחין לה בחוטמה: בר נירא. עול קטן שמניחין ל) לעגל בצוארו שיהיה למוד לכוף ראשו לכשיגדל: דלא למציוה יאלי. שלא ינקוה עלוקה שקורין סנשוא"ש: בין לנוי בין לשמר אסור. דכל נטירותא יתירתא אמרי' משאוי הוא: (מתנו) בכולי סדר מועד כל כי האי זוגא. ארבעתן יחד: חלופי ר' יוחנן. יש מחליפין ר' יוחנן ומעיילי ר' יונתן: נתפש. נענש על עבירות שבידן: בכל העולם כולו. בכל ישראל כגון מלך ונשיא שאפשר לו למחות שיראין מפניו ומקיימין דבריו: זקנים

תוספות

מאי טעמא דילמא נפיל ואתי לאתויי. אע"ג דאוקימנא לעיל דאיירי בקשורה הכא מפרש לפום משמעות ריהטא דמתני' ומשום שהאריך לעיל לא חש להאריך הכא ומתוך פי' הקונט' משמע דל"ג דילמא נפיל ואתי לאתויי: משום דמיחזי כמאן דאזיל לחינגא. אבל משוי אינו שבטל אגב אפסר ומשום דילמא נפיל נמי ליכא למיחש כדאיים גבי זוג ברים במה אשה (לקמן דף נח: ושם) דהכא מיירי באריג ואמר התם כל שהוא אריג לא גזרו: דלא למציוה יאלי. פירש"י שאנשוא"ש דהיינו עלוקה ואין נראה דאין מוללות אלא דם ועוד דהוה ליה למימר עלוקות ולא אשכחן דקרי להו יאלי בשום מקום ונראה דיאלי היינו נמי קופר דמתני' כדאמר בריש בבא בתרא (דף ד.) גבי הורדוס אהדר ליה כלילא דיאלי ונקרינהו לעיניה והאנקה מתרגמינן יאלי (ויקרא יא) והוא שקורין הירצו"ן: הוה מעשר ר' אלעזר בן עזריה כל שתא ושתא. הקשה ר"ת דאמר בפ' בתרא דבכורות (דף נג: ושם) דאין מעשר בהמה נוהג אחר החורבן מפני התקלה א"כ בזמן הבית הוה מעשר ומסתמא בן י"ג שנה היה כשעישר וא"כ מאי קאמר דהוה מעשר כל שתא ושתא דע"כ לא היה בשעת חורבן הבית לכל היותר כי אם בן י"ד או ט"ו שהרי רבי יוחנן בן זכאי משך נשיאותו אחר החורבן שנה או שנתים דכמה תקנות תקן אחר החורבן כדתנן מ) משחרב בהמ"ק התקין רבי יוחנן בן זכאי ואחריו ר"ג היה נשיא שנתים או ג' קודם שמינו רבי אלעזר בן עזריה כדאמר בפרק תפלת השחר (דף כח:) אשתקד נעריה נ) לרבי צדוק וקודם לכן נעריה לרבי יהושע על תקנת המועדות וכשהעמידוהו נשיא היה בן י"ח שנה כדאמר התם הרי בשעת החורבן היה בן י"ד או ט"ו לכל היותר וי"ל דקודם גזרה הוה מעשר אי נמי אפוטרופוס הוה מעשר בקטנותו ° והר"ר אלחנן מפרש הוה מעשר אחר חורבן בהמת ארונא למלך ס): רב ור' חנינא ור' יוחנן ורב חביבא מתני. פירוש מתני הך שמעתא דאמר בסמוך והשתא פסק הש"ס למילתיה וקאמר בכולי ע) (הש"ס) (א) כל כה"ג זוגא מיחלפא רבי יוחנן כו' ולא קאי מתני' אחילוף כך קבל רבינו שמואל בשם רבינו שלמה ששמע מרבי אליעזר רבו: ואף

עין משפט נר מצוה

לח א ב מיי' פ"כ מהל' שבת הלכה י יא סמג לאוין סה טוש"ע א"ח סי' שה סעיף יז [ורב אלפס ב"מ עז.]:
לט ג מיי' פ"ו מהל' דיעות הלכה ז סמג עשין יא:

רבינו חננאל

וראש האפסר (בין) [ביד] המושך הבהמה אותו וביני ביני יגביהנו שלא יהא קרוב לקרקע טפח. וכן הלכה. פי' מטולטת צפיחה. פי' דלא נחמטה שלא יעלה כעין עיפוש באליה. חנונות עץ ושמו עץ וחנון. ומניחין קיסם ממנו בחוטמו כדי שתתעטש ויפלו דרני ראשה. שמעון נזירא אומר כו'. גמון עץ קטן כמו עול. לא פרה בעור הקופר ברצועה שבין קרניה אי לרב בין כך ובין כך אסור אי לשמואל לשמר מותר לנוי אסור וזה היתה לנוי: כל מי שיש בידו ספק למחות ואינו מוחה נתפס עליו כו'. ה' במשפט יבא עם זקני עמו ושריו אם שרים חטאו זקנים מה חטאו אלא על שלא מיחו:

רב נסים גאון

אמר ליה רב נחמן אם כן עשיתה ילתא היא אשתו של רב נחמן ותגד דאלך (א) בסוף פרק שלשה שאכלו כאחת (ברכות דף נא) עולא בר רב איקלע לבי רב נחמן בריך וכו' שמעא ילתא ואיקפדה ובעשרה יוחסין (קדושין דף ע) אמר רב נחמן לרב יהודה נישדר מר שלמא לילתא:

חשק שלמה על רב נסים גאון

א) הוראתו ותמלא זה:

גליון הש"ס

תוס' ד"ה הוה מעשר וכו' והר"ר אלחנן מפרש. עי' מ"ל רפ"ו מהלכות בכורות:

תורה אור השלם

א) הֲכָזֶה יִהְיֶה צוֹם אֶבְחָרֵהוּ יוֹם עַנּוֹת אָדָם נַפְשׁוֹ הֲלָכֹף כְּאַגְמֹן רֹאשׁוֹ וְשַׂק וָאֵפֶר יַצִּיעַ הֲלָזֶה תִּקְרָא צוֹם וְיוֹם רָצוֹן לַייָ: [ישעיה נח, ה]

ב) יְיָ בְּמִשְׁפָּט יָבוֹא עִם זִקְנֵי עַמּוֹ וְשָׂרָיו וְאַתֶּם בִּעַרְתֶּם הַכֶּרֶם גְּזֵלַת הֶעָנִי בְּבָתֵּיכֶם: [ישעיה ג, יד]

מסורת הש"ס

א) [לעיל נג.], ב) [לקמן סד:], ג) [גיר' הערוך הקופד], ד) [לעיל נג.], ה) עדיו' פ"ג מ"ב ביצה דף כג., ו) לעיל נג., ז) [לעיל ע"א וביצה לג.], ח) גירס' רש"ל רב נחמן, ט) [לעיל נב.], י) ביצה כג., כ) סוכה ד: מגילה ז., ל) בד"א שמנהיגין, מ) [ר"ה דף כט:], נ) [במעשה דרבי לדוק כל"ל], ס) [וע' תוספות בכורות נג. ד"ה אלא וכו' שם דאו פי' זה וגם לתי' דאפוטרופוס ע"ש אבל בבילה כג. ד"ה תליסר וכו' כתבו כמו הכא וע"ע תוס' ע"ז יג. ותוס' יומא סו. ד"ה אין מקדישין], ע) [נ"ל סדר מועד].

הגהות הב"ח

(א) תוס' ד"ה רב וכו' בכולי' סדר מועד כל כי האי זוגא מיחלפא:

ליקוטי רש"י

מרדעת. העשויה כמין כר [בראשית לא, לד]. בשטי"ל ומניחין אותו כל היום על החמור לחממו דאמרי אינשי חמרא אפילו בתקופת תמוז קריר ליה [לעיל נב:]. ולא בזוג אף על פי שהוא פקוק. ואינו מוליד קול לא תלא בהמה בו וטעמא פרישנא בפרק במה בהמה (נד:) משום דמיחזי כאזיל לחינגא [לקמן סד:]. הקופר. האנקה מתרגמינן ילא (ויקרא יא) והוא שרץ שקורין הרצו"ן ושערו קשה כמחטין [ב"ב ד.]. קפוד. הריצו"ן בלע"ז [ישעיה יד, כג ועי' כאן ברש"י ובתוס' ד"ה דלא]. ברצועה שבין קרניה. לנוי ואמור רבנן משאוי הוא ואינו תכשיט לה [ביצה כג.]. כמאן דאזיל לחינגא. אסרו חכמים משום מראית העין שלא יחשדוהו באיסור [לקמן שם]. חינגא. מחול ועל שם שבני אדם סובבים והולכים בשוק כעין סובבות במחולות קרי ליה חנגא [ביצה לג.]. ע"ש שסובבין את השוק מחולות מחולות עגולות של בני אדם [לעיל ע"א]. ילתא. אשת רב נחמן והיא בת הנשיא ואשת אב בית דין וחשובה כדאמרי' בהעור והרוטב (חולין קכד.) דרב נחמן חתנא דבי נשיאה הוה [גיטין סז:]. הלכוף כאגמון ראשו. הלכוף. ה"א זו תמיהא כלומר שמא לכוף כאגמון ראשו אני צריך. אגמון הוא כמין מחט כפוף וצדין בו דגים וקורין לו איי"ם בלע"ז [ישעיה נח, ה]. לנוי. שצובעה וקולעה לנוי בין קרניה כמין קליעה מקרן לקרן ואינו אוחזה בה. לשמר. שאוחזה בה. אסור. דפרה מינטרא בלא אחיזה אלא מוליכה לפניו וקסבר נטירותא יתירתא משוי הוא. לשמר מותר. קסבר נטירותא יתירתא לאו משוי הוא [לעיל נב.]. רב ור' חנינא ור' יוחנן ורב חביבא מתנו. להך מילתא דלקמן [סוכה ד:]. הא דאמרינן לקמן [מגילה ז.]. בכוליה דמתניתין סדר מועד. כל היכא דאמרינן האי זוגא כי הדדי בשמעתא איכא אמוראי

The Mishnah continued:

וְלֹא פָּרָה בְּעוֹר הַקּוּפָּר – A COW may NOT go out WITH A HEDGEHOG SKIN.

The Gemara explains the purpose of this skin:

דְּעָבְדֵי לָהּ כִּי הֵיכִי דְּלָא לִמְצִיוֹהָ יַאלֵי – It is a shield **that they make for [a cow] so that leeches**[29] **do not suck** milk **from her.**[30]

The Mishnah continued:

וְלֹא בִרְצוּעָה שֶׁבֵּין קַרְנֶיהָ – AND a cow may NOT go out WITH A STRAP BETWEEN ITS HORNS.

The Gemara explains:

אִי לְרַב דְּאָמַר – This can be interpreted **either according to Rav,** בֵּין לְנוֹי בֵּין לְשַׁמֵּר אָסוּר – **who said** that **whether** the strap is **for decoration or to control** the cow, it is **forbidden,** אִי לִשְׁמוּאֵל – **or according to Shmuel,** דְּאָמַר לְנוֹי אָסוּר לְשַׁמֵּר מוּתָּר – **who said** that if it is **for decoration it is forbidden, but** if it is **to control** the cow **it is permitted.**[31]

The Gemara quotes the end of our Mishnah:

פָּרָתוֹ שֶׁל רַבִּי אֶלְעָזָר בֶּן עֲזַרְיָה – THE COW OF R' ELAZAR BEN AZARYAH . . .

The Gemara asks:

וַחֲדָא פָּרָה הֲוָיָא לֵיהּ – **But did he have** only **one cow?** וְהָא אָמַר רַב – **But Rav said** – וְאָמְרֵי לָהּ אָמַר רַב יְהוּדָה אָמַר רַב – **and some say Rav Yehudah said** it **in the name of Rav:** תְּרֵיסַר אַלְפֵי עֶגְלֵי הֲוָה מְעַשֵּׂר רַבִּי אֶלְעָזָר בֶּן עֲזַרְיָה מֵעֶדְרֵיהּ כָּל שַׁתָּא וְשַׁתָּא – **R' Elazar ben Azaryah used to tithe twelve thousand calves from his herd every year!**[32]

The Gemara answers:

תָּנָא לֹא שֶׁלּוֹ הָיְתָה אֶלָּא שֶׁל שְׁכֵנְתּוֹ הָיְתָה – **It is taught** in a Baraisa: IT WAS NOT HIS cow, BUT that OF A FEMALE NEIGHBOR OF HIS;[33] וּמִתּוֹךְ שֶׁלֹּא מִיחָה בָּהּ נִקְרֵאת עַל שְׁמוֹ – HOWEVER, BECAUSE HE DID NOT PROTEST AGAINST HER, IT WAS CALLED HIS cow.

The Gemara cites a series of statements by the Sages on the importance of protesting against the transgressions of fellow Jews:

רַב וְרַבִּי חֲנִינָא וְרַבִּי יוֹחָנָן וְרַב חֲבִיבָא מַתְנוּ – **Rav and R' Chanina and R' Yochanan and Rav Chaviva taught . . .**

The Gemara interrupts to comment on this group of sages:

בְּכוּלֵּיהּ דְּסֵדֶר מוֹעֵד כָּל כִּי הַאי זוּגָא חַלּוּפֵי רַבִּי יוֹחָנָן וּמְעַיֵּיל רַבִּי יוֹנָתָן – **Throughout the Order of** ***Moed*** **wherever this group** is mentioned there are those who **remove** the name **R' Yochanan and insert R' Yonasan.**

The Gemara now cites the teaching of these sages:

כָּל מִי שֶׁאֶפְשָׁר לִמְחוֹת לְאַנְשֵׁי בֵיתוֹ וְלֹא מִיחָה – **Whoever has the ability to protest against the members of his household**[34] **but does not protest** נִתְפָּס עַל אַנְשֵׁי בֵיתוֹ – **is punished for** the transgressions of **the members of his household.** בְּאַנְשֵׁי עִירוֹ – Similarly, one who can protest **against the people of his town** but does not do so נִתְפָּס עַל אַנְשֵׁי עִירוֹ – **is punished for** the transgressions of **the people of his town.** בְּכָל הָעוֹלָם כּוּלּוֹ – Further, one who can protest **against the entire world**[35] but does not protest נִתְפָּס עַל כָּל הָעוֹלָם כּוּלּוֹ – **is punished for** the transgressions of **the entire world.**

An addendum to this teaching:

אָמַר רַב פַּפָּא – **Rav Pappa said:** וְהָנֵי דְּבֵי רֵישׁ גָּלוּתָא נִתְפְּסוּ עַל כּוּלֵּי עָלְמָא – **And these** officials **of the house of the Exilarch**[36] **are punished for** the transgressions of **the entire** Jewish **world** if they fail to protest.

Scriptural support is adduced for these teachings:

כִּי הָא דְּאָמַר רַבִּי חֲנִינָא – And it is **like that which R' Chanina said:** מַאי דִּכְתִיב „ה׳ בְּמִשְׁפָּט יָבוֹא עִם־זִקְנֵי עַמּוֹ וְשָׂרָיו" – **What** is the meaning **of that which is written:**[37] ***Hashem will enter into judgment with the elders of His people and its rulers?*** אִם שָׂרִים חָטְאוּ – **If the rulers sinned,**

NOTES

29. *Rashi;* cf. *Tosafos*, who translate יַאלֵי as hedgehogs.

30. It was customary to cover a cow's udders with hedgehog skin to prevent leeches from sucking the milk (*Rashi*). When leeches [or other rodents (see note 6)] would attempt to suck the milk, they would be repelled by the sharp spines of the hedgehog skin.

31. These two opinions were discussed above, 52a.

32. This refers to the mitzvah of *maaser beheimah,* the animal tithe, wherein one annually separates a tenth of his newborn animals and offers them on the Altar.

Once an animal has been designated a tithe, it is consecrated as an offering and cannot be used for any other purpose. However, if it becomes blemished (one is forbidden to blemish it deliberately), it loses its sanctity and can be eaten like any other animal. On the Scriptural level the mitzvah of tithing animals is in force even when the Temple is not standing. Although they could not be offered at that time, the tithed animals could simply be left to pasture until they became blemished or died. However, after the Destruction the Rabbis decreed that animal tithes should not be separated, lest they be accidentally eaten (or shorn, or worked) while still unblemished.

Tosafos point out that R' Elazar ben Azaryah could not have been more than fourteen or fifteen years old when the Temple was destroyed. How, then, can the Gemara say that he tithed his animals every year? After all, before he reached the age of legal competence (thirteen) he could not separate tithes, and by the time of the Destruction he was at most fifteen!

Tosafos answer that the Rabbinic suspension of tithing did not occur until some years after the Destruction. Alternatively, while R' Elazar ben Azaryah was still a minor, the trustee of his estate tithed on his behalf.

33. *Tos. R' Akiva Eiger* on the Mishnah notes that the Baraisa here implies that women also are required to rest their animals on the Sabbath.

34. I.e. there exists the possibility that they will heed his admonitions.

35. "The entire world" means the entire Jewish nation, and the Gemara refers to someone like the king or *nasi* (head of the nation), who has the power to protest because the people fear and obey him (*Rashi*).

36. He was the leader of the exiled Jewish community in Babylonia. His authority was such that his protests could have borne fruit.

37. *Isaiah* 3:14.

אֶלָּא וּזְקֵנִים מֶה חָטְאוּ – still, **what sin did the elders commit?**[1] אֵימָא עַל זְקֵנִים שֶׁלֹּא מִיחוּ בַּשָּׂרִים – **Rather, say** that Scripture speaks **about elders who did not protest against** the sinful actions of **the leaders,** and were therefore brought to judgment by God.

The Gemara relates an anecdote that throws further light on the subject of protesting against wrongdoing:

רַב יְהוּדָה הֲוָה יָתִיב קַמֵּיהּ דִּשְׁמוּאֵל – **Rav Yehudah was** once **sitting before Shmuel** to observe him judging cases of law. אֲתַאי הַהִיא אִיתְּתָא – **A certain woman entered** the court קָא צָוְוחָה קַמֵּיהּ – **and cried out before him** about an injustice committed against her, וְלָא הֲוָה מַשְׁגַּח בָּהּ – **but [Shmuel] paid no attention to her.** אָמַר לֵיהּ לָא סָבַר לֵיהּ מַר – [Rav Yehudah] thereupon **said to [Shmuel]: Does master not hold**[2] that ,,אֹטֵם אָזְנוֹ מִזַּעֲקַת־דָּל גַּם־הוּא יִקְרָא וְלֹא יֵעָנֶה'' – *he who closes his ears to the outcry of the poor – he, too, will call and not be answered?*[3] אָמַר לֵיהּ שִׁינָּנָא – **[Shmuel] replied to him: Sharp one!**[4] רֵישָׁךְ בְּקָרִירֵי – **Your head is in cool water;** רֵישָׁא דְּרֵישָׁךְ בְּחַמִּימֵי – it is **your head's head** that **is in hot water,**[5] הָא יָתִיב מַר עוּקְבָא אַב בֵּית דִּין – **for Mar Ukva is sitting** and judging cases **as president of the Rabbinical court,** and so the ultimate responsibility is his, דִּכְתִיב ,,בֵּית דָּוִד כֹּה אָמַר ה' דִּינוּ לַבֹּקֶר מִשְׁפָּט וְהַצִּילוּ גָזוּל מִיַּד עוֹשֵׁק פֶּן־תֵּצֵא כָאֵשׁ חֲמָתִי וּבָעֲרָה וְאֵין מְכַבֶּה מִפְּנֵי רֹעַ מַעַלְלֵיהֶם וגו' '' – **as it is written:**[6] *O House of David, thus said Hashem: Execute judgment in the morning and rescue the robbed from the hand of the oppressor, lest My wrath go forth like fire, and consume that none can quench* [it], *because of the evil of their deeds* **etc.**[7]

The Gemara further discusses the importance of protesting against wrongdoing:

אָמַר לֵיהּ רַבִּי זֵירָא לְרַבִּי סִימוֹן – **R' Zeira** once **said to R' Simon:** לוֹכְחִינְהוּ מַר לְהָנֵי דְּבֵי רֵישׁ גָּלוּתָא – **Master should reprove these** officials **of the House of the Exilarch** for their transgressions! אָמַר לֵיהּ לָא מְקַבְּלֵי מִינָּאִי – **[R' Simon] said to him** in reply: **They do not accept** reproof **from me.** אָמַר לֵיהּ אַף עַל גַּב דְּלָא מְקַבְּלֵי לוֹכְחִינְהוּ מַר – **[R' Zeira]** thereupon **said to [R' Simon]: Even though they do not accept** it, **master should** nonetheless **reprove them,**[8] דְּאָמַר רַבִּי אַחָא בְּרַבִּי חֲנִינָא – **for R' Acha the son of R' Chanina said:** מֵעוֹלָם לֹא יָצְתָה מִדָּה טוֹבָה מִפִּי הַקָּדוֹשׁ בָּרוּךְ הוּא וְחָזַר בָּהּ לְרָעָה – **A good decree never issued from the mouth of the Holy One, Blessed is He, and** then **He retracted it for bad** חוּץ מִדָּבָר זֶה – **except** in **this matter** of failing to rebuke,[9] דִּכְתִיב ,,וַיֹּאמֶר ה' אֵלָיו עֲבֹר בְּתוֹךְ הָעִיר בְּתוֹךְ יְרוּשָׁלָיִם וְהִתְוִיתָ תָּו עַל מִצְחוֹת הָאֲנָשִׁים הַנֶּאֱנָחִים וְהַנֶּאֱנָקִים עַל כָּל הַתּוֹעֵבוֹת הַנַּעֲשׂוֹת בְּתוֹכָהּ וגו' '' – **as it is written:**[10] *Hashem said to* [the angel]: *Pass through the city, through Jerusalem, and mark the letter tav on the foreheads of the people who sigh and moan over all the abominations that are done in its midst.*[11]

R' Acha explains this verse:

אָמַר לוֹ הַקָּדוֹשׁ בָּרוּךְ הוּא לְגַבְרִיאֵל – **The Holy One, Blessed is He, said to** the angel **Gavriel:** לֵךְ וּרְשׁוֹם עַל מִצְחָן שֶׁל צַדִּיקִים תָּיו שֶׁל דְּיוֹ – **Go and mark a** *tav* **of ink on the foreheads of the righteous,** שֶׁלֹּא יִשְׁלְטוּ בָּהֶם מַלְאֲכֵי חַבָּלָה – **so that the angels of destruction** that I wish to send upon the city **shall have no power over them;** וְעַל מִצְחָם שֶׁל רְשָׁעִים תָּיו שֶׁל דָּם – **and on the foreheads of the wicked** set **a** *tav* **of blood,**[12] כְּדֵי שֶׁיִּשְׁלְטוּ בָּהֶן מַלְאֲכֵי חַבָּלָה – **so that the angels of destruction shall have power over them.** אָמְרָה מִדַּת הַדִּין לִפְנֵי הַקָּדוֹשׁ בָּרוּךְ הוּא – **Said the Attribute of** Strict **Justice before the Holy One, Blessed is He:** רִבּוֹנוֹ שֶׁל עוֹלָם מַה נִּשְׁתַּנּוּ אֵלּוּ מֵאֵלּוּ – **Master of the Universe, what is the difference between these and these?** אָמַר לָהּ הַלָּלוּ צַדִּיקִים גְּמוּרִים וְהַלָּלוּ רְשָׁעִים גְּמוּרִים – **[God] replied: These are completely righteous and these are completely wicked.** אָמְרָה לְפָנָיו – **[Strict Justice]** then **said before [God]:** רִבּוֹנוֹ שֶׁל עוֹלָם הָיָה בְּיָדָם לְמַחוֹת וְלֹא מִיחוּ – **Master of the Universe, [the righteous] had the opportunity to protest** the abominations, **but they did not protest!** אָמַר לָהּ גָּלוּי וְיָדוּעַ לְפָנַי שֶׁאִם מִיחוּ בָּהֶם לֹא יְקַבְּלוּ מֵהֶם – **[God] said to [Strict Justice]** in reply: **It is revealed and known to Me that if they had protested against**

NOTES

1. "Elders" refers to the members of the Sanhedrin (*Rashi*).

The commentators ask: How did R' Chanina know that the "elders" mentioned in the verse did not also sin? *Maharsha* explains that while it is true that some elders (Torah scholars) did sin before the destruction of the First Temple (see *Ezekiel* 8:12), nevertheless, in this passage of *Isaiah* the prophet speaks only about the sins of the rulers (see ibid. 1:23). R' Chanina thus infers that our verse refers to those elders who did not sin (for another answer, see *Rif* to *Ein Yaakov*).

2. *Maharsha* asks: How could Rav Yehudah ask whether Shmuel "holds" like the verse? Of course he must! Rather, Rav Yehudah should have phrased his question differently: "Does the verse not say . . .?" *Maharsha* explains that the verse refers primarily to one who refuses to give charity. Rav Yehudah therefore asked Shmuel: "Does master not hold" that the verse refers also to one who refuses to judge the case of a pauper?

3. *Proverbs* 21:13.

4. Shmuel often called Rav Yehudah by this sobriquet because the latter possessed sharp analytical ability (*Mesoras HaShas* to *Chagigah* 15b).

5. Shmuel replied: I, who am your head (i.e. your teacher), will not be scalded. However, Mar Ukva, who as president of the *Beis Din* is the head over both you and me – he will be scalded by hot water (*Rashi;* see *Meiri*), since he is the one with the power to help this woman.

6. *Jeremiah* 21:12.

7. From this verse, argued Shmuel, we learn that Hashem punishes only those who have the power to judge (*Rashi*).

Mar Ukva was descended from King David. Since the verse, which was addressed to the House of David, speaks of a "consuming fire," Shmuel's reply to Rav Yehudah was couched in the metaphor of scalding (*Maharsha*).

8. R' Zeira urged R' Simon to rebuke the errant officials because there was some chance that they might listen. However, where it is known for certain that the transgressors will not listen, one should not reprove them, but should follow the principle: "Leave them be – it is better that they sin unintentionally than sin intentionally" (*Tosafos;* see *Chidushei HaRan*). See *Orach Chaim* 608:2 for the halachic parameter of this law; see also *Rosh Yosef* and *Sfas Emes* here; and see *Yevamos* 65.

9. Which is mentioned in the following verses, where Hashem issued a favorable decree and then retracted it in order to punish those who failed to rebuke (*Rashi*).

10. *Ezekiel* 9:4, which appears in a passage that describes Ezekiel's vision of angels of destruction arriving in Jerusalem and Hashem commanding them to wreak havoc among the people.

11. These are the righteous (*Rashi*).

12. *Tosafos* point out that the verse mentions only that the righteous are marked with a *tav*. How does R' Acha know that the wicked were also marked? *Tosafos* answer that R' Acha derived it logically; however, *Tosafos* does not explain the logic.

Maharsha questions why it was even necessary to mark the wicked. Once the righteous were set apart for salvation, it was visually obvious to the angels who deserved destruction. *Maharsha* explains that it was necessary to mark both the righteous and the wicked because there existed a third group – the intermediates (*beinonim*) – that deserved neither salvation nor total destruction. This middle category is intimated in the Gemara below, where Hashem says of the two groups to be marked: "These are completely righteous and these are completely wicked."

Maharsha also finds an allusion to the wicked in the verse, which mentions the people *who sigh and moan.* That is, the righteous will *sigh* about the abominations committed in Jerusalem, and the wicked will *moan* after their deaths.

זקנים מה חטאו אלא אימא על זקנים שלא מיחו בשרים • רב יהודה הוה יתיב קמיה דשמואל אתאי ההיא איתתא קא צווחה קמיה ולא הוה משגח בה א"ל לא סבר ליה מר א) אוטם אזנו מזעקת דל גם הוא יקרא ולא יענה א"ל ב) שיננא רישך בקרירי רישא דרישך בחמימי הא יתיב מר עוקבא אב ב"ד דכתיב ב) בית דוד כה אמר ה' דינו לבקר משפט והצילו גזול מיד עושק פן תצא כאש חמתי ובערה ואין מכבה מפני רוע מעלליהם וגו' • א"ל ר' זירא לר' סימון לוכחינהו מר להני דבי ריש גלותא א"ל לא מקבלי מינאי א"ל אע"ג דלא מקבלי לוכחינהו מר דא"ר אחא בר' חנינא מעולם לא יצתה מדה טובה מפי הקב"ה וחזר בה לרעה חוץ מדבר זה דכתיב ג) ויאמר ה' אליו עבור בתוך העיר בתוך ירושלים והתוית תיו על מצחות האנשים הנאנחים והנאנקים על כל התועבות הנעשות בתוכה וגו' א"ל הקב"ה לגבריאל לך ורשום על מצחן של צדיקים תיו של דיו שלא ישלטו בהם מלאכי חבלה ועל מצחם של רשעים תיו של דם כדי שישלטו בהן מלאכי חבלה אמרה מדת הדין לפני הקב"ה רבש"ע מה נשתנו אלו מאלו אמר לה הללו צדיקים גמורים והללו רשעים גמורים אמרה לפניו רבש"ע היה בידם למחות ולא מיחו אמר לה גלוי וידוע לפני שאם מיחו בהם לא יקבלו מהם (ג) אמר) לפניו רבש"ע אם לפניך גלוי להם מי גלוי והיינו דכתיב ד) זקן בחור ובתולה טף ונשים תהרגו למשחית ועל כל איש אשר עליו התיו אל תגשו וממקדשי תחלו וכתיב ה) ויחלו באנשים הזקנים אשר לפני הבית ג) תני רב יוסף אל תקרי מקדשי אלא מקודשי אלו בני אדם שקיימו את התורה כולה מאלף ועד תיו ומיד ה) והנה ששה אנשים באים מדרך שער העליון אשר מפנה צפונה ואיש כלי מפצו בידו ואיש אחד בתוכם לבוש הבדים וקסת הסופר במתניו ויבאו ויעמדו אצל מזבח הנחושת מזבח הנחושת מי הוה אמר להו הקב"ה התחילו ממקום שאומרים שירה לפני ומאן נינהו ששה אנשים א"ר חסדא קצף אף וחימה ומשחית ומשבר ומכלה ומ"ש תיו אמר רב תיו תחיה תיו תמות ושמואל אמר תמה זכות אבות ורבי יוחנן אמר תחון זכות אבות ור"ל אמר תיו סוף חותמו של הקב"ה ד) דאמר רבי חנינא חותמו של הקב"ה אמת (אמר) ר' שמואל בר נחמני ה) אלו בני אדם שקיימו את התור' כולה מאלף ועד תיו מאימתי תמה זכות אבות • אמר רב מימות הושע בן בארי שנא' ו) אגלה את נבלתה לעיני מאהביה ואיש לא יצילנה מידי ושמואל אמר מימי חזאל שנאמר ז) וחזאל מלך ארם לחץ את ישראל כל ימי יהואחז וכתיב ח) ויחן ה' אותם וירחמם ויפן אליהם למען בריתו את אברהם יצחק ויעקב ולא אבה השחיתם ולא השליכם מעל פניו עד עתה ר' יהושע בן לוי אמר מימי אליהו שנאמר ט) ויהי בעלות המנחה ויגש אליהו הנביא ויאמר ה' אלהי אברהם יצחק וישראל היום יודע כי אתה אלהים בישראל ואני עבדך ובדברך עשיתי [את] כל הדברים האלה וגו' ורבי יוחנן אמר מימי חזקיהו שנאמר י) למרבה המשרה ולשלום אין קץ על כסא דוד ועל ממלכתו להכין אותה ולסעדה במשפט ובצדקה מעתה ועד עולם קנאת ה' צבאות תעשה זאת וגו': אמר רב אמי אין מיתה בלא חטא ואין יסורין בלא עון אין מיתה בלא חטא דכתיב כ) הנפש החוטאת היא תמות בן לא ישא בעון האב ואב לא ישא בעון הבן צדקת הצדיק עליו תהיה ורשעת הרשע עליו תהיה וגו' אין יסורין בלא עון דכתיב ל) ופקדתי בשבט פשעם ובנגעים עונם מיתיבי

רש"י

זקנים. סנהדרין: רישך בקרירי. אני שאני רבך איני נכוה אבל מר עוקבא שהוא ראש לי ולך ואב ב"ד יכווה בחמין: דכתיב בית דוד וגו'. לא ענש אלא מי שבידו לשפוט: חוץ מדבר זה. שנא' במקרא זה שהוציא דבור לטובה ומפני עונש תוכחה חזר בו: והתוית תיו על מצחות האנשים הנאנחים והנאנקים על כל התועבות הנעשות בתוכה. אלו לדיקים: שלא ישלטו בהם מלאכי חבלה. שאני רוצה לשלוח בעיר: היינו דכתיב. מעיקרא ועל כל איש אשר עליו התיו אל תגשו ולבסוף וממקדשי תחלו: ממקודשי. שהודה למקטרג מדת הדין וחזר מן הטוב: מי הוה מזבח הנחשת. בימי יחזקאל והלא שלמה גנזו ועשה מזבח אבנים של ל"ב אמה דכתיב (מלכים א ח) כי מזבח הנחשת אשר לפני ה' קטן מהכיל ו) כאדם האומר לחבירו ננס פלוני ופסול לעבודה: ממקום שאומרים שירה. מן הלוים שאומרים שיר בכלי נחשת: תיו תמות. לרשעים: חותמו של הקב"ה אמת. אמצעית לאותיות וראשון ואחרון על שם אני ראשון ואני אחרון ואני הוא: אלו בני אדם שקיימו התורה כולה. התיו סימן להם שקיימו התורה מראש עד סוף: ואיש לא יצילנה. שאין עוד זכות לאבות שאכלוה: ויפן אליהם למען בריתו את אברהם וגו' ולא השליכם מעל פניו עד עתה. אבל מכאן ואילך השליכם ולא פנה אל ברית אבות: ה' אלהי אברהם ואלהי יצחק וישראל היום יודע. שאתה זוכר ברית אברהם יצחק וישראל מדקאמר היום יודע ותו לא מכלל דתמה ועל ידי רחמים החזרה להם בימי חזאל: בימי חזקיהו. דכתיב מעתה ועד עולם קנאת ה' צבאות תעשה זאת ולא זכות אבות: בלא חטא. וחטאו של אדם גורם לו מיתה: בשבט ובנגעים. היינו יסורים וקאמר שאין באין אלא משום פקידת עון:

בעטיו

תוספות

ואע"ג דלא מקבלי לוכחינהו מר. היינו היכא דספק אי מקבלי כדאמר בסמוך לפניהם מי גלוי אבל היכא דודאי לא מקבלי הנח להם מוטב שיהו שוגגין ואל יהיו מזידין כדאמרינן בהמביא כדי יין (ביצה דף ל. ושם) ובפרק שואל (לקמן דף קמח:) גבי תוספת יוה"כ ז):

ועל הרשעים תיו של דם. לא מקרא קאמר הכי אלא מסברא' דהא דכתיב והתוית תיו על מצחות האנשים הנאנחים והנאנקים על כל התועבות הנעשות בתוכה היינו בצדיקים גמורים: מזבח נחשת בימי שלמה מי הוה. כדכתיב שלמה הסירו כי היה קטן מהכיל וא"ת והא כתיב בדברי הימים (ב ד) ויעש שלמה את מזבח הנחשת וי"ל דדרשינן ליה כי הכא מזבח שאומרים לפניו • שירה בכלי נחשת:

קצף אף וחימה. קשה לרשב"א דאמר בפ"ק דמסכת ע"ג (דף ד. ושם) כתיב חימה אין לי וכתיב נוקם ה' ובעל חימה ומשני כאן לישראל כאן לנכרים אלמא דאין להקב"ה חימה על ישראל והאיא דמס' ע"ג קשה דבס"פ ארבעה נדרים (דף לב.) אמר חימה משה הרגו דכתיב חימה אין לי ופריך והא כתיב כי יגורתי מפני האף והחימה ומשני תרי חימה הוו:

ושמואל אמר תמה זכות אבות ורבי יוחנן אמר תחון זכות אבות. אומר רבינו תם דזכות אבות תמה אבל ברית אבות לא תמה דהא כתיב (ויקרא כו) וזכרתי את בריתי יעקוב אף לאחר גלות ואנן אין אנו מזכירין זכות אבות אלא הברית • ומפרש דשמואל דאמר מימי חזאל דייק מדכתיב למען בריתו ולא למען זכותו ואומר ר"י דבויקרא רבה (פ' לו) דייק מעד עתה כדפי' בקונטרס ולר"י נראה דלא פליגי שמואל ור"י אלא שמואל קאמר דלרשעים תמה אבל לצדיקים לא תמה ובצדיקים איירי ר"י תדע דהא ר"י אמר בסמוך דמימי חזקי' תמה זכות אבות והכא קאמר דאף בשעת חורבן דבתר הכי תחון זכות אבות ועל זה אנו סומכין להזכיר זכות אבות ובשלהי ויקרא רבה רבי אחא אומר לעולם זכות אבות קיימת ולעולם אנו מזכירים אותם וכן הוא אומר כי אל רחום וגו' ולא ישכח את ברית אבותיך וגו':

אין מיתה בלא חטא. פי' (מיתה) לפי שהגזרה באה אף על השגגה ואין יסורים בלא עון של מזיד כדאמר ביומא (דף לו:) חטאים אלו השגגות עונות אלו הזדונות ואף על גב דאמר (שבועות דף ח:) גבי שעיר של יוה"כ להגין עליו מן היסורים משמע דיסורים באים על שוגג הכא מיירי ביסורי נגעים שהן מכוערים כדמייתי קרא:

ארבעה

מסורת הש"ס

א) [לקמן קנג. וש"נ ועי' מ"ש בחגיגה טו: על הגליון], ב) [נ"ל אמרה], ג) [ע"ז ד. ע"ש], ד) יומא סט: סנהדרין סד., ה) [נ"ל אמר אלו וכו'], ו) [זבחים נט:], ז) [וע"ע תוס' ב"ב ס: ד"ה מוטב ובתוס' ע"ז ד. ד"ה שהיה בידם].

גליון הש"ס

גמ' ר"י הוה יתיב. עי' ב"ב דף י ע"ב תוס' ד"ה עליונים: שם א"ל ר"ז לר' סימון לוכחינהו. עי' מדרש רבה איכה שני ד"ה ולא זכר הדום רגליו: שם אמר רב מימות הושע בן בארי. ירושלמי פרק חלק. ושם איתא הך לימוד בשם שמואל: תוס' ד"ה מזבח נחושת וכו' שירה בכלי נחושת. עי' זבחים דף ס ע"א תוס' ד"ה ה"ק: שם ד"ה ושמואל וכו' ומפרש דשמואל דאמר מימי חזאל. אולם בירושלמי פ' חלק מסיים עד עתה עד אותה שעה הזכות קיימת והיינו כפי' רש"י:

תורה אור השלם

א) אטם אזנו מזעקת דל גם הוא יקרא ולא יענה: [משלי כא, יג]

ב) בית דוד כה אמר ה' דינו לבקר משפט והצילו גזול מיד עושק פן תצא כאש חמתי ובערה ואין מכבה מפני רע מעלליכם: [ירמיה כא, יב]

ג) ויאמר ה' אליו עבר בתוך העיר בתוך ירושלים והתוית תו על מצחות האנשים הנאנחים והנאנקים על כל התועבות הנעשות בתוכה: [יחזקאל ט, ד]

ד) זקן בחור ובתולה וטף ונשים תהרגו למשחית ועל כל איש אשר עליו התו אל תגשו וממקדשי תחלו ויחלו באנשים הזקנים אשר לפני הבית: [יחזקאל ט, ו]

ה) והנה ששה אנשים באים מדרך שער העליון אשר מפנה צפונה ואיש כלי מפצו בידו ואיש אחד בתוכם לבש בדים וקסת הספר במתניו ויבאו ויעמדו אצל מזבח הנחשת: [יחזקאל ט, ב]

ו) ועתה אגלה את נבלתה לעיני מאהביה ואיש לא יצילנה מידי: [הושע ב, יב]

ז) וחזאל מלך ארם לחץ את ישראל כל ימי יהואחז: [מלכים ב' יג, כב]

ח) ויחן ה' אתם וירחמם ויפן אליהם למען בריתו את אברהם יצחק ויעקב ולא אבה השחיתם ולא השליכם מעל פניו עד עתה: [מלכים ב' יג, כג]

ט) ויהי בעלות המנחה ויגש אליהו הנביא ויאמר ה' אלהי אברהם יצחק וישראל היום יודע כי אתה אלהים בישראל ואני עבדך ובדברך עשיתי את כל הדברים האלה: [מלכים א' יח, לו]

י) למרבה המשרה ולשלום אין קץ על כסא דוד ועל ממלכתו להכין אתה ולסעדה במשפט ובצדקה מעתה ועד עולם קנאת ה' צבאות תעשה זאת: [ישעיה ט, ו]

כ) הנפש החטאת היא תמות בן לא ישא בעון האב ואב לא ישא בעון הבן צדקת הצדיק עליו תהיה ורשעת הרשע עליו תהיה: [יחזקאל יח, כ]

ל) ופקדתי בשבט פשעם ובנגעים עונם: [תהלים פט, לג]

רבינו חננאל

ד' מתו בעטיו של נחש כבר פירשנוהו:

רב נסים גאון

דאמר ר' חנינא חותמו של הקב"ה אמת. תמצא עיקר דברי ר' חנינא בפרק בא לו כהן גדול (דף סט) במס' יומא ובפ' ד' מיתות (דף סד) במס' סנהדרין ובתלמוד ארץ ישראל במסכת סנהדרין (בראש פ"א) אמרו בדבר זה טעם נאה ביותר ונראה לי לכתבה הנה והכי אמרו מהו חותמו של הקב"ה רב ביבי בשם ר' ראובן אמר אמת מהו אמת אמר ר' אבין שהוא אלהים חיים ומלך עולם אמר ר' שמעון בן לקיש אלף ראשה דאלפא ביתא מם באמצעיתה תיו בסופ' לומר (ישעי' מד) אני ה' ראשון שלא קיבלתי מלכותי מאחר ומבלעדי אין אלהים שאין לי שותף ואת אחרונים אני הוא שאין אני עתיד למוסרה לאחר ואיתא נמי בבראשית [רבה] דר' אושעיא (פרשה פא):

ליקוטי רש"י

מיד עושק. טעמו למטה שאינו שם דבר אלא שם הגזלן העושק את אחרים. ואין מכבה. שלא ימלט לכם שריד [ירמיה כא, יב]. והתוית תיו. ורשמת רושם. על מצחות האנשים. הצדיקים כדי להיות לאות שלא יפגעו בם המשחיתים [יחזקאל ט, ד]. וממקדשי תחלו. מן העומדי' לפני מקדשי ורבותינו אמרו אל תקרי ממקדשי אלא ממקודשי מן המקודשים לי הם אותם חקוקי התיו שהתרה בהם מלהזיקם חזר והוה לחבלם לפי שאמרה מדת הדין לפניו מה נשתנו אלו מאלו הרי לא מיחו בהם כדאיתא במסכת שבת [שם, ו]. גבי [ששה] משחיתים שבאו להשחית את ירושלים כתיב ביחזקאל [ע"ז ד.]. מפצו. שהוא משבר את הכל כמו ונפץ את עולליך (תהלים קלז). וקסת הסופר. פנקס הם לוחות שמחופין בשעוה וחורתין בם בעט [יחזקאל שם, ב]. ואיש לא יצילנה מידי. אף זכות אבותם תמה [הושע ב, יב]. ובדברך עשיתי. שהקרבתי בבמה בשעת איסור הבמות [מ"א יח, לו]. מעתה ועד עולם. עולמו של חזקיהו כל ימיו וכן מצינו שאמרה חנה על שמואל וישב שם עד עולם. קנאת ה' צבאות. שקנא לציון על אשר יעץ עליה ארם ופקח. תעשה זאת. ולא אתו ראוי לכך ואף זכות אבות תמה [ישעיה ט, ו עיי"ש].

[the sinners], [the latter] would not have accepted any reproof **from them.** אָמְרָה לְפָנָיו – **[Strict Justice]** then **said before [God]:** אִם לְפָנֶיךָ גָּלוּי לָהֶם מִי גָּלוּי – **If it is revealed before You, is it revealed to [the righteous]?!**[13]

With this argument the Attribute of Strict Justice "persuaded" the Holy One, Blessed is He, to rescind His decision to spare the righteous. The Gemara shows how this change is reflected in the verses:

וְהַיְינוּ דִּכְתִיב – **And this is what is written:**[14] "זָקֵן בָּחוּר וּבְתוּלָה וְ]טַף וְנָשִׁים תַּהַרְגוּ לְמַשְׁחִית וְעַל־כָּל־אִישׁ אֲשֶׁר־עָלָיו הַתָּו אַל תִּגַּשׁוּ" – ***Slay utterly the old man, the young man and the maiden, children and women, but do not approach any man upon whom is the mark of the tav.*** Here Hashem commands the angels to spare the righteous, but in the following words this instruction is revoked: "וּמִמִּקְדָּשִׁי תָּחֵלּוּ" – ***and begin with My sanctuary.***[15]

The Gemara explains how the second verse refers to the righteous:

וּכְתִיב "וַיָּחֵלּוּ בָּאֲנָשִׁים הַזְּקֵנִים אֲשֶׁר לִפְנֵי הַבָּיִת" – **And it is written** [in the continuation of the same verse]: ***And they began with the elders who were before the House.*** תָּנֵי רַב יוֹסֵף – **Rav Yosef taught:** אַל תִּקְרֵי "מִקְדָּשִׁי" אֶלָּא מְקוּדָּשַׁי – **Do not read** מִקְדָּשִׁי as ***My sanctuary,*** **but** as **"My sanctified ones";** אֵלּוּ בְּנֵי אָדָם שֶׁקִּיְּימוּ אֶת הַתּוֹרָה כּוּלָּהּ מֵאָלֶף וְעַד תָּיו – **these are the people who observed the entire Torah, from** ***alef*** **to** ***tav.***[16]

The Gemara continues to expound the passage in *Ezekiel:*

וּמִיַּד – **And immediately** the verse states:[17] "וְהִנֵּה שִׁשָּׁה אֲנָשִׁים בָּאִים מִדֶּרֶךְ־שַׁעַר הָעֶלְיוֹן אֲשֶׁר מָפְנֶה צָפוֹנָה וְאִישׁ כְּלִי מַפָּצוֹ בְּיָדוֹ וְאִישׁ־אֶחָד בְּתוֹכָם לָבֻשׁ (ה)בַּדִּים וְקֶסֶת הַסֹּפֵר בְּמָתְנָיו וַיָּבֹאוּ וַיַּעַמְדוּ אֵצֶל מִזְבַּח הַנְּחשֶׁת" – ***And, behold, six men came in through the upper gate, which faces northward, every man with his shattering weapon in his hand; and among them was one man dressed in linen,***[18] ***with a scribe's inkwell on his loin. They came in and stood by the copper Altar.***

The Gemara objects:

מִזְבַּח הַנְּחשֶׁת מִי הֲוָה – **Was there a copper Altar** in the Temple in the days of Ezekiel?![19]

The Gemara answers:

אָמַר לְהוּ הַקָּדוֹשׁ בָּרוּךְ הוּא הַתְחִילוּ מִמָּקוֹם שֶׁאוֹמְרִים שִׁירָה לְפָנַי – **The Holy One, Blessed is He, said to [the angels of destruction]: Begin from the place where they recite songs before Me.**[20]

Having cited the passage in *Ezekiel,* the Gemara discusses other aspects of the passage that are incidental to the main theme of rebuke:

וּמַאן נִינְהוּ "שִׁשָּׁה אֲנָשִׁים" – **And who are** the ***six men,*** i.e. the six destroying angels mentioned in the verse? אָמַר רַב חִסְדָּא – **Rav Chisda said:** קֶצֶף אַף וְחֵימָה וּמַשְׁחִית וּמְשַׁבֵּר וּמְכַלֶּה – They are: **Fury, Anger and Wrath, Destroyer and Breaker and Annihilator.**

The Gemara asks:

וּמַאי שְׁנָא תָּיו – **And what is unique about** the letter ***tav,*** that God chose it to be the mark on the foreheads of the righteous?

The Gemara cites five Amoraic answers:

אָמַר רַב תָּיו תִּחְיֶה תָּיו תָּמוּת – **Rav said:** ***Tav*** intimates **"you** (the righteous) **shall live"** and ***tav*** also intimates **"you** (the wicked) **shall die."**[21] וּשְׁמוּאֵל אָמַר תַּמָּה זְכוּת אָבוֹת – **And Shmuel said:** *Tav* alludes to **"the merit of the Patriarchs has expired."**[22] וְרַבִּי יוֹחָנָן אָמַר תָּחוֹן זְכוּת אָבוֹת – **R' Yochanan said:** *Tav* suggests **"the merit of the Patriarchs confers grace."** וְרֵישׁ לָקִישׁ אָמַר תָּיו סוֹף חוֹתָמוֹ שֶׁל הַקָּדוֹשׁ בָּרוּךְ הוּא – **Reish Lakish said:** ***Tav*** **is the conclusion** [i.e. the final letter] **of the seal of the Holy One, Blessed is He,** דְּאָמַר רַבִּי חֲנִינָא חוֹתָמוֹ שֶׁל הַקָּדוֹשׁ בָּרוּךְ הוּא אֱמֶת – **as R' Chanina said: The signet of the Holy One, Blessed is He,** is the word **"Truth."**[23] (אמר) רַבִּי שְׁמוּאֵל בַּר נַחְמָנִי [אָמַר] – **R'**

NOTES

13. Since the righteous were not certain that their rebuking would meet deaf ears, they erred in failing to rebuke (see above, note 8).

In *Midrash Tanchuma* (*Tazria,* end of §9) the Attribute of Strict Justice adds: "Therefore, [the righteous] should have protested against [the transgressors]; [it was incumbent upon the righteous] to be reviled for the sanctification of Your Name; to accept upon themselves and to suffer beatings from the Jewish people, as the prophets suffered at the hands of the Jewish people; for Jeremiah suffered many troubles from the Jewish people, and likewise Isaiah, as it is written (*Isaiah* 50:6): *I gave over my body to those who administered blows, and my cheeks to those who plucked out [hairs];* and also the other prophets." (And see *Hagahos Maimonios* §5 to *Hilchos De'os* 6:7, who cites the Midrash as proof that [if there is a chance of being effective] one must protest until the transgressor strikes him.)

14. *Ezekiel* 9:6.

15. With these words Hashem accepted the argument of the Attribute of Strict Justice, and revoked His favorable decree upon the righteous (*Rashi*).

16. God commanded the angels of destruction to begin with *My sanctuary.* The angels responded by beginning with *the elders* – i.e. the judges of the Sanhedrin, who were righteous individuals. From this Rav Yosef concludes that *My sanctuary* should be interpreted "My sanctified ones" (*Rif* to *Ein Yaakov*). That is, instead of sparing the righteous, Hashem decreed that they be punished first.

17. *Ezekiel* 9:2. This verse appears before the one just quoted by the Gemara, and would thus seem to be out of chronological order. However, Scripture placed it first to show that the six angels were already prepared to carry out the decree mentioned later in the passage [i.e. they were prepared to destroy, but only later was it decided whom they would destroy]. This is why the Gemara says, "And immediately" (*Maharsha*).

18. This was the angel Gavriel (*Midrash Tanchuma, Parashas Tazria,* end of §9).

19. Indeed, it had been concealed much earlier, for Scripture states (*I Kings* 8:64) that when King Solomon consecrated the Temple he found the copper Altar too small to receive all the offerings, and so replaced it with a larger one made of stone (*Rashi,* based on *Zevachim* 59b).

20. I.e. begin with the Levites, who sing in the Temple accompanied by musical instruments of copper (*Rashi*). The Altar mentioned in the verse was the stone one installed by King Solomon, but Scripture calls it the "copper" Altar because of the copper instruments. Here again we see that the most sanctified people (the Levites) were the first to be punished.

21. [*Tav* is the first letter in each Hebrew word.] Rav first speaks of the *tav* of ink and then of the *tav* of blood (*Maharsha*).

22. *Tav* is the first letter in this expression as well.

Previously, Jews were saved from Divine retribution by the merit of the Patriarchs – Abraham, Isaac and Jacob. By Ezekiel's time that merit had been exhausted (*Rashi* ד״ה ואיש), and could no longer save them.

Tosafos raise the question: If the merit of the Patriarchs has expired, why do we still invoke it in our prayers? *Tosafos* offer two explanations: (a) Although the merit of the Patriarchs has expired, the covenant that Hashem made with them has not (*Rabbeinu Tam*). (b) The merit of the Patriarchs has expired in that it no longer protects the wicked; however, it still shields the righteous. According to this second explanation, R' Yochanan, who says below that *tav* suggests "the merit of the Patriarchs confers grace," does not disagree with Shmuel, who said that *tav* implies "the merit of the Patriarchs has expired." R' Yochanan referred to the righteous, while Shmuel referred to the wicked (*Ri*). See *Maharsha*; see also *Dibros Moshe* 43:15.

23. When a king approves of an enactment drawn up by his subjects, he applies his seal to it. Similarly, the word אֱמֶת, *truth,* is – as it were – God's seal of approval (see *Sanhedrin* 64a with *Rashi* ד״ה חותמו).

Why did God choose this word? Because it begins with the first letter of the alphabet (א), continues with the middle letter (מ), and ends with the final letter (ת), thus alluding to the verses (*Isaiah* 44:6), *I am the first and I am the last, and other than Me there is no God,* and (ibid. 41:4), *I, Hashem, am first, and with the last, I am He* (*Rashi;* see also *Rabbeinu Nissim Gaon*).

מסורת הש"ס

א) [לקמן קנב. וש"נ ועי' מ"ש בחגיגה טו: על הגליון], ב) [נ"ל אמרה], ג) [ע"ז ד. ע"ש], ד) יומא סט: סנהדרין סד., ה) [נ"ל אמר אלו וכו'], ו) [זבחים נט:], ז) [וע"ע תוס' ב"ב ס: ד"ה מוטב ובתוס' ע"ז ד. ד"ה שהיה בידם].

גליון הש"ס

גמ' ר"י הוה יתיב. עי' ב"ב דף י ע"ב תוס' ד"ה עליונים: שם א"ל ר"ז לר' סימון לוכחינהו. עי' מדרש רבה איכה שני ד"ה ולא זכר הדום רגליו: שם אמר רב מימות הושע בן בארי. ירושלמי פרק חלק. ושם איתא הך לימוד בשם שמואל: תוס' ד"ה מזבח נחושת וכו' שירה בכלי נחושת. עי' זבחים דף ס ע"א תוס' ד"ה ה"ק: שם ד"ה ושמואל וכו' ומפרש דשמואל דאמר מימי חזאל. אולם בירושלמי פ' חלק מסיים עד עתה עד אותה שעה הזכות קיימת והיינו כפי' רש"י:

תורה אור השלם

א) אֹטֵם אָזְנוֹ מִזַּעֲקַת דָּל גַּם הוּא יִקְרָא וְלֹא יֵעָנֶה: [משלי כא, יג]

ב) בֵּית דָּוִד כֹּה אָמַר יְיָ דִּינוּ לַבֹּקֶר מִשְׁפָּט וְהַצִּילוּ גָזוּל מִיַּד עוֹשֵׁק פֶּן תֵּצֵא כָאֵשׁ חֲמָתִי וּבָעֲרָה וְאֵין מְכַבֶּה מִפְּנֵי רֹעַ מַעַלְלֵיכֶם: [ירמיה כא, יב]

ג) וַיֹּאמֶר יְיָ אֵלָיו עֲבֹר בְּתוֹךְ הָעִיר בְּתוֹךְ יְרוּשָׁלָיִם וְהִתְוִיתָ תָּו עַל מִצְחוֹת הָאֲנָשִׁים הַנֶּאֱנָחִים וְהַנֶּאֱנָקִים עַל כָּל הַתּוֹעֵבוֹת הַנַּעֲשׂוֹת בְּתוֹכָהּ: [יחזקאל ט, ד]

ד) זָקֵן בָּחוּר וּבְתוּלָה וְטַף וְנָשִׁים תַּהַרְגוּ לְמַשְׁחִית וְעַל כָּל אִישׁ אֲשֶׁר עָלָיו הַתָּו אַל תִּגַּשׁוּ וּמִמִּקְדָּשִׁי תָּחֵלּוּ וַיָּחֵלּוּ בָּאֲנָשִׁים הַזְּקֵנִים אֲשֶׁר לִפְנֵי הַבָּיִת: [יחזקאל ט, ו]

ה) וְהִנֵּה שִׁשָּׁה אֲנָשִׁים בָּאִים מִדֶּרֶךְ שַׁעַר הָעֶלְיוֹן אֲשֶׁר מָפְנֶה צָפוֹנָה וְאִישׁ כְּלִי מַפָּצוֹ בְּיָדוֹ וְאִישׁ אֶחָד בְּתוֹכָם לָבֻשׁ בַּדִּים וְקֶסֶת הַסֹּפֵר בְּמָתְנָיו וַיָּבֹאוּ וַיַּעַמְדוּ אֵצֶל מִזְבַּח הַנְּחֹשֶׁת: [יחזקאל ט, ב]

ו) וְעַתָּה אֲגַלֶּה אֶת נַבְלֻתָהּ לְעֵינֵי מְאַהֲבֶיהָ וְאִישׁ לֹא יַצִּילֶנָּה מִיָּדִי: [הושע ב, יב]

ז) וַחֲזָאֵל מֶלֶךְ אֲרָם לָחַץ אֶת יִשְׂרָאֵל כֹּל יְמֵי יְהוֹאָחָז: [מלכים ב' יג, כב]

ח) וַיָּחָן יְיָ אֹתָם וַיְרַחֲמֵם וַיִּפֶן אֲלֵיהֶם לְמַעַן בְּרִיתוֹ אֶת אַבְרָהָם יִצְחָק וְיַעֲקֹב וְלֹא אָבָה הַשְׁחִיתָם וְלֹא הִשְׁלִיכָם מֵעַל פָּנָיו עַד עָתָּה: [מלכים ב' יג, כג]

ט) וַיְהִי בַּעֲלוֹת הַמִּנְחָה וַיִּגַּשׁ אֵלִיָּהוּ הַנָּבִיא וַיֹּאמַר יְיָ אֱלֹהֵי אַבְרָהָם יִצְחָק וְיִשְׂרָאֵל הַיּוֹם יִוָּדַע כִּי אַתָּה אֱלֹהִים בְּיִשְׂרָאֵל וַאֲנִי עַבְדֶּךָ וּבִדְבָרְךָ עָשִׂיתִי אֵת כָּל הַדְּבָרִים הָאֵלֶּה: [מלכים א' יח, לו]

י) לְמַרְבֵּה הַמִּשְׂרָה וּלְשָׁלוֹם אֵין קֵץ עַל כִּסֵּא דָוִד וְעַל מַמְלַכְתּוֹ לְהָכִין אֹתָהּ וּלְסַעֲדָהּ בְּמִשְׁפָּט וּבִצְדָקָה מֵעַתָּה וְעַד עוֹלָם קִנְאַת יְיָ צְבָאוֹת תַּעֲשֶׂה זֹּאת: [ישעיה ט, ו]

כ) הַנֶּפֶשׁ הַחֹטֵאת הִיא תָמוּת בֵּן לֹא יִשָּׂא בַּעֲוֹן הָאָב וְאָב לֹא יִשָּׂא בַּעֲוֹן הַבֵּן צִדְקַת הַצַּדִּיק עָלָיו תִּהְיֶה וְרִשְׁעַת הָרָשָׁע עָלָיו תִּהְיֶה: [יחזקאל יח, כ]

ל) וּפָקַדְתִּי בְשֵׁבֶט פִּשְׁעָם וּבִנְגָעִים עֲוֹנָם: [תהלים פט, לג]

גמרא

זקנים מה חטאו אלא אימא על זקנים שלא מיחו בשרים ° רב יהודה הוה יתיב קמיה דשמואל אתאי ההיא איתתא קא צווחה קמיה ולא הוה משגח בה א"ל לא סבר ליה מר א) אוטם אזנו מזעקת דל גם הוא יקרא ולא יענה א"ל א) שיננא רישך בקרירי רישא דרישך בחמימי הא יתיב מר עוקבא אב ב"ד דכתיב ב) בית דוד כה אמר ה' דינו לבקר משפט והצילו גזול מיד עושק פן תצא כאש חמתי ובערה ואין מכבה מפני רוע מעלליהם וגו' ° א"ל ר' זירא לר' סימון לוכחינהו מר להני דבי ריש גלותא א"ל לא מקבלי מינאי א"ל אע"ג דלא מקבלי לוכחינהו מר דא"ר אחא בר' חנינא מעולם לא יצתה מדה טובה מפי הקב"ה וחזר בה לרעה חוץ מדבר זה דכתיב ג) ויאמר ה' אליו עבור בתוך העיר בתוך ירושלים והתוית תיו על מצחות האנשים הנאנחים והנאנקים על כל התועבות הנעשות בתוכה וגו' א"ל הקב"ה לגבריאל לך ורשום על מצחן של צדיקים תיו של דיו שלא ישלטו בהם מלאכי חבלה ועל מצחם של רשעים תיו של דם כדי שישלטו בהן מלאכי חבלה אמרה מדת הדין לפני הקב"ה רבש"ע מה נשתנו אלו מאלו אמר לה הללו צדיקים גמורים והללו רשעים גמורים אמרה לפניו רבש"ע היה בידם למחות ולא מיחו אמר לה גלוי וידוע לפני שאם מיחו בהם לא יקבלו מהם (ב) אמר) לפניו רבש"ע אם לפניך גלוי להם מי גלוי והיינו דכתיב ד) זקן בחור ובתולה טף ונשים תהרגו למשחית ועל כל איש אשר עליו התיו אל תגשו וממקדשי תחלו וכתיב ד) ויחלו באנשים הזקנים אשר לפני הבית ג) תני רב יוסף אל תקרי מקדשי אלא מקודשי אלו בני אדם שקיימו את התורה כולה מאלף ועד תיו ומיד ה) והנה ששה אנשים באים מדרך שער העליון אשר מפנה צפונה ואיש כלי מפצו בידו ואיש אחד בתוכם לבוש הבדים וקסת הסופר במתניו ויבאו ויעמדו אצל מזבח הנחושת מזבח הנחושת מי הוה אמר להו הקב"ה התחילו ממקום שאומרים שירה לפני ומאן נינהו ששה אנשים א"ר חסדא קצף אף וחימה ומשחית ומשבר ומכלה ומ"ש תיו אמר רב תיו תחיה תיו תמות ושמואל אמר תמה זכות אבות ורבי יוחנן אמר תחון זכות אבות ור"ל אמר תיו סוף חותמו של הקב"ה ד) דאמר רבי חנינא חותמו של הקב"ה אמת (אמר) ר' שמואל בר נחמני ה) אלו בני אדם שקיימו את התור' כולה מאלף ועד תיו מאימתי תמה זכות אבות ° אמר רב מימות הושע בן בארי שנא' ו) אגלה את נבלתה לעיני מאהביה ואיש לא יצילנה מידי ושמואל אמר מימי חזאל שנאמר ז) וחזאל מלך ארם לחץ את ישראל כל ימי יהואחז וכתיב ח) ויחן ה' אותם וירחמם ויפן אליהם למען בריתו את אברהם יצחק ויעקב ולא אבה השחיתם ולא השליכם מעל פניו עד עתה ר' יהושע בן לוי אמר מימי אליהו שנאמר ט) ויהי בעלות המנחה ויגש אליהו הנביא ויאמר ה' אלהי אברהם יצחק וישראל היום יודע כי אתה אלהים בישראל ואני עבדך ובדברך עשיתי [את] כל הדברים האלה וגו' ורבי יוחנן אמר מימי חזקיהו שנאמר י) למרבה המשרה ולשלום אין קץ על כסא דוד ועל ממלכתו להכין אותה ולסעדה במשפט ובצדקה מעתה ועד עולם קנאת ה' צבאות תעשה זאת וגו': אמר רב אמי אין מיתה בלא חטא ואין יסורין בלא עון אין מיתה בלא חטא דכתיב כ) הנפש החוטאת היא תמות בן לא ישא בעון האב ואב לא ישא בעון הבן צדקת הצדיק עליו תהיה ורשעת הרשע עליו תהיה וגו' אין יסורין בלא עון דכתיב ל) ופקדתי בשבט פשעם ובנגעים עונם מיתיבי

רש"י

זקנים. סנהדרין: רישך בקרירי. אני שאני רבך איני נכוה אבל מר עוקבא שהוא ראש לי ולך ואב ב"ד יכווה בחמין: דכתיב בית דוד וגו'. לא ענש אלא מי שבידו לשפוט: חוץ מדבר זה. שנא' במקרא זה שהוציא דבור לטובה ומפני ענש תוכחה חזר בו: והתוית תיו על מצחות האנשים הנאנחים והנאנקים על כל התועבות הנעשות בתוכה. אלו לדיקים: שלא ישלטו בהם מלאכי חבלה. שאני רוצה לשלוח בעיר: היינו דכתיב. מעיקרא ועל כל איש אשר עליו התיו אל תגשו ולבסוף וממקדשי תחלו: ממקודשי. שהודה למקטרג מדת הדין וחזר מן הטוב: מי הוה מזבח הנחשת. בימי יחזקאל והלא שלמה גנזו ועשה מזבח אבנים של ל"ב אמה דכתיב (מלכים א ח) כי מזבח הנחשת אשר לפני ה' קטן מהכיל ו) כאדם האומר לחבירו ננס פלוני ופסול לעבודה: ממקום שאומרים שירה. מן הלוים שאומרים שיר בכלי נחשת: תיו תמות. לרשעים: חותמו של הקב"ה אמת. אמצעית לאותיות וראשון ואחרון על שם אני ראשון ואני אחרון ואני הוא: אלו בני אדם שקיימו התורה כולה. התיו סימן להם שקיימו התורה מראש עד סוף: ואיש לא יצילנה. שאין עוד זכות לאבות שאכלוה: ויפן אליהם למען בריתו את אברהם וגו' ולא השליכם מעל פניו עד עתה. אבל מכאן ואילך השליכם ולא פנה אל ברית אבות: ה' אלהי אברהם ואלהי יצחק וישראל היום יודע. שאתה זוכר ברית אברהם יצחק וישראל מדקאמר היום יודע ותו לא מכלל דתמה ועל ידי רחמים הוזכרה להם בימי חזאל: בימי חזקיהו. דכתיב מעתה ועד עולם קנאת ה' צבאות תעשה זאת ולא זכות אבות: בלא חטא. וחטאו של אדם גורם לו מיתה: בשבט ובנגעים. היינו יסורים וקאמר שאין באין אלא משום פקידת עון: בעטיו

תוספות

ואע"ג דלא מקבלי לוכחינהו מר. היינו היכא דספק אי מקבלי כדאמר בסמוך לפניהם מי גלוי אבל היכא דודאי לא מקבלי הנח להם מוטב שיהו שוגגין ואל יהיו מזידין כדאמרינן בהמביא כדי יין (ביצה דף ל. ושם) ובפרק שואל (לקמן דף קמח:) גבי תוספת יוה"כ ז):

ועל הרשעים תי"ו של דם. לא מקרא קאמר הכי אלא מסבר' דהא דכתיב והתוית תיו על מצחות האנשים הנאנחים והנאנקים על כל התועבות הנעשות בתוכה היינו בצדיקים גמורים: **מזבח** נחשת בימי שלמה מי הוה. כדכתיב ששלמה הסירו כי היה קטן מהכיל וא"ת והא כתיב בדברי הימים (ב ד) ויעש שלמה את מזבח הנחשת וי"ל דדרשינן ליה כי הכא מזבח שאומרים לפניו ° שירה בכלי נחשת:

קצף אף וחימה. קשה לרשב"א דאמר בפ"ק דמסכת ע"ג (דף ד. ושם) כתיב חימה אין לי וכתיב נוקם ה' ובעל חימה ומשני כאן לישראל כאן לנכרים אלמא דאין להקב"ה חימה על ישראל והההיא דמס' ע"ג קשה דבס"פ ארבעה נדרים (דף לב.) אמר חימה משה הרגו דכתיב חימה אין לי ופריך והא כתיב כי יגורתי מפני האף והחימה ומשני תרי חימה הוו:

ושמואל אמר תמה זכות אבות ורבי יוחנן אמר תחון זכות אבות. אומר רבינו תם דזכות אבות תמה אבל ברית אבות לא תמה דהא כתיב (ויקרא כו) וזכרתי את בריתי יעקוב אף לאחר גלות ואנן אין אנו מזכירין זכות אבות אלא הברית ° ומפרש דשמואל דאמר מימי חזאל דייק מדכתיב למען בריתו ולא למען זכותו ואומר ר"י דבויקרא רבה (פ' לו) דייק מעד עתה כדפי' בקונטרס ולר"י נראה דלא פליגי שמואל ור"י אלא שמואל קאמר דלרשעים תמה אבל לצדיקים לא תמה ובצדיקים איירי ר"י תדע דהא ר"י אמר בסמוך דמימי חזקי' תמה זכות אבות והכא קאמר דאף בשעת חורבן דבתר הכי תחון זכות אבות ועל זה אנו סומכין להזכיר זכות אבות ובשלהי ויקרא רבה רבי אחא אומר לעולם זכות אבות קיימת ולעולם אנו מזכירים אותם וכן הוא אומר כי אל רחום וגו' ולא ישכח את ברית אבותיך וגו':

אין מיתה בלא חטא. פי' (מיתה) לפי שהגזירה באה אף על השגגה ואין יסורים בלא עון של מזיד כדאמר ביומא (דף לו:) חטאים אלו השגגות עונות אלו הזדונות ואף על גב דאמר (שבועות דף ח:) גבי שעיר של יה"כ להגין עליו מן היסורים משמע דיסורים באים על שוגג הכא איירי ביסורי נגעים שהן מכוערים כדמייתי קרא: ארבעה

רבינו חננאל

ד' מתו בעטיו של נחש כבר פירשנוהו:

רב נסים גאון

דאמר ר' חנינא חותמו של הקב"ה אמת. תמצא עיקר דברי ר' חנינא בפרק בא לו כהן גדול (דף סט) במס' יומא ובפ' ד' מיתות (דף סד) במס' סנהדרין ובתלמוד ארץ ישראל במסכת סנהדרין (בראש פ"א) אמרו בדבר זה טעם נאה ביותר ונראה לי לכתבה הנה והכי אמרו מהו חותמו של הקב"ה רב ביבי בשם ר' ראובן אמו אמת נחו אמת אומר ר' אבין שהוא אלהים חיים ומלך עולם אמר ר' שמעון בן לקיש אלף ראשה דאלפא ביתא מם באמצעיתה תיו בסופ' לומר (ישעי' מד) אני ה' ראשון שלא קיבלתי מלכותי מאחר ומבלעדי אין אלהים שאין לי שותף ואת אחרונים אני הוא שאין אני עתיד למוסרה לאחר ואיתא נמי בבראשית [רבה] דר' אושעיא (פרשה פא):

ליקוטי רש"י

מיד עושק. טעמו למטה שאינו שם דבר אלא שם הגוזלן העושק את אחרים. ואין מכבה. שלא ימלט לכם שריד [ירמיה כא, יב]. והתוית תיו. ורשמת רושם. על מצחות האנשים. הצדיקים כדי להיות לאות שלא יפגעו בם המשחיתים [יחזקאל ט, ד]. וממקדשי תחלו. מן העומדי' לפני מקדשי ורבותינו אמרו אל תקרי ממקדשי אלא ממקודשי מן המקודשים לי הם אותם חקוקי התיו שהתרה בהם מלהוכיח חזר והוה לחבלם לפי שאמרה מדת הדין לפניו מה נשתנו אלו מאלו הרי לא מיחו בהם כדאיתא במסכת שבת [שם, ו]. גבי [ששה] משחיתים שבאו להשחית את ירושלים כתיב ביחזקאל [ע"ז ד.]. מפצו. שהוא משבר את הכל כמו ונפץ את עולליך (תהלים קלז). וקסת הסופר. פנקס הם לוחות שמחופין בשעוה וחורתין בם בעט [יחזקאל שם, ב]. ואיש לא יצילנה מידי. אף זכות אבותם תמה [הושע ב, יב]. ובדברך עשיתי. שהקרבתי בבמה בשעת איסור הבמות [מ"א יח, לו]. מעתה ועד עולם. עולמו של חזקיהו כל ימיו וכן מצינו שאמרה חנה על שמואל וישב שם עד עולם. קנאת ה' צבאות. שקנא לציון על אשר יעץ עליה ארם ופקח. תעשה זאת. ולא אחז ראוי לכך ואף זכות אבות תמה [ישעיה ט, ו עיי"ש].

Shmuel bar Nachmani said: **אֵלוּ בְּנֵי אָדָם שֶׁקִּיְּמוּ אֶת הַתּוֹרָה כּוּלָּהּ מֵאָלֶף וְעַד תָּיו** – *Tav* intimates: **"These** [the ones marked with the *tav*] **are people who observed the entire Torah, from** ***alef*** **to** ***tav.*"**

The Gemara asks with regard to Shmuel's interpretation: **מֵאֵימָתַי תַּמָּה זְכוּת אָבוֹת** – **When did the merit of the Patriarchs expire?**

The Gemara cites four Amoraic answers:

אָמַר רַב מִימוֹת הוֹשֵׁעַ בֶּן בְּאֵרִי – **Rav said:** It has not existed **since the days of** the prophet **Hoshea ben B'eiri,** **שֶׁנֶּאֱמַר ,,אֲגַלֶּה אֶת־נַבְלֻתָהּ לְעֵינֵי מְאַהֲבֶיהָ וְאִישׁ לֹא־יַצִּילֶנָּה מִיָּדִי״** – **as it is stated:** *I shall uncover her* [the Jewish nation's] *disgrace in the sight of her lovers, and no one will rescue her from My hand.*[24] **וּשְׁמוּאֵל אָמַר מִימֵי חֲזָאֵל** – **Shmuel said: Since the days of Chazael,** **שֶׁנֶּאֱמַר ,,וַחֲזָאֵל מֶלֶךְ אֲרָם לָחַץ אֶת־יִשְׂרָאֵל כֹּל יְמֵי יְהוֹאָחָז״** – **as it is stated:**[25] ***And Chazael, King of Aram, oppressed Israel all the days of Yehoachaz,*** **וּכְתִיב ,,וַיָּחָן ה׳ אוֹתָם וַיְרַחֲמֵם וַיִּפֶן אֲלֵיהֶם לְמַעַן בְּרִיתוֹ אֶת־אַבְרָהָם יִצְחָק וְיַעֲקֹב וְלֹא אָבָה הַשְׁחִיתָם וְלֹא־הִשְׁלִיכָם מֵעַל־פָּנָיו עַד־עָתָּה״** – **and it is written** in the next verse: ***And Hashem was gracious unto them, and had compassion on them, and turned to them for the sake of His covenant with Abraham, Isaac and Jacob, and desired not to destroy them, and did not cast them from before Him, until now.***[26]

The third and fourth answers:

רַבִּי יְהוֹשֻׁעַ בֶּן לֵוִי אָמַר מִימֵי אֵלִיָּהוּ – **Rabbi Yehoshua ben Levi said:** There has been no Patriarchal merit **since the days of Elijah,** **שֶׁנֶּאֱמַר ,,וַיְהִי בַּעֲלוֹת הַמִּנְחָה וַיִּגַּשׁ אֵלִיָּהוּ הַנָּבִיא וַיֹּאמַר ה׳ אֱלֹהֵי אַבְרָהָם יִצְחָק וְיִשְׂרָאֵל הַיּוֹם יִוָּדַע כִּי־אַתָּה אֱלֹהִים בְּיִשְׂרָאֵל וַאֲנִי עַבְדְּךָ וּבִדְבָרְךָ עָשִׂיתִי [אֵת] כָּל־הַדְּבָרִים הָאֵלֶּה וגו׳ ״** – **as it is stated:**[27] ***And it came to pass at the time of the afternoon offering that Elijah the Prophet came near and said: Hashem, God of Abraham, Isaac and Israel, let it be known this day that You are the God in Israel and that I am Your servant, and by Your word have I done all these things etc.***[28] **וְרַבִּי יוֹחָנָן אָמַר מִימֵי חִזְקִיָּהוּ** – **And R' Yochanan said: Since the days of Chizkiyahu,** **שֶׁנֶּאֱמַר ,,לְמַרְבֵּה הַמִּשְׂרָה וּלְשָׁלוֹם אֵין־קֵץ עַל־כִּסֵּא דָוִד וְעַל־מַמְלַכְתּוֹ לְהָכִין אֹתָהּ וּלְסַעֲדָהּ בְּמִשְׁפָּט וּבִצְדָקָה מֵעַתָּה וְעַד־עוֹלָם קִנְאַת ה׳ צְבָאוֹת תַּעֲשֶׂה־זֹּאת וגו׳ ״** – **as it is stated:**[29] ***For the increase of sovereignty, and for endless peace, upon the throne of David and upon his kingdom, to establish it and uphold it with justice and righteousness, from now and forever – the zeal of the Lord of Hosts will accomplish this etc.***[30]

The Gemara has stated that even the completely righteous are punished if they fail to reprove transgressors. It now discusses whether suffering and death come to those who are free of all sin:

אָמַר רַב אַמִּי: אֵין מִיתָה בְּלֹא חֵטְא וְאֵין יִסּוּרִין בְּלֹא עָוֹן – **Said Rav Ami: There is no death without transgression, and there is no suffering without sin.**[31]

Rav Ami adduces Scriptural support for his statement:

אֵין מִיתָה בְּלֹא חֵטְא דִּכְתִיב – **There is no death without transgression, as it is written:**[32] **,,הַנֶּפֶשׁ הַחֹטֵאת הִיא תָמוּת בֵּן לֹא־יִשָּׂא בַּעֲוֹן הָאָב וְאָב לֹא יִשָּׂא בַּעֲוֹן הַבֵּן צִדְקַת הַצַּדִּיק עָלָיו תִּהְיֶה וְרִשְׁעַת הָרָשָׁע עָלָיו תִּהְיֶה וגו׳ ״** – ***The soul that sins – it shall die; the son shall not bear the iniquity of the father, nor shall the father bear the iniquity of the son. The righteousness of the righteous one shall be upon him, and the wickedness of the wicked shall be upon him*** etc. **אֵין יִסּוּרִין בְּלֹא עָוֹן דִּכְתִיב** – **There is no suffering without sin, as it is written:**[33] **,,וּפָקַדְתִּי בְשֵׁבֶט פִּשְׁעָם וּבִנְגָעִים עֲוֹנָם״** – ***I shall visit their transgression with the rod, and their iniquity with plagues.***[34]

NOTES

24. *Hosea* 2:12, which implies that no one can save the nation because they have exhausted the merit of the Patriarchs (*Rashi*).

25. *II Kings* 13:22.

26. The words *until now* imply that from then on Hashem did cast them away and did not pay heed to the covenant of the Patriarchs (*Rashi*).

It would seem according to *Rashi* that the covenant of the Patriarchs expired at this time. This opinion conflicts with that of *Rabbeinu Tam,* who maintains (see above, note 22) that while the merit of the Patriarchs eventually expired, their covenant lasts forever.

According to *Rabbeinu Tam,* then, Shmuel's interpretation is based not on the phrase *until now,* but on the phrase, *for the sake of His covenant with Abraham, Isaac and Jacob,* which implies that the Jews were saved only on account of the covenant, inasmuch as the Patriarchal merit had already been depleted (*Tosafos*).

27. *I Kings* 18:36.

28. Elijah in essence petitions: *Let it be known this day* that You remember the covenant of Abraham, Isaac and Jacob. The implication is that beyond "this day" Hashem will not remember the covenant, for it will have expired. And as to why God "remembered" the Jews at a later time, in the days of Chazael, He did so only out of compassion for them (*Rashi*).

29. *Isaiah* 9:6. This prophecy describes the reign of King Chizkiyahu.

30. The conclusion of the verse, *from now and forever – the zeal of the Lord of Hosts will accomplish this,* implies that from Chizkiyahu's time onward the salvation of the Jewish people will come through *the zeal of the Lord of Hosts,* not through the merit of the Patriarchs (*Rashi*).

31. A person's transgression is what causes his death (*Rashi*), and suffering comes only as punishment for sin.

Even the righteous die because of their transgressions, for *there is no righteous man on the earth who does (only) good and does not sin* (*Ecclesiastes* 7:20). As for children who are too young to be held responsible, they die for the sins of their parents (*Iyun Yaakov*).

The Gemara in *Yoma* (36b) teaches that the term חֵטְא ("transgression") refers to an unintentional wrongdoing, while an עָוֹן ("sin") is intentional. Thus, our Gemara implies that the death penalty is meted out even for unintentional transgressions, while suffering is the consequence of only intentional misdeeds. Although the Gemara in *Shevuos* (8b) implies that suffering can result from an unintentional violation, that Gemara refers to ordinary sufferings; however, our Gemara refers to loathsome sufferings, such as the plagues mentioned in the verse below (*Tosafos*).

[Thus, according to Rav Ami, death and ordinary suffering are occasioned by even unintentional wrongdoing, while loathsome suffering results from intentional wrongdoing.]

32. *Ezekiel* 18:20.

33. *Psalms* 89:33.

34. *The rod* and the *plagues* are sufferings, which are visited upon man as punishment for his sins (*Rashi*). [The word פֶּשַׁע refers to rebellious violations (*Yoma* 36b).]

זקנים מה חטאו אלא אימא על זקנים שלא מיחו בשרים ° רב יהודה הוה יתיב קמיה דשמואל אתאי ההיא איתתא קא צווחה קמיה ולא הוה משגח בה א"ל לא סבר ליה מר א) אוטם אזנו מזעקת דל גם הוא יקרא ולא יענה א"ל ו) שיננא רישך בקרירי רישא דרישך בחמימי הא יתיב מר עוקבא אב ב"ד דכתיב ב) בית דוד כה אמר ה' דינו לבקר משפט והצילו גזול מיד עושק פן תצא כאש חמתי ובערה ואין מכבה מפני רוע מעלליהם וגו' ° א"ל ר' זירא לר' סימון לוכחינהו מר להני דבי ריש גלותא א"ל לא מקבלי מינאי א"ל אע"ג דלא מקבלי לוכחינהו מר דא"ר אחא בר' חנינא מעולם לא יצתה מדה טובה מפי הקב"ה וחזר בה לרעה חוץ מדבר זה דכתיב ג) ויאמר ה' אליו עבור בתוך העיר בתוך ירושלים והתוית תיו על מצחות האנשים הנאנחים והנאנקים על כל התועבות הנעשות בתוכה וגו' א"ל הקב"ה לגבריאל לך ורשום על מצחן של צדיקים תיו של דיו שלא ישלטו בהם מלאכי חבלה ועל מצחם של רשעים תיו של דם כדי שישלטו בהן מלאכי חבלה אמרה מדת הדין לפני הקב"ה רבש"ע מה נשתנו אלו מאלו אמר לה הללו צדיקים גמורים והללו רשעים גמורים אמרה לפניו רבש"ע היה בידם למחות ולא מיחו אמר לה גלוי וידוע לפני שאם מיחו בהם לא יקבלו מהם (ג אמר) לפניו רבש"ע אם לפניך גלוי להם מי גלוי והיינו דכתיב ד) זקן בחור ובתולה טף ונשים תהרגו למשחית ועל כל איש אשר עליו התיו אל תגשו וממקדשי תחלו וכתיב ד) ויחלו באנשים הזקנים אשר לפני הבית ג) תני רב יוסף אל תקרי מקדשי אלא מקודשי אלו בני אדם שקיימו את התורה כולה מאלף ועד תיו ומיד ה) והנה ששה אנשים באים מדרך שער העליון אשר מפנה צפונה ואיש כלי מפצו בידו ואיש אחד בתוכם לבוש הבדים וקסת הסופר במתניו ויבאו ויעמדו אצל מזבח הנחושת מזבח הנחושת מי הוה אמר להו הקב"ה התחילו ממקום שאומרים שירה לפני ומאן נינהו ששה אנשים א"ר חסדא קצף אף וחימה ומשחית ומשבר ומכלה ומ"ש תיו אמר רב תיו תחיה תיו תמות ושמואל אמר תמה זכות אבות ורבי יוחנן אמר תחון זכות אבות ור"ל אמר תיו סוף חותמו של הקב"ה ד) דאמר רבי חנינא חותמו של הקב"ה אמת (אמר) ר' שמואל בר נחמני ה) אלו בני אדם שקיימו את התור' כולה מאלף ועד תיו מאימתי תמה זכות אבות ° אמר רב מימות הושע בן בארי שנא' ו) אגלה את נבלתה לעיני מאהביה ואיש לא יצילנה מידי ושמואל אמר מימי חזאל שנאמר ז) וחזאל מלך ארם לחץ את ישראל כל ימי יהואחז וכתיב ח) ויחן ה' אותם וירחמם ויפן אליהם למען בריתו את אברהם יצחק ויעקב ולא אבה השחיתם ולא השליכם מעל פניו עד עתה ר' יהושע בן לוי אמר מימי אליהו שנאמר ט) ויהי בעלות המנחה ויגש אליהו הנביא ויאמר ה' אלהי אברהם יצחק וישראל היום יודע כי אתה אלהים בישראל ואני עבדך ובדברך עשיתי [את] כל הדברים האלה וגו' ורבי יוחנן אמר מימי חזקיהו שנאמר י) למרבה המשרה ולשלום אין קץ על כסא דוד ועל ממלכתו להכין אותה ולסעדה במשפט ובצדקה מעתה ועד עולם קנאת ה' צבאות תעשה זאת וגו': אמר רב אמי אין מיתה בלא חטא ואין יסורין בלא עון אין מיתה בלא חטא דכתיב כ) הנפש החוטאת היא תמות בן לא ישא בעון האב ואב לא ישא בעון הבן צדקת הצדיק עליו תהיה ורשעת הרשע עליו תהיה וגו' אין יסורין בלא עון דכתיב ל) ופקדתי בשבט פשעם ובנגעים עונם מיתיבי

זקנים. סנהדרין: רישך בקרירי. אני שאני רבך איני נכוה אבל מר עוקבא שהוא ראש לי ולך ואב ב"ד יכווה בחמין: דכתיב בית דוד וגו'. לא ענש אלא מי שבידו לשפוט: חוץ מדבר זה. שנא' במקרא זה שהוליא דבור לטובה ומפני עונש תוכחה חזר בו: והתוית תיו על מצחות האנשים הנאנחים והנאנקים על כל התועבות הנעשות בתוכה. אלו לדיקים: שלא ישלטו בהם מלאכי חבלה. שאני רוצה לשלוח בעיר: היינו דכתיב. מעיקרא ועל כל איש אשר עליו התיו אל תגשו ולבסוף וממקדשי תחלו: ממקודשי. שהודה למקטרג מדת הדין וחזר מן הטוב: מי הוה מזבח הנחשת. בימי יחזקאל והלא שלמה גנזו ועשה מזבח אבנים של ל"ב אמה דכתיב (מלכים א ח) כי מזבח הנחשת אשר לפני ה' קטן מהכיל ו) כאדם האומר לחבירו ננס פלוני ופסול לעבודה: ממקום שאומרים שירה. מן הלוים שאומרים שיר בכלי נחשת: תיו תמות. לרשעים: חותמו של הקב"ה אמת. אמלעית לאותיות וראשון ואחרון על שם אני ראשון ואני אחרון ואני הוא: אלו בני אדם שקיימו התורה כולה. התיו סימן להם שקיימו התורה מראש עד סוף: ואיש לא יצילנה. שאין עוד זכות לאבות שאכלוה: ויפן אליהם למען בריתו את אברהם וגו' ולא השליכם מעל פניו עד עתה. אבל מכאן ואילך השליכם ולא פנה אל ברית אבות: ה' אלהי אברהם ואלהי יצחק וישראל היום יודע. שאתה זוכר ברית אברהם יצחק וישראל מדקאמר היום יודע ותו לא מכלל דתמה ועל ידי רחמים הוחכרה להם בימי חזאל: בימי חזקיהו. דכתיב מעתה ועד עולם קנאת ה' צבאות תעשה זאת ולא זכות אבות: בלא חטא. וחטאו של אדם גורם לו מיתה: בשבט ובנגעים. היינו יסורים וקאמר שאין באין אלא משום פקידת עון:
בעטיו

ואע"ג דלא מקבלי לוכחינהו מר. היינו היכא דספק אי מקבלי כדאמר בסמוך לפניהם מי גלוי אבל היכא דודאי לא מקבלי הנח להם מוטב שיהו שוגגין ואל יהיו מזידין כדאמרינן בהמביא כדי יין (ביצה דף ל. ושם) ובפרק שואל (לקמן דף קמח:) גבי תוספת יוה"כ ז):

ועל הרשעים תיו של דם. לא מקרא קאמר הכי אלא מסבר' דהא דכתיב והתוית תיו על מצחות האנשים הנאנחים והנאנקים על כל התועבות הנעשות בתוכה היינו בצדיקים גמורים: מזבח נחשת בימי שלמה מי הוה. כדכתיב ששלמה הסירו כי היה קטן מהכיל וא"ת והא כתיב בדברי הימים (ב ד) ויעש שלמה את מזבח הנחשת וי"ל דדרשינן ליה כי הכא מזבח שאומרים לפניו ° שירה בכלי נחשת:

קצף אף וחימה. קשה לרשב"א דאמר בפ"ק דמסכת ע"ג (דף ד. ושם) כתיב חימה אין לי וכתיב נוקם ה' ובעל חימה ומשני כאן לישראל כאן לנכרים אלמא דאין להקב"ה חימה על ישראל והאי דמס' ע"ג קשה דבס"פ ארבעה נדרים (דף לב.) אמר חימה משה הרגו דכתיב חימה אין לי ופריך והא כתיב כי יגורתי מפני האף והחימה ומשני תרי חימה הוו:

ושמואל אמר תמה זכות אבות ורבי יוחנן אמר תחון זכות אבות. אומר רבינו תם דזכות אבות תמה אבל ברית אבות לא תמה דהא כתיב (ויקרא כו) וזכרתי את בריתי יעקוב אף לאחר גלות ואנן אין אנו מזכירין זכות אבות אלא הברית ° ומפרש דשמואל דאמר מימי חזאל דייק מדכתיב למען בריתו ולא למען זכותו ואומר ר"י דבויקרא רבה (פ' לו) דייק מעד עתה כדפי' בקונטרס ולר"י נראה דלא פליגי שמואל ור"י אלא שמואל קאמר דלרשעים תמה אבל לצדיקים לא תמה ובצדיקים איירי ר"י תדע דהא ר"י אמר בסמוך דמימי חזקי' תמה זכות אבות והכא קאמר דאף בשעת חורבן דבתר הכי תחון זכות אבות ועל זה אנו סומכין להזכיר זכות אבות ובשלהי ויקרא רבה רבי אחא אומר לעולם זכות אבות קיימת ולעולם אנו מזכירים אותם וכן הוא אומר כי אל רחום וגו' ולא ישכח את ברית אבותיך וגו':

אין מיתה בלא חטא. פי' (מיתה) לפי שהגזרה באה אף על השגגה ואין יסורים בלא עון של מזיד כדאמר ביומא (דף לו:) חטאים אלו השגגות עונות אלו הזדונות ואף על גב דאמר (שבועות דף ח.) גבי שעיר של יה"כ להגין עליו מן היסורים משמע דיסורים באים על שוגג הכא מיירי ביסורי נגעים שהן מכוערים כדמייתי קרא:
ארבעה

מסורת הש"ס

א) [לקמן קנג. וש"נ ועי' מ"ש בחגיגה טו: על הגליון], ב) [נ"ל אמרה], ג) [ע"ז ד. ע"ש], ד) יומא סט: סנהדרין סד., ה) [נ"ל אמר אלו וכו'], ו) [זבחים נט:], ז) [וע"ע תוס' ב"ב ס: ד"ה מוטב ובתוס' ע"ז ד. ד"ה שהיה בידם].

גליון הש"ס

גמ' ר"י הוה יתיב. עי' ב"ב דף י ע"ב תוס' ד"ה עלוונים: שם א"ל ר"ז לר' סימון לוכחינהו. עי' מדרש רבה איכה שני ד"ה ולא זכר הדום רגליו: שם אמר רב מימות הושע בן בארי. ירושלמי פרק חלק. ושם איתא הך לימוד בשם שמואל: תוס' ד"ה מזבח נחושת וכו' שירה בכלי נחושת. עי' זבחים דף ס ע"א תוס' ד"ה ה"ק: שם ד"ה ושמואל וכו' ומפרש דשמואל דאמר מימי חזאל. אולם בירושלמי פ' חלק מסיים על עתה עד אותה שעה הזכות קיימת והיינו כפי' רש"י:

תורה אור השלם

א) אֹטֵם אָזְנוֹ מִזַּעֲקַת דָּל גַּם הוּא יִקְרָא וְלֹא יֵעָנֶה: [משלי כא, יג]

ב) בֵּית דָּוִד כֹּה אָמַר יְיָ דִּינוּ לַבֹּקֶר מִשְׁפָּט וְהַצִּילוּ גָזוּל מִיַּד עוֹשֵׁק פֶּן תֵּצֵא כָאֵשׁ חֲמָתִי וּבָעֲרָה וְאֵין מְכַבֶּה מִפְּנֵי רֹעַ מַעַלְלֵיכֶם: [ירמיה כא, יב]

ג) וַיֹּאמֶר יְיָ אֵלָיו עֲבֹר בְּתוֹךְ הָעִיר בְּתוֹךְ יְרוּשָׁלָיִם וְהִתְוִיתָ תָּו עַל מִצְחוֹת הָאֲנָשִׁים הַנֶּאֱנָחִים וְהַנֶּאֱנָקִים עַל כָּל הַתּוֹעֵבוֹת הַנַּעֲשׂוֹת בְּתוֹכָהּ: [יחזקאל ט, ד]

ד) זָקֵן בָּחוּר וּבְתוּלָה וְטַף וְנָשִׁים תַּהַרְגוּ לְמַשְׁחִית וְעַל כָּל אִישׁ אֲשֶׁר עָלָיו הַתָּו אַל תִּגַּשׁוּ וּמִמִּקְדָּשִׁי תָּחֵלּוּ וַיָּחֵלּוּ בָּאֲנָשִׁים הַזְּקֵנִים אֲשֶׁר לִפְנֵי הַבָּיִת: [יחזקאל ט, ו]

ה) וְהִנֵּה שִׁשָּׁה אֲנָשִׁים בָּאִים מִדֶּרֶךְ שַׁעַר הָעֶלְיוֹן אֲשֶׁר מָפְנֶה צָפוֹנָה וְאִישׁ כְּלִי מַפָּצוֹ בְּיָדוֹ וְאִישׁ אֶחָד בְּתוֹכָם לָבֻשׁ בַּדִּים וְקֶסֶת הַסֹּפֵר בְּמָתְנָיו וַיָּבֹאוּ וַיַּעַמְדוּ אֵצֶל מִזְבַּח הַנְּחֹשֶׁת: [יחזקאל ט, ב]

ו) וְעַתָּה אֲגַלֶּה אֶת נַבְלֻתָהּ לְעֵינֵי מְאַהֲבֶיהָ וְאִישׁ לֹא יַצִּילֶנָּה מִיָּדִי: [הושע ב, יב]

ז) וַחֲזָאֵל מֶלֶךְ אֲרָם לָחַץ אֶת יִשְׂרָאֵל כֹּל יְמֵי יְהוֹאָחָז: [מלכים ב' יג, כב]

ח) וַיָּחָן יְיָ אֹתָם וַיְרַחֲמֵם וַיִּפֶן אֲלֵיהֶם לְמַעַן בְּרִיתוֹ אֶת אַבְרָהָם יִצְחָק וְיַעֲקֹב וְלֹא אָבָה הַשְׁחִיתָם וְלֹא הִשְׁלִיכָם מֵעַל פָּנָיו עַד עָתָּה: [מלכים ב' יג, כג] ט) וַיְהִי בַּעֲלוֹת הַמִּנְחָה וַיִּגַּשׁ אֵלִיָּהוּ הַנָּבִיא וַיֹּאמַר יְיָ אֱלֹהֵי אַבְרָהָם יִצְחָק וְיִשְׂרָאֵל הַיּוֹם יִוָּדַע כִּי אַתָּה אֱלֹהִים בְּיִשְׂרָאֵל וַאֲנִי עַבְדֶּךָ וּבִדְבָרְךָ עָשִׂיתִי אֵת כָּל הַדְּבָרִים הָאֵלֶּה: [מלכים א' יח, לו] י) לְמַרְבֵּה הַמִּשְׂרָה וּלְשָׁלוֹם אֵין קֵץ עַל כִּסֵּא דָוִד וְעַל מַמְלַכְתּוֹ לְהָכִין אֹתָהּ וּלְסַעֲדָהּ בְּמִשְׁפָּט וּבִצְדָקָה מֵעַתָּה וְעַד עוֹלָם קִנְאַת יְיָ צְבָאוֹת תַּעֲשֶׂה זֹּאת: [ישעיה ט, ו] כ) הַנֶּפֶשׁ הַחֹטֵאת הִיא תָמוּת בֵּן לֹא יִשָּׂא בַּעֲוֹן הָאָב וְאָב לֹא יִשָּׂא בַּעֲוֹן הַבֵּן צִדְקַת הַצַּדִּיק עָלָיו תִּהְיֶה וְרִשְׁעַת הָרָשָׁע עָלָיו תִּהְיֶה: [יחזקאל יח, כ] ל) וּפָקַדְתִּי בְשֵׁבֶט פִּשְׁעָם וּבִנְגָעִים עֲוֹנָם: [תהלים פט, לג]

רבינו חננאל

ד' מתו בעטיו של נחש כבר פירשנוהו:

רב נסים גאון

דאמר ר' חנינא חותמו של הקב"ה אמת. תמצא עיקר דברי ר' חנינא בפרק בא לו כהן גדול (דף סט) במס' יומא ובפ' ד' מיתות (דף סד) במס' סנהדרין ובתלמוד ארץ ישראל במסכת סנהדרין (בראש פ"א) אמרו בדבר זה טעם נאה ביותר ונראה לי לכתבה הנה והכי אמרו מהו חותמו של הקב"ה רב ביבי בשם ר' ראובן אמר אמת מהו אמת אמר ר' אבין שהוא אלהים חיים ומלך עולם אמר ר' שמעון בן לקיש אלף ראשה דאלפא ביתא מם באמצעיתה תיו בסופ' לומר (ישעי' מד) אני ה' ראשון שלא קיבלתי מלכותי מאחר ומבלעדי אין אלהים שאין לי שותף ואת אחרונים אני הוא שאין אני עתיד למוסרה לאחר ואיתא נמי בבראשית [רבה] דר' אושעיא (פרשה פא):

ליקוטי רש"י

מיד עושק. טעמו למטה שאינו שם דבר אלא שם הגזלן העושק את אחרים. ואין מכבה. שלא ימלט לכם שריד [ירמיה כא, יב]. והתוית תיו. ורשמת רושם. על מצחות האנשים. הלדיקים כדי להיות לאות שלא יפגעו בם המשחיתים [יחזקאל ט, ד]. וממקדשי תחלו. מן העומדי' לפני מקדשי ורבותינו אמרו אל תקרי ממקדשי אלא ממקודשי מן המקודשים לי הם אותם מקוקי התיו שהתרה בהם מלהזיקם חזר וצוה לחבלם לפי שאמרה מדת הדין לפניו מה נשתנו אלו מאלו הרי לא מיחו בהם כדאיתא במסכת שבת [שם, ו]. גבי [ששה] משחיתים שבאו להשחית את ירושלים כתיב ביחזקאל [ע"ז ד.]. מפצו. שהוא משבר את הכל כמו ונפץ את עולליך (תהלים קלז). וקסת הסופר. פנקס הם לוחות שמחופין בשעוה וחורתין בם בעט [יחזקאל שם, ב]. ואיש לא יצילנה מידי. אף זכות אבותם תמה [הושע ב, יב]. ובדברך עשיתי. שהקרבתי בבמה בשעת איסור הבמות [מ"א יח, לו]. מעתה ועד עולם. עולמו של חזקיהו כל ימיו וכן מלינו שאמרה חנה על שמואל וישב שם עד עולם. קנאת ה' צבאות. שקנא לציון על אשר יען עליה ארם ופקח. תעשה זאת. ולא אתו ראוי לכך ואף זכות אבות תמה [ישעיה ט, ו עיי"ש].

מיתיבי אמרו מלאכי השרת לפני הקב"ה רבונו של עולם מפני מה קנסת מיתה על אדם הראשון אמר להם מצוה קלה צויתיו ועבר עליה א"ל והלא משה ואהרן שקיימו כל התורה כולה ומתו א"ל א) מקרה אחד לצדיק ולרשע לטוב וגו' הוא דאמר כי האי תנא דתניא ר"ש בן אלעזר אומר אף משה ואהרן בחטאם מתו שנא' ב) יען לא האמנתם בי א) הא האמנתם בי עדיין לא הגיע זמנכם ליפטר מן העולם מיתיבי ב) ארבעה מתו בעטיו של נחש ואלו הן בנימין בן יעקב ועמרם אבי משה וישי אבי דוד וכלאב בן דוד וכולהו גמרא לבר מישי אבי דוד דמפרש ביה קרא דכתיב ג) ואת עמשא שם אבשלום תחת יואב (ג) שר) הצבא ועמשא בן איש ושמו יתרא הישראלי אשר בא אל אביגיל בת נחש אחות צרויה אם יואב וכי בת נחש הואי והלא בת ישי הואי דכתיב ד) ואחיותיהן צרויה ואביגיל אלא בת מי שמת בעטיו של נחש מני אילימא תנא דמלאכי השרת והא איכא משה ואהרן אלא לאו ר"ש בן אלעזר היא וש"מ יש מיתה בלא חטא ויש יסורין בלא עון ותיובתא דרב אמי ° תיובתא: א"ר שמואל בר נחמני א"ר יונתן כל האומר ראובן חטא אינו אלא טועה שנאמר ה) ויהיו בני יעקב שנים עשר מלמד שכולן שקולים כאחת אלא מה אני מקיים ה) וישכב את בלהה פילגש אביו מלמד שבלבל מצעו של אביו ומעלה עליו הכתוב כאילו שכב עמה תניא ר"ש בן אלעזר אומר מוצל אותו צדיק מאותו עון ולא בא מעשה זה לידו אפשר עתיד זרעו לעמוד על הר עיבל ולומר ו) ארור שוכב עם אשת אביו ויבא חטא זה לידו אלא מה אני מקיים וישכב את בלהה פילגש אביו עלבון אמו תבע אמר אם אחות אמי היתה צרה לאמי שפחת אחות אמי תהא צרה לאמי עמד ובלבל את מצעה אחרים אומרים שתי מצעות בלבל אחת של שכינה ואחת של אביו והיינו דכתיב ז) אז חללת יצועי עלה ד) (אל תקרי יצועי אלא יצועיי) כתנאי ז) פחז כמים אל תותר ר' אליעזר אומר פזתה חבתה זלתה ר' יהושע אומר פסעתה על דת חטאת זנית ר"ג אומר פיללתה חלתה זרחה תפלתך אמר ר"ג עדיין צריכין אנו למודעי ר' אלעזר המודעי אומר הפוך את התיבה ודורשה ה) זעזעתה הרתעתה פרחה חטא ממך רבא אמר ואמרי לה ר' ירמיה בר אבא זכרת עונשו של דבר חלית עצמך חולי גדול פירשת מלחטוא: ראובן בני עלי בני שמואל דוד ושלמה ויואש ו) סימן: ז) אמר ר' שמואל בר נחמני א"ר יונתן כל האומר בני עלי חטאו אינו אלא טועה שנאמר ח) ושם שני בני עלי (עם ארון ברית האלהים) חפני ופנחס כהנים לה' סבר לה כרב דאמר רב פנחס לא חטא מקיש חפני לפנחס מה פנחס לא חטא אף חפני לא חטא אלא מה אני מקיים ט) אשר ישכבון את הנשים מתוך ששהו את קיניהן שלא הלכו אצל בעליהן מעלה עליהן הכתוב כאילו שכבום גופא אמר רב פנחס לא חטא שנאמר י) ואחיה בן אחיטוב אחי אי כבוד בן פנחס בן עלי כהן ה' וגו' אפשר חטא בא לידו והכתוב מייחסו והלא כבר נאמר כ) יכרת ה' לאיש אשר יעשנה ער ועונה מאהלי יעקב ומגיש מנחה לה' צבאות ט) אם ישראל הוא לא יהיה לו ער בחכמים ולא עונה בתלמידים ואם כהן הוא לא יהיה לו בן מגיש מנחה אלא לאו שמע מינה פנחס לא חטא אלא הא כתיב ט) אשר ישכבון ח) ישכבן כתיב והכתיב ל) אל בני כי לא טובה השמועה א"ר נחמן בר יצחק בני כתיב והכתיב ל) מעבירים א"ר הונא בריה דרב יהושע מעבירם כתיב והכתיב מ) בני בליעל מתוך שהיה לו לפנחס למחות לחפני ולא מיחה מעלה עליו הכתוב כאילו חטא א"ר שמואל בר נחמני א"ר יונתן כל האומר

בני

רש"י

בעטיו של נחש. בעצתו של נחש שהשיא לחוה ולא בחטא אחר שלא חטאו. בעטיו כמו עטא וטעם (דניאל ב): **ואחיותיהם.** בבני ישי משתעי: **אלא לאו ר"ש בן אלעזר.** דאמר משה ואהרן בחטאם מתו ומודה בהני: **כל האומר ראובן חטא.** במעשה בלהה: **דכתיב.** בההוא קרא: **ויהיו בני יעקב וגו'.** להוציא מלבך שלא תחשדנו: **ויבא חטא זה לידו.** ויגזור הקב"ה שיהיו מן המקללים: **אחת של שכינה.** כך היה יעקב עושה בארבעה אהלי נשיו מעמיד מטה לשכינה ובאותו אהל שהוא רואה בו השכינה הוא בא ולן אותו הלילה: **חללת.** אותו שם שעלה על יצועי דהיינו שכינה מדלא כתיב יצועי עלית טעם אחר עד שלא נבנה אהל מועד היתה שכינה מצויה באהלי צדיקים: **פחז.** נוטריקון הוא: **פזתה.** לשון עמא פזיזא (לקמן דף פח.). פזתה מיהרת בעצמך וחטאת: **זלתה.** זלזלת: **פיללת.** להנצל מן החטא: **חלתה.** י) ויחל משה (שמות לב): **זעזעת'.** יראת לחטוא לר' אליעזר ור' יהושע חטא ולרבן גמליאל ולמודעי בקש לחטוא ולא חטא: **חלית.** חולי גדול להתאפק לכבוש יצרך: **כל האומר בני עלי חטאו.** באשת איש אינו אלא טועה ומיהו בבזיון קדשים חטאו: **דאמר רב.** לקמן בשמעתין פנחס לא חטא וליף לה מקרא ור' יונתן יליף לה לחפני מהאי קרא דמקיש חפני לפנחס: **ששהו את קיניהן.** שהיו מסרבין להקריב שום קרבן אלא בקושי כדכתיב (שמואל א ב) גם בטרם יקטירון את החלב וגו' וכשהיו זבות ויולדות באות ממקום אחר לשילה להקריב את קיניהן והן היו משהין מלהקריבם והנשים לא היו יכולין לסמוך עליהם שיקריבו והיו שוהות שם ולא היו חוזרות אצל בעליהן עד שראו קיניהן קרבין והיו טהורות לקדשים וליכנס לעזרה לפיכך מעלה עליהם כאילו שכבום שהיו מונעים אותן מפריה ורביה: **פנחס לא חטא.** באשת איש דאשר ישכבון את הנשים אינו אלא חפני לבדו: **ואחיה בן אחיטוב וגו' כהן ה'.** בשילה נושא אפוד הרי שמיחסו לשבח ומזכיר עליו שם פנחס אבי אביו: **אפשר בא חטא לידו והכתוב מייחסו.** לשבח ואת בן בנו מייחסו אחריו והכתיב גבי עבירה דנואפים יכרת ה' לאיש וגו' והאי קרא בבא על הנכרית ועל הזונה מישתעי כדדרשינן ליה באלו הן הנשרפין כ) דכתיב לעיל מיניה כי חלל יהודה קדש ה' אשר אהב ובעל בת אל נכר ודרשינן כי חלל יהודה קדש זו זונה וכן הוא אומר לא תהיה קדשה וגו': **ער.** חריף להבין ולהורות בין החכמים כדאמרי' בעירובין (דף נג:) אהרנית ערנית: **ואם כהן הוא כו'.** וכאן מייחס כהן מגיש מנחה אחר פנחס: **והכתיב אל בני כי לא טובה השמועה אשר אנכי שומע מעבירים עם ה'** אביהם היה מוכיחם: **והא כתיב מעבירים אמר** ל) **רב הונא בריה דרב יהושע מעבירם כתיב.** קשה בעיני שם החכם הנזכר כאן כי אומר אני שטעות גדול הוא ול"ג לה להא מילתא שהרי בספרים מוגהים כתיב מעבירים וגם במסורה הגדולה במקום שמניין שם כל התיבות דלא כתיב בהן יו"ד וקורין ולא נמנה זה והם מנויין ע"פ החשבון וזו אינה קשיא דהאי מעבירים לאו לשון עבירה הוא אלא לשון ויעבירו קול במחנה (שמות לו) וה"ק להו לא טובה השמועה אשר אנכי שומע את עם ה' מעבירים ומכריזין וקובלים עליכם והאי מעבירים לשון רבים הוא ואעם ה' קאי ולאו אבני עלי שהרי הם היו עוברים ולא היו מעבירים את אחרים:

בני

תוספות

ארבעה מתו בעטיו של נחש. והא דכתיב (קהלת ז) כי אדם אין צדיק בארץ וגו' ברוב בני אדם קאמר: **וש"מ** יש מיתה בלא חטא ויש יסורים בלא עון. ואע"ג דבמאי דקאמר אין יסורין בלא עון לא איתותב: **כל** האומר בני עלי חטאו אינו אלא טועה. פירוש במאי דכתיב אשר ישכבון לא חטאו אלא מבזים קדשים היו כדכתיב (שמואל א ב) בטרם יקטירון החלב וגו': **מעבירם** כתיב. הש"ס שלנו חולק על ספרים שלנו שכתוב בהם (מ) מעבירים) וכן מצינו בירושלמי בשמשון והוא שפט את ישראל ארבעים שנה מלמד שהיו פלשתים יראים ממנו כ' שנה אחר מותו כמו בחייו ° ובכל ספרים שלנו כתיב כ' שנה (שופטים טז): **מתוך** שהיה לו לפנחס למחות. ופליג אר' יונתן דאמר שניהם לא חטאו:

שהיה

תורה אור השלם

א) הַכֹּל כַּאֲשֶׁר לַכֹּל מִקְרֶה אֶחָד לַצַּדִּיק וְלָרָשָׁע לַטּוֹב וְלַטָּהוֹר וְלַטָּמֵא וְלַזֹּבֵחַ וְלַאֲשֶׁר אֵינֶנּוּ זֹבֵחַ כַּטּוֹב כַּחֹטֶא הַנִּשְׁבָּע כַּאֲשֶׁר שְׁבוּעָה יָרֵא: [קהלת ט, ב]

ב) וַיֹּאמֶר יְיָ אֶל מֹשֶׁה וְאֶל אַהֲרֹן יַעַן לֹא הֶאֱמַנְתֶּם בִּי לְהַקְדִּישֵׁנִי לְעֵינֵי בְּנֵי יִשְׂרָאֵל לָכֵן לֹא תָבִיאוּ אֶת הַקָּהָל הַזֶּה אֶל הָאָרֶץ אֲשֶׁר נָתַתִּי לָהֶם: [במדבר כ, יב]

ג) וְאֶת עֲמָשָׂא שָׂם אַבְשָׁלֹם תַּחַת יוֹאָב עַל הַצָּבָא וַעֲמָשָׂא בֶן אִישׁ וּשְׁמוֹ יִתְרָא הַיִּשְׂרְאֵלִי אֲשֶׁר בָּא אֶל אֲבִיגַל בַּת נָחָשׁ אֲחוֹת צְרוּיָה אֵם יוֹאָב: [שמואל ב' יז, כה]

ד) וְאַחְיוֹתֵיהֶם צְרוּיָה וַאֲבִיגָיִל וּבְנֵי צְרוּיָה אַבְשַׁי וְיוֹאָב וַעֲשָׂה אֵל שְׁלשָׁה: [דברי הימים א' ב, טז]

ה) וַיְהִי בִּשְׁכֹּן יִשְׂרָאֵל בָּאָרֶץ הַהִוא וַיֵּלֶךְ רְאוּבֵן וַיִּשְׁכַּב אֶת בִּלְהָה פִּילֶגֶשׁ אָבִיו וַיִּשְׁמַע יִשְׂרָאֵל וַיִּהְיוּ בְנֵי יַעֲקֹב שְׁנֵים עָשָׂר: [בראשית לה, כב]

ו) אָרוּר שֹׁכֵב עִם אֵשֶׁת אָבִיו כִּי גִלָּה כְּנַף אָבִיו וְאָמַר כָּל הָעָם אָמֵן: [דברים כז, כ]

ז) פַּחַז כַּמַּיִם אַל תּוֹתַר כִּי עָלִיתָ מִשְׁכְּבֵי אָבִיךָ אָז חִלַּלְתָּ יְצוּעִי עָלָה: [בראשית מט, ד]

ח) וְעָלָה הָאִישׁ הַהוּא מֵעִירוֹ מִיָּמִים יָמִימָה לְהִשְׁתַּחֲוֺת וְלִזְבֹּחַ לַייָ צְבָאוֹת בְּשִׁלֹה וְשָׁם שְׁנֵי בְנֵי עֵלִי חָפְנִי וּפִנְחָס כֹּהֲנִים לַייָ: [שמואל א' א, ג]

ט) וְעֵלִי זָקֵן מְאֹד וְשָׁמַע אֵת כָּל אֲשֶׁר יַעֲשׂוּן בָּנָיו לְכָל יִשְׂרָאֵל וְאֵת אֲשֶׁר יִשְׁכְּבוּן אֶת הַנָּשִׁים הַצֹּבְאוֹת פֶּתַח אֹהֶל מוֹעֵד: [שמואל א' ב, כב]

י) וַאֲחִיָּה בֶן אֲחִטוּב אֲחִי אִיכָבוֹד בֶּן פִּינְחָס בֶּן עֵלִי כֹּהֵן יְיָ בְּשִׁלוֹ נֹשֵׂא אֵפוֹד וְהָעָם לֹא יָדַע כִּי הָלַךְ יוֹנָתָן: [שמואל א' יד, ג]

כ) יַכְרֵת יְיָ לָאִישׁ אֲשֶׁר יַעֲשֶׂנָּה עֵר וְעֹנֶה מֵאָהֳלֵי יַעֲקֹב וּמַגִּישׁ מִנְחָה לַייָ צְבָאוֹת: [מלאכי ב, יב]

ל) אַל בָּנָי כִּי לוֹא טוֹבָה הַשְּׁמֻעָה אֲשֶׁר אָנֹכִי שֹׁמֵעַ מַעֲבִרִים עַם יְיָ: [שמואל א' ב, כד]

מ) וּבְנֵי עֵלִי בְּנֵי בְלִיָּעַל לֹא יָדְעוּ אֶת יְיָ: [שמואל א' ב, יב]

מסורת הש"ס

א) [יומא פז.], ב) ב"ב יז., ג) [צ"ל על], ד) רש"ל מ"ז ועי' רש"י, ה) לשון רתת, ו) צ"ל ויאשיהו, ז) יומא ט., ח) סנהדרין פב., ט) [עיין תוספות סנהדרין ד. ד"ה ורבנן], י) [צ"ל כמו ויחל משה], כ) [סנהדרין דף פג.], ל) מהרש"א גורס רבא, מ) [צ"ל מעברים].

גליון הש"ס

גמ' ד' מתו בעטיו של נחש כו'. בזוה"ק פ' בראשית ועל דא יהושע לא מת אלא בעטיו דנחש וכו'. ובזוה"ק פ' בראשית בפסוק וינחם ה' תלתא דאיסתלקו בגין ההוא עטיא דנחש עמרם לוי בנימין ואית דאמרי אף ישי: **שם תיובתא.** עי' ברא"מ פ' וישלח ד"ה אומרא ובפ' שופטים ד"ה ריה"ג: **תוס' ד"ה מעבירם כתיב וכו' ובכל ספרים שלנו.** וכן מצינו בנדה דף לג ע"א תוס' ד"ה והנושא שכתבו דהמסורת שלנו מחולק עם הש"ס. ובמגילה דף כב ע"א כתבו תוס' דויחל הוא ג' פסוקים סמוך לפרשה שלפניו וכן והקרבתם ובמ"ת שלנו ויחל הוא ד' פסוקים מהפרשה וכן והקרבתם ג"פ וכמ"ש מהרש"א שם. ובפסחים דף קיז ע"א בתוס' ד"ה שעומדים כתבו שלא יתכן שיהיה מזמור ב' פסוקים ואלו בספרים שלנו מזמור קיז הוא ב' פסוקים. עי' מהרש"א שם ע"א. ובסנהדרין דף ד ע"א פירש"י שם דבכבשה דיחיד כתיב קרנות מלא ובמ"ת שלנו כתיב חסר. ובדף ד ע"ב כ' רש"י דבפרשה והיה כי יביאך כתיב לטטפת חסר ובפ' והיה אם שמע כתיב מלא. ובמ"ת שלנו גם בפ' והיה כי יביאך כתיב מלא. ובדף כ ע"א כתי' להכרית וקרי להכרו' ובספרים שלנו גם הכתיב להכרות. עוד שם דף קג ע"א ויחתר לו ויעתר לו מיבעיא ליה. ובספרים שלנו כתיב ויעתר. ובב"ב דף ט ע"א הלא פרוש בשין ובספרים שלנו כתיב בסין. ועי' בח"א שם במהרש"א. ובקדושין דף ל ע"א. והתגלח תליין של פסוקי' ובתיקונים בפ' לו בפסוק ויאפוד לו בו ליין דשם חצי התורה בפסוקים. ובירושלמי שהביא תוס' בכתובות דף ז ע"ב דבמקהלת ברכו אלהים חסר. ובספרים שלנו כתיב מלא. וברש"י בחומש פ' תרומה ואת כל אשר אצוה הוא וי"ו יתירה ולפנינו כתיב את בלא ו'. עי' ברא"ם שם. ובמדרש רבה שיר השירים בפסוק אחזו לנו שועלים שעלים א"ר ברכיה קדמאה מלא תניינא חסר. ובמסורה אינו כן אלא תרוייהו חסר. ובברכות דף ז ע"ב כתי' לכלותו ובספרי' שלנו בד"ה א יז כתיב לבלותו. (ובפסחים דף ג ע"א ו' דטהור. ובספרים

ליקוטי רש"י

מקרה אחד. שסוף הכל אשר צדיק ואשר רשע למות ומקרה אחד יש בעולם הזה לכולם [קהלת ט, ב]. **יען לא האמנתם בי.** גלה הכתוב שאלולי חטא זה בלבד היו נכנסין לארץ כדי שלא יאמרו עליהם כעון שאר דור המדבר שנגזר עליהם שלא יכנסו לארץ כך היה עון משה ואהרן [במדבר כ, יב]. **בעטיו של נחש.** בעצתו של נחש כלומר לא היו ראוין למות אלא שנגזרה גזירת מיתה על כל תולדותיו של אדם הראשון בעצתו של נחש בעטיו תרגום של עצתו כדכתיב (דניאל ו) אתייעטו כל וגו' וכן התיב עטא וטעם (שם ב). **ואחיותיהן.** בנות ישי כתיב [ב"ב יז.]. **בת נחש.** הוא ישי אבי דוד רבותינו אמרו שמת בלא עון בעטיו של נחש [ש"ב יז, כה]. **ויהיו בני יעקב שנים עשר.** ורבותינו דרשו ללמדנו בא שכולן שוין וכולן צדיקים שלא חטא ראובן. **וישכב את בלהה פילגש אביו וכו'.** מתוך שבלבל משכבו מעלה עליו הכתוב כאלו שכבה. ולמה בלבל וחלל יצועיו שכשמתה רחל נטל יעקב מטתו שהיתה נתונה תדיר באהל רחל ולא בשאר אהלים ונתנה באהל בלהה בא ראובן ותבע עלבון אמו אמר אם אחות אמי היתה צרה לאמי שפחת אחות אמי תהא צרה לאמי לכן בלבל [בראשית לה, כב]. **אז חללת.** אותו שם שעלה על יצועי והיא השכינה שהיה דרכה להיות עולה על יצועי. **יצועי.** לשון משכב על שם שמציעים אותו על ידי לבדין וסדינין והרבה דומים לו (תהלים סג, ז) אם זכרתיך על יצועי (שם קלב, ג) אם אעלה על ערש יצועי. **פחז כמים.** הפחז והבהלה אשר מהרת להראות כעסך כמים הללו הממהרים למרוצתם, לכך. **אל תותר.** אל תרבה ליטול כל היתרות הללו שהיו ראויות לך. **פחז.** שם דבר הוא לפיכך טעמו למעלה וכולו נקוד פת"ח ואלו היה לשון עבר היה נקוד חציו קמ"ץ וחציו פת"ח וטעמו למטה [שם מט, ד]. **אשר ישכבון.** כמשמעו ורבותינו אמרו מתוך ששהו את קיניהן והם היו ממתינות עד שתראן קיניהן קריבין מעלה עליהם כאלו שכבום [ש"א ב, כב]. **ששהו את קיניהן.** שהיו מביאות במלאות ימי לידתן ליטהר לאכול בקדשים והם היו בעלי [גאוה] והיו מתרשלין בהקרבתן והנשים ממתינות שם עד שיקריבום ומשהות מלחזור למקומן אצל בעליהן ומבטלין את הנשים מפריה ורביה [יומא ט:].

The Gemara challenges Rav Ami's statement:

מֵיתִיבֵי – **They objected** on the basis of the following Baraisa: אָמְרוּ מַלְאֲכֵי הַשָּׁרֵת לִפְנֵי הַקָּדוֹשׁ בָּרוּךְ הוּא – THE MINISTERING ANGELS SAID BEFORE THE HOLY ONE, BLESSED IS HE: רִבּוֹנוֹ שֶׁל עוֹלָם מִפְּנֵי מָה קָנַסְתָּ מִיתָה עַל אָדָם הָרִאשׁוֹן – "MASTER OF THE UNIVERSE, WHY DID YOU DECREE THE PENALTY OF DEATH UPON Adam, THE FIRST MAN?"[1] אָמַר לָהֶם מִצְוָה קַלָּה צִוִּיתִיו וְעָבַר עָלֶיהָ – [GOD] ANSWERED THEM: "I GAVE HIM ONE EASY COMMANDMENT, AND HE TRANSGRESSED IT."[2] אָמְרוּ לוֹ וַהֲלֹא מֹשֶׁה וְאַהֲרֹן שֶׁקִּיְּימוּ כָּל הַתּוֹרָה כּוּלָּהּ וָמֵתוּ – THEY then SAID TO HIM: "BUT MOSES AND AARON OBSERVED THE ENTIRE TORAH, AND THEY DIED!" אָמַר לָהֶם ,,מִקְרֶה אֶחָד לַצַּדִּיק וְלָרָשָׁע לַטּוֹב וגו׳ ״ – HE SAID TO THEM: *ONE EVENT,* [death, happens] *TO THE RIGHTEOUS AND TO THE WICKED,* TO THE GOOD etc. [*and to the pure and to the impure . . . the good just like the sinner* . . .].[3] Hashem's reply indicates that there *is* death without sin – contrary to the statement of Rav Ami. – ? –

The Gemara replies:

הוּא דְּאָמַר כִּי הַאי תַּנָּא – **He** (i.e. Rav Ami), who has ruled that there is no death without sin, **has stated** his ruling **in accordance with this** other **Tanna,** דְּתַנְיָא רַבִּי שִׁמְעוֹן בֶּן אֶלְעָזָר אוֹמֵר – **for it is taught in** a **Baraisa:** R' SHIMON BEN ELAZAR SAYS: אַף מֹשֶׁה וְאַהֲרֹן בְּחֶטְאָם מֵתוּ – MOSES AND AARON ALSO DIED ON ACCOUNT OF THEIR TRANSGRESSION, שֶׁנֶּאֱמַר ,,יַעַן לֹא־הֶאֱמַנְתֶּם בִּי״ – AS IT IS STATED: *BECAUSE YOU DID NOT BELIEVE IN ME to sanctify Me in the eyes of the Children of Israel, therefore you will not bring this congregation to the land that I have given them.*[4] הָא הֶאֱמַנְתֶּם בִּי עֲדַיִין לֹא הִגִּיעַ זְמַנְּכֶם לִיפָּטֵר מִן הָעוֹלָם – Hashem thus implies: HAD YOU BELIEVED IN ME, YOUR TIME TO DEPART FROM THE WORLD WOULD NOT HAVE ARRIVED. From here we see that Moses and Aaron also died because of a transgression. R' Shimon ben Elazar's opinion thus provides the basis for Rav Ami's statement that there is no death without transgression.

The Gemara again challenges Rav Ami:

מֵיתִיבֵי – **They objected** on the basis of the following Baraisa: אַרְבָּעָה מֵתוּ בְּעֶטְיוֹ שֶׁל נָחָשׁ – FOUR DIED only AS A RESULT OF THE SERPENT'S COUNSEL,[5] וְאֵלּוּ הֵן בִּנְיָמִין בֶּן יַעֲקֹב וְעַמְרָם אֲבִי מֹשֶׁה וְיִשַׁי אֲבִי דָוִד וְכִלְאָב בֶּן דָּוִד – AND THESE ARE THEY: BENJAMIN THE SON OF JACOB, AMRAM THE FATHER OF MOSES, YISHAI THE FATHER OF DAVID, AND KILAV THE SON OF DAVID. וְכוּלְּהוּ גְּמָרָא לְבַר מִיִּשַׁי אֲבִי דָוִד – AND with regard to ALL OF THEM this fact is an oral TRADITION – EXCEPT FOR YISHAI THE FATHER OF DAVID, דִּמְפָרֵשׁ בֵּיהּ קְרָא – CONCERNING WHOM THE VERSE IS EXPLICIT, דִּכְתִיב ,,וְאֶת־עֲמָשָׂא שָׂם אַבְשָׁלוֹם תַּחַת יוֹאָב (שר) [עַל־]הַצָּבָא וַעֲמָשָׂא בֶן־אִישׁ וּשְׁמוֹ יִתְרָא הַיִּשְׂרְאֵלִי אֲשֶׁר־בָּא אֶל־אֲבִיגַל בַּת־נָחָשׁ אֲחוֹת צְרוּיָה אֵם יוֹאָב״ – FOR IT IS WRITTEN:[6] *AND AVSHALOM SET AMASA OVER THE ARMY INSTEAD OF YOAV; NOW, AMASA WAS THE SON OF A MAN WHOSE NAME WAS YISRA THE ISRAELITE, WHO COHABITED WITH AVIGAL* (Avigayil), *THE DAUGHTER OF NACHASH [AND] THE SISTER OF TZERUYAH, THE MOTHER OF YOAV.*

The Baraisa asks rhetorically:

וְכִי בַּת נָחָשׁ הֲוַאי – BUT WAS [AVIGAYIL] really THE DAUGHTER OF NACHASH? וַהֲלֹא בַּת יִשַׁי הֲוַאי – BUT WAS SHE NOT THE DAUGHTER OF YISHAI, דִּכְתִיב ,,וְאַחְיוֹתֵיהֶם צְרוּיָה וַאֲבִיגָיִל״ – AS IT IS WRITTEN:[7] *AND THEIR SISTERS WERE TZERUYAH AND AVIGAYIL?* אֶלָּא בַּת מִי שֶׁמֵּת בְּעֶטְיוֹ שֶׁל נָחָשׁ – RATHER, Scripture calls her the daughter of Nachash (Hebrew for *serpent*) because she was THE DAUGHTER OF SOMEONE (viz. Yishai) WHO DIED only AS A RESULT OF THE SERPENT'S COUNSEL.

The Gemara concludes its challenge:

מַנִּי – Now, **who** authored the foregoing Baraisa? אִילֵימָא תַּנָּא דְּמַלְאֲכֵי הַשָּׁרֵת – **If we say** it was authored by the **Tanna of** the Baraisa that recorded God's dialogue with **the ministering angels,** that cannot be – וְהָא אִיכָּא מֹשֶׁה וְאַהֲרֹן – **for** according to that Tanna **there are Moses and Aaron,** who also died without sin![8] אֶלָּא לָאו רַבִּי שִׁמְעוֹן בֶּן אֶלְעָזָר הִיא – **Rather,** must we **not** say that **[the second Baraisa] is** in accord with **R' Shimon ben Elazar?** וּשְׁמַע מִינַּהּ יֵשׁ מִיתָה בְּלֹא חֵטְא וְיֵשׁ יִסּוּרִין בְּלֹא עָוֹן – **And derive from it** that **there is death without transgression and there is suffering without sin** even according to him, וּתְיוּבְתָּא דְּרַב אַמִי – **and** so this is **a refutation of Rav Ami!**[9]

The Gemara concludes:

תְּיוּבְתָּא – It is indeed **a refutation.**

The Gemara explained above (54b) that the Mishnah attributed the sin of a neighbor to R' Elazar ben Azaryah (on account of his failure to protest). The Gemara now continues with the theme of apparent transgressions:

אָמַר רַבִּי שְׁמוּאֵל בַּר נַחְמָנִי אָמַר רַבִּי יוֹנָתָן – **R' Shmuel bar Nachmani said in the name of R' Yonasan:** כָּל הָאוֹמֵר רְאוּבֵן חָטָא אֵינוֹ אֶלָּא טוֹעֶה – **Whoever says** that **Reuven sinned is simply mistaken,**[10] שֶׁנֶּאֱמַר ,,וַיִּהְיוּ בְנֵי־יַעֲקֹב שְׁנֵים עָשָׂר״ – **for it**

NOTES

1. The angels wondered: Since Adam is the work of Your hands, it does not seem fitting to punish him with death for a relatively minor sin. Moreover, it is not Your way to punish for the first sin, as it is written: *Behold, God does all these things two or three times with a man, to return his soul from destruction* (*Job* 33:29-30); nevertheless, You decreed death upon Adam for his very first sin (*Iyun Yaakov* to *Ein Yaakov*).

2. Hashem replied: I Myself commanded Adam regarding the Tree of Knowledge, and one who was personally commanded by the King cannot be compared to one was was commanded by an intermediary. [Therefore, for Adam's disobedience the penalty must be severe] (*Iyun Yaakov*. Moreover, Adam was the only one to receive this commandment. If many people are given a commandment and one violates it, the word of Hashem is not annulled, for the others can still observe it. But if only one person is commanded and he transgresses, the word of Hashem is de facto annulled, and this requires a more severe punishment (*Anaf Yosef* to *Ein Yaakov,* in the name of *Sefer Kol Nehi*).

3. *Ecclesiastes* 9:2.

4. *Numbers* 20:12. If Moses had spoken to the rock as commanded instead of striking it, the people's belief in Hashem would have been strengthened (*Rashi* ibid.; cf. *Ramban,* et al., ibid.). [For a discussion of how the Tanna Kamma deals with this, see *Maharsha* and *Sfas Emes.*]

5. These four were without sin, and died only because the serpent incited Eve to violate Hashem's command, thus bringing death to the world (*Rashi*).

As for the verse, *There is no righteous man on the earth who does good and does not sin* (see above, 55a note 31), that refers to the majority of people, but not to these four (*Tosafos*; see also *Meirii*).

6. *II Samuel* 17:25.

7. *I Chronicles* 2:16, which refers to the sisters of Yishai's sons (*Rashi*).

8. The Tanna Kamma of the first Baraisa held that Moses and Aaron died without sin. If he is the Tanna of the second Baraisa as well, he would have stated that six people – not merely four – died only because of the incitement of the serpent.

9. The Tanna Kamma of the first Baraisa holds that Moses and Aaron died without sin, and although R' Shimon ben Elazar disagrees about Moses and Aaron, he agrees that four others did die without sin. Thus, according to both of these Tannaim there is death without sin, and so there is no Tannaic basis for the contrary opinion of the Amora, Rav Ami. [See, however, *Tosafos* and *Chasam Sofer*; see also *Berachos* 5a,b.]

10. [Literally: is nothing but one who makes a mistake.] It is a mistake to think that Reuven sinned in the incident of Bilhah [*Genesis* 35:22] (*Rashi*).

Rashi's point is that Reuven did not commit the actual deed that the Torah seems to attribute to him (lying with Bilhah, his father's concubine). However, he did transgress by "disturbing" his father's bed, as explained by the Gemara below (*Maharsha*).

ארבעה מתו בעטיו של נחש ואלו הן בנימין בן יעקב ועמרם אבי משה וישי אבי דוד וכלאב בן דוד וכולהו גמרא לבר מישי אבי דוד דמפרש ביה קרא דכתיב ג) ואת עמשא שם אבשלום תחת יואב (ג) שר) הצבא ועמשא בן איש ושמו יתרא הישראלי אשר בא אל אביגיל בת נחש אחות צרויה אם יואב וכי בת נחש הואי והלא בת ישי הואי דכתיב ד) ואחיותיהן צרויה ואביגיל אלא בת מי שמת בעטיו של נחש מני אילימא תנא דמלאכי השרת והא איכא משה ואהרן אלא לאו ר"ש בן אלעזר היא וש"מ יש מיתה בלא חטא ויש יסורין בלא עון ותיובתא דרב אמי ° תיובתא:

מיתיבי אמרו מלאכי השרת לפני הקב"ה רבונו של עולם מפני מה קנסת מיתה על אדם הראשון אמר להם מצוה קלה צויתיו ועבר עליה א"ל והלא משה ואהרן שקיימו כל התורה כולה ומתו א"ל א) מקרה אחד לצדיק ולרשע לטוב וגו' הוא דאמר כי האי תנא דתניא ר"ש בן אלעזר אומר אף משה ואהרן בחטאם מתו שנא' ב) יען לא האמנתם בי א) הא האמנתם בי עדיין לא הגיע זמנכם ליפטר מן העולם מיתיבי ° ג) ארבעה מתו בעטיו של נחש ואלו הן בנימין בן יעקב ועמרם אבי משה וישי אבי דוד וכלאב בן דוד וכולהו גמרא לבר מישי אבי דוד דמפרש

א"ר שמואל בר נחמני א"ר יונתן כל האומר ראובן חטא אינו אלא טועה שנאמר ה) ויהיו בני יעקב שנים עשר מלמד שכולן שקולים כאחת אלא מה אני מקיים ה) וישכב את בלהה פילגש אביו מלמד שבלבל מצעו של אביו ומעלה עליו הכתוב כאילו שכב עמה תניא ר"ש בן אלעזר אומר מוצל אותו צדיק מאותו עון ולא בא מעשה זה לידו אפשר עתיד זרעו לעמוד על הר עיבל ולומר ו) ארור שוכב עם אשת אביו ויבא חטא זה לידו אלא מה אני מקיים וישכב את בלהה פילגש אביו עלבון אמו תבע אמר אם אחות אמי היתה צרה לאמי שפחת אחות אמי תהא צרה לאמי עמד ובלבל את מצעה אחרים אומרים שתי מצעות בלבל אחת של שכינה ואחת של אביו והיינו דכתיב ז) אז חללת יצועי עלה ד) (אל תקרי יצועי אלא יצועיי) כתנאי ז) פחז כמים אל תותר ר' אליעזר אומר פזתה חבתה זלתה ר' יהושע אומר פסעתה על דת חטאת זנית ר"ג אומר פיללתה חלתה זרחה תפלתך אמר ר"ג עדיין צריכין אנו למודעי ר' אלעזר המודעי אומר הפוך את התיבה ודורשה ה) זעזעתה הרתעתה פרחה חטא ממך רבא אמר ואמרי לה ר' ירמיה בר אבא זכרת עונשו של דבר חלית עצמך חולי גדול פירשת מלחטוא: ראובן בני עלי בני שמואל דוד ושלמה ויואש ו) סימן:

ז) אמר ר' שמואל בר נחמני א"ר יונתן כל האומר בני עלי חטאו אינו אלא טועה שנאמר ח) ושם שני בני עלי (עם ארון ברית האלהים) חפני ופנחס כהנים לה' סבר לה כרב דאמר רב פנחס לא חטא מקיש חפני לפנחס מה פנחס לא חטא אף חפני לא חטא אלא מה אני מקיים ט) אשר ישכבון את הנשים מתוך ששהו את קיניהן שלא הלכו אצל בעליהן מעלה עליהן הכתוב כאילו שכבום גופא אמר רב פנחס לא חטא שנאמר י) ואחיה בן אחיטוב אחי אי כבוד בן פנחס בן עלי כהן ה' וגו' אפשר חטא בא לידו והכתוב מייחסו והלא כבר נאמר כ) יכרת ה' לאיש אשר יעשנה ער ועונה מאהלי יעקב ומגיש מנחה לה' צבאות ח) אם ישראל הוא לא יהיה לו ער בחכמים ולא עונה בתלמידים ואם כהן הוא לא יהיה לו בן מגיש מנחה אלא לאו שמע מינה פנחס לא חטא אלא הא כתיב ט) אשר ישכבון ט) ישכבן כתיב והכתיב ל) אל בני כי לא טובה השמועה א"ר נחמן בר יצחק בני כתיב והכתיב ל) מעבירים א"ר הונא בריה דרב יהושע מעבירם כתיב והכתיב מ) בני בליעל מתוך שהיה לו לפנחס למחות לחפני ולא מיחה מעלה עליו הכתוב כאילו חטא א"ר שמואל בר נחמני א"ר יונתן כל האומר

בני

תוספות

ארבעה מתו בעטיו של נחש. והא דכתיב (קהלת ז) כי אדם אין צדיק בארץ וגו' ברוב בני אדם קאמר: **וש"מ** יש מיתה בלא חטא ויש יסורים בלא עון. ואע"ג דבמאי דקאמר אין יסורין בלא עון לא איתותב: **כל** האומר בני עלי חטאו אינו אלא טועה. פירוש במאי דכתיב אשר ישכבון לא חטאו אלא מבזים קדשים היו כדכתיב (שמואל א ב) בטרם יקטירון החלב וגו': **מעבירם** כתיב. הש"ס שלנו חולק על ספרים שלנו שכתוב בהם (מ) מעבירים) וכן מצינו בירושלמי בשמשון והוא שפט את ישראל ארבעים שנה מלמד שהיו פלשתים יראים ממנו כ' שנה אחר מותו כמו בחייו ° ובכל ספרים שלנו כתיב כ' שנה (שופטים טו): **מתוך** שהיה לו לפנחס למחות. ופליג אר' יונתן דאמר שניהם לא חטאו:

שהיה

השמועה אשר אנכי שומע מעבירים עם ה' אביהם היה מוכיחם: **והא כתיב מעבירים אמר** ל) **רב הונא בריה דרב יהושע מעבירם כתיב.** קשה בעיני שם החכם הנזכר כאן כי אומר אני שטעות גדול הוא ול"ג לה להא מילתא שהרי בספרים מוגהים כתיב מעבירים וגם במסורה הגדולה במקום שמנויין שם כל התיבות דלא כתיב בהן יו"ד וקורין ולא נמנה זה והם מנויין ע"פ החשבון וזו אינה קשיא דהאי מעבירים לאו לשון עבירה הוא אלא לשון ויעבירו קול במחנה (שמות לו) וה"ק להו לא טובה השמועה אשר אנכי שומע את עם ה' מעבירים ומכריזין וקובלים עליכם והאי מעבירים לשון רבים הוא ואעם ה' קאי ולאו אבני עלי שהרי הם היו עוברים ולא היו מעבירים את אחרים:

רש"י

בעטיו של נחש. בעצתו של נחש שהשיא לחוה ולא בחטא אחר שלא חטאו. בעטיו כמו עטא וטעם (דניאל ב): **ואחיותיהם.** בבני ישי משתעי: **אלא לאו ר"ש בן אלעזר.** דאמר משה ואהרן בחטאם מתו ומודה בהני: **כל האומר ראובן חטא.** במעשה בלהה: **דכתיב.** בההוא קרא: **ויהיו בני יעקב וגו'.** להוציא מלבך שלא תחשדנו: **ויבא חטא זה לידו.** ויגזור הקב"ה שיהיו מן המקללים: **אחת של שכינה.** כך היה יעקב עושה בארבעה אהלי נשיו מעמיד מטה לשכינה ובאותו אהל שהוא רואה בו השכינה הוא בא ולן אותו הלילה: **חללת.** אותו שם שעלה על יצועי דהיינו שכינה מדלא כתיב יצועי עלית טעם אחר עד שלא נבנה אהל מועד היתה שכינה מצויה באהלי צדיקים: **פחז.** נוטריקון הוא: **פזתה.** לשון עמא פזיזא (לקמן דף פח.). פזתה מיהרת בעצמך וחטאת: **זלתה.** זלזלת: **פיללת.** להנצל מן החטא: **חלתה.** י) ויחל משה (שמות לב): **זעזעת'.** יראת לחטוא לר' אליעזר ור' יהושע חטא ולרבן גמליאל ולמודעי בקש לחטוא ולא חטא: **חלית.** חולי גדול להתאפק לכבוש יצרך: **כל האומר בני עלי חטאו.** באשת איש אינו אלא טועה ומיהו בבזיון קדשים חטאו: **דאמר רב.** לקמן בשמעתין פנחס לא חטא ויליף לה מקרא ור' יונתן יליף לה לחפני מהאי קרא דמקיש חפני לפנחס: **ששהו את קיניהן.** שהיו מסרבין להקריב שום קרבן אלא בקושי כדכתיב (שמואל א ב) גם בטרם יקטירון את החלב וגו' וכשהיו זבות ויולדות באות ממקום אחר לשילה להקריב את קיניהן והן היו משהין מלהקריבם והנשים לא היו יכולין לסמוך עליהם שיקריבו והיו שוהות שם ולא היו חוזרות אצל בעליהן עד שראו קיניהן קרבין והיו טהורות לקדשים וליכנס לעזרה לפיכך מעלה עליהם כאילו שכבום שהיו מונעים אותן מפריה ורביה: **פנחס לא חטא.** באשת איש דאשר ישכבון את הנשים אינו אלא חפני לבדו: **ואחיה בן אחיטוב וגו' כהן ה'.** בשילה נושא אפוד הרי שמיחסו לשבח ומזכיר עליו שם פנחס אבי אביו: **אפשר בא חטא לידו והכתוב מייחסו.** לשבח ואת בן בנו מייחסו אחריו והכתיב גבי עבירה דנואפים יכרת ה' לאיש וגו' והאי קרא בבא על הנכרית ועל הזונה מישתעי כדדרשינן ליה באלו הן הנשרפין ס) דכתיב לעיל מיניה כי חלל יהודה קדש ה' אשר אהב ובעל בת אל נכר ודרשינן כי חלל יהודה קדש זו זונה וכן הוא אומר לא תהיה קדשה וגו': **ער.** חריף להבין ולהורות בין החכמים כדאמרי' בעירובין (דף נג:) אהרנית ערנית: **ואם כהן הוא כו'.** וכאן מייחס כהן מגיש מנחה אחר פנחס: **והכתיב אל בני כי לא טובה**

בני

תורה אור השלם

א) הַכֹּל כַּאֲשֶׁר לַכֹּל מִקְרֶה אֶחָד לַצַּדִּיק וְלָרָשָׁע לַטּוֹב וְלַטָּהוֹר וְלַטָּמֵא וְלַזֹּבֵחַ וְלַאֲשֶׁר אֵינֶנּוּ זֹבֵחַ כַּטּוֹב כַּחֹטֶא הַנִּשְׁבָּע כַּאֲשֶׁר שְׁבוּעָה יָרֵא: [קהלת ט, ב]

ב) וַיֹּאמֶר יְיָ אֶל מֹשֶׁה וְאֶל אַהֲרֹן יַעַן לֹא הֶאֱמַנְתֶּם בִּי לְהַקְדִּישֵׁנִי לְעֵינֵי בְּנֵי יִשְׂרָאֵל לָכֵן לֹא תָבִיאוּ אֶת הַקָּהָל הַזֶּה אֶל הָאָרֶץ אֲשֶׁר נָתַתִּי לָהֶם: [במדבר כ, יב]

ג) וְאֶת עֲמָשָׂא שָׂם אַבְשָׁלֹם תַּחַת יוֹאָב עַל הַצָּבָא וַעֲמָשָׂא בֶן אִישׁ וּשְׁמוֹ יִתְרָא הַיִּשְׂרְאֵלִי אֲשֶׁר בָּא אֶל אֲבִיגַל בַּת נָחָשׁ אֲחוֹת צְרוּיָה אֵם יוֹאָב: [שמואל ב' יז, כה]

ד) וְאַחְיוֹתֵיהֶם צְרוּיָה וַאֲבִיגָיִל וּבְנֵי צְרוּיָה אַבְשַׁי וְיוֹאָב וַעֲשָׂה־אֵל שְׁלֹשָׁה: [דברי הימים א' ב, טז]

ה) וַיְהִי בִּשְׁכֹּן יִשְׂרָאֵל בָּאָרֶץ הַהִוא וַיֵּלֶךְ רְאוּבֵן וַיִּשְׁכַּב אֶת בִּלְהָה פִּילֶגֶשׁ אָבִיו וַיִּשְׁמַע יִשְׂרָאֵל וַיִּהְיוּ בְנֵי יַעֲקֹב שְׁנֵים עָשָׂר: [בראשית לה, כב]

ו) אָרוּר שֹׁכֵב עִם אֵשֶׁת אָבִיו כִּי גִלָּה כְּנַף אָבִיו וְאָמַר כָּל הָעָם אָמֵן: [דברים כז, כ]

ז) פַּחַז כַּמַּיִם אַל תּוֹתַר כִּי עָלִיתָ מִשְׁכְּבֵי אָבִיךָ אָז חִלַּלְתָּ יְצוּעִי עָלָה: [בראשית מט, ד]

ח) וְעָלָה הָאִישׁ הַהוּא מֵעִירוֹ מִיָּמִים יָמִימָה לְהִשְׁתַּחֲוֹת וְלִזְבֹּחַ לַייָ צְבָאוֹת בְּשִׁלֹה וְשָׁם שְׁנֵי בְנֵי עֵלִי חָפְנִי וּפִנְחָס כֹּהֲנִים לַייָ: [שמואל א' א, ג]

ט) וְעֵלִי זָקֵן מְאֹד וְשָׁמַע אֵת כָּל אֲשֶׁר יַעֲשׂוּן בָּנָיו לְכָל יִשְׂרָאֵל וְאֵת אֲשֶׁר יִשְׁכְּבוּן אֶת הַנָּשִׁים הַצֹּבְאוֹת פֶּתַח אֹהֶל מוֹעֵד: [שמואל א' ב, כב]

י) וַאֲחִיָּה בֶן אֲחִטוּב אֲחִי אִיכָבוֹד בֶּן פִּינְחָס בֶּן עֵלִי כֹּהֵן יְיָ בְּשִׁלוֹ נֹשֵׂא אֵפוֹד וְהָעָם לֹא יָדַע כִּי הָלַךְ יוֹנָתָן: [שמואל א' יד, ג]

כ) יַכְרֵת יְיָ לָאִישׁ אֲשֶׁר יַעֲשֶׂנָּה עֵר וְעֹנֶה מֵאָהֳלֵי יַעֲקֹב וּמַגִּישׁ מִנְחָה לַייָ צְבָאוֹת: [מלאכי ב, יב]

ל) אַל בָּנָי כִּי לוֹא טוֹבָה הַשְּׁמֻעָה אֲשֶׁר אָנֹכִי שֹׁמֵעַ מַעֲבִרִים עַם יְיָ: [שמואל א' ב, כד]

מ) וּבְנֵי עֵלִי בְּנֵי בְלִיָּעַל לֹא יָדְעוּ אֶת יְיָ: [שמואל א' ב, יב]

מסורת הש"ס

א) [יומא פז.], ב) ב"ב יז., ג) [צ"ל על], ד) רש"ל מ"ז ועי' רש"י, ה) לשון רתת, ו) צ"ל ויאשיהו, ז) יומא ע., ח) סנהדרין פב., ט) [עיין תוספות סנהדרין ד. ד"ה ורבנן], י) [צ"ל כמו ויחל משה], כ) [סנהדרין דף פג.], ל) מהרש"א גורס רבה, מ) [צ"ל מעברים].

גליון הש"ס

גמ' ד' מתו בעטיו של נחש כו'. בזוה"ק פ' בראשית ועל דא יהושע לא מת אלא בעטיו דנחש וכו'. ובזוה"ק פ' בראשית בפסוק וינחם ה' תלתא דאיסתלקו בגין ההוא עטיא דנחש עמרם לוי בנימין ואית דאמרי אף ישי: **שם תיובתא.** עי' ברא"מ פ' וישלח ד"ה אומרא ובפ' שופטים ד"ה ריה"ג: תוס' ד"ה מעבירים כתיב וכו' ובכל ספרים שלנו. וכן מצינו בנדה דף לג ע"א תוס' ד"ה והנושא שכתבו דהמסורת שלנו מחולק עם הש"ס. ובמגילה דף כב ע"א כתבו תוס' דויחל הוא ג' פסוקים סמוך לפרשה שלפניו וכן והקרבתם ובס"ת שלנו ויחל הוא ד' פסוקים מהפרשה וכן והקרבתם ג"פ וכמ"ש מהרש"א שם. ובפסחים דף קיז ע"א בתוס' ד"ה שעומדים כתבו שלא יתכן שיהיה מזמור ב' פסוקים ואלו בספרים שלנו מזמור קיז הוא ב' פסוקים. עי' מהרש"א שם ע"א. ובסנהדרין דף ד ע"א פירש"י שם דבכבשה דיחיד כתיב קרנות מלא ובס"ת שלנו כתיב חסר. ובדף ד ע"ב כ' רש"י דבפרשה והיה כי יביאך כתיב לטטפת חסר ובפ' והיה אם שמע כתיב מלא. ובס"ת שלנו גם בפ' והיה כי יביאך כתיב מלא. ובדף כ ע"א כתי' להכרית וקרי להכרו' ובספרים שלנו גם הכתיב להכרות. עוד שם דף קג ע"א ויחתר לו ויעתר לו מיבעיא ליה. ובספרים שלנו כתיב ויעתר. ובב"ב דף ט ע"א הלא פרוש בסין ובספרים שלנו כתיב בסין. ועי' בח"א שם במהרש"א. ובקדושין דף ל ע"א. והתגלח חציין של פסוקי' ובמיקונים בפ' לו בפסוק ויאפוד לו בו ליין דשם חצי התורה בפסוקים. ובירושלמי שהביא תוס' בכתובות דף ז ע"ב דבמקהלת ברכו אלהים חסר. ובספרים שלנו כתיב מלא. וברש"י בחומש פ' תרומה ואת כל אשר אצוה הוא וי"ו יתירה ולפנינו כתיב את בלא ו'. עי' ברא"ם שם. ובמדרש רבה שיר השירים בפסוק אחזו לנו שועלים שעלים א"ר ברכיה קדמאה מלא תניינא חסר. ובמסורה אינו כן אלא תרוייהו חסר. ובברכות דף ז ע"ב כתי' לכלותו ובספרי' שלנו בד"ה א יז כתיב לבלותו. (ובפסחים דף ג ע"א ו' דטהור. ובספרים

ליקוטי רש"י

מקרה אחד. שסוף הכל אשר צדיק ואשר רשע למות ומקרה אחד יש בעולם הזה לכולם [קהלת ט, ב]. **יען לא האמנתם בי.** גלה הכתוב שאלולי חטא זה בלבד היו נכנסין לארץ כדי שלא יאמרו עליהם כעון שאר דור המדבר שנגזר עליהם שלא יכנסו לארץ כך היה עון משה ואהרן [במדבר כ, יב]. **בעטיו של נחש.** בעצתו של נחש כלומר לא היו ראוין למות אלא שנגזרה גזירת מיתה על כל תולדותיו של אדם הראשון בעצתו של נחש בעטיו תרגום של עצתו כדכתיב (דניאל ו) אתייעטו כל וגו' וכן התיב עטא וטעם (שם ב). **ואחיותיהן.** בבני ישי כתיב [ב"ב יז.]. **בת נחש.** הוא ישי אבי דוד רבותינו אמרו שמת בלא עון בעטיו של נחש [ש"ב יז, כה]. **ויהיו בני יעקב שנים עשר.** ורבותינו דרשו ללמדנו בא שכולן שוין וכולן צדיקים שלא חטא ראובן. **וישכב את בלהה פילגש אביו וכו'.** מתוך שבלבל משכבו מעלה עליו הכתוב כאלו שכבה. ולמה בלבל וחלל יצועיו שכשמתה רחל נטל יעקב מטתו שהיתה נתונה תדיר באהל רחל ולא בשאר אהלים ונתנה באהל בלהה בא ראובן ותבע עלבון אמו אמר אם אחות אמי היתה צרה לאמי שפחת אחות אמי תהא צרה לאמי לכן בלבל [בראשית לה, כב]. **אז חללת.** אותו שם שעלה על יצועי והיא השכינה שהיה דרכה להיות עולה על יצועי. **יצועי.** לשון משכב על שם שמציעים אותו על ידי לבדין וסדינין והרבה דומים לו (תהלים סג, ז) אם זכרתיך על יצועי (שם קלב, ג) אם אעלה על ערש יצועי. **פחז כמים.** הפחז והבהלה אשר מהרת להראות כעסך כמים הללו הממהרים למרוצתם, לכך. **אל תותר.** אל תרבה ליטול כל היתרות הללו שהיו ראויות לך. **פחז.** שם דבר הוא לפיכך טעמו למעלה וכולו נקוד פת"ח ואלו היה לשון עבר היה נקוד חציו קמ"ץ וחציו פת"ח וטעמו למטה [שם מט, ד]. **אשר ישכבון.** כמשמעו ורבותינו אמרו מתוך ששהו את קיניהן והם היו ממתינות עד שתראן קיניהן קריבין מעלה עליהם כאלו שכבום [ש"א ב, כב]. **ששהו את קיניהן.** שהיו מביאות במלאות ימי לידתן ליטהר לאכול בקדשים והם היו בעלי [גאוה] והיו מתרשלין בהקרבתן והנשים ממתינות שם עד שיקריבום ומשתהות מלחזור למקומן אצל בעליהן ומבטלין את הנשים מפריה ורביה [יומא ט:].

is stated: *And the sons of Jacob were twelve,*[11] מְלַמֵּד שֶׁכּוּלָּן שְׁקוּלִים כְּאַחַת – which teaches that all twelve **were equal.**[12]

R' Yonasan continues expounding this verse:

"אֶלָּא מָה אֲנִי מְקַיֵּים ,,וַיִּשְׁכַּב אֶת־בִּלְהָה פִּילֶגֶשׁ אָבִיו – But how, then, **do I establish** the beginning of that verse: ***And*** [Reuven] ***lay with Bilhah, the concubine of his father?* מְלַמֵּד שֶׁבִּלְבֵּל מַצָּעוֹ שֶׁל אָבִיו – It teaches that** [Reuven] **disturbed his father's bed,**[13] **וּמַעֲלֶה עָלָיו הַכָּתוּב כְּאִילּוּ שָׁכַב עִמָּהּ – and Scripture regards him as if he lay with her.**

The Gemara elaborates on Reuven's indiscretion:

תַּנְיָא רַבִּי שִׁמְעוֹן בֶּן אֶלְעָזָר אוֹמֵר – It is taught in a Baraisa: R' SHIMON BEN ELAZAR SAYS: מוּצָּל אוֹתוֹ צַדִּיק מֵאוֹתוֹ עָוֹן – THAT RIGHTEOUS PERSON [Reuven] **WAS SAVED FROM THAT SIN, וְלֹא בָא מַעֲשֶׂה זֶה לְיָדוֹ – FOR THIS DEED DID NOT COME TO HIS HAND.**[14]

R' Shimon ben Elazar offers proof:

"אֶפְשָׁר עָתִיד זַרְעוֹ לַעֲמוֹד עַל הַר עֵיבָל וְלוֹמַר ,,אָרוּר שֹׁכֵב עִם־אֵשֶׁת אָבִיו – IS IT POSSIBLE THAT [REUVEN'S] DESCENDANTS WOULD IN THE FUTURE STAND ON MT. EIVAL AND DECLARE, *CURSED IS HE WHO LIES WITH HIS FATHER'S WIFE*,[15] **וְיָבֹא חֵטְא זֶה לְיָדוֹ – AND THIS** very **SIN WOULD COME TO HIS HAND?!**[16] **"אֶלָּא מָה אֲנִי מְקַיֵּים ,,וַיִּשְׁכַּב אֶת־בִּלְהָה פִּילֶגֶשׁ אָבִיו – BUT HOW,** then, **DO I UPHOLD** the beginning of that verse: ***AND*** [Reuven] ***LAY WITH BILHAH, THE CONCUBINE OF HIS FATHER?*** **עֶלְבּוֹן אִמּוֹ תָּבַע –** It informs us that **[REUVEN] SOUGHT** to redress **THE AFFRONT TO HIS MOTHER,** Leah. **אָמַר אִם אֲחוֹת אִמִּי הָיְתָה צָרָה לְאִמִּי – HE SAID: IF MY MOTHER'S SISTER** [Rachel] **WAS A RIVAL TO MY MOTHER, שִׁפְחַת אֲחוֹת אִמִּי תְּהֵא צָרָה לְאִמִּי – SHALL THE MAIDSERVANT** [Bilhah] **OF MY MOTHER'S SISTER BE A RIVAL TO MY MOTHER?** No! **עָמַד וּבִלְבֵּל אֶת מַצָּעָהּ – HE** thereupon **ROSE AND DISTURBED [LEAH'S] BED** – i.e. he moved Jacob's bed to her tent.[17]

The Baraisa continues:

אֲחֵרִים אוֹמְרִים שְׁתֵּי מַצָּעוֹת בִּלְבֵּל – OTHERS SAY: [REUVEN] MIXED UP TWO BEDS – אַחַת שֶׁל שְׁכִינָה וְאַחַת שֶׁל אָבִיו – ONE bed **OF THE DIVINE PRESENCE,**[18] **AND ONE** bed **OF HIS FATHER,** Jacob. **"וְהַיְינוּ דִּכְתִיב ,,אָז חִלַּלְתָּ יְצוּעִי עָלָה – AND THIS IS** the meaning of **WHAT IS WRITTEN** in Jacob's rebuke of Reuven:[19] ***THEN YOU DESECRATED THE ONE WHO ASCENDED MY BED.***[20] **(אַל תִּקְרֵי ,,יְצוּעִי" אֶלָּא יְצוּעַיי – DO NOT READ *MY BED,* BUT "MY BEDS.")**

The Gemara cites a Tannaic dispute regarding whether Reuven cohabited with Bilhah:

כְּתַנָּאֵי – This question whether Reuven sinned or not is a matter of dispute between **Tannaim** recorded in the following Baraisa: **"פַּחַז כַּמַּיִם אַל־תּוֹתַר,, –** At the beginning of the aforementioned verse Jacob says of Reuven: ***WATER-LIKE IMPETUOSITY – YOU SHALL NOT BE FOREMOST.*** You lost your right to national leadership because of the impetuosity you displayed in rushing to vent your anger in the matter of Bilhah. The Baraisa regards the word פַּחַז (*impetuosity*) as an acronym,[21] and interprets the verse accordingly: **רַבִּי אֱלִיעֶזֶר אוֹמֵר – R' ELIEZER SAYS** that this word represents: **פַּזְתָּה – (פ) YOU ACTED HASTILY, חַבְתָּה – (ח) YOU BECAME LIABLE, זַלְתָּה – (ז) YOU BELITTLED.**[22] **רַבִּי יְהוֹשֻׁעַ אוֹמֵר פָּסַעְתָּה עַל דָּת – R' YEHOSHUA SAYS** that the word suggests: **(פ) YOU TRAMPLED ON THE LAW, חָטָאתָ – (ח) YOU SINNED, זָנִיתָ – (ז) YOU ACTED LEWDLY.**[23] **רַבָּן גַּמְלִיאֵל אוֹמֵר פִּילַּלְתָּה – RABBAN GAMLIEL SAYS** that the word implies: **(פ) YOU PRAYED, חִלִּתָה – (ח) YOU ENTREATED, זָרְחָה תְּפִלָּתְךָ – (ז) YOUR PRAYER SHONE FORTH.**[24] **אָמַר רַבָּן גַּמְלִיאֵל עֲדַיִין צְרִיכִין אָנוּ לַמּוֹדָעִי –** Nevertheless, **RABBAN GAMLIEL SAID: WE STILL NEED** the exegesis **of THE** sage from Mt. **MODA'I,**[25] **רַבִּי אֶלְעָזָר הַמּוֹדָעִי אוֹמֵר הֲפוֹךְ אֶת הַתֵּיבָה וְדוֹרְשֶׁהָ – for R' ELAZAR OF** Mt. **MODA'I**[26] **SAYS: REVERSE**

NOTES

11. *Genesis* 35:22. At the conclusion of the selfsame verse that records the incident with Bilhah the Torah writes: *And the sons of Jacob were twelve,* to prevent one from thinking that Reuven actually committed the immoral act attributed to him (*Rashi*).

The text in a Torah scroll is divided into paragraphs (*parashiyos*). A new paragraph invariably begins with a new verse. However, in our case a new paragraph begins in the middle of the aforementioned verse, with the words: *And the sons of Jacob were twelve.* The Torah does not begin a new verse here, to indicate that although these words begin a new topic, they also shed light on the first part of the verse, the part that relates Reuven's apparent sin with Bilhah (*Maharsha*).

12. All the sons – including Reuven – were righteous (*Rashi* on the verse). Just as the other sons were not disgraced by lying with Bilhah, so Reuven did not actually incur this disgrace (*Maharsha*).

13. He moved Jacob's bed from Bilhah's tent to that of his mother Leah (see *Rashi* on the verse).

14. I.e. Reuven never actually cohabited with Bilhah.

15. *Deuteronomy* 27:20. This is one of the twelve curses instituted in the ceremony of blessings and curses at Mt. Eival and Mt. Grizim. The Tribe of Reuven was one of the six tribes assigned to stand on Mt. Eival to affirm the curses.

16. If Reuven had actually cohabited with Bilhah, surely Hashem would not have decreed that his tribe be among those who affirmed this curse (*Rashi;* see *Melo HaRo'im*; cf. *Maharsha*).

17. [Perhaps the Gemara calls it "her bed" because (according to Reuven) it was Leah's right to have Jacob's bed in her tent.]

18. Jacob would set up a bed for the Divine Presence in each of his four wives' tents, and every night he would sleep in whichever tent where he saw the Divine Presence (*Rashi*; see *Sfas Emes*).

19. *Genesis* 49:4.

20. Had the verse stated: יְצוּעִי עָלִיתָ, "you ascended my bed," it would have taught that Reuven ascended upon Jacob's conjugal couch. However, since it states: יְצוּעִי עָלָה, *He ascended my bed,* it refers to the Divine Presence and is to be interpreted: [Then you desecrated] that Name which ascended my bed, i.e. the Divine Presence. An alternative interpretation: Until the Tabernacle was built, the Divine Presence dwelt in the tents of the righteous. [Hence, when Reuven moved Jacob's bed, the Divine Presence was also displaced] (*Rashi*).

Apparently the phrase, "Do not read 'my bed,' but 'my beds,' " did not appear in *Rashi's* text of the Gemara, since he offered two different interpretations of the verse (*Maharsha*).

One could say that the Baraisa's teaching is derived from an earlier part of the same verse: עָלִיתָ מִשְׁכְּבֵי אָבִיךָ, *you ascended the beds of your father.* The plural מִשְׁכְּבֵי, *beds,* implies the beds of Reuven's two fathers – his earthly father Jacob, and his Heavenly Father, Hashem (*Maharsha; Rif* to *Ein Yaakov*).

21. This is one of the thirty-two methods of Biblical exegesis (*Eitz Yosef,* citing *Yefas To'ar*). Its use is justified here because according to the plain meaning the verse should have said: פָּחַזְתָּ, "You were impetuous" (*Maharsha*).

22. "You acted hastily" to violate two prohibitions, namely: "You became liable" for having relations with the wife of your father, and "you belittled" his honor (*Maharsha*).

23. See *Maharsha.*

24. "You prayed" to be saved from the sin (*Rashi*).

One might have interpreted Rabban Gamliel as saying that Reuven committed the sin but then prayed for forgiveness. *Rashi* thus comes to preclude such an interpretation, for the Gemara below reveals that Rabban Gamliel held that Reuven was tempted to sin, but overcame the temptation. Thus, Rabban Gamliel means: "You prayed [to be restrained from committing adultery], you entreated [to be restrained from belittling your father's honor], and your prayer shone forth" and saved you from committing both sins (*Maharsha*).

25. Rabban Gamliel states that because his exegesis can still imply that Reuven prayed for forgiveness *after* sinning, the exegesis of R' Elazar of Mt. Moda'i is needed to establish unequivocally that Reuven did not sin (*Maharsha*).

26. R' Elazar hailed from Mt. Moda'i, near Jerusalem (*Rashi* to *Bava Basra* 10b).

מיתיבי אמרו מלאכי השרת לפני הקב"ה רבונו של עולם מפני מה קנסת מיתה על אדם הראשון אמר להם מצוה קלה צויתיו ועבר עליה א"ל והלא משה ואהרן שקיימו כל התורה כולה ומתו א"ל א) מקרה אחד לצדיק ולרשע לטוב וגו' הוא דאמר כי האי תנא דתניא ר"ש בן אלעזר אומר אף משה ואהרן בחטאם מתו שנא' ב) יען לא האמנתם בי א) הא האמנתם בי עדיין לא הגיע זמנכם ליפטר מן העולם מיתיבי ° ג) ארבעה מתו בעטיו של נחש ואלו הן בנימין בן יעקב ועמרם אבי משה וישי אבי דוד וכלאב בן דוד וכולהו גמרא לבר מישי אבי דוד דמפרש ביה קרא דכתיב ג) ואת עמשא שם אבשלום תחת יואב (ג) שר) הצבא ועמשא בן איש ושמו יתרא הישראלי אשר בא אל אביגיל בת נחש אחות צרויה אם יואב וכי בת נחש הואי והלא בת ישי הואי דכתיב ד) ואחיותיהן צרויה ואביגיל אלא בת מי שמת בעטיו של נחש מני אילימא תנא דמלאכי השרת והא איכא משה ואהרן אלא לאו ר"ש בן אלעזר היא וש"מ יש מיתה בלא חטא ויש יסורין בלא עון ותיובתא דרב אמי ° תיובתא: א"ר שמואל בר נחמני א"ר יונתן כל האומר ראובן חטא אינו אלא טועה שנאמר ה) ויהיו בני יעקב שנים עשר מלמד שכולן שקולים כאחת אלא מה אני מקיים ה) וישכב את בלהה פילגש אביו מלמד שבלבל מצעו של אביו ומעלה עליו הכתוב כאילו שכב עמה תניא ר"ש בן אלעזר אומר מוצל אותו צדיק מאותו עון ולא בא מעשה זה לידו אפשר עתיד זרעו לעמוד על הר עיבל ולומר ו) ארור שוכב עם אשת אביו ויבא חטא זה לידו אלא מה אני מקיים וישכב את בלהה פילגש אביו עלבון אמו תבע אמר אם אחות אמי היתה צרה לאמי שפחת אחות אמי תהא צרה לאמי עמד ובלבל את מצעה אחרים אומרים שתי מצעות בלבל אחת של שכינה ואחת של אביו והיינו דכתיב ז) אז חללת יצועי עלה ז) (אל תקרי יצועי אלא יצועיי) כתנאי ז) פחז כמים אל תותר ר' אליעזר אומר פזתה חבתה זלתה ר' יהושע אומר פסעתה על דת חטאת זנית ר"ג אומר פיללתה חלתה זרחה תפלתך אמר ר"ג עדיין צריכין אנו למודעי ר' אלעזר המודעי אומר הפוך את התיבה ודורשה ט) זעזעתה הרתעתה פרחה חטא ממך רבא אמר ואמרי לה ר' ירמיה בר אבא זכרת עונשו של דבר חלית עצמך חולי גדול פירשת מלחטוא: ראובן בני עלי בני שמואל דוד ושלמה ויואש י) סימן: י) אמר ר' שמואל בר נחמני א"ר יונתן כל האומר בני עלי חטאו אינו אלא טועה שנאמר ח) ושם שני בני עלי (עם ארון ברית האלהים) חפני ופנחס כהנים לה' סבר לה כרב דאמר רב פנחס לא חטא מקיש חפני לפנחס מה פנחס לא חטא אף חפני לא חטא אלא מה אני מקיים ט) אשר ישכבון את הנשים מתוך ששהו את קיניהן שלא הלכו אצל בעליהן מעלה עליהן הכתוב כאילו שכבום גופא אמר רב פנחס לא חטא שנאמר י) ואחיה בן אחיטוב אחי אי כבוד בן פנחס בן עלי כהן ה' וגו' אפשר חטא בא לידו והכתוב מייחסו והלא כבר נאמר כ) יכרת ה' לאיש אשר יעשנה ער ועונה מאהלי יעקב ומגיש מנחה לה' צבאות כ) אם ישראל הוא לא יהיה לו ער בחכמים ולא עונה בתלמידים ואם כהן הוא לא יהיה לו בן מגיש מנחה אלא לאו שמע מינה פנחס לא חטא אלא הא כתיב ט) אשר ישכבון ט) ישכבן כתיב והכתיב ל) אל בני כי לא טובה השמועה א"ר נחמן בר יצחק בני כתיב והכתיב ל) מעבירים א"ר הונא בריה דרב יהושע מעבירם כתיב והכתיב מ) בני בליעל מתוך שהיה לו לפנחס למחות לחפני ולא מיחה מעלה עליו הכתוב כאילו חטא א"ר שמואל בר נחמני א"ר יונתן כל האומר בני

בעטיו של נחש. בעלתו של נחש שהשיא לחוה ולא בחטא אחר שלא חטאו. בעטיו כמו עטא וטעם (דניאל ב): ואחיותיהם. בבני ישי משתעי: אלא לאו ר"ש בן אלעזר. דאמר משה ואהרן בחטאם מתו ומודה בהני: כל האומר ראובן חטא. במעשה בלהה: דכתיב. בההוא קרא: ויהיו בני יעקב וגו'. להוציא מלבך שלא תחשדנו: ויבא חטא זה לידו. ויגזור הקב"ה שיהיו מן המקללים: אחת של שכינה. כך היה יעקב עושה בארבעה אהלי נשיו מעמיד מטה לשכינה ובאותו אהל שהוא רואה בו השכינה הוא בא ולן אותו הלילה: חללת. אותו שם שעלה על יצועי דהיינו שכינה מדלא כתיב יצועי עלית טעם אחר עד שלא נבנה אהל מועד היתה שכינה מצויה באהלי צדיקים: פחז. נוטריקון הוא: פזתה. לשון עמא פזיזא (לקמן דף פח.). פזתה מיהרת בעלמך וחטאת: זלתה. זלזלת: פיללת. להנצל מן החטא: חלתה. י) ויחל משה (שמות לב): זעזעת'. יראת לחטוא לר' אליעזר ור' יהושע חטא ולרבן גמליאל ולמודעי בקש לחטוא ולא חטא: חלית. חולי גדול להתאפק לכבוש יצרך: כל האומר בני עלי חטאו. באשת איש אינו אלא טועה ומיהו בבזיון קדשים חטאו: דאמר רב. לקמן בשמעתין פנחס לא חטא ויליף לה מקרא ור' יונתן יליף לה לחפני מהאי קרא דמקיש חפני לפנחס: ששהו את קיניהן. שהיו מסרבין להקריב שום קרבן אלא בקושי כדכתיב (שמואל א ב) גם בטרם יקטירון את החלב וגו' וכשהיו זבות ויולדות באות ממקום אחר לשילה להקריב את קיניהן והן היו משהין מלהקריבם והנשים לא היו יכולין לסמוך עליהם שיקריבו והיו שוהות שם ולא היו חוזרות אצל בעליהן עד שראו קיניהן קרבין והיו טהורות לקדשים וליכנס לעזרה לפיכך מעלה עליהם כאילו שכבום שהיו מונעים אותן מפריה ורביה: פנחס לא חטא. באשת איש דאשר ישכבון את הנשים אינו אלא חפני לבדו: ואחיה בן אחיטוב וגו' כהן ה'. בשילה נושא אפוד הרי שמיחסו לשבח ומזכיר עליו שם פנחס אבי אביו: אפשר בא חטא לידו והכתוב מייחסו. לשבח ואת בן בנו מייחסו אחריו והכתיב גבי עבירה דנואפים יכרת ה' לאיש וגו' והאי קרא בבא על הנכרית ועל הזונה מישתעי כדדרשינן ליה באלו הן הנשרפין ל) דכתיב לעיל מיניה כי חלל יהודה קדש ה' אשר אהב ובעל בת אל נכר ודרשינן כי חלל יהודה קדש זו זונה וכן הוא אומר לא תהיה קדשה וגו': ער. חריף להבין ולהורות בין החכמים כדאמרי' בעירובין (דף נג:) אהרנית ערנית: ואם כהן הוא כו'. וכאן מייחס כהן מגיש מנחה אחר פנחס: והכתיב אל בני כי לא טובה השמועה אשר אנכי שומע מעבירים עם ה' אביהם היה מוכיחם: והא כתיב מעבירים אמר ל) רב הונא בריה דרב יהושע מעבירם כתיב.

ארבעה מתו בעטיו של נחש. והא דכתיב (קהלת ז) כי אדם אין צדיק בארץ וגו' ברוב בני אדם קאמר: וש"מ יש מיתה בלא חטא ויש יסורים בלא עון. ואע"ג דבמאי דקאמר אין יסורין בלא עון לא איתותב: כל האומר בני עלי חטאו אינו אלא טועה. פירוש במאי דכתיב אשר ישכבון לא חטאו אלא מבזים קדשים היו כדכתיב (שמואל א ב) בטרם יקטירון החלב וגו': מעבירם כתיב. הש"ס שלנו חולק על ספרים שלנו שכתוב בהם (מ) מעבירים) וכן מצינו בירושלמי בשמשון והוא שפט את ישראל ארבעים שנה מלמד שהיו פלשתים יראים ממנו כ' שנה אחר מותו כמו בחייו ° ובכל ספרים שלנו כתיב כ' שנה (שופטים טו): מתוך שהיה לו לפנחס למחות. ופליג אר' יונתן דאמר שניהם לא חטאו:

שהיה קשה בעיני שם החכם הנזכר כאן כי אומר אני שטעות גדול הוא ול"ג לה להא מילתא שהרי בספרים מוגהים כתיב מעבירים וגם במסורה הגדולה במקום שמנויין שם כל התיבות דלא כתיב בהן יו"ד וקורין ולא נמנה זה והם מנויין ע"פ החשבון וזו אינה קשיא דהאי מעבירים לאו לשון עבירה הוא אלא לשון ויעבירו קול במחנה (שמות לו) וה"ק להו לא טובה השמועה אשר אנכי שומע את עם ה' מעבירים ומכריזין וקובלים עליכם והאי מעבירים לשון רבים הוא ואעם ה' קאי ולאו אבני עלי שהרי הם היו עוברים ולא היו מעבירים את אחרים:

תורה אור השלם

א) הַכֹּל כַּאֲשֶׁר לַכֹּל מִקְרֶה אֶחָד לַצַּדִּיק וְלָרָשָׁע לַטּוֹב וְלַטָּהוֹר וְלַטָּמֵא וְלַזֹּבֵחַ וְלַאֲשֶׁר אֵינֶנּוּ זֹבֵחַ כַּטּוֹב כַּחֹטֶא הַנִּשְׁבָּע כַּאֲשֶׁר שְׁבוּעָה יָרֵא: [קהלת ט, ב]

ב) וַיֹּאמֶר יְיָ אֶל מֹשֶׁה וְאֶל אַהֲרֹן יַעַן לֹא הֶאֱמַנְתֶּם בִּי לְהַקְדִּישֵׁנִי לְעֵינֵי בְּנֵי יִשְׂרָאֵל לָכֵן לֹא תָבִיאוּ אֶת הַקָּהָל הַזֶּה אֶל הָאָרֶץ אֲשֶׁר נָתַתִּי לָהֶם: [במדבר כ, יב]

ג) וְאֶת עֲמָשָׂא שָׂם אַבְשָׁלֹם תַּחַת יוֹאָב עַל הַצָּבָא וַעֲמָשָׂא בֶן אִישׁ וּשְׁמוֹ יִתְרָא הַיִּשְׂרְאֵלִי אֲשֶׁר בָּא אֶל אֲבִיגַל בַּת נָחָשׁ אֲחוֹת צְרוּיָה אֵם יוֹאָב: [שמואל ב' יז, כה]

ד) וְאַחְיוֹתֵיהֶם צְרוּיָה וַאֲבִיגָיִל וּבְנֵי צְרוּיָה אַבְשַׁי וְיוֹאָב וַעֲשָׂה־אֵל שְׁלֹשָׁה: [דברי הימים א' ב, טז]

ה) וַיְהִי בִּשְׁכֹּן יִשְׂרָאֵל בָּאָרֶץ הַהִוא וַיֵּלֶךְ רְאוּבֵן וַיִּשְׁכַּב אֶת בִּלְהָה פִּילֶגֶשׁ אָבִיו וַיִּשְׁמַע יִשְׂרָאֵל וַיִּהְיוּ בְנֵי יַעֲקֹב שְׁנֵים עָשָׂר: [בראשית לה, כב]

ו) אָרוּר שֹׁכֵב עִם אֵשֶׁת אָבִיו כִּי גִלָּה כְּנַף אָבִיו וְאָמַר כָּל הָעָם אָמֵן: [דברים כז, כ]

ז) פַּחַז כַּמַּיִם אַל תּוֹתַר כִּי עָלִיתָ מִשְׁכְּבֵי אָבִיךָ אָז חִלַּלְתָּ יְצוּעִי עָלָה: [בראשית מט, ד]

ח) וְעָלָה הָאִישׁ הַהוּא מֵעִירוֹ מִיָּמִים יָמִימָה לְהִשְׁתַּחֲוֹת וְלִזְבֹּחַ לַייָ צְבָאוֹת בְּשִׁלֹה וְשָׁם שְׁנֵי בְנֵי עֵלִי חָפְנִי וּפִנְחָס כֹּהֲנִים לַייָ: [שמואל א' א, ג]

ט) וְעֵלִי זָקֵן מְאֹד וְשָׁמַע אֵת כָּל אֲשֶׁר יַעֲשׂוּן בָּנָיו לְכָל יִשְׂרָאֵל וְאֵת אֲשֶׁר יִשְׁכְּבוּן אֶת הַנָּשִׁים הַצֹּבְאוֹת פֶּתַח אֹהֶל מוֹעֵד: [שמואל א' ב, כב]

י) וַאֲחִיָּה בֶן אֲחִטוּב אֲחִי אִיכָבוֹד בֶּן פִּינְחָס בֶּן עֵלִי כֹּהֵן יְיָ בְּשִׁלוֹ נֹשֵׂא אֵפוֹד וְהָעָם לֹא יָדַע כִּי הָלַךְ יוֹנָתָן: [שמואל א' יד, ג]

כ) יַכְרֵת יְיָ לָאִישׁ אֲשֶׁר יַעֲשֶׂנָּה עֵר וְעֹנֶה מֵאָהֳלֵי יַעֲקֹב וּמַגִּישׁ מִנְחָה לַייָ צְבָאוֹת: [מלאכי ב, יב]

ל) אַל בָּנָי כִּי לוֹא טוֹבָה הַשְּׁמֻעָה אֲשֶׁר אָנֹכִי שֹׁמֵעַ מַעֲבִרִים עַם יְיָ: [שמואל א' ב, כד]

מ) וּבְנֵי עֵלִי בְּנֵי בְלִיָּעַל לֹא יָדְעוּ אֶת יְיָ: [שמואל א' ב, יב]

מסורת הש"ס

א) [יומא פז.], ב) ב"ב יז., ג) [נ"ל על], ד) רש"ל מ"ז ועי' רש"י, ה) לשון רמת, ו) נ"ל ויאשיהו, ז) יומא ט., ח) סנהדרין פב., ט) [עיין תוספות סנהדרין ד. ד"ה ורבנן], י) [נ"ל כמו ויחל משה], כ) [סנהדרין דף פג.], ל) מהרש"א גורס רבה, מ) [נ"ל מעברים].

גליון הש"ס

גמ' ד' מתו בעטיו של נחש כו'. בזוה"ק פ' בראשית ועל דא יהושע לא מת אלא בעטיו דנחש וכו'. ובזוה"ק פ' בראשית בפסוק וינחם ה' תלתא דאיסתלקו בגין ההוא עטיא דנחש עמרם לוי בנימין ואית דאמרי אף ישי: שם תיובתא. עי' ברא"מ פ' וישלח ד"ה אומרא ובפ' שופטים ד"ה ריה"ג: תוס' ד"ה מעבירם כתיב וכו' ובכל ספרים שלנו. וכן מצינו בנדה דף לג ע"א תוס' ד"ה והנושא שכתבו דהמסורת שלנו מחולק עם הש"ס. ובמגילה דף כב ע"א כתבו תוס' דויחל הוא ג' פסוקים סמוך לפרשה שלפניו וכן והקרבתם ובס"ת שלנו ויחל הוא ד' פסוקים מהפרשה וכן והקרבתם ג"פ וכמ"ש מהרש"א שם. ובפסחים דף קיז ע"א בתוס' ד"ה שעומדים כתבו שלא יתכן שיהיה מזמור ג' פסוקים ואלו בספרים שלנו מזמור קיז הוא ב' פסוקים. עי' מהרש"א שם ע"א. ובסנהדרין דף ד ע"א פירש"י שם דבכבשה דיחיד כתיב קרנות מלא ובס"ת שלנו כתיב חסר. ובדף ד ע"א כ' רש"י דבפרשה והיה כי יביאך כתיב לטטפת חסר ובפ' והיה אם שמע כתיב מלא. ובס"ת שלנו גם בפ' והיה כי יביאך כתיב מלא. ובדף כ ע"א כתי' להכרית וקרי להכרו' ובספרים שלנו גם הכתיב להכרות. עוד שם דף קג ע"א ויחתר לו ויעתר לו מיבעיא ליה. ובספרים שלנו כתיב ויעתר. ובב"ב דף ט ע"א הלא פרוס בשין ובספרים שלנו כתיב בסין. ועי' בח"א שם במהרש"א. ובקדושין דף ל ע"א. והתגלח חציין של פסוקי' ובתיקונים בפ' לו בפסוק ויאפוד לו בו ליין דשם חצי התורה בפסוקים. ובירושלמי שהביא תוס' בכתובות דף ז ע"ב דבמקהלת ברכו אלהים חסר. ובספרים שלנו כתיב מלא. וברש"י בחומש פ' תרומה ואת כל אשר אצוה הוא וי"ו יתירה ולפנינו כתיב את בלא ו'. עי' ברא"ם שם. ובמדרש רבה שיר השירים בפסוק אחז לנו שועלים שעלים א"ר ברכיה קדמאה מלא תניינא חסר. ובמסורה אינו כן אלא תרוייהו חסר. ובברכות דף ז ע"ב כתי' לכלותו ובספרי' שלנו בד"ה א יז כתיב לבלותו. (ובפסחים דף ג ע"א ו' דטהור. ובספרים

ליקוטי רש"י

מקרה אחד. שסוף הכל אשר לדיק ואשר רשע למות ומקרה אחד יש בעולם הזה לכולם [קהלת ט, ב]. יען לא האמנתם בי. גלה הכתוב שאלולי חטא זה בלבד היו נכנסין לארץ כדי שלא יאמרו עליהם כעון שאר דור המדבר שנגזר עליהם שלא יכנסו לארץ כך היה עון משה ואהרן [במדבר כ, יב]. בעטיו של נחש. בעלתו של נחש כלומר לא היו ראוין למות אלא שנגזרה גזירת מיתה על כל תולדותיו של אדם הראשון בעלתו של נחש בעטיו תרגום של עלתו כדכתיב (דניאל ו) אתייעטו כל וגו' וכן התיב עטא וטעם (שם ב). ואחיותיהן. בבני ישי כתיב [ב"ב יז.]. בת נחש. הוא ישי אבי דוד רבותינו אמרו שמת בלא עון בעטיו של נחש [ש"ב יז, כה]. ויהיו בני יעקב שנים עשר. ורבותינו דרשו ללמדנו בא שכולן שוין וכולן לדיקים שלא חטא ראובן. וישכב את בלהה פילגש אביו וכו'. מתוך שבלבל משכבו מעלה עליו הכתוב כאלו שכבה. ולמה בלבל וחלל יצועיו שכשמתה רחל נטל יעקב מטתו שהיתה נתונה תדיר באהל רחל ולא בשאר אהלים ונתנה באהל בלהה בא ראובן ותבע עלבון אמו אמר אם אחות אמי היתה צרה לאמי שפחת אחות אמי תהא צרה לאמי לכן בלבל [בראשית לה, כב]. אז חללת. אותו שם שעלה על יצועי והיא השכינה שהיה דרכה להיות עולה על יצועי. יצועי. לשון משכב על שם שמציעים אותו על ידי לבדין וסדינין והרבה דומים לו (תהלים סג, ז) אם זכרתיך על יצועי (שם קלב, ג) אם אעלה על ערש יצועי. פחז כמים. הפחז והבהלה אשר מהרת להראות כעסך כמים הללו הממהרים למרוצתם, לכך. אל תותר. אל תרבה ליטול כל היתרות הללו שהיו ראויות לך. פחז. שם דבר הוא לפיכך טעמו למעלה וכולו נקוד פת"ח ואלו היה לשון עבר היה נקוד חציו קמ"ץ וחציו פת"ח וטעמו למטה [שם מט, ד]. אשר ישכבון. כמשמעו ורבותינו אמרו מתוך ששהו את קיניהן והם היו ממתינות עד שתראן קיניהן קריבין מעלה עליהם כאלו שכבום [ש"א ב, כב]. ששהו את קיניהן. שהיו מביאות במלאות ימי לידתן ליטהר לאכול בקדשים והם היו בעלי [גאוה] והיו מתרשלין בהקרבתן והנשים ממתינות שם עד שיקריבום ומשתהות מלחזור למקומן אצל בעליהן ומבטלין את הנשים מפריה ורביה [יומא ט:].

THE WORD פָּחַז AND EXPOUND IT thus: וְזָעַתָּה – (ז) YOU TREMBLED,[27] הִרְתַּעְתָּה – (ה) YOU DREW BACK, פָּרְחָה חֵטְא מִמְּךָ – (פ) THE SIN FLEW AWAY FROM YOU.

The Gemara presents a similar exegesis by an Amora:

רָבָא אָמַר וְאָמְרֵי לָהּ רַבִּי יִרְמְיָה בַּר אַבָּא – **Rava said – and some say it** in the name of **R' Yirmiyah bar Abba:** פָּחַז is a reverse acronym for: זָכַרְתָּ עוֹנְשׁוֹ שֶׁל דָּבָר – (ז) **You remembered the punishment for this matter,** חָלִיתָ עַצְמְךָ חוֹלִי גָּדוֹל – (ח) **you made yourself sick with a great sickness,**[28] פֵּירַשְׁתָּ מִלַּחֲטוֹא – (פ) **you held back from sinning.**

The Gemara devotes the remainder of the chapter to a continuation of this discussion of Biblical personalities regarding whom Scripture gave a false impression of having sinned grievously. It first offers an aid for remembering the personalities treated:

רְאוּבֵן בְּנֵי עֵלִי בְּנֵי שְׁמוּאֵל דָּוִד וּשְׁלֹמֹה וְיוֹאָשׁ סִימָן – **Reuven, the sons of Eli, the sons of Samuel, David and Solomon, and Yoash – a mnemonic.**

Having discussed Reuven, the Gemara now turns to the next subject:

אָמַר רַבִּי שְׁמוּאֵל בַּר נַחְמָנִי אָמַר רַבִּי יוֹנָתָן – **R' Shmuel bar Nachmani said in the name of R' Yonasan:** כֹּל הָאוֹמֵר בְּנֵי עֵלִי חָטְאוּ אֵינוֹ אֶלָּא טוֹעֶה – **Whoever says** that **the sons of Eli,** the Kohen Gadol, **sinned**[29] **is simply mistaken,**[30] שֶׁנֶּאֱמַר ,,וְשָׁם שְׁנֵי בְנֵי־עֵלִי (עם ארון ברית האלהים) חָפְנִי וּפִנְחָס כֹּהֲנִים לַה׳ " – **for it is stated:** ***And the two sons of Eli, Chafni and Pinchas, were there – priests unto Hashem.***[31]

The Gemara explains how R' Yonasan expounds this verse:

סָבַר לָהּ כְּרַב – **[R' Yonasan] holds like Rav,** דְּאָמַר רַב פִּנְחָס לֹא חָטָא – **for Rav said: Pinchas did not sin;**[32] מַקִּישׁ חָפְנִי לְפִנְחָס – and he holds that **[our verse] compares Chafni to Pinchas,** מַה פִּנְחָס לֹא חָטָא אַף חָפְנִי לֹא חָטָא – to teach that **just as Pinchas did not sin, so Chafni did not sin.**[33]

R' Yonasan continues expounding the verse:

אֶלָּא מָה אֲנִי מְקַיֵּים ,,אֲשֶׁר־יִשְׁכְּבֻן אֶת־הַנָּשִׁים" – **But how,** then, **do I uphold** the verse, *Now, Eli . . . heard . . . **that they** [his sons] **were lying with the women** who came as a host to the door of the Tent of Meeting,*[34] which ostensibly indicates that Pinchas and Chafni were not innocent of the sin of adultery? מִתּוֹךְ שֶׁשִּׁהוּ אֶת קִינֵּיהֶן שֶׁלֹּא הָלְכוּ אֵצֶל בַּעֲלֵיהֶן – It means that **since [Pinchas and Chafni] delayed [the women's] bird offerings, so that they did not go** home immediately **to their husbands,** מַעֲלֶה עֲלֵיהֶן הַכָּתוּב כְּאִילּוּ שְׁכָבוּם – Scripture regards [Eli's sons] as if they had lain with [these women].[35]

The Gemara returns to the subject of Rav's exegesis:

גּוּפָא אָמַר רַב – Let us examine that earlier statement **itself. Rav said:** פִּנְחָס לֹא חָטָא – **Pinchas did not sin,**[36] שֶׁנֶּאֱמַר ,,וַאֲחִיָּה בֶן־אֲחִטוּב אֲחִי אִיכָבוֹד בֶּן־פִּינְחָס בֶּן־עֵלִי כֹּהֵן ה׳ וגו׳ " – **for it is stated:** ***And Achiyah, the son of Achituv, the brother of Ichavod, the son of Pinchas, the son of Eli, the priest of Hashem*** *at Shiloh, was wearing an ephod.*[37] אֶפְשָׁר חֵטְא בָּא לְיָדוֹ וְהַכָּתוּב מְיַיחֲסוֹ – Now, **is it possible** that **[Pinchas] sinned and Scripture includes him in the** honorable priestly **lineage** of his grandson, Achiyah?! וַהֲלֹא כְּבָר נֶאֱמַר ,,יַכְרֵת ה׳ לָאִישׁ אֲשֶׁר יַעֲשֶׂנָּה עֵר וְעֹנֶה מֵאָהֳלֵי יַעֲקֹב וּמַגִּישׁ מִנְחָה לַה׳ צְבָאוֹת" – **But has it not already been stated:**[38] ***Hashem will cut off the man who does this,***[39] ***he who is alert or responsive from the tents of Jacob, and who presents a meal offering to the Lord of Hosts?***

Rav expounds the verse:

אִם יִשְׂרָאֵל הוּא לֹא יִהְיֶה לוֹ ,,עֵר" בַּחֲכָמִים וְלֹא ,,עֹנֶה" בַּתַּלְמִידִים – **If [the adulterer] is an Israelite** (i.e. not a Kohen), **he will not have** a descendant who is ***alert***[40] **among the sages, or *responsive***[41] **among the students;** וְאִם כֹּהֵן הוּא לֹא יִהְיֶה לוֹ בֵּן ,,מַגִּישׁ

NOTES

27. You were afraid of sinning (*Rashi*).

[Although הִרְתַּעְתָּה begins with ה and not ח, these two letters are interchangeable since they are somewhat similar in both shape and pronunciation.]

According to R' Eliezer and R' Yehoshua, Reuven actually sinned; according to Rabban Gamliel and R' Elazar of Mt. Moda'i, he was tempted to sin but did not (*Rashi*). This is the Tannaic dispute to which the Gemara referred. See *Maharsha*.

28. "You made yourself sick with a great sickness," restraining yourself and conquering your evil inclination (*Rashi*).

29. Scripture relates that the two sons of Eli, Pinchas and Chafni, were *wicked men, and did not know Hashem* (וּבְנֵי עֵלִי בְּנֵי בְלִיָּעַל לֹא יָדְעוּ אֶת־ה׳ ; *I Samuel* 2:12). Among other wrongdoings reported by Scripture, the verse states that they committed adultery with women who came to the Temple (ibid. v. 22). Our Gemara probes this matter.

30. Whoever thinks they actually committed the sin of adultery is mistaken; however, they did dishonor the sacrificial offerings, as Scripture reports there in vs. 13-17 (*Rashi, Tosafos*).

31. *I Samuel* 1:3. The words in parentheses, עִם אֲרוֹן בְּרִית הָאֱלֹקִים, "with the Ark of the Covenant of God," do not appear in the verse and should be deleted from the text.

32. The Gemara below will explain how Rav derives from Scripture that Pinchas did not sin. R' Yonasan here builds upon that exegesis to derive that Chafni likewise did not sin, since our verse equates Pinchas and Chafni (*Rashi*).

33. The verse, *the two sons of Eli, Chafni and Pinchas,* appears superfluous and unrelated to its context; R' Yonasan thus understands that it comes to equate Chafni to Pinchas (*Maharsha*).

34. *I Samuel* 2:22.

35. Pinchas and Chafni would impose obstacles and delays before bringing any Temple offering, as described by *I Samuel* 2:15-16 [which relates how people would beseech the two Kohanim to perform their offerings, and Chafni and Pinchas would refuse to do so until they had extorted meat from the owners]. Thus, when women from distant places would come to the Tabernacle at Shiloh to bring obligatory bird offerings after giving birth or after recovering from the status of *zavah,* Pinchas and Chafni would delay these offerings. The women, having no confidence that the Kohanim would attend to the matter on their own, would remain in Shilo [overnight or longer] and would not return to their husbands until they had seen that their sacrifices had indeed been offered – for only then could they be sure they were henceforth permitted to touch sanctified food or enter the Tabernacle Courtyard. Therefore, Scripture regards Pinchas and Chafni as having committed adultery, for they prevented the women from returning to their husbands and engaging in the the mitzvah of procreation (*Rashi*).

36. That is, Pinchas did not commit adultery, for the verse, *they were lying with the women,* refers only to Chafni (*Rashi;* see also *Tosafos* ד״ה מתוך). [According to *Rashi,* Rav disagrees with R' Yonasan, who held that neither brother actually committed adultery; cf. *Rif* and *Eitz Yosef* to *Ein Yaakov.*]

Pinchas did, however, dishonor the offerings. Otherwise, the Gemara, which asks below why the plural form is used in reference to the adultery, would have also asked why the plural is used in reference to the dishonoring of the offerings (*Maharsha*).

37. *I Samuel* 14:3. This verse speaks in praise of Achiyah, mentioning that he had the honor of wearing the *ephod,* the special garment of the High Priest; and it also mentions that Achiyah was the grandson of Pinchas (*Rashi*).

38. *Malachi* 2:12.

39. I.e. any person who engages in illicit relations. The Gemara (*Sanhedrin* 82a) proves that the verse refers to a Jewish man who cohabits with a non-Jewish woman (*Rashi*). [The punishment mentioned in the verse would presumably apply to one who committed adultery with a Jewish woman (see *Rashi*).]

40. Sharp witted, and thus capable of understanding the Torah and rendering halachic decisions among the sages (*Rashi*).

41. Capable of answering students' questions [in the *beis midrash,* the *tents of Jacob*] (*Maharsha* to *Sanhedrin* 82a).

ארבעה מתו בעטיו של נחש. והא דכתיב (קהלת ז) כי אדם אין צדיק בארץ וגו' ברוב בני אדם קאמר: **וש"מ** יש מיתה בלא חטא ויש יסורים בלא עון. ואע"ג דמאי דקאמר אין יסורין בלא עון לא איתותב: **כל** האומר בני עלי חטאו אינו אלא טועה. פירוש במאי דכתיב אשר ישכבון לא חטאו אלא מבזים קדשים היו כדכתיב (שמואל א ב) בטרם יקטירון החלב וגו':

בעטיו של נחש. בעלתו של נחש שהסיאה לחוה ולא בחטא אחר שלא חטאו. בעטיו כמו עטא וטעם (דניאל ב): **ואחיותיהם.** בבני ישי משתעי: **אלא לאו ר"ש בן אלעזר.** דאמר משה ואהרן בחטאם מתו ומודה בהני: **כל האומר ראובן חטא.** במעשה בלהה: **דכתיב.** בההוא קרא: **ויהיו בני יעקב וגו'.** להוציא מלבך שלא תחשדנו: **ויבא חטא זה לידו.** ויגזור הקב"ה שיהיו מן המקללים: **אחת של שכינה.** כך היה יעקב עושה בארבעה אהלי נשיו מעמיד מטה לשכינה ובאותו אהל שהוא רואה בו השכינה הוא בא ולן אותו הלילה: **חללת.** אותו שם שעלה על יצועי דהיינו שכינה מדלא כתיב יצועי עלית טעם אחר עד שלא נבנה אהל מועד היתה שכינה מצויה באהלי צדיקים: **פחז.** נוטריקון הוא: **פזתה.** לשון עמא פזיזא (לקמן דף פח.). פזתה מיהרת בעצמך וחטאת: **זלתה.** זלזלת: **פיללת.** להנצל מן החטא: **חלתה.** ויחל משה (שמות לב): **זעזעת.** יראת לחטוא לר' אליעזר ור' יהושע חטא ולרבן גמליאל ולמודעי בקש לחטוא ולא חטא: **חלית.** חולי גדול להתאפק לכבוש יצרך: **כל האומר בני עלי חטאו.** באשת איש אינו אלא טועה ומיהו בבזיון קדשים חטאו: **דאמר רב.** לקמן בשמעתין פנחס לא חטא ויליף לה מקרא ור' יונתן יליף לה לחפני מהאי קרא דמקיש חפני לפנחס: **ששהו את קיניהן.** שהיו מסרבין להקריב שום קרבן אלא בקושי כדכתיב (שמואל א ב) גם בטרם יקטירון את החלב וגו' וכשהיו זבות ויולדות באות ממקום אחר לשילה להקריב את קיניהן והן היו משהין מלהקריבם והנשים לא היו יכולין לסמוך עליהם שיקריבו והיו שוהות שם ולא היו חוזרות אצל בעליהן עד שראו קיניהן קרבין והיו טהורות לקדשים וליכנס לעזרה לפיכך מעלה עליהם כאילו שכבום שהיו מונעים אותן מפריה ורביה: **פנחס לא חטא.** באשת איש דאשר ישכבון את הנשים אינו אלא חפני לבדו: **ואחיה בן אחיטוב וגו' כהן ה'.** בשילה נושא אפוד הרי שמייחסו לשבח ומזכיר עליו שם פנחס אבי אביו: **אפשר בא חטא לידו והכתוב מייחסו.** לשבח ואת בן בנו מייחסו אחריו והכתיב גבי עבירה דנואפים יכרת ה' לאיש וגו' והאי קרא בבא על הנכרית ועל הזונה מישתעי כדדרשינן ליה באלו הן הנשרפין ° דכתיב לעיל מיניה כי חלל יהודה קדש ה' אשר אהב ובעל בת אל נכר ודרשינן כי חלל יהודה קדש זו זונה וכן הוא אומר לא תהיה קדשה וגו': **ער.** חריף להבין ולהורות בין החכמים כדאמרי' בעירובין (דף נג:) אהרנית ערנית: **ואם כהן הוא כו'.** וכאן מייחס כהן מגיש מנחה אחר פנחס: **והכתיב אל בני כי לא טובה השמועה אשר אנכי שומע מעבירים עם ה'** אביהם היה מוכיחם: **והא כתיב מעבירים אמר** ל) **רב הונא בריה דרב יהושע מעבירם כתיב.**

מעבירם כתיב. הש"ס שלנו חולק על ספרים שלנו שכתוב בהם (מ) מעבירים) וכן מצינו בירושלמי בשמשון והוא שפט את ישראל ארבעים שנה מלמד שהיו פלשתים יראים ממנו כ' שנה אחר מותו כמו בחייו ° ובכל ספרים שלנו כתיב כ' שנה (שופטים טו): **מתוך** שהיה לו לפנחס למחות. ופליג אר' יונתן דאמר שניהם לא חטאו:

שהיה

מיתיבי אמרו מלאכי השרת לפני הקב"ה רבונו של עולם מפני מה קנסת מיתה על אדם הראשון אמר להם מצוה קלה צויתיו ועבר עליה א"ל והלא משה ואהרן שקיימו כל התורה כולה ומתו א"ל א) מקרה אחד לצדיק ולרשע לטוב וגו' הוא דאמר כי האי תנא דתניא ר"ש בן אלעזר אומר אף משה ואהרן בחטאם מתו שנא' ב) יען לא האמנתם בי א) הא האמנתם בי עדיין לא הגיע זמנכם ליפטר מן העולם מיתיבי ° ב) ארבעה מתו בעטיו של נחש ואלו הן בנימין בן יעקב ועמרם אבי משה וישי אבי דוד וכלאב בן דוד וכולהו גמרא לבר מישי אבי דוד דמפרש ביה קרא דכתיב ג) ואת עמשא שם אבשלום תחת יואב (ג) שר) הצבא ועמשא בן איש ושמו יתרא הישראלי אשר בא אל אביגיל בת נחש אחות צרויה אם יואב וכי בת נחש הואי והלא בת ישי הואי דכתיב ד) ואחיותיהן צרויה ואביגיל אלא בת מי שמת בעטיו של נחש מני אילימא תנא דמלאכי השרת והא איכא משה ואהרן אלא לאו ר"ש בן אלעזר היא וש"מ יש מיתה בלא חטא ויש יסורין בלא עון ותיובתא דרב אמי ° תיובתא: א"ר שמואל בר נחמני א"ר יונתן כל האומר ראובן חטא אינו אלא טועה שנאמר ה) ויהיו בני יעקב שנים עשר מלמד שכולן שקולים כאחת אלא מה אני מקיים ה) וישכב את בלהה פילגש אביו מלמד שבלבל מצעו של אביו ומעלה עליו הכתוב כאילו שכב עמה תניא ר"ש בן אלעזר אומר מוצל אותו צדיק מאותו עון ולא בא מעשה זה לידו אפשר עתיד זרעו לעמוד על הר עיבל ולומר ו) ארור שוכב עם אשת אביו ויבא חטא זה לידו אלא מה אני מקיים וישכב את בלהה פילגש אביו עלבון אמו תבע אמר אם אחות אמי היתה צרה לאמי שפחת אחות אמי תהא צרה לאמי עמד ובלבל את מצעה אחרים אומרים שתי מצעות בלבל אחת של שכינה ואחת של אביו והיינו דכתיב ז) אז חללת יצועי עלה ד) (אל תקרי יצועי אלא יצועיי) כתנאי ז) פחז כמים אל תותר ר' אליעזר אומר פזתה חבתה זלתה ר' יהושע אומר פסעתה על דת חטאת זנית ר"ג אומר פיללתה חלתה זרחה תפלתך אמר ר"ג עדיין צריכין אנו למודעי ר' אלעזר המודעי אומר הפוך את התיבה ודורשה ה) זעזעתה הרתעתה פרחה חטא ממך רבא אמר ואמרי לה ר' ירמיה בר אבא זכרת עונשו של דבר חלית עצמך חולי גדול פירשת מלחטוא: ראובן בני עלי בני שמואל דוד ושלמה ויואש ו) סימן: ז) אמר ר' שמואל בר נחמני א"ר יונתן כל האומר בני עלי חטאו אינו אלא טועה שנאמר ח) ושם שני בני עלי (עם ארון ברית האלהים) חפני ופנחס כהנים לה' סבר לה כרב דאמר רב פנחס לא חטא מקיש חפני לפנחס מה פנחס לא חטא אף חפני לא חטא אלא מה אני מקיים ט) אשר ישכבון את הנשים מתוך ששהו את קיניהן שלא הלכו אצל בעליהן מעלה עליהן הכתוב כאילו שכבום גופא אמר רב פנחס לא חטא שנאמר י) ואחיה בן אחיטוב אחי אי כבוד בן פנחס בן עלי כהן ה' וגו' אפשר חטא בא לידו והכתוב מייחסו והלא כבר נאמר כ) יכרת ה' לאיש אשר יעשנה ער ועונה מאהלי יעקב ומגיש מנחה לה' צבאות ט) אם ישראל הוא לא יהיה לו ער בחכמים ולא עונה בתלמידים ואם כהן הוא לא יהיה לו בן מגיש מנחה אלא לאו שמע מינה פנחס לא חטא אלא הא כתיב ט) אשר ישכבון ט) ישכבן כתיב והכתיב ל) אל בני כי לא טובה השמועה א"ר נחמן בר יצחק בני כתיב והכתיב ל) מעבירים א"ר הונא בריה דרב יהושע מעבירם כתיב והכתיב מ) בני בליעל מתוך שהיה לו לפנחס למחות לחפני ולא מיחה מעלה עליו הכתוב כאילו חטא א"ר שמואל בר נחמני א"ר יונתן כל האומר

בני

קשה בעיני שם החכם הנזכר כאן כי אומר אני שטעות גדול הוא ול"ג לה להא מילתא שהרי בספרים מוגהים כתיב מעבירים וגם במסורה הגדולה במקום שמנויין שם כל התיבות דלא כתיב בהן יו"ד וקורין ולא נמנה זה והם מנויין ע"פ החשבון וזו אינה קושיא דהאי מעבירים לאו לשון עבירה הוא אלא לשון ויעבירו קול במחנה (שמות לו) וה"ק להו לא טובה השמועה אשר אנכי שומע את עם ה' מעבירים ומכריזין וקובלים עליכם והאי מעבירים לשון רבים הוא ואעם ה' קאי ולאו אבני עלי שהרי הם היו עוברים ולא היו מעבירים את אחרים:

בני

תורה אור השלם

א) הַכֹּל כַּאֲשֶׁר לַכֹּל מִקְרֶה אֶחָד לַצַּדִּיק וְלָרָשָׁע לַטּוֹב וְלַטָּהוֹר וְלַטָּמֵא וְלַזֹּבֵחַ וְלַאֲשֶׁר אֵינֶנּוּ זֹבֵחַ כַּטּוֹב כַּחֹטֶא הַנִּשְׁבָּע כַּאֲשֶׁר שְׁבוּעָה יָרֵא: [קהלת ט, ב]

ב) וַיֹּאמֶר יְיָ אֶל מֹשֶׁה וְאֶל אַהֲרֹן יַעַן לֹא הֶאֱמַנְתֶּם בִּי לְהַקְדִּישֵׁנִי לְעֵינֵי בְּנֵי יִשְׂרָאֵל לָכֵן לֹא תָבִיאוּ אֶת הַקָּהָל הַזֶּה אֶל הָאָרֶץ אֲשֶׁר נָתַתִּי לָהֶם: [במדבר כ, יב]

ג) וְאֶת עֲמָשָׂא שָׂם אַבְשָׁלֹם תַּחַת יוֹאָב עַל הַצָּבָא וַעֲמָשָׂא בֶן אִישׁ וּשְׁמוֹ יִתְרָא הַיִּשְׂרְאֵלִי אֲשֶׁר בָּא אֶל אֲבִיגַל בַּת נָחָשׁ אֲחוֹת צְרוּיָה אֵם יוֹאָב: [שמואל ב' יז, כה]

ד) וְאַחְיֹתֵיהֶם צְרוּיָה וַאֲבִיגָיִל וּבְנֵי צְרוּיָה אַבְשַׁי וְיוֹאָב וַעֲשָׂה־אֵל שְׁלֹשָׁה: [דברי הימים א' ב, טז]

ה) וַיְהִי בִּשְׁכֹּן יִשְׂרָאֵל בָּאָרֶץ הַהִוא וַיֵּלֶךְ רְאוּבֵן וַיִּשְׁכַּב אֶת בִּלְהָה פִּילֶגֶשׁ אָבִיו וַיִּשְׁמַע יִשְׂרָאֵל וַיִּהְיוּ בְנֵי יַעֲקֹב שְׁנֵים עָשָׂר: [בראשית לה, כב]

ו) אָרוּר שֹׁכֵב עִם אֵשֶׁת אָבִיו כִּי גִלָּה כְּנַף אָבִיו וְאָמַר כָּל הָעָם אָמֵן: [דברים כז, כ]

ז) פַּחַז כַּמַּיִם אַל תּוֹתַר כִּי עָלִיתָ מִשְׁכְּבֵי אָבִיךָ אָז חִלַּלְתָּ יְצוּעִי עָלָה: [בראשית מט, ד]

ח) וְעָלָה הָאִישׁ הַהוּא מֵעִירוֹ מִיָּמִים יָמִימָה לְהִשְׁתַּחֲוֹת וְלִזְבֹּחַ לַייָ צְבָאוֹת בְּשִׁלֹה וְשָׁם שְׁנֵי בְנֵי עֵלִי חָפְנִי וּפִנְחָס כֹּהֲנִים לַייָ: [שמואל א' א, ג]

ט) וְעֵלִי זָקֵן מְאֹד וְשָׁמַע אֵת כָּל אֲשֶׁר יַעֲשׂוּן בָּנָיו לְכָל יִשְׂרָאֵל וְאֵת אֲשֶׁר יִשְׁכְּבוּן אֶת הַנָּשִׁים הַצֹּבְאוֹת פֶּתַח אֹהֶל מוֹעֵד: [שמואל א' ב, כב]

י) וַאֲחִיָּה בֶן אֲחִטוּב אֲחִי אִיכָבוֹד בֶּן פִּינְחָס בֶּן עֵלִי כֹּהֵן יְיָ בְּשִׁלוֹ נֹשֵׂא אֵפוֹד וְהָעָם לֹא יָדַע כִּי הָלַךְ יוֹנָתָן: [שמואל א' יד, ג]

כ) יַכְרֵת יְיָ לָאִישׁ אֲשֶׁר יַעֲשֶׂנָּה עֵר וְעֹנֶה מֵאָהֳלֵי יַעֲקֹב וּמַגִּישׁ מִנְחָה לַייָ צְבָאוֹת: [מלאכי ב, יב]

ל) אַל בָּנָי כִּי לוֹא טוֹבָה הַשְּׁמֻעָה אֲשֶׁר אָנֹכִי שֹׁמֵעַ מַעֲבִרִים עַם יְיָ: [שמואל א' ב, כד]

מ) וּבְנֵי עֵלִי בְּנֵי בְלִיָּעַל לֹא יָדְעוּ אֶת יְיָ: [שמואל א' ב, יב]

ליקוטי רש"י

מקרה אחד. שסוף הכל אשר צדיק ואשר רשע למות ומקרה אחד יש בעולם הזה לכולם [קהלת ט, ב]. **יען לא האמנתם בי.** גלה הכתוב שאלולי חטא זה בלבד היו נכנסין לארץ כדי שלא יאמרו עליהם כעון שאר דור המדבר שנגזר עליהם שלא יכנסו לארץ כך היה עון משה ואהרן [במדבר כ, יב]. **בעטיו של נחש.** בעלתו של נחש כלומר לא היו ראוין למות אלא שנגזרה גזירת מיתה על כל תולדותיו של אדם הראשון בעלתו של נחש בעטיו תרגום של עלתו כדכתיב (דניאל ו) אתייעטו כל וגו' וכן התיב עטא וטעם (שם ב). **ואחיותיהן.** בבני ישי כתיב [ב"ב יז.]. **בת נחש.** הוא ישי אבי דוד רבותינו אמרו שמת בלא עון בעטיו של נחש [ש"ב יז, כה]. **ויהיו בני יעקב שנים עשר.** ורבותינו דרשו ללמדנו בא שכולן שוין וכולן צדיקים שלא חטא ראובן. **וישכב את בלהה פילגש אביו וכו'.** מתוך שבלבל משכבו מעלה עליו הכתוב כאלו שכבה. ולמה בלבל וחלל יצועיו שכשמתה רחל נטל יעקב מטתו שהיתה נתונה תדיר באהל רחל ולא בשאר אהלים ונתנה באהל בלהה בא ראובן ותבע עלבון אמו אמר אם אחות אמי היתה צרה לאמי שפחת אחות אמי תהא צרה לאמי לכן בלבל [בראשית לה, כב]. **אז חללת.** אותו שם שעלה על יצועי והיא השכינה שהיה דרכה להיות עולה על יצועי. **יצועי.** לשון משכב על שם שמציעים אותו על ידי לבדין וסדינין והרבה דומים לו (תהלים סג, ז) אם זכרתיך על יצועי (שם קלב, ג) אם אעלה על ערש יצועי. **פחז כמים.** הפחז והבהלה אשר מהרת להראות כעסך כמים הללו הממהרים למרוצתם, לכך. **אל תותר.** אל תרבה ליטול כל היתרות הללו שהיו ראויות לך. **פחז.** שם דבר הוא לפיכך טעמו למעלה וכולו נקוד פת"ח ואלו היה לשון עבר היה נקוד חציו קמ"ץ וחציו פת"ח וטעמו למטה [שם מט, ד]. **אשר ישכבון.** כמשמעו ורבותינו אמרו מתוך ששהו את קיניהן והם היו ממתינות עד שתראן קיניהן קריבין מעלה עליהם כאלו שכבום [ש"א ב, כב]. **ששהו את קיניהן.** שהיו מביאות במלאות ימי לידתן ליטהר לאכול בקדשים והם היו בעלי [גאוה] והיו מתרשלין בהקרבתן והנשים ממתינות שם עד שיקריבום ומשהות מלחזור למקומן אצל בעליהן ומבטלין את הנשים מפריה ורביה [יומא ט:].

מסורת הש"ס

א) [יומא פז.], ב) ב"ב יז., ג) [צ"ל על], ד) רש"ל מ"ז ועי' רש"י, ה) לשון רמת, ו) צ"ל ויאשיהו, ז) יומא ט., ח) סנהדרין פב., ט) [עיין תוספות סנהדרין ד. ד"ה ורבנן], י) [צ"ל כמו ויחל משה], כ) [סנהדרין דף פג.], ל) מהרש"א גורס רבא, מ) [צ"ל מעברים].

גליון הש"ס

גמ' ד' מתו בעטיו של נחש כו'. בזוה"ק פ' בראשית ועל דא יהושע לא מת אלא בעטיו דנחש וכו'. ובזוה"ק פ' בראשית בפסוק וינחם ה' תלתא דאיסתלקו בגין ההוא עטיא דנחש עמרם לוי בנימין ואית דאמרי אף ישי: **שם תיובתא.** עי' ברא"מ פ' וישלח ד"ה אומרא ובפ' שופטים ד"ה ריה"ג: **תוס' ד"ה מעבירם כתיב וכו' ובכל ספרים שלנו.** וכן מצינו בנדה דף לג ע"א תוס' ד"ה והנושא שכתבו דהמסורת שלנו מחולק עם הש"ס. ובמגילה דף כב ע"א כתבו תוס' דויחל הוא ב' פסוקים סמוך לפרשה שלפניו וכן והקרבתם ובס"ת שלנו ויחל הוא ד' פסוקים מהפרשה וכן והקרבתם ג"פ וכמ"ש מהרש"א שם. ובפסחים דף קיז ע"א בתוס' ד"ה שעומדים כתבו שלא יתכן שיהיה מזמור ב' פסוקים ואלו בספרים שלנו מזמור קיז הוא ב' פסוקים. עי' מהרש"א שם ע"א. ובסנהדרין דף ד ע"א פירש"י שם דבכבשה דיחיד כתיב קרנות מלא ובס"ת שלנו כתיב חסר. ובדף ד ע"א כ' רש"י דבפרשה והיה כי יביאך כתיב לטטפת חסר ובפ' והיה אם שמע כתיב מלא. ובס"ת שלנו גם בפ' והיה כי יביאך כתיב מלא. ובדף כ ע"א כתי' להכרית וקרי להכרו' ובספרים שלנו גם הכתיב להכרות. עוד שם דף קג ע"א ויחתר לו ויעתר לו מיבעיא ליה. ובספרים שלנו כתיב ויעתר. ובב"ב דף ט ע"א הלא פרוס בשין ובספרים שלנו כתיב בסין. ועי' בח"א שם במהרש"א. ובקדושין דף ל ע"א. והתגלח חציין של פסוקי' ובתיקונים בפ' לו בפסוק ויאפוד לו בו ליין דשם חצי התורה בפסוקים. ובירושלמי שהביא תוס' בכתובות דף ז ע"ב דבמקהלת ברכו אלהים חסר. ובספרים שלנו כתיב מלא. וברש"י בחומש פ' תרומה ואת כל אשר אצוה הוא וי"ו יתירה ולפנינו כתיב את בלא ו'. עי' ברא"ם שם. ובמדרש רבה שיר השירים בפסוק אחזו לנו שועלים שעלים א"ר ברכיה קדמאה מלא תניינא חסר. ובמסורה אינו כן אלא תרוייהו חסר. ובברכות דף ז ע"ב כתי' לכלותו ובספרי' שלנו בד"ה א יז כתיב לבלותו. (ובפסחים דף ג ע"א ו' דטהור. ובספרים

מִנְחָה" – and if he is a Kohen, he will not have any son [descendant] who will *present a meal offering.*[42]

Rav concludes:

אֶלָּא לָאו שְׁמַע מִינָּהּ פִּנְחָס לֹא חָטָא – Rather, does one not derive from [this verse] in *Malachi* that **Pinchas did not sin?**

The Gemara asks:

אֶלָּא הָא כְּתִיב ,,אֲשֶׁר־יִשְׁכְּבֻן" – But it is written: . . . *that they were lying with the women!*[43] – ? –

The Gemara answers:

יִשְׁכָּבֶן כְּתִיב – [The verb] is written in a way that could be read: **"He lay with them."**[44]

The Gemara again challenges Rav's interpretation:

וְהָכְתִיב ,,אַל בָּנָי כִּי לו[א]־טוֹבָה הַשְּׁמֻעָה" – But it is written that Eli said to his sons:[45] ***Do not, my sons,***[46] ***for the report** that I hear the Lord's people spreading **is not good!***[47] – ? –

The Gemara answers:

אָמַר רַב נַחְמָן בַּר יִצְחָק בְּנִי כְּתִיב – Rav Nachman bar Yitzchak said: [The word] is written in a way that could be read: **"my son."**[48]

The Gemara asks again:

וְהָכְתִיב ,,מַעֲבִירִים" – But it is written in that same verse: *You* [plural] ***are causing** the people **to transgress!***[49] – ? –

The Gemara answers:

אָמַר רַב הוּנָא בְּרֵיהּ דְּרַב יְהוֹשֻׁעַ מַעֲבִירָם כְּתִיב – Rav Huna the son of Rav Yehoshua said: [The word] is written in a way that could be read: **"You** [singular] **are causing [the people] to transgress."**[50]

One final challenge to Rav's interpretation:

וְהָכְתִיב ,,בְּנֵי בְלִיָּעַל" – But it is written: *And the sons of Eli were **wicked men!***[51] – ? –

The Gemara answers:

מִתּוֹךְ שֶׁהָיָה לוֹ לְפִנְחָס לְמַחוֹת לְחָפְנִי וְלֹא מִיחָה – Since Pinchas should have protested against Chafni but did not protest, מַעֲלֶה עָלָיו הַכָּתוּב כְּאִילוּ חָטָא – Scripture regards him as if he had sinned.[52]

The Gemara discusses other people regarding whom Scripture gave a false impression of having sinned grievously:

אָמַר רַבִּי שְׁמוּאֵל בַּר נַחְמָנִי אָמַר רַבִּי יוֹנָתָן – R' Shmuel bar Nachmani said in the name of R' Yonasan:

כֹּל הָאוֹמֵר – Whoever says

NOTES

42. [I.e. none of his descendants will serve as Kohanim in the Temple.] Nevertheless, the verse in *Samuel* states that Pinchas had a descendant who served in the Tabernacle (*Rashi*).

43. The plural form implies that both sons were guilty.

44. The verb is written without the letter ו, as יִשְׁכְּבֻן. Were it not for the oral tradition regarding its pronunciation, the word could be read in the singular, as יִשְׁכָּבֶן. Rav expounds the written form of the word to derive that only Chafni sinned.

45. *I Samuel* 2:24. [Regarding the translation of this verse, see below, notes 49-50.]

46. I.e. do not continue doing these evil things (*Metzudas David*).

47. The plural, *my sons,* implies that both Pinchas and Chafni sinned.

Maharsha asks: Why does the Gemara assume that Eli's reproach concerns adultery? Perhaps it refers only to their dishonoring the offerings? *Maharsha* answers that Eli's reproach immediately follows the verse about adultery, and must thus pertain to it.

48. Were it not for the oral tradition regarding its pronunciation, the word could be read in the singular, as בְּנִי, "my son" – a reference to Chafni.

49. Verse 24 states in full: אַל בָּנָי כִּי לוֹא־טוֹבָה הַשְּׁמֻעָה אֲשֶׁר אָנֹכִי שֹׁמֵעַ מַעֲבִרִים עַם־ה׳. The Gemara here assumes that the word מַעֲבִרִים means *you are causing* [the people] *to transgress.* [The verse would then be translated: "Do not, my sons, for the report that I hear, that you are causing the Lord's people to transgress, is not good"; but see following note.] Since מַעֲבִירִים appears in the plural, the Gemara infers that both sons were guilty.

50. The Gemara states that מַעֲבִירָם is written with no letter י before the final ם. Hence, were it not for the oral tradition regarding how to pronounce it, it could be vocalized מַעֲבִירָם, meaning: "You (singular) are causing [the people] to transgress," and can be expounded as referring to Chafni. See *Sfas Emes.*

Rashi and *Tosafos* point out that in the authenticated text of the Book of *Samuel* this word is written: מַעֲבִרִים, with a י indeed appearing before the final ם. Thus, one must conclude either that the Gemara's text of *Samuel* differed in this detail from the authenticated text (*Tosafos;* see *Gilyon HaShas,* and *Yad Malachi* §293), or that this particular challenge to Rav (involving the word מַעֲבִרִים) is an error and should be deleted from the Gemara; indeed, *Rashi* points out that the whole basis of the Gemara's challenge is invalid, for the subject of the verb מַעֲבִרִים is not the sons of Eli and the word does not mean "cause [the people] to sin"; rather, the word means "publicize" and its subject is "the people." Thus, the correct translation of the verse would be: "Do not, my sons, for the report that I hear the Lord's people spreading is not good!"

51. See above, note 29. The term בְּנֵי בְלִיָּעַל, *wicked men,* is written in the plural, and there is no way it could be pronounced in the singular. It thus implies that both sons were guilty.

Maharsha asks: Why does the Gemara assume that the term *wicked men* refers to the sin of adultery? After all, it is not written in the passage that speaks about adultery, but in the passage that mentions the dishonoring of the offerings, a sin committed by both sons! *Maharsha* answers by demonstrating that in the Torah the term בְּנֵי בְלִיָּעַל usually refers to carnal sins.

52. The Gemara thus concludes that, in Rav's view, only Chafni actually committed adultery. R' Yonasan holds, on the other hand, that neither brother was guilty of that sin (*Tosafos;* see note 36 above; see also *Melo HaRo'im*).

בְּנֵי שְׁמוּאֵל חָטְאוּ אֵינוֹ אֶלָּא טוֹעֶה – that **the sons of Shmuel sinned is simply mistaken,**[1] **שֶׁנֶּאֱמַר** ,,וַיְהִי (כִּי זָקֵן שְׁמוּאֵל וּבָנָיו לֹא הָלְכוּ) בִּדְרָכָיו" – **as it is stated,**[2] ***When Shmuel became old ... his sons did not go in his ways,*** **בִּדְרָכָיו הוּא דְּלֹא הָלְכוּ** – which teaches that **it was in his** lofty **ways that they did not go; מִיחְטָא נַמִּי לֹא חָטְאוּ** – however, **they also did not sin.**

R' Yonasan continues expounding this verse:

אֶלָּא מָה אֲנִי מְקַיֵּים ,,וַיִּטּוּ אַחֲרֵי הַבָּצַע" – **But how,** then, **do I establish** the continuation of that verse: ***They turned aside after monetary gain,*** *took bribery, and perverted justice?* **שֶׁלֹּא עָשׂוּ כְּמַעֲשֵׂה אֲבִיהֶם** – It means **that they did not act in accordance with the deeds of their father, שֶׁהָיָה שְׁמוּאֵל הַצַּדִּיק מְחַזֵּר בְּכָל מְקוֹמוֹת יִשְׂרָאֵל וְדָן אוֹתָם בְּעָרֵיהֶם** – **for Shmuel the Righteous used to travel throughout all the Jewish areas and judge [the people] in their cities, שֶׁנֶּאֱמַר** ,,וְהָלַךְ מִדֵּי שָׁנָה בְּשָׁנָה וְסָבַב בֵּית־אֵל וְהַגִּלְגָּל וְהַמִּצְפָּה וְשָׁפַט אֶת־יִשְׂרָאֵל" – **as it is stated:**[3] ***He went every year and made a circuit of Beis El, Gilgal and Mitzpah, and judged Israel.*** **וְהֵם לֹא עָשׂוּ כֵּן** – **However, [his sons] did not do likewise; אֶלָּא יָשְׁבוּ בְּעָרֵיהֶם** – **rather, they sat in their cities** and judged **כְּדֵי לְהַרְבּוֹת שָׂכָר לְחַזָּנֵיהֶן וּלְסוֹפְרֵיהֶן** – **in order to increase the income of their attendants and scribes.**[4]

R' Yonasan taught that the sons of Shmuel did not actually pervert justice. The Gemara reports that this view is not universally held:

כְּתַנָּאֵי – The question of whether Shmuel's sons actually perverted justice **is** a matter **of** the following dispute between **Tannaim:**

,,וַיִּטּוּ אַחֲרֵי הַבָּצַע" – Scripture states: ***THEY TURNED ASIDE AFTER MONETARY GAIN.*** **רַבִּי מֵאִיר אוֹמֵר חֶלְקָם שָׁאֲלוּ בְּפִיהֶם** – **R' MEIR SAYS:** This means that **THEY EXPLICITLY REQUESTED THEIR PORTION** of the crops.[5] **רַבִּי יְהוּדָה אוֹמֵר מְלַאי הִטִּילוּ עַל בַּעֲלֵי בָתִּים** – **R' YEHUDAH SAYS: THEY JOBBED OUT MERCHANDISE TO HOUSEHOLDERS.**[6] **רַבִּי עֲקִיבָא אוֹמֵר קוּפָּה יְתֵירָה שֶׁל מַעֲשֵׂר נָטְלוּ בִּזְרוֹעַ** – **R' AKIVA SAYS: THEY FORCIBLY TOOK AN EXCESSIVE QUANTITY**[7] **OF TITHES.**[8] **רַבִּי יוֹסֵי אוֹמֵר מַתָּנוֹת נָטְלוּ בִּזְרוֹעַ** – **R' YOSE SAYS: THEY FORCIBLY TOOK THE** Torah-mandated **GIFTS.**[9]

The Gemara now discusses the sin attributed to King David:

אָמַר רַבִּי שְׁמוּאֵל בַּר נַחְמָנִי אָמַר רַבִּי יוֹנָתָן – **R' Shmuel bar Nachmani said in the name of R' Yonasan: כָּל הָאוֹמֵר דָּוִד חָטָא אֵינוֹ אֶלָּא טוֹעֶה** – **Whoever says** that **David sinned is simply mistaken,**[10] **שֶׁנֶּאֱמַר** ,,וַיְהִי דָוִד לְכָל־דְּרָכָו מַשְׂכִּיל וַה׳ עִמּוֹ וגו׳" – **for it is stated: *David was successful in all his ways, and Hashem was with him* etc.**[11] **אֶפְשָׁר חֵטְא בָּא לְיָדוֹ וּשְׁכִינָה עִמּוֹ** – Now, **is it possible that [David] sinned and the Divine Presence was with him?** Certainly not! **אֶלָּא מָה אֲנִי מְקַיֵּים** ,,מַדּוּעַ בָּזִיתָ אֶת־דְּבַר ה׳ לַעֲשׂוֹת הָרַע" – **But how,** then, **do I establish** the verse in which the prophet Nassan rebukes David: ***Why have you despised the word of Hashem, to do*** *that which is* ***evil*** *in My eyes?*[12] **שֶׁבִּיקֵּשׁ לַעֲשׂוֹת וְלֹא עָשָׂה** – It means **that [David] sought to do** a sinful act with Bathsheba,[13] **but** in fact **did not do** it.

The Gemara cites further evidence that David did not sin:

אָמַר רַב – **Rav said: רַבִּי דְּאָתֵי מִדָּוִד מְהַפֵּךְ וְדָרִישׁ בִּזְכוּתֵיהּ דְּדָוִד** – **Rebbi, who was descended from David,**[14] **sought to expound**

NOTES

1. Whoever says they sinned by taking bribery and perverting justice is mistaken (*Rashi*). However, they did do wrong, as the Gemara proceeds to explain.

2. *I Samuel* 8:1 and 8:3. The verses actually read: ... וַיְהִי כַּאֲשֶׁר זָקֵן שְׁמוּאֵל וְלֹא־הָלְכוּ בָנָיו בִּדְרָכָו (*Mesoras HaShas*).

[The Gemara (*Makkos* 11a) teaches that Eli cursed Shmuel conditionally, stating that if Shmuel did not reveal to him Hashem's prophecy, Shmuel would be like Eli – i.e. he would have errant sons. Even though the condition was never met, the curse was fulfilled.]

3. Ibid. 7:16.

4. Shmuel's sons paid their attendants to travel throughout the land and summon litigants to court, and they paid scribes to prepare legal documents such as שְׁטָרֵי בֵּירוּרִין [agreements as to which judges would adjudicate the case] and אִגְּרוֹת שׁוּם [certificates of the estimated worth of property] (*Rashi*). Shmuel's sons incurred the added expense of dispatching their attendants to summon litigants in order to be able to remain at home and tend to their private businesses. They thus demonstrated their love of lucre, for if they had followed their father's example, their financial fortunes would have suffered (*Rif* to *Ein Yaakov*).

5. Literally, they requested their portion with their mouths. The sons of Shmuel were Levites, and so were entitled to receive tithes (*maaser rishon*). Since they were leaders of the generation and its judges, the people could not refuse their forthright solicitations. The result was that other, impoverished Levites suffered from not receiving tithes.

According to R' Meir, Shmuel's sons were not guilty of actually perverting justice (*Rashi*).

6. Shmuel's sons provided various individuals with merchandise to sell, and in return received the profits. Thus, when these individuals appeared in court as litigants, the judges were partial toward them and rendered prejudiced verdicts (*Rashi*). Hence, according to R' Yehudah, Shmuel's sons indeed perverted justice. R' Yehudah, then, is the Tanna who opposes R' Yonasan's view.

7. Literally: basket.

8. They took more *maaser* than was proper (*Rashi*) [i.e. more than one-tenth of the crop]. This is theft (see *Rashi* to *Chullin* 133a ד״ה חלקם שאלו; cf. *Maharsha;* see also *Dibros Moshe* 43:18).

9. One who slaughters a non-sacred animal for his own consumption is required to give the foreleg, jaw and maw to a Kohen (*Deuteronomy* 18:3). The sons of Shmuel, even though they were not *Kohanim,* took these priestly gifts by force. [This, too, is theft (see *Dibros Moshe* ibid.).]

Another interpretation: They forcibly took the gifts of tithes that were due to them as Levites. [Although this is not theft] it is forbidden, for the Gemara derives (*Chullin* 133a) that a Kohen (or Levite) should not appropriate the gifts, but should wait until the owner gives them (*Rashi*).

10. It is a mistake to think that David cohabited with Bathsheba before she had received a divorce (*Rashi*). That is, it is a mistake to think that David committed adultery with her, for by the time he had relations with her she had already received her divorce, as the Gemara will explain below.

11. *I Samuel* 18:14. This verse describes the situation that existed long before the incident with Bathsheba. If so, why does the Gemara cite it as proof that David never sinned with her? *Rif* to *Ein Yaakov* explains that the word מַשְׂכִּיל also means cogitate, and so the verse teaches that David always kept the Divine Presence in mind when planning his deeds. Hence, it was impossible for him to commit so grave a sin as adultery.

Anaf Yosef there offers a different explanation: The Gemara in *Sanhedrin* (93b) teaches that the phrase, *Hashem was with him,* means that David was such a great Torah scholar that the halachah follows his ruling. Now, the Gemara in *Sotah* (21a) states that when one reaches this level of scholarship "he is saved from all" – i.e. no sin will come about through him. This is why our Gemara infers that David certainly could not have committed adultery.

12. *II Samuel* 12:9.

13. David sought to cohabit with Bathsheba before she received a bill of divorce from Uriah, her husband, who was sending it from the battlefront.

As the Gemara states below, all warriors who took part in the wars of King David gave bills of divorce to their wives, so that (a) if the husband died childless, the wife would not be subject to a levirate marriage (*yibum*) with his brother; or (b) if the husband was killed without witnesses or captured, the wife would not become an *agunah,* a woman who cannot remarry because she remains legally bound to her husband (*Rashi*; see *Rashash and Cheshek Shlomo*).

14. See *Megadim Chadashim.*

בני שמואל חטאו אינו אלא טועה שנאמר א) ויהי (א) כי זקן שמואל ב) ובניו לא הלכו) בדרכיו בדרכיו הוא דלא הלכו מיחטא נמי לא חטאו אלא מה אני מקיים ב) ויטו אחרי הבצע שלא עשו כמעשה אביהם שהיה שמואל הצדיק מחזר בכל מקומות ישראל ודן אותם בעריהם שנאמר ג) והלך מדי שנה בשנה וסבב בית אל והגלגל והמצפה ושפט את ישראל והם לא עשו כן אלא ישבו בעריהם א כדי להרבות שכר לחזניהן ולסופריהן כתנאי ב) ויטו אחרי הבצע ר' מאיר אומר חלקם שאלו בפיהם רבי יהודה אומר מלאי הטילו על בעלי בתים ר' עקיבא אומר קופה יתירה של מעשר נטלו בזרוע ר' יוסי אומר מתנות נטלו בזרוע: א"ר שמואל בר נחמני אמר ר' יונתן כל האומר דוד חטא אינו אלא טועה שנאמר ד) ויהי דוד לכל דרכיו משכיל וה' עמו וגו' אפשר חטא בא לידו ושכינה עמו אלא מה אני מקיים ה) מדוע בזית את דבר ה' לעשות הרע שביקש לעשות ולא עשה אמר רב רבי דאתי מדוד מהפך ודריש בזכותיה דדוד מדוע בזית את דבר ה' לעשות הרע רבי אומר משונה רעה זו מכל רעות שבתורה שכל רעות שבתורה כתיב בהו ויעש וכאן כתיב לעשות שביקש לעשות ולא עשה ה) את אוריה החתי הכית בחרב ° שהיה לך לדונו בסנהדרין ולא דנת ה) ואת אשתו לקחת לך לאשה ליקוחין יש לך בה ג) דא"ר שמואל בר נחמני א"ר יונתן כל היוצא למלחמת בית דוד כותב גט כריתות לאשתו שנאמר ו) ואת עשרת חריצי החלב האלה תביא לשר האלף ואת אחיך תפקוד לשלום ואת ערובתם תקח מאי ערובתם תני רב יוסף דברים המעורבים בינו לבינה ה) ואותו הרגת בחרב בני עמון ד) מה חרב בני עמון אי אתה נענש עליו אף אוריה החתי אי אתה נענש עליו מאי טעמא ב מורד במלכות הוה דאמר ליה ז) ואדוני יואב ועבדי אדוני על פני השדה חונים אמר רב כי מעיינת ביה בדוד לא משכחת ביה בר מדאוריה דכתיב (א) ח) רק בדבר אוריה החתי אביי קשישא רמי דרב אדרב מי אמר רב הכי ה) והאמר רב קיבל דוד לשון הרע קשיא גופא רב אמר קיבל דוד לשון הרע דכתיב ט) ויאמר לו המלך איפוא הוא ויאמר ציבא אל המלך הנה הוא בית מכיר בן עמיאל ו) (בלא) דבר וכתיב י) וישלח המלך ויקחהו מבית מכיר בן עמיאל ז) (מלא) דבר מכדי חזייה דשקרא הוא כי הדר אלשין עילויה מ"ט קיבלה מיניה דכתיב כ) ויאמר המלך ח) (אל ציבא איה) בן אדוניך ויאמר ציבא אל המלך הנה (הוא) יושב בירושלים וגו' ומנא לן דקיבל מיניה דכתיב ל) ויאמר המלך הנה לך כל אשר למפיבושת ויאמר ציבא השתחויתי אמצא חן ט) (בעיני) המלך ושמואל אמר לא קיבל דוד לשון הרע דברים הניכרים חזא ביה דכתיב מ) ומפיבושת בן שאול ירד י) (לפני) המלך לא עשה רגליו ולא עשה שפמו ואת בגדיו לא כיבס וגו' וכתיב נ) ויהי כי בא ירושלים לקראת המלך ויאמר לו המלך למה לא הלכת עמי מפיבושת ויאמר אדוני המלך עבדי רמני כי אמר עבדך אחבשה לי החמור וארכב עליה ואלך את המלך כי פסח עבדך

בני שמואל חטאו. במקח שוחד והטיית דין: לחזניהם. שמשיהם שסוכרין אותן לילך ולהזמין את הנקראים לדין: ולסופריהם. לשטרי בירורין ואגרות שום: מלאי הטילו על בעלי בתים. נותנים להן פרגמטיא לעסוק בה ולתת להם השכר ומתוך כך היה נמשך לבם להטות דין כשבאין לפניהם לדון והיינו חטאם: חלקם שאלו בפיהם. מעשר ראשון הראוי להם שלוים היו שאלו בפיהם מתוך שהיו גדולי הדור ושופטים לא היו מונעים מהם ושאר לוים עניים מצטערים ולר' מאיר לא חטאו בהטיית משפט: קופה יתירה. יותר מן הראוי: מתנות. זרוע לחיים וקיבה והם לא היו כהנים ל"א מתנות לויה כגון מעשר וקרא כתיב ונתן לכהן ודרשינן ולא שיטול מעצמו בשחיטת חולין בפ' הזרוע (דף קלג.) וה"ה לכל מתנות כהונה ולויה: דוד חטא. בבת שבע קודם שקבלה גט: שבקש. לשכב עמה קודם שקבלה גט שהיה בעלה שולח לה מן המלחמה שאם ימות לא תזקק ליבום או שמא יהרג ואין מעיד עליו ותתעגן אשתו או שמא יהא שבוי כדאמרינן לקמן כל היוצא למלחמת בית דוד כו': משונה רעה זו. בכתיבתה ובלשונה: שהיה לך לדונו. על שמרד במלכות כדלקמן: ליקוחין יש לך בה. קדושין תופסין בה שאינה אשת איש כדשמואל כו': גט כריתות. על תנאי שאם ימות תהא מגורשת מעכשיו ופעמים שהוא טרוד בבאתו ושולחו מן המלחמה: ואת ערובתם תקח. במלחמת שאול כתיב: דברים המעורבים ביניהם. היינו קדושין תקח תבטל ע"י גט שתביא להם מן המלחמה: בחרב בני עמון. כאותן שהורגים בני עמון שלא מדעתך: ואדוני יואב. לאו אורח ארעא לקבל עליו מרות אחרים בפני המלך: רק בדבר אוריה. מקרא כתיב כך בדבר אוריה שגרם לו שיהרג אבל בבת שבע לא חטא: לשון הרע. לקמיה מפרש: בלא דבר. אינו חכם בתורה והוא מלאו מלא דבר וחכם בתורה: חזייא דשקרא הוה. מתחילה מלאו שקרן בכך: כי הדר אלשין עליה. ליבא על מפיבושת כשהיה דוד בורח מפני אבשלום מאי טעמא קביל מיניה: איה בן אדוניך ויאמר הנה יושב בירושלים. כי אמר היום ישיבו לי את ממלכת אבי: דברים הניכרים חזא ביה. במפיבושת כשנהרג אבשלום וחזר דוד למלכותו ובא לפניו לא עשה רגליו ולא עשה שפמו כסבור דוד שניכרים דברי ציבא שנצטער על שחזר דוד ולא קישט עצמו ° ועוד היה מצפה שכשיושיבוהו במלכות יתנאה ויספר לכך לא קבל דבריו ואמר לו אתה וציבא תחלקו השדה והוא השיבו קשה אין לי לצעוק אלא על מי שהביאך הלום הנה שמצטער על שובו ואם לא שראה בו דברים הניכרים היה חוזר ממה שאמר הנה לך כל אשר למפיבושת ואע"פ שמיהר ואמר לו מתחלה הנה לך כל אשר למפיבושת אין זו קבלה כי כל זמן שלא היה דוד שב למלכותו יודע היה שאין מתנתו מתנה ולא אמר לו אלא על תנאי אם יראה אמת בדבריו:

שהיה לך לדונו בסנהדרין. קשה לר"י דפ"ק דמגילה (דף יד: ושם) אמרינן גבי נבל דמורד במלכות לא בעי למדייניה ואוריה מורד במלכות הוה כדאמר בסמוך ויש לומר דודאי צריך לדונו ולידע אם הוא מורד במלכות אבל לעיין בדינו ולעשות הלנת דין ולהמתין עד למחר אין צריך וכן משמע דבסנהדרין (דף לו. ושם) אמר שדן דוד את נבל בסנהדרין מויחגרו איש חרבו וגו':

ליקוחין יש לך בה. אף על גב דאפילו חטא נמי יש לו בה ליקוחין דהא אנוסה היתה ושריא לבעל וה"ה לבועל מ"מ ליקוחין יש לך בה משמע לא היה לך בה עבירה:

גט כריתות כותב לאשתו. פרש"י על תנאי שאם ימות במלחמה תהא מגורשת מעכשיו וצריך לומר לפירושו דאף על גב דאוריה בא מן המלחמה התנאי היה שאם לא ישוב בסוף המלחמה שיהא גט אך קשה דתנן במי שאחזו (גיטין דף עג. ושם) מה היא באותן הימים רבי יהודה אומר הרי היא כאשת איש לכל דבריה ואם כן לר' יהודה היתה אשת איש גמורה ונראה לר"ת שהיה מגרשה לגמרי בלא שום תנאי והא דאמרינן בהזהב (ב"מ דף נט. ושם) מוטב שיבעול אדם ספק אשת איש ואל ילבין פני חבירו ברבים מנלן מדוד קרי לה ספק אשת איש לפי שהיו מגרשים בצנעה והעולם סבורים שהיא אשת איש:

דאמר ליה ואדוני יואב. פרש"י דמורד במלכות הוה משום דקאמר ואדוני יואב ° ואין נראה דאין זה מורד שלא היה בלבו להמליכו ולקרותו מלך אלא כמו שפירש רבינו מאיר דהוי מורד משום דבקיפא דקרא כתיב ואני אבא אל ביתי לאכול ולשתות ולשכב עם אשתי וגו' שדוד אמר לו לעשות ולא רצה לעשות:

רק בדבר אוריה החתי. קשה דהא איכא מעשה דהסתה בריש פ"ב דיומא (דף כב:) וי"ל דלא חשיב ליה דלא הוי כל כך עון גדול וגם שגג: אלא על

מ א מיי' פכ"ג מהל' סנהדרין הלכה ג סמג לאוין רח טוש"ע ח"מ סי' ט סעיף ד:

מא ב מיי' פ"ג מהל' מלכים הלכה ח:

תורה אור השלם

א) וַיְהִי כַּאֲשֶׁר זָקֵן שְׁמוּאֵל וַיָּשֶׂם אֶת בָּנָיו שֹׁפְטִים לְיִשְׂרָאֵל: [שמואל א' ח, א]

ב) וְלֹא הָלְכוּ בָנָיו בִּדְרָכָיו וַיִּטּוּ אַחֲרֵי הַבָּצַע וַיִּקְחוּ שֹׁחַד וַיַּטּוּ מִשְׁפָּט: [שמואל א' ח, ג]

ג) וְהָלַךְ מִדֵּי שָׁנָה בְּשָׁנָה וְסָבַב בֵּית אֵל וְהַגִּלְגָּל וְהַמִּצְפָּה וְשָׁפַט אֶת יִשְׂרָאֵל אֵת כָּל הַמְּקוֹמוֹת הָאֵלֶּה: [שמואל א' ז, טז]

ד) וַיְהִי דָוִד לְכָל דְּרָכָו מַשְׂכִּיל וַייָ עִמּוֹ: [שמואל א' יח, יד]

ה) מַדּוּעַ בָּזִיתָ אֶת דְּבַר יְיָ לַעֲשׂוֹת הָרַע בְּעֵינַי אֵת אוּרִיָּה הַחִתִּי הִכִּיתָ בַחֶרֶב וְאֶת אִשְׁתּוֹ לָקַחְתָּ לְּךָ לְאִשָּׁה וְאֹתוֹ הָרַגְתָּ בְּחֶרֶב בְּנֵי עַמּוֹן: [שמואל ב' יב, ט]

ו) וְאֵת עֲשֶׂרֶת חֲרִצֵי הֶחָלָב הָאֵלֶּה תָּבִיא לְשַׂר הָאָלֶף וְאֶת אַחֶיךָ תִּפְקֹד לְשָׁלוֹם וְאֶת עֲרֻבָּתָם תִּקָּח: [שמואל א' יז, יח]

ז) וַיֹּאמֶר אוּרִיָּה אֶל דָּוִד הָאָרוֹן וְיִשְׂרָאֵל וִיהוּדָה יֹשְׁבִים בַּסֻּכּוֹת וַאדֹנִי יוֹאָב וְעַבְדֵי אֲדֹנִי עַל פְּנֵי הַשָּׂדֶה חֹנִים וַאֲנִי אָבוֹא אֶל בֵּיתִי לֶאֱכֹל וְלִשְׁתּוֹת וְלִשְׁכַּב עִם אִשְׁתִּי חַיֶּךָ וְחֵי נַפְשֶׁךָ אִם אֶעֱשֶׂה אֶת הַדָּבָר הַזֶּה: [שמואל ב' יא, יא]

ח) אֲשֶׁר עָשָׂה דָוִד אֶת הַיָּשָׁר בְּעֵינֵי יְיָ וְלֹא סָר מִכֹּל אֲשֶׁר צִוָּהוּ כֹּל יְמֵי חַיָּיו רַק בִּדְבַר אוּרִיָּה הַחִתִּי: [מלכים א' טו, ה]

ט) וַיֹּאמֶר לוֹ הַמֶּלֶךְ אֵיפֹה הוּא וַיֹּאמֶר צִיבָא אֶל הַמֶּלֶךְ הִנֵּה הוּא בֵּית מָכִיר בֶּן עַמִּיאֵל בְּלוֹ דְבָר: [שמואל ב' ט, ד]

י) וַיִּשְׁלַח הַמֶּלֶךְ דָּוִד וַיִּקָּחֵהוּ מִבֵּית מָכִיר בֶּן עַמִּיאֵל מִלּוֹ דְבָר: [שמואל ב' ט, ה]

כ) וַיֹּאמֶר הַמֶּלֶךְ וְאַיֵּה בֶּן אֲדֹנֶיךָ וַיֹּאמֶר צִיבָא אֶל הַמֶּלֶךְ הִנֵּה יוֹשֵׁב בִּירוּשָׁלַיִם כִּי אָמַר הַיּוֹם יָשִׁיבוּ לִי בֵּית יִשְׂרָאֵל אֵת מַמְלְכוּת אָבִי: [שמואל ב' טז, ג]

ל) וַיֹּאמֶר הַמֶּלֶךְ לְצִבָא הִנֵּה לְךָ כֹּל אֲשֶׁר לִמְפִיבֹשֶׁת וַיֹּאמֶר צִיבָא הִשְׁתַּחֲוֵיתִי אֶמְצָא חֵן בְּעֵינֶיךָ אֲדֹנִי הַמֶּלֶךְ: [שמואל ב' טז, ד]

מ) וּמְפִבֹשֶׁת בֶּן שָׁאוּל יָרַד לִקְרַאת הַמֶּלֶךְ וְלֹא עָשָׂה רַגְלָיו וְלֹא עָשָׂה שְׂפָמוֹ וְאֶת בְּגָדָיו לֹא כִבֵּס לְמִן הַיּוֹם לֶכֶת הַמֶּלֶךְ עַד הַיּוֹם אֲשֶׁר בָּא בְשָׁלוֹם: [שמואל ב' יט, כה]

נ) וַיְהִי כִּי בָא יְרוּשָׁלַםִ לִקְרַאת הַמֶּלֶךְ וַיֹּאמֶר לוֹ הַמֶּלֶךְ לָמָּה לֹא הָלַכְתָּ עִמִּי מְפִיבֹשֶׁת: וַיֹּאמַר אֲדֹנִי הַמֶּלֶךְ עַבְדִּי רִמָּנִי כִּי אָמַר עַבְדְּךָ אֶחְבְּשָׁה לִּי הַחֲמוֹר וְאֶרְכַּב עָלֶיהָ וְאֵלֵךְ אֶת הַמֶּלֶךְ כִּי פִסֵּחַ עַבְדֶּךָ: [שמואל ב' יט, כו-כז]

א) [נ"ל כאשר זקן שמואל ולא הלכו בניו], ב) [חולין קלג. תוספ' סוטה פי"ד], ג) כתובות ט:, ד) קידושין מג., ה) יומא כב:, ו) [נ"ל בלו], ז) [נ"ל מלו וע' במהרש"א], ח) [נ"ל ואיה], ט) [נ"ל בעיניך אדוני], י) [נ"ל לקראת], כ) רש"י מפ' דעת אמיתים של מפיבושת דהא דלא קישט היינו משום שעוד היה מצפה שכשישיבו לדוד במלכות יתנאה [כ"מ] ורש"ל גרס ועד עתה הי' מצפה.

הגהות הב"ח

(א) גמ' לא משכחת ביה רק בדבר אוריה כצ"ל ותיבת בר מדאורי' דכתי' נמחק:

גליון הש"ס

גמ' (ויהי כי זקן). שלנו כתיב טהר חסר ו'). ובנדרים דף לז ע"ב את דהוגד הוגד קרי ולא כתיב. ובספרים שלנו הוא קרי וכתיב כמ"ש הר"ן שם. ובפסוק אני ה' אלהיך אשר הוצאתיך איתא בירושלמי פ"ה דסוכה דחסר י'. ובספרים שלפנינו הוא מלא יו"ד. ובמדרש ויקרא רבה פ' ט' ושם דרך. א"ר ינאי ושם כתיב ובספרים שלנו כתיב בשין. ובפירש"י בחומש בראשית כ"ד הפילגשם חסר כתיב ובכל הספרים איתא מלא. ובמדרש בראשית רבה פרשה ע"ז ר"ל אמר הנתרת כתיב ובכל הספרים שלנו כתיב הנותרת. ובערכין דף לב ע"א בתוספות ד"ה אשר דרש"י כ' דהכתיב ויקרא כ"ה אשר לוא חומה והם כתבו דהכתיב אשר לו והקרי לא ובספרים שלנו הכתיב לא באל"ף והקרי לו כמ"ש המי"ט שם: גמ' שהיה לך לדונו בסנהדרין. עי' מגילה דף יד ע"ב תוס' ד"ה מורד במלכות: תוס' ד"ה דאמר ליה וכו' ואין נראה. עיין יומא דף סו ע"ב תוס' ד"ה מהו להציל:

ליקוטי רש"י

חלקם שאלו בפיהם. שלא היה עבירת גזל בידם אלא חלק לויה כגון מעשר ראשון היו שואלין בפיהם [חולין קלג.]. מלאי הטילו על בעלי בתים. פרקמטיא שלהם על בעלי בתים היודעים בטיב סחורה שישתכרו על ידו [סוטה מז:]. משכיל. מצליח [ש"א יח, יד]. כל היוצא למלחמת בית דוד כותב גט כריתות לאשתו. שאם ימות במלחמה יהא גט מיום כתיבתו והרי מת אוריה במלחמה. שנאמר. במלחמת שאול ואת אחיך כו' ודוד למד מישי אביו להנהיג שאף היוצאין למלחמותיו עושין כן [כתובות ט:]. חריצי החלב. גובנין דחלבא. לשר האלף. אני אומר לשר של אותו אלף שאחיו ממנו שלכל השבטים היו שרי אלפים לפי אלפיהם ואני שמעתי לשר האלף זה יהונתן שאמר עליו ואלף היו עם יונתן בגבעת בנימין. דברים המעורבים בינו לבינה. גט כריתות יקח מאתם ויביא לנשותיהם להפריד עירוב שבינו לבינה [ש"א יז, יח]. אלו קדושין, תקח, תטול מביניהם על ידי גט [כתובות שם]. ואדוני יואב. זהו מרד שקראו אדון בפני המלך [קידושין מג.]. לשון הרע. על מפיבושת מפי ציבא [יומא כב:]. ציבא. עבד כנעני של מפיבושת הוה [יבמות סב.]. לא עשה רגליו. לשון תקון הוא העברת שער שבין הרגלים. שפמו. גרנו"ן בלע"ז [ש"ב יט, כה]. למה לא הלכת עמי. לצאת מירושלים כשיצאתי [שם, כו]. כי פסח עבדך. ואיני יכול לילך ברגלי [שם, כז].

the verse **in defense of David,** as follows: "מַדּוּעַ בָּזִיתָ אֶת דְּבַר ה׳ לַעֲשׂוֹת הָרַע" – Although the prophet reproached David, ***Why have you despised the word of Hashem, to do** that which is **evil,*** **רַבִּי אוֹמֵר מְשׁוּנָּה רָעָה זוֹ מִכָּל רָעוֹת שֶׁבַּתּוֹרָה – Rebbi says: This "evil" is different from all the "evils" in the Torah,**[15] **שֶׁכָּל רָעוֹת שֶׁבַּתּוֹרָה כְּתִיב בְּהוּ "וַיַּעַשׂ"** – for regarding **all** other **"evils" in the Torah it is written, *He did*** *that which is evil,*[16] **וְכָאן כְּתִיב "לַעֲשׂוֹת"** – **while here it is written,** ***...to do*** *that which is evil,*[17] **שֶׁבִּיקֵּשׁ לַעֲשׂוֹת וְלֹא עָשָׂה** – which teaches **that [David] sought to do** a sinful act with Bathsheba, **but** in fact **did not do** it.

Rebbi continues to expound this verse:

"אֵת אוּרִיָּה הַחִתִּי הִכִּיתָ בַחֶרֶב" – The prophet now particularizes the "evil" that David did: ***You struck Uriah the Hittite***[18] ***with the sword.*** Nassan here seems to charge David with murder, but he actually means to say **שֶׁהָיָה לְךָ לְדוּנוֹ בְּסַנְהֶדְרִין וְלֹא דַּנְתָּ** – **that "you should have judged [Uriah] in the Sanhedrin** for his act of rebellion against you,"[19] **but you did not** so **judge** him.[20] **"וְאֶת־אִשְׁתּוֹ לָקַחְתָּ לְּךָ לְאִשָּׁה"** – Nassan further stated: ***and you took his wife unto yourself for a wife.*** This seems to charge David with adultery, but Nassan actually meant: **לִיקּוּחִין יֵשׁ לְךָ בָּהּ** – **You may** legally **take her** in marriage.[21]

The Gemara now explains why David's relationship with Bathsheba was not adulterous:

דְּאָמַר רַבִּי שְׁמוּאֵל בַּר נַחְמָנִי אָמַר רַבִּי יוֹנָתָן – For R' Shmuel bar Nachmani said in the name of R' Yonasan: כׇּל הַיּוֹצֵא לְמִלְחֶמֶת בֵּית דָּוִד כּוֹתֵב גֵּט כְּרִיתוּת לְאִשְׁתּוֹ – Whoever goes out to fight **a war of the House of David writes a bill of divorce for his wife,**[22] **שֶׁנֶּאֱמַר "וְאֵת עֲשֶׂרֶת חֲרִיצֵי הֶחָלָב הָאֵלֶּה תָּבִיא לְשַׂר הָאָלֶף וְאֶת־אַחֶיךָ תִּפְקֹד לְשָׁלוֹם וְאֶת עֲרֻבָּתָם תִּקָּח"** – **for it is stated** that Yishai said to his son David: ***And bring these ten cheeses to the captain of the thousand, and look into your brothers' wellbeing, and ascertain their safety.***[23]

The Gemara asks how R' Yonasan expounds the verse:

מַאי "עֲרֻבָּתָם" – Now, **what** is meant by ***"their safety"***?

The Gemara answers:

תָּנֵי רַב יוֹסֵף דְּבָרִים הַמְעוֹרָבִים בֵּינוֹ לְבֵינָהּ – Rav Yosef teaches: It refers to **matters that are comingled between him and her.**[24]

Rebbi continues to expound the aforementioned rebuke by Nassan (*II Samuel* 12:9) in David's favor:

"וְאֹתוֹ הָרַגְתָּ בְּחֶרֶב בְּנֵי עַמּוֹן" – Nassan the prophet told David, ***and you have slain him*** [Uriah] ***with the sword of the Ammonites,***[25] which suggests: **מָה חֶרֶב בְּנֵי עַמּוֹן אִי אַתָּה נֶעֱנָשׁ עָלָיו – Just as you,** David, **are not punished for** the killings

NOTES

15. This verse, which reports that David did evil, is written and phrased differently than other Scriptural reports of a person's wrongdoing (*Rashi*).

16. [The phrase, וַיַּעַשׂ הָרַע, *he did evil,* appears dozens of times in Scripture, especially in connection with kings.]

17. [The phrase, לַעֲשׂוֹת הָרַע, *to do evil,* also appears many times in Scripture, but very rarely is it found in connection with a report of deeds already performed. For that reason Rebbe expounds it here as referring to desire rather than deed.]

We do find the term לַעֲשׂוֹת הָרַע used in connection with other kings, but there Scripture also states וַיַּעַשׂ הָרַע. In connection with David's actions we do not find this latter term (*Maharsha*).

18. Uriah, Bathsheba's husband, was called "the Hittite" because he was a Hittite convert, or because he had lived with the Hittites (*Radak*).

19. The Gemara will explain below how Uriah rebelled against the king.

20. *Tosafos* cite the Gemara in *Megillah* (14b), which seems to indicate that the king may summarily execute one who rebels against him, and no trial is necessary. If so, why does our Gemara say that Uriah should have been tried by the Sanhedrin? *Tosafos* (here and to *Sanhedrin* 36a) answer that the Sanhedrin is certainly required to hear witnesses and determine whether the accused actually rebelled. The Gemara in *Megillah* means only that the court need not make a special effort to find exonerating evidence for him, or redeliberate a guilty verdict overnight, which is required in all other capital cases (see *Sanhedrin* 32a).

Rambam (*Hilchos Melachim* 3:8) apparently rules, however, that a Jewish king has the unilateral right to execute anyone who rebels against him. If so, why did Nassan remonstrate that Uriah should have been judged in the Sanhedrin? *Iyun Yaakov* to *Ein Yaakov* explains that in this particular case David should certainly have had the Sanhedrin determine Uriah's guilt, so that no one would unjustly suspect David of having Uriah killed in order to marry his wife.

21. Literally: taking [in marriage] you have in her.] The phrase *you took [her] for a wife* implies that David's marriage to Bathsheba was legal from the beginning, even before Uriah died; this can only be true if Bathsheba was already divorced from Uriah at that time, as the Gemara states below (Rashi; see *Maharsha*).

Tosafos apparently translates לִיקּוּחִין יֵשׁ לְךָ בָּהּ as *you have the right to marry her; Tosafos* notes further that although in this instance Bathsheba would have been permitted to David even if he *had* committed adultery (for the prohibition against marriage to an adulterer applies only when the woman consented to the relations, which was not the case with Bathsheba), the verse nevertheless implies that David did not sin – for the prophet meant to tell David: "You have done no sin with this woman" (see *Tosafos, Rashash* and *Hagahos R' Elazar Moshe Horowitz;* see also *Dibros Moshe* 43:19).

22. This was a conditional divorce, which took effect retroactively if the husband died in battle ["This is your divorce from now, if I die" – see *Gittin* 72a] or disappeared (see *Rashi* ד״ה שבקש and *Tosafos, Kesubos* 9b ד״ה כל היוצא). Sometimes a departing soldier was too busy to give a bill of divorce, and would later send it to his wife from the battlefield (*Rashi;* and see above, note 13).

Tosafos take issue with *Rashi's* interpretation, for the following reason: Even if Uriah did give Bathsheba a conditional divorce, when David first cohabited with her Uriah was still alive; and according to one Tanna (R' Yehudah in *Gittin* 73a,b) the recipient of a conditional divorce is considered a married woman in every respect until the condition is fulfilled. Hence, David's liaison with Bathsheba should be considered completely adulterous (see also *Tosafos* to *Kesubos* 9b). If so, how can our Gemara state that David did not sin?

Tosafos therefore cite Rabbeinu Tam, who maintains that a soldier's divorce was unconditional; hence, Bathsheba was a completely divorced woman when David had relations with her. [According to this interpretation, the soldier would divorce his wife in secret, so that no one would try to marry her while he was away. If he returned alive from the war, he could remarry her (see *Tosafos* to *Gittin* 73b-74a ד״ה אמר).]

Rashi, however, rejects the view that according to R' Yehudah the recipient of a conditional divorce is ever considered a married woman in every respect. On the contrary, *Rashi* holds that according to all Tannaim, once the husband dies, the woman is considered to have been a completely divorced woman from the moment she received the document (see *Rashi* to *Gittin* 73a,ד״ה לא תתיחד , and *Tosafos* there, ד״ה לא).

23. *I Samuel* 17:18. King Shaul was waging war against the Philistines. David's brothers were at the front, and Yishai sent David to visit them and bring back a firsthand report on their welfare.

24. The word עֲרֻבָּתָם derives from the root ערב, "to commingle." Thus, עֲרֻבָּתָם can also connote "their betrothals," since marriage creates a commingling between a man and a woman. Further, the word for *ascertain* (תִּקָּח) literally means "take." Thus, וְאֶת־עֲרֻבָּתָם תִּקָּח is interpreted: "Take [i.e. take back, annul] their betrothals" by bringing back bills of divorce from your brothers for their wives (*Rashi*). And David learned from his father Yishai to institute this practice as a custom for all those who went forth to fight his wars (*Rashi* to *Kesubos* 9b ד״ה דכתיב).

25. This phrase is superfluous, since the beginning of the verse states: *You struck Uriah the Hittite with the sword.* It was for that reason that Rebbi expounded it (*Maharsha*).

בני שמואל חטאו אינו אלא טועה שנאמר א) ויהי (א) כי זקן שמואל ב) ובניו לא הלכו) בדרכיו בדרכיו הוא דלא הלכו מיחטא נמי לא חטאו אלא מה אני מקיים ב) ויטו אחרי הבצע שלא עשו כמעשה אביהם שהיה שמואל הצדיק מחזר בכל מקומות ישראל ודן אותם בעריהם שנאמר ג) והלך מדי שנה בשנה וסבב בית אל והגלגל והמצפה ושפט את ישראל והם לא עשו כן אלא ישבו בעריהם [א]כדי להרבות שכר לחזניהן ולסופריהן כתנאי ב) ויטו אחרי הבצע ר' מאיר אומר חלקם שאלו בפיהם רבי יהודה אומר מלאי הטילו על בעלי בתים ר' עקיבא אומר קופה יתירה של מעשר נטלו בזרוע ר' יוסי אומר מתנות נטלו בזרוע: א"ר שמואל בר נחמני אמר ר' יונתן כל האומר דוד חטא אינו אלא טועה שנאמר ד) ויהי דוד לכל דרכיו משכיל וה' עמו וגו' אפשר חטא בא לידו ושכינה עמו אלא מה אני מקיים ה) מדוע בזית את דבר ה' לעשות הרע שביקש לעשות ולא עשה אמר רב רבי דאתי מדוד מהפך ודריש בזכותיה דדוד מדוע בזית את דבר ה' לעשות הרע רבי אומר משונה רעה זו מכל רעות שבתורה שכל רעות שבתורה כתיב בהו ויעש וכאן כתיב לעשות שביקש לעשות ולא עשה ה) את אוריה החתי הכית בחרב ° שהיה לך לדונו בסנהדרין ולא דנת ה) ואת אשתו לקחת לך לאשה ליקוחין יש לך בה [ג]דא"ר שמואל בר נחמני א"ר יונתן כל היוצא למלחמת בית דוד כותב גט כריתות לאשתו שנאמר ו) ואת עשרת חריצי החלב האלה תביא לשר האלף ואת אחיך תפקוד לשלום ואת ערובתם תקח מאי ערובתם תני רב יוסף דברים המעורבים בינו לבינה ה) ואותו הרגת בחרב בני עמון ו) מה חרב בני עמון אי אתה נענש עליו אף אוריה החתי אי אתה נענש עליו מאי טעמא [ב]מורד במלכות הוה דאמר ליה ז) ואדוני יואב ועבדי אדוני על פני השדה חונים אמר רב כי מעיינת ביה בדוד לא משכחת ביה בר מדאוריה דכתיב (א) ח) רק בדבר אוריה החתי אביי קשישא רמי דרב אדרב מי אמר רב הכי ו) והאמר רב קיבל דוד לשון הרע קשיא גופא רב אמר קיבל דוד לשון הרע דכתיב ט) ויאמר לו המלך איפוא הוא ויאמר ציבא אל המלך הנה הוא בית מכיר בן עמיאל ו) (בלא) דבר וכתיב י) וישלח המלך ויקחהו מבית מכיר בן עמיאל ו) (מלא) דבר מכדי חזייה דשקרא הוא כי הדר אלשין עילויה מ"ט קיבלה מיניה דכתיב כ) ויאמר המלך ט) (אל ציבא איה) בן אדוניך ויאמר ציבא אל המלך הנה (הוא) יושב בירושלים וגו' ומנא לן דקיבל מיניה דכתיב ל) ויאמר המלך הנה לך כל אשר למפיבושת ויאמר ציבא השתחויתי אמצא חן ט) (בעיני) המלך ושמואל אמר לא קיבל דוד לשון הרע דברים הניכרים חזא ביה דכתיב מ) ומפיבושת בן שאול ירד ו) (לפני) המלך לא עשה רגליו ולא עשה שפמו ואת בגדיו לא כיבס וגו' וכתיב נ) ויהי כי בא ירושלים לקראת המלך ויאמר לו המלך למה לא הלכת עמי מפיבושת ויאמר אדוני המלך עבדי רמני כי אמר עבדך אחבשה לי החמור וארכב עליה ואלך את המלך כי פסח עבדך

רש"י

בני שמואל חטאו. במקח שוחד והטיית דין: לחזניהם. שמשיהם שטוכרין אותן לילך ולהזמין את הנקראים לדין: ולסופריהם. לשטרי בירורין ולאגרות שום: מלאי הטילו על בעלי בתים. נותנים להן פרגמטיא לעסוק בה ולתת להם השכר ומתוך כך היה נמשך לבם להטות דין כשבאין לפניהם לדון והיינו חטאם: חלקם שאלו בפיהם. מעשר ראשון הראוי להם שלוים היו שאלו בפיהם מתוך שהיו גדולי הדור ושופטים לא היו מונעים מהם ושאר לוים עניים מצטערים ולר' מאיר לא חטאו בהטיית משפט: קופה יתירה. יותר מן הראוי: מתנות. זרוע לחיים וקיבה והם לא היו כהנים ל"א מתנות לויה כגון מעשר וקרא כתיב ונתן לכהן ודרשינן ולא שיטול מעצמו בשחיטת חולין בפ' הזרוע (דף קלג.) וה"ה לכל מתנות כהונה ולויה: דוד חטא. בבת שבע קודם שקבלה גט: שבקש. לשכב עמה קודם שקבלה גט שהיה בעלה שולח לה מן המלחמה שאם ימות לא תזקק ליבום או שמא יהרג ואין מעיד עליו ותתעגן אשתו או שמא יהא שבוי כדאמרינן לקמן כל היוצא למלחמת בית דוד כו': משונה רעה זו. בכתיבתה ובלשונה: שהיה לך לדונו. על שמרד במלכות כדלקמן: ליקוחין יש לך בה. קדושין תופסין בה שאינה אשת איש כדשמואל כו': גט כריתות. על תנאי שאם ימות תהא מגורשת מעכשיו ופעמים שהוא טרוד בצאתו ושולחו מן המלחמה: ואת ערובתם תקח. במלחמת שאול כתיב: דברים המעורבים בינהם. היינו קדושין תקח תבטל ע"י גט שתביא להם מן המלחמה: בחרב בני עמון. כאותן שהורגים בני עמון שלא מדעתך: ואדוני יואב. לאו אורח ארעא לקבל עליו מרות אחרים בפני המלך: רק בדבר אוריה. מקרא כתיב כך בדבר אוריה שגרם לו שיהרג אבל בבת שבע לא חטא: לשון הרע. לקמיה מפרש: בלא דבר. אינו חכם בתורה והוא מלאו מלא דבר וחכם בתורה: חזייה דשקרא הוה. מתחילה מלאו שקרן בכך: כי הדר אלשין עליה. ליבא על מפיבושת כשהיה דוד בורח מפני אבשלום מאי טעמא קביל מיניה: איה בן אדוניך ויאמר הנה יושב בירושלים. כי אמר היום ישיבו לי את ממלכת אבי: דברים הניכרים חזא ביה. במפיבושת כשנהרג אבשלום וחזר דוד למלכותו ובא לפניו לא עשה רגליו ולא עשה שפמו כסבור דוד שניכרים דברי ליבא שנצטער על שחזר דוד ולא קישט עצמו [כ]ועוד היה מצפה שכשיושיבוהו במלכות יתנאה ויספר לכך לא קבל דבריו ואמר לו אתה וליבא תחלקו השדה והוא השיבו קשה אין לי לצעוק אלא על מי שהביאך הלום הנה שמצטער על שובו ואם לא שראה בו דברים הניכרים היה חוזר ממה שאמר הנה לך כל אשר למפיבושת ואע"פ שמיהר ואמר לו מתחלה הנה לך כל אשר למפיבושת אין זו קבלה כי כל זמן שלא היה דוד שב למלכותו יודע היה שאין מתנתו מתנה ולא אמר לו אלא על תנאי אם יראה אמת בדבריו:

על

תוספות

שהיה לך לדונו בסנהדרין. קשה לר"י דפ"ק דמגילה (דף יד: ושם) אמרינן גבי נבל דמורד במלכות לא בעי למדייניה ואוריה מורד במלכות הוה כדאמר בסמוך ויש לומר דודאי צריך לדונו ולידע אם הוא מורד במלכות אבל לעיין בדינו ולעשות הלנת דין ולהמתין עד למחר אין צריך וכן משמע דבסנהדרין (דף לו. ושם) אמר שדן דוד את נבל בסנהדרין מויחגרו איש חרבו וגו':

ליקוחין יש לך בה. אף על גב דאפילו חטא נמי יש לו בה ליקוחין דהא אנוסה היתה ושריא לבעל וה"ה לבועל מ"מ ליקוחין יש לך בה משמע לא היה לך בה עבירה:

גט כריתות כותב לאשתו. פרש"י על תנאי שאם ימות במלחמה תהא מגורשת מעכשיו וצריך לומר לפירושו דאף על גב דאוריה בא מן המלחמה התנאי היה שאם לא ישוב בסוף המלחמה שיהא גט אך קשה דתנן במי שאחזו (גיטין דף עג. ושם) מה היא באותן הימים רבי יהודה אומר הרי היא כאשת איש לכל דבריה ואם כן לר' יהודה היתה אשת איש גמורה ונראה לר"ת שהיה מגרשה לגמרי בלא שום תנאי והא דאמרינן בהזהב (ב"מ דף נט. ושם) מוטב שיבעול אדם ספק אשת איש ואל ילבין פני חבירו ברבים מנלן מדוד קרי לה ספק אשת איש לפי שהיו מגרשים בצנעה והעולם סבורים שהיא אשת איש:

דאמר ליה ואדוני יואב. פרש"י דמורד במלכות הוה משום דקאמר ואדוני יואב ° ואין נראה דאין זה מורד שלא היה בלבו להמליכו ולקרותו מלך אלא כמו שפירש רבינו מאיר דהוי מורד משום דבסיפא דקרא כתיב ואני אבא אל ביתי לאכול ולשתות ולשכב עם אשתי וגו' שדוד אמר לו לעשות ולא רצה לעשות:

רק בדבר אוריה החתי. קשה דהא איכא מעשה דהסתה בריש פ"ב דיומא (דף כב:) וי"ל דלא חשיב ליה דלא הוי כל כך עון גדול וגם שגג:

אלא

מסורת הש"ס

א) [נ"ל כאשר זקן שמואל ולא הלכו בניו], ב) [חולין קלג. תוספ' סוטה פי"ד], ג) כתובות ט:, ד) קידושין מג., ה) יומא כב:, ו) [נ"ל בלו], ז) [נ"ל מלו וע' במהרש"א], ח) [נ"ל ואיה], ט) [נ"ל בעיניך אדוני], י) [נ"ל לקראת], כ) רש"י מפ' דעת אמיתים של מפיבושת דהא דלא קישט היינו משום שעוד היה מצפה שכשישיבו לדוד במלכות יתנאה [כ"מ] ורש"ל גרס ועד עתה הי' מצפה.

הגהות הב"ח

(א) גמ' לא משכחת ביה רק בדבר אוריה כצ"ל ותיבת בר מדאורי' דכתי' נמחק:

גליון הש"ס

שלנו כתיב טהר חסר ו'). ובנדרים דף לז ע"ב את דהוגד הוגד קרי ולא כתיב. ובספרים שלנו הוא קרי וכתיב כמ"ש הר"ן שם. ובפסוק אני ה' אלהיך אשר הוצאתיך איתא בירושלמי פ"ה דסוכה דחסר י'. ובספרים שלפנינו הוא מלא יו"ד. ובמדרש ויקרא רבה פ' ט' ושם דרך. א"ר ינאי ושם כתיב ובספרים שלנו כתיב בשין. ובפירש"י בחומש בראשית כ"ד הפילגשם חסר כתיב ובכל הספרים איתא מלא. ובמדרש בראשית רבה פרשה ע"ז ר"ל אמר הנותרת כתיב ובכל הספרים שלנו כתיב הנותרת. ובערכין דף לב ע"א בתוספות ד"ה אשר דרש"י כ' דהכתיב ויקרא כ"ה אשר לוא חומה והם כתבו דהכתיב אשר לו והקרי לא ובספרים שלנו הכתיב לא באל"ף והקרי לו כמ"ש המי"ט שם: גמ' שהיה לך לדונו בסנהדרין. עי' מגילה דף יד ע"ב תוס' ד"ה מורד במלכות: תוס' ד"ה דאמר ליה וכו' ואין נראה. עיין יומא דף סו ע"ב תוס' ד"ה מהו להציל:

ליקוטי רש"י

חלקם שאלו בפיהם. שלא היה עבירת גזל בידם אלא חלק לויה כגון מעשר ראשון היו שואלין בפיהם [חולין קלג.]. מלאי הטילו על בעלי בתים. פרקמטיא שלהם על בעלי בתים היודעים בטיב סחורה שישתכרו על ידו [סוטה מז:]. משכיל. מצליח [ש"א יח, יד]. כל היוצא למלחמת בית דוד כותב גט כריתות לאשתו. שאם ימות במלחמה יהא גט מיום כתיבתו והרי מת אוריה במלחמה. שנאמר. במלחמת שאול ואת אחיך כו' ודוד למד מישי אביו להנהיג שאף היוצאין למלחמותיו עושין כן [כתובות ט:]. חריצי החלב. גובנין דמלבא. לשר האלף. אני אומר לשר של אותו אלף שאחיו ממנו שלכל השבטים היו שרי אלפים לפי אלפיהם ואני שמעתי לשר האלף זה יהונתן שאמר עליו ואלף היו עם יונתן בגבעת בנימין. דברים המעורבים בינו לבינה. גט כריתות יקח מאתם ויביא לנשותיהם להפריד עירוב שבינו לבינה [ש"א יז, יח]. אלו קדושין, תקח, תטול מביניהם על ידי גט [כתובות שם]. ואדוני יואב. זהו מרד שקראו אדון בפני המלך [קידושין מג.]. לשון הרע. על מפיבושת מפי ציבא [יומא כב:]. ציבא. עבד כנעני של מפיבושת הוה [יבמות סב.]. לא עשה רגליו. לשון תקון הוא העברת שער שבין הרגלים. שפמו. גרנו"ן בלע"ז [ש"ב יט, כה]. למה לא הלכת עמי. לצאת מירושלים כשיצאתי [שם, כו]. כי פסח עבדך. ואיני יכול לילך ברגלי [שם, כז].

עין משפט נר מצוה

נ א מיי' פכ"ג מהל' סנהדרין הלכה ג סמג לאוין רח טוש"ע ח"מ סי' ט סעיף ד:

נא ב מיי' פ"ג מהל' מלכים הלכה ח:

תורה אור השלם

א) ויהי כאשר זקן שמואל וישם את בניו שפטים לישראל: [שמואל א' ח, א]

ב) ולא הלכו בניו בדרכיו ויטו אחרי הבצע ויקחו שחד ויטו משפט: [שמואל א' ח, ג]

ג) והלך מדי שנה בשנה וסבב בית אל והגלגל והמצפה ושפט את ישראל את כל המקומות האלה: [שמואל א' ז, טז]

ד) ויהי דוד לכל דרכו משכיל וי' עמו: [שמואל א' יח, יד]

ה) מדוע בזית את דבר י' לעשות הרע בעיני את אוריה החתי הכית בחרב ואת אשתו לקחת לך לאשה ואתו הרגת בחרב בני עמון: [שמואל ב' יב, ט]

ו) ואת עשרת חרצי החלב האלה תביא לשר האלף ואת אחיך תפקד לשלום ואת ערבתם תקח: [שמואל א' יז, יח]

ז) ויאמר אוריה אל דוד הארון וישראל ויהודה ישבים בסכות ואדני יואב ועבדי אדני על פני השדה חנים ואני אבוא אל ביתי לאכל ולשתות ולשכב עם אשתי חיך וחי נפשך אם אעשה את הדבר הזה: [שמואל ב' יא, יא]

ח) אשר עשה דוד את הישר בעיני י' ולא סר מכל אשר צוהו כל ימי חייו רק בדבר אוריה החתי: [מלכים א' טו, ה]

ט) ויאמר לו המלך איפה הוא ויאמר ציבא אל המלך הנה הוא בית מכיר בן עמיאל בלו דבר: [שמואל ב' ט, ד]

י) וישלח המלך דוד ויקחהו מבית מכיר בן עמיאל מלו דבר: [שמואל ב' ט, ה]

כ) ויאמר המלך ואיה בן אדניך ויאמר ציבא אל המלך הנה יושב בירושלים כי אמר היום ישיבו לי בית ישראל את ממלכות אבי: [שמואל ב' טז, ג]

ל) ויאמר המלך לצבא הנה לך כל אשר למפיבשת ויאמר ציבא השתחויתי אמצא חן בעיניך אדני המלך: [שמואל ב' טז, ד]

מ) ומפבשת בן שאול ירד לקראת המלך ולא עשה רגליו ולא עשה שפמו ואת בגדיו לא כבס למן היום לכת המלך עד היום אשר בא בשלום: [שמואל ב' יט, כה] נ) ויהי כי בא ירושלם לקראת המלך ויאמר לו המלך למה לא הלכת עמי מפיבשת: ויאמר אדני המלך עבדי רמני כי אמר עבדך אחבשה לי החמור וארכב עליה ואלך את המלך כי פסח עבדך: [שמואל ב' יט, כו-כז]

wrought by **the sword of the Ammonites,**[26] **אַף אוּרִיָּה הַחִתִּי אִי אַתָּה נֶעֱנָשׁ עָלָיו** – so **too, you are not punished for** the killing of **Uriah the Hittite.**[27]

The Gemara asks:

מַאי טַעְמָא – **What is the reason** that David was not punished for the killing of Uriah?

The Gemara answers:

מוֹרֵד בְּמַלְכוּת הֲוָה – **[Uriah] was** considered **a rebel against the monarchy,** **דְּאָמַר לֵיהּ ,,וַאדֹנִי יוֹאָב וְעַבְדֵי אֲדֹנִי עַל־פְּנֵי הַשָּׂדֶה חֹנִים"** – **for** when King David summoned him from the war and told him to return to his wife, **[Uriah] said to [the king]:** ***And my master Yoav and the servants of my master*** [King David] ***are encamped in the open field;*** *shall I then come to my house to eat and drink and lie with my wife? By your life and the life of your soul I shall not do this thing!*[28]

The Gemara has presented a number of defenses of King David's righteousness, cited by Rav in the name of Rebbi. Now Rav himself discusses this topic:

אָמַר רַב כִּי מְעַיְינַת בֵּיהּ בְּדָוִד לֹא מַשְׁכַּחַתְּ בֵּיהּ בַּר מִדְּאוּרִיָּה – **Rav said: When you study** the life of **David, you do not find** any sin **except for that of Uriah,**[29] **דִּכְתִיב ,,רַק בִּדְבַר אוּרִיָּה הַחִתִּי"** – **as it is written:**[30] *David did that which was just in the eyes of Hashem, and did not swerve from all that He commanded him, all the days of his life,* ***except for the matter of Uriah the Hittite.***

The Gemara examines this dictum of Rav:

אַבַּיֵי קַשִּׁישָׁא רָמֵי דְּרַב אַדְּרַב – **Abaye the Elder contrasted** this statement **of Rav with** another statement **of Rav,** **מִי אָמַר רַב הָכִי** – asking rhetorically: **Did Rav** really **say thus?** **וְהָאָמַר רַב קִיבֵּל דָּוִד לָשׁוֹן הָרַע** – **But Rav has** also **said: David accepted a slanderous report,** and believing slander is sinful.

The Gemara concludes:

קַשְׁיָא – The contradiction between Rav's statements is indeed **difficult.**

The Gemara elaborates on Rav's second statement:

גּוּפָא – Let us consider that statement **itself:** **רַב אָמַר קִיבֵּל דָּוִד לָשׁוֹן הָרַע** – **Rav said: David accepted a slanderous report,** **דִּכְתִיב ,,וַיֹּאמֶר לוֹ הַמֶּלֶךְ אֵיפֹה הוּא וַיֹּאמֶר צִיבָא אֶל הַמֶּלֶךְ הִנֵּה־הוּא בֵּית מָכִיר בֶּן־עַמִּיאֵל בְּלוֹ דְבָר"** – **for it is written:** ***And the king said to him*** [Tziva]: ***Where is he*** [Mefiboshes]? ***And Tziva said to the king: Behold, he is in the house of Machir ben Amiel, in Lo Devar;***[31] **וּכְתִיב ,,וַיִּשְׁלַח הַמֶּלֶךְ וַיִּקָּחֵהוּ מִבֵּית מָכִיר בֶּן עַמִּיאֵל מִלוֹ דְבָר"** – **and it is written** in the next verse: ***And the king sent and took him*** [Mefiboshes] ***from the house of Machir ben Amiel, from Lo Devar.***[32]

Rav asks:

מִכְּדִי חַזְיֵיהּ דְּשַׁקְרָא הוּא – **Since [David] saw that [Tziva] was lying** about Mefiboshes, **כִּי הֲדַר אַלְשִׁין עִילָּוֵיהּ מַאי טַעְמָא קִיבְּלָהּ מִינֵּיהּ** – **when [Tziva] again slandered [Mefiboshes], why did [David] accept [the report] from him?**

Rav cites verses to show how Tziva later slandered Mefiboshes:

דִּכְתִיב ,,וַיֹּאמֶר הַמֶּלֶךְ (אל ציבא) [וְ]אַיֵּה בֶּן־אֲדֹנֶיךָ וַיֹּאמֶר צִיבָא אֶל־הַמֶּלֶךְ הִנֵּה יוֹשֵׁב בִּירוּשָׁלַםִ וגו' " – **For it is written**[33] concerning the time Tziva brought supplies to David, who was then fleeing from his son Avshalom: ***And the king said to Tziva: Where is the son of your master?***[34] ***And Tziva said to the king: Behold, he abides in Jerusalem*** **etc.** [*for he has said: Today the House of Israel will restore to me the kingdom of my father*].[35]

Rav explains:

וּמְנָא לָן דְּקִיבֵּל מִינֵּיהּ – **And from where** do **we know that [David] accepted** this false report of Mefiboshes' treason **from [Tziva]?** **דִּכְתִיב ,,וַיֹּאמֶר הַמֶּלֶךְ [לְצִבָא] הִנֵּא לְךָ כֹּל אֲשֶׁר לִמְפִיבֹשֶׁת וַיֹּאמֶר צִיבָא הִשְׁתַּחֲוֵיתִי אֶמְצָא חֵן בְּעֵינֶיךָ אֲדֹנִי הַמֶּלֶךְ"** – **Because it is written** in the following verse: ***And the king said*** *to Tziva:* ***Behold, everything that belongs to Mefiboshes is yours; and Tziva said: I prostrate myself; may I find favor in your eyes, my lord the king.***[36]

Shmuel takes issue with Rav:

וּשְׁמוּאֵל אָמַר לֹא קִיבֵּל דָּוִד לָשׁוֹן הָרַע – **But Shmuel said: David did not** knowingly **accept** any **slanderous report.** **דְּבָרִים הַנִּיכָּרִים חֲזָא בֵּיהּ** – If so, why did he promise Mefiboshes' property to Tziva? Because **he saw recognizable signs in [Mefiboshes],** signs that seemed to confirm Tziva's accusation, **דִּכְתִיב ,,וּמְפִבֹשֶׁת בֶּן־שָׁאוּל יָרַד לִקְרַאת הַמֶּלֶךְ וְלֹא־עָשָׂה רַגְלָיו וְלֹא־עָשָׂה שְׂפָמוֹ וְאֶת־בְּגָדָיו לֹא כִבֵּס וגו' "** – **for it is written**[37] that after the defeat of Avshalom David returned to Jerusalem, ***and Mefiboshes the son of Shaul***[38] ***went down to meet the king, and he neither dressed his feet nor trimmed his beard and nor laundered his***

NOTES

26. Just as you are not punished for the killings perpetrated by the Ammonites in war, which occurred without your knowledge or consent (*Rashi*).

27. You are not liable to even a small punishment for indirectly causing his death (*Maharsha*).

28. *II Samuel* 11:11. It was not proper for Uriah to refer to Yoav as "my master" in front of David (*Rashi*), thus equating Yoav with King David, whom he also called "my master" (*Maharsha*). This constitutes a rebellion against the monarchy, and subjected Uriah to the death penalty.

The above is also the interpretation of *Tosafos* to *Yoma* 66b ד"ה מהו. However, *Tosafos* here [and to *Kiddushin* 43a] question whether this action is sufficient to be termed a rebellion, since Uriah did not call Yoav "king," nor did he intend to accept Yoav as such. Therefore, *Tosafos* maintain that Uriah's rebellious sentiments were expressed in the second part of the verse, where he refuses to obey King David's command to go home to his wife. [See also *Rambam, Hilchos Melachim* 3:8.]

29. I.e. that which David indirectly caused Uriah's death; however, David was completely innocent in the matter of Bathsheba (*Rashi*).

30. *I Kings* 15:5.

31. *II Samuel* 9:4. After David's monarchy was established, the king sought out the descendants of Shaul, in order to honor them for the sake of his covenant with Shaul's son Yehonasan. David discovered that there remained from the house of Shaul a slave named Tziva, who in turn informed David that one son of Yehonasan – Mefiboshes – still lived.

The actual verse reads בְּלוֹ דְּבָר, with a *vav,* but the Gemara expounds it as if it is written בְּלֹא דְבָר, with an *aleph.* The phrase *in Lo Devar* (literally: in no thing) intimates that Tziva told David that Mefiboshes was devoid of Torah knowledge (*Rashi*).

32. Ibid. v. 5. The actual verse reads מִלוֹ דְּבָר, but here again the Gemara expounds it as if it is written מְלֹא דְבָר, with an *aleph.* The phrase *from Lo Devar* can be interpreted as "full of words" or "full of things" [since if vowelized מָלֵא, the word means *full*]. It thus intimates that David found Mefiboshes to be learned in Torah (*Rashi*).

33. *II Samuel* 16:3.

34. I.e. why has Mefiboshes not come to join me?

35. Tziva claimed that Mefiboshes was hoping that when the people saw the conflicts between David and his sons, they would coronate him (*Metzudas David*).

36. David believed the slander and promised all of Mefiboshes' property to Tziva.

37. *II Samuel* 19:25.

38. Mefiboshes was not the son of Shaul, but of Yehonasan. However, the verse associates him with Shaul to hint that he emulated the deeds of Shaul, who hated David, rather than those of Yehonasan, who loved David. Because of this hint, Shmuel expounds the verses as revealing "recognizable signs" of Mefiboshes' hostility (*Iyun Yaakov* to *Ein Yaakov*).

בני שמואל חטאו אינו אלא טועה שנאמר א) ויהי (א) כי זקן שמואל ב) ובניו לא הלכו) בדרכיו בדרכיו הוא דלא הלכו מיחטא נמי לא חטאו אלא מה אני מקיים ב) ויטו אחרי הבצע שלא עשו כמעשה אביהם שהיה שמואל הצדיק מחזר בכל מקומות ישראל ודן אותם בעריהם שנאמר ג) והלך מדי שנה בשנה וסבב בית אל והגלגל והמצפה ושפט את ישראל והם לא עשו כן אלא ישבו בעריהם א כדי להרבות שכר לחזניהן ולסופריהן כתנאי ב) ויטו אחרי הבצע ר' מאיר אומר חלקם שאלו בפיהם רבי יהודה אומר מלאי הטילו על בעלי בתים ר' עקיבא אומר קופה יתירה של מעשר נטלו בזרוע ר' יוסי אומר מתנות נטלו בזרוע: א"ר שמואל בר נחמני אמר ר' יונתן כל האומר דוד חטא אינו אלא טועה שנאמר ד) ויהי דוד לכל דרכיו משכיל וה' עמו וגו' אפשר חטא בא לידו ושכינה עמו אלא מה אני מקיים ה) מדוע בזית את דבר ה' לעשות הרע שביקש לעשות ולא עשה אמר רב רבי דאתי מדוד מהפך ודריש בזכותיה דדוד מדוע בזית את דבר ה' לעשות הרע רבי אומר משונה רעה זו מכל רעות שבתורה שכל רעות שבתורה כתיב בהו ויעש וכאן כתיב לעשות שביקש לעשות ולא עשה ה) את אוריה החתי הכית בחרב ° שהיה לך לדונו בסנהדרין ולא דנת ה) ואת אשתו לקחת לך לאשה ליקוחין יש לך בה ג) דא"ר שמואל בר נחמני א"ר יונתן כל היוצא למלחמת בית דוד כותב גט כריתות לאשתו שנאמר ו) ואת עשרת חריצי החלב האלה תביא לשר האלף ואת אחיך תפקוד לשלום ואת ערובתם תקח מאי ערובתם תני רב יוסף דברים המעורבים בינו לבינה ה) ואותו הרגת בחרב בני עמון ד) מה חרב בני עמון אי אתה נענש עליו אף אוריה החתי אי אתה נענש עליו מאי טעמא ב מורד במלכות הוה דאמר ליה ז) ואדוני יואב ועבדי אדוני על פני השדה חונים אמר רב כי מעיינת ביה בדוד לא משכחת ביה בר מדאוריה דכתיב (א) ח) רק בדבר אוריה החתי אביי קשישא רמי דרב אדרב מי אמר רב הכי ה) והאמר רב קיבל דוד לשון הרע קשיא גופא רב אמר קיבל דוד לשון הרע דכתיב ט) ויאמר לו המלך איפוא הוא ויאמר ציבא אל המלך הנה הוא בית מכיר בן עמיאל ו) (בלא) דבר וכתיב י) וישלח המלך ויקחהו מבית מכיר בן עמיאל ו) (מלא) דבר מכדי חזייה דשקרא הוא כי הדר אלשין עילויה מ"ט קיבלה מיניה דכתיב כ) ויאמר המלך ח) (אל ציבא איה) בן אדונך ויאמר ציבא אל המלך הנה (הוא) יושב בירושלים וגו' ומנא לן דקיבל מיניה דכתיב ל) ויאמר המלך הנה לך כל אשר למפיבושת ויאמר ציבא השתחויתי אמצא חן ט) (בעיני) המלך ושמואל אמר לא קיבל דוד לשון הרע דברים הניכרים חזא ביה דכתיב מ) ומפיבושת בן שאול ירד י) (לפני) המלך לא עשה רגליו ולא עשה שפמו ואת בגדיו לא כיבס וגו' וכתיב נ) ויהי כי בא ירושלים לקראת המלך ויאמר לו המלך למה לא הלכת עמי מפיבושת ויאמר אדוני המלך עבדי רמני כי אמר עבדך אחבשה לי החמור וארכב עליה ואלך את המלך כי פסח עבדך

רש"י

בני שמואל חטאו. במקח שוחד והטיית דין: לחזניהם. שמשיהם ששוכרין אותן לילך ולהזמין את הנקראים לדין: ולסופריהם. לשטרי בירורין ולאגרות שום: מלאי הטילו על בעלי בתים. נותנים להן פרגמטיא לעסוק בה ולתת להם השכר ומתוך כך היה נמשך לבם להטות דין כשבאין לפניהם לדון והיינו חטאם: חלקם שאלו בפיהם. מעשר ראשון הראוי להם שלוים היו שאלו בפיהם מתוך שהיו גדולי הדור ושופטים לא היו מונעים מהם ושאר לוים עניים מצטערים ולר' מאיר לא חטאו בהטיית משפט: קופה יתירה. יותר מן הראוי: מתנות. זרוע לחיים וקיבה והם לא היו כהנים ל"א מתנות לויה כגון מעשר וקרא כתיב ונתן לכהן ודרשינן ולא שיטול מעצמו בשחיטת חולין בפ' הזרוע (דף קלג.) וה"ה לכל מתנות כהונה ולויה: דוד חטא. בבת שבע קודם שקבלה גט: שבקש. לשכב עמה קודם שקבלה גט שהיה בעלה שולח לה מן המלחמה שאם ימות לא תיזקק ליבום או שמא יהרג ואין מעיד עליו ותתעגן אשתו או שמא יהא שבוי כדאמרינן לקמן כל היוצא למלחמת בית דוד כו': משונה רעה זו. בכתיבתה ובלשונה: שהיה לך לדונו. על שמרד במלכות כדלקמן: ליקוחין יש לך בה. קדושין תופסין בה שאינה אשת איש כדשמואל כו': גט כריתות. על תנאי שאם ימות תהא מגורשת מעכשיו ופעמים שהוא טרוד בלאתו ושולחו מן המלחמה: ואת ערובתם תקח. במלחמת שאול כתיב: דברים המעורבים ביניהם. היינו קדושין תקח תבטל ע"י גט שתביא להם מן המלחמה: בחרב בני עמון. כאותן שהורגים בני עמון שלא מדעתך: ואדוני יואב. לאו אורח ארעא לקבל עליו מרות אחרים בפני המלך: רק בדבר אוריה. מקרא כתיב כך בדבר אוריה שגרם לו שיהרג אבל בבת שבע לא חטא: לשון הרע. לקמיה מפרש: בלא דבר. אינו חכם בתורה והוא מלאו מלא דבר וחכם בתורה: חזייא דשקרא הוה. מתחילה מלאו שקרן בכך: כי הדר אלשין עליה. ליבא על מפיבושת כשהיה דוד בורח מפני אבשלום מאי טעמא קביל מיניה: איה בן אדוניך ויאמר הנה יושב בירושלים. כי אמר היום ישיבו לי את ממלכת אבי: דברים הניכרים חזא ביה. במפיבושת כשנהרג אבשלום וחזר דוד למלכותו ובא לפניו לא עשה רגליו ולא עשה שפמו כסבור דוד שניכרים דברי ציבא שנצטער על שחזר דוד ולא קישט עצמו (כ) ועוד היה מצפה שכשיושיבוהו במלכות יתגאה ויספר לכך לא קבל דבריו ואמר לו אתה וציבא תחלקו השדה והוא השיבו קשה אין לי לצעוק אלא על מי שהביאך הלום הנה שמצטער על שובו ואם לא שראה בו דברים הניכרים היה חוזר ממה שאמר הנה לך כל אשר למפיבושת ואע"פ שמיהר ואמר לו מתחלה הנה לך כל אשר למפיבושת אין זו קבלה כי כל זמן שלא היה דוד שב למלכותו יודע היה שאין מתנתו מתנה ולא אמר לו אלא על תנאי אם יראה אמת בדבריו: על

תוספות

שהיה לך לדונו בסנהדרין. קשה לר"י דפ"ק דמגילה (דף יד: ושם) אמרינן גבי נבל דמורד במלכות לא בעי למדייניה ואוריה מורד במלכות הוה כדאמר בסמוך ויש לומר דודאי צריך לדונו ולידע אם הוא מורד במלכות אבל לעיין בדינו ולעשות הלנת דין ולהמתין עד למחר אין צריך וכן משמע דבסנהדרין (דף לו. ושם) אמר שדן דוד את נבל בסנהדרין מויחגרו איש חרבו וגו':

ליקוחין יש לך בה. אף על גב דאפילו חטא נמי יש לו בה ליקוחין דהא אנוסה היתה ושריא לבעל וה"ה לבועל מ"מ ליקוחין יש לך בה משמע לא היה לך בה עבירה:

גט כריתות כותב לאשתו. פרש"י על תנאי שאם ימות במלחמה תהא מגורשת מעכשיו וצריך לומר לפירושו דאף על גב דאוריה בא מן המלחמה התנאי היה שאם לא ישוב בסוף המלחמה שיהא גט אך קשה דתנן במי שאחזו (גיטין דף עג. ושם) מה היא באותן הימים רבי יהודה אומר הרי היא כאשת איש לכל דבריה ואם כן לר' יהודה היתה אשת איש גמורה ונראה לר"ת שהיה מגרשה לגמרי בלא שום תנאי והא דאמרינן בהזהב (ב"מ דף נט. ושם) מוטב שיבעול אדם ספק אשת איש ואל ילבין פני חבירו ברבים מנלן מדוד קרי לה ספק אשת איש לפי שהיו מגרשים בצנעה והעולם סבורים שהיא אשת איש:

דאמר ליה ואדוני יואב. פרש"י דמורד במלכות הוה משום דקאמר ואדוני יואב ° ואין נראה דאין זה מורד שלא היה בלבו להמליכו ולקרותו מלך אלא כמו שפירש רבינו מאיר דהוי מורד משום דבסיפא דקרא כתיב ואני אבא אל ביתי לאכול ולשתות ולשכב עם אשתי וגו' שדוד אמר לו לעשות ולא רצה לעשות:

רק בדבר אוריה החתי. קשה דהא איכא מעשה דהסתה בריש פ"ב דיומא (דף כב:) וי"ל דלא חשיב ליה דלא הוי כל כך עון גדול וגם שגג: אלא

מסורת הש"ס

א) [נ"ל כאשר זקן שמואל ולא הלכו בניו], ב) [חולין קלג. תוספ' סוטה פי"ד], ג) כתובות ט:, ד) קידושין מג., ה) יומא כב:, ו) [נ"ל בלו], ז) [נ"ל מלו וע' במהרש"א], ח) [נ"ל ואיה], ט) [נ"ל בעיניך אדוני], י) [נ"ל לקראת], כ) רש"י מפ' דעת אחימית של מפיבושת דהא דלא קיסט היינו משום שעוד היה מצפה שכשיושיבוהו לדוד במלכות יתגאה [כ"מ] ורש"ל גרס ועד עתה הי' מצפה.

הגהות הב"ח

(א) גמ' לא משכחת ביה רק בדבר אוריה כצ"ל ותיבת בר מדאורי' דכתי' נמחק:

גליון הש"ס

שלנו כתיב טהר ספר ו'). ובנדרים דף לז ע"ב את דשוהו הוגד קרי ולא כתיב. ובספרים שלנו הוא קרי וכתיב. ובמס' סופרים פ"ז הכ"ן שם. ובפסוק אני ה' אלהיך אשר הוצאתיך איתא בירושלמי פ"ה דסוטה דחסר י'. ובספרים שלפנינו הוא מלא יו"ד. ובמדרש ויקרא רבה פ' ט' ושם דלק. א"ר ינאי ושם הוא כתיב ובספרים שלנו כתיב בכין. ובפירש"י בחומש בראשית כ"ד הפילגשים חסר ובכל הספרים איתא מלא. ובמדרש בראשית רבה פרשה ע"ט אמר ר"ל אמר הנחרמת כתיב ובכל הספרים שלנו כתיב הנותרת. ובערכין דף לב ע"ב אשר לא חומה כתיב לא ויקרא כ"ה אשר לוא חומה והם כתבו דהכתיב אשר לו והקרי לא ובספרים שלנו הכתיב לא באל"ף והקרי לו כמ"ש המי"ט שם: גמ' שהיה לך לדונו בסנהדרין. עי' מגילה דף יד ע"ב תוס' ד"ה מורד במלכות: תוס' ד"ה דאמר ליה וכו' ואין נראה. עיין יומא דף סו ע"ב תוס' ד"ה מהו להליל:

ליקוטי רש"י

חלקם שאלו בפיהם. שלא היה עבירת גזל בידם אלא חלק לויה כגון מעשר ראשון היו שואלין בפיהם [חולין קלג.]. מלאי הטילו על בעלי בתים. פרקמטיא שלהם על בעלי בתים היודעים בטיב סחורה שישתכרו על ידו [סוטה מז:]. משכיל. מצליח [ש"א יח, יד]. כל היוצא למלחמת בית דוד כותב גט כריתות לאשתו. שאם ימות במלחמה יהא גט מיום כתיבתו והרי מת אוריה במלחמה. שנאמר. במלחמת שאול ואת אחיך כו' ודוד למד מישי אביו להנהיג שאף היוצאין למלחמותיו עושין כן [כתובות ט:]. חריצי החלב. גובנין דחלבא. לשר האלף. אני אומר לשר של אותו אלף שאחיו ממנו שלכל השבטים היו שרי אלפים לפי אלפיהם ואני שמעתי לשר האלף זה יהונתן שאמר עליו ואלף היו עם יונתן בגבעת בנימין. דברים המעורבים בינו לבינה. גט כריתות יקח מאתם ויביא לנשותיהם להפריד עירוב שבינו לבינה [ש"א יז, יח]. אלו קדושין, תקח, תטול מביניהם על ידי גט [כתובות שם]. ואדוני יואב. זהו מרד שקראו אדון בפני המלך [קידושין מג.]. לשון הרע. על מפיבושת מפי ציבא [יומא כב:]. ציבא. עבד כנעני של מפיבושת הוה [יבמות סב.]. לא עשה רגליו. לשון תקון הוא העברת שער שבין הרגלים. שפמו. גרנו"ן בלע"ז [ש"ב יט, כה]. למה לא הלכת עמי. לצאת מירושלים כשיצאתי [שם, כה]. כי פסח עבדך. ואיני יכול לילך ברגלי [שם, כז].

עין משפט נר מצוה

מ א מיי' פ"כ מהל' סנהדרין הלכה ג סמג לאוין רח טוש"ע ח"מ סי' ע סעיף ד:

מא ב מיי' פ"ג מהל' מלכים הלכה ח:

תורה אור השלם

א) ויהי כאשר זקן שמואל וישם את בניו שפטים לישראל: [שמואל א' ח, א]

ב) ולא הלכו בניו בדרכיו ויטו אחרי הבצע ויקחו שחד ויטו משפט: [שמואל א' ח, ג]

ג) והלך מדי שנה בשנה וסבב בית אל והגלגל והמצפה ושפט את ישראל את כל המקומות האלה: [שמואל א' ז, טז]

ד) ויהי דוד לכל דרכו משכיל וה' עמו: [שמואל א' יח, יד]

ה) מדוע בזית את דבר ה' לעשות הרע בעיני את אוריה החתי הכית בחרב ואת אשתו לקחת לך לאשה ואתו הרגת בחרב בני עמון: [שמואל ב' יב, ט]

ו) ואת עשרת חרצי החלב האלה תביא לשר האלף ואת אחיך תפקד לשלום ואת ערבתם תקח: [שמואל א' יז, יח]

ז) ויאמר אוריה אל דוד הארון וישראל ויהודה ישבים בסכות ואדני יואב ועבדי אדני על פני השדה חנים ואני אבוא אל ביתי לאכל ולשתות ולשכב עם אשתי חיך וחי נפשך אם אעשה את הדבר הזה: [שמואל ב' יא, יא]

ח) אשר עשה דוד את הישר בעיני ה' ולא סר מכל אשר צוהו כל ימי חייו רק בדבר אוריה החתי: [מלכים א' טו, ה]

ט) ויאמר לו המלך איפה הוא ויאמר ציבא אל המלך הנה הוא בית מכיר בן עמיאל בלו דבר: [שמואל ב' ט, ד]

י) וישלח המלך דוד ויקחהו מבית מכיר בן עמיאל מלו דבר: [שמואל ב' ט, ה]

כ) ויאמר המלך ואיה בן אדניך ויאמר ציבא אל המלך הנה יושב בירושלם כי אמר היום ישיבו לי בית ישראל את ממלכות אבי: [שמואל ב' טז, ג]

ל) ויאמר המלך לצבא הנה לך כל אשר למפיבשת ויאמר ציבא השתחויתי אמצא חן בעיניך אדני המלך: [שמואל ב' טז, ד]

מ) ומפבשת בן שאול ירד לקראת המלך ולא עשה רגליו ולא עשה שפמו ואת בגדיו לא כבס למן היום לכת המלך עד היום אשר בא בשלום: [שמואל ב' יט, כה]

נ) ויהי כי בא ירושלם לקראת המלך ויאמר לו המלך למה לא הלכת עמי מפיבשת: ויאמר אדני המלך עבדי רמני כי אמר עבדך אחבשה לי החמור וארכב עליה ואלך את המלך כי פסח עבדך: [שמואל ב' יט, כו-כז]

clothes* etc.** [*from the day the king departed until the day he came home in peace*].[39] וּכְתִיב ,,וַיְהִי כִּי־בָא יְרוּשָׁלַם לִקְרַאת הַמֶּלֶךְ וַיֹּאמֶר לוֹ הַמֶּלֶךְ לָמָּה לֹא־הָלַכְתָּ עִמִּי מְפִיבֹשֶׁת – **And it is written** in the following verses:[40] ***And when [Mefiboshes] ***came to Jerusalem to meet the king, the king said to him: Why did you not go with me, Mefiboshes?***[41] וַיֹּאמַר אֲדֹנִי הַמֶּלֶךְ עַבְדִּי רִמָּנִי כִּי־אָמַר עַבְדְּךָ אֶחְבְּשָׁה־לִּי הַחֲמוֹר וְאֶרְכַּב עָלֶיהָ וְאֵלֵךְ אֶת־הַמֶּלֶךְ – ***And he said: My lord the king, my slave deceived me; for your servant said: I shall saddle the donkey, that I may ride on it and go with the king.*** כִּי פִסֵּחַ –

NOTES

39. Mefiboshes refrained from properly grooming himself until David regained the throne. However, David took Mefiboshes' unkempt appearance as a sign that Tziva had spoken the truth, and that Mefiboshes was distressed over David's return. Thus, David did not accept Mefiboshes' explanation, and told him: *You and Tziva shall divide the field.* Mefiboshes then replied: *Let him take all, since my lord the king is returning in peace to his house.* The Gemara below (56b) interprets this as a harsh reply, meaning: 'I have no one to complain against except He Who brought you to this point' (i.e. God). This reply revealed to David that Mefiboshes was distressed over David's return (see *Sfas Emes,* who discusses Mefiboshes' true mindset). However, if David had not seen these "recognizable signs," he would have retracted his earlier promise to Tziva (*Behold, everything that belongs to Mefiboshes is yours*). That pronouncement did not constitute an acceptance of a slanderous report, for even Tziva knew that the grant was ineffective, for David had not yet been reinstalled as king, and the grant had been given only on condition that David found Tziva's accusation true (*Rashi*).

40. *II Samuel* 19:26-31.

41. I.e. when David went into exile.

בני שמואל חטאו אינו אלא טועה שנאמר
א) ויהי (א) כי זקן שמואל ב) ובניו לא הלכו)
בדרכיו בדרכיו הוא דלא הלכו מיחטא נמי
לא חטאו אלא מה אני מקיים ב) ויטו אחרי
הבצע שלא עשו כמעשה אביהם שהיה
שמואל הצדיק מחזר בכל מקומות ישראל
ודן אותם בעריהם שנאמר ג) והלך מדי שנה
בשנה וסבב בית אל והגלגל והמצפה ושפט
את ישראל והם לא עשו כן אלא ישבו
בעריהם א כדי להרבות שכר לחזניהן
ולסופריהן כתנאי ויטו אחרי הבצע ר' מאיר
אומר חלקם שאלו בפיהם רבי יהודה אומר
מלאי הטילו על בעלי בתים ר' עקיבא אומר
קופה יתירה של מעשר נטלו בזרוע ר' יוסי
אומר מתנות נטלו בזרוע: א"ר שמואל בר
נחמני אמר ר' יונתן כל האומר דוד חטא אינו
אלא טועה שנאמר ד) ויהי דוד לכל דרכיו
משכיל וה' עמו וגו' אפשר חטא בא לידו
ושכינה עמו אלא מה אני מקיים ה) מדוע בזית
את דבר ה' לעשות הרע שביקש לעשות ולא
עשה אמר רב רבי דאתי מדוד מהפך ודריש
בזכותיה דדוד מדוע בזית את דבר ה'
לעשות הרע רבי אומר משונה רעה זו מכל
רעות שבתורה שכל רעות שבתורה כתיב
בהו ויעש וכאן כתיב לעשות שביקש לעשות
ולא עשה ה) את אוריה החתי הכית בחרב
ב שהיה לך לדונו בסנהדרין ולא דנת ה) ואת
אשתו לקחת לך לאשה ליקוחין יש לך בה
ג דא"ר שמואל בר נחמני א"ר יונתן כל היוצא
למלחמת בית דוד כותב גט כריתות לאשתו
שנאמר ו) ואת עשרת חריצי החלב האלה
תביא לשר האלף ואת אחיך תפקוד לשלום
ואת ערובתם תקח מאי ערובתם תני רב יוסף
דברים המעורבים בינו לבינה ה) ואותו הרגת
בחרב בני עמון ז) מה חרב בני עמון אי אתה
נענש עליו אף אוריה החתי אי אתה נענש עליו מאי טעמא ד מורד במלכות
הוה דאמר ליה ז) ואדוני יואב ועבדי אדוני על פני השדה חונים אמר רב כי
מעיינת ביה בדוד לא משכחת ביה בר מדאוריה דכתיב (א) ח) רק בדבר אוריה
החתי אביי קשישא רמי דרב אדרב מי אמר רב הכי ט) והאמר רב קיבל
דוד לשון הרע קשיא גופא רב אמר קיבל דוד לשון הרע דכתיב ט) ויאמר לו
המלך איפוא הוא ויאמר ציבא אל המלך הנה הוא בית מכיר בן עמיאל
ח) (בלא) דבר וכתיב י) וישלח המלך ויקחהו מבית מכיר בן עמיאל ט) (מלא) דבר
מכדי חזייה דשקרא הוא כי הדר אלשין עילויה מ"ט קיבלה מיניה דכתיב
כ) ויאמר המלך י) (אל ציבא איה) בן אדוניך ויאמר ציבא אל המלך הנה (הוא)
יושב בירושלים וגו' ומנא לן דקיבל מיניה דכתיב ל) ויאמר המלך הנה לך כל
אשר למפיבושת ויאמר ציבא השתחויתי אמצא חן ט) (בעיני) המלך ושמואל
אמר לא קיבל דוד לשון הרע דברים הניכרים חזא ביה דכתיב מ) ומפיבושת
בן שאול ירד י) (לפני) המלך לא עשה רגליו ולא עשה שפמו ואת
בגדיו לא כיבס וגו' וכתיב נ) ויהי כי בא ירושלים לקראת המלך ויאמר לו
המלך למה לא הלכת עמי מפיבושת ויאמר אדוני המלך עבדי רמני כי
אמר עבדך אחבשה לי החמור וארכב עליה ואלך את המלך כי פסח
עבדך

בני שמואל חטאו. במקח שוחד והטיית דין: **לחזניהם.** שמשיהם שסוכרין אותן לילך ולהזמין את הנקראים לדין: **ולסופריהם.** לשטרי בירורין ולאגרות שום: **מלאי הטילו על בעלי בתים.** נותנים להן פרגמטיא לעסוק בה ולתת להם השכר ומתוך כך היה נמשך לבם להטות דין כשבאין לפניהם לדון והיינו חטאם: **חלקם שאלו בפיהם.** מעשר ראשון הראוי להם שלוים היו שאלו בפיהם מתוך שהיו גדולי הדור ושופטים לא היו מונעים מהם ושאר לוים עניים מצטערים ולר' מאיר לא חטאו בהטיית משפט: **קופה יתירה.** יותר מן הראוי: **מתנות.** זרוע לחיים וקיבה והם לא היו כהנים ל"א מתנות לויה כגון מעשר וקרא כתיב ונתן לכהן ודרשינן ולא שיטול מעצמו בשחיטת חולין בפ' הזרוע (דף קלג.) וה"ה לכל מתנות כהונה ולויה: **דוד חטא.** בבת שבע קודם שקבלה גט: **שבקש.** לשכב עמה קודם שקבלה גט שהיה בעלה שולח לה מן המלחמה שאם ימות לא תזקק ליבום או שמא יהרג ואין מעיד עליו ותתעגן אשתו או שמא יהא שבוי כדאמרינן לקמן כל היוצא למלחמת בית דוד כו': **משונה רעה זו.** בכתיבתה ובלשונה: **שהיה לך לדונו.** על שמרד במלכות כדלקמן: **ליקוחין יש לך בה.** קדושין תופסין בה שאינה אשת איש כדשמואל כו': **גט כריתות.** על תנאי שאם ימות תהא מגורשת מעכשיו ופעמים שהוא טרוד בצאתו ושולחו מן המלחמה: **ואת ערובתם תקח.** במלחמת שאול כתיב: **דברים המעורבים בינידם.** היינו קדושין תקח תבטל ע"י גט שתביא להם מן המלחמה: **בחרב בני עמון.** כאותן שהורגים בני עמון שלא מדעתך: **ואדוני יואב.** לאו אורח ארעא לקבל עליו מרות אחרים בפני המלך: **רק בדבר אוריה.** מקרא כתיב כך בדבר אוריה שגרם לו שיהרג אבל בבת שבע לא חטא: **לשון הרע.** לקמיה מפרש: **בלא דבר.** אינו חכם בתורה והוא מצאו מלא דבר וחכם בתורה: **חזייא דשקרא הוה.** מתחילה מצאו שקרן בכך: **כי הדר אלשין עליה.** ציבא על מפיבושת כשהיה דוד בורח מפני אבשלום מאי טעמא קביל מיניה: **איה בן אדוניך ויאמר הנה יושב בירושלים.** כי אמר היום ישיבו לי את ממלכת אבי: **דברים הניכרים חזא ביה.** במפיבושת כשנהרג אבשלום וחזר דוד למלכותו ובא לפניו לא עשה רגליו ולא עשה שפמו כסבור דוד שניכרים דברי ציבא שנצטער על שחזר דוד ולא קישט עצמו ט) ועוד היה מצפה שכשיושיבוהו במלכות יתנאה ויתפאר לכך לא קבל דבריו ואמר לו אתה וציבא תחלקו השדה והוא השיבו קשה אין לי לצעוק אלא על מי שהביאך הלום הנה שמצטער על שובו ואם לא שראה בו דברים הניכרים היה חוזר ממה שאמר הנה לך כל אשר למפיבושת ואע"פ שמיהר ואמר לו מתחלה הנה לך כל אשר למפיבושת אין זו קבלה כי כל זמן שלא היה דוד שב למלכותו יודע היה שאין מתנתו מתנה ולא אמר לו אלא על תנאי אם יראה אמת בדבריו:
על

שהיה לך לדונו בסנהדרין. קשה לר"י דפ"ק דמגילה (דף יד: ושם) אמרינן גבי נבל דמורד במלכות לא בעי למדייניה ואוריה מורד במלכות הוה כדאמר בסמוך ויש לומר דודאי צריך לדונו ולידע אם הוא מורד במלכות אבל לעיין בדינו ולעשות הלנת דין ולהמתין עד למחר אין צריך וכן משמע דבסנהדרין (דף לו. ושם) אמר שדן דוד את נבל בסנהדרין מויחגרו איש חרבו וגו':

ליקוחין יש לך בה. אף על גב דאפילו חטא נמי יש לו בה ליקוחין דהא אנוסה היתה ושריא לבעל וה"ה לבועל מ"מ ליקוחין יש לך בה משמע לא היה לך בה עבירה:

גט כריתות כותב לאשתו. פרש"י על תנאי שאם ימות במלחמה תהא מגורשת מעכשיו וצריך לומר לפירושו דאף על גב דאוריה בא מן המלחמה התנאי היה שאם לא ישוב בסוף המלחמה שיהא גט אך קשה דתנן במי שאחזו (גיטין דף עג. ושם) מה היא באותן הימים רבי יהודה אומר הרי היא כאשת איש לכל דבריה ואם כן לר' יהודה היתה אשת איש גמורה ונראה לר"ת שהיה מגרשה לגמרי בלא שום תנאי והא דאמרינן בהזהב (ב"מ דף נט. ושם) מוטב שיבעול אדם ספק אשת איש ואל ילבין פני חבירו ברבים מנלן מדוד קרי לה ספק אשת איש לפי שהיו מגרשים בצנעה והעולם סבורים שהיא אשת איש:

דאמר ליה ואדוני יואב. פרש"י דמורד במלכות הוה משום דקאמר ואדוני יואב ° ואין נראה דאין זה מורד שלא היה בלבו להמליכו ולקרותו מלך אלא כמו שפירש רבינו מאיר דהוי מורד משום דבסיפא דקרא כתיב ואני אבא אל ביתי לאכול ולשתות ולשכב עם אשתי וגו' שדוד אמר לו לעשות ולא רצה לעשות:

רק בדבר אוריה החתי. קשה דהא איכא מעשה דהסתה בריש פ"ב דיומא (דף כב:) וי"ל דלא חשיב ליה דלא הוי כל כך עון גדול וגם שגג:
אלא

עין משפט נר מצוה

מ א מיי' פכ"ג מהל' סנהדרין הלכה ג סמג לאוין רח טוש"ע ח"מ סי' ט סעיף ד:

מא ב מיי' פ"ג מהל' מלכים הלכה ח:

תורה אור השלם

א) וַיְהִי כַּאֲשֶׁר זָקֵן שְׁמוּאֵל וַיָּשֶׂם אֶת בָּנָיו שֹׁפְטִים לְיִשְׂרָאֵל: [שמואל א' ח, א]

ב) וְלֹא הָלְכוּ בָנָיו בִּדְרָכָיו וַיִּטּוּ אַחֲרֵי הַבָּצַע וַיִּקְחוּ שֹׁחַד וַיַּטּוּ מִשְׁפָּט: [שמואל א' ח, ג]

ג) וְהָלַךְ מִדֵּי שָׁנָה בְּשָׁנָה וְסָבַב בֵּית אֵל וְהַגִּלְגָּל וְהַמִּצְפָּה וְשָׁפַט אֶת יִשְׂרָאֵל אֵת כָּל הַמְּקוֹמוֹת הָאֵלֶּה: [שמואל א' ז, טז]

ד) וַיְהִי דָוִד לְכָל דְּרָכָו מַשְׂכִּיל וַיְיָ עִמּוֹ: [שמואל א' יח, יד]

ה) מַדּוּעַ בָּזִיתָ אֶת דְּבַר יְיָ לַעֲשׂוֹת הָרַע בְּעֵינַי אֵת אוּרִיָּה הַחִתִּי הִכִּיתָ בַחֶרֶב וְאֶת אִשְׁתּוֹ לָקַחְתָּ לְּךָ לְאִשָּׁה וְאֹתוֹ הָרַגְתָּ בְּחֶרֶב בְּנֵי עַמּוֹן: [שמואל ב' יב, ט]

ו) וְאֵת עֲשֶׂרֶת חֲרִצֵי הֶחָלָב הָאֵלֶּה תָּבִיא לְשַׂר הָאָלֶף וְאֶת אַחֶיךָ תִּפְקֹד לְשָׁלוֹם וְאֶת עֲרֻבָּתָם תִּקָּח: [שמואל א' יז, יח]

ז) וַיֹּאמֶר אוּרִיָּה אֶל דָּוִד הָאָרוֹן וְיִשְׂרָאֵל וִיהוּדָה יֹשְׁבִים בַּסֻּכּוֹת וַאדֹנִי יוֹאָב וְעַבְדֵי אֲדֹנִי עַל פְּנֵי הַשָּׂדֶה חֹנִים וַאֲנִי אָבוֹא אֶל בֵּיתִי לֶאֱכֹל וְלִשְׁתּוֹת וְלִשְׁכַּב עִם אִשְׁתִּי חַיֶּךָ וְחֵי נַפְשֶׁךָ אִם אֶעֱשֶׂה אֶת הַדָּבָר הַזֶּה: [שמואל ב' יא, יא]

ח) אֲשֶׁר עָשָׂה דָוִד אֶת הַיָּשָׁר בְּעֵינֵי יְיָ וְלֹא סָר מִכֹּל אֲשֶׁר צִוָּהוּ כֹּל יְמֵי חַיָּיו רַק בִּדְבַר אוּרִיָּה הַחִתִּי: [מלכים א' טו, ה]

ט) וַיֹּאמֶר לוֹ הַמֶּלֶךְ אֵיפֹה הוּא וַיֹּאמֶר צִיבָא אֶל הַמֶּלֶךְ הִנֵּה הוּא בֵּית מָכִיר בֶּן עַמִּיאֵל בְּלוֹ דְבָר: [שמואל ב' ט, ד]

י) וַיִּשְׁלַח הַמֶּלֶךְ דָּוִד וַיִּקָּחֵהוּ מִבֵּית מָכִיר בֶּן עַמִּיאֵל מִלּוֹ דְבָר: [שמואל ב' ט, ה]

כ) וַיֹּאמֶר הַמֶּלֶךְ וְאַיֵּה בֶּן אֲדֹנֶיךָ וַיֹּאמֶר צִיבָא אֶל הַמֶּלֶךְ הִנֵּה יוֹשֵׁב בִּירוּשָׁלַיִם כִּי אָמַר הַיּוֹם יָשִׁיבוּ לִי בֵּית יִשְׂרָאֵל אֵת מַמְלְכוּת אָבִי: [שמואל ב' טז, ג]

ל) וַיֹּאמֶר הַמֶּלֶךְ לְצִבָא הִנֵּה לְךָ כֹּל אֲשֶׁר לִמְפִיבֹשֶׁת וַיֹּאמֶר צִיבָא הִשְׁתַּחֲוֵיתִי אֶמְצָא חֵן בְּעֵינֶיךָ אֲדֹנִי הַמֶּלֶךְ: [שמואל ב' טז, ד]

מ) וּמְפִבֹשֶׁת בֶּן שָׁאוּל יָרַד לִקְרַאת הַמֶּלֶךְ וְלֹא עָשָׂה רַגְלָיו וְלֹא עָשָׂה שְׂפָמוֹ וְאֶת בְּגָדָיו לֹא כִבֵּס לְמִן הַיּוֹם לֶכֶת הַמֶּלֶךְ עַד הַיּוֹם אֲשֶׁר בָּא בְשָׁלוֹם: [שמואל ב' יט, כה] נ) וַיְהִי כִּי בָא יְרוּשָׁלַםִ לִקְרַאת הַמֶּלֶךְ וַיֹּאמֶר לוֹ הַמֶּלֶךְ לָמָּה לֹא הָלַכְתָּ עִמִּי מְפִיבֹשֶׁת: וַיֹּאמַר אֲדֹנִי הַמֶּלֶךְ עַבְדִּי רִמָּנִי כִּי אָמַר עַבְדְּךָ אֶחְבְּשָׁה לִּי הַחֲמוֹר וְאֶרְכַּב עָלֶיהָ וְאֵלֵךְ אֶת הַמֶּלֶךְ כִּי פִסֵּחַ עַבְדֶּךָ: [שמואל ב' יט, כו-כז]

מסורת הש"ס

א) [צ"ל כאשר זקן שמואל ולא הלכו בניו], ב) [חולין קלג. תוספ' סוטה פי"ד], ג) כתובות ט:, ד) קידושין מג., ה) יומא כב:, ו) [צ"ל בלו], ז) [צ"ל מלו וע' במהרש"א], ח) [צ"ל ואיה], ט) [צ"ל בעיניך אדוני], י) [צ"ל לקראת], כ) רש"י מפ' דעת אמיתית של מפיבושת דהא דלא קישט היינו משום שעוד היה מצפה שכשיושיבו לדוד במלכות יתנאה [כ"מ] ורש"ל גרס ועד עתה הי' מצפה.

הגהות הב"ח

(א) גמ' לא משכחת ביה רק בדבר אוריה כצ"ל ותיבת בר מדאורי' דכתי' נמחק:

גליון הש"ס

שלנו כתיב טהר חסר ו'). ובנדרים דף לז ע"ב אמ דהוגד הוגד קרי ולא כתיב. ובספרים שלנו הוא קרי וכתיב כמ"ש הר"ן שם. ובפסוק אני ה' אלהיך אשר הוצאתיך איתא בירושלמי פ"ה דסוכה דחסר י'. ובספרים שלפנינו הוא מלא יו"ד. ובמדרש ויקרא רבה פ' ט' ושם דרך. א"ר ינאי ושם כתיב ובספרים שלנו כתיב בסין. ובפירש"י בחומש בראשית כ"ד הפילגשם חסר כתיב ובכל הספרים איתא מלא. ובמדרש בראשית רבה פרשה ע"ז ר"ל אמר הנתרת כתיב ובכל הספרים שלנו כתיב הנותרת. ובערכין דף לב ע"א בתוספות ד"ה אשר דרש"י כ' דהכתיב ויקרא כ"ה אשר לוא חומה והם כתבו דהכתיב אשר לו והקרי לא ובספרים שלנו הכתיב לא באל"ף והקרי לו כמ"ש התי"ט שם: גמ' שהיה לך לדונו בסנהדרין. עי' מגילה דף יד ע"ב תוס' ד"ה מורד במלכות: תוס' ד"ה דאמר ליה וכו' ואין נראה. עיין יומא דף סו ע"ב תוס' ד"ה מהו להביא:

ליקוטי רש"י

חלקם שאלו בפיהם. שלא היה עבירת גזל בידם אלא חלק לויה כגון מעשר ראשון היו שואלין בפיהם [חולין קלג.]. **מלאי הטילו על בעלי בתים.** פרקמטיא שלהם על בעלי בתים היודעים בטיב סחורה שישתכרו על ידו [סוטה מז:]. **משכיל.** מצליח [ש"א יח, יד]. **כל היוצא למלחמת בית דוד כותב גט כריתות לאשתו.** שאם ימות במלחמה יהא גט מיום כתיבתו והרי מת אוריה במלחמה. **שנאמר.** במלחמת שאול ואת אחיך כו' ודוד למד מישי אביו להנהיג שאף היוצאין למלחמותיו עושין כן [כתובות ט:]. **חריצי החלב.** גובנין דחלבא. **לשר האלף.** אני אומר לשר של אותו אלף שאחיו ממנו שלכל השבטים היו שרי אלפים לפי אלפיהם ואני שמעתי לשר האלף זה יהונתן שאמר עליו ואלף היו עם יונתן בגבעת בנימין. **דברים המעורבים בינו לבינה.** גט כריתות יקח מאתם ויביא לנשותיהם להפריד עירוב שבינו לבינה [ש"א יז, יח]. אלו קדושין, תקח, תטול מביניהם על ידי גט [כתובות שם]. **ואדוני יואב.** זהו מרד שקראו אדון בפני המלך [קידושין מג.]. **לשון הרע.** על מפיבושת מפי ציבא [יומא כב:]. **ציבא.** עבד כנעני של מפיבושת הוה [יבמות סב.]. **לא עשה רגליו.** לשון תקון הוא העברת שער שבין הרגלים. **שפמו.** גרעו"ן בלע"ז [ש"ב יט, כה]. **למה לא הלכת עמי.** לצאת מירושלים כשיצאתי [שם, כו]. **כי פסח עבדך.** ואיני יכול לילך ברגלי [שם, כז].

עבדך א) וירגל בעבדך אל אדוני המלך ואדוני המלך כמלאך האלהים ועשה הטוב בעיניך ב) ויאמר לו המלך למה תדבר עוד דבריך אמרתי אתה וציבא תחלקו את השדה ויאמר מפיבשת אל המלך גם את הכל יקח אחרי אשר בא אדוני המלך בשלום אל ביתו אמר לו אני אמרתי מתי תבא בשלום ואתה עושה לי כך לא עליך יש לי תרעומות אלא על מי שהביאך בשלום היינו דכתיב ג) ובן יהונתן מריב בעל וכי מריב בעל שמו והלא מפיבשת שמו אלא מתוך שעשה מריבה עם בעליו יצתה בת קול ואמרה לו נצא בר נצא נצא הא דאמרן בר נצא דכתיב ד) ויבא שאול עד עיר עמלק וירב בנחל אמר רבי מני על עסקי נחל א) אמר רב יהודה אמר רב בשעה שאמר דוד למפיבשת ב) אתה וציבא תחלקו את השדה יצתה בת קול ואמרה לו רחבעם וירבעם יחלקו את המלוכה אמר רב יהודה אמר רב אילמלי ג) לא קיבל דוד לשון הרע לא נחלקה מלכות בית דוד ולא עבדו ישראל ע"ז ולא גלינו מארצנו: אמר ר' שמואל בר נחמני א"ר יונתן כל האומר שלמה חטא אינו אלא טועה שנאמר ה) ולא היה לבבו שלם עם ה' אלהיו כלבב דוד אביו הוא דלא הוה מיחטא נמי לא חטא אלא מה אני מקיים ה) ויהי לעת זקנת שלמה נשיו הטו את לבבו ההיא כרבי נתן דר' נתן רמי כתיב ויהי לעת זקנת שלמה נשיו הטו את לבבו והכתיב כלבב דוד אביו כלבב דוד אביו הוא דלא הוה מיחטא נמי לא חטא הכי קאמר ויהי לעת זקנת שלמה נשיו הטו את לבבו ללכת אחרי אלהים אחרים ולא הלך והכתיב ו) אז יבנה שלמה במה לכמוש שקוץ מואב שבקש לבנות ולא בנה אלא מעתה ז) אז יבנה יהושע מזבח לה' שבקש לבנות ולא בנה אלא דבנה הכא נמי דבנה אלא כדתניא רבי יוסי אומר ח) ואת הבמות אשר על פני ירושלים אשר מימין להר ג) המשחה אשר בנה שלמה מלך ישראל לעשתרות שקוץ צדונים וגו' ד) אפשר בא אסא ולא ביערם יהושפט ולא ביערם עד שבא יאשיה וביערם והלא כל ע"ז שבארץ ישראל אסא ויהושפט ביערום אלא מקיש ראשונים לאחרונים מה אחרונים לא עשו ותלה בהן לשבח אף ראשונים לא עשו ותלה בהן לגנאי והכתיב ט) ויעש שלמה הרע בעיני ה' אלא מפני שהיה לו למחות בנשיו ולא מיחה מעלה עליו הכתוב כאילו חטא אמר רב יהודה אמר שמואל נוח לו לאותו צדיק שיהא שמש לדבר אחר ואל יכתב בו ויעש הרע בעיני ה' ה) אמר רב יהודה אמר שמואל בשעה שנשא שלמה את בת פרעה הכניסה לו אלף מיני זמר ואמרה לו כך עושין לעבודה זרה פלונית וכך עושים לע"ז פלונית ולא מיחה בה ו) אמר רב יהודה אמר שמואל בשעה שנשא שלמה את בת פרעה ירד גבריאל ונעץ קנה בים ועלה בו שירטון ועליו נבנה כרך גדול [של רומי] במתניתא תנא אותו היום שהכנים ירבעם שני עגלי זהב אחד בבית אל ואחד בדן נבנה צריף אחד וזהו איטליאה של יון: א"ר שמואל בר נחמני א"ר יונתן כל האומר יאשיהו חטא אינו אלא טועה שנאמר י) ויעש הישר בעיני ה' וילך בכל דרך דוד אביו אלא מה אני מקיים כ) וכמוהו לא היה לפניו מלך אשר שב וגו' ז) שכל דין שדן מבן שמונה עד שמונה עשרה החזירן להן שמא תאמר נטל מזה ונתן לזה תלמוד לומר כ) בכל מאודו שנתן להם משלו ופליגא דרב דאמר רב אין לך גדול בבעלי תשובה יותר מיאשיהו בדורו ואחד בדורנו ומנו אבא אבוה דרבי ירמיה ח) בר אבא ואמרי לה אחא אחוה דאבא אבוה דרב ירמיה בר אבא דאמר מר רבי אבא ואחא אחי הוו אמר רב יוסף ועוד אחד בדורנו ומנו עוקבן בר נחמיה ריש גלותא והיינו ט) נתן דצוציתא אמר רב יוסף הוה יתיבנא בפירקא והוה קא מנמנם וחזאי בחילמא דקא פשט ידיה וקבליה:

הדרן עלך במה בהמה

תוספות

אלא מעתה אז יבנה יהושע כו'. הקשה הר"ר אלחנן דבחלק (סנהדרין דף צא:) מפקינן מדכתיב אז יבנה יהושע ולא כתב אז בנה מכאן לתחיית המתים מן התורה אם כן אתא לדרשה ה"נ אתא לדרשה דהכא ואומר ר"י דמ"מ פריך מדלא כתיב שבקש לבנות אלא יבנה ש"מ שרוצה לומר שבנה כההוא דיהושע דודאי בנה:

מה אחרונים לא עשו ותלה בהן כו'. לא שייך למימר הכא מקום הניחו לו אבותיו להתגדל בו כדאמר בפ"ק דחולין (דף ז. ושם:) גבי נחש נחשת שביער חזקיה דהתם לא ביערוהו אבותיו שהיו יראים לבערו לפי שעשאו משה על פי הדבור אבל הכא למה היו מניחים מלבערם: **דצוציתא.** אומר ר"ת דאמר במדרש שהיה נר דולק ° על ראשו:

הדרן עלך במה בהמה

רש"י

על עסקי נחל. ומה על נפש אחת אמרה תורה הבא עגלה ערופה בנחל נפשות הללו על אחת כמה וכמה אם גדולים חטאו קטנים מה חטאו ט): ולא עבדו ישראל עבודה זרה. שעל ידי שנחלקה המלכות העמיד ירבעם העגלים שלא יעלו ישראל ירושלים לממשלתו של רחבעם: שלמה חטא. בע"ז: כדר' נתן. דשני קרא הטו ללכת והוא לא הלך: הכא נמי דבנה. קשיא היא: אלא. מהכא תילף דלא בנה כדתניא רבי יוסי אומר כו': להר המשחה. לשון שמן דמתרגמינן משחא והוא הר הזיתים: מקיש ראשונים. מקיש את בנינו של שלמה לביעורו של יאשיהו מה יאשיהו לא עשה ביעור זה ותלו בו מן השמים לשבח הואיל וביער השאר שנעשה משמת יהושפט אף שלמה לא עשה בנין זה ותלו בו לגנות מתוך שלא מיחה בנשיו: שמש. לחטוב עצים ולשאוב מים בשכר לע"ז: ואל יכתב בו דבר זה. ללמדך שקשה התוכחה במי שבידו לימחות: מיני זמר. כלי שיר: נעץ קנה. ושרטון מדבק בו עד שנוסף והולך וגדל שרטון חול ורפש וטיט שהים גורש: כרך גדול של רומי. שהוא מיצר לישראל והוא (איטליא) של יון במסכת מגילה (דף ו:): ביום שהעמיד ירבעם את העגלים נבנה צריף אחד. באותו שרטון שגדל שם בימי שלמה. צריף כוך קטן מליידין שעושין מן קנים ומן ערבה ומאז נתוספו בתים על בתים: איטליאה. שם העיר והיא ממדינת יון וכשנטלה רומי מלכות יוונים לכדוהו והפך להם: יאשיהו חטא. דכתיב שב אל ה' משמע דחטא מעיקרא: מבן ח'. שישב על כסא מלכותו דכתיב בן ח' שנה וגו': עד בן י"ח. שמצא חלקיה את הספר ועיין ודקדק בתורה ובדיניה בכתב ובעל פה והבין שמא טעה בדינא: נטל מזה. ממי שנתן לו תחילה: ה"ג ואמרי לה אחא אחוה דאבא אבוה דרב ירמיה בר אבא: נתן דצוציתא. על שם ניצוצין דנורא שהמלאך פשט את ידו וקיבל תשובתו לישנא אחרינא על שאחזו המלאך בציצית ראשו:

הדרן עלך במה בהמה

עין משפט נר מצוה

מב א טוש"ע ח"מ סי' ז' סעיף ג:

רב נסים גאון

נצא בר נצא [נצא] הא דאמרן בר נצא דכתיב (ש"א טו) ויבא שאול עד עיר (שלמה) [עמלק] וירב בנחל אמר ר' מני על עסקי נחל בשעה שאמר הקב"ה לשאול ועתה לך והכיתה את עמלק נשא שאול קל וחומר בעצמו ואמר ומה על נפש אחת אמרה תורה הבא עגלה ערופה בנחל המאבד נפשות הרבה על אחת כמה וכמה ועוד אם אדם חטא בהמה מה חטאת אם גדולים חטאו קטנים מה חטאו:

סליק פרק במה בהמה

גליון הש"ס

תוס' ד"ה דצוציתא וכו' על ראשו. עי' סנהדרין דף לא ע"ב ברש"י ד"ה לדזיו ליה:

ליקוטי רש"י

מריב בעל. זה מפיבושת [דה"א ט, לט]. **וירב בנחל.** וילחם בנחל ורבותינו אמרו על עסקי נחל רב ודן את עצמו ומה בשביל נפש אחת אמרה תורה ערוף עגלה בנחל בשביל כל הנפשות הללו לא כ"ש אם אדם חטא בהמה מה חטאת [ש"א טו, ה]. **אז יבנה שלמה במה וכו'.** פירשו בו חכמי ישראל שבקש לבנות ולא בנה למדנו שהיו"ד על שם המחשבה נאמרה [שמות טו, א]. **צריף.** כוך של ציידין שאורבין בה את העופות ועשוי ככוורת שמשפעת והולכת שגגו וקירותיו אחד [סוכה יט:]. **איטליאה של יון.** מאיי אלישה (יחזקאל כז) מתרגמינן מנגוות איטליא [מגילה ו:]. **נתן דצוציתא.** ומצאתי בספר הגדה שהיה מר עוקבא בעל תשובה שנתן עיניו באשה אחת והעלה לבו טינא ונפל בחולי ואשת איש היתה לימים נצרכה ללות ממנו ומתוך דוחקה נתרצית לו וכבש יצרו ופטרה לשלום ונתרפא וכשהיה יוצא לשוק היה נר דולק בראשו מן השמים ועל שם כך קרי ליה ר' נתן צוציתא במסכת שבת [סנהדרין לא: עי"ש].

מסורת הש"ס

א) יומא כב:, ב) [עי' תוספות מגילה כא.], ג) [בקרא כתיב המשחית וגם בע"י איתא כך ועי' פירש"י במלכים שכתב הוא הר המשחה וכיון שהזכיר את שמו ע"י ע"ז שינו שמו לגנאי עכ"ל], ד) [חולין ו: ועי' תוס' שם ז. ד"ה אלא], ה) בכ"י הגי' ואמר וכן לקמן, ו) סנהדרין כא: ע"ש, ז) ע' ברכת הזבח כריתות כה:, ח) [ועמ"ש רש"י סנהדרין לא: ד"ה לדזיו וכו' שהיה מר עוקבא בעל תשובה שנתן עינו וכו' וכשהוא יוצא לשוק היה נר דולק בראשו מן השמים ועל שם כך קרא ליה רבי נתן צוציתא וכו'], ט) [כדמפרש ביומא כב:].

תורה אור השלם

א) וַיְרַגֵּל בְּעַבְדְּךָ אֶל אֲדֹנִי הַמֶּלֶךְ וַאדֹנִי הַמֶּלֶךְ כְּמַלְאַךְ הָאֱלֹהִים וַעֲשֵׂה הַטּוֹב בְּעֵינֶיךָ: [שמואל ב' יט, ה]

ב) וַיֹּאמֶר לוֹ הַמֶּלֶךְ לָמָּה תְּדַבֵּר עוֹד דְּבָרֶיךָ אָמַרְתִּי אַתָּה וְצִיבָא תַּחְלְקוּ אֶת הַשָּׂדֶה: וַיֹּאמֶר מְפִיבֹשֶׁת אֶל הַמֶּלֶךְ גַּם אֶת הַכֹּל יִקָּח אַחֲרֵי אֲשֶׁר בָּא אֲדֹנִי הַמֶּלֶךְ בְּשָׁלוֹם אֶל בֵּיתוֹ: [שמואל ב' יט, ל-לא]

ג) וּבֶן יְהוֹנָתָן מְרִיב בָּעַל וּמְרִיב בַּעַל הוֹלִיד אֶת מִיכָה: [דברי הימים א' ח, לד]

ד) וַיָּבֹא שָׁאוּל עַד עִיר עֲמָלֵק וַיָּרֶב בַּנָּחַל: [שמואל א' טו, ה]

ה) וַיְהִי לְעֵת זִקְנַת שְׁלֹמֹה נָשָׁיו הִטּוּ אֶת לְבָבוֹ אַחֲרֵי אֱלֹהִים אֲחֵרִים וְלֹא הָיָה לְבָבוֹ שָׁלֵם עִם יְיָ אֱלֹהָיו כִּלְבַב דָּוִיד אָבִיו: [מלכים א' יא, ד]

ו) אָז יִבְנֶה שְׁלֹמֹה בָּמָה לִכְמוֹשׁ שִׁקֻּץ מוֹאָב בָּהָר אֲשֶׁר עַל פְּנֵי יְרוּשָׁלָיִם וּלְמֹלֶךְ שִׁקֻּץ בְּנֵי עַמּוֹן: [מלכים א' יא, ז]

ז) אָז יִבְנֶה יְהוֹשֻׁעַ מִזְבֵּחַ לַייָ אֱלֹהֵי יִשְׂרָאֵל בְּהַר עֵיבָל: [יהושע ח, ל]

ח) וְאֶת הַבָּמוֹת אֲשֶׁר עַל פְּנֵי יְרוּשָׁלַיִם אֲשֶׁר מִימִין לְהַר הַמַּשְׁחִית אֲשֶׁר בָּנָה שְׁלֹמֹה מֶלֶךְ יִשְׂרָאֵל לְעַשְׁתֹּרֶת שִׁקֻּץ צִידֹנִים וְלִכְמוֹשׁ שִׁקֻּץ מוֹאָב וּלְמִלְכֹּם תּוֹעֲבַת בְּנֵי עַמּוֹן טִמֵּא הַמֶּלֶךְ: [מלכים ב' כג, יג]

ט) וַיַּעַשׂ שְׁלֹמֹה הָרַע בְּעֵינֵי יְיָ וְלֹא מִלֵּא אַחֲרֵי יְיָ כְּדָוִד אָבִיו: [מלכים א' יא, ו]

י) וַיַּעַשׂ הַיָּשָׁר בְּעֵינֵי יְיָ וַיֵּלֶךְ בְּכָל דֶּרֶךְ דָּוִד אָבִיו וְלֹא סָר יָמִין וּשְׂמֹאול: [מלכים ב' כב, ב]

כ) וְכָמֹהוּ לֹא הָיָה לְפָנָיו מֶלֶךְ אֲשֶׁר שָׁב אֶל יְיָ בְּכָל לְבָבוֹ וּבְכָל נַפְשׁוֹ וּבְכָל מְאֹדוֹ כְּכֹל תּוֹרַת מֹשֶׁה וְאַחֲרָיו לֹא קָם כָּמֹהוּ: [מלכים ב' כג, כה]

עַבְדֶּךָ – *for your servant is lame.* וַיְרַגֵּל בְּעַבְדְּךָ אֶל־אֲדֹנִי הַמֶּלֶךְ וַאדֹנִי הַמֶּלֶךְ כְּמַלְאַךְ הָאֱלֹהִים וַעֲשֵׂה הַטּוֹב בְּעֵינֶיךָ . . . – ***And he*** [Tziva] ***has slandered your servant to my lord the king, and my lord the king is like an angel of God; do therefore what is good in your eyes . . .*** וַיֹּאמֶר לוֹ הַמֶּלֶךְ לָמָּה תְּדַבֵּר עוֹד דְּבָרֶיךָ אָמַרְתִּי אַתָּה וְצִיבָא תַּחְלְקוּ אֶת־הַשָּׂדֶה. – ***And the king said to him: Why do you go on speaking your words? I have said: You and Tziva shall divide the field.*** וַיֹּאמֶר מְפִיבֹשֶׁת אֶל־הַמֶּלֶךְ גַּם אֶת הַכֹּל יִקָּח אַחֲרֵי אֲשֶׁר־בָּא אֲדֹנִי הַמֶּלֶךְ בְּשָׁלוֹם אֶל־בֵּיתוֹ. – ***And Mefiboshes said to the king: Let him take all, since my lord the king is returning in peace to his house.***

The Gemara interprets Mefiboshes' words:

אָמַר לוֹ אֲנִי אָמַרְתִּי מָתַי תָּבֹא בְּשָׁלוֹם – **[Mefiboshes]** in essence **said to [David]: "I said: 'When will [the king] return in peace?'** I was yearning for the day when you would return in peace, וְאַתָּה עוֹשֶׂה לִי כָּךְ – **and you treat me thus?!** לֹא עָלֶיךָ יֵשׁ לִי תַּרְעוֹמוֹת – **My complaint is not against you,** אֶלָּא עַל מִי שֶׁהֱבִיאֲךָ בְּשָׁלוֹם – **but against He Who brought you back in peace!"**[1]

The Gemara cites further evidence that Mefiboshes complained against Heaven:

הַיְינוּ דִּכְתִיב ,,וּבֶן־יְהוֹנָתָן מְרִיב בָּעַל'' – **This is** the meaning of **what is written:** ***And the son of Yehonasan was Meriv Baal.***[2] וְכִי מְרִיב בַּעַל שְׁמוֹ – **Is his name** really **Meriv Baal?** וַהֲלֹא מְפִיבֹשֶׁת שְׁמוֹ – **But is his name not Mefiboshes?!**[3] אֶלָּא מִתּוֹךְ שֶׁעָשָׂה מְרִיבָה עִם בְּעָלָיו – **Rather, because he conducted a quarrel with his Master** [Hashem],[4] יָצְתָה בַּת קוֹל וְאָמְרָה לוֹ נַצָּא בַּר נַצָּא – **a heavenly voice issued forth and said to him: Quarreler, son of a quarreler!** נַצָּא הָא דַּאֲמָרָן – That Mefiboshes was called a **quarreler** is because of **that which we have** just **said** – i.e. he complained against Heaven because of David's return. בַּר נַצָּא – That he was called **son of a quarreler** דִּכְתִיב ,,וַיָּבֹא שָׁאוּל עַד־עִיר עֲמָלֵק וַיָּרֶב בַּנָּחַל'' – is **because it is written:** ***And Shaul came to the city of Amalek, and he contended in the riverbed.***[5]

The Gemara expounds this verse:

אָמַר רַבִּי מָנִי עַל עִסְקֵי נַחַל – **R' Mani said:** It means that Shaul quarreled **about the matter of a riverbed.**[6]

The Gemara has explained Shmuel's position, that David did not believe the slander about Mefiboshes. It now elaborates on Rav's contrary opinion:

אָמַר רַב יְהוּדָה אָמַר רַב – **Rav Yehudah said in the name of Rav:** בְּשָׁעָה שֶׁאָמַר דָּוִד לִמְפִיבֹשֶׁת ,,אַתָּה וְצִיבָא תַּחְלְקוּ אֶת־הַשָּׂדֶה'' – **At the moment David said to Mefiboshes, *You and Tziva shall divide the field,*** יָצְתָה בַּת קוֹל וְאָמְרָה לוֹ רְחַבְעָם וְיָרָבְעָם יַחְלְקוּ אֶת הַמְּלוּכָה – **a heavenly voice issued forth and said to him: Rechavam and Yarovam shall divide the kingdom.**[7]

The Gemara cites another statement by Rav on this topic:

אָמַר רַב יְהוּדָה אָמַר רַב אִילְמָלֵי לֹא קִיבֵּל דָּוִד לָשׁוֹן הָרַע – **Rav Yehudah said in the name of Rav: If David had not accepted a slanderous report,** לֹא נֶחְלְקָה מַלְכוּת בֵּית דָּוִד – **the kingdom of the House of David would not have been divided,** וְלֹא עָבְדוּ יִשְׂרָאֵל עֲבוֹדָה זָרָה – **and Israel would not have worshiped idols,** וְלֹא גָּלִינוּ מֵאַרְצֵנוּ – **and we would not have been exiled from our land.**[8]

The Gemara now discusses the apparent sin of King Shlomo:

אָמַר ר' שְׁמוּאֵל בַּר נַחְמָנִי אָמַר ר' יוֹנָתָן – **R' Shmuel Bar Nachmani said in the name of R' Yonasan:** כָּל הָאוֹמֵר שְׁלֹמֹה חָטָא אֵינוֹ אֶלָּא טוֹעֶה – **Whoever says that Shlomo sinned is simply mistaken,**[9] שֶׁנֶּאֱמַר ,,וְלֹא־הָיָה לְבָבוֹ שָׁלֵם עִם־ה' אֱלֹהָיו כִּלְבַב דָּוִיד אָבִיו'' – **for it is stated:**[10] ***And his heart was not perfect with Hashem his God, as was the heart of David his father,*** כִּלְבַב דָּוִד אָבִיו הוּא דְּלֹא הֲוָה – which implies: **It is** only **that [his heart] was not like the heart of his father David;** מֵיחְטָא נַמִּי לֹא חָטָא – however, **he also did not sin.**

The Gemara asks:

אֶלָּא מָה אֲנִי מְקַיֵּים ,,וַיְהִי לְעֵת זִקְנַת שְׁלֹמֹה נָשָׁיו הִטּוּ אֶת־לְבָבוֹ'' – **But how,** then, **do I uphold** the beginning of that verse: ***And it came to pass, at the time of Shlomo's old age, that his wives turned his heart aside*** *after other gods*?

The Gemara answers:

הַהִיא כְּרַבִּי נָתָן – **That** verse is interpreted **according to** the teaching of **R' Nassan,** דְּרַבִּי נָתָן רָמֵי – **for R' Nassan contrasted**[11] two verses, as follows: כְּתִיב ,,וַיְהִי לְעֵת זִקְנַת שְׁלֹמֹה נָשָׁיו הִטּוּ אֶת־לְבָבוֹ'' – **It is written: *And it came to pass, at the time***

NOTES

1. Mefiboshes should have pleaded with the king for his property. Instead, he replied: *Let him take all, since my lord the king is returning.* This is a non sequitur: The fact that David was returning in peace was no reason for Tziva to take all. Therefore, Mefiboshes' reply is interpreted by the Gemara as being a "harsh" one. When David saw that Mefiboshes was grumbling against Heaven, he realized that Mefiboshes' heart was not with him (*Maharsha*).

If Mefiboshes had said, "Since my lord the king is returning, let [Tziva] take all," it would have meant that in his joy over David's return Mefiboshes regarded his own property as unimportant. However, since he began with the words; *Let him take all,* his reaction is seen as an expression of anger and complaint (*Rif* to *Ein Yaakov*).

2. *I Chronicles* 8:34 and 9:40.

3. Since the Book of *Samuel* tells us that Yehonasan had a son named Mefiboshes, while the Book of *Chronicles* relates that Yehonasan had only one son, calling him Meriv Baal, it follows that Mefiboshes and Meriv Baal are one and the same person (*Maharsha*).

4. *Meriv* means "quarrel," and *Baal* means "master."

5. *I Samuel* 15:5. Hashem had commanded Shaul to attack the nation of Amalek and obliterate it – men, women, children and even their animals.

6. Shaul was reluctant to execute Hashem's command. He reasoned: When just one person is found slain, the Torah prescribes an entire procedure, wherein a calf is beheaded in a dry, rocky riverbed (the mitzvah of *eglah arufah;* see *Deuteronomy* 21:1-9; see also *Rashi* to *Deuteronomy* 21:4; cf. *Rambam, Hil. Rotzeach* 9:2); all the more so, then, must the Torah oppose the destruction of so many lives. After all, even if the adults sinned, what sin did the children commit? (*Rashi,* based on *Yoma* 22b).

The Gemara does not take our verse literally because the Torah states elsewhere (*Numbers* 14:45) that the Amalekites lived on a mountain, not in a riverbed. Therefore, R' Mani expounds the verse as referring to a quarrel based on the matter of the riverbed, i.e. the mitzvah of *eglah arufah* (*Maharsha* to *Yoma* 22b).

7. After the death of David's son Shlomo, the monarchy was divided between Shlomo's son Rechavam and Shlomo's slave Yarovam (see *I Kings* chs. 11-12).

According to Rav, David was being punished measure for measure: Because David believed slander and divided Mefiboshes' property between master [Mefiboshes] and slave [Tziva], Hashem divided David's kingdom between king [Rechavam] and slave [Yarovam] (*Maharsha*; cf. *Chidushei Geonim* in *Ein Yaakov*).

8. If the kingdom had not been split, Yarovam would not have set up golden calves for Israel to worship to prevent them from making the pilgrimage to Jerusalem (*Rashi;* and see *I Kings* 12:25 ff). This in turn led to exile, for the Gemara above (33a) states that the sin of idol worship leads to exile (*Maharsha*).

9. It is a mistake to think that Shlomo committed the sin of idolatry (*Rashi*). However, he did sin either by not protesting the sins of his wives, or by marrying foreign women (*Maharsha*; cf. *Ahavas Eisan* in *Ein Yaakov*).

10. *I Kings* 11:4.

11. Literally: he threw [i.e. he threw one verse against the other].

עבדך א) וירגל בעבדך אל אדוני המלך ואדוני המלך כמלאך האלהים ועשה הטוב בעיניך ב) ויאמר לו המלך למה תדבר עוד דבריך אמרתי אתה וציבא תחלקו את השדה ויאמר מפיבשת אל המלך גם את הכל יקח אחרי אשר בא אדוני המלך בשלום אל ביתו אמר לו אני אמרתי מתי תבא בשלום ואתה עושה לי כך לא עליך יש לי תרעומות אלא על מי שהביאך בשלום היינו דכתיב ג) ובן יהונתן מריב בעל וכי מריב בעל שמו והלא מפיבשת שמו אלא מתוך שעשה מריבה עם בעליו יצתה בת קול ואמרה לו נצא בר נצא נצא הא דאמרן בר נצא דכתיב ד) ויבא שאול עד עיר עמלק וירב בנחל אמר רבי מני על עסקי נחל א) אמר רב יהודה אמר רב בשעה שאמר דוד למפיבשת ב) אתה וציבא תחלקו את השדה יצתה בת קול ואמרה לו רחבעם וירבעם יחלקו את המלוכה אמר רב יהודה אמר רב אילמלי ג) לא קיבל דוד לשון הרע לא נחלקה מלכות בית דוד ולא עבדו ישראל ע"ז ולא גלינו מארצנו: אמר ר' שמואל בר נחמני א"ר יונתן כל האומר שלמה חטא אינו אלא טועה שנאמר ה) ולא היה לבבו שלם עם ה' אלהיו כלבב דוד אביו כלבב דוד אביו הוא דלא הוה מיחטא נמי לא חטא אלא מה אני מקיים ה) ויהי לעת זקנת שלמה נשיו הטו את לבבו ההיא כרבי נתן דר' נתן רמי כתיב ויהי לעת זקנת שלמה נשיו הטו את לבבו והכתיב כלבב דוד אביו כלבב דוד אביו הוא דלא הוה מיחטא נמי לא חטא הכי קאמר ויהי לעת זקנת שלמה נשיו הטו את לבבו ללכת אחרי אלהים אחרים ולא הלך והכתיב ו) אז יבנה שלמה במה לכמוש שקוץ מואב שבקש לבנות ולא בנה אלא מעתה ז) אז יבנה יהושע מזבח לה' שבקש לבנות ולא בנה אלא דבנה הכא נמי דבנה אלא כדתניא רבי יוסי אומר ח) ואת הבמות אשר על פני ירושלים אשר מימין להר ג) המשחה אשר בנה שלמה מלך ישראל לעשתרות שקוץ צדונים וגו' ד) אפשר בא אסא ולא ביערם יהושפט ולא ביערם עד שבא יאשיה וביערם והלא כל ע"ז שבארץ ישראל אסא ויהושפט ביערום אלא מקיש ראשונים לאחרונים מה אחרונים לא עשו ותלה בהן לשבח אף ראשונים לא עשו ותלה בהן לגנאי והכתיב ט) ויעש שלמה הרע בעיני ה' אלא מפני שהיה לו למחות בנשיו ולא מיחה מעלה עליו הכתוב כאילו חטא אמר רב יהודה אמר שמואל נוח לו לאותו צדיק שיהא שמש לדבר אחר ואל יכתב בו ויעש הרע בעיני ה' ה) אמר רב יהודה אמר שמואל בשעה שנשא שלמה את בת פרעה הכניסה לו אלף מיני זמר ואמרה לו כך עושין לעבודה זרה פלונית וכך עושים לע"ז פלונית ולא מיחה בה ו) אמר רב יהודה אמר שמואל בשעה שנשא שלמה את בת פרעה ירד גבריאל ונעץ קנה בים ועלה בו שירטון ועליו נבנה כרך גדול [של רומי] במתניתא תנא אותו היום שהכנים ירבעם שני עגלי זהב אחד בבית אל ואחד בדן נבנה צריף אחד וזהו איטליאה של יון: א"ר שמואל בר נחמני א"ר יונתן כל האומר יאשיהו חטא אינו אלא טועה שנאמר י) ויעש הישר בעיני ה' וילך בכל דרך דוד אביו אלא מה אני מקיים כ) וכמוהו לא היה לפניו מלך אשר שב וגו' ז) שכל דיין שדן מבן שמנה עד שמנה עשרה החזירן להן שמא תאמר נטל מזה ונתן לזה תלמוד לומר כ) בכל מאודו שנתן להם משלו ופליגא דרב דאמר רב אין לך גדול בבעלי תשובה יותר מיאשיהו בדורו ואחד בדורנו ומנו אבא אבוה דרבי ירמיה ח) בר אבא ואמרי לה אחא אחוה דאבא אבוה דרב ירמיה בר אבא דאמר מר רבי אבא ואחא אחי הוו אמר רב יוסף ועוד אחד בדורנו ומנו עוקבן בר נחמיה ריש גלותא והיינו ט) נתן דצוציתא אמר רב יוסף הוה יתיבנא בפירקא והוה קא מנמנם וחזאי בחילמא דקא פשט ידיה וקבליה:

הדרן עלך במה בהמה

י) וַיַּעַשׂ הַיָּשָׁר בְּעֵינֵי יְיָ וַיֵּלֶךְ בְּכָל דֶּרֶךְ דָּוִד אָבִיו וְלֹא סָר יָמִין וּשְׂמֹאול: [מלכים ב' כב, ב]

כ) וְכָמֹהוּ לֹא הָיָה לְפָנָיו מֶלֶךְ אֲשֶׁר שָׁב אֶל יְיָ בְּכָל לְבָבוֹ וּבְכָל נַפְשׁוֹ וּבְכָל מְאֹדוֹ כְּכֹל תּוֹרַת מֹשֶׁה וְאַחֲרָיו לֹא קָם כָּמֹהוּ: [מלכים ב' כג, כה]

רש"י

על עסקי נחל. ומה על נפש אחת אמרה תורה הבא עגלה ערופה בנחל נפשות הללו על אחת כמה וכמה אם גדולים חטאו קטנים מה חטאו ט): ולא עבדו ישראל עבודה זרה. שעל ידי שנחלקה המלכות העמיד ירבעם העגלים שלא יעלו ישראל ירושלים לממשלתו של רחבעם: שלמה חטא. בע"ז: כדר' נתן. דשני קרא הטו ללכת והוא לא הלך: הכא נמי דבנה. קשיא היא: אלא. מהכא תילף דלא בנה כדתניא רבי יוסי אומר כו': להר המשחה. לשון שמן דמתרגמינן משחא והוא הר הזיתים: מקיש ראשונים. מקיש את בנינו של שלמה לביעורו של יאשיהו מה יאשיהו לא עשה ביעור זה ותלו בו מן השמים לשבח הואיל וביער השאר שנעשה משמת יהושפט אף שלמה לא עשה בנין זה ותלו בו לגנות מתוך שלא מיחה בנשיו: שמש. לחטוב עצים ולשאוב מים בשכר לע"ז: ואל יכתב בו דבר זה. ללמדך שקשה התוכחה במי שבידו לימחות: מיני זמר. כלי שיר: נעץ קנה. ושרטון מדבק בו עד שנוסף והולך וגדל שרטון חול ורפש וטיט שהים גורש: כרך גדול של רומי. שהוא מיצר לישראל והוא (איטליא) של יון במסכת מגילה (דף ו:): ביום שהעמיד ירבעם את העגלים נבנה צריף אחד. באותו שרטון שגדל שם בימי שלמה. צריף כוך קטן מליידין שעושין מן קנים ומן ערבה ומאז נתוספו בתים על בתים: איטליאה. שם העיר והיא ממדינת יון וכשנטלה רומי מלכות יוונים לכדוהו ונהפך להם: יאשיהו חטא. דכתיב שב אל ה' משמע דחטא מעיקרא: מבן ח'. שישב על כסא מלכותו דכתיב בן ח' שנה וגו': עד בן י"ח. שמצא חלקיה את הספר ועיין ודקדק בתורה ובדיניה בכתב ובעל פה והבין שמא טעה בדינא: נטל מזה. ממי שנתן לו תחילה: ה"ג ואמרי לה אחא אחוה דאבא אבוה דרב ירמיה בר אבא: נתן דצוציתא. על שם ניצוץ דנורא שהמלאך פשט את ידו וקיבל תשובתו ליטנא אחרינא על שאחזו המלאך בבלורית ראשו:

הדרן עלך במה בהמה

תוספות

אלא מעתה אז יבנה יהושע כו'. הקשה הר"ר אלחנן דבחלק (סנהדרין דף מה:) מפקינן מדכתיב אז יבנה יהושע ולא כתב אז בנה מכאן לתחיית המתים מן התורה אם כן אתא לדרשה ה"נ אתא לדרשה דהכא ואומר ר"י דמ"מ פריך מדלא כתיב שבקש לבנות אלא יבנה ש"מ שרוצה לומר שבנה כההוא דיהושע דודאי בנה:

מה אחרונים לא עשו ותלה בהן כו'. לא שייך למימר הכא מקום הניחו לו אבותיו להתגדר בו כדאמר בפ"ק דחולין (דף ז. ושם:) גבי נחש נחשת שביער חזקיה דהתם לא ביערוהו אבותיו שהיו יראים לבערו לפי שעשאו משה על פי הדבור אבל הכא למה היו מניחים מלבערם: דצוציתא. אומר ר"ת דאמר במדרש שהיה נר דולק ה) על ראשו:

הדרן עלך במה בהמה

עין משפט נר מצוה

מב א טוש"ע ח"מ סי' ז' סעיף ג:

רב נסים גאון

נצא בר נצא [נצא] הא דאמרן בר נצא דכתיב (ש"א טו) ויבא שאול עד עיר (שלמה) [עמלק] וירב בנחל אמר ר' מני על עסקי נחל בשעה שאמר הקב"ה לשאול ועתה לך והכיתה את עמלק נשא שאול קל וחומר בעצמו ואמר ומה על נפש אחת אמרה תורה הבא עגלה ערופה בנחל המאבד נפשות הרבה על אחת כמה וכמה ועוד אם אדם חטא בהמה מה חטאת אם גדולים חטאו קטנים מה חטאו:

סליק פרק במה בהמה

מסורת הש"ס

א) יומא כב:, ב) [עי' תוספות מגילה כא.], ג) [בקרא כתיב המשחית וגם בע"י איתא כך ועי' פירש"י במלכים שכתב הוא הר המשחה וכיון שהזכיר את שמו ע"י ע"ז שינו שמו לגנאי עכ"ל], ד) [חולין ו: ועי' תוס' שם ז. ד"ה אלא], ה) בכ"י הגי' ואמר וכן לקמן, ו) סנהדרין כא: ע"ש, ז) ע' ברכת הזבח כריתות כה:, ח) [ועמ"ש רש"י סנהדרין לא: ד"ה לדזיו וכו' שהיה מר עוקבא בעל תשובה שנתן עינו וכו' וכשהוא יוצא לשוק היה נר דולק בראשו מן השמים ועל שם כך קרא ליה רבי נתן צוציתא וכו'], ט) [כדמפרש ביומא כב:].

גליון הש"ס

תוס' ד"ה דצוציתא וכו' על ראשו. עי' סנהדרין דף לא ע"ב ברש"י ד"ה לדזיו ליה:

ליקוטי רש"י

מריב בעל. זה מפיבושת [דה"א ט, לט]. וירב בנחל. וילחם בנחל ורבותינו אמרו על עסקי נחל רב ודן את עצמו ומה בשביל נפש אחת אמרה תורה ערוף עגלה בנחל בשביל כל הנפשות האלו לא כ"ש אם אדם חטא בהמה מה חטאת [ש"א טו, ה]. אז יבנה שלמה במה וכו'. פירשו בו חכמי ישראל שבקש לבנות ולא בנה למדנו שהיו"ד על שם המחשבה נאמרה [שמות טו, א]. צריף. כוך של ליידין שאורבין בה את העופות ועשוי ככורת שמשפעת והולכת שגגו וקירותיו אחד [סוכה יט:]. איטליאה של יון. מאיי אלישה (יחזקאל כז) מתרגמינן מנגוות איטליא [מגילה ו:]. נתן דצוציתא. ומצאתי בספר הגדה שהיה מר עוקבא בעל תשובה שנתן עיניו באשה אחת והעלה לבו טינא ונפל בחולי ואשת איש היתה לימים נצרכה ללוות ממנו ומתוך דוחקה נתרצית לו וכבש יצרו ופטרה לשלום ונתרפא וכשהיה יוצא לשוק היה נר דולק בראשו מן השמים ועל שם כך קרי ליה ר' נתן צוציתא במסכת שבת [סנהדרין לא: עי"ש].

תורה אור השלם

א) וַיְרַגֵּל בְּעַבְדְּךָ אֶל אֲדֹנִי הַמֶּלֶךְ וַאדֹנִי הַמֶּלֶךְ כְּמַלְאַךְ הָאֱלֹהִים וַעֲשֵׂה הַטּוֹב בְּעֵינֶיךָ: [שמואל ב' יט, ה]

ב) וַיֹּאמֶר לוֹ הַמֶּלֶךְ לָמָּה תְּדַבֵּר עוֹד דְּבָרֶיךָ אָמַרְתִּי אַתָּה וְצִיבָא תַּחְלְקוּ אֶת הַשָּׂדֶה: וַיֹּאמֶר מְפִיבֹשֶׁת אֶל הַמֶּלֶךְ גַּם אֶת הַכֹּל יִקָּח אַחֲרֵי אֲשֶׁר בָּא אֲדֹנִי הַמֶּלֶךְ בְּשָׁלוֹם אֶל בֵּיתוֹ: [שמואל ב' יט, ל-לא]

ג) וּבֶן יְהוֹנָתָן מְרִיב בָּעַל וּמְרִיב בַּעַל הוֹלִיד אֶת מִיכָה: [דברי הימים א' ח, לד]

ד) וַיָּבֹא שָׁאוּל עַד עִיר עֲמָלֵק וַיָּרֶב בַּנָּחַל: [שמואל א' טו, ה]

ה) וַיְהִי לְעֵת זִקְנַת שְׁלֹמֹה נָשָׁיו הִטּוּ אֶת לְבָבוֹ אַחֲרֵי אֱלֹהִים אֲחֵרִים וְלֹא הָיָה לְבָבוֹ שָׁלֵם עִם יְיָ אֱלֹהָיו כִּלְבַב דָּוִיד אָבִיו: [מלכים א' יא, ד]

ו) אָז יִבְנֶה שְׁלֹמֹה בָּמָה לִכְמוֹשׁ שִׁקֻּץ מוֹאָב בָּהָר אֲשֶׁר עַל פְּנֵי יְרוּשָׁלָיִם וּלְמֹלֶךְ שִׁקֻּץ בְּנֵי עַמּוֹן: [מלכים א' יא, ז]

ז) אָז יִבְנֶה יְהוֹשֻׁעַ מִזְבֵּחַ לַייָ אֱלֹהֵי יִשְׂרָאֵל בְּהַר עֵיבָל: [יהושע ח, ל]

ח) וְאֶת הַבָּמוֹת אֲשֶׁר עַל פְּנֵי יְרוּשָׁלַיִם אֲשֶׁר מִימִין לְהַר הַמַּשְׁחִית אֲשֶׁר בָּנָה שְׁלֹמֹה מֶלֶךְ יִשְׂרָאֵל לְעַשְׁתֹּרֶת שִׁקֻּץ צִידֹנִים וְלִכְמוֹשׁ שִׁקֻּץ מוֹאָב וּלְמִלְכֹּם תּוֹעֲבַת בְּנֵי עַמּוֹן טִמֵּא הַמֶּלֶךְ: [מלכים ב' כג, יג]

ט) וַיַּעַשׂ שְׁלֹמֹה הָרַע בְּעֵינֵי יְיָ וְלֹא מִלֵּא אַחֲרֵי יְיָ כְּדָוִד אָבִיו: [מלכים א' יא, ו]

of Shlomo's old age, that his wives turned his heart aside to go *after other gods;* וְהָכְתִיב – **and yet it is** also **written:** ,,כִּלְבַב דָּוִד אָבִיו'' – *And his heart was not perfect with Hashem his God,* ***as was the heart of David his father,*** כִּלְבַב דָּוִד אָבִיו הוּא דְּלָא הֲוָה מִיחְטָא נַמֵּי לֹא חָטָא – which implies: **It is only that [Shlomo's heart] was not like the heart of his father David;** however, **he also did not sin. – ? –**

R' Nassan resolves the contradiction:

הָכִי קָאָמַר – **[The first verse]** in essence **states thus:** ,,וַיְהִי לְעֵת זִקְנַת שְׁלֹמֹה נָשָׁיו הִטּוּ אֶת־לְבָבוֹ'' לָלֶכֶת ,,אַחֲרֵי אֱלֹהִים אֲחֵרִים'' – ***And it came to pass, at the time of Shlomo's old age, that his wives turned his heart aside*** *[to go]* ***after other gods,*** וְלֹא הָלַךְ – **but he did not** actually **go** after those gods.

The Gemara asks:

וְהָכְתִיב ,,אָז יִבְנֶה שְׁלֹמֹה בָּמָה לִכְמוֹשׁ שִׁקֻּץ מוֹאָב'' – **But it is written:**[12] ***Then Shlomo built an altar for Kemosh, the abomination*** [idol] ***of Moav.*** This seems to indicate that Shlomo did worship "other gods." – ? –

The Gemara answers:

שֶׁבִּקֵּשׁ לִבְנוֹת וְלֹא בָּנָה – The verse means **that he sought to build** such an altar, **but did not build** it.[13]

The Gemara objects:

אֶלָּא מֵעַתָּה – **But if** this is **so,** it follows that the verse, ,,אָז יִבְנֶה יְהוֹשֻׁעַ מִזְבֵּחַ לַה' '' – ***Then Joshua built an altar for Hashem,***[14] in which the word *built* is written in what appears to be the future tense (יִבְנֶה), must mean שֶׁבִּקֵּשׁ לִבְנוֹת וְלֹא בָּנָה – **that [Joshua] sought to build the** mandated altar **but did not build** it. אֶלָּא דְּבָנָה – **However,** it is certainly the case **that [Joshua] built** the altar! הָכָא נַמֵּי דְּבָנָה – **Here, too,** regarding Shlomo, it must be the case **that he** actually **built** an altar for Kemosh.[15] – ? –

The Gemara resolves the difficulty for R' Nassan:

אֶלָּא כִּדְתַנְיָא – **Rather,** from the following we can derive that Shlomo did not build an altar for idolatry, **for it was taught in a Baraisa:** רַבִּי יוֹסֵי אוֹמֵר – **R' YOSE SAYS:** ,,וְאֶת־הַבָּמוֹת אֲשֶׁר עַל־פְּנֵי יְרוּשָׁלַיִם אֲשֶׁר מִימִין לְהַר־(הַמִּשְׁחָה) [הַמַּשְׁחִית][17] אֲשֶׁר בָּנָה שְׁלֹמֹה מֶלֶךְ־יִשְׂרָאֵל לְעַשְׁתֹּרֶת שִׁקֻּץ צִידוֹנִים וגו' '' – Scripture states[16] that when King Yoshiyahu took measures to eradicate all vestiges of idolatry in his kingdom, *the king defiled* ***THE ALTARS THAT FACED JERUSALEM, WHICH WERE ON THE RIGHT SIDE OF THE MOUNT OF OIL,***[17] ***WHICH SHLOMO THE KING OF ISRAEL BUILT TO ASHTORES THE ABOMINATION OF THE ZIDONITES etc.*** אֶפְשָׁר בָּא אָסָא וְלֹא בִיעֲרָם יְהוֹשָׁפָט וְלֹא בִיעֲרָם – Now, **IS IT POSSIBLE THAT** the righteous King **ASA CAME** to power **AND DID NOT DESTROY [THESE ALTARS],** or that the righteous King **YEHOSHAFAT** came to power **AND DID NOT DESTROY THEM,** עַד שֶׁבָּא יֹאשִׁיָּה וּבִיעֲרָם – **UNTIL YOSHIYAH CAME AND DESTROYED THEM?** וַהֲלֹא כָּל עֲבוֹדָה זָרָה שֶׁבְּאֶרֶץ יִשְׂרָאֵל אָסָא וִיהוֹשָׁפָט בִּיעֲרוּם – **BUT DID ASA AND YEHOSHAFAT NOT DESTROY ALL THE IDOLATRY IN THE LAND OF ISRAEL** before Yoshiyahu ascended the throne?![18] אֶלָּא מַקִּישׁ רִאשׁוֹנִים לָאַחֲרוֹנִים – **RATHER,** our verse **COMPARES THE EARLIER ONES** [the early kings, i.e. Shlomo] **WITH THE LATER ONES** [i.e. Yoshiyahu], as follows: מָה אַחֲרוֹנִים לֹא עָשׂוּ וְתָלָה בָּהֶן לְשֶׁבַח – **JUST AS THE LATER ONES** [Yoshiyahu] **DID NOT** actually **DO** what the verse says they did, **YET [SCRIPTURE] ATTRIBUTES** the destruction of the altars **TO THEM, TO** their **PRAISE,** אַף רִאשׁוֹנִים לֹא עָשׂוּ וְתָלָה בָּהֶן לִגְנַאי – so **TOO, THE EARLIER ONES** [Shlomo] **DID NOT** actually **DO** what the verse says they did, **YET [SCRIPTURE] ATTRIBUTES** the building of the altars **TO THEM, TO** their **DISGRACE.**[19]

The Gemara asks:

וְהָכְתִיב ,,וַיַּעַשׂ שְׁלֹמֹה הָרַע בְּעֵינֵי ה' '' – **But it is written:** ***And Shlomo did evil in the eyes of Hashem.***[20]

The Gemara answers:

אֶלָּא מִפְּנֵי שֶׁהָיָה לוֹ לִמְחוֹת בְּנָשָׁיו וְלֹא מִיחָה – Indeed, Shlomo did not build the altars, **but because he should have protested against his wives,** who worshiped idols, **and he did not protest,** מַעֲלֶה עָלָיו הַכָּתוּב כְּאִילּוּ חָטָא – **Scripture regards him as if he had sinned** by building altars for idolatry.

The Gemara further discusses King Shlomo:

אָמַר רַב יְהוּדָה אָמַר שְׁמוּאֵל – **Rav Yehudah said in the name of Shmuel:** נוֹחַ לוֹ לְאוֹתוֹ צַדִּיק שֶׁיְּהֵא שַׁמָּשׁ לְדָבָר אַחֵר – **It would have been better for that righteous person to be an attendant of "something else"** [i.e. an idol][21] וְאַל יִכָּתֵב בּוֹ ,,וַיַּעַשׂ . . . הָרַע בְּעֵינֵי ה' '' – **and it would not be written of him:** ***And*** [Shlomo] ***did evil in the eyes of Hashem.***[22]

The Gemara details the idolatrous activities of one of Shlomo's wives:

אָמַר רַב יְהוּדָה אָמַר שְׁמוּאֵל – **Rav Yehudah said in the name of Shmuel:** בְּשָׁעָה שֶׁנָּשָׂא שְׁלֹמֹה אֶת בַּת פַּרְעֹה – **At the time Shlomo married Pharaoh's daughter,** הִכְנִיסָה לוֹ אֶלֶף מִינֵי זֶמֶר – **she brought in to him a thousand musical instruments,** וְאָמְרָה לוֹ כָּךְ עוֹשִׂין לַעֲבוֹדָה זָרָה פְּלוֹנִית – **and she said to him: This is how one performs** the worship **for such-and-such idol,** וְכָךְ עוֹשִׂים לַעֲבוֹדָה זָרָה פְּלוֹנִית – **and this is how one performs** the worship **for such-and-such idol,** וְלֹא מִיחָה בָּהּ – **and he did not protest against her.**

The Gemara reveals the consequences:

אָמַר רַב יְהוּדָה אָמַר שְׁמוּאֵל – **Rav Yehudah said in the name of Shmuel:** בְּשָׁעָה שֶׁנָּשָׂא שְׁלֹמֹה אֶת בַּת פַּרְעֹה – **At the time**

NOTES

12. *I Kings* 11:17.

13. The usual way to write "he built" is בָּנָה. Here Scripture states יִבְנֶה, which resembles the future construct and indicates intent rather than action (*Rashi* to *Exodus* 15:1).

14. *Joshua* 8:30. The Torah (*Deuteronomy* 27:5) commands the Jews who crossed the Jordan River into the Land of Israel to build an altar. Our verse describes how Joshua fulfilled that commandment.

15. [See *Tosafos* ד"ה אלא and see *Lashon HaZahav.*] This presents a difficulty [for R' Nassan] (*Rashi*), who said that Shlomo did not actually worship other gods.

16. *II Kings* 23:13.

17. This refers to the Mount of Olives (*Rashi*).

In Scripture the words הַר הַמַּשְׁחִית (Mt. of the Destroyer) actually appear. *Rashi* there explains that the reference is to הַר הַמִּשְׁחָה, the Mt. of Oil (i.e. of Olives), but since the verse speaks of idolatry, it modifies the name in a derogatory manner (see *Mesoras HaShas*).

18. See *I Kings* 15:9 ff and ibid. 22:41 ff.

19. The verse equates the act of building attributed to Shlomo with the act of destroying attributed to Yoshiyahu. Yoshiyahu did not destroy all the altars mentioned in the verse; however, because he demolished the ones that were built after the death of Yehoshafat, Scripture praises him as if he had dismantled them all. Similarly, Shlomo did not build the altars, but Scripture disparages him as if he had done so. As the Gemara will presently explain, Scripture censures Shlomo thus because he did not protest against his wives' building them (*Rashi*; see *Pnei Yehoshua,* who explains this Gemara differently).

20. Ibid. 11:6. The Gemara is challenging R' Yose's exegesis: How can he expound the verse in *II Kings* as teaching that Shlomo did not actually build the altars, when this verse explicitly states that he "did evil"?

21. It would have been better for Shlomo to cut firewood and draw water as a hired worker of idolaters (*Rashi*; see *Hagahos R' Elazar Moshe Horowitz*).

22. This teaches how severely one is rebuked for failing to protest a wrongdoing (*Rashi*).

עבדך א) וירגל בעבדך אל אדוני המלך ואדוני המלך כמלאך האלהים ועשה הטוב בעיניך ב) ויאמר לו המלך למה תדבר עוד דבריך אמרתי אתה וציבא תחלקו את השדה ויאמר מפיבשת אל המלך גם את הכל יקח אחרי אשר בא אדוני המלך בשלום אל ביתו אמר לו אני אמרתי מתי תבא בשלום ואתה עושה לי כך לא עליך יש לי תרעומות אלא על מי שהביאך בשלום היינו דכתיב ג) ובן יהונתן מריב בעל וכי מריב בעל שמו והלא מפיבשת שמו אלא מתוך שעשה מריבה עם בעליו יצתה בת קול ואמרה לו נצא בר נצא נצא הא דאמרן בר נצא דכתיב ד) ויבא שאול עד עיר עמלק וירב בנחל אמר רבי מני על עסקי נחל א) אמר רב יהודה אמר רב בשעה שאמר דוד למפיבשת ב) אתה וציבא תחלקו את השדה יצתה בת קול ואמרה לו רחבעם וירבעם יחלקו את המלוכה אמר רב יהודה אמר רב אילמלי ג) לא קיבל דוד לשון הרע לא נחלקה מלכות בית דוד ולא עבדו ישראל ע"ז ולא גלינו מארצנו: אמר ר' שמואל בר נחמני א"ר יונתן כל האומר שלמה חטא אינו אלא טועה שנאמר ה) ולא היה לבבו שלם עם ה' אלהיו כלבב דוד אביו הוא דלא הוה מיחטא נמי לא חטא אלא מה אני מקיים ה) ויהי לעת זקנת שלמה נשיו הטו את לבבו ההיא כרבי נתן דר' נתן רמי כתיב ויהי לעת זקנת שלמה נשיו הטו את לבבו והכתיב כלבב דוד אביו כלבב דוד אביו הוא דלא הוה מיחטא נמי לא חטא הכי קאמר ויהי לעת זקנת שלמה נשיו הטו את לבבו ללכת אחרי אלהים אחרים ולא הלך והכתיב ו) אז יבנה שלמה במה לכמוש שקוץ מואב שבקש לבנות ולא בנה אלא מעתה ז) אז יבנה יהושע מזבח לה' שבקש לבנות ולא בנה אלא דבנה הכא נמי דבנה אלא כדתניא רבי יוסי אומר ח) ואת הבמות אשר על פני ירושלים אשר מימין להר ג) המשחה אשר בנה שלמה מלך ישראל לעשתרות שקוץ צדונים וגו' ד) אפשר בא אסא ולא ביערם יהושפט ולא ביערם עד שבא יאשיה וביערם והלא כל ע"ז שבארץ ישראל אסא ויהושפט ביערום אלא מקיש ראשונים לאחרונים מה אחרונים לא עשו ותלה בהן לשבח אף ראשונים לא עשו ותלה בהן לגנאי והכתיב ט) ויעש שלמה הרע בעיני ה' אלא מפני שהיה לו למחות בנשיו ולא מיחה מעלה עליו הכתוב כאילו חטא אמר רב יהודה אמר שמואל נוח לו לאותו צדיק שיהא שמש לדבר אחר ואל יכתב בו ויעש הרע בעיני ה' ה) אמר רב יהודה אמר שמואל בשעה שנשא שלמה את בת פרעה הכניסה לו אלף מיני זמר ואמרה לו כך עושין לעבודה זרה פלונית וכך עושים לע"ז פלונית ולא מיחה בה ו) אמר רב יהודה אמר שמואל בשעה שנשא שלמה את בת פרעה ירד גבריאל ונעץ קנה בים ועלה בו שירטון ועליו נבנה כרך גדול [של רומי] במתניתא תנא אותו היום שהכניס ירבעם שני עגלי זהב אחד בבית אל ואחד בדן נבנה צריף אחד וזהו איטליאה של יון: א"ר שמואל בר נחמני א"ר יונתן כל האומר יאשיהו חטא אינו אלא טועה שנאמר י) ויעש הישר בעיני ה' וילך בכל דרך דוד אביו אלא מה אני מקיים כ) וכמוהו לא היה לפניו מלך אשר שב וגו' ז) שכל דין שדן מבן שמנה עד שמנה עשרה החזירן להן שמא תאמר נטל מזה ונתן לזה תלמוד לומר כ) בכל מאודו שנתן להם משלו ופליגא דרב דאמר רב אין לך גדול בבעלי תשובה יותר מיאשיהו בדורו ואחד בדורנו ומנו אבא אבוה דרבי ירמיה ח) בר אבא ואמרי לה אחא אחוה דאבא אבוה דרב ירמיה בר אבא דאמר מר רבי אבא ואחא אחי הוו אמר רב יוסף ועוד אחד בדורנו ומנו עוקבן בר נחמיה ריש גלותא והיינו ט) נתן דצוציתא אמר רב יוסף הוה יתיבנא בפירקא והוה קא מנמנם וחזאי בחילמא דקא פשט ידיה וקבליה:

הדרן עלך במה בהמה

י) וַיַּעַשׂ הַיָּשָׁר בְּעֵינֵי יְיָ וַיֵּלֶךְ בְּכָל דֶּרֶךְ דָּוִד אָבִיו וְלֹא סָר יָמִין וּשְׂמֹאול: [מלכים ב' כב, ב] כ) וְכָמֹהוּ לֹא הָיָה לְפָנָיו מֶלֶךְ אֲשֶׁר שָׁב אֶל יְיָ בְּכָל לְבָבוֹ וּבְכָל נַפְשׁוֹ וּבְכָל מְאֹדוֹ כְּכֹל תּוֹרַת מֹשֶׁה וְאַחֲרָיו לֹא קָם כָּמֹהוּ: [מלכים ב' כג, כה]

רש"י

על עסקי נחל. ומה על נפש אחת אמרה תורה הבא עגלה ערופה בנחל נפשות הללו על אחת כמה וכמה אם גדולים חטאו קטנים מה חטאו ט): ולא עבדו ישראל עבודה זרה. שעל ידי שנחלקה המלכות העמיד ירבעם העגלים שלא יעלו ישראל ירושלים לממשלתו של רחבעם: שלמה חטא. בע"ז: כדר' נתן. דשני קרא הטו ללכת והוא לא הלך: הכא נמי דבנה. קשיא היא: אלא. מהכא תילף דלא בנה כדתניא רבי יוסי אומר כו': להר המשחה. לשון שמן דמתרגמינן משחא והוא הר הזיתים: מקיש ראשונים. מקיש את בנינו של שלמה לביעורו של יאשיהו מה יאשיהו לא עשה ביעור זה ותלו בו מן השמים לשבח הואיל וביער השאר שנעשה משמת יהושפט אף שלמה לא עשה בנין זה ותלו בו לגנות מתוך שלא מיחה בנשיו: שמש. לחטוב עצים ולשאוב מים בשכר לע"ז: ואל יכתב בו דבר זה. ללמדך שקשה התוכחה במי שבידו לימחות: מיני זמר. כלי שיר: נעץ קנה. ושרטון מדבק בו עד שנוסף והולך וגדל שרטון חול ורפש וטיט שהים גורש: כרך גדול של רומי. שהוא מיצר לישראל והוא (איטליא) של יון במסכת מגילה (דף ו:): ביום שהעמיד ירבעם את העגלים נבנה צריף אחד. באותו שרטון שגדל שם בימי שלמה. צריף כוך קטן מליידין שעושין מן קנים ומן ערבה ומאז נתוספו בתים על בתים: איטליאה. שם העיר והיא ממדינת יון וכשנטלה רומי מלכות יוונים לכדוהו ונהפך להם: יאשיהו חטא. דכתיב שב אל ה' משמע דחטא מעיקרא: מבן ח'. שישב על כסא מלכותו דכתיב בן ח' שנה וגו': עד בן י"ח. שמצא חלקיה את הספר ועיין ודקדק בתורה ובדיניה בכתב ובעל פה והבין שמא טעה בדינא: נטל מזה. ממי שנתן לו תחילה: ה"ג ואמרי לה אחא אחוה דאבא אבוה דרב ירמיה בר אבא: נתן דצוציתא. על שם ניצוץ דנורא שהמלאך פשט את ידו וקיבל תשובתו לישנא אחרינא על שאחזו המלאך בציצית ראשו:

הדרן עלך במה בהמה

תוספות

אלא מעתה אז יבנה יהושע כו'. הקשה הר"ר אלחנן דבחלק (סנהדרין דף נא:) מפקינן מדכתיב אז יבנה יהושע ולא כתיב אז בנה מכאן לתחיית המתים מן התורה אם כן אתא לדרשה ה"נ אתא לדרשה דהכא ואומר ר"י דמ"מ פריך מדלא כתיב שבקש לבנות אלא יבנה ש"מ שרוצה לומר שבנה כההוא דיהושע דודאי בנה:

מה אחרונים לא עשו ותלה בהן כו'. לא שייך למימר הכא מקום הניחו לו אבותיו להתגדל בו כדאמר בפ"ק דחולין (דף ז. ושם:) גבי נחש נחשת שביער חזקיה דהתם לא ביערוהו אבותיו שהיו יראים לבערו לפי שעשאו משה על פי הדבור אבל הכא למה היו מניחים מלבערם: דצוציתא. אומר ר"ת דאמר במדרש שהיה נר דולק ס) על ראשו:

הדרן עלך במה בהמה

עין משפט נר מצוה

מב א טוש"ע ח"מ סי' ז' סעיף ג:

רב נסים גאון

נצא בר נצא [נצא] הא דאמרן בר נצא דכתיב (ש"א טו) ויבא שאול עד עיר (שלמה) [עמלק] וירב בנחל אמר ר' מני על עסקי נחל בשעה שאמר הקב"ה לשאול ועתה לך והכיתה את עמלק נשא שאול קל וחומר בעצמו ואמר ומה על נפש אחת אמרה תורה הבא עגלה ערופה בנחל המאבד נפשות הרבה על אחת כמה וכמה ועוד אם אדם חטא בהמה מה חטאת אם גדולים חטאו קטנים מה חטאו:

סליק פרק במה בהמה

גליון הש"ס

תוס' ד"ה דצוציתא וכו' על ראשו. ע' סנהדרין דף לא ע"ב ברש"י ד"ה לדזיו ליה:

ליקוטי רש"י

מריב בעל. זה מפיבושת [דה"א ט, לט]. וירב בנחל. וילחם בנחל ורבותינו אמרו על עסקי נחל רב ודן את עצמו ומה בשביל נפש אחת אמרה תורה ערוף עגלה בנחל בשביל כל הנפשות האלו לא כ"ש אם אדם חטא בהמה מה חטאת [ש"א טו, ה]. אז יבנה שלמה במה וכו'. פירשו בו חכמי ישראל שבקש לבנות ולא בנה למדנו שהיו"ד על שם המחשבה נאמרה [שמות טו, א]. צריף. כוך של ליידין שאורגין בה את העופות ועשוי ככוורת שמשפעת והולכת שגגו וקירותיו אחד [סוכה יט:]. איטליאה של יון. מאיי אלישה (יחזקאל כז) מתרגמינן מנגוות איטליא [מגילה ו:]. נתן דצוציתא. ומצאתי בספר הגדה שהיה מר עוקבא בעל תשובה שנתן עיניו באשה אחת והעלה לבו טינא ונפל בחולי ואשת איש היתה לימים נצרכה ללות ממנו ומתוך דוחקה נתרצית לו וכבש יצרו ופטרה לשלום ונתרפא וכשהיה יוצא לשוק היה נר דולק בראשו מן השמים ועל שם כך קרי ליה ר' נתן צוציתא במסכת שבת [סנהדרין לא: עי"ש].

מסורת הש"ס

א) יומא כב:, ב) [עי' תוספות מגילה כא.], ג) [בקרא כתיב המשחית וגם בע"י איתא כך ועי' פירש"י במלכים שכתב הוא הר המשחה וכיון שהזכיר את שמו ע"י ע"ז שינו שמו לגנאי עכ"ל], ד) [חולין ו: ועי' תוס' שם ז. ד"ה אלא], ה) בכ"י הגי' ואמר וכן לקמן, ו) סנהדרין כא: ע"ש, ז) ע' ברכת הזבח כריתות כה:, ח) [ועמ"ש רש"י סנהדרין לא: ד"ה לדזיו וכו' שהיה מר עוקבא בעל תשובה שנתן עינו וכו' וכשהוא יוצא לשוק היה נר דולק בראשו מן השמים ועל שם כך קרא ליה רבי נתן צוציתא וכו'], ט) [כדמפרש ביומא כב:].

תורה אור השלם

א) וַיְרַגֵּל בְּעַבְדְּךָ אֶל אֲדֹנִי הַמֶּלֶךְ וַאדֹנִי הַמֶּלֶךְ כְּמַלְאַךְ הָאֱלֹהִים וַעֲשֵׂה הַטּוֹב בְּעֵינֶיךָ: [שמואל ב' יט, ה]

ב) וַיֹּאמֶר לוֹ הַמֶּלֶךְ לָמָּה תְּדַבֵּר עוֹד דְּבָרֶיךָ אָמַרְתִּי אַתָּה וְצִיבָא תַּחְלְקוּ אֶת הַשָּׂדֶה: וַיֹּאמֶר מְפִיבֹשֶׁת אֶל הַמֶּלֶךְ גַּם אֶת הַכֹּל יִקָּח אַחֲרֵי אֲשֶׁר בָּא אֲדֹנִי הַמֶּלֶךְ בְּשָׁלוֹם אֶל בֵּיתוֹ: [שמואל ב' יט, ל-לא]

ג) וּבֶן יְהוֹנָתָן מְרִיב בָּעַל וּמְרִיב בַּעַל הוֹלִיד אֶת מִיכָה: [דברי הימים א' ח, לד]

ד) וַיָּבֹא שָׁאוּל עַד עִיר עֲמָלֵק וַיָּרֶב בַּנָּחַל: [שמואל א' טו, ה]

ה) וַיְהִי לְעֵת זִקְנַת שְׁלֹמֹה נָשָׁיו הִטּוּ אֶת לְבָבוֹ אַחֲרֵי אֱלֹהִים אֲחֵרִים וְלֹא הָיָה לְבָבוֹ שָׁלֵם עִם יְיָ אֱלֹהָיו כִּלְבַב דָּוִיד אָבִיו: [מלכים א' יא, ד]

ו) אָז יִבְנֶה שְׁלֹמֹה בָּמָה לִכְמוֹשׁ שִׁקֻּץ מוֹאָב בָּהָר אֲשֶׁר עַל פְּנֵי יְרוּשָׁלָיִם וּלְמֹלֶךְ שִׁקֻּץ בְּנֵי עַמּוֹן: [מלכים א' יא, ז]

ז) אָז יִבְנֶה יְהוֹשֻׁעַ מִזְבֵּחַ לַייָ אֱלֹהֵי יִשְׂרָאֵל בְּהַר עֵיבָל: [יהושע ח, ל]

ח) וְאֶת הַבָּמוֹת אֲשֶׁר עַל פְּנֵי יְרוּשָׁלַיִם אֲשֶׁר מִימִין לְהַר הַמַּשְׁחִית אֲשֶׁר בָּנָה שְׁלֹמֹה מֶלֶךְ יִשְׂרָאֵל לְעַשְׁתֹּרֶת שִׁקֻּץ צִידֹנִים וְלִכְמוֹשׁ שִׁקֻּץ מוֹאָב וּלְמִלְכֹּם תּוֹעֲבַת בְּנֵי עַמּוֹן טִמֵּא הַמֶּלֶךְ: [מלכים ב' כג, יג]

ט) וַיַּעַשׂ שְׁלֹמֹה הָרַע בְּעֵינֵי יְיָ וְלֹא מִלֵּא אַחֲרֵי יְיָ כְּדָוִד אָבִיו: [מלכים א' יא, ו]

Shlomo married Pharaoh's daughter יָרַד גַּבְרִיאֵל וְנָעַץ קָנֶה בַּיָּם – the archangel **Gavriel descended and thrust a reed-pole into the sea,** וְעָלָה בּוֹ שִׂירְטוֹן – **and a sandbank formed around it**[23] וְעָלָיו נִבְנָה כְּרַךְ גָּדוֹל [שֶׁל רוֹמִי] – **and upon it was built the great metropolis of Rome,**[24] the tormentor of Israel.

A Baraisa amplifies this theme:

בְּמַתְנִיתָא תָּנָא – **[A Tanna] taught in a Baraisa:** אוֹתוֹ הַיּוֹם שֶׁהִכְנִיס יָרָבְעָם שְׁנֵי עֶגְלֵי זָהָב – ON THAT DAY WHEN King YAROVAM INSTALLED TWO GOLDEN CALVES, אֶחָד בְּבֵית אֵל וְאֶחָד בְּדָן – ONE IN BEIS EL AND ONE IN DAN,[25] נִבְנָה צְרִיף אֶחָד וְזֶהוּ אִיטַלְיָאָה שֶׁל יָוָן – ONE HUT WAS BUILT,[26] AND THIS IS what became ITALIA OF YAVAN.[27]

The Gemara now discusses the apparent sin of King Yoshiyahu:

אָמַר רַבִּי שְׁמוּאֵל בַּר נַחְמָנִי אָמַר רַבִּי יוֹנָתָן – **R' Shmuel bar Nachmani said in the name of R' Yonasan:** כֹּל הָאוֹמֵר יֹאשִׁיָּהוּ חָטָא אֵינוֹ אֶלָּא טוֹעֶה – **Whoever says that Yoshiyahu sinned is simply mistaken,**[28] שֶׁנֶּאֱמַר ,,וַיַּעַשׂ הַיָּשָׁר בְּעֵינֵי ה׳ וַיֵּלֶךְ בְּכָל־דֶּרֶךְ דָּוִד אָבִיו'' – **for it is stated**[29] regarding him: ***He did that which was right in the eyes of Hashem, and walked in all the way of his father David,*** *and did not turn aside to the right or to the left.*

R' Yonasan continues:

אֶלָּא מָה אֲנִי מְקַיֵּים ,,וְכָמֹהוּ לֹא־הָיָה לְפָנָיו מֶלֶךְ אֲשֶׁר־שָׁב וגו׳ '' – **But how,** then, **do I uphold** the verse,[30] ***And before him there had been no one like him – a king who returned*** **etc.** [*to Hashem with all his heart and with all his soul and with all his possessions*], which implies that Yoshiyahu had previously sinned, for if not he had no need to repent?

R' Yonasan answers:

שֶׁכָּל דִּינ[נ]ִין שֶׁדָּן מִבֶּן שְׁמֹנֶה עַד שְׁמֹנֶה עֶשְׂרֵה – This verse intimates that for **all cases that [Yoshiyahu] judged from** the age of **eight**[31] **until** the **eighteenth** year of his reign, הֶחֱזִירָן לָהֶן – **he returned [the disputed monies or properties] to [the losing litigants].**[32] שֶׁמָּא תֹּאמַר נָטַל מִזֶּה וְנָתַן לָזֶה – And **lest you say** that **he took** the monetary award **from this** winning party **and gave** it **to that** losing party, תַּלְמוּד לוֹמַר ,,בְּכָל־מְאֹדוֹ'' – **Scripture says: . . .** ***with all his possessions,*** שֶׁנָּתַן לָהֶם מִשֶּׁלּוֹ – which teaches **that [Yoshiyahu] gave to [the losing parties] from his own** money.[33]

The Gemara cites a contrary opinion:

וּפְלִיגָא דְּרַב – **And [R' Yonasan] disagrees with** the opinion **of Rav,** דְּאָמַר רַב אֵין לְךָ גָּדוֹל בְּבַעֲלֵי תְשׁוּבָה יוֹתֵר מִיֹּאשִׁיָּהוּ בְּדוֹרוֹ וְאֶחָד בְּדוֹרֵנוּ – **for Rav said: You have no greater penitents than Yoshiyahu in his generation and one in our generation.**[34]

The Gemara asks:

וּמַנּוּ – **And who is he,** the great penitent of our generation?

The Gemara answers:

אַבָּא אֲבוּהַ דְּרַבִּי יִרְמְיָה בַּר אַבָּא – He is **Abba, the father of R' Yirmiyah bar Abba.** וְאָמְרֵי לַהּ אַחָא אֲחוּהַ דְּאַבָּא אֲבוּהַ דְּרַב יִרְמְיָה בַּר אַבָּא – **And some say it** as follows: He is **Acha, the brother of Abba,** who is **the father of Rav Yirmiyah bar Abba,** דְּאָמַר מַר – **for the master said:** אַבָּא וְאַחָא אַחֵי הֲווּ – **Abba and Acha were brothers.**

Another contemporary is cited for his penitence:

אָמַר רַב יוֹסֵף – **Rav Yosef said:** וְעוֹד אֶחָד בְּדוֹרֵנוּ – **And** there was **another one,** another great penitent **in our generation.**

The Gemara asks:

וּמַנּוּ – **And who is he?**

The Gemara answers:

עוּקְבָן בַּר נְחֶמְיָה רֵישׁ גָּלוּתָא – He is **Ukvan, the son of Nechemiah the Exilarch,** וְהַיְינוּ נָתָן דְּצוּצִיתָא – **and this is the**

NOTES

23. Sand, waste material and mud ejected by the sea adhered to the reed-pole, and in this manner the material accumulated and a landmass progressively grew (*Rashi*).

24. This is Italia of Yavan, the enormous Roman city described in *Megillah* 6b (*Rashi*).

Shlomo's marriage to Pharaoh's daughter was the beginning of idolatry in Jerusalem, and hence the beginning of the Temple's destruction. On the supernatural level, the angel Gavriel was given the task of destroying the Temple with fire (see *Yoma* 77a). Therefore, it was he who thrust the reed-pole into the sea, thus setting in motion the growth of Rome, which destroyed the earthly Temple (*Maharsha* to *Sanhedrin* 21b). [Although Rome did not wreak the first destruction, it did wreak the second and more enduring one.]

25. See *I Kings* 12:25 ff.

26. This hut, a little hunter's blind made of reeds and willows, was built on the very sandbar that formed in the days of Shlomo (see Gemara above); and from that time onward the construction of houses continued unabated, until a city developed (*Rashi*).

27. Italia was the name of the city, and it was located in the country called Yavan (Greece, but see *Rashash*). When the Romans usurped the Greeks' sovereignty, they captured this city and it became theirs (*Rashi*).

28. Since Scripture says that King Yoshiyahu wholeheartedly returned to Hashem (see *II Kings* 23:25 and the Gemara below), one could infer that he had previously sinned (*Rashi*).

29. *II Kings* 22:2.

30. Ibid. 23:25.

31. Yoshiyahu was eight years old when he became king (*Rashi,* based on *II Kings* 22:1).

32. When Yoshiyahu was twenty-six (in the eighteenth year of his reign), Chilkiah the High Priest discovered a Torah scroll that had been hidden in the Temple (see *II Kings* 22:8 ff). King Yoshiyahu carefully studied this scroll and its laws, both written as well as oral, and then realized that he might have erred in his previous judgments (*Rashi*; see *Maharsha*; see also *Rashash,* who deletes the word בֶּן from the heading of *Rashi's* commentary).

However, see *Tur* and *Shulchan Aruch, Choshen Mishpat* 7:3, who derive from our Gemara that a man is not allowed to act as judge until he reaches the age of eighteen. [Apparently, they understood the Gemara to be saying that Yoshiyahu returned the monies from all cases that he had judged *until he was eighteen years of age.* This is a Rabbinic requirement; on the Scriptural level even a child may serve as judge if his knowledge and intelligence are sufficient – see *Bach* there.] Even though Yoshiyahu's verdicts may have been correct, the very fact that he had served as judge before the age of eighteen was a violation of this Rabbinic enactment. Therefore, in monetary cases that he adjudicated, he made restitution to the losing party.

This was Yoshiyahu's "repentance"; however, he never committed a Biblical transgression.

33. An earlier verse (*II Kings* 23:3) states that Yoshiyahu and the people made a covenant before Hashem to follow His laws *with all the heart and with all the soul.* Our verse adds: *with all his possessions.* From this addition R' Yonasan deduced that the "return" (repentance) performed by Yoshiyahu was solely "with all his possessions," for he had not sinned with his heart or soul. The phrase, *with all his heart and with all his soul,* refers to the earlier covenant, but not to Yoshiyahu's personal repentance. Rav, who disputes R' Yonasan below, understands that the entire phrase, *with all his heart and with all his soul and with all his possessions,* refers to Yoshiyahu's repentance. Hence, he deduces that the king needed to repent not only for serving as a judge before the age of eighteen, but for other matters as well (*Maharsha*).

34. Since Rav calls Yoshiyahu one of the two greatest penitents, he implies that Yoshiyahu had sinned.

מב א טוש"ע ח"מ סי' ז' סעיף ג:

עבדך [א] וירגל בעבדך אל אדוני המלך ואדוני המלך כמלאך האלהים ועשה הטוב בעיניך [ב] ויאמר לו המלך למה תדבר עוד דבריך אמרתי אתה וציבא תחלקו את השדה ויאמר מפיבשת אל המלך גם את הכל יקח אחרי אשר בא אדוני המלך בשלום אל ביתו אמר לו אני אמרתי מתי תבא בשלום ואתה עושה לי כך לא עליך יש לי תרעומות אלא על מי שהביאך בשלום היינו דכתיב [ג] ובן יהונתן מריב בעל וכי מריב בעל שמו והלא מפיבשת שמו אלא מתוך שעשה מריבה עם בעליו יצתה בת קול ואמרה לו נצא בר נצא נצא הא דאמרן בר נצא דכתיב [ד] ויבא שאול עד עיר עמלק וירב בנחל אמר רבי מני על עסקי נחל [א] אמר רב יהודה אמר רב בשעה שאמר דוד למפיבשת [ב] אתה וציבא תחלקו את השדה יצתה בת קול ואמרה לו רחבעם וירבעם יחלקו את המלוכה אמר רב יהודה אמר רב אילמלי [ג] לא קיבל דוד לשון הרע לא נחלקה מלכות בית דוד ולא עבדו ישראל ע"ז ולא גלינו מארצנו: אמר ר' שמואל בר נחמני א"ר יונתן כל האומר שלמה חטא אינו אלא טועה שנאמר [ה] ולא היה לבבו שלם עם ה' אלהיו כלבב דוד אביו כלבב דוד אביו הוא דלא הוה מיחטא נמי לא חטא אלא מה אני מקיים [ה] ויהי לעת זקנת שלמה נשיו הטו את לבבו ההיא כרבי נתן דר' נתן רמי כתיב ויהי לעת זקנת שלמה נשיו הטו את לבבו והכתיב כלבב דוד אביו כלבב דוד אביו הוא דלא הוה מיחטא נמי לא חטא הכי קאמר ויהי לעת זקנת שלמה נשיו הטו את לבבו ללכת אחרי אלהים אחרים ולא הלך והכתיב [ו] אז יבנה שלמה במה לכמוש שקוץ מואב שבקש לבנות ולא בנה אלא מעתה [ז] אז יבנה יהושע מזבח לה' שבקש לבנות ולא בנה אלא דבנה הכא נמי דבנה אלא כדתניא רבי יוסי אומר [ח] ואת הבמות אשר על פני ירושלים אשר מימין להר [ג] המשחה אשר בנה שלמה מלך ישראל לעשתרות שקוץ צדונים וגו' [ד] אפשר בא אסא ולא ביערם יהושפט ולא ביערם עד שבא יאשיה וביערם והלא כל ע"ז שבארץ ישראל אסא ויהושפט ביערום אלא מקיש ראשונים לאחרונים מה אחרונים לא עשו ותלה בהן לשבח אף ראשונים לא עשו ותלה בהן לגנאי והכתיב [ט] ויעש שלמה הרע בעיני ה' אלא מפני שהיה לו למחות בנשיו ולא מיחה מעלה עליו הכתוב כאילו חטא אמר רב יהודה אמר שמואל נוח לו לאותו צדיק שיהא שמש לדבר אחר ואל יכתב בו ויעש הרע בעיני ה' [ה] אמר רב יהודה אמר שמואל בשעה שנשא שלמה את בת פרעה הכניסה לו אלף מיני זמר ואמרה לו כך עושין לעבודה זרה פלונית וכך עושים לע"ז פלונית ולא מיחה בה [ו] אמר רב יהודה אמר שמואל בשעה שנשא שלמה את בת פרעה ירד גבריאל ונעץ קנה בים ועלה בו שירטון ועליו נבנה כרך גדול [של רומי] במתניתא תנא אותו היום שהכנים ירבעם שני עגלי זהב אחד בבית אל ואחד בדן נבנה צריף אחד וזהו איטליאה של יון: א"ר שמואל בר נחמני א"ר יונתן כל האומר יאשיהו חטא אינו אלא טועה שנאמר [י] ויעש הישר בעיני ה' וילך בכל דרך דוד אביו אלא מה אני מקיים [כ] וכמוהו לא היה לפניו מלך אשר שב וגו' [ז] שכל דין שדן מבן שמנה עד שמנה עשרה החזירן להן שמא תאמר נטל מזה ונתן לזה תלמוד לומר [כ] בכל מאודו שנתן להם משלו ופליגא דרב דאמר רב אין לך גדול בבעלי תשובה יותר מיאשיהו בדורו ואחד בדורנו ומנו אבא אבוה דרבי ירמיה [ח] בר אבא ואמרי לה אחא אחוה דאבא אבוה דרב ירמיה בר אבא דאמר מר רבי אבא ואחא אחי הוו אמר רב יוסף ועוד אחד בדורנו ומנו עוקבן בר נחמיה ריש גלותא והיינו [ט] נתן דצוציתא אמר רב יוסף הוה יתיבנא בפירקא והוה קא מנמנם וחזאי בחילמא דקא פשט ידיה וקבליה:

הדרן עלך במה בהמה

אלא מעתה אז יבנה יהושע כו'. הקשה הר"ר אלחנן דבחלק (סנהדרין דף צא:) מפקינן מדכתיב אז יבנה יהושע ולא כתב אז בנה מכאן לתחיית המתים מן התורה אם כן אתא לדרשה ה"נ אתא לדרשה דהכא ואומר ר"י דמ"מ פריך מדלא כתיב שבקש לבנות אלא יבנה ש"מ שרוצה לומר שבנה כההוא דיהושע דודאי בנה:

מה אחרונים לא עשו ותלה בהן כו'. לא שייך למימר הכא מקום הניחו לו אבותיו להתגדר בו כדאמר בפ"ק דחולין (דף ז. ושם:) גבי נחש הנחשת שביער חזקיה דהתם לא ביערוהו אבותיו שהיו יראים לבערו לפי שעשאו משה על פי הדבור אבל הכא למה היו מניחים מלבערם: **דצוציתא.** אומר ר"ת דאמר במדרש שהיה נר דולק [ט] על ראשו:

הדרן עלך במה בהמה

על עסקי נחל. ומה על נפש אחת אמרה תורה הבא עגלה ערופה בנחל נפשות הללו על אחת כמה וכמה אם גדולים חטאו קטנים מה חטאו [ט]: ולא עבדו ישראל עבודה זרה. שעל ידי שנחלקה המלכות העמיד ירבעם העגלים שלא יעלו ישראל ירושלים לממשלתו של רחבעם: שלמה חטא. בע"ז: כדר' נתן. דשני קרא הטו ללכת והוא לא הלך: הכא נמי דבנה. קשיא היא: אלא. מהכא תילף דלא בנה כדתניא רבי יוסי אומר כו': להר המשחה. לשון שמן דמתרגמינן משחא והוא הר הזיתים: מקיש ראשונים. מקיש את בנינו של שלמה לביעורו של יאשיהו מה יאשיהו לא עשה ביעור זה ותלו בו מן השמים לשבח הואיל וביער השאר שנעשה משמת יהושפט אף שלמה לא עשה בנין זה ותלו בו לגנות מתוך שלא מיחה בנשיו: שמש. לחטוב עצים ולשאוב מים בשכר לע"ז: ואל יכתב בו דבר זה. ללמדך שקשה התוכחה במי שבידו לימחות: מיני זמר. כלי שיר: נעץ קנה. ושרטון מדבק בו עד שנוסף והולך וגדל שרטון חול ורפש וטיט שהים גורש: כרך גדול של רומי. שהוא מיצר לישראל והוא (איטליא) של יון במסכת מגילה (דף ו:): ביום שהעמיד ירבעם את העגלים נבנה צריף אחד. באותו שרטון שגדל שם בימי שלמה. צריף כוך קטן מליידין שעושין מן קנים ומן ערבה ומאז נתוספו בתים על בתים: איטליאה. שם העיר והיא ממדינת יון וכשנטלה רומי מלכות יוונים לכדוהו ונהפך להם: יאשיהו חטא. דכתיב שב אל ה' משמע דחטא מעיקרא: מבן ח'. שישב על כסא מלכותו דכתיב בן ח' שנה וגו': עד בן י"ח. שמצא חלקיה את הספר ועיין ודקדק בתורה ובדיניה בכתב ובעל פה והבין שמא טעה בדינא: נטל מזה. ממי שנתן לו תחילה: ה"ג ואמרי לה אחא אחוה דאבא אבוה דרב ירמיה בר אבא: נתן דצוציתא. על שם ניצוץ דנורא שהמלאך פשט את ידו וקיבל תשובתו ליטנא אחרינא על שאחזו המלאך בציצית ראשו:

הדרן עלך במה בהמה

רב נסים גאון

נצא בר נצא [נצא] הא דאמרן בר נצא דכתיב (ש"א טו) ויבא שאול עד עיר (שלמה) [עמלק] וירב בנחל אמר ר' מני על עסקי נחל בשעה שאמר הקב"ה לשאול ועתה לך והכיתה את עמלק נשא שאול קל וחומר בעצמו ואמר ומה על נפש אחת אמרה תורה הבא עגלה ערופה בנחל המאבד נפשות הרבה על אחת כמה וכמה ועוד אם אדם חטא בהמה מה חטאת אם גדולים חטאו קטנים מה חטאו:

סליק פרק במה בהמה

גליון הש"ס

תוס' ד"ה דצוציתא וכו' על ראשו. עי' סנהדרין דף לא ע"ב ברש"י ד"ה לדזיו ליה:

ליקוטי רש"י

מריב בעל. זה מפיבושת [דה"א ט, לט]. **וירב בנחל.** וילחם בנחל ורבותינו אמרו על עסקי נחל רב ודן את עצמו ומה בשביל נפש אחת אמרה תורה ערוף עגלה בנחל בשביל כל הנפשות האלו לא כ"ש אם אדם חטא בהמה מה חטאת [ש"א טו, ה]. **אז יבנה שלמה במה וכו'.** פירשו בו חכמי ישראל שבקש לבנות ולא בנה למדנו שהיו"ד על שם המחשבה נאמרה [שמות טו, א]. **צריף.** כוך של ציידין שאורבין בה את העופות ועשוי ככוורת שמשפעת והולכת שגגו וקירותיו אחד [סוכה יט:]. **איטליאה של יון.** מארץ אלישה (יחזקאל כז) מתרגמינן מנגוות איטליא [מגילה ו:]. **נתן דצוציתא.** ומצאתי בספר הגדה שהיה מר עוקבא בעל תשובה שנתן עיניו באשה אחת והעלה לבו טינא ונפל בחולי ואשת איש היתה לימים נצרכה ללות ממנו ומתוך דוחקה נתרצית לו וכבש יצרו ופטרה לשלום ונתרפא וכשהיה יוצא לשוק היה נר דולק בראשו מן השמים ועל שם כך קרי ליה ר' נתן צוציתא במסכת שבת [סנהדרין לא: עי"ש].

מסורת הש"ס

א) יומא כב:, ב) [עי' תוספות מגילה כא.], ג) [בקרא כתיב המשחית וגם בע"י איתא כך ועי' פירש"י במלכים שכתב הוא הר המשחה וכיון שהזכיר את שמו ע"י ע"ז שינו שמו לגנאי עכ"ל], ד) [חולין ו: ועי' תוס' שם ז. ד"ה אלא], ה) בכ"י הגי' ואמר וכן לקמן, ו) סנהדרין כא: ע"ש, ז) ע' ברכת הזבח כריתות כה:, ח) [ועמ"ש רש"י סנהדרין לא: ד"ה לדזיו וכו' שהיה מר עוקבא בעל תשובה שנתן עינו וכו' וכשהוא יוצא לשוק היה נר דולק בראשו מן השמים ועל שם כך קרא ליה רבי נתן צוציתא וכו'], ט) [כדמפרש ביומא כב:].

תורה אור השלם

א) וַיְרַגֵּל בְּעַבְדְּךָ אֶל אֲדֹנִי הַמֶּלֶךְ וַאדֹנִי הַמֶּלֶךְ כְּמַלְאַךְ הָאֱלֹהִים וַעֲשֵׂה הַטּוֹב בְּעֵינֶיךָ: [שמואל ב' יט, כח]

ב) וַיֹּאמֶר לוֹ הַמֶּלֶךְ לָמָּה תְּדַבֵּר עוֹד דְּבָרֶיךָ אָמַרְתִּי אַתָּה וְצִיבָא תַּחְלְקוּ אֶת הַשָּׂדֶה: וַיֹּאמֶר מְפִיבֹשֶׁת אֶל הַמֶּלֶךְ גַּם אֶת הַכֹּל יִקָּח אַחֲרֵי אֲשֶׁר בָּא אֲדֹנִי הַמֶּלֶךְ בְּשָׁלוֹם אֶל בֵּיתוֹ: [שמואל ב' יט, ל-לא]

ג) וּבֶן יְהוֹנָתָן מְרִיב בָּעַל וּמְרִיב בַּעַל הוֹלִיד אֶת מִיכָה: [דברי הימים א' ח, לד]

ד) וַיָּבֹא שָׁאוּל עַד עִיר עֲמָלֵק וַיָּרֶב בַּנָּחַל: [שמואל א' טו, ה]

ה) וַיְהִי לְעֵת זִקְנַת שְׁלֹמֹה נָשָׁיו הִטּוּ אֶת לְבָבוֹ אַחֲרֵי אֱלֹהִים אֲחֵרִים וְלֹא הָיָה לְבָבוֹ שָׁלֵם עִם יְיָ אֱלֹהָיו כִּלְבַב דָּוִיד אָבִיו: [מלכים א' יא, ד]

ו) אָז יִבְנֶה שְׁלֹמֹה בָּמָה לִכְמוֹשׁ שִׁקֻּץ מוֹאָב בָּהָר אֲשֶׁר עַל פְּנֵי יְרוּשָׁלָיִם וּלְמֹלֶךְ שִׁקֻּץ בְּנֵי עַמּוֹן: [מלכים א' יא, ז]

ז) אָז יִבְנֶה יְהוֹשֻׁעַ מִזְבֵּחַ לַייָ אֱלֹהֵי יִשְׂרָאֵל בְּהַר עֵיבָל: [יהושע ח, ל]

ח) וְאֶת הַבָּמוֹת אֲשֶׁר עַל פְּנֵי יְרוּשָׁלַיִם אֲשֶׁר מִימִין לְהַר הַמַּשְׁחִית אֲשֶׁר בָּנָה שְׁלֹמֹה מֶלֶךְ יִשְׂרָאֵל לְעַשְׁתֹּרֶת שִׁקֻּץ צִידֹנִים וְלִכְמוֹשׁ שִׁקֻּץ מוֹאָב וּלְמִלְכֹּם תּוֹעֲבַת בְּנֵי עַמּוֹן טִמֵּא הַמֶּלֶךְ: [מלכים ב' כג, יג]

ט) וַיַּעַשׂ שְׁלֹמֹה הָרַע בְּעֵינֵי יְיָ וְלֹא מִלֵּא אַחֲרֵי יְיָ כְּדָוִד אָבִיו: [מלכים א' יא, ו]

י) וַיַּעַשׂ הַיָּשָׁר בְּעֵינֵי יְיָ וַיֵּלֶךְ בְּכָל דֶּרֶךְ דָּוִד אָבִיו וְלֹא סָר יָמִין וּשְׂמֹאול: [מלכים ב' כב, ב]

כ) וְכָמֹהוּ לֹא הָיָה לְפָנָיו מֶלֶךְ אֲשֶׁר שָׁב אֶל יְיָ בְּכָל לְבָבוֹ וּבְכָל נַפְשׁוֹ וּבְכָל מְאֹדוֹ כְּכֹל תּוֹרַת מֹשֶׁה וְאַחֲרָיו לֹא קָם כָּמֹהוּ: [מלכים ב' כג, כה]

very one known as **Nassan of Tzutzisa.**[35] **אָמַר רַב יוֹסֵף – Rav Yosef said: הֲוָה יָתִיבְנָא בְּפִירְקָא וַהֲוָה קָא מְנַמְנֵם – I was sitting in a** talmud **lecture and was dozing off, וַחֲזַאי בְּחֶילְמָא דְּקָא פָּשֵׁט יְדֵיהּ וְקַבְּלֵיהּ – and I saw in a dream that [an angel] stretched forth its hand and accepted [Nassan's repentance].**

הדרן עלך במה בהמה

WE SHALL RETURN TO YOU, BAMEH BEHEIMAH

NOTES

35. The name Tzutzisa alludes to the sparks (*nitzutzin*) of fire that shot out when the angel in Rav Yosef's dream [mentioned by the Gemara below] stretched forth its hand and accepted Nassan's repentance (*Rashi*); or to a light that shone upon Nassan from heaven whenever he walked in the street (*Rashi* to *Sanhedrin* 31b). Alternatively, the name refers to Nassan's sidelocks, the *tzitzis* of his head (ציצית ראשו, as in *Ezekiel* 8:3), inasmuch as the angel in the dream grasped his sidelocks [when accepting Nassan's repentance, figuratively bringing him closer to God] (*Rashi*).

Chapter Six

Introduction

As was discussed in the first chapter of this tractate, transferring objects on the Sabbath, either from a private domain to a public domain, or from a public domain to a private domain, or for a distance of four cubits within a public domain, is prohibited by the Torah and is the thirty-ninth *melachah* enumerated in the mishnah (73a). This prohibition applies only to objects being transferred from one domain to another, not to items of apparel worn by a person going from one domain to the other.[1]

Not all items worn by a person are considered apparel. The item must serve one of three functions: (a) to clothe, i.e. to cover the person's body, e.g. shirt, pants, dress; (b) to protect one's body from elements (snow, rain, cold, heat) or from injury, e.g. winter coat, raincoat, shoes, boots;[2] (c) to ornament the person, e.g. necktie, jewelry. [Additionally, any item which helps fasten or otherwise abet the wearing of one of these three types of garments, is also considered an item of apparel; e.g. a belt or tie clip.] Any item which does not serve one of these three functions, e.g. a key, may not be taken from domain to domain even if it is fastened to one's garments [unless it also assists in one of these three functions] (see *Shulchan Aruch* 301:11).

This is the Torah law. The Rabbis, however, noticed that people occasionally took off certain items while in the public domain for various reasons, and then forgetfully continued walking while still carrying those items (rather than putting them on again). To prevent inadvertent desecration of the Sabbath (by carrying four *amos* in a public domain), the Rabbis deemed it necessary to prohibit wearing, when going out, those ornaments or accessories which one might normally take off in the public domain. This chapter discusses various accessories worn by men and women, and details the Biblical or Rabbinic prohibitions that pertain to the wearing of some of these items.

NOTES

1. Needless to say, only items of apparel actually being worn are exempted from this prohibition. One who *carries* his clothing is just as liable as one who carries any other object.

2. An item whose sole purpose is to protect one's *clothing* from damage or dirt is not considered apparel and may not be worn from one domain to another as this is tantamount to carrying the item. However, an article which is generally worn to protect a *person*, e.g., a raincoat, may be worn even when the intention is only to protect one's clothing. Only an item never worn except to protect one's clothing is forbidden for such a purpose (see *Shulchan Aruch* 301:13,14).

Chapter Six

Mishnah Having dealt in the previous chapter with those items that animals may go out with on the Sabbath, the Mishnah turns its attention to the ornaments that may be worn by people on the Sabbath:[1]

בַּמֶּה אִשָּׁה יוֹצְאָה – **With what** accessories **may a woman go outside** on the Sabbath וּבַמָּה אֵינָהּ יוֹצְאָה – **and with what** accessories **may she not go outside** on the Sabbath?[2] לֹא תֵצֵא אִשָּׁה – **A woman may not go out** לֹא בְחוּטֵי צֶמֶר – **either with woolen strands,** וְלֹא בְחוּטֵי פִשְׁתָּן – **linen strands,** וְלֹא בִרְצוּעוֹת שֶׁבְּרֹאשָׁהּ – **or straps that are on her head;**[3] וְלֹא תִטְבּוֹל בָּהֶן עַד שֶׁתְּרַפֵּם – **and she may not immerse herself** in a *mikveh* **while wearing them, until she loosens them.**[4] וְלֹא בְטוֹטֶפֶת וְלֹא בְסַרְבִּיטִין – **And** she may **not** go out **with a frontlet or with head bangles,**[5] בִּזְמַן שֶׁאֵינָן תְּפוּרִים – **as long as they are not sewn** to her hat.[6] וְלֹא בְכָבוּל לִרְשׁוּת הָרַבִּים – **And** she may **not** go out **with a woolen cap**[7] **into the public domain.**[8] וְלֹא בְעִיר שֶׁל זָהָב – **Nor** may she go out **with a "city of gold";**[9] וְלֹא בְקַטְלָא – **nor with a** ***katla;***[10] וְלֹא בִנְזָמִים – **nor with nose rings;**[11]

NOTES

1. The preceding chapter, which discusses what gear animals may wear outside on the Sabbath, was taught before this chapter, which deals with people's accessories, because it was common in agricultural societies for animals to go out earlier in the morning than most people (*Tiferes Yisrael*). [This follows the observation of *Tosafos* (to 2a ד״ה יציאות השבת) that the early chapters of our tractate are arranged in chronological sequence, beginning with things forbidden on Friday afternoon in preparation for the Sabbath and moving on to the laws governing the Sabbath day itself.] Alternatively, the laws concerning the gear of animals are fewer and less complex, and also less severe. Therefore, they are dealt with first (*Meleches Shlomo,* beginning of ch. 5; *Sfas Emes* here).

2. The Mishnah speaks of accessories worn as ornaments (e.g. jewelry), not those that are carried [such as a purse or handbag]. Thus, there is certainly no Biblical prohibition to go out while wearing them. The Rabbis, however, prohibited wearing certain accessories in the street on the Sabbath out of concern that a woman might remove one of them while outside in order to show it to a friend, and unwittingly carry it four *amos* in the *reshus harabim* [which *is* Biblically prohibited] (*Rashi,* from Gemara below, 59b). [Similarly, there is concern that she might carry the article she removed into her house and thus transgress the prohibition against transferring from domain to domain; the Gemara below, however, mentions the transgression that is more likely to occur (see *Tosafos* to *Rosh Hashanah* 29b ד״ה שמא).] This decree also applies to accessories that might be removed for other reasons, as the Gemara will explain below.

[The precise parameters of the prohibition to "go out" will be discussed below – see note 8.]

3. *Rashi* explains that all of the three cases taught in the Mishnah – woolen strands, linen strands, and straps – refer to ties that are woven into the braids of the woman's hair (see also *Tos. HaRid*). *Tosafos, Rosh, Ramban,* and others, however, understand the Mishnah to be referring only to accessories that are tied *around* the hair; strands that are woven into the braids, however, may be worn outside on the Sabbath. This dispute will be discussed further below (see note 20).

The Gemara will explain why these accessories may not be worn outside on the Sabbath (*Rashi*).

4. Immersion in a *mikveh* is not valid unless the water of the *mikveh* comes into contact with the entire body of the person who is immersing (see *Eruvin* 4b, where the source for this law is derived). Any object that forms a barrier between the water and a part of the body thus invalidates the immersion (see below, note 16). [Such a barrier is termed a חֲצִיצָה, *chatzitzah* (literally: interposition).] Accordingly, the Mishnah rules that if a woman is wearing one of the hair ties mentioned here, and she wishes to immerse herself in a *mikveh* to purify herself from *tumah,* she must first loosen the tie so that the water can penetrate between the strands and her hair (*Rashi*). [This law applies to *any* immersion, whether it is performed on the Sabbath or on a weekday. The Gemara will explain why this law is stated in our Mishnah.]

5. The Gemara below (57b) describes these two somewhat similar ornaments (*Rashi*).

6. As explained in note 2, the Rabbis prohibited wearing ornaments because of the concern that a woman might remove them once outside to show to a friend. This decree, therefore, applies only to those items that a woman might conceivably remove in the street. Accordingly, frontlets and head bangles are prohibited only if they are not attached to the hat that covers her hair; if they are attached, however, they may be worn, for the woman cannot remove them without removing her hat as well – and she would not uncover her hair in public (*Rashi*). [Some authorities rule that this permit applies only to a married woman, who may not go out in public with uncovered hair; a single girl, however, who may uncover her hair in public, may not go out with these ornaments even if they are attached to her hat (see *Rama, Orach Chaim* 303:2).]

7. This was a loosely woven cap worn under the hat; it projected slightly from beneath the hat, and was worn as an ornament (see *Rashi* to 57b ד״ה אבל, and note 22 there; see also *Orach Chaim* 303:3).

[Our translation of כָּבוּל, *kavul,* as a woolen cap reflects the apparent conclusion of the Gemara on 58a; it is also the explanation found in *Shulchan Aruch* (ibid.). However, another interpretation is advanced by the Gemara on 57b.]

8. The Mishnah states that a *kavul* may not be worn *in a public domain,* which indicates that it *may* be worn outside the house, e.g. in a courtyard [even if an *eruv* has not been made to permit carrying between the houses and the courtyard – see *Shaar HaTziyun* 303:53]. However, with respect to the other adornments, the Mishnah simply states that a woman may not go out wearing them; these ornaments may not even be worn in a courtyard, for the Sages were concerned that a woman wearing them in a courtyard would unwittingly carry them into the public domain, where she might remove them and then carry them four *amos.* In the case of a *kavul,* however, the Sages were more lenient, and they allowed a woman to wear the *kavul* in a courtyard, for they felt that if they would prohibit the wearing of *all* adornments outside on the Sabbath, women might appear unattractive in the eyes of their husbands on the Sabbath [see Gemara below, 64b] (*Rashi*). [*Rashi* mentions that the decree forbidding the wearing of these ornaments is a *single* decree – i.e. the Sages did not merely forbid the wearing of ornaments *outside* the home due to the possibility that a woman might come to carry an adornment in the public domain; rather, they decreed that the ornaments should not be worn *at all* (see *Dibros Moshe* 53:1 at length – see also *Rashi* to 64b ד״ה אסור). This explains why the prohibition to wear these ornaments is not considered a Rabbinic decree enacted as a safeguard to another Rabbinic decree [גְּזֵירָה לִגְזֵירָה] (see *Ritva MHK* ed.).] Many Rishonim, however, are of the opinion that the Sages only decreed that the ornaments should not be worn *outside* the home; they did not prohibit women from wearing them (see *Ramban, Rashba, Ritva* et al. below, 64b, for the various positions; see also *Rambam, Hil. Shabbos* 19:8, and *Beur Halachah* to 303:18; and see below, 64b note 26).

9. This was a gold ornament engraved with a likeness of the city of Jerusalem (see *Rashi* and Gemara 59a). *Rashi* writes that the ornament was a type of clasp; *Tosafos* to 59a ד״ה ולא explain that it was a tiara. See also below, 59b note 1.

10. The Gemara below (59b) explains that this was an ornament that was worn tightly around the neck; see below, 57b notes 1 and 3, and 59b note 38, where this is discussed further. [According to some, the name derives from the Aramaic word קָטַל, *kill* – i.e., a choker (see *Rav* to *Keilim* 11:8 and *Aruch* ע׳ קטל). Others trace it to a Latin root (*Mussaf HeAruch* ibid.).]

11. Earrings, however, may be worn outside on the Sabbath, for the ears were usually covered by the bands [that encircled the hair], making it difficult to remove the earrings. The Sages were therefore not concerned that a woman might remove her earrings in the street to show to a friend (*Rashi* to 59b ד״ה נזמי האף).

א) **במה** א אשה יוצאה ובמה אינה יוצאה לא תצא אשה לא בחוטי צמר ולא בחוטי פשתן ולא ברצועות שבראשה ולא תטבול בהן עד שתרפם ולא בטוטפת ולא בסרביטין בזמן שאינן תפורים ולא בכבול לרה"ר ולא ג) בעיר של זהב ולא בקטלא ולא בנזמים ב ולא בטבעת שאין עליה חותם ולא במחט שאינה נקובה ואם יצאת אינה חייבת חטאת: **גמ'** טבילה מאן דכר שמה אמר רב נחמן בר יצחק אמר רבה בר אבוה מה טעם קאמר מה טעם לא תצא אשה לא בחוטי צמר ולא בחוטי פשתן מפני שאמרו חכמים בחול לא תטבול בהן עד שתרפם וכיון דבחול לא תטבול בהן עד שתרפם בשבת לא תצא דילמא מיתרמי לה טבילה של מצוה ושריא להו ואתי לאתויינהו ד' אמות ברה"ר בעא מיניה רב כהנא מרב ° תיכי חלילתא מאי א"ל אריג קאמרת כל שהוא אריג לא גזרו איתמר נמי ג) אמר רב הונא בריה דרב יהושע ג כל שהוא אריג לא גזרו ואיכא דאמרי אמר רב הונא בריה דרב יהושע חזינא לאחוותי דלא קפדן עלייהו מאי איכא בין הך לישנא ובין הך לישנא איכא בינייהו דטניפן להך לישנא דאמר כל שהוא אריג לא גזרו הני נמי ארוג ולהך לישנא דאמרת משום קפידא ד כיון דטניפא מקפד קפדא עלייהו ד) תנן התם ואלו חוצצין באדם חוטי צמר וחוטי פשתן והרצועות שבראשי הבנות ר' יהודה אומר של צמר ושל שער אין חוצצין מפני שהמים באין בהן אמר רב הונא וכולן בראשי הבנות שנינו מתקיף לה רב יוסף למעוטי מאי אילימא למעוטי דצואר ודמאי אילימא למעוטי דצמר השתא רך על גבי קשה חוצץ רך על גבי רך מיבעיא ואלא למעוטי דחוטי פשתן השתא קשה על גבי קשה חוצץ קשה על גבי רך מיבעיא אלא אמר רב יוסף היינו טעמא דרב הונא ה לפי שאין אשה חונקת את עצמה איתיביה אביי הבנות יוצאות בחוטין שבאזניהן אבל לא בחבקין שבצואריהן ואי אמרת אין אשה חונקת עצמה חבקין שבצואריהן אמאי לא י אמר רבינא הכא

במה אשה יוצאה. דהוי תכשיט ולא משוי ואיכא דהוי תכשיט וגזור ביה רבנן דילמא שלפא ומחויא לחברתה חשיבותו ודילמא אתי לאיתויי ד' אמות: **לא בחוטי צמר ופשתן ורצועה שבראשה.** שקולעת בהן שערה: **שבראשה.** אכולהו קאי ובגמ' מפרש טעמא: **ולא תטבול בהן.** משום חצילה: **עד שתרפם.** שתתירם קצת שיהיו רפויין ויכנסו המים ביניהם לשער: **טוטפת וסרביטין.** מפרש בגמרא ותשובין הן וחיישינן דילמא שלפא ומחויא לחברתה: **בזמן שאין תפורין.** עם השבכה שקורין שקופיי"א אבל תפורין ליכא למיחש לאחויי שאינה נוטלת השבכה מראשה ברה"ר שתגלה כל שערה: **כבול.** מפרש בגמ': **לרה"ר.** אבל לחצר שרי וכל הנזכרים למעלה אסורים אף לחצר שמא תרגילם ברה"ר ותלא גזירה היא דגזור בהם שלא תתקשט בהם בשבת כלל ובכבול התירו כדמפרש לקמן בפרקין (דף סד:) שלא לאסור את כל תכשיטיה ותתגנה על בעלה: **עיר של זהב.** כמין נושקא ומציירין בה כמין עיר: **קטלא.** מפרש בגמרא (לקמן דף נט:): **חותם.** צורה לחתום בה איגרת או כל דבר סגור: **שאינה נקובה.** כגון אישפיגל"א: **ואם יצאת אינה חייבת חטאת.** דכולהו תכשיטין נינהו ורבנן הוא דגזור בהו דילמא שלפא ומחויא: **גמ' טבילה מאן דכר שמה.** מה ענין טבילה אצל הלכות שבת: **ושריא להו.** ומתרת אותם לטבול בשבת שעל הטבילה לא גזרו כדאמרינן במסכת ביצה (דף יח.) אדם נראה כמיקר ואין נראה כמתקן עצמו: **תיכי חלילתא.** שרשרות של חוטין חלולות ועגולות: **מהו.** לקלוע בהן שערה ולצאת בשבת שאינה יכולה למותחן ולדוחקן על השער בחזקה והמים נכנסין בה ומיבעיא ליה מי הוי חצילה ולא תצא בהן בשבת משום גזירת טבילת מצוה או לא הוי חצילה: **כל שהוא אריג לא גזרו.** לצאת בו בשבת דלענין חצילה לא חייץ דלא מצי לאהדוקי שפיר: **לאחוותי דלא קפדן עלייהו.** ליטלן מראשן כשהן רוחצות בחמין אלמא עיילי בהו מיא שפיר אפילו להנאת רחיצה וכיון שכן לענין טבילה נמי לא צריכין להתירן ומותר לצאת בהן בשבת דהא אי מתרמי טבילה לא שרו להו לא משום חצילה ולא משום קפידא: **דמיטנפי.** שנטנפו הנך תיכי בטיט: **הא נמי אריג הוא.** והא קאמר לא גזרו כלל לצאת ולהאי לישנא דלא קפדי משמע דאי קפדי לנטלן מראשן כשהן רוחצות אסור לצאת בהן בשבת ואע"ג דלענין איהדוקי לא חיילי ומותרות לטבול בהן הלכך הני כיון דמיטנפי מקפד קפדן שלא להיות בראשן בשעת טבילתן מפני שהמים ממחין את הטיט ומלכלך בשרן בעלייתן מן הטבילה ואע"ג דחצילה לא הוי דהא עיילי בהו מיא מיהו כיון דשקלי לה משום טינוף אתי לאיתויינהו ואסור לצאת בהן וללישנא קמא לא גזרו אלא במידי דחייץ לטבילה ורבותי מפרשין הך קפידא לענין חצילה כדקי"ל רובו ומקפיד עליו חוצץ (עירובין דף ד:) וקשיא לי בגוה טובא חדא דכי איתמר ההוא במידי דמיהדק איתמר ואשמעינן דאע"ג דלא עיילי ביה מיא כיון דלא קפיד עליה חשיב כגופיה ובטל לגבי שערו אבל במידי דלא מיהדק ועיילי ביה מיא מאי חוצץ איכא למימר הא לאו חוצץ הוא ואי אתית למימר דההוא חוצץ דהתם לא דק בלישניה ומיהו כל מידי דקפיד עלייהו אסור היכי אמרינן הכא האי נמי אריג הוא ומותר כיון דפשיטא לן דהיכא דמיטנפי מקפד קפדן על כרחיך חייץ דהא רב הונא בריה דרב יהושע אהלכה למשה מסיני לא אתא לאיפלוגי: **ואלו חוצצין באדם.** משום דתני התם אלו חוצצין בכלים תני לענין טבילת אדם ואלו חוצצין באדם: **של צמר ושל שער אין חוצצין.** דלא מיהדק על גבי שער: **הבנות.** קטנות. אורחא דמילתא נקט: **וכולן בראשי הבנות שנינו.** לא תימא שבראשי הבנות ארצועות לחודייהו קאי אלא אחוטין נמי קאי: **למעוטי מאי.** אשמעינן רב הונא דחוטין נמי בראשי הבנות שנינו: **אילימא למעוטי.** חוטין הקשורין בצוארן דלא חיילי: **ודמאי.** הי חוטין אתא למעוטי דלא חיילי בצואר: למר קרוי רך לגבי פשתן ולגבי שער: **על גבי קשה.** שער: **ע"ג רך.** בשר: **מיבעיא.** בתמיה הא ודאי על גבי רך טפי מיהדק: **לפי שאין אשה חונקת עצמה.** להדק חוטין בצוארה וקושרתן בריוח שיהו רפין: **בחוטין שבאזנידם.** שנותנין שם שלא יסתם הנקב: **חבקין.** ענקי רצועות שאינן מוזהבות רחבות דלאו לתכשיט עבידן דומיא דחוטין שבאזניהן: **חבקין.** לשון קילקלי וחבק (לקמן דף סד.) לינגל"א לאסור בו סוס:
בקטלא

במה אשה כו' לא בחוטי צמר. מפרש בגמ' משום דילמא מיתרמי לה טבילה של מצוה ושרי להו ואתי לאתויינהו ארבע אמות ברה"ר אומר ר"י דהיינו דוקא בחוטין שאינן נתונין בקליעת השער אבל חוטין הנתונין בקליעת השער יוצאה בהן דבהנהו ליכא למיגזר דילמא שריא להו כדתנן בהמצניע (לקמן דף צד:) דאיכא לכל הפחות איסור שבות בגודלת וסברא הוא דכי היכי דיש איסור בעשיית קליעה ה"נ יש איסור בסתירת קליעה וא"ת מהאי טעמא תהא אשה אסורה לצאת בטלית דהא ודאי שריא לה בשעת טבילה וניחוש דילמא אתי לאתויי וי"ל דבדברים שהם עיקר מלבוש ליכא למיגזר דאפילו בחול אין דרך ללכת כלל ממקומו עד שילבישם אלא דוקא בדברים קטנים יש לחוש שאין מקפיד אם אינם עליו ורגילות הוא בחול כשמתירן פעמים נושאן בידו עד ביתו ונראה לר"י דדוקא בדברים שרגילות להסירן כדי להראותן או משום חצילה או משום קפידא גזרו שלא לצאת דשמא כשיסיר ישכח שהוא שבת ואתי לאתויי אבל דברים שמותר לצאת בהן שאין רגילות להסירן מותר לקשור ולהתיר ברה"ר דליכא למיחש למידי דאם יהא זכור שבת בשעת התרה לא אתי לאתויי ואם לא יהיה זכור שבת אפילו נאסר להתיר ולהסיר לא יועיל וכ"מ לקמן (דף סא.) דקתני בברייתא וקושר ומתיר קמיע אפילו ברה"ר והא דאיצטריך התם לאשמעי' דשרי אע"פ שכל דבר מותר להסיר כדפרישית איצטריך לאשמעינן דלא אסרינן משום דמיחזי דקושרו עליו שלא לרפואה ומתכוין להוציא כי היכי דאסור בפילפל וגרגיר מלח לכתחילה לתת בפה בשבת או להחזיר אלא כמלבוש גמור חשיב מחמת הרפואה:
השתא רך על גבי קשה חוצץ כו'. וא"ת דילמא רב הונא נקט וכולן בראשי הבנות לרבותא דאפילו בראשי הבנות דהוי רך ע"ג קשה חוצץ ואור"י דבלאו רב הונא הוה ידעינן דבכל מקום חוצצין אפילו בראש אלא ודאי למעוטי שום דבר אתא: **השתא** קשה ע"ג קשה חוצץ. סבר הש"ס דקשה ע"ג רך חייץ טפי מקשה ע"ג קשה ורך ע"ג קשה לא חייץ כקשה ע"ג קשה דהא לר' יהודה חוטי למר אין חוצצין דהוי רך על גבי קשה וחוטי פשתן דהוי קשה ע"ג קשה חוצצין וחוטי שיער דהוי נמי קשה על גבי קשה לכ"ע אין חוצצין אף על פי שחוטי פשתן חוצצין לכולי עלמא: **אלא** א"ר יוסף. לפי שרב יוסף בעצמו מקשה שייך לומר אלא:
הכא

א) [נדרים ב: מיר ב.], ב) [עי' תוס' לקמן נט. ד"ה ולא], ג) לקמן נח., ד) מקוואות פ"ט מ"א.

גליון הש"ס
גמ' תיכי חלילתא מאי. עי' זבחים דף לד ע"א תוס' ד"ה מקנחת:

ליקוטי רש"י
בקטלא. מוסטניל"א והוא בגד שיש לו שנצים כעין מכנסים ומכנסת בו רצועה רחבה וקושרת סביב צוארה והבגד תלוי על לבה והוא חשוב ומצוייר בזהב ויש מפרשים כמין חצי עגול עשוי כמין כלבוס ואוחזת בו מפתחי חלוקה והפגם בולע צוארה והוא של זהב [רש"י לקמן נט:]. **בגד חשוב** לתלות בצוארה כנגד לבה שלא יפול מה שהיא אוכלת על בגדיה ויש לו מקום שנצים כעין שעושים למכנסים ותוחב בו רצועה רחבה ומוללתו סביב הרצועה שהבגד רחב הרבה וקושרת הרצועה סביב צוארה [לקמן ע"ב ע"ש עוד ובתוס' שם]. **ולא במחט שאינה נקובה.** לענין הוצאת שבת יש חילוק בין נקובה לשאינו נקובה דנקובה קתני חייב חטאת ובשאינה נקובה כגון אישפיגל"א שהיא תכשיט קתני אינו חייב חטאת בפרק במה אשה (שבת נז:) [לעיל נב:]. **בחוטין שבאזניהן.** הבנות קטנות שמנקבות אזניהם ואין עושין נזמים עד שיגדלו ונותנין חוטין או קסמים באזניהם שלא יסתמו אזניהם [רש"י לקמן סה.].

עין משפט נר מצוה
א א מיי' פי"ט מהל' שבת הל' ו' ומיי' פ"ב מהל' מקוואות הל' ה סמג לאוין סה וסמג עשין רמח טוש"ע א"ח סי' שג סעיף א וטוש"ע י"ד סי' קלח סעיף ב:
ב ב מיי' פי"ט מהל' שבת הלכה ד' טוש"ע א"ח סי' שג סעיף י וסעיף יח:
ג ג ד מיי' שם הלכה ט טוש"ע א"ח סי' שג סעיף א וטוש"ע י"ד סי' קלח סעיף ג:
ד ה ו מיי' שם הלכה ז י טוש"ע א"ח שם סעיף ב וטוש"ע י"ד שם סעיף ב:

רבינו חננאל
במה אשה יוצאה ובמה אינה יוצאה. לא תצא אשה בחוטי כו'. אוקמה רב נחמן גזירה שמא תזדמן לה טבילה של מצוה ומשום שחוצצת מתרתן ומהלכת בהן ד' אמות ברה"ר. אבל תיכי חלילתא לא גזרו בהו רבנן דהא אחוותיה דרב הונא בריה דר' יהושע הוו טבלי בדמחתן הני תיכי חלילתא בראשיהן ולא הוו קפדי וכיון דלא הוו קפדי שרו. וה"מ תיכי חלילתא אבל תיכי טמימתא לא דחוצצות ואסיק' דחוטי שיער אינן חוצצין ואפילו הן קשורין בראש הבנות ואע"פ שהראש קשה הוא המים נכנסין בשיער ואין חוצצין אבל חוטי צמר וחוטי פשתן בראש הבנות חוצצין וכ"ש אם הן קשורין בצואר שמשתקעין בבשר ואין המים באין תחתיהן. ולפיכך חוצצין. כיוצא בהן החבקין שבצוארי הבנות ואוקימנא

וְלֹא בְּטַבַּעַת שֶׁאֵין עָלֶיהָ חוֹתָם – nor with a ring that has no signet;[12] **וְלֹא בְּמַחַט שֶׁאֵינָהּ נְקוּבָה – nor with a needle that is not pierced.**[13] **וְאִם יָצְאת – But if she went out** wearing any of these on the Sabbath, **אֵינָהּ חַיֶּיבֶת חַטָּאת – she is not liable to a *chatas*** offering.[14]

Gemara The Gemara notes that the Mishnah's ruling concerning immersion appears to be unrelated to the Mishnah's topic, and questions its inclusion in the Mishnah: **טְבִילָה מַאן דְּכַר שְׁמָהּ – Who made mention of immersion**[15] that the Tanna saw fit to state that a woman may not immerse herself in a *mikveh* before loosening any woolen or linen strands or straps in her hair? This ruling seemingly has nothing to do with the prohibition against going out while wearing such ornaments on the Sabbath. Why, then, did the Tanna include it in our Mishnah?

The Gemara answers:

אָמַר רַב נַחְמָן בַּר יִצְחָק אָמַר רַבָּה בַּר אֲבוּהּ – Rav Nachman bar Yitzchak said in the name of Rabbah bar Avuha: מַה טַּעַם קָאָמַר – [The Mishnah] is saying this law of immersion in the sense of **"what is the reason?" מַה טַּעַם לֹא תֵצֵא אִשָּׁה לֹא בְּחוּטֵי צֶמֶר וְלֹא בְּחוּטֵי פִשְׁתָּן** – That is, the Mishnah wishes to explain: **What is the reason that a woman may not go out either with woolen strands nor with linen strands** etc.? **מִפְּנֵי שֶׁאָמְרוּ חֲכָמִים – For the Sages have said בְּחוֹל לֹא תִטְבּוֹל בָּהֶן עַד שֶׁתְּרַפֵּם** – that even **on weekdays she may not immerse herself** in a *mikveh* **while wearing them until she loosens them;**[16] **וְכֵיוָן דִּבְחוֹל לֹא תִטְבּוֹל בָּהֶן עַד שֶׁתְּרַפֵּם – and since** the law is that even **on weekdays she may not immerse herself while wearing them until she loosens them, בְּשַׁבָּת לֹא תֵצֵא** – the Sages decreed that **on the Sabbath she may not go out** while wearing them. **דִּילְמָא מִיתְרְמֵי לָהּ טְבִילָה שֶׁל מִצְוָה** – For **perhaps an obligatory immersion will come her way** on the Sabbath, i.e. a situation will arise in which she is obligated to immerse herself in a *mikveh* on the Sabbath,[17] **וְשָׁרְיָא לְהוּ – and she will untie them** in order to properly perform the immersion;[18] **וְאָתֵי לְאַתּוּיִינְהוּ אַרְבַּע אַמּוֹת בִּרְשׁוּת הָרַבִּים – and she will come** unintentionally **to carry them four *amos* in the public domain.**[19] Thus, the law of immersion was stated in the Mishnah to explain why a woman may not go out with such hair accessories on the Sabbath.[20]

The Gemara cites a related inquiry:

בְּעָא מִינֵּיהּ רַב כַּהֲנָא מֵרַב – Rav Kahana inquired of Rav: תִּיכְּי חֲלִילְתָא מַאי – If a woman ties her hair with **chains** made **of open-link threads,**[21] **what** is the law? May she go out with them on the Sabbath or not?[22] **אָמַר לֵיהּ – [Rav] replied to him:**

NOTES

12. I.e. a ring that lacks an engraved seal of the type that was commonly used to seal letters and packages (*Rashi*). A ring without a seal is simply ornamental, and it is therefore only *Rabbinically* forbidden to wear it outside on the Sabbath. This is not to imply that a woman is permitted to go out wearing a ring *with* a seal on the Sabbath; on the contrary, the Mishnah speaks only of a ring without a seal because it is *Biblically* forbidden for a woman to go out with a signet ring on the Sabbath. Such a ring is not an ornament for a woman, and is thus considered merely an item being carried on the finger, as the Mishnah states below (62a).

13. I.e. a needle without an eye. Such a needle is only an ornament; it cannot be used for sewing and the like. Thus, wearing it outside is only Rabbinically forbidden. [A needle *with* an eye, however, would be Biblically forbidden; see Mishnah below (62a).]

14. I.e. even if she went out into the *reshus harabim* wearing one of these ornaments, she is not liable to a *chatas* offering; for, as explained above, the prohibition against doing so is only Rabbinic (*Rashi*).

[The list of items which may not be worn outside on the Sabbath continues into the next three Mishnahs; the five Mishnahs following those three will detail the items that may be worn outside.]

Although the Mishnah teaches that the wearing of jewelry and ornaments in the street is forbidden, it has been the custom of Jewish women to wear jewelry in the public domain even as far back as the times of the Geonim. The reason for this is the subject of much discussion; see *Tosafos* to 64b ד״ה רב ענני, and *Rishonim* there; see also *Orach Chaim* 303:18 and *Aruch HaShulchan* 303:21,22 for explanations of the prevailing custom; see also below, 64b note 26.]

15. Literally: immersion, who mentioned its name?

16. [The interposition of a hair ornament only invalidates an immersion on a Rabbinic level, as in order to invalidate an immersion Biblically, an interposition must cover a majority of the person who is immersing (see *Eruvin* 4b and Rishonim there). Thus, the loosening of such an ornament before immersion is mandated only on the Rabbinic level.]

17. I.e. it is possible that a woman who is a *niddah* and requires immersion to become *tahor* will wish to perform her immersion on the Sabbath; alternatively, perhaps a woman who is *tamei* and wishes to partake of *tahor* foods will come to immerse herself on the Sabbath [such immersions are all referred to as "obligatory immersions" – see *Rashash* and *Hagahos R' Elazar Moshe Horowitz*].

Although the Sages prohibited the immersion of *tamei* utensils in a *mikveh* on the Sabbath because they likened it to a "repair" of the vessel, they did not prohibit the immersion of a person because that appears to be merely a refreshing dip, rather than a "repair" (see *Beitzah* 18a). Accordingly, they banned wearing hair strands to prevent them from being carried by a woman who immersed (*Rashi*).

18. I.e. in order to ensure that the hair ties will not interpose between the water and her hair, she will remove them prior to her immersion (see next note).

19. Although a woman can avoid the problem of חֲצִיצָה by simply loosening the ties, the Sages were concerned that she might remove them completely. Were she to do so, the concern exists that after the immersion she might forget to retie them in her hair, and inadvertently carry them four *amos* in the public domain.

The Rishonim point out that this concern applies only to those small items that a woman would be likely to absentmindedly carry along with her after her immersion. The decree does not apply to her regular clothing, since she would definitely not walk in the street after her immersion without putting on all of her clothes (*Tosafos, Ritva MHK* ed., *Ran MHK* ed. et al.).

20. It emerges, then, that the accessories mentioned in the Mishnah fall into two groups: the hair accessories, which are prohibited because a woman may take them off prior to an immersion, and the jewelry, which is prohibited due to the concern that a woman will take it off to show to a friend.

As mentioned above (note 3), there is a dispute between *Rashi* and *Tosafos* as to the nature of the hair ties being discussed in the Mishnah. *Tosafos* are of the opinion that only strands that are worn around the hair are prohibited, for it is only such strands that may be removed prior to an immersion. Strands that are woven into the hair, however, may not be removed on the Sabbath; for just as braiding hair is prohibited on the Sabbath, at least on the Rabbinic level, because it is considered "building" [which is one of the thirty-nine *avos melachos*] (see Gemara below, 94b), unbraiding the hair to remove the strands is prohibited, because it is considered "demolishing." And since such strands cannot be removed on the Sabbath, there is no reason to prohibit a woman from wearing them on the Sabbath (see also *Rosh, Rashba, Ritva MHK* ed.). *Rashi,* however, states clearly that the prohibition in the Mishnah applies to strands woven into the braids. The commentators suggest various solutions to the difficulty raised by *Tosafos;* see *Tos. Rid, Or Zarua* vol. II, 84:1, *Pnei Yehoshua;* see also *Bach* to *Orach Chaim* §303; *Magen Avraham* 303:3; *Taz* 303:1. See also *Chelkas Binyamin* for a novel interpretation of *Rashi.*

21. *Rashi; Raavad* (cited by *Rama, Yoreh Deah* 198:4) explains this to be a type of meshwork. *Chidushei HaRan* understands that the chains were hollow tubes of woven material that could not be tightly fastened due to their *thickness.*

22. These chains cannot be tightened completely against the hair, due to their open construction; thus, the water would likely be able to penetrate them and reach the hair of the woman during the immersion. Rav Kahana inquired if nevertheless we must assume that they constitute a *chatzitzah,* which would mean that a woman would be prohibited

מסורת הש"ס

א) [נדרים ג: מיר ג.], ב) [עי' תוס' לקמן נט. ד"ה ולא], ג) לקמן נח., ד) מקוואות פ"ט מ"א.

עין משפט נר מצוה

א א מיי' פי"ט מהל' שבת הל' ו' ומיי' פ"ב מהל' מקואות הל' ה סמג לאוין סה וסמג עשין רמח טוש"ע א"ח סי' שג סעיף א וטוש"ע י"ד סי' קלא סעיף ב:

ב ב מיי' פי"ט מהל' שבת הלכה ד' טוש"ע א"ח סי' שג סעיף י וסעיף יח:

ג ג ד מיי' שם הלכה ט טוש"ע א"ח סי' שג סעיף א וטוש"ע י"ד סי' קלא סעיף ג:

ד ה ו מיי' שם הלכה ז י טוש"ע א"ח שם סעיף ב וטוש"ע י"ד שם סעיף ב:

מתני'

א) **במה** אאשה יוצאה ובמה אינה יוצאה לא תצא אשה לא בחוטי צמר ולא בחוטי פשתן ולא ברצועות שבראשה ולא תטבול בהן עד שתרפם ולא בטוטפת ולא בסרביטין בזמן שאינן תפורים ולא בכבול לרה"ר ולא ב) בעיר של זהב ולא בקטלא ולא בנזמים בולא בטבעת שאין עליה חותם ולא במחט שאינה נקובה ואם יצאת אינה חייבת חטאת:

גמ' טבילה מאן דכר שמה אמר רב נחמן בר יצחק אמר רבה בר אבוה מה טעם קאמר מה טעם לא תצא אשה לא בחוטי צמר ולא בחוטי פשתן מפני שאמרו חכמים בחול לא תטבול בהן עד שתרפם וכיון דבחול לא תטבול בהן עד שתרפם בשבת לא תצא דילמא מיתרמי לה טבילה של מצוה ושריא להו ואתי לאתויינהו ד' אמות ברה"ר בעא מיניה רב כהנא מרב ° תיכי חלילתא מאי א"ל אריג קאמרת כל שהוא אריג לא גזרו איתמר נמי ג) אמר רב הונא בריה דרב יהושע גכל שהוא אריג לא גזרו ואיכא דאמרי אמר רב הונא בריה דרב יהושע חזינא לאחוותי דלא קפדן עלייהו מאי איכא בין הך לישנא ובין הך לישנא איכא בינייהו דטניפן להך לישנא דאמר כל שהוא אריג לא גזרו הני נמי ארוג ולהך לישנא דאמרת משום קפידא דכיון דטניפא מקפד קפדא עלייהו ד) תנן התם ואלו חוצצין באדם חוטי צמר וחוטי פשתן והרצועות שבראשי הבנות ר' יהודה אומר של צמר ושל שער אין חוצצין מפני שהמים באין בהן אמר רב הונא וכולן בראשי הבנות שנינו מתקיף לה רב יוסף למעוטי מאי אילימא למעוטי דצואר ודמאי אילימא למעוטי דצמר השתא רך על גבי קשה חוציץ רך על גבי רך מיבעיא ואלא למעוטי דחוטי פשתן השתא קשה על גבי קשה חוציץ קשה על גבי רך מיבעיא אלא אמר רב יוסף היינו טעמא דרב הונא הלפי שאין אשה חונקת את עצמה איתיביה אביי הבנות יוצאות בחוטין שבאזניהן אבל לא בחבקין שבצואריהן ואי אמרת אין אשה חונקת עצמה חבקין שבצואריהן אמאי לא ואמר רבינא הכא

רש"י

במה אשה יוצאה. דהוי תכשיט ולא משוי ואיכא דהוי תכשיט וגזור ביה רבנן דילמא שלפא ומחויא לחברתה חשיבותו ודילמא אתי לאיתויי ד' אמות: **לא בחוטי צמר ופשתן ורצועה שבראשה**. שקולעת בהן שערה: **שבראשה**. אכולהו קאי ובגמ' מפרש טעמא: **ולא תטבול בהן**. משום חצילה: **עד שתרפם**. שתתירם קלת שיהיו רפויין ויכנסו המים ביניהם לשער: **טוטפת וסרביטין**. מפרש בגמרא ותשובין הן וחיישינן דילמא שלפא ומחויא לחברתה: **בזמן שאין תפורין**. עם השבכה שקורין שקופיי"א אבל תפורין ליכא למיחש לאחוויי שאינה נוטלת השבכה מראשה ברה"ר שתגלה כל שערה: **כבול**. מפרש בגמ': **לרה"ר**. אבל לחצר שרי וכל הנזכרים למעלה אסורים אף לחצר שמא תרגילם ברה"ר וחדא גזירה היא דגזור בהם שלא תתקשט בהם בשבת כלל ובכבול התירו כדמפרש לקמן בפרקין (דף סד:) שלא לאסור את כל תכשיטיה ותתגנה על בעלה: **עיר של זהב**. כמין נושקא ומציירין בה כמין עיר: **קטלא**. מפרש בגמרא (לקמן דף נט:): **חותם**. צורה לחתום בה איגרת או כל דבר סגור: **שאינה נקובה**. כגון אישפיגל"א: **ואם יצאת אינה חייבת חטאת**. דכולהו תכשיטין נינהו ורבנן הוא דגזור בהו דילמא שלפא ומחויא: **גמ' טבילה מאן דכר שמה**. מה ענין טבילה אצל הלכות שבת: **ושריא להו**. ומתרת אותם לטבול בשבת שעל הטבילה לא גזרו כדאמרינן במסכת ביצה (דף יח.) אדם נראה כמיקר ואין נראה כמתקן עצמו: **תיכי חלילתא**. שרשרות של חוטין חלולות ועגולות: **מהו**. לקלוע בהן שערה ולצאת בשבת שאינה יכולה למותחן ולדוחקן על השער בחזקה והמים נכנסין בה ומיבעיא ליה מי הוי חצילה ולא תצא בהן בשבת משום גזירת טבילת מצוה או לא הוי חצילה: **כל שהוא אריג לא גזרו**. לצאת בו בשבת דלענין חצילה לא חיין דלא מצי לאהדוקי שפיר: **לאחוותי דלא קפדן עלייהו**. ליטלן מראשן כשהן רוחצות בחמין אלמא עיילי בהו מיא שפיר אפילו להנאת רחיצה וכיון שכן לענין טבילה נמי לא צריכין להתירן ומותר לצאת בהן בשבת דהא אי מתרמי טבילה לא שרו להו לא משום חצילה ולא משום קפידא: **דמיטנפי**. שנטנפו הנך תיכי בטיט: **הא נמי אריג הוא**. והא קאמר לא גזרו כלל לצאת ולהאי לישנא דלא קפדי משמע דאי קפדי לנטלן מראשן כשהן רוחצות אסור לצאת בהן בשבת ואע"ג דלענין איהדוקי לא חיילי ומותרות לטבול בהן הלכך הני כיון דמיטנפי מקפד קפדן שלא להיות בראשן בשעת טבילתן מפני שהמים ממחין את הטיט ומלכלך בשרן בעלייתן מן הטבילה ואע"ג דחצילה לא הוי דהא עיילי בהו מיא מיהו כיון דשקלי לה משום טינוף אתי לאיתויינהו ואסור לצאת בהן וללישנא קמא לא גזרו אלא במידי דחיין לטבילה ורבותי מפרשין הך קפידא לענין חצילה כדקי"ל רובו ומקפיד עליו חוצץ (עירובין דף ד:) וקשיא לי בגוה טובא חדא דכי איתמר ההוא במידי דמיהדק איתמר ואשמעינן דאע"ג דלא עיילי ביה מיא כיון דלא קפיד עליה חשיב כגופיה ובטל לגבי שערו אבל במידי דלא מיהדק ועיילי ביה מיא מאי חוצץ איכא למימר הא לאו חוצץ הוא ואי אתית למימר דההוא חוצץ דהתם לא דק בלישניה ומיהו כל מידי דקפיד עלייהו אסור היכי אמרינן הכא האי נמי אריג הוא ומותר כיון דפשיטא לן דהיכא דמיטנפי מקפד קפדן על כרחיך חיין דהא רב הונא בריה דרב יהושע אהלכה למשה מסיני לא אתא לאיפלוגי: **ואלו חוצצין באדם**. משום דתני התם אלו חוצצין בכלים תני לענין טבילת אדם ואלו חוצצין באדם: **של צמר ושל שער אין חוצצין**. דלא מיהדק על גבי שער: **הבנות**. קטנות. אורחא דמילתא נקט: **וכולן בראשי הבנות שנינו**. לא תימא שבראשי הבנות ארצועות לחודייהו קאי אלא אחוטין נמי קאי: **למעוטי מאי**. אשמעינן רב הונא דחוטין נמי בראשי הבנות שנינו: **אילימא למעוטי**. חוטין הקשורין בצוארן דלא חיילי: **ודמאי**. הי חוטין אתא למעוטי דלא חיילי בצואר: למר קרוי רך לגבי פשתן ולגבי שער: **על גבי קשה**. שער: **ע"ג רך**. בשר: **מיבעיא**. בתמיה הא ודאי על גבי רך טפי מיהדק: **לפי שאין אשה חונקת עצמה**. להדק חוטין בצוארה וקושרתן בריוח שיהו רפין: **בחוטין שבאזניהם**. שנותנין שם שלא יסתם הנקב: **חבקין**. ענקי רצועות שאינן מחהבות רחבות דלאו לתכשיט עבידן דומיא דחוטין שבאזניהן: **חבקין**. לשון קילקלי וחבק (לקמן דף סד.) ליגל"א לאסור בו סוס:

בקטלא

תוספות

במה אשה כו' לא בחוטי צמר. מפרש בגמ' משום דילמא מיתרמי לה טבילה של מצוה ושרי להו ואתי לאתויינהו ארבע אמות ברה"ר אומר ר"י דהיינו דוקא בחוטין שאינן נתונין בקליעת השער אבל חוטין הנתונין בקליעת השער יוצאה בהן דבהנהו ליכא למיגזר דילמא שריא להו כדתנן בהמצניע (לקמן דף צד:) דאיכא לכל הפחות איסור שבות בגודלת וסברא הוא דכי היכי דיש איסור בעשיית קליעה ה"נ יש איסור בסתירת קליעה וא"ת מהאי טעמא תהא אשה אסורה לצאת בטלית דהא ודאי שריא לה בשעת טבילה וניחוש דילמא אתי לאתויי וי"ל דבדברים שהם עיקר מלבוש ליכא למיגזר דאפילו בחול אין דרך ללכת כלל ממקומו עד שילבישם אלא דוקא בדברים קטנים יש לחוש שאין מקפיד אם אינם עליו ורגילות הוא בחול כשמתירן פעמים נושאן בידו עד ביתו ונראה לר"י דדוקא בדברים שרגילות להסירן כדי להראותן או משום חצילה או משום קפידא גזרו שלא לצאת דשמא כשיסיר ישכח שהוא שבת ואתי לאתויי אבל דברים שמותר לצאת בהן שאין רגילות להסירן מותר לקשור ולהתיר ברה"ר דליכא למיחש למידי דאם יהא זכור שבת בשעת התרה לא אתי לאתויי ואם לא יהיה זכור שבת אפילו נאסר להתיר ולהסיר לא יועיל וכ"מ לקמן (דף סא.) דקתני בברייתא וקושר ומתיר קמיע אפילו ברה"ר והא דאיצטריך התם לאשמעי' דשרי אע"פ שכל דבר מותר להסיר כדפרישית איצטריך לאשמעינן דלא אסרינן משום דמיחזי דקושרו עליו שלא לרפואה ומתכוין להוציא כי היכי דאסור בפילפל וגרגיר מלח לכתחילה לתת בפה בשבת או להחזיר אלא כמלבוש גמור חשיב מחמת הרפואה:

השתא רך על גבי קשה חוציץ כו'. וא"ת דילמא רב הונא נקט וכולן בראשי הבנות לרבותא דאפילו בראשי הבנות דהוי רך ע"ג קשה חוצץ ואור"י דבלאו רב הונא הוה ידעינן דבכל מקום חוצצין אפילו בראש אלא ודאי למעוטי שום דבר אתא:

השתא קשה ע"ג קשה חוציץ. סבר הש"ס דקשה ע"ג רך חיין טפי מקשה ע"ג קשה ורך ע"ג קשה לא חיין כקשה ע"ג קשה דהא לר' יהודה חוטי למר אין חוצצין דהוי רך על גבי קשה וחוטי פשתן דהוי קשה ע"ג קשה חוצצין וחוטי שיער דהוי נמי קשה על גבי קשה לכ"ע אין חוצצין אף על פי שחוטי פשתן חוצצין לכולי עלמא:

אלא א"ר יוסף. לפי שרב יוסף בעצמו מקשה שייך לומר אלא:

הכא

גליון הש"ס

גמ' תיכי חלילתא מאי. עי' זבחים דף לד ע"א תוס' ד"ה מקנחת:

ליקוטי רש"י

בקטלא. מוטטניל"א והוא בגד שיש לו שנצים כעין מכנסים ומכנסת בו רצועה רחבה וקושרת סביב צוארה והבגד תלוי על לבה והוא חשוב ומצוייר בזהב ויש מפרשים כמין חצי עגול עשוי כמין כלבום ואוחזת בו מפתחי חלוקה והפגם בולע צוארה והוא של זהב לוי"ה [לקמן נט:]. בגד חשוב לתלות בצוארה כנגד לבה שלא יפול מה שהיא אוכלת על בגדיה ויש לו מקום שנצים כעין שעושים למכנסים ואוחז בו רצועה רחבה ומוללתו סביב הרצועה שהבגד רחב הרבה וקושרת הרצועה סביב צוארה [לקמן ע"ב ע"ש עוד ובתוס' שם]. **ולא במחט שאינה נקובה.** לענין הוצאת שבת יש חילוק בין נקובה לשאינו נקובה דנקובה קתני חייב חטאת ובשאינה נקובה כגון אישפיגל"א שהיא תכשיט קתני אינו חייב חטאת בפרק במה אשה (שבת נז:) [לעיל נב:]. **בחוטין שבאזניהן.** הבנות קטנות שמנקבות אזניהם ואין עושין נזמים עד שיגדלו ונותנין חוטין או קסמים באזניהם שלא יסתמו אזניהם לוי"ה [לקמן סה.].

רבינו חננאל

במה אשה יוצאה ובמה אינה יוצאה. לא תצא אשה בחוטי כו'. אוקמה רב נחמן גזירה שמא תזדמן לה טבילה של מצוה ומשום שחוצצת מתרתן ומהלכת בהן ד' אמות ברה"ר. אבל תיכי חלילתא לא גזרו בהו רבנן דהא אחוותיה דרב הונא בריה דר' יהושע הוו טבלי בדמחתן הני תיכי חלילתא בראשיהן ולא הוו קפדי וכיון דלא הוו קפדי שרו. וה"מ תיכי חלילתא אבל תיכי טמימתא לא דחוצצות ואסיק' דחוטי שיער אינן חוצצין ואפילו הן קשורין בראש הבנות ואע"פ שהראש קשה הוא המים נכנסין בשיער ואין חוצצין אבל חוטי צמר וחוטי פשתן בראש הבנות חוצצין וכ"ש אם הן קשורין בצואר שמשתקעין בבשר ואין המים באין תחתיהן. ולפיכך חוצצין. כיוצא בהן החבקין שבצוארי הבנות ואוקימנא

כֹּל שֶׁהוּא אָרִיג קָאָמְרַתְּ – **You inquire about a woven article?** כֹּל שֶׁהוּא אָרִיג לֹא גָּזְרוּ – **Whatever is woven was not** included **in [the Sages'] decree** concerning hair bands.[23]

The Gemara cited a corroboratory ruling:

אִיתְּמַר נַמִּי – And **it was also stated** elsewhere: אָמַר רַב הוּנָא בְּרֵיהּ דְּרַב יְהוֹשֻׁעַ – **Rav Huna the son of Rav Yehoshua said:** כֹּל שֶׁהוּא אָרִיג לֹא גָּזְרוּ – **Whatever is a woven article was not** included **in [the Sages'] decree** concerning hair bands.

Another version of Rav Huna's statement is cited:

וְאִיכָּא דְּאָמְרֵי – **And some say:** אָמַר רַב הוּנָא בְּרֵיהּ דְּרַב יְהוֹשֻׁעַ – **Rav Huna the son of Rav Yehoshua said:** חֲזֵינָא לְאַחְוָותִי דְּלָא קָפְדָן עֲלַיְיהוּ – **I have seen** that **my sisters do not insist upon** removing **these** thread chains before they bathe; obviously, then, water penetrates them, and they need not be removed before an immersion. Accordingly, women may go out while wearing them on the Sabbath.[24]

The Gemara analyzes the difference between these two versions:

מַאי אִיכָּא בֵּין הָךְ לִישָּׁנָא וּבֵין הָךְ לִישָּׁנָא – **What is the** practical **difference between this version** of Rav Huna's statement **and that version** of his statement? In both versions, he rules that a woman may immerse herself and go out on the Sabbath with woven thread chains in her hair!

The Gemara answers:

אִיכָּא בֵּינַיְיהוּ דְּטִנּוּפָן – **There is** a difference **between them** in a case **where [the chains] are soiled.**[25] לְהָךְ לִישָּׁנָא דְּאָמַר כֹּל שֶׁהוּא אָרִיג לֹא גָּזְרוּ – **According to that version in which [Rav Huna]** simply **said, "Whatever is a woven article was not** included **in [the Sages'] decree,"** הָנֵי נַמִּי אָרוּג – **these** soiled chains, **too, are woven,** and thus a woman may go out while wearing them on the Sabbath.[26] וּלְהָךְ לִישָּׁנָא דְּאָמְרַתְּ מִשּׁוּם קְפֵידָא – **But according** to **that version** in **which you said that** the Sages' decree forbidding the wearing of hair bands was made **due to** a woman's **insistence** upon removing them prior to bathing,[27] כֵּיוָן דְּטִנּוּפָא – **since [these chains] are soiled,** מִקְפַּד קָפְדָא עֲלַיְיהוּ – **[women] insist upon** removing **them** prior to bathing. Thus, they would also remove them prior to immersing in a *mikveh.* Accordingly, they may not go out while wearing them on the Sabbath, for fear that they will remove them and then carry them.[28]

The Gemara cites a Mishnah that discusses which types of hair ties must be removed before immersion:

תְּנַן הָתָם – **We learned in a Mishnah there:**[29] וְאֵלּוּ חוֹצְצִין בְּאָדָם – AND THESE are the items that INTERPOSE between the water of a *mikveh* and the body when A PERSON immerses, thus invalidating the immersion: חוּטֵי צֶמֶר וְחוּטֵי פִשְׁתָּן וְהָרְצוּעוֹת שֶׁבְּרָאשֵׁי הַבָּנוֹת – WOOLEN STRANDS, LINEN STRANDS AND THE STRAPS that are worn ON THE HEADS OF GIRLS.[30] רַבִּי יְהוּדָה אוֹמֵר – R' YEHUDAH, however, SAYS: שֶׁל צֶמֶר וְשֶׁל שֵׂעָר אֵין חוֹצְצִין – Strands OF WOOL OR OF HAIR[31] DO NOT INTERPOSE, מִפְּנֵי שֶׁהַמַּיִם בָּאִין בָּהֶן –

NOTES

to wear them outside on the Sabbath due to the possibility that she might remove them to perform an immersion; or perhaps they do not constitute a *chatzitzah,* since they cannot be tied tightly enough to [completely] bar the water (*Rashi;* see *Sfas Emes*).

23. [Literally: Whatever is a woven article, the Sages did not decree.] Woven chains were not included in the Sages' decree against wearing hair bands on the Sabbath because they do not form a barrier to water and thus need not be removed (*Rashi;* see *Ritva MHK* ed.).

[The term "woven" is used here loosely; these chains were not woven but made of interlocking links. The Gemara, however, uses the term אָרִיג, *woven article,* to refer to anything made of interlocked threads, be they woven, braided or linked (*Rashi* to 64a ד״ה ותולה בצואר בתו; see further, note 28).

24. When a woman bathes, she certainly wants the water to come in contact with all of her hair. Thus, if women do not insist upon removing such chains before they bathe, it is a clear indication that they do not pose a barrier to the water. Accordingly, they need not be removed before an immersion, and can therefore be worn outside on the Sabbath (*Rashi*).

25. *Rashi;* cf. *Rosh* §2.

26. Thread chains do not constitute a *chatzitzah* even if they are soiled, for the water is able to penetrate under them. However, if they are soiled [with clay or other dried dirt], there is a possibility that a woman will wish to remove them before immersing; for the water may soften the clay during the immersion, and she will become soiled with this mud as she ascends from the *mikveh.* Now, according to the first version of Rav Huna's ruling, the sole criterion considered by the Sages in deciding whether to prohibit the wearing of hair accessories on the Sabbath is whether or not the accessory poses a *chatzitzah* to immersion; no other variables regarding the immersion are considered. Thus, since thread chains do not interpose, they may be worn outside on the Sabbath, and we do not consider the possibility that the woman may remove them for other reasons (*Rashi;* see note 28).

27. That is, the second version of Rav Huna's ruling, in which he stated that thread chains are permitted because women do not insist upon removing them before immersing. This phraseology implies that the Sages did not restrict their decree only to those items that would be removed because they interpose; rather, the decree extends to items which would be removed before an immersion *for any reason* (see *Rashi* and next note; of course, this only applies to small items which she might come to carry absentmindedly after the immersion, as explained above in note 19).

28. According to the second version of Rav Huna's ruling, the Sages' decree applies to *any* item that a woman will remove before her immersion, even for reasons other than a *chatzitzah* (as explained in the previous note). Thus, even though thread chains do not serve as a barrier against the water, since they are soiled, a woman would remove them before immersing herself to avoid becoming soiled with the wetted dirt. Consequently, soiled bands cannot be worn outside on the Sabbath (*Rashi's* preferred explanation).

[*Rashi* also cites another explanation in the name of his teachers, according to which the fact that women insist upon removing soiled bands before an immersion actually renders them a *chatzitzah* that can invalidate an immersion. *Rashi* himself questions this view strongly, for he is of the opinion that if the bands do not bar the water from reaching the hair beneath, they cannot be viewed as a *chatzitzah,* the fact that the woman insists upon removing them notwithstanding; see also *Ritva* (*MHK* ed.), who challenges this interpretation. However, *Rama* to *Yoreh Deah* 198:4 appears to accept this view as halachah. See *Beis Yosef* ibid §198; see also *Ben Uri* (ד״ה אמנם).]

[It should be noted that although the Gemara here seems to state categorically that *any* "woven" band does not constitute a *chatzitzah,* some commentators interpret this as referring only to open bands, such as the bands discussed by Rav and R' Huna the son of R' Yehoshua. *Solid* woven material, however, would be a *chatzitzah* (*Yoreh Deah* 198:3, citing *Raavad;* see also *Ran MHK* ed. and *Meiri* here). In truth, however, the view of the *Shulchan Aruch* in this matter is unclear, for in *Orach Chaim* 303:1 he makes no such distinction. This seeming contradiction is noted by both *Magen Avraham* (§4 ibid.) and *Shach* (to *Yoreh Deah,* 198:5); see *Chasam Sofer* and *Ben Uri* for resolutions.]

29. *Mikvaos* 9:1. [The Mishnahs later in that chapter list items that are a *chatzitzah* in regard to utensils. Thus, the beginning of the chapter, which lists the items that form a *chatzitzah* in the case of *a person,* prefaces that list with the statement, "These are the items that interpose in the case of a person" (*Rashi*).]

30. These are the very strands that were mentioned in our Mishnah; the Mishnah there teaches its ruling concerning strands worn by girls only because such strands were most commonly worn by young girls (*Rashi*).

31. These are bands made of strands of hair that were twined together for use as hair ties (*Meiri*).

[א] **במה** [א] אשה יוצאה ובמה אינה יוצאה לא תצא אשה לא בחוטי צמר ולא בחוטי פשתן ולא ברצועות שבראשה ולא תטבול בהן עד שתרפם ולא בטוטפת ולא בסרביטין בזמן שאינן תפורים ולא בכבול לרה"ר ולא [ב] בעיר של זהב ולא בקטלא ולא בנזמים [ב] ולא בטבעת שאין עליה חותם ולא במחט שאינה נקובה ואם יצאת אינה חייבת חטאת: **גמ'** טבילה מאן דכר שמה אמר רב נחמן בר יצחק אמר רבה בר אבוה מה טעם קאמר מה טעם לא תצא אשה לא בחוטי צמר ולא בחוטי פשתן מפני שאמרו חכמים בחול לא תטבול בהן עד שתרפם וכיון דבחול לא תטבול בהן עד שתרפם בשבת לא תצא דילמא מיתרמי לה טבילה של מצוה ושריא להו ואתי לאתויינהו ד' אמות ברה"ר בעא מיניה רב כהנא מרב ° תיכי חלילתא מאי א"ל אריג קאמרת כל שהוא אריג לא גזרו איתמר נמי [ג] אמר רב הונא בריה דרב יהושע [ג] כל שהוא אריג לא גזרו ואיכא דאמרי אמר רב הונא בריה דרב יהושע חזינא לאחוותי דלא קפדן עלייהו מאי איכא בין הך לישנא ובין הך לישנא איכא בינייהו דטניפן להך לישנא דאמר כל שהוא אריג לא גזרו הני נמי ארוג ולהך לישנא דאמרת משום קפידא [ד] כיון דטניפא מקפד קפדא עלייהו [ד] תנן התם ואלו חוצצין באדם חוטי צמר וחוטי פשתן והרצועות שבראשי הבנות ר' יהודה אומר של צמר ושל שער אין חוצצין מפני שהמים באין בהן אמר רב הונא וכולן בראשי הבנות שנינו מתקיף לה רב יוסף למעוטי מאי אילימא למעוטי דצואר ודמאי אילימא למעוטי דצמר השתא רך על גבי קשה חוצץ רך על גבי רך מיבעיא ואלא למעוטי דחוטי פשתן השתא קשה על גבי קשה חוצץ קשה על גבי רך מיבעיא אלא אמר רב יוסף היינו טעמא דרב הונא [ה] לפי שאין אשה חונקת את עצמה איתיביה אביי הבנות יוצאות בחוטין שבאזניהן אבל לא בחבקין שבצואריהן ואי אמרת אין אשה חונקת עצמה חבקין שבצואריהן אמאי לא [ו] אמר רבינא הכא

במה אשה יוצאה. דהוי תכשיט ולא משוי ואיכא דהוי תכשיט וגזור ביה רבנן דילמא שלפא ומחויא לחברתה חשיבותו ודילמא אתי לאיתויי ד' אמות: **לא בחוטי צמר ופשתן ורצועה שבראשה.** שקולעת בהן שערה: **שבראשה.** אכולהו קאי ובגמ' מפרש טעמא: **ולא תטבול בהן.** משום חציצה: **עד שתרפם.** שתתירם קצת שיהיו רפויין ויכנסו המים ביניהם לשער: **טוטפת וסרביטין.** מפרש בגמרא וחשובין הן וחיישינן דילמא שלפא ומחויא לחברתה: **בזמן שאין תפורין.** עם השבכה שקורין שקופיי"א אבל תפורין ליכא למיחש לאחוויי שאינה נוטלת השבכה מראשה ברה"ר שתגלה כל שערה: **כבול.** מפרש בגמ': **לרה"ר.** אבל לחצר שרי וכל הנזכרים למעלה אסורים אף לחצר שמא תרגילם ברה"ר וחדא גזירה היא לגזור בהם שלא תתקשט בהם בשבת כלל ובכבול התירו כדמפרש לקמן בפרקין (דף סד:) שלא לאסור את כל תכשיטיה ותתגנה על בעלה: **עיר של זהב.** כמין נושקא ומציירין בה כמין עיר: **קטלא.** מפרש בגמרא (לקמן דף נט:): **חותם.** צורה לחתום בה איגרת או כל דבר סגור: **שאינה נקובה.** כגון איספיגל"א: **ואם יצאת אינה חייבת חטאת.** דכולהו תכשיטין נינהו ורבנן הוא דגזור בהו דילמא שלפא ומחויא: **גמ' טבילה מאן דכר שמה.** מה ענין טבילה אצל הלכות שבת: **ושריא להו.** ומתרת אותם לטבול בשבת שעל הטבילה לא גזרו כדאמרינן במסכת ביצה (דף יח.) אדם נראה כמיקר ואין נראה כמתקן עצמו: **תיכי חלילתא.** שרשרות של חוטין חלולות ועגולות: **מהו.** לקלוע בהן שערה ולצאת בשבת שאינה יכולה למותחן ולדוחקן על השער בחזקה והמים נכנסין בה ומיבעיא ליה מי הוי חציצה ולא תצא בהן בשבת משום גזירת טבילת מצוה או לא הוי חציצה: **כל שהוא אריג לא גזרו.** לצאת בו בשבת דלענין חציצה לא חייץ דלא מצי להדוקי שפיר: **לאחוותי דלא קפדן עלייהו.** ליטלן מראשן כשהן רוחצות בחמין אלמא עיילי בהו מיא שפיר אפילו להנאת רחיצה וכיון שכן לענין טבילה נמי לא צריכין להתירן ומותר לצאת בהן בשבת דהא אי מתרמי טבילה לא שרו להו לא משום חציצה ולא משום קפידא: **דמיטנפי.** שנטנפו הנך תיכי בטיט: **הא נמי אריג הוא.** והא קאמר לא גזרו כלל לצאת ולהאי לישנא דלא קפדי משמע דאי קפדי לנטלן מראשן כשהן רוחצות אסור לצאת בהן בשבת ואע"ג דלענין איהדוקי לא חיילי ומותרות לטבול בהן הלכך הני כיון דמיטנפי מקפד קפדן שלא להיות בראשן בשעת טבילתן מפני שהמים ממחין את הטיט ומלכלך בשרן בעלייתן מן הטבילה ואע"ג דחציצה לא הוי דהא עיילי בהו מיא מיהו כיון דשקלי לה משום טינוף אתי לאיתויינהו ואסור לצאת בהן וללישנא קמא לא גזרו אלא במידי דחייץ לטבילה ורבותי מפרשין הך קפידא לענין חציצה כדקי"ל רובו ומקפיד עליו חוצץ (עירובין דף ד:) וקשיא לי בגוה טובא חדא דכי איתמר ההוא במידי דמיהדק איתמר ואשמעינן דאע"ג דלא עיילי ביה מיא כיון דלא קפיד עליה חשיב כגופיה ובטל לגבי שערו אבל במידי דלא מיהדק ועיילי ביה מיא מאי חוצץ איכא למימר הא לאו חוצץ הוא ואי אתית למימר דההוא חוצץ דהתם לא דק בלישניה ומיהו כל מידי דקפיד עלייהו אסור היכי אמרינן הכא האי נמי אריג הוא ומותר כיון דפשיטא לן דהיכא דמיטנפי מקפד קפדן על כרחיך חייץ דהא רב הונא בריה דרב יהושע אהלכה למשה מסיני לא אתא לאיפלוגי: **ואלו חוצצין באדם.** משום דתני התם אלו חוצצין בכלים תני לענין טבילת אדם ואלו חוצצין באדם: **של צמר ושל שער אין חוצצין.** דלא מיהדק על גבי שער: **הבנות.** קטנות. אורחא דמילתא נקט: **וכולן בראשי הבנות שנינו.** לא תימא שבראשי הבנות ארצועות לחודייהו קאי אלא אחוטין נמי קאי: **למעוטי מאי.** אשמעינן רב הונא דחוטין נמי בראשי הבנות שנינו: **אילימא למעוטי.** חוטין הקשורין בצוארן דלא חיילי: **ודמאי.** הי חוטין אתא למעוטי דלא חיילי בצואר: **למר** קרוי רך לגבי פשתן ולגבי שער: **על גבי קשה.** שער: **ע"ג רך.** בשר: **מיבעיא.** בתמיה הא ודאי על גבי רך טפי מיהדק: **לפי שאין אשה חונקת עצמה.** להדק חוטין בצוארה וקושרתן בריוח שיהו רפין: **בחוטין שבאזניהם.** שנותנין שם שלא יסתם הנקב: **חבקין.** ענקי רצועות שאינן מוזהבות רחבות דלאו לתכשיט עבידן דומיא דחוטין שבאזניהן: **חבקין.** לשון קילקלי וחבק (לקמן דף סד.) לינגל"א לאסור בו סוס:

בקטלא

במה אשה כו' לא בחוטי צמר. מפרש בגמ' משום דילמא מיתרמי לה טבילה של מצוה ושרי להו ואתי לאתויינהו ארבע אמות ברה"ר אומר ר"י דהיינו דוקא בחוטין שאינן נתונין בקליעת השער אבל חוטין הנתונין בקליעת השער יוצאה בהן דבהנהו ליכא למיגזר דילמא שריא להו כדתנן בהמצניע (לקמן דף צד:) דאיכא לכל הפחות איסור שבות בגודלת וסברא הוא דכי היכי דיש איסור בעשיית קליעה ה"נ יש איסור בסתירת קליעה וא"ת מהאי טעמא תהא אשה אסורה לצאת בטלית דהא ודאי שריא לה בשעת טבילה וניחוש דילמא אתי לאתויי וי"ל דבדברים שהם עיקר מלבוש ליכא למיגזר דאפילו בחול אין דרך ללכת כלל ממקומו עד שילבישם אלא דוקא בדברים קטנים יש לחוש שאין מקפיד אם אינם עליו ורגילות הוא בחול כשמתירן פעמים נושאן בידו עד ביתו ונראה לר"י דדוקא בדברים שרגילות להסירן כדי להראותן או משום חציצה או משום קפידא גזרו שלא לצאת דשמא כשיסיר ישכח שהוא שבת ואתי לאתויי אבל דברים שמותר לצאת בהן שאין רגילות להסירן מותר לקשור ולהתיר ברה"ר דליכא למיחש למידי דאם יהא זכור שבת בשעת התרה לא אתי לאתויי ואם לא יהיה זכור שבת אפילו נאסר להתיר ולהסיר לא יועיל וכ"מ לקמן (דף סא.) דקתני בברייתא וקושר ומתיר קמיע אפילו ברה"ר והא דאיצטריך התם לאשמעי' דשרי אע"פ שכל דבר מותר להסיר כדפרישית איצטריך לאשמעינן דלא אסרינן משום דמיחזי דקושרו עליו שלא לרפואה ומתכוין להוציא כי היכי דאסור בפילפל וגרגיר מלח לכתחילה לתת בפה בשבת או להחזיר אלא כמלבוש גמור חשיב מחמת הרפואה: **השתא** רך על גבי קשה חוצץ כו'. וא"ת דילמא רב הונא נקט וכולן בראשי הבנות לרבותא דאפילו בראשי הבנות דהוי רך ע"ג קשה חוצץ ואור"י דבלאו רב הונא הוה ידעינן דבכל מקום חוצצין אפילו בראש אלא ודאי למעוטי שום דבר אתא: **השתא** קשה ע"ג קשה חוצץ. סבר הש"ס דקשה ע"ג רך חייץ טפי מקשה ע"ג קשה ורך ע"ג קשה לא חייץ כקשה ע"ג קשה דהא לר' יהודה חוטי למר אין חוצצין דהוי רך על גבי קשה וחוטי פשתן דהוי קשה ע"ג קשה חוצצין וחוטי שיער דהוי נמי קשה על גבי קשה לכ"ע אין חוצצין אף על פי שחוטי פשתן חוצצין לכולי עלמא: **אלא** א"ר יוסף. לפי שרב יוסף בעצמו מקשה שייך לומר אלא:

הכא

מסורת הש"ס

א) [נדרים ב: נזיר ב.], ב) [עי' תוס' לקמן נט. ד"ה ולא], ג) לקמן נח., ד) מקוואות פ"ט מ"א.

גליון הש"ס

גמ' תיכי חלילתא מאי. עי' זבחים דף לד ע"א תוס' ד"ה מקנחת:

ליקוטי רש"י

בקטלא. מוסטניל"א והוא בגד שיש לו שנצים כעין מכנסים ומכנסת בו רצועה רחבה וקושרת סביב צוארה והבגד תלוי על לבה והוא חשוב ומצוייר בזהב ויש מפרשים כמין חצי עגול עשוי כמין כלבוס ואוחזת בו מפתחי חלוקה והפגם בולע צוארה והוא של זהב לוי"ה [לקמן נט:]. **בגד חשוב** לתלות בצוארה כנגד לבה שלא יפול מה שהיא אוכלת על בגדיה ויש לו מקום שנצים כעין שעושים למכנסים ותוחב בו רצועה רחבה ומוללתו סביב הרצועה שהבגד רחב הרבה וקושרת הרצועה סביב צוארה [לקמן ע"ב ע"ש עוד ובתוס' שם]. **ולא במחט שאינה נקובה.** לענין הוצאת שבת יש חילוק בין נקובה לשאינו נקובה דנקובה קתני חייב חטאת ושאינה נקובה כגון איספיגל"א שהיא תכשיט קתני אינו חייב חטאת בפרק במה אשה (שבת נז:) [לעיל נב:]. **בחוטין שבאזניהן.** הבנות קטנות שמנקבות אזניהם ואין עושין נזמים עד שיגדלו ונותנין חוטין או קסמים באזניהם שלא יסתמו אזניהם לוי"ה [לקמן סה.].

עין משפט נר מצוה

א א מיי' פי"ט מהל' שבת הל' ו' ומיי' פ"ב מהל' מקוואות הל' ה סמג לאוין סה וסמג עשין רמח טוש"ע א"ח סי' שג סעיף א וטוש"ע י"ד סי' קלח סעיף ב:
ב ב מיי' פי"ט מהל' שבת הלכה ד' טוש"ע א"ח סי' שג סעיף י וסעיף יח:
ג ג ד מיי' שם הלכה ט טוש"ע א"ח סי' שג סעיף א וטוש"ע י"ד סי' קלח סעיף ג:
ד ה ו מיי' שם הלכה ז י טוש"ע א"ח שם סעיף ב וטוש"ע י"ד שם סעיף ב:

רבינו חננאל

במה אשה יוצאה ובמה אינה יוצאה. לא תצא אשה בחוטי כו'. אוקמה רב נחמן גזירה שמא תזדמן לה טבילה של מצוה ומשום שחוצצת מתרתן ומהלכת בהן ד' אמות ברה"ר. אבל תיכי חלילתא לא גזרו בהו רבנן דהא אחוותיה דרב הונא בריה דר' יהושע הוו טבלי בדמחתן הני תיכי חלילתא בראשיהן ולא הוו קפדי וכיון דלא הוו קפדי שרו. וה"מ תיכי חלילתא אבל תיכי טמימתא לא דחוצצות ואסיק' דחוטי שיער אינן חוצצין ואפילו הן קשורין בראש הבנות ואע"פ שהראש קשה הוא המים נכנסין בשיער ואין חוצצין אבל חוטי צמר וחוטי פשתן בראש הבנות חוצצין וכ"ש אם הן קשורין בצואר שמשתקעין בבשר ואין המים באין תחתיהן. ולפיכך חוצצין. כיוצא בהן החבקין שבצוארי הבנות ואוקימנא

BECAUSE THE WATER PENETRATES THEM.[32]

The Gemara cites a statement made in explanation of this Mishnah, and proceeds to analyze it:

אָמַר רַב הוּנָא – Rav Huna said: וְכוּלָּן בְּרָאשֵׁי הַבָּנוֹת שָׁנִינוּ – And all of these (i.e. even the woolen and linen strands) **we learned** in regard to items worn **on the heads of girls.**[33]

Rav Huna's statement is questioned:

מַתְקִיף לָהּ רַב יוֹסֵף – Rav Yosef challenged the necessity of Rav Huna's statement, asking: **לְמַעוּטֵי מַאי – What** other possibility does Rav Huna's statement come **to exclude?** I.e. where on the body can woolen or linen strands be worn during an immersion without invalidating it?[34] **אִילֵימָא לְמַעוּטֵי דְּצַוָּאר – If** you wish **to say** that Rav Huna wishes **to exclude** strands worn **on the neck,** for he is of the opinion that such strands would *not* be an interposition, this cannot be; **וּדְמַאי – for of what** material are the strands he is excluding made? **אִילֵימָא לְמַעוּטֵי דְּצֶמֶר – If** you wish **to say** he is **excluding** strands made **of wool,** and ruling that such strands pose an interposition when worn on the hair but not on the neck, this is untenable. **הַשְׁתָּא רַךְ עַל גַּבֵּי קָשֶׁה חוֹצֵץ – For now, if** a **soft** material (wool) tied **onto** a **hard** surface (hair) **is an interposition,**[35] **רַךְ עַל גַּבֵּי רַךְ מִיבַּעְיָא – can there be any question** that a **soft** material tied **onto** a **soft** surface (skin) will interpose as well?[36] **וְאֶלָּא לְמַעוּטֵי דְּחוּטֵי פִשְׁתָּן – And** if you will say, **rather,** that Rav Huna wishes **to exclude** the case **of linen strands** worn on the neck,[37] a similar difficulty arises: **הַשְׁתָּא קָשֶׁה עַל גַּבֵּי קָשֶׁה חוֹצֵץ – For now, if** a **hard** material (linen) tied **onto** a **hard** surface (hair) **is** deemed **an interposition, קָשֶׁה עַל גַּבֵּי רַךְ מִיבַּעְיָא – can there be any question** that a **hard** material (linen) tied **onto** a **soft** surface (skin) will pose an interposition?[38]

Rav Yosef offers his own understanding of Rav Huna's statement:

אֶלָּא אָמַר רַב יוֹסֵף – Rather, Rav Yosef said: Indeed, Rav Huna did mean to exclude strands worn around the neck. **הַיְינוּ טַעְמָא דְּרַב הוּנָא –** And **this is the reason for Rav Huna's** ruling that such ties do not interpose: **לְפִי שֶׁאֵין אִשָּׁה חוֹנֶקֶת אֶת עַצְמָהּ – Because a woman will not strangle herself** by tying the strands around her neck too tightly.[39]

The Gemara objects:

אֵיתִיבֵיהּ אַבַּיֵי – Abaye challenged this explanation **from the** following **Baraisa: הַבָּנוֹת יוֹצְאוֹת בְּחוּטִין שֶׁבְּאָזְנֵיהֶן – GIRLS MAY GO OUT** on the Sabbath **WITH STRANDS THAT ARE IN THEIR EARS,**[40] **אֲבָל לֹא בַחֲבָקִין שֶׁבְּצַוְּארֵיהֶן – BUT NOT WITH DRAWSTRINGS THAT ARE ON THEIR NECKS.**[41] Now, this Baraisa implies that the Sages' decree included even strands that are worn on the neck; **וְאִי אָמְרַתְּ אֵין אִשָּׁה חוֹנֶקֶת עַצְמָהּ – but if you say** that **a woman will not choke herself** by tying strings too tightly around her neck, **חֲבָקִין שֶׁבְּצַוְּארֵיהֶן אַמַּאי לֹא – why** does the Baraisa rule that young girls may **not** go out with **drawstrings that are on their necks?** Since they are not an interposition with respect to immersion, they should not have been included in the Sages' decree. – ? –

The Gemara answers:

אָמַר רָבִינָא – Ravina said:

NOTES

32. R' Yehudah is of the opinion that these bands do not lay tightly against the hair and the water can penetrate beneath them; accordingly, they do not constitute a *chatzitzah* (*Rashi;* cf. *Ran MHK* ed. who states that according to R' Yehudah woolen strands do not interpose because they *absorb* the water, which goes *through* them and onto the hair; see also *Sfas Emes*).

The Gemara below (57b) discusses whether the Tanna Kamma disputes R' Yehudah's ruling concerning bands made of hair.

33. I.e. the Tanna Kamma's words, "on the heads of the girls," do not refer only to the straps but to the two preceding cases as well (*Rashi*).

34. Rav Huna stated that the Tanna Kamma's ruling invalidating woolen and linen strands is limited to strands worn on the hair. This implies that were they to be worn on another part of the body, the Tanna Kamma would hold that they do *not* constitute a *chatzitzah.*

35. Even according to Rav Huna, the Tanna Kamma certainly considers woolen strands tied onto the hair an interposition. [The Gemara considers wool a soft substance in comparison to linen or hair, which are stiffer (*Rashi*).]

36. Since skin is softer than hair, an item that is tied around skin will sink into it more readily. The item will thus provide a greater barrier against the penetration of water when tied on the skin than it would if it were tied around hair (*Rashi*). Accordingly, if the Tanna Kamma rules that woolen and linen strands tied around the hair hold tightly enough to form an interposition to immersion, strands of these materials tied against the skin would certainly do so. Therefore, this cannot be the case that Rav Huna meant to exclude.

37. [For flax is a harder substance than wool. Perhaps, then, it does not lay as tightly against the skin as does wool, and strands of linen worn against the neck would *not* interpose.]

38. For whether the material being used as a tie is hard or soft, the fact remains that if it is tied around a soft surface, it will cut into that surface more deeply than it would cut into a stiffer surface. Accordingly, if the Tanna Kamma rules than linen threads interpose when they are tied around hair, he will certainly hold that they interpose if they are tied around skin. This, then, can also not be the case that Rav Huna means to exclude from the Tanna Kamma's ruling.

39. Rather, she will tie them loosely, so they do not cause her discomfort (*Rashi*). Thus, by stating that the Tanna Kamma refers only to strands worn on the hair, Rav Huna is teaching that the Tanna Kamma will concur that these strands do not interpose when worn around the neck (for they will not be tied tightly enough to prevent the water from penetrating).

40. After young girls have their ears pierced, strings are placed in the holes so that they will not close up (*Rashi;* see also *Rashi* below, 65a ד״ה ואפילו). These strings are not usually removed, and therefore they may be worn outside on the Sabbath.

41. The Gemara presently understands that these drawstrings are functional rather than ornamental – i.e. narrow, undecorated straps which serve to lace up clothing. The Baraisa rules that they may not be worn outside on the Sabbath, seemingly because we are concerned that they will be fastened tightly around the neck, which will necessitate their removal before an immersion and possibly result in a forbidden transport of the drawstrings in the *reshus harabim* (*Rashi,* as explained by *Rashash;* see also below, 57b note 1).

במה אשה פרק ששי שבת

(א) **במה** [א] אשה יוצאה ובמה אינה יוצאה לא תצא אשה לא בחוטי צמר ולא בחוטי פשתן ולא ברצועות שבראשה ולא תטבול בהן עד שתרפם ולא בטוטפת ולא בסרביטין בזמן שאינן תפורים ולא בכבול לרה"ר ולא (ב) בעיר של זהב ולא בקטלא ולא בנזמים [ב] ולא בטבעת שאין עליה חותם ולא במחט שאינה נקובה ואם יצאת אינה חייבת חטאת: **גמ'** טבילה מאן דכר שמה אמר רב נחמן בר יצחק אמר רבה בר אבוה מה טעם קאמר מה טעם לא תצא אשה לא בחוטי צמר ולא בחוטי פשתן מפני שאמרו חכמים בחול לא תטבול בהן עד שתרפם וכיון דבחול לא תטבול בהן עד שתרפם בשבת לא תצא דילמא מיתרמי לה טבילה של מצוה ושריא להו ואתי לאתויינהו ד' אמות ברה"ר בעא מיניה רב כהנא מרב ° תיכי חלילתא מאי א"ל אריג קאמרת כל שהוא אריג לא גזרו איתמר נמי (ג) אמר רב הונא בריה דרב יהושע [ג] כל שהוא אריג לא גזרו ואיכא דאמרי אמר רב הונא בריה דרב יהושע חזינא לאחוותי דלא קפדן עלייהו מאי איכא בין הך לישנא ובין הך לישנא איכא בינייהו דטניפן להך לישנא דאמר כל שהוא אריג לא גזרו הני נמי ארוג ולהך לישנא דאמרת משום קפידא [ד] כיון דטניפא מקפד קפדא עלייהו (ד) תנן התם ואלו חוצצין באדם חוטי צמר וחוטי פשתן והרצועות שבראשי הבנות ר' יהודה אומר של צמר ושל שער אין חוצצין מפני שהמים באין בהן אמר רב הונא וכולן בראשי הבנות שנינו מתקיף לה רב יוסף למעוטי מאי אילימא למעוטי דצואר ודמאי אילימא למעוטי דצמר השתא רך על גבי קשה חוצץ רך על גבי רך מיבעיא ואלא למעוטי דחוטי פשתן השתא קשה על גבי קשה חוצץ קשה על גבי רך מיבעיא אלא אמר רב יוסף היינו טעמא דרב הונא [ה] לפי שאין אשה חונקת את עצמה איתיביה אביי הבנות יוצאות בחוטין שבאזניהן אבל לא בחבקין שבצואריהן ואי אמרת אין אשה חונקת עצמה חבקין שבצואריהן אמאי לא [ו] אמר רבינא

הכא

במה אשה יוצאה. דהוי תכשיט ולא משוי ואיכא דהוי תכשיט וגזור ביה רבנן דילמא שלפא ומחויא לחברתה חשיבותו ודילמא אתי לאיתויי ד' אמות: **לא בחוטי צמר** ופשתן ורצועה שבראשה. שקולעת בהן שערה: **שבראשה**. אכולהו קאי ובגמ' מפרש טעמא: **ולא תטבול בהן**. משום חלילה: **עד שתרפם**. שתתירם קלת שיהיו רפויין ויכנסו המים ביניהם לשער: **טוטפת וסרביטין**. מפרש בגמרא וחשובין הן וחיישינן דילמא שלפא ומחויא לחברתה: **בזמן שאין תפורין**. עם השבכה שקורין שקופיי"א אבל תפורין ליכא למיחש לאחויי שאינה נוטלת השבכה מראשה ברה"ר שתגלה כל שערה: **כבול**. מפרש בגמ': **לרה"ר**. אבל לחצר שרי וכל הנזכרים למעלה אסורים אף לחצר שמא תרגילם ברה"ר וחדא גזירה היא דגזור בהם שלא תתקשט בהם בשבת כלל ובכבול התירו כדמפרש לקמן בפרקין (דף סד:) שלא לאסור את כל תכשיטיה ותתגנה על בעלה: **עיר של זהב**. כמין נוסקא ומציירין בה כמין עיר: **קטלא**. מפרש בגמרא (לקמן דף נט:): **חותם**. צורה לחתום בה איגרת או כל דבר סגור: **שאינה נקובה**. כגון איספיגל"א: **ואם יצאת אינה חייבת חטאת**. דכולהו תכשיטין נינהו ורבנן הוא דגזור בהו דילמא שלפא ומחויא: **גמ' טבילה מאן דכר שמה**. מה ענין טבילה אצל הלכות שבת: **ושריא להו**. ומתרת אותם לטבול בשבת שעל הטבילה לא גזרו כדאמרינן במסכת ביצה (דף יח.) אדם נראה כמיקר ואין נראה כמתקן עצמו: **תיכי חלילתא**. שרשרות של חוטין חלולות ועגולות: **מהו**. לקלוע בהן שערה ולצאת בשבת שאינה יכולה למותחן ולדוחקן על השער בחזקה והמים נכנסין בה ומיבעיא ליה מי הוי חלילה ולא תצא בהן בשבת משום גזירת טבילת מצוה או לא הוי חלילה: **כל שהוא אריג לא גזרו**. לצאת בו בשבת דלענין חלילה לא חיין דלא מצי להדוקי שפיר: **לאחוותי דלא קפדן עלייהו**. ליטלן מראשן כשהן רוחצות בחמין אלמא עיילי בהו מיא שפיר אפילו להנאת רחילה וכיון שכן לענין טבילה נמי לא צריכין להתירן ומותר לצאת בהן בשבת דהא אי מתרמי טבילה לא שרו להו לא משום חלילה ולא משום קפידא: **דמיטנפי**. שנטנפו הנך תיכי בטיט: **הא נמי אריג הוא**. והא קאמר לא גזרו כלל לצאת ולהאי לישנא דלא קפדי משמע דאי קפדי לנטלן מראשן כשהן רוחצות אסור לצאת בהן בשבת ואע"ג דלענין איהדוקי לא חיילי ומותרות לטבול בהן הלכך הני כיון דמיטנפי מקפד קפדן שלא להיות בראשן בשעת טבילתן מפני שהמים ממחין את הטיט ומלכלך בשרן בעלייתן מן הטבילה ואע"ג דחלילה לא הוי דהא עיילי בהו מיא מיהו כיון דשקלי לה משום טינוף אתי לאיתויינהו ואסור לצאת בהן וללישנא קמא לא גזרו אלא במידי דחיין לטבילה ורבותי מפרשין הך קפידא לענין חלילה כדקי"ל רובו ומקפיד עליו חוצץ (עירובין דף ד:) וקשיא לי בגוה טובא חדא דכי איתמר ההוא במידי דמיהדק איתמר ואשמעינן דאע"ג דלא עיילי ביה מיא כיון דלא קפיד עליה חשיב כגופיה ובטל לגבי שערו אבל במידי דלא מיהדק ועיילי ביה מיא מאי חוצץ איכא למימר הא לאו חוצץ הוא ואי אתית למימר דההוא חוצץ דהתם לא דק בלישניה ומיהו כל מידי דקפיד עלייהו אסור היכי אמרינן הכא האי נמי אריג הוא ומותר כיון דפשיטא לן דהיכא דמיטנפי מקפד קפדן על כרחיך חיין דהא רב הונא בריה דרב יהושע אהלכה למשה מסיני לא אתא לאיפלוגי: **ואלו חוצצין באדם**. משום דתני התם אלו חוצצין בכלים תני לענין טבילת אדם ואלו חוצצין באדם: **של צמר ושל שער אין חוצצין**. דלא מיהדק על גבי שער: **הבנות**. קטנות. אורחא דמילתא נקט: **וכולן בראשי הבנות שנינו**. לא תימא שבראשי הבנות ארצועות לחודייהו קאי אלא אחוטין נמי קאי: **למעוטי מאי**. אשמעינן רב הונא דחוטין נמי בראשי הבנות שנינו: **אילימא למעוטי**. חוטין הקשורין בצוארן דלא חיילי: **ודמאי**. הי חוטין אתא למעוטי דלא חיילי בצואר: צמר קרוי רך לגבי פשתן ולגבי שער: **על גבי קשה**. שער: **ע"ג רך**. בשר: **מיבעיא**. בתמיה הא ודאי על גבי רך טפי מיהדק: **לפי שאין אשה חונקת עצמה**. להדק חוטין בצוארה וקושרתן בריוח שיהו רפין: **בחוטין שבאזניהם**. שנותנין שם שלא יסתם הנקב: **חבקין**. ענקי רצועות שאינן מוזהבות רחבות דלאו לתכשיט עבידן דומיא דחוטין שבאזניהן: **חבקין**. לשון קילקלי וחבק (לקמן דף סד.) ליגגל"א לאסור בו סוס:

בקטלא

במה אשה כו' לא בחוטי צמר. מפרש בגמ' משום דילמא מיתרמי לה טבילה של מצוה ושרי להו ואתי לאתויינהו ארבע אמות ברה"ר אומר ר"י דהיינו דוקא בחוטין שאין נתונין בקליעת השער אבל חוטין הנתונין בקליעת השער יוצאה בהן דבהנהו ליכא למיגזר דילמא שריא להו כדתנן בהמצניע (לקמן דף צד:) דאיכא לכל הפחות איסור שבות בגודלת וסברא הוא דכי היכי דיש איסור בעשיית קליעה ה"נ יש איסור בסתירת קליעה וא"ת מהאי טעמא תהא אשה אסורה לצאת בטלית דהא ודאי שריא לה בשעת טבילה וניחוש דילמא אתי לאתויי וי"ל דבדברים שהם עיקר מלבוש ליכא למיגזר דאפילו בחול אין דרך ללכת כלל ממקומו עד שילבישם אלא דוקא בדברים קטנים יש לחוש שאין מקפיד אם אינם עליו ורגילות הוא בחול כשמתירן פעמים נושאן בידו עד ביתו ונראה לר"י דדוקא בדברים שרגילות להסירן כדי להראותן או משום חלילה או משום קפידא גזרו שלא לצאת דשמא כשיסיר ישכח שהוא שבת ואתי לאתויי אבל דברים שמותר לצאת בהן שאין רגילות להסירן מותר לקשור ולהתיר ברה"ר דליכא למיחש למידי דאם יהא זכור שבת בשעת התרה לא אתי לאתויי ואם לא יהיה זכור שבת אפילו נאסר להתיר ולהסיר לא יועיל וכ"מ לקמן (דף סא.) דקתני בברייתא וקושר ומתיר קמיע אפילו ברה"ר והא דאיצטריך התם לאשמעי' דשרי אע"פ שכל דבר מותר להסיר כדפרישית איצטריך לאשמעינן דלא אסרינן משום דמיחזי דקושרו עליו שלא לרפואה ומתכוין להוציא כי היכי דאסור בפילפל וגרגיר מלח לכתחילה לתת בפה בשבת או להחזיר אלא כמלבוש גמור חשיב מחמת הרפואה:

השתא רך על גבי קשה חוצץ כו'. וא"ת דילמא רב הונא נקט וכולן בראשי הבנות לרבותא דאפילו בראשי הבנות דהוי רך ע"ג קשה חוצץ ואור"י דבלאו רב הונא הוה ידעינן דבכל מקום חוצצין אפילו בראש אלא ודאי למעוטי שום דבר אתא: **השתא** קשה ע"ג קשה חוצץ. סבר הש"ס דקשה ע"ג רך חיין טפי מקשה ע"ג קשה ורך ע"ג קשה לא חיין כקשה ע"ג קשה דהא לר' יהודה חוטי צמר אין חוצצין דהוי רך על גבי קשה וחוטי פשתן דהוי קשה ע"ג קשה חוצצין וחוטי שיער דהוי נמי קשה על גבי קשה לכ"ע אין חוצצין אף על פי שחוטי פשתן חוצצין לכולי עלמא: **אלא** א"ר יוסף. לפי שרב יוסף בעצמו מקשה שייך לומר אלא:

הכא

א א מיי' פי"ט מהל' שבת הל' ו' ומיי' פ"ב מהל' מקוואות הל' ה סמג לאוין סה וסמג עשין רמח טוש"ע א"ח סי' שג סעיף א וטוש"ע י"ד סי' קלח סעיף ב:

ב ב מיי' פי"ט מהל' שבת הלכה ד' טוש"ע א"ח סי' שג סעיף י וסעיף יח:

ג ג ד מיי' שם הלכה ט טוש"ע א"ח סי' שג סעיף א וטוש"ע י"ד סי' קלח סעיף ג:

ד ה ו מיי' שם הלכה ז י טוש"ע א"ח שם סעיף ב וטוש"ע י"ד שם סעיף ב:

רבינו חננאל

במה אשה יוצאה ובמה אינה יוצאה. לא תצא אשה בחוטי כו'. אוקמה רב נחמן גזירה שמא תזדמן לה טבילה של מצוה ומשום שחוצצת מתרתן ומהלכת בהן ד' אמות ברה"ר. אבל תיכי חלילתא לא גזרו בהו רבנן דהא אחוותיה דרב הונא בריה דר' יהושע הוו טבלי בדמחתן הני תיכי חלילתא בראשיהן ולא הוו קפדי וכיון דלא הוו קפדי שרו. וה"מ תיכי חלילתא אבל תיכי טמימתא לא דחוצצות ואסיק' דחוטי שיער אינן חוצצין ואפילו הן קשורין בראש הבנות ואע"פ שהראש קשה הוא המים נכנסין בשיער ואין חוצצין אבל חוטי צמר וחוטי פשתן בראש הבנות חוצצין וכ"ש אם הן קשורין בצואר שמשתקעין בבשר ואין המים באין תחתיהן. ולפיכך חוצצין. כיוצא בהן החבקין שבצוארי הבנות ואוקימנא

מסורת הש"ס

א) [נדרים ג: מיר ב.], ב) [עי' תוס' לקמן נט. ד"ה ולא], ג) לקמן נח., ד) מקוואות פ"ט מ"א.

גליון הש"ס

גמ' תיכי חלילתא מאי. עי' זבחים דף לד ע"א תוס' ד"ה מקנחת:

ליקוטי רש"י

בקטלא. מוסטניי"א והוא בגד שיש לו שנצים כעין מכנסים ומכנסת בו רצועה רחבה וקושרת סביב צוארה והבגד תלוי על לבה והוא חשוב ומצוייר בזהב ויש מפרשים כמין חצי עגול עשוי כמין כלבוש ואוחזת בו מפתחי חלוקה והפגם בולע צוארה והוא של זהב [לקמן נט:]. בגד חשוב לתלות בצוארה כנגד לבה שלא יפול מה שהיא אוכלת על בגדיה ויש לו מקום שנצים כעין שעושים למכנסים ותוחב בו רצועה רחבה ומוללתו סביב הרצועה שהבגד רחב הרבה וקושרת הרצועה סביב צוארה [לקמן ע"ב ע"ש עוד ובתוס' שם]. **ולא במחט שאינה נקובה**. לענין הוצאת שבת יש חילוק בין נקובה לשאינו נקובה דנקובה קתני חייב חטאת ושאינה נקובה כגון איספיגל"א שהיא תכשיט קתני אינו חייב חטאת בפרק במה אשה (שבת נז:) [לעיל נב:]. **בחוטין שבאזניהן**. הבנות קטנות שמנקבות אזניהם ואין עושין נזמים עד שיגדלו ונותנין חוטין או קסמים באזניהם שלא יסתמו אזניהם רש"י [לקמן סה.].

הכא בקטלא עסקינן ° דאשה חונקת את עצמה דניחא לה שתראה כבעלת בשר: ר' יהודה אומר של צמר ושל שער אין חוצצין מפני שהמים באין בהן: אמר רב יוסף אמר רב יהודה אמר שמואל הלכה כרבי יהודה בחוטי שער [א] א"ל אביי הלכה מכלל דפליגי וכי תימא אי לאו דשמעינן מתנא קמא דאיירי בחוטי שער איהו נמי לא הוה מיירי ודילמא כשם קאמר להו כי היכי דמודיתו לי בחוטי שער אודו לי נמי בחוטי צמר [ב] איתמר אמר רב נחמן אמר שמואל [א] מודים חכמים לרבי יהודה בחוטי שער תניא נמי הכי חוטי צמר חוצצין חוטי שער אין חוצצין ר' יהודה אומר של צמר ושל שער אין חוצצין אמר רב נחמן בר יצחק מתניתין נמי דיקא [ג] דקתני יוצאה אשה בחוטי שער בין משלה בין משל חברתה מני אילימא רבי יהודה אפילו חוטי צמר נמי אלא לאו רבנן היא וש"מ בחוטי שער לא פליגי ש"מ: לא בטוטפת: מאי טוטפת א"ר יוסף חומרתא דקטיפתא א"ל אביי [ב] תהוי כקמיע מומחה ותשתרי אלא אמר רב יהודה משמיה דאביי [ד] אפוזיינו תניא נמי הכי [ג] יוצאה אשה בסבכה המוזהבת ובטוטפת ובסרביטין הקבועין בה איזו טוטפת ואיזו סרביטין א"ר אבהו טוטפת המוקפת לה מאזן לאזן סרביטין המגיעין לה עד לחייה אמר רב הונא עניות עושין אותן של מיני צבעונין עשירות עושין אותן של כסף ושל זהב: ולא בכבול: אמר רבי ינאי כבול זה איני יודע מהו אי כבלא דעבדא תנן אבל כיפה של צמר שפיר דמי או דילמא כיפה של צמר תנן וכ"ש כבלא דעבדא [ה] אמר רבי אבהו מסתברא כמ"ד [ד] כיפה של צמר תנן ותניא נמי הכי יוצאה אשה בכבול ובאיסטמא לחצר ר"ש בן אלעזר אומר [ו] אף בכבול לרה"ר כלל ° אמר רשב"א כל שהוא למטה מן השבכה יוצאין בו כל שהוא למעלה מן השבכה אין יוצאין בו מאי איסטמא א"ר אבהו ביזיוני מאי ביזיוני אמר אביי אמר רב כליא פרוחי ת"ר [ז] ג' דברים נאמרו באיסטמא [ה] אין בה משום כלאים [י] ואינה מטמאה בנגעים ואין יוצאין בה לרה"ר משום ר"ש אמרו אף

אין

רש"י

בקטלא עסקינן. בגד חשוב לתלות בצוארה כנגד לבה שלא יפול מה שהיא אוכלת על בגדיה ויש לו מקום שנים כעין שעושים למכנסים ותוחב בו רצועה רחבה ומוללתו סביב הרצועה שהבגד רחב הרבה וקושרת הרצועה סביב צוארה וחונקת עצמה בחוזק כדי שתהא בשרה בולטת ותראה בעלת בשר ומתוך שהרצועה חלקה ורחבה אינה מזיקתה: מכלל דפליגי. בתמיה והא ת"ק לא איירי בשערה שמע מינה בשער מודה דלא מיהדק על גבי שער: דילמא. האי דאדכר שער: כשם קאמר להו. כשם שאתם מודים לי בחוטי שער אודו לי בחוטי צמר (א): חומרתא דקטיפתא. קשר שעושין לרפואות קיטוף עין רע שלא תשלוט: ותיהוי כקמיע מומחה. דקתני מתני' ולא בקמיע בזמן שאינו מן המומחה הא מומחה שפיר דמי: אפוזייני. פרונטי"ל של זהב: שבכה. קופיי"ה דאי שלפא ליה מיגליא ראשה: המוקפת. את הפדחת מאזן לאזן: המגיעים עד לחייה. על ראשה כורכתו ותולה לה על לחייה מכאן ומכאן: אי כבלא דעבדא תנן. חותם שעושין לעבד בכסותו לסימן הוכחה שהוא עבד ובההוא קתני מתני' דשפחה לא תצא בו: אבל כיפה של צמר. ככובע שתחת השבכה דמקרי נמי כבול ומתקשטת בו: שפיר דמי. דכיון דמיגליא שערה לא שלפא ומחויא: או דילמא כיפה תנן. דלא תצא דחיישינן דילמא שלפא ומחויא מתחת השבכה ואינה מגלה וכל שכן כבלא דעבדא: בכבול ובאסטמא. לקמיה מפרש מאי אסטמא ומדקתני כל שהוא למטה מן השבכה ש"מ כיפה תנן: כליא פרוחי. מצנפת קטנה לאחר קישוריה שקולעת ראשה וכסתה יש שערות קטנות שיוצאין חוץ לקישוריה והן נקראין פרוחי על שמפריחין ויוצאין לחוץ ואוגדתן לתחת קישוריה ע"י מצנפת קלרה: כליא. מונעת אותן שערות מלצאת: אין בה משום כלאים. שעשויה כמין לבד שקורין פולטר"א ואינה טוויה: ואינה מטמאה בנגעים. מהאי טעמא גופיה דגבי נגעים כתיב נמי בגד ויליף מכלאים שוע וטווי:

אין

תוספות

הכא בקטלא עסקינן. תימה דמשמע דקטלא טעמא משום חלילה וא"כ אמאי תני (ב) במתניתין בסיפא בהדי חוטי למר ברישא הוה ליה למיתנייה ואומר רשב"א דקטלא נמי דבר של נוי הוא ויש לחוש דילמא שליף ומחויא ומיירי מתני' ברפוי דליכא חלילה ולכך אין לאוסרו אלא משום תכשיט אבל ברייתא דהכא איירי במיהדק דליכא למיחש דילמא שלפא שאינה מסירה לפי שלא תראה בעלת בשר וא"ת ומאי דוחקיה לאוקמא ברייתא משום חלילה לוקמא ברפוי ומשום משלפא כמתני' וי"ל דברייתא משמע ליה דטעמא משום חלילה דומיא דרישא דקתני הבנות יוצאות בחוטין שבאזניהם דלא איצטריך דליכא למיחש דילמא שלפא ומחויא דפשיטא הוא דמאי נוי שייך בחוטין אלא איצטריך לאשמעינן דאין בו חלילה ואינה מסירתן בשעת טבילה וה"נ סיפא טעמא משום חלילה: **תניא** נמי הכי כו'. מדתני (ג) וסרביטין הקבועים בה ודרך לקבוע אפזיינו בסבכה אבל חומרתא דקטיפתא אין קובעין: **אי** כבלא דעבדא תנן. תימה אי כבלא דעבדא תנן אמאי קתני טפי גבי אשה וי"ל דבעי למיתני בסיפא דמתני' יוצאה בכבול ובפאה נכרית לחצר ופאה נכרית לא שייכא אלא באשה וא"ת אמאי לא תני נמי ברישא פאה נכרית בהדי כבול דאין יוצאין בה לרה"ר ויש לומר דמילתא דפשיטא היא דאסור לצאת בה לרה"ר דודאי משלפה משום דמחכו עלה וא"ת אי כבלא דעבדא תנן אמאי שרי בחצר טפי משאר דברים אבל אי כיפה של צמר תנן ניחא דשרי בחצר שלא תתגנה על בעלה כדמפרש עולא לקמן (דף סד:) וי"ל דכבלא דעבדא שרי כדי לעשות בו קורת רוח לרבו שאם היה כל היום בלא כבול אפילו בחצר בדבר מועט שיעשה העבד כנגד רבו סבור רבו שדעתו למרוד בו ואתי לידי קטטה ולקמן [ח] דפירש"י דבסיפא מודו כ"ע דכבול כיפה של למר היא קשה לר"י דהא משמע הכא למ"ד כבלא דעבדא תנן שרי כיפה של למר אף לרה"ר: **אין** בה משום כלאים. פרש"י משום שאינה טווי וריב"א אומר דמשום הכי אין להתיר דהתנן [ט] הלבדים אסורין מפני שהן שועין אלא משום דאיסטמא דבר קשה הוא ובדבר קשה לא אסרו רבנן משום כלאים כדאמר בפרק קמא דבילה (דף טו. ושם) א"ר הונא בריה דרב יהושע האי נמטא גמדא דנרש שריא אע"ג דשאר לבדים אסורין האי שריא לפי שהיא קשה וכן משמע ביומא פרק בא לו (דף סט.) רב אשי אמר בגדי כהונה קשין הן ולכך שרי להציע תחתיהם כי הא דאמר רב הונא בריה דרב יהושע האי נמטא גמדא דנרש שריא וקשה לר"ת דאמרינן בפ"ק דערכין (דף ג:) הכל חייבים בציצית כהנים לוים וישראלים ופריך פשיטא ומשני כהנים איצטריך ליה סד"א הואיל ואישתרי כלאים לגבייהו כו' לא ליחייבי והשתא היכי אישתרי להו והא בגדי כהונה קשין הן וכה"ג לישראל נמי שרי ואומר ר"ת דדבר שהוא שוע טווי ונוז [ובדרך מלבוש והעלאה] דאסור מן התורה אין חילוק בין רך לקשה דבכל ענין אסור מן התורה אבל בכלאים דרבנן כגון לבדים שאינם אלא שוע שרי בקשין אפילו ללבוש כיון דאין בהו כלאים אלא מדרבנן ובגדי כהונה נמי כיון דשרי מדאורייתא [י] להציע תחתיהן כדתניא לא יעלה עליך אבל אתה מותר להציעו תחתיך אבל אמרו חכמים אסור לעשות כן כו' שרי אפילו מדרבנן כיון דקשין הן דבקשין לא גזרו רבנן כלל ובדבר רך נמי היכא דלא שכיח כריכה מותר להציעו תחתיך כגון מרדעת החמור וכרים וכסתות ומילי אחריני דחשיב במס' כלאים ועל אותן קוטש פורפונטש השיב ר' יצחק שאם יש בתוכן בלאי בגדים של למר ושל פשתן ונתחב בהן המחט שתי תפירות דאסורין בהעלאה אפילו חוט התפירה של קנבוס או של משי שלא התירו כרים וכסתות אלא בהצעה אבל בהעלאה לא אבל אם אין בתוכן רק גיזי למר יכול להיות דמותר אף בהעלאה שאין חוט התפירה מחבר לבגד כלל אלא שמחבר ומקרב שני הבגדים של פשתן שהן כסוי הקוטש משני לדדין ומתוך כך מתהדק הלמר שבינתים ואין זה חיבור כחיבור אריג או תפירה או קשירת חבלים דמה בהמה: **ואינה** מטמאה בנגעים. קשה לר"י מאי איריא בנגעים אפי' במת ושרץ לא מטמא דבעינן טווי ואריג כדאמר לקמן (דף סד.) ואומר ר"י דמטמאה במת ושרצים מק"ו דפכין קטנים שטהורין בזב וטמאים במת ושרץ איסטמא שטמאה בזב דשייך בה מדרס כמו בכפה דאמר (כלים פרק כ"ח משנה ה) כפה שנתנתו לס"ת טהור מן המדרס אינו דין שיטמא במת ושרץ ובערוך פי' איסטמא חתיכה של בגד מוזהב וקובעין בה אבנים טובות ומרגליות ולפ"ז ניחא דמטמא במת ושרצים כשאר תכשיט אבל בנגעים לא שאין הבגד עיקר כ"א הזהב ואבנים טובות ומהאי טעמא נמי אין בה משום כלאים:

והאמר

עין משפט נר מצוה

ה א מיי' פ"ב מהל' מקואות הלכה ה סמג עשין רמח טור וש"ע יו"ד סי' קצח סעיף ד:
ו ב (מיי' פי"ט מהל' שבת הל' ד) טוש"ע א"ח סי' שג סעיף טו:
ז ג מיי' פי"ט מהל' שבת הלכה יו"ד סמג לאוין סה טור וש"ע א"ח סי' שג סעיף טו:
ח ד מיי' שם הלכה ז טוש"ע שם סעיף ג:
ט ה מיי' פ"י מהל' כלאים הלכה כ סמג לאוין רפג טור וש"ע י"ד סי' שא סעיף יד:
י ו מיי' פי"ג מהל' טומאת צרעת הלכה א:

גליון הש"ס

גמ' דאשה חונקת את עצמה. ומזה הטעם נקרא קטלא. הרע"ב פי"א מ"ח דכלים: שם כלל אמר רבי שמעון בן אלעזר כל שהוא למטה מן השבכה. לקמן דף סה ע"א:

רבינו חננאל

בקטלא ומשום דאשה חונקת עצמה כדי שתראה בעלת בשר. פירש רב יוסף טוטפת חומרתא דקטיפתא יש מי שאומרים כי הוא ממיני מרגליות שתולות הנשים בצואריהן משום עין רעה. ונדחו דבריו. ואיתוקמא מאי טוטפת אבזייני כלומר אב שיש בו מינין הרבה. כי מינין תרגם זני דכתיב (דניאל ג) כל זני זמרא פירוש כל מיני זמר והיא נקראת טוטפת מפני שנותנות למעלה מן המצח במקום הטוטפת כדתניא יוצאה אשה בסבכה המוזהבת ובטוטפת ובסרביטין ואוקמה ר' אבהו טוטפת המוקפת מאוזן לאוזן סרבוטין המגיעין לה עד לחייה: ולא בכבול אוקמה ר' אבהו כיפה של צמר דתניא יוצאה אשה בכבול ובאיצטמא לחצר ר' שמעון בן אלעזר אומר בכבול אף לרה"ר כו' דייקינן דכבול דומיא דאיצטמא מה איצטמא כיפה אף כבול כיפה. וכדגרסינן (חולין קלח ע"א) כיפה של צמר היה מונח בראש כ"ג ועליו הציץ שנאמר ושמת אותו על פתיל תכלת. והן חוטין גדילין מעשה עבות רחבין בשתים ושלש אצבעות כגון אבנט ולית הלכתא כשמואל דאמר כבלא דעבדא דאין עושין בדבר של תורה להקל מספקא אלא הכבול שאסרה משנתנו היא כיפה של צמר וכ"ש כבלא דעבדא שאסור. איצטמא היא ביזוני. כלומר חוטין הרבה ממיני צבעונין ותולין אותן בפני הכלה שלא יצערוה הזבובין שמתביישת להסיר הזבובין מעליה ותולין זה בפניה ונקראת כליא דיבי והוא כגון אותה ששנינו (מדות פ"ד מ"ו) אמה כולה עורב. לפי שבמקדש [ראשון] שהיתה קדושתו בכל הקהל והיתה השכינה שרויה בו לא היו עופות פורחות עליו אבל במקדש שני פחדו שמא אין קדושתו כקדושת ראשון ושמא יפרחו העופות על המקדש וישליכו שם דבר טומאה ועשו צורה להבריח העופות מגגי ההיכל וקראו אותה כולה עורב כלומר זו מונעת העורבי מלפרוח בגג ההיכל וזו צורה כדרך שעושין עכשיו שומרי הזרעים: ת"ר שלשה דברים נאמרו באצטמא אין יוצאין בה לרה"ר לפי שאינה כליו כמשאוי חשוב ואין בה משום כלאים לפי שלא אריג הוא ואינה מטמאה בנגעים שאין ב

מסורת הש"ס

א) [לקמן קו: ושם נסמן], ב) ס"א אלא מודי' אתמר אמר רב יוסף אמר ר"י אמר שמואל, ג) לקמן סד:, ד) פי' לין [ובערוך ערך אב פי' אב זיינא], ה) ס"א איתמר רב אמר כיפה של צמר תנן ושמואל אמר כבלא דעבדא תנן אבל כיפה של צמר שפיר דמי, ו) בכבול אף לרה"ר כל"ל, ז) [תוספתא פ"ה], ח) [דף סד:], ט) [פ"ט מ"ט דכלאים], י) להציע כלאים תחתיהן כל"ל.

הגהות הב"ח

(א) רש"י ד"ה כשם קאמר וכו' למר הס"ד ואח"כ מה"ד אלא מודים איתמר כו' ה"ג בספר הישן הס"ד ונ"ב שהוא ס"א: (ב) תוס' ד"ה הכא וכו' אמאי תני לקטלא במתניתין: (ג) ד"ה תניא וכו' מדתני ובטוטפת וסרביטין:

ליקוטי רש"י

בחוטי שער. שקולעת בהן שערה. בין משלה. תלושין [לקמן סד:]. תהוי כקמיע. שכותבין וטוענין לרפואה. ותשתרי. דתכשיט הוא לחולה כאחד ממלבושיו [שם ס.]. כיפה. כמו כובע של צמר לבן שקורין פילטר"א [סוטה מט:]. כעין כובע של צמר וטומנות הנשים תחת לעיף קישוריהן כדאמרי' בבמה אשה יוצאה [גיטין כ.]. כובע קטן פלטרי"א [חולין קלח.]. למטה מן השבכה. כגון שבכה גם של צמר. יוצאין בו. דלא חיישינן דילמא שלפא ומחוייא דמיגלי שערה ומגולה בה שהשבכה נוי הוא לשער [לקמן סה.].

רב נסים גאון

פ"ו תנו רבנן שלשה דברים נאמרו באיסטמא וכו' לדברי תנא קמא אין בה משום עטרת חתנים ולדברי ר' שמעון בן אלעזר אין בה משום עטרות כלות הוא מחמת הטעם שאמרו במס' סוטה בפרק האחרון (דף מט) בפולמוס של אספסינוס גזרו על עטרות חתנים בפולמוס של טיטוס גזרו על עטרות כלות ובפ"ב מן גיטין (דף ז) אמרו אמר ליה ריש גלותא לרב הונא כלילא מנלן דאסיר אמר ליה מרבנן דתנן בפולמוס של אספסינוס קיסר גזרו על עטרות חתנים ועל האירוס אדהכי קם רב הונא לאיפנויי אמר ליה רב חסדא קרא כתיב (יחזקאל כא) כה אמר ה' הסר המצנפת והרים העטרה וגו' וכי מה מצנפת אצל עטרה לומר לך בזמן שהמצנפת בראש כהן גדול תהא עטרה בראש חתנים נסתלק מצנפת מראש כהן גדול תסתלק העטרה מראש כל אדם אדהכי אתא רב הונא אשכחינהו דהוו יתבי וקאמרי שמעתא אמר להו האלהים מדרבנן הוא דאסור:

הָכָא בְּקַטְלָא עָסְקִינַן – **here** in the Baraisa, **we are speaking of** the drawstrings of a ***katla;***[1] and in this case, the drawstrings do interpose, דְּאִשָּׁה חוֹנֶקֶת אֶת עַצְמָהּ – **for a woman will** tighten these straps and appear to **choke herself** with them, דְּנִיחָא לָהּ שֶׁתֵּרָאֶה כְּבַעֲלַת בָּשָׂר – **for it is agreeable to her that she appear** to be **a well-fleshed woman.**[2] Thus, such drawstrings may not be worn outside on the Sabbath, as a woman may remove them before an immersion and inadvertently transport them four *amos* in the public domain.[3]

The Gemara cites a section of the Mishnah in *Mikvaos* that was cited above:

רַבִּי יְהוּדָה אוֹמֵר – R' YEHUDAH SAYS: שֶׁל צֶמֶר וְשֶׁל שֵׂעָר אֵין חוֹצְצִין – Strands OF WOOL OR OF HAIR tied around one's hair DO NOT INTERPOSE, מִפְּנֵי שֶׁהַמַּיִם בָּאִין בָּהֶן – BECAUSE THE WATER PENETRATES THEM.

The Mishnah cites only R' Yehudah's view regarding strands of hair; the Tanna Kamma's view is not known. The Gemara discusses this further:

אָמַר רַב יוֹסֵף אָמַר רַב יְהוּדָה אָמַר שְׁמוּאֵל – **Rav Yosef said in the name of Rav Yehudah who said in the name of Shmuel:** הֲלָכָה כְּרַבִּי יְהוּדָה בְּחוּטֵי שֵׂעָר – **The halachah accords with R' Yehudah regarding** bindings made of **strands of hair;** i.e. they do not interpose.

R' Yosef's statement is questioned:

אָמַר לֵיהּ אַבַּיֵּי – **Abaye said to [Rav Yosef]:** הֲלָכָה מִכְּלָל דִּפְלִיגֵי – You use the term **"the halachah accords." Are we to infer that they** (the Tanna Kamma and R' Yehudah) **disagree** whether strands of hair tied around one's hair are an interposition? But the Tanna Kamma does not discuss such strands at all![4] וְכִי תֵימָא – **And if you will say** that the Tanna Kamma must hold that strands of hair are an interposition – אִי לָאו דְּשָׁמְעִינַן מִתַּנָּא קַמָּא דְּאַיְירֵי בְּחוּטֵי שֵׂעָר – for **if it had not been understood from the Tanna Kamma that he was referring to strands of hair** as well, אִיהוּ נַמִּי לֹא הֲוָה מַיְירֵי – **[R' Yehudah] too would not have referred to them**[5] – this is not a compelling argument. וְדִילְמָא כְּשֵׁם קָאָמַר לְהוּ – **For perhaps [R' Yehudah] is replying to [the Tanna Kamma]** in the form of **"Just as . . .,"** as follows: כִּי הֵיכִי דְּמוֹדֵיתוּ לִי בְּחוּטֵי שֵׂעָר – **Just as you agree with me with respect to strands of hair** that they do not interpose, אוֹדוּ לִי נַמִּי בְּחוּטֵי צֶמֶר – **agree with me also with respect to strands of wool** that they too do not interpose![6] Thus, there is no reason to assume that the Tanna Kamma disputes R' Yehudah's ruling concerning strands of hair; hence, there is no reason to state that the halachah accords with R' Yehudah in that case.

The Gemara cites support for Abaye's contention that the Tanna Kamma and R' Yehudah both agree that strands of hair do not interpose:

אִיתְּמַר – **It was stated:** אָמַר רַב נַחְמָן אָמַר שְׁמוּאֵל – **Rav Nachman said in the name of Shmuel:** מוֹדִים חֲכָמִים לְרַבִּי יְהוּדָה בְּחוּטֵי שֵׂעָר – **The Sages** (i.e. the Tanna Kamma) **agree with R' Yehudah with respect to strands** made **of hair** that they are not an interposition.[7] תַּנְיָא נַמִּי הָכִי – And **this has been taught in a Baraisa as well,** for the Baraisa states: חוּטֵי צֶמֶר חוֹצְצִין – STRANDS OF WOOL ARE AN INTERPOSITION; חוּטֵי שֵׂעָר אֵין חוֹצְצִין – STRANDS OF HAIR, however, DO NOT INTERPOSE. This is the view of the Tanna Kamma. רַבִּי יְהוּדָה אוֹמֵר – R' YEHUDAH, however, SAYS: שֶׁל צֶמֶר וְשֶׁל שֵׂעָר אֵין חוֹצְצִין – Both strands OF WOOL AND those OF HAIR DO NOT INTERPOSE. The Baraisa clearly

NOTES

1. In Talmudic times, a woman would sometimes wear an ornate bib (called a *katla*) to protect her clothing from being soiled by the food that she would eat. The bib was tied around the neck by means of straps that laced through loops at the top of the bib. Women wearing such bibs would wind the straps tightly around the neck, so as to force the skin of the neck forward and create the appearance of a double chin. The straps, being wide and smooth, would not [cut into the skin and] injure her, even though they were wound tightly around her neck (*Rashi;* see also below, notes 2 and 3).

2. [In Talmudic times, a well-fleshed appearance was considered a mark of health and prosperity. Thus, it was desirable to appear plump, and women would purposely tie the straps of their bibs tightly to achieve this effect.]

3. This, however, is only true of the strings of such a bib; other strands, however, are not wound tightly around the neck. Therefore, they need not be removed before an immersion, and they may be worn outside on the Sabbath. Thus, Rav Yosef's explanation of Rav Huna's statement (given above, on 57a) is not contradicted by the Baraisa. For Rav Yosef stated that Rav Huna meant to teach that strands of wool or linen worn on the neck do not interpose, for they are not tightly wound around the neck; and although the Baraisa implies that drawstrings worn around the neck *do* interpose, that Baraisa speaks only of the wide straps of a bib-like garment which was fastened tightly, as explained above.

An apparent difficulty: According to the Gemara's conclusion, the Baraisa teaches that the *katla* (bib) may not be worn outside on the Sabbath due to the concern that its straps will be tied tightly, and thereby necessitate its removal before immersion. But the Mishnah above also taught that a *katla* may not be worn outside on the Sabbath – and the Mishnah listed the *katla* among the items of jewelry that may not be worn, implying that the reason for its prohibition is because a woman may remove it to show it to a friend! The Rishonim offer different resolutions to this problem. *Tosafos* answer that both reasons are applicable to a *katla,* depending on how it is being worn. If the *katla* is being worn tightly, it interposes, and thus may not be worn outside lest it be removed before an immersion; there is no concern that it will be taken off and shown to a friend, however, because the wearer will not wish to loosen it and thereby reveal that she is not as well fleshed as she appears. When the *katla* is being worn loosely merely as an ornament it does not interpose, for the water can penetrate beneath it; it still may not be worn outside, however, due to the concern that it will be taken off and shown to a friend. Thus, the Mishnah teaches that a loosely worn *katla* may not be worn outside because it is jewelry that may be removed for showing; and the Baraisa teaches that a tightly fastened *katla* may not be worn because it must be removed prior to an immersion.

Other Rishonim explain that there are two distinct kinds of *katla*. The Mishnah deals with a *katla* made of gold or silver which was *not* fastened tightly against the skin; therefore, it would not interpose, and it is forbidden only due to the possibility of its being removed for display. The Baraisa, however, deals with a *katla* made of fabric, which was not ornamental and would not be taken off for showing; the Baraisa teaches that wearing it, too, was prohibited, due to the fact that it was wound tightly around the neck, creating an interposition that must be removed prior to an immersion (see *Rashba, Ran MHK* ed.; see there for a variant text cited in the name of *Rabbeinu Tam;* see also *Sfas Emes, Chelkas Binyamin* and *Hagahos R' Elazar Moshe Horowitz*).

4. Thus, from the fact that he states that wool and linen ties are *chatzitzah* but he does not so list strands of hair, it can seemingly be derived that he concurs with R' Yehudah that strands of hair [are *not chatzitzah* because they] cannot be fastened tightly against the hair [and thus do not interpose] (*Rashi*).

5. I.e. it can be argued that the Tanna Kamma *must* have expressed the opinion that strands of hair do interpose [and it was inadvertently omitted from the Mishnah], for if the Tanna Kamma had not discussed the subject of strands of hair at all, why would R' Yehudah have mentioned them in his rejoinder?

6. I.e. the fact that R' Yehudah included mention of strands of hair in his rejoinder to the Tanna Kamma is no proof that the Tanna Kamma held an opposite opinion; rather, R' Yehudah mentioned the case of strands of hair to support his argument, as he was aware that the Tanna Kamma concurred with him in this case.

7. [See the marginal gloss that cites an alternate text which presents this statement as a corrected version of the original statement attributed to Rav Yosef; see also *Bach* §1, who ascribes this version of the text to *Rashi* as well.] See also *Sfas Emes.*

הכא בקטלא עסקינן [ה] דאשה חונקת את עצמה דניחא לה שתראה כבעלת בשר: ר' יהודה אומר של צמר ושל שער אין חוצצין מפני שהמים באין בהן: אמר רב יוסף אמר רב יהודה אמר שמואל הלכה כרבי יהודה בחוטי שער [א] א"ל אביי הלכה מכלל דפליגי וכי תימא אי לאו דשמעינן מתנא קמא דאיירי בחוטי שער איהו נמי לא הוה מיירי ודילמא כשם קאמר להו כי היכי דמודיתו לי בחוטי שער אודו לי נמי בחוטי צמר [ב] איתמר אמר רב נחמן אמר שמואל [א] מודים חכמים לרבי יהודה בחוטי שער תניא נמי הכי חוטי צמר חוצצין חוטי שער אין חוצצין ר' יהודה אומר של צמר ושל שער אין חוצצין אמר רב נחמן בר יצחק מתניתין נמי דיקא [ג] דקתני יוצאה אשה בחוטי שער בין משלה בין משל חברתה מני אילימא רבי יהודה אפילו חוטי צמר נמי אלא לאו רבנן היא וש"מ בחוטי שער לא פליגי ש"מ: לא בטוטפת: מאי טוטפת א"ר יוסף חומרתא דקטיפתא א"ל אביי [ב] תהוי כקמיע מומחה ותשתרי אלא אמר רב יהודה משמיה דאביי [ד] אפוזיינו תניא נמי הכי [ג] יוצאה אשה בסבכה המוזהבת ובטוטפת ובסרביטין הקבועין בה איזו טוטפת ואיזו סרביטין א"ר אבהו טוטפת המוקפת לה מאזן לאזן סרביטין המגיעין לה עד לחייה אמר רב הונא עניות עושין אותן של מיני צבעונין עשירות עושין אותן של כסף ושל זהב: ולא בכבול: אמר רבי ינאי כבול זה איני יודע מהו אי כבלא דעבדא תנן אבל כיפה של צמר שפיר דמי או דילמא כיפה של צמר תנן וכ"ש כבלא דעבדא [ה] אמר רבי אבהו מסתברא כמ"ד [ד] כיפה של צמר תנן ותניא נמי הכי יוצאה אשה בכבול ובאיסטמא לחצר ר"ש בן אלעזר אומר [ו] אף בכבול לרה"ר כלל [ז] אמר רשב"א כל שהוא למטה מן השבכה יוצאין בו כל שהוא למעלה מן השבכה אין יוצאין בו מאי איסטמא א"ר אבהו ביזיוני מאי ביזיוני אמר אביי אמר רב כליא פרוחי ת"ר [ח] ג' דברים נאמרו באיסטמא [ה] אין בה משום כלאים [ו] ואינה מטמאה בנגעים ואין יוצאין בה לרה"ר משום ר"ש אמרו אף אין

רש"י

בקטלא עסקינן. בגד חשוב לתלות בצוארה כנגד לבה שלא יפול מה שהיא אוכלת על בגדיה ויש לו מקום שנצים כעין שעושים למכנסים ותוחב בו רצועה רחבה ומוללתו סביב הרצועה שהבגד רחב הרבה וקושרת הרצועה סביב צוארה וחונקת עצמה בחוזק כדי שתהא בשרה בולטת ותראה בעלת בשר ומתוך שהרצועה חלקה ורחבה אינה מזיקתה: מכלל דפליגי. בתמיה והא ת"ק לא איירי בשערה שמע מינה בשער מודה דלא מיהדק על גבי שער: דילמא. האי דאדכר שער: כשם קאמר להו. כשם שאתם מודים לי בחוטי שער אודו לי בחוטי צמר (א): חומרתא דקטיפתא. קשר שעושין לרפואות קיטוף עין רע שלא תשלוט: ותיהוי כקמיע מומחה. דקתני מתני' ולא בקמיע בזמן שאינו מן המומחה הא מומחה שפיר דמי: אפוזייני. פרונטי"ל של זהב: שבכה. קופיי"ה דאי שלפא ליה מיגליא ראשה: המקפת. את הפדחת מאזן לאזן: המגיעים עד לחייה. על ראשה כורכתו ותולה לה על לחייה מכאן ומכאן: אי כבלא דעבדא תנן. חותם שעושין לעבד בכסותו לסימן הוכחה שהוא עבד ובההוא קתני מתני' דשפחה לא תצא בו: אבל כיפה של צמר. ככובע שתחת השבכה דמקרי נמי כבול ומתקשטת בו: שפיר דמי. דכיון דמיגליא שערה לא שלפא ומחויא: או דילמא כיפה תנן. דלא תצא דחיישינן דילמא שלפא ומחויא מתחת השבכה ואינה מגלה וכל שכן כבלא דעבדא: בכבול ובאסטמא. לקמיה מפרש מאי אסטמא ומדקתני כל שהוא למטה מן השבכה ש"מ כיפה תנן: כליא פרוחי. מגנפת קטנה לאחר קישוריה שקולעת ראשה וכסתה יש שערות קטנות שיוצאין חוץ לקישוריה והן נקראין פרוחי על שמפריחין ויוצאין לחוץ ואוגדתן לתחת קישוריה ע"י מגנפת קטנה: כליא. מונעת אותן שערות מלצאת: אין בה משום כלאים. שעשויה כמין לבד שקורין פולטר"א ואינה טוויה: ואינה מטמאה בנגעים. מהאי טעמא גופיה דגבי נגעים כתיב נמי בגד ויליף מכלאים שוע וטווי: אין

תוספות

הכא בקטלא עסקינן. תימה דמשמע דקטלא טעמא משום חנילה וא"כ אמאי תני (ג) במתניתין בסיפא בהדי חוטי צמר ברישא הוה ליה למיתנייה ואומר רשב"א דקטלא נמי דבר של נוי הוא ויש לחוש דילמא שליף ומחויא ומיירי מתני' ברפוי דליכא חנילה ולכך אין לאוסרו אלא משום תכשיט אבל ברייתא דהכא איירי במיהדק דליכא למיחש דילמא שלפא שאינה מסירה לפי שלא תראה בעלת בשר וא"ת ומאי דוחקיה לאוקמא ברייתא משום חנילה לוקמא ברפוי ומשום משלפא כמתני' וי"ל דברייתא משמע ליה דטעמא משום חנילה דומיא דרישא דקתני הבנות יוצאות בחוטין שבאזניהם דלא איצטריך דליכא למיחש דילמא שלפא ומחויא דפשיטא הוא דמאי נוי שייך בחוטין אלא איצטריך לאשמעינן דאין בו חנילה ואינה מסירתן בשעת טבילה וה"נ סיפא טעמא משום חנילה: תניא נמי הכי כו'. מדתני (ג) וסרביטין הקבועים בה ודרך לקבוע אפזיינו בסבכה אבל חומרתא דקטיפתא אין קובעין: אי כבלא דעבדא תנן. תימה אי כבלא דעבדא תנן אמאי קתני טפי גבי אשה וי"ל דבעי למיתני בסיפא דמתני' יוצאה בכבול ובפאה נכרית לחצר ופאה נכרית לא שייכא אלא באשה וא"ת אמאי לא תני נמי ברישא פאה נכרית בהדי כבול דאין יוצאין בה לרה"ר ויש לומר דמילתא דפשיטא היא דאסור לצאת בה לרה"ר דודאי משלפה משום דמחכו עלה וא"ת אי כבלא דעבדא תנן אמאי שרי בחצר טפי משאר דברים אבל אי כיפה של צמר תנן ניחא דשרי בחצר שלא תתגנה על בעלה כדמפרש עולא לקמן (דף סד:) וי"ל דכבלא דעבדא שרי כדי לעשות בו קורת רוח לרבו שאם היה כל היום בלא כבול אפילו בחצר בדבר מועט שיעשה העבד כנגד רבו סבור רבו שדעתו למרוד בו ואתי לידי קטטה ולקמן [ח] דפירש"י דבסיפא מודו כ"ע דכבול כיפה של צמר היא קשה לר"י דהא משמע הכא למ"ד כבלא דעבדא תנן שרי כיפה של צמר אף לרה"ר: אין בה משום כלאים. פרש"י משום שאינה טווי וריב"א אומר דמשום הכי אין להתיר דהתנן [ט] הלבדים אסורין מפני שהן שועין אלא משום דאיסטמא דבר קשה הוא ובדבר קשה לא אסרו רבנן משום כלאים כדאמר בפרק קמא דביצה (דף טו. ושם) א"ר הונא בריה דרב יהושע האי נמטא גמדא דנרש שריא אע"ג דשאר לבדים אסורין האי שריא לפי שהיא קשה וכן משמע ביומא פרק בא לו (דף סט.) רב אשי אמר בגדי כהונה קשין הן ולכך שרי להציע תחתיהם כי הא דאמר רב הונא בריה דרב יהושע האי נמטא גמדא דנרש שריא וקשה לר"ת דאמרינן בפ"ק דערכין (דף ג:) הכל חייבים בציצית כהנים לוים וישראלים ופריך פשיטא ומשני כהנים איצטריך ליה סד"א הואיל ואישתרי כלאים לגבייהו כו' לא ליחייבי והשתא היכי אישתרי להו והא בגדי כהונה קשין הן וכה"ג לישראל נמי שרי ואומר ר"ת דדבר שהוא שוע טווי ונוז [ובדרך מלבוש והעלאה] דאסור מן התורה אין חילוק בין רך לקשה דבכל ענין אסור מן התורה אבל בכלאים דרבנן כגון לבדים שאינם אלא שוע שרי בקשין אפילו ללבוש כיון דאין בהו כלאים אלא מדרבנן ובגדי כהונה נמי כיון דשרי מדאורייתא [י] להציע תחתיהן כדתניא לא יעלה עליך אבל אתה מותר להציעו תחתיך אבל אמרו חכמים אסור לעשות כן כו' שרי אפילו מדרבנן כיון דקשין הן דבקשין לא גזרו רבנן כלל ובדבר רך נמי היכא דלא שכיח כריכה מותר להציעו תחתיך כגון מרדעת החמור וכרים וכסתות ומילי אחריני דחשיב במס' כלאים ועל אותן קוטש פורפונטש השיב ר' יצחק שאם יש בתוכן בלאי בגדים של צמר ושל פשתן ונתחב בהן המחט שתי תפירות דאסורין בהעלאה אפילו חוט התפירה של קנבוס או של משי שלא התירו כרים וכסתות אלא בהצעה אבל בהעלאה לא אבל אם אין בתוכן רק גיזי צמר יכול להיות דמותר אף בהעלאה שאין חוט התפירה מחבר לבגד כלל אלא שמחבר ומקרב שני הבגדים של פשתן שהן כסוי הקוטש משני צדדין ומתוך כך מתהדק הצמר שבינתים ואין זה חיבור כחיבור אריג או תפירה או קשירת חבלים דבמה בהמה: ואינה מטמאה בנגעים. קשה לר"י מאי איריא בנגעים אפי' במת ושרץ לא מטמא דבעינן טווי ואריג כדאמר לקמן (דף סד.) ואומר ר"י דמטמאה במת ושרצים מק"ו דפכין קטנים שטהורין בזב וטמאים במת ושרץ איסטמא שטמא בזב דשייך בה מדרס כמו בכפה דאמר (כלים פרק כ"ח משנה ה) כפה שנתנתו לס"ת טהור מן המדרס אינו דין שיטמא במת ושרץ ובערוך פי' איסטמא חתיכה של בגד מוזהב וקובעין בה אבנים טובות ומרגליות ולפ"ז ניחא דמטמא במת ושרצים כשאר תכשיט אבל בנגעים לא שאין הבגד עיקר כ"א הזהב והאבנים טובות ומהאי טעמא נמי אין בה משום כלאים:

והאמר

עין משפט נר מצוה

ה א מיי' פ"ב מהל' מקואות הלכה ה סמג עשין רמח טור וש"ע יו"ד סי' קצח סעיף ד:
ו ב (מיי' פי"ט מהל' שבת הלי"ד) טוש"ע א"ח סי' שג סעיף טו:
ז ג מיי' פי"ט מהל' שבת הלכה יו"ד סמג לאוין סה טור וש"ע א"ח סי' שג סעיף טו:
ח ד מיי' שם הלכה ז טוש"ע שם סעיף ג:
ט ה מיי' פ"י מהל' כלאים הלכה כ סמג לאוין רפג טור וש"ע י"ד סי' שא סעיף יד:
י ו מיי' פי"ג מהל' טומאת צרעת הלכה א:

גליון הש"ס

גמ' דאשה חונקת את עצמה. ומזה הטעם נקרא קטלא. הרע"ב פי"א מ"ח דכלים: שם כלל אמר רבי שמעון בן אלעזר כל שהוא למטה מן השבכה. לקמן דף סה ע"א:

רבינו חננאל

בקטלא ומשום דאשה חונקת עצמה כדי שתראה בעלת בשר. פירש רב יוסף טוטפת חומרתא דקטיפתא יש מי שאומרים כי הוא ממיני מרגליות שתולות הנשים בצואריהן משום עין רעה. ונדחו דבריו. ואיתוקמא מאי טוטפת אבזייני כלומר אב שיש בו מינין הרבה. כי מינין תרגם זני דכתיב (דניאל ג) זני זמרא פירוש כל מיני זמר והיא נקראת טוטפת מפני שנותנת למעלה מן המצח במקום הטוטפת כדתניא יוצאה אשה בסבכה המוזהבת ובטוטפת ובסרביטין ואוקמה ר' אבהו טוטפת המוקפת מאוזן לאוזן סרבוטין המגיעין לה עד לחייה: ולא בכבול אוקמה ר' אבהו כיפה של צמר דתניא יוצאה אשה בכבול ובאיצטמא לחצר ר' שמעון בן אלעזר אומר בכבול אף לרה"ר כו' דייקינן דכבול דומיא דאיצטמא מה איצטמא כיפה אף כבול כיפה. וכדגרסינן (חולין קלח ע"א) כיפה של צמר היה מונח בראש כ"ג ועליו הציץ שנאמר ושמת אותו על פתיל תכלת. והן חוטין גדילין מעשה עבות רחבין בשתים ושלש אצבעות כגון אבנט ולית הלכתא כשמואל דאמר כבלא דעבדא דאין עושין בדבר של תורה להקל מספקא אלא הכבול שאסרה משנתנו היא כיפה של צמר וכ"ש כבלא דעבדא שאסור. איצטמא היא ביזני. כלומר חוטין הרבה ממיני צבעונין ותולין אותן בפני הכלה שלא יצערוה הזבובין שמתביישת להסיר הזבובין מעליה ותולין זה בפניה ונקראת כליא דיבי והוא כגון אותה ששנינו (מדות פ"ד מ"ו) אמה כולה עורב. לפי שבמקדש [ראשון] שהיתה קדושתו בכל הקהל והיתה השכינה שרויה בו לא היו עופות פורחות עליו אבל במקדש שני פחדו שמא אין קדושתו כקדושת ראשון ושמא יפרחו העופות על המקדש וישליכו שם דבר טומאה ועשו צורה להבריח העופות מגגי ההיכל וקראו אותה כולה עורב כלומר זו מונעת הערוב מלפרוח בגג ההיכל וזו צורה כדרך שעושין עכשיו שומרי הזרעים: ת"ר שלשה דברים נאמרו באצטמא אין יוצאין בה לרה"ר לפי שאינה כליו כמשאוי חשוב ואין בה משום כלאים דלא אריג הוא ואינה מטמאה בנגעים שאין

מסורת הש"ס

א) [לקמן קו: ושם נסמן], ב) ס"א אלא מודי' אתמר אמר רב יוסף אמר ר"י אמר שמואל, ג) לקמן סד:, ד) פי' לין [ובערוך ערך אב פי' אב זיינא], ה) ס"א איתמר רב אמר כיפה של צמר תנן ושמואל אמר כבלא דעבדא תנן אבל כיפה של צמר שפיר דמי, ו) בכבול אף לרה"ר כצ"ל, ז) [תוספתא פ"ה], ח) [דף סד:], ט) [פ"ט מ"ע דכלאים], י) להציע כלאים תחתיהן כצ"ל.

הגהות הב"ח

(א) רש"י ד"ה כשם קאמר וכו' לצמר הס"ד ואח"כ מה"ד אלא מודים איתמר כו' ה"ג בספר הישן הס"ד ונ"ב שהוא ס"א: (ב) תוס' ד"ה הכא וכו' אמאי תני לקטלא במתניתין: (ג) ד"ה תניא וכו' מדתני ובטוטפת וסרביטין:

ליקוטי רש"י

בחוטי שער. שקולעת בהן שערה. בין משלה. תלושין [לקמן סד:]. תהוי בקמיע. שכותבין וטוענין לרפואה. ותשתרי. דתכשיט הוא למולה כאחד ממלבושיו [שם ס.]. כיפה. כמו כובע של צמר לבן שקורין פילטר"א [סוטה מט:]. כעין כובע של צמר ונותנות הנשים תחת לשיף קישוריהן כדאמרי' בבמה אשה יוצאה [גיטין כ.]. כובע קטן פלטרי"י [חולין קלח.]. למטה מן השבכה. כגון כיפה של צמר. יוצאין בו. דלא חיישינן דילמא שלפא ומחויא דמיגלי שערה ומגניא בה שהשבכה נוי הוא לשער [לקמן סה.].

רב נסים גאון

פ"ו תנו רבנן שלשה דברים נאמרו באיסטמא וכו' לדבר תנא קמא אין בה משום עטרת חתנים ולדברי ר' שמעון בן אלעזר אין בו משום עטרות כלות הוא מחמת הטעם שאמר במס' סוטה בפרק האחרון (דף מט) בפולמוס של אספסינוס גזרו על עטרות חתנים בפולמוס של טיטוס גזרו על עטרות כלות ובפ' א' מן גיטין (דף ז) אמר אמר ליה ריש גלותא לרב הונא כלילא מנלן דאסיר אמר ליה מרבנן דתניא בפולמוס של אספסינוס קיסר גזרו על עטרות חתנים ועל האירוס אדהכי קם רב הונא לאיפנויי אמר ליה רב חסדא קרא כתיב (יחזקאל כא) כה אמר ה' הסר המצנפת וכי מה מצנפת אצל העטרה לומר לך בזמן שהמצנפת בראש כהן גדול תהא עטרה בראש חתנים נסתלק מצנפת מראש כהן גדול תסתלק העטרה מראש כל אדם אדהכי אתא רב הונא אשכחינהו דהוו יתבי וקאמרי להא שמעתא אמר להו האלהים מדרבנן היא דאסור:
הזוג

states that even according to the Tanna Kamma strands of hair are not an interposition.

The Gemara derives support for this position from a Mishnah later in this chapter:

אָמַר רַב נַחְמָן בַּר יִצְחָק – Rav Nachman bar Yitzchak said: **מַתְנִיתִין נַמֵּי דַּיְקָא** – Support for **this** explanation **can also be derived through** a **precise** reading **of the Mishnah** below. **דְּקָתָנֵי – For [the Mishnah] teaches** there:[8] **יוֹצְאָה אִשָּׁה בְּחוּטֵי שֵׂעָר בֵּין מִשֶּׁלָּהּ בֵּין מִשֶּׁל חֲבֶרְתָּהּ** – A WOMAN MAY GO OUT WITH STRANDS OF HAIR tied around her hair, WHETHER they are fashioned OF HER OWN hair OR OF the hair of HER COMPANION. **מַנִּי** – Now, **whose** opinion does this Mishnah reflect? **אִילֵימָא רַבִּי יְהוּדָה** – **If** you wish **to say** that it follows the opinion of **R' Yehudah,** **אֲפִילּוּ חוּטֵי צֶמֶר נַמֵּי** – then why does the Mishnah permit only strands of hair? **Even strands of wool** should **also** be permitted![9] **אֶלָּא לָאו רַבָּנָן הִיא – Rather, is it not** clear that the Mishnah reflects of the view of **the Rabbis?** **וּשְׁמַע מִינָּהּ בְּחוּטֵי שֵׂעָר לֹא פְּלִיגֵי – Therefore, learn from this that [the Rabbis] do not dispute** R' Yehudah's opinion **with regard to strands of hair.** **שְׁמַע מִינָּהּ** – Indeed, **learn from this.**[10]

The Mishnah stated:

לֹא בְּטוֹטֶפֶת – And she may NOT go out WITH A *TOTEFES* . . .[11]

The Gemara asks:

מַאי טוֹטֶפֶת – What is a *totefes*?

The Gemara explains:

אָמַר רַב יוֹסֵף – Rav Yosef said: **חוּמַרְתָּא דְּקַטִיפְתָּא** – A *totefes* is **a charm packet** worn to ward off the effects of an evil eye.[12]

This explanation is challenged:

אָמַר לֵיהּ אַבַּיֵי – Abaye said to [Rav Yosef]: **תֶּהֱוֵי כְּקָמֵיעַ מוּמְחֶה וְתִשְׁתְּרֵי** – But **let [such a necklace] be** treated **as an amulet that is effective, and let it** therefore **be permitted!**[13] **אֶלָּא אָמַר רַב יְהוּדָה מִשְּׁמֵיהּ דְּאַבַּיֵי – Rather, Rav Yehudah said in the name of Abaye:** **אַפּוּזָיְינוּ** – A *totefes* is **a frontlet.**[14]

The Gemara cites a Baraisa which supports this definition of *totefes*:

תַּנְיָא נַמֵּי הָכִי – This was also taught in a Baraisa, which states: **יוֹצְאָה אִשָּׁה בִּסְבָכָה הַמּוּזְהֶבֶת** – A WOMAN MAY GO OUT WITH A HAT decorated WITH GOLD,[15] **וּבְטוֹטֶפֶת וּבְסַרְבִּיטִין הַקְּבוּעִין בָּהּ** – AND WITH A FRONTLET OR HEAD BANGLES THAT ARE ATTACHED TO IT.[16]

The Gemara identifies each of these two somewhat similar ornaments:

אֵיזוֹ טוֹטֶפֶת וְאֵיזוֹ סַרְבִּיטִין – What is a frontlet and what are head bangles? **אָמַר רַבִּי אַבָּהוּ – R' Abahu said:** **טוֹטֶפֶת הַמּוּקֶּפֶת לָהּ מֵאֹזֶן לְאֹזֶן** – **A frontlet** is an ornamental plate **which wraps around her** forehead **from ear to ear,**[17] **סַרְבִּיטִין הַמַּגִּיעִין לָהּ עַד לְלֶחָיֶיהָ** – while **head bangles are** wrapped around the head and hung over the temples on either side, **reaching until her cheeks.**

A further identification:

אָמַר רַב הוּנָא – Rav Huna said: **עֲנִיּוֹת עוֹשִׂין אוֹתָן שֶׁל מִינֵי צִבְעוֹנִין – Poorer women fashion [these ornaments] out of colored fabrics,** **עֲשִׁירוֹת עוֹשִׂין אוֹתָן שֶׁל כֶּסֶף וְשֶׁל זָהָב** – while **wealthy women fashion them of silver or gold.**[18]

The Mishnah stated:

וְלֹא בְּכָבוּל – AND she may NOT go out WITH A *KAVUL* . . .[19]

NOTES

8. Below, 64b.

9. [The Mishnah there permits the wearing of strands of hair because they would not be taken off and shown, and they also do not interpose; thus, there is no reason for a woman to remove them while wearing them outside. Now, according to R' Yehudah this is true of strands of wool as well, for he is of the opinion that woolen strands also do not interpose. Accordingly, the Mishnah below cannot reflect R' Yehudah's view, for it would then have permitted strands of wool to be worn outside as well.]

10. *Rashba* notes that although the Gemara concludes that even according to the Tanna Kamma strands of hair do not interpose, this is only when they are tied on the hair; strands of hair tied on the skin, however, would interpose. [With regard to hairs that are knotted, see *Ran MHK* ed.]

11. In the Mishnah, this word was translated as "frontlet"; this was based on the Gemara's conclusion here.

12. *Rashi* explains that this was a packet worn to ward off the evil eye and prevent it from having an effect (see also *Rashash* and *Orach Chaim* 303:15); *Rif* adds that it was worn suspended from the neck. *Rabbeinu Chananel,* however, understands this to refer to a necklace of pearls which women wore around their necks to ward off the evil eye (see next note).

13. The Mishnah below (60a) rules that a person who is ill may not wear an amulet outside if it has not been prepared by an expert. (Such amulets were composed of either a piece of parchment with Names of God written thereon or certain combinations of herbs – see below, 61a.) The Gemara above (53b) derived from this ruling that if the amulet *was* prepared by an expert, it would be permitted [as it is viewed as an ornament being worn by the ill person] (see *Rashi* to 60a ד״ה שאינו). In addition, any amulet known to be effective is permitted, even if it was not prepared by an expert (see further below, 61a-b). Abaye asked Rav Yosef why a necklace that was commonly worn to ward off the evil eye would not be similarly permitted. [The contents of the *totefes* were known to be effective in warding off the evil eye – therefore, Abaye compared it to an effective amulet (*Mishnah Berurah* 303:39; cf. *Shaar HaTziyun* there).]

See *Sfas Emes,* who discusses why Rav Yosef held that wearing such a packet would be forbidden.

14. I.e. an ornament worn on the forehead (*Rashi*); the Gemara will provide a more complete description below (see note 17).

[*Yefei Einayim* notes that Rav Yehudah was older than Abaye and would not usually cite him; he reverses the attribution of the ruling, and reads: *Abaye said in the name of Rav Yehudah.* See also *Hagahos Yaavetz* and *Hagahos Ben Aryeh. Dikdukei Soferim* suggests that the correct reading should be *Mar Yehudah* (in place of Rav Yehudah). Mar Yehudah was a contemporary of Abaye; see *Avodah Zarah* 16b.]

15. Although the hat is ornamental in nature, the Sages were not concerned that a woman would remove it to show it to a friend, for she would not uncover her hair in the street (*Rashi;* see above, 57a note 6).

[The word שְׂבָכָה carries the connotation of a hair *net* (see *I Kings* 7:1 with *Ralbag* and *Radak Shorashim;* see also *Rashi* to *II Kings* 1: However, our Gemara is clearly referring to a head covering that is opaque, as its purpose is to hide the hair from view. Accordingly, we have used the more generic term "hat" (see also *Rashi* to *I Kings* 7:17, and *Targum HaLaaz* by *Dayan I. Gukovitzki*).]

16. From this Baraisa it can be seen that a *totefes* is a frontlet, rather than a packet worn to ward off the evil eye, for such a packet would not be attached to the hat (*Tosafos;* see *Maharam,* who explains why a similar proof could not be brought from the Mishnah).

The Mishnah, which prohibits the wearing of these ornaments outside, speaks of frontlets and head bangles that are *not* attached to the hat; see there. See also *Beur Halachah* to 303:2 ד״ה והוא.

17. This ornament was similar in form to the צִיץ, the golden forehead plate worn by the Kohen Gadol (see *Rashi* ד״ה מקפת; see also *Tiferes Yisrael* to the Mishnah). *Rabbeinu Chananel* suggests that the name טוֹטֶפֶת derives from the fact that this ornament was worn *above* the forehead, in the place that tefillin (which are called *totafos* in Scripture) are worn (see also *Yefeh Einayim*).

18. *Ritva* (*MHK* ed.) notes that by making this identification, Rav Huna is teaching that a wealthy woman would be permitted to wear frontlets or head bangles made of colored fabrics outside on the Sabbath, since she is unlikely to wish to show such an ornament to her friends, as ornaments of this nature are not deemed impressive to a woman of her stature. *Tos. HaRosh* disagrees, and maintains that Rav Huna means to rule that wearing even frontlets and head bangles of colored fabric is forbidden [to *all* women], for they are all ornaments that may be shown to a friend.

19. In the Mishnah, this word was translated as, "a woolen cap," reflecting the apparent conclusion of the Gemara below (on 58a).

הכא בקטלא עסקינן ° דאשה חונקת את עצמה דניחא לה שתראה כבעלת בשר: ר' יהודה אומר של צמר ושל שער אין חוצצין מפני שהמים באין בהן: אמר רב יוסף אמר רב יהודה אמר שמואל הלכה כרבי יהודה בחוטי שער [א] א"ל אביי הלכה מכלל דפליגי וכי תימא אי לאו דשמעינן מתנא קמא דאיירי בחוטי שער איהו נמי לא הוה מיירי ודילמא כשם קאמר להו כי היכי דמודיתו לי בחוטי שער אודו לי נמי בחוטי צמר [ב] איתמר אמר רב נחמן אמר שמואל [א] מודים חכמים לרבי יהודה בחוטי שער תניא נמי הכי חוטי צמר חוצצין חוטי שער אין חוצצין ר' יהודה אומר של צמר ושל שער אין חוצצין אמר רב נחמן בר יצחק מתניתין נמי דיקא [ג] דקתני יוצאה אשה בחוטי שער בין משלה בין משל חברתה מני אילימא רבי יהודה אפילו חוטי צמר נמי אלא לאו רבנן היא וש"מ בחוטי שער לא פליגי ש"מ: לא בטוטפת: מאי טוטפת א"ר יוסף חומרתא דקטיפתא א"ל אביי [ב] תהוי כקמיע מומחה ותשתרי אלא אמר רב יהודה משמיה דאביי [ד] אפוזיינו תניא נמי הכי [ג] יוצאה אשה בסבכה המוזהבת ובטוטפת ובסרביטין הקבועין בה איזו טוטפת ואיזו סרביטין א"ר אבהו טוטפת המוקפת לה מאזן לאזן סרביטין המגיעין לה עד לחייה אמר רב הונא עניות עושין אותן של מיני צבעונין עשירות עושין אותן של כסף ושל זהב: ולא בכבול: אמר רבי ינאי כבול זה איני יודע מהו אי כבלא דעבדא תנן אבל כיפה של צמר שפיר דמי או דילמא כיפה של צמר תנן וכ"ש כבלא דעבדא [ה] אמר רבי אבהו מסתברא כמ"ד [ד] כיפה של צמר תנן ותניא נמי הכי יוצאה אשה בכבול ובאיסטמא לחצר ר"ש בן אלעזר אומר [ו] אף בכבול לרה"ר כלל ° אמר רשב"א כל שהוא למטה מן השבכה יוצאין בו כל שהוא למעלה מן השבכה אין יוצאין בו מאי איסטמא א"ר אבהו ביזיוני מאי ביזיוני אמר אביי אמר רב כליא פרוחי ת"ר [ז] ג' דברים נאמרו באיסטמא [ה] אין בה משום כלאים [ו] ואינה מטמאה בנגעים ואין יוצאין בה לרה"ר משום ר"ש אמרו אף אין

רש"י

בקטלא עסקינן. בגד חשוב לתלות בצוארה כנגד לבה שלא יפול מה שהיא אוכלת על בגדיה ויש לו מקום שנצים כעין שעושים למכנסים ותוחב בו רצועה רחבה ומוללתו סביב הרצועה שהבגד רחב הרבה וקושרת הרצועה סביב צוארה וחונקת עצמה בחוזק כדי שתהא בשרה בולטת ותראה בעלת בשר ומתוך שהרצועה חלקה ורחבה אינה מזיקתה: מכלל דפליגי. בתמיה והא ת"ק לא איירי בשערה שמע מינה בשער מודה דלא מיהדק על גבי שער: דילמא. האי דאדכר שער: כשם קאמר להו. כשם שאתם מודים לי בחוטי שער אודו לי בחוטי צמר (א): חומרתא דקטיפתא. קשר שעושין לרפואות קיטוף עין רע שלא תשלוט: ותיהוי כקמיע מומחה. דקתני מתני' ולא בקמיע בזמן שאינו מן המומחה הא מומחה שפיר דמי: אפוזייני. פרונטי"ל של זהב: שבכה. קופי"ה דאי שלפא ליה מיגליא ראשה: המקפת. את הפדחת מאזן לאזן: המגיעים עד לחייה. על ראשה כורכתו ותולה לה על לחייה מכאן ומכאן: אי כבלא דעבדא תנן. חותם שעושין לעבד בכסותו לסימן הוכחה שהוא עבד ובההוא קתני מתני' דשפחה לא תצא בו: אבל כיפה של צמר. כובע שתחת השבכה דמקרי נמי כבול ומתקשטת בו: שפיר דמי. דכיון דמיגליא שערה לא שלפא ומחויא: או דילמא כיפה תנן. דלא תצא דחיישינן דילמא שלפא ומחויא מתחת השבכה ואינה מגלה וכל שכן כבלא דעבדא: בכבול ובאסטמא. לקמיה מפרש מאי אסטמא ומדקתני כל שהוא למטה מן השבכה ש"מ כיפה תנן: כליא פרוחי. מגנפת קטנה לאחר קישוריה שקולעת ראשה וכסתה יש שערות קטנות שיוצאין חוץ לקישוריה והן נקראין פרוחי על שמפריחין ויוצאין לחוץ ואוגדתן לתחת קישוריה ע"י מגנפת קצרה: כליא. מונעת אותן שערות מלצאת: אין בה משום כלאים. שעשויה כמין לבד שקורין פולטר"א ואינה טוויה: ואינה מטמאה בנגעים. מהאי טעמא גופיה דגבי נגעים כתיב נמי בגד ויליף מכלאים שוע וטווי: אין

תוספות

הכא בקטלא עסקינן. תימה דמשמע דקטלא טעמא משום חציצה וא"כ אמאי תני (ב) במתניתין בסיפא בהדי חוטי למר ברישא הוה ליה למיתנייה ואומר רשב"א דקטלא נמי דבר של נוי הוא ויש לחוש דילמא שליף ומחויא ומיירי מתני' ברפוי דליכא חציצה ולכך אין לאוסרו אלא משום תכשיט אבל ברייתא דהכא איירי במיהדק דליכא למיחש דילמא שלפא שאינה מסירה לפי שלא תראה בעלת בשר וא"ת ומאי דוחקיה לאוקמא ברייתא משום חציצה לוקמא ברפוי ומשום משלפא כמתני' וי"ל דברייתא משמע ליה דטעמא משום חציצה דומיא דרישא דקתני הבנות יוצאות בחוטין שבאזניהם דלא איצטריך דליכא למיחש דילמא שלפא ומחויא דפשיטא הוא דמאי נוי שייך בחוטין אלא איצטריך לאשמעינן דאין בו חציצה ואינה מסירתן בשעת טבילה וה"נ סיפא טעמא משום חציצה: תניא נמי הכי כו'. מדתני (ג) וסרביטין הקבועים בה ודרך לקבוע אפויינו בסבכה אבל חומרתא דקטיפתא אין קובעין: אי כבלא דעבדא תנן. תימה אי כבלא דעבדא תנן אמאי קתני טפי גבי אשה וי"ל דבעי למיתני בסיפא דמתני' יוצאה בכבול ובפאה נכרית לחצר ופאה נכרית לא שייכא אלא באשה וא"ת אמאי לא תני נמי ברישא פאה נכרית בהדי כבול דאין יוצאין בה לרה"ר ויש לומר דמילתא דפשיטא היא דאסור לצאת בה לרה"ר דודאי משלפה משום דמחכו עלה וא"ת אי כבלא דעבדא תנן אמאי שרי בחצר טפי משאר דברים אבל אי כיפה של צמר תנן ניחא דשרי בחצר שלא תתגנה על בעלה כדמפרש עולא לקמן (דף סד:) וי"ל דכבלא דעבדא שרי כדי לעשות בו קורת רוח לרבו שאם היה כל היום בלא כבול אפילו בחצר בדבר מועט שיעשה העבד כנגד רבו סבור רבו שדעתו למרוד בו ואתי לידי קטטה ולקמן [ח] דפירש"י דבסיפא מודו כ"ע דכבול כיפה של צמר היא קשה לר"י דהא משמע הכא למ"ד כבלא דעבדא תנן שרי כיפה של צמר אף לרה"ר: אין בה משום כלאים. פרש"י משום שאינה טווי וריב"א אומר דמשום הכי אין להתיר דהתנן [ט] הלבדים אסורין מפני שהן שועין אלא משום דאיסטמא דבר קשה הוא ובדבר קשה לא אסרו רבנן משום כלאים כדאמר בפרק קמא דביצה (דף טו. ושם) א"ר הונא בריה דרב יהושע האי נמטא גמדא דנרש שריא אע"ג דשאר לבדים אסורין האי שריא לפי שהיא קשה וכן משמע ביומא פרק בא לו (דף סט.) רב אשי אמר בגדי כהונה קשין הן ולכך שרי להניע תחתיהם כי הא דאמר רב הונא בריה דרב יהושע האי נמטא גמדא דנרש שריא וקשה לר"ת דאמרינן בפ"ק דערכין (דף ג:) הכל חייבים בציצית כהנים לוים וישראלים ופריך פשיטא ומשני כהנים איצטריך ליה סד"א הואיל ואישתרי כלאים לגבייהו כו' לא ליחייבי והשתא היכי אישתרי להו והא בגדי כהונה קשין הן וכה"ג לישראל נמי שרי ואומר ר"ת דדבר שהוא שוע טווי ונוז [ובדרך מלבוש והעלאה] דאסור מן התורה אין חילוק בין רך לקשה דבכל ענין אסור מן התורה אבל בכלאים דרבנן כגון לבדים שאינם אלא שוע שרי בקשין אפילו ללבוש כיון דאין בהו כלאים אלא מדרבנן ובגדי כהונה נמי כיון דשרי מדאורייתא [י] להניע תחתיהן כדתניא לא יעלה עליך אבל אתה מותר להציעו תחתיך אבל אמרו חכמים אסור לעשות כן כו' שרי אפילו מדרבנן כיון דקשין הן דבקשין לא גזרו רבנן כלל ובדבר רך נמי היכא דלא שכיח כריכה מותר להציעו תחתיך כגון מרדעת החמור וכרים וכסתות ומילי אחריני דחשיב במס' כלאים ועל אותן קוטש פורפונטש השיב ר' יצחק שאם יש בתוכן בלאי בגדים של צמר ושל פשתן ונתחב בהן המחט שתי תפירות דאסורין בהעלאה אפילו חוט התפירה של קנבוס או של משי שלא התירו כרים וכסתות אלא בהצעה אבל בהעלאה לא אבל אם אין בתוכן רק גיזי צמר יכול להיות דמותר אף בהעלאה שאין חוט התפירה מחברן לבגד כלל אלא שמחבר ומקרב שני הבגדים של פשתן שהן כסוי הקוטש משני צדדין ומתוך כך מתהדק הצמר שבינתים ואין זה חיבור כחיבור אריג או תפירה או קשירת חבלים דבמה בהמה: ואינה מטמאה בנגעים. קשה לר"י מאי איריא בנגעים אפי' במת ושרץ לא מטמא דבעינן טווי ואריג כדאמר לקמן (דף סד.) ואומר ר"י דמטמא במת ושרצים מק"ו דפכין קטנים שטהורין בזב וטמאים במת ושרץ איסטמא שטמא בזב דשייך בה מדרס כמו בכפה דאמר (כלים פרק כ"ח משנה ה) כפה שנתנתו לס"ת טהור מן המדרס אינו דין שיטמא במת ושרץ ובערוך פי' איסטמא חתיכה של בגד מוזהב וקובעין בה אבנים טובות ומרגליות ולפ"ז ניחא דמטמא במת ושרצים כשאר תכשיט אבל בנגעים לא שאין הבגד עיקר כ"א הזהב ואבנים טובות ומהאי טעמא נמי אין בה משום כלאים:

והאמר

עין משפט נר מצוה

ה א מיי' פ"ב מהל' מקואות הלכה ה סמג עשין רמח טור וש"ע יו"ד סי' קלח סעיף ד:

ו ב (מיי' פי"ט מהל' שבת הל' י"ד) טוש"ע א"ח סי' שג סעיף טו:

ז ג מיי' פי"ט מהל' שבת הלכה יו"ד סמג לאוין סה טור וש"ע א"ח סי' שג סעיף טו:

ח ד מיי' שם הלכה ז טוש"ע שם סעיף ג:

ט ה מיי' פ"י מהל' כלאים הלכה כ סמג לאוין רפג טור וש"ע י"ד סי' שא סעיף יד:

י ו מיי' פי"ג מהל' טומאת צרעת הלכה א:

גליון הש"ס

גמ' דאשה חונקת את עצמה. ומזה הטעם נקרא קטלא. הרע"ב פי"א מ"ח דכלים: שם כלל אמר רבי שמעון בן אלעזר כל שהוא למטה מן השבכה. לקמן דף סה ע"א:

רבינו חננאל

בקטלא ומשום דאשה חונקת עצמה כדי שתראה בעלת בשר. פירש רב יוסף טוטפת חומרתא דקטיפתא יש מי שאומרים כי הוא ממיני מרגליות שתולות הנשים בצואריהן משום עין רעה. ונדחו דבריו. ואיתוקמא מאי טוטפת אבזייני כלומר אב שיש בו מינין הרבה. כי מינין תרגם זני דכתיב (דניאל ג) זני זמרא פירוש כל מיני זמר והיא נקראת טוטפת מפני שנותנת למעלה מן המצח במקום הטוטפת כדתניא יוצאה אשה בסבכה המוזהבת ובטוטפת ובסרביטין ואוקמה ר' אבהו טוטפת המוקפת מאוזן לאוזן סרבוטין המגיעין לה עד לחייה: ולא בכבול אוקמה ר' אבהו כיפה של צמר דתניא יוצאה אשה בכבול ובאיצטמא לחצר ר' שמעון בן אלעזר אומר בכבול אף לרה"ר כו' דייקינן דכבול דומיא דאיצטמא מה איצטמא כיפה אף כבול כיפה. וכדגרסינן (חולין קלח ע"א) כיפה של צמר היה מונח בראש כ"ג ועליו הציץ שנאמר ושמת אותו על פתיל תכלת. והן חוטין גדילין מעשה עבות רחבין בשתים ושלש אצבעות כגון אבנט ולית הלכתא כשמואל דאמר כבלא דעבדא דאין עושין בדבר של תורה להקל מספקא אלא הכבול שאסרה משנתנו היא כיפה של צמר וכ"ש כבלא דעבדא שאסור. איצטמא היא ביזני. כלומר חוטין הרבה ממיני צבעונין ותולין אותן בפני הכלה שלא יצערוה הזבובין שמתביישת להסיר הזבובין מעליה ותולין זה בפניה ונקראת כליא דיבי והוא כגון אותה ששנינו (מדות פ"ד מ"ו) אמה כולה עורב. לפי שבמקדש [ראשון] שהיתה קדושתו בכל הקהל והיתה השכינה שרויה בו לא היו עופות פורחות עליו אבל במקדש שני פחדו שמא אין קדושתו כקדושת ראשון ושמא יפרחו העופות על המקדש וישליכו שם דבר טומאה ועשו צורה להבריח העופות מגגי ההיכל וקראו אותה כולה עורב כלומר זו מונעת העורב מלפרוח בגג ההיכל וזו צורה כדרך שעושין עכשיו שומרי הזרעים: ת"ר שלשה דברים נאמרו באצטמא אין יוצאין בה לרה"ר לפי שאינה כליו כמשארי חשוב ואין בה משום כלאים דלא אריג הוא ואינה מטמאה בנגעים שאין

מסורת הש"ס

א) [לקמן קו: ושם נסמן], ב) ס"א אלא מודי' אתמר אמר רב יוסף אמר ר"י אמר שמואל, ג) לקמן סד:, ד) פי' לין [ובערוך ערך אב פי' אב זיינא], ה) ס"א איתמר רב אמר כיפה של צמר תנן ושמואל אמר כבלא דעבדא תנן אבל כיפה של צמר שפיר דמי, ו) בכבול אף לרה"ר כל"ל, ז) [תוספתא פ"ה], ח) [דף סד:], ט) [פ"ט מ"ט דכלאים], י) להציע כלאים תחתיהן כל"ל.

הגהות הב"ח

(א) רש"י ד"ה כשם קאמר וכו' למר הס"ד ואח"כ מה"ד אלא מודים איתמר כו' ה"ג בספר הישן הס"ד וג"ב שהוא ס"א: (ב) תוס' ד"ה הכא וכו' אמאי תני לקטלא במתניתין: (ג) ד"ה תניא וכו' מדתני ובטוטפת וסרביטין:

ליקוטי רש"י

בחוטי שער. שקולעו בהן שערה. בין משלה. תלושין [לקמן סד:]. תהוי כקמיע. שכותבין וטוענין לרפואה. ותשתרי דתכשיט הוא לתולה כאחד ממלבושיו [שם ס.]. כיפה. כמו כובע של צמר לבן שקורין פילטר"א [סוטה מט:]. כעין כובע של צמר ונותנות הנשים תחת לעיף קישוריהן כדאמרי' בבמה אשה יוצאה [גיטין כ.]. כובע קטן פלטר"א [חולין קלח.]. למטה מן השבכה. כגון כיפה של צמר. יוצאין בו. לא חיישינן דילמא שלפא ומחויא דמיגלי שערה ומגניא בה שהשבכה טפי הוא לשער [לקמן סה.].

רב נסים גאון

פ"ו תנו רבנן שלש דברים נאמרו באיסטמא וכו' לדברי תנא קמא אין בה משום עטרת חתנים ולדברי שמעון בן אלעזר אין בה משום עטרות כלות הוא מחמת הטעם שאמרו במס' סוטה בפרק האחרון (דף מט) בפולמוס של אספסיינוס גזרו על עטרות חתנים בפולמוס של טיטוס גזרו על עטרות כלות ובפ' מן גיטין (דף ז) אמר ליה ריש גלותא לרב הונא כלילא מנלן דאסור אמר ליה מרבנן דתנן בפולמוס של אספסינוס קיסר גזרו על עטרות חתנים ועל האירוס אדהכי קם רב הונא לאיפנויי אמר ליה רב חסדא קרא כתיב (יחזקאל כא) כה אמר ה' הסר המצנפת וכי מה מצנפת אצל העטרה לומר בזמן שהמצנפת בראש כהן גדול תהא עטרה בראש חתנים נסתלקה מצנפת מראש כהן גדול תסתלק העטרה מראש כל אדם אדהכי אתא רב הונא אשכחינהו דהוו יתבי וקאמרי לה שמעתא אמר להו האלהים מדרבנן הוא דאסור:

הזוג

The Gemara discusses the meaning of the word *kavul*:

אָמַר רַבִּי יַנַּאי – **R' Yannai said:** כָּבוּל זֶה אֵינִי יוֹדֵעַ מַהוּ – **I do not know what this *kavul*** mentioned in the Mishnah **is.** אִי כַּבְלָא דְּעַבְדָּא תְּנַן – For I am uncertain **if the Mishnah refers to a slave's *kavla*,**[20] and teaches that a slavewoman may not go out wearing it on the Sabbath,[21] אֲבָל כִּיפָּה שֶׁל צֶמֶר שַׁפִּיר דָּמֵי – **but an** ornamental **woolen cap may indeed be** worn outside on the Sabbath;[22] אוֹ דִּילְמָא כִּיפָּה שֶׁל צֶמֶר תְּנַן – **or perhaps the Mishnah's** ruling **refers to a** woman's ornamental **woolen cap,**[23] וְכָל שֶׁכֵּן כַּבְלָא דְּעַבְדָּא – **and** it **certainly** refers to **a slave's *kavla*** as well.[24]

The Gemara cites one view:

אָמַר רַבִּי אַבָּהוּ – **R' Abahu said:** מִסְתַּבְּרָא כְּמַאן דְּאָמַר כִּיפָּה שֶׁל צֶמֶר תְּנַן – **It is more reasonable to explain** the Mishnah **according to those who say** that **the Mishnah is referring to a woolen cap.**[25] וְתַנְיָא נַמִּי הָכִי – **And this was taught in a Baraisa as well.** For a Baraisa taught: יוֹצְאָה אִשָּׁה בְּכָבוּל וּבְאִיסְטְמָא לֶחָצֵר – A WOMAN MAY GO OUT WITH A *KAVUL* OR AN *ISTEMA*[26] INTO A COURTYARD ON THE SABBATH – but not into the public domain. רַבִּי שִׁמְעוֹן בֶּן אֶלְעָזָר אוֹמֵר – R' SHIMON BEN ELAZAR SAYS: אַף בְּכָבוּל לִרְשׁוּת הָרַבִּים – She may go out WITH A *KAVUL* EVEN INTO THE PUBLIC DOMAIN.[27] כְּלָל אָמַר רַבִּי שִׁמְעוֹן בֶּן אֶלְעָזָר – A GENERAL RULE WAS STATED BY R' SHIMON BEN ELAZAR: כֹּל שֶׁהוּא לְמַטָּה מִן הַשְּׂבָכָה – ANY ORNAMENT THAT IS worn UNDERNEATH THE HAT, יוֹצְאִין בּוֹ – [A WOMAN] MAY GO OUTSIDE WITH IT on the Sabbath; כֹּל שֶׁהוּא לְמַעְלָה מִן הַשְּׂבָכָה – but ANY ORNAMENT THAT IS worn OVER THE HAT, אֵין יוֹצְאִין בּוֹ – [A WOMAN] MAY NOT GO OUTSIDE WITH IT on the Sabbath.[28] Since R' Shimon ben Elazar states that a woman may go out with a *kavul* because it is worn under the hat, it is evident that he understands a *kavul* to be an ornamental woolen cap, and not a slave's emblem.[29]

The Gemara turns to define the other ornament mentioned in the Baraisa:

מַאי אִיסְטְמָא – **What is an *istema*?** אָמַר רַבִּי אַבָּהוּ בִּיזְיוֹנֵי – **R' Abahu said:** It is a ***bizyonei.*** מַאי בִּיזְיוֹנֵי – **And what is a *bizyonei*?** אָמַר אַבָּיֵי אָמַר רַב – **Abaye said in the name of Rav:** כַּלְיָא פָּרוּחֵי – It is a scarf worn for **holding back stray hairs.**[30]

The Gemara cites a Baraisa that discusses this ornament further:

תָּנוּ רַבָּנָן – **The Rabbis taught in a Baraisa:** שְׁלוֹשָׁה דְּבָרִים נֶאֶמְרוּ בְּאִיסְטְמָא – THREE THINGS WERE SAID CONCERNING AN *ISTEMA.* אֵין בָּהּ מִשּׁוּם כִּלְאַיִם – IT IS NOT SUBJECT TO THE LAWS OF *SHAATNEZ;*[31] וְאֵינָהּ מִטַּמְּאָה בִּנְגָעִים – IT CANNOT BECOME *TAMEI*

NOTES

20. I.e. an emblem placed on the clothing of a slave as identification of his status as a slave (*Rashi;* see next note).

21. The Gemara will explain below (58a) why, and in what circumstances, the Sages prohibited the wearing of a slave's emblem. [The Gemara knew that both of these items were called *kavul;* the question raised by R' Yannai is to which of them the Tanna of the Mishnah referred.]

[According to this interpretation, the Mishnah includes this ruling in the list of items that *women* may not wear outside in order to teach this law as it applies to female slaves (see *Rashi*); see *Ritva MHK* ed. for other resolutions; see also *Tzlach.*]

22. As explained above (57a note 7), the ornamental woolen cap projected slightly from beneath the hat (see *Ran MHK* ed., *Rashba*), and was considered an ornament in its own right. Nevertheless, it is possible that the Sages did not prohibit wearing such a cap because they considered it unlikely that a woman would remove it in public for fear of exposing her hair (see *Rashi;* see also below, note 27).

23. I.e. perhaps the Mishnah actually rules that it is *forbidden* to wear this woolen cap outside, due to the possibility that the woman will pull the woolen cap from beneath the hat while holding the hat in place, so that her hair will not be uncovered (*Rashi;* for another explanation see *Chidushei HaRan*).

24. [I.e. if the Mishnah is referring to a woolen cap (which is only occasionally called a *kavul* – see *Rashi* ד"ה אבל), then certainly it can be assumed that it refers to a slave's *kavla* (which is the standard meaning of *kavul*) (see *Sfas Emes;* see also *Dibros Moshe* 53:4).]

Tosafos ask: The Mishnah states that the Sages were more lenient with respect to a *kavul* than with respect to other ornaments, permitting it to be worn within a courtyard. Now, if a *kavul* is an ornamental woolen cap that women wear, then this distinction is understandable; for, as explained above (see 57a note 8), the Sages did not wish for women to appear unattractive to their husbands. But what reason would the Sages have to accord special leniency in the case of a slave's *kavla*?

They answer that the Sages were concerned that a slave, once released from the obligation to wear the emblem, would act in a disrespectful manner toward his master on the Sabbath, and the master, seeing that the slave was not wearing his emblem, would mistakenly interpret the slave's act as an act of rebellion; this would lead to strife. Other Rishonim answer that while the Sages had to extend the prohibition against wearing ornaments even to courtyards because they knew that permitting women to wear ornaments in courtyards would lead to their being worn in the public domain, they did not need to do this with regard to a slave's mark; for a slave will certainly take off a slave's mark whenever he has an excuse to do so (*Ritva MHK* ed., *Rashba*).

25. R' Abahu held that it is more reasonable to explain the Mishnah as teaching a prohibition that applies to *all* women, and not just to female slaves (*Sfas Emes*). [See *Ritva MHK* ed., who notes that (to this point) the Gemara has not even cited a dispute in this matter, and cites a variant version of the text. Alternatively, he suggests that R' Abahu was aware that a dispute existed in the matter (see also *Rif* and marginal gloss to the Gemara).] See also *Tzlach.*

26. The Gemara will identify this ornament below.

27. R' Shimon ben Elazar is of the opinion that a woman will not remove her woolen cap in the street, and therefore he rules that it was not included in the Sages' decree. [*Ran* (*MHK* ed.) suggests that R' Shimon ben Elazar holds that although a woman can pull her cap from beneath her hat without uncovering her hair, she is not likely to do so, for she knows that she will be unable to *replace* the cap without taking off the hat. See also *Ramban* and *Ritva MHK* ed.]

28. For any ornament that is over the hat may be removed without uncovering the hair; such ornaments are included in the Sages' decree forbidding ornaments that may be removed for showing. Any ornament that is worn under the hat, though, cannot be removed (and replaced) without uncovering the hair; it is therefore not included in the Sages' decree, according to R' Shimon ben Elazar.

29. *Rashi;* cf. *Rabbeinu Chananel*

30. After a woman has completed braiding and putting up her hair, there are invariably stray hairs that escape the braids and protrude from whatever hat or cap she is wearing. In order to cover these stray hairs, a woman would wind a small scarf around her head below the brim of her hat. This scarf is called כַּלְיָא פָּרוּחֵי, *one that holds back those that fly,* because it holds back the stray hairs from protruding (*Rashi*). The Rabbis prohibited the wearing of this scarf in the public domain because they were concerned that a woman might remove it to show; however, they permitted a woman to wear it in a courtyard (along with the *kavul*).

[It should be noted that *Rashi's* explanation is not the one given by most commentators. *Rabbeinu Chananel, Rif* and *Rosh* explain that this is a strip of colored cloth that was hung in front of a bride to keep away flying insects that she would be embarrassed to brush away herself; see *Chelkas Binyamin* for other interpretations.]

[The attribution of this statement – Abaye in the name of Rav – is somewhat problematic; *Rif* and *Rosh* omit it entirely.]

31. An *istema* was made of a felt-like material that consisted of compacted fibers that had not been spun into thread. [Thus, they are not subject to the prohibition against *shaatnez* (a forbidden mixture of wool and linen threads – see Glossary), for that prohibition is limited to fibers that have been spun (*Rashi*). Although there is a Rabbinic

עין משפט נר מצוה

ה א מיי' פ"ב מהל' מקואות הלכה ה סמג עשין רמח טור וש"ע יו"ד סי' קצח סעיף ד:
ו ב (מיי' פי"ט מהל' שבת הלי"ד) טוש"ע א"ח סי' שג סעיף טו:
ז ג מיי' פי"ט מהל' שבת הלכה יו"ד סמג לאוין סה טור וש"ע א"ח סי' שג סעיף טו:
ח ד מיי' שם הלכה ז טוש"ע שם סעיף ג:
ט ה מיי' פ"י מהל' כלאים הלכה כ סמג לאוין רפג טור וש"ע י"ד סי' שא סעיף יד:
י ו מיי' פי"ג מהל' טומאת צרעת הלכה א:

גליון הש"ס

גמ' דאשה חונקת את עצמה. ומזה הטעם נקרא קטלא. הרע"ב פי"א מ"ח דכלים: שם כלל אמר רבי שמעון בן אלעזר כל שהוא למטה מן השבכה. לקמן דף סה ע"א:

רבינו חננאל

בקטלא ומשום דאשה חונקת עצמה כדי שתראה בעלת בשר. פירש רב יוסף טוטפת חומרתא דקטיפתא יש מי שאומרים כי הוא ממיני מרגליות שתולות הנשים בצואריהן משום עין רעה. ונדחו דבריו. ואיתוקמא מאי טוטפת אבזייני כלומר אב שיש בו מינין הרבה. כי מינין תרגם זני דכתיב (דניאל ג) זני זמרא פירוש כל מיני זמר והיא נקראת טוטפת מפני שנותנת למעלה מן המצח במקום הטוטפת כדתניא יוצאה אשה בסבכה המוזהבת ובטוטפת ובסרביטין ואוקמה ר' אבהו טוטפת המוקפת מאוזן לאוזן סרבוטין המגיעין לה עד לחייה: ולא בכבול אוקמה ר' אבהו כיפה של צמר דתניא יוצאה אשה בכבול ובאיצטמא לחצר ר' שמעון בן אלעזר אומר בכבול אף לרה"ר כו' דייקינן דכבול דומיא דאיצטמא מה איצטמא כיפה אף כבול כיפה. וכדגרסינן (חולין קלח ע"א) כיפה של צמר היה מונח בראש כ"ג ועליו הציץ שנאמר ושמת אותו על פתיל תכלת. והן חוטין גדילין מעשה עבות רחבין בשתים ושלש אצבעות כגון אבנט ולית הלכתא כשמואל דאמר כבלא דעבדא דאין עושין בדבר של תורה להקל מספקא אלא הכבול שאסרה משנתנו היא כיפה של צמר וכ"ש כבלא דעבדא שאסור. איצטמא היא ביזני. כלומר חוטין הרבה ממיני צבעונין ותולין אותן בפני הכלה שלא יצערוה הזבובין שמתביישת להסיר הזבובין מעליה ותולין זה בפניה ונקראת כליא דיבי והוא כגון אותה ששנינו (מדות פ"ד מ"ו) אמה כולה עורב. לפי שבמקדש [ראשון] שהיתה קדושתו בכל הקהל והיתה השכינה שרויה בו לא היו עופות פורחות עליו אבל במקדש שני פחדו שמא אין קדושתו כקדושת ראשון ושמא יפרחו העופות על המקדש וישליכו שם דבר טומאה ועשו צורה להבריח העופות מגגי ההיכל וקראו אותה כולה עורב כלומר זו מונעת העורבים מלפרוח בגג ההיכל וזו צורה כדרך שעושין עכשיו שומרי הזרעים: ת"ר שלשה דברים נאמרו באצטמא אין יוצאין בה לרה"ר לפי שאינה כליו כמשאוי חשוב ואין בה משום כלאים דלא אריג הוא ואינה מטמאה בנגעים שאין בה

גמרא

הכא בקטלא עסקינן דאשה חונקת את עצמה דניחא לה שתראה כבעלת בשר: ר' יהודה אומר של צמר ושל שער אין חוצצין מפני שהמים באין בהן: אמר רב יוסף אמר רב יהודה אמר שמואל הלכה כרבי יהודה בחוטי שער א"ל אביי הלכה מכלל דפליגי וכי תימא אי לאו דשמעינן מתנא קמא דאיירי בחוטי שער איהו נמי לא הוה מיירי ודילמא כשם קאמר להו כי היכי דמודיתו לי בחוטי שער אודו לי נמי בחוטי צמר איתמר אמר רב נחמן אמר שמואל מודים חכמים לרבי יהודה בחוטי שער תניא נמי הכי חוטי צמר חוצצין חוטי שער אין חוצצין ר' יהודה אומר של צמר ושל שער אין חוצצין אמר רב נחמן בר יצחק מתניתין נמי דיקא דקתני יוצאה אשה בחוטי שער בין משלה בין משל חברתה מני אילימא רבי יהודה אפילו חוטי צמר נמי אלא לאו רבנן היא וש"מ בחוטי שער לא פליגי ש"מ: לא בטוטפת: מאי טוטפת א"ר יוסף חומרתא דקטיפתא א"ל אביי תהוי בקמיע מומחה ותשתרי אלא אמר רב יהודה משמיה דאביי אפזיינו תניא נמי הכי יוצאה אשה בסבכה המוזהבת ובטוטפת ובסרביטין הקבועין בה איזו טוטפת ואיזו סרביטין א"ר אבהו טוטפת המוקפת לה מאזן לאזן סרביטין המגיעין לה עד לחייה אמר רב הונא עניות עושין אותן של מיני צבעונין עשירות עושין אותן של כסף ושל זהב: ולא בכבול: אמר רבי ינאי כבול זה איני יודע מהו אי כבלא דעבדא תנן אבל כיפה של צמר שפיר דמי או דילמא כיפה של צמר תנן וכ"ש כבלא דעבדא אמר רבי אבהו מסתברא כמ"ד כיפה של צמר תנן ותניא נמי הכי יוצאה אשה בכבול ובאיסטמא לחצר ר"ש בן אלעזר אומר אף בכבול לרה"ר כלל אמר רשב"א כל שהוא למטה מן השבכה יוצאין בו כל שהוא למעלה מן השבכה אין יוצאין בו מאי איסטמא א"ר אבהו ביזיוני מאי ביזיוני אמר אביי אמר רב כליא פרוחי ת"ר ג' דברים נאמרו באיסטמא אין בה משום כלאים ואינה מטמאה בנגעים ואין יוצאין בה לרה"ר משום ר"ש אמרו אף

אין

רש"י

בקטלא עסקינן. בגד חשוב לתלות בצוארה כנגד לבה שלא יפול מה שהיא אוכלת על בגדיה ויש לו מקום שנצים כעין שעושים למכנסים ותוחב בו רצועה רחבה ומוללתו סביב הרצועה שהבגד רחב הרבה וקושרת הרצועה סביב צוארה וחונקת עצמה בחוזק כדי שתהא בשרה בולטת ותראה בעלת בשר ומתוך שהרצועה חלקה ורחבה אינה מזיקתה: מכלל דפליגי. בתמיה והא ת"ק לא איירי בשערה שמע מינה בשער מודה דלא מיהדק על גבי שער: דילמא. האי דאדכר שער: כשם קאמר להו. כשם שאתם מודים לי בחוטי שער אודו לי בחוטי צמר (א): חומרתא דקטיפתא. קשר שעושין לרפואות קיטוף עין רע שלא תשלוט: ותיהוי בקמיע מומחה. דקתני מתני' ולא בקמיע בזמן שאינו מן המומחה הא מומחה שפיר דמי: אפזייני. פרונטי"ל של זהב: שבכה. קופיי"ה דאי שלפא ליה מיגליא ראשה: המקפת. את הפדחת מאזן לאזן: המגיעים עד לחייה. על ראשה כורכתו ותולה לה על לחייה מכאן ומכאן: אי כבלא דעבדא תנן. חותם שעושין לעבד בכסותו לסימן הוכחה שהוא עבד ובההוא קתני מתני' דשפחה לא תצא בו: אבל כיפה של צמר. ככובע שתחת השבכה דמקרי נמי כבול ומתקשטת בו: שפיר דמי. דכיון דמיגליא שערה לא שלפא ומחויא: או דילמא כיפה תנן. דלא תצא דחיישינן דילמא שלפא ומחויא מתחת השבכה ואינה מגלה וכל שכן כבלא דעבדא: בכבול ובאסטמא. לקמיה מפרש מאי אסטמא ומדקתני כל שהוא למטה מן השבכה ש"מ כיפה תנן: כליא פרוחי. מצנפת קטנה לאחר קישוריה שקולעת ראשה וכסתה יש שערות קטנות שיוצאין חוץ לקישוריה והן נקראין פרוחי על שמפריחין ויוצאין לחוץ ואוגדתן לתחת קישוריה ע"י מצנפת קלרה: כליא. מונעת אותן שערות מלצאת: אין בה משום כלאים. שעשויה כמין לבד שקורין פולטר"א ואינה טוויה: ואינה מטמאה בנגעים. מהאי טעמא גופיה דגבי נגעים כתיב נמי בגד וילפינן מכלאים שוע וטווי:

אין

תוספות

הכא בקטלא עסקינן. תימה דמשמע דקטלא טעמא משום חציצה וא"כ אמאי תני (ג) במתניתין בסיפא בהדי חוטי צמר ברישא הוה ליה למיתנייה ואומר רשב"א דקטלא נמי דבר של נוי הוא ויש לחוש דילמא שליף ומחויא ומיירי מתני' ברפוי דליכא חציצה ולכך אין לאוסרו אלא משום תכשיט אבל ברייתא דהכא איירי במיהדק דליכא למיחש דילמא שלפא שאינה מסירה לפי שלא תראה בעלת בשר וא"ת ומאי דוחקיה לאוקמא ברייתא משום חציצה לוקמא ברפוי ומשום משלפא כמתני' וי"ל דברייתא משמע ליה דטעמא משום חציצה דומיא דרישא דקתני הבנות יוצאות בחוטין שבאזניהם דלא איצטריך דליכא למיחש דילמא שלפא ומחוייא דפשיטא הוא דמאי נוי שייך בחוטין אלא איצטריך לאשמעינן דאין בו חציצה ואינה מסירתן בשעת טבילה וה"נ סיפא טעמא משום חציצה: **תניא** נמי הכי כו'. מדתני (ג) וסרביטין הקבועים בה ודרך לקבוע אפזיינו בסבכה אבל חומרתא דקטיפתא אין קובעין: **אי** כבלא דעבדא תנן. תימה אי כבלא דעבדא תנן אמאי קתני טפי גבי אשה וי"ל דבעי למיתני בסיפא דמתני' יוצאה בכבול ובפאה נכרית לחצר ופאה נכרית לא שייכא אלא באשה וא"ת אמאי לא תני נמי ברישא פאה נכרית בהדי כבול דאין יוצאין בה לרה"ר ויש לומר דמילתא דפשיטא היא דאסור לצאת בה לרה"ר דודאי משלפה משום דמחכו עלה וא"ת אי כבלא דעבדא תנן אמאי שרי בחצר טפי משאר דברים אבל אי כיפה של צמר תנן ניחא דשרי בחצר שלא תתגנה על בעלה כדמפרש עולא לקמן (דף סד:) וי"ל דכבלא דעבדא שרי כדי לעשות בו קורת רוח לרבו שאם היה כל היום בלא כבול אפילו בחצר בדבר מועט שיעשה העבד כנגד רבו סבור רבו שדעתו למרוד בו ואתי לידי קטטה ולקמן ח) דפירש"י דבסיפא מודו כ"ע דכבול כיפה של צמר היא קשה לר"י דהא משמע הכא למ"ד כבלא דעבדא תנן שרי כיפה של צמר אף לרה"ר: **אין** בה משום כלאים. פרש"י משום שאינה טווי וריב"א אומר דמשום הכי אין להתיר דהתנן ט) הלבדים אסורין מפני שהן שועין אלא משום דאיסטמא דבר קשה הוא ודבר קשה לא אסרו רבנן משום כלאים כדאמר בפרק קמא דביצה (דף טו. ושם) א"ר הונא בריה דרב יהושע האי נמטא גמדא דנרש שריא אע"ג דשאר לבדים אסורין האי שריא לפי שהיא קשה וכן משמע ביומא פרק בא לו (דף סט.) רב אשי אמר בגדי כהונה קשין הן ולכך שרי להציע תחתיהם כי הא דאמר רב הונא בריה דרב יהושע האי נמטא גמדא דנרש שריא וקשה לר"ת דאמרינן בפ"ק דערכין (דף ג:) הכל חייבים בציצית כהנים לוים וישראלים ופריך פשיטא ומשני כהנים איצטריך ליה סד"א הואיל ואישתרי כלאים לגבייהו כו' לא ליחייבי והשתא היכי אישתרי להו והא בגדי כהונה קשין הן וכה"ג לישראל נמי שרי ואומר ר"ת דדבר שהוא שוע טווי ונוז [ובדרך מלבוש והעלאה] דאסור מן התורה אין חילוק בין רך לקשה דבכל ענין אסור מן התורה אבל בכלאים דרבנן כגון לבדים שאינם אלא שוע שרי בקשין אפילו ללבוש כיון דאין בהו כלאים אלא מדרבנן ובגדי כהונה נמי כיון דשרי מדאורייתא י) להציע תחתיהן כדתניא לא יעלה עליך אבל אתה מותר להציעו תחתיך אבל אמרו חכמים אסור לעשות כן כו' שרי אפילו מדרבנן כיון דקשין הן לא גזרו רבנן כלל ובדבר רך נמי היכא דלא שכיח כריכה מותר להציעו תחתיך כגון מרדעת החמור וכרים וכסתות ומילי אחריני דחשיב במס' כלאים ועל אותן קוטש פורפונטש השיב ר' יצחק שאם יש בתוכן בלאי בגדים של צמר ושל פשתן ונתחב בהן המחט שתי תפירות דאסורין בהעלאה אפילו חוט התפירה של קנבוס או של משי שלא התירו כרים וכסתות אלא בהצעה אבל בהעלאה לא אבל אם אין בתוכן רק גיזי צמר יכול להיות דמותר אף בהעלאה שאין חוט התפירה מחברן לבגד כלל אלא שמחבר ומקרב שני הבגדים של פשתן שהן כסוי הקוטש משני צדדין ומתוך כך מתהדק הצמר שבינתים ואין זה חיבור כחיבור אריג או תפירה או קשירת חבלים דבמה בהמה: **ואינה** מטמאה בנגעים. קשה לר"י מאי איריא בנגעים אפי' במת ושרץ לא מטמא דבעינן טווי ואריג כדאמר לקמן (דף סד.) ואומר ר"י דמטמאה במת ושרצים מק"ו דפכין קטנים שטהורין בזב וטמאים במת ושרץ איסטמא שטמאה בזב דשייך בה מדרס כמו בכפה דאמר (כלים פרק כ"ח משנה ה) כפה שנתנתו לס"ת טהור מן המדרס אינו דין שיטמא במת ושרץ ובערוך פי' איסטמא חתיכה של בגד מוזהב וקבועין בה אבנים טובות ומרגליות ולפ"ז ניחא דמטמאה במת ושרצים כשאר תכשיט אבל בנגעים לא שאין הבגד עיקר כ"א הזהב והאבנים טובות ומהאי טעמא נמי אין בה משום כלאים:

והאמר

מסורת הש"ס

א) [לקמן קו: ושם נסמן], ב) ס"א אלא מודי' אתמר אמר רב יוסף אמר ר"י אמר שמואל, ג) לקמן סד:, ד) פי' לוין [ובערוך ערך אב פי' אב זיינא], ה) ס"א איתמר רב אמר כיפה של צמר תנן ושמואל אמר כבלא דעבדא תנן אבל כיפה של צמר שפיר דמי, ו) בכבול אף לרה"ר כצ"ל, ז) [תוספתא פ"ה], ח) [דף סד:], ט) [פ"ט מ"ט דכלאים], י) להציע כלאים תחתיהן כצ"ל.

הגהות הב"ח

(א) רש"י ד"ה כשם קאמר וכו' צמר הס"ד ואח"כ מה"ד אלא מודים איתמר כו' ה"ג בספר הישן הס"ד ונ"ב שהוא ס"א: (ב) תוס' ד"ה הכא וכו' אמאי תני לקטלא במתניתין: (ג) ד"ה תניא וכו' מדתני ובטוטפת וסרביטין:

ליקוטי רש"י

בחוטי שער. שקולעת בהן שערה. בין משלה. תלושין [לקמן סד:]. תהוי בקמיע. שכותבין וטוענין לרפואה. ותשתרי. דתכשיט הוא לחולה כאחד ממלבושיו [שם ס.]. כיפה. כמו כובע של צמר לבן שקורין פילטר"א [סוטה מט:]. כעין כובע של צמר ונותנות הנשים תחת לעיף קישוריהן כדאמרי' בבמה אשה יוצאה [גיטין כ.]. כובע קטן פלטרי"י [חולין קלח.]. למטה מן השבכה. כגון כיפה של צמר. יוצאין בו. דלא חיישינן דילמא שלפא ומחויא דמיגלי שערה ומגניא בה שהשבכה נוי הוא לשער [לקמן סה.].

רב נסים גאון

פ"ו תנו רבנן שלשה דברים נאמרו באיסטמא וכו' ולדברי ר' תנא קמא אין בה משום עטרת חתנים ולדברי ר' שמעון בן אלעזר יש בה משום עטרות כלות הוא מחמת הטעם שאמרו במס' סוטה בפרק האחרון (דף מט) בפולמוס של אספסינוס גזרו על עטרות חתנים בפולמוס של טיטוס גזרו על עטרות כלות ובפ' א' מן גיטין (דף ז) אמרו אמר ליה ריש גלותא לרב הונא כלילא מנלן דאסיר אמר ליה מרבנן דתנן בפולמוס של אספסינוס קיסר גזרו על עטרות חתנים ועל האירוס אדהכי קם רב הונא לאיפנויי אמר ליה רב חסדא קרא כתיב (יחזקאל כא) כה אמר ה' הסר המצנפת וכי מה מצנפת אצל עטרה אלא לומר לך בזמן שהמצנפת בראש כהן גדול תהא עטרה בראש חתנים נסתלקה מצנפת מראש כהן גדול תסתלק העטרה מראש כל אדם אדהכי אתא רב הונא יתבי וקאמרי להא שמעתא אמר להו האלהים מדרבנן הוא דאסור:

הזוג

THROUGH *TZARAAS;*[32] וְאֵין יוֹצְאִין בָּהּ לִרְשׁוּת הָרַבִּים – AND [A WOMAN] MAY NOT GO OUT WITH IT INTO THE PUBLIC DOMAIN on the Sabbath. מִשּׁוּם רַבִּי שִׁמְעוֹן אָמְרוּ – THEY SAID IN THE NAME OF R' SHIMON: אַף – ALSO,

NOTES

prohibition against making garments of such material (see *Kilayim* 9:9), in this case no such prohibition applies, because it does not provide any warmth [or protection] to the wearer at all (*Ramban, Chidushei HaRan;* see also *Tosafos*). Others explain that the *istema* is not subject to the *shaatnez* laws because it is not woven (see *Ramban*). And although some authorities are of the opinion that unwoven *shaatnez* is *Biblically* forbidden (see *Rambam, Hil. Kilayim* 10:2 with *Raavad*), in this case the prohibition does not apply, because the *istema* is providing no warmth or protection and is being worn as an ornament rather than clothing (see *Ramban* and *Meiri;* see also *Tosafos* citing *Aruch*).

32. Regarding clothing that is subject to the laws of *tzaraas,* the Torah states (*Leviticus* 13:47) that the *tzaraas* must be found *in a garment.* And in regard to the prohibition against *shaatnez* as well, the Torah specifies (ibid. 19:19) that *a garment* of mixed fibers is prohibited. Thus we derive from *shaatnez* that only a garment of the type subject to the Biblical prohibition against *shaatnez* is subject to *tzaraas* affliction (*Rashi;* see *Tosafos,* who discusses the status of an *istema* with regard to other forms of *tumah*). See *Ritva* (*MHK* ed.), however, who cites *Toras Kohanim* (*Tazria* 13:3) as ruling that *tzaraas* can only affect *white* clothing, thus excluding an *istema,* which is made of colored cloth (see also other interpretation in *Tosafos;* and see *Chelkas Binyamin*).

אֵין בָּהּ מִשּׁוּם עַטְרוֹת כַּלּוֹת – IT (an *istama*) IS NOT SUBJECT TO the Rabbinic decree forbidding **"CROWNS OF BRIDES."**[1]

Above, the Gemara cited R' Abahu, who explained that the word *kavul* in our Mishnah refers to an ornamental woolen cap. The Gemara now cites a dissenting view:

וּשְׁמוּאֵל אָמַר – **But Shmuel said:** כַּבְלָא דְעַבְדָּא תְּנַן – **The Mishnah refers to a slave's *kavla*** (emblem), and teaches that a slavewoman may not wear such an emblem in the public domain on the Sabbath. An ornamental woolen cap, however, may be worn even in the public domain.[2]

The Gemara asks:

וּמִי אָמַר שְׁמוּאֵל הָכִי – **But did Shmuel** indeed **say this?** וְהָאָמַר שְׁמוּאֵל – **Why, Shmuel has said:** יוֹצֵא הָעֶבֶד בְּחוֹתָם שֶׁבְּצַוָּארוֹ – **A slave may go out** on the Sabbath **with an emblem that is on** (i.e. tied around) **his neck,** אֲבָל לֹא בְּחוֹתָם שֶׁבִּכְסוּתוֹ – **but not with an emblem that is on** (i.e. attached to) **his clothing!**[3] Thus, Shmuel explicitly states that a slave *may* go out with an emblem on the Sabbath. How, then, can he explain the Mishnah's prohibition as referring to a slave's emblem?[4]

The Gemara answers:

לֹא קַשְׁיָא – This is **not a difficulty.** הָא דְּעָבֵד לֵיהּ רַבֵּיהּ – **This** ruling of Shmuel, which permits a slave to wear an emblem, speaks of **one made for him by his master,** which he will not remove; הָא דְּעָבֵד אִיהוּ לְנַפְשֵׁיהּ – while **this** other statement of Shmuel, that explains the Mishnah as referring to a slave's emblem, refers to **where [the slave] made** an emblem **for himself.**[5] In such a case, Shmuel states that the Mishnah prohibits wearing an emblem.[6]

This resolution is challenged:

בְּמַאי אוֹקִימְתָּא לְהָא דִּשְׁמוּאֵל – **How have you construed this** second ruling **of Shmuel,** which permits a slave to carry an emblem? דְּעָבֵד לֵיהּ רַבֵּיהּ – In a case **where his master made it for him.** בְּחוֹתָם שֶׁבִּכְסוּתוֹ אַמַּאי לֹא – In that case, **why** may he **not** wear **an emblem that is on his clothing?** Since his master made it for him, he will not remove it in any case!

The Gemara answers that it is forbidden for another reason: דִּילְמָא מִיפְּסִק – Shmuel holds that such an emblem may not be worn outside on the Sabbath because **it may perhaps become detached,**[7] וּמִירְתַת וּמִיקַפֵּל לֵיהּ – **and [the slave] will be frightened** of his master[8] **and will fold [his cloak]** וּמַחֵית לֵיהּ אַכַּתְפֵיהּ – **and place it on his shoulder,**[9] so that the place where the emblem had been attached is not visible.[10] כִּדְרַב יִצְחָק בַּר יוֹסֵף – By wearing his cloak folded in this manner, the slave will transgress a Biblical prohibition, **as** can be seen from the ruling **of Rav Yitzchak bar Yosef.** דְּאָמַר רַב יִצְחָק בַּר יוֹסֵף אָמַר רַבִּי יוֹחָנָן – **For Rav Yitzchak bar Yosef said in the name of R' Yochanan:** הַיּוֹצֵא בְּטַלִּית מְקֻפֶּלֶת וּמוּנַּחַת לוֹ עַל כְּתֵפָיו בְּשַׁבָּת – **One who goes out on the Sabbath with a cloak that is folded and resting on his shoulder** חַיָּיב חַטָּאת – **is liable to a *chatas*** offering.[11] Thus, although Shmuel holds that we are not concerned that a slave will remove an emblem made by his master, he nevertheless forbids going out with an emblem attached to clothing, for fear that it will result in the Biblically prohibited carrying of an improperly folded cloak.[12]

NOTES

1. At the time of the events leading to the destruction of the Temple, the Rabbis decreed that certain public demonstrations of joyous celebration be curtailed to express our mourning over this great loss. Among the decrees was an edict forbidding brides from wearing crowns at their weddings (see *Sotah* 49a-b). The Baraisa teaches that an *istama* is not included in this edict (*Rashi*). *Ritva* (*MHK* ed.) explains that the decree only applied to crowns made of [precious] metal; thus, an *istama,* which was made of fabric, was not prohibited.

2. For, as explained above (57b note 22), a woman will not remove such a cap in the street.

3. [The reason for this distinction will be explained below.]

The חוֹתָם, *emblem,* was made of [stamped] clay (*Rashi;* but see Gemara below). It is identical to the כַּבְלָא דְעַבְדָּא mentioned above (*Rashi*).

4. The Gemara does not attempt to reconcile Shmuel's ruling with the Mishnah by interpreting the Mishnah as referring specifically to an emblem attached to the slave's clothing, for it is preferable to explain the Mishnah as referring to all slave's emblems [regardless of where they are worn] (*Tosafos;* see also *Chidushei HaRan*). Alternatively, the Gemara knew that the word *kavul* referred specifically to the type of emblem worn around the neck (*Ramban*). [*Ramban* notes that this explanation fits well with *Rashi's* commentary in ד״ה חותם שבצוארו; however, from *Rashi* above, 57b ד״ה אי כבלא it appears that *Rashi* does not accord with this view. See also *Ritva MHK* ed. and *Shabbos Shel Mi* to *Rashi* on 57b ibid.; see also *Hagahos R' Elazar Moshe Horowitz* here and to 57b.]

5. The Sages prohibited wearing a slave's emblem outside on the Sabbath due to the possibility that the slave will remove it and carry it in his hand [so as to conceal the fact that he is a slave]. Shmuel rules that this concern does not exist when the emblem was fashioned by the master, for the slave will be afraid of removing it lest he incur his master's wrath. When the slave fashioned the emblem himself, however, the master is not as insistent that the slave wear it at all times; thus, wearing it outside on the Sabbath may indeed lead to its being carried in the slave's hand, and the Sages therefore prohibited it (see *Rashi;* see also next note).

6. However, even in the case of an emblem fashioned by the slave himself, the master desires that the slave wear it; therefore, the Sages were lenient and allowed him to wear the emblem in a courtyard, so as not to lead to strife between the slave and the master (*Tosafos;* see above, 57b note 24).

7. And then fall off the slave's garment and break (*Rashi*). [Commonly, these emblems were made of clay or earthenware, and they would shatter if they fell off a garment. This will be discussed in greater detail below.]

8. The slave will fear that his master will accuse him of having deliberately destroyed the emblem, to conceal the fact that he is a slave.

9. I.e. he will fold his cloak over so that a panel of the cloak covers the spot where the missing emblem had been attached, thereby hiding the fact that he is no longer wearing the emblem. This can result in a Biblical prohibition, as the Gemara will proceed to explain (*Rashi;* see note 11).

10. Although folding over a cloak so that a slave's emblem is not visible (even if it is still in place) can also be construed by a master as an act of rebellion, the slave still prefers not to walk with the cloak unfolded and the emblem missing; for if he does so the master will assume that he *purposely* detached the emblem (*Tosafos*); moreover, if the master merely sees a folded cloak, he may not realize that the emblem is missing at all (*Rashi*).

11. An [unusually] folded cloak, even if worn, is viewed as a burden rather than a garment (*Rashi*). [Since the cloak is not usually worn in this manner, the person cannot be said to be wearing the garment (see *Orach Chaim* 301:29, 30).] Thus, if one goes from a *reshus hayachid* to a *reshus harabim* while wearing the cloak in this manner, he has transgressed the *melachah* of *transferring from domain to domain,* and he is liable to a *chatas* offering for an inadvertent transgression.

12. [I.e. the slave will walk four *amos* in the public domain wearing the improperly folded cloak, which is also Biblically forbidden.]

Shmuel admits, however, that an emblem made by the master can be worn around the neck, because if it were to fall off, no transgression would result. This is because the slave will not be tempted to carry it in his hand, for doing so will not appease his master, since carrying an emblem in one's hand does not indicate that he is a slave (*Rashi* below ד״ה יוצא). [Moreover, the clay emblem is worthless once it breaks, and the slave will not feel compelled to save it (see below, note 25).]

[The Rishonim note that if Shmuel had been referring to an emblem fashioned by the slave, the distinction between an emblem worn around the neck and one sewn to clothing could have been more easily explained; for it would be possible to say that although we are not concerned that a slave would deliberately remove an emblem from around his neck, we are concerned that he would fold his cloak to hide such an emblem, since this is not as blatant an act of rebellion. However, since Shmuel's rulings were interpreted as referring to emblems fashioned by the

אין בה משום עטרות כלות ושמואל אמר כבלא דעבדא תנן ומי אמר שמואל הכי והאמר שמואל יוצא העבד בחותם שבצוארו אבל לא בחותם שבכסותו לא קשיא [א]הא דעבד ליה רביה הא דעבד איהו לנפשיה במאי אוקימתא להא דשמואל דעבד ליה רביה בחותם שבכסותו אמאי לא דילמא מיפסק ומירתת ומיקפל ליה ומחית ליה אכתפיה כדרב יצחק בר יוסף דא"ר יצחק בר יוסף א"ר יוחנן (א) היוצא בטלית מקופלת ומונחת לו על כתפיו בשבת חייב חטאת וכי הא דא"ל שמואל לרב חיננא בר שילא כולהו רבנן דבי ריש גלותא לא ליפקו בסרבלי חתימי לבר מינך דלא קפדי עליך דבי ריש גלותא: גופא אמר שמואל יוצא העבד בחותם שבצוארו אבל לא בחותם שבכסותו תניא נמי הכי [ב]יוצא העבד בחותם שבצוארו אבל לא בחותם שבכסותו ורמינהו לא יצא העבד בחותם שבצוארו ולא בחותם שבכסותו [ג]זה וזה אין מקבלין טומאה ולא בזוג שבצוארו אבל יוצא הוא בזוג שבכסותו [ד]זה וזה מקבלין טומאה [ה]ולא תצא בהמה לא בחותם שבצוארה ולא בחותם שבכסותה ולא בזוג שבכסותה ולא בזוג שבצוארה זה וזה אין מקבלין טומאה לימא הא דעבד ליה רביה הא דעבד איהו לנפשיה לא אידי ואידי דעבד ליה רביה וכאן [ו]בשל מתכת וכאן בשל טיט וכדרב נחמן אמר רבה בר אבוה דבר המקפיד עליו רבו אין יוצאין בו דבר שאין מקפיד עליו יוצאין בו ה"נ מסתברא מדקתני זה וזה אין מקבלין טומאה אי אמרת בשלמא של מתכת הני הוא דלא מקבלי טומאה הא כלים דידהו מקבלי טומאה אלא אי אמרת בשל טיט תנן הני הוא דלא מקבלי טומאה הא כלים דידהו מקבלי טומאה והא (ב) תניא [ז]כלי אבנים כלי גללים וכלי אדמה אין מקבלין טומאה לא מדברי תורה ולא מדברי סופרים אלא ש"מ של מתכת ש"מ: אמר מר ולא בזוג שבצוארו אבל יוצא הוא בזוג שבכסותו (ג) זוג שבצוארו אמאי לא דילמא מיפסיק ואתא לאיתויי זוג שבכסותו נמי ליחוש דילמא מיפסיק ואתי לאיתויי הכא במאי עסקינן דמיחא ביה מומחא וכדרב הונא בריה דרב יהושע דאמר (ד) רב הונא בריה דרב יהושע כל שהוא ארוג לא גזרו: אמר מר לא תצא בהמה לא בחותם שבצוארה ולא בחותם שבכסותה ולא בזוג שבצוארה ולא בזוג שבכסותה זה וזה אין מקבלין טומאה וזוג דבהמה אין מקבלין טומאה ורמינהו זוג של בהמה טמאה ושל

רש"י

אין בה משום עטרות כלות. דגזרו עליהן שלא תלא בהן מחורבן ואילך משום לער במס' סוטה (דף מט.): ושמואל אמר. כבול דמתני' כבלא דעבדא ופליג אדר' אבהו: חותם שבצוארו. הוא כבלא דעבדא והיו עושין אותו משל טיט: דעביד ליה רביה. אית ליה אימתא ולא שקיל ליה מצוארו להוליכו בידו: מיפסק. החותם ונשבר ומירתת מרבו שלא יאמר שהוא נטלו להראות בשוק שהוא בן חורין: ומקפל ליה. הטלית על כתפיו כדי שלא יראה מקום החותם ולא ידינו שנפל ודמי הטלית על כתפו כמשוי: חייב חטאת. דאינו תכשיט אלא בזמן שלובשו דרך מלבוש: כולהו רבנן לא ליפקו בסרבלי חתימי. היו עושין חותמות לטליתות שלהן כעין עבדים להראות שהן כפופין לריש גלותא לא ליפקו דאי מפסקי מרתתי ומקפלי להו: דלא קפדי עלך. אם תלך בלא חותם: יוצא העבד בחותם שבצוארו. ובשל טיט דלא קפיד עליה לאתויי ואי משום דמירתת מאי חורבא נפקא מינה משום אימתא דרביה לא מייתי ליה בידיה דהא לאו הוכחה היא לעבדות אלא כשישנו על צוארו או בכסותו: וזה וזה אין מקבלין טומאה. דלאו לנוי עביד שיהא טמא משום תכשיט ואע"ג דבשל מתכת מוקמינן לה להא לקמן מיהו לאו לנוי דיליה הוא אלא לגנאי וכלי תשמיש נמי לא הוי: זוג. לנוי עביד: ולא בזוג שבצוארו אבל יוצא הוא בזוג שבכסותו. לקמיה מפרש טעמא: מקבלין טומאה. שתכשיט הוא: שבכסותה. עושים לסוסים מעילין שלא יטנפו: לא תצא. כדאמרינן באידך פרקין (דף נד:) דמתחזי כמאן דאזיל לחינגא: אין מקבלין טומאה. דאין תכשיט לבהמה: לא אידי ואידי דעבד ליה רביה. דאע"ג דכבול דמתניתין אוקימנא בדעבד איהו לנפשיה התם הוא דאיכא לאוקמיה בסתם חותמות של טיט דאי מיתבר אין מקפיד עליו להביא שבריו לבית אדונו הלכך ליכא לאוקמיה בדעבד ליה רביה דאי עבד ליה רביה לא הוה מיתסר דכל זמן שלא נפסק לא שקיל ליה מצוארו משום אימתא דרביה ואי מיפסק לא קפיד עליה בעליו משום פסידא דליכא פסידא הלכך לא מייתי ליה אבל הך לא איכא לאוקמא בשל טיט כדמסתברא לקמן מסיפא הלכך אפילו עבד ליה רביה נמי אסור דאי מיפסק קפיד עליה משום פסידא ומירתת עבד ומייתי ליה בידיה: דבר המקפיד עליו רבו. אם יאבד לא ילא דאי מפסיק מייתי ליה: מסתברא. דבשל מתכת קאי מדאיצטריך למיתני אין מקבלין טומאה וטעמא משום דלאו לנוי עבידא: הני הוא דלא מקבלין טומאה. משום דלאו כלים נינהו הא שאר כלי מתכות מקבלין: כלים דידהו. דמתכות: אלא אי אמרת. כלים דידהו כלי העשוי מטיט כזה שאינו מצרפו בכבשן מעשה ידי יוצר דניהוי קרוי כלי חרס אלא כלי אדמה מי מקבל טומאה בתמיה: כלי גללים. [ה]לפיעי בקר שעשה מהן כלי: דמיחא מומחא. שארגו בבגד ותו לא מיפסיק: לא גזרו. לצאת בו ודרב הונא לענין אריג כי האי גוונא נמי איתמר דאשמעינן דלא חיישינן תו לדלמא מיפסק:

ושל

תוספות

והאמר שמואל יוצא העבד בחותם כו'. ולא בעי לאוקמי מתניתין בחותם שבכסותו דניחא ליה לאוקמה בדעבד איהו לנפשיה ואיירי מתני' בכל חותמות: הא דעבד איהו לנפשיה. קשה לרשב"א אמאי שריא מתני' בדעבד איהו לנפשיה בחלר כיון דליכא קפידא דרבו וי"ל דאיכא קלת קפידא אבל לא כל כך כמו בעבד ליה רביה: במאי אוקימתא להא דשמואל בדעבד ליה רביה כו'. אבל אי מיירי בדעבד איהו לנפשיה אתי שפיר דבלוארו ליכא למיחש דלמא פסיק ליה בידים כדי שלא יבינו הרואין שהוא עבד אבל בכסותו איכא למיחש דלמא מקפל טליתו לכסות החותם ולא ידע דיש בזה חיוב חטאת אבל בדעבד ליה רביה משום אימתא דרביה ירא לקפל והשתא נמי ידע הש"ם לדרב ילחק אלא דלא ידע שיש לחוש דילמא מיפסיק ובתר דמשני מייתי דרב ילחק ונחת לפרושי שיש חיוב חטאת בקיפול: דילמא מיפסק ומרתת ומקפל ליה. דניחא ליה טפי שיהיה מקופל משיראה רבו שנפסק לגמרי ויסבור שבמזיד פסקו למרוד בו: לא תצא בהמה כו'. דמיחזי כמאן דאזיל לחינגא כדפי' בקונ' דלא מצינן למימר משום דילמא מיפסיק ואתי לאתויי דהא לעיל (דף נד:) מפרש דזוג אסור משום דמיחזי כמאן דאזיל לחינגא ולא קאמר דלמא מיפסק דומיא דחותם: מאי שנא זוג שבצוארו דלמא מיפסיק ואתי לאתויי. והא דתנן לקמן (דף סו:) בני מלכים יולאין בזוגין וכל אדם אלא שדברו חכמים בהווה אומר ר"י דמיירי בזוגין יקרים שיולאין בהן בני מלכים כגון של כסף ושל זהב דליכא למיחש בהו דילמא מיפסיק דמסתמא תקועין הן יפה בשלשלאות של כסף והכא מיירי בזוג דעלמא דומיא דזוג של בהמה ולמאי דמוקי לה בגמרא באריג בכסותו אתי נמי שפיר: הב"ע דמחי. וא"ת כי היכי דזוג איירי במחי הכי נמי איירי חותם שבכסותו במחי ואם כן אמאי אסור וי"ל דזוג מותר לפי שדרך לאורגו בבגד שאין שום בגד שלא יהא ראוי לנוי ותכשיט כזה ולא הטריחוהו לפוסקו מכל בגדים ולגנות הבגד אבל חותם אין דרך לעשותו בכל הבגדים שאינו יפוי הבגד ולכך גזרו חכמים אפילו בארוג בכסותו שיהא לריך לפוסקו אטו היכא שאין ארוג וא"ת אדמפליג בין זוג שבלוארו לזוג שבכסותו ליפלוג בזוג שבכסותו גופיה בין מחי ללא מחי ויש לומר דניחא ליה לאשמעינן דזוג שבלוארו אסור אפילו בחתיכת הבגד שסביב לוארו ואינה יכולה ליפול אלא ע"י חתיכה: כדרב הונא כו'. ואע"ג דמילתא דרב הונא איירי לעיל (דף נז.) גבי חלילה מדקאמר כל שהוא אריג משמע דה"ק בין לענין חלילה בין לענין דלמא מיפסיק לא חיישינן באריג: (ה) אע"פ שחברו בדלת וקבעו במסמרים טמא. והא דאמר בהקומץ רבה (מנחות דף כד.) סדין שעשאו וילון טהור מן המדרס לאו משום קביעות גרידא טהור אלא מיירי שעשה שום שינוי מעשה. והא דאמר בנגמר הדין (סנהדרין דף מח:) כפה שנתנתו לספר טהור מן המדרס אף על פי שלא עשתה שום שינוי מעשה כיון דנאסר בהנאה ע"י כן חשוב כשינוי מעשה:

אין

עין משפט נר מצוה

יא א ב מיי' פי"ט מהל' שבת הל' יח [ועיין בכ"מ] סמג לאוין סה טוש"ע א"ח סי' דש סעיף א' בהג"ה:
יב ג מיי' פ"ח מהל' כלים הלכה ט:
יג ד שם הלכה ח:
יד ה מיי' פ"כ מהל' שבת הלכה י סמג לאוין סה טוש"ע א"ח סי' שה סעיף יב:
טו ו מיי' פי"ט מהל' שבת הלכה יח סמג שם טוש"ע א"ח סי' דש סעיף א בהג"ה:
טז ז מיי' פ"א מהל' כלים הלכה ו:

רבינו חננאל

שתי וערב. [אמר] רב הונא טוטפת עניות עושות של מיני צבעונין עשירות עושות אותן של כסף ושל זהב: הא דאמר שמואל יוצא העבד בשבת בחותם שבצוארו אבל לא בחותם שבכסותו הא והא בחותם דעבד ליה רביה ובחותם שבכסותו אמאי לא נפיק חיישינן דלמא מיפסק ומירתת מרביה ומכפל לכסותיה ומנח ליה אכתפיה וכר' יוחנן דאמר היוצא בטלית מקופלת ומונחת לו על כתיפו בשבת חייב חטאת וכדאמרו ליה לרב חנניא בר שילא רבנן כולהו לא ליפקו בסרבלא חתימה פי' דת המלך היתה באותה העת כל הקונה סרבלא מייתי לה גבי מוכס ויהיב ליה מיכסיה וחתים עליה במטבע של אינך כדי לידע שניטל מיכסא וכל טלית שנמצאת בלא חותם אינך נתפש לובשה כגנב המכס הלכך מתיירא כל אדם לצאת בטלית שתלוי עליה חותם זה חיישינן שמא יפסק החותם ומפני פחדו מן המוכס יסירה מעליה ויקפלה וישאנה על כתיפו כמשא לפיכך אסורה לכל אדם לצאת בטלית שיש עליה חותם אבל רב חנינה בר שילא שיש לו נשיאות פנים ואינו חושש מן המוכס מותר לו לצאת בטלית שיש בה חותם שאם יחתך החותם אינו חושש שאינו מתיירא מן המוכס ולא מזולתו ומפני זה הטעם אסר שמואל לצאת העבד בחותם שעשה לו רבו בכסותו. תנ"ה יוצא העבד בחותם שבצוארו אבל לא בחותם שבכסותו איני והא תנינן לא יצא העבד לא בחותם שבצוארו ולא בחותם שבכסותו וזה וזה אין מקבלין טומאה כו' ושנינן הא והא דעביד ליה רביה. ולא קשיא א) הא דתני

חשק שלמה על רבינו חננאל

א) נראה דחסר כאן וכל"ל ולא קשיא כאן בשל מתכת וכאן בשל טיט אמר מר לא תצא בהמה וכו' זה וזה אין מקבלין טומאה ורמינהו זוג של בהמה טמאה לא קשיא וכו':

מסורת הש"ס

א) לקמן קמז., ב) [כלים פי"ג מ"א ע"ש] מנחות סט: [ושם איתא דבר זה בשם דאמר מר כלי אבנים], ג) מ"ש זוג שבצוארו דלא דילמא כו' כצ"ל רש"ל, ד) [לעיל נז.], ה) שייך לע"ב.

גליון הש"ס

רש"י ד"ה כלי גללים צפיעי בקר. ע"ל דף טז ע"ב ברש"י ד"ה גללים. ועי' מנחות דף סט ע"ב תד"ה כלי גללים:

ליקוטי רש"י

בטלית מקופלת. לאחר שנתנה על ראשו הגביה שיפוליה על כתפיו. חייב חטאת. שאין זה דרך מלבוש [לקמן קמז.]. כלי גללים. כלי גללי בהמה [מנחות סט: עיי"ש בתוס' ובהגרי"ב]. לפיעי בקר מפרש להו במנחות בפרק ר' ישמעאל (סט:) [יומא ב.]. שיש [לעיל טז: עיי"ש בב"ח ובגה"ש כאן ושם]. כלי אדמה. שאין עשויין ככלי חרס בכבשן אלא מן האדמה היא שהוא כאבן רכה ומוקקין ממנה כלים [יומא שם]. דלאו על ידי גיבול הוא ככלי נתר וכלי חרס. אין מקבלין טומאה. שאינם קרויים כלים לענין קבלת טומאה [לעיל שם].

The Gemara recounts an incident which illustrates this very concern:

וְכִי הָא דְּאָמַר לֵיהּ שְׁמוּאֵל לְרַב חִינָּנָא בַּר שֵׁילָא – **And this is similar to that which Shmuel said to Rav Chinana bar Shila:** כּוּלְּהוּ רַבָּנָן דְּבֵי רֵישׁ גָּלוּתָא – **All the rabbis of the house of the Exilarch**[13] לֹא לִיפְּקוּ בְּסַרְבָּלֵי חֲתִימֵי – **may not go out** on the Sabbath **with cloaks that carry** the Exilarch's **emblem** on them,[14] for if the emblems become detached they may fold their cloaks to conceal the empty place, לְבַר מִינָּךְ – **except for you;** דְּלֹא קָפְדֵי עֲלָךְ דְּבֵי רֵישׁ גָּלוּתָא – **for the house of the Exilarch would not object to you** going out without an emblem upon your cloak,[15] and therefore you would not be tempted to fold your cloak over the place of a missing emblem. This statement of Shmuel illustrates that the reason an emblem attached to clothing cannot be worn outside on the Sabbath is because we are concerned that it will lead to the carrying of a folded cloak on one's shoulder.

The Gemara now directs its attention to an analysis of Shmuel's ruling:[16]

גּוּפָא – **The ruling itself** that was cited above stated: אָמַר שְׁמוּאֵל – **Shmuel said:** יוֹצֵא הָעֶבֶד בְּחוֹתָם שֶׁבְּצַוָּארוֹ – **A slave may go out** on the Sabbath **with an emblem that is on his neck,** אֲבָל לֹא בְּחוֹתָם שֶׁבִּכְסוּתוֹ – **but not with an emblem that is on his clothing.**

The Gemara cites a Baraisa that corroborates this ruling:

תַּנְיָא נַמִּי הָכִי – **This was taught in a Baraisa as well.** For a Baraisa states: יוֹצֵא הָעֶבֶד בְּחוֹתָם שֶׁבְּצַוָּארוֹ – A SLAVE MAY GO OUT on the Sabbath WITH AN EMBLEM THAT IS ON HIS NECK, אֲבָל לֹא בְּחוֹתָם שֶׁבִּכְסוּתוֹ – BUT NOT WITH AN EMBLEM THAT IS ON HIS CLOTHING.

The Gemara notes that this Baraisa is contradicted by a second Baraisa:

וּרְמִינְהוּ – **But contrast this** Baraisa with the following Baraisa, which states: לֹא יֵצֵא הָעֶבֶד בְּחוֹתָם שֶׁבְּצַוָּארוֹ – A SLAVE MAY NOT GO OUT on the Sabbath WITH AN EMBLEM THAT IS ON HIS NECK, וְלֹא בְּחוֹתָם שֶׁבִּכְסוּתוֹ – NOR may he go out WITH AN EMBLEM THAT IS ON HIS CLOTHING; זֶה וָזֶה אֵין מְקַבְּלִין טוּמְאָה – AND BOTH THIS type of emblem AND THIS type of emblem ARE NOT SUSCEPTIBLE TO *TUMAH*.[17] וְלֹא בְּזוּג שֶׁבְּצַוָּארוֹ – NOR may the slave go out WITH A BELL THAT IS ON (i.e. tied around) HIS NECK; אֲבָל יוֹצֵא הוּא בְּזוּג שֶׁבִּכְסוּתוֹ – BUT HE MAY GO OUT WITH A BELL THAT IS ON (i.e. attached to) HIS CLOTHING;[18] זֶה וָזֶה מְקַבְּלִין טוּמְאָה – and both THIS type of bell AND THIS type of bell ARE SUSCEPTIBLE TO *TUMAH*.[19] וְלֹא תֵצֵא בְּהֵמָה לֹא בְּחוֹתָם שֶׁבְּצַוָּארָהּ וְלֹא בְּחוֹתָם שֶׁבִּכְסוּתָהּ – BUT AN ANIMAL MAY NOT GO OUT EITHER WITH AN EMBLEM THAT IS ON ITS NECK OR WITH AN EMBLEM THAT IS ON ITS CLOTHING;[20] וְלֹא בְּזוּג שֶׁבִּכְסוּתָהּ וְלֹא בְּזוּג שֶׁבְּצַוָּארָהּ – NOR may it go out WITH A BELL THAT IS ON ITS CLOTHING NOR WITH A BELL THAT IS ON ITS NECK.[21] זֶה וָזֶה אֵין מְקַבְּלִין טוּמְאָה – And BOTH THIS (the emblems) AND THIS (the bells) ARE NOT SUSCEPTIBLE TO *TUMAH*.[22] At any rate, the first section of this Baraisa states that a slave may *not* go out with an emblem that is around his neck, thus contradicting the first Baraisa's ruling that permits this – ? –

The Gemara suggests a possible resolution:

לֵימָא הָא דְּעָבַד לֵיהּ רַבֵּיהּ – **Shall we say** that **this** first Baraisa speaks of an emblem **that was made for him by his master,** הָא דְּעָבַד אִיהוּ לְנַפְשֵׁיהּ – **and this** second Baraisa speaks of an emblem **that the slave made for himself?**[23]

The Gemara replies:

לֹא – **No!** It is not necessary to explain the second Baraisa as

NOTES

master (so that they would not conflict with the Mishnah's ruling), this distinction is apparently untenable – for hiding an emblem fashioned by the master would be an act of rebellion whether it is accomplished by removing the emblem *or* hiding it beneath the cloak! The Gemara therefore prefaced its question by saying, "now that we have interpreted Shmuel as referring to an emblem fashioned by the master . . ." And the Gemara answers that, indeed, we are not concerned that the slave will *hide* the emblem by folding the cloak – rather, we are concerned that the emblem will fall off and the slave will fold the cloak to cover the empty spot (*Tosafos, Rashba, Ritva MHK* ed., et al.).]

13. [The *Reish Galusa* (Exilarch) was the leader of the Jewish community in Babylonia.]

14. The rabbis of the Exilarch's court were required to wear emblems on their cloaks similar to those worn by slaves, to demonstrate their subservience to the Exilarch (*Rashi*). Other Rishonim understand that the purpose of the emblems was to show that the taxes due on the cloak had already been paid (*Rabbeinu Chananel, Rashba;* see also *Ran MHK* ed.), or to show that the person wearing the cloak was exempt from the taxes levied by the king (*Ritva MHK* ed.).

15. Rav Chinana had a close relationship with the Exilarch, and his loyalty was unquestioned; thus, the Exilarch would not object were he to be seen without an emblem upon his cloak, and Rav Chinana would not be tempted to fold his cloak if the emblem were to fall off. [According to those Rishonim who interpret the Gemara as referring to a mark intended to exempt from taxes, Rav Chinana was the exception because he was a distinguished man to whom the tax collectors would defer, and thus he would not attempt to hide the fact that the emblem was missing from his cloak.]

16. I.e. the second ruling of Shmuel, which has been interpreted as referring to an emblem fashioned by the master.

17. A [non-food] item can only be susceptible to *tumah* if it is either a utensil, a garment, or an ornament. The emblem of a slave is none of these, for it is neither a utensil nor a garment, and it is not considered an ornament, inasmuch as it diminishes the status of the one who wears it (see *Rashi*).

[The contradiction to the first Baraisa is apparent from this section of the Baraisa, since the first Baraisa permits a slave to go out with a neck emblem whereas the Baraisa here prohibits it. The Gemara, however, cites the Baraisa in its entirety before addressing the question.]

18. I.e. bells attached to a slave's clothing as ornaments (*Rashi*). [The reason for the distinction between bells worn on the neck and bells worn on clothing is explained by the Gemara below.]

19. Since these bells are ornamental in nature, they are susceptible to *tumah* [as any other ornament] (*Rashi*).

20. The "clothing" of animals mentioned here refers to blankets and the like that were used to cover horses so they would not become dirty (*Rashi;* see *Ishei Yisrael;* see also next note).

21. An animal may not go out with these items on the Sabbath because when an animal is marked or adorned in this fashion, it gives the impression that the owner is taking it to market to be sold [which is forbidden on the Sabbath] (*Rashi,* from above, 54b). [From *Rashi* it seems that this reason applies even to an emblem, although the Gemara he cites refers only to bells (see also *Rashi* printed alongside *Rif,* folio 26b. This is also the view of *Tosafos,* as understood by *Ishei Yisrael;* see, however, *Maharsha*).]

22. Although the bells are ornamental in nature, this does not render them susceptible to acquiring *tumah,* because an ornament used to adorn an animal does not attain the status of an "ornament" with regard to *tumah* (*Rashi;* see Gemara 58b, where this law is discussed further; see also *Keilim* 12:1). [The emblems are certainly not susceptible to *tumah,* for they are neither utensils nor ornaments.]

23. [This Baraisa would seem to state the very same ruling as the Mishnah does (according to Shmuel) – namely, that a slave may not go out on the Sabbath with an emblem anywhere on his person. Why, then, asks the Gemara, should we not explain the Baraisa as we did the Mishnah – as referring to an emblem fashioned by the slave himself, which cannot be worn outside due to the concern that the slave may remove it and come to carry it?]

אין בה משום עטרות כלות ושמואל אמר כבלא דעבדא תנן ומי אמר שמואל הכי והאמר שמואל יוצא העבד בחותם שבצוארו אבל לא בחותם שבכסותו לא קשיא [א] הא דעביד ליה רביה הא דעביד איהו לנפשיה במאי אוקימתא להא דשמואל דעביד ליה רביה בחותם שבכסותו אמאי לא דילמא מיפסק ומירתת ומיקפל ליה ומחית ליה אכתפיה כדרב יצחק בר יוסף דא"ר יצחק בר יוסף א"ר יוחנן א) היוצא בטלית מקופלת ומונחת לו על כתפיו בשבת חייב חטאת וכי הא דא"ל שמואל לרב חיננא בר שילא כולהו רבנן דבי ריש גלותא לא ליפקו בסרבלי חתימי לבר מינך דלא קפדי עליך דבי ריש גלותא: גופא אמר שמואל יוצא העבד בחותם שבצוארו אבל לא בחותם שבכסותו תניא נמי הכי [ב] יוצא העבד בחותם שבצוארו אבל לא בחותם שבכסותו ורמינהו לא יצא העבד בחותם שבצוארו ולא בחותם שבכסותו [ג] זה וזה אין מקבלין טומאה ולא בזוג שבצוארו אבל יוצא הוא בזוג שבכסותו [ד] זה וזה מקבלין טומאה [ה] ולא תצא בהמה לא בחותם שבצוארה ולא בחותם שבכסותה ולא בזוג שבכסותה ולא בזוג שבצוארה זה וזה אין מקבלין טומאה לימא הא דעביד ליה רביה הא דעביד איהו לנפשיה לא אידי ואידי דעביד ליה רביה וכאן [ו] בשל מתכת וכאן בשל טיט וכדרב נחמן אמר רבה בר אבוה דבר המקפיד עליו רבו אין יוצאין בו דבר שאין מקפיד עליו יוצאין בו ה"נ מסתברא מדקתני זה וזה אין מקבלין טומאה אי אמרת בשלמא של מתכת הני הוא דלא מקבלי טומאה הא כלים דידהו מקבלי טומאה אלא אי אמרת בשל טיט תנן הני הוא דלא מקבלי טומאה הא כלים דידהו מקבלי טומאה והא [ז] תניא [ז] כלי אבנים כלי גללים וכלי אדמה אין מקבלין טומאה לא מדברי תורה ולא מדברי סופרים אלא ש"מ של מתכת ש"מ: אמר מר ולא בזוג שבצוארו אבל יוצא הוא בזוג שבכסותו [ח] זוג שבצוארו אמאי לא דילמא מיפסיק ואתא לאיתויי זוג שבכסותו נמי ליחוש דילמא מיפסיק ואתי לאיתויי הכא במאי עסקינן דמיחא ביה מומחא וכדרב הונא בריה דרב יהושע דאמר [ט] רב הונא בריה דרב יהושע כל שהוא ארוג לא גזרו: אמר מר לא תצא בהמה לא בחותם שבצוארה ולא בחותם שבכסותה ולא בזוג שבכסותה ולא בזוג שבצוארה זה וזה אין מקבלין טומאה ורמינהו זוג של בהמה טמאה ושל

רש"י

אין בה משום עטרות כלות. דגזרו עליהן שלא תצא בהן מתורגמן ואלך משום לער במס' סוטה (דף מט.): **ושמואל אמר.** כבלא דעבדא ופליג אדר' אבהו: **חותם שבצוארו.** הוא כבלא דעבדא והיו עושין אותו משל טיט: **דעביד ליה רביה.** אית ליה אימתא ולא שקיל ליה מלואריה להוליכו בידו: **מיפסק.** החותם ושבר ומירתת מרבו שלא יאמר שהוא נטלו להראות בשוק שהוא בן חורין: **ומקפל ליה.** הטלית על כתפיו כדי שלא יראה מקום החותם ולא יבינו שנפל ודמי הטלית על כתפו כמשוי: **חייב חטאת.** דלאו מכשיט אלא בזמן שלובשו דרך מלבוש: **כולהו רבנן לא ליפקו בסרבלי חתימי.** היו עושין חותמות לטליתות שלהן כעין עבדים להראות שהן כפופין לריש גלותא לא ליפקו דלמא מפסקי מרתתי ומקפלי להו: **דלא קפדי עלך.** אם תלך בלא חותם: **יוצא העבד בחותם שבצוארו.** ובשל טיט דלא קפיד עליה לאתויי ולאו משום דמירתת מאי הורלא נפקא מינה משום אימתא דרביה לא מייתי ליה בידיה דהא לאו הוכחה היא לעבדות אלא כשישנו על צוארו או בכסותו: **וזה וזה אין מקבלין טומאה.** דלאו תכשיט עביד שיהא טמא משום תכשיט ואע"ג דבשל מתכת מוקמינן לה להא לקמן מיהו לאו לנוי דיליה הוא אלא לגנאי וכלי תשמיש נמי לא הוי: **זוג.** לנוי עביד: **ולא בזוג שבצוארו אבל יוצא הוא בזוג שבכסותו.** לקמיה מפרש טעמא: **מקבלין טומאה.** שתכשיט הוא: **שבכסותה.** עושים לסוסים מעילין שלא יטנפו: **לא תצא.** כדאמרינן בפירקין (דף נד:) דמחזי כמאן דאזיל לחינגא: **אין מקבלין טומאה.** דלאו תכשיט נינהו לבהמה: **לא אידי ואידי דעביד ליה רביה.** דאע"ג דכבול דמתניתין אוקימנא בדעביד איהו לנפשיה התם הוא דליכא לאוקמיה בהתם חותמות של טיט דלאי מיתבר אין מקפיד עליו להביא שבריו לבית אדונו הלכך ליכא לאוקמיה בדעביד ליה רביה דאי עבד ליה רביה לא הוה מיתסר דכל זמן שלא נפסק לא שקיל ליה מלואריה משום אימתא דרביה ואי מיפסק לא קפיד עליה בעליו משום פסידא דליכא פסידא הלכך לא מייתי ליה אבל הך לא איכא לאוקמא בשל טיט כדמסתברא לקמן מסיפא הלכך אפילו עבד ליה רביה נמי אסור דאי מיפסק קפיד עליה משום פסידא ומירתת עבד ומייתי ליה בידיה: **דבר המקפיד עליו רבו.** אם יאבד לא יצא דאי מפסיק מייתי ליה: **מסתברא.** דבשל מתכת קאי מדאיצטריך למיתני אין מקבלין טומאה וטעמא משום דלאו לנוי עבידה: **הני הוא דלא מקבלין טומאה.** משום דלאו כלים נינהו הא שאר כלי מתכות מקבלין: **כלים דידהו.** דמתכות: **אלא אי אמרת.** כלים דידהו כלי העשוי מטיט כזה שאינו מצרפו בכבשן מעשה ידי יוצר דניהוי קרוי כלי חרס אלא כלי אדמה מי מקבל טומאה בתמיה: **כלי גללים.** [ט] לפיעי בקר שעשה מהן כלי: **דמיחא מומחא.** שארגו בבגד ותו לא מיפסק: **לא גזרו.** לצאת בו ודרב הונא לענין ארוג כי האי גוונא נמי איתמר דלאשמעינן דלא חיישינן תו לדלמא מיפסק:

ושל

תוספות

והאמר שמואל יוצא העבד בחותם כו'. ולא בעי לאוקמי מתניתין בחותם שבכסותו דניחא ליה לאוקמה בדעבד איהו לנפשיה ולאיירי מתני' בכל חותמות: **הא דעבד איהו לנפשיה.** קשה לרשב"א אמאי שריא מתני' בדעבד איהו לנפשיה כיון דליכא קפידא דרבו וי"ל דליכא קלא קפידא אבל לא כל כך כמו בעבד ליה רביה: **במאי אוקימתא להא דשמואל בדעבד ליה רביה כו'.** אבל אי איירי בדעבד איהו לנפשיה אתי שפיר דבלוארו ליכא למיחש דלמא פסיק ליה בידים כדי שלא יבינו הרואין שהוא עבד אבל בכסותו איכא למיחש דלמא מקפל טליתו לכסות החותם ולא ידע דיש בזה חיוב חטאת אבל בדעבד ליה רביה משום אימתא דרביה ירא לקפל והשתא נמי לא ידע הש"ס לדרב יצחק אלא דלא ידע שיש לחוש דילמא מיפסיק ובתר דמשני מייתי לדרב יצחק ונקט לפרושי שיש חיוב חטאת בקיפול: **דילמא מיפסק ומרתת ומקפל ליה.** דניחא ליה טפי שיהיה מקופל משירלה רבו שנפסק לגמרי ויסבור שבמזיד פסקו למרוד בו: **לא תצא בהמה כו'.** דמיחזי כמאן דאזיל לחינגא כדפי' בקונ' דלא מצינן למימר משום דילמא מיפסיק ואתי לאתויי דהא לעיל (דף נד:) מפרש דזוג אסור משום דמיחזי כמאן דאזיל לחינגא ולא קאמר דלמא מיפסק דומיא לחותם: **מאי שנא זוג שבצוארו דלמא מיפסיק ואתי לאתויי.** והא דתנן לקמן (דף סו:) בני מלכים יולאין בזוגין וכל אדם אלא שדברו חכמים בהווה אומר ר"י דמיירי בזוגין יקרים שיולאין בהן בני מלכים כגון של כסף ושל זהב דליכא למיחש בהו דילמא מיפסיק דמסתמא תקועין הן יפה בשלשלאות של כסף והכא מיירי בזוג דעלמא דומיא דזוג של בהמה ולמאי דמוקי לה בגמרא בארוג בכסותו אתי נמי שפיר: **הב"ע דמחי.** וא"ת כי היכי דמיירי במחי הכי נמי לוקמי חותם שבכסותו במחי ואם כן אמאי אסור וי"ל דזוג מותר לפי שדרך לאורגו בבגד שאין שום בגד שלא יהא ראוי לנוי ותכשיט הוא ולא הטריחוהו לפוסקו מכל בגדים ולגנות הבגד אבל כל חותם אין דרך לעשותו בכל הבגדים שאינו יופי הבגד ולכך גזרו חכמים אפילו בארוג בכסותו שיהא לריך לפוסקו מטו היכא שאין ארוג ולא"ת דמפליג בין זוג שבצוארו לזוג שבכסותו ליפלוג בזוג שבכסותו גופיה בין מחי ללא מחי ויש לומר דניחא ליה לאשמעינן דזוג שבצוארו אסור אפילו בחתיכת הבגד שסביב צוארו ואינה יכולה ליפול אלא ע"י חתיכה: **כדרב הונא כו'.** ואע"ג דמילתא דרב הונא איתי לעיל (דף נז.) גבי חליצה מדקאמר כל שהוא ארוג משמע דה"ק בין לענין חליצה בין לענין דלמא מיפסיק לא חיישינן בארוג: **אע"פ** שחברו בדלת וקבעו במסמרים טמא. והא דאמר בהקומץ רבה (מנחות דף מב.) סדין שעשאו וילון טהור מן המדרס לאו משום קביעות גרידא טהור אלא מיירי שעשה שום שינוי מעשה. והא דאמר בנגמר הדין (סנהדרין דף מח:) כפה שנתנתו לספר טהור מן המדרס אף על פי שלא עשתה שום שינוי מעשה כיון דנאסר בהנאה ע"י כן חשוב כשינוי מעשה:

אין

מסורת הש"ס

א) לקמן קמז., ב) [כלים פי"ב מ"א ע"ש] מנחות סט: [ושם איתא דבר זה בשם דאמר מר כלי אבנים], ג) מ"ש זוג שבצוארו דלא דילמא כו' כל"ל רש"ל, ד) [לעיל נז.], ה) שייך לע"ב.

גליון הש"ס

רש"י ד"ה כלי גללים צפיעי בקר. ע"ל דף טז ע"ב ברש"י ד"ה גללים. ועי' מנחות דף סט ע"ב תד"ה כלי גללים:

ליקוטי רש"י

בטלית מקופלת. לאחר שנתנה על ראשו הגביה שיפוליה על כתפיו. **חייב חטאת.** שאין זה דרך מלבוש [לקמן קמז.]. **כלי גללים.** כלי גללי בהמה [מנחות סט: עיי"ש בתוס' ובהגרי"ב]. לפיעי בקר מפרש להו במנחות בפרק ר' ישמעאל (סט:) [יומא ב.]. שייש [לעיל טז: עיי"ש בב"ח ובגה"ש כאן ושם]. **כלי אדמה.** שאין עשוין ככלי חרס בכבשן אלא מן האדמה היא שהוא כאבן רכה וחוקקין ממנה כלים [יומא שם]. דלאו על ידי גיבול הוא ככלי נתר וכלי חרס. **אין מקבלין טומאה.** שאינם קרויים כלים לענין קבלת טומאה [לעיל שם].

עין משפט נר מצוה

יא א ב מיי' פי"ט מהל' שבת הל' יח [ועיין במ"מ] סמג לאוין סה טוש"ע א"ח סי' דש סעיף א' בהג"ה:

יב ג מיי' פ"ח מהל' כלים הלכה ט:

יג ד שם הלכה ח:

יד ה מיי' פ"כ מהל' שבת הלכה י סמג לאוין סה טוש"ע א"ח סי' שה סעיף יב:

טו ו מיי' פי"ט מהל' שבת הלכה יח סמג שם טוש"ע א"ח סי' דש סעיף א בהג"ה:

טז ז מיי' פ"א מהל' כלים הלכה ו:

רבינו חננאל

שתי וערב. [אמר] רב הונא טוטפת עניות עושות של מיני צבעונין עשירות עושות אותן של כסף ושל זהב: **הא דאמר** שמואל יוצא העבד בשבת בחותם שבצוארו אבל לא בחותם שבכסותו הא והא בחותם דעבד ליה רביה ובחותם שבכסותו אמאי לא נפיק חיישינן דלמא מיפסק ומירתת מרביה ומכפל לכסותיה ומנח ליה אכתפיה וכר' יוחנן דאמר היוצא בטלית מקופלת ומונחת לו על כתיפו בשבת חייב חטאת וכדאמרו ליה לרב חנניא בר שילא רבנן כולהו לא ליפקו בסרבלא חתימה פי' דת המלך היתה באותה העת כל הקונה סרבלא מייתי לה גבי מוכס ויהיב ליה מיכסיה וחותים עליה במטבע של אינך כדי לידע שניטל מיכסא וכל טלית שנמצאת בלא חותם אינך נתפש לובשה כגנב המכס הלכך מתיירא כל אדם לצאת בטלית שתלוי עליה חותם זה חיישינן שמא יפסק החותם ומפני פחדו מן המוכס יסירה מעליה ויקפלה וישאנה על כתיפו כמשא לפיכך אסורה לכל אדם לצאת בטלית שיש עליה חותם אבל רב חנינה בר שילא שיש לו נשיאות פנים ואינו חושש מן המוכס מותר לו לצאת בטלית שיש בה חותם שאם יחתך החותם אינו חושש שאינו מתיירא מן המוכס ולא מזולתו ומפני זה הטעם אסר שמואל לצאת העבד בחותם שעשה לו רבו בכסותו. תנ"ה יוצא העבד בחותם שבצוארו אבל לא בחותם שבכסותו איני והא תנינן לא יצא העבד לא בחותם שבצוארו ולא בחותם שבכסותו וזה וזה אין מקבלין טומאה כו' ושנינן הא והא דעביד ליה רביה. ולא קשיא א) הא דתני

חשק שלמה על רבינו חננאל

א) נראה דחסר כאן וכל"ל ולא קשיא כאן בשל מתכת וכאן בשל טיט אמר מר לא תצא בהמה וכו' זה וזה אין מקבלין טומאה ורמינהו זוג של בהמה טמאה לא קשיא וכו':

referring only to an emblem made by the slave himself. אִידִי וְאִידִי דְּעָבַד לֵיהּ רַבֵּיהּ – Rather, **both this** first Baraisa **and this** second Baraisa speak even **of** an emblem **that was made for him by his master.**[24] וְכָאן בְּשֶׁל מַתֶּכֶת – **And** yet there is no contradiction, for **here,** in the second Baraisa, we are speaking **of** an emblem **made of metal,** וְכָאן בְּשֶׁל טִיט – **while here,** in the first Baraisa, we are speaking of an emblem **made of clay.** וְכִדְרַב נַחְמָן אָמַר רַבָּה בַּר אֲבוּהָ – **And** this distinction is made **in accordance with** that which **Rav Nachman** stated **in the name of Rabbah bar Avuha:** דָּבָר הַמַּקְפִּיד עָלָיו רַבּוֹ אֵין יוֹצְאִין בּוֹ – **An item** whose loss **[a slave's] master is particular about, [a slave] may not go out** with it on the Sabbath, for if it becomes detached he might carry it home with him out of fear of his master. דָּבָר שֶׁאֵין מַקְפִּיד עָלָיו יוֹצְאִין בּוֹ – But **an item that he is not particular about, [the slave] may go out** wearing it, for he will not carry it home if it becomes detached.[25] Thus, the first Baraisa permits a slave to go out with an emblem of clay fashioned by his master around his neck, for his master will not object to its loss if it becomes detached;[26] and the second Baraisa forbids a slave to go out with an emblem made of metal around his neck, for the master will object to its loss if it becomes detached, and the slave may therefore carry it home in order to avoid his master's displeasure.[27]

The Gemara provides proof from within the second Baraisa itself that the Baraisa speaks of an emblem made of metal:

הָכִי נַמִּי מִסְתַּבְּרָא – **And this** explanation of the second Baraisa as referring to an emblem of metal **is indeed more reasonable,** מִדְּקָתָנֵי זֶה וָזֶה אֵין מְקַבְּלִין טוּמְאָה – as can be seen **from the fact that the Baraisa taught** concerning the emblems worn by a slave: BOTH THIS AND THIS ARE NOT SUSCEPTIBLE TO *TUMAH.* This ruling implies that although the emblem is made of a material which normally would be susceptible to *tumah,* the emblem is nevertheless not susceptible.[28] אִי אָמְרַת בִּשְׁלָמָא שֶׁל מַתֶּכֶת – Now, **if you say** that the emblem being discussed is **made of metal, this is understandable,** הָנֵי הוּא דְּלָא מְקַבְּלֵי טוּמְאָה – for **it is** then only **these** [i.e. emblems] **that are not susceptible to *tumah,*** הָא כֵּלִים דִּידְהוּ מְקַבְּלֵי טוּמְאָה – **but utensils made of their** material – metal – ***are* susceptible to *tumah*** – and the Baraisa's ruling would then contain an element of novelty. אֶלָּא אִי אָמְרַת בְּשֶׁל טִיט תְּנַן – **But if you say** that **the Baraisa speaks of** an emblem **made of clay,** the Baraisa's ruling seems puzzling; הָנֵי הוּא דְּלָא מְקַבְּלֵי טוּמְאָה – for can you say that **it is** only **these** [the emblems of clay] **that are not susceptible to *tumah,*** הָא כֵּלִים דִּידְהוּ מְקַבְּלֵי טוּמְאָה – **but utensils made of their** material **are susceptible to *tumah*?** וְהָא תַּנְיָא – **But a Baraisa was taught:** כְּלֵי אֲבָנִים – STONEWARE, כְּלֵי גְלָלִים – DUNGWARE,[29] וּכְלֵי אֲדָמָה – AND UTENSILS OF unbaked CLAY[30] אֵין מְקַבְּלִין טוּמְאָה לֹא מִדִּבְרֵי תוֹרָה וְלֹא מִדִּבְרֵי סוֹפְרִים – ARE NOT SUSCEPTIBLE TO *TUMAH* EITHER BY TORAH LAW OR BY RABBINIC LAW. Thus, if the Baraisa speaks of emblems of clay, it would be superfluous to state that they are not susceptible to *tumah* as emblems. אֶלָּא שְׁמַע מִינָּהּ שֶׁל מַתֶּכֶת – **Rather, learn from this** that the Baraisa speaks of emblems **made of metal.** שְׁמַע מִינָּהּ – Indeed, you can **learn** it **from this.**[31]

The Gemara cites a segment of the second Baraisa:

אָמַר מַר – **The master stated** in the Baraisa: וְלֹא בְּזוּג שֶׁבְּצַוָּארוֹ – NOR may the slave go out WITH A BELL THAT IS ON HIS NECK; אֲבָל יוֹצֵא הוּא בְּזוּג שֶׁבִּכְסוּתוֹ – BUT HE MAY GO OUT WITH A BELL THAT IS ON HIS CLOTHING.

The Gemara questions this distinction:

זוּג שֶׁבְּצַוָּארוֹ אַמַּאי לֹא – **Why** is it that a slave may **not** go out **with a bell that is on his neck?** דִּילְמָא מִפְּסִיק וְאָתָא לְאֵיתוּיֵי – Presumably, it is because we are concerned that **[a bell] will perhaps become detached, and [the slave] will come to carry it** home. זוּג שֶׁבִּכְסוּתוֹ נַמִּי – But then in the case of **a bell that is on his clothing as well,** לֵיחוּשׁ דִּילְמָא מִפְּסִיק וְאָתֵי לְאֵיתוּיֵי – **let**

NOTES

24. I.e. there is a way to interpret this second Baraisa, which prohibits the wearing of an emblem worn around the neck, as referring even to a case where the master fashioned the emblem. [See also next note.]

25. [With this answer the Gemara is introducing a new element into the question of whether a slave may wear an emblem on the Sabbath – the possibility that the slave will want to save an emblem that becomes detached and therefore carry it home with him.] This concern, however, applies only to emblems that are worth saving, and not to the common emblems that were made of clay (*Rashi*).

26. [Furthermore, the slave will not carry the emblem in his hand to appease his master, for carrying an emblem does not indicate his slave status, as explained above (note 12).]

27. The Gemara above could have resolved the conflict between Shmuel's ruling and the Mishnah in this manner as well; i.e. the Gemara could have interpreted the Mishnah as referring to a case where the master fashioned an emblem of metal, and the prohibition to wear an emblem is due to the possibility that it will fall off and the slave will carry it home. The Gemara did not interpret the Mishnah this way because it preferred to explain the Mishnah as referring to the more common emblems that are made of clay, which a slave would *not* attempt to save. [The Gemara therefore explained the Mishnah to be referring to an emblem fashioned by the slave himself.] The only reason that the Gemara explains the second Baraisa as referring to a metal emblem is that there are internal indications within that Baraisa that metal emblems are being discussed, as the Gemara will explain below (see *Rashi;* cf. *Tosafos* ד״ה והאמר שמואל and *Maharsha* there; see also below, note 31).

28. I.e. the Baraisa teaches that the emblems are not susceptible to *tumah* because they are merely emblems and not utensils. There would be no reason for the Baraisa to teach this, however, unless they could be susceptible to *tumah* if they were utensils – which can only be true if they are made of a material that becomes *tamei* (*Rashi*).

29. I.e. vessels made out of dried dung (*Rashi;* cf. *Rashi* above, 16b ד״ה גללים; see also *Meromei Sadeh* there).

30. Literally: utensils of earth. These differ from כְּלֵי חֶרֶס, *earthenware,* in that earthenware is baked in a kiln, while כְּלֵי אֲדָמָה are not (*Rashi*). Rather, they are dried in the sun, which results in an inferior product (*Rav* to *Keilim* 3:2, 4:4; *Mishnah Berurah* 159:4).

31. Thus, the resolution advanced by the Gemara above – that the first Baraisa speaks of emblems of clay, while the second speaks of emblems of metal – is accepted.

In summary: This concludes the Gemara's discussion regarding the wearing of slaves' emblems outside on the Sabbath. The laws that emerge from the preceding discussion can be summarized as follows: (a) An emblem made of *metal* may *never* be worn outside on the Sabbath, for the slave will want to save it if it falls off, and he may come to carry it home with him. (This is the law taught in the second Baraisa.) (b) An emblem made of *clay* that was fashioned by the master may be worn by a slave around his neck, for he will be afraid to remove it, and if it should fall off, he will not be tempted to save it; there is therefore never any reason for him to carry it. He may not wear such an emblem on his cloak, however, for if the emblem were to fall off, the slave might fold his cloak (and wear it in a manner that constitutes carrying) to hide the place of the missing emblem. (These are the laws taught by Shmuel.) (c) If the emblem was fashioned by the slave himself, it may not be worn at all, even around his neck – for we are concerned that he will remove it and carry it to conceal the fact that he is a slave. (This is the law taught in the Mishnah.)

[This summary reflects the view of most Rishonim – see *Rosh, Meiri, Ramban, Ritva MHK* ed., and *Ran MHK* edition. *Rif,* however, does not mention the last law at all. Seemingly, he maintains that even if the slave fashioned a clay emblem himself, he may go outside with it on the Sabbath if it is around his neck; this also seems to be the view of *Rambam* (see *Hil. Shabbos* 19:8 with *Maggid Mishneh*) and *Tur* §304 as well. See *Ran, Chelkas Binyamin* and *Shabbos Shel Mi,* who discuss this further.]

אין בה משום עטרות כלות ושמואל אמר כבלא דעבדא תנן ומי אמר שמואל הכי והאמר שמואל יוצא העבד בחותם שבצוארו אבל לא בחותם שבכסותו לא קשיא [א]הא דעבד ליה רביה הא דעבד איהו לנפשיה במאי אוקימתא להא דשמואל דעבד ליה רביה בחותם שבכסותו אמאי לא דילמא מיפסק ומירתת ומיקפל ליה ומחית ליה אכתפיה כדרב יצחק בר יוסף דא"ר יצחק בר יוסף א"ר יוחנן [א]היוצא בטלית מקופלת ומונחת לו על כתפיו בשבת חייב חטאת וכי הא דא"ל שמואל לרב חיננא בר שילא כולהו רבנן דבי ריש גלותא לא ליפקו בסרבלי חתימי לבר מינך דלא קפדי עליך דבי ריש גלותא: גופא אמר שמואל יוצא העבד בחותם שבצוארו אבל לא בחותם שבכסותו תניא נמי הכי [ב]יוצא העבד בחותם שבצוארו אבל לא בחותם שבכסותו ורמינהו לא יצא העבד בחותם שבצוארו ולא בחותם שבכסותו [ג]זה וזה אין מקבלין טומאה ולא בזוג שבצוארו אבל יוצא הוא בזוג שבכסותו [ד]זה וזה מקבלין טומאה [ה]ולא תצא בהמה לא בחותם שבצוארה ולא בחותם שבכסותה ולא בזוג שבכסותה ולא בזוג שבצוארה זה וזה אין מקבלין טומאה לימא הא דעבד ליה רביה הא דעבד איהו לנפשיה לא אידי ואידי דעבד ליה רביה וכאן [ו]בשל מתכת וכאן בשל טיט וכדרב נחמן אמר רבה בר אבוה דבר המקפיד עליו רבו אין יוצאין בו דבר שאין מקפיד עליו יוצאין בו ה"נ מסתברא מדקתני זה וזה אין מקבלין טומאה אי אמרת בשלמא של מתכת הני הוא דלא מקבלי טומאה הא כלים דידהו מקבלי טומאה אלא אי אמרת בשל טיט תנן הני הוא דלא מקבלי טומאה הא כלים דידהו מקבלי טומאה והא [ג]תניא [ז]כלי אבנים כלי גללים וכלי אדמה אין מקבלין טומאה לא מדברי תורה ולא מדברי סופרים אלא ש"מ של מתכת ש"מ: אמר מר ולא בזוג שבצוארו אבל יוצא הוא בזוג שבכסותו [ג]זוג שבצוארו אמאי לא דילמא מיפסיק ואתא לאיתויי זוג שבכסותו נמי ליחוש דילמא מיפסיק ואתי לאיתויי הכא במאי עסקינן דמיחא ביה מומחא וכדרב הונא בריה דרב יהושע דאמר [ד]רב הונא בריה דרב יהושע כל שהוא ארוג לא גזרו: אמר מר לא תצא בהמה לא בחותם שבצוארה ולא בחותם שבכסותה ולא בזוג שבצוארה ולא בזוג שבכסותה זה וזה אין מקבלין טומאה וזוג דבהמה אין מקבלין טומאה ורמינהו זוג של בהמה טמאה ושל

רש"י

אין בה משום עטרות כלות. דגזרו עליהן שלא תלא כהן מחורבן ואילך משום לער במס' סוטה (דף מט.): ושמואל אמר. כבול דמתני' כבלא דעבדא ופליג אדר' אבהו: חותם שבצוארו. הוא כבלא דעבדא והיו עושין אותו משל טיט: דעביד ליה רביה. אית ליה אימתא ולא שקיל ליה מצוארו להוליכו בידו: מיפסק. החותם ונשבר ומירתת מרבו שלא יאמר שהוא נטלו להראות בשוק שהוא בן חורין: ומקפל ליה. הטלית על כתפיו כדי שלא יראה מקום החותם ולא יבינו שנפל ודמי הטלית על כתפו כמשוי: חייב חטאת. דאינו תכשיט אלא בזמן שלובשו דרך מלבוש: כולהו רבנן לא ליפקו בסרבלי חתימי. היו עושין חותמות לטליתות שלהן כעין עבדים להראות שהן כפופין לריש גלותא לא ליפקו דאי מפסקי מרתתי ומקפלי להו: דלא קפדי עלך. אם תלך בלא חותם: יוצא העבד בחותם שבצוארו. ובשל טיט דלא קפיד עליה לאתויי ואי משום דמירתת מאי הורבא נפקא מינה משום אימתא דרביה לא מייתי ליה בידיה דהא לאו הוכחה היא דעבדות אלא כשישנו על צוארו או בכסותו: וזה וזה אין מקבלין טומאה. דלאו לנוי עביד שיהא טמא משום תכשיט ואע"ג דבשל מתכת מוקמינן לה להא לקמן מיהו לאו לנוי דיליה הוא אלא לגנאי וכלי תשמיש נמי לא הוי: זוג. לנוי עביד: ולא בזוג שבצוארו אבל יוצא הוא בזוג שבכסותו. לקמיה מפרש טעמא: מקבלין טומאה. שתכשיט הוא: שבכסותה. עושים לסוסים מעילין שלא יטנפו: לא תצא. כדאמרינן באידך פרקין (דף נד:) דמתחזי כמאן דאזיל לחינגא: אין מקבלין טומאה. דאין תכשיט לבהמה: לא אידי ואידי דעבד ליה רביה. דאע"ג דכבול דמתניתין אוקימנא בדעבד איהו לנפשיה התם הוא דאיכא לאוקמיה בשתם חותמות של טיט דאי מיתבר אין מקפיד עליו להביא שבריו לבית אדונו הלכך ליכא לאוקמיה בדעבד ליה רביה דאי עבד ליה רביה לא הוה מיתסר דכל זמן שלא נפסק לא שקיל ליה מצוארו משום אימתא דרביה ואי מיפסק לא קפיד עליה בעליו משום פסידא דליכא פסידא הלכך לא מייתי ליה אבל הך לא איכא לאוקמא בשל טיט כדמסתברא לקמן מסיפא הלכך אפילו עבד ליה רביה נמי אסור דאי מיפסק קפיד עליה משום פסידא ומירתת עבד ומייתי ליה בידיה: דבר המקפיד עליו רבו. אם יאבד לא יצא דאי מפסיק מייתי ליה: מסתברא. דבשל מתכת קאי מדאיצטריך למיתני אין מקבלין טומאה וטעמא משום דלאו לנוי עבידא: הני הוא דלא מקבלין טומאה. משום דלאו כלים נינהו הא שאר כלי מתכות מקבלין: כלים דידהו. דמתכות: אלא אי אמרת. כלים דידהו כלי העשוי מטיט כזה שאינו מצרפו בכבשן מעשה ידי יוצר דניהוי קרוי כלי חרס אלא כלי אדמה מי מקבל טומאה בתמיה: כלי גללים. [ה]לפיעי בקר שעשה מהן כלי: דמיחא מומחא. שארגו בבגד ותו לא מיפסיק: לא גזרו. לצאת בו ודרב הונא לענין אריג כי האי גוונא נמי איתמר דאשמעינן דלא חיישינן תו לדלמא מיפסק:

תוספות

והאמר שמואל יוצא העבד בחותם כו'. ולא בעי לאוקמי מתניתין בחותם שבכסותו דניחא ליה לאוקמה בדעבד איהו לנפשיה ואיירי מתני' בכל חותמות: הא דעבד איהו לנפשיה. קשה לרשב"א אמאי שריא מתני' בדעבד איהו לנפשיה בחצר כיון דליכא קפידא דרבו וי"ל דאיכא קצת קפידא אבל לא כל כך כמו בעבד ליה רביה: במאי אוקימתא להא דשמואל בדעבד ליה רביה כו'. אבל אי מיירי בדעבד איהו לנפשיה אתי שפיר דבצוארו ליכא למיחש דלמא פסיק ליה בידים כדי שלא יבינו הרואין שהוא עבד אבל בכסותו איכא למיחש דלמא מקפל טליתו לכסות החותם ולא ידע דיש בזה חיוב חטאת אבל בדעבד ליה רביה משום אימתא דרביה ירא לקפל והשתא נמי ידע הש"ס לדרב יצחק אלא דלא ידע שיש לחוש דילמא מיפסיק ובתר דמשני מייתי דרב יצחק ונחת לפרושי שיש חיוב חטאת בקיפול: דילמא מיפסק ומרתת ומקפל ליה. דניחא ליה טפי שיהיה מקופל משיראה רבו שנפסק לגמרי ויסבור שבמזיד פסקו למרוד בו: לא תצא בהמה כו'. דמיחזי כמאן דאזיל לחינגא כדפי' בקונ' דלא מלינן למימר משום דילמא מיפסיק ואתי לאתויי דהא לעיל (דף נד:) מפרש דזוג אסור משום למיחזי כמאן דאזיל לחינגא ולא קאמר דלמא מיפסק דומיא דחותם: מאי שנא זוג שבצוארו דלמא מיפסיק ואתי לאתויי. והא דתנן לקמן (דף סו:) בני מלכים יוצאין בזוגין וכל אדם אלא שדברו חכמים בהווה אומר ר"י דמיירי בזוגין יקרים שיוצאין בהן בני מלכים כגון של כסף ושל זהב דליכא למיחש בהו דילמא מיפסיק דמסתמא תקועין הן יפה בשלשלאות של כסף והכא מיירי בזוג דעלמא דומיא דזוג של בהמה ולמאי דמוקי לה בגמרא באריג בכסותו אתי נמי שפיר: הב"ע דמחי. וא"ת כי היכי דזוג איירי במחי הכי נמי איירי חותם שבכסותו במחי ואם כן אמאי אסור וי"ל דזוג מותר לפי שדרך לאורגו בבגד שאין שום בגד שלא יהא ראוי לנוי ותכשיט כזה ולא הטריחוהו לפוסקו מכל בגדים ולגנות הבגד אבל חותם אין דרך לעשותו בכל הבגדים שאינו יפוי הבגד ולכך גזרו חכמים אפילו באריג בכסותו שיהא צריך לפוסקו אטו היכא שאין ארוג וא"ת אדמפליג בין זוג שבצוארו לזוג שבכסותו ליפלוג בזוג שבכסותו גופיה בין מחי ללא מחי ויש לומר דניחא ליה לאשמעינן דזוג שבצוארו אסור אפילו בחתיכת הבגד שסביב צוארו ואינה יכולה ליפול אלא ע"י חתיכה: כדרב הונא כו'. ואע"ג דמילתא דרב הונא איתי לעיל (דף נז.) גבי חלילה מדקאמר כל שהוא אריג משמע דה"ק בין לענין חלילה בין לענין דלמא מיפסיק לא חיישינן באריג: [ה]אע"פ שחברו בדלת וקבעו במסמרים טמא. והא דאמר בהקומץ רבה (מנחות דף כד.) סדין שעשאו וילון טהור מן המדרס לאו משום קביעות גרידא טהור אלא מיירי שעשה שום שינוי מעשה. והא דאמר בנגמר הדין (סנהדרין דף מח:) כפה שנתנתו לספר טהור מן המדרס אף על פי שלא עשתה שום שינוי מעשה כיון דנאסר בהנאה ע"י כן חשוב כשינוי מעשה:

אין

עין משפט נר מצוה

יא א ב מיי' פי"ט מהל' שבת הל' יח [ועיין בכ"מ] סמג לאוין סה טוש"ע א"ח סי' דש סעיף א' בהג"ה:
יב ג מיי' פ"ח מהל' כלים הלכה ט:
יג ד שם הלכה ח:
יד ה מיי' פ"כ מהל' שבת הלכה י סמג לאוין סה טוש"ע א"ח סי' שה סעיף יב:
טו ו מיי' פי"ט מהל' שבת הלכה יח סמג שם טוש"ע א"ח סי' דש סעיף א בהג"ה:
טז ז מיי' פ"א מהל' כלים הלכה ו:

רבינו חננאל

שתי וערב. [אמר] רב הונא טוטפת עניות עושות של מיני צבעונין עשירות עושות אותן של כסף ושל זהב: **הא דאמר** שמואל יוצא העבד בשבת בחותם שבצוארו אבל לא בחותם שבכסותו הא והא בחותם דעבד ליה רביה ובחותם שבכסותו אמאי לא נפיק חיישינן דלמא מיפסק ומירתת מרביה ומכפל לכסותיה ומנח ליה אכתפיה וכר' יוחנן דאמר היוצא בטלית מקופלת ומונחת לו על כתיפו בשבת חייב חטאת וכדאמרו ליה לרב חנניא בר שילא רבנן כולהו לא ליפקו בסרבלא חתימה פי' דת המלך היתה באותה העת כל הקונה סרבלא מייתי לה גבי מוכס ויהיב ליה מיכסיה וחתים עליה במטבע של אינך כדי לידע שניטל מיכסא וכל טלית שנמצאת בלא חותם אינך נתפש לובשה כגנב המכס הלכך מתיירא כל אדם לצאת בטלית שתלוי עליה חותם זה חיישינן שמא יפסק החותם ומפני פחדו מן המוכס יסירה מעליה ויקפלה וישאנה על כתיפו כמשא לפיכך אסורה לכל אדם לצאת בטלית שיש עליה חותם אבל רב חנינה בר שילא שיש לו נשיאות פנים ואינו חושש מן המוכס מותר לו לצאת בטלית שיש בה חותם שאם יחתך החותם אינו חושש שאינו מתיירא מן המוכס ולא מזולתו ומפני זה הטעם אסר שמואל לצאת העבד בחותם שעשה לו רבו בכסותו. תנ"ה יוצא העבד בחותם שבצוארו אבל לא בחותם שבכסותו איני והא תנינן לא יצא העבד לא בחותם שבצוארו ולא בחותם שבכסותו וזה וזה אין מקבלין טומאה כו' ושנינן הא והא דעביד ליה רביה. ולא קשיא [א] הא דתני

חשק שלמה על רבינו חננאל

[א] נראה דחסר כאן וכצ"ל ולא קשיא כאן בשל מתכת וכאן בשל טיט אמר מר לא תצא בהמה וכו' זה וזה אין מקבלין טומאה ורמינהו זוג של בהמה טמאה לא קשיא וכו':

מסורת הש"ס

א) לקמן קמז., ב) [כלים פי"ג מ"א ע"ש] מנחות סט: [ושם איתא דבר זה בשם דאמר מר כלי אבנים], ג) מ"ש זוג שבצוארו דלא דילמא כו' כצ"ל רש"ל, ד) [לעיל נז.], ה) שייך לע"ב.

גליון הש"ס

רש"י ד"ה כלי גללים צפיעי בקר. ע"ל דף טז ע"ב ברש"י ד"ה גללים. ועי' מנחות דף סט ע"ב מד"ה כלי גללים:

ליקוטי רש"י

בטלית מקופלת. לאחר שנתנה על ראשו הגביה שיפוליה על כתפיו. חייב חטאת. שאין זה דרך מלבוש [לקמן קמז.]. כלי גללים. כלי גללי בהמה [מנחות סט: עיי"ש בתוס' ובהגרי"ב]. לפיעי בקר מפרש להו במנחות בפרק ר' ישמעאל (סט:) [יומא ב.]. שיש [לעיל טז: עיי"ש בב"ח ובגה"ש כאן ושם]. כלי אדמה. שאין עשויין ככלי חרס בכבשן אלא מן האדמה היא שהוא לאבן רכה וחוקקין ממנה כלים [יומא שם]. דלאו על ידי גיבול הוא ככלי נתר וכלי חרס. אין מקבלין טומאה. שאינם קרויים כלים לענין קבלת טומאה [לעיל שם].

us be concerned that **it will perhaps become detached and [the slave] will come to carry it** home! Why, then, is a bell attached to clothing permitted?

The Gemara answers:

הָכָא בְּמַאי עַסְקִינַן – Here in the Baraisa, **with what** case **are we dealing? דְּמִיחָא בֵּיהּ מוּמְחָא** – With a case **where the bell is sewn onto [the garment].**[32] **וּכְדְרַב הוּנָא בְּרֵיהּ דְּרַב יְהוֹשֻׁעַ – And** this ruling **accords with** that which **Rav Huna the son of Rav Yehoshua** said. **דְּאָמַר רַב הוּנָא בְּרֵיהּ יְהוֹשֻׁעַ – For Rav Huna the son of Rav Yehoshua said: כֹּל שֶׁהוּא אָרוּג לֹא גָּזְרוּ – Whatever is woven** was **not** included in **[the Sages'] decree.**[33]

The Gemara cites the latter portion of the Baraisa:

אָמַר מַר – The master said in the Baraisa: **לֹא תֵּצֵא בְּהֵמָה – AN ANIMAL MAY NOT GO OUT** on the Sabbath **לֹא בְּחוֹתָם שֶׁבְּצַוָּארָהּ – EITHER WITH AN EMBLEM THAT IS ON ITS NECK וְלֹא בְּחוֹתָם שֶׁבִּכְסוּתָהּ – OR WITH AN EMBLEM THAT IS ON ITS CLOTHING; וְלֹא בְּזוּג שֶׁבְּצַוָּארָהּ וְלֹא בְּזוּג שֶׁבִּכְסוּתָהּ – NOR** may it go out **WITH A BELL THAT IS ON ITS NECK NOR WITH A BELL THAT IS ON ITS CLOTHING. זֶה וָזֶה אֵין מְקַבְּלִין טוּמְאָה** – And **BOTH THESE** (the emblems) **AND THESE** (the bells) **ARE NOT SUSCEPTIBLE TO *TUMAH*.**[34]

The Gemara notes a difficulty with the final law stated in the Baraisa:

וְזוּג דִּבְהֵמָה אֵין מְקַבְּלִין טוּמְאָה – And is the bell of an animal not susceptible to *tumah*? וּרְמִינְהוּ – But contrast this with the ruling in another Baraisa: **זוּג שֶׁל בְּהֵמָה טְמֵאָה – THE BELL OF AN ANIMAL IS** susceptible to ***TUMAH;***

NOTES

32. In this case, we are not concerned that the bell will become detached (*Rashi;* see *Shiltei HaGiborim* [folio 30b in *Rif*]).

An apparent difficulty: If bells that are sewn onto clothing are permitted, why does the Baraisa forbid the wearing of emblems on one's clothing (a prohibition that seemingly includes even emblems that are sewn on)? *Tosafos* explain that since all items of clothing can be decorated with bells, the Sages did not trouble people to remove bells from clothing and degrade them due to the somewhat remote possibility that people would come to wear bells that were not sewn on. Emblems, however, are not worn on all cloaks, for they do not adorn the cloaks to which they are attached. Therefore, the Sages required that they be removed even when sewn on, due to the fact that people might wear the emblems outside even when they were not sewn on. Cf. *Ritva MHK* ed. and *Ran MHK* ed.

33. This statement was actually cited above (57a) as referring to the question of whether woven items constitute a *chatzitzah.* However, Rav Huna issued this statement with regard to this question as well – stating that if an item is sewn on ("woven"), the Sages do not prohibit wearing it outside on the Sabbath, for we need not concern ourselves that it will become detached (*Rashi;* see *Tosafos,* who states that this dual application of Rav Huna's teaching is based on the fact that Rav Huna stated that the Sages did not decree regarding *any* woven item [which implies that Rav Huna's teaching applies to *both* contexts discussed in the Mishnah – interpositions to immersion and items that may not be worn on the Sabbath]; see also *Ran MHK* ed.).

34. See above, note 22.

אין בה משום עטרות כלות ושמואל אמר כבלא דעבדא תנן ומי אמר שמואל הכי והאמר שמואל יוצא העבד בחותם שבצוארו אבל לא בחותם שבכסותו לא קשיא [א]הא דעבד ליה רביה הא דעבד איהו לנפשיה במאי אוקימתא להא דשמואל דעבד ליה רביה בחותם שבכסותו אמאי לא דילמא מיפסק ומירתת ומיקפל ליה ומחית ליה אכתפיה כדרב יצחק בר יוסף דא"ר יצחק בר יוסף א"ר יוחנן [א] היוצא בטלית מקופלת ומונחת לו על כתפיו בשבת חייב חטאת וכי הא דא"ל שמואל לרב חיננא בר שילא כולהו רבנן דבי ריש גלותא לא ליפקו בסרבלי חתימי לבר מינך דלא קפדי עליך דבי ריש גלותא: גופא אמר שמואל יוצא העבד בחותם שבצוארו אבל לא בחותם שבכסותו תניא נמי הכי [ב]יוצא העבד בחותם שבצוארו אבל לא בחותם שבכסותו ורמינהו לא יצא העבד בחותם שבצוארו ולא בחותם שבכסותו [ג]זה וזה אין מקבלין טומאה ולא בזוג שבצוארו אבל יוצא הוא בזוג שבכסותו [ד]זה וזה מקבלין טומאה [ה]ולא תצא בהמה לא בחותם שבצוארה ולא בחותם שבכסותה ולא בזוג שבכסותה ולא בזוג שבצוארה זה וזה אין מקבלין טומאה לימא הא דעבד ליה רביה הא דעבד איהו לנפשיה לא אידי ואידי דעבד ליה רביה וכאן [ו]בשל מתכת וכאן בשל טיט וכדרב נחמן אמר רבה בר אבוה דבר המקפיד עליו רבו אין יוצאין בו דבר שאין מקפיד עליו יוצאין בו ה"נ מסתברא מדקתני זה וזה אין מקבלין טומאה אי אמרת בשלמא של מתכת הני הוא דלא מקבלי טומאה הא כלים דידהו מקבלי טומאה אלא אי אמרת בשל טיט תנן הני הוא דלא מקבלי טומאה הא כלים דידהו מקבלי טומאה והא [ב] תניא [ז]כלי אבנים כלי גללים וכלי אדמה אין מקבלין טומאה לא מדברי תורה ולא מדברי סופרים אלא ש"מ של מתכת ש"מ: אמר מר ולא בזוג שבצוארו אבל יוצא הוא בזוג שבכסותו [ג] זוג שבצוארו אמאי לא דילמא מיפסיק ואתא לאיתויי זוג שבכסותו נמי ליחוש דילמא מיפסיק ואתי לאיתויי הכא במאי עסקינן דמיחא ביה מומחא וכדרב הונא בריה דרב יהושע דאמר [ד]רב הונא בריה דרב יהושע כל שהוא ארוג לא גזרו: אמר מר לא תצא בהמה לא בחותם שבצוארה ולא בחותם שבכסותה ולא בזוג שבצוארה ולא בזוג שבכסותה זה וזה אין מקבלין טומאה וזוג דבהמה אין מקבלין טומאה ורמינהו זוג של בהמה טמאה ושל

אין בה משום עטרות כלות. דגזרו עליהן שלא תלא כהן מחורבן ואילך משום לער במס' סוטה (דף מט.): **ושמואל אמר.** כבול דמתני' כבלא דעבדא ופליג אדר' אבהו: **חותם שבצוארו.** הוא כבלא דעבדא והיו עושין אותו משל טיט: **דעביד ליה רביה.** אית ליה אימתא ולא שקיל ליה מצוארו להוליכו בידו: **מיפסק.** החותם ונשבר ומירתת מרבו שלא יאמר שהוא נטלו להראות בשוק שהוא בן חורין: **ומקפל ליה.** הטלית על כתפיו כדי שלא יראה מקום החותם ולא יבינו שנפל ודמי הטלית על כתפו כמשוי: **חייב חטאת.** דאינו תכשיט אלא בזמן שלובשו דרך מלבוש: **כולהו רבנן לא ליפקו בסרבלי חתימי.** היו עושין חותמות לטליתות שלהן כעין עבדים להראות שהן כפופין לריש גלותא לא ליפקו דאי מפסקי מרתתי ומקפלי להו: **דלא קפדי עלך.** אם תלך בלא חותם: **יוצא העבד בחותם שבצוארו.** ובשל טיט דלא קפיד עליה לאתויי ואי משום דמירתת מאי חורבא נפקא מינה משום אימתא דרביה לא מייתי ליה בידיה דהא לאו הוכחה היא לעבדות אלא כשישנו על צוארו או בכסותו: **וזה וזה אין מקבלין טומאה.** דלאו לנוי עביד שיהא טמא משום תכשיט ואע"ג דבשל מתכת מוקמינן לה להא לקמן מיהו לאו לנוי דיליה הוא אלא לגנאי וכלי תשמיש נמי לא הוי: **זוג.** לנוי עביד: **ולא בזוג שבצוארו אבל יוצא הוא בזוג שבכסותו.** לקמיה מפרש טעמא: **מקבלין טומאה.** שתכשיט הוא: **שבכסותה.** עושים לסוסים מעילין שלא יטנפו: **לא תצא.** כדאמרינן באידך פרקין (דף נד:) דמתחזי כמאן דאזיל לחינגא: **אין מקבלין טומאה.** דאין תכשיט לבהמה: **לא אידי ואידי דעבד ליה רביה.** דאע"ג דכבול דמתניתין אוקימנא בדעבד איהו לנפשיה התם הוא דאיכא לאוקמיה בהתם חותמות של טיט דאי מיתבר אין מקפיד עליו להביא שבריו לבית אדונו הלכך ליכא לאוקמיה בדעבד ליה רביה דאי עבד ליה רביה לא הוה מיתסר דכל זמן שלא נפסק לא שקיל ליה מצוארו משום אימתא דרביה ואי מיפסק לא קפיד עליה בעליו משום פסידא דליכא פסידא הלכך לא מייתי ליה אבל הך לא איכא לאוקמא בשל טיט כדמסתברא לקמן מסיפא הלכך אפילו עבד ליה רביה נמי אסור דאי מיפסק קפיד עליה משום פסידא ומירתת עבד ומייתי ליה בידיה: **דבר המקפיד עליו רבו.** אם יאבד לא יצא דאי מפסיק מייתי ליה: **מסתברא.** דבשל מתכת קאי מדאיצטריך למיתני אין מקבלין טומאה וטעמא משום דלאו לנוי עבידא: **הני הוא דלא מקבלין טומאה.** משום דלאו כלים נינהו הא שאר כלי מתכות מקבלין: **כלים דידהו.** דמתכות: **אלא אי אמרת.** כלים דידהו כלי העשוי מטיט כמה שאינו מצרפו בכבשן מעשה ידי יוצר דניהוי קרוי כלי חרס אלא כלי אדמה מי מקבל טומאה בתמיה: **כלי גללים.** [ה] לפיעי בקר שעשה מהן כלי: **דמיחא מומחא.** שארגו בבגד ותו לא מיפסיק: **לא גזרו.** לצאת בו ודרב הונא לענין ארוג כי האי גוונא נמי איתמר דאשמעינן דלא חיישינן תו לדלמא מיפסק:

והאמר שמואל יוצא העבד בחותם כו'. ולא בעי לאוקמי מתניתין בחותם שבכסותו דניחא ליה לאוקמה בדעבד איהו לנפשיה ואיירי מתני' בכל חותמות: **הא** דעבד איהו לנפשיה. קשה לרשב"א אמאי שריא מתני' בדעבד איהו לנפשיה בחצר כיון דליכא קפידא דרבו וי"ל דאיכא קצת קפידא אבל לא כל כך כמו בעבד ליה רביה: **במאי** אוקימתא להא דשמואל בדעבד ליה רביה כו'. אבל אי מיירי בדעבד איהו לנפשיה אתי שפיר דבצוארו ליכא למיחש דלמא פסיק ליה בידים כדי שלא יבינו הרואין שהוא עבד אבל בכסותו איכא למיחש דלמא מקפל טליתו לכסות החותם ולא ידע דיש בזה חיוב חטאת אבל בדעבד ליה רביה משום אימתא דרביה ירא לקפל והשתא נמי ידע הש"ס לדרב יצחק אלא דלא ידע שיש לחוש דילמא מיפסיק ובתר דמשני מייתי דרב יצחק ונחת לפרושי שיש חיוב חטאת בקיפול: **דילמא** מיפסק ומרתת ומקפל ליה. דניחא ליה טפי שיהיה מקופל משיראה רבו שנפסק לגמרי ויסבור שבמזיד פסקו למרוד בו: **לא** תצא בהמה כו'. דמיחזי כמאן דאזיל לחינגא כדפי' בקונ' דלא מצינן למימר משום דילמא מיפסיק ואתי לאתויי דהא לעיל (דף נד:) מפרש דזוג אסור משום דמיחזי כמאן דאזיל לחינגא ולא קאמר דלמא מיפסק דומיא דחותם: **מאי** שנא זוג שבצוארו דלמא מיפסיק ואתי לאתויי. והא דתנן לקמן (דף סו:) בני מלכים יוצאין בזוגין וכל אדם אלא שדברו חכמים בהווה אומר ר"י דמיירי בזוגין יקרים שיוצאין בהן בני מלכים כגון של כסף ושל זהב דליכא למיחש בהו דילמא מיפסיק דמסתמא תקועין הן יפה בשלשלאות של כסף והכא מיירי בזוג דעלמא דומיא דזוג של בהמה ולמאי דמוקי לה בגמרא באריג בכסותו אתי נמי שפיר: **הב"ע** דמחי. וא"ת כי היכי דזוג איירי במחי הכי נמי איירי חותם שבכסותו במחי ואם כן אמאי אסור וי"ל דזוג מותר לפי שדרך לאורגו בבגד שאין שום בגד שלא יהא ראוי לנוי ותכשיט כזה ולא הטריחוהו לפוסקו מכל בגדים ולגנות הבגד אבל חותם אין דרך לעשותו בכל הבגדים שאינו יפוי הבגד ולכך גזרו חכמים אפילו בארוג בכסותו שיהא צריך לפוסקו אטו היכא שאין ארוג וא"ת אדמפליג בין זוג שבצוארו לזוג שבכסותו ליפלוג בזוג שבכסותו גופיה בין מחי ללא מחי ויש לומר דניחא ליה לאשמעינן דזוג שבצוארו אסור אפילו בחתיכת הבגד שסביב צוארו ואינה יכולה ליפול אלא ע"י חתיכה: **כדרב** הונא כו'. ואע"ג דמילתא דרב הונא אייתי לעיל (דף נז.) גבי אלילה מדקאמר כל שהוא ארוג משמע דה"ק בין לענין אלילה בין לענין דלמא מיפסיק לא חיישינן בארוג: [ו] **אע"פ** שחברו בדלת וקבעו במסמרים טמא. והא דאמר בהקומץ רבה (מנחות דף כז.) סדין שעשאו וילון טהור מן המדרס לאו משום קביעות גרידא טהור אלא מיירי שעשה שום שינוי מעשה. והא דאמר בנגמר הדין (סנהדרין דף מח:) כפה שנתנתו לספר טהור מן המדרס אף על פי שלא עשתה שום שינוי מעשה כיון דנאסר בהנאה ע"י כן חשוב כשינוי מעשה:

אין / ושל

עין משפט נר מצוה

יא א ב מיי' פי"ט מהל' שבת הל' יח [ועיין במ"מ] סמג לאוין סה טוש"ע א"ח סי' דש סעיף א' בהג"ה:

יב ג מיי' פ"א מהל' כלים הלכה ט:

יג ד שם הלכה ח:

יד ה מיי' פ"כ מהל' שבת הלכה י סמג לאוין סה טוש"ע א"ח סי' שה סעיף יב:

טו ו מיי' פי"ט מהל' שבת הלכה יח סמג שם טוש"ע א"ח סי' דש סעיף א בהג"ה:

טז ז מיי' פ"א מהל' כלים הלכה ו:

רבינו חננאל

שתי וערב. [אמר] רב הונא טוטפת עניות עושות של מיני צבעונין עשירות עושות אותן של כסף ושל זהב: **הא דאמר** שמואל יוצא העבד בשבת בחותם שבצוארו אבל לא בחותם שבכסותו הא והא בחותם דעבד ליה רביה ובחותם שבכסותו אמאי לא נפיק חיישינן דלמא מיפסק ומירתת מרביה ומכפל לכסותיה ומנח ליה אכתפיה וכר' יוחנן דאמר היוצא בטלית מקופלת ומונחת לו על כתיפו בשבת חייב חטאת וכדאמרו ליה לרב חנניא בר שילא רבנן כולהו לא ליפקו בסרבלא חתימה פי' דת המלך היתה באותה העת כל הקונה סרבלא מייתי לה גבי מוכס ויהיב ליה מיכסיה וחתים עליה במטבע של אינך כדי לידע שניטל מיכסא וכל טלית שנמצאת בלא חותם אינך נתפש לובשה כגנב המכס הלכך מתיירא כל אדם לצאת בטלית שתלוי עליה חותם זה חיישינן שמא יפסק החותם ומפני פחדו מן המוכס יסירה מעליה ויקפלה וישאנה על כתיפו כמשא לפיכך אסורה לכל אדם לצאת בטלית שיש עליה חותם אבל רב חנינה בר שילא שיש לו נשיאות פנים ואינו חושש מן המוכס מותר לו לצאת בטלית שיש בה חותם שאם יחתך החותם אינו חושש שאינו מתיירא מן המוכס ולא מזולתו ומפני זה הטעם אסר שמואל לצאת העבד בחותם שעשה לו רבו בכסותו. תנ"ה יוצא העבד בחותם שבצוארו אבל לא בחותם שבכסותו איני והא תנינן לא יצא העבד לא בחותם שבצוארו ולא בחותם שבכסותו וזה וזה אין מקבלין טומאה כו' ושנינן הא והא דעביד ליה רביה. ולא קשיא א) הא דתני

חשק שלמה על רבינו חננאל

א) נראה דחסר כאן וכל"ל ולא קשיא כאן בשל מתכת וכאן בשל טיט אמר מר לא תצא בהמה וכו' זה וזה אין מקבלין טומאה ורמינהו זוג של בהמה טומאה לא קשיא וכו'.

מסורת הש"ס

א) לקמן קמז., ב) [כלים פי"מ ע"ש] מנחות סט: [ושם איתא דבר זה בשם דאמר מר כלי אבנים], ג) מ"ש זוג שבצוארו דלא דילמא כו' כצ"ל רש"ל, ד) [לעיל מ.], ה) שייך לע"ב.

גליון הש"ס

רש"י ד"ה כלי גללים צפיעי בקר. ע"ל דף טז ע"ב ברש"י ד"ה גללים. ועי' מנחות דף סט ע"ב תד"ה כלי גללים:

ליקוטי רש"י

בטלית מקופלת. לאחר שנתנה על ראשו הגביה שיפוליה על כתפיו. **חייב חטאת.** שאין זה דרך מלבוש [לקמן קמז.]. **כלי גללים.** כלי גללי בהמה [מנחות סט: עיי"ש בתוס' ובהגרי"ב]. לפיעי בקר מפרש להו במנחות בפרק ר' ישמעאל (סט:) [יומא ב.]. שיש [לעיל טז: עיי"ש בב"ח ובגה"ש כאן ושם]. **כלי אדמה.** שאין עשויין ככלי חרס בכבשן אלא מן האדמה היא שהוא כאבן רכה ומוקקין ממנה כלים [יומא שם]. דלאו על ידי גיבול הוא ככלי נתר וכלי חרס. **אין מקבלין טומאה.** שאינם קרויים כלים לענין קבלת טומאה [לעיל שם].

עין משפט נר מצוה

יז א מיי' פ"ח מהל' כלים הלכה יג:
יח ב מיי' פ"ח מהל' כלים הלכה ז:
יט ג מיי' פ' יב מהל' פרה הלכה ט:

ושל דלת טהורה [א]של דלת ועשאו לבהמה טמאה של בהמה ועשאו לדלת אף על פי שחיברו לדלת וקבעו במסמרים טמא שכל הכלים [א]יורדין לידי טומאתן במחשבה ואין עולין מידי טומאתן אלא בשינוי מעשה לא קשיא הא דאית ליה עינבל הא דלית ליה עינבל מה נפשך אי מנא הוא אע"פ דלית ליה עינבל אי לאו מנא הוא עינבל משוי ליה מנא אין כדר' שמואל בר נחמני א"ר יונתן [ב]דאמר ר' שמואל בר נחמני אמר ר' יונתן מנין למשמיע קול בכלי מתכות שהוא טמא שנאמר [א]כל דבר אשר יבא באש תעבירו באש אפי' דיבור יבא באש במאי אוקימתא בדלית ליה עינבל אימא מציעתא ולא בזוג שבצוארו אבל יוצא הוא בזוג שבכסותו וזה וזה מקבלין טומאה אי דלית ליה עינבל מי מקבלי טומאה ורמינהו [ג][ב]העושה זגין למכתשת ולעריסה ולמטפחות ספרים ולמטפחות תינוקות יש להם עינבל טמאין אין להם עינבל טהורין ניטלו עינבליהן עדיין טומאתן עליהם ה"מ בתינוק דלקלא עבידי ליה אבל גדול תכשיט הוא ליה אע"ג דלית ליה עינבל: אמר מר ניטלו עינבליהן עדיין טומאתן עליהן למאי חזו אמר אביי הואיל שההדיוט יכול להחזירו מתיב רבא [ד][ג]הזוג והעינבל חיבור וכי תימא הכי קאמר אע"ג דלא מחבר כמאן דמחבר דמי והתניא [ה]מספורת של פרקים ואיזמל של רהיטני חיבור לטומאה ואין חיבור להזאה ואמרינן מה נפשך אי חיבור הוא אפילו להזאה (א) ואי לא חיבור הוא אפילו לטומאה נמי לא ואמר רבה דבר תורה בשעת מלאכה חיבור בין לטומאה בין להזאה שלא בשעת מלאכה אינו חיבור לא לטומאה ולא להזאה וגזרו על טומאה שלא בשעת מלאכה משום טומאה שהיא בשעת מלאכה ועל הזאה שהיא בשעת מלאכה משום הזאה שלא בשעת מלאכה אלא אמר רבא הואיל

רש"י

ושל דלת טהור. דלת מחובר לבית הוא שהוא חבור לקרקע ואינו כלי לקבל טומאה וזוג העשוי לו בטיל לגביה כדאמרי' בריש פרקין דלעיל [ו] כל המחובר לו הרי הוא כמוהו: של דלת ועשאו לבהמה טמאה. מכאן ולהבא ואע"פ דלא עבד ביה מעשה אלא שחישב עליו ותלאו ותלייה לאו מעשה היא שכל הכלים יורדים לידי תורת טומאה במחשבה שלו: של בהמה ועשאו לדלת טמא. ואפי' מכאן ולהבא יקבל טומאה שאין חיבורו מעשה עד שישנהו מכמות שהיה: שאין עולין מטומאתן. מתורת טומאה שירדה להן ואע"פ שעדיין לא נטמאו משנמלך עליהן אין עולין מלקבל טומאה אלא בשינוי מעשה: עינבל. בטדי"ל שעשוי בתוכו להשמיע קול: אי מנא הוא. דתכשיט חשיב ליה: עינבל משוי ליה מנא. בתמיה משום העינבל מי הוי תכשיט: אין. עינבל משוי ליה מנא ולא משום תכשיט אלא משום כלי: כל דבר שיבא באש. בכלי מתכות משתעי במעשה מדין: אימא מציעתא. זוג דאדם: מי מקבל טומאה. אפי' דאדם: העושה זגין למכתשת. שמפטמין בה סממנין להקטיר לריח דקיי"ל בכריתות (פ"א ד' ו:) שהקול יפה לבשמים: ולעריסה. שהתינוק שוכב בתוכה שקורין בירל"ה ותולה בו זגין לקשקש כדי שישמע התינוק ויישן: ולמטפחות ספרים. כשנושאין אותן לבית הכנסת שהתינוקות של בית רבן קורין שם מקשקשין הזגין והתינוקות שומעין ובאין: ולמטפחות תינוקות. שתולין בצוארן: ניטלו עינבליהם כו'. [ז](אם ניטלו קודם שנטמאו תורת טומאה עליהם ומקבלין טומאה כדמפרש טעמא לקמיה מעיקרא כי אין להם עינבל דקתני טהורין (ב) דעדיין לא נגמרה מלאכתן אבל משירדה להם תורת טומאה לא בטל שם כלי מעליהם בנטילת העינבל) ואם ניטל לאחר שנטמאו עדיין טומאתן עליהן דלא הוי ככלי שנשבר ובטל מתורת כלי ליטהר מטומאתו: הדיוט. שאין צריך אומן: הזוג והעינבל חיבור. כשהן יחד הרי הן כלי אחד נטמא זה נטמא זה הזה על זה טהור זה וכיון דקרי ליה חיבור שמע מינה דכי נתפרדו הוי כלי שניטל מקלתו ואף על גב דהדיוט יכול להחזירו כל כמה דלא אהדריה לאו שלם הוא: וכי תימא. דהאי חיבור דקאמר הכי קאמר אפי' מפורדים קרינן ליה חיבור ואתא לאשמעי' דאם נתפרדו משנטמאו לא עלו מטומאתן: הא תניא. גבי ההיא: מספורת של פרקים. ששני סכינים שלה מתפרדין: ואיזמל של רהיטני. פלינה של אומנים תריסים שנותנים האיזמל לתוך בין שני עצים העשוין לכך ולאחר מלאכתו נוטלו ומצניעו: חיבור לטומאה. ואם נטמא זה נטמא זה: שלא בשעת מלאכה. הואיל ואין צריכין להיות מחוברין הוו להו כשני כלים ואין חיבור ואף על פי שמחוברין דע"כ שלא בשעת מלאכה דומיא דשעת מלאכה קאמר ובשעת מלאכה מחוברין הן אלמא במחוברין עסקינן וגזרו לחומרא על הטומאה דליהוי חיבור ועל הזאה דלא ליהוי חיבור ומשום הכי קתני חיבור לטומאה לעולם ואין חיבור להזאה לעולם: אלא אמר רבא. לא תימא הואיל והדיוט יכול להחזיר דולאי (ג) חד מנא הואי כדקתני בברייתא הזוג והעינבל חיבור וכי מיפרדי הוי כלי שניטל מקלתו [ח]ואינו מקבל טומאה העינבל לעצמו אבל הזוג טמא לעצמו דלא בטל ליה מתורת כלי:

הואיל

תוספות

אין כדר' שמואל כו'. דחשיב ליה כלי תשמיש לאדם משום דבעי ליה לקלא דע"י הזוג ששומע יודע היכן בהמתו עומדת ומוצאה ע"י כך ° והוי כמקל של בהמה של מתכת דטמאה הואיל ואדם רודה בה וכ"מ לקמן גבי בירית טהורה דמשמיע [קול] בכלי מתכות אינו טמא אלא היכא דבעי ליה לקלא והא דמשני הא דאית ביה עינבל הא דלית ביה עינבל ולא מחלק באית ביה עינבל בין בעי ליה לקלא בין לא בעי אומר ר"י דלא שכיח שיעשו עינבל אלא אם כן בעי ליה לקלא:

כל דבר אשר יבא. ואע"ג דהאי קרא לא לגבי טומאה כתיב אלא לגבי הגעלה מסתברא דהתם אין דיבור מעלה ומוריד ואם אינו ענין להגעלה תנהו לענין טומאה:

מתיב רבא הזוג והעינבל חיבור. פי' בקונטרס מדקרי ליה חיבור ש"מ דכי נתפרדו הוי כלי שניטל מקלתו ואע"ג דהדיוט יכול להחזיר כל כמה דלא אהדרי' לאו שלם הוא וקשה לר"י דהא מעיקרא נמי הוי ידענא דהוי כלי שניטל מקלתו ולהכי פריך למאי חזו ומשני דודאי באפי נפשה לא חזו לא זוג ולא עינבל אלא משום דהדיוט יכול להחזירו ומה שפירש נמי והתניא כו' גבי ההיא מספורת של פרקים לא עיין דההוא דזוג ועינבל משנה היא במסכת פרה (פי"ב משנה ח) וההיא דמספורת בתוספתא דכלים ומפרש הרב פור"ת בשם ר' שמואל הואיל והדיוט יכול להחזירם ואע"ג דהשתא בלא עינבל לא חזי מידי כיון דהדיוט יכול בקל להחזירה כמאן דמיחברי דמי ואם נטמא העינבל נטמא גם הזוג כאילו הן מחוברין נפקא מינה דלכשיתחברו יטמא הזוג את הנוגע בו ומיהו בלא חיבור לא יטמא כי אם העינבל לבדו שנגע בטומאה והכי משמע לישנא דקאמר וכי תימא ה"ק אע"ג דלא מיחברי כמאן דמיחברי דמי משמע דאביי הכי סבירא ליה דמדתלי טעמא בחזרת הדיוט משמע דסבר דלא חזי השתא למידי ואי לאו כמחובר חשיב ליה היאך יקבל טומאה מאחר דלא חזי מידי בלא חזרה: [ט]מתיב רבא הזוג והעינבל חיבור. שאם נטמא זה נטמא זה וה"מ כשמחוברים אבל שלא בשעת חיבור אם נטמא זה לא נטמא זה ולא חיישינן להדיוט יכול להחזיר דהשתא מיהא לאו מחוברין נינהו וממשנה זו אין לנו להוכיח דמיירי בשעת חיבור כדקאמר וכי תימא כו' אבל מכח ברייתא מוכיח דבשעת חיבור מיירי ומברייתא גרידתא הוה מצי רבא לאותוביה לאביי אלא דניחא ליה לאקשויי מהך דמיירי בזוג ועינבל בהדיא לאביי דאיירי נמי בזוג ועינבל: [י](וכי תימא כו') והתניא מספורת של פרקים ואיזמל של רהיטני. שתי ברייתות הן במסכת כלים [כ]כל אחד בפני עצמה וברישא קתני בהדיא דכשאינן מחוברין מקבל כל א' טומאה בפני עצמו וגזרו על טומאה שלא בשעת מלאכה שיהא חיבור לטומאה ליטמא זה כשניטמא זה משום דדמי לשעת מלאכה אבל שלא בחיבורין משמע דאפי' גזירה דרבנן ליכא ואם נטמא זה לא נטמא זה דלא חיים למה שהדיוט יכול להחזירו: [ל](אלא) אמר רבא הואיל ויכול להקישו. פי' מקבל טומאה הזוג אבל עינבל דאין ראוי להקישו לא ומספורת ואיזמל נמי בלא חיבור ראויין למעין מלאכה ראשונה ומקבלי טומאה כל אחד בפני עצמו כדתני בתוספתא: אלא אמר רבא כו'. פירש בקונטרס דטומאה לא פרח הימנו כשנפרד משקיבל הואיל וראוי להקישו והוה ליה ככלי (עץ) שניקב בפחות ממוציא רמון דלא טהר מטומאה ומשמע שרוצה לומר דמכאן ואילך לא מקבל טומאה וקשה לר"י דלמה לא יקבל טומאה כיון דנפחת פחות מכשיעור דהוי כאילו שלם לגמרי ונראה לר"י דודאי גם מקבל טומאה מכאן ולהבא ולקונטרס דחקו לפרש כן משום דכשלא היה להם עינבל טהורין ולא מקבלי טומאה אף על גב דראוי להקישו ואינו דומה דכשלא היה בו עינבל מעולם ודאי טהור דכיון שעומד ליתן בו עינבל דהא עביד לקלא והוי גולמי כלי מתכות אבל משנגמר שהיה בו עינבל אף על פי שניטל מקבל טומאה שלא בטל מתורת כלי שהיה עליו קודם לכן והר"ס הביא ראיה מחמת שתפרה ושייר פחות ממוציא רמון דטהורה (חולין קלח.) אע"ג דחמת שלם שנקרע

פחות

רבינו חננאל

אין מקבלין טומאה בדלית ליה עינבל והא דתני טמא בזוג שיש לו עינבל פי' עינבל הברזל שבתוך הזוג המקיש בדופני הזוג ומשמיע הקול וכי הא דאמר כו' מנין למשמיע קול בכלי מתכות שטמא שנאמר כל דבר אשר יבא באש אפילו דבור במשמע ואקשינן במאי אוקימנא להא דתני בזוג בהמה אין מקבלין טומאה בדלית לה עינבל אימ' מציעתא אין העבד יוצא בזוג שבצוארו אבל יוצא בזוג שבכסותו וזה וזה מקבלין טומאה ואי לית ליה עינבל מי מקבלי טומאה והתנן העושה זגין למכתשת ולעריסה ולמטפחות ספרים ולמטפחת תינוקו' כולן יש להן עינבליהן טמאין אין להן עינבליהן טהורין כו'. ושנינן הא בתינוק דלקלא עבידי אבל גדול כגון העבד דלתכשיט עביד ליה רביה אע"ג דלית ליה עינבל מקבל טומאה ואקשינן ניטלו עינבליהן עדיין טומאתן עליהן אי נטלו עינבליהן למאי חזו ושנינן בזה דכיון דההדיוט יכול להחזירו אע"פ שעדיין לא החזירו כמוחזר דמי. איני והא תנינן מספורת של פרקים ואיזמל של רהיטני כו' וכבר פירשנו למעלה (מח:) ומשני

רב נסים גאון

הזוג והעינבל חיבור. ראוי לידע כי זה הזוג זולתי הזוג הנאמר גבי נזיר ותמצא פי' דבר זה במסכת נזירות בפ' ג' מינין (דף לד) חרצנים אלו החיצונים הזגין אלו הפנימיים דברי ר' יהודה ר' יוסי אומר שלא תטעה בזוג של בהמה החיצון זוג והפנימי עינבל:

מסורת הש"ס

א) כלים פכ"ה מ"ט סוכה יג: לעיל נב: קדושין נט. [מנחות סט.], ב) לקמן סג:, ג) תוספ' דכלים ב"מ פ"א, ד) פרה פי"ב מ"ח, ה) לעיל מח: [תוספ' כלים ב"מ פ"ג], ו) דף נג:, ז) רש"ל מוחק כ"ז, ח) ואינו מקבל טומאה הזוג לעצמו אבל לענין מפרש טומאה לא פרחה מיניה משקבלה כצ"ל והשאר נמחק רש"ל, ט) רש"ל ומהר"מ כתבו דכל הנך דיבורי תוס' הם דיבו' אחד מן מתיב רבא עד סוף ד"ה אלא וכו' כדתני בתוספתא, י) ר"מ מ"ז, כ) [בפ"ג דבבא מציעא], ל) ר"מ מ"ז.

הגהות הב"ח

(א) גמ' אפי' להזאה נמי ואי לאו חיבור: (ב) רש"י ד"ה ניטלו עינבליה' וכו' ומעיקרא כי אין להם עינבל דקתני טהורין משום דעדיין: (ג) ד"ה אלא אמר וכו' דודאי לאו חד מנא:

גליון הש"ס

תוס' ד"ה אין וכו' הוי כמקל של בהמה. לעיל נג ע"ב:

תורה אור השלם

א) כָּל דָּבָר אֲשֶׁר יָבֹא בָאֵשׁ תַּעֲבִירוּ בָאֵשׁ וְטָהֵר אַךְ בְּמֵי נִדָּה יִתְחַטָּא וְכֹל אֲשֶׁר לֹא יָבֹא בָּאֵשׁ תַּעֲבִירוּ בַמָּיִם: [במדבר לא, כג]

ליקוטי רש"י

שכל הכלים יורדין לידי טומאתן במחשבה. כגון גולמי כלים דאמר בהכל שוחטין (חולין כה.) כל שעתיד לשוף לשבץ ולגרר ואמר התם דאכתי חסרון מלאכה הוא וטהורים ואם חישב עליה שלא לשוף ושלא לשבץ הביאתו מחשבה זו לידי גמר מלאכה מכאן ולהבא [קידושין נט.]. [משחישב] עליו שזה יהא גמר מלאכתן כגון שעידבו לדרגש או לדולבקי כיון שעידבו מקבל טומאה ואלמלי עידבו לרצועות וסנדלין אין מקבלים טומאה עד שיגמרו למלאכת הסנדלין [סוכה יד.]. מאחר שחישב עליו שיניחנו כמות שהוא עכשיו ולא יוסיף תיקון אחר הוא גמר מלאכתן ומקבל טומאה [לעיל נב:]. ואין עולין מידי טומאתן. משקבלוה [קידושין שם]. ממחשבת תורת קבלת טומאה אין עולין במחשבה כגון עידבו לשלחן ולדרגש וחישב עליו לרצועות וסנדלין אין מחשבתו מבטלתן מתורת קבלת טומאה [סוכה שם]. מאחר שחישב על העור לעשות שטיח ירד לידי טומאה ואם חזר וחישב עליו לרצועות וסנדלים לא בטל מתורת כלי [לטהר] בכך עד שיתן בו איזמל דהוי שינוי מעשה [לעיל שם]. אלא בשינוי מעשה. שיעשה בה מעשה לקלקלם שישברם או ינקבם וכן עד שלא יקבלו טומאה אין עולין מתורת קבלת טומאה שירדו במחשבה זו אלא בשינוי מעשה עד שיתחיל לשוף לשבץ ולגרר [קידושין שם]. עד שיתן בו איזמל [סוכה שם]. איזמל של רהיטני. פליינ"ה בלע"ז של עץ וברזל חד נעוץ בתוכו ובהן משוה פני רוחב הקרש ומחליקה [לקמן צז.]. פליינ"א שממחקים בה את התריסין ונותנין הברזל לתוך דפוס של עץ המתוקן לו ולאחר מלאכתו נוטלו הימנו. ואין חיבור להזאה. ולריך להיות על שניהם [לעיל מח:]. וגזרו על טומאה שלא בשעת מלאכה. שיהא חיבור. ועל הזאה שהיא בשעת מלאכה. שלא יהא חיבור הלכך חיבור לטומאה לעולם ואין חיבור להזאה כלל [שם מט.].

וְשֶׁל דֶּלֶת טְהוֹרָה – BUT the bell OF A DOOR IS *TAHOR,* i.e. it is not susceptible to *tumah.*[1] שֶׁל דֶּלֶת וַעֲשָׂאוֹ לִבְהֵמָה – If it was originally the bell OF A DOOR AND HE MADE IT INTO a bell FOR AN ANIMAL, טְמֵאָה – IT IS SUSCEPTIBLE TO *TUMAH* as soon as its function is changed.[2] שֶׁל בְּהֵמָה וַעֲשָׂאוֹ לְדֶלֶת – But if it was originally the bell OF AN ANIMAL AND HE MADE IT INTO a bell for A DOOR, אַף עַל פִּי שֶׁחִיבְּרוֹ לְדֶלֶת וּקְבָעוֹ בְּמַסְמְרִים – EVEN IF HE ATTACHED IT TO THE DOOR AND FIXED IT in place WITH NAILS, טָמֵא – it remains SUSCEPTIBLE TO *TUMAH.*[3] שֶׁכָּל הַכֵּלִים יוֹרְדִין לִידֵי טוּמְאָתָן בְּמַחֲשָׁבָה – And the reason for this distinction[4] is THAT ALL UTENSILS DESCEND [i.e. become susceptible] TO *TUMAH* even THROUGH THOUGHT,[5] וְאֵין עוֹלִין מִידֵי טוּמְאָתָן אֶלָּא בְּשִׁינּוּי מַעֲשֶׂה – BUT THEY DO NOT EMERGE FROM THEIR susceptibility to *TUMAH* EXCEPT THROUGH A PHYSICAL CHANGE.[6] At any rate, this Baraisa teaches that the bell of an animal is susceptible to acquiring *tumah,* while the Baraisa cited above taught that it is not. – ? –

The Gemara responds:

לֹא קַשְׁיָא – This is **not a difficulty.** הָא דְּאִית לֵיהּ עִינְבָּל – **This** second Baraisa speaks of **[a bell] that has a clapper,** הָא דְּלֵית לֵיהּ עִינְבָּל – while **this** first Baraisa speaks of **[a bell] that has no clapper.**[7]

The Gemara protests:

מַה נַּפְשָׁךְ – But **whichever way you wish** to explain the reason that a bell can contract *tumah,* this distinction is difficult to understand. אִי מָנָא הוּא – For **if [a bell] is** deemed **a utensil** due to its ornamental nature, אַף עַל פִּי דְּלֵית לֵיהּ עִינְבָּל – then **even if it does not have a clapper** it should be susceptible to acquiring *tumah.*[8] אִי לָאו מָנָא הוּא – And **if it is not** deemed **a utensil,** עִינְבָּל מְשַׁוֵּי לֵיהּ מָנָא – **can the clapper make it** into **a utensil?**[9]

The Gemara answers:

אִין – **Yes.** It is precisely the addition of the clapper that gives the bell the status of a utensil; כִּדְרַבִּי שְׁמוּאֵל בַּר נַחְמָנִי אָמַר רַבִּי יוֹנָתָן – and this is **in accordance with** the ruling that **R' Shmuel bar Nachmani said in the name of R' Yonasan.**[10] דְּאָמַר רַבִּי שְׁמוּאֵל בַּר נַחְמָנִי אָמַר רַבִּי יוֹנָתָן – **For R' Shmuel bar Nachmani said in the name of R' Yonasan:** מִנַּיִן לְמַשְׁמִיעַ קוֹל בִּכְלֵי מַתָּכוֹת שֶׁהוּא טָמֵא – **From where do we know** concerning **a utensil of metal designed to produce sound that it is susceptible to *tumah*?** שֶׁנֶּאֱמַר – **For [the verse] states:**[11] ,,כָּל־דָּבָר אֲשֶׁר־יָבֹא בָאֵשׁ תַּעֲבִירוּ בָאֵשׁ" – ***Any item that has come into the fire,** you **shall pass through the fire*** and it will be purified. אֲפִילוּ דִּיבּוּר יָבֹא בָאֵשׁ – The seemingly superfluous word דָּבָר, *item,* is expounded to teach that **even** an item that produces **sound must come into the fire** to be purified, for it can acquire *tumah.*[12] Thus, we see that it is possible for an item to be classified as a utensil because of its ability to produce

NOTES

1. The door of a house is itself not susceptible to *tumah*, for it is fixed to the ground, and items that are fixed to the ground do not become *tamei*. The Baraisa teaches that a doorbell is considered a part of the door rather than a separate entity, and it is therefore not susceptible to *tumah*. This is in keeping with the rule taught in the previous chapter (48b): *Any (subsidiary) object that is attached to a (primary) item is treated as that item* (*Rashi*; see also *Keilim* 12:2).

2. Although the bell was not physically changed in any way, merely removing it from the door and hanging it from the neck of the animal renders it susceptible to *tumah* from that point onward. This is not because of the action involved in hanging it from the animal's neck – for this is not legally deemed a physical change – but rather because even *intent* to use the bell for such a function is sufficient to render it susceptible to *tumah* [as the Baraisa goes on to explain] (*Rashi*). See *Mishnah Acharonah to Keilim* 25:9 ד״ה יורדין.

3. Fixing the bell to the door with nails is not deemed a physical change, for the bell itself is unaffected and did not undergo any physical change; thus, its status as an article that can contract *tumah* remains unchanged, and it can become *tamei* even while affixed to the door (see *Rashi*). The Baraisa will explain why a physical change is required.

4. I.e. the fact that a doorbell can become susceptible to *tumah* by virtue of mere intent, while a cowbell cannot lose its susceptibility to *tumah* without physical change.

5. I.e. any utensil that cannot contract *tumah* due to a status that it possesses (e.g. it is attached to the ground, or it is a utensil whose initial construction has not been completed) can be removed from that status (and rendered susceptible to *tumah*) by virtue of even a thought, i.e. intent. Thus, if the owner of a utensil attached to the ground decides that he wishes to detach the utensil and use it in an unattached state, the decision alone is sufficient to render the item susceptible to *tumah* (see *Mishnah Acharonah* to *Keilim* ibid., and to *Machshirin* 1:2 ד״ה ואת שבו). Similarly, if a craftsman mentally decides that he will not refine an unfinished utensil any further, and he will use it in its present, unrefined state, the vessel is viewed as completed, and it becomes susceptible to *tumah* (see *Rashi* to *Kiddushin* 59a ד״ה יורדין).

6. Once an item has become susceptible to *tumah*, mere intent to perform an act that will remove it from that status (e.g. to attach it to the ground) does not serve to render it insusceptible to *tumah*; rather, its state of susceptibility remains in place until the act is actually performed, and it can contract *tumah* even after the decision to perform such an act was reached (*Rashi*). [This rule applies also to items that have actually contracted *tumah*; the intent to perform an act that would remove the *tumah* (breaking the utensil, or piercing it so that it cannot perform its function) is not sufficient to remove the *tumah*; the act must actually be performed (see *Rashi* to *Kiddushin* ibid. ד״ה אלא).]

This rule is the explanation for the distinction made in the Baraisa. For a doorbell is not susceptible to *tumah*, and the intent to make it into a cowbell (which *is* susceptible to *tumah*) is sufficient to render it susceptible. But a cowbell, which is already susceptible to *tumah,* cannot be removed from that status unless a physical change is made to the bell.

7. A bell that has a clapper is susceptible to *tumah* because it has a useful purpose (this will be explained further in the Gemara below). Thus, the second Baraisa rules concerning such a bell that it can contract *tumah*. A bell that has no clapper, however, serves no purpose, and the first Baraisa therefore rules that it is not susceptible to *tumah*. [The first Baraisa's ruling concerning bells worn by a slave will be discussed in the Gemara below.]

8. I.e. if we are to assume that the only reason a bell can contract *tumah* is because it serves as an ornament [just as jewelry contracts *tumah* as a result of its ornamental status], the fact that the bell is lacking a clapper should be of no consequence, because the lack of the clapper does not affect its appearance at all (see *Rashi*; see also *Sfas Emes*).

9. [If the bell is not viewed as an ornament, then it should not be susceptible to *tumah* at all, even if it has a clapper; for] how can the clapper make the bell more ornamental [being inside the bell, where it cannot even be seen]? (*Rashi*).

10. The Gemara answers that a bell with a clapper is susceptible to *tumah not* because it is an ornament, but because it is deemed a useful utensil. As the Gemara will explain, this status is contingent upon the bell's ability to produce sound, and therefore it is restricted only to a bell that has a clapper.

11. *Numbers* 31:23. The verse speaks of the methods by which utensils taken as spoils in the Midianite war could be purified for use by their new Jewish owners (see next note).

12. The word דָּבָר, *item*, is similar in form to the word דִיבּוּר, which means *speech* or *sound*. Thus, the verse is expounded as teaching that any item that produces sound must be purified.

Although this verse speaks of purification from the absorption of forbidden substances through purging, rather than purification from *tumah* (ritual contamination), the law taught by this exposition is interpreted as applying to ritual *tumah* rather than to purging, for the fact that an item can produce sound is not at all relevant to whether it needs purging or not (see *Tosafos* and *Rashba*). [This interpretation of the exposition is further supported by the fact that the end of the verse does speak of ritual *tumah* – for the verse reads: *but it must be purified with the water of sprinkling* (in addition to being purged, if it was *tamei*); – see *Ran MHK* ed.]

ושל דלת טהורה [א] של דלת ועשאו לבהמה טמאה של בהמה ועשאו לדלת אף על פי שחיברו לדלת וקבעו במסמרים טמא שכל הכלים (א) יורדין לידי טומאתן במחשבה ואין עולין מידי טומאתן אלא בשינוי מעשה לא קשיא הא דאית ליה עינבל הא דלית ליה עינבל מה נפשך אי מנא הוא אע"פ דלית ליה עינבל אי לאו מנא הוא עינבל משוי ליה מנא אין כדר' שמואל בר נחמני א"ר יונתן (ג) דאמר ר' שמואל בר נחמני אמר ר' יונתן מנין למשמיע קול בכלי מתכות שהוא טמא שנאמר (א) כל דבר אשר יבא באש תעבירו באש אפי' דיבור יבא באש במאי אוקימתא בדלית ליה עינבל אימא מציעתא ולא בזוג שבצוארו אבל יוצא הוא בזוג שבכסותו וזה וזה מקבלין טומאה אי דלית ליה עינבל מי מקבלי טומאה ורמינהו (ג) [ב] העושה זגין למכתשת ולעריסה ולמטפחות ספרים ולמטפחות תינוקות יש להם עינבל טמאין אין להם עינבל טהורין ניטלו עינבליהן עדיין טומאתן עליהם ה"מ בתינוק דלקלא עבידי ליה אבל גדול תכשיט הוא ליה אע"ג דלית ליה עינבל: אמר מר ניטלו עינבליהן עדיין טומאתן עליהן למאי חזו אמר אביי הואיל שההדיוט יכול להחזירו מתיב רבא (ד) [ג] הזוג והעינבל חיבור וכי תימא הכי קאמר אע"ג דלא מחבר כמאן דמחבר דמי והתניא (ה) מספורת של פרקים ואיזמל של רהיטני חיבור לטומאה ואין חיבור להזאה ואמרינן מה נפשך אי חיבור הוא אפילו להזאה (א) ואי לא חיבור הוא אפילו לטומאה נמי לא ואמר רבה דבר תורה בשעת מלאכה חיבור בין לטומאה בין להזאה שלא בשעת מלאכה אינו חיבור לא לטומאה ולא להזאה וגזרו על טומאה שלא בשעת מלאכה משום טומאה שהיא בשעת מלאכה ועל הזאה שהיא בשעת מלאכה משום הזאה שלא בשעת מלאכה אלא אמר רבא הואיל

רש"י

ושל דלת טהור. דלת מחובר לבית הוא שהוא חבור לקרקע ואינו כלי לקבל טומאה וזוג העשוי לו בטיל לגביה כדאמרי' בריש פרקין דלעיל (ו) כל המחובר לו הרי הוא כמוהו: של דלת ועשאו לבהמה טמאה. מכאן ולהבא ואע"פ דלא עבד ביה מעשה אלא שחישב עליו ותלאו ותלייה לאו מעשה היא שכל הכלים יורדים לידי תורת טומאה במחשבה שלו: של בהמה ועשאו לדלת טמא. ואפי' מכאן ולהבא יקבל טומאה שאין חיבורו מעשה עד שישנהו מכמות שהיה: שאין עולין מטומאתן. מתורת טומאה שירדה להן ואע"פ שעדיין לא נטמאו משנמלך עליהן אין עולין מלקבל טומאה אלא בשינוי מעשה: עינבל. בטדי"ל שעשוי בתוכו להשמיע קול: אי מנא הוא. דתכשיט חשיב ליה: עינבל משוי ליה מנא. בתמיה משום העינבל מי הוי תכשיט: אין. עינבל משוי ליה מנא ולא משום תכשיט אלא משום כלי: כל דבר שיבא באש. בכלי מתכות משתעי במעשה מדין: אימא מציעתא. זוג לאדם: מי מקבל טומאה. אפי' לאדם: העושה זגין למכתשת. שמפטמין בה סממנין להקטיר לריח דקיי"ל בכריתות (פ"א ד' ו:) שהקול יפה לבשמים: ולעריסה. שהתינוק שוכב בתוכה שקורין בירל"ה ותולה בו זגין לקשקש כדי שישמע התינוק ויישן: ולמטפחות ספרים. כשנושאין אותן לבית הכנסת שהתינוקות של בית רבן קורין שם מקשקשין הזגין והתינוקות שומעין ובאין: ולמטפחות תינוקות. שתולין בצוארן: ניטלו עינבליהם כו'. (ז) (אם ניטלו קודם שנטמאו תורת טומאה עליהם ומקבלין טומאה כדמפרש טעמא לקמיה מעיקרא כי אין להם עינבל דקתני טהורין (ב) דעדיין לא נגמרה מלאכתן אבל משירדה להם תורת טומאה לא בטל שם כלי מעליהם בנטילת העינבל) ואם ניטל לאחר שנטמאו עדיין טומאתן עליהן דלא הוי ככלי שנשבר ובטל מתורת כלי ליטהר מטומאתו: הדיוט. שאין צריך אומן: הזוג והעינבל חיבור. כשהן יחד הרי הן כלי אחד נטמא זה נטמא זה הזה על זה טהור זה וכיון דקרי ליה חיבור שמע מינה דכי נתפרדו הוי כלי שניטל מקלתו ואף על גב דהדיוט יכול להחזירו כל כמה דלא אהדריה לאו שלם הוא: וכי תימא. דהאי חיבור דקאמר הכי קאמר אפי' מפורדים קרינן ליה חיבור ואתא לאשמעי' דאם נתפרדו משנטמאו לא עלו מטומאתן: הא תניא. גבי ההיא: מספורת של פרקים. שתי סכינים שלה מתפרדין: ואיזמל של רהיטני. פלינה של אומנים תריסים שנותנים האיזמל לתוך בין שני עצים העשוין לכך ולאחר מלאכתו נוטלו ומצניעו: חיבור לטומאה. ואם נטמא זה נטמא זה: שלא בשעת מלאכה. הואיל ואין צריכין להיות מחוברין הוו להו כשני כלים ואין חיבור ואף על פי שמחוברין דע"כ שלא בשעת מלאכה דומיא דשעת מלאכה קאמר ובשעת מלאכה מחוברין הן אלמא במחוברין עסקינן וגזרו לחומרא על הטומאה דליהוי חיבור ועל הזאה דלא ליהוי חיבור ומשום הכי קתני חיבור לטומאה לעולם ואין חיבור להזאה לעולם: אלא אמר רבא. לא תימא הואיל והדיוט יכול להחזיר דודאי (ג) חד מנא הואי כדקתני בברייתא הזוג והעינבל חיבור וכי מיפרדי הוי כלי שניטל מקלתו (ח) ואינו מקבל טומאה העינבל לעצמו אבל הזוג טמא לעצמו דלא בטל ליה מתורת כלי:

תוספות

אין כדר' שמואל כו'. דחשיב ליה כלי תשמיש דאדם משום דבעי ליה לקלא דע"י הזוג ששומע יודע היכן בהמתו עומדת ומוצאה ע"י כך (°) והוי כמקל של בהמה של מתכת דטמאה הואיל ואדם רודה בה וכ"מ לקמן גבי בירית טהורה דמשמיע [קול] בכלי מתכות אינו טמא אלא היכא דבעי ליה לקלא והא דמשני הא דאית ביה עינבל הא דלית ביה עינבל ולא מחלק באית ביה עינבל בין בעי ליה לקלא בין לא בעי אומר ר"י דלא שכיח שיעשו עינבל אלא אם כן בעי ליה לקלא:

כל דבר אשר יבא. ואע"ג דהאי קרא לא לגבי טומאה כתיב אלא לגבי הגעלה מסתברא דהתם אין דיבור מעלה ומוריד ואם אינו ענין להגעלה תנהו לענין טומאה:

מתיב רבא הזוג והעינבל חיבור. פי' בקונטרס מדקרי ליה חיבור ש"מ דכי נתפרדו הוי כלי שניטל מקלתו ואע"ג דהדיוט יכול להחזיר כל כמה דלא אהדרי' לאו שלם הוא וקשה לר"י דהא מעיקרא נמי הוי ידענא דהוי כלי שניטל מקלתו ולהכי פריך למאי חזו ומשני דודאי באפי נפשה לא חזו לא זוג ולא עינבל אלא משום דהדיוט יכול להחזירו ומה שפירש נמי והתניא כו' גבי ההיא מספורת של פרקים לא עיין דההוא דזוג ועינבל משנה היא במסכת פרה (פי"ב משנה ח) וההיא דמספורת בתוספתא דכלים ומפרש הרב פור"ת בשם ר' שמואל הואיל והדיוט יכול להחזירם ואע"ג דהשתא בלא עינבל לא חזי מידי כיון דהדיוט יכול בקל להחזירה כמאן דמיחברי דמי ואם נטמא העינבל נטמא גם הזוג כאילו הן מחוברין נפקא מינה דלכשיתחברו יטמא הזוג את הנוגע בו ומיהו בלא חיבור לא יטמא כי אם העינבל לבדו שנגע בטומאה והכי משמע לישנא דקאמר וכי תימא ה"ק אע"ג דלא מיחברי כמאן דמיחברי דמי משמע דאביי הכי סבירא ליה דמדתלי טעמא בחזרת הדיוט משמע דסבר דלא חזי השתא למידי ואי לאו כמחובר חשיב ליה היאך יקבל טומאה מאחר דלא חזי מידי בלא חזרה: (ט) **מתיב** רבא הזוג והעינבל חיבור. שאם נטמא זה נטמא זה וה"מ כשמחוברים אבל שלא בשעת חיבור אם נטמא זה לא נטמא זה ולא חיישינן להדיוט יכול להחזיר דהשתא מיהא לאו מחוברין נינהו וממשנה זו אין לנו להוכיח דמיירי בשעת חיבור כדקאמר וכי תימא כו' אבל מכח ברייתא מוכיח דבשעת חיבור מיירי ומברייתא גרידתא הוה מצי רבא לאותוביה לאביי אלא דניחא ליה לאקשויי מהך דמיירי בזוג ועינבל בהדיא לאביי דאיירי נמי בזוג ועינבל: (י) **(וכי** תימא כו') והתניא מספורת של פרקים ואיזמל של רהיטני. שתי ברייתות הן במסכת כלים (כ) כל אחד בפני עצמה ובריש' קתני בהדיא דכשאין מחוברין מקבל כל א' טומאה בפני עצמו וגזרו על טומאה שלא בשעת מלאכה שיהא חיבור לטומאה ליטמא זה כשניטמא זה משום דדמי לשעת מלאכה אבל שלא בחיבורין משמע דאפי' גזירה דרבנן ליכא ואם נטמא זה לא נטמא זה דלא חיישינן למה שהדיוט יכול להחזירו: (ל) **(אלא)** אמר רבא הואיל ויכול להקישו. פי' מקבל טומאה הזוג אבל עינבל דאין ראוי להקישו לא ומספורת ואיזמל נמי בלא חיבור ראויין למעין מלאכה ראשונה ומקבלי טומאה כל אחד בפני עצמו כדתני בתוספתא: **אלא** אמר רבא כו'. פירש בקונטרס דטומאה לא פרח הימנו כשנפרד משקיבל הואיל וראוי להקישו והוה ליה ככלי (עץ) שניקב בפחות ממוציא רמון דלא טהר מטומאה ומשמע שרוצה לומר דמכאן ואילך לא מקבל טומאה וקשה לר"י דלמה לא יקבל טומאה כיון דנפחת פחות מכשיעור דהוי כאילו שלם לגמרי ונראה לר"י דודאי גם מקבל טומאה מכאן ולהבא ולקונטרס דחקו לפרש כן משום דכשלא היה להם עינבל טהורין ולא מקבלי טומאה אף על גב דראוי להקישו ואינו דומה דכשלא היה בו עינבל מעולם ודאי טהור דכיון שעומד ליתן בו עינבל דהא עביד לקלא והוי גולמי כלי מתכות אבל משנגמר שהיה בו עינבל אף על פי שניטל מקבל טומאה שלא בטל מתורת כלי שהיה עליו קודם לכן והר"ס הביא ראיה מחטאת שתפרה ושייר פחות ממוציא רמון דטהורה (חולין קלח.) אע"ג דחטאת שלם שנקרע פחות

מסורת הש"ס

א) כלים פכ"ה מ"ט סוכה יג: לעיל נב: קדושין נט. [מנחות סט.], ב) לקמן סג:, ג) תוספ' דכלים ב"מ פ"א, ד) פרה פי"ב מ"ח, ה) לעיל מח: [תוספ' כלים ב"מ פ"ג], ו) דף נב:, ז) רש"ל מוחק כ"ז, ח) ואינו מקבל טומאה הזוג לעצמו אבל לענין מפרח טומאה לא פרחה מיניה משקבלה כצ"ל והשאר נמחק רש"ל, ט) רש"ל ומהר"מ כתבו דכל הנך דיבורי תוס' הם דיבו' אחד מן מתיב רבא עד סוף ד"ה אלא וכו' כדתני בתוספתא, י) ר"מ מ"ז, כ) [בפ"ג דבבא מציעא], ל) ר"מ מ"ז.

הגהות הב"ח

(א) גמ' אפי' להזאה נמי ואי לאו חיבור: (ב) רש"י ד"ה ניטלו עינבליה' וכו' ומעיקרא כי אין להם עינבל דקתני טהורין משום דעדיין: (ג) ד"ה אלא אמר וכו' דודאי לאו חד מנא:

ליקוטי רש"י

שכל הכלים יורדין לידי טומאתן במחשבה. כגון גולמי כלים דאמר בהכל שוחטין (חולין כה.) כל שעתיד לשוף לשבץ ולגרר ואמר התם דלאכי חסרון מלאכה הוא וטהורים ואם חישב עליה שלא לשוף ושלא לשבץ הביאתו מחשבה זו לידי גמר מלאכה מכאן ולהבא [קידושין נט.]. [משחישב עליו שזה יהא גמר מלאכתן כגון שעידו לדרגש או לדולבקי כיון שעידו מקבל טומאה ואלמלי עידו לרצועות וסנדלין אין מקבלים טומאה עד שיגמרו למלאכת הסנדלין [סוכה יד.]. מאחר שחישב עליו שיניחנו כמות שהוא עכשיו ולא יוסיף תיקון אחר הוא גמר מלאכתן ומקבל טומאה [לעיל נב:]. **ואין עולין מידי טומאתן.** משקבלוה [קידושין שם]. ממחשבת תורת קבלת טומאה אין עולין במחשבה כגון עידו לשלחן ולדרגש וחישב עליו לרצועות וסנדלין אין מחשבתו מבטלתן מתורת קבלת טומאה [סוכה שם]. מאחר שחישב על העור לעשות שטיח ירד לידי טומאה ואם חזר וחישב עליו לרצועות וסנדלים לא בטל מתורת כלי [לטהר] בכך עד שיתן בו אזמל דהוי שינוי מעשה [לעיל שם]. **אלא בשינוי מעשה.** שיעשה בה מעשה לקלקלם שישברם או ינקבם וכן עד שלא יקבלו טומאה אין עולין מתורת קבלת טומאה שירדו במחשבה זו אלא בשינוי מעשה עד שיתחיל לשוף לשבץ ולגרר [קידושין שם]. עד שיתן בו איזמל [סוכה שם]. **איזמל של רהיטני.** פליינ"ה בלע"ז של עץ וברזל חד נעוץ בתוכו ובהן משוה פני רוחב הקרש (°) ומחליקה [לקמן צז.]. פליינ"א שממחקים בה את התריסין ונותנין הברזל לתוך דפוס של עץ המתוקן לו ולאחר מלאכתו נוטלו הימנו. **ואין חיבור להזאה.**

עין משפט נר מצוה

יז א מיי' פ"ח מהל' כלים הלכה יב:
יח ב מיי' פ"ח מהל' כלים הלכה ז:
יט ג מיי' פ' יב מהל' פרה הלכה ט:

רבינו חננאל

אין מקבלין טומאה בדלית ליה עינבל והא דתני טמא בזוג שיש לו עינבל פי' עינבל הברזל שבתוך הזוג המקיש בדופני הזוג ומשמיע הקול וכי הא דאמר כו' מנין למשמיע קול בכלי מתכות שטמא שנאמר כל דבר אשר יבא באש אפילו דבור במשמע ואקשינן במאי אוקימנא להא דתני בזוג בהמה אין מקבלין טומאה בדלית לה עינבל אימ' מציעתא אין העבד יוצא בזוג שבצוארו אבל יוצא בזוג שבכסותו וזה וזה מקבלין טומאה ואי לית ליה עינבל מי מקבלי טומאה והתנן העושה זגין למכתשת ולעריסה ולמטפחות ספרים ולמטפחת תינוקו' כולן יש להן עינבליהן טמאין אין להן עינבליהן טהורין כו'. ושנינן הא בתינוק דלקלא עבידי אבל גדול כגון העבד דלתכשיט עביד ליה רביה אע"ג דלית ליה עינבל מקבל טומאה ואקשינן ניטלו עינבליהן עדיין טומאתן עליהן אי נטלו עינבליהן למאי חזו ושנינן בזה דכיון דהדיוט יכול להחזירו אע"פ שעדיין לא החזירו כמוחזר דמי. איני והא תנינן מספורת של פרקים ואיזמל של רהיטני כו' וכבר פירשנו למעלה (מח:) ומשני

רב נסים גאון

הזוג והעינבל חיבור. ראוי לידע כי זה הזוג זולתי הזוג הנאמר גבי נזיר ותמצא פי' דבר זה במסכת נזירות בפ' ג' מינין (דף לד) חרצנים אלו החיצונים הזגין אלו הפנימיים דברי ר' יהודה ר' יוסי אומר שלא תטעה בזוג של בהמה החיצון זוג והפנימי עינבל:

גליון הש"ס

תוס' ד"ה אין וכו' הוי כמקל של בהמה. לעיל נג ע"ב:

תורה אור השלם

א) כָּל דָּבָר אֲשֶׁר יָבֹא בָאֵשׁ תַּעֲבִירוּ בָאֵשׁ וְטָהֵר אַךְ בְּמֵי נִדָּה יִתְחַטָּא וְכֹל אֲשֶׁר לֹא יָבֹא בָּאֵשׁ תַּעֲבִירוּ בַמָּיִם: [במדבר לא, כג]

וצריך להזות על שניהם [לעיל מח:]. וגזרו על טומאה שלא בשעת מלאכה. שיהא חיבור. ועל הזאה שהיא בשעת מלאכה. שלא יהא חיבור הלכך חיבור לטומאה לעולם ואין חיבור להזאה כלל [שם מט.].

sound;[13] hence, it is plausible to say that a bell with a clapper is susceptible to acquiring *tumah,* while a bell with no clapper is not.[14]

The Gemara points out a difficulty with this resolution:

בְּמַאי אוֹקִימְתָּא – **How have you interpreted** the first Baraisa – בִּדְלֵית לֵיהּ עִינְבָּל – **as referring to [a bell] that has no clapper?** אֵימָא מְצִיעָתָא – But **cite the middle case** of the Baraisa, which speaks of bells worn by a slave: וְלֹא בְּזוּג שֶׁבְּצַוָּארוֹ – NOR may the slave go out WITH THE BELL THAT IS AROUND HIS NECK; אֲבָל יוֹצֵא הוּא בְּזוּג שֶׁבִּכְסוּתוֹ – BUT HE MAY GO OUT WITH THE BELL THAT IS ON HIS CLOTHING. וְזֶה וָזֶה מְקַבְּלִין טוּמְאָה – AND BOTH THIS bell AND THIS bell ARE SUSCEPTIBLE TO *TUMAH.* אִי דְּלֵית לֵיהּ עִינְבָּל – Now, **if** the Baraisa speaks of **[a bell] that does not have a clapper,** as you have suggested, מִי מְקַבְּלֵי טוּמְאָה – **would it be susceptible to *tumah*?**[15] וּרְמִינְהוּ – **But note a contradiction** to this in the following Baraisa:[16] הָעוֹשֶׂה זַגִּין לְמַכְתֶּשֶׁת – IF ONE MAKES BELLS FOR A MORTAR,[17] וְלַעֲרִיסָה – OR FOR A CRADLE,[18] וּלְמִטְפְּחוֹת סְפָרִים וּלְמִטְפְּחוֹת תִּינוֹקוֹת – OR FOR THE COVERINGS OF study SCROLLS[19] OR FOR THE COVERINGS OF CHILDREN,[20] the rule is: יֵשׁ לָהֶם עִינְבָּל טְמֵאִין – IF THEY HAVE CLAPPERS, THEY ARE susceptible to acquiring *TUMAH;* אֵין לָהֶם עִינְבָּל טְהוֹרִין – IF THEY HAVE NO CLAPPERS, THEY ARE *TAHOR.*[21] נִיטְּלוּ עִינְבְּלֵיהֶן – If they originally had clappers, but THEIR CLAPPERS WERE REMOVED, עֲדַיִין טוּמְאָתָן עֲלֵיהֶם – THEIR *TUMAH* STILL REMAINS UPON THEM.[22] This Baraisa states clearly that a bell that never had a clapper is not susceptible to acquiring *tumah.* How, then, can we explain the middle case of the first Baraisa?[23]

The Gemara answers:

הָנֵי מִילֵּי בְּתִינוֹק – **Where do the words** of the Baraisa just cited **apply? To** bells that are on the clothing of **children,** דִּלְקָלָא עֲבִידִי לֵיהּ – **for [those bells] are made for** the purpose of producing **sound,**[24] and thus without a clapper they are useless and are not deemed utensils. אֲבָל גָּדוֹל – **But** a bell worn by **a grown person,** such as the slave discussed in the first Baraisa, תַּכְשִׁיט הוּא לֵיהּ – **it is an ornament for him,** אַף עַל גַּב דְּלֵית לֵיהּ עִינְבָּל – and thus it is susceptible to acquiring *tumah* **even if it does not have a clapper.**[25]

The Gemara examines the final ruling in the Baraisa that was just cited:

אָמַר מַר – **The master stated** in the Baraisa above: נִיטְּלוּ עִינְבְּלֵיהֶן – If the bells originally had clappers, but THEIR CLAPPERS WERE REMOVED, עֲדַיִין טוּמְאָתָן עֲלֵיהֶן – THEIR *TUMAH* STILL REMAINS UPON THEM.

The Gemara asks:

לְמַאי חֲזוּ – But **for what** use **are they fit** in this state? Seemingly, the fact that they cannot be used any longer should cause them to emerge from their *tumah* status.[26] – ? –

NOTES

13. *Tosafos* explain that the sound-producing bell derives its *tumah* from the fact that it is viewed as a utensil that serves man, due to the fact that the man uses the sound to ascertain the whereabouts of his animal (see *Maharam;* see also *Rashba*).

14. At this point the Gemara assumes that a bell is *not* considered an ornament; it can only contract *tumah* by virtue of its sound-producing capabilities. Thus, a bell with a clapper is susceptible to *tumah*, while a bell without a clapper, which cannot produce sound, is not.

15. [It can be assumed that all the bells mentioned in the Baraisa are of the same type; thus, if the cowbells spoken of in the Baraisa are bells without clappers, then the slave's bells discussed in the middle cases of the Baraisa are also bells without clappers. And] if the only reason that a bell can acquire *tumah* is because it produces sound, even a slave's bell that has no clapper should not be susceptible to *tumah*! (see *Rashi*).

16. [I.e. apart from the fact that according to the Gemara's present understanding there is no reason why a slave's bell without a clapper should be susceptible to *tumah*, there is a second difficulty; viz. the Baraisa's ruling that a slave's bell is susceptible to *tumah* cannot be speaking of a bell without a clapper, for another Baraisa (cited presently) states clearly that such a bell is *not* susceptible to *tumah*!]

17. A mortar and pestle used for grinding aromatic spices were often equipped with bells, for the Gemara (*Kereisos* 6b) states that the presence of sound during the grinding process enhances the aroma of the spices (*Rashi*).

18. Bells were attached to infants' cradles so that their tinkling would lull the babies to sleep (*Rashi*).

19. The scrolls that schoolchildren used for study texts were covered with mantles hung with bells; when the teachers would carry them to the study hall, they would ring, signaling to the children that it was time to come and study (*Rashi*).

20. Bells were hung [on bib-like garments that were worn] around the necks of children (*Rashi*; see below, note 24).

21. Bells without clappers are deemed utensils that have not been completed, and they therefore are not susceptible to *tumah* (*Rashi*; see next note).

22. If they were *tamei* at the time that their clappers were removed, they remain *tamei*; they are not viewed as utensils that have been broken, which would no longer be *tamei*. [The reason for this is explained in the Gemara below.] And if they were not *tamei*, but were merely *susceptible* to *tumah*, they retain that status, and can still contract *tumah* although they no longer have clappers (*Rashi*). [It should be noted that we will explain *Rashi* throughout this passage in consonance with the version of *Rashi* that appears in our texts, which is *not* the version cited by *Tosafos* and most Rishonim. In their texts, *Rashi* writes that although *tamei* bells that have their clappers removed remain *tamei*, *tahor* bells that have their clappers removed can no longer contract *tumah*; see *Tosafos*, *Rashba,* and *Ran MHK* ed., who enumerate the difficulties inherent in this position. *Maharshal* emends our version of *Rashi* in several places to conform with their understanding of *Rashi*; however, see *Maharam* and *Pnei Yehoshua*, who explain *Rashi* as it appears in our texts.] The Gemara below will explain why such bells retain their *tumah* even though they have undergone a physical change.

23. For that Baraisa clearly states (according to the interpretation currently favored by the Gemara) that a slave's bell without a clapper *is* susceptible to *tumah*!

[Originally, the Gemara was not bothered by the fact that the first Baraisa rules that a cowbell is not susceptible to *tumah* while a slave's bell is, for the Gemara understood that the *tumah* of the bell derives from its classification as an ornament; and while the ornament of a person is deemed a utensil with respect to *tumah*, a cowbell is not, for there is no such thing as an animal's "ornament" (see above, 58a note 22). But once the Gemara established that a bell derives its susceptibility to *tumah* from its sound-producing properties, the Gemara can no longer distinguish between a slave's bell and a cow's bell in this manner.]

24. [The main purpose of the bells placed on the children was to alert adults to their whereabouts; indeed, all of the bells mentioned in the Baraisa are also for the purpose of producing sound (see also *Dibros Moshe* 53:10).]

25. The Gemara now retracts its current position and maintains that there are two ways that a bell can achieve *tumah* susceptibility – either by virtue of being a utensil whose purpose is to produce sound, or by virtue of its ornamental nature. However, the status of the bell hinges on the purpose for which it was intended. If it was primarily fashioned to produce sound – as in the case of a cowbell or a child's bell – then it is susceptible to *tumah* only if it was made with a clapper and can produce sound. Thus, the first Baraisa rules that a cowbell without a clapper is *tahor*, and the third Baraisa rules that a child's bell without a clapper is *tahor*. But if it was fashioned as an ornament – such as a slave's bell – it is susceptible to *tumah* even if it does not have a clapper (as the first Baraisa states regarding a slave's bell).

26. As explained above, a physical change is sufficient to remove an item from susceptibility to *tumah*, and it is also sufficient to remove *tumah* from an item that actually became *tamei* if it renders the item unsuitable for its original function (see note 6). Removal of a bell's clapper should seemingly accomplish this, as it renders the bell incapable of producing sound (and this Baraisa speaks of bells that are susceptible to *tumah* because of their ability to produce sound, as explained above).

ושל דלת טהורה [א] של דלת ועשאו לבהמה טמאה של בהמה ועשאו לדלת אף על פי שחיברו לדלת וקבעו במסמרים טמא שכל הכלים [א] יורדין לידי טומאתן במחשבה ואין עולין מידי טומאתן אלא בשינוי מעשה לא קשיא הא דאית ליה עינבל הא דלית ליה עינבל מה נפשך אי מנא הוא אע"פ דלית ליה עינבל אי לאו מנא הוא עינבל משוי ליה מנא אין כדר' שמואל בר נחמני א"ר יונתן [ב] דאמר ר' שמואל בר נחמני אמר ר' יונתן מנין למשמיע קול בכלי מתכות שהוא טמא שנאמר [א] כל דבר אשר יבא באש תעבירו באש אפי' דיבור יבא באש במאי אוקימתא בדלית ליה עינבל אימא מציעתא ולא בזוג שבצוארו אבל יוצא הוא בזוג שבכסותו וזה וזה מקבלין טומאה אי דלית ליה עינבל מי מקבלי טומאה ורמינהו [ג] [ב] העושה זגין למכתשת ולעריסה ולמטפחות ספרים ולמטפחות תינוקות יש להם עינבל טמאין אין להם עינבל טהורין ניטלו עינבליהן עדיין טומאתן עליהם ה"מ בתינוק דלקלא עבידי ליה אבל גדול תכשיט הוא ליה אע"ג דלית ליה עינבל: אמר מר ניטלו עינבליהן עדיין טומאתן עליהן למאי חזו אמר אביי הואיל שההדיוט יכול להחזירו מתיב רבא [ד] [ג] הזוג והעינבל חיבור וכי תימא הכי קאמר אע"ג דלא מחבר כמאן דמחבר דמי והתניא [ה] מספורת של פרקים ואיזמל של רהיטני חיבור לטומאה ואין חיבור להזאה ואמרינן מה נפשך אי חיבור הוא אפילו להזאה (א) ואי לא חיבור הוא אפילו לטומאה נמי לא ואמר רבה דבר תורה בשעת מלאכה חיבור בין לטומאה בין להזאה שלא בשעת מלאכה אינו חיבור לא לטומאה ולא להזאה וגזרו על טומאה שלא בשעת מלאכה משום טומאה שהיא בשעת מלאכה ועל הזאה שהיא בשעת מלאכה משום הזאה שלא בשעת מלאכה אלא אמר רבא הואיל

רש"י

ושל דלת טהור. דלת מחובר לבית הוא שהוא חבור לקרקע ואינו כלי לקבל טומאה וזוג העשוי לו בטיל לגביה כדאמרי' בריש פרקין דלעיל [י] כל המחובר לו הרי הוא כמוהו: של דלת ועשאו לבהמה טמאה. מכאן ולהבא ואע"פ דלא עבד ביה מעשה אלא שחישב עליו ותלאו ותלייה לאו מעשה היא שכל הכלים יורדים לידי תורת טומאה במחשבה שלו: של בהמה ועשאו לדלת טמא. ואפי' מכאן ולהבא יקבל טומאה שאין חיבורו מעשה עד שישנהו מכמות שהיה: שאין עולין מטומאתן. מתורת טומאה שירדה להן ואע"פ שעדיין לא נטמאו משנמלך עליהן אין עולין מלקבל טומאה אלא בשינוי מעשה: עינבל. בטדי"ל שעשוי בתוכו להשמיע קול: אי מנא הוא. דתכשיט חשיב ליה: עינבל משוי ליה מנא. בתמיה משום העינבל מי הוי תכשיט: אין. עינבל משוי ליה מנא ולא משום תכשיט אלא משום כלי: כל דבר שיבא באש. בכלי מתכות משתעי במעשה מדין: אימא מציעתא. זוג דאדם: מי מקבל טומאה. אפי' דאדם: העושה זגין למכתשת. שמפטמין בה סממנין להקטיר לריח דקיי"ל בכריתות (פ"א ד' ו:) שהקול יפה לבשמים: ולעריסה. שהתינוק שוכב בתוכה שקורין בירצ"ה ותולה בו זגין לקשקש כדי שישמע התינוק ויישן: ולמטפחות ספרים. כשנושאין אותן לבית הכנסת שהתינוקות של בית רבן קורין שם מקשקשין הזגין והתינוקות שומעין ובאין: ולמטפחות תינוקות. שתולין בצוארן: ניטלו עינבליהם כו'. [ז] (אם ניטלו קודם שנטמאו תורת טומאה עליהם ומקבלין טומאה כדמפרש טעמא לקמיה מעיקרא כי אין להם עינבל דקתני טהורין (ב) דעדיין לא נגמרה מלאכתן אבל משירדה להם תורת טומאה לא בטל שם כלי מעליהם בנטילת העינבל) ואם ניטל לאחר שנטמאו עדיין טומאתן עליהן דלא הוי ככלי שנשבר ובטל מתורת כלי ליטהר מטומאתו: הדיוט. שאין צריך אומן: הזוג והעינבל חיבור. כשהן יחד הרי הן כלי אחד נטמא זה נטמא זה הזה על זה טהור זה וכיון דקרי ליה חיבור שמע מינה דכי נתפרדו הוי כלי שניטל מקלתו ואף על גב דהדיוט יכול להחזירו כל כמה דלא אהדריה לאו שלם הוא: וכי תימא. דהאי חיבור דקאמר הכי קאמר אפי' מפורדים קרינן ליה חיבור ואתא לאשמעי' דאם נתפרדו משנטמאו לא עלו מטומאתן: הא תניא. גבי ההיא: מספורת של פרקים. שסכינים שלה מתפרדין: ואיזמל של רהיטני. פלינה של אומנים תריסים שנותנים האיזמל לתוך בין שני עצים העשוין לכך ולאחר מלאכתו נוטלו ומצניעו: חיבור לטומאה. ואם נטמא זה נטמא זה: שלא בשעת מלאכה. הואיל ואין צריכין להיות מחוברין הוו להו כשני כלים ואין חיבור ואף על פי שמחוברין דע"כ שלא בשעת מלאכה דומיא דשעת מלאכה קאמר ובשעת מלאכה מחוברין הן אלמא במחוברין עסקינן וגזרו לחומרא על הטומאה דליהוי חיבור ועל הזאה דלא ליהוי חיבור ומשום הכי קתני חיבור לטומאה לעולם ואין חיבור להזאה לעולם: אלא אמר רבא. לא תימא הואיל והדיוט יכול להחזיר דודאי (ג) חד מנא הוא כדקתני בברייתא הזוג והעינבל חיבור וכי מיפרדי הוי כלי שניטל מקלתו [ח] ואינו מקבל טומאה העינבל לעצמו אבל הזוג טמא לעצמו דלא בטל ליה מתורת כלי:

הואיל

תוספות

אין כדר' שמואל כו'. דחשיב ליה כלי תשמיש לאדם משום דבעי ליה לקלא דע"י הזוג שומע יודע היכן בהמתו עומדת ומוצאה ע"י כך ° והוי כמקל של בהמה של מתכת דטמאה הואיל ואדם רודה בה וכ"מ לקמן גבי בירית טהורה דמשמיע [קול] בכלי מתכות אינו טמא אלא היכא דבעי ליה לקלא והא דמשני הא דאית ביה עינבל הא דלית ביה עינבל ולא מחלק באית ביה עינבל בין בעי ליה לקלא בין לא בעי אומר ר"י דלא שכיח שיעשו עינבל אלא אם כן בעי ליה לקלא:

כל דבר אשר יבא. ואע"ג דהאי קרא לא לגבי טומאה כתיב אלא לגבי הגעלה מסתברא דהתם אין דיבור מעלה ומוריד ואם אינו ענין להגעלה תנהו לענין טומאה:

מתיב רבא הזוג והעינבל חיבור. פי' בקונטרס מדקרי ליה חיבור ש"מ דכי נתפרדו הוי כלי שניטל מקלתו ואע"ג דהדיוט יכול להחזיר כל כמה דלא אהדרי' לאו שלם הוא וקשה לר"י דהא מעיקרא נמי הוי ידענא דהוי כלי שניטל מקלתו ולהכי פריך למאי חזו ומשני דודאי באפי נפשה לא חזו לא זוג ולא עינבל אלא משום דהדיוט יכול להחזירו ומה שפירש נמי והתניא כו' גבי ההיא מספורת של פרקים לא עיין דההוא דזוג ועינבל משנה היא במסכת פרה (פי"ב משנה ח) וההיא דמספורת בתוספתא דכלים ומפרש הרב פור"ת בשם ר' שמואל הואיל והדיוט יכול להחזירם ואע"ג דהשתא בלא עינבל לא חזי מידי כיון דהדיוט יכול בקל להחזירה כמאן דמיחברי דמי ואם נטמא העינבל נטמא גם הזוג כאילו הן מחוברין נפקא מינה דלכשיתחברו יטמא הזוג את הנוגע בו ומיהו בלא חיבור לא יטמא כי אם העינבל לבדו שנגע בטומאה והכי משמע לישנא דקאמר וכי תימא ה"ק אע"ג דלא מיחברי כמאן דמיחברי דמי משמע דאביי הכי סבירא ליה דמדתלי טעמא בחזרת הדיוט משמע דסבר דלא חזי השתא למידי ואי לאו כמחובר חשיב ליה היאך יקבל טומאה מאחר דלא חזי מידי בלא חזרה: [ט] מתיב רבא הזוג והעינבל חיבור. שאם נטמא זה נטמא זה וה"מ כשמחוברים אבל שלא בשעת חיבור אם נטמא זה לא נטמא זה ולא חיישינן להדיוט יכול להחזיר דהשתא מיהא לאו מחוברין נינהו וממשנה זו אין לנו להוכיח דמיירי בשעת חיבור כדקאמר וכי תימא כו' אבל מכח ברייתא מוכיח דבשעת חיבור מיירי ומברייתא גרידתא הוה מצי רבא לאותוביה לאביי אלא דניחא ליה לאקשויי מהך דמיירי בזוג ועינבל בהדיא לאביי דאיירי נמי בזוג ועינבל: [י] (וכי תימא כו') והתניא מספורת של פרקים ואיזמל של רהיטני. שתי ברייתות הן במסכת כלים [כ] כל אחד בפני עצמה וברישא קתני בהדיא דכשאין מחוברין מקבל כל א' טומאה בפני עצמו וגזרו על טומאה שלא בשעת מלאכה שיהא חיבור לטומאה ליטמא זה כשניטמא זה משום דדמי לשעת מלאכה אבל שלא בחיבורין משמע דאפי' גזירה דרבנן ליכא ואם נטמא זה לא נטמא זה דלא חיים למה שהדיוט יכול להחזירו: [ל] (אלא) אמר רבא הואיל ויכול להקישו. פי' מקבל טומאה הזוג אבל עינבל דאין ראוי להקישו לא ומספורת ואיזמל נמי בלא חיבור ראויין למעין מלאכה ראשונה ומקבלי טומאה כל אחד בפני עצמו כדתני בתוספתא: אלא אמר רבא כו'. פירש בקונטרס דטומאה לא פרח הימנו כשנפרד משקישקל הואיל וראוי להקישו והוה ליה ככלי (עץ) שניקב בפחות ממוציא רמון דלא טהר מטומאה ומשמע שרוצה לומר דמכאן ואילך לא מקבל טומאה וקשה לר"י דלמה לא יקבל טומאה כיון דנפחת פחות מכשיעור דהוי כאילו שלם לגמרי ונראה לר"י דודאי גם מקבל טומאה מכאן ולהבא ולקונטרס דחקו לפרש כן משום דכשלא היה להם עינבל טהורין ולא מקבלי טומאה אף על גב דראוי להקישו ואינו דומה דכשלא היה בו עינבל מעולם ודאי טהור דכיון שעומד ליתן בו עינבל דהא עביד לקלא והוי גולמי כלי מתכות אבל משנגמר שהיה בו עינבל אף על פי שניטל מקבל טומאה שלא בטל מתורת כלי שהיה עליו קודם לכן והר"ס הביא ראיה מחמת שתפרה ושייר פחות ממוציא רמון דטהורה (חולין קלח.) אע"ג דחמת שלם שנקרע פחות

עין משפט נר מצוה

יז א מיי' פ"ח מהל' כלים הלכה יג:

יח ב מיי' פ"ח מהל' כלים הלכה ז:

יט ג מיי' פ' יב מהל' פרה הלכה ט:

רבינו חננאל

אין מקבלין טומאה בדלית ליה עינבל והא דתני טמא בזוג שיש לו עינבל פי' עינבל הברזל שבתוך הזוג המקיש בדופני הזוג ומשמיע הקול וכי הא דאמר כו' מנין למשמיע קול בכלי מתכות שטמא שנאמר כל דבר אשר יבא באש אפילו דבור במשמע ואקשינן במאי אוקימנא להא דתני בזוג בהמה אין מקבלין טומאה בדלית לה עינבל אימ' מציעתא אין העבד יוצא בזוג שבצוארו אבל יוצא בזוג שבכסותו וזה וזה מקבלין טומאה ואי לית ליה עינבל מי מקבלי טומאה והתנן העושה זגין למכתשת ולעריסה ולמטפחות ספרים ולמטפחת תינוק' כולן יש להן עינבליהן טמאין אין להן עינבליהן טהורין כו'. ושנינן הא בתינוק דלקלא עבידי אבל גדול כגון העבד דלתכשיט עביד ליה רביה אע"ג דלית ליה עינבל מקבל טומאה ואקשינן ניטלו עינבליהן עדיין טומאתן עליהן אי נטלו עינבליהן למאי חזו ושנינן בזה דכיון דהדיוט יכול להחזירו אע"פ שעדיין לא החזירו כמוחזר דמי. איני והא תנינן מספורת של פרקים ואיזמל של רהיטני כו' וכבר פירשנו למעלה (מח:) ומשני

רב נסים גאון

הזוג והעינבל חיבור. ראוי לידע כי זה הזוג זולתי הזוג הנאמר גבי נזיר ותמצא פי' דבר זה במסכת נזירות בפ' ג' מינין (דף לד) חרצנים אלו החיצונים הזגין אלו הפנימיים דברי ר' יהודה ר' יוסי אומר שלא תטעה בזוג של בהמה החיצון זוג והפנימי עינבל:

גליון הש"ס

תוס' ד"ה אין וכו' הוי כמקל של בהמה. לעיל נב ע"ב:

תורה אור השלם

א) כָּל דָּבָר אֲשֶׁר יָבֹא בָאֵשׁ תַּעֲבִירוּ בָאֵשׁ וְטָהֵר אַךְ בְּמֵי נִדָּה יִתְחַטָּא וְכֹל אֲשֶׁר לֹא יָבֹא בָּאֵשׁ תַּעֲבִירוּ בַמָּיִם: [במדבר לא, כג]

מסורת הש"ס

א) כלים פכ"ה מ"ט סוכה יג: לעיל נב: קדושין נט. [מנחות סט.], ב) לקמן סג:, ג) תוספ' דכלים ב"מ פ"א, ד) פרה פי"ב מ"ח, ה) לעיל מח: [תוספ' כלים ב"מ פ"ג], ו) דף נב:, ז) רש"ל מוחק כ"ז, ח) ואינו מקבל טומאה הזוג לעצמו אבל לענין מפרח טומאה לא פרחה מיניה משקבלה כצ"ל והשאר נמחק רש"ל, ט) רש"ל ומהר"מ כתבו דכל הנך דיבורי תוס' הם דיבו' אחד מן מתיב רבא עד סוף ד"ה אלא וכו' כדתני בתוספתא, י) ר"מ מ"ז, כ) [בפ"ג דבבא מליעא], ל) ר"מ מ"ז.

הגהות הב"ח

(א) גמ' אפי' להזאה נמי ואי לאו חיבור: (ב) רש"י ד"ה ניטלו עינבליה' וכו' ומעיקרא כי אין להם עינבל דקתני טהורין משום דעדיין: (ג) ד"ה אלא אמר וכו' דודאי לאו חד מנא:

ליקוטי רש"י

שכל הכלים יורדין לידי טומאתן במחשבה. כגון גולמי כלים דאמר בהכל שוחטין (חולין כה.) כל שעתיד לשוף לשבץ ולגרר ואמר התם דלאכתי חסרון מלאכה הוא וטהורים ואם חישב עליה שלא לשוף ושלא לשבץ הביאתו מחשבה זו לידי גמר מלאכה מכאן ולהבא [קידושין נט.]. [משחישב] עליו שזה יהא גמר מלאכתן כגון שעידו לדרגש או לדולבקי כיון שעידו מקבל טומאה ואלמלי עידו לרצועות וסנדלין אין מקבלים טומאה עד שיגמרו למלאכת הסנדלין [סוכה יד.]. מאחר שחישב עליו שיניחנו כמות שהוא עכשיו ולא יוסיף תיקון אחר הוא גמר מלאכתן ומקבל טומאה [לעיל נב:]. ואין עולין מידי טומאתן. משקבלוה [קידושין שם]. ממחשבת תורת קבלת טומאה אין עולין במחשבה כגון עידו לשלחן ולדרגש וחישב עליו לרצועות וסנדלין אין מחשבתו מבטלתן מתורת קבלת טומאה [סוכה שם]. מאחר שחישב על העור לעשות שטיח ירד לידי טומאה ואם חזר וחישב עליו לרצועות וסנדלים לא בטל מתורת כלי [לטהר] בכך עד שיתן בו אזמל דהוי שינוי מעשה [לעיל שם]. אלא בשינוי מעשה. שיעשה בה מעשה לקלקלם שישברם או ינקבם וכן עד שלא יקבלו טומאה אין עולין מתורת קבלת טומאה שירדו במחשבה זו אלא בשינוי מעשה עד שיתחיל לשוף לשבץ ולגרר [קידושין שם]. עד שיתן בו אזמל [סוכה שם]. איזמל של רהיטני. פליי"ה בלע"ז של עץ וברזל חד נעוץ בתוכו ובהן משוה פני רוחב הקרש ומחליקה [לקמן צז.]. פליי"א שממחקים בה את התריסין ונותנין הברזל לתוך דפוס של עץ המתוקן לו ולאחר מלאכתו נוטלו הימנו. ואין חיבור להזאה. וצריך להזות על שניהם [לעיל מח:]. וגזרו על טומאה שלא בשעת מלאכה. שיהא חיבור. ועל הזאה שהיא בשעת מלאכה. שלא יהא חיבור הלכך חיבור לטומאה לעולם ואין חיבור להזאה כלל [שם מט.].

The Gemara offers an explanation:

אָמַר אַבַּיֵי – **Abaye said:** הוֹאִיל שֶׁהֶדְיוֹט יָכוֹל לְהַחֲזִירוֹ – The bell is still considered a utensil, **because** even **a layman** who is unskilled at smithing **would be able to return [the clapper]** to its place inside the bell. Since the bell is so easily repaired, the fact that it is temporarily unusable does not detract from its status as a utensil.

This explanation is challenged:

מֵתִיב רָבָא – **Rava objected** to Abaye's explanation on the basis of the following Mishnah: הַזּוּג וְהָעִינְבָּל חִיבּוּר – THE BELL AND THE CLAPPER ARE treated as ATTACHED, and if one of them comes in contact with an *av hatumah,* both of them become *tamei* as a result.[27] This Baraisa shows that a clapper is deemed an integral part of the bell;[28] accordingly, if it is removed, the bell should be viewed as an incomplete utensil even if it can be replaced easily, and it should emerge from its *tumah* status.[29] – ? –

The Gemara anticipates a possible reply:

וְכִי תֵּימָא הָכִי קָאָמַר – **And if you wish to say** that **this is what [the Mishnah] is saying** when it teaches that the bell and the clapper are "attached" – אַף עַל גַּב דְּלָא מְחַבַּר כְּמַאן דִּמְחַבַּר דָּמֵי – that **even when they are not attached,** we nevertheless view them **as if they were attached**[30] – וְהָתַנְיָא – **but** this cannot be correct, for **it has been taught in a Baraisa:**[31] מִסְפּוֹרֶת שֶׁל פְּרָקִים וְאִיזְמֵל שֶׁל רְהִיטְנִי – A SCISSORS OF TWO SECTIONS[32] AND the blade and handle of A CARPENTER'S PLANE[33] חִיבּוּר לְטוּמְאָה וְאֵין חִיבּוּר לְהַזָּאָה – ARE CONSIDERED ATTACHED WITH REGARD TO *TUMAH* BUT NOT WITH REGARD TO SPRINKLING.[34] וְאַמְרִינַן – **And we said,** analyzing this Baraisa: מַה נַּפְשָׁךְ – **Whichever way you wish** to view these utensils, this distinction is difficult to explain. אִי חִיבּוּר הוּא – For **if [their attachment] is** viewed as a legal **attachment,** אֲפִילּוּ לְהַזָּאָה – then this should hold true **even with regard to sprinkling.** וְאִי לֹא חִיבּוּר הוּא – **And if it is not** viewed as **an attachment,** אֲפִילּוּ לְטוּמְאָה נַמִּי לֹא – then they should **not** be treated as attached **even with regard to *tumah*!**[35] וְאָמַר רַבָּה – **And Rabbah said,** in explanation of the Baraisa: דְּבַר תּוֹרָה – By **Torah law,** בִּשְׁעַת מְלָאכָה – **while** the scissors and plane are **in use,** when they must be connected to perform their functions, חִיבּוּר – they are considered **attached** בֵּין לְטוּמְאָה בֵּין לְהַזָּאָה – **both with regard to *tumah* and with regard to sprinkling.**[36] שֶׁלֹּא בִּשְׁעַת מְלָאכָה – And **while they are not in use,** and therefore it is unnecessary for them to be connected, אֵינוֹ חִיבּוּר – **they are not** treated as **attached,** לֹא לְטוּמְאָה וְלֹא לְהַזָּאָה – **neither with regard to *tumah* nor with regard to sprinkling.**[37] וְגָזְרוּ עַל טוּמְאָה שֶׁלֹּא בִּשְׁעַת מְלָאכָה – **But [the Rabbis] decreed** that we should rule stringently **with respect to *tumah*** that occurred **when they are not in use** מִשּׁוּם טוּמְאָה שֶׁהִיא בִּשְׁעַת מְלָאכָה – **because of** the fear that one might incorrectly rule leniently with respect to ***tumah*** that occurred **when they are in use;**[38] וְעַל הַזָּאָה שֶׁהִיא בִּשְׁעַת מְלָאכָה – **likewise,** they decreed that we should rule stringently **with respect to sprinkling** that was performed **when they are in use** מִשּׁוּם הַזָּאָה שֶׁלֹּא בִּשְׁעַת מְלָאכָה – **because of** the fear that one might incorrectly rule leniently with respect to **sprinkling that** occurred **when they were not in use.**[39] For this reason, Rabbah

NOTES

27. [*Rashi* identifies this as a Baraisa; however, *Tosafos* and other Rishonim point out that it is actually a Mishnah found in *Parah* (12:8).] Although the *tamei* item did not touch both the bell and the clapper, they are both *tamei*; similarly, when the bell and clapper are sprinkled with *mei chatas* (see Glossary) as part of the purification process, they both become *tahor* even if the water touches only one of them (*Rashi*).

28. [If the bell and the clapper were not deemed a single unit, and only the bell was touched by the *tumah*, the clapper would remain *tahor*; although the bell obviously touches it, this is of no consequence, because a utensil cannot transmit *tumah* (other than corpse *tumah* – see *Oholos* ch. 1) to another utensil.]

29. *Rashi*. [*Tosafos* and *Ritva MHK* ed. ask: Although it can be logically proven from this Mishnah that when a clapper is detached from a bell it is an incomplete utensil, Abaye did not dispute this – he merely stated that the fact that it can be easily repaired causes us to deem it as whole with respect to the *tumah* status that it acquired while together, since it can easily be replaced – and this logic is *not* necessarily disproven from the Mishnah! *Ritva* therefore understands the Gemara's question as follows: The Mishnah's ruling that the bell and the clapper are deemed one utensil seemingly stems from the fact that they can be reconnected only by a craftsman – thus, the Mishnah directly contradicts Abaye's explanation. For a defense of *Rashi's* position, see *Chiddushei HaRan, Maginei Shlomo* and *Shabbos Shel Mi*; see also below, note 42; see also *Tosafos*.]

30. I.e. perhaps the Mishnah can be interpreted as teaching the very law taught by Abaye – that even though the bell and the clapper are presently *not* attached, they are deemed as being attached – i.e. they maintain their former status (of *tumah* or susceptibility to *tumah*) [due to the fact that they can be easily reattached] (see *Rashi*).

31. [The Baraisa quoted here in the Gemara is actually a composite of two Baraisos in *Tosefta Keilim,* section II, 3:2 and 3:6. It was cited in the Gemara above (48b-49a).]

32. I.e. a scissors whose two blades can be taken apart (*Rashi*).

33. A carpenter's plane consisted of a blade that was inserted into a groove cut into a wooden handle; the blade was inserted into the handle when the tool was used, and it was removed and stored away afterwards (*Rashi*). [Both the scissors and the plane were put together for use; however, even when they were taken apart, the separate sections could be used to some extent (see *Tosefta Keilim* ibid.).]

34. If a *tamei* object touched one of the scissors' blades or one of the parts of the plane, both sections become *tamei*; but if the scissors or plane was *tamei* with corpse *tumah,* and *mei chatas* sprinkled on them to purify them touched only one of the sections, the other section would not be purified (see *Rashi*).

35. That is, if their attachment is sufficient reason to view them as a single unit, then sprinkling on one section of either of these utensils should be sufficient to purify both sections. And if they are not deemed a single unit, then *tumah* that touches one section should not render the second section *tamei*! There is seemingly no explanation for treating them as a single unit with regard to *tumah* and two units with regard to the purification process.

36. Thus, on the Biblical level, a sprinkling that touches only one section of the utensil *would* serve to purify the second section as well.

37. Since it is not necessary for them to be connected while they are not in use [and they are often taken apart when not in use] they are Biblically viewed as two separate units, even if they are in fact connected at the time; accordingly, if *tumah* touches one of the sections, the other should not become *tamei* (*Rashi*). [*Rashi* notes further that Rabbah does not refer to utensils that have *actually* been taken apart, for Rabbah draws a distinction between the utensils at the time that they are being used and those same utensils at the time that they are not being used, which implies that there is no difference in the *physical* state of the utensils.]

38. The Sages were concerned that if *tumah* would touch one section of one of these utensils when it was not being used, and we were to rule that the other section is *tahor*, people would mistakenly think that the untouched section *never* becomes *tamei*, even if the utensil was touched by the *tumah* while it was being used (in which case the untouched section would be Biblically *tamei*). Therefore, they decreed that the second section should always be ruled *tamei*, even if the *tumah* occurred while the utensil was not being used.

39. Sprinkling on one section of such a utensil does not purify the untouched section if the sprinkling occurs when the utensil is not being used. But the Sages were concerned that if people were to see that the sprinkling *does* purify the entire utensil when the sprinkling was done during the time of its use, they would mistakenly assume that the sprinkling purifies the entire utensil in all cases. Accordingly, they decreed that the sprinkling *never* purifies the untouched section of the utensil.

ושל דלת טהורה [א] של דלת ועשאו לבהמה טמאה של בהמה ועשאו לדלת אף על פי שחיברו לדלת וקבעו במסמרים טמא שכל הכלים (א) יורדין לידי טומאתן במחשבה ואין עולין מידי טומאתן אלא בשינוי מעשה לא קשיא הא דאית ליה עינבל הא דלית ליה עינבל מה נפשך אי מנא הוא אע"פ דלית ליה עינבל אי לאו מנא הוא עינבל משוי ליה מנא אין כדר' שמואל בר נחמני א"ר יונתן (ב) דאמר ר' שמואל בר נחמני אמר ר' יונתן מנין למשמיע קול בכלי מתכות שהוא טמא שנאמר (א) כל דבר אשר יבא באש תעבירו באש אפי' דיבור יבא באש במאי אוקימתא בדלית ליה עינבל אימא מציעתא ולא בזוג שבצוארו אבל יוצא הוא בזוג שבכסותו וזה וזה מקבלין טומאה אי דלית ליה עינבל מי מקבלי טומאה ורמינהו (ג) [ב] העושה זגין למכתשת ולעריסה ולמטפחות ספרים ולמטפחות תינוקות יש להם עינבל טמאין אין להם עינבל טהורין ניטלו עינבליהן עדיין טומאתן עליהם ה"מ בתינוק דלקלא עבידי ליה אבל גדול תכשיט הוא ליה אע"ג דלית ליה עינבל: אמר מר ניטלו עינבליהן עדיין טומאתן עליהן למאי חזו אמר אביי הואיל שההדיוט יכול להחזירו מתיב רבא (ד) [ג] הזוג והעינבל חיבור וכי תימא הכי קאמר אע"ג דלא מחבר כמאן דמחבר דמי והתניא (ה) מספורת של פרקים ואיזמל של רהיטני חיבור לטומאה ואין חיבור להזאה ואמרינן מה נפשך אי חיבור הוא אפילו להזאה (א) ואי לא חיבור הוא אפילו לטומאה נמי לא ואמר רבה דבר תורה בשעת מלאכה חיבור בין לטומאה בין להזאה שלא בשעת מלאכה אינו חיבור לא לטומאה ולא להזאה וגזרו על טומאה שלא בשעת מלאכה משום טומאה שהיא בשעת מלאכה ועל הזאה שהיא בשעת מלאכה משום הזאה שלא בשעת מלאכה אלא אמר רבא הואיל

רש"י

ושל דלת טהור. דלא מחובר לבית הוא שהוא חבור לקרקע ואינו כלי לקבל טומאה וזוג העשוי לו בטיל לגביה כדאמרי' בריש פרקין דלעיל [ו] כל המחובר לו הרי הוא כמוהו: **של דלת ועשאו לבהמה טמאה.** מכאן ולהבא ואע"פ דלא עבד ביה מעשה אלא שחישב עליו ותלאו ותלייה לאו מעשה היא שכל הכלים יורדים לידי תורת טומאה במחשבה שלו: **של בהמה ועשאו לדלת טמא.** ואפי' מכאן ולהבא יקבל טומאה שאין חיבורו מעשה עד שישנהו מכמות שהיה: **שאין עולין מטומאתן.** מתורת טומאה שירדה להן ואע"פ שעדיין לא נטמאו משנמלך עליהן אין עולין מלקבל טומאה אלא בשינוי מעשה: **עינבל.** בטדי"ל שעשוי בתוכו להשמיע קול: **אי מנא הוא.** דתכשיט חשיב ליה: **עינבל משוי ליה מנא.** בתמיה משום העינבל מי הוי תכשיט: **אין.** עינבל משוי ליה מנא ולא משום תכשיט אלא משום כלי: **כל דבר שיבא באש.** בכלי מתכות משתעי במעשה מדין: **אימא מציעתא.** זוג דאדם: **מי מקבל טומאה.** אפי' דאדם: **העושה זגין למכתשת.** שמפטמין בה סממנין להקטיר לריח דקיי"ל בכריתות (פ"א ד' ו:) שהקול יפה לבשמים: **ולעריסה.** שהתינוק שוכב בתוכה שקורין בירצ"ה ותולה בו זגין לקשקש כדי שישמע התינוק ויישן: **ולמטפחות ספרים.** כשנושאין אותן לבית הכנסת שהתינוקות של בית רבן קורין שם מקשקשין הזגין והתינוקות שומעין ובאין: **ולמטפחות תינוקות.** שתולין בצוארן: **ניטלו עינבליהם כו'.** [ז] (אם ניטלו קודם שנטמאו תורת טומאה עליהם ומקבלין טומאה כדמפרש טעמא לקמיה מעיקרא כי אין להם עינבל דקתני טהורין (ג) דעדיין לא נגמרה מלאכתן אבל משירדה להם תורת טומאה לא בטל שם כלי מעליהם בנטילת העינבל) ואם ניטל לאחר שנטמאו עדיין טומאתן עליהן דלא הוי ככלי שנשבר ובטל מתורת כלי ליטהר מטומאתו: **הדיוט.** שאין צריך אומן: **הזוג והעינבל חיבור.** כשהן יחד הרי הן כלי אחד נטמא זה נטמא זה הזה על זה טהור זה וכיון דקרי ליה חיבור שמע מינה דכי נתפרדו הוי כלי שניטל מקלתו ואף על גב דהדיוט יכול להחזירו כל כמה דלא אהדריה לאו שלם הוא: **וכי תימא.** דהאי חיבור דקאמר הכי קאמר אפי' מפורדים קרינן ליה חיבור ואתא לאשמעי' דאם נתפרדו משנטמאו לא עלו מטומאתן: **הא תניא.** גבי ההיא: **מספורת של פרקים.** שני סכינים שלה מתפרדין: **ואיזמל של רהיטני.** פלינה של אומנים תריסים שנותנים האיזמל לתוך בין שני עצים העשוין לכך ולאחר מלאכתו נוטלו ומצניעו: **חיבור לטומאה.** ואם נטמא זה נטמא זה: **שלא בשעת מלאכה.** הואיל ואין צריכין להיות מחוברין הוו להו כשני כלים ואין חיבור ואף על פי שמחוברין דע"כ שלא בשעת מלאכה דומיא דשעת מלאכה קאמר ובשעת מלאכה מחוברין הן אלמא במחוברין עסקינן וגזרו לחומרא על הטומאה דליהוי חיבור ועל הזאה דלא ליהוי חיבור ומשום הכי קתני חיבור לטומאה לעולם ואין חיבור להזאה לעולם: **אלא אמר רבא.** לא תימא הואיל והדיוט יכול להחזיר דודאי (ג) חד מנא הואי כדקתני בברייתא הזוג והעינבל חיבור וכי מיפרדי הוי כלי שניטל מקלתו [ח] ואינו מקבל טומאה העינבל לעצמו אבל הזוג טמא לעצמו דלא בטל ליה מתורת כלי:

הואיל

תוספות

אין כדר' שמואל כו'. דחשיב ליה כלי תשמיש דאדם משום דבעי ליה לקלא דע"י הזוג ששומע יודע היכן בהמתו עומדת ומולאה ע"י כך ° והוי כמקל של בהמה של מתכת דטמאה הואיל ואדם רודה בה וכ"מ לקמן גבי בירית טהורה דמשמיע [קול] בכלי מתכות אינו טמא אלא היכא דבעי ליה לקלא והא דמשני הא דאית ביה עינבל הא דלית ביה עינבל ולא מחלק באית ביה עינבל בין בעי ליה לקלא בין לא בעי אומר ר"י דלא שכיח שיעשו עינבל אלא אם כן בעי ליה לקלא:

כל דבר אשר יבא. ואע"ג דהאי קרא לא לגבי טומאה כתיב אלא לגבי הגעלה מסתברא דהתם אין דיבור מעלה ומוריד ואם אינו ענין להגעלה תנהו לענין טומאה:

מתיב רבא הזוג והעינבל חיבור. פי' בקונטרס מדקרי ליה חיבור ש"מ דכי נתפרדו הוי כלי שניטל מקלתו ואע"ג דהדיוט יכול להחזיר כל כמה דלא אהדרי' לאו שלם הוא וקשה לר"י דהא מעיקרא נמי הוי ידענא דהוי כלי שניטל מקלתו ולהכי פריך למאי חזו ומשני דודאי באפי נפשה לא חזו לא זוג ולא עינבל אלא משום דהדיוט יכול להחזירו ומה שפירש נמי והתניא כו' גבי ההיא מספורת של פרקים לא עיין דההוא דזוג ועינבל משנה היא במסכת פרה (פי"ב משנה ח) וההיא דמספורת בתוספתא דכלים ומפרש הרב פור"ת בשם ר' שמואל הואיל והדיוט יכול להחזירם ואע"ג דהשתא בלא עינבל לא חזי מידי כיון דהדיוט יכול בקל להחזירה כמאן דמיחברי דמי ואם נטמא העינבל נטמא גם הזוג כאילו הן מחוברין נפקא מינה דלכשיתחברו יטמא הזוג את הנוגע בו ומיהו בלא חיבור לא יטמא כי אם העינבל לבדו שנגע בטומאה והכי משמע לישנא דקאמר וכי תימא ה"ק אע"ג דלא מיחברי כמאן דמיחברי דמי משמע דאביי הכי סבירא ליה דמדתלי טעמא בחזרת הדיוט משמע דסבר דלא חזי השתא למידי ואי לאו כמחובר חשיב ליה היאך יקבל טומאה מאחר דלא חזי מידי בלא חזרה:

(ט) **מתיב** רבא הזוג והעינבל חיבור. שאם נטמא זה נטמא זה וה"מ כשמחוברים אבל שלא בשעת חיבור אם נטמא זה לא נטמא זה ולא חיישינן להדיוט יכול להחזיר דהשתא מיהא לאו מחוברין נינהו וממשנה זו אין לנו להוכיח דמיירי בשעת חיבור כדקאמר וכי תימא כו' אבל מכח ברייתא מוכיח דבשעת חיבור מיירי ומברייתא גרידתא הוה מצי רבא לאותוביה לאביי אלא דניחא ליה לאקשויי מהך דמיירי בזוג ועינבל בהדיא לאביי דאיירי נמי בזוג ועינבל:

(י) **(וכי** תימא כו') והתניא מספורת של פרקים ואיזמל של רהיטני. שתי ברייתות הן במסכת כלים (כ) כל אחד בפני עצמה וברישא קתני בהדיא דכשאינן מחוברין מקבל כל א' טומאה בפני עצמו וגזרו על טומאה שלא בשעת מלאכה שיהא חיבור לטומאה ליטמא זה כשניטמא זה משום דדמי לשעת מלאכה אבל שלא בחיבורין משמע דאפי' גזירה דרבנן ליכא ואם נטמא זה לא נטמא זה דלא חיים למה שהדיוט יכול להחזירו:

(ל) **(אלא)** אמר רבא הואיל ויכול להקישו. פי' מקבל טומאה הזוג אבל עינבל דאין ראוי להקישו לא ומספורת ואיזמל נמי בלא חיבור ראויין למעין מלאכה ראשונה ומקבלי טומאה כל אחד בפני עצמו כדתני בתוספתא:

אלא אמר רבא כו'. פירש בקונטרס דטומאה לא פרח הימנו כשנפרד משקיבל הואיל וראוי להקישו והוה ליה ככלי (עץ) שניקב בפחות ממוציא רמון דלא טהר מטומאה ומשמע שרוצה לומר דמכאן ואילך לא מקבל טומאה וקשה לר"י דלמה לא יקבל טומאה כיון דנפחת פחות מכשיעור דהוי כאילו שלם לגמרי ונראה לר"י דודאי גם מקבל טומאה מכאן ולהבא ולקונטרס דחקו לפרש כן משום דכשלא היה להם עינבל טהורין ולא מקבלי טומאה אף על גב דראוי להקישו ואינו דומה דכשלא היה בו עינבל מעולם ודאי טהור דכיון שעומד ליתן בו עינבל דהא עביד לקלא והוי גולמי כלי מתכות אבל משנגמר שהיה בו עינבל אף על פי שניטל מקבל טומאה שלא בטל מתורת כלי שהיה עליו קודם לכן והר"ס הביא ראיה מחמת שתפרה ושייר פחות ממוציא רמון דטהורה (חולין קלח.) אע"ג דחמת שלם שנקרע

פחות

עין משפט נר מצוה

יז א מיי' פ"ח מהל' כלים הלכה יב:

יח ב מיי' פ"ח מהל' כלים הלכה ז:

יט ג מיי' פ' יב מהל' פרה הלכה ט:

רבינו חננאל

אין מקבלין טומאה בדלית ליה עינבל והא דתני טמא בזוג שיש לו עינבל פי' עינבל הברזל שבתוך הזוג המקיש בדופני הזוג ומשמיע הקול וכי הא דאמר כו' מנין למשמיע קול בכלי מתכות שטמא שנאמר כל דבר אשר יבא באש אפילו דבור במשמע ואקשינן במאי אוקימנא להא דתני בזוג בהמה אין מקבלין טומאה בדלית לה עינבל אימ' מציעתא אין העבד יוצא בזוג שבצוארו אבל יוצא בזוג שבכסותו וזה וזה מקבלין טומאה ואי לית ליה עינבל מי מקבלי טומאה והתנן העושה זגין למכתשת ולעריסה ולמטפחות ספרים ולמטפחת תינוקו' כולן יש להן עינבליהן טמאין אין להן עינבליהן טהורין כו'. ושנינן הא בתינוק דלקלא עבידי אבל גדול כגון העבד דלתכשיט עביד ליה רביה אע"ג דלית ליה עינבל מקבל טומאה ואקשינן ניטלו עינבליהן עדיין טומאתן עליהן אי נטלו עינבליהן למאי חזו ושנינן בזה דכיון דההדיוט יכול להחזירו אע"פ שעדיין לא החזירו כמוחזר דמי. איני והא תנינן מספורת של פרקים ואיזמל של רהיטני כו' וכבר פירשנו למעלה (מח:) ומשני

רב נסים גאון

הזוג והעינבל חיבור. ראוי לידע כי זה הזוג זולתי הזוג הנאמר גבי נזיר ותמצא פי' דבר זה במסכת נזירות בפ' ג' מינין (דף לד:) חרצנים אלו החיצונים הזגין אלו הפנימיים דברי ר' יהודה ר' יוסי אומר שלא תטעה בזוג של בהמה החיצון זוג והפנימי עינבל:

גליון הש"ס

תוס' ד"ה אין וכו' הוי כמקל של בהמה. לעיל נב ע"ב:

תורה אור השלם

א) כָּל דָּבָר אֲשֶׁר יָבֹא בָאֵשׁ תַּעֲבִירוּ בָאֵשׁ וְטָהֵר אַךְ בְּמֵי נִדָּה יִתְחַטָּא וְכֹל אֲשֶׁר לֹא יָבֹא בָּאֵשׁ תַּעֲבִירוּ בַמָּיִם: [במדבר לא, כג]

מסורת הש"ס

א) כלים פכ"ה מ"ט סוכה יג: לעיל נב: קדושין נט. [מנחות סט.], ב) לקמן סג., ג) תוספ' דכלים ב"מ פ"א, ד) פרה פי"ב מ"ח, ה) לעיל מח: [תוספ' כלים ב"מ פ"ג], ו) דף נב:, ז) רש"ל מוחק כ"ז, ח) ואינו מקבל טומאה הזוג לעצמו אבל לענין מפרח טומאה לא פרחה מיניה משקבלה כצ"ל והשאר נמחק רש"ל, ט) רש"ל ומהר"מ כתבו דכל הנך דיבורי תוס' הם דיבו' אחד מן מתיב רבא עד סוף ד"ה אלא וכו' כדתני בתוספתא, י) ר"מ מ"ז, כ) [בפ"ג דבבא מליעא], ל) ר"מ מ"ז.

הגהות הב"ח

(א) גמ' אפי' להזאה נמי ואי לאו חיבור: (ב) רש"י ד"ה ניטלו עינבליה' וכו' ומעיקרא כי אין להם עינבל דקתני טהורין משום דעדיין: (ג) ד"ה אלא אמר וכו' דודאי לאו חד מנא:

ליקוטי רש"י

שכל הכלים יורדין לידי טומאתן במחשבה. כגון גולמי כלים דאמר בהכל שוחטין (חולין כה.) כל שעתיד לשוף לשבץ ולגרר ואמר התם דלאכתי חסרון מלאכה הוא וטהורים ואם חישב עליה שלא לשוף ושלא לשבץ הביאתו מחשבה זו לידי גמר מלאכה מכאן ולהבא [קידושין נט.]. [משחישב] עליו שזה יהא גמר מלאכתן כגון שעידנו לדרגש או לדולבקי כיון שעידנו מקבל טומאה ואלמלי עידו לרצועות וסנדלין אין מקבלים טומאה עד שיגמרו למלאכת הסנדלין [סוכה יד.]. מאחר שחישב עליו שיניחנו כמות שהוא עכשיו ולא יוסיף תיקון אחר הוא גמר מלאכתן [לעיל נב.]. ואין עולין מידי טומאתן. משקבלוה [קידושין שם]. ממחשבת תורת קבלת טומאה אין עולין ממחשבה כגון עידנו לשלחן ולדרגש וחישב עליו לרצועות וסנדלין אין מחשבתו מבטלתו מתורת קבלת טומאה [סוכה שם]. לא מאחר שחישב על העור לעשות שטיח לידי טומאה ואם חזר וחישב עליו לרצועות וסנדלים לא בטל מתורת כלי [illegible] אלא בשינוי מעשה. [illegible] איזמל של רהיטני. פליי"נא בלע"ז [illegible] שממחקים בה הנסרים ונותנין הברזל לתוך דפוס של עץ המתוקן לו ולאחר מלאכתו נוטלו הימנו. ואין חיבור להזאה. וצריך להזות על שניהם [לעיל מח:]. וגזרו על טומאה שלא בשעת מלאכה. שיהא חיבור. ועל הזאה שהיא בשעת מלאכה. שלא יהא חיבור הלכך חיבור לטומאה לעולם ואין חיבור להזאה כלל [שם מט.].

explained, the Baraisa states that these utensils are treated as connected with respect to *tumah* but are not treated as connected with respect to sprinkling.[40] At any rate, it is clear from this Baraisa that such utensils are treated as one only when they are connected;[41] but if they were separated, even if they could be easily reattached, they would certainly be viewed as two separate utensils.[42] – ? –

The Gemara therefore offers another explanation for the Baraisa's ruling that a bell that has its clapper removed does not emerge from its *tumah* status:

אֶלָּא אָמַר רָבָא – Rather, Rava said:

NOTES

40. The Baraisa thus reflects the Rabbinic law (see notes 38 and 39).

41. See end of note 37.

42. The Baraisa states that the two sections of the scissors and the plane are viewed as a single unit on the Biblical level when they are in use, and on the Rabbinic level when they are not in use. This implies that if the two sections were actually detached, they would not be viewed as a single unit to any degree, even on the Rabbinic level. Certainly, then, when the Mishnah in *Parah* states unequivocally that the bell and clapper are considered attached [and thus a single utensil], it follows that when the clapper is removed we would view the bell as a broken utensil (the fact that it can be easily repaired notwithstanding even to the extend that it would lose its *tumah* status). Accordingly, this Baraisa poses a challenge to Abaye, who maintained above that the fact that a layman can repair the bell causes us to view the bell and the clapper as a single [unbroken] unit even when they are not attached. See *Chidushei HaRan* and *Ritva MHK* ed.; see also *Shabbos Shel Mi*.

[The Gemara assumes that both the Mishnah in *Parah* and the Baraisa use the word חִיבּוּר to refer to items that are actually attached. *Rashi* apparently attributes this to the fact that the two were taught together (see *Rashi* ד״ה הא תניא); see, however, note 27 above. Cf. *Tosafos* and *Ritva MHK* ed., who provide other reasons for this assumption; see also *Shabbos Shel Mi*.]

הוֹאִיל וְרָאוּי לְהַקִּישׁוֹ עַל גַּבֵּי חֶרֶס – A bell that has had its clapper removed does not lose its *tumah* status **because it is** still **fit to strike against an earthenware** pot.[1] אִיתְּמַר נַמִּי אָמַר רַבִּי יוֹסֵי בְּרַבִּי חֲנִינָא – **It was also stated** that **R' Yose the son of R' Chanina said:** הוֹאִיל וְרָאוּי לְהַקִּישׁוֹ עַל גַּבֵּי חֶרֶס – The bell retains its *tumah* status **because it is** still **fit to strike against an earthenware** pot.[2]

The Gemara cites a different explanation:

רַבִּי יוֹחָנָן אָמַר – But **R' Yochanan said:** הוֹאִיל וְרָאוּי לְגַמֵּע בּוֹ מַיִם לְתִינוֹק – The bell retains its *tumah* status **because it is fit to give** a **drink** of **water to a child in it.**[3] Thus, although it no longer can produce sound, the fact that the bell still has a function causes it to retain its *tumah* status.[4]

The Gemara notes a difficulty with R' Yochanan's position:

וְרַבִּי יוֹחָנָן לֹא בָּעֵי מֵעֵין מְלָאכָה רִאשׁוֹנָה – **But** is it true that **R' Yochanan does not require** that a utensil be usable for **a semblance of its original function** in order for it to retain its *tumah* status? וְהָתַנְיָא – **Why, we have been taught** otherwise **in a Baraisa,** which states: ,,וְכָל־[הַ]כְּלִי אֲשֶׁר־יֵשֵׁב עָלָיו וגו׳ " – The verse states with regard to *midras tumah*:[5] *Any bedding upon which the zav will recline will become tamei;* **AND ANY UTENSIL** ***UPON WHICH HE WILL SIT*** **etc.** [*will become tamei*]. יָכוֹל כָּפָה סְאָה וְיָשַׁב עָלֶיהָ – **IT MIGHT HAVE BEEN THOUGHT** that **IF [A *ZAV*] TURNED OVER A *SE'AH*-sized** barrel **AND SAT UPON IT,** כָּפָה תַּרְקַב וְיָשַׁב עָלֶיהָ – or if he turned over **A HALF-*SE'AH***[6] barrel **AND SAT UPON IT,** יְהֵא טָמֵא – **IT WOULD BE *TAMEI*;**[7] תַּלְמוּד לוֹמַר – to dispel this notion **[THE TORAH] STATES:** ,,אֲשֶׁר־יֵשֵׁב עָלָיו (הַזָּב)"[8] – ***AND ANY UTENSIL UPON WHICH [THE ZAV] WILL SIT.*** מִי שֶׁמְּיוּחָד לִישִׁיבָה – The use of the future tense, *upon which he will sit,* implies that this *tumah* is contracted only by **[A UTENSIL] THAT IS RESERVED FOR SITTING** upon;[9] יָצָא זֶה – **EXCLUDED,** then, **IS THIS** kind of container, שֶׁאוֹמְרִים לוֹ עֲמוֹד וְנַעֲשֶׂה מְלַאכְתֵּנוּ – **FOR WE SAY TO [THE *ZAV*]** who is sitting upon it, **"STAND, AND LET US DO OUR WORK"** with the container!"[10]

In regard to this Baraisa the Gemara cites a dispute between R' Elazar and R' Yochanan as to when this principle is applied:

רַבִּי אֶלְעָזָר אוֹמֵר – **R' Elazar says:** בְּמִדְרָסוֹת אוֹמְרִים עֲמוֹד וְנַעֲשֶׂה מְלַאכְתֵּנוּ – **with regard to *tumos* of *midras,* we say, "Stand, and let us do our work!"**[11] וְאֵין אוֹמְרִים בְּטָמֵא מֵת עֲמוֹד וְנַעֲשֶׂה מְלַאכְתֵּנוּ – **But with respect to corpse *tumah,* we do not say, "Stand, and let us do our work";** that is, an item that has contracted corpse *tumah* does not lose its *tamei* status just because

NOTES

1. According to Rava, a bell that has had its clapper removed retains its *tumah* status as long as it can still perform a semblance of its original function (even if it cannot be repaired easily). Since the function of a bell is to produce sound, and a bell can still produce sound if struck against a pot, it remains susceptible to *tumah.* This is similar to the case of a [wooden] utensil that was punctured with a hole smaller than a pomegranate, which retains its *tumah* status (even if it was previously used to store smaller objects) because it can still be used to store pomegranates (*Rashi;* see *Keilim* 17:1 with commentaries).

Tosafos (to 58b ד״ה (אלא) אמר רבא) and *Ritva* (*MHK* ed.) point out that this reasoning would apply only to the susceptibility to *tumah* of the bell and not to that of the clapper. (Abaye's reasoning, by contrast, would apply to both the bell and the clapper.)

2. The laws concerning the *tumah* of a bell can thus be summarized as follows: (a) A bell worn by an animal is not susceptible to *tumah* if it does not have a clapper, for it is not a utensil, and an item worn by an animal cannot attain the status of an ornament with regard to contracting *tumah* (this is the law taught in the first Baraisa, on 58a). (b) A bell worn by an animal that has a clapper is susceptible to *tumah,* for the clapper renders it a utensil used by man, as it produces sound and enables the man to locate the animal (this is the law taught by the second Baraisa). (c) A bell worn by a man (e.g. a slave) is susceptible to *tumah* even if it was made with no clapper, for it is an ornament (this law is taught in the first Baraisa as well). (d) A bell worn by a child is susceptible to *tumah* only if it has a clapper, since its primary purpose is the production of sound; if such a bell has not yet had a clapper installed, it is not susceptible to *tumah,* for it is regarded as an unfinished utensil (this law appears in the third Baraisa). (e) If such a bell had a clapper, but it was removed, the bell retains its *tumah* status [see above, 58b note 22] (*Rashi*). [There is some question as to whether the bell of an animal retains its *tumah* status if its clapper is removed. *Sfas Emes* states that according to *Rashi* it would not; see, however, *Rambam* (in his commentary to *Keilim* 8:7) and *Chasam Sofer* here.]

3. The bell, being hollow, can be turned over and used as a cup.

4. R' Yochanan is of the opinion that the bell retains its *tumah* status as long as it still is useful, even if it is only useful as a cup. Rava, however, would hold that the fact that the bell can be used as a cup would not cause it to retain its *tumah* status, because it is not similar to the original sound-producing function of the bell. R' Yochanan's position will be discussed further in the Gemara below.

Tosafos note that *Rashi* below (95b) rules that an earthenware utensil retains its *tumah* status when it is fit for a secondary use only if it is *designated* for that use. But the Gemara here seems to say that the bell retains its *tumah* status because it is *fit* for use as a cup, which implies that this use is considered significant even without designation for this use! They explain that it is only in the case of the bell, which, in addition to having a secondary use, can also be easily repaired, that merely being fit for another use can be said to be sufficient to allow it to retain its *tumah* status (see also *Ritva MHK* ed.).

5. *Midras tumah* is *tumah* transmitted when a person who is *tamei* due to a bodily emission or affliction (e.g. a *zav, zavah, niddah,* or a woman who has given birth) sits or leans on a bed, chair, or other such utensil (even if the *tamei* person does not come into direct contact with the bed or chair); the utensil becomes an *av hatumah.* The verse expounded in the Baraisa is found in *Leviticus* 15:4 (*Rashi's* first and preferred explanation).

6. The word *tarkav,* which means half a *se'ah,* is a combination of the words *trei* and *kav,* interpreted as "*two* (*kavs*) plus a *kav*" (*Rashi*). [A *se'ah* equals six *kavs.*]

7. I.e. one might have thought that since the container is being used as a chair, it would become *tamei* with *midras tumah.*

8. Emendation follows *Rashi* and *Bach* (§1).

9. The verse should seemingly have stated: "Any bedding upon which the *zav* reclined . . . and any utensils upon which he sat are *tamei.*" Instead, the verse phrases the law in the future tense, stating that the *tumah* descends upon any bedding or utensils that the zav *will* recline or sit on. This teaches us that in order for a utensil to be eligible to contract *midras tumah,* it must not only be a utensil that the *zav* reclined or sat upon, but one that will also be available for him to recline or sit upon in the future (*Rashi*). This excludes a container that the *zav* happened to use for a seat, as the Gemara proceeds to explain.

10. Since the primary function of the barrel is to be used as a container, the *zav* will not always be able to sit on it, for he will be asked to rise so the barrel can fulfill its primary function. Thus, the barrel is not a utensil that the *zav will* sit upon, and the verse (as expounded here) excludes it from *midras tumah.*

[This interpretation of the Baraisa's exposition follows the first explanation of *Rashi;* see there for another explanation, which *Rashi* rejects.]

11. *Rashi* explains that with respect to *midras tumah* the rule of "Stand, and let us do our work" has two applications. The first is the one outlined in the Baraisa: A utensil cannot contract *midras tumah* unless it is reserved for sitting (or leaning etc.). The second application of this principle concerns an item that was reserved for sitting that already has contracted *midras tumah.* The rule of "Stand, and let us do our work" teaches here that if the *tamei* utensil is changed in such a way that it can no longer be used for its original function (so that no one can say concerning it, "Stand, and let us use it for its [original] work"), this suffices to *remove* it from its *tumah.* Thus, for instance, if a mat measuring 3x3 handbreadths that was reserved for sitting contracted *midras tumah,* and then it was cut in half (so that it can no longer be used for sitting), it is *tahor* from the *midras tumah,* although it can still be used for other purposes [and it can contract other types of *tumah* as long as it still measures 3 x 3 fingerbreadths] (*Rashi*). [According to *Rashi,* the principle of "Stand, and let us do our work" thus has two different meanings (see *Chidushei R' Mordechai Banet*); cf. *Tosafos* and *Rishonim* et al., who understand that the two are linked.]

הואיל וראוי להקישו על גבי חרס איתמר נמי אמר ר' יוסי בר' חנינא הואיל וראוי להקישו על גבי חרס ר' יוחנן אמר הואיל וראוי לגמע בו מים לתינוק ור' יוחנן לא בעי מעין מלאכה ראשונה (א) והתניא (א) וכל כלי אשר ישב עליו וגו' (א) יכול כפה סאה וישב עליה כפה תרקב וישב עליה יהא טמא תלמוד לומר (א) אשר ישב עליו הזב מי שמיוחד לישיבה יצא זה שאומרים לו עמוד ונעשה מלאכתנו ר' אלעזר אומר במדרסות אומרים עמוד ונעשה מלאכתנו ואין אומרים בטמא מת עמוד ונעשה מלאכתנו ור' יוחנן אמר אף אומר בטמא מת עמוד ונעשה מלאכתנו איפוך קמייתא ומאי חזית דאפכת קמייתא איפוך בתרייתא הא שמעינן ליה לרבי יוחנן דבעי מעין מלאכה ראשונה (ג) דתניא (ג) סנדל של בהמה של מתכת טמא למאי חזי אמר רב ראוי לשתות בו מים במלחמה ור' חנינא אמר ראוי לסוך בו שמן במלחמה ור' יוחנן אמר בשעה שבורח מן הקרב מניחו ברגליו ורץ על קוצין ועל הברקנים מאי בין רב לר' חנינא איכא בינייהו דמאים בין ר' יוחנן לר' חנינא איכא בינייהו דיקיר: (ב) ולא בעיר של זהב: מאי בעיר של זהב רבה בר בר חנה א"ר יוחנן ירושלים דדהבא כדעבד

רש"י

הואיל וראוי להקישו ע"ג חרס. ומשמיע קול כבתחלה ולא בטל ליה ממלאכה ראשונה והוה ליה ככלי שניקב בפחות ממוציא רימון דקיי"ל דלא טיהר מטומאתו משום דראוי למלאכתו והשתא איתרצו כולהו דבהמה טהורה בלא עינבל כדקתני במתני' קמייתא דלאו מנא הוא ובעינבל טמא כדאוקמינן בתרייתא דעינבל משוי לה מנא ודאדם גדול אף בלא עינבל טמא דלתכשיט הוא ולא בעי עינבל והיינו דקתני בקמייתא דמקבלין טומאה ודקטנים דלקלא עביד קבולי הוא דלא קביל בלא עינבל כדקתני אין להם עינבל טהורים בשלא היה לו עינבל מעולם דלא נגמרה מלאכתן (ד) נטלו עינבלין בין לפני טומאה בין לאחר טומאה טמאים דלא נשתברו כשיעור: ה"ג לה בת"כ וכל הכלי אשר ישב עליו. רישא דקרא וכל המשכב וגו' יכול כל כלי במשמע ואפי' אין עשוי לישיבה: תרקב. חצי סאה פי' תרי וקב: ת"ל אשר ישב. מדלא כתיב גבי משכב אשר שכב וגבי מושב אשר ישב וכתיב ישכב ישב משמע שישכב עליו תמיד וישב עליו תמיד במיוחד לשכיבה ולישיבה וגבי משכב נמי דריש ליה התם הכי ובכל הספרים כתיב והיושב על הכלי אשר ישב עליו וקרא אחר הוא ומפרשים אותו התלמידים מדכתיב היושב על הכלי אשר ישב עליו שתי ישיבות ריבה הכתוב ללמדך דבמיוחד לישיבה קאמר ולא היא דשתי ישיבות דקאמר טובא צריכי כדמפרש התם יושב אע"פ שלא נגע אלא ישב או נתלה ולא נגע טמא דאיצטריך למיכתב גבי זב שטימא כלי בישיבתו ואע"פ שלא נגע ואיצטריך גבי טהור נמי שנטמא גם הוא ביושבו עליו אע"פ שלא נגע ועוד בת"כ לאו אההוא קרא קתני לה: ר' אלעזר אומר במדרסות כו'. בין בתחלת טומאה לענין שאמרנו דאינו מטמא מדרס למיהוי אב הטומאה בין בסוף טומאה כגון ג' על ג' שנטמאו מדרס למיהוי אב הטומאה ונחלקו טהור מן המדרס דאמרינן בו עמוד ונעשה מלאכתנו הראשונה שהיה ראוי לישיבה והרי עתה אינו ראוי לכך הלכך טהור מן המדרס ואע"ג דאית בכל חד שלש על שלש והוי כלי לקבל טומאה מיהו מתורת אב הטומאה טיהר לו: ואין אומרים. לענין אב הטומאה של טומאת מת עמוד ונעשה מלאכתנו כלומר אם נטמא ונשבר ועודהו ראוי למלאכה בעלמא שאין מעין מלאכה ראשונה טמא ולא אמרי' עמוד ונעשה מלאכתנו ראשונה וכיון דלא חזי להכי יהא טהור וכ"ש דבתחלת טומאה אין אומרים עמוד ונעשה מלאכתנו ראשונה דנימא אם אינו מיוחד למת לא יקבל טומאת מת דהא כלי מעשה כתיב: אומר כו'. דאי לא עביד מעין מלאכה ראשונה טהור ועל כרחיך לא איתמר דר' יוחנן אלא לענין שנשבר ולטהרו כדפרישית דליכא לפרושא כי ההיא דמדרסות ולמימרא דכלי שאינו עשוי למת לא יטמא במת דהא כתיב (במדבר יט) והזה על האהל ועל כל הכלים: איפוך קמייתא. דר' יוסי בר' חנינא לר' יוחנן: סנדל של בהמה. שלא ליזוק בפרסותיה באבנים: למאי חזי. אי משום בהמה אין תכשיט לבהמה: מניחו ברגליו. הוא בעצמו אלמא הואיל ולשם סנדל עשאו אי לאו דראוי לנעילה לא הוה מטמא ליה ר' יוחנן: איכא בינייהו דמאים. לרב לא מטמא דאין ראוי לשתות ורב סיכה לית ליה קסבר אין מוליכין שמן למלחמה לסוך וה"ה בין רב (בין) לר' יוחנן נמי איכא בינייהו דמאים: בין ר' חנינא וכו' איכא בינייהו דיקיר. כבד ואין ראוי בו לברוח:

כדעבד

תוספות

פחות ממוציא רימון מקבל טומאה ועוד קשה לר"י לפי' הקונטרס דלטומאה שהיתה עליהן שלא תפרח מהני שפיר טעמא דהדיוט יכול להחזירו בלא טעמא דראוי להקישו כדאשכחן בפ' שלשה שאכלו (ברכות נ:) גבי מטה דאפי' מפורקת לא פרחה טומאה מינה אא"כ נגנבה או שאבדה חציה או שחלקוה אחים או שותפים שאין סופן לחברה ולא איצטריך כלל לטעמא דהקשה אלא לענין לקבל טומאה מכאן ולהבא דהאי טעמא הואיל והדיוט יכול להחזירו לא מהני לקבל בה טומאה כדקתני התם החזירוה מקבלת טומאה מכאן ולהבא ולאביי נמי הוה בעי למימר דמשום דהדיוט יכול להחזירו מקבלין שניהן זוג והעינבל טומאה מכאן ולהבא וריב"א הביא ראיה לפי' הקונט' דתניא בתוספתא דמסכת כלים בפ' רשב"ג העושה זוג למכתשת ולעריסה ולמטפחות תינוקות נטלו עינבליהן טהורין משמע דזגין טהורין ולפירוש הקונט' ניחא דטהורין דלא מקבלי טומאה מכאן ולהבא אבל לפר"י קשה אמאי טהורין ור"י השיב דכמה ברייתות יש בתוספתא דפליגי אש"ס שלנו: **ורבי** יוחנן אמר הואיל וראוי לגמע בו מים לתינוק. קשה לרשב"א דע"כ בלא ייחדו איירי מדקאמר הואיל וראוי משמע בראוי בעלמא אפי' בלא ייחוד ועוד דביחדו לכך לא הוה פליג ר' יוסי בר' חנינא ועוד דביחדו אפי' לא היה לו עינבל מעולם נמי מקבל טומאה ועוד אי ביחדו מיירי מאי פריך דר' יוחנן אדר' יוחנן הא התם ע"כ איירי בלא ייחדו דביחדו אפי' במדרסות נמי אין אומרים עמוד ונעשה מלאכתנו ולקמן בס"פ המצניע (דף צה: ושם) גבי ניקב כמוציא זית טהור מלקבל בו זיתים ועדיין כלי הוא לקבל בו רימונים ופי' בקונטרס אם ייחדו לרימונים ואי לאו פי' הקונט' דהתם הוה ניחא וי"ל דאפי' לפירוש הקונטרס הכא חזי טפי ע"י גימוע משום דהואיל דמעיקרא הוה כלי גמור וגם עתה הדיוט יכול להחזירו אית לן למימר דע"י דבר מועט שעדיין ראוי לגמוע בו מים חשיב כלי אפי' בלא יחוד ולמ"ד נמי הואיל וראוי להקישו דבעי מעין מלאכה ראשונה אתי שפיר בכל ענין דאפי' לא בעינן בעלמא ייחוד הכא אתי שפיר דלא מהני גמוע מים משום שעומד עדיין למלאכתו ראשונה להחזיר בו העינבל ואומר לו עמוד ונעשה מלאכתנו וכ"ש דאי בעינן בעלמא ייחוד דאתי טפי שפיר: **ואין** אומרים בטמא מת עמוד ונעשה מלאכתנו. לפירוש הקונט' קשה לר"י למה ליה לאתויי ברייתא דתרקב כיון דלא שייכא למילתיה דר' אלעזר ור' יוחנן אלא נראה לר' יצחק כפירוש ריב"א אומרים במדרסות עמוד מעל תרקב זה ונעשה מלאכתנו שאינו יכול להיות טמא מדרס ע"י שאתה יושב עליו הואיל ואינו מיוחד לכך כדקתני בברייתא ואין אומרים בטמא מת עמוד מגמוע מים בזה הזוג או בזה הסנדל של בהמה ונעשה מלאכתנו ליתן בו העינבל כדי להשמיע הקול וליתן סנדל ברגלי הבהמה אלא טמא טומאת מת על ידי הגימוע אע"פ שאינו מיוחד לכך והוי בר קבולי טומאה דחשיב כלי ע"י גימוע מים ור' יוחנן אמר אף אומר כו' דבעינן שיהא ראוי למלאכתו ראשונה ולא מהני ליה מידי לקבולי טומאה מה שראוי למלאכה אחרת אבל הקשת זוג ע"ג החרס והנחת סנדל של בהמה ברגלו כשבורח מן הקרב הוי מעין מלאכה ראשונה ולהכי הוי בר קבולי טומאה ולא שייך למימר ביה עמוד ונעשה מלאכתנו דהיינו נמי מלאכתו: **סנדל** של בהמה של מתכת. ושל עץ אינו ראוי לכל הני דברים דנפרש בסמוך דדרך הבהמה לקלקלו ורבינו שמואל גריס סנדל של בהמה ושל מתכת ומיירי בסנדל של סיידין דלקמן (סו.): **הואיל** וראוי לשתות בו מים במלחמה. וא"ת והא בזוג שלא היה בו עינבל מעולם לא מטמינן משום דחזי לגמוע והכא חשוב כמו זוג שלא היה בו עינבל מעולם דכיון דנעשה לצורך בהמה אינו מקבל טומאה וי"ל דתחלתו נמי עשוי לשתות בו מים במלחמה או לסוך אלא שעיקרו עומד לבהמה ואומר לו עמוד ונעשה מלאכתנו למאן דבעי מעין במלאכה ראשונה: **בשעה** שבורח מן הקרב מניחו ברגליו. תימה א"כ יטמא מדרס ותניא בתוספתא דכלים פרק כיפה ג' סנדלים הם של אדם טמא מדרס של מתכת ושל בהמה טמא טומאת מת משמע אבל מן המדרס טהור: (ה) **ולא** בעיר של זהב. אור"ת דלאו היינו נושקא כדפי' בקונט' דהא אמרי' בפרק בתרא דסוטה (דף מט:) מאי עטרות כלות עיר של זהב משמע דעשוי הוא כעין עטרה ואע"ג דאמרי' התם בפולמוס של טיטוס גזרו על עטרות חתנים וכלות והכא לא אסרו אלא בשבת אור"ת דדוקא לחתנים וכלות גזרו ולא לשאר בני אדם(ו):

מאן

עין משפט נר מצוה

כ א מיי' פ"ז מהל' משכב ומושב הלכה ח:

כא ב מיי' פי"ט מהל' שבת הלכה ו סמג לאוין סה טור וש"ע א"ח סי' שג סעיף ד:

רבינו חננאל

רבא הואיל וראוי להקישו התינוק ע"ג חרס ולהשמיע קול. ר' יוחנן אמר הואיל וראוי לגמע בו מים לתינוק עדיין תורת כלי עליהן ולפיכך עדיין טומאתו עליהן ואקשינן וכי ר' יוחנן לא בעי (שישא) [שיהא] בכלי המשמש מעין מלאכתו [והתניא] והיושב על הכלי אשר ישב עליו הזב יטמא יכול כפה סאה וישב עליה כפה כו' עד ור' יוחנן אמר בטומאת מת עמוד ונעשה מלאכתנו הנה בפי' ר' יוחנן אמר כי אין הכלי מקבל טומאה אלא אם הוא ראוי למלאכתו שנעשה בו ואפיך קמייתא ואימא ר' יוחנן אמר הואיל וראוי להקישו ע"ג חרס משום דשמעינן ליה לר' יוחנן בהדיא דבעי מעין מלאכתו ראשונה דתניא סנדל של מתכת של בהמה טמא ואמרינן למאי חזית [רב] אמר חזי לשתות מים. ר' חנינא אמר ראוי לסוך בו שמן ר' יוחנן [אמר] ראוי להניחו ברגליו כשבורח ורץ על הקוצי' ועל הברקנים הנה שמענו לר' יוחנן דבעי מעין מלאכתו ראשונה כשם שמתחלה למנעל הרגל כך באחרונה: מתניתין ולא תצא אשה בעיר של זהב. מאי עיר של זהב. ירושלים דדהבא

רב נסים גאון

מאי עיר של זהב אמר רבה בר בר חנה אמר ר' יוחנן ירושלים דדהבא כי דעביד לה (ר' יוחנן) [ר"ע] לדביתהו תמצא במס' נדרים בפרק הנודר מן המבושל (ד' נ) ר' עקיבא איקדשא ליה ברתיה דבר כלבא שבוע שמע אבוהא אדרא הנאה מכל נכסיה אזלא ואיתנסיבא ליה בסיתוא הוה גנו בי תיבנא הוה מנקיט לה תיבנא מן מזייה אמר לה אי הואי לי רמינא ליך ירושלם דדהבא והזכירו אחר כך שהגיע לעושר גדול כמו שאמרו מן ו' מילי איעתר ר' עקיבא ולאחר שהגיעה ידו שילם לה נדרו ועשה לה ירושלם דדהבא ובגמ' דהדין פירקא דבני מערבא אמרי מעשה ברבי עקיבא שעשה לאשתו עיר של זהב חמתה איתתיה דרבן גמליאל וקניאת בה אתת ואמרה קמי בעלה אמר לה מה הוית עבדא לי כמה דהוות עבדא ליה דהוות מזבנא מן קלעיתה דשערה ויהיבא ליה והוא לעי באורייתא:

מסורת הש"ס

א) חגיגה כג: נדה מט:, ב) [נ"ל דתנן], ג) [כלים פי"ד מ"ה], ד) נטלו עינבלין אחרי טומאתן טמאין דלא כצ"ל רש"ל, ה) [שייך במשנה דלעיל נז.], ו) [מפני שיש להן שמחה בכן ועי' תוס' גיטין ז. ד"ה עטרות].

הגהות הב"ח

(א) גמ' תלמוד לומר וכל הכלי אשר ישב:

תורה אור השלם

א) כָּל הַמִּשְׁכָּב אֲשֶׁר יִשְׁכַּב עָלָיו הַזָּב יִטְמָא וְכָל הַכְּלִי אֲשֶׁר יֵשֵׁב עָלָיו יִטְמָא: [ויקרא טו, ד]

ליקוטי רש"י

תרקב. חצי סאה תרי וקב דהיינו שלש קבין שהן חצי סאה [ערכין כה.]. ת"ל אשר ישב עליו. יֵשֵׁב לא נאמר אלא אשר יֵשֵׁב עליו הזב במיוחד תמיד לכך [ויקרא טו, ד]. מדלא קרינן אשר יָשַׁב למדנו שאינו מדבר אלא באשר מיוחד לישב שם תמיד [חגיגה כג:]. מי שמיוחד לישיבה. הוא דהוי אב הטומאה דכתיב וכבס בגדיו וגו'. יצא זה. סאה ותרקב שאין מדרס הזב לטמא אדם וכלים אבל טמאין הם טומאת מגע הזב להיות ראשונים וכמת נעשין אב הטומאה [נדה מט:]. ירושלים דדהבא. ירושלים של זהב כמין נפש שמצויירת בכל ענייני ירושלים [נדרים נ.]. תכשיט של זהב שירושלים מצוייר בה [ר"ן שם].

it is no longer usable for its original function, as long as it still has a valid function as a utensil.[12] **וְרַבִּי יוֹחָנָן אָמַר – But R' Yochanan said: אַף אוֹמֵר בְּטְמֵא מֵת עֲמוֹד וְנַעֲשֶׂה מְלַאכְתֵּנוּ – Even with respect to corpse *tumah*, we say, "Stand, and let us do our work."**[13] We see from this that according to R' Yochanan, corpse *tumah* can be removed if an item is changed so that it can no longer be used for its original function.[14] Why, then, did R' Yochanan rule above that a bell that had its clapper removed is still *tamei* because it can be used as a cup? Seemingly, it should be *tahor* because it cannot be used for its original function![15] – ? –

The Gemara concedes the point, and responds:

אֵיפוּךְ קַמַּיְיתָא – Reverse the attributions of **the first** rulings, which were cited with respect to a bell, and cite R' Yochanan as ruling that a bell retains its *tumah* status when its clapper is removed because it can still produce sound when struck against an earthenware pot.[16]

The Gemara asks:

וּמַאי חֲזֵית דְּאַפַּכְתְּ קַמַּיְיתָא – But what did you see that made **you** decide to **reverse the first** ruling of R' Yochanan? **אֵיפוּךְ בַּתְרַיְיתָא** – Perhaps you should **reverse the last** ruling of R' Yochanan that was cited in regard to the Baraisa![17]

The Gemara replies:

הָא שַׁמְעִינַן לֵיהּ לְרַבִּי יוֹחָנָן דְּבָעֵי מֵעֵין מְלָאכָה רִאשׁוֹנָה – We prefer to reverse the first ruling of R' Yochanan, for **we have learned concerning R' Yochanan that he requires** that a utensil be usable for a **semblance of its original function** in order for it to retain its *tumah* status.[18] **דְּתַנְיָא – For we have learned in a Mishnah:**[19] **סַנְדָּל שֶׁל בְּהֵמָה שֶׁל מַתֶּכֶת טָמֵא – THE METAL SHOE OF AN ANIMAL**[20] **IS SUSCEPTIBLE TO TUMAH.**[21] **לְמַאי חֲזֵי** – And the question was raised: **For what** use **is [such a shoe] fit?**[22] **אָמַר רַב – Rava said: רָאוּי לִשְׁתּוֹת בּוֹ מַיִם בְּמִלְחָמָה – It is fit to drink water with it during war.**[23] **וְרַבִּי חֲנִינָא אָמַר – And R' Chanina said: רָאוּי לָסוּךְ בּוֹ שֶׁמֶן בְּמִלְחָמָה – It is fit to anoint oil with it during war.**[24] **וְרַבִּי יוֹחָנָן אָמַר – But R' Yochanan** said: **בְּשָׁעָה שֶׁבּוֹרֵחַ מִן הַקְּרָב** – These shoes are susceptible to *tumah* due to the fact that, **when [a person] flees from battle, מַנִּיחוֹ בְּרַגְלָיו – he places [them] on his feet, וְרָץ עַל קוֹצִין וְעַל הַבַּרְקָנִים – and** he is then able to **run over thorns and thistles.**[25] We see from this statement that R' Yochanan deems the shoe susceptible

NOTES

12. I.e. the *second* application of the principle (as outlined in the previous note) cannot be applied to items that have contracted corpse *tumah;* rather, the corpse *tumah* remains in force as long as the utensil can be used in any fashion (*Rashi*). [It goes without saying that the *first* application of the principle of "Stand, and let us do our work" cannot be applied to corpse *tumah,* for that would mean that corpse *tumah* could not be contracted except by utensils that were reserved for the corpse – a conclusion which is clearly untenable, as the Torah states (*Numbers* 31:51) that corpse *tumah* devolves upon any utensil that has a function (see *Rashi*).]

13. R' Yochanan disagrees with R' Elazar, and maintains that even corpse *tumah* may be removed if a utensil is changed so that it is no longer usable for its primary function. [This is the second application of the rule of "Stand, and let us do our work," as explained above.] However, even R' Yochanan concedes that this rule cannot limit the contracting of corpse *tumah* to utensils reserved for the corpse, as the verse clearly states (*Numbers* 19:18) concerning corpse *tumah*: *and he shall sprinkle* (the *mei chatas*) *upon the tent and upon all the vessels,* which implies that *all* vessels found in the tent require purification. [See *Rashash,* who wonders why *Rashi* did not cite *Numbers* 31:51, the verse that he cited before (see previous note) to prove that any utensil that has a function can contract corpse *tumah* (and see *Rashi* to 84a ד״ה טמאה, where he cites a *third* verse!).]

14. For this is the law that results from the application of the rule of "Stand, and let us do our work" to the laws of corpse *tumah,* as explained above (note 13).

15. For, as explained, R' Yochanan is of the opinion that a *tamei* item can become *tahor* if it is changed in a way that renders it unusable for its original function.

[*Tosafos* note that according to the explanation of the Gemara advanced by *Rashi,* R' Yochanan and R' Elazar only dispute the question of whether the *second* application of the rule of "Stand, and let us do our work" can be applied to the laws of corpse *tumah;* they both agree that the *first* application cannot be applied to those laws. Why, then, ask *Tosafos,* does the Gemara cite the Baraisa concerning the case of a *zav* who sits upon a barrel to introduce their dispute? This is an instance of the *first* application of the rule (see above, note 11), and both R' Yochanan and R' Elazar agree that this application is not relevant to the laws of corpse *tumah*! *Tosafos* therefore interpret the dispute between R' Elazar and R' Yochanan differently; according to their interpretation, the two applications of the principle of "Stand, and let us do our work" are interdependent (as mentioned above, note 11), and thus, the citation of the Baraisa as an introduction of the dispute does not pose a difficulty. See there.]

16. Thus, the two rulings of R' Yochanan both teach that a *tamei* item retains its *tumah* status only as long as it can be used for its primary purpose. [According to the reversed attributions, R' Yose the son of R' Chanina would hold that the bell retains its *tumah* status as long as it is usable for any function.]

17. I.e perhaps the rulings of R' Elazar and R' Yochanan should be reversed, and it is R' Yochanan who *is* consistently of the opinion that a *tamei* item remains *tamei* as long as it can be used for *any* function.

18. Thus, to conform to all of the rulings of R' Yochanan, we must reverse the attributions of the rulings cited regarding bells; for there are *two* rulings of R' Yochanan that indicate that he is of the opinion that a utensil retains its *tumah* status only if it can be used for a semblance of its original function (and we would sooner reverse one ruling than two).

19. *Keilim* 14:5. [The marginal gloss emends דְּתַנְיָא to read דְּתְנַן.]

20. I.e. a [removable] shoe worn by an animal so its hoofs will not be damaged by the stones upon which it walks (*Rashi*). [Unlike horseshoes, the shoes spoken of here were cup shaped, as is evident from the Gemara which follows.]

[*Tosafos* cites a variant text which cites the Mishnah as speaking of two cases – the shoe of an animal, or the metal shoe of a seller of lime. See also *Rashash.*]

21. The Gemara will presently explain why this is so.

22. As mentioned above, an item worn by an animal cannot contract *tumah* as an ornament (*Rashi*); nor can it be classified as the animal's clothing. An item that serves an animal can contract *tumah* only if it serves man as well – see above, 52b, and see *Mishnah Acharonah* to *Keilim* 14:5 ד״ה של מתכת.

23. Rav is of the opinion that a secondary use of a utensil is sufficient to accord it the status of a utensil that is susceptible to *tumah* even if that use does not resemble the primary use of that utensil. Thus, although the shoe is not usually used as a cup, it can contract *tumah* because it is occasionally used for that purpose.

[It does not follow from this ruling that any utensil of an animal that can sometimes be used by man will contract *tumah* (or that a bell that never had a clapper should contract *tumah* because it can be used as a cup); the case of the animal's metal shoe is different, since it is *originally made* with the intent that it will sometimes incidentally be used as a cup (see *Tosafos* and *Tos. HaRosh*).]

24. Rav, however, is of the opinion that since oil for anointing is not usually available during wartime, such a use will not classify the animal's shoe as a utensil (*Rashi* ד״ה איכא).

[R' Chanina concurs with Rav that a secondary use of the utensil need not resemble its primary use in order for the utensil to retain its *tumah* status.]

25. *Tosafos* wonder why such a shoe should not be susceptible to *midras tumah* (and *Tosefta* to *Bava Basra* 2:4 clearly states that it is not), since it is used as a shoe by men! They offer no resolution; see, however, *Ben Uri* and *Hagahos R' Elazar Moshe Horowitz;* see also *Maginei Shlomo.*

הואיל וראוי להקישו על גבי חרס איתמר נמי אמר ר' יוסי בר' חנינא הואיל וראוי להקישו על גבי חרס ר' יוחנן אמר הואיל וראוי לגמע בו מים לתינוק ור' יוחנן לא בעי מעין מלאכה ראשונה (א) והתניא (א) וכל כלי אשר ישב עליו וגו' (א) יכול כפה סאה וישב עליה כפה תרקב וישב עליה יהא טמא תלמוד לומר (א) אשר ישב עליו הזב מי שמיוחד לישיבה יצא זה שאומרים לו עמוד ונעשה מלאכתנו ר' אלעזר אומר במדרסות אומרים עמוד ונעשה מלאכתנו ואין אומרים בטמא מת עמוד ונעשה מלאכתנו ור' יוחנן אמר אף אומר בטמא מת עמוד ונעשה מלאכתנו איפוך קמייתא ומאי חזית דאפכת קמייתא איפוך בתרייתא הא שמעינן ליה לרבי יוחנן דבעי מעין מלאכה ראשונה (ג) דתניא (ג) סנדל של בהמה של מתכת טמא למאי חזי אמר רב ראוי לשתות בו מים במלחמה ור' חנינא אמר ראוי לסוך בו שמן במלחמה ור' יוחנן אמר בשעה שבורח מן הקרב מניחו ברגליו ורץ על קוצין ועל הברקנים מאי בין רב לר' חנינא איכא בינייהו דמאים בין ר' יוחנן לר' חנינא איכא בינייהו דיקיר: (ב) ולא בעיר של זהב: מאי בעיר של זהב רבה בר בר חנה א"ר יוחנן ירושלים דדהבא כדעבד

רש"י

הואיל וראוי להקישו ע"ג חרס. ומשמיע קול כבתחלה ולא בטל ליה ממלאכה ראשונה והוה ליה ככלי שניקב בפחות ממוציא רימון דקיי"ל דלא טיהר מטומאתו משום דראוי למלאכתו והשתא איתרצו כולהו דבהמה טהורה בלא עינבל כדקתני במתני' קמייתא דלאו מנא הוא ובעינבל טמא כדאוקמינן בבתרייתא דעינבל משוי לה מנא ודאדם גדול אף בלא עינבל טמא דלתכשיט הוא ולא בעי עינבל והיינו דקתני בקמייתא דמקבלין טומאה ודקטנים דלקלא עביד קבולי הוא דלא קביל בלא עינבל כדקתני אין להם עינבל טהורים בשלא היה לו עינבל מעולם דלא נגמרה מלאכתן (ד) נטלו עינבלין בין לפני טומאה בין לאחר טומאה טמאים דלא נשתברו כשיעור: ה"ג לה בת"כ וכל הכלי אשר ישב עליו. רישא דקרא וכל המשכב וגו' יכול כל כלי במשמע ואפי' אין עשוי לישיבה: תרקב. חצי סאה פי' תרי וקב: ת"ל אשר ישב. מדלא כתיב גבי משכב אשר שכב וגבי מושב אשר ישב וכתיב ישכב ישב משמע שישכב עליו תמיד וישב עליו תמיד במיוחד לשכיבה ולישיבה וגבי משכב נמי דריש ליה התם הכי ובכל הספרים כתיב והיושב על הכלי אשר ישב עליו וקרא אחר הוא ומפרשים אותו התלמידים מדכתיב היושב על הכלי אשר ישב עליו שתי ישיבות ריבה הכתוב ללמדך דבמיוחד לישיבה קאמר ולא היא דשתי ישיבות דקאמר טובא צריכי כדמפרש התם יושב אע"פ שלא נגע אלא ישב או נתלה ולא נגע טמא דאיצטריך למיכתב גבי זב שטימא כלי בישיבתו ואע"פ שלא נגע ואיצטריך גבי טהור נמי שנטמא גם הוא ביושבו עליו אע"פ שלא נגע ועוד בת"כ לאו אההוא קרא קתני לה: ר' אלעזר אומר במדרסות כו'. בין בתחלת טומאה לענין שאמרנו דאינו מטמא מדרס למיהוי אב הטומאה בין בסוף טומאה כגון ג' על ג' שנטמאו מדרס למיהוי אב הטומאה ונחלקו טהור מן המדרס דאמרינן בו עמוד ונעשה מלאכתנו הראשונה שהיה ראוי לישיבה והרי עתה אינו ראוי לכך הלכך טהור מן המדרס ואע"ג דאית בכל חד שלש על שלש והוי כלי לקבל טומאה מיהו מתורת אב הטומאה טיהר לו: ואין אומרים. לענין אב הטומאה של טומאת מת עמוד ונעשה מלאכתנו כלומר אם נטמא ונשבר ועודהו ראוי למלאכה בעלמא שאין מעין מלאכה ראשונה טמא ולא אמרי' עמוד ונעשה מלאכתנו ראשונה וכיון דלא חזי להכי יהא טהור וכ"ש דבתחלת טומאה אין אומרים עמוד ונעשה מלאכתנו ראשונה דנימא אם אינו מיוחד למת לא יקבל טומאת מת דהא כלי מעשה כתיב: אומר כו'. דאי לא עביד מעין מלאכה ראשונה טהור ועל כרחיך לא איתמר דר' יוחנן אלא לענין שנשבר ולטהרו כדפרישית דליכא לפרושא כי ההיא דמדרסות ולמימרא דכלי שאינו עשוי למת לא יטמא במת דהא כתיב (במדבר יט) והזה על האהל ועל כל הכלים: איפוך קמייתא. דר' יוסי בר' חנינא לר' יוחנן: סנדל של בהמה. שלא ליזוק בפרסותיה באבנים: למאי חזי. אי משום בהמה אין תכשיט לבהמה: מניחו ברגליו. הוא בעצמו אלמא הואיל ולשם סנדל עשאו אי לאו דראוי לנעילה לא הוה מטמא ליה ר' יוחנן: איכא בינייהו דמאים. לרב לא מטמא דאין ראוי לשתות ורב סיכה לית ליה קסבר אין מוליכין שמן למלחמה לסוך וה"ה בין רב (בין) לר' יוחנן נמי איכא בינייהו דמאים: בין ר' חנינא וכו' איכא בינייהו דיקיר. כבד ואין ראוי בו לברוח:

תוספות

פחות ממוציא רימון מקבל טומאה ועוד קשה לר"י לפי' הקונטרס דלטומאה שהיתה עליהן שלא תפרח מהני שפיר טעמא דהדיוט יכול להחזירו בלא טעמא דראוי להקישו כדאשכחן בפ' שלשה שאכלו (ברכות נ:) גבי מטה דאפי' מפורקת לא פרחה טומאה מינה אא"כ נגנבה או שאבדה חציה או שחלקוה אחים או שותפים שאין סופן לחברה ולא איצטריך כלל לטעמא דהקשה אלא לענין לקבל טומאה מכאן ולהבא דהאי טעמא הואיל והדיוט יכול להחזירו לא מהני לקבל בה טומאה כדקתני התם החזירוה מקבלת טומאה מכאן ולהבא ולאביי נמי הוה בעי למימר דמשום דהדיוט יכול להחזירו מקבלין שניהן זוג והעינבל טומאה מכאן ולהבא וריצב"א הביא ראיה לפי' הקונט' דתניא בתוספתא דמסכת כלים בפ' רשב"ג העושה זוג למכתשת ולעריסה ולמטפחות תינוקות ניטלו עינבליהן טהורין משמע דזגין טהורין ולפירוש הקונט' ניחא דטהורין דלא מקבלי טומאה מכאן ולהבא אבל לפר"י קשה אמאי טהורין ור"י השיב דכמה ברייתות יש בתוספתא דפליגי אש"ס שלנו: **ורבי** יוחנן אמר הואיל וראוי לגמע בו מים לתינוק. קשה לרשב"א דע"כ בלא ייחדו איירי מדקאמר הואיל וראוי משמע בראוי בעלמא אפי' בלא ייחוד ועוד דביחדו לכך לא הוה פליג ר' יוסי בר' חנינא ועוד דביחדו אפי' לא היה לו עינבל מעולם נמי מקבל טומאה ועוד אי ביחדו איירי מאי פריך דר' יוחנן אדר' יוחנן הא התם ע"כ איירי בלא ייחדו דביחדו אפי' במדרסות נמי אין אומרים עמוד ונעשה מלאכתנו ולקמן בס"פ המצניע (דף צה: ושם) גבי ניקב כמוציא זית טהור מלקבל בו זיתים ועדיין כלי הוא לקבל בו רימונים ופי' בקונטרס אם ייחדו לרימונים ואי לאו פי' הקונט' דהתם הוה ניחא וי"ל דאפי' לפירוש הקונטרס הכא חזי טפי ע"י גימוע משום דהואיל דמעיקרא הוה כלי גמור וגם עתה הדיוט יכול להחזירו אית לן למימר דע"י דבר מועט שעדיין ראוי לגמוע בו מים חשיב כלי אפי' בלא ייחוד ולמ"ד נמי הואיל וראוי להקישו דבעי מעין מלאכה ראשונה אתי שפיר בכל ענין דאפי' לא בעינן בעלמא ייחוד הכא אתי שפיר דלא מהני גמוע מים משום שעומד עדיין למלאכתו ראשונה להחזיר בו העינבל ואומר לו עמוד ונעשה מלאכתנו וכ"ש דאי בעינן בעלמא ייחוד דאתי טפי שפיר: **ואין** אומרים בטמא מת עמוד ונעשה מלאכתנו. לפירוש הקונט' קשה לר"י למה ליה לאתויי ברייתא דתרקב כיון דלא שייכא למילתיה דר' אלעזר ור' יוחנן אלא נראה לר' יצחק כפירוש ריב"א אומרים במדרסות עמוד מעל תרקב זה ונעשה מלאכתנו שאינו יכול להיות טמא מדרס ע"י שאתה יושב עליו הואיל ואינו מיוחד לכך כדקתני בברייתא ואין אומרים בטמא מת עמוד מגמוע מים בזה הזוג או בזה הסנדל של בהמה ונעשה מלאכתנו ליתן בו העינבל כדי להשמיע הקול וליתן סנדל ברגלי הבהמה אלא טמא טומאת מת על ידי הגימוע אע"פ שאינו מיוחד לכך והוי בר קבולי טומאה דחשיב כלי ע"י גימוע מים ור' יוחנן אמר אף אומר כו' דבעינן שיהא ראוי למלאכתו ראשונה ולא מהני ליה מידי לקבולי טומאה מה שראוי למלאכה אחרת אבל הקשת זוג ע"ג החרס והנחת סנדל של בהמה ברגלו כשבורח מן הקרב הוי מעין מלאכה ראשונה ולהכי הוי בר קבולי טומאה ולא שייך למימר ביה עמוד ונעשה מלאכתנו דהיינו נמי מלאכתו: **סנדל** של בהמה של מתכת. ושל עץ אינו ראוי לכל הני דברים דמפרש בסמוך דדרך הבהמה לקלקלו ורבינו שמואל גרים סנדל של בהמה ושל מתכת ומיירי בסנדל של סיידין דלקמן (ס.): **הואיל** וראוי לשתות בו מים במלחמה. וא"ת והא בזוג שלא היה בו עינבל מעולם לא מטמינן משום דחזי לגמוע והכא חשוב כמו זוג שלא היה בו עינבל מעולם דכיון דנעשה לצורך בהמה אינו מקבל טומאה וי"ל דתחלתו נמי עשוי לשתות בו מים במלחמה או לסוך אלא שעיקרו עומד לבהמה ואומר לו עמוד ונעשה מלאכתנו למאן דבעי מעין במלאכה ראשונה: **בשעה** שבורח מן הקרב מניחו ברגליו. תימה א"כ יטמא מדרס ותניא בתוספתא דכלים פרק כיפה ג' סנדלים הם של אדם טמא מדרס של מתכת ושל בהמה טמא טומאת מת משמע אבל מן המדרס טהור: (ה) **ולא** בעיר של זהב. אור"ת דלאו היינו נושקא כדפי' בקונט' דהא אמרי' בפרק בתרא דסוטה (דף מט:) מאי עטרות כלות עיר של זהב משמע דעשוי הוא כעין עטרה ואע"ג דאמרי' התם בפולמוס של טיטוס גזרו על עטרות חתנים וכלות והכא לא אסרו אלא בשבת אור"ת דדוקא לחתנים וכלות גזרו ולא לשאר בני אדם (ו):

מאן

עין משפט נר מצוה

כ א מיי' פ"ז מהל' משכב ומושב הלכה ח:

כא ב מיי' פי"ט מהל' שבת הלכה ו סמג לאוין סה טור וש"ע א"ח סי' שג סעיף ד:

רבינו חננאל

רבא הואיל וראוי להקישו התינוק ע"ג חרס ולהשמיע קול. ר' יוחנן אמר הואיל וראוי לגמע בו מים לתינוק עדיין תורת כלי עליהן ולפיכך עדיין טומאתו עליהן ואקשינן וכי ר' יוחנן לא בעי (שישא) [שיהא] בכלי המשמש מעין מלאכתו [והתניא] והיושב על הכלי אשר ישב עליו הזב יטמא יכול כפה סאה וישב עליה כפה כו' עד ור' יוחנן אמר בטומאת מת עמוד ונעשה מלאכתנו הנה בפי' ר' יוחנן אמר כי אין הכלי מקבל טומאה אלא אם הוא ראוי למלאכתו שנעשה בו ואפיך קמייתא ואימא ר' יוחנן אמר הואיל וראוי להקישו ע"ג חרס משום דשמעינן ליה לר' יוחנן בהדיא דבעי מעין מלאכתו ראשונה דתניא סנדל של מתכת של בהמה טמא ואמרינן למאי חזית [רב] אמר חזי לשתות מים. ר' חנינא אמר ראוי לסוך בו שמן ר' יוחנן [אמר] ראוי להניחו ברגליו כשבורח ורץ על הקוצי' ועל הברקנים הנה שמענו לר' יוחנן דבעי מעין מלאכתו ראשונה כשם שמתחלה למנעל הרגל כך באחרונה: מתניתין ולא תצא אשה בעיר של זהב. מאי עיר של זהב. ירושלים דדהבא

רב נסים גאון

מאי עיר של זהב אמר רבה בר בר חנה אמר ר' יוחנן ירושלים דדהבא כי דעביד לה (ר' יוחנן) [ר"ע] לדביתהו תמצא במס' נדרים בפרק הנודר מן המבושל (ד' נ) ר' עקיבא איקדשא ליה ברתיה דבר כלבא שבוע שמע אבוהא אדרא הנאה מכל נכסיה אזלא ואיתנסיבא ליה בסיתוא הוה גנו בי תיבנא הוה מנקיט לה תיבנא מן מזייה אמר לה אי הואי לי רמינא ליך ירושלם דדהבא והזכירו אחר כך שהגיע לעושר גדול כמו שאמרו מן ו' מילי איעתר ר' עקיבא ולאחר שהגיעה ידו שילם לה נדרו ועשה לה ירושלם דדהבא ובגמ' דהדין פירקא דבני מערבא אמרי מעשה ברבי עקיבא שעשה לאשתו עיר של זהב חמתה איתתיה דרבן גמליאל וקניאת בה אתת ואמרה קמי בעלה אמר לה מה הוית עבדא לי כמה דהוות עבדא ליה דהות מזבנא מן קלעיתה דשערה ויהיבא ליה והוא לעי באורייתא:

מסורת הש"ס

א) חגיגה כג: נדה מט:, ב) [צ"ל דתנן], ג) [כלים פי"ד מ"ה], ד) נטלו עינבלין אחרי טומאתן טמאין דלא כצ"ל רש"ל, ה) [שייך במשנה דלעיל נז.], ו) [מפני שיש להן שמחה בהן ועי' תוס' גיטין ז. ד"ה עטרות].

הגהות הב"ח

(א) גמ' תלמוד לומר וכל הכלי אשר ישב:

תורה אור השלם

א) כָּל הַמִּשְׁכָּב אֲשֶׁר יִשְׁכַּב עָלָיו הַזָּב יִטְמָא וְכָל הַכְּלִי אֲשֶׁר יֵשֵׁב עָלָיו יִטְמָא: [ויקרא טו, ד]

ליקוטי רש"י

תרקב. חצי סאה תרי וקב דהיינו שלש קבין שהן חצי סאה [ערכין כה.]. ת"ל אשר ישב עליו. ישב לא נאמר אלא אשר ישב עליו הזב במיוחד תמיד לכך [ויקרא טו, ד]. מדלא קרינן אשר ישב למדנו שאינו מדבר אלא באשר מיוחד לישב שם תמיד [חגיגה כג:]. מי שמיוחד לישיבה. הוא דהוו אב הטומאה דכתיב וכבס בגדיו וגו'. יצא זה. סאה ותרקב שאין מדרס הזב לטמא אדם וכלים אבל טמאין הם טומאת מגע הזב להיות ראשונים וכמת נעשין אב הטומאה [נדה מט:]. ירושלים דדהבא. ירושלים של זהב כמין נפש שמצויירת בכל ענייני ירושלים [נדרים נ.]. תכשיט של זהב שירושלים מצוייר בה [ר"ן שם].

to *tumah* only if it can be used in a manner resembling its regular function.[26] Accordingly, when faced with a discrepancy in R' Yochanan's position, the Gemara prefers to reverse the single ruling that does not conform rather than having to reverse two rulings.

The Gemara seeks a practical difference between the three reasons given for the *tumah* of an animal's metal shoe:

מַאי בֵּין רַב לְרַבִּי חֲנִינָא – **What is** the practical difference **between** the reason of **Rav and** that of **R' Chanina?** אִיכָּא בֵּינַיְיהוּ דְּמָאִיס – **There is** a practical difference **between them where [the shoe] is repulsive.**[27] According to Rav, it would not be susceptible to *tumah,* while according to R' Chanina it would be susceptible.[28] And what difference is there **between R' Yochanan and R' Chanina?**[29] בֵּין רַבִּי יוֹחָנָן לְרַבִּי חֲנִינָא אִיכָּא בֵּינַיְיהוּ דְּיַקִּיר – **There is** a practical difference **between them where [the shoe] is heavy,** and it cannot be used while fleeing. According to R' Chanina, the shoe is susceptible to *tumah,* while according to R' Yochanan it is not.

The Mishnah stated:

וְלֹא בְּעִיר שֶׁל זָהָב – AND a woman may NOT go out WITH A CITY OF GOLD.

The Gemara asks:

מַאי בְּעִיר שֶׁל זָהָב – **What** does the Mishnah mean when it says WITH A CITY OF GOLD? רַבָּה בַּר בַּר חָנָה אָמַר רַבִּי יוֹחָנָן – **Rabbah bar bar Chanah said in the name of R' Yochanan:** יְרוּשְׁלַיִם דְּדַהֲבָא – The Mishnah refers to **a golden** ornament engraved with a likeness **of** the city of **Jerusalem,**

NOTES

26. Although the rulings of R' Yochanan are not exactly identical – e.g. his ruling concerning the bell states that an item does not retain its *tumah* status unless it can be used for a semblance of its original use, and his ruling regarding an animal's shoe states that an item cannot be deemed susceptible to *tumah* on account of a secondary use unless that use resembles its primary use – the Gemara nevertheless sees them as two different ramifications of the same basic rule: A secondary use of an item cannot be accorded the same significance as that item's primary usage unless the secondary usage is similar to the primary usage (see *Ritva MHK* ed.).

27. E.g. it became soiled, so that one would not drink from it.

28. Even if the shoe is soiled, it can still be used to spread oil over one's body; thus, according to R' Chanina the shoe would be susceptible to *tumah. Rashi* notes that according to Rav Yochanan, too, such a shoe would be susceptible to *tumah* [for it is normal for a man to wear even a soiled shoe when fleeing battle].

29. Both of these Tannaim agree that a soiled shoe would be susceptible to *tumah.* What is the case where their views diverge?

הואיל וראוי להקישו על גבי חרס איתמר נמי אמר ר' יוסי בר' חנינא הואיל וראוי להקישו על גבי חרס ר' יוחנן אמר הואיל וראוי לגמע בו מים לתינוק ור' יוחנן לא בעי מעין מלאכה ראשונה (א) והתניא (א) וכל כלי אשר ישב עליו וגו' (א) יכול כפה סאה וישב עליה כפה תרקב וישב עליה יהא טמא תלמוד לומר (א) אשר ישב עליו הזב מי שמיוחד לישיבה יצא זה שאומרים לו עמוד ונעשה מלאכתנו ר' אלעזר אומר במדרסות אומרים עמוד ונעשה מלאכתנו ואין אומרים בטמא מת עמוד ונעשה מלאכתנו ור' יוחנן אמר אף אומר בטמא מת עמוד ונעשה מלאכתנו איפוך קמייתא ומאי חזית דאפכת קמייתא איפוך בתרייתא הא שמעינן ליה לרבי יוחנן דבעי מעין מלאכה ראשונה (ג) דתניא (ג) סנדל של בהמה של מתכת טמא למאי חזי אמר רב ראוי לשתות בו מים במלחמה ור' חנינא אמר ראוי לסוך בו שמן במלחמה ור' יוחנן אמר בשעה שבורח מן הקרב מניחו ברגליו ורץ על קוצין ועל הברקנים מאי בין רב לר' חנינא איכא בינייהו דמאים בין ר' יוחנן לר' חנינא איכא בינייהו דיקיר: (ב) ולא בעיר של זהב: מאי בעיר של זהב רבה בר בר חנה א"ר יוחנן ירושלים דדהבא כדעבד

רש"י

הואיל וראוי להקישו ע"ג חרס. ומשמיע קול כבתחלה ולא בטל ליה ממלאכה ראשונה והוה ליה ככלי שניקב בפחות ממוציא רימון דקי"ל דלא טיהר מטומאתו משום דראוי למלאכתו והשתא איתרלו כולהו דבהמה טהורה בלא עינבל כדקתני במתני' קמייתא דלאו מנא הוא ובעינבל טמא כדאוקמינן בבתרייתא דעינבל משוי לה מנא ודאדם גדול אף בלא עינבל טמא דלתכשיט הוא ולא בעי עינבל והיינו דקתני בקמייתא דמקבלין טומאה ודקטנים דלקלא עביד קבולי הוא דלא קביל בלא עינבל כדקתני אין להם עינבל טהורים בשלא היה לו עינבל מעולם דלא נגמרה מלאכתן (ד) נטלו עינבלין בין לפני טומאה בין לאחר טומאה טמאים דלא נשתברו כשיעור: ה"ג לה בת"כ וכל הכלי אשר ישב עליו. רישא דקרא וכל המשכב וגו' יכול כל כלי במשמע ואפי' אין עשוי לישיבה: תרקב. חצי סאה פי' תרי וקב: ת"ל אשר ישב. מדלא כתיב גבי משכב אשר שכב וגבי מושב אשר ישב וכתיב ישכב ישב משמע שישכב עליו תמיד וישב עליו תמיד במיוחד לשכיבה ולישיבה וגבי משכב נמי דריש ליה התם הכי ובכל הספרים כתיב והיושב על הכלי אשר ישב עליו וקרא אחר הוא ומפרשים אותו התלמידים מדכתיב היושב על הכלי אשר ישב עליו שתי ישיבות ריבה הכתוב ללמדך דבמיוחד לישיבה קאמר ולא היא דשתי ישיבות דקאמר טובא צריכי כדמפרש התם יושב אע"פ שלא נגע אלא ישב או נתלה ולא נגע טמא דאיצטריך למיכתב גבי זב שטימא כלי בישיבתו ואע"פ שלא נגע ואיצטריך גבי טהור נמי שנטמא גם הוא ביושבו עליו אע"פ שלא נגע ועוד בת"כ לאו אההוא קרא קתני לה: ר' אלעזר אומר במדרסות כו'. בין בתחלת טומאה לענין שאמרנו דאינו מטמא מדרס למיהוי אב הטומאה בין בסוף טומאה כגון ג' על ג' שנטמאו מדרס למיהוי אב הטומאה ונחלקו טהור מן המדרס דאמרינן בו עמוד ונעשה מלאכתנו הראשונה שהיה ראוי לישיבה והרי עתה אינו ראוי לכך הלכך טהור מן המדרס ואע"ג דאית בכל חד שלש על שלש והוי כלי לקבל טומאה מיהו מתורת אב הטומאה טיהר לו: ואין אומרים. לענין אב הטומאה של טומאת מת עמוד ונעשה מלאכתנו כלומר אם נטמא ונשבר ועודהו ראוי למלאכה בעלמא שאין מעין מלאכה ראשונה טמא ולא אמרי' עמוד ונעשה מלאכתנו ראשונה וכיון דלא חזי להכי יהא טהור וכ"ש דבתחלת טומאה אין אומרים עמוד ונעשה מלאכתנו ראשונה דנימא אם אינו מיוחד למת לא יקבל טומאת מת דהא כלי מעשה כתיב: אומר כו'. דאי לא עביד מעין מלאכה ראשונה טהור ועל כרחיך לא איתמר דר' יוחנן אלא לענין שנשבר ולטהרו כדפרישית דליכא לפרושא כי ההיא דמדרסות ולמימרא דכלי שאינו עשוי למת לא יטמא במת דהא כתיב (במדבר יט) והזה על האהל ועל כל הכלים: איפוך קמייתא. דר' יוסי בר' חנינא לר' יוחנן: סנדל של בהמה. שלא ליזוק בפרסותיה באבנים: למאי חזי. אי משום בהמה אין תכשיט לבהמה: מניחו ברגליו. הוא בעצמו אלמא הואיל ולשם סנדל עשאו אי לאו דראוי לנעילה לא הוה מטמא ליה ר' יוחנן: איכא בינייהו דמאים. לרב לא מטמא דאין ראוי לשתות ורב סיכה לית ליה קסבר אין מוליכין שמן למלחמה לסוך וה"ה בין רב (בין) לר' יוחנן נמי איכא בינייהו דמאים: בין ר' חנינא וכו' איכא בינייהו דיקיר. כבד ואין ראוי בו לברוח:

תוספות

פחות ממוציא רימון מקבל טומאה ועוד קשה לר"י לפי' הקונטרס דלטומאה שהיתה עליהן שלא תפרח מהני שפיר טעמא דהדיוט יכול להחזירו בלא טעמא דראוי להקישו כדאשכחן בפ' שלשה שאכלו (ברכות נ:) גבי מטה דאפי' מפורקת לא פרחה טומאה מינה אא"כ נגנבה או שאבדה חציה או שחלקוה אחים או שותפים שאין סופן לחברה ולא איצטריך כלל לטעמא דהקשה אלא לענין לקבל טומאה מכאן ולהבא דהאי טעמא הואיל והדיוט יכול להחזירו לא מהני לקבל בה טומאה כדקתני התם החזירוה מקבלת טומאה מכאן ולהבא ולאביי נמי הוה בעי למימר דמשום דהדיוט יכול להחזירו מקבלין שניהן זוג והעינבל טומאה מכאן ולהבא וריצב"א הביא ראיה לפי' הקונט' דתניא בתוספתא דמסכת כלים בפ' רשב"ג העושה זוג למכתשת ולעריסה ולמטפחות תינוקות ניטלו עינבליהן טהורין משמע דזוגין טהורין ולפירוש הקונט' ניחא דטהורין דלא מקבלי טומאה מכאן ולהבא אבל לפר"י קשה אמאי טהורין ור"י השיב דכמה ברייתות יש בתוספתא דפליגי אש"ס שלנו: **ורבי** יוחנן אמר הואיל וראוי לגמע בו מים לתינוק. קשה לרשב"א דע"כ בלא ייחדו מיירי מדקאמר הואיל וראוי משמע בראוי בעלמא אפי' בלא ייחוד ועוד דביחדו לכך לא הוה פליג ר' יוסי בר' חנינא ועוד דביחדו אפי' לא היה לו עינבל מעולם נמי מקבל טומאה ועוד אי ביחדו מיירי מאי פריך דר' יוחנן אדר' יוחנן הא התם ע"כ איירי בלא ייחדו דביחדו אפי' במדרסות נמי אין אומרים עמוד ונעשה מלאכתנו ולקמן בס"פ המצניע (דף צה: ושם) גבי ניקב כמוציא זית טהור מלקבל בו זיתים ועדיין כלי הוא לקבל בו רימונים ופי' בקונטרס אם ייחדו לרימונים ואי לאו פי' הקונט' דהתם הוה ניחא וי"ל דאפי' לפירוש הקונטרס הכא חזי טפי ע"י גימוע משום דהואיל דמעיקרא הוה כלי גמור וגם עתה הדיוט יכול להחזירו אית לן למימר דע"י דבר מועט שעדיין ראוי לגמוע בו מים חשיב כלי אפי' בלא ייחוד ולמ"ד נמי הואיל וראוי להקישו דבעי מעין מלאכה ראשונה אתי שפיר בכל ענין דאפי' לא בעינן בעלמא ייחוד הכא אתי שפיר דלא מהני גמוע מים משום שעומד עדיין למלאכתו ראשונה להחזיר בו העינבל ואומר לו עמוד ונעשה מלאכתנו וכ"ש דאי בעינן בעלמא ייחוד דאתי טפי שפיר: **ואין** אומרים בטמא מת עמוד ונעשה מלאכתנו. לפירוש הקונט' קשה לר"י למה ליה לאתויי ברייתא דתרקב כיון דלא שייכא למילתיה דר' אלעזר ור' יוחנן אלא נראה לר' יצחק כפירוש ריב"א אומרים במדרסות עמוד מעל תרקב זה ונעשה מלאכתנו שאינו יכול להיות טמא מדרס ע"י שאתה יושב עליו הואיל ואינו מיוחד לכך כדקתני בברייתא ואין אומרים בטמא מת עמוד מגמוע מים בזה הזוג או בזה הסנדל של בהמה ונעשה מלאכתנו ליתן בו העינבל כדי להשמיע הקול וליתן סנדל ברגלי הבהמה אלא טמא טומאת מת על ידי הגימוע אע"פ שאינו מיוחד לכך והוי בר קבולי טומאה דחשיב כלי ע"י גימוע מים ור' יוחנן אמר אף אומר כו' דבעינן שיהא ראוי למלאכתו ראשונה ולא מהני ליה מידי לקבולי טומאה מה שראוי למלאכה אחרת אבל הקשת זוג ע"ג החרס והנחת סנדל של בהמה ברגלו כשבורח מן הקרב הוי מעין מלאכה ראשונה ולהכי הוי בר קבולי טומאה ולא שייך למימר ביה עמוד ונעשה מלאכתנו דהיינו נמי מלאכתו: **סנדל** של בהמה של מתכת. ושל עץ אינו ראוי לכל הני דברים דמפרש בסמוך לדרך הבהמה לקלקלו ורבינו שמואל גרים סנדל של בהמה ושל מתכת ומיירי בסנדל של סיידין דלקמן (ס.): **הואיל** וראוי לשתות בו מים במלחמה. וא"ת והא בזוג שלא היה בו עינבל מעולם לא מטמינן משום דחזי לגמוע והכא חשוב כמו זוג שלא היה בו עינבל מעולם דכיון דנעשה לצורך בהמה אינו מקבל טומאה וי"ל דתחלתו נמי עשוי לשתות בו מים במלחמה או לסוך אלא שעיקרו עומד לבהמה ואומר לו עמוד ונעשה מלאכתנו למאן דבעי מעין במלאכה ראשונה: **בשעה** שבורח מן הקרב מניחו ברגליו. תימה א"כ יטמא מדרס ותניא בתוספתא דכלים פרק כיפה ג' סנדלים הם של אדם טמא מדרס של מתכת ושל בהמה טמא טומאת מת משמע אבל מן המדרס טהור: (ו) **ולא** בעיר של זהב. אור"ת דלאו היינו נושקא כדפי' בקונט' דהא אמרי' בפרק בתרא דסוטה (דף מט:) מאי עטרות כלות עיר של זהב משמע דעשוי הוא כעין עטרה ואע"ג דאמרי' התם בפולמוס של טיטוס גזרו על עטרות חתנים וכלות והכא לא אסרו אלא בשבת אור"ת דדוקא לחתנים וכלות גזרו ולא לשאר בני אדם (ז):

מאן

מסורת הש"ס

א) חגיגה כג: נדה מט., ב) [נ"ל דתנן], ג) [כלים פי"ד מ"ה], ד) נטלו עינבלין אחרי טומאתן טמאין דלא כנ"ל רש"ל, ה) [שייך במשנה לעיל נז.], ו) [מפני שיש להן שמחה בהן ועי' תוס' גיטין ז. ד"ה עטרות].

הגהות הב"ח

(א) גמ' תלמוד לומר וכל הכלי אשר ישב:

תורה אור השלם

א) כָּל הַמִּשְׁכָּב אֲשֶׁר יִשְׁכַּב עָלָיו הַזָּב יִטְמָא וְכָל הַכְּלִי אֲשֶׁר יֵשֵׁב עָלָיו יִטְמָא: [ויקרא טו, ד]

ליקוטי רש"י

תרקב. חצי סאה תרי וקב דהיינו שלש קבין שהן חצי סאה [ערכין כה.]. ת"ל אשר ישב עליו. ישב לא נאמר אלא אשר ישב עליו הזב במיוחד תמיד לכך [ויקרא טו, ד]. מדלא קרינן אשר ישב למדנו שאינו מדבר אלא באשר מיוחד לישב שם תמיד [חגיגה כג:]. מי שמיוחד לישיבה. הוא דהוי אב הטומאה דכתיב וכבס בגדיו וגו'. יצא זה. סאה ותרקב שאין מדרס הזב לטמא אדם וכלים אבל טמאין הם טומאת מגע הזב להיות ראשונים וכמת ונעשין אב הטומאה [נדה מט:]. ירושלים דדהבא. ירושלים של זהב כמי נפש שמצויירת בכל ענייני ירושלים [נדרים נ.]. תכשיט של זהב שירושלים מצוייר בה [ר"ן שם].

עין משפט נר מצוה

כ א מיי' פ"ז מהל' משכב ומושב הלכה ח:
כא ב מיי' פי"ט מהל' שבת הלכה ו סמג לאוין סה טור וש"ע א"ח סי' שג סעיף ד:

רבינו חננאל

רבא הואיל וראוי להקישו התינוק ע"ג חרס ולהשמיע קול. ר' יוחנן אמר הואיל וראוי לגמע בו מים לתינוק עדיין תורת כלי עליהן ולפיכך עדיין טומאתו עליהן ואקשינן וכי ר' יוחנן לא בעי (שישא) [שיהא] בכלי המשמש מעין מלאכתו [והתניא] והיושב על הכלי אשר ישב עליו הזב יטמא יכול כפה סאה וישב עליה כפה כו' עד ור' יוחנן אמר בטומאת מת עמוד ונעשה מלאכתנו הנה בפי' ר' יוחנן אמר כי אין הכלי מקבל טומאה אלא אם הוא ראוי למלאכתו שנעשה בו ואפיך קמייתא ואימא ר' יוחנן אמר הואיל וראוי להקישו ע"ג חרס משום דשמעינן ליה לר' יוחנן בהדיא דבעי מעין מלאכתו ראשונה דתניא סנדל של מתכת של בהמה טמא ואמרינן למאי חזית [רב] אמר חזי לשתות מים. ר' חנינא אמר ראוי לסוך בו שמן ר' יוחנן [אמר] ראוי להניחו ברגליו כשבורח ורץ על הקוצי' ועל הברקנים הנה שמענו לר' יוחנן דבעי מעין מלאכתו ראשונה כשם שמתחלה למנעל הרגל כך באחרונה: **מתניתין** ולא תצא אשה בעיר של זהב. מאי עיר של זהב. ירושלים דדהבא

רב נסים גאון

מאי עיר של זהב אמר רבה בר בר חנה אמר ר' יוחנן ירושלים דדהבא כי דעביד לה (ר' יוחנן) [ר"ע] לדביתהו תמצא במס' נדרים בפרק הנודר מן המבושל (ד' נ) ר' עקיבא איקדשא ליה ברתיה דבר כלבא שבוע שמע אבוהא אדרא הנאה מכל נכסיה אזלא ואיתנסיבא ליה בסיתוא הוה גנו בי תיבנא הוה מנקיט לה תיבנא מן מזייה אמר לה אי הואי לי רמינא ליך ירושלם דדהבא והזכירו אחר כך שהגיע לעושר גדול כמו שאמרו מן ו' מילי איעתר ר' עקיבא ולאחר שהגיעה ידו שילם לה נדרו ועשה לה ירושלם דדהבא ובגמ' דהדין פירקא דבני מערבא אמרי מעשה ברבי עקיבא שעשה לאשתו עיר של זהב חמתה איתתיה דרבן גמליאל וקניאת בה אתת ואמרה קמי בעלה אמר לה מה הוית עבדא לי כמה דהוות עבדא ליה דהוות מזבנא מן קלעיתה דשערה ויהיבא ליה והוא לעי באורייתא:

כדעבד ליה רבי עקיבא לדביתהו [א] ת"ר לא תצא אשה בעיר של זהב ואם יצתה חייבת חטאת דברי רבי מאיר וחכמים אומרים לא תצא ואם יצתה פטורה [ב] רבי אליעזר אומר יוצאה אשה בעיר של זהב לכתחלה במאי קמיפלגי ר"מ סבר משוי הוא ורבנן סברי תכשיט הוא דילמא שלפא ומחויא ליה ואתיא לאתויי ור"א סבר מאן דרכה למיפק בעיר של זהב אשה חשובה ואשה חשובה לא משלפא ומחויא כלילא רב אסר ושמואל [א] שרי דאניסכא כולי עלמא לא פליגי דאסור כי פליגי דארוקתא מר סבר אניסכא עיקר ומר סבר ארוקתא עיקר רב אשי מתני לקולא [ב] דארוקתא דכולי עלמא לא פליגי דשרי כי פליגי דאניסכא מר סבר דילמא שלפא ומחויא ואתי לאתויי ומר סבר מאן דרכה למיפק בכלילא אשה חשובה ואשה חשובה לא שלפא ומחויא ° א"ל רב שמואל בר בר חנה לרב יוסף בפירוש אמרת לן משמיה דרב כלילא שרי [ג] אמרו ליה לרב אתא גברא רבה אריכא לנהרדעא ומטלע ודרש כלילא שרי אמר מאן גברא רבה אריכא [דאיטלע] לוי ש"מ נח נפשיה דרבי אפס ויתיב ר' חנינא ברישא ולא הוה ליה איניש ללוי למיתב גביה (א) וקאתי להכא ודילמא נח נפשיה דרבי חנינא ור' אפס כדקאי קאי ולא הוה ליה איניש ללוי למיתב גביה וקאתי להכא אם איתא דרבי חנינא שכיב לוי לר' אפס מיכף הוה כייף ליה ותו דרבי חנינא לא סגי דלא מליך דכי הוה קא ניחא נפשיה דרבי אמר חנינא בר' חמא יתיב בראש וכתיב בהו בצדיקים [א] ותגזר אומר ויקם לך וגו' דרש לוי בנהרדעא כלילא שרי נפיק עשרין וארבע כלילי מכולה נהרדעא דרש רבה בר אבוה [רב] במחוזא כלילא שרי ונפקו תמני סרי כלילי מחדא מבואה אמר רב יהודה אמר רב שמואל קמרא שרי איכא דאמרי דארוקתא ואמר רב ספרא מידי דהוה אטלית מוזהבת ואיכא דאמרי [ג] דאניסכא ואמר רב ספרא מידי דהוה אאבנט של מלכים א"ל רבינא לרב אשי קמרא עילוי המיינא מאי א"ל [ד] תרי המייני קאמרת אמר רב אשי [ה] האי רסוקא אי אית ליה מפרחייתא שרי ואי לא אסיר: ולא בקטלא: מאי קטלא מנקטא פארי: נזמים: [ו] נזמי האף: ולא בטבעת שאין עליה חותם: הא יש עליה חותם חייבת אלמא לאו תכשיט הוא ורמינהו [ז] תכשיטי נשים טמאים ואלו הן תכשיטי נשים קטלאות נזמים וטבעות וטבעת בין שיש עליה חותם בין שאין עליה חותם ונזמי האף ואמר רבי זירא לא קשיא הא ר' נחמיה הא רבנן [ח] דתניא [ט] היא של מתכת וחותמה של אלמוג טמאה היא של אלמוג וחותמה של מתכת טהורה ורבי נחמיה מטמא שהיה ר' נחמיה אומר בטבעת הלך אחר חותמה בעול הלך אחר סמלוניו בקולב

כדעבד ליה ר' עקיבא לדביתהו. במסכת נדרים (דף נ.): **כלילא.** על פדחתה היא קושרתו מאזן לאזן יש שכולו טס זהב שקורין לימ"א ויש שעושין ממשי טווי עם הזהב שקורין פריז"ש: **דניסכא.** טס העשוי כולו מניסכא דהיינו זהב או כסף דבר הניתך: **דאסיר.** מגו דחשיב גזירה דילמא שלפא ומחוייא: **דארוקתא.** רצועה שמצויירת בזהב ובאבנים טובות: **אניסכא.** דאית ביה עיקר ומחויא ליה ומר סבר ארוקתא הוא עיקר דידיה ולא חשיב ליה ולא מחויא ליה: **כולי עלמא לא פליגי דשרי.** דארוקתא עיקר: **בפירוש אמרת לן משמיה דרב.** לפני חלייך קודם ששכחת תלמודך: **כלילא שרי.** אלמא דרב אשי עיקר דמוקי פלוגתא בדניסכא אבל בארוקתא מודה רב ואיכא לאוקמי לדידיה בארוקתא: **גברא רבה אריכא ומטלע.** לוי איטלע דאחוי קידה קמיה דרבי (ז): **נח נפשיה דרבי אפס.** במסכת כתובות בהנושא (קג:) אמרינן דכי שכיב רבי אמר רבי חנינא בר חמא ישב בראש ולא קיבל עליו רבי חנינא שהיה רבי אפס גדול ממנו שתי שנים (ב) ויתיב רבי אפס ברישא ומתוך שהיה רבי חנינא חשוב לא נכנס לבית מדרשו והיה יושב בחוץ ומשום כבודו ישב לו לוי אצלו: **וקאתי להכא.** שלא היה רבי חנינא גדול הימנו לא בתורה ולא בשנים ולא ניכף ליה לוי ובא לכאן: **לוי לרבי אפס מיכף הוה כייף ליה.** שהרי זקן ממנו: **קמרא.** אבנט חשוב יש שעושין אותו טס של זהב ויש שעושין אותו רצועה משבצות זהב ואבנים קבועות בו: **מידי דהוה אטלית מוזהבת.** דהוי תכשיט ושריא ולמישלף ואחויי נמי לא חיישינן שאין דרך להתיר אזורו בשוק ויפלו בגדיו: **אאבנט של מלכים.** שעשוי כולו דניסכא ° וכל ישראל בני מלכים ראוים לו: **תרי המייני קאמרת.** הא ודאי משאוי הוא ואסור לשון תלמידי רבינו יצחק (ג) נ"ע [ובתלמידי] רבינו הלוי מצאתי מותר והראשון נראה לי משום דגבי הצלת דליקה מנינן לר' יוסי שמנה עשר כלים והתם חד חגור הוא דמנינן בכל כתבי הקדש (לקמן דף קכ.) ואי שני חגורות שרי לכתחילה נימני התם תרי: **רסוקי.** חתיכת מעיל רחבה: **אי אית ליה מפרחייתא.** רצועות קצרות תלויות בה לקושרה בהם ולהדקה סביבותיו: **שרי.** דמיהדק שפיר וליכא למיחש דילמא משתרי קטרי ונפיל ואתי לאיתויי: **מפרחייתא.** פינדל"א בלע"ז: **מנקטא פארי** (ד). מוסטניל"א והוא בגד שיש לו שנצים כעין מכנסים ומכנסת בו רצועה רחבה וקושרת סביב צוארה והבגד תלוי על לבה והוא חשוב ומצוייר בזהב וי"מ כמין חלי עגול עשוי כמין כלבוס [ס] (ה) אוחזת בו מפתחי חלוקה והפגם בולע צוארה והוא של זהב לוי"ה: **נזמי האף.** אבל נזמי האוזן מותרין לכתחלה דטריחא לה מילתא למישלף ואחויי מפני שאזניה מכוסות בקישורין: **ולא בטבעת שאין עליה חותם.** קתני מתניתין דאם יצאת פטורה דתכשיט הוא לה ומשום דילמא משלפא ומחויא הוא דמיתסר: **הא יש עליה חותם חייבת חטאת.** דלאו תכשיט הוא והוי משאוי: **נזמים.** נזמי האוזן: **וטבעת בין שיש כו'.** כלומר וטבעת שאמרנו בין שיש עליה כו': **הא רבי נחמיה.** דאמר עיקר טבעת אדעתא דחותם הוא חייבת חטאת דחותם לאשה לאו תכשיט הוא דאין דרך לאשה לחתום ולשלוח שלוחים שאין חותם עשוי אלא לאדם גדול וממונה והא דקתני תכשיט הוא רבנן דאמרי גופה של טבעת עיקר ואדעתא דטבעת נפקא ביה וטבעת ודאי תכשיט הוא: **טמאה.** דטבעת עיקר והוה ליה פשוטי כלי מתכות: **היא של אלמוג וחותמה של מתכת טהורה.** דהוה ליה פשוטי כלי עץ: **הלך אחר סמלוניו.** ואם של מתכות הם טמא: **סמלוניו.** העול שלהם לא היה פגום כשלנו אלא חלק ונוקבים בו שני נקבים וביניהם כעודי עורף השור ותוחבין בהן שתי יתדות והם סימלונין: בקולב

מאן דרכה למיפק בכלילא אשה חשובה. אומר ר"י דדוקא בכלילא שרי שמואל הכא וכן רבי אליעזר דוקא בעיר של זהב שאין כל הנשים רגילות בהן אלא אשה חשובה אבל שאר תכשיטי נשים אסירי אפי' לאשה חשובה דאין לחלק בין הנשים והביא ראיה מס"פ כירה (לעיל דף מו:) דקאמר עולא מה טעם הואיל ואיכא תורת כלי עליהן ומה דחק לומר כן כיון דחזי לנשים חשובות דאפי' לרבנן דאסרי בעיר של זהב לאשה חשובה מודו בשאר תכשיטים אליבא דשמואל דשרי כלילא אפילו לרבנן:

אאבנט של מלכים. שמלבושם הוא ואין להם אבנט אחר ה"נ שרי האי קמרא לאיתתא דמלבושה היא ולא משלפא ומחויא:

תרי המייני קאמרת. לשון אחד פי' בקונטרס לאיסור ואע"ג דחשיב בפ' כל כתבי (לקמן דף קכ:) בי"ח כלים פונדא וחגור ופי' התם בקונט' דפונדא הוא אזור היינו כגון שיש בגד מפסיק בינתים אבל תרי המייני זה על גב זה אסור ולא דמי לכמה מלבושים שאדם לובש בשביל הקור אבל תרי המייני מה הנאה יש ואין דרך לחגור ומשוי הוא:

מנקטא פארי. פירורי הפת ותכשיט הוא:

נזמי האף. ונזמי האוזן שרו כדפי' בקונטרס ואע"ג דאמר לקמן [ט] הבנות יוצאות בחוטין שבאזניהן ואמר בגמ' דשל מיני צבעונים אסירי דילמא משלפי הואיל ותכשיט נינהו התם יותר קל ° ליטלם מנזמי האוזן:

הא יש עליה חותם חייבת חטאת. אסיפא סמיך [י] דקתני בהדיא דחייבת חטאת:

רבי נחמיה מטמא. נראה לר"י דברישא מטהר דלא בעי למימר הלך אף אחר חותמה אלא דוקא אחר חותמה שהוא עיקר וכן משמע בהדיא בתוספתא דמסכת כלים [כ] דתניא טבעת של מתכת וחותמה של אלמוג רבי נחמיה מטהר שהיה רבי נחמיה אומר בטבעת הלך אחר חותמה:

עין משפט נר מצוה

כב א ב מיי' פי"ט מהל' שבת הלכה י' טוש"ע א"ח סי' שג סעיף ה:
כג ג מיי' שם הל' ב' סמג לאוין כה:
כד ד טוש"ע א"ח סי' שא סעיף לו:
כה ה טוש"ע א"ח סי' שג סעיף ו:
כו ו מיי' שם הלכה ז טוש"ע שם סעיף ח:

רבינו חננאל

כדעבד ר' עקיבא לדביתהו. ת"ר לא תצא אשה בעיר של זהב ואם יצא חייבת חטאת דברי ר' מאיר וחכ"א לא תצא ואם יצאת פטורה. ר' אליעזר אומר יוצאה אשה בעיר של זהב לכתחלה: **כלילא** רב אסר ושמואל שרי. פי' נסכא חוטין מלשון המסכת (כלים פכ"א). רוקתא מטלית. וקיי"ל כרב אשי דהוא בתראה דאמר ארוקתא כו' כ"ע לא פליגי דשרי כי פליגא כלילא דאניסכא רב אסר ושמואל שרי וקיי"ל כרב באיסורי ואע"ג דאיכא למימר מעשה רב והא דדרש [לוי] כלילא [שרי] ונפקו כ"ד כלילי מנהרדעא וכן הא דדרש רבה בר אבוה במחוזא כלילא שרי כלילא דאניסכא דרשו דשרי. כיון דלא איתמרא בהדיא לא שרינן לה דדלמא לא שרי אלא דארוקתא: אמר רב ששת קמרא שרי הוא חגור שבמתנים כגון אבנט רחב מדבעא רבינא מרב אשי קמרא עילוי המיינא מאי ואמר ליה תרי המייני קאמרת ש"מ דקמרא המיינא הוא והא דרב אשי אתמר בה תרי לישני ולישנא בתראה אניסכא שרי פי' כלילא וקמרא. חתיכות חתיכות של זהב נקובות ובהן מרגלית ומעמידין בחוטין שמכניסין בנקבין. נמצא דאניסכא כגון מלאכת אבנט של מלכים כי כן מלאכתן להיעשות בחוטין. רוקתא מטלית. שנמצא בין כלילא בין קמרא חתיכות של זהב נקובות ומרגלית קבוער' במטלי' שנמצאת מלאכתן כגון מלאכת טלית מוזהבת. אמר רב אשי

רב נסים גאון

גברא רבא אריכא אתא לנהרדעאי ומטלע פירוש והוא צולע על ירכו כדמתרגמינן והוא מטלע והדבר שגרם לו זה מפורש בפ' ג' דתענית (דף כה) לוי גזר תעניתא בעא רחמי ולא אתא מיטרא אמר לפניו רבונו של עולם עלית וישבת למעלה במרום ואי אתה משגיח על בניך ואתא מיטרא ואיטלע אמר ר' אלעזר אל יטיח אדם דברים כלפי למעלה שהרי אדם גדול הטיח דברים כלפי למעלה ואטלע ובמסכת סוכה (דף נג) בפ' החליל קאמרי לוי אחוי קידה קמיה דר' ואטלע ואמרו בפירוקה הא והא גרמא ליה אבל מעשה דר' אפס ור' חנינא בר חמא ומה דאמר רבנו הקדוש בצוויו חנינא בר חמא ישב בראש כו' (מעשה כמפורש) [מפורש] בפרק הנושא

מסורת הש"ס

א) [לקמן קלח. תוספתא פ"ה], ב) עדיות פ"ב מ"ז, ג) כתובות קג:, ד) [כלים פרק יא מ"ח ע"ש], ה) [בכלים פי"ג מ"ו לא מכר פלוגתא דר' נחמי' הלכך שפיר גרסי' דתניא], ו) לעיל נב: תוספתא דכלי' ב"מ פ"ג כלים פי"ג מ"ו, ז) [סוכה נג.], ח) מה

ט) [דף סה.], י) [לקמן סב.], כ) [פ"ג בבא מציעא].

הגהות הב"ח

(א) גמ' למיתב גבי' וקם וקאתי: (ב) רש"י ד"ה נח נפשיה וכו' שתי שנים ומאלה ויתיב: (ג) ד"ה תרי וכו' ר' יצחק בר יהודה נ"ע: (ד) ד"ה מנקטא פארי. נ"ב ע"ל בדף נז ע"ב במה שפירש"י: (ה) בא"ד כמין כלבוס כזה:

גליון הש"ס

גמ' א"ל רב שמואל בר בר חנה לרב יוסף. לקמן קמו ע"ב: רש"י ד"ה אאבנט וכו' וכל ישראל בני מלכים. עיין לקמן דף קיא ע"א: תוס' ד"ה נזמי האף וכו' ליטלם מנזמי האזן. עיין תשו' ב"ח המחדשות סי' מ"א:

תורה אור השלם

א) וְתִגְזַר אֹמֶר וְיָקָם לָךְ וְעַל דְּרָכֶיךָ נָגַהּ אוֹר: [איוב כב, כח]

ליקוטי רש"י

ר"מ סבר. דלאו תכשיט הוא אלא משוי. **תכשיט הוא.** ולכתחילה אסור דילמא שלפא ומחויא [לקמן קלח.]. **גברא רבה אריכא [דאיטלע].** פסח היה כדאמרינן בעלמא (סוכה נג.) לוי אחוי קידה ואטלע [כתובות קג:]. נעשה חיגר [סוכה נג.]. שנצלע בקידה [תענית כה.]. נצלע בגופא דאטמא [מגילה כב:]. **וקאתי להכא.** לבבל. **מיכף הוה כייף ליה.** קודם שיגלה ממקומו אבל לר' חנינא לא כייף [כתובות שם]. **מאי קטלא מנקטא פארי.** בגד חשוב לתלות בצוארה כנגד לבה שלא יפול מה שהיא אוכלת על בגדיה ויש לו מקום שנצים כעין שעושים למכנסים ותוחב בו רצועה רחבה ומוללתו סביב הרצועה שהבגד רחב הרבה וקושרת הרצועה סביב צוארה [לעיל נז: עיי"ש עוד ובתוס' שם]. **ותגזר אומר.** מה שתבקש מן היוצר יעשה [ב"מ קו.]. **ויקם לך.** כמו ויקום לך [איוב כב, כח]. **אלמוג.** עצי אלמוגים והוא נאה. **טמאה.** דבתר טבעת אזלינן ופשוטי כלי מתכות טמאים [לעיל נב:].

כִּדְעָבַד לֵיהּ רַבִּי עֲקִיבָא לִדְבֵיתְהוּ – **like [the ornament] R' Akiva fashioned for his wife.**[1]

The Gemara cites a Tannaic dispute concerning the wearing of such an ornament outside on the Sabbath:

תָּנוּ רַבָּנָן – **The Rabbis taught in a Baraisa:** לֹא תֵצֵא אִשָּׁה בְּעִיר שֶׁל זָהָב – A WOMAN MAY NOT GO OUT on the Sabbath while WEARING A "CITY OF GOLD"; וְאִם יָצְתָה חַיֶּיבֶת חַטָּאת – AND IF SHE WENT OUT wearing it, SHE IS LIABLE TO A *CHATAS* offering.[2] דִּבְרֵי רַבִּי מֵאִיר – These are THE WORDS OF R' MEIR.[3] וַחֲכָמִים אוֹמְרִים – BUT THE SAGES SAY: לֹא תֵצֵא – SHE MAY NOT GO OUT wearing such an ornament on the Sabbath, וְאִם יָצְתָה פְּטוּרָה – BUT IF SHE DID GO OUT wearing it, SHE IS EXEMPT from a *chatas* offering.[4] רַבִּי אֱלִיעֶזֶר אוֹמֵר – R' ELIEZER SAYS: יוֹצְאָה אִשָּׁה בְּעִיר שֶׁל זָהָב לְכַתְּחִלָּה – A WOMAN MAY GO OUT WITH A "CITY OF GOLD" on the Sabbath even IN THE FIRST PLACE; i.e. it is completely permitted.

The Gemara explains the reasoning of each Tanna in the Baraisa:

בְּמַאי קָמִיפַּלְגֵי – **In what** issue **do [these Tannaim] disagree?** רַבִּי מֵאִיר סָבַר מַשּׂוֹי הוּא – **R' Meir holds that [the "city of gold"] is a burden,** rather than an ornament; thus, it is Biblically prohibited to wear it outside on the Sabbath.[5] וְרַבָּנָן סָבְרִי תַּכְשִׁיט הוּא – **And the Sages hold** that **it is an ornament;** thus, it is not Biblically prohibited to wear outside, – דִּילְמָא שָׁלְפָא וּמַחְוְיָא לֵיהּ – but the Rabbis were concerned that **a woman might remove it to show it** to a friend, וְאַתְיָא לְאַתּוּיֵי – **and come to carry it** four *amos* in the public domain. Therefore, wearing this ornament is Rabbinically prohibited.[6] וְרַבִּי אֱלִיעֶזֶר סָבַר – **And R' Eliezer holds** that a woman is permitted to wear this ornament on the Sabbath, מַאן דַּרְכָּהּ לְמֵיפַּק בְּעִיר שֶׁל זָהָב – for **who is accustomed to go out wearing a "city of gold"** ornament? אִשָּׁה חֲשׁוּבָה – **A distinguished woman,**[7] וְאִשָּׁה חֲשׁוּבָה לֹא מִשַּׁלְפָא וּמַחְוְיָא – **and a distinguished woman is not** likely **to remove her ornaments and show** them to others.[8] Thus, there was no reason for the Rabbis to forbid the wearing of a "city of gold."[9]

The Gemara discusses another ornament:

כְּלִילָא – Whether **a tiara**[10] may be worn outside on the Sabbath is a matter of dispute: רַב אָסַר וּשְׁמוּאֵל שָׁרֵי – **Rav prohibits** it, **while Shmuel permits** it.

The Gemara qualifies the dispute:

דְּאַנִיסְכָּא כּוּלֵּי עָלְמָא לֹא פְּלִיגֵי דְּאָסוּר – Concerning a tiara fashioned **of a hammered plate** of gold or silver, **there is no dispute; all agree that** wearing **it is prohibited.**[11] כִּי פְּלִיגֵי – **When do they argue?** דְּאַרוּקְתָא – Concerning a tiara made **of fabric** studded with gold pieces and precious stones. מַר סָבַר אַנִיסְכָּא עִיקָר – One **master** (Rav) **holds that the** gold **pieces** in the tiara **are the primary part** of the ornament, and thus it is a significant item that a woman would wish to show to a friend; accordingly, he rules that wearing it is prohibited. וּמַר סָבַר אַרוּקְתָא עִיקָר – **But** the other **master** (Shmuel) **holds** that **the fabric is the main part** of the ornament, and therefore it is not considered a significant ornament; accordingly, it may be worn on the Sabbath.[12]

The Gemara presents another explanation of the dispute:

רַב אַשִׁי מַתְנֵי לְקוּלָּא – **Rav Ashi taught a more lenient interpretation** of the dispute: דְּאַרוּקְתָא דְּכוּלֵּי עָלְמָא לֹא פְּלִיגֵי דְּשָׁרֵי – In his opinion, **there is no dispute** concerning a tiara made **of fabric** studded with gold and stones; **all agree that** wearing **it is permitted.**[13] כִּי פְּלִיגֵי דְּאַנִיסְכָּא – **When do they argue?** Concerning a tiara fashioned **of a hammered** metal **plate.**

NOTES

1. The Gemara in *Nedarim* (50a) relates that R' Akiva was married to the daughter of the wealthy Kalba Savua, who refused to support the young couple (because at that point R' Akiva was as yet unlearned). R' Akiva sought to console his wife during their time of hardship by promising her that when he was able, he would fashion for her a golden ornament engraved with the likeness of Jerusalem (see *Rashi*). [The Gemara in *Nedarim* does not explicitly state that R' Akiva in fact fashioned the ornament; *Ran, Rosh* and *Tosafos* (to *Nedarim* ibid.) all state that this is known from our Gemara.]

[*Tosafos* (to 59a ד״ה ולא) notes that although the wearing of "crowns of brides" was forbidden at the time of the Destruction of the Temple (see above, 58a note 1), and the Gemara in *Sotah* (49b) explains "crowns of brides" to be referring to a crown engraved with the likeness of the city of Jerusalem, this does not pose a contradiction to our Mishnah, which forbids wearing such crowns only on the Sabbath; for the edict forbidding such crowns applied only to brides, and not to other women. This difficulty does not arise according to *Rashi* (to 57a ד״ה עיר), for he understands our Gemara to be referring to a *clasp* engraved with a likeness of Jerusalem, rather than a crown. See *Chidushei R' Mordechai Banet;* see also *Rashash*.

2. I.e. if she wore it outside thinking that doing so was permitted, or not realizing that it was the Sabbath, she is liable to a *chatas* offering to atone for the inadvertent transgression of the Sabbath (see next note).

3. The Gemara below explains that according to R' Meir it is Biblically prohibited to wear this ornament outside on the Sabbath, and therefore if a woman does so inadvertently she must bring a *chatas* offering. [The Gemara will explain R' Meir's reasoning below as well.]

4. For the Sages are of the opinion that wearing this ornament outside on the Sabbath is only Rabbinically prohibited. Accordingly, no liability to a *chatas* is incurred for an inadvertent transgression. [This is the view of the Tanna of our Mishnah as well.] The Gemara below will explain their reasoning.

5. Since R' Meir deems the "city of gold" a burden rather than an ornament, he holds that wearing it is akin to carrying it; and it is no different than carrying any other burden, which is Biblically forbidden.

Tos. HaRosh explains that according to R' Meir the "city of gold" is not deemed an ornament because it was not really worn for purposes of adornment; it was simply a very heavy piece of engraved gold that was worn chiefly to advertise the great wealth of the wearer (see also *Rashba*). Cf. *Rashash;* see also *Pnei Yehoshua* and *Orach Chaim* 303:9.

6. According to the Sages, there is no difference between a "city of gold" ornament and any of the other ornaments mentioned in the Mishnah (e.g. frontlets, nose rings); wearing it outside is Rabbinically prohibited because a woman may remove it to show to a friend and come to carry it four *amos* in the public domain.

7. This ornament was very expensive, and only wealthy and important women wore it.

8. It is beneath the dignity of a distinguished woman to show her jewelry to others in the street; therefore, there is no reason to fear that she will come to carry the ornament (see also next note).

9. R' Eliezer concurs, however, that even a distinguished woman may not wear those ornaments that most women wear, the fact that she is not likely to remove them notwithstanding – for once the Rabbis prohibited the wearing of regular ornaments, their edict extended to all women equally. It was only in the case of an ornament like a "city of gold," that is *only* worn by distinguished women who will not remove it, that the Rabbis did not issue their edict at all (*Tosafos* ד״ה מאן, *Ritva MHK* ed. *Rashba,* et al.).

10. The Gemara below describes this ornament, which was fastened across the woman's forehead, in greater detail (see *Rashi*).

11. See *Rashi.* Since this tiara is a significant ornament, the Rabbis prohibited wearing it outside on the Sabbath, lest a woman remove it to show it to her friend and come to carry it four *amos* in the public domain. Cf. *Rabbeinu Chananel.*

12. A woman will only show her friend an ornament that she considers worthy of showing off. According to Shmuel, a tiara that consists of jewel-studded fabric was not considered a fancy ornament, and a woman would not be likely to remove it in the public domain; thus, it was not included in the Rabbinic edict against wearing an ornament outside on the Sabbath (see *Rashi*).

13. According to this explanation of the dispute, both Rav and Shmuel agree that a tiara made of jewel-studded fabric is not considered a fancy ornament that a woman would remove and show to her friend.

כדעבד ליה רבי עקיבא לדביתהו [א] ת"ר לא תצא אשה בעיר של זהב ואם יצתה חייבת חטאת דברי רבי מאיר וחכמים אומרים לא תצא ואם יצתה פטורה [ב] רבי אליעזר אומר יוצאה אשה בעיר של זהב לכתחלה במאי קמיפלגי ר"מ סבר משוי הוא ורבנן סברי תכשיט הוא דילמא שלפא ומחויא ליה ואתיא לאתויי ור"א סבר מאן דרכה למיפק בעיר של זהב אשה חשובה ואשה חשובה לא משלפא ומחויא כלילא רב אסר ושמואל [א] שרי דאניסכא כולי עלמא לא פליגי דאסור כי פליגי דארוקתא מר סבר אניסכא עיקר ומר סבר ארוקתא עיקר רב אשי מתני לקולא [ב] דארוקתא דכולי עלמא לא פליגי דשרי כי פליגי דאניסכא מר סבר דילמא שלפא ומחויא ואתי לאתויי ומר סבר מאן דרכה למיפק בכלילא אשה חשובה ואשה חשובה לא שלפא ומחויא א"ל רב שמואל בר בר חנה לרב יוסף בפירוש אמרת לן משמיה דרב כלילא שרי [ג] אמרו ליה לרב אתא גברא רבה אריכא לנהרדעא ומטלע ודרש כלילא שרי אמר מאן גברא רבה אריכא [דאיטלע] לוי ש"מ נח נפשיה דרבי אפס ויתיב ר' חנינא ברישא ולא הוה ליה איניש ללוי למיתב גביה (א) וקאתי להכא ודילמא נח נפשיה דרבי חנינא ור' אפס כדקאי קאי ולא הוה ליה איניש ללוי למיתב גביה וקאתי להכא אם איתא דרבי חנינא שכיב לוי לר' אפס מיכף הוה כייף ליה ותו דרבי חנינא לא סגי דלא מליך דכי הוה קא ניחא נפשיה דרבי אמר חנינא בר' חמא יתיב בראש וכתיב בהו בצדיקים [א] ותגזר אומר ויקם לך וגו' דרש לוי בנהרדעא כלילא שרי נפיק עשרין וארבע כלילי מכולה נהרדעא דרש רבה בר אבוה

רב

במחוזא כלילא שרי ונפקו תמני סרי כלילי מחדא מבואה אמר רב יהודה אמר רב שמואל קמרא שרי איכא דאמרי דארוקתא ואמר רב ספרא מידי דהוה אטלית מוזהבת ואיכא דאמרי [ג] דאניסכא ואמר רב ספרא מידי דהוה אאבנט של מלכים א"ל רבינא לרב אשי קמרא עילוי המיינא מאי א"ל [ד] תרי המייני קאמרת אמר רב אשי [ה] האי רסוקא אי אית ליה מפרחייתא שרי ואי לא אסיר: ולא בקטלא: מאי קטלא מנקטא פארי: נזמים: [ו] נזמי האף: ולא בטבעת שאין עליה חותם: הא יש עליה חותם חייבת אלמא לאו תכשיט הוא ורמינהו [ז] תכשיטי נשים טמאים ואלו הן תכשיטי נשים קטלאות נזמים וטבעות וטבעת בין שיש עליה חותם בין שאין עליה חותם ונזמי האף ואמר רבי זירא לא קשיא הא ר' נחמיה הא רבנן [ח] דתניא [ט] היא של מתכת וחותמה של אלמוג טמאה היא של אלמוג וחותמה של מתכת טהורה ורבי נחמיה מטמא שהיה ר' נחמיה אומר בטבעת הלך אחר חותמה בעול סמלוניו

בקולב

רש"י

כדעבד ליה ר' עקיבא לדביתהו. במסכת נדרים (דף נ): כלילא. על פדחתה היא קושרתו מאוזן לאוזן יש שכולו טס זהב שקורין לימ"א ויש שעושין ממשי טווי עם הזהב שקורין פריז"ש: דניסכא. טס העשוי כולו מניסכא דהיינו זהב או כסף דבר הניתך: דאסיר. מגו דחשיב גזירה דילמא שלפא ומחוייא: דארוקתא. רצועה שמצויירת בזהב ובאבנים טובות: אניסכא. דאית ביה עיקר ומחויא ליה ומר סבר ארוקתא הוא עיקר דידיה ולא חשיב ליה ולא מחויא ליה: כולי עלמא לא פליגי דשרי. דארוקתא עיקר: בפירוש אמרת לן משמיה דרב. לפני חלייך קודם ששכחת תלמודך: כלילא שרי. אלמא דרב אשי עיקר דמוקי פלוגתא בדניסכא אבל בארוקתא מודה רב ואיכא לאוקמי לדידיה בארוקתא: גברא רבה אריכא ומטלע. לוי איטלע לאחוי קידה קמיה דרבי[י]: נח נפשיה דרבי אפס. במסכת כתובות בהנושא (קג:) אמרינן דכי שכיב רבי אמר רבי חנינא בר חמא ישב בראש ולא קיבל עליו רבי חנינא שהיה רבי אפס גדול ממנו שתי שנים (ב) ויתיב רבי אפס ברישא ומתוך שהיה רבי חנינא חשוב לא נכנס לבית מדרשו והיה יושב בחוץ ומשום כבודו ישב לו לוי אצלו: וקאתי להכא. שלא היה רבי חנינא גדול הימנו לא בתורה ולא בשנים ולא ניכף ליה לוי ובא לכאן: לוי לרבי אפס מיכף הוה כייף ליה. שהרי זקן ממנו: קמרא. אבנט חשוב יש שעושין אותו טס של זהב ויש שעושין אותו רצועה משבצות זהב ואבנים קבועות בו: מידי דהוה אטלית מוזהבת. דהוי תכשיט ושריא ולמישלף ואחויי נמי לא חיישינן שאין דרך להתיר אזורו בשוק ויפלו בגדיו: אאבנט של מלכים. שעשוי כולו דניסכא [ה] וכל ישראל בני מלכים ראוים לו: תרי המייני קאמרת. הא ודאי משאוי הוא ואסור לשון תלמידי רבינו יצחק (ג) נ"ע [ובתלמידי] רבינו הלוי מצאתי מותר והראשון נראה לי משום דגבי הצלת דליקה מנינן לר' יוסי שמנה עשר כלים והתם חד חגור הוא דמנינן בכל כתבי הקדש (לקמן דף קכ.) ואי שני חגורות שרי לכתחילה נימני התם תרי: רסוקי. חתיכת מעיל רחבה: אי אית ליה מפרחייתא. רצועות קצרות תלויות בה לקושרה בהם ולהדקה סביבותיו: שרי. דמיהדק שפיר וליכא למיחש דילמא משתרי קטרי ונפיל ואתי לאיתויי: מפרחייתא. פינדל"א בלע"ז: מנקטא פארי (ד). מוסטניל"א והוא בגד שיש לו שנצים כעין מכנסים ומכנסת בו רצועה רחבה וקושרת סביב צוארה והבגד תלוי על לבה והוא חשוב ומצוייר בזהב וי"מ כמין חצי עגול עשוי כמין כלבוס [ס] (ה) אוחזת בו מפתחי חלוקה והפגם בולע צוארה והוא של זהב לוי"ה: נזמי האף. אבל נזמי האוזן מותרין לכתחלה דטריחא לה מילתא למישלף ואחויי מפני שאזניה מכוסות בקישורין: ולא בטבעת שאין עליה חותם. קתני מתניתין דאם יצאת פטורה דתכשיט הוא לה ומשום דילמא משלפא ומחויא הוא דמיתסר: הא יש עליה חותם חייבת חטאת. דלאו תכשיט הוא והוי משאוי: נזמים. נזמי האוזן: וטבעת בין שיש כו'. כלומר וטבעת שאמרנו בין שיש עליה כו': הא רבי נחמיה. דאמר עיקר טבעת אדעתא דחותם הוא חייבת חטאת דחותם לאשה לאו תכשיט הוא דאין דרך לאשה לחתום ולשלוח שלוחים שאין חותם עשוי אלא לאדם גדול וממונה והא דקתני תכשיט הוא רבנן דאמרי גופה של טבעת עיקר ואדעתא דטבעת נפקא ביה וטבעת ודאי תכשיט הוא: טמאה. דטבעת עיקר והוה ליה פשוטי כלי מתכות: היא של אלמוג וחותמה של מתכת טהורה. דהוה ליה פשוטי כלי עץ: הלך אחר סמלוניו. ואם של מתכות הם טמא: סמלוניו. העול שלהם לא היה פגום כשלנו אלא חלק ונוקבים בו שני נקבים וביניהם כעובי עורף השור ותוחבין בהן שתי יתדות והם סימלונין:

בקולב

תוספות

מאן דרכה למיפק בכלילא אשה חשובה. אומר ר"י דדוקא בכלילא שרי שמואל הכא וכן רבי אליעזר דוקא בעיר של זהב שאין כל הנשים רגילות בהן אלא אשה חשובה אבל שאר תכשיטי נשים אסירי אפי' לאשה חשובה דאין לחלק בין הנשים והביא ראיה מס"פ כירה (לעיל דף מו:) דקאמר עולא מה טעם הואיל ואיכא תורת כלי עליהן ומה דחק לומר כן כיון דחזי לנשים חשובות דאפי' לרבנן דאסרי בעיר של זהב לאשה חשובה מודו בשאר תכשיטים אליבא דשמואל דשרי כלילא אפילו לרבנן:

אאבנט של מלכים. שמלבושם הוא ואין להם אבנט אחר ה"נ שרי האי קמרא לאיתתא דמלבושה היא ולא משלפא ומחויא:

תרי המייני קאמרת. לשון אחד פי' בקונטרס לאיסור ואע"ג דחשיב בפ' כל כתבי (לקמן דף קכ:) בי"ח כלים פונדא וחגור ופי' התם בקונט' דפונדא הוא אזור היינו כגון שיש בגד מפסיק בינתים אבל תרי המייני זה על גב זה אסור ולא דמי לכמה מלבושים שאדם לובש בשביל הקור אבל תרי המייני מה הנאה יש ואין דרך לחגור ומשוי הוא:

מנקטא פארי. פירורי הפת ותכשיט הוא:

נזמי האף. ונזמי האוזן שרו כדפי' בקונטרס ואע"ג דאמר לקמן [ס] הבנות יוצאות בחוטין שבאזניהן ואמר בגמ' דשל מיני צבעונים אסירי דילמא משלפי הואיל ותכשיט נינהו התם יותר קל ליטלם מנזמי האוזן:

הא יש עליה חותם חייבת חטאת. אסיפא סמיך [י] דקתני בהדיא דחייבת חטאת:

רבי נחמיה מטמא. נראה לר"י דברישא מטהר דלא בעי למימר הלך אף אחר חותמה אלא דוקא אחר חותמה שהוא עיקר וכן משמע בהדיא בתוספתא דמסכת כלים [כ] דתניא טבעת של מתכת וחותמה של אלמוג רבי נחמיה מטהר שהיה רבי נחמיה אומר בטבעת הלך אחר חותמה:

עין משפט נר מצוה

כב א ב מיי' פי"ט מהל' שבת הלכה י' טוש"ע א"ח סי' שג סעיף ה:
כג ג מיי' שם הל' ב' סמג לאוין כה:
כד ד טוש"ע א"ח סי' שא סעיף לו:
כה ה טוש"ע א"ח סי' שג סעיף ו:
כו ו מיי' שם הלכה ז טוש"ע שם סעיף ח:

רבינו חננאל

כדעבד ר' עקיבא לדביתהו. ת"ר לא תצא אשה בעיר של זהב ואם יצא חייבת חטאת דברי ר' מאיר וחכ"א לא תצא ואם יצאת פטורה. ר' אליעזר אומר יוצאה אשה בעיר של זהב לכתחלה: כלילא רב אסר ושמואל שרי. פי' נסכא חוטין מלשון המסכת (כלים פכ"א). רוקתא מטלית. וקיי"ל כרב אשי דהוא בתראה דאמר ארוקתא כו' כ"ע לא פליגי דשרי כי פליגא כלילא דאניסכא רב אסר ושמואל שרי וקיי"ל כרב באיסורי ואע"ג דאיכא למימר מעשה רב והא דדרש [לוי] כלילא [שרי] ונפקו כ"ד כלילי מנהרדעא וכן הא דדרש רבה בר אבוה במחוזא כלילא שרי כלילא דאניסכא דרשו דשרי. כיון דלא איתמרא בהדיא לא שרינן לה דדלמא לא שרי אלא דארוקתא: אמר רב ששת קמרא שרי הוא חגור שבמתנים כגון אבנט רחב מדבעא רבינא מרב אשי קמרא עילוי המיינא מאי ואמר ליה תרי המייני קאמרת ש"מ דקמרא המיינא הוא והא דרב אשי אתמר בה תרי לישני ולישנא בתראה אניסכא שרי פי' כלילא וקמרא. חתיכות חתיכות של זהב נקובות ובהן מרגלית ומעמידין בחוטין שמכניסין בנקבין. נמצא דאניסכא כגון מלאכת אבנט של מלכים כי כן מלאכתן להיעשות בחוטין. רוקתא מטלית. שנמצא בין כלילא בין קמרא חתיכות של זהב נקובות ומרגלית קבוער' במטלי' שנמצאת מלאכתן כגון מלאכת טלית מוזהבת. אמר רב אשי

רב נסים גאון

גברא רבא אריכא אתא לנהרדעאי ומטלע פירוש והוא צולע על ירכו כדמתרגמינן והוא מטלע והדבר שגרם לו זה מפורש בפ' ג' דתענית (דף כה) לוי גזר תעניתא בעא רחמי ולא אתא מיטרא אמר לפניו רבונו של עולם עלית וישבת למעלה במרום ואי אתה משגיח על בניך ואתא מיטרא ואיטלע אמר ר' אלעזר אל יטיח אדם דברים כלפי למעלה שהרי אדם גדול הטיח דברים כלפי למעלה ואטלע ובמסכת סוכה (דף נג) בפ' החליל קאמרי לוי אחוי קידה קמיה דר' ואטלע ואמרו בפירוקה הא והא גרמא ליה אבל מעשה דר' אפס ור' חנינא בר חמא ומה דאמר רבנו הקדוש בצוויו חנינא בר חמא ישב בראש כו' (מעשה כמפורש) [מפורש] בפרק הנושא

מסורת הש"ס

א) [לקמן קלח. תוספתא פ"ה], ב) עדיות פ"ב מ"ז, ג) כתובות קג:, ד) [כלים פרק יא מ"ח ע"ש], ה) [בכלים פי"ג מ"ו לא מזכר פלוגתא דר' נחמי' הלכך שפיר גרסי' דתניא], ו) לעיל נג: תוספתא דכלי' ב"מ פ"ג כלים פי"ג מ"ו, ז) [סוכה נג.], ח) מה

ט) [דף סה.], י) [לקמן סב.], כ) [פ"ג בבא מציעא].

הגהות הב"ח

(א) גמ' למיתב גבי' וקם וקאתי: (ב) רש"י ד"ה נח נפשיה וכו' שתי שנים ומאלה ויתיב: (ג) ד"ה תרי וכו' ר' יצחק בר יהודה נ"ע: (ד) ד"ה מנקטא פארי. נ"ב ע"ל בדף נז ע"ב במה שפירש"י: (ה) בא"ד כמין כלבוס כזה:

גליון הש"ס

גמ' א"ל רב שמואל בר בר חנה לרב יוסף. לקמן קמו ע"ב: רש"י ד"ה אאבנט וכו' וכל ישראל בני מלכים. עיין לקמן דף קיא ע"א: תוס' ד"ה נזמי האף וכו' ליטלם מנזמי האזן. עיין תשו' ב"ח החדשות סי' מ"א:

תורה אור השלם

א) וְתִגְזַר אֹמֶר וְיָקָם לָךְ וְעַל דְּרָכֶיךָ נָגַהּ אוֹר: [איוב כב, כח]

ליקוטי רש"י

ר"מ סבר. דלאו תכשיט הוא אלא משוי. תכשיט הוא. ולכתחילה אסור דילמא שלפא ומחויא [לקמן קלח.]. גברא רבה אריכא [דאיטלע]. פסח היה כדאמרינן בעלמא (סוכה נג.) לוי אחוי קידה ואטלע [כתובות קג:]. נעשה חיגר [סוכה נג.]. שנצלע בקידה [תענית כה.]. נצלע בגוקא לאטמא [מגילה כב:]. וקאתי להכא. לבבל. מיכף הוה כייף ליה. קודם שיגלה ממקומו אבל לר' חנינא לא כייף [כתובות שם]. מאי קטלא מנקטא פארי. בגד חשוב לתלות בצוארה כנגד לבה שלא יפול מה שהיא אוכלת על בגדיה ויש לו מקום שנצים כעין שעושים למכנסים ותוחב בו רצועה רחבה ומוללתו סביב הרצועה שהבגד רחב הרבה וקושרת הרצועה סביב צוארה [לעיל נז: עיי"ש עוד ובתוס' שם]. ותגזר אומר. מה שתבקש מן היוצר יעשה [ב"מ קו.]. ויקם לך. כמו ויקום לך [איוב כב, כח]. אלמוג. עצי אלמוגים והוא נאה. טמאה. דנתר טבעת אזלינן ופשוטי כלי מתכות טמאים [לעיל נב:].

מַר סָבַר דִּילְמָא שָׁלְפָא וּמַחְוְיָא – One **master** (Rav) **holds** that [a **woman**] **might remove** such a tiara in the street **and show it** to a friend, וְאָתֵי לְאַתוּיֵי – **and come to carry** it four *amos* in the public domain; thus, wearing it is prohibited. וּמַר סָבַר – **But** the other **master** (Shmuel) **holds** that it is permitted; מַאן דַּרְכָּהּ לְמֵיפַּק בִּכְלִילָא – for **who is accustomed to go out wearing** such **a tiara?** אִשָּׁה חֲשׁוּבָה – **A distinguished woman,** וְאִשָּׁה חֲשׁוּבָה לֹא שָׁלְפָא וּמַחְוְיָא – **and a distinguished woman is not** likely **to remove** her tiara **and show it** to another woman in the street.[14]

The Gemara cites support for the latter interpretation:

אָמַר לֵיהּ רַב שְׁמוּאֵל בַּר בַּר חָנָה לְרַב יוֹסֵף – **Rav Shmuel bar bar Chanah said to Rav Yosef:** בְּפֵירוּשׁ אָמַרְתְּ לָן מִשְּׁמֵיהּ דְּרַב כְּלִילָא שָׁרֵי – **You explicitly told us**[15] **in Rav's name** that wearing **a tiara is permitted** on the Sabbath; thus, you obviously subscribed to Rav Ashi's interpretation of the dispute, for according to Rav Ashi, Rav permits the wearing of a studded fabric tiara.[16]

The Gemara cites other instances where rulings permitting the wearing of tiaras on the Sabbath were issued:

אָמְרוּ לֵיהּ לְרַב – **[The Sages] said to Rav:** אָתָא גַּבְרָא רַבָּה אֲרִיכָא לִנְהַרְדְּעָא – **A great man who was** very **tall came to Nehardea,** וּמַטְלַע – **and he was limping;** וְדָרַשׁ כְּלִילָא שָׁרֵי – **and he taught** that wearing **a tiara** outside on the Sabbath **is permitted.**[17]

Rav identified the anonymous sage:

אָמַר – **Rav said:** מַאן גַּבְרָא רַבָּה אֲרִיכָא [דְּאִיטְּלַע] – **Who is a great man that is** very **tall and limps?** לֵוִי – It is **Levi.**[18]

Rav commented further:

שְׁמַע מִינָּהּ נָח נַפְשֵׁיהּ דְּרַבִּי אֲפֵס – And **from this,** i.e. the fact that Levi has come, **we can deduce** that **R' Afeis,** who was the head of the academy in Eretz Yisrael, **must have died,** וִיתֵיב רַבִּי חֲנִינָא בְּרֵישָׁא – **and R' Chanina,** with whom Levi had been studying,[19] **is now the head**[20] of the academy; וְלָא הֲוָה לֵיהּ אִינִישׁ לְלֵוִי לְמֵיתַב גַּבֵּיהּ – **and [Levi] did not have anyone with whom he could sit** and study, וְקָאָתֵי לְהָכָא – **so he came here** to Nehardea to seek a teacher.[21]

The Gemara questions Rav's conclusion:

וְדִילְמָא נָח נַפְשֵׁיהּ דְּרַבִּי חֲנִינָא – **But** how did Rav know that R' Afeis had died? **Perhaps** it was **R' Chanina** who **died,** וְרַבִּי אֲפֵס כִּדְקָאֵי קָאֵי – **and R' Afeis still stands in his place** as the head of the Eretz Yisrael academy; וְלָא הֲוָה לֵיהּ אִינִישׁ לְלֵוִי לְמֵיתַב גַּבֵּיהּ – **but** as a result of R' Chanina's death, **[Levi] had no Sage with whom he could sit** and study,[22] וְקָאָתֵי לְהָכָא – **and** that is why **he came here** to Nehardea!?

The Gemara explains why Rav rejected this possibility:

אִם אִיתָא דְּרַבִּי חֲנִינָא שְׁכִיב – Rav reasoned that **if it were so that R' Chanina had died,** לֵוִי לְרַבִּי אֲפֵס מֵיכַף הֲוָה כָּיֵיף לֵיהּ – **Levi would have** subordinated **himself to** the authority of **R' Afeis,** who was older than Levi.[23] Thus, it must have been R' Afeis who died.[24] וְתוּ – **And furthermore,** Rav knew that R' Chanina had not died, דְּרַבִּי חֲנִינָא לָא סַגִּי דְּלָא מָלֵיךְ – for **it could not be that R' Chanina would never head** the academy;[25] דְּכִי הֲוָה קָא נִיחָא נַפְשֵׁיהּ דְּרַבִּי אָמַר – **for when Rebbi was dying, he said:** חֲנִינָא בְּרַבִּי חָמָא יָתִיב בְּרֹאשׁ – **"Chanina the son of R' Chama shall sit at the head** of the academy";[26] וּכְתִיב בְּהוּ בְּצַדִּיקִים – **and it is written regarding the righteous,** "וְתִגְזַר־אֹמֶר וְיָקָם לָךְ וגו׳" – **"*And you will make a plan and it will succeed for you etc.*"**[27] Thus, it had to be that R' Chanina would head the academy at some point; Levi's coming to Nehardea could therefore only be a result of the death of R' Afeis.

The Gemara recounts the reaction to Levi's exposition:

דָּרַשׁ לֵוִי בִּנְהַרְדְּעָא כְּלִילָא שָׁרֵי – **Levi taught in Nehardea** that wearing **a tiara** on the Sabbath **is permitted,** נְפִיק עֶשְׂרִין וְאַרְבַּע כְּלִילֵי מִכּוּלָּהּ נְהַרְדְּעָא – and **twenty-four tiaras emerged**[28] **from all of Nehardea.** דָּרַשׁ רַבָּה בַּר אֲבוּהָ בִּמְחוֹזָא כְּלִילָא שָׁרֵי – **Rabbah bar Avuha taught in Mechoza** that wearing **a tiara** on

NOTES

14. See above, note 8.

There is a dispute among the Rishonim whether Shmuel's ruling permitting a tiara of metal plate is linked to the ruling of R' Eliezer (cited in the Gemara above) that permits the wearing of a "city of gold." *Meiri* suggests that Shmuel's ruling is indeed based on R' Eliezer's ruling; see also *Piskei Rid. Tosafos, Ritva MHK* ed., *Rashba* and other Rishonim maintain that Shmuel holds that a tiara is a *more* significant ornament than a "city of gold," and even the Rabbis who prohibit the wearing of that ornament would permit the wearing of a tiara of metal plate. [Similarly, Shmuel agrees that a frontlet made of gold that is worn on the forehead may not be worn outside on the Sabbath if it is not attached to her hat, because the frontlet is an ornament worn by many women, and it was therefore included in the Rabbis' edict, unlike the more exclusive tiara (*Chelkas Binyamin;* see also *Dibros Moshe* 53:12).

15. Rav Yosef became ill and forgot much of his Talmudic knowledge. His disciples would often remind him of statements he had made before his illness (*Rashi;* see, for example, *Makkos* 4a).

16. According to the first interpretation of the dispute, however, Rav forbids the wearing of *any* tiara [and even Shmuel permits only a fabric tiara].

17. [The Sages told Rav that a sage had arrived from Eretz Yisrael and cited a ruling issued there that permitted the wearing of a tiara outside on the Sabbath; they did not, however, know the identity of the sage.] *Ritva* explains that the sage taught that wearing a tiara made of jewel-studded fabric was permitted; thus, his teaching conformed with Rav's opinion according to Rav Ashi's interpretation of the dispute between Rav and Shmuel (in line with the general rule that when Rav and Shmuel dispute a matter of ritual law, the halachah accords with Rav); he maintains that this is the view of *Rashi* as well.

18. Levi became lame as a result of an injury he suffered while demonstrating an intricate form of ritual prostration before Rebbi (*Rashi,* from *Succah* 53a; see Gemara there).

19. *Rashi* (citing *Kesubos* 103b) supplies the historical background to this situation. Rebbi, who was the head of the academy in Eretz Yisrael, had stated on his deathbed that R' Chanina was to head the academy after him. When Rebbi passed away, however, R' Chanina refused to assume the position, because he did not wish to subject R' Afeis, who was two-and-one-half years his senior (see *Bach* §2), to the embarrassment of being subordinate to his junior. R' Afeis then assumed the position, and R' Chanina, who was [at least] R' Afeis' equal in wisdom, studied outside the academy. So that a scholar of R' Chanina's stature would not be left to study alone, Levi, who was a colleague of his, would study with him rather than under R' Afeis (see also Gemara below).

20. Literally: R' Chanina sits at the head.

21. Levi was the equal of R' Chanina in both years and scholarship, and he therefore did not feel beholden to remain with R' Chanina once R' Chanina had assumed the position at the head of the academy [and was no longer studying alone] (*Rashi*).

22. For he had been studying with R' Chanina, as explained above.

23. [R' Afeis was certainly Levi's senior (see *Rashi*), and Levi would have studied under him if R' Chanina had passed away, rather than leaving Eretz Yisrael.]

24. And Levi did not remain to study under R' Chanina, as explained above (note 21).

25. Literally: it would not be enough for R' Chanina if he were not to rule [the academy].

26. See above, note 19.

27. *Job* 22:28. The Gemara uses this verse, which speaks of the special treatment God accords the righteous, to describe the power of the declaration of a righteous person (see also below, 63a). [Although the position was indeed offered to R' Chanina, and he refused the appointment of his own volition, Rav was confident that Rebbi's statement ("Chanina . . . shall head the academy") would be fulfilled at some point during R' Chanina's lifetime.]

28. I.e. twenty-four tiaras were worn outside on the Sabbath.

כדעבד ליה רבי עקיבא לדביתהו (א) ת"ר לא תצא אשה בעיר של זהב ואם יצתה חייבת חטאת דברי רבי מאיר וחכמים אומרים לא תצא ואם יצתה פטורה (ב) רבי אליעזר אומר יוצאה אשה בעיר של זהב לכתחלה במאי קמיפלגי ר"מ סבר משוי הוא ורבנן סברי תכשיט הוא דילמא שלפא ומחויא ליה ואתיא לאתויי ור"א סבר מאן דרכה למיפק בעיר של זהב אשה חשובה ואשה חשובה לא משלפא ומחויא כלילא רב אסר ושמואל (א) שרי דאניסכא כולי עלמא לא פליגי דאסור כי פליגי דארוקתא מר סבר אניסכא עיקר ומר סבר ארוקתא עיקר רב אשי מתני לקולא (ג) דארוקתא דכולי עלמא לא פליגי דשרי כי פליגי דאניסכא מר סבר דילמא שלפא ומחויא ואתי לאתויי ומר סבר מאן דרכה למיפק בכלילא אשה חשובה ואשה חשובה לא שלפא ומחויא (ה) א"ל רב שמואל בר בר חנה לרב יוסף בפירוש אמרת לן משמיה דרב כלילא שרי (ג) אמרו ליה לרב אתא גברא רבה אריכא לנהרדעא ומטלע ודרש כלילא שרי אמר מאן גברא רבה אריכא [דאיטלע] לוי ש"מ נח נפשיה דרבי אפס ויתיב ר' חנינא ברישא ולא הוה ליה איניש ללוי למיתב גביה (א) וקאתי להכא ודילמא נח נפשיה דרבי חנינא ור' אפס כדקאי קאי ולא הוה ליה איניש ללוי למיתב גביה וקאתי להכא אם איתא דרבי חנינא שכיב לוי לר' אפס מיכף הוה כייף ליה ותו דרבי חנינא לא סגי דלא מליך דכי הוה קא ניחא נפשיה דרבי אמר חנינא בר' חמא יתיב בראש וכתיב בהו בצדיקים (א) ותגזר אומר ויקם לך וגו' דרש לוי בנהרדעא כלילא שרי נפיק עשרין וארבע כלילי מכולה נהרדעא דרש רבה בר אבוה במחוזא כלילא שרי ונפקו תמני סרי כלילי מחדא מבואה אמר רב יהודה אמר רב שמואל קמרא שרי איכא דאמרי דארוקתא ואמר רב ספרא מידי דהוה אטלית מוזהבת ואיכא דאמרי (ג) דאניסכא ואמר רב ספרא מידי דהוה אאבנט של מלכים א"ל רבינא לרב אשי קמרא עילוי המיינא מאי א"ל (ד) תרי המייני קאמרת אמר רב אשי (ה) האי רסוקא אי אית ליה מפרחייתא שרי ואי לא אסיר: ולא בקטלא: מאי קטלא מנקטא פארי: נזמים: (י) נזמי האף: ולא בטבעת שאין עליה חותם: הא יש עליה חותם חייבת אלמא לאו תכשיט הוא ורמינהו (ז) תכשיטי נשים טמאים ואלו הן תכשיטי נשים קטלאות נזמים וטבעות וטבעת בין שיש עליה חותם בין שאין עליה חותם ונזמי האף ואמר רבי זירא לא קשיא הא ר' נחמיה הא רבנן (ח) דתניא (ו) היא של מתכת וחותמה של אלמוג טמאה היא של אלמוג וחותמה של מתכת טהורה ורבי נחמיה מטמא שהיה ר' נחמיה אומר בטבעת הלך אחר חותמה בעול הלך אחר סמלוניו

בקולב

רש"י

כדעבד ליה ר' עקיבא לדביתהו. במסכת נדרים (דף נ.): כלילא. על פדחתה היא קושרתו מאזן לאזן יש שכולו טס זהב שקורין לימ"א ויש שעושין ממשי טווי עם הזהב שקורין פריז"ש: דניסכא. טס העשוי כולו מניסכא דהיינו זהב או כסף דבר הניתך: דאסיר. מגו דחשיב גזירה דילמא שלפא ומחוייא: דארוקתא. רצועה שמצויירת בזהב ובאבנים טובות: אניסכא. דאית ביה עיקר ומחויא ליה ומר סבר ארוקתא הוא עיקר דידיה ולא חשיב ליה ולא מחויא ליה: כולי עלמא לא פליגי דשרי. דארוקתא עיקר: בפירוש אמרת לן משמיה דרב. לפני חלייך קודם ששכחת תלמודך: כלילא שרי. אלמא דרב אשי עיקר דמוקי פלוגתא בדניסכא אבל בארוקתא מודה רב ואיכא לאוקמי לדידיה בארוקתא: גברא רבה אריכא ומטלע. לוי איטלע דאחוי קידה קמיה דרבי[ז]: נח נפשיה דרבי אפס. במסכת כתובות בהנושא (קג:) אמרינן דכי שכיב רבי אמר רבי חנינא בר חמא ישב בראש ולא קיבל עליו רבי חנינא שהיה רבי אפס גדול ממנו שתי שנים (ב) ויתיב רבי אפס ברישא ומתוך שהיה רבי חנינא חשוב לא נכנס לבית מדרשו והיה יושב בחוץ ומשום כבודו ישב לו לוי אצלו: וקאתי להכא. שלא היה רבי חנינא גדול הימנו לא בתורה ולא בשנים ולא ניכף ליה לוי ובא לכאן: לוי לרבי אפס מיכף הוה כייף ליה. שהרי זקן ממנו: קמרא. אבנט חשוב יש שעושין אותו טס של זהב ויש שעושין אותו רצועה משבצות זהב ואבנים קבועות בו: מידי דהוה אטלית מוזהבת. דהוי תכשיט ושריא ולמישלף ואחויי נמי לא חיישינן שאין דרך להתיר אזורו בשוק ויפלו בגדיו: אאבנט של מלכים. שעשוי כולו דניסכא ° וכל ישראל בני מלכים ראוים לו: תרי המייני קאמרת. הא ודאי משאוי הוא ואסור לשון תלמידי רבינו יצחק (ג) נ"ע [ובתלמידי] רבינו הלוי מצאתי מותר והראשון נראה לי משום דגבי הצלת דליקה מנינן לר' יוסי שמנה עשר כלים והתם חד חגור הוא דמנינן בכל כתבי הקדש (לקמן דף קכ.) ואי שני חגורות שרי לכתחילה נימני התם תרי: רסוקי. חתיכת מעיל רחבה: אי אית ליה מפרחייתא. רצועות קצרות תלויות בה לקושרה בהם ולהדקה סביבותיו: שרי. דמיהדק שפיר וליכא למיחש דילמא משתרי קטרי ונפיל ואתי לאיתויי: מפרחייתא. פינדל"א בלע"ז: מנקטא פארי (ד). מוסטניל"א והוא בגד שיש לו שנצים כעין מכנסים ומכנסת בו רצועה רחבה וקושרת סביב צוארה והבגד תלוי על לבה והוא חשוב ומצוייר בזהב וי"מ כמין חצי עגול עשוי כמין כלבוס (ה) (ס) אוחזת בו מפתחי חלוקה והפגם בולע צוארה והוא של זהב לרי"ה: נזמי האף. אבל נזמי האזן מותרין לכתחלה דטריחא לה מילתא למישלף ואחויי מפני שאזניה מכוסות בקישורין: ולא בטבעת שאין עליה חותם. קתני מתניתין דאם יצאת פטורה דתכשיט הוא לה ומשום דילמא משלפא ומחויא הוא דמיתסר: הא יש עליה חותם חייבת חטאת. דלאו תכשיט הוא והוי משאוי: נזמים. נזמי האזן: וטבעת בין שיש כו'. כלומר וטבעת שאמרנו בין שיש עליה כו': הא רבי נחמיה. דאמר עיקר טבעת אדעתא דחותם הוא חייבת חטאת דחותם לאשה לאו תכשיט הוא דאין דרך לאשה לחתום ולשלוח שלוחים שאין חותם עשוי אלא לאדם גדול וממונה והא דקתני תכשיט הוא רבנן דאמרי גופה של טבעת עיקר ואדעתא דטבעת נפקא ביה וטבעת ודאי תכשיט הוא: טמאה. דטבעת עיקר והוה ליה פשוטי כלי מתכות: היא של אלמוג וחותמה של מתכת טהורה. דהוה ליה פשוטי כלי עץ: הלך אחר סמלוניו. ואם של מתכות הם טמא: סמלוניו. העול שלהם לא היה פגום כשלנו אלא חלק ונוקבים בו שני נקבים וביניהם כעובי עורף השור ותוחבין בהן שתי יתדות והם סימלונין:

בקולב

תוספות

מאן דרכה למיפק בכלילא אשה חשובה. אומר ר"י דדוקא בכלילא שרי שמואל הכא וכן רבי אליעזר דוקא בעיר של זהב שאין כל הנשים רגילות בהן אלא אשה חשובה אבל שאר תכשיטי נשים אסירי אפי' לאשה חשובה דאין לחלק בין הנשים והביא ראיה מס"פ כירה (לעיל דף מו:) דקאמר עולא מה טעם הואיל ואיכא תורת כלי עליהן ומה דחק לומר כן כיון דחזי לנשים חשובות דאפי' לרבנן דאסרי בעיר של זהב לאשה חשובה מודו בשאר תכשיטים אליבא דשמואל דשרי כלילא אפילו לרבנן:

אאבנט של מלכים. שמלובשם הוא ואין להם אבנט אחר ה"נ שרי האי קמרא לאיתתא דמלבושה היא ולא משלפא ומחויא:

תרי המייני קאמרת. לשון אחד פי' בקונטרס לאיסור ואע"ג דחשיב בפ' כל כתבי (לקמן דף קכ:) בי"ח כלים פונדא וחגור ופי' התם בקונט' דפונדא הוא אזור היינו כגון שיש בגד מפסיק בינתים אבל תרי המייני זה על גב זה אסור ולא דמי לכמה מלבושים שאדם לובש בשביל הקור אבל תרי המייני מה הנאה יש ואין דרך לחגור ומשוי הוא:

מנקטא פארי. פירורי הפת ותכשיט הוא:

נזמי האף. ונזמי האזן שרו כדפי' בקונטרס ואע"ג דאמר לקמן (ט) הבנות יוצאות בחוטין שבאזניהן ואמר בגמ' דשל מיני צבעונים אסירי דילמא משלפי הואיל ותכשיט נינהו התם יותר קל ° ליטלם מנזמי האזן:

הא יש עליה חותם חייבת חטאת. אסיפא סמיך (י) דקתני בהדיא דחייבת חטאת:

רבי נחמיה מטמא. נראה לר"י דברישא מטהר דלא בעי למימר הלך אף אחר חותמה אלא דוקא אחר חותמה שהוא עיקר וכן משמע בהדיא בתוספתא דמסכת כלים (כ) דתניא טבעת של מתכת וחותמה של אלמוג רבי נחמיה מטהר שהיה רבי נחמיה אומר בטבעת הלך אחר חותמה:

עין משפט נר מצוה

כב א ב מיי' פי"ט מהל' שבת הלכה י' טוש"ע א"ח סי' שג סעיף ה:
כג ג מיי' שם הל' ב' סמג לאוין סה:
כד ד טוש"ע א"ח סי' שא סעיף לו:
כה ה טוש"ע א"ח סי' שג סעיף ו:
כו ו מיי' שם הלכה ז טוש"ע שם סעיף ח:

רבינו חננאל

כדעבד ר' עקיבא לדביתהו. ת"ר לא תצא אשה בעיר של זהב ואם יצא חייבת חטאת דברי ר' מאיר וחכ"א לא תצא ואם יצאת פטורה. ר' אליעזר אומר יוצאה אשה בעיר של זהב לכתחלה: כלילא רב אסר ושמואל שרי. פי' נסכא חוטין מלשון המסכת (כלים פכ"א). רוקתא מטלית. וקיי"ל כרב אשי דהוא בתראה דאמר ארוקתא כו' כ"ע לא פליגי דשרי כי פליגא כלילא דאניסכא רב אסר ושמואל שרי וקיי"ל כרב באיסורי ואע"ג דאיכא למימר מעשה רב והא דדרש [לוי] כלילא [שרי] ונפקו כ"ד כלילי מנהרדעא וכן הא דדרש רבה בר אבוה במחוזא כלילא שרי כלילא דאניסכא דרשו דשרי. כיון דלא איתמרא בהדיא לא שרינן לה דדלמא לא שרי אלא דארוקתא: אמר רב ששת קמרא שרי הוא חגור שבמתנים כגון אבנט רחב מדבעא רבינא מרב אשי קמרא עילוי המיינא מאי ואמר ליה תרי המייני קאמרת ש"מ דקמרא המיינא הוא והא דרב אשי אתמר בה תרי לישני ולישנא בתראה אניסכא שרי פי' כלילא וקמרא. חתיכות חתיכות של זהב נקובות ובהן מרגלית ומעמידין בחוטין שמכניסין בנקבין. נמצא דאניסכא כגון מלאכת אבנט של מלכים כי כן מלאכתן להיעשות בחוטין. רוקתא מטלית. שנמצא בין כלילא בין קמרא חתיכות של זהב נקובות ומרגלית קבוע' במטלי' שנמצאת מלאכתן כגון מלאכת טלית מוזהבת. אמר רב אשי

רב נסים גאון

גברא רבא אריכא אתא לנהרדעאי ומטלע פירוש והוא צולע על ירוכו כדמתרגמינן והוא מטלע והדבר שגרם לו זה מפורש בפ' ג' דתענית (דף כה) לוי גזר תעניתא בעא רחמי ולא אתא מיטרא אמר לפניו רבונו של עולם עלית וישבת למעלה במרום ואי אתה משגיח על בניך ואתא מיטרא ואיטלע אמר ר' אלעזר אל יטיח אדם דברים כלפי למעלה שהרי אדם גדול הטיח דברים כלפי למעלה ואטלע ובמסכת סוכה (דף נג) בפ' החליל קאמרי לוי אחוי קידה קמיה דר' ואטלע ואמרו בפירוקה הא והא גרמא ליה אבל מעשה דר' אפס ור' חנינא בר חמא ומה דאמר רבנו הקדוש בצוויו חנינא בר חמא ישב בראש כו' (מעשה כמפורש) [מפורש] בפרק הנושא

מסורת הש"ס

א) [לקמן קלח. תוספתא פ"ה], ב) עדיות פ"ב מ"ז, ג) כתובות קג:, ד) [כלים פרק יא מ"ח ע"ש], ה) [בכלים פי"ג מ"ו לא מזכר פלוגתא דר' נחמי' הלכך שפיר גרסי' דתניא], ו) לעיל נג: תוספתא דכלי' ב"מ פ"ג כלים פי"ג מ"ו, ז) [סוכה נג.], ח) כח

ט) [דף סה.], י) [לקמן סב.], כ) [פ"ג בבא מציעא].

הגהות הב"ח

(א) גמ' למיתב גבי' וקם וקאתי: (ב) רש"י ד"ה נח נפשיה וכו' שתי שנים ומחלה ויתיב: (ג) ד"ה תרי וכו' ר' יצחק בר יהודה נ"ע: (ד) ד"ה מנקטא פארי. נ"ב ע"ל בדף נז ע"ב במה שפירש"י: (ה) בא"ד כמין כלבוס כזה:

גליון הש"ס

גמ' א"ל רב שמואל בר בר חנה לרב יוסף. לקמן קמו ע"ב: רש"י ד"ה אאבנט וכו' וכל ישראל בני מלכים. עיין לקמן דף קיא ע"א: תוס' ד"ה נזמי האף וכו' ליטלם מנזמי האזן. עיין תשו' ב"ח המדשות סי' מ"א:

תורה אור השלם

א) וְתִגְזַר אֹמֶר וְיָקָם לָךְ וְעַל דְּרָכֶיךָ נָגַהּ אוֹר: [איוב כב, כח]

ליקוטי רש"י

ר"מ סבר. דלאו תכשיט הוא אלא משוי. תכשיט הוא. ולכתחילה אסור דילמא שלפא ומחויא [לקמן קלח.]. גברא רבה אריכא [דאיטלע]. פסח היה כדאמרינן בעלמא (סוכה נג.) לוי אחוי קידה ואטלע [כתובות קג:]. נעשה חיגר [סוכה נג.]. שנצלע בקידה [תענית כה.]. נצלע בבוקא דאטמא [מגילה כב:]. וקאתי להכא. לבבל. מיכף הוה כייף ליה. קודם שיגלה ממקומו אבל לר' חנינא לא כייף [כתובות שם]. מאי קטלא מנקטא פארי. בגד חשוב לתלות בצוארה כנגד לבה שלא יפול מה שהיא אוכלת על בגדיה ויש לו מקום שנצים כעין שעושים למכנסים ותוחב בו רצועה רחבה ומוללתו סביב הרצועה שהבגד רחב הרבה וקושרת הרצועה סביב צוארה [לעיל נז: עיי"ש עוד ובתוס' שם]. ותגזר אומר. מה שתבקש מן היוצר יעשה [ב"מ קו.]. ויקם לך. כמו ויקום לך [איוב כב, כח]. אלמוג. עצי אלמוגים והוא נאה. טמאה. דבתר טבעת אזלינן ופשוטי כלי מתכות טמאים [לעיל נב:].

the Sabbath **is permitted,** וְנָפְקוּ תְּמָנֵי סְרֵי כְּלִילֵי מֵחֲדָא מְבוֹאָה – **and eighteen tiaras emerged from a single *mavoi*** in the town.[29]

The Gemara discusses another ornament:

אָמַר רַב יְהוּדָה אָמַר רַב שְׁמוּאֵל – **Rav Yehudah said in the name of Rav Shmuel:**[30] קַמְרָא שְׁרֵי – Wearing **an ornate belt**[31] outside on the Sabbath **is permitted.**

The Gemara presents two interpretations of this ruling:

אִיכָּא דְּאָמְרֵי דְּאַרוּקְתָּא – **There are those that say** that Rav Yehudah's ruling refers **to a fabric** belt studded with gold and precious stones; וְאָמַר רַב סַפְרָא – **and Rav Safra said** in explanation of the ruling מִידֵי דַּהֲוָה אַטַּלִּית מוּזְהֶבֶת – that wearing such a belt is permitted **just as** wearing **a cloak decorated with gold** is permitted.[32] וְאִיכָּא דְּאָמְרֵי דְּאַנִּיסְכָּא – **And there are those who say** that Rav Yehudah's ruling refers to a belt made **of hammered** gold; וְאָמַר רַב סַפְרָא – **and Rav Safra said** in explanation of the ruling מִידֵי דַּהֲוָה אַאַבְנֵט שֶׁל מְלָכִים – that wearing this belt is permitted **just as a** hammered golden **belt of kings** may be worn.[33]

The Gemara raises an inquiry regarding such a belt:

אָמַר לֵיהּ רָבִינָא לְרַב אַשִׁי – **Ravina said to Rav Ashi:** קַמְרָא עִילָּוֵי הֶמְיָינָא מַאי – If one wishes to wear **an ornate belt on top of a** regular **belt, what** is the law? May he wear the belt in this manner or not?[34] אָמַר לֵיהּ – **[Rav Ashi] replied to [Ravina]:** תְּרֵי הֶמְיָינֵי קָאָמְרַת – **Do you speak of two belts** worn one directly atop the other?! Such wearing is certainly forbidden, for one does not usually wear a second belt over the first.[35]

A related ruling:

אָמַר רַב אַשִׁי – **Rav Ashi said:** הַאי רְסוּקָא – **This corset,**[36] אִי אִית לֵיהּ מַפְרְחָיָיתָא שְׁרֵי – **if it has ties** attached to it, wearing **it** outside on the Sabbath **is permitted;** וְאִי לֹא אָסִיר – **but if not,** wearing **it is prohibited.**[37]

The Mishnah stated:

וְלֹא בְּקַטְלָא – AND she may NOT go out WITH A *KATLA*.

The Gemara asks:

מַאי קַטְלָא – **What is a "*katla*"?**

The Gemara explains:

מְנִקְטָא פָּארֵי – A "*katla*" is an ornate bib worn tightly around the neck as **a crumb-catcher.**[38]

NOTES

29. Mechoza was a much wealthier town than Nehardea (see *Bava Kamma* 119 and *Rosh Hashanah* 17b). Thus, the women in a single *mavoi* of Mechoza possessed almost as many tiaras as the entire female population of Nehardea. Cf. *Chasam Sofer.*

[The commentators differ as to the halachah in the dispute between Rav and Shmuel concerning the wearing of tiaras on the Sabbath. *Rosh, Ramban,* and *Tur* §303 are of the opinion that the halachah follows Rav, as explained by Rav Ashi; thus, a fabric tiara is permitted, while a tiara of metal plate is forbidden. (This follows the general rule that we decide the halachah in accordance with Rav in matters of ritual law – *Ritva MHK* ed.) *Rif* and *Rambam* (*Hil. Shabbos* 19:10), however, permit the wearing of both fabric and metal tiaras, in accordance with Shmuel's view. See *Chelkas Binyamin* for a discussion of this dispute.

30. *Rosh* cites this ruling as *Rav Yehudah in the name of Rav; Rif* cites it as *Rav Yehudah in the name of Rav Sheishess.*

31. The Gemara below describes this ornament in more detail (see also next note).

32. I.e. just as a cloak decorated with gold is an ornament [rather than a burden], so too an ornate jewel-studded belt is an ornament and not a burden, and it may be worn on the Sabbath. Nor is there any concern that a person will remove the belt to show it, for if he removes his belt, his clothes will fall (*Rashi*). [*Rashi's* statement here is somewhat problematic, for there is seemingly no reason to assume that a belt would be considered a burden (indeed, it should be viewed as an item of clothing!); so why would a comparison to a decorated cloak be necessary? *Ritva* (*MHK* ed.) therefore states that the comparison to the decorated cloak is made only to indicate that just as we do not concern ourselves with the possibility that a person will remove his cloak to show to others (as he will not remove his clothing in the street), we do not concern ourselves with the possibility that a person will remove his belt in the street (see also Rishonim to the Mishnah on 57a).]

[From *Rashi's* comments here it seems that the Gemara is referring to a belt being worn by a *man* rather than a woman (see *Ran* and *Shabbos Shel Mi*). This is indeed the position of most Rishonim; *Tosafos,* however, maintains that the Gemara is discussing a belt worn by a woman (see next note).]

33. That is, just as a [Jewish] king may wear a belt made of hammered gold on the Sabbath, so too any person may wear such a belt on the Sabbath (although this type of belt was usually only worn by those associated with the monarchy – see *Aruch* ע׳ קמר, citing *Rav Sherira Gaon*); for any Jew is entitled to wear the clothing of royalty [as he is considered royalty] (*Rashi;* this logic is actually subject to dispute in the Gemara later in the tractate [see below, Mishnah 111a]; Rav Yehudah's ruling follows the view of R' Shimon stated there [see *Ritva MHK* ed.]).

Ramban (to 57a) explains that the belt is permitted because it is considered an item of clothing, and a man will not remove his clothes in the street. He infers from this Gemara that purely *ornamental* items worn by men cannot be worn outside on the Sabbath, due to the possibility that a man might remove them to show them to his friends. Other Rishonim, however (see *Ritva MHK* ed. *Rashba,* et al.), explain that the belt being discussed here is considered an ornament, and the reason that the Sages were not concerned for the possibility that the man might remove the belt and show it to a friend is because the Sages did not issue their edict upon men's ornaments at all, as men are not wont to show off their ornaments. [In their view, the Gemara is only explaining why the belt is not considered a burden.] The edict extended only to the ornaments of women, who would often remove their ornament to show them to friends. [*Rashi* is clearly of the opinion that men's ornaments are included in the Sages' decree, as he excludes the fabric belt only because it holds up the man's clothes; see also *Rashi* below, 62a ד״ה אמר עולא. Cf. *Tosafos* there ד״ה וחילופיהן; see *Ran MHK* ed. and *Chelkas Binyamin;* see also *Beur HaGra* to *Orach Chaim* 301:9.]

[These two versions of Rav Safra's statement do not necessarily argue a point of law; it is possible that both types of belts may be worn for the reasons stated (see *Meiri*).]

34. Although the Gemara stated that an ornate belt is considered an ornament, perhaps this is only true when it is worn alone (as kings wear it). The Gemara questions whether it can be worn in a case where it is not functioning as a belt at all (for the belt beneath it is performing that function), but only as an ornament – for perhaps when it is worn in such a fashion, it is a burden (see *Ritva MHK* ed.; see also next note).

35. Even though an ornate belt is considered an ornament, it can only be taken outside when it is being *worn.* Wearing it on top of another belt is tantamount to carrying it, and this is therefore prohibited [as is carrying any ornament] (*Rashi's* preferred explanation; see there for an alternate explanation). See *Mishnah Berurah* 301:133.

The Gemara's statement that wearing two belts is prohibited applies only when the two belts are serving the same function; i.e. they are tied upon the same garment. However, if one belt ties an inner garment and another ties an outer garment, both are permitted, for each is serving a useful purpose (see *Tosafos*).

36. A wide strap of material [that was tied around one's body] (*Rashi*).

37. The narrow ties of the corset allow it to be tied tightly around the body; thus the Sages were not concerned that it would loosen and fall and the person would come to carry it in the public domain. If it had no ties, however, it could not be tied tightly around the body (due to the width of the strap – see *Chidushei HaRan*), and the Sages prohibited its wearing due to the fear that it would fall off in the street and a person would carry it home (*Rashi;* cf. *Rabbeinu Chananel, Rif*).

38. This was an ornate bib that was fastened to a woman's neck by means of a wide strap that was strung through loops on the bib and tied tightly around the neck (see above, 57b note 3); it was decorated with gold and was of an ornamental nature. Alternatively, the *katla* was an open-ended half-circle of precious metal that was placed around a woman's neck, securing the open corners of her shirt (*Rashi*). [According to the first explanation, the word פארי means *crumbs* (see *Tosafos* ד״ה מנקטא); according to the second explanation, it refers to the *neck* (see *Mussaf HeAruch* ע׳ מנקטא).]

כדעבד ליה רבי עקיבא לדביתהו א) ת"ר לא תצא אשה בעיר של זהב ואם יצתה חייבת חטאת דברי רבי מאיר וחכמים אומרים לא תצא ואם יצתה פטורה ב) רבי אליעזר אומר יוצאה אשה בעיר של זהב לכתחלה במאי קמיפלגי ר"מ סבר משוי הוא ורבנן סברי תכשיט הוא דילמא שלפא ומחויא ליה ואתיא לאתויי ור"א סבר מאן דרכה למיפק בעיר של זהב אשה חשובה ואשה חשובה לא משלפא ומחויא כלילא רב אסר ושמואל א שרי דאניסכא כולי עלמא לא פליגי דאסור כי פליגי דארוקתא מר סבר אניסכא עיקר ומר סבר ארוקתא עיקר רב אשי מתני לקולא ב דארוקתא דכולי עלמא לא פליגי דשרי כי פליגי דאניסכא מר סבר דילמא שלפא ומחויא ואתי לאתויי ומר סבר מאן דרכה למיפק בכלילא אשה חשובה ואשה חשובה לא שלפא ומחויא ° א"ל רב שמואל בר בר חנה לרב יוסף בפירוש אמרת לן משמיה דרב כלילא שרי ג) אמרו ליה לרב אתא גברא רבה אריכא לנהרדעא ומטלע ודרש כלילא שרי אמר מאן גברא רבה אריכא [דאיטלע] לוי ש"מ נח נפשיה דרבי אפס ויתיב ר' חנינא ברישא ולא הוה ליה איניש ללוי למיתב גביה (א) וקאתי להכא ודילמא נח נפשיה דרבי חנינא ור' אפס כדקאי קאי ולא הוה ליה איניש ללוי למיתב גביה וקאתי להכא אם איתא דרבי חנינא שכיב לוי לר' אפס מיכף הוה כייף ליה ותו דרבי חנינא לא סגי דלא מליך דכי הוה קא ניחא נפשיה דרבי אמר חנינא בר' חמא יתיב בראש וכתיב בהו בצדיקים א) ותגזר אומר ויקם לך וגו' דרש לוי בנהרדעא כלילא שרי נפיק עשרין וארבע כלילי מכולה נהרדעא דרש רבה בר אבוה רב במחוזא כלילא שרי ונפקו תמני סרי כלילי מחדא מבואה אמר רב יהודה אמר רב שמואל קמרא שרי איכא דאמרי דארוקתא ואמר רב ספרא מידי דהוה אטלית מוזהבת ואיכא דאמרי ג דאניסכא ואמר רב ספרא מידי דהוה אאבנט של מלכים א"ל רבינא לרב אשי קמרא עילוי המיינא מאי א"ל ד תרי המייני קאמרת אמר רב אשי ה האי רסוקא אי אית ליה מפרחייתא שרי ואי לא אסיר: ולא בקטלא: מאי קטלא מנקטא פארי: נזמים: ו נזמי האף: ולא בטבעת שאין עליה חותם: הא יש עליה חותם חייבת אלמא לאו תכשיט הוא ורמינהו ז תכשיטי נשים טמאים ואלו הן תכשיטי נשים קטלאות נזמים וטבעות וטבעת בין שיש עליה חותם בין שאין עליה חותם ונזמי האף ואמר רבי זירא לא קשיא הא ר' נחמיה הא רבנן ח) דתניא ט) היא של מתכת וחותמה של אלמוג טמאה היא של אלמוג וחותמה של מתכת טהורה ורבי נחמיה מטמא שהיה ר' נחמיה אומר בטבעת הלך אחר חותמה בעול הלך אחר סמלוניו בקולב

רש"י

כדעבד ליה ר' עקיבא לדביתהו. במסכת נדרים (דף נ.): כלילא. על פדחתה היא קושרתו מאזן לאזן יש שכולו טס זהב שקורין לימ"א ויש שעושין ממשי טווי עם הזהב שקורין פריז"ש: דניסכא. טס העשוי כולו מניסכא דהיינו זהב או כסף דבר הניתך: דאסיר. מגו דחשיב גזירה דילמא שלפא ומחוייא: דארוקתא. רצועה שמצויירת בזהב ובאבנים טובות: אניסכא. דאית ביה עיקר ומחויא ליה ומר סבר ארוקתא הוא עיקר דידיה ולא חשיב ליה ולא מחויא ליה: כולי עלמא לא פליגי דשרי. דארוקתא עיקר: בפירוש אמרת לן משמיה דרב. לפני חלייך קודם ששכחת תלמודך: כלילא שרי. אלמא דרב אשי עיקר דמוקי פלוגתא בדניסכא אבל בארוקתא מודה רב ואיכא לאוקמי לדידיה בארוקתא: גברא רבה אריכא ומטלע. לוי איטלע דאחוי קידה קמיה דרבי י): נח נפשיה דרבי אפס. במסכת כתובות בהנושא (קג:) אמרינן דכי שכיב רבי אמר רבי חנינא בר חמא ישב בראש ולא קיבל עליו רבי חנינא שהיה רבי אפס גדול ממנו שתי שנים (ב) ויתיב רבי אפס ברישא ומתוך שהיה רבי חנינא חשוב לא נכנס לבית מדרשו והיה יושב בחוץ ומשום כבודו ישב לו לוי אצלו: וקאתי להכא. שלא היה רבי חנינא גדול הימנו לא בתורה ולא בשנים ולא ניכף ליה לוי ובא לכאן: לוי לרבי אפס מיכף הוה כייף ליה. שהרי זקן ממנו: קמרא. אבנט חשוב יש שעושין אותו טס של זהב ויש שעושין אותו רצועה משבצות זהב ואבנים קבועות בו: מידי דהוה אטלית מוזהבת. דהוי תכשיט ושריא ולמישלף ואחויי נמי לא חיישינן שאין דרך להתיר אזורו בשוק ויפלו בגדיו: אאבנט של מלכים. שעשוי כולו דניסכא ° וכל ישראל בני מלכים ראוים לו: תרי המייני קאמרת. הא ודאי משאוי הוא ואסור לשון תלמידי רבינו יצחק (ג) נ"ע [ובתלמידי] רבינו הלוי מצאתי מותר והראשון נראה לי משום דגבי הצלת דליקה מנינן לר' יוסי שמנה עשר כלים והתם חד חגור הוא דמנינן בכל כתבי הקדש (לקמן דף קכ.) ואי שני חגורות שרי לכתחילה נימני התם תרי: רסוקי. חתיכת מעיל רחבה: אי אית ליה מפרחייתא. רצועות קצרות תלויות בה לקושרה בהם ולהדקה סביבותיו: שרי. דמיהדק שפיר וליכא למיחש דילמא משתרי קטרי ונפיל ואתי לאיתויי: מפרחייתא. פינדל"א בלע"ז: מנקטא פארי (ד). מושטניל"א והוא בגד שיש לו שנצים כעין מכנסים ומכנסת בו רצועה רחבה וקושרת סביב צוארה והבגד תלוי על לבה והוא חשוב ומצוייר בזהב ו"מ כמין חלי עגול עשוי כמין כלבוס ח) (ה) אוחזת בו מפתחי חלוקה והפגם בולע צוארה והוא של זהב לוי"ה: נזמי האף. אבל נזמי האוזן מותרין לכתחלה דטריחא לה מילתא למישלף ואחויי מפני שאזניה מכוסות בקישורין: ולא בטבעת שאין עליה חותם. קתני מתניתין דאם יצאת פטורה דתכשיט הוא לה ומשום דילמא משלפא ומחויא הוא דמיתסר: הא יש עליה חותם חייבת חטאת. דלאו תכשיט הוא והוי משאוי: נזמים. נזמי האוזן: וטבעת בין שיש כו'. כלומר וטבעת שאמרנו בין שיש עליה כו': הא רבי נחמיה. דאמר עיקר טבעת אדעתא דחותם הוא חייבת חטאת דחותם לאשה לאו תכשיט הוא דאין דרך לאשה לחתום ולשלוח שלוחים שאין חותם עשוי אלא לאדם גדול וממונה והא דקתני תכשיט הוא רבנן דאמרי גופה של טבעת עיקר ולאדעתא דטבעת נפקא ביה וטבעת ודאי תכשיט הוא: טמאה. דטבעת עיקר והוה ליה פשוטי כלי מתכות: היא של אלמוג וחותמה של מתכת טהורה. דהוה ליה פשוטי כלי עץ: הלך אחר סמלוניו. ואם של מתכות הם טמא: סמלוניו. העול שלהם לא היה פגום כשלנו אלא חלק ונוקבים בו שני נקבים וביניהם כעובי עורף השור ותוחבין בהן שתי יתדות והם סימלונין: בקולב

תוספות

מאן דרכה למיפק בכלילא אשה חשובה. אומר ר"י דדוקא בכלילא שרי שמואל הכא וכן רבי אליעזר דוקא בעיר של זהב שאין כל הנשים רגילות בהן אלא אשה חשובה אבל שאר תכשיטי נשים אסירי אפי' לאשה חשובה דאין לחלק בין הנשים והביא ראיה מס"פ כירה (לעיל דף מו:) דקאמר עולא מה טעם הואיל ואיכא תורת כלי עליהן ומה דחק לומר כן כיון דחזי לנשים חשובות דאפי' לרבנן דאסרי בעיר של זהב לאשה חשובה מודו בשאר תכשיטים אליבא דשמואל דשרי כלילא אפילו לרבנן:

אאבנט של מלכים. שמלבושם הוא ואין להם אבנט אחר ה"נ שרי האי קמרא לאיתתא דמלבושה היא ולא משלפא ומחויא:

תרי המייני קאמרת. לשון אחד פי' בקונטרס לאיסור ואע"ג דחשיב בפ' כל כתבי (לקמן דף קכ:) בי"ח כלים פונדא וחגור ופי' התם בקונט' דפונדא הוא אזור היינו כגון שיש בגד מפסיק בינתים אבל תרי המייני זה על גב זה אסור ולא דמי לכמה מלבושים שאדם לובש בשביל הקור אבל תרי המייני מה הנאה יש ואין דרך לחגור ומשוי הוא:

מנקטא פארי. פירורי הפת ותכשיט הוא:

נזמי האף. ונזמי האוזן שרו כדפי' בקונטרס ואע"ג דאמר לקמן ט) הבנות יוצאות בחוטין שבאזניהן ואמר בגמ' דשל מיני צבעונים אסירי דילמא משלפי הואיל ותכשיט נינהו התם יותר קל ° ליטלם מנזמי האוזן:

הא יש עליה חותם חייבת חטאת. אסיפא סמיך י) דקתני בהדיא דחייבת חטאת:

רבי נחמיה מטמא. נראה לר"י דברישא מטהר דלא בעי למימר הלך אף אחר חותמה אלא דוקא אחר חותמה שהוא עיקר וכן משמע בהדיא בתוספתא דמסכת כלים כ) דתניא טבעת של מתכת וחותמה של אלמוג רבי נחמיה מטהר שהיה רבי נחמיה אומר בטבעת הלך אחר חותמה:

עין משפט נר מצוה

כב א ב מיי' פי"ט מהל' שבת הלכה י' טוש"ע א"ח סי' שג סעיף ה:
כג ג מיי' שם הל' ב' סמג לאוין כה:
כד ד טוש"ע א"ח סי' שא סעיף לו:
כה ה טוש"ע א"ח סי' שג סעיף ו:
כו ו מיי' שם הלכה ז טוש"ע שם סעיף ח:

רבינו חננאל

כדעבד ר' עקיבא לדביתהו. ת"ר לא תצא אשה בעיר של זהב ואם יצא חייבת חטאת דברי ר' מאיר וחכ"א לא תצא ואם יצאת פטורה. ר' אליעזר אומר יוצאה אשה בעיר של זהב לכתחלה: כלילא רב אסר ושמואל שרי. פי' נסכא חוטין מלשון המסכת (כלים פכ"א). רוקתא מטלית. וקיי"ל כרב אשי דהוא בתראה דאמר ארוקתא כו' כ"ע לא פליגי דשרי כי פליגא כלילא דאניסכא רב אסר ושמואל שרי וקיי"ל כרב באיסורי ואע"ג דאיכא למימר מעשה רב והא דדריש [לוי] כלילא [שרי] ונפקו כ"ד כלילי מנהרדעא וכן הא דדרש רבה בר אבוה במחוזא כלילא שרי כלילא דאניסכא דרשו דשרי. כיון דלא איתמרא בהדיא לא שרינן לה דדלמא לא שרי אלא דארוקתא: אמר רב ששת קמרא שרי הוא חגור שבמתנים כגון אבנט רחב מדבעא רבינא מרב אשי קמרא עילוי המיינא מאי ואמר ליה תרי המייני קאמרת ש"מ דקמרא המיינא הוא והא דרב אשי אתמר בה תרי לישני ולישנא בתראה אניסכא שרי פי' כלילא וקמרא. חתיכות חתיכות של זהב נקובות ובהן מרגלית ומעמידין בחוטין שמכניסין בנקבין. נמצא דאניסכא כגון מלאכת אבנט של מלכים כי כן מלאכתן להיעשות בחוטין. רוקתא מטלית. שנמצא בין כלילא בין קמרא חתיכות של זהב נקובות ומרגלית קבוע' במטלי' שנמצאת מלאכתן כגון מלאכת טלית מוזהבת. אמר רב אשי

רב נסים גאון

גברא רבא אריכא אתא לנהרדעאי ומטלע פירוש והוא צולע על יריכו כדמתרגמינן והוא מטלע והדבר שגרם לו זה מפורש בפ' ג' דתענית (דף כה) לוי גזר תעניתא בעא רחמי ולא אתא מיטרא אמר לפניו רבונו של עולם עלית וישבת למעלה במרום ואי אתה משגיח על בניך ואתא מיטרא ואיטלע אמר ר' אלעזר אל יטיח אדם דברים כלפי למעלה שהרי אדם גדול הטיח דברים כלפי למעלה ואטלע ובמסכת סוכה (דף נג) בפ' החליל קאמרי לוי אחוי קידה קמיה דר' ואטלע ואמרו בפירוקה הא והא גרמא ליה אבל מעשה דר' אפס ור' חנינא בר חמא ומה דאמר רבנו הקדוש בצוויו חנינא בר חמא ישב בראש כו' (מעשה כמפורש) [מפורש] בפרק הנושא

מסורת הש"ס

א) [לקמן קלח. תוספתא פ"ה], ב) עדיות פ"ב מ"ז, ג) כתובות קג:, ד) [כלים פרק יא מ"ח ע"ש], ה) [בכלים פי"ג מ"ו לא מצא פלוגתא דר' נחמי' הלכך שפיר גרסי' דתניא], ו) לעיל נב: תוספתא דכלי' ב"מ פ"ג כלים פי"ג מ"ו, ז) [סוכה נג.], ח) סה, ט) [דף סה.], י) [לקמן סב.], כ) [פ"ג בבא מציעא].

הגהות הב"ח

(א) גמ' למיתב גבי' וקם וקאתי: (ב) רש"י ד"ה נח נפשיה וכו' שתי שנים ומחצה ויתיב: (ג) ד"ה תרי וכו' ר' יצחק בר יהודה נ"ע: (ד) ד"ה מנקטא פארי. נ"ב ע"ל בדף נז ע"ב במה שפירש"י: (ה) בא"ד כמין כלבוס כזה:

גליון הש"ס

גמ' א"ל רב שמואל בר בר חנה לרב יוסף. לקמן קמו ע"ב: רש"י ד"ה אאבנט וכו' וכל ישראל בני מלכים. עיין לקמן דף קיא ע"א: תוס' ד"ה נזמי האף וכו' ליטלם מנזמי האזן. עיין תשו' ב"מ החדשות סי' מ"א:

תורה אור השלם

א) וְתִגְזַר אֹמֶר וְיָקָם לָךְ וְעַל דְּרָכֶיךָ נָגַהּ אוֹר: [איוב כב, כח]

ליקוטי רש"י

ר"מ סבר. דלאו תכשיט הוא אלא משוי. תכשיט הוא. ולכתחילה אסור דילמא שלפא ומחויא [לקמן קלח.]. גברא רבה אריכא [דאיטלע]. פסח היה כדאמרינן בעלמא (סוכה נג.) לוי אחוי קידה ואטלע [כתובות קג:]. נעשה חיגר [סוכה נג.]. שנגלע בקידה [תענית כה.]. נגלע בכוקא דאטמא [מגילה כב:]. וקאתי להכא. לבבל. מיכף הוה כייף ליה. קודם שיגלה ממקומו אבל לר' חנינא לא כייף [כתובות שם]. מאי קטלא מנקטא פארי. בגד חשוב לתלות בצוארה כנגד לבה שלא יפול מה שהיא אוכלת על בגדיה ויש לו מקום שנצים כעין שעושים למכנסים ותוחב בו רצועה רחבה ומוללתו סביב הרצועה שהבגד רחב הרבה וקושרת הרצועה סביב צוארה [לעיל נז: עיי"ש עוד ובתוס' שם]. ותגזר אומר. מה שתבקש מן היוצר יעשה [ב"מ קו.]. ויקם לך. כמו ויקום לך [איוב כב, כח]. אלמוג. עצי אלמוגים והוא נאה. טמאה. דבתר טבעת אזלינן ופשוטי כלי מתכות טמאים [לעיל נב:].

The Mishnah stated:
נְזָמִים – NOR may she go out WITH RINGS ...

The Gemara explains:
נִזְמֵי הָאַף – The Mishnah's ruling refers only to **nose rings;** earrings, however, are permitted.[39]

The Mishnah stated:
וְלֹא בְּטַבַּעַת שֶׁאֵין עָלֶיהָ חוֹתָם – AND she may NOT go out WITH A RING THAT BEARS NO SIGNET ...

The Mishnah teaches that a woman is Rabbinically prohibited from wearing a ring that bears no signet. The Gemara infers another law from this teaching, and challenges it:
הָא יֵשׁ עָלֶיהָ חוֹתָם חַיֶּיבֶת – The Mishnah implies that **if** a woman were to wear **a ring that bore a signet, she would be liable** to a *chatas.*[40] אַלְמָא לָאו תַּכְשִׁיט הוּא – **We see,** then, **that [such a ring] is not** deemed **an ornament** for a woman.[41] וּרְמִינְהוּ – **But contrast this** with the law that we learn in the following Mishnah:[42] תַּכְשִׁיטֵי נָשִׁים טְמֵאִים – The ORNAMENTS OF WOMEN ARE SUSCEPTIBLE TO *TUMAH.* וְאֵלּוּ הֵן תַּכְשִׁיטֵי נָשִׁים – AND THESE ARE THE ORNAMENTS OF WOMEN: קַטְלָאוֹת – CHOKERS, נְזָמִים – EARRINGS,[43] וְטַבָּעוֹת – AND RINGS. וְטַבַּעַת – AND THE RING spoken of here בֵּין שֶׁיֵּשׁ עָלֶיהָ חוֹתָם בֵּין שֶׁאֵין עָלֶיהָ חוֹתָם – is susceptible to *tumah* WHETHER IT BEARS A SIGNET OR IT DOES NOT BEAR A SIGNET – וְנִזְמֵי הָאַף – AND NOSE RINGS. This Mishnah clearly states that even a ring that bears a signet is considered an ornament. – ? –

The Gemara offers a resolution:
וְאָמַר רַבִּי זֵירָא[44] – **R' Zeira said:** לֹא קַשְׁיָא – This is **not a difficulty,** הָא רַבִּי נְחֶמְיָה – for **this** inference that you drew from our Mishnah, that a signet ring is not an ornament, **accords with** the view of **R' Nechemyah,**[45] הָא רַבָּנַן – while **this** Mishnah, which states that a signet ring is an ornament, **accords with** the view of **the Rabbis** who dispute him.[46]

The Gemara cites the dispute between R' Nechemyah and the Rabbis:
דְּתַנְיָא – **For it was taught in a Baraisa:** הִיא שֶׁל מַתֶּכֶת וְחוֹתָמָהּ שֶׁל אַלְמוֹג – If [THE RING] was made OF METAL AND ITS SIGNET was made OF *ALMOG* wood, טְמֵאָה – it IS SUSCEPTIBLE TO *TUMAH;* הִיא שֶׁל אַלְמוֹג וְחוֹתָמָהּ שֶׁל מַתֶּכֶת – if IT was made OF *ALMOG* wood[47] AND ITS SIGNET was made OF METAL, טְהוֹרָה – IT IS *TAHOR,* i.e. not susceptible to *tumah.* This is the view of the Rabbis.[48] וְרַבִּי נְחֶמְיָה מְטַמֵּא – BUT R' NECHEMYAH DECLARES a wooden ring with a metal signet *TAMEI;* שֶׁהָיָה רַבִּי נְחֶמְיָה אוֹמֵר – FOR R' NECHEMYAH WOULD SAY: בְּטַבַּעַת הַלֵּךְ אַחַר חוֹתָמָהּ – When deciding the *tumah* status OF A RING, FOLLOW AFTER THE composition of ITS SIGNET;[49] בְּעוֹל הַלֵּךְ אַחַר סְמָלוֹנָיו – when deciding the *tumah* status OF A YOKE, FOLLOW AFTER the composition of ITS PEGS;[50]

NOTES

39. For it is difficult for her to remove them and show them to others, as her ears are covered with the bands [that encircle her hair] (*Rashi*). [*Tosafos* note that colored threads inserted into the ears are more easily removed, and they are therefore forbidden, as the Gemara teaches below (65a); see also *Chidushei HaRan.*]

40. [This inference is actually not a compelling one, for one could just as easily deduce from the fact that it is a ring without a signet which is Rabbinically prohibited, that a ring with a signet is not prohibited at all! However, the Gemara's assumption is based on the fact that the Mishnah below (62a) explicitly states that a woman who wears a signet ring outside on the Sabbath is liable to a *chatas* (*Tosafos,* as explained by *Maharsha*). The Rishonim note further that the Gemara could have eschewed the inference altogether and simply cited the law from the Mishnah below; however, it is common for the Gemara to deduce a law from an earlier Mishnah even when it is explicitly stated in a later Mishnah (*Ramban, Rashba,* et al.). Cf. *Baal HaMaor.*]

41. [Since a woman does not usually wear a signet ring (*Mishnah Berurah* 303:26)] it is not considered an ornament when she wears it, but rather a burden; [therefore, she is Biblically forbidden to wear it] (*Rashi;* see also Gemara below, 62a).

42. *Keilim* 11:8; see *Rashi* above, 52a ד״ה טמאה.

43. *Rashi.* [Nose rings too are included in this category, as the Baraisa explicitly states below.]

44. Translation follows *Ritva* (*MHK* ed.), who reads אָמַר in place of וְאָמַר.

45. As the Gemara proceeds to explain, R' Nechemyah is of the opinion that the *tumah* status of a ring is determined by the composition of its signet. Accordingly, R' Nechemyah would hold that the question of whether a signet ring is a burden or an ornament also depends upon whether the wearer uses the *signet* portion of the ring or not; and since a woman rarely uses a signet (for a signet was generally used to seal missives and packages, and was most often used only by men of authority), the ring is considered a burden (*Rashi*).

46. The Rabbis dispute R' Nechemyah (as recorded in the Baraisa cited in the Gemara below), and maintain that the *tumah* status of a ring is determined by the composition of the ring, rather than the signet. Thus, they will hold that the question of whether the ring is a burden or an ornament is decided based on the status of the ring itself rather than the signet; and since a woman often wears rings as ornaments, a signet ring too is deemed an ornament (*Rashi*).

47. A type of cedar; see above, 52b note 33.

48. A ring made of wood is not susceptible to *tumah,* for it has no receptacle, and it is therefore in the class of פְּשׁוּטֵי כְּלֵי עֵץ, *flat wooden utensils,* which cannot acquire *tumah* (see, however, *Tosafos* above, 52b ד״ה היא, and *Ritva MHK* ed. here at length). Flat *metal* utensils, however, are susceptible to *tumah* (*Rashi*). Thus, according to the Rabbis, who determine the *tumah* status of the signet ring following the ring rather than the signet, if the ring was wooden, it is *tahor,* and if it was metal, it can become *tamei.*

49. According to R' Nechemyah, the signet is the portion of the ring that determines its *tumah* status; thus, if the signet is made of metal, the ring is susceptible to *tumah,* even if the ring itself is made of wood. [R' Nechemyah also disputes the first ruling of the Rabbis, and holds that a metal ring with a wooden signet is *not* susceptible to *tumah;* this is clearly stated in *Tosefta* (*Tosafos*), as well as in *Yerushalmi,* where it is stated that R' Nechemyah *reverses* (מַחֲלִיף) the rulings of the Rabbis (*Ritva MHK* ed., *Rashba,* et al.).

50. The yokes made in Talmudic times did not follow the contours of the oxen's necks as ours do today; rather, they were straight bars that were placed over and under the necks of the oxen. The bars were connected with straight pegs that fit into holes in the bars on either side of the oxen and; these pegs held the bars in place, and enabled the yoke to function; it is these pegs to which the Baraisa refers (*Rashi;* see diagram).

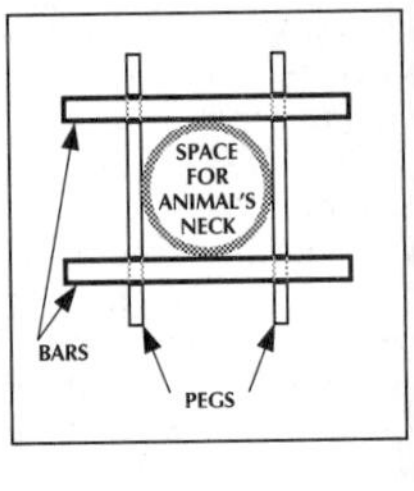

בְּקוּלָב – when deciding the *tumah* status of **A DISPLAY BOARD,** **הַלֵּךְ אַחַר מַסְמְרוֹתָיו** – **FOLLOW AFTER ITS NAILS;**[1] **בְּסוּלָם** – when deciding the *tumah* status of **A LADDER,** **הַלֵּךְ אַחַר שְׁלִיבוֹתָיו** – **FOLLOW AFTER ITS RUNGS;**[2] **בְּעַרְסִי** – when deciding the *tumah* status of **A BALANCE SCALE,** **הַלֵּךְ אַחַר שַׁלְשְׁלוֹתָיו** – **FOLLOW AFTER ITS CHAINS.**[3] **וַחֲכָמִים אוֹמְרִים** – **BUT THE SAGES SAY:** **הַכֹּל הוֹלֵךְ אַחַר הַמַּעֲמִיד** – **ALL** decisions concerning the *tumah* status of these items **FOLLOW THE** portion of the item that provides **SUPPORT.**[4] Thus, according to the Rabbis, a signet ring's *tumah* status depends upon the composition of the ring itself, while according to R' Nechemyah we follow the composition of the signet; hence, a signet ring worn by a woman is an ornament according to the Rabbis and a burden according to R' Nechemyah.[5]

The Gemara offers a second resolution of the contradiction:

רָבָא אָמַר – **Rava said:** **לִצְדָדִים קָתָנֵי** – **The** statement of the **Mishnah** in *Keilim* that a ring is an ornament whether it has a signet or not **was taught** in reference **to** two **separate cases.**[6] **יֵשׁ עָלֶיהָ חוֹתָם** – For **if [the ring] has a seal,** **תַּכְשִׁיט דְּאִישׁ** – **it is an ornament for a man;**[7] **אֵין עָלֶיהָ חוֹתָם תַּכְשִׁיט דְּאִשָּׁה** – if it **has no seal,** it is **an ornament for a woman.** Thus, even the Mishnah in *Keilim* agrees that a signet ring is not deemed an ornament for a woman, and she is Biblically prohibited from wearing it on the Sabbath.[8]

A third resolution is offered:

רַב נַחְמָן בַּר יִצְחָק אָמַר – **Rav Nachman bar Yitzchak said:** **טוּמְאָה אַשַּׁבָּת קָרָמֵית** – **Do you** attempt to **contrast** the laws of ***tumah*** **with** the laws of the **Sabbath?**[9] This is not a valid comparison, for the criteria for the classification of an **item** as *tamei* differ from the criteria for prohibiting the wearing of an item on the Sabbath.[10] **טוּמְאָה** – With respect to ***tumah,*** **,,כְּלִי מַעֲשֶׂה" אָמַר רַחֲמָנָא** – **the Merciful One states** in His Torah that an item is susceptible to *tumah* if it falls into the category **of *a fashioned vessel;***[11] **וּכְלִי הוּא** – **and** a ring with a signet is therefore susceptible to *tumah,* for although it is not an ornament for a woman, **it is a** fashioned **vessel.**[12] **שַׁבָּת** – But with respect to wearing an item outside on the **Sabbath,** **מִשּׁוּם מַשּׂוֹי אָמַר רַחֲמָנָא** – **the Merciful One states** that an item may not be worn outside on the Sabbath **if it is a burden;** thus there is a distinction depending upon the type of ring that the woman is wearing. **אֵין עָלֶיהָ חוֹתָם תַּכְשִׁיט** – **If it has no seal it is an ornament,** and it is Rabbinically prohibited; **יֵשׁ עָלֶיהָ חוֹתָם מַשּׂוֹי** – **if it** does **have a seal,** it is **a burden,** and it is Biblically prohibited.[13]

NOTES

1. The display board was a sort of pillar, wide at the bottom and narrow at the top, that sellers of belts and straps would stand in front of the windows of their shops. The pillar was studded with nails, and the shopkeepers would hang their merchandise on the nails to display them (*Rashi*). R' Nechemyah rules that if the nails were made of metal, the display board was susceptible to *tumah* [even though the pillar itself was a flat wooden utensil, which would not be susceptible to *tumah* in its own right].

2. [If the rungs are made of metal, R' Nechemyah declares the ladder susceptible to *tumah* even if the sides of the ladder were made of wood.]

3. I.e. the chains from which the pans of the scale are suspended. [The balance scale being discussed here is a large wooden scale that was used to weigh commodities such as wool, wax or copper (*Rashi*). It consisted of the following four components: (a) a vertical bar that stands on the ground or is suspended from the ceiling; (b) a horizontal bar, known as the *beam* (קָנֶה); (c) A mechanism with which the beam is attached at its midpoint to the vertical bar so that it pivots when either end is weighted down. This mechanism is the *fulcrum* of the scale. (d) two *pans* (כַּפּוֹת) suspended by *chains* (שַׁלְשְׁלָאוֹת) at either end of the beam. See diagrams.]

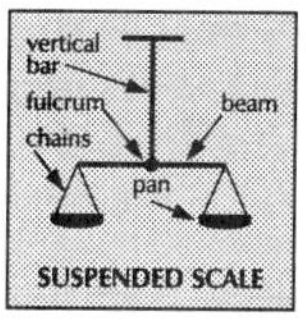

SUSPENDED SCALE

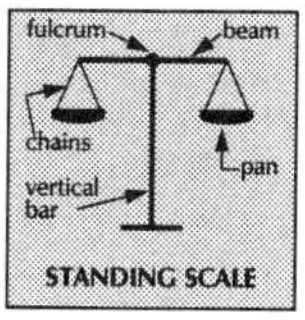

STANDING SCALE

4. According to the Sages, the part of the object which provides support for the other components of the object is considered its most essential component, and it is that part's composition that determines the object's *tumah* status. Thus, in the case of a signet ring, we consider the composition of the ring itself [for it supports the seal]; in the case of a yoke, we consider the composition of the bars [for it is the pegs that are attached to the bars, and not vice versa]; in the case of a ladder, we consider the composition of the ladder's stiles (sides) [for the rungs are attached to them]; in the case of the balance scale, we follow the composition of the beam [for it is the central part of the balance, to which all the other parts of the scale – i.e. the fulcrum, the vertical bar, and the chains, from which the pans are suspended – are attached] (*Rashi,* as understood by *Bach* and *Maharshal;* see also *Maharam*).

5. See above, 59b notes 46 and 48.

6. I.e. when the Mishnah in *Keilim* states that a ring is an ornament whether it has a seal or not, it is not referring to its earlier statement that a ring is considered a woman's ornament; for in truth, a ring with a seal is *not* considered an ornament for a woman. Rather, the Mishnah is stating that rings with seals and those without seals can both be ornaments, albeit in different cases; for the signet ring is an ornament when worn by a man, and the ring with no seal is an ornament when worn by a woman [this is what the Mishnah mentioned in its earlier ruling] (*Rashi;* see also below, note 7). A signet ring is *not* an ornament for a woman, however, as our Mishnah implies (and the Mishnah below states explicitly), and she is Biblically prohibited from wearing one outside on the Sabbath.

[*Rashi's* mention of the *Baraisa* is seemingly imprecise, as he is citing the Mishnah in *Keilim;* see *Rashash.*]

7. [That is, it is susceptible to *tumah* because it is an ornament. Whether it can be worn by the man on the Sabbath depends on whether or not the Sages were concerned that men would remove ornaments in the street to show them to their friends; this question is the subject of a dispute in the Rishonim, as noted above (see 59b note 33).]

8. *Tos. HaRosh* states that Rava does not agree with R' Zeira's extension of the dispute between R' Nechemyah and the Sages to the laws of the Sabbath; rather, he is of the opinion that both the Sages and R' Nechemyah agree that with respect to the laws of the Sabbath a woman's signet ring is not an ornament. Cf. *Tosafos.*

9. The initial contradiction raised by the Gemara (on 59b) contrasted the implication of our Mishnah (that a woman's signet ring is not an ornament with respect to wearing it outside on the Sabbath) with the ruling of the Mishnah in *Keilim* (which seems to say that even a woman's signet ring is susceptible to *tumah* because it is an ornament). Rav Nachman resolves the contradiction by modifying our understanding of the Mishnah in *Keilim* (see further, note 12).

10. For a ring can be *tamei without* being an ornament, as the Gemara will now derive [and the Mishnah in *Keilim,* which describes a ring as an ornament, refers to a ring without a signet].

11. *Numbers* 31:51. The verse speaks of the golden vessels [which were contaminated with corpse *tumah*], which were taken from the plunder of the Midianite war, that the leaders of the Jewish army offered to God as thanksgiving for the fact that they suffered no casualties during the battle (see *Rashi* to *Numbers* loc. cit.; see also Gemara below, 63b-64a, where this derivation is elaborated).

12. According to Rav Nachman, when the Mishnah in *Keilim* stated that "the ring of which we speak means a ring with a seal as well as a ring without a seal," it was not [referring to its earlier ruling and] stating that a ring is *a woman's ornament* whether it has a seal or not; rather, it was merely stating that a ring is *tamei* whether it has a seal or not, because even a signet ring, that is *not* an ornament for a woman, is still *tamei,* as it is "a fashioned vessel." The Mishnah's earlier ruling, that stated that a ring was a woman's ornament, refers only to a ring that has no seal (*Rashi;* see *Ritva MHK* ed.). Thus, the fact that the Mishnah in *Keilim* equates signet rings and rings without seals is not a contradiction to our Mishnah; for that Mishnah equates the rings only with regard to *tumah,* while our Mishnah [implicitly] differentiates between them with regard to the laws of Shabbos, where the criteria are different.

13. [The Rishonim dispute whether Rav Nachman rules that a signet ring is a burden only according to R' Nechemyah or even according to the Sages of the Baraisa cited above (see note 8).]

בקולב הלך אחר מסמרותיו בסולם הלך אחר שליבותיו בערסי הלך אחר שלשלותיו וחכמים אומרים [א] הכל הולך אחר המעמיד רבא אמר לצדדים קתני יש עליה חותם תכשיט דאיש אין עליה חותם תכשיט דאשה רב נחמן בר יצחק אמר [ב] טומאה אשבת קרמית טומאה [א] כלי מעשה אמר רחמנא וכלי הוא שבת משום משוי אמר רחמנא אין עליה חותם תכשיט יש עליה חותם משוי: ולא במחט שאינה נקובה: [א] למאי חזיא אמר רב יוסף הואיל ואשה [ג] אוגרת בה שערה א"ל אביי ותהוי כבירית טהורה ותשתרי אלא תרגמא רב אדא נרשאה קמיה דרב יוסף הואיל ואשה חולקת בה שערה בשבת למאי חזיא אמר רבא טס של זהב יש לה על ראשה בחול חולקת בה שערה בשבת מניחתה כנגד פדחתה: **מתני'** [ב] לא יצא האיש בסנדל המסומר ולא [ג] ביחיד בזמן שאין ברגלו מכה ולא בתפילין [ד] ולא בקמיע בזמן שאינו מן המומחה [ה] ולא בשריון ולא בקסדא ולא במגפיים ואם יצא אינו חייב חטאת: **גמ'** סנדל המסומר מאי טעמא אמר שמואל שלפי הגזרה היו והיו נחבאין במערה ואמרו הנכנס יכנס והיוצא אל יצא נהפך סנדלו של אחד מהן כסבורין הם אחד מהן יצא וראוהו אויבים ועכשיו באין עליהן דחקו זה בזה והרגו זה את זה יותר ממה שהרגו בהם אויבים רבי אילעאי בן אלעזר אומר במערה היו יושבין ושמעו קול מעל גבי המערה כסבורין היו שבאו עליהם אויבים דחקו זה בזה והרגו זה את זה יותר ממה שהרגו בהן אויבים רמי בר יחזקאל אמר בבהכ"נ היו יושבין ושמעו קול מאחורי בהכ"נ כסבורין היו שבאו עליהם אויבים דחקו זה בזה והרגו זה את זה יותר ממה שהרגו בהן אויבים באותה שעה אמרו אל יצא אדם בסנדל המסומר אי הכי בחול נמי ליתסר מעשה כי הוה בשבת הוה ביום טוב לישתרי אלמה תנן משלחין

רש"י

בקולב. הוא כמין עמוד רחב מלמטה ודק מלמעלה ומיטלטל והחנוני מעמידו לפני חלון חנותו ומסמרין תחובין בו ותולין בהן אבנטים ורצועות למכור: **בערסה.** אישתרייד"א בלע"ז והן מאזנים גדולות לשקול צמר ושעוה ונחשת והן של עץ: **הלך אחר שלשלותיו.** שתלוי בהן ואם של מתכת הן טמאות: **המעמיד.** גוף הטבעת מעמיד החותם והעול מעמיד את סמלוניו והקולב את מסמרותיו והסולם את שליבותיו שהרי בהם קבועים והערסה הוא עץ (א) ארוך שהקנה שקורין יי"ש"א והלשון תחוב בו והשלשלות קבועות בקנה וכולן העץ ארוך מעמידן שהוא פליי"ל ששתי כפות המאזנים תלויות בב' ראשין: **רבא אמר.** ברייתא דקתני וטבעת הוי תכשיט בין שיש עליה חותם בין שאין עליה חותם לאו ארישא דאיירי בתכשיטי נשים קיימי תרוייהו אלא חד תכשיט דאיש וחד תכשיט דאשה ולצדדין קתני: **טומאה אשבת קרמית.** הא דקתני וטבעת בין שיש עליה כו' לאו ארישא קאי דקרי ליה תכשיט נשים אלא הכי קאמר וטבעת שאמרו שנטמאת בין שיש עליה חותם דלאו תכשיט הוא מיהו כלי מעשה הוא בין שאין עליה חותם דהוי תכשיט וכי קתני רישא תכשיטי נשים אשאין עליה חותם: **למאי חזיא.** לתכשיט דקתני אינה חייבת חטאת: **אוגרת בה שערה.** היוצא חוץ לקישוריה כורכתו סביב המחט ותוחבת המחט בשבכה מתחתיה שלא יראה שערה: **ותיהוי כבירית.** דתנא מתניתין (לקמן דף סג.) בירית טהורה מלטמא ויוצאין בה והיא כמין אצעדה שעושה לשוקיה מעל בתי שוקיה להדקן שלא יפלו על רגלה: **טהורה.** דלאו תכשיט היא אלא תשמיש לבתי שוקיה והוי (ב) כטבעת הכלים דאמרן טהורות בפרקין דלעיל ויוצאין בה שצריך לה עם בתי שוקיה ולא הוי משאוי ויוצאין דכיון דלצניעותא היא לא שלפא ומחוי והאי מחט נמי לצניעות דשער באשה ערוה ולא מחויא ואמאי לא תנא לכתחילה: **חולקת.** לכאן ולכאן באמצע ראשה שקורין גריוו"א בלע"ז: **ובשבת למאי חזיא.** הרי בשבת אינה חולקת שערה: **טס של זהב יש לה על ראשה.** האחד והשני עוקץ הוי: **בחול חולקת שערה.** בעוקץ: **ובשבת.** תוחבת העוקץ בשבכה והטס שבראשה השני מונח על פדחתה: **מתני' סנדל המסומר.** של עץ הוא ותוחבין מסמרות (ג) למעלה לחזק התחתון עם העליון [ה] (העץ עם העור שלמעלה הימנו ויש לו שתי פיות ותוחב רגלו בו) ובגמרא מפרש מאי טעמא גזרו ביה: **ולא ביחיד.** ולא בסנדל יחיד: **בזמן שאין ברגלו מכה.** בש"ס ירושלמי מפרש דלא ליחשדיה דטעין ליה לחבריה תותי כנפיה ולשון רבותי דילמא מחייכי עליה ושקיל דשליף ליה ומתטי ליה בידי' בשכחת שבת ומיהו בזמן שיש ברגלו מכה שרי ובגמרא בעי בהי מינייהו יהיב ליה: **ולא בתפילין.** כדמפרש טעמא בגמרא (לקמן דף סא.): **ולא בקמיע.** שכותבין וטוענין לרפואה: **שאינו מן המומחה.** אבל בקמיע מומחה שרי דתכשיט הוא לחולה כאחד ממלבושיו: **שריון קסדא ומגפיים.** מפרש בגמרא: **אינו חייב חטאת.** דכולהו מין מלבושין נינהו בחול למלחמה: **גמ' שלפי הגזירה היו.** בני אדם הנשמטים מן הגזירה היו: **הנכנס יכנס.** הרוצה ליכנס שהנכנס יראה תחלה שאין אדם רואה: **והיוצא אל יצא.** שמא יש אויבים מבחוץ והוא לא ידע ויראוהו ויבינו שאנו כאן: **נהפך סנדלו.** שיש לו שתי פיות ויכול לנועלו מב' צדדין אבל ניכר מי הוא לפנים ומי הוא לאחור וכשנועלו זה הפוך נראה הנכנס כאילו הוא יוצא וניכר מקומו בקרקע: **והרגו זה את זה.** בדחיקתן שהיו סנדליהן מסומרין כעין אותם שעושין לרגלי הסוסים לאחיזתן עבים: **אל יצא.** האיש בשבת כדמפרש לקמיה דבשבת היה מעשה ומענין המאורע אסרו: **אלמה תנן.** במסכת ביצה: משלחין

תוספות

רב נחמן בר יצחק אמר טומאה אשבת קא רמית. דאפילו בלאו טעמא דהוי תכשיט לאיש היא טמאה מכל כלי מעשה והשתא בין לרבא בין לרב נחמן בר יצחק מוקמי תרוייהו כרבי נחמיה ולא מטמא מטעם תכשיט דאשה אלא מטעם תכשיט דאיש או מטעם דהוי כלי מעשה ולצדדין קתני בין לרבא בין לרב נחמן בר יצחק:

למאי חזיא. פי' בקונטרס למאי חזיא והא משוי הוא וקשה לר"י דאם כן מאי משני הואיל ואשה חולקת בה שערה אטו משום הכי לא הוי משוי והא אינו לא מלבוש ולא תכשיט אלא נראה לפרש למאי חזיא למה היא רגילה לצאת בה בחול אמר רב יוסף כו' ובתר הכי פריך ובשבת למאי חזיא נהי שרגילה לנושאה בשביל שצריכה לחלק בה שערה בשבת תיהוי משוי כיון דאינו לא מלבוש ולא תכשיט ובקונטרס פי' בסמוך בשבת למאי חזיא והלא בשבת אינה חולקת שערה וקשה לר"י חדא דהא מנא ליה דאסור לחלק בה שיער בשבת ועוד דלמאי פריך והא אסור אפילו יהא מותר תקשה והא משוי הוא:

הואיל ואשה אוגרת בה שערה. נראה לר"י שתוחבת המחט בתוך הסבכה ודוחקת את הסבכה כדי שלא יפלו שערותיה חוץ לקישוריה והשתא אתי שפיר דהויא כעין בירית שאוחזת בתי שוקיה שלא יפלו ולא כפירוש הקונטרס:

ותיהוי כבירית טהורה ותשתרי. פירש בקונטרס דכי היכי דהתם לא חיישי לדילמא משלפא ומחויא הואיל ולצניעותא עבידא ה"נ לא ניחוש למישלף ואחוויי מהאי טעמא וקשה לר"י דהא כבלים אין יוצאין בהן בשבת דחיישינן דילמא משלפא להו משום דהוי תכשיט כמו שאפרש אע"ג דלצניעותא עבידא כמו בירית דהכל ענין אחד אלא שבירית באחת וכבלים בשתים כדאמרינן לקמן (דף סג:) ועוד דלמה לו להזכיר כאן טהרת בירית הוה ליה למימר ותיהוי כבירית ותשתרי ונראה לר"י דה"פ ותהוי כבירית שיוצאין בה לפי שהיא טהורה משום שאינה תכשיט דאינה נוי לאשה כיון דאינה כ"א באחת והויא כטבעת הכלים דאינה כ"א לצורך בתי שוקים ה"נ האי מחט שהיא טהורה לפי שאינה אלא כטבעת הכלים תשתרי דאינה תכשיט וא"ת אמאי לא משני השתא כמין טס של זהב יש לה בראשה כדמשני לאידך שינויא דבסמוך וי"ל דאם היתה אוגרת בה שערה לא היתה מניחתה לעולם כנגד פדחתה ואינה חשובה תכשיט אלא טס וקשה לרשב"א לפירוש זה דכיון דמחט שאוגרת בה שערה היא טהורה היכי קאמר לעיל (דף נג:) אבל לענין טומאה דא ודא אחת היא הרי יש חילוק אפילו בשלימה דאותה שאינה אוגרת בה טמאה ואותה שאוגרת בה טהורה וצריך לומר דלטומאה נמי פריך ותיהוי טהורה כבירית שהיא טהורה גם תשתרי לצאת בה:

ומניחתה כנגד פדחתה. השתא לא היה צריך לומר שחולקת בה שערה כלל אלא האמת מפרש: **וישמעו** קול מעל גבי המערה. קול של סנדל המסומר: (שייך לע"ב) **לא** [ו] בסנדל המסומר ולא [ו] במנעל שאינו תפור. תימה לר"י והא קתני סיפא זה הכלל כל שניאותין בו משלחין אותו ביו"ט ומפרש בגמ' דכל שנאותין בו בחול קאמר וסנדל המסומר ניאותין בו בחול ואמאי אין משלחין אותו בי"ט וי"ל דהחמירו בו לפי שבא תקלה על ידו כי היכי דאסר ליה בשמעתין ר' אלעזר בר' שמעון לטלטלו לכסות בו את הכלי או לסמוך בו כרעי המטה אע"פ [ח] שאר כלים שמלאכתן לאיסור שרי לטלטלן לצורך גופן ומקומן וזה הכלל דקתני התם לא קאי אלא אמנעל שאינו תפור ונראה לר"י דאפי' לרבנן דר' אלעזר דשרי לטלטל לצורך גופו ומקומו אסור לשלוח בו בי"ט אע"ג דשלוח משום שמחת י"ט חשיב כמו לצורך גופו מדשרי לשלוח דברים שמלאכתן לאיסור כיון שבאת תקלה על ידו ליכא שמחת י"ט:

עין משפט נר מצוה

כז א מיי' פי"ט מהל' שבת הלכה ה סמג לאוין סה טוש"ע א"ח סי' שג סעיף ט:

כח ב מיי' פי"ט מהל' שבת הלכה ב:

כט ג מיי' שם הלכה טו סמג שם טוש"ע א"ח סי' שא סעיף ו:

רבינו חננאל

ריסוקא. פי' חגור של עור אי אית ביה מפרחייתא שרי ותכשיט הוא ואי לא אסור פי' אם יש לו מפרחייתא חתיכות יוצאות ועודפות ממנו לימינו ולשמאלו תכשיט הוא ואי לא אינו מלאכת תכשיט ואסור לצאת בו בשבת כי אינו כלי. קטלא תכשיט בצואר. כגון ענק והיא בלשון ערבי מכנקא. נזמים יש נזמי האף ונזמים שבאזנים: **ולא** בטבעת שאין עליה חותם הא יש עליה חותם משאוי ואם תצא בו חייבת חטאת. אלמא לאו תכשיט הוא איני והתניא תכשיטי נשים עיר של זהב קטלאות נזמים וטבעת אחת טבעת שיש עליה חותם ואחת טבעת שאין עליה חותם ונזמי האף [טמאים] ומשני ר' זירא בטבעת של אלמוג וחותמה של מתכת ומתניתין [כרבנן] בכלים פרק י"ג דאמרי טהורה. [וכיון] לענין טומאה לאו כלי הוא לענין שבת נמי לאו כלי הוא. ומשוי הוא. הא ברייתא ר' נחמיה היא דמשוי ליה לענין [טומאה] מנא לענין שבת נמי תכשיט הוא דתנינן טבעת של מתכת וחותמה של אלמוג [טמאה היא של אלמוג] וחותמה של מתכת טהורה. ור' נחמיה מטמא: סימלוניו פי' רצועות שהן בעול דתנינן בתורת כהנים מיד בא ושיבר העול וקיצץ סימלונין כדכתיב ה' צדיק קצץ עבות רשעים. קולב. יש מי שאומרים ממיני תכשיט הוא להשמיע קול כדורך בגת ומחזקו במסמרים: **שליבות** ושלשלאות פשוטות הן. רבא אמר הא מתניתא לצדדין קתני אין עליה חותם תכשיט דאשה יש עליה חותם תכשיט דאיש והדין כך הוא. שיהא האיש מותר לצאת בטבעת שיש עליה חותם והאשה בטבעת שאין עליה חותם. מפני שתכשיט הוא להן וכל תכשיט שרי אלא משום גזירה א) דרבא כדבעינן למימר לקמן (סב.) דאמר פעמים שהאשה נותנת לבעלה טבעת שאין עליה חותם להוליכה אצל האומן ומניחה באצבעו עד שמגיע אל האומן. ופעמים שהאיש נותן לאשתו טבעת שיש עליה חותם להניחה בקופסא ומניחתה באצבעתה עד שמגעת לקופסא. לפיכך אסרו אחד האיש ואחד האשה לצאת בין בטבעת שיש עליה חותם בין בטבעת שאין עליה חותם. רב נחמן בר יצחק אמר כו' טומאה אשבת קרמית כו'. ולא במחט שאינה נקובה כדתניא כמין טס של זהב יש לה על ראשה. בחול חולקת בה שערה בשבת מנחת על פדחתה. ונרי הוא: לא יצא בסנדל מסומר כו'. מ"ט שלפי השמד כו' פשוטה היא.

מסורת הש"ס

א) [לעיל עו:], ב) לקמן קכב., ג) [גי' הערוך בערך אגד אוגרת], ד) [לעיל נג:], ה) רש"ל מוחק זה, ו) [צ"ל סנדל], ז) [צ"ל מנעל], ח) [לקמן קכד.].

הגהות הב"ח

(א) רש"י ד"ה המעמיד וכו' והערסה הוא עץ הארוך שהוא קנה שקורין: (ב) ד"ה טהורה וכו' והוי הוא כטבעת: (ג) ד"ה סנדל וכו' מסמרות למזק כצ"ל ותיבת למעלה נמחק:

גליון הש"ס

מתני' ולא בשריון. עי' לקמן סד ע"ב ברש"י ד"ה כל שאמרו:

תורה אור השלם

א) וַיִּקַּח מֹשֶׁה וְאֶלְעָזָר הַכֹּהֵן אֶת הַזָּהָב מֵאִתָּם כֹּל כְּלִי מַעֲשֶׂה: [במדבר לא, נא]

ליקוטי רש"י

בסנדל המסומר. סנדל של עץ מלופה עור ומסמרות קבועין בו שגזרו חכמים עליו שלא לנעלו בשבת וביום טוב משום מעשה שהיה ידיו במסכת שבת (ס.) [ביצה יד:]. ולא בקמיע. כתב לרפואת חולי. מומחה. שריפא כבר שלש פעמים [לעיל נג.]. ולא בשריון ולא במגפיים. שאמרו חכמים משום מראית העין שלא יחשדוהו באיסור [לקמן סד:].

חשק שלמה על רבינו חננאל

א) עי' בהגש"ס שמתה ע"ד רבינו בזה:

The Mishnah stated:

וְלֹא בְּמַחַט שֶׁאֵינָהּ נְקוּבָה – AND she may NOT go out WITH A NEEDLE THAT IS NOT PIERCED . . .

The Gemara asks:

לְמַאי חַזְיָא – **For what is [such a needle] used?**[14]

The Gemara answers:

אָמַר רַב יוֹסֵף – **Rav Yosef said:** הוֹאִיל וְאִשָּׁה אוֹגֶרֶת בָּהּ שְׂעָרָהּ – Such a needle is useful **because a woman collects her** stray **hairs with it.**[15]

The Gemara persists:

אָמַר לֵיהּ אַבַּיֵי – **Abaye said to [Rav Yosef]:** וְתֶהֱוֵי כְּבִירִית טְהוֹרָה – **But** if this is the function of the needle, **let it be** viewed as **similar to a garter that is *tahor*,**[16] וְתִשְׁתְּרֵי – **and let** wearing **it** outside on the Sabbath **be permitted.**[17]

The Gemara concedes the point, and offers another explanation:

אֶלָּא תַּרְגְּמָהּ רַב אַדָּא נַרְשָׁאָה קַמֵּיהּ דְּרַב יוֹסֵף – **Rather, Rav Adda** from **Narash explained this before Rav Yosef** as follows: הוֹאִיל וְאִשָּׁה חוֹלֶקֶת בָּהּ שְׂעָרָהּ – The needle is useful **because a woman parts her hair with it.**[18]

The Gemara questions this explanation:

בְּשַׁבָּת לְמַאי חַזְיָא – **But of what use is [such a needle] on the Sabbath?**[19]

The Gemara answers:

אָמַר רָבָא – **Rava said:** טַס שֶׁל זָהָב יֵשׁ לָהּ עַל רֹאשָׁהּ – **[This needle] has a bar of gold on** one of **its ends.**[20] Thus, it is a useful accessory at all times; בְּחוֹל חוֹלֶקֶת בָּהּ שְׂעָרָהּ – **during the weekdays,** a woman **will part her hair with it** using the sharp end, בְּשַׁבָּת מַנִּיחַתָּהּ כְּנֶגֶד פַּדַּחְתָּהּ – and **on the Sabbath she** sticks the sharp end into her hat and **places [the gold bar] upon her forehead** as an ornament.[21]

Mishnah

The Mishnah lists those items which a man may not wear outside on the Sabbath: לֹא יֵצֵא הָאִישׁ בְּסַנְדָּל הַמְּסוּמָּר – **A man may not go outside** on the Sabbath **with a hobnailed sandal;**[22] וְלֹא בְּיָחִיד – **and** he may **not** go out **with a single** sandal[23] בִּזְמַן שֶׁאֵין בְּרַגְלוֹ מַכָּה – **when there is no wound on his foot;**[24] וְלֹא בִּתְפִילִּין – **and** he may **not** go out **with tefillin;**[25] וְלֹא בְקָמֵיעַ בִּזְמַן שֶׁאֵינוֹ מִן הַמּוּמְחֶה – **and not with an amulet when it is not from an expert;**[26] וְלֹא בְשִׁרְיוֹן – **nor with a coat of mail;** וְלֹא בְקַסְדָּא – **nor with a helmet;**[27] וְלֹא בְמַגָּפַיִים – **nor with shin guards.**[28] וְאִם יָצָא – **But if he went out** wearing any of these items, אֵינוֹ חַיָּיב חַטָּאת – **he is not liable to a *chatas*** offering.[29]

NOTES

14. From the fact that our Mishnah states that a woman who wears a needle without an eye into the public domain is not liable to a *chatas,* we can derive that it is only Rabbinically prohibited for her to do so. Obviously, then, the needle is not a burden [which would be Biblically prohibited]; and this would only be so if it can be classified as an ornament or accessory of some sort. Accordingly, the Gemara asks: What is the function of such a needle? (see *Rashi;* cf. *Tosafos, Ritva MHK* ed.; see also *Chelkas Binyamin*).

15. When stray hairs protrude from beneath her hair coverings, she winds the hairs around the needle, and then thrusts the needle into the underside of her hat, so that the hairs are hidden beneath it and are no longer visible (*Rashi;* cf. *Tosafos*).

16. The Mishnah below (63a) states that a woman may go out wearing a garter on the Sabbath. [A garter is a band that encircles the top of a woman's stocking and prevents the stocking from falling down.] The garter is not considered a burden, for the woman needs it to keep her stocking in place; and we are not concerned that a woman will remove it in the street to show to a friend, for she will not wish her stocking to fall down (*Rashi,* as understood by *Chidushei HaRan;* see next note).

The Gemara's mention of the fact that the garter is *tahor* — a law taught in the Mishnah below — is not relevant to the Gemara's question according to *Rashi;* it is merely mentioned here incidentally (*Ritva MHK* ed.). [The *reason* that the garter is *tahor* is because its function is to assist the function of another article (the stocking); as such, it is considered similar to the rings attached to utensils that are used to hang those utensils, which are not susceptible to *tumah,* as the Gemara stated in the previous chapter (*Rashi;* see above, 52a,b).]

17. Just as a woman may go outside wearing the garter because it keeps her stocking in place, and we are not concerned that she will remove it, a woman should be permitted to go out with a needle that she uses to tuck stray hairs under her hat, for she will not remove the needle, as she will thereby allow the stray hairs to protrude again and it is not permitted for a woman to uncover her hair in the street (see *Rashi;* see also above, 57a note 6; see also *Responsa Chasam Sofer, Orach Chaim* §36). Cf. *Tosafos, Ritva MHK* ed. *Rashba,* et al., who understand the Gemara's question differently.

18. I.e. she uses it to part her hair in the center of her head, combing her hair out from the center towards either side (*Rashi;* see next note).

19. A woman does not comb her hair on the Sabbath (*Rashi*). Thus, the Gemara asks that the needle should still be considered a burden on the Sabbath, as there is no reason for the woman to have it with her.

[*Tosafos* and other Rishonim take exception to *Rashi's* explanation, noting that the Gemara above (50b) and the Gemara in *Nazir* (42a) seem to permit combing of the hair on the Sabbath. Furthermore, they note that even the original answer of the Gemara [that the needle can be used as a comb] requires explanation; for the fact that the needle is functional certainly is not sufficient reason to allow it to be worn on the Sabbath! They therefore explain this entire passage differently. For a defense of *Rashi's* position, see *Meromei Sadeh* and *Chelkas Binyamin.*

20. That is, on one end (the tip) the needle is sharp, but on the other end (the head) there is a wide bar of gold (*Rashi*).

21. Accordingly, it is Rabbinically prohibited to wear this needle on the Sabbath, for she may remove it to show the ornamental head to a friend. [A needle being used to hold stray hairs in place, however, may be worn outside on the Sabbath, as it will not be removed (see *Maharsha*).]

22. This is a wooden sandal whose leather uppers are attached to its sole with nails [that protrude through the sole to its underside]. The Gemara will explain why the Sages prohibited the wearing of such sandals on the Sabbath (*Rashi*). [Although the Mishnah states only that one may not go out while wearing these sandals, the Sages extended the decree to prohibit one from wearing them altogether on the Sabbath (see *Chidushei HaRan* to 60b; see also *Rambam, Hil. Shabbos* 19:2, *Tos. Yom Tov* to *Beitzah* 1:10, and *Sfas Emes* to *Beitzah* 15a).]

23. [This refers to *any* sandal, not only a hobnailed one.]

24. *Rashi* cites two possible explanations for this prohibition: (a) The Sages were concerned that people would suspect a person wearing a single sandal of carrying its mate underneath his clothing (cited in the name of *Yerushalmi*). (b) The Sages were concerned that people would make fun of him, and he would take off the single sandal and carry it (cited in the name of *Rashi's* teachers). This prohibition applies, however, only if there is no wound on his foot (the Gemara below, 61a, discusses whether the sandal is being worn on the foot with the wound or the other foot; see there for further discussion of this law).

25. The reason for this prohibition is explained in the Gemara below (61a).

26. An amulet (worn to cure or prevent disease) may not be worn unless its efficacy can be assumed, in which case it is an accessory and similar to the clothing of the person wearing it (*Rashi;* see *Sfas Emes,* who discusses why wearing an amulet that is not from an expert is not Biblically prohibited). The Gemara below (61a-b) discusses the criteria for classifying an amulet as effective.

27. See Gemara below, 62a.

28. I.e. sections of armor that protect the legs (Gemara below, 62a).

29. Wearing these items is not Biblically prohibited, for they are all *worn,* rather than carried. [The mail, helmet and shin guards are normal clothing during times of war (*Rashi;* see also *Rashi* to 64b ד״ה כל שאסרו [ב׳], who explains why wearing these items is Rabbinically prohibited; see also below, 62a note 13.]

בקולב הלך אחר מסמרותיו בסולם הלך אחר שליבותיו בערסי הלך אחר שלשלותיו וחכמים אומרים [א] הכל הולך אחר המעמיד רבא אמר לצדדים קתני יש עליה חותם תכשיט דאיש אין עליה חותם תכשיט דאשה רב נחמן בר יצחק אמר [ג] טומאה אשבת קרמית טומאה [א] כלי מעשה אמר רחמנא וכלי הוא שבת משום משוי אמר רחמנא אין עליה חותם תכשיט יש עליה חותם משוי: ולא במחט שאינה נקובה: [א] למאי חזיא אמר רב יוסף הואיל ואשה [ג] אוגרת בה שערה א"ל אביי ותהוי כבירית טהורה ותשתרי אלא תרגמא רב אדא נרשאה קמיה דרב יוסף הואיל ואשה חולקת בה שערה בשבת למאי חזיא אמר רבא טס של זהב יש לה על ראשה בחול חולקת בה שערה בשבת מניחתה כנגד פדחתה: **מתני'** [ב] לא יצא האיש בסנדל המסומר ולא [ג] ביחיד בזמן שאין ברגלו מכה ולא בתפילין [ד] ולא בקמיע בזמן שאינו מן המומחה [ה] ולא בשריון ולא בקסדא ולא במגפיים ואם יצא אינו חייב חטאת: **גמ'** סנדל המסומר מאי טעמא אמר שמואל שלפי הגזרה היו והיו נחבאין במערה ואמרו הנכנס יכנס והיוצא אל יצא נהפך סנדלו של אחד מהן כסבורין הם אחד מהן יצא וראוהו אויבים ועכשיו באין עליהן דחקו זה בזה והרגו זה את זה יותר ממה שהרגו בהם אויבים רבי אילעאי בן אלעזר אומר במערה היו יושבין ושמעו קול מעל גבי המערה כסבורין היו שבאו עליהם אויבים דחקו זה בזה והרגו זה את זה יותר ממה שהרגו בהן אויבים רמי בר יחזקאל אמר בבהכ"נ היו יושבין ושמעו קול מאחורי בהכ"נ כסבורין היו שבאו עליהם אויבים דחקו זה בזה והרגו זה את זה יותר ממה שהרגו בהן אויבים באותה שעה אמרו אל יצא אדם בסנדל המסומר אי הכי בחול נמי ליתסר מעשה כי הוה בשבת הוה ביום טוב לישתרי אלמה תנן משלחין

רש"י

בקולב. הוא כמין עמוד רחב מלמטה ודק מלמעלה ומיטלטל והחנוני מעמידו לפני חלון חנותו ומסמרין תחובין בו ותולין בהן אבנטים ורצועות למכור: **בערסה.** אישתרייד"א בלע"ז והן מאזנים גדולות לשקול צמר ושעוה ונחשת והן של עץ: **הלך אחר שלשלותיו.** שתלוי בהן ואם של מתכת הן טמאות: **המעמיד.** גוף הטבעת מעמיד החותם והעול מעמיד את סמלוניו והקולב את מסמרותיו והסולם את שליבותיו שהרי בהם קבועים והערסה הוא עץ (א) ארוך שהקנה שקורין יי"א והלשון תחוב בו והשלשלות קבועות בקנה וכולן העץ ארוך מעמידן שהוא פליי"ל ששתי כפות המאזנים תלויות בב' ראשין: **רבא אמר.** ברייתא דקתני וטבעת הוי תכשיט בין שיש עליה חותם בין שאין עליה חותם לאו ארישא דאיירי בתכשיטי נשים קיימי תרווייהו אלא חד תכשיט דאיש וחד תכשיט דאשה ולצדדין קתני: **טומאה אשבת קרמית.** הא דקתני וטבעת בין שיש עליה כו' לאו ארישא קאי דקרי ליה תכשיט נשים אלא הכי קאמר וטבעת שאמרו שנטמאת בין שיש עליה חותם דלאו תכשיט הוא מיהו כלי מעשה הוא בין שאין עליה חותם דהוי תכשיט וכי קתני רישא תכשיטי נשים אשאין עליה חותם: **למאי חזיא.** לתכשיט דקתני אינה חייבת חטאת: **אוגרת בה שערה.** היוצא חוץ לקישוריה כורכתו סביב המחט ותוחבת המחט בשבכה מתחתיה שלא יראה שערה: **ותיהוי כבירית.** דתנא מתניתין (לקמן דף סג.) בירית טהורה מלטמא ויוצאין בה והיא כמין אצעדה שעושה לשוקיה מעל בתי שוקיה להדקן שלא יפלו על רגלה: **טהורה.** דלאו תכשיט היא אלא תשמיש לבתי שוקיה והוי (ב) כטבעת הכלים דאמרן טהורות בפרקין דלעיל ויוצאין בה שצריך לה עם בתי שוקיה ולא הוי משאוי ויוצאין דכיון דלצניעותא היא לא שלפא ומחוי והאי מחט נמי לצניעות דשער באשה ערוה ולא מחויא ואמאי לא תצא לכתחילה: **חולקת.** לכאן ולכאן באמצע ראשה שקורין גריוו"א בלע"ז: **ובשבת למאי חזיא.** הרי בשבת אינה חולקת שערה: **טס של זהב יש לה על ראשה.** האחד והשני עוקץ הוי: **בחול חולקת שערה.** בעוקץ: **ובשבת.** תוחבת העוקץ בשבכה והטס שבראשה השני מונח על פדחתה: **מתני' סנדל המסומר.** של עץ הוא ותוחבין מסמרות (ג) למעלה לחזק התחתון עם העליון [ה] (העץ עם העור שלמעלה הימנו ויש לו שתי פיות ותוחב רגלו בו) ובגמרא מפרש מאי טעמא גזרו ביה: **ולא ביחיד.** ולא בסנדל יחיד: **בזמן שאין ברגלו מכה.** בש"ס ירושלמי מפרש דלא ליחשדיה דטעין ליה לחבריה תותי כנפיה ולשון רבותי דילמא מחייכי עליה ושקיל דשליף ליה וממטי ליה בידי' בשכחת שבת ומיהו בזמן שיש ברגלו מכה שרי ובגמרא בעי בהי מינייהו יהיב ליה: **ולא בתפילין.** כדמפרש טעמא בגמרא (לקמן דף סא.): **ולא בקמיע.** שכותבין וטוענין לרפואה: **שאינו מן המומחה.** אבל בקמיע מומחה שרי דתכשיט הוא לחולה כאחד ממלבושיו: **שריון קסדא ומגפיים.** מפרש בגמרא: **אינו חייב חטאת.** דכולהו מין מלבושין נינהו בחול למלחמה: **גמ' שלפי הגזירה היו.** בני אדם הנשמטים מן הגזירה היו: **הנכנס יכנס.** הרוצה ליכנס יכנס שהנכנס יראה תחלה שאין אדם רואה: **והיוצא אל יצא.** שמא יש אויבים מבחוץ והוא לא ידע ויראוהו ויבינו שאנו כאן: **נהפך סנדלו.** שיש לו שתי פיות ויכול לנועלו מב' צדדין אבל ניכר מי הוא לפנים ומי הוא לאחור וכשנועלו זה הפוך נראה הנכנס כאילו הוא יוצא וניכר מקומו בקרקע: **והרגו זה את זה.** בדחיקתן שהיו סנדליהן מסומרין כעין אותם שעושין לרגלי הסוסים ראשיהן עבים: **אל יצא.** האיש בשבת כדמפרש לקמיה דבשבת היה מעשה ומעין המאורע אסרו: **אלמה תנן.** במסכת ביצה: משלחין

תוספות

רב נחמן בר יצחק אמר טומאה אשבת קא רמית. דאפילו בלאו טעמא דהוי תכשיט לאיש היא טמאה מכל כלי מעשה והשתא בין לרבא בין לרב נחמן בר יצחק מוקמי תרווייהו כרבי נחמיה ולא מטמא מטעם תכשיט דאשה אלא מטעם תכשיט דאיש או מטעם דהוי כלי מעשה ולצדדין קתני בין לרבא בין לרב נחמן בר יצחק:

למאי חזיא. פי' בקונטרס למאי חזיא והא משוי הוא וקשה לר"י דאם כן מאי משני הואיל ואשה חולקת בה שערה אטו משום הכי לא הוי משוי והא אינו לא מלבוש ולא תכשיט אלא נראה לפרש למאי חזיא למה היא רגילה לצאת בה בחול אמר רב יוסף כו' ובתר הכי פריך ובשבת למאי חזיא נהי שרגילה לנושאה בשביל שצריכה לחלק בה שערה בשבת תיהוי משוי כיון דאינו לא מלבוש ולא תכשיט ובקונטרס פי' בסמוך בשבת למאי חזיא והלא בשבת אינה חולקת שערה וקשה לר"י חדא דהא מנא ליה דאסור לחלק בה שיער בשבת ועוד דאמאי פריך והא אסור אפילו יהא מותר תקשה והא משוי הוא:

הואיל ואשה אוגרת בה שערה. נראה לר"י שתוחבת המחט בתוך הסבכה ודוחקת את הסבכה כדי שלא יפלו שערותיה חוץ לקישוריה והשתא אתי שפיר דהויא כעין בירית שאוחזת בתי שוקיה שלא יפלו ולא כפירוש הקונטרס:

ותיהוי כבירית טהורה ותשתרי. פירש בקונטרס דכי היכי דהתם לא חיישי לדילמא משלפא ומחויא הואיל ולצניעותא עבידא ה"נ לא ניחוש למישלף ואחווי מהאי טעמא וקשה לר"י דהא בכלים אין יוצאין בהן בשבת דחיישינן דילמא משלפא להו משום דהוי תכשיט כמו שאפרש אע"ג דלצניעותא עבידא כמו בירית דהכל ענין אחד אלא שבירית באחת וכבלים בשתים כדאמרינן לקמן (דף סג:) ועוד דלמה לו להזכיר כאן טהרת בירית הוה ליה למימר ותיהוי כבירית ותשתרי ונראה לר"י דה"פ ותהוי כבירית שיוצאין בה לפי שהיא טהורה משום שאינה תכשיט דאינה נוי לאשה כיון דאינה כ"א באחת והויא כטבעת הכלים דאינה כ"א לצורך בתי שוקים ה"נ האי מחט שהיא טהורה לפי שאינה אלא כטבעת הכלים תשתרי דאינה תכשיט וא"ת אמאי לא משני השתא כמין טס של זהב יש לה בראשה כדמשני לאידך שינויא דבסמוך וי"ל דאם היתה אוגרת בה שערה לא היתה מניחתה לעולם כנגד פדחתה ואינה חשובה תכשיט אלא טס וקשה לרשב"א לפירוש זה דכיון דמחט שאוגרת בה שערה היא טהורה היכי קאמר לעיל (דף נז:) אבל לענין טומאה דא ודא אחת היא הרי יש חילוק אפילו בשלימה דאותה שאינה אוגרת בה טמאה ואותה שאוגרת בה טהורה וצריך לומר דאטומאה נמי פריך ותיהוי טהורה כבירית שהיא טהורה גם תשתרי לצאת בה:

ומניחתה כנגד פדחתה. השתא לא היה צריך לומר שחולקת בה שערה כלל אלא האמת מפרש:

ושמעו קול מעל גבי המערה. קול של סנדל המסומר: (שייך לע"ב)

לא [ו] בסנדל המסומר ולא [ז] במנעל שאינו תפור. תימה לר"י והא קתני סיפא זה הכלל כל שנאותין בו משלחין אותו ביו"ט ומפרש בגמ' דכל שנאותין בו בחול קאמר וסנדל המסומר נאותין בו בחול ואמאי אין משלחין אותו בי"ט וי"ל דהחמירו בו לפי שבא תקלה על ידו כי היכי דאסר ליה בשמעתין ר' אלעזר בר' שמעון לטלטלו לכסות בו את הכלי או לסמוך בו כרעי המטה אע"פ [ח] שאר כלים שמלאכתן לאיסור שרי לטלטלן לצורך גופן ומקומן וזה הכלל דקתני התם לא קאי אלא אמנעל שאינו תפור ונראה לר"י דאפי' לרבנן דר' אלעזר דשרי לטלטל לצורך גופו ומקומו אסור לשלחו בי"ט אע"ג דשילוח משום שמחת י"ט חשיב כמו לצורך גופו מדשרי' לשלוח דברים שמלאכתן לאיסור כיון שבאת תקלה על ידו ליכא שמחת י"ט:

אין

עין משפט נר מצוה

כז א מיי' פי"ט מהל' שבת הלכה ה סמג לאוין סה טוש"ע א"ח סי' שג סעיף ט:

כח ב מיי' פי"ט מהל' שבת הלכה ג:

כט ג מיי' שם הלכה טו סמג שם טוש"ע א"ח סי' שא סעיף ו:

רבינו חננאל

ריסוקא. פי' חגור של עור אי אית ביה מפרחייתא שרי ותכשיט הוא ואי לא אסור פי' אם יש לו מפרחייתא חתיכות יוצאות ועודפות ממנו לימינו ולשמאלו תכשיט הוא ואי לא אינו מלאכת תכשיט ואסור לצאת בו בשבת כי אינו כלי. קטלא תכשיט בצואר. כגון ענק והיא בלשון ערבי מכנקא. נזמים יש נזמי האף ונזמים שבאזנים: **ולא** בטבעת שאין עליה חותם הא יש עליה חותם משאוי ואם תצא בו חייבת חטאת. אלמא לאו תכשיט הוא איני והתניא תכשיטי נשים עיר של זהב קטלאות נזמים וטבעת אחת טבעת שיש עליה חותם ואחת טבעת שאין עליה חותם ונזמי האף [טמאים] ומשני ר' זירא בטבעת של אלמוג וחותמה של מתכת ומתניתין [כרבנן] בכלים פרק י"ג דאמרי טהורה. [וכיון] לענין טומאה לאו כלי הוא לענין שבת נמי לאו כלי הוא. ומשוי הוא. הא ברייתא ר' נחמיה היא דמשוי ליה לענין [טומאה] מנא לענין שבת נמי תכשיט הוא דתנינן טבעת של מתכת וחותמה של אלמוג [טמאה היא של אלמוג] וחותמה של מתכת טהורה. ור' נחמיה מטמא: סימלוניו פי' רצועות שהן בעול דתנינן בתורת כהנים מיד בא ושיבר העול וקיצץ סימלונין כדכתיב ה' צדיק קצץ עבות רשעים. קולב. יש מי שאומרים ממיני תכשיט הוא להשמיע קול כדורך בגת ומחזקו במסמרים: **שליבות** ושלשלאות פשוטות הן. רבא אמר הא מתניתא לצדדין קתני אין עליה חותם תכשיט דאשה יש עליה חותם תכשיט דאיש והדין כך הוא. שיהא האיש מותר לצאת בטבעת שיש עליה חותם והאשה בטבעת שאין עליה חותם. מפני שתכשיט הוא להן וכל תכשיט שרי אלא משום גזירה א) דרבא כדבעינן למימר לקמן (סב.) דאמר פעמים שהאשה נותנת לבעלה טבעת שאין עליה חותם להוליכה אצל האומן ומניחה באצבעו עד שמגיע אל האומן. ופעמים שהאיש נותן לאשתו טבעת שיש עליה חותם להניחה בקופסא ומניחתה באצבעתה עד שמגעת לקופסא. לפיכך אסרו אחד האיש ואחד האשה לצאת בין בטבעת שיש עליה חותם בין בטבעת שאין עליה חותם. רב נחמן בר יצחק אמר טומאה אשבת קרמית כו'. ולא במחט שאינה נקובה אוקימנא כדתניא כמין טס של זהב יש לה על ראשה. בחול חולקת בה שערה בשבת מנחת על פדחתה. ונוי הוא לה: **לא** יצא בסנדל מסומר כו'. מ"ט שלפי השמד כו' פשוטה היא.

מסורת הש"ס

א) [לעיל טו:], ב) לקמן קכג., ג) [גי' הערוך בערך אגד אוגדת], ד) [לעיל נג:], ה) רש"ל מוחק זה, ו) [נ"ל סנדל], ז) [נ"ל מנעל], ח) [לקמן קכד.].

הגהות הב"ח

(א) רש"י ד"ה המעמיד וכו' והערסה הוא עץ הארוך שהוא קנה שקורין: (ב) ד"ה טהורה וכו' והרי הוא כטבעת: (ג) ד"ה סנדל וכו' מסמרות לחזק כצ"ל ותיבת למעלה נמחק:

גליון הש"ס

מתני' ולא בשריון. עי' לקמן סד ע"ב ברש"י ד"ה כל שאסרו:

תורה אור השלם

א) וַיִּקַּח מֹשֶׁה וְאֶלְעָזָר הַכֹּהֵן אֶת הַזָּהָב מֵאִתָּם כֹּל כְּלִי מַעֲשֶׂה: [במדבר לא, נא]

ליקוטי רש"י

בסנדל המסומר. סנדל של עץ מצופה עור ומסמרות קבועין בו שגזרו חכמים עליו שלא לנעלו בשבת וביום טוב משום מעשה שהיה שנהרגו הרוגים בשבת על ידיו במסכת שבת (ס.) [ביצה יד:]. **ולא בקמיע.** כתב לרפואת חולי. **מומחה.** שריפא כבר שלש פעמים [לעיל נג.]. **ולא בשריון ולא בקסדא ולא במגפיים.** שאסרו חכמים משום מראית העין שלא יחשדוהו באיסור [לקמן סד:].

חשק שלמה על רבינו חננאל

א) עי' ברש"א שמחק ע"ד רבינו כזה.

Gemara The Gemara seeks the reason for the first ruling of the Mishnah:

סַנְדָּל הַמְסוּמָּר מַאי טַעְמָא – What is the reason that one may not wear **a hobnailed sandal** on the Sabbath? **אָמַר שְׁמוּאֵל – Shmuel said:** The Rabbis decreed that such sandals not be worn due to the following unfortunate incident. **שְׁלְפֵי הַגְּזֵרָה הָיוּ – They were fugitives from the** anti-Jewish **decree**[30] **וְהָיוּ נֶחְבָּאִין בִּמְעָרָה – and they were hiding in a cave. וְאָמְרוּ – And [the fugitives] said: הַנִּכְנָס יִכָּנֵס – He who** wishes **to enter, may enter; וְהַיּוֹצֵא אַל יֵצֵא – but** he who wishes **to leave, may not leave.**[31] **נֶהְפַּךְ סַנְדָּלוֹ שֶׁל אֶחָד מֵהֶן – The sandal of one of them became reversed,**[32] and when he came into the cave, he left footprints which appeared to lead *away* from the cave.[33] **כִּסְבוּרִין הֵם אֶחָד מֵהֶן יָצָא** – When they saw these footprints, **they thought** that **one of [the fugitives] had exited** the cave, **וְרָאוּהוּ אוֹיְבִים – and** they feared that **the enemy had seen him, וְעַכְשָׁיו בָּאִין עֲלֵיהֶן – and were now coming upon** the cave to capture **them. דָּחֲקוּ זֶה בָּזֶה** – In their panic, **they pushed** and kicked **at each other וְהָרְגוּ זֶה אֶת זֶה יוֹתֵר מִמַּה שֶּׁהָרְגוּ בָּהֶם אוֹיְבִים – and** they **killed more of each other than the enemies did.**[34] Since this was due in part to hobnailed sandals that they were wearing,[35] the Sages decreed that these sandals should not be worn on the Sabbath.[36]

The Gemara offers a second version of the incident that prompted the Sages' decree:

רַבִּי אִילְעַאי בֶּן אֶלְעָזָר אוֹמֵר – R' Il'ai the son of Elazar says: בִּמְעָרָה הָיוּ יוֹשְׁבִין – [The fugitives] were hiding[37] **in a cave, וְשָׁמְעוּ קוֹל מֵעַל גַּבֵּי הַמְּעָרָה – and they heard a noise above the cave. כִּסְבוּרִין הָיוּ שֶׁבָּאוּ עֲלֵיהֶם אוֹיְבִים – They** mistakenly **thought that their enemies were coming to** capture **them, דָּחֲקוּ זֶה בָּזֶה** – and, in their panic, **they pushed** and kicked **at each other, וְהָרְגוּ זֶה אֶת זֶה יוֹתֵר מִמַּה שֶּׁהָרְגוּ בָּהֶן אוֹיְבִים – and they killed more of each other than the enemies did.** Since this was due in part to the hobnailed sandals, the Sages decreed that hobnailed sandals not be worn on the Sabbath.[38]

The Gemara cites a third version of the incident that prompted the Sages' decree:

רָמִי בַּר יְחֶזְקֵאל אָמַר – Rami bar Yecheskel said: בְּבֵית הַכְּנֶסֶת הָיוּ יוֹשְׁבִין – [The fugitives] were sitting in the synagogue, וְשָׁמְעוּ קוֹל מֵאֲחוֹרֵי בֵּית הַכְּנֶסֶת – and they heard noises from behind the synagogue. כִּסְבוּרִין הָיוּ שֶׁבָּאוּ עֲלֵיהֶם אוֹיְבִים – They thought that **their enemies were coming to capture them, דָּחֲקוּ זֶה בָּזֶה** – and, in their panic, **they pushed at each other וְהָרְגוּ זֶה אֶת זֶה יוֹתֵר מִמַּה שֶּׁהָרְגוּ בָּהֶן אוֹיְבִים – and killed more of each other than the enemies did.**[39] **בְּאוֹתָהּ שָׁעָה אָמְרוּ – At that time, [the Sages] stated: אַל יֵצֵא אָדָם בְּסַנְדָּל הַמְסוּמָּר – A man may not go out with a hobnailed sandal** on the Sabbath.

The Gemara asks the obvious question:

אִי הָכִי – But **if this** is the reason for the decree, **בְּחוֹל נַמִּי לִיתְסַר – let it** (the wearing of such sandals) **be forbidden even on weekdays!**[40]

The Gemara answers:

מַעֲשֶׂה כִּי הֲוָה בְּשַׁבָּת הֲוָה – When this incident occurred, it was on the Sabbath that it occurred; and the Sages prohibited the wearing of these sandals only in circumstances similar to those in which the incident occurred.[41]

The Gemara persists:

בְּיוֹם טוֹב לִישְׁתְּרֵי – But if this is true, **let it be permitted** to wear such sandals **on a Yom Tov!**[42] **אַלְמָה תְּנַן – Why,** then, **we have learned in a Mishnah:**[43]

NOTES

30. The word "הַגְּזֵרָה," the decree, is the censor's corruption of the text, which originally read "הַשְּׁמַד" (*Dikdukei Soferim*). The term שְׁמַד, which means religious persecutions in general, is used by the Sages specifically in reference to the unbearable persecutions by the Roman Emperor Hadrian (117-138 C.E.) which followed the collapse of the Bar Kochba revolt (see *Bereishis Rabbah* 79:6 and *Shir HaShirim Rabbah* 2:5).

The word שְׁלְפֵי is interpreted in other places as "the end of" (e.g. *Yevamos* 116b and *Rashi* there; see also *Rabbeinu Perachyah*). An alternate reading is שְׁלְהֵי, which also means "the end of" (*Chidushei HaRan*). According to this interpretation, the event took place toward the end of that terrible era.

31. The fugitives were concerned that anyone leaving the hiding place would be observed as he came out, revealing their refuge to the enemy. They were not concerned about those entering, as no one would enter unless he first checked to see that he was not being watched (*Rashi*).

32. [This was a hobnailed sandal, as is evident from the Gemara below (see note 35).] The sandal was constructed so that one could insert his foot into it from either end; however, the sandal's design was not symmetrical front to back; thus, if one wore it backwards, the footprints he would leave would appear to be those of a person walking in the opposite direction (*Rashi*).

33. As the footprints of the reversed sandal appeared to lead in the opposite direction from which the man had actually walked (see previous note).

34. Literally: than the enemies killed of them.

35. The hobnailed sandals were thick and studded with nails, similar to those that horses were shod with – thus, they were capable of inflicting considerable damage (*Rashi*).

36. The Gemara below (60b) will explain why the Sages restricted their decree to the Sabbath.

37. Literally: sitting.

38. See notes 35 and 36.

39. Due to the hobnailed sandals they were wearing (see note 35). [This follows *Rashi's* explanation of the Gemara. *Tosafos*, however, explain that the noise that was heard above the cave (and, presumably, the noise that was made behind the synagogue in Rami bar Yecheskel's version of the incident) was made by the hobnailed sandals of passersby, and it was for this reason that the Sages prohibited wearing them [and *not* because the fugitives were wearing the hobnailed sandals] (see *Rambam, Commentary to the Mishnah,* and *Meiri; cf. Ben Yehoyada*). [*Tosafos* do not explain the problem caused by the hobnailed sandal in Shmuel's version of the incident; *Maharam* suggests that it was the asymmetrical design of the nails in the sandals that made the reversed footprints seem to be leading away from the refuge.]

[*Sfas Emes* suggests that in fact all three of these incidents occurred, and the Sages' decree was based on the cumulative destruction caused by hobnailed sandals.]

40. If the Sages were concerned that a repetition of this incident would occur, why did they only prohibit the wearing of such sandals on the Sabbath? They should have forbidden wearing them at any time!

41. I.e. the Sages were not concerned that the tragedy would occur another time; they merely wished to prevent people from being saddened by the memory of the calamity. They accomplished this by prohibiting the wearing of these sandals on a day similar to the day upon which the tragedy occurred (see *Rashi, Chidushei HaRan,* and *Ritva MHK* ed.; see also *Ishei Yisrael* and *Ben Yehoyada*).

42. [For the incident did not occur on Yom Tov, and if the Sages only wished to extend the prohibition to days similar to the one upon which the tragedy occurred, the prohibition should not apply to Yom Tov.]

43. *Beitzah* 14b.

בקולב הלך אחר מסמרותיו בסולם הלך אחר שליבותיו בערסי הלך אחר שלשלותיו וחכמים אומרים (א) הכל הולך אחר המעמיד רבא אמר לצדדים קתני יש עליה חותם תכשיט דאיש אין עליה חותם תכשיט דאשה רב נחמן בר יצחק אמר (ג) טומאה אשבת קרמית טומאה (א) כלי מעשה אמר רחמנא וכלי הוא שבת משום משוי אמר רחמנא אין עליה חותם תכשיט יש עליה חותם משוי: ולא במחט שאינה נקובה: א למאי חזיא אמר רב יוסף הואיל ואשה (ג) אוגרת בה שערה א"ל אביי ותהוי כבירית טהורה ותשתרי אלא תרגמא רב אדא נרשאה קמיה דרב יוסף הואיל ואשה חולקת בה שערה בשבת למאי חזיא אמר רבא טס של זהב יש לה על ראשה בחול חולקת בה שערה בשבת מניחתה כנגד פדחתה: **מתני'** ב לא יצא האיש בסנדל המסומר ולא ג ביחיד בזמן שאין ברגלו מכה ולא בתפילין (ד) ולא בקמיע בזמן שאינו מן המומחה (ה) ולא בשריון ולא בקסדא ולא במגפיים ואם יצא אינו חייב חטאת: **גמ'** סנדל המסומר מאי טעמא אמר שמואל שלפי הגזרה היו והיו נחבאין במערה ואמרו הנכנס יכנס והיוצא אל יצא נהפך סנדלו של אחד מהן כסבורין הם אחד מהן יצא וראוהו אויבים ועכשיו באין עליהן דחקו זה בזה והרגו זה את זה יותר ממה שהרגו בהם אויבים רבי אילעאי בן אלעזר אומר במערה היו יושבין ושמעו קול מעל גבי המערה כסבורין היו שבאו עליהם אויבים דחקו זה בזה והרגו זה את זה יותר ממה שהרגו בהן אויבים רמי בר יחזקאל אמר בבהכ"נ היו יושבין ושמעו קול מאחורי בהכ"נ כסבורין היו שבאו עליהם אויבים דחקו זה בזה והרגו זה את זה יותר ממה שהרגו בהן אויבים באותה שעה אמרו אל יצא אדם בסנדל המסומר אי הכי בחול נמי ליתסר מעשה כי הוה בשבת הוה ביום טוב לישתרי אלמה תנן

משלחין

רש"י

בקולב. הוא כמין עמוד רחב מלמטה ודק מלמעלה ומיטלטל והחנוני מעמידו לפני חלון חנותו ומסמרין תחובין בו ותולין בהן אבנטים ורצועות למכור: **בערסה.** אישתרייד"א בלע"ז והן מאזנים גדולות לשקול נמר ושעוה ונחשת והן של עץ: **הלך אחר שלשלותיו.** שתלוי בהן ואם של מתכת הן טמאות: **המעמיד.** גוף הטבעת מעמיד החותם והעול מעמיד את סמלוניו והקולב את מסמרותיו והסולם את שליבותיו שהרי בהם קבועים והערסה הוא עץ (א) ארוך שהקנה שקורין יימ"א והלשון תחוב בו והשלשלות קבועות בקנה וכולן העץ ארוך מעמידן שהוא פליי"ל ששתי כפות המאזנים תלויות בב' ראשין: **רבא אמר.** ברייתא דקתני וטבעת הוי תכשיט בין שיש עליה חותם בין שאין עליה חותם לאו ארישא דאיירי בתכשיטי נשים קיימי תרוייהו אלא חד תכשיט דאיש וחד תכשיט דאשה ולצדדין קתני: **טומאה אשבת קרמית.** הא דקתני וטבעת בין שיש עליה כו' לאו ארישא קאי דקרי ליה תכשיט נשים אלא הכי קאמר וטבעת שאמרו שנטמאת בין שיש עליה חותם דלאו תכשיט הוא מיהו כלי מעשה הוא בין שאין עליה חותם דהוי תכשיט וכי קתני רישא תכשיטי נשים אשאין עליה חותם: **למאי חזיא.** לתכשיט דקתני אינה חייבת חטאת: **אוגרת בה שערה.** היוצא חוץ לקישוריה כורכתו סביב המחט ותוחבת המחט בשבכה מתחתיה שלא יראה שערה: **ותיהוי כבירית.** דתנא מתניתין (לקמן דף סג.) בירית טהורה מלטמא ויוצאין בה והיא כמין אצעדה שעושה לשוקיה מעל בתי שוקיה להדקן שלא יפלו על רגלה: **טהורה.** דלאו תכשיט היא אלא תשמיש לבתי שוקיה והוי (ב) כטבעת הכלים דאמרן טהורות בפרקין דלעיל ויוצאין בה שצריך לה עם בתי שוקיה ולא הוי משאוי ויוצאין דכיון דלצניעותא היא לא שלפא ומחוי והאי מחט נמי לצניעות דשער באשה ערוה ולא מחויא ואמאי לא תצא לכתחילה: **חולקת.** לכאן ולכאן באמצע ראשה שקורין גריוו"א בלע"ז: **ובשבת למאי חזיא.** הרי בשבת אינה חולקת שערה: **טס של זהב יש לה על ראשה.** האחד והשני עוקץ הוי: **בחול חולקת שערה.** בעוקץ: **ובשבת.** תוחבת העוקץ בשבכה והטס שבראשה השני מונח על פדחתה: **מתני' סנדל המסומר.** של עץ הוא ותוחבין מסמרות (ג) למעלה לחזק התחתון עם העליון (ה) (העץ עם העור שלמעלה הימנו ויש לו שתי פיות ותוחב רגלו בו) ובגמרא מפרש מאי טעמא גזרו ביה: **ולא ביחיד.** ולא בסנדל יחיד: **בזמן שאין ברגלו מכה.** בש"ס ירושלמי מפרש דלא ליחשדיה דטעין ליה לחבריה תותי כנפיה ולשון רבותי דילמא מחייכי עליה ושקיל דשליף ליה וממטי ליה בידי' בשכחת שבת ומיהו בזמן שיש ברגלו מכה שרי ובגמרא בעי בהי מינייהו יהיב ליה: **ולא בתפילין.** כדמפרש טעמא בגמרא (לקמן דף סא.): **ולא בקמיע.** שכותבין וטוענין לרפואה: **שאינו מן המומחה.** אבל בקמיע מומחה שרי דתכשיט הוא לחולה כאחד ממלבושיו: **שריון קסדא ומגפיים.** מפרש בגמרא: **אינו חייב חטאת.** דכולהו מין מלבושין נינהו בחול למלחמה: **גמ' שלפי הגזירה היו.** בני אדם הנשמטים מן הגזירה היו: **הנכנס יכנס.** הרוצה ליכנס יכנס שהנכנס יראה תחלה שאין אדם רואה: **והיוצא אל יצא.** שמא יש אויבים מבחוץ והוא לא ידע ויראוהו ויבינו שאנו כאן: **נהפך סנדלו.** שיש לו שתי פיות ויכול לנועלו מב' צדדין אבל ניכר מי הוא לפנים ומי הוא לאחור וכשנועלו זה הפוך נראה הנכנס כאילו הוא יוצא וניכר מקומו בקרקע: **והרגו זה את זה.** בדחיקתן שהיו סנדליהן מסומרין כעין אותם שעושין לרגלי הסוסים ראשיהן עבים: **אל יצא.** האיש בשבת כדמפרש לקמיה דבשבת היה מעשה ומעין המאורע אסרו: **אלמה תנן.** במסכת ביצה:

משלחין

תוספות

רב נחמן בר יצחק אמר טומאה אשבת קא רמית. דאפילו בלאו טעמא דהוי תכשיט לאיש היא טמאה מכל כלי מעשה והשתא בין לרבא בין לרב נחמן בר יצחק מוקמי תרוייהו כרבי נחמיה ולא מטמא מטעם תכשיט דאשה אלא מטעם תכשיט דאיש או מטעם דהוי כלי מעשה ולצדדין קתני בין לרבא בין לרב נחמן בר יצחק:

למאי חזיא. פי' בקונטרס למאי חזיא והא משוי הוא וקשה לר"י דאם כן מאי משני הואיל ואשה חולקת בה שערה אטו משום הכי לא הוי משוי והא אינו לא מלבוש ולא תכשיט אלא נראה לפרש למאי חזיא למה היא רגילה לצאת בה בחול אמר רב יוסף כו' ובתר הכי פריך ובשבת למאי חזיא נהי שרגילה לנושאה בשביל שצריכה לחלק בה שערה בשבת תיהוי משוי כיון דאינו לא מלבוש ולא תכשיט ובקונטרס פי' בסמוך בשבת למאי חזיא והלא בשבת אינה חולקת שערה וקשה לר"י חדא דהא מנא ליה דאסור לחלק בה שיער בשבת ועוד דאמאי פריך והא אסור אפילו יהא מותר תקשה והא משוי הוא:

הואיל ואשה אוגרת בה שערה. נראה לר"י שתוחבת המחט בתוך הסבכה ודוחקת את הסבכה כדי שלא יפלו שערותיה חוץ לקישוריה והשתא אתי שפיר דהויא כעין בירית שאוחזת בתי שוקיה שלא יפלו ולא כפירוש הקונטרס:

ותיהוי כבירית טהורה ותשתרי. פירש בקונטרס דכי היכי דהתם לא חיישי לדילמא משלפא ומחויא הואיל ולצניעותא עבידא ה"נ לא ניחוש למישלף ואחוויי מהאי טעמא וקשה לר"י דהא כבלים אין יוצאין בהן בשבת דחיישינן דילמא משלפא להו משום דהוי תכשיט כמו שאפרש אע"ג דלצניעותא עבידא כמו בירית דהכל ענין אחד אלא שבירית באחת וכבלים בשתים כדאמרינן לקמן (דף סג:) ועוד דלמה לו להזכיר כאן טהרת בירית הוה ליה למימר ותיהוי כבירית ותשתרי ונראה לר"י דה"פ ותהוי כבירית שיוצאין בה לפי שהיא טהורה משום שאינה תכשיט דאינה נוי לאשה כיון דאינה כ"א באחת והויא כטבעת הכלים דאינה כ"א לצורך בתי שוקים ה"נ האי מחט שהיא טהורה לפי שאינה אלא כטבעת הכלים תשתרי דאינה תכשיט וא"ת אמאי לא משני השתא כמין טס של זהב יש לה בראשה כדמשני לאידך שינויא דבסמוך וי"ל דאם היתה אוגרת בה שערה לא היתה מניחתה לעולם כנגד פדחתה ואינה חשובה תכשיט אלא טס וקשה לרשב"א לפירוש זה דכיון דמחט שאוגרת בה שערה היא טהורה היכי קאמר לעיל (דף נב:) אבל לענין טומאה דא ודא אחת היא הרי יש חילוק אפילו בשלימה דאותה שאינה אוגרת בה טמאה ואותה שאוגרת בה טהורה וצריך לומר דאטומאה נמי פריך ותיהוי טהורה כבירית שהיא טהורה גם תשתרי לצאת בה:

ומניחתה כנגד פדחתה. השתא לא היה צריך לומר שחולקת בה שערה כלל אלא האמת מפרש:

ושמעו קול מעל גבי המערה. קול של סנדל המסומר: (שייך לע"ב)

לא (ו) בסנדל המסומר ולא (ז) במנעל שאינו תפור. תימה לר"י והא קתני סיפא זה הכלל כל שנאותין בו משלחין אותו ביו"ט ומפרש בגמ' דכל שנאותין בו בחול קאמר וסנדל המסומר נאותין בו בחול ואמאי אין משלחין אותו בי"ט וי"ל דהחמירו בו לפי שבאת תקלה על ידו כי היכי דאסר ליה בשמעתין ר' אלעזר בר' שמעון לטלטלו לכסות בו את הכלי או לסמוך בו כרעי המטה אע"פ (ח) שאר כלים שמלאכתן לאיסור שרי לטלטלן לצורך גופן ומקומן וזה הכלל דקתני התם לא קאי אלא אמנעל שאינו תפור ונראה לר"י דאפי' לרבנן דר' אלעזר דשרי לטלטל לצורך גופו ומקומו אסור לשלחו בי"ט אע"ג דשילוח משום שמחת י"ט חשיב כמו לצורך גופו מדשרי' לשלוח דברים שמלאכתן לאיסור כיון שבאת תקלה על ידו ליכא שמחת י"ט:

אין

מסורת הש"ס

א) [לעיל טו:], ב) לקמן קכג., ג) [גי' הערוך בערך אגד אוגדת], ד) [לעיל נג:], ה) רש"ל מוחק זה, ו) [צ"ל סנדל], ז) [צ"ל מנעל], ח) [לקמן קכד.].

הגהות הב"ח

(א) רש"י ד"ה המעמיד וכו' והערסה הוא עץ הארוך שהוא קנה שקורין: (ב) ד"ה טהורה וכו' והרי הוא כטבעת: (ג) ד"ה סנדל וכו' מסמרות לחזק כצ"ל ותיבת למעלה נמחק:

גליון הש"ס

מתני' ולא בשריון. עי' לקמן סד ע"ב ברש"י ד"ה כל שאסרו:

תורה אור השלם

א) וַיִּקַּח מֹשֶׁה וְאֶלְעָזָר הַכֹּהֵן אֶת הַזָּהָב מֵאִתָּם כֹּל כְּלִי מַעֲשֶׂה: [במדבר לא, נא]

ליקוטי רש"י

בסנדל המסומר. סנדל של עץ מלופה עור ומסמרות קבועין בו שגזרו חכמים עליו שלא לנעלו בשבת וביום טוב משום מעשה שהיה שנהרגו הרוגים בשבת על ידיו במסכת שבת (ס.) [ביצה יד:]. **ולא בקמיע.** כתב לרפואת חולי. **מומחה.** שריפא כבר שלש פעמים [לעיל נג.]. **ולא בשריון ולא בקסדא ולא במגפיים.** שאסרו חכמים משום מראית העין שלא יחשדוהו באיסור [לקמן סד:].

חשק שלמה על רבינו חננאל

א) עי' ברשב"א שתמה ע"ד רבינו בזה:

עין משפט נר מצוה

כז א מיי' פי"ט מהל' שבת הלכה ה סמג לאוין סה טוש"ע א"ח סי' שג סעיף ט:

כח ב מיי' פי"ט מהל' שבת הלכה ג:

כט ג מיי' שם הלכה טו סמג שם טוש"ע א"ח סי' שא סעיף ו:

רבינו חננאל

ריסוקא. פי' חגור של עור אי אית ביה מפרחייתא שרי ותכשיט הוא ואי לא אסור פי' אם יש לו מפרחייתא חתיכות יוצאות ועודפות ממנו לימינו ולשמאלו תכשיט הוא ואי לא אינו מלאכת תכשיט ואסור לצאת בו בשבת כי אינו כלי. קטלא תכשיט בצואר. כגון ענק והיא בלשון ערבי מכנקא. נזמים יש נזמי האף ונזמים שבאזנים: **ולא** בטבעת שאין עליה חותם הא יש עליה חותם משאוי ואם תצא בו חייבת חטאת. אלמא לאו תכשיט הוא איני והתניא תכשיטי נשים עיר של זהב קטלאות נזמים וטבעת אחת טבעת שיש עליה חותם ואחת טבעת שאין עליה חותם ונזמי האף [טמאים] ומשני ר' זירא בטבעת של אלמוג וחותמה של מתכת ומתניתין [כרבנן] בכלים פרק י"ג דאמרי טהורה. [וכיון] לענין טומאה לאו כלי הוא לענין שבת נמי לאו כלי הוא. ומשוי הוא. הא ברייתא ר' נחמיה היא דמשוי ליה לענין [טומאה] מנא לענין שבת נמי תכשיט הוא דתנינן טבעת של מתכת וחותמה של אלמוג [טמאה היא של אלמוג] וחותמה של מתכת טהורה. ור' נחמיה מטמא: סימלוניו פי' רצועות שהן בעול דתנינן בתורת כהנים מיד בא ושיבר העול וקיצץ סימלונין כדכתיב ה' צדיק קצץ עבות רשעים. קולב. יש מי שאומרים ממיני תכשיט הוא להשמיע קול כדורך בגת ומחזקו במסמרים: **שליבות** ושלשלאות פשוטות הן. רבא אמר הא מתניתא לצדדין קתני אין עליה חותם תכשיט דאשה יש עליה חותם תכשיט דאיש והדין כך הוא. שיהא האיש מותר לצאת בטבעת שיש עליה חותם והאשה בטבעת שאין עליה חותם. מפני שתכשיט הוא להן וכל תכשיט שרי אלא משום גזירה א) דרבא כדבעינן למימר לקמן (סב.) דאמר פעמים שהאשה נותנת לבעלה טבעת שאין עליה חותם להוליכה אצל האומן ומניחה באצבעו עד שמגיע אל האומן. ופעמים שהאיש נותן לאשתו טבעת שיש עליה חותם להניחה בקופסא ומניחתה באצבעתה עד שמגעת לקופסא. לפיכך אסרו אחד האיש ואחד האשה לצאת בין בטבעת שיש עליה חותם בין בטבעת שאין עליה חותם. רב נחמן בר יצחק אמר טומאה אשבת קרמית כו'. ולא במחט שאינה נקובה אוקימנא כדתניא כמין טס של זהב יש לה על ראשה. בחול חולקת בה שערה בשבת מנחת על פדחתה. ונוי הוא לה: **לא** יצא בסנדל מסומר כו'. מ"ט שלפי השמד כו' פשוטה היא.

משנה (גמרא):

א) (ג) משלחין א כלים בי"ט בין תפורין בין שאינן תפורין) ב אבל לא סנדל המסומר ולא מנעל שאינו תפור (ג בי"ט) בשבת מ"ט דאיכא כינופיא בי"ט נמי איכא כינופיא תענית צבור איכא כינופיא ליתסר מעשה כי הוה בכינופיא דאיסורא הכא כינופיא דהתירא הוה ואפילו לר' ד) חנינא בן עקיבא ה) דאמר לא אסרו אלא בירדן ובספינה וכמעשה שהיה הני מילי ירדן דשאני משאר נהרות אבל י"ט ושבת כי הדדי נינהו ו) דתנן אין בין י"ט לשבת אלא אוכל נפש בלבד א"ר יהודה אמר שמואל ג לא שנו אלא לחזק אבל לנוי מותר וכמה לנוי ר' יוחנן אמר חמש בזה וחמש בזה ור' חנינא אמר שבע בזה ושבע בזה א"ל ר' יוחנן לרב שמן בר אבא אסברא לך לדידי שתים מכאן ושתים מכאן ואחת בתרסיותיו לר' חנינא ג' מכאן וג' מכאן ואחת בתרסיותיו מיתיבי סנדל הנוטה עושה לו שבע דברי רבי נתן ורבי מתיר בי"ג בשלמא לרבי חנינא הוא דאמר כרבי נתן אלא רבי יוחנן דאמר כמאן הוא דאמר כר' נהוראי דתניא ר' נהוראי אומר ה' מותר ושבע אסור א"ל איפה לרבה בר בר חנה אתון תלמידי רבי יוחנן עבידו כר' יוחנן אנן נעביד כרבי חנינא בעא מיניה רב הונא מרב אשי חמש מהו א"ל אפילו ז' מותר ט' מאי א"ל אפילו ח' אסור בעא מיניה ההוא רצענא מרבי אמי תפרו מבפנים מהו א"ל מותר ולא ידענא מ"ט אמר (א) רב אשי ולא ידע מר מ"ט כיון דתפרו מבפנים הוי ליה מנעל בסנדל גזרו ביה רבנן במנעל לא גזרו ביה רבנן בעא מיניה ר' אבא בר זבדא מר' אבא בר אבינא עשאו כמין ז) כלבוס מהו א"ל מותר איתמר נמי אמר רבי יוסי בר' חנינא עשאו כמין כלבוס מותר א"ר ששת חיפהו כולו במסמרות כדי שלא תהא קרקע אוכלתו מותר תניא כוותיה דרב ששת ח) לא יצא האיש בסנדל המסומר ולא יטייל מבית לבית אפילו ממטה למטה אבל מטלטלין אותו לכסות בו את הכלי ולסמוך בו כרעי המטה ור' אלעזר בר' שמעון אוסר נשרו רוב ממסמרותיו ונשתייר בו ד' או ה' מותר ורבי מתיר עד שבע ט) חיפהו בעור מלמטה וקבע לו מסמרות מלמעלה מותר עשאו (ב) כמין כלבוס או כמין טס או כמין יתד או שחיפהו כולו במסמרות כדי שלא תהא קרקע אוכלתו מותר הא גופה קשיא אמרת נשרו רוב מסמרותיו אע"ג דנשתיירו ביה טובא והדר תני ארבע או חמש אין טפי לא א"ר ששת לא קשיא כאן שנגממו כאן שנעקרו: ארבע או חמש מותר: השתא חמש שרי ארבע מיבעיא א"ר חסדא ארבע מסנדל קטן וחמש מסנדל גדול: ורבי מתיר עד שבע: והתניא רבי מתיר עד שלש עשרה נוטה שאני השתא דאתית להכי לרבי יוחנן נמי לא קשיא נוטה שאני אמר רב מתנה ואמרי לה אמר רב אחדבוי בר מתנה אמר רב מתנה אין הלכה כר' אלעזר בר' שמעון פשיטא י) יחיד ורבים הלכה כרבים מהו דתימא מסתברא טעמא דרבי אלעזר ברבי שמעון בהא קמ"ל אמר רבי חייא אי לאו דקרו לי בבלאי שרי איסורי שרינא ביה טובא וכמה בפומבדיתא אמרין עשרין וארבע בסורא אמרין עשרין ותרתין אמר רב נחמן בר יצחק וסימניך עד דאתא מפומבדיתא לסורא חסר תרתי: ולא ביחיד בזמן שאין ברגלו מכה: הא

תוספות:

אין בין יו"ט לשבת כו'. ואע"פ דבפ' משילין (ביצה דף לז. ושם) ולקמן בפ' כל הכלים (דף קכד. ושם) מוקמינן לה כב"ש דאי כב"ה הא אמרי מתוך שהותרה הבערה לצורך הותרה נמי שלא לצורך מ"מ דמי טפי יו"ט לשבת הואיל ולא שריא שאר דברים אלא מטעם שהותרה לצורך אוכל נפש:

השתא חמש שרינן כו'. בפרק קמא דסוכה (ד' ג: ושם) גבי רבי יהודה מכשיר עד ארבעים וחמשים אמה לא פריך השתא חמשים כו' וכן בריש אע"פ (כתובות דף נז. ושם) גבי אבל חכמים אומרים משהה אדם עם אשתו אפילו שתים ושלש שנים בלא כתובה ונראה לר"י דכל היכא דפשיטא ליה דבעי למימר אפי' טובא לא פריך אבל הכא ליכא לפרושי ד' וה' אפילו טובא דא"כ התרתה סנדל המסומר וכן בפרק בנות כותים (נדה דף לז: ושם) פריך [גבי] וכמה היא קישויה ר' מאיר אומר אפילו מ' וג' יום דליכא למימר אפילו טובא דאין סברא שיחשב דם קישוי מיום תחילת עיבורה ומשמע ליה בכל הני דשיעורא בתרא דוקא ולהכי פריך דלימא שיעורא בתרא ולא לימא שיעורא קמא ולקמן בפרק מפנין ד' וה' קופות (דף קכו:) פריך נמי השתא חמש שרי ד' כו' משמע ליה דטפי לא שרינן משום טורח שבת ומשני רב חסדא ד' מאוצר קטן חמש מאוצר גדול ושמואל משני ד' וה' אפילו טובא כדאמרי אינשי דסבר אפילו טובא מצי לפנות ובלבד שלא יגמור את האוצר פי' קרקעית האוצר משום אשוויי גומות וכדאמרן התם וא"ת דבפרק אע"פ (כתובות דף ס. ושם) אמרינן תינוק יונק והולך אפילו ד' וה' שנים ולא פריך אף על גב דהוי דוקא מדפריך התם מחבילתו על כתפו ומשני אידי ואידי חד שיעורא וי"ל הא בכחוש הא בבריא והא דאמרינן בפרק הזרוע (חולין דף קלג:) כהן טבח שתים וג' שבתות פטור מן המתנות מכאן ואילך חייב במתנות אומר ר"י דנקט שתים לרבי דאית ליה בהבא על יבמתו (יבמות דף סד:) דבתרי זימני הויא חזקה וג' לרשב"ג מ):

רש"י:

משלחין כלים ביו"ט בין תפורין בין שאינן תפורין אבל לא סנדל המסומר. אלמא לאו בר מנעלי' ביו"ט הוא דהא קתני התם כל שנאותין בו ביו"ט משלחין אותו: **איכא כינופיא.** שאין עושין מלאכה ונקבצין לבתי כנסיות ולבתי מדרשות כי ההיא מעשה דהוה כינופיא: דאיסורא. בעשיית מלאכה: **ואפילו לרבי חנינא בן עקיבא.** בפרק חומר בקדש גבי נושא מי חטאת ואפר חטאת בירדן ובספינה שנמצא כזית מן המת תחוב בקרקעית' של ספינה ° ונטמאו וקאמרי רבנן דגזרו שלא יעביר אדם מי חטאת בספינה ולא על הגשר ולא ישוט על פני המים אחד ירדן ואחד שאר נהרות ופליג ר' חנינא ואמר לא אסרו אלא בירדן ובספינה ולא גשר ושאר נהרות דגזירה שגזרו מחמת מאורע אין להם לגזור אלא מעין המאורע: **דשאני משאר נהרות.** ברוחב או בעומק: **אלא לחזק.** שמסמרותיו נעשו לחזק העקב שקורין שול"א עם הפנתא שקורין אינפייל"א אבל לנוי מותר דלא גזרו אלא מעין המאורע והנהו לחזק היו כשהם מסמרים דסנדל: **שתים מכאן.** לצד חילון אחד בראשו לצד האצבעות ואחד לצד עקיבו ושתים מכאן לצד פנימי לעבר בין הרגלים: **תרסיותיו.** רצועותיו: **סנדל הנוטה.** שתחתון שלו אינו שוה שעב מצד זה ודק מצד זה וכשדורס נוטה לצד הדק וצריך להגביהו שיהא שוה לצד שכנגדו: **איפה.** שם חכם ובנו של ר' רחבה דפומבדיתא הוה כ): **תפרו מבפנים.** שנתן מנעל של עור לפנים מן הסנדל. תפרו פורדרי"ן בלע"ז: **מותר.** שמעתי מרבי יוחנן וטעמא לא ידענא: **מותר.** לקבוע בו מסמרים מבחוץ: **עשאו.** למסמר כמין כלבוס בלע"ז טינפיילו"ן שני ראשין חדין וכפופין ונועץ שני ראשים בעץ כדאמרי' בסוטה (יט:) כלבוס של ברזל מטילין לה לתוך פיה: **מותר.** הואיל ונשתנה משאר מסמרים דלא גזרו אלא מעין המאורע: **חיפהו.** מלמטה: **אבל מטלטלין אותו.** דתורת כלי עליו: **אוסר.** דילמא אתי לנועלו: **נשרו רוב מסמרותיו כו'.** לקמן מפרש לה: **מותר.** הואיל ונשתנה מכמו שהיה דמעין המאורע גזרו: **עשאו.** לראש מסמר רחב כמין טס או שעשאו חד כמין יתד: **אע"ג דאישתאר טובא.** ובלבד שיהיו מעוט: **שנגממו.** מלמעלה ורשומו ניכר בתוך העץ אפילו טובא דהא מינכר שאינו כברייתו: **שנעקרו.** לגמרי שאין ניכר שהיה בו יותר ד' או ה' [אין] טפי לא לר"ה ולשון חבירו איפכא: **נוטה שאני.** שכולן צריכין לו להשוותו ואין אחד מהן לחזק: **השתא דאתית להכי.** לחלק בין נוטה לשאין נוטה: **לרבי יוחנן נמי.** דקפרכת לעיל מינה ואמרי דאמר כמאן איכא נמי לתרוצי לעולם כרבי נתן ונוטה שאני דהתם מתיר עד שבע אבל אין נוטה ה' ותו לא: **מסתברא טעמא.** דאסור לטלטל שמא ינעלנו: **בבלאי שרי איסורי.** דר' חייא מבבל הוה כדאמרינן בסוכה ל) עלו ר' חייא ובניו ויסדוה: **עד דאתא רבי חייא.** כשעלה מבבל לארץ ישראל ובא דרך סוריא מפומבדיתא: **חסר תרתי.** נפלו שתים ממסמרותיו בדרך: **לסורא חסר.** (תרתי) דומה אבל דומה: הא

עין משפט נר מצוה

ל א טוש"ע א"ח סי' שכו סעיף ג:

לא ב ג מיי' פ' יט מהל' שבת הלכה ג:

רבינו חננאל

ואסיקנא בסנדל מסומר **אחד** שבת ואחד יו"ט **אסור** דיו"ט ושבת כי **הדדי** ניהו: **הא** דר' **חנינא** בן עקיבא דאמר לא **אסרו** אלא בירדן **ובספינה.** וכמעשה שהיה **מפורש** ביבמות פרק **האשה** שהלכה היא **ובעלה** למדינת הים. **מעשה** באחד שהיה **מעביר** מי חטאת ואפר **חטאת** בירדן ובספינה **תמצאת** כזית מת תחוב **בקרקעיתה** של ספינה. **באותה** שעה אמרו לא **ישא אדם** מי חטאת ואפר **חטאת** ויעבירם בירדן **ובספינה** [וצריך לעיין] **התם** כדי שיתברר לו **השמועה** היטב: קי"ל **סנדל המסומר** לחזק אסור **לנוי** מותר כרב יהודה **אמר** שמואל דהא דייקי **אשמעתיה** לאוקומה **דאמרינן** וכמה לנוי דשרי **ר' יוחנן** אמר ב' מכאן וב' **מכאן** וא' בתרסיותיו ר' **חנינא** אמר ג' מיכן ג' **מכאן** וא' בתרסיותיו וכר' **חנינא** קיי"ל דר' יוחנן **לגבי** ר' חנינא תלמיד **הוא.** והא דאמר ליה איפה **לרבה** בר בר חנה אתון **תלמידי** דר' יוחנן (אתון) **עבידו** כר' יוחנן לאו **משום** דהלכה כר' יוחנן **אלא** משום דבאתריה דר' **יוחנן** ביותר מחמש נהגו **בו** איסור. ודברים **המותרים** ואחרים נהגו **בהן** איסור אי אתה רשאי **להתירן** בפניהם. א) ור' **אמי** נמי קם ליה כר' **חנינא** דשבע מותר והא **דקתני** ר' מתיר עד י"ג **בנוטה** הוא. כגון שניטל **עקיבו** ולדברי הכל. ור' **חייא** מתיר בה הרבה. **בסורא** אמרו כ"ב **בפומבדיתא** אמרי כ"ד. **תפרו** לסנדל מבפנים שרי **משום** דהוי ליה מנעל **ואסנדל** גזרו רבנן אמנעל **לא** גזרו. כמין כלבוס **מותר.** אמר רב ששת **חיפהו** כולו במסמרים כדי **שלא** יהא קרקע אוכל **ממנו** מותר תניא כוותיה **דרב ששת** לא יצא האיש **בסנדל** מסומר ולא יטייל **בו** מבית לבית כו': **ולא** ביחיד בזמן שאין ברגלו **מכה.** ירושלמי אמר ר' **אבא** מפני חשד שלא **יאמרו** איש פלוני נפסק **סנדלו** ותלאו בבית שחיו:

חשק שלמה על רבינו חננאל

א) מדברי רבינו נראה שהיה גורס בעי מיניה רב הונא מרב אמי וכו':

גליון הש"ס

רש"י ד"ה ואפי' לר"ח בן עקביא וכו' ונטמאו. עי' זבחים לג ע"א תוס' ד"ה מי חטאת:

מסורת הש"ס

א) ביצה יד:, ב) רש"ל מ"ז, ג) [במשנה ליתא], ד) בכ"י חנניא בן עקביא, ה) [תוספתא פרה פ"ח] יבמות קטז: חגיגה כג., ו) לקמן קכד. קלז: מגילה ז: ביצה כח. לז: [תוספ' דמגילה פ"א], ז) סה

ח) [תוספתא פ"ה ותוספתא יומא פ"ד], ט) [שם ע"ש], י) [ברכות דף ט. וש"נ], כ) [סנהדרין יז:], ל) [דף כ.], מ) [וע"ע תוס' עירובין ג. ד"ה עד ותוס' יומא כג. ד"ה שתים ותוס' סוכה ב: ד"ה עד ותוס' כתובות נז. ד"ה שתים ודף ס. ד"ה רבי יהושע ותוס' ב"מ ע"ט: ד"ה השתא ותוס' נדה לו: ד"ה ארבעים.

הגהות הב"ח

(א) גמ' אמר ליה רב אשי ולא: (ב) שם מלמעלה מותר עשאו כמין טס כצ"ל ותיבות כמין כלבוס או נמחק:

רב נסים גאון

הנושא את האשה בכתובות (קג): **ואפי' לר'** חנניא בר עקיבא דאמר לא אסרו אלא בירדן וספינה וכמעשה שהיה. זה המעשה **עיקרו** במעשה חגיגה בפ' חומר בקודש (דף כג) **וביבמות** בפרק האשה [שהלכה] היא ובעלה למדינת הים שלום בינה לבינה (קטז) מאי מעשה שהיה **דאמר** רב יהודה אמר רב מעשה באדם אחד שהיה מעביר מי חטאת ואפר **חטאת** בירדן ובספינה **ונמצא** כזית מת תחוב בקרקעית' של ספינה באותה שעה אמרו לא ישא אדם מי חטאת ואפר חטאת ויעבירם בירדן ובספינה: **ולא** ביחיד **בזמן** שאין ברגלו מכה גרסי. דבני מערבא אמר ר' **אבא**

ליקוטי רש"י

משלחין כלים. בגדים. **ולא מנעל שאינו תפור.** דלא חזי למידי [ביצה יד:]. **ואפילו לר' חנינא בן עקיבא.** דאמר כל מקום שגזרו חכמים על דבר על מעשה שהיה לא גזרו אלא כדוגמת המעשה וכאותו דבר [חגיגה כג.]. **אין בין יו"ט לשבת.** להיות מותר לכתחלה ביום טוב מה שאסור בשבת אבל לענין עונשין יש הרבה שזה בסקילה וכרת וזה בלאו גרידא [מגילה ז:]. **כלבום.** שני שניים יש לו [סוטה יט:]. כמין חצי עגול [לעיל נט:]. **הלכה כרבים.** דאמרי רבים להטות כתיב (שמות כג) [ב"ק קטז.].

(מְשַׁלְּחִין כֵּלִים בְּיוֹם טוֹב – WE MAY SEND GARMENTS as gifts ON YOM TOV,[1] בֵּין תְּפוּרִין בֵּין שֶׁאֵינָן תְּפוּרִין – WHETHER the garments are SEWN OR NOT SEWN;[2]) אֲבָל לֹא סַנְדָּל הַמְּסוּמָּר – BUT we may NOT send A HOBNAILED SANDAL, וְלֹא מִנְעָל שֶׁאֵינוֹ תָּפוּר בְּיוֹם טוֹב – AND we may NOT send AN UNSEWN SHOE as gifts **on Yom Tov.**[3] This Mishnah is proof that a hobnailed sandal may *not* be worn on Yom Tov![4] – ? –

The Gemara answers:

בְּשַׁבָּת מַאי טַעְמָא – **What is the reason** that the Sages forbade the wearing of hobnailed sandals **on the Sabbath?** דְּאִיכָּא כִּינּוּפְיָא – **Because there is a gathering** of people at that time.[5] בְּיוֹם טוֹב נַמִּי אִיכָּא כִּינּוּפְיָא – **On Yom Tov, there is also a gathering** of people; thus, the Sages extended the decree to include Yom Tov as well.

The Gemara persists:

תַּעֲנִית צִבּוּר אִיכָּא כִּינּוּפְיָא – But **on a public fast** day **there is** also **a gathering** of people;[6] לִיתְּסַר – **let it** therefore **be prohibited** to wear hobnailed sandals on fast days as well. – ? –

The Gemara explains why fast days were not included in the decree:

מַעֲשֶׂה כִּי הֲוָה בְּכִינּוּפְיָא דְאִיסּוּרָא – **The incident occurred on** the Sabbath, a day when there is **a gathering due to** a **prohibition** against performing labor; הָכָא – **here** in the case of a fast day, however, כִּינּוּפְיָא דְהֶתֵּירָא הֲוָה – **the gathering is** one **of** people that are **permitted** to do work.[7] Since the "gathering" on fast days is not similar to the "gathering" of the Sabbath and Yom Tov, the decree was not extended to include fast days.[8]

The Gemara notes that the inclusion of Yom Tov in the decree is defensible even according to those who hold that Rabbinic decrees are applied to similar cases very narrowly:

וַאֲפִילּוּ לְרַבִּי חֲנִינָא בֶּן עֲקִיבָא – **And even according to R' Chanina the son of Akiva,** דְּאָמַר לֹא אָסְרוּ אֶלָּא בַּיַּרְדֵּן וּבִסְפִינָה – **who said** that **[the Sages] did not prohibit** the transporting of *mei chatas* over water **except for** crossing over **the Jordan, and** only when traveling **in a boat**[9] – וּכְמַעֲשֶׂה שֶׁהָיָה – **and** this is because, in his opinion, the Sages only issued their decree to forbid transport **similar to the** transport that was used in the unfortunate **incident that transpired**[10] – still, in our case he would concur that Yom Tov should be included in the decree. הָנֵי מִילֵּי יַרְדֵּן דְּשָׁאנֵי מִשְּׁאָר נְהָרוֹת – For **this** limitation **is** defensible **in the case of the Jordan, as it is** clearly **different from other rivers;**[11] אֲבָל יוֹם טוֹב וְשַׁבָּת כִּי הֲדָדֵי נִינְהוּ – **but Yom Tov and the Sabbath are alike,** דִּתְנַן – **as we have learned in a Mishnah:**[12] אֵין בֵּין יוֹם טוֹב לְשַׁבָּת אֶלָּא אוֹכֶל נֶפֶשׁ בִּלְבַד – THERE IS NO DIFFERENCE BETWEEN THE SABBATH AND YOM TOV, EXCEPT with regard to FOOD preparation.[13] Thus, there is no rationale for excluding Yom Tov from the decree against wearing hobnailed sandals.

The Gemara discusses the specifics of the decree prohibiting the wearing of hobnailed sandals:

אָמַר רַב יְהוּדָה אָמַר שְׁמוּאֵל – **Rav Yehudah said in the name of Shmuel:** לֹא שָׁנוּ אֶלָּא לְחַזֵּק – **We did not learn** that such sandals are prohibited **except** where the nails are there **to strengthen** the sandal;[14] אֲבָל לְנוֹי מוּתָּר – **but** if they were only

NOTES

1. [The general rule is that one may send presents to another person on Yom Tov only if those presents are usable (see note 3 below); if they cannot be used, the sender's effort is viewed as having been expended needlessly on the holy day (see *Beitzah* ibid. and *Meiri* there).] See *Orach Chaim* 516:1,3 and *Mishnah Berurah* §4 and §12.

2. Sewn garments may be sent on Yom Tov, as they are suitable for wearing immediately; even unsewn garments may be sent, for the recipient can use them to cover himself, or to sit on (*Beitzah* ibid.). [This section of the Mishnah is not relevant to the Gemara's discussion here, and is cited only incidentally; *Maharshal* deletes it from the text.]

3. A hobnailed sandal, as the Gemara will explain, may not be worn on Yom Tov. [Although the Sages permitted the sending of items that would be usable only on *weekdays* (see *Mishnah Berurah* 516:12, who explains why), they forbade the sending of a hobnailed sandal entirely – see *Tosafos* to 60a ד״ה לא, and *Ritva MHK* ed. and *Chasam Sofer* here.]

An unsewn shoe is not usable at all (*Rashi* to *Beitzah* ibid.); thus, it may not be sent, as the sender's effort is thereby needlessly expended on Yom Tov (see note 1).

4. Seemingly, then, the Sages *did* include Yom Tov in the decree forbidding the wearing of hobnailed sandals. But if the Sages' decree was meant to apply only in circumstances similar to those in which the incident occurred, why did they extend the decree to Yom Tov?

5. *Melachah* is forbidden on the Sabbath, and people would customarily gather in the synagogues and study halls on the Sabbath day. These gatherings were the impetus for the Sages' decree forbidding the wearing of these sandals on the Sabbath, for the incident that occurred involved a group of people who were gathered on the Sabbath [as explained above, 60a] (*Rashi*; see also below, note 7).

6. On public fast days the people would gather in the synagogue to [repent and] and recite special prayers (see *Orach Chaim* 575:2, 576:16).

7. [There is no prohibition against performing labor on a public fast day.] See *R' Akiva Eiger* to the Mishnah (§82) and next note.

8. *Chidushei HaRan* explains that on the Sabbath and on Yom Tov, the people are enjoined to refrain from labor and instead celebrate the holy day; the Sages were concerned that the wearing of hobnailed sandals would call to mind the tragedy that had occurred under similar circumstances, and dampen the joyous mood of the day. On a public fast day, however, where no such commandment to celebrate the day exists, the Sages did not issue their decree. [For this reason, even during those fast days on which the Sages did prohibit the performance of labor (see *Taanis* 12b), they did not prohibit the wearing of hobnailed sandals.]

9. The Gemara in *Chagigah* (23a) relates that the Sages prohibited the transport of *mei chatas* (see Glossary) or ashes of the *parah adumah* across a body of water. They promulgated this decree because of an incident that once occurred, where *mei chatas* was transported across the Jordan River in a boat, and it was later discovered that an olive-sized piece of a corpse had lodged in the flooring of the boat, and rendered the precious *mei chatas* and ashes useless (see *Tosafos* to *Chagigah* ibid. ד״ה מת and to *Zevachim* 93a ד״ה מי). The Gemara there cites a dispute as to the extent of this decree. The Rabbis maintain that the decree applies to any body of water, and to any mode of transportation (e.g. the *mei chatas* may not be thrown over a bridge [see *Maharam*] or carried across a river by a swimmer). R' Chanina disagrees, and maintains that the Sages only prohibited transporting of these items over *the Jordan* River *by boat* (*Rashi*; see next note).

10. In the incident that occurred, the *mei chatas* was being transported over the Jordan River on a boat; R' Chanina holds that the Sages only issued their decree in those same circumstances (*Rashi*).

11. One can clearly differentiate between the Jordan River and other rivers, as it is unique in its width or in its depth (*Rashi*).

12. *Megillah* 7b.

13. I.e. whatever types of labor are forbidden on the Sabbath are forbidden on Yom Tov as well, with the exception of certain types of labor that are required for the preparation of food. Such labor is generally permitted on Yom Tov but forbidden on the Sabbath (see *Rashi* to *Beitzah* 23b ד״ה אין צדין, *Tosafos* to *Beitzah* 3a ד״ה גזירה, and *Rambam, Hil. Yom Tov* 1:5-8). [Although, according to Beis Hillel, this permit is extended on Yom Tov to permit those types of labor even when they are not being performed for food preparation (see *Beitzah* 12a; indeed, the Gemara below [124a] suggests that the Mishnah cited in our Gemara reflects Beis Shammai's view), the Sabbath and Yom Tov are alike in that all *other types* of labor are prohibited (see *Tosafos* and *Ritva MHK* ed.).]

14. I.e. to strengthen the bonding of the wooden sole of the sandal to its leather upper portion (*Rashi*). [The sandal's upper portion was attached to the sole with stitching; the nails served to strengthen that attachment.]

עין משפט
נר מצוה

ל א טוש"ע א"ח סי' תקטו סעיף ג:
לא ב ג מיי' פ' יט מהל' שבת הלכה ג:

(א) (ג) משלחין א כלים בי"ט בין תפורין בין שאינן תפורין) ב אבל לא סנדל המסומר ולא מנעל שאינו תפור (ג בי"ט) בשבת מ"ט דאיכא כינופיא בי"ט נמי איכא כינופיא תענית צבור איכא כינופיא ליתסר מעשה כי הוה בכינופיא דאיסורא הכא כינופיא דהתירא הוה ואפילו לר' ד) חנינא בן עקיבא ה) דאמר לא אסרו אלא בירדן ובספינה וכמעשה שהיה הני מילי ירדן דשאני משאר נהרות אבל י"ט ושבת כי הדדי נינהו ו) דתנן אין בין י"ט לשבת אלא אוכל נפש בלבד א"ר יהודה אמר שמואל ג לא שנו אלא לחזק אבל לנוי מותר וכמה לנוי ר' יוחנן אמר חמש בזה וחמש בזה ור' חנינא אמר שבע בזה ושבע בזה א"ל ר' יוחנן לרב שמן בר אבא אסברא לך לדידי שתים מכאן ושתים מכאן ואחת בתרסיותיו לר' חנינא ג' מכאן וג' מכאן ואחת בתרסיותיו מיתיבי סנדל הנוטה עושה לו שבע דברי רבי נתן ורבי מתיר בי"ג בשלמא לרבי חנינא הוא דאמר כרבי נתן אלא רבי יוחנן דאמר כמאן הוא דאמר כר' נהוראי דתניא ר' נהוראי אומר ה' מותר ושבע אסור א"ל איפה לרבה בר בר חנה אתון תלמידי רבי יוחנן עבידו כר' יוחנן אנן נעביד כרבי חנינא בעא מיניה רב הונא מרב אשי חמש מהו א"ל אפילו ז' מותר ט' מאי א"ל אפילו ח' אסור בעא מיניה ההוא רצענא מרבי אמי תפרו מבפנים מהו א"ל מותר ולא ידענא מ"ט אמר (א) רב אשי ולא ידע מר מ"ט כיון דתפרו מבפנים הוי ליה מנעל בסנדל גזרו ביה רבנן במנעל לא גזרו ביה רבנן בעא מיניה ר' אבא בר זבדא מר' אבא בר אבינא עשאו כמין ז) כלבוס מהו א"ל מותר איתמר נמי אמר רבי יוסי בר' חנינא עשאו כמין כלבוס מותר א"ר ששת חיפהו כולו במסמרות כדי שלא תהא קרקע אוכלתו מותר תניא כוותיה דרב ששת ח) לא יצא האיש בסנדל המסומר ולא יטייל מבית לבית אפילו ממטה למטה אבל מטלטלין אותו לכסות בו את הכלי ולסמוך בו כרעי המטה ור' אלעזר בר' שמעון אוסר נשרו רוב ממסמרותיו ונשתייר בו ד' או ה' מותר ורבי מתיר עד שבע ט) חיפהו בעור מלמטה וקבע לו מסמרות מלמעלה מותר עשאו (ב) כמין כלבוס או כמין טס או כמין יתד או שחיפהו כולו במסמרות כדי שלא תהא קרקע אוכלתו מותר הא גופה קשיא אמרת נשרו רוב מסמרותיו אע"ג דנשתיירו ביה טובא והדר תני ארבע או חמש אין טפי לא א"ר ששת לא קשיא כאן שנגממו כאן שנעקרו: ארבע או חמש מותר: השתא חמש שרי ארבע מיבעיא א"ר חסדא ארבע מסנדל קטן וחמש מסנדל גדול: ורבי מתיר עד שבע: והתניא רבי מתיר עד שלש עשרה נוטה שאני השתא דאתית להכי לרבי יוחנן נמי לא קשיא נוטה שאני אמר רב מתנה ואמרי לה אמר רב אחדבוי בר מתנה אמר רב מתנה אין הלכה כר' אלעזר בר' שמעון פשיטא י) יחיד ורבים הלכה כרבים מהו דתימא מסתברא טעמא דרבי אלעזר ברבי שמעון בהא קמ"ל אמר רבי חייא אי לאו דקרו לי בבלאי שרי איסורי שרינא ביה טובא וכמה בפומבדיתא אמרין עשרין וארבע בסורא אמרין עשרין ותרתין אמר רב נחמן בר יצחק וסימניך עד דאתא מפומבדיתא לסורא חסר תרתי: ולא ביחיד בזמן שאין ברגלו מכה:
הא

משלחין כלים ביו"ט בין תפורין בין שאינן תפורין אבל לא סנדל המסומר. אלמא לאו בר מנעלי' ביו"ט הוא דהא קתני התם כל שנאותין בו ביו"ט משלחין אותו: איכא כינופיא. שאין עושין מלאכה ונקבצין לבתי כנסיות ולבתי מדרשות כי ההיא מעשה דהוה כינופיא דאיסורא. בעשיית מלאכה: ואפילו לרבי חנינא בן עקיבא. בפרק חומר בקדש גבי נושא מי חטאת ואפר חטאת בירדן ובספינה שנמצא כזית מן המת תחוב בקרקעית' של ספינה ° ונטמאו וקאמרי רבנן דגזרו שלא יעביר אדם מי חטאת בספינה ולא על הגשר ולא ישיטם על פני המים אחד ירדן ואחד שאר נהרות ופליג ר' חנינא ואמר לא אסרו אלא בירדן ובספינה ולא גשר ושאר נהרות דגזירה שגזרו מחמת מאורע אין להם לגזור אלא מעין המאורע: דשאני משאר נהרות. ברוחב או בעומק: אלא לחזק. שמסמרותיו נעשו לחזק העקב שקורין שול"א עם הפנתא שקורין אינפיי"לא אבל לנוי מותר דלא גזרו אלא מעין המאורע והנהו לחזק היו כשתם מסמרים דסנדל: שתים מכאן. לצד חילון אחד בראשו לצד האצבעות ואחד לצד עקיבו ושתים מכאן לצד פנימי לעבר בין הרגלים: תרסיותיו. רצועותיו: סנדל הנוטה. שתחתון שלו אינו שוה שעב מצד זה ודק מצד זה וכשדורס נוטה לצד הדק וצריך להגביהו שיהא שוה לצד שכנגדו: איפה. שם חכם ובנו של ר' רחבה דפומבדיתא הוה (כ): תפרו מבפנים. שנתן מנעל של עור לפנים מן הסנדל. תפרו פורדרי"ן בלע"ז: מותר. שמעתי מרבי יוחנן וטעמא לא ידענא: מותר. לקבוע בו מסמרים מבחוץ: עשאו. למסמר כמין כלבוס בלע"ז טינפיילו"ן שני ראשין חדין וכפופין ונועץ שני ראשים בעץ כדאמרי' בסוטה (יט:) כלבוס של ברזל מטילין לה לתוך פיה: מותר. הואיל ונשתנה משאר מסמרים דלא גזרו אלא מעין המאורע: חיפהו. מלמטה: אבל מטלטלין אותו. דתורת כלי עליו: אוסר. דילמא אתי לנועלו: נשרו רוב מסמרותיו כו'. לקמן מפרש לה: מותר. הואיל ונשתנה מכמו שהיה דמעין המאורע גזרו: עשאו. לראש מסמר רחב כמין טס או שעשאו חד כמין יתד: אע"ג דאישתאר טובא. ובלבד שיהיו מעוט: שנגממו. מלמעלה ורשומו ניכר בתוך העץ אפילו טובא דהא מינכר שאינו כברייתו: שנעקרו. לגמרי שאין ניכר שהיה בו יותר ד' או ה' [אין] טפי לא לר"ה ולשון חבירו איפכא: נוטה שאני. שכולן צריכין לו להשוותו ואין אחד מהן לחזק: השתא דאתית להכי. לחלק בין נוטה לשאין נוטה: לרבי יוחנן נמי. דקפרכת לעיל מינה ואמרי דאמר כמאן איכא נמי לתרוצי לעולם כרבי נתן ונוטה שאני דהתם מתיר עד שבע אבל אין נוטה ה' ותו לא: מסתברא טעמא. דאסור לטלטל שמא ינעלנו: בבלאי שרי איסורי. דר' חייא מבבל הוה כדאמרינן בסוכה (ל) עלו ר' חייא ובניו ויסדוה: עד דאתא רבי חייא. כשעלה מבבל לארץ ישראל ובא דרך סוריא מפומבדיתא: חסר תרתי. נפלו שתים ממסמרותיו בדרך: לסורא חסר. (תרתי) דומה אלא דומה:
הא

אין בין יו"ט לשבת כו'. ואע"פ דבפ' משילין (ביצה דף לז. ושם) ולקמן בפ' כל הכלים (דף קכד. ושם) מוקמינן לה כב"ש דאי כב"ה הא אמרי מתוך שהותרה הבערה לצורך הותרה נמי שלא לצורך מ"מ דמי טפי יו"ט לשבת הואיל ולא שריא שאר דברים אלא מטעם שהותרה לצורך אוכל נפש:

השתא חמש שרינן כו'. בפרק קמא דסוכה (ד' ג: ושם) גבי רבי יהודה מכשיר עד ארבעים וחמשים אמה לא פריך השתא חמשים כו' וכן בריש אע"פ (כתובות דף נז. ושם) גבי אבל חכמים אומרים משהה אדם עם אשתו אפילו שתים ושלש שנים בלא כתובה ונראה לר"י דכל היכא דפשיטא ליה דבעי למימר אפי' טובא לא פריך אבל הכא ליכא לפרושי ד' וה' אפילו טובא דא"כ התרתה סנדל המסומר וכן בפרק בנות כותים (נדה דף לז: ושם) פריך [גבי] וכמה היא קישויה ר' מאיר אומר אפילו מ' וכ' יום דליכא למימר אפילו טובא דאין סברא שיחשב דם קישוי מיום תחילת עיבורה ומשמע ליה בכל הני דשיעורא בתרא דוקא ולהכי פריך דלימא שיעורא בתרא ולא לימא שיעורא קמא ולקמן בפרק מפנין ד' וה' קופות (דף קכו:) פריך נמי השתא חמש שרי ד' כו' משמע ליה דטפי לא שרינן משום טורח שבת ומשני רב חסדא ד' מאוצר קטן חמש מאוצר גדול ושמואל משני ד' וה' אפילו טובא כדאמרי אינשי דסבר אפילו טובא מלי לפנות ובלבד שלא יגמור את האוצר פי' קרקעית האוצר משום אשויי גומות וכדאמרן התם וא"ת דבפרק אע"פ (כתובות דף ס. ושם) אמרינן תינוק יונק והולך אפילו ד' וה' שנים ולא פריך אף על גב דהוי דוקא מדפריך התם מחבילתו על כתפו ומשני אידי ואידי חד שיעורא וי"ל הא בכחוש הא בבריא והא דאמרינן בפרק הזרוע (חולין דף קלב:) כהן טבח שתים וג' שבתות פטור מן המתנות מכאן ואילך חייב במתנות אומר ר"י דנקט שתים לרבי דאית ליה בהבא על יבמתו (יבמות דף סד:) דבתרי זימני הויא חזקה וג' לרשב"ג (מ):
דעבד

רבינו חננאל

ואסיקנא בסנדל מסומר אחד שבת ואחד יו"ט אסור דיו"ט ושבת כי הדדי נינהו: הא דר' חנינא בן עקיבא דאמר לא אסרו אלא בירדן ובספינה. וכמעשה שהיה מפורש ביבמות פרק האשה שהלכה היא ובעלה למדינת הים. מעשה באחד שהיה מעביר מי חטאת ואפר חטאת בירדן ובספינה ונמצאת כזית מת תחוב בקרקעיתה של ספינה. באותה שעה אמרו לא ישא אדם מי חטאת ואפר חטאת ויעבירם בירדן ובספינה [וצריך לעיין] התם כדי שיתברר לו השמועה היטב: קי"ל סנדל המסומר לחזק אסור לנוי מותר כרב יהודה אמר שמואל דהא דייקי אשמעתיה לאוקומה דאמרינן וכמה לנוי דשרי ר' יוחנן אמר ב' מכאן וב' מכאן וא' בתרסיותיו ר' חנינא אמר ג' מכן ג' מכאן וא' בתרסיותיו וכר' חנינא קיי"ל דר' יוחנן לגבי ר' חנינא תלמיד הוא. והא דאמר ליה איפה לרבה בר בר חנה אתון תלמידי דר' יוחנן (אתון) עבידו כר' יוחנן לאו משום דהלכה כר' יוחנן אלא משום דבאתריה דר' יוחנן ביותר מחמש נהגו בו איסור. ודברים המותרים ואחרים נהגו בהן איסור אי אתה רשאי להתירן בפניהם. א) ור' אמי נמי קם ליה כר' חנינא דשבע מותר והא דקתני ר' מתיר עד י"ג בנוטה הוא. כגון שניטל עקיבו ולדברי הכל. ור' חייא מתיר בה הרבה. בסורא אמרו כ"ב בפומבדיתא אמרי כ"ד. תפרו לסנדל מבפנים שרי משום דהוי ליה מנעל ואסנדל גזרו רבנן אמנעל לא גזרו. כמין כלבוס מותר. אמר רב ששת חיפהו כולו במסמרים כדי שלא יהא קרקע אוכל ממנו מותר תניא כוותיה דרב ששת לא יצא האיש בסנדל מסומר ולא יטייל בו מבית לבית כו': ולא ביחיד בזמן שאין ברגלו מכה. ירושלמי אמר ר' אבא מפני חשד שלא יאמרו איש פלוני נפסק סנדלו ותלאו בבית שחיו:

חשק שלמה
על רבינו חננאל

א) מדברי רבינו נראה שהיה גורס בעי מיניה רב הונא מרב אמי וכו':

גליון הש"ס

רש"י ד"ה ואפי' לר"ח בן עקביא וכו' ונטמאו. עי' זבחים לג ע"א תוס' ד"ה מי חטאת:

מסורת הש"ם

א) ביצה יד:, ב) רש"ל מ"ז, ג) [במשנה ליתא], ד) בכ"י חנניא בן עקביא, ה) [תוספתא פרה פ"ח] יבמות קטז: חגיגה כג., ו) לקמן קכד. קלז: מגילה ז: ביצה כח. לו: [תוספ' דמגילה פ"א], ז) כזה

ח) [תוספתא פ"ה ותוספתא יומא פ"ד], ט) [שם ע"ש], י) [ברכות דף ט. וש"נ], כ) [סנהדרין יז:], ל) [דף כ.], מ) [וע"ע תוס' עירובין ב. ד"ה עד ותוס' יומא כג. ד"ה שתים ותוס' סוכה ב: ד"ה עד ותוס' כתובות נז. ד"ה שתים ודף ס. ד"ה רבי יהושע ותוס' ב"מ ע"ט: ד"ה השתא ותוס' נדה לז: ד"ה ארבעים.

הגהות הב"ח

(א) גמ' אמר ליה רב אשי ולא: (ב) שם מלמעלה מותר עשאו כמין טס כצ"ל ותיבות כמין כלבוס או נמחק:

רב נסים גאון

הנושא את האשה בכתובות (קג): ואפי' לר' חנניא בר עקיבא דאמר לא אסרו אלא בירדן וספינה וכמעשה שהיה. זה המעשה עיקרו במעשה חגיגה בפ' חומר בקודש (דף כג) וביבמות בפרק האשה [שהלכה] היא ובעלה למדינת הים שלום בינה לבינה (קטז) מאי מעשה שהיה דאמר רב יהודה אמר רב מעשה באדם אחד שהיה מעביר מי חטאת ואפר חטאת בירדן ובספינה ונמצא כזית מת תחוב בקרקעית' של ספינה באותה שעה אמרו לא ישא אדם מי חטאת ואפר חטאת ויעבירם בירדן ובספינה: ולא ביחיד בזמן שאין ברגלו מכה גרסי. דבני מערבא אמר ר' אבא

ליקוטי רש"י

משלחין כלים. בגדים. ולא מנעל שאינו תפור. דלא חזי למידי [ביצה יד:]. ואפילו לר' חנינא בן עקיבא. דאמר כל מקום שגזרו חכמים על דבר על מעשה שהיה לא גזרו אלא כדוגמת המעשה וכאותו דבר [חגיגה כג.]. אין בין יו"ט לשבת. להיות מותר לכתחלה ביום טוב מה שאסור בשבת אבל לענין עונשין יש הרבה שזה בסקילה וכרת וזה בלאו גרידא [מגילה ז:]. כלבוס. שני שניים יש לו [סוטה יט:]. כמין חצי עגול [לעיל נט:]. הלכה כרבים. דאחרי רבים להטות כתיב (שמות כג) [ב"ק קטז.].

made **to beautify** the sandal, wearing it is **permitted.**[15] וְכַמָּה לְנוֹי – **And how many** nails are put into a sandal only **to beautify** it?[16] רַבִּי יוֹחָנָן אָמַר – **R' Yochanan said:** חָמֵשׁ בָּזֶה וְחָמֵשׁ בָּזֶה – **Five nails in this** sandal, **and five** more **in this** second sandal; וְרַבִּי חֲנִינָא אָמַר – **but R' Chanina said:** שֶׁבַע בָּזֶה וְשֶׁבַע בָּזֶה – **Seven** nails **in this** sandal, **and seven** more **in this** second sandal.[17]

The Gemara explains how the nails are placed:

אָמַר לֵיהּ רַבִּי יוֹחָנָן לְרַב שֶׁמֶן בַּר אַבָּא – **R' Yochanan said to Rav Shemen bar Abba:** אַסְבְּרָא לָךְ – **I will explain to you** where the nails are placed according to each view. לְדִידִי – **According to my view,** that five nails are permitted, שְׁתַּיִם מִכָּאן וּשְׁתַּיִם מִכָּאן – **two** are placed **on one side** of the sandal;[18] **two** are placed **on the other side** of the sandal,[19] וְאַחַת בְּתַרְסִיּוֹתָיו – **and one where the straps** are fastened.[20] לְרַבִּי חֲנִינָא – And **according to R' Chanina,** who holds that seven nails are permitted, שָׁלֹשׁ מִכָּאן וְשָׁלֹשׁ מִכָּאן – **three** are placed **on this side** of the sandal **and three** are placed **on the other side,** וְאַחַת בְּתַרְסִיּוֹתָיו – **and one where the straps** are fastened.

The Gemara questions R' Yochanan's view from a Baraisa:

מֵיתִיבֵי – **They challenged** R' Yochanan's view from the following Baraisa: סַנְדָּל הַנּוֹטֶה – If one has A SANDAL with an uneven sole THAT LEANS to one side,[21] עוֹשֶׂה לוֹ שֶׁבַע – HE MAY MAKE SEVEN nails for it; דִּבְרֵי רַבִּי נָתָן – these are THE WORDS OF R' NASSAN.[22] וְרַבִּי מַתִּיר בִּשְׁלֹשׁ עֶשְׂרֵה – AND REBBI PERMITS even a sandal WITH UP TO THIRTEEN nails. בִּשְׁלָמָא לְרַבִּי חֲנִינָא – Now, **this** Baraisa's ruling **is understandable according to R' Chanina,** הוּא דְּאָמַר כְּרַבִּי נָתָן – for **he stated** his ruling **in accord with** that of **R' Nassan.** אֶלָּא רַבִּי יוֹחָנָן דְּאָמַר כְּמַאן – **But according to whom does R' Yochanan state** his ruling? Both Tannaim in the Baraisa agree that more than five nails may be used in each sandal![23] – ? –

The Gemara answers that R' Yochanan too states his ruling in accord with a Tannaic view:

הוּא דְּאָמַר כְּרַבִּי נְהוֹרַאי – **[R' Yochanan] stated** his ruling **in accord with the view of R' Nehorai.** דְּתַנְיָא – **For it was taught in a Baraisa:** רַבִּי נְהוֹרַאי אוֹמֵר – R' NEHORAI SAYS: חָמֵשׁ מוּתָּר – A sandal that has FIVE nails is PERMITTED, וְשֶׁבַע אָסוּר – BUT a sandal with SEVEN nails in it is PROHIBITED.[24]

The Gemara discusses the halachah in this dispute:

אָמַר לֵיהּ אֵיפָה לְרַבָּה בַּר בַּר חָנָה – **Eifah**[25] **said to Rabbah bar bar Chanah:** אַתּוּן תַּלְמִידֵי רַבִּי יוֹחָנָן – **You [and your colleagues], who are disciples of R' Yochanan,** עֲבִידוּ כְּרַבִּי יוֹחָנָן – should **do as R' Yochanan** rules, and allow only five nails in each sandal. אֲנַן נַעֲבִיד כְּרַבִּי חֲנִינָא – But **we,** who are not disciples of R' Yochanan, **may do as R' Chanina** rules, and allow even seven nails in each sandal.

The Gemara cites another ruling issued concerning this issue:

בְּעָא מִינֵּיהּ רַב הוּנָא מֵרַב אַשִׁי – **Rav Huna inquired of Rav Ashi:** חָמֵשׁ מַהוּ – If there are **five** nails in each sandal, **what is [the law]?** May it be worn on the Sabbath or not? אָמַר לֵיהּ – **[Rav Ashi] replied to him:** אֲפִילּוּ שֶׁבַע מוּתָּר – **Even** a sandal with seven nails is **permitted.**[26] Rav Huna then asked: תֵּשַׁע מַאי – **What** is the law if a sandal has **nine** nails in it? אָמַר לֵיהּ – **[Rav Ashi] replied to him:** אֲפִילּוּ שְׁמוֹנָה אָסוּר – **Even** a sandal with **eight** nails **is prohibited.**[27]

The Gemara cites a related inquiry:

בְּעָא מִינֵּיהּ הַהוּא רַצְעָנָא מֵרַבִּי אַמִּי – **A certain shoemaker inquired of R' Ami:** תְּפָרוֹ מִבִּפְנִים מַהוּ – **If he sewed [a shoe] onto the inside** of a sandal,[28] **what is [the law]?** May it be worn or not? אָמַר לֵיהּ מוּתָּר – **[R' Ami] replied to him:** It is **permitted,** וְלָא יָדַעְנָא מַאי טַעְמָא – **but I do not know what the reason** is.[29] אָמַר רַב אַשִׁי – **Rav Ashi** thereupon **said** to R' Ami: וְלֹא יָדַע מַר מַאי טַעְמָא – **But does the master not know what the reason** for this law **is?** כֵּיוָן דִּתְפָרוֹ מִבִּפְנִים הָוֵי לֵיהּ מִנְעָל – **Since the shoe is sewn onto the inside, [the footwear] is now** deemed **a shoe** rather than a sandal; accordingly, wearing it is permitted, בְּסַנְדָּל גָּזְרוּ בֵּיהּ רַבָּנָן – for **the Rabbis only decreed** that such **a sandal** should not be worn, בְּמִנְעָל לֹא גָּזְרוּ בֵּיהּ רַבָּנָן – **but they did not decree** anything **about a shoe.**[30]

The Gemara cites another related inquiry:

בְּעָא מִינֵּיהּ רַבִּי אַבָּא בַּר זַבְדָּא מֵרַבִּי אַבָּא בַּר אֲבִינָא – **R' Abba bar**

NOTES

15. When the Sages issued their decree, they only prohibited sandals similar to those that were being worn during the time of the original incident; and the nails in the sandal that were being worn when the incident occurred were for the purpose of strengthening the sandal [this was the most common reason for putting nails in such sandals] (*Rashi;* see *Yevamos* 116b). Accordingly, a sandals with nails that are only for purposes of beautification was not included in the decree. [However, this is only so if the number of nails in the sandal clearly indicates that they were placed only to beautify the sandal (see next note).]

16. In order for the sandal to be permitted, it must be evident that the nails in the sandal are for purposes of beautification and not to strengthen the sandal. Accordingly, the Gemara asks: What is the maximum number of nails that one may put into a sandal without creating the impression that the nails are there to strengthen the sandal? (*Ritva MHK* ed.; see also *Sfas Emes*).

17. The Gemara will explain where the nails are placed according to each view.

18. I.e. on the outside of his foot; one nail is situated near the top of the sandal near the wearer's toes, while the other is near the heel (*Rashi*).

19. I.e. on the instep of the sandal; one nail near the toes and the other near the heel (*Rashi*).

20. At the point that the straps (that were used to tie the sandal to the wearer's foot) were fixed to the sole of the sandal, there was also a nail driven into the sole.

21. If the sole of a sandal is thicker on one side than the other, the sandal will "lean" to the thinner side when it is worn. Thus, nails must be pounded into the thinner side, so that that side will be lifted up and the sandal will be level (see *Rashi*).

22. [At this point, the Gemara assumes that according to R' Nassan, when a sandal with an uneven sole contains seven nails, those nails are clearly not intended to strengthen the sandal, and therefore the sandal is not included in the Sages' decree. See, however, the Gemara below, on this *amud*.]

23. When R' Chanina stated that a sandal with up to seven nails may be worn, he was expressing a view that is supported by the Tannaic ruling of R' Nassan. But R' Yochanan would seem to state a ruling that is not supported by *any* Tannaic view!

24. Thus, R' Yochanan's ruling too is supported by a Tannaic ruling. [R' Nehorai and R' Yochanan do not speak of a sandal that has *six* nails, for the sandal always has one nail to hold its straps, and thus the sandal usually has an odd number of nails (see *Ran MHK* ed.; see also *Sfas Emes*).]

25. Eifah was the son of R' Rechavah of Pumbedisa (*Rashi;* see *Sanhedrin* 17b).

26. [Rav Ashi concurs with the view expressed by R' Nassan and R' Chanina, as cited above.]

27. [As noted above, sandals do not usually have an even number of nails; Rav Ashi merely wished to underscore the point that the maximum amount of nails that is permitted is seven (*Ran MHK* ed.).]

28. I.e. he inserted a formed upper of soft leather into the sandal and sewed it into place (*Rashi*; cf. *Ritva MHK* ed.).

29. Rav Ami told the shoemaker that he had heard from R' Yochanan that such a sandal was permitted, but he did not know R' Yochanan's reason (*Rashi*).

30. As explained above, the Sages prohibited only the wearing of sandals similar to those that were worn during the incident that precipitated the decree. R' Yochanan ruled that in this case, the soft leather sewn onto the sandal transforms it into a shoe [sandals were usually made of stiff leather – see *Yevamos* 101a], and therefore the decree does not apply

א) (ג) משלחין א כלים בי"ט בין תפורין בין שאינן תפורין) ב אבל לא סנדל המסומר ולא מנעל שאינו תפור (ג בי"ט) בשבת מ"ט דאיכא כינופיא בי"ט נמי איכא כינופיא תענית צבור איכא כינופיא ליתסר מעשה כי הוה בכינופיא דאיסורא הכא כינופיא דהתירא הוה ואפילו לר' ד) חנינא בן עקיבא ה) דאמר לא אסרו אלא בירדן ובספינה וכמעשה שהיה הני מילי ירדן דשאני משאר נהרות אבל י"ט ושבת כי הדדי נינהו ו) דתנן אין בין י"ט לשבת אלא אוכל נפש בלבד א"ר יהודה אמר שמואל ג לא שנו אלא לחזק אבל לנוי מותר וכמה לנוי ר' יוחנן אמר חמש בזה וחמש בזה ור' חנינא אמר שבע בזה ושבע בזה א"ל ר' יוחנן לרב שמן בר אבא אסברא לך לדידי שתים מכאן ושתים מכאן ואחת בתרסיותיו לר' חנינא ג' מכאן וג' מכאן ואחת בתרסיותיו מיתיבי סנדל הנוטה עושה לו שבע דברי רבי נתן ורבי מתיר בי"ג בשלמא לרבי חנינא הוא דאמר כרבי נתן אלא רבי יוחנן דאמר כמאן הוא דאמר כר' נהוראי דתניא ר' נהוראי אומר ה' מותר ושבע אסור א"ל איפה לרבה בר בר חנה אתון תלמידי רבי יוחנן עבידו כר' יוחנן אנן נעביד כרבי חנינא בעא מיניה רב הונא מרב אשי חמש מהו א"ל אפילו ז' מותר ט' מאי א"ל אפילו ח' אסור בעא מיניה ההוא רצענא מרבי אמי תפרו מבפנים מהו א"ל מותר ולא ידענא מ"ט אמר (א) רב אשי ולא ידע מר מ"ט כיון דתפרו מבפנים הוי ליה מנעל בסנדל גזרו ביה רבנן במנעל לא גזרו ביה רבנן בעא מיניה ר' אבא בר זבדא מר' אבא בר אבינא עשאו כמין ז) כלבוס מהו א"ל מותר איתמר נמי אמר רבי יוסי בר' חנינא עשאו כמין כלבוס מותר א"ר ששת חיפהו כולו במסמרות כדי שלא תהא קרקע אוכלתו מותר תניא כוותיה דרב ששת ח) לא יצא האיש בסנדל המסומר ולא יטייל מבית לבית אפילו ממטה למטה אבל מטלטלין אותו לכסות בו את הכלי ולסמוך בו כרעי המטה ור' אלעזר בר' שמעון אוסר נשרו רוב ממסמרותיו ונשתייר בו ד' או ה' מותר ורבי מתיר עד שבע ט) חיפהו בעור מלמטה וקבע לו מסמרות מלמעלה מותר עשאו (ב) כמין כלבוס או כמין טס או כמין יתד או שחיפהו כולו במסמרות כדי שלא תהא קרקע אוכלתו מותר הא גופה קשיא אמרת נשרו רוב מסמרותיו אע"ג דנשתיירו ביה טובא והדר תני ארבע או חמש אין טפי לא א"ר ששת לא קשיא כאן שנגממו כאן שנעקרו: ארבע או חמש מותר: השתא חמש שרי ארבע מיבעיא א"ר חסדא ארבע מסנדל קטן וחמש מסנדל גדול: ורבי מתיר עד שבע: והתניא רבי מתיר עד שלש עשרה נוטה שאני השתא דאתית להכי לרבי יוחנן נמי לא קשיא נוטה שאני אמר רב מתנה ואמרי לה אמר רב אחדבוי בר מתנה אמר רב מתנה אין הלכה כר' אלעזר בר' שמעון פשיטא י) יחיד ורבים הלכה כרבים מהו דתימא מסתברא טעמא דרבי אלעזר ברבי שמעון בהא קמ"ל אמר רבי חייא אי לאו דקרו לי בבלאי שרי איסורי שרינא ביה טובא וכמה בפומבדיתא אמרין עשרין וארבע בסורא אמרין עשרין ותרתין אמר רב נחמן בר יצחק וסימניך עד דאתא מפומבדיתא לסורא חסר תרתי: ולא ביחיד בזמן שאין ברגלו מכה:

הא

משלחין כלים ביו"ט בין תפורין בין שאינן תפורין אבל לא סנדל המסומר. אלמא לאו בר מנעלי' ביו"ט הוא דהא קתני התם כל שנאותין בו ביו"ט משלחין אותו: איכא כינופיא. שאין עושין מלאכה ונקבצין לבתי כנסיות ולבתי מדרשות כי ההיא מעשה דהוה כינופיא: דאיסורא. בעשיית מלאכה: ואפילו לרבי חנינא בן עקיבא. בפרק חומר בקדש גבי נושא מי חטאת ואפר חטאת בירדן ובספינה שנמצא כזית מן המת תחוב בקרקעית' של ספינה ° ונטמאו וקאמרי רבנן דגזרו שלא יעביר אדם מי חטאת בספינה ולא על הגשר ולא ישיטם על פני המים אחד ירדן ואחד שאר נהרות ופליג ר' חנינא ואמר לא אסרו אלא בירדן ובספינה ולא גשר ושאר נהרות דגזירה שגזרו מחמת מאורע אין להם לגזור אלא מעין המאורע: דשאני משאר נהרות. ברוחב או בעומק: אלא לחזק. שמסמרותיו נעשו לחזק העקב שקורין שול"א עם הפנתא שקורין אינפיי"א אבל לנוי מותר דלא גזרו אלא מעין המאורע והנהו לחזק היו כשתם מסמרים דסנדל: שתים מכאן. לצד חילון אחד בראשו לצד האצבעות ואחד לצד עקיבו ושתים מכאן לצד פנימי לעבר בין הרגלים: תרסיותיו. רצועותיו: סנדל הנוטה. שתחתון שלו אינו שוה שעב מצד זה ודק מצד זה וכשדורס נוטה לצד הדק וצריך להגביהו שיהא שוה לצד שכנגדו: איפה. שם חכם ובנו של ר' רחבה דפומבדיתא הוה ס): תפרו מבפנים. שנתן מנעל של עור לפנים מן הסנדל. תפרו פורדרי"ץ בלע"ז: מותר. שמעתי מרבי יוחנן וטעמא לא ידענא: מותר. לקבוע בו מסמרים מבחוץ: עשאו. למסמר כמין כלבוס בלע"ז טינפיילו"ן שני ראשין חדין וכפופין ונועץ שני ראשים בעץ כדאמרי' בסוטה (יט:) כלבוס של ברזל מטילין לה לתוך פיה: מותר. הואיל ונשתנה משאר מסמרים דלא גזרו אלא מעין המאורע: חיפהו. מלמטה: אבל מטלטלין אותו. דתורת כלי עליו: אוסר. דילמא אתי לנועלו: נשרו רוב מסמרותיו כו'. לקמן מפרש לה: מותר. הואיל ונשתנה מכמו שהיה דמעין המאורע גזרו: עשאו. לראש מסמר רחב כמין טס או שעשאו חד כמין יתד: אע"ג דאישתאר טובא. ובלבד שיהיו מעוט: שנגממו. מלמעלה ורשומו ניכר בתוך העץ אפילו טובא דהא מינכר שאינו כברייתו: שנעקרו. לגמרי שאין ניכר שהיה בו יותר ד' או ה' [אין] טפי לא לרי"ה ולשון חבירו איפכא: נוטה שאני. שכולן צריכין לו להשוותו ואין אחד מהן לחזק: השתא דאתית להכי. לחלק בין נוטה לשאין נוטה: לרבי יוחנן נמי. דקפרכת לעיל מינה ואמרי דאמר כמאן איכא נמי לתרולי לעולם כרבי נתן ונוטה שאני דהתם מתיר עד שבע אבל אין נוטה ה' ותו לא: מסתברא טעמא. דאסור לטלטל שמא ינעלנו: בבלאי שרי איסורי. דר' חייא מבבל הוה כדאמרינן בסוכה ל) עלו ר' חייא ובניו ויסדוה: עד דאתא רבי חייא. כשעלה מבבל לארץ ישראל ובא דרך סוריא מפומבדיתא: חסר תרתי. נפלו שתים ממסמרותיו בדרך: לסורא חסר. (תרתי) דומה אבל דומה:

הא

אין בין יו"ט לשבת כו'. ואע"פ דבפ' משילין (ביצה דף לז. ושם) ולקמן בפ' כל הכלים (דף קכד. ושם) מוקמינן לה כב"ש דאי כב"ה הא אמרי מתוך שהותרה הבערה לצורך הותרה נמי שלא לצורך מ"מ דמי טפי יו"ט לשבת הואיל ולא שריא שאר דברים אלא מטעם שהותרה לצורך אוכל נפש:

השתא חמש שרינן כו'. בפרק קמא דסוכה (ד' ג: ושם) גבי רבי יהודה מכשיר עד ארבעים וחמשים אמה לא פריך השתא חמשים כו' וכן בריש אע"פ (כתובות דף נז. ושם) גבי אבל חכמים אומרים משהה אדם עם אשתו אפילו שתים ושלש שנים בלא כתובה ונראה לר"י דכל היכא דפשיטא ליה דבעי למימר אפי' טובא לא פריך אבל הכא ליכא לפרושי ד' וה' אפילו טובא דא"כ התרתה סנדל המסומר וכן בפרק בנות כותים (נדה דף לו: ושם) פריך [גבי] וכמה היא קישוייה ר' מאיר אומר אפילו מ' וכ' יום דליכא למימר אפילו טובא דאין סברא שיחשב דם קישוי מיום תחילת עיבורה ומשמע ליה בכל הני דשיעורא בתרא דוקא ולהכי פריך דלימא שיעורא בתרא ולא לימא שיעורא קמא ולקמן בפרק מפנין ד' וה' קופות (דף קכו:) פריך נמי השתא חמש שרי ד' כו' משמע ליה דטפי לא שרינן משום טורח שבת ומשני רב חסדא ד' מאוצר קטן חמש מאוצר גדול ושמואל משני ד' וה' אפילו טובא כדאמרי אינשי דסבר אפילו טובא מצי לפנות ובלבד שלא יגמור את האוצר פי' קרקעית האוצר משום אשוויי גומות וכדאמרן התם וא"ת דבפרק אע"פ (כתובות דף ס. ושם) אמרינן תינוק יונק והולך אפילו ד' וה' שנים ולא פריך אף על גב דהוי דוקא מדפריך התם מחבילתו על כתפו ומשני אידי ואידי חד שיעורא וי"ל הא בכחוש הא בבריא והא דאמרינן בפרק הזרוע (חולין דף קלג:) כהן טבח שתים וג' שבתות פטור מן המתנות מכאן ואילך חייב במתנות אומר ר"י דנקט שתים לרבי דאית ליה בהבא על יבמתו (יבמות דף סד:) דבתרי זימני הויא חזקה וג' לרשב"ג מ):

דעבד

ל א טוש"ע א"ח סי' תקטו סעיף ג:
לא ב ג מיי' פ' יט מהל' שבת הלכה ב:

רבינו חננאל

ואסיקנא בסנדל מסומר אחד שבת ואחד יו"ט אסור דיו"ט ושבת כי הדדי נינהו: הא דר' חנינא בן עקיבא דאמר לא אסרו אלא בירדן ובספינה. וכמעשה שהיה מפורש ביבמות פרק האשה שהלכה היא ובעלה למדינת הים. מעשה באחד שהיה מעביר מי חטאת ואפר חטאת בירדן ובספינה ונמצאת כזית מת תחוב בקרקעיתה של ספינה. באותה שעה אמרו לא ישא אדם מי חטאת ואפר חטאת ויעבירם בירדן ובספינה [וצריך לעיין] התם כדי שיתבאר לו השמועה היטב: קי"ל סנדל המסומר לחזק אסור לנוי מותר כרב יהודה אמר שמואל דהא דייקי אשמעתיה לאוקומה דאמרינן וכמה לנוי דשרי ר' יוחנן אמר ב' מכאן וב' מכאן וא' בתרסיותיו ר' חנינא אמר ג' מיכן ג' מכאן וא' בתרסיותיו וכר' חנינא קיי"ל דר' יוחנן לגבי ר' חנינא תלמיד הוא. והא דאמר ליה איפה לרבה בר בר חנה אתון תלמידי דר' יוחנן (אתון) עבידו כר' יוחנן לאו משום דהלכה כר' יוחנן אלא משום דבאתריה דר' יוחנן ביותר מחמש נהגו בו איסור. ודברים המותרים ואחרים נהגו בהן איסור אי אתה רשאי להתירן בפניהם. א) ור' אמי נמי קם ליה כר' חנינא דשבע מותר והא דקתני ר' מתיר עד י"ג בנוטה הוא. כגון שניטל עקיבו ולדברי הכל. ור' חייא מתיר בה הרבה. בסורא אמרו כ"ב בפומבדיתא אמרי כ"ד. תפרו לסנדל מבפנים שרי משום דהוי ליה מנעל ואסנדל גזרו רבנן אמנעל לא גזרו. כמין כלבוס מותר. אמר רב ששת חיפהו כולו במסמרים כדי שלא יהא קרקע אוכל ממנו מותר תניא כוותיה דרב ששת לא יצא האיש בסנדל מסומר ולא יטייל בו מבית לבית כו': ולא ביחיד בזמן שאין ברגלו מכה. ירושלמי אמר ר' אבא מפני חשד שלא יאמרו איש פלוני נפסק סנדלו ותלאו בבית שחיו:

חשק שלמה
על רבינו חננאל

א) מדברי רבינו נראה שהיה גורס בעי מיניה רב הונא מרב אמי וכו':

גליון הש"ס

רש"י ד"ה ואפי' לר"ח בן עקביא וכו' ונטמאו. עי' זבחים לג ע"א תוס' ד"ה מי חטאת:

מסורת הש"ס

א) ביצה יד:, ב) רש"ל מ"ז, ג) [במשנה ליתא], ד) בכ"י חנניא בן עקביא, ה) [תוספתא פרה פ"ח] יבמות קטז: חגיגה כג., ו) לקמן קכד. קלז: מגילה ז: ביצה כח. לו: [תוספ' דמגילה פ"א], ז) סוה

כ

ח) [תוספתא פ"ה ותוספתא יומא פ"ד], ט) [שם ע"ש], י) [ברכות דף ט. וש"נ], כ) [סנהדרין יז:], ל) [דף כ.], מ) [וע"ע תוס' עירובין ב. ד"ה עד ותוס' יומא כג. ד"ה שתים ותוס' סוכה ב: ד"ה עד ותוס' כתובות נז. ד"ה שתים ודף ס. ד"ה רבי יהושע ותוס' ב"מ ע"ט: ד"ה השתא ותוס' נדה לו: ד"ה ארבעים.

הגהות הב"ח

(א) גמ' אמר ליה רב אשי ולא: (ב) שם מלמעלה מותר עשאו כמין טס כצ"ל ותיבות כמין כלבוס או נמחק:

רב נסים גאון

הנושא את האשה בכתובות (קג): ואפי' לר' חנניא בר עקיבא דאמר לא אסרו אלא בירדן וספינה וכמעשה שהיה. זה המעשה עיקרו במעשה חגיגה בפ' חומר בקודש (דף כג) וביבמות בפרק האשה [שהלכה] היא ובעלה למדינת הים שלום בינה לבינה (קטז) מאי מעשה שהיה דאמר רב יהודה אמר רב מעשה באדם אחד שהיה מעביר מי חטאת ואפר חטאת בירדן ובספינה ונמצא כזית מת תחוב בקרקעית' של ספינה באותה שעה אמרו לא ישא אדם מי חטאת ואפר חטאת ויעבירם בירדן ובספינה: ולא ביחיד בזמן שאין ברגלו מכה גרסי. דבני מערבא אמר ר' אבא

ליקוטי רש"י

משלחין כלים. בגדים. ולא מנעל שאינו תפור. דלא חזי למידי [ביצה יד:]. ואפילו לר' חנינא בן עקיבא. דאמר כל מקום שגזרו חכמים על דבר על מעשה שהיה לא גזרו אלא כדוגמת המעשה וכאותו דבר [חגיגה כג.]. אין בין יו"ט לשבת. להיות מותר לכתחלה ביום טוב מה שאסור בשבת אבל לענין עונשין יש הרבה שזה בסקילה וכרת וזה בלאו גרידא [מגילה ז:]. כלבום. שני שניים יש לו [סוטה יט:]. כמין חצי עגול [לעיל נט:]. הלכה כרבים. דאמרי רבים להטות כתיב (שמות כג) [ב"ק קטז.].

Zavda inquired of R' Abba bar Avina: עֲשָׂאוֹ כְּמִין כְּלְבּוּס מַהוּ – **If he shaped [each nail] like tongs,**[31] **what is [the law]?** May the sandal be worn or not? אֲמַר לֵיהּ – **[R' Abba bar Avina] replied:** מוּתָּר – It is **permitted.**[32] אִיתְּמַר נַמִּי אָמַר רַבִּי יוֹסֵי בְּרַבִּי חֲנִינָא – **It was also stated** that **R' Yose the son of R' Chanina** explicitly **said:** עֲשָׂאוֹ כְּמִין כְּלְבּוּס מוּתָּר – **If he shaped [each nails] like tongs,** it is **permitted** to wear the sandal on the Sabbath.

The Gemara cited another instance where wearing a hobnailed sandal is permitted:

אָמַר רַב שֵׁשֶׁת – **Rav Sheishess said:** חִיפָּהוּ כּוּלּוֹ בְּמַסְמְרוֹת – **If he covered the entire** sole of the sandal **with nails** כְּדֵי שֶׁלֹּא תְּהֵא קַרְקַע אוֹכַלְתּוֹ – **so that the ground not consume it,**[33] מוּתָּר – wearing it is **permitted.**[34]

The Gemara cites a Baraisa to support this ruling:[35]

תַּנְיָא כְּוָותֵיהּ דְּרַב שֵׁשֶׁת – **A Baraisa was taught in accordance with the view of Rav Sheishess:** לֹא יֵצֵא הָאִישׁ בְּסַנְדָּל הַמְּסוּמָּר – A MAN MAY NOT GO OUT on the Sabbath WEARING A HOBNAILED SANDAL, וְלֹא יְטַיֵּיל מִבַּיִת לְבַיִת – AND HE MAY NOT WALK FROM one HOUSE TO another HOUSE wearing such a sandal,[36] אֲפִילּוּ מִמִּטָּה לְמִטָּה – and EVEN wearing it to walk FROM one BED TO another BED within the house is forbidden; אֲבָל מְטַלְטְלִין אוֹתוֹ לְכַסּוֹת בּוֹ אֶת הַכְּלִי – BUT WE MAY CARRY IT TO COVER A UTENSIL WITH IT, וְלִסְמוֹךְ בּוֹ כַּרְעֵי הַמִּטָּה – OR TO SUPPORT THE LEGS OF A BED WITH IT.[37] וְרַבִּי אֶלְעָזָר בְּרַבִּי שִׁמְעוֹן אוֹסֵר – BUT R' ELAZAR THE SON OF R' SHIMON FORBIDS THIS.[38] נָשְׁרוּ רוֹב מַסְמְרוֹתָיו – If A MAJORITY OF [THE SANDAL'S] NAILS HAVE FALLEN OUT, וְנִשְׁתַּיֵּיר בּוֹ אַרְבַּע אוֹ חָמֵשׁ – AND only FOUR OR FIVE nails ARE STILL embedded IN IT, מוּתָּר – IT IS PERMITTED.[39] וְרַבִּי מַתִּיר עַד שֶׁבַע – AND REBBI PERMITS the wearing of such a sandal even if it has UP TO SEVEN nails left in it.[40] חִיפָּהוּ בְּעוֹר מִלְּמַטָּה – If HE COVERED THE UNDERSIDE OF [THE SOLE] WITH LEATHER, וְקָבַע לוֹ מַסְמְרוֹת מִלְמַעְלָה – AND HE AFFIXED NAILS TO THE UPPER SECTION of the shoe, מוּתָּר – wearing IT IS PERMITTED.[41] עֲשָׂאוֹ כְּמִין כְּלְבּוּס – IF HE SHAPED [EACH NAIL] LIKE TONGS, אוֹ כְּמִין טַס – OR if the heads of the nails were shaped LIKE A BAR אוֹ כְּמִין יָתֵד – OR LIKE A STAKE,[42] אוֹ שֶׁחִיפָּהוּ כּוּלּוֹ בְּמַסְמְרוֹת – OR IF HE COVERED THE ENTIRE sole WITH NAILS כְּדֵי שֶׁלֹּא תְּהֵא קַרְקַע אוֹכַלְתּוֹ – SO THAT THE GROUND NOT CONSUME IT, מוּתָּר – wearing IT IS PERMITTED.[43] The final ruling of this Baraisa supports the ruling of Rav Sheishess cited above.

The Gemara notes a contradiction within the Baraisa:

הָא גּוּפָהּ קַשְׁיָא – But **this** Baraisa **itself is difficult!** אָמְרַתְּ נָשְׁרוּ רוֹב מַסְמְרוֹתָיו – **You said** in the Baraisa that a hobnailed sandal may be worn **if a majority of its nails have fallen out;** אַף עַל גַּב דְּנִשְׁתַּיְּירוּ בֵּיהּ טוּבָא – this implies that the sandal may be worn **even if many nails remain** in the sandal, as long as less than half of the nails remain. וַהֲדַר תָּנֵי – **And then the Baraisa teaches** אַרְבַּע אוֹ חָמֵשׁ אִין – that if **four or five** nails remain, then **yes** – it may be worn, טְפֵי לֹא – but if **more** than five nails remain, it may **not** be worn – even if most of the nails have fallen out![44]

The Gemara resolves the contradiction:

אָמַר רַב שֵׁשֶׁת – **Rav Sheishess said:** לֹא קַשְׁיָא – There is **no difficulty.** כָּאן שֶׁנִּגְמְמוּ – **Here,** when the Baraisa rules that even many nails are permitted as long as more than half have fallen out, it refers to a case **where [the nails] wore down** to the point that they are level with the sole;[45] כָּאן שֶׁנֶּעֶקְרוּ – while **here,** when the Baraisa limits the amount of permissible nails to four or five, it refers to a case **where [the nails] were** completely **extracted.**[46]

The Gemara now cites a section of the Baraisa just quoted:

אַרְבַּע אוֹ חָמֵשׁ מוּתָּר – If most of the nails have fallen out, and FOUR OR FIVE remain, wearing the sandal is PERMITTED.

The Gemara seeks to clarify this ruling:

הַשְׁתָּא חָמֵשׁ שְׁרֵי – But **now, if it is permitted** to wear a sandal that has **five** nails remaining, אַרְבַּע מִיבַּעְיָא – **need it be said** that a sandal with **four** remaining nails may be worn?![47]

NOTES

31. I.e. he took a nail with two sharp heads and bent it into a semicircular shape [similar to a curved staple]; he then drove both sharp heads of the nail into the sandal (see *Rashi*).

32. Since semicircular nails are different from the standard nails used in most sandals, sandals with these nails were not included in the Sages' decree (*Rashi*).

33. I.e. so that the wooden sole of the sandal would not rot due to exposure to the ground.

34. In this case too the nails in the sandal do not serve the same purpose (of strengthening the sandal) that the nails in the sandal forbidden by the Sages did; accordingly, such a sandal was not included in the Sages' decree.

35. [The support to Rav Sheishess is found in the final ruling of the Baraisa; however, the Gemara cites the Baraisa in its entirety.]

36. Even if he does not go out into the public domain (see *Tos. Yom Tov* to *Beitzah* 1:10).

37. [For although the Sages prohibited the wearing of the sandal even inside the house,] it is still classified as an article [of clothing] (*Rashi*). It may therefore be used as any article that is normally used for a purpose forbidden on the Sabbath (כְּלִי שֶׁמְּלַאכְתּוֹ לְאִיסוּר).]

38. R' Shimon ben Elazar is of the opinion that the Sages prohibited any use of the sandal, lest one come to wear it (*Rashi*).

39. For it is no longer similar to the sandal that the Sages prohibited. This ruling will be explained in the Gemara below.

40. [The Gemara below will discuss the apparent contradiction between this ruling of Rebbi and the ruling he issued in the case of the uneven sandal (where he permitted up to thirteen nails).]

41. Such a sandal differs significantly from the sandal worn when the incident occurred; thus, the Sages did not include it in their decree.

42. I.e. instead of the nails being shaped with the standard round flat heads, they had wide bar-shaped heads or sharp heads like those of stakes (*Rashi*).

43. See note 41.

44. Thus, the Baraisa contradicts itself, for it establishes two contradictory criteria for permitting such a sandal. This contradiction is illustrated in a case where the sandal originally had fifteen nails and eight of them fell out. On the one hand, the sandal should be permitted, for most of the nails have fallen out; on the other hand, it should be forbidden, because more than five nails remain! [See *Sfas Emes*, who discusses why the Gemara did not simply assume that *both* conditions must be met to permit the wearing of the sandal.]

45. When the nails are merely leveled, a remnant of each nail is still visible in the sole; thus, the sandal is permitted if most of the nails have fallen out (even if many nails remain), because it is still clear that this sandal originally contained many more nails and is not in its original state (*Rashi*; see next note).

46. When the nails are extracted, there is no visible indication that more nails were ever in the sandal; thus, only a number of nails that can initially be permitted is allowed (see *Sfas Emes*). Hence, the Baraisa only permits four or five nails in that case. [This explanation follows *Rashi's* first explanation; cf. *Rashi's* second explanation; see also *Ritva MHK* ed.]

[According to this understanding of the Baraisa, it is understood as follows: If a majority of the sandal's nails wore down, or if the nails were extracted and four or five remained, the sandal may be worn.]

47. The Baraisa should have stated that a sandal containing five nails may be worn, and we would know that a sandal with four nails is permitted!

[The Gemara does not always ask this question when two numbers are used in this manner (see, for example, *Kesubos* 60a); see *Tosafos* and *Ritva MHK* ed., who discuss the criteria for determining whether this is a valid challenge in each context.]

א) (ג) משלחין א כלים בי״ט בין תפורין בין שאינן תפורין) ב אבל לא סנדל המסומר ולא מנעל שאינו תפור (ג) בי״ט) בשבת מ״ט דאיכא כינופיא בי״ט נמי איכא כינופיא תענית צבור איכא כינופיא ליתסר מעשה כי הוה בכינופיא דאיסורא הכא כינופיא דהתירא הוה ואפילו לר׳ ד) חנינא בן עקיבא ה) דאמר לא אסרו אלא בירדן ובספינה וכמעשה שהיה הני מילי ירדן דשאני משאר נהרות אבל י״ט ושבת כי הדדי נינהו ו) דתנן אין בין י״ט לשבת אלא אוכל נפש בלבד א״ר יהודה אמר שמואל ג לא שנו אלא לחזק אבל לנוי מותר וכמה לנוי ר׳ יוחנן אמר חמש בזה וחמש בזה ור׳ חנינא אמר שבע בזה ושבע בזה א״ל ר׳ יוחנן לרב שמן בר אבא אסברא לך לדידי שתים מכאן ושתים מכאן ואחת בתרסיותיו לר׳ חנינא ג׳ מכאן וג׳ מכאן ואחת בתרסיותיו מיתיבי סנדל הנוטה עושה לו שבע דברי רבי נתן ורבי מתיר בי״ג בשלמא לרבי חנינא הוא דאמר כרבי נתן אלא רבי יוחנן דאמר כמאן הוא דאמר כר׳ נהוראי דתניא ר׳ נהוראי אומר ה׳ מותר ושבע אסור א״ל איפה לרבה בר בר חנה אתון תלמידי רבי יוחנן עבידו כר׳ יוחנן אנן נעביד כרבי חנינא בעא מיניה רב הונא מרב אשי חמש מהו א״ל אפילו ז׳ מותר ט׳ מאי א״ל אפילו ח׳ אסור בעא מיניה ההוא רצענא מרבי אמי תפרו מבפנים מהו א״ל מותר ולא ידענא מ״ט אמר (א) רב אשי ולא ידע מר מ״ט כיון דתפרו מבפנים הוי ליה מנעל בסנדל גזרו ביה רבנן במנעל לא גזרו ביה רבנן בעא מיניה ר׳ אבא בר זבדא מר׳ אבא בר אבינא עשאו כמין ז) כלבום מהו א״ל מותר איתמר נמי אמר רבי יוסי בר׳ חנינא עשאו כמין כלבום מותר א״ר ששת חיפהו כולו במסמרות כדי שלא תהא קרקע אוכלתו מותר תניא כוותיה דרב ששת ח) לא יצא האיש בסנדל המסומר ולא יטייל מבית לבית אפילו ממטה למטה אבל מטלטלין אותו לכסות בו את הכלי ולסמוך בו כרעי המטה ור׳ אלעזר בר׳ שמעון אוסר נשרו רוב ממסמרותיו ונשתייר בו ד׳ או ה׳ מותר ורבי מתיר עד שבע ט) חיפהו בעור מלמטה וקבע לו מסמרות מלמעלה מותר עשאו (ב) כמין כלבום או כמין טס או כמין יתד או שחיפהו כולו במסמרות כדי שלא תהא קרקע אוכלתו מותר הא גופה קשיא אמרת נשרו רוב מסמרותיו אע״ג דנשתיירו ביה טובא והדר תני ארבע או חמש אין טפי לא א״ר ששת לא קשיא כאן שנגממו כאן שנעקרו: ארבע או חמש מותר: השתא חמש שרי ארבע מיבעיא א״ר חסדא ארבע מסנדל קטן וחמש מסנדל גדול: ורבי מתיר עד שבע: והתניא רבי מתיר עד שלש עשרה נוטה שאני השתא דאתית להכי לרבי יוחנן נמי לא קשיא נוטה שאני אמר רב מתנה ואמרי לה אמר רב אחדבוי בר מתנה אמר רב מתנה אין הלכה כר׳ אלעזר בר׳ שמעון פשיטא י) יחיד ורבים הלכה כרבים מהו דתימא מסתברא טעמא דרבי אלעזר ברבי שמעון בהא קמ״ל אמר רבי חייא אי לאו דקרו לי בבלאי שרי איסורי שרינא ביה טובא וכמה בפומבדיתא אמרין עשרין וארבע בסורא אמרין עשרין ותרתין אמר רב נחמן בר יצחק וסימניך עד דאתא מפומבדיתא לסורא חסר תרתי: ולא ביחיד בזמן שאין ברגלו מכה:

הא

רש״י

משלחין כלים ביו״ט בין תפורין בין שאינן תפורין אבל לא סנדל המסומר. אלמא לאו בר מנעלי׳ ביו״ט הוא דהא קתני התם כל שנאותין בו ביו״ט משלחין אותו: איכא כינופיא. שאין עושין מלאכה ונקבצין לבתי כנסיות ולבתי מדרשות כי ההיא מעשה דהוה כינופיא דאיסורא. בעשיית מלאכה: ואפילו לרבי חנינא בן עקיבא. בפרק חומר בקדש גבי נושא מי חטאת ואפר חטאת בירדן ובספינה שנמצא כזית מן המת תחוב בקרקעית׳ של ספינה ° ונטמאו וקאמרי רבנן דגזרו שלא יעביר אדם מי חטאת בספינה ולא על הגשר ולא ישוט על פני המים אחד ירדן ואחד שאר נהרות ופליג ר׳ חנינא ואמר לא אסרו אלא בירדן ובספינה ולא גשר ושאר נהרות דגזירה שגזרו מחמת מאורע אין להם לגזור אלא מעין המאורע: דשאני משאר נהרות. ברוחב או בעומק: אלא לחזק. שמסמרותיו נעשו לחזק העקב שקורין שול״א עם הפנתא שקורין אינפיי״א אבל לנוי מותר דלא גזרו אלא מעין המאורע והנהו לחזק היו כשתם מסמרים דסנדל: שתים מכאן. לצד חילון אחד בראשו לצד האצבעות ואחד לצד עקיבו ושתים מכאן לצד פנימי לעבר בין הרגלים: תרסיותיו. רצועותיו: סנדל הנוטה. שתחתון שלו אינו שוה שעב מצד זה ודק מצד זה וכשדורס נוטה לצד הדק וצריך להגביהו שיהא שוה לצד שכנגדו: איפה. שם חכם ובנו של ר׳ רחבה דפומבדיתא הוה כ): תפרו מבפנים. שנתן מנעל של עור לפנים מן הסנדל. תפרו פורדרי״ן בלע״ז: מותר. שמעתי מרבי יוחנן וטעמא לא ידענא: מותר. לקבוע בו מסמרים מבחוץ: עשאו. למסמר כמין כלבום בלע״ז טינפיילו״ן שני ראשין חדין וכפופין ונועץ שני ראשים בעץ כדאמרי׳ בסוטה (יט:) כלבום של ברזל מטילין לה לתוך פיה: מותר. הואיל ונשתנה משאר מסמרים דלא גזרו אלא מעין המאורע: חיפהו. מלמטה: אבל מטלטלין אותו. דתורת כלי עליו: אוסר. דילמא אתי לנועלו: נשרו רוב מסמרותיו כו׳. לקמן מפרש לה: מותר. הואיל ונשתנה מכמו שהיה דמעין המאורע גזרו: עשאו. לראש מסמר רחב כמין טס או שעשאו חד כמין יתד: אע״ג דאישתאר טובא. ובלבד שיהיו מעוט: שנגממו. מלמעלה ורשומו ניכר בתוך העץ אפילו טובא דהא מינכר שאינו כברייתו: שנעקרו. לגמרי שאין ניכר שהיה בו יותר ד׳ או ה׳ [אין] טפי לא לוי״ה ולשון חבירו איפכא: נוטה שאני. שכולן צריכין לו להשוותו ואין אחד מהן לחזק: השתא דאתית להכי. לחלק בין נוטה לשאין נוטה: לרבי יוחנן נמי. דקפרכת לעיל מינה ואמרי דאמר כמאן איכא נמי לתרוצי לעולם כרבי נתן ונוטה שאני דהתם מתיר עד שבע אבל אין נוטה ה׳ ותו לא: מסתברא טעמא. דאסור לטלטל שמא ינעלנו: בבלאי שרי איסורי. דר׳ חייא מבבל הוה כדאמרינן בסוכה ל) עלו ר׳ חייא ובניו ויסדוה: עד דאתא רבי חייא. כשעלה מבבל לארץ ישראל ובא דרך סוריא מפומבדיתא: חסר תרתי. נפלו שתים ממסמרותיו בדרך: לסורא חסר. (תרתי) דומה אלא דומה:

הא

תוספות

אין בין יו״ט לשבת כו׳. ואע״פ דבפ׳ משילין (ביצה דף לז. ושם) ולקמן בפ׳ כל הכלים (דף קכד. ושם) מוקמינן לה כב״ש דאי כב״ה הא אמרי מתוך שהותרה הבערה לצורך הותרה נמי שלא לצורך מ״מ דמי טפי יו״ט לשבת הואיל ולא שריא שאר דברים אלא מטעם שהותרה לצורך אוכל נפש:

השתא חמש שרינן כו׳. בפרק קמא דסוכה (ד׳ ג: ושם) גבי רבי יהודה מכשיר עד ארבעים וחמשים אמה לא פריך השתא חמשים כו׳ וכן בריש אע״פ (כתובות דף נז. ושם) גבי אבל חכמים אומרים משהה אדם עם אשתו אפילו שתים ושלש שנים בלא כתובה ונראה לר״י דכל היכא דפשיטא ליה דבעי למימר אפי׳ טובא לא פריך אבל הכא ליכא לפרושי ד׳ וה׳ אפילו טובא דא״כ התרתה סנדל המסומר וכן בפרק בנות כותים (נדה דף לו: ושם) פריך [גבי] וכמה היא קישוייה ר׳ מאיר אומר אפילו מ׳ ונ׳ יום דליכא למימר אפילו טובא דאין סברא שיחשב דם קישוי מיום תחלת עיבורה ומשמע ליה בכל הני דשיעורא בתרא דוקא ולהכי פריך דלימא שיעורא בתרא ולא לימא שיעורא קמא ולקמן בפרק מפנין ד׳ וה׳ קופות (דף קכו:) פריך נמי השתא חמש שרי ד׳ כו׳ משמע ליה דטפי לא שרינן משום טורח שבת ומשני רב חסדא ד׳ מאוצר קטן חמש מאוצר גדול ושמואל משני ד׳ וה׳ אפילו טובא כדאמרי אינשי דסבר אפילו טובא מלי לפנות ובלבד שלא יגמור את האוצר פי׳ קרקעית האוצר משום אשווי גומות וכדאמרן התם וא״ת דבפרק אע״פ (כתובות דף ס. ושם) אמרינן תינוק יונק והולך אפילו ד׳ וה׳ שנים ולא פריך אף על גב דהוי דוקא מדפריך התם מחבילתו על כתפו ומשני אידי ואידי חד שיעורא וי״ל הא בכחוש הא בבריא והא דאמרינן בפרק הזרוע (חולין דף קלב:) כהן טבח שתים וג׳ שבתות פטור מן המתנות מכאן ואילך חייב במתנות אומר ר״י דנקט שתים לרבי דאית ליה בהבא על יבמתו (יבמות דף סד:) דבתרי זימני הויא חזקה וג׳ לרשב״ג מ):

דעבד

עין משפט נר מצוה

ל א טוש״ע א״ח סי׳ תקכו סעיף ג:
לא ב ג מיי׳ פ׳ יט מהל׳ שבת הלכה ג:

רבינו חננאל

ואסיקנא בסנדל מסומר אחד שבת ואחד יו״ט אסור דיו״ט ושבת כי הדדי נינהו: הא דר׳ חנינא בן עקיבא דאמר לא אסרו אלא בירדן ובספינה. וכמעשה שהיה מפורש ביבמות פרק האשה שהלכה היא ובעלה למדינת הים. מעשה באחד שהיה מעביר מי חטאת ואפר חטאת בירדן ובספינה ונמצאת כזית מת תחוב בקרקעיתה של ספינה. באותה שעה אמרו לא ישא אדם מי חטאת ואפר חטאת ויעבירם בירדן ובספינה [וצריך לעיין] התם כדי שיתברר לו השמועה היטב: קי״ל סנדל המסומר לחזק אסור לנוי מותר כרב יהודה אמר שמואל דהא דייקי אשמעתיה לאוקומה דאמרינן וכמה לנוי דשרי ר׳ יוחנן אמר ב׳ מכאן וב׳ מכאן וא׳ בתרסיותיו ר׳ חנינא אמר ג׳ מיכן ג׳ מכאן וא׳ בתרסיותיו וכר׳ חנינא קיי״ל דר׳ יוחנן לגבי ר׳ חנינא תלמיד הוא. והא דאמר ליה איפה לרבה בר בר חנה אתון תלמידי דר׳ יוחנן (אתון) עבידו כר׳ יוחנן לאו משום דהלכה כר׳ יוחנן אלא משום דבאתריה דר׳ יוחנן ביותר מחמש נהגו בו איסור. ודברים המותרים ואחרים נהגו בהן איסור אי אתה רשאי להתירן בפניהם. א) ור׳ אמי נמי קם ליה כר׳ חנינא דשבע מותר והא דקתני ר׳ מתיר עד י״ג בנוטה הוא. כגון שניטל עקיבו ולדברי הכל. ור׳ חייא מתיר בה הרבה. בסורא אמרו כ״ב בפומבדיתא אמרי כ״ד. תפרו לסנדל מבפנים שרי משום דהוי ליה מנעל ואסנדל גזרו רבנן אמנעל לא גזרו. כמין כלבוס מותר. אמר רב ששת חיפהו כולו במסמרים כדי שלא יהא קרקע אוכל ממנו מותר תניא כוותיה דרב ששת לא יצא האיש בסנדל מסומר ולא יטייל בו מבית לבית כו׳: ולא ביחיד בזמן שאין ברגלו מכה. ירושלמי אמר ר׳ אבא מפני חשד שלא יאמרו איש פלוני נפסק סנדלו ותלאו בבית שחיו:

חשק שלמה על רבינו חננאל

א) מדברי רבינו נראה שהיה גורס כאן בגמ׳ מתניה רב הונא מרב אמי וכו׳:

גליון הש״ס

רש״י ד״ה ואפי׳ לר״ח בן עקיבא וכו׳ ונטמאו. ע׳ זבחים כג ע״ב תוס׳ ד״ה מי חטאת:

מסורת הש״ס

א) ביצה יד:, ב) רש״ל מ״ז, ג) [במשנה ליתא], ד) בכ״י חנניא בן עקביא, ה) [תוספתא פרה פ״ח] יבמות קטז: חגיגה כג., ו) לקמן קכד. קלז: מגילה ז: ביצה כח. לו: [תוספ׳ דמגילה פ״א], ז) כה

ח) [תוספתא פ״ה ותוספתא יומא פ״ד], ט) [שם ע״ש], י) [ברכות דף ט. וש״נ], כ) [סנהדרין יז:], ל) [דף כ.], מ) [וע״ע תוס׳ עירובין ב. ד״ה עד ותוס׳ יומא כג. ד״ה שתים ותוס׳ סוכה ב: ד״ה עד ותוס׳ כתובות נז. ד״ה שתים ודף ס. ד״ה רבי יהושע ותוס׳ ב״מ ע״ט: ד״ה השתא ותוס׳ נדה לו: ד״ה ארבעים.

הגהות הב״ח

(א) גמ׳ אמר ליה רב אשי ולא: (ב) שם מלמעלה מותר עשאו כמין טס כצ״ל ותיבות כמין כלבום או נמחק:

רב נסים גאון

הנושא את האשה בכתובות (קג): ואפי׳ לר׳ חנניא בר עקיבא דאמר לא אסרו אלא בירדן וספינה וכמעשה שהיה. זה המעשה עיקרו במעשה חגיגה בפ׳ חומר בקודש (דף כג) וביבמות בפרק האשה [שהלכה] היא ובעלה למדינת הים שלום בינה לבינה (קטז) מאי מעשה שהיה דאמר רב יהודה אמר רב מעשה באדם אחד שהיה מעביר מי חטאת ואפר חטאת בירדן ובספינה ונמצא כזית מת תחוב בקרקעית׳ של ספינה באותה שעה אמרו לא ישא אדם מי חטאת ואפר חטאת ויעבירם בירדן ובספינה: ולא ביחיד בזמן שאין ברגלו מכה גרסי. דבני מערבא אמר ר׳ אבא

ליקוטי רש״י

משלחין כלים. בגדים. ולא מנעל שאינו תפור. דלא חזי למידי [ביצה יד:]. ואפילו לר׳ חנינא בן עקיבא. דאמר כל מקום שגזרו חכמים על דבר על מעשה שהיה לא גזרו אלא כדוגמת המעשה וכאותו דבר [חגיגה כג.]. אין בין יו״ט לשבת. להיות מותר לכתחלה ביום טוב מה שאסור בשבת אבל לענין עונשין יש הרבה שזה בסקילה ובכרת וזה בלאו גרידא [מגילה ז:]. כלבום. שני שניים יש לו [סוטה יט:]. כמין חלי עגול [לעיל נט:]. הלכה כרבים. דאחרי רבים להטות כתיב (שמות כג) [ב״ק קטז.].

The Gemara answers:

אָמַר רַב חִסְדָּא – **Rav Chisda said:** אַרְבַּע מִסַּנְדָּל קָטָן – This is what the Baraisa means: **Four** nails may remain **from** the nails of **a small sandal,** וְחָמֵשׁ מִסַּנְדָּל גָּדוֹל – **and five** may remain **from** the nails **of a large sandal.**[48]

The Gemara goes on to cite the next ruling from the Baraisa: וְרַבִּי מַתִּיר עַד שֶׁבַע – AND REBBI PERMITS the wearing of a sandal that has lost most of its nails even if it has UP TO SEVEN nails left in it.

The Gemara contrasts this ruling of Rebbi with another ruling of Rebbi that was cited above regarding an uneven sandal: וְהָתַנְיָא – **But we have been taught in the Baraisa** that was cited above:[49] רַבִּי מַתִּיר עַד שְׁלֹשׁ עֶשְׂרֵה – And REBBI PERMITS even a sandal WITH UP TO THIRTEEN nails!

The Gemara answers:

נוֹטֶה שָׁאנִי – **A sandal that** is uneven and **leans** to one side **is different,** for the extra nails are needed to even out the sole.[50]

The Gemara notes that this distinction can also be used to resolve a difficulty that the Gemara raised in its previous discussion:

הַשְׁתָּא דְּאָתֵית לְהָכִי – **Now that you have come to this conclusion** (that an uneven sandal may have more nails than an even sandal), לְרַבִּי יוֹחָנָן נַמִּי לָא קַשְׁיָא – the Baraisa, which states that both Tannaim permit at least seven nails, **does not pose a difficulty to R' Yochanan** (who holds that only five nails are permitted) **either;**[51] נוֹטֶה שָׁאנִי – for we can say that he, too, agrees that **a sandal that leans is different,** and he would therefore concur that seven nails are permitted in that case.

Above, the Baraisa cited a dispute as to whether a hobnailed sandal may be moved on the Sabbath to cover a utensil or support the legs of a bed. The Gemara discusses which view is accepted as halachah:

אָמַר רַב מַתְנָה – **Rav Masnah said** – וְאָמְרִי לָהּ אָמַר רַב אַחְדְּבוֹי בַּר מַתְנָה אָמַר רַב מַתְנָה – **and some say that Rav Achadvoi bar Masnah said in the name of Rav Masnah:** אֵין הֲלָכָה כְּרַבִּי אֶלְעָזָר בְּרַבִּי שִׁמְעוֹן – **The halachah does not follow** the view of **R' Elazar the son of R' Shimon;** rather, it follows the opinion of the Tanna Kamma, who allows the sandal to be moved for these purposes.

The Gemara asks:

פְּשִׁיטָא – But **this is obvious!** יָחִיד וְרַבִּים הֲלָכָה כְּרַבִּים – For we have a rule that when there is a dispute between **an individual and a majority,**[52] **the halachah follows** the view of **the majority!** Why was it necessary, then, to state that the halachah does not follow R' Elazar the son of R' Shimon?

The Gemara answers:

מַהוּ דְּתֵימָא – **You might have said** מִסְתַּבְּרָא טַעְמָא דְּרַבִּי אֶלְעָזָר בְּרַבִּי שִׁמְעוֹן בְּהָא – that **in this case the reasoning of R' Elazar the son of R' Shimon is sound,**[53] and therefore this law might be an exception to the general rule; קָמַשְׁמַע לָן – [Rav Masnah] **therefore informs us** that this is not the case.

The Gemara cites a more lenient view regarding the numbers of nails permitted in a hobnailed sandal:

אָמַר רַבִּי חִיָּיא – **R' Chiya said:** אִי לָאו דְּקָרוּ לִי בַּבְלָאִי שָׁרֵי אִיסוּרֵי – **If not for the fact that people would call me "the Babylonian that permits forbidden things,"**[54] שָׁרֵינָא בֵּיהּ טוּבָא – **I would permit** a hobnailed sandal that has **many** nails **in it.**[55]

The Gemara seeks to clarify R' Chiya's position:

וְכַמָּה – **And how many** would R' Chiya have permitted? בְּפוּמְבְּדִיתָא אָמְרִין עֶשְׂרִין וְאַרְבַּע – **In Pumbedisa, they said** that R' Chiya would have permitted **twenty-four** nails in each sandal; בְּסוּרָא אָמְרִין עֶשְׂרִין וְתַרְתֵּין – **in Sura, they said** he would have permitted up to **twenty-two** in each sandal.[56] אָמַר רַב נַחְמָן בַּר יִצְחָק – **Rav Nachman bar Yitzchak said:** וְסִימָנָיךְ – **And your mnemonic,** that will remind you which opinion was held by which academy, is the following sentence: עַד דַּאֲתָא מִפּוּמְבְּדִיתָא לְסוּרָא חֲסַר תַּרְתֵּי – **"Until he came from Pumbedisa to Sura, he lost two."**[57]

The Mishnah stated:

וְלֹא בְּיָחִיד בִּזְמַן שֶׁאֵין בְּרַגְלוֹ מַכָּה – AND he may NOT go out WITH A SINGLE sandal, WHEN THERE IS NO WOUND ON HIS FOOT.

NOTES

48. [*Hagahos R' Elazar Moshe Horowitz* explains that "a small sandal" refers to a sandal tight enough to be worn without straps; hence, it would have one nail less, for the fifth nail was used to fasten the straps, as explained above.]

49. [This Baraisa was cited earlier on this *amud*.]

50. These nails are clearly not intended to strengthen the sandal, and therefore the sandal is not similar to the sandal that the Sages prohibited (*Rashi*).

51. [Above, the Gemara answered this question by citing another Tannaic opinion (that of R' Nehorai) which accorded with that of R' Yochanan; the Gemara now suggests that R' Yochanan's opinion can be reconciled with the opinion of R' Nassan (*Rashi*). See *Rashash* and *Leshon HaZahav.*]

52. Literally: an individual and many.

53. For it is indeed likely that once a person is permitted to handle the sandal, he may come to wear it.

54. R' Chiya was born in Babylonia, and ascended to Eretz Yisrael (*Rashi*, from *Succah* 20a).

55. [R' Chiya was of the opinion that a true hobnailed sandal had a large number of nails in it, and even a sandal with many more than seven nails would be recognizable as a sandal *decorated* with nails, rather than a hobnailed sandal.] The Gemara below discusses exactly how many nails R' Chiya would allow.

56. I.e. there was a dispute between the two Babylonian Talmudic academies of Pumbedisa and Sura as to the extent of R' Chiya's opinion.

57. When R' Chiya traveled from Babylonia to Eretz Yisrael (see note 54), his route passed first through Pumbedisa and then through Sura. Now, it was common for the nails in these sandals to wear down or fall out due to the rigors of travel; thus, it would be likely that [had Rav Chiya been wearing such a sandal during his trip] the sandal would lose some nails during the trip from Pumbedisa to Sura. Rav Nachman used these facts as the basis for his mnemonic, which serves to remind one that the academy of Sura had R' Chiya permitting less nails than did the academy of Pumbedisa. Furthermore, the wording of the mnemonic itself prevents one from confusing the order of the towns (and saying "until he came from *Sura* to *Pumbedisa* he loses two") because the Hebrew word for *lost* (חסר) is placed next to the similar word Sura (*Rashi,* as understood by *Rashash;* cf. *Maharshal* and *Shabbos Shel Mi*).

The Gemara draws an inference from the Mishnah's ruling:

הָא יֵשׁ בְּרַגְלוֹ מַכָּה – **This** ruling[1] implies that **if there was a wound in his foot,** נָפִיק – **he may go out** wearing a single sandal.[2]

The Gemara seeks a clarification:

בְּהֵי מִינַּיְיהוּ נָפִיק – **On which of [his feet] may he** wear the single sandal and **go out?**

The Gemara offers the first of two interpretations:

אָמַר רַב הוּנָא – **Rav Huna said:** בְּאוֹתָהּ שֶׁיֵּשׁ בָּהּ מַכָּה – He may go out wearing the single sandal **on [the foot] that has the wound in it.**

The Gemara identifies the basic premise of this interpretation:

אַלְמָא – **We see** from Rav Huna's interpretation קָסָבַר סַנְדָּל לְשׁוּם צַעַר עֲבִיד – that **he is of the opinion that a sandal is worn**[3] **for the purpose of** protecting the foot from **pain;**[4] accordingly, even a single sandal may be worn to protect the wounded foot.[5]

The second interpretation:

וְחִיָּיא בַּר רַב אָמַר – **But Chiya bar Rav said:** בְּאוֹתָהּ שֶׁאֵין בָּהּ מַכָּה – He may go out wearing the single sandal **on [the foot] that does *not* have the wound in it.**

The Gemara explains Chiya bar Rav's reasoning:

אַלְמָא קָסָבַר לְשׁוּם תַּעֲנוּג עֲבִיד – **We see** that **[Chiya bar Rav] holds** that **[a sandal] is worn for the purpose of** providing **comfort,**[6] וְזוֹ שֶׁיֵּשׁ בָּהּ מַכָּה – **and this** foot **that has a wound in it** need not be wearing a sandal, מַכָּתָהּ מוֹכַחַת עָלֶיהָ – for **its wound attests to it.**[7]

The Gemara cites support for the first interpretation:

וְאַף רַבִּי יוֹחָנָן סָבַר לָהּ לְהָא דְּרַב הוּנָא – **And R' Yochanan also concurs with the opinion of Rav Huna,** as can be seen from the following incident: דְּאָמַר לֵיהּ רַבִּי יוֹחָנָן לְרַב שֶׁמֶן בַּר אַבָּא – **For R' Yochanan** once **said to Rav Shemen bar Abba:** הַב לִי מְסָנַאי – **"Give me my shoes."** יְהַב לֵיהּ דְּיָמִין – **[Rav Shemen] gave [R' Yochanan] his right shoe.**[8] אָמַר לֵיהּ – **[R' Yochanan]** thereupon **said to him:** עֲשִׂיתוֹ מַכָּה – **"You have made [my foot]** resemble one that has **a wound!"** Presumably, R' Yochanan meant that since he would be wearing just his right shoe,[9] it would appear as if he has a wound on that foot.[10] Obviously, then, R' Yochanan agrees with Rav Huna that a single shoe (or sandal) would be worn on the foot that has the wound.

The Gemara argues that this proof is not compelling:

וְדִילְמָא כְּחִיָּיא בַּר רַב סְבִירָא לֵיהּ – **But** this is not conclusive, for **perhaps [R' Yochanan] concurs with Chiya bar Rav,** who holds that a single shoe would be worn on the foot *without* the *wound.* וְהָכִי קָאָמַר – **And this is what [R' Yochanan] was saying:** עֲשִׂיתָ שֶׁל שְׂמֹאל מַכָּה – If I were to put on my right shoe first, **you have made my *left* foot** resemble one that has **a wound;** for I will be wearing only my right shoe, just as I would if my left foot had a wound.[11] Thus, R' Yochanan's comment does not prove that he concurs with Rav Huna.

In both versions of R' Yochanan's statement, he would not put on his left shoe once he had already put on his right shoe.[12] The Gemara notes that this is consistent with another ruling issued by R' Yochanan:

וְאַזְדָּא רַבִּי יוֹחָנָן לְטַעְמֵיהּ – **And R' Yochanan is consistent** in this **with his own reasoning** as expressed elsewhere, דְּאָמַר רַבִּי יוֹחָנָן – **for R' Yochanan said:** כִּתְפִילִּין כָּךְ מִנְעָלִין – **As** one dons **tefillin, so** should he put on his **shoes;** מַה תְּפִילִּין בִּשְׂמֹאל – i.e. **just as tefillin** are worn **on the left** hand,[13] אַף מִנְעָלִין בִּשְׂמֹאל

NOTES

1. I.e. the Mishnah's ruling that one may not go out on the Sabbath wearing just one sandal where there is no wound on his foot.

2. For the Mishnah limits the prohibition to the case where there is no wound on one's foot.

3. Literally: made.

4. That is, a sandal is worn for the purpose of protecting one's feet from the pain that would result from stepping upon projections or rocks in the road (*Rashi;* see next note).

5. Above (60a note 24), two possible explanations were offered as to why one may not go out with a single sandal on the Sabbath; either because people will suspect him of carrying the other sandal under his clothing, or because we are afraid that people will ridicule him and he will remove the single sandal and carry it. According to Rav Huna, who holds that the sandal is worn for the purpose of avoiding pain, neither of these concerns apply in the case of a sandal worn on a wounded foot, for the following reasons: He will not be suspected of carrying the other sandal, for people who see him limping will assume that he is a man who has calloused soles and usually goes barefoot; they will attribute the single sandal that he wears to the fact that the foot he wears the shoe on must be wounded. [If, however, he would be wearing a single sandal on the *unwounded* foot, and leaving his wounded foot unshod, he is demonstrating that he does not need to protect his feet, and the single shoe that he *is* wearing is [similar to] a burden (*Ritva MHK* ed.; cf. *Milchamos*).] Nor are we concerned that he will remove the single sandal when people [who do not realize that he is wounded] jeer at him, for he will not expose himself to additional pain by exposing the wounded foot to the projections in the road (*Rashi*).

6. According to Chiya bar Rav, sandals are not worn for protection from pain; rather, they are worn by more delicate individuals for the purpose of cushioning the feet (*Rashi;* see next note).

7. A person who wears a single sandal has identified himself as one who desires the level of comfort provided by sandals; he therefore may not wear only one sandal, for the absence of its mate will lead others to suspect him of carrying it (according to the first explanation), or cause them to jeer at him for this abnormal behavior (according to the second explanation). One who has a wound on his foot, however, may leave that foot unshod; for he will not be suspected or laughed at, as all will see the wound that prevents him from putting on the second sandal (*Rashi*). [If he only wears the sandal on the foot that has the wound, however, he has no excuse not to wear the second sandal, and he may be suspected of carrying it or jeered at for his behavior.]

[The Rishonim dispute the halachah in this matter. *Rif, Milchamos and Rambam* (*Hil. Shabbos* 19:15) rule in accordance with Chiya bar Rav, while *Baal HaMaor* and *Or Zarua* rule in accordance with Rav Huna. See *Chelkas Binyamin,* who discusses this dispute at length.]

8. Literally: [the shoe] of the right [foot].

9. As the Gemara will explain below, R' Yochanan held that one should put on his left shoe first. Thus, if he would put on his right shoe first, he would not put on his left shoe, and he would go out wearing a single sandal on his right foot (*Rashi;* see *Chidushei HaRan;* see also *Meromei Sadeh* and *Dibros Moshe* 53:18).

10. For one who has a wound on his foot goes out with a shoe *on that foot.* This is the basis of the Gemara's proof; for seemingly, R' Yochanan said that wearing a shoe on his right foot made him resemble a person with a wound on *his right foot*!

11. R' Yochanan's rebuke was not explicitly worded; thus, it is possible that he was comparing his [potential] appearance to a person with a wound on his *left* foot. If this was his intention, he concurs with Chiya bar Rav that one would wear a single sandal on the foot that is *not* wounded.

12. This can be derived from the fact that R' Yochanan compared his situation to one who has a wounded foot, as explained above (*Rashi;* see above, note 9).

13. This is derived by the Gemara in *Menachos* (37a) from the verse (*Exodus* 13:16) that states: ...וְהָיָה לְאוֹת עַל־יָדְכָה, *and it* (the tefillin) *shall be a sign upon your arm* . . . The unusual spelling of the word יָדְכָה, *your arm* (normally, it would be spelled יָדְךָ), is expounded as if it reads יַד כֵּהָה, which means *the weaker hand.* Thus expounded, the verse reads: "And [the tefillin] shall be a sign upon your weaker hand . . ." This teaches that the tefillin are to be placed on the person's left hand, which is his weaker hand when it comes to doing work (*Rashi*). [This is of course referring to a right-handed person; a left-handed person puts tefillin on his right hand, for that is his "left" (i.e. weaker) hand.]

הא יש ברגלו מכה נפיק בהי מינייהו נפיק אמר רב הונא באותה שיש בה מכה אלמא קסבר סנדל לשום צער עביד וחייא בר רב אמר [א]באותה שאין בה מכה אלמא קסבר לשום תענוג עביד וזו שיש בה מכה מכתה מוכחת עליה ואף רבי יוחנן סבר לה להא דרב הונא דאמר ליה ר' יוחנן לרב שמן בר אבא הב לי מסנאי יהב ליה דימין אמר ליה עשיתו מכה ודילמא כחייא בר רב ס"ל והכי קאמר עשית של שמאל מכה ואזדא רבי יוחנן לטעמיה דאמר ר' יוחנן כתפילין כך מנעלין מה תפילין בשמאל אף מנעלין בשמאל מיתיבי כשהוא נועל נועל של ימין ואחר כך נועל של שמאל אמר רב יוסף השתא דתניא הכי ואמר רבי יוחנן הכי דעבד הכי עבד ודעבד הכי עבד אמר ליה אביי דילמא רבי יוחנן הא מתני' [א]לא הוה שמיע ליה ואי הוה שמיע ליה הוה הדר ביה ואי נמי שמיע ליה וקסבר אין הלכה כאותה משנה [ב]אמר רב נחמן בר יצחק ירא שמים יוצא ידי שתיהן ומנו מר בריה דרבנא [ב]היכי עביד סיים דימיניה ולא קטר וסיים דשמאליה וקטר והדר קטר דימיניה אמר רב אשי חזינא לרב כהנא דלא קפיד תנו רבנן [ג]כשהוא נועל נועל של ימין ואחר כך נועל של שמאל [ג]כשהוא חולץ חולץ של שמאל ואח"כ חולץ של ימין [ד]כשהוא רוחץ רוחץ של ימין ואח"כ רוחץ של שמאל כשהוא סך סך של ימין ואח"כ של שמאל והרוצה לסוך כל גופו סך ראשו תחילה מפני שהוא מלך על כל איבריו: [ה]ולא בתפילין: אמר רב ספרא לא תימא אליבא דמ"ד [ד]שבת לאו זמן תפילין הוא אלא אפילו למ"ד שבת זמן תפילין הוא לא יצא דילמא אתי לאיתויי ברה"ר ואיכא דמתני לה אסיפא ואם יצא אינו חייב חטאת אמר רב ספרא לא תימא אליבא דמ"ד [ה]שבת זמן תפילין הוא אלא אפילו למ"ד שבת לאו זמן תפילין הוא אינו חייב חטאת מ"ט דרך מלבוש עבידא: [ו]ולא בקמיע בזמן שאינו מן המומחה: אמר רב פפא [ז]לא תימא עד דמומחה גברא ומומחה קמיע אלא כיון דמומחה גברא אף על גב דלא מומחה קמיע דיקא נמי דקתני ולא בקמיע בזמן שאינו מן המומחה ולא קתני בזמן שאינו מומחה ש"מ: [ח]ת"ר [ו]איזהו קמיע מומחה כל שריפא ושנה ושלש אחד קמיע של כתב ואחד קמיע של עיקרין אחד חולה שיש בו סכנה ואחד חולה שאין בו סכנה לא שנכפה אלא שלא יכפה וקושר ומתיר אפילו ברה"ר ובלבד שלא יקשרנו

בשיר

רש"י

הא יש ברגלו מכה. איכא למידק דנפיק ביחיד והשתא בעי תלמודא בהי מרגליו נפיק: **סנדל לשם צער עביד.** שלא ינגף ביתדות הדרכים ויצטער הילכך כשרואין אותו נועל ויודעין שיש ברגלו מכה אין חושדין אותו שטוען את השני בידו אלא מכירין בו לפי מעשיו שפרסותיו קשות ואינו מצטער ביתדות הדרכים ולא נועלו אלא משום מכה ודיו בזה לבדו וללשון רבותי אי נמי מחכו עלה דלא חזו למכה לא שליף לה דמצטער ביתדות הדרכים מחמת המכה: **לשום תענוג עביד.** אדם איסטניס ורך ומכירין מתוך מעשיו שנעל נעלו אחת שהוא איסטניס וזו מכתה מוכחת עלה ומבינין שהמכה מונעתו מלנעול ולא חשדי ליה ולענין אחוכי נמי לא מחייכי עליה: **עשיתו מכה.** ורבי יוחנן סבירא ליה דהנועל סנדלים נועל של שמאל תחילה ואח"כ של ימין וקס"ד דהכי קאמר ליה א"כ שאנעול זה שוב לא אנעול של שמאל אחריו והנני יוצא ביחיד ועשית את זו של ימין כאילו היתה בה מכה אלמא קסבר באותה שיש בה מכה נועל: **ודילמא כר' חייא סבירא ליה.** דאמר באותה שאין בה מכה נועל והכי קאמר ליה א"כ הריני יוצא ביחיד בזו של ימין ועשית את רגלי של שמאל כאילו יש בה מכה דאלא ביחיד באותה שאין בה מכה: **ואזדא ר' יוחנן.** דאמר עשית מכה דשמעינן מינה דאי הוה נעיל דימין ברישא תו לא הוה נעיל דשמאל בתריה לטעמיה דאמר דשמאל חשיבא: **תפילין בשמאל.** כדילפינן במנחות (דף לז.) מעל ידכה מלא יד כהה דהיינו שמאל שהיא כהה לענין תשמיש: **הוה הדר ביה.** ולא עבדינן כר' יוחנן: **אין הלכה.** וכרבי יוחנן בעינן למעבד: **יוצא ידי שניהם.** עביד כתרוייהו: **וסיים דשמאליה וקטר.** נמצא נעילת ימין קודמת לשמאל כי מתניתא וקשירת שמאל לשל ימין כר' יוחנן: **חולץ של שמאל.** דזהו כבודו של ימין בכולהו גרסינן של ימין ברישא חוץ מחולץ: **לא תימא כו'.** בפרק בתרא דעירובין (ד' נה:) מייתינן פלוגתייהו בגמרא: **דילמא.** שקיל להו מרישא אם בא לפנות וממטי להו ד' אמות: **דמומחה גברא ומומחה קמיע.** שעשה אדם זה קמיע זו לג' אנשים דנעשה אדם זה מומחה שריפא ג' אנשים והקמיע מומחה שריפא כתב זה ג' אנשים א"נ שכתב אדם זה ג' מיני קמיעים של ג' מיני חלאים לג' אנשים היינו איתמחי גברא בכל קמיעים שיעשה לעולם ומומחה קמיעה שנעשית [קמיע זו] לג' אנשים מחולי זה בין שכתבה רופא זה בין שכתבה רופא אחר נעשה הקמיע מומחה: **אלא כיון דאיתמחי גברא.** בג' מיני קמיעות לג' בני אדם אע"ג דלא איתמחי קמיע שלא ריפא קמיע זה אדם מעולם: **מן המומחה.** משמע מאדם מומחה: **ולא קתני בזמן שאינו מומחה.** דליהוו משמע דקפיד אמומחה קמיע עצמו. קמיע אינו אלא לשון קשר ודעיקרין של שרשי סממנין נמי קרוין קמיע: **ולא שנכפה.** כלומר לא תימא דלא יצא אלא מי שבא עליו החולי כבר פעם אחת: **נכפה.** היינו חולי שאדם נופל מחמתו לארץ ומכהו בראשו במוחו ומפילו: **אלא שלא יכפה.** שבא ממשפחת נכפין ודואג שלא יכפה:

תוספות

דעבד הכי עבד. פירוש דברייתא לא פליגא ארבי יוחנן ולא ר' יוחנן אברייתא וה"פ כתפילין אע"ג דימין חשובה לענין בהן יד ובהן רגל וכן לענין חליצה יכול לנעול של שמאל תחילה ברייתא נמי קמ"ל דאע"ג דשמאל חשובה לתפילין יכול לנעול של ימין תחילה וא"ת א"כ אמאי הקפיד רבי יוחנן על רב שמן שנתן לו של ימין כיון דיכול לנעול איזה שירלה תחילה ונראה לר"י דה"פ דעבד הכי עבד מי שרוצה לחבב של שמאל משום מצות תפילין הרשות בידו ומי שרוצה לחבב של ימין יותר משום חשיבות של ימין הרשות בידו ורבי יוחנן היה דרכו לחבב כל שעה של שמאל יותר ורב שמן בר אבא (לא) היה יודע מנהגו:

וסיים דשמאליה וקטר. אומר ריב"א דדוקא לענין קשירה הוא דחשיבא של שמאל טפי משום דחשיבות תפילין הוא בקשירה אבל איפכא לא ולהאי טעמא יש לנעול של ימין תחלה במנעלים שאין בהן קשירה: **דילמא** מיפסקי ואתי לאתויינהו ד' אמות ברה"ר. קשה לר"י דאפילו לא חיישינן דילמא מיפסקו אסור משום דזימנין דאיצטריך לבה"כ ואתי לאתויינהו ד"א ברה"ר דהכי אמר לקמן גבי קמיע ומתוך פי' הקונטרס משמע דלא גרס דילמא מיפסקו ופי' דילמא שקיל להו מרשו אם בא ליפנות והקדוש מקורבי"ל אומר דגרסינן לה שפיר ואיצטריך טעמא דמיפסקו לתפילין של יד דאין צריך לחלוץ כשצריך [ס] לבה"כ אלא של ראש משום שי"ן: **עד** דמימחי גברא ומימחי קמיע. נראה לר"י שאם כתב לחש אחד בשלש איגרות וריפאו שלשתן ג' בני אדם כל אחד אדם אחד היינו מומחי גברי וכאשר רפאו שלשתן אדם אחד בעיא היא בסמוך אי מימחי גברא או לא ודוקא לאותו לחש הוא מומחה אבל לשאר לחשים לא ודוקא שכתבם הוא אבל אחר לא ואם כל אחת מאיגרות ריפא שלש פעמים אפילו אדם אחד מומחות שלשתן ואין הלחש מומחה כל מקום שהוא אלא דווקא איגרת לבדה שהומחת והיינו מומחה גברא ומומחה קמיע שקמיע זה הומחה שריפא שלש פעמים וכתבו אדם מומחה שכתב שלשה קמיעין והועילו שלשתן: **אע"ג** דלא מימחי קמיע. נראה דכל שכן מימחי קמיע ולא גברא שהמחאת קמיע עדיפא מהמחאת הרופא כדמוכח לקמן דבהמחאת קמיע פשיטא ליה דאיתמחי אפילו בחד גברא ובאיתמחי גברא מספקא ליה אי איתמחי בתלת קמיע לחד גברא אי לא: **אע"ג** דלא מימחי קמיע. קשה לרשב"א היכי משכחת לה דאתמחי גברא ולא קמיע כיון שהאיש מומחה לכתוב לחש זה א"כ אגרת זו שכתב ודאי תועיל ואומר ר"י דנ"מ שאם אבדה מחאתו שכתב ג' קמיעים ולא הועילו אם הומחה הקמיע מועיל אפילו אבד אדם מחאתו: **ולא** קתני בזמן שאינו מומחה. קשה לרשב"א דילמא לעולם בעינן תרוייהו ואי הוה תני הכי הוה משמע מומחה קמיע ולא גברא וי"ל דאינו מומחה משמע שפיר בין אגברא בין אקמיע דהא לקמן תניא איזהו קמיע מומחה כו' ומוקמינן לה לאמחויי גברא:

כל

מסורת הש"ס

א) [לעיל דף יט: וש"נ], ב) [ברכות לט:], ג) [מס' ד"א פ"י], ד) [עירובין צה: צו. מנחות לו:], ה) [שם ולקמן סב.], ו) [תוספתא פ"ה].

רב נסים גאון

אבא מפני החשד שלא יהו אומרים איש פלוני נפסק סנדלו ותלאו בבית שחיו: **אמר** רב ספרא לא תימא אליבא דמאן דאמר שבת לאו זמן תפילין הוא וכו'. משתכח עיקר דילה במס' עירובין בפרק המוצא תפילין (דף צו) דתניא ושמרת את החקה הזאת למועדה מימים ימימה ימים ולא לילות מימים ולא כל הימים פרט לשבתות ולימים טובים דברי ר' יוסי הגלילי ור' עקיבא כר' יוסי הגלילי סבירא ליה דאמר שבת לאו זמן תפילין הוא כמו שאמרה הברייתא דתניא ר' עקיבא אומר יכול יניח אדם תפילין בשבתות וימים טובים ת"ל והיה לך לאות על ידך מי שצריכין אות יצאו שבתות וימים טובים שהן גופן אות וחקרו בתלמוד לידע איזה תנא דקסבר שבת לאו זמן תפילין ונשאו ונתנו בדבר זה הרבה עד שקיימו כי הוא ר' מאיר כדאמרינן בסיפא אלא האי תנא הוא דתניא המוצא תפילין מכניסן זוג זוג אחד איש ואחד אשה כו' עד כאן לא פליגי אלא בחדשות ובישנות אבל באשה לא פליגי דקסברי תפילין מצות עשה שלא הזמן גרמא הוא ונשים חייבות ומכלל דבריהם למדנו שר' מאיר ור' יהודה סברי שבת זמן תפילין הוא ועל דעת מי שסבר שבת לאו זמן תפילין הוא הויא לה מצות עשה שהזמן גרמא לפי שהיא נוהגת בחול בלבד ואלו שחייבו הנשים בה סברו כי חובתה נוהגת בכל עת ואינה מיוחדת בזמן ידוע ובפ' האשה נקנית (קידושין לה) אמרו מאן שמעת ליה דאמר תפילין מצות עשה שלא הזמן גרמה ר' מאיר היא ואמרו עוד ולר' יהודה דאמר ב' כתובין הבאין כאחד מלמדין ותפילין מצות עשה שלא הזמן גרמא מאי איכא למימר זה הברייתא דפליגו בה ר' יוסי הגלילי ור' עקיבא עם הברייתא בתראה דהיא דברי ר' עקיבא אשכחנן במס' דמנחות בפ' הקומץ את המנחה (לו) ואשכחנן עוד בגמ' דלא תצא אשה במחט נקובה (לקמן סב) אקשייה אביי לרב יוסף מדברי הברייתא ואותביה רב יוסף התם קסבר ר"מ לילה זמן תפילין ושבת זמן תפילין:

מותיב

גליון הש"ס

תוס' ד"ה דילמא מיפסקי וכו' **אלא של ראש משום שי"ן.** עי' מנחות דף לה ע"ב תוס' ד"ה אלו תפילין:

עין משפט נר מצוה

לב א מיי' פי"ט מהל' שבת הלכה טו סמג לאוין סה טוש"ע א"ח סי' שא סעיף ז:
לג ב טוש"ע א"ח סי' ב סעיף ד:
לד ג שם סעיף ה:
לה ד טוש"ע א"ח סי' ד סעיף י:
לו ה מיי' פי"ט מהל' שבת הלכה יד סמג לאוין סה טוש"ע א"ח סי' שא סעיף ז:
לז ו ז ח מיי' וסמג שם טוש"ע א"ח שם סעיף כה:

רבינו חננאל

סוגיא כחייא בר רב דאמר נועל הרגל (עראי) [שאין] בה הכאה. כי הרגל שיש בה הכאה המכה מוכחת עליה. א) דר' יוחנן קאי כוותיה הלא תראה כיון שהביא לו רב שמן בר אבא הסנדל של ימין והיה ראוי לו [להביא] של שמאל שהדין לנעול השמאל תחלה אמר לו עשיתה השמאל מכה ואמרת בדעתך כיון שהשמאל מוכה אין לה נעילת סנדל לפיכך הבאתה לי של ימין ש"מ דסבר ר' יוחנן כי מי שאין עליה מכה היא שיש בה נעילת סנדל. ומי שיש בה מכה היא נשארת יחיפה. ואזדא ר' יוחנן לטעמיה דאמר כתפילין מה תפילין בשמאל אף מנעל בשמאל. ואסקא רב אשי דזמנין חזינא לרב כהנא דנועל של שמאל תחלה ואח"כ של ימין וזמנין חזינא דנועל של ימין תחלה ואח"כ של שמאל. ולא קפיד וקיי"ל כוותיה דרב אשי דהוא בתרא: **ולא** בתפילין ואם יצא אינו חייב חטאת. אסיקא לישנא בתרא. אמר רב ספרא לא תימא מתניתין דקתני אם יצא אינו חייב חטאת אליבא דמאן דאמר שבת זמן תפילין היא אלא אפילו למ"ד שבת לאו זמן תפילין הוא חיוב חטאת ליכא מ"ט דרך מלבוש עבידן. והוצאה דרך מלבוש אינו חייב ומפורש בפרק אחרון דעירובין: **ולא בקמיע** בזמן שאינו מן המומחה. אוקמה רב פפא אי אתמחי גברא אע"ג דלא אתמחי קמיעא שרי למיפק ביה בשבת ודייק ממתניתין דקתני בזמן שאינו מן המומחה ולא קתני בזמן שאינו (מן המומחה) [מומחה] הקמיע עצמו.

חשק שלמה על רבינו חננאל

א) נראה מזה כי רבינו הי' לו גירסא אחרת בסוגיא דר"י ע"כ ס"ל כחייא בר רב וצ"ע:

ליקוטי רש"י

לא הוה שמיע ליה. שאין הכל בקיאין בברייתא וגם האמורא עצמו זימנין דלא ידע לה [רשב"ם פסחים קא:]. **דרך מלבוש עבידא.** משום דתכשיט הוא לגביה ולאו משאוי [עירובין צה:]. **נכפה.** חולי שממנו נופל לארץ ויש לו זמן לבא [כתובות עז:].

– so too one who puts on his **shoes** should begin **with the left** shoe.[14] It was for this reason that R' Yochanan would not put on his left shoe after his right shoe.

The Gemara objects to R' Yochanan's ruling:

מֵיתִיבֵי – **They challenged this** ruling **from the** following **Baraisa:** כְּשֶׁהוּא נוֹעֵל – WHEN [A PERSON] PUTS ON his SHOES, נוֹעֵל שֶׁל יָמִין וְאַחַר כָּךְ נוֹעֵל שֶׁל שְׂמֹאל – HE PUTS ON HIS RIGHT SHOE first AND AFTER THIS, HE PUTS ON HIS LEFT SHOE.[15] The Baraisa clearly states that it is the *right* shoe that should be put on first. – ? –

The Gemara cites a halachic ruling issued as a result of this objection:

אָמַר רַב יוֹסֵף – **Rav Yosef said:** הַשְׁתָּא דְּתַנְיָא הָכִי – **Now that the Baraisa has taught this** order (right foot first) וְאָמַר רַבִּי יוֹחָנָן הָכִי – **and R' Yochanan has stated that** order (left foot first), the halachah is that דְּעָבֵד הָכִי עָבֵד – **he who does it this way has done** correctly, וּדְעָבֵד הָכִי עָבֵד – **and he who does it that way has** also **done** correctly; i.e. either way is acceptable.[16]

The Gemara cites a dissenting opinion:

אָמַר לֵיהּ אַבָּיֵי – **Abaye said to [Rav Yosef]:** דִּילְמָא רַבִּי יוֹחָנָן הָא מַתְנִיתָא לֹא הֲוָה שְׁמִיעַ לֵיהּ – But **perhaps R' Yochanan** had **never heard of this Baraisa** – וְאִי הֲוָה שְׁמִיעַ לֵיהּ – **and if he had heard of it,** הֲוָה הָדַר בֵּיהּ – **he would have retracted** his ruling![17] וְאִי נַמִּי שְׁמִיעַ לֵיהּ – **Furthermore,** perhaps **he** *did* **hear of [the Baraisa],** וְקָסָבַר אֵין הֲלָכָה כְּאוֹתָהּ מִשְׁנָה – **but he holds that the halachah does not accord with that Baraisa!**[18] Since it is possible that R' Yochanan's ruling and the ruling in the Baraisa are not complementary, how can we rule that either way is acceptable?

The Gemara notes another possible solution:

אָמַר רַב נַחְמָן בַּר יִצְחָק – **Rav Nachman bar Yitzchak said:** יְרֵא שָׁמַיִם יוֹצֵא יְדֵי שְׁתֵּיהֶן – **One who fears Heaven can fulfill both** directives.[19] וּמַנּוּ – **And who was it** that followed this practice? מַר בְּרֵיהּ דְּרַבָנָא – **Mar the son of Rabana.**

The Gemara asks:

הֵיכִי עָבִיד – **How did he accomplish this?**[20]

The Gemara explains:

סָיֵים דִּימִינֵיהּ וְלֹא קָטַר – **He would put on his right** shoe, **but** he would **not tie it;** וְסָיֵים דִּשְׂמָאלֵיהּ וְקָטַר – **and** then **he would put on his left** shoe **and tie it;** וַהֲדַר קָטַר דִּימִינֵיהּ – **and then he would tie his right** shoe. Thus, he put on his right shoe first, as the Baraisa directs, and he tied his left shoe first, in accordance with R' Yochanan's ruling.[21]

The Gemara records the practice followed by another Amora:

אָמַר רַב אַשִׁי – **Rav Ashi said:** חֲזֵינָא לְרַב כַּהֲנָא דְּלָא קָפֵיד – **I have seen that Rav Kahana is not particular** about the order in which he puts on his shoes.[22]

The Gemara cites a Baraisa that discusses the precedence of right over left with regard to various actions:

תָּנוּ רַבָּנָן – **The Rabbis taught in a Baraisa:** כְּשֶׁהוּא נוֹעֵל – WHEN [A PERSON] PUTS ON his SHOES, נוֹעֵל שֶׁל יָמִין וְאַחַר כָּךְ נוֹעֵל שֶׁל שְׂמֹאל – HE SHOULD PUT ON HIS RIGHT SHOE first, AND AFTER THIS, HE SHOULD PUT ON HIS LEFT SHOE.[23] כְּשֶׁהוּא חוֹלֵץ – WHEN HE REMOVES his SHOES, חוֹלֵץ שֶׁל שְׂמֹאל וְאַחַר כָּךְ חוֹלֵץ שֶׁל יָמִין – HE SHOULD REMOVE HIS LEFT SHOE first, AND AFTER THIS, HE SHOULD REMOVE HIS RIGHT SHOE.[24] כְּשֶׁהוּא רוֹחֵץ – WHEN HE WASHES, רוֹחֵץ שֶׁל יָמִין וְאַחַר כָּךְ רוֹחֵץ שֶׁל שְׂמֹאל – HE SHOULD WASH HIS RIGHT hand first AND AFTERWARDS HE SHOULD WASH HIS LEFT hand.[25] כְּשֶׁהוּא סָךְ – WHEN HE ANOINTS his hands with oil, סָךְ שֶׁל יָמִין וְאַחַר כָּךְ שֶׁל שְׂמֹאל – HE SHOULD ANOINT HIS RIGHT hand first AND AFTERWARDS HE SHOULD ANOINT HIS LEFT hand. וְהָרוֹצֶה לָסוּךְ כָּל גּוּפוֹ – AND ONE WHO WISHES TO ANOINT

NOTES

14. [Seemingly, there is no connection between putting on shoes and putting on tefillin; furthermore, tefillin are put *only* on the left hand! However, R' Yochanan teaches that by showing preference to the left side, one is demonstrating that the mitzvah of tefillin (where the left side is significant) is dear to him (see *Dibros Moshe* 53:18). See, however, notes 16 and 22 below.]

15. [With respect to many of the Torah laws, there is a general rule that the right side is given precedence (see, for example, *Leviticus* ch. 14, and *Zevachim* 24b). See *Meiri,* who explains the symbolism involved.]

16. Rav Yosef reasoned that R' Yochanan would not have issued a ruling that was the very opposite of the Baraisa's unless he had Tannaic support for his view. Thus, he viewed the contradiction between the Baraisa and R' Yochanan as an indication of a Tannaic dispute as to the proper order of putting on one's shoes; and, in the absence of any halachic decision, he ruled that either opinion could be followed (*Chidushei HaRan;* see also *Chelkas Binyamin*). Alternatively, Rav Yosef is suggesting that in truth the Baraisa and R' Yochanan do not dispute each other; for the Baraisa suggests that the right hand should be favored because it is the primary one, and R' Yochanan suggests that the left foot can be favored nevertheless, just as the left hand is favored regarding tefillin. Accordingly, Rav Yosef stated that one is entitled to favor either foot, as long as he favors the same foot consistently, and does not switch back and forth from one foot to the other (*Tosafos;* see *Maharsha;* cf. *Beis Yoshef* to *Orach Chaim* §2; see also below, note 22). According to this version, R' Yochanan refused to put on his left shoe after his right because his practice was to always put on his left shoe first.

17. Thus, how can you state that one who follows R' Yochanan has acted correctly? Perhaps R' Yochanan himself would have retracted his view in the face of the Baraisa! (*Rashi*; see *Chidushei HaRav*).

18. Thus, how can you state that one who follows the practice stated in the Baraisa has acted correctly? Perhaps we should follow R' Yochanan's view (or, the view of the Tanna that supports him – see note 16, first explanation) that the halachah does not accord with the Baraisa (see *Rashi*).

[Although the wording of the Gemara mentions that R' Yochanan does not agree with the *Mishnah,* the Gemara is referring to the Baraisa cited above. See *Rashash* to 83b ד״ה שהרי.]

19. The Gemara below will explain how this is accomplished.

20. [Literally: How did he act?] Seemingly, it is impossible to put on both the left shoe and the right shoe first!

21. *Rashi. Tosafos* explain that tying the left shoe first is akin to the act of tying on the tefillin, and therefore by tying the left shoe first, one [demonstrates that the mitzvah of tefillin is dear to him, and] fulfills the directive of R' Yochanan; thus, they state (in the name of *Riva*) that if one wears shoes that have no laces, the right shoe should be put on first, for there is no basis to compare them to tefillin. [See *Beis Yosef* to *Orach Chaim* §2 ד״ה ואיכא.]

22. That is, sometimes he puts his right shoe on first, while sometimes he puts his left shoe on first (*Rabbeinu Chananel*).

[The commentators differ as to Rav Kahana's reasoning. *Beis Yosef* (*Orach Chaim* §2) explains that Rav Kahana agrees with Rav Yosef that the Baraisa and R' Yochanan do not argue. *Bach* rejects this understanding, arguing that even Rav Yosef held that one should be consistent in his practice, and Rav Kahana was not particular at all! He therefore explains that Rav Kahana disagrees with both Abaye and Rav Yosef, and maintains that one need not concern himself with this matter at all; this opinion is also held by *Ritva* (*MHK* ed.; see there). The halachah in this matter is also subject to dispute; *Tur* (*Orach Chaim* ibid.) and *Rabbeinu Yonah* rule that one should follow the practice of Mar the son of Rabana, while *Rabbeinu Chananel and Beis Yosef* rule in accordance with Rav Kahana (see *Chelkas Binyamin,* who discusses this dispute at length).]

23. [This Baraisa echoes the ruling of the previously cited Baraisa, which taught that the right foot is favored.]

24. When one is removing his shoes, one should remove the less important shoe first, for this is an honor to the more important shoe; thus, this Baraisa holds that the left shoe is removed first (see *Rashi*).

25. [One should wash the more important hand first.] This law is cited in *Orach Chaim* 4:10 with respect to the washing of one's hands upon rising; see there.

גמרא

הא יש ברגלו מכה נפיק בהי מינייהו נפיק אמר רב הונא באותה שיש בה מכה אלמא קסבר סנדל לשום צער עביד וחייא בר רב אמר [א]באותה שאין בה מכה אלמא קסבר לשום תענוג עביד וזו שיש בה מכה מכתה מוכחת עליה ואף רבי יוחנן סבר לה להא דרב הונא דאמר ליה ר' יוחנן לרב שמן בר אבא הב לי מסנאי יהב ליה דימין אמר ליה עשיתו מכה ודילמא כחייא בר רב ס"ל והכי קאמר עשית של שמאל מכה ואזדא רבי יוחנן לטעמיה דאמר ר' יוחנן כתפילין כך מנעלין מה תפילין בשמאל אף מנעלין בשמאל מיתיבי כשהוא נועל נועל של ימין ואחר כך נועל של שמאל אמר רב יוסף השתא דתניא הכי ואמר רבי יוחנן הכי דעבד הכי עבד ודעבד הכי עבד אמר ליה אביי דילמא רבי יוחנן הא מתני' [א]לא הוה שמיע ליה ואי הוה שמיע ליה הוה הדר ביה ואי נמי שמיע ליה וקסבר אין הלכה כאותה משנה [ב]אמר רב נחמן בר יצחק ירא שמים יוצא ידי שתיהן ומנו מר בריה דרבנא [ב]היכי עביד סיים דימיניה ולא קטר וסיים דשמאליה וקטר והדר קטר דימיניה אמר רב אשי חזינא לרב כהנא דלא קפיד תנו רבנן [ג]כשהוא נועל נועל של ימין ואחר כך נועל של שמאל [ג]כשהוא חולץ חולץ של שמאל ואח"כ חולץ של ימין [ד]כשהוא רוחץ רוחץ של ימין ואח"כ רוחץ של שמאל כשהוא סך סך של ימין ואח"כ של שמאל והרוצה לסוך כל גופו סך ראשו תחילה מפני שהוא מלך על כל איבריו: [ה]ולא בתפילין: אמר רב ספרא לא תימא אליבא דמ"ד [ד]שבת לאו זמן תפילין הוא אלא אפילו למ"ד שבת זמן תפילין הוא לא יצא דילמא אתי לאיתויי ברה"ר ואיכא דמתני לה אסיפא ואם יצא אינו חייב חטאת אמר רב ספרא לא תימא אליבא דמ"ד [ה]שבת זמן תפילין הוא אלא אפילו למ"ד שבת לאו זמן תפילין הוא אינו חייב חטאת מ"ט דרך מלבוש עבידא: [ו]ולא בקמיע בזמן שאינו מן המומחה: אמר רב פפא [ז]לא תימא עד דמומחה גברא ומומחה קמיע אלא כיון דמומחה גברא אף על גב דלא מומחה קמיע דיקא נמי דקתני ולא בקמיע בזמן שאינו מן המומחה ולא קתני בזמן שאינו מומחה ש"מ: [ח]ת"ר [ו]איזהו קמיע מומחה כל שריפא ושנה ושלש אחד קמיע של כתב ואחד קמיע של עיקרין אחד חולה שיש בו סכנה ואחד חולה שאין בו סכנה לא שנכפה אלא שלא יכפה וקושר ומתיר אפילו ברה"ר ובלבד שלא יקשרנו בשיר

רש"י

הא יש ברגלו מכה. היכא למידק דנפיק ביחיד והשתא בעי תלמודא בהי מרגליו נפיק: סנדל לשם צער עביד. שלא ינגף ביתדות הדרכים וילטער הילך כשרואין אותו נועל ויודעין שיש ברגליו מכה אין חושדין אותו שטוען את השני בידו אלא מכירין בו לפי מעשיו שפרסותיו קשות ואינו מצטער ביתדות הדרכים ולא נועלו אלא משום מכה ודיו בזה לבדו וללשון רבותי אי נמי מחכו עלה דלא חזו למכה לא שליף לה דמצטער ביתדות הדרכים מחמת המכה: לשום תענוג עביד. אדם איסטניס ורך ומכירין מתוך מעשיו שנעל נעלו אחת שהוא איסטניס וזו מכתה מוכחת עלה ומבינין שהמכה מונעתו מלנעול ולא חשדי ליה ולענין אחוכי נמי לא מחייכי עליה: עשיתו מכה. ורבי יוחנן סבירא ליה דהנועל סנדלים נועל של שמאל תחילה ואח"כ של ימין וקס"ד דהכי קאמר ליה א"כ שאנעול זה שוב לא אנעול של שמאל אחריו והנני יוצא ביחיד ועשית את זו של ימין כאילו היתה בה מכה אלמא קסבר באותה שיש בה מכה נועל: ודילמא כר' חייא סבירא ליה. דאמר באותה שאין בה מכה נועל והכי קאמר ליה א"כ הריני יוצא ביחיד בזו של ימין ועשית את רגלי של שמאל כאילו יש בה מכה דהלא ביחיד באותה שאין בה מכה: ואזדא ר' יוחנן. דאמר עשית מכה דשמעינן מינה דאי הוה נעיל דימין ברישא תו לא הוה נעיל דשמאל בתריה לטעמיה דאמר דשמאל חשיבא: תפילין בשמאל. כדילפינן במנחות (דף לז.) מעל ידכה מלא יד כהה דהיינו שמאל שהיא כהה לענין תשמיש: הוה הדר ביה. ולא עבדינן כר' יוחנן: אין הלכה. וכרבי יוחנן בעינן למעבד: יוצא ידי שניהם. עביד כתרוייהו: וסיים דשמאליה וקטר. נמצא נעילת ימין קודמת לשמאל כי מתניתא וקשירת שמאל לשל ימין כר' יוחנן: חולץ של שמאל. דזהו כבודו של ימין בכולהו גרסינן של ימין ברישא חוץ מחולץ: לא תימא כו'. בפרק בתרא דעירובין (ד' צה:) מייתין פלוגתייהו בגמרא: דילמא. שקיל להו מרישא אם בא לפנות וממטי להו ד' אמות: דמומחה גברא ומומחה קמיע. שעשה אדם זה קמיע זו לג' אנשים דנעשה אדם זה מומחה שריפא ג' אנשים והקמיע מומחה שריפא כתב זה ג' אנשים א"נ שכתב אדם זה ג' מיני קמיעים של ג' מיני חלאים לג' אנשים היינו איתמחי גברא בכל קמיעים שיעשה לעולם ומומחה קמיעה שנעשית [קמיע זו] לג' אנשים מחולי זה בין שכתבה רופא זה בין שכתבה רופא אחר נעשה הקמיע מומחה: אלא כיון דאיתמחי גברא. בג' מיני קמיעות לג' בני אדם אע"ג דלא איתמחי קמיע שלא ריפא קמיע זה אדם מעולם: מן המומחה. משמע מאדם מומחה: ולא קתני בזמן שאינו מומחה. דליהוו משמע דקפיד אמומחה קמיע עצמו. קמיע אינו אלא לשון קשר ודעיקרין של שרשי סממנין נמי קרוין קמיע: ולא שנכפה. כלומר לא תימא דלא יצא אלא מי שבא עליו החולי כבר פעם אחת: נכפה. היינו חולי שאדם נופל מחמתו לארץ ומכהו בראשו במוחו ומפילו: אלא שלא יכפה. שבא ממשפחת נכפין ודואג שלא יכפה:

בשיר

תוספות

דעבד הכי עבד. פירוש דברייתא לא פליגא ארבי יוחנן ולא ר' יוחנן אברייתא וה"פ כתפילין אע"ג דימין חשובה לענין בהן יד ובהן רגל וכן לענין חליצה יכול לנעול של שמאל תחילה ברייתא נמי קמ"ל דאע"ג דשמאל חשובה לתפילין יכול לנעול של ימין תחילה וא"ת א"כ אמאי הקפיד רבי יוחנן על רב שמן שנתן לו של ימין כיון דיכול לנעול איזה שירצה תחילה ונראה לר"י דה"פ דעבד הכי עבד מי שרוצה לחבב של שמאל משום מצות תפילין הרשות בידו ומי שרוצה לחבב של ימין יותר משום חשיבות של ימין הרשות בידו ורבי יוחנן היה דרכו לחבב כל שעה של שמאל יותר ורב שמן בר אבא (לא) היה יודע מנהגו:

וסיים דשמאליה וקטר. אומר ריב"א דדוקא לענין קשירה הוא דחשיבא של שמאל טפי משום דחשיבות תפילין הוא בקשירה אבל איפכא לא ולהאי טעמא יש לנעול של ימין תחלה במנעלים שאין בהן קשירה: דילמא מיפסקי ואתי לאתויינהו ד' אמות ברה"ר. קשה לר"י דאפילו לא חיישינן דילמא מיפסקו אסור משום דזימנין דאיצטריך לבה"כ ואתי לאתויינהו ד"א ברה"ר דהכי אמר לקמן גבי קמיע ומתוך פי' הקונטרס משמע דלא גרס דילמא מיפסקו ופי' דילמא שקיל להו מראשו אם בא ליפנות והקדוש מקורבי"ל אומר דגרסינן לה שפיר ואיצטריך טעמא דמיפסקו לתפילין של יד דאין צריך לחלוץ כשנכנס [°] לבה"כ אלא של ראש משום שי"ן:

עד דמימחי גברא ומימחי קמיע. נראה לר"י שאם כתב לאחד בשלש איגרות וריפאו שלשתן ג' בני אדם כל אחד אדם אחד היינו מומחי גברי וכאשר רפאו שלשתן אדם אחד בעיא היא בסמוך אי מימחי גברא או לא ודוקא לאותו לחש הוא מומחה אבל לשאר לחשים לא ודוקא שכתבם הוא אבל אחר לא ואם כל אחת מאיגרות ריפא שלש פעמים אפילו אדם אחד מומחות שלשתן ואין הלחש מומחה כל מקום שהוא אלא דווקא איגרת לבדה שהומחת והיינו מומחה גברא ומומחה קמיע שקמיע זה הומחה שריפא שלש פעמים וכתבו אדם מומחה שכתב שלשה קמיעין והועילו שלשתן:

אע"ג דלא מימחי קמיע. נראה דכל שכן מימחי קמיע ולא גברא שהמחאת קמיע עדיפא מהמחאת הרופא כדמוכח לקמן דבהמחאת קמיע פשיטא ליה דאיתמחי אפילו בחד גברא ובאיתמחי גברא מספקא ליה אי איתמחי בתלת קמיע לחד גברא אי לא:

אע"ג דלא מימחי קמיע. קשה לרשב"א היכי משכחת לה דאתמחי גברא ולא קמיע כיון שהאיש מומחה לכתוב לחש זה א"כ אגרת זו שכתב ודאי תועיל ואומר ר"י דנ"מ שאם אבדה מאחתו שכתב ג' קמיעים ולא הועילו אם הומחה הקמיע מועיל אפילו אבד אדם מאחתו: ולא קתני בזמן שאינו מומחה. קשה לרשב"א דילמא לעולם בעינן תרוייהו ואי הוה תני הכי הוה משמע מומחה קמיע ולא גברא וי"ל דאינו מומחה משמע שפיר בין אגברא בין אקמיע דהא לקמן תניא איזהו קמיע מומחה כו' ומוקמינן לה לאתמויי גברא:

כל

מסורת הש"ס

א) [לעיל דף יט: וש"נ], ב) [ברכות לט:], ג) [מס' ד"א פ"י], ד) [עירובין צה: צו. מנחות לו:], ה) [שם ולקמן סב.], ו) [תוספתא פ"ה].

רב נסים גאון

אבא מפני החשד שלא יהו אומרים איש פלוני נפסק סנדלו ותלאו בבית שחיו: אמר רב ספרא לא תימא אליבא דמאן דאמר שבת לאו זמן תפילין הוא וכו'. משתכח עיקר דילה במס' עירובין בפרק המוצא תפילין (דף צו) דתניא ושמרת את החקה הזאת למועדה מימים ימימה ימים ולא לילות מימים ולא כל הימים פרט לשבתות ולימים טובים דברי ר' יוסי הגלילי ור' עקיבא כר' יוסי הגלילי סבירא ליה דאמר שבת לאו זמן תפילין הוא כמו שאמרה הברייתא דתניא ר' עקיבא אומר יכול יניח אדם תפילין בשבתות וימים טובים ת"ל והיה לך לאות על ידך מי שצריכין אות יצאו שבתות וימים טובים שהן גופן אות וחקרו בתלמוד לידע איזה תנא דקסבר שבת לאו זמן תפילין ונשאו ונתנו בדבר זה הרבה עד שקיימו כי הוא ר' מאיר כדאמרינן בסיפא אלא האי תנא הוא דתניא המוצא תפילין מכניסן זוג זוג אחד איש ואחד אשה כו' עד כאן לא פליגי אלא בחדשות ובישנות אבל באשה לא פליגי דקסברי תפילין מצות עשה שלא הזמן גרמא הוא ונשים חייבות ומכלל דבריהם למדנו שר' מאיר ור' יהודה סברי שבת זמן תפילין הוא ועל דעת מי שסבר שבת לאו זמן תפילין הוא הויא לה מצות עשה שהזמן גרמא לפי שהיא נוהגת בחול בלבד ואלו שחייבו הנשים בה סברו כי חובתה נוהגת בכל עת ואינה מיוחדת בזמן ידוע ובפ' האשה נקנית (קידושין לה) אמרו מאן שמעת ליה דאמר תפילין מצות עשה שלא הזמן גרמה ר' מאיר היא ואמרו עוד ולר' יהודה דאמר ב' כתובין הבאין כאחד מלמדין ותפילין מצות עשה שלא הזמן גרמא מאי איכא למימר זה הברייתא דפליגו בה ר' יוסי הגלילי ור' עקיבא עם הברייתא בתראה דהיא דברי ר' עקיבא אשכחנן במס' דמנחות בפ' הקומץ את המנחה (לו) ואשכחנן עוד בגמ' דלא תצא אשה במחט נקובה (לקמן סב) אקשייה אביי לרב יוסף מדברי הברייתא ואותביה רב יוסף התם קסבר ר"מ לילה זמן תפילין ושבת זמן תפילין:

מותיב

גליון הש"ס

תוס' ד"ה דילמא מיפסקי וכו' אלא של ראש משום שי"ן. עי' מנחות דף לה ע"ב תוס' ד"ה אלו תפילין:

עין משפט נר מצוה

לב א מיי' פי"ט מהל' שבת הלכה טו סמג לאוין סה טוש"ע א"ח סי' שא סעיף ז:

לג ב טוש"ע א"ח סי' ב סעיף ד:

לד ג שם סעיף ה:

לה ד טוש"ע א"ח סי' ד סעיף י:

לו ה מיי' פי"ט מהל' שבת הלכה יד סמג לאוין סה טוש"ע א"ח סי' שא סעיף ז:

לז ו ז ח מיי' וסמג שם טוש"ע א"ח שם סעיף כה:

רבינו חננאל

סוגיא כחייא בר רב דאמר נועל הרגל (עראי) [שאין] בה הכאה. כי הרגל שיש בה הכאה המכה מוכחת עליה. א) דר' יוחנן קאי כוותיה הלא תראה כיון שהביא לו רב שמן בר אבא הסנדל של ימין והיה ראוי לו [להביא] של שמאל שהדין לנעול השמאל תחלה אמר לו עשיתה השמאל מכה ואמרת בדעתך כיון שהשמאל מוכה אין לה נעילת סנדל לפיכך הבאתה לי של ימין ש"מ דסבר ר' יוחנן כי מי שאין עליה מכה היא שיש בה נעילת סנדל. ומי שיש בה מכה היא נשארת יחיפה. ואזדא ר' יוחנן לטעמיה דאמר כתפילין מה תפילין בשמאל אף מנעל בשמאל. ואסקא רב אשי דזמנין חזינא לרב כהנא דנועל של שמאל תחלה ואח"כ של ימין וזמנין חזינא דנועל של ימין תחלה ואח"כ של שמאל. ולא קפיד וקיי"ל כוותיה דרב אשי דהוא בתרא: ולא בתפילין ואם יצא אינו חייב חטאת. אסיקא לישנא בתרא. אמר רב ספרא לא תימא מתניתין דקתני אם יצא אינו חייב חטאת אליבא דמאן דאמר שבת זמן תפילין היא אלא אפילו למ"ד שבת לאו זמן תפילין הוא חיוב חטאת ליכא מ"ט דרך מלבוש עבידן. והוצאה דרך מלבוש אינו חייב ומפורש בפרק אחרון דעירובין: ולא בקמיע בזמן שאינו מן המומחה. אוקמה רב פפא אי אתמחי גברא אע"ג דלא אתמחי קמיעא שרי למיפק ביה בשבת ודייק ממתניתין דקתני בזמן שאינו מן המומחה ולא קתני בזמן שאינו (מן המומחה) [מומחה] הקמיע עצמו.

חשק שלמה על רבינו חננאל

א) נראה מזה כי רבינו הי' לו גירסא אחרת בסוגיא דר"י ע"כ ס"ל מזיא בר רב ול"ע:

ליקוטי רש"י

לא הוה שמיע ליה. שאין הכל בקיאין בברייתא וגם האמורא עצמו זימנין דלא ידע לה [רשב"ם פסחים קא:]. דרך מלבוש עבידא. משום דמכסיא הוא לגביה ולאו משאוי [עירובין צה:]. נכפה. חולי שמפילו ונופל לארץ ויש לו זמן לבא [כתובות עז:].

HIS ENTIRE BODY with oil סָךְ רֹאשׁוֹ תְּחִילָּה – **SHOULD ANOINT HIS HEAD FIRST,** מִפְּנֵי שֶׁהוּא מֶלֶךְ עַל כָּל אֵיבָרָיו – **FOR [THE HEAD] IS THE RULER OF ALL OF ONE'S LIMBS.**[26]

The Mishnah stated:

וְלֹא בִּתְפִילִּין – **AND** he may **NOT** go out **WITH TEFILLIN . . .**

The Gemara notes that this ruling is *not* dependent upon a particular dispute:

אָמַר רַב סַפְרָא – **Rav Safra said:** לֹא תֵּימָא – **Do not say** אַלִּיבָּא דְּמַאן דְּאָמַר שַׁבָּת לָאו זְמַן תְּפִילִּין הוּא – that the Mishnah prohibits the wearing of tefillin only **according to the one who says that the Sabbath is not a time for tefillin.**[27] אֶלָּא אֲפִילּוּ לְמַאן דְּאָמַר שַׁבָּת זְמַן תְּפִילִּין הוּא – **Rather,** the law is that **even according to the one who says** that **the Sabbath is a time for tefillin,** לֹא יֵצֵא – **one may not go out** while wearing them; דִּילְמָא אָתֵי לְאִיתּוּיֵי בִּרְשׁוּת הָרַבִּים – for the Sages were concerned that **perhaps he will** remove them in the street[28] and **come to carry them** four *amos* **in a public domain.**[29]

The Gemara cites a second version of Rav Safra's statement:

וְאִיכָּא דְּמַתְנֵי לָהּ אַסֵּיפָא – **And there are those who teach [Rav Safra's statement] as referring to the latter ruling** in the Mishnah, which states: וְאִם יָצָא אֵינוֹ חַיָּיב חַטָּאת – **BUT IF HE GOES OUT** wearing any of these items, **HE IS NOT LIABLE TO A** *CHATAS.*[30] אָמַר רַב סַפְרָא – And **Rav Safra said** in explanation of this ruling: לֹא תֵּימָא – **Do not say** אַלִּיבָּא דְּמַאן דְּאָמַר שַׁבָּת זְמַן תְּפִילִּין הוּא – that the Mishnah exempts one who goes out with tefillin from liability to a *chatas* only **according to the one who says** that **the Sabbath is a time for tefillin.**[31] אֶלָּא אֲפִילּוּ לְמַאן דְּאָמַר שַׁבָּת לָאו זְמַן תְּפִילִּין הוּא – **Rather,** the law is that **even according to the one who says** that **the Sabbath is *not* a time for tefillin,** אֵין חַיָּיב חַטָּאת – **one is not liable to a** *chatas* if he wears them outside on the Sabbath. מַאי טַעְמָא – And **what is the reason** for this? דֶּרֶךְ מַלְבּוּשׁ עֲבִידָא – Because **[the tefillin] are worn in the manner of clothing.**[32]

The Mishnah stated:

וְלֹא בְקָמֵיעַ בִּזְמַן שֶׁאֵינוֹ מִן הַמּוּמְחֶה – **AND** he may **NOT** go out **WITH AN AMULET, AS LONG AS IT IS NOT FROM AN EXPERT . . .**

The Gemara clarifies the Mishnah's ruling:

אָמַר רַב פַּפָּא – **Rav Pappa said:** לֹא תֵּימָא – **Do not say** עַד דְּמוּמְחֶה גַּבְרָא וּמוּמְחֶה קָמֵיעַ – that one may not wear an amulet **until the man** who wrote the amulet **is a** proven **expert and the amulet** has been proven **effective;**[33] אֶלָּא כֵּיוָן דְּמוּמְחֶה גַּבְרָא – **rather, once the man** who wrote the amulet **is a** proven **expert,**[34] אַף עַל גַּב דְּלָא מוּמְחֶה קָמֵיעַ – **even if the amulet** has **not** been proven **effective,**[35] it may be worn.[36]

The Gemara notes that this clarification is supported by the Mishnah's phrasing:

דַּיְקָא נַמִּי – And **this can also be inferred through** a **precise** reading of the Mishnah, דְּקָתָנֵי – **for the Mishnah taught:**

NOTES

26. I.e. it is the most important portion of the body, and therefore it must be treated with deference. [This would appear to apply to one who washes his entire body as well – see *Darkei Moshe* to *Tur Orach Chaim* ibid.]

[See *Kuntres Ish Itair,* who discusses proper conduct for a left-handed person with regard to these and many other laws.]

27. There is a Tannaic dispute whether the mitzvah of tefillin applies even on the Sabbath. [This dispute is discussed at length in Tractate *Eruvin* (95b-96b).] One might have thought that the Mishnah's ruling forbidding the wearing of tefillin was stated only according to the Tanna who holds that there is no mitzvah to wear tefillin on the Sabbath, for it is understandable that this Tanna would view the tefillin as items that cannot be worn – as they would be considered [at least on the Rabbinic level] a burden. But according to the Tanna who holds that one fulfills the mitzvah of tefillin on the Sabbath, it could be logically assumed that wearing the tefillin should be permitted, for they should be viewed as part of the person's attire! Rav Safra therefore informs us that this is not the case.

28. I.e. perhaps he will feel the need to relieve himself, and he will remove the tefillin before doing so (*Rashi*). [*Tosafos* cite a text that states that we are concerned that one of the straps of the tefillin will break and he will come to carry the tefillin; they explain that the possibility that he will remove the tefillin to relieve himself applies only to the tefillin worn on the head, which must be removed because of the engraved letter *shin* on the outside of the tefillin case itself (see below, 62a); the tefillin on the hand, however, may be worn even while one relieves himself. *Magen Avraham* (*Orach Chaim* 43:1), however, maintains that even the tefillin worn on the arm must be removed before one relieves himself (see also *Rashi* above, 28b ד״ה שי״ן, *Chidushei HaRan,* and *Chelkas Binyamin;* see also *Dibros Moshe* 53:19).]

29. [Most bathrooms in Talmudic times were located out of doors, in the fields (*Rashi* to 61b).] Thus, even according to the Tanna who holds that the mitzvah of tefillin applies on the Sabbath [in whose opinion the tefillin can be considered part of a person's attire], the Sages decreed that the tefillin cannot be worn on the Sabbath; accordingly, the Mishnah's ruling is unanimously held. [See *Tos. Yom Tov* ד״ה ולא בתפילין, *Chelkas Binyamin,* and *Orach Chaim* 301:7 with *Magen Avraham* and *Gra* as to whether this decree was necessary according to the opinion that the Sabbath is *not* a time when the mitzvah of tefillin can be fulfilled.]

30. For, as explained above (60a note 29), going outside while wearing any of the items listed in the Mishnah (including tefillin) is not Biblically prohibited.

31. It would have been possible to assume that tefillin are Biblically permitted only according to the Tanna who holds that one can fulfill the mitzvah of tefillin on the Sabbath, for in his view the tefillin are not a burden. In the view of the Tanna who holds that one cannot fulfill the mitzvah of tefillin on the Sabbath, one could assume that the tefillin would be considered a burden, and it would be Biblically prohibited to wear them outside on the Sabbath.

32. [Literally: they are made in the manner of clothing.] I.e. since they are items that are worn during the week (when the mitzvah of tefillin can be fulfilled), they are viewed as being worn [rather than carried] on the Sabbath as well (see *Ritva MHK* ed.).

33. *Rashi* offers two explanations of this scenario: (a) A person healed three different people from the same disease with the same type of amulet. Thus, the person is a proven expert, for he has cured three people, and this amulet is proven effective because it has cured three people (see *Tosafos* to 61b ד״ה תלת [ב׳], and *Ran MHK* ed.). [According to this explanation, the person is *not* proven to be expert with regard to curing other diseases, but the amulet is proven effective even if written by a different person (see below, 61b note 15). (b) A person wrote three amulets for three different diseases, and each one of the amulets cured three different people (nine cures in all – this case will be discussed further below, on 61b). Thus, the person is proven an expert with regard to curing *any* disease with an amulet (see 61b note 9, where this is discussed further), and the amulets, which have each cured three people, are proven effective to cure those diseases, whether they are written by this person or by another healer (*Rashi*). These laws will be discussed at length in the Gemara below (61b); see also *Ran MHK* ed. and *Chidushei HaRan* here).

34. E.g. if the man was proven expert by virtue of his having cured three different people with three different types of amulets [each amulet having been used only once] (*Rashi*).

35. [Not only if the amulet has cured only once or twice in the past, but even if he wrote] a new amulet that has as of yet never cured anyone (*Rashi;* see *Tosafos* ד״ה אע״ג).

36. For we assume that any amulet written by an expert healer is effective, and therefore it may be worn on the Sabbath (see *Chidushei HaRan*).

Tosafos and other Rishonim note that if the amulet is proven but the healer is not, it may certainly be worn on the Sabbath; the Gemara speaks of the case where the amulet is not proven because the permit in such a case is a greater novelty [since the effectiveness of the very object being worn is in question]. See also *Sfas Emes.*

מסורת הש"ס

א) [לעיל דף יט: וש"נ], ב) [ברכות לט:], ג) [מס' ד"א פ"י], ד) [עירובין לה: צו. מנחות לו:], ה) [שם ולקמן סב.], ו) [תוספתא פ"ה].

רב נסים גאון

אבא מפני החשד שלא יהו אומרים איש פלוני נפסק סנדלו ותלאו בבית שחיו: **אמר** רב ספרא לא תימא אליבא דמאן דאמר שבת לאו זמן תפילין הוא וכו'. משתכח עיקר דילה במס' עירובין בפרק המוצא תפילין (דף צו) דתניא ושמרת את החקה הזאת למועדה מימים ימימה ימים ולא לילות מימים ולא כל הימים פרט לשבתות ולימים טובים דברי ר' יוסי הגלילי ור' עקיבא כר' יוסי הגלילי סבירא ליה דאמר שבת לאו זמן תפילין הוא כמו שאמרה הברייתא דתניא ר' עקיבא אומר יכול יניח אדם תפילין בשבתות וימים טובים ת"ל והיה לך לאות על ידך מי שצריכין אות יצאו שבתות וימים טובים שהן גופן אות וחקרו בתלמוד לידע איזה תנא דקסבר שבת לאו זמן תפילין ונשאו ונתנו בדבר זה הרבה עד שקימו כי הוא ר' מאיר כדאמרינן בסיפא אלא האי תנא הוא דתניא המוצא תפילין מכניסן זוג זוג אחד איש ואחד אשה כו' עד כאן לא פליגי אלא בחדשות ובישנות אבל באשה לא פליגי דקסברי תפילין מצות עשה שלא הזמן גרמא הוא ונשים חייבות ומכלל דבריהם למדנו שר' מאיר ור' יהודה סברי שבת זמן תפילין הוא ועל דעת מי שסבר שבת לאו זמן תפילין הוא הויא לה מצות עשה שהזמן גרמא לפי שהיא נוהגת בחול בלבד ואלו שחייבו הנשים בה סברו כי חובתה נוהגת בכל עת ואינה מיוחדת בזמן ידוע ובפ' האשה נקנית (קידושין לה) אמרו מאן שמעת ליה דאמר תפילין מצות עשה שלא הזמן גרמה ר' מאיר היא ואמרו עוד ולר' יהודה דאמר ב' כתובין הבאין כאחד מלמדין ותפילין מצות עשה שלא הזמן גרמא מאי איכא למימר זה הברייתא דפליגו בה ר' יוסי הגלילי ור' עקיבא עם הברייתא בתראה דהיא דברי ר' עקיבא אשכחנן במס' דמנחות בפ' הקומץ את המנחה (לו) ואשכחנן עוד בגמ' דלא תצא אשה במחט נקובה (לקמן סב) אקשייה אביי לרב יוסף מדברי הברייתא ואותביה רב יוסף התם קסבר ר"מ לילה זמן תפילין ושבת זמן תפילין: מוחיב

גליון הש"ס

תוס' ד"ה דילמא מיפסקי וכו' אלא של ראש משום שי"ן. עי' מנחות דף לה ע"ב תוס' ד"ה אלו תפילין:

גמרא

הא יש ברגלו מכה נפיק בהי מינייהו נפיק אמר רב הונא באותה שיש בה מכה אלמא קסבר סנדל לשום צער עביד וחייא בר רב אמר [א] באותה שאין בה מכה אלמא קסבר לשום תענוג עביד וזו שיש בה מכה מכתה מוכחת עליה ואף רבי יוחנן סבר לה להא דרב הונא דאמר ליה ר' יוחנן לרב שמן בר אבא הב לי מסנאי יהב ליה דימין אמר ליה עשיתו מכה ודילמא כחייא בר רב ס"ל והכי קאמר עשית של שמאל מכה ואזדא רבי יוחנן לטעמיה דאמר ר' יוחנן כתפילין כך מנעלין מה תפילין בשמאל אף מנעלין בשמאל מיתיבי כשהוא נועל נועל של ימין ואחר כך נועל של שמאל אמר רב יוסף השתא דתניא הכי ואמר רבי יוחנן הכי דעבד הכי עבד ודעבד הכי עבד אמר ליה אביי דילמא רבי יוחנן הא מתני' [א] לא הוה שמיע ליה ואי הוה שמיע ליה הוה הדר ביה ואי נמי שמיע ליה וקסבר אין הלכה כאותה משנה [ג] אמר רב נחמן בר יצחק ירא שמים יוצא ידי שתיהן ומנו מר בריה דרבנא [ב] היכי עביד סיים דימיניה ולא קטר וסיים דשמאליה וקטר והדר קטר דימיניה אמר רב אשי חזינא לרב כהנא דלא קפיד תנו רבנן [ג] כשהוא נועל נועל של ימין ואחר כך נועל של שמאל [ג] כשהוא חולץ חולץ של שמאל ואח"כ חולץ של ימין [ד] כשהוא רוחץ רוחץ של ימין ואח"כ רוחץ של שמאל כשהוא סך סך של ימין ואח"כ של שמאל והרוצה לסוך כל גופו סך ראשו תחילה מפני שהוא מלך על כל איבריו: [ה] ולא בתפילין: אמר רב ספרא לא תימא אליבא דמ"ד [ד] שבת לאו זמן תפילין הוא אלא אפילו למ"ד שבת זמן תפילין הוא לא יצא דילמא אתי לאיתויי ברה"ר ואיכא דמתני לה אסיפא ואם יצא אינו חייב חטאת אמר רב ספרא לא תימא אליבא דמ"ד [ה] שבת זמן תפילין הוא אלא אפילו למ"ד שבת לאו זמן תפילין הוא אינו חייב חטאת מ"ט דרך מלבוש עבידא: [ו] ולא בקמיע בזמן שאינו מן המומחה: אמר רב פפא [ז] לא תימא עד דמומחה גברא ומומחה קמיע אלא כיון דמומחה גברא אף על גב דלא מומחה קמיע דיקא נמי דקתני ולא בקמיע בזמן שאינו מן המומחה ולא קתני בזמן שאינו מומחה ש"מ: [ח] ת"ר [ו] איזהו קמיע מומחה כל שריפא ושנה ושלש אחד קמיע של כתב ואחד קמיע של עיקרין אחד חולה שיש בו סכנה ואחד חולה שאין בו סכנה לא שנכפה אלא שלא יכפה וקושר ומתיר אפילו ברה"ר ובלבד שלא יקשרנו

בשיר

רש"י

הא יש ברגלו מכה. איכא למידק דנפיק ביחיד והשתא בעי תלמודא בהי מרגליו נפיק: סנדל לשם צער עביד. שלא ינגף ביתדות הדרכים ויצטער הילכך כשרואין אותו נועל ויודעין שיש ברגליו מכה אין חושדין אותו שטוען את השני בידו אלא מכירין בו לפי מעשיו שפרסותיו קשות ואינו מצטער ביתדות הדרכים ולא נועלו אלא משום מכה ודיו בזה לבדו וללשון רבותי אי נמי מחכו עלה דלא חזו למכה לא שליף לה דמצטער ביתדות הדרכים מחמת המכה: לשום תענוג עביד. אדם איסטניס ורך ומכירין מתוך מעשיו שנעל נעלו אחת שהוא איסטניס וזו מכתה מוכחת עלה ומבינין שהמכה מונעתו מלנעול ולא חשדי ליה ולענין אחוכי נמי לא מחייכי עליה: עשיתו מכה. ורבי יוחנן סבירא ליה דהנועל סנדלים נועל של שמאל תחילה ואח"כ של ימין וקס"ד דהכי קאמר ליה א"כ שאנעול זה שוב לא אנעול של שמאל אחריו והנני יוצא ביחיד ועשית את זו של ימין כאילו היתה בה מכה אלמא קסבר באותה שיש בה מכה נועל: ודילמא כר' חייא סבירא ליה. דאמר באותה שאין בה מכה נועל והכי קאמר ליה א"כ הריני יוצא ביחיד בזו של ימין ועשית את רגלי של שמאל כאילו יש בה מכה דאלא ביחיד באותה שאין בה מכה: ואזדא ר' יוחנן. דאמר עשית מכה דשמעינן מינה דאי הוה נעיל דימין ברישא תו לא הוה נעיל דשמאל בתריה לטעמיה דאמר דשמאל חשיבא: תפילין בשמאל. כדילפינן במנחות (דף לז.) מעל ידכה מלא יד כהה דהיינו שמאל שהיא כהה לענין תשמיש: הוה הדר ביה. ולא עבדינן כר' יוחנן: אין הלכה. וכרבי יוחנן בעינן למעבד: יוצא ידי שניהם. עביד כתרוייהו: וסיים דשמאליה וקטר. נמצא נעילת ימין קודמת לשמאל כי מתניתא וקשירת שמאל לשל ימין כר' יוחנן: חולץ של שמאל. דזהו כבודו של ימין בכולהו גרסינן של ימין ברישא חוץ מחולץ: לא תימא כו'. בפרק בתרא דעירובין (ד' צה:) מייתינן פלוגתייהו בגמרא: דילמא. שקיל להו מרישא אם בא לפנות וממטי להו ד' אמות: דמומחה גברא ומומחה קמיע. שעשה אדם זה קמיע זו לג' אנשים דנעשה אדם זה מומחה שריפא ג' אנשים והקמיע מומחה שריפא כתב זה ג' אנשים א"נ שכתב אדם זה ג' מיני קמיעים של ג' מיני חלאים לג' אנשים היינו איתמחי גברא בכל קמיעים שיעשה לעולם ומומחה קמיעה שנעשית [קמיע זו] לג' אנשים מחולי זה בין שכתבה רופא זה בין שכתבה רופא אחר נעשה הקמיע מומחה: אלא כיון דאיתמחי גברא. בג' מיני קמיעות לג' בני אדם אע"ג דלא איתמחי קמיע שלא ריפא קמיע זה אדם מעולם: מן המומחה. משמע מאדם מומחה: ולא קתני בזמן שאינו מומחה. דליהוו משמע דקפיד אמומחה קמיע עצמו. קמיע אינו אלא לשון קשר ודעיקרין של שרשי סממנין נמי קרוין קמיע: ולא שנכפה. כלומר לא תימא דלא יצא אלא מי שבא עליו החולי כבר פעם אחת: נכפה. היינו חולי שאדם נופל מחמתו לארץ ומכהו בראשו במוחו ומפילו: אלא שלא יכפה. שבא ממשפחת נכפין ודואג שלא יכפה:

בשיר

תוספות

דעבד הכי עבד. פירוש דברייתא לא פליגא ארבי יוחנן ולא ר' יוחנן אברייתא וה"פ כתפילין אע"ג דימין חשובה לענין בהן יד ובהן רגל וכן לענין חליצה יכול לנעול של שמאל תחילה ברייתא נמי קמ"ל דאע"ג דשמאל חשובה לתפילין יכול לנעול של ימין תחילה וא"ת א"כ אמאי הקפיד רבי יוחנן על רב שמן שנתן לו של ימין כיון דיכול לנעול איזה שירצה תחילה ונראה לר"י דה"פ דעבד הכי עבד מי שרוצה לחבב של שמאל משום מצות תפילין הרשות בידו ומי שרוצה לחבב של ימין יותר משום חשיבות של ימין הרשות בידו ורבי יוחנן היה דרכו לחבב כל שעה של שמאל יותר ורב שמן בר אבא (לא) היה יודע מנהגו: **וסיים** דשמאליה וקטר. אומר ריב"א דדוקא לענין קשירה הוא דחשיבא של שמאל טפי משום דחשיבות תפילין הוא בקשירה אבל איפכא לא ולהאי טעמא יש לנעול של ימין תחלה במנעלים שאין בהן קשירה: **דילמא** מיפסקי ואתי לאתויינהו ד' אמות ברה"ר. קשה לר"י דאפילו לא חיישינן דילמא מיפסקו אסור משום דזימנין דאיצטריך לבה"כ ואתי לאתויינהו ד"א ברה"ר דהכי אמר לקמן גבי קמיע ומתוך פי' הקונטרס משמע דלא גרס דילמא מיפסקו ופי' דילמא שקיל להו מרישא אם בא ליפנות והקדוש מקורביי"ל אומר דגרסינן לה שפיר ואיצטריך טעמא דמיפסקו לתפילין של יד דאין צריך לחלוץ כשצריך ° לבה"כ אלא של ראש משום שי"ן: **עד** דמימחי גברא ומימחי קמיע. נראה לר"י שאם כתב לאדם אחד בשלש איגרות וריפאו שלשתן ג' בני אדם כל אחד אדם אחד היינו מומחי גברי וכאשר רפאו שלשתן אדם אחד בעיא היא בסמוך אי מימחי גברא או לא ודוקא לאותו לחש הוא מומחה אבל לשאר לחשים לא ודוקא שכתבם הוא אבל אחר לא ואם כל אחת מאיגרות ריפא שלש פעמים אפילו אדם אחד מומחות שלשתן ואין הלחש מומחה כל מקום שהוא אלא דווקא איגרת לבדה שהומחת והיינו מומחה גברא ומומחה קמיע שקמיע זה הומחה שריפא שלש פעמים וכתבו אדם מומחה שכתב שלשה קמיעין והועילו שלשתן: **אע"ג** דלא מימחי קמיע. נראה דכל שכן מימחי קמיע ולא גברא שהמחאת קמיע עדיפא מהמחאת הרופא כדמוכח לקמן דבהמחאת קמיע פשיטא ליה דאיתמחי אפילו בחד גברא ובאיתמחי גברא מספקא ליה אי איתמחי בתלת קמיע לחד גברא אי לא: **אע"ג** דלא מימחי קמיע. קשה לרשב"א היכי משכחת לה דאתמחי גברא ולא קמיע כיון שהאיש מומחה לכתוב לחש זה א"כ אגרת זו שכתב ודאי תועיל ואומר ר"י דנ"מ שאם אבדה מאאתו שכתב ג' קמיעים ולא הועילו אם הומחה הקמיע מועיל אפילו אבד אדם מאאתו: **ולא** קתני בזמן שאינו מומחה. קשה לרשב"א דילמא לעולם בעינן תרוייהו ואי הוה תני הכי הוה משמע מומחה קמיע ולא גברא וי"ל דאינו מומחה משמע שפיר בין אגברא בין אקמיע דהא לקמן תניא איזהו קמיע מומחה כו' ומוקמינן לה לאמחויי גברא:

כל

עין משפט נר מצוה

לב א מיי' פי"ט מהל' שבת הלכה טו סמג לאוין סה טוש"ע א"ח סי' שא סעיף ז:
לג ב טוש"ע א"ח סי' ב סעיף ד:
לד ג שם סעיף ה:
לה ד טוש"ע א"ח סי' ד סעיף י:
לו ה מיי' פי"ט מהל' שבת הלכה יד סמג לאוין סה טוש"ע א"ח סי' שא סעיף ז:
לז ו ז ח מיי' וסמג שם טוש"ע א"ח שם סעיף כה:

רבינו חננאל

סוגיא כחייא בר רב דאמר נועל הרגל (עראי) [שאין] בה הכאה. כי הרגל שיש בה הכאה המכה מוכחת עליה. א) דר' יוחנן קאי כוותיה הלא תראה כיון שהביא לו רב שמן בר אבא הסנדל של ימין והיה ראוי לו [להביא] של שמאל שהדין לנעול השמאל תחלה אמר לו עשיתה השמאל מכה ואמרת בדעתך כיון שהשמאל מוכה אין לה נעילת סנדל לפיכך הבאתה לי של ימין ש"מ דסבר ר' יוחנן כי מי שאין עליה מכה היא שיש בה נעילת סנדל. ומי שיש בה מכה היא נשארת יחיפה. ואזדא ר' יוחנן לטעמיה דאמר כתפילין מה תפילין בשמאל אף מנעל בשמאל. ואסקא רב אשי דזמנין חזינא לרב כהנא דנועל של שמאל תחלה ואח"כ של ימין וזמנין חזינא דנועל של ימין תחלה ואח"כ של שמאל. ולא קפיד וקיי"ל כוותיה דרב אשי דהוא בתרא: **ולא** בתפילין ואם יצא אינו חייב חטאת. אסיקא לישנא בתרא. אמר רב ספרא לא תימא מתניתין דקתני אם יצא אינו חייב חטאת אליבא דמאן דאמר שבת זמן תפילין היא אלא אפילו למ"ד שבת לאו זמן תפילין הוא חיוב חטאת ליכא מ"ט דרך מלבוש עבידן. והוצאה דרך מלבוש אינו חייב ומפורש בפרק אחרון דעירובין: **ולא בקמיע** בזמן שאינו מן המומחה. אוקמה רב פפא אי אתמחי גברא אע"ג דלא אתמחי קמיעא שרי למיפק ביה בשבת ודייק ממתניתין דקתני בזמן שאינו מן המומחה ולא קתני בזמן שאינו (מן המומחה) [מומחה] הקמיע עצמו.

חשק שלמה על רבינו חננאל

א) נראה מזה כי רבינו הי' לו גירסא אחרת בסוגיא דר"י ע"כ ס"ל כחייא בר רב וצ"ע:

ליקוטי רש"י

לא הוה שמיע ליה. שאין הכל בקיאין בברייתא וגם האמורא עצמו זימנין דלא ידע לה [רשב"ם פסחים קא:]. **דרך מלבוש עבידא.** משום דתכשיט הוא לגביה ולאו משאוי [עירובין צה:]. **נכפה.** חולי שממנו נופל לארץ ויש לו זמן לבא [כתובות עז.].

וְלֹא בְקָמֵיעַ בִּזְמַן שֶׁאֵינוֹ מִן הַמּוּמְחֶה – AND he may NOT go out WITH AN AMULET AS LONG AS IT IS NOT *FROM* AN EXPERT – וְלָא קָתָנֵי – **and it did not teach** that the amulet may not be worn בִּזְמַן שֶׁאֵינוֹ מוּמְחֶה – **"as long as it is not** proven **effective."** The phrasing used by the Mishnah indicates that if the amulet was *from* an expert, this is sufficient reason to permit one to wear it, even if the amulet itself is not proven.[37] שְׁמַע מִינָּהּ – Indeed, **derive from this** that any amulet written by an expert may be worn.

The Gemara cites a Baraisa that identifies the "effective amulet" which one may wear on the Sabbath:

תָּנוּ רַבָּנָן – **The Rabbis taught in a Baraisa:** אֵיזֶהוּ קָמֵיעַ מוּמְחֶה – WHICH AMULET IS considered AN EFFECTIVE AMULET? כֹּל שֶׁרִיפֵּא וְשָׁנָה וְשִׁלֵּשׁ – ANY amulet THAT HAS CURED an illness one time, AND CURED the same illness AGAIN, AND CURED the same illness A THIRD TIME.[38] אֶחָד קָמֵיעַ שֶׁל כְּתָב וְאֶחָד קָמֵיעַ שֶׁל עִיקָּרִין – It can be EITHER AN AMULET OF WRITING OR AN AMULET OF ROOTS of herbs.[39] אֶחָד חוֹלֶה שֶׁיֵּשׁ בּוֹ סַכָּנָה – It may be worn EITHER BY A DANGEROUSLY ILL PERSON וְאֶחָד חוֹלֶה שֶׁאֵין בּוֹ סַכָּנָה – OR BY ONE WHO IS NOT DANGEROUSLY ILL.[40] לֹא שֶׁנִּכְפָּה – Its use is NOT restricted to ONE THAT HAS ALREADY FALLEN[41] due to disease; אֶלָּא שֶׁלֹּא יִכָּפֶה – RATHER, one may wear it SO THAT HE DOES NOT FALL.[42] וְקוֹשֵׁר וּמַתִּיר אֲפִילּוּ בִּרְשׁוּת הָרַבִּים – AND HE MAY TIE IT AND UNTIE IT EVEN while he is IN THE PUBLIC DOMAIN;[43] וּבִלְבַד שֶׁלֹּא יִקְשְׁרֶנּוּ – AND this is so AS LONG AS HE DOES NOT TIE IT

NOTES

37. If the Mishnah had written that the amulet may not be worn "as long as it is not expert," we might have translated this to mean that both the amulet *and* the healer must be proven, for both of these requirements are indicated by the expression "as long as it is not expert." Since the Mishnah chose instead to teach that wearing the amulet is forbidden as long as it is not *from* an expert, we see that if the healer is a proven expert, this alone is sufficient (see *Tosafos* and *Shabbos Shel Mi*).

38. [Initially, the Gemara (on 61b) assumes that the Baraisa is teaching only that the amulet is expert even if it cured one person three times (see *Rashi* to 61b ד״ה והתניא; cf. *Tosafos* there ד״ה כל); see Gemara there, where this is discussed further.]

39. [The word קָמֵיעַ literally means *bundle* or *packet;* thus it can refer equally to a piece of parchment or to a packet of herbs (see *Rashi*).]

40. [Even a person who is not dangerously ill considers the amulet as part of his attire; thus, he too may go out while wearing it.] See *Meiri* (to 61b), who discusses why amulets were not forbidden under the general Rabbinic prohibition against healing on the Sabbath.

41. I.e. one who already suffers from a disease [as an example, the Gemara uses the disease of epilepsy, whose fits cause one to fall to the ground] and must be cured (*Rashi*).

42. Even a person who has never suffered from a disease, but has reason to believe that he may be predisposed to the disease (e.g. he comes from a family with a history of epilepsy), may wear the amulet on the Sabbath as a preventive measure [as he too will not remove it] (see *Rashi*).

43. See *Tosafos* to 57a ד״ה במה, who explain why we are not concerned that he will carry the amulet.

גמרא

הא יש ברגלו מכה נפיק בהי מינייהו נפיק אמר רב הונא באותה שיש בה מכה אלמא קסבר סנדל לשום צער עביד וחייא בר רב אמר [א] באותה שאין בה מכה אלמא קסבר לשום תענוג עביד וזו שיש בה מכה מכתה מוכחת עליה ואף רבי יוחנן סבר לה להא דרב הונא דאמר ליה ר' יוחנן לרב שמן בר אבא הב לי מסנאי יהב ליה דימין אמר ליה עשיתו מכה ודילמא כחייא בר רב ס"ל והכי קאמר עשית של שמאל מכה ואזדא רבי יוחנן לטעמיה דאמר ר' יוחנן כתפילין כך מנעלין מה תפילין בשמאל אף מנעלין בשמאל מיתיבי כשהוא נועל נועל של ימין ואחר כך נועל של שמאל אמר רב יוסף השתא דתניא הכי ואמר רבי יוחנן הכי דעבד הכי עבד ודעבד הכי עבד אמר ליה אביי דילמא רבי יוחנן הא מתני' [א] לא הוה שמיע ליה ואי הוה שמיע ליה הוה הדר ביה ואי נמי שמיע ליה וקסבר אין הלכה כאותה משנה [ב] אמר רב נחמן בר יצחק ירא שמים יוצא ידי שתיהן ומנו מר בריה דרבנא [ב] היכי עביד סיים דימיניה ולא קטר וסיים דשמאליה וקטר והדר קטר דימיניה אמר רב אשי חזינא לרב כהנא דלא קפיד תנו רבנן [ג] כשהוא נועל נועל של ימין ואחר כך נועל של שמאל [ג] כשהוא חולץ חולץ של שמאל ואח"כ חולץ של ימין [ד] כשהוא רוחץ רוחץ של ימין ואח"כ רוחץ של שמאל כשהוא סך סך של ימין ואח"כ של שמאל והרוצה לסוך כל גופו סך ראשו תחילה מפני שהוא מלך על כל איבריו: [ה] ולא בתפילין: אמר רב ספרא לא תימא אליבא דמ"ד [ד] שבת לאו זמן תפילין הוא אלא אפילו למ"ד שבת זמן תפילין הוא לא יצא דילמא אתי לאיתויי ברה"ר ואיכא דמתני לה אסיפא ואם יצא אינו חייב חטאת אמר רב ספרא לא תימא אליבא דמ"ד [ה] שבת זמן תפילין הוא אלא אפילו למ"ד שבת לאו זמן תפילין הוא אינו חייב חטאת מ"ט דרך מלבוש עבידא: [ו] ולא בקמיע בזמן שאינו מן המומחה: אמר רב פפא [ז] לא תימא עד דמומחה גברא ומומחה קמיע אלא כיון דמומחה גברא אף על גב דלא מומחה קמיע דיקא נמי דקתני ולא בקמיע בזמן שאינו מן המומחה ולא קתני בזמן שאינו מומחה ש"מ: [ח] ת"ר [ו] איזהו קמיע מומחה כל שריפא ושנה ושלש אחד קמיע של כתב ואחד קמיע של עיקרין אחד חולה שיש בו סכנה ואחד חולה שאין בו סכנה לא שנכפה אלא שלא יכפה וקושר ומתיר אפילו ברה"ר ובלבד שלא יקשרנו

בשיר

רש"י

הא יש ברגלו מכה. איכא למידק דנפיק ביחיד והשתא בעי תלמודא בהי מרגליו נפיק: סנדל לשם צער עביד. שלא ינגף ביתדות הדרכים וילטער הילך כשרואין אותו צולע ויודעין שיש ברגליו מכה אין חושדין אותו שטוען את השני בידו אלא מכירין בו לפי מעשיו שפרסותיו קשות ואינו מצטער ביתדות הדרכים ולא נועלו אלא משום מכה ודיו בזה לבדו וללשון רבותי אי נמי מחכו עלה דלא חזו למכה לא שליף לה דמצטער ביתדות הדרכים מחמת המכה: לשום תענוג עביד. אדם איסטניס ורך ומכירין מתוך מעשיו שנעל נעלו אחת שהוא איסטניס וזו מכתה מוכחת עלה ומבינין שהמכה מונעתו מלנעול ולא חשדי ליה ולענין אחוכי נמי לא מחייכי עליה: עשיתו מכה. ורבי יוחנן סבירא ליה דהנועל סנדלים נועל של שמאל תחילה ואח"כ של ימין וקס"ד דהכי קאמר ליה א"כ שאנעול זה שוב לא אנעול של שמאל אחריו והנני יוצא ביחיד ועשית את זו של ימין כאילו היתה בה מכה אלמא קסבר באותה שיש בה מכה נועל: ודילמא כר' חייא סבירא ליה. דאמר באותה שאין בה מכה נועל והכי קאמר ליה א"כ הריני יוצא ביחיד בזו של ימין ועשית את רגלי של שמאל כאילו יש בה מכה דאלא ביחיד באותה שאין בה מכה: ואזדא ר' יוחנן. דאמר עשית מכה דשמעינן מינה דאי הוה נעיל דימין ברישא תו לא הוה נעיל דשמאל בתריה לטעמיה דאמר דשמאל חשיבא: תפילין בשמאל. כדילפינן במנחות (דף לז.) מעל ידכה מלא יד כהה דהיינו שמאל שהיא כהה לענין תשמיש: הוה הדר ביה. ולא עבדינן כר' יוחנן: אין הלכה. וכרבי יוחנן בעינן למעבד: יוצא ידי שניהם. עביד כתרוייהו: וסיים דשמאליה וקטר. נמצא נעילת ימין קודמת לשמאל כי מתניתא וקשירת שמאל לשל ימין כר' יוחנן: חולץ של שמאל. דזהו כבודו של ימין בכולהו גרסינן של ימין ברישא חוץ מחולץ: לא תימא כו'. בפרק בתרא דעירובין (ד' צה:) מייתינן פלוגתייהו בגמרא: דילמא. שקיל להו מרישא אם בא לפנות וממטי להו ד' אמות: דמומחה גברא ומומחה קמיע. שעשה אדם זה קמיע זו לג' אנשים דנעשה אדם זה מומחה שריפא ג' אנשים והקמיע מומחה שריפא כתב זה ג' אנשים א"נ שכתב אדם זה ג' מיני קמיעים של ג' מיני חלאים לג' אנשים היינו איתמחי גברא בכל קמיעים שיעשה לעולם ומומחה קמיעה שנעשית [קמיע זו] לג' אנשים מחולי זה בין שכתבה רופא זה בין שכתבה רופא אחר נעשה הקמיע מומחה: אלא כיון דאיתמחי גברא. בג' מיני קמיעות לג' בני אדם אע"ג דלא איתמחי קמיע שלא ריפא קמיע זה אדם מעולם: מן המומחה. משמע מאדם מומחה: ולא קתני בזמן שאינו מומחה. דליהוו משמע דקפיד אמומחה קמיע עצמו. קמיע אינו אלא לשון קשר ודעיקרין של שרשי סממנין נמי קרויין קמיע: ולא שנכפה. כלומר לא תימא דלא יצא אלא מי שבא עליו החולי כבר פעם אחת: נכפה. היינו חולי שאדם נופל מחמתו לארץ ומכהו בראשו במוחו ומפילו: אלא שלא יכפה. שבא ממשפחת נכפין ודואג שלא יכפה:

בשיר

תוספות

דעבד הכי עבד. פירוש דברייתא לא פליגא ארבי יוחנן ולא ר' יוחנן אברייתא וה"פ כתפילין אע"ג דימין חשובה לענין בהן יד ובהן רגל וכן לענין חליצה יכול לנעול של שמאל תחילה ברייתא נמי קמ"ל דאע"ג דשמאל חשובה לתפילין יכול לנעול של ימין תחילה וא"ת א"כ אמאי הקפיד רבי יוחנן על רב שמן שנתן לו של ימין כיון דיכול לנעול איזה שירצה תחילה ונראה לר"י דה"פ דעבד הכי עבד מי שרוצה לחבב של שמאל משום מצות תפילין הרשות בידו ומי שרוצה לחבב של ימין יותר משום חשיבות של ימין הרשות בידו ורבי יוחנן היה דרכו לחבב כל שעה של שמאל יותר ורב שמן בר אבא (לא) היה יודע מנהגו:

וסיים דשמאליה וקטר. אומר ריב"א דדוקא לענין קשירה הוא דחשיבא של שמאל טפי משום דחשיבות תפילין הוא בקשירה אבל איפכא לא ולהאי טעמא יש לנעול של ימין תחלה במנעלים שאין בהן קשירה:

דילמא מיפסקי ואתי לאתוייניהו ד' אמות ברה"ר. קשה לר"י דאפילו לא חיישינן דילמא מיפסקו אסור משום דזימנין דאיצטריך לבה"כ ואתי לאתוייניהו ד"א ברה"ר דהכי אמר לקמן גבי קמיע ומתוך פי' הקונטרס משמע דלא גרס דילמא מיפסקו ופי' דילמא שקיל להו מרישיה אם בא ליפנות והקדוש מקורבי"ל אומר דגרסינן לה שפיר ואיצטריך טעמא דמיפסקו לתפילין של יד דאין צריך לחלוץ כשנצריך ° לבה"כ אלא של ראש משום ש"ן:

עד דמימחי גברא ומימחי קמיע. נראה לר"י שאם כתב לחש אחד בשלש איגרות וריפאו שלשתן ג' בני אדם כל אחד אדם אחד היינו מומחי גברי וכאשר רפאו שלשתן אדם אחד בעיא היא בסמוך אי מימחי גברא או לא ודוקא לאותו לחש הוא מומחה אבל לשאר לחשים לא ודוקא שכתבם הוא אבל אחר לא ואם כל אחת מאיגרות ריפא שלש פעמים אפילו אדם אחד מומחות שלשתן ואין הלחש מומחה כל מקום שהוא אלא דווקא איגרת לבדה שהומחת והיינו מומחה גברא ומומחה קמיע שקמיע זה הומחה שריפא שלש פעמים וכתבו אדם מומחה שכתב שלשה קמיעין והועילו שלשתן:

אע"ג דלא מימחי קמיע. נראה דכל שכן מימחי קמיע ולא גברא שהמחאת קמיע עדיפא מהמחאת הרופא כדמוכח לקמן דבהמחאת קמיע פשיטא ליה דאיתמחי אפילו בחד גברא ובאיתמחי גברא מספקא ליה אי איתמחי בתלת קמיע לחד גברא אי לא:

אע"ג דלא מימחי קמיע. קשה לרשב"א היכי משכחת לה דאתמחי גברא ולא קמיע כיון שהאיש מומחה לכתוב לחש זה א"כ אגרת זו שכתב ודאי תועיל ואומר ר"י דנ"מ שאם אבדה מחאתו שכתב ג' קמיעים ולא הועילו אם הומחה הקמיע מועיל אפילו אבד אדם מחאתו:

ולא קתני בזמן שאינו מומחה. קשה לרשב"א דילמא לעולם בעינן תרוייהו ואי הוה תני הכי הוה משמע מומחה קמיע ולא גברא וי"ל דאינו מומחה משמע שפיר בין אגברא בין אקמיע דהא לקמן תניא איזהו קמיע מומחה כו' ומוקמינן לה לאמחויי גברא:

כל

עין משפט נר מצוה

לב א מיי' פי"ט מהל' שבת הלכה טו סמג לאוין סה טוש"ע א"ח סי' שא סעיף ז:
לג ב טוש"ע א"ח סי' ב סעיף ד:
לד ג שם סעיף ה:
לה ד טוש"ע א"ח סי' ד סעיף י:
לו ה מיי' פי"ט מהל' שבת הלכה יד סמג לאוין סה טוש"ע א"ח סי' שא סעיף ז:
לז ו ז ח מיי' וסמג שם טוש"ע א"ח שם סעיף כה:

רבינו חננאל

סוגיא כחייא בר רב דאמר נועל הרגל (עראי) [שאין] בה הכאה. כי הרגל שיש בה הכאה המכה מוכחת עליה. א) דר' יוחנן קאי כוותיה הלא תראה כיון שהביא לו רב שמן בר אבא הסנדל של ימין והיה ראוי לו [להביא] של שמאל שהדין לנעול השמאל תחלה אמר לו עשיתה השמאל מכה ואמרת בדעתך כיון שהשמאל מוכה אין לה נעילת סנדל לפיכך הבאתה לי של ימין ש"מ דסבר ר' יוחנן כי מי שאין עליה מכה היא שיש בה נעילת סנדל. ומי שיש בה מכה היא נשארת יחיפה. ואזדא ר' יוחנן לטעמיה דאמר כתפילין מה תפילין בשמאל אף מנעל בשמאל. ואסקא רב אשי דזמנין חזינא לרב כהנא דנועל של שמאל תחלה ואח"כ של ימין וזמנין חזינא דנועל של ימין תחלה ואח"כ של שמאל. ולא קפיד וקיי"ל כוותיה דרב אשי דהוא בתרא: ולא בתפילין ואם יצא אינו חייב חטאת. אסיקא לישנא בתרא. אמר רב ספרא לא תימא מתניתין דקתני אם יצא אינו חייב חטאת אליבא דמאן דאמר שבת זמן תפילין היא אלא אפילו למ"ד שבת לאו זמן תפילין הוא חיוב חטאת ליכא מ"ט דרך מלבוש עבידן. והוצאה דרך מלבוש אינו חייב ומפורש בפרק אחרון דעירובין: ולא בקמיע בזמן שאינו מן המומחה. אוקמה רב פפא אי אתמחי גברא אע"ג דלא אתמחי קמיעא שרי למיפק ביה בשבת ודייק ממתניתין דקתני בזמן שאינו מן המומחה ולא קתני בזמן שאינו (מן המומחה) [מומחה] הקמיע עצמו.

חשק שלמה על רבינו חננאל

א) נראה מזה כי רבינו הי' לו גירסא אחרת בסוגיא דר"י ע"כ ס"ל כחייא בר רב ול"ע:

ליקוטי רש"י

לא הוה שמיע ליה. שאין הכל בקיאין בברייתא וגם האמורא עצמו זימנין דלא ידע לה [רשב"ם פסחים קא:]. **דרך מלבוש עבידא.** משום דתכשיט הוא לגביה ולאו משאוי [עירובין צה:]. **נכפה.** חולי שממנו נופל לארץ ויש לו זמן לבא [כתובות עז:].

מסורת הש"ס

א) [לעיל דף יט: וש"נ], ב) [ברכות לט:], ג) [מס' ד"א פ"י], ד) [עירובין צה: צו. מנחות לו:], ה) [שם ולקמן סב.], ו) [תוספתא פ"ה].

רב נסים גאון

אבא מפני החשד שלא יהו אומרים איש פלוני נפסק סנדלו ותלאו בבית שחיו: **אמר** רב ספרא לא תימא אליבא דמאן דאמר שבת לאו זמן תפילין הוא וכו'. משתכח עיקר דילה במס' עירובין בפרק המוצא תפילין (דף צו) דתניא ושמרת את החקה הזאת למועדה מימים ימימה ימים ולא לילות מימים ולא כל הימים פרט לשבתות ולימים טובים דברי ר' יוסי הגלילי ור' עקיבא כר' יוסי הגלילי סבירא ליה דאמר שבת לאו זמן תפילין הוא כמו שאמרה הברייתא דתניא ר' עקיבא אומר יכול יניח אדם תפילין בשבתות וימים טובים ת"ל והיה לך לאות על ידך מי שצריכין אות יצאו שבתות וימים טובים שהן גופן אות וחקרו בתלמוד לידע איזה תנא דקסבר שבת לאו זמן תפילין ונשאו ונתנו בדבר זה הרבה עד שקיימו כי הוא ר' מאיר כדאמרינן בסיפא אלא האי תנא הוא דתניא המוצא תפילין מכניסן זוג זוג אחד איש ואחד אשה כו' עד כאן לא פליגי אלא בחדשות ובישנות אבל באשה לא פליגי דקסברי תפילין מצות עשה שלא הזמן גרמא הוא ונשים חייבות ומכלל דבריהם למדנו שר' מאיר ור' יהודה סברי שבת זמן תפילין הוא ועל דעת מי שסבר שבת לאו זמן תפילין הוא הויא לה מצות עשה שהזמן גרמא לפי שהיא נוהגת בחול בלבד ואלו שחייבו הנשים בה סברו כי חובתה נוהגת בכל עת ואינה מיוחדת בזמן ידוע ובפ' האשה נקנית (קידושין לה) אמרו מאן שמעת ליה דאמר תפילין מצות עשה שלא הזמן גרמא ר' מאיר היא ואמרו עוד ולר' יהודה דאמר ב' כתובין הבאין כאחד מלמדין ותפילין מצות עשה שלא הזמן גרמא הוא מי איכא למימר זה הברייתא דפליגו בה ר' יוסי הגלילי ור' עקיבא עם הברייתא בתראה דהיא במס' דמנחות בפ' הקומץ את המנחה (לו) ואשכחנן עוד בגמ' דלא תצא אשה במחט נקובה (לקמן סב) אקשיה אביי לרב יוסף מדברי הברייתא ואותביה רב יוסף התם קסבר ר"מ לילה זמן תפילין ושבת זמן תפילין:

מותיב

גליון הש"ס

תוס' ד"ה דילמא מיפסקי וכו' אלא של ראש משום ש"ן. עי' מנחות דף לה ע"ב תוס' ד"ה אלו תפילין:

בשיר ובטבעת ויצא בו ברשות הרבים משום מראית העין והתניא איזהו קמיע מומחה כל שריפא ג' בני אדם כאחד לא קשיא הא למחויי גברא הא למחויי קמיעא אמר רב פפא פשיטא לי תלת קמיע לתלת גברי תלתא תלתא זימני איתמחי גברא א) ואתמחי קמיע תלתא קמיע לתלתא גברי חד חד זימנא גברא איתמחי קמיעא לא איתמחי חד קמיע לתלתא גברי קמיעא איתמחי גברא לא איתמחי בעי רב פפא תלתא קמיע לחד גברא מאי קמיעא ודאי לא איתמחי גברא איתמחי או לא איתמחי מי אמרינן הא אסי ליה או דילמא א מזלא דהאי גברא הוא דקא מקבל כתבא תיקו: איבעיא להו קמיעין יש בהן משום קדושה או דילמא אין בהן משום קדושה למאי הילכתא אילימא לאצולינהו מפני הדליקה ת"ש א) הברכות והקמיעין אע"פ שיש בהן אותיות ומענינות הרבה שבתורה אין מצילין אותן מפני הדליקה ונשרפים במקומן אלא לענין גניזה ג) ת"ש היה ב כתוב על ידות הכלים ועל כרעי המטה ג) יגוד ויגנזנו אלא ליכנס בהן בבית הכסא מאי יש בהן קדושה ואסיר או דילמא אין בהן קדושה ושרי ת"ש ולא בקמיע בזמן שאינו מן המומחה הא מן המומחה נפיק ואי אמרת קמיעין יש בהן משום קדושה זמנין דמיצטריך לבית הכסא ואתי לאיתויינהו ד' אמות ברה"ר הכא במאי עסקינן בקמיע של עיקרין והתניא אחד קמיע של כתב ואחד קמיע של עיקרין אלא הכא במאי עסקינן בחולה שיש בו סכנה והתניא אחד חולה שיש בו סכנה ואחד חולה שאין בו סכנה אלא כיון דמסי אף על גב דנקיט ליה בידיה נמי שפיר דמי

והתניא

בשיר. אלעדה: מפני מראית העין. דלא מיחזי כמאן דבעי ליה לרפואה אלא לתכשיט ולאו תכשיט הוא אלא מחמת דאגת חולי: והתניא כל שריפא ג' בני אדם. ולעיל קתני כל שריפא ושנה ושילש ואפילו אדם אחד: הא לאמחויי גברא כו'. הא דקתני ג' בני אדם משום דקתם ג' בני אדם שלשה מיני חלאים ואיירי בג' מיני קמיעין שאינן דומין זה לזה ולאמחויי גברא שנעשה מומחה בכל קמיעים שיעשה לעולם כדאמרינן בב"ק (דף לז.) נגח שור וחמור וגמל נעשה מועד לכל אבל הקמיע אינו מומחה אם יכתוב רופא אחר אחד מהן: והא. דקתני כל שריפא ושנה ושילש מיירי בחולי אחד וכתבו זה הלחש וריפא ג' פעמים או לאדם אחד או לשלשה ולאיתמחויי קמיעא מיירי דנעשה הקמיע לבדו מומחה על יד אדם זה או אם כתבוס שלשה רופאים נעשה קמיע של לחש זה מומחה מיד כל אדם: תלתא קמיעי. ג' מיני לחש: תלתא תלתא זימני. כל לחש ריפא שלשה פעמים ואפילו אדם אחד: אתמחי גברא. בכל קמיעות לעולם שהרי הומחה בשלשה מיני קמיעים: ואתמחי קמיע. שלשה קמיעין הללו נעשים מומחים מיד כל אדם שהרי ריפא כל אחד ג"פ ואין לומר מזל הרופא גורם דאין הדבר תלוי במזל הרופא אלא בחכמתו ואין לומר נמי (א) החולה גרס שמתרפא על ידי קמיעין שהרי בשלשה אנשים הוחזק: קמיעא לא אתמחי. לבא מיד רופא אחר: חד קמיע לתלתא גברי. לחולי אחד: קמיעא איתמחי. מיד כל אדם: גברא לא איתמחי. לקמיע אחר שאינו של לחש [זה] ושל חולי זה: תלתא קמיעי. של שלש מיני חולי: קמיעא ודאי לא איתמחי. מיד אדם אחר שהרי לא ריפא אלא פעם אחת: מזליה דהאי גברא. מלאכו של חולי זה דמקבל קמיעא וא"ת ממתני' דלעיל שמעינן לה דקתני כל שריפא ושנה ושילש דמשמע לאדם אחד ואוקימנא דאיתמחי קמיעא ולא אמרינן מזליה הוא לא דמי התם חד קמיעא הוא וליכא למיתלייה במזלא דגברא אלא בקמיע הני ודאי בגברא תלוי או ברופא או במתרפא הלכך מיבעיא לן במאי ניתליה: לאצולינהו. בשבת ° לחצר ד) המעורבת כשאר כתבי הקדש: הברכות. שתקנו חכמים כגון תשעה של ר"ה שיש בהן מלכיות וזכרונות ושופרות: מענינות. מפרשיות הרבה שכותבין בהן את מקראות של רפואה: היה כתוב שם יגוד. ה) יקוץ מקום השם ויגנזנו: סתם בית הכסא שלהן בשדות: שיש בו סכנה. אי שקיל ליה מיניה דשרי למיעל בהן לבית הכסא משום פקוח נפש: אף על גב דנקיט ליה בידיה. תכשיטו הוא הלכך אי נמי מייתי ליה ד' אמות בידים לא מחייב:

שלא

כל שריפא שלשה בני אדם כאחד. נראה לר"י דגרסינן כאחד והכי פירושו מדקתני כאחד אלמא משמע דבג' קמיעים איירי ולעיל קתני כל שריפא ושנה ושילש משמע קמיע אחד ומשני דההוא דלעיל לאמחויי קמיע והך לאמחויי גברא וה"ה אפילו לא נתרפאו יחד אלא הא דנקט כאחד לאשמעינן דבג' קמיעין איירי ולאמחויי גברא:

תלתא קמיעין לג' גברי תלת תלת זימני. פירוש שכתב לחש אחד בג' איגרות וכל אחת הועילה לג' אנשים או לאחד שלש פעמים קשה לרשב"א קמיע ג' היכי איתמחי הלא מיד כשנתרפא האדם שלישי בקמיע ג' [פעם א'] איתמחי גברא וכיון דאתמחי גברא ודאי שאותה האיגרת תועיל מכאן ואילך וי"ל כגון דשני קמיעין הללו ריפאו תלת זימני לתרי גברי וקמיע שלישי לחד מהנך תרי גברי תרי זימני והשתא מימחו כבר תרי קמיעי וגברא וקמיע שלישי אכתי לא איתמחי וחזר וריפא קמיע שלישי אדם שלישי דהשתא בא בבת אחת המחאת גברא והמחאת קמיע:

תלת תלת זימני. הוה מצי למימר חד תלת זימני ואינך חד זימנא אלא בעי למימר שיהיו שלשה קמיעין מומחין: חד קמיע לתלת גברי. נראה לר"י דה"ה לחד גברא תלת זימני דודאי לגבי המחאת גברא הוא דמבעיא ליה בסמוך אי אתמחי בחד גברא מתלת קמיעי אבל לענין המחאת קמיע דעדיף לא קא מיבעיא ליה דפשיטא דתלינן בהמחאת קמיע ולא אמרינן מזליה דהאי גברא הוא דמקבל כתבא והאי דנקט לתלתא גברי משום רבותא דאפילו הכי גברא לא אתמחי: תלת קמיע לחד גברא מאי. תימה תיפשוט ליה מדתני לעיל איזהו קמיע מומחה כל שריפא שלשה בני אדם ומוקמינן לה לאמחויי גברא משמע דוקא תלת גברי אבל חד גברא לא מדלא קתני כל שריפא אדם א' בג' קמיעין ובקונטרס פי' בפי' א' מימחי גברא מימחי קמיע שעשה אדם זה קמיע לשלשה אנשים דנעשה אדם זה מומחה שריפא שלשה אנשים והקמיע מומחה שריפא כתב זה ג' אנשים ולהאי פירושא נמי לא אימחי גברא אלא דוקא לאותו לחש וקשה לר"י לפירוש זה דהא אמרינן לקמן חד קמיע לתלתא גברי קמיע איתמחי ב) גברא לא איתמחי ויש ליישב לשון הקונטרס דה"ק שעשה אדם זה לחש זה בשלשה איגרות לג' אנשים דנעשה אדם זה מומחה שריפא לג' אנשים והלחש מומחה שריפא לחש זה ג' אנשים וגם זה אין נראה לר"י דאם בענין זה נמי קרוי חד קמיע לתלתא גברא הדרא קושיא לדוכתיה ואם הוא קרוי בענין זה תלתא קמיע לתלתא גברי חד חד זימנא הא אמרינן לקמן דגברא איתמחי ולא קמיע לכך נראה לר"י כדפירש וכן פירוש אחר שפי' בקונטרס מיושב מן הראשון:

הא לאמחויי קמיע. פירש בקונטרס דנעשה הקמיע לבדו מומחה ע"י אדם זה תימה דהוא עצמו פירש בסמוך גבי תלת תלת זימני דכל לחש שריפא ג' פעמים נעשו ג' קמיעות הללו מומחים מיד כל אדם אע"פ שרוצה לומר הקונטרס שרופא אחד כתבם מדפירש ואין לומר שמזל הרופא גרס וכן נראה ודאי עיקר דלא ע"י אדם זה לבד נעשה הקמיע מומחה אלא אף מיד כל אדם דהא אמרינן בסמוך תלתא קמיע לתלתא גברי תלת תלת זימני איתמחי גברא ואיתמחי קמיע והאי תלתא קמיעי לתלתא גברי דקאמר איירי שרופא אחד עשאם דבענין אחר לא איתמחי גברא וא"כ האי דקאמר נמי תלת תלת זימני איירי נמי ברופא אחד כמו רישא וקאמר דאיתמחי קמיע והיינו ע"כ מיד כל אדם דאי מיד רופא זה הא בלאו הכי הוא מומחה בכל קמיעין שבעולם וממה שפירש נמי גבי תלת תלת זימני כל לחש ריפא ג' פעמים ואפילו אדם אחד חזר בו מזה דפירש איתמחי קמיע ואין לומר מזל החולה גרס שמתרפא ע"י קמיעתא שהרי בשלשה אנשים הוחזק משמע דלא אמרינן איתמחי קמיע אלא א"כ ריפא ג' אנשים:

איתמחי קמיע. פירש הקונטרס ואין לומר מזל הרופא גרס דאין הדבר תלוי במזל הרופא אלא בחכמתו משמע שרוצה ליתן טעם אמאי איתמחי קמיע במזל הרופא היה לנו לתלות שכבר הומחה שריפא ג' אנשים בג' מיני קמיעים ולא היה לנו לתלות בקמיע ולא ידע רשב"א מה טעם נותן על זה דהא לא איתמחו שאר קמיעין של שאר חולאים אע"ג דהרופא איתמחי בכל קמיעין שבעולם ה"נ אלו ג' קמיעים נמי לתלות ברופא אלא צריך לתרץ כמו שפירשתי ללשון ר"י בענין שיבא המחאת קמיע והמחאת גברא בבת אחת:

והתניא

עין משפט נר מצוה

לח א מיי' וסמג שם טוש"ע א"ח סי' שא סעיף כה:

לט ב מיי' פ"ו מהל' יסודי התורה הלכה ו סמג לאוין ג:

רבינו חננאל

וכדתניא איזהו קמיע מומחה כל שריפא ג' בני אדם כאחד. בעי רב פפא תלתא גווני קמיע רפאו לאחד ג' מיני חלאים כל קמיע ריפא חולי מאי קמיעא ודאי לא אתמחאי גברא מאי מי אמרינן הא מסי ליה ג' זמני או דלמא מזלא דהאי גברא דמקבל קמיעא ועלתה בתיקו. ולא אתמחי לא גברא ולא קמיעא. ירושלמי נאמן אדם לומר קמיעא זו ריפאתי בו ב' וג' פעמים. קמיעין יש בהן משום קדושה ואסור למיעל בהו לבית הכסא אי לא [לגניזה] לא קא מיבעי לן דלא גרעי הקמיעין מן הכלים שאם היה שם כתוב עליהן תנינן הרי זה יגור ויגנז [כי] קא מיבעיא לן למיעל בהו לבהכ"ס.

מסורת הש"ס

א) לקמן דף קטו: וש"נ, ב) ערכין ו. [מס' סופרים פ"ה הי"ג], ג) [גיר' הערוך יגור], ד) לאצר שאינה מעורבת כצ"ל וכ"ה ברש"י שבאלפס, ה) וגי' הערוך יגור ברי"ם פי' יגור אותו במגירה רש"ל, ו) שייך לעיל קודם ד"ה תלתא.

תוספות ישנים

א) ק"ק דאכתי לא משכחת שיתמחי הקמיע הג'. אמ"ל דגברא אתמחי אפילו בג' קמיעין לחד גברא והיכי קאמר פשיטא לי דמשמע נמי דקאי אקמיע שלישית מדקאמר תלת זימני משמע דהומחו שלשתן. וי"ל אע"ג דכבר אתמחי גברא כי ריפא כל אחד ג"פ יש לנו לתלות גם בקמיע דעדיף כל מה שאנו יכולין למימחי קמיע ולא גברא כגון שכתב זה ריפא תלתא זימנא חד גברא ואתמחי גברא ולא קמיע כגון שריפא בג' אגרות לג' אנשים:
ב) גברא לא איתמחי. ולהאי פי' היינו דלא איתמחי אפילו ללחש זה כצ"ל:

הגהות הב"ח

(א) רש"י ד"ה ואיתמחי כו' נמי מזל החולה גרס:

גליון הש"ס

רש"י ד"ה לאצולינהו בשבת לחצר המעורבת. עי' לקמן דף קטו ע"א ברש"י ד"ה מצילין אותן וצ"ע:

ליקוטי רש"י

מזלא דהאי גברא. מלאך שלו ומליץ עליו [לעיל נג:]. הברכות. מטבע ברכות שטבעו חכמים כגון שמונה עשרה ושאר ברכות. ומעניינות הרבה. מפרשיות שהיו כותבין בקמיעין פסוקים ללחש כגון כל המחלה וכגון לא תירא מפחד לילה. במקומן. אם נפלה דליקה בשבת [לקמן קטו:]. יגוד. יחתוך כמו (דניאל ד) גודו אילנא [בכורות מד.]. יחתוך מקום השם ויגנזנו החתיכה וישתמש במותר [ערכין ו.]. שכל דבר קדש טעון גניזה [לקמן צ.]. אסור להניחן במקום הפקר [שם קטו.].

וְיֵצֵא בּוֹ בִּרְשׁוּת הָרַבִּים בְּשֵׁיר וּבְטַבַּעַת – TO A BRACELET OR A RING – AND GO OUT WITH IT TO THE PUBLIC DOMAIN;[1] מִשּׁוּם מַרְאִית הָעַיִן – this is forbidden BECAUSE OF THE APPEARANCE of wrongdoing.[2]

The Baraisa just cited states that an amulet is proven effective if it has cured three times. The Gemara questions this ruling:

וְהָתַנְיָא – **But it has been taught in a** second **Baraisa:** אֵיזֶהוּ קָמֵיעַ מוּמְחֶה – WHICH amulet IS considered AN EFFECTIVE AMULET? כֹּל שֶׁרִיפֵּא שְׁלוֹשָׁה בְּנֵי אָדָם כְּאֶחָד – ANY amulet THAT HAS CURED THREE MEN AS ONE.[3] This Baraisa seems to state that an amulet is proven effective only if it cures three *different* people, while the first Baraisa states that it is proven effective as long as it has healed three times, even if the same person was healed each time.[4] – ? –

The Gemara resolves this difficulty:

לֹא קַשְׁיָא – There is **no difficulty.** הָא – **This** second Baraisa, which requires that three different people be cured, לְמַחוּיֵי גַּבְרָא – speaks of the prerequisite **for proving the man** (i.e. the healer who wrote the amulet) **expert;**[5] this is only accomplished if he wrote three different amulets that healed three different people.[6] הָא – And **this** Baraisa, which requires only that the amulet cure three times, לְמַחוּיֵי קָמֵיעָא – speaks of the prerequisite **for establishing the amulet** as **effective;** this can be accomplished even by healing one person three times.[7]

The Gemara delineates the guidelines for establishing healers and amulets as expert:

אָמַר רַב פַּפָּא – **Rav Pappa said:** פְּשִׁיטָא לִי – **It is obvious to me** תְּלָת קָמֵיעַ לִתְלָת גַּבְרֵי – that if a healer wrote **three** different types of **amulets for three** different **people,** תְּלָתָא תְּלָתָא זִימְנֵי – and **each one** of the amulets cured **three times,**[8] אִיתְמַחִי גַּבְרָא וְאִתְמַחִי קָמֵיעַ – **the man is proven expert and the amulet is proven effective.**[9] תְּלָתָא קָמֵיעַ לִתְלָתָא גַּבְרֵי – It is also obvious

NOTES

1. [I.e. the amulet must be tied to the body; it may not be fastened to another piece of jewelry, such as a bracelet or a ring. The Gemara will explain why this is so.]

2. If one wears an amulet attached to a bracelet or a ring, it appears as if the amulet is being worn as an ornament; and this is forbidden, for in truth the amulet is *not* an ornament, since it is only being worn for the purpose of avoiding illness (*Rashi*, see also *Ritva MHK* ed.).

3. [*Rashi's* text apparently did not contain the word כְּאֶחָד, *as one*; see *Chidushei HaRan*, and *Rosh Yosef*.]

4. *Rashi*. Cf. *Tosafos*, who explain the Gemara's question differently.

5. The Gemara revises its original understanding of the second Baraisa, and concludes that it is *not* teaching how an amulet is proven effective; rather, it is teaching how the *writer* of the amulet is proven expert at writing all types of amulets (*Rashi*; see next note). [Although the Baraisa states אֵיזֶהוּ קָמֵיעַ מוּמְחֶה, which is normally translated as "which is an effective amulet?", these words can also be translated as referring to the *writer* of the amulet (see above, 61a note 37, citing *Tosafos*; see also *Chidushei HaRan* here).]

6. In order for a writer of an amulet to be proven expert at writing *all* manner of amulets, he must write three different types of amulets, and use them to cure three different ailments. Once he has accomplished this, it can be assumed that he is a proficient writer of amulets, and any amulet that he writes is presumed effective. [*Rashi* likens this to the case of an ox that gored three different types of animals; the ox is thereby considered a *mu'ad* ox with regard to *any* type of animal that it gores, since it has demonstrated that its aggressive behavior is not limited to attacks against a single species. Similarly, once a writer of amulets has demonstrated his ability to cure three different illnesses, we assume that he is expert in curing *all* illnesses. [Cf. *Tosafos* and *Rosh*, who question *Rashi's* comparison to a *muad* ox; see *Ritva, MHK* ed. for a resolution. See also *Chidushei HaRan*, citing *Rabbeinu Yehonasan*, who relates the efficacy of amulets to the healer's abilities with regard to praying for the ill person, and explains the *sugya* that follows on this basis.] Thus, the second Baraisa is teaching that a writer of amulets is proven expert if his amulets cured three people that had three different diseases [although the second Baraisa speaks only of curing three people, three people are assumed to have three different diseases unless specified otherwise] (see *Rashi*). [The question of whether a writer of amulets is proven effective if three of his amulets cure *one person* of three different ailments is discussed in the Gemara below.]

[Note that in the case of the second Baraisa, where each amulet healed only one person, none of the amulets are proven effective, and even identical amulets may not be worn outside on the Sabbath if they are written by another healer (*Rashi*).]

7. If an amulet cures even *one* person three times from the same illness, that amulet itself is proven effective; if the same healer writes another, identical amulet, it may be worn outside on the Sabbath. This is the law that the first Baraisa teaches: If an amulet cures three times, it is proven effective. If the amulet cured three *different* people of the same ailment, the amulet is proven effective to the extent that we presume that an identical amulet will be effective to heal the same illness even if it was written by another healer. Furthermore, if three identical amulets were written by three different healers, then even if the three amulets cured *one* person three times from the same illness, the amulet is proven effective no matter who writes it; for the fact that three healers used the amulet effectively demonstrates that it can be used effectively by any healer (*Rashi*, as explained by *Tos. HaRosh*; cf. *Tosafos*). [It should be noted that the upcoming passage of Gemara and *Rashi's* commentary thereon are complex and somewhat obscure; the Rishonim and later commentators struggle to explain the Gemara, and grapple with several seemingly contradictory statements within *Rashi's* commentary, offering several possible interpretations (see especially *Ritva*, *MHK* ed. and *Maharsha*, and commentaries to *Orach Chaim* 301:25 (see *Beru Halachah*) and *Tur* ibid.). We have explained the Gemara with *Rashi* as understood by *Tos. HaRosh*; see there for a systematic explication of *Rashi's* approach to the entire passage.]

8. I.e. a total of nine cures were accomplished by the three amulets, each one curing one of three different diseases three times. This can occur in one of two ways: (a) Each of three people suffered from three different diseases, so that each amulet healed three different people; or (b) each of three people suffered from a different disease, and each amulet cured one person three times from a single disease (see *Rashi*).

9. The writer of the three amulets is proven expert at writing all manner of amulets, as three of his amulets were effective in curing three different diseases (see above, note 6). And the three amulets are proven effective no matter who writes them, because each of them has cured three times (*Rashi*).

[That the amulets are proven effective regardless of the writer is certainly true in the first scenario [case (a)] described in the previous note, where each amulet cured three people of a disease, for it has already been explained that once an amulet has cured three different people, we presume it to be effective no matter who writes it (see above, second case of note 7). And even in the second scenario described in the previous note [case (b)] where each amulet cured one person three times from a single disease, the amulets *still* are proven effective no matter who writes them, *if* the same healer performed this feat with three different amulets. Although above (first case of note 7) it was explained that if a single amulet cured one person three times, the amulet is only presumed effective if it is written by the same healer, this is because the healer has not yet demonstrated proficiency in identifying effective amulets in general, and it is possible that only *he* can cure with this amulet. Once a healer has cured with three different amulets, however, we identify him as a person that is knowledgeable in identifying effective amulets; from that point on, any amulet that comes from his hands and cures three times, even if it only cured the same person three times, is assumed to be an effective cure that will heal even if prepared by another person (see *Rashi* and *Tos. HaRosh*; see also below, end of note 14).

[The Rishonim (*Tosafos*, *Ritva MHK* ed. et al.) ask: Once the healer has been established as an expert by writing three amulets that cured three people even *one* time each (as explained in the second Baraisa cited above), how can it be subsequently proven that any amulet he uses is effective in its own right, and can be used by any healer? Perhaps the amulet is not effective to that degree, and the only reason that the amulet is working is because the healer is an expert! Some Rishonim answer that indeed, an amulet can only be proven totally effective if the proof of its effectiveness (i.e. its cure of a third person) precedes, or is

בשיר ובטבעת ויצא בו ברשות הרבים משום מראית העין והתניא איזהו קמיע מומחה כל שריפא ג' בני אדם כאחד לא קשיא הא למחויי גברא הא למחויי קמיעא אמר רב פפא פשיטא לי תלת קמיע לתלת גברי תלתא תלתא זימני איתמחי גברא א) ואתמחי קמיע תלתא קמיע לתלתא גברי חד חד זימנא גברא איתמחי קמיעא לא איתמחי חד קמיע לתלתא גברי קמיעא איתמחי גברא לא איתמחי בעי רב פפא תלתא קמיע לחד גברא מאי קמיעא ודאי לא איתמחי גברא איתמחי או לא איתמחי מי אמרינן הא אסי ליה או דילמא [א] מזלא דהאי גברא הוא דקא מקבל כתבא תיקו: איבעיא להו קמיעין יש בהן משום קדושה או דילמא אין בהן משום קדושה למאי הילכתא אילימא לאצולינהו מפני הדליקה ת"ש [ד] הברכות והקמיעין אע"פ שיש בהן אותיות ומענינות הרבה שבתורה אין מצילין אותן מפני הדליקה ונשרפים במקומן אלא לענין גניזה [ה] ת"ש היה [ב] כתוב על ידות הכלים ועל כרעי המטה [ג] יגוד ויגנזנו אלא ליכנם בהן בבית הכסא מאי יש בהן קדושה ואסיר או דילמא אין בהן קדושה ושרי ת"ש ולא בקמיע בזמן שאינו מן המומחה הא מן המומחה נפיק ואי אמרת קמיעין יש בהן משום קדושה זמנין דמיצטריך לבית הכסא ואתי לאיתויינהו ד' אמות ברה"ר הכא במאי עסקינן בקמיע של עיקרין והתניא אחד קמיע של כתב ואחד קמיע של עיקרין אלא הכא במאי עסקינן בחולה שיש בו סכנה והתניא אחד חולה שיש בו סכנה ואחד חולה שאין בו סכנה אלא כיון דמסי אף על גב דנקיט ליה בידיה נמי שפיר דמי

והתניא

כל שריפא שלשה בני אדם כאחד. נראה לר"י דגרסינן כאחד והכי פירושו מדקתני כאחד אלמא משמע דבג' קמיעים מיירי ולעיל קתני כל שריפא ושנה ושילש משמע קמיע אחד ומשני דההוא דלעיל לאמחויי קמיע והך לאמחויי גברא וה"ה אפילו לא נתרפאו יחד אלא הא דנקט כאחד לאשמעינן דבג' קמיעין מיירי ולאמחויי גברא:

תלתא קמיעין לג' גברי תלת תלת זימני. פירוש שכתב לחש אחד בג' איגרות וכל אחת הועילה לג' אנשים או לאחד שלש פעמים קשה לרשב"א קמיע ג' היכי איתמחי הלא מיד כשנתרפא האדם שלישי בקמיע ג' [פעם א'] איתמחי גברא וכיון דאתמחי גברא ודאי שאותה האיגרת תועיל מכאן ואילך וי"ל כגון דשני קמיעין הללו ריפאו תלת זימני לתרי גברי וקמיע שלישי לחד מהנך תרי גברי תרי זימני והשתא מימחו כבר תרי קמיעי וגברא וקמיע שלישי אכתי לא איתמחי וחזר וריפא קמיע שלישי אדם שלישי דהשתא בא בבת אחת המחאת גברא והמחאת קמיע:

תלת תלת זימני. הוה מצי למימר חד תלת זימני ואיך חד זימנא אלא בעי למימר שיהיו שלשה קמיעין מומחין: **חד** קמיע לתלת גברי. נראה לר"י דה"ה לחד גברא תלת זימני דודאי לגבי המחאת גברא הוא דמבעיא ליה בסמוך אי אתמחי בחד גברא מתלת קמיעי אבל לענין המחאת קמיע דעדיף לא קא מיבעיא ליה דפשיטא דתלינן בהמחאת קמיע ולא אמרינן מזליה דהאי גברא הוא דמקבל כתבא והאי דנקט לתלתא גברי משום רבותא דאפילו הכי גברא לא אתמחי: **תלת** קמיע לחד גברא מאי. תימה תיפשוט ליה מדתני לעיל איזהו קמיע מומחה כל שריפא שלשה בני אדם ומוקמינן לה לאמחויי גברא משמע דוקא תלת גברי אבל חד גברא לא מדלא קתני כל שריפא אדם א' בג' קמיעין ובקונטרס פי' בפי' א' מימחי גברא מימחי קמיע שעשה אדם זה קמיע לשלשה אנשים דנעשה אדם זה מומחה שריפא שלשה אנשים והקמיע מומחה שריפא כתב זה ג' אנשים ולהאי פירושא נמי לא אימחי גברא אלא דוקא לאותו לחש וקשה לר"י לפירוש זה דהא אמרינן לקמן חד קמיע לתלתא גברי קמיע איתמחי ב) גברא לא איתמחי ויש ליישב לשון הקונטרס דה"ק שעשה אדם זה לחש זה בשלשה איגרות לג' אנשים דנעשה אדם זה מומחה שריפא לג' אנשים והלחש מומחה שריפא לחש זה ג' אנשים וגם זה אין נראה לר"י דאם בענין זה נמי קרוי חד קמיע לתלתא גברא הדרא קושיא לדוכתיה ואם הוא קרוי בענין זה תלתא קמיע לתלתא גברי חד חד זימנא הא אמרינן לקמן דגברא איתמחי ולא קמיע לכך נראה לר"י כדפירש וכן פירוש אחר שפי' בקונטרס מיושב מן הראשון: [ו] **הא** לאמחויי קמיע. פירש בקונטרס דנעשה הקמיע לבדו מומחה ע"י אדם זה תימה דהוא עצמו פירש בסמוך גבי תלת תלת זימני דכל לחש שריפא ג' פעמים נעשו ג' קמיעות הללו מומחים מיד כל אדם אע"פ שרוצה לומר הקונטרס שרופא אחד כתבם מדפירש ואין לומר שמזל הרופא גרס וכן נראה ודאי עיקר דלא ע"י אדם זה לבד נעשה הקמיע מומחה אלא אף מיד כל אדם דהא אמרינן בסמוך תלתא קמיע לתלתא גברי תלת תלת זימני איתמחי גברא ואיתמחי קמיע והאי תלתא קמיעי לתלתא גברי דקאמר איירי שרופא אחד עשאם דבענין אחר לא איתמחי גברא וא"כ האי דקאמר נמי תלת תלת זימני איירי נמי ברופא אחד כמו רישא וקאמר דאיתמחי קמיע והיינו ע"כ מיד כל אדם דאי מיד רופא זה הא בלאו הכי הוא מומחה בכל קמיעין שבעולם וממה שפירש נמי גבי תלת תלת זימני כל לחש ריפא ג' פעמים ואפילו אדם אחד חזר בו מזה דפירש איתמחי קמיע ואין לומר מזל החולה גרס שמתרפא ע"י קמיעתא שהרי בשלשה אנשים הוחזק משמע דלא אמרינן איתמחי קמיע אלא א"כ ריפא ג' אנשים:

איתמחי קמיע. פירש הקונטרס ואין לומר מזל הרופא גרס דאין הדבר תלוי במזל הרופא אלא בחכמתו משמע שרוצה ליתן טעם אמאי איתמחי קמיע במזל הרופא היה לנו לתלות שכבר הומחה שריפא ג' אנשים בג' מיני קמיעים ולא היה לנו לתלות בקמיע ולא ידע רשב"א מה טעם נותן על זה דהא לא איתמחו שאר קמיעין של שאר חולאים אע"ג דהרופא איתמחי בכל קמיעין שבעולם ה"נ אלו ג' קמיעים נמי לתלות ברופא אלא צריך לתרץ כמו שפירשתי ללשון ר"י בענין שיבא המחאת קמיע והמחאת גברא בבת אחת:

בשיר. אלעדה: מפני מראית העין. דלא מיחזי כמאן דבעי ליה לרפואה אלא לתכשיט ולאו תכשיט הוא אלא מחמת דאגת חולי: והתניא כל שריפא ג' בני אדם. ולעיל קתני כל שריפא ושנה ושילש ואפילו אדם אחד: הא לאמחויי גברא כו'. הא דקתני ג' בני אדם משום דקתם ג' בני אדם שלשה מיני חלאים ואיירי בג' מיני קמיעין שאין דומין זה לזה ולאמחויי גברא שנעשה מומחה בכל קמיעים שיעשה לעולם כדאמרינן בב"ק (דף לז.) נגח שור וחמור וגמל נעשה מועד לכל אבל הקמיע אינו מומחה אם יכתוב רופא אחר אחד מהן: והא. דקתני כל שריפא ושנה ושילש מיירי בחולי אחד וכתבו זה הלחש וריפא ג' פעמים או לאדם אחד או לשלשה ולאיתמחויי קמיעא מיירי דנעשה הקמיע לבדו מומחה על יד אדם זה או אם כתבוס שלשה רופאים נעשה קמיע של לחש זה מומחה מיד כל אדם: תלתא קמיעי. ג' מיני לחש: תלתא תלתא זימני. כל לחש ריפא שלשה פעמים ואפילו אדם אחד: אתמחי גברא. בכל קמיעות לעולם שהרי הומחה בשלשה מיני קמיעים: ואתמחי קמיע. שלשה קמיעין הללו נעשים מומחים מיד כל אדם שהרי ריפא כל אחד ג"פ ואין לומר מזל הרופא גורס דאין הדבר תלוי במזל הרופא אלא בחכמתו ואין לומר נמי (א) החולה גרס שמתרפא על ידי קמיעין שהרי בשלשה אנשים הוחזק: קמיעא לא אתמחי. לבא מיד רופא אחר: חד קמיע לתלתא גברי. לחולי אחד: קמיעא איתמחי. מיד כל אדם: גברא לא איתמחי. לקמיע אחר שאינו של לחש [זה] ושל חולי זה: תלתא קמיעי. של שלש מיני חולי: קמיעא ודאי לא איתמחי. מיד אדם אחר שהרי לא ריפא אלא פעם אחת: מזליה דהאי גברא. מלאכו של חולי זה דמקבל קמיעא וא"ת ממתני' דלעיל שמעינן לה דקתני כל שריפא ושנה ושילש דמשמע לאדם אחד ואוקימנא דאיתמחי קמיעא ולא אמרינן מזליה הוא לא דמי התם חד קמיעא הוא וליכא למיתלייה במזלא דגברא אלא בקמיע הני ודאי בגברא תלוי או ברופא או במתרפא הלכך מיבעיא לן במאי ניתליה: לאצולינהו. בשבת [ו] לחצר [ז] המעורבת כשאר כתבי הקדש: הברכות. שתקנו חכמים כגון תשעה של ר"ה שיש בהן מלכיות חכרונות ושופרות: מענינות. מפרשיות הרבה שכותבין בהן את מקראות של רפואה: היה כתוב שם יגוד. [ה] יקוץ מקום השם ויגנזנו: סתם בית הכסא שלהן בשדות: שיש בו סכנה. אי שקיל ליה מיניה דשרי למיעל בהן לבית הכסא משום פקוח נפש: אף על גב דנקיט ליה בידיה. תכשיטו הוא הלכך אי נמי מייתי ליה ד' אמות בידים לא מחייב:

שלא

עין משפט נר מצוה

לח א מיי' וסמג שם טוש"ע א"ח סי' שא סעיף כה:

לט ב מיי' פ"ו מהל' יסודי התורה הלכה ו סמג לאוין ג:

רבינו חננאל

וכדתניא איזהו קמיע מומחה כל שריפא ג' בני אדם כאחד. בעי רב פפא תלתא גוני קמיע רפאו לאחד ג' מיני חלאים כל קמיע ריפא חולי מאי קמיעא ודאי לא אתמחאי גברא מאי מי אמרינן הא מסי ליה ג' זמני או דלמא מזלא דהאי גברא דמקבל קמיעא ועלתה בתיקו. ולא אתמחי לא גברא ולא קמיעא. ירושלמי נאמן אדם לומר קמיעא זו ריפאתי בו ב' וג' פעמים. קמיעין יש בהן משום קדושה ואסור למיעל בהו לבית הכסא אי לא [לגניזה] לא קא מיבעי לן דלא גרעי הקמיעין מן הכלים שאם היה שם כתוב עליהן תנינן הרי זה יגור ויגנז [כי] קא מיבעיא לן למיעל בהו לבהכ"ס.

מסורת הש"ס

א) לקמן דף קטו: וש"נ, ב) ערכין ו. [מס' סופרים פ"ה הי"ג], ג) [גיר' הערוך יגור], ד) לאחר שאינה מעורבת כצ"ל וכ"ה ברש"י שבאלפס, ה) וגי' הערוך יגור ברי"ש פי' יגור אותו במגירה רש"ל, ו) שייך לעיל קודם ד"ה תלתא.

תוספות ישנים

א) ק"ק דאכתי לא משכחת שיתמחי הקמיע הג'. את"ל דגברא אתמחי אפילו בג' קמיעין לחד גברא והיכי קאמר פשיטא לי דמשמע נמי דקאי אקמיע שלישית מדקאמר תלת זימני משמע דהומחו שלשתן. וי"ל אע"ג דכבר אתמחי גברא כי ריפא כל אחד ג"פ יש לנו לתלות גם בקמיע דעדיף כל מה שאנו יכולין למימחי קמיע ולא גברא כגון שכתב זה ריפא תלתא זימנא חד גברא ואתמחי גברא ולא קמיע כגון שריפא בג' אגרות לג' אנשים:

ב) גברא לא איתמחי. ולהאי פי' היינו דלא איתמחי אפילו ללחש זה כצ"ל:

הגהות הב"ח

(א) רש"י ד"ה ואיתמחי כו' נמי מזל החולה גרס:

גליון הש"ס

רש"י ד"ה לאצולינהו בשבת לחצר המעורבת. עי' לקמן דף קטו ע"א ברש"י ד"ה מצילין אותן וצ"ע:

ליקוטי רש"י

מזלא דהאי גברא. מלאך שלו ומליץ עליו [לעיל נג:]. **הברכות.** מטבע ברכות שטבעו חכמים כגון שמונה עשרה ושאר ברכות. **ומענינות הרבה.** מפרשיות שהיו כותבין בקמיעין פסוקים ללחש כגון כל המחלה וכגון לא תירא מפחד לילה. **ונשרפים במקומן.** אם נפלה דליקה בשבת [לקמן קטו:]. **יגוד.** יחתוך כמו (דניאל ד) גודו אילנא [בכורות מד.]. יחתוך מקום השם ויגנוז החתיכה וישתמש במותר [ערכין ו.]. **ויגנזנו.** שכל דבר קדש טעון גניזה [לקמן צ.]. אסור להניחן במקום הפקר [שם קטו.].

that if a healer wrote **three** different **amulets for three** different **people,** חַד חַד זִימְנָא – and **each one** of the amulets cured **one time,** גַּבְרָא אִיתְמַחִי – **the man is proven expert,** קָמֵיעָא לֹא אִיתְמַחִי – but each **amulet is not proven effective.**[10] חַד קָמֵיעַ לִתְלָתָא גַּבְרֵי – Furthermore, it is obvious that if the healer wrote **one amulet for** each of **three people** suffering from the same illness, and they were all cured, קָמֵיעָא אִיתְמַחִי – the **amulet is proven effective,**[11] גַּבְרָא לֹא אִיתְמַחִי – but the **man who** wrote the amulet **is not proven expert.**[12]

The Gemara cites one case that was the subject of an inquiry:

בָּעֵי רַב פַּפָּא – **Rav Pappa inquired:** תְּלָתָא קָמֵיעַ לְחַד גַּבְרָא – If one wrote **three** different **amulets for a single person** who suffered from three different illnesses, and cured him of all three illnesses, מַאי – **what** is the law?

The Gemara clarifies the inquiry:

קָמֵיעָא וַדַּאי לֹא אִיתְמַחִי – Each **amulet is certainly not proven effective,** for each amulet has cured only one time. Rav Pappa's question was: גַּבְרָא אִיתְמַחִי אוֹ לֹא אִיתְמַחִי – **Is the man proven expert, or is he not proven expert?**

The Gemara explains the two sides of the question:

מִי אָמְרִינַן – **Do we say** הָא אַסֵּי לֵיהּ – that **this** healer **has cured him** three times, and therefore the healer should be proven expert; אוֹ דִּילְמָא – **or perhaps** we say מַזָּלָא דְּהַאי גַּבְרָא הוּא דְּקָא מְקַבֵּל כְּתָבָא – it is **the *mazal***[13] **of that man that accepts** the cure of **amulets?**[14]

The Gemara does not attempt to resolve the inquiry, and concludes:

תֵּיקוּ – **Let [this question] stand.**[15]

The Gemara continues its discussion of amulets:

אִיבַּעְיָא לְהוּ – **They inquired:** קָמֵיעִין יֵשׁ בָּהֶן מִשּׁוּם קְדוּשָּׁה – Shall we say that **amulets have intrinsic sanctity,** אוֹ דִּילְמָא אֵין בָּהֶן מִשּׁוּם קְדוּשָּׁה – **or perhaps [amulets] do not have intrinsic sanctity?**[16]

The Gemara seeks to clarify the inquiry:

לְמַאי הִילְכְתָא – With respect **to what law** was this question raised?[17] אִילֵימָא לְאַצּוּלִינְהוּ מִפְּנֵי הַדְּלֵיקָה – **If** you wish **to say** that the question concerned whether or not one is permitted **to save them from a fire**[18] on the Sabbath, this question is easily resolved, תָּא שְׁמַע – for we can **come and learn** the answer from the following Baraisa: הַבְּרָכוֹת וְהַקְּמֵיעִין – BLESSINGS[19] AND AMULETS, אַף עַל פִּי שֶׁיֵּשׁ בָּהֶן אוֹתִיּוֹת וּמֵעִנְיָנוֹת הַרְבֵּה שֶׁבַּתּוֹרָה – ALTHOUGH THEY CONTAIN LETTERS of God's Names [20] AND verses FROM MANY SECTIONS OF THE TORAH,[21] אֵין מַצִּילִין אוֹתָן מִפְּנֵי הַדְּלֵיקָה – WE DO NOT SAVE THEM FROM A BONFIRE, וְנִשְׂרָפִים בִּמְקוֹמָן – AND THEY are allowed to BURN IN THEIR PLACE. This

NOTES

concurrent with, the proof that the healer is expert (see *Tosafos* ד״ה תלתא and *Ritva* (*MHK* ed.), who explain the various cases). Others differ, and maintain that even if a healer has been proven expert, the fact that an amulet cures three different people accords it the status of an effective amulet in its own right, and we do not use the status of the healer to explain the amulet's efficiency (see *Chidushei HaRan* ד״ה מי אמרינן, citing *Re'ah*).]

10. The writer of the amulets is proven expert with respect to all types of amulets, for he has written three different amulets that cured three different illnesses (see note 6); however, the amulets are not proven effective [and if they are written by another healer, they may not be worn on the Sabbath], for each of them has only healed one time (see *Rashi*).

11. Even if written by another healer; for once it cured three different people, it is established as an effective amulet for that illness no matter who writes it (see *Rashi* and *Tos. HaRosh*).

12. I.e. the healer is not proven expert to write other amulets besides this one [he (or anyone else) can, however, write this type of amulet for the sickness that it has cured in three different people] (see *Rashi*).

13. *Rashi* translates *mazal* in this context as "guardian angel"; i.e. perhaps it is the Heavenly merits of the ill person that allow the amulets to heal him, even if they would not heal another person (see *Rashi*).

14. [Literally: writings.] If this is the case, then the person should not be proven expert to the extent that another person would be permitted to wear an amulet written by him, for perhaps his cures are effective only for this person.

[*Rashi* himself notes that the first Baraisa cited above states that an amulet is proven effective if it cures the same person three times; why, then, does the Gemara not prove from that Baraisa that we do *not* consider the possibility that the merit of the ill person is the reason for a cure? He answers that in that case, when the same amulet cured three times, it is logical to attribute the cures to the amulet rather than to the person. But in the case of Rav Pappa's inquiry, where three separate amulets each effected a cure once, so that we do *not* attribute the cure to the amulet itself, we do not know whether to attribute the healing either to the merit of the healer or the merit of the ill person; accordingly, the Gemara inquires whether the healer is proven expert or not. See also *Ritva MHK* ed.]

[Although Rav Pappa posits that when a single person is cured of three diseases by one healer there is perhaps no proof that the healer is expert, he agrees that if the healer performs this feat three times (i.e. he cures each of three people from three diseases using three amulets for each person – case (a) in note 8, above), the healer *is* proven expert, and we definitely do *not* attribute the cures to the merit of the ill persons. For once three different people have been cured, it is not likely that all three of them had such merit (*Rashi*, end of ד״ה ואתמחי קמיע, as explained by *Tos. HaRosh*; cf. *Tosafos* and *Ritva MHK* ed.).]

15. **In summary:** These are the guidelines for establishing healers and amulets as expert, according to *Rashi* as understood by *Tos. HaRosh*: (1) If a healer heals one person three times from the same disease with the same type of amulet, the amulet is proven effective for any person suffering from that disease, if it is written by that healer; the healer is not proven expert with regard to any other amulet. (2) If a healer heals each of three people suffering from the same disease (one time each) with the same type of amulet, *or* if three healers each heal the same person from the same disease with the same type of amulet, the amulet is proven effective for any person suffering from that disease, no matter who writes the amulet; the healer(s) are not proven expert with regard to any other amulets. (3) If a healer heals three different people who each suffer from a different disease by giving each one a different amulet (each amulet curing only once), the healer is proven expert and can write any amulet for any disease; the amulets are not presumed effective when written by another healer. (4) If a healer heals each of three people from three different diseases three times (nine cures) using three amulets, either by curing each of them three times from the same disease (one amulet to each person), or by curing each of them from each of three different diseases (each amulet curing three people), the healer is proven expert with regard to all amulets, and each of the three amulets is proven expert no matter who writes it. (5) If a healer heals one person from three illnesses with three different amulets, the amulets are not proven effective; the Gemara is uncertain as to whether the healer is proven expert (see further in sources cited in note 7).

16. [Amulets often contained verses of the Torah or Names of God. The Gemara therefore wonders if they are accorded the sanctity of holy scrolls.]

17. I.e. Regarding what law is there a difference whether amulets possess intrinsic sanctity or not?

18. I.e. to remove them from a burning house into a courtyard, even if there was no *eruv* [in which case such carrying is Rabbinically prohibited] (*Rashi*, as emended by marginal gloss; see also *Rashi* printed alongside *Rif*; cf. *Rashash*; see also *Dibros Moshe* 53:20). [The Sages permitted saving other holy scrolls in such a manner; see below, 115a,b and *Orach Chaim* 334:17.]

19. I.e. blessings that the Sages instituted [as sections of prayer that contain verses from the Scriptures], such as the nine blessings found in the *Amidah* prayer said on Rosh Hashanah, which contain verses that discuss the three subjects of kingship, remembrance, and *shofar* blasts (*Rashi*; cf. *Rashi* below, 115b ד״ה הברכות).

20. See *Ritva* (*MHK* ed.).

21. Many amulets contained verses of the Torah which speak of healing (*Rashi*; see also *Rashi* below, 115b ד״ה ומעניינות).

בשיר ובטבעת ויצא בו ברשות הרבים משום מראית העין והתניא איזהו קמיע מומחה כל שריפא ג' בני אדם כאחד לא קשיא הא למחויי גברא הא למחויי קמיעא אמר רב פפא פשיטא לי תלת קמיע לתלת גברי תלתא תלתא זימני איתמחי גברא [א] ואתמחי קמיע תלתא קמיע לתלתא גברי חד חד זימנא גברא איתמחי קמיעא לא איתמחי חד קמיע לתלתא גברי קמיעא איתמחי גברא לא איתמחי בעי רב פפא תלתא קמיע לחד גברא מאי קמיעא ודאי לא איתמחי גברא איתמחי או לא איתמחי מי אמרינן הא אסי ליה או דילמא [א]מזלא דהאי גברא הוא דקא מקבל כתבא תיקו: איבעיא להו קמיעין יש בהן משום קדושה או דילמא אין בהן משום קדושה למאי הילכתא אילימא לאצולינהו מפני הדליקה ת"ש [ו] הברכות והקמיעין אע"פ שיש בהן אותיות ומענינות הרבה שבתורה אין מצילין אותן מפני הדליקה ונשרפים במקומן אלא לענין גניזה [ז] ת"ש היה [ב]כתוב על ידות הכלים ועל כרעי המטה [ג]יגוד ויגנזנו אלא ליכנס בהן בבית הכסא מאי יש בהן קדושה ואסיר או דילמא אין בהן קדושה ושרי ת"ש ולא בקמיע בזמן שאינו מן המומחה הא מן המומחה נפיק ואי אמרת קמיעין יש בהן משום קדושה זמנין דמיצטריך לבית הכסא ואתי לאיתויינהו ד' אמות ברה"ר הכא במאי עסקינן בקמיע של עיקרין והתניא אחד קמיע של כתב ואחד קמיע של עיקרין אלא הכא במאי עסקינן בחולה שיש בו סכנה והתניא אחד חולה שיש בו סכנה ואחד חולה שאין בו סכנה אלא כיון דמסי אף על גב דנקיט ליה בידיה נמי שפיר דמי

והתניא

רש"י

בשיר. אלעדה: מפני מראית העין. דלא מיחזי כמאן דבעי ליה לרפואה אלא לתכשיט ולאו תכשיט הוא אלא מחמת דאגת חולי: והתניא כל שריפא ג' בני אדם. ולעיל קתני כל שריפא ושנה ושילש ואפילו אדם אחד: הא לאמחויי גברא כו'. הא דקתני ג' בני אדם משום דסתם ג' בני אדם שלשה מיני חלאים ואיירי בג' מיני קמיעין שאין דומין זה לזה ולאמחויי גברא שנעשה מומחה בכל קמיעים שיעשה לעולם כדאמרינן בב"ק (דף לז.) נגח שור וחמור וגמל נעשה מועד לכל אבל הקמיע אינו מומחה אם יכתוב רופא אחר אחד מהן: והא. דקתני כל שריפא ושנה ושילש איירי בחולי אחד וכתבו זה הלחש וריפא ג' פעמים או לאדם אחד או לשלשה ולאיתמחויי קמיעא איירי דנעשה הקמיע לבדו מומחה על יד אדם זה או אם כתבוס שלשה רופאים נעשה קמיע של לחש זה מומחה מיד כל אדם: תלתא קמיעי. ג' מיני לחש: תלתא תלתא זימני. כל לחש ריפא שלשה פעמים ואפילו אדם אחד: אתמחי גברא. בכל קמיעות לעולם שהרי הומחה בשלשה מיני קמיעים: ואתמחי קמיע. שלשה קמיעין הללו נעשים מומחים מיד כל אדם שהרי ריפא כל אחד ג"פ ואין לומר מזל הרופא גורם דאין הדבר תלוי במזל הרופא אלא בחכמתו ואין לומר נמי (א) החולה גרם שמתרפא על ידי קמיעין שהרי בשלשה אנשים הוחזק: קמיעא לא אתמחי. לבא מיד רופא אחר: חד קמיע לתלתא גברי. לחולי אחד: קמיעא איתמחי. מיד כל אדם: גברא לא איתמחי. לקמיע אחר שאינו של לחש [זה] ושל חולי זה: תלתא קמיעי. של שלש מיני חולי: קמיעא ודאי לא איתמחי. מיד אדם אחר שהרי לא ריפא אלא פעם אחת: מזליה דהאי גברא. מלאכו של חולי זה דמקבל קמיעא וא"ת ממתני' דלעיל שמעינן לה דקתני כל שריפא ושנה ושילש דמשמע לאדם אחד ואוקימנא דאיתמחי קמיעא ולא אמרינן מזליה הוא לא דמי התם חד קמיעא הוא וליכא למיתלייה במזלא דגברא אלא בקמיע הני ודאי בגברא תלוי או ברופא או במתרפא הלכך מיבעיא לן במאי ניתליה: לאצולינהו. בשבת °לחצר [ד] המעורבת כשאר כתבי הקדש: הברכות. שתקנו חכמים כגון תשעה של ר"ה שיש בהן מלכיות וזכרונות ושופרות: מעינות. מפרשיות הרבה שכותבין בהן את מקראות של רפואה: היה כתוב שם יגוד. [ה] יקוץ מקום השם ויגנזנו: סתם בית הכסא שלהן בשדות: שיש בו סכנה. אי שקיל ליה מיניה דשרי למיעל בהן לבית הכסא משום פקוח נפש: אף על גב דנקיט ליה בידיה. תכשיטו הוא הלכך אי נמי מייתי ליה ד' אמות בידים לא מחייב:

שלא

תוספות

כל שריפא שלשה בני אדם כאחד. נראה לר"י דגרסינן כאחד והכי פירושו מדקתני כאחד אלמא משמע דבג' קמיעים איירי ולעיל קתני כל שריפא ושנה ושילש משמע קמיע אחד ומשני דההוא דלעיל לאמחויי קמיע והך לאמחויי גברא וה"ה אפילו לא נתרפאו יחד אלא הא דנקט כאחד לאשמעינן דבג' קמיעין איירי ולאמחויי גברא:

תלתא קמיעין לג' גברי תלת תלת זימני. פירוש שכתב לחש אחד בג' איגרות וכל אחת הועילה לג' אנשים או לאחד שלש פעמים קשה לרשב"א קמיע ג' היכי איתמחי הלא מיד כשנתרפא האדם שלישי בקמיע ג' [פעם א'] איתמחי גברא וכיון דאתמחי גברא ודאי שאותה איגרת תועיל מכאן ואילך וי"ל כגון דשני קמיעין הללו ריפאו תלת זימני לתרי גברי וקמיע שלישי לחד מהנך תרי גברי תרי זימני והשתא מימחו כבר תרי קמיעי וגברא וקמיע שלישי אכתי לא איתמחי וחזר וריפא קמיע שלישי אדם שלישי דהשתא בא בבת אחת המחאת גברא והמחאת קמיע:

תלת תלת זימני. הוה מצי למימר חד תלת זימני ואינך חד זימנא אלא בעי למימר שיהיו שלשה קמיעין מומחין: חד קמיע לתלת גברי. נראה לר"י דה"ה לחד גברא תלת זימני דודאי לגבי המחאת גברא הוא דמבעיא ליה בסמוך אי אתמחי בחד גברא מתלת קמיעי אבל לענין המחאת קמיע דעדיף לא קא מיבעיא ליה דפשיטא דתלינן בהמחאת קמיע ולא אמרינן מזליה דהאי גברא הוא דמקבל כתבא והאי דנקט לתלתא גברי משום רבותא דאפילו הכי גברא לא אתמחי: תלת קמיע לחד גברא מאי. תימה תיפשוט ליה מדתני לעיל איזהו קמיע מומחה כל שריפא שלשה בני אדם ומוקמינן לה לאמחויי גברא משמע דוקא תלת גברי אבל חד גברא לא מדלא קתני כל שריפא אדם א' בג' קמיעין ובקונטרס פי' בפי' א' מימחי גברא מימחי קמיע שעשה אדם זה קמיע לשלשה אנשים דנעשה אדם זה מומחה שריפא שלשה אנשים והקמיע מומחה שריפא כתב זה ג' אנשים ולהאי פירושא נמי לא אימחי גברא אלא דוקא לאותו לחש וקשה לר"י לפירוש זה דהא אמרינן לקמן חד קמיע לתלתא גברי קמיע איתמחי [ב] גברא לא איתמחי ויש ליישב לשון הקונטרס דה"ק שעשה אדם זה לחש זה בשלשה איגרות לג' אנשים דנעשה אדם זה מומחה שריפא לג' אנשים והלחש מומחה שריפא לחש זה ג' אנשים וגם זה אין נראה לר"י דאם בענין זה נמי קרוי חד קמיע לתלתא גברא הדרא קושיא לדוכתיה ואם הוא קרוי בענין זה תלתא קמיע לתלתא גברי חד חד זימנא הא אמרינן לקמן דגברא איתמחי ולא קמיע לכך נראה לר"י כדפירש וכן פירוש אחר שפי' בקונטרס מיושב מן הראשון: [ו] הא לאמחויי קמיע. פירש בקונטרס דנעשה הקמיע לבדו מומחה ע"י אדם זה תימה דהוא עצמו פירש בסמוך גבי תלת תלת זימני דכל לחש שריפא ג' פעמים נעשו ג' קמיעות הללו מומחים מיד כל אדם אע"פ שרוצה לומר הקונטרס שרופא אחד כתבם מדפירש ואין לומר שמזל הרופא גרם וכן נראה ודאי עיקר דלא ע"י אדם זה לבד נעשה הקמיע מומחה אלא אף מיד כל אדם דהא אמרינן בסמוך תלתא קמיע לתלתא גברי תלת תלת זימני איתמחי גברא ואיתמחי קמיע והאי תלתא קמיעי לתלתא גברי דקאמר איירי שרופא אחד עשאם דבענין אחר לא איתמחי גברא וא"כ האי דקאמר נמי תלת תלת זימני איירי נמי ברופא אחד כמו רישא וקאמר דאיתמחי קמיע והיינו ע"כ מיד כל אדם דאי מיד רופא זה הא בלאו הכי הוא מומחה בכל קמיעין שבעולם וממה שפירש נמי גבי תלת תלת זימני כל לחש ריפא ג' פעמים ואפילו אדם אחד חזר בו מזה דפירש איתמחי קמיע ואין לומר מזל החולה גרם שמתרפא ע"י קמיעתא שהרי בשלשה אנשים הוחזק משמע דלא אמרינן איתמחי קמיע אלא א"כ ריפא ג' אנשים:

איתמחי קמיע. פירש הקונטרס ואין לומר מזל הרופא גרם דאין הדבר תלוי במזל הרופא אלא בחכמתו משמע שרוצה ליתן טעם אמאי איתמחי קמיע במזל הרופא היה לנו לתלות שכבר הומחה שריפא ג' אנשים בג' מיני קמיעים ולא היה לנו לתלות בקמיע ולא ידע רשב"א מה טעם נותן על זה דהא לא איתמחו שאר קמיעין של שאר חולאים אע"ג דהרופא איתמחי בכל קמיעין שבעולם ה"נ אלו ג' קמיעים נמי לתלות ברופא אלא צריך לתרץ כמו שפירשתי ללשון ר"י בענין שיבא המחאת קמיע והמחאת גברא בבת אחת:

והתניא

לח א מיי' וסמג שם טוש"ע א"ח סי' שא סעיף כה:
לט ב מיי' פ"ו מהל' יסודי התורה הלכה ו סמג לאוין ג:

רבינו חננאל

וכדתניא איזהו קמיע מומחה כל שריפא ג' בני אדם כאחד. בעי רב פפא תלתא גווני קמיע רפאו לאחד ג' מיני חלאים כל קמיע ריפא חולי מאי קמיעא ודאי לא אתמחאי גברא מאי מי אמרינן הא מסי ליה ג' זמני או דלמא מזלא דהאי גברא דמקבל קמיעא ועלתה בתיקו. ולא אתמחי לא גברא ולא קמיעא. ירושלמי נאמן אדם לומר קמיעא זו ריפאתי בו ב' וג' פעמים. קמיעין יש בהן משום קדושה ואסור למיעל בהו לבית הכסא אי לא [לגניזה] לא קא מיבעי לן דלא גרעי הקמיעין מן הכלים שאם היה שם כתוב עליהן תנינן הרי זה יגור ויגנז [כי] קא מיבעיא לן למיעל בהו לבהכ"ס.

א) לקמן דף קטו: וש"נ, ב) ערכין ו. [מס' סופרים פ"ה ה"ג], ג) [גיר' הערוך יגור], ד) לחצר שאינה מעורבת כצ"ל וכ"ה ברש"י שבאלפס, ה) וגי' הערוך יגור ברי"ש פי' יגור אותו במגירה רש"ל, ו) שייך לעיל קודם ד"ה תלתא.

תוספות ישנים

א) ק"ק דלכתי לא משכחת שיתמחי הקמיע הג'. אמ"ל דגברא אתמחי אפילו בג' קמיעין לחד גברא והיכי קאמר פשיטא לי דמשמע נמי דקאי אקמיע שלישית מדקאמר תלת זימני משמע דהומחו שלשתן. וי"ל אע"ג דכבר אתמחי גברא כי ריפא כל אחד ג"פ יש לנו לתלות גם בקמיע דעדיף כל מה שאנו יכולין למימחי קמיע ולא גברא כגון שכתב זה ריפא תלתא זימנא חד גברא ואתמחי גברא ולא קמיע כגון שריפא בג' אגרות לג' אנשים:
ב) גברא לא איתמחי. ולהאי פי' היינו דלא איתמחי אפילו ללחש זה כצ"ל:

הגהות הב"ח

(א) רש"י ד"ה ואיתמחי כו' נמי מזל החולה גרס:

גליון הש"ס

רש"י ד"ה לאצולינהו בשבת לחצר המעורבת. עי' לקמן דף קטו ע"א ברש"י ד"ה מצילין אותן וצ"ע:

ליקוטי רש"י

מזלא דהאי גברא. מלאך שלו ומליץ עליו [לעיל נג:]. הברכות. מטבע ברכות שטבעו חכמים כגון שמונה עשרה ושאר ברכות. ומעניינות הרבה. מפרשיות שהיו כותבין בקמיעין פסוקים ללחש כגון כל המחלה וכגון לא תירא מפחד לילה. ונשרפים במקומן. אם נפלה דליקה בשבת [לקמן קטו:]. יגוד. יחתוך כמו (דניאל ד) גודו אילנא [בכורות מד.]. יחתוך מקום השם ויגנוז החתיכה וישתמש במותר [ערכין ו.]. ויגנזנו. שכל דבר קדש טעון גניזה [לקמן צ.]. אסור להניחן במקום הפקר [שם קטו.].

Baraisa clearly states that amulets may *not* be saved.[22] אֶלָּא לְעִנְיַן גְּנִיזָה – And if you will say, **rather,** that the question was raised **concerning the hiding away** of worn-out amulets,[23] this too can be easily resolved, תָּא שְׁמַע – for we can **come and learn** the answer from the following Baraisa: הָיָה כָּתוּב עַל יְדוֹת הַכֵּלִים – IF [ONE OF THE NAMES OF GOD] WAS WRITTEN ON THE HANDLES OF UTENSILS וְעַל כַּרְעֵי הַמִּטָּה – OR ON THE LEGS OF A BED, יָגוֹד וְיִגְנְזֶנּוּ – HE MUST CUT that section OFF AND HIDE IT AWAY.[24] We see from this Baraisa that Names of God must be stored away; this would apply to amulets as well. אֶלָּא לִיכָּנֵס בָּהֶן בְּבֵית הַכִּסֵּא – **Rather,** the inquiry was raised concerning whether one is permitted **to enter a latrine while wearing [amulets].** מַאי – **What** is the law? יֵשׁ בָּהֶן קְדוּשָּׁה וַאֲסִיר – Do we say that **[amulets] have intrinsic sanctity and it is** therefore **forbidden** to enter a bathroom while wearing them?[25] אוֹ דִילְמָא אֵין בָּהֶן קְדוּשָּׁה וּשְׁרֵי – **Or perhaps [amulets] do not have intrinsic sanctity, and it is permitted** to wear them into a bathroom?

The Gemara attempts to bring a proof from our Mishnah:

תָּא שְׁמַע – **Come, learn** a proof from our Mishnah, which states: וְלֹא בְּקָמֵיעַ בִּזְמַן שֶׁאֵינוֹ מִן הַמּוּמְחֶה – AND he may NOT go out WITH AN AMULET, WHEN IT IS NOT FROM AN EXPERT. הָא מִן הַמּוּמְחֶה נָפֵיק – Now, **this** ruling implies that if the amulet was **from an expert, it may be taken outside.** וְאִי אָמְרַתְּ קְמֵיעִין יֵשׁ בָּהֶן מִשּׁוּם קְדוּשָּׁה – **But if you say** that **amulets have intrinsic sanctity,** and cannot be taken into a bathroom, the wearing of amulets from experts should also be prohibited; זִמְנִין דְּמִיצְטְרִיךְ לְבֵית הַכִּסֵּא – for **sometimes he** (i.e. the wearer of the amulet) **will need to use the latrine,** and he will remove the amulet, וְאָתֵי לְאַיְתּוּיֵינְהוּ אַרְבַּע אַמּוֹת בִּרְשׁוּת הָרַבִּים – **and he will** inadvertently **come to carry it four *amos* in the public domain!**[26] From the fact that the Mishnah does not seem to be concerned with this possibility, we see that amulets do not have intrinsic sanctity.[27] – ? –

The Gemara deflects the proof:

הָכָא בְּמַאי עַסְקִינַן – **Here** in the Mishnah, **with what are we dealing?** בְּקָמֵיעַ שֶׁל עִיקָּרִין – **With an amulet made of roots** of herbs, that definitely has no sanctity. Thus, it cannot be proven from our Mishnah that amulets do not have sanctity.[28]

The Gemara persists:

וְהָתַנְיָא – **But it was taught in a Baraisa:**[29] אֶחָד קָמֵיעַ שֶׁל כְּתָב וְאֶחָד קָמֵיעַ שֶׁל עִיקָּרִין – An effective amulet may be EITHER AN AMULET OF WRITING OR AN AMULET OF ROOTS of herbs. This Baraisa teaches that one may wear even an amulet of writing if it is proven effective.[30] – ? –

The Gemara offers another answer:

אֶלָּא הָכָא בְּמַאי עַסְקִינַן – **Rather, what are we dealing with here** in the Mishnah? בְּחוֹלֶה שֶׁיֵּשׁ בּוֹ סַכָּנָה – **With a person who is dangerously ill,** who will certainly wear his amulet at all times.[31]

The Gemara questions this answer as well:

וְהָתַנְיָא – **But it was taught in that** same **Baraisa** אֶחָד חוֹלֶה שֶׁיֵּשׁ בּוֹ סַכָּנָה – that an effective amulet may be worn EITHER BY A PERSON WHO IS DANGEROUSLY ILL וְאֶחָד חוֹלֶה שֶׁאֵין בּוֹ סַכָּנָה – OR BY A PERSON WHO IS NOT DANGEROUSLY ILL! Thus, the original proof still stands.[32] – ? –

The Gemara offers a third possible answer:

אֶלָּא – **Rather,** כֵּיוָן דְּמַסֵּי – **since [the amulet] cures him,**[33] אַף עַל גַּב דְּנָקֵיט לֵיהּ בִּידֵיהּ נַמִּי שַׁפִּיר דָּמֵי – **even if he holds it in his hand, it is fine;** i.e. it is permitted. Thus, even if the amulet has intrinsic sanctity, one would be permitted to wear it outside.[34]

NOTES

22. [See Chapter 16 of this tractate, and *Orach Chaim* 334:11, regarding what *can* be done to save amulets.]

23. I.e. the Gemara was inquiring whether worn-out amulets (that often contained Names of God) needed to be hidden away just as holy scrolls are hidden away when they wear out. [This inquiry would then have no connection to the laws of the Sabbath (*Chidushei HaRan*).]

24. I.e. they may not be treated as regular utensils (this is so even if amulets do *not* have intrinsic sanctity – see *Meiri*).

25. [It is forbidden to bring items that have sanctity into an outhouse – see *Berachos* 23a ff.]

26. [Most latrines in Talmudic times were out of doors (*Rashi*).]

27. Since the Mishnah rules that an amulet from an expert may be worn, it must be that the Sages were not concerned that the wearer would remove it before going to the bathroom; and this can only be explained if we assume that an amulet has no intrinsic sanctity and therefore need not be removed.

28. For it is possible that written amulets are indeed prohibited, as a person may remove them [due to their sanctity] before using the bathroom; and the Mishnah's ruling permitting amulets would be interpreted as referring only to amulets of herbs.

29. This Barasia was cited above, on 61a.

30. Accordingly, the original proof is reinstated; for if the written amulet can be worn in the street, obviously the Sages were not concerned that a person would remove it before relieving himself; and this can only be true if amulets have no intrinsic sanctity.

31. Thus, he may wear his amulet into the latrine as well, and the Sages were not concerned that he would remove it (*Rashi*). Hence, it is still possible to say that amulets possess intrinsic sanctity. See *Sfas Emes*.

32. For the Mishnah is teaching that an effective amulet may be worn even by a moderately ill person; obviously, then, the Sages were not concerned that a person would remove it before relieving himself, and this would only be true if amulets have no intrinsic sanctity.

33. [Or prevents him from becoming ill (see above, 61a).]

34. For an amulet is considered the accessory of the ill person, and it is considered part of his attire [and the Gemara now assumes that this is true even if it must be carried to effect the cure (see *Sfas Emes* to 62a ד״ה והתניא).] Thus, even if the amulet has intrinsic sanctity, the Sages were not concerned that the person would take it off and carry it in the street, for even if he did so, he would not be liable (*Rashi*).

The Gemara objects:

רַבִּי אוֹשַׁעְיָא וְהָתַנְיָא – But we have been taught in a Baraisa: R' OSHAYA SAYS: **אוֹמֵר** – **וּבִלְבַד שֶׁלֹּא יֹאחֲזֶנּוּ בְּיָדוֹ** – One may wear an amulet that comes from an expert, AS LONG AS HE DOES NOT HOLD IT IN HIS HAND **וְיַעֲבִירֶנּוּ אַרְבַּע אַמּוֹת בִּרְשׁוּת הָרַבִּים** – AND CARRY IT FOUR *AMOS* IN THE PUBLIC DOMAIN.[1] This Baraisa clearly states that an amulet may *not* be carried, even though it cures the ill person. Thus, we can still prove from the Mishnah that amulets do not possess intrinsic sanctity.[2] – ? –

The Gemara deflects the proof by reinterpreting the Mishnah's teaching that amulets may be worn on the Sabbath:

[אֶלָּא] הָכָא בְּמַאי עַסְקִינַן – **Rather, with what are we dealing here,** in the Mishnah? **בִּמְחוּפֶּה עוֹר** – **With** an amulet **covered with hide.** A person wearing such an amulet need not remove it before entering a latrine;[3] thus, it cannot be proven from the Mishnah's ruling permitting the wearing of amulets on the Sabbath that amulets have no intrinsic sanctity.[4]

The Gemara takes issue with the assumption that one need not remove an amulet before entering a latrine if the amulet is covered with leather:

וַהֲרֵי תְּפִילִּין דִּמְחוּפֶּה עוֹר – **But there are tefillin, which are covered with leather,**[5] **וְתַנְיָא** – **and** yet **it has been taught in a Baraisa: הַנִּכְנָס לְבֵית הַכִּסֵּא** – ONE WHO IS ENTERING A LATRINE **חוֹלֵץ תְּפִילִּין בְּרִחוּק אַרְבַּע אַמּוֹת וְנִכְנָס** – SHOULD REMOVE HIS TEFILLIN AT A DISTANCE OF FOUR *AMOS* from it, AND then ENTER. We see from this Baraisa that items possessing sanctity may not be brought into a latrine even if they are covered with leather. Thus, the proof from the Mishnah that amulets do not possess sanctity is reinstated.[6] – ? –

The Gemara answers:

הָתָם מִשּׁוּם שִׁי״ן – In truth, an amulet covered with leather may be carried into a latrine.[7] But **there** in the case of tefillin, they may not be worn in a bathroom **because of the** Hebrew letter ***shin*** that appears on the *outside* of the leather casing of the tefillin.[8] **דְּאָמַר אַבַּיֵּי** – **For Abaye said: שִׁי״ן שֶׁל תְּפִילִּין הֲלָכָה לְמֹשֶׁה מִסִּינַי** – **The *shin*** that protrudes from the leather box **of the tefillin is** known from **a Halachah Le'Moshe MiSinai.** Amulets, however, may be taken into a latrine if they are covered.[9]

The Gemara cites other, related laws of tefillin that are derived from oral tradition:

וְאָמַר אַבַּיֵּי – **And Abaye** also **said: דל״ת שֶׁל תְּפִילִּין הֲלָכָה לְמֹשֶׁה מִסִּינַי** – **The *dalet*** formed by the straps **of** the **tefillin** worn on the head[10] **is** known from **a Halachah Le'Moshe MiSinai. וְאָמַר אַבַּיֵּי** – **And Abaye** also **said: יו״ד שֶׁל תְּפִילִּין הֲלָכָה לְמֹשֶׁה מִסִּינַי** – **The** letter ***yud*** formed by the straps **of** the **tefillin** worn on the arm **is** known from **a Halachah Le'Moshe MiSinai.**[11]

The Mishnah stated:

וְלֹא בְשִׁרְיוֹן וְלֹא בְקַסְדָּא וְלֹא בְמַגָּפַיִים – AND he may NOT go out WITH A COAT OF MAIL (*shiryon*),[12] NOR with A HELMET, NOR with SHIN GUARDS.

The Gemara identifies these items:

שִׁרְיוֹן זַרְדָּא – ***Shiryon*** refers to **a coat of mail. קַסְדָּא** – **A helmet** – **אָמַר רַב סַנְוָארְתָּא** – **Rav said:** This refers to the **leather helmet** worn under the armor helmet. **מַגָּפַיִים** – **Shin guards** – **אָמַר רַב פֻּזְמְקֵי** – **Rav said:** This refers to **leggings of iron** worn during times of war.[13]

NOTES

1. For an amulet is considered an accessory only when it is being worn [i.e. hung around the neck] (*Rashi;* see *Chidushei HaRan* and *Sfas Emes*); when it is carried in the hand, however, it is a burden, and carrying it is Biblically prohibited.

2. For the Mishnah allows an ill person to go out with an expert's amulet, which indicates that the Sages were not concerned that he would remove the amulet before entering a latrine; and the reason that the Sages were not concerned is perforce because amulets do not have inherent sanctity (and therefore they need not be removed before one enters a latrine).

[*Tosafos* ask: Perhaps carrying an expert's amulet is only Rabbinically prohibited (just as tying an amulet to a ring is Rabbinically prohibited; see 61b note 2), and the reason the Sages were not concerned that one would come to carry the amulet is because even if one *were* to remove the amulet [due to its inherent sanctity] before entering the latrine, no Biblical prohibition would result; thus, even if amulets *do* have inherent sanctity, the Mishnah's ruling would still be correct! They answer that R' Oshaya's categorical statement implies that it is forbidden to carry the amulet out in one's hand even if it is held in his closed fist, where it cannot be seen; thus, he must be speaking not of a Rabbinic prohibition due to appearances, but of a Biblical prohibition (see *Tosafos;* see also *Ritva MHK* ed. and *Dibros Moshe* 53:21).]

3. Since the amulet is covered, it is not demeaning to bring it into a latrine, and he need not remove it (*Rashi*). [*Ritva* (*MHK* ed.) notes that simply placing the amulet or any other holy item in a bag does not allow a person to bring it into a latrine, unless there is a *tefach* of open space around the item within the bag (see *Berachos* 23a). It is only a casing which is not often removed, such as the covering of an amulet (which is sewn shut), that serves to permit the bringing in of the item. See also *Ran* (*MHK* ed.), and *Sfas Emes; Magen Avraham* to *Orach Chaim* 43:13; and *Rashba* and *Pnei Yehoshua* to *Berachos* ibid.]

4. For it is possible that the Mishnah permits going out only with an amulet that is covered; an uncovered amulet, however, may possibly be prohibited, due to the fact that one might come to remove it before entering a latrine because of its inherent sanctity (see *Chidushei HaRan*).

5. The parchments on which the four Torah passages of tefillin are written are encased in the leather boxes of the tefillin (*Rashi*).

6. For the Mishnah permits wearing an amulet on the Sabbath, which indicates that the Sages were not concerned that the amulet would be removed before the wearer enters a latrine; and since this unconcern cannot be due to the fact that the amulet is covered [as it has been established that the covering is not effective], it must be because the amulet possesses no inherent sanctity!

7. Thus, the proof from the Mishnah is not valid, as explained above (see note 4).

8. Three creases in the shape of the Hebrew letter *shin* are worked into the outer surface of the leather box that encases the tefillin worn on the head (see *Orach Chaim* 32:42). This *shin* combines with the Hebrew letter *dalet* that is formed by the knot in the strap of the tefillin worn on the head (see note 10), and the *yud* formed by the strap of the tefillin worn on the arm, to form the Hebrew word ש־די, one of the Names of God (see *Rashi*). The *shin* is not covered, and it is because of the *shin* that the tefillin may not be worn into a latrine. [This applies to the tefillin worn on the head. As regards tefillin worn on the arm, *Tosafos* hold that they need not be removed before entering a latrine; *Rashi* apparently disagrees (see below, note 11). See also above, 61a note 25, and *Pnei Yehoshua* and *Chasam Sofer* there.] A covered amulet, however, may indeed be worn into a latrine.

9. See note 7.

10. The knot in the straps of the tefillin worn on the head was tied so that the two sections forming the knot were at right angles to each other, thus forming the shape of the letter *dalet* (see *Rashi;* see also *Rashash* and *Shabbos Shel Mi*).

11. The strap of the tefillin worn on the arm is knotted onto itself, to form the semblance of the letter *yud* (see *Rashi;* see also *Rashi* printed alongside *Rif* with *Hagahos HaBach;* see also *Menachem Meishiv Nefesh*).

[*Tosafos* and other Rishonim (see *Ran MHK* ed.) delete these two statements of Abaye from the text. (This is consistent with their position that tefillin worn on the arm need not be removed before entering the bathroom; see above, note 8.) See above, 28b; see also *Chelkas Binyomin* to 61a (to *Tosafos* ד״ה דילמא).]

12. The word *shiryon* was translated in the Mishnah in reflection of the Gemara's conclusion here.

13. These items are clothing worn in battle; thus, it is Biblically permitted to wear them on the Sabbath. The Sages prohibited them lest

והתניא רבי אושעיא אומר ובלבד שלא יאחזנו בידו ויעבירנו ארבע אמות ברשות הרבים [אלא] א הכא במאי עסקינן במחופה עור והרי תפילין דמחופה עור ותניא (א) ב הנכנס לבית הכסא חולץ תפילין ברחוק ארבע אמות ונכנס התם משום שי"ן דאמר אביי [ב] ג) שי"ן של תפילין הלכה למשה מסיני ואמר אביי ד' של תפילין הלכה למשה מסיני ואמר אביי יו"ד של תפילין הלכה למשה מסיני: ולא בשריון ולא בקסדא ולא במגפיים: שריון ג) זרדא קסדא אמר רב סנוארתא מגפיים אמר רב פזמקי: **מתני'** ג לא תצא אשה במחט הנקובה ולא בטבעת שיש עליה חותם ולא בכוליאר ולא ד) בכובלת ולא בצלוחית של פלייטון ° ואם יצתה חייבת חטאת דברי ר' מאיר וחכמים פוטרין בכובלת ובצלוחית של פלייטון: **גמ'** ד אמר עולא וחילופיהן באיש אלמא קסבר עולא כל מידי דחזי לאיש לא חזי לאשה ומידי דחזי לאשה לא חזי לאיש מתיב רב יוסף ה) הרועים יוצאין בשקין ולא הרועים בלבד אמרו ה אלא כל אדם אלא שדרכן של הרועים לצאת בשקין [אלא] אמר רב יוסף קסבר עולא נשים עם בפני עצמן הן איתיביה אביי [ה] ו) המוצא תפילין מכניסן זוג זוג אחד האיש ואחד האשה ואי אמרת נשים עם בפני עצמן הן והא מצות עשה שהזמן גרמא הוא ז) וכל מצות עשה שהזמן גרמא נשים פטורות התם קסבר ר"מ לילה זמן תפילין הוא ח) ושבת זמן תפילין הוא הוה ליה מצות עשה שלא הזמן גרמא וכל מצות עשה שלא הזמן גרמא נשים חייבות והא הוצאה כלאחר יד היא אמר רבי ירמיה באשה גזברית עסקינן אמר ט) רבה (בר בר חנה אמר רבי יוחנן) תרצת אשה איש מאי איכא למימר אלא אמר רבא ו פעמים שאדם נותן לאשתו טבעת שיש עליה חותם להוליכה לקופסא ומניחתה בידה עד שמגעת לקופסא ופעמים שהאשה נותנת לבעלה טבעת שאין עליה חותם להוליכה אצל אומן לתקן ומניחה בידו עד שמגיע אצל אומן: ז ולא בכוליאר ולא בכובלת: מאי כוליאר א"ר י) מכבנתא כובלת אמר רב חומרתא דפילון וכן אמר רב אסי חומרתא כ) דפילון ת"ר לא תצא בכובלת ואם יצתה חייבת חטאת דברי ר"מ וחכמים אומרים ח לא תצא ואם יצתה פטורה רבי אליעזר אומר יוצאה אשה בכובלת לכתחלה במאי קמיפלגי רבי מאיר סבר משאוי הוא ורבנן סברי תכשיט הוא ודילמא שלפא ומחויא ואתיא לאיתויה ורבי אליעזר סבר מאן דרכה למירמיה אשה שריחה רע לא שלפא ומחויא ולא אתיא לאתוייה ארבע אמות ברשות הרבים ° והתניא ל) ר' אליעזר פוטר בכובלת ובצלוחית של פלייטון לא קשיא הא מ) כי קאי אדרבי מאיר הא כי קאי אדרבנן כי קאי אדרבי מאיר דאמר חייב חטאת אמר ליה פטור כי קאי אדרבנן דאמרי פטור אבל אסור אמר איהו מותר לכתחלה

ומאי

רש"י

שלא יאחזנו. דלא הוי תכשיט שלו אלא דרך מלבוש: במכוסה עור. דליכא גנותא אי מעייל לבית הכסא ולא בעי למיסקליה: חולץ תפילין. ואע"ג דמכוסה עור שהארבע אגרות שהפרשיות כתובות בהן תחובות בדפוסין של עור: התם משום שי"ן. שעשויה מעור הסילון עצמו קומט בו ג' קמטין כעין שי"ן משדי והדלי"ת והיו"ד עשויין בקשר שקושר הרצועה (א) אחת לצפון ואחת למזרח כמין ד' ורצועה קטנה מאד תלויה בה ואין בה אלא כפיפה כמין יו"ד וכופאה בעוד העור לח והיא כפופה לעולם: זרדא. ברוני"א: סנוארתא. כובע עור תחת כובע המתכת: פזמקי. אנפלייאות של ברזל במלחמה: מתני' בכוליאר. מפרש בגמרא וכן כובלת: פלייטון. בלסמ"א משחא דאפרסמא: חייבת חטאת. קסבר לאו תכשיט נינהו: גמ' אמר עולא וחילופיהן באיש. אטבעת קאי דטבעת שיש עליו חותם אם יצא פטור ואם אין עליו חותם ויצא חייב חטאת: בשקין. שמתכסין בהן מפני הגשמים שקין מלבוש שק: אלא כל אדם. אלמא אע"ג דלא רגילי ביה מגו דלגבי האי תכשיט לגבי האי נמי תכשיט הוא: המוצא תפילין. בשבת בשוק או בדרך: מכניסן. לעיר דרך מלבוש: זוג זוג. כדרך שהוא לובש בחול אחד בראש ואחד בזרוע וחולצן וחוזר ומניח זוג אחר ומכניסן וכן כולן: ואחד האשה. ואע"ג דלאו תכשיט דאשה נינהו מגו דהוו תכשיט לאיש שרי אף לאשה: לילה זמן תפילין הוא וכן שבת. הלכך לעולם זמנם הוא ואין להם זמן קבוע שתהא מצותן מצות עשה שהזמן גרמא להפטר נשים מהן הלכך נקט לילה ושבת משום דפלוגתא בתרווייהו ואי הוי סבירא ליה לרבי מאיר בחד מינייהו דלאו זמן תפילין הוא נמצא זמן קבוע לתפילין והוו להו נשים פטורות: נשים חייבות. הלכך תכשיטין הן לה: והא הוצאה כלאחר יד הוא. אמתני' קאי והוצאת טבעת שמוציאתה דרך מלבוש באצבע זה שאינו תכשיט לה אמאי חייבת חטאת הרי לא הוציאה כדרך כל המוציאין שכל המוציא דבר שאינו תכשיט לו מוציאין אותו בידים ולא דרך מלבוש: גזברית. שעולת חותמות תמיד לממונין תחתיה לאמר תנו כך וכך מעות לפלוני והרי חותמה בידה הלכך רגילה היא להניחה באצבעה ומיהו תכשיט לא הוי לדידה דאין דרך נשים בכך ומיהו דרך הוצאתה של זו בכך: איש מאי איכא למימר. דקאמר עולא וחילופיהם באיש דמחייב אטבעת שאין עליה חותם והא הוצאה כלאחר יד הוא שאין דרכו להוציא בזו דרך מלבוש: לקופסא. איסקריינ"ה בלע"ז כדי להצניעה שם וי"מ שהקופסא חתומה בו וכשפותחה חוזרה וחותמת בה ולא נהירא דאם כן מנחתה באצבעה עד שמחזירתה לבעלה מיבעי ליה: אצל אומן לתקנה ומניחה באצבעו. אלמא דרך הוצאה היא: מכבנתא. נושקא"ה י) ע"ש שמכבנת וקושרת מפתחי החלוק: חומרתא דפילון. קשר שקשור בו ° סם ששמו פילון וריחו ערב ובלע"ז בלסמ"ו ואשה שריחה רע טוענתו עליה: ורבנן סברי תכשיט הוא. הלכך אם יצאת פטורה ומיהו לכתחלה לא תצא דילמא שלפא ומחויא: למרמיה. להניח בצוארה כמו שקיל ורמי: ה"ג ואשה שריחה רע לא שלפא ומחויא. שגנות הוא לה: והתניא ר' אליעזר פוטר. והכא שרי לכתחלה: הא. דקתני פוטר: כי קאי אר' מאיר. בההיא מתניתא לא איירו רבנן אלא ר"מ לחודיה וגבי חיוב דר"מ שייך למיתני רבי אליעזר פוטר ואע"פ שהוא מתיר לכתחלה: הא כי קאי ארבנן. במתניתא דלעיל דאיירו רבנן בה ואמרו פטור פריש ר' אליעזר בהדיא למילתיה לאיפלוגי עלייהו ואמר יוצאה לכתחלה:

ומאי

תוספות

והתניא ר' אושעיא אומר ובלבד כו'. תימה לר"י דילמא משום מראית העין דוקא הוא אסור מדרבנן כמו קושר בשיר ובטבעת דהשתא ליכא למיגזר דאפילו מייתי לה ליכא איסורא מדאורייתא ואומר ר"י דשלא יאחזנו בידו משמע אפילו בקומצו דליכא מראית העין אלא איסורא דאורייתא איכא ואפילו למ"ד כל דבר שאסרו חכמים משום מראית העין אפילו בחדרי חדרים אסור הכא לא שייך למיגזר דאפילו עומד בשוק ונושאן בקומצו אין כאן מראית העין:

שי"ן של תפילין. ול"ג דלי"ת ויו"ד של תפילין כו' כדמוכח בפ' במה מדליקין (לעיל כח:) גבי הא דתני רב יוסף לא הוכשרו למלאכת שמים כו' ומוקי לה לרצועותיהן ולא פריך דלי"ת של תפילין הלכה למשה מסיני כדפריך גבי שי"ן [פ]:

וחילופיהן באיש. ° אור"ת דלאחיוב חטאת קאי:

וכל מצות עשה שהזמן גרמא נשים פטורות. פירוש דהוי משוי וליתסר וא"ת והא הוצאה כלאחר יד היא ושריא משום בזיון תפילין וי"ל כיון דמשוי הוא ויכול לבא לידי חיוב חטאת היכא דמוציא בלא שינוי משום בזיון לא שרינן ליה:

אין

עין משפט נר מצוה

מ א מיי' פ"י מהל' ס"ת הלכה ה טוש"ע י"ד סי' רפב סעיף ו:

מא ב מיי' פ"ד מהל' תפילין הלכה יז סמג עשין כב טוש"ע א"ח סי' מג סעיף ה:

[מא] [ב] [מיי' שם פ"ג הלכה א' טוש"ע א"ח סי' לב סעיף מב נב]:

מב ג ד מיי' פי"ט מהל' שבת הלכה ד ה סמג לאוין סה טור א"ח סי' שג סעיף ט י וסי' שא סעיף ח ט:

מג ה מיי' שם הלכה יח טוש"ע א"ח סי' שא סעיף כא:

[מג] [ה] [מיי' פי"ט מהל' שבת הלכה כג טוש"ע א"ח סי' שא סעיף מב]:

מד ו מיי' פי"ט שם הלכה ג:

מה ז ח מיי' פי"ט שם הלכה ז סמג שם טוש"ע א"ח סי' שג סעיף יא:

רבינו חננאל

ופשטינא אם מחופין עור (כיון) שפיר דמי והא דתניא לא יכנס אדם בתפילין לבית הכסא קבע אפי' להשתין מים התם משום שי"ן דאמר אביי שי"ן של תפילין הל"מ. ת"ר איזהו קמיע מומחה כל שריפה ושנה ושלש אחד קמיע של כתב ואחד קמיע של עקרין אחד חולה שיש בו סכנה ואחד חולה שאין בו סכנה [ולא] שנכפה אלא שלא יכפה וקושר ומתיר. ואפילו ברה"ר ובלבד שלא יקשרנו בשיר או בטבעת ויוצא בו לרה"ר מפני מראית העין: שירין זרדא: **לא** תצא אשה במחט נקובה. ולא בטבעת שיש עליה חותם. אמר עולא חילופיהן באיש כלומר האיש אסור בטבעת שאין עליה חותם ופטור בטבעת שיש עליה חותם. וכי קאמר עולא וחילופיהן באיש בטבעת בלבד קאמר מותבינן אמאי חייב חטאת והא הוצאה כלאחר יד היא כלומר באצבעה היא מוציאה ואין דרך המוציאין דבר להוציאה דרך מלבוש. ומוקים לה ר' ירמיה באשה גזברית עסקינן שכן דרכה להיות הטבעת באצבעה כדי שתהא חותמת בו כיסים ובתים. הוצאה בכוונה היא לחתום בו ולאו משום תכשיט הוא ודחינן תרצת אשה איש בטבעת שאין עליה חותם אמאי חייב חטאת. ואוקמה רבא לעולם באשה שאינה גזברית ומשום הכי חייבת חטאת דפעמים אדם [נותן] טבעת שיש עליה חותם לאשתו להוליכה לקופסא ומנחתה באצבעה עד שמגעת לקופסא שנמצאת הוצאה בכוונה כדרכה. והאשה נמי פעמים שנותנת כו' וקיי"ל טבעת שיש עליה חותם תכשיט לאיש ולא לאשה ושאין עליה חותם תכשיט לאשה ולא לאיש. ובדין הוא להיות כל אחד ואחד מותר במה שהוא תכשיט לו אלא גזרו משום דרבא שכבר פרשנהו למעלה (ס.): בכולייר. תכשיט שמסבב הראש כולה כדגרסינן ביומא (כה.) הכהנים היו מוקפין ועומדין ככולייר. כובלת חומרתא דפילון. פי' בשמים בלולין כדמתרגם בלולה דפילא. צלוחית של פלייטון

ראשית

מסורת הש"ס

א) ברכות כג., ב) לעיל כח:, מנחות לה., ג) פירוש שריון מטכעות קטנו', ד) [גיר' הערוך בכובלת], ה) [תוספת' פ"ו מדרים נה:], ו) עירובין צו: תוס' דעירובין פ"ח ביצה טו., ז) [קידושין כט. ושם נסמן], ח) [לעיל דף סא. וש"נ], ט) נ"ל רבא, י) [עמוס' ב"ב קט: ד"ה כבינתי], כ) [רב אלפס פי' מלשון בלולה בשמן מתרגמינן דפילא במשח וכי"א בהרא"ש], ל) [לקמן סה. תוספתא פ"ה ע"ש], מ) [עי' תוס' לעיל ג. סד"ה בר מהני], נ) עי' רש"י יומא כה. ד"ה בכוליאר, ס) [וע"ע תוס' ברכות ו. ד"ה אלו וכו'].

הגהות הב"ח

(א) רש"י ד"ה התם וכו' הרצוע' שבראש אחת לצפון:

גליון הש"ס

מתני' ואם יצתה חייבת חטאת. עי' לעיל דף יא ע"ב תוס' ד"ה ואם יצא: גמ' והתניא ר"א פוטר. עיין לעיל דף ג ע"א תוס' ד"ה בר מהני: רש"י ד"ה חומרתי דפילון וכו' סם ששמו פילון. עיין סוטה דף טו ע"א תוס' ד"ה כמין חומר: תוס' ד"ה וחילופיהן באיש. אור"ת דאחיוב חטאת קאי. עיין עירובין דף סט ע"א תוס' ד"ה כיון דחזיא:

ליקוטי רש"י

תפילין דמחופה עור. עור דפוס שלהן שהכתבים של פרשיות מונחים בו [לעיל כח:]. חולץ תפילין ברחוק ארבע אמות. ויאחז תפילין בידו כדאמרינן לקמן ובקבוע נמי אוחזן בידו אלא שצריך לחלצן ברחוק ארבע אמות שבזמן שהם בראשו הם בגלוי ונגלי הדבר [ברכות כג.]. שי"ן של תפילין וכו' ד' של תפילין וכו'. שי"ן של תפילין שיהא העור נקמט מבחוץ שלשה קמטין ודומה לשי"ן והרצועה נקשרת כמין דלי"ת ויש רצועה כפופה כמין י' דהיינו שדי [לעיל שם ועי' במסוה"ש שם]. שישים הרצועות על ראשו [כעין] דל"ת כדי שיהא שדי נראה עליהן דשי"ן נראה בקמט בית חיצונה שכפל הקלף כעין שי"ן ודל"ת נראה בקשר ויו"ד נראה באותו של יד כמין רצועה קטנה וראשה כפוף מעט כמין יו"ד [מנחות לה:]. הלכה למשה מסיני היאך הוא עשוי שדומה לדל"ת וכתפירתן עשוי כמין שי"ן ורצועה קטנה קבועה בהן וראשה כפוף ודומה ליו"ד הרי שדי [עירובין צז.]. במחט הנקובה. לענין הוצאת שבת יש חילוק בין נקובה לשאינו נקובה דנקובה קתני חייב חטאת ובשאינה נקובה כגון איספינגל"א שהיא תכשיט קתני אינו חייב חטאת בפרק במה אשה (שבת נז:) [לעיל נב:]. ולא בטבעת שיש עליה חותם. דלאו תכשיט הוא והוי משאוי. דחותם לאשה לאו תכשיט הוא דאין דרך לאשה לחתום ולשלוח שלוחים שאין חותם עשוי אלא לאדם גדול וממונה [שם נט:]. חותם. צורה לחתום בה איגרת או כל דבר סגור [שם נז.]. בכוליאר. עגול שקורין נושק"א [יומא כה.]. פלייטון. בושם שריחו נודף ואינו אפרסמון [סנהדרין קח. ועיין במלוא הרועים]. המוצא תפילין. בשדה במקום שנאבדין. מכניסן. לעיר ולבית. זוג זוג. אחד בראש ואחד בזרוע והיינו זוג כדרך שלובשן בחול וחוזר תמיד ומכניסן זוג אחר זוג עד שיכלו [עירובין צה.]. נותן בראשו אחד ואחד בזרועו כדרך הנחתן בחול ומכניסן וחוזר והולך ולובש זוג אחר ומכניסן, תפילין של ראש ושל זרוע קרי זוג זוג [ביצה טו.]. מצות עשה שהזמן גרמא. נפקא לן בפרק קמא דקידושין (כט.) דנשים פטורות [פסחים מג:]. שהזמן גרמא. שהזמן גורם לה שתבא [קידושין כט.]. מכבנתא. כמין קרסי מתכת לחבר הבגד כמו תנתן כבינתי לבתי (גיטין טו.) וכמו (גיטין יד:) תנתן כבנתי לבתי פרמוי"ל והוא [בית] נפש שקורין נושק"א שמחברין בה פתיחות פי החלוק [שבועות ו:]. חומרתא דפילון. בוטין שהנשים תולות בצואריהן של זהב או של כסף ונותן בו שמן שמעורב בו מין בושם ששמו פילון ודומה לעלי גפנים כדתניא בת"כ שלא יערב קימוס כמר מי גלובקיא בשמן עלי גפנים כפילון [גיטין סט:].

Mishnah The Mishnah lists those items that a woman is Biblically forbidden to wear outside on the Sabbath: לֹא תֵצֵא אִשָּׁה בְּמַחַט הַנְּקוּבָה – **A woman may not go out** on the Sabbath **with a needle that is pierced;**[14] וְלֹא בְטַבַּעַת שֶׁיֵּשׁ עָלֶיהָ חוֹתָם – **and** she may **not** go out **while wearing a ring that has a signet;** וְלֹא בְכוּלְיָאר – **and not with a brooch,**[15] וְלֹא בְכוֹבֶלֶת – **and not** wearing **a spice bundle,**[16] וְלֹא בִצְלוֹחִית שֶׁל פַּלְיָיטוֹן – **and not** wearing **a flask of balsam oil.**[17] וְאִם יָצְתָה – **And if she went out** wearing any of these items, חַיֶּיבֶת חַטָּאת – **she is liable to a *chatas*** offering; דִּבְרֵי רַבִּי מֵאִיר – these are **the words of R' Meir.**[18] וַחֲכָמִים פּוֹטְרִין בְּכוֹבֶלֶת – **But the Sages exempt** her from a *chatas* if she goes out **with a spice bundle** וּבִצְלוֹחִית שֶׁל פַּלְיָיטוֹן – **or with a flask of balsam oil.**[19]

Gemara In the first Mishnah of the chapter, it was taught that it is Rabbinically forbidden for a woman to go out with a ring that has no seal; in our Mishnah it is taught that it is Biblically forbidden for a woman to go out with a ring that has a seal.

The Gemara notes that these laws apply specifically to women: אָמַר עוּלָּא – **Ulla said:** וְחִילּוּפֵיהֶן בְּאִישׁ – **And the** very **opposite** of these laws applies when the ring is worn outside **by a man.** That is, it is Rabbinically forbidden for a man to go out wearing a signet ring, while it is Biblically forbidden for him to go out wearing a ring without a signet.[20]

The Gemara attempts to explain Ulla's reasoning:

אַלְמָא קָסָבַר עוּלָּא – **We see** from this ruling **that Ulla holds** כָּל מִידֵי דַּחֲזֵי לְאִישׁ – that **any item that is fit** as an accessory **for a man** לֹא חֲזֵי לְאִשָּׁה – **is not** thereby considered **fit** as an accessory **for a woman,** וּמִידֵי דַּחֲזֵי לְאִשָּׁה – **and any item that is fit** as an accessory **for a woman** לֹא חֲזֵי לְאִישׁ – **is not** thereby considered **fit** as an accessory **for a man.**[21]

The Gemara objects to this reasoning:

מָתִיב רַב יוֹסֵף – **Rav Yosef challenged this** reasoning **from the Baraisa,** which states: הָרוֹעִים יוֹצְאִין בְּשַׂקִּין – SHEPHERDS MAY GO OUT on the Sabbath WITH clothes of SACKCLOTH;[22] וְלֹא הָרוֹעִים בִּלְבַד אָמְרוּ – AND [THE SAGES] DID NOT SAY THIS CONCERNING ONLY SHEPHERDS; אֶלָּא כָּל אָדָם – RATHER, they stated this permit TO ALL PEOPLE – אֶלָּא שֶׁדַּרְכָּן שֶׁל הָרוֹעִים לָצֵאת בְּשַׂקִּין – and the Mishnah speaks of shepherds ONLY BECAUSE IT IS THE CUSTOM OF SHEPHERDS TO WEAR clothes made of SACKCLOTH.[23] We see from this Baraisa that any man may wear clothing of sackcloth, because shepherds normally wear them. Why, then, can a man not wear a ring without a seal (on the Biblical level) simply because a woman can wear it?

The Gemara answers:

[אֶלָּא] אָמַר רַב יוֹסֵף – **Rather,**[24] **Rav Yosef said:** קָסָבַר עוּלָּא נָשִׁים עַם בִּפְנֵי עַצְמָן הֵן – **Ulla holds** that **women are viewed as a nation unto themselves** vis-a-vis men;[25] thus, although an item that is worn by *some* men (e.g. shepherds) may be worn by *all* men, the fact that a woman wears an item does not cause it to be permitted to be worn by men.[26]

The Gemara questions this logic from a Mishnah:

אֵיתִיבֵיהּ אַבָּיֵי – **Abaye challenged this** reasoning from the

NOTES

people think that the wearer was going forth on the Sabbath to wage war (see *Rashi* to 64b). *Dibros Moshe* (53:34) notes that although it is generally permissible to participate in a national war even on the Sabbath, our fear is that an onlooker might suspect the wearer of preparing for a private feud in a time of national peace.

[*Chidushei HaRan* notes that these three items of armor were worn together to effect a complete covering of the body, for the helmet covered the head, the coat of mail covered the torso, and the leggings covered the person from the waist down.]

14. I.e. a needle that has an eye and is used for sewing; such a needle is a burden rather than an ornament, and it may not be taken out even if it is thrust into the woman's clothing, for this is a common way of carrying such a needle (see *Chidushei HaRan;* see also *Tosafos* to 11b ד״ה ואם).

15. The nature of this ornament is discussed in the Gemara.

16. I.e. a hollow pendant [made of silver or gold (see below, note 50)] in which spices were placed (see below, note 44). The Gemara will describe this ornament in more detail.

17. *Rashi;* see *Melo HaRo'im;* cf. *Rambam, Commentary to the Mishnah.*

18. R' Meir considers all of these items as burdens rather than accessories (*Rashi*). Therefore, going out with them on the Sabbath is Biblically prohibited, and one who does go out is liable to a *chatas.* [The pierced needle and the signet ring are not ornamental; and the other items mentioned in the Mishnah are not considered ornaments in R' Meir's view, since the majority of women do not wear such items (see *Rashash*).]

19. The Sages regard these two items as ornaments (see below, note 49); therefore taking them out is permitted on the Biblical level. However, the Sages prohibited wearing them because they were afraid that a woman would remove them to show to her friend and come to carry them in the public domain (see Gemara below).

20. Biblically, it is permitted for a man to wear a signet ring outside on the Sabbath, for it is considered an ornament for him; the Sages prohibited this, however, for fear that a man would remove it to show to a friend and come to carry it in the public domain. A ring without a signet, however, is considered a burden for a man (in those places where men do not usually wear rings – see *Beur Halachah* to 301:9 ד״ה ואם יצא), and wearing it outside is Biblically prohibited (see *Rashi, Rif*). [This follows *Rashi's* view expressed in this chapter, that the Sages' decree concerning wearing ornaments on the Sabbath extends to the ornaments of men as well. Cf. *Tosafos,* who explain that the Gemara is referring only to the law of liability to a *chatas;* that is, while a woman is liable to a *chatas* only if she goes out with a ring that has a signet (which is deemed a burden to her), a man is liable to a *chatas* only if he goes out with a ring that has no signet. The Rabbinic prohibition, however, applies only to women in their view.]

[From *Rashi* it seems that Ulla's statement applies only to rings; *Rif* and *Rambam* (*Hil. Shabbos* 19:5), however, understand it as applying to needles as well. See *Rosh* and *Korban Nesanel* §200 where this is discussed further; see also *Orach Chaim* 301:8.]

21. That is, Ulla holds that the fact that a man normally wears a signet ring does not remove such a ring from its status as a burden for a woman who wears it; and the fact that a woman normally wears a ring without a seal does does not remove such a ring from its status as a burden for a man who wears it. Accordingly, it is possible that concerning rings, the laws of men and women can be opposite.

22. *Rashi;* see *Rama, Orach Chaim* 361:21. Shepherds would often wear this thick clothing to keep out the rains that fell while they were in the field. See also *Mishnah Berurah* 301:73. Thus, they are viewed as regular clothing, and they may be worn even when there is no threat of rain (see *Rosh* to *Nedarim* 55b).

23. [Although most people never wear clothes of sackcloth, nevertheless, the fact that shepherds do is sufficient to permit the wearing of such clothes for any person (see *Tos. HaRosh*).]

24. [Although Rav Yosef is not stating a *new* answer, since he was the one asking the question, the preface אֶלָּא is appropriate for introducing his own answer (see *Tosafos* above, 57a ד״ה אלא).]

25. That is, we cannot determine whether an item is considered an accessory or a burden for a man by examining how women use that item, for women are looked upon as a separate group, and their actions prove nothing with respect to men.

26. Thus, wearing a ring without a seal is Biblically forbidden for a man, even though it is [Biblically] permitted for a woman; and wearing a ring with a seal is Biblically forbidden for a woman, even though it is [Biblically] permitted for a man.

והתניא רבי אושעיא אומר ובלבד שלא יאחזנו בידו ויעבירנו ארבע אמות ברשות הרבים [אלא] א הכא במאי עסקינן במחופה עור והרי תפילין דמחופה עור ותניא (א) ב הנכנס לבית הכסא חולץ תפילין ברחוק ארבע אמות ונכנס התם משום שי"ן דאמר אביי [ב] ג) שי"ן של תפילין הלכה למשה מסיני ואמר אביי ד' של תפילין הלכה למשה מסיני ואמר אביי יו"ד של תפילין הלכה למשה מסיני: ולא בשריון ולא בקסדא ולא במגפיים: שריון ג) זרדא קסדא אמר רב סנוארתא מגפיים אמר רב פזמקי: **מתני'** ג לא תצא אשה במחט הנקובה ולא בטבעת שיש עליה חותם ולא בכוליאר ולא ד) בכובלת ולא בצלוחית של פלייטון ° ואם יצתה חייבת חטאת דברי ר' מאיר וחכמים פוטרין בכובלת ובצלוחית של פלייטון: **גמ'** ד אמר עולא וחילופיהן באיש אלמא קסבר עולא כל מידי דחזי לאיש לא חזי לאשה ומידי דחזי לאשה לא חזי לאיש מתיב רב יוסף ה) הרועים יוצאין בשקין ולא הרועים בלבד אמרו ה אלא כל אדם אלא שדרכן של הרועים לצאת בשקין [אלא] אמר רב יוסף קסבר עולא נשים עם בפני עצמן הן איתיביה אביי [ה] ו) המוצא תפילין מכניסן זוג זוג אחד האיש ואחד האשה ואי אמרת נשים עם בפני עצמן הן והא מצות עשה שהזמן גרמא הוא ו) וכל מצות עשה שהזמן גרמא נשים פטורות התם קסבר ר"מ לילה זמן תפילין הוא ח) ושבת זמן תפילין הוא הוה ליה מצות עשה שלא הזמן גרמא וכל מצות עשה שלא הזמן גרמא נשים חייבות והא הוצאה כלאחר יד היא אמר רבי ירמיה באשה גזברית עסקינן אמר ט) רבה (בר בר חנה אמר רבי יוחנן) תרצת אשה איש מאי איכא למימר אלא אמר רבא ו פעמים שאדם נותן לאשתו טבעת שיש עליה חותם להוליכה לקופסא ומניחתה בידה עד שמגעת לקופסא ופעמים שהאשה נותנת לבעלה טבעת שאין עליה חותם להוליכה אצל אומן לתקן ומניחה בידו עד שמגיע אצל אומן: ז ולא בכוליאר ולא בכובלת: מאי כוליאר א"ר י) מכבנתא כובלת אמר רב חומרתא דפילון וכן אמר רב אסי חומרתא כ) דפילון ת"ר לא תצא בכובלת ואם יצתה חייבת חטאת דברי ר"מ וחכמים אומרים ח לא תצא ואם יצתה פטורה רבי אליעזר אומר יוצאה אשה בכובלת לכתחלה במאי קמיפלגי רבי מאיר סבר משאוי הוא ורבנן סברי תכשיט הוא ודילמא שלפא ומחויא ואתיא לאיתוייה ורבי אליעזר סבר מאן דרכה למירמיה אשה שריחה רע לא שלפא ומחויא ולא אתיא לאתוייה ארבע אמות ברשות הרבים ° והתניא ל) ר' אליעזר פוטר בכובלת ובצלוחית של פלייטון לא קשיא הא מ) כי קאי אדרבי מאיר הא כי קאי אדרבנן כי קאי אדרבי מאיר דאמר חייב חטאת אמר ליה פטור כי קאי אדרבנן דאמרי פטור אבל אסור אמר איהו מותר לכתחלה ומאי

רש"י

שלא יאחזנו. דלא הוי תכשיט שלו אלא דרך מלבוש: במכוסה עור. דליכא גנותא אי מעייל לבית הכסא ולא בעי למישקליה: חולץ תפילין. ואע"ג דמכוסה עור שהארבע אגרות שהפרשיות כתובות בהן תחובות בדפוסין של עור: התם משום שי"ן. שעשויה מעור החילון עצמו קומטו בו ג' קמטין כעין שי"ן מש"די והדלי"ת והיו"ד עשוין בקשר שקושר הרצועה (א) אחת לצפון ואחת למזרח כמין ד' ורצועה קטנה מאד תלויה בה ואין בה אלא כפיפה כמין יו"ד וכופאה בעוד העור לח והיא כפופה לעולם: זרדא. ברוני"א: סנוארתא. כובע עור תחת כובע המתכת: פזמקי. אנפלייאות של ברזל במלחמה: מתני' בכוליאר. מפרש בגמרא וכן כובלת: פלייטון. בלסמ"א משחא דאפרסמא: חייבת חטאת. קסבר לאו תכשיט נינהו: גמ' אמר עולא וחילופיהן באיש. אטבעת קאי דטבעת שיש עליו חותם אם יצא פטור ואם אין עליו חותם ויצא חייב חטאת: בשקין. שמתכסין בהן מפני הגשמים שקין מלבוש שק: אלא כל אדם. אלמא אע"ג דלא רגילי ביה מגו דלגבי האי תכשיט לגבי האי נמי תכשיט הוא: המוצא תפילין. בשבת בשוק או בדרך: מכניסן. לעיר דרך מלבוש: זוג זוג. כדרך שהוא לובש בחול אחד בראש ואחד בזרוע וחולצן וחוזר ומניח זוג אחר ומכניסן וכן כולן: ואחד האשה. ואע"ג דלאו תכשיט דאשה נינהו מגו דהוו תכשיט לאיש שרי אף לאשה: לילה זמן תפילין הוא וכן שבת. הלכך לעולם זמנם הוא ואין להם זמן קבוע שתהא מצותן מצות עשה שהזמן גרמא להפטר נשים מהן הלכך נקט לילה ושבת משום דפלוגתא בתרווייהו ואי הוי סבירא ליה לרבי מאיר בחד מינייהו דלאו זמן תפילין הוא נמצא זמן קבוע לתפילין והוו להו נשים פטורות: נשים חייבות. הלכך תכשיטין הן לה: והא הוצאה כלאחר יד הוא. אמתני' קאי והוצאת טבעת שמוציאתה דרך מלבוש באצבע חיה שאינו תכשיט לה אמאי חייבת חטאת הרי לא הוציאה כדרך כל המוציאין שכל המוציא דבר שאינו תכשיט לו מוציאין אותו בידים ולא דרך מלבוש: גזברית. ששולחת חותמות תמיד לממונין תחתיה לאמר תנו כך וכך מעות לפלוני והרי חותמה בידה הלכך רגילה היא להניחה באצבעה ומיהו תכשיט לא הוי לדידה דאין דרך נשים בכך ומיהו דרך הוצאתה של זו בכך: איש מאי איכא למימר. דקאמר עולא וחילופיהם באיש דמחייב אטבעת שאין עליה חותם והא הוצאה כלאחר יד הוא שאין דרכו להוציא בזו דרך מלבוש: לקופסא. איסקריי"ה בלע"ז כדי להצניעה שם וי"מ שהקופסא חתומה בו וכשפותחה חוזרה וחותמת בה ולא נהירא דאם כן מנחתה באצבעה עד שמחזירתה לבעלה מיבעי ליה: אצל אומן לתקנה ומניחה באצבעו. אלמא דרך הוצאה היא: מכבנתא. נושקא"ה י) ע"ש שמכבנת וקושרת מפתחי החלוק: חומרתא דפילון. קשר שקושר בו ° סם ששמו פילון וריחו ערב ובלע"ז בלסמ"ו ואשה שריחה רע טוענתו עליה: ורבנן סברי תכשיט הוא. הלכך אם יצאת פטורה ומיהו לכתחלה לא תצא דילמא שלפא ומחויא: למרמיה. להניח בצוארה כמו שקיל ורמי: ה"ג ואשה שריחה רע לא שלפא ומחויא. שגנות הוא לה: והתניא ר' אליעזר פוטר. והכא שרי לכתחלה: הא. דקתני פוטר: כי קאי אר' מאיר. בההיא מתנית' לא איירו רבנן אלא ר"מ לחודיה וגבי חיוב דר"מ שייך למיתני רבי אליעזר פוטר ואע"פ שהוא מתיר לכתחלה: הא כי קאי ארבנן. במתנית' דלעיל דאיירו רבנן בה ואמרו פטור פריש ר' אליעזר בהדיא למילתיה לאיפלוגי עלייהו ואמר יוצאה לכתחלה:

תוספות

והתניא ר' אושעיא אומר ובלבד כו'. תימה לר"י דילמא משום מראית העין דוקא הוא אסור מדרבנן כמו קושר בשיר ובטבעת דהשתא ליכא למיגזר דאפילו מייתי לה ליכא איסורא מדאורייתא ואומר ר"י דשלא יאחזנו בידו משמע אפילו בקומצו דליכא מראית העין אלא איסורא דאורייתא איכא ואפילו למ"ד כל דבר שאסרו חכמים משום מראית העין אפילו בחדרי חדרים אסור הכא לא שייך למיגזר דאפילו עומד בשוק ונושאן בקומצו אין כאן מראית העין: שי"ן של תפילין. ול"ג דלי"ת ויו"ד של תפילין כו' כדמוכח בפ' במה מדליקין (לעיל כח:) גבי הא דתני רב יוסף לא הוכשרו למלאכת שמים כו' ומוקי לה לרצועותיהן ולא פריך דלי"ת של תפילין הלכה למשה מסיני כדפריך גבי שי"ן ס): וחילופיהן באיש. ° אור"ת דלאחיוב חטאת קאי: וכל מצות עשה שהזמן גרמא נשים פטורות. פירוש דהוי משוי וליתסר וא"ת והא הוצאה כלאחר יד היא ושריא משום בזיון תפילין וי"ל כיון דמשוי הוא ויכול לבא לידי חיוב חטאת היכא דמוציא בלא שינוי משום בזיון לא שרינן ליה:

מסורת הש"ס

א) ברכות כג., ב) לעיל כח: מנחות לה., ג) פירוש שריון מטבעות קטנו', ד) [גירס' הערוך בכובלת], ה) [תוספת' פ"ו מדרים נה:], ו) עירובין צו: תוס' לעירובין פ"ח ביצה טו., ז) [קידושין כט. ושם נסמן], ח) [לעיל דף סא. וש"נ], ט) ל"ל רבא, י) [עתוס' ב"ע קנו: ד"ה כבינתי], כ) [כל אלפס פי' מלשון בלולה בשמן מתרגמינן פילא במשח וכ"ה בהערו"ש], ל) [לקמן סה. תוספתא פ"ה], מ) [עי' תוס' לעיל ג. ד"ה בר מהני], נ) עי' רש"י יומא סה. ד"ה בכוליאר, ס) [וע"ע תוס' ברכות ו. ד"ה אלו וכו'].

הגהות הב"ח

(א) רש"י ד"ה התם וכו' הרצוע' שבראש אחת לצפון:

גליון הש"ס

מתני' ואם יצתה חייבת חטאת. עי' לעיל דף נט ע"ב תוס' ד"ה ואם יצא: גמ' והתניא ר"א פוטר. עיין לעיל דף ג ע"א תוס' ד"ה בר מהני: רש"י ד"ה חומרתא דפילון וכו' סם ששמו פילון. עיין סוטה דף יב ע"א תוס' ד"ה כמין תומר: תוס' ד"ה וחילופיהן באיש. אור"ת דאחיוב חטאת קאי. עיין עירובין דף סט ע"א תוס' ד"ה כיון דחזיא:

עין משפט נר מצוה

מ א מיי' פ"ד מהל' ס"ת הלכה ט טוש"ע י"ד סי' רפב סעיף ו:
מא ב מיי' פ"ד מהל' תפילין הלכה יח סמג עשין כב טוש"ע א"ח סי' מג סעיף ה:
[מא] [ב] [מיי' שם פ"ג הלכה א' טוש"ע א"ח סי' לב סעיף מב נב]:
מב ג ד מיי' פי"ט מהל' שבת הלכה ד ה סמג לאוין סה טוש"ע א"ח סי' שא סעיף ט י וסי' שא סעי' ט:
מג ה מיי' שם הלכה יח טוש"ע א"ח סי' שא סעיף כג:
[מג] [ה] [מיי' פי"ט מהל' שבת הלכה כג טוש"ע א"ח סי' שא סעיף מב]:
מד ו מיי' פי"ט שם הלכה ג:
מה ז ח מיי' פי"ט שם הלכה ז סמג שם טוש"ע א"ח סי' שג סעיף יח:

רבינו חננאל

ופשטינא אם מחופין עור (כיון) שפיר דמי והא דתניא לא יכנס אדם בתפילין לבית הכסא קבע אפי' להשתין מים התם משום שי"ן דאמר אביי שי"ן של תפילין הל"מ. ת"ר איזהו קמיע מומחה כל שריפה ושנה ושלש אחד קמיע של כתב ואחד קמיע של עקרין אחד חולה שיש בו סכנה ואחד חולה שאין בו סכנה [ולא] שנכפה אלא שלא יכפה וקושר ומתיר. ואפילו ברה"ר ובלבד שלא יקשרנו בשיר או בטבעת ויוצא בו לרה"ר מפני מראית העין: שיריין זרדא: לא תצא אשה במחט נקובה. ולא בטבעת שיש עליה חותם. אמר עולא חילופיהן באיש כלומר האיש אסור בטבעת שאין עליה חותם ופטור בטבעת שיש עליה חותם. וכי קאמר עולא וחילופיהן באיש בטבעת בלבד קאמר מותבינן אמאי חייב חטאת והא הוצאה כלאחר יד היא כלומר באצבעה היא מרציאה ואין דרך המרציאין דבר להוציאה דרך מלבוש. ומוקים לה ר' ירמיה באשה גזברית עסקינן שכן דרכה להיות הטבעת באצבעה כדי שתהא חותמת בו כיסים ובתים. הרצאה בכוונה היא לחתום בו ולאו משום תכשיט הוא ודחינן תרצת אשה איש בטבעת שאין עליה חותם אמאי חייב חטאת. ואוקמה רבא לעולם באשה שאינה גזברית ומשום הכי חייבת חטאת דפעמים אדם [נותן] טבעת שיש עליה חותם לאשתו להוליכה לקופסא ומנחתה באצבעה עד שמגעת לקופסא שנמצאת הרצאה בכוונה כדרכה. והאשה נמי פעמים שנותנת כו' וקיי"ל טבעת שיש עליה חותם תכשיט לאיש ולא לאשה ושאין עליה חותם תכשיט לאשה ולא לאיש. ובדין הוא להיות כל אחד ואחד מותר במה שהוא תכשיט לו אלא גזרו משום דרבא שכבר פרשנוהו למעלה (ס.): בכולייר. תכשיט שמסבב הראש כולה כדגרסינן ביומא (כה.) הכהנים היו מוקפין ועומדין ככולייר. כובלת חומרתא דפילון. פי' בשמים בלולין כדמתרגם בלולה דפילא. צלוחית של פלייטון ראשית

ליקוטי רש"י

תפילין דמחופה עור. עור דפוס שלהן שהכתבים של פרשיות מונחים בו [לעיל כח:]. חולץ תפילין ברחוק ארבע אמות. ואלו תפילין בידו כדאמרינן לקמן ובקבוע נמי אוחזן בידו אלא שצריך לחלצן ברחוק ארבע אמות שבזמן שהם בראשו הם בגלוי וגנאי הדבר [ברכות כג.]. שי"ן של תפילין וכו' ד' של תפילין וכו'. שי"ן של תפילין שיהא העור נקמט מבחוץ שלושה קמטין ודומה לשי"ן והרצועה נקשרת כמין דלי"ת ויש רצועה כפופה כמין י' דהיינו שדי [לעיל שם ועי' במסור"ש שם]. שישים הרצועות על ראשו [כעין] דל"ת כדי שיהא שדי נראה עליהן דשי"ן נראה בקמט בית חיצונה שכפל הקלף כעין שי"ן ודל"ת נראה בקשר ויו"ד נראה באותו של יד כמין רצועה קטנה וראשה כפוף מעט כמין יו"ד [מנחות לה:]. הלכה למשה מסיני היאך הוא עשוי שדומה לדל"ת ובתפירתן עשוי כמין שי"ן ורצועה קטנה קבועה בהן וראשה כפוף ודומה ליו"ד הרי שדי [עירובין צז.]. במחט הנקובה. לענין הוצאת שבת יש חילוק בין נקובה לשאינו נקובה דנקובה קתני חייב חטאת ושאינה נקובה כגון איספיגל"א שהיא תכשיט קתני אינו חייב חטאת בפרק במה אשה (שבת נז:) [לעיל נב:]. ולא בטבעת שיש עליה חותם. דלאו תכשיט הוא והוי משאוי. דחותם לאשה לאו תכשיט הוא דאין דרך לאשה לחתום ולשלוח שלוחים שאין חותם עשוי אלא לאדם גדול וממונה [שם נט:]. חותם. צורה לחתום בה איגרת או כל דבר סגור [שם נז.]. בכוליאר. עגול שקורין נושק"א [יומא כה.]. פלייטון. בושם שריחו נודף ואינו אפרסמון [סנהדרין קח. ועיין במלוא הרועים]. המוצא תפילין. בשדה במקום שנאבדין. מכניסן. לעיר ולבית. זוג זוג. אחד בראש ואחד בזרוע והיינו זוג כדרך שלובשן בחול וחוזר תמיד ומכניסן זוג אחר זוג עד שיכלו [עירובין צה.]. נותן בראשו אחד ואחד בזרועו כדרך הנחתן בחול ומכניסן וחוזר והולך ולובש זוג אחר ומכניסן, תפילין של ראש ושל זרוע קרי זוג זוג [ביצה טו.]. מצות עשה שהזמן גרמא. נפקא לן בפרק קמא דקידושין (כט.) דנשים פטורות [פסחים מג:]. שהזמן גורם לה שתבא [קידושין כט.]. מכבנתא. כמין קרסי מתכת לחבר הבגד כמו תנהן כבינתי לבתי (גיטין טו.) נושק"א בלע"ז [לעיל נד.]. לשון הרחלים יוצאות כבונות (שבת נג:) וכמו (גיטין יד:) תנהן כבנתי לבתי פרמוי"ל והוא [בית] נפש שקורין נושקא שמחברין בה פתיחות פי החלוק [שבועות ו:]. חומרתא דפילון. בוטון שהנשים תולות בצואריהן של זהב או של כסף ונותן בו שמן שמעורב בו מין בושם ששמו פילון ודומה לעלי גפנים כדתניא בת"כ שלא יערב קימוס במר מי גלובקיא בשמן עלי גפנים בפילון [גיטין סט:].

following Baraisa: הַמּוֹצֵא תְּפִילִּין – ONE WHO FINDS TEFILLIN on the Sabbath in the marketplace or in a field[27] מַכְנִיסָן זוּג זוּג – SHOULD put them on and BRING THEM IN PAIR BY PAIR,[28] אֶחָד הָאִישׁ וְאֶחָד הָאִשָּׁה – WHETHER IT IS A MAN OR A WOMAN that found them. We see from this Baraisa that, Biblically, a woman may go out with tefillin on the Sabbath. וְאִי אָמְרַתְּ נָשִׁים עַם בִּפְנֵי עַצְמָן הֵן – **But if you say** that **women are** viewed as **a separate nation unto themselves,** why may she do so? וְהָא מִצְוַת עֲשֵׂה שֶׁהַזְּמַן גְּרָמָא הוּא – **But [tefillin] is a positive commandment that time causes** – וְכָל מִצְוַת עֲשֵׂה שֶׁהַזְּמַן גְּרָמָא נָשִׁים פְּטוּרוֹת – **and** the rule is that with respect to **any positive commandment that time causes, women are exempt!**[29] It must be, then, that a woman may go out with tefillin on the Sabbath because they are considered accessories for men. We see, then, that women are *not* viewed as a separate nation.[30] – ? –

The Gemara answers:

הָתָם – **There** in the Baraisa, קָסָבַר רַבִּי מֵאִיר לַיְלָה זְמַן תְּפִילִּין הוּא – **R' Meir**[31] **holds** that **night is a time for tefillin,** וְשַׁבָּת זְמַן תְּפִילִּין הוּא – **and** he also holds that the **Sabbath is a time for tefillin.** הֲוָה לֵיהּ מִצְוַת עֲשֵׂה שֶׁלֹּא הַזְּמַן גְּרָמָא – Accordingly, **the mitzvah** of tefillin **is a positive commandment that is not caused by time**[32] – וְכָל מִצְוַת עֲשֵׂה שֶׁלֹּא הַזְּמַן גְּרָמָא נָשִׁים חַיָּיבוֹת – **and** the rule is that with respect to **any positive commandment that is not caused by time, women are obligated!**[33] For this reason, a woman may wear the tefillin on the Sabbath.[34]

The Gemara now returns to the Mishnah's ruling that it is Biblically forbidden for a woman to wear a signet ring outside on the Sabbath:

The Gemara asks:

וְהָא הוֹצָאָה כִּלְאַחַר יָד הִיא – **But this is** an act of **transferring** from one domain to another **in an unusual manner!**[35] How, then, can it be Biblically prohibited?[36]

The Gemara replies:

אָמַר רַבִּי יִרְמְיָה – **R' Yirmiyah said:** בְּאִשָּׁה גִּזְבָּרִית עָסְקִינַן – **We are dealing** in the Mishnah **with a woman** who is an **overseer;** hence, it is normal for her to wear a signet ring in this manner.[37]

The Gemara notes that a difficulty still remains:

אָמַר רַבָּה (בַּר בַּר חָנָה אָמַר רַבִּי יוֹחָנָן) – **Rabbah said:**[38] תֵּרַצְתְּ אִשָּׁה – **You have answered** the case of **a woman** who goes out with a signet ring.[39] אִישׁ מַאי אִיכָּא לְמֵימַר – But concerning the case of **a man,** where Ulla ruled that it is Biblically forbidden for a man to go out with a ring that has no seal, **what is there to say?** Since a man does not usually wear such a ring, going out while wearing it should be considered transferring in an unusual manner, and it should not be Biblically prohibited. – ? –

The Gemara concedes the point, and offers a different interpretation:

אֶלָּא אָמַר רָבָא – **Rather, Rava said:** פְּעָמִים שֶׁאָדָם נוֹתֵן לְאִשְׁתּוֹ טַבַּעַת שֶׁיֵּשׁ עָלֶיהָ חוֹתָם – **There are times when a man will give his wife a ring that has a signet** לְהוֹלִיכָהּ לְקוּפְסָא – **to take it to put in [its] chest,**[40] וּמַנִּיחָתָהּ בְּיָדָהּ עַד שֶׁמַּגַּעַת לְקוּפְסָא – **and she puts it on her hand until she reaches the chest;** וּפְעָמִים שֶׁהָאִשָּׁה נוֹתֶנֶת לְבַעְלָהּ טַבַּעַת שֶׁאֵין עָלֶיהָ חוֹתָם – **and sometimes a woman will give her husband a ring that has no seal** לְהוֹלִיכָהּ אֵצֶל אוּמָּן לְתַקֵּן – **to take it to a craftsman to repair,** וּמַנִּיחָהּ בְּיָדוֹ עַד שֶׁמַּגִּיעַ אֵצֶל אוּמָּן – **and he puts it on his hand until he reaches the craftsman.** Thus, both men and women do at least occasionally carry both types of rings by wearing them; accordingly, wearing a ring can never be deemed a transfer made in an unusual manner.[41]

The Mishnah stated:

וְלֹא בְּכוּלְיָאר וְלֹא בְּכוֹבֶלֶת – AND she may NOT go out WITH A *CULYAR*[42] AND NOT wearing A SPICE BUNDLE.

NOTES

27. E.g. in a place where one is not permitted to carry and where the tefillin are in danger of being destroyed or desecrated (see *Beitzah* 15a).

28. He should don them as he would to perform the mitzvah of tefillin and walk to a safe shelter in the city, remove them, and then repeat this procedure until he has recovered and secured all of the tefillin (*Rashi*).

29. The Gemara in *Kiddushin* (34a-35a) derives this rule from Scripture.

30. See *Rashi.* Thus, Ulla's statement concerning rings cannot be explained as R' Yosef did above, and we have no satisfactory explanation of why all men can wear shepherd's clothes, but not rings that have no seals.

[The Gemara cannot answer that women are permitted to bring in the tefillin because they are being carried in an unusual manner (being worn rather than carried), and such carrying, which is normally only Rabbinically forbidden (see below, note 35), was permitted so that the tefillin should not be desecrated. This is because the Mishnah only permits the wearing of the tefillin *in pairs,* and if the permit was based on the fact that the carrying is being done in an unusual manner, carrying even many at once should be permitted! Obviously, then, the permit is based on the fact that the tefillin are an accessory when worn properly (*Rashba, Ran MHK* ed.; cf. *Tosafos*).]

31. [R' Meir is not mentioned in the Baraisa; however, the Gemara in *Eruvin* (95b) states that R' Meir (who is presumed to be the Tanna of anonymous Mishnahs) is the Tanna of the Mishnah there that parallels the Baraisa being discussed here.]

32. For there is no time that one is not able to fulfill the mitzvah, since one can fulfill the mitzvah both at night *and* on the Sabbath (see *Rashi*).

33. This is derived from Scripture in *Kiddushin* (ibid.) as well.

34. And the reason that she may bring in the tefillin is *not* because they are considered the accessories of a man, but because they are considered accessories for *her.*

35. Literally: with the back of the hand. If one performs a forbidden labor (*av melachah*) on the Sabbath, he is not Biblically liable if he did not perform the *melachah* in the manner in which it is usually performed (however, it is still Rabbinically prohibited). See General Introduction.

36. The Mishnah teaches that a woman who goes out with a signet ring is liable to a *chatas,* which means that this act is Biblically prohibited. But if a woman does not usually wear such a ring, the act of wearing it outside should only be Rabbinically forbidden, since a burden is usually carried in the hand, and this burden is being "carried" on the finger (see *Rashi*).

37. For a woman who is an overseer needs a signet ring to seal the missives and packages that she sends to her underlings; she will often place the ring on her finger. For this reason, it is considered a normal act of carrying for her to go out with the ring on her finger, and she is Biblically liable. [The ring is not considered an *accessory* for her, however, because most women do not have signet rings, and the status of the ring is determined by the way that it is used (or not used) by *most* women (*Rashi*).]

38. [See marginal gloss that emends this attribution to read אָמַר רָבָא, *Rava said.*]

39. In that case, the Gemara has successfully explained that one is liable to a *chatas* even though such a ring is not normally worn by a woman, for we are dealing with the case of a woman overseer, who *does* wear a ring in such a manner.

40. A box used for storing jewelry and other accessories (*Aruch*).

41. Therefore, it is Biblically prohibited for a woman to wear a signet ring, as it is deemed a burden for her, and she is carrying it in a normal way. A ring *without* a seal is permitted Biblically because it is an ornament for her; it is Rabbinically prohibited, however, lest she remove it to show to others. It is Rabbinically prohibited for a man to go out with a signet ring for this same reason (according to *Rashi;* see note 20); and it is Biblically prohibited for a man to wear a ring with no seal, for it is a burden for him, and he is carrying it in a normal way.

42. In the Mishnah, this word was translated as "a brooch," reflecting the Gemara's conclusion here.

והתניא רבי אושעיא אומר ובלבד שלא יאחזנו בידו ויעבירנו ארבע אמות ברשות הרבים [אלא] [א]הכא במאי עסקינן במחופה עור והרי תפילין דמחופה עור ותניא (א) [ב]הנכנס לבית הכסא חולץ תפילין ברחוק ארבע אמות ונכנס התם משום שי"ן דאמר אביי [ב] (ג) שי"ן של תפילין הלכה למשה מסיני ואמר אביי ד' של תפילין הלכה למשה מסיני ואמר אביי יו"ד של תפילין הלכה למשה מסיני: ולא בשריון ולא בקסדא ולא במגפיים: שריון (ג) זרדא קסדא אמר רב סנוארתא מגפיים אמר רב פזמקי: **מתני'** [ג]לא תצא אשה במחט הנקובה ולא בטבעת שיש עליה חותם ולא בכוליאר ולא (ד) בכובלת ולא בצלוחית של פלייטון ° ואם יצתה חייבת חטאת דברי ר' מאיר וחכמים פוטרין בכובלת ובצלוחית של פלייטון: **גמ'** [ד]אמר עולא וחילופיהן באיש אלמא קסבר עולא כל מידי דחזי לאיש לא חזי לאשה ומידי דחזי לאשה לא חזי לאיש מתיב רב יוסף (ה) הרועים יוצאין בשקין ולא הרועים בלבד אמרו [ה]אלא כל אדם אלא שדרכן של הרועים לצאת בשקין [אלא] אמר רב יוסף קסבר עולא נשים עם בפני עצמן הן איתיביה אביי [ה] (ו) המוצא תפילין מכניסן זוג זוג אחד האיש ואחד האשה ואי אמרת נשים עם בפני עצמן הן והא מצות עשה שהזמן גרמא הוא (ז) וכל מצות עשה שהזמן גרמא נשים פטורות התם קסבר ר"מ לילה זמן תפילין הוא (ח) ושבת זמן תפילין הוא הוה ליה מצות עשה שלא הזמן גרמא וכל מצות עשה שלא הזמן גרמא נשים חייבות והא הוצאה כלאחר יד היא אמר רבי ירמיה באשה גזברית עסקינן אמר (ט) רבה (בר בר חנה אמר רבי יוחנן) תרצת אשה איש מאי איכא למימר אלא אמר רבא [י]פעמים שאדם נותן לאשתו טבעת שיש עליה חותם להוליכה לקופסא ומניחתה בידה עד שמגעת לקופסא ופעמים שהאשה נותנת לבעלה טבעת שאין עליה חותם להוליכה אצל אומן לתקן ומניחה בידו עד שמגיע אצל אומן: [ז]ולא בכוליאר ולא בכובלת: מאי כוליאר א"ר (י) מכבנתא כובלת אמר רב חומרתא דפילון וכן אמר רב אסי חומרתא (כ) דפילון ת"ר לא תצא בכובלת ואם יצתה חייבת חטאת דברי ר"מ וחכמים אומרים [ח]לא תצא ואם יצתה פטורה רבי אליעזר אומר יוצאה אשה בכובלת לכתחלה במאי קמיפלגי רבי מאיר סבר משאוי הוא ורבנן סברי תכשיט הוא ודילמא שלפא ומחויא ואתיא לאיתויה ורבי אליעזר סבר מאן דרכה למירמיה אשה שריחה רע לא שלפא ומחויא ולא אתיא לאתויה ארבע אמות ברשות הרבים ° והתניא (ל) ר' אליעזר פוטר בכובלת ובצלוחית של פלייטון לא קשיא הא (מ) כי קאי אדרבי מאיר הא כי קאי אדרבנן כי קאי אדרבי מאיר דאמר חייב חטאת אמר ליה פטור כי קאי אדרבנן דאמרי פטור אבל אסור אמר איהו מותר לכתחלה

ומאי

רש"י

שלא יאחזנו. דלא הוי תכשיט שלו אלא דרך מלבוש: **במכוסה עור.** דליכא גנותא אי מעייל לבית הכסא ולא בעי למישקליה: **חולץ תפילין.** ואע"ג דמכוסה עור שהארבע אגרות שהפרשיות כתובות בהן תחובות בדפוסין של עור: **התם משום שי"ן.** שעשויה מעור החילון עצמו קומט בו ג' קמטין כעין שי"ן משדי והדלי"ת והיו"ד עשויין בקשר שקושר הרצועה (א) אחת לצפון ואחת למזרח כמין ד' ורצועה קטנה מאד תלויה בה ואין בה אלא כפיפה כמין יו"ד וכופלא בעוד העור לח והיא כפופה לעולם: **זרדא.** ברוני"א: **סנוארתא.** כובע עור תחת כובע המתכת: **פזמקי.** אנפלייאות של ברזל במלחמה: **מתני' בכוליאר.** מפרש בגמרא וכן כובלת: **פלייטון.** בלסמ"א משחא דאפרסמא: **חייבת חטאת.** קסבר לאו תכשיט נינהו: **גמ' אמר עולא וחילופיהן באיש.** אטבעת קאי דטבעת שיש עליו חותם אם יצא פטור ואם אין עליו חותם ויצא חייב חטאת: **בשקין.** שמתכסין בהן מפני הגשמים שקין מלבוש שק: **אלא כל אדם.** אלמא אע"ג דלא רגילי ביה מגו דלגבי האי תכשיט לגבי האי נמי תכשיט הוא: **המוצא תפילין.** בשבת בשוק או בדרך: **מכניסן.** לעיר דרך מלבוש: **זוג זוג.** כדרך שהוא לובש בחול אחד בראש ואחד בזרוע וחולצן וחוזר ומניח זוג אחר ומכניסן וכן כולן: **ואחד האשה.** ואע"ג דלאו תכשיט דאשה נינהו מגו דהוו תכשיט לאיש שרי אף לאשה: **לילה זמן תפילין הוא וכן שבת.** הלכך לעולם זמנם הוא ואין להם זמן קבוע שתהא מצותן מצות עשה שהזמן גרמא להפטר נשים מהן הלכך נקט לילה ושבת משום דפלוגתא בתרווייהו ואי הוי סבירא ליה לרבי מאיר בחד מינייהו דלאו זמן תפילין הוא נמצא זמן קבוע לתפילין והוו להו נשים פטורות: **נשים חייבות.** הלכך תכשיטין הן לה: **והא הוצאה כלאחר יד הוא.** אמתני' קאי והוצאת טבעת שמוציאתה דרך מלבוש באצבע וזה שאינו תכשיט לה אמאי חייבת חטאת הרי לא הוציאה כדרך כל המוציאין שכל המוציא דבר שאינו תכשיט לו מוציאין אותו בידים ולא דרך מלבוש: **גזברית.** שסולחת חותמות תמיד לממונין תחתיה לאמר תנו כך וכך מעות לפלוני והרי חותמה בידה הלכך רגילה היא להניחה באצבעה ומיהו תכשיט לא הוי לדידה דאין דרך נשים בכך ומיהו דרך הוצאתה של זו בכך: **איש מאי איכא למימר.** דקאמר עולא וחילופיהם באיש דמחייב אטבעת שאין עליה חותם והא הוצאה כלאחר יד הוא שאין דרכו להוציא בזו דרך מלבוש: **לקופסא.** אישקריי"ה בלע"ז כדי להצניעה שם וי"מ שהקופסא חתומה בו וכשפותחה חוזרת וחותמת בה ולא נהירא דאם כן מנחתה באצבעה עד שמחזירתה לבעלה מיבעי ליה: **אצל אומן לתקנה ומניחה באצבעו.** אלמא דרך הוצאה היא: **מכבנתא.** נוסקא"ה ע"ש שמכבנת וקושרת מפתחי החלוק: **חומרתא דפילון.** קשר שקשור בו ° סם ששמו פילון וריחו ערב ובלע"ז בלסמ"ו ואשה שריחה רע טוענתו עליה: **ורבנן סברי תכשיט הוא.** הלכך אם יצאת פטורה ומיהו לכתחלה לא תצא דילמא שלפא ומחויא: **למרמיה.** להניח בצוארה כמו שקיל ורמי: ה"ג **ואשה שריחה רע לא שלפא ומחויא.** שגנות הוא לה: **והתניא ר' אליעזר פוטר.** והכא שרי לכתחלה: **הא.** דקתני פוטר: **כי קאי אר' מאיר.** בההיא מתנית' לא איירו רבנן אלא ר"מ לחודיה וגבי חיוב דר"מ שייך למיתני רבי אליעזר פוטר ואע"פ שהוא מתיר לכתחלה: **הא כי קאי ארבנן.** במתנית' דלעיל דאיירו רבנן בה ואמרו פטור פריש ר' אליעזר בהדיא למילתיה לאיפלוגי עלייהו ואמר יוצאה לכתחלה:

תוספות

והתניא ר' אושעיא אומר ובלבד כו'. תימה לר"י דילמא משום מראית העין דוקא הוא אסור מדרבנן כמו קושר בשיר ובטבעת דהשתא ליכא למיגזר דאפילו מייתי לה ליכא איסורא מדאורייתא ואומר ר"י דשלא יאחזנו בידו משמע אפילו בקומצו דליכא מראית העין אלא איסורא דאורייתא איכא ואפילו למ"ד כל דבר שאסרו חכמים משום מראית העין אפילו בחדרי חדרים אסור הכא לא שייך למיגזר דאפילו עומד בשוק ונושאן בקומצו אין כאן מראית העין:

שי"ן של תפילין. ול"ג דלי"ת ויו"ד של תפילין כו' כדמוכח בפ' במה מדליקין (לעיל כח:) גבי הא דתני רב יוסף לא הוכשרו למלאכת שמים כו' ומוקי לה לרצועותיהן ולא פריך דלי"ת של תפילין הלכה למשה מסיני כדפריך גבי שי"ן (פ):

וחילופיהן באיש. ° אור"ת דאחיוב חטאת קאי:

וכל מצות עשה שהזמן גרמא נשים פטורות. פירוש דהוי משוי וליתסר וא"ת והא הוצאה כלאחר יד היא ושריא משום בזיון תפילין וי"ל כיון דמשוי הוא ויכול לבא לידי חיוב חטאת היכא דמוציא בלא שינוי משום בזיון לא שרינן ליה:

אין

עין משפט נר מצוה

מ א מיי' פ"י מהל' ק"ש הלכה ה טוש"ע י"ד סי' רפב סעיף ו:
מא ב מיי' פ"ד מהל' תפילין הלכה יז סמג עשין כב טוש"ע א"ח סי' מג סעיף ה:
[מא] [ב] [מיי' שם פ"ג הלכה א' טוש"ע א"ח סי' לב סעי' נב]:
מב ג ד מיי' פי"ט מהל' שבת הלכה ה ו סמג לאוין סה טור א"ח סי' שג סעיף ט וסי' שא סעיף ח:
מג ה מיי' שם הלכה יז טוש"ע א"ח סי' שא סעיף כב:
[מג] [ה] [מיי' פ"ט מהל' שבת הלכה כג טוש"ע א"ח סי' שא סעיף מב]:
מד ו מיי' פי"ט שם הלכה ג:
מה ז ח מיי' פי"ט שם הלכה ז סמג שם טוש"ע א"ח סי' שג סעיף יא:

רבינו חננאל

ופשטינא אם מחופין עור (כיון) שפיר דמי והא דתניא לא יכנס אדם בתפילין לבית הכסא קבע אפי' להשתין מים התם משום שי"ן דאמר אביי שי"ן של תפילין הל"מ. ת"ר איזהו קמיע מומחה כל שריפה ושנה ושלש אחד קמיע של כתב ואחד קמיע של עקרין אחד חולה שיש בו סכנה ואחד חולה שאין בו סכנה [ולא] שנכפה אלא שלא יכפה וקושר ומתיר. ואפילו ברה"ר ובלבד שלא יקשרנו בשיר או בטבעת ויוצא בו לרה"ר מפני מראית העין: שירין זרדא: **לא** תצא אשה במחט נקובה. ולא בטבעת שיש עליה חותם. אמר עולא חילופיהן באיש כלומר האיש אסור בטבעת שאין עליה חותם ופטור בטבעת שיש עליה חותם. וכי קאמר עולא וחילופיהן באיש בטבעת בלבד קאמר מותבינן אמאי חייב חטאת והא הוצאה כלאחר יד היא כלומר באצבעה היא מוציאה ואין דרך המוציאין דבר להוציאה דרך מלבוש. ומוקים לה ר' ירמיה באשה גזברית עסקינן שכן דרכה להיות הטבעת באצבעה כדי שתהא חותמת בו כיסים ובתים. הוצאה בכוונה היא לחתום בו ולאו משום תכשיט הוא ודחינן תרצת אשה איש בטבעת שאין עליה חותם אמאי חייב חטאת. ואוקמה רבא לעולם באשה שאינה גזברית ומשום הכי חייבת חטאת דפעמים אדם [נותן] טבעת שיש עליה חותם לאשתו להוליכה לקופסא ומנחתה באצבעה עד שמגעת לקופסא שנמצאת הוצאה בכוונה כדרכה. והאשה נמי פעמים שנותנת כו' וקיי"ל טבעת שיש עליה חותם תכשיט לאיש ולא לאשה ושאין עליה חותם תכשיט לאשה ולא לאיש. ובדין הוא להיות כל אחד ואחד מותר במה שהוא תכשיט לו אלא גזרו משום דרבא שכבר פרשנוהו למעלה (ס.): בכולייר. תכשיט שמסבב הראש כולה כדגרסינן ביומא (כה.) הכהנים היו מוקפין ועומדין ככולייר. כובלת חומרתא דפילון. פי' בשמים בלולין כדמתרגם בלולה דפילא. צלוחית של פלייטון

ראשית

מסורת הש"ס

א) ברכות כג., ב) לעיל כח: מנחות לה., ג) פירוש הערוך מטבעות קטנו', ד) [גיר' הערוך בכובלת], ה) [תוספ' פ"ה], ו) עירובין צו: [תוס' דעירובין פ"ח] ביצה טו., ז) [קידושין כט. ושם נסמן], ח) [לעיל דף סב. וש"נ], ט) נ"ל רבא, י) [ערוך ע' כמכינת], כ) [כל אלפס פי' מלשון בלולה בשמן מתרגמינן פילה במשח וכ"ה בערוך], ל) [לקמן סה. תוספתא פ"ה ע"ש], מ) [ע' תוס' לעיל ג. סד"ה בר מהני], נ) ע' רש"י יומא כה. ד"ה כבוליאר, ס) [וע"ע תוס' ברכות ו. ד"ה אלו וכו'].

הגהות הב"ח

(א) רש"י ד"ה התם וכו' הרצוע' שבראשו אחת לצפון:

גליון הש"ס

מתני' ואם יצתה חייבת חטאת. עי' לעיל דף נז ע"ב תוס' ד"ה ולא יצא: גמ' והתניא ר"א פוטר. עיין לעיל דף ג ע"א תוס' ד"ה בר מהני: רש"י ד"ה חומרתי דפילון וכו' בסם ששמו פילון. עיין סוטה דף טו ע"א תוס' ד"ה כמין סומך: תוס' ד"ה וחילופיהן באיש. אור"ת דאחיוב חטאת קאי. עיין עירובין דף סט ע"א תוס' ד"ה כיון דמזיד:

ליקוטי רש"י

תפילין דמחופה עור. עור דפוס שלהן שהכתובים מונחים בו [לעיל כח:]. **חולץ תפילין ברחוק ארבע אמות.** ואחר תפילין בידו כדאמרינן לקמן ובקבעא נמי אוחזן בידו [ברכות כג:]. **שי"ן של תפילין.** שי"ן של תפילין שיהא העור נקמט מבחוץ שלשה קמטין כמין שי"ן והרצועה נקשרת כמין דלי"ת לאחוריו וקשר של יד כמין יו"ד [מנחות לה:]. **הלכה למשה מסיני** היא הוא עשוי שדומה לדל"ת ובתפירתן עשוי כמין שי"ן ורצועה קטנה קבועה בהן ורצשה כפוף ודומה ליו"ד הרי שדי [עירובין צז.]. **במחט הנקובה.** לענין הוצאת שבת יש חילוק בין נקובה לשאינו נקובה דנקובה קתני חייב חטאת ושאינה נקובה כגון אישפיגל"א שהיא תכשיט קתני אינו חייב חטאת בפרק במה אשה (שבת נז:) [לעיל נב:]. **ולא בטבעת שיש עליה חותם.** דלאו תכשיט הוא והוי משאוי. דחותם לאשה לאו תכשיט הוא דאין דרך לאשה לחתום ולשלוח שלוחים שאין חותם עשוי אלא לאדם גדול וממונה [שם נט:]. **חותם.** צורה לחתום בה איגרת או כל דבר סגור [שם נז.]. **בכוליאר.** עגול שקורין נושק"א [יומא כה.]. **פלייטון.** בושם שריחו נודף ואינו אפרסמון [סנהדרין קח. ועיין במלוא הרועים]. **המוצא תפילין.** בשדה במקום שנאבדין. **מכניסן.** לעיר ולבית. **זוג זוג.** אחד בראש ואחד בזרוע והיינו זוג כדרך שלובשן בחול וחוזר תמיד ומכניסן זוג אחר זוג עד שיכלו [עירובין צה.]. **נותן** בראשו אחד ואחד בזרועו כדרך הנחתן בחול ומכניסן וחוזר והולך ולובש זוג אחר ומכניסן, תפילין של ראש ושל זרוע קרי זוג זוג [ביצה טו.]. **מצות עשה שהזמן גרמא.** נפקא לן בפרק קמא דקידושין (כט.) דנשים פטורות [פסחים מג:]. **שהזמן גרמא.** שהזמן גורם לה שתבא [קידושין כט.]. **מכבנתא.** כמין קרסי מתכת לחבר הבגד כמו תנתן כבינתי לבתי (גיטין טו.) נושק"א בלע"ז [לעיל נד.]. לשון הרחלים יוצאות כבונות (שבת נג:) וכמו (גיטין יד:) תנתן כבנתי לבתי פרמוי"ל והוא [בית] נפש שקורין נושקא שמחברין בה פתיחות פי החלוק [שבועות ו:]. **חומרתא דפילון.** בוטון שהנשים תולות בצואריהן של זהב או של כסף ונותן בו שמן שמעורב בו מין בושם ששמו פילון ודומה לעלי גפנים כדתניא בת"כ שלא יערב קימום במר מי גלובקיא בשמן עלי גפנים בפילון [גיטין סט:].

The Gemara seeks to identify these ornaments:

מַאי כּוּלְיָאר – What is a *culyar*? **אָמַר רַב – Rav said:** **מַכְבַּנְתָּא** – It is **a brooch** used to close the open ends of a woman's blouse.[43] **כּוּבֶלֶת** – And what is **a spice bundle? אָמַר רַב – Rav said: חוּמַרְתָּא דְפִילוֹן – A packet containing *pilon*.**[44] **וְכֵן אָמַר רַב אַסִּי חוּמַרְתָּא דְפִילוֹן – And Rav Assi also said:** The Mishnah refers to **a pendant containing *pilon*.**

The Gemara cites the Baraisa that records a dispute concerning the wearing of spice bundles on the Sabbath:

תָּנוּ רַבָּנָן – The Rabbis taught in a Baraisa: לֹא תֵצֵא בְכוּבֶלֶת – [A WOMAN] MAY NOT GO OUT WITH A SPICE BUNDLE, **וְאִם יָצְתָה חַיֶּיבֶת חַטָּאת** – AND IF SHE DID GO OUT with such a bundle, SHE IS LIABLE TO A *CHATAS* offering; **דִּבְרֵי רַבִּי מֵאִיר** – these are THE WORDS OF R' MEIR.[45] **וַחֲכָמִים אוֹמְרִים** – BUT THE SAGES SAY: **לֹא תֵצֵא** – SHE MAY NOT GO OUT wearing the bundle, **וְאִם יָצְתָה פְּטוּרָה** – BUT IF SHE GOES OUT wearing it, SHE IS NOT LIABLE TO A *CHATAS*.[46] **רַבִּי אֱלִיעֶזֶר אוֹמֵר** – R' ELIEZER SAYS: **יוֹצְאָה אִשָּׁה בְּכוּבֶלֶת לְכַתְּחִלָּה** – A WOMAN MAY GO OUT WITH A SPICE BUNDLE even IN THE FIRST PLACE.[47]

The Gemara ask:

בְּמַאי קָמִיפַּלְגֵי – In what point **do they argue?**

The Gemara explains the dispute:

רַבִּי מֵאִיר סָבַר מַשּׂאוֹי הוּא – R' Meir holds that **[the spice bundle]** is considered **a burden,**[48] and therefore wearing it is Biblically forbidden, **וְרַבָּנָן סָבְרֵי תַּכְשִׁיט הוּא – while the Rabbis hold** that **[the spice bundle]** is considered **an ornament;**[49] **וְדִילְמָא שָׁלְפָא וּמַחְוְיָא – and** the Sages were concerned that **perhaps [the woman] will remove it and show it** to her friend,[50] **וְאַתְיָא לְאַיְתוּיֵיהּ – and she will come to carry it** four *amos* in the public domain; therefore, going out with the spice bundle is Rabbinically prohibited. **וְרַבִּי אֱלִיעֶזֶר סָבַר – And R' Eliezer holds** that wearing it is permitted for the following reason: **מַאן דַּרְכָּהּ לְמִירְמֵיהּ – Who is accustomed to put on [a spice bundle]? אִשָּׁה שֶׁרֵיחָהּ רַע – A woman whose odor is unpleasant.**[51] **אִשָּׁה שֶׁרֵיחָהּ רַע לֹא שָׁלְפָא וּמַחְוְיָא** – Now, **a woman whose odor is unpleasant will not remove** the bundle **and show** it to a friend,[52] **וְלֹא אַתְיָא לְאַתּוּיֵיהּ אַרְבַּע אַמּוֹת בִּרְשׁוּת הָרַבִּים – and** therefore **she will not come to carry it four *amos* in the public domain.** Therefore, the wearing of a spice bundle on the Sabbath is permitted.

The Gemara cites a Baraisa that has R' Eliezer subscribing to a different view:

וְהָתַנְיָא – But we have been taught in a Baraisa: רַבִּי אֱלִיעֶזֶר פּוֹטֵר בְּכוּבֶלֶת וּבִצְלוֹחִית שֶׁל פַּלְיָיטוֹן – R' ELIEZER EXEMPTS her from *chatas* liability if she goes out WITH A SPICE BUNDLE OR A FLASK OF BALSAM OIL. This Baraisa would seem to intimate that according to R' Eliezer going out with these items is Rabbinically prohibited;[53] while the previous Baraisa stated that R' Eliezer holds that the wearing of a spice bundle is completely permitted!

The Gemara answers:

לֹא קַשְׁיָא – This is **not a difficulty.** In truth, R' Eliezer holds that going out while wearing a spice bundle is completely permitted; **הָא כִּי קָאֵי אַדְּרַבִּי מֵאִיר** – but he stated **this** ruling (which implies only exemption from a *chatas*) **when his opinion is** contrasted **with that of R' Meir,**[54] **הָא כִּי קָאֵי אַדְּרַבָּנָן** – and he stated **this** ruling (completely permitted) **when his opinion is** contrasted **with that of the Rabbis.**

The Gemara elaborates:

כִּי קָאֵי אַדְּרַבִּי מֵאִיר דְּאָמַר חַיָּיב חַטָּאת – When [R' Eliezer's ruling] is being contrasted **with the view of R' Meir, who said** that going out while wearing a spice bundle is Biblically prohibited and the wearer is **liable to a *chatas*, אָמַר לֵיהּ פָּטוּר – [R' Eliezer] said to [R' Meir]:** She is **exempt;** there is no liability to a *chatas*.[55] **כִּי קָאֵי אַדְּרַבָּנָן דְּאָמְרֵי פָּטוּר אֲבָל אָסוּר** – But **when it is** being contrasted **with the view of the Rabbis, who said** that going out wearing a spice bundle is **Rabbinically prohibited, אָמַר אִיהוּ מוּתָּר לְכַתְּחִלָּה – [R' Eliezer] said** that **it is permitted** even **in the first place.**[56]

NOTES

43. *Rashi;* see also *Rashi* to *Yoma* 25a ד״ה בכוליאר, where he states that this ornament is round in shape; cf. *Rabbeinu Chananel* and *Aruch,* who define this ornament as a band worn around the head. It is deemed a burden because most women do not wear it (see *Chidushei HaRan;* see *Rashash;* see also *Mishnah Berurah* 303:29).

44. The packet was a hollow pendant which was worn by women who suffered from unpleasant body odor. They would place an aromatic spice called *pilon* in the pendant, and its aroma would mask the unpleasant odor (*Rashi;* cf. *Rabbeinu Chananel* and *Rosh,* who explain that *pilon* is a mixture of spices – in their opinion, the word *pilon* derives from the Aramaic word for *mixed*.

45. The Gemara will explain the reasoning of each of the disputants below.

46. According to the Rabbis, wearing the spice bundle is only Rabbinically prohibited; thus, there is no liability to a *chatas* if the woman wears it on the Sabbath.

47. According to R' Eliezer, a spice bundle was not included in the Sages' decree prohibiting the wearing of accessories on the Sabbath (the Gemara will explain why), and therefore it may be worn.

[Although this permit is stated only with regard to a spice bundle, the Gemara will assume that it applies to a flask of balsam oil as well (see *Ritva MHK* ed. and *Chidushei HaRan*).]

48. [Since the overwhelming majority of women do not wear these pendants (only women with unpleasant body odors do), R' Meir considers it a burden rather than an ornament.]

49. [Although the majority of women do not wear such pendants, the Sages hold that since most women who suffer from unpleasant odors *do* wear them, they are considered an accessory for those women (see *Meiri*). Therefore, wearing them is not Biblically prohibited.]

50. [According to the Sages, the spice pendant is treated as are the items of jewelry listed in the Mishnah on 57a; it may not be worn outside on the Sabbath, for she may remove the pendant (which was made of precious metal – see *Chidushei HaRan*) to show to a friend. However, one who does wear it is not liable to a *chatas*.]

51. For the purpose of the spice bundle is to mask the offensive odor, as explained above.

52. For showing this ornament to a friend is embarrassing to her, as doing so calls attention to the fact that the wearer is trying to mask an offensive odor (see *Rashi*); accordingly, she is not likely to call attention to this by showing the pendant to a friend.

53. [The word פָּטוּר generally refers to an act that is Rabbinically prohibited (see above, 3a).]

54. I.e. in a Baraisa that states only R' Eliezer's opinion and that of R' Meir (this Baraisa will be cited in the Gemara below), R' Eliezer did not explicitly state that he completely permits the wearing of spice bundles; he merely took issue with R' Meir's ruling that the wearer is liable to a *chatas*. In truth, however, he is of the opinion that there is no restriction at all, and the spice bundle may be worn without reservation (see *Rashi*).

55. R' Eliezer does not explicitly mention the greater novelty (that wearing the bundle is completely permitted) in this Baraisa; he merely wished to dispute R' Meir's contention that the wearer is liable to a *chatas* (see *Tos. HaRosh* and *Tosafos* to 3a ד״ה בר).

56. In the Baraisa cited by the Gemara above, where the intermediate view of the Sages is cited as well, R' Eliezer states that he disagrees with them as well, and that in his opinion wearing the spice bundle is completely permitted.

והתניא רבי אושעיא אומר ובלבד שלא יאחזנו בידו ויעבירנו ארבע אמות ברשות הרבים [אלא] הכא במאי עסקינן במחופה עור והרי תפילין דמחופה עור ותניא הנכנס לבית הכסא חולץ תפילין ברחוק ארבע אמות ונכנס התם משום שי"ן דאמר אביי [ב] שי"ן של תפילין הלכה למשה מסיני ואמר אביי ד' של תפילין הלכה למשה מסיני ואמר אביי יו"ד של תפילין הלכה למשה מסיני: ולא בשריון ולא בקסדא ולא במגפיים: שריון זרדא קסדא אמר רב סנוארתא מגפיים אמר רב פזמקי: **מתני'** לא תצא אשה במחט הנקובה ולא בטבעת שיש עליה חותם ולא בכוליאר ולא בכובלת ולא בצלוחית של פלייטון ואם יצתה חייבת חטאת דברי ר' מאיר וחכמים פוטרין בכובלת ובצלוחית של פלייטון: **גמ'** אמר עולא וחילופיהן באיש אלמא קסבר עולא כל מידי דחזי לאיש לא חזי לאשה ומידי דחזי לאשה לא חזי לאיש מתיב רב יוסף הרועים יוצאין בשקין ולא הרועים בלבד אמרו אלא כל אדם אלא שדרכן של הרועים לצאת בשקין [אלא] אמר רב יוסף קסבר עולא נשים עם בפני עצמן הן איתיביה אביי [ה] המוצא תפילין מכניסן זוג זוג אחד האיש ואחד האשה ואי אמרת נשים עם בפני עצמן הן והא מצות עשה שהזמן גרמא הוא וכל מצות עשה שהזמן גרמא נשים פטורות התם קסבר ר"מ לילה זמן תפילין הוא ושבת זמן תפילין הוא הוה ליה מצות עשה שלא הזמן גרמא וכל מצות עשה שלא הזמן גרמא נשים חייבות והא הוצאה כלאחר יד היא אמר רבי ירמיה באשה גזברית עסקינן אמר רבה (בר בר חנה אמר רבי יוחנן) תרצת אשה איש מאי איכא למימר אלא אמר רבא פעמים שאדם נותן לאשתו טבעת שיש עליה חותם להוליכה לקופסא ומניחתה בידה עד שמגעת לקופסא ופעמים שהאשה נותנת לבעלה טבעת שאין עליה חותם להוליכה אצל אומן לתקן ומניחה בידו עד שמגיע אצל אומן: ולא בכוליאר ולא בכובלת: מאי כוליאר א"ר מכבנתא כובלת אמר רב חומרתא דפילון וכן אמר רב אסי חומרתא דפילון ת"ר לא תצא בכובלת ואם יצתה חייבת חטאת דברי ר"מ וחכמים אומרים לא תצא ואם יצתה פטורה רבי אליעזר אומר יוצאה אשה בכובלת לכתחלה במאי קמיפלגי רבי מאיר סבר משאוי הוא ורבנן סברי תכשיט הוא ודילמא שלפא ומחויא ואתיא לאיתוייה ורבי אליעזר סבר מאן דרכה למירמיה אשה שריחה רע לא שלפא ומחויא ולא אתיא לאתוייה ארבע אמות ברשות הרבים והתניא ר' אליעזר פוטר בכובלת ובצלוחית של פלייטון לא קשיא הא כי קאי אדרבי מאיר הא כי קאי אדרבנן כי קאי אדרבי מאיר דאמר חייב חטאת אמר ליה פטור כי קאי אדרבנן דאמרי פטור אבל אסור אמר איהו מותר לכתחלה ומאי

רש"י

שלא יאחזנו. דלא הוי תכשיט שלו אלא דרך מלבוש: במכוסה עור. דליכא גנותא אי מעייל לבית הכסא ולא בעי למישקליה: חולץ תפילין. ואע"ג דמכוסה עור שהארבע אגרות שהפרשיות כתובות בהן תחובות בדפוסין של עור: התם משום שי"ן. שעשויה מעור החילון עצמו קומט בו ג' קמטין כעין שי"ן משדי והדלי"ת והיו"ד עשויין בקשר שקושר הרצועה (א) אחת לצפון ואחת למזרח כמין ד' ורצועה קטנה מאד תלויה בה ואין בה אלא כפיפה כמין יו"ד וכופפה בעוד העור לח והיא כפופה לעולם: זרדא. ברוני"א: סנוארתא. כובע עור תחת כובע המתכת: פזמקי. אנפלייאות של ברזל במלחמה: **מתני'** בכוליאר. מפרש בגמרא וכן כובלת: פלייטון. בלשמ"א משחא דאפרסמא: חייבת חטאת. קסבר לאו תכשיט נינהו: **גמ'** אמר עולא וחילופיהן באיש. אטבעת קאי דטבעת שיש עליו חותם אם יצא פטור ואם אין עליו חותם ויצא חייב חטאת: בשקין. שמתכסין בהן מפני הגשמים שקין מלבוש שק: אלא כל אדם. אלמא אע"ג דלא רגילי ביה מגו דלגבי האי תכשיט לגבי האי נמי תכשיט הוא: המוצא תפילין. בשבת בשוק או בדרך: מכניסן. לעיר דרך מלבוש: זוג זוג. כדרך שהוא לובש בחול אחד בראש ואחד בזרוע וחולצן וחוזר ומניח זוג אחר ומכניסן וכן כולן: ואחד האשה. ואע"ג דלאו תכשיט דאשה נינהו מגו דהוו תכשיט לאיש שרי אף לאשה: לילה זמן תפילין הוא וכן שבת. הלכך לעולם זמנם הוא ואין להם זמן קבוע שתהא מצותן מצות עשה שהזמן גרמא להפטר נשים מהן הלכך נקט לילה ושבת משום דפלוגתא בתרווייהו ואי הוי סבירא ליה לרבי מאיר בחד מינייהו דלאו זמן תפילין הוא נמצא זמן קבוע לתפילין והוו להו נשים פטורות: נשים חייבות. הלכך תכשיטין הן לה: והא הוצאה כלאחר יד הוא. אמתני' קאי והוצאת טבעת שמוציאתה דרך מלבוש באצבע וזה שאינו תכשיט לה אמאי חייבת חטאת הרי לא הוציאה כדרך כל המוציאין שכל המוציא דבר שאינו תכשיט לו מוציאין אותו בידים ולא דרך מלבוש: גזברית. שעולחת חותמות תמיד לממונין תחתיה לאמר תנו לך וכך מעות לפלוני והרי חותמה בידה הלכך רגילה היא להניחה באצבעה ומיהו תכשיט לא הוי לדידה דאין דרך נשים בכך ומיהו דרך הוצאתה של זו בכך: איש מאי איכא למימר. דקאמר עולא וחילופיהם באיש דמחייב אטבעת שאין עליה חותם והא הוצאה כלאחר יד הוא שאין דרכו להוציא בזו דרך מלבוש: לקופסא. אישקריי"ה בלע"ז כדי להצניעה שם וי"מ שהקופסא פתוחה בו וכשפותחה חוזרה וחותמת בה ולא נהירא דאם כן מנחתה באצבעה עד שמחזירתה לבעלה מיבעי ליה: אצל אומן לתקנה ומניחה באצבעו. אלמא דרך הוצאה היא: מכבנתא. נושקא"ה ע"ש שמכבנת וקושרת מפתחי החלוק: חומרתא דפילון. קשר שקשור בו סם ששמו פילון וריחו ערב ובלע"ז בלסמ"ו ואשה שריחה רע טוענתו עליה: ורבנן סברי תכשיט הוא. הלכך אם יצאת פטורה ומיהו לכתחלה לא תצא דילמא שלפא ומחויא: למרמיה. להניח בצוארה כמו שקיל ורמי: ה"ג ואשה שריחה רע לא שלפא ומחויא. שגגות הוא לה: והתניא ר' אליעזר פוטר. והכא שרי לכתחלה: הא. דקתני פוטר: כי קאי אר' מאיר. בההיא מתנית' לא איירו רבנן אלא ר"מ לחודיה וגבי חיוב דר"מ שייך למיתני רבי אליעזר פוטר ואע"פ שהוא מתיר לכתחלה: הא כי קאי ארבנן. במתנית' דלעיל דאיירו רבנן בה ואמרו פטור פריש ר' אליעזר בהדיא למילתיה לאיפלוגי עלייהו ואמר יוצאה לכתחלה:

ומאי

תוספות

והתניא ר' אושעיא אומר ובלבד כו'. תימה לר"י דילמא משום מראית העין דוקא הוא אסור מדרבנן כמו קושר בשיר ובטבעת דהשתא ליכא למיגזר דאפילו מייתי לה ליכא איסורא מדאורייתא ואומר ר"י דשלא יאחזנו בידו משמע אפילו בקומצו דליכא מראית העין אלא איסורא דאורייתא איכא ואפילו למ"ד כל דבר שאסרו חכמים משום מראית העין אפילו בחדרי חדרים אסור הכא לא שייך למיגזר דאפילו עומד בשוק ונושאן בקומצו אין כאן מראית העין:

שי"ן של תפילין. ול"ג דלי"ת ויו"ד של תפילין כו' כדמוכח בפ' במה מדליקין (לעיל כח:) גבי הא דתני רב יוסף לא הוכשרו למלאכת שמים כו' ומוקי לה לרצועותיהן ולא פריך דלי"ת של תפילין הלכה למשה מסיני כדפריך גבי שי"ן:

וחילופיהן באיש. אור"ת דאחיוב חטאת קאי:

וכל מצות עשה שהזמן גרמא נשים פטורות. פירוש דהוי משוי וליתסר וא"ת והא הוצאה כלאחר יד היא ושריא משום בזיון תפילין וי"ל כיון דמשוי הוא ויכול לבא לידי חיוב חטאת היכא דמוליא בלא שינוי משום בזיון לא שרינן ליה:

אין

עין משפט נר מצוה

מ א מיי' פי"י מהל' ס"ת הלכה ה טוש"ע י"ד סי' רפב סעיף ו:

מא ב מיי' פ"ד מהל' תפילין הלכה יז סמג עשין כב טוש"ע א"ח סי' מג סעיף ה:

[מא] [ב] [מיי' שם פ"ג הלכה א' טוש"ע א"ח סי' לב סעיף מב נב]:

מב ג ד מיי' פי"ט מהל' שבת הלכה ד ה סמג לאוין סה טור א"ח סי' שג סעיף ט י וסי' שא סעיף ח ט:

מג ה מיי' שם הלכה יח טוש"ע א"ח סי' שא סעיף כא:

[מג] [ה] [מיי' פי"ט מהל' שבת הלכה כג טוש"ע א"ח סי' שא סעיף מב]:

מד ו מיי' פי"ט שם הלכה ג:

מה ז ח מיי' פי"ט שם הלכה ז סמג שם טוש"ע א"ח סי' שג סעיף יא:

רבינו חננאל

ופשטינא אם מחופין עור (כיון) שפיר דמי והא דתניא לא יכנס אדם בתפילין לבית הכסא קבע אפי' להשתין מים התם משום שי"ן דאמר אביי שי"ן של תפילין הל"מ. ת"ר איזהו קמיע מומחה כל שריפה ושנה ושלש אחד קמיע של כתב ואחד קמיע של עקרין אחד חולה שיש בו סכנה ואחד חולה שאין בו סכנה [ולא] שנכפה אלא שלא יכפה וקושר ומתיר. ואפילו ברה"ר ובלבד שלא יקשרנו בשיר או בטבעת ויוצא בו לרה"ר מפני מראית העין: שירין זרדא: לא תצא אשה במחט נקובה. ולא בטבעת שיש עליה חותם. אמר עולא חילופיהן באיש כלומר האיש אסור בטבעת שאין עליה חותם ופטור בטבעת שיש עליה חותם. וכי קאמר עולא וחילופיהן באיש בטבעת בלבד קאמר מותבינן אמאי חייב חטאת והא הוצאה כלאחר יד היא כלומר באצבעה היא מוציאה ואין דרך המוציאין דבר להוציאה דרך מלבוש. ומוקים לה ר' ירמיה באשה גזברית עסקינן שכן דרכה להיות הטבעת באצבעה כדי שתהא חותמת בו כיסים ובתים. הוצאה בכוונה היא לחתום בו ולאו משום תכשיט הוא ודחינן תרצת אשה איש בטבעת שאין עליה חותם אמאי חייב חטאת. ואוקמה רבא לעולם באשה שאינה גזברית ומשום הכי חייבת חטאת דפעמים אדם [נותן] טבעת שיש עליה חותם לאשתו להוליכה לקופסא ומנחתה באצבעה עד שמגעת לקופסא שנמצאת הוצאה בכוונה כדרכה. והאשה נמי פעמים שנותנת כו' וקיי"ל טבעת שיש עליה חותם תכשיט לאיש ולא לאשה ושאין עליה חותם תכשיט לאשה ולא לאיש. ובדין הוא להיות כל אחד ואחד מותר במה שהוא תכשיט לו אלא גזרו משום דרבא שכבר פרשנוהו למעלה (ס.): בכולייר. תכשיט שמסבב הראש כולה כדגרסינן ביומא (כה.) הכהנים היו מוקפין ועומדין ככולייר. כובלת חומרתא דפילון. פי' בשמים בלולין כדמתרגם בלולה דפילא. צלוחית של פלייטון ראשית

מסורת הש"ס

א) ברכות כג., ב) לעיל כח: מנחות לה., ג) פירוש שריון מטכעות קטנו', ד) [גיר' הערוך בכובלת], ה) [תוספת' פ"ו מדרים נה:], ו) עירובין לו: תוס' דעירובין פ"ח בילה טו., ז) [קידושין כט. ושם נסמן], ח) [לעיל דף סא. וש"נ], ט) נ"ל רבא, י) [עתוס' ב"ב קט: ד"ה כבינתי], כ) [רב אלפס פי' מלשון בלולה בשמן מתרגמינן דפילא במשח וכ"א בהרא"ש], ל) [לקמן סה. תוספתא פ"ה ע"ש], מ) [עי' תוס' לעיל ג. סד"ה בר מהני], נ) עי' רש"י יומא כה. ד"ה בכוליאר, ס) [וע"ע תוס' ברכות ו. ד"ה אלו וכו'].

הגהות הב"ח

(א) רש"י ד"ה התם וכו' הרצוע' שבראש אחת לצפון:

גליון הש"ס

מתני' ואם יצתה חייבת חטאת. עי' לעיל דף יא ע"ב תוס' ד"ה ואם יצא: גמ' והתניא ר"א פוטר. עיין לעיל דף ג ע"א תוס' ד"ה בר מהני: רש"י ד"ה חומרתי דפילון וכו' סם ששמו פילון. עיין סוטה דף טו ע"א תוס' ד"ה כמין מומר: תוס' ד"ה וחילופיהן באיש. אור"ת דאחיוב חטאת קאי. עיין עירובין דף סט ע"א תוס' ד"ה כיון דמזיד.

ליקוטי רש"י

תפילין דמחופה עור. עור דקות שלבן שהכתבים פרשיות מונחים בו [לעיל כח:]. חולץ תפילין ברחוק ארבע אמות. [illegible] סמוך לבית הכסא צריך לחלוץ ברחוק ארבע אמות [illegible] וגנאי הדבר [ברכות כג.]. שי"ן של תפילין וכו' ד' של תפילין וכו'. שי"ן של תפילין [illegible] ודומה לשי"ן והרצועה נקשרת כמין דל"ת [illegible] כמין יו"ד [illegible] [לעיל שם ועי' במסורה"ש שם]. [illegible] שי"ן ודל"ת נראה בקשר ויו"ד נראה [illegible] [מנחות לה:]. הלכה למשה מסיני. [illegible] ודומה ליו"ד הרי שדי [עירובין צז.]. במחט הנקובה. [illegible] נקובה לשאינו נקובה דנקובה קתני חייב חטאת ובשאינה נקובה כגון אישפינגל"א שהיא תכשיט קתני אינו [illegible] מה אשה (שבת נז:) [לעיל נב:]. ולא בטבעת שיש עליה חותם. דלאו תכשיט הוא והוי משאוי. [illegible] שיט הוא דאין דרך לאשה לחתום ולשלוח שלוחים שאין חותם עשוי אלא לאדם גדול וממונה [שם נט:]. [illegible] בה איגרת או כל דבר סגור [שם נז.]. בכוליאר. עגול שקורין טשק"א [יומא כה.]. פליימון. בושם [illegible] ריסמון [סנהדרין קח. ועיין במלוא הרועים]. המוצא תפילין. בשדה במקום שנאבדין. מכניסן. לעיר ולבית. זוג זוג. אחד בראש ואחד בזרוע והיינו זוג כדרך שלובשן בחול וחוזר תמיד ומכניסן זוג אחר זוג עד שיכלו [עירובין צה.]. נותן בראשו ואחד בזרועו [illegible] דרך הנחתן בחול ומכניסן וחוזר והולך ולובש זוג אחר ומכניסן, תפילין של ראש ושל זרוע קרי זוג זוג [ביצה טו.]. מצות עשה שהזמן גרמא. נפקא לן בפרק קמא דקידושין (כט.) דנשים פטורות [פסחים מג:]. שהזמן גורם [illegible] מכבנתא. [illegible] חומרתא דפילון. [illegible]

ומאי ר' מאיר דתניא [א] לא תצא אשה במפתח שבידה ואם יצאת חייבת חטאת דברי רבי מאיר רבי אליעזר פוטר [ב] בכובלת ובצלוחית של פלייטון כובלת מאן דכר שמה חסורי מחסרא והכי קתני וכן בכובלת וכן בצלוחית של פלייטון לא תצא ואם יצאה חייבת חטאת דברי רבי מאיר רבי אליעזר פוטר בכובלת ובצלוחית של פלייטון [ג] במה דברים אמורים כשיש בהם בושם אבל אין בהם בושם חייבת אמר רב אדא בר אהבה זאת אומרת המוציא אוכלין פחות מכשיעור בכלי חייב דהא אין בה בושם כפחות מכשיעור בכלי דמי וקתני חייבת רב אשי אמר בעלמא אימא לך פטור ושאני הכא דליתיה לממשא כלל: א) וראשית שמנים ימשחו אמר רב יהודה אמר שמואל זה פלייטון מתיב רב יוסף [ד] אף על פלייטון גזר רבי יהודה בן בבא ולא הודו לו ואי אמרת משום תענוג אמאי לא הודו לו אמר ליה אביי ולטעמיך הא דכתיב א) השותים במזרקי יין ר' אמי ור' אסי חד אמר קנישקנין וחד אמר שמזרקין כוסותיהן זה לזה הכי נמי דאסיר והא [ה] רבה בר רב הונא איקלע לבי ריש גלותא ושתה בקנישקנין ולא אמר ליה ולא מידי אלא כל מידי דאית ביה תענוג ואית ביה שמחה גזרו רבנן אבל מידי דאית ביה תענוג ולית ביה שמחה לא גזרו רבנן: ב) השוכבים על מטות שן וסרוחים על ערשותם [ו] אמר רבי יוסי ברבי חנינא מלמד שהיו משתינין מים בפני מטותיהן ערומים מגדף בה ר' אבהו אי הכי היינו דכתיב ג) לכן עתה יגלו בראש גולים משום דמשתינין מים בפני מטותיהם ערומים יגלו בראש גולים אלא א"ר אבהו אלו בני אדם שהיו אוכלים ושותים זה עם זה ודובקין מטותיהן זו בזו ומחליפין נשותיהן זה עם זה ומסריחין ערסותם בשכבת זרע שאינו שלהן א"ר אבהו ואמרי לה במתניתא תנא ג' דברים מביאין את האדם לידי עניות ואלו הן המשתין מים בפני מטתו ערום ° ומזלזל בנטילת ידים ושאשתו מקללתו בפניו המשתין מים בפני מטתו ערום אמר רבא לא אמרן אלא דמהדר אפיה לפורייה אבל לבראי לית לן בה ומהדר אפיה לפורייה נמי לא אמרן אלא לארעא אבל במנא לית לן בה [ז] ומזלזל בנטילת ידים אמר רבא לא אמרן אלא דלא משא ידיה כלל אבל משא ולא משא לית לן בה ולאו מילתא היא דאמר רב חסדא אנא משאי מלא חפני מיא ויהבו לי מלא חפני טיבותא ושאשתו מקללתו בפניו אמר רבא על עסקי תכשיטיה והני מילי דאית ליה ולא עביד: דרש רבא בריה דרב עילאי מאי [ח] דכתיב ד) ויאמר ה' יען כי גבהו בנות ציון שהיו מהלכות בקומה זקופה ד) ותלכנה נטויות גרון שהיו מהלכות עקב בצד גודל ד) ומשקרות עינים דהוה מלאן כוחלא לעינייהו ומרמזן ד) הלוך וטפוף שהיו מהלכות ארוכה בצד קצרה ד) וברגליהן תעכסנה אמר רב יצחק דבי ר' אמי מלמד שמטילות מור ואפרסמון במנעליהן ומהלכות בשוקי ירושלים וכיון שמגיעות אצל בחורי ישראל בועטות בקרקע ומתיזות עליהם ומכניסות בהן יצר הרע כארס [ט] בכעוס מאי פורענותיהם כדדריש רבה בר עולא ה) והיה תחת בושם מק יהיה מקום שהיו מתבשמות בו נעשה נמקים נמקים ה) ותחת חגורה נקפה מקום שהיו חגורות בצלצול נעשה נקפים נקפים ה) ותחת מעשה מקשה קרחה מקום שהיו מתקשטות בו נעשה קרחים קרחים ה) ותחת פתיגיל מחגורת שק פתחים המביאין לידי גילה יהיו למחגורת שק ה) כי תחת יופי אמר רבא היינו דאמרי אינשי חלופי שופרא כיבא ו) [י] (וספח) ה' קדקד בנות ציון אמר רבי יוסי ברבי חנינא מלמד שפרחה בהן צרעת כתיב הכא ושפח וכתיב התם ז) לשאת ולספחת ו) וה' פתהן יערה רב ושמואל חד אמר שנשפכו כקיתון וחד אמר שנעשו פתחיהן כיער אמר רב יהודה אמר רב אנשי ירושלים אנשי שחץ היו אדם אומר לחבירו במה סעדת היום בפת עמילה או בפת שאינה עמילה ביין גורדלי או ביין

ומאי רבי מאיר. היכא אשכחן דאיירי בה רבי מאיר בלא רבנן ופליג רבי אליעזר עליה: בד"א. דרבי אליעזר פוטר והאי פוטר היינו מותר לכתחלה כדאוקימנא: כשיש בה בושם. פלייטון יש בההוא חומרתא העשויה כקמיע דכיון דיש בה בושם תכשיט היא לזו שריחה רע ולמשלף ולאיתויי נמי לא חייש כדאמרן דגנות הוא לה: אבל אין בה בושם. חומרתא לחודא לאו תכשיט הוא וחייבת: זאת אומרת. הא דקתני אין בה בושם חייבת אלמא דקסבר רבי אליעזר המוציא אוכלין בשבת בכלי פחות מכשיעור דלא מיחייב על הוצאת אוכלין פחות מגרוגרת כדלקמן (דף ע:) חייב מיהא על הכלי ולא אמרינן הכלי טפל להן ולא מיחייב עליה שלא נתכוין להוציא אלא משום אוכלין ופלוגתא היא על סתם משנה השנויה בפרק המצניע (לקמן דף צג:) דקתני פטור אף על הכלי: דהא אין בו בושם כפחות מכשיעור דמי. שהכלי קלט את הריח ושיעור הוצאת בשמים בכל שהוא וכיון שאינו כל שהוא הוי ריחה פחות מכשיעור (הוא) וקתני חייבת ולא אמרינן נעשה כלי טפל לריח שבתוכו והריחה לא מיחייב דפחות מכשיעור הוא: ושאני הכא. ליכא למימר נעשה כלי טפל לריח שאין בו שום ממש ואפילו פחות מכשיעור לא מיקרי אבל פחות מכשיעור בדבר שיש בו ממש נעשה כלי טפל לו ופטור: ראשית שמנים. מובחר שבשמנים: גזר. משום לעז חורבן: ואי אמרת. זה פלייטון והאי קרא בתענוג משתעי שלא היו נותנים לב לדברי הנביאים הניבאים על הפורענות ועסוקים בתענוגים: ולטעמיך הא דכתיב. בהאי ענינא השותים במזרקי יין ורבי אמי ורבי אסי פירשו ° זהו קנישקנין כלי זכוכית ארוך ולו שני פיות ויין נזרק מזה לזה: שמזרקין. על ידי אומנות כדאמר בהחליל (סוכה דף נג.) מטייל בתמני כסי: הכי נמי דאסור. למשתי השתא בקנישקנין: משתינין. דדייק מסרוחים: לידי עניות. דאמרינן בע"פ (פסחים דף קיא:) שרא דעניותא נביל שמיה ונביל קרי ליה ואוהב מקום מיאוס ומשתין מים לפני מטתו היינו מיאוס: ערום. אורחא דמילתא נקט מתוך שהוא ערום אינו יוצא לחוץ להשתין דטורח הוא לו ללבוש ולצאת: אבל לבראי לית לן בה. שהקילוח ארוך וניתז למרחוק: משא ולא משא. שאינו רוחץ ומשפשף יפה אלא מעט מים כגון רביעית מלומלם: על עסקי תכשיטיה. שאינו רוצה לקנות לה: גבהו. היינו קומה זקופה: ותלכנה נטויות גרון שהיו הולכות עקב בצד גודל. למעט בהילוכם שהיו מסתכלין בה והיא שוהה בפסיעותיה ודרך נוטין גרון לילך בנחת לפי שאינו רואה לרגליו: ומשקרות עינים דמליין כוחלא. לשון סיקרא: ומרמזן. את הבחורים: סיקור. לשון הבטה: הלוך וטפוף שהיו מהלכות ארוכה בצד קצרה. שתראה נאה על ראש חברתה והוא נוי לה ונשואות היו לפיכך מספר בגנותן: וטפוף. כמו על דאטפת אטפוך (אבות פ"ב מ"ו): תעכסנה. כמו וכעכס אל מוסר אויל (משלי ז) והוא ארס של נחש וקרי ליה עכס על שם שאינו מטילו אלא על ידי כעס: בכעוס. נחש כעוסה: נמקים. כמו המק בשרו (זכריה יד): צלצול. בנדי"ל נאה: נקפים. חבורות לשון המנקף רגלו וניקף סבכי היער (ישעיה י): מתקשטות. היינו שער שסורקות ומפרכסות: מתקשטות. דומה למקשה כעין נוטריקון: פתיגיל. נוטריקון פתח גילה אותו מקום: כי תחת יופי. כי כל אלה יבא לך תחת יפייך: כיבא. קיוטור"א ליחה כמו שיחנא וכיבי דקודשין דפלימו (דף פא:): פתהן. כמו פתחיהן: שנשפכו בקיתון. שופכות דם זיבה: יערה. כמו ותער כדה (בראשית כד): כיער. נתמלאו שער ונמאסות לתשמיש: אנשי שחץ. מדברים בלשון גאוה ולעגי שפה: סעדת. תשמיש: פת עמילה. בעולה: שאינה עמילה. בתולה: פת עמילה. ברייאי"ה בלע"ז: גורדלי. לבן היה:

ביין

עין משפט נר מצוה

מו א טוש"ע א"ח סי' רמא:

מז ב ג מיי' פ"ו מהל' ברכות הלכה יט טוש"ע א"ח סי' קנח סעיף ט:

מח ד מיי' פכ"א מהל' איסורי ביאה הלכה ב' טוש"ע אה"ע סי' כא סעיף א:

רבינו חננאל

ראשית שמנים כמשמעו ואפילו מאן דפטר לא פטר אלא בשיש בה בושם. אבל אין בה בושם חייבת. קנישקנין כוס שיש בה שתי פיות ושותין ממנה שנים בבת אחת. מסקרות עינים. דהוו מליין כוחלא רמזא. ארס בכעוס. פי' החיה כשתכעוס גוררת ומשלכת. ארס קשה. פי' פת עמילה. אשה בעולה ופת שאינה עמילה בתולה. וכולן על זה הענין: צלצול חגור. כדגרסינן בסוף מנחות (דף קט:):

רב נסים גאון

מותיב רב יוסף אף על פליאטון גזר ר' יהודה בן בבא. עיקר זאת הברייתא בתוספ' סוטה בסוף המסכת בפולמוס האחרון גזרו על חופת חתנים אלו זהוריות המוזהבות כו' אף על פליאטון גזר ר' יהודה בן בבא ולא הודו לו:

תורה אור השלם

א) הַשֹּׁתִים בְּמִזְרְקֵי יַיִן וְרֵאשִׁית שְׁמָנִים יִמְשָׁחוּ וְלֹא נֶחְלוּ עַל שֵׁבֶר יוֹסֵף: [עמוס ו, ו]

ב) הַשֹּׁכְבִים עַל מִטּוֹת שֵׁן וּסְרֻחִים עַל עַרְשׂוֹתָם וְאֹכְלִים כָּרִים מִצֹּאן וַעֲגָלִים מִתּוֹךְ מַרְבֵּק: [עמוס ו, ד]

ג) לָכֵן עַתָּה יִגְלוּ בְּרֹאשׁ גֹּלִים וְסָר מִרְזַח סְרוּחִים: [עמוס ו, ז]

ד) וַיֹּאמֶר יְיָ יַעַן כִּי גָבְהוּ בְּנוֹת צִיּוֹן וַתֵּלַכְנָה נְטוּיוֹת גָּרוֹן וּמְשַׂקְּרוֹת עֵינָיִם הָלוֹךְ וְטָפֹף תֵּלַכְנָה וּבְרַגְלֵיהֶם תְּעַכַּסְנָה: [ישעיה ג, טז]

ה) וְהָיָה תַחַת בֹּשֶׂם מַק יִהְיֶה וְתַחַת חֲגוֹרָה נִקְפָּה וְתַחַת מַעֲשֶׂה מִקְשֶׁה קָרְחָה וְתַחַת פְּתִיגִיל מַחֲגֹרֶת שָׂק כִּי תַחַת יֹפִי: [ישעיה ג, כד]

ו) וְשִׂפַּח אֲדֹנָי קָדְקֹד בְּנוֹת צִיּוֹן וַיְיָ פָּתְהֵן יְעָרֶה: [ישעיה ג, יז]

ז) וְלַשְׂאֵת וְלַסַּפַּחַת וְלַבֶּהָרֶת: [ויקרא יד, נו]

מסורת הש"ס

א) [תוספתא פ"ה ע"ש], ב) [לקמן דף סה.], ג) [תוספתא שם ע"ש], ד) [תוספ' דסוטה פט"ו], ה) [ע"ז דף עב: ע"ש], ו) קדושין עא., ז) נדה יז., ח) [יומא דף ע: ע"ש], ט) [עי' ערוך ערך ארס], י) [נ"ל ושפח].

גליון הש"ס

גמ' ומזלזל בנט"י. עי' סוטה ד ע"ב תוס' ד"ה נעקר: רש"י ד"ה ולטעמיך וכו' זהו קנישקנין. עי' ע"ז דף עב ע"ב ברש"י ד"ה קניסקנין:

ליקוטי רש"י

וראשית שמנים. מובחר שבשמנים והוא אפרסמון. השותים במזרקי יין. יש מרבותינו שאומרים במסכת שבת שהיו זורקין כוסותיהן זה לזה וי"מ על שם כלי שהיו לו שתי פיות והוא ארוך ושותה זה מכאן וזה מכאן הוא נזרק מפיו אל פיו [עמוס ו, ו]. קנישקנין. כלי רחב ויש לו שני קנין או שלשה יוצאין מלידו ונמשכין ועולין כנגד גובהו וכשנותנין יין בפיו מתמלאין כל הקנים ויכולין כמה בני אדם לשתות בו ביחד וכאן קורין לו קרוגל"א מפני שמוקף קנים כמחולות הללו [ע"ז עב:]. ויאמר ה'. על הנשים אשר משלו בעמי יען כי גבהו וגו'. הלוך וטפוף. לשון דבר לף על גבי חבירו כמו (דברים יא) אשר הציף ומתרגמינן דאטיף כך היתה ארוכה מהלכת בין שתי קצרות כדי שתהא נראית צפה למעלה מהם. וברגליהן תעכסנה. להבעיר בו יצר הרע כעכס זה של נחש, עכס הוא ארס של נחש [ישעיה ג, טז]. והיה תחת בושם מק. מקום שהיו מתבשמות בו יהיה נימק. ותחת חגורה נקפה. מקום שחגרה שם יהיה ניקף נחתך בחבורות ורשומי מכות כמו ואחר עורי נקפו (איוב יט) ונקף סבכי היער (ישעיה י). ותחת מעשה מקשה. מקום שהיו עושות בו המעשה האמור למעלה הלוך וטפוף תלכנה והוא בגובה הראש שם תהיה מקשה קרחה מכה המקרחת את הראש מקשה ל' דא לדא נקשן (דניאל ה) ואני הייתי מפרשו תחת המעשה מקשה מקום שהיו שם חגורות נותנות עדי הזהב העשויות מקשה בטדי"ך בלע"ז אלא שהוא נקוד פתח והוא במסורה בעשרה נקודים פתח ואין אחד מהם דבוק לתיבה של אחריו וכל מעשה שהוא דבק לתיבה של אחריו נקוד קמץ. ותחת פתיגיל. הוא בית הרחם האמור למעלה פתהן חלוף אותה גילה תהיה מחגורת שק בכל מתניה. כי תחת יופי. כי זאת הוגנת להיות להם תחת יופי שהיו משתחצות בו [שם, כד]. ושפח. לשון צרעת כמו (ויקרא יג) מספחת היא ועל שנכתב בשי"ן דרשו בו רבותינו שמעשנה שפחות מכודות ויש שדרשוהו שהרבה בהן משפחות משפחות של כנים. פתהן יערה. הן היו אומרות ימהר יחישה מעשהו של רואה אותי ונוטל אותי כשבא הפורענות היו שרי נ"נ נוטלין אותן להיות לנשים מחמת יופין ורמז הקב"ה והיו שופעות כאדם המערה מכלי אל כלי וכאשר נענשו בדם נדה והיו נמאסות עליהן ומשליכין אותן לארץ מעל קרונות שלהן [שם, יז]. פת עמילה. שאינה ממהרת להחמיץ שעמילתה מעכבתה עמילה ברייר"א [פסחים לז:].

The Gemara continues its elaboration:

וּמַאי רַבִּי מֵאִיר – And in **what** place is R' Eliezer's ruling contrasted with that of **R' Meir?**[1] **דְּתַנְיָא – It is that which was taught in a Baraisa:** **לֹא תֵּצֵא אִשָּׁה בְּמַפְתֵּחַ שֶׁבְּיָדָהּ** – A WOMAN MAY NOT GO OUT on the Sabbath WITH A KEY THAT IS IN HER HAND; **וְאִם יָצְאת חַיֶּיבֶת חַטָּאת** – AND IF SHE GOES OUT, SHE IS LIABLE TO A *CHATAS* offering.[2] **דִּבְרֵי רַבִּי מֵאִיר** – These are THE WORDS OF R' MEIR. **רַבִּי אֱלִיעֶזֶר פּוֹטֵר בְּכוֹבֶלֶת וּבִצְלוֹחִית שֶׁל פַּלְיָיטוֹן** – R' ELIEZER EXEMPTS her IN THE CASE OF A SPICE BUNDLE OR A FLASK OF BALSAM OIL.[3]

The Gemara immediately objects:

כּוֹבֶלֶת מַאן דְּכַר שְׁמַהּ – Who made mention of a spice bundle, that R' Eliezer saw fit to issue his ruling exempting the wearer? A spice bundle is not discussed in the Baraisa at all!

The Gemara answers by emending the Mishnah:

חַסּוּרֵי מִחַסְּרָא – We must say that **[the Mishnah] is missing words** in the Tanna Kamma's ruling, **וְהָכִי קָתָנֵי – and this is what it should say:** **וְכֵן בְּכוֹבֶלֶת וְכֵן בִּצְלוֹחִית שֶׁל פַּלְיָיטוֹן לֹא תֵּצֵא** – A woman may not go out with a key; AND ALSO WITH A SPICE BUNDLE, AND ALSO WITH A FLASK OF BALSAM OIL SHE MAY NOT GO OUT;[4] **וְאִם יָצְאָה חַיֶּיבֶת חַטָּאת** – AND IF SHE GOES OUT with any of these items, SHE IS LIABLE TO A *CHATAS*. **דִּבְרֵי רַבִּי מֵאִיר** – These are THE WORDS OF R' MEIR. **רַבִּי אֱלִיעֶזֶר פּוֹטֵר בְּכוֹבֶלֶת וּבִצְלוֹחִית שֶׁל פַּלְיָיטוֹן** – But R' ELIEZER EXEMPTS her IN THE CASE OF A SPICE BUNDLE OR A FLASK OF BALSAM OIL. Thus corrected, this Baraisa is where we find R' Eliezer's ruling contrasted with that of R' Meir.[5]

The Gemara cites the continuation of the Baraisa, in which R' Eliezer qualifies his ruling:

בַּמֶּה דְּבָרִים אֲמוּרִים – In WHAT CASE WERE THESE WORDS STATED? **כְּשֶׁיֵּשׁ בָּהֶם בּוֹשֶׂם** – WHEN THEY (the spice bundle or flask) HAVE SPICE or oil IN THEM. **אֲבָל אֵין בָּהֶם בּוֹשֶׂם** – BUT IF THERE IS NO SPICE or oil IN THEM, and a woman wears them when they are empty, **חַיֶּיבֶת** – SHE IS LIABLE to A *CHATAS*.[6]

The Gemara attempts to derive a point of law from this ruling:

אָמַר רַב אַדָּא בַּר אַהֲבָה – Rav Adda bar Ahavah said: **זֹאת אוֹמֶרֶת – This** ruling of R' Eliezer **teaches** us[7] the following law: **הַמּוֹצִיא אוֹכָלִין פָּחוֹת מִכַּשִּׁיעוּר בִּכְלִי – One who takes out less than the minimum quantity of food**[8] **in a utensil** on the Sabbath **חַיָּיב – is liable** for taking out the utensil, even though he is not liable for taking out the food.[9] **דְּהָא אֵין בָּהּ בּוֹשֶׂם כְּפָחוֹת מִכַּשִּׁיעוּר בִּכְלִי דָּמֵי – For** taking out a spice bundle or flask **that has no spice** or oil in it **is comparable to** taking out **less than the minimum quantity** of food in a utensil, since the aroma of the spices still linger;[10] **וְקָתָנֵי חַיֶּיבֶת – and the Baraisa teaches** that in that case the wearer is **liable!** Thus, in the case of one who takes out less than the minimum quantity of food in a utensil, he should also be liable.

The Gemara rejects the comparison:

רַב אַשִׁי אָמַר – Rav Ashi said: **בְּעָלְמָא אֵימָא לָךְ פָּטוּר – With regard to** the **general** case of less than the minimum quantity of food in a utensil, **I can say** to you that one is **exempt;**[11] **וְשָׁאנֵי הָכָא – but here** in the case of an empty spice bundle of flask, **it is different,** **דְּלֵיתֵיהּ לְמַמָּשָׁא כְּלָל – because there is no substance** in it **at all.**[12]

The Gemara discusses balsam oil in a different context:

"וְרֵאשִׁית שְׁמָנִים יִמְשָׁחוּ" – Scripture states:[13] ***And they anoint themselves with the finest of oils.*** **אָמַר רַב יְהוּדָה אָמַר שְׁמוּאֵל – Rav Yehudah said in the name of Shmuel:** **זֶה פַּלְיָיטוֹן – This refers to balsam.**

This interpretation is challenged:

מְתִיב רַב יוֹסֵף – Rav Yosef objected to it on the basis of the following Baraisa,[14] which lists practices that were banned because of the Temple's destruction:[15] **אַף עַל פַּלְיָיטוֹן גָּזַר רַבִּי יְהוּדָה בֶּן בָּבָא** – EVEN AGAINST the use of BALSAM DID R' YEHUDAH BEN BAVA DECREE. **וְלֹא הוֹדוּ לוֹ** – BUT [THE SAGES] DID NOT

NOTES

1. I.e. in what place do we find a dispute between R' Meir and R' Eliezer in the matter of a spice bundle, where the intermediate view of the Sages is *not* recorded? (*Rashi;* see *Sfas Emes*).

2. [This ruling would seem to be patently obvious; see, however, *Tosefta* (5:10) where the text reads: "A woman may not go out . . . with a key that is on her *finger.*" According to this reading, R' Meir teaches that although the key is being *worn,* it still may not be carried out (see *Orach Chaim* 301:11 with *Rama*).]

3. [In this instance, although R' Eliezer uses the word פָּטוּר, he actually holds that it is completely permitted,as stated above [on 62a] (*Rashi*).]

4. Thus, R' Meir actually issued rulings on all three cases: a key, a spice bundle and a flask of balsam oil.

5. See above, 62a note 54.

6. The pendant itself is not considered an ornament when it is empty, for it is usually not worn empty; therefore, one who wears it outside on the Sabbath is liable to a *chatas* (*Rashi*).

7. Literally: this says.

8. In order to be Biblically liable for taking out an item on the Sabbath, one must take out a significant or useful quantity of that item. The minimum amounts for many common items are discussed in the seventh and eighth chapters of this tractate; in general, the minimum amount for most foodstuffs is a piece the size of a dried fig (*Rashi;* see Mishnah below, 76b).

9. It might have been thought that a utensil containing food should be deemed subordinate to the food (since it is only being carried out to contain the food), and hence inconsequential; accordingly, in an instance where one cannot be liable for the food, such as where it is less than the minimum amount, one would not be not liable for the utensil either [though if he carried out the utensil for its own sake, he *would* be liable]. Indeed, the view of the anonymous Mishnah below (93b) is that in such a case one *is not* liable for taking out the utensil. Rav Adda states that R' Eliezer argues with that Mishnah (*Rashi;* see *Ritva MHK* ed. and *Chidushei HaRan*). The Gemara below explains the parallel between the two cases.

10. Some of the aroma of the spices clings to the walls of the pendant. Now, with regard to spices, even a minuscule amount is enough to satisfy the minimum for the prohibition against carrying; when there is nothing but a scent, however, it is compared by Rav Adda to a case where less than the minimum quantity remains. Accordingly, the fact that R' Eliezer rules that one who goes out wearing an empty spice bundle on the Sabbath is liable to a *chatas* is proof that he does *not* view the pendant as subordinate to the aroma within it; accordingly, he would hold one liable for taking out a utensil containing less than the minimum quantity of food as well (*Rashi;* see also *Dibros Moshe* 53:23, who explains the Gemara's original position).

11. For, in truth, we do not regard the utensil as significant when it is being taken out only to hold the food within it, even where there is a less-than-minimum quantity of food in the utensil.

12. In this case, Rav Ashi states that we cannot view the pendant as inconsequential with regard to the spice that is within it, for there *is no* spice within it, only an aroma. The aroma is *not* considered as a less-than-minimum quantity; rather, it is disregarded entirely, and the pendant is deemed completely empty. Accordingly, one who wears it on the Sabbath is liable. In the case of the food, however, it is possible that R' Eliezer would concur with the view of the Mishnah below (93b; see note 9) and exempt one who takes out such a utensil, for there the utensil can be deemed inconsequential with respect to the small quantity of food that is in it (*Rashi*).

13. *Amos* 6:6. The prophet rebukes the people for ignoring prophecies of their retribution and continuing instead to indulge in luxuries (*Rashi* ד״ה ואי אמרת).

14. *Tosefta Sotah* 15:4.

15. The Sages banned certain joyful practices in order to impress upon the people the gravity of the tragedy that had befallen them (see *Sotah* 49a-b, *Bava Basra* 60b; see also *Shulchan Aruch Orach Chaim* 560).

עין משפט
נר מצוה

מז א טוש"ע א"ח סי' רמא:
מז ב ג מיי' פ"ו מהל' ברכות הלכה יט טוש"ע א"ח סי' קנח סעיף ט:
מח ד מיי' פכ"א מהל' איסורי ביאה הלכה ב' טוש"ע אה"ע סי' כא סעיף א:

ומאי ר' מאיר דתניא (א) לא תצא אשה במפתח שבידה ואם יצאת חייבת חטאת דברי רבי מאיר רבי אליעזר פוטר (ב) בכובלת ובצלוחית של פלייטון כובלת מאן דכר שמה חסורי מחסרא והכי קתני וכן בכובלת וכן בצלוחית של פלייטון לא תצא ואם יצאה חייבת חטאת דברי רבי מאיר רבי אליעזר פוטר בכובלת ובצלוחית של פלייטון (ג) במה דברים אמורים כשיש בהם בושם אבל אין בהם בושם חייבת אמר רב אדא בר אהבה זאת אומרת המוציא אוכלין פחות מכשיעור בכלי חייב דהא אין בה בושם כפחות מכשיעור בכלי דמי וקתני חייבת רב אשי אמר בעלמא אימא לך פטור ושאני הכא דליתיה לממשא כלל: (א) וראשית שמנים ימשחו אמר רב יהודה אמר שמואל זה פלייטון מתיב רב יוסף (ד) אף על פלייטון גזר רבי יהודה בן בבא ולא הודו לו ואי אמרת משום תענוג אמאי לא הודו לו אמר ליה אביי ולטעמיך הא דכתיב (א) השותים במזרקי יין ר' אמי ור' אסי חד אמר קנישקנין וחד אמר שמזרקין כוסותיהן זה לזה הכי נמי דאסיר והא (ה) רבה בר רב הונא איקלע לבי ריש גלותא ושתה בקנישקנין ולא אמר ליה ולא מידי אלא כל מידי דאית ביה תענוג ואית ביה שמחה גזרו רבנן אבל מידי דאית ביה תענוג ולית ביה שמחה לא גזרו רבנן: (ב) השוכבים על מטות שן וסרוחים על ערשותם (ו) אמר רבי יוסי ברבי חנינא מלמד שהיו משתינין מים בפני מטותיהן ערומים מגדף בה ר' אבהו אי הכי היינו דכתיב (ג) לכן עתה יגלו בראש גולים משום דמשתינין מים בפני מטותיהם ערומים יגלו בראש גולים אלא א"ר אבהו אלו בני אדם שהיו אוכלים ושותים זה עם זה ודובקין מטותיהן זו בזו ומחליפין נשותיהן זה עם זה ומסריחין ערסותם בשכבת זרע שאינו שלהן א"ר אבהו ואמרי לה במתניתא תנא ג' דברים מביאין את האדם לידי עניות ואלו הן (ז) המשתין מים בפני מטתו ערום ° ומזלזל בנטילת ידים ושאשתו מקללתו בפניו °המשתין מים בפני מטתו ערום אמר רבא לא אמרן אלא דמהדר אפיה לפורייה אבל לבראי לית לן בה ומהדר אפיה לפורייה נמי לא אמרן אלא לארעא אבל במנא לית לן בה °ומזלזל בנטילת ידים אמר רבא לא אמרן אלא דלא משא ידיה כלל אבל משא ולא משא לית לן בה ולאו מלתא היא דאמר רב חסדא °אנא משאי מלא חפני מיא ויהבו לי מלא חפני טיבותא ושאשתו מקללתו בפניו אמר רבא על עסקי תכשיטיה וה"מ הוא דאית ליה ולא עביד: דרש רבא בריה דרב עילאי מאי (ח) דכתיב (ד) ויאמר ה' יען כי גבהו בנות ציון שהיו מהלכות בקומה זקופה (ד) ותלכנה נטויות גרון שהיו מהלכות עקב בצד גודל (ד) ומשקרות עינים דהוה מלאן כוחלא לעיניהו ומרמזן (ד) הלוך וטפוף שהיו מהלכות ארוכה בצד קצרה (ד) וברגליהן תעכסנה אמר רב יצחק דבי ר' אמי °מלמד שמטילות מור ואפרסמון במנעליהן ומהלכות בשוקי ירושלים וכיון שמגיעות אצל בחורי ישראל בועטות בקרקע ומתיזות עליהם ומכניסות בהן יצר הרע כארס (ט) בכעוס מאי פורענותיהם כדדריש רבה בר עולא (ה) והיה תחת בושם מק יהיה מקום שהיו מתבשמות בו נעשה נמקים (ה) ותחת חגורה נקפה מקום שהיו חגורות בצלצול נעשה נקפים נקפים (ה) ותחת מעשה מקשה קרחה מקום שהיו מתקשטות בו נעשה קרחים קרחים (ה) ותחת פתיגיל מחגורת שק פתחים המביאין לידי גילה יהיו למחגורת שק (ה) כי תחת יופי אמר רבא היינו דאמרי אינשי חלופי שופרא כיבא (ו) (י) (וספח) ה' קדקוד בנות ציון אמר רבי יוסי ברבי חנינא מלמד שפרחה בהן צרעת כתיב הכא ושפח וכתיב התם (ז) לשאת ולספחת (ו) וה' פתהן יערה רב ושמואל חד אמר שנשפכו כקיתון וחד אמר שנעשו פתחיהן כיער אמר רב יהודה אמר רב אנשי ירושלים אנשי שחץ היו אדם אומר לחברו במה סעדת היום בפת עמילה או בפת שאינה עמילה ביין גורדלי או ביין

ומאי רבי מאיר. היכא אשכחן דאיירי בה רבי מאיר בלא רבנן ופליג רבי אליעזר עליה: בד"א. דרבי אליעזר פוטר והאי פוטר היינו מותר לכתחלה כדאוקימנא: כשיש בה בושם. פלייטון יש בההוא אומרתא העשויה כקמיע דכיון דיש בה בושם תכשיט היא לזו שריחה רע ולמשלף ואיתויי נמי לא חייש כדאמרן דגנות הוא לה: אבל אין בה בושם. אומרתא לחודא לאו תכשיט הוא וחייבת: זאת אומרת. הא דקתני אין בה בושם חייבת אלמא דקסבר רבי אליעזר המוציא אוכלין בשבת בכלי פחות מכשיעור דלא מיחייב על הוצאת אוכלין פחות מגרוגרת כדלקמן (דף עו:) חייב מיהא על הכלי ולא אמרינן הכלי טפל להן ולא מיחייב עליה שלא נתכוין להוציא אלא משום אוכלין ופלוגתא היא על סתם משנה השנויה בפרק המצניע (לקמן דף צג:) דקתני פטור אף על הכלי: דהא אין בו בושם כפחות מכשיעור דמי. שהכלי קלט את הריח ושיעור הוצאת בשמים בכל שהוא וכיון שאינו כל שהוא הוי ריחה פחות מכשיעור (הוא) וקתני חייבת ולא אמרינן נעשה כלי טפל לריח שבתוכו והריחא לא מיחייב דפחות מכשיעור הוא: ושאני הכא. ליכא למימר נעשה כלי טפל לריח שאין בו שום ממש ואפילו פחות מכשיעור לא מיקרי אבל פחות מכשיעור בדבר שיש בו ממש נעשה כלי טפל לו ופטור: ראשית שמנים. מובחר שבשמנים: גזר. משום לער חורבן: ואי אמרת. זה פלייטון והאי קרא בתענוג משתעי שלא היו נותנים לב לדברי הנביאים הניבאים על הפורענות ועסוקים בתענוגים: ולטעמיך הא דכתיב. בהאי עניינא השותים במזרקי יין ורבי אמי ורבי אסי פירשו ° זהו קנישקנין כלי זכוכית ארוך ולו שני פיות ויין נזרק מזה לזה: שמזרקין. על ידי אומנות כדאמר בהחליל (סוכה דף נג.) מטייל בתמני כסי: הכי נמי דאסור. למשתי השתא בקנישקנין: משתינין. דדייק מסרוחים: לידי עניות. דאמרינן בע"פ (פסחים דף קיא:) שרא דעניותא נביל שמיה ונביל קרי ליה ואוהב מקום מיאוס ומשתין מים לפני מטתו היינו מיאוס: ערום. אורחא דמילתא נקט מתוך שהוא ערום אינו יוצא לחוץ להשתין דטורח הוא לו ללבוש ולצאת: אבל לבראי לית לן בה. שהקילוח ארוך וניתז למרחוק: משא ולא משא. שאינו רוחץ ומשפשף יפה אלא מעט מים כגון רביעית מצומצם: על עסקי תכשיטיה. שאינו רוצה לקנות לה: גבהו. היינו קומה זקופה: ותלכנה נטויות גרון שהיו הולכות עקב בצד גודל. למעט בהילוכם שהיו מסתכלין בה והיא שוהה בפסיעותיה ודרך נוטין גרון לילך בנחת לפי שאינו רואה לרגליו: ומשקרות עינים דמליין כוחלא. לשון סיקרא: ומרמזן. את הבחורים: סיקור. לשון הבטה: הלוך וטפוף שהיו מהלכות ארוכה בצד קצרה. שתראה לפה על ראש חברתה והוא נוי לה ונשואות היו לפיכך מספר בגנותן: וטפוף. כמו על דלטפשת לטפוף (אבות פ"ב מ"ו): תעכסנה. כמו וכעכס אל מוסר אויל (משלי ז) והוא ארס של נחש וקרי ליה עכס על שם שאינו מטילו אלא על ידי כעס: בכעוס. נחש כעוסה: נמקים. כמו המק בשרו (זכריה יד): צלצול. בנדי"ל נאה: נקפים. חבורות לשון המנקף רגלו וניקף סבכי היער (ישעיה י): מתקשטות. היינו שער שסורקות ומפרכסות: מתקשטות. דומה למקשה כעין נוטריקון: פתיגיל. נוטריקון פתח גילה אותו מקום: כי תחת יופי. כי כל אלה יבא לך תחת יפייך: כיבא. קיטור"א ליחה כמו שיחנא וכיבי דקדושין דפלימו (דף פא:): פתהן. כמו פתחיהן: שנשפכו כקיתון. שופכות דם זיבה: יערה. כמו ותער כדה (בראשית כד): כיער. נתמלאו שער ונמאסות לתשמיש: אנשי שחץ. מדברים בלשון גאוה ולעגי שפה: סעדת. תשמיש: פת עמילה. בעולה: שאינה עמילה. בתולה: פת עמילה. ברייא"ה בלע"ז: גורדלי. לבן היה:
ביין

רבינו חננאל

ראשית שמנים כמשמעו ואפילו מאן דפטר לא פטר אלא בשיש בה בושם. אבל אין בה בושם חייבת. קנישקנין כוס שיש בה שתי פיות ושותין ממנה שנים בבת אחת. מסקרות עינים. דהוו מליין כוחלא רמזא. ארס בכעוס. פי' החיה כשתכעוס גוררת ומשלכת. ארס קשה. פי' פת עמילה. אשה בעולה ופת שאינה עמילה בתולה. וכולן על זה הענין: צלצול חגור. כדגרסינן בסוף מנחות (דף קט:):

רב נסים גאון

מותיב רב יוסף אף על פליאטון גזר ר' יהודה בן בבא. עיקר זאת הברייתא בתוספ' סוטה בסוף המסכת בפולמוס האחרון גזרו על חופת חתנים אלו זהוריות המוזהבות כו' אף על פליאטון גזר ר' יהודה בן בבא ולא הודו לו:

תורה אור השלם

א) הַשֹּׁתִים בְּמִזְרְקֵי יַיִן וְרֵאשִׁית שְׁמָנִים יִמְשָׁחוּ וְלֹא נֶחְלוּ עַל שֵׁבֶר יוֹסֵף: [עמוס ו, ו]
ב) הַשֹּׁכְבִים עַל מִטּוֹת שֵׁן וּסְרֻחִים עַל עַרְשׂוֹתָם וְאֹכְלִים כָּרִים מִצֹּאן וַעֲגָלִים מִתּוֹךְ מַרְבֵּק: [עמוס ו, ד]
ג) לָכֵן עַתָּה יִגְלוּ בְּרֹאשׁ גֹּלִים וְסָר מִרְזַח סְרוּחִים: [עמוס ו, ז]
ד) וַיֹּאמֶר יְיָ יַעַן כִּי גָבְהוּ בְּנוֹת צִיּוֹן וַתֵּלַכְנָה נְטוּיוֹת גָּרוֹן וּמְשַׂקְּרוֹת עֵינָיִם הָלוֹךְ וְטָפֹף תֵּלַכְנָה וּבְרַגְלֵיהֶם תְּעַכַּסְנָה: [ישעיה ג, טז]
ה) וְהָיָה תַחַת בֹּשֶׂם מַק יִהְיֶה וְתַחַת חֲגוֹרָה נִקְפָּה וְתַחַת מַעֲשֶׂה מִקְשֶׁה קָרְחָה וְתַחַת פְּתִיגִיל מַחֲגֹרֶת שָׂק כִּי תַחַת יֹפִי: [ישעיה ג, כד]
ו) וְשִׂפַּח אֲדֹנָי קָדְקֹד בְּנוֹת צִיּוֹן וַייָ פָּתְהֵן יְעָרֶה: [ישעיה ג, יז]
ז) וְלַשְׂאֵת וְלַסַּפַּחַת וְלַבֶּהָרֶת: [ויקרא יד, נו]

מסורת הש"ס

א) [תוספתא פ"ה ע"ש], ב) [לקמן דף סה.], ג) [תוספתא שם ע"ש], ד) [תוספ' דסוטה פט"ו], ה) [ע"ז דף עב: ע"ש], ו) קדושין עא:, ז) נדה יז., ח) [יומא דף ט: ע"ש], ט) [עי' ערוך ערך ארס], י) [נ"ל ושפח].

גליון הש"ס

גמ' ומזלזל בנט"י. עי' סוטה ד ע"ב תוס' ד"ה נעקר: רש"י ד"ה ולטעמיך וכו' זהו קנישקנין. עי' ע"ז דף עב ע"ב ברש"י ד"ה קנישקנין:

ליקוטי רש"י

וראשית שמנים. מובחר שבשמנים והוא אפרסמון. השותים במזרקי יין. יש מרבותינו שאומרים במסכת שבת שהיו זורקין כוסותיהן זה לזה וי"מ על שם כלי שהיו לו שתי פיות והוא ארוך ושותה זה מכאן וזה מכאן הוא נזרק מפיו אל פיו [עמוס ו, ו]. קנישקנין. כלי רחב ויש לו שני קנין או שלשה יוצאין מלידו ונמשכין ועולין כנגד גובהו וכשנותנין יין בפיו מתמלאין כל הקנים ויכולין כמה בני אדם לשתות בו ביחד וכאן קורין לו קרוגל"א מפני שמוקף קנים כמחולות הללו [ע"ז עב:]. ויאמר ה'. על הנשים אשר משלו בעמי יען כי גבהו וגו'. הלוך וטפוף. לשון דבר לף על גבי חבירו כמו (דברים יא) אשר הציף ומתרגמינן דאטיף כך היתה ארוכה מהלכת בין שתי קצרות כדי שתהא נראית צפה למעלה מהם. וברגליהן תעכסנה. להבעיר בו יצר הרע כעכס זה של נחש, עכס הוא ארס של נחש [ישעיה ג, טז]. והיה תחת בושם מק. מקום שהיו מתבשמות בו יהיה נימק. ותחת חגורה נקפה. מקום שחגרה שם יהיה ניקף נתתך בחבורות ורשומי מכות כמו ואחר עורי נקפו (איוב יט) ונקף סבכי היער (ישעיה י). ותחת מעשה מקשה. מקום שהיו עושות בו המעשה האמור למעלה הלוך וטפוף תלכנה והוא בגובה הראש שם תהיה מקשה קרחה מכה המקרחת את הראש מקשה ל' דא לדא נקשן (דניאל ה) ואני הייתי מפרשו תחת המעשה מקשה מקום שהיו שם חגורות עושות עדי הזהב העשויות מקשה בטדי"ך בלע"ז אלא שהוא נקוד פתח והוא במסורה בעשרה נקודים פתח ואין אחד מהם דבוק לתיבה של אחריו וכל מעשה שהוא דבק לתיבה של אחריו נקוד קמץ. ותחת פתיגיל. הוא בית הרחם האמור למעלה פתהן חלוף אותה גילה תהיה מחגורת שק בכל מתניה. כי תחת יופי. כי זאת הוגנת להיות להם תחת יופי שהיו משתחצות בו [שם, כד]. ושפח. לשון צרעת כמו (ויקרא יג) מספחת היא ועל שנכתב בשי"ן דרשו בו רבותינו שתעשנה שפחות מכודנות ויש שדרשוהו שהרבה בהן משפחות משפחות של כנים. פתהן יערה. הן היו אומרות ימהר יחישה מעשהו שנראה אותו ונוטל אותי כשבא הפורענות היו שרי נ"נ נוטלין אותן להיות לנשים מחמת יופין ורמז הקב"ה והיו שופעות כאדם המערה מכלי אל כלי וכאשר נענשו בדם נדה והיו נמאסות עליהן ומשליכין אותן לארץ מעל קרונות שלהן [שם, יז]. פת עמילה. שאינה ממהרת להחמיץ שעמילתה מעכבתה עמילה ברייר"א [פסחים לז:].

AGREE WITH HIM. וְאִי אָמְרַתְּ מִשּׁוּם תַּעֲנוּג – Now if you say that the aforementioned verse refers to balsam, and hence it is evident that balsam is used **for purposes of pleasure,**[16] אַמַּאי לֹא הוֹדוּ לוֹ – **why did [the Sages] not agree with [R' Yehudah ben Bava],** who banned the use of balsam?[17]

This argument is refuted:

אָמַר לֵיהּ אַבַּיֵי – **Abaye said to [Rav Yosef]:** וּלְטַעְמֵיךְ – **But according to your reasoning,** that all the activities listed in this verse should be forbidden, הָא דִּכְתִיב – a problem arises with **the following** phrase, **which is written** in the same verse: "הַשֹּׁתִים בְּמִזְרְקֵי יַיִן" – *who drink out of bowls of wine.* רַבִּי אַמִּי וְרַבִּי אַסִּי – **R' Ami and R' Assi** gave different interpretations of this phrase. חַד אָמַר קְנִישְׁקָנִין – **One said** it refers to ***ken-ishkanin,***[18] וְחַד אָמַר שֶׁמְּזָרְקִין כּוֹסוֹתֵיהֶן זֶה לָזֶה – **and one said** it means **that they threw their cups to each other.**[19] הָכִי נַמִּי דְּאָסִיר – Therefore, **here too,** regarding each of these activities, you should say **that it is forbidden** because it is included in the verse. וְהָא רַבָּה בַּר רַב הוּנָא אִיקְלַע לְבֵי רֵישׁ גָּלוּתָא – **But** this is not so, for when **Rabbah bar Rav Huna visited the house of the Exilarch** וְשָׁתָה בִּקְנִישְׁקָנִין – **and [the Exilarch] was drinking out of *kenishkanin,*** וְלֹא אָמַר לֵיהּ וְלֹא מִידֵי – **[Rabbah bar Rav Huna] did not say anything to him at all** by way of rebuke.[20] Thus, we see that not everything listed in the verse is prohibited.[21]

Abaye concludes:

אֶלָּא – **Rather,** the criteria for prohibition are as follows: כָּל מִידֵי דְּאִית בֵּיהּ תַּעֲנוּג – **Everything that involves pleasure** וְאִית בֵּיהּ שִׂמְחָה – **and** also **involves joy,** גָּזְרוּ רַבָּנָן – **the Rabbis decreed** against its use. אֲבָל מִידֵי דְּאִית בֵּיהּ תַּעֲנוּג – **But something that involves** only **pleasure** וְלֵית בֵּיהּ שִׂמְחָה – **and does not involve joy,** לֹא גָּזְרוּ רַבָּנָן – **the Rabbis did not decree** against it use.[22]

The Gemara interprets another verse from that passage: "הַשֹּׁכְבִים עַל־מִטּוֹת שֵׁן וּסְרֻחִים עַל־עַרְשׂוֹתָם" – ***Who lie upon beds of ivory, stretched out on their couches.***[23] אָמַר רַבִּי יוֹסֵי בְּרַבִּי חֲנִינָא – **R' Yose the son of R' Chanina said:** מְלַמֵּד שֶׁהָיוּ מַשְׁתִּינִין מַיִם בִּפְנֵי מִטּוֹתֵיהֶן עֲרוּמִּים – **[This verse] teaches that they would urinate before their beds** while **naked.**[24]

This interpretation is rejected and a different one proposed:

מְגַדֵּף בָּהּ רַבִּי אֲבָהוּ – **R' Abahu scoffed at it,** saying: אִי הָכִי הַיְינוּ דִּכְתִיב – **If so,**[25] there is a difficulty with **that which is written** in a following verse:[26] "לָכֵן עַתָּה יִגְלוּ בְּרֹאשׁ גֹּלִים" – ***Therefore, now they shall go into exile at the head of the exiles.*** מִשּׁוּם דְּמַשְׁתִּינִין מַיִם בִּפְנֵי מִטּוֹתֵיהֶם עֲרוּמִּים – Now, can you say that **because they urinate before their beds** while **naked,** יִגְלוּ בְּרֹאשׁ גּוֹלִים – **they will go into exile at the head of the exiles?!**[27] Clearly, this punishment is too severe for such an act. אֶלָּא אָמַר רַבִּי אֲבָהוּ – **Rather, said R' Abahu,** אֵלּוּ בְּנֵי אָדָם שֶׁהָיוּ אוֹכְלִים וְשׁוֹתִים זֶה עִם זֶה – **these are people who eat and drink with each other,** וְדוֹבְקִין מִטּוֹתֵיהֶן זוֹ בָּזוֹ – **and attach their beds one to the other,** וּמַחֲלִיפִין נְשׁוֹתֵיהֶן זֶה עִם זֶה – **and exchange their wives with each other,** וּמַסְרִיחִין עַרְסוֹתָם בְּשִׁכְבַת זֶרַע שֶׁאֵינוֹ שֶׁלָּהֶן – **and defile their couches with semen that is not theirs.**[28]

The Gemara now states the punishment for urinating before one's bed:

אָמַר רַבִּי אֲבָהוּ – **R' Abahu said,** וְאָמְרִי לָהּ בְּמַתְנִיתָא תָּנָא – **and some say** that **a Tanna taught it in a Baraisa:** שְׁלוֹשָׁה דְּבָרִים מְבִיאִין אֶת הָאָדָם לִידֵי עֲנִיּוּת – **Three things bring a person to poverty.** וְאֵלּוּ הֵן – **They are:** הַמַּשְׁתִּין מַיִם בִּפְנֵי מִטָּתוֹ עָרוֹם – **Urinating before one's bed naked;**[29] וּמְזַלְזֵל בִּנְטִילַת יָדַיִם – **treating** the mitzvah of **washing the hands**[30] **lightly;** וְשֶׁאִשְׁתּוֹ מְקַלַּלְתּוֹ בְּפָנָיו – **and being cursed by one's wife in one's own presence.**

NOTES

16. For the verse enumerates luxuries in which the people indulged at that time (*Rashi;* see note 13).

17. [Rav Yosef assumes that all the activities listed in that passage should be forbidden on account of the Temple's destruction, since Scripture recognizes them as luxuries.]

18. A tall glass vessel with two spouts (*Rashi*). Two people could drink out of it simultaneously (*Rabbeinu Chananel;* see *Rashi* to *Avodah Zarah* 72b).

19. This was a skillful trick in which two people would juggle [cups of wine] between themselves (see *Rashi*).

Both opinions interpret the phrase מִזְרְקֵי יַיִן (literally: bowls of wine) to mean "throwers of wine." [מִזְרָק is similar to זָרַק, *throw.*] The first opinion understands it as denoting a multispouted vessel in which wine would be "thrown" (i.e. pass) from one spout to the other. The second understands it as referring to throwing (i.e. juggling) cups of wine.

20. This narrative proves that the use of *kenishkanin* is permitted.

21. Rav Yehudah is therefore justified in explaining the phrase (*they anoint themselves with the finest of oils*) as referring to balsam, although balsam was not later forbidden as a luxury.

22. תַּעֲנוּג, *pleasure,* denotes sensual gratification; שִׂמְחָה, *joy,* signifies gaiety and jubilation. The Rabbis banned only those activities that inspire both of these emotions. Hence, the activities listed in the verse in *Amos,* which involve "pleasure" but not necessarily "joy" (e.g. balsam oil), are not all prohibited. [The use of *kenishkanin,* too, was not prohibited because its purpose was primarily to enhance the pleasure of the *drinking* of the wine.]

23. *Amos* 6:4.

24. That is, if they needed to urinate while they were still in their beds, they would not bother to get dressed and go outside. Instead they would urinate onto the floor next to their beds (see *Rashi* ד״ה ערום and note 29).

R' Yose bases this interpretation on the word סְרֻחִים, which he relates to סָרַח, *foul* (*Rashi*).

25. I.e. if the word סְרֻחִים in this context refers to those who urinate before their beds.

26. Ibid. v. 7.

27. The entire verse reads: לָכֵן עַתָּה יִגְלוּ בְּרֹאשׁ גֹּלִים וְסָר מִזְרַח סְרוּחִים, *Therefore, now they shall go into exile at the head of the exiles, and the revelry of those who stretched themselves out shall pass away.* The word סְרוּחִים, *those who stretched themselves out,* refers back to the phrase discussed above (v. 4): וּסְרֻחִים עַל־עַרְשׂוֹתָם, *stretched out on their beds* (*Ibn Ezra* ad loc.), which R' Yose interpreted as referring to urinating before one's bed. The verse thus implies that the punishment of exile is particularly appropriate for those who engaged in this act.

28. Those who engaged in this behavior were indeed deserving of going into exile before anyone else. A Baraisa cited above (33a) states: "For the sin of forbidden sexual relations . . . exile comes to the world" (*Melo HaRo'im*). [R' Abahu, too, links סְרֻחִים to סָרַח, *foul,* but he interprets it differently.]

See *Iyun Yaakov* and *Ben Yehoyada,* who suggest defenses for R' Yose's understanding of the verse.

29. The Gemara in *Pesachim* (111b) states that the "angel" of poverty is called נָבָל, which connotes repulsiveness. This means that poverty is occasioned by repulsive behavior, such as urinating before one's bed (*Rashi*).

The Gemara specifies "naked" only because that is the typical circumstance. When a person is lying in bed naked, he would urinate next to his bed rather than go to the trouble of getting dressed and going outside (*Rashi*). However, the same applies to one who urinates before his bed while clothed.

According to this reasoning, a "bed" is also mentioned only because it is the most common example. Indeed, urinating in any place where it is repulsive, such as next to one's table, would also cause poverty (*Maharsha*).

30. It is a Rabbinic obligation to wash one's hands in a certain manner before eating a meal (see *Shulchan Aruch Orach Chaim* 158 ff).

ומאי ר' מאיר דתניא לא תצא אשה במפתח שבידה ואם יצתה חייבת חטאת דברי רבי מאיר רבי אליעזר פוטר בכובלת ובצלוחית של פלייטון כובלת מאן דכר שמה חסורי מחסרא והכי קתני וכן בכובלת וכן בצלוחית של פלייטון לא תצא ואם יצאה חייבת חטאת דברי רבי מאיר רבי אליעזר פוטר בכובלת ובצלוחית של פלייטון במה דברים אמורים כשיש בהם בושם אבל אין בהם בושם חייבת אמר רב אדא בר אהבה זאת אומרת המוציא אוכלין פחות מכשיעור בכלי חייב דהא אין בה בושם כפחות מכשיעור בכלי דמי וקתני חייבת רב אשי אמר בעלמא אימא לך פטור ושאני הכא דליתיה לממשא כלל: וראשית שמנים ימשחו אמר רב יהודה אמר שמואל זה פלייטון מתיב רב יוסף אף על פלייטון גזר רבי יהודה בן בבא ולא הודו לו ואי אמרת משום תענוג אמאי לא הודו לו אמר ליה אביי ולטעמיך הא דכתיב השותים במזרקי יין ר' אמי ור' אסי חד אמר קנישקנין וחד אמר שמזרקין כוסותיהן זה לזה הכי נמי דאסיר והא רבה בר רב הונא איקלע לבי ריש גלותא ושתה בקנישקנין ולא אמר ליה ולא מידי אלא כל מידי דאית ביה תענוג ואית ביה שמחה גזרו רבנן אבל מידי דאית ביה תענוג ולית ביה שמחה לא גזרו רבנן: השוכבים על מטות שן וסרוחים על ערשותם אמר רבי יוסי ברבי חנינא מלמד שהיו משתינין מים בפני מטותיהן ערומים מגדף בה ר' אבהו אי הכי היינו דכתיב לכן עתה יגלו בראש גולים משום דמשתינין מים בפני מטותיהם ערומים יגלו בראש גולים אלא א"ר אבהו אלו בני אדם שהיו אוכלים ושותים זה עם זה ודובקין מטותיהן זו בזו ומחליפין נשותיהן זה עם זה ומסריחין ערסותם בשכבת זרע שאינו שלהן א"ר אבהו ואמרי לה במתניתא תנא ג' דברים מביאין את האדם לידי עניות ואלו הן המשתין מים בפני מטתו ערום ומזלזל בנטילת ידים ושאשתו מקללתו בפניו המשתין מים בפני מטתו ערום אמר רבא לא אמרן אלא דמהדר אפיה לפורייה אבל לבראי לית לן בה ומהדר אפיה לפורייה נמי לא אמרן אלא לארעא אבל במנא לית לן בה ומזלזל בנטילת ידים אמר רבא לא אמרן אלא דלא משא ידיה כלל אבל משא ולא משא לית לן בה ולאו מלתא היא דאמר רב חסדא אנא משאי מלא חפני מיא ויהבו לי מלא חפני טיבותא ושאשתו מקללתו בפניו אמר רבא על עסקי תכשיטיה וה"מ הוא דאית ליה ולא עביד: דרש רבא בריה דרב עילאי מאי דכתיב ויאמר ה' יען כי גבהו בנות ציון שהיו מהלכות בקומה זקופה ותלכנה נטויות גרון שהיו מהלכות עקב בצד גודל ומשקרות עינים דהוה מלאן כוחלא לעינייהו ומרמזן הלוך וטפוף שהיו מהלכות ארוכה בצד קצרה וברגליהן תעכסנה אמר רב יצחק דבי ר' אמי מלמד שמטילות מור ואפרסמון במנעליהן ומהלכות בשוקי ירושלים וכיון שמגיעות אצל בחורי ישראל בועטות בקרקע ומתיזות עליהם ומכניסות בהן יצר הרע כארס בכעוס מאי פורענותיהם כדדריש רבה בר עולא והיה תחת בושם מק יהיה מקום שהיו מתבשמות בו נעשה נמקים נמקים ותחת חגורה נקפה מקום שהיו חגורות בצלצול נעשה נקפים נקפים ותחת מעשה מקשה קרחה מקום שהיו מתקשטות בו נעשה קרחים קרחים ותחת פתיגיל מחגורת שק פתחים המביאין לידי גילה יהיו למחגורת שק כי תחת יופי אמר רבא היינו דאמרי אינשי חלופי שופרא כיבא (וספחה) ה' קדקד בנות ציון אמר רבי יוסי ברבי חנינא מלמד שפרחה בהן צרעת כתיב הכא ושפח וכתיב התם לשאת ולספחת וה' פתהן יערה רב ושמואל חד אמר שנשפכו כקיתון וחד אמר שנעשו פתחיהן כיער אמר רב יהודה אמר רב אנשי ירושלים אנשי שחץ היו אדם אומר לחברו במה סעדת היום בפת עמילה או בפת שאינה עמילה ביין גורדלי או ביין

ומאי רבי מאיר. היכא אשכחן דאיירי בה רבי מאיר בלא רבנן ופליג רבי אליעזר עליה: בד"א. דרבי אליעזר פוטר והאי פוטר היינו מותר לכתחלה כדאוקימנא: כשיש בה בושם. פלייטון יש בההוא מורסא העשויה כקמיע דכיון דיש בה בושם תכשיט היא לגו שריחה רע ולמשלף ולאיתויי נמי לא חייש כדאמרן דגנות הוא לה: אבל אין בה בושם. מורסא לחודה לאו תכשיט הוא וחייבת: זאת אומרת. הא דקתני אין בה בושם חייבת אלמא דקסבר רבי אליעזר המוציא אוכלין בשבת בכלי פחות מכשיעור דלא מיחייב על הוצאת אוכלין פחות מגרוגרת כדלקמן (דף צ:) חייב מיהא על הכלי ולא אמרינן הכלי טפל להן ולא מיחייב עליה שלא נתכוין להוציא אלא משום אוכלין ופלוגתא היא על סתם משנה השנויה בפרק המצניע (לקמן דף צג:) דקתני פטור אף על הכלי: דהא אין בו בושם כפחות מכשיעור דמי. שהכלי קלטו את הריח ושיעור הוצאת בשמים בכל שהוא וכיון שאינו כל שהוא הוי ריחה פחות מכשיעור (הוא) וקתני חייבת ולא אמרינן נעשה כלי טפל לריח שבתוכו והריחה לא מיחייב דפחות מכשיעור הוא: ושאני הכא. ליכא למימר נעשה כלי טפל לריח שאין בו שום ממש ואפילו פחות מכשיעור לא מיקרי אבל פחות מכשיעור בדבר שיש בו ממש נעשה כלי טפל לו ופטור: ראשית שמנים. מובחר שבשמנים: גזר. משום צער חורבן: ואי אמרת. זה פלייטון והאי קרא בתענוג משתעי שלא היו נותנים לב לדברי הנביאים הניבאים על הפורענות ועסוקים בתענוגים: ולטעמיך הא דכתיב. בהאי ענינא השותים במזרקי יין ורבי אמי ורבי אסי פירשו זהו קנישקנין כלי זכוכית ארוך ולו שני פיות ויין נזרק מזה לזה: שמזרקין. על ידי אומנות כדאמר בהחליל (סוכה דף נג.) מטייל בתמני כסי: הכי נמי דאסור. למשתי השתא בקנישקנין: משתינין. דדייק מסרוחים: לידי עניות. דאמרינן בע"פ (פסחים דף קיא:) שרא דעניותא נביל שמיה ונביל קרי ליה ואוהב מקום מיאוס ומשתין מים לפני מטתו היינו מיאוס: ערום. אורחא דמילתא נקט מתוך שהוא ערום אינו יוצא לחוץ להשתין דטורח הוא לו ללבוש ולצאת: אבל לבראי לית לן בה. שהקילוח ארוך ונימז למרחוק: משא ולא משא. שאינו רוחץ ומשפשף יפה אלא מעט מים כגון רביעית מצומצם: על עסקי תכשיטיה. שאינו רוצה לקנות לה: גבהו. היינו קומה זקופה: ותלכנה נטויות גרון שהיו הולכות עקב בצד גודל. למעט בהילוכם שהיו מטפלות בה והיא גוהה בפסיעותיה ולדרך נוטין גרון ליגל בנחת לפי שאינו רואה לרגליו: ומשקרות עינים דמליין כוחלא. לשון סיקרא: ומרמזן. את הבחורים: סיקור. לשון הבטה: הלוך וטפוף שהיו מהלכות ארוכה בצד קצרה. שתראה לפה על ראש חברתה והוא נוי לה ונשואות היו לפיכך מספר בגנותן: וטפוף. כמו על דאטפת אטפוך (אבות פ"ב מ"ו): תעכסנה. כמו וכעכס אל מוסר אויל (משלי ז) והוא ארס של נחש וקרי ליה עכס על שם שאינו מטיל אלא על ידי כעס: בכעוס. נחש כעוסה: נמקים. כמו המק בשרו (זכריה יד): צלצול. בנד"ל נאה: נקפים. חבורות לשון המנקף רגלו וינקף סבכי היער (ישעיה י): מתקשטות. היינו שער סרוקות ומפרכסות: מתקשטות. דומה למקשה כעין נוטריקון: פתיגיל. נוטריקון פתח גילה אותו מקום: כי תחת יופי. כי כל אלה יבא לך תחת יופייך: כיבא. קיטור"א ליחה כמו שיחנה וכיבי דקדוסין דפלימו (דף פ:): פתהן. כמו פתחיהן: שנשפכו כקיתון. שופכות דם זיבה: יערה. כמו ותער כדה (בראשית כד): כיער. נתמלאו שער ונעשות לתשמיש: אנשי שחץ. מדברים בלשון גאוה ולעגי שפה: סעדת. תשמיש: פת עמילה. בעולה. שאינה עמילה. בתולה: פת עמילה. ברייא"ה בלע"ז: גורדלי. לבן היה: ביין

עין משפט נר מצוה

מו א טוש"ע א"ח סי' רמה:

מז ב ג מיי' פ"ו מהל' ברכות הלכה יט טוש"ע א"ח סי' קנח סעיף ט:

מח ד מיי' פכ"א מהל' איסורי ביאה הלכה ב' טוש"ע אה"ע סי' כא סעיף א:

רבינו חננאל

ראשית שמנים כמשמעו ואפילו מאן דפטר לא פטר אלא בשיש בה בושם. אבל אין בה בושם חייבת. קנישקנין כוס שיש בה שתי פיות ושותין בה שנים בבת אחת. משקרות עינים. דהוו מליין כוחלא ומזא. ארס בכעוס. פי' החיה כשתכעוס גוררת ומשלכת. ארס קשה. פי' פת עמילה. אשה בעולה ופת שאינה עמילה בתולה. וכולן על זה הענין. צלצול חגור. כדגרסינן בסוף מנחות (דף קט.):

רב נסים גאון

מותיב רב יוסף אף על פלייטון גזר ר' יהודה בן בבא. עיקר זאת הברייתא בתוספ' סוטה בסוף המסכת בפולמוס האחרון גזרו על חופת חתנים אלו זהורית המוזהבות כו' אף על פלייטון גזר ר' יהודה בן בבא ולא הודו לו:

תורה אור השלם

א) הַשֹּׁתִים בְּמִזְרְקֵי יַיִן וְרֵאשִׁית שְׁמָנִים יִמְשָׁחוּ וְלֹא נֶחְלוּ עַל שֵׁבֶר יוֹסֵף: [עמוס ו, ו]

ב) הַשֹּׁכְבִים עַל מִטּוֹת שֵׁן וּסְרֻחִים עַל עַרְשׂוֹתָם וְאֹכְלִים כָּרִים מִצֹּאן וַעֲגָלִים מִתּוֹךְ מַרְבֵּק: [עמוס ו, ד]

ג) לָכֵן עַתָּה יִגְלוּ בְּרֹאשׁ גֹּלִים וְסָר מִרְזַח סְרוּחִים: [עמוס ו, ז]

ד) וַיֹּאמֶר יְיָ יַעַן כִּי גָבְהוּ בְּנוֹת צִיּוֹן וַתֵּלַכְנָה נְטוּוֹת גָּרוֹן וּמְשַׂקְּרוֹת עֵינָיִם הָלוֹךְ וְטָפוֹף תֵּלַכְנָה וּבְרַגְלֵיהֶם תְּעַכַּסְנָה: [ישעיה ג, טז]

ה) וְהָיָה תַחַת בֹּשֶׂם מַק יִהְיֶה וְתַחַת חֲגוֹרָה נִקְפָּה וְתַחַת מַעֲשֶׂה מִקְשֶׁה קָרְחָה וְתַחַת פְּתִיגִיל מַחֲגֹרֶת שָׂק כִּי תַחַת יֹפִי: [ישעיה ג, כד]

ו) וְשִׂפַּח אֲדֹנָי קָדְקֹד בְּנוֹת צִיּוֹן וַיְיָ פָּתְהֵן יְעָרֶה: [ישעיה ג, יז]

ז) וְלַשְׂאֵת וְלַסַּפַּחַת וְלַבֶּהָרֶת: [ויקרא יד, נו]

מסורת הש"ס

א) [תוספתא פ"ה ע"ש], ב) [לקמן דף סה.], ג) [תוספתא שם ע"ש], ד) [תוספ' דסוטה פט"ו], ה) [ע"ז דף עב: ע"ש], ו) קדושין עא., ז) נדה יז., ח) [יומא דף עז: ע"ש], ט) [ע' ערוך ערך ארס], י) [נ"ל ושפח].

גליון הש"ס

גמ' ומזלזל בנט"י. עי' סוטה ד ע"ב תוס' ד"ה נעקר: רש"י ד"ה ולטעמיך וכו' זהו קנישקנין. עי' ע"ז דף עב ע"ב ברש"י ד"ה קנישקנין:

ליקוטי רש"י

וראשית שמנים. מובחר שבשמנים והוא אפרסמון. השותים במזרקי יין. יש מרבותינו שאומרים במסכת שבת שהיו זורקין כוסותיהן זה לזה וי"מ על שם כלי שהיו לו שני פיות והוא ארוך ושותה זה מכאן וזה מכאן הוא נזרק מפיו לפיו [עמוס ו, ו]. קנישקנין. כלי רחב יש לו שני קנין או שלשה יוצאין מצדיו ומנסכין ועולין כנגד גובהו ושותין יין בפיו ממקומות כל הקנים ויכולין כמה בני אדם לשתות בו ביחד ומדה קורין לו קרוג"א מפני שמוקף קנים כמחולות [ע"ז עב:]. ויאמר ה'. על הנשים אשר משלו בעמי יען כי גבהו וגו'. הלוך וטפוף. לשון דבר קל על גבי חבירו כמו (דברים יא) אשר הציף ומתרגמינן דאטיף כך היתה הארוכה מהלכת בין שתי קצרות כדי שתהא נראית צפה למעלה מהם. וברגליהן תעכסנה. להבעיר בהן יצר הרע כעכס זה של נחש. עכס ארס של נחש [ישעיה ג, טז]. והיה תחת בושם מק. מקום שהיו מתבשמות בו יהיה נימק. ותחת חגורה נקפה. מקום שהיו חגורות בחגורות יהיו שם נקפות וחבורות ורשומי מכות כמו ואחר עורי נקפו (איוב יט) ונקף סבכי היער (ישעיה י). ותחת מעשה מקשה. מקום שהיו עושות בו מעשה המקשה האמור למעלה הלוך וטפוף תלכנה והוא גובהו הראש שם תהיה מקשה קרחה מכה המקשה את הראש מקשה ל' דא לדא נקשן (דניאל ה) ואני הייתי מפרשו מקום תחת המעשה מקשה מקום שהיו שם מגורות נותנות עדי הזהב העשויות מקשה כמו בנדי"ן בלע"ז. ותחת פתיגיל. לשון פתח וגיל במשולה עבירה נקודים פתח והוא מוקף בא אחר מהם לדבק למינה של אחריו וכל אל פתח גיל לדבק לגיל מגיל נקוד קמץ. ותחת פתיגיל. הוא בית הרחם האמור למעלה פתחן פתחים לפתוח אותה הגילה תהיה מחגרת שק בכל מתניה. כי תחת יופי. כי זאת הוגנת להיות להם תחת יופי שהיו משתמשות בו [שם, כד]. ושפח. לשון צרעת כמו (ויקרא יג) מספחת היא ועל שנכתב בשי"ן דרשו בו רבותינו שתעשנה שפחות מכודנות ויש שדרשוהו שהרבה בהן משפחות משפחות של כינים. פתהן יערה. [illegible] [שם, יז]. פת עמילה. שאינה ממהרת להתמיד שעמילתה מעכבתה עמילה ברייר"א [פסחים לז:].

Rava elaborates on each of these cases:
הַמַּשְׁתִּין מַיִם בִּפְנֵי מִטָּתוֹ עָרוֹם – Regarding **one who urinates before his bed naked,** אָמַר רָבָא – **Rava said:** לֹא אֲמָרָן אֶלָּא דִּמְהַדַּר אַפֵּיהּ לְפוּרְיֵיהּ – **We do not say** that this leads to poverty **except where he turns his face toward his bed** while urinating, אֲבָל לְבָרַאי לֵית לָן בָּהּ – **but** if he faces **outward, we have no** objection **to it.**[31] וּמְהַדַּר אַפֵּיהּ לְפוּרְיֵיהּ נַמִּי – **And even** regarding **one who turns his face toward his bed** while urinating, לֹא אֲמָרָן – **we do not say** that this leads to poverty, אֶלָּא לְאַרְעָא – **except** where he urinates **onto the ground,** אֲבָל בְּמָנָא לֵית לָן בָּהּ – **but** if he urinates **into a vessel, we have no** objection **to it.**

Rava discusses the second cause of poverty:
וּמְזַלְזֵל בִּנְטִילַת יָדַיִם – **And** regarding **one who treats** the mitzvah of **washing the hands lightly,** אָמַר רָבָא – **Rava said:** לֹא אֲמָרָן – **We do not say** that this leads to poverty אֶלָּא דְּלֹא מָשָׁא יְדֵיהּ כְּלָל – **except where he does not wash** his hands **at all.** אֲבָל מָשָׁא וְלֹא מָשָׁא – **But** where **he does wash** his hands, although **he does not wash** them well,[32] לֵית לָן בָּהּ – **we have no** objection **to it.**

The Gemara rejects this teaching:
וְלָאו מִלְּתָא הִיא – **But it is not correct,** דְּאָמַר רַב חִסְדָּא – **for Rav Chisda said:** אֲנָא מְשָׁאִי מְלֹא חָפְנֵי מַיָּא – **I washed** my hands **with full handfuls of water,** וִיהֲבוּ לִי מְלֹא חָפְנֵי טֵיבוּתָא – **and I was given full handfuls of prosperity.**[33]

Rava elaborates upon the third cause of poverty listed above:
וְשֶׁאִשְׁתּוֹ מְקַלַּלְתּוֹ בְּפָנָיו – **And** regarding **one whose wife curses him in his presence,** אָמַר רָבָא – **Rava said:** עַל עִסְקֵי תַּכְשִׁיטֶיהָ – the case is that she curses him **concerning matters of her adornments,** i.e. for not providing her with adornments. וְהָנֵי מִילֵּי הוּא דְּאִית לֵיהּ – **And this teaching** (namely, that such a curse causes poverty) **applies** only **where he has** enough money to buy adornments for her[34] וְלֹא עָבִיד – **but does not do** so.[35]

The Gemara presents a phrase-by-phrase interpretation of a Scriptural verse which rebukes Jewish women for flaunting their beauty:
דָּרַשׁ רָבָא בְּרֵיהּ דְּרַב עִילַּאי – **Rava the son of Rav Ilai expounded:** מַאי דִּכְתִיב – **What is** the meaning of **that which is written?** "וַיֹּאמֶר ה׳ יַעַן כִּי גָבְהוּ בְּנוֹת צִיּוֹן" – ***Hashem said: Because the daughters of Zion are haughty ...***?[36] שֶׁהָיוּ מְהַלְּכוֹת בְּקוֹמָה זְקוּפָה – It means **that they would walk with erect posture.**[37]

"וַתֵּלַכְנָה נְטוּיוֹת גָּרוֹן" – ***... walking with outstretched necks*** – שֶׁהָיוּ מְהַלְּכוֹת עָקֵב בְּצַד גּוּדָל – this means **that they would walk** with short steps, putting the **heel** of one foot **next to the big toe** of the other.[38]

"וּמְשַׂקְּרוֹת עֵינַיִם" – ***... and with gazing eyes*** – דַּהֲוָה מְלָאן כּוּחְלָא לְעֵינַיְיהוּ וּמְרַמְּזָן – this means **that they would fill their eyes with makeup and beckon** to the young men.[39]

"הָלוֹךְ וְטָפוֹף" – ***... floating as they walked*** – שֶׁהָיוּ מְהַלְּכוֹת אֲרוּכָּה בְּצַד קְצָרָה – this means **that a tall woman would walk next to a short woman.**[40]

"וּבְרַגְלֵיהֶן תְּעַכַּסְנָה" – ***... and with their feet they would spew venom.*** אָמַר רַב יִצְחָק דְּבֵי רַבִּי אַמֵּי – **R' Yitzchak said in the name of R' Ami:** מְלַמֵּד שֶׁמְּטִילוֹת מוֹר וַאֲפַרְסְמוֹן בְּמִנְעֲלֵיהֶן – **[This] teaches that they would put myrrh and balsam in their shoes,** וּמְהַלְּכוֹת בְּשׁוּקֵי יְרוּשָׁלַיִם – **and walk in the market-places of Jerusalem,** וְכֵיוָן שֶׁמַּגִּיעוֹת אֵצֶל בַּחוּרֵי יִשְׂרָאֵל – **and when they reached unmarried Jewish youths,** בּוֹעֲטוֹת בַּקַּרְקַע – **they would stamp on the ground,** וּמַתִּיזוֹת עֲלֵיהֶם – **and spray** the perfume **over them,** וּמַכְנִיסוֹת בָּהֶן יֵצֶר הָרַע כְּאֶרֶס בִּכְעוּס – **driving the Evil Inclination into them like the venom of an angry [snake].**[41]

The Gemara interprets each phrase of another verse in that passage which delineates the punishments of these women:
מַאי פּוּרְעָנוּתֵיהֶם – **What are their punishments?** כִּדְדָרִישׁ רַבָּה בַּר עוּלָּא – It is **as Rabbah bar Ulla expounded:** "וְהָיָה תַחַת בֹּשֶׂם מַק יִהְיֶה" – ***And it shall be that instead of fragrance there will be decay***[42] – מָקוֹם שֶׁהָיוּ מִתְבַּשְּׂמוֹת בּוֹ נַעֲשָׂה נְמָקִים נְמָקִים – **the** very **place where they perfumed themselves became full of decay.**

"וְתַחַת חֲגוֹרָה נִקְפָּה" – ***... and instead of the belt, bruising*** – מָקוֹם שֶׁהָיוּ חֲגוּרוֹת בִּצִלְצוֹל נַעֲשָׂה נְקָפִים נְקָפִים – **the** very **place where they girded themselves with a belt became full of bruises.**

"וְתַחַת מַעֲשֶׂה מִקְשֶׁה קָרְחָה" – ***... and instead of carved items** of jewelry,*[43] ***baldness*** – מָקוֹם שֶׁהָיוּ מִתְקַשְּׁטוֹת בּוֹ נַעֲשָׂה קְרָחִים קְרָחִים – **the** very **place where they adorned themselves**[44]

NOTES

31. If one urinates with his back to the bed, the urine will fall some distance away from it (*Rashi*).

32. He uses only a small amount of water, e.g. a *reviis* [the minimum required to satisfy the obligation (see *Mishnah Berurah* 158:37)], which is not enough for a thorough washing (*Rashi*).

33. In the merit of washing his hands with a generous amount of water, Rav Chisda was granted prosperity. [Since he enhanced his performance of the preparations required before eating food, he was blessed with an abundance of food.]

Rav Chisda implies that the more water one uses the more one will be blessed. He thus contradicts Rava's statement, "But where he does wash his hands, although he does not wash them well, we have *no* objection to it," which indicates that one has nothing to lose by using the minimum amount of water.

[However, to avoid *poverty,* Rav Chisda could well agree that using the minimum suffices. Hence, he would agree that the aforementioned teaching: "Three things cause poverty ... treating the mitzvah of washing the hands lightly," applies only to one who uses *less* than the minimum, as Rava stated (see *Bach Orach Chaim* 158).]

34. See *Maharsha.*

35. Since he did not take care of his wife's needs, his needs will not be provided for and he will be reduced to poverty (see *Meiri* and *Chidushei HaRan*).

36. *Isaiah* 3:16. God warns that because these women are haughty, they will be punished with the afflictions enumerated in the following verses.

37. This interpretation understands the word גָּבְהוּ (they are haughty) in its literal sense, i.e. they are tall (see *Rashi* and *Maharsha*).

38. They would walk slowly so that people could gaze at them.

This interpretation is related to the words of the verse, *walking with outstretched necks,* because one who walks with his neck outstretched proceeds slowly and deliberately since he cannot see his feet (*Rashi*).

39. The word of the verse, מְשַׂקְּרוֹת, *mesakros,* is interpreted here in two ways: (a) It is related to סִיקְרָא, *sikra* – eye makeup. (b) It derives from the verb סקר, *look* [for the women would cast their eyes at the men in a beckoning manner] (*Rashi; Maharsha*).

40. [Literally: they would walk, a tall woman next to a short woman.] The taller woman would appear to "float" above the shorter one, thus enhancing her attractiveness.

The verse speaks of this disparagingly, because it refers to married women (*Rashi*). [For a single woman, who is seeking a husband, such behavior is not always inappropriate (see *Taanis* 26b and 31a).]

41. This exposition links the word used in the verse תְּעַכַּסְנָה to עֶכֶס, *the venom of a snake.* A snake's venom is called עֶכֶס because it is secreted only when the snake is angered (*Rashi*). עֶכֶס is similar to כַּעַס, *anger* (see *Maharsha*).

42. Ibid. v. 24.

43. [See *Rashi* ibid. and *Maharsha.*] מִקְשֶׁה means formed by carving out a solid block, as opposed to attaching pieces together (see *Rashi* to *Exodus* 25:18).

44. I.e. the hair, which a woman combs and lacquers.

This interpretation is based on a play on words. מִתְקַשְּׁטוֹת, *miskashtos,* is similar to מַעֲשֶׂה מִקְשֶׁה, *maaseh miksheh* (*Rashi;* cf. *Maharsha*).

ומאי ר' מאיר דתניא [א] לא תצא אשה במפתח שבידה ואם יצאת חייבת חטאת דברי רבי מאיר רבי אליעזר פוטר [ב] בכובלת ובצלוחית של פלייטון כובלת מאן דכר שמה חסורי מחסרא והכי קתני וכן בכובלת וכן בצלוחית של פלייטון לא תצא ואם יצאה חייבת חטאת דברי רבי מאיר רבי אליעזר פוטר בכובלת ובצלוחית של פלייטון [ג] במה דברים אמורים כשיש בהם בושם אבל אין בהם בושם חייבת אמר רב אדא בר אהבה זאת אומרת המוציא אוכלין פחות מכשיעור בכלי חייב דהא אין בה בושם כפחות מכשיעור בכלי דמי וקתני חייבת רב אשי אמר בעלמא אימא לך פטור ושאני הכא דליתיה לממשא כלל: [א] וראשית שמנים ימשחו אמר רב יהודה אמר שמואל זה פלייטון מתיב רב יוסף [ד] אף על פלייטון גזר רבי יהודה בן בבא ולא הודו לו ואי אמרת משום תענוג אמאי לא הודו לו אמר ליה אביי ולטעמיך הא דכתיב [א] השותים במזרקי יין ר' אמי ור' אסי חד אמר קנישקנין וחד אמר שמזרקין כוסותיהן זה לזה הכי נמי דאסיר והא [ה] רבה בר רב הונא איקלע לבי ריש גלותא ושתה בקנישקנין ולא אמר ליה ולא מידי אלא כל מידי דאית ביה תענוג ואית ביה שמחה גזרו רבנן אבל מידי דאית ביה תענוג ולית ביה שמחה לא גזרו רבנן: [ב] השוכבים על מטות שן וסרוחים על ערשותם [ו] אמר רבי יוסי ברבי חנינא מלמד שהיו משתינין מים בפני מטותיהן ערומים מגדף בה ר' אבהו אי הכי היינו דכתיב [ג] לכן עתה יגלו בראש גולים משום דמשתינין מים בפני מטותיהם ערומים יגלו בראש גולים אלא א"ר אבהו אלו בני אדם שהיו אוכלים ושותים זה עם זה ודובקין מטותיהן זו בזו ומחליפין נשותיהן זה עם זה ומסריחין ערסותם בשכבת זרע שאינו שלהן א"ר אבהו ואמרי לה במתניתא תנא ג' דברים מביאין את האדם לידי עניות ואלו הן [ז] המשתין מים בפני מטתו ערום ° ומזלזל בנטילת ידים ושאשתו מקללתו בפניו [א] המשתין מים בפני מטתו ערום אמר רבא לא אמרן אלא דמהדר אפיה לפורייה אבל לבראי לית לן בה ומהדר אפיה לפורייה נמי לא אמרן אלא לארעא אבל במנא לית לן בה [ב] ומזלזל בנטילת ידים אמר רבא לא אמרן אלא דלא משא ידיה כלל אבל משא ולא משא לית לן בה ולאו מלתא היא דאמר רב חסדא [ג] אנא משאי מלא חפני מיא ויהבו לי מלא חפני טיבותא ושאשתו מקללתו בפניו אמר רבא על עסקי תכשיטיה וה"מ הוא דאית ליה ולא עביד: דרש רבא בריה דרב עילאי מאי [ח] דכתיב [ד] ויאמר ה' יען כי גבהו בנות ציון שהיו מהלכות בקומה זקופה [ד] ותלכנה נטויות גרון שהיו מהלכות עקב בצד גודל [ד] ומשקרות עינים דהוה מלאן כוחלא לעינייהו ומרמזן [ד] הלוך וטפוף שהיו מהלכות ארוכה בצד קצרה [ד] וברגליהן תעכסנה אמר רב יצחק דבי ר' אמי [ד] מלמד שמטילות מור ואפרסמון במנעליהן ומהלכות בשוקי ירושלים וכיון שמגיעות אצל בחורי ישראל בועטות בקרקע ומתיזות עליהם ומכניסות בהן יצר הרע כארס [ט] בכעוס מאי פורענותיהם כדדריש רבה בר עולא [ה] והיה תחת בושם מק יהיה מקום שהיו מתבשמות בו נעשה נמקים [ה] ותחת חגורה נקפה מקום שהיו חגורות בצלצול נעשה נקפים נקפים [ה] ותחת מעשה מקשה קרחה מקום שהיו מתקשטות בו נעשה קרחים קרחים [ה] ותחת פתיגיל מחגורת שק פתחים המביאין לידי גילה יהיו למחגורת שק [ה] כי תחת יופי אמר רבא היינו דאמרי אינשי חלופי שופרא כיבא [ו] [י] (וספח) ה' קדקוד בנות ציון אמר רבי יוסי ברבי חנינא מלמד שפרחה בהן צרעת כתיב הכא ושפח וכתיב התם [ז] לשאת ולספחת [ו] וה' פתהן יערה רב ושמואל חד אמר שנשפכו כקיתון וחד אמר שנעשו פתחיהן כיער אמר רב יהודה אמר רב אנשי ירושלים אנשי שחץ היו אדם אומר לחברו במה סעדת היום בפת עמילה או בפת שאינה עמילה ביין גורדלי או ביין

ומאי רבי מאיר. היכא אשכחן דאיירי בה רבי מאיר בלא רבנן ופליג רבי אליעזר עליה: בד"א. דרבי אליעזר פוטר והאי פוטר היינו מותר לכתחלה כדאוקימנא: כשיש בה בושם. פלייטון יש בההוא חומרתא העשויה כקמיע דכיון דיש בה בושם תכשיט היא לזו שריחה רע ולמשלף ולאיתויי נמי לא חייש כדאמרן דגנות הוא לה: אבל אין בה בושם. חומרתא לחודא לאו תכשיט הוא וחייבת: זאת אומרת. הא דקתני אין בה בושם חייבת אלמא דקסבר רבי אליעזר המוציא אוכלין בשבת בכלי פחות מכשיעור דלא מיחייב על הוצאת אוכלין פחות מגרוגרת כדלקמן (דף עו:) חייב מיהא על הכלי ולא אמרינן הכלי טפל להן ולא מיחייב עליה שלא נתכוין להוציא אלא משום אוכלין ופלוגתא היא על סתם משנה השנויה בפרק המצניע (לקמן דף צג:) דקתני פטור אף על הכלי: דהא אין בו בושם כפחות מכשיעור דמי. שהכלי קלט את הריח ושיעור הוצאת בשמים בכל שהוא וכיון שאינו כל שהוא הוי ריחה פחות מכשיעור (הוא) וקתני חייבת ולא אמרינן נעשה כלי טפל לריח שבתוכו ואריחא לא מיחייב דפחות מכשיעור הוא: ושאני הכא. ליכא למימר נעשה כלי טפל לריח שאין בו שום ממש ואפילו פחות מכשיעור לא מיקרי אבל פחות מכשיעור בדבר שיש בו ממש נעשה כלי טפל לו ופטור: ראשית שמנים. מובחר שבשמנים: גזר. משום לער חורבן: ואי אמרת. זה פלייטון והאי קרא בתענוג משתעי שלא היו נותנים לב לדברי הנביאים הניבאים על הפורענות ועסוקים בתענוגים: ולטעמיך הא דכתיב. בהאי ענינא השותים במזרקי יין ורבי אמי ורבי אסי פירשו ° זהו קנישקנין כלי זכוכית ארוך ולו שני פיות ויין נזרק מזה לזה: שמזרקין. על ידי אומנות כדאמר בהחליל (סוכה דף נג.) מטייל בתמני כסי: הכי נמי דאסור. למשתי השתא בקנישקנין: משתינין. דדייק מסרוחים: לידי עניות. דאמרינן בע"פ (פסחים דף קיא:) שרא דעניותא נביל שמיה ונביל קרי ליה ואוהב מקום מיאוס ומשתין מים לפני מטתו היינו מיאוס: ערום. אורחא דמילתא נקט מתוך שהוא ערום אינו יוצא לחוץ להשתין דטורח הוא לו ללבוש ולצאת: אבל לבראי לית לן בה. שהקילוח ארוך וניתז למרחוק: משא ולא משא. שאינו רוחץ ומשפשף יפה אלא מעט מים כגון רביעית מלומלם: על עסקי תכשיטיה. שאינו רוצה לקנות לה: גבהו. היינו קומה זקופה: ותלכנה נטויות גרון שהיו הולכות עקב בצד גודל. למעט בהילוכם שהיו מסתכלין בה והיא שוהה בפסיעותיה ודרך נוטין גרון לילך בנחת לפי שאינו רואה לרגליו: ומשקרות עינים דמליין כוחלא. לשון סיקרא: ומרמזן. את הבחורים: סיקור. לשון הבטה: הלוך וטפוף שהיו מהלכות ארוכה בצד קצרה. שתראה לפה על ראש חברתה והוא נוי לה ונשואות היו לפיכך מספר בגנותן: וטפוף. כמו על דאטפת אטפוך (אבות פ"ב מ"ו): תעכסנה. כמו וכעכס אל מוסר אויל (משלי ז) והוא ארס של נחש וקרי ליה עכס על שם שאינו מטילו אלא על ידי כעס: בכעוס. נחש כעוסה: נמקים. כמו המק בשרו (זכריה יד): צלצול. בנדי"ל נאה: נקפים. חבורות לשון המנקף רגלו וניקף סבכי היער (ישעיה י): מתקשטות. היינו שער שסורקות ומפרכסות: מתקשטות. דומה למקשה כעין נוטריקון: פתיגיל. נוטריקון פתח גילה אותו מקום: כי תחת יופי. כי כל אלה יבא לך תחת יפייך: כיבא. קיטור"א ליחה כמו שיחנא וכיבי דקדושין דפלימו (דף פא:): פתהן. כמו פתחיהן: שנשפכו כקיתון. שופכות דם זיבה: יערה. כמו ותער כדה (בראשית כד): כיער. נתמלאו שער ונמאסות לתשמיש: אנשי שחץ. מדברים בלשון גאוה ולעגי שפה: סעדת. תשמיש: פת עמילה. בעולה: שאינה עמילה. בתולה: פת עמילה. ברייאי"ה בלע"ז: גורדלי. לבן היה: ביין

מסורת הש"ס

א) [תוספתא פ"ה ע"ש], ב) [לקמן דף סה.], ג) [תוספתא שם ע"ש], ד) [תוספ' דסוטה פט"ו], ה) [ע"ז דף עב: ע"ש], ו) קדושין עא:, ז) נדה יז., ח) [יומא דף ט: ע"ש], ט) [עי' ערוך ערך ארס], י) [נ"ל ושפח].

גליון הש"ס

גמ' ומזלזל בנט"י. עי' סוטה ד ע"ב תוס' ד"ה נעקר: רש"י ד"ה ולטעמיך וכו' זהו קנישקנין. עי' ע"ז דף עב ע"ב ברש"י ד"ה קנישקנין:

ליקוטי רש"י

וראשית שמנים. מובחר שבשמנים והוא אפרסמון. השותים במזרקי יין. יש מרבותינו שאומרים במסכת שבת שהיו זורקין כוסותיהן זה לזה וי"מ על שם כלי שהיו לו שתי פיות והוא ארוך ושותה זה מכאן וזה מכאן הוא נזרק מפיו אל פיו [עמוס ו, ו]. קנישקנין. כלי רחב ויש לו שני קנין או שלשה יוצאין מלידו ונמשכין ועולין כנגד גובהו וכשנותנין יין בפיו מתמלאין כל הקנים ויכולין כמה בני אדם לשתות בו ביחד וכאן קורין לו קרוגל"א מפני שמוקף קנים כמחולות הללו [ע"ז עב:]. ויאמר ה'. על הנשים אשר משלו בעמי יען כי גבהו וגו'. הלוך וטפוף. לשון דבר לף על גבי חבירו כמו (דברים יא) אשר הציף ומתרגמינן דאטיף כך היתה ארוכה מהלכת בין שתי קצרות כדי שתהא נראית צפה למעלה מהם. וברגליהן תעכסנה. להבעיר בו יצר הרע כעכס זה של נחש, עכס הוא ארס של נחש [ישעיה ג, טז]. והיה תחת בושם מק. מקום שהיו מתבשמות בו יהיה נימק. ותחת חגורה נקפה. מקום שחגרה שם יהיה ניקף נחתך בחבורות ורשומי מכות כמו ואחר עורי נקפו (איוב יט) ונקף סבכי היער (ישעיה י). ותחת מעשה מקשה. מקום שהיו עושות בו המעשה האמור למעלה הלוך וטפוף תלכנה והוא בגובה הראש שם תהיה מקשה קרחה מכה המקרחת את הראש מקשה ל' דא לדא נקשן (דניאל ה) ואני הייתי מפרשו תחת המעשה מקשה מקום שהיו שם מגורות נותנות טסי הזהב העשויות מקשה בטדי"ן בלע"ז אלא שהוא נקוד פתח והוא במסורה בעשרה נקודים פתח ואין אחד מהם דבוק לתיבה של אחריו וכל מעשה שהוא דבק לתיבה של אחריו נקוד קמץ. ותחת פתיגיל. הוא בית הרחם האמור למעלה פתהן חלוף אותה גילה תהיה מחגורת שק בכל מתניה. כי תחת יופי. כי זאת הוגנת להיות להם תחת יופי שהיו משתחצות בו [שם, כד]. ושפח. לשון לרעת כמו (ויקרא יג) מספחת היא ועל שנכתב בשי"ן דרשו בו רבותינו שמעשנה שפחות מכודנות ויש שדרשוהו שהרבה בהן משפחות משפחות של כנים. פתהן יערה. הן היו אומרות ימהר יחישה מעשהו שר רואה אותי ונוטל אותי כשבא הפורענות היו שרי נ"נ נוטלין אותן להיות לנשים מחמת יופין ורמז הקב"ה והיו שופעות כאדם המערה מכלי אל כלי וכאשר נגעו בדם נדה והיו נמאסות עליהן ומשליכין אותן לארץ מעל קרונות שלהן [שם, יז]. פת עמילה. שאינה ממהרת להחמיץ שעמילתה מעכבתה עמילה ברייר"א [פסחים לז:].

עין משפט נר מצוה

מו א טוש"ע א"ח סי' רמא:
מז ב ג מיי' פ"ו מהל' ברכות הלכה יט טוש"ע א"ח סי' קנח סעיף ט:
מח ד מיי' פכ"א מהל' איסורי ביאה הלכה ב' טוש"ע אה"ע סי' כא סעיף א:

רבינו חננאל

ראשית שמנים כמשמעו ואפילו מאן דפטר לא פטר אלא בשיש בה בושם. אבל אין בה בושם חייבת. קנישקנין כוס שיש בה שתי פיות ושותין ממנה שנים בבת אחת. מסקרות עינים. דהוו מליין כוחלא רמזא. ארס בכעוס. פי' החיה כשתכעוס גוררת ומשלכת. ארס קשה. פי' פת עמילה. אשה בעולה ופת שאינה עמילה בתולה. וכולן על זה הענין: צלצול חגור. כדגרסינן בסוף מנחות (דף קט:):

רב נסים גאון

מותיב רב יוסף אף על פליאטון גזר ר' יהודה בן בבא. עיקר זאת הברייתא בתוספ' סוטה בסוף המסכת בפולמוס האחרון גזרו על חופת חתנים אלו זהוריות המוזהבות כו' אף על פליאטון גזר ר' יהודה בן בבא ולא הודו לו:

תורה אור השלם

א) הַשֹּׁתִים בְּמִזְרְקֵי יַיִן וְרֵאשִׁית שְׁמָנִים יִמְשָׁחוּ וְלֹא נֶחְלוּ עַל שֵׁבֶר יוֹסֵף: [עמוס ו, ו]

ב) הַשֹּׁכְבִים עַל מִטּוֹת שֵׁן וּסְרֻחִים עַל עַרְשׂוֹתָם וְאֹכְלִים כָּרִים מִצֹּאן וַעֲגָלִים מִתּוֹךְ מַרְבֵּק: [עמוס ו, ד]

ג) לָכֵן עַתָּה יִגְלוּ בְּרֹאשׁ גֹּלִים וְסָר מִרְזַח סְרוּחִים: [עמוס ו, ז]

ד) וַיֹּאמֶר יְיָ יַעַן כִּי גָבְהוּ בְּנוֹת צִיּוֹן וַתֵּלַכְנָה נְטוּיוֹת גָּרוֹן וּמְשַׂקְּרוֹת עֵינָיִם הָלוֹךְ וְטָפֹף תֵּלַכְנָה וּבְרַגְלֵיהֶם תְּעַכַּסְנָה: [ישעיה ג, טז]

ה) וְהָיָה תַחַת בֹּשֶׂם מַק יִהְיֶה וְתַחַת חֲגוֹרָה נִקְפָּה וְתַחַת מַעֲשֶׂה מִקְשֶׁה קָרְחָה וְתַחַת פְּתִיגִיל מַחֲגֹרֶת שָׂק כִּי תַחַת יֹפִי: [ישעיה ג, כד]

ו) וְשִׂפַּח אֲדֹנָי קָדְקֹד בְּנוֹת צִיּוֹן וַיְיָ פָּתְהֵן יְעָרֶה: [ישעיה ג, יז]

ז) וְלַשְׂאֵת וְלַסַּפַּחַת וְלַבֶּהָרֶת: [ויקרא יד, נו]

became full of bald patches.

,,וְתַחַת פְּתִיגִיל מַחֲגֹרֶת שָׂק״ – *. . . and instead of the sash, a belt of sackcloth* – **פְּתָחִים הַמְּבִיאִין לִידֵי גִילָה יִהְיוּ לְמַחֲגֹרֶת שָׂק** – the **openings that lead to gladness**[45] **will be for a girding of sackcloth.**

,,כִּי תַחַת יֹפִי״ – *. . . for* [all these things will befall you] ***instead of beauty*** – **אָמַר רָבָא** – **Rava said: הַיְינוּ דְּאָמְרֵי אִינְשֵׁי** – **This** verse reflects the maxim **that people say: ,,חֲלוּפֵי שׁוּפְרָא כִּיבָא״** – **"In exchange for beauty – sores."**[46]

The Gemara expounds upon another verse that describes the punishment of these women:

,,וְשִׂפַּח ה׳ קָדְקֹד בְּנוֹת צִיּוֹן״ – ***The Lord will afflict the heads of the daughters of Zion with lesions.***[47] **אָמַר רַבִּי יוֹסֵי בְּרַבִּי חֲנִינָא** – **R' Yose the son of R' Chanina said: מְלַמֵּד שֶׁפָּרְחָה בָּהֶן צָרַעַת** – **[This] teaches that *tzaraas***[48] **broke out in them. כְּתִיב הָכָא** – For **it is written here: ,,וְשִׂפַּח״** – ***He shall afflict with lesions*** (*v'sipach*): **וּכְתִיב הָתָם** – **and it is written there,** in reference to *tzaraas*: **,,וְלַשְׂאֵת וְלַסַּפַּחַת״** – ***and*** [the laws] ***of the s'eis and of the sapachas.***[49]

The verse continues:

,,וַה׳ פָּתְהֵן יְעָרֶה״ – ***And Hashem will cause their openings to pour.***[50] **רַב וּשְׁמוּאֵל** – **Rav and Shmuel** gave different interpretations of this phrase: **חַד אָמַר** – **One said** it means **שֶׁנִּשְׁפְּכוּ כְּקִיתוֹן** – **that they were poured out like a pitcher.**[51] **וְחַד אָמַר** – **And one said** it means **שֶׁנַּעֲשׂוּ פִּתְחֵיהֶן כְּיַעַר** – **that their openings became like a forest.**[52]

Having discussed the haughtiness of the women of Jerusalem, the Gemara now turns to the men:

אָמַר רַב יְהוּדָה אָמַר רַב – **Rav Yehudah said in the name of Rav: אַנְשֵׁי יְרוּשָׁלַיִם אַנְשֵׁי שַׁחַץ הָיוּ** – **The men of Jerusalem were men of pretentiousness.**[53] **אָדָם אוֹמֵר לַחֲבֵרוֹ** – **A man would ask his fellow: בַּמֶּה סָעַדְתָּ הַיּוֹם** – **On what did you dine**[54] **today? בְּפַת עֲמִילָה אוֹ בְּפַת שֶׁאֵינָהּ עֲמִילָה** – Did you dine **on bread that was well kneaded**[55] **or on bread that was not well kneaded?**[56] **בְּיֵין גּוֹרְדְּלִי אוֹ** – **On *gordeli* wine or**

NOTES

45. פְּתִיגִיל is understood as a contraction of the two words פֶּתַח, *opening,* and גִּילָה, *gladness.* It thus refers to the private parts (*Rashi*).

46. כִּי (literally: for) is taken as an abbreviation of כִּיבָא, *sore* (*Maharsha*).

47. *Isaiah* 3:17.

48. *Tzaraas* is the skin affliction described in *Leviticus* ch. 13.

49. *Leviticus* 14:56. The Gemara connects שִׂפַּח (*sipach*) to the similar word סַפַּחַת (*sapachas*). *S'eis* and *sapachas* denote various forms of the skin discoloration associated with *tzaraas* (see *Rambam, Hil. Tumas Tzaraas* 1:2).

50. פָּתְהֵן is translated as a contraction of פִּתְחֵיהֶן, *their openings* [i.e. their private parts] (*Rashi*).

51. They are afflicted with an abnormal flow of blood (*Rashi*).

52. Their private parts became full of hair, making intercourse repulsive (*Rashi*).

This interpretation links יְעָרֶה, *y'areh* (literally: he will pour) to יַעַר, *ya'ar* (forest).

53. They would speak in an arrogant, gilded tongue (*Rashi*). [I.e. they would mask their low behavior by alluding to it with a high-class manner of speech.]

54. This refers to cohabitation (*Rashi*).

55. A non-virgin (*Rashi*).

56. A virgin (*Rashi*).

אָמַר רַחֲבָה אָמַר רַבִּי יְהוּדָה – **Rachavah said in the name of R' Yehudah:** עֲצֵי יְרוּשָׁלַיִם שֶׁל קִינָּמוֹן הָיוּ – **The logs** used **in Jerusalem** as fuel **were of** the **cinnamon** tree. וּבְשָׁעָה שֶׁהָיוּ מַסִּיקִין מֵהֶן – **When they would burn some of [those logs],** רֵיחָן נוֹדֵף בְּכָל אֶרֶץ יִשְׂרָאֵל – **their fragrance would waft through all of Eretz Yisrael.** וּמִשֶּׁחָרְבָה יְרוּשָׁלַיִם נִגְנְזוּ – **But when Jerusalem was destroyed, they were hidden** וְלֹא נִשְׁתַּיֵּיר אֶלָּא כִּשְׂעוֹרָה – **and only** a piece **the size of a barley grain remained,** וּמִשְׁתַּכַּח בְּגִנְזַאי דְצִימְצְמַאי מַלְכְּתָא – **which is found in the storehouses of Queen Tzimtzemai.**[4]

בְּמֵסַב רָחָב אוֹ בְּמֵסַב קָצָר – Did you recline **on a wide couch or a narrow couch?**[2] בְּחָבֵר טוֹב אוֹ בְּחָבֵר רַע – Did you dine **with a good companion or a poor companion?**[3]

The Gemara explains:

אָמַר רַב חִסְדָּא – **Rav Chisda said:** וְכוּלָּן לִזְנוּת – **And all [these questions] pertain to illicit sexual relations.**

This section concludes with another narrative about the fragrances of Jerusalem:

Mishnah לֹא יֵצֵא הָאִישׁ לֹא בְסַיִיף וְלֹא בְקֶשֶׁת וְלֹא בִתְרִיס וְלֹא בְאַלָּה וְלֹא בְרוֹמַח – **A man may not go out** into the public domain **with a sword, nor with a bow, nor with a shield, nor with an** ***alah,***[5] **nor with a spear,** וְאִם יָצָא חַיָּיב חַטָּאת – **and if he did go out** with one of these implements of war, **he is liable for a** ***chatas*** **offering.**[6] רַבִּי אֱלִיעֶזֶר אוֹמֵר תַּכְשִׁיטִין הֵן לוֹ – **R' Eliezer says: They are ornaments for him,** since they enhance his appearance. וַחֲכָמִים אוֹמְרִים אֵינָן אֶלָּא לִגְנַאי – **But the Sages**[7] **say: They are nothing but a disgrace,** שֶׁנֶּאֱמַר ,,וְכִתְּתוּ חַרְבוֹתָם לְאִתִּים וַחֲנִיתוֹתֵיהֶם לְמַזְמֵרוֹת לֹא־יִשָּׂא גוֹי אֶל־גּוֹי חֶרֶב וְלֹא־יִלְמְדוּ עוֹד מִלְחָמָה'' – **as it is stated:** ***They shall beat their swords into plowshares, and their spears into pruning shears; nation shall not lift up a sword against nation, neither shall they learn war anymore.***[8]

בִּירִית טְהוֹרָה וְיוֹצְאִין בָּהּ בְּשַׁבָּת – **A garter is** ***tahor,***[9] **and one may go out with it on the Sabbath.**[10] כְּבָלִים טְמֵאִים וְאֵין יוֹצְאִין בָּהֶן בְּשַׁבָּת – **Leg chains are** susceptible to ***tumah,*** **and one may not go out with them on the Sabbath.**[11]

Gemara The Gemara asks regarding one of the weapons mentioned in the Mishnah:

מַאי בְּאַלָּה – **What is** meant by the phrase, "nor **WITH AN** ***ALAH***"?

The Gemara answers:

קוּלְפָּא – It refers to **a mace.**[12]

The Gemara quotes the next opinion in the Mishnah:

רַבִּי אֱלִיעֶזֶר אוֹמֵר תַּכְשִׁיטִין הֵן לוֹ – **R' ELIEZER SAYS: THEY ARE ORNAMENTS FOR HIM.**

The Gemara elaborates on the debate between R' Eliezer and the Sages:

תַּנְיָא אָמְרוּ לוֹ לְרַבִּי אֱלִיעֶזֶר – **It was taught in a Baraisa: [THE SAGES] SAID TO R' ELIEZER:** וְכִי מֵאַחַר דְּתַכְשִׁיטִין הֵן לוֹ – **INASMUCH AS [THESE WEAPONS] ARE ORNAMENTS FOR HIM,** מִפְּנֵי מָה הֵן בְּטֵלִין לִימוֹת הַמָּשִׁיחַ – **WHY WILL THEY BE ELIMINATED IN THE MESSIANIC ERA?**[13] אָמַר לָהֶן לְפִי שֶׁאֵינָן צְרִיכִין – **[R' ELIEZER] SAID TO THEM** in reply: **BECAUSE THEY WILL NOT BE NEEDED** for war, שֶׁנֶּאֱמַר ,,לֹא־יִשָּׂא גוֹי אֶל־גּוֹי חֶרֶב'' – **AS IT IS STATED:** ***NATION SHALL NOT LIFT UP A SWORD AGAINST NATION.***

The Gemara asks:

וְתֶהֱוֵי לְנוֹי בְּעָלְמָא – **But let it be** worn **merely for an adornment!** Even when weapons for war are no longer needed, they could be used as ornaments.

The Gemara answers:

אָמַר אַבַּיֵי מִידִי דַּהֲוָה אַשְׁרָגָא בְּטִיהֲרָא – **Abaye said:** A useless weapon is **something that is similar to a lamp in broad daylight.**[14]

The Gemara notes:

וּפְלִיגָא דִּשְׁמוּאֵל – **And [our Baraisa] disagrees with** the opinion **of Shmuel,**[15] דְּאָמַר שְׁמוּאֵל אֵין בֵּין הָעוֹלָם הַזֶּה לִימוֹת הַמָּשִׁיחַ אֶלָּא

NOTES

1. *Gordali* wine is white, whereas *chardali* wine is black. That is to say: Was the woman fair or dark? (*Rashi*).

2. A מֵסַב is a couch on which people would recline while eating. The question meant: Was the woman fat or thin? (*Rashi*).

3. I.e. was the woman attractive? (*Rashi*).

4. That was her name (*Rashi*; see *Maharatz Chayes*).

Maharsha suggests that צִימְצְמַאי is a verb meaning *adorn.* Thus, the Gemara means that the last piece of cinnamon wood was stored in the treasure house of a certain king and was used only as a perfume for the queen.

5. The Gemara below will define this term.

6. Since these items are neither clothing nor ornaments they are a burden, and one who carries them from the private to the public domain has performed the Biblically forbidden labor of הוֹצָאָה, *transferring.*

7. The Sages do not represent a third view, but merely explain that of the Tanna Kamma (*Tos. Yom Tov*).

Except for the sword, which is worn hanging from the belt, the weapons mentioned by our Mishnah are carried in the hand. Why, then, does R' Eliezer rule that one is not liable to a sin offering? After all, going out into the public domain with an ornament is permitted only if one is wearing it; one certainly should incur liability if he carries it! *Tiferes Yisrael* explains that an ornament that is normally worn (e.g. a ring) is indeed considered a burden when carried. However, certain items function as an adornment only when carried in the hand (e.g. a fancy walking stick). The other weapons in the Mishnah fall into this category, and therefore are not considered burdens (see also *Magen Avraham* 301:27).

Does R' Eliezer permit going out with these weapons on the Sabbath in the first place, or does he only rule that, after the fact, one is exempt from bringing a *chatas* offering? This question is debated by *Tiferes Yisrael* and *Magen Avraham* ibid. (see also *Mishnah Berurah* 301:66, and Gemara below, 138a).

8. *Isaiah* 2:4. If these weapons also functioned as adornments, they would not be consigned to oblivion in the future (*Rashi*).

9. [I.e. it is not susceptible to *tumah.*] The Gemara will discuss this case below (63b); see note 10 there.

10. This is permitted because there is no danger that a woman will remove the garter to show a friend, for if she did her legs would be exposed (*Rashi*).

11. The Gemara below (ibid.) will discuss this case as well.

12. This is a metal club with a round, studded ball at its head (*Aruch;* see *Rashi*).

13. Scripture expressly states that they will be converted into agricultural tools.

14. Since a lamp in broad daylight is useless, it is not attractive. [Similarly, when weapons will no longer be needed, they will lose their appeal as ornaments, and subsequently will be beaten into hoes and pruning shears.] But in our day, which is an era of war, weapons are ornaments (*Rashi*).

15. Our Baraisa, which assumes that weapons will become obsolete in the Messianic era, conflicts with Shmuel, who holds that weapons will still be needed then (*Rashi*).

It is surprising for the Gemara to say that a Baraisa disagrees with an Amora. Normally, the Gemara would challenge Shmuel's view by saying that a Baraisa contradicts it. However, perhaps this Baraisa was not

ביין חרדלי במסב רחב או במסב קצר בחבר טוב או בחבר רע א"ר חסדא וכולן לזנות אמר רחבה אמר רבי יהודה עצי ירושלים של קינמון היו ובשעה שהיו מסיקין מהן ריחן נודף בכל ארץ ישראל ומשחרבה ירושלים נגנזו ולא נשתייר אלא כשעורה ומשתכח בגנזאי דצימצמאי מלכתא:

מתני' לא יצא האיש לא בסייף ולא בקשת ולא בתרים ולא באלה ולא ברומח ואם יצא חייב חטאת רבי אליעזר אומר תכשיטין הן לו וחכ"א אינן אלא לגנאי שנאמר א) וכתתו חרבותם לאתים וחניתותיהם למזמרות ולא ישא גוי אל גוי חרב ולא ילמדו עוד מלחמה בירית טהורה ויוצאין בה בשבת כבלים טמאים ואין יוצאין בהן בשבת: **גמ'** מאי באלה קולפא: ר' אליעזר אומר תכשיטין הן לו: תניא אמרו לו לרבי אליעזר וכי מאחר דתכשיטין הן לו מפני מה הן בטלין לימות המשיח אמר להן לפי שאינן צריכין שנאמר א) לא ישא גוי אל גוי חרב ותהוי לנוי בעלמא אמר אביי מידי דהוה אשרגא בטיהרא ופליגא דשמואל דאמר שמואל אין בין העולם הזה לימות המשיח אלא שיעבוד גליות בלבד שנאמר ב) כי לא יחדל אביון מקרב הארץ מסייע ליה לרבי חייא בר אבא דא"ר חייא בר אבא כל הנביאים לא נתנבאו אלא לימות המשיח אבל לעולם הבא ג) עין לא ראתה אלהים זולתך ואיכא דאמרי אמרו לו לר' אליעזר וכי מאחר דתכשיטין הן לו מפני מה הן בטלין לימות המשיח אמר להן אף לימות המשיח אינן בטלין היינו דשמואל ופליגא דר' חייא בר אבא א"ל אביי לרב דימי ואמרי לה לרב אויא ואמרי לה רב יוסף לרב דימי ואמרי לה לרב אויא ואמרי לה אביי לרב יוסף מ"ט דר"א דאמר תכשיטין הן לו דכתיב ד) חגור חרבך על ירך גבור הודך והדרך א"ל רב כהנא למר בריה דרב הונא האי בדברי תורה כתיב א"ל אין מקרא יוצא מידי פשוטו א"ר כהנא כד הוינא בר תמני סרי שנין והוה גמירנא ליה לכוליה הש"ס ולא הוה ידענא דאין מקרא יוצא מידי פשוטו עד השתא מאי קמ"ל דליגמר איניש והדר ליסבר: סימן זרות: א"ר ירמיה א"ר אלעזר שני תלמידי חכמים המחדדין זה לזה בהלכה הקב"ה מצליח להם שנאמר ה) והדרך צלח אל תקרי והדרך אלא וחדדך ולא עוד אלא שעולין לגדולה שנאמר ה) צלח רכב יכול אפילו שלא לשמה תלמוד לומר ה) על דבר אמת יכול אם הגים דעתו ת"ל ה) וענוה צדק ואם עושין כן זוכין לתורה שניתנה בימין שנאמר ה) ותורך נוראות ימינך רב נחמן בר יצחק אמר זוכין לדברים שנאמרו בימינה של תורה דאמר רבא בר רב שילא ואמרי לה אמר רב יוסף בר חמא א"ר ששת מאי דכתיב ו) אורך ימים בימינה בשמאלה עושר וכבוד אלא בימינה אורך ימים איכא עושר וכבוד ליכא אלא למיימינין בה אורך ימים איכא וכ"ש עושר וכבוד למשמאילים בה עושר וכבוד איכא אורך ימים ליכא א"ר ירמיה אמר ר' שמעון בן לקיש שני תלמידי חכמים הנוחין זה לזה בהלכה הקדוש ברוך הוא מקשיב להן שנאמר ז) אז נדברו יראי ה' וגו' אין דיבור אלא נחת שנאמר ח) ידבר עמים תחתינו מאי ולחושבי שמו א"ר אמי אפילו חישב לעשות מצוה ונאנס ולא עשאה מעלה עליו הכתוב כאילו עשאה א"ר חיננא בר אידי כל העושה מצוה כמאמרה אין מבשרין אותו בשורות רעות שנאמר ט) שומר מצוה לא ידע דבר רע א"ר אסי ואיתימא ר' חנינא אפילו הקב"ה גוזר גזירה הוא מבטלה שנאמר י) באשר דבר מלך שלטון ומי יאמר לו מה תעשה וסמיך ליה ט) שומר מצוה לא ידע דבר רע אמר רבי אבא אמר רבי שמעון בן לקיש שני תלמידי חכמים המקשיבים זה לזה בהלכה הקדוש ב"ה שומע לקולן שנאמר כ) היושבת בגנים חברים מקשיבים לקולך השמיעני ואם אין עושין כן גורמין לשכינה שמסתלקת מישראל שנאמר ל) ברח דודי ודמה וגו' אמר רבי אבא א"ר שמעון בן לקיש שני ת"ח המדגילים זה לזה בהלכה הקדוש ברוך הוא אוהבן שנאמר מ) ודגלו עלי אהבה אמר רבא והוא דידעי צורתא דשמעתא והוא דלית להו רבה במתא למיגמר מיניה (א"ר) אבא א"ר שמעון בן לקיש גדול המלוה יותר מן העושה צדקה ומטיל בכים יותר מכולן (א"ר) אבא אמר ר' שמעון בן לקיש אם תלמיד חכם נוקם ונוטר כנחש הוא חגריהו על מתניך אם עם הארץ הוא חסיד אל תדור בשכונתו אמר רב כהנא אמר רבי שמעון בן לקיש ואמרי לה אמר רב אסי אמר (ריש לקיש) ואמרי לה אמר רבי אבא אמר רבי שמעון בן לקיש כל המגדל כלב רע בתוך ביתו מונע חסד מתוך ביתו שנאמר נ) למס

מרעהו

רש"י

ביין חרדלי. שחור כלומר לבנה או שחורה: במסב רחב. מיסב מטה שמיסב עליה בשעת אכילה ולענין ניאוף אשה שמנה: קצר. כחושה: חבר טוב. אשה טובת מראה: דצימצמאי מלכתא. כך שמה: מתני' באלה. מפרש בגמ' קולפא מלוק"ה בלע"ז: וכתתו חרבותם. ואי תכשיטין נינהו לא יהו בטלין לעתיד: בירית. בגמרא מפרש: טהורה. אינה מקבלת טומאה: ויוצאין בה. דלא שלפא ומחויא שלא יראה שוקה: כבלין טמאין. בגמ' מפרש לה: גמ' שרגא בטיהרא. נר בצהרים מתוך שאינו צריך אינו נאה אבל בזמן הזה שהוא עת מלחמה תכשיטין הן: ופליגא. הא דקתני בטלין לימות המשיח פליגא דשמואל דלשמואל אין בטלין לימות המשיח: לא יחדל. משמע לעולם אלמא יש עניות ועשירות ש"מ נחמות שנתנבאו הנביאים ולא יהיה כנעני עוד (זכריה יד) לא לימות המשיח נתנבאו שהן מן העולם הזה דאם כן חדל לך אביון: מסייע ליה. ברייתא דקתני בטלין לימות המשיח לרבי חייא בר אבא: לא נתנבאו. דברי נחמות שלהן: עין לא ראתה. עין של נביאים לא שלטה לראותו: בדברי תורה כתיב. הוי זהיר לחזור על משנתך שתהא מזומנת לך בשעת הדין להביא ראיה כחרב על ירך גבור לנצח במלחמה והוא הודך והדרך: דליגמר איניש. לגרוס שמעתא מרביה ואף על גב דלא ידע לכולהו טעמיה: והדר ליסבר. טעמיה דהא קשה ליה לרב כהנא ולא הוה ידע להאי טעמא ותלמודיה הוה קים ליה מדהוה בר תמני סרי: המחדדין. שואלין ומשיבין ולא לקפח אלא להתחדד: והדרך. כמו וחדדך: ותורך. ותלמדך (א): למיימינין. של תורה שמפשפשין טעמיהן בדקדוק ובוררין כימין המיומנת למלאכה: עושר וכבוד ליכא. בתמיה כיון דאיכא אורך ימים כ"ש עושר וכבוד: למשמאילין בה. שאין יגעים בה כל צרכן אי נמי מיימינין בה עוסקין לשמה משמאילים שלא לשמה: הנוחין זה לזה. נושאין ונותנין בה בנחת רוח מתעסקין כדי שילמדו זה מזה: ידבר עמים תחתינו. ישפיל וכל שפלות בנחת ל"א הנוחין מנהיגין זה את זה להבנתה של הלכה כמו לך נחה (שמות לב) ידבר תרגום של ינהג: ומי יאמר לו מה תעשה. שומר מצות יוכל לומר לו: המקשיבין. מלמדים זה את זה ומבינים זה מזה ולישנא דקרא נקט: בגנים. בתי מדרשות: חבירים מקשיבים. זה לזה להם אני אומר שישמיעוני קולם ואענם: ברח דודי. בתריה כתיב: המדגילים. מאספין זה את זה ואומרים בא ונלמוד ונבין בין שנינו הואיל ואין לנו רב ללמדנו: צורתא. שורש הדבר קצת למדו מרבם: גדול המלוה. לפי שאין העני בוש בדבר: ומטיל לכים. מעות ומלאי להשתכר בהן למחצית שכר ואידי דאיירי רבי אבא אמר ריש לקיש נקט כל הני מילי דאגדתא דאמר להו ר' אבא משמיה: חוגרו. הדבק בו שסופך ליהנות מתלמודו: אל תדור בשכונתו. שאינו יודע בדקדוקי מצות ואין חסידותו שלם וסופך ללמוד ממנו: מונע חסד. שאינו מניח העניים לבא לפתחו: למס. דהיינו כלב:

מרעהו

תוספות

אין בין העוה"ז לימות המשיח. אע"ג דהשתא אין ירושלים ואין בהמ"ק ואילו לימות המשיח יהיה הכל בנוי נ"ל דהאי אין בין לאו דוקא ק):

ואילו

עין משפט נר מצוה

מט א מיי' פי"ט מהל' שבת הלכה א סמג לאוין סה טוש"ע א"ח סי' ש"א סעיף ז:

נ ב מיי' פי"ב מהל' מלכים הלכה ב:

נא ג מיי' פ"ח מהל' תשובה הלכה ז:

נב ד מיי' פ"י מהל' מ"ע הלכה ח טוש"ע י"ד סי' רמט סעיף ו:

נג ה מיי' פ"ו מהל' דעות הלכה א ב:

נד ו מיי' פי"א מהל' רוצח הלכה ד:

ליקוטי רש"י

ולא בתרים. תריסין. מגינים [בכורות לו.]. **וכתתו חרבותם לאתים.** קולטר"ש בלע"ז. **למזמרות.** שרפ"ש בלע"ז שזומרין בהן הכרמים [ישעיה ב, ד]. **בירית טהורה.** מלטמא ויוצאין בה והיא כמין אצעדה שעושה לשוקיה מעל בתי שוקיה להדקן שלא יפלו על רגלה. טהורה, דלאו תכשיט היא אלא תשמיש לבתי שוקיה [והרי הוא] כטבעת הכלים דאמרן טהורות בפרקין דלעיל ויוצאין בה שצריך לה עם בתי שוקיה ולא הוי משאוי ויוצאין דכיון דלצניעותא היא לא שלפא ומחוי [לעיל ס.]. **קולפא.** מקל לרדות [ברכות נח.]. **שרגא בטיהרא.** נר בצהרים אינו מאיר [חולין ס:]. **ופליגא דשמואל.** דאמר ימות המשיח אין משתנין משל עכשיו [פסחים סח.]. **לא נתנבאו.** טובה לישראל [סנהדרין צט.]. הטובות והנחמות [ברכות לד:]. **עין לא ראתה.** זולתי עין של הקב"ה את אשר יעשה למחכה לו לא נראה כבוד וגדולה דוגמתה [ע"ז סה.]. דאין קץ לדבר [סנהדרין שם]. לא נראית ולא נגלית לשום נביא [ברכות שם]. עין שום נביא לא ראתה את אשר יעשה הקב"ה למחכה לו זולתי עיניך אתה אלהים [ישעיה סד, ג]. **האי בדברי תורה כתיב.** חגור חרבך על ירך להלחם מלחמתה של תורה והוא הודך והוא הדרך [תהלים מה, ד]. **אין מקרא יוצא מידי פשוטו.** ואע"ג דדרשינן ליה לדרשא מידי פשוטו מיהו לא נפיק לגמרי [יבמות כד.]. **על דבר אמת.** להורות כדת ולהתנהג בענות צדק [תהלים מה, ה עיין במהרש"א ח"א]. **בימינה.** למיימינים בה ועוסקים בה לשמה אורך ימים וכ"ש עושר וכבוד ולמשמאילים בה שעוסקי' בה שלא לשמה מ"מ עושר וכבוד יש [משלי ג, טז ועי' דה"ב א, יב]. **למיימינין.** עסוקים בכל כחם וטרודים לדעת סודה כאדם המשתמש ביד ימינו שהיא עיקר [לקמן פח:]. **ידבר עמים תחתינו.** ומנחם חבר ידבר ל' הנהגה [תהלים מז, ד]. ינהל עמים תחתינו [מכות יא.]. **שומר מצוה לא ידע דבר רע.** אם שומר מצוה אתה לא תדע דבר רע ולא תבוקך. **באשר דבר מלך שלטון.** בשביל אשר דבר הקב"ה מושל הוא ומי יאמר לו מה תעשה [קהלת ח, ד]. **נוקם.** נקמתו. **ונוטר כנחש.** נוטר איבה כנחש בלבו [יומא כג.].

מסורת הש"ס

א) פי' מגן, ב) נ"ל לא, ג) [גיר' הערוך מאי אלה קופל פי' דומה למקל וכו' וראשו עגול כמו כדור וכו' ע"ש], ד) [פי' שבט שמכין בו וראשו עב], ה) [במיכה כתיב ישאו], ו) חולין ס:, ז) ברכות לד: לקמן קנא: פסחים סח. סנהדרין צא: צט., ח) י"כ דרבינא, ט) [יבמות דף יא: כד.], י) מכות יא., כ) ברכות ו. קדושין מ. ע"ש, ל) [מ"ק טז: ב"מ פה.], מ) [עי' תוס' ע"ז כב: ד"ה רגלא וכו' שהשיגו אפירוש רש"י דהכא], נ) [עתו' ע"ז שם], ס) [נ"ל וא"ר], ע) פסחים נג:, פ) [נ"ל וא"ר], צ) [נ"ל ר' שמעון בן לקיש], ק) [ועי' תוס' תענית יג: ד"ה מאי שייר ותוס' מגילה ח. ד"ה אין בין ומ"ש שם על הגליון].

הגהות הב"ח

(א) רש"י ד"ה ותורך ותלמדך הס"ד ואח"כ מ"ה עושר וכבוד וכו' עושר וכבוד הס"ד ואח"כ מ"ה למיימינין בה שמפשפשין כצ"ל ותיבת של תורה נמחק ונ"ב ע"ל בדף פח ע"ב:

גליון הש"ס

גמ' **אלא שעבוד גליות.** עי' פסחים נ ע"ב:

תורה אור השלם

א) וְשָׁפַט בֵּין הַגּוֹיִם וְהוֹכִיחַ לְעַמִּים רַבִּים וְכִתְּתוּ חַרְבוֹתָם לְאִתִּים וַחֲנִיתוֹתֵיהֶם לְמַזְמֵרוֹת לֹא יִשָּׂא גוֹי אֶל גּוֹי חֶרֶב וְלֹא יִלְמְדוּ עוֹד מִלְחָמָה: [ישעיה ב, ד]

ב) כִּי לֹא יֶחְדַּל אֶבְיוֹן מִקֶּרֶב הָאָרֶץ עַל כֵּן אָנֹכִי מְצַוְּךָ לֵאמֹר פָּתֹחַ תִּפְתַּח אֶת יָדְךָ לְאָחִיךָ לַעֲנִיֶּךָ וּלְאֶבְיֹנְךָ בְּאַרְצֶךָ: [דברים טו, יא]

ג) וּמֵעוֹלָם לֹא שָׁמְעוּ לֹא הֶאֱזִינוּ עַיִן לֹא רָאָתָה אֱלֹהִים זוּלָתְךָ יַעֲשֶׂה לִמְחַכֵּה לוֹ: [ישעיה סד, ג]

ד) חֲגוֹר חַרְבְּךָ עַל יָרֵךְ גִּבּוֹר הוֹדְךָ וַהֲדָרֶךָ: [תהלים מה, ד]

ה) וַהֲדָרְךָ צְלַח רְכַב עַל דְּבַר אֱמֶת וְעַנְוָה צֶדֶק וְתוֹרְךָ נוֹרָאוֹת יְמִינֶךָ: [תהלים מה, ה]

ו) אֹרֶךְ יָמִים בִּימִינָהּ בִּשְׂמֹאולָהּ עֹשֶׁר וְכָבוֹד: [משלי ג, טז]

ז) אָז נִדְבְּרוּ יִרְאֵי יְיָ אִישׁ אֶל רֵעֵהוּ וַיַּקְשֵׁב יְיָ וַיִּשְׁמָע וַיִּכָּתֵב סֵפֶר זִכָּרוֹן לְפָנָיו לְיִרְאֵי יְיָ וּלְחֹשְׁבֵי שְׁמוֹ: [מלאכי ג, טז]

ח) יַדְבֵּר עַמִּים תַּחְתֵּינוּ וּלְאֻמִּים תַּחַת רַגְלֵינוּ: [תהלים מז, ד]

ט) שׁוֹמֵר מִצְוָה לֹא יֵדַע דָּבָר רָע וְעֵת וּמִשְׁפָּט יֵדַע לֵב חָכָם: [קהלת ח, ה]

י) בַּאֲשֶׁר דְּבַר מֶלֶךְ שִׁלְטוֹן וּמִי יֹאמַר לוֹ מַה תַּעֲשֶׂה: [קהלת ח, ד] כ) הַיּוֹשֶׁבֶת בַּגַּנִּים חֲבֵרִים מַקְשִׁיבִים לְקוֹלֵךְ הַשְׁמִיעִנִי: [שיר השירים ח, יג] ל) בְּרַח דּוֹדִי וּדְמֵה לְךָ לִצְבִי אוֹ לְעֹפֶר הָאַיָּלִים עַל הָרֵי בְשָׂמִים: [שיר השירים ח, יד]

מ) הֱבִיאַנִי אֶל בֵּית הַיָּיִן וְדִגְלוֹ עָלַי אַהֲבָה: [שיר השירים ב, ד] נ) לַמָּס מֵרֵעֵהוּ חָסֶד וְיִרְאַת שַׁדַּי יַעֲזוֹב: [איוב ו, יד]

שִׁיעְבּוּד גָּלֻיּוֹת בִּלְבַד – **for Shmuel said: There is no** difference **between this world and the Messianic era except the subjugation of** the Jews in the various **exiles,**[16] שֶׁנֶּאֱמַר ,,כִּי לֹא־יֶחְדַּל אֶבְיוֹן מִקֶּרֶב הָאָרֶץ״ – **as it is stated:** ***For the poor will not cease from the midst of the land.***[17] מְסַיֵּיעַ לֵיהּ לְרַבִּי חִיָּיא בַּר אַבָּא – On the other hand, **[our Baraisa],** which holds that *Isaiah* 2:4 and the prophetic consolations relate to the Messianic era, **supports** the opinion of **R' Chiya bar Abba,** דְּאָמַר רַבִּי חִיָּיא בַּר אַבָּא כָּל הַנְּבִיאִים לֹא נִתְנַבְּאוּ אֶלָּא לִימוֹת הַמָּשִׁיחַ – for R' Chiya bar Abba said: All the prophets prophesied only about the Messianic era, אֲבָל לָעוֹלָם הַבָּא ,,עַיִן לֹא־רָאָתָה אֱלֹהִים זוּלָתְךָ״ – but regarding the World to Come it is said: ***No eye has seen, O God, except You,*** *that which He will do for one who waits for Him.*[18]

The Gemara cites a different version of the foregoing Baraisa: וְאִיכָּא דְּאָמְרֵי אָמְרוּ לוֹ לְרַבִּי אֱלִיעֶזֶר – **But there are those who say** that the Baraisa reads as follows: [THE SAGES] SAID TO R' ELIEZER: וְכִי מֵאַחַר דְּתַכְשִׁיטִין הֵן לוֹ – INASMUCH AS [THESE WEAPONS] ARE ORNAMENTS FOR HIM, מִפְּנֵי מָה הֵן בְּטֵלִין לִימוֹת הַמָּשִׁיחַ – WHY WILL THEY BE ELIMINATED IN THE MESSIANIC ERA? אָמַר לָהֶן אַף לִימוֹת הַמָּשִׁיחַ אֵינָן בְּטֵלִין – [R' ELIEZER] SAID TO THEM: THEY WILL NOT BE ELIMINATED EVEN IN THE MESSIANIC ERA.

The Gemara comments on this second version of the Baraisa: הַיְינוּ דִּשְׁמוּאֵל – **This** opinion of R' Eliezer **is** consistent with the opinion **of Shmuel,** who said that the Messianic era will not usher in any change in the natural order, and so weapons will still be needed; וּפְלִיגָא דְּרַבִּי חִיָּיא בַּר אַבָּא – **and it disagrees with** the opinion **of R' Chiya bar Abba,** who holds that all the prophecies, including *nation shall not lift up a sword against nation,* refer to the Messianic era.

The Gemara cites the basis for R' Eliezer's opinion: אָמַר לֵיהּ אַבַּיֵּי לְרַב דִּימִי – **Abaye said to Rav Dimi;** וְאָמְרֵי לָהּ לְרַב אַוְיָא – **and some say that** Abaye said it **to Rav Avya;** וְאָמְרֵי לָהּ רַב יוֹסֵף לְרַב דִּימִי – **and some say that Rav Yosef** said it **to Rav Dimi;** וְאָמְרֵי לָהּ לְרַב אַוְיָא – **and some say that** Rav Yosef said it **to Rav Avya;** וְאָמְרֵי לָהּ אַבַּיֵּי לְרַב יוֹסֵף – and some say **that: Abaye** said **to Rav Yosef:** מַאי טַעְמָא דְּרַבִּי אֱלִיעֶזֶר דְּאָמַר תַּכְשִׁיטִין הֵן לוֹ – What is the reason of R' Eliezer, who said that [weapons] **are ornaments for [a man]?** דִּכְתִיב ,,חֲגוֹר־חַרְבְּךָ עַל־יָרֵךְ גִּבּוֹר הוֹדְךָ וַהֲדָרֶךָ״ – **Because it is written** in a psalm praising the king of Israel:[19] ***Gird your sword upon [your] thigh, O mighty one,*** [for it is] ***your glory and your splendor.***

An objection is raised to this choice of verse: אָמַר לֵיהּ רַב כַּהֲנָא לְמַר בְּרֵיהּ דְּרַב הוּנָא – **Rav Kahana said to Mar, the son of Rav Huna:** הַאי בְּדִבְרֵי תוֹרָה כְּתִיב – **This is written regarding words of Torah,**[20] and is not to be taken literally, as pertaining to weapons.

The Gemara defends the proof: אָמַר לֵיהּ – **[Mar, the son of Rav Huna] said to [Rav Kahana]:** אֵין מִקְרָא יוֹצֵא מִידֵי פְשׁוּטוֹ – **A verse never departs from its plain meaning.**[21]

Rav Kahana accepts this point: אָמַר רַב כַּהֲנָא כַּד הֲוֵינָא בַּר תַּמְנֵי סְרֵי שְׁנִין – **Rav Kahana said: When I was eighteen years of age** וַהֲוָה גְּמִירְנָא לֵיהּ לְכוּלֵּיהּ (הש״ס) [תַּלְמוּדָא] – **I had learned the entire Talmud,**[22] וְלָא הֲוָה יָדַעְנָא דְּאֵין מִקְרָא יוֹצֵא מִידֵי פְשׁוּטוֹ עַד הַשְׁתָּא – **but I did not know that a verse never departs from its plain meaning until now.**

The Gemara draws a lesson from this statement: מַאי קָא מַשְׁמַע לָן – **What does [Rav Kahana] teach us?** דְּלִיגְמַר אִינִישׁ וַהֲדַר לִיסְבַּר – **That a person should** first **learn, and afterward reason.**[23]

The Gemara offers an aid for remembering the forthcoming discussions:

סִימָן זָרוֹת – **A mnemonic:** ***Zaros.***[24]

The first discussion, in which the previously cited passage from *Psalms* is further expounded: אָמַר רַבִּי יִרְמְיָה אָמַר רַבִּי אֶלְעָזָר – **R' Yirmiyah said in the name of R' Elazar:** שְׁנֵי תַלְמִידֵי חֲכָמִים הַמְחַדְּדִין זֶה לָזֶה בַּהֲלָכָה – When

NOTES

established as authoritive. Or perhaps, since the topic is Aggadic, Shmuel is empowered to challenge the Baraisa (*Rashash*).

16. Shmuel maintains that the Messianic era does not usher in any change in the natural order. What *will* change is that all Jews will return to Eretz Yisrael from the lands of their exile and dwell there in complete security and independence (see also *Rambam, Hil. Melachim* chs. 11-12 at length). [Hence, the need for weapons will exist only for the other nations, who will still battle one another (*Maharsha* here). According to Shmuel, then, *Isaiah* 2:4 (*They shall beat their swords* etc.) does not describe the circumstances of the Messianic era. See following note.] Cf. *Ritva, MHK* ed.

Tosafos note that Shmuel's dictum is not to be taken literally: To be sure, there will be other differences between this world and the Messianic era – the existence of a rebuilt Jerusalem and Holy Temple not the least of these!

17. *Deuteronomy* 15:11. This verse implies that in this world there will always be poverty and wealth – and the Messianic era is part of this world. Therefore, the consolations of the prophets [e.g. וְלֹא־יִהְיֶה כְנַעֲנִי עוֹד, *There shall no more be paupers* (*Zechariah* 14:21)] do not refer to the Messianic era (*Rashi*). Rather, they refer to the next world. Likewise, our verse (*Isaiah* 2:4), which foretells the end of wars, refers to the next world.

However, according to Shmuel "the next world" does not mean the world of souls, where the righteous will sit with "crowns" on their heads delighting in the radiance of the Divine Presence (*Berachos* 17a), for in that world there is no bodily activity. *Isaiah* 2:4, on the other hand, implies that people will still use hoes and pruning shears. Hence, "the next world" of *Isaiah* 2:4 and the verses of consolation must be the time of the Resurrection of the Dead, when there will be bodily activity, as distinguished from the world of souls, where there is only spiritual existence (*Maharsha*).

18. *Isaiah* 64:3. [Even] the eyes of the prophets were not capable of seeing the World to Come (*Rashi*).

19. *Psalms* 45:4.

20. The verse states metaphorically: Be careful to review your learning so that it will be a ready source of proof for you when debating the law, just as a sword stands ready upon the thigh of a mighty warrior, with which he triumphs in battle; and this ability to recall your learning is *your glory and your splendor* (*Rashi*).

21. Even when a verse is expounded exegetically, its literal meaning is not completely discarded (*Rashi* to *Yevamos* 24a). Hence, R' Eliezer is justified in using the literal meaning of this verse as a proof.

22. Emendation follows *Dikdukei Soferim*.

23. One should first learn the Talmud from his teacher, even though he does not understand the rationale of every statement, and only afterward should he probe for the reasoning. Rav Kahana himself exemplifies this principle, for he did not understand how the verse provided the basis for R' Eliezer's opinion, and did not know the reason given by our Gemara [namely, that a verse never departs from its plain meaning] – and yet he had known the entire Talmud since the age of eighteen (*Rashi*). See also *Maharatz Chayes*.

24. The Gemara will now present a series of dicta on the topic of Torah study, many of them reported by R' Yirmiyah and R' Abba in the name of R' Elazar or Reish Lakish. The mnemonic זרות, *zaros,* is actually an acronym that suggests the four aforementioned Amoraim: ר׳ אֶלְעָזָר = ז (z = R' Elazar); רֵישׁ לָקִישׁ = ר (r = **R**eish Lakish); וְתַלְמִידֵיהֶן = ות [the letters ו and ת **(os)** are the first two letters of *and their students,* which alludes to R' Yirmiyah and R' Abba, who were disciples of R' Elazar and Reish Lakish] (*R' David Pardo,* cited by *Toldos Tannaim v'Amoraim* in "*Simanei HaShas*").

בייו חרדלי במסב רחב או במסב קצר בחבר טוב או בחבר רע א"ר חסדא וכולן לזנות אמר רחבה אמר רבי יהודה עצי ירושלים של קינמון היו ובשעה שהיו מסיקין מהן ריחן נודף בכל ארץ ישראל ומשחרבה ירושלים נגנזו ולא נשתייר אלא כשעורה ומשתכח בגזאי דצימצמאי מלכתא:

מתני' א) לא יצא האיש לא בסייף ולא בקשת ולא א) בתרים ולא באלה ולא ברומח ואם יצא חייב חטאת רבי אליעזר אומר תכשיטין הן לו וחכ"א אינן אלא לגנאי שנאמר א) וכתתו חרבותם לאתים וחניתותיהם למזמרות ב) ולא ישא גוי אל גוי חרב ולא ילמדו עוד מלחמה בירית טהורה ויוצאין בה בשבת כבלים טמאים ואין יוצאין בהן בשבת: גמ' ג) מאי באלה ד) קולפא: ר' אליעזר אומר תכשיטין הן לו: תניא אמרו לו לרבי אליעזר וכי מאחר דתכשיטין הן לו מפני מה הן בטלין לימות המשיח אמר להן לפי שאינן צריכין שנאמר א) לא ה) ישא גוי אל גוי חרב ותהוי לנוי בעלמא אמר אביי מידי דהוה ו) אשרגא בטיהרא ופליגא דשמואל דאמר שמואל ז) ב אין בין העולם הזה לימות המשיח אלא שיעבוד גליות בלבד שנאמר ב) כי לא יחדל אביון מקרב הארץ מסייע ליה לרבי חייא בר אבא דא"ר חייא בר אבא ג כל הנביאים לא נתנבאו אלא לימות המשיח אבל לעולם הבא ג) עין לא ראתה אלהים זולתך ואיכא דאמרי אמרו לו לר' אליעזר וכי מאחר דתכשיטין הן לו מפני מה הן בטלין לימות המשיח אמר להן אף לימות המשיח אינן בטלין היינו דשמואל ופליגא דר' חייא בר אבא א"ל אביי לרב דימי ואמרי לה לרב אויא ואמרי לה רב יוסף לרב דימי ואמרי לה לרב אויא ואמרי לה אביי לרב יוסף מ"ט דר"א דאמר תכשיטין הן לו דכתיב ד) חגור חרבך על ירך גבור הודך והדרך א"ל רב כהנא למר בריה ח) דרב הונא האי בדברי תורה כתיב א"ל ט) אין מקרא יוצא מידי פשוטו א"ר כהנא כד הוינא בר תמני סרי שנין והוה גמירנא ליה לכוליה הש"ס ולא הוה ידענא דאין מקרא יוצא מידי פשוטו עד השתא מאי קמ"ל דליגמר איניש והדר ליסבר: סימן זרות: א"ר ירמיה א"ר אלעזר שני תלמידי חכמים המחדדין זה לזה בהלכה הקב"ה מצליח להם שנאמר ה) והדרך צלח אל תקרי והדרך אלא וחדדך ולא עוד אלא שעולין לגדולה שנאמר ה) צלח רכב יכול אפילו שלא לשמה תלמוד לומר ה) על דבר אמת יכול אם הגים דעתו ת"ל ה) וענוה צדק ואם עושין כן זוכין לתורה שניתנה בימין שנאמר ה) ותורך נוראות ימינך רב נחמן בר יצחק אמר זוכין לדברים שנאמרו בימינה של תורה דאמר רבא בר רב שילא ואמרי לה אמר רב יוסף בר חמא א"ר ששת מאי דכתיב ו) אורך ימים בימינה בשמאלה עושר וכבוד אלא בימינה אורך ימים איכא עושר וכבוד ליכא אלא למיימינין בה אורך ימים איכא וכ"ש עושר וכבוד למשמאילים בה עושר וכבוד איכא אורך ימים ליכא א"ר ירמיה אמר ר' שמעון בן לקיש שני תלמידי חכמים הנוחין זה לזה בהלכה הקדוש ברוך הוא מקשיב להן שנאמר ז) אז נדברו יראי ה' וגו' י) אין דיבור אלא נחת שנאמר ח) ידבר עמים תחתינו כ) מאי ל) ולחושבי שמו א"ר אמי אפילו חישב לעשות מצוה ונאנס ולא עשאה מעלה עליו הכתוב כאילו עשאה א"ר חיננא בר אידי כל העושה מצוה כמאמרה אין מבשרין אותו בשורות רעות שנאמר ט) שומר מצוה לא ידע דבר רע א"ר אסי ואיתימא ר' חנינא אפילו הקב"ה ל) גוזר גזירה הוא מבטלה שנאמר י) באשר דבר מלך שלטון ומי יאמר לו מה תעשה וסמיך ליה ט) שומר מצוה לא ידע דבר רע אמר רבי אבא אמר רבי שמעון בן לקיש שני תלמידי חכמים המקשיבים זה לזה בהלכה הקדוש ב"ה שומע לקולן שנאמר כ) היושבת בגנים חברים מקשיבים לקולך השמיעני ואם אין עושין כן גורמין לשכינה שמסתלקת מישראל שנאמר ל) ברח דודי ודמה וגו' אמר רבי אבא א"ר שמעון בן לקיש שני ת"ח מ) המדגילים זה לזה בהלכה הקדוש ברוך הוא אוהבן שנאמר מ) ודגלו עלי אהבה אמר רבא והוא דידעי צורתא דשמעתא נ) והוא דלית להו רבה במתא למיגמר מיניה (פ) א"ר) אבא א"ר שמעון בן לקיש ד גדול המלוה יותר מן העושה צדקה ע) ומטיל בכים יותר מכולן (פ) א"ר) אבא אמר ר' שמעון בן לקיש ה אם תלמיד חכם נוקם ונוטר כנחש הוא חגריהו על מתניך אם עם הארץ הוא חסיד אל תדור בשכונתו אמר רב כהנא אמר רבי שמעון בן לקיש ואמרי לה אמר רב אסי אמר (צ) ריש לקיש) ואמרי לה אמר רבי אבא אמר רבי שמעון בן לקיש ו כל המגדל כלב רע בתוך ביתו מונע חסד מתוך ביתו שנאמר נ) למס מרעהו

רש"י

בייו חרדלי. שחור כלומר לבנה או שחורה: במסב רחב. מיסב מטה שמיסב עליה בשעת אכילה ולענין ניאוף אשה שמנה: קצר. כחושה: חבר טוב. אשה טובת מראה: דצימצמאי מלכתא. כך שמה: מתני' באלה. מפרש בגמ' קולפא מלוק"ה בלע"ז: וכתתו חרבותם. ואי תכשיטין נינהו לא יהו בטלין לעתיד: בירית. בגמרא מפרש: טהורה. אינה מקבלת טומאה: ויוצאין בה. דלא שלפא ומחויא שלא יראה שוקה: כבלין טמאין. בגמ' מפרש לה: גמ' שרגא בטיהרא. נר בצהרים מתוך שאינו צריך אינו נאה אבל בזמן הזה שהוא עת מלחמה תכשיטין הן: ופליגא. הא דקתני בטלין לימות המשיח פליגא דשמואל דלשמואל אין בטלין לימות המשיח: לא יחדל. משמע לעולם אלמא יש עניות ועשירות ש"מ נחמות שנתנבאו הנביאים ולא יהיה כנעני עוד (זכריה יד) לא לימות המשיח נתנבאו שהן מן העולם הזה דאם כן חדל לך אביון: מסייע ליה. ברייתא דקתני בטלין לימות המשיח לרבי חייא בר אבא: לא נתנבאו. דברי נחמות שלהן: עין לא ראתה. עין של נביאים לא שלטה לראותו: בדברי תורה כתיב. הוי זהיר לחזור על משנתך שתהא מזומנת לך בשעת הדין להביא ראיה כחרב על ירך גבור לנצח במלחמה והוא הודך והדרך: דליגמר איניש. לגרוס שמעתא מרביה ואף על גב דלא ידע לכולהו טעמיה: והדר ליסבר. טעמיה דהא קשה ליה לרב כהנא ולא הוה ידע להאי טעמא ותלמודיה הוה קים ליה מדהוה בר תמני סרי: המחדדין. שואלין ומשיבין ולא לקפח אלא להתחדד: והדרך. כמו וחדדך: ותורך. ותלמדך (א): למיימינין. של תורה שמפספסין טעמיהן בדקדוק וזוררין כימין המיומנת למלאכה: עושר וכבוד ליכא. בתמיה כיון דאיכא אורך ימים כ"ש עושר וכבוד: למשמאילין בה. שאין יגעים בה כל צרכן אי נמי מיימינין בה עוסקין לשמה משמאילים שלא לשמה: הנוחין זה לזה. נושאין ונותנין בה בנחת רוח מתעסקין כדי שילמדו זה מזה: ידבר עמים תחתינו. ישפיל וכל שפלות בנחת ל"א הנוחין מנהיגין זה את זה להבנתה של הלכה כמו לך נחה (שמות לב) ידבר תרגום של ינהג: ומי יאמר לו מה תעשה. שומר מצות יוכל לומר לו: המקשיבין. מלמדים זה את זה ומבינים זה מזה ולישנא דקרא נקט: בגנים. בתי מדרשות: חבירים מקשיבים. זה לזה להם אני אומר שישמיעוני קולם ולענם: ברח דודי. בתריה כתיב: המדגילים. מאספין זה את זה ואומרים בא ונלמוד ונבין בין שנינו הואיל ואין לנו רב ללמדנו: צורתא. שורש הדבר קצת למדו מרבם: גדול המלוה. לפי שאין העני בוש בדבר: ומטיל לכים. מעות ומלאי להשתכר בהן למחצית שכר ואיידי דאיירי רבי אבא אמר ריש לקיש נקט כל הני מילי דאגדתא דאמר להו ר' אבא משמיה: חוגרו. הדבק בו שסופך ליהנות מתלמודו: אל תדור בשכונתו. שאינו יודע בדקדוקי מצות ואין חסידותו שלם וסופך ללמוד ממנו: מונע חסד. שאינו מניח העניים לבא לפתחו: למס. דהיינו כלב:

תוספות

אין בין העוה"ז לימות המשיח. אע"ג דהשתא אין ירושלים ואין בהמ"ק ואילו לימות המשיח יהיה הכל בנוי צ"ל דהאי אין בין לאו דוקא ק): ואילו

עין משפט נר מצוה

מט א מיי' פי"ט מהל' שבת הלכה א סמג לאוין סה טוש"ע א"ח סי' ש"א סעיף ז:
נ ב מיי' פי"ב מהל' מלכים הלכה ב:
נא ג מיי' פ"ח מהל' תשובה הלכה ז:
נב ד מיי' פ"י מהל' מ"ע הלכה ח טוש"ע י"ד סי' רמט סעיף ו:
נג ה מיי' פ"ו מהל' דעות הלכה א ג:
נד ו מיי' פי"א מהל' רוצח הלכה ד:

ליקוטי רש"י

ולא בתרים. תריסין. מגינים [בכורות לו.]. וכתתו חרבותם לאתים. קולטר"ש בלע"ז. למזמרות. שרפ"ש בלע"ז שזומרין בהן הכרמים [ישעיה ב, ד]. בירית טהורה. אלטמא ויוצאין בה והיא כמין אצעדה שעושה לשוקיה מעל בתי שוקיה להדקן שלא יפלו על רגלה. טהורה, דלאו תכשיט היא אלא תשמיש לבתי שוקיה [והרי הוא] כטבעת הכלים דאמרן טהורות בפרקין דלעיל ויוצאין בה שצריך לה עם בתי שוקיה ולא הוי משאוי ויוצאין דכיון דלצניעותא היא לא שלפא ומחוי [לעיל ס.]. קולפא. מקל לרדות [ברכות נח.]. שרגא בטיהרא. נר בצהרים אינו מאיר [חולין ס:]. ופליגא דשמואל. דאמר ימות המשיח אין משתנין משל עכשיו [פסחים סח.]. לא נתנבאו. טובה לישראל [סנהדרין צט.]. הטובות והנחמות [ברכות לד:]. עין לא ראתה. זולתי עין של הקב"ה את אשר יעשה למחכה לו לא נראה כבוד וגדולה דוגמתה [ע"ז סה.]. דאין קץ לדבר [סנהדרין שם]. לא נראית ולא נגלית לשום נביא [ברכות שם]. עין שום נביא לא ראתה את אשר יעשה הקב"ה למחכה לו זולתי עיניך אתה אלהים [ישעיה סד, ג]. האי בדברי תורה כתיב. חגור חרבך על ירך להלחם מלחמתה של תורה והוא הודך והוא הדרך [תהלים מה, ד]. אין מקרא יוצא מידי פשוטו. ואע"ג דדרשינן ליה לדרשא מידי פשוטו מיהו לא נפיק לגמרי [יבמות כד.]. על דבר אמת. להורות כדת ולהתנהג בענות לדק [תהלים מה, ה עיין במהרש"א ח"א]. בימינה. למיימינים בה ועוסקים בה לשמה אורך ימים וכ"ש עושר וכבוד ולמשמאילים בה שעוסקי' בה שלא לשמה מ"מ עושר וכבוד יש [משלי ג, טז ועי' דה"ב א, יב]. למיימינין. עסוקים בכל כחם וטרודים לדעת סודה כאדם המשתמש ביד ימינו שהיא עיקר [לקמן פח:]. ידבר עמים תחתינו. ומנחם חבר ידבר ל' הנהגה [תהלים מז, ד]. ינהל עמים תחתינו [מכות יא.]. שומר מצוה לא ידע דבר רע. אם שומר מצוה אתה לא תדע דבר רע ולא תבואך. באשר דבר מלך שלטון. בשביל אשר דבר הקב"ה מושל הוא ומי יאמר לו מה תעשה [קהלת ח, ד]. נוקם. נקמתו. ונוטר כנחש. נוטר איבה כנחש בלבו [יומא כג.].

מסורת הש"ס

א) פי' מגן, ב) נ"ל לא, ג) [גיר' הערוך מאי אלה קופל פי' דומה למקל וכו' וראשו עגול כמו כדור וכו' ע"ש], ד) [פי' שבט שמכין בו וראשו עב], ה) [במיכה כתיב ישאו], ו) חולין ס., ז) ברכות לד: לקמן קנא: פסחים סח. סנהדרין צא: צט., ח) י"ג דרבינא, ט) [יבמות דף יא: כד.], י) מכות יא., כ) ברכות ו. קדושין מ. ע"ש, ל) [מ"ק טז: ב"מ פה.], מ) [עי' תוס' ע"ז כב: ד"ה רגלא וכו' שהשיגו אפירוש רש"י דהכא], נ) [עתו' ע"ז שם], ס) [נ"ל וא"ר], ע) פסחים נג:, פ) [נ"ל וא"ר], צ) [נ"ל ר' שמעון בן לקיש], ק) [ועי' תוס' תענית יג: ד"ה מאי שייר ותוס' מגילה ח. ד"ה אין בין ומ"ש שם על הגליון].

הגהות הב"ח

(א) רש"י ד"ה ותורך ותלמדך הס"ד ואח"כ מ"ה עושר וכבוד וכו' עושר וכבוד הס"ד ואח"כ מ"ה למיימינין בה שמפספסין כצ"ל ותיבת של תורה נמחק וכ"ב ע"ל בדף פח ע"ב:

גליון הש"ס

גמ' אלא שעבוד גליות. עי' פסחים נ ע"ב:

תורה אור השלם

א) וְשָׁפַט בֵּין הַגּוֹיִם וְהוֹכִיחַ לְעַמִּים רַבִּים וְכִתְּתוּ חַרְבוֹתָם לְאִתִּים וַחֲנִיתוֹתֵיהֶם לְמַזְמֵרוֹת לֹא יִשָּׂא גוֹי אֶל גּוֹי חֶרֶב וְלֹא יִלְמְדוּ עוֹד מִלְחָמָה: [ישעיה ב, ד]
ב) כִּי לֹא יֶחְדַּל אֶבְיוֹן מִקֶּרֶב הָאָרֶץ עַל כֵּן אָנֹכִי מְצַוְּךָ לֵאמֹר פָּתֹחַ תִּפְתַּח אֶת יָדְךָ לְאָחִיךָ לַעֲנִיֶּךָ וּלְאֶבְיֹנְךָ בְּאַרְצֶךָ: [דברים טו, יא]
ג) וּמֵעוֹלָם לֹא שָׁמְעוּ לֹא הֶאֱזִינוּ עַיִן לֹא רָאָתָה אֱלֹהִים זוּלָתְךָ יַעֲשֶׂה לִמְחַכֵּה לוֹ: [ישעיה סד, ג]
ד) חֲגוֹר חַרְבְּךָ עַל יָרֵךְ גִּבּוֹר הוֹדְךָ וַהֲדָרֶךָ: [תהלים מה, ד]
ה) וַהֲדָרְךָ צְלַח רְכַב עַל דְּבַר אֱמֶת וְעַנְוָה צֶדֶק וְתוֹרְךָ נוֹרָאוֹת יְמִינֶךָ: [תהלים מה, ה]
ו) אֹרֶךְ יָמִים בִּימִינָהּ בִּשְׂמֹאולָהּ עֹשֶׁר וְכָבוֹד: [משלי ג, טז]
ז) אָז נִדְבְּרוּ יִרְאֵי יְיָ אִישׁ אֶל רֵעֵהוּ וַיַּקְשֵׁב יְיָ וַיִּשְׁמָע וַיִּכָּתֵב סֵפֶר זִכָּרוֹן לְפָנָיו לְיִרְאֵי יְיָ וּלְחֹשְׁבֵי שְׁמוֹ: [מלאכי ג, טז]
ח) יַדְבֵּר עַמִּים תַּחְתֵּינוּ וּלְאֻמִּים תַּחַת רַגְלֵינוּ: [תהלים מז, ד]
ט) שׁוֹמֵר מִצְוָה לֹא יֵדַע דָּבָר רָע וְעֵת וּמִשְׁפָּט יֵדַע לֵב חָכָם: [קהלת ח, ה]
י) בַּאֲשֶׁר דְּבַר מֶלֶךְ שִׁלְטוֹן וּמִי יֹאמַר לוֹ מַה תַּעֲשֶׂה: [קהלת ח, ד]
כ) הַיּוֹשֶׁבֶת בַּגַּנִּים חֲבֵרִים מַקְשִׁיבִים לְקוֹלֵךְ הַשְׁמִיעִנִי: [שיר השירים ח, יג]
ל) בְּרַח דּוֹדִי וּדְמֵה לְךָ לִצְבִי אוֹ לְעֹפֶר הָאַיָּלִים עַל הָרֵי בְשָׂמִים: [שיר השירים ח, יד]
מ) הֱבִיאַנִי אֶל בֵּית הַיָּיִן וְדִגְלוֹ עָלַי אַהֲבָה: [שיר השירים ב, ד]
נ) לַמָּס מֵרֵעֵהוּ חָסֶד וְיִרְאַת שַׁדַּי יַעֲזוֹב: [איוב ו, יד]

two Torah scholars sharpen[25] each other in the Law, הַקָּדוֹשׁ בָּרוּךְ הוּא מַצְלִיחַ לָהֶם – the Holy One, Blessed is He, grants them success, שֶׁנֶּאֱמַר ,,וַהֲדָרְךָ צְלַח'' – as it is stated:[26] *And with your splendor, succeed.* אַל תִּקְרֵי ,,וַהֲדָרְךָ'' אֶלָּא ,,וַחֲדָרְךָ'' – Read not *your splendor,* but "your sharpening."[27] וְלֹא עוֹד אֶלָּא שֶׁעוֹלִין לִגְדוּלָּה – And not only that, but they rise to greatness, to positions of power and influence, שֶׁנֶּאֱמַר ,,צְלַח רְכַב'' – as it is stated in the same verse: *Succeed, ride [on royal steeds].*[28] יָכוֹל אֲפִילּוּ שֶׁלֹּא לִשְׁמָהּ – One might think that success and greatness are bestowed even if they are studying for ulterior motives; תַּלְמוּד לוֹמַר ,,עַל דְּבַר אֱמֶת'' – to dispel this notion the Torah states in the same verse: *for the sake of truth.* יָכוֹל אִם הֵגִיס דַּעְתּוֹ – One might also think that these blessings come even if [the scholar] is arrogant; תַּלְמוּד לוֹמַר ,,וְעַנְוָה צֶדֶק'' – to dispel this notion the Torah states in the same verse: *and righteous humility.* וְאִם עוֹשִׂין כֵּן זוֹכִין לְתוֹרָה שֶׁנִּיתְּנָה בְּיָמִין – And if they do this, if they study humbly and altruistically, they will merit to achieve the Torah, which was given with the right hand,[29] שֶׁנֶּאֱמַר ,,וְתוֹרְךָ נוֹרָאוֹת יְמִינֶךָ'' – as it is stated also in that verse: *and your right hand will teach you awesome things.*

Another Amora expounds the verse differently:

רַב נַחְמָן בַּר יִצְחָק אָמַר – Rav Nachman bar Yitzchak said: זוֹכִין לִדְבָרִים שֶׁנֶּאֶמְרוּ בִּימִינָהּ שֶׁל תּוֹרָה – [Two Torah scholars who "sharpen" each other in the Law] merit to receive things that are ascribed to the right hand of the Torah, דְּאָמַר רָבָא בַּר רַב שִׁילָא וְאָמְרֵי לָהּ אָמַר רַב יוֹסֵף בַּר חָמָא אָמַר רַב שֵׁשֶׁת – for Rava bar Rav Shila said, and some say: Rav Yosef bar Chama said in the name of Rav Sheishess: מַאי דִּכְתִיב ,,אֹרֶךְ יָמִים בִּימִינָהּ בִּשְׂמֹאלָהּ עֹשֶׁר וְכָבוֹד'' – What is the meaning of that which is written:[30] *Length of days is in her* [the Torah's] *right hand, in her left hand are wealth and honor?* אֶלָּא בִּימִינָהּ אוֹרֶךְ יָמִים אִיכָּא עוֹשֶׁר וְכָבוֹד לֵיכָּא – But can it mean that in her right hand there is length of days but there is no wealth or honor?! Of course not![31] אֶלָּא לַמַּיְימִינִין בָּהּ – Rather, the verse means that for those who deal with her right-handedly[32] אוֹרֶךְ יָמִים אִיכָּא וְכָל שֶׁכֵּן עוֹשֶׁר וְכָבוֹד – there is length of days and, all the more so, wealth and honor. לַמַּשְׂמְאִילִים בָּהּ – However, for those who deal with her left-handedly[33] עוֹשֶׁר וְכָבוֹד אִיכָּא אוֹרֶךְ יָמִים לֵיכָּא – there is wealth and honor, but there is no length of days.

The Gemara continues discussing the topic of Torah study:

אָמַר רַבִּי יִרְמְיָה אָמַר רַבִּי שִׁמְעוֹן בֶּן לָקִישׁ – R' Yirmiyah said in the name of R' Shimon ben Lakish: שְׁנֵי תַלְמִידֵי חֲכָמִים הַנּוֹחִין זֶה לָזֶה בַּהֲלָכָה – When two Torah scholars are pleasant toward one another in the course of debating the Law,[34] הַקָּדוֹשׁ בָּרוּךְ הוּא מַקְשִׁיב לָהֶן – the Holy One, Blessed is He, listens to them,[35] שֶׁנֶּאֱמַר ,,אָז נִדְבְּרוּ יִרְאֵי ה' וגו' '' – as it is stated:[36] *Then those who fear Hashem will speak* etc. [*with one another, and Hashem will hearken and hear*].

The Gemara explicates the verse:

אֵין דִּיבּוּר אֶלָּא נַחַת – The word דִּיבּוּר implies only pleasantness, שֶׁנֶּאֱמַר ,,יַדְבֵּר עַמִּים תַּחְתֵּינוּ'' – as it is stated: *He shall humble peoples beneath us, and nations under our feet.*[37]

The Gemara expounds the final words of the aforecited verse in *Malachi*:[38]

מַאי ,,וּלְחוֹשְׁבֵי שְׁמוֹ'' – What is the meaning of *and for those who ponder His Name?* אָמַר רַבִּי אַמִי אֲפִילּוּ חִישֵּׁב לַעֲשׂוֹת מִצְוָה וְנֶאֱנַס וְלֹא עֲשָׂאָהּ – R' Ami said: Even if one merely thought to perform a commandment of the Torah but was unavoidably prevented from doing so, מַעֲלֶה עָלָיו הַכָּתוּב כְּאִילּוּ עֲשָׂאָהּ – Scripture regards and rewards him as if he had performed it.

The Gemara pursues the theme of performing mitzvos:

אָמַר רַב חִינָּנָא בַּר אִידִי – Rav Chinana bar Idi said: כָּל הָעוֹשֶׂה מִצְוָה כְּמַאֲמָרָהּ – Regarding anyone who performs a commandment according to its utterance[39] – אֵין מְבַשְּׂרִין אוֹתוֹ בְּשׂוֹרוֹת רָעוֹת – they will never inform him of evil tidings, שֶׁנֶּאֱמַר ,,שׁוֹמֵר מִצְוָה לֹא יֵדַע דָּבָר רָע'' – as it is stated:[40] *He who guards a commandment shall know no evil thing.*[41] אָמַר רַב אַסִּי וְאִיתֵּימָא רַבִּי חֲנִינָא – Rav Assi – and some say R' Chanina – said: אֲפִילּוּ הַקָּדוֹשׁ בָּרוּךְ הוּא גּוֹזֵר גְּזֵירָה – Even if the Holy One, Blessed is He, decrees a harsh punishment, הוּא מְבַטְּלָהּ – [one who performs a mitzvah "according to its utterance"] can cancel it, שֶׁנֶּאֱמַר ,,בַּאֲשֶׁר דְּבַר־מֶלֶךְ שִׁלְטוֹן וּמִי יֹאמַר־לוֹ מַה־תַּעֲשֶׂה'' – for it is stated,[42] *For the word of the king has authority, and who can say to him, "What are you doing?"*

NOTES

25. They pose [challenging] questions and respond to one another – not in order to overpower the other, but to become sharper [in their understanding of the Law] (*Rashi*).

26. *Psalms* 45:5.

27. The word וַהֲדָרְךָ (*your splendor*) appears superfluous, since it is mentioned at the end of the previous verse; for that reason the Sages expounded it. The letters ר and ד may be interchanged since they are similar in shape (*Maharsha*). [Similarly, the letters ה and ח may be interchanged.]

28. *Targum* adds the words in brackets.

29. The word "Torah" suggests the rendering of halachic decisions (*moreh horaah*). That is, each of these scholars will merit to become a sage capable of rendering halachic decisions for the public. The Torah was given with the right hand, as it states (*Deuteronomy* 33:2): מִימִינוֹ אֵשׁ דָּת לָמוֹ, *From His right hand, a fiery Law for them* (*Maharsha*).

30. *Proverbs* 3:16.

31. If there is length of days, then all the more so should there be wealth and honor (*Rashi*).

32. Those who search out the precise reasons behind the Torah's teachings, examining and clarifying everything – like the right hand, which performs skillfully (*Rashi*).

33. Those who do not labor sufficiently in the Torah. Alternatively, "those who deal with her right-handedly" learn Torah for its own sake, while "those who deal with her left-handedly" learn for ulterior motives (*Rashi*).

34. They engage in Torah study with the intent to learn from each other (*Rashi*).

35. The Divine Presence is with them (*Berachos* 6a).

36. *Malachi* 3:16.

37. *Psalms* 47:4. The word יַדְבֵּר (*humble*) in this verse and the word נִדְבְּרוּ (*will speak*) in *Malachi* are both forms of דִּיבּוּר. Since the *Psalms* variant means *he shall humble,* one can expound the verse in *Malachi* as referring to a humble, pleasant manner of Talmudic discourse (*Rashi*; see *Hagahos R' Elazar Moshe Horowitz*).

Alternatively, the phrase הַנּוֹחִין זֶה לָזֶה בַּהֲלָכָה can be rendered *those who lead each other* [to the correct understanding of] the law [in which case the verse in *Psalms* 47 is translated: *He shall cause peoples to be led by us*] (ibid.).

38. *Malachi* 3:16 states in full: אָז נִדְבְּרוּ יִרְאֵי יהוה אִישׁ אֶל־רֵעֵהוּ וַיַּקְשֵׁב יהוה וַיִּשְׁמָע וַיִּכָּתֵב סֵפֶר זִכָּרוֹן לְפָנָיו לְיִרְאֵי יהוה וּלְחֹשְׁבֵי שְׁמוֹ, *Then those who fear Hashem will speak with one another, and Hashem will hearken and hear, and a Book of Remembrance will be written before Him for those who fear Hashem and for those who ponder His Name.*

39. I.e. for its own sake (*Maharsha*); alternatively, as it was meant to be done, without any deficiency (*Maharal, Chidushei Aggados*; see *Sfas Emes*).

40. *Ecclesiastes* 8:5.

41. The verse states *he who guards* rather than "he who performs" because one can "perform" a mitzvah even with an ulterior motive; however, "guarding" it implies that one preserves the mitzvah as it was originally uttered. That is, he performs it for its own sake (*Maharsha*).

42. *Ecclesiastes* 8:4.

ביין חרדלי במסב רחב או במסב קצר בחבר טוב או בחבר רע א"ר חסדא וכולן לזנות אמר רחבה אמר רבי יהודה עצי ירושלים של קינמון היו ובשעה שהיו מסיקין מהן ריחן נודף בכל ארץ ישראל ומשחרבה ירושלים נגנזו ולא נשתייר אלא כשעורה ומשתכח בגנזי דצימצמאי מלכתא:

מתני' לא יצא האיש לא בסייף ולא בקשת ולא בתרים ולא באלה ולא ברומח ואם יצא חייב חטאת רבי אליעזר אומר תכשיטין הן לו וחכ"א אינן אלא לגנאי שנאמר וכתתו חרבותם לאתים וחניתותיהם למזמרות ולא ישא גוי אל גוי חרב ולא ילמדו עוד מלחמה בירית טהורה ויוצאין בה בשבת כבלים טמאים ואין יוצאין בהן בשבת:

גמ' מאי באלה קולפא: ר' אליעזר אומר תכשיטין הן לו: תניא אמרו לו לרבי אליעזר וכי מאחר דתכשיטין הן לו מפני מה הן בטלין לימות המשיח אמר להן לפי שאינן צריכין שנאמר לא ישא גוי אל גוי חרב ותהוי לנוי בעלמא אמר אביי מידי דהוה אשרגא בטיהרא ופליגא דשמואל דאמר שמואל אין בין העולם הזה לימות המשיח אלא שיעבוד גליות בלבד שנאמר כי לא יחדל אביון מקרב הארץ מסייע ליה לרבי חייא בר אבא דא"ר חייא בר אבא כל הנביאים לא נתנבאו אלא לימות המשיח אבל לעולם הבא עין לא ראתה אלהים זולתך ואיכא דאמרי אמרו לו לר' אליעזר וכי מאחר דתכשיטין הן לו מפני מה הן בטלין לימות המשיח אמר להן אף לימות המשיח אינן בטלין היינו דשמואל ופליגא דר' חייא בר אבא א"ל אביי לרב דימי ואמרי לה לרב אויא ואמרי לה רב יוסף לרב דימי ואמרי לה לרב אויא ואמרי לה אביי לרב יוסף מ"ט דר"א דאמר תכשיטין הן לו דכתיב חגור חרבך על ירך גבור הודך והדרך א"ל רב כהנא למר בריה דרב הונא האי בדברי תורה כתיב א"ל אין מקרא יוצא מידי פשוטו א"ר כהנא כד הוינא בר תמני סרי שנין והוה גמירנא ליה לכוליה הש"ס ולא הוה ידענא דאין מקרא יוצא מידי פשוטו עד השתא מאי קמ"ל דליגמר איניש והדר ליסבר: סימן זרות: א"ר ירמיה א"ר אלעזר שני תלמידי חכמים המחדדין זה לזה בהלכה הקב"ה מצליח להם שנאמר והדרך צלח אל תקרי והדרך אלא וחדדך ולא עוד אלא שעולין לגדולה שנאמר צלח רכב יכול אפילו שלא לשמה תלמוד לומר על דבר אמת יכול אם הגיס דעתו ת"ל וענוה צדק ואם עושין כן זוכין לתורה שניתנה בימין שנאמר ותורך נוראות ימינך רב נחמן בר יצחק אמר זוכין לדברים שנאמרו בימינה של תורה דאמר רבא בר רב שילא ואמרי לה אמר רב יוסף בר חמא א"ר ששת מאי דכתיב אורך ימים בימינה בשמאלה עושר וכבוד אלא בימינה אורך ימים איכא עושר וכבוד ליכא אלא למיימינין בה אורך ימים איכא וכ"ש עושר וכבוד למשמאילים בה עושר וכבוד איכא אורך ימים ליכא א"ר ירמיה אמר ר' שמעון בן לקיש שני תלמידי חכמים הנוחין זה לזה בהלכה הקדוש ברוך הוא מקשיב להן שנאמר אז נדברו יראי ה' וגו' אין דיבור אלא נחת שנאמר ידבר עמים תחתינו מאי ולחושבי שמו א"ר אמי אפילו חישב לעשות מצוה ונאנס ולא עשאה מעלה עליו הכתוב כאילו עשאה א"ר חיננא בר אידי כל העושה מצוה כמאמרה אין מבשרין אותו בשורות רעות שנאמר שומר מצוה לא ידע דבר רע ואיתימא ר' חנינא אפילו הקב"ה גוזר גזירה הוא מבטלה שנאמר באשר דבר מלך שלטון ומי יאמר לו מה תעשה וסמיך ליה שומר מצוה לא ידע דבר רע אמר רבי אבא אמר רבי שמעון בן לקיש שני תלמידי חכמים המקשיבים זה לזה בהלכה הקדוש ב"ה שומע לקולן שנאמר היושבת בגנים חברים מקשיבים לקולך השמיעני ואם אין עושין כן גורמין לשכינה שמסתלקת מישראל שנאמר ברח דודי ודמה וגו' אמר רבי אבא א"ר שמעון בן לקיש שני ת"ח המדגילים זה לזה בהלכה הקדוש ברוך הוא אוהבן שנאמר ודגלו עלי אהבה אמר רבא והוא דידעי צורתא דשמעתא והוא דלית להו רבה במתא למיגמר מיניה (א"ר) אבא א"ר שמעון בן לקיש גדול המלוה יותר מן העושה צדקה ומטיל בכים יותר מכולן (א"ר) אבא אמר ר' שמעון בן לקיש אם תלמיד חכם נוקם ונוטר כנחש הוא חגריהו על מתניך אם עם הארץ הוא חסיד אל תדור בשכונתו אמר רב כהנא אמר רבי שמעון בן לקיש ואמרי לה אמר רב אסי אמר (ריש לקיש) ואמרי לה אמר רבי אבא אמר רבי שמעון בן לקיש כל המגדל כלב רע בתוך ביתו מונע חסד מתוך ביתו שנאמר למס מרעהו

תוספות

אין בין העוה"ז לימות המשיח. אע"ג דהשתא אין ירושלים ואין בהמ"ק ואילו לימות המשיח יהיה הכל בנוי צ"ל דהאי אין בין לאו דוקא: ואילו

רש"י

ביין חרדלי. שחור כלומר לבנה או שחורה: במסב רחב. מיסב מטה שמיסב עליה בשעת אכילה ולענין ניאוף אשה שמנה: קצר. כחושה: חבר טוב. אשה טובת מראה: דצימצמאי מלכתא. כך שמה: מתני' באלה. מפרש בגמ' קולפא מלוק"ה בלע"ז: וכתתו חרבותם. ואי תכשיטין נינהו לא יהו בטלין לעתיד: בירית. בגמרא מפרש: טהורה. אינה מקבלת טומאה: ויוצאין בה. דלא שלפא ומחויא שלא יראה שוקה: כבלין טמאין. בגמ' מפרש לה: גמ' שרגא בטיהרא. נר בצהרים מתוך שאינו צריך אינו נאה אבל בזמן הזה שהוא עת מלחמה תכשיטין הן: ופליגא. הא דקתני בטלין לימות המשיח פליגא דשמואל דלשמואל אין בטלין לימות המשיח: לא יחדל. משמע לעולם אלמא יש עניות ועשירות ש"מ נחמות שנתנבאו הנביאים ולא יהיה כנעני עוד (זכריה יד) לא לימות המשיח נתנבאו שהן מן העולם הזה דאם כן חדל לך אביון: מסייע ליה. ברייתא דקתני בטלין לימות המשיח לרבי חייא בר אבא: לא נתנבאו. דברי נחמות שלהן: עין לא ראתה. עין של נביאים לא שלטה לראותו: בדברי תורה כתיב. הוי זהיר לחזור על משנתך שתהא מזומנת לך בשעת הדין להביא ראיה כחרב על ירך גבור לנצח במלחמה והוא הודך והדרך: דליגמר איניש. לגרוס שמעתא מרביה ואף על גב דלא ידע לכולהו טעמיה: והדר ליסבר. טעמיה דהא קשה ליה לרב כהנא ולא הוה ידע להאי טעמא ותלמודיה הוה קים ליה מדהוה בר תמני סרי: המחדדין. שואלין ומשיבין ולא לקפח אלא להתחדד: והדרך. כמו וחדדך: ותורך. ותלמדך (א): למיימינין. של תורה שמפספסין טעמיהן בדקדוק וזורזין כימין המיומנת למלאכה: עושר וכבוד ליכא. בתמיה כיון דאיכא אורך ימים כ"ש עושר וכבוד: למשמאילין בה. שאין יגעים בה כל צרכן אי נמי מיימינין בה עוסקין לשמה משמאילים שלא לשמה: הנוחין זה לזה. נושאין ונותנין בה בנחת רוח מתעסקין כדי שילמדו זה מזה: ידבר עמים תחתינו. ישפיל וכל שפלות בנחת ל"א הנוחין מנהיגין זה את זה להבנתה של הלכה כמו לך נחה (שמות לב) ידבר תרגום של ינהג: ומי יאמר לו מה תעשה. שומר מצות יוכל לומר לו: המקשיבין. מלמדים זה את זה ומבינים זה מזה ולישנא דקרא נקט: בגנים. בתי מדרשות: חבירים מקשיבים. זה לזה להם אני אומר שישמיעוני קולם ואענם: ברח דודי. בתריה כתיב: המדגילים. מאספין זה את זה ואומרים בא ונלמוד ונבין בין שנינו הואיל ואין לנו רב ללמדנו: צורתא. שורש הדבר קצת למדו מרבם: גדול המלוה. לפי שאין העני בוש בדבר: ומטיל לכיס. מעות ומלאי להשתכר בהן למחצית שכר ואיידי דאיירי רבי אבא אמר ריש לקיש נקט כל הני מילי דאגדתא דאמר להו ר' אבא משמיה: חוגרו. הדבק בו שסופך ליהנות מתלמודו: אל תדור בשכונתו. שאינו יודע בדקדוקי מצות ואין חסידותו שלם וסופך ללמוד ממנו: מונע חסד. שאינו מניח העניים לבא לפתחו: למס. דהיינו כלב: מרעהו

עין משפט נר מצוה

מט א מיי' פי"ט מהל' שבת הלכה א סמג לאוין סה טוש"ע א"ח סי' ש"א סעיף ז:
נ ב מיי' פי"ב מהל' מלכים הלכה ב:
נא ג מיי' פ"ח מהל' תשובה הלכה ז:
נב ד מיי' פ"י מהל' מ"ע הלכה ח טוש"ע י"ד סי' רמט סעיף ו:
נג ה מיי' פ"ו מהל' דעות הלכה א ב:
נד ו מיי' פי"א מהל' רוצח הלכה ד:

ליקוטי רש"י

ולא בתרים. תריסין. מגינים [בכורות לו.]. וכתתו חרבותם לאתים. קולטר"ש בלע"ז. למזמרות. שרפ"ש בלע"ז שזומרין בהן הכרמים [ישעיה ב, ד]. בירית טהורה. אצעדה ויוצאין בה והיא כמין אצעדה שעושה לשוקיה מעל בתי שוקיה להדקן שלא יפלו על רגלה. טהורה, דלאו תכשיט היא אלא תשמיש לבתי שוקיה [והרי הוא] כטבעת הכלים דאמרן טהורות בפרקין דלעיל ויוצאין בה שצריך לה עם בתי שוקיה ולא הוי משאוי ויוצאין דכיון דלצניעותא היא לא שלפא ומחוי [לעיל ס.]. קולפא. מקל לרדות [ברכות נח.]. שרגא בטיהרא. נר בצהרים אינו מאיר [חולין ס:]. ופליגא דשמואל. דאמר ימות המשיח אין משתנין משל עכשיו [פסחים סח.]. לא נתנבאו. טובה לישראל [סנהדרין צט.]. הטובות והנחמות [ברכות לד:]. עין לא ראתה. זולתי עין של הקב"ה את אשר יעשה למחכה לו לא נראה כבוד וגדולה דוגמתה [ע"ז סה.]. דאין קץ לדבר [סנהדרין שם]. לא נראית ולא נגלית לשום נביא [ברכות שם]. עין שום נביא לא ראתה את אשר יעשה הקב"ה למחכה לו זולתי עיניך אתה אלהים [ישעיה סד, ג]. האי בדברי תורה כתיב. חגור חרבך על ירך להלחם מלחמתה של תורה והוא הודך והוא הדרך [תהלים מה, ד]. אין מקרא יוצא מידי פשוטו. ואע"ג דדרשינן ליה לדרשא מידי פשוטו מיהו לא נפיק לגמרי [יבמות כד.]. על דבר אמת. להורות כדת ולהתנהג בענות לדק [תהלים מה, ה עיין במהרש"א ח"א]. בימינה. למיימינים בה ועוסקים בה לשמה אורך ימים וכ"ש עושר וכבוד ולמשמאילים בה שעוסקי' בה שלא לשמה מ"מ עושר וכבוד יש [משלי ג, טז ועי' דה"ב א, יב]. למיימינין. עסוקים בכל כחם וטרודים לדעת סודה כאדם המשתמש ביד ימינו שהיא עיקר [לקמן פח:]. ידבר עמים תחתינו. ומנחם חבר ידבר ל' הנהגה [תהלים מז, ד]. ינהל עמים תחתינו [מכות יא.]. שומר מצוה לא ידע דבר רע. אם שומר מצוה אתה לא תדע דבר רע ולא תנזק. באשר דבר מלך שלטון. בשביל אשר דבר הקב"ה מושל הוא ומי יאמר לו מה תעשה [קהלת ח, ד]. נוקם. נקמתו. ונוטר כנחש. נוטר איבה כנחש בלבו [יומא כג.].

מסורת הש"ס

א) פי' מגן, ב) נ"ל לא, ג) [גיר' הערוך מאי אלה קופל פי' דומה למקל וכו' וראשו עגול כמו כדור וכו' ע"ש], ד) [פי' שבט שמכין בו וראשו עב], ה) [במיכה כתיב ישאו], ו) חולין ס:, ז) ברכות לד: לקמן קנא: פסחים סח. סנהדרין צא: צט., ח) י"ג דרבינא, ט) [יבמות דף יא: כד.], י) מכות יא., כ) ברכות ו. קדושין מ. ע"ש, ל) [מ"ק טז: ב"מ פה.], מ) [עי' תוס' ע"ז כב: ד"ה רגלא וכו' שהשיגו אפירוש רש"י דהכא], נ) [עתו' ע"ז שם], ס) [נ"ל וא"ר], ע) פסחים נג:, פ) [נ"ל וא"ר], צ) [נ"ל ר' שמעון בן לקיש], ק) [ועי' תוס' תענית יג: ד"ה מאי שייר ותוס' מגילה ח. ד"ה אין בין ומ"ש שם על הגליון].

הגהות הב"ח

(א) רש"י ד"ה ותורך ותלמדך הס"ד ואח"כ מ"ה עושר וכבוד וכו' עושר וכבוד הס"ד ואח"כ מ"ה למיימינין בה שמפספסין כצ"ל ותיבת של תורה נמחק ונ"ב ע"ל בדף פח ע"ב:

גליון הש"ס

גמ' אלא שעבוד גליות. עי' פסחים נ ע"ב:

תורה אור השלם

א) וְשָׁפַט בֵּין הַגּוֹיִם וְהוֹכִיחַ לְעַמִּים רַבִּים וְכִתְּתוּ חַרְבוֹתָם לְאִתִּים וַחֲנִיתוֹתֵיהֶם לְמַזְמֵרוֹת לֹא יִשָּׂא גוֹי אֶל גּוֹי חֶרֶב וְלֹא יִלְמְדוּ עוֹד מִלְחָמָה: [ישעיה ב, ד]
ב) כִּי לֹא יֶחְדַּל אֶבְיוֹן מִקֶּרֶב הָאָרֶץ עַל כֵּן אָנֹכִי מְצַוְּךָ לֵאמֹר פָּתֹחַ תִּפְתַּח אֶת יָדְךָ לְאָחִיךָ לַעֲנִיֶּךָ וּלְאֶבְיֹנְךָ בְּאַרְצֶךָ: [דברים טו, יא]
ג) וּמֵעוֹלָם לֹא שָׁמְעוּ לֹא הֶאֱזִינוּ עַיִן לֹא רָאָתָה אֱלֹהִים זוּלָתְךָ יַעֲשֶׂה לִמְחַכֵּה לוֹ: [ישעיה סד, ג]
ד) חֲגוֹר חַרְבְּךָ עַל יָרֵךְ גִּבּוֹר הוֹדְךָ וַהֲדָרֶךָ: [תהלים מה, ד]
ה) וַהֲדָרְךָ צְלַח רְכַב עַל דְּבַר אֱמֶת וְעַנְוָה צֶדֶק וְתוֹרְךָ נוֹרָאוֹת יְמִינֶךָ: [תהלים מה, ה]
ו) אֹרֶךְ יָמִים בִּימִינָהּ בִּשְׂמֹאולָהּ עֹשֶׁר וְכָבוֹד: [משלי ג, טז]
ז) אָז נִדְבְּרוּ יִרְאֵי יְיָ אִישׁ אֶל רֵעֵהוּ וַיַּקְשֵׁב יְיָ וַיִּשְׁמָע וַיִּכָּתֵב סֵפֶר זִכָּרוֹן לְפָנָיו לְיִרְאֵי יְיָ וּלְחֹשְׁבֵי שְׁמוֹ: [מלאכי ג, טז]
ח) יַדְבֵּר עַמִּים תַּחְתֵּינוּ וּלְאֻמִּים תַּחַת רַגְלֵינוּ: [תהלים מז, ד]
ט) שׁוֹמֵר מִצְוָה לֹא יֵדַע דָּבָר רָע וְעֵת וּמִשְׁפָּט יֵדַע לֵב חָכָם: [קהלת ח, ה]
י) בַּאֲשֶׁר דְּבַר מֶלֶךְ שִׁלְטוֹן וּמִי יֹאמַר לוֹ מַה תַּעֲשֶׂה: [קהלת ח, ד]
כ) הַיּוֹשֶׁבֶת בַּגַּנִּים חֲבֵרִים מַקְשִׁיבִים לְקוֹלֵךְ הַשְׁמִיעִנִי: [שיר השירים ח, יג]
ל) בְּרַח דּוֹדִי וּדְמֵה לְךָ לִצְבִי אוֹ לְעֹפֶר הָאַיָּלִים עַל הָרֵי בְשָׂמִים: [שיר השירים ח, יד]
מ) הֱבִיאַנִי אֶל בֵּית הַיָּיִן וְדִגְלוֹ עָלַי אַהֲבָה: [שיר השירים ב, ד]
נ) לַמָּס מֵרֵעֵהוּ חָסֶד וְיִרְאַת שַׁדַּי יַעֲזוֹב: [איוב ו, יד]

Who can question the decrees of God? וּסְמִיךְ לֵיהּ ,,שׁוֹמֵר מִצְוָה לֹא יֵדַע דָּבָר רָע" – **And adjacent to [this verse] Scripture says,** ***He who guards a commandment shall know no evil thing.*** That is, he will suffer no harsh decrees.[43]

The Gemara returns to the topic of two Torah scholars who learn together:

אָמַר רַבִּי אַבָּא אָמַר רַבִּי שִׁמְעוֹן בֶּן לָקִישׁ – **R' Abba said in the name of R' Shimon ben Lakish:** שְׁנֵי תַּלְמִידֵי חֲכָמִים הַמַּקְשִׁיבִים זֶה לָזֶה בַּהֲלָכָה – **When two Torah scholars listen to each other in the Law,**[44] הַקָּדוֹשׁ בָּרוּךְ הוּא שׁוֹמֵעַ לְקוֹלָן – **the Holy One, Blessed is He, hears their voice,** שֶׁנֶּאֱמַר ,,הַיּוֹשֶׁבֶת בַּגַּנִּים חֲבֵרִים מַקְשִׁיבִים לְקוֹלֵךְ הַשְׁמִיעִנִי" – **as it is stated,** ***You who dwell in the gardens, the companions hearken to your voice; let Me hear [it].***[45] וְאִם אֵין עוֹשִׂין כֵּן גּוֹרְמִין לַשְּׁכִינָה שֶׁמִּסְתַּלֶּקֶת מִיִּשְׂרָאֵל – **And if they do not do so, they cause the Divine Presence to depart from Israel,** שֶׁנֶּאֱמַר ,,בְּרַח דּוֹדִי וּדְמֵה וגו' " – **as it is stated** in the very next verse, ***Flee, my Beloved, and be like*** **etc.** [*a deer or a young gazelle*].

The Gemara has spoken about two Torah scholars who "sharpen" each other, "are pleasant" toward each other, and who "listen" to each other. Now, it discusses a fourth type of relationship:

אָמַר רַבִּי אַבָּא אָמַר רַבִּי שִׁמְעוֹן בֶּן לָקִישׁ – **R' Abba said in the name of R' Shimon ben Lakish:** שְׁנֵי תַּלְמִידֵי חֲכָמִים הַמַּדְגִּילִים זֶה לָזֶה בַּהֲלָכָה – **When two Torah scholars "gather" each other in the Law,** הַקָּדוֹשׁ בָּרוּךְ הוּא אוֹהֲבָן – **the Holy One, Blessed is He, loves them,** שֶׁנֶּאֱמַר ,,וְדִגְלוֹ עָלַי אַהֲבָה" – **as it is stated:** ***And his banner over me is love.***[46] אָמַר רָבָא וְהוּא דְּיָדְעֵי צוּרְתָא דִשְׁמַעְתָּא – **Rava said:** The above applies **provided that they know the** basic **features of the subject,**[47] וְהוּא דְלֵית לְהוּ רַבָּה בְּמָתָא לְמִיגְמַר מִינֵּיהּ – **and provided that they do not have a teacher in the city from whom to learn.** I.e. they once had a teacher from whom they learned the basic concepts, but there is no longer any teacher available.

Having already presented two dicta on the subject of Torah study by R' Abba in the name of R' Shimon ben Lakish, the Gemara cites other Aggadic lessons that R' Abba taught in Reish Lakish's name:

אָמַר רַבִּי אַבָּא אָמַר רַבִּי שִׁמְעוֹן בֶּן לָקִישׁ – **R' Abba said in the name of R' Shimon ben Lakish:** גָּדוֹל הַמַּלְוֶה יוֹתֵר מִן הָעוֹשֶׂה צְדָקָה – **A lender is greater than one who gives charity,**[48] וּמֵטִיל בַּכִּיס יוֹתֵר מִכּוּלָּן – **and one who puts** working capital **in the pocket** of a pauper[49] **is more** outstanding **than them all.**[50] אָמַר רַבִּי אַבָּא אָמַר רַבִּי שִׁמְעוֹן בֶּן לָקִישׁ – **R' Abba** also **said in the name of R' Shimon ben Lakish:** אִם תַּלְמִיד חָכָם נוֹקֵם וְנוֹטֵר כְּנָחָשׁ הוּא – Even **if a Torah scholar exacts revenge and bears a grudge like a serpent,** חַגְרֵיהוּ עַל מָתְנֶיךָ – **gird him to your loins;**[51] אִם עַם הָאָרֶץ הוּא חָסִיד – however, even **if an unlearned man is** ostensibly **pious,** אַל תָּדוּר בִּשְׁכוּנָתוֹ – **do not dwell in his neighborhood.**[52]

The Gemara cites another Aggadic teaching of R' Shimon ben Lakish:

אָמַר רַב כַּהֲנָא אָמַר רַבִּי שִׁמְעוֹן בֶּן לָקִישׁ – **Rav Kahana said in the name of R' Shimon ben Lakish;** וְאָמְרֵי לָהּ אָמַר רַב אַסִּי אָמַר (ריש) [רַבִּי שִׁמְעוֹן בֶּן] לָקִישׁ – **and some say it** as follows: **Rav Assi said in the name of R' Shimon ben Lakish;** וְאָמְרֵי לָהּ אָמַר רַבִּי אַבָּא אָמַר רַבִּי שִׁמְעוֹן בֶּן לָקִישׁ – **and some say it: R' Abba said in the name of R' Shimon ben Lakish:** כָּל הַמְגַדֵּל כֶּלֶב רַע בְּתוֹךְ בֵּיתוֹ – **Whoever raises a bad dog in his house** מוֹנֵעַ חֶסֶד מִתּוֹךְ בֵּיתוֹ – **prevents kindness from** coming **into his house,**[53] שֶׁנֶּאֱמַר לַמָּס – **as it is stated:** [*Whoever keeps*] **a** [*bad*] ***dog***

NOTES

43. The juxtaposition implies that "he who guards a commandment" can say to God, "What are You doing?" (*Rashi*). [That is, the Holy One, Blessed is He, empowers him to "question," as it were, and repeal the decree.]

A mitzvah is inherently good, and any defect in the mitzvah is evil. When one performs a mitzvah flawlessly, he removes himself from the realm of evil, and therefore does not receive evil tidings. Likewise, since he is attached to a level where there is no evil, he can cancel a harsh decree, which is an evil thing (*Maharal, Chidushei Aggados*).

44. When they teach each other and gain understanding from each other (*Rashi*).

45. *Song of Songs* 8:13. The "gardens" are houses of study, the "companions" are Torah scholars, and the "voice" is one of Torah and prayer. The verse is therefore expounded as follows: The Holy One, Blessed is He, says: "When you [the Congregation of Israel] sit in the houses of study as [scholarly] companions and listen [to each other, then I say in reference] to your voice: 'Let Me hear [it]' – i.e. let Me hear your prayers, and I shall answer them" (*Rashi*).

46. *Song of Songs* 2:4. [A banner, around which people rally, symbolizes the concept of gathering, which the verse associates with love.] From here the Gemara expounds that when two Torah scholars "gather" each other – i.e. they say to one another: "Come, let us learn, and between the two of us we shall understand, since we do not have a teacher" – Hashem loves them [even though they may not understand as well as if they had a teacher] (see *Rashi;* cf. *Tosafos* to *Avodah Zarah* 22b ד״ה רגלא).

47. I.e. provided that at a bare minimum they had learned from their teacher the basic concepts of the Talmudic subject they are studying (*Rashi*).

48. A pauper is embarrassed to accept charity, but not a loan [since he expects to repay the loan] (*Rashi*).

49. He gives the pauper merchandise or money with which to do business, and receives a percentage of the profits (*Rashi*).

50. One generally does not lend great sums of money, since he needs funds to conduct his own business. Consequently, the borrower receives only what is required to satisfy his immediate needs, and may therefore suffer embarrassment while he struggles to accumulate sufficient funds for repayment. An investor, on the other hand, transfers a large sum of money – enough for the pauper to do business and support himself from the profits, and to use the capital to repay the loan promptly. Hence, the investor does not cause the pauper any embarrassment at all (*Maharsha*; see also *Meiri*).

51. [Even if his character is less than perfect] attach yourself to him, for in the end you will benefit from his scholarship (*Rashi*; cf. *Maharatz Chayes*).

52. Since he does not know the fine details of the mitzvos and his piety is [perforce] incomplete [see *Avos* 2:5 (*Maharsha*)], in the end you will be adversely influenced by him (*Rashi*).

53. For a wild dog will not let the poor approach one's door (*Rashi*).

ביין חרדלי במסב רחב או במסב קצר בחבר טוב או בחבר רע א"ר חסדא וכולן לזנות אמר רחבה אמר רבי יהודה עצי ירושלים של קינמון היו ובשעה שהיו מסיקין מהן ריחן נודף בכל ארץ ישראל ומשחרבה ירושלים נגנזו ולא נשתייר אלא כשעורה ומשתכח בגזאי דצימצמאי מלכתא:

מתני' [א]לא יצא האיש לא בסייף ולא בקשת ולא [א]בתרים ולא באלה ולא ברומח ואם יצא חייב חטאת רבי אליעזר אומר תכשיטין הן לו וחכ"א אינן אלא לגנאי שנאמר [א]וכתתו חרבותם לאתים וחניתותיהם למזמרות [ב]ולא ישא גוי אל גוי חרב ולא ילמדו עוד מלחמה בירית טהורה ויוצאין בה בשבת כבלים טמאים ואין יוצאין בהן בשבת: גמ' [ג]מאי באלה [ד]קולפא: ר' אליעזר אומר תכשיטין הן לו: תניא אמרו לו לרבי אליעזר וכי מאחר דתכשיטין הן לו מפני מה הן בטלין לימות המשיח אמר להן לפי שאינן צריכין שנאמר [א]לא [ה]ישא גוי אל גוי חרב ותהוי לנוי בעלמא אמר אביי מידי דהוה [ו]אשרגא בטיהרא ופליגא דשמואל דאמר שמואל [ז]ב אין בין העולם הזה לימות המשיח [°]אלא שיעבוד גליות בלבד שנאמר [ב]כי לא יחדל אביון מקרב הארץ מסייע ליה לרבי חייא בר אבא דא"ר חייא בר אבא [ג]כל הנביאים לא נתנבאו אלא לימות המשיח אבל לעולם הבא [ג]עין לא ראתה אלהים זולתך ואיכא דאמרי אמרו לו לר' אליעזר וכי מאחר דתכשיטין הן לו מפני מה הן בטלין לימות המשיח אמר להן אף לימות המשיח אינן בטלין היינו דשמואל ופליגא דר' חייא בר אבא א"ל אביי לרב דימי ואמרי לה לרב אויא ואמרי לה רב יוסף לרב דימי ואמרי לה לרב אויא ואמרי לה אביי לרב יוסף מ"ט דר"א דאמר תכשיטין הן לו דכתיב [ד]חגור חרבך על ירך גבור הודך והדרך א"ל רב כהנא למר בריה [ח]דרב הונא האי בדברי תורה כתיב א"ל [ט]אין מקרא יוצא מידי פשוטו א"ר כהנא כד הוינא בר תמני סרי שנין והוה גמירנא ליה לכוליה הש"ס ולא הוה ידענא דאין מקרא יוצא מידי פשוטו עד השתא מאי קמ"ל דליגמר איניש והדר ליסבר: סימן זרות: א"ר ירמיה א"ר אלעזר שני תלמידי חכמים המחדדין זה לזה בהלכה הקב"ה מצליח להם שנאמר [ה]והדרך צלח אל תקרי והדרך אלא וחדדך ולא עוד אלא שעולין לגדולה שנאמר [ה]צלח רכב יכול אפילו שלא לשמה תלמוד לומר [ה]על דבר אמת יכול אם הגיס דעתו ת"ל [ה]וענוה צדק ואם עושין כן זוכין לתורה שניתנה בימין שנאמר [ה]ותורך נוראות ימינך רב נחמן בר יצחק אמר זוכין לדברים שנאמרו בימינה של תורה דאמר רבא בר רב שילא ואמרי לה אמר רב יוסף בר חמא א"ר ששת מאי דכתיב [ו]אורך ימים בימינה בשמאלה עושר וכבוד אלא בימינה אורך ימים איכא עושר וכבוד ליכא אלא למיימינין בה אורך ימים איכא וכ"ש עושר וכבוד למשמאילים בה עושר וכבוד איכא אורך ימים ליכא א"ר ירמיה אמר ר' שמעון בן לקיש שני תלמידי חכמים הנוחין זה לזה בהלכה הקדוש ברוך הוא מקשיב להן שנאמר [ז]אז נדברו יראי ה' וגו' [י]אין דיבור אלא נחת שנאמר [ח]ידבר עמים תחתינו [כ]מאי [י]ולחושבי שמו א"ר אמי אפילו חישב לעשות מצוה ונאנס ולא עשאה מעלה עליו הכתוב כאילו עשאה א"ר חיננא בר אידי כל העושה מצוה כמאמרה אין מבשרין אותו בשורות רעות שנאמר [ט]שומר מצוה לא ידע דבר רע א"ר אסי ואיתימא ר' חנינא אפילו הקב"ה [ל]גוזר גזירה הוא מבטלה שנאמר [י]באשר דבר מלך שלטון ומי יאמר לו מה תעשה וסמיך ליה [ט]שומר מצוה לא ידע דבר רע אמר רבי אבא אמר רבי שמעון בן לקיש שני תלמידי חכמים המקשיבים זה לזה בהלכה הקדוש ב"ה שומע לקולן שנאמר [כ]היושבת בגנים חברים מקשיבים לקולך השמיעני ואם אין עושין כן גורמין לשכינה שמסתלקת מישראל שנאמר [ל]ברח דודי ודמה וגו' אמר רבי אבא א"ר שמעון בן לקיש שני ת"ח [מ]המדגילים זה לזה בהלכה הקדוש ברוך הוא אוהבן שנאמר [מ]ודגלו עלי אהבה אמר רבא והוא דידעי צורתא דשמעתא [י]והוא דלית להו רבה במתא למיגמר מיניה ([ס]א"ר) אבא א"ר שמעון בן לקיש [ד]גדול המלוה יותר מן העושה צדקה [ע]ומטיל בכיס יותר מכולן ([פ]א"ר) אבא אמר ר' שמעון בן לקיש [ה]אם תלמיד חכם נוקם ונוטר כנחש הוא חגריהו על מתניך אם עם הארץ הוא חסיד אל תדור בשכונתו אמר רב כהנא אמר רבי שמעון בן לקיש ואמרי לה אמר רב אסי אמר ([צ]ריש לקיש) ואמרי לה אמר רבי אבא אמר רבי שמעון בן לקיש [י]כל המגדל כלב רע בתוך ביתו מונע חסד מתוך ביתו שנאמר [נ]למס מרעהו

אין בין העוה"ז לימות המשיח. אע"ג דהשתא אין ירושלים ואין בהמ"ק ואילו לימות המשיח יהיה הכל בנוי צ"ל דהאי אין בין לאו דוקא [ק]: ואילו

ביין חרדלי. שחור כלומר לבנה או שחורה: במסב רחב. מיסב מטה שמיסב עליה בשעת אכילה ולענין ניאוף אשה שמנה: קצר. כחושה: חבר טוב. אשה טובת מראה: דצימצמאי מלכתא. כך שמה: מתני' באלה. מפרש בגמ' קולפא מלוק"ה בלע"ז: וכתתו חרבותם. ואי תכשיטין נינהו לא יהו בטלין לעתיד: בירית. בגמרא מפרש: טהורה. אינה מקבלת טומאה: ויוצאין בה. דלא שלפא ומחויא שלא יראה שוקה: כבלין טמאין. בגמ' מפרש לה: גמ' שרגא בטיהרא. נר בצהרים מתוך שאינו צריך אינו נאה אבל בזמן הזה שהוא עת מלחמה תכשיטין הן: ופליגא. הא דקתני בטלין לימות המשיח פליגא דשמואל דלשמואל אין בטלין לימות המשיח: לא יחדל. משמע לעולם אלמא יש עניות ועשירות ש"מ נחמות שנתנבאו הנביאים ולא יהיה כנעני עוד (זכריה יד) לא לימות המשיח נתנבאו שהן מן העולם הזה דאם כן חדל לך אביון: מסייע ליה. ברייתא דקתני בטלין לימות המשיח לרבי חייא בר אבא: לא נתנבאו. דברי נחמות שלהן: עין לא ראתה. עין של נביאים לא שלטה לראותו: בדברי תורה כתיב. הוי זהיר לחזור על משנתך שתהא מזומנת לך בשעת הדין להביא ראיה כחרב על ירך גבור לנצח במלחמה והוא הודך והדרך: דליגמר איניש. לגרוס שמעתא מרביה ואף על גב דלא ידע לכולהו טעמיה: והדר ליסבר. טעמיה דהא קשה ליה לרב כהנא ולא הוה ידע להאי טעמא ותלמודיה הוה קים ליה מדהוה בר תמני סרי: המחדדין. שואלין ומשיבין ולא לקפח אלא להתחדד: והדרך. כמו וחדדך: ותורך. ותלמדך (א): למיימינין. של תורה שמפשפשין טעמיהן בדקדוק וזוררין כימין המיומנת למלאכה: עושר וכבוד ליכא. בתמיה כיון דאיכא אורך ימים כ"ש עושר וכבוד: למשמאילין בה. שאין יגעים בה כל צרכן אי נמי מיימינין בה עוסקין לשמה משמאילים שלא לשמה: הנוחין זה לזה. נושאין ונותנין בה בנחת רוח מתעסקין כדי שילמדו זה מזה: ידבר עמים תחתינו. ישפיל וכל שפלות בנחת ל"א הנוחין מנהיגין זה את זה להבנתה של הלכה כמו לך נחה (שמות לב) ידבר תרגום של ינהג: ומי יאמר לו מה תעשה. שומר מצות יוכל לומר לו: המקשיבין. מלמדים זה את זה ומבינים זה מזה ולישנא דקרא נקט: בגנים. בתי מדרשות: חבירים מקשיבים. זה לזה להם אני אומר שישמיעוני קולם וענם: ברח דודי. בתריה כתיב: המדגילים. מאספין זה את זה ואומרים בא ונלמוד ונבין בין שנינו הואיל ואין לנו רב ללמדנו: צורתא. שורש הדבר קצת למדו מרבם: גדול המלוה. לפי שאין העני בוש בדבר: ומטיל לכיס. מעות ומלאי להשתכר בהן למחצית שכר ואיידי דאיירי רבי אבא אמר ריש לקיש נקט כל הני מילי דאגדתא דאמר להו ר' אבא משמיה: חוגרו. הדבק בו שסופך ליהנות מתלמודו: אל תדור בשכונתו. שאינו יודע בדקדוקי מצות ואין חסידותו שלם וסופך ללמוד ממנו: מונע חסד. שאינו מניח העניים לבא לפתחו: למס. דהיינו כלב:

מסורת הש"ס
א) פי' מגן, ב) נ"ל לא, ג) [גיר' הערוך מאי אלה קופל פי' דומה למקל וכו' וראשו עגול כמו כדור וכו' ע"ש], ד) [פי' שבט שמכין בו וראשו עב], ה) [במיכה כתיב ישאו], ו) חולין ס:, ז) ברכות לד: לקמן קנא: פסחים סח. סנהדרין צא: צט., ח) י"ג דרבינא, ט) [יבמות דף יא: כד.], י) מכות יא., כ) ברכות ו. קדושין מ. ע"ש, ל) [מ"ק טז: ב"מ פה.], מ) [עי' תוס' ע"ז כב: ד"ה רגלא וכו' שהשיגו אפירוש רש"י דהכא], נ) [עמו' ע"ז שם], ס) [נ"ל וא"ר], ע) פסחים נג:, פ) [נ"ל וא"ר], צ) [נ"ל ר' שמעון בן לקיש], ק) [ועי' תוס' תענית יג: ד"ה מאי שייר ותוס' מגילה ח. ד"ה אין בין ומ"ש שם על הגליון].

הגהות הב"ח
(א) רש"י ד"ה ותורך ותלמדך הס"ד ואח"כ מ"ה עושר וכבוד וכו' עושר וכבוד הס"ד ואח"כ מ"ה למיימינין בה שמפשפשין כצ"ל ותיבת של תורה נמחק ונ"ב ע"ל בדף פח ע"ב:

גליון הש"ס
גמ' אלא שעבוד גליות. עי' פסחים נ ע"ב:

תורה אור השלם
א) וְשָׁפַט בֵּין הַגּוֹיִם וְהוֹכִיחַ לְעַמִּים רַבִּים וְכִתְּתוּ חַרְבוֹתָם לְאִתִּים וַחֲנִיתוֹתֵיהֶם לְמַזְמֵרוֹת לֹא יִשָּׂא גוֹי אֶל גּוֹי חֶרֶב וְלֹא יִלְמְדוּ עוֹד מִלְחָמָה: [ישעיה ב, ד]
ב) כִּי לֹא יֶחְדַּל אֶבְיוֹן מִקֶּרֶב הָאָרֶץ עַל כֵּן אָנֹכִי מְצַוְּךָ לֵאמֹר פָּתֹחַ תִּפְתַּח אֶת יָדְךָ לְאָחִיךָ לַעֲנִיֶּךָ וּלְאֶבְיֹנְךָ בְּאַרְצֶךָ: [דברים טו, יא]
ג) וּמֵעוֹלָם לֹא שָׁמְעוּ לֹא הֶאֱזִינוּ עַיִן לֹא רָאָתָה אֱלֹהִים זוּלָתְךָ יַעֲשֶׂה לִמְחַכֵּה לוֹ: [ישעיה סד, ג]
ד) חֲגוֹר חַרְבְּךָ עַל יָרֵךְ גִּבּוֹר הוֹדְךָ וַהֲדָרֶךָ: [תהלים מה, ד]
ה) וַהֲדָרְךָ צְלַח רְכַב עַל דְּבַר אֱמֶת וְעַנְוָה צֶדֶק וְתוֹרְךָ נוֹרָאוֹת יְמִינֶךָ: [תהלים מה, ה]
ו) אֹרֶךְ יָמִים בִּימִינָהּ בִּשְׂמֹאולָהּ עֹשֶׁר וְכָבוֹד: [משלי ג, טז]
ז) אָז נִדְבְּרוּ יִרְאֵי יְיָ אִישׁ אֶל רֵעֵהוּ וַיַּקְשֵׁב יְיָ וַיִּשְׁמָע וַיִּכָּתֵב סֵפֶר זִכָּרוֹן לְפָנָיו לְיִרְאֵי יְיָ וּלְחֹשְׁבֵי שְׁמוֹ: [מלאכי ג, טז]
ח) יַדְבֵּר עַמִּים תַּחְתֵּינוּ וּלְאֻמִּים תַּחַת רַגְלֵינוּ: [תהלים מז, ד]
ט) שׁוֹמֵר מִצְוָה לֹא יֵדַע דָּבָר רָע וְעֵת וּמִשְׁפָּט יֵדַע לֵב חָכָם: [קהלת ח, ה]
י) בַּאֲשֶׁר דְּבַר מֶלֶךְ שִׁלְטוֹן וּמִי יֹאמַר לוֹ מַה תַּעֲשֶׂה: [קהלת ח, ד]
כ) הַיּוֹשֶׁבֶת בַּגַּנִּים חֲבֵרִים מַקְשִׁיבִים לְקוֹלֵךְ הַשְׁמִיעִנִי: [שיר השירים ח, יג]
ל) בְּרַח דּוֹדִי וּדְמֵה לְךָ לִצְבִי אוֹ לְעֹפֶר הָאַיָּלִים עַל הָרֵי בְשָׂמִים: [שיר השירים ח, יד]
מ) הֱבִיאַנִי אֶל בֵּית הַיָּיִן וְדִגְלוֹ עָלַי אַהֲבָה: [שיר השירים ב, ד]
נ) לַמָּס מֵרֵעֵהוּ חָסֶד וְיִרְאַת שַׁדַּי יַעֲזוֹב: [איוב ו, יד]

עין משפט נר מצוה
מט א מיי' פי"ט מהל' שבת הלכה א סמג לאוין סה טוש"ע א"ח סי' ש"א סעיף ז:
נ ב מיי' פי"ב מהל' מלכים הלכה ב:
נא ג מיי' פ"ח מהל' תשובה הלכה ז:
נב ד מיי' פ"י מהל' מ"ע הלכה ח טוש"ע י"ד סי' רמט סעיף ו:
נג ה מיי' פ"ו מהל' דעות הלכה א ב:
נד ו מיי' פי"א מהל' רוצח הלכה ד:

ליקוטי רש"י
ולא בתרים. תריסין. מגינים [בכורות לו.]. וכתתו חרבותם לאתים. קולטר"ש בלע"ז. למזמרות. שרפ"ש בלע"ז שזומרין בהן הכרמים [ישעיה ב, ד]. בירית טהורה. מלטמא ויוצאין בה והיא כמין אצעדה שעושה לשוקיה מעל בתי שוקיה להדקן שלא יפלו על רגלה. טהורה, דלאו תכשיט היא אלא תשמיש לבתי שוקיה [והרי הוא] כטבעת הכלים דאמרן טהורות בפרקין דלעיל ויוצאין בה שצריך לה עם בתי שוקיה ולא הוי משאוי ויוצאין דכיון דלצניעותא היא לא שלפא ומחוי [לעיל ס.]. קולפא. מקל לרדות [ברכות נח.]. שרגא בטיהרא. נר בצהרים אינו מאיר [חולין ס:]. ופליגא דשמואל. דאמר ימות המשיח אין משתנין משל עכשיו [פסחים סח.]. לא נתנבאו. טובה לישראל [סנהדרין צט.]. הטובות והנחמות [ברכות לד:]. עין לא ראתה. זולתי עין של הקב"ה את אשר יעשה למחכה לו לא נראה כבוד וגדולה דוגמתה [ע"ז סה.]. דאין קץ לדבר [סנהדרין שם]. לא נראית ולא נגלית לשום נביא [ברכות שם]. עין שום נביא לא ראתה את אשר יעשה הקב"ה למחכה לו זולתי עיניך אתה אלהים [ישעיה סד, ג]. האי בדברי תורה כתיב. חגור חרבך על ירך להלחם מלחמתה של תורה והוא הודך והוא הדרך [תהלים מה, ד]. אין מקרא יוצא מידי פשוטו. ואע"ג דדרשינן ליה לדרשא מידי פשוטו מיהו לא נפיק לגמרי [יבמות כד.]. על דבר אמת. להורות כדת ולהתנהג בענות לדק [תהלים מה, ה עיין במהרש"א ח"א]. בימינה. למיימינים בה ועוסקים בה לשמה אורך ימים וכ"ש עושר וכבוד ולמשמאילים בה שעוסקי' בה שלא לשמה מ"מ עושר וכבוד יש [משלי ג, טז ועי' דה"ב א, יב]. למיימינין. עסוקים בכל כחם וטרודים לדעת סודה כאדם המשתמש ביד ימינו שהיא עיקר [לקמן פח:]. ידבר עמים תחתינו. ומנהם חבר ידבר ל' הנהגה [תהלים מז, ד]. ינהל עמים תחתינו [מכות יא.]. שומר מצוה לא ידע דבר רע. אם שומר מצוה אתה לא תדע דבר רע ולא תבואך. באשר דבר מלך שלטון. בשביל אשר דבר הקב"ה מושל הוא ומי יאמר לו מה תעשה [קהלת ח, ד]. נוקם. נקמתו. ונוטר כנחש. נוטר איבה כנחש בלבו [יומא כג.].

עין משפט
נר מצוה

נה א מיי' פ"ט מהל' שבת הלכה ה ו ומיי' פ"ט מהל' כלים הלכה ד סמג לאוין סה טוש"ע א"ח סי' שג סעיף טו:
נו ב מיי' פ"ט מהל' כלי המקדש הלכה א סמג עשין קעג:
נז ג מיי' פ"א מהל' כלים הלכה יא ופכ"ב הלכה א:

מרעהו חסד • שכן בלשון יונית קורין לכלב למס רב נחמן בר יצחק אמר אף פורק ממנו יראת שמים שנאמר א) ויראת שדי יעזוב ההיא א) איתתא דעיילא לההוא ביתא למיפא נבח בה כלבא איתעקר ולדה אמר לה מרי דביתא לא תידחלי דשקילי ניביה ושקילין טופריה אמרה ליה ג) שקולא טיבותיך ושדיא אחיזרי כבר נד ולד אמר רב הונא מאי דכתיב ב) שמח בחור בילדותך ויטיבך לבך בימי בחורותיך והלך בדרכי לבך ובמראה עיניך ודע כי על כל אלה יביאך האלהים במשפט עד כאן דברי יצר הרע מכאן ואילך דברי יצר טוב ריש לקיש אמר • עד כאן לדברי תורה מכאן ואילך למעשים טובים: א בירית טהורה: אמר רב יהודה בירית זו אצעדה מתיב רב יוסף בירית טהורה ויוצא בה בשבת ואילו אצעדה טמאה היא ה"ק בירית תחת אצעדה עומדת יתיב רבין ורב הונא • קמיה דרב ירמיה ויתיב רב ירמיה וקא מנמנם ויתיב רבין וקאמר בירית באחת כבלים בשתים א"ל רב הונא אלו ואלו בשתים ומטילין שלשלת ביניהן ונעשו כבלים ושלשלת שבו משויא ליה מנא וכ"ת כרבי שמואל בר נחמני ג) דאמר רבי שמואל בר נחמני א"ר ד) יוחנן מניין למשמיע קול בכלי מתכות שהוא טמא שנאמר ג) כל דבר אשר יבא באש אפילו דיבור במשמע בשלמא התם קא בעו לה לקלא וקעביד מעשה הכא מאי מעשה קעביד הכא נמי קא עביד מעשה דאמר רבה בר בר חנה א"ר יוחנן משפחה אחת היתה בירושלים שהיו פסיעותיהן גסות והיו בתולותיהן נושרות עשו להן כבלים והטילו שלשלת ביניהן שלא יהיו פסיעותיהן גסות ולא היו בתולותיהן נושרות איתער בהו ר' ירמיה אמר להו ה) יישר וכן א"ר יוחנן כי אתא רב דימי א"ר יוחנן מניין לאריג כל שהוא שהוא טמא מציץ א"ל אביי וציץ אריג הוא והתניא ו) ציץ ב כמין טס של זהב ורוחב שתי אצבעות ומוקף מאוזן לאוזן וכתוב עליו בב' שיטין יו"ד ה"א למעלה וקודש למ"ד למטה ואמר ר' אליעזר בר' יוסי אני ראיתיו בעיר רומי וכתוב קדש לה' בשיטה אחת כי סליק רב דימי לנהרדעא שלח להו ז) דברים שאמרתי לכם טעות הם בידי ברם כך אמרו משום רבי יוחנן מניין לתכשיט כ"ש שהוא טמא מציץ ומניין לאריג כ"ש שהוא טמא ח) מאו בגד תנו רבנן ג אריג כ"ש טמא ותכשיט כ"ש טמא אריג ותכשיט כ"ש טמא מוסף שק על הבגד שטמא משום אריג אמר רבא אריג כל שהוא טמא מאו בגד תכשיט כל שהוא טמא מציץ אריג ותכשיט כל שהוא טמא ה) מכל כלי מעשה א"ל ההוא מרבנן לרבא ההוא במדין כתיב א"ל גמר כלי

מניין

רש"י

מרעהו. מונע חסד ולע"ג דלא כתיב מונע ממילא משמע שכל תיבה שראשה מ"ם משמשת נטילה היא כמו ויקח מידם (שמות לב) אבדו גוים מארצו (תהלים י): למיפא. לאפות עיסה שהשאיל בעה"ב תנורו: שקילי ניביה. נטולות ד' שיניו שהוא נושך בהן אותן שיניים קרי ניבין כדאמרינן באלו טרפות (חולין דף נט.) גמל ניבי אית ליה: שקילי טופריה. נטולות לפרניו מלסרוט: שקולא. נטולה טובתך ומוטלת על הקולים: טיבותיך. טובת הנאת נחמתך כמו מחזיק טוב הגרי"א בלע"ז: עד כאן. עד ודע כי על כל אלה וגו': עד כאן לתורה. שמח בתלמודך למוד משמחה ומטוב לב והלך בדרכי לבך להבין מה בלבך לפי ראות עיניך: מכאן ואילך למעשים טובים. ודע כי על כל אלה על כל מה שלמדת סופך ליתן את הדין אם לא תקיים: אצעדה. של זרוע: ואילו אצעדה טמאה היא. דכתיב (במדבר לא) במעשה מדין אצעדה ולמיד וגו' וכתיב תתחטאו אתם ושביכם: תחת אצעדה. שבזרוע עומדת בשוק להחזיק בתי שוקיה שלא יפלו ויראו שוקיה הלכך טהורה דלאו לנוי היא וכלי תשמיש נמי לא הוי אלא כלי המשמש כלי דומיא לטבעות הכליס דאמרינן בפרקין דלעיל דטהורין ויוצאין בהם דלורך לבישה היא ומישלף ואחויי נמי ליכא למיחש דלא מיגליא לשוקה: בירית באחת. משוקיה: ושלשלת משוי להו מנא. בתמיה דקתני כבלים טמאים: וכי תימא כדר' שמואל כו': משמיע קול בכלי מתכות. בריש פרקין: ועשו להן שלשלת כו'. הלכך שלשלת תשמיש אדם הוא ולאו תשמיש כלי דלא תקבל טומאה ואין יוצאין בהן דילמא שלפא לשלשלת שהיא של זהב ומחויא דכי שקלה לשלשלת לא מיגליא שוקה שהרי בירית במקומה עומדת: יישר וכן אמר ר' יוחנן. יפה אמרת וכן שמעתי מר' יוחנן: מציץ. שהוא דבר מועט ומנאו עם תכשיטי כהן: יו"ד ה"א מלמעלה קדש למ"ד מלמטה. כלומר השם שלם בשיטה עליונה וקדש למ"ד בשיטה תחתונה שלא להקדים שאר אותיות למעלה מן השם מאחר ששני שיטין היו ורבינו הלוי שונה ח) קודש לה' מלמטה והיא היא: אני ראיתיו ברומי. שנכנס לאוצר המלך ליטול מה שירצה במס' מעילה (דף יז:) במעשה בן תלמיון: כי סליק רב דימי לנהרדעא. חזר בו ממה שאמר ציץ אריג הוא: מאו בגד. דכתיב גבי שרצים או בגד או עור או ריבוי הוא: אריג ותכשיט כל שהוא. חציו אריג וחציו תכשיט שאינו אריג וכולו הוי כל שהוא כלומר דבר קטן: מוסיף שק על הבגד. בדבר זה שהשק טמא משום אריג ולקמיה מפרש ליה: ההוא במדין כתיב. גבי טומאת מת ושרץ ממת לא יליף להחמיר דמה למת שכן טומאתו חמורה:

כלי

תוספות

ואילו אצעדה טמאה היא. פ"ה דכתיב במעשה מדין אצעדה וצמיד וגו' וכתיב תתחטאו אתם ושביכם ולא נהירא דע"כ תתחטאו לא אכל השבי קאי דהא בהמות נמי הוו בשבי ולאו בני קבולי טומאה נינהו לכן נ"ל משום דכתיב אצעדה וצמיד וכתיב בתריה ויקח ט) (מהם) כל כלי מעשה דקאי אכל הכלים שנלקחו וילפינן לקמן כלי כלי משרצים:

בירית תחת אצעדה עומדת. פי' בקונטרס (א) בשוק להחזיק בתי שוקיה שלא יפלו ויראו שוקיה וקשה לפי' זה דא"כ בכבלים אמאי אין יוצאין למאי דס"ד השתא דאין חילוק בין בירית לכבלים אלא שזה באחת וזה בשתים לכן נ"ל דאפשר ליטלן בלא גילוי שוקים ומש"ה כבלים אין יוצאין בהן דילמא שלפא ומחויא דתכשיט לנוי הם אבל בירית שהיא באחת לא שלפא ומחויא דאין זה תכשיט דכיון שאין לה אלא באחת גנאי היא לה ומש"ה ניחא דבירית טהורה דלאו תכשיט לנוי הוא וכלי תשמיש נמי לא הוי אלא כלי המשמש כלי דומיא דטבעת הכלי דאמר לעיל דטהור וכן פירש הקונטרס וטעמא דכבלים טמאים משום דתכשיט הם לנוי כדפי':

וכתוב עליו בשני שיטין יו"ד ה"א מלמעלה וקדש למ"ד למטה. נראה לר"ת שהיה כתוב יו"ד ה"א בסוף שיטה ראשונה וקדש ל' בתחלת שיטה שניה והשתא נקרא יפה ואין לפרש כמשמעו דא"כ אינו נקרא כהלכתו:

מניין לאריג כל שהוא שהוא טמא ת"ל או בגד. וא"ת והא לעיל בפרק במה מדליקין (דף כו. ושם) לא מרבינן אלא ג' על ג' וי"ל דהתם מיירי בבא מבגד גדול אבל הכא מיירי באריג כל שהוא דמתחלה לא היה דעתו להוסיף עליו ותרווייהו שמעינן מאו בגד דשקולים הם דחשיב כל שהוא אריג מתחלה כמו ג' על ג' מבגד גדול י) וא"ת ואכתי בגד כל שהוא למה הוא טמא והא בעינן שיטלטל מלא וריקן דומיא דשק וי"ל • דראוי הוא לכוף ולקפל וליקח בו מרגלית או מחט ואם תאמר א"כ פשוטי כלי עור אמאי טהורין הרי ראויין הם לקפל בו שום דבר כמו הכא וי"ל דמיירי בעור חלוק שהוא קשה:

מניין לתכשיט כל שהוא טמא. ואם תאמר תיפוק ליה דתכשיט כל שהוא טמא מדכתיב בכלי מדין טבעת ויש לומר דאפשר שהטבעת היא עבה וגדולה מאד ולא הוי כל שהוא:

אריג ותכשיט. פי' חציו אריג וחציו תכשיט טמא מכאן משמע דמ"מ בעינן שיעור קצת דאל"כ חציו דכ"ש מאי הוי:

ההוא במדין כתיב. פ"ה ובמדין הויא טומאת מת ושרץ ממת לא יליף להחמיר דמה למת שכן טומאה חמורה ומשני גמר כלי כלי משרץ פירוש מה כלי האמור בשרץ מטמא בשרץ אף כלי האמור כאן מטמא בשרץ וקשה דא"כ הוה ליה למיפרך ההוא בטומאת מת כתיב ועוד כי משני גמר כלי כלי הוה ליה לשנויי גמר בגד ועור לג"ש לכן נ"ל דההוא במדין כתיב בשלל מדין ולא מיירי הך פרשה בטומאה כלל והיכי יליף דאריג ותכשיט כל שהוא טמא מכל כלי מעשה ומשני גמר כלי כלי פי' כי היכי דכלי דכתיב גבי שרצים מיירי לענין טומאה הכי נמי כלי דכתיב גבי מדין לענין טומאה:

רבינו חננאל

בירית זו אצעדה. אוקימנא בשתי ירוכות בלא שלשלת נקראת בירית. ואם יש בהן שלשלת נקרא כבלים. הא דתניא ציץ דומה כמין טס של זהב רחב ב' אצבעות ומוקף מאוזן לאוזן וכתוב עליו בב' שיטין יו"ד ה"א מלמעלה קדש למ"ד מלמטה. א"ר אלעזר בר' יוסי אני הייתי ברומי כו':

רב נסים גאון

אמר ר' אלעזר בר' יוסי אני ראיתיו ברומי וכתוב עליו קודש לה' בשיטה אחת. ותניא כוותיה במס' דיומא בפ' הוציאו לו את הכף (דף נז) אמר ר' אלעזר בר' יוסי אני ראיתיה ברומי והיו עליה כמה טיפי דמים והדבר שגרם לו לצאת לרומי מפורש במס' מעילה בפ' קדשי מזבח (דף יז) שאל ר' מתיה בן חרש את ר' שמעון בן יוחי ברומי מניין לדם שרצים שהוא טמא אמר ליה דאמר קרא וזה לכם הטמא אמרו לו תלמידיו (גזר עליו) [חכים ליה] רשב"י אמר להם תלמוד ערוך הוא מפיו של ר' אלעזר בר' יוסי פעם אחת גזרה מלכות הרשעה גזרה על ישראל שלא ישמרו את השבת ושלא ימולו בניהם ושיבעלו נשותיהם כשהן נדות הלך ר' ראובן בן איצטרובולי וספר קומי והלך וישב עמהם אמר להם מי שיש לו אויב רוצה שיעשיר או שיעני אמרו לו יעני אמר להן אם כן לא יעשו מלאכה בשבת כדי שיענו אמרו לו טבות אמר ובטלוה חזר ואמר להן מי שיש לו אויב יכחיש או יבריא אמרו לו יכחיש אמר אם כן ימלו בניהם לח' ימים כדי שיכחישו אמרו טבות אמר ובטלוה חזר ואמר מי שיש לו אויב ירבה או ימעיט אמרו ימעיט אמר להם (לא) אם כן לא יבעלו נשותיהם כשהן נדות ובטלוה הכירו בו שהוא יהודי החזירום אמרו מי ילך ויבטל את הגזירה ילך ר' שמעון בן יוחי שהוא מלומד בנסים וילך עמו ר' אלעזר בר' יוסי וכו' על לבי גזא אשכחוה להההוא אגרתא שקלוה וקרעוה והיינו דאמר ר' אלעזר אני ראיתיה ברומי והיו עליה כמה טיפי דמים ובתוספ' מקואות (פרק ד) אמר ר' אלעזר בר' יוסי הלכה זו הוריתי ברומי לטהרה וכשבאתי אצל חברי אמרו לי יפה הוריתה ובמס' נדה בפ' הרואה כתם (דף נח) תניא כוותיה אמר ר' אלעזר בר' יוסי הלכה זו כו':

הניחא

מסורת הש"ס

א) ב"ק פג., ב) [ביצה כט: כתובות נג. בבא קמא פג. ב"מ סג:], ג) לעיל נח., ד) [שם אי' יונתן], ה) [לעיל נג. ברכות מג: עירובין לב: פסחים נג: ב"מ נח. סנהדרין ק. שבועות מ. מה: חולין יח: עה: עו:], ו) סוכה ה., ז) [ברכות לג: עירובין טז: קד. יבמות כ: עו. ב"ב קמ. קלא. סנהדרין סא. מכות ח: זבחים לד. מנחות יב: לז. חולין ע. נדה סח.], ח) קודש מלמטה לה' מלמעלה כצ"ל וכ"כ הרמב"ם בפ"ט מהל' כה"מ וגם גי' הירושלמי פ' טרף בקלפי סוטה קך, ט) [צ"ל מאתם], י) [ע' תוס' לעיל כו. ד"ה אין בו וכו'].

הגהות הב"ח

(א) תוס' ד"ה בירית וכו' פי' בקונט' עומדת בשוק:

גליון הש"ס

גמ' שכן בל' יונית. וכן סוכה לה ע"א. וסנהדרין ד ע"ב טט בכתפי שתים וכו': שם ע"ב לדברי תורה. עי' ערכין יא ע"א תוס' ד"ה משמח: שם קמיה דר' ירמיה ויתיב ר"י וקא מנמנם. גיטין יא ע"ב. ונדרים כט ע"ב: תוס' ד"ה מנין לאריג וכו'. דראוי הוא לכוף. ק"ל ממתני' פ' כ"ו מ"ב דכלים לרור המרגלית. ועי' ברמב"ם ור"ש שם והרי מ"מ הוא בכלל אפשר לקפל ולהניח בו מעות כמקדש. ולע"ג:

תורה אור השלם

א) לַמָּס מֵרֵעֵהוּ חָסֶד וְיִרְאַת שַׁדַּי יַעֲזוֹב: [איוב ו, יד]

ב) שְׂמַח בָּחוּר בְּיַלְדוּתֶךָ וִיטִיבְךָ לִבְּךָ בִּימֵי בְחוּרוֹתֶךָ וְהַלֵּךְ בְּדַרְכֵי לִבְּךָ וּבְמַרְאֵה עֵינֶיךָ וְדָע כִּי עַל כָּל אֵלֶּה יְבִיאֲךָ הָאֱלֹהִים בַּמִּשְׁפָּט: [קהלת יא, ט]

ג) כָּל דָּבָר אֲשֶׁר יָבֹא בָאֵשׁ תַּעֲבִירוּ בָאֵשׁ וְטָהֵר אַךְ בְּמֵי נִדָּה יִתְחַטָּא וְכֹל אֲשֶׁר לֹא יָבֹא בָּאֵשׁ תַּעֲבִירוּ בַמָּיִם: [במדבר לא, כג]

ד) וְכֹל אֲשֶׁר יִפֹּל עָלָיו מֵהֶם בְּמֹתָם יִטְמָא מִכָּל כְּלִי עֵץ אוֹ בֶגֶד אוֹ עוֹר אוֹ שָׂק כָּל כְּלִי אֲשֶׁר יֵעָשֶׂה מְלָאכָה בָּהֶם בַּמַּיִם יוּבָא וְטָמֵא עַד הָעֶרֶב וְטָהֵר: [ויקרא יא, לב]

ה) וַיִּקַּח מֹשֶׁה וְאֶלְעָזָר הַכֹּהֵן אֶת הַזָּהָב מֵאִתָּם כֹּל כְּלִי מַעֲשֶׂה: [במדבר לא, נא]

ליקוטי רש"י

ניביה. ינייב"ש לע"א ארבע שיני הכלב הארוכות שבהן נושך כך שמעתי (חולין דף נט.) (בבכורות) [ב"ק פג.]. שקולא טיבותיך. אין אנו מחזיקין לך טובה בכך נטולה היא טובתך ומוטלת על הקוצים (שלא קשרת את הכלב) מה שאתה מנחמני הבל. כבר נד. ונעקר ממקומו [ב"ק שם]. טיבותיך, גרי"ר בלע"ז [ביצה כט:]. חיזוק טובותיך שאתה סבור שנחזיק לך טובה בזו נטולה היא ממך ומוטלת על החרולים [כתובות נג:]. נטולה היא טובתך ומוטלת על הקוצים. כל דבר אשר יבא באש. בכלי מתכות משתעי במעשה מדין [לעיל נח:]. ומוקף מאוזן לאוזן. מקיף על המצח מאוזן לאוזן [שמות כח, לו].

שֶׁבֵּן "מֵרֵעֵהוּ חָסֶד" – [withholds] ***kindness from his fellow;***[1] בְּלָשׁוֹן יְוָנִית קוֹרִין לְכֶלֶב לַמָּס – **for in the Greek language they call a dog** ***lamas.***[2] רַב נַחְמָן בַּר יִצְחָק אָמַר – **Rav Nachman bar Yitzchak said:** אַף פּוֹרֵק מִמֶּנּוּ יִרְאַת שָׁמַיִם – **He also casts off from himself the fear of Heaven,** שֶׁנֶּאֱמַר ,,וְיִרְאַת שַׁדַּי יַעֲזוֹב" – **as it is stated** at the conclusion of that verse: ***. . .and he abandons the fear of God.***

The Gemara illustrates this point with an anecdote:

הַהִיא אִיתְּתָא דְּעַיְילָא לְהָהוּא בֵּיתָא לְמֵיפָא – **A certain pregnant woman came into a particular house to bake.**[3] נְבַח בָּהּ כַּלְבָּא – The owner's **dog barked at her,** אִיתְעֲקַר וַלְדָהּ – **and** because of the sudden fright **her fetus was uprooted** from its place in the womb. אָמַר לָהּ מָרֵי דְּבֵיתָא – **The owner of the house said to her:** לָא תִידְחֲלִי – **"Don't be afraid,** דִּשְׁקִילֵי נִיבֵיהּ וּשְׁקִילִין טוּפְרֵיהּ – **for [the dog's] fangs**[4] **and its claws have been removed,** and so it can neither bite nor scratch." אָמְרָה לֵיהּ – **She said to him** in reply: שְׁקוּלָא טֵיבוּתֵיךְ וְשַׁדְיָא אַחִיזְרֵי – **The gratitude for your** reassurance **is taken away and cast onto thorns;** כְּבָר נָד וָלָד – **the fetus has already been dislodged."**

The Gemara cites another Aggadic teaching of R' Shimon ben Lakish – this time in a dispute with Rav Huna:

אָמַר רַב הוּנָא מַאי דִּכְתִיב – **Rav Huna said: What is** the meaning of that **which is written:**[5] ,,שְׂמַח בָּחוּר בְּיַלְדוּתֶךָ וִיטִיבְךָ לִבְּךָ בִּימֵי בְחוּרוֹתֶיךָ וְהַלֵּךְ בְּדַרְכֵי לִבְּךָ וּבְמַרְאֵה עֵינֶיךָ וְדָע כִּי עַל־כָּל־אֵלֶּה יְבִיאֲךָ הָאֱלֹהִים בַּמִּשְׁפָּט" – ***Rejoice, young man, in your childhood, and let your heart cheer you in the days of your youth, and go in the ways of your heart and after the sight of your eyes – but know that for all these things God will bring you to judgment.*** Rav Huna answers his own question: עַד כָּאן דִּבְרֵי יֵצֶר הָרַע – **Until here**[6] **are the words of the Evil Inclination;** מִכָּאן וְאֵילָךְ דִּבְרֵי יֵצֶר טוֹב – **from here onward are the words of the Good Inclination.** רֵישׁ לָקִישׁ אָמַר – **Reish Lakish said:** עַד כָּאן לְדִבְרֵי תוֹרָה – **Until here**[6] the verse refers **to the words of the Torah;**[7] מִכָּאן וְאֵילָךְ לְמַעֲשִׂים טוֹבִים – **from here onward** it refers **to good deeds.**[8]

The Gemara quotes the next part of the Mishnah:

בִּירִית טְהוֹרָה – A GARTER IS *TAHOR*[9] and one may go out with it on the Sabbath. Leg chains are [susceptible to *tumah,* and one may not go out with them on the Sabbath].

The Gemara more precisely describes the items mentioned in this part of the Mishnah:

אָמַר רַב יְהוּדָה – **Rav Yehudah said:** בִּירִית זוֹ אֶצְעָדָה – A GARTER – **this** refers to **an arm band.**

The Gemara objects to this definition:

מַתִיב רַב יוֹסֵף – **Rav Yosef retorted** by quoting our Mishnah: בִּירִית טְהוֹרָה וְיוֹצְאִין בָּהּ בְּשַׁבָּת – A GARTER IS *TAHOR*, AND ONE MAY GO OUT WITH IT ON THE SABBATH, וְאִילּוּ אֶצְעָדָה טְמֵאָה הִיא – **whereas an arm band is** susceptible to ***tumah!***[10] Hence, the "garter" mentioned in the Mishnah cannot be an arm band. – ? –

The Gemara reinterprets the statement of Rav Yehudah:

הָכִי קָאָמַר – **He** actually **said thus:** בִּירִית תַּחַת אֶצְעָדָה עוֹמֶדֶת – **A garter stands in place of an arm band.**[11]

NOTES

1. *Job* 6:14.

2. The plain meaning of the word מָס is "withhold," so that the verse would ordinarily be translated: *To he who withholds* (לַמָּס) *kindness from his fellow* (מֵרֵעֵהוּ חָסֶד). However, the Gemara expounds לַמָּס to mean "a dog," so that the verse now reads: "A dog (לַמָּס) – from his fellow kindness (מֵרֵעֵהוּ חָסֶד)." The word "from" implies a taking away of something from someone; hence, even though the word "withhold" is not actually written according to the Gemara's interpretation, the verse is construed to mean that one who raises a wild dog withholds kindness from his fellow (*Rashi*).

3. The owner of the house had given her permission to use his oven (*Rashi*).

4. The term נִיבֵיהּ refers to the four teeth with which a dog bites (*Rashi*).

5. *Ecclesiastes* 11:9.

6. Until, but not including, the words *. . .but know that for all these things God will bring you to judgment* (*Rashi*).

7. *Rejoice* in your Torah studies – learn joyfully and contentedly; *and go in the ways of your heart,* to understand what is in your heart according to *the sight of your eyes* (*Rashi*). That is, follow your most sincere understanding of what the Torah intends.

8. *But know that for all these things* – for all the things you have learned – in the end you will be judged if you do not fulfill them (*Rashi*).

9. I.e. it is not susceptible to *tumah.*

10. Following the war against Midian, Moshe told the soldiers that they and their booty would have to be purified from the *tumah* of corpses. (Soldiers who had killed Midianites with the sword became *tamei,* as did the articles of booty removed from the corpses.) For Moshe told them: *Become purified. . .you and your booty* (תִּתְחַטְּאוּ. . .אַתֶּם וּשְׁבִיכֶם; *Numbers* 31:19). A later verse relates that the soldiers offered the booty to the Tabernacle treasury, and included in that gift were *arm bands* (אֶצְעָדָה; ibid. v.50). This establishes that arm bands are susceptible to *tumah* (*Rashi*).

Tosafos take issue with *Rashi's* proof: The mere fact that arm bands are listed among the booty does not establish that they are susceptible to *tumah,* for live animals were also listed, and surely they are not susceptible to *tumah. Tosafos* therefore offer a different proof: *Numbers* 31:50 mentions arm bands among the booty. The following verse refers to the booty in general as *every fashioned article* (כָּל כְּלִי מַעֲשֶׂה). Since the Gemara below derives exegetically from the word כְּלִי (*article*) that all the booty items were susceptible to *tumah,* it is apparent that the arm bands were also susceptible to *tumah.*

11. According to this version the "garter" of the Mishnah is a band worn on the calf of the leg, and thus resembles an arm band. However, while an arm band beautifies, this "garter" is worn solely to hold up a woman's stockings. This explains why the garter is not susceptible to *tumah* – for it is neither an ornament nor a utensil directly serving the woman. Rather, it is a utensil that serves a garment (the stockings). Thus, it is legally similar to a ring used to hang a utensil, and the Gemara states above (end of 52a) that such a ring is not susceptible to *tumah.* And why is a woman permitted to go out on the Sabbath wearing this garter? Because it is part of her clothing. Moreover, there is no danger that she will remove it to show to a friend, for she will not wish to expose her leg (*Rashi.*)

Tosafos object to *Rashi's* interpretation, for the Gemara below postulates that the only difference between the "garter" and the "leg chains" (*kevalim*) of the Mishnah is that the garter is a single band while the *kevalim* are an unattached pair. If *Rashi's* definition of garter is correct, why does our Mishnah forbid going out with *kevalim*? These, too, the woman would not take off to show a friend, since her stockings would fall! (See *Ran,* who quotes *Tosafos* as asking why, according to *Rashi,* the *kevalim* are susceptible to *tumah;* and see *Hagahos R' Elazar Moshe Horowitz* for a defense of *Rashi.*)

Tosafos therefore explain that although the sole function of a garter (single leg band) is to help hold up the stockings, and that is why it is not susceptible to *tumah;* nevertheless even if the garter is removed, the stockings will not immediately fall (see *Mordechai*). Why, then, is a woman permitted to go out with a garter but not with *kevalim*? The answer is that since the garter is a single band, it is an embarrassment, not an ornament. Hence, a woman would not remove it to show to a friend. [*Mordechai* explains that her friends would laugh at her because she does not have one on the other leg.] The *kevalim,* on the other hand, are a pair of bands, and as such are ornamental. Hence, they are susceptible to *tumah.* Moreover, since a woman might remove one to show to a friend and subsequently carry it four *amos* in the public domain, she may not go out with them on the Sabbath. (See *Ran* for a different explanation of the distinction between a garter and *kevalim.*)

מרעהו חסד • שכן בלשון יונית קורין לכלב למס רב נחמן בר יצחק אמר אף פורק ממנו יראת שמים שנאמר א) ויראת שדי יעזוב ההיא א) איתתא דעיילא להווא ביתא למיפא נבח בה כלבא איתעקר ולדה אמר לה מרי דביתא לא תידחלי דשקילי ניביה ושקילין טופריה אמרה ליה ג) שקולא טיבותיך ושדיא אחיזרי כבר נד ולד אמר רב הונא מאי דכתיב ב) שמח בחור בילדותך ויטיבך לבך בימי בחורותיך והלך בדרכי לבך ובמראה עיניך ודע כי על כל אלה יביאך האלהים במשפט עד כאן דברי יצר הרע מכאן ואילך דברי יצר טוב ריש לקיש אמר • עד כאן לדברי תורה מכאן ואילך למעשים טובים: א בירית טהורה: אמר רב יהודה בירית זו אצעדה מתיב רב יוסף בירית טהורה ויוצא בה בשבת ואילו אצעדה טמאה היא ה"ק בירית תחת אצעדה עומדת יתיב רבין ורב הונא • קמיה דרב ירמיה ויתיב רב ירמיה וקא מנמנם ויתיב רבין וקאמר בירית באחת כבלים בשתים א"ל רב הונא אלו ואלו בשתים ומטילין שלשלת ביניהן ונעשו כבלים ושלשלת שבו משויא ליה מנא וכ"ת כרבי שמואל בר נחמני ג) דאמר רבי שמואל בר נחמני א"ר ד) יוחנן מניין למשמיע קול בכלי מתכות שהוא טמא שנאמר ג) כל דבר אשר יבא באש אפילו דיבור במשמע בשלמא התם קא בעו לה לקלא וקעביד מעשה הכא מאי מעשה קעביד הכא נמי קא עביד מעשה דאמר רבה בר בר חנה א"ר יוחנן משפחה אחת היתה בירושלים שהיו פסיעותיהן גסות והיו בתולותיהן נושרות עשו להן כבלים והטילו שלשלת ביניהן שלא יהיו פסיעותיהן גסות ולא היו בתולותיהן נושרות איתער בהו ר' ירמיה אמר להו ה) יישר וכן א"ר יוחנן כי אתא רב דימי א"ר יוחנן מניין לאריג כל שהוא שהוא טמא מציץ א"ל אביי וציץ אריג הוא והתניא ו) ציץ ב כמין טס של זהב ורוחב שתי אצבעות ומוקף מאוזן לאוזן וכתוב עליו בב' שיטין יו"ד ה"א למעלה וקודש למ"ד למטה ואמר ר' אליעזר בר' יוסי אני ראיתיו בעיר רומי וכתוב קדש לה' בשיטה אחת כי סליק רב דימי לנהרדעא שלח להו י) דברים שאמרתי לכם טעות הם בידי ברם כך אמרו משום רבי יוחנן מניין לתכשיט כ"ש שהוא טמא מציץ ומניין לאריג כ"ש שהוא טמא ד) מאו בגד תנו רבנן ג אריג כ"ש טמא ותכשיט כ"ש טמא אריג ותכשיט כ"ש טמא מוסף שק על הבגד שטמא משום אריג אמר רבא אריג כל שהוא טמא מאו בגד תכשיט כל שהוא טמא מציץ אריג ותכשיט כל שהוא טמא ה) מכל כלי מעשה א"ל ההוא מרבנן לרבא ההוא במדין כתיב א"ל גמר כלי

רש"י

מרעהו. מונע חסד ולע"ג דלא כתיב מונע ממילא משמע שכל תיבה שראשה מ"ם משמשת נטילה היא כמו ויקח מידם (שמות לב) אבדו גוים מארצו (תהלים י): למיפא. לאפות עיסה שהשאיל בעה"ב תנורו: שקילי ניביה. נטולות ד' שיניו שהוא נושך בהן אותן שיניים קרי ניבין כדאמרינן באלו טרפות (חולין דף נט.) גמל ניבי אית ליה: שקילי טופריה. נטולות צפרניו מלסרוט: שקולא. נטולה טובתך ומוטלת על הקוצים: טיבותיך. טובת הנאה נחמתך כמו מחזיק טוב הגרי"א בלע"ז: עד כאן. עד ודע כי על כל אלה וגו': עד כאן לתורה. שמח בתלמודך למוד משמחה ומטוב לב והלך בדרכי לבך להבין מה בלבך לפי ראות עיניך: מכאן ואילך למעשים טובים. ודע כי על כל אלה על כל מה שלמדת סופך ליתן את הדין אם לא תקיים: אצעדה. של זרוע: ואילו אצעדה טמאה היא. דכתיב (במדבר לא) במעשה מדין אצעדה וצמיד וגו' וכתיב תתחטאו אתם ושביכם: תחת אצעדה. שבזרוע עומדת בשוק להחזיק בתי שוקיה שלא יפלו ויראו שוקיה הלכך טהורה דלאו לנוי היא וכלי תשמיש נמי לא הוי אלא כלי המשמש כלי דומיא דטבעות הכלים דאמרינן בפרקין דלעיל דטהורין ויוצאין בהם דלורך לבישה היא ומישלף ואחויי נמי ליכא למיחש דלא מיגליא לשוקה: בירית באחת. משוקיה: ושלשלת משוי להו מנא. בתמיה דקתני כבלים טמאים: וכי תימא כדר' שמואל כו': משמיע קול בכלי מתכות. ברים פרקין: ועשו להן שלשלת כו'. הלכך שלשלת תשמיש אדם הוא ולאו תשמיש כלי דלא תקבל טומאה ואין יוצאין בהן דילמא שלפא לשלשלת שהיא של זהב ומחויא דכי שקלה לשלשלת לא מיגליא שוקה שהרי בירית במקומה עומדת: יישר וכן אמר ר' יוחנן. יפה אמרת וכן שמעתי מר' יוחנן: מציץ. שהוא דבר מועט ומנאו עם תכשיטי כהן: יו"ד ה"א מלמעלה קדש למ"ד מלמטה. כלומר השם שלם בשיטה עליונה וקדש למ"ד בשיטה תחתונה שלא להקדים שאר אותיות למעלה מן השם מאחר ששני שיטין היו ורבינו הלוי שונה ח) קודש לה' מלמטה והיא היא: אני ראיתיו ברומי. שנכנס לאולר המלך ליטול מה שירצה במס' מעילה (דף יז:) במעשה בן תלמיון: כי סליק רב דימי לנהרדעא. חזר בו ממה שאמר ציץ אריג הוא: מאו בגד. דכתיב גבי שרצים או בגד או עור או ריבוי הוא: אריג ותכשיט כל שהוא. חציו אריג וחציו תכשיט שאינו אריג וכולו הוי כל שהוא כלומר דבר קטן: מוסף שק על הבגד. בדבר זה שהשק טמא משום אריג ולקמיה מפרש ליה: ההוא במדין כתיב. גבי טומאת מת ושרץ ממת לא יליף להחמיר דמה למת שכן טומאתו חמורה: כלי כלי פי' כי היכי דכלי דכתיב גבי שרצים מיירי לענין טומאה הכי נמי כלי דכתיב גבי מדין לענין טומאה:

מניין

תוספות

ואילו אצעדה טמאה היא. פ"ה דכתיב במעשה מדין אצעדה וצמיד וגו' וכתיב תתחטאו אתם ושביכם ולא נהירא דע"כ תתחטאו לא אכל השבי קאי דהא בהמות נמי הוו בשבי ולאו בני קבולי טומאה נינהו לכן נ"ל משום דכתיב אצעדה וצמיד וכתיב בתריה ויקח ט) (מהם) כל כלי מעשה דקאי אכל הכלים שנלקחו וילפינן לקמן כלי כלי משרצים:

בירית תחת אצעדה עומדת. פי' בקונטרס (א) בשוק להחזיק בתי שוקיה שלא יפלו ויראו שוקיה וקשה לפי' זה דא"כ בכבלים אמאי אין יוצאין למאי דס"ד השתא דאין חילוק בין בירית לכבלים אלא שזה באחת וזה בשתים לכן נ"ל דאפשר ליטלן בלא גילוי שוקים ומש"ה כבלים אין יוצאין בהן דילמא שלפא ומחויא דתכשיט לנוי הם אבל בירית שהיא באחת לא שלפא ומחויא דאין זה תכשיט דכיון שאין לה אלא באחת גנאי היא לה ומש"ה ניחא דבירית טהורה דלאו תכשיט לנוי הוא וכלי תשמיש נמי לא הוי אלא כלי המשמש כלי דומיא דטבעת הכלי דאמר לעיל דטהור וכן פירש הקונטרס וטעמא דכבלים טמאים משום דתכשיט הם לנוי כדפי':

וכתוב עליו בשני שיטין יו"ד ה"א מלמעלה וקדש למ"ד למטה. נראה לר"ת שהיה כתוב יו"ד ה"א בסוף שיטה ראשונה וקדש ל' בתחלת שיטה שניה והשתא נקרא יפה ואין לפרש כמשמעו דא"כ אינו נקרא כהלכתו:

מניין לאריג כל שהוא שהוא טמא ת"ל או בגד. וא"ת והא לעיל בפרק במה מדליקין (דף כו. ושם) לא מרבינן אלא ג' על ג' וי"ל דהתם מיירי בבא מבגד גדול אבל הכא מיירי באריג כל שהוא דמתחלה לא היה דעתו להוסיף עליו ותרוייהו שמעינן מאו בגד דשקולים הם דחשיב כל שהוא אריג מתחלה כמו ג' על ג' מבגד גדול י) וא"ת ואכתי בגד כל שהוא למה הוא טמא והא בעינן שיטלטל מלא וריקן דומיא דשק וי"ל • דראוי הוא לכוף ולקפל וליקח בו מרגלית או מחט ואם תאמר א"כ פשוטי כלי עור אמאי טהורין הרי ראויין הם לקפל בו שום דבר כמו הכא וי"ל דמיירי בעור שלוק שהוא קשה:

מניין לתכשיט כל שהוא טמא. ואם תאמר תיפוק ליה דתכשיט כל שהוא טמא מדכתיב בכלי מדין טבעת ויש לומר דאפשר שהטבעת היא עבה וגדולה מאד ולא הוי כל שהוא:

אריג ותכשיט. פי' חציו אריג וחציו תכשיט טמא מכאן משמע דמ"מ בעינן שיעור קצת דאל"כ חציו דכ"ש מאי הוי:

ההוא במדין כתיב. פ"ה ובמדין הויא טומאת מת ושרץ ממת לא יליף להחמיר דמה למת שכן טומאה חמורה ומשני גמר כלי כלי משרץ פירוש מה כלי האמור בשרץ מטמא בשרץ אף כלי האמור כאן מטמא בשרץ וקשה דא"כ הוה ליה למיפרך ההוא בטומאת מת כתיב ועוד כי משני גמר כלי כלי הוה ליה לשנויי גמר בגד ועור לג"ש לכן נ"ל דההוא במדין כתיב בשלל מדין ולא מיירי הך פרשה בטומאה כלל והיכי יליף דאריג ותכשיט כל שהוא טמא מכל כלי מעשה ומשני גמר כלי כלי

עין משפט נר מצוה

נה א מיי' פי"ט מהל' שבת הלכה ה ו ומיי' פ"ט מהל' כלים הלכה ד סמג לאוין סה טוש"ע א"ח סי' שג סעיף טו:
נו ב מיי' פ"ט מהל' כלי המקדש הלכה א סמג עשין קעג:
נז ג מיי' פ"א מהל' כלים הלכה יא ופכ"ב הלכה א:

רבינו חננאל

בירית זו אצעדה. אוקימנא בשתי ירכות בלא שלשלת נקראת בירית. ואם יש בהן שלשלת נקרא כבלים. הא דתניא ציץ דומה כמין טס של זהב רחב ב' אצבעות ומוקף מאוזן לאוזן וכתוב עליו בב' שיטין יו"ד ה"א מלמעלה קדש למ"ד מלמטה. א"ר אלעזר בר' יוסי אני הייתי ברומי כו':

רב נסים גאון

אמר ר' אלעזר בר' יוסי אני ראיתיו ברומי וכתוב עליו קודש לה' בשיטה אחת. ותניא כוותיה במס' יומא בפ' הוציאו לו את הכף (דף נז) אמר ר' אלעזר בר' יוסי אני ראיתיה ברומי והיו עליה כמה טיפי דמים והדבר שגרם לו לצאת לרומי מפורש במס' מעילה בפ' קדשי מזבח (דף יז) שאל ר' מתיה בן חרש את ר' שמעון בן יוחי ברומי מניין לדם שרצים שהוא טמא אמר ליה דאמר קרא וזה לכם הטמא אמרו לו תלמידיו (גזר עליו) [חכים ליה] רשב"י אמר להם תלמוד ערוך הוא מפיו של ר' אלעזר בר' יוסי פעם אחת גזרה מלכות הרשעה גזרה על ישראל שלא ישמרו את השבת ושלא ימולו בניהם ושיבעלו נשותיהם כשהן נדות הלך ר' ראובן בן איצטרובולי וספר קומי והלך וישב עמהם אמר להם מי שיש לו אויב רוצה שיעשיר או שיעני אמרו לו יעני אמר להן אם כן לא יעשו מלאכה בשבת כדי שיענו אמרו לו טבות אמר ובטלוה חזר ואמר להן מי שיש לו אויב יכחיש או יבריא אמרו לו יכחיש אמר אם כן ימלו בניהם לח' ימים כדי שיכחישו אמרו טבות אמר ובטלוה חזר ואמר מי שיש לו אויב ירבה או ימעיט אמרו ימעיט אמר להם (לא) אם כן לא יבעלו נשותיהם כשהן נדות ובטלוה הכירו בו שהוא יהודי החזירום אמרו מי ילך ויבטל את הגזירה ילך ר' שמעון בן יוחי שהוא מלומד בנסים וילך עמו ר' אלעזר בר' יוסי וכו' על לבי גזא אשכחוה לההוא אגרתא שקלוה וקרעוה והיינו דאמר ר' אלעזר אני ראיתיה ברומי והיו עליה כמה טיפי דמים ובתוספ' מקואות (פרק ד) אמר ר' אלעזר בר' יוסי הלכה זו הוריתי ברומי לטהרה וכשבאתי אצל חברי אמרו לי יפה הוריתה ובמס' נדה בפ' הרואה כתם (דף נח) תניא כוותיה אמר ר' אלעזר בר' יוסי הלכה זו כו':

הניחא

מסורת הש"ס

א) ב"ק פג., ב) [ביצה כט: כתובות נג. בבא קמא פג. ב"מ סג:], ג) לעיל נח:, ד) [שם א' יונתן], ה) [לעיל נג. ברכות מב: עירובין לב: פסחים נג: ב"מ נא. סנהדרין ק. שבועות מ. מה: חולין יח: עה: עו:], ו) סוכה ה., ז) [ברכות לו: עירובין טז: קד. יבמות כ: עו. ב"ב קמ. קלא. סנהדרין סא. מכות ח: זבחים לד. מנחות יב: לז. חולין ע. נדה סח.], ח) קודש מלמטה לה' מלמעלה כצ"ל וכ"כ הרמב"ם בפ"ט מהל' כה"מ וגם גי' הירושלמי פ' טרף בקלפי סוטה קך, ט) [צ"ל מאתם], י) [ע' תוס' לעיל כו. ד"ה אין בו וכו'].

הגהות הב"ח

(א) תום' ד"ה בירית וכו' פי' בקונט' עומדת בשוק:

גליון הש"ס

גמ' שכן בל' יונית. וכן סוכה לה ע"א. וסנהדרין ד ע"ב טט בכתפי שתים וכו': שם ע"ב לדברי תורה. עי' ערכין יא ע"א תוס' ד"ה משמח: שם קמיה דר' ירמיה ויתיב ר"י וקא מנמנם. גיטין יא ע"ב. ונדרים כט ע"ב: תוס' ד"ה מנין לאריג וכו'. דראוי הוא לכוף. ק"ל ממתני' פ' כ"ו מ"ב דכלים לגרור המרגלית. ועי' ברמב"ם ור"ש שם והרי מ"מ הוא בכלל אפשר לקפל ולהניח בו מעות כמקדש. ולע"ג:

תורה אור השלם

א) לַמָּס מֵרֵעֵהוּ חָסֶד וְיִרְאַת שַׁדַּי יַעֲזוֹב: [איוב ו, יד]

ב) שְׂמַח בָּחוּר בְּיַלְדוּתֶךָ וִיטִיבְךָ לִבְּךָ בִּימֵי בְחוּרוֹתֶךָ וְהַלֵּךְ בְּדַרְכֵי לִבְּךָ וּבְמַרְאֵה עֵינֶיךָ וְדָע כִּי עַל כָּל אֵלֶּה יְבִיאֲךָ הָאֱלֹהִים בַּמִּשְׁפָּט: [קהלת יא, ט]

ג) כָּל דָּבָר אֲשֶׁר יָבֹא בָאֵשׁ תַּעֲבִירוּ בָאֵשׁ וְטָהֵר אַךְ בְּמֵי נִדָּה יִתְחַטָּא וְכֹל אֲשֶׁר לֹא יָבֹא בָּאֵשׁ תַּעֲבִירוּ בַּמָּיִם: [במדבר לא, כג]

ד) וְכֹל אֲשֶׁר יִפֹּל עָלָיו מֵהֶם בְּמֹתָם יִטְמָא מִכָּל כְּלִי עֵץ אוֹ בֶגֶד אוֹ עוֹר אוֹ שָׂק כָּל כְּלִי אֲשֶׁר יֵעָשֶׂה מְלָאכָה בָּהֶם בַּמַּיִם יוּבָא וְטָמֵא עַד הָעֶרֶב וְטָהֵר: [ויקרא יא, לב]

ה) וַיִּקַּח מֹשֶׁה וְאֶלְעָזָר הַכֹּהֵן אֶת הַזָּהָב מֵאִתָּם כֹּל כְּלִי מַעֲשֶׂה: [במדבר לא, נא]

ליקוטי רש"י

ניביה. יניבי"ש ל"א ארבע שיני הכלב הארוכות שבהן נושך כך שמעתי (חולין דף נט.) (בבכורות) [ב"ק פג.]. שקולא טיבותיך. אין אנו מחזיקין לך טובה בכך נטולה היא טובתך ומוטלת על הקוצים. טיבותיך, גרי"ר בלע"ז [ביצה כט:]. חיזוק טובותיך שאתה סבור שנחזיק לך טובה בזו נטולה היא ממך ומוטלת על הקוצים [כתובות נג:]. נטולה היא טובתך ומוטלת על הקוצים (שלא קשרת את הכלב) מה שאתה מנחמני הבל. [ב"ק שם]. כבר נד. ונעקר ממקומו [ב"ק שם]. כל דבר אשר יבא באש. בכלי מתכות משתעי במעשה מדין [לעיל נח:]. ומוקף מאוזן לאוזן. מקיף על המצח מאוזן לאוזן [שמות כח, לו].

The Gemara records another discussion about these two items: יָתִיב רָבִין וְרַב הוּנָא קַמֵּיהּ דְּרַב יִרְמְיָה – Ravin and Rav Huna[12] were sitting before Rav Yirmiyah, וְיָתִיב רַב יִרְמְיָה וְקָא מְנַמְנֵם – and Rav Yirmiyah was sitting and dozing; וְיָתִיב רָבִין וְקָאָמַר – and Ravin sat and said: בִּירִית בְּאַחַת כְּבָלִים בִּשְׁתַּיִם – The **garter** is worn **on one** leg, while ***kevalim*** are worn **on both** legs.[13]

Rav Huna disagrees:

אָמַר לֵיהּ רַב הוּנָא – **Rav Huna said to [Ravin]:** אֵלּוּ וָאֵלּוּ בִּשְׁתַּיִם – **These** garters **and those** *kevalim* are worn **on both** legs, וּמַטִּילִין שַׁלְשֶׁלֶת בֵּינֵיהֶן וְנַעֲשׂוּ כְּבָלִים – **but one puts a chain between them and they become leg chains.** When they are worn without a chain connecting them, they are called garters; while with the chain, they are called *kevalim* (leg chains).

The Gemara asks:

וְשַׁלְשֶׁלֶת שֶׁבּוֹ מְשַׁוְּיָא לֵיהּ מָנָא – **But does the chain on it render it a utensil?!**[14]

The Gemara proposes and rejects an explanation of why the chain would render the *kevalim* susceptible to *tumah:*

וְכִי תֵימָא כְּרַבִּי שְׁמוּאֵל בַּר נַחְמָנִי – **And should you say** that Rav Huna's opinion **accords with** that of **R' Shmuel bar Nachmani,** דְּאָמַר רַבִּי שְׁמוּאֵל בַּר נַחְמָנִי אָמַר רַבִּי יוֹחָנָן – **for R' Shmuel bar Nachmani said in the name of R' Yochanan:**[15] מִנַּיִין לְמַשְׁמִיעַ קוֹל בִּכְלֵי מַתָּכוֹת שֶׁהוּא טָמֵא – **From where** do we know concerning **a metal utensil** designed **to produce sound that it is** susceptible to ***tumah?*** שֶׁנֶּאֱמַר ,,כָּל־דָּבָר אֲשֶׁר־יָבֹא בָאֵשׁ" – **For it is stated**[16] regarding the ritual purification of the booty captured from Midian: ***Any item that has come into the fire*** *you shall pass through the fire, and it will be purified.* אֲפִילּוּ דִּיבּוּר בְּמַשְׁמַע – The seemingly superfluous word דָּבָר, *item,* **implies** that **even** an item that produces **sound** (e.g. a bell) can acquire *tumah.* Thus, we see that an item can be classified as a utensil because of its ability to produce sound. Hence, one might say that *kevalim* likewise are a utensil.[17]

The Gemara rejects this explanation:

בִּשְׁלָמָא הָתָם – **It is understandable** that the bell discussed **there** should be susceptible to *tumah,* קָא בָּעוּ לָהּ לְקָלָא וְקָעָבִיד מַעֲשֶׂה – since **one wants it for the sound** it makes, **and it performs a task** for him. הָכָא מַאי מַעֲשֶׂה קָעָבִיד – But **here** in the case of the chain, inasmuch as he has no need for the sound, **what task does it perform** for him?

The Gemara explains why *kevalim can* be considered a utensil:

הָכָא נַמִּי קָא עָבִיד מַעֲשֶׂה – **Here too, [the chain] performs a task,** דְּאָמַר רַבָּה בַּר בַּר חָנָה אָמַר רַבִּי יוֹחָנָן – **for Rabbah bar bar Chanah said in the name of R' Yochanan:** מִשְׁפָּחָה אַחַת הָיְתָה בִּירוּשָׁלַיִם שֶׁהָיוּ פְּסִיעוֹתֵיהֶן גַּסּוֹת – **There was one family in Jerusalem whose strides were large** (they took long steps when they walked), וְהָיוּ בְּתוּלוֹתֵיהֶן נוֹשְׁרוֹת – **and** consequently **the hymenal membranes** of the young girls in this family **would fall out.**[18] עָשׂוּ לָהֶן כְּבָלִים וְהִטִּילוּ שַׁלְשֶׁלֶת בֵּינֵיהֶן – **[The elders]** eventually **made garters for them and put a chain between [the bands],** thereby connecting one to the other, שֶׁלֹּא יִהְיוּ פְּסִיעוֹתֵיהֶן גַּסּוֹת – **so that their strides would not be large,** וְלֹא הָיוּ בְּתוּלוֹתֵיהֶן נוֹשְׁרוֹת – **and** the result was that **their hymenal membranes did not fall out.**[19]

R' Yirmiyah confirms this interpretation:

אִיתְּעַר בְּהוּ רַבִּי יִרְמְיָה – **R' Yirmiyah** thereupon **awoke** אָמַר לְהוּ יִישַׁר וְכֵן אָמַר רַבִּי יוֹחָנָן – and **said to [Ravin and Rav Huna]: Well said! – and so said R' Yochanan.**

The Gemara presents another statement of R' Yochanan regarding *tumah* susceptibility.[20]

כִּי אֲתָא רַב דִּימִי אָמַר רַבִּי יוֹחָנָן – **When Rav Dimi came** to Babylonia from Eretz Yisrael he said **in the name of R' Yochanan:** מִנַּיִין לְאָרִיג כָּל שֶׁהוּא שֶׁהוּא טָמֵא – **From where** do we learn **that a woven article of any size is susceptible to *tumah*?** מִצִּיץ – **From the *tzitz*** (headplate) worn by the Kohen Gadol.[21] Just as the *tzitz*, which is of small size,[22] is considered significant enough to be counted as one of the priestly vestments, so too with respect to the laws of *tumah,* a woven article of small size can be considered significant and therefore be susceptible to *tumah.*

NOTES

12. This cannot be the Rav Huna usually mentioned by the Gemara, for that sage was much greater than Rav Yirmiyah and would not have "sat before him" as a disciple (*Tosafos* to *Gittin* 11b ד״ה יתיב).

13. The garter is a single band that is worn on one leg, while *kevalim* are a pair of bands, one worn on each leg (see above, note 11).

14. The Mishnah states that *kevalim* are susceptible to *tumah,* which implies they must be a utensil that serves the woman herself. However, why should adding a chain to a pair of garters render them a utensil? (*Rashi*). [At this point the Gemara apparently assumes that the only purpose of the chain is to serve the pair of garters – i.e. to prevent them from becoming separated and lost, or to help them hold up the stockings.]

15. For an explanation of R' Shmuel bar Nachmani's dictum, see above, 58b notes 11-13.

16. *Numbers* 31:23.

17. Even though *kevalim* do not directly serve a woman, their chain does produce a sound (see *Meiri*). Perhaps that is sufficient to render the *kevalim* a utensil.

18. This was unfortunate, since an intact hymenal membrane serves as proof of a bride's virginity.

19. Unlike garters, which serve only the stockings, the chain serves the woman herself, and so *kevalim* are susceptible to *tumah.* Moreover, she is forbidden to go out wearing *kevalim* on the Sabbath, for the chain is made of gold, and she may remove it to show to a friend [which would not cause her stockings to fall, since the bands remains in place] (*Rashi*).

According to one interpretation cited by *Meiri,* the chain makes a sound when the steps are too rapid and forceful; thus, the sound itself reminded the girls to take more delicate steps.

20. To understand the next Gemara, a brief introduction is necessary:

אָרִיג – **a woven article:** We learned above (26b-27a) that a cloth is not ordinarily susceptible to *tumah* unless it measures at least three fingerbreadths [אֶצְבָּעוֹת] by three fingerbreadths (or, in some cases and according to some opinions, three handbreadths [טְפָחִים] by three handbreadths). This is the smallest size cloth considered to be significant and thus the smallest size capable of contracting *tumah*. A Mishnah in *Keilim* (27:1) teaches, however, that an article woven for the specific purpose of being used in a smaller size is susceptible to *tumah* regardless of its size. [The three by three minimum mentioned above thus refers only to a piece of cloth that comes from a larger cloth (*Tosafos, Ramban; Rashba; Rambam, Hil. Keilim* 22:1). This law is relevant not only to unusually small items, but also to such common items as a cloth belt which, though it is more than three fingerbreadths long, is less than three wide and thus not susceptible to *tumah* under the regular three by three standard (*Rambam Commentary* to *Keilim* 27:1; see *Pnei Yehoshua*).] Such an article is referred to as an אָרִיג, *woven article.* The Gemara will now quote R' Yochanan's statement regarding the source for this law.

21. The Torah (*Exodus* chapter 28) lists eight vestments worn by the Kohen Gadol, one of which is the *tzitz*, a headplate worn on his forehead. The Gemara presently assumes R' Yochanan to have held that the *tzitz* was made of woven cloth; thus, its recognition as a significant item of apparel serves as a model for other woven articles (see *Chidushei HaRan* and *Pnei Yehoshua*). [Although the verse in *Exodus* 28:36 states explicitly that the *tzitz* was made from gold, the Gemara now assumes this to mean that it was made from gold thread (*Sfas Emes*).] See also *Ritva MHK* ed.

22. It is only two fingerbreadths wide (Gemara below).

עין משפט נר מצוה

נה א מיי' פ"ט מהל' שבת הלכה ה ו ומיי' פ"ט מהל' כלים הלכה ד סמג לאוין סה טוש"ע א"ח סי' שג סעיף טו:
נו ב מיי' פ"ט מהל' כלי המקדש הלכה א סמג עשין קעג:
נז ג מיי' פ"א מהל' כלים הלכה יא ופכ"ב הלכה א:

רבינו חננאל

בירית זו אצעדה. אוקימנא בשתי ירכות בלא שלשלת נקראת בירית. ואם יש בהן שלשלת נקרא כבלים. הא דתניא ציץ דומה כמין טס של זהב רחב ב' אצבעות ומוקף מאוזן לאוזן וכתוב עליו בב' שיטין יו"ד ה"א מלמעלה קדש למ"ד מלמטה. א"ר אלעזר בר' יוסי אני הייתי ברומי כו':

רב נסים גאון

אמר ר' אלעזר בר' יוסי אני ראיתיו ברומי וכתוב עליו קודש לה' בשיטה אחת. ותניא כוותיה במס' דיומא בפ' הוציאו לו את הכף (דף נז) אמר ר' אלעזר בר' יוסי אני ראיתיה ברומי והיו עליה כמה טיפי דמים והדבר שגרם לו לצאת לרומי מפורש במס' מעילה בפ' קדשי מזבח (דף יז) שאל ר' מתיה בן חרש את ר' שמעון בן יוחי ברומי מניין לדם שרצים שהוא טמא אמר ליה דאמר קרא וזה לכם הטמא אמרו לו תלמידיו (גזר עליו) [חכים ליה] רשב"י אמר להם תלמוד ערוך הוא מפיו של ר' אלעזר בר' יוסי פעם אחת גזרה מלכות הרשעה גזרה על ישראל שלא ישמרו את השבת ושלא ימולו בניהם ושיבעלו נשותיהם כשהן נדות הלך ר' ראובן בן איצטרובולי וספר קומי והלך וישב עמהם אמר להם מי שיש לו אויב רוצה שיעשיר או שיעני אמרו לו יעני אמר להן אם כן לא יעשו מלאכה בשבת כדי שיענו אמרו לו טבות אמר ובטלוה חזר ואמר להן מי שיש לו אויב יכחיש או יבריא אמרו לו יכחיש אמר אם כן ימלו בניהם לח' ימים כדי שיכחישו אמרו טבות אמר ובטלוה חזר ואמר מי שיש לו אויב ירבה או ימעיט אמרו ימעיט אמר להם (לא) אם כן לא יבעלו נשותיהם כשהן נדות ובטלוה הכירו בו שהוא יהודי החזירום אמרו מי ילך ויבטל את הגזירה ילך ר' שמעון בן יוחי שהוא מלומד בנסים וילך עמו ר' אלעזר בר' יוסי וכו' על לבי גזא אשכחוה להַהוא אגרתא שקלוה וקרעוה והיינו דאמר ר' אלעזר אני ראיתיה ברומי והיו עליה כמה טיפי דמים ובתוספ' מקואות (פרק ד) אמר ר' אלעזר בר' יוסי הלכה זו הוריתי ברומי לטהרה וכשבאתי אצל חברי אמרו לי יפה הוריתה ובמס' נדה בפ' הרואה כתם (דף נח) תניא כוותיה אמר ר' אלעזר בר' יוסי הלכה זו כו':

הניחא

ואילו אצעדה טמאה היא. פ"ה דכתיב במעשה מדין אצעדה וצמיד וגו' וכתיב תתחטאו אתם ושביכם ולא נהירא דע"כ תתחטאו לא אכל השבי קאי דהא בהמות נמי הוו בשבי ולאו בני קבולי טומאה נינהו לכן נ"ל משום דכתיב אצעדה וצמיד וכתיב בתריה ויקח ט) (מהם) כל כלי מעשה דקאי אכל הכלים שנלקחו וילפינן לקמן כלי כלי משרצים: **בירית** תחת אצעדה עומדת. פי' בקונטרס (א) בשוק להחזיק בתי שוקיה שלא יפלו ויראו שוקיה וקשה לפי' זה דא"כ בכבלים אמאי אין יוצאין למאי דס"ד השתא דאין חילוק בין בירית לכבלים אלא שזה באחת וזה בשתים לכן נ"ל דאפשר ליטלן בלא גילוי שוקים ומש"ה כבלים אין יוצאין בהן דילמא שלפא ומחויא דתכשיט לנוי הם אבל בירית שהיא באחת לא שלפא ומחויא דאין זה תכשיט דכיון שאין לה אלא באחת גנאי היא לה ומש"ה ניחא דבירית טהורה דלאו תכשיט לנוי הוא וכלי תשמיש נמי לא הוי אלא כלי המשמש כלי דומיא דטבעת הכלי דאמר לעיל דטהור וכן פירש הקונטרס וטעמא דכבלים טמאים משום דתכשיט הם לנוי כדפי': **וכתוב** עליו בשני שיטין יו"ד ה"א מלמעלה וקדש למ"ד למטה. נראה לר"ת שהיה כתוב יו"ד ה"א בסוף שיטה ראשונה וקדש ל' בתחלת שיטה שניה והשתא נקרא יפה ואין לפרש כמשמעו דא"כ אינו נקרא כהלכתו: **מניין** לאריג כל שהוא שהוא טמא ת"ל או בגד. וא"ת והא לעיל בפרק במה מדליקין (דף כו. ושם) לא מרבינן אלא ג' על ג' וי"ל דהתם מיירי בבא מבגד גדול אבל הכא מיירי באריג כל שהוא דמתחלה לא היה דעתו להוסיף עליו ותרוייהו שמעינן מאו בגד דשקולים הם לחשיב כל שהוא אריג מתחלה כמו ג' על ג' מבגד גדול י) וא"ת ואכתי בגד כל שהוא למה הוא טמא והא בעינן שיטלטל מלא וריקן דומיא דשק וי"ל • דראוי הוא לכוף ולקפל וליקח בו מרגלית או מחט ואם תאמר א"כ פשוטי כלי עור אמאי טהורין הרי ראויין הם לקפל בו שום דבר כמו הכא וי"ל דמיירי בעור שלוק שהוא קשה: **מניין** לתכשיט כל שהוא טמא. ואם תאמר תיפוק ליה דתכשיט כל שהוא טמא מדכתיב בכלי מדין טבעת ויש לומר דאפשר שהטבעת היא עבה וגדולה מאד ולא הוי כל שהוא: **אריג** ותכשיט. פי' חליו אריג וחליו תכשיט טמא מכאן משמע דמ"מ בעינן שיעור קצת דאל"כ חליו דכ"ש מאי הוי: **ההוא** במדין כתיב. פ"ה ובמדין הויא טומאת מת ושרץ ממת לא יליף להחמיר דמה למת שכן טומאה חמורה ומשני גמר כלי כלי משרץ פירוש מה כלי האמור בשרץ מטמא בשרץ אף כלי האמור כאן מטמא בשרץ וקשה דא"כ הוה ליה למיפרך ההוא בטומאת מת כתיב ועוד כי משני גמר כלי כלי הוה ליה לשנויי גמר בגד ועור לג"ש לכן נ"ל דההוא במדין כתיב בשלל מדין ולא מיירי הך פרשה בטומאה כלל והיכי יליף דאריג ותכשיט כל שהוא טמא מכל כלי מעשה ומשני גמר כלי כלי פי' כי היכי דכלי דכתיב גבי שרצים מיירי לענין טומאה הכי נמי כלי דכתיב גבי מדין לענין טומאה:

מרעהו חסד • שכן בלשון יונית קורין לכלב למס רב נחמן בר יצחק אמר אף פורק ממנו יראת שמים שנאמר א) ויראת שדי יעזוב ההיא א) איתתא דעיילא להַהוא ביתא למיפא נבח בה כלבא איתעקר ולדה אמר לה מרי דביתא לא תידחלי דשקילי ניביה ושקילין טופריה אמרה ליה ג) שקולא טיבותיך ושדיא אחיזרי כבר נד ולד אמר רב הונא מאי דכתיב ב) שמח בחור בילדותך ויטיבך לבך בימי בחורותיך והלך בדרכי לבך ובמראה עיניך ודע כי על כל אלה יביאך האלהים במשפט עד כאן דברי יצר הרע מכאן ואילך דברי יצר טוב ריש לקיש אמר • עד כאן לדברי תורה מכאן ואילך למעשים טובים: א בירית טהורה: אמר רב יהודה בירית זו אצעדה מתיב רב יוסף בירית טהורה ויוצא בה בשבת ואילו אצעדה טמאה היא ה"ק בירית תחת אצעדה עומדת יתיב רבין ורב הונא • קמיה דרב ירמיה ויתיב רב ירמיה וקא מנמנם ויתיב רבין וקאמר בירית באחת כבלים בשתים א"ל רב הונא אלו ואלו בשתים ומטילין שלשלת ביניהן ונעשו כבלים ושלשלת שבו משויא ליה מנא וכ"ת כרבי שמואל בר נחמני ג) דאמר רבי שמואל בר נחמני א"ר ד) יוחנן מניין למשמיע קול בכלי מתכות שהוא טמא שנאמר ג) כל דבר אשר יבא באש אפילו דיבור במשמע בשלמא התם קא בעו לה לקלא וקעביד מעשה הכא מאי מעשה קעביד הכא נמי קא עביד מעשה דאמר רבה בר בר חנה א"ר יוחנן משפחה אחת היתה בירושלים שהיו פסיעותיהן גסות והיו בתולותיהן נשרות עשו להן כבלים והטילו שלשלת ביניהן שלא יהיו פסיעותיהן גסות ולא היו בתולותיהן נשרות איתער בהו ר' ירמיה אמר להו ה) יישר וכן א"ר יוחנן כי אתא רב דימי א"ר יוחנן מניין לאריג כל שהוא שהוא טמא מציץ א"ל אביי וציץ אריג הוא והתניא ו) ציץ ב כמין טס של זהב ורוחב שתי אצבעות ומוקף מאוזן לאוזן וכתוב עליו בב' שיטין יו"ד ה"א למעלה וקודש למ"ד למטה ואמר ר' אליעזר בר' יוסי אני ראיתיו בעיר רומי וכתוב קדש לה' בשיטה אחת כי סליק רב דימי לנהרדעא שלח להו ז) דברים שאמרתי לכם טעות הם בידי ברם כך אמרו משום רבי יוחנן מניין לתכשיט כ"ש שהוא טמא מציץ ומניין לאריג כ"ש שהוא טמא ד) מאו בגד תנו רבנן ג אריג כ"ש טמא ותכשיט כ"ש טמא אריג ותכשיט כ"ש טמא מוסף שק על הבגד שטמא משום אריג אמר רבא אריג כל שהוא טמא מאו בגד תכשיט כל שהוא טמא מציץ אריג ותכשיט כל שהוא טמא ה) מכל כלי מעשה א"ל ההוא מרבנן לרבא ההוא במדין כתיב א"ל גמר כלי

מרעהו. מונע חסד ואע"ג דלא כתיב מונע ממילא משמע שכל תיבה שראשה מ"ם משמשת נטילה היא כמו ויקח מידם (שמות לב) אבדו גוים מארצו (תהלים י): **למיפא.** לאפות עיסה שהשאיל בעה"ב תנורו: **שקילי ניביה.** נטולות ד' שיניו שהוא נושך בהן אותן שיניים קרי ניבין כדאמרינן באלו טרפות (חולין דף נט.) גמל ניבי אית ליה: **שקילי טופריה.** נטולות צפרניו מלסרוט: **שקולא.** נטולה טובתך ומוטלת על הקוצים: **טיבותיך.** טובת הנאת נחמתך כמו מחזיק טוב הגרי"א בלע"ז: **עד כאן.** עד ודע כי על כל אלה וגו': **עד כאן לתורה.** שמח בתלמודך למוד משמחה ומטוב לב והלך בדרכי לבך להבין מה בלבך לפי ראות עיניך: **מכאן ואילך למעשים טובים.** ודע כי על כל אלה על כל מה שלמדת סופך ליתן את הדין אם לא תקיים: **אצעדה.** של זרוע: **ואילו אצעדה טמאה היא.** דכתיב (במדבר לא) במעשה מדין אצעדה וצמיד וגו' וכתיב תתחטאו אתם ושביכם: **תחת אצעדה.** שבזרוע עומדת בשוק להחזיק בתי שוקיה שלא יפלו ויראו שוקיה הלכך טהורה דלאו לנוי היא וכלי תשמיש נמי לא הוי אלא כלי המשמש כלי דומיא דטבעות הכלים דאמרינן בפרקין דלעיל דטהורין ויוצאין בהם דלורך לבישה היא ומישלף ואחויי נמי ליכא למיחש דלא מיגליא לשוקה: **בירית באחת.** משוקיה: **ושלשלת משוי להו מנא.** בתמיה דקתני כבלים טמאים: **וכי תימא כדר' שמואל כו': משמיע קול בכלי מתכות.** בריש פרקין: **ועשו להן שלשלת כו'.** הלכך שלשלת תשמיש אדם הוא ולאו תשמיש כלי דלא תקבל טומאה ואין יוצאין בהן דילמא שלפא לשלשלת שהיא של זהב ומחויא דכי שקלה לשלשלת לא מיגליא שוקה שהרי בירית במקומה עומדת: **יישר וכן אמר ר' יוחנן.** יפה אמרת וכן שמעתי מר' יוחנן: **מציץ.** שהוא דבר מועט ומנאו עם תכשיטי כהן: **יו"ד ה"א מלמעלה קדש למ"ד מלמטה.** כלומר השם שלם בשיטה עליונה וקדש למ"ד בשיטה תחתונה שלא להקדים שאר אותיות למעלה מן השם מאחר ששני שיטין היו ורבינו הלוי שונה ח) קודש לה' מלמטה והיא היא: **אני ראיתיו ברומי.** שנכנס לאוצר המלך ליטול מה שירצה במס' מעילה (דף יז:) במעשה בן תלמיון: **כי סליק רב דימי לנהרדעא.** חזר בו ממה שאמר ציץ אריג הוא: **מאו בגד.** דכתיב גבי שרצים או בגד או עור או ריבוי הוא: **אריג ותכשיט כל שהוא.** חליו אריג וחליו תכשיט שאינו אריג וכולו הוי כל שהוא כלומר דבר קטן: **מוסיף שק על הבגד.** בדבר זה שהשק טמא משום אריג ולקמיה מפרש ליה: **ההוא במדין כתיב.** גבי טומאת מת ושרץ ממת לא יליף להחמיר דמה למת שכן טומאתו חמורה:

כלי

מסורת הש"ס

א) ב"ק פג., ב) [ביצה כט: כתובות נג. בבא קמא פג. ב"מ סג:], ג) לעיל נח:, ד) [שם אי' יונתן], ה) [לעיל נג. ברכות מב: עירובין לב: פסחים נג: ב"מ נא. סנהדרין ק. שבועות מ. מה: חולין יח: עה: עו:], ו) סוכה ה., ז) [ברכות לא: עירובין נח: קד. יבמות כ: עו. ב"ב קמ. קלא. סנהדרין סא. מכות ח: זבחים לד. מנחות יב: לז. חולין נו. נדה סח.], ח) קודש מלמטה לה' מלמעלה כצ"ל וכ"כ הרמב"ם בפ"ט מהל' כה"מ וגם גי' הירושלמי פ' טרף בקלפי נוטה כך, ט) [נ"ל מאתם], י) [ע' תוס' לעיל כו. ד"ה אין בו וכו'].

הגהות הב"ח

(א) תוס' ד"ה בירית וכו' פי' בקונט' עומדת בשוק:

גליון הש"ס

גמ' שכן בל' יונית. וכן סוכה לה ע"א. וסנהדרין ד ע"ב טט בכתפי שתים וכו': שם ע"ב לדברי תורה. עי' ערכין יא ע"א תוס' ד"ה משמח: שם קמיה דר' ירמיה ויתיב ר"י וקא מנמנם. גיטין יא ע"ב. ונדרים כט ע"ב: תוס' ד"ה מנין לאריג וכו'. דראוי הוא לכוף. ק"ל ממתני' פ' כ"ו מ"ב דכלים לרור המרגלית. ועי' ברמב"ם ור"ש שם והרי מ"מ הוא בכלל אפשר לקפל ולהניח בו מעות כמקדם. ולע"ג:

תורה אור השלם

א) לַמָּס מֵרֵעֵהוּ חָסֶד וְיִרְאַת שַׁדַּי יַעֲזוֹב: [איוב ו, יד]

ב) שְׂמַח בָּחוּר בְּיַלְדוּתֶךָ וִיטִיבְךָ לִבְּךָ בִּימֵי בְחוּרוֹתֶךָ וְהַלֵּךְ בְּדַרְכֵי לִבְּךָ וּבְמַרְאֵה עֵינֶיךָ וְדָע כִּי עַל כָּל אֵלֶּה יְבִיאֲךָ הָאֱלֹהִים בַּמִּשְׁפָּט: [קהלת יא, ט]

ג) כָּל דָּבָר אֲשֶׁר יָבֹא בָאֵשׁ תַּעֲבִירוּ בָאֵשׁ וְטָהֵר אַךְ בְּמֵי נִדָּה יִתְחַטָּא וְכֹל אֲשֶׁר לֹא יָבֹא בָּאֵשׁ תַּעֲבִירוּ בַמָּיִם: [במדבר לא, כג]

ד) וְכֹל אֲשֶׁר יִפֹּל עָלָיו מֵהֶם בְּמֹתָם יִטְמָא מִכָּל כְּלִי עֵץ אוֹ בֶגֶד אוֹ עוֹר אוֹ שָׂק כָּל כְּלִי אֲשֶׁר יֵעָשֶׂה מְלָאכָה בָּהֶם בַּמַּיִם יוּבָא וְטָמֵא עַד הָעֶרֶב וְטָהֵר: [ויקרא יא, לב]

ה) וַיִּקַּח מֹשֶׁה וְאֶלְעָזָר הַכֹּהֵן אֶת הַזָּהָב מֵאִתָּם כֹּל כְּלִי מַעֲשֶׂה: [במדבר לא, נא]

ליקוטי רש"י

ניביה. יניבי"ש ל"א ארבע שיני הכלב הארוכות שבהן נושך כך שמעתי (חולין דף נט.) (בבכורות) [ב"ק פג.]. שקולא טיבותיך. אין אנו מחזיקין לך טובה בכך נטולה היא טובתך ומוטלת על הקולים. טיבותיך, גרי"ר בלע"ז [ביצה כט:]. חיזוק טובותיך שאתה סבור שנחזיק לך טובה בזו נטולה היא ממך ומוטלת על החרולים [כתובות נג:]. נטולה היא טובתך ומוטלת על הקולים (שלא קשרת את הכלב) מה שאתה מנחמני הבל. כבר נד. ונעקר ממקומו [ב"ק שם]. כל דבר אשר יבא באש. בכלי מתכות משתעי במעשה מדין [לעיל נח:]. ומוקף מאוזן לאוזן. מקיף על המצח מאוזן לאוזן [שמות כח, לז].

The derivation is challenged:

אָמַר לֵיהּ אַבַּיֵי – Abaye asked [Rav Dimi]: וְצִיץ אָרִיג הוּא – Was the *tzitz* a woven article? וְהָתַנְיָא – But we have learned in a Baraisa otherwise: צִיץ כְּמִין טַס שֶׁל זָהָב – THE *TZITZ* WAS A SORT OF GOLD PLATE, וְרוֹחַב שְׁתֵּי אֶצְבָּעוֹת – TWO FINGER-BREADTHS WIDE, וּמוּקָּף מֵאוֹזֶן לְאוֹזֶן – WHICH ENCIRCLED the Kohen Gadol's forehead FROM EAR TO EAR. וְכָתוּב עָלָיו בִּשְׁתֵּי שִׁיטִין ,,יו״ד הֵא״ לְמַעְלָה וְ,,קוֹדֶשׁ למ״ד״ לְמַטָּה – AND INSCRIBED ON IT, ON TWO separate LINES, were the words "HASHEM" (i.e. the Tetragrammaton)[23] ON THE UPPER line AND "HOLY TO" ON THE LOWER line.[24] וְאָמַר רַבִּי אֱלִיעֶזֶר בְּרַבִּי יוֹסֵי – AND R' ELIEZER THE SON OF R' YOSE SAID: אֲנִי רְאִיתִיו בְּעִיר רוֹמִי – I SAW IT IN THE CITY OF ROME וְכָתוּב ,,קֹדֶשׁ לַה׳ ״ בְּשִׁיטָה אַחַת – AND the words "HOLY TO HASHEM" WERE all INSCRIBED ON ONE LINE.[25] It is clear from this Baraisa that the *tzitz* was a plate of gold and was not a weave. How then can the dimensions of the *tzitz* serve as the source for the law that a woven article is susceptible to *tumah* in any size?

Rav Dimi accepted this objection:

כִּי סָלִיק רַב דִּימִי לִנְהַרְדְּעָא שָׁלַח לְהוּ – When Rav Dimi traveled to Nehardea he sent back **to them** the following message.[26] **דְּבָרִים שֶׁאָמַרְתִּי לָכֶם טָעוּת הֵם בְּיָדִי – The statement that I** previously **made to you** (that the *tumah* susceptibility of a diminutive woven article is derived from the *tzitz*) **was a mistake on my part. בְּרַם כָּךְ אָמְרוּ מִשּׁוּם רַבִּי יוֹחָנָן – In truth, this is what they said in the name of R' Yochanan: מִנַּיִין לְתַכְשִׁיט כָּל שֶׁהוּא טָמֵא – From where do we know that an ornament of any size is** susceptible to ***tumah*?**[27] **מִצִּיץ – From the *tzitz*** which was a diminutive ornament and was nevertheless counted among the priestly vestments. So too, with respect to the laws of *tumah,* a diminutive ornament has sufficient significance to be subject to *tumah.* **וּמִנַּיִין לְאָרִיג כָּל שֶׁהוּא טָמֵא – And from where do we know that a woven article of any size is** susceptible to ***tumah*? מֵ,,אוֹ בֶגֶד״ – From** the verse: ***or a garment.***[28]

The Gemara cites a Baraisa concerning the law just learned:

תָּנוּ רַבָּנָן – The Rabbis taught in a Baraisa: אָרִיג כָּל שֶׁהוּא טָמֵא – A WOVEN ARTICLE OF ANY SIZE IS susceptible to *TUMAH;* וְתַכְשִׁיט כָּל שֶׁהוּא טָמֵא – AND AN ORNAMENT OF ANY SIZE IS SUSCEPTIBLE TO *TUMAH.* אָרִיג וְתַכְשִׁיט כָּל שֶׁהוּא טָמֵא – An article that is partly A WEAVE AND partly AN ORNAMENT, OF ANY SIZE, IS SUSCEPTIBLE TO *TUMAH.*[29] מוּסָף שַׂק עַל הַבֶּגֶד שֶׁטָּמֵא מִשּׁוּם אָרִיג – SACK cloth (i.e. cloth made of goats' hair) IS MORE susceptible to *tumah* THAN GARMENT cloth (i.e. cloth made of ordinary fibers)[30]

NOTES

23. I.e. the full four-letter Name of God [*yud, kah, vav, keh*] (*Rashi*). [The Baraisa, however, merely mentions the first two letters to avoid spelling out the entire name (see *Tosafos, Avodah Zarah* 18a ד״ה הוגה השם).]

24. Thereby forming the phrase קֹדֶשׁ לַה׳, *Holy to Hashem.* In deference to the sanctity of the Divine Name, however, the word "Hashem" was inscribed on the upper line and "Holy to" on the lower line. Since the words were to be inscribed on two lines, putting קֹדֶשׁ לְ, *Holy to,* first would have resulted in another word being placed above the Name of God, which would have been inappropriate. The natural sequence of the words was therefore reversed so that the word "Hashem" should be on the top line (*Rashi* as explained by *Ritva MHK* edition; see diagram).

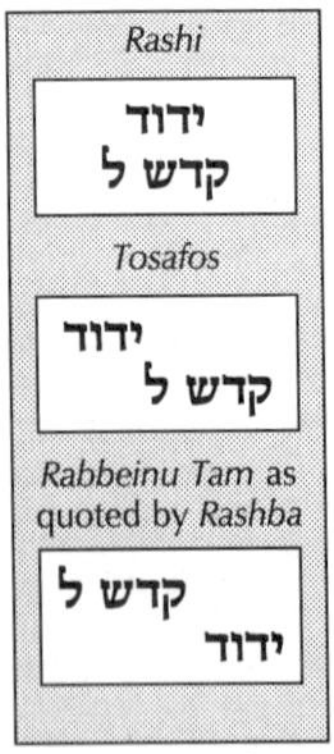

Tosafos challenge this explanation on the grounds that reversing the order of the words would prevent them from being read properly. *Tosafos* therefore assert that the word "Hashem" was inscribed at the *end* of the upper line and קֹדֶשׁ לְ, *Holy to,* was inscribed at the *beginning* of the lower line, so that the phrase could be read in its proper sequence (see diagram). Still others assert that the words קֹדֶשׁ לְ appeared at the end of the top line and the word "Hashem" at the beginning of the bottom line. According to this view, the words לְמַעְלָה, לְמַטָּה should be translated as *earlier* and *later* rather than *upper* and *lower* (*Rashba* citing *Rabbeinu Tam; Rabbinu Bachya* to *Exodus* 28:36 citing *Raavad*, quoted by *Maharam, Succah* 5a; *Tosafos* here attribute the second view to *Rabbeinu Tam*).

[*Rashi*, quoting *Rabbeinu HaLevi*, cites another version of the Baraisa that reads קֹדֶשׁ (*Holy*) on one line and לַה׳ (*to Hashem*) on the other line; i.e. the *lamed* was kept together with the word "Hashem." This is also *Rambam's* version of the Baraisa.]

25. R' Eliezer the son of R' Yose earned the gratitude of the emperor and was allowed into the royal treasury to choose his reward. While inside he saw many of the vessels of the Temple, which had been carried off by the Romans when they destroyed it. (The circumstances surrounding his visit to Rome are recounted in *Me'ilah* 17b and the way in which he earned the emperor's gratitude is more fully elaborated by *Rashi, Yoma* 57a.)

[It is interesting to note that although R' Eliezer the son of R' Yose gave an eyewitness account, the Sages still did not accept his opinion but relied on their tradition. This is because even according to the Sages a *tzitz* is acceptable after the fact (בְּדִיעֲבַד) even if both words were inscribed on one line. The Sages felt that the *tzitz* observed by R' Eliezer did not disprove their tradition (see *Rambam, Klei HaMikdash* 9:1 with *Kesef Mishneh*).]

26. [When Rav Dimi came to Babylonia, he reported R' Yochanan's teaching to the Yeshiva of Pumbedisa, as is evident from the fact that Abaye (who studied in and later headed this Yeshiva) challenged Rav Dimi's account. Thus, when Rav Dimi later traveled to Nehardea and reconsidered what he had said, he sent a message back to the Yeshiva of Pumbedisa to correct his error.]

27. The law that an ornament is susceptible to *tumah* is derived from the verse regarding the jewelry captured by the Israelites during their retaliation against the Midianites (*Rashi* above ד״ה ואילו אצעדה and 52a ד״ה טמאה; see *Numbers* 31:50). The Gemara's inquiry here concerns the source for the law that an ornament of even minuscule size is susceptible to *tumah*.

Although ordinary utensils do not require any minimum size to be susceptible to *tumah* (e.g. even a needle contracts *tumah*), ornaments are not considered regular utensils since they are not *used* in the performance of any task, but merely hang decoratively. Thus, it is necessary to derive their susceptibility and size separately (*Pnei Yehoshua* in explanation of *Rashi;* see *Rashi* 64a ד״ה כל כלי; see also *Mishnah Acharonah* to *Keilim* 11:8 ד״ה כל תכשיטי נשים).

[See *Tosafos, Rashba* and *Ritva* (*MHK* ed.) for a discussion of why the Gemara did not simply derive the rule for undersized ornaments from the ring mentioned among the adornments captured from the Midianites.]

28. *Leviticus* 11:32. The verse speaks of the various objects that are subject to the *tumah* of *sheretz* (any of the eight creeping creatures listed in *Leviticus* 11:29-30). The verse in its entirety states: וְכֹל אֲשֶׁר־יִפֹּל־עָלָיו מֵהֶם בְּמֹתָם יִטְמָא מִכָּל־כְּלִי־עֵץ אוֹ בֶגֶד אוֹ עוֹר אוֹ שָׂק כָּל־כְּלִי אֲשֶׁר־יֵעָשֶׂה מְלָאכָה בָּהֶם בַּמַּיִם יוּבָא וְטָמֵא עַד־הָעֶרֶב וְטָהֵר, *And anything upon which a part of them falls when they are dead shall become tamei, whether any wooden utensil, or a garment, or a hide, or a sack – every utensil with which work is done – shall be brought into the water and remain tamei until evening and then become tahor*. The word אוֹ, *or,* is extra [since the verse could have said וּבֶגֶד rather than אוֹ בֶגֶד] and is thus understood to be inclusionary of something else – namely, an אָרִיג, *woven article* (*Rashi*) [which is like a garment but lacks its minimum size].

[Thus, R' Yochanan actually said two laws regarding articles being susceptible to *tumah* in any size, one in regard to ornaments and one in regard to woven articles. Rav Dimi in his original citation mistakenly telescoped the two laws, quoting the law about woven articles together with the source given by R' Yochanan for ornaments.]

29. Even though neither part is functional on its own and thus cannot qualify for *tumah* under either of the previous categories (*Rashi* as explained by *Ritva* and *Chazon Ish, Keilim* 30:27; cf. *Rashba*). See note 32.

30. [Whether this refers specifically to cloth made of wool or linen, or even to cloth made of other fibers, was discussed by the Gemara above, 26b-27a.]

מרעהו חסד ° שכן בלשון יונית קורין לכלב למס רב נחמן בר יצחק אמר אף פורק ממנו יראת שמים שנאמר א) ויראת שדי יעזוב ההיא ה) איתתא דעיילא להדוא ביתא למיפא נבח בה כלבא איתעקר ולדה אמר לה מרי דביתא לא תידחלי דשקילי ניביה ושקילין טופריה אמרה ליה ג) שקולא טיבותיך ושדיא אחיזרי כבר נד ולד אמר רב הונא מאי דכתיב ב) שמח בחור בילדותך ויטיבך לבך בימי בחורותיך והלך בדרכי לבך ובמראה עיניך ודע כי על כל אלה יביאך האלהים במשפט עד כאן דברי יצר הרע מכאן ואילך דברי יצר טוב ריש לקיש אמר ° עד כאן לדברי תורה מכאן ואילך למעשים טובים: א בירית טהורה: אמר רב יהודה בירית זו אצעדה מתיב רב יוסף בירית טהורה ויוצא בה בשבת ואילו אצעדה טמאה היא ה"ק בירית תחת אצעדה עומדת יתיב רבין ורב הונא ° קמיה דרב ירמיה ויתיב רב ירמיה וקא מנמנם ויתיב רבין וקאמר בירית באחת כבלים בשתים א"ל רב הונא אלו ואלו בשתים ומטילין שלשלת ביניהן ונעשו כבלים ושלשלת שבו משויא ליה מנא וכ"ת כרבי שמואל בר נחמני ג) דאמר רבי שמואל בר נחמני א"ר ד) יוחנן מניין למשמיע קול בכלי מתכות שהוא טמא שנאמר ג) כל דבר אשר יבא באש אפילו דיבור במשמע בשלמא התם קא בעו לה לקלא וקעביד מעשה הכא מאי מעשה קעביד הכא נמי קא עביד מעשה דאמר רבה בר בר חנה א"ר יוחנן משפחה אחת היתה בירושלים שהיו פסיעותיהן גסות והיו בתולותיהן נושרות עשו להן כבלים והטילו שלשלת ביניהן שלא יהיו פסיעותיהן גסות ולא היו בתולותיהן נושרות איתער בהו ר' ירמיה אמר להו ה) יישר וכן א"ר יוחנן כי אתא רב דימי א"ר יוחנן מניין לאריג כל שהוא שהוא טמא מציץ א"ל אביי וציץ אריג הוא והתניא ו) ציץ ב כמין טס של זהב ורוחב שתי אצבעות ומוקף מאוזן לאוזן וכתוב עליו בב' שיטין יו"ד ה"א למעלה וקודש למ"ד למטה ואמר ר' אליעזר בר' יוסי אני ראיתיו בעיר רומי וכתוב קדש לה' בשיטה אחת כי סליק רב דימי לנהרדעא שלח להו ז) דברים שאמרתי לכם טעות הם בידי ברם כך אמרו משום רבי יוחנן מניין לתכשיט כ"ש שהוא טמא מציץ ומניין לאריג כ"ש שהוא טמא ד) מאו בגד תנו רבנן ג אריג כ"ש טמא ותכשיט כ"ש טמא אריג ותכשיט כ"ש טמא מוסף שק על הבגד שטמא משום אריג אמר רבא אריג כל שהוא טמא מאו בגד תכשיט כל שהוא טמא מציץ אריג ותכשיט כל שהוא טמא ה) מכל כלי מעשה א"ל ההוא מרבנן לרבא ההוא במדין כתיב א"ל גמר כלי

כלי

רש"י

מרעהו. מונע חסד ולא"ג דלא כתיב מונע ממילא משמע שכל תיבה שראשה מ"ס משמשת נטילה היא כמו ויקח מידם (שמות לג) אבדו גוים מארצו (תהלים י): למיפא. לאפות עיסה שהשאיל בעה"ב תנורו: שקילי ניביה. נטולות ד' שיניו שהוא נושך בהן אותן שיניים קרי ניבין כדאמרינן באלו טרפות (חולין דף נט.) גמל ניבי אית ליה: שקילי טופריה. נטולות לפרניו מלסרוט: שקולא. נטולה טובתך ומוטלת על הקוצים: טיבותיך. טובת הנאה נחמתך כמו מחזיק טוב הגרי"א בלע"ז: עד כאן. עד ודע כי על כל אלה וגו': עד כאן לתורה. שמח בתלמודך למוד משמחה ומטוב לב והלך בדרכי לבך להבין מה בלבך לפי ראות עיניך: מכאן ואילך למעשים טובים. ודע כי על כל אלה על כל מה שלמדת סופך ליתן את הדין אם לא תקיים: אצעדה. של זרוע: ואילו אצעדה טמאה היא. דכתיב (במדבר לא) במעשה מדין אצעדה וצמיד וגו' וכתיב תתחטאו אתם ושביכם: תחת אצעדה. שבזרוע עומדת בשוק להחזיק בתי שוקיה שלא יפלו ויראו שוקיה הלכך טהורה דלאו לנוי היא וכלי תשמיש נמי לא הוי אלא כלי המשמש כלי דומיא דטבעות הכלים דאמרינן בפרקין דלעיל דטהורין ויוצאין בהם דלורך לבישה היא ומישלף ואחוויי נמי ליכא למיחש דלא מיגליא לשוקה: בירית באחת. משוקיה: ושלשלת משוי להו מנא. בתמיה דקתני כבלים טמאים: וכי תימא כדר' שמואל כו': משמיע קול בכלי מתכות. בריש פרקין: ועשו להן שלשלת כו'. הלכך שלשלת תשמיש אדם הוא ולאו תשמיש כלי דלא תקבל טומאה ואין יוצאין בהן דילמא שלפא לשלשלת שהיא של זהב ומחויא דכי שקלה לשלשלת לא מיגליא שוקה שהרי בירית במקומה עומדת: יישר וכן אמר ר' יוחנן. יפה אמרת וכן שמעתי מר' יוחנן: מציץ. שהוא דבר מועט ומנאו עם תכשיטי כהן: יו"ד ה"א מלמעלה קדש למ"ד מלמטה. כלומר השם שלם בשיטה עליונה וקדש למ"ד בשיטה תחתונה שלא להקדים שאר אותיות למעלה מן השם מאחר ששני שיטין היו ורבינו הלוי שונה ח) קודש לה' מלמטה והיא היא: אני ראיתיו ברומי. שנכנס לאוצר המלך ליטול מה שירצה במס' מעילה (דף יז:) במעשה בן תלמיון: כי סליק רב דימי לנהרדעא. חזר בו ממה שאמר ציץ אריג הוא: מאו בגד. דכתיב גבי שרצים או בגד או עור או ריבוי הוא: אריג ותכשיט כל שהוא. חליו אריג וחליו תכשיט שאינו אריג וכולו הוי כל שהוא כלומר דבר קטן: מוסיף שק על הבגד. בדבר זה שהשק טמא משום אריג ולקמיה מפרש ליה: ההוא במדין כתיב. גבי טומאת מת ושרץ ממת לא יליף להחמיר דמה למת שכן טומאתו חמורה:

כלי

תוספות

ואילו אצעדה טמאה היא. פ"ה דכתיב במעשה מדין אצעדה וצמיד וגו' וכתיב תתחטאו אתם ושביכם ולא נהירא דע"כ תתחטאו לא אכל השבי קאי דהא בהמות נמי הוו בשבי ולאו בני קבולי טומאה נינהו לכן נ"ל משום דכתיב אצעדה וצמיד וכתיב בתריה ויקח ט) (מהם) כל כלי מעשה דקאי אכל הכלים שנלקחו וילפינן לקמן כלי כלי משרצים: בירית תחת אצעדה עומדת. פי' בקונטרס (א) בשוק להחזיק בתי שוקיה שלא יפלו ויראו שוקיה וקשה לפי' זה דא"כ בכבלים אמאי אין יוצאין למאי דס"ד השתא דאין חילוק בין בירית לכבלים אלא שזה באחת וזה בשתים לכן נ"ל דאפשר ליטלן בלא גילוי שוקים ומש"ה כבלים אין יוצאין בהן דילמא שלפא ומחויא דתכשיט לנוי הם אבל בירית שהיא באחת לא שלפא ומחויא דאין זה תכשיט דכיון שאין לה אלא באחת גנאי היא לה ומש"ה ניחא דבירית טהורה דלאו תכשיט לנוי הוא וכלי תשמיש נמי לא הוי אלא כלי המשמש כלי דומיא דטבעת הכלי דאמר לעיל דטהור וכן פירש הקונטרס וטעמא דכבלים טמאים משום דתכשיט הם לנוי כדפי': וכתוב עליו בשני שיטין יו"ד ה"א מלמעלה וקדש למ"ד למטה. נראה לר"ת שהיה כתוב יו"ד ה"א בסוף שיטה ראשונה וקדש ל' בתחלת שיטה שניה והשתא נקרא יפה ואין לפרש כמשמעו דא"כ אינו נקרא כהלכתו: מניין לאריג כל שהוא שהוא טמא ת"ל או בגד. וא"ת והא לעיל בפרק במה מדליקין (דף כו. ושם) לא מרבינן אלא ג' על ג' וי"ל דהתם מיירי בבא מבגד גדול אבל הכא מיירי באריג כל שהוא דמתחלה לא היה דעתו להוסיף עליו ותרוייהו שמעינן מאו בגד דשקולים הם דחשיב כל שהוא אריג מתחלה כמו ג' על ג' מבגד גדול י) וא"ת ואכתי בגד כל שהוא למה הוא טמא והא בעינן שיטלטל מלא וריקן דומיא דשק וי"ל ° דראוי הוא לכוף ולקפל וליקח בו מרגלית או מחט ואם תאמר א"כ פשוטי כלי עור אמאי טהורין הרי ראויין הם לקפל בו שום דבר כמו הכא וי"ל דמיירי בעור שלוק שהוא קשה: מניין לתכשיט כל שהוא טמא. ואם תאמר תיפוק ליה דתכשיט כל שהוא טמא מדכתיב בכלי מדין טבעת ויש לומר דאפשר שהטבעת היא עבה וגדולה מאד ולא הוי כל שהוא: אריג ותכשיט. פי' חליו אריג וחליו תכשיט טמא מכאן משמע דמ"מ בעינן שיעור קצת דאל"כ חליו דכ"ש מאי הוי: ההוא במדין כתיב. פ"ה ובמדין הויא טומאת מת ושרץ ממת לא יליף להחמיר דמה למת שכן טומאה חמורה ומשני גמר כלי כלי משרץ פירוש מה כלי האמור בשרץ מטמא בשרץ אף כלי האמור כאן מטמא בשרץ וקשה דא"כ הוה ליה למיפרך ההוא בטומאת מת כתיב ועוד כי משני גמר כלי כלי הוה ליה לשנויי גמר בגד ועור לג"ש לכן נ"ל דההוא במדין כתיב בשלל מדין ולא מיירי הך פרשה בטומאה כלל והיכי יליף דאריג ותכשיט כל שהוא טמא מכל כלי מעשה ומשני גמר כלי כלי פי' כי היכי דכלי דכתיב גבי שרצים מיירי לענין טומאה הכי נמי כלי דכתיב גבי מדין לענין טומאה:

מניין

עין משפט נר מצוה

נה א מיי' פ"ט מהל' שבת הלכה ה ו ומיי' פ"ט מהל' כלים הלכה ד סמג לאוין סה טוש"ע א"ח סי' שג סעיף טו:

נו ב מיי' פ"ט מהל' כלי המקדש הלכה א סמג עשין קעג:

נז ג מיי' פ"א מהל' כלים הלכה יא ופכ"ב הלכה א:

רבינו חננאל

בירית זו אצעדה. אוקימנא בשתי ירוכות בלא שלשלת נקראת בירית. ואם יש בהן שלשלת נקרא כבלים. הא דתניא ציץ דומה כמין טס של זהב רחב ב' אצבעות ומוקף מאוזן לאוזן וכתוב עליו בב' שיטין יו"ד ה"א מלמעלה קדש למ"ד מלמטה. א"ר אלעזר בר' יוסי אני הייתי ברומי כו':

רב נסים גאון

אמר ר' אלעזר בר' יוסי אני ראיתיו ברומי וכתוב עליו קודש לה' בשיטה אחת. ותניא כוותיה במס' יומא בפ' הוציאו לו את הכף (דף נז) אמר ר' אלעזר בר' יוסי אני ראיתיה ברומי והיו עליה כמה טיפי דמים והדבר שגרם לו לצאת לרומי מפורש במס' מעילה בפ' קדשי מזבח (דף יז) שאל ר' מתיה בן חרש את ר' שמעון בן יוחי ברומי מניין לדם שרצים שהוא טמא אמר ליה דאמר קרא וזה לכם הטמא אמרו לו תלמידיו (גזר עליו) [חכים ליה] רשב"י אמר להם תלמוד ערוך הוא מפיו של ר' אלעזר בר' יוסי פעם אחת גזרה מלכות הרשעה גזרה על ישראל שלא ישמרו את השבת ושלא ימולו בניהם ושיבעלו נשותיהם כשהן נדות הלך ר' ראובן בן איצטרובולי וספר קומי והלך וישב עמהם אמר להם מי שיש לו אויב רוצה שיעשיר או שיעני אמרו לו יעני אמר להן אם כן לא יעשו מלאכה בשבת כדי שיענו אמרו לו טבות אמר ובטלוה חזר ואמר להן מי שיש לו אויב יכחיש או יבריא אמרו לו יכחיש אמר אם כן ימלו בניהם לח' ימים כדי שיכחישו אמרו טבות אמר ובטלוה חזר ואמר מי שיש לו אויב ירבה או ימעיט אמרו ימעיט אמר להם (לא) אם כן לא יבעלו נשותיהם כשהן נדות ובטלוה הכירו בו שהוא יהודי החזירום אמרו מי ילך ויבטל את הגזירה ילך ר' שמעון בן יוחי שהוא מלומד בנסים וילך עמו ר' אלעזר בר' יוסי וכו' על לבי גזא אשכחוה להההוא אגרתא שקלוה וקרעוה והיינו דאמר ר' אלעזר אני ראיתיה ברומי והיו עליה כמה טיפי דמים ובתוספ' מקואות (פרק ד) אמר ר' אלעזר בר' יוסי הלכה זו הוריתי ברומי לטהרה וכשבאתי אצל חברי אמרו לי יפה הוריתה ובמס' נדה בפ' הרואה כתם (דף נח) תניא כוותיה אמר ר' אלעזר בר' יוסי הלכה זו כו':

הניחא

מסורת הש"ס

א) ב"ק פג., ב) [ביצה כט: כתובות נג. בבא קמא פג. ב"מ סג:], ג) לעיל נח:, ד) [שם אי' יונתן], ה) [לעיל נג. ברכות מב: עירובין לג: פסחים נג: ב"מ נח. סנהדרין ק. שבועות מ. מה: חולין יח: עה: עו:], ו) סוכה ה., ז) [ברכות לו: עירובין טז: קד. יבמות כ: עו. ב"ב קמ. קלא. סנהדרין סא. מכות ח: זבחים לד. מנחות יב: לז. חולין ע. נדה סח.], ח) קודש מלמטה לה' מלמעלה כצ"ל וכ"כ הרמב"ם בפ"ט מהל' כה"מ וגם גי' הירושלמי פ' טרף בקלפי נטה קך, ט) [צ"ל מאתם], י) [ע' תוס' לעיל כו. ד"ה אין בו וכו'].

הגהות הב"ח

(א) תוס' ד"ה בירית וכו' פי' בקונט' עומדת בשוק:

גליון הש"ס

גמ' שכן בל' יונית. וכן סוכה לה ע"א. וסנהדרין ד ע"ב טט בכתפי שתים וכו': שם ע"ב לדברי תורה. עי' ערכין יא ע"א תוס' ד"ה משמש: שם קמיה דר' ירמיה ויתיב ר"י וקא מנמנם. גיטין יא ע"ב. ונדרים כט ע"ב: תוס' ד"ה מנין לאריג וכו'. דראוי הוא לכוף. ק"ל ממתני' פ' כ"ו מ"ב דכלים לרור המרגלית. ועי' ברמב"ם ור"ש שם והרי מ"מ הוא בכלל אפשר לקפל ולהניח בו מעות כמקדש. ולע"ג:

תורה אור השלם

א) לַמָּס מֵרֵעֵהוּ חָסֶד וְיִרְאַת שַׁדַּי יַעֲזוֹב: [איוב ו, יד]

ב) שְׂמַח בָּחוּר בְּיַלְדוּתֶךָ וִיטִיבְךָ לִבְּךָ בִּימֵי בְחוּרוֹתֶךָ וְהַלֵּךְ בְּדַרְכֵי לִבְּךָ וּבְמַרְאֵה עֵינֶיךָ וְדָע כִּי עַל כָּל אֵלֶּה יְבִיאֲךָ הָאֱלֹהִים בַּמִּשְׁפָּט: [קהלת יא, ט]

ג) כָּל דָּבָר אֲשֶׁר יָבֹא בָאֵשׁ תַּעֲבִירוּ בָאֵשׁ וְטָהֵר אַךְ בְּמֵי נִדָּה יִתְחַטָּא וְכֹל אֲשֶׁר לֹא יָבֹא בָּאֵשׁ תַּעֲבִירוּ בַמָּיִם: [במדבר לא, כג]

ד) וְכֹל אֲשֶׁר יִפֹּל עָלָיו מֵהֶם בְּמֹתָם יִטְמָא מִכָּל כְּלִי עֵץ אוֹ בֶגֶד אוֹ עוֹר אוֹ שָׂק כָּל כְּלִי אֲשֶׁר יֵעָשֶׂה מְלָאכָה בָּהֶם בַּמַּיִם יוּבָא וְטָמֵא עַד הָעֶרֶב וְטָהֵר: [ויקרא יא, לב]

ה) וַיִּקַּח מֹשֶׁה וְאֶלְעָזָר הַכֹּהֵן אֶת הַזָּהָב מֵאִתָּם כֹּל כְּלִי מַעֲשֶׂה: [במדבר לא, נא]

ליקוטי רש"י

ניביה. יינייד"ש ל"א ארבע שיני הכלב הארוכות שבהן נושך כך שמעתי (חולין דף נט.) (בבכורות) [ב"ק פג.]. שקולא טיבותיך. אין אתו מחזיקין לך טובה בכך נטולה היא טובתך ומוטלת על הקוצים. טיבותיך, גרי"ר בלע"ז [ביצה כט:]. חיזוק טובותיך שאתה סבור שנחזיק לך טובה בזו נטולה היא ממך ומוטלת על החרולים [כתובות נג:]. נטולה היא טובתך ומוטלת על הקוצים (שלא קשרת את הכלב) מה שאתה מנחמני הבל. כבר נד. ונעקר ממקומו [ב"ק שם]. כל דבר אשר יבא באש. בכלי מתכות משתעי במעשה מדין [לעיל נח:]. ומוקף מאוזן לאוזן. מקיף על המצח מאוזן לאוזן [שמות כח, לו].

IN THAT IT [sack cloth] IS SUSCEPTIBLE TO *TUMAH* AS A WOVEN ARTICLE.[31]

The Gemara cites the Scriptural sources for the Baraisa's rulings:

אָמַר רָבָא – Rava said: אָרִיג כָּל שֶׁהוּא טָמֵא מֵ,,אוֹ בֶגֶד״ – The law that **a woven article of any size is susceptible to *tumah* is** derived **from** the verse: ***or a garment,*** as stated above. תַּכְשִׁיט כָּל שֶׁהוּא טָמֵא מִצִּיץ – The law that **an ornament of any size is susceptible to *tumah*** is derived **from the *tzitz,*** as stated above. אָרִיג וְתַכְשִׁיט כָּל שֶׁהוּא טָמֵא ,,מִכֹּל כְּלִי מַעֲשֶׂה״ – The law that an article that is partly **a weave and** partly **an ornament, of any size, is** susceptible to ***tumah*** is derived **from** the verse: ***every fashioned vessel.***[32]

This last derivation is questioned:

אָמַר לֵיהּ הַהוּא מֵרַבָּנָן לְרָבָא – **One of the Rabbis asked Rava** regarding this derivation: הַהוּא בְּמִדְיָן כְּתִיב – **That** verse, *every fashioned vessel*, **is stated in** the passage concerning the war with **the Midianites,** in which the Torah is dealing with corpse *tumah*. How do we know to apply this law to the *tumah* of a *sheretz* which is a more lenient form of *tumah?*[33]

Rava replies:

אָמַר לֵיהּ – [Rava] answered him: גָּמַר – **It is derived**

NOTES

31. This ruling will be explained by the Gemara on 64a.

32. [*Numbers* 31:51 – *And Moses and Elazar the Kohen took the gold from them, every fashioned vessel.* The verse refers to the jewelry captured from the Midianites. Since they were taken in battle they are assumed to have come in contact with a corpse. Thus, they are included in the laws of corpse *tumah* taught in that passage (see *Rashi* above ד״ה ואילו אצעדה). The word כֹּל, *every*, is inclusionary and thus teaches that the law of the ornament applies even to something that is only partially an ornament.]

Seemingly, this combination article was used as an ornament. Why then should a new derivation be required for its *tumah*? Possibly, since the law for undersized ornaments is derived from the *tzitz,* we can only learn from it the susceptibility of undersized metal ornaments. [Thus, since the metal part of this combined piece does not serve as an ornament in its own right, the susceptibility of the piece as a whole must be separately derived.] See *Ritva* MHK ed.; see also *Tosafos* ד״ה אריג ותכשיט.

33. For one who contracts *tumah* from a *sheretz* immerses in a *mikveh* and is *tahor* that evening, whereas one who contracts corpse *tumah* remains *tamei* for at least seven days (see *Rashi* 64a ד״ה אם היקל). Since the law of corpse *tumah* is more stringent, any stringencies stated in connection with that law cannot be assumed to apply to less stringent forms of *tumah* (*Rashi* from Baraisa 64a).

,,כְּלִי" ,,כְּלִי" מֵהָתָם – by means of a *gezeirah shavah* between the words ***utensil*** and ***utensil***, **from there** – the utensils taken from the Midianites.[1]

The Gemara cites the final ruling of the Baraisa quoted above: מוּסָף שַׂק עַל הַבֶּגֶד שֶׁטָּמֵא מִשּׁוּם אָרִיג – SACK cloth (i.e. cloth made from goats' hair)[2] IS MORE susceptible to *tumah* THAN GARMENT cloth (i.e. cloth made of other fibers)[3] IN THAT IT [sack cloth] IS SUSCEPTIBLE TO *TUMAH* AS A WOVEN ARTICLE.

The Gemara understands the Baraisa to be saying that an undersized piece of sack cloth is subject to *tumah* as a woven article, whereas a regular cloth is not. The Gemara therefore asks: אַטּוּ בֶּגֶד לָאו אָרִיג הוּא – **Is then a garment not** also **a woven article?** Why should an ordinary cloth not also be susceptible to *tumah* if it is woven to be used specifically as an undersized item?[4]

The Gemara answers:

הָכִי קָאָמַר – **This is what [the Baraisa]** means to **say:** מוּסָף שַׂק עַל הַבֶּגֶד – **Sack** cloth (i.e. goats' hair fabric) **is more** susceptible to *tumah* **than a garment** (ordinary fabric) אַף עַל פִּי שֶׁאֵינוֹ אָרִיג טָמֵא – in that **it is susceptible to *tumah* even though it is *not* a woven article** but merely braided.[5]

The Gemara asks:

לְמַאי חָזֵי – **For what is [braided sackcloth] fit?**[6]

The Gemara answers:

אָמַר רַבִּי יוֹחָנָן – **R' Yochanan said:** שֶׁכֵּן עָנִי קוֹלֵעַ שָׁלֹשׁ נִימִין – **For a poor man will braid three strands** (i.e. threads) **of** goats' hair together וְתוֹלֶה בְּצַוַּאר בִּתּוֹ – **and hang it around his daughter's neck.**[7]

The Gemara cites a Baraisa:

תָּנוּ רַבָּנָן – **The Rabbis taught in a Baraisa:** The verse lists among the articles that acquire *tumah* from a dead *sheretz*: ,,שַׂק" – A *SACK*.[8] אֵין לִי אֶלָּא שַׂק – From this I KNOW ONLY that A SACK is susceptible to *tumah*. מִנַּיִין לְרַבּוֹת אֶת הַקִּילְקְלִי וְאֶת הַחֲבָק – FROM WHERE do I know TO INCLUDE A BREAST STRAP AND A GIRTH[9] in the law of susceptibility to *tumah*? תַּלְמוּד לוֹמַר – To teach this [THE TORAH] STATES: ,,אוֹ שָׂק" – *OR A SACK.*[10] יָכוֹל שֶׁאֲנִי מְרַבֶּה אֶת הַחֲבָלִים וְאֶת הַמְּשִׁיחוֹת – Now IT MIGHT BE thought on this basis THAT I should also INCLUDE ROPES AND MEASURING STRINGS[11] among the goats'-hair items that are susceptible to *tumah*. תַּלְמוּד לוֹמַר ,,שַׂק" – To dispel this notion [THE TORAH] STATES the specific example of a *SACK*: מָה שַׂק טָווּי וְאָרִיג – JUST AS A SACK IS made of SPUN AND WOVEN thread, אַף כָּל טָווּי וְאָרִיג – SO TOO, ALL other items produced from goats' hair are only susceptible to *tumah* if they are made of SPUN AND WOVEN thread. This excludes ropes, for they are not made from spun thread.[12]

The above discussion concerned *tumah* transmitted by a *sheretz*. The Baraisa now examines the law for these materials in regard to corpse *tumah*:

הֲרֵי הוּא אוֹמֵר בְּמֵת – NOW, THE [VERSE] STATES IN REGARD TO utensils that come in contact with A CORPSE: ,,וְכָל־כְּלִי־עוֹר וְכָל־מַעֲשֵׂה עִזִּים וגו׳ תִּתְחַטָּאוּ" – *AND EVERY UTENSIL OF HIDE, AND*

NOTES

1. The Torah states in regard to the utensils that can be contaminated by a *sheretz* that they are כָּל־כְּלִי אֲשֶׁר־יֵעָשֶׂה מְלָאכָה בָּהֶם, *every utensil with which work is done* (*Rashi*, from *Leviticus* 11:32; see above, 63b note 30). The word כְּלִי, *utensil*, in this verse connects to the word כְּלִי, *utensil*, in the verse concerning the Midianite vessels cited above, to form a *gezeirah shavah* from which we may learn that the law taught in the latter verse in regard to corpse *tumah* applies for the *tumah* of *sheretz* as well.

The *tumah* of a utensil that is part weave and part ornament cannot be learned (without the *gezeirah shavah*) simply from the text of the *sheretz* verse itself, which speaks of *every utensil with which work is done*, for this description applies only to utensils with which *work is done* (i.e. to something else), not to an article of adornment, which is merely decorative (*Rashi*; see 63b note 27). [Thus, since the combination of weave and ornament is used merely as an ornament, its susceptibility to the *tumah* of *sheretz* must be derived separately from the *gezeirah shavah.*]

2. The word שַׂק, *sack*, refers specifically to material made of goats' hair (*Rashi* here and *Zevachim* 93b ד״ה שק).

3. [The word "garment" in this context does not refer to an article of clothing specifically, but rather to fabric (see *Keilim* 27:1 and above, 26b-27b).]

4. [Indeed, since the special law of a "woven article" is derived from the extra word in the phrase *or a garment* (אוֹ בֶגֶד), as we learned on 63b, this law must surely apply to ordinary cloth as well.]

5. The Baraisa should thus be understood as follows: "Sackcloth is susceptible to *tumah* as a woven article – even when it is not actually woven but merely braided." The reason for this is that it is customary for goats' hair to be used in this manner [as the Gemara will shortly explain] (*Rashi*). Other fibers, however [such as wool and linen], are susceptible to *tumah* as woven articles only when they are actually woven.

6. [For a woven fabric to be susceptible to *tumah* even though it is less than three fingers wide it must have been made to be used in this small size (see 63b). The Gemara therefore wonders what purpose is served by such a small piece of braided goats' hair that people would actually bother to make it.]

7. I.e. a poor man makes a necklace for his daughter out of a few threads of dyed goats' hair which he then braids together. [The Gemara does not mean that he makes them out of three hairs, but rather out of three *threads* of spun goats' hair.] This string serves as the band of a necklace, from which pendants are hung. Since braided goats'-hair necklaces are used by the poor as adornments, they qualify for susceptibility to *tumah* under the category of "woven articles." Although they are not actually woven, their braiding is considered tantamount to weaving (*Rashi*, who cites as a parallel the case of the "chains of open-link threads" mentioned on 57a, which the Gemara calls a "woven article" even though it was made of just linked loops of thread).

[Since the Gemara is giving this as an illustration of goats' hair's greater susceptibility to *tumah* as a "woven article," it is clear that this necklace is not being defined as susceptible to *tumah* because it is a תַּכְשִׁיט, *ornament*, but rather because it is an אָרִיג, *woven article*. A fabric must by definition qualify for *tumah* under the rules of fabrics (see, however, *Meiri* and *Chidushei HaRan*). Nevertheless, this braided piece of goats' hair is considered a *useful* woven article because it serves a function as part of a necklace.]

[Necklaces of this sort were made by the poor specifically from goats'-hair thread because wool and linen threads are thinner and a braid made of three threads would not form a substantial necklace (*Raavad* to *Eduyos* 3:4 ד״ה חוץ מן הצמרים).]

8. *Leviticus* 11:32. (The verse was quoted in its entirety on 63b note 30.) The sacks of Biblical times were made of goats' hair spun into a coarse thread (see above, note 2).

9. These items are woven from spun goats'-hair thread. The breast strap binds the harness of a horse or donkey to the animal's chest below the neck; the girth (or bellyband) is a strap attached to a harness or saddle that is passed beneath the belly of the animal to fasten it from underneath (see *Rashi* and *Targum HaLaaz*). [Although made from goats'-hair thread, these items are not like sacks, for they are never used as garments by humans, whereas] sacks are sometimes used to outfit shepherds (*Rashi*). Thus, an additional source is required to teach their susceptibility to *tumah*.

10. [The word אוֹ, *or*, in this verse is redundant (since a simple *vav* would have sufficed to serve as the conjunction). It is thus understood to add things that are similar to a sack, namely, items woven from goats' hair that had been spun into thread.]

11. I.e. long strings [of fixed lengths] used to measure distances [somewhat like our modern tape measures]. These measuring strings and ropes were made of goats' hair that had not been spun but merely twisted together to form a cord (*Rashi*).

12. The breast strap and girth, however, are made of spun and woven thread and thus are included in the law of *tumah*. Similarly, the braided threads used to make necklaces were also made from spun goats'-hair thread. Although the threads were not woven together, their braiding serves in place of weaving and renders them susceptible to *tumah* (*Rashi*; see note 7 above).

א) כלי כלי מהתם: מוסף א שק על הבגד שטמא משום אריג: אטו בגד לאו אריג הוא הכי קאמר מוסף שק על הבגד אף על פי שאינו אריג טמא למאי חזי אמר רבי יוחנן שכן עני קולע שלש נימין ותולה בצואר בתו (א) תנו רבנן א) שק אין לי אלא שק ב מניין לרבות את הקילקלי ואת החבק ת"ל או שק ג יכול שאני מרבה את החבלים ואת המשיחות ת"ל שק מה שק טווי ואריג אף כל טווי ואריג הרי הוא אומר במת ב) וכל כלי עור וכל מעשה עזים וגו' תתחטאו לרבות הקילקלי ואת החבק יכול שאני מרבה את החבלים ואת המשיחות ודין הוא טימא בשרץ וטימא במת מה כשטימא בשרץ לא טימא אלא טווי ואריג אף כשטימא במת לא טימא אלא טווי ואריג הן אם היקל בטמא שרץ שהיא קלה נקיל בטומאת המת שהיא חמורה תלמוד לומר בגד ועור בגד ועור לגזירה שוה נאמר א) בגד ועור בשרץ ונאמר ב) בגד ועור במת מה בגד ועור האמור בשרץ לא טימא אלא טווי ואריג אף בגד ועור האמור במת לא טימא אלא טווי ואריג ומה בגד ועור האמור במת טמא כל מעשה עזים אף בגד ועור האמור בשרץ טמא כל מעשה עזים אין לי אלא דבר הבא מן העזים ד מניין לרבות דבר הבא מזנב הסוס ומזנב הפרה תלמוד לומר א) או שק והא אפיקתיה לקילקלי וחבק הני מילי מקמי דליתיה ג"ש השתא דאתי גזירה שוה אייתור ליה ואין לי אלא בשרץ בטומאת מת מניין ודין הוא טימא במת וטימא בשרץ מה כשטימא בשרץ עשה דבר הבא מזנב הסוס ומזנב הפרה כמעשה עזים אף כשטימא במת עשה דבר הבא מזנב הסוס ומזנב הפרה כמעשה עזים הן אם הרבה בטומאת ערב שהיא מרובה נרבה בטומאת שבעה שהיא מועטת תלמוד לומר בגד ועור בגד ועור לגזירה שוה נאמר בגד ועור בשרץ ונאמר בגד ועור במת מה בגד ועור האמור בשרץ עשה דבר הבא מזנב הסוס ומזנב הפרה כמעשה עזים אף בגד ועור האמור במת עשה דבר הבא מזנב הסוס ומזנב הפרה כמעשה עזים ומופנה דאי לאו מופנה איכא למיפרך מה לשרץ שכן מטמא בכעדשה ה לאי אפנויי מופני ו מכדי שרץ איתקש לשכבת זרע דכתיב ג) איש אשר תצא ממנו שכבת זרע וסמיך ליה ד) איש אשר יגע בכל שרץ וכתיב ביה בשכבת זרע ה) וכל בגד וכל עור אשר יהיה עליו שכבת זרע בגד ועור דכתב רחמנא בשרץ למה לי שמע מינה לאפנויי ואכתי מופנה מצד אחד הוא הניחא למאן דאמר ז מופנה מצד אחד למידין ואין משיבין אלא למאן דאמר ח למידין ומשיבין מאי איכא למימר דמת נמי אפנויי מופנה מכדי מת אתקש לשכבת זרע דכתיב ג) והנוגע בכל טמא נפש או איש אשר תצא ממנו שכבת זרע וכתיב בשכבת זרע וכל בגד וכל עור בגד ועור דכתב רחמנא במת למה לי ש"מ לאפנויי: ו) ונקרב את קרבן ה' איש אשר מצא כלי זהב אצעדה וצמיד טבעת עגיל וכומז א"ר אלעזר ט עגיל זה דפוס של דדין כומז זה דפוס של בית הרחם אמר רב יוסף אי הכי היינו דמתרגמינן מחוך דבר המביא לידי גיחוך אמר ליה רבה מגופיה דקרא ש"מ כומז כאן מקום זימה: ז) ויקצוף משה על פקודי החיל אמר רב נחמן אמר רבה בר אבוה אמר להן משה לישראל שמא חזרתם לקלקולכם הראשון אמרו לו ח) לא נפקד ממנו איש אמר להן אם כן כפרה למה אמרו לו אם מידי עבירה יצאנו מידי הרהור לא יצאנו מיד ו) ונקרב את קרבן ה' תנא דבי רבי ישמעאל מפני מה הוצרכו ישראל שבאותו הדור כפרה מפני

שזנו

רש"י

כלי כלי. בשרצים כתיב כל כלי אשר יעשה מלאכה וגו' ומגופיה דקרא דשרצים לא מצי יליף דאשר יעשה מלאכה לאו כלי תכשיט משמע: שק. הוא עשוי מנוצה של עזים שאף על פי שאינו אריג אלא קלע קטן עשה מנוצה של עזים לתלות בו בתי נפש לצואר בתו טמא שדרכו בכך ותכשיט הוא וה"ק שהוא טמא משום אריג ואע"פ שאינו אריג: קולע ג' נימין כו'. ג' חוטין של מטוה של נוצה של עזים לבועה: ותולה בצואר בתו. וקליעתה זו היא אריגתו מאחר שהוא טווי כדאמרן גבי תיכי חלילתא בריש פירקין דקרי להו אריג והא דקאמר אע"פ שאינו אריג כלומר לאו אריג ממש: אין לי אלא שק. העשוי ללבוש רועים: קילקלי. מסרך של סוס שקורין פייטרא"ל: חבק. ליגגלא של סרגא ואוכף ועושין אותה מנוצה של עזים טווי ואריג: יכול שאני מרבה החבלים והמשיחות. לציא"ל שעושין למדוד וקולעין מן הנוצה כמו שנתלשה ואינו טווי ולא דמי לקולע שלש נימין דלעיל דהתם טווי הוא וזו היא אריגתו: יכול שאני מרבה כו'. הואיל וכתיב כל: ודין הוא שלא נרבה. ולא צריך קרא למעוטי: הן. תמיה הוא וכי דברים כוונים הם: אם היקל בטומאת שרץ שהיא קלה. כלומר אם היקל מלטמא חבלים ומשיחות היקל לך בשרץ שטומאתו קלה טומאת ערב: נקל. גם אנחנו בבנין אב זה במת שטומאתו חמורה טומאת ז': השתא דאתיא גזירה שוה. וכי היכי דיליף מת משרץ למעוטי חבלים ומשיחות יליף נמי שרץ ממת לכל מעשה עזים לרבות קילקלי וחבק: אין לי אלא בשרץ. דלא שק התם כתיב: אם ריבה. לטמא דבר הבא מזנב הסוס בטומאת ערב הוא דריבה: שהיא מרובה. שכל המגעות טומאת ערב הן בין דשרץ ונבילה ושכבת זרע מגע הזב ומגע טמא מת: נרבה אנו בטומאת ז' שכן מועטת היא. שאינה בכל המגעות אלא במגע המת בלבד: מופנה. צריך שתהא גזירה שוה זו מב' תיבות דבגד ועור מופנין למדרש זה שלא יהו צריכין לגופן ומאחר שמופנין ללמוד גזירה שוה ה"ל כמאן דכתיב דרשא בקרא בהדיא ואין משיבין עליה: דאי לאו מופנה. אמרינן לגופן באו ולא ילפינן להא מילתא מינייהו: דאיכא למיפרך כו'. וה"ה דמצי למימר הכי אגזירה שוה קמייתא ומיהו אסקי לכולה ברייתא ברישא ופריך אהא דסליק מינה ובשינויא דמשנינן בהא מיתרצא נמי קמייתא: לאי. באמת: וכתיב ביה בשכבת זרע. דבגד ועור טמאים הם בו: מצד אחד. הכתובין בשרץ מופנים כדאמרן אבל הכתובין במת אין מופנין: הניחא למ"ד כו'. פלוגתא דרבי ישמעאל ורבנן היא במסכת נדה בהמפלת (דף כב:): אלא למאן דאמר למידין. אם אין תשובה: ומשיבין. אם יש להשיב: מאי איכא למימר. הרי יש להשיב שכן מטמא בכעדשה: והנוגע בכל טמא נפש או איש אשר תצא ממנו שכבת זרע: דפוס של דדין. שמונחות בו: גיחוך. ליצנות: לקלקולכם. של מעשה שטים לזנות את בנות מואב שמא כך עשיתם במדין לכך אתם צריכין קרבן: לא נפקד. לא נחסר מדת יהודית:

שזנו

תוספות

מניין לרבות את הקילקלי והחבק. ואם תאמר והא לא מיטלטל מלא וריקן ואי משום דאפשר לקפלה אם אינו עשוי לכך לאו כלום הוא כדאמר לקמן גבי קב הקיטע דאע"ג דיש לו בית קיבול לראש שוקו אם אינו עשוי לקבל טהור וי"ל דהני נמי לשם כל צורכן הן עשוין מתחלה אך קשה דלעיל פ' במה מדליקין (דף כ. ושם) מפיק דבר הבא מן העזים דמטמא בשרצים מאו בגד וקילקלי וחבק באין מן העזים ומפיק להן הכא מאו שק ועו"ק דהתם מרבה לנוצה של עזים לג' על ג' ואילו שק שיעורו בד' ואומר ר"י דתרי גווני נוצה של עזים הוו והתם מיירי [בדקה] שעושים ממנה בגדים חשובים והלכך איתרבו לשלשה על שלשה כמו שאר בגדים והכא מיירי בנוצה גסה שממנה עושין קילקלי וחבק וחבלים ומשיחות ושק: שמע מינה לאפנויי. הקשה ה"ר אליעזר ממיץ כיון דאיתקש שרץ ומת לשכבת זרע א"כ ג"ש דבגד ועור ל"ל דכל מה שיהיה במת ניתן בשכבת זרע וכל מה שיהיה בשכבת זרע ניתן בשרץ וכן להפך דהא קי"ל ז) דבר הבא מן ההיקש חוזר ומלמד בהיקש חוץ מן הקדשים: מידי הרהור מי יצאנו. וא"ת והא אפילו (א) יפת תואר הותרה להם וי"ל דמכל מקום שייך בה איסור כדאמרינן (קדושין דף כב.) ותשקת בה ולא בחברתה:

וכמון

עין משפט נר מצוה

נח א ב ג ד מיי' פ"א מהל' כלים הלכה יב:

רבינו חננאל

קילקלי. מלשון יון הוא והוא עשוי בגד [(גליון) משיער של עזים והוא קשה עשוי להצניעו תחת הכרים והכסתות. חבקים כסוי הכסאות (ת"ל) או בגד או עור או שק אין לי אלא] שק בלבד מנין לרבות הקילקלי וחבק ת"ל או שק פי' מרבינן להו מאו כלומר הוה ליה למימר שק. או דכתב רחמנא למה לי לרבויי קילקלי וחבק. יכול שאני מרבה חבלים ומשיחין שיטמאו ת"ל שק מה שק טווי ואריג אף כל טווי ואריג הרי הוא אמר במת כל מעשה עזים יכול שאני מרבה חבלים ומשיחים דין הוא טימא בשרץ טימא במת כו'. ודחינן ואם היקל בטומאת שרץ שהיא קלה פי' טומאת שרץ קלה היא שהיא טומאת ערב אבל טומאת מת חמורה היא שהיא טומאת שבעה לא נתרבה ת"ל (או) בגד ועור בגד ועור לג"ש נאמר בגד ועור בשרץ ונאמר בגד ועור במת. פי' דין ג"ש ב' פסוקים וכל פסוק ופסוק כתוב מלין שאינן צריכין לפסוק ואין מילין פטיין לא נכתבו אלא בתוך פסוקים אלו אלא לדון מהם ג"ש להיות כל דין שמפורש באחד מהן שיהא גם השני כמותו וזהו שכתוב בענייננו בגד ועור בשרץ בגד ועור במת וצריכין להיות אלו בגד ועור מופנים בשני הפסוקים. שאם הן בפסוק אחד יתירין כגון שלמדו טומאת בגד ועור בשרץ משכבת זרע ונמצא בגד ועור האמור בשרץ מופנה כגון זה למידין ואם יש פירכא משיבין ופורכין ואם הן אלו פסוקים בגד ועור יתירין בשרץ ובמת למידין במת מן השרץ זהו טמאין במת דבר הבא מזנב הסוס מזנב הפרה כשם שמטמאין בשרץ ואין משיבין ואע"ג דאיכא למפרך ואם ריבה בטומאת שרץ שהיא מרובה. פי' טומאת שרץ (נותנת) [נוהגת] בשמנה שרצים. נרבה טומאת מת שהיא מועטת שאינה אלא במת בלבד ואוקימנא כיון שהן מופנה משני צדדין למידין ואין משיבין. ואלו הדברים הל"מ להדרש בענין הזה מסורת בידי חכמים:

רב נסים גאון

הניחא למאן [דאמר] מופנה מצד א' למדין ואין משיבין אלא למאן דאמר למידין ומשיבין מאי איכא למימר. מחלוקת בין ר' ישמעאל ורבנן ועיקר דילה במס' נדה בפרק המפלת (דף כב) אמר רב יהודה אמר שמואל משום ר' כל גזירה שוה שאינה מופנה כל עיקר אין למידין ממנה מופנה מצד אחד לר' ישמעאל למידין ואין משיבין לרבנן למידין ומשיבין: אמר להם משה לישראל שמא חזרתם לקלקולכם הראשון אמרו לו לא נפקד ממנו איש. במס' יבמות בפרק הבא על יבמתו (דף סא) אמרו ור' שמעון לא נפקד ממנו איש לעבירה ולדבר זה נתכונו בהם בתשובה זו:

קסבר

מסורת הש"ס

א) ת"כ פ' שמיני, ב) [בערוך איתא לאיי ומפרש דלשון יון הוא ע"ש], ג) [ב"ק כה:], ד) [נדה כב:], ה) [לקמן קלא. יבמות ע: עד. נדה כב:], ו) [מס' כלה], ז) [זבחים מט:].

הגהות הב"ח

(א) תוס' ד"ה מידי וכו' אפי' ליקח יפת תואר:

תורה אור השלם

א) וְכֹל אֲשֶׁר יִפֹּל עָלָיו מֵהֶם בְּמֹתָם יִטְמָא מִכָּל כְּלִי עֵץ אוֹ בֶגֶד אוֹ עוֹר אוֹ שָׂק כָּל כְּלִי אֲשֶׁר יֵעָשֶׂה מְלָאכָה בָּהֶם בַּמַּיִם יוּבָא וְטָמֵא עַד הָעֶרֶב וְטָהֵר: [ויקרא יא, לב]

ב) וְכָל בֶּגֶד וְכָל כְּלִי עוֹר וְכָל מַעֲשֵׂה עִזִּים וְכָל כְּלִי עֵץ תִּתְחַטָּאוּ: [במדבר לא, כ]

ג) אִישׁ אִישׁ מִזֶּרַע אַהֲרֹן וְהוּא צָרוּעַ אוֹ זָב בַּקֳּדָשִׁים לֹא יֹאכַל עַד אֲשֶׁר יִטְהָר וְהַנֹּגֵעַ בְּכָל טְמֵא נֶפֶשׁ אוֹ אִישׁ אֲשֶׁר תֵּצֵא מִמֶּנּוּ שִׁכְבַת זָרַע: [ויקרא כב, ד]

ד) אוֹ אִישׁ אֲשֶׁר יִגַּע בְּכָל שֶׁרֶץ אֲשֶׁר יִטְמָא לוֹ אוֹ בְאָדָם אֲשֶׁר יִטְמָא לוֹ לְכֹל טֻמְאָתוֹ: [ויקרא כב, ה]

ה) וְכָל בֶּגֶד וְכָל עוֹר אֲשֶׁר יִהְיֶה עָלָיו שִׁכְבַת זָרַע וְכֻבַּס בַּמַּיִם וְטָמֵא עַד הָעָרֶב: [ויקרא טו, יז]

ו) וַנַּקְרֵב אֶת קָרְבַּן יְיָ אִישׁ אֲשֶׁר מָצָא כְלִי זָהָב אֶצְעָדָה וְצָמִיד טַבַּעַת עָגִיל וְכוּמָז לְכַפֵּר עַל נַפְשֹׁתֵינוּ לִפְנֵי יְיָ: [במדבר לא, נ]

ז) וַיִּקְצֹף מֹשֶׁה עַל פְּקוּדֵי הֶחָיִל שָׂרֵי הָאֲלָפִים וְשָׂרֵי הַמֵּאוֹת הַבָּאִים מִצְּבָא הַמִּלְחָמָה: [במדבר לא, יד]

ח) וַיֹּאמְרוּ אֶל מֹשֶׁה עֲבָדֶיךָ נָשְׂאוּ אֶת רֹאשׁ אַנְשֵׁי הַמִּלְחָמָה אֲשֶׁר בְּיָדֵנוּ וְלֹא נִפְקַד מִמֶּנּוּ אִישׁ: [במדבר לא, מט]

ליקוטי רש"י

קילקלי. ליגגל"ש לקשור האוכף במכיסת החמור. חבק. פוטרי"ל וצרכי רכיבה הן [רשב"ם ב"ב עח.]. ליגגל"א לאסור בו סוס [לעיל נז.]. למידין ואין משיבין. ואפילו יש להשיב [נדה כב:]. בכל טמא נפש. כמי שנטמא במת [ויקרא כב, ד]. אצעדה. אלו צמידים של רגל. וצמיד. של יד. וכומז. דפוס של בית הרחם לכפר על הרהור הלב של בנות מדין [במדבר לא, נ]. דפוס של בית הרחם. כלי זהב הוא נתון כנגד אותו מקום לאשה ורבותינו פירשו שם כומז כאן מקום זמה [שמות לה, כב]. שהיו עושין לבנותיהן ונוקבין כתלי בית הרחם כדרך שנוקבין את האזנים ותוחבין אותו כדי שלא יזדקקו להן זכרים [ברכות כד.]. על פקודי החיל. ממונים על החיל [במדבר שם, יד].

EVERYTHING MADE FROM GOATS ETC. *YOU SHALL PURIFY.*[13] לְרַבּוֹת הַקִּילְקְלִי וְאֶת הַחֲבָק – The word "*everything*" serves TO INCLUDE THE BREAST STRAP AND THE GIRTH and teaches that they too are susceptible to corpse *tumah.* יָכוֹל שֶׁאֲנִי מְרַבֶּה אֶת הַחֲבָלִים וְאֶת הַמְּשִׁיחוֹת – Now IT MIGHT BE thought THAT I SHOULD also INCLUDE THE ROPE AND THE MEASURING STRING in the law of susceptibility to corpse *tumah.*[14]

Before presenting the Scriptural text that excludes them from *tumah* susceptibility, the Baraisa first attempts to exclude them by simple analogy to the law of *sheretz* cited above:

וְדִין הוּא – BUT IT IS only LOGICAL to assume the reverse, i.e. that we do *not* include the rope and the measuring string. טִימֵּא בְּשֶׁרֶץ – For [THE TORAH] DECLARED goats' hair SUSCEPTIBLE TO *TUMAH* IN the case of A *SHERETZ,* וְטִימֵּא בְּמֵת – AND [THE TORAH] DECLARED goats' hair SUSCEPTIBLE TO *TUMAH* IN the case of A CORPSE. מַה כְּשֶׁטִּימֵּא בְּשֶׁרֶץ – JUST AS WHEN [THE TORAH] DECLARED *TUMAH* IN the case of A *SHERETZ,* לֹא טִימֵּא אֶלָּא טָווּי וְאָרִיג – IT DECLARED articles of goats' hair SUSCEPTIBLE TO *TUMAH* ONLY if they are made of goats' hair that was SPUN AND WOVEN, as expounded by the Baraisa above, אַף כְּשֶׁטִּימֵּא בְּמֵת – SO TOO WHEN IT DECLARED *TUMAH* IN the case of A CORPSE, לֹא טִימֵּא אֶלָּא טָווּי וְאָרִיג – IT also DECLARED SUSCEPTIBLE TO *TUMAH* ONLY articles made of goats' hair that was SPUN AND WOVEN.[15]

The Baraisa rejects this analogy:

הֵן – INDEED? Is this analogy compelling? אִם הֵיקֵל בְּטָמֵא שֶׁרֶץ שֶׁהִיא קַלָּה – IF [THE TORAH] WAS LENIENT WITH RESPECT TO SOMETHING CONTAMINATED BY A *SHERETZ,*[16] WHICH IS a more LENIENT form of *tumah,*[17] נָקֵיל בְּטוּמְאַת הַמֵּת – SHOULD WE therefore BE LENIENT WITH RESPECT TO CORPSE *TUMAH,* שֶׁהִיא חֲמוּרָה – WHICH IS a more STRINGENT form of *tumah*? Certainly not! Therefore, even though ropes and measuring strings are excluded from the *tumah* of a *sheretz,* they are perhaps still susceptible to the more stringent corpse *tumah.*

The Baraisa therefore cites a *gezeirah shavah* to exclude ropes and measuring strings from corpse *tumah:*

תַּלְמוּד לוֹמַר – For this reason [THE TORAH] STATES the words: "בֶּגֶד וְעוֹר" "בֶּגֶד וְעוֹר" לִגְזֵירָה שָׁוָה – *GARMENT* AND *HIDE* and *GARMENT* AND *HIDE* – TO establish A *GEZEIRAH SHAVAH.* נֶאֱמַר "בֶּגֶד וְעוֹר" בְּשֶׁרֶץ – IT IS STATED IN REGARD TO the *tumah* of a *SHERETZ: whether* ... A GARMENT OR A HIDE ...[18] וְנֶאֱמַר "בֶּגֶד וְעוֹר" בְּמֵת – AND IT IS STATED IN REGARD TO CORPSE *tumah: and every* GARMENT AND *every utensil of* HIDE...[19] מַה "בֶּגֶד וְעוֹר" הָאָמוּר בְּשֶׁרֶץ – JUST AS in the case of THE *GARMENT* AND *HIDE* STATED IN connection with A *SHERETZ,* לֹא טִימֵּא אֶלָּא טָווּי וְאָרִיג – [THE TORAH] DECLARED goats' hair articles SUSCEPTIBLE TO *TUMAH* ONLY if they are made of goats'-hair that was SPUN AND WOVEN, אַף "בֶּגֶד וְעוֹר" הָאָמוּר בְּמֵת – SO TOO in the case of THE *GARMENT* AND *HIDE* STATED IN connection with A CORPSE, לֹא טִימֵּא אֶלָּא טָווּי וְאָרִיג – [THE TORAH] DECLARED goats'-hair articles SUSCEPTIBLE TO *TUMAH* ONLY if they are made of goats' hair that was SPUN AND WOVEN. This excludes ropes and measuring strings, which are made from unspun goats' hair.

The Baraisa now uses this *gezeirah shavah* to derive a law from corpse *tumah* to *tumas sheretz*:

וּמַה "בֶּגֶד וְעוֹר" הָאָמוּר בְּמֵת – AND JUST AS in the case of THE *GARMENT* AND *HIDE* STATED IN connection with A CORPSE, טִמֵּא כָּל מַעֲשֵׂה עִזִּים – [THE TORAH] DECLARED SUSCEPTIBLE TO *TUMAH* ANYTHING MADE FROM GOATS' hair[20] such as a breast strap and girth, אַף בֶּגֶד וְעוֹר הָאָמוּר בְּשֶׁרֶץ – SO TOO in the case of THE *GARMENT* AND *HIDE* STATED IN connection with A *SHERETZ,* טִמֵּא כָּל מַעֲשֵׂה עִזִּים – [THE TORAH] DECLARED SUSCEPTIBLE TO *TUMAH* ANYTHING MADE FROM GOATS' hair, such as a breast strap and girth.[21]

The Baraisa derives another law from the verse concerning corpse *tumah*:

אֵין לִי אֶלָּא דָּבָר הַבָּא מִן הָעִזִּים – From the exegesis given above I KNOW ONLY that SOMETHING MADE FROM GOATS' hair is susceptible to *tumah*. מִנַּיִן לְרַבּוֹת דָּבָר הַבָּא מִזְּנַב הַסּוּס וּמִזְּנַב הַפָּרָה – FROM WHERE do I know TO INCLUDE THINGS MADE OF THE TAIL OF A HORSE OR THE TAIL OF A COW? תַּלְמוּד לוֹמַר "אוֹ שָׂק" – [THE TORAH] therefore STATES in regard to the *tumah* of a *sheretz: OR A SACK.* The word *or* serves to include articles produced from horse tail or cow tail.[22]

The Gemara interrupts the Baraisa to ask:

וְהָא אַפִּיקְתֵּיהּ לְקִילְקְלִי וַחֲבָק – But we have already used that word – *or* – **to** teach that **a breast strap and girth** are susceptible to the *tumah* of a *sheretz.* How then can it be used to include sacks made from horse tails or cow tails?

The Gemara answers:

הָנֵי מִילֵּי מִקַּמֵּי דְּלֵיתְיֵיהּ גְּזֵרָה שָׁוָה – That was so only before the *gezeirah shavah* was introduced;[23] **הַשְׁתָּא דְּאָתְיָא גְּזֵירָה שָׁוָה** – but **now that the *gezeirah shavah* has been introduced,** **אַיְיתּוּר לֵיהּ** – the word ***[or]* is superfluous** and is therefore free to include sacks made of horse or cow tail.[24]

NOTES

13. *Numbers* 31:20. [The verse speaks of the utensils captured from the Midianites. Since these were taken in battle, they are assumed to have come in contact with a corpse (see *Pnei Yehoshua*).] The verse in its entirety states: וְכָל־בֶּגֶד וְכָל־כְּלִי־עוֹר וְכָל־מַעֲשֵׂה עִזִּים וְכָל־כְּלִי־עֵץ תִּתְחַטָּאוּ, *And every garment, and every utensil of hide* [i.e. leather utensil], *and everything made from goats, and every utensil of wood, you shall purify.*

14. Since these are also made of goats' hair, they too should be included in the teaching: "*everything made from goats*" (*Rashi*).

15. [*Ritva* (*MHK* ed.) asks how the Baraisa could think to exclude the rope and measuring string on the basis of such an analogy (בִּנְיַן אָב) when the reason to *include* them would be the extra word כָּל, *everything.* Surely, a teaching derived from an extra word overrides what we conclude from logic alone! *Ritva* answers that since the word כָּל, *everything,* is in any event expounded to include the breast strap and the girth, the logic of analogy can serve to *limit* this inclusion to just those items, and not to the ropes and strings that the logic of comparison would exclude (cf. *Chidushei HaRan*).

16. By declaring that ropes and measuring strings are *not* susceptible to *tumah.*

17. One who contracts *tumah* from a *sheretz,* immerses in a *mikveh* and is *tahor* that evening, whereas one who contracts corpse *tumah* remains *tamei* for at least seven days (*Rashi*).

18. See note 63b note 30.

19. See note 13.

20. Provided it is spun and woven, as taught in the previous exposition.

21. [The Baraisa already derived this point above from the word אוֹ, *or.* The Gemara will shortly explain why the Baraisa offers another derivation for this law.]

22. [These articles are considered similar to sackcloth because these animal hairs are also used to make sacks (see version of this Baraisa found in *Toras Kohanim, Parashas Shemini, perek* 8).]

23. [The correct reading of the Gemara here would seem to be מִקַּמֵּי דְּתֵיתֵי גְּזֵירָה שָׁוָה (rather than דְּלֵיתְיֵיהּ) – see *Dikdukei Soferim.* Our translation follows that reading.]

24. [I.e. the word אוֹ, *or,* was expounded to teach that a breast strap and girth are susceptible to the *tumah* of a *sheretz* only before we knew of the *gezeirah shavah* to corpse *tumah.* But once the Baraisa taught that there is a *gezeirah shavah* equating the susceptibility to *tumas sheretz* with that of corpse *tumah,* there is no longer any need to independently derive the susceptibility of a breast strap and girth to *tumas sheretz,* for it can now be derived from corpse *tumah* by means of the *gezeirah shavah.* The word אוֹ, *or,* is therefore now available to teach a different lesson – namely, the susceptibility to *tumah* of sacks made of horse or cow tail.]

אא) כלי כלי מהתם: מוסף אשק על הבגד שטמא משום אריג: אטו בגד לאו אריג הוא הכי קאמר מוסף שק על הבגד אף על פי שאינו אריג טמא למאי חזי אמר רבי יוחנן שכן עני קולע שלש נימין ותולה בצואר בתו

א) תנו רבנן א) שק אין לי אלא שק במניין לרבות את הקילקלי ואת החבק ת"ל או שק גיכול שאני מרבה את החבלים ואת המשיחות ת"ל שק מה שק טווי ואריג אף כל טווי ואריג הרי הוא אומר במת ב) וכל כלי עור וכל מעשה עזים וגו' תתחטאו לרבות הקילקלי ואת החבק יכול שאני מרבה את החבלים ואת המשיחות ודין הוא טימא בשרץ וטימא במת מה כשטימא בשרץ לא טימא אלא טווי ואריג אף כשטימא במת לא טימא אלא טווי ואריג הן אם היקל בטמא שרץ שהיא קלה נקיל בטומאת המת שהיא חמורה תלמוד לומר בגד ועור בגד ועור לגזירה שוה נאמר א) בגד ועור בשרץ ונאמר ב) בגד ועור במת מה בגד ועור האמור בשרץ לא טימא אלא טווי ואריג אף בגד ועור האמור במת לא טימא אלא טווי ואריג ומה בגד ועור האמור במת טמא כל מעשה עזים אף בגד ועור האמור בשרץ טמא כל מעשה עזים אין לי אלא דבר הבא מן העזים דמניין לרבות דבר הבא מזנב הסוס ומזנב הפרה תלמוד לומר א) או שק והא אפיקתיה לקילקלי וחבק הני מילי מקמי דליתיה ג"ש השתא דאתי גזירה שוה אייתור ליה ואין לי אלא בשרץ בטומאת מת מניין ודין הוא טימא במת וטימא בשרץ מה כשטימא בשרץ עשה דבר הבא מזנב הסוס ומזנב הפרה כמעשה עזים אף כשטימא במת עשה דבר הבא מזנב הסוס ומזנב הפרה כמעשה עזים הן אם הרבה בטומאת ערב שהיא מרובה נרבה בטומאת שבעה שהיא מועטת תלמוד לומר בגד ועור בגד ועור לגזירה שוה נאמר בגד ועור בשרץ ונאמר בגד ועור במת מה בגד ועור האמור בשרץ עשה דבר הבא מזנב הסוס ומזנב הפרה כמעשה עזים אף בגד ועור האמור במת עשה דבר הבא מזנב הסוס ומזנב הפרה כמעשה עזים ומופנה דאי לאו מופנה איכא למיפרך מה לשרץ שכן מטמא בכעדשה ולאי אפנויי מופני גמכדי שרץ איתקש לשכבת זרע דכתיב ג) איש אשר תצא ממנו שכבת זרע וסמיך ליה ד) איש אשר יגע בכל שרץ וכתיב ביה בשכבת זרע ה) וכל בגד וכל עור אשר יהיה עליו שכבת זרע בגד ועור דכתב רחמנא בשרץ למה לי שמע מינה לאפנויי ואכתי מופנה מצד אחד הוא הניחא למאן דאמר דמופנה מצד אחד למידין ואין משיבין אלא למאן דאמר הלמידין ומשיבין מאי איכא למימר דמת נמי אפנויי מופנה מכדי מת אתקש לשכבת זרע דכתיב ג) והנוגע בכל טמא נפש או איש אשר תצא ממנו שכבת זרע וכתיב בשכבת זרע וכל בגד וכל עור בגד ועור דכתב רחמנא במת למה לי ש"מ לאפנויי: ו) ונקרב את קרבן ה' איש אשר מצא כלי זהב אצעדה וצמיד טבעת עגיל וכומז א"ר אלעזר ועגיל זה דפוס של דדין כומז זה דפוס של בית הרחם אמר רב יוסף אי הכי היינו דמתרגמינן מחוך דבר המביא לידי גיחוך אמר ליה רבה מגופיה דקרא ש"מ כומז כאן מקום זימה: ז) ויקצוף משה על פקודי החיל אמר רב נחמן אמר רבה בר אבוה אמר להן משה לישראל שמא חזרתם לקלקולכם הראשון אמרו לו ח) לא נפקד ממנו איש אמר להן אם כן כפרה למה אמרו לו אם מידי עבירה יצאנו מידי הרהור לא יצאנו מיד ו) ונקרב את קרבן ה' תנא דבי רבי ישמעאל מפני מה הוצרכו ישראל שבאותו הדור כפרה מפני

שזנו

רש"י

כלי כלי. בשרלים כתיב כל כלי אשר יעשה מלאכה וגו' ומגופיה דקרא דשרלים לא מצי יליף דאשר יעשה מלאכה לאו כלי תכשיט משמע: שק. הוא עשוי מנולה של עזים שאף על פי שאינו אריג אלא קלע קטן עשה מנולה של עזים לתלות בו בתי נפש לצואר בתו טמא שדרכו בכך ותכשיט הוא וה"ק שהוא טמא משום אריג ואע"פ שאינו אריג: קולע ג' נימין כו'. ג' חוטין של מטוה של נולה של עזים לבועה: ותולה בצואר בתו. וקליעתה זו היא אריגתו מאחר שהוא טווי כדאמרן גבי תיכי חלילתא ברים פירקין דקרי להו אריג והא דקאמר אע"פ שאינו אריג כלומר לאו אריג ממש: אין לי אלא שק. העשוי ללבוש רועים: קילקלי. מסרך של סוס שקורין פייטרא"ל: חבק. לינגלא של סרגא ואוכף ועושין אותה מנולה של עזים טווי ואריג: יכול שאני מרבה החבלים והמשיחות. לגיא"ל שעושין למדוד וקולעין מן הנולה כמו שנתלשה ואינו טווי ולא דמי לקולע שלש נימין דלעיל דהתם טווי הוא חו היא אריגתו: יכול שאני מרבה כו'. הואיל וכתיב כל: ודין הוא שלא נרבה. ולא לריך קרא למעוטי: הן. תמיה הוא וכי דברים כוונים הם: אם היקל בטומאת שרץ שהיא קלה. כלומר אם היקל מלטמא חבלים ומשיחות היקל לך בשרץ שטומאתו קלה טומאת ערב: נקל. גם אנחנו בבנין אב זה במת שטומאתו חמורה טומאת ז': השתא דאתיא גזירה שוה. וכי היכי דיליף מת משרץ למעוטי חבלים ומשיחות יליף נמי שרץ ממת לכל מעשה עזים לרבות קילקלי וחבק: אין לי אלא בשרץ. דאו שק התם כתיב: אם ריבה. לטמא דבר הבא מזנב הסוס בטומאת ערב הוא דריבה: שהיא מרובה. שכל המגעות טומאת ערב הן בין דשרץ ונבילה ושכבת זרע מגע הזב ומגע טמא מת: נרבה אנו בטומאת ז' שכן מועטת היא. שאינה בכל המגעות אלא במגע המת בלבד: מופנה. לריך שתהא גזירה שוה זו מב' תיבות דבגד ועור מופנין למדרש זה שלא יהו לריכין לגופן ומאחר שמופנין ללמוד גזירה שוה ה"ל כמאן דכתיב דרשא בקרא בהדיא ואין משיבין עליה: דאי לאו מופנה. אמרינן לגופן באו ולא ילפינן להא מילתא מינייהו: דאיכא למיפרך כו'. וה"ה דמלי למימר הכי אגזירה שוה קמייתא ומיהו אסקי לכולה ברייתא ברישא ופריך אהא דסליק מינה ובשינויא דמשנינן בהא מיתרלה נמי קמייתא: לאי. באמת: וכתיב ביה בשכבת זרע. דבגד ועור טמאים הם בו: מצד אחד. הכתובין בשרץ מופנים כדאמרן אבל הכתובין במת אין מופנין: הניחא למ"ד כו'. פלוגתא דרבי ישמעאל ורבנן היא במסכת נדה בהמפלת (דף כב:): אלא למאן דאמר למידין. אם אין תשובה: ומשיבין. אם יש להשיב: מאי איכא למימר. הרי יש להשיב שכן מטמא בכעדשה: והנוגע בכל טמא נפש או איש אשר תלא ממנו שכבת זרע: דפוס של דדין. שמונחות בו: גיחוך. ליצנות: לקלקולכם. של מעשה שטים לזנות את בנות מואב שמא כך עשיתם במדין לכך אתם לריכין קרבן: לא נפקד. לא נחסר מדת יהודית:

שזנו

תוספות

מניין לרבות את הקילקלי והחבק. ואם תאמר והא לא מיטלטל מלא וריקן ואי משום דאפשר לקפלה אם אינו עשוי לכך לאו כלום הוא כדאמר לקמן גבי קב הקיטע דאע"ג דיש לו בית קיבול לראש שוקו אם אינו עשוי לקבל טהור וי"ל דהני נמי לשם כל צורכן הן עשוין מתחלה אך קשה דלעיל פ' במה מדליקין (דף כ. ושם) מפיק דבר הבא מן העזים דמטמא בשרלים מאו בגד וקילקלי וחבק באין מן העזים ומפיק להן הכא מאו שק וע"ק דהתם מרבה לנולה של עזים לג' על ג' ואילו שק שיעורו בד' ואומר ר"י דתרי גווני נולה של עזים הוו והתם מיירי [בדקה] שעושים ממנה בגדים חשובים והלכך איתרבו לשלשה על שלשה כמו שאר בגדים והכא מיירי בנולה גסה שממנה עושין קילקלי וחבק וחבלים ומשיחות ושק: שמע מינה לאפנויי. הקשה ה"ר אליעזר ממיץ כיון דאיתקש שרץ ומת לשכבת זרע א"כ ג"ש דבגד ועור ל"ל דכל מה שיהיה במת ניתן בשכבת זרע וכל מה שיהיה בשכבת זרע ניתן בשרץ וכן להפך דהא קי"ל ז) דבר הבא מן ההיקש חוזר ומלמד בהיקש חוץ מן הקדשים: מידי הרהור מי יצאנו. וא"ת והא אפילו (א) יפת תואר הותרה להם וי"ל דמכל מקום שייך בה איסור כדאמרינן (קדושין דף כב.) וחשקת בה ולא בחברתה:

וכמון

עין משפט נר מצוה

נח א ב ג ד מיי' פ"א מהל' כלים הלכה יב:

רבינו חננאל

קילקלי. מלשון יון הוא והוא עשוי בגד [(גליון) משיער של עזים והוא קשה עשוי להצניעו תחת הכרים והכסתות. חבקים כסוי הכסאות (ת"ל) או בגד או עור או שק אין לי אלא] שק בלבד מנין לרבות הקילקלי וחבק ת"ל או שק פי' מרבינן להו מאו כלומר הוה ליה למימר שק. או דכתב רחמנא למה לי לרבויי קילקלי וחבק. יכול שאני מרבה חבלים ומשיחין שיטמאו ת"ל שק מה שק טווי ואריג אף כל טווי ואריג הרי הוא אמר במת כל מעשה עזים יכול שאני מרבה חבלים ומשיחים דין הוא טימא בשרץ טימא במת כו'. ודחינן ואם היקל בטומאת שרץ שהיא קלה פי' טומאת שרץ קלה היא שהיא טומאת ערב אבל טומאת מת חמורה היא שהיא טומאת שבעה לא נתרבה ת"ל (או) בגד ועור בגד ועור לג"ש נאמר בגד ועור בשרץ ונאמר בגד ועור במת. פי' דין ג"ש ב' פסוקים וכל פסוק ופסוק כתוב מלין שאינן צריכין לפסוק ואין מילין פטיין לא נכתבו אלא בתוך פסוקים אלו אלא לדון מהם ג"ש להיות כל דין שמפורש באחד מהן שיהא גם השני כמותו וזהו שכתוב בעניננו בגד ועור בשרץ בגד ועור במת וצריכין להיות אלו בגד ועור מופנים בשני הפסוקים. שאם הן בפסוק אחד יתירין כגון שלמדו טומאת בגד ועור בשרץ משכבת זרע ונמצא בגד ועור האמור בשרץ מופנה כגון זה למידין ואם יש פירכא משיבין ופורכין ואם הן אלו פסוקים בגד ועור יתירין בשרץ ובמת למידין במת מן השרץ זהו טמאין במת דבר הבא מזנב הסוס מזנב הפרה כשם שמטמאין בשרץ ואין משיבין ואע"ג דאיכא למפרך ואם ריבה בטומאת שרץ שהיא מרובה. פי' טומאת שרץ (נותנת) [נוהגת] בשמנה שרצים. נרבה טומאת מת שהיא מועטת שאינה אלא במת בלבד ואוקימנא כיון שהן מופנה משני צדדין למידין ואין משיבין. ואלו הדברים הל"מ להדרש בענין הזה מסורת בידי חכמים:

רב נסים גאון

הניחא למאן [דאמר] מופנה מצד א' למדין ואין משיבין אלא למאן דאמר למידין ומשיבין מאי איכא למימר. מחלוקת בין ר' ישמעאל ורבנן ועיקר דילה במס' נדה בפרק המפלת (דף כב) אמר רב יהודה אמר שמואל משום ר' כל גזירה שוה שאינה מופנה כל עיקר אין למידין ממנה מופנה מצד אחד לר' ישמעאל למידין ואין משיבין לרבנן למידין ומשיבין: אמר להם משה לישראל שמא חזרתם לקלקולכם הראשון אמרו לו לא נפקד ממנו איש. במס' יבמות בפרק הבא על יבמתו (דף סא) אמרו ור' שמעון לא נפקד ממנו איש לעבירה ולדבר זה נתכוונו בהם בתשובה זו:

קסבר

מסורת הש"ס

א) מ"כ פ' שמיני, ב) [בערוך איתא לאיי ומפרש דלשון יון הוא ע"ש], ג) [ב"ק כה:], ד) [נדה כב:], ה) [לקמן קלא. יבמות ע: עד. נדה כב:], ו) [מס' כלה], ז) [זבחים מט:].

הגהות הב"ח

(א) תוס' ד"ה מידי וכו' אפי' ליקח יפת תואר:

תורה אור השלם

א) וְכֹל אֲשֶׁר יִפֹּל עָלָיו מֵהֶם בְּמֹתָם יִטְמָא מִכָּל כְּלִי עֵץ אוֹ בֶגֶד אוֹ עוֹר אוֹ שָׂק כָּל כְּלִי אֲשֶׁר יֵעָשֶׂה מְלָאכָה בָּהֶם בַּמַּיִם יוּבָא וְטָמֵא עַד הָעֶרֶב וְטָהֵר: [ויקרא יא, לב]

ב) וְכָל בֶּגֶד וְכָל כְּלִי עוֹר וְכָל מַעֲשֵׂה עִזִּים וְכָל כְּלִי עֵץ תִּתְחַטָּאוּ: [במדבר לא, כ]

ג) אִישׁ אִישׁ מִזֶּרַע אַהֲרֹן וְהוּא צָרוּעַ אוֹ זָב בַּקֳּדָשִׁים לֹא יֹאכַל עַד אֲשֶׁר יִטְהָר וְהַנֹּגֵעַ בְּכָל טְמֵא נֶפֶשׁ אוֹ אִישׁ אֲשֶׁר תֵּצֵא מִמֶּנּוּ שִׁכְבַת זָרַע: [ויקרא כב, ד]

ד) אוֹ אִישׁ אֲשֶׁר יִגַּע בְּכָל שֶׁרֶץ אֲשֶׁר יִטְמָא לוֹ אוֹ בְאָדָם אֲשֶׁר יִטְמָא לוֹ לְכֹל טֻמְאָתוֹ: [ויקרא כב, ה]

ה) וְכָל בֶּגֶד וְכָל עוֹר אֲשֶׁר יִהְיֶה עָלָיו שִׁכְבַת זָרַע וְכֻבַּס בַּמַּיִם וְטָמֵא עַד הָעָרֶב: [ויקרא טו, יז]

ו) וַנַּקְרֵב אֶת קָרְבַּן יְיָ אִישׁ אֲשֶׁר מָצָא כְלִי זָהָב אֶצְעָדָה וְצָמִיד טַבַּעַת עָגִיל וְכוּמָז לְכַפֵּר עַל נַפְשֹׁתֵינוּ לִפְנֵי יְיָ: [במדבר לא, נ]

ז) וַיִּקְצֹף מֹשֶׁה עַל פְּקוּדֵי הֶחָיִל שָׂרֵי הָאֲלָפִים וְשָׂרֵי הַמֵּאוֹת הַבָּאִים מִצְּבָא הַמִּלְחָמָה: [במדבר לא, יד]

ח) וַיֹּאמְרוּ אֶל מֹשֶׁה עֲבָדֶיךָ נָשְׂאוּ אֶת רֹאשׁ אַנְשֵׁי הַמִּלְחָמָה אֲשֶׁר בְּיָדֵנוּ וְלֹא נִפְקַד מִמֶּנּוּ אִישׁ: [במדבר לא, מט]

ליקוטי רש"י

קילקלי. לינגל"ש לקשור האוכף בחגישת החמור. חבק. פוטרי"ל ולרמי רלינה הן [רשב"ם ב"ב עח.]. לינגל"א לאסור בו סוס [לעיל נז.]. למידין ואין משיבין. ואפילו יש להשיב [נדה כב:]. בכל טמא נפש. במי שנטמא במת [ויקרא כב, ד]. אצעדה. אלו למידים של רגל. וצמיד. של יד. וכומז. דפוס של בית הרחם לכפר על הרהור הלב של בנות מדין [במדבר לא, נ]. דפוס של בית הרחם. כלי זהב הוא נתון כנגד אותו מקום לאשה ורבותינו פירשו שם כומז כאן מקום זמה [שמות לה, כב]. שהיו עושין לבנותיהן ונוקבין כמלי בית הרחם כדרך שנוקבין את האזנים ותוחבין אותו כדי שלא יזדקקו להן זכרים [ברכות כד.]. על פקודי החיל. ממונים על החיל [במדבר שם, יד].

The Gemara returns to the Baraisa:

וְאֵין לִי אֶלָּא בְּשֶׁרֶץ – **NOW** from this **I KNOW ONLY** horse and cow-tail articles **IN REGARD TO** the *tumah* of a ***SHERETZ.*** בְּטוּמְאַת מֵת מִנַּיִין – **FROM WHERE** do I know to include them **IN REGARD TO CORPSE** ***TUMAH?***

The Baraisa first attempts to prove this point by analogy: וְדִין הוּא – **NOW IT IS ONLY LOGICAL** to say they are subject to corpse *tumah*. טִימֵּא בְּמֵת – For **[THE TORAH] DECLARED** sackcloth **SUSCEPTIBLE TO** ***TUMAH*** **IN** the case of **A CORPSE,** וְטִימֵּא בְּשֶׁרֶץ – **AND [THE TORAH] DECLARED** sackcloth **SUSCEPTIBLE TO** ***TUMAH*** **IN** the case of **A** ***SHERETZ.*** מָה כְּשֶׁטִּימֵּא בְּשֶׁרֶץ – **JUST AS WHEN [THE TORAH] DECLARED** ***TUMAH*** **IN** the case of **A** ***SHERETZ*** עָשָׂה דָּבָר הַבָּא מִזְּנַב הַסּוּס וּמִזְּנַב הַפָּרָה כְּמַעֲשֵׂה עִזִּים – **[THE TORAH] TREATED THINGS MADE FROM THE TAIL OF A HORSE OR THE TAIL OF A COW THE SAME AS THINGS MADE FROM GOATS'** hair, and declared both susceptible to *tumah,* as we learned above, אַף כְּשֶׁטִּימֵּא בְּמֵת – **SO TOO WHEN [THE TORAH] DECLARED** ***TUMAH*** **IN** the case of **A CORPSE** עָשָׂה דָּבָר הַבָּא מִזְּנַב הַסּוּס וּמִזְּנַב הַפָּרָה כְּמַעֲשֵׂה עִזִּים – **[THE TORAH] TREATED THINGS MADE FROM THE TAIL OF A HORSE OR THE TAIL OF A COW THE SAME AS THINGS MADE FROM GOATS'** hair and declared both susceptible to *tumah.*

The Baraisa rejects this analogy:

הֵן – **INDEED!** Is this analogy compelling? אִם הִרְבָּה בְּטוּמְאַת עֶרֶב – **IF [THE TORAH] ADDED** articles made of horse and cow tail to the list of things subject **TO THE** ***TUMAH*** **OF NIGHTFALL,** שֶׁהִיא מְרוּבָּה – **WHICH IS** a **MORE COMMON** form of *tumah,*[25] נַרְבֶּה בְּטוּמְאַת שִׁבְעָה – **SHOULD WE** therefore **ADD** it on our own to the list of things subject **TO SEVEN-DAY** ***TUMAH,*** שֶׁהִיא מוּעֶטֶת – **WHICH IS** a **RARE** form of *tumah*? Certainly not![26] Therefore, even though articles made from horse or cow tail are included in the *tumah* of a *sheretz,* perhaps they are not susceptible to the less common form of *tumah* that is corpse *tumah.*

The Baraisa therefore cites a *gezeirah shavah* to teach this:

תַּלְמוּד לוֹמַר – To teach this **[THE TORAH] STATES:** ,,בֶּגֶד וְעוֹר'' ,,בֶּגֶד וְעוֹר'' לִגְזֵירָה שָׁוָה – ***GARMENT*** **AND** ***HIDE*** and ***GARMENT*** **AND** ***HIDE*** – **TO** establish **A** ***GEZEIRAH SHAVAH.*** נֶאֱמַר ,,בֶּגֶד וְעוֹר'' בְּשֶׁרֶץ – **IT IS STATED IN REGARD TO** the *tumah* of **A** ***SHERETZ:*** *whether it is* **A** ***GARMENT OR HIDE;*** וְנֶאֱמַר ,,בֶּגֶד וְעוֹר'' בְּמֵת – **AND IT IS STATED IN REGARD TO** the *tumah* of **A CORPSE:** *and every* ***GARMENT AND*** *every utensil of* ***HIDE.*** מָה ,,בֶּגֶד וְעוֹר'' הָאָמוּר בְּשֶׁרֶץ – **JUST AS** in the case of **THE** ***GARMENT*** **AND** ***HIDE*** **STATED IN** connection with **A** ***SHERETZ,*** עָשָׂה דָּבָר הַבָּא מִזְּנַב הַסּוּס וּמִזְּנַב הַפָּרָה כְּמַעֲשֵׂה עִזִּים – **[THE TORAH] TREATED THINGS MADE FROM THE TAIL OF A HORSE OR THE TAIL OF A COW THE SAME AS THINGS MADE FROM GOATS'** hair, and declared both susceptible to *tumah,* אַף ,,בֶּגֶד וְעוֹר'' הָאָמוּר בְּמֵת – **SO TOO** in the case of **THE** ***GARMENT*** **AND** ***HIDE*** **STATED IN** connection with **A CORPSE,** עָשָׂה דָּבָר הַבָּא מִזְּנַב הַסּוּס וּמִזְּנַב הַפָּרָה כְּמַעֲשֵׂה עִזִּים – **[THE TORAH] TREATED THINGS MADE FROM THE TAIL OF A HORSE OR THE TAIL OF A COW THE SAME AS THINGS MADE FROM GOATS'** hair and declared them both susceptible to *tumah.*[27]

The Gemara comments on this *gezeirah shavah*:

וּמוּפְנֶה – **And** the words ***[garment*** **and** ***hide***] upon which this *gezeirah shavah* is based **are** perforce **free** (i.e. superfluous) for exposition;[28] דְּאִי לָאו מוּפְנֶה – **For if they were not free** אִיכָּא לְמִיפְרַךְ – **one could challenge** this *gezeirah shavah* on the following grounds: מָה לְשֶׁרֶץ שֶׁכֵּן מְטַמֵּא בְּכַעֲדָשָׁה – **What** comparison can be made **to** ***tumas sheretz,*** **when [*sheretz*] conveys** ***tumah*** even if it is only **the size of a lentil,** whereas in the case of corpse *tumah,* a piece at least the size of an olive is needed to convey *tumah.*[29] Thus, we can argue that *tumas sheretz,* which is more stringent than corpse *tumah* in this respect, conveys *tumah* to articles made from horse or cow tail, but corpse *tumah* does not.[30]

The Gemara confirms this supposition:

לָאִי אַפְנוּיֵי מוּפְנֵי – **In truth** the words ***[garment*** **and** ***hide***] found in the passage of *sheretz* **are certainly free,** as will now be demonstrated. מִכְּדִי – **Now,** let us see: שֶׁרֶץ אִיתְקַשׁ לְשִׁכְבַת זֶרַע – The *tumah* of **sheretz is compared** by the Torah **to** the *tumah* of **semen,** דִּכְתִיב ,,אִישׁ אֲשֶׁר־תֵּצֵא מִמֶּנּוּ שִׁכְבַת־זָרַע'' – **as it is written:** ***"or a man from whom there shall issue semen,"***[31] וּסְמִיךְ לֵיהּ ,,אִישׁ אֲשֶׁר יִגַּע בְּכָל־שֶׁרֶץ'' – **and** immediately **next to it is written:** ***or a man who will touch any sheretz.***[32] וּכְתִיב בֵּיהּ בְּשִׁכְבַת זֶרַע ,,וְכָל־בֶּגֶד וְכָל־עוֹר אֲשֶׁר־יִהְיֶה עָלָיו שִׁכְבַת־זָרַע'' – **Now it is written concerning semen:** ***And any garment or hide on which there shall be semen*** *shall be immersed in water and remain tamei until evening.*[33] ,,בֶּגֶד וְעוֹר'' דִּכְתַב רַחֲמָנָא בְּשֶׁרֶץ לָמָּה לִי – Accordingly, **why do I need** the words ***garment*** **and**

NOTES

25. With most sources of *tumah* (e.g. a *sheretz, neveilah,* semen, *zav*) the person or object who touched and thereby contracts *tumah* from them can immediately immerse in a *mikveh* and become *tahor* at nightfall. The only exception is one who touches a corpse – where the *tumah* lasts seven days (*Rashi*).

26. [For we see that the Torah was sparing in its application of seven-day *tumah,* limiting it to contact with a corpse. Thus, it is possible that the Torah was also more stinting in regard to the types of articles it subjected to this rare form of *tumah* and did not extend it to horse and cow tail articles (see the fuller version of this Baraisa found in *Toras Kohanim* to this verse).]

27. **To summarize:** The Torah teaches in connection with both *tumas sheretz* and corpse *tumah* that "sack" is susceptible to *tumah.* The Baraisa derives from a series of expositions that breast straps and girths are *included* along with sacks in both types of *tumah,* that ropes and measuring strings (which are made from unspun goats' hair) are *excluded* from both, and that articles made of (spun and woven) horse or cow tail are *included* in both types of *tumah.* The susceptibility of breast straps and girths is derived in the first place (according to the Baraisa's conclusion) from the verse *everything made from goats* stated in the passage concerning corpse *tumah,* and it is extended from corpse *tumah* to *tumas sheretz* by means of a *gezeirah shavah.* The exclusion of articles made of unspun goats' hair (such as ropes and measuring strings) is derived in the first place from the word *sack* stated in the *sheretz* passage and then extended to corpse *tumah* by means of the *gezeirah shavah.* The inclusion of articles made of horse and cow tail is derived in the first place from the word או (*or*) stated in the *sheretz* passage and then extended to corpse *tumah* by means of the *gezeirah shavah.*

28. I.e. they are not needed for the plain meaning of the passage or to teach another law. A *gezeirah shavah* that is based on words that are otherwise superfluous is immune to refutation, for it is as if the law derived via the *gezeirah shavah* is stated explicitly in the context. If, however, the words of the *gezeirah shavah* are needed for other teachings, the *gezeirah shavah* is subject to challenge (*Rashi*). [See *Rosh Yosef* who explains how a *gezeirah shavah* can be challenged when it is necessarily based on Oral Sinaitic tradition.]

29. [Although the Baraisa itself cited a different stringency of *sheretz* over corpse *tumah* – namely, that it is a more common form of *tumah* – the Gemara feels that a more profound distinction is necessary to upset a *gezeirah shavah* (*Chidushei HaRan, Maharsha*).]

30. Actually, the Gemara could have posed this challenge after the Baraisa derived its first law from the *gezeirah shavah.* The Gemara, however, preferred to quote the Baraisa in its entirety and then pose the challenge from the last law cited. The Gemara's answer to this challenge – that this *gezeirah shavah* is indeed based on otherwise superfluous words and is hence immune to refutation – suffices to answer any possible challenge to the derivations of the earlier laws (*Rashi;* see *Maharsha*).

31. *Leviticus* 22:4.

32. Ibid. v. 5. The juxtaposition of these two verses establishes a *hekeish* between them.

33. Ibid. 15:17.

[א] כלי כלי מהתם: מוסף [א] שק על הבגד שטמא משום אריג: אטו בגד לאו אריג הוא הכי קאמר מוסף שק על הבגד אף על פי שאינו אריג טמא למאי חזי אמר רבי יוחנן שכן עני קולע שלש נימין ותולה בצואר בתו [א] תנו רבנן [א] שק אין לי אלא שק [ב] מניין לרבות את הקילקלי ואת החבק ת"ל או שק [ג] יכול שאני מרבה את החבלים ואת המשיחות ת"ל שק מה שק טווי ואריג אף כל טווי ואריג הרי הוא אומר במת [ב] וכל כלי עור וכל מעשה עזים וגו' תתחטאו לרבות הקילקלי ואת החבק יכול שאני מרבה את החבלים ואת המשיחות ודין הוא טימא בשרץ וטימא במת מה כשטימא בשרץ לא טימא אלא טווי ואריג אף כשטימא במת לא טימא אלא טווי ואריג הן אם היקל בטמא שרץ שהיא קלה נקיל בטומאת המת שהיא חמורה תלמוד לומר בגד ועור בגד ועור לגזירה שוה נאמר [א] בגד ועור בשרץ ונאמר [ב] בגד ועור במת מה בגד ועור האמור בשרץ לא טימא אלא טווי ואריג אף בגד ועור האמור במת לא טימא אלא טווי ואריג ומה בגד ועור האמור במת טמא כל מעשה עזים אף בגד ועור האמור בשרץ טמא כל מעשה עזים אין לי אלא דבר הבא מן העזים [ד] מניין לרבות דבר הבא מזנב הסוס ומזנב הפרה תלמוד לומר [א] או שק והא אפיקתיה לקילקלי וחבק הני מילי מקמי דליתיה ג"ש השתא דאתי גזירה שוה אייתור ליה ואין לי אלא בשרץ בטומאת מת מניין ודין הוא טימא בשרץ וטימא במת מה כשטימא בשרץ עשה דבר הבא מזנב הסוס ומזנב הפרה כמעשה עזים אף כשטימא במת עשה דבר הבא מזנב הסוס ומזנב הפרה כמעשה עזים הן אם הרבה בטומאת ערב שהיא מרובה נרבה בטומאת שבעה שהיא מועטת תלמוד לומר בגד ועור בגד ועור לגזירה שוה נאמר בגד ועור בשרץ ונאמר בגד ועור במת מה בגד ועור האמור בשרץ עשה דבר הבא מזנב הסוס ומזנב הפרה כמעשה עזים אף בגד ועור האמור במת עשה דבר הבא מזנב הסוס ומזנב הפרה כמעשה עזים ומופנה דאי לאו מופנה איכא למיפרך מה לשרץ שכן מטמא בכעדשה [ה] לאי אפנויי מופני [ג] מכדי שרץ איתקש לשכבת זרע דכתיב [ג] איש אשר תצא ממנו שכבת זרע וסמיך ליה [ד] איש אשר יגע בכל שרץ וכתיב ביה בשכבת זרע [ה] וכל בגד וכל עור אשר יהיה עליו שכבת זרע בגד ועור דכתב רחמנא בשרץ למה לי שמע מינה לאפנויי ואכתי מופנה מצד אחד הוא הניחא למאן דאמר [ו] מופנה מצד אחד למידין ואין משיבין אלא למאן דאמר [ז] למידין ומשיבין מאי איכא למימר דמת נמי אפנויי מופנה מכדי מת אתקש לשכבת זרע דכתיב [ג] והנוגע בכל טמא נפש או איש אשר תצא ממנו שכבת זרע וכתיב בשכבת זרע וכל בגד וכל עור בגד ועור דכתב רחמנא במת למה לי ש"מ לאפנויי: [ו] ונקרב את קרבן ה' איש אשר מצא כלי זהב אצעדה וצמיד טבעת עגיל וכומז א"ר אלעזר [ו] עגיל זה דפוס של דדין כומז זה דפוס של בית הרחם אמר רב יוסף אי הכי היינו דמתרגמינן מחוך דבר המביא לידי גיחוך אמר ליה רבה מגופיה דקרא ש"מ כומז כאן מקום זימה: [ז] ויקצוף משה על פקודי החיל אמר רב נחמן אמר רבה בר אבוה אמר להן משה לישראל שמא חזרתם לקלקולכם הראשון אמרו לו [ח] לא נפקד ממנו איש אמר להן אם כן כפרה למה אמרו לו אם מידי עבירה יצאנו מידי הרהור לא יצאנו מיד [ו] ונקרב את קרבן ה' תנא דבי רבי ישמעאל מפני מה הוצרכו ישראל שבאותו הדור כפרה מפני

שזנו

רש"י

כלי כלי. בשרצים כתיב כל כלי אשר יעשה מלאכה וגו' ומגופיה דקרא דשרצים לא מצי יליף דאשר יעשה מלאכה לאו כלי תכשיט משמע: שק. הוא עשוי מנוצה של עזים שאף על פי שאינו אריג אלא קלע קטן עשה מנוצה של עזים לתלות בו בתי נפש לצואר בתו טמא שדרכו בכך ותכשיט הוא וה"ק שהוא טמא משום אריג ואע"פ שאינו אריג: קולע ג' נימין כו'. ג' חוטין של מטוה של נוצה של עזים צבועה: ותולה בצואר בתו. וקליעתה זו היא אריגתו מאחר שהוא טווי כדאמרן גבי תיכי חלילתא בריש פירקין דקרי להו אריג והא דקאמר אע"פ שאינו אריג כלומר לאו אריג ממש: אין לי אלא שק. העשוי ללבוש רועים: קילקלי. מסרך של סוס שקורין פייטרא"ל: חבק. צינגלא של סרגא ואוכף ועושין אותה מנוצה של עזים טווי ואריג: יכול שאני מרבה החבלים והמשיחות. לציא"ל שעושין למדוד וקולעין מן הנוצה כמו שנתלשה ואינו טווי ולא דמי לקולע שלש נימין דלעיל דהתם טווי הוא חו היא אריגתו: יכול שאני מרבה כו'. הואיל וכתיב כל: ודין הוא שלא נרבה. ולא צריך קרא למעוטי: הן. תמיה הוא וכי דברים כוונים הם: אם היקל בטומאת שרץ שהיא קלה. כלומר אם היקל מלטמא חבלים ומשיחות היקל לך בשרץ שטומאתו קלה טומאת ערב: נקל. גם אנחנו בבנין אב זה במת שטומאתו חמורה טומאת ז': השתא דאתיא גזירה שוה. וכי היכי דיליף מת משרץ למעוטי חבלים ומשיחות יליף נמי שרץ ממת לכל מעשה עזים לרבות קילקלי וחבק: אין לי אלא בשרץ. דהא שק התם כתיב: אם ריבה. לטמא דבר הבא מזנב הסוס בטומאת ערב הוא דריבה: שהיא מרובה. שכל המגעות טומאת ערב הן בין דשרץ ונבילה ושכבת זרע מגע הזב ומגע טמא מת: נרבה אנו בטומאת ז' שכן מועטת היא. שאינה בכל המגעות אלא במגע המת בלבד: מופנה. צריך שתהא גזירה שוה זו מב' תיבות דבגד ועור מופנין למדרש זה שלא יהו צריכין לגופן ומאחר שמופנין ללמוד גזירה שוה ה"ל כמאן דכתיב דרשא בקרא בהדיא ואין משיבין עליה: דאי לאו מופנה. אמרינן לגופן באו ולא ילפינן להא מילתא מינייהו: דאיכא למיפרך כו'. וה"ה דמצי למימר הכי אגזירה שוה קמייתא ומיהו אסקי לכולה ברייתא ברישא ופריך אהא דסליק מינה ובשינויא דמשנינן בהא מיתרצה נמי קמייתא: לאי. באמת: וכתיב ביה בשכבת זרע. דבגד ועור טמאים הם בו: מצד אחד. הכתובין בשרץ מופנים כדאמרן אבל הכתובין במת אין מופנין: הניחא למ"ד כו'. פלוגתא דרבי ישמעאל ורבנן היא במסכת נדה בהמפלת (דף כב:): אלא למאן דאמר למידין. אם אין תשובה: ומשיבין. אם יש להשיב: מאי איכא למימר. הרי יש להשיב שכן מטמא בכעדשה: והנוגע בכל טמא נפש או איש אשר תצא ממנו שכבת זרע: דפוס של דדין. שמונחות בו: גיחוך. ליצנות: לקלקולכם. של מעשה שטים לזנות את בנות מואב שמא כך עשיתם במדין לכך אתם צריכין קרבן: לא נפקד. לא נחסר מדת יהודית:

שזנו

תוספות

מניין לרבות את הקילקלי והחבק. ואם תאמר והא לא מיטלטל מלא וריקן ואי משום דאפשר לקפלה אם אינו עשוי לכך לאו כלום הוא כדאמר לקמן גבי קב הקיטע דאע"ג דיש לו בית קיבול לראש שוקו אם אינו עשוי לקבל טהור וי"ל דהני נמי לשם כל צורכן הן עשוין מתחלה אך קשה דלעיל פ' במה מדליקין (דף כ. ושם) מפיק דבר הבא מן העזים דמטמא בשרצים מאו בגד וקילקלי וחבק באין מן העזים ומפיק להן הכא מאו שק וע"ק דהתם מרבה לנוצה של עזים לג' על ג' ואילו שק שיעורו בד' ואומר ר"י דתרי גווני נוצה של עזים הוו והתם מיירי [בדקה] שעושים ממנה בגדים חשובים והלכך איתרבו לשלשה על שלשה כמו שאר בגדים והכא מיירי בנוצה גסה שממנה עושין קילקלי וחבק וחבלים ומשיחות ושק: שמע מינה לאפנויי. הקשה ה"ר אליעזר ממיץ כיון דאיתקש שרץ ומת לשכבת זרע א"כ ג"ש דבגד ועור ל"ל דכל מה שיהיה במת ניתן בשכבת זרע וכל מה שיהיה בשכבת זרע ניתן בשרץ וכן להפך דהא קי"ל [ז] דבר הבא מן ההיקש חוזר ומלמד בהיקש חוץ מן הקדשים: מידי הרהור מי יצאנו. וא"ת והא אפילו (א) יפת תואר הותרה להם וי"ל דמכל מקום שייך בה איסור כדאמרינן (קדושין דף כב.) וחשקת בה ולא בחברתה:

וכמוך

עין משפט נר מצוה

נח א ב ג ד מיי' פ"א מהל' כלים הלכה יב:

רבינו חננאל

קילקלי. מלשון יון הוא והוא עשוי בגד [(גליון) משיער של עזים והוא קשה עשוי להצניעו תחת הכרים והכסתות. חבקים כסוי הכסאות (ת"ל) או בגד או עור או שק אין לי אלא] שק בלבד מנין לרבות הקילקלי וחבק ת"ל או שק פי' מרבינן להו מאו כלומר הוה ליה למימר שק. או דכתב רחמנא למה לי לרבויי קילקלי וחבק. יכול שאני מרבה חבלים ומשיחין שיטמאו ת"ל שק מה שק טווי ואריג אף כל טווי ואריג הרי הוא אמר במת כל מעשה עזים יכול שאני מרבה חבלים ומשיחים דין הוא טימא בשרץ טימא במת כו'. דחינן ואם היקל בטומאת שרץ שהיא קלה פי' טומאת שרץ קלה היא שהיא טומאת ערב אבל טומאת מת חמורה היא שהיא טומאת שבעה לא נתרבה ת"ל (או) בגד ועור בגד ועור לג"ש נאמר בגד ועור בשרץ ונאמר בגד ועור במת. פי' דין ג"ש ב' פסוקים וכל פסוק ופסוק כתוב מלין שאינן צריכין לפסוק ואין מילין פטיין לא נכתבו אלא בתוך פסוקים אלו אלא לדון מהם ג"ש להיות כל דין שמפורש באחד מהן שיהא גם השני כמותו וזהו שכתוב בעניננו בגד ועור בשרץ בגד ועור במת וצריכין להיות אלו בגד ועור מופנים בשני הפסוקים. שאם הן בפסוק אחד יתירין כגון שלמדו טומאת בגד ועור בשרץ משכבת זרע ונמצא בגד ועור האמור בשרץ מופנה כגון זה למידין ואם יש פירכא משיבין ופורכין ואם הן אלו פסוקים בגד ועור יתירין בשרץ ובמת למידין במת מן השרץ זהו טמאין במת דבר הבא מזנב הסוס מזנב הפרה כשם שמטמאין בשרץ ואין משיבין ואע"ג דאיכא למפרך ואם ריבה בטומאת שרץ שהיא מרובה. פי' טומאת שרץ (נותנת) [נוהגת] בשמנה שרצים. נרבה טומאת מת שהיא מועטת שאינה אלא במת בלבד ואוקימנא כיון שהן מופנה משני צדדין למידין ואין משיבין. ואלו הדברים הל"מ להדרש בענין הזה מסורת בידי חכמים:

רב נסים גאון

הניחא למאן [דאמר] מופנה מצד א' למדין ואין משיבין אלא למאן דאמר למידין ומשיבין מאי איכא למימר. מחלוקת בין ר' ישמעאל ורבנן ועיקר דילה במס' נדה בפרק המפלת (דף כב) אמר רב יהודה אמר שמואל משום ר' כל גזירה שוה שאינה מופנה כל עיקר אין למידין ממנה מופנה מצד אחד לר' ישמעאל למידין ואין משיבין לרבנן למידין ומשיבין: אמר להם משה לישראל שמא חזרתם לקלקולכם הראשון אמרו לו לא נפקד ממנו איש. במס' יבמות בפרק הבא על יבמתו (דף סא) אמרו ור' שמעון לא נפקד ממנו איש לעבירה ולדבר זה נתכוונו בהם בתשובה זו:

קסבר

מסורת הש"ס

א) ת"כ פ' שמיני, ב) [בערוך איתא לאיי ומפרש דלשון יון הוא ע"ש], ג) [ב"ק כה:], ד) [נדה כב:], ה) [לקמן קלא. יבמות ע: עד. נדה כב:], ו) [מס' כלה], ז) [זבחים מט:].

הגהות הב"ח

(א) תוס' ד"ה מידי וכו' אפי' ליקח יפת תואר:

תורה אור השלם

א) וְכֹל אֲשֶׁר יִפֹּל עָלָיו מֵהֶם בְּמֹתָם יִטְמָא מִכָּל כְּלִי עֵץ אוֹ בֶגֶד אוֹ עוֹר אוֹ שָׂק כָּל כְּלִי אֲשֶׁר יֵעָשֶׂה מְלָאכָה בָּהֶם בַּמַּיִם יוּבָא וְטָמֵא עַד הָעֶרֶב וְטָהֵר: [ויקרא יא, לב]

ב) וְכָל בֶּגֶד וְכָל כְּלִי עוֹר וְכָל מַעֲשֵׂה עִזִּים וְכָל כְּלִי עֵץ תִּתְחַטָּאוּ: [במדבר לא, כ]

ג) אִישׁ אִישׁ מִזֶּרַע אַהֲרֹן וְהוּא צָרוּעַ אוֹ זָב בַּקֳּדָשִׁים לֹא יֹאכַל עַד אֲשֶׁר יִטְהָר וְהַנֹּגֵעַ בְּכָל טְמֵא נֶפֶשׁ אוֹ אִישׁ אֲשֶׁר תֵּצֵא מִמֶּנּוּ שִׁכְבַת זָרַע: [ויקרא כב, ד]

ד) אוֹ אִישׁ אֲשֶׁר יִגַּע בְּכָל שֶׁרֶץ אֲשֶׁר יִטְמָא לוֹ אוֹ בְאָדָם אֲשֶׁר יִטְמָא לוֹ לְכֹל טֻמְאָתוֹ: [ויקרא כב, ה]

ה) וְכָל בֶּגֶד וְכָל עוֹר אֲשֶׁר יִהְיֶה עָלָיו שִׁכְבַת זָרַע וְכֻבַּס בַּמַּיִם וְטָמֵא עַד הָעָרֶב: [ויקרא טו, יז]

ו) וַנַּקְרֵב אֶת קָרְבַּן יְיָ אִישׁ אֲשֶׁר מָצָא כְלִי זָהָב אֶצְעָדָה וְצָמִיד טַבַּעַת עָגִיל וְכוּמָז לְכַפֵּר עַל נַפְשֹׁתֵינוּ לִפְנֵי יְיָ: [במדבר לא, נ]

ז) וַיִּקְצֹף מֹשֶׁה עַל פְּקוּדֵי הֶחָיִל שָׂרֵי הָאֲלָפִים וְשָׂרֵי הַמֵּאוֹת הַבָּאִים מִצְּבָא הַמִּלְחָמָה: [במדבר לא, יד]

ח) וַיֹּאמְרוּ אֶל מֹשֶׁה עֲבָדֶיךָ נָשְׂאוּ אֶת רֹאשׁ אַנְשֵׁי הַמִּלְחָמָה אֲשֶׁר בְּיָדֵנוּ וְלֹא נִפְקַד מִמֶּנּוּ אִישׁ: [במדבר לא, מט]

ליקוטי רש"י

קילקלי. צינגל"ש לקשור האוכף בחגישת החמור. חבק. פוטרי"ל ולרכי רכיבה הן [רשב"ם ב"ב עח.]. צינגל"א לאסור בו סוס [לעיל נז.]. למידין ואין משיבין. ואפילו יש להשיב [נדה כב:]. בכל טמא נפש. כמי שנטמא במת [ויקרא כב, ד]. אצעדה. אלו צמידים של רגל. וצמיד. של יד. וכומז. דפוס של בית הרחם לכפר על הרהור הלב של בנות מדין [במדבר לא, נ]. דפוס של בית הרחם. כלי זהב הוא נתון כנגד אותו מקום לאשה ורבותינו פירשו שם כומז כאן מקום זמה [שמות לה, כב]. שהיו עושין לבנותיהן ונוקבין כתלי בית הרחם כדרך שנוקבין את האזנים ותוחבין אותו כדי שלא יזדקקו להן זכרים [ברכות כד.]. על פקודי החיל. ממונים על החיל [במדבר שם, יד].

hide **that the Merciful One wrote** in His Torah **concerning** ***sheretz*** (since their susceptibility to *tumas sheretz* can be derived from the *hekeish* comparison of *sheretz* to semen)? שְׁמַע מִינָּהּ לְאַפְנוּיֵי – **Learn from this** that the Torah wrote those words in regard to *sheretz* **to make them free to establish a** *gezeirah shavah* with the passage of corpse *tumah*.

The Gemara asks:

וְאַכַּתִּי מוּפְנֶה מִצַּד אֶחָד הוּא – **But still,** this makes it **free only on one side.**[34] הָנִיחָא לְמַאן דְּאָמַר מוּפְנֶה מִצַּד אֶחָד לְמֵידִין וְאֵין מְשִׁיבִין – **This** situation **is satisfactory according to the one who says** that **we may derive** laws from a *gezeirah shavah* that is **free on only one side, and we cannot raise** any **objections** to refute it.[35] אֶלָּא לְמַאן דְּאָמַר לְמֵידִין וּמְשִׁיבִין מַאי אִיכָּא לְמֵימַר – **However, according to the one who says that we may derive laws** from such a *gezeirah shavah* only when no objection can be made, **but we may raise** logical **objections,** if possible, to refute the derivation, **what is there to say?**[36]

The Gemara answers:

דְּמֵת נַמִּי אַפְנוּיֵי מוּפְנֶה – The [***garment*** **and** ***hide***] found in the context **of a corpse is surely free as well,** as we will now demonstrate: מִכְּדֵי מֵת אִתְקַשׁ לְשִׁכְבַת זֶרַע – **Now,** let us examine this: **Corpse** *tumah* **is compared** by the Torah **to semen** *tumah;* דִּכְתִיב ,,וְהַנֹּגֵעַ בְּכָל־טְמֵא־נֶפֶשׁ אוֹ אִישׁ אֲשֶׁר־תֵּצֵא מִמֶּנּוּ שִׁכְבַת־זָרַע" – **as it is written:** ***Or one who touches anyone made tamei by a corpse or a man from whom there shall issue semen.***[37] וּכְתִיב בְּשִׁכְבַת זֶרַע ,,וְכָל־בֶּגֶד וְכָל־עוֹר" – **Now it is written concerning semen:** ***And any garment or hide*** *on which there shall be semen shall be immersed in water and remain tamei until evening.* This would suffice to teach that corpse *tumah* too can be transmitted to "garment and hide." ,,בֶּגֶד וְעוֹר" דִּכְתַב רַחֲמָנָא בְּמֵת לָמָּה לִי – Accordingly, **why do I need the** words ***garment*** **and** ***hide*** **that the Merciful One wrote** in His Torah **concerning corpse** ***tumah?*** שְׁמַע מִינָּהּ לְאַפְנוּיֵי – **Learn from this** that the Torah wrote them concerning corpse *tumah* **to make** them **free** and available to establish a *gezeirah shavah*. Thus, the words *garment* and *hide* are free on both the *sheretz* and corpse sides of *gezeirah shavah,* making it immune to refutation. We can therefore derive from it that articles made from the horse or cow tail are susceptible to corpse *tumah*.

The Gemara digresses to expound homiletically a verse stated in the same passage as the verse cited above in regard to corpse *tumah:* ,,וַנַּקְרֵב אֶת־קָרְבַּן ה' אִישׁ אֲשֶׁר מָצָא כְלִי־זָהָב אֶצְעָדָה וְצָמִיד טַבַּעַת עָגִיל וְכוּמָז" – The verse states:[38] ***So we have brought an offering for God, what any man found of gold vessels, anklet and bracelet, ring, an "agil" and "kumaz"*** *to atone for our souls before God.* אָמַר רַבִּי אֶלְעָזָר – **R' Elazar said:** ,,עָגִיל" זֶה דְּפוּס שֶׁל דַּדִּין – ***Agil*** **is an** ornamental **cast of** women's **breasts** worn over them; ,,כּוּמָז" זֶה דְּפוּס שֶׁל בֵּית הָרֶחֶם – ***kumaz*** **is an** ornamental **cast of the womb.**

Support for this identification is cited from *Targum Onkelos'* translation of this word:

אָמַר רַב יוֹסֵף – **Rav Yosef remarked:** אִי הָכִי הַיְינוּ דְּמִתַּרְגְּמִינַן ,,מָחוֹךְ" – **If so** (that *kumaz* refers to a cast of the womb), **this is why** the word *kumaz* **is translated** as ***machoch*** – דָּבָר הַמֵּבִיא לִידֵי גִיחוּךְ – i.e. **a thing that leads to** ***gichuch*** (levity).[39]

Further support:

אָמַר לֵיהּ רַבָּה – **Rabbah said to him:** מִגּוּפֵיהּ דִּקְרָא שְׁמַע מִינָּהּ – **This** meaning **can be inferred from** the wording of **the verse itself;** כּוּמָז כָּאן מְקוֹם זִימָּה – for the word *kumaz* can be understood to be an acronym for the words ***kan mekom zimah*** (here is the place of lewdness).[40]

The Gemara explains another verse from this passage:

,,וַיִּקְצֹף מֹשֶׁה עַל פְּקוּדֵי הֶחָיִל" – The verse states:[41] ***Moses was angry with the commanders of the army***. What caused this anger? אָמַר רַב נַחְמָן אָמַר רַבָּה בַּר אֲבוּהָ – **Rav Nachman said in the name of Rabbah bar Avuha:** אָמַר לָהֶן מֹשֶׁה לְיִשְׂרָאֵל – Upon seeing the commanders offer an atonement gift[42] to the Mishkan, **Moses said to them:** שֶׁמָּא חֲזַרְתֶּם לְקִלְקוּלְכֶם הָרִאשׁוֹן – **"Did you perhaps revert to your previous misconduct** with the Moabite women and sin with the Midianite women?"[43] אָמְרוּ לוֹ ,,לֹא־נִפְקַד מִמֶּנּוּ אִישׁ" – **[The commanders] replied to him:** "We took a census of the men who went to war and ***not a man among us was missing,***"[44] i.e. not one of us was found to be lacking in the observance of Jewish law.[45] אָמַר לָהֶן אִם כֵּן כַּפָּרָה לָמָּה – **[Moses] said to them: "If so, why do you require an atonement?"** אָמְרוּ לוֹ – **They replied to [Moses]:** אִם מִידֵי עֲבֵירָה יָצָאנוּ – **"If we have escaped** committing **a sin** in deed, מִידֵי הִרְהוּר לֹא יָצָאנוּ – **we have not escaped improper thoughts."** מִיָּד ,,וַנַּקְרֵב אֶת־קָרְבַּן ה' " – Therefore, **immediately** afterwards it states: ***We have brought an offering to God*** – i.e. to atone for these thoughts.

A similar approach:

תָּנָא דְּבֵי רַבִּי יִשְׁמָעֵאל – **A Baraisa of the academy of R' Yishmael has taught:** מִפְּנֵי מָה הוּצְרְכוּ יִשְׂרָאֵל שֶׁבְּאוֹתוֹ הַדּוֹר כַּפָּרָה – **Why did** the **Jews of that generation** (following the campaign against Midian) **require an atonement?** מִפְּנֵי – **Because**

NOTES

34. A *gezeirah shavah* is established by the appearance of a common expression "on two sides" (i.e. in two passages). In the present case, the two sides are *sheretz* and corpse. True, you have shown that the expression "garment" and "hide" on the *sheretz* side is superfluous; but you have not shown that this expression on the corpse side is similarly superfluous.

35. This is the opinion of R' Yishmael (see *Niddah* 22b).

36. This is the opinion of the Sages (ibid.). They hold that a *gezeirah shavah* is immune to refutation only if the common expression is free on both sides.

37. *Leviticus* 22:4. [By speaking of contact with *either* a person who touched a corpse *or* a person from whom semen issued, the Torah in effect equates the *tumah* acquired from either of these two sources.]

38. *Numbers* 31:50. The Torah recounts how the Moabites and the Midianites, on Bilaam's counsel, had sent their daughters to seduce the Israelites to debauchery in an attempt to undermine the sanctity of the Jewish people. This resulted in a plague that killed 24,000 Jews. God then instructed Israel to wage war against the Midianites as a punitive action.

Upon returning from this successful campaign, the army commanders offered an atonement gift to the Mishkan from the jewelry which was taken from Midianite women. The verse cited here delineates this gift.

39. [Rav Yosef understands the Aramaic name for this ornament, *machoch,* to be based on the Aramaic word *gichuch,* which literally means *laughter* – thus, *machach* is an object that brings about laughter.] In this case the intent is that it causes לֵיצָנוּת, *levity* (*Rashi*), i.e. lewdness (see next statement of the Gemara). [The word *laughter,* like the word *levity,* is used here by the Sages as a euphemism for lewd behavior; see *Avodah Zarah* 44a and *Rashi* to *Exodus* 32:6.]

40. [I.e. the place encased by this ornament is the part of the body which is the focus of lewdness.]

41. Ibid. 31:14.

42. See note 38.

43. I.e. is this the reason for your offering an atonement gift? (*Rashi*).

The commentaries find *Rashi's* explanation problematic because the sequence of the verses has Moses becoming angry *before* the atonement gift was offered. *Maharsha* therefore suggests that Moses' anger was aroused by the fact that they had allowed the womenfolk to live (see verse 15 there). [However, the Gemara's reconstruction below of the exchange between Moses and the commanders indicates that the Gemara here is explaining Moses' anger to be related to the atonement gift brought by the commanders (see *Maharsha* who explains this according to his interpretation).]

44. Ibid. 31:49.

45. [The verse is thus construed to mean, "Not a man among us was found to be lacking anything of what *he* had been at the time he went out to war"; none of us has been diminished by sin.]

א) כלי כלי מהתם: מוסף [א] שק על הבגד שטמא משום אריג: אטו בגד לאו אריג הוא הכי קאמר מוסף שק על הבגד אף על פי שאינו אריג טמא למאי חזי אמר רבי יוחנן שכן עני קולע שלש נימין ותולה בצואר בתו [א] תנו רבנן א) שק אין לי אלא שק [ב] מניין לרבות את הקילקלי ואת החבק ת"ל או שק [ג] יכול שאני מרבה את החבלים ואת המשיחות ת"ל שק מה שק טווי ואריג אף כל טווי ואריג הרי הוא אומר במת ב) וכל כלי עור וכל מעשה עזים וגו' תתחטאו לרבות הקילקלי ואת החבק יכול שאני מרבה את החבלים ואת המשיחות ודין הוא טימא בשרץ וטימא במת מה כשטימא בשרץ לא טימא אלא טווי ואריג אף כשטימא במת לא טימא אלא טווי ואריג הן אם היקל בטמא שרץ שהיא קלה נקיל בטומאת המת שהיא חמורה תלמוד לומר בגד ועור בגד ועור לגזירה שוה נאמר א) בגד ועור בשרץ ונאמר ב) בגד ועור במת מה בגד ועור האמור בשרץ לא טימא אלא טווי ואריג אף בגד ועור האמור במת לא טימא אלא טווי ואריג ומה בגד ועור האמור במת טמא כל מעשה עזים אף בגד ועור האמור בשרץ טמא כל מעשה עזים אין לי אלא דבר הבא מן העזים [ד] מניין לרבות דבר הבא מזנב הסוס ומזנב הפרה תלמוד לומר א) או שק והא אפיקתיה לקילקלי וחבק הני מילי מקמי דליתיה ג"ש השתא דאתי גזירה שוה אייתור ליה ואין לי אלא בשרץ בטומאת מת מניין ודין הוא טימא במת וטימא בשרץ מה כשטימא בשרץ עשה דבר הבא מזנב הסוס ומזנב הפרה כמעשה עזים אף כשטימא במת עשה דבר הבא מזנב הסוס ומזנב הפרה כמעשה עזים הן אם הרבה בטומאת ערב שהיא מרובה נרבה בטומאת שבעה שהיא מועטת תלמוד לומר בגד ועור בגד ועור לגזירה שוה נאמר בגד ועור בשרץ ונאמר בגד ועור במת מה בגד ועור האמור בשרץ עשה דבר הבא מזנב הסוס ומזנב הפרה כמעשה עזים אף בגד ועור האמור במת עשה דבר הבא מזנב הסוס ומזנב הפרה כמעשה עזים ומופנה דאי לאו מופנה איכא למיפרך מה לשרץ שכן מטמא בכעדשה [ה] לאי אפנויי מופני [ו] מכדי שרץ איתקש לשכבת זרע דכתיב ג) איש אשר תצא ממנו שכבת זרע וסמיך ליה ד) איש אשר יגע בכל שרץ וכתיב ביה בשכבת זרע ה) וכל בגד וכל עור אשר יהיה עליו שכבת זרע בגד ועור דכתב רחמנא בשרץ למה לי שמע מינה לאפנויי ואכתי מופנה מצד אחד הוא הניחא למאן דאמר [ד] מופנה מצד אחד למידין ואין משיבין אלא למאן דאמר [ה] למידין ומשיבין מאי איכא למימר דמת נמי אפנויי מופנה מכדי מת אתקש לשכבת זרע דכתיב ג) והנוגע בכל טמא נפש או איש אשר תצא ממנו שכבת זרע וכתיב בשכבת זרע וכל בגד וכל עור בגד ועור דכתב רחמנא במת למה לי ש"מ לאפנויי: ו) ונקרב את קרבן ה' איש אשר מצא כלי זהב אצעדה וצמיד טבעת עגיל וכומז א"ר אלעזר [ו] עגיל זה דפוס של דדין כומז זה דפוס של בית הרחם אמר רב יוסף אי הכי היינו דמתרגמינן מחוך דבר המביא לידי גיחוך אמר ליה רבה מגופיה דקרא ש"מ כומז כאן מקום זימה: ז) ויקצוף משה על פקודי החיל אמר רב נחמן אמר רבה בר אבוה אמר להן משה לישראל שמא חזרתם לקלקולכם הראשון אמרו לו ח) לא נפקד ממנו איש אמר להן אם כן כפרה למה אמרו לו אם מידי עבירה יצאנו מידי הרהור לא יצאנו מיד ו) ונקרב את קרבן ה' תנא דבי רבי ישמעאל מפני מה הוצרכו ישראל שבאותו הדור כפרה מפני

שזנו

רש"י

כלי כלי. בשרצים כתיב כל כלי אשר יעשה מלאכה וגו' ומגופיה דקרא דשרצים לא מצי יליף דאשר יעשה מלאכה לאו כלי תכשיט משמע: שק. הוא עשוי מנוצה של עזים שאף על פי שאינו אריג אלא קלע קטן עשה מנוצה של עזים לתלות בו בתי נפש לצואר בתו טמא שדרכו בכך ותכשיט הוא וה"ק שהוא טמא משום אריג ואע"פ שאינו אריג: קולע ג' נימין כו'. ג' חוטין של מטוה של נוצה של עזים לצועה: ותולה בצואר בתו. וקליעתה זו היא אריגתו מאחר שהוא טווי כדאמרן גבי תיכי חלילתא בריש פירקין דקרי להו אריג והא דקאמר אע"פ שאינו אריג כלומר לאו אריג ממש: אין לי אלא שק. העשוי ללבוש רועים: קילקלי. מסרך של סוס שקורין פייטרא"ל: חבק. צינגלא של סרגא ואוכף ועושין אותה מנוצה של עזים טווי ואריג: יכול שאני מרבה החבלים והמשיחות. לציא"ל שעושין למדוד וקולעין מן הנוצה כמו שנתלשה ואינו טווי ולא דמי לקולע שלש נימין דלעיל דהתם טווי הוא חו היא אריגתו: יכול שאני מרבה כו'. הואיל וכתיב כל: ודין הוא שלא נרבה. ולא צריך קרא למעוטי: הן. תמיה הוא וכי דברים כוונים הם: אם היקל בטומאת שרץ שהיא קלה. כלומר אם היקל מלטמא חבלים ומשיחות היקל לך בשרץ שטומאתו קלה טומאת ערב: נקל. גם אנחנו בבנין אב זה במת שטומאתו חמורה טומאת ז': השתא דאתיא גזירה שוה. וכי היכי דיליף מת משרץ למעוטי חבלים ומשיחות יליף נמי שרץ ממת לכל מעשה עזים לרבות קילקלי וחבק: אין לי אלא בשרץ. דאו שק התם כתיב: אם ריבה. לטמא דבר הבא מזנב הסוס בטומאת ערב הוא דריבה: שהיא מרובה. שכל המגעות טומאת ערב הן בין דשרץ ונבילה ושכבת זרע מגע הזב ומגע טמא מת: נרבה אנו בטומאת ז' שכן מועטת היא. שאינה בכל המגעות אלא במגע המת בלבד: מופנה. צריך שתהא גזירה שוה זו מב' תיבות דבגד ועור מופנין למדרש זה שלא יהו צריכין לגופן ומאחר שמופנין ללמוד גזירה שוה ה"ל כמאן דכתיב דרשא בקרא בהדיא ואין משיבין עליה: דאי לאו מופנה. אמרינן לגופן באו ולא ילפינן להא מילתא מינייהו: דאיכא למיפרך כו'. וה"ה דמצי למימר הכי אגזירה שוה קמייתא ומיהו אסקי לכולה ברייתא ברישא ופריך אהא דסליק מינה ובשינויא דמשנינן בהא מיתרצה נמי קמייתא: לאי. באמת: וכתיב ביה בשכבת זרע. דבגד ועור טמאים הם בו: מצד אחד. הכתובין בשרץ מופנים כדאמרן אבל הכתובין במת אין מופנין: הניחא למ"ד כו'. פלוגתא דרבי ישמעאל ורבנן היא במסכת נדה בהמפלת (דף כב:): אלא למאן דאמר למידין. אם אין תשובה: ומשיבין. אם יש להשיב: מאי איכא למימר. הרי יש להשיב שכן מטמא בכעדשה: והנוגע בכל טמא נפש או איש אשר תצא ממנו שכבת זרע: דפוס של דדין. שמונחות בו: גיחוך. ליצנות: לקלקולכם. של מעשה שטים לזנות את בנות מואב שמא כך עשיתם במדין לכך אתם צריכין קרבן: לא נפקד. לא נחסר מדת יהודית:

שזנו

תוספות

מניין לרבות את הקילקלי והחבק. ואם תאמר והא לא מיטלטל מלא וריקן ואי משום דאפשר לקפלה אם אינו עשוי לכך לאו כלום הוא כדאמר לקמן גבי קב הקיטע דאע"ג דיש לו בית קיבול לראש שוקו אם אינו עשוי לקבל טהור וי"ל דהני נמי לשם כל צורכן הן עשוין מתחלה אך קשה דלעיל פ' במה מדליקין (דף כ. ושם) מפיק דבר הבא מן העזים דמטמא בשרצים מאו בגד וקילקלי וחבק באין מן העזים ומפיק להן הכא מאו שק וע"ק דהתם מרבה לנוצה של עזים לג' על ג' ואילו שק שיעורו בד' ואומר ר"י דתרי גווני נוצה של עזים הוו והתם מיירי [בדקה] שעושים ממנה בגדים חשובים והלכך איתרבו לשלשה על שלשה כמו שאר בגדים והכא מיירי בנוצה גסה שממנה עושין קילקלי וחבק וחבלים ומשיחות ושק: שמע מינה לאפנויי. הקשה ה"ר אליעזר ממיץ כיון דאיתקש שרץ ומת לשכבת זרע א"כ ג"ש דבגד ועור ל"ל דכל מה שיהיה במת ניתן בשכבת זרע וכל מה שיהיה בשכבת זרע ניתן בשרץ וכן להפך דהא קי"ל [ז] דבר הבא מן ההיקש חוזר ומלמד בהיקש חוץ מן הקדשים: מידי הרהור מי יצאנו. וא"ת והא אפילו (א) יפת תואר הותרה להם וי"ל דמכל מקום שייך בה איסור כדאמרינן (קדושין דף כב.) ותשקת בה ולא בחברתה:

וכמוך

מסורת הש"ס

א) ת"כ פ' שמיני, ב) [בערוך איתא לאיי ומפרש דלשון יון הוא ע"ש], ג) [ב"ק כה:], ד) [נדה כב:], ה) [לקמן קלא. יבמות ע: עד. נדה כב:], ו) [מס' כלה], ז) [זבחים מט:].

הגהות הב"ח

(א) תוס' ד"ה מידי וכו' אפי' ליקח יפת תואר:

תורה אור השלם

א) וְכֹל אֲשֶׁר יִפֹּל עָלָיו מֵהֶם בְּמֹתָם יִטְמָא מִכָּל כְּלִי עֵץ אוֹ בֶגֶד אוֹ עוֹר אוֹ שָׂק כָּל כְּלִי אֲשֶׁר יֵעָשֶׂה מְלָאכָה בָּהֶם בַּמַּיִם יוּבָא וְטָמֵא עַד הָעֶרֶב וְטָהֵר: [ויקרא יא, לב]

ב) וְכָל בֶּגֶד וְכָל כְּלִי עוֹר וְכָל מַעֲשֵׂה עִזִּים וְכָל כְּלִי עֵץ תִּתְחַטָּאוּ: [במדבר לא, כ]

ג) אִישׁ אִישׁ מִזֶּרַע אַהֲרֹן וְהוּא צָרוּעַ אוֹ זָב בַּקֳּדָשִׁים לֹא יֹאכַל עַד אֲשֶׁר יִטְהָר וְהַנֹּגֵעַ בְּכָל טְמֵא נֶפֶשׁ אוֹ אִישׁ אֲשֶׁר תֵּצֵא מִמֶּנּוּ שִׁכְבַת זָרַע: [ויקרא כב, ד]

ד) אוֹ אִישׁ אֲשֶׁר יִגַּע בְּכָל שֶׁרֶץ אֲשֶׁר יִטְמָא לוֹ אוֹ בְאָדָם אֲשֶׁר יִטְמָא לוֹ לְכֹל טֻמְאָתוֹ: [ויקרא כב, ה]

ה) וְכָל בֶּגֶד וְכָל עוֹר אֲשֶׁר יִהְיֶה עָלָיו שִׁכְבַת זָרַע וְכֻבַּס בַּמַּיִם וְטָמֵא עַד הָעָרֶב: [ויקרא טו, יז]

ו) וַנַּקְרֵב אֶת קָרְבַּן יְיָ אִישׁ אֲשֶׁר מָצָא כְלִי זָהָב אֶצְעָדָה וְצָמִיד טַבַּעַת עָגִיל וְכוּמָז לְכַפֵּר עַל נַפְשֹׁתֵינוּ לִפְנֵי יְיָ: [במדבר לא, נ]

ז) וַיִּקְצֹף מֹשֶׁה עַל פְּקוּדֵי הֶחָיִל שָׂרֵי הָאֲלָפִים וְשָׂרֵי הַמֵּאוֹת הַבָּאִים מִצְּבָא הַמִּלְחָמָה: [במדבר לא, יד]

ח) וַיֹּאמְרוּ אֶל מֹשֶׁה עֲבָדֶיךָ נָשְׂאוּ אֶת רֹאשׁ אַנְשֵׁי הַמִּלְחָמָה אֲשֶׁר בְּיָדֵנוּ וְלֹא נִפְקַד מִמֶּנּוּ אִישׁ: [במדבר לא, מט]

ליקוטי רש"י

קילקלי. צינגל"ש לקשור האוכף בתכישת החמור. חבק. פוטרי"ל ולרכי רכיבה הן [רשב"ם ב"ב עח.]. צינגל"א לאסור בו סוס [לעיל נז.]. למידין ואין משיבין. ואפילו יש להשיב [נדה כב:]. בכל טמא נפש. כמי שנטמא במת [ויקרא כב, ד]. אצעדה. אלו צמידים של רגל. וצמיד. של יד. וכומז. דפוס של בית הרחם לכפר על הרהור הלב של בנות מדין [במדבר לא, נ]. דפוס של בית הרחם. כלי זהב הוא נתון כנגד אותו מקום לאשה ורבותינו פירשו שם כומז כאן מקום זמה [שמות לה, כב]. שהיו עושין לבנותיהן ונוקבין כתלי בית הרחם כדרך שנוקבין את האזנים ותוחבין אותו כדי שלא יזדקקו להן זכרים [ברכות כד.]. על פקודי החיל. ממונים על החיל [במדבר שם, יד].

עין משפט נר מצוה

נח א ב ג ד מיי' פ"א מהל' כלים הלכה יב:

רבינו חננאל

קילקלי. מלשון יון הוא והוא עשוי בגד [(גליין) משיער של עזים והוא קשה עשוי להצניעו תחת הכרים והכסתות. חבקים כסוי הכסאות (ת"ל) או בגד או עור או שק אין לי אלא] שק בלבד מנין לרבות הקילקלי וחבק ת"ל או שק פי' מרבינן להו מאו כלומר הוה ליה למימר שק. או דכתב רחמנא למה לי לרבויי קילקלי וחבק. יכול שאני מרבה חבלים ומשיחין שיטמאו ת"ל שק מה שק טווי ואריג אף כל טווי ואריג הרי הוא אמר במת כל מעשה עזים יכול שאני מרבה חבלים ומשיחים דין הוא טימא בשרץ טימא במת כו'. ודחינן ואם היקל בטומאת שרץ שהיא קלה פי' טומאת שרץ קלה היא שהיא טומאת ערב אבל טומאת מת חמורה היא שהיא טומאת שבעה לא נתרבה ת"ל (או) בגד ועור בגד ועור לג"ש נאמר בגד ועור בשרץ ונאמר בגד ועור במת. פי' דין ג"ש ב' פסוקים וכל פסוק ופסוק כתוב מלין שאינן צריכין לפסוק ואין מילין פטיין לא נכתבו אלא בתוך פסוקים אלו אלא לדון מהם ג"ש להיות כל דין שמפורש באחד מהן שיהא גם השני כמותו וזהו שכתוב בעניננו בגד ועור בשרץ בגד ועור במת וצריכין להיות אלו בגד ועור מופנים בשני הפסוקים. שאם הן בפסוק אחד יתירין כגון שלמדו טומאת בגד ועור בשרץ משכבת זרע ונמצא בגד ועור האמור בשרץ מופנה כגון זה למידין ואם יש פירכא משיבין ופורכין ואם הן אלו פסוקים בגד ועור יתירין בשרץ ובמת למידין במת מן השרץ זהו טמאין במת דבר הבא מזנב הסוס מזנב הפרה כשם שמטמאין בשרץ ואין משיבין ואע"ג דאיכא למפרך ואם ריבה בטומאת שרץ שהיא מרובה. פי' טומאת שרץ (נותנת) [נוהגת] בשמנה שרצים. נרבה טומאת מת שהיא מועטת שאינה אלא במת בלבד ואוקימנא כיון שהן מופנה משני צדדין למידין ואין משיבין. ואלו הדברים הל"מ להדרש בענין הזה מסורת בידי חכמים:

רב נסים גאון

הניחא למאן [דאמר] מופנה מצד א' למדין ואין משיבין אלא למאן דאמר למידין ומשיבין מאי איכא למימר. מחלוקת בין ר' ישמעאל ורבנן ועיקר דילה במס' נדה בפרק המפלת (דף כב) אמר רב יהודה אמר שמואל משום ר' כל גזירה שוה שאינה מופנה כל עיקר אין למידין ממנה מופנה מצד אחד לר' ישמעאל למידין ואין משיבין לרבנן למידין ומשיבין: אמר להם משה לישראל שמא חזרתם לקלקולכם הראשון אמרו לו לא נפקד ממנו איש. במס' יבמות בפרק הבא על יבמתו (דף סא) אמרו ור' שמעון לא נפקד ממנו איש לעבירה ולדבר זה נתכוונו בהם בתשובה זו:

קסבר

שזנו עיניהם מן הערוה אמר רב ששת [א] א מפני מה מנה הכתוב תכשיטין שבחוץ עם תכשיטין שבפנים לומר לך כל המסתכל באצבע קטנה של אשה כאילו מסתכל במקום התורפה: **מתני'** [ב] ב יוצאה אשה בחוטי שער בין משלה בין משל חבירתה בין משל בהמה ובטוטפת ובסרביטין בזמן שהן תפורין בכבול ובפאה נכרית לחצר במוך שבאזנה ובמוך שבסנדלה ובמוך שהתקינה לנדתה ג בפילפל [ג] ובגלגל מלח וכל דבר שניתן לתוך פיה ובלבד שלא תתן לכתחלה בשבת ואם נפל לא תחזיר שן תותבת שן של זהב רבי מתיר וחכמים אוסרים: **גמ'** וצריכא דאי אשמעינן דידה משום דלא מאיס אבל חבירתה דמאיס אימא לא ואי אשמעינן דחבירתה דבת מינה הוא אבל דבהמה לאו בר מינה הוא אימא לא צריכא תנא ד ובלבד שלא תצא ילדה בשל זקנה וזקנה בשל ילדה בשלמא זקנה בשל ילדה שבח הוא לה [ד] אלא ילדה בשל זקנה אמאי גנאי הוא לה איידי דתנא זקנה בשל ילדה תנא נמי ילדה בשל זקנה: בכבול ובפאה נכרית לחצר: אמר רב כל ה שאסרו חכמים לצאת בו לרה"ר אסור לצאת בו לחצר [ה] חוץ מכבול ופאה נכרית רבי ענני בר ששון משמיה [ו] דר' ישמעאל אמר הכל ככבול תנן בכבול ובפאה נכרית לחצר בשלמא לרב ניחא אלא לרבי ענני בר ששון קשיא רבי ענני בר ששון משמיה דמאן קאמר ליה משמיה דר' ישמעאל בר יוסי רבי ישמעאל בר יוסי תנא הוא ופליג ורב מאי שנא הני אמר עולא כדי שלא תתגנה על בעלה כדתניא [א] והדוה בנדתה זקנים הראשונים אמרו שלא תכחול ולא תפקוס ולא תתקשט בבגדי צבעונין עד שבא ר"ע ולימד י אם כן אתה מגנה על בעלה ונמצא בעלה מגרשה אלא מה ת"ל והדוה בנדתה ז בנדתה תהא עד שתבא במים [ז] אמר רב יהודה אמר רב כל מקום שאסרו חכמים מפני מראית העין אפילו בחדרי חדרים אסור [ח] תנן ולא בזוג אע"פ שפקוק ותניא [ט] אידך [י] פוקק לה זוג בצווארה ומטייל עמה בחצר תנאי היא דתניא

שוטחן

שזנו. לשון מזון שנהנו במראית העין: תכשיטין שבחוץ. טבעת: תכשיטין שבפנים. כומז: לומר לך המסתכל באצבע. שהיא מקום טבעת כמסתכל במקום כומז שהרי כפרה זו על שנסתכלו בה: **מתני'** בחוטי שער. שקולעת בהן שערה: בין משלה. תלושין: בין משל בהמה. כגון של סוס: שהן תפורין. לסבכה דתו לא שלפא להו לאחוויי: לחצר. אכבול ופיאה נכרית קאי דאסרו לעיל למיפק בה לרה"ר ואיצטריך לאשמעינן דלחצר מותר וכבול דסיפא דמתני' לא איפלגו בה אמוראי דלכולי עלמא כיפה של צמר: פיאה נכרית. קליעת שער תלושה ומוברתה על שערה עם קליעתה שתראה בעלת שער: במוך שבאזנה. שנותנת לבלוע ליחה של צואת האוזן: שבסנדלה. לתענוג: לנדתה. באותו מקום שיבלע בו הדם ולא יטנף בגדיה: פלפל. פלפל ארוך נותנת אשה בפיה שריחה רע: גלגל מלח. כמו גרגיר מלח לרפואת חולי שינים: שנתנה לתוך פיה. מבעוד יום: שן תותבת. נותנת בלחייה ממקום אחר והיא של זהב: רבי מתיר. לצאת בה: וחכמים אוסרין. דכיון דמשונה משאר השינים דילמא מחייכי עלה ושקלה לה מהתם וממטי לה בידה ובגמרא אמרינן דשל זהב נקט דווקא ל"א שן תותבת שן של אדם היתה ואהיתירא דלעיל קאי ולאו אפלוגתא דרבי ורבנן והכי קאמר בפלפל ובגלגל מלח ושן תותבת שן של זהב רבי מתיר כו': **גמ'** דלא מאים. וליכא למימר דמשלפא ליה משום דמחכו עלה וממטי ליה בידיה: דבת מינה הוא. ולא מינכר ולא מחייכי עלה: ובלבד שלא תצא זקנה. בחוטי שער של ילדה וילדה בשל זקנה דלבנות על שחורות או שחורות על לבנות מאים ואתי למישלף: כל שאסרו חכמים. בריש פרקין חוטי צמר ופשתן טוטפת ושאר השנויים במשנה שאסור ללכת בהן לרה"ר: אסור לצאת לחצר. ואף על גב דשרי לטלטולינהו דתורת כלי עליהן כדאמרן הרי הן ככל הכלים הניטלים בחצר מיהו דרך מלבוש אסור דמרגלה ליה ונפקא ביה לרה"ר: חוץ מכבול ופיאה. שמותר לחצר כדתנן במתניתין וטעמא מפרש לקמיה: הכל ככבול. כל הנאסרים לא נאסרו אלא לרה"ר אבל לחצר מותרים ככבול: בשלמא לרב ניחא. מדנקט הני ושבקינהו לאינך דמיתני בהדייהו לאיסורא ברישא דמתניתין מכלל דכולהו אף לחצר באיסורייהו קיימי: כדי שלא תתגנה. התירו לה קלת קישוטים הנאים: כדתניא. דחשו רבנן להכי: בנדתה. היו דורשין הראשונים כמשמעו כדבר המנודה ומרחיקה מבעלה: שלא תכחול. עיניה: ולא תפקוס. [כ] סרק על פניה טינפאנ"ל בלע"ז והוא אדום: תהא בנדתה. בטומאתה: עד שתבא במים. לטבול ואע"פ שעברו ז' שלה ופסק מעיינה: כל שאסרו חכמים משום מראית העין. שלא יחשדוהו באיסור כגון שריון וקסדא ומגפיים או לא יקשור גמלים זה בזה דמיחזי כאזיל לחינגא: ולא בזוג אע"פ שהוא פקוק. ואינו מוליד קול לא תצא בהמה בו וטעמא פרישנא בפ' במה בהמה (לעיל דף נד:) משום דמיחזי כאזיל לחינגא: ותניא. בברייתא דבחצר דליכא מראית העין מותר:

שוטחן

ובמוך שהתקינה לנדתה. פ"ה באותו מקום שיבלע בו הדם ולא יטנפו בגדיה ול"נ דא"כ אצולי טינוף הוא ומשוי הוא כדאמר בפ"ק (דף יא:) דכל אצולי טינוף לא חשיב ומשוי הוא לכן נ"ל שלא יפול על בשרה ותייבש עליה ונמצא מצטערה:

ובלבד שלא תתן לכתחלה בשבת. פירש הר"ר פורת גזירה משום שחיקת סממנים כיון דלרפואה הוא ול"נ דאם כן אם נפל אמאי לא תחזיר האמר בפרק בתרא דעירובין (דף קב: ושם) מחזירין רטיה במקדש אבל לא במדינה וע"כ לא אסרינן להחזיר הרטיה אלא משום שמא ימרח והכא לא שייך מירוח דאין שייך מירוח אלא בדבר לח כגון רטיה אבל בפלפלין ובגלגלא לא שייך מירוח לכן נ"ל ובלבד שלא תתן לכתחלה מפני שנראה כמערמת להוציאה ולפירוש זה כל הנך דלעיל מוך שבאזנה ושבסנדלה אסורין לתת לכתחלה וא"ת א"כ היכי שרו לקמן פורפת על האבן או על האגוז והא נראה כמערמת וי"ל דהתם ניכר הדבר והכל יודעין דלכך צריכה וליכא שום חששא אבל בדבר שהיא נותנת בתוך פיה אינם יודעין למה היא נותנת:

ובלבד שלא תצא זקנה בשל ילדה וילדה בשל זקנה. כך היא עיקר הגירסא והשתא פריך שפיר בשלמא זקנה בשל ילדה שבח הוא לה פירוש ומשום הכי איצטריך לאשמעינן שלא תצא דאפילו הכי מחכו עלה אלא ילדה בשל זקנה אמאי גנאי הוא לה פירוש אמאי איצטריך לאשמעינן דלא תצא פשיטא דכיון דגנאי הוא לה ודאי מחכו עלה ושקלה להו וכיון דתנא זקנה בשל ילדה אסור כל שכן ילדה בשל זקנה ודוחק הוא לומר זו וא"צ לומר זו קתני ואית דגרסי איפכא ובלבד שלא תצא ילדה בשל זקנה וזקנה בשל ילדה ואינו מיושב דא"כ אמאי פריך ילדה בשל זקנה אמאי שהרי כך הוא דרך הש"ס לשנות הפשוט תחלה והרב פורת מיישב גירסא זו וה"פ אלא ילדה בשל זקנה אמאי איצטריך גנאי הוא לה דלעולם לא תצא בהן אפילו בחול:

רבי ענני ברבי ששון אמר הכל ככבול. ונראה דהלכה כרבי ענני [ל] מדאמר מילתיה משמיה דרבי ישמעאל בר' יוסי ור' ישמעאל תנא הוא ופליג ועוד דבשל סופרים הלך אחר המיקל ור' ענני דמתיר בחצר היינו אפילו בחצר שאינה מעורבת דבחצר מעורבת ליכא שום חדוש אם כן נשים מותרות להתקשט בבית ובחצר בטבעות ובתכשיטין ואנו שאין לנו רה"ר גמור דכל רה"ר שלנו כרמלית היא שהרי אין מבואות שלנו רחבות י"ו אמה ולא ס' ריבוא בוקעים בו הרי הוא כחצר שאינה מעורבת ומותרות נשים שלנו להתקשט בטבעות ובתכשיטים כפר"ת והקשה ר"י דאפילו אי רה"ר שלנו חשיב ככרמלית היכי שרו כמו חצר והאמר לקמן פרק כל כתבי (דף קכ.) גבי דליקה דמותר להציל בחצר שאינה מעורבת ולא בכרמלית ואומר רבינו ברוך כיון דלדידהו הוו להו רה"ר גמורה לא מדמו כרמלית לחצר שאינה מעורבת ואסרינן כרמלית משום רה"ר אבל אנו שאין לנו רה"ר כלל ° אין להחמיר בכרמלית כ"כ וה"ר שמשון מלא כתוב בשם רבינו שר שלום דדבר שהוא רגילות להראות זו לזו אסור וכשאינם רגילות מותרות ונשי דידן אין מראות תכשיטיהן וטבעותיהן ומש"ה מותרות לצאת בהן וסוף דבר אמרו הקדמונים דמותרות לצאת בהן דמוטב יהו שוגגות ואל יהו מזידות:

אמר

עין משפט נר מצוה

נט א מיי' פכ"א מהל' איסורי ביאה הלכה ב סמג לאוין קכו טוש"ע אה"ע סי' כא סעיף א:

ס ב מיי' פי"ט מהל' שבת הלכה ט סמג לאוין סה טוש"ע א"ח סי' שג סעיף יד:

סא ג מיי' שם הלכה יב טוש"ע שם סעיף טו:

סב ד מיי' שם הלכה ט טוש"ע שם סעיף יד:

סג ה מיי' שם הלכה ח טוש"ע שם סעיף יח:

סד ו מיי' פי"א מהל' איסורי ביאה הלכה יט סמג לאוין קיא טוש"ע י"ד סימן קצה סעיף ט:

סה ז מיי' פ"ד שם הלכה ג ופי"א הלכה טו סמג שם טוש"ע שם סעי' א וסי' קנז סעי' א:

רבינו חננאל

מתני' **יוצאה** אשה בחוטי שיער כו'. אמר [רב] כל שאסרו חכמים לצאת בו לרה"ר אסור לצאת בו אפילו לחצר חוץ מכבול ופאה נכרית כדי שלא תתגנה על בעלה. והלכתא כותיה דרב ואע"ג דאמרינן ר' ישמעאל ב"ר יוסי תנא הוא ופליג לית הלכתא כוותיה. אמר רב יהודה אמר רב כל מקום שאסרו חכמים מפני מראית העין אפי' בחדרי חדרים אסור. ואקשינן עליה תנן בפרקין דקמי דין תנן לא בזוג אע"פ שהוא פקוק ותניא פוקקין לה זוג ומטיילתא בחצר. ומשני תנאי היא דתניא מי שנשרו כליו

גליון הש"ס

תוס' ד"ה ר' ענני כו' **אין** להחמיר בכרמלית. עי' כתובות דף ז ע"א תוס' ד"ה מתוך:

תורה אור השלם

א) וְהַדָּוָה בְּנִדָּתָהּ וְהַזָּב אֶת זוֹבוֹ לַזָּכָר וְלַנְּקֵבָה וּלְאִישׁ אֲשֶׁר יִשְׁכַּב עִם טְמֵאָה: [ויקרא טו, לג]

מסורת הש"ס

א) ברכות כד., ב) [לעיל נז:], ג) [גיר' הערוך ובגרגר וכן איתא במשנה שבמשניות], ד) בס"י הגיר' ואתיא לאחווי, ה) [עי' תוס' מנחות לו: ד"ה אי קסבר], ו) [נ"ל דר' ישמעאל בר' יוסי], ז) לקמן קמו: בילה ט. ע"ז יב., ח) לעיל נד:, ט) [ס"א עלה], י) לעיל נג., כ) עי' לקמן לד: רש"י ד"ה וכן הפוקסת ובמ"ק ט: תוס' ד"ה פוקסת, ל) [עי' תוס' במנחות לו: ד"ה אין].

ליקוטי רש"י

תכשיטין שבחוץ. אצעדה וצמיד הן הביאו אותן על כפרת הרהור עבירה שנסתכלו בבנות מדין [ברכות כד.]. **בזמן שהן תפורין.** עם השבכה שקורין שקופי"א כו' ליכא למיחש לאחוויי שאינה נוטלת השבכה מראשה ברשות הרבים שתגלה כל שערה [לעיל נז.]. **פיאה נכרית.** גדיל של שערות דעלמא שעושין לנוי [סנהדרין קיב.]. רגילות היו נשים כששערן מועט לקשור שיער נשים נכריות לשערן והוא פיאה נכרית. פיאה. קליעה [ערכין ז:]. **שן תותבת.** שנפלה שינה והושיבה שן אחר באותו מקום [נדרים סו:]. **שלא תכחול.** כוחלת. נותנת כחול בין עיניה כדי שדומות נאים. **ולא תפקום.** פוקסת. מחלקת שערה לכאן ולכאן [מו"ק ט: עיי"ש בתוס']. פוקסת. מעברת שרק על פניה [כתובות ד: עיי"ש בתוס']. יש מרבותי אומרים מתקנת שערה במסרק או בידי' ויש שמפרשין טחה כמין בצק על פניה וכשנוטלו מאדים הבשר [לקמן צד: עיי"ש בתוס']. **בנדתה תהא.** ועד שתבא במים לטבילה היא בנדתה דמרבינן מתהיה בנדתה בהוייתה תהא עד שתבא במים בתורת כהנים [לעיל יג:]. **כל מקום שאסרו חכמים.** דבר המותר ואסרוהו מפני מראית העין שהרואהו חושדו בדבר עבירה. **אפילו בחדרי חדרים אסור.** במקום שאין אדם רואה אסרוהו [ע"ז יב.]. **בזוג.** אישקליט"א. **אף על פי.** שמלאו פקוק במוכין שאין העינבל שלו מקשקש להשמיע קול. **פקוק.** סתום [לעיל נד:]. **פוקק לה זוג.** אבל כשאינו פקוק אפילו בחצר לא תצא מפני שהעינבל שבתוכה מקשקש ומוליד קול לכך פוקק בצמר או במוכין שלא יקשקש העינבל שבתוכה. **זוג.** אישקלי"ט. עינבל. בטדי"ל. **ומטייל.** באותו זוג בחצר אבל לא תצא בו לרשות הרבים כדמפרש לקמן בפרקין (נד:) דמיחזי כמאן דאזיל לחינגא [שם נג.].

כָּל jewelry (e.g. the *kumaz*)?[1] **לוֹמַר לְךָ – To teach you** that **הַמִּסְתַּכֵּל בְּאֶצְבַּע קְטַנָּה שֶׁל אִשָּׁה – whoever gazes at** even **the little finger of a woman** (the place where the ring is worn) **כְּאִילוּ מִסְתַּכֵּל בִּמְקוֹם הַתּוֹרְפָּה** – is considered to be **like one who gazes at the place of** her **nakedness** (the place where the *kumaz* is worn).[2]

שֶׁזָּנוּ עֵינֵיהֶם מִן הָעֶרְוָה – they feasted their eyes on lewdness in their conquest of Midian.

Another comment on the ornaments of the verse:

אָמַר רַב שֵׁשֶׁת – Rav Sheishess said: מִפְּנֵי מָה מָנָה הַכָּתוּב תַּכְשִׁיטִין שֶׁבַּחוּץ עִם תַּכְשִׁיטִין שֶׁבִּפְנִים – Why did [the Torah] list the outer jewelry (e.g. the ring) **together with the inner**

Mishnah The following Mishnah enumerates the items with which a woman is permitted to go out on the Sabbath: **יוֹצְאָה אִשָּׁה – A woman may go out** on the Sabbath **בְּחוּטֵי שֵׂעָר – with** her hair braided with **strands of hair,**[3] **בֵּין מִשֶּׁלָּהּ – whether** the strands are **of her own** hair,[4] **בֵּין מִשֶּׁל חֲבֵירְתָּהּ – whether** they are **of [the hair] of her companion, בֵּין מִשֶּׁל בְּהֵמָה** – or **whether** they are **of [the hair] of an animal;**[5] **וּבְטוֹטֶפֶת וּבְסַרְבִיטִין בִּזְמַן שֶׁהֵן תְּפוּרִין – with a frontlet or with head bangles when they are sewn** to her hat;[6] **בְּכָבוּל וּבְפֵאָה נָכְרִית לֶחָצֵר – with** an ornamental **woolen cap or with a wig,**[7] **into the courtyard;**[8] **בְּמוֹךְ שֶׁבְּאָזְנָהּ – with a wad in her ear,**[9] **וּבְמוֹךְ שֶׁבְּסַנְדָּלָהּ – with a wad in her sandal,**[10] **וּבְמוֹךְ שֶׁהִתְקִינָה לְנִדָּתָהּ – or with a wad that she prepared for her menses;**[11] **בְּפִלְפֵּל – with a peppercorn,**[12] **וּבְגַלְגַּל מֶלַח – with a lump of salt,**[13] **וְכָל דָּבָר שֶׁנּוֹתֵן לְתוֹךְ פִּיהָ** – **or** with **anything** else **that was placed in her mouth,**[14] **וּבִלְבַד שֶׁלֹּא תִּתֵּן לְכַתְּחִלָּה בְּשַׁבָּת – but provided that she does not initially place** it there **on the Sabbath,**[15] **וְאִם נָפַל לֹא תַּחֲזִיר – and** that, **if it fell** from her mouth, **she does not return** it there.[16]

NOTES

1. [There was no need to list the specific types of ornaments donated by the returning soldiers; the Torah could simply have said that they donated every piece of jewelry.] The specific listings were included to allude to the *reason* for the gift, namely, their desire to atone for having feasted their eyes on lewdness and having indulged in improper thoughts. But if so, the verse should only have listed the intimate items of jewelry that gave rise to these sins, such as the *agil* and *kumaz*. Why does the verse also list the articles of "outer jewelry," such as rings? (see *Rashi* ד״ה לומר לך and *Maharsha*).

2. [I.e. to teach that it is forbidden to gaze even at a woman's little finger.] See *Shulchan Aruch Even HaEzer* 21:1 with commentators for the parameters of this law.

3. Strands of hair cannot be drawn tightly enough around a woman's own hair to keep water from passing through. Since they therefore need not be removed during immersion in a *mikveh,* we do not fear that a woman might remove and carry them on such an occasion (see above 57b).

4. I.e. loose strands of her own hair (*Rashi*).

5. E.g. strands of horsehair (*Rashi*).

6. For since they are sewn to her hat, she cannot show them to her friends without removing her hat entirely, leaving her hair uncovered. A woman will certainly not do this, since a married woman is forbidden to expose her hair to public view (*Rashi* here and to 57a ד״ה בזמן). [*Rama* (*Orach Chaim* 303:2) therefore rules that a maiden, whose hair need not be covered, is forbidden to go out with a frontlet or head bangles even if they are sewn to her hat, lest she remove the entire hat, and inadvertently carry it in the public domain.]

7. [Literally: a foreign lock (of hair).] This is a plait braided of the hair of another which a woman piles upon her own hair so that she will appear well-endowed with hair (*Rashi*).

8. I.e. an ornamental woolen cap and a wig are permitted only in a courtyard, but are prohibited in a public domain. Since the first Mishnah in the chapter forbids one to wear a woolen cap (a *kavul*) in a public domain, the Mishnah must now inform us that it is permitted in a courtyard (*Rashi*). [The Gemara below will explain why these items are permissible in a courtyard.]

The reason a woman is forbidden to wear a wig in a public domain is that it may subject her to ridicule, causing her to remove it and carry it, in violation of the Sabbath (*Tosafos* above, 57b ד״ה אי כבלא דעבדא תנן; see below, note 27).

[Although the Gemara above (57b, 58a) cited a dispute concerning the identity of the *kavul* mentioned in the first Mishnah of the chapter, all agree that the *kavul* of our Mishnah is certainly a woman's woolen cap, and not a slave's emblem (*Rashi;* cf. *Ramban, Ritva,* and *Rashba;* cf. also *Tosafos* above, 57b ד״ה אי כבלא דעבדא תנן; see *Pnei Yehoshua* ad loc. for an answer to *Tosafos'* challenge to *Rashi*). This is because the Mishnah's equating of a *kavul* and a wig suggests that they are permissible for the same reason – to safeguard a woman's attractiveness to her husband (see Gemara below). This reason obviously pertains only to a woman's woolen cap, and not to a slave's emblem (*Pnei Yehoshua*).]

9. I.e. she may go out with a wad [of absorbent material] that she inserts in her ear to absorb the wax when it runs (*Rashi*).

10. Which she inserts there to make her shoe more comfortable (*Rashi*). [Of course, this wad and the one inserted into one's ear are permissible for a man as well as a woman (see below, 65a; see *Shabbos Shel Mi*).

11. I.e. a wad which she prepared to absorb her menstrual blood in order to keep it from soiling her clothing (*Rashi;* cf. *Tosafos,* explained by *Melo HaRo'im;* see also *Ran;* see *Shulchan Aruch, Orach Chaim* 301:13,14 and 303:15; see *Maginei Shlomo,* and *Dibros Moshe* 53:32 for an elucidation of *Rashi's* opinion). [The Gemara will discuss whether or not these various wads need be tied.]

12. I.e. she may go out with a peppercorn placed in her mouth to combat bad breath (*Rashi*).

13. Which she places in her mouth to heal a diseased tooth (*Rashi*).

14. I.e. she may go out with anything placed in her mouth for medicinal purposes (*Chidushei HaRan;* see also *Beis Yosef, Orach Chaim* 303:15 ד״ה וכתב בספר המצוות; cf. *Tiferes Yisrael*). [Since these items are serving a therapeutic function in her mouth, they do not legally constitute a burden, but are viewed as accessories; they thus may be taken outside. Obviously, a man as well as a woman may go out with these items.]

15. For if she initially places one of these items in her mouth on the Sabbath, one who observes her doing so, not knowing of her need for a remedy, might assume that her true intention is to transport the item to another domain. The observer might therefore be led to believe that such a transfer is permissible, and might thereby come to violate the Sabbath (*Tosafos,* second explanation; see *Rashi, Eruvin* 102b ד״ה אבל לא במדינה, and *Tosafos* ad loc.; see also *Magen Avraham* 303:11; see below, 65a note 23). *Tosafos* point out that according to this explanation, this stipulation forbids one as well to insert wadding in one's ear or sandal initially on the Sabbath, since that too might be taken as a subterfuge designed to transport items from one domain to another. Others, however, maintain that in that case it would be obvious to anyone watching that her intention is not to transport the wadding; one would consequently be permitted to insert it even on the Sabbath (see *Mishnah Berurah* 103:49; see also *Dibros Moshe* 53:33; see *Yerushalmi* with *Korban HaEidah* regarding the question of wadding).

[Alternatively, one is forbidden to place these items in one's mouth on the Sabbath because they are remedies, and one is forbidden to engage in healing on the Sabbath (*Tosafos,* first explanation, quoting *R' Poras*). According to this explanation, this stipulation might apply only to the lump of salt and other remedies, since only they are actually being used for their curative properties [רְפוּאָה]. However, it may be permissible to place a peppercorn in one's mouth even on the Sabbath, since it is not truly a remedy, but serves only to conceal bad breath (see *Beis Yosef* ibid.; see also *Or Zarua;* see also *Tosafos R' Akiva Eiger* §85). It is certainly permissible to place wadding in one's ear or shoe according to this explanation, as they are not remedies at all.]

16. For one who witnesses her returning it to her mouth will assume she intends to transport it to another domain (*Tosafos;* see previous note).

[The above accords with the first explanation presented in the previ-

שזנו עיניהם מן הערוה אמר רב ששת א) א מפני מה מנה הכתוב תכשיטין שבחוץ עם תכשיטין שבפנים לומר לך כל המסתכל באצבע קטנה של אשה כאילו מסתכל במקום התורפה: **מתני'** ג) ב יוצאה אשה בחוטי שער בין משלה בין משל חבירתה בין משל בהמה ובטוטפת ובסרביטין בזמן שהן תפורין בכבול ובפאה נכרית לחצר במוך שבאזנה ובמוך שבסנדלה ובמוך שהתקינה לנדתה ג בפילפל ג) ובגלגל מלח וכל דבר שניתן לתוך פיה ובלבד שלא תתן לכתחלה בשבת ואם נפל לא תחזיר שן תותבת שן של זהב רבי מתיר וחכמים אוסרים: **גמ'** וצריכא דאי אשמעינן דידה משום דלא מאים אבל חבירתה דמאים אימא לא ואי אשמעינן דחבירתה דבת מינה הוא אבל דבהמה לאו בר מינה הוא אימא לא צריכא תנא ד ובלבד שלא תצא ילדה בשל זקנה וזקנה בשל ילדה בשלמא זקנה בשל ילדה שבח הוא לה ד) אלא ילדה בשל זקנה אמאי גנאי הוא לה איידי דתנא זקנה בשל ילדה תנא נמי ילדה בשל זקנה: בכבול ובפאה נכרית לחצר: אמר רב כל ה שאסרו חכמים לצאת בו לרה"ר אסור לצאת בו לחצר ה) חוץ מכבול ופאה נכרית רבי ענני בר ששון משמיה ו) דר' ישמעאל אמר הכל ככבול תנן בכבול ובפאה נכרית לחצר בשלמא לרב ניחא אלא לרבי ענני בר ששון קשיא רבי ענני בר ששון משמיה דמאן קאמר ליה משמיה דר' ישמעאל בר יוסי רבי ישמעאל בר יוסי תנא הוא ופליג ורב מאי שנא הני אמר עולא כדי שלא תתגנה על בעלה כדתניא א) והדוה בנדתה זקנים הראשונים אמרו שלא תכחול ולא תפקוס ולא תתקשט בבגדי צבעונין עד שבא ר"ע ולימד ו אם כן אתה מגנה על בעלה ונמצא בעלה מגרשה אלא מה ת"ל והדוה בנדתה ז בנדתה תהא עד שתבא במים ז) אמר רב יהודה אמר רב כל מקום שאסרו חכמים מפני מראית העין אפילו בחדרי חדרים אסור ח) תנן ולא בזוג אע"פ שפקוק ותניא ט) אידך י) פוקק לה זוג בצוארה ומטייל עמה בחצר תנאי היא דתניא

שוטחן

רש"י

שזנו. לשון מזון שנהנו במראית העין: **תכשיטין שבחוץ.** טבעת: **תכשיטין שבפנים.** כומז: **לומר לך המסתכל באצבע.** שהיא מקום טבעת כמסתכל במקום כומז שהרי כפרה זו על שנסתכלו בה: **מתני' בחוטי שער.** שקולעת בהן שערה: **בין משלה.** תלושין: **בין משל בהמה.** כגון של סוס: **שהן תפורין.** לסבכה דתו לא שלפא להו לאחוויי: **לחצר.** אכבול ופיאה נכרית קאי דאסרו לעיל למיפק בה לרה"ר ואיצטריך לאשמעינן דלחצר מותר וכבול דסיפא דמתני' לא איפלגו בה אמוראי דלכולי עלמא כיפה של צמר: **פיאה נכרית.** קליעת שער תלושה ומוברתה על שערה עם קליעתה שתראה בעלת שער: **במוך שבאזנה.** שנותנת לבלוע ליחה של צואת האוזן: **שבסנדלה.** לתענוג: **לנדתה.** באותו מקום שיבלע בו הדם ולא יטנף בגדיה: **פלפל.** פלפל ארוך נותנת אשה בפיה שריחה רע: **גלגל מלח.** כמו גרגיר מלח לרפואת חולי שינים: **שנתנה לתוך פיה.** מבעוד יום: **שן תותבת.** נותנת בלחייה ממקום אחר והיא של זהב: **רבי מתיר.** לצאת בה: **וחכמים אוסרין.** דכיון דמשונה משאר השינים דילמא מיחייכי עלה ושקלה לה מהתם וממטי לה בידה ובגמרא אמרינן דשל זהב נקט דווקא לי"א שן תותבת שן של אדם היתה ואהיתירא דלעיל קאי ולאו אפלוגתא דרבי ורבנן והכי קאמר בפלפל ובגלגל מלח ושן תותבת שן של זהב רבי מתיר כו': **גמ' דלא מאים.** וליכא למימר דמשלפא ליה משום דמחכו עלה וממטי ליה בידיה: **דבת מינה הוא.** ולא מינכר ולא מחייכי עלה: **ובלבד שלא תצא זקנה.** בחוטי שער של ילדה וילדה בשל זקנה דלבנות על שחורות או שחורות על לבנות מאים ואתי למישלף: **כל שאסרו חכמים.** ברים פרקין חוטי צמר ופשתן טוטפת ושאר השנויים במשנה שאסור ללכת בהן לרה"ר: **אסור לצאת לחצר.** ואף על גב דשרי לטלטולינהו דתורת כלי עליהן כדאמרן הרי הן ככל הכלים הניטלים בחצר מיהו דרך מלבוש אסור דמרגלא ליה ונפקא ביה לרה"ר: **חוץ מכבול ופיאה.** שמותר לחצר כדתנן במתניתין וטעמא מפרש לקמיה: **הכל ככבול.** כל הנאסרים לא נאסרו אלא לרה"ר אבל לחצר מותרים ככבול: **בשלמא לרב ניחא.** מדנקט הני ושבקינהו לאינך דמיתני בהדייהו לאיסורא ברישא דמתניתין מכלל דכולהו אף לחצר באיסורייהו קיימי: **כדי שלא תתגנה.** התירו לה קצת קישוטים הנאים: **כדתניא.** דחשו רבנן להכי: **בנדתה.** היו דורשין הראשונים כמשמעו כדבר המנודה ומרחיקה מבעלה: **שלא תכחול.** עיניה: **ולא תפקוס.** ס) שרק על פניה טינפאנ"ל בלע"ז והוא אדום: **תהא בנדתה.** בטומאתה: **עד שתבא במים.** לטבול ואע"פ שעברו ז' שלה ופסק מעיינה: **כל שאסרו חכמים משום מראית העין.** שלא יחשדוהו באיסור כגון שרין וקסדא ומגפיים או לא יקשור גמלים זה בזה דמיחזי כאזיל לחינגא: **ולא בזוג אע"פ שהוא פקוק.** ואינו מוליד קול לא תצא בהמה בו וטעמא פרישנא בפ' במה בהמה (לעיל דף נד:) משום דמיחזי כאזיל לחינגא: **ותניא.** בברייתא דבחצר דליכא מראית העין מותר:

שוטחן

תוספות

ובמוך שהתקינה לנדתה. פ"ה באותו מקום שיבלע בו הדם ולא יטנפו בגדיה ול"נ דא"כ אצולי טינוף הוא ומשוי הוא כדאמר בפ"ק (דף יא:) דכל אצולי טינוף לא חשיב ומשוי הוא לכן נ"ל שלא יפול על בשרה ותייבש עליה ונמצא מצערה:

ובלבד שלא תתן לכתחלה בשבת. פירש הר"ר פורת גזירה משום שחיקת סממנים כיון דלרפואה הוא ול"נ דאם כן אם נפל אמאי לא תחזיר האמר בפרק בתרא דעירובין (דף קב: ושם) מחזירין רטיה במקדש אבל לא במדינה וע"כ לא אסרינן להחזיר הרטיה אלא משום שמא ימרח והכא לא שייך מירוח דאין שייך מירוח אלא בדבר לח כגון רטיה אבל בפלפלין ובגלגלא לא שייך מירוח לכן נ"ל ובלבד שלא תתן לכתחלה מפני שנראה כמערמת להוציאה ולפירוש זה כל הנך דלעיל מוך שבאזנה ושבסנדלה אסורין לתת לכתחלה וא"ת א"כ היכי שרו לקמן פורפת על האבן או על האגוז והא נראה כמערמת וי"ל דהתם ניכר הדבר והכל יודעין דלכך צריכה וליכא שום חששא אבל בדבר שהיא נותנת בתוך פיה אינם יודעין למה היא נותנת:

ובלבד שלא תצא זקנה בשל ילדה וילדה בשל זקנה. כך היא עיקר הגירסא והשתא פריך שפיר בשלמא זקנה בשל ילדה שבח הוא לה פירוש ומשום הכי איצטריך לאשמעינן שלא תצא דאפילו הכי מחכו עלה אלא ילדה בשל זקנה אמאי גנאי הוא לה פירוש אמאי איצטריך לאשמעינן דלא תצא פשיטא דכיון דגנאי הוא לה ודאי מחכו עלה ושקלה להו וכיון דתנא זקנה בשל ילדה אסור כל שכן ילדה בשל זקנה ודוחק הוא לומר זו וא"צ לומר זו קתני ואית דגרסי איפכא ובלבד שלא תצא ילדה בשל זקנה וזקנה בשל ילדה ואינו מיושב דא"כ אמאי פריך ילדה בשל זקנה אמאי שהרי כך הוא דרך הש"ס לשנות הפשוט תחלה והרב פורת מיישב גירסא זו וה"פ אלא ילדה בשל זקנה אמאי איצטריך גנאי הוא לה דלעולם לא תצא בהן אפילו בחול:

רבי ענני ברבי ששון אמר הכל ככבול. ונראה דהלכה כרבי ענני ל) מדאמר מילתיה משמיה דרבי ישמעאל בר' יוסי ור' ישמעאל תנא הוא ופליג ועוד דבשל סופרים הלך אחר המיקל ור' ענני דמתיר בחצר היינו אפילו בחצר שאינה מעורבת דבחצר מעורבת ליכא שום חדוש אם כן נשים מותרות להתקשט בבית ובחצר בטבעות ובתכשיטין ואנו שאין לנו רה"ר גמור דכל רה"ר שלנו כרמלית היא שהרי אין מבואות שלנו רחבות י"ו אמה ולא ס' ריבוא בוקעים בו הרי הוא כחצר שאינה מעורבת ומותרות נשים שלנו להתקשט בטבעות ובתכשיטים כפר"ת והקשה ר"י דאפילו אי רה"ר שלנו חשיב ככרמלית היכי שרו כמו חצר והאמר לקמן פרק כל כתבי (דף קכ.) גבי דליקה דמותר להציל בחצר שאינה מעורבת ולא בכרמלית ואומר רבינו ברוך כיון דלדידהו הוו להו רה"ר גמורה לא מדמו כרמלית לחצר שאינה מעורבת ואסרינן כרמלית משום רה"ר אבל אנו שאין לנו רה"ר כלל ° אין להחמיר בכרמלית כ"כ וה"ר שמשון מצא כתוב בשם רבינו שר שלום דדבר שהוא רגילות להראות זו לזו אסור וכשאינם רגילות מותרות ונשי דידן אין מראות תכשיטיהן וטבעותיהן ומש"ה מותרות לצאת בהן וסוף דבר אמרו הקדמונים דמותרות לצאת בהן דמוטב יהו שוגגות ואל יהו מזידות:

אמר

עין משפט נר מצוה

נט א מיי' פכ"א מהל' איסורי ביאה הלכה ג סמג לאוין קכו טוש"ע אה"ע סי' כא סעיף א:

ס ב מיי' פי"ט מהל' שבת הלכה ט סמג לאוין סה טוש"ע א"ח סי' שג סעיף יד:

סא ג מיי' שם הלכה יב טוש"ע שם סעיף טו:

סב ד מיי' שם הלכה ט טוש"ע שם סעיף יד:

סג ה מיי' שם הלכה ח טוש"ע שם סעיף יח:

סד ו מיי' פי"א מהל' איסורי ביאה הלכה יט סמג לאוין קיא טוש"ע י"ד סימן קצה סעיף ט:

סה ז מיי' פ"ד שם הלכה ג ופי"א הלכה טז סמג שם טוש"ע שם סעי' א וסי' קנז סעי' א:

רבינו חננאל

מתני' **יוצאה** אשה בחוטי שיער כו'. אמר [רב] כל שאסרו חכמים לצאת בו לרה"ר אסור לצאת בו אפילו לחצר חוץ מכבול ופאה נכרית כדי שלא תתגנה על בעלה. והלכתא כותיה דרב ואע"ג דאמרינן ר' ישמעאל ב"ר יוסי תנא הוא ופליג לית הלכתא כוותיה. אמר רב יהודה אמר רב כל מקום שאסרו חכמים מפני מראית העין אפי' בחדרי חדרים אסור. ואקשינן עליה תנן בפרקין דקמי דין תנן לא בזוג אע"פ שהוא פקוק ותניא פוקקין לה זוג ומטיילתא בחצר. ומשני תנאי היא דתניא מי שנשרו כליו

גליון הש"ס

תוס' ד"ה ר' ענני כו' **אין** להחמיר בכרמלית. עי' כתובות דף ז ע"א תוס' ד"ה מתוך:

תורה אור השלם

א) וְהַדָּוָה בְּנִדָּתָהּ וְהַזָּב אֶת זוֹבוֹ לַזָּכָר וְלַנְּקֵבָה וּלְאִישׁ אֲשֶׁר יִשְׁכַּב עִם טְמֵאָה: [ויקרא טו, לג]

מסורת הש"ס

א) ברכות כד., ב) [לעיל נז:], ג) [גיר' הערוך ובגרגר וכן איתא במשנה שבמשניות], ד) בס"יהגיר' **ואתיא** לאחוויי, ה) [עי' תוס' מנחות לו: ד"ה אי קסבר], ו) [נ"ל דר' **ישמעאל בר'** יוסי], ז) לקמן קמו: ביצה ט. ע"ז יב., ח) לעיל נד:, ט) [ס"א עלה], י) לעיל נג., כ) עי' לקמן לד: רש"י ד"ה וכן הפוקסת ובמ"ק ט: תוס' ד"ה פוקסת, ל) [עי' תוס' במנחות לו: ד"ה אי].

ליקוטי רש"י

תכשיטין שבחוץ. אצעדה וצמיד הן הביאו אותן על כפרת הרהור עבירה שנסתכלו בבנות מדין [ברכות כד.]. **בזמן שהן תפורין.** עם השבכה שקורין שקופי"א כו' ליכא למיחש לאחוויי שאינה נוטלת השבכה מראשה ברשות הרבים שתגלה כל שערה [לעיל נז.]. **פיאה נכרית.** גדיל של שערות דעלמא שעושין לנוי [סנהדרין קיב.]. רגילות היו נשים כששערן מועט לקשור שיער נשים נכריות לשערן והוא פיאה נכרית. פיאה. קליעה [ערכין ז:]. **שן תותבת.** שנפלה שינה והושיבה שן אחר באותו מקום [נדרים סו:]. **שלא תכחול.** כוחלת. נותנת כחול בין עיניה כדי שדומות נאים. **ולא תפקום.** פוקסת. מחלקת שערה לכאן ולכאן [מו"ק ט: עיי"ש בתוס']. פוקסת. מעברת שרק על פניה [כתובות ד: עיי"ש בתוס']. יש מרבותי אומרים מתקנת שערה במסרק או בידי' ויש שמפרשין טחה כמין בצק על פניה וכשנוטלו מאדים הבשר [לקמן צד: עיי"ש בתוס']. **בנדתה תהא.** ועד שתבא במים לטבילה היא בנדתה דמרבינן מתהיה בנדתה בהוייתה תהא עד שתבא במים בתורת כהנים [לעיל יג:]. **כל מקום שאסרו חכמים.** דבר המותר ואסרוהו מפני מראית העין שהרואהו חושדו בדבר עבירה. **אפילו בחדרי חדרים אסור.** במקום שאין אדם רואה אסרוהו [ע"ז יב.]. **בזוג.** אישקליט"א. **אף על פי.** שמללו פקוק במוכין שאין העינבל שלו מקשקש להשמיע קול. **פקוק.** סתום [לעיל נד:]. **פוקק לה זוג.** אבל כשאינו פקוק אפילו בחצר לא תצא מפני שהעינבל שבתוכה מקשקש ומוליד קול לכך פוקק בצמר או במוכין שלא יקשקש העינבל שבתוכה. **זוג.** אישקליי"ט. **עינבל.** בטדי"ל. **ומטייל.** באותו זוג בחצר אבל לא תצא בו לרשות הרבים כדמפרש לקמן בפרקין (נד:) דמיחזי כמאן דאזיל לחינגא [שם נג.].

A dispute:

שֵׁן תּוֹתֶבֶת שֵׁן שֶׁל זָהָב – **A false tooth made of gold:**[17] רַבִּי מַתִּיר – **Rebbi permits** one to go out with it, וַחֲכָמִים אוֹסְרִים – **but the Sages forbid** it.[18]

Gemara The Gemara explains why the Mishnah deems it necessary to enumerate three sorts of hair strands – her own, that of a companion, and that of an animal:

וּצְרִיכָא – **It is necessary** for the Mishnah to enumerate all three sorts of hair strands. דְּאִי אַשְׁמְעִינַן דִּידָהּ – **For if [the Mishnah] would** only **have informed us** that a woman is permitted to go out with her hair braided with loose strands of **her own** hair, I would have said that מִשּׁוּם דְּלָא מְאִיס – this is **because [wearing these strands] is not** considered a **repugnant** practice. אֲבָל חֲבֶירְתָּהּ דִּמְאִיס – **But** in the case of a woman wearing strands of the hair of **her companion, which is** generally viewed as a **repugnant** practice, אֵימָא לֹא – **I would have said** that she is **not** permitted to go out, since people might ridicule her, thereby leading her to remove the strands and carry them. The Mishnah must therefore state that a woman is permitted to go out with strands of another woman's hair entwined in her own. וְאִי אַשְׁמְעִינַן דַּחֲבֶירְתָּהּ – **And if [the Mishnah] would have informed us** that a woman is permitted to go out wearing strands **of** the hair of **her companion,** I would have said that דְּבַת מִינָהּ הוּא – this is **because [these strands] are of like kind with [her own]** hair; since the strands are therefore not noticeable, they will not lead others to ridicule her. אֲבָל דִּבְהֵמָה – **But** in the case of a woman wearing strands **of animal** hair, לַאו בַּר מִינָהּ הוּא – which **is not of like kind with [her own]** hair, אֵימָא לֹא – **I would have said** that she is **not** permitted to go out.[19] צְרִיכָא – **It is** therefore **necessary** for the Mishnah to state explicitly that a woman may go out with her hair braided with strands of animal hair.[20]

The Gemara cites a Baraisa regarding the wearing of strands of hair on the Sabbath:

תָּנָא – **A Baraisa has taught:** וּבִלְבַד שֶׁלֹּא תֵּצֵא יַלְדָּה בְּשֶׁל זְקֵנָה – It is permissible for a woman to go out on the Sabbath wearing strands of hair PROVIDED THAT A YOUNG GIRL DOES NOT GO OUT WITH strands of [THE HAIR] OF AN ELDERLY WOMAN, וּזְקֵנָה בְּשֶׁל יַלְדָּה – AND THAT AN ELDERLY WOMAN DOES NOT GO OUT WITH strands of [THE HAIR] OF A YOUNG GIRL, lest they remove the strands and carry them because of ridicule.[21]

The Gemara questions the need for the Baraisa to state explicitly that a young girl may not go out while wearing the hair of an elderly woman:

בִּשְׁלָמָא זְקֵנָה בְּשֶׁל יַלְדָּה – **It is understandable** that the Baraisa deems it necessary to teach that **an elderly woman** may not go out **with** strands of **[the hair] of a young girl.** שֶׁבַח הוּא לָהּ – For since **[the hair of a young girl] is** considered **an enhancement for [an elderly woman],** one might think that an elderly woman is permitted to go out on the Sabbath while wearing strands of it, as she certainly will not be subject to ridicule for doing so. The Baraisa must therefore inform us that an elderly woman is in fact forbidden to go out with the hair of a young girl.[22] אֶלָּא יַלְדָּה בְּשֶׁל זְקֵנָה – **But** with regard to **a young girl** going out **with** strands of **[the hair] of an elderly woman,** אַמַּאי – **why** is it necessary for the Baraisa to teach that she may not go out? גְּנַאי הוּא לָהּ – **[The hair of an elderly woman] is** considered **a repulsive thing for [a young girl],** and will certainly subject her to ridicule! It is therefore obvious that she may not go out with such strands! – ? –

The Gemara answers:

אַיְּידֵי דִּתְנָא זְקֵנָה בְּשֶׁל יַלְדָּה – **Since the Mishnah taught** the necessary law of **an elderly woman** who goes out **with** strands **of [the hair] of a young girl,** תְּנָא נַמִּי יַלְדָּה בְּשֶׁל זְקֵנָה – **it also taught** the incidental law of **a young girl** who goes out **with** strands **of [the hair] of an elderly woman.**

The Mishnah states:

בְּכָבוּל וּבְפֵאָה נָכְרִית לֶחָצֵר – [A woman may go out . . .] WITH AN ornamental WOOLEN CAP OR WITH A WIG INTO THE COURTYARD.

The Gemara cites a dispute between Amoraim:

אָמַר רַב – **Rav said:** כֹּל שֶׁאָסְרוּ חֲכָמִים לָצֵאת בּוֹ לִרְשׁוּת הָרַבִּים – **Anything which the Sages prohibited one to go out with into a public domain,** אָסוּר לָצֵאת בּוֹ לֶחָצֵר – one is similarly **prohibited to go out with into the courtyard,**[23]

NOTES

ous note. According to the second explanation, one is forbidden to initially place these items into one's mouth because of the prohibition against healing, and *returning* them to one's mouth is like placing them there initially (*Mishnah Berurah* ibid. §50). See *Tosafos, Eruvin* (102b ד״ה רטיה), who draw a distinction, according to this explanation, between an item that fell from one's mouth to the floor and one that fell onto some other article [such as a piece of furniture] (see also *Magen Avraham* ibid., and *Mishnah Berurah* ibid.; see above, 38b, for a similar distinction).]

17. [Literally: a foreign tooth, a tooth of gold.]

18. For since a gold tooth stands out among a woman's natural teeth, it might be noticed by others, who may subject her to ridicule for wearing it; she might therefore remove the tooth from her mouth and carry it in her hand, thus violating the Sabbath (*Rashi;* cf. *Ramban* and *Rashba;* note that the explanation we have given follows the view of *Rashi's* teachers cited below, 65a note 12; see there for *Rashi's* own view). Rebbi holds that people generally will not ridicule one who wears a gold tooth (*Rashi* to 65a).

[The translation of שֵׁן תּוֹתֶבֶת שֵׁן שֶׁל זָהָב as *a false tooth made of gold* follows the first explanation of *Rashi.* Alternatively, *Rashi* splits the phrase in two (*a false tooth, a tooth made of gold),* assigning each segment to another part of the Mishnah. Thus, with the words *a false tooth,* which refer to a substitute human tooth, the Mishnah resumes the enumeration of items with which a woman is permitted to go out on the Sabbath, teaching that a woman may go out with another person's tooth set into her jaw (see below, 65a note 12 for discussion of the permissibility of a substitute human tooth). It then presents the case of *a tooth made of gold,* which is the subject of the dispute between Rebbi and the Sages (cf. *Ramban, Ritva MHK* ed., *Rashba*).]

19. For since animal hair stands out against her own hair, people will notice it, and might ridicule her, causing her to remove the strands (see *Rashi* ד״ה דבת מינה הוא).

20. For although she may be subject to ridicule for wearing animal hair, since she has gone to the trouble of braiding the strands into her hair, we are confident that she will not remove them (*Chidushei HaRan*).

21. For people find repugnant the contrast of white hair against dark, or dark against white, and may ridicule a woman whose hair is bound in this fashion (*Rashi;* see *Shabbos Shel Mi;* cf. *Rambam, Shabbos* 19:9; see *Maggid Mishneh* ad loc.).

22. For although some people see the hair of a young girl as an enhancement for an elderly woman, others will ridicule her for wearing it. She therefore may not go out with it on the Sabbath, lest she be led to remove and carry it (*Tosafos; Ran*).

23. I.e. all those things mentioned in the previous Mishnahs with which a person is forbidden to go out into a public domain [e.g. woolen threads, linen threads, a frontlet], one is likewise prohibited to go out with into the courtyard.

The Rabbis prohibited wearing these items in a courtyard [which is a

שזנו עיניהם מן הערוה אמר רב ששת [א] א מפני מה מנה הכתוב תכשיטין שבחוץ עם תכשיטין שבפנים לומר לך כל המסתכל באצבע קטנה של אשה כאילו מסתכל במקום התורפה: **מתני'** [ב] ב יוצאה אשה בחוטי שער בין משלה בין משל חבירתה בין משל בהמה ובטוטפת ובסרביטין בזמן שהן תפורין בכבול ובפאה נכרית לחצר במוך שבאזנה ובמוך שבסנדלה ובמוך שהתקינה לנדתה ג בפילפל [ג] ובגלגל מלח וכל דבר שניתן לתוך פיה ובלבד שלא תתן לכתחלה בשבת ואם נפל לא תחזיר שן תותבת שן של זהב רבי מתיר וחכמים אוסרים: **גמ'** וצריכא דאי אשמעינן דידה משום דלא מאים אבל חבירתה דמאים אימא לא ואי אשמעינן דחבירתה דבת מינה הוא אבל דבהמה לאו בר מינה הוא אימא לא צריכא תנא ד ובלבד שלא תצא ילדה בשל זקנה וזקנה בשל ילדה בשלמא זקנה בשל ילדה שבח הוא לה [ד] אלא ילדה בשל זקנה אמאי גנאי הוא לה איידי דתנא זקנה בשל ילדה תנא נמי ילדה בשל זקנה: בכבול ובפאה נכרית לחצר: אמר רב כל ה שאסרו חכמים לצאת בו לרה"ר אסור לצאת בו לחצר [ה] חוץ מכבול ופאה נכרית רבי ענני בר ששון משמיה [ו] דר' ישמעאל אמר הכל ככבול תנן בכבול ובפאה נכרית לחצר בשלמא לרב ניחא אלא לרבי ענני בר ששון קשיא רבי ענני בר ששון משמיה דמאן קאמר ליה משמיה דר' ישמעאל בר יוסי רבי ישמעאל בר יוסי תנא הוא ופליג ורב מאי שנא הני אמר עולא כדי שלא תתגנה על בעלה כדתניא [א] והדוה בנדתה זקנים הראשונים אמרו שלא תכחול ולא תפקוס ולא תתקשט בבגדי צבעונין עד שבא ר"ע ולימד ו אם כן אתה מגנה על בעלה ונמצא בעלה מגרשה אלא מה ת"ל והדוה בנדתה ז בנדתה תהא עד שתבא במים [ז] אמר רב יהודה אמר רב כל מקום שאסרו חכמים מפני מראית העין אפילו בחדרי חדרים אסור [ח] תנן ולא בזוג אע"פ שפקוק ותניא [ט] אידך [י] פוקק לה זוג בצוארה ומטייל עמה בחצר תנאי היא דתניא

שוטחן

רש"י

שזנו. לשון מזון שנהנו במראית העין: תכשיטין שבחוץ. טבעת: תכשיטין שבפנים. כומז: לומר לך המסתכל באצבע. שהיא מקום טבעת כמסתכל במקום כומז שהרי כפרה זו על שנסתכלו בה: מתני' בחוטי שער. שקולעת בהן שערה: בין משלה. תלושין: בין משל בהמה. כגון של סוס: שהן תפורין. לסבכה דתו לא שלפא להו לאחוויי: לחצר. אכבול ופיאה נכרית קאי דאסרו לעיל למיפק בה לרה"ר ואיצטריך לאשמעינן דלחצר מותר וכבול דסיפא דמתני' לא איפלגו בה אמוראי דלכולי עלמא כיפה של צמר: פיאה נכרית. קליעת שער תלושה ונותנתה על שערה עם קליעתה שתראה בעלת שער: במוך שבאזנה. שנותנת לבלוע ליחה של צואת האוזן: שבסנדלה. לתענוג: לנדתה. באותו מקום שיבלע בו הדם ולא יטנף בגדיה: פלפל. פלפל ארוך נותנת אשה בפיה שריחה רע: גלגל מלח. כמו גרגיר מלח לרפואת חולי שינים: שנתנה לתוך פיה. מבעוד יום: שן תותבת. נותנת בלחייה ממקום אחר והיא של זהב: רבי מתיר. לצאת בה: וחכמים אוסרין. דכיון דמשונה משאר השינים דילמא מחייכי עלה ושקלה לה מהתם וממטי לה בידה ובגמרא אמרינן דשל זהב נקט דווקא ל"א שן תותבת שן של אדם היתה ואהיתירא דלעיל קאי ולאו אפלוגתא דרבי ורבנן והכי קאמר בפלפל ובגלגל מלח ושן תותבת שן של זהב רבי מתיר כו': גמ' דלא מאים. וליכא למימר דמשלפא ליה משום דמחכו עלה וממטי ליה בידיה: דבת מינה הוא. ולא מינכר ולא מחייכי עלה: ובלבד שלא תצא זקנה. בחוטי שער של ילדה וילדה בשל זקנה דלבנות על שחורות או שחורות על לבנות מאיס ואתי למישלף: כל שאסרו חכמים. בריש פרקין חוטי צמר ופשתן טוטפת ושאר השנויים במשנה שאסור ללכת בהן לרה"ר: אסור לצאת לחצר. ואף על גב דשרי לטלטולינהו דתורת כלי עליהן כדאמרן הרי הן ככל הכלים הניטלים בחצר מיהו דרך מלבוש אסור דמרגלא ליה ונפקא ביה לרה"ר: חוץ מכבול ופיאה. שמותר לחצר כדתנן במתניתין וטעמא מפרש לקמיה: הכל ככבול. כל הנאסרים לא נאסרו אלא לרה"ר אבל לחצר מותרים ככבול: בשלמא לרב ניחא. מדנקט הני ושבקינהו לאינך דמיתני בהדייהו לאיסורא ברישא דמתניתין מכלל דכולהו אף לחצר באיסורייהו קיימי: כדי שלא תתגנה. התירו לה קצת קישוטים הנאים: כדתניא. דחשו רבנן להכי: בנדתה. היו דורשין הראשונים כמשמעו כדבר המנודה ומרחיקה מבעלה: שלא תכחול. עיניה: ולא תפקוס. [כ] שרק על פניה טינפאנ"ל בלע"ז והוא אדום: תהא בנדתה. בטומאתה: עד שתבא במים. לטבול ואע"פ שעברו ז' שלה ופסק מעיינה: כל שאסרו חכמים משום מראית העין. שלא יחשדוהו באיסור כגון שרין וקסדא ומגפיים או לא יקשור גמלים זה בזה דמיחזי כאזיל לחינגא: ולא בזוג אע"פ שהוא פקוק. ואינו מוליד קול לא תצא בהמה בו וטעמא פרישנא בפ' במה בהמה (לעיל דף נד:) משום דמיחזי כאזיל לחינגא: ותניא. בברייתא דבחצר דליכא מראית העין מותר:

שוטחן

תוספות

ובמוך שהתקינה לנדתה. פ"ה באותו מקום שיבלע בו הדם ולא יטנפו בגדיה ול"נ דא"כ אפילו טינוף הוא ומשוי הוא כדאמר בפ"ק (דף יא:) דכל אפילו טינוף לא חשיב ומשוי הוא לכן נ"ל שלא יפול על בשרה ותייבש עליה ונמצא מצטערה:

ובלבד שלא תתן לכתחלה בשבת. פירש הר"ר פורת גזירה משום שחיקת סממנים כיון דלרפואה הוא ול"נ דאם כן אם נפל אמאי לא תחזיר האמר בפרק בתרא דעירובין (דף קב: ושם) מחזירין רטיה במקדש אבל לא במדינה וע"כ לא אסרינן להחזיר הרטיה אלא משום שמא ימרח והכא לא שייך מירוח דאין שייך מירוח אלא בדבר לח כגון רטיה אבל בפלפלין ובגלגלא לא שייך מירוח לכן נ"ל ובלבד שלא תתן לכתחלה מפני שנראה כמערמת להוציאה ולפירוש זה כל הנך דלעיל מוך שבאזנה ושבסנדלה אסורין לתת לכתחלה וא"ת א"כ היכי שרו לקמן פורפת על האבן או על האגוז והא נראה כמערמת וי"ל דהתם ניכר הדבר והכל יודעין דלכך צריכה וליכא שום חששא אבל בדבר שהיא נותנת בתוך פיה אינם יודעין למה היא נותנת:

ובלבד שלא תצא זקנה בשל ילדה וילדה בשל זקנה. כך היא עיקר הגירסא והשתא פריך שפיר בשלמא זקנה בשל ילדה שבח הוא לה פירוש ומשום הכי איצטריך לאשמעינן שלא תצא דאפילו הכי מחכו עלה אלא ילדה בשל זקנה אמאי גנאי הוא לה פירוש אמאי איצטריך לאשמעינן דלא תצא פשיטא דכיון דגנאי הוא לה ודאי מחכו עלה ושקלה להו וכיון דתנא זקנה בשל ילדה אסור כל שכן ילדה בשל זקנה ודוחק הוא לומר זו וא"צ לומר זו קתני ואית דגרסי איפכא ובלבד שלא תצא ילדה בשל זקנה וזקנה בשל ילדה ואינו מיושב דא"כ אמאי פריך ילדה בשל זקנה אמאי שהרי כך הוא דרך הש"ס לשנות הפשוט תחלה והרב פורת מיישב גירסא זו וה"פ אלא ילדה בשל זקנה אמאי איצטריך גנאי הוא לה דלעולם לא תצא בהן אפילו בחול:

רבי ענני ברבי ששון אמר הכל ככבול. ונראה דהלכה כרבי ענני [ל] מדאמר מילתיה משמיה דרבי ישמעאל בר' יוסי ור' ישמעאל תנא הוא ופליג ועוד דבשל סופרים הלך אחר המיקל ור' ענני דמתיר בחצר היינו אפילו בחצר שאינה מעורבת דבחצר מעורבת ליכא שום חדוש אם כן נשים מותרות להתקשט בבית ובחצר בטבעות ובתכשיטין ואנו שאין לנו רה"ר גמור דכל רה"ר שלנו כרמלית היא שהרי אין מבואות שלנו רחבות י"ו אמה ולא ס' ריבוא בוקעים בו הרי הוא כחצר שאינה מעורבת ומותרות נשים שלנו להתקשט בטבעות ובתכשיטים כפר"ת והקשה ר"י דאפילו אי רה"ר שלנו חשיב ככרמלית היכי שרו כמו חצר והאמר לקמן פרק כל כתבי (דף קכ.) גבי דליקה דמותר להציל בחצר שאינה מעורבת ולא בכרמלית ואומר רבינו ברוך כיון דלדידהו הוו להו רה"ר גמורה לא מדמו כרמלית לחצר שאינה מעורבת ואסרינן כרמלית משום רה"ר אבל אנו שאין לנו רה"ר כלל ° אין להחמיר בכרמלית כ"כ וה"ר שמשון מצא כתוב בשם רבינו שר שלום דדבר שהוא רגילות להראות זו לזו אסור וכשאינם רגילות מותרות ונשי דידן אינן מראות תכשיטיהן וטבעותיהן ומש"ה מותרות לצאת בהן וסוף דבר אמרו הקדמונים דמותרות לצאת בהן דמוטב יהו שוגגות ואל יהו מזידות:

אמר

עין משפט נר מצוה

נט א מיי' פכ"א מהל' איסורי ביאה הלכה ב סמג לאוין קכו טוש"ע אה"ע סי' כא סעיף א:
ס ב מיי' פי"ט מהל' שבת הלכה ט סמג לאוין סה טוש"ע א"ח סי' שג סעיף יד:
סא ג מיי' שם הלכה יב טוש"ע שם סעיף טו:
סב ד מיי' שם הלכה ט טוש"ע שם סעיף יד:
סג ה מיי' שם הלכה ח טוש"ע שם סעיף יח:
סד ו מיי' פי"א מהל' איסורי ביאה הלכה יט סמג לאוין קיא טוש"ע י"ד סימן קצה סעיף ט:
סה ז מיי' פ"ד שם הלכה ג ופי"א הלכה טז סמג שם טוש"ע שם סעי' א וסי' קצז סעי' א:

רבינו חננאל

מתני' **יוצאה** אשה בחוטי שיער כו'. אמר [רב] כל שאסרו חכמים לצאת בו לרה"ר אסור לצאת בו אפילו לחצר חוץ מכבול ופאה נכרית כדי שלא תתגנה על בעלה. והלכתא כותיה דרב ואע"ג דאמרינן ר' ישמעאל ב"ר יוסי תנא הוא ופליג לית הלכתא כוותיה. אמר רב יהודה אמר רב כל מקום שאסרו חכמים מפני מראית העין אפי' בחדרי חדרים אסור. ואקשינן עליה תנן בפרקין דקמי דין תנן לא בזוג אע"פ שהוא פקוק ותניא פוקקין לה זוג ומטיילתא בחצר. ומשני תנאי היא דתניא מי שנשרו כליו

גליון הש"ס

תוס' ד"ה ר' ענני כו' אין להחמיר בכרמלית. עי' כתובות דף ז ע"א תוס' ד"ה מתוך:

תורה אור השלם

א) וְהַדָּוָה בְּנִדָּתָהּ וְהַזָּב אֶת זוֹבוֹ לַזָּכָר וְלַנְּקֵבָה וּלְאִישׁ אֲשֶׁר יִשְׁכַּב עִם טְמֵאָה: [ויקרא טו, לג]

מסורת הש"ס

א) ברכות כד., ב) [לעיל נז:], ג) [גיר' הערוך ובגרגר וכן איתא במשנה שבמשניות], ד) בס"י הגיר' ואתיא לאחויי, ה) [עי' תוס' מנחות לו: ד"ה אי קסבר], ו) [נ"ל דר' ישמעאל בר' יוסי], ז) לקמן קמו: בילה ט. ע"ז יב., ח) לעיל נד:, ט) [ס"א עלה], י) לעיל נג., כ) עי' לקמן לד: רש"י ד"ה וכן הפוקסת ובמ"ק ט: תוס' ד"ה פוקסת, ל) [עי' תוס' במנחות לו: ד"ה אין].

ליקוטי רש"י

תכשיטין שבחוץ. אצעדה וצמיד הן הביאו אותן על כפרת הרהור עבירה שנסתכלו בבנות מדין [ברכות כד.]. **בזמן שהן תפורין.** עם השבכה שקורין שקופי"א כו' ליכא למיחש לאחוויי שאינה נוטלת השבכה מראשה ברשות הרבים שתגלה כל שערה [לעיל נז.]. **פיאה נכרית.** גדיל של שערות דעלמא שעושין לנוי [סנהדרין קיב.]. רגילות היו נשים כששערן מועט לקשור שיער נשים נכריות לשערן והוא פיאה נכרית. פיאה. קליעה [ערכין ז:]. **שן תותבת.** שנפלה שינה והושיבה שן אחר באותו מקום [נדרים סו:]. **שלא תכחול.** כוחלת. נותנת כחול בין עיניה כדי שדומות נאים. **ולא תפקוס.** פוקסת. מחלקת שערה לכאן ולכאן [מו"ק ט: עיי"ש בתוס']. פוקסת. מעברת סרק על פניה [כתובות ד: עיי"ש בתוס']. יש מרבותי אומרים מתקנת שערה במסרק או בידי' ויש שמפרשין טחה כמין בצק על פניה וכשנוטלו מאדים הבשר [לקמן צד: עיי"ש בתוס']. **בנדתה תהא.** ועד שתבא במים לטבילה היא בנדתה דמרבינן מתהיה בנדתה בהוייתה תהא עד שתבא במים בתורת כהנים [לעיל יג:]. **כל מקום שאסרו חכמים.** דבר המותר ואסרוהו מפני מראית העין שהרואהו חושדו בדבר עבירה. **אפילו בחדרי חדרים אסור.** במקום שאין אדם רואה אסרוהו [ע"ז יב.]. **בזוג.** אישקליט"א. **אף על פי.** שחללו פקוק במוכין שאין העינבל שלו מקשקש להשמיע קול. **פקוק.** סתום [לעיל נד:]. **פוקק לה זוג.** אבל כשאינו פקוק אפילו בחצר לא תצא מפני שהעינבל שבתוכה מקשקש ומוליד קול לכך פוקק בצמר או במוכין שלא יקשקש העינבל שבתוכה. זוג. אישקלי"ט. עינבל. בטדי"ל. **ומטייל.** באותו זוג בחצר אבל לא תצא בו לרשות הרבים כדמפרש לקמן בפרקין (נד:) דמיחזי כמאן דאזיל לחינגא [שם נג.].

חוּץ מִכָּבוּל וּפֵאָה נָכְרִית – except for a woolen cap or a wig.[24]

A dissenting opinion:

רַבִּי עֲנָנִי בַּר שָׂשׂוֹן מִשְּׁמֵיהּ דְּרַבִּי יִשְׁמָעֵאל [בְּרַבִּי יוֹסֵי] אָמַר – R' Anani bar Sasson said in the name of R' Yishmael the son of R' Yose: הַכֹּל כְּכָבוּל – All of the items that the Sages prohibited **are like a woolen cap,** i.e. they are prohibited in a public domain, but are permitted in a courtyard.

The Gemara challenges R' Anani's ruling:

תְּנַן – We have learned in our Mishnah: בְּכָבוּל וּבְפֵאָה נָכְרִית לְחָצֵר – [A woman may go out . . .] **WITH A WOOLEN CAP OR WITH A WIG INTO THE COURTYARD.** This implies that only a woolen cap or a wig is permitted in a courtyard; all other prohibited items, however, are prohibited even in a courtyard.[25] **בִּשְׁלָמָא לְרַב נִיחָא – This is understandable according to Rav's** opinion, which **fits well** with this implication of the Mishnah. **אֶלָּא לְרַבִּי עֲנָנִי בַּר שָׂשׂוֹן – But according to R' Anani bar Sason's** opinion, which permits *all* of the prohibited articles in a courtyard, **קַשְׁיָא – there is a difficulty!** For his ruling is contradicted by the implication of our Mishnah! – ? –

The Gemara answers:

רַבִּי עֲנָנִי בַּר שָׂשׂוֹן מִשְּׁמֵיהּ דְּמַאן קָאָמַר לֵיהּ – In whose name did R' Anani bar Sason say [his ruling]? מִשְּׁמֵיהּ דְּרַבִּי יִשְׁמָעֵאל בְּרַבִּי יוֹסֵי – He said it **in the name of R' Yishmael the son of R' Yose. רַבִּי יִשְׁמָעֵאל בְּרַבִּי יוֹסֵי תַּנָּא הוּא וּפָלִיג – R' Yishmael the son of R' Yose is a Tanna, and he disagrees** with our Mishnah![26]

The Gemara turns to Rav's ruling:

וְרַב מַאי שְׁנָא הָנֵי – But according to **Rav, why are these** (a woolen cap and a wig) **different** from the other items in that they alone are permitted in a courtyard?

The Gemara answers:

אָמַר עוּלָּא – Ulla said: כְּדֵי שֶׁלֹּא תִּתְגַּנֶּה עַל בַּעְלָהּ – The Rabbis permitted these ornaments **in order** to ensure **that [a woman] will not become repulsive to her husband** through her complete lack of adornment.[27] **כִּדְתַנְיָא – For so it has been taught in a Baraisa** with regard to the adornments of a menstruating woman: "וְהַדָּוָה בְּנִדָּתָהּ" – The Torah states, in enumerating those who become contaminated through bodily emissions: ***AND***

NOTES

private domain] for fear that one will become accustomed to wearing them, and will unthinkingly walk out with them into a public domain. [Thus, the restriction concerns only *wearing* the articles; *carrying* them, however, is permissible (as is evident from the Gemara at the beginning of 46b; see *Ran* and *Ritva MHK* ed. for a further connection between that Gemara and our Gemara)] (*Rashi*). Now, according to Rav one is prohibited to wear these items not only in a courtyard, which is owned jointly with others, but inside one's own house as well. This is because the Rabbis did not differentiate in their injunction between where a woman wears these articles, but simply forbade a woman to adorn herself with them on the Sabbath altogether, even indoors or in a courtyard, lest she inadvertently wear them into a public domain (*Rashi* to Mishnah 57a; *Ramban,* first explanation; *Ritva MHK* ed.).

[Other Rishonim hold that the reason these articles are prohibited in a courtyard is not because one might inadvertently wear them into a public domain, but because a courtyard, since it is used by the public, is itself similar to a public domain. Therefore, if these items were permitted in a courtyard, one could mistakenly come to believe that they are permitted in a public domain as well (*Ra'ah,* quoted in *Chidushei HaRan; Ramban,* second explanation). One would therefore be permitted to wear these items in a house, since it will not be mistaken for a public domain. *Rambam* (*Shabbos* 19:8) maintains that the only courtyard in which these items are forbidden is one without an *eruv chatzeiros* (an *eruv* that turns a jointly owned courtyard into a private domain), for only such a courtyard is similar to a public domain (see *Ran's* elucidation of *Rambam;* cf. *Ramban;* see *Orach Chaim* 303:18).]

24. Which are prohibited in a public domain, but are permitted in a courtyard (*Rashi*).

25. For the Mishnah groups the woolen cap and wig with the other items when it issues its prohibition (57a), but singles them out for permissibility in a courtyard! Evidently, it is only these two articles which are permitted in a courtyard (*Rashi*).

26. *Rabbeinu Tam* (cited in *Tosafos* ד״ה רבי ענני) rules in accordance with R' Anani, and therefore prohibits the articles enumerated in this chapter in a public domain only. He thereby resolves the question that vexed many commentators: Why do women adorn themselves on the Sabbath with many of the articles mentioned in this chapter [e.g. rings, hair ornaments], both in the house and in public, in the face of what appears to be an explicit injunction prohibiting these ornaments? *Rabbeinu Tam* explains that present-day streets are not true public domains, since they are either less than sixteen *amos* wide or do not have 600,000 people passing through them each day. They therefore possess only the status of *karmelis* (an area which is neither a public nor a private domain, but one is forbidden to carry there by Rabbinic decree). Since according to R' Anani the Rabbinic decree prohibiting these articles was enacted only with regard to a public domain, present-day streets are not included in the decree. Thus, for all practical purposes, these ornaments are permitted (see *Rabbeinu Yitzchak's* challenge to *Rabbeinu Tam,* cited in *Tosafos* ibid.; see *Rabbeinu Baruch's* defense, cited there). Other Rishonim, however (see *Ritva MHK* ed.) rule in accordance with Rav, who prohibits wearing these items even in a private domain, and certainly in a *karmelis*! How, then, do we explain the prevalent custom for women to adorn themselves on the Sabbath with the articles prohibited in this chapter?

Rabbeinu Baruch (cited in *Ritva MHK* ed.) explains that since the purpose of the decree was to prevent women from inadvertently carrying in a public domain, the Rabbis enacted it only in areas where true public domains exist; since they rarely exist nowadays, the decree is not pertinent. Another explanation of the custom is that this injunction was not enacted as an irrevocable decree. Rather, it was meant only for the women of that time and place, who were vain and took pride in showing their finery to others; the Rabbis therefore felt it necessary to prohibit their adornments, lest they unthinkingly carry them. Nowadays, however, women generally do not remove their finery to show it, and are therefore permitted to wear it (*Ritva MHK* ed. from *HaGaon R' Shalom;* see *Tosafos* for a similar explanation). *Rama (Orach Chaim* 303:18) explains in a similar vein that the decree was intended for a time when jewelry was not common, and was therefore proudly shown to others. Nowadays, though, when jewelry is relatively common, women are unlikely to show it, and therefore will not come to carry it (see *Aruch HaShulchan* ad loc. §22, who expands upon this explanation). Finally, there are those who maintain that even today, one is forbidden to wear the items discussed in this chapter on the Sabbath. We do not, however, publicize this law, since many women will not obey, and it is better that they sin inadvertently than deliberately [מוּטָב שֶׁיִּהְיוּ שׁוֹגְגִים וְאַל יִהְיוּ מְזִידִים] (*Tosafos,* in the name of the *Kadmonim; Ritva MHK* ed.; see *Orach Chaim* ibid. with *Beur Halachah;* see *Orach Chaim* 608:2 with *Beur Halachah* for the conditions under which the rule, "It is better that they sin inadvertently etc." is applied). [Obviously, some of these explanations apply only with regard to items prohibited because of the chance that they may be shown to others; according to these explanations, items forbidden because they are legally considered a burden, or because they will cause one to be ridiculed, are prohibited (see *Orach Chaim* 303:18).]

27. In order to maintain a woman's attractiveness to her husband, the Rabbis permitted her two of her more beautiful adornments [at home or in her courtyard, where she is with her husband] (*Rashi;* see *Ramban*). *Pnei Yehoshua* asks: The reason a wig is prohibited in a public domain is because it will subject one who wears it to ridicule. Yet, the Rabbis considered this item essential in preserving a woman's beauty! How can this be? He answers that this sort of wig was generally worn by a woman whose own hair was rather sparse – it was therefore a vitally important component of her wardrobe. Nonetheless, some observers might ridicule one for wearing it, since it reveals one's shortcoming (*Pnei Yehoshua* to *Tosafos* 57b ד״ה כבלא דעבדא תנן; see *Rashba* to 65a ד״ה אמר אביי).

[It is worth noting that *Shiltei HaGiborim* (29a in *dafei HaRif*) views our Mishnah and Gemara as a source for the prevalent custom whereby married women, who must cover their hair, do so with wigs. See, however, *Be'er Sheva* (§18) at length who takes sharp issue with *Shiltei HaGiborim,* and prohibits the use of wigs; see also *Darkei Moshe* (303:6) and *Magen Avraham* 75:5.]

שזנו עיניהם מן הערוה אמר רב ששת ו) א מפני מה מנה הכתוב תכשיטין שבחוץ עם תכשיטין שבפנים לומר לך כל המסתכל באצבע קטנה של אשה כאילו מסתכל במקום התורפה: מתני' ב) ב יוצאה אשה בחוטי שער בין משלה בין משל חבירתה בין משל בהמה ובטוטפת ובסרביטין בזמן שהן תפורין בכבול ובפאה נכרית לחצר במוך שבאזנה ובמוך שבסנדלה ובמוך שהתקינה לנדתה ג) בפילפל ובגלגל מלח וכל דבר שניתן לתוך פיה ובלבד שלא תתן לכתחלה בשבת ואם נפל לא תחזיר שן תותבת שן של זהב רבי מתיר וחכמים אוסרים: גמ' וצריכא דאי אשמעינן דידה משום דלא מאיס אבל חבירתה דמאיס אימא לא ואי אשמעינן דחבירתה דבת מינה הוא אבל דבהמה לאו בר מינה הוא אימא לא צריכא תנא ד) ובלבד שלא תצא ילדה בשל זקנה וזקנה בשל ילדה בשלמא זקנה בשל ילדה שבח הוא לה ז) אלא ילדה בשל זקנה אמאי גנאי הוא לה איידי דתנא זקנה בשל ילדה תנא נמי ילדה בשל זקנה: בכבול ובפאה נכרית לחצר: אמר רב כל ה) שאסרו חכמים לצאת בו לרה"ר אסור לצאת בו לחצר ט) חוץ מכבול ופאה נכרית רבי ענני בר ששון משמיה ו) דר' ישמעאל אמר הכל ככבול תנן בכבול ובפאה נכרית לחצר בשלמא לרב ניחא אלא לרבי ענני בר ששון קשיא רבי ענני בר ששון משמיה דמאן קאמר ליה משמיה דר' ישמעאל בר יוסי רבי ישמעאל בר יוסי תנא הוא ופליג ורב מאי שנא הני אמר עולא כדי שלא תתגנה על בעלה כדתניא א) והדוה בנדתה זקנים הראשונים אמרו שלא תכחול ולא תפקוס ולא תתקשט בבגדי צבעונין עד שבא ר"ע ולימד י) אם כן אתה מגנה על בעלה ונמצא בעלה מגרשה אלא מה ת"ל והדוה בנדתה י) בנדתה תהא עד שתבא במים ז) אמר רב יהודה אמר רב כל מקום שאסרו חכמים מפני מראית העין אפילו בחדרי חדרים אסור ח) תנן ולא בזוג אע"פ שפקוק ותניא ט) אידך י) פוקק לה זוג בצוארה ומטייל עמה בחצר תנאי היא דתניא

שוטחן

רש"י

שזנו. לשון מזון שנהנו במראית העין: תכשיטין שבחוץ. טבעת: תכשיטין שבפנים. כומז: לומר לך המסתכל באצבע. שהיא מקום טבעת כמסתכל במקום כומז שהרי כפרה זו על שנסתכלו בה: מתני' בחוטי שער. שקולעת בהן שערה: בין משלה. תלושין: בין משל בהמה. כגון של סוס: שהן תפורין. לסבכה דתו לא שלפא להו לאחוויי: לחצר. אכבול ופיאה נכרית קאי דאסרו לעיל למיפק בה לרה"ר ואיצטריך לאשמעינן דלחצר מותר וכבול דסיפא דמתני' לא איפלגו בה אמוראי דלכולי עלמא כיפה של צמר: פיאה נכרית. קליעת שער תלושה ומוברתה על שערה עם קליעתה שתראה בעלת שער: במוך שבאזנה. שנותנת לבלוע ליחה של צואת האוזן: שבסנדלה. לתענוג: לנדתה. באותו מקום שיבלע בו הדם ולא יטנף בגדיה: פלפל. פלפל ארוך נותנת אשה בפיה שריחה רע: גלגל מלח. כמו גרגיר מלח לרפואת חולי שיניים: שנתנה לתוך פיה. מבעוד יום: שן תותבת. נותנת בלחייה ממקום אחר והיא של זהב: רבי מתיר. לצאת בה: וחכמים אוסרין. דכיון דמשונה משאר השינים דילמא מחייכי עלה ושקלה לה מהתם וממטי לה בידה ובגמרא אמרינן דשל זהב נקט דווקא ל"א שן תותבת שן של אדם היתה ואהיתירא דלעיל קאי ולאו אפלוגתא דרבי ורבנן והכי קאמר בפלפל ובגלגל מלח ושן תותבת שן של זהב רבי מתיר כו': גמ' דלא מאיס. וליכא למימר דמשלפא ליה משום דמחכו עלה וממטי ליה בידיה: דבת מינה הוא. ולא מינכר ולא מחייכי עלה: ובלבד שלא תצא זקנה. בחוטי שער של ילדה וילדה בשל זקנה דלבנות על שחורות או שחורות על לבנות מאיס ואתי למישלף: כל שאסרו חכמים. בריש פרקין חוטי צמר ופשתן טוטפת ושאר השנויים במשנה שאסור ללכת בהן לרה"ר: אסור לצאת לחצר. ואף על גב דשרי לטלטולינהו דתורת כלי עליהן כדאמרן הרי הן ככל הכלים הנטלים בחצר מיהו דרך מלבוש אסור דמרגלה ליה ונפקא ביה לרה"ר: חוץ מכבול ופיאה. שמותר לחצר כדתנן במתניתין וטעמא מפרש לקמיה: הכל ככבול. כל הנאסרים לא נאסרו אלא לרה"ר אבל לחצר מותרים ככבול: בשלמא לרב ניחא. מדנקט הני ושבקינהו לאינך דמיתני בהדייהו לאיסורא ברישא דמתניתין מכלל דכולהו אף לחצר באיסורייהו קיימי: כדי שלא תתגנה. התירו לה קצת קישוטים הנאים: כדתניא. דחשו רבנן להכי: בנדתה. היו דורשין הראשונים כמשמעו כדבר המנודה ומרחיקה מבעלה: שלא תכחול. עיניה: ולא תפקוס. כ) שרק על פניה טינפאצ"ל בלע"ז והוא אדום: תהא בנדתה. בטומאתה: עד שתבא במים. לטבול ואע"פ שעברו ז' שלה ופסק מעיינה: כל שאסרו חכמים משום מראית העין. שלא יחשדוהו באיסור כגון שריון וקסדא ומגפיים או לא יקשור גמלים זה בזה דמיחזי כאזיל לחינגא: ולא בזוג אע"פ שהוא פקוק. ואינו מוליד קול לא תצא בהמה בו וטעמא פרישנא בפ' במה בהמה (לעיל דף נד:) משום דמיחזי כאזיל לחינגא: ותניא. בברייתא דבחצר דליכא מראית העין מותר:

שוטחן

אמר

תוספות

ובמוך שהתקינה לנדתה. פ"ה באותו מקום שיבלע בו הדם ולא יטנפו בגדיה ול"נ דא"כ אצולי טינוף הוא ומשוי הוא כדאמר בפ"ק (דף יא:) דכל אצולי טינוף לא חשיב ומשוי הוא לכן נ"ל שלא יפול על בשרה ותייבש עליה ונמצא מצטערה:

ובלבד שלא תתן לכתחלה בשבת. פירש הר"ר פורת גזירה משום שחיקת סממנים כיון דלרפואה הוא ול"נ דאם כן אם נפל אמאי לא תחזיר האמר בפרק בתרא דעירובין (דף קב: ושם) מחזירין רטיה במקדש אבל לא במדינה וע"כ לא אסרינן להחזיר הרטיה אלא משום שמא ימרח והכא לא שייך מירוח דאין שייך מירוח אלא בדבר לח כגון רטיה אבל בפלפלין ובגלגלא לא שייך מירוח לכן נ"ל ובלבד שלא תתן לכתחלה מפני שנראה כמערמת להוציאה ולפירוש זה כל הנך דלעיל מוך שבאזנה ושבסנדלה אסורין לתת לכתחלה וא"ת א"כ היכי שרו לקמן פורפת על האבן או על האגוז והא נראה כמערמת וי"ל דהתם ניכר הדבר והכל יודעין דלכך צריכה וליכא שום חששא אבל בדבר שהיא נותנת בתוך פיה אינם יודעין למה היא נותנת:

ובלבד שלא תצא זקנה בשל ילדה וילדה בשל זקנה. כך היא עיקר הגירסא והשתא פריך שפיר בשלמא זקנה בשל ילדה שבח הוא לה פירוש ומשום הכי איצטריך לאשמעינן שלא תצא דאפילו הכי מחכו עלה אלא ילדה בשל זקנה אמאי גנאי הוא לה פירוש אמאי איצטריך לאשמעינן דלא תצא פשיטא דכיון דגנאי הוא לה ודאי מחכו עלה ושקלה להו וכיון דתנא זקנה בשל ילדה אסור כל שכן ילדה בשל זקנה ודוחק הוא לומר זו וא"צ לומר זו קתני ואית דגרסי איפכא ובלבד שלא תצא ילדה בשל זקנה וזקנה בשל ילדה ואינו מיושב דא"כ אמאי פריך ילדה בשל זקנה אמאי שהרי כך הוא דרך הש"ס לשנות הפשוט תחלה והרב פורת מיישב גירסא זו וה"פ אלא ילדה בשל זקנה אמאי איצטריך גנאי הוא לה דלעולם לא תצא בהן אפילו בחול:

רבי ענני ברבי ששון אמר הכל ככבול. ונראה דהלכה כרבי ענני ל) מדאמר מילתיה משמיה דרבי ישמעאל בר' יוסי ור' ישמעאל תנא הוא ופליג ועוד דבשל סופרים הלך אחר המיקל ור' ענני דמתיר בחצר היינו אפילו בחצר שאינה מעורבת דבחצר מעורבת ליכא שום חדוש אם כן נשים מותרות להתקשט בבית ובחצר בטבעות ובתכשיטין ואנו שאין לנו רה"ר גמור דכל רה"ר שלנו כרמלית היא שהרי אין מבואות שלנו רחבות י"ו אמה ולא ס' ריבוא בוקעים בו הרי הוא כחצר שאינה מעורבת ומותרות נשים שלנו להתקשט בטבעות ובתכשיטים כפר"ת והקשה ר"י דאפילו אי רה"ר שלנו חשיב ככרמלית היכי שרו כמו חצר והאמר לקמן פרק כל כתבי (דף קכ.) גבי דליקה דמותר להציל בחצר שאינה מעורבת ולא בכרמלית ואומר רבינו ברוך כיון דלדידהו הוו להו רה"ר גמורה לא מדמו כרמלית לחצר שאינה מעורבת ואסרינן כרמלית משום רה"ר אבל אנו שאין לנו רה"ר כלל ° אין להחמיר בכרמלית כ"כ וה"ר שמשון מצא כתוב בשם רבינו שר שלום דלדבר שהוא רגילות להראות זו לזו אסור וכשאינם רגילות מותרות ונשי דידן אינן מראות תכשיטיהן וטבעותיהן ומש"ה מותרות לצאת בהן וסוף דבר אמרו הקדמונים דמותרות לצאת בהן דמוטב יהו שוגגות ואל יהו מזידות:

עין משפט נר מצוה

נט א מיי' פכ"א מהל' איסורי ביאה הלכה ב סמג לאוין קכו טוש"ע אה"ע סי' כא סעיף א:
ס ב מיי' פי"ט מהל' שבת הלכה ט סמג לאוין סה טוש"ע א"ח סי' שג סעיף יד:
סא ג מיי' שם הלכה יב טוש"ע שם סעיף טו:
סב ד מיי' שם הלכה ט טוש"ע שם סעיף יד:
סג ה מיי' שם הלכה ח טוש"ע שם סעיף יח:
סד ו מיי' פי"א מהל' איסורי ביאה הלכה יט סמג לאוין קיא טוש"ע י"ד סימן קצה סעיף ט:
סה ז מיי' פ"ד שם הלכה ג ופי"א הלכה טו סמג שם טוש"ע שם סעי' א וסי' קנז סעי' א:

רבינו חננאל

מתני' יוצאה אשה בחוטי שיער כו'. אמר [רב] כל שאסרו חכמים לצאת בו לרה"ר אסור לצאת בו אפילו לחצר חוץ מכבול ופאה נכרית כדי שלא תתגנה על בעלה. והלכתא כותיה דרב ואע"ג דאמרינן ר' ישמעאל ב"ר יוסי תנא הוא ופליג לית הלכתא כוותיה. אמר רב יהודה אמר רב כל מקום שאסרו חכמים מפני מראית העין אפי' בחדרי חדרים אסור. ואקשינן עליה תנן בפרקין דקמי דין תנן לא בזוג אע"פ שהוא פקוק ותניא פוקקין לה זוג ומטיילתא בחצר. ומשני תנאי היא דתניא מי שנשרו כליו

גליון הש"ס

תוס' ד"ה ר' ענני כו' אין להחמיר בכרמלית. עי' כתובות דף ז ע"א תוס' ד"ה מתוך:

תורה אור השלם

א) וְהַדָּוָה בְּנִדָּתָהּ וְהַזָּב אֶת זוֹבוֹ לַזָּכָר וְלַנְּקֵבָה וּלְאִישׁ אֲשֶׁר יִשְׁכַּב עִם טְמֵאָה: [ויקרא טו, לג]

מסורת הש"ס

א) ברכות כד., ב) [לעיל מז:], ג) [גיר' הערוך ובגרגר וכן איתא במשנה שבמשניות], ד) כפ"י הגיר' ואתיא לאחוויי, ה) [עי' תוס' מנחות לו: ד"ה אי קסבר], ו) [נ"ל דר' ישמעאל בר' יוסי], ז) לקמן קמו: ביצה ט. ע"ז יב., ח) לעיל נד:, ט) [ס"א עלה], י) לעיל נג., כ) עי' לקמן לד: רש"י ד"ה וכן הפוקסת ובמ"ק ט: תוס' ד"ה פוקסת, ל) [עי' תוס' במנחות לו: ד"ה אי].

ליקוטי רש"י

תכשיטין שבחוץ. אצעדה וצמיד הן הביאו אותן על כפרת הרהור עבירה שנסתכלו בבנות מדין [ברכות כד.]. בזמן שהן תפורין. עם השבכה שקורין שקופי"א כו' ליכא למיחש לאחוויי שאינה נוטלת השבכה מראשה ברשות הרבים שתגלה כל שערה [לעיל נז.]. פיאה נכרית. גדיל של שערות דעלמא שעושין לנוי [סנהדרין קיב.]. רגילות היו נשים כששערן מועט לקשור שיער נשים נכריות לשערן והוא פיאה נכרית. פיאה. קליעה [ערכין ז:]. שן תותבת. שנפלה שינה והושיבה שן אחר באותו מקום [נדרים סו:]. שלא תכחול. כוחלת. נותנת כחול בין עיניה כדי שדומות נאים. ולא תפקום. פוקסת. מחלקת שערה לכאן ולכאן [מו"ק ט: עיי"ש בתוס']. פוקסת. מעברת שרק על פניה [כתובות ד: עיי"ש בתוס']. יש מרבותי אומרים מתקנת שערה במסרק או בידי' ויש שמפרשין טחה כמין בצק על פניה וכשנוטלו מאדים הבשר [לקמן צד: עיי"ש בתוס']. בנדתה תהא. ועד שתבא במים לטבילה היא בנדתה דמרבינן מתהיה בנדתה בהוייתה תהא עד שתבא במים בתורת כהנים [לעיל יג:]. כל מקום שאסרו חכמים. דבר המותר ואסרוהו מפני מראית העין שהרואהו חושדו בדבר עבירה. אפילו בחדרי חדרים אסור. במקום שאין אדם רואה אסרוהו [ע"ז יב.]. בזוג. אישקליט"א. אף על פי. שחללו פקוק במוכין שאין העינבל שלו מקשקש להשמיע קול. פקוק. סתום [לעיל נד:]. פוקק לה זוג. אבל כשאינו פקוק אפילו בחצר לא תצא מפני שהעינבל שבתוכה מקשקש ומוליד קול לכך פוקק בצמר או במוכין שלא יקשקש העינבל שבתוכה. זוג. אישקלי"ט. עינבל. בטדי"ל. ומטייל. באותו זוג בחצר אבל לא תצא בו לרשות הרבים כדמפרש לקמן בפרקין (נד:) דמיחזי כמאן דאזיל לחינגא [שם נג.].

THE MENSTRUATING WOMAN IN HER STATE OF NIDDAH.[28] זְקֵנִים הָרִאשׁוֹנִים אָמְרוּ – Based on the words *in her state of niddah* (i.e. separation), THE EARLY ELDERS DECREED שֶׁלֹּא תִּכְחוֹל – THAT [A MENSTRUATING WOMAN] MAY NEITHER APPLY EYE MAKEUP, וְלֹא תִּפְקוֹס – NOR APPLY ROUGE,[29] וְלֹא תִתְקַשֵּׁט בְּבִגְדֵי צִבְעוֹנִין – NOR ADORN HERSELF WITH COLORFUL CLOTHING, so that she will remain in a state of separation from her husband.[30] עַד שֶׁבָּא רַבִּי עֲקִיבָא וְלִימֵּד – This decree remained in force UNTIL R' AKIVA CAME AND TAUGHT: אִם כֵּן אַתָּה מְגַנָּהּ עַל בַּעְלָהּ – IF SO, YOU WILL MAKE HER REPULSIVE TO HER HUSBAND, וְנִמְצָא בַּעְלָהּ מְגָרְשָׁהּ – AND HER HUSBAND WILL CONSEQUENTLY DIVORCE HER! אֶלָּא מַה תַּלְמוּד לוֹמַר "וְהַדָּוָה בְּנִדָּתָהּ" – RATHER, WHAT DOES [THE TORAH] mean to SAY with *AND THE MENSTRUATING WOMAN IN HER STATE OF NIDDAH?* בְּנִדָּתָהּ תְּהֵא עַד שֶׁתָּבֹא בַּמַּיִם – That SHE REMAINS IN HER STATE OF *NIDDAH* (i.e. *tumah*) UNTIL SHE IMMERSES herself IN the WATER of a *mikveh.*[31] She is permitted, however, to adorn herself even during the period of her menses.

We see, then, that R' Akiva went so far as to rescind a decree in order to ensure that women remain attractive to their husbands. Likewise with regard to the decree dealt with in our Mishnah, the Rabbis limited the decree by permitting ornamental woolen caps and wigs in a courtyard. They thus ensured that women would remain attractive in their husbands' eyes.

The Gemara presents another of Rav's rulings:[32]

אָמַר רַב יְהוּדָה אָמַר רַב – **Rav Yehudah said in the name of Rav:** כָּל מָקוֹם שֶׁאָסְרוּ חֲכָמִים מִפְּנֵי מַרְאִית הָעַיִן – **Wherever the Sages prohibited** an act **because** they were concerned that it might give the **appearance** of wrongdoing,[33] אֲפִילּוּ בְּחַדְרֵי חֲדָרִים אָסוּר – **[the act] is prohibited even in one's most private chambers.**[34]

The Gemara challenges this ruling:

וְלֹא בְזוּג אַף עַל פִּי שֶׁפָּקוּק תְּנַן – **We have learned in a Mishnah:**[35] AND a donkey may NOT go out into a public domain WITH A BELL on the Sabbath, EVEN IF [THE BELL] IS PLUGGED.[36] Since animals on their way to market are often adorned with bells, a bell would give the impression that this donkey too is being taken to market, which is prohibited on the Sabbath. It is thus forbidden to hang the bell because of the appearance of wrongdoing. וְתַנְיָא אִידָךְ – **Yet it has also been taught in a Baraisa:** פּוֹקֵק לָהּ זוּג בְּצַוָּארָהּ – ONE MAY PLUG A BELL FOR [THE DONKEY], and hang it ON ITS NECK, וּמְטַיֵּיל עִמָּהּ בֶּחָצֵר – AND then WALK WITH [THE DONKEY] ABOUT A COURTYARD, where there are no onlookers, since where there are none to see, there can be no appearance of wrongdoing!

We see then that an act prohibited because of the appearance of wrongdoing is in fact permitted where it will not be seen! How then can Rav say that it is prohibited even in one's private chambers?[37]

The Gemara answers:

תַּנָּאֵי הִיא – **[This issue] is** actually the subject of a dispute between **Tannaim.** דְּתַנְיָא – **For it has been taught in a Baraisa:**

NOTES

28. *Leviticus* 15:33.

29. A reddish facial cosmetic (*Rashi;* see *Rashi* below, 94b ד״ה וכן הפוקסת).

30. The Early Elders expounded the word בְּנִדָּתָהּ (*beniddasah*) according to the literal meaning of the root *niddah* (נִדָּה), which is *separation* [of a menstruating woman from her husband]. They therefore enacted a decree [based on this verse] designed to ensure a woman's separation from her husband during her menstrual period — they forbade her to make herself desirable in his eyes (*Rashi; Sfas Emes*).

31. R' Akiva, in order to ensure that women would remain attractive to their husbands, rescinded the decree of the Early Elders (see *Sfas Emes*). He accordingly expounded the word בְּנִדָּתָהּ according to the secondary meaning of the word *niddah,* namely, *tumah* (*Rashi*). Thus, the verse teaches that a woman remains in her state of *tumah* even after her menstrual flow has ceased, until she immerses herself in a *mikveh.*

[The Early Elders certainly agreed that a woman remains *tamei* until she immerses in a *mikveh;* however, they derived this law from another source (for a discussion concerning their source, see *Ritva* and *Rashba* here, and *Tosafos, Yoma* 78a and *Chagigah* 11a). See *Hagahos R' Yaakov Emden, Chasam Sofer,* and *Meromei Sadeh* for why the Early Elders were not concerned with the possibility of divorce.]

32. See *Pnei Yehoshua,* who suggests a connection between this ruling and the one cited above.

33. And thereby cause the perpetrator to be suspected of illegal activity . . .

For example, one may not don mail, a battle helmet, or iron leggings (see above, 60a) because they give the appearance that one is preparing to engage in battle, an activity forbidden on the Sabbath. Likewise, one may not rope camels together and lead them on the Sabbath (see above, 54a), for fear that he will be suspected of taking them to market (*Rashi*).

34. [Literally: rooms of rooms.] Accordingly, on the Sabbath, one may not don battle dress, or rope beasts together even in a private place, where there are none to see (*Rashi*).

[The reason this sort of decree extends even to places where no one will see is that the Rabbis feared that if they allowed this activity in a private place, one might mistakenly come to believe that it is permissible in a public place as well. Alternatively, they knew that there can occasionally be an onlooker even in the most private place (*Ran* to *Beitzah* [4b-5a in *dafei HaRif*; cf. *Mishnah Berurah* 301:165).]

35. Above, 54b.

36. Even if the bell is stuffed with rags, and therefore will not emit sound, one may not hang it upon his animal lest an onlooker suspect that he is taking it to market (*Rashi*). [However, if the bell is not plugged, it is forbidden to hang it on the animal because of the tinkling sound it emits (see *Magen Avraham* 305:5).]

37. [The Rishonim debate the following question: Does Rav's principle apply even to an act prohibited because of the appearance of violating a Rabbinic decree [דְּרַבָּנָן], or only to an act prohibited because of the appearance of violating a Biblical decree [דְּאוֹרַיְיתָא]? (see *Tosafos* to *Kesubos* 60a ד״ה ממעכן, *Rosh* to Gemara below, 146b, and *Ran* to *Beitzah* cited in note 34). Now the act of taking an animal to market is in fact prohibited only by Rabbinic decree (see *Magen Avraham* 306:15). Since the Gemara nonetheless cites the permissibility of this act in a courtyard as a challenge to Rav, it evidently holds that his principle pertains even to Rabbinically prohibited actions, thus contradicting those Rishonim that take the opposite view! *Magen Avraham* (301:56) suggests that according to these Rishonim our Gemara is actually at odds over this issue with the Gemara in *Kesubos* 60a, which limits Rav's principle to Biblically prohibited actions; see, however, *Chidushei R' Akiva Eiger,* who resolves the contradiction by identifying a Biblical element to the prohibition against taking an animal to market.]

שׁוֹטְחָן בַּחַמָּה – If one's clothes became soaked with rainwater on the Sabbath, ONE MAY SPREAD THEM OUT IN THE SUN to dry in a secluded area, **אֲבָל לֹא כְּנֶגֶד הָעָם** – BUT NOT BEFORE PEOPLE, i.e. in an area open to public view, lest onlookers suspect him of having washed his clothes on the Sabbath.[1] **רַבִּי [אֶלְעָזָר] (אליעזר) וְרַבִּי שִׁמְעוֹן אוֹסְרִין** – But R' ELAZAR AND R' SHIMON FORBID one to spread clothes to dry even in a secluded area, because they hold that an act prohibited because of the appearance of wrongdoing is prohibited even in one's private chambers.

Thus, this issue is the subject of a Tannaic dispute; the aforecited Baraisa is in accordance with the opinion of the Tanna Kamma, whereas Rav follows the opinion of R' Elazar and R' Shimon.

The Mishnah continues:

וּבְמוֹךְ שֶׁבְּאָזְנָהּ – [A woman may go out . . .] WITH A WAD IN HER EAR.

The Gemara qualifies this statement:

תָּנֵי רָמִי בַּר יְחֶזְקֵאל – **Rami bar Yechezkel taught** a Baraisa: **וְהוּא שֶׁקָּשׁוּר בְּאָזְנָהּ** – BUT THIS IS true only IF [THE WAD] IS TIED TO HER EAR; otherwise, she may not go out with it on the Sabbath, lest it fall and she be led to carry it in a public domain.[2]

The Mishnah continues:

וּבְמוֹךְ שֶׁבְּסַנְדָּלָהּ – [A woman may go out . . .] WITH A WAD IN HER SANDAL.

The Gemara qualifies this statement as well:

תָּנֵי רָמִי בַּר יְחֶזְקֵאל – **Rami bar Yechezkel taught** a Baraisa: **וְהוּא שֶׁקָּשׁוּר לָהּ בְּסַנְדָּלָהּ** – BUT THIS IS true only IF [THE WAD] IS TIED TO HER SANDAL; otherwise, she may not go out with it on the Sabbath, lest it fall to the ground and she be led to carry it.[3]

The Mishnah continues:

וּבְמוֹךְ שֶׁהִתְקִינָה לָהּ לְנִדָּתָהּ – [A woman may go out . . .] WITH A WAD THAT SHE PREPARED FOR HER MENSES.

The Gemara considers qualifying this statement as well:

סָבַר רָמִי בַּר חָמָא לְמֵימַר – **Rami bar Chama thought to say:** **וְהוּא שֶׁקְּשׁוּרָה לָהּ בֵּין יְרֵיכוֹתֶיהָ** – **But this is** true only **if [the wad] is tied between her thighs,** so that it will not fall; otherwise, she may not go out with it on the Sabbath.

The Gemara dismisses this assumption:

אָמַר רָבָא – **Rava said:** **אַף עַל פִּי שֶׁאֵינוֹ קָשׁוּר לָהּ** – No! She may go out with this wad **even if it is not tied to her,** **כֵּיוָן דְּמָאִיס לֹא אַתְיָא לְאַיְתוּיֵי** – for **since it is** a **repulsive** article, she will not wish to take hold of it, and **she will** therefore **not come to carry it** even if it does fall.

The Gemara inquires in the case of a wad possessing a handle:

בְּעָא מִינֵּיהּ רַבִּי יִרְמְיָה מֵרַבִּי אַבָּא – **R' Yirmiyah inquired of R' Abba:** **עֲשָׂתָה לָהּ בֵּית יָד מַהוּ** – **If [a woman] fashioned a handle for [a wad prepared for her menses],** thereby making it less disgusting to hold, **what is [the law]?** Is she permitted to go out with this wad without tying it, or is she forbidden to do so, lest she grasp it by its handle, and carry it home?[4] **אָמַר לֵיהּ** – **[R' Abba] replied to [R' Yirmiyah]:** **מוּתָּר** – **She is permitted** to go out even with this wad, for since it is repulsive to take hold of even by its handle, she certainly will not be led to carry it.

The Gemara supports R' Abba's ruling:

אִיתְּמַר [נַמִּי] – **It has similarly been said:** **אָמַר רַב נַחְמָן בַּר אוֹשַׁעְיָא אָמַר רַבִּי יוֹחָנָן** – **Rav Nachman bar Oshaya said in the name of R' Yochanan:** **עֲשָׂתָה לָהּ בֵּית יָד מוּתָּר** – Even if **[a woman] fashioned a handle for a [wad prepared for her menses], she is permitted** to go out with it on the Sabbath.

The Gemara recounts an incident regarding a wad inserted in the ear:

רַבִּי יוֹחָנָן נָפִיק [בֵּיהּ] (בהו)[5] לְבֵי מִדְרְשָׁא – **R' Yochanan went out to the House of Study with [a wad in his ear],** but did not tie it, **וַחֲלוּקִין עָלָיו חֲבֵרָיו** – **and his colleagues took issue with him** over this action.[6]

A similar incident:

רַבִּי יַנַּאי נָפִיק בְּהוּ לְכַרְמְלִית – **R' Yannai went out into a** ***karmelis***[7] **with [these items]** (a wad in his ear and a wad in his shoe), but did not tie them, **וַחֲלוּקִין עָלָיו כָּל דּוֹרוֹ** – **and all** the scholars of **his generation took issue with him** over this action.[8]

The Gemara questions R' Yochanan's action:

וְהָתָנֵי רָמִי בַּר יְחֶזְקֵאל – **But Rami bar Yechezkel taught** the following Baraisa: **וְהוּא שֶׁקָּשׁוּר לָהּ בְּאָזְנָהּ** – BUT THIS (i.e. the ruling that permits a woman to go out with a wad in her ear) IS true only IF [THE WAD] IS TIED TO HER EAR; otherwise, she may not go out with it! How then could R' Yochanan have gone out with a wad that was not tied?!

The Gemara answers:

לֹא קַשְׁיָא – **It is not a difficulty.** **הָא דְּמִיהֲדַק** – **In [R' Yochanan's case], [the wad] was pressed tightly** into his ear, and therefore did not require tying;[9] **הָא דְּלֹא מִיהֲדַק** – **this**

NOTES

1. This Tanna holds that an act prohibited because of the appearance of wrongdoing is prohibited only in a public place, but not in a private one (*Rashi*).

2. [For although this wad does not legally constitute a burden when worn, the Rabbis feared that one might be led to carry it.]

3. See previous note. *Ritva* (*MHK* ed.) states that this ruling pertains only to a sandal or any other open shoe; a wad placed into a completely closed shoe, however, need not be tied, since it will certainly not fall out (see *Beis Yosef, Orach Chaim* 303:15 ד"ה וכתב בספר המצוות).

[*Meiri* writes that what the Rabbis feared was not that these wads would fall, but that the wearer would unthinkingly remove them for some reason. According to his explanation, even a wad in a closed shoe would presumably be prohibited.]

4. I.e. do we say that since the handle makes the wad less repugnant to hold, she may be led to retrieve it if it falls, [or is it repulsive enough even with the handle to prevent her from carrying it]? (*Rashi;* cf. *Rashba, Chidushei HaRan*).

5. [Emendation follows *Rashi.*]

6. R' Yochanan used a wad because he was old, and suffered from excessive ear wax. The route he took to the House of Study passed through a public domain. His colleagues therefore took issue with him, for they held that since the wad was not tied, he should not have gone out with it into a public domain (*Rashi;* see note 9 for an alternative explanation).

7. [A *karmelis* is an area that classifies as neither a public nor a private domain (see Glossary). The prohibition against carrying there on the Sabbath is of Rabbinic origin.] R' Yannai held that the Rabbis enacted their decree prohibiting various articles of attire with regard to a public domain only [much as R' Anani bar Sasson holds on 64b]; since a *karmelis* is not a public domain, one is permitted to wear these articles there (*Ritva MHK* ed.; see *Lashon HaZahav;* see above, 64b, note 23).

8. For all but R' Yannai held that this decree was enacted with regard to a *karmelis* as well; one therefore may not go out into a *karmelis* with these wads unless they are tied (*Ritva MHK* ed.; see following note for why R' Yannai was opposed by *all* the scholars of his generation, whereas R' Yochanan faced only the opposition of his colleagues).

9. A wad that is pressed tightly into the ear need not be tied, since it certainly will not fall. Therefore, R' Yochanan went into a public domain with a wad that was not tied (*Rashi*). [He therefore was opposed only by his colleagues, who held that it does not suffice for the wad to be pressed in; it must be tied. R' Yannai, by contrast, went out with a wad that was neither tied *nor* pressed in; he therefore faced universal opposition (*Ritva MHK* ed.).]

[We have explained the Gemara according to *Rashi's* first, and preferred, explanation. Alternatively, the incident concerned a wad *tied* to R' Yochanan's ear, and he did not go out into a public domain, but only into a private one, since his House of Study was near his home, with no

שוטחן בחמה אבל לא כנגד העם רבי אליעזר ורבי שמעון אוסרין: ובמוך שבאזנה: תני רמי בר יחזקאל והוא שקשור באזנה: ובמוך שבסנדלה: תני רמי בר יחזקאל והוא שקשור לה בסנדלה: ובמוך שהתקינה לה לנדתה: סבר רמי בר חמא למימר והוא שקשורה לה בין ירכותיה אמר רבא אע"פ שאינו קשור לה כיון דמאים לא אתיא לאיתויי בעא מיניה רבי ירמיה מרבי אבא עשתה לה בית יד מהו א"ל מותר איתמר [נמי] אמר רב נחמן בר אושעיא א"ר יוחנן עשתה לה בית יד מותר רבי יוחנן נפיק בהו לבי מדרשא וחלוקין עליו חבריו רבי ינאי נפיק בהו לכרמלית וחלוקין עליו כל דורו והתני רמי בר יחזקאל והוא שקשור לה באזנה לא קשיא הא דמיהדק הא דלא מיהדק: בפלפל ובגלגל מלח: פלפל לריח הפה גלגל מלח לדורשיני: וכל דבר שנותנת לתוך פיה: זנגבילא אי נמי דרצונא: שן תותבת שן של זהב רבי מתיר וחכמים אוסרין: א"ר זירא לא שנו אלא של זהב אבל בשל כסף דברי הכל מותר תניא נמי הכי בשל כסף ד"ה מותר של זהב רבי מתיר וחכמים אוסרין אמר אביי רבי ור' אליעזר ור' שמעון בן אלעזר כולהו סבירא להו דכל מידי דמיגניא ביה לא אתיא לאחויי רבי הא דאמרן ר' אליעזר דתניא ר' אליעזר פוטר בכובלת ובצלוחית של פלייטון ר' שמעון בן אלעזר דתניא כלל אמר רבי שמעון בן אלעזר כל שהוא למטה מן הסבכה יוצאה בו למעלה מן הסבכה אינה יוצאה בו:

מתני' יוצאה בסלע שעל הצינית הבנות קטנות יוצאות בחוטין ואפי' בקיסמין שבאזניהם ערביות יוצאות רעולות ומדיות פרופות וכל אדם אלא שדברו חכמים בהוה פורפת על האבן ועל האגוז ועל המטבע ובלבד שלא תפרוף לכתחלה בשבת: גמ' מאי צינית בת ארעא ומאי שנא סלע אילימא כל מידי דאקושא מעלי לה ליעבד לה חספא אלא משום שוכתא ליעבד לה טסא אלא משום צורתא ליעבד לה פולסא אמר אביי שמע מינה כולהו מעלין לה: הבנות יוצאות בחוטין: אבוה דשמואל לא שביק להו לבנתיה דנפקי בחוטין ולא שביק להו גניאן גבי הדדי ועביד להו מקוואות ביומי ניסן ומפצי ביומי תשרי לא שביק להו יוצאות בחוטין והאנן תנן הבנות יוצאות בחוטין בנתיה דאבוה דשמואל דצבעונין הוו לא שביק להו גניאן גבי הדדי לימא מסייע ליה לרב הונא דאמר ר"ה נשים המסוללות זו בזו

פסולות

שוטחן בחמה. מי שנשרו כליו בדרך במי גשמים: אבל לא כנגד העם. שלא יאמרו כבסן בשבת האי תנא סבר דמידי דמשום מראית העין מותר בחדרים: אוסרין. כרב: עשתה לו בית יד. למוך שבאותו מקום מהו למיסריה דילמא שקלה וממטיא לה בידים דלא מאיס לאוחזה בבית יד שלה: עשתה לה בית יד מותר. דלא אמרינן לא מאיס אלא אפילו בבית יד מאיס: רבי יוחנן נפיק ביה לבי מדרשא. במוך שבאזנו שהיה זקן והיתה לו צואת האוזן מרובה: וחלוקין עליו חבריו. מפני שלא היה קשור באזנו והוא יוצא בו לרה"ר: הא דמיהדק. דר' יוחנן היה מותב באזנו יפה ומהדק ולא בעי קשירה ודרמי בר יחזקאל בדלא מיהדק ל"א מתלמידי רבינו הלוי דרבי יוחנן קשור הוה ובית מדרשו סמוך לביתו הוה ולא היתה רה"ר מפסקת: והא תני רמי והוא שקשור כו'. וכי קשור מיהא אפילו לרה"ר מותר ואמאי קאמר לבי מדרשו ולא קאמר לרשות הרבים ומשני דר' יוחנן קשור ולא מיהדק הקשר ולשון ראשון מיושב מזה: לדורשיני. לחולי השינים: זנגבילא. גינזירו: דרצונא. קנמון: לא שנו. דחכמים אוסרין אלא של זהב שמשונה במראה משאר שינים ודילמא מבזו לה ושקלה לה בידה וממטיא: אבל של כסף. שדומה לשאר השינים דברי הכל מותר לשון רבותי ולי נראה טעמא דשל זהב משום דחשיבא ואתי' לאחויי לכך אסור אבל של כסף לא חשיבא ולא אתי' לאחויי וללשון רבותי קשיא לי הא דאמר אביי רבי ור"ש בן אלעזר כו' ואי טעמא דרבנן משום דחייכי עלה הוא מאי שנא רבי (א) דקחשיב ליה רבנן נמי לאו לאחויי חיישי ויש לתרץ דרבנן מיסר קאסרי מכל מקום ורבי מתיר דקסבר לא חייכו עלה ולא שלפא להו ומיהו ה"ל למיחש דלמא שלפא לה משום אחויי אלא לא שלפא משום דלא מחוי לה גנותא היא: רבי הא דאמרן. דלא חיש דילמא שלפא: פוטר בכובלת. ואוקימנא דהאי פוטר מותר לכתחילה הוא ואמר טעמא מאן דרכה למיפק בכובלת אשה שריחה רע ולא שלפא ומחויא גנותה: למטה מן הסבכה. כגון כיפה של צמר: יוצאה בה. דלא חיישינן דילמא שלפא ומחויא דמיגלי שערה ומגניא בה שהשבכה נוי הוא לשער: מתני' סלע. מטבע הוא: צינית. מפרש בגמ': הבנות קטנות. שמנקבות אזניהם ואין עושין נזמים עד שיגדלו ונותנין חוטין או קסמים באזניהם שלא יסתמו אזניהם לנ"ה: ואפילו. רבותא קאמר דלא"ג דלאו תכשיט נוי הוא אורחא בהכי ולא משאוי הוא ויש מפרשין חוטין שקולעת בהן שערה דאסרינן לגדולה בריש פרקין התם משום דשכיחא בהו טבילה אבל קטנות דלא שכיחא בהו טבילה שרי ולשון ראשון הגון מזה חדא דקטנות נמי צריכות טבילה לטומאת מגע משום טהרות ואף נדות נמי שכיחות בהו כדתניא (נדה דף לב.) מעשה שהיה והטבילוה קודם לאמה ועוד מדקתני אפי' בקיסמין איכא למישמע דחוטין נמי באזנים קיימי דאי חוטי הראש לא שייך למיתני אפי' בקסמין: ערביות. נשים ישראליות שבערב: יוצאות רעולות. דרך ערביות להיות מעוטפות ראשן ופניהם חוץ מן העינים וקרי לה בלשון ערבי רעולות היינו הרעלות דכתיב גבי תכשיטי נשים בספר ישעיה (ג): מדיות. נשים ישראליות שבמדי: פרופות. שמעטפות בטלית ותולה הרצועה בשפתה האחת כנגד צוארה ובשפתה השנית כורכת אבן או אגוז וקושרת הרצועה בכרך ואין הטלית נופל מעליה: פורפת. כמו קרסים דמתרגמינן פורפין כל המחבר בגד לחבירו קרי פריפה: ובלבד שלא תפרוף לכתחלה בשבת. ובגמ' פריך והאמרת רישא פורפת: גמ' בת ארעא. מכה שהיא תחת פרסת הרגל וקושר בה סלע לרפואה: דאקושא. שהיא קשה ומגינה על המכה מקוצים ויתדות דרכים: שוכתא. ליחלוחית היוצא מן הכסף ובלע"ז רוי"ל ויפה למכה שוכתא כמו דשתך טפי דאלו מגילות (ב"מ דף כו.) ומשתכין כנחשת דתענית (דף ח.): ליעבד טסא. דכספא טיבעא למה לי אלא משום צורתא דטיבעא מעליא למכה ולאו שוכתא: ליעבד פולסא. עגול של עץ ויצור עליו: אמר אביי ש"מ. ממתני' דנקט סלע: כולהו בהדדי מעלו לה. ולהכי נקט סלע דאיתנהו לכולהו אקושא ושוכתא וצורתא: לא שביק להו לבנתיה כו'. מפרש לקמן טעמא דכולהו: גניאן גבי הדדי. ליגן זו אצל זו בעודן בתולות: מקואות ביומי ניסן. של מים מכונסין או סמוך לנהר וממשיך לתוכן מי הנהר וטובלות שם: ומפצי ביומי תשרי. שטובלות בפרת ומפני הטיט שלא יהא חצילה נותנות המפץ תחת רגליהן: דצבעונין. וחיש למישלף ואחויי: המסוללות. מתחככות משום תאות תשמיש:

פסולות

לעיל אמר רב כל מקום שאסרו חכמים כו'. י"מ דאין הלכה כרב מדתני בחולין (דף מא.) אין שוחטין לתוך גומא ברשות הרבים שלא יחקה האפיקורסים ובחצר מותר ומיהו אין זה ראיה דבחצר מותר דאף הרואה אותו אומר לנקר חצרו הוא צריך אבל בעלמא שאם יראה אדם הרואה יחשדנו אפילו בחדרי חדרים אסור:

ליעבד לה פולסא. פ"ה חתיכה של עץ ויצור עליה צורה ולפירושו (ב) ניחא מה שמקשים דבעלמא אמר מאי אסימון פולסא ופ"ה התם היינו דבר שאין עליו צורה וקשה דהכא משמע דפולסא הוא דבר שיש עליו צורה ולפירש"י ניחא דפירש ליעבד פולסא בלא צורה ויצור עליו הצורה אבל לפיר"ת קשה דפירש אסימון הוי של מתכת ויש עליו צורה אבל אינה חשובה ואינה יוצאה אם כן הכא מאי איריא סלע אפילו אסימון ושמא י"ל דצורת סלע צריך:

ומפצי ביומי תשרי. פ"ה מפני הטיט שלא יהיה חצילה ונותנות המפץ תחת רגליהן ורבינו תם פירש שהיו נותנות מפצי זקופות שלא יראו אותן העולם ויתביישו מהם ולא יטבלו היטב:

פסולות

א) ביצה ט. [לקמן קמו:], ב) [צ"ל אלעזר], ג) [גיר' הערוך ערך דר ה' לדור שיני ע"ש], ד) [לעיל סב. תוספתא פ"ה ע"ש], ה) [לעיל מז:], ו) [נדרים מ:] בכורות נה: נדה סז., ז) יבמות עו., ח) [עיין תוספות לקמן קמו: ד"ה מי שנשרו ותוספות ביצה לה: ד"ה מי. שהשיגו על פרש"י דהכא אבל לקמן קמו: במשנה וביצה לה: עולה פירושו כפירוש תוספות וביצה ט. פרש"י כדהכא], ט) [ב"מ מז:], י) [וע"ע תוס' נדה סו: ד"ה אשה].

הגהות הב"ח

(א) רש"י ד"ה אבל של כסף וכו' ומאי שנא רבי דקא שרי ליה משום דלא אתיא לאחויי רבנן נמי: (ב) תום' ד"ה ליעבד וכו' ולפירושו. נ"ב ובתוס' פ' בכל מערבין דף לא ע"ב כתבו בענין אחר ע"ש בד"ה שפדאו:

ליקוטי רש"י

שוטחן בחמה. ליבשן [לקמן קמו: עיי"ש עוד ובמסוה"ש כאן]. מי שנשרו כליו בדרך במי גשמים שוטחן בחמה והן נוגבין מאליהן. אבל לא כנגד העם. שלא יאמרו כבסן בשבת אלמא מידי דמשום מראית העין מותר במקום צנוע [ביצה ט.]. שיחשדוהו שכבסן [לקמן שם]. בכובלת. תומרתא דפילון, קשר שקשור בו סם ששמו פילון וריחו ערב ובלע"ז בלסמ"ו ואשה שריחה רע טוענתו עליה [לעיל סב.]. בושם שהנשים תולות בצואריהן של זהב או של כסף ונותן בו שמן שמעורב בו מין בושם ששמו פילון ודומה לעלי גפנים כדתניא במ"כ שלא יערב קימום במר מי גלוקקיא בשמן עלי גפנים כפילון [גיטין סט:]. פלייטון. בלסמ"א משחא דאפרסמא [לעיל שם]. בושם שריחו נודף ואינו אפרסמון [סנהדרין קח. וע"ש במלוא הרועים]. רעולות. לפי שמנליפות כל פרצופיהם חוץ מגלגל העין ל"א והרעלות מיני פרכלים נאים להתעטף בהן ובל' משנה יש מדיות רעולות במס' שבת [ישעיה ג, יט]. רעל לשון עטיפה הוא כמו והברושים הרעלו (נחום ב) ובלשון משנה מדיות רעולות [תהלים ס, ה]. מעוטפין ודומה לו (ישעיה ג) הנטיפות והשרות והרעלות ובל' משנה שנינו מדיות רעולות מסכת שבת [נחום ב, ד]. בת ארעא וכו'. ומי שיש לו מכה בפיסת רגלו מתחת קושר מהס שם דמעליא ליה סלודה דידהו ואורחא דידהו כדאמרינן במסכת שבת [כתובות צג.]. פולסא. מחוסר צורה וקורין לו פלדו"ן [ב"מ מז: ועיין תוס' כאן]. ביומי ניסן. מקוה מים חיים [זוחלין] נובעים בבית ולא היה מניחן לטבול בנהרות [בכורות נה:]. מקוה מים מכונסין ואינן טובלות בנהר [נדה סז.]. שמפני שהיה חושש להפשרת שלגים לא היה מניחן לטבול בזוחלין [ר"ן נדרים מ:]. ומפצי ביומי תשרי. שבתשרי מתמעטין הנהרות מן כל ימות השנה ומעלין טיט והיה נותן המפץ בקרקעית הנהר שלא יכנס הטיט ברגליהן ויהא חצילה [רש"י נדרים שם]. כשהיו טובלות בנהר ביומי תשרי הי' עושה להם מחצלות של קנים שקורין קלוי"ש ומשליכן לתוך המים ועומדות עליהן וטובלות לפי שבימי תשרי יש טיט רק בנהרות אבל שפתם וחושש שמא יעלה טיט למעלה על רגליהן ויהיה חוצץ [בכורות שם]. שטובלין בנהר שהזוחלין מרובין אבל מפני חצילת הטיט נותן מחצלות בנהר שעוברות עליהן [נדה שם]. בנהר היה נותן תחת כפות רגליהן משום טיט דלא ליהוי חצילה א"נ לצניעותא בעלמא והיה מניחן לטבול בנהר משום דביומי תשרי ליכא למיחש (לזוחלין) [לנוטפין] ומאי דקאמר ביומי ניסן מניסן ועד תשרי קאמר וכ"ש בימות הגשמים כך פירשו ואין הלשון נוח לי דהוה ליה למימר עביד להו מקוואות לבנתיה כולה שתא ומפצי ביומי תשרי לפיכך נ"ל דבנתיה דאבוה דשמואל בקמות לא היו טובלות בנהר משום נדה אלא במקוואות שבבתיהן וביומי ניסן דרויח עלמא היו מתחילות לטבול בנהרות והיה מתקן להם אהיהם שם בתחילת ניסן מקוואות שהיו טובלות בהן עד תשרי וביומי תשרי לא היה מצריכן למקוואות משום דליכא למיחש לנוטפין ולפיכך היה מתקן להן מפצי ובשעוברין ימי תשרי כבר היו חוזרות לטבול בבתיהם משום נדה [ר"ן נדרים שם]. המסוללות. דרך תשמיש זכר ונקבה מששפות נקבתן זו לזו וכן המסוללת בבנה קטן דסנהדרין (סט:) [יבמות עו.].

סו א ב ג ד מיי' פי"ט מהל' שבת הלכה יא סמג לאוין סה טוש"ע א"ח סי' שג סעיף טו:
סז ה ו מיי' שם הל' ז טוש"ע שם סעי' יב:
סח ז מיי' שם הלכה יג סמג שם טוש"ע א"ח סימן שא סעיף כח:
סט ח מיי' שם הלכה יב סמג שם טוש"ע א"ח סימן שג סעיף כ:
ע ט מיי' שם טוש"ע שם סעיף כא:
עא י מיי' פ"א מהל' מקואות הלכה יא טוש"ע י"ד סימן קצח סעיף לג לד:
עב כ מיי' פי"ט מהל' שבת הל' י סמג לאוין סה טוש"ע א"ח סימן שג סעיף כ:
עג ל מיי' פכ"א מהל' איסורי ביאה הלכה ח סמג לאוין קכו טוש"ע אה"ע סי' כ סעיף ב:

רבינו חננאל

שוטחן בחמה אבל לא כנגד העם ור' אלעזר ורבי שמעון אוסרין ואיהו דאמר כר' אלעזר ורבי שמעון: במוך שבאזנה תני רמי [בר יחזקאל] והוא שקשור באזנה. ובמוך שבסנדלה והוא שקשור בעקבה. במוך שהתקינה לנדתה והוא שקשור בירכותיה ורבא אמר אע"פ שאינו קשור כיון דמאיס לה לא אתיא לאחוריה. אמר רבא עשתה לה בית יד מותר. פי' בית יד שעושה לידה שתכסה אותה כדי שתבדוק מוך לנדתה ולא תגע בו ולא תטנף בו. והא דאמר במוך שבאזנה ותני רמי בר יחזקאל והוא שקשור באזנה אוקמה במהדק ואי לא מהדק אסור: ושן תותבת של כסף דברי הכל מותר: ר' שמתיר בשל זהב ור' אלעזר שמתיר בצלוחית של פלייטון ור' שמעון בן אלעזר שמתיר בכל שהוא למטה מן הסבכה אלו כולן סבירא להו כל מידי דגנאי הוא לא אתא לאחוריה והני שיטה נינהו ולית הלכתא כחד מינייהו: מתני' יוצאין בסלע שעל הצינית סילעיא שיש עליה צורת מטבע ומעלא לצינית שהוא מכה תחת הרגל. ציניתא בת ארעא. הבנות יוצאות בחוטין אפילו בקסמים שבאזניהן. בנתיה דאבוה דשמואל תלתא גווני צבעונין הוו חוטי דידהו ולא שביק להו למיפק בהו סבר דילמא שלפא ומחויא לחברתה

גליון הש"ס

תוס' ד"ה אמר רב וכו' מדתני בחולין. ראיה זו כתבו תוספות בחולין בשם ירושלמי:

Baraisa, however, discusses a wad **that is not squeezed tightly** into the ear; it therefore must be tied to ensure that it will not fall.

The Mishnah continues:
בְּפִלְפֵּל וּבְגַלְגַּל מֶלַח – [A woman may go out . . .] **WITH A PEPPERCORN OR WITH A LUMP OF SALT** [in her mouth].

The Gemara explains the function of these items:
פִּלְפֵּל לְרֵיחַ הַפֶּה – **A peppercorn is** used **for mouth odor;** גַּלְגַּל מֶלַח לְדוּרְשִׁינֵי – **a lump of salt is** used **for tooth disease.**[10]

The Mishnah continues:
וְכָל דָּבָר [שֶׁנִּיתַּן] (שנותנת) לְתוֹךְ פִּיהָ – **AND** a woman may go out **WITH ANYTHING** else **THAT WAS PLACED IN HER MOUTH.**

The Gemara gives examples of items that may be carried outside in one's mouth:
זַנְגְּבִילָא – One may carry **ginger,** אִי נַמִּי דַּרְצוּנָא – and **likewise cinnamon,** outside in one's mouth on the Sabbath, since these items serve a therapeutic function.[11]

The Mishnah continues:
שֵׁן תּוֹתֶבֶת שֵׁן שֶׁל זָהָב – **A FALSE TOOTH MADE OF GOLD:** רַבִּי מַתִּיר וַחֲכָמִים אוֹסְרִין – **REBBI PERMITS** a woman to go out with it, **BUT THE SAGES FORBID** it.

The Gemara addresses the ruling of the Sages:
אָמַר רַבִּי זֵירָא – **R' Zeira said:** לֹא שָׁנוּ אֶלָּא שֶׁל זָהָב – **They** (the Sages of the Mishnah) **taught this** ruling **only** with regard to a false tooth made **of gold,** which, because of its value, a woman might wish to show to her companions, אֲבָל בְּשֶׁל כֶּסֶף – **but in** the case of a tooth made **of silver,** which is not all that valuable, דִּבְרֵי הַכֹּל מוּתָּר – **all agree that it is permissible** for a woman to go out with it on the Sabbath.[12]

The Gemara supports R' Zeira's statement with a Baraisa:
תַּנְיָא נַמִּי הָכִי – **This has also been taught in a Baraisa:** בְּשֶׁל כֶּסֶף דִּבְרֵי הַכֹּל מוּתָּר – **IN** the case of a false tooth made **OF SILVER, ALL AGREE** that **IT IS PERMISSIBLE** for a woman to go out with it on the Sabbath. שֶׁל זָהָב – But in the case of a tooth made **OF GOLD,** רַבִּי מַתִּיר וַחֲכָמִים אוֹסְרִין – **REBBI PERMITS** a woman to go out with it, **BUT THE SAGES FORBID** it.

The reason Rebbi permits a woman to go out with a tooth made of gold is that he holds that a person will never show off an object if doing so would be cause for embarrassment. He accordingly does not suspect that a woman will remove her gold tooth to show it to others, since doing so would underline the embarrassing fact that she is missing a tooth. The Gemara now lists two others who agree with Rebbi's principle:
אָמַר אַבַּיֵי – **Abaye said:** רַבִּי וְרַבִּי אֱלִיעֶזֶר וְרַבִּי שִׁמְעוֹן בֶּן אֶלְעָזָר כּוּלְּהוּ – **Rebbi, R' Eliezer, and R' Shimon the son of Elazar** סְבִירָא לְהוּ דְּכָל מִידִי דְּמִיגַּנְיָא בֵּיהּ – **all hold that any item that causes one embarrassment,** לֹא אַתְיָא לְאַחְוּוייֵ – **one will never come to show** and thus inadvertently carry; one therefore can be trusted to go out with such items on the Sabbath.

The Gemara cites the instances in which each of these three Tannaim rule in accordance with this principle:
רַבִּי הָא דַּאֲמָרַן – We see **Rebbi** agrees with this principle from **this** case of a gold tooth **that we have** just **discussed.**[13] רַבִּי אֱלִיעֶזֶר – We see **R' Eliezer** agrees with it from the following Baraisa: דְּתַנְיָא – **For a Baraisa has taught** with regard to ornamental items worn to prevent body odor: רַבִּי אֱלִיעֶזֶר פּוֹטֵר בְּכוּבֶּלֶת וּבִצְלוֹחִית שֶׁל פַּלְיָיטוֹן – **R' ELIEZER EXEMPTS** a woman who enters a public domain wearing **A SPICE BUNDLE OR A FLASK OF BALSAM OIL** on the Sabbath,[14] for since showing others these ornaments would reveal the embarrassing fact of her body odor, she

NOTES

public domain intervening. The Gemara questions why the official version of this incident takes care to inform us, by mentioning the House of Study, that R' Yochanan went only into a private domain. For since Rami bar Yechezkel permits one to go into a public domain with a tied wad, R' Yochanan could legally have entered a public domain just as well! The Gemara answers that one is permitted to enter a public domain with a wad only if the knot with which it is bound was tied tightly [קֶשֶׁר מְהוּדָּק]. The knot fastening the wad to R' Yochanan's ear, however, was not bound tightly; he therefore could not enter a public domain while wearing his wad (*Rashi,* in the name of the students of *Rabbeinu HaLevi;* see ruling in *Orach Chaim* 303:15, which mandates a wad tightly knotted to the ear; cf. however, *Rosh Yosef's* understanding of this ruling). R' Yochanan's colleagues, however, held that one is permitted to enter even a public domain with a wad that is not tightly knotted (*Rashi,* as explained by *Beur HaGra* to *Orach Chaim* 303:15; see *Korban Nesanel* §10 to *Rosh* §14).]

10. *Rashi;* see *Aruch* (5) ערך דר, and *Hagahos R' Yaakov Emden.* [Items used for these purposes do not constitute a burden, but are legally viewed as accessories, or garments; one therefore may go out with them on the Sabbath.]

11. *Chidushei HaRan* to the Mishnah. [Therapeutic items do not legally constitute a burden,] and since they are needed for healing, one will not come to remove, and inadvertently carry, them (ibid.).

12. Since she certainly will not bother to show such an item to her friends (*Rashi*).

[Our explanation that the reason the Sages forbid a gold tooth is for fear that she will show it follows *Rashi's* own view; alternatively, what the Sages suspect is not that she will remove the tooth to show it, but that others will notice it and ridicule her for wearing it, causing her to remove and carry it (see above 64b note 18). The reason the Sages permit a silver tooth according to this explanation is because it is similar in color to a human tooth; since it is therefore not noticeable, it will not subject one to ridicule. Rebbi, however, holds that even a gold tooth is not an object of derision (*Rashi,* in the name of his teachers). Others offer yet a third explanation for the Sages' opinion: They are concerned that the gold tooth may fall from the woman's mouth, and she will then retrieve it and carry it home. However, they are confident that she will not bother to retrieve a silver tooth that falls, since it is an inexpensive item, and easily replaced (*Rashba* to the Mishnah; see *Rambam, Shabbos* 19:7, and *Rosh Yosef*).]

[A substitute human tooth is permissible according to both explanations offered by *Rashi,* for it is not an item that one would show, and, since it is not noticeable, it will not subject one to ridicule (see *Rosh* and *Orach Chaim* 303:12). *Rashba* and *Rambam* (ibid.), however, prohibit wearing such a tooth, for fear that if it falls, one will retrieve it and carry it home (see *Rosh Yosef*).]

13. For the reason Rebbi permits a woman to go out with a gold tooth is that he is certain that because of embarrassment she will not show it (*Rashi*).

[*Rashi* questions the explanation offered by his teachers (see note 12) as follows: By including only Rebbi in this list, Abaye implies that the Sages do not agree with this principle that a person will not display that which will embarrass him. But according to *Rashi's* teachers, the Sages forbid a gold tooth *only* because the woman might remove it in embarrassment, and *not* because she might show it! Since they are confident that she will not show the gold tooth, they evidently hold that one will not show others that which may cause embarrassment! Why then did Abaye imply that the Sages do not admit to the truth of this principle? *Rashi* explains that Abaye lists only those who not only agree with this principle, but who actually put it into use by permitting the wearing of an ornament whose display will cause embarrassment. Since Rebbi permits a gold tooth, and does not suspect that she will show it [or that others will ridicule her], Abaye includes him; since the Sages do not in fact permit a gold tooth, Abaye does not list them here despite the fact that they agree that she will not show the tooth (see *Maharsha* and *Rosh Yosef*).]

14. Although this Baraisa states only that R' Eliezer *exempts* one who goes out with these items, implying that one should preferably not wear them, R' Eliezer actually rules that it is entirely proper for one to go out wearing these ornaments on the Sabbath, since there is absolutely no reason to suspect that one will come to show them to others (*Rashi;* see *Rashash;* see above, 62a, for why the Baraisa employs the term "exempts" [פּוֹטֵר]).

[א] שוטחן בחמה אבל לא כנגד העם רבי [ב] אליעזר ורבי שמעון אוסרין: [א] ובמוך שבאזנה: תני רמי בר יחזקאל והוא שקשור באזנה: [ב] ובמוך שבסנדלה: תני רמי בר יחזקאל והוא שקשור לה בסנדלה: ובמוך שהתקינה לה לנדתה: סבר רמי בר חמא למימר והוא שקשורה לה בין ירכותיה אמר רבא [ג] אע"פ שאינו קשור לה כיון דמאים לא אתיא לאיתויי בעא מיניה רבי ירמיה מרבי אבא עשתה לה בית יד מהו א"ל [ד] מותר איתמר [נמי] אמר רב נחמן בר אושעיא א"ר יוחנן עשתה לה בית יד מותר רבי יוחנן נפיק בהו לבי מדרשא וחלוקין עליו חבריו רבי ינאי נפיק בהו לכרמלית וחלוקין עליו כל דורו והתני רמי בר יחזקאל והוא שקשור לה באזנה לא קשיא הא דמיהדק הא דלא מיהדק: בפלפל ובגלגל מלח: פלפל לריח הפה גלגל מלח [ג] לדורשיני: וכל דבר שנותנת לתוך פיה: זנגבילא אי נמי דרצונא: שן תותבת שן של זהב רבי מתיר [ה] וחכמים אוסרין: א"ר זירא [ו] לא שנו אלא של זהב אבל בשל כסף דברי הכל מותר תניא נמי הכי בשל כסף ד"ה מותר של זהב רבי מתיר וחכמים אוסרין אמר אביי רבי ור' אליעזר ור' שמעון בן אלעזר כולהו סבירא להו דכל מידי דמיגניא ביה לא אתיא לאחויי רבי הא דאמרן ר' אליעזר [ד] דתניא ר' אליעזר פוטר בכובלת ובצלוחית של פלייטון ר' שמעון בן אלעזר דתניא [ה] כלל אמר רבי שמעון בן אלעזר כל שהוא למטה מן הסבכה יוצאה בו למעלה מן הסבכה אינה יוצאה בו: מתני' [ז] יוצאה בסלע שעל הצינית [ח] הבנות קטנות יוצאות בחוטין ואפי' בקיסמין שבאזניהם [ט] ערביות יוצאות רעולות ומדיות פרופות וכל אדם אלא שדברו חכמים בהוה פורפת על האבן ועל האגוז ועל המטבע ובלבד שלא תפרוף לכתחלה בשבת: גמ' מאי צינית בת ארעא ומאי שנא סלע אילימא כל מידי דאקושא מעלי לה ליעבד לה חספא אלא משום שוכתא ליעבד לה טסא אלא משום צורתא ליעבד לה פולסא אמר אביי שמע מינה כולהו מעלין לה: הבנות יוצאות בחוטין: אבוה דשמואל לא שביק להו לבנתיה דנפקי בחוטין ולא שביק להו גניאן גבי הדדי [ו] ועביד להו מקוואות ביומי ניסן [י] ומפצי ביומי תשרי לא שביק להו יוצאות בחוטין והאנן תנן הבנות יוצאות בחוטין דאבוה דשמואל [כ] דצבעונין הוו לא שביק להו גניאן גבי הדדי לימא מסייע ליה לרב הונא [ז] דאמר ר"ה [ל] נשים המסוללות זו בזו

פסולות

רש"י

שוטחן בחמה. מי שנשרו כליו בדרך [ח] במי גשמים: אבל לא כנגד העם. שלא יאמרו כבסן בשבת האי תנא סבר דמידי דמשום מראית העין מותר בחדרים: אוסרין. כרב: עשתה לו בית יד. למוך שבאותו מקום מהו למיסריה דילמא שקלה וממטא לה בידים דלא מאיס לאוחזה בבית יד שלה: עשתה לה בית יד מותר. דלא אמרינן לא מאיס אלא אפילו בבית יד מאיס: רבי יוחנן נפיק ביה לבי מדרשא. במוך שבאזנו שהיה זקן והיתה לו צואת האוזן מרובה: וחלוקין עליו חבריו. מפני שלא היה קשור באזנו והוא יוצא בו לרה"ר: הא דמיהדק. דר' יוחנן היה תוחב באזנו יפה ומהדק ולא בעי קשירה ודרמי בר יחזקאל בדלא מיהדק ל"א מתלמידי רבינו הלוי דרבי יוחנן קשור הוה ובית מדרשו סמוך לביתו הוה ולא היתה רה"ר מפסקת: והא תני רמי והוא שקשור כו'. וכי קשור מיהא אפילו לרה"ר מותר ואמאי קאמר לבי מדרשו ולא קאמר לרשות הרבים ומשני דר' יוחנן קשור ולא מיהדק הקשר ולשון ראשון מיושב מזה: לדורשיני. לחולי השינים: זנגבילא. גינזירו: דרצונא. קנמון: לא שנו. דחכמים אוסרין אלא של זהב שמשונה במראה משאר שינים ודילמא מבזו לה ושקלה לה בידה וממטיא: אבל של כסף. שדומה לשאר השינים דברי הכל מותר לשון רבותי ולי נראה טעמא דשל זהב משום דחשיבא ואתי' לאחויי לכך אסור אבל של כסף לא חשיבא ולא אתי' לאחויי וללשון רבותי קשיא לי הא דאמר אביי רבי ור"ש בן אלעזר כו' ואי טעמא דרבנן משום דחייכי עלה הוא מאי שנא רבי (א) דקחשיב ליה רבנן נמי לאו לאחויי חיישי ויש לתרץ דרבנן מיסר קאסרי מכל מקום ורבי מתיר דקסבר לא חייכו עלה ולא שלפא להו ומיהו ה"ל למיחש דלמא שלפא לה משום אחויי אלא לא שלפא משום דאי מחוי לה גנותא היא: רבי הא דאמרן. דלא חייש דילמא שלפא: פוטר בכובלת. ואוקימנא דהאי פוטר מותר לכתחילה הוא ואמר טעמא מאן דרכה למיפק בכובלת אשה שריחה רע ולא שלפא ומחויא גנותה: למטה מן הסבכה. כגון כיפה של צמר: יוצאה בה. דלא חיישינן דילמא שלפא ומחויא דמיגלי שערה ומגניא בה שהסבכה נוי הוא לשער: מתני' סלע. מטבע הוא: צינית. מפרש בגמ': הבנות קטנות. שמנקבות אזניהם ואין עושין נזמים עד שיגדלו ונותנין חוטין או קסמים באזניהם שלא יסתמו אזניהם לו"ה: ואפילו. רבותא קאמר דאע"ג דלאו תכשיט נוי הוא אורחא בהכי ולא משאוי הוא ויש מפרשין חוטין שקולעת בהן שערה דאסרינן לגדולה בריש פרקין התם משום דשכיחא בהו טבילה אבל קטנות דלא שכיחא בהו טבילה שרי ולשון ראשון הגון מזה חדא דקטנות נמי צריכות טבילה לטומאת מגע משום טהרות ואף נדות נמי שכיחות בהו כדתניא (נדה דף לב.) מעשה שהיה והטבילוה קודם לאמה ועוד מדקתני אפי' בקיסמין איכא למישמע דחוטין נמי באזנים קיימי דאי חוטי הראש לא שייך למיתני אפי' בקסמין: ערביות. נשים ישראליות שבערב: יוצאות רעולות. דרך ערביות להיות מעוטפות ראשן ופניהם חוץ מן העינים וקרי לה בלשון ערבי רעולות היינו הרעלות דכתיב גבי תכשיטי נשים בספר ישעיה (ג): מדיות. נשים ישראליות שבמדי: פרופות. שמעטפות בטלית ותולה הרצועה בשפתה האחת כנגד צוארה ובשפתה השנית כורכת אבן או אגוז וקושרת הרצועה בכרך ואין הטלית נופל מעליה: פורפת. כמו קרסים דמתרגמינן פורפין כל המחבר בגד לחבירו קרי פריפה: ובלבד שלא תפרוף לכתחלה בשבת. ובגמ' פריך והאמרת רישא פורפת: גמ' בת ארעא. מכה שהיא תחת פרסת הרגל וקושר בה סלע לרפואה: דאקושא. שהיא קשה ומגינה על המכה מקוצים ויתדות דרכים: שוכתא. ליחלוחית היוצא מן הכסף ובלע"ז רוי"ל ויפה למכה שוכתא כמו דשתך טפי דאלו מציאות (ב"מ דף כו.) ומשתכין כנחשת דתענית (דף ח.): ליעבד טסא. דכספא טיבעא למה לי אלא משום צורתא דטיבעא מעליא למכה ולאו שוכתא: ליעבד פולסא. עגול של עץ ויצור עליו: אמר אביי ש"מ. ממתני' דנקט סלע: כולהו בהדדי מעלו לה. ולהכי נקט סלע דאיתנהו לכולהו אקושא ושוכתא וצורתא: לא שביק להו לבנתיה כו'. מפרש לקמן טעמא דכולהו: גניאן גבי הדדי. לישן זו אצל זו בעודן בתולות: מקואות ביומי ניסן. של מים מכונסין או סמוך לנהר וממשיך לתוכן מי הנהר וטובלות שם: ומפצי ביומי תשרי. שטובלות בפרת ומפני הטיט שלא יהא חציצה נותנות המפץ תחת רגליהן: דצבעונין. וחייש למישלף ואחויי: המסוללות. מתחככות משום תאות תשמיש:

פסולות

תוספות

אמר רב כל מקום שאסרו חכמים כו'. י"מ דאין הלכה כרב [ט] מדתני בחולין (דף מא.) אין שוחטין לתוך גומא ברשות הרבים שלא יחקה האפיקורסים ובחצר מותר ומיהו אין זה ראיה דבחצר מותר דאף הרואה אותו אומר לנקר חצרו הוא צריך אבל בעלמא שאם יראה אדם הרואה יחשדנו אפילו בחדרי חדרים אסור:

ליעבד לה פולסא. פ"ה חתיכה של עץ ויצור עליה צורה ולפירושו (ג) ניחא מה שמקשים דבעלמא אמר [ט] מאי אסימון פולסא ופ"ה התם היינו דבר שאין עליו צורה וקשה דהכא משמע דפולסא הוא דבר שיש עליו צורה ולפירש"י ניחא דפירש ליעבד פולסא בלא צורה ויצור עליו הצורה אבל לפר"ת קשה דפירש אסימון הוי של מתכת ויש עליו צורה אבל אינה חשובה ואינה יוצאה אם כן הכא מאי איריא סלע אפילו אסימון ושמא י"ל דצורת סלע צריך:

ומפצי ביומי תשרי. פ"ה מפני הטיט שלא יהיה חציצה ונותנות המפץ תחת רגליהן ורבינו תם פירש שהיו נותנות מפצי זקופות שלא יראו אותן העולם ויתביישו מהם ולא יטבלו היטב [י]:

פסולות

מסורת הש"ס

א) ביצה ט. [לקמן קמו:], ב) [ג"ל אלעזר], ג) [גיר' הערוך ערך דר ה' לדור שיני ע"ש], ד) [לעיל סב. תוספתא פ"ה ע"ש], ה) [לעיל מו:], ו) [נדרים מ: בכורות נה: נדה סו.], ז) יבמות עו., ח) [עיין תוספות לקמן קמו: ד"ה מי שנשרו ותוספות ביצה ט: ד"ה מי. שהשיגו על פרש"י דהכא אבל לקמן קמו: במשנה וביצה לה: עולה פירושו כפירוש תוספות וביצה ט. פרש"י דהכא], ט) [ב"מ מז:], י) [וע"ע תוס' נדה סו: ד"ה אשה].

הגהות הב"ח

(א) רש"י ד"ה אבל של כסף וכו' ומאי שנא רבי דקא שרי ליה משום דלא אתיא לאחויי רבנן נמי: (ג) תום' ד"ה ליעבד וכו' ולפירושו. נ"ב ובתוס' פ' כל מערבין דף לא ע"ב כתבו בענין אחר ע"ש בד"ה שפלטו:

ליקוטי רש"י

שוטחן בחמה. ליבשן [לקמן קמו: עיי"ש עוד ובמסה"ש כאן]. מי שנשרו כליו בדרך במי גשמים שוטחן בחמה והן נוגבין מאליהן. אבל לא כנגד העם. שלא יאמרו כבסן בשבת שאלמא מידי דמשום מראית העין מותר במקום צנוע [ביצה ט.]. שיחשדוהו שכבסן [לקמן שם]. בכובלת. מומרתא דפילון, קשר שקשור בו סם ששמו פילון וריחו ערב ובלע"ז בלסמ"ו ואשה שריחה רע טוענתו עליה [לעיל סב.]. בושן שהסמים תולות בצואריהן של זהב או של כסף ונותן בו שמן מעורב בו מין בושם ששמו פילון ודומה לעלי גפנים כדאמר במ"ב שלא יערב קימום במר מי גלוקיא בשמן עלי גפנים כפילון [גיטין סט:]. פליוטון. בלסמ"ו משחא דאפרסמא [לעיל שם]. בושם שריחו נודף ואינו אפרסמון [סנהדרין קח. ועיי"ש בלוא הרעים]. רעולות. לניף שמלניפים כל פרצופיהם חוץ מגלגל העין ל"א הרעלות מיני פרבלים נאים להתעטף בהן ובכל' משנה יש מדיות רעולות במס' שבת [ישעיה ג, יט]. רעל לשון עטיפה הוא כמו והברושים הרעלו [נחום ב] ובלשון משנה מדיות רעולות [תהלים ס, ה]. מעוטפין ודומה לו [ישעיה ג] הנטיפות והשרות והרעלות ובל' משנה שנינו מדיות רעולות מסכת שבת [נחום ב, ד]. בת ארעא וכו'. ומי שיש לו מכה בפיסת רגלו מתחת קושר מהם שם דמעלי ליה לגלודה ולורתא דידהו [כתובות צג.]. פולסא. מחסר לורה וקורין לו פלדו"ן [ב"מ מז: ועיין תוס' כאן]. ביומי ניסן. מקוה מים חיים [זוחלין] טובעים בבית ולא היה מניחן לטבול בנהרות [בכורות נה:]. מקוה מים מכונסין ואינן טובלות בנהר [נדה סז.]. שמפני שהיה חושש להפשרת שלגים לא היה מניחן לטבול בזוחלין [ר"ן נדרים מ:]. ומפצי ביומי תשרי. שבתשרי מתמעטין הנהרות מן כל ימות השנה ומעלין טיט והיה נותן המפץ בקרקעית הנהר שלא יכנס הטיט ברגליהן ויהא חציצה [רש"י נדרים שם]. כשהיו טובלות בנהר ביומי תשרי הי' עושה להם מחצלות של קנים שקורין קלוי"ש ומשליכן לתוך המים ועומדות עליהן וטובלות לפי שבימי תשרי יש טיט רך בנהרות אצל שפתם וחושש שמא יעלה טיט למעלה על רגליהן ויהיה חוצץ [בכורות שם]. שטובלין בנהר שהזוחלין מרובין אבל מפני חציצת הטיט נותן מחצלות בנהר שעוברות עליהן [נדה שם]. בנהר היה נותן תחת כפות רגליהן משום טיט דלא ליהוי חציצה א"נ לצניעותא בעלמא והיה מניחן לטבול בנהר משום דביומי תשרי ליכא למיחש (לזוחלין) [לנוטפין] ומאי דקאמר ביומי ניסן מניסן ועד תשרי קאמר וכ"ש בימות הגשמים כך פירשו ואין הלשון נוח לי דהוה ליה למימר עביד להו מקוואות לבנתיה כולה שתא ומפצי ביומי תשרי לפיכך נ"ל דבנתיה דאבוה דשמואל בסתוא לא היו טובלות בנהר משום נזה אלא במקוואות שבבתיהן וביומי ניסן דרוב עלמא היו מתחילות לטבול בנהרות והיה מתקן להם אביהם שם בתחילת ניסן מקוואות שהיו טובלות בהן עד תשרי וביומי תשרי לא היה מצריכן למקוואות משום דליכא למיחש לנוטפין ולפיכך היה מתקן להן מפצי וכשעוברין ימי תשרי כבר היו חוזרות לטבול בבתיהם משום נזה [ר"ן נדרים שם]. המסוללות. דרך תשמיש זכר ונקבה משפשפות נקבתן זו לזו וכן המסוללת בבנה קטן דסנהדרין (סט:) [יבמות עו.].

עין משפט נר מצוה

סו א ב ג ד מיי' פי"ט מהל' שבת הלכה יא סמג לאוין סה טוש"ע א"ח סי' שג סעיף טו:

סז ה ו מיי' שם הל' ז טוש"ע שם סעי' יג:

סח ז מיי' שם הלכה יג סמג שם טוש"ע א"ח סימן שא סעיף כח:

סט ח מיי' שם הלכה יב סמג שם טוש"ע א"ח סימן שג סעיף כ:

ע ט מיי' שם טוש"ע שם סעיף כא:

עא י מיי' פ"א מהל' מקוואות הלכה יא טוש"ע י"ד סימן קלח סעיף לג לד:

עב כ מיי' פי"ט מהל' שבת הל' י סמג לאוין סה טוש"ע א"ח סימן שג סעיף כ:

עג ל מיי' פכ"א מהל' איסורי ביאה הלכה ח סמג לאוין קכו טוש"ע אה"ע סי' כ סעיף ב:

רבינו חננאל

שוטחן בחמה אבל לא כנגד העם ור' אלעזר ורבי שמעון אוסרין ואיהו דאמר כר' אלעזר ורבי שמעון: במוך שבאזנה תני רמי [בר יחזקאל] והוא שקשור באזנה. ובמוך שבסנדלה והוא שקשור בעקבה. במוך שהתקינה לנדתה והוא שקשור בירכותיה ורבא אמר אע"פ שאינו קשור כיון דמאיס לה לא אתיא לאחוייה. אמר רבא עשתה לה בית יד מותר. פי' בית יד שעושה לידה שתכסה אותה כדי שתבדוק מוך לנדתה ולא תגע בו ולא תטנף בו. והא דאמר במוך שבאזנה ותני רמי בר יחזקאל והוא שקשור באזנה אוקמה במהדק ואי לא מהדק אסור: ושן תותבת של כסף דברי הכל מותר: ר' שמתיר בשל זהב ור' אלעזר שמתיר בצלוחית של פלייטון ור' שמעון בן אלעזר שמתיר בכל שהוא למטה מן הסבכה אלו כולן סבירא להו כל מידי דגנאי הוא לא אתא לאחווייה והני שיטה נינהו ולית הלכתא כחד מינייהו: מתני' יוצאין בסלע שעל הצינית סילעיא שיש עליה צורת מטבע ומעלא לצינית שהוא מכה תחת הרגל. ציניתא בת ארעא. הבנות יוצאות בחוטין אפילו בקסמים שבאזניהן. בנתיה דאבוה דשמואל תלתא גווני צבעונים הוו חוטי דידהו ולא שביק להו למיפק בהו סבר דילמא שלפא ומחויא לחברתה

גליון הש"ס

תוס' ד"ה אמר רב וכו' מדתני בחולין. ראיה זו כתבו תוספות בחולין בשם ירושלמי:

certainly will not show them off. רַבִּי שִׁמְעוֹן בֶּן אֶלְעָזָר – We see that **R' Shimon the son of Elazar** agrees with this principle from the following Baraisa: דְּתַנְיָא – **For a Baraisa has taught:** כְּלָל אָמַר רַבִּי שִׁמְעוֹן בֶּן אֶלְעָזָר – **R' SHIMON THE SON OF ELAZAR STATED A RULE:** כֹּל שֶׁהוּא לְמַטָּה מִן הַסְּבָכָה יוֹצְאָה בּוֹ – **[A WOMAN] MAY GO OUT** on the Sabbath **WITH ANYTHING THAT IS** worn **BENEATH THE HAT;**[15] לְמַעְלָה מִן הַסְּבָכָה אֵינָהּ יוֹצְאָה בּוֹ – **BUT SHE MAY NOT GO OUT** on the Sabbath **WITH ANYTHING WORN ABOVE THE HAT.** Items worn below a woman's hat are permitted, since in slipping these items from beneath her hat to show them, a woman will presumably expose some of her hair. This she certainly will not do, since revealing her uncovered hair would cause her embarrassment.[16]

We see, then, that these three Tannaim all agree on this issue – we need not suspect that a woman will show an article if doing so will cause her embarrassment.

Mishnah The following Mishnah enumerates additional items with which a woman may go out on the Sabbath:

יוֹצְאָה בְּסֶלַע שֶׁעַל הַצִּינִית – **[A woman] may go out** on the Sabbath **with a *sela* that is** bound **upon a *tzinis*.**[17] הַבָּנוֹת קְטַנּוֹת יוֹצְאוֹת בְּחוּטִין – **The young girls may go out** on the Sabbath **with threads,** וַאֲפִילוּ בְּקֵיסָמִין – **and even with splinters,** שֶׁבְּאָזְנֵיהֶם – **that are** passed through holes **in their ears.**[18] עַרְבִיּוֹת יוֹצְאוֹת רְעוּלוֹת – **Arabian women may go out** on the Sabbath **wrapped** in headcloths,[19] וּמָדִיּוֹת פְּרוּפוֹת – **and Median women** with their cloaks **fastened** on stones or nuts.[20] וְכָל אָדָם – **And** this is actually true of **any person,**[21] אֶלָּא שֶׁדִּבְּרוּ חֲכָמִים בַּהֹוֶה – **however, the Sages spoke in** regard to **the prevalent** custom.[22]

The Mishnah permits various unconventional sorts of fasteners:

פּוֹרֶפֶת עַל הָאֶבֶן – **[A woman] may fasten** her cloak **on a stone,** וְעַל הָאֱגוֹז – **on a nut,** וְעַל הַמַּטְבֵּעַ – **or on a coin** on the Sabbath,[23] וּבִלְבַד שֶׁלֹּא תִּפְרוֹף לְכַתְּחִלָּה בְּשַׁבָּת – **but provided that she does not initially fasten** with it **on the Sabbath.**[24]

NOTES

15. Such as the ornamental woolen cap [כִּיפָּה שֶׁל צֶמֶר] that is worn under a woman's hat (*Rashi*).

16. For a married woman is required to keep her hair covered in public; she will therefore feel shame if her hair is exposed to public view (see *Rashi*).

Although all agree that a woman generally will not expose her hair by showing her ornaments (see above 64b), Abaye deliberately chooses to present the ruling of R' Shimon the son of Elazar to illustrate this phenomenon. This is because only R' Shimon rules that in a case in which only a small amount of hair will be exposed (since the woman attempts to slip the ornament from under her hat without removing the hat – see above, 57b), a woman will nonetheless avoid even the comparatively *minor* embarrassment of exposing a small amount of hair. Since R' Shimon's ruling is thus comparable to that of the other Tannaim here, who likewise speak of comparatively minor embarrassments (i.e. a missing tooth, body odor), Abaye selects it for inclusion in this list (*Ritva MHK* ed.; see *Ritva MHK* ed. to 60a ד״ה הואיל ואשה; cf. *Rashba*).

17. A *sela* is a particular coin. The Gemara will explain what a *tzinis* is (*Rashi*).

18. It was customary for girls to pierce their ears when young, but not to acquire earrings until maturity. To keep the holes in their earlobes from closing, they would insert threads or splinters in place of earrings (*Rashi*). The threads and splinters are inserted only loosely into the ear, and do not keep water from passing through. Since they therefore need not be removed during immersion in a *mikveh,* we do not fear that a girl will remove and inadvertently carry them on such an occasion (*Rashba,* in explanation of *Rashi*).

When the Mishnah says, "and *even* with splinters," it implies that there is good reason to assume that splinters would *not* be permitted. This is because splinters worn in the ear are not ornamental in any way, and could thus be thought to constitute a burden. The Mishnah must therefore state explicitly that one is permitted to go out even with splinters, for since it is common practice to do so, they are not considered a burden (*Rashi;* cf. *Tosafos HaRosh*).

[Others maintain that the case of threads refers to threads braided into the girls' hair, and that the Mishnah is differentiating between adult women, who, as the Mishnah teaches on 57a, are forbidden to wear threads in their hair, and minors, who are permitted to do so. The reason to differentiate is that mature women (who are subject to menstrual bleeding) must use a *mikveh* regularly; the Rabbis therefore prohibited them from wearing threads in their hair, lest they remove and carry the threads on such an occasion. Young girls, by contrast, rarely require immersion; the Rabbis therefore did not promulgate this decree with regard to them. *Rashi* rejects this explanation because, while it is true that young girls are less likely to experience menstrual bleeding than are grown women, they are equally susceptible to *tumah* spread by *tamei* objects, and often require immersion to purify themselves of such *tumah* (so that they might handle food that must be kept *tahor*). Moreover (says *Rashi*), even young girls often experience menstrual bleeding (see *Niddah* 32a); the Rabbis therefore certainly included them in their decree. Finally, the term "and even with splinters" equates the case of threads with that of splinters, and implies that with regard to both, the Mishnah discusses a single case – an item passed through a hole in the ear (see *Rashba;* cf. *Ramban* from *Yerushalmi;* cf. also *Rambam, commentary to Mishnah*; see *Rosh Yosef*).]

19. I.e. Jewish women who reside in Arabia may go out wrapped in headcloths. It was the custom in Arabia for women to wrap their heads and faces with a cloth, leaving only their eyes exposed (*Rashi;* see *Rashi, Isaiah* 3:19; cf. *Rambam, Commentary to Mishnah*). The Mishnah teaches that a cloth worn in this unusual manner is not legally considered a burden, but a garment; one is therefore permitted to go out in this fashion on the Sabbath (*Mishnah Berurah* 303:71).

20. I.e. Jewish women who reside in Media may go out in this manner. It was customary in Media to secure one's cloak by means of a strap attached to one of the upper corners; a stone or nut [functioning as a button] was wrapped into the cloak's opposite upper corner, and the strap was wound about it (*Rashi*). [The makeshift button is not considered a burden, but a part of the garment; it is thus permissible to wear it outside.]

[Media was a province of Persia.]

21. [I.e. anyone may go out on the Sabbath wrapped in a headcloth, or wearing a cloak fastened with a makeshift button.] However, this holds true only if these items are an accepted mode of dress; otherwise, they are viewed as a burden, and are prohibited to be worn outside on the Sabbath (*Ritva MHK* ed. to 64b סד״ה ר׳ עניני). Thus, only a woman may go out with a headcloth, since it is primarily a woman's garment; both men and women, however, may fasten their cloaks upon stones or nuts, since this practice is commonly followed by individuals of either gender (see *Orach Chaim* 303:21-23 with *Mishnah Berurah* §76).

22. [I.e. to the custom that prevailed during the time of the Mishnah, when these manners of dress were prevalent mainly among Arabian and Median women.]

23. For we do not fear that one observing her action will suspect that she is using a subterfuge to transport the makeshift button to another domain. Rather, it is obvious to anyone watching that her intention is to fasten her cloak, and not to transport the item (*Tosafos* to 64b ד״ה ובלבד שלא תתן; see also *Mishnah Berurah* 303:72; see 64b note 15).

24. [The Gemara (65b) will discuss this passage.]

שוטחן בחמה אבל לא כנגד העם רבי אליעזר ורבי שמעון אוסרין: ובמוך שבאזנה: תני רמי בר יחזקאל והוא שקשור באזנה: ובמוך שבסנדלה: תני רמי בר יחזקאל והוא שקשור לה בסנדלה: ובמוך שהתקינה לה לנדתה: סבר רמי בר חמא למימר והוא שקשורה לה בין ירכותיה אמר רבא אע"פ שאינו קשור לה כיון דמאים לא אתיא לאיתויי בעא מיניה רבי ירמיה מרבי אבא עשתה לה בית יד מהו א"ל מותר איתמר [נמי] אמר רב נחמן בר אושעיא א"ר יוחנן עשתה לה בית יד מותר רבי יוחנן נפיק בהו לבי מדרשא וחלוקין עליו חבריו רבי ינאי נפיק בהו לכרמלית וחלוקין עליו כל דורו והתני רמי בר יחזקאל והוא שקשור לה באזנה לא קשיא הא דמיהדק הא דלא מיהדק: בפלפל ובגלגל מלח: פלפל לריח הפה גלגל מלח לדורשיני: וכל דבר שנותנת לתוך פיה: זנגבילא אי נמי דרצונא: שן תותבת שן של זהב רבי מתיר וחכמים אוסרין: א"ר זירא לא שנו אלא של זהב אבל בשל כסף דברי הכל מותר תניא נמי הכי בשל כסף ד"ה מותר של זהב רבי מתיר וחכמים אוסרין אמר אביי רבי ור' אליעזר ור' שמעון בן אלעזר כולהו סבירא להו דכל מידי דמיגניא ביה לא אתיא לאחויי רבי הא דאמרן ר' אליעזר דתניא ר' אליעזר פוטר בכובלת ובצלוחית של פלייטון ר' שמעון בן אלעזר דתניא כלל אמר רבי שמעון בן אלעזר כל שהוא למטה מן הסבכה יוצאה בו למעלה מן הסבכה אינה יוצאה בו: מתני' יוצאה בסלע שעל הצינית הבנות קטנות יוצאות בחוטין ואפי' בקיסמין שבאזניהם ערביות יוצאות רעולות ומדיות פרופות וכל אדם אלא שדברו חכמים בהווה פורפת על האבן ועל האגוז ועל המטבע ובלבד שלא תפרוף לכתחלה בשבת: גמ' מאי צינית בת ארעא ומאי שנא סלע אילימא כל מידי דאקושא מעלי לה ליעבד לה חספא אלא משום שוכתא ליעבד לה טסא אלא משום צורתא ליעבד לה פולסא אמר אביי שמע מינה כולהו מעלין לה: הבנות יוצאות בחוטין: אבוה דשמואל לא שביק להו לבנתיה דנפקי בחוטין ולא שביק להו גניאן גבי הדדי ועביד להו מקואות ביומי ניסן ומפצי ביומי תשרי לא שביק להו יוצאות בחוטין והאנן תנן הבנות יוצאות בחוטין בנתיה דאבוה דשמואל דצבעונין הוו לא שביק להו גניאן גבי הדדי לימא מסייע ליה לרב הונא דאמר ר"ה נשים המסוללות זו בזו פסולות

שוטחן בחמה. מי שנשרו כליו בדרך במי גשמים: אבל לא כנגד העם. שלא יאמרו כבסן בשבת האי תנא סבר דמידי דמשום מראית העין מותר בחדרים: אוסרין. כרב: עשתה לו בית יד. למוך שבאותו מקום מהו למיסריה דילמא שקלה וממטיא לה בידים דלא מאים לאוחזה בבית יד שלה: עשתה לה בית יד מותר. דלא אמרינן לא מאים אלא אפילו בבית יד מאים: רבי יוחנן נפיק ביה לבי מדרשא. במוך שבאזנו שהיה זקן והיתה לו צואת האוזן מרובה: וחלוקין עליו חבריו. מפני שלא היה קשור באזנו והוא יוצא בו לרה"ר: הא דמיהדק. דר' יוחנן היה תוחב באזנו יפה ומהדק ולא בעי קשירה ודרמי בר יחזקאל בדלא מיהדק ל"א מתלמידי רבינו הלוי דרבי יוחנן קשור הוה ובית מדרשו סמוך לביתו הוה ולא היתה רה"ר מפסקת: והא תני רמי והוא שקשור כו'. וכי קשור מיהא אפילו לרה"ר מותר ואמאי קאמר לבי מדרשו ולא קאמר לרשות הרבים ומשני דר' יוחנן קשור ולא מיהדק הקשר ולשון ראשון מיושב מזה: לדורשיני. לחולי השיניים: זנגבילא. גינזירו: דרצונא. קנמון: לא שנו. דחכמים אוסרין אלא של זהב שמשונה במראה משאר שיניים ודילמא מבזו לה ושקלה לה בידה וממטיא: אבל של כסף. שדומה לשאר השיניים דברי הכל מותר לשון רבותי ולי נראה טעמא דשל זהב משום דחשיבא ואתי' לאחויי לכך אסור אבל של כסף לא חשיבא ולא אתי' לאחויי וללשון רבותי קשיא לי הא דאמר אביי רבי ור"ש בן אלעזר כו' ולי טעמא דרבנן משום דחייכי עלה הוא מאי שנא רבי (א) דקחשיב ליה רבנן נמי לאו לאחויי חיישי ויש לתרץ דרבנן מיסר קאסרי מכל מקום ורבי מתיר דקסבר לא חייכו עלה ולא שלפא להו ומיהו ה"ל למיחש דלמא שלפא לה משום אחויי אלא לא שלפא משום דאי מחוי לה גנותא היא: רבי הא דאמרן. דלא חייש דילמא שלפא: פוטר בכובלת. ואוקימנא דהאי פוטר מותר לכתחילה הוא ואמר טעמא מאן דרכה למיפק בכובלת אשה שריחה רע ולא שלפא ומחויא גנותה: למטה מן הסבכה. כגון כיפה של צמר: יוצאה בה. דלא חיישינן דילמא שלפא ומחוויא דמיגלי שערה ומגניא בה שהשבכה נוי הוא לשער: מתני' סלע. מטבע הוא: צינית. מפרש בגמ': הבנות קטנות. שמנקבות אזניהם ואין עושין נזמים עד שיגדלו ונותנין חוטין או קסמים באזניהם שלא יסתמו אזניהם לוי"ה: ואפילו. רבותא קאמר דלע"ג דלאו תכשיט נוי הוא אורחא בהכי ולא משאוי הוא ויש מפרשין חוטין שקולעת בהן שערה דאסרינן לגדולה בריש פרקין התם משום דשכיחא בהו טבילה אבל קטנות דלא שכיחא בהו טבילה שרי ולשון ראשון הגון מזה חדא דקטנות נמי צריכות טבילה לטומאת מגע משום טהרות ואף נדות נמי שכיחות בהו כדתניא (נדה דף לב.) מעשה שהיה והטבילוה קודם לאמה ועוד מדקתני אפי' בקיסמין איכא למישמע דחוטין נמי אאזנים קיימי דאי חוטי הראש לא שייך למיתני אפי' בקסמין: ערביות. נשים ישראליות שבערב: יוצאות רעולות. דרך ערביות להיות מעוטפות ראשן ופניהם חוץ מן העינים וקרי לה בלשון ערבי רעולות היינו הרעלות דכתיב גבי תכשיטי נשים בספר ישעיה (ג): מדיות. נשים ישראליות שבמדי: פרופות. שמעטפות בטלית ותולה הרלועה בשפתה האחת כנגד צוארה ובשפתה השנית כורכת אבן או אגוז וקושרת הרלועה בכרך ואין הטלית נופל מעליה: פורפת. כמו קרסים דמתרגמינן פורפין כל המחבר בגד לחבירו קרי פריפה: ובלבד שלא תפרוף לכתחלה בשבת. ובגמ' פריך והאמרת רישא פורפת: גמ' בת ארעא. מכה שהיא תחת פרסת הרגל וקושר בה סלע לרפואה: דאקושא. שהיא קשה ומגינה על המכה מקוצים ויתדות דרכים: שוכתא. ליחלוחית היוצא מן הכסף ובלע"ז רוי"ל ויפה למכה שוכתא כמו דשתך טפי דאלו מגילות (ב"מ דף כו.) ומשתכין כנחשת דתענית (דף ח.): ליעבד טסא. דכספא טיבעא למה לי אלא משום צורתא דטיבעא מעליא למכה ולאו שוכתא: ליעבד פולסא. עגול של עץ ויצור עליו: אמר אביי ש"מ. ממתני' דנקט סלע: כולהו בהדדי מעלו לה. ולהכי נקט סלע דאיתנהו לכולהו אקושא ושוכתא וצורתא: לא שביק להו לבנתיה כו'. מפרש לקמן טעמא דכולהו: גניאן גבי הדדי. ליישן זו אצל זו בעודן בתולות: מקואות ביומי ניסן. של מים מכונסין או סמוך לנהר וממשיך לתוכן מי הנהר וטובלות שם: ומפצי ביומי תשרי. שטובלות בפרת ומפני הטיט שלא יהא חציצה נותנות המפץ תחת רגליהן: דצבעונין. וחיישי למישלף ואחויי: המסוללות. מתחככות משום תאות תשמיש:
פסולות

אמר רב כל מקום שאסרו חכמים כו'. י"מ דאין הלכה כרב מדתני בחולין (דף מא.) אין שוחטין לתוך גומא ברשות הרבים שלא יחקה האפיקורסים ובחצר מותר ומיהו אין זה ראיה דבחצר מותר דאף הרואה אותו אומר לנקר חצרו הוא צריך אבל בעלמא שאם יראה אדם הרואה יחשדנו אפילו בחדרי חדרים אסור:

ליעבד לה פולסא. פ"ה חתיכה של עץ ויצור עליה צורה ולפירושו (ב) ניחא מה שמקשים דבעלמא אמר ט) מאי אסימון פולסא ופ"ה התם היינו דבר שאין עליו צורה וקשה דהכא משמע דפולסא הוא דבר שיש עליו צורה ולפירש"י ניחא דפירש ליעבד פולסא בלא צורה ויצור עליו הצורה אבל לפר"ת קשה דפירש אסימון הוי של מתכת ויש עליו צורה אבל אינה חשובה ואינה יוצאה אם כן הכא מאי איריא סלע אפילו אסימון ושמא י"ל דצורת סלע צריך:

ומפצי ביומי תשרי. פ"ה מפני הטיט שלא יהיה חציצה ונותנות המפץ תחת רגליהן ורבינו תם פירש שהיו נותנות מפצי זקופות שלא יראו אותן העולם ויתביישו מהם ולא יטבלו היטב י):
פסולות

מסורת הש"ס

א) ביצה ט. [לקמן קמו:], ב) [ג"א אליעזר], ג) [גיר' הערוך ערך דר ג' דדור שיני ע"ש], ד) [לעיל סב. תוספתא פ"ה ע"ש], ה) [לעיל מ:], ו) [נדרים מ:] בכורות נה: נדה סז., ז) יבמות עו., ח) [עיין תוספות לקמן קמו: ד"ה מי שנשרו ותוספות ביצה ט. ד"ה מי. שהשיגו על פרש"י דהכא אבל לקמן קמו: במשנה ובביצה ט: עולה פירושו כפירוש דהכא], ט) [ב"מ מז:], י) [וע"ע תוס' נדה סז: ד"ה משום].

הגהות הב"ח

(א) רש"י ד"ה אבל של כסף וכו' ומאי שנא רבי דקא שרי ליה משום דלא אתיא לאחווי רבנן נמי: (ב) תוס' ד"ה ליעבד וכו' ולפירושו. נ"ב ובתוס' פ' כל מערבין דף לא ע"ב כתבו בענין אחר ע"ש בד"ה שפלאו:

ליקוטי רש"י

שוטחן בחמה. ליבשן [לקמן קמו: עיי"ש עוד ובמסורה"ש כאן]. מי שנשרו כליו בדרך במי גשמים שוטחן בחמה והן נוגבין מאליהן. אבל לא כנגד העם. שלא יאמרו כבסן בשבת אלמא מידי דמשום מראית העין מותר במקום צנוע [ביצה ט.]. שיחשדוהו שכבסן [לקמן שם]. בכובלת. מומרתא דפילון, קשר שקושר בו סם ששמו פילון וריחו ערב ובלע"ז בלסמ"ו ואשה שריחה רע טוענתו עליה [לעיל סב.]. בוטון שהנשים תולות בצואריהן של זהב או של כסף ונותן בו שמן שמעורב בו מין בושם ששמו פילון ודומה לעלי גפנים כדתניא בת"כ שלא יערב קימום במר מי גלובקיא בשמן עלי גפנים בפילון [גיטין סט:]. פלייטון. בלסמ"א משחא דאפרסמא [לעיל שם]. בושם שריחו נודף ואינו אפרסמון [סנהדרין קח. וע"ש במלוא הרועים]. רעולות. לניף שמלניפות כל פרצופיהם חוץ מגלגל העין ל"א והרעלות מיני סרבלים נאים להתעטף בהן ובל' משנה יש מדיות רעולות במס' שבת [ישעיה ג, יט]. רעל לשון עטיפה הוא כמו והברושים הרעלו (נחום ב) ובלשון משנה מדיות רעולות [תהלים ס, ה]. מעוטפין ודומה לו (ישעיה ג) הנטיפות והשרות והרעלות ובל' משנה שנינו מדיות רעולות מסכת שבת [נחום ב, ד]. בת ארעא וכו'. ומי שיש לו מכה בפיסת רגלו מתחת קושר מהם שם דמעליא ליה אלודה דידהו ולורתא דידהו כדאמרינן במסכת שבת [כתובות צג.]. פולסא. מסוכר לורה וקורין לו פלדו"ן [ב"מ מז: ועיין תוס' כאן]. ביומי ניסן. מקוה מים [זוחלין] נובעים בבית ולא היה מניחן לטבול בנהרות [בכורות נה:]. מקוה מים מכונסין ואין טובלות בנהר [נדה סז.]. שמפני שהיה חושש להפשרת שלגים לא היה מניחן לטבול בזוחלין [ר"ן נדרים מ:]. ומפצי ביומי תשרי. שבתשרי מתמעטין הנהרות מן כל ימות השנה ומעלין טיט והיה נותן המפץ בקרקעית הנהר שלא יכנס הטיט ברגליהן ויהא חציצה [רש"י נדרים שם]. כשהיו טובלות בנהר ביומי תשרי הי' עושה להם מחצלות של קנים שקורין קלויי"ש ומשליכן לתוך המים ועומדות עליהן וטובלות לפי שבימי תשרי יש טיט רק בנהרות אבל שפתם וחושש שמא יעלה הטיט ויהיה חוצץ [בכורות שם]. שטובלין בנהר שהזוחלין מרובין אבל מפני חלילת הטיט נותן מחצלות בנהר שעוברות עליהן [נדה שם]. בנהר היה נותן תחת כפות רגליהן משום טיט דלא ליהוי חציצה א"נ לצניעותא בעלמא והיה מניחן לטבול בנהר משום דליכא למיחש (לזוחלין) [לנוטפין] ומאי דקאמר ביומי ניסן מניחן ועד תשרי קאמר וכ"ש בימות הגשמים כך פירשו ואין הלשון נוח לי דהוה ליה למימר עביד להו מקוואות לבנתיה כולה שתא ומפצי ביומי תשרי לפיכך נ"ל דבנתיה דאבוה דשמואל בשתא לא היו טובלות בנהר משום לנה אלא במקוואות שבבתיהן וביומי ניסן דרוית עלמא היו מתחילות לטבול בנהרות והיה מתקן להם אביהם שם בתחילת ניסן מקוואות שהיו טובלות בהן עד תשרי וביומי תשרי לא היה מצריכן למקוואות משום דליכא למיחש לנוטפין ולפיכך היה מתקן להן מפצי וכשעוברין ימי תשרי כבר היו חוזרות לטבול בבתיהם משום לנה [ר"ן נדרים שם]. המסוללות. דרך תשמיש זכר ונקבה משפשפות נקבתן זו לזו וכן המסוללת בבנה קטן דסנהדרין (סט:) [יבמות עו.].

עין משפט נר מצוה

סו א ב ג ד מיי' פי"ט מהל' שבת הלכה יד סמג לאוין סה טוש"ע א"ח סי' שג סעיף טו:
סז ה ו מיי' שם הל' ז טוש"ע שם סעי' יג:
סח ז מיי' שם הלכה יג סמג שם טוש"ע א"ח סימן שא סעיף כח:
סט ח מיי' שם הלכה יב סמג שם טוש"ע א"ח סימן שג סעיף כ:
ע ט מיי' שם טוש"ע א"ח סעיף כד:
עא י מיי' פ"א מהל' מקוואות הלכה יא טוש"ע י"ד סימן קצח סעיף לג:
עב כ מיי' פי"ט מהל' שבת הל' י סמג לאוין סה טוש"ע א"ח סימן שג סעיף כ:
עג ל מיי' פכ"א מהל' איסורי ביאה הלכה ח סמג לאוין קמ טוש"ע אה"ע סי' כ סעיף ב:

רבינו חננאל

שוטחן בחמה אבל לא כנגד העם ור' אלעזר ורבי שמעון אוסרין ואיתו דאמר כר' אלעזר ורבי שמעון: במוך שבאזנה תני רמי [בר יחזקאל] והוא שקשור באזנה. ובמוך שבסנדלה והוא שקשור בעקבה. במוך שהתקינה לנדתה והוא שקשור בירכותיה ורבא אמר אע"פ שאינו קשור כיון דמאים לה לא אתיא לאחוויה. אמר רבא עשתה לה בית יד מותר. פי' בית יד שעושה לידה שתכסה אותה כדי שתבדוק מוך לנדה ולא תגע בו ולא תטנף בו. והא דאמר במוך שבאזנה ותני רמי בר יחזקאל והוא שקשור באזנה אוקמה במהדק ואי לא מהדק אסור: ושן תותבת של כסף דברי הכל מותר: ר' שמתיר בשל זהב וזה ור' אלעזר שמתיר בצלוחית של פלייטון ור' שמעון בן אלעזר שמתיר בכל שהוא למטה מן הסבכה אלו כולן סבירא להו כל מידי דגנאי הוא לא אתא לאחוויה ולית הלכתא כחד מינייהו: מתני' יוצאה בסלע שעל הצינית סלעיא שיש עליה צורת מטבע ומעלא לצינית שהוא מכה תחת הרגל. צינית בת ארעא. הבנות יוצאות בחוטין אפילו בקסמים שבאזניהן. בנתיה דאבוה דשמואל תלתא גווני צבעונים הוו חוטי דידהו ולא שביק להו למיפק בהו דסבר דילמא שלפא ומחויא לחברתה

גליון הש"ס

תוס' ד"ה אמר רב וכו' מדתני בחולין. ראיה זו כתבו תוספות בחולין בשם ירושלמי:

Gemara The Gemara inquires after the identity of a *tzinis*: מַאי צִינִית – **What is a *tzinis*?**

The Gemara answers:

בַּת אַרְעָא – It is **a wound on the sole of the foot** upon which a *sela* is bound for therapeutic reasons. Since this coin is being used for healing, it is not considered a burden, and one may go out with it on the Sabbath.

The Gemara questions why the Mishnah specifies a coin:

וּמַאי שְׁנָא סֶלַע – **And what is special about a *sela*** that the Mishnah specifies its use? אִילֵימָא כָּל מִידִי דְּאַקּוּשָׁא מְעַלֵּי לָהּ – **If you will say** that **anything that is hard is beneficial for [the wound],** since it protects it,[25] לֵיעֲבֵד לָהּ חַסְפָּא – then **let [the woman] fashion** an **earthenware** shard, which is also of hard material, into a shield **for [the wound]!** Why must she use a coin? אֶלָּא מִשּׁוּם שׁוּכְתָּא – **Rather,** then, perhaps you will say that this coin is beneficial not because it is hard, but **because** its silver generates **moisture.**[26] לֵיעֲבֵד לָהּ טַסָּא – But then **let her fashion** silver **plating** into a covering **for [the wound]!** Why must she use minted coinage? אֶלָּא מִשּׁוּם צוּרְתָא – **Rather,** then, perhaps you will say that the *sela* is beneficial not because of its moisture, but **because of the image** stamped upon it.[27] לֵיעֲבֵד לָהּ פּוּלְסָא – But then **let her fashion a disk** of wood into a covering **for [the wound]** and etch an image into it![28] Why must she use a coin?

The Gemara concludes:

אָמַר אַבַּיֵי – **Abaye said:** שְׁמַע מִינָּהּ כּוּלְּהוּ מְעַלִּין לָהּ – **We learn from this** that only an object combining **all [these three]** qualities (i.e. hardness, moisture and a graven image) **is beneficial for [this wound].** However, an object with only one or two of these qualities will not heal this wound; since it would accordingly be considered a burden, one may not go out with it on the Sabbath. The Mishnah therefore specifies a *sela* for this wound.[29]

The Mishnah states:

הַבָּנוֹת יוֹצְאוֹת בְּחוּטִין – THE [YOUNG] GIRLS MAY GO OUT WITH THREADS ... [in their ears].

The Gemara recounts the practice of the father of Shmuel regarding this issue and two others:

אֲבוּהּ דִּשְׁמוּאֵל לֹא שָׁבִיק לְהוּ לִבְנָתֵיהּ דְּנָפְקֵי בְּחוּטִין – **The father of Shmuel did not let his daughters go out** on the Sabbath **with threads** in their ears, וְלָא שָׁבִיק לְהוּ גַּנְיָאן גַּבֵּי הֲדָדֵי – **and did not let them sleep next to one another** while they were virgins. וְעָבִיד לְהוּ מִקְוָאוֹת בְּיוֹמֵי נִיסָן – **And he prepared *mikvaos* for them** to immerse in **during the days of Nissan,** rather than allow them to immerse in the Euphrates River,[30] וּמַפָּצֵי בְּיוֹמֵי תִשְׁרֵי – **and mats** for immersing in the Euphrates **during the days of Tishrei.**[31]

The Gemara questions the first ruling of the father of Shmuel:

לֹא שָׁבִיק לְהוּ יוֹצְאוֹת בְּחוּטִין – **He did not let [his daughters] go out with threads** in their ears. וְהָאֲנַן תְּנַן – **But our Mishnah has taught:** הַבָּנוֹת יוֹצְאוֹת בְּחוּטִין – THE [YOUNG] GIRLS MAY GO OUT WITH THREADS in their ears! Why then did Shmuel's father forbid his daughters to do so?

The Gemara answers:

בְּנָתֵיהּ דַּאֲבוּהּ דִּשְׁמוּאֵל דִּצְבְעוֹנִין הֲוו – **[The threads]** worn by **the daughters of the father of Shmuel were colored ones,** so he feared that his daughters would remove the threads in order to show them to their companions, and inadvertently carry them.[32]

The Gemara addresses the second ruling of the father of Shmuel:

לָא שָׁבִיק לְהוּ גַּנְיָאן גַּבֵּי הֲדָדֵי – **He did not let them sleep next to one another** while they were yet virgins. לֵימָא מְסַיַּיע לֵיהּ לְרַב הוּנָא – **Let us say that [this practice] supports** the statement made by **Rav Huna.** דְּאָמַר רַב הוּנָא – **For Rav Huna said:** נָשִׁים הַמְסוֹלְלוֹת זוֹ בָּזוֹ – **Women who rub one another** to satisfy a desire for sexual intercourse

NOTES

25. From thorns and from nails on the road (*Rashi*).

26. Which promotes healing (*Rashi*).

27. [It was widely believed in earlier times that certain graven images were useful in healing (see *Rashba, Responsa* §413).]

28. *Rashi*; cf. *Tosafos*; see there for *Tosafos'* version of *Rashi*.

29. *Rashi,* as explained by *Rosh Yosef.* We see from this ruling that an object bound to a wound for no other reason than to protect it is viewed as a burden. One therefore would not be permitted to go out with such an object on the Sabbath unless it also serves to heal the wound (see *Orach Chaim* 301:28 with *Magen Avraham* and *Pri Megadim;* see also *Mishnah Berurah* ibid. §108).

30. The Gemara below will explain the reasons for these practices (*Rashi*).

31. The mats were intended to prevent the mud on the river bottom from covering the girls' feet and thus invalidating their immersion through interposition [חֲצִיצָה] (*Rashi;* cf. *Tosafos,* et al.; see also *Rambam, Mikvaos* 1:11 and 9:13). [It will become clear in the course of the Gemara why they immersed in the Euphrates only during the days of Tishrei.]

32. [The threads discussed in our Mishnah, by contrast, are plain ones, which a girl would have no reason to show her companion.]

[Although *Rashi* to the Gemara above (59b) rules that a woman generally will not remove her earrings to show them to her companions, he speaks there of a married woman, who customarily binds her hair with a kerchief that reaches till below her ears. She therefore will not show her earrings, since it is too much trouble for her to loosen the knots of the kerchief and remove the earrings. The daughters of the father of Shmuel, however, were maidens, and therefore did not cover their hair; since it was therefore no trouble for them to remove the colorful threads, their father forbade them to wear them (see *Magen Avraham* 303:16; see *Beur Halachah* to 303:20 ד״ה אבל אם הם צבועים; see also *Tosafos* above, 59b ד״ה נזמי).]

שוטחן בחמה אבל לא כנגד העם רבי אליעזר ורבי שמעון אוסרין: ובמוך שבאזנה: תני רמי בר יחזקאל והוא שקשור באזנה: ובמוך שבסנדלה: תני רמי בר יחזקאל והוא שקשור לה בסנדלה: ובמוך שהתקינה לה לנדתה: סבר רמי בר חמא למימר והוא שקשורה לה בין ירכותיה אמר רבא אע"פ שאינו קשור לה כיון דמאים לא אתיא לאיתויי בעא מיניה רבי ירמיה מרבי אבא עשתה לה בית יד מהו א"ל מותר איתמר [נמי] אמר רב נחמן בר אושעיא א"ר יוחנן עשתה לה בית יד מותר רבי יוחנן נפיק בהו לבי מדרשא וחלוקין עליו חבריו רבי ינאי נפיק בהו לכרמלית וחלוקין עליו כל דורו והתני רמי בר יחזקאל והוא שקשור לה באזנה לא קשיא הא דמיהדק הא דלא מיהדק: בפלפל ובגלגל מלח: פלפל לריח הפה גלגל מלח לדורשיני: וכל דבר שנותנת לתוך פיה: זנגבילא אי נמי דרצונא: שן תותבת שן של זהב רבי מתיר וחכמים אוסרין: א"ר זירא לא שנו אלא של זהב אבל בשל כסף דברי הכל מותר תניא נמי הכי בשל כסף ד"ה מותר של זהב רבי מתיר וחכמים אוסרין אמר אביי רבי ור' אליעזר ור' שמעון בן אלעזר כולהו סבירא להו דכל מידי דמיגניא ביה לא אתיא לאחויי רבי הא דאמרן ר' אליעזר דתניא ר' אליעזר פוטר בכובלת ובצלוחית של פלייטון ר' שמעון בן אלעזר דתניא כלל אמר רבי שמעון בן אלעזר כל שהוא למטה מן הסבכה יוצאה בו למעלה מן הסבכה אינה יוצאה בו:

מתני' יוצאה בסלע שעל הצינית הבנות קטנות יוצאות בחוטין ואפי' בקיסמין שבאזניהם ערביות יוצאות רעולות ומדיות פרופות וכל אדם אלא שדברו חכמים בהוה פורפת על האבן ועל האגוז ועל המטבע ובלבד שלא תפרוף לכתחלה בשבת: גמ' מאי צינית בת ארעא ומאי שנא סלע אילימא כל מידי דאקושא מעלי לה ליעבד לה חספא אלא משום שוכתא ליעבד לה טסא אלא משום צורתא ליעבד לה פולסא אמר אביי שמע מינה כולהו מעלין לה: הבנות יוצאות בחוטין: אבוה דשמואל לא שביק להו לבנתיה דנפקי בחוטין ולא שביק להו גניאן גבי הדדי ועביד להו מקואות ביומי ניסן ומפצי ביומי תשרי לא שביק להו יוצאות בחוטין והאנן תנן הבנות יוצאות בחוטין בנתיה דאבוה דשמואל דצבעונין הוו לא שביק להו גניאן גבי הדדי לימא מסייע ליה לרב הונא דאמר ר"ה נשים המסוללות זו בזו פסולות

רש"י

שוטחן בחמה. מי שנשרו כליו בדרך במי גשמים: אבל לא כנגד העם. שלא יאמרו כבסן בשבת האי תנא סבר דמידי דמשום מראית העין מותר בחדרים: אוסרין. כרב: עשתה לו בית יד. למוך שבאזנו מקום מהו למיסריה דילמא שקלה וממטיא לה בידים דלא מאים לאוחזה בבית יד שלה: עשתה לה בית יד מותר. דלא אמרינן לא מאים אלא אפילו בבית יד מאים: רבי יוחנן נפיק ביה לבי מדרשא. במוך שבאזנו שהיה זקן והיתה לו צואת האזן מרובה: וחלוקין עליו חבריו. מפני שלא היה קשור באזנו והוא יוצא בו לרה"ר: הא דמיהדק. דר' יוחנן היה תוחב באזנו יפה ומהדק ולא בעי קשירה ודרמי בר יחזקאל בדלא מיהדק ל"א מתלמידי רבינו הלוי דרבי יוחנן קשור הוה ובית מדרשו סמוך לביתו הוה ולא היתה רה"ר מפסקת: והא תני רמי והוא שקשור כו'. וכי קשור מיהא אפילו לרה"ר מותר ואמאי קאמר לבי מדרשו ולא קאמר לרשות הרבים ומשני דר' יוחנן קשור ולא מיהדק הקשר ולשון ראשון מיושב מזה: לדורשיני. לחולי השינים: זנגבילא. גינזירו: דרצונא. קנמון: לא שנו. דחכמים אוסרין אלא של זהב שמשונה במראה משאר שינים ודילמא מבזו לה ושקלה לה בידה וממטיא: אבל של כסף. שדומה לשאר השינים דברי הכל מותר לשון רבותי ולי נראה טעמא דשל זהב משום דחשיבא ואתי' לאחווי לכך אסור אבל של כסף לא חשיבא ולא אתי' לאחווי וללשון רבותי קשיא לי הא דאמר אביי רבי ור"ש בן אלעזר כו' ואי טעמא דרבנן משום דחייכי עלה הוא מאי שנא רבי (א) דקחשיב ליה רבנן נמי לאו לאחווי חיישי ויש לתרץ דרבנן מיסר קאסרי מכל מקום ורבי מתיר דקסבר לא חייכו עלה ולא שלפא להו ומיהו ה"ל למיחש דלמא שלפא לה משום אחווי אלא לא שלפא משום דלאי מחוי לה גנותא היא: רבי הא דאמרן. דלא חייש דילמא שלפא: פוטר בכובלת. ואוקימנא דהאי פוטר מותר לכתחילה הוא ואמר טעמא מאן דרכה למיפק בכובלת אשה שריחה רע ולא שלפא ומחויא גנותה: למטה מן הסבכה. כגון כיפה של צמר: יוצאה בה. דלא חיישינן דילמא שלפא ומחויא דמיגלי שערה ומגניא בה שהסבכה נוי הוא לשער: מתני' סלע. מטבע הוא: צינית. מפרש בגמ': הבנות קטנות. שמנקבות אזניהם ואין עושין נזמים עד שיגדלו ונותנין חוטין או קסמים באזניהם שלא יסתמו אזניהם לר"ה: ואפילו. רבותא קאמר דאע"ג דלאו תכשיט נוי הוא אורחא בהכי ולא משאוי הוא ויש מפרשין חוטין שקולעת בהן שערה דאסרינן לגדולה בריש פרקין התם משום דשכיחא בהו טבילה אבל קטנות דלא שכיחא בהו טבילה שרי ולשון ראשון הגון מזה חדא דקטנות נמי צריכות טבילה לטומאת מגע משום טהרות ואף נדות נמי שכיחות בהו כדתניא (נדה דף לב.) מעשה שהיה והטבילוה קודם לאמה ועוד מדקתני אפי' בקיסמין איכא למישמע דחוטין נמי באזנים קיימי דאי חוטי הראש לא שייך למיתני אפי' בקסמין: ערביות. נשים ישראליות שבערב: יוצאות רעולות. דרך ערביות להיות מעוטפות ראשן ופניהם חוץ מן העינים וקרי לה בלשון ערבי רעולות היינו הרעלות דכתיב גבי תכשיטי נשים בספר ישעיה (ג): מדיות. נשים ישראליות שבמדי: פרופות. שמעטפות בטלית ותולה הרלועה בשפתה האחת כנגד צוארה ובשפתה השנית כורכת אבן או אגוז וקושרת הרלועה בכרך ואין הטלית נופל מעליה: פורפת. כמו קרסים דמתרגמינן פורפין כל המחבר בגד לחבירו קרי פריפה: ובלבד שלא תפרוף לכתחלה בשבת. ובגמ' פריך והאמרת רישא פורפת: גמ' בת ארעא. מכה שהיא תחת פרסת הרגל וקושר בה סלע לרפואה: דאקושא. שהיא קשה ומגינה על המכה מקוצים ויתדות דרכים: שוכתא. ליחלוחית היוצא מן הכסף ובלע"ז רוי"ל ויפה למכה שוכתא כמו דשתך טפי דלאו מגילות (ב"מ דף כו.) ומשתכין כנחשת דתענית (דף ח.): ליעבד טסא. דכספא טיבעא למה לי אלא משום צורתא דטיבעא מעליא למכה ולאו שוכתא: ליעבד פולסא. עגול של עץ ויצור עליו: אמר אביי ש"מ. ממתני' דנקט סלע: כולהו בהדדי מעלו לה. ולהכי נקט סלע דאיתנהו לכולהו אקושא ושוכתא וצורתא: לא שביק להו לבנתיה כו'. מפרש לקמן טעמא דכולהו: גניאן גבי הדדי. לישן זו אצל זו בעודן בתולות: מקואות ביומי ניסן. של מים מכונסין או סמוך לנהר וממשיך לתוכן מי הנהר וטובלות שם: ומפצי ביומי תשרי. שטובלות בפרת ומפני הטיט שלא יהא חלילה נותנות המפץ תחת רגליהן: דצבעונין. וחיים למישלף ואחווי: המסוללות. מתחככות משום תאות תשמיש:
פסולות

תוספות

אמר רב כל מקום שאסרו חכמים כו'. י"מ דאין הלכה כרב מדתני בחולין (דף מא.) אין שוחטין לתוך גומא ברשות הרבים שלא יחקה האפיקורסים ובחצר מותר ומיהו אין זה ראיה דבחצר מותר דאף הרואה אותו אומר לנקר חצרו הוא צריך אבל בעלמא שאם יראה אדם הרואה יחשדנו אפילו בחדרי חדרים אסור:

ליעבד לה פולסא. פ"ה חתיכה של עץ ויצור עליה צורה ולפירושו (ב) ניחא מה שמקשים דבעלמא אמר מאי אסימון פולסא ופ"ה התם היינו דבר שאין עליו צורה וקשה דהכא משמע דפולסא הוא דבר שיש עליו צורה ולפירש"י ניחא דפירש ליעבד פולסא בלא צורה ויצור עליו הצורה אבל לפיר"ת קשה דפירש אסימון הוי של מתכת ויש עליו צורה אבל אינה חשובה ואינה יוצאה אם כן הכא מאי איריא סלע אפילו אסימון ושמא י"ל דצורת סלע צריך:

ומפצי ביומי תשרי. פ"ה מפני הטיט שלא יהיה חלילה ונותנות המפץ תחת רגליהן ורבינו תם פירש שהיו נותנות מפצי זקופות שלא יראו אותן העולם ויתביישו מהם ולא יטבלו היטב:
פסולות

מסורת הש"ס

א) ביצה ט. [לקמן קמו:], ב) [נ"ל אלעזר], ג) [גיר' הערוך ערך דר ה' לדור שיני ע"ש], ד) [לעיל סב. תוספתא פ"ה ע"ש], ה) [לעיל מ:], ו) [נדרים מ:] בכורות נה: נדה סז., ז) יבמות עו., ח) [עיין תוספות לקמן קמו: ד"ה מי שנשרו ותוספות ביצה לה: ד"ה מי. שהשיגו על פרש"י דהכא אבל לקמן קמו: במשנה וביצה לה: עולה פירושו כפירוש תוספות וביצה ט. פרש"י כדהכא], ט) [ב"מ מז:], י) [וע"ע תוס' נדה סו: ד"ה אשה].

הגהות הב"ח

(א) רש"י ד"ה אבל של כסף וכו' ומאי שנא רבי דקא שרי ליה משום דלא אתיא לאחווי רבנן נמי: (ב) תוס' ד"ה ליעבד וכו' ולפירושו. נ"ב ובתוס' פ' בכל מערבין דף לא ע"ב כתבו בענין אחר ע"ש בד"ה שפדאו:

ליקוטי רש"י

שוטחן בחמה. ליבשן [לקמן קמו: עיי"ש עוד ובמסוה"ש כאן]. מי שנשרו כליו בדרך במי גשמים שוטחן בחמה והן נוגבין מאליהן. אבל לא כנגד העם. שלא יאמרו כבסן בשבת אלמא מידי דמשום מראית העין מותר במקום צנוע [ביצה ט.]. שיחשדוהו שכבסן [לקמן שם]. בכובלת. מומרתא דפילון, קשר שקשור בו סם ששמו פילון וריחו ערב ובלע"ז בלסמ"ו ולאשה שריחה רע טוענתו עליה [לעיל סב.]. כוטון שהנשים תולות בצואריהן של זהב או של כסף ונותן בו שמן שמעורב בו מין בושם ששמו פליטון ודומה לעלי גפנים כדמיה בת"כ שלא יערב קיומו כמו מי גלובקיה בשמן של גפנים פליטון [גיטין סט.]. פלייטון. בלסמ"א משחא דאפרסמא [לעיל שם]. בושם שריחו נודף והיינו אפרסמון [סנהדרין קח. וע"ש במלוא הרועים]. רעולות. לניף שמעטיפות כל פרצופיהם חוץ מגלגל העין ל"א והרעלות מיני פרצלים נאים להתעטף בהן ובל' משנה יש מדיות רעולות במס' שבת [ישעיה ג, יט]. רעל לשון עטיפה הוא כמו והברושים הרעלו (נחום ב) ובלשון משנה מדיות רעולות [תהלים ס, ה]. מעוטפין ודומה לו (ישעיה ג) הנטיפות והשרות והרעלות ובל' משנה שנינו מדיות רעולות מסכת שבת [נחום ב, ד]. בת ארעא וכו'. ומי שיש לו מכה בפיסת רגלו מתחת קושר מהם שם דמעליא ליה סלודה דידהו וצורתא דידהו כדאמרינן במסכת שבת [כתובות צג.]. פולסא. מטבע צורה וקורין לו פלדו"ן [ב"מ מז: ועיין תוס' כאן]. ביומי ניסן. מקוה מים חיים [זוחלין] טובעים בבית ולא היה מניין לטבול בנהרות [בכורות נה:]. מקוה מים מכונסין ואין טובלות בנהר [נדה סו.]. שמפני שהיה חושש להפשרת שלגים לא היה מניחן לטבול בזוחלין [ר"ן נדרים מ:]. ומפצי ביומי תשרי. שבתשרי מתמעטין הנהרות מן כל ימות השנה ומעלין טיט והיה נותן המפץ בקרקעית הנהר שלא יכנס הטיט ברגליהן ויהא חלילה [רש"י נדרים שם]. כשהיו טובלות בנהר ביומי תשרי הי' עושה להם מחצלות של קנים שקורין קלויי"ש ומשליכן לתוך המים ועומדות עליהן וטובלות לפי שבימי תשרי יש טיט רך בנהרות אבל שפתם וחושש שמא יעלה טיט למעלה על רגליהן ויהיה חוצץ [בכורות שם]. שטובלין בנהר שהזוחלין מרובין אבל מפני חלילת הטיט נותן מחצלות בנהר שעוברות עליהן [נדה שם]. בנהר היה נותן תחת כפות רגליהן משום טיט דלא ליהוי חלילה א"נ לצניעותא בעלמא והיה מניחן לטבול בנהר משום דביומי תשרי ליכא למיחש (לזוחלין) [לנוטפין] ומאי דקאמר ביומי ניסן מניחן ועד תשרי קאמר וכ"ש בימות הגשמים כך פירשו ואין הלשון נוח לי דהוה ליה למימר עביד להו מקוואות לבנתיה כולה שתא ומפצי ביומי תשרי לפיכך נ"ל דבנתיה דאבוה דשמואל בקמות לא היו טובלות בנהר משום גנה אלא במקוואות שבבתיהן וביומי ניסן דרוית עלמא היו מתחילות לטבול בנהרות והיה מתקן להם אביהם שם בתחילת ניסן מקוואות שהיו טובלות בהן עד תשרי וביומי תשרי לא היה מצריכן למקוואות משום דליכא למיחש לנוטפין ולפיכך היה מתקן להן מפצי ובשעוברין ימי תשרי כבר היו חוזרות לטבול בבתיהם משום גנה [ר"ן נדרים שם]. המסוללות. דרך תשמיש זכר ונקבה משפשפות נקבתן זו לזו וכן המסוללת בבנה קטן דסנהדרין (סט:) [יבמות עו.].

עין משפט נר מצוה

סו א ב ג ד מיי' פי"ט מהל' שבת הלכה יא סמג לאוין סה טוש"ע א"ח סי' שג סעיף טו:
סז ה ו מיי' שם הל' ז טוש"ע שם סעי' יג:
סח ז מיי' שם הלכה יג סמג שם טוש"ע א"ח סימן שא סעיף כח:
סט ח מיי' שם הלכה יב סמג שם טוש"ע א"ח סימן שג סעיף כ:
ע ט מיי' שם טוש"ע שם סעיף כא:
עא י מיי' פ"א מהל' מקואות הלכה יא טוש"ע י"ד סימן קצח סעיף לג לד:
עב כ מיי' פי"ט מהל' שבת הל' י סמג לאוין סה טוש"ע א"ח סימן שג סעיף כ:
עג ל מיי' פכ"א מהל' איסורי ביאה הלכה ח סמג לאוין קכו טוש"ע אה"ע סי' כ סעיף ב:

רבינו חננאל

שוטחן בחמה אבל לא כנגד העם ור' אלעזר ורבי שמעון אוסרין ואיהו דאמר כר' אלעזר ורבי שמעון: במוך שבאזנה תני רמי [בר יחזקאל] והוא שקשור באזנה. ובמוך שבסנדלה והוא שקשור בעקבה. במוך שהתקינה לנדתה והוא שקשור בירכותיה ורבא אמר אע"פ שאינו קשור כיון דמאיס לה לא אתיא לאחוריה. אמר רבא עשתה לה בית יד מותר. פי' בית יד שעושה לידה שתכסה אותה כדי שתבדוק מוך לנדתה ולא תגע בו ולא תטנף בו. והא דאמר במוך שבאזנה ותני רמי בר יחזקאל והוא שקשור באזנה אוקמה במהדק ואי לא מהדק אסור: ושן תותבת של כסף דברי הכל מותר: ר' שמתיר בשל זהב ור' אלעזר שמתיר בצלוחית של פלייטון ור' שמעון בן אלעזר שמתיר בכל שהוא למטה מן הסבכה אלו כולן סבירא להו כל מידי דגנאי הוא לא אתא לאחוויה והני שיטה נינהו ולית הלכתא כחד מינייהו: מתני' יוצאין בסלע שעל הצינית סילעיא שיש עליה צורת מטבע ומעלא לצינית שהוא מכה תחת הרגל. ציניתא בת ארעא. הבנות יוצאות בחוטין אפילו בקסמים שבאזניהן. בנתיה דאבוה דשמואל תלתא גווני צבעונים הוו חוטי דידהו ולא שביק להו למיפק בהו סבר דילמא שלפא ומחויא לחברתה

גליון הש"ס

תוס' ד"ה אמר רב וכו' מדתני בחולין. ראיה זו כתבו תוספות בחולין בשם ירושלמי:

פסולות לכהונה לא סבר כי היכי דלא לילפן גופא נוכראה [א]ועביד להו מקוה ביומי ניסן מסייע ליה לרב דאמר רב [א] מטרא במערבא סהדא רבה פרת [ב]סבר שלא ירבו הנוטפין על הזוחלין ופליגא דשמואל דאמר שמואל נהרא מכיפיה מיברך ופליגא דידיה אדידיה דאמר שמואל אין המים מטהרין בזוחלין אלא פרת ביומי תשרי בלבד: [ג]פורפת על האבן כו': והאמרת רישא פורפת אמר אביי [ד]סיפא אתאן למטבע בעי אביי [ה]אשה מהו שתערים ותפרוף על האגוז להוציא לבנה קטן בשבת תיבעי למ"ד [ג] (א) מערימין תיבעי למאן דאמר אין מערימין תיבעי למאן דאמר מערימין בדליקה התם הוא דאי לא שרית ליה אתי לכבויי אבל הכא אי לא שרית ליה לא אתי לאפוקי או דלמא אפילו למאן דאמר אין מערימין בדליקה התם דרך הוצאה בכך אבל הכא אין דרך הוצאה בכך אימא שפיר דמי תיקו: **מתני'** [ג] הקיטע יוצא בקב שלו דברי ר' מאיר ורבי

רש"י

פסולות לכהונה. לכהן גדול דלא הויא בתולה שלימה דאע"ג דכהן גדול ביומיה לא הוה הואיל ודרך זנות חשיב ליה לאו אורח ארעא: **דלא לילפן גופא נוכראה.** ויתאוו לשכב עם איש: **מטרא במערבא.** בארץ ישראל: **סהדא רבה פרת.** פרת מעיד בדבר שהוא יורד מארץ ישראל לבבל וגדל ממי הגשמים ויודעין בני בבל שירדו גשמים בהרי ארץ ישראל ושמחים על אחיהם ואבוה דשמואל נמי כרב סבירא ליה דאמר פרת גדל ומימיו מתברכין ע"י גשמים: **וסבר שמא ירבו נוטפים.** היינו גשמים על הזוחלין הנובעין ותנן במסכת מקואות (פ"ה מ"ה) הזוחלין כמעיין והנוטפין כמקוה ושנינו בת"כ אך מעין ובור מקוה מים יכול מילא על כתפו ועשה מקוה בתחילה יהא טהור ת"ל מעיין מה מעיין בידי שמים אף מקוה בידי שמים אי מה מעיין מטהר בזוחלין אף מקוה מטהר בזוחלין תלמוד לומר אך מעיין המעיין מטהר בזוחלין ומקוה מטהר באשבורן ומהו אשבורן דקוו וקיימי לאפוקי שאם הטביל בו כלים דרך זחילתו כשהן נמשכין ויורדים למקוה לא עלתה להם טבילה דבור ומקוה כתיב דקוו וקיימי אבל נובעין מטהרין כמו שהן זוחלין ומושכין מגבוה לנמוך כדרך כל הנהרות הלכך ביומי ניסן שהנהרות גדילים ממי הגשמים של ימי החורף ומהפשרת השלגים חייש שמא ירבו הנוטפין על הזוחלין שניתוספו בנהר (ב) מן הגשמים על הזוחלים החיים ובטלו הזוחלין החיים בנוטפים ואין תורת מעיין עליהן לטהר בזוחלין אלא באשבורן ועביד להו מקוואות דקוו וקיימי ואני קבלתי מרבינו הלוי משום דספק זיבות נינהו וזבה טעונה מים חיים ואי אפשר להעמיד שמועתו משום דאמרינן[ז] חומר בזב מבזבה שהזב טעון מים חיים וזבה אינה טעונה מים חיים וחזרתי ודקדקתי לפרשה וכן נראה בעיני כמו שפירשתי ורובא דעלמא מפרשים נוטפין כשאובין ולאו מילתא היא דתנן הנוטפין כמקוה: דהוו להו שאובין ל"ג: **מכיפיה מיברך.** משפתו וממקורו ומסלעו סלע מתרגמינן כיפה מכיפיה מיברך ולא ממי הגשמים: **ופליגא דידיה אדידיה.** דשמואל אשמואל: **אין המים מטהרין בזוחלין.** אין מטהרין אדם וכלים הטובלין בהן דרך זחילה וצריך להמשיכן למקוה ולטבול במקוה: **אלא פרת ביומי תשרי.** שחדלו הגשמים ורבו הזוחלין עליהם ויש תורת מעיין על נהרות המושכין אלמא סבירא ליה שגדלין ממי הגשמים ואני שמעתי בבכורות מטהרין בזוחלין שהנוטפין שבתוכן מטהרין בריבוי הזוחלין ויתבטלו הנוטפין בהן להיות זב וזבה טובלין בהן בשביל הזוחלין: **והא אמרת רישא פורפת.** והיא ודאי לכתחלה קאמר בשבת דאי מבעוד יום ולאשמועינן דיוצאה בו בשבת הא תנא רישא מדיות פרופות: **סיפא.** דקתני לא תפרוף: **אתאן למטבע.** דלאו בר טלטול הוא אבל אבן שהקצה לכך ראוי לטלטול: **להוציא לבנה הקטן.** לאוכלו: **תיבעי למאן דאמר.** פלוגתא בכל כתבי הקדש (לקמן דף קכ.) לובש כל מה שיכול ללבוש דברי רבי מאיר ואפילו עשרה חלוקים זה על זה רבי יוסי אומר שמונה עשר כלים כדרך שהוא לובש בחול: **דרך הוצאה בכך.** כגון מוכרי כסות מוציאין אותו דרך מלבוש: **מתני'** הקיטע. שנקטעה רגלו [ה]: **יוצא בקב שלו.** דמנעל דידיה הוא: ורבי

תוספות

פסולות לכהונה. פי' לכהונה גדולה דלאו בתולה שלימה היא ואע"ג דכהן גדול בימי [ו]שמואל לא הוה היה מחמיר וי"מ משום זונה ופסולות אף לכהן הדיוט וכן משמע בפ' הערל (יבמות עו.) דקאמר התם לית הלכתא [לא כברא ולא] כאבא (עד דקאמר) [וקאמר] ואפילו לרבי אלעזר דאמר פנוי הבא על הפנויה שלא לשם אישות עשאה זונה כו' משמע דטעמא משום זונה: **סהדא** רבה פרת. פי' הקונטרס פרת מעיד (ג) שהוא יורד מא"י לבבל וגדל ממי גשמים ולא נהירא שהרי בבל במזרח א"י קאי וכל הנהרות יורדים ממזרח למערב לכך פר"ת שהיו מכירים שירדו הגשמים לא"י ע"י שחוזר פרת לאחוריו על ידי גדילתו בא"י מתוך הגשמים: **שמא** ירבו הנוטפים. פירוש מי גשמים על מי נהרות שהיו זוחלין והוו להו מקוה ואמרינן דאין מקוה מטהר בזוחלין כ"א באשבורן דתנן במסכת מקוואות (פ"ה מ"ה) הזוחלין כמעיין והנוטפין כמקוה ותניא בת"כ יכול מילא מים על כתיפו ועשאו מקוה בתחילה יהא טהור תלמוד לומר מעיין מה מעיין בידי שמים אף מקוה בידי שמים אי מה מעיין מטהר בזוחלין אף מקוה מטהר בזוחלין פי' אף בזוחלין וכ"ש באשבורן תלמוד לומר אך מעיין מטהר בזוחלין ומקוה באשבורן ומהו אשבורן דקוו וקיימי ויש מפרשים שלא היה רוצה להטבילן בהן משום דהוו להו ספק זבות וזב וזבה טעונים מים חיים ושמא ירבו הנוטפין והוו להו מכונסין ולא נהירא חדא דמ"מ עביד להו מקוואות והא בעינן מים חיים ועוד (דבת"כ) [דבתוספתא פ"ג דזבים] קאמר חומר בזב מבזבה שהזב טעון מים חיים והזבה אינה טעונה מים חיים וא"ת ולשמואל דאמר אין המים מטהרין בזוחלין אלא פרת ביומי תשרי זב דבעי מים חיים איך יטבול ביומי ניסן וי"ל במעיין מכוסה שאין מי גשמים יורדין בתוכו וא"ת אמאי חיישינן שמא ירבו הנוטפים לימא קמא קמא בטיל כדאמר בפ"ה דמסכת ע"ז (דף עג.) המערה יין נסך לבור אפילו כל היום כולו כשר דאמרינן קמא קמא בטיל וי"ל דלא מהני טעמא דקמא קמא בטיל כיון שהאיסור רבה מכשיעור והתם דיין נסך דקאמר קמא קמא בטיל היינו קודם שרבה האיסור עד כדי נתינת טעם בהיתר: **דאמר** שמואל נהרא מכיפיה מיתבריך. פי' ממקומו ומסלעו סלע מתרגם כיפיה מנביעתו מיתבריך ולא ממי גשמים וא"ת והא קא חזינן שמחמת הגשמים הם גדילים וי"ל כדאמר במסכת תענית (דף כה:) שאין לך טפח יורד מלמעלה שאין טפחיים עולים כנגדו מלמטה ואור"ת דהילכתא כוותיה דשמואל ומייתי ראיה מפרק בתרא דבכורות (דף נה:) דתניא רבי מאיר אומר לא פרת שמו אלא יובל שמו ולמה נקרא שמו פרת שמימיו פרין ורבין ולאו דוקא נקט פרת דה"ה לכל נהרות והא דנקט פרת משום שהוא גדול מכל נהרות ולפי שהוא מא"י וקאמר התם מסייע ליה לשמואל דאמר נהרא מכיפיה מיתבריך ועל זה אנו סומכין לטבול בנהרות אפילו אם גדלו מאד: **הקיטע** יוצא בקב שלו. פ"ה קיטע שנקטעה רגלו עושה כמין דפוס רגל וחוקק בו מעט לשום ראש שוקו בתוכו ואינו [ס"א והוא] נסמך עליו ומש"ה יוצא בקב שלו דמנעל דידיה הוא ור' יוסי אוסר דלאו תכשיט הוא ואינו מנעל והוי משוי והקשה רבינו תם דבמסכת יומא (דף עח: ושם) משמע דלכ"ע מנעל הוא ואסור לנעול בו ביוה"כ ולענין שבת בהא הוא דפליגי דרבי יוסי גזר דילמא מיפסיק ואתי לאתויי ורבי מאיר לא גזר וי"ל דה"נ בהא פליגי דטעמא דר' יוסי דכיון דלא הוי של עור לא מיהדק ואיכא למיחש דילמא מיפסיק ואתי לאתויי אך קשה מהא דאמר בגמרא חלצה בסנדל כו' חליצתו כשרה ואמר שמואל ר"מ הוא משמע דלר' יוסי חליצתו פסולה ואמאי כיון דמנעל הוא וי"ל דהאי נמי בהא תליא דכיון דלענין שבת גזר דילמא מיפסיק אינו ראוי להלך בו ודמי לקטן שחלץ במנעל גדול דחליצתו פסולה כדאיתא בפ' מצות חליצה (יבמות קג:) משום דנעלו כתיב נעלו הראוי לו וא"ת היכי גזרי דילמא נפיל ואתי לאתויי הלא אין לו אלא רגל אחד ואי נפיל לא יזוז ממקומו ואומר ר"י דמיירי שנושא בידו מקל ועיקר הליכתו היא בסמיכת המקל והשתא אי נמי מיפסיק יוכל להלך מכאן יש להתיר למי שכווצו גידי שוקיו ללכת במקלו בשבת והרב פור"ת פי' דקיטע יש לו סמך שקושר בכרעו ומגיע לארץ והשוק כפופה לאחוריה ובראש השוק במקום הרגל עושה לו קב (ד) להראות כמו שיש לו רגל ובהא פליגי ר' יוסי סבר כיון שאינו נסמך עליו אלא תלוי באויר חיישינן דילמא נפיל ור"מ לא חייש ולפי זה אין ראיה להתיר לקיטע לצאת במקלו אמנם יש להתיר מסיפא דמתניתין דאינו אוסר אלא סמוכות שלו לפי ששוקיו תלויין באויר ודילמא נפיל ואתי לאתויי (אבל הכסא) והספסלים שבידו אינו אוסר ואינהו הוו דומיא דמקל וק"ק לפי זה אמאי מטמא ליה רבא משום מדרס כיון שאינו נסמך עליו ושמא כשהוא יושב פעמים הוא נסמך עליו ולכך עושה לו בית קבול כתיתין שלא יוזק בקשר העץ שהוא יושב: סנדל

עין משפט נר מצוה

עד א ב מיי' פ"ט מהל' מקוואות הלכה יג סמג עשין רמח טוש"ע י"ד סי' רא סעיף ג:
עה ג ד מיי' פי"ט מהל' שבת הלכה יז סמג לאוין סה טוש"ע א"ח סי' שג סעיף כג:
עו ה מיי' שם טוש"ע שם סעיף כג:

רבינו חננאל

לחברתה ולא הוה שביק להו דגנייו גבי הדדי סבר דלא לילפו גופא נוכראה (ואמר רב הונא נשים המסוללות זו בזו פסולות לכהונה) והוה עביד לבנתי' מקוה (ביום) [ביומי] ניסן ולא היה מניחן לטבול בפרת מפני שרוב מי פרת בניסן מי מטר הן כרב דאמר מטרא במערבא שהדא רבה פרת. כלומר כיון שתראה כי רבו מי פרת עדות היא שהוגשמה ארץ המערב וסבר אבוה דשמואל שמא ירבו נוטפין שהן מי גשמים הנוטפין מן הגגות ונעשו שאובין על מי הפרת שהן זוחלין כדתני במקוואות בפ' ה' הזוחלין כמעין והנוטפין כמקוה העיד ר' (יצחק) [צדוק] על הזוחלין שרבו על הנוטפין שמכשירין ושאמר שמואל נהרא מכיפיה מתברך כלומר הנהר הגדול מן הסלע שיוצא ממנו משום נרבת מליאתו ולא ממי המטר פליגא על אבוה דשמואל ועל רב ועוד דברי שמואל סותרין זה את זה בכאן אמר כי מי המטר אינם ממלאים הנהר אלא מכיפיה מיברך ועוד אמר אין המים מטהרין בזוחלין אלא פרת ביומי תשרי בלבד מכלל דבשאר החדשים זולתי תשרי נוטפין הם דגשמים רבו עליהן ומפצי ביומי תשרי הוא מסתירו לבנותיו במפצי מפני בני אדם שעל שפת הנהר וטובלת בפרת כי דברי הכל בתשרי זוחלין הן ולמה במפצי דלית להו טהרה במקוה: פורפת על האבן ועל האגוז ועל המטבע מע"ש. פי' נותנת אבן או אגוז או מטבע בקצה הסדין כמין קרס בלולאות שלא ישמט הסדין מעליה כדי שתהא מתעטפת באותו סדין ונותנת זה שעשאתו כמין קרס. נשים מדיות מנהגן לצאת בענין הזה פרופות. ובלבד שלא תפרוף בתחלה בשבת על מנהגן לצאת רעלות ופי' רעלות בירושלמי בליכריאה והן כמו כסוי פנים כדכתיב (ישעיה ג) השרות והרעלות. ר"א זוג ללמדך שבמקומות הללו כך היה מנהגם ומותר להם וכל אשר מותר בכך אלא שדברו חכמים בהווה: בעי אביי אשה מהו שתערים ותפרוף באגוז להוציא לבנה קטן בשבת ועלתה בתיקו: [מתני'] הקיטע יוצא בקב שלו דברי רבי מאיר ורבי

רב נסים גאון

קסבר שמא ירבו הנוטפין על הזוחלין. עיקר דילה בתורת כהנים אי מה מעין מטהר בזוחלין אף מקוה מטהר בזוחלין תלמוד לומר אך המעין מטהר בזוחלין והמקוה מטהר באשבורן ובמסכת מקואות (פרק ה משנה ה) הזוחלין כמעין והנוטפין כמקוה העיד רבי צדוק על הזוחלין שרבו על הנוטפין שהן כשרים ותישתכח בפרק ד' דעדיות הנוטפין שרבו על הזוחלין אינן כשירים: **תיבעי** למאן דאמר (מדליקין) [מערימין] בדליקה תיבעי למאן דאמר אין מערימין. עיקר דיליה בפרק כל כתבי הקודש (דף קכ) דתנן לובש כל שהוא יכול ללבוש ועוטף כל מה שהוא יכול להתעטף רבי יוסי אומר י"ח כלי מכלל דתנא קמא סבר מותר ללבוש ולהציל אפילו יתר מי"ח כלי ואף על פי שהוא מערים בכך:

סמיכות

מסורת הש"ס

א) נדרים מ: בכורות נה: ע"ש, ב) לקמן דספק הב"ח סימן של"ד והר"ן דהתם מיירי לתלר המעורכת קשה לפרש הך סוגיא. ואין ענין כלל להך דהכא ולמאי דכוונת הסוגיא דפליגי בתוספתא פ"ד מגילין מפני הדליקה כו' יזמין ואת"ל יגיל כו' ואין מערימין בכך ר"ח מערימין. מהרש"ל הג' ר' בנימין קארנגאלד ז"ל, ג) יומא עח: [יבמות קג:], ד) [בתוספתא מגילה פ"א ותוספתא דזבים פ"ג, ה) [ע' רש"י ברכות נח: ד"ה קטע], ו) [צ"ל אבוה דשמואל].

הגהות הב"ח

(א) גמ' תיבעי למ"ד מערימין בדליקה תיבעי למ"ד אין מערימין בדליקה תיבעי: (ב) רש"י ד"ה וסבר שמא וכו' שניתוספו בנהר מי הגשמים: (ג) תוספות ד"ה סהדא וכו' מעיד בדבר שהוא: (ד) תוס' ד"ה הקיטע וכו' עושה לו קב כמין סנדל להראות כמו שיש:

ליקוטי רש"י

פסולות לכהונה. משום זונות [יבמות עו.]. **מטרא במערבא סהדא רבה פרת.** פרת יורד מא"י לבבל וכשהגשמים יורדין בא"י מעיד פרת שהוא גדל יותר בבבל שירדו גשמים במערבא לפי שגדל מחמת הגשמים [בכורות נה:]. כשנהר פרת גדול יש עדות שגשמים שיורדין לא"י לא גבוה מכל הארצות ובאין גשמים ונוטפים בפרת ומתגדל מהן והאי דאמרי' נהרא מתגדל ממי גשמים הוי פלוגתא דשמואל [נדרים מ:]. כשירד מטר בא"י מעיד עליו פרת בבבל שהוא גדל בידוע שבא"י ירדו גשמים ונפקא מינה שאסור לטבול בו לפי שאין מי גשמים הנוטפין מטהרין בזוחלין אלא באשבורן כלומר דקוו וקיימי כדתניא בספרי כולהו מה מעין מטהר בזוחלין אף מקוה מטהר בזוחלין ת"ל אך מעין ובור מקוה מים מטהר בזוחלין ומקוה באשבורן הילכך היכא דאיכא למיחש שמא רבו נוטפין על הזוחלין אסור והיינו כשהנהר גדל הרבה אבל אם היה הולך לאטו או מתגדלה אלא מעט דליכא למיפסקי ברובא ברביית נוטפין שרי בתוספתא העיד ר' אלעזר בר צדוק על הזוחלין שרבו על הנוטפין שהם כשרים [ר"ן שם]. **סבר שלא ירבו הנוטפין על הזוחלין.** לפי שבימי ניסן רבין נוטפין על הזוחלין מחמת הגשמים שהרי על השלגים והקרח [illegible]

סלא ואפי' מי גשמי' מכונסים שלא מלינו מים חיים אלא לזב בלבד שנאמר בו מים חיים [illegible]
דוקא דכל נשים בזמן הזה זבות נינהו [רש"י שם:]. שבימות הגשמים ירדו גשמים הרבה וחייש [illegible]
מעבים לתוך הנהר שהם זוחלים דלא חזו להן משום דהוו להו ספק זבות ובזב כתיב מים חיים [illegible]
שנפלו מן העבים לקרקע ומן הקרקע זחלו וקילחו לתוך הנהר דאי לא נוטפים משום זוחלים [illegible]
ראשון דתמורה (יב.) השאובה מיטהרת בהמשכה דהיינו שממשיך מים שאובים לתוך המקוה על יד[illegible]
לפי שרבו המים בימות הגשמים מגשמים שנפלו וחייש שמא ירבו נוטפין על הזוחלין ותניא בתו[illegible]
מטהר בזוחלין אף מקוה מטהר בזוחלין כלומר שמטבילין במכונסין דרך זחילתן קודם שנקוו ונחו [illegible]
מעין מטהר בזוחלין והמקוה מטהר באשבורן ומהו אשבורן דקוו וקיימי דאין מטבילין במכונסים אלא משנקוו למקווייהם ונחו מזחילתן ותנן במסכת מקוואות (פ"ה מ"ה) הזוחלין כמעין כלומר זוחלין שבנהרות כמעין והנוטפין [illegible]
מההרים הרי הן כמקוה ואין מטהרים בזחילה הילכך בימי ניסן שנתרבה הנהר על ידי גשמים חיישינן שמא רבו נוטפין שבו על חיים שבו ובטלו זוחלין ואין מטהרין את הטמא הטובל בהן דרך זחילה וכל הנהרות לעולם הן הולכ[illegible]
להו מקוה באשבורן לטבול בתוכו יש מפרשים דבעינן מים חיים לזבה ולאו מילתא היא דתניא בתוספתא (דמגילה פ"א) חומר בזב מבזבה שהזב טעון מים חיים כו' [נדה סו.]. [המשך בדף סו.]

פְּסוּלוֹת לִכְהוּנָּה – are disqualified from marriage **to a Kohen Gadol**[1] because of their immoral behavior. Presumably, the father of Shmuel feared that his daughters might be led to engage in such behavior, and therefore forbade them to sleep together. Evidently, he agrees with Rav Huna's ruling!

The Gemara dismisses this assumption:

לֹא סָבַר כִּי הֵיכִי דְּלֹא לֵילְפָן גּוּפָא נוּכְרָאָה – No! He held that this restriction was necessary **so that [his daughters] would not become accustomed to** lying against **the body of another,** and thereby become desirous of lying with a man.[2]

The Gemara addresses the third ruling of the father of Shmuel:

וְעָבִיד לְהוּ מִקְוֶה בְּיוֹמֵי נִיסָן – And he prepared ***mikvaos* for them** to immerse in **during the days of Nissan.** **מְסַיֵּיע לֵיהּ לְרַב – This** practice **supports** the opinion of **Rav.** **דְּאָמַר רַב – For Rav said:** **מִטְרָא בְּמַעֲרָבָא** – When **rain** falls **in the West,** i.e. in Eretz Yisrael, **סַהֲדָא רַבָּה פְּרָת – the Euphrates bears great witness,**[3] as it becomes swollen with the rainwater. **סָבַר [שֶׁמָּא] (שלא)**[4] **יִרְבּוּ הַנּוֹטְפִין עַל הַזּוֹחֲלִין** – Accordingly, **[the father of Shmuel] held** that **perhaps the** volume of **rainwater** in the Euphrates **will increase** during the month of Nissan[5] **over** that of **the flowing** river **water** and nullify it,[6] giving the entire Euphrates River the legal status of rainwater. Since flowing rainwater does not purify one from *tumah* contamination,[7] the river will be rendered invalid for ritual immersion! He therefore did not allow his daughters to immerse themselves in the Euphrates, and instead built *mikvaos* for use during that period.[8]

The Gemara presents a dissenting opinion:

וּפְלִיגָא דִּשְׁמוּאֵל – And this practice of the father of Shmuel **is at odds with** the opinion **of Shmuel.** **דְּאָמַר שְׁמוּאֵל – For Shmuel said:** **נַהֲרָא מִכֵּיפֵיהּ מִיבָּרַךְ – A river is increased** primarily **from its source,**[9] not from rainwater![10] There is thus no reason to suspect that even a swollen river contains more rainwater than river water.[11]

The Gemara records an apparent contradiction in the opinion of Shmuel:

וּפְלִיגָא דִּידֵיהּ אַדִּידֵיהּ – And [Shmuel's] opinion in this matter **is at odds with his own** opinion elsewhere! **דְּאָמַר שְׁמוּאֵל – For Shmuel said:** **אֵין הַמַּיִם מְטַהֲרִין בְּזוֹחֲלִין – No flowing water**

NOTES

1. [Literally: to (one of) the priesthood (כְּהוּנָּה).]

A Kohen Gadol may not marry a woman who is not a virgin [בְּתוּלָה]. Although the lewd behavior of the women discussed by Rav Huna obviously does not constitute actual sexual intercourse [בִּיאָה], one who indulges in behavior of this sort cannot be considered pure and virginal, but bears in some degree the taint of her actions. The Kohen Gadol, by virtue of his unique holiness, was therefore forbidden [by Rabbinic decree] to enter into marital union with such a woman (*Rashi*; see *Dibros Moshe* 53:35). Although there was no Kohen Gadol in the time of the father of Shmuel, who lived after the destruction of the Holy Temple, he nonetheless deemed it necessary to guard his daughters from being led into this activity, since Rav Huna had designated it lewd and immoral behavior (*Rashi*; cf. *Tosafos*).

2. [Thus, the practice of the father of Shmuel in this matter is not necessarily in consonance with the ruling of Rav Huna. Indeed, *Rambam* (*Isurei Biah* 21:8) and *Shulchan Aruch* (*Even HaEzer* 20:2) do not rule according to Rav Huna, but permit a Kohen Gadol to marry a woman who took part in licentious behavior with another woman. However, they do forbid a woman to engage in such conduct on the basis of a specific prohibition (see there)! See *Dibros Moshe* (ibid.) at length for why the Gemara did not attribute the practice of the father of Shmuel to this prohibition.]

3. The Euphrates River [lies upon the northern boundary of Eretz Yisrael (see *Deuteronomy* 11:24 with *Ramban* and *Joshua* 1:4) and] runs eastward from Eretz Yisrael to Babylonia. When the Babylonian Jews would see the swelling of the Euphrates, they would rejoice, knowing that it signified rainfall for their brethren in Eretz Yisrael (*Rashi*; cf. *Tosafos;* see *Ritva MHK* ed. for an answer to *Tosafos'* challenge; see also *Rashash*). [The Euphrates represents the northern border of *Greater* Eretz Yisrael (i.e. the area promised to Abraham – see *Genesis* 15:18-21); however, Jews never actually conquered and settled the land as far north as that, due to their fear of the gentiles.]

4. Emendation follows *Rashi*.

5. When the Euphrates becomes swollen with the winter rains and the melted snow [that runs off the mountains] (*Rashi*).

6. [Through the legal principle of *nullification by the majority* (בִּטּוּל בְּרוֹב); however, see *Ramban*; see also *Baalei HaNefesh L'HaRaavad*, beginning of *Shaar HaMayim*].

7. The Torah, when teaching the law of purification by immersion, states: *Only a spring or a pit, a gathering of water, shall be tahor* (*Leviticus* 11:36; see *Rashi* there), thus validating two bodies of water for purification from *tumah* – a natural spring, and a gathering of water, i.e. a *mikveh*. One essential legal difference between a spring and a *mikveh* is that a spring can be used for immersion even while it is flowing, whereas a *mikveh* must be still water, gathered in one place. A river is fed by springs; it therefore can be used for ritual immersion even though it is composed of running water. Rainwater, by contrast, does not emanate from a spring, and is therefore invalid for immersion if it is flowing (*Rashi*, from *Mikvaos* 5:5, and *Toras Kohanim* to *Leviticus* ibid.). Therefore, if the river contains more rainwater than spring water, and the river is flowing, it cannot be used for immersion, since the rainwater nullifies the spring water. [See *Rashi* and *Tosafos,* who mention an alternative explanation for the Gemara, but immediately dismiss it.]

[*Terumas HaDeshen* (§254) asks: We know that if מַיִם שְׁאוּבִים, *drawn water* [which is invalid for ritual immersion], falls into a *mikveh*, even if its volume is many times greater than the water in the *mikveh*, it does not nullify the *mikveh* water, but is rather rendered immediately suitable for immersion itself (see *Yoreh Deah* 201:15). This transformation is achieved through the phenomenon known as *hashakah* [הַשָּׁקָה – literally: the kissing (of water to water)], by which any water in even minimal contact with a *mikveh* becomes like a *mikveh* – i.e. valid for ritual immersion. Likewise, the rainwater that falls into the river should not nullify the water of the river, but should rather be itself rendered valid for immersion through contact with the river! See there for an answer; see *Taz, Yoreh Deah* 201:3 for a discussion of this question.]

8. He would dig a pit and allow it to become filled with rainwater; alternatively, he would dig a pit close by the river, and then break a channel through to the river, allowing its water to fill the pit (*Rashi* to 65a). [During the month of Tishrei, however, which climaxed the dry season, there was little rainwater in the Euphrates (see below); Shmuel's father therefore allowed his daughters to immerse in the river itself during that period, and prepared mats to facilitate their immersion, as was explained on 65a.]

[*Ran* (to *Nedarim* 40b ד״ה אבוה דשמואל) finds odd the statement that Shmuel's father required *mikvaos* during the month of Nissan, for since Tishrei was the *only* time he allowed use of the river, the Gemara should have said that he required *mikvaos* all year long, with the exception of the Tishrei dry season! *Ran* explains that the Gemara is only discussing the period in which it is warm enough to immerse *outdoors*, which begins in Nissan. The Gemara therefore states that during Nissan he would build outdoor *mikvaos*, in which his daughters would immerse until Tishrei, when he was confident that the Euphrates did not contain a majority of rainwater. At that point, the girls would commence immersing in the Euphrates itself. In cold weather, however, they would not immerse outdoors at all.]

9. Literally: its bedrock [from where the springs that feed it flow] (*Rashi*; see *Targum Yonasan* to *Judges* 15:8 and *Isaiah* 32:2).

10. I.e. rivers can become swollen from their feeder springs alone, without experiencing any rainfall at all (see *Rashi* to *Bechoros* 55b ד״ה פרין ורבין). [In fact, R' Meir teaches that this is how the Euphrates, which in Hebrew is called Peras (פְּרָת), got its name. For the word Peras connotes fruitfulness and increase (as in פְּרוּ וּרְבוּ – *Genesis* 1:28); since the Euphrates is the most blessed of all rivers in this respect, it was given a name evocative of this quality (see *Bechoros* ibid.; see also *Tosafos* there ד״ה מסייע ליה).]

11. For while it is true that rivers often experience enormous swelling during the rainy season and the spring thaw, the greater part of this increase comes from their feeder springs, which flow with redoubled strength during this season (*Tosafos* from *Taanis* 25b).

גמרא

פסולות לכהונה לא סבר כי היכי דלא לילפן גופא נוכראה [א]ועביד להו מקוה ביומי ניסן מסייע ליה לרב דאמר רב [ה] מטרא במערבא סהדא רבה פרת [ב]סבר שלא ירבו הנוטפין על הזוחלין ופליגא דשמואל דאמר שמואל נהרא מכיפיה מיברך ופליגא דידיה אדידיה דאמר שמואל אין המים מטהרין בזוחלין אלא פרת ביומי תשרי בלבד: [ג]פורפת על האבן כו': והאמרת רישא פורפת אמר אביי [ד]סיפא אתאן למטבע בעי אביי [ה]אשה מהו שתערים ותפרוף על האגוז להוציא לבנה קטן בשבת תיבעי למ"ד [ג] (א) מערימין תיבעי למאן דאמר אין מערימין תיבעי למאן דאמר מערימין בדליקה התם הוא דאי לא שרית ליה אתי לכבויי אבל הכא אי לא שרית ליה לא אתי לאפוקי או דלמא אפילו למאן דאמר אין מערימין בדליקה התם דרך הוצאה בכך אבל הכא אין דרך הוצאה בכך אימא שפיר דמי תיקו:

מתני' [ג] הקיטע יוצא בקב שלו דברי ר' מאיר ורבי

רש"י

פסולות לכהונה. לכהן גדול דלא הויא בתולה שלימה דאע"ג דכהן גדול ביומיה לא הוה הואיל ודרך זנות חשיב ליה לאו אורח ארעא: דלא לילפן גופא נוכראה. ויתאוו לשכב עם איש: מטרא במערבא. בארץ ישראל: סהדא רבה פרת. פרת מעיד בדבר שהוא יורד מארץ ישראל לבבל וגדל ממי הגשמים ויודעין בני בבל שירדו גשמים בהרי ארץ ישראל ושמחים על אחיהם ואבוה דשמואל נמי כרב סבירא ליה דאמר פרת גדל ומימיו מתברכין ע"י גשמים: וסבר שמא ירבו נוטפים. היינו גשמים על הזוחלין הנובעין ותנן במסכת מקואות (פ"ה מ"ה) הזוחלין כמעיין והנוטפין כמקוה ושנינו בת"כ אך מעין ובור מקוה מים יכול מילא על כתפו ועשה מקוה בתחילה יהא טהור ת"ל מעיין מה מעיין בידי שמים אף מקוה בידי שמים אי מה מעיין מטהר בזוחלין אף מקוה מטהר בזוחלין תלמוד לומר אך מעיין המעיין מטהר בזוחלין ומקוה מטהר באשבורן ומהו אשבורן דקוו וקיימי לאפוקי שאם הטביל בו כלים דרך זחילתו כשהן נמשכין ויורדים למקוה לא עלתה להם טבילה דבור ומקוה כתיב דקוו וקיימי אבל נובעין מטהרין כמו שהן זוחלין ומושכין מגבוה לנמוך כדרך כל הנהרות הלכך ביומי ניסן שהנהרות גדילים ממי הגשמים של ימי החורף ומהפשרת השלגים חייש שמא ירבו הנוטפין על הזוחלין שניתוספו בנהר (ב) מן הגשמים על הזוחלים החיים ובטלו הזוחלין החיים בנוטפים ואין תורת מעיין עליהן לטהר בזוחלין אלא באשבורן ועביד להו מקוואות דקוו וקיימי ואני קבלתי מרבינו הלוי משום דספק זיבות ניהו וזבה טעונה מים חיים ואי אפשר להעמיד שמועתו משום דאמרינן[ז] חומר בזב מבזבה שהזב טעון מים חיים וזבה אינה טעונה מים חיים וחזרתי ודקדקתי לפרשה וכן נראה בעיני כמו שפירשתי ורובא דעלמא מפרשים נוטפין כשאובין ולאו מילתא היא דתנן הנוטפין כמקוה: דהוו להו שאובין ל"ג: מכיפיה מיברך. משפתו וממקורו ומסלעו סלע מתרגמינן כיפה מכיפיה מיברך ולא ממי הגשמים: ופליגא דידיה אדידיה. דשמואל אשמואל: אין המים מטהרין בזוחלין. אין מטהרין אדם וכלים הטובלין בהן דרך זחילה וצריך להמשיכן למקוה ולטבול במקוה: אלא פרת ביומי תשרי. שחדלו הגשמים ורבו הזוחלין עליהם ויש תורת מעיין על נהרות המושכין אלמא סבירא ליה שגדילין ממי הגשמים ואני שמעתי בבכורות מטהרין בזוחלין שהנוטפין שבתוכן מטהרין בריבוי הזוחלין ויתבטלו הנוטפין בהן להיות זב וזבה טובלין בהן בשביל הזוחלין: והא אמרת רישא פורפת. והיא ודאי לכתחלה קאמר בשבת דאי מבעוד יום ולאשמועינן דיוצאה בו בשבת הא תנא רישא מדיות פרופות: סיפא. דקתני לא תפרוף: אתאן למטבע. דלאו בר טלטול הוא אבל אבן שהקצה לכך ראוי לטלטול: להוציא לבנה הקטן. לאוכלו: תיבעי למאן דאמר. פלוגתא בכל כתבי הקדש (לקמן דף קכ.) לובש כל מה שיכול ללבוש דברי רבי מאיר ואפילו עשרה חלוקים זה על זה רבי יוסי אומר שמונה עשר כלים כדרך שהוא לובש בחול: דרך הוצאה בכך. כגון מוכרי כסות מוליכין אותו דרך מלבוש: מתני' הקיטע. שנקטעה רגלו [ה]: יוצא בקב שלו. דמנעל דידיה הוא:

תוספות

פסולות לכהונה. פי' לכהונה גדולה דלאו בתולה שלימה היא ואע"ג דכהן גדול בימי [ו] שמואל לא הוה היה מחמיר וי"מ משום זונה ופסולות אף לכהן הדיוט וכן משמע בפ' הערל (יבמות עו.) דקאמר התם לית הלכתא [לא כברא ולא] כאבא (עד דקאמר) [וקאמר] ואפילו לרבי אלעזר דאמר פנוי הבא על הפנויה שלא לשם אישות עשאה זונה כו' משמע דטעמא משום זונה:

סהדא רבה פרת. פי' הקונטרס פרת מעיד (ג) שהוא יורד מא"י לבבל וגדל ממי גשמים ולא נהירא שהרי בבל במזרח א"י קאי וכל הנהרות יורדים ממזרח למערב לכך פר"ת שהיו מכירים שירדו הגשמים לא"י ע"י שחוזר פרת לאחוריו על ידי גדילתו בא"י מתוך הגשמים:

שמא ירבו הנוטפים. פירוש מי גשמים על מי נהרות שהיו זוחלין והוו להו מקוה ואמרינן דאין מקוה מטהר בזוחלין כ"א באשבורן דתנן במסכת מקוואות (פ"ה מ"ה) הזוחלין כמעיין והנוטפין כמקוה ותניא בת"כ יכול מילא מים על כתיפו ועשאו מקוה בתחילה יהא טהור תלמוד לומר מעיין מה מעיין בידי שמים אף מקוה בידי שמים אי מה מעיין מטהר בזוחלין אף מקוה מטהר בזוחלין פי' אף בזוחלין וכ"ש באשבורן תלמוד לומר אך מעיין מעיין מטהר בזוחלין ומקוה באשבורן ומהו אשבורן דקוו וקיימי ויש מפרשים שלא היה רוצה להטבילן בהן משום דהוו להו ספק זבות וזב וזבה טעונים מים חיים ושמא ירבו הנוטפין והוו להו מכונסין ולא נהירא חדא דמ"מ עביד להו מקוואות והא בעינן מים חיים ועוד (דבת"כ) [דבתוספתא פ"ג דזבים] קאמר חומר בזב מבזבה שהזב טעון מים חיים והזבה אינה טעונה מים חיים וא"ת ולשמואל דאמר אין המים מטהרין בזוחלין אלא פרת ביומי תשרי זב דבעי מים חיים איך יטבול ביומי ניסן וי"ל במעיין מכוסה שאין מי גשמים יורדין בתוכו וא"ת אמאי חיישינן שמא ירבו הנוטפים לימא קמא קמא בטיל כדאמר בפ"ה דמסכת ע"ז (דף עג.) המערה יין נסך לבור אפילו כל היום כולו כשר דאמרינן קמא קמא בטיל וי"ל דלא מהני טעמא דקמא קמא בטיל כיון שהאיסור רבה מכשיעור והיא דיין נסך דקאמר קמא קמא בטיל היינו קודם שרבה האיסור עד כדי נתינת טעם בהיתר:

דאמר שמואל נהרא מכיפיה מיתבריך. פי' ממקומו ומסלעו סלע מתרגם כיפיה מנביעתו מיתבריך ולא ממי גשמים וא"ת והא קא חזינן שמחמת הגשמים הם גדילים וי"ל כדאמר במסכת תענית (דף כה:) שאין לך טפח יורד מלמעלה שאין טפחיים עולים כנגדו מלמטה ואור"ת דהילכתא כוותיה דשמואל ומייתי ראיה מפרק בתרא דבכורות (דף נה:) דתניא רבי מאיר אומר לא פרת שמו אלא יובל שמו ולמה נקרא שמו פרת שמימיו פרין ורבין ולאו דוקא נקט פרת דה"ה לכל נהרות והא דנקט פרת משום שהוא גדול מכל נהרות ולפי שהוא מא"י וקאמר התם מסייע ליה לשמואל דאמר נהרא מכיפיה מיתבריך ועל זה אנו סומכין לטבול בנהרות אפילו אם גדלו מאד:

הקיטע יוצא בקב שלו. פ"ה קיטע שנקטעה רגלו עושה כמין דפוס רגל וחוקק בו מעט לשום ראש שוקו בתוכו ואינו [ס"א והוא] נסמך עליו ומש"ה יוצא בקב שלו דמנעל דידיה הוא ור' יוסי אוסר דלאו תכשיט הוא ואינו מנעל והוי משוי והקשה רבינו תם דבמסכת יומא (דף עח: ושם) משמע דלכ"ע מנעל הוא ואסור לנעול בו ביוה"כ ולענין שבת בהא הוא דפליגי דרבי יוסי גזר דילמא מיפסיק ואתי לאתויי ורבי מאיר לא גזר וי"ל דה"נ בהא פליגי דטעמא דר' יוסי דכיון דלא הוי של עור לא מיהדק ואיכא למיחש דילמא מיפסיק ואתי לאתויי אך קשה מהא דאמר בגמרא חלצה בסנדל כו' חליצתו כשרה ואמר שמואל ר"מ הוא משמע דלר' יוסי חליצתו פסולה ואמאי כיון דמנעל הוא וי"ל דהאי נמי בהא תליא דכיון דלענין שבת גזר דילמא מיפסיק אינו ראוי להלך בו ודמי לקטן שחלץ במנעל גדול דחליצתו פסולה כדאיתא בפ' מצות חליצה (יבמות קג:) משום דנעלו כתיב נעלו הראוי לו וא"ת היכי גזרי דילמא נפיל ואתי לאתויי הלא אין לו אלא רגל אחד ואי נפיל לא יזוז ממקומו ואומר ר"י דמיירי שנושא בידו מקל ועיקר הליכתו היא בסמיכת המקל והשתא אי נמי מיפסיק יוכל להלך מכאן יש להתיר למי שכווצו גידי שוקיו ללכת במקלו בשבת והרב פור"ת פי' דקיטע יש לו סמך שקושר בכרעו ומגיע לארץ והשוק כפופה לאחוריה ובראש השוק במקום הרגל עושה לו קב (ד) להראות כמו שיש לו רגל ובהא פליגי ר' יוסי סבר כיון שאינו נסמך עליו אלא תלוי באויר חיישינן דילמא נפיל ור"מ לא חייש ולפי זה אין ראיה להתיר לקיטע לצאת במקלו אמנם יש להתיר מסיפא דמתניתין דאינו אוסר אלא סמוכות שלו לפי ששוקיו תלויין באויר ודילמא נפיל ואתי לאתויי (אבל הכסא) והספסלים שבידו אינו אוסר ואינהו הוו דומיא דמקל וק"ק לפי זה אמאי מטמא ליה רבא משום מדרס כיון שאינו נסמך עליו ושמא כשהוא יושב פעמים הוא נסמך עליו ולכך עושה לו בית קבול כתיתין שלא יוזק בקשר העץ שהוא יושב:

סנדל

עין משפט נר מצוה

עד א ב מיי' פ"ט מהל' מקוואות הלכה יג סמג עשין רמח טוש"ע י"ד סי' רא סעיף ג:

עה ג ד מיי' פי"ט מהל' שבת הלכה יז סמג לאוין סה טוש"ע א"ח סי' שג סעיף כב:

עו ה מיי' שם טוש"ע שם סעיף כג:

רבינו חננאל

לחברתה ולא הוה שביק להו דגנייו גבי הדדי סבר דלא לילפו גופא נוכראה (ואמר רב הונא נשים המסוללות זו בזו פסולות לכהונה) והוה עביד לבנתי' מקוה (ביום) [ביומי] ניסן ולא היה מניחן לטבול בפרת מפני שרוב מי פרת בניסן מי מטר הן כרב דאמר מטרא במערבא שהדא רבה פרת. כלומר כיון שתראה כי רבו מי פרת עדות היא שהוגשמה ארץ המערב וסבר אבוה דשמואל שמא ירבו נוטפין שהן מי גשמים הנוטפין מן הגגות ונעשו שאובין על מי הפרת שהן זוחלין כדתני במקוואות בפ' ה' הזוחלין כמעין והנוטפין כמקוה העיד ר' (יצחק) [צדוק] על הזוחלין שרבו על הנוטפין שמכשירין ושאמר שמואל נהרא מכיפיה מתברך כלומר הנהר הגדול מן הסלע שיוצא ממנו משום נרבת מליאתו ולא ממי המטר פליגא על אבוה דשמואל ועל רב ועוד דברי שמואל סותרין זה את זה בכאן אמר כי מי המטר אינם ממלאים הנהר אלא מכיפיה מיבריך ועוד אמר אין המים מטהרין בזוחלין אלא פרת ביומי תשרי בלבד מכלל דבשאר החדשים זולתי תשרי כנוטפין הם דגשמים רבו עליהן ומפצי ביומי תשרי היה מסתירו לבנותיו במפצי מפני בני אדם שעל הנהר וטובלת בפרת כי דברי הכל בתשרי זוחלין הן ולמה במפצי דלית להו טהרה במקוה: **פורפת** על האבן ועל האגוז ועל המטבע מע"ש. פי' נותנת אבן או אגוז או מטבע בקצה הסדין כמין קרס בלולאות שלא ישמט הסדין מעליה כדי שתהא מתעטפת באותו סדין ונותנת זה שעשאתו כמין קרס. נשים מדיות מנהגן לצאת בענין הזה פרופות. ובלבד שלא תפרוף בתחלה בשבת על המטבע. והנשים הערביות מנהגן לצאת רעלות ופי' רעלות בירושלמי בליכריאה והן כמו כסוי פנים כדכתיב (ישעיה ג) השרות והרעלות. וי"א זוג ללמדך שבמקומות הללו כך היה מנהגם ומותר להם וכל אדם מותר בכך אלא שדברו חכמים בהווה: **בעי** אביי אשה מהו שתערים ותפרוף באגוז להוציא לבנה קטן בשבת ועלתה בתיקו: [מתני'] הקיטע יוצא בקב שלו דברי רבי מאיר ורבי

רב נסים גאון

קסבר שמא ירבו הנוטפין על הזוחלין. עיקר דילה בתורת כהנים אי מה מעין מטהר בזוחלין אף מקוה מטהר בזוחלין תלמוד לומר אך המעין מטהר בזוחלין והמקוה מטהר באשבורן ובמסכת מקואות (פרק ה משנה ה) הזוחלין כמעין והנוטפין כמקוה העיד רבי צדוק על הזוחלין שרבו על הנוטפין שהן כשרים ותישתכח בפרק ז' דעדיות הנוטפין שרבו על הזוחלין אינן כשירים: **תיבעי** למאן דאמר (מדליקין) [מערימין] בדליקה תיבעי למאן דאמר אין מערימין. עיקר דיליה בפרק כל כתבי הקדש (דף קכ) דתנן לובש כל שהוא יכול ללבוש ועוטף כל מה שהוא יכול להתעטף רבי יוסי אומר י"ח כלי מכלל דתנא קמא סבר מותר ללבוש ולהציל אפילו יותר מי"ח כלי ואף על פי שהוא מערים בכך:

סמיכות

מסורת הש"ס

א) נדרים מ: בכורות נה: ע"ש, ב) לא דפסק הב"י סימן של"ד והר"ן דהתם מיירי לאסר המעורבת קשה לפרש הך סוגיא. ואין ענין כלל להך דהכא ואפלע"ד דכוונת הסוגיא לאי דפליגי בתוספתא פי"ד אלילן מפני הדליקה כו' יחמין ואח"כ יליל כו' ואין מערימין בכך רי"א מערימין. מהרב הג' ר' בנימין קארנגאלד ז"ל, ג) יומא עח: [יבמות קג:], ד) [בתוספתא מגילה פ"א ותוספתא זבים פ"ג], ה) [עי' רש"י ברכות נח: ד"ה קטע], ו) [צ"ל אבוה דשמואל].

הגהות הב"ח

(א) גמ' תיבעי למ"ד מערימין בדליקה תיבעי למ"ד אין מערימין בדליקה תיבעי: (ב) רש"י ד"ה וסבר שמא וכו' שניתוספו בנהר מי הגשמים: (ג) תוספות ד"ה סהדא וכו' מעיד בדבר שהוא: (ד) תום' ד"ה הקיטע וכו' עושה לו קב כמין סנדל להראות כמו שיש:

ליקוטי רש"י

פסולות לכהונה. משום זנות [יבמות עו.]. **מטרא במערבא סהדא רבה פרת.** פרת יורד מא"י לבבל וכשהגשמים יורדין בא"י סהדא רבה הוי פרת בבבל שירדו גשמים במערבא לפי שגדל מחמת הגשמים [בכורות נה:]. כשנהר פרת גדול הוי עדות לגשמים שיורדין לא"י דא"י גבוה מכל הארצות ובאין גשמים ונופלין בפרת ומתגדל מהן והאי דאמרי' דנהר מתגדל ממי גשמים הוי פלוגתא אדשמואל [נדרים מ.]. כשיורד מטר בא"י מעיד עליו פרת בבבל שכל שהוא גדול בידוע שאע"פ שלא ירדו גשמים כאן ירדו גשמים בא"י ונפקא מינה שאסור לטבול בו לפי שאין מי גשמים הנוטפין מטהרין בזוחלין אלא באשבורן כלומר דקוו וקיימי כדתניא בספרי אי מה מעיין מטהר בזוחלין אף מקוה מטהר בזוחלין ת"ל אך מעין ובור מעיין מטהר בזוחלין ומקוה באשבורן הילכך כל היכא דאיכא למיחש שמא רבו נוטפין על הזוחלין אסור והיינו כשהנהר גדול הרבה אבל אם היה הולך לאטו או שלא נתרבה אלא מעט דליכא לספוקי ברביית נוטפין שרי כדתניא בתוספתא העיד ר' אלעזר בר צדוק על הזוחלין שרבו על הנוטפין שהם כשרים [ר"ן שם]. **סבר שלא ירבו הנוטפין על הזוחלין.** לפי שביומי ניסן רבין נוטפין על הזוחלין מחמת הגשמים שהרי כל השלגים והקרח (ש)נתפשרו [ו]באין המים דרך דרך צינורות דהוו להו שאובין אבל [אם] לא באין דרך צינורות אלא מאליהן שוטפין ובאין טובלין בהן כדאמר זבה ונדה ויולדת טבילתן במי מקוה של מ' סאה ואפי' מי גשמי' מכונסים שלא מלינו מים חיים אלא לזב בלבד שנאמר בו מים חיים והמפרש לא פירש הכי ולאו דוקא דכל נשים בזמן הזה זבות ניהו [רש"י שם:]. שבימות הגשמים ירדו גשמים הרבה וחייש שמא ירבו מים שנוטפים מעבים לתוך הנהר שהם זוחלים דלא חזו להן משום דהוו להו ספק זבות ובזב כתיב מים חיים ל"א על הזוחלים על אותם שנפלו מן העבים לקרקע ומן הקרקע זחלו וקילחו לתוך הנהר דאי לא נוטפים משום זוחלים לא מיפסלי דאמרינן בפ' ראשון דתמורה (יב.) השאובה מיטהרת בהמשכה דהיינו שממשיך מים שאובים לתוך המקוה על ידי צנורות [בכורות שם]. לפי שרבו המים בימות הגשמים מגשמים שנפלו וחייש שמא ירבו נוטפין על הזוחלין ותניא בתורת כהנים אי מה מעין מטהר בזוחלין אף מקוה מטהר בזוחלין כלומר שמטבילין במכונסין דרך זחילתן קודם שנקוו ונחו במקוה ת"ל אך מעין מטהר בזוחלין והמקוה מטהר באשבורן ומהו אשבורן דקוו וקיימי דאין מטבילין במכונסים אלא משנקוו למקוויהם ונחו מזחילתן ותנן במסכת מקוואות (פ"ה מ"ה) הזוחלין כמעין כלומר זוחלין שבנהרות כמעין והנוטפין כמקוה מהטהרים הרי הן כמקוה ואין מטהרים בזוחלה הילכך ביומי ניסן שנתרבה הנהר על ידי גשמים חייש שמא רבו נוטפין שבו על חיים שבו ובטלו זוחלין ואין מטהרין את הטמא הטובל בהן דרך זחילה וכל הנהרות לעולם הן הולכים וזוחלין לפיכך עביד להו מקוה באשבורן לטבול בתוכו יש מפרשים דבעינן מים חיים לזבה ולאו מילתא היא דתניא בתוספתא (דמגילה פ"א) חומר בזב מבזבה שהזב טעון מים חיים כו' [נדה סז.]. [המשך בדף סו.]

purifies articles from contamination, אֶלָּא פְּרָת בְּיוֹמֵי תִּשְׁרֵי בִּלְבַד – **except** for **the Euphrates River during the days of Tishrei alone,** when it contains only a very small amount of rainwater.[12] We see, then, that during most of the year, Shmuel actually forbids the use of rivers for ritual immersion, since he suspects that they contain a greater volume of rainwater than river water. His opinion is thus at odds with the opinion attributed to him above.[13]

The Mishnah continues:

פּוֹרֶפֶת עַל הָאֶבֶן כו׳ – [A WOMAN] MAY FASTEN her cloak ON A STONE, [on a nut, or on a coin, provided that she does not initially fasten with it on the Sabbath].

The Gemara questions the stipulation prohibiting a woman from initially fastening with these items on the Sabbath:

וְהָאָמְרַת רֵישָׁא פּוֹרֶפֶת – **But the first segment** of this ruling **states:** [A WOMAN] MAY FASTEN, which implies permission to fasten with these items on the Sabbath itself![14] How can the Mishnah then forbid this very activity in the second segment of the ruling?!

The Gemara answers:

אָמַר אַבַּיֵי – **Abaye said:** סֵיפָא אֲתָאן לְמַטְבֵּעַ – The law taught in **the second segment** of the ruling **comes only** with regard **to a coin,** which one is forbidden to fasten with initially on the Sabbath because it is *muktzeh*![15] However, it does not concern a stone or a nut used for fastening, for since these items are not *muktzeh,* they may be used initially for this purpose on the Sabbath itself.[16]

The Gemara presents an inquiry:

בָּעֵי אַבַּיֵי – **Abaye inquired:** אִשָּׁה מַהוּ שֶׁתַּעֲרִים וְתִפְרוֹף עַל הָאֱגוֹז לְהוֹצִיא לִבְנָהּ קָטָן בְּשַׁבָּת – **What is [the law]** regarding **whether a woman may employ a subterfuge and fasten** her cloak **on a nut in order to take it out to her young son on the Sabbath?**[17] תִּיבָּעֵי לְמַאן דְּאָמַר מַעֲרִימִין – **He inquires according to the [Tanna] who says** in another case that **one may employ a subterfuge** to evade a Sabbath prohibition, תִּיבָּעֵי לְמַאן דְּאָמַר אֵין מַעֲרִימִין – and **he inquires according to the [Tanna] who says** in that other case that **one may not employ a subterfuge** to evade a Sabbath prohibition.

The Gemara explains:

תִּיבָּעֵי לְמַאן דְּאָמַר מַעֲרִימִין בִּדְלֵיקָה – **He inquires according to the [Tanna] who says** that **in** the event of **a fire one may employ a subterfuge** to rescue clothing by donning many articles of clothing at once, and wearing them outside.[18] הָתָם הוּא – For

NOTES

12. By Tishrei, the rainwaters have generally abated, and are of lesser volume than the river water. Shmuel therefore allows use of the river for immersion at that time. This is true not only of the Euphrates, but of all rivers (*Rashi*; see *Ran, Nedarim* 40b ד״ה אלא פרת and *Baalei HaNefesh LeHaRaavad* ibid., as to why Shmuel discusses the Euphrates in particular).

[*Ran* (ibid.) explains that the reason Shmuel limits river immersion to Tishrei is because that is the only period during which one can be absolutely sure that the river water has not been nullified by rainwater. However, if one knows that a particular river has not experienced an increase, but is at its Tishrei level, one may use it for immersion even during other periods of the year.]

13. *Ran* (ibid. ד״ה ולענין הלכה) states that the two statements of Shmuel are not in fact a contradiction; rather, although Shmuel holds in theory that the increase of a river is generated primarily by its feeder springs, he rules stringently in actual practice, because of the possibility that his disputants may be correct.

14. For it cannot be that the first segment of the ruling is discussing a stone or nut that was wrapped into the cloak *before* the Sabbath, and is teaching that it does not legally constitute a burden, for that law was already taught in the earlier section of the Mishnah, which permitted Median women to go out with their cloaks fastened with a makeshift button! Perforce, the Mishnah means to permit one to wrap these items into a corner of one's cloak, and to fasten with them on the Sabbath itself [and we do not fear that an onlooker will view this act as a subterfuge designed to transport the item – see above, 65a note 23] (*Rashi;* see *Ritva MHK* ed.). [The Gemara at this point assumes that the Mishnah's prohibition concerns the act of wrapping and fastening, mandating that it be performed before the Sabbath. The Gemara therefore challenges this requirement from the ruling's first segment, which permits one to perform this act on the Sabbath itself.]

15. [*Muktzeh* literally means *set aside,* and refers to a class of objects whose use on the Sabbath was unanticipated, and which therefore may not be handled on the Sabbath. Since monetary transactions are forbidden on the Sabbath, one does not anticipate using a coin;] it is therefore *muktzeh*, and may not be handled (*Rashi*). [The Gemara now realizes that the Mishnah's stipulation does not in fact concern the act of fastening, since that is certainly permissible on the Sabbath. Rather, the Mishnah is concerned with the permissibility of handling the object being used as a button, and therefore stipulates (in the case of a coin) that it be an object used previously for this purpose, so that it will not be forbidden as *muktzeh.*] For the only way to remove *muktzeh* status from the coin is to make actual use of it as a button – merely designating it as a button, whether orally or in one's mind, will not render it permissilbe. This is because a coin is a significant item of intrinsic value, and is not generally employed for the insignificant use of fastening a cloak (*Pnei Yehoshua*); a mere oral designation therefore does not suffice to effect a legal change in the coin's status (see following note).

However, if the coin was actually *used* as a button before the Sabbath, it may subsequently be used even on the Sabbath. This is because a change in use inaugurated by an *action* does suffice to remove the coin from its previous use to a new one as a button; its use on the Sabbath was therefore anticipated, and it is not *muktzeh* (*Orach Chaim* 303:22; *Mishnah Berurah* ibid. §75).

[The above holds true with regard to a coin designated as a button for a single Sabbath only. However, if one designates a coin for use as a button for all time, even oral designation or intention suffices to make it into a button, thereby permitting its use on the Sabbath itself (see *Mishnah Berurah* 303:73,74; see also *Orach Chaim* 308:22 with *Mishnah Berurah*).

16. Although a stone that was never set to any particular use would also be *muktzeh*, the Mishnah refers to a stone that was designated [orally or in one's mind – see *Mishnah Berurah* 308:93] for use as a button before the Sabbath (*Rashi*). [Since it thereby "becomes" a button, it is not *muktzeh* (see previous note for why oral designation does not remove *muktzeh* from a coin).]

Mishnah Berurah (303:73) writes that oral designation can only render a stone a button if the stone is ideally shaped for button use [e.g. a round stone]. However, this is true only if one intends to use the stone as a button for no more than a single Sabbath. If, however, one intends the stone to remain a button for all time, it may be used even if it is poorly shaped for button use (*Mishnah Berurah* 303:73,74).

17. [The boy stands in a public domain; the woman wishes to carry the nut to him from a private domain. She obviously may not do so in normal fashion, and therefore wraps the nut into a corner of her cloak, and then fastens her cloak upon it. She then walks to the boy and gives him the nut. However, since the woman's purpose is obviously to transport the nut, this act might give the *appearance* of a violation of the prohibition against transporting objects from one domain to another on the Sabbath (see *Mishnah Berurah* 303:76), and may thus lead one to look lightly upon this prohibition! Abaye is therefore unsure whether one is permitted to perform this action.]

18. [This case is the subject of a Tannaic dispute in a Mishnah below (120a). The dispute concerns the Rabbinic decree that limits the property one is permitted to carry into a courtyard in the event of a fire. For although it is generally permissible to carry into a courtyard, the Rabbis feared that if one were permitted to rescue all one's belongings, in the tumult and confusion of doing so, one might come to extinguish the fire. They therefore limited rescue to certain items essential to one's existence over the Sabbath. With regard to rescuing clothing, however, R' Meir holds that one may don *any* number of garments and wear them into a courtyard to save them from a fire. This is because the restriction attached to the rescue – i.e. that

פסולות לכהונה לא סבר כי היכי דלא לילפן גופא נוכראה א ועביד להו מקוה ביומי ניסן מסייע ליה לרב דאמר רב א) מטרא במערבא סהדא רבה פרת ב סבר שלא ירבו הנוטפין על הזוחלין ופליגא דשמואל דאמר שמואל נהרא מכיפיה מיברך ופליגא דידיה אדידיה דאמר שמואל אין המים מטהרין בזוחלין אלא פרת ביומי תשרי בלבד: ג פורפת על האבן כו': והאמרת רישא פורפת אמר אביי ד סיפא אתאן למטבע בעי אביי ה אשה מהו שתערים ותפרוף על האגוז להוציא לבנה קטן בשבת תיבעי למ"ד ג) (א) מערימין תיבעי למאן דאמר אין מערימין תיבעי למאן דאמר מערימין בדליקה התם הוא דאי לא שרית ליה אתי לכבויי אבל הכא אי לא שרית ליה לא אתי לאפוקי או דלמא אפילו למאן דאמר אין מערימין בדליקה התם דרך הוצאה בכך אבל הכא אין דרך הוצאה בכך אימא שפיר דמי תיקו: מתני' ג) הקיטע יוצא בקב שלו דברי ר' מאיר ורבי

רש"י

פסולות לכהונה. לכהן גדול דלא הויא בתולה שלימה דאע"ג דכהן גדול ביומיה לא הוה הואיל ודרך זנות חשיב ליה לאו אורח ארעא: **דלא לילפן גופא נוכראה.** ויתאוו לשכב עם איש: **מטרא במערבא.** בארץ ישראל: **סהדא רבה פרת.** פרת מעיד בדבר שהוא יורד מארץ ישראל לבבל וגדל ממי הגשמים ויודעין בני בבל שירדו גשמים בהרי ארץ ישראל ושמחים על אחיהם ואבוה דשמואל נמי כרב סבירא ליה דאמר פרת גדל ומימיו מתברכין ע"י גשמים: **וסבר שמא ירבו נוטפים.** היינו גשמים על זוחלין הנובעין ותנן במסכת מקוואות (פ"ה מ"ה) הזוחלין כמעיין והנוטפין כמקוה ושנינו בת"כ אך מעין ובור מקוה מים יכול מילא על כתפו ועשה מקוה בתחילה יהא טהור ת"ל מעיין מה מעיין בידי שמים אף מקוה בידי שמים אי מה מעיין מטהר בזוחלין אף מקוה מטהר בזוחלין תלמוד לומר אך מעיין המעיין מטהר בזוחלין ומקוה מטהר באשבורן ומהו אשבורן דקוו וקיימי לאפוקי שאם הטביל בו כלים דרך זחילתו כשהן נמשכין ויורדים למקוה לא עלתה להם טבילה דבור ומקוה כתיב דקוו וקיימי אבל נובעין מטהרין כמו שהן זוחלין ומושכין מגבוה לנמוך כדרך כל הנהרות הלכך ביומי ניסן שהנהרות גדילים ממי הגשמים של ימי החורף ומהפשרת השלגים חייש שמא ירבו הנוטפין על הזוחלין שניתוספו בנהר (ב) מן הגשמים על הזוחלים החיים ובטלו הזוחלין החיים בנוטפים ואין תורת מעיין עליהן לטהר בזוחלין אלא באשבורן ועביד להו מקוואות דקוו וקיימי ואני קבלתי מרבינו הלוי משום דספק זיבות נינהו וזבה טעונה מים חיים ואי אפשר להעמיד שמועתו משום דאמרינן ז) חומר בזב מבזבה שהזב טעון מים חיים וזבה אינה טעונה מים חיים וחזרתי ובדקתי לפרשה וכן נראה בעיני כמו שפירשתי ורובא דעלמא מפרשים נוטפין כשאובין ולאו מילתא היא דתנן הנוטפין כמקוה: דהוו להו שאובין ל"ג: **מכיפיה מיברך.** משפתו וממקורו ומסלעו סלע מתרגמינן כיפה מכיפיה מיברך ולא ממי הגשמים: **ופליגא דידיה אדידיה.** דשמואל אשמואל: **אין המים מטהרין בזוחלין.** אין מטהרין אדם וכלים הטובלין בהן דרך זחילה וצריך להמשיכן למקוה ולטבול במקוה: **אלא פרת ביומי תשרי.** שחדלו הגשמים ורבו הזוחלין עליהם ויש תורת מעיין על נהרות המושכין אלמא סבירא ליה שגדלין ממי הגשמים ואני שמעתי בבכורות מטהרין בזוחלין שהנוטפין שבתוכן מטהרין ברבוי הזוחלין ויתבטלו הנוטפין בהן להיות זב וזבה טובלין בהן בשביל הזוחלין: **והא אמרת רישא פורפת.** והיא ודאי לכתחלה קאמר בשבת דאי מבעוד יום ולאשמועינן דיוצאה בו בשבת הא תנא רישא מדיות פרופות: **סיפא.** דקתני לא תפרוף: **אתאן למטבע.** דלאו בר טלטול הוא אבל אבן שהקצה לכך ראוי לטלטול: **להוציא לבנה הקטן.** לאוכלו: **תיבעי למאן דאמר.** פלוגתא בכל כתבי הקדש (לקמן דף קכ.) לובש כל מה שיכול ללבוש דברי רבי מאיר ואפילו עשרה חלוקים זה על זה רבי יוסי אומר שמונה עשר כלים כדרך שהוא לובש בחול: **דרך הוצאה בכך.** כגון מוכרי כסות מוליאין אותו דרך מלבוש: **מתני' הקיטע.** שנקטעה רגלו ה): **יוצא בקב שלו.** דמנעל דידיה הוא: ורבי

תוספות

פסולות לכהונה. פי' לכהונה גדולה דלאו בתולה שלימה היא ואע"ג דכהן גדול בימי י) שמואל לא הוה היה מחמיר וי"מ משום זונה ופסולות אף לכהן הדיוט וכן משמע בפ' הערל (יבמות עו.) דקאמר התם לית הלכתא [לא כברא ולא] כאבא (עד דקאמר) [וקאמר] ואפילו לרבי אלעזר דאמר פנוי הבא על הפנויה שלא לשם אישות עשאה זונה כו' משמע דטעמא משום זונה: **סהדא** רבה פרת. פי' הקונטרס פרת מעיד (ג) שהוא יורד מא"י לבבל וגדל ממי גשמים ולא נהירא שהרי בבל במזרח א"י קאי וכל הנהרות יורדים ממזרח למערב לכך פר"ת שהיו מכירים שירדו הגשמים לא"י ע"י שחוזר פרת לאחוריו על ידי גדילתו בא"י מתוך הגשמים: **שמא** ירבו הנוטפים. פירוש מי גשמים על מי נהרות שהיו זוחלין והוו להו מקוה ואמרינן דאין מקוה מטהר בזוחלין כ"א באשבורן דתנן במסכת מקוואות (פ"ה מ"ה) הזוחלין כמעיין והנוטפין כמקוה ותניא בת"כ יכול מילא מים על כתיפו ועשאו מקוה בתחילה יהא טהור תלמוד לומר מעיין מה מעיין בידי שמים אף מקוה בידי שמים אי מה מעיין מטהר בזוחלין אף מקוה מטהר בזוחלין פי' אף בזוחלין וכ"ש באשבורן תלמוד לומר אך מעיין מטהר בזוחלין ומקוה באשבורן ומהו אשבורן דקוו וקיימי ויש מפרשים שלא היה רוצה להטבילן בהן משום דהוו להו ספק זבות וזב וזבה טעונים מים חיים ושמא ירבו הנוטפין והוו להו מכונסין ולא נהירא חדא דמ"מ עביד להו מקוואות והא בעינן מים חיים ועוד (דבת"כ) [דבתוספתא פ"ג דזבים] קאמר חומר בזב מבזבה שהזב טעון מים חיים והזבה אינה טעונה מים חיים וא"ת ולשמואל דאמר אין המים מטהרין בזוחלין אלא פרת ביומי תשרי זב דבעי מים חיים איך יטבול ביומי ניסן וי"ל במעיין מכוסה שאין מי גשמים יורדין בתוכו וא"ת אמאי חיישינן שמא ירבו הנוטפים לימא קמא קמא בטיל כדאמר בפ"ה דמסכת ע"ז (דף עג.) המערה יין נסך לבור אפילו כל היום כולו כשר דאמרינן קמא קמא בטיל וי"ל דלא מהני טעמא דקמא קמא בטיל כיון שהאיסור רבה מכשיעור וההיא דיין נסך דקאמר קמא קמא בטיל היינו קודם שרבה האיסור עד כדי נתינת טעם בהיתר: **דאמר** שמואל נהרא מכיפיה מיתבריך. פי' ממקומו ומסלעו סלע מתרגם כיפיה מנביעתו מיתבריך ולא ממי גשמים וא"ת והא קא חזינן שמחמת הגשמים הם גדילים וי"ל כדאמר במסכת תענית (דף כה:) שאין לך טפח יורד מלמעלה שאין טפחיים עולים כנגדו מלמטה ואור"ת דהילכתא כוותיה דשמואל ומייתי ראיה מפרק בתרא דבכורות (דף נה:) דתניא רבי מאיר אומר לא פרת שמו אלא יובל שמו ולמה נקרא שמו פרת שמימיו פרין ורבין ולאו דוקא נקט פרת דה"ה לכל נהרות והא דנקט פרת משום שהוא גדול מכל נהרות ולפי שהוא מא"י וקאמר התם מסייע ליה לשמואל דאמר נהרא מכיפיה מיתבריך ועל זה אנו סומכין לטבול בנהרות אפילו אם גדלו מאד: **הקיטע** יוצא בקב שלו. פ"ה קיטע שנקטעה רגלו עושה כמין דפוס רגל וחוקק בו מעט לשום ראש שוקו בתוכו ואינו [ס"א והוא] נסמך עליו ומש"ה יוצא בקב שלו דמנעל דידיה הוא ור' יוסי אוסר דלאו תכשיט הוא ואינו מנעל והוי משוי והקשה רבינו תם דבמסכת יומא (דף עח: ושם) משמע דלכ"ע מנעל הוא ואסור לנעול בו ביוה"כ ולענין שבת בהא הוא דפליגי דרבי יוסי גזר דילמא מיפסיק ואתי לאתויי ורבי מאיר לא גזר וי"ל דה"נ בהא פליגי דטעמא דר' יוסי דכיון דלא הוי של עור לא מיהדק ואיכא למיחש דילמא מיפסיק ואתי לאתויי אך קשה מהא דאמר בגמרא חליצה בסנדל כו' חליצתו כשרה ואמר שמואל ר"מ הוא משמע דלר' יוסי חליצתו פסולה ואמאי כיון דמנעל הוא וי"ל דהאי נמי בהא תליא דכיון דלענין שבת גזר דילמא מיפסיק אינו ראוי להלך בו ודמי לקטן שחלץ במנעל גדול דחליצתו פסולה כדאיתא בפ' מצות חליצה (יבמות קג:) משום דנעלו כתיב נעלו הראוי לו וא"ת היכי גזרי דילמא נפיל ואתי לאתויי הלא אין לו אלא רגל אחד ואי נפיל לא יזוז ממקומו ואומר ר"י דמיירי שנושא בידו מקל ועיקר הליכתו היא בסמיכת המקל והשתא אי נמי מיפסיק יוכל להלך מכאן יש להתיר למי שכוולו גידי שוקיו ללכת במקלו בשבת והרב פור"ת פי' דקיטע יש לו סמך שקושר בכרעו ומגיע לארץ והשוק כפופה לאחוריה ובראש השוק במקום הרגל עושה לו קב (ד) להראות כמו שיש לו רגל ובהא פליגי ר' יוסי סבר כיון שאינו נסמך עליו אלא תלוי באויר חיישינן דילמא נפיל ור"מ לא חייש ולפי זה אין ראיה להתיר לקיטע לצאת במקלו אמנם יש להתיר מסיפא דמתניתין דאינו אוסר אלא סמוכות שלו לפי שוקיו תלויין באויר ודילמא נפיל ואתי לאתויי (אבל הכסא) והספסלים שבידו אינו אוסר ואינהו הוו דומיא דמקל וק"ק לפי זה אמאי מטמא ליה רבא משום מדרס כיון שאינו נסמך עליו ושמא כשהוא יושב פעמים הוא נסמך עליו ולכך עושה לו בית קבול כתיתין שלא יוזק בקשר העץ שהוא יושב: סנדל

עין משפט נר מצוה

עד א ב מיי' פ"ט מהל' מקוואות הלכה יג סמג עשין רמח טוש"ע י"ד סי' רא סעיף ג:

עה ג ד מיי' פי"ט מהל' שבת הלכה יז סמג לאוין סה טוש"ע א"ח סי' שג סעיף כב:

עו ה מיי' שם טוש"ע שם סעיף כג:

רבינו חננאל

לחברתה ולא הוה שביק להו דגנייו גבי הדדי סבר דלא לילפו גופא נוכראה (ואמר רב הונא נשים המסוללות זו בזו פסולות לכהונה) והוה עביד לבנתי' מקוה (ביום) [ביומי] ניסן ולא היה מניחן לטבול בפרת מפני שרוב מי פרת בניסן מי מטר הן כרב דאמר מטרא במערבא שהדא רבה פרת. כלומר כיון שתראה כי רבו מי פרת עדות היא שהוגשמה ארץ המערב וסבר אבוה דשמואל שמא ירבו נוטפין שהן מי גשמים הנוטפין מן הגגות ונעשו שאובין על מי הפרת שהן זוחלין כדתני במקוואות בפ' ה' הזוחלין כמעין והנוטפין כמקוה העיד ר' (יצחק) [צדוק] על הזוחלין שרבו על הנוטפין שמכשירין ושאמר שמואל נהרא מכיפיה מתברך כלומר הנהר הגדול מן הסלע שיוצא ממנו משום נרבת מליאתו ולא ממי המטר פליגא על אבוה דשמואל ועל רב ועוד דברי שמואל סותרין זה את זה בכאן אמר כי מי המטר אינם ממלאים הנהר אלא מכיפיה מיבריך ועוד אמר אין המים מטהרין בזוחלין אלא פרת ביומי תשרי בלבד מכלל דבשאר החדשים זולתי תשרי כנוטפין הם דגשמים רבו עליהן ומפצי ביומי תשרי היה מסתירו לבנותיו במפצי מפני בני אדם שעל הנהר וטובלת בפרת כי דברי הכל בתשרי זוחלין הן ולמה במפצי דלית להו טהרה במקוה: **פורפת** על האבן ועל האגוז ועל המטבע מע"ש. פי' נותנת אבן או אגוז או מטבע בקצה הסדין כמין קרס בלולאות שלא ישמט הסדין מעליה כדי שתהא מתעטפת באותו סדין ונותנת זה שעשאתו כמין קרס. נשים מדיות מנהגן לצאת בענין הזה פרופות. ובלבד שלא תפרוף בתחלה בשבת על המטבע. והנשים הערביות מנהגן לצאת רעלות ופי' רעלות בירושלמי בליכריאה והן כמו כסוי פנים כדכתיב (ישעיה ג) השרות והרעלות. וי"א זוג ללמדך שבמקומות הללו כך היה מנהגם ומותר להם וכל אדם מותר בכך אלא שדברו חכמים בהווה: **בעי** אביי אשה מהו שתערים ותפרוף באגוז להוציא לבנה קטן בשבת ועלתה בתיקו: [**מתני'**] הקיטע יוצא בקב שלו דברי רבי מאיר ורבי

רב נסים גאון

קסבר שמא ירבו הנוטפין על הזוחלין. עיקר דילה בתורת כהנים אי מה מעין מטהר בזוחלין אף מקוה מטהר בזוחלין תלמוד לומר אך המעין מטהר בזוחלין והמקוה מטהר באשבורן ובמסכת מקואות (פרק ה משנה ה) הזוחלין כמעין והנוטפין כמקוה העיד רבי צדוק על הנוטפין שהן כשרים ותישתכח בפרק ד' דעדיות הנוטפין שרבו על הזוחלין אינן כשירים: **תיבעי** למאן דאמר (מדליקין) [מערימין] בדליקה תיבעי למאן דאמר אין מערימין. עיקר דיליה בפרק כל כתבי הקודש (דף קכ) דתנן לובש כל שהוא יכול ללבוש ועוטף כל מה שהוא יכול להתעטף רבי יוסי אומר י"ח כלי מכלל דתנא קמא סבר מותר ללבוש ולהציל אפילו יתר מי"ח כלי ואף על פי שהוא מערים בכך:

סמיכות

מסורת הש"ס

א) נדרים מ: בכורות נה: ע"ש, ב) לאמי דספק הב"י סימן של"ד והר"ן דהתם מיירי לאגר המעורבת קשה לפרש הך סוגיא. ואין ענין כלל להך דהכא ואפלע"ד דכוונת הסוגיא לאמי דפליגי בתוספתא פי"ד מגילין מפני הדליקה כו' יחמין ואח"כ יליל כו' ואין מערימין בכך רי"א מערימין. מהרב הגו' ר' בנימין קארנגאלד ז"ל, ג) יומא עח: [יבמות קג:], ד) [תוספתא מגילה פ"א ותוספתא זבים פ"ג], ה) [ע' רש"י ברכות נח: ד"ה קטע], ו) [נ"ל אבוה דשמואל].

הגהות הב"ח

(א) גמ' תיבעי למ"ד מערימין בדליקה תיבעי למ"ד אין מערימין בדליקה תיבעי: (ב) רש"י ד"ה וסבר שמא וכו' שניתוספו בנהר מי הגשמים: (ג) תוספות ד"ה סהדא וכו' מעיד בדבר שהוא: (ד) תוס' ד"ה הקיטע וכו' עושה לו קב כמין סנדל להראות כמו שיש:

ליקוטי רש"י

פסולות לכהונה. משום זונות [יבמות עו.]. **מטרא במערבא סהדא רבה פרת.** פרת יורד מא"י לבבל וכשהגשמים יורדין בא"י סהדא רבה הוי פרת בבבל שירדו גשמים במערבא לפי שגדל מחמת הגשמים [בכורות נה:]. כשנהר פרת גדול הוי עדות לגשמים שיורדין לא"י דא"י גבוה מכל הארצות ובאין גשמים ונופלין בפרת ומתגדל מהן והאי דאמרי' דנהר מתגדל ממי גשמים הוי פלוגתא אדשמואל [נדרים מ.]. כשיורד מטר בא"י מעיד עליו פרת בבבל שכל שהוא גדול בידוע שאע"פ שלא ירדו גשמים כאן ירדו גשמים בא"י ונפקא מינה שאסור לטבול בו לפי שאין מי גשמים הנוטפין מטהרין בזוחלין אלא באשבורן כלומר דקוו וקיימי כדתניא בספרי אי מה מעיין מטהר בזוחלין אף מקוה מטהר בזוחלין ת"ל אך מעין ובור מעיין מטהר בזוחלין ומקוה באשבורן הילכך כל היכא דאיכא למיחש שמא רבו נוטפין על הזוחלין אסור והיינו כשהנהר גדול הרבה אבל אם היה הולך לאטו או שלא נתרבה אלא מעט דליכא לספוקי ברביית נוטפין שרי כדתניא בתוספתא העיד ר' אלעזר בר צדוק על הזוחלין שרבו על הנוטפין שהם כשרים [ר"ן שם]. **סבר שלא ירבו הנוטפין על הזוחלין.** לפי שביומי ניסן רבין נוטפין על הזוחלין מחמת הגשמים שהרי כל השלגים והקרח (ש)נתפשרו [ו]באין המים דרך לך ליגורות דהוו להו שאובין אבל [אם] לא באין דרך ליגורות אלא מאליהן שוטפין ובאין טובלין בהן כדאמר זבה ונדה ויולדת טבילתן במי מקוה של מ' סאה ואפי' מי גשמי' מכונסים שלא מליאו מים חיים אלא לזב בלבד שנאמר בו מים חיים והמפרש לא פירש הכי ולאו דוקא דכל נשים בזמן הזה זבות נינהו [רש"י שם:]. שבימות הגשמים ירדו גשמים הרבה וחייש שמא ירבו מים שנוטפין מעבים לתוך הנהר שהם זוחלים דלא חזו להן משום דהוו להו ספק זבות וזב כתיב מים חיים לא"ל על הזוחלים על אותם שנפלו מן העבים לקרקע ומן הקרקע זחלו וקילחו לתוך הנהר דאי לא נוטפים משום זוחלים לא מיפסלי דאמרינן בפ' ראשון דתמורה (יב.) השאובה מיטהרת בהמשכה דהיינו שממשיך מים שאובים לתוך המקוה על ידי צנורות [בכורות שם]. לפי שרבו המים בימות הגשמים מגשמים שנפלו וחייש שמא ירבו נוטפין על הזוחלין ותניא בתורת כהנים אי מה מעין מטהר בזוחלין אף מקוה מטהר בזוחלין כלומר שמטבילין במכונסין דרך זחילתן קודם שנקוו ונחו במקוה ת"ל אך מעין מעין מטהר בזוחלין והמקוה מטהר באשבורן ומהו אשבורן דקוו וקיימי דאין מטבילין במכונסים אלא משנקוו למקוויהם ונחו מזחילתן ותנן במסכת מקוואות (פ"ה מ"ה) הזוחלין כמעין כלומר זוחלין שבנהרות כמעין והנוטפין כמקוה ומים הנוטפין מההרים הרי הן כמקוה ואין מטהרים בזחילה הילכך בימי ניסן שנתרבה הנהר על ידי גשמים חייש שמא רבו נוטפין שבו על חיים שבו ובטלו זוחלין ואין מטהרין את הטמא הטובל בהן דרך זחילה וכל הנהרות לעולם הן הולכים וזוחלין לפיכך עביד להו מקוה באשבורן לטבול בתוכו יש מפרשים דבעינן מים חיים לזבה ולאו מילתא היא דתניא בתוספתא (דמגילה פ"א) חומר בזב מבזבה שהזב טעון מים חיים כו' [נדה סז.]. [המשך בדף סו.]

perhaps **it is** only **there** that a subterfuge is permitted, **דְּאִי לָא שָׁרֵית לֵיהּ אָתֵי לְכַבּוּיֵי** – **since, if we do not permit one** to wear the clothing outside, **one may come to extinguish [the fire]** so as not to lose one's belongings. **אֲבָל הָכָא** – **But here** (regarding taking a nut outside for a child), **אִי לָא שָׁרֵית לֵיהּ לָא אָתֵי לְאַפּוּקֵי** – even **if we do not permit one** to employ a subterfuge, **one will not come to take it out** illegally, since it is not of vital importance that the boy receive the nut. Therefore, even the Tanna who permits one to don many articles of clothing in order to save them might agree that one would not be permitted to fasten one's cloak upon a nut in order to take it out on the Sabbath. **אוֹ דִּלְמָא אֲפִילוּ לְמַאן דְּאָמַר אֵין מַעֲרִימִין בִּדְלֵיקָה** – **Or perhaps, even according to the [Tanna] who says** that **in** the event of **a fire one may not employ a subterfuge** of donning many articles of clothing, in the case of taking a nut to a child one may indeed employ a subterfuge to do so. **הָתָם דֶּרֶךְ הוֹצָאָה בְּכָךְ** – For **there** (in the case of donning many articles of clothing) **it is an** accepted **method of transporting** clothing;[19] this Tanna therefore prohibits it, for fear that it might lead one to transport items illegally on the Sabbath.[20] **אֲבָל הָכָא אֵין דֶּרֶךְ הוֹצָאָה בְּכָךְ** – **But here** (in the case of fastening one's cloak on a nut), since **this is not an** accepted **method of transporting** articles,[21] **אֵימָא שַׁפִּיר דָּמֵי** – **I would say it is all right** to employ this method as a subterfuge. Thus, even the Tanna who does not permit one to don a surfeit of garments in order to save them might agree that one is permitted to fasten one's cloak on a nut in order to take it out on the Sabbath.

The Gemara responds to Abaye's inquiry:

תֵּיקוּ – **Let [the question]** posed by Abaye **stand;** it remains unresolved.[22]

Mishnah

This Mishnah presents several laws concerning the various appurtenances of three types of crippled individuals:

הַקִּיטֵּעַ יוֹצֵא בְּקַב שֶׁלּוֹ – **An amputee may go out** on the Sabbath **with his wooden foot,** as it is considered to be his shoe.[23] **דִּבְרֵי רַבִּי מֵאִיר** – **These are the words of R' Meir.**

NOTES

the clothing be worn, not carried – will help one to remember that it is the Sabbath, and will thus prevent one from extinguishing the fire. R' Yose, however, forbids one to don more than a normal complement of clothing (see below for R' Yose's reason).]

19. For example, garment sellers will often employ this method to transport their merchandise [donning many layers of clothing in order to carry them from place to place] (*Rashi*). Since wearing extra garments is not an accepted manner of dress, but *is* an accepted method of transporting clothing, the extra garments are viewed as a burden [by Rabbinic decree], and may not be worn into a public domain (see *Rashi* above, 59b ד״ה תרי המייני קאמרת; see also *Rama, Orach Chaim* 301:36, with *Beur HaGra* ad loc. ד״ה ויש אוסרין; see also *Mishnah Berurah* ad loc. §133 and *Dibros Moshe* 53:37).

20. [For since wearing excess garments is a regular method of transport, the Sages forbade a subterfuge of this sort [inasmuch as it is actually carrying] (see *Ritva MHK* ed.). See also *Ran* (45a in *dafei HaRif*) ד״ה וטעמיה.]

21. [But is rather an indirect form of transport (הוֹצָאָה כִּלְאַחַר יָד – see *Ritva MHK* ed.). One therefore will not draw a comparison between this irregular form of transport and other, established forms of transport.]

22. For the halachic ruling, see *Rosh* with *Korban Nesanel;* see also *Orach Chaim* 303:23; see also *Rosh Yosef*.

23. It is common practice for one whose foot has been severed to insert the stump of his lower leg into a piece of wood carved to resemble a foot. The purpose of this wooden foot is not to support the cripple's weight, but to conceal the fact that he is maimed (*Rashi, Yevamos* 102b ד״ה בקב הקיטע, and as quoted in *Tosafos,* but see *Maharsha;* see *Rashi* to the *Rif;* see explanation of *Rashi* by *Rosh,* and by *Rabbeinu Yitzchak* in *Tosafos, Yoma* 78b ד״ה הקיטע יוצא [ב׳]). His weight is borne by either a wooden stump strapped to his lower leg, or by a hand-held crutch (*Rashi, Yevamos* ibid.; see *Tosafos, Yoma* ibid.). R' Meir holds that [although shoes are generally made of leather, wooden shoes too are considered normal footwear;] this false foot is therefore viewed as the crippled individual's shoe, and may be worn on the Sabbath (*Rashi;* see 66a note 1).

וְרַבִּי יוֹסֵי אוֹסֵר – **But R' Yose prohibits** an amputee from going out with his wooden foot, as it is not considered a shoe.[1] וְאִם יֵשׁ לוֹ בֵּית קִיבּוּל כְּתִיתִין טָמֵא – **If [the wooden foot] possesses a receptacle for rags, it is susceptible to** contamination with ***tumah***.[2]

Three laws concerning another case of a crippled individual:

סָמוֹכוֹת שֶׁלוֹ – **The** leather **supports** for the lower legs **of [a double amputee]** טְמֵאִין מִדְרָס – **are susceptible to** contamination with ***midras tumah,***[3] וְיוֹצְאִין בָּהֶן בְּשַׁבָּת – **and one may go out with them on the Sabbath,**[4] וְנִכְנָסִין בָּהֶן בָּעֲזָרָה – **and one may enter the Temple Courtyard with them.**[5]

Three laws concerning a third case of a crippled individual:

כִּסֵּא וְסָמוֹכוֹת שֶׁלוֹ – **The chair and** the leg **supports of [one whose lower legs have atrophied]** טְמֵאִין מִדְרָס – **are susceptible to** contamination with ***midras tumah,***[6] וְאֵין יוֹצְאִין בָּהֶן בְּשַׁבָּת – **and one may not go out with them on the Sabbath,**[7] וְאֵין נִכְנָסִין בָּהֶן בָּעֲזָרָה – **and one may not enter the Temple Courtyard**

NOTES

1. R' Yose holds that only shoes made of the prevalent material – leather – are considered customary footwear. A shoe made of wood, however, is not a typical shoe, and is therefore classified not as a garment, but as a burden, whose transport is prohibited on the Sabbath. Accordingly, a cripple's wooden foot is considered a burden, and he may not go out with it on the Sabbath. Although an amputee wears this foot to conceal his infirmity, it is not considered an ornament, since the general public would not utilize this item for ornamental wear (*Rashi*, as explained by *Tosafos, Yoma* 78b [ד״ה ורבי יוסי אוסר ;[ד״ה הקיטע יוצא א׳]; *Rashi, Yoma* 78b see *Tosafos, Yevamos* 103a ד״ה הקיטע וד״ה באנפיליא; see Gemara below; see below, end of note 24). Although an item that is absolutely essential to ambulation may even be *carried* outside [e.g. a crutch for one with a broken leg – see below, notes 4 and 7], this wooden foot does not qualify as such an item, since its function is not weight bearing, but cosmetic (*Rashi,* as explained by *Rabbeinu Yitzchak* in *Tosafos, Yoma* 78b ד״ה הקיטע יוצא [ב׳]; see, however, note 24 below).

[Although R' Yose prohibits one to go out with a wooden foot, one who does so will not be liable to a *chatas*, for since this is not the usual method of transporting articles, it is forbidden only by Rabbinic decree, and not by Biblical law (see *Rambam, Shabbos* 19:15, and *Mishnah Berurah* 301:70).]

[We have stated that the reason R' Yose does not accord wooden footwear the legal status of shoes is because shoes are not usually crafted of wood. However, the Gemara in *Yevamos* 102b with *Rashi* 103a (ד״ה קב הקיטע) seemingly attributes R' Yose's ruling to a Scriptural verse (*Ezekiel* 16:10) that characterizes footwear as shoes made of leather! See, however, *Rosh* to *Yevamos* 102b, who states that the Gemara does not mean this verse to serve as the actual *source* for R' Yose's ruling, but only as a support upon which he can loosely base his reasoning (אַסְמַכְתָּא). See also *Dibros Moshe* 53:38 for discussion of this issue.]

2. I.e. if the cavity into which the cripple inserts his leg was cut large enough to provide space for a cushion of soft rags, the wooden foot is susceptible to contamination with *tumah* transmitted by contact. However, if the cavity is only large enough to contain the stump of the cripple's lower leg, but has no extra space for rags, the wooden foot will not become *tamei*. This is because wooden utensils do not acquire *tumah* through contact unless they can be classified as containers [כְּלֵי קִיבּוּל] – which are defined in *Toras Kohanim* (to *Leviticus* 11:32) as vessels whose use entails that they are carried while laden with other objects. Any wooden vessel that does not meet this criterion [e.g. a wooden implement that does not possess a receptacle, or a vessel too large to be carried when laden] will not be susceptible to *tumah* spread by contact (such as *tumas meis* or *tumas sheretz*). Hence, a wooden foot carved to contain rags will be susceptible to *tumah*, as it is in fact a utensil that is carried while laden (i.e. with rags). However, a wooden foot that was not sized for rags, since it serves no carrying function, is no better than a wooden utensil without any receptacle at all [פְּשׁוּטֵי כְּלֵי עֵץ]. It is therefore not susceptible to *tumah*.

Although the cavity of the wooden foot does *contain* the cripple's leg, it does not *carry* it; rather, the wooden foot is itself carried by his leg, to which it is attached (*Rashi*; see *Tosafos* to 81a ד״ה חפי and *Ritva MHK* ed. for further elucidation of this point. See *Chazon Ish*, *Keilim* 3:5, and 21:7).

Now, one might object that since even a wooden foot that was not made to contain rags *could* be put to use as a container, it too should be susceptible to *tumah*! The answer is that only a wooden vessel *made* for use as a container attains *tumah* susceptibility; it does not suffice that it can be adapted to such use (*Tosafos* 64a ד״ה מניין; see *Rashi* 123b ד״ה ואמאי).

The source from which we know that a wooden utensil is not susceptible to *tumah* unless it can be classified as a container, is from a verse (*Leviticus* 11:32) that enumerates the items susceptible to *tumas sheretz*. The verse states: *whether it is a wooden utensil, or a garment, or a hide or a sack,* thus equating through *hekeish* a wooden utensil to a sack, and thereby teaching that just as a sack is an item that is carried laden as well as empty, so too must wooden utensils be the sort that are carried laden as well as empty in order to be susceptible to *tumah* (see *Toras Kohanim* to *Leviticus* ibid.; see below, 83b and 123b). Other varieties of contact-generated *tumah* are derived from *tumas sheretz.*

[*Rashi* explains this ruling in accordance with Abaye's opinion in the Gemara below; Rava, however, understands this ruling to be discussing *tumas midras* as well as *tumah* transmitted by contact – see below for the particulars of this dispute.]

3. One who has had both feet severed cannot walk with crutches, and therefore must propel himself while in a kneeling position, using his knees and lower legs. One maimed in this manner will often fashion leather pads [i.e. supports] for his shins and knees. Since these pads are made to support one's weight, they will become *tamei* with *midras tumah* in the event that the cripple is a *zav* [i.e. one *tamei* as the result of a particular sort of gonorrheal emission] (*Rashi*; cf. *Tosafos, Yoma* 78b ד״ה הקיטע יוצא [ב׳]).

[*Midras* (literally: treading) *tumah* is the *tumah* acquired by an object when one *tamei* as the result of a bodily emission (e.g. a *zav, zavah* or *niddah*) rests his or her weight upon it, whether by sitting, lying, standing or leaning.] Not every object can become *tamei* in this manner – rather, it must be an object whose intended use is to support the weight of a human being (see above, 59a). Since the pads of a double amputee are intended for support, they are susceptible to *tumas midras* (*Rashi*).

4. [For since this individual cannot propel himself at all without these pads,] they are legally considered an ornament for him, and not a burden (*Rashi*).

5. The Mishnah in *Berachos* (54a) states: *One may not enter the Temple Mount with his stick, or with his shoe*, thus prohibiting one to wear shoes on the Temple Mount, and certainly in the Temple Courtyard. Our Mishnah teaches that although a double amputee's supporting pad functions as a shoe, it is not legally considered a shoe, and may therefore be worn into the Temple Courtyard. This is because an article of footwear does not have legal status as a shoe unless it is worn at the end of one's limb [i.e. upon one's foot, or at the tip of an amputee's stump]. These pads, by contrast, run along the length of the cripple's legs, being affixed to his shins and knees; they therefore are not considered shoes, and may be worn into the Temple (*Rashi*).

[See *Tosafos, Yoma* ibid. for why the Mishnah does not discuss whether one may enter the Temple with a wooden foot.]

6. One whose lower leg muscles and tendons have atrophied cannot even walk on his knees and lower legs. One crippled in this manner generally propels himself by means of a low chair strapped onto him from behind. He holds short bench-like crutches in his hands, and, using the crutches, pushes himself up and forward, coming to rest again in a sitting position. This person's feet, or leg stumps, are encased in wooden or leather supports, since in the action of pushing forward, he will use his legs to momentarily support his weight.

Since the chair and leg supports are used to support his weight, they become *tamei* with *tumas midras* [in the event that the cripple is a *zav*] (*Rashi*).

7. I.e. one may not go out with the leg supports, for since one's legs dangle over the side of the chair, but do not rest upon the ground, the supports are easily dislodged, and may fall, leading one to inadvertently transport them on the Sabbath (*Rashi,* second and preferred explanation). [However, one may certainly go out with the chair and short crutches, for since one cannot even walk without them, one surely

ורבי יוסי אוסר ואם יש לו בית קיבול כתיתין טמא סמוכות שלו טמאין מדרס ויוצאין בהן בשבת ונכנסין בהן בעזרה כסא וסמוכות שלו טמאין מדרס ואין יוצאין בהן בשבת ואין נכנסין בהן בעזרה (א) לוקטמין טהורין ואין יוצאין בהן: **גמ'** אמר ליה רבא לרב נחמן היכי תנן אמר ליה לא ידענא הילכתא מאי אמר ליה לא ידענא איתמר אמר שמואל אין הקיטע וכן אמר רב הונא אין הקיטע אמר רב יוסף הואיל ואמר שמואל אין הקיטע ואמר רב הונא אין הקיטע אנן נמי ניתני אין הקיטע מתקיף לה רבא בר שירא לא שמיע להו הא דמתני ליה רב חנן בר רבא לחייא בר רב קמיה דרב בקיטונא דבי רב אין הקיטע יוצא בקב שלו דברי ר' מאיר ור' יוסי מתיר ומחוי ליה רב איפוך אמר רב נחמן בר יצחק וסימנא סמך סמך (א) ואף שמואל הדר ביה דתנן חלצה בסנדל שאינו שלו בסנדל של עץ או של שמאל בימין חליצה כשרה ואמרינן מאן תנא אמר שמואל ר"מ היא דתנן הקיטע יוצא בקב שלו דברי ר"מ ר' יוסי אוסר ואף רב הונא הדר ביה דתניא סנדל של סיידין טמא מדרס ואשה חולצת בו ויוצאין בו בשבת דברי ר"ע ולא הודו לו [א] והתניא הודו לו אמר רב הונא מאן הודו לו ר' מאיר ומאן לא הודו לו ר' יוסי ° (אמר רב יוסף) מאן לא הודו לו ר' יוחנן בן נורי דתנן [ב] כוורת של קש ושפופרת של קנים ר"ע מטמא ור' יוחנן בן נורי מטהר אמר מר סנדל של סיידין טמא מדרס הא לאו להילוכא עבדי אמר רב אחא בר רב עולא שכן הסייד מטייל בו עד שמגיע לביתו: ואם יש לו בית קיבול כתיתין טמא: אמר אביי טמא טומאת מת ואין טמא מדרס רבא אמר אף טמא מדרס אמר רבא מנא אמינא לה דתנן עגלה של קטן טמאה מדרס ואביי אמר התם סמיך עילויה הכא לא סמיך עילויה אמר אביי מנא אמינא לה דתניא מקל של זקנים טהור מכלום ורבא התם

לתרוצי

רש"י

ור' יוסי אוסר. דלאו תכשיט הוא: ואם יש לו בית קבול כתיתין. שנחקק בו כדי קיבול כתיתין של בגדים רכין ומוכין להניח ראש שוקו עליהן: טמא. מקבל טומאת מגע אבל אם אין לו אלא בית קבול ראש שוקו ואינו מניח שם כתיתין לאו בית קבול לטומאה (ב) והוה ליה כפשוטי כלי עץ ודומיא דשק בעינן שקבול שלו עשוי לטלטל על ידו מה שנותנין לתוכו ° אבל שוקו אינו מיטלטל ע"ג הכלי: סמוכות שלו. סמוכות של קיטע יש קיטע בשתי רגליו מהלך על שוקיו ועל ארכובותיו ועושה סמוכות של עור לשוקיו: טמאין מדרס. אם זב הוא דהא לסמיכת גופו עביד ומדרס הזב עושה אב הטומאה: ויוצאין בהן בשבת. דתכשיט דידיה הוא: ונכנסין בהן לעזרה. דאע"ג דתנן (ברכות דף נד.) לא יכנס אדם להר הבית במנעלו הני לאו מנעל נינהו דלאו בראש רגלו הן: כסא. יש קיטע שיבשו וכווצו גידי שוקיו ואפי' על ארכובותיו אינו יכול לילך ועושין כמין כסא נמוך ויושב עליו וכשהוא מהלך נסמך על ידיו בספסלים קטנים ועוקר גופו מן הארץ ונדחף לפניו וחוזר ונח על אחוריו והכסא קשור לו מאחוריו: סמוכות. של אותו קיטע עושה לה סמוכות של עור או של עץ לראשי שוקיו או רגליו התלויין וכשהוא נשען על ידיו ועוקר עצמו נשען גם על רגליו קצת: ואין יוצאין בהן בשבת. רבותינו אומרים מפני שאינם צריכין לו כל כך ולא נהירא לי טעמא ואיכא למימר דאיידי דתלו ולא מנחי אארעא זימנין דמשתלפי: ואין נכנסין בהן בעזרה. דמנעל נינהו: לוקטמין. טלמשק"א נעשין לשחוק להבעית תינוקות: טהורים. מלקבל טומאה דאינו לא כלי תשמיש ולא תכשיט: גמ' היכי תנן. הקיטע יוצא ורבי יוסי אוסר או אין הקיטע יוצא ורבי יוסי מתיר: בר שירא: קיטונא. חדר קטן של בית המדרש: סמך סמך. ר' יוסי אוסר שתי תיבות שיש בהן סמך סמך זו אצל זו: או של שמאל בימין. סנדל של שמאל נעל בימין וחלצה דחליצה בימין הוא דגמר רגל רגל ממצורע: מאן תנא. דסנדל של עץ חשיב נעלו: סנדל של סיידין. מוכרי סיד וכשמתעסקין בו נועלין אותו ושל עץ הוא מפני שהסיד שורף את העור: ואמר רב הונא גרסי': מאן הודו לו ר' מאיר. דאמר הקיטע יוצא בקב שלו: ור' יוחנן בן נורי מטהר. דלאו אורחא לעשות מקש אלא מקנים ומנעל נמי לאו אורחיה מעץ אלא מעור זה לשון רבותי ולי נראה סנדל של סיידין של קש הוא ור' יוחנן בן נורי מטהר בכלי קש דלאו עץ נינהו ור' עקיבא כעץ חשיב להו דקשין הן: קש. זנבות השבלים: ואין טמא מדרס. דלא מסתמיך עליה הא דנקט טומאת מת ה"ה לכל טומאת מגע אלא משום דאמר אין טמא מדרס שהוא אב הטומאה נקט נמי טומאת מת והכי קאמר נעשה אב הטומאה ע"י מת דכלי עץ שיש לו בית קבול הוא ומקבל כל טומאת מגע ואהל ועל ידי כל הטומאות הוא נעשה ראשון ועל ידי מת שהוא אבי אבות הטומאה נעשה אב הטומאה ואין נעשה אב הטומאה ע"י מדרס דקסבר לאו לסמיכה עבידי אלא לתכשיט ואומרים לו עמוד ונעשה מלאכתנו: עגלה של קטן. לשחק בה ולטלטלו עליה: טמאה מדרס. הואיל ופעמים שיושב עליה והאי נמי זימנין דמסתמיך עליה: טהור מכלום. לא מדרס ולא שאר טומאה לא מטמא מדרס משום דלאו לסמיכה עביד שעל רגלו מהלך ואע"ג דמיסתמיך עליה לפרקים ושאר טומאה נמי לא דפשוטי כלי עץ הוא אלמא אע"ג דזימנין דמסתמיך עליה הואיל ועיקר עשייתה אינה לכך אינה טמאה מדרס ואין לומר משום דפשוט הוא יהא טהור ממדרס דלא הוזכרה טהרת פשוטי כלי עץ אלא לטומאת מגע ואהל דטעמא משום דאיתקש לשק הוא וגבי מת ושרצים הויא היקישא:

לתרוצי

תוספות

סנדל של סיידין. פ"ה מוכרי הסיד וכשמתעסקין בסיד נועלין אותו ושל עץ הוא מפני שהסיד שורף את העור זה לשון רבותי ול"נ סנדל סיידין של קש הוא וכפי' זה נראה דהכי תניא בתוספתא סנדל של קש ר' עקיבא מטמא כו':

טמא מדרס ולא הודו לו. וא"ת ואמאי לא הודו לו ומי גרע מכופת שאור שיחדו לישיבה דקיי"ל (ז) דטמא מדרס דגבי מדרס לא בעינן דומיא דשק דכל דבר המיוחד למדרס טמא מדרס וי"ל דללשון שפירש רש"י של קש הוא ניחא דכיון דלאו בר קיימא הוא אינו טמא ולא דמי לכופת שאור שהוא בר קיימא והכי אשכחן במשניות (ק) דקתני גבי האלון והאגוז ורימון שחקקום תינוקות למוד בהן עפר שמקבלין טומאה ואילו גבי לפת ואתרוג שחקקו קתני שאינן מקבלין טומאה לפי שאינן מתקיימין וללשון שפירש שסנדל הוי של עץ קשה שהרי ראוי הוא להתקיים כיון שהוא של עץ וטמא י"ל דהיינו טעמא דמטהר סנדל דלא חשיב עביד להילוכא מה שמטייל בו הואיל ואין רגילות לעשות מנעל להילוך כמותו דכוותה בשפופרת כיון שאין רגילות לעשותה מקנים לא חשיבה כלי ולא דמי לכופה שרגילות לעשות לישיבה כמותה: כוורת הקש ושפופרת של קנים ר"ע מטמא. ואם תאמר והיכי מטמא (ל) לענין טמא מת) כיון דלא חזי לישיבה לא מטמא מדרס ולענין טומאת מת הא לא כתיב בפרשה אלא כלי עץ ועור ובגד ושק וי"ל דקש נמי חשיב של עץ כדאמר (ברכות דף מ.) פרי שאכל אדם הראשון חטה היתה אי נמי הך טומאה דרבנן היא: ורבי יוחנן מטהר. לפירוש אחרון שפי' בקונטרס דסנדל של קש הוא מדמי שפיר כוורת לסנדל של סיידין ולאידך פירושא שפי' דסנדל של עץ הוא צ"ל דמייתי הכי דכי היכי דר' יוחנן מטהר בכוורת של קש לפי שאין רגילות לעשותה מקש הכי נמי במנעל של סיידין לפי שאין רגילות לעשות מנעל של עץ מטהר: והא לאו להילוכא עביד. הקשה הר"ר אליעזר ממיץ לרשב"א מאי פריך והלא משעת מלאכתו הוא מהלך בו ולכך הוא נעשה ותירץ לו דסנדל של סיידין לאו לנעול עשוי אלא אחד מכלי אומנותו של סיידין הוא ועשוי כעין סנדל ויכול לתת רגלו בתוכו לנועלו אך אין עשוי רק לטוח בו את הבית ופעמים שנועל בו ומטייל בו עד שיגיע לביתו ולהכי פריך והא לאו להילוכא כו' ור"י פירש הואיל ואין עשוי כלל לנעילה רק לשמור מנעליו שלא ישרפו בסיד לאו להילוכא עביד ומכל מקום משני לו שכן הסייד כו': רבא אמר אף טמא טומאת מדרס. פי' הרב פור"ת הא דלא קתני ברישא דמתניתין ואם יש לו בית קיבול כתיתין טמא מדרס כדקתני בסיפא משום דהוה משמע אבל אם אין לו בית קיבול טהור מן המדרס אבל טמא טומאת מת ולא היא דהא פשוטי כלי עץ הוא ולהכי תנא טמא סתמא דבכה"ג טמא הא אין לו בית קיבול כתיתין טהור לגמרי וא"ת למה לי בית קיבול כתיתין תיפוק ליה דכל הטמא מדרס טמא טומאת מת (מ) וי"ל דבית קיבול כתיתין עושין אותו ראוי למדרס: עגלה של קטן. פ"ה עגלה שהקטן יושב עליה ול"נ דא"כ מאי קמ"ל פשיטא דאין לך מיוחד למדרס גדול מזה לכך נ"ל דהיינו עגלה שעושין לקטן להתלמד להלך טמאה מדרס דנשען עליה:

קישורי

עין משפט נר מצוה

עז א מיי' פי"ט מהל' שבת הלכה טז סמג לאוין סה טוש"ע א"ח סימן שא סעיף טו:
עח ב שם סעיף טז:
עט ג מיי' פכ"ה מהל' כלים הלכה יח:
פ ד ה שם הלכה יט:
פא ו שם הלכה טז:
פב ז שם הלכה יז:

ליקוטי רש"י

ופליגא דשמואל דאמר שמואל נהרא מכיפיה מיברך. שנובע מגדותיו ולא ממי גשמים [רש"י נדרים שם]. מכיפיה מסלעו כלומר ממקורו הוא מתגדל שאע"פ שאנו רואים שכשהגשמים יורדין נהרות מתרבים עיקר רבויין ממקורן הוא כדאמרי' בפרק סדר תעניות (כה:) אין לך כל טפח וטפח יורד מלמעלה שאין תהום עולה לקראתו טפחיים ונמצא שלעולם זוחלין רבין על הנוטפין דהא לטפח של גשמים איכא טפחיים דמעיין הלכך לשמואל מותר לטבול בנהרות לעולם אפי' כשרואה לעין שנתרבו הרבה מחמת המטר. אין המים מטהרין בזוחלין. דאיכא למיחש לרבו הנוטפין [ר"ן שם]. [דבכל] שעה הוו מים נוטפין רבין עליהן [בכורות שם]. אלא פרת ביומי תשרי בלבד. דכל ימות השנה רבין נוטפין על הזוחלין מן הגשמים שיורדין לתוכו ומן השלגים שמתפשרין כל ימות החמה אבל בתשרי כבר פסקו השלגים ונתפשרו כולן והלכו להן מטהרין הזוחלין ואין בנהרות אלא מימיו שנובעין בלבד [רש"י נדרים שם:]. לפי שאינו עת גשמים ולא זמן הפשרת שלגים ולא למיסר כל הנהרות חוץ מפרת אתא ולא למיסר נמי פרת בכל השנה אלא וכו' קאמר שמואל שאין המים מטהרין בזוחלין אלא פרת וכיוצא בו שאינו מכזב לעולם ולמעוטי מים המכזבין הוא דקאמר פרת ופרת וכיוצא בו קאמר וקאמר נמי דבפרת וכיוצא בו שאינו מכזב אינו מותר לטבול בו מן הפסח בכל השנה כולה מי שאינו בקי בו אלא ביומי תשרי בלבד לפי שביומי תשרי אינו עת גשמים ולא זמן הפשרת שלגים ולפיכך אפי' מי שאינו בקי בו אין לו לחוש שמא רבו עליו נוטפין אבל אין ה"נ דמי שבקי בפרת וכיוצא בו כל השנה כל שהוא רואה שלא נתרבה על מה שהוא זוחל בתשרי בכדי שיהא ראוי לחוש לרבוי נוטפין טובל בו בכל השנה וכן נמי אם רואה בתשרי שנתרבה כל כך עד שאפשר לו לחוש שמא רבו בו נוטפין אפי' בתשרי אינו טובל בו אלא שמואל סתמא קאמר דמי שאינו מכיר אפי' בנהרות שאין מכזבין יש לו לחוש כל השנה ברבייתן וביומי תשרי אין לו לחוש כן נ"ל וראיתי מי שכתב בהפך ולא נראו לי דבריו [ר"ן שם]. שפרת היו מימיו פרין ורבין וזוחלין [ונובעין] ממעיינות מרובין ועוד שתשרי סוף ימי הקיץ ולא ירדו גשמים (הרי) [לזמן] מרובה אלמא נהרות מתרבין ממימי גשמים ולעיל אמר מכיפיה מיבריך לישנא אחרינא הא דאבוה דשמואל הוה עביד [לבנתיה] מקוואות ביומי ניסן מפני שהוא סוף החורף שירדו גשמים מרובים אבל באמצע החורף לא הוה עביד ופליגא אדשמואל דהוא אומר דכל שעה בעינן מקוואות אלא פרת ביומי תשרי [בכורות שם].

הקיטע. היכא דקתני קטע לחוד משמע דרגלים כדתנן (שבת סה:) הקטע יוצא בקב שלו [ברכות נח: עיי"ש]. הקיטע יוצא בקב שלו. עושין לו כמין דפוס רגל וחוקק בו מעט לתת ראש שוקו לתוכו ואינו נסמך עליו ולכך יצא בקב שלו דמנעל דידיה הוא [רש"י ברי"ף ועי' בתוס' כאן]. בקב הקיטע שנקטעה רגלו עושה כמין דפוס רגל ויש בה בית קיבול קטן ומכניס שם ראש שוקו ואין נסמך עליו והוא קרוי קב ולמשענת הליכה יש לו אשקצ"א קשורה בשוקיו ומשענת ידיו שקורין קרוק"א [יבמות קב:]. קב הקיטע נעל הוא לצאת בו בשבת [שם קג:]. קב. אשקצ"א [יומא עח:] [ע"כ שייך לדף סה:]. כתיתין. חתיכות דקות של מוכין ועור רך [יבמות קב:]. חתיכות בגדים קטנות שהם נוחות לו לסמוך שוקו עליהם. טמא. מקבל טומאה דלאו פשוטי כלי עץ הוא [יומא עח:]. או של שמאל בימין חליצה כשרה. שהחליצה ברגל ימיני ואם נעל בו סנדל שמאל וחלצה כשר [לקמן קיב:]. אבל חליצה של שמאל קתני בפירקין (יבמות קד.) פלוגתא [יבמות קא.]. מאן תנא. סנדל של עץ דקתני מתני' חליצתה כשרה מני. רבי מאיר היא. דאמר קב הקיטע נעל הוא לצאת בו בשבת [שם קג:]. עגלה של קטן. שעושין לו לשחוק ויושב עליה ומטלטלין אותו עליה. טמאה מדרס. אם התינוק זב נעשית העגלה אב הטומאה דמיוחדת לישיבה היא דהא סומך קטן עליה נמצאת שהיא מיוחדת לו לישיבה ואין אומרים לו עמוד ונעשה מלאכתנו דאילו לא מיוחדא להכי לא הוה אב הטומאה כדתניא יכול כפה סאה וישב עליה כו' (שבת נט.) [ביצה כג:].

מסורת הש"ס

א) [במשנה שבמשניות איתא אנקטמין וערוך כתב לדהכא], ב) [שבועות מו.], ג) [שם], ד) יבמות קא., ה) עדיות פ"ב מ"ח תוספתא דכלים ב"ב פ"ד [ע"ש], ו) [נ"ל רב יוסף אמר], ז) שם, ח) [בפי"ז דכלים מי"ז תנן מחצלת הקש ושפופרת הקש ר"ע מטמא ור"י בן נורי מטהר וע"ש בפי' הר"ש ד"ה ר"ע ולכאורה נראה שצ"ל דתניא כוורת וכו'], ט) ביצה כג:, תוספתא דכלים ב"ב פ"ד, י) [חולין קכט.], כ) [כלים פי"ז מט"ו], ל) בס"י ליתא, מ) [כדאיתא נדה מט.].

הגהות הב"ח

(א) גמרא וסימנא סמך סמך. נ"ב עי' בפ' ח' שרצים דף קי ע"א במ"ש התוספו' בד"ה סיפאי: (ב) רש"י ד"ה טמא מקבל וכו' לטומאה הוא והוה וכו' ודומיא דשק:

גליון הש"ס

גמ' אמר רב יוסף מאן לא הודו לו. ברמב"ן במלחמות רפ"ח דיומא גרס כאן רבה אמר: רש"י ד"ה טמא וכו' אבל שוקו אינו מיטלטל. עיין לקמן דף פא ע"א תוס' ד"ה חפי פוחתת:

הגהות הגר"א

[א] גמ' והתניא. נ"ב וסתם. מתני' בעדיות: [ב] שם (כוורת של קש ושפופרת של קנים). תא"מ וכ"ב מחצלת הקש ושפופרת הקש ועיין בפי"ז דכלים:

רבינו חננאל

ורבי יוסי אוסר וכדאוקמוה (א) ומחתי בה סימנא סמך סמך כלומר ר' יוסי אוסר (סבר) [דכ"ע סברי] הקב של קיטע (אינו) חשוב כסנדל ואסור לצאת בו ביוה"כ והיינו טעמא דר' יוסי דאסר בשבת גזרה דלמא משתמיט ואתי לאתויי ד' אמות ברה"ר (כו') ושמואל נמי ורב יוסף (לפנינו הגי' רב הונא) הדרו ואוקמוה למתני' הקטע יוצא דברי ר"מ: סנדל של סיידין. פי' הסייד כשהוא סד קרקעית הבית בסיד נועל סנדלו של עץ ברגלו כדי שלא יהא הסיד אוכל ברגלו. בית קבול כתיתין. פי' חקוק בתוך הקב חקיקה להיות

חשק שלמה על רבינו חננאל

א) הובא בא"ז בשם רבינו:

רב נסים גאון

סמיכות שלו אין נכנסין בהן לעזרה. מחמת מה שנאמרה בפ' הרואה מקום במסכת ברכות (דף נד) ולא יכנס בה להר הבית במקל

with them.[8]

The Mishnah now presents two laws concerning *lokitmin*:

לוּקְטָמִין טְהוֹרִין וְאֵין יוֹצְאִין בָּהֶן – ***Lokitmin* are not susceptible to** contamination with ***tumah*****, and one may not go out with them** on the Sabbath.[9]

Gemara The Gemara presents two questions regarding the dispute between R' Meir and R' Yose. The first question concerns the true reading of the Mishnah:

אָמַר לֵיהּ רָבָא לְרַב נַחְמָן – **Rava said to Rav Nachman:** **הֵיכִי תְּנַן** – **How was** the dispute actually **taught in our Mishnah?** Did the Mishnah say that R' Meir permits an amputee to go out with a wooden foot, whereas R' Yose forbids it, or was it the other way around? **אָמַר לֵיהּ** – **[Rav Nachman] replied to him:** **לֹא יָדְעְנָא** – **I do not know.**

Rava's second question:

הִילְכְתָא מַאי – **What is** in fact **the halachah?** May an amputee go out with his wooden foot or not? **אָמַר לֵיהּ** – **[Rav Nachman] replied to [Rava]:** **לֹא יָדְעְנָא** – **I do not know.**

The Gemara addresses Rava's first question:

אִיתְּמַר – **It has been said** with regard to the Mishnah's reading: **אָמַר שְׁמוּאֵל** – **Shmuel said:** **אֵין הַקִּיטֵּעַ** – The Mishnah's true reading is: AN AMPUTEE MAY NOT [go out with his wooden foot on the Sabbath. These are the words of R' Meir. But R' Yose permits it]. **וְכֵן אָמַר רַב הוּנָא** – **And so too Rav Huna said:** **אֵין הַקִּיטֵּעַ** – The Mishnah's true reading is: AN AMPUTEE MAY NOT [go out with his wooden foot on the Sabbath. These are the words of R' Meir. But R' Yose permits it]. Thus, according to the reading of both Shmuel and Rav Huna, R' Meir prohibits an amputee to go out with his wooden foot, whereas R' Yose permits him to do so!

Rav Yosef concurs with this reading:

אָמַר רַב יוֹסֵף – **Rav Yosef said:** **הוֹאִיל וְאָמַר שְׁמוּאֵל אֵין הַקִּיטֵּעַ** – **Since Shmuel said** that the Mishnah reads: AN AMPUTEE MAY NOT [go out . . . these are the words of R' Meir], **וְאָמַר רַב הוּנָא אֵין הַקִּיטֵּעַ** – **and Rav Huna** as well **said** that the Mishnah reads: AN AMPUTEE MAY NOT [go out . . . these are the words of R' Meir], **אֲנַן נַמִּי נִיתְנֵי אֵין הַקִּיטֵּעַ** – **we too will learn** that the Mishnah reads: AN AMPUTEE MAY NOT [go out . . . these are the words of R' Meir]. Thus, Rav Yosef agrees that according to the Mishnah's true reading, R' Meir prohibits an amputee to go out with his wooden foot, while R' Yose permits him to do so.

This reading is challenged:

מַתְקִיף לָהּ רָבָא בַּר שִׁירָא – **Rava bar Shira objected to [Rav Yosef's concurrence]:** **לֹא שְׁמִיעַ לְהוּ הָא דְּמַתְנֵי לֵיהּ רַב חָנָן בַּר רָבָא לְחִיָּיא בַּר רַב קַמֵּיהּ דְּרַב בְּקִיטוֹנָא דְּבֵי רַב** – **Did they** (i.e. Rav Yosef and his students) **not hear of [the incident]** in **which Rav Chanan bar Rava taught [our Mishnah] to Chiya bar Rav before Rav in the small chamber of Rav's academy** as follows: **אֵין הַקִּיטֵּעַ יוֹצֵא בְּקַב שֶׁלּוֹ** – AN AMPUTEE MAY NOT GO OUT WITH HIS WOODEN FOOT. **דִּבְרֵי רַבִּי מֵאִיר** – THESE ARE THE WORDS OF R' MEIR. **וְרַבִּי יוֹסֵי מַתִּיר** – BUT R' YOSE PERMITS him to do so; **וּמַחֲוֵי לֵיהּ רַב אֵיפּוּךְ** – **whereupon Rav signaled to him**[10] (Rav Chanan bar Rava) to **reverse** the opinions, and to say instead that R' Meir permits a wooden foot, while R' Yose prohibits it?! We see from this incident that Rav disputes Shmuel's reading; why then does Rav Yosef follow it?

The Gemara presents a mnemonic for Rav's reading:

אָמַר רַב נַחְמָן בַּר יִצְחָק – **Rav Nachman bar Yitzchak said:** **וְסִימָנָא סמך סמך** – **And the mnemonic** for Rav's reading **is *samech*, *samech***, since the phrase, "R' Yose prohibits" (*R' Yose osair*) has two words containing a *samech*.[11]

The Gemara now demonstrates that even Shmuel admits to Rav's reading:

וְאַף שְׁמוּאֵל הֲדַר בֵּיהּ – **And even Shmuel retracted** his opinion regarding this issue. **דִּתְנַן** – **For we have learned in a Mishnah:**[12] **חָלְצָה בְּסַנְדָּל שֶׁאֵינוֹ שֶׁלּוֹ** – If [A *YEVAMAH*] PERFORMED *CHALITZAH* WITH A SANDAL THAT WAS NOT [THE *YAVAM'S*] property, **בְּסַנְדָּל שֶׁל עֵץ** – WITH A SANDAL OF WOOD, **אוֹ שֶׁל שְׂמֹאל בְּיָמִין** – OR WITH A LEFT shoe from UPON THE *yavam's* RIGHT foot, **חֲלִיצָה כְּשֵׁרָה** – THE *CHALITZAH* IS VALID.[13] **וְאָמְרִינַן** – **And we said:** **מַאן תַּנָּא** – **Who is this Tanna** who holds that a wooden sandal is legally considered a shoe?[14] **אָמַר שְׁמוּאֵל** – **Shmuel said:** **רַבִּי מֵאִיר הִיא** – **It is R' Meir.** **דִּתְנַן** – **For we have learned in a Mishnah:** **הַקִּיטֵּעַ יוֹצֵא בְּקַב שֶׁלּוֹ** – AN AMPUTEE MAY GO OUT on the Sabbath WITH HIS WOODEN FOOT. **דִּבְרֵי רַבִּי מֵאִיר** – THESE ARE THE WORDS OF R' MEIR. **רַבִּי יוֹסֵי אוֹסֵר** – BUT R' YOSE PROHIBITS him to do so. Thus, R' Meir holds that with regard to the laws of Sabbath, a wooden shoe is legally considered a shoe. Likewise, with regard to the laws of *chalitzah*, it is R' Meir who holds that a wooden sandal is legally considered a shoe.[15]

NOTES

will not come to transport them (see *Tosafos* to 65b ד"ה הקיטע).]

Alternatively, the reason the leg supports are prohibited is because they are not absolutely essential to this method of ambulation; they therefore constitute a burden and may not be worn outside. The chair and the short crutches, by contrast, are permitted, since this sort of cripple absolutely cannot propel himself without these items (*Rashi*, in the name of his teachers; *Tosafos, Yoma* ibid.).

8. I.e. with the leg supports, for since they are worn upon one's foot, or at the tip of one's stump, they are considered shoes, and therefore may not be worn into the Temple (*Rashi*). [The chair, however, is obviously not considered a shoe.]

[In a case where the leg supports were fashioned of wood, R' Yose would of course maintain that they may be worn into the Temple, in accordance with his opinion that wooden shoes do not have legal status as shoes (*Ritva MHK* ed.).]

9. *Rashi* states that *lokitmin* are masks used in a playful manner to frighten small children [see, however, two alternative explanations in the Gemara (66b)]. Since masks are neither utensils nor ornaments, they cannot become *tamei* (*Rashi*). And since they are neither ornaments nor garments, one may not go out wearing them on the Sabbath, as they constitute a burden (*Mishnah Berurah* 301:70).

10. [When the Gemara recounts a similar incident in *Yoma* (19b), it explains that the reason Rav signaled to Rav Chanan bar Rava instead of speaking to him was because he was engaged in reciting the *Krias Shema*, and could not interrupt.]

11. [One can thus jog one's memory as to the correct version by making a mental note that the proper reading contains two consecutive words containing a *samech* (for further discussion of this particular mnemonic, see *Sfas Emes*).]

12. *Yevamos* 101a.

13. *Chalitzah* is the rite performed by a *yavam* who does not wish to fulfill the *mitzvah* of *yibum* (the levirate marriage to his childless brother's widow). In this rite, the *yevamah* (the widow) removes the *yavam's* shoe before the court, and spits before him, and declares: כָּכָה יֵעָשֶׂה לָאִישׁ אֲשֶׁר לֹא־יִבְנֶה אֶת־בֵּית אָחִיו, *So should be done to the man who will not build his brother's house* (see *Deuteronomy* 25:5-10). This Mishnah, which deals with the details of the *chalitzah* rite, discusses the sort of shoe suitable for it.

14. [For the Torah (ibid. v. 9) demands that the *yevamah* remove the *yavam's* shoe (וְחָלְצָה נַעֲלוֹ); since this Tanna validates a *chalitzah* performed with a wooden shoe, he evidently holds that even an article of wooden footwear qualifies as a shoe!]

15. [However, see *Yevamos* 103b, where the father of Shmuel offers an alternative explanation of that Mishnah – that it discusses a wooden shoe covered with leather, which both R' Meir and R' Yose agree is considered a shoe.]

ורבי יוסי [א]אוסר ואם יש לו בית קיבול כתיתין טמא סמוכות שלו טמאין מדרס [ב]ויוצאין בהן בשבת ונכנסין בהן בעזרה כסא וסמוכות שלו טמאין מדרס ואין יוצאין בהן בשבת ואין נכנסין בהן בעזרה (א) לוקטמין טהורין ואין יוצאין בהן: **גמ'** אמר ליה רבא לרב נחמן [ב]היכי תנן אמר ליה לא ידענא [ג]הילכתא מאי אמר ליה לא ידענא איתמר אמר שמואל אין הקיטע וכן אמר רב הונא אין הקיטע אמר רב יוסף הואיל ואמר שמואל אין הקיטע ואמר רב הונא אין הקיטע אנן נמי ניתני אין הקיטע מתקיף לה רבא בר שירא לא שמיע להו הא דמתני ליה רב חנן בר רבא לחייא בר רב קמיה דרב בקיטונא דבי רב אין הקיטע יוצא בקב שלו דברי ר' מאיר ור' יוסי מתיר ומחוי ליה רב איפוך אמר רב נחמן בר יצחק וסימנא סמך סמך (א) ואף שמואל הדר ביה דתנן [ד]חלצה בסנדל שאינו שלו בסנדל של עץ או של שמאל בימין חליצה כשרה ואמרינן מאן תנא אמר שמואל ר"מ היא דתנן הקיטע יוצא בקב שלו דברי ר"מ ר' יוסי אוסר ואף רב הונא הדר ביה דתניא [ה]סנדל של סיידין טמא מדרס ואשה חולצת בו ויוצאין בו בשבת דברי ר"ע ולא הודו לו [א] והתניא הודו לו אמר רב הונא מאן הודו לו ר' מאיר ומאן לא הודו לו ר' יוסי (ו) אמר רב יוסף) מאן לא הודו לו ר' יוחנן בן נורי [ז]דתנן [ב] [ח]כוורת של קש ושפופרת של קנים ר"ע מטמא ור' יוחנן בן נורי מטהר אמר מר [ג]סנדל של סיידין טמא מדרס הא לאו להילוכא עבדי אמר רב אחא בר רב עולא שכן הסייד מטייל בו עד שמגיע לביתו: [ד]ואם יש לו בית קיבול כתיתין טמא: אמר אביי טמא טומאת מת ואין טמא מדרס רבא אמר [ה]אף טמא מדרס אמר רבא מנא אמינא לה [ט]דתנן [ו]עגלה של קטן טמאה מדרס ואביי אמר התם סמיך עילויה הכא לא סמיך עילויה אמר אביי מנא אמינא לה דתניא [ז]מקל של זקנים טהור מכלום ורבא התם לתרוצי

רש"י

ור' יוסי אוסר. דלאו תכשיט הוא: **ואם יש לו בית קבול כתיתין.** שנחקק בו כדי קיבול כתיתין של בגדים רכין ומוכין להניח ראש שוקו עליהן: **טמא.** מקבל טומאת מגע אבל אם אין לו אלא בית קבול ראש שוקו ואינו מניח שם כתיתין לאו בית קבול לטומאה (ב) והוה ליה כפשוטי כלי עץ ודומיא דשק בעינן שקבול שלו עשוי לטלטל על ידו מה שנותנין לתוכו [°] אבל שוקו אינו מיטלטל ע"ג הכלי: **סמוכות שלו.** סמוכות של קיטע יש קיטע בשתי רגליו מהלך על שוקיו ועל ארכובותיו ועושה סמוכות של עור לשוקיו: **טמאין מדרס.** אם זב הוא דהא לסמיכת גופו עביד ומדרס הזב עושה אב הטומאה: **ויוצאין בהן בשבת.** דתכשיט דידיה הוא: **ונכנסין בהן לעזרה.** דאע"ג דתנן (ברכות דף נד.) לא יכנס אדם להר הבית במנעלו הני לאו מנעל נינהו דלאו בראש רגלו הן: **כסא.** יש קיטע שיבשו וכווצו גידי שוקיו ואפי' על ארכובותיו אינו יכול לילך ועושין כמין כסא נמוך ויושב עליו וכשהוא מהלך נסמך על ידיו בספסלים קטנים ועוקר גופו מן הארץ ונדחף לפניו וחוזר ונח על אחוריו והכסא קשור לו מאחוריו: **סמוכות.** של אותו קיטע עושה לה סמוכות של עור או של עץ לראשי שוקיו או רגליו התלויין וכשהוא נשען על ידיו ועוקר עצמו נשען גם על רגליו קצת: **ואין יוצאין בהן בשבת.** רבותינו אומרים מפני שאינם צריכין לו כל כך ולא נהירא לי טעמא ואיכא למימר דאיידי דתלו ולא מנחי אארעא זימנין דמשתלפי: **ואין נכנסין בהן בעזרה.** דמנעל נינהו: **לוקטמין.** טלמשק"א נעשין לשחוק להבעית תינוקות: **טהורים.** מלקבל טומאה דאינו לא כלי תשמיש ולא תכשיט: **גמ' היכי תנן.** הקיטע יוצא ורבי יוסי אוסר או אין הקיטע יוצא ורבי יוסי מתיר: **בר שירא:** **קיטונא.** חדר קטן של בית המדרש: **סמך סמך.** ר' יוסי אוסר שתי תיבות שיש בהן סמך סמך זו אצל זו: **או של שמאל בימין.** סנדל של שמאל נעל בימין וחלצה דחליצה בימין הוא דגמר רגל רגל ממצורע: **מאן תנא.** דסנדל של עץ חשיב נעלו: **סנדל של סיידין.** מוכרי סיד וכשמתעסקין בו נועלין אותו ושל עץ הוא מפני שהסיד שורף את העור: **ואמר רב הונא גרסי': מאן הודו לו ר' מאיר.** דאמר הקיטע יוצא בקב שלו: **ור' יוחנן בן נורי מטהר.** דלאו אורחא לעשות מקש אלא מקנים ומנעל נמי לאו אורחיה מעץ אלא מעור זה לשון רבותי ולי נראה סנדל של סיידין של קש הוא ור' יוחנן בן נורי מטהר בכלי קש דלאו עץ נינהו ור' עקיבא כעץ חשיב להו דקשין הן: **קש.** זנבות השבלים: **ואין טמא מדרס.** דלא מסתמיך עליה הא דנקט טומאת מת ה"ה לכל טומאת מגע אלא משום דאמר אין טמא מדרס שהוא אב הטומאה נקט נמי טומאת מת והכי קאמר נעשה אב הטומאה ע"י מת דכלי עץ שיש לו בית קבול הוא ומקבל כל טומאת מגע ואהל ועל ידי כל הטומאות הוא נעשה ראשון ועל ידי מת שהוא אבי אבות הטומאה נעשה אב הטומאה ואין נעשה אב הטומאה ע"י מדרס דקסבר לאו לסמיכה עבידי אלא לתכשיט ואומרים לו עמוד ונעשה מלאכתנו: **עגלה של קטן.** לצחק בה ולטלטלו עליה: **טמאה מדרס.** הואיל ופעמים שיושב עליה והאי נמי זימנין דמסתמיך עליה: **טהור מכלום.** לא מדרס ולא שאר טומאה לא מטמא מדרס משום דלאו לסמיכה עביד שעל רגלו מהלך ואע"ג דמיסתמיך עליה לפרקים ושאר טומאה נמי לא דפשוטי כלי עץ הוא אלמא אע"ג דזימנין דמסתמיך עליה הואיל ועיקר עשייתה אינה לכך אינה טמאה מדרס ואין לומר משום דפשוט הוא יהא טהור ממדרס דלא הוזכרה טהרת פשוטי כלי עץ אלא לטומאת מגע ואהל דטעמא משום דאיתקש לשק הוא וגבי מת ושרצים הויא היקישא:

תוספות

סנדל של סיידין. פ"ה מוכרי הסיד וכשמתעסקין בסיד נועלין אותו ושל עץ הוא מפני שהסיד שורף את העור זה לשון רבותי ול"נ סנדל סיידין של קש הוא וכפי' זה נראה דהכי תניא בתוספתא סנדל של קש ר' עקיבא מטמא כו':

טמא מדרס ולא הודו לו. וא"ת ואמאי לא הודו לו ומי גרע מכופת שאור שיחדו לישיבה דקיי"ל [י] דטמא מדרס דגבי מדרס לא בעינן דומיא דשק דכל דבר המיוחד למדרס טמא מדרס וי"ל דללשון שפירש רש"י של קש הוא ניחא דכיון דלאו בר קיימא הוא אינו טמא ולא דמי לכופת שאור שהוא בר קיימא והכי אשכחן במשניות [כ] דקתני גבי האלון והאגוז ורימון שחקקום תינוקות למוד בהן עפר שמקבלין טומאה ואילו גבי לפת ואתרוג שחקקו קתני שאינן מקבלין טומאה לפי שאינן מתקיימין וללשון שפירש שסנדל הוי של עץ קשה שהרי ראוי הוא להתקיים כיון שהוא של עץ ושמא י"ל דהיינו טעמא דמטהר סנדל דלא חשיב עביד להילוכא מה שמטייל בו הואיל ואין רגילות לעשות מנעל להילוך כמותו דכוותה בשפופרת כיון שאין רגילות לעשותה מקנים לא חשיבה כלי ולא דמי לכופה שרגילות לעשות לישיבה כמותה: **כוורת** הקש ושפופרת של קנים ר"ע מטמא. ואם תאמר והיכי מטמא ([ל] לענין טמא מת) כיון דלא חזי לישיבה לא מטמא מדרס ולענין טומאת מת הא לא כתיב בפרשה אלא כלי עץ ועור ובגד ושק וי"ל דקש נמי חשיב של עץ כדאמר (ברכות דף מ.) פרי שאכל אדם הראשון חטה היתה אי נמי הך טומאה דרבנן היא: **ורבי** יוחנן מטהר. לפירוש אחרון שפי' בקונטרס דסנדל של קש הוא מדמי שפיר כוורת לסנדל של סיידין ולאידך פירושא שפי' דסנדל של עץ הוא צ"ל דמייתי הכי דכי היכי דר' יוחנן מטהר בכוורת של קש לפי שאין רגילות לעשותה מקש הכי נמי במנעל של סיידין לפי שאין רגילות לעשות מנעל של עץ מטהר: **והא** לאו להילוכא עביד. הקשה הר"ר אליעזר ממיץ לרשב"א מאי פריך והלא משעת מלאכתו הוא מהלך בו ולכך הוא נעשה ותירץ לו דסנדל של סיידין לאו לנעול עשוי אלא אחד מכלי אומנותו של סיידין הוא ועשוי כעין סנדל ויכול לתת רגלו בתוכו לנועלו אך אין עשוי רק לטוח בו את הבית ופעמים שנועל בו ומטייל בו עד שיגיע לביתו ולהכי פריך והא לאו להילוכא כו' ור"י פירש הואיל ואין עשוי כלל לנעילה רק לשמור מנעליו שלא ישרפו בסיד לאו להילוכא עביד ומכל מקום משני לו שכן הסייד כו':

רבא אמר אף טמא טומאת מדרס. פי' הרב פור"ת הא דלא קתני ברישא דמתניתין ואם יש לו בית קיבול כתיתין טמא מדרס כדקתני בסיפא משום דהוה משמע אבל אם אין לו בית קיבול טהור מן המדרס אבל טמא טומאת מת ולא היא דהא פשוטי כלי עץ הוא ולהכי תנא טמא סתמא דבכה"ג טמא הא אין לו בית קיבול כתיתין טהור לגמרי וא"ת למה לי בית קיבול כתיתין תיפוק ליה דלכל הטמא מדרס טמא טומאת מת [מ] וי"ל דבית קיבול כתיתין עושין אותו ראוי למדרס:

עגלה של קטן. פ"ה עגלה שהקטן יושב עליה ול"נ דא"כ מאי קמ"ל פשיטא דאין לך מיוחד למדרס גדול מזה לכך נ"ל דהיינו עגלה שעושין לקטן להתלמד להלך טמאה מדרס דנשען עליה:

קיסורי

עין משפט נר מצוה

עז א מיי' פי"ט מהל' שבת הלכה טז סמג לאוין סה טוש"ע א"ח סימן שא סעיף טו:
עח ב שם סעיף טז:
עט ג מיי' פכ"ה מהל' כלים הלכה יח:
פ ד ה שם הלכה יט:
פא ו שם הלכה טז:
פב ז שם הלכה יז:

ליקוטי רש"י

ופליגא דשמואל דאמר שמואל נהרא מכיפיה מיברך. שנובע מגדותיו ולא ממי גשמים [רש"י נדרים שם.]. מכיפיה מקלעו כלומר ממקורו הוא מתגדל שאע"פ שאנו רואים שכשהגשמים יורדין נהרות מתרבים עיקר רבויין ממקורן הוא כדאמרי' בפרק סדר תעניות (כה:) אין לך כל טפח וטפח יורד מלמעלה שאין תהום עולה לקראתו טפחיים ונמצא שלעולם זוחלין רבין על הנוטפין דהא לטפח של גשמים איכא טפחיים דמעיין הלכך לשמואל מותר לטבול בנהרות לעולם אפי' כשראה לעין שנתרבו הרבה מחמת המטר. **אין המים מטהרין בזוחלין.** דאיכא למיחש לרבו הנוטפין [ר"ן שם]. [דבכל] שעה הוו מים נוטפין רבין עליהן [בכורות שם]. **אלא פרת ביומי תשרי בלבד.** דכל ימות השנה רבין נוטפין על הזוחלין מן הגשמים שיורדין לתוכו ומן השלגים שמתפשרין כל ימות החמה אבל בתשרי כבר פסקו השלגים ונתפשרו כולן והלכו להן מטהרין הזוחלין ואין בנהרות אלא מימיו שנובעין בלבד [רש"י נדרים שם:]. לפי שאינו עת גשמים ולא זמן הפשרת שלגים ולא למיסר כל הנהרות חוץ מפרת אתא ולא למיסר נמי פרת כל השנה אלא ... שמואל שאין המים מטהרין בזוחלין אלא פרת וכיוצא בו שאינו מכזב לעולם ... תשרי אין לו לחוש כן נ"ל ורלאיתי מי שכתב בהפך ולא נראו לי דבריו [ר"ן שם]. שפרת היו מימיו פרין ורבין וזוחלין [ונובעין] ממעיינות מרובין ועוד שתשרי סוף ימי הקיץ ולא ירדו גשמים (הרי) [לזמן] מרובה אלמא נהרות מתרבין ממימי גשמים ולעיל אמר מכיפיה מיברך לישנא

מסורת הש"ס

א) [במשנה שבמשניות איתא אנקטמין ובערוך כתב כדהכא], ב) [שבועות מז.], ג) [שם], ד) יבמות קא., ה) עדיות פ"ב מ"ח תוספתא דכלים ב"ב פ"ד [ע"ש], ו) [נ"א רב יוסף אמר], ז) שם, ח) [בפי"ז דכלים מי"ז תנן מחצלת הקש ושפופרת הקש ר"ע מטמא ור"י בן נורי מטהר וע"ש בפי' הר"ש ד"ה ר"ע ולכאורה נראה שצ"ל דתניא כוורת וכו'], ט) ביצה כג:, תוספתא דכלים ב"ב פ"ד, י) [חולין קכט.], כ) [כלים פי"ז מט"ו], ל) בס"י ליתא, מ) [כדאיתא נדה מט.].

הגהות הב"ח

(א) גמרא וסימנא סמך סמך. נ"ב עי' בפ' ח' שרלים דף קי ע"א במ"ש התוספו' בד"ה סיקאני: (ב) רש"י ד"ה טמא מקבל וכו' לטומאה הוא והוה וכו' דדומיא דשק:

גליון הש"ס

גמ' אמר רב יוסף מאן לא הודו לו. ברמב"ן במלחמות רפ"ח דיומא גרס כאן רבא אמר: רש"י ד"ה טמא וכו' אבל שוקו אינו מיטלטל. עיין לקמן דף פא ע"א תוס' ד"ה חפי פותחת:

הגהות הגר"א

[א] גמ' והתניא. נ"ב והתנן. מתני' בעדיות: [ב] שם (כוורת של קש ושפופרת של קנים). תא"מ ונ"ב מחצלת הקש ושפופרת הקש ועיין בפי"ז דכלים:

רבינו חננאל

ורבי יוסי אוסר וכדאוקמוה (א) ומחתי בה סימנא סמך סמך כלומר ר' יוסי אוסר (סבר) [דכ"ע סברי] הקב של קיטע (אינו) חשוב כסנדל ואסור לצאת בו ביוה"כ והיינו טעמא דר' יוסי דאסר בשבת גזרה דלמא משתמיט ואתי לאתויי ד' אמות ברה"ר (כו') ושמואל נמי ורב יוסף (לפנינו ליתא רב הונא) הדרו ואוקמוה למתני' הקיטע יוצא דברי ר"מ. סנדל של סיידין. פי' הסייד כשהוא סד קרקעית הבית בסיד נועל סנדלו של עץ ברגלו שלא יהא הסיד אוכל ברגלו. בית קבול כתיתין. פי' חקוק בתוך הקב חקיקה להיות

חשק שלמה על רבינו חננאל

א) הוכח בא"ו בשם רבינו:

רב נסים גאון

סמיכות שלו אין נכנסין בהן לעזרה. מחמת מה שנאמרה בפ' הרואה מקום במסכת ברכות (דף נד) ולא יכנס בה להר הבית במקל

לתרוצי

אמרינא הא דאבוה דשמואל הוה עביד [לבנתיה] מקוואות ביומי ניסן מפני שהוא סוף החורף שירדו גשמים מרובים אבל באמצע החורף לא הוה עביד ופליגא אדשמואל דהוא אומר דכל שעה בעינן מקוואות אלא פרת ביומי תשרי [בכורות שם]. **הקיטע.** היכא דקתני קטע לחוד משמע דרגליו כדתנן (שבת סה:) הקיטע יוצא בקב שלו [ברכות נח: עיי"ש]. **הקיטע יוצא בקב שלו.** עושין לו כמין דפוס רגל וחוקק בו מעט לתת ראש שוקו לתוכו ואינו נסמך עליו ולכך יצא בקב שלו דמנעל דידיה הוא [רש"י בר"ף ועי' בתוס' כאן]. בקב הקיטע שנקטעה רגלו עושה כמין דפוס רגל ויש בה בית קיבול קטן ומכניס שם ראש שוקו ואין נסמך עליו והוא קרוי קב ולמשענת הליכה יש לו אשקצ"א קשורה בשוקיו ומשענת ידיו שקורין קרוק"א [יבמות קב:]. קב הקיטע נעל הוא לצאת בו בשבת [שם קג:]. **קב.** אשקצ"א [יומא עח:] [ע"כ שייך לדף סה:]. **כתיתין.** חתיכות דקות של מוכין ועור רך [יבמות קב:]. חתיכות בגדים קטנות שהם נוחות לו לסמוך שוקו עליהם. **טמא.** מקבל טומאה דלאו פשוטי כלי עץ הוא [יומא עח:]. **או של שמאל בימין חליצה כשרה.** שהחליצה ברגל ימיני ואם נעל בו סנדל שמאל וחלצה כשר [לקמן קיב.]. אבל חליצה של שמאל קתני בפירקין (יבמות קד.) פלוגתא [יבמות קא.]. **מאן תנא.** סנדל של עץ דקתני מתני' חליצתו כשרה מני. **רבי מאיר היא.** דאמר קב הקיטע נעל הוא לצאת בו בשבת [שם קג:]. **עגלה של קטן.** שעושין לו לשחוק ויושב עליה ומטלטלין אותו עליה. **טמאה מדרס.** אם התינוק זב נעשית העגלה אב הטומאה דמיוחדת לישיבה היא דהא סומך קטן עליה נמצאת שהיא מיוחדת לו לישיבה ואין אומרים לו עמוד ונעשה מלאכתנו דאילו לא מיוחדא להכי לא הוה אב הטומאה כדתניא יכול כפה סאה וישב עליה כו' (שבת נט.) [ביצה כג:].

We see, then, that Shmuel also holds that it is R' Meir who permits an amputee to go out on the Sabbath with his wooden foot, not R' Yose! Apparently, he retracted his opinion in favor of Rav's reading.

The Gemara now demonstrates that Rav Huna too admits to Rav's reading:

וְאַף רַב הוּנָא הֲדַר בֵּיהּ – **And even Rav Huna retracted** his opinion regarding this issue. דְּתַנְיָא – **For a Baraisa has taught:** סַנְדָּל שֶׁל סַיָּידִין – A PLASTER SELLERS' straw SANDAL[16] טָמֵא מִדְרָס – IS SUSCEPTIBLE TO contamination with *MIDRAS TUMAH,* וְאִשָּׁה חוֹלֶצֶת בּוֹ – AND A WOMAN MAY PERFORM *CHALITZAH* WITH IT, וְיוֹצְאִין בּוֹ בְּשַׁבָּת – AND ONE MAY GO OUT WITH IT ON THE SABBATH, since it has legal status as a shoe. דִּבְרֵי רַבִּי עֲקִיבָא – THESE ARE THE WORDS OF R' AKIVA.[17] וְלֹא הוֹדוּ לוֹ – BUT [THE SAGES] DID NOT ACQUIESCE TO HIM, for since it is not common practice to use straw for footwear, a shoe made of straw is not legally considered a shoe.[18] [וְהָתְנַן] (והתניא) – **But we have learned in a Mishnah,**[19] in a seeming contradiction to this Baraisa: הוֹדוּ לוֹ – [THE SAGES] DID ACQUIESCE TO [R' AKIVA]![20] אָמַר רַב הוּנָא – To resolve this apparent contradiction, **Rav Huna said:** מַאן הוֹדוּ לוֹ – **Who is one** of those **who acquiesced to [R' Akiva]?** רַבִּי מֵאִיר – It is **R' Meir,** who holds in our Mishnah that one may go out on the Sabbath with a wooden foot, thus ruling that even a shoe made of material not commonly used for footwear is accorded legal status as a shoe. He therefore agrees with R' Akiva that although straw is not commonly used for footwear, a sandal made of straw is legally considered a shoe. וּמַאן לֹא הוֹדוּ לוֹ – **And who is one** of those **who did not acquiesce to [R' Akiva]?** רַבִּי יוֹסֵי – It is **R' Yose,** who holds in our Mishnah that one may not go out on the Sabbath with a wooden foot, for since footwear is not commonly crafted of wood, wooden shoes are not legally considered shoes. Likewise, a sandal made of straw is not accorded legal status as a shoe.

We see, then, that Rav Huna holds that it is R' Meir who in our Mishnah permits an amputee to go out with his wooden foot, and R' Yose who does not! Apparently, he retracted his opinion in favor of the reading of Rav. Thus, all agree that R' Meir permits a wooden foot, while R' Yose prohibits it, in accordance with Rav's reading.

Having cited Rav Huna's statement that R' Yose is one of those who disputes R' Akiva in the aforecited Baraisa, the Gemara now identifies another of R' Akiva's disputants:

אָמַר רַב יוֹסֵף – **Rav Yosef said:** מַאן לֹא הוֹדוּ לוֹ – **Who is** another **one** of those **who did not acquiesce to [R' Akiva's]** ruling? רַבִּי יוֹחָנָן בֶּן נוּרִי – It is **R' Yochanan ben Nuri.** דִּתְנַן – **For we have learned in a Mishnah:** [מַחֲצֶלֶת הַקַּשׁ וּשְׁפוֹפֶרֶת הַקַּשׁ] (כוורת של קש ושפופרת של קנים) – A STRAW MAT OR A STRAW TUBE[21] – רַבִּי עֲקִיבָא מְטַמֵּא – R' AKIVA HOLDS that THEY ARE SUSCEPTIBLE TO contamination with *TUMAH,*[22] וְרַבִּי יוֹחָנָן בֶּן נוּרִי מְטַהֵר – BUT R' YOCHANAN BEN NURI HOLDS that THEY ARE NOT SUSCEPTIBLE TO contamination with *TUMAH,* since they are made of straw, which is insusceptible to *tumah.*[23] Since a plaster seller's sandal is also made of straw, R' Yochanan ben Nuri must hold that it too is not susceptible to *tumah;* evidently, he is one of R' Akiva's disputants![24]

NOTES

16. Which plaster sellers wear over their leather shoes to keep the plaster from burning their shoes (*Rashi*; see *Tosafos*).

17. [R' Akiva holds that despite the fact that straw is not generally used for shoes, a shoe made of straw is nonetheless considered normal footwear. Therefore, it is susceptible to *tumas midras*, it is suitable for *chalitzah*, and one is permitted to go out with it on the Sabbath (see following note).]

18. Therefore, this straw sandal is not susceptible to *tumas midras,* is not suitable for *chalitzah*, and will be considered a burden with respect to going out with it on the Sabbath.] The reason it is not susceptible to *tumas midras* is because even an article whose intended use is to support human weight, such as a sandal, will not be susceptible to *tumas midras* unless it is commonly used for this purpose. Since it is certainly not common practice to make shoes of straw, this sandal is not viewed as an item meant to bear a person's weight, and therefore is not susceptible to *tumas midras* (see *Tosafos* ד״ה טמא מדרס, second explanation; see note 24 below).

19. *Eduyos* 2:8. Emendation follows *Hagahos HaGra*.

20. [In this Mishnah, R' Akiva states that a straw sandal of the sort worn by plaster sellers is susceptible to *tumas midras*, and the Sages agree that this is true. Evidently, they too hold that a shoe made of straw has legal status as a shoe! Although the Mishnah does not discuss going out with this sandal on the Sabbath, or using it for *chalitzah*, it can be assumed that the Sages agree with R' Akiva with regard to those laws as well, since his reasoning regarding those laws parallels his reasoning regarding *midras*.]

21. *Keilim* 17:17. Emendation follows *Hagahos HaGra*, and is implicit in *Rashi* as well.

22. The straw mat discussed in this Mishnah is one designated for lying upon; it is therefore susceptible even to *tumas midras*. *A straw tube* refers to a small tube-shaped basket [which, because it is a container, is susceptible to *tumah* transmitted by contact] (*Rash, Keilim* 17:17).

23. Articles susceptible to *tumah* are listed in *Leviticus* (11:32) as follows: *a wooden utensil, or a garment, or a hide or a sack*. Thus, articles made of straw [which is not listed in the verse] are not susceptible to *tumah* (*Rashi*; see *Tosafos*; but see also *Pnei Yehoshua* to *Tosafos*). R' Akiva, however, holds that straw can be classified as wood, for it is stiff and hard, and thus resembles wood (*Rashi*). *Tosafos*, in a similar vein, classifies straw as wood because of the Gemara in *Berachos* (40a), which states [according to one opinion] that the "tree" of whose fruit Adam ate was the wheat stalk; accordingly, Scripture refers to straw as wood (see above, bottom of 27b; see also note 35 ad loc.).

[The verse cited above speaks explicitly only of *tumas sheretz,* which is *tumah* transmitted by contact; R' Yochanan ben Nuri, however, discusses even *tumas midras* (in the case of a straw mat), which is not transmitted by contact! Apparently, *Rashi* holds that *tumas midras* is also derived from this verse (see *Dibros Moshe* 53:38). However, *Rash* (*Keilim* 17:17) takes issue with *Rashi's* assertion that *tumas midras* is derived from this verse, and poses a number of challenges to *Rashi*; see *Dibros Moshe* (ibid.) for responses to these challenges.]

24. Our elucidation of the Gemara has followed *Rashi's* own understanding of the Baraisa concerning a plaster seller's sandal. However, *Rashi* offers an alternative explanation in the name of his teachers. They maintain that the plaster seller's sandal mentioned in the Baraisa is made not of straw, but of wood. R' Akiva renders this sandal susceptible to *tumas midras*, allows its use in the *chalitzah* rite, and permits one to wear it outside on the Sabbath because he holds that even articles of wooden footwear are legally considered shoes. Those who do not acquiesce to him hold that wooden footwear is not accorded legal status as shoes. Thus, Rav Huna says, the dispute between those who agree with R' Akiva and those who do not parallels that of R' Meir and R' Yose in our Mishnah. Rav Yosef then points out that one of those who disagree with R' Akiva is R' Yochanan ben Nuri, who disputes R' Akiva in the matter of straw mats and straw tubes, and rules that these items are not susceptible to *tumah.* His reason is that no utensil is susceptible to *tumah* unless it is one commonly used for the purpose for which it was designated (see above, note 18). Mats and basket-tubes, however, are not commonly crafted of straw, but of reeds; those crafted of straw are therefore insusceptible to *tumah*. Likewise, since shoes are normally crafted of leather, a sandal made of wood is not susceptible to *tumah.* He thus disputes R' Akiva.

In our entire *sugya,* we have explained the dispute between R' Meir and R' Yose according to *Rashi*. However, many Rishonim take issue with *Rashi*, and say that both R' Meir and R' Yose agree that a wooden shoe has legal status as a shoe, and is not viewed as a burden on the Sabbath at all! According to them, the reason R' Yose does not allow a cripple to go out with a wooden foot is because he fears that the foot may fall from the cripple's stump, and the cripple will then inadvertently carry it home in violation of the Sabbath (*Rabbeinu Tam*, quoted in *Tosafos* 65b; *Ramban*; *Ritva MHK* ed.; *Rashba*). [The same is true of the wooden shoe of any individual

ורבי יוסי [א]אוסר ואם יש לו בית קיבול כתיתין טמא סמוכות שלו טמאין מדרס [ב]ויוצאין בהן בשבת ונכנסין בהן בעזרה כסא וסמוכות שלו טמאין מדרס ואין יוצאין בהן בשבת ואין נכנסין בהן בעזרה (א)לוקטמין טהורין ואין יוצאין בהן: גמ' אמר ליה רבא לרב נחמן (ב)היכי תנן אמר ליה לא ידענא (ג)הילכתא מאי אמר ליה לא ידענא איתמר אמר שמואל אין הקיטע וכן אמר רב הונא אין הקיטע אמר רב יוסף הואיל ואמר שמואל אין הקיטע ואמר רב הונא אין הקיטע אנן נמי ניתני אין הקיטע מתקיף לה רבא בר שירא לא שמיע להו הא דמתני ליה רב חנן בר רבא לחייא בר רב קמיה דרב בקיטונא דבי רב אין הקיטע יוצא בקב שלו דברי ר' מאיר ור' יוסי מתיר ומחוי ליה רב איפוך אמר רב נחמן בר יצחק וסימנא סמך סמך (א) ואף שמואל הדר ביה דתנן (ד)חליצה בסנדל שאינו שלו בסנדל של עץ או של שמאל בימין חליצה כשרה ואמרינן מאן תנא אמר שמואל ר"מ היא דתנן הקיטע יוצא בקב שלו דברי ר"מ ר' יוסי אוסר ואף רב הונא הדר ביה דתניא (ה)סנדל של סיידין טמא מדרס ואשה חולצת בו ויוצאין בו בשבת דברי ר"ע ולא הודו לו [א] והתניא הודו לו אמר רב הונא מאן הודו לו ר' מאיר ומאן לא הודו לו ר' יוסי ° ((ו)אמר רב יוסף) מאן לא הודו לו ר' יוחנן בן נורי (ז)דתנן [ב] (ח)כוורת של קש ושפופרת של קנים ר"ע מטמא ור' יוחנן בן נורי מטהר אמר מר [ג]סנדל של סיידין טמא מדרס הא לאו להילוכא עבדי אמר רב אחא בר רב עולא שכן הסייד מטייל בו עד שמגיע לביתו: [ד]ואם יש לו בית קיבול כתיתין טמא: אמר אביי טמא טומאת מת ואין טמא מדרס רבא אמר [ה]אף טמא מדרס אמר רבא מנא אמינא לה (ט)דתנן [ו]עגלה של קטן טמאה מדרס ואביי אמר התם סמיך עילויה הכא לא סמיך עילויה אמר אביי מנא אמינא לה דתניא [ז]מקל של זקנים טהור מכלום ורבא התם

לתרוצי

רש"י

ור' יוסי אוסר. דלאו תכשיט הוא: ואם יש לו בית קבול כתיתין. שנחקק בו כדי קיבול כתיתין של בגדים רכין ומוכין להניח ראש שוקו עליהן: טמא. מקבל טומאת מגע אבל אם אין לו אלא בית קבול ראש שוקו ואינו מניח שם כתיתין לאו בית קבול לטומאה (ב) והוה ליה כפשוטי כלי עץ ודומיא דשק בעינן שקבול שלו עשוי לטלטל על ידו מה שנותנין לתוכו ° אבל שוקו אינו מיטלטל ע"ג הכלי: סמוכות שלו. סמוכות של קיטע יש קיטע בשתי רגליו מהלך על שוקיו ועל ארכובותיו ועושה סמוכות של עור לשוקיו: טמאין מדרס. אם זב הוא דהא לסמיכת גופו עביד ומדרס הזב עושה אב הטומאה: ויוצאין בהן בשבת. דתכשיט דידיה הוא: ונכנסין בהן לעזרה. דאע"ג דתנן (ברכות דף נד.) לא יכנס אדם להר הבית במנעלו הני לאו מנעל נינהו דלאו בראש רגלו הן: כסא. יש קיטע שיבשו וכווצו גידי שוקיו ואפי' על ארכובותיו אינו יכול לילך ועושין כמין כסא נמוך ויושב עליו וכשהוא מהלך נסמך על ידיו בספסלים קטנים ועוקר גופו מן הארץ ונדחף לפניו וחוזר ונח על אחוריו והכסא קשור לו מאחוריו: סמוכות. של אותו קיטע עושה לה סמוכות של עור או של עץ לראשי שוקיו או רגליו התלויין וכשהוא נשען על ידיו ועוקר עצמו נשען גם על רגליו קצת: ואין יוצאין בהן בשבת. רבותינו אומרים מפני שאינם צריכין לו כל כך ולא נהירא לי טעמא ואיכא למימר דאיידי דתלו ולא מנחי אארעא זימנין דמשתלפי: ואין נכנסין בהן בעזרה. דמנעל נינהו: לוקטמין. טלמשק"א נעשין לשחוק להבעית תינוקות: טהורים. מלקבל טומאה דאינו לא כלי תשמיש ולא תכשיט: גמ' היכי תנן. הקיטע יוצא ורבי יוסי אוסר או אין הקיטע יוצא ורבי יוסי מתיר: בר שירא: קיטונא. חדר קטן של בית המדרש: סמך סמך. ר' יוסי אוסר שתי תיבות שיש בהן סמך סמך זו אצל זו: או של שמאל בימין. סנדל של שמאל נעל בימין וחלצה דחליצה בימין הוא דגמר רגל רגל ממצורע: מאן תנא. דסנדל של עץ חשיב נעלו: סנדל של סיידין. מוכרי סיד וכשמתעסקין בו נועלין אותו ושל עץ הוא מפני שהסיד שורף את העור: ואמר רב הונא גרסי': מאן הודו לו ר' מאיר. דאמר הקיטע יוצא בקב שלו: ור' יוחנן בן נורי מטהר. דלאו אורחא לעשות מקש אלא מקנים ומנעל נמי לאו אורחיה מעץ אלא מעור זה לשון רבותי ולי נראה סנדל של סיידין של קש הוא ור' יוחנן בן נורי מטהר בכלי קש דלאו עץ נינהו ור' עקיבא כעץ חשיב להו דקשין הן: קש. זנבות השבלים: ואין טמא מדרס. דלא מסתמיך עליה הא דנקט טומאת מת ה"ה לכל טומאת מגע אלא משום דאמר אין טמא מדרס שהוא אב הטומאה נקט נמי טומאת מת והכי קאמר נעשה אב הטומאה ע"י מת דכלי עץ שיש לו בית קבול הוא ומקבל כל טומאת מגע ואהל ועל ידי כל הטומאות הוא נעשה ראשון ועל ידי מת שהוא אבי אבות הטומאה נעשה אב הטומאה ואין נעשה אב הטומאה ע"י מדרס דקסבר לאו לסמיכה עבידי אלא לתכשיט ואומרים לו עמוד ונעשה מלאכתנו: עגלה של קטן. לשחק בה ולטלטלו עליה: טמאה מדרס. הואיל ופעמים שיושב עליה והאי נמי זימנין דמסתמיך עליה: טהור מכלום. לא מדרס ולא שאר טומאה לא מטמא מדרס משום דלאו לסמיכה עביד שעל רגלו מהלך ואע"ג דמיסתמיך עליה לפרקים ושאר טומאה נמי לא דפשוטי כלי עץ הוא אלמא אע"ג דזימנין דמסתמיך עליה הואיל ועיקר עשייתה אינה לכך אינה טמאה מדרס ואין לומר משום דפשוט הוא יהא טהור ממדרס דלא הוזכרה טהרת פשוטי כלי עץ אלא לטומאת מגע ואהל דטעמא משום דאיתקש לשק הוא וגבי מת ושרצים הויא היקישא:

לתרוצי

תוספות

סנדל של סיידין. פ"ה מוכרי הסיד וכשמתעסקין בסיד נועלין אותו ושל עץ הוא מפני שהסיד שורף את העור זה לשון רבותי ול"נ סנדל סיידין של קש הוא וכפי' זה נראה דהכי תניא בתוספתא סנדל של קש ר' עקיבא מטמא כו':

טמא מדרס ולא הודו לו. וא"ת ואמאי לא הודו לו ומי גרע מכופת שאור שיחדו לישיבה דקי"ל(י) דטמא מדרס דגבי מדרס לא בעינן דומיא דשק דכל דבר המיוחד למדרס טמא מדרס וי"ל דללשון שפירש רש"י של קש הוא ניחא דכיון דלאו בר קיימא הוא אינו טמא ולא דמי לכופת שאור שהוא בר קיימא והכי אשכחן במשניות(כ) דקתני גבי האלון והאגוז ורימון שחקקום תינוקות למוד בהן עפר שמקבלין טומאה ואילו גבי לפת ואתרוג שחקקו קתני שאינן מקבלין טומאה לפי שאינן מתקיימין וללשון שפירש שסנדל הוי של עץ קשה שהרי ראוי הוא להתקיים כיון שהוא של עץ ושמא י"ל דהיינו טעמא דמטהר סנדל דלא חשיב עביד להילוכא מה שמטייל בו הואיל ואין רגילות לעשות מנעל להילוך כמותו דכוותה בשפופרת כיון שאין רגילות לעשותה מקנים לא חשיבה כלי ולא דמי לכופה שרגילות לעשות לישיבה כמותה:

כוורת הקש ושפופרת של קנים ר"ע מטמא. ואם תאמר והיכי מטמא ((ל)לענין טמא מת) כיון דלא חזי לישיבה לא מטמא מדרס ולענין טומאת מת הא לא כתיב בפרשה אלא כלי עץ ועור ובגד ושק וי"ל דקש נמי חשיב של עץ כדאמר (ברכות דף מ.) פרי שאכל אדם הראשון חטה היתה אי נמי הך טומאה דרבנן היא:

ורבי יוחנן מטהר. לפירוש אחרון שפי' בקונטרס דסנדל של קש הוא מדמי שפיר כוורת לסנדל של סיידין ולאידך פירושא שפי' דסנדל של עץ הוא צ"ל דמייתי הכי דכי היכי דר' יוחנן מטהר בכוורת של קש לפי שאין רגילות לעשותה מקש הכי נמי במנעל של סיידין לפי שאין רגילות לעשות מנעל של עץ מטהר:

והא לאו להילוכא עביד. הקשה הר"ר אליעזר ממיץ לרשב"א מאי פריך והלא משעת מלאכתו הוא מהלך בו ולכך הוא נעשה ותירץ לו דסנדל של סיידין לאו לנעול עשוי אלא אחד מכלי אומנותו של סיידין הוא ועשוי כעין סנדל ויכול לתת רגלו בתוכו לנועלו אך אין עשוי רק לטוח בו את הבית ופעמים שנועל בו ומטייל בו עד שיגיע לביתו ולהכי פריך והא לאו להילוכא כו' ור"י פירש הואיל ואין עשוי כלל לנעילה רק לשמור מנעליו שלא ישרפו בסיד לאו להילוכא עביד ומכל מקום משני לו שכן הסייד כו':

רבא אמר אף טמא טומאת מדרס. פי' הרב פור"ת הא דלא קתני ברישא דמתניתין ואם יש לו בית קיבול כתיתין טמא מדרס כדקתני בסיפא משום דהוה משמע אבל אם אין לו בית קיבול טהור מן המדרס אבל טמא טומאת מת ולא היא דהא פשוטי כלי עץ הוא ולהכי תנא טמא סתמא דבכה"ג טמא הא אין לו בית קיבול כתיתין טהור לגמרי וא"ת למה לי בית קיבול כתיתין תיפוק ליה דכל הטמא מדרס טמא טומאת מת(מ) וי"ל דבית קיבול כתיתין עושין אותו ראוי למדרס:

עגלה של קטן. פ"ה עגלה שהקטן יושב עליה ול"נ דא"כ מאי קמ"ל פשיטא דאין לך מיוחד למדרס גדול מזה לכך נ"ל דהיינו עגלה שעושין לקטן להתלמד להלך טמאה מדרס דנשען עליה:

קישורי

עין משפט נר מצוה

עז א מיי' פי"ט מהל' שבת הלכה טז סמג לאוין סה טוש"ע א"ח סימן שא סעיף טו:
עח ב שם סעיף טז:
עט ג מיי' פכ"ה מהל' כלים הלכה יח:
פ ד ה שם הלכה יט:
פא ו שם הלכה טז:
פב ז שם הלכה יז:

ליקוטי רש"י

ופליגא דשמואל דאמר שמואל נהרא מכיפיה מיברך. שנובע מגדותיו ולא ממי גשמים [רש"י נדרים שם.]. מכיפיה מקלעו כלומר ממקורו הוא מתגדל שאע"פ שאנו רואים שכשהגשמים יורדין נהרות מתרבים עיקר רבויין ממקורן הוא כדאמרי' בפרק סדר תעניות (כה:) אין לך כל טפח וטפח יורד מלמעלה שאין תהום עולה לקראתו טפחיים ונמצא שלעולם זוחלין רבין על הנוטפין דהא לטפח של גשמים איכא טפחיים דמעיין הלכך לשמואל מותר לטבול בנהרות לעולם אפי' כשראה לעין שנתרבו הרבה מחמת המטר. אין המים מטהרין בזוחלין. דאיכא למיחש לרבו הנוטפין [ר"ן שם]. [דבכל] שעה הוו מים נוטפין רבין עליהן [בכורות שם]. אלא פרת ביומי תשרי בלבד. דכל ימות השנה רבין נוטפין על הזוחלין מן הגשמים שיורדין לתוכו ומן השלגים שמתפשרין כל ימות החמה אבל בתשרי כבר פסקו השלגים ונתפשרו כולן והלכו להן מטהרין הזוחלין ואין בנהרות אלא מימיו שנובעין בלבד [רש"י נדרים שם:]. לפי שאינו עת גשמים ולא זמן הפשרת שלגים ולא למיסר כל הנהרות חוץ מפרת אתא ולא למיסר נמי פרת בכל השנה אלא וכו' קאמר שמואל שאין המים מטהרין בזוחלין אלא פרת וכיוצא בו שאינו מכזב לעולם ולמעוטי מים המכזבין הוא דקאמר פרת ופרת וכיוצא בו קאמר וקאמר נמי דבפרת וכיוצא בו שאינו מכזב אינו מותר לטבול בו מן הסתם בכל השנה כולה מי שאינו בקי בו אלא ביומי תשרי בלבד לפי שביומי תשרי אינו עת גשמים ולא זמן הפשרת שלגים ולפיכך אפי' מי שאינו בקי בו אין לו לחוש שמא רבו עליו נוטפין אבל אין ה"נ דמי שבקי בפרת וכיוצא בו כל השנה כולה שהוא רואה שלא נתרבה על מה שהוא זוחל בתשרי בכדי שיהא ראוי לחוש לרבוי נוטפין טובל בו בכל השנה וכן נמי אם רואה בתשרי שנתרבה כל כך עד שאפשר לו לחוש שמא רבו בו נוטפין אפי' בתשרי אינו טובל בו אלא שמואל סתמא קאמר דמי שאינו מכיר אפי' בנהרות שאין מכזבין יש לו לחוש כל השנה ברבייתן וביומי תשרי אין לו לחוש כן נ"ל ורָאיתי מי שכתב בהפך ולא נראו לי דבריו [ר"ן שם]. שפרת היו מימיו פרין ורבין חוזלין [ונובעין] ממעיינות מרובין ועוד שתשרי סוף ימי הקיץ ולא ירדו גשמים (הרי) [לזמן] מרובה אלמא נהרות מתרבין ממימי גשמים ולעיל אמר מכיפיה מיבריך ליישנא אחרינא הא דאבוה דשמואל הוה עביד [לבנתיה] מקוואות ביומי ניסן מפני שהוא סוף החורף שירדו גשמים מרובים אבל באמצע החורף לא הוה עביד ופליגא אדשמואל דהוא אומר דכל שעה בעינן מקוואות אלא פרת ביומי תשרי [בכורות שם]. הקיטע. היכא דקתני קטע לחוד משמע דרגלים כדתנן (שבת סה:) הקטע יוצא בקב שלו [ברכות נח: עיי"ש]. הקיטע יוצא בקב שלו. עושין לו כמין דפוס רגל וחוקק בו מעט לתת ראש שוקו לתוכו ואינו נסמך עליו ולכך יצא בקב שלו דמנעל דידיה הוא [רש"י ברי"ף ועי' בתוס' כאן]. בקב הקיטע שנקטעה רגלו עושה כמין דפוס רגל ויש בה בית קיבול קטן ומכנים שם ראש שוקו ואין נסמך עליו והוא קרוי קב ולמשענת הליכה יש לו אשקיצ"א קשורה בשוקיו ומשענת ידיו שקורין קרוק"א [יבמות קב:]. קב הקיטע נעל הוא לצאת בו בשבת [שם קג:]. קב. אשקל"א [יומא עח:]. [ע"כ שייך לדף סה:]. כתיתין. מתיכות דקות של מוכין ועור רך [יבמות קב:]. מתיכות בגדים קטנות שהם נוחות לו לסמוך שוקו עליהם. טמא. מקבל טומאה דלאו פשוטי כלי עץ הוא [יומא עח:]. או של שמאל בימין חליצה כשרה. שהחליצה ברגל ימיני ואם נעל בו סנדל שמאל וחלצה כשר [לקמן קיב.]. אבל חליצה של שמאל קתני בפירקין (יבמות קד.) פלוגתא [יבמות קא.]. מאן תנא. סנדל של עץ דקתני מתני' חליצתה כשרה מני. רבי מאיר היא. דאמר קב הקיטע נעל הוא לצאת בו בשבת [שם קג:]. עגלה של קטן. שעושין לו לשחוק ויושב עליה ומטלטלין אותו עליה. טמאה מדרס. אם התינוק זב נעשית העגלה אב הטומאה דמיוחדת לישיבה היא דהא סומך קטן עליה נמצאת שהיא מיוחדת לו לישיבה ואין אומרים לו עמוד ונעשה מלאכתנו דאילו לא מיוחדא להכי לא הוית אב הטומאה כדתניא יכול כפה סאה וישב עליה כו' (שבת נט.) [ביצה כג:].

מסורת הש"ס

א) [במשנה שבמשניות איתא אנקטמין ובערוך כתב כדהכא], ב) [שבועות מז.], ג) [שם], ד) יבמות קא., ה) עדיות פ"ב מ"ח תוספתא דכלים ב"ב פ"ד [ע"ש], ו) [צ"ל רב יוסף אמר], ז) שם, ח) [בפי"ז דכלים מי"ז תנן מחצלת הקש ושפופרת הקש ר"ע מטמא ור"י בן נורי מטהר וע"ש בפי' הר"ש ד"ה ר"ע ולכאורה נראה שצ"ל דתניא כוורת וכו'], ט) ביצה כג:, תוספתא דכלים ב"ב פ"ד, י) [חולין קכט.], כ) [כלים פי"ז מט"ו], ל) בס"י ליתא, מ) [כדאיתא נדה מט.].

הגהות הב"ח

(א) גמרא וסימנא סמך סמך. נ"ב עי' בפ' ח' שרצים דף קי ע"א במ"ש התוספו' בד"ה סיקאי: (ב) רש"י ד"ה טמא מקבל וכו' לטומאה הוא והוה וכו' דדומיא דשק:

גליון הש"ס

גמ' אמר רב יוסף מאן לא הודו לו. ברמב"ן במלחמות רפ"ח דיומא גרס כאן רבא אמר: רש"י ד"ה טמא וכו' אבל שוקו אינו מיטלטל. עיין לקמן דף פא ע"א תוס' ד"ה חפי פותחת:

הגהות הגר"א

[א] גמ' והתניא. נ"ב והתנן. מתני' בעדיות: [ב] שם (כוורת של קש ושפופרת של קנים). תא"מ ונ"ב מחצלת הקש ושפופרת הקש ועיין בפי"ז דכלים:

רבינו חננאל

ורבי יוסי אוסר וכדאוקמוה א) ומחתי בה סימנא סמך סמך כלומר ר' יוסי אוסר (סבר) [דכ"ע סברי] הקב של קיטע (אינו) חשוב כסנדל ואסור לצאת בו ביוה"כ והיינו טעמא דר' יוסי דאסר בשבת גזרה דלמא משתמיט ואתי לאתויי ד' אמות ברה"ר (כו') ושמואל נמי ורב יוסף (לפנינו הגי' רב הונא) הדרו ואוקמוה למתני' הקטע יוצא דברי ר"מ: סנדל של סיידין. פי' הסייד כשהוא סד קרקעית הבית בסיד נועל סנדלו של עץ ברגלו כדי שלא יהא הסיד אוכל ברגלו. בית קבול כתיתין. פי' חקוק בתוך הקב חקיקה להיות

חשק שלמה על רבינו חננאל

א) הובא בא"ז בשם רבינו:

רב נסים גאון

סמיכות שלו אין נכנסין בהן לעזרה. מחמת מה שנאמרה בפ' הרואה מקום במסכת ברכות (דף נד) ולא יכנס בה להר הבית במקל

Having cited R' Akiva's ruling in the case of a plaster seller's sandal, the Gemara now questions it:
אָמַר מַר – **The master** (R' Akiva) **stated in the Baraisa:** סַנְדָּל שֶׁל סַיָּידִין טָמֵא מִדְרָס – A PLASTER SELLERS' SANDAL IS SUSCEPTIBLE TO contamination with *MIDRAS TUMAH.* הָא לָאו לְהִילוּכָא עָבְדִי – **But [a plaster seller's sandal] is not made for walking,** but only to protect one's shoes from being burned by the plaster! It therefore should not be susceptible to *midras tumah*![25] – ? –

The Gemara answers:
אָמַר רַב אַחָא בַּר רַב עוּלָּא – **Rav Acha bar Rav Ulla said:** שֶׁכֵּן הַסַּיָּיד מְטַיֵּיל בּוֹ עַד שֶׁמַּגִּיעַ לְבֵיתוֹ – The reason this sort of sandal is susceptible to *midras tumah* is **because** even after work, **the plaster seller will** often continue to **walk in it until he reaches his home.**[26]

The Mishnah states:
וְאִם יֵשׁ לוֹ בֵּית קִיבּוּל כְּתִיתִין טָמֵא – IF [THE WOODEN FOOT] POSSESSES A RECEPTACLE FOR RAGS, IT IS SUSCEPTIBLE TO contamination with *TUMAH.*

The Gemara presents an Amoraic dispute concerning the sort of *tumah* to which a wooden foot with a receptacle is susceptible:
אָמַר אַבָּיֵי – **Abaye said:** טָמֵא טוּמְאַת מֵת – If the wooden foot possesses a receptacle for rags, **it is susceptible to** contamination with **corpse *tumah*,**[27] וְאֵין טָמֵא מִדְרָס – **but it is not susceptible to** contamination with ***midras tumah*,** since its primary purpose is not to support the cripple's weight, but to disguise the fact that he is missing a foot.[28] רָבָא אָמַר – But **Rava said:** אַף טָמֵא מִדְרָס – If the wooden foot possesses a receptacle, **it is susceptible even to** contamination with ***midras tumah*,** since the cripple sometimes uses it to support his weight.[29]

Rava explains his reason for ruling as he does:
אָמַר רָבָא – **Rava said:** מְנָא אֲמִינָא לָהּ – **From where do I** find a source to **say this?** דִּתְנַן – **For we have learned in a Mishnah:**[30] עֲגָלָה שֶׁל קָטָן טְמֵאָה מִדְרָס – A CHILD'S WAGON[31] IS SUSCEPTIBLE TO contamination with *MIDRAS TUMAH* even though it is used only occasionally to bear the weight of the child! We see that even occasional use as a support renders an article susceptible to *midras tumah.* A wooden foot is likewise susceptible, since it is sometimes used to support the cripple's weight.

Abaye differentiates between a wagon and a wooden foot:
וְאַבָּיֵי אָמַר – **But Abaye said:** הָתָם סָמִיךְ עִילָּוֵיהּ – **There** (in the case of a child's wagon) the child **supports** itself **upon it** often; it therefore is susceptible to *midras tumah.* הָכָא לֹא סָמִיךְ עִילָּוֵיהּ – But **here** (in the case of a wooden foot) the crippled person **does not support** himself **upon it** often; it therefore is not susceptible to *midras tumah.*

Abaye explains his reason for ruling as he does:
אָמַר אַבָּיֵי – **Abaye said:** מְנָא אֲמִינָא לָהּ – **From where do I** find a source to **say this?** דְּתַנְיָא – **For a Baraisa has taught:** מַקֵּל שֶׁל זְקֵנִים טָהוֹר מִכְּלוּם – A walking STICK used BY ELDERLY PEOPLE IS NOT SUSCEPTIBLE TO contamination with ANY SORT OF *TUMAH,*[32] including *midras tumah.* For although its users occasionally put their weight upon it, its primary purpose is not to support one's weight. We see, then, that an item used only occasionally for support is not susceptible to *midras tumah.*

The Gemara explains how Rava will differentiate between a walking stick and a wooden foot:
וְרָבָא – **But Rava** will answer: הָתָם – **There** (in the case of a walking stick)

NOTES

Since such a shoe is rigid, and does not grip one's foot as a leather shoe would, R' Yose fears that it might easily fall from one's foot, and be carried home.] The source for these Rishonim is the Gemara in *Yoma* (78b), where Rava proves that this is indeed R' Yose's reasoning. [According to these Rishonim, the Gemara's citation of R' Yochanan ben Nuri takes on great significance; see *Ramban* and *Rashba* for particulars.]

Rashi, however, did not explain the dispute in this manner because he holds that the Amoraim of our Gemara are actually at odds with Rava, and hold that R' Yose does consider a wooden shoe a burden! The reason our Gemara does not present Rava's proof is that it relies upon the Gemara in *Yoma*, which does (*Ritva MHK* ed.).

A major distinction between *Rashi's* explanation and that of the other Rishonim is that according to *Rashi* any wooden shoe is forbidden, since it constitutes a burden, whereas according to the Rishonim, a shoe that fits well is permitted, as we are confident that it will not fall off the foot (see *Rama, Orach Chaim* 301:16).

25. *Rashi*, as explained by *Rabbeinu Yitzchak*, cited in *Tosafos*; cf. *R' Eliezer MiMetz*, cited ad loc.; see *Ritva MHK* ed., and *Rashba*. The Gemara's question is based upon the Gemara above (59a) that limits *midras tumah* to objects whose function is to support the weight of a human being. Although the plaster seller certainly rests his weight upon this sandal, that is not the reason he wears it — he simply wishes to avoid ruining his shoes! Since the sandal's function is accordingly not a weight-bearing one, it should not be susceptible to *midras tumah* (see *Tosafos*)!

26. [The fact that the plaster seller will often continue wearing these sandals even after his work is done is proof that he views them not only as protection for his normal shoes, but as shoes in their own right. They are thus considered objects whose function is to bear weight, and are therefore susceptible to *midras tumah*.]

27. [Which is transmitted by contact.]

28. For Abaye holds that in order for an object to acquire *tumas midras*, its *primary* function must be to bear a person's weight. The fact that that is its occasional function does not suffice to render it susceptible to *midras*. Accordingly, a cripple's wooden foot, whose primary purpose is merely cosmetic, will be susceptible to *tumas meis*, but not to *tumas midras*. See *Sfas Emes*.

Now, Abaye of course does not mean to single out *tumas meis*, for he in fact holds that the wooden foot is susceptible to any sort of *tumah* transmitted through contact [e.g. *tumas sheretz*]. He chooses *tumas meis* as his example only as a parallel to *tumas midras*, since both possess the ability to render an object an *av hatumah* (literally: father of *tumah*) (*Rashi*). [Other sorts of contact-generated *tumah*, by contrast, generate *tumah* of only a lesser degree].

29. [Rava holds that even secondary weight-bearing use is sufficient to render an object susceptible to *tumas midras*. Therefore, since the cripple occasionally rests his weight upon this foot, it is susceptible.]

The reason the wooden foot will not be susceptible to *tumas midras* unless it possesses a receptacle for rags is that without cushioning for the amputee's stump, it is not considered a fit support for his weight (*Tosafos*; see *R' Poras*, cited in *Tosafos*, for why the Mishnah does not state explicitly that the foot is susceptible to *tumas midras;* see *Maharshal*).

30. *Beitzah* 23b.

31. Which is used in play, and to carry the child (*Rashi*; cf. *Tosafos*).

32. It is not susceptible to *tumas midras* because it is not used *primarily* for supporting one's weight. It is not susceptible to *tumah* transmitted through contact [e.g. *tumas meis*] because it is not a container (see above, note 2).

[*Rashi* notes that some may wish to challenge Abaye's proof by saying that the reason the stick is not susceptible to *tumas midras* is not because its primary use is not for support, but for the same reason that it is insusceptible to *tumas meis* — because it has no receptacle! *Rashi* rejects this challenge, since the *hekeish* from which the requirement of a receptacle is derived (see above, note 2) applies only to *tumah* transmitted through contact. *Tumas midras*, however, is not included in this *hekeish*; it therefore can affect even utensils without receptacles. (Although, as noted above (note 23), the verse from which receptacles are derived *does* apply to *tumas midras* with regard to certain laws, *tumas midras* is nonetheless not included in this *hekeish* — see *Dibros Moshe* 53:38 for an explanation.)]

ורבי יוסי [א]אוסר ואם יש לו בית קיבול כתיתין טמא סמוכות שלו טמאין מדרס [ב]ויוצאין בהן בשבת ונכנסין בהן בעזרה כסא וסמוכות שלו טמאין מדרס ואין יוצאין בהן בשבת ואין נכנסין בהן בעזרה [א]לוקטמין טהורין ואין יוצאין בהן: גמ' אמר ליה רבא לרב נחמן [ג]היכי תנן אמר ליה לא ידענא [ג]הילכתא מאי אמר ליה לא ידענא איתמר אמר שמואל אין הקיטע וכן אמר רב הונא אין הקיטע אמר רב יוסף הואיל ואמר שמואל אין הקיטע ואמר רב הונא אין הקיטע אנן נמי ניתני אין הקיטע מתקיף לה רבא בר שירא לא שמיע להו הא דמתני ליה רב חנן בר רבא לחייא בר רב קמיה דרב בקיטונא דבי רב אין הקיטע יוצא בקב שלו דברי ר' מאיר ור' יוסי מתיר ומחוי ליה רב איפוך אמר רב נחמן בר יצחק וסימנא סמך סמך (א) ואף שמואל הדר ביה דתנן [ד]חליצה בסנדל שאינו שלו בסנדל של עץ או של שמאל בימין חליצה כשרה ואמרינן מאן תנא אמר שמואל ר"מ היא דתנן הקיטע יוצא בקב שלו דברי ר"מ ר' יוסי אוסר ואף רב הונא הדר ביה דתניא [ה]סנדל של סיידין טמא מדרס ואשה חולצת בו ויוצאין בו בשבת דברי ר"ע ולא הודו לו [א] והתניא הודו לו אמר רב הונא מאן הודו לו ר' מאיר ומאן לא הודו לו ר' יוסי ° ([ו]אמר רב יוסף מאן לא הודו לו ר' יוחנן בן נורי [ז]דתנן [ב] [ח]כוורת של קש ושפופרת של קנים ר"ע מטמא ור' יוחנן בן נורי מטהר אמר מר [ג]סנדל של סיידין טמא מדרס הא לאו להילוכא עבדי אמר רב אחא בר רב עולא שכן הסייד מטייל בו עד שמגיע לביתו: [ד]ואם יש לו בית קיבול כתיתין טמא: אמר אביי טמא טומאת מת ואין טמא מדרס רבא אמר [ה]אף טמא מדרס אמר רבא מנא אמינא לה [ט]דתנן [ו]עגלה של קטן טמאה מדרס ואביי אמר התם סמיך עילויה הכא לא סמיך עילויה אמר אביי מנא אמינא לה דתניא [ז]מקל של זקנים טהור מכלום ורבא התם לתרוצי

רש"י

ור' יוסי אוסר. דלאו תכשיט הוא: ואם יש לו בית קבול כתיתין. שנחקק בו כדי קיבול כתיתין של בגדים רכין ומוכן להניח ראש שוקו עליהן: טמא. מקבל טומאת מגע אבל אם אין לו אלא בית קבול ראש שוקו ואינו מניח שם כתיתין לאו בית קבול לטומאה (ב) והוה ליה כפשוטי כלי עץ ודומיא דשק בעינן שקבול שלו עשוי לטלטל על ידו מה שנותנין לתוכו ° אבל שוקו אינו מיטלטל ע"ג הכלי: סמוכות שלו. סמוכות של קיטע יש קיטע בשתי רגליו מהלך על שוקיו ועל ארכובותיו ועושה סמוכות של עור לשוקיו: טמאין מדרס. אם זב הוא דהא לסמיכת גופו עביד ומדרס הזב עושה אב הטומאה: ויוצאין בהן בשבת. דתכשיט דידיה הוא: ונכנסין בהן לעזרה. דאע"ג דתנן (ברכות דף נד.) לא יכנס אדם להר הבית במנעלו הני לאו מנעל נינהו דלאו בראש רגלו הן: כסא. יש קיטע שיבשו וכווצו גידי שוקיו ואפי' על ארכובותיו אינו יכול לילך ועושין כמין כסא נמוך ויושב עליו וכשהוא מהלך נסמך על ידיו בספסלים קטנים ועוקר גופו מן הארץ ונדחף לפניו וחוזר ונח על אחוריו והכסא קשור לו מאחוריו: סמוכות. של אותו קיטע עושה לה סמוכות של עור או של עץ לראשי שוקיו או רגליו התלוין וכשהוא נשען על ידיו ועוקר עצמו נשען גם על רגליו קצת: ואין יוצאין בהן בשבת. רבותינו אומרים מפני שאינם צריכין לו כל כך ולא נהירא לי טעמא ואיכא למימר דאידי דתלו ולא מנחי אארעא זימנין דמשתלפי: ואין נכנסין בהן בעזרה. דמנעל נינהו: לוקטמין. טלמסק"א נעשין לשחוק להבעית תינוקות: טהורים. מלקבל טומאה דאינו לא כלי תשמיש ולא תכשיט: גמ' היכי תנן. הקיטע יוצא ורבי יוסי אוסר או אין הקיטע יוצא ורבי יוסי מתיר: בר שירא: קיטונא. חדר קטן של בית המדרש: סמך סמך. ר' יוסי אוסר שתי תיבות שיש בהן סמך סמך זו אצל זו: או של שמאל בימין. סנדל של שמאל נעל בימין וחלצה דחליצה בימין הוא דגמר רגל רגל ממצורע: מאן תנא. דסנדל של עץ חשיב נעלו: סנדל של סיידין. מוכרי סיד וכשמתעסקין בו נועלין אותו ושל עץ הוא מפני שהסיד שורף את העור: ואמר רב הונא גרסי': מאן הודו לו ר' מאיר. דאמר הקיטע יוצא בקב שלו: ור' יוחנן בן נורי מטהר. דלאו אורחא לעשות מקש אלא מקנים ומנעל נמי לאו אורחיה מעץ אלא מעור זה לשון רבותי ולי נראה סנדל של סיידין של קש הוא ור' יוחנן בן נורי מטהר בכלי קש דלאו עץ נינהו ור' עקיבא כעץ חשיב להו דקשין הן: קש. זנבות השבלים: ואין טמא מדרס. דלא מסתמיך עליה הא דנקט טומאת מת ה"ה לכל טומאת מגע אלא משום דאמר אין טמא מדרס שהוא אב הטומאה נקט נמי טומאת מת והכי קאמר נעשה אב הטומאה ע"י מת דכלי עץ שיש לו בית קבול הוא ומקבל כל טומאת מגע ואהל ועל ידי כל הטומאות הוא נעשה ראשון ועל ידי מת שהוא אבי אבות הטומאה נעשה אב הטומאה ואין נעשה אב הטומאה ע"י מדרס דקסבר לאו לסמיכה עבידי אלא לתכשיט ואומרים לו עמוד ונעשה מלאכתנו: עגלה של קטן. לשחק בה ולטלטלו עליה: טמאה מדרס. הואיל ופעמים שיושב עליה והאי נמי זימנין דמסתמיך עליה: טהור מכלום. לא מדרס ולא שאר טומאה לא מטמא מדרס משום דלאו לסמיכה עביד שעל רגלו מהלך ואע"ג דמיסתמיך עליה לפרקים ושאר טומאה נמי לא דפשוטי כלי עץ הוא אלמא אע"ג דזימנין דמסתמיך עליה הואיל ועיקר עשייתה אינה לכך אינה טמאה מדרס ואין לומר משום דפשוט הוא יהא טהור ממדרס דלא הוזכרה טהרת פשוטי כלי עץ אלא לטומאת מגע ואהל דטעמא משום דאיתקש לשק הוא וגבי מת ושרצים הויא היקישא:
לתרולי

תוספות

סנדל של סיידין. פ"ה מוכרי הסיד וכשמתעסקין בסיד נועלין אותו ושל עץ הוא מפני שהסיד שורף את העור זה לשון רבותי ול"נ סנדל סיידין של קש הוא וכפי' זה נראה דהכי תניא בתוספתא סנדל של קש ר' עקיבא מטמא כו':

טמא מדרס ולא הודו לו. וא"ת ואמאי לא הודו לו ומי גרע מכופת שאור שיחדו לישיבה דקי"ל[י] דטמא מדרס דגבי מדרס לא בעינן דומיא דשק דכל דבר המיוחד למדרס טמא מדרס וי"ל דללשון שפירש רש"י של קש הוא ניחא דכיון דלאו בר קיימא הוא אינו טמא ולא דמי לכופת שאור שהוא בר קיימא והכי אשכחן במשניות[כ] דקתני גבי האלון והאגוז ורימון שחקקום תינוקות למוד בהן עפר שמקבלין טומאה ואילו גבי לפת ואתרוג שחקקו קתני שאינן מקבלין טומאה לפי שאינן מתקיימין וללשון שפירש שסנדל הוי של עץ קשה שהרי ראוי הוא להתקיים כיון שהוא של עץ ושמא י"ל דהיינו טעמא דמטהר סנדל דלא חשיב עביד להילוכא מה שמטייל בו הואיל ואין רגילות לעשות מנעל להילוך כמותו דכוותה בשפופרת כיון שאין רגילות לעשותה מקנים לא חשיבה כלי ולא דמי לכופה שרגילות לעשות לישיבה כמותה: כוורת הקש ושפופרת של קנים ר"ע מטמא. ואם תאמר והיכי מטמא ([ל]לענין טמא מת) כיון דלא חזי לישיבה לא מטמא מדרס ולענין טומאת מת הא לא כתיב בפרשה אלא כלי עץ ועור ובגד ושק וי"ל דקש נמי חשיב של עץ כדאמר (ברכות דף מ.) פרי שאכל אדם הראשון חטה היתה אי נמי הך טומאה דרבנן היא: ורבי יוחנן מטהר. לפירוש אחרון שפי' בקונטרס דסנדל של קש הוא מדמי שפיר כוורת לסנדל של סיידין ולאידך פירושא שפי' דסנדל של עץ הוא צ"ל דמייתי הכי דכי היכי דר' יוחנן מטהר בכוורת של קש לפי שאין רגילות לעשותה מקש הכי נמי במנעל של סיידין לפי שאין רגילות לעשות מנעל של עץ מטהר: והא לאו להילוכא עביד. הקשה הר"ר אליעזר ממיץ לרשב"א מאי פריך והלא משעת מלאכתו הוא מהלך בו ולכך הוא נעשה ותירץ לו דסנדל של סיידין לאו לנעול עשוי אלא אחד מכלי אומנותו של סיידין הוא ועשוי כעין סנדל ויכול לתת רגלו בתוכו לנועלו אך אין עשוי רק לטוח בו את הבית ופעמים שנועל בו ומטייל בו עד שיגיע לביתו ולהכי פריך והא לאו להילוכא כו' ור"י פירש הואיל ואין עשוי כלל לנעילה רק לשמור מנעליו שלא ישרפו בסיד לאו להילוכא עביד ומכל מקום משני לו שכן הסייד כו':

רבא אמר אף טמא טומאת מדרס. פי' הרב פור"ת הא דלא קתני ברישא דמתניתין ואם יש לו בית קיבול כתיתין טמא מדרס כדקתני בסיפא משום דהוה משמע אבל אם אין לו בית קיבול טהור מן המדרס אבל טמא טומאת מת ולא היא דהא פשוטי כלי עץ הוא ולהכי תנא טמא סתמא דבכה"ג טמא הא אין לו בית קיבול כתיתין טהור לגמרי וא"ת למה לי בית קיבול כתיתין תיפוק ליה דכל הטמא מדרס טמא טומאת מת[מ] וי"ל דבית קיבול כתיתין עושין אותו ראוי למדרס:

עגלה של קטן. פ"ה עגלה שהקטן יושב עליה ול"נ דא"כ מאי קמ"ל פשיטא דאין לך מיוחד למדרס גדול מזה לכך נ"ל דהיינו עגלה שעושין לקטן להתלמד להלך טמאה מדרס דנשען עליה:
קישורי

עז א מיי' פי"ט מהל' שבת הלכה טז סמג לאוין סה טוש"ע א"ח סימן שא סעיף טו:
עח ב שם סעיף טז:
עט ג מיי' פכ"ה מהל' כלים הלכה יח:
פ ד ה שם הלכה יט:
פא ו שם הלכה טז:
פב ז שם הלכה יז:

ליקוטי רש"י

ופליגא דשמואל דאמר שמואל נהרא מכיפיה מיברך. שנובע מגדותיו ולא ממי גשמים [רש"י נדרים שם.]. מכיפיה מסלעו כלומר ממקורו הוא מתגדל שאע"פ שאנו רואים שכשהגשמים יורדין נהרות מתרבים עיקר רבויין ממקורן הוא כדאמרי' בפרק סדר תעניות (כה:) אין לך כל טפח וטפח יורד מלמעלה שאין תהום עולה לקראתו טפחיים ונמצא שלעולם זוחלין רבין על הנוטפין דהא לטפח של גשמים איכא טפחיים דמעיין הלכך לשמואל מותר לטבול בנהרות לעולם אפי' כשראה לעין שנתרבו הרבה מחמת המטר. אין המים מטהרין בזוחלין. דאיכא למיחש לרבו הנוטפין [ר"ן שם]. [דבכל] שעה הוו מים נוטפין רבין עליהן [בכורות שם]. אלא פרת ביומי תשרי בלבד. דכל ימות השנה רבין נוטפין על הזוחלין מן הגשמים שיורדין לתוכו ומן השלגים שמתפשרין כל ימות החמה אבל בתשרי כבר פסקו השלגים ונתפשרו כולן והלכו להן מטהרין הזוחלין ואין בנהרות אלא מימיו שנובעין בלבד [רש"י נדרים שם:]. לפי שאינו עת גשמים ולא זמן הפשרת שלגים ולא למיסר כל הנהרות חוץ מפרת אתא ולא למיסר נמי פרת בכל השנה אלא וכו' קאמר שמואל שאין המים מטהרין בזוחלין אלא פרת וכיוצא בו שאינו מכזב לעולם ולמעוטי מים המכזבין הוא דקאמר פרת ופרת וכיוצא בו קאמר וקאמר נמי דבפרת וכיוצא בו שאינו מכזב אינו מותר לטבול בו מן הסתם בכל השנה כולה מי שאינו בקי בו אלא ביומי תשרי בלבד לפי שביומי תשרי אינו עת גשמים ולא זמן הפשרת שלגים ולפיכך אפי' מי שאינו בקי בו אין לו לחוש שמא רבו עליו נוטפין אבל אין ה"נ דמי שבקי בפרת וכיוצא בו כל השנה כל שהוא רואה שלא נתרבה על מה שהוא זוחל בתשרי בכדי שיהא ראוי לחוש לרבוי נוטפין טובל בו בכל השנה וכן נמי אם רואה בתשרי שנתרבה כל כך עד שאפשר לו לחוש שמא רבו בו נוטפין אפי' בתשרי אינו טובל בו אלא שמואל סתמא קאמר דמי שאינו מכיר אפי' בנהרות שאין מכזבין יש לו לחוש כל השנה ברבייתן וביומי תשרי אין לו לחוש כן נ"ל וראיתי מי שכתב בהפך ולא נראו לי דבריו [ר"ן שם]. שפרת היו מימיו פרין ורבין וזוחלין [ונובעין] ממעיינות מרובין ועוד שתשרי סוף ימי הקיץ ולא ירדו גשמים (הרי) [לזמן] מרובה אלמא נהרות מתרבין ממימי גשמים ולעיל אמר מכיפיה מיברך לישנא אחרינא הא דאבוה דשמואל הוה עביד [לבנתיה] מקוואות ביומי ניסן מפני שהוא סוף החורף שירדו גשמים מרובים אבל באמצע החורף לא הוה עביד ופליגא אדשמואל דהוא אומר דכל שעה בעינן מקוואות אלא פרת ביומי תשרי [בכורות שם].
הקיטע. היכא דקתני קטע לחוד משמע דרגלים כדתנן (שבת סה:) הקטע יוצא בקב שלו [ברכות נח: עיי"ש]. הקיטע יוצא בקב שלו. עושין לו כמין דפוס רגל וחוקק בו מעט לתת ראש שוקו לתוכו ואינו נסמך עליו ולכך יוצא בקב שלו דמנעל דידיה הוא [רש"י בר"ף ועי' בתוס' כאן]. בקב הקיטע שנקטעה רגלו עושה כמין דפוס רגל ויש בה בית קיבול קטן ומכניס שם ראש שוקו ואין נסמך עליו והוא קרוי קב ולמשענת הליכה יש לו אשקי"א קשורה בשוקיו ומשענת ידיו שקורין קרוק"א [יבמות קב:]. קב הקיטע נעל הוא ללאת בו בשבת [שם קג:]. קב. אשקל"א [יומא עח:]. [ע"כ שייך לדף סה:]. כתיתין. חתיכות דקות של מוכין ועור רך [יבמות קב:]. חתיכות בגדים קטנות שהם נוחות לו לסמוך שוקו עליהם. טמא. מקבל טומאה דלאו פשוטי כלי עץ הוא [יומא עח:]. או של שמאל בימין חליצה כשרה. שהחליצה ברגל ימיני ואם נעל בו סנדל שמאל וחלצה כשר [לקמן קיב.]. אבל חליצה של שמאל קתני בפירקין (יבמות קד.) פלוגתא [יבמות קא.]. מאן תנא. סנדל של עץ דקתני מתני' חליצתה כשרה מני. רבי מאיר היא. דאמר קב הקיטע נעל הוא ללאת בו בשבת [שם קג:]. עגלה של קטן. שעושין לו לשחוק ויושב עליה ומטלטלין אותו עליה. טמאה מדרס. אם התינוק זב נעשית העגלה אב הטומאה דמיוחדת לישיבה היא דהא סומך קטן עליה נמצאת שהיא מיוחדת לו לישיבה ואין אומרים לו עמוד ונעשה מלאכתנו דאילו לא מיוחדא להכי לא הוה אב הטומאה כדתניא יכול כפה סאה ויושב עליה כו' (שבת נט.) [ביצה כג:].

א) [במשנה שבמשניות איתא אנקטמין ובערוך כתב כדהכא], ב) [שבועות מז.], ג) [שם], ד) יבמות קא., ה) עדיות פ"ב מ"ח תוספתא דכלים ב"ב פ"ד [ע"ש], ו) [ל"ל רב יוסף אמר], ז) שם, ח) [בפי"ז דכלים מי"ז תנן מחצלת הקש ושפופרת הקש ר"ע מטמא ור"י בן נורי מטהר וע"ש בפי' הר"ש ד"ה ר"ע ולכאורה נראה של"ל דתניא כוורת וכו'], ט) ביצה כג: תוספתא דכלים ב"ב פ"ד, י) [חולין קכט.], כ) [כלים פי"ז מט"ו], ל) בס"י ליתא, מ) [כדאיתא נדה מט.].

הגהות הב"ח

(א) גמרא וסימנא סמך סמך. נ"ב עי' בפ' ח' שרצים דף קי ע"א במ"ש התוספו' בד"ה סיפאי: (ב) רש"י ד"ה טמא מקבל וכו' לטומאה הוא והוה וכו' לדומיא דשק:

גליון הש"ס

גמ' אמר רב יוסף מאן לא הודו לו. ברמב"ן במלחמות רפ"ח דיומא גרס כאן רבא אמר: רש"י ד"ה טמא וכו' אבל שוקו אינו מיטלטל. עיין לקמן דף פא ע"א תוס' ד"ה חפי פותחת:

הגהות הגר"א

[א] גמ' והתניא. נ"ב והתנן. מתני' בעדיות: [ב] שם (כוורת של קש ושפופרת של קנים). תא"מ ונ"ב מחצלת הקש ושפופרת הקש ועיין בפי"ז דכלים:

רבינו חננאל

ורבי יוסי אוסר וכדאוקמוה א) ומחתי בה סימנא סמך סמך כלומר ר' יוסי אוסר (סבר) [דכ"ע סברי] הקב של קיטע (אינו) חשוב כסנדל ואסור לצאת בו ביוה"כ והיינו טעמא דר' יוסי דאסר בשבת גזרה דלמא משתמיט ואתי לאתויי ד' אמות ברה"ר (כו') ושמואל נמי ורב יוסף (לפנינו הגי' רב הונא) הדרו ואוקמוה למתני' הקטע יוצא דברי ר"מ: סנדל של סיידין. פי' הסייד כשהוא סד קרקעית הבית בסיד נועל סנדלו של עץ ברגלו כדי שלא יהא הסיד אוכל ברגלו. בית קבול כתיתין. פי' חקוק בתוך הקב חקיקה להיות

חשק שלמה על רבינו חננאל

א) הובא בא"ז בשם רבינו:

רב נסים גאון

סמיכות שלו אין נכנסין בהן לעזרה. מחמת מה שנאמרה בפ' הרואה מקום במסכת ברכות (דף נד) ולא יכנס בה להר הבית במקל

ח) לתרוצי סוגיא עבידא הכא לסמוך עילויה הוא דעבידא וסמיך עליה: (א) טמאין מדרס ואין יוצאין בהן בשבת ואין נכנסין בהן לעזרה: תני תנא קמיה דר' יוחנן נכנסין בהן לעזרה א"ל אני שונה אשה חולצת בו ואת אמרת נכנסין תני אין נכנסין בהן לעזרה: לוקטמין טהורה: מאי לוקטמין אמר ר' אבהו א חמרא דאכפא ג) רבא בר פפא אמר ב קשירי בני רבא בר רב הונא אמר ג) ג פרמי: **מתני'** הבנים יוצאין בקשרים ובני מלכים בזוגין וכל אדם אלא שדברו חכמים בהווה: **גמ'** מאי קשרים אמר אדא מרי אמר רב נחמן בר ברוך אמר רב אשי בר אבין אמר רב יהודה קשורי פואה אמר אביי ד) אמרה לי אם תלתא מוקמי חמשה מסו שבעה אפילו לכשפים מעלי אמר רב אחא בר יעקב והוא דלא חזי ליה שמשא וסיהרא ולא חזי מיטרא ולא שמיע ליה קול ברזלא וקל תרנגולתא וקל ניגרי אמר רב נחמן בר יצחק ה) נפל פותא בבירא מאי איריא בנים אפי' בנות נמי מאי איריא קטנים אפי' גדולים נמי אלא מאי קשרים כי הא דאמר אבין בר הונא א"ר חמא בר גוריא בן שיש (ב) געגועין על אביו נוטל רצועה ממנעל של ימין וקושר לו בשמאלו אמר רב נחמן בר יצחק וסימניך תפילין וחילופא סכנתא אמר אבין בר הונא אמר רב חמא בר גוריא ד סחופי כסא אטיבורי בשבתא שפיר דמי ואמר אבין בר הונא אמר רב חמא בר גוריא ה מותר לסוך שמן ומלח בשבת כי הא דרב הונא מבי רב ורב מבי ר' חייא ור' חייא מבי רבי כי הוו מיבסמי מייתי משחא ומילחא ושייפי להו לגויתא דידייהו וגוייתא דכרעייהו ואמרי כי היכי דציל הא מישחא ליציל חמריה דפלניא בר פלניתא ואי לא מייתי שיעא דדנא ושרי ליה במיא ואמר כי היכי דליציל האי שיעא ליציל חמריה דפלניא בר פלניתא ואמר אבין בר הונא אמר רב חמא בר גוריא ו מותר לחנק בשבת ואמר אבין בר הונא אמר רב חמא בר גוריא ו) ז לפופי ינוקא בשבתא שפיר דמי רב פפא מתני בנים רב זביד מתני בן רב פפא מתני בנים ותרוייהו מתני להו באבין בר הונא רב זביד מתני בן קמייתא מתני באבין בר הונא והאי מתני לה ברבה בר בר חנה דאמר ז) רבה בר בר חנה לפופי ינוקא בשבתא שפיר דמי אמר אביי אמרה לי אם כל מנייני בשמא דאימא וכל קטרי בשמאלא ואמר אביי אמרה לי אם כל מנייני דמפרשי כדמפרשי ודלא מפרשי ארבעין וחד זימני ת"ר ח יוצאין באבן תקומה בשבת משום ר"מ אמרו ט אף במשקל אבן תקומה ולא שהפילה אלא שמא תפיל ולא שעיברה אלא שמא תתעבר ותפיל אמר רב יימר בר שלמיא משמיה דאביי והוא דאיכוון ואיתקל בעי אביי משקל דמשקל מאי תיקו ואמר אביי אמרה לי אם לאשתא בת יומא לישקול זוזא חיוורא וליזיל למלחתא וליתקול מתקליה מילחא ולצייריה בחללא דבי צואר בנירא ברקא ואי לא ליתוב אפרשת דרכים וכי חזי שומשמנא גמלא דדרי מידי לישקליה ולישדייה בגובתא דנחשא וליסתמיה באברא וליחתמי בשיתין גושפנקי ולברזוליה ולידריה ולימא ליה טעונך עלי וטעונאי עלך אמר ליה רב אחא בריה דרב הונא לרב אשי ודילמא איניש אשכחיה ואיפסק ביה אלא לימא ליה טעונאי וטעונך עלך ואי לא לישקול כוזא חדתא וליזיל לנהרא ולימא ליה נהרא נהרא אוזפן כוזא דמיא לאורחא דאיקלע לי ולהדר שב זימני על רישיה ולשדיין לאחוריה ולימא ליה נהרא נהרא שקול מיא דיהבת לי דאורחא דאיקלע לי ביומיה אתא וביומיה אזל אמר רב הונא

לאשתא

תוספות

קישורי. פי' הקונטרס אשקל"ש והקשה בקונטרס ור"י תירץ דכיון שאינם עשויים אלא ללכת דרך העברה בטיט ס) אינו טמא מדרס ובערוך י) פירש דקישורי היינו אשקל"ש שעושין הליצנים והן גבוהין מאד ואינן אלא לרקד עליהן ולא להילוך עבידי כ):

רש"י

לתרוצי סוגיא. לתקן פסיעותיו ולזקוף קומה מפני שרגליו ושוקיו רותתות ולא לסמיכת כל גופו: אני שונה אשה חולצת בהן. אלמא נעל קרינא ביה: חמרא דאכפא. חמור הנישא בכתפיים הליצנים עושין אותו ונראה כמי שרוכב עליו ובמקומנו נקרא אורדפיס"א: קישורי. אשקל"ש שמהלכין בהם במקום טיט וקשיא לי נהי דטהורין מטומאת מגע דפשוטי כלי עץ נינהו אבל מן המדרס למה טהורין: פרמי. טלמוסא הנקשרת על הפרצוף להבעית הבנים קטנים: **מתני'** בקשרים. מפרש בגמרא: בזגין. איסקליט"ש של זהב לנוי: **גמ'** אדא מרי. כך שמו: קשרי פואה. גרנצ"א קושרים בקשרים ותולין בצואר לרפואה ולא ידעתי לאיזה חולי: מוקמי. מעמידין החולי שלא יגדל: ה'. קשרים: מסו. מתרפאין: נגרי. פסיעות: נפל פותא בבירא. נפל רפואת הפואה בבור דאין אדם נזהר בכל אלו: מאי איריא בנים. לרב יהודה פריך אי קישורין דמתני' לרפואת חולי נינהו מאי איריא בנים: געגועין. ברמור"ט מגעגע עליו ואינו יכול ליפרד ממנו ורפואה זו לא שייכא בנקבות שאין האב מחבבן כל כך מתחילתן שיהיו מגעגעין עליו: תפילין. שיד ימינו קושרתו לשמאלו זהו סימן לגירסא: סכנתא. שמגעגע יותר מדאי: סחופי כסא. כוס שיש בו הבל כגון שעירו ממנו מים חמין וכופהו על הטיבור למי שחש במעיו ואוחז הכוס את הבשר ומושך אליו את המעיים ומושיבן במקומן: לסוך. בכפות ידיו ורגליו: דרב הונא מבי רב. שהיה בא מבי רב שהוא רבו וכן רב מבי ר' חייא ור' חייא מבי רבי: מבסמי. שכורין שהיו משקין את התלמידים ואלו מפני שחשובין הן היו עושין להן דבר להפג את יינן: לגוייתא דידייהו. תוכי ידיהם דהיינו כף: דצייל. שהולך ונעשה צלול כל שעה מחום הבשר: שיעא דדנא. מגופת החבית: דציל האי שיעא. מחמת המים: ליחנק. מי שנפרקה חוליא של מפרקת צוארו (ג) ונופלת בגרונו תולין אותו בראשו שיהא צוארו נפשט ודומה לחניקה: לפופי. לכורכו בבגדים וקושרו בחגורה רחבה ומתיישבין פרקי אבריו שהן רכין ונשמטין בחבלי הלידה וקורין אנמלטויי"ר בלע"ז: מתני בנים. שתי שמועות דאיירי בקטנים היה שונה בשם רבי (ח) אבא) בר הונא משמיה דרב חמא בר גוריא: בן. חדא שמעתא דאיירי בקטן מתני בשמיה: תרוייהו. געגועין ולפופי: כל מנייני. כל לחשות ומפני שכופלין אותן יש ג' פעמים ויש יותר קרי להו מנייני: בשמא דאמא. פלוני בן פלונית: דמיפרשי. כל לחשים שמפורש מניין כמה פעמים שיאמרו ויכפלו אותו: כדמפרשי. כופלין אותו כפי מניינו ודלא מיפרשי בהם סתם כפילתן ארבעין וחד זימנין: אבן תקומה. אבן שנושאות אותה נשים עוברות שלא יפילו וקורין לה קוטאנ"א בלע"ז: במשקל. שום דבר ששקלוהו כנגדה: ולא שהפילה. ולא תאמר שלא התירו לצאת בה אלא לאשה שעלולה להפיל עוברה שהפילה כבר עובר אחר: ולא שעיברה. שידוע לה שהיא מעוברת: והוא דאיכוון ותקל. שנמלא החפץ מאליו למשקל האבן ולא שחיסרו ממנו או הוסיפו עליו לכוונו: בת יומא. שאחזתו בכל יום: זוזא חיוורא. צרוף וחדש: למלחתא. למקום שריפת המים שעושין נגרים על שפת הים להמשיך מים לבריכות רחבות העשויות לכך וכשנתמלאו סותם החריצין והשמש שורף את המים שמלוחין הן ונעשה מלח: בחללא דבי צוארו. תחת גרונו כנגד מפתחי חלוקו לשון רבינו הלוי: נירא ברקא. נימא של שער: פרשת דרכים. מקום ששני דרכים מתפרשים: שומשמנא גמלא. נמלה גדולה מ): דדרי מידי. שטוען כלום: לישקליה. לשומשמנא: בגובתא דנחשא. כמין קנה של נחשת: ולסתמיה באברא. יסתום פיה בעופרת: גושפנקי. חותמות ולאו דוקא שיתין נקט ולאו דוקא חותמות של צורה אלא סתימות הרבה זו על זו שטוח על העופרת ושוב זפת ושוב טיט: וליברזוליה. ינענענו: ולידריה. ישאנו: ולימא ליה. לשומשמנא: טעונך עלי. מה שהיית נושא אשאנו: וטעונאי. החולי שלי: איניש אשכחיה ואיפסק ביה. חולי מה שזה עושה וכי אמר ליה טעונך עלי זהו חולי של חברו: כוזא חדתא. כלי חרס קטן חדש: אוזפן. הלויני: ולהדריה ז' זימני ארישיה. יקיפנו סביבות ראשו:

לאשתא

עין משפט נר מצוה

פג א ב ג מיי' פי"ט מהל' שבת הלכה טו סמג לאוין סה טוש"ע א"ח סימן שא סעיף כ:

פד ד מיי' פכ"א מהל' שבת הל' לא סמג לאוין סה טוש"ע א"ח סי' שכח סעיף מ וסעי' מג:

פה ה מיי' שם הל' כג טוש"ע שם סעי' מא:

פו ו ז מיי' פכ"א שם הלכה לא:

פז ח ט מיי' פי"ט שם הלכה יד סמג שם טוש"ע א"ח סימן שג סעיף כד:

רבינו חננאל

הכתיתין ומוגלא הזבה מרגלו זבין מתקבצין באותה החקיקה ולא יהו מצערין אותו בארכובותיו אמר אביי טמא טומאת מת מפני שיש בו בית קבול והוי כלי. רבא אמר אף טמא מדרס כמו עגלה של קטן יוצאין בהן בשבת כי אינם (משא וכלים הם) [משתמטים] תני תנא קמיה דרבי יוחנן נכנסין בהן לעזרה כלומר אינם סנדל כי אסור אדם ליכנס בסנדל בעזרה כדתנן (ברכות נד.) לא יכנס אדם להר הבית במקל ובמנעלו כו' א"ל אני שונה אשה חולצת בסנדל של עץ ואתה שונה נכנסין תני אין נכנסין: **לוקטמין** חמרא דאכפי. גידם מי שידיו קצוצות עושין לו יד של עץ ונקרא חמרא דאכפי: **פרמי.** פי' פרמו יש מי שאומרים חתיכה של בגד שקושרין לזקנים א) ששפתותיהן מתרפטות: **קשרים** קשרי פואה משום רפואה. בן שיש לו געגועין על אביו יש מי שאומרים כי כשיגדל עצב הבן במיתת אביו נוטל רצועה ממנעל אביו הימין וקושרה בשמאל הבן ואומרים שמשקיט לבו ואם יחליף אומרים שהוא סכנה וסימניך תפילין והן שעל היד השמאל: **סחופי** כסא אטיבורא. פי' אם בולט טיבורו של אדם בחוץ ממעיו או אם ניקב מניחין שם [כוס] קטן על טיבורו כדי שלא יבלוט ויתבקע ומניחין אותו עד שיתרפא הא דשרו לבסימא לסוך מלח ושמן לכרעייהו פשוטה היא פי' לחנק פי' לפופי ינוקא. אבן תקומה פי' אומרים כי יש אבן ידועה כשהיא תלויה על אשה הרה אינה מפלת וגם המשקל שכנגד אותו האבן מועלת ומותר לצאת בהן בשבת אבל

חשק שלמה על רבינו חננאל

א) עי' בגליון בשס הערוך וכ"ה בא"ז בשם רבינו:

גליון הש"ס

תוס' ד"ה קישורי וכו' **אינו טמא מדרס.** עיין מנחות דף לא ע"א תוספות ד"ה שידה.

מסורת הש"ס

א) [תרגום של ובמישור ובתרלותא ועי' בערוך ערך תרן], ב) בד' פפד"מ רפרם וכ"ה ברי"ף, ג) [פרמאי פי' חתיכה של בגד שקושרין לזקנים על פיהם למען רירם מפני ששפתותיהן מתרפטות ערוך ערך אנקטמין וע"ע בערוך ערך פרמא], ד) [קידושין לא: וש"נ], ה) [ברכות נו.], ו) [פי' שמחברין איבריו כמו ויחבר תרגומו ולפוף ערוך], ז) [לקמן קמז: ע"ש], ח) [נ"ל אבין], ט) בלשון ארמית אומר לכל דבר גדול גמלא. הרמב"ם בפי' המשנה כלאים פ"ג מ"ב, י) [ערך אנקטמין], כ) [וע"ע תוספות מנחות לא. תד"ה שידה].

הגהות הב"ח

(א) גמ' כסא וסמוכות שלו טמאין מדרס: (ב) שם בן שיש לו געגועין: (ג) רש"י ד"ה ליחנק וכו' צוארו. נ"ב ס"א או נפלה לו ערלת הגרון ונופל בגרונו וכו':

רב נסים גאון

ובמנעלו: רב פפא מתני בנים תרווייהו. כלומר שהיה שונה הראשונה בן שיש לו געגועין על אביו וזו האחרת לפופי משום אבון בר הונא אמר רב חמא בר גוריא והיה רב זביד שוה עמו בשמועה ראשונה בן שיש לו געגועין על אביו וחלוק עליו בשמועה שניה לפופי ינוקא והיה רב זביד אומרה משם רבה בר בר חנה אמר רבי יוחנן ולפי שהיתה השמועה הראשונה בן שיש לו געגועין על אביו והשניה לפופי ינוקא ואמר על שניהם מתני בנים זה הוא פירושם והוזקקתי לכותבו הנה מפני שראיתיו קשה לתלמידים ובארתיו כדי שיתגלה לכל:

סליק פרק במה אשה

ליקוטי רש"י

סחופי כסא. כפיית הכלי [יבמות מז.]. **לפופי.** אנמליו"ן בלע"ז ולאו היינו אסוכי ינוקא דאמרן לעיל בפרק כל הכלים (קכג.) דהא שמעינן ליה לרב נחמן דאסר אלא לפופי בעלמא כמו שעושין בחגורות ופסיקיאות [לקמן קכט:]. **לפופי.** אונמלוטי"א כמו שעושין לקטן שיתיישבו אבריו ולא יתעקם [שם קמז:]. **מלחתא.** משרפות מים דמתרגמינן חרילי ימא (יהושע א) שממשיך לתוכו מים מן הים והחמה שורפתן והן נעשין מלח ואותו חריץ קרי מילחתא [לקמן עג:]. על שפת הים חרילין עשוין שמי הים נכנסים בהן והחומה מייבשתן ועושין מלח והן משרפות מים האמורין במקרא (יהושע יא) ומתרגמינן חרילי ימא [כתובות עט:]. **נירא ברקא.** ליל"א של שיער בהמה [ע"ז כח:]. **גובתא.** קנה חלול [ברכות ו.].

לְתָרוּצֵי סוּגְיָא עֲבִידָא – it is never used to support one's *full weight,* but **is** meant solely **to straighten one's steps** by bearing a part of one's weight; it therefore is not susceptible to *midras tumah.*[1] הָכָא לִסְמוֹךְ עִילָוֵיהּ הוּא דַּעֲבִידָא – But **here** (in the case of a wooden foot) **it is made** not only for cosmetic reasons, but also **to** occasionally **support** one's full weight **upon it,** וְסָמִיךְ עֲלֵיהּ – **and** indeed **[those who use it]** do **support** their full weight **upon it** from time to time! It is therefore susceptible to *midras tumah.*

The Mishnah continues:

טְמֵאִין מִדְרָס – [The chair and the leg supports of one whose lower legs have atrophied] **ARE SUSCEPTIBLE TO** contamination with ***MIDRAS TUMAH,*** וְאֵין יוֹצְאִין בָּהֶן בְּשַׁבָּת – **AND ONE MAY NOT GO OUT WITH THEM ON THE SABBATH,** וְאֵין נִכְנָסִין בָּהֶן לָעֲזָרָה – **AND ONE MAY NOT ENTER THE TEMPLE COURTYARD WITH THEM.**

The Gemara presents a Baraisa that contradicts the Mishnah:

תָּנֵי תַּנָּא קַמֵּיהּ דְּרַבִּי יוֹחָנָן – **A teacher of Baraisos**[2] **taught** the following **in the presence of R' Yochanan:** נִכְנָסִין בָּהֶן לָעֲזָרָה – **ONE MAY ENTER THE TEMPLE COURTYARD WITH [THE LEG SUPPORTS]** of one whose lower legs have atrophied.

R' Yochanan objects:

אָמַר לֵיהּ – **[R' Yochanan] said to him:** אֲנִי שׁוֹנֶה אִשָּׁה חוֹלֶצֶת בּוֹ – **I learn** in another Baraisa: **A WOMAN MAY PERFORM *CHALITZAH* WITH** such **[A LEG SUPPORT],** since it is legally considered a shoe, וְאַתְּ אָמְרַת נִכְנָסִין – **and you are quoting: ONE MAY ENTER** the Temple Courtyard with a leg support, since it is *not* considered a shoe! Obviously, you are teaching this Baraisa incorrectly! תְּנֵי – Rather, then, **teach** in the text of the Baraisa as follows: אֵין נִכְנָסִין בָּהֶן לָעֲזָרָה – **ONE MAY NOT ENTER THE TEMPLE COURTYARD WITH [THESE LEG SUPPORTS],** since they are considered shoes.

The Mishnah continues:

לוּקְטְמִין טְהוֹרָה – ***LOKITMIN*** **ARE NOT SUSCEPTIBLE TO** contamination with ***TUMAH*** [and one may not go out with them on the Sabbath].

The Gemara inquires about the identity of *lokitmin*:

מַאי לוּקְטְמִין – **What are *lokitmin*?**

The Gemara answers:

אָמַר רַבִּי אַבָּהוּ – **R' Avahu said:** חֲמָרָא דְּאַכְּפָא – They are wooden **donkeys that are** carried **upon the shoulders** of clowns.[3]

Another opinion:

רָבָא בַּר פַּפָּא אָמַר – **Rava bar Pappa said:** קְשִׁירֵי – They are **stilts** used to walk in muddy areas.[4]

A third opinion:

רָבָא בַּר רַב הוּנָא אָמַר – **Rava bar Rav Huna said:** פְּרָמֵי – They are **masks** used to frighten children.[5]

Mishnah

This Mishnah lists two additional items with which one may go out on the Sabbath: הַבָּנִים יוֹצְאִין בִּקְשָׁרִים – Young **boys may go out** on the Sabbath **with knots,**[6] וּבְנֵי מְלָכִים בְּזוּגִין – **and princes with** ornamental golden **bells.** וְכָל אָדָם – **And** this is actually true of **any person,** אֶלָּא שֶׁדִּבְּרוּ חֲכָמִים בַּהֹוֶה – **however, the Sages spoke in** regard to **the prevalent** custom.[7]

Gemara

The Gemara inquires after the knots mentioned in the Mishnah:

מַאי קְשָׁרִים – **What are** these **knots** discussed in the Mishnah? אָמַר אַדָּא מָרִי אָמַר רַב נַחְמָן בַּר בָּרוּךְ אָמַר רַב אַשִׁי בַּר אָבִין אָמַר רַב יְהוּדָה – **Adda Mari said in the name of Rav Nachman bar Baruch, who said in the name of Rav Ashi bar Avin, who said in the name of Rav Yehudah:** קְשׁוּרֵי פּוּאָה – **They are knots of** the **madder** plant, which are hung about the neck for their curative properties.[8]

Abaye recounts a bit of lore concerning these knots:

אָמַר אַבַּיֵי – **Abaye said:** אֲמָרָה לִי אֵם – **Mother told me**[9] regarding knots of madder: תְּלָתָא מוֹקְמֵי – **Three** knots **contain** the

NOTES

1. For an article cannot acquire *tumas midras* unless it is used to bear the greater part of one's weight (*Rashi;* see *Zavim* 4:4 with *Rash;* see also *Toras Kohanim* to *Leviticus* 15:23; but cf. *Rashi* to *Sanhedrin* 48a ד״ה שהוא טמא מדרס). An elderly person's cane, however, is used only as an additional support, to keep its user's back from hunching, and his legs from wobbling because of weakness in his legs. It is not meant to support his body's full weight (*Rashi*).

2. In this context the word תַּנָּא, *Tanna,* refers to an Amora who would memorize the Tannaic texts and repeat them verbatim for scholars.

3. These clowns were street performers, who would incorporate this device into their acts (*Aruch* ע׳ אנקטמין). The donkey would be suspended between the performer's legs, giving the impression that he was riding it, but it actually hung from his shoulders (*Rashi*). Since it is not a utensil, it is not susceptible to *tumah* [that is transmitted by contact] (*Aruch* ibid.). [It is not susceptible to *tumas midras* because it does not truly bear the clown's weight.] The reason one may not go out with it on the Sabbath is because since it is not a garment, it constitutes a burden; however, one who does go out with it will not be liable, since this is not a regular method of transport (*Mishnah Berurah* 301:70; see above, 66a note 1).

4. The reason these stilts are not susceptible to *tumah* transmitted by contact is because they are wooden implements that do not possess receptacles [פְּשׁוּטֵי כְּלֵי עֵץ] (see above, 66a note 2) (*Rashi*). *Rashi* has difficulty, however, explaining why they are not susceptible to *tumas midras* (and, by extension, to contact-generated *tumah* – see Mishnah, *Niddah* 49a, and *Hagahos R' Yaakov Emden* here). For since they are used for walking upon, they are seemingly a perfect example of an article made to support one's weight! *Rabbeinu Yitzchak* (cited in *Tosafos*) answers that although their *use* entails support of one's weight, their true *purpose* is not to bear weight, for they are only used occasionally to enable one to walk easily in deep mud. They therefore are not susceptible to *tumas midras* (see also *Tosafos* to *Menachos* 31a ד״ה שידה).

[*Ritva* (*MHK* ed.) poses an obvious challenge to *Rabbeinu Yitzchak's* answer: How do these stilts differ from a plaster seller's sandal (above, 66a), whose true purpose is not to bear weight, but is only worn occasionally when going home, and which nonetheless is susceptible to *tumas midras*? He answers that a plaster seller's sandal is different in that it has the form of a regular shoe; stilts, by contrast, are no more than simple slats of wood, and therefore are not susceptible to *tumas midras.*]

[The literal translation of the term קְשִׁירֵי is *knots.* The stilts are given this name because their upper segments are bound to the wearer's leg (see *Aruch* ע׳ אנקטמין).]

For why these stilts may not be worn outside on the Sabbath, see previous note.

5. See above, 66a note 9. (For another interpretation of פְּרָמֵי, see *Aruch* ibid.).

6. [The Gemara will explain what manner of knots these are and why they are restricted to young boys.]

7. [I.e. commoners too are actually permitted to go out on the Sabbath adorned with bells; however, it is customary only for the nobility, or for those who are wealthy, to do so.] See *Tosafos* above, 58a ד״ה מאי שנא, and Gemara below, 67a; see also *Orach Chaim* 301:23 with *Beur Halachah* ד״ה דוקא.

8. *Rashi*, as explained by *Targum HaLaaz* §558. [Madder is a plant with whorled leaves and yellowish flowers whose root is used to produce a red dye.] It was customary to knot madder stems and hang them about one's neck as a cure (*Rashi*; *Aruch* [ע׳ פאה [ג]). *Rashi* states that he does not know for which sickness these knots were used; see, however, *Korban HaEidah* ד״ה בקשרי פואה, who cites proof that they are beneficial for all illnesses. [Since they are worn for healing purposes, they do not constitute a burden; one is therefore permitted to go out with them on the Sabbath.]

9. Abaye's mother died while giving birth to him. Thus, whenever Abaye

לתרוצי סוגיא עבידא הכא לסמוך עילויה הוא דעבידא וסמיך עליה: (א) טמאין מדרס ואין יוצאין בהן בשבת ואין נכנסין בהן לעזרה: תני תנא קמיה דר' יוחנן נכנסין בהן לעזרה א"ל אני שונה אשה חולצת בו ואת אמרת נכנסין תני אין נכנסין בהן לעזרה: לוקטמין טהורה: מאי לוקטמין אמר ר' אבהו [א]חמרא דאכפא [ג]רבא בר פפא אמר [ב]קשירי בני רבא בר רב הונא אמר [ג][ג]פרמי: **מתני'** הבנים יוצאין בקשרים ובני מלכים בזוגין וכל אדם אלא שדברו חכמים בהווה: **גמ'** מאי קשרים אמר אדא מרי אמר רב נחמן בר ברוך אמר רב אשי בר אבין אמר רב יהודה קשורי פואה אמר אביי [ד]אמרה לי אם תלתא מוקמי חמשה מסו שבעה אפילו לכשפים מעלי אמר רב אחא בר יעקב והוא דלא חזי ליה שמשא וסיהרא ולא חזי מיטרא ולא שמיע ליה קול ברזלא וקל תרנגולתא וקל ניגרי אמר רב נחמן בר יצחק [ה]נפל פותא בבירא מאי איריא בנים אפי' בנות נמי מאי איריא קטנים אפי' גדולים נמי אלא מאי קשרים כי הא דאמר אבין בר הונא א"ר חמא בר גוריא בן שיש (ב) געגועין על אביו נוטל רצועה ממנעל של ימין וקושר לו בשמאלו אמר רב נחמן בר יצחק וסימניך תפילין וחילופא סכנתא אמר אבין בר הונא אמר רב חמא בר גוריא [ד]סחופי כסא אטיבורי בשבתא שפיר דמי ואמר אבין בר הונא אמר רב חמא בר גוריא [ה]מותר לסוך שמן ומלח בשבת כי הא דרב הונא מבי רב ורב מבי ר' חייא ור' חייא מבי רבי כי הוו מיבסמי מייתי משחא ומילחא ושייפי להו לגוייתא דידייהו וגוייתא דכרעייהו ואמרי כי היכי דציל הא מישחא ליציל חמריה דפלניא בר פלניתא ואי לא מייתי שיעא דדנא ושרי ליה במיא ואמר כי היכי דליציל האי שיעא ליציל חמריה דפלניא בר פלניתא ואמר אבין בר הונא אמר רב חמא בר גוריא [ו]מותר לחנק בשבת ואמר אבין בר הונא אמר רב חמא בר גוריא [ז][ז]לפופי ינוקא בשבתא שפיר דמי רב פפא מתני בנים רב זביד מתני בן רב פפא מתני בנים ותרוייהו מתני להו באבין בר הונא רב זביד מתני בן קמייתא מתני באבין בר הונא והאי מתני לה ברבה בר בר חנה דאמר [ח]רבה בר בר חנה לפופי ינוקא בשבתא שפיר דמי אמר אביי אמרה לי אם כל מנייני בשמא דאימא וכל קטרי בשמאלא ואמר אביי אמרה לי אם כל מנייני דמפרשי כדמפרשי ודלא מפרשי ארבעין וחד זימני ת"ר [ח]יוצאין באבן תקומה בשבת משום ר"מ אמרו [ט]אף במשקל אבן תקומה ולא שהפילה אלא שמא תפיל ולא שעיברה אלא שמא תתעבר ותפיל אמר רב יימר בר שלמיא משמיה דאביי והוא דאיכוון ואיתקל בעי אביי משקל דמשקל מאי תיקו ואמר אביי אמרה לי אם לאשתא בת יומא לישקול זוזא חיוורא וליזיל למלחתא וליתקול מתקליה מילחא ולצייריה בחללא דבי צואר בנירא ברקא ואי לא ליתוב אפרשת דרכים וכי חזי שומשמנא גמלא דדרי מידי לישקליה ולישדייה בגובתא דנחשא וליסתמיא באברא וליחתמי בשיתין גושפנקי ולברזוליה ולידריה ולימא ליה טעונך עלי וטעונאי עלך אמר ליה רב אחא בריה דרב הונא לרב אשי ודילמא איניש אשכחיה ואיפסק ביה אלא לימא ליה טעונאי וטעונך עלך ואי לא לישקול כוזא חדתא וליזיל לנהרא ולימא ליה נהרא נהרא אוזפן כוזא דמיא לאורחא דאיקלע לי ולהדר שב זימני על רישיה ולשדיין לאחוריה ולימא ליה נהרא נהרא שקול מיא דיהבת לי דאורחא דאיקלע לי ביומיה אתא וביומיה אזל אמר רב הונא לאשתא

רש"י

לתרוצי סוגיא. לתקן פסיעותיו ולזקוף קומה מפני שרגליו ושוקיו רותתות ולא לסמיכת כל גופו: אני שונה אשה חולצת בהן. אלמא נעל קרינא ביה: חמרא דאכפא. חמור הנישא בכתפיים הליצנים עושין אותו ונראה כמי שרוכב עליו ובמקומנו נקרא אורדפיס"א: קישורי. אשקצ"ש שמהלכין בהם במקום טיט וקשיא לי נהי דטהורין מטומאת מגע דפשוטי כלי עץ נינהו אבל מן המדרס למה טהורין: פרמי. טלמושא הנקשרת על הפרצוף להבעית הבנים קטנים: מתני' בקשרים. מפרש בגמרא: בזגין. אישקליט"ש של זהב לנוי: גמ' אדא מרי. כך שמו: קשרי פואה. גרנצ"א קושרים בקשרים ותולין בצואר לרפואה ולא ידעתי לאיזה חולי: מוקמי. מעמידין החולי שלא יגדל: ה'. קשרים: מסו. מתרפאין: נגרי. פסיעות: נפל פותא בבירא. נפל רפואת הפואה בבור דאין אדם נזהר בכל אלו: מאי איריא בנים. לרב יהודה פריך אי קישורין דמתני' לרפואת חולי נינהו מאי איריא בנים: געגועין. ברמור"ט מגעגע עליו ואינו יכול ליפרד ממנו ורפואה זו לא שייכא בנקבות שאין האב מחבבן כל כך מתחילתן שיהיו מגעגעין עליו: תפילין. שיד ימינו קושרתו לשמאלו זהו סימן לגירסא: סכנתא. שמגעגע יותר מדאי: סחופי כסא. כוס שיש בו הבל כגון שעירו ממנו מים חמין וכופהו על הטיבור למי שחש במעיו ואוחז הכוס את הבשר ומושך אליו את המעיים ומושיבן במקומן: לסוך. בכפות ידיו ורגליו: דרב הונא מבי רב. שהיה בא מבי רב שהוא רבו וכן רב מבי ר' חייא ור' חייא מבי רבי: מבסמי. שכורין שהיו משקין את התלמידים ואלו מפני שחשובין הן היו עושין להן דבר להפג את יינן: לגוייתא דידיהו. תוכי ידיהם דהיינו כף: דצייל. שהולך ונעשה צלול כל שעה מחום הבשר: שיעא דדנא. מגופת החבית: דציל האי שיעא. מחמת המים: ליחנק. מי שנפרקה חוליא של מפרקת צוארו (ג) ונופלת בגרונו תולין אותו בראשו שיהא צוארו נפשט ודומה לחניקה: לפופי. לכורכו בבגדים וקושרו בחגורה רחבה ומתיישבין פרקי אבריו שהן רכין ונשמטין בחבלי הלידה וקורין אנמלטוויי"ר בלע"ז: מתני בנים. שתי שמועות דאיירי בקטנים היה שונה בשם רבי ([ח]אבא) בר הונא משמיה דרב חמא בר גוריא: בן. חדא שמעתא דאיירי בקטן מתני בשמיה: תרוייהו. געגועין ולפופי: כל מנייני. כל לחשים ומפני שכופלין אותן יש ג' פעמים ויש יותר קרי להו מנייני: בשמא דאמא. פלוני בן פלונית: דמיפרשי. כל לחשים שמפורש מניין כמה פעמים שיאמרו ויכפלו אותו: כדמפרשי. כופלין אותו כפי מניינו ודלא מיפרשי בהם סתם כפילתן ארבעין וחד זימנין: אבן תקומה. אבן שנושאות אותה נשים עוברות שלא יפילו וקורין לה קוטאנ"א בלע"ז: במשקל. שום דבר ששקלוהו כנגדה: ולא שהפילה. ולא תאמר שלא התירו לצאת בה אלא לאשה שעלולה להפיל עוברה שהפילה כבר עובר אחר: ולא שעיברה. שידוע לה שהיא מעוברת: והוא דאיכוון ותקל. שנמצא החפץ מאליו למשקל האבן ולא שחיסרו ממנו או הוסיפו עליו לכוונו: בת יומא. שאחזתו בכל יום: זוזא חיוורא. צרוף וחדש: למלחתא. למקום שריפת המים שעושין נגרים על שפת הים להמשיך מים לבריכות רחבות העשויות לכך וכשנתמלאו סותם החריצין והשמש שורף את המים שמלוחין הן ונעשה מלח: בחללא דבי צוארו. תחת גרונו כנגד מפתחי חלוקו לשון רבינו הלוי: נירא ברקא. נימא של שער: פרשת דרכים. מקום ששני דרכים מתפרשים: שומשמנא גמלא. נמלה גדולה[ט]: דדרי מידי. שטוען כלום: לישקליה. לשומשמנא: בגובתא דנחשא. כמין קנה של נחשת: וליסתמייה באברא. יסתום פיה בעופרת: גושפנקי. חותמות ולאו דוקא שיתין נקט ולאו דוקא חותמות של צורה אלא סתימות הרבה זו על זו שעוה על העופרת ושוב זפת ושוב טיט: וליברזוליה. ינענעו: ולידריה. ישאנו: ולימא ליה. לשומשמנא: טעונך עלי. מה שהיית נושא אשאנו: וטעונאי. החולי שלי: איניש אשכחיה ואיפסק ביה. חולי כזה שזה עושה וכי אמר ליה טעונך עלי זהו חולי של חברו: כוזא חדתא. כלי חרס קטן חדש: אוזפן. הלוני: ולהדריה ז' זימני ארישיה. יקיפנו סביבות ראשו: לאשתא

תוספות

קישורי. פי' הקונטרס אשקצ"ש והקשה בקונטרס ור"י תירץ דכיון שאינם עשויים אלא ללכת דרך העברה בטיט [ס]אינו טמא מדרס ובערוך [י]פירש דקישורי היינו אשקצ"ש שעושין הליצנים והן גבוהין מאד ואינן אלא לרקד עליהן ולא להילוך עבידי[כ]:

עין משפט נר מצוה

פג א ב ג מיי' פי"ט מהל' שבת הלכה טו סמג לאוין סה טוש"ע א"ח סימן שא סעיף כ:
פד ד מיי' פכ"א מהל' שבת הל' לא סמג לאוין סה טוש"ע א"ח סי' שכח סעיף מ וסעי' מג:
פה ה מיי' שם הל' כג טוש"ע שם סעי' מא:
פו ו ז מיי' פכ"א שם הלכה לא:
פז ח ט מיי' פי"ט שם הלכה יד סמג שם טוש"ע א"ח סימן שג סעיף כד:

רבינו חננאל

הכתיתין ומוגלא הזבה מרגלו זבין מתקבצין באותה החקיקה ולא יהו מצערין אותו בארכובותיו אמר אביי טמא טומאת מת מפני שיש בו בית קבול והוי כלי. רבא אמר אף טמא מדרס כמו עגלה של קטן יוצאין בהן בשבת כי אינם (משא וכלים הם) [משתמטים] תני תנא קמיה דרבי יוחנן נכנסין בהן לעזרה כלומר אינם סנדל כי אסור אדם ליכנס בסנדל בעזרה כדתנן (ברכות נד.) לא יכנס אדם להר הבית במקל ובמנעלו כו' א"ל אני שונה אשה חולצת בסנדל של עץ ואתה שונה נכנסין תני אין נכנסין: **לוקטמין** חמרא דאכפי. גידם מי שידיו קצוצות עושין לו יד של עץ ונקרא חמרא דאכפי: **פרמי.** פי' פרמו יש מי שאומרים חתיכה של בגד שקושרין לזקנים א) ששפתותיהן מתרפטות: **קשרים** קשרי פואה משום רפואה. בן שיש לו געגועין על אביו יש מי שאומרים כי כשיגדל עצב הבן במיתת אביו נוטל רצועה ממנעל אביו הימין וקושרה בשמאל הבן ואומרים שמשקיט לבו ואם יחליף אומרים שהוא סכנה וסימניך תפילין והן שעל היד השמאל: **סחופי** כסא אטיבורא. פי' אם בולט טיבורו של אדם בחוץ ממעיו או אם ניקב מניחין שם [כוס] קטן על טיבורו כדי שלא יבלוט ויתבקע ומניחין אותו עד שיתרפא הא דשרו לבסימא לסוך מלח ושמן לכרעייהו פשוטה היא פי' לחנק פי' לפופי ינוקא. אבן תקומה פי' אומרים כי יש אבן ידועה כשהיא תלויה על אשה הרה אינה מפלת וגם המשקל שכנגד אותו האבן מועלת ומותר לצאת בהן בשבת אבל

חשק שלמה על רבינו חננאל

א) עי' בגליון בשם הערוך וכ"ה בא"ז בשם רביט:

גליון הש"ס

תוס' ד"ה קישורי וכו' אינו טמא מדרס. עיין מנחות דף לא ע"א תוספות ד"ה שידה:

מסורת הש"ס

א) [תרגום של ובמישור ובתרגומא ועי' בערוך ערך תרן], ב) כד' פפד"מ רפרם וכ"ה ברי"ף, ג) [פרמאי פי' חתיכה של בגד שקושרין לזקנים על פיהם למען ריחם מפני ששפתותיהן מתרפטות ערוך ערך אנקטמין וע"ע בערוך ערך פרמא], ד) [קידושין לא: וש"נ], ה) [ברכות נו.], ו) [פי' שמחברין איבריו כמו ויחבר תרגומו ולפוף ערוך], ז) [לקמן קמז: ע"ש], ח) [נ"ל אבין], ט) בלשון ארמית אומר לכל דבר גדול גמלא. הרמב"ם בפי' המשנה כלאים פ"ג מ"ב, י) [ערך אנקטמין], כ) [וע"ע תוספות מנחות לא. תד"ה שידה].

הגהות הב"ח

(א) גמ' כסא וסמוכות שלו טמאין מדרס: (ב) שם בן שיש לו געגועין: (ג) רש"י ד"ה ליחנק וכו' צוארו. נ"ב ס"א או נפלה לו ערלת הגרון ונופל בגרונו וכו':

רב נסים גאון

ובמנעלו: **רב** פפא מתני בנים תרווייהו. כלומר שהיה שונה הראשונה בן שיש לו געגועין על אביו וזו האחרת לפופי משום אבון בר הונא אמר רב חמא בר גוריא והיה רב זביד שוה עמו בשמועה ראשונה בן שיש לו געגועין על אביו וחלוק עליו בשמועה שניה לפופי ינוקא והיה רב זביד אומרה משם רבה בר בר חנה אמר רבי יוחנן ולפי שהיתה השמועה הראשונה בן שיש לו געגועין על אביו והשניה לפופי ינוקא ואמר על שניהם מתני בנים זה הוא פירושם והוזקקתי לכותבו הנה מפני שראיתיו קשה לתלמידים וביארתיו כדי שיתגלה לכל:
סליק פרק במה אשה

ליקוטי רש"י

סחופי כסא. כפיית הכלי [יבמות מז.]. לפופי. אנמליו"ן בלע"ז ולאו היינו אסוקי ינוקא דאמרן לעיל בפרק כל הכלים (קכג.) דהא שמעינן ליה לרב נחמן דאסר אלא לפופי בעלמא כמו שעושין בחגורות ופסיקיאות [לקמן קכט:]. לפופי. אונמלוטי"א כמו שעושין לקטן שיתיישבו אבריו ולא יתעקם [שם קמז:]. מלחתא. משרפות מים דמתרגמינן חרילי ימא (יהושע א) שממשיך לתוכו מים מן הים והחמה שורפתן והן נעשין מלח ואותו חריץ קרי מילחתא [לקמן עג:]. על שפת הים חריצין עשויין שמי הים נכנסים בהן והחמה מייבשתן ועושין מלח והן משרפות מים האמורין במקרא (יהושע יא) ומתרגמינן חרילי ימא [כתובות עט:]. נירא ברקא. נימא של שיער בהמה [ע"ז כח:]. גובתא. קנה חלול [ברכות ו.].

illness, חֲמִשָּׁה מַסּוּ – **five heal** it, שִׁבְעָה אֲפִילוּ לִכְשָׁפִים מְעַלֵּי – and **seven are beneficial even for** warding off **witchcraft.**

The Gemara presents conditions for the use of knots of madder: אָמַר רַב אַחָא בַּר יַעֲקֹב – **Rav Acha bar Yaakov said:** וְהוּא דְּלָא חָזֵי לֵיהּ שִׁמְשָׁא וְסִיהֲרָא – **And this is** true [i.e. that knots of madder heal] only **if [the knots] are not exposed**[10] **to sunlight or moonlight,** וְלָא חָזֵי מִיטְרָא – **and if they are not exposed to rain,** וְלָא שָׁמִיעַ לֵיהּ קוֹל בַּרְזְלָא – **and if they are not exposed**[11] **to the sound of metal** clanking, וְקַל תַּרְנְגוֹלְתָּא – **or** to **the sound of a rooster** crowing, וְקַל נִיגְרֵי – **or** to **the sound of footsteps.**

Rav Nachman bar Yitzchak responds to Rav Acha's conditions: אָמַר רַב נַחְמָן בַּר יִצְחָק – **Rav Nachman bar Yitzchak said:** נְפַל פּוּתָא בְּבֵירָא – If so, the remedy of **madder** knots **has fallen into a pit!** It is useless, since it is impossible to comply with all these conditions![12]

The Gemara now challenges those who explain that the Mishnah refers to knots of madder:

מַאי אִירְיָא בָּנִים – If, indeed, the Mishnah refers to knots of madder, then for **what reason** does **it teach** this law only with regard to **boys,** thus implying that only they are permitted to go out on the Sabbath with these knots? אֲפִילוּ בָּנוֹת נַמִּי – **Even girls too** should be permitted to go out in this manner, since madder knots constitute a remedy for them as well!

A further challenge:

מַאי אִירְיָא קְטַנִּים – Moreover, if the Mishnah refers to knots of madder, then for **what reason** does it **teach** this law only with regard to **minors?** אֲפִילוּ גְּדוֹלִים נַמִּי – **Even adults too** should be permitted to go out with these knots! Obviously, the Mishnah is not discussing therapeutic knots of madder, but knots used for some other purpose!

The Gemara presents a different explanation:

אֶלָּא מַאי קְשָׁרִים – **Rather, what are** the **knots** spoken of by our Mishnah? כִּי הָא דְּאָמַר אָבִין בַּר הוּנָא אָמַר רַב חָמָא בַּר גּוּרְיָא – **They are like those that Avin bar Huna spoke of in the name of Rav Chama bar Gurya.** He said: בֵּן שֶׁיֵּשׁ [לוֹ] גַּעְגּוּעִין עַל אָבִיו – To comfort **a son who yearns after his father** who is parting from him, נוֹטֵל רְצוּעָה מִמִּנְעָל שֶׁל יָמִין – **[the father] takes a strap from [his own] right shoe,** וְקוֹשֵׁר לוֹ בִּשְׂמֹאלוֹ – **and knots it to [the boy's] left** arm. This will alleviate the boy's sadness.[13]

Rav Nachman bar Yitzchak offers a mnemonic for review: אָמַר רַב נַחְמָן בַּר יִצְחָק – **Rav Nachman bar Yitzchak said:** וְסִימָנֵיךְ תְּפִילִּין – **And your mnemonic** for this practice **is tefillin,** which are also straps knotted onto one's left arm with the right hand.

The Gemara explains why it is important to perform this therapy properly:

וְחִילּוּפָא סַכַּנְתָּא – **For the opposite,** i.e. a strap from the left shoe knotted to the right arm, constitutes **a danger,** as it will cause the boy excessive yearning, and perhaps plunge him into dangerous melancholia.

Having cited one ruling from Avin bar Huna in the name of Rav Chama bar Gurya concerning healing on the Sabbath, the Gemara now continues with a series of such rulings:

אָמַר אָבִין בַּר הוּנָא אָמַר רַב חָמָא בַּר גּוּרְיָא – **Avin bar Huna said in the name of Rav Chama bar Gurya:** סְחוּפֵי כָּסָא אַטִּיבּוּרֵי בְּשַׁבְּתָא שַׁפִּיר דָּמֵי – **It is all right** for one **to invert a** hot **cup upon the navel on the Sabbath.**[14]

A second ruling:

וְאָמַר אָבִין בַּר הוּנָא אָמַר רַב חָמָא בַּר גּוּרְיָא – **And Avin bar Huna said in the name of Rav Chama bar Gurya:** מוּתָּר לָסוּךְ שֶׁמֶן וּמֶלַח בְּשַׁבָּת – **It is permissible to smear** a mixture of **oil and salt** upon the palms of one's hands and the soles of one's feet **on the Sabbath** to relieve one's inebriation.[15]

The Gemara records several instances where this practice was employed to relieve inebriation:

כִּי הָא דְּרַב הוּנָא מִבֵּי רַב – **As in [the case] of Rav Huna** when he would come **from the house of** his teacher **Rav,** וְרַב מִבֵּי רַבִּי חִיָּיא – **and Rav** when he would come **from the house of** his

NOTES

quotes from his mother, he is actually referring to his nursemaid, who raised him (*Kiddushin* 31b).

10. Literally: if they do not see [sunlight or moonlight].

11. Literally: if they do not hear [the sound of metal, of a rooster crowing, or of footsteps].

12. *Rashi*. *Aruch* (ibid.) explains differently: These conditions render the remedy useless, since only knots stored at the bottom of a dark pit could possibly conform to all these conditions. [See *Magen Avraham* to *Orach Chaim* 155:3 for an interesting exchange regarding this Gemara.]

13. [The boy therefore may go out with these knots on the Sabbath, as they constitute healing for him.] Girls, however, may not wear them outside, for since the love a father feels for his daughter is not as powerful as that he feels for his son, she experiences considerably less trauma upon his departure, and does not require knot therapy. For her, then, the knots are simply a burden, and are therefore forbidden to wear on the Sabbath (*Rashi*).

[*Rambam* to the Mishnah agrees that these knots are used in the event that one's father must leave for a considerable length of time. However, *Rabbeinu Chananel* and *Aruch* (ע׳ געגע [א׳]) maintain that the knots are meant to relieve melancholy that falls upon a boy upon the death of his father, while *Chidushei HaRan* states that they are used as a preventive measure – they prevent a son from becoming overly attached to a seriously ill father, lest the father die, and the son be plunged into depression.]

[There are conflicting opinions regarding the proper performance of this therapy. Our translation follows *Rabbeinu Chananel* and *Rambam*; however, *Meiri* maintains that the leather strap is taken from the son's shoe and tied onto the father's arm, while *Chidushei HaRan* states that it is taken from the son's own right shoe and tied to his own left arm.]

[*Meiri* implies that these knots are not actually effective (see below, 67a note 32), but may nonetheless be worn on the Sabbath. Since it is the custom to wear them, they do not legally constitute a burden.]

14. The Gemara refers to a cup that was first filled with hot liquid, and was then emptied and placed upon the navel to relieve stomach pain. The heat draws one's flesh towards it, thereby returning one's intestines to their proper place (*Rashi*). Now, the use of most remedies is prohibited on the Sabbath by Rabbinic decree, since the Rabbis feared that one might be led to grind ingredients for potions [שְׁחִיקַת סַמָּנִים], which is forbidden on the Sabbath. The reason this particular remedy is permitted is because it involves only the manual manipulation of body parts, and not the use of potions; we are therefore confident that no such transgression will occur. However, even remedies involving only manipulation of the body are generally prohibited because they constitute weekday activity [עוּבְדָּא דְחוֹל]; for illnesses that cause one severe pain, however, as does the stomach ailment discussed here, these remedies are permitted (*Rambam, Shabbos* 21:31; *Orach Chaim* 328:43; *Magen Avraham* ad loc. §48). [*Chidushei HaRan* states that the reason this remedy is permitted is because this stomach ailment is a life-threatening one.]

[One must pour the hot liquid from the cup before placing it on the patient's stomach so that it will not spill onto his stomach, and thereby give the impression that he is violating the prohibition against washing on the Sabbath. Moreover, the patient is in danger of receiving a serious burn should boiling water splash onto his stomach! (see above, 40b with *Rashi*).

Although *Rashi* speaks of a cup that was heated by the liquid that filled it, one is permitted as well to simply heat an empty cup and place it upon one's stomach (*Orach Chaim* 326:6; *Mishnah Berurah* ad loc.).]

15. For sobering one who is intoxicated does not qualify as healing, and is therefore not included in the Rabbinic decree that prohibits healing (*Taz, Orach Chaim* ibid. §27; see *Eliyah Rabbah* ad loc.).

א) לתרוצי סוגיא עבידא הכא לסמוך עילויה הוא דעבידא וסמיך עליה: (א) טמאין מדרס ואין יוצאין בהן בשבת ואין נכנסין בהן לעזרה: תני תנא קמיה דר' יוחנן נכנסין בהן לעזרה א"ל אני שונה אשה חולצת בו ואת אמרת נכנסין תני אין נכנסין בהן לעזרה: לוקטמין טהורה: מאי לוקטמין אמר ר' אבהו א חמרא דאכפא ב) רבא בר פפא אמר ב קשירי רבא בר רב הונא אמר ג) ג פרמי: מתני' הבנים יוצאין בקשרים ובני מלכים בזוגין וכל אדם אלא שדברו חכמים בהווה: גמ' מאי קשרים אמר אדא מרי אמר רב נחמן בר ברוך אמר רב אשי בר אבין אמר רב יהודה קשורי פואה אמר אביי ד) אמרה לי אם תלתא מוקמי חמשה מסו שבעה אפילו לכשפים מעלי אמר רב אחא בר יעקב והוא דלא חזי ליה שמשא וסיהרא ולא חזי מיטרא ולא שמיע ליה קול ברזלא וקל תרנגולתא וקל ניגרי אמר רב נחמן בר יצחק ה) נפל פותא בבירא מאי איריא בנים אפי' בנות נמי מאי איריא קטנים אפי' גדולים נמי אלא מאי קשרים כי הא דאמר אבין בר הונא א"ר חמא בר גוריא בן שיש (ב) געגועין על אביו נוטל רצועה ממנעל של ימין וקושר לו בשמאלו אמר רב נחמן בר יצחק וסימניך תפילין וחילופא סכנתא אמר אבין בר הונא אמר רב חמא בר גוריא ד סחופי כסא אטיבורי בשבתא שפיר דמי ואמר אבין בר הונא אמר רב חמא בר גוריא ה מותר לסוך שמן ומלח בשבת כי הא דרב הונא מבי רב ורב מבי ר' חייא ור' חייא מבי רבי כי הוו מיבסמי מייתי משחא ומילחא ושייפי להו לגוייתא דידייהו וגוייתא דכרעייהו ואמרי כי היכי דציל הא מישחא ליציל חמריה דפלניא בר פלניתא ואי לא מייתי שיעא דדנא ושרי ליה במיא ואמר כי היכי דליציל האי שיעא ליציל חמריה דפלניא בר פלניתא ואמר אבין בר הונא אמר רב חמא בר גוריא ו מותר לחנק בשבת ואמר אבין בר הונא אמר רב חמא בר גוריא ו) ז לפופי ינוקא בשבתא שפיר דמי רב פפא מתני בנים רב זביד מתני בן רב פפא מתני בנים ותרוייהו מתני להו באבין בר הונא רב זביד מתני בן קמייתא מתני באבין בר הונא והאי מתני לה ברבה בר בר חנה דאמר ז) רבה בר בר חנה לפופי ינוקא בשבתא שפיר דמי אמר אביי אמרה לי אם כל מנייני בשמא דאימא וכל קטרי בשמאלא ואמר אביי אמרה לי אם כל מנייני דמפרשי כדמפרשי ודלא מפרשי ארבעין וחד זימני ת"ר ח יוצאין באבן תקומה בשבת משום ר"מ אמרו ט אף במשקל אבן תקומה ולא שהפילה אלא שמא תפיל ולא שעיברה אלא שמא תתעבר ותפיל אמר רב יימר בר שלמיא משמיה דאביי והוא דאיכוון ואיתקל בעי אביי משקל דמשקל מאי תיקו ואמר אביי אמרה לי אם לאשתא בת יומא לישקול זוזא חיוורא וליזיל למלחתא וליתקול מתקליה מילחא ולציירה בחללא דבי צואר בנירא ברקא ואי לא ליתוב אפרשת דרכים וכי חזי שומשמנא גמלא דדרי מידי לישקליה ולישדייה בגובתא דנחשא וליסתמיא באברא וליחתמי בשיתין גושפנקי ולברזוליה ולידריה ולימא ליה טוענך עלי וטעונאי עלך אמר ליה רב אחא בריה דרב הונא לרב אשי ודילמא איניש אשכחיה ואיפסק ביה אלא לימא ליה טעונאי וטעונך עלך ואי לא לישקול כוזא חדתא וליזיל לנהרא ולימא ליה נהרא נהרא אוזפן כוזא דמיא לאורחא דאיקלע לי ולהדר שב זימני על רישיה ולשדיין לאחוריה ולימא ליה נהרא נהרא שקול מיא דיהבת לי דאורחא דאיקלע לי ביומיה אתא וביומיה אזל אמר רב הונא
לאשתא

רש"י

לתרוצי סוגיא. לתקן פסיעותיו ולזקוף קומה מפני שרגליו ושוקיו רותתות ולא לסמיכת כל גופו: אני שונה אשה חולצת בהן. אלמא נעל קרינא ביה: חמרא דאכפא. חמור הנישא בכתפיים הליצנים עושין אותו ונראה כמי שרוכב עליו ובמקומנו נקרא אורדפיי"א: קישורי. אשקצ"ש שמהלכין בהם במקום טיט וקשיא לי נהי דטהורין מטומאת מגע דפשוטי כלי עץ ניהו אבל מן המדרס למה טהורין: פרמי. טלמוסא הנקשרת על הפרצוף להבעית הבנים קטנים: מתני' בקשרים. מפרש בגמרא: בזגין. אישקליט"ש של זהב לנוי: גמ' אדא מרי. כך שמו: קשרי פואה. גרנצ"א קושרים בקשרים ותולין בצואר לרפואה ולא ידעתי לאיזה חולי: מוקמי. מעמידין החולי שלא יגדל: ה'. קשרים: מסו. מתרפאין: נגרי. פסיעות: נפל פותא בבירא. נפל רפואת הפואה בבור דאין אדם נזהר בכל אלו: מאי איריא בנים. לרב יהודה פריך אי קישורין דמתני' לרפואת חולי נינהו מאי איריא בנים: געגועין. ברמור"ט מגעגע עליו ואינו יכול ליפרד ממנו ורפואה זו לא שייכא בנקבות שאין האב מחבבן כל כך מתחילתן שיהיו מגעגעין עליו: תפילין. שיד ימינו קושרתו לשמאלו זהו סימן לגירסא: סכנתא. שמגעגע יותר מדאי: סחופי כסא. כוס שיש בו הבל כגון שעירו ממנו מים חמין וכופהו על הטיבור למי שחש במעיו ואוחז הכוס את הבשר ומושך אליו את המעיים ומושיבן במקומן: לסוך. בכפות ידיו ורגליו: דרב הונא מבי רב. שהיה בא מבי רב שהוא רבו וכן רב מבי ר' חייא ור' חייא מבי רבי: מבסמי. שכורין שהיו משקין את התלמידים ואלו מפני שחשובין הן היו עושין להן דבר להפג את יינן: לגוייתא דידייהו. תוכי ידיהם דהיינו כף: דצייל. שהולך ונעשה צלול כל שעה מחום הבשר: שיעא דדנא. מגופת החבית: דציל האי שיעא. מחמת המים: ליחנק. מי שנפרקה חוליא של מפרקת צוארו (ג) ונופלת בגרונו תולין אותו בראשו שיהא צוארו נפשט ודומה לחניקה: לפופי. לכורכו בבגדים וקושרו בחגורה רחבה ומתיישבין פרקי אבריו שהן רכין ונשמטין בחבלי הלידה וקורין אנמלטוי"ר בלע"ז: מתני בנים. שתי שמועות דאיירי בקטנים היה שונה בשם רבי (ט) אבא) בר הונא משמיה דרב חמא בר גוריא: בן. חדא שמעתא דאיירי בקטן מתני בשמיה: תרוייהו. געגועין ולפופי: כל מנייני. כל לחשים ומפני שכופלין אותן יש ג' פעמים ויש יותר קרי להו מנייני: בשמא דאמא. פלוני בן פלונית: דמיפרשי. כל לחשים שמפורש מניין כמה פעמים שיאמרו ויכפלו אותו: כדמפרשי. כופלין אותו כפי מניינו ודלא מיפרשי בהם סתם כפילתן ארבעין וחד זימנין: אבן תקומה. אבן שנושאות אותה נשים עוברות שלא יפילו וקורין לה קוטאנ"א בלע"ז: במשקל. שום דבר ששקלוהו כנגדה: ולא שהפילה. ולא תאמר שלא התירו לצאת בה אלא לאשה שעלולה להפיל עוברה שהפילה כבר עובר אחר: ולא שעיברה. שידוע לה שהיא מעוברת: והוא דאיכוון ותקל. שנמצא החפץ מאליו למשקל האבן ולא שחיסרו ממנו או הוסיפו עליו לכוונו: בת יומא. שאחזתו בכל יום: זוזא חיוורא. צרוף וחדש: למלחתא. למקום שריפת המים שעושין נגרים על שפת הים להמשיך מים לבריכות רחבות העשויות לכך וכשנתמלאו סותם החריצין והשמש שורף את המים שמלוחין הן ונעשה מלח: בחללא דבי צוארו. תחת גרונו כנגד מפתחי חלוקו לשון רבינו הלוי: נירא ברקא. ליצ"א של שער: פרשת דרכים. מקום ששני דרכים מתפרשים: שומשמנא גמלא. נמלה גדולה (ט): דדרי מידי. שטוען כלום: לישקליה. לשומשמנא: בגובתא דנחשא. כמין קנה של נחשת: ולסתמייה באברא. יסתום פיה בעופרת: גושפנקי. חותמות ולאו דוקא שיתין נקט ולאו דוקא חותמות של צורה אלא סתימות הרבה זו על זו שעוה על העופרת ושוב זפת ושוב טיט: וליברזוליה. ינענענו: ולידריה. ישאנו: ולימא ליה. לשומשמנא: טוענך עלי. מה שהיית נושא אשאנו: וטעונאי. החולי שלי: איניש אשכחיה ואיפסק ביה. חולי כזה שזה עושה וכי אמר ליה טוענך עלי זהו חולי של חברו: כוזא חדתא. כלי חרס קטן חדש: אוזפן. הלוני: ולהדריה ז' זימני ארישיה. יקיפנו סביבות ראשו:
לאשתא

תוספות

קישורי. פי' הקונטרס אשקצ"ש והקשה בקונטרס ור"י תירץ דכיון שאינם עשויים אלא ללכת דרך העברה בטיט ° אינו טמא מדרס ובערוך י) פירש דקישורי היינו אשקצ"ש שעושין הליצנים והן גבוהין מאד ואינן אלא לרקד עליהן ולא להילוך עבידי כ):

בני

עין משפט נר מצוה

פג א ב ג מיי' פי"ט מהל' שבת הלכה טו סמג לאוין סה טוש"ע א"ח סימן שא סעיף כ:

פד ד מיי' פכ"א מהל' שבת הל' לא סמג לאוין סה טוש"ע א"ח סי' שכח סעיף מ וסעי' מג:

פה ה מיי' שם הל' כג טוש"ע שם סעי' מא:

פו ו ז מיי' פכ"א שם הלכה לא:

פז ח ט מיי' פי"ט שם הלכה יד סמג שם טוש"ע א"ח סימן שג סעיף כד:

רבינו חננאל

הכתיתין ומוגלא הזבה מרגלו זבין מתקבצין באותה החקיקה ולא יהו מצערין אותו בארכובותיו אמר אביי טמא טומאת מת מפני שיש בו בית קבול והוי כלי. רבא אמר אף טמא מדרס כמו עגלה של קטן יוצאין בהן בשבת כי אינם (משא וכלים הם) [משתמטים] תני תנא קמיה דרבי יוחנן נכנסין בהן לעזרה כלומר אינם סנדל כי אסור אדם ליכנס בסנדל בעזרה כדתנן (ברכות נד.) לא יכנס אדם להר הבית במקל ובמנעלו כו' א"ל אני שונה אשה חולצת בסנדל של עץ ואתה שונה נכנסין תני אין נכנסין: לוקטמין חמרא דאכפי. גידם מי שידיו קצוצות עושין לו יד של עץ ונקרא חמרא דאכפי: פרמי. פי' פרמו יש מי שאומרים חתיכה של בגד שקושרין לזקנים א) ששפתותיהן מתרפטות: קשרים קשרי פואה משום רפואה. בן שיש לו געגועין על אביו יש מי שאומרים כי כשיגדל עצב הבן במיתת אביו נוטל רצועה ממנעל אביו הימין וקושרה בשמאל הבן ואומרים שמשקיט לבו ואם יחליף אומרים שהוא סכנה וסימניך תפילין והן שעל היד השמאל: סחופי כסא אטיבורא. פי' אם בולט טיבורו של אדם בחוץ ממעיו או אם ניקב מניחין שם [כוס] קטן על טיבורו כדי שלא יבלוט ויתבקע ומניחין אותו עד שיתרפא הא דשרו לבסימא לסוך מלח ושמן לכרעייהו פשוטה היא פי' לחנק פי' לפופי ינוקא. אבן תקומה פי' אומרים כי יש אבן ידועה כשהיא תלויה על אשה הרה אינה מפלת וגם המשקל שכנגד אותו האבן מועלת ומותר לצאת בהן בשבת
אבל

חשק שלמה על רבינו חננאל

א) עי' בגליון בשם הערוך וכ"ה בא"ז בשם רבינו:

גליון הש"ס

תוס' ד"ה קישורי וכו' אינו טמא מדרס. עיין מנחות דף לא ע"א תוספות ד"ה שידה:

מסורת הש"ס

א) [תרגום של ובמישור ובתרצותא ועי' בערוך ערך תרן], ב) כל' פפד"מ רפרם וכ"ה ברי"ף, ג) [פרמאי פי' חתיכה של בגד שקושרין לזקנים על פיהם למען רירם מפני ששפתותיהן מתרפטות ערוך ערך אנקטמין וע"ע בערוך ערך פרמא], ד) [קידושין לא: וש"נ], ה) [ברכות נו.], ו) [פי' שמחברין איבריו כמו ויחבר תרגומו ולפוף ערוך], ז) [לקמן קמז: ע"ש], ח) [צ"ל אבין], ט) בלשון ארמית אומר לכל דבר גדול גמלא. הרמב"ם בפי' המשנה כלאים פ"ג מ"ב, י) [ערך אנקטמין], כ) [וע"ע תוספות מנחות לא. תד"ה שידה].

הגהות הב"ח

(א) גמ' כסא וסמוכות שלו טמאין מדרס: (ב) שם בן שיש לו געגועין: (ג) רש"י ד"ה ליחנק וכו' צוארו. נ"ב ס"א או נפלה לו ערלת הגרון ונופל בגרונו וכו':

רב נסים גאון

ובמנעלו: רב פפא מתני בנים תרווייהו. כלומר שהיה שונה הראשונה בן שיש לו געגועין על אביו וזו האחרת לפופי משום אבון בר הונא אמר רב חמא בר גוריא והיה רב זביד שוה עמו בשמועה ראשונה בן שיש לו געגועין על אביו וחלוק עליו בשמועה שניה לפופי ינוקא והיה רב זביד אומרה משם רבה בר בר חנה אמר רבי יוחנן ולפי שהיתה השמועה הראשונה בן שיש לו געגועין על אביו והשניה לפופי ינוקא ואמר על שניהם מתני בנים זה הוא פירושם והוזקקתי לכותבו הנה מפני שראיתיו קשה לתלמידים וביארתיו כדי שיתגלה לכל:

סליק פרק במה אשה

ליקוטי רש"י

סחופי כסא. כפיית הכלי [יבמות מז.]. לפופי. אנמליו"ן בלע"ז ולאו היינו אסובי ינוקא דאמרן לעיל בפרק כל הכלים (קכג.) דהא שמעינן ליה לרב נחמן דאסר אלא לפופי בעלמא כמו שעושין בחגורות ופסיקיאות [לקמן קכט:]. לפופי. אונמלוטי"א כמו שעושין לקטן שיתיישבו אבריו ולא יתעקם [שם קמז:]. מלחתא. משרפות מים דמתרגמינן חרילי ימא (יהושע א) שממשיך לתוכו מים מן הים והחמה שורפתן והן נעשין מלח ואותו חריץ קרי מילחתא [לקמן עג:]. על שפת הים חרילין עשויין שמי הים נכנסים בהן והחומה מייבשתן ועושין מלח והן משרפות מים האמורין במקרא (יהושע יא) ומתרגמינן חרילי ימא [כתובות עט:]. נירא ברקא. ליצ"א של שיער בהמה [ע"ז כח:]. גובתא. קנה חלול [ברכות ו.].

teacher **R' Chiya,** וְרַבִּי חִיָּיא מִבֵּי רַבִּי – **and R' Chiya** when he would come **from the house of** his teacher **Rebbi.** כִּי הֲווּ מִיבַּסְמֵי – **If they were inebriated,**[16] מַיְיתֵי מִשְׁחָא וּמִילְחָא – [their teachers] **would bring** a mixture of **oil and salt,** וְשָׁיְיפֵי לְהוּ לְגַוְּויָתָא דִּידַיְיהוּ וְגַוְּויָתָא דְּכַרְעַיְיהוּ וְאָמְרֵי – **and would smear it for them upon the palms of their hands and the soles of their feet,**[17] **and they would say:** כִּי הֵיכִי דְּצָלִיל הָא מִישְׁחָא – **"Just as this oil is thinning out** because of the warmth of this person's body, לִיצִיל חַמְרֵיהּ דִּפְלָנְיָא בַּר פְּלָנִיתָא – so too **should the wine** causing the inebriation **of** this person, **so-and-so the son of [the woman] so-and-so, become thin** and impotent." וְאִי לָא – **And if** oil and salt were **not** available, מַיְיתֵי שִׁיעָא דְּדַנָּא וְשָׁרֵי לֵיהּ בְּמַיָּא וְאָמַר – **they would bring the** clay **seal of a barrel, and soak it in water, and say:** כִּי הֵיכִי דְּלִיצִיל הַאי שִׁיעָא – **"Just as** the clay of **this seal is thinning** because of the water, לִיצִיל חַמְרֵיהּ דִּפְלָנְיָא בַּר פְּלָנִיתָא – so too **let the wine** causing the **inebriation of** this person, **so-and-so the son of [the woman] so-and-so, become thin** and impotent."

A third ruling from Avin bar Huna in the name of Rav Chama bar Gurya:

וְאָמַר אָבִין בַּר הוּנָא אָמַר רַב חָמָא בַּר גּוּרְיָא – **And Avin bar Huna said in the name of Rav Chama bar Gurya:** מוּתָּר לְחַנֵּק בְּשַׁבָּת – **It is permissible to perform "strangling"** therapy **on the Sabbath.**[18]

A fourth ruling:

וְאָמַר אָבִין בַּר הוּנָא אָמַר רַב חָמָא בַּר גּוּרְיָא – **And Avin bar Huna said in the name of Rav Chama bar Gurya:** לְפוּפֵי יְנוּקָא בְּשַׁבְּתָא שַׁפִּיר דָּמֵי – **It is all right** for one **to wrap an infant on the Sabbath** in order to straighten its bones.[19]

The Gemara cites a difference of opinion regarding the source of the previous ruling:

רַב פַּפָּא מַתְנֵי בָּנִים – When repeating these rulings of Avin bar Huna in the name of Rav Chama bar Gurya, **Rav Pappa taught "children"** (plural), i.e. he taught two rulings regarding healing children. רַב זְבִיד מַתְנֵי בֵּן – However, **Rav Zevid taught "child"** (singular), i.e. he taught only one ruling regarding healing children in the name of Avin bar Huna from Rav Chama bar Gurya.

The Gemara explains:

וְתַרְוַיְיהוּ רַב פַּפָּא מַתְנֵי בָּנִים – **Rav Pappa taught "children,"** מַתְנֵי לְהוּ בְּאָבִין בַּר הוּנָא – because **he taught both** the ruling concerning knots to alleviate a boy's melancholy, and that concerning wrapping an infant, **in** the name of **Avin bar Huna,** since both these rulings were transmitted to him in Avin bar Huna's name. רַב זְבִיד מַתְנֵי בֵּן – However, **Rav Zevid taught "child,"** קַמַּיְיתָא מַתְנֵי בְּאָבִין בַּר הוּנָא – because while **he** indeed **taught the first ruling** (regarding knot therapy) **in** the name of **Avin bar Huna** in whose name it was transmitted to him, וְהָאי מַתְנֵי לָהּ בְּרַבָּה בַּר בַּר חָנָה – **he taught this** second ruling (regarding wrapping an infant) **in** the name of **Rabbah bar bar Chanah,** since it was transmitted to him in Rabbah's name. דְּאָמַר רַבָּה בַּר בַּר חָנָה – **For Rabbah bar bar Chanah said:** לְפוּפֵי יְנוּקָא בְּשַׁבְּתָא שַׁפִּיר דָּמֵי – **It is all right** for one **to wrap an infant on the Sabbath** in order to straighten its bones. Thus, Rav Pappa attributes the ruling concerning wrapping an infant to Avin bar Huna, whereas Rav Zevid attributes it to Rabbah bar bar Chanah.

The Gemara now presents several rules concerning incantations and talismans that were taught to Abaye by his nursemaid:[20]

אָמַר אַבַּיֵי – **Abaye said:** אָמְרָה לִי אֵם – **Mother told me:** כָּל מְנְיָינֵי בִּשְׁמָא דְּאִימָּא – **All incantations**[21] are recited **with the name of the** sufferer's **mother,**[22] וְכָל קִטְרֵי בִּשְׂמָאלָא – **and all knots are** tied **upon the left arm.**[23]

Another rule:

וְאָמַר אַבַּיֵי – **And Abaye said:** אָמְרָה לִי אֵם – **Mother told me:** כָּל מְנְיָינֵי דִּמְפָרְשֵׁי כִּדְמִפָּרְשֵׁי – **Any [incantations] whose number** of repetitions **are stated** in their formulae **are** to be repeated as often **as stated.** וּדְלָא מִפָּרְשֵׁי אַרְבְּעִין וְחַד זִימְנֵי – **And those [whose number of repetitions] are not stated** are to be repeated **forty-one times.**

The Gemara interrupts with a Baraisa that teaches of another item with which a woman may go out on the Sabbath:

תָּנוּ רַבָּנָן – **The Rabbis taught in a Baraisa:** יוֹצְאִין בְּאֶבֶן תְּקוּמָה בְּשַׁבָּת – [A WOMAN] MAY GO OUT ON THE SABBATH WITH A PRESERVING STONE,[24] i.e. a stone that preserves her pregnancy,

NOTES

16. It was common practice for teachers to give wine to young scholars [so as to enable them to comprehend the depths of Torah] (*Rashi*; see *Mahadura Basra* to 67b, from *Sanhedrin* 38a). [Sometimes the students would become intoxicated;] since these three students were of great stature, their teachers would seek to relieve their inebriation before they left (*Rashi*).

17. [Literally: upon the insides of their hands, and upon the insides of their feet.]

18. This refers to the manual manipulation of one's neck bone. If a vertebra from the neck bone slipped forward towards one's throat, the practice was to hang one by the head, thus stretching the neck, so that the vertebra would return to its proper place. It is called strangling therapy because it resembles strangulation (*Rashi*). It is permissible because it does not involve the use of potions, and because slippage of this vertebra causes severe pain (*Rambam* ibid.; see above, note 14). [*Chidushei HaRan* cites others who maintain that this remedy involved actual strangulation, in which one's air supply was momentarily cut off as a remedy for a particular illness.]

19. An infant's bones, which are soft, are often bent because of the forceful contractions it experiences at birth. The custom was to swaddle the infant tightly in a wide band of fabric, thus straightening its bent limbs (*Rashi*; see Gemara below, 123a, and *Rashi* 129b ד״ה מלפפין for a procedure which, although similar, is nonetheless prohibited; see also *Tosafos* 123a ד״ה אסובי ינוקא). This remedy too is permitted because it does not involve the use of potions, and because the infant experiences severe pain from the bent limbs (*Rambam* ibid.). It is permissible not only when the child is newly born, but for as long as it is needed (*Meiri*).

20. See below, 67a note 32, for conflicting opinions regarding the efficacy of the cures presented by our Gemara.

21. Literally: all countings. Incantations are referred to as מְנְיָינֵי, *countings,* because they must be repeated, some only three times, some more often (*Rashi*).

22. I.e. the sufferer is referred to in the course of the incantation as so-and-so the son of his mother so-and-so, and not as the son of his father so-and-so (*Rashi*; see *R' Tzadok HaKohen's Machshevos Charutz*, p. 39, for an explanation; see also *Hagahos Yaavetz* here). [It is noteworthy that when praying for the well-being of one who is ill, we likewise refer to one as the son or daughter of one's mother, although when praying for one who has died, we employ the name of the deceased's father (see *Mekor Chesed* §1 to *Sefer Chasidim* §242 for a reason for this distinction).]

23. [I.e. the knots mentioned above that alleviate a young boy's melancholy (however, see *Sefer Chasidim* §1153 with *Mekor Chesed* §3).] See *Haggadah Simchas Yaabetz, ArtScroll* 1993, pp. 241-243, for an interesting insight into the connection between these two pieces of advice.

24. This is a hollowed-out chunk of gravel that contains a second stone within its cavity like a clapper in a bell. The stone must be found this way, not fashioned by hand (*Eliyah Rabbah* to *Orach Chaim* 303:77, from *Maharshal*). However, *Chidushei HaRan* names this stone a diamond, and describes it as an exceptionally hard stone, which cannot be broken even with blows from a hammer. He adds that its name אֶבֶן תְּקוּמָה derives from this quality, as it is *preserved* in the face of any attempt to destroy it. *Rashba*, though, writes [in *Responsa* 1:413] that the preserving stone is one that was imbued with its capacity to prevent miscarriage by undergoing a certain happening, though he does not state what happening that is. [*Rabbeinu Bachya* to *Exodus* 28:15 states that a balas, or a ruby, is efficacious in preventing miscarriage (see there at some length).]

א) לתרוצי סוגיא עבידא הכא לסמוך עילויה הוא דעבידא וסמיך עליה: (א) טמאין מדרס ואין יוצאין בהן בשבת ואין נכנסין בהן לעזרה: תני תנא קמיה דר' יוחנן נכנסין בהן לעזרה א"ל אני שונה אשה חולצת בו ואת אמרת נכנסין תני אין נכנסין בהן לעזרה: לוקטמין טהורה: מאי לוקטמין אמר ר' אבהו א חמרא דאכפא ג) רבא בר פפא אמר ב קשירי בני רבא בר רב הונא אמר ג ג) פרמי: **מתני'** הבנים יוצאין בקשרים ובני מלכים בזוגין וכל אדם אלא שדברו חכמים בהווה: **גמ'** מאי קשרים אמר אדא מרי אמר רב נחמן בר ברוך אמר רב אשי בר אבין אמר רב יהודה קשורי פואה אמר אביי ד) אמרה לי אם תלתא מוקמי חמשה מסו שבעה אפילו לכשפים מעלי אמר רב אחא בר יעקב והוא דלא חזי ליה שמשא וסיהרא ולא חזי מיטרא ולא שמיע ליה קול ברזלא וקל תרנגולתא וקל ניגרי אמר רב נחמן בר יצחק ה) נפל פותא בבירא מאי איריא בנים אפי' בנות נמי מאי איריא קטנים אפי' גדולים נמי אלא מאי קשרים כי הא דאמר אבין בר הונא א"ר חמא בר גוריא בן שיש (ב) געגועין על אביו נוטל רצועה ממנעל של ימין וקושר לו בשמאלו אמר רב נחמן בר יצחק וסימניך תפילין וחילופא סכנתא אמר אבין בר הונא אמר רב חמא בר גוריא ד סחופי כסא אטיבורי בשבתא שפיר דמי ואמר אבין בר הונא אמר רב חמא בר גוריא ה מותר לסוך שמן ומלח בשבת כי הא דרב הונא מבי רב ורב מבי ר' חייא ור' חייא מבי רבי כי הוו מיבסמי מייתי משחא ומילחא ושייפי להו לגוייתא דידייהו וגוייתא דכרעייהו ואמרי כי היכי דציל הא מישחא ליציל חמריה דפלניא בר פלניתא ואי לא מייתי שיעא הדנא ושרי ליה במיא ואמר כי היכי דליציל האי שיעא ליציל חמריה דפלניא בר פלניתא ואמר אבין בר הונא אמר רב חמא בר גוריא ו מותר לחנק בשבת ואמר אבין בר הונא אמר רב חמא בר גוריא ו) ז לפופי ינוקא בשבתא שפיר דמי רב פפא מתני בנים רב זביד מתני בן רב פפא מתני בנים ותרוייהו מתני להו באבין בר הונא רב זביד מתני בן קמייתא מתני באבין בר הונא והאי מתני לה ברבה בר בר חנה דאמר ח) רבה בר בר חנה לפופי ינוקא בשבתא שפיר דמי אמר אביי אמרה לי אם כל מנייני בשמא דאימא וכל קטרי בשמאלא ואמר אביי אמרה לי אם כל מנייני דמפרשי כדמפרשי ודלא מפרשי ארבעין וחד זימני ת"ר ח יוצאין באבן תקומה בשבת משום ר"מ אמרו ט אף במשקל אבן תקומה ולא שהפילה אלא שמא תפיל ולא שעיברה אלא שמא תתעבר ותפיל אמר רב יימר בר שלמיא משמיה דאביי והוא דאיכוון ואיתקל בעי אביי משקל דמשקל מאי תיקו ואמר אביי אמרה לי אם לאשתא בת יומא לישקול זוזא חיוורא וליזיל למלחתא וליתקול מתקליה מילחא ולציירה בחללא דבי צואר בנירא ברקא ואי לא ליתוב אפרשת דרכים וכי חזי שומשמנא גמלא דדרי מידי לישקליה ולישדייה בגובתא דנחשא וליסתמיא באברא וליחתמי בשיתין גושפנקי ולברזוליה ולידריה ולימא ליה טעונך עלי וטעונאי עלך אמר ליה רב אחא בריה דרב הונא לרב אשי ודילמא איניש אשכחיה ואיפסק ביה אלא לימא ליה טעונאי וטעונך עלך ואי לא לישקול כוזא חדתא וליזיל לנהרא ולימא ליה נהרא נהרא אוזפן כוזא דמיא לאורחא דאיקלע לי ולהדר שב זימני על רישיה ולשדיין לאחוריה ולימא ליה נהרא נהרא שקול מיא דיהבת לי דאורחא דאיקלע לי ביומיה אתא וביומיה אזל אמר רב הונא לאשתא

קישורי. פי' הקונטרס אשקל"ש והקשה בקונטרס ור"י תירץ דכיון שאינם עשויים אלא ללכת דרך העברה בטיט ° אינו טמא מדרס ובערוך י) פירש דקישורי היינו אשקל"ש שעושין הליצנים והן גבוהין מאד ואינן אלא לרקד עליהן ולא להילוך עבידי כ):

לתרוצי סוגיא. לתקן פסיעותיו ולזקוף קומה מפני שרגליו ושוקיו רותתות ולא לסמיכת כל גופו: **אני שונה אשה חולצת בהן.** אלמא נעל קרינא ביה: **חמרא דאכפא.** חמור הנישא בכתפיים הליצנים עושין אותו ונראה כמי שרוכב עליו ובמקומנו נקרא אורדפיש"א: **קישורי.** אשקל"ש שמהלכין בהם במקום טיט וקשיא לי נהי דטהורין מטומאת מגע דפשוטי כלי עץ נינהו אבל מן המדרס למה טהורין: **פרמי.** מפרש בגמרא: **בזגין.** אישקליט"ש של זהב לנוי: **גמ' אדא מרי.** כך שמו: **קשרי פואה.** גרנצ"א קושרים בקשרים ותולין בצואר לרפואה ולא ידעתי לאיזה חולי: **מוקמי.** מעמידין החולי שלא יגדל: **ה'.** קשרים: **מסו.** מתרפאין: **נגרי.** פסיעות: **נפל פותא בבירא.** נפל רפואת הפואה בבור דאין אדם נזהר בכל אלו: **מאי איריא בנים.** לרב יהודה פריך אי קישורין דמתני' לרפואת חולי נינהו מאי איריא בנים: **געגועין.** ברמור"ט מגעגע עליו ואינו יכול ליפרד ממנו ורפואה זו לא שייכא בנקבות שאין האב מחבבן כל כך מתחילתן שיהיו מגעגעין עליו: **תפילין.** שיד ימינו קושרתו לשמאלו זהו סימן לגירסא: **סכנתא.** שמגעגע יותר מדאי: **סחופי כסא.** כוס שיש בו הבל כגון שעירו ממנו מים חמין וכופהו על הטיבור למי שחש במעיו ואוחז הכוס את הבשר ומושך אליו את המעיים ומושיבן במקומן: **לסוך.** בכפות ידיו ורגליו: **דרב הונא מבי רב.** שהיה בא מבי רב שהוא רבו וכן רב מבי ר' חייא ור' חייא מבי רבי: **מבסמי.** שכורין שהיו משקין את התלמידים ואלו מפני שחשובין הן היו עושין להן דבר להפג את יינן: **לגוייתא דידייהו.** תוכי ידיהם דהיינו כף: **דצייל.** שהולך ונעשה צלול כל שעה מחום הבשר: **שיעא דדנא.** מגופת החבית: **דציל האי שיעא.** מחמת המים: **ליחנק.** מי שנפרקה חוליא של מפרקת צוארו (ג) ונופלת בגרונו תולין אותו בראשו שיהא צוארו נפשט ודומה לחניקה: **לפופי.** לכורכו בבגדים וקושרו בחגורה רחבה ומתיישבין פרקי אבריו שהן רכין ונשמטין בחבלי הלידה וקורין אנמלטוויי"ר בלע"ז: **מתני בנים.** שתי שמועות דאיירי בקטנים היה שונה בשם רבי (ס) (אבא) בר הונא משמיה דרב חמא בר גוריא: **בן.** חדא שמעתא דאיירי בקטן מתני בשמיה: **תרוייהו.** געגועין ולפופי: **כל מנייני.** כל לחישות ומפני שכופלין אותן יש ג' פעמים ויש יותר קרי להו מנייני: **בשמא דאמא.** פלוני בן פלונית: **דמיפרשי.** כל לחשים שמפורש מניין כמה פעמים שיאמרו ויכפלו אותו: **כדמפרשי.** כופלין אותו כפי מניינו ודלא מיפרשי בהם סתם כפילתן ארבעין וחד זימנין: **אבן תקומה.** אבן שנושאות אותה נשים עוברות שלא יפילו וקורין לה קוטאנ"א בלע"ז: **במשקל.** שום דבר ששקלוהו כנגדה: **ולא שהפילה.** ולא תאמר שלא התירו לצאת בה אלא לאשה שעלולה להפיל עוברה שהפילה כבר עובר אחר: **ולא שעיברה.** שידוע לה שהיא מעוברת: **והוא דאיכוון ותקל.** שנמלא החפץ מאליו למשקל האבן ולא שחיסרו ממנו או הוסיפו עליו לכוונו: **בת יומא.** שאחזתו בכל יום: **זוזא חיוורא.** צרוף וחדש: **למלחתא.** למקום שריפת המים שעושין גריס על שפת הים להמשיך מים לבריכות רחבות העשויות לכך וכשנתמלאו סותם החריצין והשמש שורף את המים שמלוחין הן ונעשה מלח: **בחללא דבי צוארו.** תחת גרונו כנגד מפתחי חלוקו לשון רבינו הלוי: **נירא ברקא.** נימא של שער: **פרשת דרכים.** מקום ששני דרכים מתפרשים: **שומשמנא גמלא.** נמלה גדולה ט): **דדרי מידי.** שטוען כלום: **לישקליה.** לשומשמנא: **בגובתא דנחשא.** כמין קנה של נחשת: **וליסתמייה באברא.** יסתום פיה בעופרת: **גושפנקי.** חותמות ולאו דוקא שיתין נקט ולאו דוקא חותמות של צורה אלא סתימות הרבה זו על זו שעוה על העופרת ושוב זפת ושוב טיט: **וליברזוליה.** ינענענו: **ולידריה.** ישאנו: **ולימא ליה.** לשומשמנא: **טעונך עלי.** מה שהיית נושא אשאנו: **וטעונאי.** החולי שלי: **איניש אשכחיה ואיפסיק ביה.** חולי מה שזה עושה וכי אמר ליה טעונך עלי זהו חולי של חברו: **כוזא חדתא.** כלי חרס קטן חדש: **אוזפן.** הלוני: **וליהדריה ז' זימני ארישיה.** יקיפנו סביבות ראשו: לאשתא

עין משפט נר מצוה

פג א ב ג מיי' פי"ט מהל' שבת הלכה טו סמג לאוין סה טוש"ע א"ח סימן שא סעיף כ:

פד ד מיי' פכ"א מהל' שבת הל' לא סמג לאוין סה טוש"ע א"ח סי' שכח סעיף מ וסעי' מג:

פה ה מיי' שם הל' כג טוש"ע שם סעי' מא:

פו ו ז מיי' פכ"א שם הלכה לא:

פז ח ט מיי' פי"ט שם הלכה יד סמג שם טוש"ע א"ח סימן שג סעיף כד:

רבינו חננאל

הכתיתין ומוגלא הזבה מרגלו זבין מתקבצין באותה החקיקה ולא יהו מצערין אותו בארכובותיו אמר אביי טמא טומאת מת מפני שיש בו בית קבול והוי כלי. רבא אמר אף טמא מדרס כמו עגלה של קטן יוצאין בהן בשבת כי אינם (משא וכלים הם) [משתמטים] תני תנא קמיה דרבי יוחנן נכנסין בהן לעזרה כלומר אינם סנדל כי אסור אדם ליכנס בסנדל בעזרה כדתנן (ברכות נד.) לא יכנס אדם להר הבית במקל ובמנעלו כו' א"ל אני שונה אשה חולצת בסנדל של עץ ואתה שונה נכנסין תני אין נכנסין: **לוקטמין** חמרא דאכפי. גידם מי שידיו קצוצות עושין לו יד של עץ ונקרא חמרא דאכפי: **פרמי.** פי' פרמו יש מי שאומרים חתיכה של בגד שקושרין לזקנים א) ששפתותיהן מתרפטות: **קשרים** קשרי פואה משום רפואה. בן שיש לו געגועין על אביו יש מי שאומרים כי כשיגדל עצב הבן במיתת אביו נוטל רצועה ממנעל אביו הימין וקושרה בשמאל הבן ואומרים שמשקיט לבו ואם יחליף אומרים שהוא סכנה וסימניך תפילין והן שעל היד השמאל: **סחופי** כסא אטיבורא. פי' אם בולט טיבורו של אדם בחוץ ממעיו או אם ניקב מניחין שם [כוס] קטן על טיבורו כדי שלא יבלוט ויתבקע ומניחין אותו עד שיתרפא הא דשרו לבסימא לסוך מלח ושמן לכרעייהו פשוטה היא פי' לחנק פי' לפופי ינוקא. אבן תקומה פי' אומרים כי יש אבן ידועה כשהיא תלויה על אשה הרה אינה מפלת וגם המשקל שכנגד אותו האבן מועלת ומותר לצאת בהן בשבת אבל

חשק שלמה על רבינו חננאל

א) עי' בגליון בשם הערוך וכ"ה בא"ז בשם רבינו:

גליון הש"ס

תוס' ד"ה קישורי וכו' **אינו טמא מדרס.** עיין מנחות דף לא ע"א תוספות ד"ה שידה:

מסורת הש"ס

א) [תרגום של ובמישור ובתרלותא ועי' בערוך ערך תרן], ב) בד' פפד"מ רפרם וכ"ה בר"ף, ג) [פרמאי פי' חתיכה של בגד שקושרין לזקנים על פיהם למען רירם מפני ששפתותיהן מתרפטות ערוך ערך אנקטמין וע"ע בערוך ערך פרמא], ד) [קידושין לא: וש"נ], ה) [ברכות נו.], ו) [פי' שמחברין איבריו כמו ויחבר תרגומו ולפוף ערוך], ז) [לקמן קמז: ע"ש], ח) [צ"ל אבין], ט) בלשון ארמית אומר לכל דבר גדול גמלא. הרמב"ם בפי' המשנה כלאים פ"ג מ"ב, י) [ערך אנקטמין], כ) [וע"ע תוספות מנחות לא. תד"ה שידה].

הגהות הב"ח

(א) גמ' כסא וסמוכות שלו טמאין מדרס: (ב) שם בן שיש לו געגועין: (ג) רש"י ד"ה ליחנק וכו' צוארו. נ"ב ס"א או נפלה לו ערלת הגרון ונופל בגרונו וכו':

רב נסים גאון

ובמנעלו: **רב** פפא מתני בנים תרווייהו. כלומר שהיה שונה הראשונה בן שיש לו געגועין על אביו וזו האחרת לפופי משום אבון בר הונא אמר רב חמא בר גוריא והיה רב זביד שוה עמו בשמועה ראשונה בן שיש לו געגועין על אביו וחלוק עליו בשמועה שניה לפופי ינוקא והיה רב זביד אומרה משם רבה בר בר חנה אמר רבי יוחנן ולפי שהיתה השמועה הראשונה בן שיש לו געגועין על אביו והשניה לפופי ינוקא ואמר על שניהם מתני בנים זה הוא פירושם והוזקקתי לכותבו הנה מפני שראיתיו קשה לתלמידים וביארתיו כדי שיתגלה לכל:

סליק פרק במה אשה

ליקוטי רש"י

סחופי כסא. כפיית הכלי [יבמות מז.]. **לפופי.** אנמליו"ן בלע"ז ולאו היינו אסובי ינוקא דאמרן לעיל בפרק כל הכלים (קכג.) דהא שמעינן ליה לרב נחמן דאסר אלא לפופי בעלמא כמו שעושין בחגורות ופסקיאות [לקמן קכט:]. **לפופי.** אונמלוטי"א כמו שעושין לקטן שיתיישבו אבריו ולא יתעקס [שם קמז:]. **מלחתא.** משרפות מים דמתרגמינן חרילי ימא (יהושע א) שממשיך לתוכו מים מן הים והחמה שורפתן והן נעשין מלח ואותו חריץ קרי מילחתא [לקמן עג:]. על שפת הים חרילין עשוין שמי הים נכנסים בהן והחומה מייבשתן ועושין מלח והן משרפות מים האמורין במקרא (יהושע יא) ומתרגמינן חרילי ימא [כתובות עט:]. **נירא ברקא.** ניצ"א של שיער בהמה [ע"ז כח:]. **גובתא.** קנה חלול [ברכות ו.].

for since it prevents miscarriage, it is not viewed as a burden on the Sabbath. מִשּׁוּם רַבִּי מֵאִיר אָמְרוּ – But THEY SAID IN THE NAME OF R' MEIR: אַף בְּמִשְׁקַל אֶבֶן תְּקוּמָה – A woman may EVEN go out WITH THE COUNTERWEIGHT OF A PRESERVING STONE, i.e. an object that was weighed against such a stone, for R' Meir holds that such a counterweight is also effective in preventing miscarriage. וְלֹא שֶׁהִפִּילָה – AND this stone is permissible NOT only IF SHE MISCARRIED previously, אֶלָּא שֶׁמָּא תַּפִּיל – BUT even on the mere suspicion that SHE MAY MISCARRY. וְלֹא שֶׁעִיבְּרָה – AND the stone is permissible NOT only IF SHE knows that she HAS already BECOME PREGNANT, אֶלָּא שֶׁמָּא תִּתְעַבֵּר וְתַפִּיל – BUT even on the mere suspicion that SHE MAY BECOME PREGNANT AND MISCARRY the fetus.[25]

The Gemara attaches a condition to the ruling permitting the counterweight of a preserving stone:

אָמַר רַב יֵימַר בַּר שְׁלַמְיָא מִשְּׁמֵיהּ דְּאַבָּיֵי – Rav Yeimar bar Shelamya said in the name of Abaye: וְהוּא דְּאִיכַּוַּון וְאִיתְקַל – **But this is** only true (i.e. that the counterweight to a preserving stone is permitted) **if [the item used as a counterweight] was** exactly **equivalent** in weight to the stone **when it was weighed** against it. However, if it was necessary to add or remove from the item in order to match the weight of the stone, it is not effective, and therefore may not be worn outside on the Sabbath.

The Gemara presents an inquiry concerning this law:

בָּעֵי אַבָּיֵי – **Abaye inquired:** מִשְׁקַל דְּמִשְׁקַל מַאי – **What of the counterweight of the counterweight** of a preserving stone?[26] Is it also effective in preventing miscarriage?

The Gemara replies:

תֵּיקוּ – **Let the question stand;** it remains unanswered.

The Gemara returns to the lore taught to Abaye by his nursemaid, and presents several therapeutic talismans and incantations in her name:

וְאָמַר אַבָּיֵי – **And Abaye said:** אָמְרָה לִי אֵם – **Mother said to me:** לְאִשְׁתָּא בַּת יוֹמָא – **For a fever** that strikes **daily,** לִישְׁקוֹל זוּזָא חִיוָּורָא – **one must take a white** ***zuz*****,**[27] וְלֵיזִיל לְמַלְחָתָא – **and go** with it **to a salt evaporator,**[28] וְלִיתְקוֹל מַתְקַלֵיהּ מִילְחָא – **and weigh** against it **its weight in salt.** וּלְצַיְירֵיהּ בַּחֲלָלָא דְּבֵי צַוָּאר בְּנִירָא בַּרְקָא – **He** then **must tie** the salt **by the neck opening** of his shirt **with a strand of hair.** This will cure him of his fever.

וְאִי לָא – **And if** these items are **not** available, לֵיתוּב אַפָּרָשַׁת דְּרָכִים – **וְכִי חָזֵי שׁוּמְשְׁמָנָא** – then **he must sit at a crossroads,** גַּמְלָא דְּדָרֵי מִידֵי – **and when he sees a large ant carrying something,** לִישְׁקְלֵיהּ וְלִישַׁדְיֵיהּ בְּגוּבְתָא דְּנְחָשָׁא – **he must take [the ant] and place it into a copper tube.** וְלִיסְתְּמֵיהּ בַּאֲבָרָא – **He must** then **close [the tube] with lead,** וְלִיחְתְּמֵי[ה] בְּשִׁיתִּין גּוּשְׁפַּנְקֵי – **and seal it with sixty** different types of **seals.**[29] וְלִבַרְזוּלֵיהּ – **He must shake [the tube],** וְלִידְרֵיהּ – **and carry it,** וְלֵימָא לֵיהּ – **and** then **say to [the ant],** טְעוּנָךְ עֲלַי וּטְעוּנַאי עֲלָךְ – **"Your burden upon me, and my burden upon you!"** He thus rids himself of the burden of his daily illness.

The Gemara objects to the phrasing of the incantation:

אָמַר לֵיהּ רַב אַחָא בְּרֵיהּ דְּרַב הוּנָא לְרַב אַשִׁי – Rav Acha the son of Rav Huna said to Rav Ashi: וְדִילְמָא אִינִישׁ אַשְׁכְּחֵיהּ וְאִיפְּסַק בֵּיהּ – **But perhaps** another **person** had previously **found [this very ant] and stopped** his illness **by it,** i.e. had assigned his own illness to it; when the present sufferer now takes the ant's load upon himself, he inadvertently accepts yet another illness upon himself! This cannot be the proper manner in which to recite this incantation!

The Gemara retracts:

אֶלָּא לֵימָא לֵיהּ – **Rather, he must say to [the ant]:** טְעוּנַאי וּטְעוּנָךְ עֲלָךְ – **"My burden and your burden upon you!"** He thus rids himself of his illness, while leaving those already upon the insect where they are.

וְאִי לָא – **And if** these items are **not** available to the sufferer, לִישְׁקוֹל כּוּזָא חַדְתָּא – **he must take a small new earthenware vessel,**[30] וְלֵיזִיל לְנַהֲרָא – **and go to the river,** וְלֵימָא לֵיהּ – **and say to it:** נַהֲרָא נַהֲרָא – **"River, river!** אוֹזְפַן כּוּזָא דְמַיָּא לְאוֹרְחָא דְּאִיקְלַע לִי – **Lend me a vessel full of water to** heal **the routine** (i.e. the daily illness) **that has come upon me."** וְלִיהַדַר שַׁב זִימְנֵי עַל רֵישֵׁיהּ – **He must circle [the vessel full of water] seven times around his head,** וּלְשַׁדְיֵין לַאֲחוֹרֵיהּ – **and** then **toss [the water] behind him** into the river, וְלֵימָא לֵיהּ – **and say to [the river]:** נַהֲרָא נַהֲרָא – **"River, river!** שְׁקוֹל מַיָּא דִּיהַבְתְּ לִי – **Take** back **the water that you gave to me,** דְּאוֹרְחָא דְּאִיקְלַע לִי – **for the routine that has come upon me** – בְּיוֹמֵיהּ אָתָא וּבְיוֹמֵיהּ אָזַל – **it came upon me in its day, and it has** now **left me in its day."** He thus sloughs off his illness into the river.

The Gemara presents another talismanic remedy:

אָמַר רַב הוּנָא – **Rav Huna said:**

NOTES

25. Such as in the case of a woman genetically predisposed to this affliction (e.g. a woman from a family whose females are subject to this misfortune), who therefore fears that it may occur with her pregnancy (*Meiri*; *Chidushei HaRan*; see *Hagahos R' Elazar Moshe HaLevi Horowitz* to *Rashi*).

26. [I.e. an object that was weighed against a preserving stone's counterweight.]

27. I.e. a newly minted [silver] coin (*Rashi*). [A *zuz* is a coin of a particular denomination.]

28. This was a wide pool connected to the sea by way of a trench. The pool would be filled with salt water, after which the trench would be closed. The sun would then evaporate the water, leaving behind deposits of salt (*Rashi*).

29. For example, he must cover the lead seal with one of wax, and that one with one of pitch, and that one with one of clay, and so on. The number sixty is not meant precisely, nor must these seals be stamped with a signet. He simply must use many materials to close the straw, one on top of another (*Rashi*; the Talmud often uses the number sixty to denote a large number – see *Tosafos, Bava Metzia* 107b ד״ה שיתין).

30. *Rashi*; however, *Rashba* (*Responsa* ibid.) states that the vessel must be made of copper.

לְאֶשָּׁתָּא תִּילְתָּא – **For a fever** that strikes every **three** days[1] לַיְיתֵי שִׁבְעָה סִילְוֵי מִשִּׁבְעָה דִּיקְלֵי – **one must bring** together **seven small branches from seven date palms,** וְשִׁבְעָה צִיבֵי מִשִּׁבְעָה כְּשׁוּרֵי – **and seven splinters from seven** wooden **beams,** וְשִׁבְעָה סִיכֵּי מִשִּׁבְעָה גְּשׁוּרֵי – **and seven pegs from seven bridges,** וְשִׁבְעָה קְטִימֵי מִשִּׁבְעָה תַּנּוּרֵי – **and seven** specimens of **ash from seven ovens,** וְשִׁבְעָה עַפְרֵי מִשִּׁבְעָה סְנָרֵי – **and seven** specimens **of dirt from seven door sockets,**[2] וְשִׁבְעָה כּוּפְרֵי מִשִּׁבְעָה אַרְבֵי – **and seven** specimens **of pitch from seven ships,**[3] וְשִׁבְעָה בּוּנֵי כַּמּוֹנֵי – **and seven kernels of cumin,**[4] וְשִׁבְעָה בִּינֵי מִדִּיקְנָא דְּכַלְבָּא סָבָא – **and seven hairs from the beard of an aged dog,** וְלִצְיְירִינְהוּ בְּחַלְלָא דְּבֵי צַוָּארָא בְּנִירָא בַּרְקָא – **and he must tie these items by the neck opening** of his shirt **with a strand of hair.** This will cure him of his recurring illness.

The Gemara presents another talismanic remedy, this time combined with recitation of Scriptural verses:

אָמַר רַבִּי יוֹחָנָן – **R' Yochanan said:** לְאֶשָּׁתָּא צְמִירְתָּא – **For a burning fever**[5] לִישְׁקַל סַכִּינָא דְּכוּלָּא פַּרְזְלָא – **one must take a knife that is** made **completely of iron,** וְלֵיזִיל לְהֵיכָא דְּאִיכָּא וּורְדִּינָא – **and go to a place where there is a thornbush,**[6] וְלִיקְטַר בֵּיהּ נִירָא בַּרְקָא – **and knot upon it a strand of hair.** He must return there for three days. יוֹמָא קַמָּא לִיחְרוֹק בֵּיהּ פּוּרְתָּא וְלֵימָא – **The first day, he must notch [the bush] slightly, and recite** the following verse, which speaks of the thornbush's insusceptibility to fire: ,,וַיֵּרָא מַלְאַךְ ה׳ אֵלָיו וגו׳ ״ – ***And an angel of Hashem appeared to him*** *(Moses) in a flame of fire from within the thornbush. And he saw and behold! the thornbush was burning in the fire, but the thornbush was not consumed.*[7] לְמָחָר לִיחְרוֹק בֵּיהּ פּוּרְתָּא וְלֵימָא – **The next day he must notch [the bush] a bit** more **and recite:** ,,וַיֹּאמֶר מֹשֶׁה אָסֻרָה־נָּא וְאֶרְאֶה״ – ***And Moses said, Let me turn aside now and see*** *the great sight – why will the thornbush not be burned,*[8] which speaks as well of the bush's insusceptibility to fire. לְמָחָר לִיחְרוֹק בֵּיהּ פּוּרְתָּא וְלֵימָא – **The next day, he must notch [the bush] a bit** more, **and recite:** ,,וַיַּרְא ה׳ כִּי סָר לִרְאוֹת וגו׳ ״ – ***And Hashem saw that he turned aside to see.***[9] The phrase "turned aside" expresses the sufferer's wish that the burning fever be turned away from him as well.

The Gemara objects to the choice of verses:

אָמַר לֵיהּ רַב אַחָא בְּרֵיהּ דְּרָבָא לְרַב אַשִׁי – **Rav Acha the son of Rava said to Rav Ashi:** וְלֵימָא ,,וַיֹּאמֶר אַל־תִּקְרַב הֲלֹם וגו׳ ״ – **But let him** also **recite** the verse, ***And He said, "Do not come closer to here,"***[10] and thereby express his wish that the sickness approach him no longer!

The Gemara therefore retracts:

אֶלָּא לְיוֹמָא קַמָּא לֵימָא – **Rather,** then, **on the first day he must** first **recite:** ,,וַיֵּרָא מַלְאַךְ ה׳ אֵלָיו וגו׳ ״ – ***And an angel of Hashem appeared to him*** **etc.,** and then continue with: ,,וַיֹּאמֶר מֹשֶׁה וגו׳ ״ – ***And Moses said*** **etc.** וּלְמָחָר לֵימָא – **And on the next day, he must recite:** ,,וַיַּרְא ה׳ כִּי סָר לִרְאוֹת״ – ***And Hashem saw that he turned aside to see.*** וּלְמָחָר – **And on the next day** he indeed concludes with: ,,וַיֹּאמֶר (ה׳) אַל־תִּקְרַב הֲלֹם״ – ***And He said, "Do not come closer to here."***

The Gemara continues with the remedy:

וְכִי פָּסֵק לֵיהּ – **And when [the burning fever] has stopped** afflicting him, לִיתַתֵּיהּ וְלִפְסְקֵיהּ וְלֵימָא הָכִי – **he must bend low and** completely **sever** the bush close to the ground, **and say thus:** הַסְּנֶה הַסְּנֶה – **"The thornbush, the thornbush!** לָאו מִשּׁוּם דִּגְבִיהַת מִכָּל אִילָנֵי אַשְׁרֵי הַקָּדוֹשׁ בָּרוּךְ הוּא שְׁכִינְתֵּיהּ עֲלָךְ – **It is not because you are loftier than all** other **trees that the Holy One, Blessed is He, rested His Divine Presence upon you.**[11] אֶלָּא מִשּׁוּם דְּמָיְיכַת מִכָּל אִילָנֵי אַשְׁרֵי קוּדְשָׁא בְּרִיךְ הוּא שְׁכִינְתֵּיהּ עֲלָךְ – **Rather,** it **is because you are humbler than all** other **trees that the Holy One, Blessed is He, rested His Divine Presence upon you."** וְכִי הֵיכִי דַּחֲמִיתֵיהּ אֶשָּׁתָּא לַחֲנַנְיָה מִישָׁאֵל וַעֲזַרְיָה וַעֲרִיקַת מִן קֳדָמוֹהִי – He then continues: **"And just as the fire** into which they were thrown **beheld Chananyah, Mishael, and Azaryah,**[12] **and** then **fled from before them,** כֵּן תֶּחֱמִינֵיהּ אֶשָּׁתָּא לִפְלוֹנִי בַּר פְּלוֹנִית וְתִיעֲרוֹק מִן קֳדָמוֹהִי – **so too shall the fire** of burning fever **behold so-and-so the son of [the woman] so-and-so** (i.e. himself), **and** then **flee from before him."** Through these actions and recitations, one is cured of the illness of burning fever.[13]

The Gemara now presents several therapeutic incantations:

לְסִימְטָא לֵימָא הָכִי – **For boils one must** mention the angels that heal this illness, and **say thus:** בַּז בַּזְיָה מַס מַסְיָא כַּס כַּסְיָה שַׁרְלַאי וְאַמַּרְלַאי – **"Baz Bazyah, Mas Masya, Kas Kasyah,**[14] **Sharlai,**

NOTES

1. *Rashi* identifies this illness as *shachefes,* which he describes in *Leviticus* 26:16 as a consumptive, debilitating disease in which one's flesh first becomes swollen and then begins to waste away.

2. This is the socket in the door's threshold in which the pin that the door is hinged upon turns (*Rashi*).

3. Pitch is used to seal the hulls of ships (*Rashi*).

4. Alternatively: seven fistfuls of cumin (*Rashi*).

5. This is *kadachas,* an illness that causes one's entire body to become fevered and inflamed (*Rashi*; see *Rashi, Avodah Zarah* 28a ד״ה אישתא צמירתא with *Targum HaLaaz* §978).

6. This is the thornbush called סְנֶה in Scripture (*Rashi*; see below).

7. *Exodus* 3:2. [The verse speaks of the incident in which Hashem commanded Moses to go to Egypt and command Pharaoh to free the Jews. Moses was tending his sheep, when, arriving at Mount Sinai, he noticed a thornbush that was burning, but was not consumed by fire. The verse expresses the sufferer's wish to be free of his fiery illness.]

8. Ibid. v. 3. The significance of this verse is in its second part – *why will the thornbush not be burned* (*Rashi*).

9. Ibid. v. 4.

10. Ibid. v. 5.

11. [In the form of the Heavenly fire that took hold of the bush in Moses's time.]

12. This refers to the incident, recounted in *Daniel* ch. 3, in which Nebuchadnezzar, king of Babylon, erected an idol, and ordered all his subjects to bow before it. Three Jews – Chananyah, Mishael, and Azaryah – refused, and were thrown into a fiery furnace in punishment. They were miraculously saved from immolation, and walked unharmed among the flames.

13. Many commentators ask an obvious question regarding this Gemara. The Gemara in *Shevuos* 15b states that one is forbidden to heal oneself by reciting Scripture; how then can our Gemara recommend a remedy that makes use of Scriptural verses? *Tosafos* (*Shevuos* ibid., and *Pesachim* 111a) and *Rif* (to *Sanhedrin* 101a) answer that the illness of burning fever is different, since it is life-threatening. *Meiri* suggests that healing with Scripture is forbidden only if it is the primary remedy; here, though, it is only part of a larger remedy, and is therefore permitted. *Maharsha* says that one is only forbidden to use Torah to heal one's *physical* ailments. If, however, one recognizes that what lies at the root of every physical ailment is a *spiritual* shortcoming, one may employ Torah to remedy one's spiritual lack (see ibid. for an explanation of the verses cited here). Once one is healed in a spiritual sense, his physical symptoms will disappear of their own accord. This is why, as part of this remedy, one mentions that the Divine Presence rests only upon one who is humble. For the remedy is based upon one's recognition that if he is to be healed, he must humble himself before God.

14. These angels are named according to their function: *Baz Bazyah* – he who tears [the illness]; *Mas Masya* – he who heals [the illness]; *Kas Kasyah* – he who grinds down [the illness] (*Rashi*).

לאשתא תילתא לייתי שבעה סילוי משבעה דיקלי ושבעה ציבי משבעה כשורי ושבעה סיכי משבעה גשורי ושבעה קטימי משבעה תנורי ושבעה עפרי משבעה סנרי ושבעה כופרי משבעה ארבי ושבעה בוני כמוני ושבעה ביני מדיקנא דכלבא סבא ולציירינהו בחללא דבי צוארא בנירא ברקא א"ר יוחנן לאשתא צמירתא לישקל סכינא דכולא פרזלא וליזל להיכא דאיכא וורדינא וליקטר ביה נירא ברקא יומא קמא ליחרוק ביה פורתא ולימא וירא מלאך ה' אליו וגו' למחר ליחרוק ביה פורתא ולימא ויאמר משה אסורה נא ואראה למחר ליחרוק ביה פורתא ולימא וירא ה' כי סר לראות וגו' א"ל רב אחא בריה דרבא לרב אשי ולימא ויאמר אל תקרב הלום וגו' אלא ליומא קמא לימא וירא מלאך ה' אליו וגו' ויאמר משה וגו' ולמחר לימא וירא ה' כי סר לראות ולמחר ויאמר (ה') אל תקרב הלום וכי פסק ליה ליתתיה ולפסקי ולימא הכי הסנה הסנה לאו משום דגביהת מכל אילני אשרי הקב"ה שכינתיה עלך אלא משום דמייכת מכל אילני אשרי קודשא בריך הוא שכינתיה עלך וכי היכי דחמיתיה אשתא לחנניה מישאל ועזריה ועריקת מן קדמוהי כן תחמיניה אשתא לפלוני בר פלונית ותיערוק מן קדמוהי לסימטא לימא הכי בז בזייה מס מסייא כס כסייה שרלאי ואמרלאי אלין מלאכי דאישתלחו מארעא דסדום ולאסאה שחינא כאיבין בזך בזיך מסמסיך כמון כמיך עיניך ביך עינך ביך אתריך בך זרעיך כקלוט וכפרדה דלא פרה ולא רביא כך לא תפרה ולא תרבה בגופיה דפלוני בר פלונית לכיפה לימא הכי חרב שלופה וקלע נטושה לא שמיה יוכב חולין מכאובין לשידא לימא הכי הוית דפקיק דפקיק הוית ליטא תבור ומשומת בר טיט בר טמא בר טינא כשמגז מריגז ואיסטמאי לשידא דבית הכסא לימא הכי אקרקפי דארי ואאוסי דגורייתא אשכחתון לשידאי בר שיריקא פנדא במישרא דכרתי חבטיה בלועא דחמרא חטרתיה: ובני מלכים בזגין: מאן תנא א"ר אושעיא רבי שמעון היא דאמר כל ישראל בני מלכים הם רבא אמר באריג בכסותו ודברי הכל:

מתני' יוצאין בביצת החרגול ובשן שועל ובמסמר מן הצלוב משום רפואה דברי ר"מ וחכמים אוסרין אף בחול משום דרכי האמורי:

גמ' יוצאין בביצת החרגול דעבדי לשיחלא ובשן של שועל דעבדי לשינתא דחייא למאן דניים דמיתא למאן דלא ניים: ובמסמר מן הצלוב: דעבדי לזירפא: משום רפואה דברי רבי מאיר: אביי ורבא דאמרי תרוייהו כל דבר שיש בו משום רפואה אין בו משום דרכי האמורי הא אין בו משום רפואה יש בו משום דרכי האמורי והתניא אילן שמשיר פירותיו סוקרו (וצובע אותו) בסיקרא וטוענו באבנים בשלמא טוענו באבנים כי היכי דליכחוש חיליה אלא סוקרו בסיקרא מאי רפואה קעביד כי היכי דליחזייה אינשי וליבעו עליה רחמי כדתניא וטמא טמא יקרא צריך להודיע צערו לרבים ורבים יבקשו עליו רחמים אמר רבינא כמאן תלינן כובסי בדיקלא כי האי תנא תני תנא בפרק אמוראי קמיה דר' חייא בר אבין א"ל כולהו אית בהו משום דרכי האמורי לבר מהני מי שיש לו עצם בגרונו מביא מאותו המין ומניח ליה על קדקדו ולימא הכי חד חד נחית בלע בלע נחית חד חד אין בו משום דרכי האמורי לאדרא לימא הכי ננעצתא כמחט ננעלתא כתרים שייא שייא

האומר

רש"י

לאשתא תילתא. שחפת שלישית שבאה מג' ימים לג' ימים: סילוי. ענבים (א) קטנים: ושבעה ציבי. קסמים: כשורי. קורות: ושבעה סיכי. יתידות קייבל"ש בלע"ז: משבעה גשורי. גשרים: ז' סינרי. לנור הדלת חור האסקופה שציר הדלת סובב בו: כופרי. זפת שזופתין הספינות: ארבי. ספינות: ושבעה בוני (ב) כמוני. גרעיני כמון ל"א בוני כמון גרסי' מלא אגרוף: ושבעה ביני מדיקנא דכלבא סבא. שבעה נימי מזקן כלב זקן: אשתא צמירתא. חולי שמחממת וקודחת את הגוף: וורדינא. סנה: ליחרוק. איסקרני"ר כמו דמיבלע חירקייהו דאלו טריפות (חולין דף נט:): ויאמר משה. משום סיפיה מדוע לא יבער הסנה: כי סר. שיסור החולי: אל תקרב הלום. שלא יקרב זה החולי אליו: ליתתיה ולפסקיה. סמוך לקרקע. ליתתיה ישפיל: דמייכת. שאתה שפילה: דחמיתא אשתא. שראית האש: לסימטא. שאין קרו"ג בלע"ז: בזוזיה מסמסייה כסכסייה. שמות המלאכים על שם שקורעים וממסמסים ומכסכסים אותו. בז לשון בזעא: מארעא דסדום. כך הוא הלחש ולא מסדום באו: בזך בזיך. אין לו משמעות אלא כך הוא הלחש: עיניך ביך. מראיך בך שלא תאדים יותר: אתריך ביך. שלא תרחיב: כקלוט. שנקלט זרעו בשריי בטנו שלא יוליד: לכיפה. אונפול"ש אבעבועות כך לשון רבי יצחק ברבי מנחם נ"ע ולשון רבותי לכיפה למי שכופהו שד: לימא הכי. לחש בעלמא הוא: הוית דפקיק דפקיק הוית. לחש הוא: ליט תבר ומשומת. מקולל ונשבר ומשומת יהא שד זה ששמו בר טיט בר טינא: לשידא דבית הכסא. אם הזיק לימא לחש זה: אקרקפי דארי. בראש הארי זכר: ואאוסי דגורייתא. ובחוטם לביאה נקבה: אשכחתא לשידאי בר שריקאי פנדאי. כך שמו: במישרא דכרתי חבטיה. בערוגת כרשין הפלתיו: בלועא דחמרא חטרתיה. בלחי החמור הלקיתיו: מאן תנא. דקתני וכל אדם ואפילו עני שבישראל: רבי שמעון. בפרק שמונה שרצים: בני מלכים. הלכך לעני נמי חזיא ולא גנותא דידיה דליתחזיא כיוהרא ושליף אי נמי דמגו דחידוש הוא שליף ומחוי: באריג בכסותו. דלא שליף ליה ומחוי: מתני' דרכי האמורי. ניחוש הוא וכתיב ובחוקותיהם לא תלכו (ויקרא יח): גמ' לשיחלא. לכאב האוזן ותולין באזנו: לשינתא. יש שעשאו כדי שיישן ויש כדי שלא יישן: דחייא. של שן שועל חי: לזירפא. נפח מכה דכל פרזלא זריף ואתי מסי לזירפא: שיש בו משום רפואה. שנראית רפואתו כגון שתיית כוס ותחבושת מכה ופרכינן הא אין בו כו' כגון לחש שאין ניכר שיהא מרפא יש בו משום דרכי האמורי בתמיה: דליכחוש חיליה. שעל ידי שהוא שמן וכחו רב פירותיו נושרין: דליחזייה אינשי. ולסימנא עבדי ליה לאודעי דמשיר פירותיו: טמא טמא. הוא עצמו אומר טמא רחקו מעלי: כובסי. אשכול תמרים וסימן הוא שמשיר פירותיו: בפרק אמוראי. בפרק אחד (מ) ששנוי בתוספתא דמסכת שבת בהלכות דרכי האמורי: א"ל. רבי חייא לתנא: כולהו אית בהו. כל השנויות שם אל תטעה לומר באחד מהן אין בו משום דרכי האמורי אלא בכולן אתה שונה יש בו לבר מהני ב' אלו שאפרש לך: מי שיש לו עצם וכו' ולחש דנעלתה כמחט אלו ב' לבדם אין בהם: חד חד נחית. לחש הוא: לאדרא. עצם של דג שישב לאדם בושט: שייא שייא. לחש הוא רד רד:

האומר

תוספות

בני מלכים יוצאין בזגין מאן תנא ר"ש היא כו'. פי' הקונטרס וליכא למיחש דילמא מחייכי בהו ואתו לאתויי וא"ת מכל מקום ליחוש דילמא איפסיק ואתי לאתויי כדאמרינן לעיל גבי עבד דלא יצא בחותם שבצוארו וי"ל דהכא מיירי בתלוים בשלשלת דלא מיפסקי וריב"א פירש דבירושלמי מוקי לה בקטנים דאפילו אי פסיק ומייתי לה ליכא איסור והכי איתא בירושלמי ר' זעירא אומר בזוג שבצוארו ומהו כל אדם דקתני במתניתין בין קטנים עשירים בין קטנים עניים מתניתין פליגא עליה דרבי זעירא ולא בזוג שבצוארו כאן בגדולים כאן בקטנים פירוש ההוא דלא יצא בזוג שבצוארו בגדולים דלמא מיפסיק ואתי לאתויי והא דשרי הכא בקטנים דליכא למיחש כדפי' מ"מ יש לדקדק אמאי נקט בני מלכים כיון דליכא חששא אי מייתי להו קטן בידים וי"ל דאי לאו בני מלכים הוו מחייכו עליה בני מלכים כל שעה ואי אפשר שלא ישמע אביו מעולם ויטלם אביו בידו ואתו לאתויי אבל אי בני מלכים לא מחייכי אם כן אפילו אי מיפסיק ליכא למיחש דילמא מייתי להו אבוה דלא שכיח שיהא אביו בגלדו בשעה שיפסוק:

הדרן עלך במה אשה

עין משפט נר מצוה

פח א מיי' פי"ט מהל' שבת הלכה יח סמג לאוין סה טוש"ע א"ח סימן שא סעיף כג:

פט ב ג מיי' שם הלכה יג טוש"ע שם סעיף כז:

צ ד מיי' פי"י מהלכות טומאת צרעת הלכה ח וסמג עשין רלה:

רבינו חננאל

אבל משקל דמשקל עלתה בתיקו. וכל [תיקו] דאיסורא [לחומרא] ואין יוצאין בה בשבת בני מלכים בזוגים אוקמה (רב) [רבא] בזוג ארוג בכסות ולדברי הכל כי האי גונא שרי פר' שיח לא פצע האוזן פי' זירפא [ענביתא] (עכיבתא) אביי ורבא דאמרי תרווייהו כל שהוא משום רפואה אין בו משום דרכי האמורי: ירושלמי רבי אבהו בשם רבי יוחנן כל שמרפא אין בו משום דרכי האמורי

ליקוטי רש"י

אשתא צמירתא. חולי שקורין מלוי"י למירתא חם כמו דלמרה למורי בבבא קמא (ס.) [פסחים כה:]. חולי חמה בלע"ז מלווי"ד לשון שריפה וחמימות ודוגמתו בהכונס לאן לדיר (ב"ק ס.) דלמרא למורי. סימטא. קלו"ג בלע"ז נפח העומד באדם [ע"ז כח.]. משום דרכי האמורי. ניחוש וכתיב (שמות כג) ולא תעשה כמעשיהם [חולין עז.]. שיש בו משום רפואה. כגון משקה או סם או לחש שלוחש על המכה. אין בו משום רפואה. כגון שעושין שלא על החולי כגון קורעת שליא בפרשת דרכים וכיוצא בהם שדומין לניחוש [שם:]. דליכחוש חיליה. שמרוב שומנו הוא משירן. דליחזייה אינשי. סימן הוא שמשיר פירותיו. וטמא טמא יקרא. צועק ואומר טמא הוא [שם עח.]. כובסי. על שם שתלויים כדאמרינן כמאן תלינן כובסי בדקלא תלאי של תמרים [ב"מ קא:]. כל דבר התלוי במחובר קרי ליה כובסא כדאמר אזול גרמא וממיה לכובסא ואתר תמרי באלו הן הגולין (מכות ח.) [שבועות מא.]. הוא אשכול התמרים המקובלים יחד [מכות ח.]. כי האי תנא. לבקש עליו רבים רחמים [חולין שם].

מסורת הש"ס

א) [בערוך גרס שיבי פי' חתיכה קטנה], ב) [גירס' הערוך סוכרי פי' קברים ע"ש בערך סכר א'], ג) [עי' תוספות שבועות טו: ד"ה אסור], ד) [גיר' הערוך לביבא בערך כב ג], ה) לקמן קיא: קכח. [ב"מ קיג:], ו) [גירס' הירושל' דברי רבי יוסי ר' מאיר אוסר אף בחול], ז) חולין עז:, ח) [מלת הא ליתא בחולין ומשמע שם דהכל מדברי אביי ורבא ועי' בפירש"י דהכא ד"ה שיש וכו' ופרכינן הא אין בו וכו'], ט) מו"ק ה. [סוטה לב: חולין עח. נדה סו.], י) עי' בערוך ערך אמורי, כ) [גירסת הערוך לאדרא], ל) [גירסת הערוך שה שה פי' המם המם], מ) פ"ז ופ"ח.

הגהות הב"ח

(א) רש"י ד"ה סילוי ענפים קטנים: (ב) ד"ה ושבעה מיני כמונא גרעיני:

גליון הש"ס

גמרא ולימא וירא מלאך. עיין שבועות דף טו ע"ב תוס' ד"ה אסור. ופסחים דף קיא ע"א תוס' ד"ה נפתח: שם אביי ורבא דאמרי תרווייהו כל דבר שיש בו משום רפואה. עיין בב"מ דף כז ע"ב תוס' ד"ה ליס וארנקי: שם כולהו אית בהו משום דרכי האמורי. עיין תשובת רשב"א סימן תי"ג בארוכה:

תורה אור השלם

א) וַיֵּרָא מַלְאַךְ יְיָ אֵלָיו בְּלַבַּת אֵשׁ מִתּוֹךְ הַסְּנֶה וַיַּרְא וְהִנֵּה הַסְּנֶה בֹּעֵר בָּאֵשׁ וְהַסְּנֶה אֵינֶנּוּ אֻכָּל: [שמות ג, ב]

ב) וַיֹּאמֶר מֹשֶׁה אָסֻרָה נָּא וְאֶרְאֶה אֶת הַמַּרְאֶה הַגָּדֹל הַזֶּה מַדּוּעַ לֹא יִבְעַר הַסְּנֶה: [שמות ג, ג]

ג) וַיַּרְא יְיָ כִּי סָר לִרְאוֹת וַיִּקְרָא אֵלָיו אֱלֹהִים מִתּוֹךְ הַסְּנֶה וַיֹּאמֶר מֹשֶׁה מֹשֶׁה וַיֹּאמֶר הִנֵּנִי: [שמות ג, ד]

ד) וַיֹּאמֶר אַל תִּקְרַב הֲלֹם שַׁל נְעָלֶיךָ מֵעַל רַגְלֶיךָ כִּי הַמָּקוֹם אֲשֶׁר אַתָּה עוֹמֵד עָלָיו אַדְמַת קֹדֶשׁ הוּא: [שמות ג, ה]

ה) וְהַצָּרוּעַ אֲשֶׁר בּוֹ הַנֶּגַע בְּגָדָיו יִהְיוּ פְרֻמִים וְרֹאשׁוֹ יִהְיֶה פָרוּעַ וְעַל שָׂפָם יַעְטֶה וְטָמֵא טָמֵא יִקְרָא: [ויקרא יג, מה]

and Amarlai" אֵלִין מַלְאֲכֵי דְאִישְׁתַּלַּחוּ מֵאַרְעָא דִסְדוֹם וּלְאַסָּאָה שְׁחִינָא כְּאִיבִין – **"These are the angels sent forth from the land of Sodom**[15] **to heal painful boils."** בַּזָךְ בָּזִיךְ בַּזְבָּזִיךְ מַסְמָסִיךְ כַּמּוֹן כַּמִּיךְ – **"Bazach, Bazich, Bazbazich, Masmasich, Kamon, Kamich."**[16] עֵינֵיךְ בֵּיךְ עֵינֵיךְ בֵּיךְ – Now he addresses the boils: "May **your color** remain **as you are,** may **your color** remain **as you are,"** i.e. do not become any more red and inflamed. אַתְרֵיךְ בָּךְ – "May **your place** remain **where you are,"** i.e. do not spread any further. זַרְעֵיךְ כְּקָלוּט וּכְפִרְדָּה דְּלָא פָּרָה וְלָא רָבְיָא – "May **your seed be like** that of a ***kalut***[17] **and** like that of **a mule, who do not increase, and do not multiply** – כָּךְ לֹא תִּפְרֶה וְלֹא תִּרְבֶּה בְּגוּפֵיהּ דִּפְלוֹנִי בַּר פְּלוֹנִית – **so too may you** (the boils) **neither increase nor multiply upon the body of so-and-so the son of [the woman] so-and-so** (i.e himself)."

A second therapeutic incantation:

לְכִיבָּה לֵימָא הָכִי – **For blisters**[18] **one must say thus:** חֶרֶב שְׁלוּפָה וְקֶלַע נְטוּשָׁה – **"An unsheathed sword and a slingshot placed** in readiness." לָא שְׁמֵיהּ יוֹכָב חוּלִין מַכְאוֹבִין – **"Its name is not Yochav, painful illnesses!"** This incantation will heal the blisters.

A fourth incantation:

לְשִׁידָא לֵימָא הָכִי – To banish **a demon one must say thus:** הֲוֵית דְּפָקִיק דְּפָקִיק הֲוֵית – **"You were stopped up, stopped up you were."** לִיטָא תְבוּר וּמְשׁוּמֶּתֶת בַּר טִיט בַּר טָמֵא בַּר טִינָא כְּשַׁמְגַּז מְרִיגַז וְאִיסְטְמַאי – **"You shall be cursed, broken, and excommunicated,** you who are called, **Bar Tit, Bar Tamei, Bar Tina,**[19] **as** are **Shamgaz, Merigaz, and Istemai!"**

A fifth incantation:

לְשִׁידָא דְבֵית הַכִּסֵּא לֵימָא הָכִי – To banish **a demon of the privy** that is causing harm, **one must say thus:** אַקַּרְקַפֵּי דַאֲרִי – **"Upon the head of a lion,** וְאַאוּסֵי דְגוּרְיָיתָא – **and within the nostril of a lioness,** אַשְׁכַּחְתּוּן לְשִׁידָאי בַּר שִׁירִיקָא פַּנְדָּא – **shall be found the demon Bar Shirika Panda."**[20] בְּמִישְׁרָא דְכַרְתִּי חַבְטֵיהּ – **"Upon a field of leek I felled him,** בְּלוּעָא דַּחֲמָרָא חֲטַרְתֵּיהּ – **with the jawbone of a donkey I smote him."**

The Mishnah states:

וּבְנֵי מְלָכִים בְּזַגִּין – **AND PRINCES** [may go out on the Sabbath] **WITH BELLS.** [And this is actually true of any person etc.]

The Gemara is troubled by the statement that commoners are permitted to go out on the Sabbath wearing bells:

מַאן תַּנָּא – **Who is the Tanna** of our Mishnah who permits commoners to go out with bells? Since bells are worn exclusively by nobles, the sight of a commoner adorned with them is likely to elicit derisive comment on the part of bystanders, leading one who wears them to remove them and transport them on the Sabbath! Moreover, since bells are a novelty for a commoner, he will certainly remove them to show them to his friends! How then can the Mishnah permit a commoner to wear bells?

The Gemara explains:

אָמַר רַבִּי אוֹשַׁעְיָא – **R' Oshaya said:** רַבִּי שִׁמְעוֹן הִיא – **[The Tanna]** of our Mishnah **is R' Shimon,** דְּאָמַר כָּל יִשְׂרָאֵל בְּנֵי מְלָכִים הֵם – **who stated** in a Mishnah:[21] **ALL JEWS ARE** like **PRINCES;** since it is thus natural for them to don princely adornments, derisive comments will not faze them, nor will the novelty of the adornments unduly excite them. Therefore, since they will not remove the bells, they are permitted to wear them outside on the Sabbath.[22]

A dissenting opinion:

רָבָא אָמַר – **Rava said:** בְּאָרִיג בִּכְסוּתוֹ – The Mishnah is speaking **in** a case of bells **woven into one's garment,** וְדִבְרֵי הַכֹּל – **and** it accords with **the opinions of all** parties, i.e. both with the opinion of R' Shimon, and with that of his disputants, the Sages. For although the Sages hold that Jews are not considered princes, they agree that one may wear bells if they are woven into one's garment. For since they are securely fastened to the garment, one will not be led to remove them.[23]

NOTES

15. The angels do not actually come from Sodom; these simply happen to be the words of the incantation [which need not make conventional sense] (*Rashi*).

16. Words without conventional meaning that form the incantation (*Rashi*).

17. *Kalut* literally means: locked up, and refers to one who is sterile, whose seed is "locked" within his body (*Rashi*).

18. *Rashi* from *R' Yitzchak the son of R' Menachem*. Alternatively: for one who is possessed by a demon (*Rashi,* second explanation).

19. [Bar Tit means *son of mud*; Bar Tamei, *son of contamination*; Bar Tina, *son of clay.*]

20. This demon's name (*Rashi*).

21. Below, 111a. This Mishnah cites a dispute concerning the permissibility of smearing rose oil upon one's wound on the Sabbath. The Sages hold that a commoner may not smear rose oil upon a wound, for since it is an expensive item that one would not use if he were healthy, it is obvious that it is being used solely for healing purposes. R' Shimon, however, asserts that all Jews are like princes; therefore, they too may use rose oil.

22. *Rashi*; see *Dibros Moshe* 53:39 for elucidation of *Rashi*'s explanation of the Gemara.

Tosafos ask: The Gemara above (58a) stated that a slave may not go out with a bell hung about his neck or attached to his clothing for fear that the string holding it will break, and he will be led to carry it home, in violation of the Sabbath. Only if the bell is actually woven into the fabric of his clothing may he wear it outside. Yet in this Gemara we permit one to wear bells even if they are not woven into one's garment! *Tosafos* answer that that Gemara deals with a slave's bell, which, being an inexpensive object, is generally hung on a piece of string. Our Gemara, however, discusses precious golden bells, which are usually attached securely to a strong metal chain. Since such a chain will not break easily, one is permitted to wear bells that are hung upon it (see also *Tosafos* above, 58a ד״ה מאי שנא).

This explanation follows *Rashi*; however, *Riva* (cited by *Tosafos*) holds that no adult may go out with a bell that is not woven into a garment, lest it fall, and he inadvertently transport it. He therefore interprets our Mishnah as dealing only with minors; since they are in any case permitted to carry on the Sabbath, we allow them to wear the bells even though they may fall (see *Tosafos* for how *Riva* explains our Gemara).

23. If, however, the bells are not woven into one's clothing, one may not wear them, for fear that one will remove them to show them, or because of ridicule (*Rashi* as explained by *Dibros Moshe* ibid.). Princes, however, may wear bells even if they are not sewn to their garments, for they will not show them (see above, 59b), nor will any ridicule them (see *Shaar HaTziyun* 301:90; cf. *Rosh Yosef*).

The only bells that are permissible on the Sabbath are those without clappers; bells with clappers, however, are prohibited, because of the sound they emit (*Rama, Orach Chaim* 301:23; see *Magen Avraham* ad loc. §35). The Gemara above (58a-b) that permits a slave to go out with a bell that *is* equipped with a clapper is discussing a stuffed bell, which emits no sound (*Beur HaGra* ad loc.; cf. *Magen Avraham* ibid.; see *Beur Halachah* ad loc.).

[*Rashi,* who states here that one reason commoners should be forbidden to wear bells is because they will show them off, follows his stated opinion elsewhere that it is men as well as women who are wont to show their finery to their friends. *Rabbeinu Tam,* however, who disputes this, does not hold that this is a reason that commoners should be forbidden to wear bells; rather, the only reason is the fear that one will remove the bells because of ridicule (*Ramban* to 57a; see *Rosh* to 62a).

לאשתא תילתא לייתי שבעה סילוי משבעה דיקלי ושבעה [א] ציבי משבעה כשורי ושבעה סיכי משבעה גשורי ושבעה קטימי משבעה תנורי ושבעה עפרי משבעה [ב] סנרי ושבעה כופרי משבעה ארבי ושבעה בוני כמוני ושבעה ביני מדיקנא דכלבא סבא ולציירינהו בחללא דבי צוארא בנירא ברקא א"ר יוחנן לאשתא צמירתא לישקל סכינא דכולא פרזלא וליזל להיכא דאיכא וורדינא וליקטר ביה נירא ברקא יומא קמא ליחרוק ביה פורתא ולימא [א] וירא מלאך ה' אליו וגו' למחר ליחרוק ביה פורתא ולימא [ב] ויאמר משה אסורה נא ואראה למחר ליחרוק ביה פורתא [ג] ולימא [ג] וירא ה' כי סר לראות וגו' א"ל רב אחא בריה דרבא לרב אשי ולימא [ד] ויאמר אל תקרב הלום וגו' אלא ליומא קמא לימא וירא מלאך ה' אליו וגו' ויאמר משה וגו' ולמחר לימא וירא ה' כי סר לראות ולמחר ויאמר (ה') אל תקרב הלום וכי פסק ליה ליתתיה ולפסקי ולימא הכי הסנה הסנה לאו משום דגביהת מכל אילני אשרי הקב"ה שכינתיה עלך אלא משום דמייכת מכל אילני אשרי קודשא בריך הוא שכינתיה עלך וכי היכי דחמיתיה אשתא לחנניה מישאל ועזריה ועריקת מן קדמוהי כן תחמיניה אשתא לפלוני בר פלונית ותיערוק מן קדמוהי לסימטא לימא הכי בז בזייה מס מסייא כס כסייה שרלאי ואמרלאי אלין מלאכי דאישתלחו מארעא דסדום ולאסאה שחינא כאיבין בזך בזיך בזבזיך מסמסיך כמון כמיך עיניך ביך אתריך בך זרעיך כקלוט וכפרדה דלא פרה ולא רביא כך לא תפרה ולא תרבה בגופיה דפלוני בר פלונית [ד] לכיפה לימא הכי חרב שלופה וקלע נטושה לא שמיה יוכב חולין מכאובין לשידא לימא הכי הוית דפקיק דפקיק הוית ליטא תבור ומשומת בר טיט בר טמא בר טינא כשמגז מריגז ואיסטמאי לשידא דבית הכסא לימא הכי אקרקפי דארי ואאוסי דגורייתא אשכחתון לשידאי בר שיריקא פנדא במישרא דכרתי חבטיה בלועא דחמרא חטרתיה: ובני מלכים בזגין: מאן תנא א"ר אושעיא רבי שמעון היא דאמר [ה] כל ישראל בני מלכים הם רבא אמר [א] באריג בכסותו ודברי הכל:

מתני' [ב] יוצאין בביצת החרגול ובשן שועל ובמסמר מן הצלוב משום רפואה [ו] דברי ר"מ וחכמים אוסרין אף בחול משום דרכי האמורי: **גמ'** יוצאין בביצת החרגול דעבדי לשיחלא ובשן של שועל דעבדי לשינתא דחייא למאן דניים דמיתא למאן דלא ניים: ובמסמר מן הצלוב: דעבדי לזירפא: משום רפואה דברי רבי מאיר: [ז] אביי ורבא דאמרי תרווייהו [ג] כל דבר שיש בו משום רפואה אין בו משום דרכי האמורי [ח] הא אין בו משום רפואה יש בו משום דרכי האמורי והתניא אילן שמשיר פירותיו סוקרו (וצובע אותו) בסיקרא וטוענו באבנים בשלמא טוענו באבנים כי היכי דליכחוש חיליה אלא סוקרו בסיקרא מאי רפואה קעביד כי היכי דליחזייה אינשי וליבעו עליה רחמי כדתניא [ה] וטמא טמא יקרא [ט] [ד] צריך להודיע צערו לרבים ורבים יבקשו עליו רחמים אמר רבינא כמאן תלינן כובסי בדיקלא כי האי תנא תני תנא בפרק [י] אמוראי קמיה דר' חייא בר אבין א"ל כולהו אית בהו משום דרכי האמורי לבר מהני מי שיש לו עצם בגרונו מביא מאותו המין ומניח ליה על קדקדו ולימא הכי חד חד נחית בלע בלע נחית חד חד אין בו משום דרכי האמורי [כ] לאדרא לימא הכי נגעצתא כמחט נגעלתא כתרים [ל] שייא שייא

האומר

רש"י

לאשתא תילתא. שחפת שלישית שבאה מג' ימים לג' ימים: סילוי. ענבים (א) קטנים: ושבעה ציבי. קסמים: כשורי. קורות: ושבעה סיכי. יתידות קייבל"ש בלע"ז: משבעה גשורי. גשרים: ז' סינרי. לנור הדלת חור האסקופה שציר הדלת סובב בו: כופרי. זפת שזופתין הספינות: ארבי. ספינות: ושבעה בוני (ב) כמוני. גרעיני כמון ל"א בוני כמון גרסי' מלא אגרוף: ושבעה ביני מדיקנא דכלבא סבא. שבעה נימי מזקן כלב זקן: אשתא צמירתא. חולי שמחממת וקודחת את הגוף: וורדינא. סנה: ליחרוק. אישקרני"ר כמו דמיבלע חירקייהו דאלו טריפות (חולין דף נט:): ויאמר משה. משום סיפיה מדוע לא יבער הסנה: כי סר. שיסור החולי: אל תקרב הלום. שלא יקרב זה החולי אליו: ליתתיה ולפסקיה. סמוך לקרקע. ליתתיה ישפיל: דמייכת. שאתה שפילה: דחמיתא אשתא. שראית האש: לסימטא. שחין קרו"ג בלע"ז: בזבזייה מסמסייה כסכסייה. שמות המלאכים על שם שקורעים וממסמסים ומכסכסים אותו. בז לשון בזעא: מארעא דסדום. כך הוא הלחש ולא מסדום באו: בזך בזיך. אין לו משמעות אלא כך הוא הלחש: עיניך ביך. מראיך בך שלא תאדים יותר: אתריך ביך. שלא תרחיב: בקלוט. שנקלט זרעו בשרירי בטנו שלא יוליד: לכיפה. אונפול"ש אבעבועות כך לשון רבי יצחק ברבי מנחם נ"ע ולשון רבותי לכיפה למי שכופהו שד: לימא הכי. לחש בעלמא הוא: הוית דפקיק דפקיק הוית. לחש הוא: ליט תבר ומשומת. מקולל ונשבר ומשומת יהא שד זה ששמו בר טיט בר טינא: לשידא דבית הכסא. אם הזיק לימא לחש זה: אקרקפי דארי. בראש הארי זכר: ואאוסי דגורייתא. ובחוטם לביאה נקבה: אשכחתא לשידאי בר שריקאי פנדאי. כך שמו: במישרא דכרתי חבטיה. בערוגת כרשין הפלתיו: בלועא דחמרא חטרתיה. בלחי החמור הלקיתיו: מאן תנא. דקתני וכל אדם ואפילו עני שבישראל: רבי שמעון. בפרק שמונה שרצים: בני מלכים. הלכך לעני נמי חזיא ולא גנותא דידיה דליתחזיא כיוהרא ושליף אי נמי דמגו דחידוש הוא שליף ומחוי: באריג בכסותו. דלא שליף ליה ומחוי: **מתני'** דרכי האמורי. ניחוש הוא וכתיב ובחוקותיהם לא תלכו (ויקרא יח): **גמ'** לשיחלא. לכאב האוזן ותולין באזנו: לשינתא. יש שעשאו כדי שיישן ויש כדי שלא יישן: דחייא. של שן שועל חי: לזירפא. נפח מכה דכל פרזלא זריף והאי מסי לזירפא: שיש בו משום רפואה. שנראית רפואתו כגון שתיית כוס ותחבושת מכה ופרכינן הא אין בו כו' כגון לחש שאין ניכר שיהא מרפא יש בו משום דרכי האמורי בתמיה: דליכחוש חיליה. שעל ידי שהוא שמן וכחו רב פירותיו נושרין: דליחזויה אינשי. ולסימנא עבדי ליה לאודעי דמשיר פירותיו: טמא טמא. הוא עצמו אומר טמא רחקו מעלי: כובסי. אשכול תמרים וסימן הוא שמשיר פירותיו: בפרק אמוראי. בפרק אחד [מ] ששנוי בתוספתא דמסכת שבת בהלכות דרכי האמורי: א"ל. רבי חייא לתנא: כולהו אית בהו. כל השנויות שם אל תטעה לומר באחד מהן אין בו משום דרכי האמורי אלא בכולן אתה שונה יש בו לבר מהני ב' אלו שאפרש לך: מי שיש לו עצם וכו' ולחש דנעלתה כמחט אלו ב' לבדם אין בהם: חד חד נחית. לחש הוא: לאדרא. עצם של דג שישב לאדם בושט: שייא שייא. לחש הוא רד רד:

האומר

תוספות

בני מלכים יוצאין בזגין מאן תנא ר"ש היא כו'. פי' הקונטרס וליכא למיחש דילמא מחייכי בהו ואתו לאתויי וא"ת מכל מקום ליחוש דילמא איפסיק ואתי לאתויי כדאמרינן לעיל גבי עבד דלא יצא בחותם שבצוארו וי"ל דהכא מיירי בתלוים בשלשלת דלא מיפסקי וריב"א פירש דבירושלמי מוקי לה בקטנים דאפילו אי פסיק ומייתי לה ליכא איסור והכי איתא בירושלמי ר' זעירא אומר בזוג שבצוארו ומהו כל אדם דקתני במתניתין בין קטנים עשירים בין קטנים עניים מתניתין פליגא עליה דרבי זעירא ולא בזוג שבצוארו כאן בגדולים כאן בקטנים פירוש ההוא דלא יצא בזוג שבצוארו בגדולים דלמא מיפסיק ואתי לאתויי והא דשרי הכא בקטנים דליכא למיחש כדפי' מ"מ יש לדקדק אמאי נקט בני מלכים כיון דליכא חששא אי מייתי להו קטן בידים וי"ל דאי לאו בני מלכים הוו מחייכו עליה בני מלכים כל שעה ואי אפשר שלא ישמע אביו מעולם ויטלם אביו בידו ואתו לאתויי אבל אי בני מלכים לא מחייכי אם כן אפילו אי מיפסיק ליכא למיחש דילמא מייתי להו אבוה דלא שכיח שיהא אביו בלדו בשעה שיפסוק:

הדרן עלך במה אשה

עין משפט נר מצוה

פח א מיי' פי"ט מהל' שבת הלכה יח סמג לאוין סה טוש"ע א"ח סימן שא סעיף כג:

פט ב ג מיי' שם הלכה יג טוש"ע שם סעיף מ:

צ ד מיי' פי"י מהלכות טומאת צרעת הלכה ח וסמג עשין רלה:

רבינו חננאל

אבל משקל דמשקל עלתה בתיקו. וכל [תיקו] דאיסורא [לחומרא] ואין יוצאין בה בשבת בני מלכים בזוגים אוקמה (רב) [רבא] בזוג ארוג בכסות ולדברי הכל כי האי גוונא שרי פר' שיח לא פצע האוזן פי' זירפא [ענביתא] (עכיבתא) אביי ורבא דאמרי תרווייהו כל שהוא משום רפואה אין בו משום דרכי האמורי: ירושלמי רבי אבהו בשם רבי יוחנן כל שמרפא אין בו משום דרכי האמורי

ליקוטי רש"י

אשתא צמירתא. חולי שקורין מלוי"י למירתא חם כמו דלמרה למורי בבבא קמא (פ.) [פסחים כה:]. חולי חמה בלע"ז מלווי"ד לשון שריפה וחמימות ודוגמתו בהכונס לאן לדיר (ב"ק ס.) דלמרא למורי. סימטא. קלו"ג בלע"ז נפח העומד באדם [ע"ז כח.]. משום דרכי האמורי. ניחוש וכתיב (שמות כג) ולא תעשה כמעשיהם [חולין עז.]. שיש בו משום רפואה. כגון משקה או סם או לחש שלוחש על המכה. אין בו משום רפואה. כגון שעושין שלא על החולי כגון קבורת שליא בפרשת דרכים וכיוצא בהם שדומין לניחוש [שם:]. דליכחוש חיליה. שמרוב שומנו הוא משירן. דליחזייה אינשי. סימן הוא שמשיר פירותיו. וטמא טמא יקרא. לועק ואומר טמא הוא [שם עח.]. כובסי. על שם שתלויים כדאמרינן כמאן תלינן כובסי בדקלא תלאי של תמרים [ב"מ קא:]. כל דבר התלוי במחובר קרי ליה כובסא כדאמר אזול גרמא ומחיה לכובסא ואתר תמרי באלו הן הגולין (מכות ח.) [שבועות מא.]. הוא אשכול התמרים המקובצים יחד [מכות ח.]. כי האי תנא. לבקש עליו רבים רחמים [חולין שם].

מסורת הש"ס

א) [בערוך גרס שיבי פי' חתיכה קטנה], ב) [גירס' הערוך סוברי פי' קברים ע"ש בערך סבר א'], ג) [עי' תוספות שבועות טו: ד"ה אסור], ד) [גיר' הערוך לכיבא בערך כב ...], ה) לקמן קיא: קכח. ב"מ קיג:], ו) [גירס' ירושל' דברי רבי יוסי ר' מאיר אוסר אף בחול], ז) חולין עז:, ח) [מלת הא ליתא בחולין משמע שם דהכל מדברי אביי ורבא ועי' בפירש"י דהכא ד"ה שיש וכו' ופרכינן הא אין בו וכו'], ט) מו"ק ה. [סוטה לב:] חולין עח. נדה סו., י) עי' ערוך ערך אמורי, כ) [גירסת הערוך אדדא], ל) [גירסת הערוך שח שח פי' המס המס], מ) פ"ז ופ"ח.

הגהות הב"ח

(א) רש"י ד"ה סילוי ענבים קטנים: (ב) ד"ה שבעה מיני כמונא גרעיני:

גליון הש"ס

גמרא ולימא וירא מלאך. עיין שבועות דף טו ע"ב תוס' ד"ה אסור. פסחים דף קיא ע"א תוס' ד"ה נפתח: שם אביי ורבא דאמרי תרווייהו כל דבר שיש בו משום רפואה. עיין בב"מ דף ... ע"ב תוס' ד"ה כיס ארנקי: שם כולהו אית בהו משום דרכי האמורי. עיין תשובת רשב"א סימן תי"ג בארוכה:

תורה אור השלם

א) וַיֵּרָא מַלְאַךְ יְיָ אֵלָיו בְּלַבַּת אֵשׁ מִתּוֹךְ הַסְּנֶה וַיַּרְא וְהִנֵּה הַסְּנֶה בֹּעֵר בָּאֵשׁ וְהַסְּנֶה אֵינֶנּוּ אֻכָּל: [שמות ג, ב]

ב) וַיֹּאמֶר מֹשֶׁה אָסֻרָה נָּא וְאֶרְאֶה אֶת הַמַּרְאֶה הַגָּדֹל הַזֶּה מַדּוּעַ לֹא יִבְעַר הַסְּנֶה: [שמות ג, ג]

ג) וַיַּרְא יְיָ כִּי סָר לִרְאוֹת וַיִּקְרָא אֵלָיו אֱלֹהִים מִתּוֹךְ הַסְּנֶה וַיֹּאמֶר מֹשֶׁה מֹשֶׁה וַיֹּאמֶר הִנֵּנִי: [שמות ג, ד]

ד) וַיֹּאמֶר אַל תִּקְרַב הֲלֹם שַׁל נְעָלֶיךָ מֵעַל רַגְלֶיךָ כִּי הַמָּקוֹם אֲשֶׁר אַתָּה עוֹמֵד עָלָיו אַדְמַת קֹדֶשׁ הוּא: [שמות ג, ה]

ה) וְהַצָּרוּעַ אֲשֶׁר בּוֹ הַנֶּגַע בְּגָדָיו יִהְיוּ פְרֻמִים וְרֹאשׁוֹ יִהְיֶה פָרוּעַ וְעַל שָׂפָם יַעְטֶה וְטָמֵא טָמֵא יִקְרָא: [ויקרא יג, מה]

Mishnah This Mishnah discusses the permissibility of going out on the Sabbath with articles of talismanic healing:

יוֹצְאִין בְּבֵיצַת הַחַרְגּוֹל – **One may go out** on the Sabbath **with a locust's egg,**[24] **וּבְשֵׁן שׁוּעָל** – **with a fox's tooth, וּבְמַסְמֵר מִן הַצָּלוּב** – **or with a nail from** the gallows of **one who was hanged,**[25] **מִשּׁוּם רְפוּאָה** – **for the purpose of healing.**[26] **דִּבְרֵי רַבִּי מֵאִיר** – **These are the words of R' Meir. וַחֲכָמִים אוֹסְרִין אַף בַּחוֹל** – **But the Sages prohibit** use of these items **even during the week, מִשּׁוּם דַּרְכֵי הָאֱמוֹרִי** – **because** of the prohibition against following in **the ways of the Emorites.**[27]

Gemara The Gemara explains the therapeutic function of each of these items:

יוֹצְאִין בְּבֵיצַת הַחַרְגּוֹל דְּעָבְדֵי לְשִׁיחְלָ – **One may go out** on the abbath **with a locust's egg** hung from one's ear **because it is** sed for earache,[28] **וּבְשֵׁן שֶׁל שׁוּעָל דְּעָבְדֵי לְשִׁינְתָּא** – **and with a** ox's tooth because it is used for sleep disorders. **דְּחַיָּיא לְמַאן דְּנָיֵי** – The tooth **of a live fox** is used **by one who is** overly rowsy to keep awake, **דְּמִיתָא לְמַאן דְּלָא נָיֵים** – whereas that **of** dead fox is used **by an insomniac** to enable him to sleep.[29]

The Mishnah states:

וּבְמַסְמֵר מִן הַצָּלוּ – AND WITH A NAIL FROM the gallows of ONE HO WAS HANGED.

The Gemara explains the function of this nail:

דְּעָבְדֵי לְזִירְפָּ – One may go out with this nail on the Sabbath ecause **it is used to** heal the **swelling** of a wound.[30]

The Mishnah continues:

מִשּׁוּם רְפוּאָ – One may go out on the Sabbath with a locust's egg, fox's tooth, and a nail from a gallows FOR THE PURPOSE OF HEALING. **דִּבְרֵי רַבִּי מֵאִיר** – THESE ARE THE WORDS OF R' MEIR. [But the Sages forbid use of these items even during the week, because of the prohibition against following in the ways of the Emorites.]

The Gemara cites Abaye and Rava, who rule regarding this dispute:

אַבַּיֵי וְרָבָא דְּאָמְרֵי תַּרְוַיְיהוּ – **Abaye and Rava both say: כָּל דָּבָר שֶׁיֵּשׁ בּוֹ מִשּׁוּם רְפוּאָה אֵין בּוֹ מִשּׁוּם דַּרְכֵי הָאֱמוֹרִי** – **Any practice** that is **of** evident **therapeutic value is not** prohibited **because of** the prohibition against following in **the ways of the Emorites,** even if it is a practice that the Emorites follow.[31] Thus, both Abaye and Rava rule in accordance with R' Meir.

The Gemara asks:

הָא אֵין בּוֹ מִשּׁוּם רְפוּאָה יֵשׁ בּוֹ מִשּׁוּם דַּרְכֵי הָאֱמוֹרִי – This implies that **an** Emorite **practice** that is **not of** evident **therapeutic value** ***is*** prohibited **because of** the prohibition against following in **the ways of the Emorites.**[32] **וְהָתַנְיָא** – **But a Baraisa has taught: אִילָן שֶׁמַּשִּׁיר פֵּירוֹתָיו** – One who possesses AN overly vital

NOTES

. A *chargol* is one of the four species of locust [enumerated in *Leviticus* :22] that may be eaten (see *Chullin* 65a-b for a description of this sect). It (as well as the other items mentioned in the Mishnah) was ıng around the neck for therapeutic purposes (see *Mishnah Berurah* 1:104).

. [It was customary to hang the corpse of one executed for a capital ime upon a gallows as a lesson to others.] A nail was used to secure the rpse to the gallows. The Mishnah speaks of this nail (*Meiri*; *Chidushei aRan*). [See *Tirgeim Avraham* to *Genesis* 40:19 for the origin of the ord צָלוּב.]

. [Since these items are used for healing, they are not legally viewed burdens, but as ornaments; one may therefore go out with them on e Sabbath, as with an effective amulet (above, 61a). The Gemara will scuss the therapeutic function of each item mentioned.]

. For they are magical acts, and are therefore prohibited by the verse *eviticus* 18:3), וּבְחֻקֹּתֵיהֶם לֹא תֵלֵכוּ, *do not follow their* (the Canaanites') *stoms* (*Rashi*). *Rashi* (to *Chullin* 77a) prohibits these acts from *codus* 23:24 as well, which states: וְלֹא תַעֲשֶׂה כְּמַעֲשֵׂיהֶם, *and you shall not t according to their* (the Canaanites') *practices* (see *Ramban* ad loc.). t a third source for this prohibition is cited by *Rambam* to the ishnah, as follows: וְלֹא תֵלְכוּ בְּחֻקֹּת הַגּוֹי, *do not follow the customs of the tion* [Canaan] (*Leviticus* 20:23) (see below, note 31 and note 32 for a ll discussion of this prohibition).

[This prohibition is named *ways of the Emorites* after the verses that ach it (the Emorites were one of the Canaanite nations). However, en the practices of other nations are prohibited if they are like Emorite ıys.]

. *Rashi*; *Chidushei HaRan*; see *Yerushalmi;* cf. *Rambam* to Mishnah; *sh.*

. *Rashba* (*Responsa* 1:413) likens the inherent ability of a fox's tooth affect a person's sleep patterns to the power a magnet possesses to eate a magnetic field.

. I.e. the swelling caused by a sword wound (*Meiri*). This remedy is an pecially unusual one, since [a wound caused by] iron usually causes flammation, and this bit of iron relieves it (*Rashi*).

Rashba (ibid.) differentiates between the respective capabilities of a x's tooth and a gallows nail. The power inherent in a fox's tooth is turally inborn in it, whereas a gallows nail is imbued with its power rough the use to which it was put.

. This is because the only actions that are forbidden because of the prohibition against following in Emorite ways are those that are clearly being done to ape gentile customs (e.g. superstitions that are blindly followed without rhyme or reason), since only such practices might be taken as an admission of the rightness of gentile ways. Practices that have evident therapeutic value, by contrast, are clearly not being practiced in imitation of the gentiles, but for the benefit derived from them. One is therefore permitted to perform such acts (*Maharik* 88:1).

32. *Rashi* gives two examples of practices that have definite therapeutic value: the drinking of various potions and the bandaging of wounds with certain materials, since these acts are of evident value in healing. *Rashi's* example of a practice without therapeutic value is incantation, which is therefore prohibited by Abaye and Rava. However, *Rosh* challenges *Rashi* on the basis of the Gemara of the last two *amudim,* which recommends many incantations as efficacious [some taught by Abaye himself]! *Rosh* therefore explains that *Rashi* refers only to incantations that have no clear healing properties; these are not of evident therapeutic value, and are thus prohibited. The incantations mentioned above, however, are well known to be healing incantations; they are therefore permissible (see *Orach Chaim* 301:27 with *Beur HaGra;* see also *Rashi* to *Chullin* 77b ד״ה אין בו משום רפואה). *Mishnah Berurah* (ad loc. §105,106) adds that even incantations that are not widely known to possess therapeutic value are permissible, since an onlooker, knowing of the existence of healing incantations, will assume that these too are of this sort. Thus, the only sorts of incantations prohibited are those of which it is definitely known that they are *not* for the purpose of healing (see *Ritva MHK* ed. and *Ran*; see *Teshuvos Chavas Yair* §234; see also *Chasam Sofer* here).

There is actually a good deal of contention among the authorities concerning the nature of Emorite practices, and what Abaye and Rava mean to permit. *Meiri* writes that Emorite practices are those which have neither natural nor supernatural basis as remedies such as incantations, but which are believed to be curative by the foolish masses, who perform them as adjuncts to idol worship (this is the view of the Sages in our Mishnah). Abaye and Rava therefore ruled that practices known to be effective remedies are permissible, be they natural or supernatural [דֶּרֶךְ סְגֻלָּה]. *Meiri* then states that the various incantations recommended in our *sugya* are entirely ineffective. The Rabbis permitted these practices [he says] only because they are so obviously without merit that no one could possibly be led astray by performing them. Alternatively, the reason these practices were permitted was that since the masses believed in their efficacy, their performance was psychologically

לאשתא תילתא לייתי שבעה סילוי משבעה דיקלי ושבעה (א) ציבי משבעה כשורי ושבעה סיכי משבעה גשורי ושבעה קטימי משבעה תנורי ושבעה עפרי משבעה (ב) סנרי ושבעה כופרי משבעה ארבי ושבעה בוני כמוני ושבעה ביני מדיקנא דכלבא סבא ולצייירינהו בחללא דבי צווארא בנירא ברקא א"ר יוחנן לאשתא צמירתא לישקל סכינא דכולא פרזלא וליזל להיכא דאיכא וורדינא וליקטר ביה נירא ברקא יומא קמא ליחרוק ביה פורתא ולימא א) וירא מלאך ה' אליו וגו' למחר ליחרוק ביה פורתא ולימא ב) ויאמר משה אסורה נא ואראה למחר ליחרוק ביה פורתא (ג) ולימא ג) וירא ה' כי סר לראות וגו' א"ל רב אחא בריה דרבא לרב אשי ולימא ד) ויאמר אל תקרב הלום וגו' אלא ליומא קמא לימא וירא מלאך ה' אליו וגו' ויאמר משה וגו' ולמחר לימא וירא ה' כי סר לראות ולמחר ויאמר (ה') אל תקרב הלום וכי פסק ליה ליתתיה ולפסקי ולימא הכי הסנה הסנה לאו משום דגביהת מכל אילני אשרי הקב"ה שכינתיה עלך אלא משום דמייכת מכל אילני אשרי קודשא בריך הוא שכינתיה עלך וכי היכי דחמיתיה אשתא לחנניה מישאל ועזריה ועריקת מן קדמוהי כן תחמיניה אשתא לפלוני בר פלונית ותיערוק מן קדמוהי לסימטא לימא הכי בז בזייה מס מסייא כס כסייה שרלאי ואמרלאי אלין מלאכי דאישתלחו מארעא דסדום ולאסאה שחינא כאיבין בזך בזיך בזבזיך מסמסיך כמון כמיך עיניך ביך ביך אתריך בך זרעיך כקלוט וכפרדה דלא פרה ולא רביא כך לא תפרה ולא תרבה בגופיה דפלוני בר פלונית (ד) לכיפה לימא הכי חרב שלופה וקלע נטושה לא שמיה יוכב חולין מכאובין לשידא לימא הכי הוית דפקיק דפקיק הוית ליטא תבור ומשומת בר טיט בר טמא בר טינא כשמגז מריגז ואיסטמאי לשידא דבית הכסא לימא הכי אקרקפי דארי ואאוסי דגורייתא אשכחתון לשידאי בר שיריקא פנדא במישרא דכרתי חבטיה בלועא דחמרא חטרתיה: ובני מלכים בזגין: מאן תנא א"ר אושעיא רבי שמעון היא דאמר (ה) כל ישראל בני מלכים הם רבא אמר א בארוג בכסותו ודברי הכל:

מתני' ב יוצאין בביצת החרגול ובשן שועל ובמסמר מן הצלוב משום רפואה (ו) דברי ר"מ וחכמים אוסרין אף בחול משום דרכי האמורי: גמ' יוצאין בביצת החרגול דעבדי לשיחלא ובשן של שועל דעבדי לשינתא דחייא למאן דניים דמיתא למאן דלא ניים: ובמסמר מן הצלוב: דעבדי לזירפא: משום רפואה דברי רבי מאיר: (ז) אביי ורבא דאמרי תרווייהו ג כל דבר שיש בו משום רפואה אין בו משום דרכי האמורי (ח) הא אין בו משום רפואה יש בו משום דרכי האמורי והתניא אילן שמשיר פירותיו סוקרו (וצובע אותו) בסיקרא וטוענו באבנים בשלמא טוענו באבנים כי היכי דליכחוש חיליה אלא סוקרו בסיקרא מאי רפואה קעביד כי היכי דליחזייה אינשי וליבעו עליה רחמי כדתניא ה) וטמא טמא יקרא (ט) ד צריך להודיע צערו לרבים ורבים יבקשו עליו רחמים אמר רבינא כמאן תלינן כובסי בדיקלא כי האי תנא תני תנא בפרק (י) אמוראי קמיה דר' חייא בר אבין א"ל כולהו אית בהו משום דרכי האמורי לבר מהני מי שיש לו עצם בגרונו מביא מאותו המין ומניח ליה על קדקדו ולימא הכי חד חד נחית בלע בלע נחית חד חד אין בו משום דרכי האמורי (כ) לאדרא לימא הכי ננעצתא כמחט ננעלתא כתרים (ל) שייא שייא
האומר

רש"י

לאשתא תילתא. שאחת שלישית שבאה מג' ימים לג' ימים: סילוי. ענפים (א) קטנים: ושבעה ציבי. קסמים: כשורי. קורות: ושבעה סיכי. יתידות קייבל"ש בלע"ז: משבעה גשורי. גשרים: ז' סינרי. לנור הדלת חור האסקופה שציר הדלת סובב בו: כופרי. זפת שזופתין הספינות: ארבי. ספינות: ושבעה בוני (ב) כמוני. גרעיני כמון ל"א בוני כמון גרסי' מלא אגרוף: ושבעה ביני מדיקנא דכלבא סבא. שבעה נימי מזקן כלב זקן: אשתא צמירתא. חולי שמחממת וקודחת את הגוף: וורדיני. סנה: ליחרוק. אישקרני"ר כמו דמיבלע סירקייהו דאלו טריפות (חולין דף נט:): ויאמר משה. מאחר שסיפיה מדוע לא יבער הסנה: כי סר. שיסור החולי: אל תקרב הלום. שלא יקרב זה החולי אליו: ליתתיה ולפסקיה. סמוך לקרקע. ליתתיה ישפיל: דמייכת. שאתה שפילה: דחמיתא אשתא. שראית האש: לסימטא. שחין קרו"ג בלע"ז: בזבזייה מסמסייה כסכסייה. שמות המלאכים על שם שקורעים וממסמסים ומכסכסים אותו. בז לשון בזעא: מארעא דסדום. כך הוא הלחש ולא מסדום באו: בזך בזיך. אין לו משמעות אלא כך הוא הלחש: עיניך ביך. מראיך בך שלא תאדים יותר: אתריך ביך. שלא תרחיב: כקלוט. שנקלט זרעו בשרירי בטנו שלא יוליד: לכיפה. אונפול"ש אבעבועות כך לשון רבי יצחק ברבי מנחם נ"ע ולשון רבותי לכיפה למי שכופהו שד: לימא הכי. לחש בעלמא הוא: הוית דפקיק דפקיק הוית. לחש הוא: ליט תבר ומשומת. מקולל ונשבר ומשומת יהא שד זה ששמו בר טיט בר טינא: לשידא דבית הכסא. אם הזיק לימא לחש זה: אקרקפי דארי. בראש הארי זכר: ואאוסי דגורייתא. ובחוטם לביאה נקבה: אשכחתא לשידאי בר שריקאי פנדאי. כך שמו: במישרא דכרתי חבטיה. בערוגת כרשין הפלתיו: בלועא דחמרא חטרתיה. בלחי החמור הלקיתיו: מאן תנא. דקתני וכל אדם ואפילו עני שבישראל: רבי שמעון. בפרק שמונה שרצים: בני מלכים. הלכך לעני נמי חזיא ולא גנותא דידיה דליתחזיא כיוהרא ושליף אי נמי דמגו דחידוש הוא שליף ומחוי: באריג בכסותו. דלא שליף ליה ומחוי: מתני' דרכי האמורי. ניחוש הוא וכתיב ובחוקותיהם לא תלכו (ויקרא יח): גמ' לשיחלא. לכאב האוזן ותולין באזנו: לשינתא. יש שעושאו כדי שיישן ויש כדי שלא יישן: דחייא. של שן שועל חי: לזירפא. נפח מכה דכל פרזלא זריף והאי מסי לזירפא: שיש בו משום רפואה. שנראית רפואתו כגון שתיית כוס ותחבושת מכה ופרכינן הא אין בו כו' כגון לחש שאין ניכר שיהא מרפא יש בו משום דרכי האמורי בתמיה: דליכחוש חיליה. שעל ידי שהוא שמן וכחו רב פירותיו נושרין: דליחזויה אינשי. ולסימנא עבדי ליה לאודעי דמשיר פירותיו: טמא טמא. הוא עצמו אומר טמא רחקו מעלי: כובסי. אשכול תמרים וסימן הוא שמשיר פירותיו: בפרק אמוראי. בפרק אחד (מ) ששנוי בתוספתא דמסכת שבת בהלכות דרכי האמורי: א"ל. רבי חייא לתנא: כולהו אית בהו. כל השנויות שם אל תטעה לומר באחד מהן אין בו משום דרכי האמורי אלא בכולן אתה שונה יש בו לבר מהני ב' אלו שאפרש לך: מי שיש לו עצם וכו' ולחש דנעצתא כמחט אלו ב' לבדם אין בהם: חד חד נחית. לחש הוא: לאדרא. עצם של דג שישב לאדם בושט: שייא שייא. לחש הוא רד רד:
האומר

תוספות

בני מלכים יוצאין בזגין מאן תנא ר"ש היא כו'. פי' הקונטרס וליכא למיחש דילמא מחייכי בהו ואתו לאתויי וא"ת מכל מקום ליחוש דילמא איפסיק ואתי לאתויי כדאמרינן לעיל גבי עבד דלא יצא בחותם שבצוארו וי"ל דהכא מיירי בתלוים בשלשלת דלא מיפסקי וריב"א פירש דבירושלמי מוקי לה בקטנים דאפילו אי פסיק ומייתי לה ליכא איסור והכי איתא בירושלמי ר' זעירא אומר בזוג שבצוארו ומהו כל אדם דקתני במתניתין בין קטנים עשירים בין קטנים עניים מתניתין פליגא עליה דרבי זעירא ולא בזוג שבצוארו כאן בגדולים כאן בקטנים פירוש ההוא דלא יצא בזוג שבצוארו בגדולים דלמא מיפסיק ואתי לאתויי והא דשרי הכא בקטנים דליכא למיחש כדפי' מ"מ יש לדקדק אמאי נקט בני מלכים כיון דליכא חששא אי מייתי להו קטן בידים וי"ל דאי לאו בני מלכים הוו מחייכו עליה בני מלכים כל שעה ואי אפשר שלא ישמע אביו מעולם ויטלם אביו בידו ואתו לאתויי אבל אי בני מלכים לא מחייכי אם כן אפילו אי מיפסיק ליכא למיחש דילמא מייתי להו אבוה דלא שכיח שיהא אביו בלדו בשעה שיפסוק:

הדרן עלך במה אשה

עין משפט נר מצוה

פח א מיי' פי"ט מהל' שבת הלכה יח סמג לאוין סה טוש"ע א"ח סימן שא סעיף כג:
פט ב ג מיי' שם הלכה יג טוש"ע שם סעיף מ:
צ ד מיי' פי"י מהלכות טומאת צרעת הלכה ח וסמג עשין רלה:

רבינו חננאל

אבל משקל דמשקל עלתה בתיקו. וכל [תיקו] דאיסורא [לחומרא] ואין יוצאין בה בשבת בני מלכים בזוגים אוקמה (רב) [רבא] בזוג ארוג בכסות ולדברי הכל כי האי גונא שרי פר' שיח לא פצע האוזן פי' זירפא [ענביתא] (עכיבתא) אביי ורבא דאמרי תרווייהו כל שהוא משום רפואה אין בו משום דרכי האמורי: ירושלמי רבי אבהו בשם רבי יוחנן כל שמרפא אין בו משום דרכי האמורי

ליקוטי רש"י

אשתא צמירתא. חולי שקורין מלוי"י למירתא הם כמו דצמרה למורי בבבא קמא (ס.) [פסחים כה:]. חולי חמה בלע"ז מלווי"ד לשון שריפה וחמימות ודוגמתו בהכונס לאן לדיר (ב"ק ס.) דצמרה למורי. סימטא. קלו"ג בלע"ז נפח העומד באדם [ע"ז כח.]. משום דרכי האמורי. ניחוש וכתיב (שמות כג) ולא תעשה כמעשיהם [חולין עז.]. שיש בו משום רפואה. כגון משקה או סם או לחש שלוחש על המכה. אין בו משום רפואה. כגון שעושין שלא על החולי כגון קוברת שליא בפרשת דרכים וכיוצא בהם שדומין לניחוש [שם:]. דליכחוש חיליה. שמרוב שומנו הוא משירן. דליחזייה אינשי. סימן הוא שמשיר פירותיו. וטמא טמא יקרא. לועק ואומר טמא הוא [שם עח.]. כובסי. על שם שתלויים כדאמרינן כמאן תלינן כובסי בדקלא תלאי של תמרים [ב"מ קא:]. כל דבר התלוי במחובר קרי ליה כובסא כדאמר אזול גרמא ומחיה לכובסא ואתר תמרי באלו הן הגולין (מכות ח.) [שבועות מא.]. הוא אשכול התמרים המקובלים יחד [מכות ח.]. כי האי תנא. לבקש עליו רבים רחמים [חולין שם].

מסורת הש"ס

א) [בערוך גרס שיבי פי' חתיכה קטנה], ב) [גירס' הערוך סוכרי פי' קברים ע"ש בערך סכר א'], ג) [עי' תוספות שבועות טו: ד"ה אסור], ד) [גיר' הערוך לכיבא בערך כב ג], ה) לקמן קיא: קכח. [ב"מ קיג:], ו) [גירס' הירושל' דברי רבי יוסי ר' מאיר אוסר אף בחול], ז) חולין עז., ח) [מלת הא ליתא בחולין ומשמע שם דהכל מדברי אביי ורבא ועי' בפירש"י דהכא ד"ה שיש וכו' ופרכינן הא אין בו וכו'], ט) מו"ק ה. [סוטה לב:] חולין עח. נדה סו., י) עי' בערוך ערך אמור, כ) [גירסת הערוך לאדרא], ל) [גירסת הערוך שח שח פי' המם המם], מ) פ"ז ופ"ח.

הגהות הב"ח

(א) רש"י ד"ה סילוי ענפים קטנים: (ב) ד"ה ושבעה מיני כמונא גרעיני:

גליון הש"ס

גמרא ולימא וירא מלאך. עיין שבועות דף טו ע"ב תוס' ד"ה אסור. ופסחים דף קיא ע"א תוס' ד"ה נפחא: שם אביי ורבא דאמרי תרווייהו כל דבר שיש בו משום רפואה. עיין ב"מ דף כז ע"ב תוס' ד"ה ביה ולרנקי: שם כולהו אית בהו משום דרכי האמורי. עיין תשובת רשב"א סימן תי"ג בארוכה:

תורה אור השלם

א) וַיֵּרָא מַלְאַךְ יְיָ אֵלָיו בְּלַבַּת אֵשׁ מִתּוֹךְ הַסְּנֶה וַיַּרְא וְהִנֵּה הַסְּנֶה בֹּעֵר בָּאֵשׁ וְהַסְּנֶה אֵינֶנּוּ אֻכָּל: [שמות ג, ב]
ב) וַיֹּאמֶר מֹשֶׁה אָסֻרָה נָּא וְאֶרְאֶה אֶת הַמַּרְאֶה הַגָּדֹל הַזֶּה מַדּוּעַ לֹא יִבְעַר הַסְּנֶה: [שמות ג, ג]
ג) וַיַּרְא יְיָ כִּי סָר לִרְאוֹת וַיִּקְרָא אֵלָיו אֱלֹהִים מִתּוֹךְ הַסְּנֶה וַיֹּאמֶר מֹשֶׁה מֹשֶׁה וַיֹּאמֶר הִנֵּנִי: [שמות ג, ד]
ד) וַיֹּאמֶר אַל תִּקְרַב הֲלֹם שַׁל נְעָלֶיךָ מֵעַל רַגְלֶיךָ כִּי הַמָּקוֹם אֲשֶׁר אַתָּה עוֹמֵד עָלָיו אַדְמַת קֹדֶשׁ הוּא: [שמות ג, ה]
ה) וְהַצָּרוּעַ אֲשֶׁר בּוֹ הַנֶּגַע בְּגָדָיו יִהְיוּ פְרֻמִים וְרֹאשׁוֹ יִהְיֶה פָרוּעַ וְעַל שָׂפָם יַעְטֶה וְטָמֵא טָמֵא יִקְרָא: [ויקרא יג, מה]

TREE THAT SHEDS ITS FRUIT early, סוֹקְרוֹ (וצובע אותו) בְּסִיקְרָא – **DYES IT WITH RED PIGMENT,** וְטוֹעֲנוֹ בַּאֲבָנִים – **AND BURDENS ITS** branches **WITH ROCKS,** both Emorite practices. בִּשְׁלָמָא טוֹעֲנוֹ בַּאֲבָנִים – Now, **it is understandable** that **he** should **burden [the tree's]** branches **with rocks,** כִּי הֵיכִי דְּלִיכְחוּשׁ חֵילֵיהּ – since he does this **so that its vitality will be sapped,** and its fruit will not ripen early. אֶלָּא סוֹקְרוֹ בְּסִיקְרָא – **But** that **he dyes it with red pigment** – מַאי רְפוּאָה קָעָבִיד – **what healing has he performed** with this action? None![33] Nonetheless, this act is permitted. We see, then, that one is permitted to perform even an Emorite practice of no evident therapeutic value! – ? –

The Gemara answers:

כִּי הֵיכִי דְּלִיחֲזְיֵיהּ אִינְשֵׁי וְלִיבְעוּ עֲלֵיהּ רַחֲמֵי – No! The tree is dyed for the purpose of drawing the attention of the public, **so that people will see [his misfortune] and pray that he be shown mercy.** כִּדְתַנְיָא – **For a Baraisa has taught** with regard to the following verse: "וְטָמֵא טָמֵא יִקְרָא" – *AND HE* (a *metzora*) *SHALL CALL OUT, "[I AM] TAMEI, [I AM] TAMEI."*[34] צָרִיךְ לְהוֹדִיעַ צַעֲרוֹ לָרַבִּים – This verse teaches that **ONE MUST INFORM THE PUBLIC OF HIS MISFORTUNE,** וְרַבִּים יְבַקְּשׁוּ עָלָיו רַחֲמִים – **SO THAT THE PUBLIC WILL BEG FOR MERCY UPON HIM.** Likewise here, the function of the red dye is not to heal, but to attract attention to one's plight, so that others will pray that the health of the tree be restored.

The Gemara takes note of a similar practice:

אָמַר רָבִינָא – **Ravina said:** כְּמַאן תָּלֵינַן כּוּבְסֵי בְּדִיקְלָא – **According to whose** teaching **do we** know to **hang a bunch of dates upon a date palm** that is shedding its fruit early? כִּי הַאי תַּנָּא – **According to** the teaching of **this Tanna,** who teaches in this Baraisa that one afflicted by a misfortune is required to tell others of it, so that they will pray for mercy. We likewise hang dates upon an unhealthy palm to alert others that their prayers are needed.

The Gemara now commences a section in which it will quote a lengthy Baraisa detailing a number of acts that are prohibited because they are practiced by the Emorites:

תָּנֵי תַּנָּא בְּפֶרֶק אֱמוֹרָאֵי קַמֵּיהּ דְּרַבִּי חִיָּיא בַּר אָבִין – **A teacher of Baraisos** once **taught** several laws **from the chapter of Emorite** practices[35] **before R' Chiya bar Avin.** אֲמַר לֵיהּ – **[R' Chiya] said to him:** כּוּלְּהוּ אִית בְּהוּ משום דַּרְכֵי הָאֱמוֹרִי לְבַר מֵהָנֵי – When you teach that chapter of Baraisos, do not say that any of the practices enumerated there are permissible! Rather, be sure to teach that **all of [the practices]** enumerated there **are** prohibited **because of** the prohibition against following in **the ways of the Emorites, except for these** two that I will set forth for you.[36]

R' Chiya bar Huna will now apprise the teacher of Baraisos of the two practices that are indeed permitted, and will then continue with a selection from the Baraisa of those practices that are prohibited.

The first of the two permissible practices:

מִי שֶׁיֵּשׁ לוֹ עֶצֶם בִּגְרוֹנוֹ – **ONE WHO HAS A BONE** stuck **IN HIS THROAT,** מֵבִיא מֵאוֹתוֹ הַמִּין – **BRINGS** another bone **OF THAT SORT,** וּמַנִּיחַ לֵיהּ עַל קָדְקֳדוֹ וְלֵימָא הָכִי – **AND PUTS IT UPON** the top of **HIS SKULL, AND SAYS THUS:** חַד חַד נָחִית בָּלַע – **"ONE BY ONE, GO DOWN AND BE SWALLOWED,** בָּלַע נָחִית חַד חַד – **BE SWALLOWED AND GO DOWN, ONE BY ONE."**[37] אֵין בּוֹ מִשּׁוּם דַּרְכֵי הָאֱמוֹרִי – **THIS** practice **IS NOT** prohibited **BECAUSE OF** the prohibition against following in **THE WAYS OF THE EMORITES.**

The second of the two permissible practices:

לְאִדְרָא לֵימָא הָכִי – **FOR A FISH BONE** stuck in one's throat, **ONE MUST SAY THUS:** נִנְעַצְתָּא כְּמַחַט – **"YOU ARE EMBEDDED LIKE A NEEDLE,** נִנְעַלְתָּא כִּתְרִיס – **YOU ARE LOCKED** tightly **AS A SHUTTER,** שְׁיָיא שְׁיָיא – **GO DOWN, GO DOWN."**[38] This practice too is not prohibited because of the prohibition against following in the ways of the Emorites.

NOTES

beneficial, since they worked as a placebo for those who were ill (see *Yoreh Deah* 179:6). *Rambam* (*Avodas Kochavim* 11:16 and *Moreh Nevuchim* 3:37) states that all conjurations, charms, incantations and the like are entirely without substance, and are given credence only by fools, but are prohibited because they can lead one to witchcraft, which can in turn lead one to idol worship (see, however, *Beur HaGra* to *Yoreh Deah* ibid. §13, who takes sharp issue with *Rambam's* assertion that these matters are without substance). According to *Rambam,* the only practices that are permitted are those that have been proven by scientific inquiry, or that can be explained according to the laws of nature. *Rambam* accordingly states that the various cures of our *sugya* (e.g. a gallows' nail) were believed in the period of the Gemara to be effective according to natural law. *Rashba* (*Responsa* 1:413), however, points out many apparent contradictions in *Rambam*'s ruling. He also shows that many of the cures that the Gemara assures us are effective cannot be explained at all according to the laws of nature! He therefore permits any practice which is known to be effective, be it natural or supernatural, so long as it is performed with the recognition that all healing is in God's hands. However, practices that have no therapeutic value, or evil practices that lead one away from God, such as drinking blood in order to consort with demons, are indeed prohibited (see *Rashba* at great length).

Shiltei HaGiborim (30b-31a in *dafei HaRif*) writes that one is permitted to perform not only those practices that cure one of disease, but even those practices that are designed to prevent monetary loss [with the exception of practices meant to physically heal animals] (cf. *Riaz,* cited there; see *Tosafos, Bava Metzia* 27b ד"ה כיס וארנקי with *Rashash* and *Maharatz Chayos*).

[*Maharil* (quoted in *Ta'amei HaMinhagim* p. 561) once stated that nowadays one may not perform the remedies recommended by the Gemara, for since we are not expert in their performance, they will not prove efficacious, and may lead, God forbid, to ridicule of the Torah and its teachers. However, he did permit one remedy that was proven effective even in the present day – that presented at the bottom of this page as a remedy for a bone stuck in one's throat (for further discussion of *Maharil's* statement, see *R' Tzadok HaKohen's Likutei Maamarim* p.130).]

33. For this act is known to have no therapeutic value (*Rosh*; see beginning of previous note).

34. *Leviticus* 13:45. [A *metzora* is one who was rendered *tamei* by one of a variety of skin blemishes (*tzaraas*).] This verse teaches that such an individual must warn others of his contamination, and warn them to distance themselves from him (*Rashi).* However, if the Torah had desired to teach only this law, the words *I am tamei* should have appeared in this verse only one time! The reason the verse repeats this phrase is to teach that one is obligated to tell others of his misfortune, so that they will beg God to have mercy upon him (*Moed Katan* 5a).

35. "The chapter of Emorite practices" refers to Chapters Seven and Eight of the *Tosefta* to *Shabbos,* which deal almost exclusively with Emorite practices (*Rashi*).

36. *Rashi;* however, see below, 67b note 8 for others who explain that R' Chiya bar Huna is actually saying that *all* of the following practices [including those listed on 67b] are *not* prohibited as Emorite ways!

37. *Rashi. Aruch* reads חרחר for חַד חַד, thus translating, *into a pit go down and be swallowed, go down and be swallowed into a pit* (ע' חרחר [ד']).

38. *Rashi. Aruch* reads שַׁח שַׁח for שְׁיָיא שְׁיָיא, thus translating, *be dissolved, be dissolved* (ע' שח [ג']).

לאשתא תילתא לייתי שבעה סילוי משבעה דיקלי ושבעה [א] ציבי משבעה כשורי ושבעה סיכי משבעה גשורי ושבעה קטימי משבעה תנורי ושבעה עפרי משבעה [ב] סנרי ושבעה כופרי משבעה ארבי ושבעה בוני כמוני ושבעה ביני מדיקנא דכלבא סבא ולציירינהו בחללא דבי צווארא בנירא ברקא א"ר יוחנן לאשתא צמירתא לישקל סכינא דכולא פרזלא וליזל להיכא דאיכא וורדינא וליקטר ביה נירא ברקא יומא קמא ליחרוק ביה פורתא ולימא [א] וירא מלאך ה' אליו וגו' למחר ליחרוק ביה פורתא ולימא [ב] ויאמר משה אסורה נא ואראה למחר ליחרוק ביה פורתא [ג] ולימא [ג] וירא ה' כי סר לראות וגו' א"ל רב אחא בריה דרבא לרב אשי ולימא [ד] ויאמר אל תקרב הלום וגו' אלא ליומא קמא לימא וירא מלאך ה' אליו וגו' ויאמר משה וגו' ולמחר לימא וירא ה' כי סר לראות ולמחר ויאמר (ה') אל תקרב הלום וכי פסק ליה ליתתיה ולפסקי ולימא הכי הסנה הסנה לאו משום דגביהת מכל אילני אשרי הקב"ה שכינתיה עלך אלא משום דמייכת מכל אילני אשרי קודשא בריך הוא שכינתיה עלך וכי היכי דחמיתיה אשתא לחנניה מישאל ועזריה ועריקת מן קדמוהי כן תחמיניה אשתא לפלוני בר פלונית ותיערוק מן קדמוהי לסימטא לימא הכי בז בזייה מס מסייא כס כסייה שרלאי ואמרלאי אלין מלאכי דאישתלחו מארעא דסדום ולאסאה שחינא כאיבין בזך בזיך מסמסיך כמון כמיך עיניך ביך עינך ביך אתריך בך זרעיך כקלוט וכפרדה דלא פרה ולא רביא כך לא תפרה ולא תרבה בגופיה דפלוני בר פלונית [ד] לכיפה לימא הכי חרב שלופה וקלע נטושה לא שמיה יוכב חולין מכאובין לשידא לימא הכי הוית דפקיק דפקיק הוית ליטא תבור ומשומת בר טיט בר טמא בר טינא כשמגז מריגז ואיסטמאי לשידא דבית הכסא לימא הכי אקרקפי דארי ואאוסי דגורייתא אשכחתון לשידאי בר שיריקא פנדא במישרא דכרתי חבטיה בלועא דחמרא חטרתיה: ובני מלכים בזגין: מאן תנא א"ר אושעיא רבי שמעון היא דאמר [ה] כל ישראל בני מלכים הם רבא אמר [א] באריג בכסותו ודברי הכל:

מתני' [ב] יוצאין בביצת החרגול ובשן שועל ובמסמר מן הצלוב משום רפואה [ו] דברי ר"מ וחכמים אוסרין אף בחול משום דרכי האמורי: גמ' יוצאין בביצת החרגול דעבדי לשיחלא ובשן של שועל דעבדי לשינתא דחייא למאן דניים דמיתא למאן דלא ניים: ובמסמר מן הצלוב: דעבדי לזירפא: משום רפואה דברי רבי מאיר: [ז] אביי ורבא דאמרי תרווייהו [ג] כל דבר שיש בו משום רפואה אין בו משום דרכי האמורי [ח] הא אין בו משום רפואה יש בו משום דרכי האמורי והתניא אילן שמשיר פירותיו סוקרו (וצובע אותו) בסיקרא וטוענו באבנים בשלמא טוענו באבנים כי היכי דליכחוש חיליה אלא סוקרו בסיקרא מאי רפואה קעביד כי היכי דליחזייה אינשי וליבעו עליה רחמי כדתניא [ה] וטמא טמא יקרא [ט] [ד] צריך להודיע צערו לרבים ורבים יבקשו עליו רחמים אמר רבינא כמאן תלינן כובסי בדיקלא כי האי תנא תני תנא בפרק [י] אמוראי קמיה דר' חייא בר אבין א"ל כולהו אית בהו משום דרכי האמורי לבר מהני מי שיש לו עצם בגרונו מביא מאותו המין ומניח ליה על קדקדו ולימא הכי חד חד נחית בלע בלע נחית חד חד אין בו משום דרכי האמורי [כ] לאדרא לימא הכי ננעצתא כמחט ננעלתא כתרים [ל] שייא שייא

האומר

רש"י

לאשתא תילתא. שחפת שלישית שבאה מג' ימים לג' ימים: סילוי. ענפים (א) קטנים: ושבעה ציבי. קסמים: כשורי. קורות: ושבעה סיכי. יתידות קייבל"ש בלע"ז: משבעה גשורי. גשרים: ז' סינרי. לנור הדלת חור האסקופה שציר הדלת סובב בו: כופרי. זפת שזופתין הספינות: ארבי. ספינות: ושבעה בוני (ב) כמוני. גרעיני כמון ל"א בוני כמון גרסי' מלא אגרוף: ושבעה ביני מדיקנא דכלבא סבא. שבעה נימי מזקן כלב זקן: אשתא צמירתא. חולי שמחממת וקודחת את הגוף: וורדיני. סנה: ליחרוק. אשקרני"ר כמו דמיבלע חירקייהו דאלו טריפות (חולין דף נט:): ויאמר משה. משום סיפיה מדוע לא יבער הסנה: כי סר. שיסור החולי: אל תקרב הלום. שלא יקרב זה החולי אליו: ליתתיה ולפסקיה. סמוך לקרקע. ליתתיה ישפיל: דמייכת. שאתה שפילה: דחמיתא אשתא. שראית האש: לסימטא. שחין קרו"ג בלע"ז: בזבזיה מסמסייה כסכסייה. שמות המלאכים על שם שקורעים וממסמסים ומכסכסים אותו. בז לשון בזעא: מארעא דסדום. כך הוא הלחש ולא מסדום באו: בזך בזיך. אין לו משמעות אלא כך הוא הלחש: עיניך ביך. מראיך בין שלא תאדים יותר: אתריך ביך. שלא תרחיב: בקלוט. שנקלט זרעו בשרירי בטנו שלא יוליד: לכיפה. אונפול"ש אבעבועות כך לשון רבי יצחק ברבי מנחם נ"ע ולשון רבותי לכיפה למי שכופהו שד: לימא הכי. לחש בעלמא הוא: הוית דפקיק דפקיק הוית. לחש הוא: ליט תבר ומשומת. מקולל ונשבר ומשומת יהא שד זה ששמו בר טיט בר טינא: לשידא דבית הכסא. אם הזיק לימא לחש זה: אקרקפי דארי. בראש הארי זכר: ואאוסי דגורייתא. ובחוטם לביאה נקבה: אשכחתא לשידאי בר שריקאי פנדאי. כך שמו: במישרא דכרתי חבטיה. בערוגת כרשין הפלתיו: בלועא דחמרא חטרתיה. בלחי החמור הלקיתיו: מאן תנא. דקתני וכל אדם ואפילו עני שבישראל: רבי שמעון. בפרק שמונה שרצים: בני מלכים. הלכך לעני נמי חזיא ולא גנותא דידיה דליתחזיא כיוהרא ושליף אי נמי דמגו דחידוש הוא שליף ומחוי: באריג בכסותו. דלא שליף ליה ומחוי: מתני' דרכי האמורי. ניחוש הוא וכתיב ובחוקותיהם לא תלכו (ויקרא יח): גמ' לשיחלא. לכאב האוזן ותולין באזנו: לשינתא. יש שעושאו כדי שיישן ויש כדי שלא יישן: דחייא. של שן שועל חי: לזירפא. נפח מכה דכל פרזלא זריף והאי מסי לזירפא: שיש בו משום רפואה. שנראית רפואתו כגון שתיית כוס ותחבושת מכה ופרכינן הא אין בו כו' כגון לחש שאין ניכר שיהא מרפא יש בו משום דרכי האמורי בתמיה: דליכחוש חיליה. שעל ידי שהוא שמן וכחו רב פירותיו נושרין: דליחזיוה אינשי. ולסימנא עבדי ליה לאודעי דמשיר פירותיו: טמא טמא. הוא עצמו אומר טמא רחקו מעלי: כובסי. אשכול תמרים וסימן הוא שמשיר פירותיו: בפרק אמוראי. בפרק אחד [מ] ששנוי בתוספתא דמסכת שבת בהלכות דרכי האמורי: א"ל. רבי חייא לתנא: כולהו אית בהו. כל השנויות שם אל תטעה לומר באחד מהן אין בו משום דרכי האמורי אלא בכולן אתה שונה יש בו לבר מהני ב' אלו שאפרש לך: מי שיש לו עצם וכו' ולחש דנעלתה כמחט אלו ב' לבדם אין בהם: חד חד נחית. לחש הוא: לאדרא. עצם של דג שישב לאדם בושט: שייא שייא. לחש הוא רד רד:

האומר

תוספות

בני מלכים יוצאין בזגין מאן תנא ר"ש היא כו'. פי' הקונטרס וליכא למיחש דילמא מחייכי בהו ואתו לאתויי וא"ת מכל מקום ליחוש דילמא איפסיק ואתי לאתויי כדאמרינן לעיל גבי עבד דלא יצא בחותם שבצוארו וי"ל דהכא מיירי בתלוים בשלשלת דלא מיפסקי וריב"א פירש דבירושלמי מוקי לה בקטנים דאפילו אי פסיק ומייתי לה ליכא איסור והכי איתא בירושלמי ר' זעירא אומר בזוג שבצוארו ומהו כל אדם דקתני במתניתין בין קטנים עשירים בין קטנים עניים מתניתין פליגא עליה דרבי זעירא ולא בזוג שבצוארו כאן בגדולים כאן בקטנים פירוש ההוא דלא יצא בזוג שבצוארו בגדולים דלמא מיפסיק ואתי לאתויי והא דשרי הכא בקטנים דליכא למיחש כדפי' מ"מ יש לדקדק אמאי נקט בני מלכים כיון דליכא חששא אי מייתי להו קטן בידים וי"ל דאי לאו בני מלכים הוו מחייכו עליה בני מלכים כל שעה ואי אפשר שלא ישמע אביו מעולם ויטלם אביו בידו ואתו לאתויי אבל אי בני מלכים לא מחייכי אם כן אפילו אי מיפסיק ליכא למיחש דילמא מייתי להו אבוה דלא שכיח שיהא אביו בצדו בשעה שיפסוק:

הדרן עלך במה אשה

עין משפט נר מצוה

פח א מיי' פי"ט מהל' שבת הלכה יח סמג לאוין סה טוש"ע א"ח סימן שא סעיף כג:
פט ב ג מיי' שם הלכה יג טוש"ע שם סעיף מ:
צ ד מיי' פי"י מהלכות טומאת צרעת הלכה ח וסמג עשין רלה:

רבינו חננאל

אבל משקל דמשקל עלתה בתיקו. וכל [תיקו] דאיסורא [לחומרא] ואין יוצאין בה בשבת בני מלכים בזוגים אוקמה (רב) [רבא] בזוג ארוג בכסות ולדברי הכל כי האי גוונא שרי פר' שיח לא פצע האוזן פי' זירפא [ענביתא] (עכיבתא) אביי ורבא דאמרי תרווייהו כל שהוא משום רפואה אין בו משום דרכי האמורי: ירושלמי רבי אבהו בשם רבי יוחנן כל שמרפא אין בו משום דרכי האמורי

ליקוטי רש"י

אשתא צמירתא. חולי שקורין מלוי"י לצירתא חם כמו דאמרה לצורי בבבא קמא (פ.) [פסחים כה:]. חולי חמה בלע"ז מלווי"ד לשון שריפה ותמימות ודוגמתו בהכונס לאן לדיר (ב"ק פ.) דאמרה לצורי. סימטא. קלו"ג בלע"ז נפח העומד באדם [ע"ז כח.]. משום דרכי האמורי. ניחוש וכתיב (שמות כג) ולא תעשה כמעשיהם [חולין עז.]. שיש בו משום רפואה. כגון משקה או סם או לחש שלוחש על המכה. אין בו משום רפואה. כגון שעושין שלא על החולי כגון קוברת שליא בפרשת דרכים וכיוצא בהם שדומין לניחוש [שם:]. דליכחוש חיליה. שמרוב שומנו הוא משירן. דליחזייה אינשי. סימן הוא שמשיר פירותיו. וטמא טמא יקרא. צועק ואומר טמא הוא [שם עח.]. כובסי. על שם שתלויים כדאמרינן כמאן תלינן כובסי בדקלא תלאי של תמרים [ב"מ קא:]. כל דבר התלוי במחובר קרי ליה כובסא כדאמר אזול גרמא וממיה לכובסא ואתר תמרי באלו הן הגולין (מכות ח.) [שבועות מא.]. הוא אשכול התמרים המקובצים יחד [מכות ח.]. כי האי תנא. לבקש עליו רבים רחמים [חולין שם].

מסורת הש"ס

א) [בערוך גרס שיבי פי' חתיכה קטנה], ב) [גירס' הערוך סוכרי פי' קברים ע"ש בערך סכר א'], ג) [עי' תוספות שבועות טו: ד"ה אסור], ד) [גיר' הערוך לכיבא בערך כב ג], ה) לקמן קיא: קכח. [ב"מ קיג:], ו) [גירס' הירושל' דברי רבי יוסי ר' מאיר אוסר אף בחול], ז) חולין עז:, ח) [מלת הא ליתא בחולין ומשמע שם דהכל מדברי אביי ורבא ועי' בפירש"י דהכא ד"ה שיש וכו' ופרכינן הא אין בו וכו'], ט) מו"ק ה. [סוטה לב:] חולין עח. נדה סו., י) עי' בערוך ערך אמורי, כ) [גירסת הערוך לאדרא], ל) [גירסת הערוך שה שה פי' המס המס], מ) פ"ז ופ"ח.

הגהות הב"ח

(א) רש"י ד"ה סילוי ענפים קטנים: (ב) ד"ה ושבעה מיני כמונא גרעיני:

גליון הש"ס

גמרא ולימא וירא מלאך. עיין שבועות דף טו ע"ב תוס' ד"ה אסור. ופסחים דף קיא ע"א תוס' ד"ה נפתח: שם אביי ורבא דאמרי תרווייהו כל דבר שיש בו משום רפואה. עיין בב"מ דף כז ע"ב תוס' ד"ה כים ואנקי: שם כולהו אית בהו משום דרכי האמורי. עיין תשובת רשב"א סימן תי"ג בארוכה:

תורה אור השלם

א) וַיֵּרָא מַלְאַךְ יְיָ אֵלָיו בְּלַבַּת אֵשׁ מִתּוֹךְ הַסְּנֶה וַיַּרְא וְהִנֵּה הַסְּנֶה בֹּעֵר בָּאֵשׁ וְהַסְּנֶה אֵינֶנּוּ אֻכָּל: [שמות ג, ב]
ב) וַיֹּאמֶר מֹשֶׁה אָסֻרָה נָּא וְאֶרְאֶה אֶת הַמַּרְאֶה הַגָּדֹל הַזֶּה מַדּוּעַ לֹא יִבְעַר הַסְּנֶה: [שמות ג, ג]
ג) וַיַּרְא יְיָ כִּי סָר לִרְאוֹת וַיִּקְרָא אֵלָיו אֱלֹהִים מִתּוֹךְ הַסְּנֶה וַיֹּאמֶר מֹשֶׁה מֹשֶׁה וַיֹּאמֶר הִנֵּנִי: [שמות ג, ד]
ד) וַיֹּאמֶר אַל תִּקְרַב הֲלֹם שַׁל נְעָלֶיךָ מֵעַל רַגְלֶיךָ כִּי הַמָּקוֹם אֲשֶׁר אַתָּה עוֹמֵד עָלָיו אַדְמַת קֹדֶשׁ הוּא: [שמות ג, ה]
ה) וְהַצָּרוּעַ אֲשֶׁר בּוֹ הַנֶּגַע בְּגָדָיו יִהְיוּ פְרֻמִים וְרֹאשׁוֹ יִהְיֶה פָרוּעַ וְעַל שָׂפָם יַעְטֶה וְטָמֵא טָמֵא יִקְרָא: [ויקרא יג, מה]

האומר גד גדי וסנוק לא אשכי ובושכי יש בו משום דרכי האמורי ר' יהודה אומר גד אינו אלא לשון ע"ז שנאמר א) העורכים לגד שלחן הוא בשמה והיא בשמו יש בו משום דרכי האמורי ה) דונו דני יש בו משום דרכי האמורי ר' יהודה אומר אין דן אלא לשון ע"ז שנאמר ב) הנשבעים באשמת שומרון ואמרו חי אלהיך דן האומר ג) לעורב צרח ולעורבתא שריקי והחזירי לי זנביך לטובה יש בו משום דרכי האמורי א האומר שחטו תרנגול זה שקרא ערבית ותרנגולת שקראה גברית יש בו משום דרכי האמורי אשתה ואותיר אשתה ואותיר יש בו משום דרכי האמורי ג) המבקעת ביצים בכותל (והטח) בפני האפרוחים יש בו משום דרכי האמורי והמגים בפני אפרוחים יש בו משום דרכי האמורי המרקדת והמונה שבעים ואחד אפרוחין בשביל שלא ימותו יש בו משום דרכי האמורי המרקדת לכותח והמשתקת לעדשים והמצווחת לגריסין יש בו משום דרכי האמורי המשתנת בפני קדירתה בשביל שתתבשל מהרה יש בו משום דרכי האמורי אבל נותנין קיסם של תות ושברי זכוכית בקדירה בשביל שתתבשל מהרה וחכמים אוסרין (א) בשברי זכוכית מפני הסכנה תנו רבנן ד) נותנין בול של מלח לתוך הנר בשביל שתאיר ותדליק ונותנין טיט וחרסית תחת הנר בשביל שתמתין ותדליק אמר רב זוטרא האי מאן דמיכסי שרגא דמשחא ומגלי נפטא קעבר משום ג) בל תשחית חמרא וחיי לפום רבנן אין בו משום דרכי האמורי מעשה ברבי עקיבא שעשה משתה לבנו ועל כל כוס וכוס שהביא אמר חמרא וחיי לפום רבנן חיי וחמרא לפום רבנן ולפום תלמידיהון:

הדרן עלך במה אשה

כלל ה) גדול אמרו בשבת ב) כל השוכח עיקר שבת ועשה מלאכות הרבה בשבתות הרבה אינו חייב אלא חטאת אחת היודע עיקר שבת ועשה מלאכות הרבה בשבתות הרבה חייב על כל שבת ושבת ג) היודע שהוא שבת ועשה מלאכות הרבה בשבתות הרבה חייב על כל

רש"י

האומר גד גדי. התמזל מזלי: וסנוק לא. עיף אל תהי ו): אשכי ובושכי. יום ולילה: יש בו משום דרכי האמורי. וכן בכולן עד סוף פירקא גרסינן הרי זה מדרכי האמורי וה"ג בתוספ': הוא בשמה והיא בשמו. הוא ואשתו מחליפין שמותיהן זה בזה בלילה משום ניחוש: דונו דני. התחזקו חביותי: דן. אינו חק האמורי אלא ע"ז ממש וחייב משום קורא בשם עבודת גלולים: האומר לעורב צרח. כשהוא קורא אומר לו כן מפני שהוא מבשר בשורות ולוחש לו לחש זה: שקרא ערבית. איחר יותר משאר חביריו ול"נ שקרא כעורב: שקראה גברית. כתרנגול כמו קרא גברא (יומא דף כ:): אשתה ואותיר. כדי שתהא ברכה מצויה ביינו: המבקעת ביצים בכותל. ואית דגרסי ביליס (ב) מקבעת לאחר שיצאו האפרוחים מחזרת (ג) הקליפות במקל וקובעתן בכותל לפניהם וזהו לנחש שלא ימותו: המרקדת לכותח. כשעושה כותח מרקדת לפניו והוא ניחוש שיתחזק: המשתקת לעדשים. כשנותנת בקדרה משתקת את כל העומדים כדי שיתבשלו ולגריסין מצווחת: ה"ג אבל נותנין קיסם של תות. מורי"ר וחזק הוא כחומץ ומועיל לבשל ואין זה לנחש: ה"ג אבל אסרו חכמים בשברי זכוכית. אע"פ שמשום דרכי האמורי אין בו אסרו חכמים מפני הסכנה שלא יבלע: בול של מלח. מלא אגרוף מלח בשביל שתאיר ותדליק שאין זה ניחוש אלא מסייע ממש שהמלח נולל את השמן וימשך אחר הפתילה: טיט וחרסית. מצננין את השמן ואינו דולק מהר: דמכסי שרגא דמשחא. שעושה לו כיסוי למעלה ממהר לידלק: נפטא. כשמגלין אותו האור הולך ונמשך אליו ומבעיר: חמרא וחיי. כשמחזגין ונותנין כוס אומר כן לברכה בעלמא:

הדרן עלך במה אשה

כלל גדול. בגמרא מפרש אמאי קרי ליה גדול: השוכח עיקר שבת. כסבור אין שבת בתורה: אינו חייב אלא חטאת אחת. בגמרא (לקמן דף סט:) יליף לה שמירה אחת לשבתות הרבה ושמירה לכל שבת ושבת ומסתברא דכי כתיב שמירה אחת לשבתות הרבה כי האי גוונא כתיב דכולא חדא שגגה היא וקרבן אשוגג קאתי: היודע עיקר שבת. שיש שבת בתורה ונאסרו בה מלאכות: ועשה מלאכות הרבה בשבתות הרבה. על ידי שגגת שבת ששכח שהיום שבת היום מדקתני סיפא היודע שהוא שבת מכלל דרישא בדאין יודע שהוא שבת ועשה מלאכות הרבה בשבתות הרבה בענין זה ולא נודע לו בינתים שחטא: חייב על כל שבת ושבת. חטאת אחת לכל שבת ואע"פ שלא נודע לו בינתים והעלם אחד הוא אמרינן ימים שבינתים הוין ידיעה לחלק שא"א שלא שמע בינתים שאותו היום הויא שבת אלא שלא נזכר לו במלאכות שנעשו בו ושגגה קמייתא משום שבת הוא דהואי והא אתידע ליה ביני ביני הלכך כל חדא שבת חדא שגגה היא ומיהו על הרבה מלאכות שבכל שבת לא מיחייב אלא חדא דכולה שבת חדא שגגה דהא לא שגג אמלאכות דיודע הוא שהמלאכות אסורות אלא אשבת הוא דשגג: היודע שהוא שבת ועשה מלאכות הרבה. שלא ידע שהמלאכות הללו אסורות ועשאם כמה פעמים בכמה שבתות חייב על כל אב מלאכה חטאת אחת ואף על פי שחזר וכפלה בכמה שבתות כולה חדא שגגה היא דהא לא נודע לו בינתים ולענין שגגת שבת הוא דאיכא למימר ימים שבינתים הוין ידיעה לחלק אבל לענין שגגת מלאכות לא אמרו הכי דמשום הפסק ימים אין לו לדעת אלא אם כן ישב ועסק לפני חכמים בהלכות שבת ומיהו בחטאת אחת לא מיפטר על כל שבת דשגגה לאו בשבת הויא אלא במלאכות ושגגות טובא הוו לשבת אחת ובגמרא (לקמן דף ע.) יליף פעמים שהוא חייב על כל אחת ואחת ופעמים שאינו חייב אלא אחת על כל שבת ומסתברא דחשיבא בזדון שבת ושגגת מלאכות דאיכא שגגות טובא ופטורא בשגגת שבת וזדון מלאכות דחדא שגגה היא:

תוספות

כלל גדול. כל היודע עיקר שבת חייב על כל שבת ושבת כו'. פי' בקונטרס אע"פ שלא נודע לו בינתים אמרינן ימים שבינתים הוין ידיעה לחלק שאי אפשר שלא שמע בינתים שאותו יום שבת היה אלא שלא נזכר במלאכות וקשה לה"ר אליעזר דאמר בגמרא (לקמן דף עא.) קצר וטחן כגרוגרת בשגגת שבת וזדון מלאכות וחזר וקצר וטחן כגרוגרת בזדון שבת ושגגת מלאכות קצירה גוררת קצירה וטחינה גוררת טחינה פירוש ואינו חייב אלא אחת ובשבת אחת איירי דבשתי שבתות היה חייב שתים דימים שבינתים הוין ידיעה לחלק אלמא אע"פ שנודע לו קודם קצירה אחרונה שאותו יום שבת הוא דהא בזדון שבת קצר וטחן אפי' הכי לא הויא ידיעה וחשיב העלם אחד כיון שלא נודע לו שחטא שהרי סבור שהמלאכה מותר' וטעמא משום דכתיב או הודע אליו חטאתו שיהיה לו ידיעת חטא ועוד הקשה ריב"ס דבגמרא מפקינן לה מקרא ואי כדפי' בקונטרס שאי אפשר שלא נודע לו למה לן קרא ועוד קשה לר"י דתנן בפרק אמרו לו (כריתות דף טז.) א"ר עקיבא שאלתי את ר' אליעזר העושה מלאכות הרבה בשבתות הרבה מעין מלאכה כו' אמר ליה חייב על כל אחת ואחת ק"ו מנדה כו' ופליגי התם אמוראי בגמרא היכי בעי מיניה וקאמר בסוף שמעתא ולרב חסדא דאמר שגגת שבת וזדון מלאכות הוא דבעא מיניה אי ימים שבינתים הוין ידיעה לחלק או לא נדה מאי ימים שבינתים איכא ומשני שבא עליה וטבלה וראתה וחזר ובא עליה והתם אפילו איחרה כמה שנים ולא טבלה חשיב הכל העלם אחד אלא כשטבלה ימי היתר שבינתים אע"פ דלא ידע כמי שידע דמי ה"נ גבי שבת אע"פ שלא שמע ימי היתר שבינתים הוין ידיעה לחלק דגזרת הכתוב היא שתהא שמירה לכל שבת ותימה דהתם יליף רבי אליעזר שבת מנדה ואדרבה בשבת כתיב קרא ובנדה לא כתיב ונראה לר"י דהא דנפקא לן מקרא בגמרא היינו כרבי אליעזר ברבי שמעון דהתם דאמר לא כך שאלו רבי עקיבא לרבי אליעזר אלא הבא על הנדה והשיב לו רבי אליעזר דחייב על כל אחת ואחת ק"ו משבת:

עין משפט נר מצוה

צא א מיי' פי"א מהל' ע"ז הלכה ד סמג לאוין נא טוש"ע י"ד סימן קעט סעיף ג:

א ב מיי' פ"ז מהלכות שגגות הלכה ג:

ב ג שם הלכה ג:

רבינו חננאל

(כפסא) ת"ר נותנין בול של מלח לתוך הנר כדי שתאיר ותדליק. טיט וחרסית תחת הנר כדי שתמתין ותדליק. חמרא חייא לפום רבנן ותלמידיהון:

הדרן עלך במה אשה יוצאה

כלל גדול אמרו בשבת. אסיקנא

תורה אור השלם

א) וְאַתֶּם עֹזְבֵי יְיָ הַשְּׁכֵחִים אֶת הַר קָדְשִׁי הַעֹרְכִים לַגַּד שֻׁלְחָן וְהַמְמַלְאִים לַמְנִי מִמְסָךְ: [ישעיה סה, יא]

ב) הַנִּשְׁבָּעִים בְּאַשְׁמַת שֹׁמְרוֹן וְאָמְרוּ חֵי אֱלֹהֶיךָ דָּן וְחֵי דֶּרֶךְ בְּאֵר שָׁבַע וְנָפְלוּ וְלֹא יָקוּמוּ עוֹד: [עמוס ח, יד]

ג) כִּי תָצוּר אֶל עִיר יָמִים רַבִּים לְהִלָּחֵם עָלֶיהָ לְתָפְשָׂהּ לֹא תַשְׁחִית אֶת עֵצָהּ לִנְדֹּחַ עָלָיו גַּרְזֶן כִּי מִמֶּנּוּ תֹאכֵל וְאֹתוֹ לֹא תִכְרֹת כִּי הָאָדָם עֵץ הַשָּׂדֶה לָבֹא מִפָּנֶיךָ בַּמָּצוֹר: [דברים כ, יט]

מסורת הש"ס

א) [תוספתא פרק ח], ב) [שם פ"ז], ג) [בערוך ערך קבע איתא מקבעת ופי' כדאיתא ברש"י], ד) [תוספתא פרק ב], ה) כריתות טז., ו) פסחים ג.:

הגהות הב"ח

(א) גמרא שתתבשל מהרה אבל אסרו חכמים בשברי זכוכית: (ב) רש"י ד"ה המבקעת וכו' ואית דגרסי מקבעת כצ"ל ותיבת ביליס נמחק: (ג) בא"ד האפרוחים מחזרת הקליפות:

ליקוטי רש"י

גד גדי וסנוק לא. התגבר מזלי ואל תהי עייף. סינוק לשון עייפות [פסחים ג:]. העורכים לגד שלחן. שם עכו"ם העשוים על שם המזל ובלשון משנה יש גד גדי וסינוק לא [ישעיה סה, יא ועיין במהרש"א ח"א]. שכן עושין שמניחין שלחן ערוך במאכל ומשתה לשם אותה עבודה זרה שקורין גד [סנהדרין צב.]. חי אלהיך דן. אחד מן העגלים שהעמיד ירבעם בדן [עמוס ח, יד]. השוכח עיקר שבת. דסבור לא נכתבה שבת בתורה דהיינו העלם זה וזה בידו שגגת שבת ושגגת מלאכות. חטאת אחת. על כולן [דחדא] שגגה היא והתם ליכא למימר ימים שבינתיים הויין ידיעה דהא לא ידע לעולם עיקר שבת עד שילמוד. היודע עיקר שבת. שידע שארבעים אבות מלאכות אסורות בשבת אבל אינו יודע שהיום שבת דהיינו שגגת שבת וזדון מלאכות ועשה מלאכות הרבה בשבתות הרבה ולא נודע לו בינתיים שחטא. חייב על כל שבת ושבת. חטאת אחת משום דימים שבינתיים הויין ידיעה לענין שגגת שבת ואינו חייב על כל מלאכה ומלאכה של כל שבת ושבת דהא שגגת שבת וזדון מלאכות [אינו חייב אלא אחת] [כריתות טז:]. דלא אמרינן חדא שגגה אלא אמרינן ימים שבינתיים הויין ידיעה דדמי כמי שנודע לו בינתיים דשבת הוי והוי כעושה מלאכה אחת בכמה העלמות [שם.]. היודע שהוא שבת ועשה מלאכות הרבה בשבתות הרבה. ואותן שעשה בזו עשה בזו דשגג במלאכות הרבה כסבור מלאכה זו מותרת חייב על כל מלאכה ומלאכה על שבת [אחת] [שם:].

R' Chiya bar Huna now continues with those Emorite practices that *are* prohibited. The practices listed here are only some of those enumerated in the chapter of Emorite practices.

הָאוֹמֵר גַּד גַּדִּי – If ONE SAYS: "MAY MY CONSTELLATION *(GADI)* SHOW ME GOOD FORTUNE,[1] וְסָנוּק לֹא אַשְׁכִּי וּבוּשְׁכִּי – AND may it NOT BE WEARIED, NEITHER BY DAY NOR BY NIGHT" – יֵשׁ בּוֹ מִשּׁוּם דַּרְכֵי הָאֱמוֹרִי – THIS incantation IS prohibited BECAUSE OF the prohibition against following in THE WAYS OF THE EMORITES.

The Baraisa cites a dissenting opinion:

רַבִּי יְהוּדָה אוֹמֵר – R' YEHUDAH SAYS: גַּד אֵינוֹ אֶלָּא לְשׁוֹן עֲבוֹדָה זָרָה – *GAD* IS NONE OTHER THAN A TERM OF IDOL WORSHIP, שֶׁנֶּאֱמַר – AS IT IS STATED regarding certain Jews who worshiped idols: "הָעֹרְכִים לַגַּד שֻׁלְחָן" – *THOSE WHO SET A TABLE FOR GAD!*[2] Thus, this incantation is not merely an Emorite practice, it is a violation of the prohibition to call out in the name of an idol![3]

The Baraisa continues its list of proscribed Emorite practices: הוּא בִּשְׁמָהּ וְהִיא בִּשְׁמוֹ – If HE (a husband) is called by night WITH HER (his wife's) NAME, AND SHE is called WITH HIS NAME for the purposes of divination – יֵשׁ בּוֹ מִשּׁוּם דַּרְכֵי הָאֱמוֹרִי – THIS practice IS prohibited BECAUSE OF the prohibition against following in THE WAYS OF THE EMORITES.

דּוֹנוּ דָּנֵי – If one incants: "MAY MY BARRELS of wine BE STRENGTHENED *(DONU)*" – יֵשׁ בּוֹ מִשּׁוּם דַּרְכֵי הָאֱמוֹרִי – THIS incantation IS prohibited BECAUSE OF the prohibition against following in THE WAYS OF THE EMORITES.

R' Yehudah once again dissents:

רַבִּי יְהוּדָה אוֹמֵר – R' YEHUDAH SAYS: אֵין דָּן אֶלָּא לְשׁוֹן עֲבוֹדָה זָרָה – *DAN* IS NONE OTHER THAN A TERM OF IDOL WORSHIP, שֶׁנֶּאֱמַר – AS IT IS STATED regarding certain Jews who worshiped idols: "הַנִּשְׁבָּעִים בְּאַשְׁמַת שֹׁמְרוֹן וְאָמְרוּ חֵי אֱלֹהֶיךָ דָּן" – *THOSE WHO SWEAR BY THE INIQUITY OF SAMARIA, OR SAY, "BY THE LIFE OF YOUR GOD DAN!"*[4] This incantation is not merely one of the Emorite ways, it is a violation of the prohibition to call out in the name of an idol![5]

The Baraisa returns to its listing:

הָאוֹמֵר לְעוֹרֵב צְרַח – If ONE SAYS TO A RAVEN: "CROAK," וּלְעוֹרַבְתָּא שְׁרִיקִי וְהַחֲזִירִי לִי זַנְבֵיךְ לְטוֹבָה – OR TO A FEMALE RAVEN: "SHRIEK, AND TURN YOUR TAIL TO ME FOR my GOOD fortune" – יֵשׁ בּוֹ מִשּׁוּם דַּרְכֵי הָאֱמוֹרִי – THIS incantation IS prohibited BECAUSE OF the prohibition against following in THE WAYS OF THE EMORITES.[6]

הָאוֹמֵר שַׁחֲטוּ תַּרְנְגוֹל זֶה שֶׁקָּרָא עַרְבִית – If ONE SAYS: "SLAUGHTER THIS ROOSTER THAT CROAKED LIKE A RAVEN,[7] וְתַרְנְגוֹלֶת שֶׁקָּרְאָה גַּבְרִית – OR THIS HEN THAT CROWED LIKE A ROOSTER" – יֵשׁ בּוֹ מִשּׁוּם דַּרְכֵי הָאֱמוֹרִי – THIS practice IS prohibited BECAUSE OF the prohibition against following in THE WAYS OF THE EMORITES.[8]

אֶשְׁתֶּה וְאוֹתִיר אֶשְׁתֶּה וְאוֹתִיר – If one incants: "I WILL DRINK AND LEAVE OVER, I WILL DRINK AND LEAVE OVER," in the hope that his wine will thus be infused with blessing, so that only a small measure of it will slake one's thirst – יֵשׁ בּוֹ מִשּׁוּם דַּרְכֵי הָאֱמוֹרִי – THIS practice IS prohibited BECAUSE OF the prohibition against following in THE WAYS OF THE EMORITES.[9]

הַמְבַקַּעַת בֵּיצִים בַּכּוֹתֶל (והטח) בִּפְנֵי הָאֶפְרוֹחִים – If ONE BREAKS EGGSHELLS UPON A WALL BEFORE FLEDGLINGS so that they will not die[10] – יֵשׁ בּוֹ מִשּׁוּם דַּרְכֵי הָאֱמוֹרִי – THIS practice IS prohibited BECAUSE OF the prohibition against following in THE WAYS OF THE EMORITES.

וְהַמֵּגִיס בִּפְנֵי אֶפְרוֹחִים – If ONE STIRS BEFORE FLEDGLINGS so that they will not die – יֵשׁ בּוֹ מִשּׁוּם דַּרְכֵי הָאֱמוֹרִי – THIS practice IS prohibited BECAUSE OF the prohibition against following in THE WAYS OF THE EMORITES.

הַמְרַקֶּדֶת – If ONE DANCES before fledglings, וְהַמּוֹנָה שִׁבְעִים וְאֶחָד אֶפְרוֹחִין בִּשְׁבִיל שֶׁלֹּא יָמוּתוּ – OR if ONE COUNTS SEVENTY-ONE FLEDGLINGS so that they will not die[11] – יֵשׁ בּוֹ דַּרְכֵי הָאֱמוֹרִי – THESE practices ARE prohibited BECAUSE OF the

NOTES

1. Gad is an astrological sign (*Rashi* to *Isaiah* 65:11). [Believers in astrology held that one's fortune is dependant upon one's sign;] one thus incants so that his sign will favor him (*Rashi*).

2. *Isaiah* ibid. Gad was an idol named for the constellation Gad (*Rashi* ad loc.). It was worshiped by leaving a table set with food and drink (*Rashi, Sanhedrin* 92a ד״ה המשייר פתיתין). See *Sanhedrin* ibid.; see also *Nedarim* 56a and *Moed Katan* 27a with regard to עַרְסָא דְגַדָא; see also *Rama, Yoreh Deah* 178:3.

3. *Rashi.* One is generally forbidden to even mention the name of an idol (*Sanhedrin* 63b with *Rosh;* see *Exodus* 23:13 with *Ramban;* see *Yoreh Deah* 147:1). Although this rule does not apply to idols mentioned in Scripture (*Yoreh Deah* ibid. §4), such as Gad, this person is not merely mentioning Gad's name, but is actually calling out for Gad to help him, which is certainly prohibited!

4. *Amos* 8:14. *The iniquity of Samaria* refers to the golden calf placed by Yarovam ben Nevat, first king of the Ten Tribes, in Beis El (see *Radak* ad loc.). *Your god Dan* refers to the golden calf he placed in the tribal portion of Dan (*Rashi* ad loc.; see *I Kings* 12:28,29).

5. See above, note 3. [The words *donu* and *dan* are related. Thus, this incantation is actually a request that the idol Dan bestow good fortune upon one's wine barrels.]

6. Ravens were considered by the Emorites to be bearers of [evil] tidings; therefore, [if one hears a raven croak,] he incants thus so that it will augur well for him (*Rashi;* see *Tosefta* 7:3).

7. [Alternatively, the text reads עַרְבִית, *at night;* this incantantion thus translates as:] this rooster that crowed later than its fellows (*Rashi*). *Chidushei HaRan* translates: this rooster that crowed earlier at night than its fellows.

8. [These phenomena would strike fear into the hearts of the Emorites, since they run counter to the world's natural course (see *Taz, Yoreh Deah* 179:2). They therefore would slaughter birds that behaved in this perverse manner.]

The *Tur* and *Shulchan Aruch* (ibid. §3) rule that one is indeed forbidden to slaughter a bird for these reasons, in accordance with our Gemara. However, *Beis Yosef* (ibid.) notes that people customarily do slaughter hens that crow like roosters. The source for this custom is *R' Yehudah HeChasid,* who commanded his offspring [in his will §50] to follow this practice. *Beis Yosef* explains [from *Maharil* §111] that those who follow this custom rely upon the reading of the *Ramach,* whose version of our Gemara stated that each of the practices enumerated on this page is actually *not* prohibited as an Emorite practice (see this reading in *Chidushei HaRan* as well, quoting *Raah*). Thus, all of these practices are permitted. [According to this reading, R' Chiya bar Huna was differentiating between the practices listed in our Gemara, and the rest of the practices enumerated in the *Tosefta* – these are permitted, while those of the *Tosefta* are indeed prohibited (see *Beur HaGra* to *Yoreh Deah* ibid.; see above, 67a note 36).] *Rashi*'s reading, however, accords with the Gemara as we have it (see *Rashi* ד״ה יש בו משום דרכי האמורי; and above, 67a ד״ה כולהו אית בהו).

Rama (ibid.), however, states that the reason that those who customarily slaughter such hens are permitted to do so is because they do not say explicitly why they are slaughtering the hens, but simply announce that they will be slaughtered. In that case, the slaughter is permissible (see *Beur HaGra* ad loc., who takes sharp issue with this). *Taz* (ibid.) agrees with *Rama,* and even considers extending this reasoning to all Emorite practices. In a similar vein, *Shiltei Giborim* (to *Rif, Avodah Zarah* fol. 9a) writes that an act of conjuration and superstition is forbidden only if one states explicitly that he is performing it in accordance with a superstition. However, if one simply performs the act without stating why, it is permissible, as one is permitted to take action to avoid that which the world views as a danger (see *Mekor Chesed* §67, to *Tzavaas R' Yehudah HeChasid* §50 for further discussion and sources regarding this custom).

9. However, one is permitted to say to others, "May you drink and leave over, may you drink and leave over" (*Tosefta* 8:3), since he means this merely as a blessing (*Minchas Bikkurim* ad loc.; see Gemara below).

10. Alternatively: if one pierces eggshells and sets them into a wall before fledglings so that they will not die (*Rashi; Aruch* ערך קבע [א׳]).

11. See *Chasdei David* to *Tosefta* 7:9 for the supposed significance of the

האומר גד גדי וסנוק לא אשכי ובושכי יש בו משום דרכי האמורי ר' יהודה אומר גד אינו אלא לשון ע"ז שנאמר א) העורכים לגד שלחן הוא בשמה והיא בשמו יש בו משום דרכי האמורי א) דונו דני יש בו משום דרכי האמורי ר' יהודה אומר אין דן אלא לשון ע"ז שנאמר ב) הנשבעים באשמת שומרון ואמרו חי אלהיך דן האומר ב) לעורב צרח ולעורבתא שריקי והחזירי לי זנביך לטובה יש בו משום דרכי האמורי א האומר שחטו תרנגול זה שקרא ערבית ותרנגולת שקראה גברית יש בו משום דרכי האמורי אשתה ואותיר אשתה ואותיר יש בו משום דרכי האמורי ג) המבקעת ביצים בכותל (והטח) בפני האפרוחים יש בו משום דרכי האמורי והמגים בפני אפרוחים יש בו משום דרכי האמורי המרקדת והמונה שבעים ואחד אפרוחין בשביל שלא ימותו יש בו משום דרכי האמורי המרקדת לכותח והמשתקת לעדשים והמצווחת לגריסין יש בו משום דרכי האמורי המשתנת בפני קדירתה בשביל שתתבשל מהרה יש בו משום דרכי האמורי אבל נותנין קיסם של תות ושברי זכוכית בקדירה בשביל שתתבשל מהרה וחכמים אוסרין (א) בשברי זכוכית מפני הסכנה תנו רבנן ד) נותנין בול של מלח לתוך הנר בשביל שתאיר ותדליק ונותנין טיט וחרסית תחת הנר בשביל שתמתין ותדליק אמר רב זוטרא האי מאן דמיכסי שרגא דמשחא ומגלי נפטא קעבר משום ג) בל תשחית חמרא וחיי לפום רבנן אין בו משום דרכי האמורי מעשה ברבי עקיבא שעשה משתה לבנו ועל כל כוס וכוס שהביא אמר חמרא וחיי לפום רבנן חיי וחמרא לפום רבנן ולפום תלמידיהון:

הדרן עלך במה אשה

כלל ה) גדול אמרו בשבת ו) כל השוכח עיקר שבת ועשה מלאכות הרבה בשבתות הרבה אינו חייב אלא חטאת אחת היודע עיקר שבת ועשה מלאכות הרבה בשבתות הרבה חייב על כל שבת ושבת ג היודע שהוא שבת ועשה מלאכות הרבה בשבתות הרבה חייב על כל

רש"י

האומר גד גדי. התמזל מזלי: וסנוק לא. עיף אל תהי(ו): **אשכי** ובושכי. יום ולילה: יש בו משום דרכי האמורי. וכן בכולן עד סוף פירקא גרסינן הרי זה מדרכי האמורי וה"ג בתוספ': **הוא בשמה והיא** בשמו. הוא ואשתו מחליפין שמותיהן זה בזה בלילה משום ניחוש: דוני דני. התחזקו חביותי: דן. אינו חק האמורי אלא ע"ז ממש וחייב משום קורא בשם עבודת גלולים: **האומר לעורב צרח.** כשהוא קורא אומר לו כן מפני שהוא מבשר בשורות ולוחש לו לחש זה: **שקרא ערבית.** איחר יותר משאר חביריו ול"נ שקרא כעורב: **שקראה גברית.** כתרנגול כמו קרא גברא (יומא דף כ:): **אשתה ואותיר.** כדי שתהא ברכה מצויה ביינו: **המבקעת ביצים בכותל.** ואית דגרסי ביצים (ב) מקבעת לאחר שיצאו האפרוחים מחזרת (ג) הקליפות במקל וקובעתן בכותל לפניהם וזהו לנחש שלא ימותו: **המרקדת לכותח.** כשעושה כותח מרקדת לפניו והוא ניחוש שיתחזק: **המשתקת לעדשים.** כשנותנת בקדרה משתקת את כל העומדים כדי שיתבשלו ולגריסין מצווחת: ה"ג **אבל נותנין קיסם של תות.** מוריי"ר וחזק הוא כחומץ ומועיל לבשל ואין זה לנחש: ה"ג **אבל אסרו חכמים בשברי זכוכית.** אע"פ שמשום דרכי האמורי אין בו אסרו חכמים מפני הסכנה שלא יבלע: **בול של מלח.** מלא אגרוף מלח בשביל שתאיר ותדליק שאין זה ניחוש אלא מסייע ממש שהמלח נולל את השמן וימשך אחר הפתילה: **טיט וחרסית.** מצננין את השמן ואינו דולק מהר: **דמכסי שרגא דמשחא.** שעושה לו כיסוי למעלה ממהר לידלק: **נפטא.** כשמגלין אותו האור הולך ונמשך אליו ומבעיר: **חמרא וחיי.** כשמוזגין ונותנין כוס אומר כן לברכה בעלמא:

הדרן עלך במה אשה

כלל גדול. בגמרא מפרש אמאי קרי ליה גדול: **השוכח עיקר שבת.** כסבור אין שבת בתורה: **אינו חייב אלא חטאת אחת.** בגמרא (לקמן דף סט:) יליף לה שמירה אחת לשבתות הרבה ושמירה לכל שבת ושבת ומסתברא דכי כתיב שמירה אחת לשבתות הרבה כי האי גוונא כתיב דכולא חדא שגגה היא וקרבן אשוגג קאתי: **היודע עיקר שבת.** שיש שבת בתורה ונאסרו בה מלאכות: **ועשה מלאכות הרבה בשבתות הרבה.** על ידי שגגת שבת ששכח ששבת היום מדקתני סיפא היודע שהוא שבת מכלל דרישא בדאין יודע שהוא שבת ועשה מלאכות הרבה בשבתות הרבה בענין זה ולא נודע לו בינתים שחטא: **חייב על כל שבת ושבת.** חטאת אחת לכל שבת ואע"פ שלא נודע לו בינתים והעלם אחד הוא אמרינן ימים שבינתים הויין ידיעה לחלק שא"א שלא שמע בינתים שאותו היום היה שבת אלא שלא נזכר לו במלאכות שנעשו בו ושגגה קמייתא משום שבת הוא דהואי והא אתידע ליה ביני ביני הלכך כל חדא שבת חדא שגגה היא ומיהו על הרבה מלאכות שבכל שבת לא מיחייב אלא חדא דכולה שבת חדא שגגה דהא לא שגג אמלאכות דיודע הוא שהמלאכות אסורות אלא אשבת הוא דשגג: **היודע שהוא שבת ועשה מלאכות הרבה.** שלא ידע שהמלאכות הללו אסורות ועשאם כמה פעמים בכמה שבתות חייב על כל אב מלאכה חטאת אחת ואף על פי שחזר וכפלה בכמה שבתות כולה חדא שגגה היא דהא לא נודע לו בינתים ולענין שגגת שבת הוא דאיכא למימר ימים שבינתים הויין ידיעה לחלק אבל לענין שגגת מלאכות לא אמרו הכי דמשום הפסק ימים אין לו לדעת אלא אם כן ישב ועסק לפני חכמים בהלכות שבת ומיהו בחטאת אחת לא מיפטר על כל שבת דשגגה לאו בשבת הויא אלא במלאכות ושגגות טובא הוו לשבת אחת ובגמרא (לקמן דף ע.) יליף פעמים שהוא חייב על כל אחת ואחת ופעמים שאינו חייב אלא אחת על כל שבת ומסתברא דחיובא בזדון שבת ושגגת מלאכות דאיכא שגגות טובא ופטורא בשגגת שבת וזדון מלאכות דחדא שגגה היא:

אב

תוספות

כלל גדול. כל היודע עיקר שבת חייב על כל שבת ושבת כו'. פי' בקונטרס אע"פ שלא נודע לו בינתים אמרינן ימים שבינתים הויין ידיעה לחלק שאי אפשר שלא שמע בינתים שאותו יום שבת היה אלא שלא נזכר במלאכות וקשה לה"ר אליעזר דאמר בגמרא (לקמן דף עא.) קצר וטחן כגרוגרת בשגגת שבת וזדון מלאכות וחזר וקצר וטחן כגרוגרת בזדון שבת ושגגת מלאכות קצירה גוררת קצירה וטחינה גוררת טחינה פירוש ואינו חייב אלא אחת ובשבת אחת איירי דבשתי שבתות היה חייב שתים דימים שבינתים הויין ידיעה לחלק אלמא אע"פ שנודע לו קודם קצירה אחרונה שאותו יום שבת הוא דהא בזדון שבת קצר וטחן אפי' הכי לא הויא ידיעה וחשיב העלם אחד כיון שלא נודע לו שחטא שהרי סבור שהמלאכה מותר' וטעמא משום דכתיב או הודע אליו חטאתו שיהיה לו ידיעת חטא ועוד הקשה ריב"ם דבגמרא מפקינן לה מקרא ואי כדפי' בקונטרס שאי אפשר שלא נודע לו למה לן קרא ועוד קשה לר"י דתנן בפרק אמרו לו (כריתות דף טז.) א"ר עקיבא שאלתי את ר' אליעזר העושה מלאכות הרבה בשבתות הרבה מעין מלאכה כו' אמר ליה חייב על כל אחת ואחת ק"ו מנדה כו' ופליגי התם אמוראי בגמרא היכי בעי מיניה וקאמר בסוף שמעתא ולרב חסדא דאמר שגגת שבת וזדון מלאכות הוא דבעא מיניה אי ימים שבינתים הויין ידיעה לחלק או לא נדה מאי ימים שבינתים איכא ומשני שבא עליה וטבלה וראתה וחזר ובא עליה והתם אפילו איחרה כמה שנים ולא טבלה חשיב הכל העלם אחד אלא כשטבלה ימי היתר שבינתים אע"פ דלא ידע כמי שידע דמי ה"נ גבי שבת אע"פ שלא שמע ימי היתר שבינתים הויין ידיעה לחלק דגזרת הכתוב היא שתהא שמירה לכל שבת ותימה דהתם יליף רבי אליעזר שבת מנדה ואדרבה בשבת כתיב קרא ובנדה לא כתיב ונראה לר"י דהא דנפקא לן מקרא בגמרא היינו כרבי אליעזר ברבי שמעון דהתם דאמר לא כך שאלו רבי עקיבא לרבי אליעזר אלא הבא על הנדה והשיב לו רבי אליעזר דחייב על כל אחת ואחת ק"ו משבת:

צא א מיי' פי"א מהל' ע"ז הלכה ד סמג לאוין נא טוש"ע י"ד סימן קעט סעיף ג:

א ב מיי' פ"ז מהלכות שגגות הלכה ג:

ב ג שם הלכה ג:

רבינו חננאל

(כפסא) ת"ר נותנין בול של מלח לתוך הנר כדי שתאיר ותדליק. טיט וחרסית תחת הנר כדי שתמתין ותדליק. חמרא חייא לפום רבנן ותלמידיהון:

הדרן עלך במה אשה יוצאה

כלל גדול אמרו בשבת. אסיקנא

תורה אור השלם

א) וְאַתֶּם עֹזְבֵי יְיָ הַשְּׁכֵחִים אֶת הַר קָדְשִׁי הַעֹרְכִים לַגַּד שֻׁלְחָן וְהַמְמַלְאִים לַמְנִי מִמְסָךְ: [ישעיה סה, יא]

ב) הַנִּשְׁבָּעִים בְּאַשְׁמַת שֹׁמְרוֹן וְאָמְרוּ חֵי אֱלֹהֶיךָ דָּן וְחֵי דֶּרֶךְ בְּאֵר שָׁבַע וְנָפְלוּ וְלֹא יָקוּמוּ עוֹד: [עמוס ח, יד]

ג) כִּי תָצוּר אֶל עִיר יָמִים רַבִּים לְהִלָּחֵם עָלֶיהָ לְתָפְשָׂהּ לֹא תַשְׁחִית אֶת עֵצָהּ לִנְדֹּחַ עָלָיו גַּרְזֶן כִּי מִמֶּנּוּ תֹאכֵל וְאֹתוֹ לֹא תִכְרֹת כִּי הָאָדָם עֵץ הַשָּׂדֶה לָבֹא מִפָּנֶיךָ בַּמָּצוֹר: [דברים כ, יט]

מסורת הש"ס

א) [תוספתא פרק ח], ב) [שם פ"ז], ג) [בערוך ערך קבע איתא **מקבעת** ופי' כדאיתא ברש"י], ד) [תוספתא פרק ב], ה) כריתות טז., ו) פסחים ג.:

הגהות הב"ח

(א) **גמרא** שתתבשל מהרה אבל אסרו חכמים בשברי זכוכית: (ב) **רש"י** ד"ה המבקעת וכו' ואית דגרסי מקבעת כצ"ל ותיבת ביצים נמחק: (ג) **בא"ד** האפרוחים מחזרת הקליפות:

ליקוטי רש"י

גד גדי וסנוק לא. התגבר מזלי ואל תהי עייף. סינוק לשון עייפות [פסחים ג:]. **העורכים לגד שלחן.** שם עכו"ם העשוים על שם המזל ובלשון משנה יש גד גדי וסינוק לא [ישעיה סה, יא ועיין במהרש"א ח"א]. שכן עושין שמניחין שלחן ערוך במאכל ומשתה לשם אותה עבודה זרה שקורין גד [סנהדרין צב.]. **חי אלהיך דן.** אחד מן העגלים שהעמיד ירבעם בדן [עמוס ח, יד]. **השוכח עיקר שבת.** דסבור לא נכתבה שבת בתורה דהיינו העלם זה וזה בידו שגגת שבת ושגגת מלאכות. **חטאת אחת.** על כולן [דהדא] שגגה היא והתם ליכא למימר ימים שבינתיים הויין ידיעה דהא לא ידע לעולם עיקר שבת עד שילמוד. **היודע עיקר שבת.** שידע שארבעים אבות מלאכות אסורות בשבת אבל אינו יודע שהיום שבת דהיינו שגגת שבת וזדון מלאכות ועשה מלאכות הרבה בשבתות הרבה ולא נודע לו בינתיים שחטא. **חייב על כל שבת ושבת.** חטאת אחת משום דימים שבינתיים הויין ידיעה לענין שגגת שבת ואינו חייב על כל מלאכה ומלאכה של כל שבת ושבת דהא שגגת שבת וזדון מלאכות [אינו חייב אלא אחת] [כריתות טז:]. דלא אמרינן חדא שגגה אלא אמרינן ימים שבינתיים הויין ידיעה דדמי כמי שנודע לו בינתיים דשבת הוי והוי כעושה מלאכה אחת בכמה העלמות [שם.]. **היודע שהוא שבת ועשה מלאכות הרבה בשבתות הרבה.** ואותן שעשה בזו עשה בזו דשגג במלאכות הרבה כסבור מלאכה זו מותרת חייב על כל מלאכה ומלאכה על שבת [אחת] [שם:].

prohibition against following in THE WAYS OF THE EMORITES. הַמְרַקֶּדֶת לְכוּתָח – If [A WOMAN] DANCES BEFORE *KUTACH* so that its flavor will be strong,[12] וְהַמְשַׁתֶּקֶת לַעֲדָשִׁים – OR if [A WOMAN] SILENCES bystanders while placing LENTILS into a pot so that they will cook thoroughly, וְהַמְצַוַּוחַת לַגְּרִיסִין – OR if [A WOMAN] SHOUTS BEFORE a pot of BEANS so that they will cook thoroughly – יֵשׁ בּוֹ מִשּׁוּם דַּרְכֵי הָאֱמוֹרִי – THESE practices ARE prohibited BECAUSE OF the prohibition against following in THE WAYS OF THE EMORITES.

הַמַּשְׁתֶּנֶת בִּפְנֵי קְדֵירָתָהּ בִּשְׁבִיל שֶׁתִּתְבַּשֵּׁל מְהֵרָה – If [A WOMAN] URINATES BEFORE HER COOKPOT SO THAT [THE FOOD] WILL COOK QUICKLY – יֵשׁ בּוֹ מִשּׁוּם דַּרְכֵי הָאֱמוֹרִי – THIS practice IS prohibited BECAUSE OF the prohibition against following in THE WAYS OF THE EMORITES. אֲבָל נוֹתְנִין קֵיסָם שֶׁל תּוּת וְשִׁבְרֵי זְכוּכִית בַּקְּדֵירָה בִּשְׁבִיל שֶׁתִּתְבַּשֵּׁל מְהֵרָה – HOWEVER, ONE MAY PLACE A SPLINTER OF MULBERRY wood OR GLASS FRAGMENTS INTO A COOKPOT SO THAT [THE FOOD] WILL COOK QUICKLY, since this is not a superstition, but an actual method of speeding up cooking time.[13] וַחֲכָמִים אוֹסְרִין בְּשִׁבְרֵי זְכוּכִית מִפְּנֵי הַסַּכָּנָה – HOWEVER, THE SAGES FORBID the use of GLASS FRAGMENTS in the cookpot BECAUSE OF THE DANGER that one might come to swallow a shard of broken glass.

Having mentioned the practice of placing articles into the cookpot, the Gemara interrupts with a similar practice that is likewise not prohibited as an Emorite practice:

תָּנוּ רַבָּנָן – **The Rabbis taught in a Baraisa:** נוֹתְנִין בּוּל שֶׁל מֶלַח לְתוֹךְ הַנֵּר בִּשְׁבִיל שֶׁתָּאִיר וְתַדְלִיק – ONE MAY PLACE A FISTFUL OF SALT INTO A LAMP SO THAT IT WILL BURN more BRIGHTLY, since this is not a magical practice, but an actual method of gaining more light; וְנוֹתְנִין טִיט וְחַרְסִית תַּחַת הַנֵּר בִּשְׁבִיל שֶׁתַּמְתִּין וְתַדְלִיק – AND ONE MAY PLACE MUD OR CLAY BENEATH A LAMP SO THAT IT WILL BURN more SLOWLY, since this too is not a magical practice.[14]

Having mentioned this Baraisa, the Gemara teaches a law regarding a similar practice:

אָמַר רַב זוּטְרָא – **Rav Zutra said:** הַאי מַאן דִּמְכַסֵּי שְׁרָגָא דְּמִשְׁחָא – **A person who** needlessly **covers an oil lamp,** וּמְגַלֵּי נַפְטָא – **or** needlessly **uncovers a naphtha lamp,** thereby causing them to burn more quickly,[15] קָעָבַר מִשּׁוּם בַּל תַּשְׁחִית – **has transgressed** the command **not to destroy** useful possessions, since he caused fuel to be wasted.[16]

The Gemara continues with its quotation from the chapter of Emorite practices:

חַמְרָא וְחַיֵּי לְפוּם רַבָּנָן – If one offers a toast: "WINE AND LIFE TO THE MOUTHS OF THE RABBIS!" – אֵין בּוֹ מִשּׁוּם דַּרְכֵי הָאֱמוֹרִי – THIS practice IS NOT prohibited BECAUSE OF the prohibition against following in THE WAYS OF THE EMORITES, since it is merely meant as a blessing.[17]

The Baraisa cites an incident supporting this ruling:

מַעֲשֶׂה בְּרַבִּי עֲקִיבָא שֶׁעָשָׂה מִשְׁתֶּה לִבְנוֹ – AN INCIDENT took place WITH R' AKIVA IN WHICH HE PREPARED A FEAST FOR HIS SON, וְעַל כָּל כּוֹס וְכוֹס שֶׁהֵבִיא אָמַר – AND OVER EACH CUP THAT HE BROUGHT out, HE PROCLAIMED the following toast: חַמְרָא וְחַיֵּי לְפוּם רַבָּנָן – "WINE AND LIFE TO THE MOUTHS OF THE RABBIS, חַיֵּי וְחַמְרָא לְפוּם רַבָּנָן וּלְפוּם תַּלְמִידֵיהוֹן – LIFE AND WINE TO THE MOUTHS OF THE RABBIS AND TO THE MOUTHS OF THEIR STUDENTS!"[18] If R' Akiva uttered this toast, it obviously is not prohibited as an Emorite practice.

הדרן עלך במה אשה

WE SHALL RETURN TO YOU, BAMEH ISHAH

NOTES

number seventy-one.

12. [*Kutach* is a sauce or dip made of breadcrumbs and whey.] This charm and the ones that follow concern superstition in cooking practices; they therefore are addressed to women, who generally did the cooking (*Chasdei David, Tosefta* 7:7).

13. Mulberry wood is sharp as vinegar, and therefore speeds up the cooking process (*Rashi*).

14. Salt thins the oil, allowing it to be drawn more easily after the wick, and thus to burn more brightly. Mud and clay cool the oil, causing it to be drawn more slowly after the wick, and thus to burn for a longer period (*Rashi*).

[Our translation follows *Rashi;* however, this Baraisa is actually taught in the *Tosefta* (2:6) with regard to the Sabbath lamp. For the Sabbath lamp must be lit with fuel that will be drawn easily by a wick, so that it will burn brightly, and will not flicker (see above, 21a). Since salt causes the oil to be drawn more readily after the wick, it is proper to place it into the Sabbath lamp before the Sabbath (*Rambam, Shabbos* 5:7; *Tur* and *Rama, Orach Chaim* 264:2; see *Shulchan Aruch HaRav* 264:5). One places mud and clay beneath the Sabbath lamp so that it will continue burning well into the night (see *Tosefta*).

[Our Gemara cites this Baraisa to teach that although the brightness and longevity of this lamp may appear to have been achieved by magical means, it is actually not so, since these are in fact legitimate methods of increasing the brightness and duration of the flame.]

15. A cover causes the oil in a lamp to burn more quickly (*Rashi*). [This is because the cover contains the heat generated by the lamp; the extra warmth thins the oil, allowing it to be drawn more quickly.]

Naphtha is highly flammable. Therefore, when the cover is removed from a naphtha lamp, the fire on the wick jumps to the fuel, which abursts into flame, and is wasted (*Rashi*).

16. In describing the laws of warfare, the Torah writes (*Deuteronomy* 20:19): *When you besiege a city for many days to wage war against it to take it, you shall not destroy its trees.* The prohibition against destroying the trees actually applies at all times, and applies to the destruction of any useful article (*Rambam, Melachim* 6:8,10; see below, 129a, and *Kiddushin* 32a). Rav Zutra therefore says that one who wastes fuel has violated this command. This prohibition applies only if one destroys the article merely for the sake of destruction. If, however, one does so for a useful purpose (e.g. burning furniture when there is no other firewood), the destruction is permitted (*Shulchan Aruch HaRav, Hilchos Shemiras Guf V'Nefesh U'Bal Tashchis*). [Note that *Rambam* holds that the prohibition against destroying articles other than trees is of Rabbinic origin only; however, other Rishonim disagree.]

17. Which is itself a form of prayer (*Meiri*). Thus, says *Minchas Bikkurim* (to *Tosefta* 8:3), one is permitted to utter the customary toast of "To life!" over a beverage (see also *Midrash Tanchuma, Pikudei* §2 for the origin of this toast).

18. See *Maharsha* and *Mahadura Basra* for why R' Akiva reversed the order of "wine" and "life" in the two segments of his toast, and why only the second segment included a toast to the students.

Chapter Seven

Introduction

This chapter will list all of the *melachos* that are prohibited on the Sabbath. Before doing so, however, the first Mishnah explains the liability incurred for violating them בְּשׁוֹגֵג, *inadvertently* (*Chidushei HaRan*).

Deliberate violation of the Sabbath (מֵזִיד) is subject to the death penalty (*Exodus* 35:2, *Numbers* 15:35; Mishnah, *Sanhedrin* 66a). A court, however, may only impose this penalty if the act took place (a) in the presence of two valid witnesses, and (b) after the perpetrator had been warned by the witnesses of the transgression and its consequences. If either of these conditions is not met, the matter no longer falls under the jurisdiction of the court, but is subject to the Divine punishment known as *kares* (see *Exodus* 31:14).

An inadvertent violation [שׁוֹגֵג] of the Sabbath must be atoned for with a *chatas* offering. In general, though one is theoretically liable for each and every *melachah* he performs, one *chatas* offering suffices to atone for all inadvertent transgressions committed in a single lapse of awareness as a result of any one error. Where various violations resulted from different errors (e.g. one was unaware of the prohibition of several of the *melachos*), one is required to bring a separate *chatas* for every error that resulted in a violation.

There is one important qualification of this rule: A *chatas* offering can atone for all violations committed as a result of any one error only if they were committed without his ever having realized the error in the interim. If, however, one committed a violation inadvertently, then realized his error, and then again forgot the prohibition, any new violations committed as a result of this second episode of forgetfulness will necessitate a second *chatas*. This case is akin to committing two violations as a result of two different errors.

The law in regard to the Sabbath is somewhat more complicated. On the one hand, there is but one negative commandment against performing *melachah* on the Sabbath. On the other hand, the Gemara below (70a) will derive that there are instances in which each *av melachah* is treated as a separate prohibition, requiring its own *chatas*. Moreover, there are instances when even though a single *chatas* suffices for all the *melachos*, the violations of separate Sabbaths nevertheless require separate *chatas* offerings for each Sabbath. The first Mishnah of this chapter delineates the rules for when a single *chatas* suffices for all the violations of all Sabbaths, when a separate *chatas* is required for each Sabbath, and when a separate *chatas* is required for each category of *melachah*.

TERMS RELEVANT TO THIS CHAPTER

יְדִיעָה – awareness
הַעֲלָמָה – lapse of awareness
שִׁגְגַת שַׁבָּת – inadvertence with regard to the Sabbath
שִׁגְגַת מְלָאכָה – inadvertence with regard to the *melachos*
שׁוֹגֵג – inadvertent/inadvertent transgressor
מֵזִיד – deliberate/deliberate transgressor

עין משפט נר מצוה

צא א מיי׳ פי״א מהל׳ ע״ז הלכה ד סמג לאוין נא טוש״ע י״ד סימן קעט סעיף ג:
א ב מיי׳ פ״ז מהלכות שגגות הלכה ב:
ב ג שם הלכה ג:

רבינו חננאל

(כפסא) ת״ר נותנין בול של מלח לתוך הנר כדי שתאיר ותדליק. טיט וחרסית תחת הנר כדי שתמתין ותדליק. חמרא חייא לפום רבנן ותלמידיהון:

הדרן עלך במה אשה יוצאה

כלל גדול אמרו בשבת. אסיקנא

תורה אור השלם

א) וְאַתֶּם עֹזְבֵי יְיָ הַשְּׁכֵחִים אֶת הַר קָדְשִׁי הַעֹרְכִים לַגַּד שֻׁלְחָן וְהַמְמַלְאִים לַמְנִי מִמְסָךְ: [ישעיה סה, יא]

ב) הַנִּשְׁבָּעִים בְּאַשְׁמַת שֹׁמְרוֹן וְאָמְרוּ חֵי אֱלֹהֶיךָ דָּן וְחֵי דֶּרֶךְ בְּאֵר שָׁבַע וְנָפְלוּ וְלֹא יָקוּמוּ עוֹד: [עמוס ח, יד]

ג) כִּי תָצוּר אֶל עִיר יָמִים רַבִּים לְהִלָּחֵם עָלֶיהָ לְתָפְשָׂהּ לֹא תַשְׁחִית אֶת עֵצָהּ לִנְדֹּחַ עָלָיו גַּרְזֶן כִּי מִמֶּנּוּ תֹאכֵל וְאֹתוֹ לֹא תִכְרֹת כִּי הָאָדָם עֵץ הַשָּׂדֶה לָבֹא מִפָּנֶיךָ בַּמָּצוֹר: [דברים כ, יט]

גמרא

האומר גד גדי וסנוק לא אשכי ובושכי יש בו משום דרכי האמורי ר׳ יהודה אומר גד אינו אלא לשון ע״ז שנאמר א) העורכים לגד שלחן הוא בשמה והיא בשמו יש בו משום דרכי האמורי א) דונו דני יש בו משום דרכי האמורי ר׳ יהודה אומר אין דן אלא לשון ע״ז שנאמר ב) הנשבעים באשמת שומרון ואמרו חי אלהיך דן האומר ג) לעורב צרח ולעורבתא שריקי והחזירי לי זנביך לטובה יש בו משום דרכי האמורי א האומר שחטו תרנגול זה שקרא ערבית ותרנגולת שקראה גברית יש בו משום דרכי האמורי אשתה ואותיר אשתה ואותיר יש בו משום דרכי האמורי ג) המבקעת ביצים בכותל (והטח) בפני האפרוחים יש בו משום דרכי האמורי והמגים בפני אפרוחים יש בו משום דרכי האמורי המרקדת והמונה שבעים ואחד אפרוחין בשביל שלא ימותו יש בו משום דרכי האמורי המרקדת לכותח והמשתקת לעדשים והמצווחת לגריסין יש בו משום דרכי האמורי המשתנת בפני קדירתה בשביל שתתבשל מהרה יש בו משום דרכי האמורי אבל נותנין קיסם של תות ושברי זכוכית בקדירה בשביל שתתבשל מהרה וחכמים אוסרין (א) בשברי זכוכית מפני הסכנה תנו רבנן ד) נותנין בול של מלח לתוך הנר בשביל שתאיר ותדליק ונותנין טיט וחרסית תחת הנר בשביל שתמתין ותדליק אמר רב זוטרא האי מאן דמיכסי שרגא דמשחא ומגלי נפטא קעבר משום ג) בל תשחית חמרא וחיי לפום רבנן אין בו משום דרכי האמורי מעשה ברבי עקיבא שעשה משתה לבנו ועל כל כוס וכוס שהביא אמר חמרא וחיי לפום רבנן חיי וחמרא לפום רבנן ולפום תלמידיהון:

הדרן עלך במה אשה

כלל ה) גדול אמרו בשבת ו) כל השוכח עיקר שבת ועשה מלאכות הרבה בשבתות הרבה אינו חייב אלא חטאת אחת היודע עיקר שבת ועשה מלאכות הרבה בשבתות הרבה חייב על כל שבת ושבת ג היודע שהוא שבת ועשה מלאכות הרבה בשבתות הרבה חייב על כל

רש״י

האומר גד גדי. התמזל מזלי: וסנוק לא. עיף אל תהי׳): אשכי ובושכי. יום ולילה: יש בו משום דרכי האמורי. וכן בכולן עד סוף פירקא גרסינן הרי זה מדרכי האמורי וה״ג בתוספ׳: הוא בשמה והיא בשמו. הוא ואשתו מחליפין שמותיהן זה בזה בלילה משום ניחוש: דוני דני. התחזקו חביותי: דן. אינו חק האמורי אלא ע״ז ממש וחייב משום קורא בשם עבודת גלולים: האומר לעורב צרח. כשהוא קורא אומר לו כן מפני שהוא מבשר בשורות ולוחש לו לחש זה: שקרא ערבית. איחר יותר משאר חביריו ול״נ שקרא כעורב: שקראה גברית. כתרנגול כמו קרא גברא (יומא דף כ:): אשתה ואותיר. כדי שתהא ברכה מצויה ביינו: המבקעת ביצים בכותל. ואית דגרסי ביליס (ב) מקבעת לאחר שיצאו האפרוחים מחזרת (ג) הקליפות במקל וקובעתן בכותל לפניהם וזהו לנחש שלא ימותו: המרקדת לכותח. כשעושה כותח מרקדת לפניו והוא ניחוש שיתחזק: המשתקת לעדשים. כשנותנת בקדרה משתקת את כל העומדים כדי שיתבשלו ולגריסין מלוותת: ה״ג אבל נותנין קיסם של תות. מוריי״ר וחזק הוא כחומץ ומועיל לבשל ואין זה לנחש: ה״ג אבל אסרו חכמים בשברי זכוכית. אע״פ שמשום דרכי האמורי אין בו אסרו חכמים מפני הסכנה שלא יבלע: בול של מלח. מלא אגרוף מלח בשביל שתאיר ותדליק שאין זה ניחוש אלא מסייע ממש שהמלח נולל את השמן וימשך אחר הפתילה: טיט וחרסית. מלננין את השמן ואינו דולק מהר: דמכסי שרגא דמשחא. שעושה לו כיסוי למעלה ממהר לידלק: נפטא. כשמגלין אותו האור הולך ונמשך אליו ומבעיר: חמרא וחיי. כשמוזגין ונותנין כוס אומר כן לברכה בעלמא:

הדרן עלך במה אשה

כלל גדול. בגמרא מפרש אמאי קרי ליה גדול: השוכח עיקר שבת. כסבור אין שבת בתורה: אינו חייב אלא חטאת אחת. בגמרא (לקמן דף סט:) יליף לה שמירה אחת לשבתות הרבה ושמירה לכל שבת ושבת ומסתברא דכי כתיב שמירה אחת לשבתות הרבה כי האי גוונא כתיב דכולא חדא שגגה היא וקרבן אשוגג קאתי: היודע עיקר שבת. שיש שבת בתורה ונאסרו בה מלאכות: ועשה מלאכות הרבה בשבתות הרבה. על ידי שגגת שבת ששכח ששבת היום מדקתני סיפא היודע שהוא שבת מכלל דרישא בדאין יודע שהוא שבת ועשה מלאכות הרבה בשבתות הרבה בענין זה ולא נודע לו בינתים שחטא: חייב על כל שבת ושבת. חטאת אחת לכל שבת ואע״פ שלא נודע לו בינתים והעלם אחד הוא אמרינן ימים שבינתים הויין ידיעה לחלק שא״א שלא שמע בינתים שאותו היום הויא שבת אלא שלא נזכר לו במלאכות שנעשו בו ושגגה קמייתא משום שבת הוא דהואי והא אתידע ליה ביני ביני הלכך כל חדא שבת חדא שגגה היא ומיהו על הרבה מלאכות שבכל שבת לא מיחייב אלא חדא דכולה שבת חדא שגגה דהא לא שגג אמלאכות דיודע הוא שהמלאכות אסורות אלא אשבת הוא דשגג: היודע שהוא שבת ועשה מלאכות הרבה. שלא ידע שהמלאכות הללו אסורות ועשאם כמה פעמים בכמה שבתות חייב על כל אב מלאכה חטאת אחת ואף על פי שחזר וכפלה בכמה שבתות כולה חדא שגגה היא דהא לא נודע לו בינתים ולענין שגגת שבת הוא דאיכא למימר ימים שבינתים הויין ידיעה לחלק אבל לענין שגגת מלאכות לא אמרו הכי דמשום הפסק ימים אין לו לדעת אלא אם כן ישב ועסק לפני חכמים בהלכות שבת ומיהו בחטאת אחת לא מיפטר על כל שבת דשגגה לאו בשבת הויא אלא במלאכות ושגגות טובא הוו לשבת אחת ובגמרא (לקמן דף ע.) יליף פעמים שהוא חייב על כל אחת ואחת ופעמים שאינו חייב אלא אחת על כל שבת ומסתברא דחיובא בזדון שבת ושגגת מלאכות דאיכא שגגות טובא ופטורא בשגגת שבת וזדון מלאכות דחדא שגגה היא:

תוספות

כלל גדול. כל היודע עיקר שבת חייב על כל שבת ושבת כו׳. פי׳ בקונטרס אע״פ שלא נודע לו בינתים אמרינן ימים שבינתים הויין ידיעה לחלק שאי אפשר שלא שמע בינתים שאותו יום שבת היה אלא שלא נזכר במלאכות וקשה לה״ר אליעזר דאמר בגמרא (לקמן דף עא.) קצר וטחן כגרוגרת בשגגת שבת וזדון מלאכות וחזר וקצר וטחן כגרוגרת בזדון שבת ושגגת מלאכות קצירה גוררת קצירה וטחינה גוררת טחינה פירוש ואינו חייב אלא אחת ובשבת אחת איירי דבשתי שבתות היה חייב שתים דימים שבינתים הויין ידיעה לחלק אלמא אע״פ שנודע לו קודם קצירה אחרונה שאותו יום שבת הוא דהא בזדון שבת קצר וטחן אפי׳ הכי לא הויא ידיעה וחשיב העלם אחד כיון שלא נודע לו שחטא שהרי סבור שהמלאכה מותר׳ וטעמא משום דכתיב או הודע אליו חטאתו שיהיה לו ידיעת חטא ועוד הקשה ריב״ם דבגמרא מפקינן לה מקרא ואי כדפי׳ בקונטרס שאי אפשר שלא נודע לו למה לן קרא ועוד קשה לר״י דתנן בפרק אמרו לו (כריתות דף טז.) א״ר עקיבא שאלתי את ר׳ אליעזר העושה מלאכות הרבה בשבתות הרבה מעין מלאכה כו׳ אמר ליה חייב על כל אחת ואחת ק״ו מנדה כו׳ ופליגי התם אמוראי בגמרא היכי בעי מיניה וקאמר בסוף שמעתא ולרב חסדא דאמר שגגת שבת וזדון מלאכות הוא דבעא מיניה אי ימים שבינתים הויין ידיעה לחלק או לא נדה מאי ימים שבינתים איכא ומשני שבא עליה וטבלה וראתה וחזר ובא עליה והתם אפילו איחרה כמה שנים ולא טבלה חשיב הכל העלם אחד אלא כשטבלה ימי היתר שבינתים אע״פ דלא ידע כמי שידע דמי ה״נ גבי שבת אע״פ שלא שמע ימי היתר שבינתים הויין ידיעה לחלק דגזרת הכתוב היא שתהא שמירה לכל שבת ותימה דהתם יליף רבי אליעזר שבת מנדה ואדרבה בשבת כתיב קרא ובנדה לא כתיב ונראה לר״י דהא דנפקא לן מקרא בגמרא היינו כרבי אליעזר ברבי שמעון דהתם דאמר לא כך שאלו רבי עקיבא לרבי אליעזר אלא הבא על הנדה והשיב לו רבי אליעזר דחייב על כל אחת ואחת ק״ו משבת:

מסורת הש״ס

א) [תוספתא פרק ח], ב) [שם פ״ז], ג) [בערוך ערך קבע איתא מקבעת ופי׳ כדאיתא ברש״י], ד) [תוספתא פרק ב], ה) כריתות טז:, ו) פסחים ג.:

הגהות הב״ח

(א) גמרא שתתבשל מהרה אבל אסרו חכמים בשברי זכוכית: (ב) רש״י ד״ה המבקעת וכו׳ ואית דגרסי מקבעת כצ״ל ותיבת ביליס נמחק: (ג) בא״ד האפרוחים מחזרת הקליפות:

ליקוטי רש״י

גד גדי וסנוק לא. התגבר מזלי ואל תהי עייף. סינוק לשון עייפות [פסחים ג:]. **העורכים לגד שלחן.** שם עכו״ם העשוים על שם המזל ובלשון משנה יש גד גדי וסינוק לא [ישעיה סה, יא ועיין במהרש״א ח״א]. שכן עושין שמניחין שלחן ערוך במאכל ומשתה לשם אותה עבודה זרה שקורין גד [סנהדרין צב.]. **חי אלהיך דן.** אחד מן העגלים שהעמיד ירבעם בדן [עמוס ח, יד]. **השוכח עיקר שבת.** דסבור לא נכתבה שבת בתורה דהיינו העלם זה וזה בידו שגגת שבת ושגגת מלאכות. **חטאת אחת.** על כולן [דחדא] שגגה היא והתם ליכא למימר ימים שבינתיים הויין ידיעה דהא לא ידע לעולם עיקר שבת עד שילמוד. **היודע עיקר שבת.** שידע שארבעים אבות מלאכות אסורות בשבת אבל אינו יודע שהיום שבת דהיינו שגגת שבת וזדון מלאכות ועשה מלאכות הרבה בשבתות הרבה ולא נודע לו בינתיים שחטא. **חייב על כל שבת ושבת.** חטאת אחת משום דימים שבינתיים הויין ידיעה לענין שגגת שבת ואינו חייב על כל מלאכה ומלאכה של כל שבת ושבת דהא שגגת שבת וזדון מלאכות [אינו חייב אלא אחת] [כריתות טז:]. דלא אמרינן חדא שגגה אלא אמרינן ימים שבינתיים הויין ידיעה דדמי כמי שנודע לו בינתיים דשבת הוי והוי כעושה מלאכה אחת בכמה העלמות [שם.]. **היודע שהוא שבת ועשה מלאכות הרבה בשבתות הרבה.** ואותן שעשה בזו עשה בזו דשגג במלאכות הרבה כסבור מלאכה זו מותרת חייב על כל מלאכה ומלאכה על שבת [אחת] [שם:].

Chapter Seven

Mishnah The Mishnah delineates the rule for determining how many *chatas* offerings one is liable to for multiple inadvertent transgressions of the Sabbath:

כְּלָל גָּדוֹל אָמְרוּ בְּשַׁבָּת – **[The Sages] stated a major rule concerning the Sabbath:**[1] כָּל הַשּׁוֹכֵחַ עִיקַּר שַׁבָּת – **Anyone who forgets the essence of the Sabbath**[2] וְעָשָׂה מְלָאכוֹת הַרְבֵּה בְּשַׁבָּתוֹת הַרְבֵּה – **and** as a result **performed many *melachos* on many Sabbaths** אֵינוֹ חַיָּיב אֶלָּא חַטָּאת אַחַת – **is liable to but one *chatas*** offering for all the *melachos* that he performed.[3]

הַיּוֹדֵעַ עִיקַּר שַׁבָּת – **One who knows the essence of the Sabbath**[4] וְעָשָׂה מְלָאכוֹת הַרְבֵּה בְּשַׁבָּתוֹת הַרְבֵּה – **and** inadvertently **performed many *melachos* on many Sabbaths**[5] חַיָּיב עַל כָּל שַׁבָּת וְשַׁבָּת – **is liable to** a separate *chatas* offering **for each and every Sabbath** that he desecrated.[6]

הַיּוֹדֵעַ שֶׁהוּא שַׁבָּת – **One who knows it is the Sabbath,** וְעָשָׂה מְלָאכוֹת הַרְבֵּה בְּשַׁבָּתוֹת הַרְבֵּה – **and** inadvertently **performed many *melachos* on many Sabbaths,**[7] חַיָּיב עַל כָּל – **is liable for each and every**

NOTES

1. The Gemara will explain why this rule is called "major" (*Rashi*). The Mishnah proceeds to list the various errors a person can make about Sabbath law, and the resulting number of *chatas* offerings he is required to bring in each case.

2. I.e. he was not aware that the Torah has a law regarding the Sabbath (*Rashi*).

3. The Gemara below deduces from Scripture that under certain circumstances a person is liable to only one *chatas* offering for all the violations performed on several Sabbaths, whereas sometimes he is liable to a separate *chatas* for the violations of *each* Sabbath. Since a *chatas* is required only for an inadvertent transgression – i.e. a transgression resulting from error [see Chapter Introduction], logic dictates that the differing requirements of the verses relate to the number of errors that caused the transgressions. Thus, it is logical to assume that the verse that requires only one *chatas* for all the transgressions performed on several Sabbaths refers to a case where all the violations resulted from the person's unawareness of a *single* fact – the existence of Sabbath law (*Rashi*).

4. I.e. he knew that the Torah contains the Sabbath law, according to which various types of labor [the *melachos*] are prohibited on the Sabbath (*Rashi*).

5. Losing track of the calendar, he performed *melachos* on the Sabbath, thinking it was a weekday. He then repeated this mistake on subsequent Sabbaths without ever realizing his transgression during the intervening weekdays (*Rashi*).

[Although the Mishnah does not explicitly say that this was the cause of his error, it is evident from the next case of the Mishnah that this is so. For the Mishnah prefaces that case by saying that he knew it was the Sabbath day, implying that in the previous case he did not know (*Rashi*).]

6. Since it is highly unlikely for a person to go through an entire week without discovering what day of the week it really is, the law presumes that the person did in fact realize his mistaken calculation at some time during the intervening week but forgot again before the next Sabbath. Therefore, even though his realization did not bring with it a realization that he had been guilty of desecrating the Sabbath (because when he recognized that he had erred concerning the day of the week he did not remember having performed *melachah* on the day that was actually the Sabbath), he is still obligated to bring a separate *chatas* for each Sabbath on which he performed *melachah*. Since his initial mistake was a miscalculation of the calendar day, and this was presumably corrected some time during the week, the desecration on the next Sabbath is considered a new mistake, requiring its own *chatas*. It is in such a case that Scripture requires a separate *chatas* for each Sabbath desecrated (*Rashi; cf. Tosafos;* we have explained *Rashi's* view in accord with *Pnei Yehoshua* and *Maginei Shlomo;* see also *Even HaOzeir* at length; cf. *Chasam Sofer* and *Sfas Emes* for a different understanding of *Rashi's* view).

Nevertheless, the person is liable to only one *chatas* per Sabbath, even though he performed numerous *melachos* on each Sabbath. This is because his *chatas* liability is tied to his inadvertence, and in this case he knew that the *melachos* were forbidden on the Sabbath and erred in regard to only a single matter – the identity of the day (*Rashi*).

7. This refers to one who knew the general law of Sabbath, and also knew that it was the Sabbath day but, forgetting that certain types of labor are prohibited, inadvertently performed those *melachos* on several different Sabbaths (*Rashi*).

הָעוֹשֶׂה מְלָאכוֹת הַרְבֵּה מֵעֵין מְלָאכָה אַחַת – If **one performs many *melachos* of one** category of ***melachah,***[2] אֵינוֹ חַיָּיב אֶלָּא חַטָּאת אַחַת – **he is liable to only one *chatas.***[3]

אַב מְלָאכָה וּמְלָאכָה – ***av melachah*** that he performed.[1]

Gemara

The Gemara examines the introductory statement of the Mishnah:

מַאי טַעְמָא תָּנָא כְּלָל גָּדוֹל – **Why did [the Tanna] teach** that this is **"a major rule"?**[4]

The Gemara suggests one possible answer and notes a difficulty with it:

אִילֵימָא מִשּׁוּם דְּקָבָעֵי לְמִיתְנֵי עוֹד כְּלָל אַחֵר – **If you say that because [the Tanna] wanted to teach another,** less complex **rule** in the Mishnah below, תָּנָא כְּלָל גָּדוֹל – **he taught** the more complex rule here as **a "major rule";**[5] וְגַבֵּי שְׁבִיעִית נַמִּי – **and regarding *sheviis* as well,**[6] מִשּׁוּם דְּקָבָעֵי לְמִיתְנֵי עוֹד כְּלָל אַחֵר – where **because [the Tanna] wanted to teach another,** less complex **rule** in the next Mishnah,[7] תָּנָא כְּלָל גָּדוֹל – **he taught** the first one as **a "major rule";**[8] וְהָא גַּבֵּי מַעֲשֵׂר דְּקָתָנֵי כְּלָל אַחֵר – this cannot be the reason, **for in regard to *maaser*, where [the Tanna]** also **taught another rule** following a first rule, וְלֹא תָּנֵי כְּלָל גָּדוֹל – **he nevertheless did not teach** the first one as **a "major rule."**[9] Apparently, then, it is not the style of the Mishnah to refer to a rule as "major" simply because a less complex rule will be taught afterwards.

The Gemara therefore suggests another reason why the rule in our Mishnah is called "major":

אָמַר רַבִּי יוֹסֵי בַּר אָבִין – **R' Yose bar Avin said:** שַׁבָּת וּשְׁבִיעִית – In regard to the **Sabbath and *sheviis,*** דְּאִית בְּהוּ אָבוֹת וְתוֹלָדוֹת – **which have in them** both ***avos* and *tolados*** as part of their prohibitions,[10] תָּנָא כְּלָל גָּדוֹל – **[the Tanna] teaches** the rule as a **"major** rule."[11] מַעֲשֵׂר דְּלֵית בָּהּ אָבוֹת וְתוֹלָדוֹת – However, in regard to ***maaser,* which does not have in its** regulations ***avos* and *tolados,*** לֹא תָּנָא כְּלָל גָּדוֹל – **[the Tanna] did not teach** the rule as a **"major** rule."[12]

The Gemara rejects this explanation:

וּלְבַר קַפָּרָא – **But according to Bar Kappara,** דְּתָנֵי כְּלָל גָּדוֹל בְּמַעֲשֵׂר – **who taught** in his Baraisa the rule **regarding *maaser***

NOTES

1. I.e. he is obligated to bring a separate *chatas* for each of the thirty-nine categories of *melachah* that he violated. Though he may have violated one particular category numerous times and over several Sabbaths, he is nevertheless obligated to bring only one *chatas* to atone for all violations of that one category. Any violation, however, falling under a different category, though it may have occurred only once, necessitates a separate *chatas* (*Rashi*). [Although the term *av melachah* usually refers to a *primary labor,* in contrast to a *toladah, derivative labor,* it is here used in the sense of the category it represents rather than the specific activity it is (*Rashi*).]

This ruling is based on an exposition the Gemara makes below (70a), teaching that under certain circumstances a person is liable to bring separate *chatas* offerings for each *melachah* he performed, whereas at other times he is liable to only one *chatas* for numerous *melachos.* Logic dictates that the difference between the two verses be understood on the basis of the number of errors that contributed to the repetition of the transgressions. Thus, if the person performed numerous *melachos* unaware that it was the Sabbath, all his actions are the result of *one* error; we therefore apply to this case the verse that teaches that one is liable to only one *chatas* for numerous *melachos.* But if a person is aware of the Sabbath day but is unaware of various specific laws involved, he cannot blame his different violations on one flaw in his knowledge. Each category of *melachah* of which he is unaware represents a separate piece of incognizance. We therefore apply to this case the verse that teaches that one is liable to a *chatas* for each *melachah.* This person must therefore bring a separate *chatas* for each *category* of *melachah* he violated.

Nevertheless, he is liable to only one *chatas* per category despite the fact that he performed that *melachah* numerous times over many Sabbaths. For in regard to *this* issue, all his violations are the result of a *single* error – his lack of knowledge of the law of that *melachah.* Nor can it be argued that the days between one Sabbath and the next should create a presumption of awareness, as it does in the previous case of one who forgot the Sabbath day (see 67b note 6). Only when an error is chronological in nature can the passage of time be presumed to have corrected the error. This is because in the normal course of events one *will* likely discover which day of the week it really is. Where, however, one's error is due to a lack of Torah knowledge (i.e. he did not know certain laws of the Sabbath), there is no way for time alone to correct the error. This can be done only through study of the Sabbath laws, and there is no reason to assume that one has studied the Sabbath laws during the intervening week. Since we can make no presumption of an awareness of error having taken place between one Sabbath and the next, all violations are attributed to a single lack of knowledge and one *chatas* suffices (*Rashi*).

2. I.e. he performed an *av* and its *toladah,* or two *tolados* of one *av,* without becoming aware of his error in the interim (*Rashi*).

3. A person who repeatedly transgresses a single prohibition during one period of forgetfulness is liable to only one *chatas.* All the *tolados* of an *av melachah* are considered part of the same prohibition – that category of *melachah.* Hence, one is liable to only one *chatas* for all the transgressions he performed in that one category of *melachah* (*Rashi*). Different categories of *melachah,* however, are treated as different prohibitions. Thus, one who performs two different *melachos* because he is unaware of their laws is liable to two *chataos* – even if he performed both acts in a single period of forgetfulness.

4. The Mishnah should have merely stated that a rule was taught about the Sabbath laws. Why does it call the rule "major"?

5. In a Mishnah below (75b), the Tanna states another rule, which includes only two details. Since the rule of our Mishnah includes more details, our Mishnah calls its rule "major" (*Rashi*).

6. Every seventh year is observed as a Sabbatical year (called *shemittah* or *sheviis*). During the Sabbatical year, it is forbidden to cultivate the land of Eretz Yisrael; crops that grow on their own become sanctified and subject to various restrictions. The seventh chapter of Tractate *Sheviis* discusses what growths are subject to these *sheviis* laws. The first Mishnah there begins: כְּלָל גָּדוֹל אָמְרוּ בַּשְּׁבִיעִית, *A major rule was stated concerning sheviis.* The Gemara now explains why that Mishnah too calls its rule "major."

7. The next Mishnah in *Sheviis* (7:2) begins: וְעוֹד כְּלָל אַחֵר אָמְרוּ, *And furthermore, another rule was stated.*

8. There too the first Mishnah includes more details than the second. This justifies the use of the term "major" to refer to the rule in the first Mishnah (*Tosafos; Ramban, Rashba;* see further in *Sfas Emes*).

9. Tractate *Maasros* discusses the obligation to tithe produce grown in Eretz Yisrael. In the first Mishnah there the Tanna states two rules – the first of which contains more details than the second – without calling the first one "major" (see *Sfas Emes* in explanation of *Rashi;* cf. *Tosafos*).

10. The Sabbath laws contain thirty-nine *avos,* acts that were needed to construct the Mishkan in the Wilderness, as well as numerous *tolados,* acts that are similar in nature to the *avos* [and which are also Biblically prohibited]. Similarly, *sheviis* law consists of four activities explicitly prohibited in the Torah – sowing, reaping [grain], pruning and picking [grapes] – which are referred to as its *avos.* There are, however, related activities of the field and vineyard that are also prohibited during *sheviis;* these are called *tolados,* as taught in *Moed Katan* 3a (*Rashi*).

[Although Rava states there that the *tolados* of *sheviis* are not prohibited at the Biblical level, nevertheless, in Rabbinic law, at least, *sheviis* does contain both *avos* and *tolados* (*Tosafos*).]

11. [Due to the complexity of prohibitions having *avos* and *tolados,* the Tanna refers to the rules of the Sabbath and *sheviis* as "major."] Having referred to the first rule listed in each of these tractates as a "major rule," the Tanna saw no reason to repeat this designation in the second rule of each of these tractates, since the second rule is in each case labeled "another rule," i.e. another rule of the same type as the first (*Tosafos*).

12. [I.e., it is not sufficiently complex to be called "major."]

אב מלאכה ומלאכה (א) [א]העושה מלאכות הרבה מעין מלאכה אחת אינו חייב אלא חטאת אחת:

גמ' מ"ט תנא כלל גדול אילימא משום דקבעי למיתני עוד כלל אחר תנא כלל גדול וגבי שביעית נמי משום דקבעי למיתני עוד כלל אחר תנא כלל גדול והא גבי מעשר דקתני (א) כלל אחר ולא תני כלל גדול א"ר יוסי בר אבין שבת ושביעית דאית בהו אבות ותולדות תנא גדול מעשר דלית בה אבות ותולדות לא תנא כלל גדול ולבר קפרא דתני כלל גדול במעשר מאי אבות ומאי תולדות איכא אלא לאו היינו טעמא גדול עונשו של שבת יותר משל שביעית דאילו שבת איתא בין בתלוש בין במחובר ואילו שביעית בתלוש ליתא במחובר איתא וגדול עונשה של שביעית יותר מן המעשר דאילו שביעית איתא בין במאכל אדם בין במאכל בהמה ואילו מעשר במאכל אדם איתא במאכל בהמה ליתא ולבר קפרא דתני כלל גדול במעשר גדול עונשו של מעשר יותר משל פיאה דאילו מעשר איתא בתאנה וירק ואילו פיאה ליתא בתאנה וירק [ב]דתנן כלל אמרו בפיאה כל שהוא אוכל ונשמר וגידולו מן הארץ ולקיטתו כאחת ומכניסו לקיום חייב בפיאה אוכל למעוטי ספיחי סטים וקוצה ונשמר למעוטי הפקר וגידולו מן הארץ למעוטי כמיהין ופטריות ולקיטתו כאחת ° למעוטי תאנה ומכניסו לקיום למעוטי ירק ואילו גבי מעשר תנן [ג] כלל אמרו במעשר כל שהוא אוכל ונשמר וגידולו מן הארץ חייב במעשר ואילו לקיטתו כאחת ומכניסו לקיום לא תנן: רב ושמואל דאמרי תרוייהו מתניתין בתינוק שנשבה לבין הנכרים וגר שנתגייר לבין הנכרים אבל הכיר ולבסוף שכח חייב על כל שבת ושבת תנן השוכח עיקר שבת לאו מכלל דהויא ליה ידיעה מעיקרא לא מאי כל השוכח עיקר שבת דהיתה שכוח ממנו עיקרה של שבת אבל הכיר ולבסוף שכח מאי חייב על כל שבת ושבת אדתני היודע עיקר שבת ועשה מלאכות הרבה בשבתות הרבה חייב על כל שבת ושבת ליתני הכיר ולבסוף שכח וכ"ש הא מאי היודע עיקר שבת מי שהיה יודע עיקרה של שבת ושכחה אבל

רש"י

אב מלאכה דנקט לאו למעוטי תולדות דה"ה לתולדות ובלבד שיהו תולדות דשני אבות אלא למעוטי היכא דהוו ב' תולדות דאב אחד או אב ותולדה שלו דאינו חייב אלא אחת כדקתני סיפא העושה מלאכות הרבה מעין מלאכה אחת שתי תולדות של אב אחד אינו חייב אלא חטאת אחת דהרי הוא כעושה וחוזר ועושה בהעלם אחד ואין חילוק חטאות בהעלם אחד אלא בגופי עבירה שאינן דומין או בחילוק שבתות לענין שגגת שבת: גמ' עוד כלל אחר. לקמן בפירקין (דף עה:) ולא כלל בו אלא ב' דברים כל הכשר להצניע וכל שאינו כשר להצניע וכאן כלל יותר ומשום הכי קרי להו גדול: וגבי שביעית. בפרק [ד] (בנות שוח): גבי מעשר. בפ"ק דמסכת מעשרות: אית ביה אבות. ארבעים חסר אחת שהוצרכו למשכן ותולדות הדומות לכל אחת הויא תולדות דידיה אבות דשביעית זריעה וקצירה וזמירה ובצירה דכתיבן תולדות שאר עבודות שבשדה וכרם כדאמרינן במועד קטן בפ"ק (דף ג.): ולבר קפרא דתנא. בתוספתא דידיה במעשר מאי אבות כו': אלא לאו היינו טעמא. משום אבות ותולדות אלא דבר שנאמר בו כלל ועונשו גדול מדבר אחר שנאמר בו כלל תני ביה כלל גדול: שבת איתא. לאיסור דידה בין בדבר שהיה תלוש מבעוד יום כגון טוחן ולש בין בדבר שמחובר משקדש היום: ואילו שביעית. בדבר שהיה מחובר משקדשה שביעית איתא אבל בדבר שהיה תלוש לפני שביעית ליתא: שביעית. נמי איתיה במאכל בהמה דכתיב ולבהמתך ולחיה וגו' (ויקרא כה) מעשר ליתיה במאכל בהמה דמדאורייתא דגן תירוש ויצהר כתיב ורבנן תקון פירות האילן וירק דמאכל אדם כדקתני כל שהוא אוכל כו': איתיה בתאנה וירק. מדרבנן: כל שהוא אוכל כו'. דגבי פיאה קציר כתיב מה קציר מיוחד שיש בו כל אלו: למעוטי ספיחי סטים וקוצה. שעומדים לצבע להכי נקט ספיחים דאין דרך ללוקטן בשנה שמזרעים אלא לסוף ד' וה' שנים שהשרשין מתפשטין בארץ ומשביחין ושורש שלהן עיקר והא דנקט הני ולא נקט שאר מינים שאינן ראוין לאכילה משום דאיידי דגבי שביעית תני להו דיש להן שביעית נקט הכא דבפיאה ומעשר ליתנהו לשון רבינו הלוי. סטים ווישד"א קול' וורנצ"א: ומכניסו לקיום למעוטי ירק. כגון לפת וקפלוטות: ואילו מכניסו לקיום ולקיטתו כאחד לא תנן. דכי תקון רבנן אדידהו לא פלוג בפירות האילן ובירק בין מין למין:

מתניתין. דפטר בחד חטאת: בתינוק שנשבה. ולא ידע שבת מעולם: אבל הכיר ולבסוף שכח. הוה ליה כשוכח שהיום שבת ויודע עיקר שבת וחייב על כל שבת ושבת: שהיתה שכוחה ממנו. מעולם: לתני הכיר ולבסוף שכח. דחייב ואע"ג דליכא למימר ימים שבינתים הווין ידיעה לחלק וכ"ש הא דאיכא למימר שימים שבינתים הווין ליה ידיעה לחלק:

תוספות

וגבי שביעית נמי כו'. הכי תנן בשביעית (פ"ז מ"א) כלל גדול אמרו כל שהוא מאכל אדם ומאכל בהמה וממין הצובעין ואינו מתקיים בארץ פירות שכלה לחיה יש לו שביעית ולדמיו שביעית יש לו ביעור ולדמיו ביעור ועוד כלל אחר אמרו דקתני כל שאינו מאכל אדם ומאכל בהמה וכו' ומתקיים בארץ יש לו שביעית ולדמיו שביעית ואין לו ולדמיו ביעור דכלל הראשון גדול דיש לו ביעור ואחרון אין לו ביעור ואע"ג דקתני התם בבבא אחריתא כלל גדול אמרו בשביעית ולא קתני בתריה כלל אחר כיון דקתני כלל קטן קמיה שייך למתני בתריה כלל גדול: והא גבי מעשר דקתני עוד כלל אחר אמרו כו'. תימה למה ישנה בראשון כלל גדול כיון דאינו גדול מן השני וצ"ע: דאית ביה אבות ותולדות. ואפילו לרבא דאמר במועד קטן (דף ג:) גבי שביעית אבות אסר רחמנא תולדות לא אסר רחמנא מ"מ מדרבנן מיהא אית ביה אבות ותולדות וא"ת במעשר איכא נמי אבות ותולדות דמדאורייתא דגן ותירוש ויצהר ומדרבנן כל מילי וי"ל דלא שייך להזכיר אבות ותולדות במילי דלית ביה איסור מלאכות וא"ת ובכלל אחר דשבת ושביעית ליתני נמי כלל גדול מהאי טעמא ויש לומר דלא צריך למיתני דאכלל גדול קמא קאי וה"ק עוד כלל גדול אחר אמרו: גדול עונשו של שבת משל שביעית. לפירוש הקונטרס דמפרש בתלוש שנתלש קודם שבת וקודם שביעית משמע שרוצה לפרש שביעית במחובר איתא היינו במחובר ערב שביעית ונתלש בשביעית ומיירי באיסור פירות שביעית לאכילה וקשה לר"י דלפי' לא הוה ליה למימר אלא גדול עונשו של שבת ושביעית משל מעשר דאיתנהו במאכל בהמה מה שאין כן במעשר ולמה ליה למימר כלל גדול עונשה של שבת משל שביעית אלא נראה לר"י דבמידי דאכילה דלא שייכא לענין שבת לא שייך למימר גדול שבת לא משביעית ולא ממעשר ולהכי לא קאמר גדול שבת ושביעית ממעשר אלא קאמר גדול שבת משביעית דאיסור מלאכות איתנהו בין בתלוש בין במחובר ואילו איסור מלאכות דשביעית במחובר איתא בתלוש ליתא וכן משמע בירושלמי דקתני שהשבת חלה על הכל ושביעית לא חלה אלא על עבודת הארץ בלבד: ולבר קפרא דתני כלל גדול במעשר כו'. נראה לרשב"א דאחרים לא שנו כלל גדול במעשר לפי שאינו גדול מפאה אלא מדרבנן אבל כלל גדול דשבת גדול משביעית מדאורייתא וכן של שביעית משל מעשר: ואילו פאה ליתא בתאנה וירק. לאו דוקא תאנה דהא רוב אילנות אין לקיטתן כאחד ואין רק ה' אילנות דחשיב בפ"ק דפאה (מ"ה) דחייב בפאה אלא נקט תאנה משום דנלקטת כמה פעמים כדאמרינן בחזקת הבתים (ב"ב דף כח:) אכל ג' פירי בחד יומא כגון תאנה כו' ואומר ר"ת דמדאורייתא לא מחייב בפאה אלא בדגן ותירוש ויצהר דסתם קציר דכתיב גבי פאה הוא דגן וכתיב כי תחבוט זיתך כי תבצור כרמך והא דדריש בת"כ יכול שאני מרבה קישואין ודלועין שיהיו חייבים בפאה ת"ל ובקוצרכם את קציר ארצכם מה קציר שהוא אוכל ונשמר כו' אסמכתא היא דהתם נמי דריש מעשר ירק מקרא אע"ג דהוי מדרבנן ומה שלא תקנו פאה בירק ובתאנה ודדמי לה כמו שתקנו מעשר מהן אומר ר"ת משום דאין לקיטתן כאחד דבר מועט הוא פאה דידיה ויש הפסד לעניים בה יותר מן הריוח שמתבטלין לפי שאין יודעים זמן לקיטתן ודבר שאין מכניסו לקיום נמי לא חשיב ויפסידו יותר ממה שירויחו במקום אחר: ספיחי סטים וקוצה. הא דלא קאמר סתם למעוטי מידי דלאו אוכל אלא נקט הני אומר ר"י משום דקצת הם ראויים לאכילה וקמ"ל דאפילו הכי אין פאה נוהגת בהן וכן מצא רשב"ם בתשובת רש"י והא דנקט ספיחים משום דשמא סטים וקוצה עצמם אינם ראויים כלל לאכילת אדם ולא הוה חידוש או שמא הן אוכל גמור ולא ממעטינן: גר שנתגייר בין הנכרים. בפני ג' ולא הודיעוהו מצות שבת דאי נתגייר בינו לבין עצמו לא הוי גר כדאמרינן בהחולץ (יבמות דף מו:): אבל

עין משפט נר מצוה

ג א מיי' שם הלכה ז ופ"ז מהלכות שגגות הלכה ט:

רבינו חננאל

תנא כלל גדול הכא משום חומרא דשבת גדולה מכלל שביעית דאילו איסורא דשבת חלה בין בתלוש ובין במחובר ואיסורא דשביעית אינה אלא מן המחובר לקרקע ותוב איסורא דשביעית גדולה מאיסורא דמעשר שהשביעית חלה באוכלי אדם ובאוכלי בהמה והמעשר אינו חל [אלא] על אוכלי אדם בלבד לפיכך קתני כלל גדול בשביעית ולבר קפרא משום דעונש של מעשרות גדול מעונשה של פאה לפיכך תני כלל גדול במעשר. ותנא דידן שבת ושביעית דחומרא דאורייתא תני כלל גדול. אבל מעשר כגון ירק וכיוצא בו דחומרא דרבנן הוא לא קתני כלל גדול.

רב נסים גאון

פרק ז אמרו גדול עונשה של שבת יותר משל שביעית דאילו שבת איתא בין בתלוש ובין במחובר. ודבר זה מפורסם וברור כי אפילו המוציא מרשות לרשות בשבת חייב חטאת והרבה מן המלאכות שאינן במחובר והן ידועות ואין אנו צריכין למנותן ואילו שביעית במחובר איתא בתלוש ליתא ועיקר דילה בתורת כהנים הזרע והזמיר בכלל היו ולמה יצאו להקיש אליהן מה זרע וזמיר מיוחדין שהן עבודה בארץ ובאילן אף אין לי אלא דבר שהיא עבודה בארץ ובאילן ועיקר דילה בפרק משקין בית השלחין (מועד קטן דף ג) וגדול עונשה של שביעית יותר משל מעשר דאילו שביעית איתא בין במאכל אדם בין במאכל בהמה ועיקרה בתורה דכתיב (ויקרא כה) ולבהמתך ולחיה אשר בארצך ובמשנה (שביעית פ' ד) כלל גדול אמרו בשביעית כל שהוא מאוכל אדם ומאוכל בהמה וממין הצובעים ואינו מתקיים בארץ יש לו שביעית: ואילו מעשר במאכל אדם איתיה במאכל בהמה ליתיה. עיקר דבר זה הוא כתוב בתורה (דברים יד) עשר תעשר את כל תבואת זרעך וסמיך ליה ואכלת דבר שהוא אוכל ובמשנה (מעשרות פרק א) כל שהוא אוכל:

מסורת הש"ס

א) [כריתות טז:], ב) פאה פ"א מ"ד פסחים נו: נדה נ., ג) מעשרות פ"א מ"א נדה נ., ד) [צ"ל שביעית].

הגהות הב"ח

(א) גמרא מעשר דקתני עוד כלל אחר:

גליון הש"ס

גמרא למעוטי תאנה. עיין ר"ה דף טו ע"ב תוס' ד"ה נהגו העם:

ליקוטי רש"י

דאילו מעשר איתא בתאנה וירק. מדרבנן דמדאורייתא לא מיחייב אלא דגן ותירוש ויצהר. כל שהוא אוכל וכו'. בפאה כתיב (ויקרא יט) ובקוצרכם את קציר וגו' דומיא דקציר דמכניסו לקיום ואוכלה כל הני [נדה נ.]. ונשמר. שאינו מופקר ומקפידין עליו לשומרו. ומכניסו לקיום. שמתקיים ימים רבים [פסחים נו:]. שאדם יכול לאוצרו [נדה שם]. למעוטי ספיחי סטים וקוצה. סטים קרוי"ד בלע"ז כרכום קוצה גוד"א בלע"ז [ב"ק קא:]. דאין אוכל אלא מין צבע. סטים, קרו"ג. קוצה, ווייד"א ולא ידענא מאי נקט ספיחים וכמדומה לי שהראשונים ראויים לאכילה [נדה שם]. ספיחי סטים וקוצה קשין לאכילה אבל סטים וקוצה אינם ספיחים חזו לאכילה. סטים, מוריק"א קרו"ג. קוצה, ווייסד"א. תאנה. אינה מתבשלת כאחת אלא זו גמורה היום וזו למחרת הכוחה בלידה כל ימות הקיץ [פסחים שם]. ואילו לקיטתו כאחד. דממעט תאנה ומכניסו לקיום דממעט ירק [נדה שם]. כמיהין ופטריות. יוצאין כמות שבולים באילנות ורחבין ועגולין כגלוסקאות [עירובין כח:]. בוליי"ן בלע"ז שאלו מגדולות הגשמים [תענית כג.]. מאוירא ינקי שאין להם שרשים בארץ [נדרים נה:]. דלאו פירות הארץ נינהו [ר"ן שם]. מלחלוחית הארץ הם גדלים על העצים ועל הכלים [ברכות מ:].

with the words **"a major rule,"**[13] מַאי אָבוֹת וּמַאי תּוֹלָדוֹת אִיכָּא – **what *avos* and *tolados* are there** in regard to *maaser* law?[14] This, then, cannot be the reason why our Mishnah calls its rule "major." – ? –

The Gemara gives another reason why the rule in our Mishnah is called "major":

אֶלָּא לָאו הַיְינוּ טַעְמָא – **Rather, this is not the reason** for the use of the term "major" in our Mishnah and in *Sheviis.*[15] גָּדוֹל עוֹנְשׁוֹ שֶׁל שַׁבָּת יוֹתֵר מִשֶּׁל שְׁבִיעִית – Instead, the reason that the term "major" is used in our Mishnah is that **the punishment pertaining to the Sabbath** law **is greater than that pertaining to *sheviis*** law in the following respect: דְּאִילּוּ שַׁבָּת אִיתָא בֵּין בְּתָלוּשׁ בֵּין בִּמְחוּבָּר – **For the Sabbath** law **applies to both detached and attached** produce,[16] וְאִילּוּ שְׁבִיעִית בְּתָלוּשׁ לֵיתָא בִּמְחוּבָּר אִיתָא – **whereas *sheviis*** law **does not apply to detached** produce; **it applies** only **to** produce still **attached** at the beginning of the *sheviis* year.[17] Since the Mishnah states a rule in regard to both the Sabbath and *sheviis,* and the Sabbath rule is more severe than the *sheviis* rule, the Tanna refers to it as a "major" rule. וְגָדוֹל עוֹנְשָׁהּ שֶׁל שְׁבִיעִית יוֹתֵר מִן הַמַּעֲשֵׂר – **Furthermore, the punishment pertaining to *sheviis*** law **is greater than that of *maaser*** law in the following respect: דְּאִילּוּ שְׁבִיעִית אִיתָא בֵּין בְּמַאֲכַל אָדָם בֵּין בְּמַאֲכַל בְּהֵמָה – **For *sheviis*** law **applies to both human food and animal food,**[18] וְאִילּוּ מַעֲשֵׂר בְּמַאֲכַל אָדָם אִיתָא בְּמַאֲכַל בְּהֵמָה לֵיתָא – **whereas *maaser*** law **applies** only **to human food; it does not** apply **to animal food.**[19] The Tanna therefore refers to the rule of *sheviis* also as a major rule.

This explanation can account for the phraseology used in Bar Kappara's Baraisa as well:

וּלְבַר קַפָּרָא דְּתָנֵי כְּלָל גָּדוֹל בְּמַעֲשֵׂר – **And according to Bar Kappara, who taught** in his Baraisa the rule **regarding *maaser*** with the words **"a major rule,"** we may continue this line of reasoning as follows: גָּדוֹל עוֹנְשׁוֹ שֶׁל מַעֲשֵׂר יוֹתֵר מִשֶּׁל פֵּאָה – **The punishment pertaining to *maaser*** law **is greater than that pertaining to *pe'ah*** law in the following respect:[20] דְּאִילּוּ מַעֲשֵׂר אִיתָא בִּתְאֵנָה וְיָרָק – **For the *maaser*** obligation **applies to figs and vegetables,**[21] וְאִילּוּ פֵּאָה לֵיתָא בִּתְאֵנָה וְיָרָק – **whereas the *pe'ah*** obligation **does not apply to figs and vegetables,** as the Gemara will now demonstrate. Bar Kappara is therefore justified in using the term "major" when referring to the rule of *maaser.*

The Gemara demonstrates that the *pe'ah* obligation is more limited than that of *maaser*:

דִּתְנַן – **For we learned in a Mishnah:**[22] כְּלָל אָמְרוּ בְּפֵאָה – [THE RABBIS] STATED A RULE CONCERNING *PE'AH*:[23] כֹּל שֶׁהוּא אוֹכֶל – ANYTHING THAT IS A FOOD,[24] וְנִשְׁמָר – AND IS PROTECTED, וְגִידּוּלוֹ מִן הָאָרֶץ – AND WHOSE GROWTH IS FROM THE GROUND, וּלְקִיטָתוֹ כְּאַחַת – AND WHICH IS GATHERED ALL AS ONE, וּמַכְנִיסוֹ לְקִיּוּם – AND WHICH ONE BRINGS IN TO LAST, חַיָּיב בְּפֵאָה – IS OBLIGATED IN *PE'AH.*

The Gemara explains each of these criteria:

אוֹכֶל לְמַעוּטֵי סְפִיחֵי סָטִיס וְקוֹצָה – When the Mishnah states that it must be A FOOD it means **to exclude the aftergrowth of woad and madder;**[25] וְנִשְׁמָר לְמַעוּטֵי הֶפְקֵר – when it says PROTECTED it means **to exclude ownerless** crops;[26] וְגִידּוּלוֹ מִן הָאָרֶץ לְמַעוּטֵי כְּמֵיהִין וּפִטְרִיּוֹת – when it says that ITS GROWTH IS FROM THE GROUND it means **to exclude truffles and mushrooms;**[27] וּלְקִיטָתוֹ כְּאַחַת לְמַעוּטֵי תְּאֵנָה – when it says that IT IS GATHERED ALL AS ONE it means **to exclude a fig** crop;[28] וּמַכְנִיסוֹ לְקִיּוּם לְמַעוּטֵי יָרָק – and when it says that ONE BRINGS IT IN TO LAST it means **to exclude vegetables.**[29]

NOTES

13. Bar Kappara composed a version of *Tosefta* (*Rashi*); i.e. he arranged Baraisos based on teachings he learned from Tannaim to explain the Mishnah, which had recently been redacted by Rebbi (*Doros HaRishonim* vol. 5 ch. 33, p. 126). In his *Tosefta* on Tractate *Maasros* he calls the Mishnah's law about *maaser* a "major" rule.

14. See *Rashba* and *Ran* (*MHK* ed.) who discuss why the Gemara did not simply answer that, according to Bar Kappara, the previous answer suffices.

15. That is, the use of the term "major" is not predicated on the fact that Sabbath law includes *avos* and *tolados,* but rather on the reason that follows (*Rashi*).

[*Rashi* explains this phrase as a statement of its own and explains the next phrase as if it were prefaced with the word אֶלָּא. Perhaps *Rashi* had that word in his text of the Gemara. We have translated the Gemara here according to *Rashi's* understanding.]

16. For example, the *melachos* of grinding and kneading apply even to crops that were detached before the Sabbath began (*Rashi*).

17. The *sheviis* prohibitions (see note 10) apply only to crops that were still attached to the ground when the *sheviis* year began. Anything detached at the beginning of the *sheviis* is exempt from the *sheviis* prohibitions (*Rashi;* cf. *Tosafos;* see also *Sfas Emes*).

See *Maharsha* and *Maharam* who discuss why the Gemara did not explain that Sabbath law is subject to a greater punishment than *sheviis* law in that one is executed for desecrating the Sabbath, which is not the case in regard to *sheviis.*

18. As derived from Scripture (*Rashi;* see *Leviticus* 25:6,7).

19. Under Biblical law only grapes, olives, and the five species of grain are obligated in *maaser.* The Rabbis, however, extended the *maaser* obligation to other crops grown for human consumption (as will be taught below) but not to those fit only for animal consumption (*Rashi*).

[Actually, there is a dispute of Rishonim whether the Biblical obligation refers to the grapes and olives or only to the wine and oil. However, *Rashi's* view seems to be that the obligation refers to the grapes and olives (see *Rashi, Bava Metzia* 88b ד"ה בענבים וזיתים; see also *Minchas Chinuch* 395:2 for other views regarding which fruits are Biblically obligated in *maaser*).]

20. *Pe'ah* (literally: edge) is the portion of the crop that the Torah requires a farmer in Eretz Yisrael to leave for the poor (see *Leviticus* 19:9-10; 23:22).

21. At least by Rabbinic law (*Rashi*), as previously noted.

22. *Pe'ah* 1:4.

23. The Rabbis taught the rule that follows concerning which species are subject to *pe'ah.*

The Torah (*Leviticus* 19:9) states that the obligation of *pe'ah* applies וּבְקֻצְרְכֶם אֶת־קְצִיר אַרְצְכֶם, *when you reap the harvest of your land.* The term קָצַר, *reap* or *harvest,* refers by definition only to the harvesting of species that exhibit the five properties enumerated below by the Mishnah. Accordingly, these properties serve as the criteria for determining which species are subject to *pe'ah* (*Rashi;* see *Toras Kohanim* loc. cit.). The Gemara will explain what each criterion excludes.

24. The first condition is that the crop must be fit for human consumption in order to be subject to *pe'ah.*

25. These plants are used to make dyes, not as food. They are therefore not subject to *pe'ah* (*Rashi;* see *Sheviis* 7:1).

Rashi adds that the Gemara refers to these as "aftergrowths" because the plants themselves are generally not harvested the year they are planted; rather, they are left in the ground for four to five years to allow the roots to grow, since the roots are the principal useful part of the plant. [Thus, they appear to be aftergrowths.] The Gemara mentions these particular species rather than other inedible ones, because these are mentioned as subject to the laws of *sheviis* (see *Sheviis* 7:1). The Gemara therefore states that they are nevertheless not subject to *pe'ah* (cf. *Rashi* to *Pesachim* 56b; *Tosafos*).

26. [Being ownerless, no one tends or "protects" them.]

27. [These species of fungi lack roots and are therefore considered to draw their nourishment from the air rather than directly from the ground.]

28. To be subject to *pe'ah,* the entire crop must ripen at one time and thus be harvested as one. Figs ripen at different times; thus, each fruit is picked as it ripens, and there is no full-scale harvest.

Tosafos note that most fruit trees actually fall into this category. The Gemara chooses figs as its example because their ripening is particularly irregular.

29. Such as turnips and leeks (*Rashi*). To be subject to *pe'ah,* a species

אב מלאכה ומלאכה (א) [א]העושה מלאכות הרבה מעין מלאכה אחת אינו חייב אלא חטאת אחת: **גמ'** מ"ט תנא כלל גדול אילימא משום דקבעי למיתני עוד כלל אחר תנא כלל גדול וגבי שביעית נמי משום דקבעי למיתני עוד כלל אחר תנא כלל גדול והא גבי מעשר דקתני (א) כלל אחר ולא תני כלל גדול א"ר יוסי בר אבין שבת ושביעית דאית בהו אבות ותולדות תנא גדול מעשר דלית בה אבות ותולדות לא תנא כלל גדול ולבר קפרא דתני כלל גדול במעשר מאי אבות ומאי תולדות איכא אלא לאו היינו טעמא גדול עונשו של שבת יותר משל שביעית דאילו שבת איתא בין בתלוש בין במחובר ואילו שביעית בתלוש ליתא במחובר איתא וגדול עונשה של שביעית יותר מן המעשר דאילו שביעית איתא בין במאכל אדם בין במאכל בהמה ואילו מעשר במאכל אדם איתא במאכל בהמה ליתא ולבר קפרא דתני כלל גדול במעשר גדול עונשו של מעשר יותר משל פיאה דאילו מעשר איתא בתאנה וירק ואילו פיאה ליתא בתאנה וירק [ב]דתנן כלל אמרו בפיאה כל שהוא אוכל ונשמר וגידולו מן הארץ ולקיטתו כאחת ומכניסו לקיום חייב בפיאה אוכל למעוטי ספיחי סטים וקוצה ונשמר למעוטי הפקר וגידולו מן הארץ למעוטי כמיהין ופטריות ולקיטתו כאחת ° למעוטי תאנה ומכניסו לקיום למעוטי ירק ואילו גבי מעשר תנן [ג] כלל אמרו במעשר כל שהוא אוכל ונשמר וגידולו מן הארץ חייב במעשר ואילו לקיטתו כאחת ומכניסו לקיום לא תנן: רב ושמואל דאמרי תרוייהו מתניתין בתינוק שנשבה לבין הנכרים וגר שנתגייר לבין הנכרים אבל הכיר ולבסוף שכח חייב על כל שבת ושבת תנן השוכח עיקר שבת לאו מכלל דהויא ליה ידיעה מעיקרא לא מאי כל השוכח עיקר שבת דהיתה שכוח ממנו עיקרה של שבת אבל הכיר ולבסוף שכח מאי חייב על כל שבת ושבת אדתני היודע עיקר שבת ועשה מלאכות הרבה בשבתות הרבה חייב על כל שבת ושבת ליתני הכיר ולבסוף שכח וכ"ש הא מאי היודע עיקר שבת מי שהיה יודע עיקרה של שבת ושכחה אבל

רש"י

אב מלאכה דנקט לאו למעוטי תולדות דה"ה לתולדות ובלבד שיהו תולדות דשני אבות אלא למעוטי היכא דהוו ב' תולדות דאב אחד או אב ותולדה שלו דאינו חייב אלא אחת כדקתני סיפא העושה מלאכות הרבה מעין מלאכה אחת שתי תולדות של אב אחד אינו חייב אלא חטאת אחת דהרי הוא כעושה ואחר ועושה בהעלם אחד ואין חילוק חטאות בהעלם אחד אלא בגופי עבירה שאינן דומין או בחילוק שבתות לענין שגגת שבת: **גמ' עוד כלל אחר.** לקמן בפירקין (דף עה:) ולא כלל בו אלא ג' דברים כל הכשר להצניע וכל שאינו כשר להצניע וכאן כלל יותר ומשום הכי קרי להו גדול: **וגבי שביעית.** בפרק ז' (בנות שוח): **גבי מעשר.** בפ"ק דמסכת מעשרות: **אית ביה אבות.** ארבעים חסר אחת שהוצרכו למשכן ותולדות הדומות לכל אחת הויא תולדות דידיה אבות דשביעית זריעה וקצירה וזמירה ובצירה דכתיבן תולדות שאר עבודות שבשדה וכרם כדאמרינן במועד קטן בפ"ק (דף ג.): **ולבר קפרא דתנא.** בתוספתא דידיה במעשר מאי אבות כו': **אלא לאו היינו טעמא.** משום אבות ותולדות אלא דבר שנאמר בו כלל ועונשו גדול מדבר אחר שנאמר בו כלל תני ביה כלל גדול: **שבת איתא.** לאיסור דידה בין בדבר שהיה תלוש מבעוד יום כגון טוחן ולש בין בדבר שמחובר משקדש היום: **ואילו שביעית.** בדבר שהיה מחובר משקדשה שביעית איתא אבל בדבר שהיה תלוש לפני שביעית ליתא: **שביעית.** נמי איתיה במאכל בהמה דכתיב ולבהמתך ולחיה וגו' (ויקרא כה) מעשר ליתיה במאכל בהמה דמדאורייתא דגן תירוש ויצהר כתיב ורבנן תקון פירות האילן וירק דמאכל אדם כדקתני כל שהוא אוכל כו': **איתיה בתאנה וירק.** מדרבנן: **כל שהוא אוכל כו'.** דגבי פיאה קציר כתיב מה קציר מיוחד שיש בו כל אלו: **למעוטי ספיחי סטים וקוצה.** שעומדים לצבע להכי נקט ספיחים דאין דרך ללוקטן בשנה שזורעים אלא לסוף ד' וה' שנים שהשרשין מתפשטין בארץ ומשביחין ושורש שלהן עיקר והא דנקט הני ולא נקט שאר מינים שאינן ראוין לאכילה משום דאיידי דגבי שביעית תני להו דיש להן שביעית נקט הכא דבפיאה ומעשר ליתנהו לשון רבינו הלוי. סטים ווישד"א קול' וורנצ"א: **ומכניסו לקיום למעוטי ירק.** כגון לפת וקפלוטות: **ואילו מכניסו לקיום ולקיטתו כאחד לא תנן.** דכי תקון רבנן אדידהו לא פלוג בפירות האילן ובירק בין מין למין:

מתניתין. דפטר בחד חטאת: **בתינוק שנשבה.** ולא ידע שבת מעולם: **אבל הכיר ולבסוף שכח.** הוה ליה כשוכח שהיום שבת ויודע עיקר שבת וחייב על כל שבת ושבת: **שהיתה שכוחה ממנו.** מעולם: **לתני הכיר ולבסוף שכח.** דחייב ואע"ג דליכא למימר ימים שבינתים הווין ידיעה לחלק וכ"ש הא דאיכא למימר שימים שבינתים הווין ליה ידיעה לחלק:

תוספות

וגבי שביעית נמי כו'. הכי תנן בשביעית (פ"ז מ"א) כלל גדול אמרו כל שהוא מאכל אדם ומאכל בהמה וממין הצובעין ואינו מתקיים בארץ פירוש שכלה לחיה יש לו שביעית ולדמיו שביעית יש לו ביעור ולדמיו ביעור ועוד כלל אחר אמרו דקתני כל שאינו מאכל אדם ומאכל בהמה וכו' ומתקיים בארץ יש לו שביעית ולדמיו שביעית ואין לו ולדמיו ביעור דכלל הראשון גדול דיש לו ביעור ואחרון אין לו ביעור ואע"ג דקתני התם בבבא אחריתא כלל גדול אמרו בשביעית ולא קתני בתריה כלל אחר כיון דקתני כלל קטן קמיה שייך למתני בתריה כלל גדול: **והא** גבי מעשר דקתני עוד כלל אחר אמרו כו'. תימה למה ישנה בראשון כלל גדול כיון דאינו גדול מן השני וצ"ע:

דאית ביה אבות ותולדות. ואפילו לרבא דאמר במועד קטן (דף ג:) גבי שביעית אבות אסר רחמנא תולדות לא אסר רחמנא מ"מ מדרבנן מיהא אית ביה אבות ותולדות וא"ת במעשר איכא נמי אבות ותולדות דמדאורייתא דגן ותירוש ויצהר ומדרבנן כל מילי וי"ל דלא שייך להזכיר אבות ותולדות במילי דלית ביה איסור מלאכות וא"ת ובכלל אחר דשבת ושביעית ליתני נמי כלל גדול מהאי טעמא ויש לומר דלא צריך למיתני דאכלל גדול קמא קאי וה"ק עוד כלל גדול אחר אמרו: **גדול** ענשו של שבת משל שביעית. לפירוש הקונטרס דמפרש בתלוש שנתלש קודם שבת וקודם שביעית משמע שרוצה לפרש שביעית במחובר איתא היינו במחובר ערב שביעית ונתלש בשביעית ומיירי באיסור פירות שביעית לאכילה וקשה לר"י דלפי' לא הוה ליה למימר אלא גדול עונשו של שבת ושביעית משל מעשר דאיתנהו במאכל בהמה מה שאין כן במעשר ולמה ליה למימר כלל גדול עונשה של שבת משל שביעית אלא נראה לר"י דבמידי דאכילה דלא שייכא לענין שבת לא שייך למימר גדול שבת לא משביעית ולא ממעשר ולהכי לא קאמר גדול שבת ושביעית ממעשר אלא קאמר גדול שבת משביעית דאיסור מלאכות איתנהו בין בתלוש בין במחובר ואילו איסור מלאכות דשביעית במחובר איתא בתלוש ליתא וכן משמע בירושלמי דקתני שהשבת חלה על הכל ושביעית לא חלה אלא על עבודת הארץ בלבד: **ולבר** קפרא דתני כלל גדול במעשר כו'. נראה לרשב"א דאחרים לא שנו כלל גדול במעשר לפי שאינו גדול מפאה אלא מדרבנן אבל כלל גדול דשבת גדול משביעית מדאורייתא וכן של שביעית משל מעשר: **ואילו** פאה ליתא בתאנה וירק. לאו דוקא תאנה דהא רוב אילנות אין לקיטתן כאחד ואינן רק ה' אילנות דחשיב בפ"ק דפאה (מ"ה) דחייב בפאה אלא נקט תאנה משום דנלקטת כמה פעמים כדאמרינן בחזקת הבתים (ב"ב דף כח:) אכל ג' פירי בחד יומא כגון תאנה כו' ואומר ר"ת דמדאורייתא לא מיחייב בפאה אלא בדגן ותירוש ויצהר דסתם קציר דכתיב גבי פאה הוא דגן וכתיב כי תחבוט זיתך כי תבצור כרמך והא דדריש בת"כ יכול שאני מרבה קישואין ודלועין שיהיו חייבים בפאה ת"ל ובקוצרכם את קציר ארצכם מה קציר שהוא אוכל ונשמר כו' אסמכתא היא דהתם נמי דריש מעשר ירק מקרא אע"ג דהוי מדרבנן ומה שלא תקנו פאה בירק ובתאנה ודדמי לה כמו שתקנו מעשר מהן אומר ר"ת משום דאין לקיטתן כאחד דבר מועט הוא פאה דידיה ויש הפסד לעניים בה יותר מן הריוח שמתבטלין לפי שאין יודעים זמן לקיטתן ודבר שאין מכניסו לקיום נמי לא חשיב ויפסידו יותר ממה שירויחו במקום אחר: **ספיחי** סטים וקוצה. הא דלא קאמר סתם למעוטי מידי דלאו אוכל אלא נקט הני אומר ר"י משום דקלת הם ראויים לאכילה וקמ"ל דאפילו הכי אין פאה נוהגת בהן וכן מצא רשב"ם בתשובת רש"י והא דנקט ספיחים משום דשמא סטים וקוצה עצמם אינם ראוים כלל לאכילת אדם ולא הוה חידוש או שמא הן אוכל גמור ולא ממעטינן: **גר** שנתגייר בין הנכרים. בפני ג' ולא הודיעוהו מצות שבת דאי נתגייר בינו לבין עצמו לא הוי גר כדאמרינן בהחולץ (יבמות דף מז:): אבל

עין משפט נר מצוה

ג א מיי' שם הלכה ז ופ"ז מהלכות שבת הלכה ט:

רבינו חננאל

תנא כלל גדול הכא משום חומרא דשבת גדולה מכלל שביעית דאילו איסורא דשבת חלה בין בתלוש ובין במחובר ואיסורא דשביעית אינה אלא מן המחובר לקרקע ותוב איסורא דשביעית גדולה מאיסורא דמעשר שהשביעית חלה באוכלי אדם ובאוכלי בהמה והמעשר אינו חל [אלא] על אוכלי אדם בלבד לפיכך קתני כלל גדול בשביעית ולבר קפרא משום דעונש של מעשרות גדול מעונשה של פאה לפיכך תני כלל גדול במעשר. ותנא דידן שבת ושביעית דחומרא דאורייתא תני כלל גדול. אבל מעשר כגון ירק וכיוצא בו דחומרא דרבנן הוא לא קתני כלל גדול.

רב נסים גאון

פרק ז **אמרו** גדול עונשה של שבת יותר משל שביעית דאילו שבת איתא בין בתלוש ובין במחובר. ודבר זה מפורסם וברור כי אפילו המוציא מרשות לרשות בשבת חייב חטאת והרבה מן המלאכות שאינן במחובר והן ידועות ואין אנו צריכין למנותן ואילו שביעית במחובר איתא בתלוש ליתא ועיקר דילה בתורת כהנים הזרע והזמיר בכלל היו ולמה יצאו להקיש אליהן מה זרע וזמר מיוחדין שהן עבודה בארץ ובאילן אף אין לי אלא דבר שהיא עבודה בארץ ובאילן ועיקר דילה בפרק משקין בית השלחין (מועד קטן דף ג) וגדול עונשה של שביעית יותר משל מעשר דאילו שביעית איתא בין במאכל אדם בין במאכל בהמה ועיקרה בתורה דכתיב (ויקרא כה) ולבהמתך ולחיה אשר בארצך ובמשנה (שביעית פ' ד') כלל גדול אמרו בשביעית כל שהוא מאוכל אדם ומאוכל בהמה וממין הצובעים ואינו מתקיים בארץ יש לו שביעית ולדמיו שביעית: **ואילו** מעשר במאכל אדם איתיה במאכל בהמה ליתיה. עיקר דבר זה הוא כתוב בתורה (דברים יד) עשר תעשר את כל תבואת זרעך וסמיך ליה ואכלת דבר שהוא אוכל ובמשנה (מעשרות פרק א) כל שהוא אוכל:

מסורת הש"ס

א) [כריתות טז:], ב) פאה פ"א מ"ד פסחים נו: נדה נ., ג) מעשרות פ"א מ"א נדה נ., ד) [צ"ל שביעי].

הגהות הב"ח

(א) גמרא מעשר דקתני עוד כלל אחר:

גליון הש"ס

גמרא למעוטי תאנה. עיין ר"ה דף טו ע"ב תוס' ד"ה נהגו העם:

ליקוטי רש"י

דאילו מעשר איתא בתאנה וירק. מדרבנן דמדאורייתא לא מחייב אלא דגן ותירוש ויצהר. **כל שהוא אוכל וכו'.** בפאה כתיב (ויקרא יט) ובקוצרכם את קציר וגו' דומיא דקציר דמכניסו לקיום ואיכא כל הני [נדה נ.]. **ונשמר.** שאינו מופקר ומקפידין עליו לשומרו. **ומכניסו לקיום.** שמתקיים ימים רבים [פסחים נו:]. שאדם יכול לאוצרו [נדה שם]. **למעוטי ספיחי סטים וקוצה.** סטים קרוג"א בלע"ז כרכום קוצה גווד"א בלע"ז [ב"ק קא:]. דאין אוכל אלא מין צבע. סטים, קרו"ג. קוצה, ויטר"א ולא ידענא אמאי נקט ספיחים וכמדומה לי שהראשונים ראויים לאכילה [נדה שם]. ספיחי סטים וקוצה קשין לאכילה אבל סטים וקוצה שאינם ספיחים חזו לאכילה. סטים, מוריק"א קרו"ג. קוצה, ווייסר"א. **תאנה.** אינה מתבשלת כאחת אלא זו גמורה היום ואחרת יוצאה בנידה כל ימות הקיץ [פסחים שם]. **ואילו לקיטתו כאחד.** דממעט תאנה ומכניסו לקיום דממעט ירק [נדה שם]. **כמיהין ופטריות.** יוצאין כמות שהן בלילה אחד ורחבין ועגולין כגלוסקאות [לעיל ל:]. בולי"ן בלע"ז שיוצאו מלחלוח הגשמים [תענית כג.]. מאוירא ינקי שאין להם שרשים בארץ [נדרים נה:]. דלאו פירות הארץ נינהו [ר"ן שם]. מלחלוחית הארץ הם גדלים על העצים ועל הכלים [ברכות מ:].

The Gemara concludes its demonstration by quoting the parallel Mishnah in regard to *maaser:*

וְאִילּוּ גַּבֵּי מַעֲשֵׂר תְּנַן – However, concerning *maaser* we learned in a Mishnah:[30] **כְּלָל אָמְרוּ בְּמַעֲשֵׂר** – THEY STATED A RULE CONCERNING *MAASER*: **כֹּל שֶׁהוּא אוֹכֶל** – ANYTHING THAT IS A FOOD, **וְנִשְׁמָר** – AND IS PROTECTED, **וְגִידּוּלוֹ מִן הָאָרֶץ** – AND WHOSE GROWTH IS FROM THE GROUND, **חַיָּיב בְּמַעֲשֵׂר** – IS OBLIGATED IN *MAASER;* **וְאִילּוּ לְקִיטָתוֹ כְּאַחַת וּמַכְנִיסוֹ לְקִיּוּם לֹא תְּנַן** – **whereas** the requirements that **it be gathered as one and** that **one bring it in to last are not taught** in regard to *maaser,* making it evident that these criteria do *not* apply to *maaser.* Thus, figs and vegetables *are* subject to the *maaser* obligation.[31] Since more species of crops are subject to *maaser* than are subject to *pe'ah,* the Tanna (according to the version of Bar Kappara) called his rule about *maaser* "major."[32]

The Gemara now analyzes the first ruling of our Mishnah, which stated that a person who did not know the essence of the Sabbath is liable to only one *chatas* for his violations of numerous *melachos* over many Sabbaths:

רַב וּשְׁמוּאֵל דְּאָמְרֵי תַּרְוַויְהוּ – Rav and Shmuel both said: **מַתְנִיתִין בְּתִינוֹק שֶׁנִּשְׁבָּה לְבֵין הַנָּכְרִים** – **Our Mishnah** is dealing **with** the case of **a child who was captured** and raised **among gentiles,**[33] **וְגֵר שֶׁנִּתְגַּיֵּיר לְבֵין הַנָּכְרִים** – **or a convert who converted** and lived **among gentiles.**[34] Since such a person never knew about the Sabbath, he is liable to only one *chatas* for all his violations. **אֲבָל הִכִּיר וּלְבַסּוֹף שָׁכַח** – **But if he recognized** the Sabbath law **and eventually forgot** it, **חַיָּיב עַל כָּל שַׁבָּת וְשַׁבָּת** – **he is liable for each and every Sabbath** that he desecrated.[35]

The Gemara challenges this interpretation:

תְּנַן – **We learned in** the beginning of **our Mishnah:** **הַשּׁוֹכֵחַ עִיקַּר שַׁבָּת** – ONE WHO FORGETS THE ESSENCE OF THE SABBATH . . . is liable to but one *chatas.* **לָאו מִכְּלָל דַּהֲוָיָא לֵיהּ יְדִיעָה מֵעִיקָּרָא** – **Does this** wording **not imply that he originally had knowledge** of the Sabbath?[36]

The Gemara answers:

לֹא – **No!** **מַאי כֹּל הַשּׁוֹכֵחַ עִיקַּר שַׁבָּת** – **What** does the Mishnah mean when it says: ANYONE WHO FORGETS THE ESSENCE OF THE SABBATH? **דְּהָיְתָה שְׁכוּחַ מִמֶּנּוּ עִיקָּרָהּ שֶׁל שַׁבָּת** – It means **that the essence of the Sabbath was forgotten from him** from the very beginning, i.e. that he *never* knew it.[37]

The Gemara asks further:

אֲבָל הִכִּיר וּלְבַסּוֹף שָׁכַח מַאי – **But** if **he recognized** the essence of the Sabbath **and eventually forgot** it, **what** is the law? **חַיָּיב עַל כָּל שַׁבָּת וְשַׁבָּת** – Clearly, you are saying that **he is liable for each and every Sabbath.**[38] **אַדְּתָנֵי הַיּוֹדֵעַ עִיקַּר שַׁבָּת** – But if so, **then instead of** the Mishnah **teaching** in the second case: ONE WHO KNOWS THE ESSENCE OF THE SABBATH **וְעָשָׂה מְלָאכוֹת הַרְבֵּה בְּשַׁבָּתוֹת הַרְבֵּה** – AND yet inadvertently PERFORMED MANY *MELACHOS* ON MANY SABBATHS **חַיָּיב עַל כָּל שַׁבָּת וְשַׁבָּת** – IS LIABLE TO a separate *chatas* FOR EACH AND EVERY SABBATH,[39] **לִיתְנֵי הִכִּיר וּלְבַסּוֹף שָׁכַח** – **[the Mishnah] should teach** that **one** who **recognized** the essence of the Sabbath **and eventually forgot** it is liable for every Sabbath desecrated, **וְכָל שֶׁכֵּן הָא** – **and** we would conclude on our own that one is **certainly** liable for every

NOTES

must be able to be stored for a long time without spoiling. This excludes most vegetables, which are perishable (*Rav, Rambam* to Mishnah there).

30. *Maasros* 1:1.

31. [As stated above, according to Biblical law only grapes, olives, and the five species of grain are obligated in *maaser.*] When the Rabbis instituted the requirement that other types of crops also be tithed they did not distinguish between different types of fruits and vegetables (*Rashi*).

[*Tosafos* write that according to Biblical law the *pe'ah* requirement also applies only to grapes, olives, and the five grains. Nevertheless, when the Rabbis added other species of fruits and vegetables to the *pe'ah* requirement, they excluded fruits that do not ripen at the same time because the *pe'ah* value of such fruits is minimal. Similarly, they excluded perishable vegetables so that the poor would be induced to exert their efforts on more substantial crops.

Ritva (*MHK* ed.), however, cites *Rashbam,* who holds that all species possessing the five criteria listed in the Mishnah are subject to *pe'ah* according to Biblical law (see also *Ramban*). Accordingly, in the case of *maaser* law, where the Biblical law applies only to grains, grapes and olives, and it was the Rabbis who extended the obligation to other species, they extended it to figs and vegetables as well. For *pe'ah,* though, which applies even under Biblical law to other species, the Rabbis did not make a special enactment to include just those few items excluded from the Biblical requirement. This seems to be the view of *Rashi* here (ד״ה כל שהוא) as well, and is explicitly attributed to *Rashi* by *Tos. HaRosh* to *Niddah* (50a).]

32. However, the Mishnah's version of that law in *Maasros* does not call the rule "major" because at the Biblical level figs and vegetables are no more obligated in *maaser* than in *pe'ah.* Only where the greater stringency is Biblical does our Tanna accord it the title of "major" (*Tosafos*).

33. And he thus never learned about the mitzvah of the Sabbath (*Rashi*).

34. This cannot mean that a gentile converted to Judaism on his own; such an action has no validity. Rather, the Gemara means that when he converted, the officiating Rabbis did not tell him about the laws of the Sabbath (*Tosafos*). Thus, since he continued to live among gentiles, he never learned the law of the Sabbath.

Even though the Rabbinic court is supposed to inform the potential convert of some of the mitzvos, they are not required to inform him of all mitzvos. Thus, it is possible that they told him about mitzvos other than the Sabbath. Furthermore, even a conversion performed without informing the convert of any of the mitzvos is valid, after the fact (*Ramban;* see also *Rambam, Hil. Isurei Bi'ah* 13:17 with *Maggid Mishneh; Ritva* to *Yevamos* 47a; cf. *Ritva MHK* ed. here, and *Teshuvos Chemdas Shlomo* §29).

35. I.e. he is treated like someone who knew the law of the Sabbath but forgot that the day was the Sabbath day. Accordingly, he is liable to a separate *chatas* for every Sabbath that he desecrated (*Rashi*).

[Obviously, this would not be because of a presumption that he realized his error during the intervening days, since there is no reason to presume that he relearned the law of the Sabbath during the intervening days (see note 1 above and *Rashi* below ד״ה ליתני הכיר ולבסוף שכח). Rather, the reason is that if we explain the verse that sets forth an obligation of one *chatas* for the violations of numerous Sabbaths as referring to a case where the person *never* knew of the Sabbath, as Rav and Shmuel maintain, then it follows that the verse that obligates a separate *chatas* for each Sabbath is referring to a case where the person did once know the Sabbath law but forgot it (see 67b note 3 for the teachings of these two verses). Thus, the second verse teaches that one who knew of the Sabbath law but forgot it is liable to a separate *chatas* for each and every Sabbath (see *Pnei Yehoshua;* cf. *Rashba;* see also *Dibros Moshe* 64:7).]

36. The term שׁוֹכֵחַ, *forgets,* indicates that he forgot information that he once knew – i.e. the existence of the mitzvah of the Sabbath (*Ritva MHK* ed.; see also *Rashba*).

37. Accordingly, the Mishnah uses the term שׁוֹכֵחַ, *forgets,* loosely (*Ritva MHK* ed.; see *Meleches Shlomo* to the Mishnah).

38. Actually, there is no necessity to deduce this from the previous statement, for Rav and Shmuel said so explicitly. The Gemara's point here is that this citation of their opinion must be correct, for it follows logically from the first part of their statement (see *Ritva MHK* ed.; cf. *Rosh Yosef* who suggests that Rav and Shmuel did not actually say the words, "But if he recognized and then forgot," and that those words were merely ascribed to them by the Gemara).

39. [This was understood to mean that the person knew about the Sabbath law when he performed the *melachos* but did not realize that it was, in fact, the Sabbath day.]

אב מלאכה ומלאכה (א) [א]העושה מלאכות הרבה מעין מלאכה אחת אינו חייב אלא חטאת אחת: **גמ'** מ"ט תנא כלל גדול אילימא משום דקבעי למיתני עוד כלל אחר תנא כלל גדול וגבי שביעית נמי משום דקבעי למיתני עוד כלל אחר תנא כלל גדול והא גבי מעשר דקתני (א) כלל אחר ולא תני כלל גדול א"ר יוסי בר אבין שבת ושביעית דאית בהו אבות ותולדות תנא גדול מעשר דלית בה אבות ותולדות לא תנא כלל גדול ולבר קפרא דתני כלל גדול במעשר מאי אבות ומאי תולדות איכא אלא לאו היינו טעמא גדול עונשו של שבת יותר משל שביעית דאילו שבת איתא בין בתלוש בין במחובר ואילו שביעית בתלוש ליתא במחובר איתא וגדול עונשה של שביעית יותר מן המעשר דאילו שביעית איתא בין במאכל אדם בין במאכל בהמה ואילו מעשר במאכל אדם איתא במאכל בהמה ליתא ולבר קפר"א דתני כלל גדול במעשר גדול עונשו של מעשר יותר משל פיאה דאילו מעשר איתא בתאנה וירק ואילו פיאה ליתא בתאנה וירק [ב]דתנן כלל אמרו בפיאה כל שהוא אוכל ונשמר וגידולו מן הארץ ולקיטתו כאחת ומכניסו לקיום חייב בפיאה אוכל למעוטי ספיחי סטים וקוצה ונשמר למעוטי הפקר וגידולו מן הארץ למעוטי כמיהין ופטריות ולקיטתו כאחת ° למעוטי תאנה ומכניסו לקיום למעוטי ירק ואילו גבי מעשר תנן [ג] כלל אמרו במעשר כל שהוא אוכל ונשמר וגידולו מן הארץ חייב במעשר ואילו לקיטתו כאחת ומכניסו לקיום לא תנן: רב ושמואל דאמרי תרוייהו מתניתין בתינוק שנשבה לבין הנכרים וגר שנתגייר לבין הנכרים אבל הכיר ולבסוף שכח חייב על כל שבת ושבת תנן השוכח עיקר שבת לאו מכלל דהויא ליה ידיעה מעיקרא לא מאי כל השוכח עיקר שבת דהיתה שכוח ממנו עיקרה של שבת אבל הכיר ולבסוף שכח מאי חייב על כל שבת ושבת אדתני היודע עיקר שבת ועשה מלאכות הרבה בשבתות הרבה חייב על כל שבת ושבת ליתני הכיר ולבסוף שכח וכ"ש הא מאי היודע עיקר שבת מי שהיה יודע עיקרה של שבת ושכחה אבל

רש"י

אב מלאכה דנקט לאו למעוטי תולדות דה"ה לתולדות ובלבד שיהו תולדות דשני אבות אלא למעוטי היכא דהוו ב' תולדות דאב אחד או אב ותולדה שלו דאינו חייב אלא אחת כדקתני סיפא העושה מלאכות הרבה מעין מלאכה אחת שתי תולדות של אב אחד אינו חייב אלא חטאת אחת דהרי הוא כעושה וחוזר ועושה בהעלם אחד ואין חילוק חטאות בהעלם אחד אלא בגופי עבירה שאינן דומין או בחילוק שבתות לענין שגגת שבת: **גמ' עוד כלל אחר.** לקמן בפירקין (דף עה:) ולא כלל בו אלא ב' דברים כל הכשר להצניע וכל שאינו כשר להצניע וכאן כלל יותר ומשום הכי קרי להו גדול: **וגבי שביעית.** בפרק [ד] (בנות שוח): **גבי מעשר.** בפ"ק דמסכת מעשרות: **אית ביה אבות.** ארבעים חסר אחת שהוצרכו למשכן ותולדות הדומות לכל אחת הויא תולדות דידיה אבות דשביעית זריעה וקצירה וזמירה ובצירה דכתיבן תולדות שאר עבודות שבשדה וכרם כדאמרינן במועד קטן בפ"ק (דף ג.): **ולבר קפרא דתנא.** בתוספתא דידיה במעשר מאי אבות כו': **אלא לאו היינו טעמא.** משום אבות ותולדות אלא דבר שנאמר בו כלל ועונשו גדול מדבר אחר שנאמר בו כלל תני ביה כלל גדול: **שבת איתא.** לאיסור דידה בין בדבר שהיה תלוש מבעוד יום כגון טוחן ולש בין בדבר שמחובר משקדש היום: **ואילו שביעית.** בדבר שהיה מחובר משקדשה שביעית איתא אבל בדבר שהיה תלוש לפני שביעית ליתא: **שביעית.** נמי איתיה במאכל בהמה דכתיב ולבהמתך ולחיה וגו' (ויקרא כה) מעשר ליתיה במאכל בהמה דמדאורייתא דגן תירוש ויצהר כתיב ורבנן תקון פירות האילן וירק דמאכל אדם כדקתני כל שהוא אוכל כו': **איתיה בתאנה וירק.** מדרבנן: **כל שהוא אוכל כו'.** דגבי פיאה קציר כתיב מה קציר מיוחד שיש בו כל אלו: **למעוטי ספיחי סטים וקוצה.** שעומדים לצבע להכי נקט ספיחים דאין דרך ללוקטן בשנה שנזרעים אלא לסוף ד' וה' שנים שהשרשין מתפשטין בארץ ומשביחין ושורש שלהן עיקר והא דנקט הני ולא נקט שאר מינים שאינן ראוין לאכילה משום דאיידי דגבי שביעית תני להו דיש להן שביעית נקט הכא דבפיאה ומעשר ליתנהו לשון רבינו הלוי. סטים ווישד"א קול' וורנצ"א: **ומכניסו לקיום למעוטי ירק.** כגון לפת וקפלוטות: **ואילו מכניסו לקיום ולקיטתו כאחד לא תנן.** דכי תקון רבנן אדידהו לא פלוג בפירות האילן ובירק בין מין למין: מתניתין. דפטר בחד חטאת: **בתינוק שנשבה.** ולא ידע שבת מעולם: אבל הכיר ולבסוף שכח. הוה ליה כשוכח שהיום שבת ויודע עיקר שבת וחייב על כל שבת ושבת: **שהיתה שכוחה ממנו. מעולם: ליתני הכיר** ולבסוף שכח. דחייב ואע"ג דליכא למימר ימים שבינתים הווין ידיעה לחלק וכ"ש הא דאיכא למימר שימים שבינתים הווין ליה ידיעה לחלק: אבל

תוספות

וגבי שביעית נמי כו'. הכי תנן בשביעית (פ"ז מ"א) כלל גדול אמרו כל שהוא מאכל אדם ומאכל בהמה וממין הצובעין ואינו מתקיים בארץ פירות שכלה לחיה יש לו שביעית ולדמיו שביעית יש לו ביעור ולדמיו ביעור ועוד כלל אחר אמרו דקתני כל שאינו מאכל אדם ומאכל בהמה וכו' ומתקיים בארץ יש לו שביעית ולדמיו שביעית ואין לו ולדמיו ביעור דכלל הראשון גדול דיש לו ביעור ואחרון אין לו ביעור ואע"ג דקתני התם בבבא אחריתא כלל גדול אמרו בשביעית ולא קתני בתריה כלל אחר כיון דקתני כלל קטן קמיה שייך למתני בתריה כלל גדול: **והא** גבי מעשר דקתני עוד כלל אחר אמרו כו'. תימה למה ישנה בראשון כלל גדול כיון דאינו גדול מן השני וצ"ע:

דאית ביה אבות ותולדות. ואפילו לרבא דאמר במועד קטן (דף ג:) גבי שביעית אבות אסר רחמנא תולדות לא אסר רחמנא מ"מ מדרבנן מיהא אית ביה אבות ותולדות וא"ת במעשר איכא נמי אבות ותולדות דמדאורייתא דגן ותירוש ויצהר ומדרבנן כל מילי וי"ל דלא שייך להזכיר אבות ותולדות במילי דלית ביה איסור מלאכות וא"ת ובכלל אחר דשבת ושביעית ליתני נמי כלל גדול מהאי טעמא ויש לומר דלא צריך למיתני דאכלל גדול קמא קאי וה"ק עוד כלל גדול אחר אמרו:

גדול ענשו של שבת משל שביעית. לפירוש הקונטרס דמפרש בתלוש שנתלש קודם שבת וקודם שביעית משמע שרוצה לפרש שביעית במחובר איתא היינו במחובר ערב שביעית ונתלש בשביעית ומיירי באיסור פירות שביעית לאכילה וקשה לר"י דלפי' לא הוה ליה למימר אלא גדול עונשו של שבת ושביעית משל מעשר דאיתנהו במאכל בהמה מה שאין כן במעשר ולמה ליה למימר כלל גדול עונשה של שבת משל שביעית אלא נראה לר"י דבמידי דאכילה דלא שייכא לענין שבת לא שייך למימר גדול שבת לא משביעית ולא ממעשר ולהכי לא קאמר גדול שבת ושביעית ממעשר אלא קאמר גדול שבת משביעית דאיסור מלאכות איתנהו בין בתלוש בין במחובר ואילו איסור מלאכות דשביעית במחובר איתא בתלוש ליתא וכן משמע בירושלמי דקתני שהשבת חלה על הכל ושביעית לא חלה אלא על עבודת הארץ בלבד:

ולבר קפרא דתני כלל גדול במעשר כו'. נראה לרשב"א דאחרים לא שנו כלל גדול במעשר לפי שאינו גדול מפאה אלא מדרבנן אבל כלל גדול דשבת גדול משביעית מדאורייתא וכן של שביעית משל מעשר: **ואילו** פאה ליתא בתאנה וירק. לאו דוקא תאנה דהא רוב אילנות אין לקיטתן כאחד ואינן רק ה' אילנות דחשיב בפ"ק דפאה (מ"ה) דחייב בפאה אלא נקט תאנה משום דנלקטת כמה פעמים כדאמרינן בחזקת הבתים (ב"ב דף כח:) אכל ג' פירי בחד יומא כגון תאנה כו' ואומר ר"ת דמדאורייתא לא מיחייב בפאה אלא בדגן ותירוש ויצהר דסתם קציר דכתיב גבי פאה הוא דגן וכתיב כי תחבוט זיתך כי תבצור כרמך והא דדריש בת"כ יכול שאני מרבה קישואין ודלועין שיהיו חייבים בפאה ת"ל ובקוצרכם את קציר ארצכם מה קציר שהוא אוכל ונשמר כו' אסמכתא היא דהתם נמי דריש מעשר ירק מקרא אע"ג דהוי מדרבנן ומה שלא תקנו פאה בירק ובתאנה ודמי לה כמו שתקנו מעשר מהן אומר ר"ת משום דאין לקיטתן כאחד דבר מועט הוא פאה דידיה ויש הפסד לעניים בה יותר מן הריוח שמתבטלין לפי שאין יודעים זמן לקיטתן ודבר שאין מכניסו לקיום נמי לא חשיב ויפסידו יותר ממה שירויחו במקום אחר: **ספיחי** סטים וקוצה. הא דלא קאמר סתם למעוטי מידי דלאו אוכל אלא נקט הני אומר ר"י משום דקלא הס ראויים לאכילה וקמ"ל דאפילו הכי אין פאה נוהגת בהן וכן מלא רשב"ם בתשובת רש"י והא דנקט ספיחים משום דשמא סטים וקוצה עצמם אינם ראוים כלל לאכילת אדם ולא הוה מידום או שמא הן אוכל גמור ולא ממעטינן: **גר** שנתגייר בין הנכרים. בפני ג' ולא הודיעוהו מצות שבת דאי נתגייר בינו לבין עצמו לא הוי גר כדאמרינן בהחולץ (יבמות דף מז:): אבל

עין משפט נר מצוה

ג א מיי' שם הלכה ז ופ"ז מהלכות שבת הלכה ט:

רבינו חננאל

תנא כלל גדול הכא משום חומרא דשבת גדולה מכלל שביעית דאילו איסורא דשבת חלה בין בתלוש ובין במחובר ואיסורא דשביעית אינה אלא מן המחובר לקרקע ותוב איסורא דשביעית גדולה מאיסורא דמעשר שהשביעית חלה באוכלי אדם ובאוכלי בהמה והמעשר אינו חל [אלא] על אוכלי אדם בלבד לפיכך קתני כלל גדול בשביעית ולבר קפרא משום דעונש של מעשרות גדול מעונשה של פאה לפיכך תני כלל גדול במעשר. ותנא דידן שבת ושביעית דחומרא דאורייתא תני כלל גדול. אבל מעשר כגון ירק וכיוצא בו דחומרא דרבנן הוא לא קתני כלל גדול.

רב נסים גאון

פרק ז **אמרו** גדול עונשה של שבת יותר משל שביעית דאילו שבת איתא בין בתלוש ובין במחובר. ודבר זה מפורסם וברור כי אפילו המוציא מרשות לרשות בשבת חייב חטאת והרבה מן המלאכות שאינן במחובר והן ידועות ואין אנו צריכין למנותן ואילו שביעית במחובר איתא בתלוש ליתא ועיקר דילה בתורת כהנים הזרע והזמיר בכלל היו ולמה יצאו להקיש אליהן מה זרע וזמר מיוחדין שהן עבודה בארץ ובאילן אף אין לי אלא דבר שהיא עבודה בארץ ובאילן ועיקר דילה בפרק משקין בית השלחין (מועד קטן דף ג) וגדול עונשה של שביעית יותר משל מעשר דאילו שביעית איתא בין במאכל אדם בין במאכל בהמה ועיקרה בתורה דכתיב (ויקרא כה) ולבהמתך ולחיה אשר בארצך ובמשנה (שביעית פ' ד) כלל גדול אמרו בשביעית כל שהוא מאוכל אדם ומאוכל בהמה וממין הצובעים ואינו מתקיים בארץ יש לו שביעית ולדמיו שביעית ואילו מעשר במאכל אדם איתיה במאכל בהמה ליתיה. עיקר דבר זה הוא כתוב בתורה (דברים יד) עשר תעשר את כל תבואת זרעך וסמיך ליה ואכלת דבר שהוא אוכל ובמשנה (מעשרות פרק א) כל שהוא אוכל:

מסורת הש"ס

א) [כריתות טז:], ב) פאה פ"א מ"ד פסחים נו: נדה נ., ג) מעשרות פ"א מ"א נדה נ., ד) [צ"ל שביעי].

הגהות הב"ח

(א) גמרא מעשר דקתני עוד כלל אחר:

גליון הש"ס

גמרא למעוטי תאנה. עיין ר"ה דף טו ע"ב תוס' ד"ה נהגו העם:

ליקוטי רש"י

דאילו מעשר איתא בתאנה וירק. מדרבנן דמדאורייתא לא מיחייב אלא דגן ותירוש ויצהר. **כל שהוא אוכל וכו'.** בפאה כתיב (ויקרא יט) ובקוצרכם את קציר וגו' דומיא דקציר דמכניסו לקיום ואיכא כל הני [נדה נ.]. **ונשמר.** שאינו מופקר ומקפידין עליו לשומרו. **ומכניסו לקיום.** שמתקיים ימים רבים [פסחים נו:]. שאדם יכול לאוצרו [נדה שם]. **למעוטי ספיחי סטים וקוצה.** סטים קרוג"א בלע"ז כרכום קוצה גווד"א בלע"ז [ב"ק קא:]. דאין אוכל אלא מין צבע. סטים, קרו"ג. קוצה, ויטר"א ולא ידענא אמאי נקט ספיחים וכמדומה לי שהראשונים ראויים לאכילה [נדה שם]. ספיחי סטים וקוצה קשין לאכילה אבל סטים וקוצה שאינם ספיחים חזו לאכילה. סטים, מוריק"א קרו"ג. קוצה, ווישר"א. **תאנה.** אינה מתבשלת כאחת אלא זו גמורה היום ואחרת יוצאה בגידה כל ימות הקיץ [פסחים שם]. **ואילו לקיטתו כאחד.** דממעט תאנה ומכניסו לקיום דממעט ירק [נדה שם]. **כמיהין ופטריות.** יוצאין כמות שכן בלילה אחד ורכבין ועגולין כגלוסקאות [לעיל ל:]. בולי"ץ בלע"ז שיצאו מלחלוחית העצים [תענית כה.]. מאוירא ינקי שאין להם שרשים בארץ [נדרים נה:]. דלאו פירות הארץ נינהו [ר"ן שם]. מלחלוחית הארץ הם גדלים על העצים ועל הכלים [ברכות מ:].

Sabbath in **this** case, where even *now* he knows the essence of the Sabbath but forgot the Sabbath day![40] – ? –

The Gemara answers:

מַאי הַיּוֹדֵעַ עִיקַּר שַׁבָּת – What does the Mishnah mean when it says: ONE WHO KNOWS THE ESSENCE OF THE SABBATH? **מִי שֶׁהָיָה יוֹדֵעַ עִיקָּרָהּ שֶׁל שַׁבָּת וּשְׁכָחָהּ** – It means: **One who** *once* **knew the essence of the Sabbath and** then **forgot it.** It does not mean that the person knew about the essence of the Sabbath when he committed the violations.

NOTES

40. [It is the style of the Mishnah to teach a law in the case of its greatest novelty and to allow the reader to conclude from that ruling that the law certainly holds true in more obvious situations. Thus, if the law requiring a separate *chatas* for each Sabbath violated applies to both the case of one who forgot the essence of the Sabbath as well as to the case of one who knew the essence of the Sabbath but lost track of the days of the week, the Tanna should have taught the law of a *chatas*-per-Sabbath in the case of one who forgot the essence of the Sabbath, rather than the day of the week, since this is the more novel case.] For if the person totally forgot the law of the Sabbath, there is no reason to assume that he remembered it again during the intervening weekdays. Thus, there is no natural reason to divide his transgressions into separate errors and separate liabilities. If he is nevertheless liable to a separate *chatas* for each Sabbath that he desecrated, then he is certainly liable to multiple *chatas* offerings when he knew the essence of Sabbath but kept forgetting which day is the Sabbath. For in this case there is reason to divide his transgressions into separate liabilities, namely, the likelihood that he *did* become aware of his error concerning the day of the week during the intervening days (*Rashi*).

אב מלאכה ומלאכה (א) [א] העושה מלאכות הרבה מעין מלאכה אחת אינו חייב אלא חטאת אחת: גמ' מ"ט תנא כלל גדול אילימא משום דקבעי למיתני עוד כלל אחר תנא כלל גדול וגבי שביעית נמי משום דקבעי למיתני עוד כלל אחר תנא כלל גדול והא גבי מעשר דקתני (א) כלל אחר ולא תני כלל גדול א"ר יוסי בר אבין שבת ושביעית דאית בהו אבות ותולדות תנא גדול מעשר דלית בה אבות ותולדות לא תנא כלל גדול ולבר קפרא דתני כלל גדול במעשר מאי אבות ומאי תולדות איכא אלא לאו היינו טעמא גדול עונשו של שבת יותר משל שביעית דאילו שבת איתא בין בתלוש בין במחובר ואילו שביעית בתלוש ליתא במחובר איתא וגדול עונשה של שביעית יותר מן המעשר דאילו שביעית איתא בין במאכל אדם בין במאכל בהמה ואילו מעשר במאכל אדם איתא במאכל בהמה ליתא ולבר קפרא דתני כלל גדול במעשר גדול עונשו של מעשר יותר משל פיאה דאילו מעשר איתא בתאנה וירק ואילו פיאה ליתא בתאנה וירק [ב] דתנן כלל אמרו בפיאה כל שהוא אוכל ונשמר וגידולו מן הארץ ולקיטתו כאחת ומכניסו לקיום חייב בפיאה אוכל למעוטי ספיחי סטים וקוצה ונשמר למעוטי הפקר וגידולו מן הארץ למעוטי כמיהין ופטריות ולקיטתו כאחת ° למעוטי תאנה ומכניסו לקיום למעוטי ירק ואילו גבי מעשר תנן [ג] כלל אמרו במעשר כל שהוא אוכל ונשמר וגידולו מן הארץ חייב במעשר ואילו לקיטתו כאחת ומכניסו לקיום לא תנן: רב ושמואל דאמרי תרוייהו מתניתין בתינוק שנשבה לבין הנכרים וגר שנתגייר לבין הנכרים אבל הכיר ולבסוף שכח חייב על כל שבת ושבת תנן השוכח עיקר שבת לאו מכלל דהויא ליה ידיעה מעיקרא לא מאי כל השוכח עיקר שבת דהיתה שכוח ממנו עיקרה של שבת אבל הכיר ולבסוף שכח מאי חייב על כל שבת ושבת אדתני היודע עיקר שבת ועשה מלאכות הרבה בשבתות הרבה חייב על כל שבת ושבת ליתני הכיר ולבסוף שכח וכ"ש הא מאי היודע עיקר שבת מי שהיה יודע עיקרה של שבת ושכחה אבל

רש"י

אב מלאכה דנקט לאו למעוטי תולדות דה"ה לתולדות ובלבד שיהו תולדות דשני אבות אלא למעוטי היכא דהוו ב' תולדות דאב אחד או אב ותולדה שלו דאינו חייב אלא אחת כדקתני סיפא העושה מלאכות הרבה מעין מלאכה אחת שתי תולדות של אב אחד אינו חייב אלא חטאת אחת דהרי הוא כעושה וחוזר ועושה בהעלם אחד ואין חילוק חטאות בהעלם אחד אלא בגופי עבירה שאינן דומין או בחילוק שבתות לענין שגגת שבת: גמ' עוד כלל אחר. לקמן בפירקין (דף עה:) ולא כלל בו אלא ב' דברים כל הכשר להצניע וכל שאינו כשר להצניע וכאן כלל יותר ומשום הכי קרי להו גדול: וגבי שביעית. בפרק [ד] (בנות שוח): גבי מעשר. בפ"ק דמסכת מעשרות: אית ביה אבות. ארבעים חסר אחת שהוצרכו למשכן ותולדות הדומות לכל אחת הויא תולדות דידיה אבות דשביעית זריעה וקצירה וזמירה ובצירה דכתיבן תולדות שאר עבודות שבשדה וכרם כדאמרינן במועד קטן בפ"ק (דף ג.): ולבר קפרא דתנא. בתוספתא דידיה במעשר מאי אבות כו': אלא לאו היינו טעמא. משום אבות ותולדות אלא דבר שנאמר בו כלל ועונשו גדול מדבר אחר שנאמר בו כלל תני ביה כלל גדול: שבת איתא. לאיסור דידה בין בדבר שהיה תלוש מבעוד יום כגון טוחן ולש בין בדבר שמחובר מקודש היום: ואילו שביעית. בדבר שהיה מחובר משקדשה שביעית איתא אבל בדבר שהיה תלוש לפני שביעית ליתא: שביעית. נמי איתיה במאכל בהמה דכתיב ולבהמתך ולחיה וגו' (ויקרא כה) מעשר ליתיה במאכל בהמה דמדאורייתא דגן תירוש ויצהר כתיב ורבנן תקון פירות האילן וירק דמאכל אדם כדקתני כל שהוא אוכל כו': איתיה בתאנה וירק. מדרבנן: כל שהוא אוכל כו'. דגבי פיאה קציר כתיב מה קציר מיוחד שיש בו כל אלו: למעוטי ספיחי סטים וקוצה. שעומדים לצבע להכי נקט ספיחים דאין דרך ללוקטן בשנה שמזרעים אלא לסוף ד' וה' שנים שהשרשין מתפשטין בארץ ומשביחין ושורש שלהן עיקר והא דנקט הני ולא נקט שאר מינים שאינן ראוין לאכילה משום דאיידי דגבי שביעית תני להו דיש להן שביעית נקט הכא דבפיאה ומעשר ליתנהו לשון רבינו הלוי. סטים ווישד"א קול' וורנל"א: ומכניסו לקיום למעוטי ירק. כגון לפת וקפלוטות: ואילו מכניסו לקיום ולקיטתו כאחד לא תנן. דכי תקון רבנן אדידהו לא פלוג בפירות האילן ובירק בין מין למין:

מתניתין. דפטר בחד חטאת: בתינוק שנשבה. ולא ידע שבת מעולם: אבל הכיר ולבסוף שכח. הוה ליה כשוכח שהיום שבת ויודע עיקר שבת וחייב על כל שבת ושבת: שהיתה שכוחה ממנו. מעולם: לתני הכיר ולבסוף שכח. דחייב ואע"ג דליכא למימר ימים שבינתים הווין ידיעה לחלק וכ"ש הא דאיכא למימר שימים שבינתים הווין ליה ידיעה לחלק:

אבל

תוספות

וגבי שביעית נמי כו'. הכי תנן בשביעית (פ"ז מ"א) כלל גדול אמרו כל שהוא מאכל אדם ומאכל בהמה וממין הצובעין ואינו מתקיים בארץ פירות שכלה לחיה יש לו שביעית ולדמיו שביעית יש לו ביעור ולדמיו ביעור ועוד כלל אחר אמרו דקתני כל שאינו מאכל אדם ומאכל בהמה וכו' ומתקיים בארץ יש לו שביעית ולדמיו שביעית ואין לו ולדמיו ביעור דכלל הראשון גדול דיש לו ביעור ואחרון אין לו ביעור ואע"ג דקתני התם בבבא אחריתא כלל גדול אמרו בשביעית ולא קתני בתריה כלל אחר כיון דקתני כלל קטן קמיה שייך למתני בתריה כלל גדול: והא גבי מעשר דקתני עוד כלל אחר אמרו כו'. תימה למה ישנה בראשון כלל גדול כיון דאינו גדול מן השני וצ"ע:

דאית ביה אבות ותולדות. ואפילו לרבא דאמר במועד קטן (דף ג:) גבי שביעית אבות אסר רחמנא תולדות לא אסר רחמנא מ"מ מדרבנן מיהא אית ביה אבות ותולדות וא"ת במעשר איכא נמי אבות ותולדות דמדאורייתא דגן ותירוש ויצהר ומדרבנן כל מילי וי"ל דלא שייך להזכיר אבות ותולדות במילי דלית ביה איסור מלאכות וא"ת ובכלל אחר דשבת ושביעית ליתני נמי כלל גדול מהאי טעמא ויש לומר דלא צריך למיתני דאכלל גדול קמא קאי וה"ק עוד כלל גדול אחר אמרו:

גדול עונשו של שבת משל שביעית. לפירוש הקונטרס דמפרש בתלוש שנתלש קודם שבת וקודם שביעית משמע שרוצה לפרש שביעית במחובר איתא היינו במחובר ערב שביעית ונתלש בשביעית ומיירי באיסור פירות שביעית לאכילה וקשה לר"י דלפי' לא הוה ליה למימר אלא גדול עונשו של שבת ושביעית משל מעשר דאיתנהו במאכל בהמה מה שאין כן במעשר ולמה ליה למימר כלל גדול עונשה של שבת משל שביעית אלא נראה לר"י דבמידי דאכילה דלא שייכא לענין שבת לא שייך למימר גדול שבת לא משביעית ולא ממעשר ולהכי לא קאמר גדול שבת ושביעית ממעשר אלא קאמר גדול שבת משביעית דאיסור מלאכות איתנהו בין בתלוש בין במחובר ואילו איסור מלאכות דשביעית במחובר איתא בתלוש ליתא וכן משמע בירושלמי דקתני שהשבת חלה על הכל ושביעית לא חלה אלא על עבודת הארץ בלבד:

ולבר קפרא דתני כלל גדול במעשר כו'. נראה לרשב"א דאחרים לא שנו כלל גדול במעשר לפי שאינו גדול מפאה אלא מדרבנן אבל כלל גדול דשבת גדול משביעית מדאורייתא וכן של שביעית משל מעשר: ואילו פאה ליתא בתאנה וירק. לאו דוקא תאנה דהא רוב אילנות אין לקיטתן כאחד ואינן רק ה' אילנות דחשיב בפ"ק דפאה (מ"ה) דחייב בפאה אלא נקט תאנה משום דנלקטת כמה פעמים כדאמרינן בחזקת הבתים (ב"ב דף כח:) אכל ג' פירי בחד יומא כגון תאנה כו' ואומר ר"ת דמדאורייתא לא מחייב בפאה אלא בדגן ותירוש ויצהר דסתם קציר דכתיב גבי פאה הוא דגן וכתיב כי תחבוט זיתך כי תבצור כרמך והא דדריש בת"כ יכול שאני מרבה קישואין ודלועין שיהיו חייבים בפאה ת"ל ובקוצרכם את קציר ארצכם מה קציר שהוא אוכל ונשמר כו' אסמכתא היא דהתם נמי דריש מעשר ירק מקרא אע"ג דהוי מדרבנן ומה שלא תקנו פאה בירק ובתאנה ודדמי לה כמו שתקנו מעשר מהן אומר ר"ת משום דאין לקיטתן כאחד דבר מועט הוא פאה דידיה ויש הפסד לעניים בה יותר מן הריוח שמתבטלין לפי שאין יודעים זמן לקיטתן ודבר שאין מכניסו לקיום נמי לא חשיב ויפסידו יותר ממה שירויחו במקום אחר: ספיחי סטים וקוצה. הא דלא קאמר סתם למעוטי מידי דלאו אוכל אלא נקט הני אומר ר"י משום דקלת הם ראויים לאכילה וקמ"ל דאפילו הכי אין פאה נוהגת בהן וכן מלא רשב"ם בתשובת רש"י והא דנקט ספיחים משום דשמא סטים וקוצה עצמם אינם ראויים כלל לאכילת אדם ולא הוה חידוש או שמא הן אוכל גמור ולא ממעטינן:

גר שנתגייר בין הנכרים. בפני ג' ולא הודיעוהו מצות שבת דאי נתגייר בינו לבין עצמו לא הוי גר כדאמרינן בהחולץ (יבמות דף מז:):

אבל

מסורת הש"ס

א) [כריתות טז:], ב) פאה פ"א מ"ד פסחים נו: נדה נ., ג) מעשרות פ"א מ"א נדה נ., ד) [צ"ל שביעי].

הגהות הב"ח

(א) גמרא מעשר דקתני עוד כלל אחר:

גליון הש"ס

גמרא למעוטי תאנה. עיין ר"ה דף טו ע"ב תוס' ד"ה נהגו העם:

ליקוטי רש"י

דאילו מעשר איתא בתאנה וירק. מדרבנן דמדאורייתא לא מיחייב אלא דגן ותירוש ויצהר. כל שהוא אוכל וכו'. בפאה כתיב (ויקרא יט) ובקוצרכם את קציר וגו' דומיא דקציר דמכניסו לקיום ואיכא כל הני [נדה נ.]. ונשמר. שאינו מופקר ומקפידין עליו לשומרו. ומכניסו לקיום. שמתקיים ימים רבים [פסחים נו:]. שאדם יכול לאוצרו [נדה שם]. למעוטי ספיחי סטים וקוצה. סטים קרוג"א בלע"ז כרכום קוצה גוד"א בלע"ז [ב"ק קא:]. דאין אוכל אלא מין צבע. סטים, קרו"ג. קוצה, ויטר"א ולא ידענא אמאי נקט ספיחים וכמדומה לי שהראשונים ראויים לאכילה [נדה שם]. ספיחי סטים וקוצה קשין לאכילה אבל סטים וקוצה שאינם ספיחים חזו לאכילה. סטים, מוריק"א קרו"ג. קוצה, ווישר"א. תאנה. אינה מתבשלת כאחת אלא זו גמורה היום ואחרת יוצאה בלידה כל ימות הקיץ [פסחים שם]. ואילו לקיטתו כאחד. דממעט תאנה ומכניסו לקיום דממעט ירק [נדה שם]. כמיהין ופטריות. יוצאין כמות שהן בלילה אחד ורחבין ועגולין כגלוסקאות [לעיל ל:]. בולי"ץ בלע"ז שיוצאו מלחלוח הגשמים [תענית כג.]. מאוירא ינקי שאין להם שרשים בארץ [נדרים נה:]. דלאו פירות הארץ נינהו [ר"ן שם]. מלחלוחית הארץ הם גדלים על העצים ועל הכלים [ברכות מ:].

עין משפט נר מצוה

ג א מיי' שם הלכה ז ופ"ז מהלכות שבת הלכה ט:

רבינו חננאל

תנא כלל גדול הכא משום חומרא דשבת גדולה מכלל שביעית דאילו איסורא דשבת חלה בין בתלוש ובין במחובר ואיסורא דשביעית אינה אלא מן המחובר לקרקע ותוב איסורא דשביעית גדולה מאיסורא דמעשר שהשביעית חלה באוכלי אדם ובאוכלי בהמה והמעשר אינו חל [אלא] על אוכלי אדם בלבד לפיכך קתני כלל גדול בשביעית ולבר קפרא משום דעונש של מעשרות גדול מעונשה של פאה לפיכך תני כלל גדול במעשר. ותנא דידן שבת ושביעית דחומרא דאורייתא תני כלל גדול. אבל מעשר כגון ירק וכיוצא בו דחומרא דרבנן הוא לא קתני כלל גדול.

רב נסים גאון

פרק ז אמרו גדול עונשה של שבת יותר משל שביעית דאילו שבת איתא בין בתלוש ובין במחובר. ודבר זה מפורסם וברור כי אפילו המוציא מרשות לרשות בשבת חייב חטאת והרבה מן המלאכות שאינן במחובר והן ידועות ואין אנו צריכין למנותן ואילו שביעית במחובר איתא בתלוש ליתא ועיקר דילה בתורת כהנים הזרע והזמיר בכלל היו ולמה יצאו להקיש אליהן מה זרע חמר מיוחדין שהן עבודה בארץ ובאילן אף אין לי אלא דבר שהיא עבודה בארץ ובאילן ועיקר דילה בפרק משקין בית השלחין (מועד קטן דף ג) וגדול עונשה של שביעית יותר משל מעשר דאילו שביעית איתא בין במאכל אדם בין במאכל בהמה ועיקרה בתורה דכתיב (ויקרא כה) ולבהמתך ולחיה אשר בארצך ובמשנה (שביעית פ' ז) כלל גדול אמרו בשביעית כל שהוא מאוכל אדם ומאוכל בהמה וממין הצובעים ואינו מתקיים בארץ יש לו שביעית ולדמיו שביעית: ואילו מעשר במאכל אדם איתיה במאכל בהמה ליתיה. עיקר דבר זה הוא כתוב בתורה (דברים יד) עשר תעשר את כל תבואת זרעך וסמיך ליה ואכלת דבר שהוא אוכל ובמשנה (מעשרות פרק א) כל שהוא אוכל:

עין משפט
נר מצוה

ד א מיי' פ"ב מהלכות שגגות הלכה ו ופ"ז הלכה ג סמג עשין ריג:

רבינו חננאל

מתני' לדברי הכל בהכיר ולבסוף שכח אינו חייב אלא חטאת אחת ורב ושמואל הוסיפו אפילו קטן שנשבה לבין עו"ג כהכיר ולבסוף שכח דמי וחייב חטאת ורבי יוחנן וריש לקיש אמרי קטן שנשבה בין עו"ג פטור ואותיבנא עלייהו מהא דתניא השוכח עיקר שבת ועשה מלאכות הרבה בשבתות הרבה אינו חייב אלא חטאת אחת וחייב על ע"ז אחת. פירש אם עבד ע"ז הרבה דינו כדין שבת וכן כל מצוה ומצוה אינו חייב אלא בכל מצוה אחת ומונבז פוטר בכל ומשני רבי יוחנן וריש לקיש אנן דאמרינן כמונבז דסבר כיון דלא הויא ידיעה ליה בתחלה בעיקר שבת אף על גב דבתר דעביד מלאכות הרבה בשבתות הרבה אתיידע ליה איסורא דשבת לא מחייב וכי אמרו רבי יוחנן ור"ל דאנן כמונבז סבירא לן בהאי לחוד דפטר קטן שנשבה בין הנכרים אבל בהאי דבעי ידיעה למונבז בשעת מעשה שידע

רב נסים גאון

ורבנן כדמקרי ליה ר' יהושע בן לוי לבריה תורה אחת יהיה לכם לעושה בשגגה והנפש אשר תעשה ביד רמה הוקשה כל התורה כולה לע"ז. דע שפרשת (במדבר טו) וכי תשגו ולא תעשו ואם נפש אחת תחטא בשגגה שממנה אלו הפסוקים אמרו רבותינו ז"ל כי היא מיוחדת בע"ז ותמצא פירוש זה בספרי בע"ז הכתוב מדבר אתה אומר בע"ז או אינו אלא באחת מן המצות האמורות בתורה ת"ל והיה אם מעיני העדה נעשתה ייחד הכתוב מצוה זו בפני עצמה ואיזו זו ע"ז וכו' ובמסכת הוריות בפ' הורה כהן משיח (דף ח) אמרו דכולי עלמא הני קראי בע"ז הוא דכתיבי מנא לן אמר רבא ואיתימא ר' יהושע בן לוי ואמרי לה כדי וכי תשגו ולא תעשו את כל המצות האלה איזו היא מצוה שהיא שקולה כנגד כל המצות כולן הוי אומר זו ע"ז דבית ר' תנא אמר קרא א) את כל אשר דבר ה' אליכם ביד משה איזו היא מצוה

חשק שלמה
על רב נסים גאון

א) אשר דבר ה' אל משה את כל אשר צוה ה' אליכם ביד משה כצ"ל:

תורה אור השלם

א) הָאֶזְרָח בִּבְנֵי יִשְׂרָאֵל וְלַגֵּר הַגָּר בְּתוֹכָם תּוֹרָה אַחַת יִהְיֶה לָכֶם לָעֹשֶׂה בִּשְׁגָגָה: [במדבר טו, כט]

ב) וְהַנֶּפֶשׁ אֲשֶׁר תַּעֲשֶׂה בְּיָד רָמָה מִן הָאֶזְרָח וּמִן הַגֵּר אֶת יְיָ הוּא מְגַדֵּף וְנִכְרְתָה הַנֶּפֶשׁ הַהִוא מִקֶּרֶב עַמָּהּ: [במדבר טו, ל]

אבל לא שכחה מאי א) חייב על כל מלאכה ומלאכה אדתני היודע שהוא שבת ועשה מלאכות הרבה בשבתות הרבה חייב על כל מלאכה ומלאכה ליתני היודע עיקר שבת וכל שכן הא אלא מתניתין כשהכיר ולבסוף שכח ודרב ושמואל נמי כהכיר ולבסוף שכח דמי והכי איתמר רב ושמואל דאמרי תרווייהו [א] אפילו תינוק שנשבה בין הנכרים וגר שנתגייר לבין הנכרים כהכיר ולבסוף שכח דמי וחייב ורבי יוחנן ורבי שמעון בן לקיש דאמרי תרווייהו דוקא הכיר ולבסוף שכח אבל תינוק שנשבה בין הנכרים וגר שנתגייר לבין הנכרים פטור מיתיבי כלל גדול אמרו בשבת כל השוכח עיקר שבת ועשה מלאכות הרבה בשבתות הרבה אינו חייב אלא אחת כיצד תינוק שנשבה לבין הנכרים וגר שנתגייר בין הנכרים ועשה מלאכות הרבה בשבתות הרבה אינו חייב אלא חטאת אחת וחייב על הדם אחת ועל החלב אחת ועל ע"ז אחת ומונבז פוטר וכך היה מונבז דן לפני רבי עקיבא הואיל ומזיד קרוי חוטא ושוגג קרוי חוטא מה מזיד שהיתה לו ידיעה אף שוגג שהיתה לו ידיעה אמר לו ר' עקיבא הריני מוסיף על דבריך אי מה מזיד שהיתה הידיעה בשעת מעשה אף שוגג שהיתה לו ידיעה בשעת מעשה אמר לו הן וכל שכן שהוספת אמר לו לדבריך אין זה קרוי שוגג אלא מזיד קתני מיהא כיצד תינוק בשלמא לרב ושמואל ניחא אלא לרבי יוחנן ולרבי שמעון בן לקיש קשיא אמרי לך רבי יוחנן וריש לקיש לא מי איכא מונבז דפטר אנן דאמרינן כמונבז מאי טעמא דמונבז דכתיב א) תורה אחת יהיה לכם לעושה בשגגה וסמיך ליה ב) והנפש אשר תעשה ביד רמה הקיש שוגג למזיד מה מזיד שהיתה לו ידיעה אף שוגג שהיתה לו ידיעה ורבנן האי תורה אחת מאי עבדי ליה מיבעי להו א) לכדמקרי ליה ר' יהושע בן לוי לבריה תורה אחת יהיה לכם לעושה בשגגה וכתיב וכי

אבל לא שכחה מאי חייב על כל מלאכה ומלאכה. תימה לר"י מנא ליה למידק הכי אימא דלא שכחה נמי אינו חייב על כל מלאכה ומלאכה אלא על כל שבת ושבת כמו בהכיר ולבסוף שכח ותנא הכיר ולבסוף שכח וכ"ש הא כדפרי' ומה שפי' בקונטרס דדייק דחייב על כל מלאכה ומלאכה מדלא כייל להו אהדדי מי שידע עיקר שבת ושכחה והיודע עיקר שבת חייב על כל שבת ושבת דהוה משמע דוקא על כל שבת ושבת ולא על כל מלאכה אין נראה לר"י דא"כ היכי פריך לעיל לתני הכיר ולבסוף שכח וכל שכן הא דמשמע דהא לא איצטריך למיתני והא נמי איצטריך לאשמעינן דאינו חייב על כל מלאכה ומלאכה ונראה לר"י דלעיל דקאמר ליתני הכיר ולבסוף שכח וכ"ש הא לא בעי למימר דלא ליתני' כלל במשנה אלא ה"פ מדקתני חייב על כל שבת ושבת ולא קתני אינו חייב אלא על כל שבת דהוה משמע ולא על כל מלאכה ומלאכה משמע דעיקר מתניתין חיובא אתא לאשמעינן דחייב על כל שבת ושבת ולא פטורא דאינו חייב על כל מלאכה ואם כן ליתני הכיר ולבסוף שכח דהוי רבותא טפי וכ"ש האי דחייב על כל שבת ולא הוה צריך למתנייה בהאי בבא אלא ה"ל למיתני בתר הכי בבבא אחריתי היודע עיקר שבת אינו חייב אלא על כל שבת ושבת לאשמעינן דאינו חייב על כל מלאכה והשתא דייק שפיר אבל לא שכחה מאי חייב על כל מלאכה ומלאכה מדלא תני בבבא אחריתי דאינו חייב אלא על כל שבת ושבת ב):

ליתני היודע עיקר שבת וכ"ש הא. תימה לר"י לרבא דאמר בכריתות בסוף פרק אמרו לו (דף טז:) דבזדון שבת ושגגת מלאכות לא מיחייב אכל שבת ושבת ודייק ממתניתין דהכא דלא קתני חייב על כל אב מלאכה ומלאכה של כל שבת ושבת ולדידיה היכי פריך הכא ליתני היודע עיקר שבת הא לא מצי למיתני הכי דאם כן הוה משמע דלא מיחייב היודע עיקר שבת אכל שבת ושבת ותירץ דהכי פריך דליתני היודע עיקר שבת דחייב אכל אב מלאכה של כל שבת ושבת ורשב"א מפרש דאי הוה תני בהדיא היודע עיקר שבת חייב על כל אב מלאכה ליכא למידק דלא מיחייב אכל שבת מדלא קתני חייב על כל אב מלאכה של כל שבת ושבת דלא צריך למיתני' דמרישא שמעינן ליה דקתני בהכיר ולבסוף שכח דחייב על כל שבת ושבת כ"ש יודע עיקר שבת כדאמר לעיל: **וכ"ש** האי. ה"נ לא בעי למימר דלא לתני' כלל במשנה דאם כן הוה אמינא דחייב נמי על כל שבת ושבת ואינו כן לרבה דכריתות אלא ליתני בבא אחריתי היודע שהוא שבת אינו חייב על כל שבת:

אבל לא שכחה. לעיקר שבת אלא ששכח שהיום שבת מאי: **חייב על כל אב מלאכה.** דע"כ אי הוה סבירא ליה דאינו חייב אלא אחת לכל שבת ושבת הוה ליה (א) למיכרך ולמיתני הכי מי שידע עיקר שבת ושכחה וכן היודע עיקר שבת ועשה מלאכות הרבה בשבתות הרבה חייב על כל שבת ושבת: **ליתני היודע עיקר שבת.** דהוה שגגת שבת וזדון מלאכות הרבה חייב על כל מלאכה אע"ג דבכל שבת ליכא אלא חדא שגגה וכ"ש שגגת מלאכות וזדון שבת דאיכא שגגות הרבה: **כהכיר ולבסוף שכח דמי.** ומתניתין איצטריך למינקט הכיר ולבסוף שכח דלא תימא חייב על כל שבת ושבת: **פטור.** דקסברי רבי יוחנן ור"ל אומר מותר אנוס הוא ולא שגגה היא: **וחייב על הדם.** שאכל כל ימיו אחת וכן על כל דבר כרת שבתורה: **מזיד קרוי חוטא.** דכתיב (ויקרא ה) בשבועת העדות נפש כי תחטא ושמעה וגומר ולא כתיב ביה ונעלם: **הריני מוסיף על דבריך.** כלומר אם כך באת לדרוש ג"ש ללמד שוגג ממזיד בא ואוסיף גם אני על דבריך עוד וזה תראה אם יעמדו דבריך: **אף שוגג שהיתה לו ידיעה בשעת מעשה.** תחייבהו גם בזו חטאת: **כ"ש שהוספת.** על דברי והרי אתה מסייעני וגם בזו אני אומר שהוא חייב ולקמן מפרש במאי שגג: **קתני מיהא.** רישא תינוק שנשבה לבין הנכרים חייב: **בשלמא לרב ושמואל ניחא.** דאינהו נמי מחייבי ואיכא לאוקמי דהוא הדין להכיר ולבסוף שכח כי מתניתין וברייתא דקתני תינוק היא גופא איצטריך לאשמעינן פלוגתא דמונבז ורבנן: **מאי טעמא דמונבז.** אבנין אב ודאי לא סמיך למיעבד שוגג דומיא דמזיד דהאי שוגג חילוף דמזיד וליכא לדמוינהו דהאי חייב והאי פטור: **מקיש שוגג.** לענין חטאת למזיד לענין כרת ואף על גב דלא דמי ע"כ הקישן הכתוב: **ורבנן.** הך הקישא בעיא לכדרבי יהושע ב"ל: **תורה אחת יהיה לכם.** גבי קרבן ע"ז כתיב בפרשת שלח לך אנשים: וכי

כי הכיר ולבסוף שכח דמי. פירש בקונטרס דלהכי לא תנא במתניתין שכח מעיקרו דהיינו תינוק שנשבה דלא תימא דהכיר ולבסוף שכח חייב על כל שבת וקשה לר"י דמ"מ ליתנייה וליתני נמי בתר הכי הכיר ולבסוף שכח אינו חייב אלא אחת דכה"ג פריך לעיל ליתני הכיר ולבסוף שכח וכ"ש הא כדפרישית ונראה לר"י דודאי אי הוה תני חייב חטאת דהוה אתי לאשמעינן חיובא הוה שייך למיפרך ליתני תינוק שנשבה דהוי רבותא טפי אבל השתא דקתני אינו חייב אלא אחת אתא לאשמעינן פטורא נקט הכיר ולבסוף שכח דהוי רבותא טפי ומיהו קשה לר"י דמ"מ ליתני תינוק שנשבה דלא נטעה לומר דפטור כרבי יוחנן וריש לקיש והדר ליתני הכיר ולבסוף שכח: **אבל** תינוק שנשבה פטור. פירש בקונטרס דקסברי אומר מותר אנוס הוא ואין נראה דטעמייהו כמונבז כדאמר בסמוך וטעמא דמונבז מפרש לקמן דיליף מקרא והא דאמר בפ"ב דמכות (דף ז:) גבי גלות בשגגה פרט למזיד ומפרש (אביי) [נ"ל רבא] פרט לאומר מותר ופריך ליה (רבא) [נ"ל אביי] אומר מותר אנוס הוא לאו דוקא קאמר אנוס דבכל מקום מחייבין ליה אלא לגבי גלות דוקא ממעט (אביי) [נ"ל רבא] אומר מותר משום דטובא בשגגה כתיב התם דהא בפירקין (ב) מחייבי אומר מותר בע"ז ובחלב אע"ג דכתיב בהן בשגגה (ורבא) [נ"ל ואביי] פריך ליה אומר מותר אנוס הוא ולא הוה ליה למיתני בברייתא בשגגה פרט למזיד אלא פרט לאנוס דיותר דמי וקרוב לאנוס מלמזיד: **וחייב** על הדם אחת. אע"ג דמילתא דפשיטא היא דאכל מה שאכל דם אינו חייב אלא אחת כיון שאין בדם חילוק איסור כמו שיש בשבת חילוק מלאכות וכל אדם נמי בלא תינוק שנשבה אכל דם ודם אינו חייב אלא אחת אלא אומר ר"י דמיירי דאפי' (לקמן דף עא.) לר"י דבכמה תמחוין אכלן אפי' בהעלם אחד ובתינוק שנשבה אינו חייב אלא אחד אך קשה לרשב"א דמאי איצטריך תו לאשמעינן ולמתני ועל החלב אחד: **כל** שכן שהוספת. כדפירש בקונטרס דאף בזו מחייב ומחייב נמי כי ליכא ידיעה בשעת מעשה דהא רבי יוחנן וריש לקיש סברי כמונבז ומחייבי הכיר ולבסוף שכח ותניא נמי לקמן שגג בזה ובזה זהו שוגג האמור בתורה ומוקמינן לה כמונבז והיינו טעמא משום דסברא הוא דלא איתקש שוגג למזיד לאפוקי ליה ממשמעות שגגה דאדרבה שוגג משמע דלית ליה ידיעה בשעת מעשה ולא אתא היקשא אלא לחייב נמי כי אית ליה ידיעה בשעת מעשה ומיהו קשה לר"י דהא פטרי מהיקשא תינוק שנשבה מהאי טעמא נמי יפטור הכיר ולבסוף שכח: מה

מסורת הש"ס

א) יבמות דף ט. הוריות ח ע"א.

תוספות ישנים

א) ונוקי אחת שהיא הנה בין שגגת שבת וזדון מלאכה בין בזדון שבת ושגגת מלאכה כפי' רב נחמן לרב חייא. והנה שהיא אחת בהכיר ולבסוף שכח:

ב) לר"י דפי' דדייק מדלא קתני לה בבא אחריתי ולא שיפרש אינו חייב על כל מלאכה לא נתיישב לי דהא לא איצטריך למיתני בבא אחריתא דמסיפא שמעינן מדקתני היודע שהוא שבת חייב על כל מלאכה ומשמע הא שכחה אינו חייב על כל מלאכה. ועוד מאי פריך בסמוך ליתני היודע עיקר שבת וכ"ש הא מאי הוי צריך למיתני היודע עיקר שבת שהוא חייב על כל מלאכה והא שמעינן לה מדלא תני בבא אחריתי כדפרי'. והיה נ"ל דלעיל פריך ליתני הכיר ולבסוף שכח בהדיא וכ"ש היודע עיקר שבת ולא הוי צריך כלל למיתני דחייב על כל שבת דשמעינן מכ"ש דהכיר ולבסוף שכח שאינו חייב על כל מלאכה. מדנקט בסיפא היודע שהוא שבת כו' משמע דהיודע עיקר שבת ושכחה אינו חייב על כל מלאכה. אבל השתא דמשני דיודע עיקר שבת היינו הכיר ולבסוף שכח פריך שפיר אבל לא שכחה מאי חייב על כל מלאכה. דאי אינו חייב כמו בשכחה א"כ אמאי נקט היודע עיקר שבת דמשמע טפי דאיירי בלא שכחה ה"ל למיתני בהדיא הכיר ולבסוף שכח דהוי משמע רבותא טפי אלא ודאי בשלא שכחה חייב על כל מלאכה והוי בכלל בבא דסיפא. להכי ליכא למיטעי במאי דנקט האי לישנא דהיודע עיקר שבת ולא נקט הכיר ולבסוף שכח בהדיא אימא סיפא היודע שהוא שבת וכו'. בשלמא אי הוי תני בהדיא היודע עיקר שבת ולא שכחה בסיפא הוי ידעינן ליה מכ"ש דסיפא א"ש כדפרישית אבל השתא דהיודע עיקר שבת ולא שכחה לא שמעינן מסיפא אלא אדרבה משמע דוקא יודע שהוא שבת חייב על כל מלאכה אם כן מציעתא משמע דמיירי ביודע עיקר שבת ולא שכחה כדמשמע לישנא. ומשמע דוקא לא שכחה אבל שכחה אינו חייב על כל שבת. דאי חייב ליתני הכיר ולבסוף שכחה בהדיא וכל שכן היודע עיקר שבת ולא שכחה כדפרי' לעיל:

הגהות הב"ח

(א) רש"י ד"ה חייב על וכו' ה"ל למיתני כצ"ל ותיבת למיכרך נמחק: (ב) תוס' ד"ה אבל תינוק וכו' דהא בפירקין. נ"ב בסוף דף עב:

ליקוטי רש"י

לכדמקרי ליה ר' יהושע בן לוי לבריה תורה אחת. לענין קרבן כתיב [בפרשת] עבודת כוכבים תורה כל התורה במשמע הוקשה כל התורה לענין קרבן לעבודת כוכבים [יבמות ט.].

[מכאן שייך לדף סט.]

וכי תשגו. בעבודה זרה הכתוב מדבר או אינו אלא באחת מכל המצות תלמוד לומר את כל המצות האלה מצוה אחת שהיא ככל המצות מה העובר על כל המצות פורק עול ומפר ברית ומגלה פנים אף מצוה זו פורק בה עול ומפר ברית ומגלה פנים ואיזו זו עבודה זרה [במדבר טו, כב]. **ביד רמה.** במזיד [שם, ל]. **הוקשו כולם לע"ז.** שהוקשו כל חטאות שבתורה לחטאת עבודה זרה דכתיב תורה אחת יהיה לכם וגו' [לקמן קלז.]. דהוקשה כל התורה כולה לענין קרבן לעבודת כוכבים שנאמר בפרשת שלח לך אנשים אצל קרבן עבודת כוכבים תורה אחת יהיה לכם לעושה בשגגה כאן הוקשו כל עבירות שבתורה בשגגתן לעבודת כוכבים לענין קרבן [מכות יג:]. **מה להלן דבר שחייבים על זדונו כרת ושגגתו חטאת.** דהכא כתיב הכרת תכרת אף כו' [הוריות ח.]. כדכתיב התם והנפש אשר תעשה ביד רמה ונכרתה אלמא כולה פרשתא בדבר שזדונו כרת ושגגתו חטאת מישתעי [יבמות ט.]. **מעם.** ולא כל עם וגבי חטאת כתיב שבא [על] השוגג [חולין ה:]. **מעם הארץ.** מביא קרבן ולא כל עם הארץ [הוריות יא.]. **פרט למומר.** דאינו מביא קרבן על שגגתו דאין מקבלין מידו [שם ב.]. **ר"ש בן אלעזר אומר משום ר"ש.** מכאן אתה למד [חולין שם]. **אשר לא תעשינה בשגגה ואשם.** אשר לא תעשינה משמע שאילו ידע לא עשה אבל בשגגה עשה ואשם [יומא פ.]. וסמיך ליה או הודע אליו חטאתו אשר חטא והביא אשמו דמשמע אשר לא תעשינה אם היה יודע שהוא אסור ושגגה היתה לו וחטא ואשם הוא יביא. **השב מידיעתו.** שאם היה יודע שהוא חלב היה יושב ומבטל מעבירה זו ואית דגרים השב והוא נמי הפורש ונבדל מתחלה ואין עובר אם היה יודע שהוא אסור ובת"כ גרס היושב [חולין שם]. **לא שב מידיעתו אינו מביא קרבן על שגגתו.** ומומר לא שב מידיעתו הוא לפיכך אינו מביא קרבן על שגגתו ואמר לקמן בפ"ב מומר שאכל חלב והביא קרבן על הדם איכא בינייהו [הוריות שם].

The Gemara asks:

אֲבָל לֹא שָׁכְחָהּ מַאי – But if **he did not forget** the essence of **[the Sabbath],** but rather forgot that the day was the Sabbath day, **what** is the law?[1] חַיָּיב עַל כָּל מְלָאכָה וּמְלָאכָה – **Is he liable for each *melachah*** that he performs?[2] אַדְּתָנֵי הַיּוֹדֵעַ שֶׁהוּא שַׁבָּת – If so, **then instead of teaching** in the third case: ONE WHO KNOWS IT IS THE SABBATH but forgot which labors are forbidden, וְעָשָׂה מְלָאכוֹת הַרְבֵּה בְּשַׁבָּתוֹת הַרְבֵּה – AND as a result HE PERFORMED MANY *MELACHOS* ON MANY SABBATHS, חַיָּיב עַל כָּל מְלָאכָה וּמְלָאכָה – HE IS LIABLE FOR EACH AND EVERY *av MELACHAH* that he performed, לִיתְנֵי הַיּוֹדֵעַ עִיקַּר שַׁבָּת – **let [the Mishnah] teach** that **"One** who **knows the essence of the Sabbath** but forgot it was the Sabbath"[3] is liable for each *av melachah* performed, וְכָל שֶׁכֵּן הָא – **and** we would know on our own that he is **certainly** liable for every *melachah* in **this** case, i.e. in the case where he knew it was the Sabbath day but forgot the *melachos*![4] – ? –

The Gemara concedes and therefore retracts the entire previous explanation of the Mishnah:

אֶלָּא מַתְנִיתִין כְּשֶׁהִכִּיר וּלְבַסּוֹף שָׁכַח – **Rather,** when **our Mishnah** speaks in its first ruling of "one who forgot the essence of the Sabbath," it **is** dealing with a case of **one who** once **recognized** the essence of the Sabbath **and eventually forgot** it.[5] וּדְרַב וּשְׁמוּאֵל נַמִּי כְּהִכִּיר וּלְבַסּוֹף שָׁכַח דָּמֵי – **However,** the case **of Rav and Shmuel** – i.e. the case of one who *never* knew the Sabbath law – **is also** treated **like** a case of **one who recognized** the essence of the Sabbath **and eventually forgot** it. וְהָכִי אִיתְּמַר – **And this is what was** actually **stated** in their name: רַב וּשְׁמוּאֵל דְּאָמְרֵי תַּרְוַיְיהוּ – **Rav and Shmuel both said:** אֲפִילוּ תִּינוֹק שֶׁנִּשְׁבָּה בֵּין הַנָּכְרִים – **Even a child who was captured** and raised **among gentiles,** וְגֵר שֶׁנִּתְגַּיֵּיר לְבֵין הַנָּכְרִים – **or a convert who converted** and lived **among gentiles**, who never knew the Sabbath law, כְּהִכִּיר וּלְבַסּוֹף שָׁכַח דָּמֵי – **is like one who recognized** the Sabbath **and eventually forgot** it, וְחַיָּיב – **and he is** therefore **liable** to a single *chatas* for his Sabbath desecrations.[6]

The Gemara presents a dissenting opinion:

וְרַבִּי יוֹחָנָן וְרַבִּי שִׁמְעוֹן בֶּן לָקִישׁ דְּאָמְרֵי תַּרְוַיְיהוּ – **But R' Yochanan and R' Shimon ben Lakish both said:** דַּוְקָא הִכִּיר וּלְבַסּוֹף שָׁכַח – The Mishnah's ruling is true **only** for **one who recognized** the essence of the Sabbath **and eventually forgot** it; אֲבָל תִּינוֹק שֶׁנִּשְׁבָּה בֵּין הַנָּכְרִים – **but a child who was captured** and raised **among gentiles,** וְגֵר שֶׁנִּתְגַּיֵּיר לְבֵין הַנָּכְרִים – **or a convert who converted** and lived **among gentiles,** פָּטוּר – **is exempt** from any *chatas* whatsoever.[7]

The Gemara asks:

מֵיתִיבֵי – **They challenged** this view **from the** following **Baraisa:** כְּלָל גָּדוֹל אָמְרוּ בְּשַׁבָּת – [THE SAGES] STATED A MAJOR RULE CONCERNING THE SABBATH: כֹּל הַשּׁוֹכֵחַ עִיקַּר שַׁבָּת – ANYONE WHO FORGETS THE ESSENCE OF THE SABBATH וְעָשָׂה מְלָאכוֹת הַרְבֵּה בְּשַׁבָּתוֹת הַרְבֵּה – AND as a result PERFORMED MANY *MELACHOS* ON MANY SABBATHS אֵינוֹ חַיָּיב אֶלָּא אַחַת – IS LIABLE TO BUT ONE *chatas*. כֵּיצַד – HOW SO? תִּינוֹק שֶׁנִּשְׁבָּה לְבֵין הַנָּכְרִים – If A CHILD WAS CAPTURED and raised AMONG GENTILES, וְגֵר שֶׁנִּתְגַּיֵּיר בֵּין הַנָּכְרִים – OR A CONVERT CONVERTED and lived AMONG GENTILES and thus never learned the law of the Sabbath, וְעָשָׂה מְלָאכוֹת הַרְבֵּה בְּשַׁבָּתוֹת הַרְבֵּה – AND HE PERFORMED MANY *MELACHOS* ON MANY SABBATHS, אֵינוֹ חַיָּיב אֶלָּא חַטָּאת אַחַת – HE IS LIABLE TO BUT ONE *CHATAS* for all his Sabbath violations. וְחַיָּיב עַל הַדָּם אַחַת – AND [SUCH A PERSON] IS LIABLE TO ONE *chatas*

NOTES

1. That is, he knew that the Torah included the Sabbath law, but he forgot that the particular day on which he performed *melachos* was the Sabbath day (*Rashi*).

2. Seemingly, you are forced to say so. For if in this case too he is liable to only one *chatas* per Sabbath, the Mishnah should have combined this case with its second case and taught the following: If someone once knew the essence of the Sabbath but forgot it, or if he remembered the essence of the Sabbath [but forgot that the day was in fact the Sabbath], he is obligated to bring only one *chatas* for each Sabbath he desecrated. By not making this combined statement the Mishnah indicates that if the person was aware of the essence of the Sabbath law he would be obligated to bring a separate *chatas* for each *melachah* he performed (*Rashi;* cf. *Tosafos;* see *Maharsha;* see also *Sfas Emes*).

3. That is, he knew which *melachos* were prohibited on the Sabbath, but did not realize this day was in fact the Sabbath (*Rashi*).

4. For if a person is liable for each *av melachah* when he acted inadvertently regarding one issue – i.e. he did not realize that it was actually the Sabbath day – certainly he should be liable for each *av melachah* when he acted inadvertently as a result of having forgotten the laws of numerous *melachos* (*Rashi*).

5. [As indicated by the word שׁוֹכֵחַ, implying that he *forgot* something he once knew.] The Mishnah teaches that even though he once knew the law of the Sabbath, he is still liable to only one *chatas* for all the Sabbaths that he desecrated after he forgot the Sabbath law (*Rashi*).

6. The Mishnah, though, teaches the single-*chatas* rule in the case of a person who once knew and then forgot to make it clear that even in this case he is still obligated to bring only one *chatas* for all of the Sabbaths he desecrated (*Rashi;* see also *Chidushei HaRan*).

According to this revised version of Rav and Shmuel's teaching, the novelty of their ruling is that one who never knew the Sabbath law is nonetheless *held accountable* for his transgressions; he cannot claim exemption from a *chatas* on the grounds that he was raised among the gentiles and thus never learned the law (*Rosh Yosef*). This point will now be disputed by R' Yochanan and Reish Lakish.

The Gemara has thus reverted back to the original understanding of the Mishnah's three rulings, which should again be understood as we originally explained them in the Mishnah:

(a) If one errs in not knowing the basic Sabbath law [according to Rav and Shmuel even if he never knew it], he is obligated to bring only one *chatas* for all his Sabbath violations.

(b) If he knows all the Sabbath laws but errs in not knowing that it is the Sabbath day, he is obligated to bring one *chatas* for each Sabbath during which a violation took place.

(c) If he knows that Sabbath law exists and that the day is the Sabbath day, but errs in not knowing various specific laws of the Sabbath, he is obligated to bring a separate *chatas* for each *melachah* category he violated.

7. R' Yochanan and Reish Lakish hold that a transgression that results from thinking that something is permissible [because one never learned otherwise] is not considered an inadvertent transgression [שׁוֹגֵג]; rather, it is the legal equivalent of an אֹנֶס, *accident,* for which a person cannot be held responsible (*Rashi*). [Although every person who sins inadvertently does so because he does not realize that what he is doing is forbidden, the *root* of his transgression can usually be traced to his having *forgotten* the knowledge that would have prevented him from sinning (e.g. the Sabbath law, the day of the week) or his having *failed to learn* what he could have been expected to learn (e.g. the details of the Sabbath law). One who grew up among the gentiles, however, *never* had any knowledge that would have prevented his sin, and never had any reason to inquire about the law (since he had never learned the essence of the Sabbath and thus had no reason to inquire about its details). Thus, his transgression is traceable to no other factor than his quite reasonable assumption (under the circumstances) that what he was doing was permissible [אוֹמֵר מוּתָּר]. This, according to R' Yochanan and Reish Lakish, is not considered an inadvertent transgression (שׁוֹגֵג) but an unavoidable transgression (אֹנֶס). For a lengthy discussion of the parameters of the category of אוֹמֵר מוּתָּר, *one who says a thing is permissible,* and the difference between this and שׁוֹגֵג (*inadvertent transgression*), see the responsum of *R' Chaim Volozhiner* printed at the end of *Teshuvos Beis HaLevi* vol. 1 §3; see also *Dibros Moshe* 64:9.]

[*Tosafos* ask why *Rashi* gives this explanation of the exemption when the Gemara below will give a Scriptural source for a Tanna whose view R' Yochanan and Reish Lakish apparently follow. See *Pnei Yehoshua* and *Rosh Yosef* for defenses of *Rashi.*]

אבל לא שכחה מאי א) חייב על כל מלאכה ומלאכה אדתני היודע שהוא שבת ועשה מלאכות הרבה בשבתות הרבה חייב על כל מלאכה ומלאכה ליתני היודע עיקר שבת וכל שכן הא אלא מתניתין כשהכיר ולבסוף שכח ודרב ושמואל נמי כהכיר ולבסוף שכח דמי והכי איתמר רב ושמואל דאמרי תרווייהו אפילו תינוק שנשבה בין הנכרים וגר שנתגייר לבין הנכרים כהכיר ולבסוף שכח דמי וחייב ורבי יוחנן ורבי שמעון בן לקיש דאמרי תרווייהו דוקא הכיר ולבסוף שכח אבל תינוק שנשבה בין הנכרים וגר שנתגייר לבין הנכרים פטור מיתיבי כלל גדול אמרו בשבת כל השוכח עיקר שבת ועשה מלאכות הרבה בשבתות הרבה אינו חייב אלא אחת כיצד תינוק שנשבה לבין הנכרים וגר שנתגייר בין הנכרים ועשה מלאכות הרבה בשבתות הרבה אינו חייב אלא חטאת אחת וחייב על הדם אחת ועל החלב אחת ועל ע"ז אחת ומונבז פוטר וכך היה מונבז דן לפני רבי עקיבא הואיל ומזיד קרוי חוטא ושוגג קרוי חוטא מה מזיד שהיתה לו ידיעה אף שוגג שהיתה לו ידיעה אמר לו ר' עקיבא הריני מוסיף על דבריך אי מה מזיד שהיתה הידיעה בשעת מעשה אף שוגג שהיתה לו ידיעה בשעת מעשה אמר לו הן וכל שכן שהוספת אמר לו לדבריך אין זה קרוי שוגג אלא מזיד קתני מיהא כיצד תינוק בשלמא לרב ושמואל ניחא אלא לרבי יוחנן ולרבי שמעון בן לקיש קשיא אמרי לך רבי יוחנן וריש לקיש לא מי איכא מונבז דפטר אנן דאמרינן כמונבז מאי טעמא דמונבז דכתיב א) תורה אחת יהיה לכם לעושה בשגגה וסמיך ליה ב) והנפש אשר תעשה ביד רמה הקיש שוגג למזיד מה מזיד שהיתה לו ידיעה אף שוגג שהיתה לו ידיעה ורבנן האי תורה אחת מאי עבדי ליה מיבעי להו א) לכדמקרי ליה ר' יהושע בן לוי לבריה תורה אחת יהיה לכם לעושה בשגגה וכתיב וכי

רש"י

אבל לא שכחה. לעיקר שבת אלא ששכח שהיום שבת מאי: **חייב על כל אב מלאכה.** דע"כ אי הוה סבירא ליה דאינו חייב אלא אחת לכל שבת ושבת הוה ליה (א) למיכרך ולמיתני הכי מי שידע עיקר שבת ושכחה וכן היודע עיקר שבת ועשה מלאכות הרבה בשבתות הרבה חייב על כל שבת ושבת: **ליתני היודע עיקר שבת.** דהוה שגגת שבת וזדון מלאכות הרבה חייב על כל מלאכה אע"ג דבכל שבת ליכא אלא חדא שגגה וכ"ש שגגת מלאכות וזדון שבת דאיכא שגגות הרבה: **כהכיר ולבסוף שכח דמי.** ומתניתין איצטריך למינקט הכיר ולבסוף שכח דלא תימא חייב על כל שבת ושבת: **פטור.** דקסברי רבי יוחנן ור"ל אומר מותר אנוס הוא ולא שגגה היא: **וחייב על הדם.** שאכל כל ימיו אחת וכן על כל דבר כרת שבתורה: **מזיד קרוי חוטא.** דכתיב (ויקרא ה) בשבועת העדות נפש כי תחטא ושמעה וגומר ולא כתיב ביה ונעלם: **הריני מוסיף על דבריך.** כלומר אם כך באת לדרוש ג"ש ללמד שוגג ממזיד בא ואוסיף גם אני על דבריך עוד ובה תראה אם יעמדו דבריך: **אף שוגג שהיתה לו ידיעה בשעת מעשה.** תחייבהו גם בזו חטאת: **כ"ש שהוספת.** על דברי והרי אתה מסייעני וגם בזו אני אומר שהוא חייב ולקמן מפרש במאי שגג: **קתני מיהא.** רישא תינוק שנשבה לבין הנכרים חייב: **בשלמא לרב ושמואל ניחא.** דאינהו נמי מחייבי ואיכא לאוקמי דהוא הדין להכיר ולבסוף שכח כי מתניתין ובריית' דקתני תינוק היא גופא איצטריך לאשמעינן פלוגתא דמונבז ורבנן: **מאי טעמא דמונבז.** אבנין אב ודאי לא סמיך למיעבד שוגג דומיא דמזיד דהאי שוגג חילוף דמזיד וליכא לדמויינהו דהאי חייב והאי פטור: **מקיש שוגג.** לענין חטאת למזיד לענין כרת ואף על גב דלא דמי ע"כ הקישן הכתוב: **ורבנן.** הך הקישא בעיא לכדרבי יהושע ב"ל: **תורה אחת יהיה לכם.** גבי קרבן ע"ז כתיב בפרשת שלח לך אנשים: **וכי**

תוספות

אבל לא שכחה מאי חייב על כל מלאכה ומלאכה. תימה לר"י מנא ליה למידק הכי אימא דלא שכחה נמי אינו חייב על כל מלאכה ומלאכה אלא על כל שבת ושבת כמו בהכיר ולבסוף שכח ותנא הכיר ולבסוף שכח וכ"ש הא כדפרי' ומה שפי' בקונטרס דדייק דחייב על כל מלאכה ומלאכה מדלא כייל להו אהדדי מי שידע עיקר שבת ושכחה והיודע עיקר שבת חייב על כל שבת ושבת דהוה משמע דוקא על כל שבת ושבת ולא על כל מלאכה אין נראה לר"י דא"כ היכי פריך לעיל לתני הכיר ולבסוף שכח וכל שכן הא דמשמע דהא לא איצטריך למיתני והא נמי איצטריך לאשמעינן דאינו חייב על כל מלאכה ומלאכה ונראה לר"י דלעיל דקאמר ליתני הכיר ולבסוף שכח וכ"ש הא לא בעי למימר דלא ליתני' כלל במשנה אלא ה"פ מדקתני חייב על כל שבת ושבת ולא קתני אינו חייב אלא על כל שבת דהוה משמע ולא על כל מלאכה ומלאכה משמע דעיקר מתניתין חיובא אתא לאשמעינן דחייב על כל שבת ושבת ולא פטורא דאינו חייב על כל מלאכה ואם כן ליתני הכיר ולבסוף שכח דהוי רבותא טפי וכ"ש האי דחייב על כל שבת ולא הוה צריך למתנייה בהאי בבא אלא ה"ל למיתני בתר הכי בבבא אחריתי היודע עיקר שבת אינו חייב אלא על כל שבת ושבת לאשמעינן דאינו חייב על כל מלאכה והשתא דייק שפיר אבל לא שכחה מאי חייב על כל מלאכה ומלאכה מדלא תני בבבא אחריתי דאינו חייב אלא על כל שבת ושבת ב):

ליתני היודע עיקר שבת וכ"ש הא. תימה לר"י לרבא דאמר בכריתות בסוף פרק אמרו לו (דף טז:) דבזדון שבת ושגגת מלאכות לא מיחייב אכל שבת ושבת ודייק ממתניתין דהכא דלא קתני חייב על כל אב מלאכה ומלאכה של כל שבת ושבת ולדידיה היכי פריך הכא ליתני היודע עיקר שבת הא לא מצי למיתני הכי דאם כן הוה משמע דלא מיחייב היודע עיקר שבת אכל שבת ושבת ותירץ דהכי פריך דליתני היודע עיקר שבת דחייב אכל אב מלאכה של כל שבת ושבת ורשב"א מפרש דאי הוה תני בהדיא היודע עיקר שבת חייב על כל אב מלאכה ליכא למידק דלא מיחייב אכל שבת מדלא קתני חייב על כל אב מלאכה של כל שבת ושבת דלא צריך למיתני' דמרישא שמעינן ליה דקתני בהכיר ולבסוף שכח דחייב על כל שבת ושבת כ"ש יודע עיקר שבת כדאמר לעיל: **וכ"ש** האי. ה"נ לא בעי למימר דלא לתני' כלל במשנה דאם כן הוה אמינא דחייב נמי על כל שבת ושבת ואינו כן לרבה דכריתות אלא ליתני בבא אחריתי היודע שהוא שבת אינו חייב על כל שבת:

כי הכיר ולבסוף שכח דמי. פירש בקונטרס דלהכי לא תנא במתניתין שכח מעיקרו דהיינו תינוק שנשבה דלא תימא דהכיר ולבסוף שכח חייב על כל שבת וקשה לר"י דמ"מ ליתנייה וליתני נמי בתר הכי הכיר ולבסוף שכח אינו חייב אלא אחת דכה"ג פריך לעיל ליתני הכיר ולבסוף שכח וכ"ש הא כדפרישית ונראה לר"י דודאי אי הוה תני חייב חטאת דהוה אתי לאשמעינן חיובא הוה שייך למיפרך דליתני תינוק שנשבה דהוי רבותא טפי אבל השתא דקתני אינו חייב אלא אחת אתא לאשמעינן נקט הכיר ולבסוף שכח דהוי רבותא טפי ומיהו קשה לר"י דמ"מ ליתני תינוק שנשבה דלא נטעה לומר דפטור כרבי יוחנן וריש לקיש והדר ליתני הכיר ולבסוף שכח:

אבל תינוק שנשבה פטור. פירש בקונטרס דקסברי אומר מותר אנוס הוא ואין נראה דטעמייהו כמונבז כדאמר בסמוך וטעמא דמונבז מפרש לקמן דיליף מקרא והא דאמר בפ"ב דמכות (דף ז:) גבי גלות בשגגה פרט למזיד ומפרש (אביי) [נ"ל רבא] פרט לאומר מותר ופריך ליה (רבא) [נ"ל אביי] אומר מותר אנוס הוא לאו דוקא קאמר אנוס דבכל מקום מחייבין ליה אלא לגבי גלות דוקא ממעט (אביי) [נ"ל רבא] אומר מותר משום דטובא בשגגה כתיב התם דהא בפירקין (ג) מחייבי אומר מותר בע"ז ובחלב אע"ג דכתיב בהן בשגגה (ורבא) [נ"ל ואביי] פריך ליה אומר מותר אנוס הוא ולא הוה ליה למיתני בברייתא בשגגה פרט למזיד אלא פרט לאנוס דיותר דמי וקרוב לאנוס מלמזיד:

וחייב על הדם אחת. אע"ג דמילתא דפשיטא היא דאכל מה שאכל דם אינו חייב אלא אחת כיון שאין בדם חילוק איסור כמו שיש בשבת חילוק מלאכות וכל אדם נמי בלא תינוק שנשבה אכל דם ודם אינו חייב אלא אחת אלא אומר ר"י דמיירי דאפי' אכלן בכמה תמחויין דלר"י (לקמן דף עא.) אדם אחר חייב על כל תמחוי אפי' בהעלם אחד ובתינוק שנשבה אינו חייב אלא אחד אך קשה לרשב"א דמאי איצטריך תו לאשמעינן ולמתני ועל החלב אחד:

כל שכן שהוספת. כדפירש בקונטרס דאף בזו מחייב ומחייב נמי כי ליכא ידיעה בשעת מעשה דהא רבי יוחנן וריש לקיש סברי כמונבז ומחייבי הכיר ולבסוף שכח ותניא נמי לקמן שגג בזה ובזה זהו שוגג האמור בתורה ומוקמינן לה כמונבז והיינו טעמא משום דסברא הוא דלא איתקש שוגג למזיד לאפוקי ליה ממשמעות שגגה דאדרבה שוגג משמע דלית ליה ידיעה בשעת מעשה ולא אתא היקשא אלא לחייב נמי כי אית ליה ידיעה בשעת מעשה ומיהו קשה לר"י דהא פטרי מהיקשא תינוק שנשבה מהאי טעמא נמי יפטור הכיר ולבסוף שכח:

מה

עין משפט נר מצוה

ד א מיי' פ"ב מהלכות שגגות הלכה ו ופ"ז הלכה ב סמג עשין ריג:

רבינו חננאל

מתני' לדברי הכל בהכיר ולבסוף שכח אינו חייב אלא חטאת אחת ורב ושמואל הוסיפו אפילו קטן שנשבה לבין עו"ג כהכיר ולבסוף שכח דמי וחייב חטאת ורבי יוחנן וריש לקיש אמרי קטן שנשבה בין עו"ג פטור ואותיבנא עלייהו מהא דתניא השוכח עיקר שבת ועשה מלאכות הרבה בשבתות הרבה אינו חייב אלא חטאת אחת וחייב על ע"ז אחת. פירש אם עבד ע"ז הרבה דינו כדין שבת וכן כל מצוה ומצוה אינו חייב אלא בכל מצוה אחת ומונבז פוטר בכל ומשני רבי יוחנן וריש לקיש אנן דאמרינן כמונבז דסבר כיון דלא הויא ידיעה ליה בתחלה בעיקר שבת אף על גב דבתר דעביד מלאכות הרבה בשבתות הרבה אתיידע ליה איסורא דשבת לא מחייב וכי אמרו רבי יוחנן ור"ל דאנן כמונבז סבירא לן בהאי לחוד דפטר קטן שנשבה בין הנכרים אבל בהאי דבעי ידיעה למונבז בשעת מעשה שידע

רב נסים גאון

ורבנן כדמקרי ליה ר' יהושע בן לוי לבריה תורה אחת יהיה לכם לעושה בשגגה והנפש אשר תעשה ביד רמה הוקשה כל התורה כולה לע"ז. דע שפרשת (במדבר טו) וכי תשגו ולא תעשו ואם נפש אחת תחטא בשגגה שממנה אלו הפסוקים אמרו רבותינו ז"ל כי היא מיוחדת בע"ז ותמצא פירוש זה בספרי בע"ז הכתוב מדבר אתה אומר בע"ז או אינו אלא באחת מן המצות האמורות בתורה ת"ל והיה אם מעיני העדה נעשתה ייחד הכתוב מצוה זו בפני עצמה ואיזו זו ע"ז וכו' ובמסכת הוריות בפ' הורה כהן משיח (דף ח) אמרו דכולי עלמא הני קראי בע"ז הוא דכתיבי מנא לן אמר רבא ואיתימא ר' יהושע בן לוי ואמרי לה כדי וכי תשגו ולא תעשו את כל המצות האלה איזו היא מצוה שהיא שקולה כנגד כל המצות כולן הוי אומר זו ע"ז דבית ר' תנא אמר קרא א) את כל אשר דבר ה' אליכם ביד משה איזו היא מצוה

חשק שלמה על רב נסים גאון

א) אשר דבר ה' אל משה את כל אשר צוה ה' אליכם ביד משה כצ"ל:

תורה אור השלם

א) הָאֶזְרָח בִּבְנֵי יִשְׂרָאֵל וְלַגֵּר הַגָּר בְּתוֹכָם תּוֹרָה אַחַת יִהְיֶה לָכֶם לָעֹשֶׂה בִּשְׁגָגָה: [במדבר טו, כט]

ב) וְהַנֶּפֶשׁ אֲשֶׁר תַּעֲשֶׂה בְּיָד רָמָה מִן הָאֶזְרָח וּמִן הַגֵּר אֶת יְיָ הוּא מְגַדֵּף וְנִכְרְתָה הַנֶּפֶשׁ הַהִוא מִקֶּרֶב עַמָּהּ: [במדבר טו, ל]

מסורת הש"ס

א) יבמות דף ע. הוריות ח ע"א.

תוספות ישנים

א) ונקט אחת שהיא הנה בין שגגת שבת וזדון מלאכה בין בזדון שבת ושגגת מלאכה כפי' רב נחמן לרב חייא. והנה שהיא אחת בהכיר ולבסוף שכח:

ב) נר"י דפי' דדייק מדלא קתני לה בבא אחריתי ולא שיפרש אינו חייב על כל מלאכה לא נחייש לי דהא לא איצטריך למיתני בבא אחריתא דמסיפא שמעינן מדקתני היודע שהוא שבת חייב על כל מלאכה ומשמע הא שכחה אינו חייב על כל מלאכה. ועוד מאי פריך בסמוך ליתני היודע עיקר שבת וכ"ש הא אמאי הוי נריך למיתני היודע עיקר שבת שהוא חייב על כל מלאכה והא שמעינן לה מדלא תני בבא אחריתי כדפרי'. והיה נ"ל דלעיל פריך ליתני הכיר ולבסוף שכח בהדיא וכ"ש היודע עיקר שבת ולא הוי נריך כלל למיתני דחייב על כל שבת דשמעינן מכ"ש דהכיר ולבסוף שכח שאינו חייב על כל מלאכה. מדנקט בסיפא היודע שהוא שבת כו' משמע דהיודע עיקר שבת ושכח אינו חייב על כל מלאכה. אבל השתא דמשני דיודע עיקר שבת היינו הכיר ולבסוף שכח פריך שפיר אבל לא שכחה מאי חייב על כל מלאכה. דאי אינו חייב כמו בשכחה א"כ אמאי נקט היודע עיקר שבת דמשמע טפי דאיירי בלא שכחה ה"ל למיתני בהדיא הכיר ולבסוף שכח דהוי משמע רבותא טפי אלא ודאי בשלא שכחה חייב על כל מלאכה והוי בכלל בבא דסיפא. להכי ליכא למיטעי במאי דנקט האי לישנא דהיודע עיקר שבת ולא נקט הכיר ולבסוף שכח בהדיא אימא סיפא היודע שהוא שבת וכו'. בשלמא אי הוי תני בהדיא היודע עיקר שבת ולא שכחה בסיפא הוי ידעינן ליה מכ"ש דסיפא א"ש כדפרישית אבל השתא דהיודע עיקר שבת ולא שכחה לא שמעינן מסיפא אלא אדרבה משמע דוקא יודע שהוא שבת חייב על כל מלאכה אם כן מליעתא משמע דמיירי ביודע עיקר שבת ולא שכחה כדמשמע לישנא. ומשמע דוקא לא שכחה אבל שכחה אינו חייב על כל שבת. דאי חייב ליתני הכיר ולבסוף שכחה בהדיא וכל שכן היודע עיקר שבת ולא שכחה כדפרי' לעיל:

הגהות הב"ח

(א) רש"י ד"ה חייב על וכו' ה"ל למיתני כצ"ל ותיבת למיכרך נמחק: (ג) תוס' ד"ה אבל תינוק וכו' דהא בפירקין. נ"ב בסוף דף עב:

ליקוטי רש"י

לכדמקרי ליה ר' יהושע בן לוי לבריה תורה אחת. לענין קרבן כתיב [בפרשת] עבודת כוכבים תורה כל התורה במשמע הוקשה כל התורה לענין קרבן לעבודת כוכבים [יבמות ט.].

[מכאן שייך לדף סט.]

וכי תשגו. בעבודה זרה הכתוב מדבר או אינו אלא באחת מכל המצות תלמוד לומר את כל המצות האלה מצוה אחת שהיא ככל המצות מה העובר על כל המצות פורק עול ומפר ברית ומגלה פנים אף מצוה זו פורק בה עול ומפר ברית ומגלה פנים ואיזו זו עבודה זרה [במדבר טו, כב]. **ביד רמה.** במזיד [שם, ל]. **הוקשו כולם לע"ז.** שהוקשו כל חטאות שבתורה לחטאת עבודה זרה דכתיב תורה אחת יהיה לכם וגו' [לקמן קלז.]. דהוקשה כל התורה כולה לענין קרבן לעבודת כוכבים שנאמר בפרשת שלח לך אנשים אבל קרבן עבודת כוכבים תורה אחת יהיה לכם לעושה בשגגה כאן הוקשו כל עבירות שבתורה בשגגתן לעבודת כוכבים לענין קרבן [מכות יג:]. **מה להלן דבר שחייבים על זדונו כרת ושגגתו חטאת.** דהכא כתיב הכרת תכרת אף כו' [הוריות ח.]. כדכתיב התם והנפש אשר תעשה ביד רמה ונכרתה אלמא כולה פרשתא בדבר שזדונו כרת ושגגתו חטאת משתעי [יבמות ט.]. **מעם.** ולא כל עם וגבי חטאת כתיב שבא [על] השוגג [חולין ה:]. **מעם הארץ.** מביא קרבן ולא כל עם הארץ [הוריות יא.]. **פרט למומר.** דאינו מביא קרבן על שגגתו דלאין מקבלין מידו [שם ב.]. **ר"ש בן אלעזר אומר משום ר"ש.** מכאן אתה למד [חולין שם]. **אשר לא תעשינה בשגגה ואשם.** אשר לא תעשינה משמע שאילו ידע לא עשה אבל בשגגה עשה ואשם [יומא פ.]. וסמיך ליה או הודע אליו חטאתו אשר חטא והביא אשמו למשמע אשר לא תעשינה אם היה יודע שהוא אסור ושגגה היתה לו וחטא ואשם הוא יביא. **השב מידיעתו.** שאם היה יודע שהוא חלב היה יושב ומבטל מעבירה זו ואית דגרים השב והוא נמי הפורש ובדל מתחלה ואין עובר אם היה יודע שהוא אסור ובת"כ גרס היושב [חולין שם]. **לא שב מידיעתו אינו מביא קרבן על שגגתו.** ומומר לא שב מידיעתו הוא לפיכך אינו מביא קרבן על שגגתו ואמר לקמן בפ"ב מומר שאכל חלב והביא קרבן על הדם איכא בינייהו [הוריות שם].

for all of the times he consumed **BLOOD;**[8] **וְעַל הַחֵלֶב אַחַת – AND TO ONE FOR** all the times he consumed ***CHEILEV;*** **וְעַל עֲבוֹדָה זָרָה אַחַת – AND TO ONE FOR** all the times he was guilty of **IDOLATRY.**[9]

The Baraisa cites a dissenting view:

וּמוּנְבָּז פּוֹטֵר – BUT MUNBAZ EXEMPTS him for any *chatas* obligation.[10] **וְכָךְ הָיָה מוּנְבָּז דָּן לִפְנֵי רַבִּי עֲקִיבָא – AND THUS DID MUNBAZ ARGUE BEFORE R' AKIVA: הוֹאִיל וּמֵזִיד קָרוּי חוֹטֵא – SINCE A DELIBERATE [TRANSGRESSOR] IS CALLED** by the Torah **A SINNER,**[11] **וְשׁוֹגֵג קָרוּי חוֹטֵא – AND AN INADVERTENT [TRANSGRESSOR] IS** also **CALLED** by the Torah **A SINNER,**[12] there is an implied similarity in the quality of their sins. **מַה מֵּזִיד שֶׁהָיְתָה לוֹ יְדִיעָה** – Therefore, we say that **JUST AS THE DELIBERATE [TRANSGRESSOR]** of whom the Torah speaks **HAD KNOWLEDGE** of the prohibition he transgressed, **אַף שׁוֹגֵג שֶׁהָיְתָה לוֹ יְדִיעָה – SO TOO THE INADVERTENT [TRANSGRESSOR]** of whom the Torah speaks is one who once **HAD KNOWLEDGE** of the prohibition he transgressed.[13]

R' Akiva replies:

אָמַר לוֹ רַבִּי עֲקִיבָא – R' AKIVA SAID TO HIM: הֲרֵינִי מוֹסִיף עַל דְּבָרֶיךָ – I WILL ADD TO YOUR WORDS, i.e. extend your argument and thereby demonstrate its invalidity:[14] **אִי מַה מֵּזִיד שֶׁהָיְתָה הַיְדִיעָה בִּשְׁעַת מַעֲשֶׂה** – For **IF** this comparison is true, we should also say: **JUST AS THE DELIBERATE [TRANSGRESSOR] HAD KNOWLEDGE** of the prohibition **AT THE TIME OF THE** prohibited **ACT, אַף שׁוֹגֵג שֶׁהָיְתָה לוֹ יְדִיעָה בִּשְׁעַת מַעֲשֶׂה – SO TOO THE INADVERTENT [TRANSGRESSOR] HAD** some **KNOWLEDGE** of the prohibition **AT THE TIME OF THE ACT.**[15] **אָמַר לוֹ – [MUNBAZ] SAID TO HIM: הֵן וְכָל שֶׁכֵּן שֶׁהוֹסַפְתָּ – YES! AND YOU HAVE CERTAINLY ADDED** to my words.[16] **אָמַר לוֹ – [R' AKIVA] SAID TO [MUNBAZ]: לְדִבְרֶיךָ – ACCORDING TO YOUR REASONING, אֵין זֶה קָרוּי שׁוֹגֵג – THIS** person **IS NOT CALLED AN INADVERTENT [TRANSGRESSOR] אֶלָּא מֵזִיד – BUT A DELIBERATE [TRANSGRESSOR].**

The Gemara now explains its challenge to R' Yochanan and Reish Lakish from this Baraisa:

קָתָנֵי מִיהָא כֵּיצַד תִּינוֹק – At any rate, the Baraisa has taught: "HOW SO? A CHILD captured and raised among the gentiles . . . is liable to but one *chatas.*" **בִּשְׁלָמָא לְרַב וּשְׁמוּאֵל נִיחָא – Now, according to Rav and Shmuel all is well,** since they indeed hold such a person liable to a *chatas;* **אֶלָּא לְרַבִּי יוֹחָנָן וּלְרַבִּי שִׁמְעוֹן בֶּן לָקִישׁ קַשְׁיָא – but according to R' Yochanan and R' Shimon ben Lakish this is difficult,** since they exempt such a person from any *chatas* obligation.[17] – ? –

The Gemara answers:

אָמְרֵי לָךְ רַבִּי יוֹחָנָן וְרֵישׁ לָקִישׁ – R' Yochanan and Reish Lakish would tell you: לָא מִי אִיכָּא מוּנְבָּז דְּפָטַר – Is there not Munbaz, who exempts such a person? **אֲנַן דְּאָמְרִינַן כְּמוּנְבָּז – We stated** our ruling **in accordance with Munbaz!**[18]

The Gemara analyzes the opinion of Munbaz:

מַאי טַעְמָא דְמוּנְבָּז – What is the reason of Munbaz?[19] **דִּכְתִיב**

NOTES

8. [One who consumes animal blood deliberately is liable to *kares;* when he does so inadvertently he is liable to a *chatas.*] Since this person is liable to one *chatas* for each category of *kares*-bearing sin that he unknowingly violated as a result of his non-Jewish upbringing, he brings one *chatas* for all the times he consumed blood (see *Rashi*).

[*Tosafos* ask why the Baraisa has to add this case. It is obvious that if a person violates the same law numerous times without discovering his transgression, he is liable to only one *chatas.* This is true even for a person who once knew the law and forgot it! Only in the case of the Sabbath was it necessary for the Baraisa to teach this law because Sabbath law includes multiple *melachos,* which sometimes render the person liable to separate *chataos* for each category of *melachah.* But in the case of blood or *cheilev,* there would be no reason to think that he would be liable to more than one *chatas* for all the transgressions he committed before he learned the law.

Tos. HaRosh answers that the Baraisa means to teach that he is liable to a separate *chatas* for each *kares*-bearing prohibition he transgressed before he learned the Torah, and one *chatas* does not suffice for all sins (as it does for all *melachos*). (See *Rosh Yosef,* however, who points out that *Rashi's* language here indicates that he did not follow this approach. See *Tosafos* here for another answer.)]

9. [See *Dibros Moshe* 64:11.] *Cheilev* [the forbidden fats of an animal] and idolatry are two more examples of *kares*-bearing sins. Thus, the Baraisa teaches that this person is liable to one *chatas* for each *kares*-bearing prohibition he violated.

10. According to Munbaz a person who never knew of a certain law is not obligated to bring a *chatas* for violating it.

11. The verse states (*Leviticus* 5:1): וְנֶפֶשׁ כִּי־תֶחֱטָא, *If a person will sin,* when referring to one who swears falsely about testimony he is called to give [שְׁבוּעַת הָעֵדוּת]. Now that section refers to one who acted deliberately [מֵזִיד], since it says nothing about the violation being inadvertent. We see therefore that the Torah uses the term חֵטְא, *sin,* even for a deliberate violation (*Rashi*). [This is significant because the Torah generally uses other words for deliberate sin (e.g. פֶּשַׁע, עָוֹן) whereas חֵטְא is usually used for inadvertent sin (see *Pnei Yehoshua* ד"ה אבל תינוק שנשבה).]

12. [Most *chatas* offerings are brought for inadvertent violations, which the Torah commonly refers to as חֵטְא (see, for example, *Leviticus* 4:27).]

13. [That is, to be liable to a *chatas* for an inadvertent transgression the person must have at least once known that his act was prohibited.]

14. For if the assumption that the Torah's use of the word חוטא, *sinner,* indicates a comparison between an inadvertent sinner and a deliberate one, the following additional comparison should also be true. Since it is not, it shows that the basic argument is not valid (*Rashi*).

[*Rashi's* use of the term *gezeirah shavah* here is not meant literally, as is evident from *Rashi* himself below ד"ה מאי טעמא (*Rashash*).]

15. Thus, the comparison should teach that even in a case where the person had knowledge of the prohibition at the time he sinned, he should still be liable to a *chatas.* The Gemara below will explain in what sense this can be called an inadvertent violation if he knew the law at the time of his transgression (*Rashi*).

16. [*Tosafos* conclude from *Rashi's* explanation (see previous note) that Munbaz certainly agrees that a person is liable to a *chatas* when he was not aware of the prohibition at the time of the transgression. That is based on the literal meaning of the term שְׁגָגָה, *inadvertence,* stated in Scripture. However, from the comparison to a deliberate sinner, Munbaz derives that one can be liable to a *chatas* even when he *had* knowledge of the prohibition at the time of his transgression. See also *Ritva MHK* ed.]

17. Rav and Shmuel hold that a child raised among gentiles is liable to a *chatas* when he discovers the law. Though Rav and Shmuel state that our Mishnah speaks of a case of one who knew the law of the Sabbath and then forgot it, it may well be that the Baraisa also agrees that a person who was once aware of the Sabbath and then forgot it is liable to one *chatas* for all his violations, but the Baraisa means to add by its illustration that in the case of a child captured and raised among the gentiles there is a dispute between Munbaz and the Rabbis whether the Mishnah's law applies (*Rashi*). Thus, the Baraisa does not contradict Rav and Shmuel's interpretation of the Mishnah. However, R' Yochanan and Reish Lakish insist that the Mishnah's obligation of a *chatas* applies *only* in the case of one who knew and forgot, but one who *never* knew (e.g. a child captured and raised among the gentiles) is exempt from a *chatas.* This interpretation of the Mishnah is clearly contradicted by the opening statement of the Baraisa, which states that the Mishnah's ruling holds true for a child who *never* learned the law of the Sabbath.

18. [I.e. we follow Munbaz's view and hold that the anonymous ruling of our Mishnah reflects the view of Munbaz and not the Rabbis.]

19. The Gemara takes it for granted that Munbaz could not have based his opinion solely on the logic of the comparison mentioned in the Baraisa. For inadvertent action and deliberate action are direct opposites [particularly with respect to one's knowledge of the prohibition]. Since this distinction forms the very basis of the difference in law between them, *logic* dictates that they not be considered comparable (*Rashi*).

עין משפט
נר מצוה

ד א מיי' פ"ג מהלכות שגגות הלכה ו ופ"ז הלכה ג סמג עשין ריג:

אבל לא שכחה מאי א) חייב על כל מלאכה ומלאכה אדתני היודע שהוא שבת ועשה מלאכות הרבה בשבתות הרבה חייב על כל מלאכה ומלאכה ליתני היודע עיקר שבת וכל שכן הא אלא מתניתין כשהכיר ולבסוף שכח ודרב ושמואל נמי כהכיר ולבסוף שכח דמי והכי איתמר רב ושמואל דאמרי תרוייהו א אפילו תינוק שנשבה בין הנכרים וגר שנתגייר לבין הנכרים כהכיר ולבסוף שכח דמי וחייב ורבי יוחנן ורבי שמעון בן לקיש דאמרי תרוייהו דוקא הכיר ולבסוף שכח אבל תינוק שנשבה בין הנכרים וגר שנתגייר לבין הנכרים פטור מיתיבי כלל גדול אמרו בשבת כל השוכח עיקר שבת ועשה מלאכות הרבה בשבתות הרבה אינו חייב אלא אחת כיצד תינוק שנשבה לבין הנכרים וגר שנתגייר בין הנכרים ועשה מלאכות הרבה בשבתות הרבה אינו חייב אלא חטאת אחת וחייב על הדם אחת ועל החלב אחת ועל ע"ז אחת ומונבז פוטר וכך היה מונבז דן לפני רבי עקיבא הואיל ומזיד קרוי חוטא ושוגג קרוי חוטא מה מזיד שהיתה לו ידיעה אף שוגג שהיתה לו ידיעה אמר לו ר' עקיבא הריני מוסיף על דבריך אי מה מזיד שהיתה הידיעה בשעת מעשה אף שוגג שהיתה לו ידיעה בשעת מעשה אמר לו הן וכל שכן שהוספת אמר לו לדבריך אין זה קרוי שוגג אלא מזיד קתני מיהא כיצד תינוק בשלמא לרב ושמואל ניחא אלא לרבי יוחנן ולרבי שמעון בן לקיש קשיא אמרי לך רבי יוחנן וריש לקיש לא מי איכא מונבז דפטר אנן דאמרינן כמונבז מאי טעמא דמונבז דכתיב א) תורה אחת יהיה לכם לעושה בשגגה וסמיך ליה ב) והנפש אשר תעשה ביד רמה הקיש שוגג למזיד מה מזיד שהיתה לו ידיעה אף שוגג שהיתה לו ידיעה ורבנן האי תורה אחת מאי עבדי ליה מיבעי להו א) לכדמקרי ליה ר' יהושע בן לוי לבריה תורה אחת יהיה לכם לעושה בשגגה וכתיב וכי

רש"י

אבל לא שכחה. לעיקר שבת אלא ששכח שהיום שבת מאי: חייב על כל אב מלאכה. דע"כ אי הוה סבירא ליה דאינו חייב אלא אחת לכל שבת ושבת הוה ליה (א) למיכרך ולמיתני הכי מי שידע עיקר שבת ושכחה וכן היודע עיקר שבת ועשה מלאכות הרבה בשבתות הרבה חייב על כל שבת ושבת: ליתני היודע עיקר שבת. דהוה שגגת שבת וזדון מלאכות הרבה חייב על כל מלאכה אע"ג דבכל שבת ליכא אלא חדא שגגה וכ"ש שגגת מלאכות וזדון שבת דאיכא שגגות הרבה: כהכיר ולבסוף שכח דמי. ומתניתין איצטריך למינקט הכיר ולבסוף שכח דלא תימא חייב על כל שבת ושבת: פטור. דקסברי רבי יוחנן ור"ל אומר מותר אנוס הוא ולא שגגה היא: וחייב על הדם. שאכל כל ימיו אחת וכן על כל דבר כרת שבתורה: מזיד קרוי חוטא. דכתיב (ויקרא ה) בשבועת העדות נפש כי תחטא ושמעה וגומר ולא כתיב ביה ונעלם: הריני מוסיף על דבריך. כלומר אם כך באת לדרוש ג"ש ללמד שוגג ממזיד בא ואוסיף גם אני על דבריך עוד וזה תראה אם יעמדו דבריך: אף שוגג שהיתה לו ידיעה בשעת מעשה. תחייבהו גם בזו חטאת: כ"ש שהוספת. על דברי והרי אתה מסייעני וגם בזו אני אומר שהוא חייב ולקמן מפרש במאי שגג: קתני מיהא. רישא תינוק שנשבה לבין הנכרים חייב: בשלמא לרב ושמואל ניחא. דאינהו נמי מחייבי ואיכא לאוקמי דהוא הדין להכיר ולבסוף שכח כי מתניתין וברייתא דקתני תינוק היא גופא איצטריך לאשמעינן פלוגתא דמונבז ורבנן: מאי טעמא דמונבז. אבנין אב ודאי לא סמיך למיעבד שוגג דומיא דמזיד דהאי שוגג חילוף דמזיד וליכא לדמויינהו דהאי חייב והאי פטור: מקיש שוגג. לענין חטאת למזיד לענין כרת ואף על גב דלא דמי ע"כ הקישן הכתוב: ורבנן. הך הקישא בעיא לכדרבי יהושע ב"ל: תורה אחת יהיה לכם. גבי קרבן ע"ז כתיב בפרשת שלח לך אנשים: וכי

תוספות

אבל לא שכחה מאי חייב על כל מלאכה ומלאכה. תימה לר"י מנא ליה למידק הכי אימא דלא שכחה נמי אינו חייב על כל מלאכה ומלאכה אלא על כל שבת ושבת כמו בהכיר ולבסוף שכח ותנא הכיר ולבסוף שכח וכ"ש הא כדפרי' ומה שפי' בקונטרס דדייק דחייב על כל מלאכה ומלאכה מדלא כייל להו אהדדי מי שידע עיקר שבת ושכחה והיודע עיקר שבת חייב על כל שבת ושבת דהוה משמע דוקא על כל שבת ושבת ולא על כל מלאכה אין נראה לר"י דא"כ היכי פריך לעיל לתני הכיר ולבסוף שכח וכל שכן הא דמשמע דהא לא איצטריך למיתני והא נמי איצטריך לאשמעינן דאינו חייב על כל מלאכה ומלאכה ונראה לר"י דלעיל דקאמר ליתני הכיר ולבסוף שכח וכ"ש הא לא בעי למימר דלא ליתני' כלל במשנה אלא ה"פ מדקתני חייב על כל שבת ושבת ולא קתני אינו חייב אלא על כל שבת דהוה משמע ולא על כל מלאכה ומלאכה משמע דעיקר מתניתין חיובא אתא לאשמעינן דחייב על כל שבת ושבת ולא פטורא דאינו חייב על כל מלאכה ואם כן ליתני הכיר ולבסוף שכח דהוי רבותא טפי וכ"ש האי דחייב על כל שבת ולא הוה צריך למתנייה בהאי בבא אלא ה"ל למיתני בתר הכי בבבא אחריתי היודע עיקר שבת אינו חייב אלא על כל שבת ושבת לאשמעינן דאינו חייב על כל מלאכה והשתא דייק שפיר אבל לא שכחה מאי חייב על כל מלאכה ומלאכה מדלא תני בבבא אחריתי דאינו חייב אלא על כל שבת ושבת ב):

ליתני היודע עיקר שבת וכ"ש הא. תימה לר"י לרבא דאמר בכריתות בסוף פרק אמרו לו (דף טז:) דבזדון שבת ושגגת מלאכות לא מיחייב אכל שבת ושבת ודייק ממתניתין דהכא דלא קתני חייב על כל אב מלאכה ומלאכה של כל שבת ושבת ולדידיה היכי פריך הכא ליתני היודע עיקר שבת הא לא מצי למיתני הכי דאם כן הוה משמע דלא מיחייב היודע עיקר שבת אכל שבת ושבת ותירץ דהכי פריך דליתני היודע עיקר שבת דחייב אכל אב מלאכה של כל שבת ושבת ורשב"א מפרש דאי הוה תני בהדיא היודע עיקר שבת חייב על כל אב מלאכה ליכא למידק דלא מיחייב אכל שבת מדלא קתני חייב על כל אב מלאכה של כל שבת ושבת דלא צריך למיתני' דמרישא שמעינן ליה דקתני בהכיר ולבסוף שכח דחייב על כל שבת ושבת כ"ש יודע עיקר שבת כדאמר לעיל: וכ"ש האי. ה"נ לא בעי למימר דלא לתני' כלל במשנה דאם כן הוה אמינא דחייב נמי על כל שבת ושבת ואינו כן לרבה דכריתות אלא ליתני בבא אחריתי היודע שהוא שבת אינו חייב על כל שבת:

כי הכיר ולבסוף שכח דמי. פירש בקונטרס דלהכי לא תנא במתניתין שכח מעיקרו דהיינו תינוק שנשבה דלא תימא דהכיר ולבסוף שכח חייב על כל שבת וקשה לר"י דמ"מ ליתנייה וליתני נמי בתר הכי הכיר ולבסוף שכח אינו חייב אלא אחת דהכ"ג פריך לעיל ליתני הכיר ולבסוף שכח וכ"ש הא כדפרישית ונראה לר"י דודאי אי הוה תני חייב חטאת דהוה אתי לאשמעינן חיובא הוה שייך למיפרך דליתני תינוק שנשבה דהוי רבותא טפי אבל השתא דקתני אינו חייב אלא אחת אתא לאשמעינן פטורא אחת דפטורה נקט הכיר ולבסוף שכח דהוי רבותא טפי ומיהו קשה לר"י דמ"מ ליתני תינוק שנשבה דלא נטעה לומר דפטור כרבי יוחנן ור"ל והדר ליתני הכיר ולבסוף שכח:

אבל תינוק שנשבה פטור. פירש בקונטרס דקסברי אומר מותר אנוס הוא ואין נראה דטעמייהו כמונבז כדאמר בסמוך וטעמא דמונבז מפרש לקמן דיליף מקרא והא דאמר בפ"ב דמכות (דף ז:) גבי גלות בשגגה פרט למזיד ומפרש (אביי) [נ"ל רבא] פרט לאומר מותר ופריך ליה (רבא) [נ"ל אביי] אומר מותר אנוס הוא לאו דוקא קאמר אנוס דבכל מקום מחייבין ליה אלא לגבי גלות דוקא ממעט (אביי) [נ"ל רבא] אומר מותר משום דטובא בשגגה כתיב התם דהא בפירקין (ג) מחייבי אומר מותר בע"ז ובחלב אע"ג דכתיב בהן בשגגה (ורבא) [נ"ל ואביי] פריך ליה אומר מותר אנוס הוא ולא הוה ליה למיתני בברייתא בשגגה פרט למזיד אלא פרט לאנוס דיותר דמי וקרוב לאנוס מלמזיד: וחייב על הדם אחת. אע"ג דמילתא דפשיטא היא דאכל מה שאכל דם אינו חייב אלא אחת כיון שאין בדם חילוק איסור כמו שיש בשבת חילוק מלאכות וכל אדם נמי בלא תינוק שנשבה אכל דם ודם אינו חייב אלא אחת אלא אומר ר"י דמיירי דאפי' אכלן בכמה תמחויין דלר"י (לקמן דף עא.) אדם אחר חייב על כל תמחוי אפי' בהעלם אחד ובתינוק שנשבה אינו חייב אלא אחד אך קשה לרשב"א דמאי איצטריך תו לאשמעינן ולמתני ועל החלב אחד:

כל שכן שהוספת. כדפירש בקונטרס דאף בזו מחייב ומחייב נמי כי ליכא ידיעה בשעת מעשה דהא רבי יוחנן וריש לקיש סברי כמונבז ומחייבי הכיר ולבסוף שכח ותניא נמי לקמן שגג בזה ובזה זהו שוגג האמור בתורה ומוקמינן לה כמונבז והיינו טעמא משום דסברא הוא דלא איתקש שוגג למזיד לאפוקי ליה ממשמעות שגגה דאדרבה שוגג משמע דלית ליה ידיעה בשעת מעשה ולא אתא היקשא אלא לחייב נמי כי אית ליה ידיעה בשעת מעשה ומיהו קשה לר"י דהא פטרי מהיקשא תינוק שנשבה מהאי טעמא נמי יפטור הכיר ולבסוף שכח: מה

רבינו חננאל

מתני' לדברי הכל בהכיר ולבסוף שכח אינו חייב אלא חטאת אחת ורב ושמואל הוסיפו אפילו קטן שנשבה לבין עו"ג כהכיר ולבסוף שכח דמי וחייב חטאת ורבי יוחנן וריש לקיש אמרי קטן שנשבה בין עו"ג פטור ואותיבנא עלייהו מהא דתניא השוכח עיקר שבת ועשה מלאכות הרבה בשבתות הרבה אינו חייב אלא חטאת אחת וחייב על ע"ז אחת. פירש אם עבד ע"ז הרבה דינו כדין שבת וכן כל מצוה ומצוה אינו חייב אלא בכל מצוה אחת ומונבז פוטר בכל ומשני רבי יוחנן וריש לקיש אנן דאמרינן כמונבז דסבר כיון דלא הויא ידיעה ליה בתחלה בעיקר שבת אף על גב דבתר דעביד מלאכות הרבה בשבתות הרבה אתיידע ליה איסורא דשבת לא מחייב וכי אמרו רבי יוחנן ור"ל דאנן כמונבז סבירא לן בהאי לחוד דפטר קטן שנשבה בין הנכרים אבל בהאי דבעי ידיעה למונבז בשעת מעשה שידע

רב נסים גאון

ורבנן כדמקרי ליה ר' יהושע בן לוי לבריה תורה אחת יהיה לכם לעושה בשגגה והנפש אשר תעשה ביד רמה הוקשה כל התורה כולה לע"ז. דע שפרשת (במדבר טו) וכי תשגו ולא תעשו ואם נפש אחת תחטא בשגגה שממנה אלו הפסוקים אמרו רבותינו ז"ל כי היא מיוחדת בע"ז ותמצא פירוש זה בספרי בע"ז הכתוב מדבר אתה אומר בע"ז או אינו אלא באחת מן המצות האמורות בתורה ת"ל והיה אם מעיני העדה נעשתה ייחד הכתוב מצוה זו בפני עצמה ואיזו זו ע"ז וכו' ובמסכת הוריות בפ' הורה כהן משיח (דף ח) אמרו דכולי עלמא הני קראי בע"ז הוא דכתיבי מנא לן אמר רבא ואיתימא ר' יהושע בן לוי ואמרי לה כדי וכי תשגו ולא תעשו את כל המצות האלה איזו היא מצוה שהיא שקולה כנגד כל המצות כולן הוי אומר זו ע"ז דבית ר' תנא אמר קרא א) את כל אשר דבר ה' אליכם ביד משה איזו היא מצוה

חשק שלמה על רב נסים גאון

א) אשר דבר ה' אל משה את כל אשר צוה ה' אליכם ביד משה כצ"ל:

תורה אור השלם

א) הָאֶזְרָח בִּבְנֵי יִשְׂרָאֵל וְלַגֵּר הַגָּר בְּתוֹכָם תּוֹרָה אַחַת יִהְיֶה לָכֶם לָעֹשֶׂה בִּשְׁגָגָה: [במדבר טו, כט]

ב) וְהַנֶּפֶשׁ אֲשֶׁר תַּעֲשֶׂה בְּיָד רָמָה מִן הָאֶזְרָח וּמִן הַגֵּר אֶת יְיָ הוּא מְגַדֵּף וְנִכְרְתָה הַנֶּפֶשׁ הַהִוא מִקֶּרֶב עַמָּהּ: [במדבר טו, ל]

מסורת הש"ס

א) יבמות דף ט. הוריות ח ע"א.

תוספות ישנים

א) ותוקי אחת שהיא הנה בין שגגת שבת וזדון מלאכה בין בזדון שבת ושגגת מלאכה כפי' רב נחמן לרב חייא. והנה שהיא אחת בהכיר ולבסוף שכח:

ב) לר"י דפי' דדייק מדלא קתני לה בבא אחריתי ולא שיפרש אינו חייב על כל מלאכה לא נחייש לי דהא לא איצטריך למיתני בבא אחריתא דמסיפא שמעינן מדקתני היודע שהוא שבת חייב על כל מלאכה ומשמע הא שכחה אינו חייב על כל מלאכה. ועוד מאי פריך בסמוך ליתני היודע עיקר שבת וכ"ש הא אמאי הוי צריך למיתני היודע עיקר שבת שהוא חייב על כל מלאכה והא שמעינן לה מדלא תני בבא אחריתי כדפרי'. והיה נ"ל דלעיל פריך ליתני הכיר ולבסוף שכח בהדיא וכ"ש היודע עיקר שבת ולא הוי צריך כלל למיתני דחייב על כל שבת דשמעינן מכ"ש דהכיר ולבסוף שכח שאינו חייב על כל מלאכה. מדנקט בסיפא היודע שהוא שבת כו' משמע דהיודע עיקר שבת ושכח אינו חייב על כל מלאכה. אבל השתא דמשני דיודע עיקר שבת היינו הכיר ולבסוף שכח פריך שפיר אבל לא שכחה מאי חייב על כל מלאכה. דאי אינו חייב כמו בשכחה א"כ אמאי נקט היודע עיקר שבת דמשמע טפי דאיירי בלא שכחה ה"ל למיתני בהדיא הכיר ולבסוף שכח דהוי משמע רבותא טפי אלא ודאי בשלא שכחה חייב על כל מלאכה והוי בכלל בבא דסיפא. להכי ליכא למיטעי במאי דנקט האי לישנא דהיודע עיקר שבת ולא נקט הכיר ולבסוף שכח בהדיא אימא סיפא היודע שהוא שבת וכו'. בשלמא אי הוי תני בהדיא היודע עיקר שבת ולא שכחה בסיפא הוי ידעינן ליה מכ"ש דסיפא א"ש כדפרישית אבל השתא דהיודע עיקר שבת ולא שכחה לא שמעינן מסיפא אלא אדרבה משמע דוקא יודע שהוא שבת חייב על כל מלאכה אם כן מליעתא משמע דמיירי ביודע עיקר שבת ולא שכחה כדמשמע לישנא. ומשמע דוקא לא שכחה אבל שכחה אינו חייב על כל שבת. דאי חייב ליתני הכיר ולבסוף שכחה בהדיא וכל שכן היודע עיקר שבת ולא שכחה כדפרי' לעיל:

הגהות הב"ח

(א) רש"י ד"ה חייב על וכו' ה"ל למיתני כצ"ל ומיבת למיכרך נמחק: (ב) תוס' ד"ה אבל תינוק וכו' דהא בפירקין. נ"ב בסוף דף עב:

ליקוטי רש"י

לכדמקרי ליה ר' יהושע בן לוי לבריה תורה אחת. לענין קרבן כתיב [בפרשת] עבודת כוכבים תורה כל התורה במשמע הוקשה כל התורה לענין קרבן לעבודת כוכבים [יבמות ט.].

[מכאן שייך לדף סט.]

וכי תשגו. בעבודה זרה הכתוב מדבר או אינו אלא באחת מכל המצות תלמוד לומר את כל המצות האלה מצוה אחת שהיא ככל המצות מה העובר על כל המצות פורק עול ומפר ברית ומגלה פנים אף מצוה זו פורק בה עול ומפר ברית ומגלה פנים ואיזו זו עבודה זרה [במדבר טו, כב]. ביד רמה. במזיד [שם, ל]. הוקשו כולם לע"ז. שהוקשו כל חטאות שבתורה לחטאת עבודה זרה דכתיב תורה אחת יהיה לכם וגו' [לקמן קלז.]. דהוקשה כל התורה כולה לענין קרבן לעבודת כוכבים שנאמר בפרשת שלח לך אנשים אבל קרבן עבודת כוכבים תורה אחת יהיה לכם לעושה בשגגה כאן הוקשו כל עבירות שבתורה בשגגתן לעבודת כוכבים לענין קרבן [מכות יג:]. מה להלן דבר שחייבים על זדונו כרת ושגגתו חטאת. דהכא כתיב הכרת תכרת אף כו' [הוריות ח.]. כדכתיב התם והנפש אשר תעשה ביד רמה ונכרתה אלמא כולה פרשתא בדבר שזדונו כרת ושגגתו חטאת מישתעי [יבמות ט.]. מעם. ולא כל עם וגבי חטאת כתיב שבא [על] השוגג [חולין ה:]. מעם הארץ. מביא קרבן ולא כל עם הארץ [הוריות יא.]. פרט למומר. דאינו מביא קרבן על שגגתו דלאין מקבלין מידו [שם ב.]. ר"ש בן אלעזר אומר משום ר"ש. מכאן אתה למד [חולין שם]. אשר לא תעשינה בשגגה ואשם. אשר לא תעשינה משמע שאילו ידע לא עשה אבל בשגגה עשה ואשם [יומא פ.]. וסמיך ליה או הודע אליו חטאתו אשר חטא והביא אשמו למשמע דאשר לא תעשינה אם היה יודע שהוא אסור ושגגה היתה לו וחטא ואשם הוא יביא. השב מידיעתו. שאם היה יודע שהוא חלב היה יושב ומבטל מעבירה זו ואית דגרים השב והוא נמי הפורש ובדל מתחלה ואין עובר אם היה יודע שהוא אסור ובת"כ גרס היושב [חולין שם]. לא שב מידיעתו אינו מביא קרבן על שגגתו. ומומר לא שב מידיעתו הוא לפיכך אינו מביא קרבן על שגגתו ואמר לקמן בפ"ב מומר שאכל חלב והביא קרבן על הדם איכא בינייהו [הוריות שם].

,,תּוֹרָה אַחַת יִהְיֶה לָכֶם לָעֹשֶׂה בִּשְׁגָגָה'' – **For it is written:**[20] ***There shall be a single law for you, for one who acts with inadvertence;*** וּסְמִיךְ לֵיהּ – **and nearby to that** verse it says: ,,וְהַנֶּפֶשׁ אֲשֶׁר־תַּעֲשֶׂה בְּיָד רָמָה'' – ***But a person who shall act high-handedly . . .***[21] הִקִּישׁ שׁוֹגֵג לְמֵזִיד – **[The Torah]** thereby **compares an inadvertent [transgressor] to a deliberate [transgressor].** מַה מֵּזִיד שֶׁהָיְתָה לוֹ יְדִיעָה – **Just as the deliberate [transgressor] had knowledge** of the prohibition, אַף שׁוֹגֵג שֶׁהָיְתָה לוֹ יְדִיעָה – **so too the inadvertent [transgressor]** of whom the Torah speaks is one who **had knowledge** of the prohibition.[22]

The Gemara questions Munbaz's disputants:

וְרַבָּנָן – **Now, the Rabbis!** הַאי ,,תּוֹרָה אַחַת'' מַאי עָבְדֵי לֵיהּ – **What do they do with this** verse, ***a single law,*** and the analogy implied by it?[23]

The Gemara answers:

מִיבָּעֵי לְהוּ לִכְדְמַקְרֵי לֵיהּ רַבִּי יְהוֹשֻׁעַ בֶּן לֵוִי לִבְרֵיהּ – **They need it for that which was taught by R' Yehoshua ben Levi in a Scriptural lesson to his son:** ,,תּוֹרָה אַחַת יִהְיֶה לָכֶם לָעֹשֶׂה בִּשְׁגָגָה'' – ***There shall be a single law for you, for one who acts with inadvertence;***[24] וּכְתִיב – **and it is written** earlier in that passage:

NOTES

20. *Numbers* 15:29, with regard to the *chatas* offering brought for inadvertent idolatry.

21. In the very next verse (v. 30). This verse speaks of one who knowingly commits idolatry.

22. Thus, even though they are not logically comparable, the *hekeish* implied by the juxtaposition of these two verses teaches that we must establish an analogy between them in regard to some matter (*Rashi;* see *Ritva*). [Accordingly, the simple comparison put forth by Munbaz to R' Akiva in the Baraisa is not the main basis for his view. See *Maharam* and *Chasam Sofer* who explains why, if so, Munbaz put forth that argument to R' Akiva (cf. *Rashba*).]

23. I.e. what do the Rabbis, who disagree with Munbaz, derive from that *hekeish*? (see *Rashi*).

24. [See note 20.] The phrase תּוֹרָה אַחַת, *a single law,* literally means "a single *Torah,*" and is understood in the context of this exposition to refer to the entire Torah (see *Rashi* 69a ד״ה וכי תשגו).

"וְכִי תִשְׁגּוּ וְלֹא תַעֲשׂוּ אֵת כָּל־הַמִּצְוֹת הָאֵלֶּה" – *When you will err and will not do all of these commandments,*[1] which makes it clear that this Scriptural section refers to idolatry. וּכְתִיב "וְהַנֶּפֶשׁ אֲשֶׁר־תַּעֲשֶׂה בְּיָד רָמָה" – **And it is written** there: ***But the person who will act high-handedly*** *... will be cut off.*[2] הוּקְשׁוּ כּוּלָּם לַעֲבוֹדָה זָרָה – From the juxtaposition of these verses we learn that **all [the Torah's commandments] are compared to idolatry** with respect to *chatas* liability:[3] מַה לְהַלָּן דָּבָר שֶׁחַיָּיבִים עַל זְדוֹנוֹ כָּרֵת – **Just as there** [in the case of idolatry], the verse speaks of **something for which one is liable to *kares* for its deliberate** violation, וְשִׁגְגָתוֹ חַטָּאת – **and a *chatas* for its inadvertent** violation, אַף כָּל דָּבָר שֶׁחַיָּיבִין עַל זְדוֹנוֹ כָּרֵת – **so too** in regard to **everything** else, i.e. all other Torah laws, the law is that for **something for which one is liable to *kares* for its deliberate** violation, וְעַל שִׁגְגָתוֹ חַטָּאת – one is liable to a ***chatas* for its inadvertent** violation.[4]

The Gemara analyzes the opinion of Munbaz:

וְאֶלָּא מוּנְבַּז שְׁגָגָה בְּמַאי – **Now,** according to **Munbaz,** who holds that a person is liable to a *chatas* even if he had knowledge of the law at the time of the transgression, **regarding what was the inadvertence?**[5]

The Gemara answers:

כְּגוֹן שֶׁשָּׁגַג בְּקָרְבָּן – According to Munbaz one is obligated to bring a *chatas* **in a case where he acted with inadvertence in regard to the sacrifice,** i.e. he did not know that inadvertent violation of this prohibition requires a sacrifice to atone. He did, however, know that the act was prohibited and subject to *kares.*[6]

The Gemara explains the dissenting view of the Rabbis:

וְרַבָּנָן – **And the Rabbis:** שִׁגְגַת קָרְבָּן לֹא שְׁמָהּ שְׁגָגָה – They hold that **inadvertence concerning** the obligation to bring **a sacrifice is not considered inadvertence.**[7]

The Gemara examines the criterion for inadvertence according to the Rabbis:

וְרַבָּנָן שְׁגָגָה בְּמַאי – **Now,** according to **the Rabbis,** who hold that the inadvertence regarding the sacrifice is not sufficient, **regarding what must there be inadvertence?**[8]

The Gemara presents two views:

רַבִּי יוֹחָנָן אָמַר – **R' Yochanan said:** כֵּיוָן שֶׁשָּׁגַג בְּכָרֵת – **As long as he acted inadvertently with regard to** the ***kares*** penalty, אַף עַל פִּי שֶׁהֵזִיד בְּלָאו – **even though he acted deliberately with regard to the prohibition,** he is liable to a *chatas.*[9] וְרֵישׁ לָקִישׁ אָמַר – **But Reish Lakish said:** עַד שֶׁיִּשְׁגּוֹג בְּלָאו וְכָרֵת – He is not liable to a *chatas* **unless he acted inadvertently with regard to** both the **prohibition and** the ***kares*** penalty.[10]

The Gemara explains Reish Lakish's view:

אָמַר רָבָא – **Rava said:** מַאי טַעְמָא דְּרַבִּי שִׁמְעוֹן בֶּן לָקִישׁ – **What is the reason of R' Shimon ben Lakish?**[11] אָמַר קְרָא – For **the verse states** that the *chatas* offering is brought by someone who performs one of the acts "אֲשֶׁר לֹא־תֵעָשֶׂינָה (בִּשְׁגָגָה) וְאָשֵׁם" – ***that are not to be done – inadvertently – and he becomes***

NOTES

1. *Numbers* 15:22. [This verse introduces the *chatas* discussion of that chapter. Though it refers to a communal *chatas* obligation, it is clear from the context that the section on the personal obligation that follows (vs. 27-31) refers to the same sin mentioned in verse 22.] Now, the Gemara in *Horayos* (8a) explains that this verse speaks of idolatry, for it as the sin that is considered equivalent to violating *all* of the mitzvos combined (*Rashi*).

2. Ibid. 15:30. This verse teaches that one who is guilty of a deliberate transgression of idolatry is liable to *kares.*

3. For verse 22 (...וְכִי תִשְׁגּוּ) makes clear that the sin being discussed in this passage is the sin of idolatry, and the juxtaposition of verse 29 (תּוֹרָה אַחַת ... לָעֹשֶׂה בִּשְׁגָגָה, *there shall be a single Torah ... for one who acts inadvertently*) to verse 30 (וְהַנֶּפֶשׁ אֲשֶׁר־תַּעֲשֶׂה בְּיָד רָמָה, *but a person who shall act high-handedly ... will be cut off*) makes it clear that the liability to a *chatas* referred to in verse 29 is for a sin whose *deliberate* violation ("high-handed") is subject to *kares* (being "cut off") – i.e. full-fledged idolatry [and not the lesser forms of idolatry, such as embracing an idol, that are not subject to *kares* (*Maharam* in explanation of *Rashi*)]. Thus, when verse 29 states that there shall be *a single Torah,* we understand it to mean that the law of *chatas* throughout the Torah conforms to the model established here in the case of idolatry, as the Gemara will now elaborate (*Rashi*).

4. [From the previous verse's statement (15:29) of תּוֹרָה אַחַת, *a single Torah,* we derive through a *hekeish* to the idolatry law taught in 15:30 that other Torah laws are compared to idolatry.] Thus, we learn from this exposition that there is no *chatas* for an inadvertent transgression law unless a deliberate transgression of that prohibition is subject to *kares* – as is the case with idolatry (*Rashi*). The Rabbis use the *hekeish* given for Munbaz's law to teach this law instead.

5. Munbaz maintained in response to R' Akiva's challenge that one would indeed be liable to a *chatas* even if he had knowledge of the prohibition *at the time* of his transgression. But this is difficult to understand, for the Torah states that a *chatas* is brought for a שְׁגָגָה, *an inadvertent transgression* (*Rashi*). Thus, to be liable to a *chatas* the person must have been unaware of *something* when he sinned.

6. Munbaz holds that the Torah's concept of שְׁגָגָה, *inadvertence,* encompasses even the case of one who was aware at the time he sinned that he would be liable to the *kares* penalty for his deliberate transgression of the law but who was unaware that this sin carries a *chatas* liability for an inadvertent transgression (*Rashi*). According to Munbaz, his ignorance of the *chatas* requirement renders him a שׁוֹגֵג, *inadvertent transgressor,* with regard to this sin [since he does not fully realize all of its consequences (see *Ritva MHK* ed.)]. This is the lesson derived by Munbaz from the *hekeish* cited above.

7. According to the Rabbis a person is not liable to a *chatas* unless his inadvertence concerned the transgression itself (*Rashi*). [In this case, however, his error was not in regard to what he actually did, since he knew the prohibition, was aware of the *kares* penalty for it and nonetheless performed the transgression deliberately. His error was only in regard to the penalty for inadvertent transgression – but he did not act inadvertently but deliberately!]

8. That is, granted that the inadvertence must be in regard to the transgression [he actually performed], how mistaken must the person have been? Must he have been completely unaware that the act was forbidden, or is it sufficient that he was unaware of the *penalty* for his deliberate transgression, though he was aware of the prohibition? (*Rashi*).

9. According to R' Yochanan, the Rabbis hold that liability to a *chatas* is tied by the Torah to inadvertence about the *kares* penalty, as we see from the *hekeish* cited above, in which the verse concerning the "law for inadvertent violation" is juxtaposed to the verse describing the *kares* penalty. Therefore, even if the person realizes that the act is forbidden, but he does not know that it can lead to *kares,* he is considered a שׁוֹגֵג, *inadvertent sinner,* with respect to the *kares* and is liable to a *chatas* to atone for that part of his transgression (*Rashi*). Since no reference is made in that verse to the prohibition, we derive from the *hekeish* that the inadvertence need be only regarding *kares,* not regarding the prohibition as well (*Tosafos*).

[See *Kehillos Yaakov* §29 who cites *Yerushalmi* as maintaining that the sinner would nonetheless be liable to *malkus* for his deliberate transgression of the prohibition. He is considered "inadvertent" only with respect to the *greater severity* of this sin (i.e. the *kares* aspect) beyond that of ordinary prohibitions (those for which there is no *kares*). This greater aspect is sufficient (according to R' Yochanan) to obligate him to a *chatas* and it is for this aspect alone that it atones. *Rashi's* wording here implies a similar understanding (though there is no evidence that *Rashi* would hold him liable to *malkus* for the unatoned part of his sin).]

10. I.e. according to the Rabbis, a person is not liable to a *chatas* unless he did not know that the act was prohibited.

11. R' Yochanan's reasoning is obvious, as explained in note 9. The Gemara therefore asks why Reish Lakish disagrees (*Tosafos*).

וכי תשגו ולא תעשו את כל המצות האלה וכתיב **והנפש אשר תעשה ביד רמה** הוקשו כולם לע"ז מה להלן דבר שחייבים על זדונו כרת ושגגתו חטאת אף כל דבר שחייבין על זדונו כרת ועל שגגתו חטאת ואלא מונבז שגגה במאי כגון ששגג בקרבן ורבנן שגגת קרבן לא שמה שגגה ורבנן שגגה במאי רבי יוחנן אמר כיון ששגג בכרת אף על פי שהזיד בלאו וריש לקיש אמר עד שישגוג בלאו וכרת אמר רבא מאי טעמא דרשב"ל אמר קרא אשר לא תעשינה (בשגגה) ואשם עד שישגוג בלאו וכרת שבה ורבי יוחנן האי קרא דרשב"ל מאי עביד ליה מיבעי ליה לכדתניא מעם הארץ פרט למומר רבי שמעון בן אלעזר אומר משום רבי שמעון אשר לא תעשינה (בשגגה) ואשם השב מידיעתו מביא קרבן על שגגתו לא שב מידיעתו אינו מביא קרבן על שגגתו: תנן אבות מלאכות ארבעים חסר אחת והוינן בה מנינא למה לי ואמר ר' יוחנן שאם עשאן כולן בהעלם אחד חייב על כל אחת ואחת היכי משכחת לה בזדון שבת ושגגת מלאכות בשלמא לרבי יוחנן דאמר כיון ששגג בכרת אע"פ שהזיד בלאו משכחת לה כגון דידע לה לשבת בלאו אלא לר"ש ב"ל דאמר עד שישגוג בלאו ובכרת דידע ליה לשבת במאי דידעה בתחומין ואליבא דר"ע מאן תנא להא דתנו רבנן שגג בזה ובזה זהו שוגג האמור בתורה הזיד בזה ובזה זו היא מזיד האמור בתורה שגג בשבת והזיד במלאכות או ששגג במלאכות והזיד בשבת או שאמר יודע אני שמלאכה זו אסורה אבל איני יודע שחייבין עליה קרבן או לא חייב כמאן כמונבז אמר אביי הכל מודים בשבועת ביטוי שאין חייבין עליה קרבן עד שישגוג בלאו שבה הכל מודים מאן ר' יוחנן פשיטא כי קא"ר יוחנן היכא דאיכא כרת אבל הכא דליכא כרת לא סד"א הואיל וחייב קרבן חידוש הוא דבכל התורה כולה לא אשכחן לאו דמייתי עליה קרבן והכא מייתי כי שגג בקרבן נמי ליחייב קמ"ל

רש"י

וכי תשגו ולא תעשו את כל המצות האלה. וילפינן בהוריות (דף ח.) זו ע"ז שהיא שקולה ככל המצות וכתיב תורה אחת כל התורה במשמע: **הוקשו.** קרבנות של שגגות של כל עבירות לשל ע"ז מה ע"ז קרבן שלה אינו בא אלא על עבירה גמורה שחייב על זדונו כרת דסמיך ליה והנפש אשר תעשה ביד רמה ונכרתה: **אף כל התורה.** אין מביאין חטאת אלא על דבר שזדונו כרת: **ואלא מונבז.** דאמר לעיל דמי שהיתה לו ידיעה בשעת מעשה חייב חטאת: **דשגג במאי.** הא גבי חטאת שגגה כתיב: **דשגג בקרבן.** דיודע שחייב על זדונו כרת אבל אינו יודע שחייב עליה חטאת: **לא שמה שגגה.** עד ששגג בעבירה עצמה: **ורבנן.** דבעו שגגה בעבירה עצמה שגגה במאי קאמרי שגגה בכולה מילתא בלאו וכרת או בכרת לחודיה: **כיון ששגג בכרת אע"ג שהזיד בלאו.** שאז הקרבן על הכרת הוא בא כדאמרן לעושה בשגגה וסמיך ליה והנפש אשר תעשה וגו': **לא תעשינה.** היינו לאו: **מנינא למה לי.** ליתני אבות מלאכות הזורע והחורש כו' למה לי למיתנא ארבעים חסר אחת ליתנינהו ואנן ידעינן דמ' חסר אחת איכא: **שאם עשאן כולן כו'.** וסימנא בעלמא אשמעינן לידע כמה חטאות חייב על חילול שבת אחת: **היכי משכחת לה.** דמיחייב ע"כ לא משכחת לה אלא בזדון שבת דיודע שהוא שבת ושגגת מלאכות דאינו יודע שהמלאכות הללו אסורות דאי בזדון מלאכות ושגגת שבת דיודע שהן אסורות בשבת אבל שכח שהיום שבת הא תנן דאינו חייב אלא אחת לכל שבת וזדון שבת לא הוי אא"כ יודע אחת מהלכותיה דאי לא ידע בחדא מינייהו אין שבת חלוק לו משאר ימים וזה ששגג בכולן אין כאן זדון שבת: **בשלמא לר' יוחנן.** דאמר שגגת כרת שמה שגגה: **משכחת לה.** זדון שבת בלאוין ושגגת מלאכות בכריתות דיודע לה לשבת שהוזהר על הלאוין או של כולן או של אחת מהן: **דידע לה לשבת במאי.** הלא בכולן שגג כסבור שכל ל"ט מלאכות מותרות: **בתחומין.** דאין בקרבן: **ואליבא דר' עקיבא.** דאמר במסכת סוטה (א) תחומין דאורייתא נינהו דתנן בו ביום דרש רבי עקיבא ומדותם מחוץ לעיר כו': **זהו שוגג האמור בתורה.** כלומר היכא דשגג בשבת ובמלאכות אין כאן לא דין ולא דיין לקנתר ואין לך שוגג כזה: **הזיד בזה ובזה.** אין לך מזיד כזה: **שגג באחת מהן.** אף זה שוגג וחייבים עליה קרבן: **שבועת ביטוי.** שאוכל ולא אוכל שאכלתי ולא אכלתי חייב עליה קרבן וכתיב ביה ונעלם דהיינו שוגג הכל מודים בשוגג שלה דאם נשבע שלא אוכל ואכל אינו חייב אלא אם כן שכח שבועתו כשאכל דהשתא שגג בלאו שבה: **הכל מודים מאן רבי יוחנן.** כלומר על כרחין אביי לאו אפלוגתא דמונבז ורבנן קאי דלישמעינן דמודה מונבז בהא (דהא) [י] שגגת קרבן לא הויא שגגה דמהיכא תיתי והא ק"ו היא השתא בכל התורה כולה דליכא חידוש בקרבן דידהו אמר מונבז דמיחייב בשגגת קרבן הכא דחידוש הוא דאין בה כרת ומביא קרבן עליה לא כ"ש אלא לרבנן קאמר ואפלוגתא דר"י ור"ל קאי ומאן הכל מודים ר"י דאף על גב דבעלמא קאמר אף על פי שהזיד בלאו הכא בעינן שישגוג בלאו: **פשיטא.** כיון דאליבא דרבנן איפליג דאמרי שגגת קרבן לאו שגגה היא אי בלאו שלה הזיד במאי שגג דע"כ לא קאמר ר"י בעלמא אלא במקום כרת דשגג בכרת: **סלקא דעתך אמינא.** בשבועת ביטוי נמי קאי רבי יוחנן במילתיה דאף על פי שהזיד בלאו ודקשיא לך במאי שגג שגג בקרבן דהואיל וחידוש מודו ביה רבנן: קמ"ל

תוספות

מה ע"ז שחייבים על זדונו כרת. וא"ת מ"מ היקשא דשוגג למזיד למה לי דאפילו לא הוי כתיב התם קרא דוהנפש אשר תעשה ביד רמה ילפינן שפיר מע"ז שחייב על זדונה כרת כו' וי"ל דלית לן לאקושה לע"ז אלא במאי דכתיב בההיא פרשה כדמשמע מתוך פירוש הקונטרס ולהכי אצטריך לאתויי הכא והנפש אשר תעשה תדע דהא לא ילפינן מע"ז דניבעי על זדונו סקילה כע"ז משום דלא כתיב סקילה בההיא פרשה אלא כרת והא דממעטינן בריש פרק בתרא דמכות (דף יג:) פסח ומילה מקרבן אע"פ שיש בהן כרת משום דמה ע"ז דאמר רחמנא לא תעביד והני קום עשה ניהו היינו נמי משום דכתיב והנפש אשר תעשה ביד רמה ° דמשמע מה שצויתי שלא לעשות וא"ת רבנן דהכא ר' עקיבא ור' עקיבא אית ליה בפ"ק דכריתות (דף ז:) דהאי קרא דמגדף במברך את השם כתיב וי"ל דלישנא דנקט הכא הוקשה כל התורה כולה לע"ז נקט אליבא דרבנן דרבי עקיבא אבל לר"ע אית לן למימר דהוקשה כל התורה כולה למברך את השם וא"ת ולמונבז האי דרשא דר' יהושע בן לוי מנא ליה ואומר ר"י דנפקא ליה כדדריש רבי בפ"ק דיבמות (דף ט.) ובפ"ב דהוריות (דף ח.) נאמר כאן ונודעה החטאת אשר חטאו עליה ונאמ' ואשה אל אחותה לא תקח לצרור לגלות ערותה עליה: **אלא** למונבז שגגה במאי. לא מצי למימר ששגג בלאו והזיד בקרבן דאין סברא לחייב בהזיד בקרבן דלא שב מידיעתו הוא וליכא נמי למימר שגג בלאו וקרבן דסברא הוא דכיון דמקיש למזיד אפי' מזיד בכל דבר ושוגג רק בדבר אחד דהיינו בקרבן יש לנו לחייבו א) ומיהו היכא דאיכא סקילה בעינן שיהא שוגג גם בסקילה דאי הוה מזיד בסקילה אין לחייבו בקרבן דכיון דאינו שב מסקילה פשיטא שאפילו היה יודע שחייב גם קרבן שלא היה שב ולא שב מידיעתו הוא ואע"ג דבהזיד בכרת חשיב ליה שב מידיעתו לקרבן היינו משום דכרת אפשר בתשובה וקרבן לא אפשר בתשובה ועוד דגבי כרת שייך שפיר למימר אם היה יודע שחייב כרת עם הקרבן היה שב: **כגון** ששגג בכרת אע"פ שהזיד בלאו. וטעמא דר' יוחנן משום דלא כתיב לאו בהיקשא דר' יהושע ולא כתיב אלא כרת בההיא ענינא ולהכי בעי מ"ט דריש לקיש ולא בעי מ"ט דר' יוחנן ול"ל דרבי יוחנן מיירי אליבא דרבנן דאית להו היקשא דרבי יהושע בן לוי ° אבל לרבי דנפקא ליה מג"ש דעליה מודה רבי יוחנן דבעי עד שישגוג בלאו וכרת דהא כתיב לאו בההוא קרא ואשה אל אחותה לא תקח וגו': **אמר** קרא אשר לא תעשינה בשגגה. קשה לר"י מנא ליה לריש לקיש דרבנן דרשי הכי ובעו שגגת לאו וליכא למימר דמשמע ליה למדרש קרא הכי דהא ע"כ סבירא ליה דאין סברא לדרוש כן דהא איהו סבר כמונבז כדאמר לעיל ומונבז לא בעי שגגת לאו אלא שגגת קרבן גרידא דההיא תניא לקמן או שאמר יודע אני שמלאכה זו אסורה אבל איני יודע אם חייבים עליה קרבן אם לאו חייב ולא קאמר קרבן ומלקות אם לאו: **דידע** לה בתחומין ב). לא מצי למימר דידע לה בדאיסי דבההוא נמי חייב חטאת כדפירשתי בפרק קמא (דף ו: בד"ה הא קמ"ל) תימה לר"י דאמאי לא קאמר דידע לה לשבת בעשה דכתיב וביום השביעי תשבות וגו' (שמות כג) וכתיב נמי ושמרתם את השבת (שם לא): **עד** שישגוג בלאו שבה. כגון נשבע שלא יאכל ואכל ובשעת אכילה שכח איסור שבועה וקרינן ביה האדם בשבועה שנשבע היה יודע היטב איסור שבועה אלא שבשעת אכילה היה סבור דמותר לעבור על שבועתו ורש"י פירש דבשעת אכילה שכח שנשבע ואין נראה דאין זה קרוי שגג בלאו שבה במה שאינו זכר שנשבע: הא

עין משפט נר מצוה

ה א מיי' פ"א מהלכות שגגות הלכה ב:
ו ב ג מיי' פ"ב מהלכות שגגות הלכה ב סמג עשין רג:
ז ד מיי' שם ופ"ז ה"ג:

רבינו חננאל

שהיא מעשה שבת ויודע שהעושה מלאכה זו חייב עליה לאו וכרת וכי לא שגג אלא בקרבן בלבד וסבר כל כי האי גוונא הוא דחייב חטאת וזולתי כן פטור. וכדתניא אמר אני יודע שמלאכה זו אסורה אבל איני יודע אם חייבין עליה קרבן אם לאו חייב דאוקימנא כמונבז. בהאי סברא בתרא דמונבז רבי יוחנן ור"ל לא סבירא להו כוותיה. וקא מפרש ר' יוחנן כטעמא דרבנן כיון ששגג בכרת אע"פ שהזיד בלאו חייב חטאת. ור"ל אמר אינו חייב חטאת עד שישגוג בלאו וכרת ומותבינן על ר"ל הא דתנן אבות מלאכות ארבעים חסר אחת והוינן בה מנינא למה לי ואמר ר' יוחנן אם עשאן כולם בהעלם אחד חייב על כל אחת ואחת ואוקימנא בזדון שבת ושגגת מלאכות בשלמא לר' יוחנן כגון שהזיד בלאו פי' ידע שהיא היום שבת וידע שהעושה מלאכה (חייב כרת) [עובר בלאו] אמרי' כיון ששגג [בכרת] אף על פי שהזיד בלאו שגגה היא וחייב חטאת אלא לריש לקיש דאמר עד שישגוג בלאו וכרת זדון שבת היכי משכחת ליה ומשני כגון דידע לשבת בתחומין אמרת אין השבת אסור אלא בתחומין כדכתיב אל יצא איש ממקומו וגו' וכרבי עקיבא דסבר תחומין דאורייתא כדמפרש בסוטה פ' ה' ואף על גב דדחי התם ואמרינן (עירובין ס: א)) לית דחש להא דרבי עקיבא: **אמר** אביי הכל מודים בשבועת ביטוי שאין חייבין עליה קרבן עד שישגוג בלאו שבה. מאן הכל מודים רבי יוחנן דסבר עד שישגוג בכרת והאי כיון דלית בה כרת בעי שגגה בלאו ואמרינן פשיטא מהו דתימא הואיל וחדוש הוא דלא אשכחן בכל התורה לאו שאין בה כרת שמייתי קרבן והכא בשבועת ביטוי מייתי קרבן אע"פ שאין בה כרת הוה אמינא כי שגג בקרבן (נמי) בלבד [נמין] מחייב קמ"ל דלא מחייב רבי יוחנן עד שישגוג בלאו שבה. קיי"ל דכל לאו שבתורה שחייבין עליו מלקות בלבד ואין בו כרת אינו חייב עליו חטאת וכי אינו חייב חטאת אלא על

חשק שלמה על רבינו חננאל

א) ע"ש דלא מיירי כלל מדין תחומין דאורייתא. אכן מ"מ יש ללמוד מהתם דגם בדין תחומין דאורייתא לא קיי"ל כר"ע. ועיין תוס' שם ד"ה לית דחש:

רב נסים גאון

מצוה שהיא בדברו של הקב"ה רצוה על ידי משה הוי אומר זו ע"ז: **דידע** להו בתחומים ואליבא דרבי עקיבא כמה דאמר ר' עקיבא במסכת סוטה בפ' כשם שהמים בודקין אותה (דף כז) בו ביום דרש רבי עקיבא ומדותם מחוץ לעיר ומקרא אחד אומר מקיר העיר וחוצה אלף אמה אי אפשר לומר אלף אמה שכבר נאמר אלפים אמה ואי אפשר לומר אלפים שכבר נאמר אלף ולמה נאמר אלף ולמה נאמר אלפים אלא אלף אמה מגרש ואלפים אמה תחום שבת ר' אלעזר בנו של ר' יוסי הגלילי אלף אמה מגרש ואלפים שדות וכרמים ואמרו בגמרא במאי

מסורת הש"ס

א) [לקמן דף קנג: ע"ש], ב) יומא פ. הוריות ב. יא. ע"ש חולין ה., ג) שבועות כו: וש"נ, ד) לקמן עג. [לעיל ו:], ה) [לעיל ו:] לקמן ע. עג. לו: כריתות ג., ו) [עי' תוספות חגיגה ד"ה דמתיא ותוס' לעיל ו: ד"ה הא קמ"ל], ז) [לקמן ע. עג. קנג: סנהדרין סו.], ח) [סוטה ס: וש"נ], ט) הואיל וחידוש הוא כצ"ל רש"ל, י) נ"ל דשגגת רש"ל.

תוספות ישנים

א) הכא ולא ליכא למימר דשגג בכרת דא"כ היינו רבנן. ועוד כיון דמקיש שוגג למזיד בכרת אית לן למימר דמכרת אית ליה ידיעה בשעת מעשה. ועוד דשגגת לאו אפילו לרבנן לא מיחייבן:
ב) לא מצי למימר דידע לי' בלאו דממאמר מ"ד כפי' בתרא דאין בו חטאת דכיון דסבור דעצמו מותר בכל המלאכות כ"ש שסבור שאינו מוזהר על בהמתו. ולא מצי למימר דרבי יוסי היא בהבערה ללאו יצאת דהא קתני ליה במתניתין. וליכא למימר דידע לה בתולדה כיון דלא ידע אבות כ"ש תולדות. וליכא למימר דידע לה בשביעית דאם כן לא שב מידיעתו הוא. ואין סברא לומר כגון שטעה בשיעורין כגון דסבר דלא מחייבי אלא בהעביר ה' אמות ברשות הרבים או בתופר ג' תפירות וכותב ג' אותיות דלא שייך שכחת שאין ואמר מדעתו שיעור שאינו:

הגהות הב"ח

(א) רש"י ד"ה ואליבא דרבי עקיבא דאמר במסכת סוטה. נ"ב כלדו דף כז ע"ב ודף ל ע"ב:

גליון הש"ס

תוס' ד"ה מה ע"ז וכו' דמשמע מה שצויתי שלא לעשות. עיין בכ"ק דף קח ע"ב תוס' ד"ה מאי לאו: שם ד"ה כגון ששגג וכו' אבל לרבי דנפקא ליה מגז"ש. עיין בחידושי הר"ן שבועות דף יט ע"ב ובחי' הרמב"ן שם:

תורה אור השלם

א) וְכִי תִשְׁגּוּ וְלֹא תַעֲשׂוּ אֵת כָּל הַמִּצְוֹת הָאֵלֶּה אֲשֶׁר דִּבֶּר יְיָ אֶל מֹשֶׁה: [במדבר טו, כב]
ב) וְהַנֶּפֶשׁ אֲשֶׁר תַּעֲשֶׂה בְּיָד רָמָה מִן הָאֶזְרָח וּמִן הַגֵּר אֶת יְיָ הוּא מְגַדֵּף וְנִכְרְתָה הַנֶּפֶשׁ הַהִוא מִקֶּרֶב עַמָּהּ: [במדבר טו, ל]
ג) וְאִם נֶפֶשׁ אַחַת תֶּחֱטָא בִשְׁגָגָה מֵעַם הָאָרֶץ בַּעֲשֹׂתָהּ אַחַת מִמִּצְוֹת יְיָ אֲשֶׁר לֹא תֵעָשֶׂינָה וְאָשֵׁם: [ויקרא ד, כז]

ליקוטי רש"י

מנינא למה לי. ליתני אבות מלאכות הזורע והחורש כו' למה לי לאשמעינן מניינא הא מני להו ותני. **חייב על כל אחת ואחת.** ובא להודיעו סכום החטאות שאדם חייב באיסורי שבת בהעלם אחד ולאשמעינן [...]ת הן ותו לא שאפילו עשה תולדותיהן עמהן אינו מביא על התולדה היכא דעשאה עם אביה דהוה ליה [...]שה דכולה חדא עבירה היא [לעיל ו:]. ובא להודיעך שאם נתעלמו כל הלכות שבת ממנו כמה חטאות [...] [לקמן עג:]. **היכי משכחת לה.** דמיחייב שום אדם על כל מלאכה ומלאכה שבהעלם אחד על כרחך בזדון שבת ושגגת מלאכות הוא דבעית לאשכוחיה והכא דאיעלימו כולהו מיניה מאי זדון שבת איכא במה ניכר לו שבת משאר ימים [שם.]. דניחייב איניש אכל חדא על כרחך בזדון שבת [...] מאי זדון שבת איכא. דהא לא [...]יון דכל הלכותיה נעלמות ממנו אין חילוק היום משאר ימים. **בשלמא לרבי יוחנן וכו'.** משכחת ליה שלא נעלמו ממנו אלא הכריתות ויודע הלאוין והיינו זד[ון] [...] שמלאכות הללו אסורות אבל [...] בדבר אחד כגון דידע שאסור לצאת חוץ לתחום [כריתות ג.]. **ואליבא דרבי עקיבא.** דיליף להו מקראי במסכת סוטה (ל:). ור' עקיבא מודה נמי בתחומים ד[...] אבות מלאכות ארבעים חסר אחת ולא פליג ר' עקיבא [סנהדרין סו.]. דאמר דאורייתא נינהו והוי מחלל ומיהו אין חייבין לא על שגגתו חטאת כו' [לקמן קנג:].

guilty,[12] עַד שֶׁיִּשְׁגּוֹג בְּלָאו וְכָרֵת שֶׁבָּהּ – which implies that one is not liable to a *chatas* **unless he acts inadvertently with regard to** both the **prohibition and** the ***kares*** penalty attached **to it.**[13]

The Gemara asks:

וְרַבִּי יוֹחָנָן – **But R' Yochanan,** הַאי קְרָא דְּרַבִּי שִׁמְעוֹן בֶּן לָקִישׁ מַאי עָבֵיד לֵיהּ – **what does he do with this verse of R' Shimon ben Lakish?**

The Gemara answers:

מִיבְּעֵי לֵיהּ לִכְדְתַנְיָא – **He needs it for that which was taught in a Baraisa:** "מֵעַם הָאָרֶץ" – The verse states:[14] *If an individual will sin inadvertently* FROM AMONG THE PEOPLE OF THE LAND . . . *he shall bring his offering . . .* פְּרָט לְמוּמָר – This EXCLUDES A RENEGADE from bringing a *chatas.*[15] רַבִּי שִׁמְעוֹן בֶּן אֶלְעָזָר אוֹמֵר מִשּׁוּם רַבִּי שִׁמְעוֹן – R' SHIMON BEN ELAZAR SAID IN THE NAME OF R' SHIMON: "אֲשֶׁר לֹא־תֵעָשֶׂינָה (בִּשְׁגָגָה) וְאָשֵׁם" – It is stated in another verse [the one expounded above by Reish Lakish] that the *chatas* offering is brought by someone who performed acts *THAT ARE NOT TO BE DONE – INADVERTENTLY – AND HE BECOMES GUILTY.*[16] And the next verse states: *If his sin that he committed becomes known to him, he shall bring his offering* etc. הַשָּׁב מִידִיעָתוֹ מֵבִיא קָרְבָּן עַל שִׁגְגָתוֹ – This teaches that only ONE WHO WOULD REFRAIN from transgressing AS A RESULT OF HIS KNOWLEDGE that the act is forbidden BRINGS AN OFFERING to atone FOR HIS INADVERTENT [TRANSGRESSION]; לֹא שָׁב מִידִיעָתוֹ – but ONE WHO WOULD NOT REFRAIN from transgressing AS A RESULT OF HIS KNOWLEDGE that the act is forbidden אֵינוֹ מֵבִיא קָרְבָּן עַל שִׁגְגָתוֹ – DOES NOT BRING AN OFFERING to atone FOR HIS INADVERTENT [TRANSGRESSION].[17] R' Yochanan thus uses the verse for the exposition made by R' Shimon ben Elazar.

The Gemara attempts a proof from a Mishnah below:

תְּנַן – **We learned in the Mishnah:** אֲבוֹת מְלָאכוֹת אַרְבָּעִים חָסֵר אַחַת – THE PRIMARY LABORS ARE FORTY MINUS ONE.[18] וְהָוֵינַן בָּהּ – **Now in discussing this** we asked: מִנְיָנָא לָמָּה לִי – **Why do I need** the Tanna to specify **the number** of *melachos?*[19] וְאָמַר רַבִּי יוֹחָנָן – **And** in answer to this **R' Yochanan said:** שֶׁאִם עֲשָׂאָן כּוּלָּן בְּהֶעְלֵם אֶחָד – The Mishnah teaches **that if someone performed all** thirty-nine of them **in one lapse of awareness,** חַיָּיב עַל כָּל אַחַת וְאַחַת – **he is liable** to a separate *chatas* **for each and every one** he transgressed, a total of thirty-nine offerings.[20]

The Gemara now explains its proof:

הֵיכִי מַשְׁכַּחַתְּ לָהּ – **How is such** a case **to be found,** i.e. a case in which one would be liable to thirty-nine *chatas* offerings in a single Sabbath? בִּזְדוֹן שַׁבָּת וְשִׁגְגַת מְלָאכוֹת – Clearly, it must be in a case where he acted **with deliberateness regarding the Sabbath and inadvertence regarding the** ***melachos.***[21] בִּשְׁלָמָא לְרַבִּי יוֹחָנָן – Now **this fits well according to R' Yochanan,** דְּאָמַר כֵּיוָן שֶׁשָּׁגַג בְּכָרֵת אַף עַל פִּי שֶׁהֵזִיד בְּלָאו – **who said that as long as one acted inadvertently with regard to** the ***kares*** penalty he is liable to a *chatas* **even though he acted deliberately with regard to** the **prohibition,** מַשְׁכַּחַתְּ לָהּ כְּגוֹן דְּיָדַע לָהּ לְשַׁבָּת בְּלָאו – for **this** ruling of the Mishnah **can occur in**

NOTES

12. *Leviticus* 4:22, dealing with the special *chatas* offering of a ruler (see note 17).

[The parentheses placed around the word בִּשְׁגָגָה in the standard Vilna *Shas* – which indicate a deletion – are in error (*Rashash*). This very verse is cited in the Baraisa that follows, and wherever this Baraisa is cited, the word בִּשְׁגָגָה is included (see *Chullin* 5b, *Yoma* 80a, *Horayos* 2a, 11a). Thus, the reference is to the *prince's chatas* mentioned in *Leviticus* 4:22 and not to the similarly worded verse in *Leviticus* 4:27.]

13. The phrase לֹא־תֵעָשֶׂינָה, *not to be done,* refers to the prohibition (*Rashi*). [Thus, when the verse states אֲשֶׁר לֹא־תֵעָשֶׂינָה בִּשְׁגָגָה, *that are not to be done – inadvertently,* we see that the inadvertence relates to the prohibition.]

14. Ibid. 4:27. This verse and the following one state: וְאִם־נֶפֶשׁ אַחַת תֶּחֱטָא בִשְׁגָגָה מֵעַם הָאָרֶץ בַּעֲשֹׂתָהּ אַחַת מִמִּצְוֹת ה׳ אֲשֶׁר לֹא־תֵעָשֶׂינָה וְאָשֵׁם. אוֹ הוֹדַע אֵלָיו חַטָּאתוֹ אֲשֶׁר חָטָא וְהֵבִיא קָרְבָּנוֹ וגו׳, *If an individual will sin inadvertently – from among the people of the land – by performing one of the commandments of Hashem that are not to be done, and he becomes guilty. If the sin that he committed becomes known to him, he shall bring his offering* etc.

15. The preposition מֵ, "from among," in the expression מֵעַם הָאָרֶץ, *"from among" the people of the land,* is a restrictive term, implying that some – but not all – inadvertent sinners bring a *chatas.* The Tanna expounds this limitation to exclude a renegade (i.e. one who routinely disregards the Torah's laws; see further, *Chullin* 5a,b) from bringing a *chatas* for an inadvertent sin that he commits (see *Rashi* to *Chullin* 5b).

16. The Torah states regarding the special *chatas* of a ruler [*nasi*] (ibid. 4:22-23): אֲשֶׁר נָשִׂיא יֶחֱטָא וְעָשָׂה אַחַת מִכָּל־מִצְוֹת ה׳ אֱלֹהָיו אֲשֶׁר לֹא־תֵעָשֶׂינָה בִּשְׁגָגָה וְאָשֵׁם. אוֹ־הוֹדַע אֵלָיו חַטָּאתוֹ אֲשֶׁר חָטָא בָּהּ וְהֵבִיא אֶת־קָרְבָּנוֹ שְׂעִיר עִזִּים זָכָר תָּמִים, *When a ruler sins and commits one from among all the commandments of Hashem his God that are not to be done – inadvertently – and becomes guilty. If his sin that he committed becomes known to him, he shall bring his offering, a male goat, unblemished.*

17. According to R' Shimon, the words אֲשֶׁר לֹא־תֵעָשֶׂינָה, *that are not to be done,* do not refer to the prohibition per se, but rather to the pattern of a person's behavior. Thus, the verse is understood as follows: *When a ruler sins* and does one of those things *that are not to be done* [when one knows that they are forbidden – and he did so because he acted] *inadvertently* [i.e. because he was unaware of the prohibition] *and he becomes guilty* for this reason [which implies that had he known of the forbidden nature of his act he would *not* have become guilty;] – then, *if his sin becomes known to him, he shall bring his offering.* The implication is that *only* if the condition of the first verse (v. 22) is met does one bring the offering required by the second verse (v. 23). Hence, the combination of these two verses teaches that only a person who would not have committed that act had he known that it was forbidden, and who became guilty solely due to this unawareness, is offered the opportunity for atonement through a *chatas* offering (*Rashi, Chullin* 5b). Thus, for example, if somebody ate *cheilev* (forbidden fat), but would have refrained from doing so had he realized that it was *cheilev,* he brings a *chatas* offering. But a renegade, who would not have refrained from eating *cheilev* even if he had known that it was sinful, does not bring a *chatas* offering even though he sinned inadvertently with regard to *cheilev.*

[The Gemara in *Chullin* 5a and *Horayos* (11a) explains the case in which these Tannaim disagree. See also *Rashi* to *Chullin* 5b for two explanations of the literal meaning of the phrase שָׁב מִידִיעָתוֹ, *who would refrain as a result of his knowledge.*]

18. Below, 73a. The Mishnah then proceeds to list all thirty-nine *melachos* for which one is liable on the Sabbath.

19. Since the Mishnah lists all of them, we could count them on our own and see that there are thirty-nine. What purpose is served by the Mishnah counting them for us? (*Rashi*).

20. By stating that there are thirty-nine *avos melachos,* the Mishnah means to allude to the maximum number of *chatas* offerings a person would have to bring for desecrating one Sabbath (*Rashi*).

21. That is, the person knew that it was the Sabbath, but did not know that those *melachah* acts were prohibited on the Sabbath. It is in such a case that our Mishnah teaches that one is liable for each and every *av melachah* (the Mishnah's third rule). The teaching concerning thirty-nine *chataos* cannot, however, refer to a case in which he knew which *melachos* were prohibited but thought that it was not the Sabbath day, for in such a case he would bring only one *chatas* for *all* his *melachah* transgressions, as our Mishnah taught (in its second rule). Thus, the *only* case in which a person could be liable to a separate *chatas* for every one of the thirty-nine *melachos* is when he knew it was the Sabbath day but did not know any of the *melachos.*

Now, being aware of the Sabbath implies having *some* knowledge of Sabbath law, because otherwise Saturday is no different to him than any other day of the week. But if this person was unaware of *all* thirty-nine *melachos,* he cannot be said to have acted deliberately regarding the Sabbath (*Rashi*).

מה ע"ז שחייבים על זדונו כרת. וא"ת מ"מ היקשא דשוגג למזיד

(גמרא)

א) וכי תשגו ולא תעשו את כל המצות האלה וכתיב ב) והנפש אשר תעשה ביד רמה א) הוקשו כולם לע"ז [א]מה להלן דבר שחייבים על זדונו כרת ושגגתו חטאת אף כל דבר שחייבין על זדונו כרת ועל שגגתו חטאת ואלא מונבז שגגה במאי כגון ששגג בקרבן ורבנן [ב]שגגת קרבן לא שמה שגגה ורבנן שגגה במאי רבי יוחנן אמר [ג]כיון ששגג בכרת אף על פי שהזיד בלאו וריש לקיש אמר עד שישגוג בלאו וכרת אמר רבא מאי טעמא דרשב"ל אמר קרא ג) אשר לא תעשינה (בשגגה) ואשם עד שישגוג בלאו וכרת שבה ורבי יוחנן האי קרא דרשב"ל מאי עביד ליה מיבעי ליה ב) לכדתניא ג) מעם הארץ פרט למומר רבי שמעון בן אלעזר אומר משום רבי שמעון אשר לא תעשינה (בשגגה) ואשם ג) השב מידיעתו מביא קרבן על שגגתו לא שב מידיעתו אינו מביא קרבן על שגגתו: תנן ד) אבות מלאכות ארבעים חסר אחת והוינן בה ה) מנינא למה לי ואמר ר' יוחנן [ד]שאם עשאן כולן בהעלם אחד חייב על כל אחת ואחת היכי משכחת לה בזדון שבת ושגגת מלאכות בשלמא לרבי יוחנן דאמר כיון ששגג בכרת אע"פ שהזיד בלאו משכחת לה כגון דידע לה לשבת בלאו אלא לר"ש ב"ל דאמר עד שישגוג בלאו ובכרת דידע ליה לשבת במאי ו) דידעה ז) בתחומין ח) ואליבא דר"ע מאן תנא להא דתנו רבנן שגג בזה ובזה זהו שוגג האמור בתורה הזיד בזה ובזה זו היא מזיד האמור בתורה שגג בשבת והזיד במלאכות או ששגג במלאכות והזיד בשבת או שאמר יודע אני שמלאכה זו אסורה אבל איני יודע שחייבין עליה קרבן או לא חייב כמאן כמונבז אמר אביי הכל מודים בשבועת ביטוי שאין חייבין עליה קרבן עד שישגוג בלאו שבה הכל מודים מאן ר' יוחנן פשיטא כי קא"ר יוחנן היכא דאיכא כרת אבל הכא דליכא כרת לא סד"א ט) הואיל וחייב קרבן חידוש הוא דבכל התורה כולה לא אשכחן לאו דמייתי עליה קרבן והכא מייתי כי שגג בקרבן נמי ליחייב קמ"ל

(רש"י)

וכי תשגו ולא תעשו את כל המצות האלה. וילפינן בהוריות (דף ח.) זו ע"ז שהיא שקולה ככל המצות וכתיב תורה אחת כל התורה במשמע: הוקשו. קרבנות של שגגות של כל עבירות לשל ע"ז מה ע"ז קרבן שלה אינו בא אלא על עבירה גמורה שחייב על זדונו כרת דסמיך ליה והנפש אשר תעשה ביד רמה ונכרתה: אף כל התורה. אין מביאין חטאת אלא על דבר שזדונו כרת: ואלא מונבז. דאמר לעיל דמי שהיתה לו ידיעה בשעת מעשה חייב חטאת: דשגג במאי. הא גבי חטאת שגגה כתיב: דשגג בקרבן. דיודע שחייב על זדונו כרת אבל אינו יודע שחייב עליה חטאת: לא שמה שגגה. עד ששגג בעבירה עצמה: ורבנן. דבעו שגגה בעבירה עצמה שגגה במאי קאמרי שגגה בכולה מילתא בלאו וכרת או בכרת לחודיה: כיון ששגג בכרת אע"ג שהזיד בלאו. שאז הקרבן על הכרת הוא בא כדאמרן לעושה בשגגה וסמיך ליה והנפש אשר תעשה וגו': לא תעשינה. היינו לאו: מנינא למה לי. ליתני אבות מלאכות הזורע והחורש כו' למה לי למיתנא ארבעים חסר אחת ליתנינהו ואנן ידעינן דמ' חסר אחת איכא: שאם עשאן כולן כו'. וסימנא בעלמא אשמעינן לידע כמה חטאות חייב על חילול שבת אחת: היכי משכחת לה. דמיחייב ע"כ לא משכחת לה אלא בזדון שבת דיודע שהוא שבת ושגגת מלאכות דאינו יודע שהמלאכות הללו אסורות דאי בזדון מלאכות ושגגת שבת דיודע שהן אסורות בשבת אבל שכח שהיום שבת הא תנן דאינו חייב אלא אחת לכל שבת וזדון שבת לא הוי אא"כ יודע אחת מהלכותיה דאי לא ידע בחדא מינייהו אין שבת חלוק לו משאר ימים וזה ששגג בכולן אין כאן זדון שבת: בשלמא לר' יוחנן. דאמר שגגת כרת שמה שגגה: משכחת לה. זדון שבת בלאוין ושגגת מלאכות בכריתות דיודע לה לשבת שהוזהר על הלאוין או של כולן או של אחת מהן: דידע לה לשבת במאי. הלא בכולן שגג כסבור שכל ל"ט מלאכות מותרות: בתחומין. דאין בקרבן: ואליבא דר' עקיבא. דאמר במסכת סוטה (א) תחומין דאורייתא נינהו דתנן בו ביום דרש רבי עקיבא ומדותם מחוץ לעיר כו': זהו שוגג האמור בתורה. כלומר היכא דשגג בשבת ובמלאכות אין כאן לא דין ולא דיין לקנתר ואין לך שוגג כזה: הזיד בזה ובזה. אין לך מזיד כזה: שגג באחת מהן. אף זה שוגג וחייבים עליה קרבן: שבועת ביטוי. שאוכל ולא אוכל שאכלתי ולא אכלתי חייב עליה קרבן וכתיב ביה ונעלם דהיינו שוגג הכל מודים בשוגג שלה דאם נשבע שלא אוכל ואכל אינו חייב אלא אם כן שכח שבועתו כשאכל דהשתא שגג בלאו שבה: הכל מודים מאן רבי יוחנן. כלומר על כרחין אביי לאו אפלוגתא דמונבז ורבנן קאי דלישמעינן דמודה מונבז בהא (דהא) י) שגגת קרבן לא הויא שגגה דמהיכא תיתי והא ק"ו היא השתא בכל התורה כולה דליכא חידוש בקרבן דידהו אמר מונבז דמיחייב בשגגת קרבן הכא דחידוש הוא דאין בה כרת ומביא קרבן עליה לא כ"ש אלא לרבנן קאמר ואפלוגתא דר"י ור"ל קאי ומאן הכל מודים ר"י דאף על גב דבעלמא קאמר אף על פי שהזיד בלאו הכא בעינן שישגוג בלאו: פשיטא. כיון דאליבא דרבנן איפליג דאמרי שגגת קרבן לאו שגגה היא אי בלאו שלה הזיד במאי שגג דע"כ לא קאמר ר"י בעלמא אלא במקום כרת דשגג בכרת: סלקא דעתך אמינא. בשבועת ביטוי נמי קאי רבי יוחנן במילתיה דאף על פי שהזיד בלאו ודקשיא לך במאי שגג שגג בקרבן דהואיל וחידוש מודו ביה רבנן:

(תוספות)

מה ע"ז שחייבים על זדונו כרת. וא"ת מ"מ היקשא דשוגג למזיד למה לי דאפילו לא הוי כתיב התם קרא דוהנפש אשר תעשה ביד רמה ילפינן שפיר מע"ז שחייב על זדונה כרת כו' וי"ל דלית לן לאקושה לע"ז אלא במאי דכתיב בההיא פרשה כדמשמע מתוך פירוש הקונטרס ולהכי אצטריך לאתויי הכא והנפש אשר תעשה תדע דהא לא ילפינן מע"ז דניבעי על זדונו סקילה כע"ז משום דלא כתיב סקילה בההיא פרשה אלא כרת והא דממעטינן בריש פרק בתרא דמכות (דף יג:) פסח ומילה מקרבן אע"פ שיש בהן כרת משום דמה ע"ז דאמר רחמנא לא תעביד והני קום עשה נינהו היינו נמי משום דכתיב והנפש אשר תעשה ביד רמה ° דמשמע מה שצויתי שלא לעשות וא"ת רבנן דהכא ר' עקיבא ור' עקיבא אית ליה בפ"ק דכריתות (דף ז:) דהאי קרא דמגדף במברך את השם כתיב וי"ל דלישנא דנקט הכא הוקשה כל התורה כולה לע"ז נקט אליבא דרבנן דרבי עקיבא אבל לר"ע אית לן למימר דהוקשה כל התורה כולה למברך את השם וא"ת ולמונבז האי דרשא דר' יהושע בן לוי מנא ליה ואומר ר"י דנפקא ליה כדדריש רבי בפ"ק דיבמות (דף ט.) ובפ"ב דהוריות (דף ח.) נאמר כאן ונודעה החטאת אשר חטאו עליה ונאמ' ואשה אל אחותה לא תקח לצרור לגלות ערותה עליה: **אלא** למונבז שגגה במאי. לא מצי למימר ששגג בלאו והזיד בקרבן דאין סברא לחייב בהזיד בקרבן דלא שב מידיעתו הוא וליכא נמי למימר שגג בלאו וקרבן דסברא הוא דכיון דמקיש למזיד אפי' מזיד בכל דבר ושוגג רק בדבר אחד דהיינו בקרבן יש לנו לחייבו א) ומיהו היכא דאיכא סקילה בעינן שיהא שוגג גם בסקילה דאי הוה מזיד בסקילה אין לחייבו בקרבן דכיון דאינו שב מסקילה פשיטא שאפילו היה יודע שחייב גם קרבן שלא היה שב ולא שב מידיעתו הוא ואע"ג דבהזיד בכרת חשיב ליה שב מידיעתו לקרבן היינו משום דכרת אפשר בתשובה וקרבן לא אפשר בתשובה ועוד דגבי כרת שייך שפיר למימר אם היה יודע שחייב כרת עם הקרבן היה שב: **כגון** ששגג בכרת אע"פ שהזיד בלאו. וטעמא דר' יוחנן משום דלא כתיב לאו בהיקשא דר' יהושע ולא כתיב אלא כרת בההיא ענינא ולהכי בעי מ"ט דריש לקיש ולא בעי מ"ט דר' יוחנן וצ"ל דרבי יוחנן מיירי אליבא דרבנן דאית להו היקשא דרבי יהושע בן לוי ° אבל לרבי דנפקא ליה מג"ש דעליה מודה רבי יוחנן דבעי עד שישגוג בלאו וכרת דהא כתיב לאו בההוא קרא ואשה אל אחותה לא תקח וגו': **אמר** קרא אשר לא תעשינה בשגגה. קשה לר"י מנא ליה לריש לקיש דרבנן דרשי הכי ובעו שגגת לאו וליכא למימר דמשמע ליה למדרש קרא הכי דהא ע"כ סבירא ליה דאין סברא לדרוש כן דהא איהו סבר כמונבז כדאמר לעיל ומונבז לא בעי שגגת לאו אלא שגגת קרבן גרידא דבהדיא תניא לקמן או שאמר יודע אני שמלאכה זו אסורה אבל איני יודע אם חייבים עליה קרבן אם לאו חייב ולא קאמר קרבן ומלקות אם לאו: **דידע** לה בתחומין ב). לא מצי למימר דידע לה בדאיסי דבההוא נמי חייב חטאת כדפירשתי בפרק קמא (דף ו: בד"ה הא קמ"ל) תימה לר"י דאמאי לא קאמר דידע לה לשבת בעשה דכתיב וביום השביעי תשבות וגו' (שמות כג) וכתיב נמי ושמרתם את השבת (שם לא): **עד** שישגוג בלאו שבה. כגון נשבע שלא יאכל ואכל ובשעת אכילה שכח איסור שבועה וקרינן ביה האדם דבשעת שבועה שנשבע היה יודע היטב איסור שבועה אלא שבשעת אכילה היה סבור דמותר לעבור על שבועתו ורש"י פירש דבשעת אכילה שכח שנשבע ואין נראה דאין זה קרוי שגג בלאו שבה במה שאינו נזכר שנשבע: הא

עין משפט נר מצוה

ה א מיי' פ"א מהלכות שגגות הלכה ב:
ו ב ג מיי' פ"ב מהלכות שגגות הלכה ב סמג עשין רג:
ז ד מיי' שם ופ"ז ה"ג:

רבינו חננאל

שהיא מעשה שבת ויודע שהעושה מלאכה זו חייב עליה לאו וכרת וכי לא שגג אלא בקרבן בלבד וסבר כל כי האי גוונא הוא דחייב חטאת חולתי כן פטור. וכדתניא אמר אני יודע שמלאכה זו אסורה אבל איני יודע אם חייבין עליה קרבן אם לאו חייב דאוקימנא כמונבז. בהאי סברא בתרא דמונבז רבי יוחנן ור"ל לא סבירא להו כוותיה. וקא מפרש ר' יוחנן כטעמא דרבנן כיון ששגג בכרת אע"פ שהזיד בלאו חייב חטאת. ור"ל אמר אינו חייב חטאת עד שישגוג בלאו וכרת ומותבינן על ר"ל הא דתנן אבות מלאכות ארבעים חסר אחת והוינן בה מנינא למה לי ואמר ר' יוחנן אם עשאן כולם בהעלם אחד חייב על כל אחת ואחת ואוקימנא בזדון שבת ושגגת מלאכות בשלמא לר' יוחנן כגון שהזיד בלאו פי' ידע שהיא היום שבת וידע שהעושה מלאכה (חייב כרת) [עובר בלאו] אמרי' כיון ששגג [בכרת] אף על פי שהזיד בלאו שגגה היא וחייב חטאת אלא לריש לקיש דאמר עד שישגוג בלאו וכרת זדון שבת היכי משכחת ליה ומשני כגון דידע לשבת בתחומין אמרת אין השבת אסור אלא בתחומין כדכתיב אל יצא איש ממקומו וגו' וכרבי עקיבא דסבר תחומין דאורייתא כדמפרש בסוטה פ' ה' ואף על גב דדחי התם ואמרינן (עירובין ס: א)) לית דחש להא דרבי עקיבא: **אמר** אביי הכל מודים בשבועת ביטוי שאין חייבין עליה קרבן עד שישגוג בלאו שבה. מאן הכל מודים רבי יוחנן דסבר עד שישגוג בכרת והאי כיון דלית בה כרת בעי שגגה בלאו ואמרינן פשיטא מהו דתימא הואיל וחדוש הוא דלא אשכחן בכל התורה לאו שאין בה כרת שמייתי קרבן והכא בשבועת ביטוי מייתי קרבן אע"פ שאין בה כרת הוה אמינא כי שגג בקרבן (נמי) בלבד [נמי] מחייב קמ"ל דלא מחייב רבי יוחנן עד שישגוג בלאו שבה. קיי"ל דכל לאו שבתורה שחייבין עליו מלקות בלבד ואין בו כרת אינו חייב עליו חטאת וכי אינו חייב חטאת אלא על

חשק שלמה על רבינו חננאל

א) ע"ש דלא מיירי כלל מדין תחומין דאורייתא. אכן מ"מ יש ללמוד מהתם דגם בדין תחומין דאורייתא לא קיי"ל כר"ע. ועיין תוס' שם ד"ה לית ודו"ק:

רב נסים גאון

מצוה שהיא בדברו של הקב"ה וצוה על ידי משה הוי אומר זו ע"ז: **דידע** להו בתחומים ואליבא דרבי עקיבא כמה דאמר ר' עקיבא במסכת סוטה בפ' כשם שהמים בודקין אותה (דף כז) בו ביום דרש רבי עקיבא ומדותם מחוץ לעיר ומקרא אחד אומר מקיר העיר וחוצה אלף אמה אי אפשר לומר אלף אמה שכבר נאמר אלפים אמה ואי אפשר לומר אלפים אמה שכבר נאמר אלף ולמה נאמר אלף ולמה נאמר אלפים אלא אלף אמה מגרש ואלפים אמה תחום שבת ר' אלעזר בנו של ר' יוסי הגלילי אלף אמה מגרש ואלפים שדות וכרמים ואמרו בגמרא במאי

מסורת הש"ס

א) [לקמן דף קנג: ע"ש], ב) יומא פ. הוריות ב. יא. ע"ש חולין ה., ג) שבועות כו: וש"נ, ד) לקמן עג. [לו: ולעיל ו:], ה) לעיל ו: לקמן ע. עג. לו: כריתות ב., ו) [עי' תוספות חגיגה י: ד"ה דכתיב ותוס' לעיל ו: ד"ה הא קמ"ל], ז) [לקמן ע. עג. קנג: סנהדרין סו.], ח) [סוטה כז: וש"נ], ט) הואיל וחידוש הוא כצ"ל רש"ל, י) צ"ל דשגגת רש"ל.

תוספות ישנים

א) דהא ודאי ליכא למימר דשגג בכרת דא"כ היינו רבנן. ועוד כיון דמקיש שוגג למזיד בכרת אית לן למימר דמכרת אית ליה ידיעה בשעת מעשה. ועוד דשגגת לאו אפילו לרבנן לא חיישינן: ב) לא מצי למימר דידע לי' בלאו דממכר לא"ד בפר' בתרא דאין בו חטאת דכיון דסבור דעצמו מותר בכל המלאכות כ"ש שסבור שאינו מוזהר על בהמתו. ולא מצי למימר דידע ליה בהעברה אליבא דרבי יוסי דהא קתני ליה במתניתין. וליכא למימר דידע ליה בתולדה דכיון דלא ידע אבות כ"ש תולדות. וליכא למימר דידע לה בסקילה דאם כן לא שב מידיעתו הוא. ואין סברא לומר כגון שטעה בשיעורין כגון דסבר דלא מיחייב אלא בהעביר ה' אמות ברשות הרבים או בתופר ג' תפירות וכותב ג' אותיות דלא שכיח שיטעה ויאמר מדעתו שיעור שאינו:

הגהות הב"ח

(א) רש"י ד"ה ואליבא דרבי עקיבא דאמר במסכת סוטה. נכתב בלדו דף כז ע"ב ודף ל ע"ב:

גליון הש"ס

תוס' ד"ה מה ע"ז וכו' דמשמע מה שצויתי שלא לעשות. עיין בב"ק דף קה ע"ב תוס' ד"ה מאי לאו: שם ד"ה כגון ששגג וכו' אבל לרבי דנפקא ליה מגז"ש. עיין בחידושי הר"ן שבועות דף ה ע"ב ובחי' הרמב"ן שם:

תורה אור השלם

א) וְכִי תִשְׁגּוּ וְלֹא תַעֲשׂוּ אֵת כָּל הַמִּצְוֹת הָאֵלֶּה אֲשֶׁר דִּבֶּר יְיָ אֶל מֹשֶׁה: [במדבר טו, כב]

ב) וְהַנֶּפֶשׁ אֲשֶׁר תַּעֲשֶׂה בְּיָד רָמָה מִן הָאֶזְרָח וּמִן הַגֵּר אֶת יְיָ הוּא מְגַדֵּף וְנִכְרְתָה הַנֶּפֶשׁ הַהִוא מִקֶּרֶב עַמָּהּ: [במדבר טו, ל]

ג) וְאִם נֶפֶשׁ אַחַת תֶּחֱטָא בִשְׁגָגָה מֵעַם הָאָרֶץ בַּעֲשֹׂתָהּ אַחַת מִמִּצְוֹת יְיָ אֲשֶׁר לֹא תֵעָשֶׂינָה וְאָשֵׁם: [ויקרא ד, כז]

ליקוטי רש"י

מנינא למה לי. ליתני אבות מלאכות הזורע והחורש כו' למה לי לאשמעינן מנינא הא מני להו וקתני. **חייב על כל אחת ואחת.** וכא להודיעו סכום החטאות שאדם חייב באיסורי שבת בהעלם אחד ולאשמעינן ארבעים חסר אחת הן ותו לא שאפילו עשה תולדותיהן עמהן אינו מביא על התולדה היכא דעשאה עם אביה דהוה ליה כעושה וחוזר ועושה דכולה חדא עבירה היא [לעיל ו:]. וכא להודיעך שאם נתעלמו כל הלכות שבת ממנו כמה חטאות [חייב] עליו [לקמן עג:]. **היכי משכחת לה.** דמיחייב שום אדם על כל מלאכה ומלאכה שבהעלם אחד על כרחך בזדון שבת ושגגת מלאכות הוא דמשכחת לה דבעית לאשכוחיה והכא דאיעלימו כולהו מיניה הוא דמשכחת לה והכא מאי זדון שבת איכא. דהא לא ידע שבת במידי כיון דכל הלכותיה נעלמות ממנו אין חילוק היום משאר ימים [שם.]. דניחייב איניש אכל חדא על כרחך בזדון שבת איכא במה ניכר לו שבת משאר ימים. **בשלמא לרבי יוחנן וכו'.** משכחת ליה שלא נעלמו ממנו אלא הכריתות ויודע הלאוין והיינו זדון שבת [שם ע:]. **בתחומין.** דאינו יודע שמלאכות הללו אסורות אבל יודע [illegible] כגון דידע שאסור לצאת חוץ לתחום [כריתות ג.]. **ואליבא דרבי עקיבא.** [illegible] (סוטה כז:). [illegible] [סנהדרין סו.]. [illegible] [לקמן קנג:]. [illegible] אבות מלאכות ארבעים חסר [illegible]

a case where he knew about the Sabbath with regard to the prohibition against performing *melachos,* but he was not aware of the *kares* penalty for violating this prohibition. Thus, he is considered to have sinned inadvertently and is liable to a separate *chatas* for each *av melachah* – thirty-nine in all. אֶלָּא לְרַבִּי שִׁמְעוֹן בֶּן לָקִישׁ דְּאָמַר עַד שֶׁיִּשְׁגּוֹג בְּלָאו וּבְכָרֵת – **But according to R' Shimon ben Lakish, who said** that one is not liable to a *chatas* **unless he acted inadvertently with regard to both** the **prohibition and** the ***kares*** penalty, דְּיָדַע לֵיהּ לְשַׁבָּת בְּמַאי – **in what** respect **did he know** about **the Sabbath?** He cannot have known that the *melachos* were prohibited, since if he had, his violations would not be classed inadvertent according to Reish Lakish![22] – ? –

The Gemara answers:

דְּיָדְעָהּ בִּתְחוּמִין – **He knew** about **[the Sabbath] with regard to the *techum* law,**[23] וְאַלִּיבָּא דְּרַבִּי עֲקִיבָא – **and** this **according to R' Akiva,** who holds that the prohibition to travel beyond the *techum* on the Sabbath is Biblical.[24]

The Gemara analyzes a Baraisa related to the disagreement between Munbaz and his disputants:

מַאן תָּנָא לְהָא דְּתָנוּ רַבָּנָן – **Who** is the one who **taught that** which **the Rabbis taught in the** following **Baraisa:** שָׁגַג בָּזֶה וּבָזֶה – If HE ACTED INADVERTENTLY WITH REGARD TO both THIS [the Sabbath day] AND THIS [the *melachos*], i.e. he knew neither that it was the Sabbath day nor that his actions were prohibited on the Sabbath, זֶהוּ שׁוֹגֵג הָאָמוּר בַּתּוֹרָה – THIS IS THE INADVERTENT [TRANSGRESSOR] STATED IN THE TORAH.[25] הֵזִיד בָּזֶה וּבָזֶה – If HE ACTED DELIBERATELY WITH REGARD TO both THIS [the Sabbath] AND THIS [the *melachos*], i.e. he knew both that it was the Sabbath day and that his actions were prohibited on the Sabbath, זוֹ הִיא מֵזִיד הָאָמוּר בַּתּוֹרָה – THIS IS THE DELIBERATE [TRANSGRESSOR] STATED IN THE TORAH.[26] שָׁגַג בַּשַּׁבָּת וְהֵזִיד בַּמְּלָאכוֹת – If HE ACTED INADVERTENTLY WITH REGARD TO THE SABBATH, BUT ACTED DELIBERATELY WITH REGARD TO THE *MELACHOS*;[27] אוֹ שֶׁשָּׁגַג בַּמְּלָאכוֹת וְהֵזִיד בַּשַּׁבָּת – OR if HE ACTED INADVERTENTLY WITH REGARD TO THE *MELACHOS,* BUT ACTED DELIBERATELY WITH REGARD TO THE SABBATH;[28] אוֹ שֶׁאָמַר יוֹדֵעַ אֲנִי שֶׁמְּלָאכָה זוֹ אֲסוּרָה – OR if HE SAID, "I KNOW THAT THIS *MELACHAH* IS PROHIBITED, אֲבָל אֵינִי יוֹדֵעַ שֶׁחַיָּיבִין עָלֶיהָ קָרְבָּן אוֹ לֹא – BUT I DO NOT KNOW WHETHER ONE IS LIABLE TO A SACRIFICE FOR IT OR NOT," חַיָּיב – in each of these three cases HE IS LIABLE to a *chatas*. Thus we see that the Baraisa considers the failure to realize that a transgression is subject to a *chatas* a form of inadvertent transgression, even though the person was aware of the prohibition!

The Gemara answers:

כְּמַאן – **In accordance with whom** was this Baraisa taught? כְּמוּנְבַּז – **In accordance with Munbaz.**[29]

The Gemara relates the dispute between R' Yochanan and Reish Lakish concerning *chatas* and *kares* to another case requiring an offering:

אָמַר אַבַּיֵי – **Abaye said:** הַכֹּל מוֹדִים בִּשְׁבוּעַת בִּיטּוּי – **Everyone agrees in regard to the oath of utterance,**[30] שֶׁאֵין חַיָּיבִין עָלֶיהָ קָרְבָּן – **that one is not liable to** bring **a sacrifice for it** עַד שֶׁיִּשְׁגּוֹג בְּלָאו שֶׁבָּהּ – **unless he acted inadvertently with regard to its prohibition.**[31]

The Gemara analyzes Abaye's statement:

הַכֹּל מוֹדִים מַאן – **Who is** the one that Abaye wishes to include by stating that **everyone agrees?** רַבִּי יוֹחָנָן – **R' Yochanan,** who stated above that according to the Rabbis one is liable to a *chatas* even if he was aware of the prohibition. Nevertheless, in the case of a false oath, R' Yochanan agrees that he must have acted inadvertently regarding the prohibition to be obligated to bring a sacrifice.[32]

NOTES

22. [Thus, it is clear that he did not know of their prohibition.] But if so, in what sense did he know it was the Sabbath, when he thought that all manner of *melachah* is permitted? (*Rashi*).

[See *Ritva* (*MHK* ed.) who asks why the Gemara did not answer that he knows of the obligation to sanctify the Sabbath by making kiddush! From the fact that the Gemara does not answer this it is evident that to qualify as having "knowledge of the essence of the Sabbath" as required by our Mishnah for multiple *chatas* liabilities, a person must have knowledge of some of its *prohibitions,* and not simply its rituals.]

23. Whose violation is not subject to a sacrifice (*Rashi;* see *Maharam* who explains why Rashi emphasizes this point).

[The law of *techum* (the Sabbath boundary) limits the distance a person may travel from his place of residence on the Sabbath to two thousand *amos.*]

24. In *Sotah* (27b) R' Akiva derives that the *techum* laws are Biblical (*Rashi*). Thus, according to his view, if the person knew only this Sabbath law, it would be sufficient to call him aware of the Sabbath. Then, since he knew nothing about any of the thirty-nine *melachos,* he would be liable to one *chatas* for each.

[According to the Sages, however, the *techum* prohibition is merely Rabbinic, not Biblical. Thus, Reish Lakish is forced to say that our Mishnah follows the view of R' Akiva.] See *Ritva MHK* ed. and *Yefeh Einayim.*

25. I.e. there is no question that a *melachah* performed under these circumstances is a שׁוֹגֵג, *inadvertent transgression* (*Rashi*), for which one brings a *chatas.*

26. I.e. this is the ultimate case of a deliberate violation (*Rashi*), for which one is liable to *kares.*

27. That is, he did not realize that it was the Sabbath day, but he knew that the actions he performed were prohibited on the Sabbath.

28. He knew it was the Sabbath day, but did not know that his actions were prohibited on the Sabbath.

29. The Gemara stated above that according to Munbaz one is liable to a *chatas* even if he knew that it was the Sabbath and that his act was a *melachah,* as long as he was unaware of the *chatas* liability it incurs. The Baraisa's last ruling clearly follows this view. According to the Rabbis, though, a person is not liable unless the person was unaware that there was a *kares* penalty for deliberate violation [according to R' Yochanan], or that there is even a prohibition [according to Reish Lakish].

30. This is the oath referred to by the Torah in *Leviticus* (5:4): אוֹ נֶפֶשׁ כִּי תִשָּׁבַע לְבַטֵּא בִשְׂפָתַיִם לְהָרַע אוֹ לְהֵיטִיב לְכֹל אֲשֶׁר יְבַטֵּא הָאָדָם בִּשְׁבֻעָה וְנֶעְלַם מִמֶּנּוּ, *Or if a person swears by uttering with [his] lips to do bad or to do good, anything that a person might utter in an oath, and it is concealed from him* (and he then violates his oath). The Gemara in *Shevuos* (27a) derives that this law applies to oaths pertaining to both the past and the future. For example, if one swears that he ate when he really did not, or he swears that he will eat and does not, he is liable to the sacrifice prescribed in that section. But the verse states that this law applies only when the oath was נֶעְלַם מִמֶּנּוּ, *concealed from him* – i.e. he acted inadvertently (see *Rashi;* see below, 69b note 2). The Gemara will now discuss what needs to have been concealed from him.

31. [For example,] if someone swears that he will not eat and he does eat, he is not obligated to bring a sacrifice unless he forgot about the oath when he ate, which makes his transgression of the oath inadvertent with regard to the prohibition (*Rashi*). He would not, however, be liable if he remembered the oath and the prohibition but forgot that violating an oath makes one liable to a sacrifice.

[*Tosafos* object to *Rashi's* explanation because forgetting that one *made* the oath would not be called an inadvertence with regard to the *prohibition. Tosafos* therefore explain Abaye to refer to a case where the person remembered having made the oath but forgot that there is a Torah prohibition against violating an oath. See *Maharam* for a defense of *Rashi.*]

32. [It would seem to be quite obvious that Abaye is referring to R' Yochanan. Why then does the Gemara find it necessary to elaborate this explicitly?] The Gemara could simply have proceeded to its next question ("This is obvious!") without first making this point. *Rashi* explains that the Gemara does so because it would be possible to say

א) וכי תשגו ולא תעשו את כל המצות האלה וכתיב ב) והנפש אשר תעשה ביד רמה א) הוקשו כולם לע"ז א מה להלן דבר שחייבים על זדונו כרת ושגגתו חטאת אף כל דבר שחייבין על זדונו כרת ועל שגגתו חטאת ואלא מונבז שגגה במאי כגון ששגג בקרבן ורבנן ב שגגת קרבן לא שמה שגגה ורבנן שגגה במאי רבי יוחנן אמר ג כיון ששגג בכרת אף על פי שהזיד בלאו וריש לקיש אמר עד שישגוג בלאו וכרת אמר רבא מאי טעמא דרשב"ל אמר קרא ג) אשר לא תעשינה (בשגגה) ואשם עד שישגוג בלאו וכרת שבה ורבי יוחנן האי קרא דרשב"ל מאי עביד ליה מיבעי ליה ב) לכדתניא ג) מעם הארץ פרט למומר רבי שמעון בן אלעזר אומר משום רבי שמעון אשר לא תעשינה (בשגגה) ואשם ג) השב מידיעתו מביא קרבן על שגגתו לא שב מידיעתו אינו מביא קרבן על שגגתו: תנן ד) אבות מלאכות ארבעים חסר אחת והוינן בה ה) מנינא למה לי ואמר ר' יוחנן ד שאם עשאן כולן בהעלם אחד חייב על כל אחת ואחת היכי משכחת לה בזדון שבת ושגגת מלאכות בשלמא לרבי יוחנן דאמר כיון ששגג בכרת אע"פ שהזיד בלאו משכחת לה כגון דידע לה לשבת בלאו אלא לר"ש ב"ל דאמר עד שישגוג בלאו ובכרת דידע ליה לשבת במאי ו) דידעה ז) בתחומין ח) ואליבא דר"ע מאן תנא להא דתנו רבנן שגג בזה ובזה זהו שוגג האמור בתורה הזיד בזה ובזה זו היא מזיד האמור בתורה שגג בשבת והזיד במלאכות או ששגג במלאכות והזיד בשבת או שאמר יודע אני שמלאכה זו אסורה אבל איני יודע שחייבין עליה קרבן או לא חייב כמאן כמונבז אמר אביי הכל מודים בשבועת ביטוי שאין חייבין עליה קרבן עד שישגוג בלאו שבה הכל מודים מאן ר' יוחנן פשיטא כי קא"ר יוחנן היכא דאיכא כרת אבל הכא דליכא כרת לא סד"א ט) הואיל וחייב קרבן חידוש הוא דבכל התורה כולה לא אשכחן לאו דמייתי עליה קרבן והכא מייתי כי שגג בקרבן נמי ליחייב קמ"ל

רש"י

וכי תשגו ולא תעשו את כל המצות האלה. וילפינן בהוריות (דף ח.) זו ע"ז שהיא שקולה ככל המצות וכתיב תורה אחת כל התורה במשמע: הוקשו. קרבנות של שגגות של כל עבירות לשל ע"ז מה ע"ז קרבן שלה אינו בא אלא על עבירה גמורה שחייב על זדונו כרת דסמיך ליה והנפש אשר תעשה ביד רמה ונכרתה: אף כל התורה. אין מביאין חטאת אלא על דבר שזדונו כרת: ואלא מונבז. דאמר לעיל דמי שהיתה לו ידיעה בשעת מעשה חייב חטאת: דשגג במאי. הא גבי חטאת שגגה כתיב: דשגג בקרבן. דיודע שחייב על זדונו כרת אבל אינו יודע שחייב עליה חטאת: לא שמה שגגה. עד ששגג בעבירה עצמה: ורבנן. דבעו שגגה בעבירה עצמה שגגה במאי קאמרי שגגה בכולה מילתא בלאו וכרת או בכרת לחודיה: כיון ששגג בכרת אע"ג שהזיד בלאו. שאז הקרבן על הכרת הוא בא כדאמרן לעושה בשגגה וסמיך ליה והנפש אשר תעשה וגו': לא תעשינה. היינו לאו: מנינא למה לי. ליתני אבות מלאכות הזורע והחורש כו' למה לי למיתנא ארבעים חסר אחת ליתנינהו ואנן ידעינן דמ' חסר אחת איכא: שאם עשאן כולן כו'. וסימנא בעלמא אשמעינן לידע כמה חטאות חייב על חילול שבת אחת: היכי משכחת לה. דמיחייב ע"כ לא משכחת לה אלא בזדון שבת דיודע שהוא שבת ושגגת מלאכות דאינו יודע שהמלאכות הללו אסורות דאי בזדון מלאכות ושגגת שבת דיודע שהן אסורות בשבת אבל שכח שהיום שבת הא תנן דאינו חייב אלא אחת לכל שבת וזדון שבת לא הוי אא"כ יודע אחת מהלכותיה דאי לא ידע בחדא מינייהו אין שבת חלוק לו משאר ימים וזה ששגג בכולן אין כאן זדון שבת: בשלמא לר' יוחנן. דאמר שגגת כרת שמה שגגה: משכחת לה. זדון שבת בלאוין ושגגת מלאכות בכריתות דיודע לה לשבת שהוזהר על הלאוין או של כולן או של אחת מהן: דידע לה לשבת במאי. הא בכולן שגג כסבור שכל ל"ט מלאכות מותרות: בתחומין. דאין בקרבן: ואליבא דר' עקיבא. דאמר במסכת סוטה (א) תחומין דאורייתא נינהו דתנן בו ביום דרש רבי עקיבא ומדותם מחוץ לעיר כו': זהו שוגג האמור בתורה. כלומר היכא דשגג בשבת ובמלאכות אין כאן לא דין ולא דיין לקנתר ואין לך שוגג כזה: הזיד בזה ובזה. אין לך מזיד כזה: שגג באחת מהן. אף זה שוגג וחייבים עליה קרבן: שבועת ביטוי. שאוכל ולא אוכל שאכלתי ולא אכלתי חייב עליה קרבן וכתיב ביה ונעלם דהיינו שוגג הכל מודים בשוגג שלה דאם נשבע שלא אוכל ואכל אינו חייב אלא אם כן שכח שבועתו כשאכל דהשתא שגג בלאו שבה: הכל מודים מאן רבי יוחנן. כלומר על כרחין אביי לאו אפלוגתא דמונבז ורבנן קאי דלישמעינן דמודה מונבז בהא (דהא) י) שגגת קרבן לא הויא שגגה דמהיכא תיתי והא ק"ו היא השתא בכל התורה כולה דליכא חידוש בקרבן דידהו אמר מונבז דמיחייב בשגגת קרבן הכא דחידוש הוא דאין בה כרת ומביא קרבן עליה לא כ"ש אלא לרבנן קאמר ואפלוגתא דר"י ור"ל קאי ומאן הכל מודים ר"י דאף על גב דבעלמא קאמר אף על פי שהזיד בלאו הכא בעינן שישגוג בלאו: פשיטא. כיון דאליבא דרבנן איפליג דאמרי שגגת קרבן לאו שגגה היא אי בלאו שלה הזיד במאי שגג דע"כ לא קאמר ר"י בעלמא אלא במקום כרת דשגג בכרת: סלקא דעתך אמינא. בשבועת ביטוי נמי קאי רבי יוחנן במילתיה דאף על פי שהזיד בלאו ודקשיא לך במאי שגג שגג בקרבן דהואיל וחידוש מודו ביה רבנן:

תוספות

מה ע"ז שחייבים על זדונו כרת. וא"ת מ"מ היקשא דשוגג למזיד למה לי דאפילו לא הוי כתיב התם קרא דוהנפש אשר תעשה ביד רמה ילפינן שפיר מע"ז שחייב על זדונה כרת כו' וי"ל דלית לן לאקושה לע"ז אלא במאי דכתיב בההיא פרשה כדמשמע מתוך פירוש הקונטרס ולהכי אצטריך לאתויי הכא והנפש אשר תעשה תדע דהא לא ילפינן מע"ז דניבעי על זדונו סקילה כע"ז משום דלא כתיב סקילה בההיא פרשה אלא כרת והא דממעטינן בריש פרק בתרא דמכות (דף יג:) פסח ומילה מקרבן אע"פ שיש בהן כרת משום דמה ע"ז דאמר רחמנא לא תעביד והני קום עשה נינהו היינו נמי משום דכתיב והנפש אשר תעשה ביד רמה ° דמשמע מה שצויתי שלא לעשות וא"ת רבנן דהכא ר' עקיבא ור' עקיבא אית ליה בפ"ק דכריתות (דף ז:) דהאי קרא דמגדף במברך את השם כתיב וי"ל דלישנא דנקט הכא הוקשה כל התורה כולה לע"ז נקט אליבא דרבנן דרבי עקיבא אבל לר"ע אית לן למימר דהוקשה כל התורה כולה למברך את השם וא"ת ולמונבז האי דרשא דר' יהושע בן לוי מנא ליה ואומר ר"י דנפקא ליה כדדריש רבי בפ"ק דיבמות (דף ט.) ובפ"ב דהוריות (דף ח.) נאמר כאן ונודעה החטאת אשר חטאו עליה ונאמ' ואשה אל אחותה לא תקח לצרור לגלות ערותה עליה: **אלא** למונבז שגגה במאי. לא מצי למימר ששגג בלאו והזיד בקרבן דאין סברא לחייב בהזיד בקרבן דלא שב מידיעתו הוא וליכא נמי למימר שגג בלאו וקרבן דסברא הוא דכיון דמקיש למזיד אפי' מזיד בכל דבר ושוגג רק בדבר אחד דהיינו בקרבן יש לנו לחייבו א) ומיהו היכא דאיכא סקילה בעינן שיהא שוגג גם בסקילה דאי הוה מזיד בסקילה אין לחייבו בקרבן דכיון דאינו שב מסקילה פשיטא שאפילו היה יודע שחייב גם קרבן שלא היה שב ולא שב מידיעתו הוא ואע"ג דבהזיד בכרת חשיב ליה שב מידיעתו לקרבן היינו משום דכרת אפשר בתשובה וקרבן לא אפשר בתשובה ועוד דגבי כרת שייך שפיר למימר אם היה יודע שחייב כרת עם הקרבן היה שב: **כגון** ששגג בכרת אע"פ שהזיד בלאו. וטעמא דר' יוחנן משום דלא כתיב לאו בהיקשא דר' יהושע ולא כתיב אלא כרת בההיא ענינא ולהכי בעי מ"ט דריש לקיש ולא בעי מ"ט דר' יוחנן ול"ל דרבי יוחנן מיירי אליבא דרבנן דאית להו היקשא דרבי יהושע בן לוי ° אבל לרבי דנפקא ליה מג"ש דעליה מודה רבי יוחנן דבעי עד שישגוג בלאו וכרת דהא כתיב לאו בההוא קרא ואשה אל אחותה לא תקח וגו': **אמר** קרא אשר לא תעשינה בשגגה. קשה לר"י מנא ליה לריש לקיש דרבנן דרשי הכי ובעו שגגת לאו וליכא למימר דמשמע ליה למדרש קרא הכי דהא ע"כ סבירא ליה דאין סברא לדרוש כן דהא איהו סבר כמונבז כדאמר לעיל ומונבז לא בעי שגגת לאו אלא שגגת קרבן גרידא דבהדיא תניא לקמן או שאמר יודע אני שמלאכה זו אסורה אבל איני יודע אם חייבים עליה קרבן אם לאו חייב ולא קאמר קרבן ומלקות אם לאו: **דידע** לה בתחומין ב). לא מצי למימר דידע לה בדאיסי דבההוא נמי חייב חטאת כדפירשתי בפרק קמא (דף ו: בד"ה הא קמ"ל) תימה לר"י דאמאי לא קאמר דידע לה לשבת בעשה דכתיב וביום השביעי תשבות וגו' (שמות כג) וכתיב נמי ושמרתם את השבת (שם לא): **עד** שישגוג בלאו שבה. כגון נשבע שלא יאכל ואכל ובשעת אכילה שכח איסור שבועה וקרינן ביה האדם בשבועה שנשבע היה יודע היטב איסור שבועה אלא שבשעת אכילה היה סבור דמותר לעבור על שבועתו ורש"י פירש דבשעת אכילה שכח שנשבע ואין נראה דאין זה קרוי שגג בלאו שבה במה שאינו זוכר שנשבע: הא

מסורת הש"ס

א) [לקמן דף קנג: ע"ש], ב) [יבמות ט. הוריות ח. ע"ש חולין ה.], ג) שבועות כו: וש"נ, ד) [לקמן עג.], ה) [לעיל ו:], ו) [לקמן עג: כריתות ג:], ז) [עי' תוספות מגילה ח: ד"ה כתיב ותוס' לעיל ו: ד"ה למ"ל], ח) [לקמן עג. קנג: סנהדרין סו.], ט) [סוטה ל: וש"נ], י) הואיל וחידוש הוא כל"ל רש"ל, כ) צ"ל שגגת רש"ל.

עין משפט נר מצוה

ה א מיי' פ"ז מהלכות שגגות הלכה ב:
ו ב ג מיי' פ"ו מהלכות שגגות הלכה ג סמג עשין רג:
ז ד מיי' שם ופ"ז ה"ג:

רבינו חננאל

שהיא מעשה שבת וידע שהעושה מלאכה זו חייב עליה לאו וכרת וכי לא שגג אלא בקרבן בלבד וסבר כל כי האי גוונא הוא דחייב חטאת וחולתי כן פטור. וכדתניא אמר אני יודע שמלאכה זו אסורה אבל איני יודע אם חייבין עליה קרבן אם לאו חייב דאוקימנא כמונבז. בהאי סברא בתרא דמונבז רבי יוחנן ור"ל לא סבירא להו כוותיה. וקא מפרש ר' יוחנן כטעמא דרבנן כיון ששגג בכרת אע"פ שהזיד בלאו הרי זה חייב חטאת. ור"ל אמר אינו חייב חטאת עד שישגוג בלאו וכרת ומותבינן על ר"ל הא דתנן אבות מלאכות ארבעים חסר אחת והוינן בה מנינא למה לי ואמר ר' יוחנן אם עשאן כולם בהעלם אחד חייב על כל אחת ואחת ושגגת מלאכות בשלמא לר' יוחנן כגון שהזיד בלאו פי' ידע שהיא היום שבת וידע שהעושה מלאכה (חייב כרת) [עובר בלאו] אמר' כיון ששגג [בכרת] אף על פי שהזיד בלאו שגגה היא וחייב חטאת אלא לריש לקיש דאמר עד שישגוג בלאו וכרת זדון שבת היכי משכחת ליה ומשני כגון דידע לשבת בתחומין אמרת אין השבת אסור אלא בתחומין כדכתיב אל יצא איש ממקומו וגו' וכרבי עקיבא דסבר תחומין דאורייתא כדמפרש בסוטה פ' ה' ואף על גב דדחי התם ואמרינן (עירובין דף יז:) לית דחש להא דרבי עקיבא: אמר אביי הכל מודים בשבועת ביטוי שאין חייבין עליה קרבן עד שישגוג בלאו שבה. מאן הכל מודים רבי יוחנן דסבר עד שישגוג בכרת והאי כיון דלית בה כרת בעי שגגה בלאו ואמרינן פשיטא מהו דתימא הואיל וחדוש הוא דלא אשכחן בכל התורה לאו שאין בה כרת שמייתי קרבן והכא בשבועת ביטוי מייתי קרבן אע"פ שאין בה כרת הוה אמינא כי שגג בקרבן (נמי) מחייב קמ"ל דלא מחייב רבי יוחנן עד שישגוג בלאו שבה. קיי"ל דכל לאו שבתורה שחייבין עליו מלקות בלבד ואין בו כרת אינו חייב עליו חטאת וכי אינו חייב חטאת אלא על

חשק שלמה על רבינו חננאל

א) ע"ש דלא מיירי כלל מדין תחומין דאורייתא. אלא מ"מ יש ללמוד מהתם דגם דין תחומין דאורייתא כר"ע. ועיין תוס' שם ד"ה לית דחיש:

רב נסים גאון

מצוה שהיא בדבור של הקב"ה רצוה על ידי משה הרי אומר זו ע"ז: דידע להו לתחומים ואליבא דרבי עקיבא כמה דאמר ר' עקיבא במסכת סוטה בפ' כשם שהמים בודקין אותה (דף כז) בו ביום דרש רבי עקיבא ומדותם מחוץ לעיר ומקרא אחד אומר מקיר העיר וחוצה אלף אמה אי אפשר לומר אלף אמה שכבר נאמר אלפים אמה ואי אפשר לומר אלפים שכבר נאמר אלף ולמה נאמר אלף ולמה נאמר אלפים אלא אלף אמה מגרש ואלפים אמה תחום שבת ר' אלעזר בנו של ר' יוסי הגלילי אומר אלף אמה מגרש ואלפים שדות וכרמים ואמרו בגמרא במאי

תוספות ישנים

א) דהא ודאי ליכא למימר דשגג בכרת דא"כ היינו רבנן. ועוד כיון דמקיש לשוגג למזיד בכרת אית לן למימר דמכרת אית ליה ידיעה בשעת מעשה. ועוד דשגגת לאו אפילו לרבנן לא מיישבי:
ב) לא מצי למימר דידע לי' לאו דלא תעשה כמזיד בפ"ב בתרא דלאו בו חטאת דכיון דסבור המלאכות כ"ש סבור שלא מחלל על בהמתו. ולא מצי למימר דידע ליה בהכנסה אליבא דרבי יוסי דהא קתני ליה במתניתין. וליכא למימר דידע לה בתולדה דלא ידע להו אבות כ"ש תולדות, וליכא למימר דידע לה בקפילה דאם כן ידע מיהא ליה הוא. ואין סברא לומר כגון שטעה בשיעורין כגון בהעביר ה' אמות ברשות הרבים או כותב ג' תפירות וכותב ג' אותיות דלא ידע שיכתב שיעור בפחות מלמעבר מדעתו שיעור שלינו:

הגהות הב"ח

(א) רש"י ד"ה ואליבא דרבי עקיבא דאמר במסכת סוטה. נ"ב בנדו דף ס ע"ב ודף ע"ב:

גליון הש"ס

תוס' ד"ה מה ע"ז וכו' דמשמע מה שצויתי שלא לעשות. עיין בכ"ק דף קב ע"ב תוס' ד"ה מאי לאו: שם ד"ה אבל לרבי דנפקא ליה מגז"ש. עיין בחידושי הר"ן שבועות דף ה ע"א ובר"מ הרמב"ן שם:

תורה אור השלם

א) וְכִי תִשְׁגּוּ וְלֹא תַעֲשׂוּ אֵת כָּל הַמִּצְוֹת הָאֵלֶּה אֲשֶׁר דִּבֶּר יְיָ אֶל מֹשֶׁה: [במדבר טו, כב]
ב) וְהַנֶּפֶשׁ אֲשֶׁר תַּעֲשֶׂה בְּיָד רָמָה מִן הָאֶזְרָח וּמִן הַגֵּר אֶת יְיָ הוּא מְגַדֵּף וְנִכְרְתָה הַנֶּפֶשׁ הַהִוא מִקֶּרֶב עַמָּהּ: [במדבר טו, ל]
ג) וְאִם נֶפֶשׁ אַחַת תֶּחֱטָא בִשְׁגָגָה מֵעַם הָאָרֶץ בַּעֲשֹׂתָהּ אַחַת מִמִּצְוֹת יְיָ אֲשֶׁר לֹא תֵעָשֶׂינָה וְאָשֵׁם: [ויקרא ד, כז]

ליקוטי רש"י

מנינא למה לי. ליתני אבות מלאכות הזורע והחורש כו' למה לי לאשמעינן מניינא הא מינה להו ולומר. חייב על כל אחת ואחת. וגם להודיענו סכום החטאות שאדם חייב באיסורי שבת בהעלם אחד ולאשמעינן ארבעים חסר אחת הן ותו לא שאפילו עשה תולדותיהן עמהן אינו מביא על התולדה היכא דעשאה עם אביה דהוה ליה כולה חדא עבירה היא [לעיל ו:]. וגם להודיענו שאם נתעלמו כל הלכות שבת ממנו כמה חטאות [חייב] עליו [לקמן עג:]. היכי משכחת לה. דמיחייב שום אדם על כל מלאכה ומלאכה שבהעלם אחד על כרחך בזדון שבת ושגגת מלאכות הוא דבעית לאשכוחיה והכא דליעלימו כולהו מיניה מאי זדון שבת איכא במה ניכר לו שבת משאר ימים [שם.]. דניחייב איניש אכל חדא על כרחך בזדון שבת ושגגת מלאכות הוא דמשכחת לה והכא מאי זדון שבת איכא יודע שבת במידי שבכל הלכותיה נעלמות ממנו אין חילוק היום משאר ימים. בשלמא לרבי יוחנן וכו'. משכחת ליה שלא נעלמו ממנו אלא הכריתות ויודע הלאוין והיינו זדון שבת [שם ע:]. בתחומין. דאינו יודע שמלאכות אלו אסורות אלא בדבר אחד כגון דידע שאסור לצאת חוץ לתחום [כריתות ג.]. ואליבא דרבי עקיבא. דיליף להו מקראי במסכת סוטה (כז:). ור' עקיבא מודה נמי בתחומים דאין חייבים עליהם כרת דתנן (שבת עג.) אבות מלאכות ארבעים חסר אחת ולא פליג ר' עקיבא [סנהדרין סו.]. דאמר דאורייתא נינהו והוי מחלל ומיהו אין חייבין לא על שגגתו חטאת כו' [לקמן קנג:].

The Gemara asks:

פְּשִׁיטָא – But **this is obvious!** **כִּי קָאָמַר רַבִּי יוֹחָנָן** – **When did R' Yochanan say** that one is liable to a *chatas* even when he was aware of the prohibition? **הֵיכָא דְּאִיכָּא כָּרֵת** – Only in a case **where there is** a ***kares*** penalty; for in such a case R' Yochanan rules that the person's unawareness of the *kares* penalty classifies him as an inadvertent sinner. **אֲבָל הָכָא דְּלֵיכָּא כָּרֵת** – **But here** (in the case of a false oath), **where there is no *kares*** penalty,[33] **לֹא** – he would **not** say this.[34] Rather, R' Yochanan would clearly agree that the person must be unaware of the prohibition to be liable to a sacrifice! – **?** –

The Gemara explains the need for Abaye's statement:

סַלְקָא דַּעְתָּךְ אֲמִינָא – **I might have thought** **הוֹאִיל וְחִיּוּב קָרְבָּן חִידּוּשׁ הוּא** – that **since the liability to a sacrifice** in the case of one who swears falsely **is a novelty,** **דִּבְכָל הַתּוֹרָה כּוּלָּהּ** – **for in the entire Torah** **לֹא אַשְׁכְּחַן לָאו דְּמַיְיתִי עֲלֵיהּ קָרְבָּן** – **we do not find a** mere **prohibition for which one brings a sacrifice for its** violation,[35] **וְהָכָא מַיְיתִי** – **whereas here** (in the case of a false oath), **one does bring** a sacrifice for its violation,[36] **כִּי שָׁגַג בְּקָרְבָּן נַמִּי לִיחַיֵּיב** – therefore even **when he acted inadvertently with regard to the sacrifice he should also be liable** to a sacrifice.[37]

NOTES

that Abaye is referring not to R' Yochanan but rather to Munbaz, who holds that inadvertence regarding the sacrifice obligation suffices to classify a violator as inadvertent. Abaye would then be saying that in the case of a false oath, even Munbaz agrees that a violation is not considered inadvertent unless the person was completely unaware of the transgression. The Gemara therefore finds it necessary to state that Abaye must be referring to R' Yochanan, not Munbaz. For if Munbaz considers inadvertence regarding the sacrifice to be sufficient to classify the person as a שׁוֹגֵג, *inadvertent sinner,* even with regard to a regular *chatas,* then he certainly considers him so in regard to a false oath. This is so because the very obligation of a sacrifice in the case of a false oath is a novelty since there is no *kares* penalty associated with this prohibition. Hence, if unawareness of the usual type of sacrifice penalty is considered inadvertence according to Munbaz, certainly unawareness of the novel sacrifice of a false oath would also be considered inadvertence (see note 37). Hence, the Gemara points out that Abaye must be referring to R' Yochanan's view according to the Rabbis who dispute Munbaz.]

33. The false oath is unique in this respect, in that the Torah mandates a *chatas* for its inadvertent violation even though there is no *kares* penalty for its deliberate transgression, as the Gemara will state below.

34. On the contrary, since according to the Rabbis, inadvertence about the sacrifice penalty is never sufficient to classify a person a שׁוֹגֵג, as *inadvertent* [as Munbaz holds], and since there is no *kares* for a false oath, if the person was aware of the prohibition there would be no possible grounds for which to call him an inadvertent sinner! (*Rashi*).

35. That is, we do not find anywhere that a person is obigated to bring a *chatas* sacrifice for a prohibition that does not carry a *kares* penalty.

36. [Even though there is no *kares* penalty for swearing falsely.]

37. Since the sacrifice requirement in the case of a false oath is an exception to the general rules of such requirements, perhaps even the Rabbis would consider him to be an inadvertent sinner merely as a result of his ignorance of the sacrifice penalty (*Rashi*).

א) וכי תשגו ולא תעשו את כל המצות האלה וכתיב ב) והנפש אשר תעשה ביד רמה א) הוקשו כולם לע"ז א מה להלן דבר שחייבים על זדונו כרת ושגגתו חטאת אף כל דבר שחייבין על זדונו כרת ועל שגגתו חטאת ואלא מונבז שגגה במאי כגון ששגג בקרבן ורבנן ב שגגת קרבן לא שמה שגגה ורבנן שגגה במאי רבי יוחנן אמר ג כיון ששגג בכרת אף על פי שהזיד בלאו וריש לקיש אמר עד שישגוג בלאו וכרת אמר רבא מאי טעמא דרשב"ל אמר קרא ג) אשר לא תעשינה (בשגגה) ואשם עד שישגוג בלאו וכרת שבה ורבי יוחנן האי קרא דרשב"ל מאי עביד ליה מיבעי ליה ב) לכדתניא ג) מעם הארץ פרט למומר רבי שמעון בן אלעזר אומר משום רבי שמעון אשר לא תעשינה (בשגגה) ואשם ג) השב מידיעתו מביא קרבן על שגגתו לא שב מידיעתו אינו מביא קרבן על שגגתו: תנן ד) אבות מלאכות ארבעים חסר אחת והוינן בה ה) מנינא למה לי ואמר ר' יוחנן ד שאם עשאן כולן בהעלם אחד חייב על כל אחת ואחת היכי משכחת לה בזדון שבת ושגגת מלאכות בשלמא לרבי יוחנן דאמר כיון ששגג בכרת אע"פ שהזיד בלאו משכחת לה כגון דידע לה לשבת בלאו אלא לר"ש ב"ל דאמר עד שישגוג בלאו ובכרת דידע ליה לשבת במאי ו) דידעה ז) בתחומין ח) ואליבא דר"ע מאן תנא להא דתנו רבנן שגג בזה ובזה זהו שוגג האמור בתורה הזיד בזה ובזה זו היא מזיד האמור בתורה שגג בשבת והזיד במלאכות או ששגג במלאכות והזיד בשבת או שאמר יודע אני שמלאכה זו אסורה אבל איני יודע שחייבין עליה קרבן או לא חייב כמאן כמונבז אמר אביי הכל מודים בשבועת ביטוי שאין חייבין עליה קרבן עד שישגוג בלאו שבה הכל מודים מאן ר' יוחנן פשיטא כי קא"ר יוחנן היכא דאיכא כרת אבל הכא דליכא כרת לא סד"א ט) הואיל וחייב קרבן חידוש הוא דבכל התורה כולה לא אשכחן לאו דמייתי עליה קרבן והכא מייתי כי שגג בקרבן נמי ליחייב קמ"ל

רש"י

וכי תשגו ולא תעשו את כל המצות האלה. וילפינן בהוריות (דף ח.) זו ע"ז שהיא שקולה ככל המצות וכתיב תורה אחת כל התורה במשמע: הוקשו. קרבנות של שגגות של כל עבירות לשל ע"ז מה ע"ז קרבן שלה אינו בא אלא על עבירה גמורה שחייב על זדונו כרת דסמיך ליה והנפש אשר תעשה ביד רמה ונכרתה: אף כל התורה. אין מביאין חטאת אלא על דבר שזדונו כרת: ואלא מונבז. דאמר לעיל דמי שהיתה לו ידיעה בשעת מעשה חייב חטאת: דשגג במאי. הא גבי חטאת שגגה כתיב: דשגג בקרבן. דיודע שחייב על זדונו כרת אבל אינו יודע שחייב עליה חטאת: לא שמה שגגה. עד ששגג בעבירה עצמה: ורבנן. דבעו שגגה בעבירה עצמה שגגה במאי קאמרי שגגה בכולה מילתא בלאו וכרת או בכרת לחודיה: כיון ששגג בכרת אע"ג שהזיד בלאו. שאז הקרבן על הכרת הוא בא כדאמרן לעושה בשגגה וסמיך ליה והנפש אשר תעשה וגו': לא תעשינה. היינו לאו: מנינא למה לי. ליתני אבות מלאכות הזורע והחורש כו' למה לי למיתנא ארבעים חסר אחת ליתנינהו ואנן ידעינן דמ' חסר אחת איכא: שאם עשאן כולן כו'. וסימנא בעלמא אשמעינן לידע כמה חטאות חייב על חילול שבת אחת: היכי משכחת לה. דמיחייב ע"כ לא משכחת לה אלא בזדון שבת דיודע שהוא שבת ושגגת מלאכות דאינו יודע שהמלאכות הללו אסורות דאי בזדון מלאכות ושגגת שבת דיודע שהן אסורות בשבת אבל שכח שהיום שבת הא תנן דאינו חייב אלא אחת לכל שבת וזדון שבת לא הוי אא"כ יודע אחת מהלכותיה דאי לא ידע בחדא מינייהו אין שבת חלוק לו משאר ימים וזה ששגג בכולן אין כאן זדון שבת: בשלמא לר' יוחנן. דאמר שגגת כרת שמה שגגה: משכחת לה. זדון שבת בלאוין ושגגת מלאכות בכריתות דיודע לה לשבת שהוזהר על הלאוין או של כולן או של אחת מהן: דידע לה לשבת במאי. הלא בכולן שגג כסבור שכל ל"ט מלאכות מותרות: בתחומין. דאין בקרבן: ואליבא דר' עקיבא. דאמר במסכת סוטה (א) תחומין דאורייתא נינהו דתנן בו ביום דרש רבי עקיבא ומדותם מחוץ לעיר כו': זהו שוגג האמור בתורה. כלומר היכא דשגג בשבת ובמלאכות אין כאן לא דין ולא דיין לקנתר ואין לך שוגג כזה: הזיד בזה ובזה. אין לך מזיד כזה: שגג באחת מהן. אף זה שוגג וחייבים עליה קרבן: שבועת ביטוי. שאוכל ולא אוכל שאכלתי ולא אכלתי חייב עליה קרבן וכתיב ביה ונעלם דהיינו שוגג הכל מודים בשוגג שלה דאם נשבע שלא אוכל ואכל אינו חייב אלא אם כן שכח שבועתו כשאכל דהשתא שגג בלאו שבה: הכל מודים מאן רבי יוחנן. כלומר על כרחין אביי לאו אפלוגתא דמונבז ורבנן קאי דלישמעינן דמודה מונבז בהא (דהא) ° שגגת קרבן לא הויא שגגה דמהיכא תיתי והא ק"ו היא השתא בכל התורה כולה דליכא חידוש בקרבן דידהו אמר מונבז דמיחייב בשגגת קרבן הכא דחידוש הוא דאין בה כרת ומביא קרבן עליה לא כ"ש אלא לרבנן קאמר ואפלוגתא דר"י ור"ל קאי ומאן הכל מודים ר"י דאף על גב דבעלמא קאמר אף על פי שהזיד בלאו הכא בעינן שישגוג בלאו: פשיטא. כיון דאליבא דרבנן איפליג דאמרי שגגת קרבן לאו שגגה היא אי בלאו שלה הזיד במאי שגג דע"כ לא קאמר ר"י בעלמא אלא במקום כרת דשגג בכרת: סלקא דעתך אמינא. בשבועת ביטוי נמי קאי רבי יוחנן במילתיה דאף על פי שהזיד בלאו ודקשיא לך במאי שגג שגג בקרבן דהואיל וחידוש מודו ביה רבנן: קמ"ל

תוספות

מה ע"ז שחייבים על זדונו כרת. וא"ת מ"מ היקשא דשוגג למזיד למה לי דאפילו לא הוי כתיב התם קרא דוהנפש אשר תעשה ביד רמה ילפינן שפיר מע"ז שחייב על זדונה כרת כו' וי"ל דלית לן לאקושה לע"ז אלא במאי דכתיב בההיא פרשה כדמשמע מתוך פירוש הקונטרס ולהכי אצטריך לאתויי הכא והנפש אשר תעשה תדע דהא לא ילפינן מע"ז דניבעי על זדונו סקילה כע"ז משום דלא כתיב סקילה בההיא פרשה אלא כרת והא דממעטינן בריש פרק בתרא דמכות (דף יג:) פסח ומילה מקרבן אע"פ שיש בהן כרת משום דמה ע"ז דאמר רחמנא לא תעביד והני קום עשה נינהו היינו נמי משום דכתיב והנפש אשר תעשה ביד רמה ° דמשמע מה שצויתי שלא לעשות וא"ת רבנן דהכא ר' עקיבא ור' עקיבא אית ליה בפ"ק דכריתות (דף ז:) דהאי קרא דמגדף במברך את השם כתיב וי"ל דלישנא דנקט הכא הוקשה כל התורה כולה לע"ז נקט אליבא דרבנן דרבי עקיבא אבל לר"ע אית לן למימר דהוקשה כל התורה כולה למברך את השם וא"ת ולמונבז האי דרשא דר' יהושע בן לוי מנא ליה ואומר ר"י דנפקא ליה כדדריש רבי בפ"ק דיבמות (דף ט.) ובפ"ב דהוריות (דף ח.) נאמר כאן ונודעה החטאת אשר חטאו עליה ונאמ' ואשה אל אחותה לא תקח לצרור לגלות ערותה עליה: אלא למונבז שגגה במאי. לא מצי למימר ששגג בלאו והזיד בקרבן דאין סברא לחייב בהזיד בקרבן דלא שב מידיעתו הוא וליכא נמי למימר שגג בלאו וקרבן דסברא הוא דכיון דמקיש למזיד אפי' מזיד בכל דבר ושוגג רק בדבר אחד דהיינו בקרבן יש לנו לחייבו א) ומיהו היכא דאיכא סקילה בעינן שיהא שוגג גם בסקילה דאי הוה מזיד בסקילה אין לחייבו בקרבן דכיון דאינו שב מסקילה פשיטא שאפילו היה יודע שחייב גם קרבן שלא היה שב ולא שב מידיעתו הוא ואע"ג דבהזיד בכרת חשיב ליה שב מידיעתו לקרבן היינו משום דכרת אפשר בתשובה וקרבן לא אפשר בתשובה ועוד דגבי כרת שייך שפיר למימר אם היה יודע שחייב כרת עם הקרבן היה שב: כגון ששגג בכרת אע"פ שהזיד בלאו. וטעמא דר' יוחנן משום דלא כתיב לאו בהיקשא דר' יהושע ולא כתיב אלא כרת בההיא ענינא ולהכי בעי מ"ט דריש לקיש ולא בעי מ"ט דר' יוחנן ול"ל דרבי יוחנן מיירי אליבא דרבנן דאית להו היקשא דרבי יהושע בן לוי ° אבל לרבי דנפקא ליה מג"ש דעליה מודה רבי יוחנן דבעי עד שישגוג בלאו וכרת דהא כתיב לאו בההוא קרא ואשה אל אחותה לא תקח וגו': אמר קרא אשר לא תעשינה בשגגה. קשה לר"י מנא ליה לריש לקיש לדרשי הכי ובעו שגגת לאו וליכא למימר דמשמע ליה למדרש קרא הכי דהא ע"כ סבירא ליה דאין סברא לדרוש כן דהא איהו סבר כמונבז כדאמר לעיל ומונבז לא בעי שגגת לאו אלא שגגת קרבן גרידא דבהדיא תניא לקמן או שאמר יודע אני שמלאכה זו אסורה אבל איני יודע אם חייבים עליה קרבן אם לאו חייב ולא קאמר קרבן ומלקות אם לאו: דידע לה בתחומין ב). לא מצי למימר דידע לה בדאיסי דבההוא נמי חייב חטאת כדפירשתי בפרק קמא (דף ו: בד"ה הא קמ"ל) תימה לר"י דאמאי לא קאמר דידע לה לשבת בעשה דכתיב וביום השביעי תשבות וגו' (שמות כג) וכתיב נמי ושמרתם את השבת (שם לא): עד שישגוג בלאו שבה. כגון נשבע שלא יאכל ואכל ובשעת אכילה שכח איסור שבועה וקרינן ביה האדם דבשעת שבועה שנשבע היה יודע היטב איסור שבועה אלא שבשעת אכילה היה סבור דמותר לעבור על שבועתו ורש"י פירש דבשעת אכילה שכח שנשבע ואין נראה דאין זה קרוי שגג בלאו שבה במה שאינו נזכר שנשבע: הא

מסורת הש"ס

א) [לקמן דף קנג: ע"ש], ב) יומא פ. הוריות ב. יא. ע"ש חולין ה., ג) שבועות כו: וש"נ, ד) לקמן עג. [לו:] [לעיל ו:], ה) לעיל ו: לקמן ע: עג. לו: כריתות ב., ו) [עי' תוספות חגיגה יח: ד"ה דכתיב ותוס' לעיל ו: ד"ה הא קמ"ל], ז) [לקמן ע: עג. קנג: סנהדרין סו.], ח) [סוטה כז: וש"נ], ט) הואיל וחידוש הוא כל"ל רש"ל, י) צ"ל דשגגת רש"ל.

תוספות ישנים

א) דהא ודאי ליכא למימר דשוגג בכרת דא"כ היינו רבנן. ועוד כיון דמקיש שוגג למזיד בכרת אית לן למימר דמכרת אית ליה ידיעה בשעת מעשה. ועוד דשגגת לאו אפילו לרבנן לא מחייבין:

ב) לא מצי למימר דידע לי' בלאו דממאמר למ"ד בפ' בתרא דאין בו חטאת דכיון דסבור דעלמו מותר בכל המלאכות כ"ש שסבור שאינו מוזהר על בהמתו. ולא מצי למימר דידע ליה בהבערה אליבא דרבי יוסי דהא קתני ליה במתניתין. וליכא למימר דידע לה בתולדה דכיון דלא ידע אבות כ"ש תולדות. וליכא למימר דידע לה בסקילה דאם כן לא שב מידיעתו הוא. ואין סברא לומר כגון שטעה בשיעורין כגון דסבר דלא מיחייב אלא בהעביר ה' אמות ברשות הרבים או בתופר ג' תפירות וכותב ג' אותיות דלא שכיח שיטעה ויאמר מדעתו שיעור שאינו:

הגהות הב"ח

(א) רש"י ד"ה ואליבא דרבי עקיבא דאמר במסכת סוטה. נ"ב בלדו דף כז ע"ב ודף ל ע"ב:

גליון הש"ס

תוס' ד"ה מה ע"ז וכו' דמשמע מה שצויתי שלא לעשות. עיין בכ"ק דף קס ע"ב תוס' ד"ה מאי לאו: שם ד"ה כגון ששגג וכו' אבל לרבי דנפקא ליה מגז"ש. עיין בחידושי הר"ן שבועות דף ה ע"א ובחי' הרמב"ן שם:

תורה אור השלם

א) וְכִי תִשְׁגּוּ וְלֹא תַעֲשׂוּ אֵת כָּל הַמִּצְוֹת הָאֵלֶּה אֲשֶׁר דִּבֶּר יְיָ אֶל מֹשֶׁה: [במדבר טו, כב]

ב) וְהַנֶּפֶשׁ אֲשֶׁר תַּעֲשֶׂה בְּיָד רָמָה מִן הָאֶזְרָח וּמִן הַגֵּר אֶת יְיָ הוּא מְגַדֵּף וְנִכְרְתָה הַנֶּפֶשׁ הַהִוא מִקֶּרֶב עַמָּהּ: [במדבר טו, ל]

ג) וְאִם נֶפֶשׁ אַחַת תֶּחֱטָא בִשְׁגָגָה מֵעַם הָאָרֶץ בַּעֲשֹׂתָהּ אַחַת מִמִּצְוֹת יְיָ אֲשֶׁר לֹא תֵעָשֶׂינָה וְאָשֵׁם: [ויקרא ד, כז]

ליקוטי רש"י

מנינא למה לי. ליתני אבות מלאכות הזורע והחורש כו' למה לי לאשמעינן מנינייהו הא מני להו ואזיל. חייב על כל אחת ואחת. וכא להודיענו סכום החטאות שאדם חייב באיסורי שבת בהעלם אחד ולאשמעינן ארבעים חסר אחת הן ותו לא שאפילו עשה תולדותיהן עמהן אינו מביא על התולדה היכא דעשאה עם אביה דהוי ליה כעושה וחוזר ועושה דכולה חדא עבירה היא [לעיל ו:]. וכא להודיעך שאם נתעלמו כל הלכות שבת ממנו כמה חטאות [חייב] עליו [לקמן עג.]. היכי משכחת לה. דמיחייב שום אדם על כל מלאכה ומלאכה שבהעלם אחד על כרחך בזדון שבת ושגגת מלאכות הוא דבעית לאשכוחיה והכא דאיעלימו כולהו מיניה מאי זדון שבת איכא במה ניכר לו שבת משאר ימים [שם.]. דניחייב איניש אכל חדא על כרחך בזדון שבת ושגגת מלאכות הוא דמשכחת לה והכא מאי זדון שבת איכא. דהא לא כל הלכותיה נעלמות ממנו אין חילוק היום משאר ימים. משכחת ליה שלא נעלמו ממנו אלא הכריתות ויודע הלאוין והיינו זדון שבת [שם ע:]. בשלמא לרבי יוחנן וכו'. בתחומין. דאינו יודע שמלאכות הללו אסורות אבל אחד כגון דידע שאסור לצאת חוץ לתחום [כריתות ג.]. ואליבא דרבי עקיבא. דיליף להו מקראי במסכת סוטה (כז:). ור' עקיבא מודה נמי בתחומים דאין חייבים עליהם כרת דתנן (שבת עג.) אבות מלאכות ארבעים חסר אחת ולא פליג ר' עקיבא [סנהדרין סו.]. דאמר דאורייתא נינהו והוי מחלל ומיהו אין חייבין לא על שגגתו חטאת כו' [לקמן קנג:].

עין משפט נר מצוה

ה א מיי' פ"א מהלכות שגגות הלכה ב:
ו ב ג מיי' פ"ב מהלכות שגגות הלכה ב סמג עשין רג:
ז ד מיי' שם ופ"ז ה"ג:

רבינו חננאל

שהיא מעשה שבת ויודע שהעושה מלאכה זו חייב עליה לאו וכרת וכי לא שגג אלא בקרבן בלבד וסבר כל כי האי גוונא הוא דחייב חטאת וזולתי כן פטור. וכדתניא אמר אני יודע שמלאכה זו אסורה אבל איני יודע אם חייבין עליה קרבן אם לאו חייב דאוקימנא כמונבז. בהאי סברא בתרא דמונבז רבי יוחנן ור"ל לא סבירא להו כוותיה. וקא מפרש ר' יוחנן כטעמא דרבנן כיון ששגג בכרת אע"פ שהזיד בלאו חייב חטאת. ור"ל אמר אינו חייב חטאת עד שישגוג בלאו וכרת ומותבינן על ר"ל הא דתנן אבות מלאכות ארבעים חסר אחת והוינן בה מנינא למה לי ואמר ר' יוחנן אם עשאן כולם בהעלם אחד חייב על כל אחת ואחת ואוקימנא בזדון שבת ושגגת מלאכות בשלמא לר' יוחנן כגון שהזיד בלאו פי' ידע שהיא היום שבת וידע שהעושה מלאכה (חייב כרת) [עובר בלאו] אמרי' כיון ששגג [בכרת] אף על פי שהזיד בלאו שגגה היא וחייב חטאת אלא לריש לקיש דאמר עד שישגוג בלאו וכרת זדון שבת היכי משכחת ליה ומשני כגון דידע לשבת בתחומין אמרת אין השבת אסור אלא בתחומין כדכתיב אל יצא איש ממקומו וגו' וכרבי עקיבא דסבר תחומין דאורייתא כדמפרש בסוטה פ' ה' ואף על גב דדחי התם ואמרינן (עירובין ס: א)) לית דחש להא דרבי עקיבא: אמר אביי הכל מודים בשבועת ביטוי שאין חייבין עליה קרבן עד שישגוג בלאו שבה. מאן הכל מודים רבי יוחנן דסבר עד שישגוג בכרת והאי כיון דלית בה כרת בעי שגגה בלאו ואמרינן פשיטא מהו דתימא הואיל וחדוש הוא דלא אשכחן בכל התורה לאו שאין בה כרת שמייתי קרבן והכא בשבועת ביטוי מייתי קרבן אע"פ שאין בה כרת הוה אמינא כי שגג בקרבן (נמי) בלבד [נמין] מחייב קמ"ל דלא מחייב רבי יוחנן עד שישגוג בלאו שבה. קיי"ל דכל לאו שבתורה שחייבין עליו מלקות בלבד ואין בו כרת אינו חייב עליו חטאת וכי אינו חייב חטאת אלא על

חשק שלמה על רבינו חננאל

א) ע"ש דלא מיירי כלל מדין תחומין דאורייתא. אכן מ"מ יש ללמוד מהתם דגם בדין תחומין דאורייתא לא קיי"ל כר"ע. ועיין תוס' שם ד"ה לית דחש:

רב נסים גאון

מצוה שהיא בדברו של הקב"ה וצוה על ידי משה הוי אומר זו ע"ז: דידע להו בתחומים ואליבא דרבי עקיבא כמה דאמר ר' עקיבא במסכת סוטה בפ' כשם שהמים בודקין אותה (דף כז) בו ביום דרש רבי עקיבא ומדותם מחוץ לעיר ומקרא אחד אומר מקיר העיר וחוצה אלף אמה אי אפשר לומר אלף אמה שכבר נאמר אלפים אמה ואי אפשר לומר אלפים שכבר נאמר אלף ולמה נאמר אלף ולמה נאמר אלפים אלא אלף אמה מגרש ואלפים אמה תחום שבת ר' אלעזר בנו של ר' יוסי הגלילי אלף אמה מגרש ואלפים שדות וכרמים ואמרו בגמרא במאי

קמ"ל מיתיבי [א] איזהו [א] שגגת שבועת ביטוי לשעבר שאם אמר יודע אני ששבועה זו אסורה אבל איני יודע אם חייבין עליה קרבן או לא חייב הא מני מונבז היא (לישנא אחרינא מני אילימא מונבז פשיטא השתא בכל התורה דלאו חידוש הוא אמר (א) שגגת קרבן שמה שגגה הכא דחידוש הוא לא כ"ש אלא לאו רבנן היא ותיובתא דאביי תיובתא): ואמר אביי הכל מודים בתרומה שאין חייבין עליה חומש עד שישגוג בלאו שבה הכל מודים מאן רבי יוחנן פשיטא כי אמר רבי יוחנן היכא דאיכא כרת היכא דליכא כרת לא מהו דתימא מיתה במקום כרת עומדת וכי שגג במיתה נמי ליחייב קמ"ל רבא אמר [ב] מיתה במקום כרת עומדת וחומש במקום קרבן קאי: אמר רב הונא [ג] היה מהלך [ג] (בדרך או) במדבר ואינו יודע אימתי שבת מונה ששה ימים ומשמר יום אחד חייא בר רב אומר משמר יום אחד ומונה ששה במאי קמיפלגי מר סבר כברייתו של עולם ומר סבר כאדם הראשון מיתיבי היה מהלך בדרך ואינו יודע אימתי שבת משמר יום אחד לששה מאי לאו מונה ששה ומשמר יום אחד לא משמר יום אחד ומונה ששה אי הכי משמר יום אחד לששה משמר יום אחד ומונה ששה מיבעי ליה ועוד תניא היה מהלך בדרך או במדבר ואינו יודע אימתי שבת מונה ששה ומשמר יום אחד תיובתא [ג] (דר' חייא) בר רב תיובתא אמר רבא בכל יום ויום עושה לו כדי פרנסתו [בר מההוא יומא] וההוא יומא לימות [ד] דעביד מאתמול שתי פרנסות ודילמא מאתמול שבת הואי אלא [ד] כל יום ויום עושה לו פרנסתו אפילו ההוא יומא וההוא יומא במאי מינכר ליה בקידושא ואבדלתא אמר רבא [ה] אם היה מכיר [ה] מקצת היום שיצא בו עושה מלאכה כל היום כולו פשיטא מהו דתימא כיון דשבת לא נפיק במעלי שבתא [נמי] לא נפיק והאי אי נמי בחמשה בשבתא נפיק לישתרי ליה למיעבד מלאכה תרי יומי קא משמע לן זימנין דמשכח שיירתא ומקרי ונפיק: היודע עיקר שבת: מנהני מילי אמר רב נחמן אמר רבה בר אבוה תרי קראי כתיבי א) ושמרו בני ישראל את השבת וכתי' ב) ואת שבתותי תשמורו הא כיצד ושמרו בני ישראל את השבת שמירה אחת לשבתות הרבה ואת שבתותי תשמורו שמירה אחת לכל שבת ושבת מתקיף לה רב נחמן בר יצחק אדרבה איפכא מסתברא ושמרו בני ישראל את השבת שמירה אחת לכל שבת ושבת ואת שבתותי תשמורו שמירה אחת לשבתות הרבה: היודע שהוא שבת:

מאי

קמ"ל. אביי דמודה רבי יוחנן בה דבעינן שגגת לאו דאי הזיד בלאו תו ליכא שגגה דבהא נמי פליגי רבנן אמונבז ואמרי דאין שגגת קרבן שגגה: איזהו שבועת ביטוי לשעבר. בשלמא להבא כגון שלא אוכל משכחת לה כגון שנתעלמה השבועה ואכל אלא לשעבר כגון שאכלתי והוא לא אכל אין כאן שוגג דאי כסבור שאכל בשעה שנשבע אינו חייב קרבן דתניא בשבועות (פ"ג דף כו.) האדם בשבועה פרט לאנוס כלומר האדם בשבועה שיהא אדם בשעת שבועה שתהא דעתו עליו בשעת שבועה ופרשינן לה התם לאפוקי כי האי גוונא ומהשתא לא משכחת שגגה אלא בקרבן: אמר יודע אני שאני נשבע לשקר. ומוזהרתי על כך: אבל איני יודע כו'. דאי בנתעלמה ממנו אזהרת שבועה אין לך אונס בשעת שבועה כזה: חייב. אלמא מודו ביה רבנן דמיחייב אשגגת קרבן: הא מני מונבז היא. דאמר נמי בעלמא שמה שגגה אבל לרבנן דפליגי עליה לית להו ביטוי לשעבר דסברי כר' ישמעאל דאמר בשבועות אינו חייב אלא על העתיד לבא (שם דף כה.). יש גורסין הא מני (ב) מונבז פשיטא השתא בכל התורה אמר מונבז שגגת קרבן שמה שגגה הכא דחידוש הוא לא כ"ש אלא לאו רבנן תיובתא דאביי תיובתא ולא נהירא לי דמאי פשיטותא הא איצטריך לאשמעינן דחלוקה שגגה זו משאר שגגות דאילו בכל התורה למונבז בין ששגג בקרבן בין ששגג בלאו וכרת שמה שגגה וכאן בלשעבר אם שגג בלאו שבה לאו שגגה היא דכתיב האדם בשבועה: הכל מודים בתרומה. זר שאכל תרומה בשוגג משלם חומש על שגגתו דכתיב (ויקרא כב) ואיש כי יאכל קדש בשגגה אבל מזיד אין מוסיף חומש וחייב מיתה בידי שמים דכתיב (שם) ומתו בו כי יחללוהו וסמיך ליה וכל זר לא יאכל קדש: בלאו שבה. כסבור חולין ואין כאן לאו: מיתה. דכתיב בתרומה: במקום כרת. דשאר עבירות: וחומש. דשגגת תרומה במקום קרבן דשגגת שאר עבירות ולרבי יוחנן מיחייב חומש אשגגת מיתה: מונה ו'. מיום שטעה אל לבו שכחתו ומשמר השביעי: משמר יום אחד ומונה ו'. וכל יום שטעה אל לבו אינו משמר דשמא עשה מלאכה אבל יום המחרת משמר ולקמן מפרש דבהנך דאינו משמר לא עביד נמי מלאכה אלא כדי פרנסת היום: כברייתו של עולם. ימי חול נמנו תחלה: כאדם הראשון. שנברא בע"ש ויום ראשון למנינו שבת היה: יום אחד לששה. משמע לו' שעברו: וההוא יומא לימות. בתמיה: ודלמא אתמול שבת הוה. ונמצא מחלל שבת שלא לפקוח נפש: בקדושתא ואבדלתא. לזכרון בעלמא שיהא לו שם יום חלוק משאר ימים ולא תשתכח שבת ממנו: אם היה מכיר מקצת יום שיצא בו. לא שזכר איזה יום בשבת היה אלא זכור שהיום יום שלישי ליציאתו או רביעי ליציאתו ומתוך כך ידע שמונה ליציאתו עושה מלאכה כל יום ח' וכן לעולם ודאי זהו יום שיצא בו וקים ליה דבשבת לא יצא שהרי בישוב לא שכח את השבת: במעלי שבתא נמי לא נפיק. דאין דרך לצאת מפני כבוד השבת ועל כן כל יום ח' וט' ליציאתו לישתרו דליכא לספוקינהו בשבת: מנא הני מילי. שיש מחלל בשבתות הרבה וחייב אחת על כולן ויש מחללן וחייב על כל שבת: הכי גרסינן הא כיצד ושמרו בני ישראל את השבת שמירה אחת לשבתות הרבה ואת שבתותי תשמורו שמירה לכל שבת ושבת. דקרא קמא חדא שבת הוא דחשיב משמע שאינו מקפיד אלא על האחת והכא כתיב את שבתותי אכולהו קפיד ולא מסרן אלא לחכמים להודיען מסברא האי בשכח עיקר שבת דחדא שגגה היא והאי בשוכח שהיום שבת אבל יודע עיקר שבת דליכא למימר ימים שבינתים [הוין] ידיעה לחלק: איפכא מסתברא. ושמרו בני ישראל את השבת משמע שמירה אחת לשבת אחת ואת שבתותי תשמורו ב' שבתות ואינו מזהיר אלא על שמירה אחת ובין רב נחמן ובין רב נחמן בר יצחק לא פליגי אלא במשמעותא מאי דיליף מר מהאי קרא יליף מר מאידך:

מאי

הא מני מונבז היא. פירש בקונטרס אבל לרבנן דפליגי אמונבז לא אשכחן שגגת שבועת ביטוי לשעבר וסברי כרבי ישמעאל דאמר בשבועות דאינו חייב אלא על העתיד לבא והקשה ה"ר אליעזר לרבינו שמואל דהא רבנן דמונבז רבי עקיבא ור"ע מחייב בהדיא על לשעבר בשבועות [ו] [פ"ג וכלשון אחר שפי' בקונטרס מוכח בשבועות] בפ"ג (דף כו:) דאמר בעא מיניה רבא מרב נחמן איזהו שגגת ביטוי לשעבר אמר ליה כגון דאמר יודע אני ששבועה זו אסורה אבל איני יודע אם חייבין עליה קרבן אם לאו ופריך ליה כמאן כמונבז ומשני אפילו תימא רבנן אע"ג דבכל התורה כולה לית להו שגגה בקרבן כו' ומה שהקשה בקונטרס מאי פשיטא הא קמ"ל אף על גב דבעלמא (ג) הוי שגגה הכא לאו שגגה היא משום דהאדם בשבועה בעינן לאו פירכא היא דאי משום הא איצטריך ליתני בהדיא האדם בשבועה פרט לאנוס אלא משמע דשגגת קרבן אתא לאשמעינן שמה שגגה ומיהו קשה דבלאו הך ברייתא הוה מצי למיפרך לאביי ממתניתין דשבועות דמחייב ר"ע שבועת ביטוי לשעבר ולא משכחת לה אלא אם כן הזיד בלאו על כן נראה כפירוש רבינו שמואל שהשיב (ד) לרבנן דשגגת קרבן לאו שמה שגגה משכחת שגגת שבועת ביטוי לשעבר כגון שיודע ששבועה זו אסורה אבל אינו יודע שיש בה לאו אבל סבור שיש בה איסור עשה והשיב שפיר האדם בשבועה בענין זה וכן מוכח בשבועות (שם) דמהאדם בשבועה לא ממעט אלא כסבור בשעת שבועה שבאמת נשבע כגון תלמידי דרב דמר משתבע דהכי אמר רב כו' הלכך הא מני מונבז הוא דלרבנן הוה ליה למיתני ואינו יודע אם חייבין עליה לאו וההוא דשבועות דבעא מיניה רבא מרב נחמן פליגא אדאביי: עושה כדי פרנסתו. אבל להלך יכול כל מה שירצה רק ביום שמשמר דאי לאו הכי לא יגיע לעולם לישוב והא דקאמר במאי מינכר משום דאין זה היכר שבת במה שיושב ואינו הולך אי נמי אפי' ביום שמשמר הולך כמו שרוצה והשתא לא מינכר אלא בקידושא. הרב פור"ת:

אם

ח א מיי' פ"ג מהלכות שבועות הלכה ז:

ט ב מיי' פ"י מהלכות תרומות הלכה א:

י ג ד מיי' פ"ב מהלכות שבת הלכה כב טוש"ע א"ח סי' שדמ סעיף א:

יא ה מיי' שם טוש"ע שם סעיף ב:

רבינו חננאל

דבר שזדונו חייב כרת בשגגתו חייב חטאת זולתי המביאין על הזדון כשגגה ומותבינן עליה דר' יוחנן איזהו שבועת ביטוי לשעבר אמר אני יודע ששבועה זו אסורה אבל איני יודע אם חייבין עליה קרבן אם לאו חייב ודחי ר' יוחנן הא למונבז היא ואנא דאמרי כרבנן מיהא שמעינן דרבי יוחנן פליג עליה דמונבז בהא תו אמר אביי הכל מודים והוא ר' יוחנן בזר שאכל תרומה שאין חייבין עליה חומש עד שישגוג [בלאו] שבה מ"ט כיון דתרומה יש בה מיתה שנאמר ומתו בו כי יחללוהו אבל כרת לית בה עד שישגוג בלאו שבה דקיי"ל שגגת דכרת הויא שגגה וכל מאן דלית ליה כרת בעינן שגגה בלאו שבה ואע"ג דתרומה עון מיתה היא שגגת דמיתה אינה חשובה כשגגה דכרת אלא בעינן שגגה בלאו שבה ודחה רבא להא דאביי ואמר לעולם מיתה במקום כרת עומדת וכשם שבשאר מצות אם שגג בכרת אע"פ שהזיד בלאו לר' יוחנן מביא קרבן הכי נמי לענין תרומה אם שגג במיתה אע"פ שהזיד בלאו מוסיף חומש שחומש במקום קרבן הוא וקיי"ל כרבא. וקמייתא נמי דאמר אביי בשבועת ביטוי עד שישגוג בלאו שבה אבל שגגת קרבן לאו שמה שגגה לרבנן [אוקמינה] להא מתניתא בשבועות פר' ב' אפילו תימא רבנן בשגגת קרבן בשבועת ביטוי מחייבי דעד כאן לא פליגי רבנן עליה דמונבז אלא בעלמא אבל בשבועת ביטוי דהוא חידוש דלא אשכחן מזיד קאי בלאו בשוגג מייתי קרבן והכא בשבועת ביטוי מזיד קאי בלאו ושוגג מייתי קרבן שגגה דקרבן נמי הוא שגגה וחייב חטאת: הא דאמר רב הונא היה מהלך במדבר ואינו יודע מתי שבת כו' א) קיי"ל כרבא דאמר חושש בכל יום שמא היום שבת הוא ואעפ"כ עושה כדי פרנסתו בכל יום. ומונה ו' ימים ומשמר שביעי ואם אין לו מאין יתפרנס עושה גם בו ביום כדי פרנסתו ומינכר ליה בקידושא ובאבדלתא כלומר בו ביום מקדש ומבדיל לעשות היכר בין זה היום לשאר ששה ימים ואם מכיר סכום הימים שיצא כל יום שמיני מותר לעשות מלאכה כל היום (דלא מנפקא ליה) דודאי יום שבת לא יצא וכל יום שמיני ליציאתו הוא יום יציאתו. ואם ברי לו שלא יצא בע"ש עושה יום שמיני ויום תשיעי בלא ספק אבל אי לא ידע בבירור חיישינן דלמא אזדמן ליה שיירא ונפק בע"ש: היודע עיקר שבת ונעלם ממנו שהיום יום שבת הוא ועשה מלאכות הרבה בשבתות הרבה אינו חייב אלא חטאת אחת בכל שבת ושבת ושמעינן ליה מדכתיב ושמרתם את השבת וכתיב את שבתותי תשמורו ופשוטה היא לרבה בר אבוה כטעמיה. ולרב נחמן בר יצחק כטעמיה זה סובר [ושמרו ב"י את השבת שמירה אחת לשבתות הרבה כנגד השוכח עיקר שבת את שבתותי תשמורו שמירה לכל שבת ושבת כנגד היודע עיקר שבת וזה סובר] ושמרו בני ישראל את השבת שמירה לכל שבת ושבת כנגד היודע עיקר שבת את שבתותי תשמורו שמירה אחת לשבתות הרבה כנגד (היודע) [השוכח] עיקר שבת: היודע שהוא שבת והזיד בה ושגג במלאכות ועשה מלאכות הרבה בשבתות הרבה חייב על כל מלאכה ומלאכה ואקשינן מאי שנא בהיודע עיקר שבת דחייב על כל שבת ושבת וביודע שהיא שבת דחייב על כל מלאכה ומלאכה ופריק רב חסדא כאן מידיעת שבתות הוא פורש כו'. פי' היודע עיקר שבת ואינו יודע שהיום שבת הוא כיון שאמרו לו היום שבת היא מיד פורש נמצאת שגגתו על השבת לפי' אינו חייב אלא אחת על כל שבת ושבת אבל היודע שהיא שבת ושגג ועשה מלאכות הרבה וכיון שאומרים לו הלא מלאכה היא זו מיד פורש נמצאת שגגתו על המלאכות לפיכך חייב על כל מלאכה ומלאכה ודחה רב נחמן ואמר כלום פורש מן השבת אלא משום מלאכות כו' אלא אמר רב נחמן קרבן [דחייב רחמנא] אמאי אשגגה הוא השתא כיון

חשק שלמה על רבינו חננאל א) מן קיי"ל כרבא עד סוף הענין הובא בה"ג בשם רבינו:

מסורת הש"ס

א) שבועות כו: [ע"ש היטב], ב) [שתי תיבות הללו ליתא בהרי"ף והרא"ש והרמב"ם ובטור וש"ע], ג) [צ"ל דחייא], ד) ס"א לעביד, ה) נ"א סכום, ו) רש"ל ורש"א ומהר"ם וכ"ה בס".

הגהות הב"ח

(א) גמ' אמר מונבז שגגת קרבן: (ב) רש"י ד"ה הא מני וכו' יש גורס הא מני אילימא מונבז פשיטא השתא בכל התורה דלאו חידוש הוא אמר מונבז: (ג) תוס' ד"ה הא מני וכו' אע"ג דבעלמא שגגת לאו נמי הויא שגגה: (ד) בא"ד רבינו שמואל שהשיב להר"א דלרבנן דשגגת:

גליון הש"ס

גמ' רבא אמר מיתה במקום כרת. עי' בר"ש רפ"ו דתרומות:

תורה אור השלם

א) ושמרו בני ישראל את השבת לעשות את השבת לדרתם ברית עולם: [שמות לא, טז]

ב) איש אמו ואביו תיראו ואת שבתתי תשמרו אני יי אלהיכם: [ויקרא יט, ג]

ליקוטי רש"י

איזהו שגגת שבועת ביטוי לשעבר. כיון דבעינן אדם בשבועה היכי משכחת לה שוגג, אי דידע בשעת שבועה שהוא נשבע לשקר, מזיד הוא וקרא כתב ונעלם בשלמא להבא משכחת לה שבשעת שבועה דעתו מיושבת עליו ולאחר זמן נתעלמה ממנו שבועה [שבועות כו:]. ומקרי ונפיק. לשון ויקר מקרה (רות ב) [רשב"ם ב"ב ל:].

רב נסים גאון

במאי קמיפלגי מר סבר תחומין דאורייתא ומר סבר תחומין דרבנן: אמר אביי הכל מודים בתרומה שאין חייבין עליה חומש כו'. עיקר דבר זה הוא כתוב בתורה (ויקרא כב) ואיש כי יאכל קודש בשגגה ויסף חמישיתו עליו וכמו כן עוד חיוב המיתה הוא כתוב בתורה (שם) ומתו בו כי יחללוהו וכמה ששנינו במסכת ביכורים בפ' התרומה והביכורים חייבין עליהן מיתה וחומש ופי' אל ברייתא במסכת זבחים בפרק רבי אומר [בתוספתא דזבחים פ' י"ג] הפרש בין השוחט בפנים ובמסכת כריתות בפ' א' אלו שהן במיתה האוכל את הטבל והכהן טמא שאכל תרומה טהורה וזר שאכל את התרומה ומצאנו בתלמוד במס' סנהדרין (פג) בפ' אלו הן הנשרפין

הכא

חשק שלמה על רב נסים גאון

א) ופי' בברייתא.

קָא מַשְׁמַע לָן – [Abaye] therefore **informs us** that even in the case of a false oath R' Yochanan holds that inadvertence regarding the sacrifice is not sufficient to make someone liable to a sacrifice.[1]

The Gemara questions Abaye's statement:

מֵיתִיבֵי – **They challenged** this **from a Baraisa:** אֵיזֶהוּ שִׁגְגַת שְׁבוּעַת בִּיטּוּי לְשֶׁעָבַר – WHAT IS the case of AN INADVERTENT violation of an OATH OF UTTERANCE pertaining TO THE PAST?[2] שֶׁאִם אָמַר יוֹדֵעַ אֲנִי שֶׁשְּׁבוּעָה זוֹ אֲסוּרָה – THAT IF HE SAYS, when he knowingly swears falsely, "I KNOW THAT swearing THIS OATH IS PROHIBITED,[3] אֲבָל אֵינִי יוֹדֵעַ אִם חַיָּיבִין עָלֶיהָ קָרְבָּן אוֹ לֹא – BUT I DO NOT KNOW WHETHER OR NOT ONE IS LIABLE TO AN OFFERING ON ACCOUNT OF IT," חַיָּיב – HE IS LIABLE to an offering.[4] This contradicts Abaye's assertion. – ? –

The Gemara answers:

הָא מַנִּי – **Who is** the Tanna of **this** Baraisa? מוּנְבַּז הִיא – **It is Munbaz.**[5] The Baraisa therefore bears no relevance to R' Yochanan's explanation of the Rabbis' view.[6]

An alternative response to the question:[7]

לִישָּׁנָא אַחֲרִינָא – **Another version:** מַנִּי – **Who** does this Baraisa follow? אִילֵימָא מוּנְבַּז – **If you say Munbaz,** פְּשִׁיטָא – then **it is obvious** that one is liable to a sacrifice in this case and there is no necessity for the Baraisa to say so. הַשְׁתָּא בְּכָל הַתּוֹרָה דְּלָאו חִידּוּשׁ הוּא – For **now,** if **all through the Torah, where it** [the obligation to bring a sacrifice] **is not a novelty,** אָמַר שִׁגְגַת קָרְבָּן שְׁמָהּ שְׁגָגָה – **[Munbaz] says that inadvertence regarding a sacrifice is called inadvertence,** הָכָא דְּחִידּוּשׁ הוּא לֹא כָּל שֶׁכֵּן – then **here, where it is a novelty,**[8] **is it not certainly** considered inadvertence? אֶלָּא לָאו רַבָּנַן הִיא – **Rather, is it not** clear that **[the Baraisa] is** stating this according to **the Rabbis?**[9] וּתְיוּבְתָּא דְּאַבַּיֵי – **This** then **is a refutation of Abaye;** תְּיוּבְתָּא – **it is** indeed **a refutation.**[10]

The Gemara discusses another case of inadvertence:

וְאָמַר אַבַּיֵי – **And Abaye said:** הַכֹּל מוֹדִים בִּתְרוּמָה – **Everyone agrees in regard to** the transgression of a non-Kohen eating *terumah*[11] שֶׁאֵין חַיָּיבִין עָלֶיהָ חוֹמֶשׁ – **that one is not liable to** the **one-fifth** surcharge **for it** עַד שֶׁיִּשְׁגּוֹג בְּלָאו שֶׁבָּהּ – **unless he acted inadvertently with regard to its prohibition.**[12]

The Gemara analyzes Abaye's statement:

הַכֹּל מוֹדִים מַאן – **Who is** the one that Abaye meant to include by stating that **all agree?** רַבִּי יוֹחָנָן – **R' Yochanan,** who stated above that one can be considered to have acted inadvertently even if he was aware of the prohibition (but not of the *kares* penalty). Nevertheless, in the case of a non-Kohen eating *terumah* R'

NOTES

1. Therefore, if the sinner was aware [that he was violating] the prohibition against swearing falsely, he does not bring an offering for his transgression according to the Rabbis. Abaye teaches that the disagreement between Munbaz and the Rabbis concerning inadvertence with regard to the sacrifice extends to the law of שְׁבוּעַת בִּטּוּי, *oath of utterance,* as well (*Rashi*).

2. It is easy to find a case of an inadvertent violation of an oath of utterance pertaining to the future (e.g. "I will eat" or "will not eat"); namely, where the person subsequently forgot his oath and then violated it. It is difficult, however, to find a case of an inadvertent violation of an oath pertaining to the past (e.g. "I ate" or "I did not eat"), for if the person making the oath forgot that he had eaten and therefore swore that he had not eaten, he would *not* be liable to a sacrifice for his false oath, as taught by a Baraisa in *Shevuos* (26a). The Baraisa is based on the verse that states (*Leviticus* 5:4): אוֹ נֶפֶשׁ כִּי תִשָּׁבַע לְבַטֵּא בִשְׂפָתַיִם לְהָרַע אוֹ לְהֵיטִיב לְכֹל אֲשֶׁר יְבַטֵּא הָאָדָם בִּשְׁבֻעָה וְנֶעְלַם מִמֶּנּוּ, *Or if a person swears by uttering with [his] lips to do bad or to do good, anything that a person might utter in an oath, and it is concealed from him.* The Baraisa expounds the juxtaposition of the words הָאָדָם, *the person,* and בִּשְׁבֻעָה, *in an oath,* to teach that the oathtaker must be a "complete person in his oath," i.e. he must be fully aware of what he is doing at the time he makes the oath; if he is not (e.g. where he *thinks* he is swearing truthfully), he is not liable to a sacrifice for his false oath (*Rashi*).

3. *Rashi's* version of the Baraisa apparently read: יוֹדֵעַ אֲנִי שֶׁאֲנִי נִשְׁבָּע לַשֶּׁקֶר, *I know that I am swearing falsely,* and that it is prohibited to do so.

4. For in this case all the requirements for liability are met: Since he deliberately swore falsely, the oathtaker was a "complete person," aware of all the facts, at the time of his oath [and since he was unaware of the obligation to bring an offering, his transgression can be considered inadvertent]. Since the Baraisa states that one is indeed obligated to bring the sacrifice, we see that one is liable to a sacrifice for a false oath even when his inadvertence concerned only the sacrifice – contrary to Abaye's statement (*Rashi*).

5. Munbaz holds that inadvertence regarding the sacrifice suffices to obligate a *chatas* in all cases. This case of the false oath is therefore no different. But according to the Rabbis who dispute Munbaz's view and hold that inadvertence regarding the sacrifice does not ordinarily suffice for a *chatas* obligation, the person swearing falsely would not be liable to a *chatas* in this case either. Thus, according to those Rabbis, a person would never be obligated to bring a sacrifice for a false oath about a past event. In this they follow the view of R' Yishmael in *Shevuos* (25a), who holds that the verse about the oath of utterance refers only to oaths sworn about the future (*Rashi*), where it is possible for a person to violate his *earlier* oath by forgetting what he swore.

[*Tosafos* question this explanation on the grounds that the "Rabbis" who dispute Munbaz are R' Akiva (see Baraisa 68b), and R' Akiva is the very Tanna who disputes R' Yishmael and requires a sacrifice for a false oath concerning the past! *Tosafos* (see also *Baal HaMaor, Rashba* and *Ritva MHK* ed.) therefore reject this reading of the Gemara and favor the other reading found here (see below). See, however, *Ramban* who proposes a solution, and see *Maginei Shlomo, Pnei Yehoshua* and *Chasam Sofer* for other defenses of *Rashi.*]

6. [Abaye made his statement in regard to R' Yochanan, who was himself discussing the view of the Rabbis who dispute Munbaz and hold that inadvertence with regard to the sacrifice is not considered שׁוֹגֵג.]

7. [From *Rashi* and the other Rishonim it is clear that the Gemara itself does not give two versions of the answer; it is merely that there are two versions of what the correct reading of the Gemara's answer should be – both of which have found their way into the printed text.]

8. Because there is no *kares* penalty for deliberate violation (see above, 69a note 9).

9. [And the Rabbis hold that an oath of utterance is an exception to the general rule (because of its novelty) and in its case an inadvertency regarding the sacrifice suffices to make one liable to a sacrifice.]

10. *Rashi* writes that this "second version" cannot be an authentic part of the Gemara, because the statement that the teaching is "obvious" according to Munbaz and thus not in need of explication is not true. Even according to Munbaz the Baraisa needs to explain that the prohibition on swearing falsely differs from other prohibitions. For in the case of all other Torah laws, if a person acted inadvertently with regard to both the prohibition and sacrifice, he is liable to a *chatas*. In the case of a false oath, however, he has to have *some* awareness of the prohibition (i.e. oath), since if he does not, he would be exempt as derived from הָאָדָם בִּשְׁבֻעָה, a "complete person in the oath." See, however, *Tosafos, Ramban* and other Rishonim for a defense of this version of the Gemara.

11. If a non-Kohen eats *terumah* inadvertently, he is obligated to replace what he ate, add an additional fifth, and give it to a Kohen. However, if he eats *terumah* deliberately, he is liable to מִיתָה בִּידֵי שָׁמַיִם, *death at the hands of Heaven* [a Divine punishment somewhat less severe than *kares*] and is exempt from the one-fifth surcharge (*Rashi,* who gives the sources for these laws as *Leviticus* 22:9,14; see also *Terumos* 6:1 and 7:1).

[It should be noted that the "fifth" spoken of here is actually a חוֹמֶשׁ מִלְּבַר, *fifth from the outside,* i.e. a fifth of the principal plus penalty (see *Bava Metzia* 53b-54a). The surcharge is thus actually a fourth of the principal. For example, if the *terumah* eaten was worth 20 dinars, the person pays back the principal plus a 5-dinar surcharge. His total payment is thus 25 dinars, of which the 5-dinar surcharge represents a fifth.]

12. I.e. he ate the *terumah* thinking that it was *chullin,* which is not prohibited (*Rashi;* see *Chidushei HaRan; Maharsha, Maharam*). If, however, he is aware of the prohibition but is not aware of the Heavenly death penalty, he does not pay the one-fifth surcharge imposed on an inadvertent transgressor (see Gemara below).

קמ"ל מיתיבי א איזהו (א) שגגת שבועת ביטוי לשעבר שאם אמר יודע אני ששבועה זו אסורה אבל איני יודע אם חייבין עליה קרבן או לא חייב הא מני מונבז היא (לישנא אחרינא מני אילימא מונבז פשיטא השתא בכל התורה דלאו חידוש הוא אמר (א) שגגת קרבן שמה שגגה הכא דחידוש הוא לא כ"ש אלא לאו רבנן היא ותיובתא דאביי תיובתא): ואמר אביי הכל מודים בתרומה שאין חייבין עליה חומש עד שישגוג בלאו שבה הכל מודים מאן רבי יוחנן פשיטא כי אמר רבי יוחנן היכא דאיכא כרת היכא דליכא כרת לא מהו דתימא מיתה במקום כרת עומדת וכי שגג במיתה נמי ליחייב קמ"ל רבא אמר • ב מיתה במקום כרת עומדת וחומש במקום קרבן קאי: אמר רב הונא ג היה מהלך ד) (בדרך או) במדבר ואינו יודע אימתי שבת מונה ששה ימים ומשמר יום אחד חייא בר רב אומר משמר יום אחד ומונה ששה במאי קמיפלגי מר סבר כברייתו של עולם ומר סבר כאדם הראשון מיתיבי היה מהלך בדרך ואינו יודע אימתי שבת משמר יום אחד לששה מאי לאו מונה ששה ומשמר יום אחד לא משמר יום אחד ומונה ששה אי הכי משמר יום אחד לששה משמר יום אחד ומונה ששה מיבעי ליה ועוד תניא היה מהלך בדרך או במדבר ואינו יודע אימתי שבת מונה ששה ומשמר יום אחד תיובתא ה) (דר' חייא) בר רב תיובתא אמר רבא בכל יום ויום עושה לו כדי פרנסתו [בר מההוא יומא] וההוא יומא לימות ו) דעביד מאתמול שתי פרנסות ודילמא מאתמול שבת הואי אלא ד כל יום ויום עושה לו פרנסתו אפילו ההוא יומא וההוא יומא במאי מינכר ליה בקידושא ואבדלתא אמר רבא ה אם היה מכיר ו) מקצת היום שיצא בו עושה מלאכה כל היום כולו פשיטא מהו דתימא כיון דשבתא לא נפיק במעלי שבתא [נמי] לא נפיק והאי אי נמי בחמשה בשבתא נפיק לישתרי ליה למיעבד מלאכה תרי יומי קא משמע לן זימנין דמשכח שיירתא ומקרי ונפיק: היודע עיקר שבת: מנהני מילי אמר רב נחמן אמר רבה בר אבוה תרי קראי כתיבי א) ושמרו בני ישראל את השבת וכתי' ב) ואת שבתותי תשמורו הא כיצד ושמרו בני ישראל את השבת שמירה אחת לשבתות הרבה ואת שבתותי תשמורו שמירה אחת לכל שבת ושבת מתקיף לה רב נחמן בר יצחק אדרבה איפכא מסתברא ושמרו בני ישראל את השבת שמירה אחת לכל שבת ושבת ואת שבתותי תשמורו שמירה אחת לשבתות הרבה: היודע שהוא שבת: מאי

קמ"ל. אביי דמודה רבי יוחנן בה דבעינן שגגת לאו דאי הזיד בלאו תו ליכא שגגה דבהא נמי פליגי רבנן אמונבז ואמרי דאין שגגת קרבן שגגה: איזהו שבועת ביטוי לשעבר. בשלמא להבא כגון שלא אוכל משכחת לה כגון שנתעלמה השבועה ואכל אלא לשעבר כגון שאכלתי והוא לא אכל אין כאן שוגג דאי כסבור שאכל בשעה שנשבע אינו חייב קרבן דתניא בשבועות (פ"ג דף כו.) האדם בשבועה פרט לאנוס כלומר האדם בשבועה שיהא אדם בשעת שבועה שתהא דעתו עליו בשעת שבועה ופרשינן לה התם לאפוקי כי האי גוונא ומהשתא לא משכחת שגגה אלא בקרבן: אמר יודע אני שאני נשבע לשקר. ומוזהרתי על כך: אבל איני יודע כו'. דאי בנתעלמה ממנו אזהרת שבועה אין לך אונס בשעת שבועה כזה: חייב. אלמא מודו ביה רבנן דמיחייב אשגגת קרבן: הא מני מונבז היא. דאמר נמי בעלמא שמה שגגה אבל לרבנן דפליגי עליה לית להו ביטוי לשעבר דסברי כר' ישמעאל דאמר בשבועות אינו חייב אלא על העתיד לבא (שם דף כה.). יש גורסין הא מני (ב) מונבז פשיטא השתא בכל התורה אמר מונבז שגגת קרבן שמה שגגה הכא דחידוש הוא לא כ"ש אלא לאו רבנן תיובתא דאביי תיובתא ולא נהירא לי דמאי פשיטותא הא איצטריך לאשמעינן דחלוקה שגגה זו משאר שגגות דאילו בכל התורה למונבז בין ששגג בקרבן בין ששגג בלאו וכרת שמה שגגה וכאן בלשעבר אם שגג בלאו שבה לאו שגגה היא דכתיב האדם בשבועה: הכל מודים בתרומה. זר שאכל תרומה בשוגג משלם חומש על שגגתו דכתיב (ויקרא כב) ואיש כי יאכל קדש בשגגה אבל מזיד אין מוסיף חומש וחייב מיתה בידי שמים דכתיב (שם) ומתו בו כי יחללוהו וסמיך ליה וכל זר לא יאכל קדש: בלאו שבה. כסבור חולין ואין כאן לאו: מיתה. דכתיב בתרומה: במקום כרת. דשאר עבירות: וחומש. דשגגת תרומה במקום קרבן דשגגת שאר עבירות ולרבי יוחנן מיחייב חומש אשגגת מיתה: מונה ו'. מיום ששם אל לבו שכחתו ומשמר השביעי: משמר יום אחד ומונה ו'. וכל יום ששם אל לבו אינו משמר דשמא עשה מלאכה אבל יום המחרת משמר ולקמן מפרש דההוא דאינו משמר לא עביד נמי מלאכה אלא כדי פרנסת היום: כברייתו של עולם. ימי חול נמנו תחלה: כאדם הראשון. שנברא בע"ש ויום ראשון למנינו שבת היה: יום אחד לששה. משמע לו' שעברו: וההוא יומא לימות. בתמיה: ודלמא אתמול שבת הוה. ונמצא מחלל שבת שלא לפקוח נפש: בקידושא ואבדלתא. לזכרון בעלמא שיהא לו שם יום חלוק משאר ימים ולא תשתכח שבת ממנו: אם היה מכיר מקצת יום שיצא בו. לא שזכר איזה יום בשבת היה אלא זכור שהיום יום שלישי ליציאתו או רביעי ליציאתו ומתוך כך ידע שמונה ליציאתו עושה מלאכה כל יום ח' וכן לעולם ודאי זהו יום שיצא בו וקים ליה דבשבת לא יצא שהרי בישוב לא שכח את השבת: במעלי שבתא נמי לא נפיק. דאין דרך לצאת מפני כבוד השבת ועל כן כל יום ח' וט' ליציאתו ליתסרו דליכא לספוקינהו בשבת: מנא הני מילי. שיש מחלל בשבתות הרבה וחייב אחת על כולן ויש מחללן וחייב על כל שבת: הכי גרסינן הא כיצד ושמרו בני ישראל את השבת שמירה אחת לשבתות הרבה ואת שבתותי תשמורו שמירה לכל שבת ושבת. דקרא קמא חדא שבת הוא דכתיב משמע שאינו מקפיד אלא על האחת והכא כתיב את שבתותי אכולהו קפיד ולא מסרן אלא לחכמים להודיען מסברא האי בשכח עיקר שבת דחדא שגגה היא והאי בשוכח שהיום שבת אבל יודע עיקר שבת דאיכא למימר ימים שבינתים [הווין] ידיעה לחלק: איפכא מסתברא. ושמרו בני ישראל את השבת משמע שמירה אחת לשבת אחת ואת שבתותי תשמורו ב' שבתות ואינו מזהיר אלא על שמירה אחת ובין רב נחמן ובין רב נחמן בר יצחק לא פליגי אלא במשמעותא מאי דיליף מר מהאי קרא יליף מר מאידך: מאי

הא מני מונבז היא. פירש בקונטרס אבל לרבנן דפליגי אמונבז לא משכחן שגגת שבועת ביטוי לשעבר וסברי כרבי ישמעאל דאמר בשבועות דאינו חייב אלא על העתיד לבא והקשה ה"ר אליעזר לרבינו שמואל דהא רבנן דמונבז רבי עקיבא ור"ע מחייב בהדיא על לשעבר בשבועות י) [פ"ג וכלשון אחר שפי' בקונטרס מוכח בשבועות] בפ"ג (דף כו:) דאמר בעא מיניה רבא מרב נחמן איזהו שגגת ביטוי לשעבר אמר ליה כגון דאמר יודע אני ששבועה זו אסורה אבל איני יודע אם חייבין עליה קרבן אם לאו ופריך ליה כמאן כמונבז ומשני אפילו תימא רבנן אע"ג דבכל התורה כולה לית להו שגגה בקרבן כו' ומה שהקשה בקונטרס מאי פשיטא הא קמ"ל אף על גב דבעלמא (ג) הוי שגגה הכא לאו שגגה היא משום דהאדם בשבועה בעינן לאו פירכא היא דאי משום הא איצטריך ליתני בהדיא האדם בשבועה פרט לאנוס אלא משמע דשגגת קרבן אתא לאשמעינן שמה שגגה ומיהו קשה דבלאו הך ברייתא הוה מצי למיפרך לאביי ממתניתין דשבועות דמחייב ר"ע שבועת ביטוי לשעבר ולא משכחת לה אלא אם כן הזיד בלאו על כן נראה כפירוש רבינו שמואל שהשיב (ד) לרבנן דשגגת קרבן לאו שמה שגגה משכחת שגגת שבועת ביטוי לשעבר כגון שיודע ששבועה זו אסורה אבל אינו יודע שיש בה לאו אבל סבור שיש בה איסור עשה ותשיב שפיר האדם בשבועה בענין זה וכן מוכח בשבועות (שם) דמהאדם בשבועה לא ממעט אלא כסבור בשעת שבועה שבאמת נשבע כגון תלמידי דרב דמר משתבע דהכי אמר רב כו' הלכך הא מני מונבז הוא דלרבנן הוה ליה למיתני ואינו יודע אם חייבין עליה לאו וההוא דשבועות דבעא מיניה רבא מרב נחמן פליגא אדאביי: עושה כדי פרנסתו. אבל להלך יכול כל מה שירצה רק ביום שמשמר דאי לאו הכי לא יגיע לעולם לישוב והא דקאמר במאי מינכר משום דאין זה היכר שבת במה שיושב ואינו הולך אי נמי אפי' ביום שמשמר הולך כמו שרוצה והשתא לא מינכר אלא בקידושא. הרב פור"ת: אם

עין משפט
נר מצוה

ח א מיי' פ"ג מהלכות שבועות הלכה ז:
ט ב מיי' פ"י מהלכות תרומות הלכה א:
י ג ד מיי' פ"ב מהלכות שבת הלכה כב טוש"ע א"ח סי' שדמ סעיף א:
יא ה נמי' שם טוש"ע שם סעיף ב:

רבינו חננאל

דבר שזדונו חייב כרת בשגגתו חייב חטאת זולתי המביאין על הזדון כשגגה ומותבינן עליה דר' יוחנן איזהו שבועת ביטוי לשעבר אמר אני יודע ששבועה זו אסורה אבל איני יודע אם חייבין עליה קרבן אם לאו חייב ודחי ר' יוחנן הא למונבז היא ואנא דאמרי כרבנן מיהא שמעינן דרבי יוחנן פליג עליה דמונבז בהא תו אמר אביי הכל מודים והוא ר' יוחנן בזר שאכל תרומה שאין חייבין עליה חומש עד שישגוג [בלאו] שבה מ"ט כיון דתרומה יש בה מיתה שנאמר ומתו בו כי יחללוהו אבל כרת לית בה עד שישגוג בלאו שבה דקיי"ל שגגת דכרת הויא שגגה וכל מאן דלית ליה כרת בעינן שגגה בלאו שבה ואע"ג דתרומה עון מיתה היא שגגת דמיתה אינה חשובה כשגגה דכרת אלא בעינן שגגה בלאו שבה ודחה רבא להא דאביי ואמר לעולם מיתה במקום כרת עומדת וכשם שבשאר מצות אם שגג בכרת אע"פ שהזיד בלאו לר' יוחנן מביא קרבן הכי נמי לענין תרומה אם שגג במיתה אע"פ שהזיד בלאו מוסיף חומש שחומש במקום קרבן הוא וקיי"ל כרבא. וקמייתא נמי דאמר אביי בשבועת ביטוי עד שישגוג בלאו שבה אבל שגגת קרבן לאו שמה שגגה לרבנן [אוקמינה] להא מתניתא בשבועות פר' ב' אפילו תימא רבנן בשגגת קרבן בשבועת ביטוי מחייבי דעד כאן לא פליגי רבנן עליה דמונבז אלא בעלמא אבל בשבועת ביטוי דהוא חידוש דלא אשכחן מזיד קאי בלאו בשוגג מייתי קרבן והכא בשבועת ביטוי מזיד קאי בלאו ושוגג מייתי קרבן שגגה דקרבן נמי הוא שגגה וחייב חטאת: הא דאמר רב הונא היה מהלך במדבר ואינו יודע מתי שבת כו' א) קיי"ל כרבא דאמר חושש בכל יום שמא היום שבת הוא ואעפ"כ עושה כדי פרנסתו בכל יום. ומונה ו' ימים ומשמר שביעי ואם אין לו מאין יתפרנס עושה גם בו ביום כדי פרנסתו ומינכר ליה בקידושא ובאבדלתא כלומר בו ביום מקדש ומבדיל לעשות היכר בין זה היום לשאר ששה ימים ואם מכיר סכום הימים שיצא כל יום שמיני מותר לעשות מלאכה כל היום (דלא מנפקא ליה) דודאי יום שבת לא יצא וכל יום שמיני ליציאתו הוא יום יציאתו. ואם ברי לו שלא יצא בע"ש עושה יום שמיני ויום תשיעי בלא ספק אבל אי לא ידע בבירור חיישינן דלמא אזדמן ליה שיירא ונפק בע"ש: היודע עיקר שבת ונעלם ממנו שהיום יום שבת הוא ועשה מלאכות הרבה בשבתות הרבה אינו חייב אלא חטאת אחת בכל שבת ושבת ושמעינן ליה מדכתיב ושמרתם את השבת וכתיב את שבתותי תשמורו ופשוטה היא לרבה בר אבוה כטעמיה. ולרב נחמן בר יצחק כטעמיה זה סובר [ושמרו ב"י את השבת שמירה אחת לשבתות הרבה כנגד השוכח עיקר שבת את שבתותי תשמורו שמירה לכל שבת ושבת כנגד היודע עיקר שבת וזה סובר] ושמרו בני ישראל את השבת שמירה לכל שבת ושבת כנגד היודע עיקר שבת את שבתותי תשמורו שמירה אחת לשבתות הרבה כנגד (היודע) [השוכח] עיקר שבת: היודע שהוא שבת והזיד בה ושגג במלאכות ועשה מלאכות הרבה בשבתות הרבה חייב על כל מלאכה ומלאכה ואקשינן מאי שנא בהיודע עיקר שבת דחייב על כל שבת ושבת וביודע שהיא שבת דחייב על כל מלאכה ומלאכה ופריק רב חסדא כאן מידיעת שבתות הוא פורש כו'. פי' היודע עיקר שבת ואינו יודע שהיום שבת הוא כיון שאמרו לו היום שבת היא מיד פורש נמצאת שגגתו על השבת לפי' אינו חייב אלא אחת על כל שבת ושבת אבל היודע שהיא שבת ושגג ועשה מלאכות הרבה וכיון שאומרים לו הלא מלאכה היא זו מיד פורש נמצאת שגגתו על המלאכות לפיכך חייב על כל מלאכה ומלאכה ודחה רב נחמן ואמר כלום פורש מן השבת אלא משום מלאכות כו' אלא אמר רב נחמן קרבן [דחייב רחמנא] אמאי אשגגה הוא השתא כיון

חשק שלמה על רבינו חננאל א) מן קיי"ל כרבא עד סוף הענין הוגה כא"ז בשם רביט:

מסורת הש"ס

א) שבועות כו: [ע"ש היטב], ב) [שתי תיבות הללו ליתא בהרי"ף והרא"ש והרמב"ם ובטור וש"ע], ג) [נ"ל דחייא], ד) ס"א לעביד, ה) נ"א סכום, ו) רש"ל ורש"א ומהרש"ס וכ"ה בת"י.

הגהות הב"ח

(א) גמ' אמר מונבז שגגת קרבן: (ב) רש"י ד"ה הא מני וכו' יש גורס הא מני אילימא מונבז פשיטא השתא בכל התורה דלאו חידוש הוא אמר מונבז: (ג) תוס' ד"ה הא מני וכו' אע"ג דבעלמא שגגת לאו נמי הויא שגגה: (ד) בא"ד רבינו שמואל שהשיב להר"א דלרבנן דשגגת:

גליון הש"ס

גמ' רבא אמר מיתה במקום כרת. עי' בר"ש רפ"ו דתרומות:

תורה אור השלם

א) וְשָׁמְרוּ בְנֵי יִשְׂרָאֵל אֶת הַשַּׁבָּת לַעֲשׂוֹת אֶת הַשַּׁבָּת לְדֹרֹתָם בְּרִית עוֹלָם: [שמות לא, טז]

ב) אִישׁ אִמּוֹ וְאָבִיו תִּירָאוּ וְאֶת שַׁבְּתֹתַי תִּשְׁמֹרוּ אֲנִי יְיָ אֱלֹהֵיכֶם: [ויקרא יט, ג]

ליקוטי רש"י

איזהו שגגת שבועת ביטוי לשעבר. כיון דבעינן אדם בשבועה היכי משכחת לה שוגג, אי דידע בשעת שבועה שהוא נשבע לשקר, מזיד הוא וקרא כתב ונעלם בשלמא להבא משכחת לה שבשעת שבועה דעתו מיושבת עליו ולאחר זמן נתעלמה ממנו שבועה [שבועות כו:]. ומקרי ונפיק. לשון ויקר מקרה (רות ב) [רשב"ם ב"ב ל:].

רב נסים גאון

במאי קמיפלגי מר סבר תחומין דאורייתא ומר סבר תחומין דרבנן: אמר אביי הכל מודים בתרומה שאין חייבין עליה חומש כו'. עיקר דבר זה הוא כתוב בתורה (ויקרא כב) ואיש כי יאכל קודש בשגגה ויסף חמישיתו עליו וכמו כן עוד חיוב המיתה הוא כתוב בתורה (שם) ומתו בו כי יחללוהו וכמה ששנינו במסכת ביכורים בפ' התרומה והביכורים חייבין עליהן מיתה וחומש ופי אל א) בריתא במסכת זבחים בפרק רבי אומר [בתוספתא דזבחים פ' י"ג] הפרש בין השוחט בפנים ובמסכת כריתות בפ' א' אלו שהן במיתה האוכל את הטבל וכהן טמא שאכל תרומה טהורה וזר שאכל את התרומה ותמצאנו בתלמוד במס' סנהדרין (פג) בפ' אלו הן הנשרפין:
הכא

חשק שלמה על רב נסים גאון

א) ופי' בברייתא:

Yochanan agrees that to be liable to the surcharge, the non-Kohen must have acted inadvertently with regard to the prohibition itself. פְּשִׁיטָא – But **this is obvious!** כִּי אָמַר רַבִּי יוֹחָנָן הֵיכָא דְּאִיכָּא כָּרֵת – For **when did R' Yochanan say** that one is considered to have acted inadvertently even though he was aware of the prohibition? Only **where there is** a ***kares*** penalty of which he was not aware. הֵיכָא דְּלֵיכָּא כָּרֵת – But **where there is no *kares*** penalty, as is the case with *terumah,* לֹא – he would **not** say this. Thus, there is no need for Abaye to teach this! – ? –

The Gemara answers that Abaye's statement is needed for the following reason:

מַהוּ דְתֵימָא מִיתָה בִּמְקוֹם כָּרֵת עוֹמֶדֶת – **You might have said that death** at the hands of Heaven for eating *terumah* **stands in place of** the ***kares*** penalty in other violations, וְכִי שָׁגַג בְּמִיתָה נַמִּי לִיחַיֵּיב – **and** therefore, **when one acted inadvertently with regard to** the penalty of **death** at the hands of Heaven **he should also be liable** to the one-fifth surcharge.[13] קָא מַשְׁמַע לָן – [**Abaye**] therefore **informs us** that this is not so.[14]

The Gemara cites a dissenting opinion:

רָבָא אָמַר – **Rava said:** מִיתָה בִּמְקוֹם כָּרֵת עוֹמֶדֶת – **Death** at the hands of Heaven does **stand in the place of** the ***kares*** penalty, וְחוֹמֶשׁ בִּמְקוֹם קָרְבָּן קָאֵי – **and the one-fifth** surcharge for eating *terumah* **stands in place of the sacrifice** in other violations. Therefore, according to R' Yochanan, if a non-Kohen eats *terumah* unaware of the Heavenly death penalty, he is considered an inadvertent sinner and is liable to the one-fifth surcharge.[15]

The Gemara digresses to discuss another issue:[16]

אָמַר רַב הוּנָא – **Rav Huna said:** הָיָה מְהַלֵּךְ בַּדֶּרֶךְ אוֹ בַּמִּדְבָּר – **If someone was walking on the way or in the desert,** וְאֵינוֹ יוֹדֵעַ אֵימָתַי שַׁבָּת – **and he does not know when it is the Sabbath,** מוֹנֶה שִׁשָּׁה יָמִים וּמְשַׁמֵּר יוֹם אֶחָד – **he counts six days** from the day he realizes his unawareness[17] **and** then **observes one day** as the Sabbath. חִיָּיא בַּר רַב אוֹמֵר – **Chiya bar Rav says:** מְשַׁמֵּר יוֹם אֶחָד וּמוֹנֶה שִׁשָּׁה – **He** first **observes one day** as the Sabbath **and** then **counts six** days as weekdays.[18]

The Gemara explains the dispute:

בְּמַאי קָמִיפַּלְגֵי – **Regarding what** issue **do they disagree?** מַר סָבַר כִּבְרִיָּיתוֹ שֶׁל עוֹלָם – One **master** [Rav Huna] **holds** the person should count **like the creation of the world,** i.e., just as the Sabbath followed the six days of creation, so too does he observe the Sabbath after counting six weekdays. וּמַר סָבַר כְּאָדָם הָרִאשׁוֹן – **And** the other **master** [Chiya bar Rav] **holds** the person should count **like Adam, the first** man, i.e. just as Adam was created on Friday and the very next day was the Sabbath, so too this person observes the next day as the Sabbath.

The Gemara asks:

מֵיתִיבֵי – **They challenged** Chiya bar Rav from the following Baraisa: הָיָה מְהַלֵּךְ בַּדֶּרֶךְ – IF SOMEONE WAS WALKING ON THE WAY וְאֵינוֹ יוֹדֵעַ אֵימָתַי שַׁבָּת – AND HE DOES NOT KNOW WHEN IT IS THE SABBATH, מְשַׁמֵּר יוֹם אֶחָד לְשִׁשָּׁה – HE OBSERVES ONE DAY as Sabbath FOR every SIX days. מַאי לָאו – **Does this not** mean מוֹנֶה שִׁשָּׁה וּמְשַׁמֵּר יוֹם אֶחָד – **he** first **counts six days and** then **observes one day** as the Sabbath?[19]

The Gemara attempts to defend Chiya bar Rav:

לֹא – **No!** מְשַׁמֵּר יוֹם אֶחָד וּמוֹנֶה שִׁשָּׁה – **He** first **observes one day and** then **counts six.**

The Gemara objects:

אִי הָכִי – **If so,** מְשַׁמֵּר יוֹם אֶחָד לְשִׁשָּׁה – rather than state: **"He observes one day *for* every six,"** מְשַׁמֵּר יוֹם אֶחָד וּמוֹנֶה שִׁשָּׁה מִיבָּעֵי לֵיהּ – **it should have** said: **"He observes one day** as the Sabbath ***and counts*** **six."** וְעוֹד תַּנְיָא – **Furthermore, it was taught** explicitly **in a** second **Baraisa:** הָיָה מְהַלֵּךְ בַּדֶּרֶךְ אוֹ בַּמִּדְבָּר – IF SOMEONE WAS WALKING ON THE WAY OR IN THE DESERT, וְאֵינוֹ יוֹדֵעַ אֵימָתַי שַׁבָּת – AND HE DOES NOT KNOW WHEN IT IS THE SABBATH, מוֹנֶה שִׁשָּׁה וּמְשַׁמֵּר יוֹם אֶחָד – HE COUNTS SIX DAYS AND OBSERVES ONE DAY as the Sabbath. This clearly reflects the view of Rav Huna. – ? –

The Gemara concedes:

תְּיוּבְתָּא (דרבי חייא) [דְּחִיָּיא] בַּר רַב – **This is a refutation of Chiya bar Rav.**[20] תְּיוּבְתָּא – **It is** indeed **a refutation.**

The Gemara elaborates on this case:

אָמַר רָבָא – **Rava said:** בְּכָל יוֹם וָיוֹם עוֹשֶׂה לוֹ כְּדֵי פַּרְנָסָתוֹ – **On every day** of the six **he may work** only **enough for his sustenance,** i.e. enough to stay alive, [בַּר מֵהַהוּא יוֹמָא] – **except**

NOTES

13. [Although a non-Kohen eating *terumah* is not punishable by *kares,* he is subject to another Divine punishment – "death at the hands of Heaven" (see *Tosafos* to *Yevamos* 2a ד״ה אשת). We could therefore think that inadvertence regarding this form of Divine punishment is treated the same as inadvertence regarding *kares.* Therefore, just as a person is liable to a *chatas* when he acts inadvertently regarding *kares* even though he was aware of the prohibition and knowingly violated it, so too a person who acts inadvertently regarding "death at the hands of Heaven" should be liable to the one-fifth surcharge even though he was aware of the prohibition to eat *terumah* and knowingly violated it.]

14. [The reason that inadvertence with regard to *kares* is considered sufficient to render a person liable to a *chatas* is because the *chatas* obligation is specifically pegged to the *kares* penalty by the *hekeish* cited above (see 69a note 4); and it atones for that aspect of the transgression, as explained there. But we have no similar Scriptural source tying the one-fifth surcharge to the inadvertence regarding the Heavenly death penalty; all we know is that the Torah does not impose the surcharge on deliberate transgression. Thus, the surcharge may be simply for the inadvertent transgression of the *prohibition* and not for the inadvertent transgression of the *death penalty.* Therefore, Abaye maintains that it is not paid unless the person was inadvertent even with regard to the prohibition itself (see *Kehillos Yaakov* §29).]

15. *Rashi.* [From *Rashi* it seems that Rava adds that "the fifth stands in place of the sacrifice in other violations" to complete the correspondence between *terumah* and *kares*-bearing transgressions. I.e. just as the latter have three factors that relate to inadvertence – the prohibition, the *kares* penalty and the sacrifice for inadvertent transgression, so too *terumah* has three corresponding factors – the prohibition, the Heavenly death penalty and the one-fifth surcharge. This serves to establish a basis of comparison between the two laws and allows Rava to conclude that R' Yochanan would say the same in regard to Heavenly death as he does in regard to *kares. Ritva* (*MHK* ed.), however, states that Rava adds this to make the point that according to Munbaz one would be liable to the surcharge even if he knew of the Heavenly death penalty but failed to know the law requiring a one-fifth surcharge (see also *Sfas Emes* and *Melo HaRo'im*).]

16. [The Mishnah and Gemara discussed the rule for one who performs *melachah* as a result of having forgotten that it was the Sabbath day (שִׁגְגַת שַׁבָּת, *inadvertence with regard to the Sabbath*). In conjunction with this the Gemara now explains what one must do if he realizes that he has lost track of the days and is in an uninhabited region where he cannot possibly determine what day it is.] See *Magen Avraham* to *Orach Chaim* 344:1.

17. Including that day (*Bach, Orach Chaim* 344).

18. Here, he cannot observe the day he realized his predicament as the Sabbath, because he might have already performed *melachah* that day. He therefore observes the following day.

The Gemara will explain below what exactly is permitted on the six days [according to both views] (*Rashi*).

19. The wording of the Baraisa indicates that he counts one day for the six that already passed (*Rashi*).

20. Emendation follows *Mesoras HaShas.*

ח א מיי' פ"ג מהלכות שבועות הלכה ז:
ט ב מיי' פ"י מהלכות תרומות הלכה א:
י ג ד מיי' פ"ב מהלכות שבת הלכה כב טוש"ע א"ח סי' שדמ סעיף א:
יא ה מיי' שם טוש"ע שם סעיף ג:

רבינו חננאל

דבר שזדונו חייב כרת בשגגתו חייב חטאת זולתי המביאין על הזדון כשגגה ומותבינן עליה דר' יוחנן איזהו שבועת ביטוי לשעבר אמר אני יודע ששבועה זו אסורה אבל איני יודע אם חייבין עליה קרבן אם לאו חייב ודחי ר' יוחנן הא למונבז היא ואנא דאמרי כרבנן מיהא שמעינן דרבי יוחנן פליג עליה דמונבז בהא תו אמר אביי הכל מודים והוא ר' יוחנן בזר שאכל תרומה שאין חייבין עליה חומש עד שישגוג [בלאו] שבה מ"ט כיון דתרומה יש בה מיתה שנאמר ומתו בו כי יחללוהו אבל כרת לית בה עד שישגוג בלאו שבה דקיי"ל שגגת דכרת הויא שגגה וכל מאן דלית ליה כרת בעינן שגגה בלאו שבה ואע"ג דתרומה עון מיתה היא שגגת דמיתה אינה חשובה כשגגה דכרת אלא בעינן שגגה בלאו שבה ודחה רבא להא דאביי ואמר לעולם מיתה במקום כרת עומדת וכשם שבשאר מצות אם שגג בכרת אע"פ שהזיד בלאו לר' יוחנן מביא קרבן הכי נמי לענין תרומה אם שגג במיתה אע"פ שהזיד בלאו מוסיף חומש שחומש במקום קרבן הוא וקיי"ל כרבא. וקמייתא נמי דאמר אביי בשבועת ביטוי עד שישגוג בלאו שבה אבל שגגת קרבן לאו שמה שגגה לרבנן [אוקמינה] להא מתניתא בשבועות פר' ב' אפילו תימא רבנן בשגגת קרבן בשבועת ביטוי מחייבי דעד כאן לא פליגי רבנן עליה דמונבז אלא בעלמא אבל בשבועת ביטוי דהוא חידוש דלא אשכחן מזיד קאי בלאו בשוגג מייתי קרבן והכא בשבועת ביטוי מזיד קאי בלאו ושוגג מייתי קרבן שגגה דקרבן נמי הוא שגגה וחייב חטאת: **הא דאמר** רב הונא היה מהלך במדבר ואינו יודע מתי שבת כו' א) קיי"ל כרבא דאמר חושש בכל יום שמא היום שבת הוא ואעפ"כ עושה כדי פרנסתו בכל יום. ומונה ו' ימים ומשמר שביעי ואם אין לו מאין יתפרנס עושה גם בו ביום כדי פרנסתו ומינכר ליה בקידושא ובאבדלתא כלומר בו ביום מקדש ומבדיל לעשות היכר בין זה היום לשאר ששה ימים ואם מכיר סכום הימים שיצא כל יום שמיני מותר לעשות מלאכה כל היום (דלא מנפקא ליה) דודאי יום שבת לא יצא וכל יום שמיני ליציאתו הוא יום יציאתו. ואם ברי לו שלא יצא בע"ש עושה יום שמיני ויום תשיעי בלא ספק אבל אי לא ידע בבירור חיישינן דלמא אזדמן ליה שיירא ונפק בע"ש: **היודע** עיקר שבת ונעלם ממנו שהיום יום שבת הוא ועשה מלאכות הרבה בשבתות הרבה אינו חייב אלא חטאת אחת בכל שבת ושבת ושמעינן ליה מדכתיב ושמרתם את השבת וכתיב את שבתותי תשמורו ופשוטה היא לרבה בר אבוה כטעמיה. ולרב נחמן בר יצחק כטעמיה זה סובר [ושמרו ב"י את השבת שמירה אחת לשבתות הרבה כנגד השוכח עיקר שבת את שבתותי תשמורו שמירה לכל שבת ושבת כנגד היודע עיקר שבת וזה סובר] ושמרו בני ישראל את השבת שמירה לכל שבת ושבת כנגד היודע עיקר שבת את שבתותי תשמורו שמירה אחת לשבתות הרבה כנגד (היודע) [השוכח] עיקר שבת: היודע שהוא שבת והזיד בה ושגג במלאכות ועשה מלאכות הרבה בשבתות הרבה חייב על כל מלאכה ומלאכה ואקשינן מאי שנא בהיודע שהיא שבת דחייב על כל שבת ושבת וביודע שהיא שבת דחייב על כל מלאכה ומלאכה ופריק רב חסדא כאן מידיעת שבתות הוא פורש כו'. פי' היודע עיקר שבת ואינו יודע שהיום שבת הוא כיון שאמרו לו היום שבת היא מיד פורש נמצאת שגגתו על השבת לפי' אינו חייב אלא אחת על כל שבת ושבת אבל היודע שהיא שבת ושגג ועשה מלאכות הרבה וכיון שאומרים לו הלא מלאכה היא זו מיד פורש נמצאת שגגתו על המלאכות לפיכך חייב על כל מלאכה ומלאכה ודחה רב נחמן ואמר כלום פורש מן השבת אלא משום מלאכות כו' אלא אמר רב נחמן קרבן [דחייב רחמנא] אמאי אשגגה הוא השתא כיון

חשק שלמה על רבינו חננאל א) מן קיי"ל כרבא עד סוף הענין הובא בא"ז בשם רביט:

תוספות

הא מני מונבז היא. פירש בקונטרס אבל לרבנן דפליגי אמונבז לא אשכחן שגגת שבועת ביטוי לשעבר וסברי כרבי ישמעאל דאמר בשבועות דאינו חייב אלא על העתיד לבא והקשה ה"ר אליעזר לרבינו שמואל דהא רבנן דמונבז רבי עקיבא ור"ע מחייב בהדיא על לשעבר בשבועות ו) [פ"ג וכלשון אחר שפי' בקונטרס מוכח בשבועות] בפ"ג (דף כו:) דאמר בעא מיניה רבא מרב נחמן איזהו שגגת ביטוי לשעבר אמר ליה כגון דאמר יודע אני ששבועה זו אסורה אבל איני יודע אם חייבין עליה קרבן אם לאו ופריך ליה כמאן כמונבז ומשני אפילו תימא רבנן אע"ג דבכל התורה כולה לית להו שגגה בקרבן כו' ומה שהקשה בקונטרס מאי פשיטא הא קמ"ל אף על גב דבעלמא (ג) הוי שגגה הכא לאו שגגה היא משום דהאדם בשבועה בעינן לאו פירכא היא דאי משום הא איצטריך ליתני בהדיא האדם בשבועה פרט לאנוס אלא משמע דשגגת קרבן אתא לאשמעינן שמה שגגה ומיהו קשה דבלאו הך ברייתא הוה מצי למיפרך לאביי ממתניתין דשבועות דמחייב ר"ע שבועת ביטוי לשעבר ולא משכחת לה אלא אם כן הזיד בלאו על כן נראה כפירוש רבינו שמואל שהשיב (ד) לרבנן דשגגת קרבן לאו שמה שגגה משכחת שגגת שבועת ביטוי לשעבר כגון שיודע ששבועה זו אסורה אבל אינו יודע שיש בה לאו אבל סבור שיש בה איסור עשה וחשיב שפיר האדם בשבועה בענין זה וכן מוכח בשבועות (שם) דמהאדם בשבועה לא ממעט אלא כסבור בשעת שבועה שבאמת נשבע כגון תלמידי דרב דמר משתבע דהכי אמר רב כו' הלכך הא מני מונבז הוא דלרבנן הוה ליה למיתני ואינו יודע אם חייבין עליה לאו וההוא דשבועות דבעא מיניה רבא מרב נחמן פליגא אדאביי: **עושה** כדי פרנסתו. אבל להלך יכול כל מה שירצה רק ביום שמשמר דאי לאו הכי לא יגיע לעולם לישוב והא דקאמר במאי מינכר משום דאין זה היכר שבת במה שיושב ואינו הולך אי נמי אפי' ביום שמשמר הולך כמו שרוצה והשתא לא מינכר אלא בקידושא. הרב פור"ת: אם

גמרא

קמ"ל מיתיבי א איזהו א) שגגת שבועת ביטוי לשעבר שאם אמר יודע אני ששבועה זו אסורה אבל איני יודע אם חייבין עליה קרבן או לא חייב הא מני מונבז היא (לישנא אחרינא מני אילימא מונבז פשיטא השתא בכל התורה דלאו חידוש הוא אמר (א) שגגת קרבן שמה שגגה הכא דחידוש הוא לא כ"ש אלא לאו רבנן היא ותיובתא דאביי תיובתא): ואמר אביי הכל מודים בתרומה שאין חייבין עליה חומש עד שישגוג בלאו שבה הכל מודים מאן רבי יוחנן פשיטא כי אמר רבי יוחנן היכא דאיכא כרת היכא דליכא כרת לא מהו דתימא מיתה במקום כרת עומדת וכי שגג במיתה נמי ליחייב קמ"ל רבא אמר ב מיתה במקום כרת עומדת וחומש במקום קרבן קאי: אמר רב הונא ג היה מהלך ג) (בדרך או) במדבר ואינו יודע אימתי שבת מונה ששה ימים ומשמר יום אחד חייא בר רב אומר משמר יום אחד ומונה ששה במאי קמיפלגי מר סבר כברייתו של עולם ומר סבר כאדם הראשון מיתיבי היה מהלך בדרך ואינו יודע אימתי שבת משמר יום אחד לששה מאי לאו מונה ששה ומשמר יום אחד לא משמר יום אחד ומונה ששה אי הכי משמר יום אחד לששה משמר יום אחד ומונה ששה מיבעי ליה ועוד תניא היה מהלך בדרך או במדבר ואינו יודע אימתי שבת מונה ששה ומשמר יום אחד תיובתא ג) (דר' חייא) בר רב תיובתא אמר רבא בכל יום ויום עושה לו כדי פרנסתו [בר מההוא יומא] וההוא יומא לימות ד) דעביד מאתמול שתי פרנסות ודילמא מאתמול שבת הואי אלא ד כל יום ויום עושה לו פרנסתו אפילו ההוא יומא וההוא יומא במאי מינכר ליה בקידושא ואבדלתא אמר רבא ה אם היה מכיר ה) מקצת היום שיצא בו עושה מלאכה כל היום כולו פשיטא מהו דתימא כיון דשבת לא נפיק במעלי שבתא [נמי] לא נפיק והאי אי נמי בחמשה בשבתא נפיק לישתרי ליה למיעבד מלאכה תרי יומי קא משמע לן זימנין דמשכח שיירתא ומקרי ונפיק: היודע עיקר שבת: מנהני מילי אמר רב נחמן אמר רבה בר אבוה תרי קראי כתיבי א) ושמרו בני ישראל את השבת וכתי' ב) ואת שבתותי תשמורו הא כיצד ושמרו בני ישראל את השבת שמירה אחת לשבתות הרבה ואת שבתותי תשמורו שמירה אחת לכל שבת ושבת מתקיף לה רב נחמן בר יצחק אדרבה איפכא מסתברא ושמרו בני ישראל את השבת שמירה אחת לכל שבת ושבת ואת שבתותי תשמורו שמירה אחת לשבתות הרבה: היודע שהוא שבת: מאי

רש"י

קמ"ל. אביי דמודה רבי יוחנן בה דבעינן שגגת לאו דאי הזיד בלאו תו ליכא שגגה דבהא נמי פליגי רבנן אמונבז ואמרי דאין שגגת קרבן שגגה: **איזהו שבועת ביטוי לשעבר.** בשלמא להבא כגון שלא אוכל משכחת לה כגון שנתעלמה השבועה ואכל אלא לשעבר כגון שאכלתי והוא לא אכל אין כאן שוגג דאי כסבור שאכל בשעה שנשבע אינו חייב קרבן דתניא בשבועות (פ"ג דף כו.) האדם בשבועה פרט לאנוס כלומר האדם בשבועה שיהא אדם בשעת שבועה שתהא דעתו עליו בשעת שבועה ופרשינן לה התם לאפוקי כי האי גוונא ומהשתא לא משכחת שגגה אלא בקרבן: **אמר יודע אני שאני נשבע לשקר.** ומוזהרתי על כך: **אבל איני יודע כו'.** דאי בנתעלמה ממנו אזהרת שבועה אין לך אונס בשעת שבועה כזה: **חייב.** אלמא מודו ביה רבנן דמיחייב אשגגת קרבן: **הא מני מונבז היא.** דאמר נמי בעלמא שמה שגגה אבל לרבנן דפליגי עליה לית להו ביטוי לשעבר דסברי כר' ישמעאל דאמר בשבועות אינו חייב אלא על העתיד לבא (שם דף כה.). יש גורסין הא מני (ב) מונבז פשיטא השתא בכל התורה אמר מונבז שגגת קרבן שמה שגגה הכא דחידוש הוא לא כ"ש אלא לאו רבנן תיובתא דאביי תיובתא ולא נהירא לי דמאי פשיטותא הא איצטריך לאשמעינן דחלוקה שגגה זו משאר שגגות דאילו בכל התורה למונבז בין ששגג בקרבן בין ששגג בלאו וכרת שמה שגגה וכאן בלשעבר אם שגג בלאו שבה לאו שגגה היא דכתיב האדם בשבועה: **הכל מודים בתרומה.** זר שאכל תרומה בשוגג משלם חומש על שגגתו דכתיב (ויקרא כב) ואיש כי יאכל קדש בשגגה אבל מזיד אין מוסיף חומש וחייב מיתה בידי שמים דכתיב (שם) ומתו בו כי יחללוהו וסמיך ליה וכל זר לא יאכל קדש: **בלאו שבה.** כסבור חולין ואין כאן לאו: **מיתה.** דכתיב בתרומה: **במקום כרת.** דשאר עבירות: **וחומש.** דשגגת תרומה במקום קרבן דשגגת שאר עבירות ולרבי יוחנן מחייב חומש אשגגת מיתה: **מונה ו'.** מיום שמסך אל לבו שכחתו ומשמר השביעי: **משמר יום אחד ומונה ו'.** וכל יום שמסך אל לבו אינו משמר דשמא עשה מלאכה אבל יום המחרת משמר ולקמן מפרש דההך דאינו משמר לא עביד נמי מלאכה אלא כדי פרנסת היום: **כברייתו של עולם.** ימי חול נמנו תחלה: **כאדם הראשון.** שנברא בע"ש ויום ראשון למנינו שבת היה: **יום אחד לששה.** משמע לו' שעברו: **וההוא יומא לימות.** בתמיה: **ודלמא אתמול שבת הוה.** ונמצא מחלל שבת שלא לפקוח נפש: **בקדושתא ואבדלתא.** לזכרון בעלמא שיהא לו שם יום חלוק משאר ימים ולא תשתכח שבת ממנו: **אם היה מכיר מקצת יום שיצא בו.** לא שזוכר איזה יום בשבת היה אלא זכור שהיום יום שלישי ליציאתו או רביעי ליציאתו ומתוך כך ידע שמונה ליציאתו עושה מלאכה כל יום ח' וכן לעולם ודאי זהו יום שיצא בו וקים ליה דבשבת לא יצא שהרי בישוב לא שכח את השבת: **במעלי שבתא נמי לא נפיק.** דאין דרך לצאת מפני כבוד השבת ועל כן כל יום ח' וט' ליציאתו לישתרו דליכא לספוקינהו בשבת: **מנא הני מילי.** שיש מחלל בשבתות הרבה וחייב אחת על כולן ויש מחללן וחייב על כל שבת: **הכי גרסינן הא כיצד ושמרו בני ישראל את השבת שמירה אחת לשבתות הרבה ואת שבתותי תשמורו שמירה לכל שבת ושבת.** דקרא קמא חדא שבת הוא דחשיב משמע שאינו מקפיד אלא על האחת והכא כתיב את שבתותי אכולהו קפיד ולא מסרן אלא לחכמים להודיען מסברא האי בשכח עיקר שבת דחדא שגגה היא והאי בשוכח שהיום שבת אבל יודע עיקר שבת דאיכא למימר ימים שבינתים [הווין] ידיעה לחלק: **איפכא מסתברא.** ושמרו בני ישראל את השבת משמע שמירה אחת לשבת אחת ואת שבתותי תשמורו ב' שבתות ואינו מזהיר אלא על שמירה אחת ובין רב נחמן ובין רב נחמן בר יצחק לא פליגי אלא במשמעותא מאי דיליף מר מהאי קרא יליף מר מאידך: מאי

מסורת הש"ס

א) שבועות כו: [ע"ש היטב], ב) [שתי תיבות הללו ליתא בהרי"ף והרא"ש והרמב"ם ובטור וש"ע], ג) [נ"ל דחייא], ד) ס"א לעביד, ה) נ"א סכום, ו) רש"ל ורש"א ומהר"ם וכ"ה בח"י.

הגהות הב"ח

(א) גמ' אמר מונבז שגגת קרבן: (ב) רש"י ד"ה הא מני וכו' יש גורס הא מני אילימא מונבז פשיטא השתא בכל התורה דלאו חידוש הוא אמר מונבז: (ג) תוס' ד"ה הא מני וכו' אע"ג דבעלמא שגגת לאו נמי הויא שגגה: (ד) בא"ד רבינו שמואל שהשיב להר"א דלרבנן דשגגת:

גליון הש"ס

גמ' רבא אמר מיתה במקום כרת. עי' בר"ש רפ"ו דתרומות:

תורה אור השלם

א) וְשָׁמְרוּ בְנֵי יִשְׂרָאֵל אֶת הַשַּׁבָּת לַעֲשׂוֹת אֶת הַשַּׁבָּת לְדֹרֹתָם בְּרִית עוֹלָם: [שמות לא, טז]

ב) אִישׁ אִמּוֹ וְאָבִיו תִּירָאוּ וְאֶת שַׁבְּתֹתַי תִּשְׁמֹרוּ אֲנִי יְיָ אֱלֹהֵיכֶם: [ויקרא יט, ג]

ליקוטי רש"י

איזהו שגגת שבועת ביטוי לשעבר. כיון דבעינן אדם בשבועה היכי משכחת לה שוגג, אי דידע בשעת שבועה שהוא נשבע לשקר, מזיד הוא וקרא כתב ונעלם בשלמא להבא משכחת לה שבשעת שבועה דעתו מיושבת עליו ולאחר זמן נתעלמה ממנו שבועה [שבועות כו:]. **ומקרי ונפיק.** לשון ויקר מקרה (רות ב) [רשב"ם ב"ב ל:].

רב נסים גאון

במאי קמיפלגי מר סבר תחומין דאורייתא ומר סבר תחומין דרבנן: **אמר** אביי הכל מודים בתרומה שאין חייבין עליה חומש כו'. עיקר דבר זה הוא כתוב בתורה (ויקרא כב) ואיש כי יאכל קודש בשגגה ויסף חמישיתו עליו וכמו כן עוד חיוב המיתה הוא כתוב בתורה (שם) ומתו בו כי יחללוהו וכמה ששנינו במסכת ביכורים בפ' התרומה והביכורים חייבין עליהן מיתה וחומש ופי' אל א) בריתא במסכת זבחים בפרק רבי אומר [בתוספתא דזבחים פ' י"ג] הפרש בין השוחט בפנים ובמסכת כריתות בפ' א' אלו שהן במיתה האוכל את הטבל וכהן טמא שאכל תרומה טהורה וזר שאכל את התרומה ותמצאנו בתלמוד במס' סנהדרין (פג) בפ' אלו הן הנשרפין:

הכא

חשק שלמה על רב נסים גאון

א) ופי' בברייתא:

for that day which he counts as the Sabbath.[21]

The Gemara objects:

וְהָהוּא יוֹמָא לֵימוּת – And on that seventh **day should he die?**[22]

The Gemara answers:

דְּעָבִיד מֵאֶתְמוֹל שְׁתֵּי פַּרְנָסוֹת – He works the day before enough to supply **sustenance for two** days.

The Gemara asks:

וְדִילְמָא מֵאֶתְמוֹל שַׁבָּת הֲוַאי – But perhaps the day before was actually **the Sabbath.** How then is he allowed to work twice as much on that day?[23]

The Gemara concedes:

אֶלָּא כָּל יוֹם וָיוֹם עוֹשֶׂה לוֹ פַּרְנָסָתוֹ – Rather, every day he works enough for his sustenance, אֲפִילוּ הָהוּא יוֹמָא – even that day which he is observing as the Sabbath.[24]

The Gemara asks:

וְהָהוּא יוֹמָא בְּמַאי מִינְכַּר לֵיהּ – But how will that day be recognizable as the Sabbath?[25]

The Gemara replies:

בְּקִידּוּשָׁא וְאַבְדַּלְתָּא – By reciting the **kiddush** at the beginning of that day **and the havdalah** at the end.[26]

The Gemara elaborates further on the case of someone lost in the desert:

אָמַר רָבָא – Rava said: אִם הָיָה מַכִּיר מִקְצָת הַיּוֹם שֶׁיָּצָא בּוֹ – If he has partial knowledge of the day on which he embarked on his journey, i.e. he remembers how many days ago he left but does not recall what day of the week that was, **עוֹשֶׂה מְלָאכָה כָּל הַיּוֹם כּוּלּוֹ – he may perform *melachah* on that entire day.**[27]

The Gemara asks:

פְּשִׁיטָא – This is obvious! – ? –

The Gemara answers:

מַהוּ דְּתֵימָא – You might have thought כֵּיוָן דְּשַׁבָּת לֹא נָפִיק – since he would not depart on the Sabbath, בְּמַעֲלֵי שַׁבְּתָא [נַמִּי] לֹא נָפִיק – he also would not depart on the eve of the Sabbath [Friday].[28] **וְהַאי – Thus this** person, **אִי נַמִּי בַּחֲמִשָּׁה בְּשַׁבְּתָא נָפִיק – even if he departed on Thursday לִישְׁתְּרֵי לֵיהּ לְמֶיעְבַּד מְלָאכָה תְּרֵי יוֹמֵי – would be permitted to perform *melachah* for two days.**[29] **קָא מַשְׁמַע לָן – [Rava]** therefore **informs us זִימְנִין דְּמַשְׁכַּח שַׁיַּירְתָּא – that sometimes a caravan is available וּמִקְרֵי וְנָפִיק – and it happens that someone does depart** on Friday. Therefore, the person cannot assume that the day he left was not Friday.

The Gemara discusses the second case of the Mishnah:

הַיּוֹדֵעַ עִיקַּר שַׁבָּת – ONE WHO KNOWS THE ESSENCE OF THE SABBATH and performed many *melachos* on many Sabbaths is liable for each and every Sabbath.

The Gemara asks:

מְנָהָנֵי מִילֵּי – From where do we know these rulings, i.e. that sometimes a person is liable to only one *chatas* for desecrating many Sabbaths while other times he is liable to a separate *chatas* for each Sabbath?

The Gemara answers:

אָמַר רַב נַחְמָן אָמַר רַבָּה בַּר אֲבוּהָ – Rav Nachman said in the name of Rabbah bar Avuhah: תְּרֵי קְרָאֵי כְּתִיבֵי – Two verses are written: "וְשָׁמְרוּ בְנֵי יִשְׂרָאֵל אֶת הַשַּׁבָּת" – First:[30] ***The Children of Israel shall observe the Sabbath*** (singular). **וּכְתִיב "וְאֶת שַׁבְּתֹתַי תִּשְׁמֹרוּ" –** And also:[31] ***And My Sabbaths*** (plural) ***shall you observe.*** **הָא כֵּיצַד – How is this? "וְשָׁמְרוּ בְנֵי יִשְׂרָאֵל אֶת הַשַּׁבָּת" – *The Children of Israel shall observe the Sabbath* שְׁמִירָה אַחַת לְשַׁבָּתוֹת הַרְבֵּה –** refers to **one observance for many Sabbaths; "וְאֶת שַׁבְּתֹתַי תִּשְׁמֹרוּ" – *And My Sabbaths shall you observe* שְׁמִירָה אַחַת לְכָל שַׁבָּת וְשַׁבָּת –** refers to **one observance for each individual Sabbath.**[32]

The Gemara objects:

מַתְקִיף לָהּ רַב נַחְמָן בַּר יִצְחָק – Rav Nachman bar Yitzchak asked: אַדְּרַבָּה – On the contrary! אִיפְּכָא מִסְתַּבְּרָא – The reverse is more **logical. "וְשָׁמְרוּ בְנֵי יִשְׂרָאֵל אֶת הַשַּׁבָּת" – *The Children of Israel shall observe the Sabbath* שְׁמִירָה אַחַת לְכָל שַׁבָּת וְשַׁבָּת –** indicates **one observance for each individual Sabbath; "וְאֶת שַׁבְּתֹתַי תִּשְׁמֹרוּ" – *And My Sabbaths shall you observe* שְׁמִירָה אַחַת לְשַׁבָּתוֹת הַרְבֵּה –** indicates **one observance for many Sabbaths.**[33]

NOTES

21. Since any given day may in fact be the Sabbath, he cannot risk desecrating it by working. He may thus perform on any given day only as much work as he needs to stay alive. On the day which he actually observes as the Sabbath, however, he may not do *any* work.

22. If on the other six days he can work only enough to keep himself alive – even having to fast if he does not absolutely need to eat to stay alive – it appears that on the day he keeps as the Sabbath he cannot do even that amount of work (*Ritva MHK* ed.; see also *Beur Halachah* 344:1 ד״ה ואו).

23. By working more than he needs to stay alive that day, he will have desecrated the Sabbath for a non-life-threatening situation (*Rashi;* cf. *Gilyonei HaShas*).

24. I.e. on all days he may do only enough to keep himself alive and nothing more.

25. If he works as much on that day as on the other six, in what way does he indicate that that day is different?

26. He will perform these services as a reminder of the Sabbath, treating one day differently than the other six. In this way he will not forget about the Sabbath (*Rashi*). Ordinarily, it would be prohibited to recite the blessing for these services when there is a doubt if they are required, because it is prohibited to recite a blessing in vain. The Rabbis, though, stated that a person lost in a desert should recite these blessings to reinforce his memory of the Sabbath. Thus, even if that day happens to be a weekday, the blessing will not be in vain (*Shaar HaTziyun* 344:2, in explanation of *Rashi;* cf. *Ritva MHK* ed.).

[See *Pri Megadim* (*Mishbitzos Zahav* 344:1) and *Yad David* here for a discussion about whether the person should pray the weekday service or the Sabbath service on that day.]

27. Since he certainly would not have left on the Sabbath, he can assume that the eighth day after his departure [which is the same day of the week as the one in which he departed] is also not the Sabbath, and perform any *melachah* on that day (*Rashi*).

Ritva (*MHK* ed.) writes that it is proper for him to work that entire day to minimize the amount of work needed on the other days.

28. It is not befitting the honor of the Sabbath to embark on a journey on Friday (*Rashi*).

29. That is, he could perform *melachah* on the eighth and ninth days after the beginning of his journey (*Rashi*), the eighth because he definitely did not depart on the Sabbath, and the ninth because presumably he did not depart on a Friday either.

30. *Exodus* 31:16.

31. *Leviticus* 19:30.

32. Since the first verse mentions only one Sabbath, it indicates that he will be liable for only one Sabbath. The plural "Sabbaths" in the second verse, by contrast, indicates obligations for multiple Sabbaths. The Rabbis understood through logic that if someone forgot the essence of the Sabbath, he would be liable to only one *chatas* for all of his desecrations; whereas if he once knew about the Sabbath but then forgot about it, he is liable to a *chatas* for every Sabbath, since he presumably discovered the identity of the Sabbath during the intervening days (*Rashi*).

33. The singular "Sabbath" indicates that each Sabbath requires its own observance. [Thus, the desecration of each requires a separate

ח א מיי' פ"ג מהלכות שבועות הלכה ז:
ט ב מיי' פ"י מהלכות תרומות הלכה א:
י ג ד מיי' פ"ב מהלכות שבת הלכה כב טוש"ע א"ח סי' שדמ סעיף א:
יא ה מיי' שם טוש"ע שם סעיף ב:

קמ"ל מיתיבי א איזהו (א) שגגת שבועת ביטוי לשעבר שאם אמר יודע אני ששבועה זו אסורה אבל איני יודע אם חייבין עליה קרבן או לא חייב הא מני מונבז היא (לישנא אחרינא מני אילימא מונבז פשיטא השתא בכל התורה דלאו חידוש הוא אמר (א) שגגת קרבן שמה שגגה הכא דחידוש הוא לא כ"ש אלא לאו רבנן היא ותיובתא דאביי תיובתא): ואמר אביי הכל מודים בתרומה שאין חייבין עליה חומש עד שישגוג בלאו שבה הכל מודים מאן רבי יוחנן פשיטא כי אמר רבי יוחנן היכא דאיכא כרת היכא דליכא כרת לא מהו דתימא מיתה במקום כרת עומדת וכי שגג במיתה נמי ליחייב קמ"ל רבא אמר ∘ ב מיתה במקום כרת עומדת וחומש במקום קרבן קאי: אמר רב הונא ג היה מהלך ו) (בדרך או) במדבר ואינו יודע אימתי שבת מונה ששה ימים ומשמר יום אחד חייא בר רב אומר משמר יום אחד ומונה ששה במאי קמיפלגי מר סבר כברייתו של עולם ומר סבר כאדם הראשון מיתיבי היה מהלך בדרך ואינו יודע אימתי שבת משמר יום אחד לששה מאי לאו מונה ששה ומשמר יום אחד לא משמר יום אחד ומונה ששה אי הכי משמר יום אחד לששה משמר יום אחד ומונה ששה מיבעי ליה ועוד תניא היה מהלך בדרך או במדבר ואינו יודע אימתי שבת מונה ששה ומשמר יום אחד תיובתא ג) (דר' חייא) בר רב תיובתא אמר רבא בכל יום ויום עושה לו כדי פרנסתו [בר מההוא יומא] וההוא יומא לימות ד) דעביד מאתמול שתי פרנסות ודילמא מאתמול שבת הואי אלא ד כל יום ויום עושה לו פרנסתו אפילו ההוא יומא וההוא יומא במאי מינכר ליה בקידושא ואבדלתא אמר רבא ה אם היה מכיר ה) מקצת היום שיצא בו עושה מלאכה כל היום כולו פשיטא מהו דתימא כיון דשבת לא נפיק במעלי שבתא [נמי] לא נפיק והאי אי נמי בחמשה בשבתא נפיק לישתרי ליה למיעבד מלאכה תרי יומי קא משמע לן זימנין דמשכח שיירתא ומקרי ונפיק: היודע עיקר שבת: מנהני מילי אמר רב נחמן אמר רבה בר אבוה תרי קראי כתיבי א) ושמרו בני ישראל את השבת וכתי' ב) ואת שבתותי תשמורו הא כיצד ושמרו בני ישראל את השבת שמירה אחת לשבתות הרבה ואת שבתותי תשמורו שמירה אחת לכל שבת ושבת מתקיף לה רב נחמן בר יצחק אדרבה איפכא מסתברא ושמרו בני ישראל את השבת שמירה אחת לכל שבת ושבת ואת שבתותי תשמורו שמירה אחת לשבתות הרבה: היודע שהוא שבת: מאי

הא מני מונבז היא. פירש בקונטרס אבל לרבנן דפליגי אמונבז לא אשכחן שגגת שבועת ביטוי לשעבר וסברי כרבי ישמעאל דאמר בשבועות דאינו חייב אלא על העתיד לבא והקשה ה"ר אליעזר לרבינו שמואל דהא רבנן דמונבז רבי עקיבא ור"ע מחייב בהדיא על לשעבר בשבועות י) [פ"ג וכלשון אחר שפי' בקונטרס מוכח בשבועות] בפ"ג (דף כו:) דאמר בעא מיניה רבא מרב נחמן איזהו שגגת ביטוי לשעבר אמר ליה כגון דאמר יודע אני ששבועה זו אסורה אבל איני יודע אם חייבין עליה קרבן אם לאו ופריך ליה כמאן כמונבז ומשני אפילו תימא רבנן אע"ג דבכל התורה כולה לית להו שגגה בקרבן כו' ומה שהקשה בקונטרס מאי פשיטא הא קמ"ל אף על גב דבעלמא (ג) הוי שגגה הכא לאו שגגה היא משום דהאדם בשבועה בעינן לאו פירכא היא דאי משום הא איצטריך ליתני בהדיא האדם בשבועה פרט לאנוס אלא משמע דשגגת קרבן אתא לאשמעינן שמה שגגה ומיהו קשה דבלאו הך ברייתא הוה מצי למיפרך לאביי ממתניתין דשבועות דמחייב ר"ע שבועת ביטוי לשעבר ולא משכחת לה אלא אם כן הזיד בלאו על כן נראה כפירוש רבינו שמואל שהשיב (ד) לרבנן דשגגת קרבן לאו שמה שגגה משכחת שגגת שבועת ביטוי לשעבר כגון שיודע ששבועה זו אסורה אבל אינו יודע שיש בה לאו אבל סבור שיש בה איסור עשה וחשיב שפיר האדם בשבועה בענין זה וכן מוכח בשבועות (שם) דמהאדם בשבועה לא ממעט אלא כסבור בשעת שבועה שבאמת נשבע כגון תלמידי דרב דמר משתבע דהכי אמר רב כו' הלכך הא מני מונבז הוא דלרבנן הוה ליה למיתני ואינו יודע אם חייבין עליה לאו והוה דשבועות דבעא מיניה רבא מרב נחמן פליגא אדאביי: **עושה** כדי פרנסתו. אבל להלך יכול כל מה שירצה רק ביום שמשמר דאי לאו הכי לא יגיע לעולם לישוב והא דקאמר במאי מינכר משום דאין זה היכר שבת במה שיושב ואינו הולך אי נמי אפי' ביום שמשמר הולך כמו שרוצה והשתא לא מינכר אלא בקידושא. הרב פור"ת:
אס

קמ"ל. אביי דמודה רבי יוחנן בה דבעינן שגגת לאו דאי הזיד בלאו תו ליכא שגגה דבהא נמי פליגי רבנן אמונבז ואמרי דאין שגגת קרבן שגגה: **איזהו שבועת ביטוי לשעבר.** בשלמא להבא כגון שלא אוכל משכחת לה כגון שנתעלמה השבועה ואכל אלא לשעבר כגון שאכלתי והוא לא אכל אין כאן שוגג דאי כסבור שאכל בשעה שנשבע אינו חייב קרבן דתניא בשבועות (פ"ג דף כו.) האדם בשבועה פרט לאנוס כלומר האדם בשבועה שיהא אדם בשעת שבועה שתהא דעתו עליו בשעת שבועה ופרשינן לה התם לאפוקי כי האי גוונא ומהשתא לא משכחת שגגה אלא בקרבן: **אמר יודע אני שאני נשבע לשקר.** ומוזהרתי על כך: **אבל איני יודע כו'.** דאי בנתעלמה ממנו אזהרת שבועה אין לך אונס בשעת שבועה כזה: **חייב.** אלמא מודו ביה רבנן דמיחייב אשגגת קרבן: **הא מני מונבז היא.** דאמר נמי בעלמא שמה שגגה אבל לרבנן דפליגי עליה לית להו ביטוי לשעבר דסברי כר' ישמעאל דאמר בשבועות אינו חייב אלא על העתיד לבא (שם דף כה.). יש גורסין הא מני (ב) מונבז פשיטא השתא בכל התורה אמר מונבז שגגת קרבן שמה שגגה הכא דחידוש הוא לא כ"ש אלא לאו רבנן תיובתא דאביי תיובתא ולא נהירא לי דמאי פשיטותא הא איצטריך לאשמעינן דחלוקה שגגה זו משאר שגגות דאילו בכל התורה למונבז בין ששגג בקרבן בין ששגג בלאו וכרת שמה שגגה וכאן בלשעבר אם שגג בלאו שבה לאו שגגה היא דכתיב האדם בשבועה: **הכל מודים בתרומה.** זר שאכל תרומה בשוגג משלם חומש על שגגתו דכתיב (ויקרא כב) ואיש כי יאכל קדש בשגגה אבל מזיד אין מוסיף חומש וחייב מיתה בידי שמים דכתיב (שם) ומתו בו כי יחללוהו וסמיך ליה וכל זר לא יאכל קדש: **בלאו שבה.** כסבור חולין ואין כאן לאו: **מיתה.** דכתיב בתרומה: **במקום כרת.** דשאר עבירות: **וחומש.** דשגגת תרומה במקום קרבן דשגגת שאר עבירות ולרבי יוחנן מיחייב חומש אשגגת מיתה: **מונה ו'.** מיום ששם אל לבו שכחתו ומשמר השביעי: **משמר יום אחד ומונה ו'.** וכל יום ששם אל לבו אינו משמר דשמא עשה מלאכה אבל יום המחרת משמר ולקמן מפרש דההך דאינו משמר לא עביד נמי מלאכה אלא כדי פרנסת היום: **כברייתו של עולם.** ימי חול נמנו תחלה: **כאדם הראשון.** שנברא בע"ש ויום ראשון למנינו שבת היה: **יום אחד לששה.** משמע לו' שעברו: **וההוא יומא לימות.** בתמיה: **ודלמא אתמול שבת הוה.** ונמצא מחלל שבת שלא לפקוח נפש: **בקדושתא ואבדלתא.** לזכרון בעלמא שיהא לו שם יום חלוק משאר ימים ולא תשתכח שבת ממנו: **אם היה מכיר מקצת יום שיצא בו.** לא שזכר איזה יום בשבת היה אלא זכור שהיום יום שלישי ליציאתו או רביעי ליציאתו ומתוך כך ידע שמונה ליציאתו עושה מלאכה כל יום ח' וכן לעולם ודאי זהו יום שיצא בו וקים ליה דבשבת לא יצא שהרי בישוב לא שבק את השבת: **במעלי שבתא נמי לא נפיק.** דאין דרך לצאת מפני כבוד השבת ועל כן כל יום ח' וט' ליציאתו לישתרו דליכא לספוקינהו בשבת: **מנא הני מילי.** שיש מחלל בשבתות הרבה וחייב אחת על כולן ויש מחללן וחייב על כל שבת: **הכי גרסינן הא כיצד ושמרו בני ישראל את השבת שמירה אחת לשבתות הרבה ואת שבתותי תשמורו שמירה לכל שבת ושבת.** דקרא קמא חדא שבת הוא דחשיב משמע שאינו מקפיד אלא על האחת והכא כתיב את שבתותי אכולהו קפיד ולא מסרן אלא לחכמים להודיען מסברא האי בשכח עיקר שבת דהדא שגגה היא והאי בשוכח שהיום שבת אבל יודע עיקר שבת דאיכא למימר ימים שבינתים [הוין] ידיעה לחלק: **איפכא מסתברא.** ושמרו בני ישראל את השבת משמע שמירה אחת לשבת אחת ואת שבתותי תשמורו ב' שבתות ואינו מוזהיר אלא על שמירה אחת ובין רב נחמן בר יצחק לא פליגי אלא במשמעותא מאי דיליף מר מהאי קרא יליף מר מאידך:
מאי

רבינו חננאל

דבר שזדונו חייב כרת בשגגתו חייב חטאת זולתי המביאין על הזדון כשגגה ומותבינן עליה דר' יוחנן איזהו שבועת ביטוי לשעבר אמר אני יודע ששבועה זו אסורה אבל איני יודע אם חייבין עליה קרבן אם לאו חייב ודחי ר' יוחנן הא למונבז היא ואנא דאמרי כרבנן מיהא שמעינן דרבי יוחנן פליג עליה דמונבז בהא תו אמר אביי הכל מודים והוא ר' יוחנן בזר שאכל תרומה שאין חייבין עליה חומש עד שישגוג [בלאו] שבה מ"ט כיון דתרומה יש בה מיתה שנאמר ומתו בו כי יחללוהו אבל כרת לית בה עד שישגוג בלאו שבה דקיי"ל שגגת דכרת הויא שגגה וכל מאן דלית ליה כרת בעינן שגגה בלאו שבה ואע"ג דתרומה עון מיתה היא שגגת דמיתה אינה חשובה כשגגה דכרת אלא בעינן שגגה בלאו שבה ודחה רבא להא דאביי ואמר לעולם מיתה במקום כרת עומדת וכשם שבשאר מצות אם שגג בכרת אע"פ שהזיד בלאו לר' יוחנן מביא קרבן הכי נמי לענין תרומה אם שגג במיתה אע"פ שהזיד בלאו מוסיף חומש שחומש במקום קרבן הוא וקיי"ל כרבא. וקמייתא נמי דאמר אביי בשבועת ביטוי עד שישגוג בלאו שבה אבל שגגת קרבן לאו שמה שגגה לרבנן [אוקמינה] להא מתניתא בשבועות פר' ב' אפילו תימא רבנן בשגגת קרבן בשבועת ביטוי מחייבי דעד כאן לא פליגי רבנן עליה דמונבז אלא בעלמא אבל בשבועת ביטוי דהוא חידוש דלא אשכחן מזיד קאי בלאו בשוגג מייתי קרבן והכא בשבועת ביטוי מזיד קאי בלאו ושוגג מייתי קרבן שגגה דקרבן נמי הוא שגגה וחייב חטאת: **הא דאמר** רב הונא היה מהלך במדבר ואינו יודע מתי שבת כו' א) קיי"ל כרבא דאמר חושש בכל יום שמא היום שבת הוא ואעפ"כ עושה כדי פרנסתו בכל יום. ומונה ו' ימים ומשמר שביעי ואם אין לו מאין יתפרנס עושה גם בו ביום כדי פרנסתו ומינכר ליה בקידושא ובאבדלתא כלומר בו ביום מקדש ומבדיל לעשות היכר בין זה היום לשאר ששה ימים ואם מכיר סכום הימים שיצא כל יום שמיני מותר לעשות מלאכה כל היום (דלא מנפקא ליה) דודאי יום שבת לא יצא וכל יום שמיני ליציאתו הוא יום יציאתו. ואם ברי לו שלא יצא בע"ש עושה יום שמיני ויום תשיעי בלא ספק אבל אי לא ידע בבירור חיישינן דלמא אזדמן ליה שיירא ונפק בע"ש: **היודע** עיקר שבת ונעלם ממנו שהיום יום שבת הוא ועשה מלאכות הרבה בשבתות הרבה אינו חייב אלא חטאת אחת בכל שבת ושבת ושמעינן ליה מדכתיב ושמרתם את השבת וכתיב את שבתותי תשמורו ופשוטה היא לרבה בר אבוה כטעמיה. ולרב נחמן בר יצחק כטעמיה זה סובר [ושמרו ב"י את השבת שמירה אחת לשבתות הרבה כנגד השוכח עיקר שבת ואת שבתותי תשמורו שמירה לכל שבת ושבת כנגד היודע עיקר שבת וזה סובר] ושמרו בני ישראל את השבת שמירה לכל שבת ושבת כנגד היודע עיקר שבת את שבתותי תשמורו שמירה אחת לשבתות הרבה כנגד (היודע) [השוכח] עיקר שבת: היודע שהוא שבת והזיד בה ושגג במלאכות ועשה מלאכות הרבה בשבתות הרבה חייב על כל מלאכה ומלאכה ואקשינן מאי שנא בהיודע עיקר שבת דחייב על כל שבת ושבת וביודע שהיא שבת דחייב על כל מלאכה ומלאכה ופריק רב חסדא כאן מידיעת שבתות הוא פורש כו'. פי' היודע עיקר שבת ואינו יודע שהיום שבת הוא כיון שאמרו לו היום שבת היא מיד פורש נמצאת שגגתו על השבת לפי' אינו חייב אלא אחת על כל שבת ושבת אבל היודע שהיא שבת ושגג ועשה מלאכות הרבה וכיון שאומרים לו הלא מלאכה היא זו מיד פורש נמצאת שגגתו על המלאכות לפיכך חייב על כל מלאכה ומלאכה ודחה רב נחמן ואמר כלום פורש מן השבת אלא משום מלאכות כו' אלא אמר רב נחמן קרבן [דחייב רחמנא] אמאי אשגגה הוא השתא כיון

חשק שלמה על רבינו חננאל א) מן קיי"ל כרבא עד סוף הענין הובא בה"ג בשם רבינו:

מסורת הש"ס

א) שבועות כו: [ע"ש היטב], ב) [שתי מיתות הללו ליתא בהרי"ף והרמב"ם וטור וש"ע], ג) [נ"ל דחייא], ד) ס"א דעביד, ה) נ"ל סבום, ו) רש"ל והמהרש"א וכ"ה במ"י.

הגהות הב"ח

(א) גמ' אמר מונבז שגגת קרבן: (ב) רש"י ד"ה הא מני וכו' יש גורסין הא מני אילימא מונבז פשיטא השתא בכל התורה דלאו חידוש הוא אמר מונבז: (ג) תוס' ד"ה הא מני וכו' אע"ג דבעלמא שגגת לאו נמי הויא שגגה: (ד) בא"ד רבינו שמואל שהשיב להר"א דלרבנן דשגגת:

גליון הש"ס

גמ' רבא אמר מיתה במקום כרת. עי' כר"ש רפ"ו דתרומות:

תורה אור השלם

א) וְשָׁמְרוּ בְנֵי יִשְׂרָאֵל אֶת הַשַּׁבָּת לַעֲשׂוֹת אֶת הַשַּׁבָּת לְדֹרֹתָם בְּרִית עוֹלָם: [שמות לא, טז]

ב) אִישׁ אִמּוֹ וְאָבִיו תִּירָאוּ וְאֶת שַׁבְּתֹתַי תִּשְׁמֹרוּ אֲנִי יְיָ אֱלֹהֵיכֶם: [ויקרא יט, ג]

ליקוטי רש"י

איזהו שגגת שבועת ביטוי לשעבר. כיון דבעינן אדם בשבועה היכי משכחת לה שוגג, אי דידע בשעת שבועה שהוא נשבע לשקר, מזיד הוא וקרבן כתב ונעלם משכחת לה בשגגת שבועה שהוא דעתו מיושבת עליו ולאחר זמן נתעלמה ממנו שבועה [שבועות כו:]. **ומקרי ונפיק.** לשון ויקר מקרה (רות ב) [רשב"ם ב"ב ל:].

רב נסים גאון

במאי קמיפלגי מר סבר תחומין דאורייתא ומר סבר תחומין דרבנן. אמר אביי הכל מודים בתרומה שאין חייבין עליה חומש כו'. עיקר דבר זה הוא כתוב בתורה (ויקרא כב) ואיש כי יאכל קודש בשגגה ויסף חמישיתו עליו וכמו כן עוד חיוב המיתה הוא כתוב בתורה (שם) ומתו בו כי יחללוהו וכמה ששנינו במסכת ביכורים בפ' התרומה והביכורים חייבין עליהן מיתה וחומש ופי' אל א) בריתא במסכת זבחים בפרק רבי אומר [בתוספתא דזבחים פ' י"ג] הפרש בין השוחט בפנים ובמסכת כריתות בפ' א' אלו שהן במיתה האוכל את הטבל וכהן טמא שאכל תרומה טהורה וזר שאכל את התרומה ותמצאנו בתלמוד במס' סנהדרין (פג) בפ' אלו הן הנשרפין:
הכא

חשק שלמה על רב נסים גאון

א) ופי' בברייתא.

The Gemara discusses the third case of the Mishnah: הַיּוֹדֵעַ שֶׁהוּא שַׁבָּת – ONE WHO KNOWS IT IS THE SABBATH and performed many *melachos* on many Sabbaths is liable for each and every *av melachah.*

NOTES

chatas for atonement.] The plural "Sabbaths," on the other hand, gives only one warning to observe all the Sabbaths in total. [Therefore, desecrating many Sabbaths is subject to only one *chatas.*]

Rav Nachman and Rav Nachman bar Yitzchak agree that the Mishnah's rulings emerge from these two verses; they disagree only as to which verse teaches which ruling (*Rashi;* see also *Ritva MHK* ed.).

מַאי שְׁנָא רֵישָׁא וּמַאי שְׁנָא סֵיפָא – **What is the difference between the first** case [inadvertence regarding the Sabbath and deliberateness regarding *melachos*] **and the latter** case [deliberateness regarding the Sabbath and inadvertence regarding *melachos*]?[1]

The Gemara answers:

אָמַר רַב סַפְרָא – **Rav Safra said:** כָּאן מִידִיעַת שַׁבָּת הוּא פּוֹרֵשׁ – **Here** in the first case **he withdraws** from his work **because of the knowledge of** the **Sabbath;**[2] וְכָאן מִידִיעַת מְלָאכָה הוּא פּוֹרֵשׁ – **whereas here** in the second case **he withdraws** from his work **because of the knowledge of** the ***melachah.***[3]

The Gemara objects:

אָמַר לֵיהּ רַב נַחְמָן – **Rav Nachman said to him:** כְּלוּם פָּרִישׁ מִשַּׁבָּת אֶלָּא מִשּׁוּם מְלָאכוֹת – **Does he withdraw** from his work **because** of his awareness **of the Sabbath for any reason other than** that he also became aware of **the *melachos*?** וּכְלוּם פָּרִישׁ מִמְּלָאכוֹת אֶלָּא מִשּׁוּם שַׁבָּת – **And does he withdraw** from his work **because** of his awareness **of the *melachos* for any reason other than** that he also became aware of **the Sabbath?**[4]

Rav Nachman therefore offers another explanation:

אֶלָּא אָמַר רַב נַחְמָן – **Rather, Rav Nachman said:** קָרְבָּן דְּחַיֵּיב רַחֲמָנָא אַמַּאי – **For what did the Merciful One obligate** someone to bring **a sacrifice?** אַשְּׁגָגָה – **For inadvertence.** הָתָם חֲדָא שְׁגָגָה – **There** [inadvertence regarding the Sabbath and deliberateness regarding *melachos*], the person acts with **one inadvertence;** הָכָא טוּבָא שִׁגְגוֹת הָוְיָין – **here** [deliberateness regarding the Sabbath and inadvertence regarding *melachos*], **there are many inadvertencies.**[5]

The Gemara analyzes the Mishnah's ruling about inadvertence regarding the *melachos*:

חַיָּיב עַל כָּל מְלָאכָה וּמְלָאכָה – If someone knows it was the Sabbath, and performed many *melachos* on many Sabbaths, **HE IS LIABLE FOR EACH AND EVERY *MELACHAH*** that he performed.

The Gemara gives the source for this ruling:

חִילּוּק מְלָאכוֹת מְנָלַן – **From where do we know** the concept of the **separation of** the ***melachos*** into distinct categories of liability?[6]

אָמַר שְׁמוּאֵל – **Shmuel said:** אָמַר קְרָא ,,מְחַלְלֶיהָ מוֹת יוּמָת" – **The verse states: *One who desecrates it shall surely be put to death.***[7] הַתּוֹרָה רִבְּתָה מִיתוֹת הַרְבֵּה עַל חִילּוּל אֶחָד – **The Torah included many "deaths" for one desecration.**[8]

The Gemara objects:

הַאי בְּמֵזִיד כְּתִיב – **This is written about one who acts deliberately!**[9] Hence, nothing can be derived from there to a case where someone violates the Sabbath inadvertently. – ? –

The Gemara answers:

אִם אֵינוֹ עִנְיָן לְמֵזִיד – **If [this verse] has no application to one who acts deliberately,** דִּכְתִיב ,,כָּל־הָעֹשֶׂה . . . מְלָאכָה יוּמָת" – **for it is already written: *whoever does work on it shall be put to death,***[10] תְּנֵהוּ עִנְיָן לְשׁוֹגֵג – **assign it an application to one who acts inadvertently.** וּמַאי ,,יוּמָת" – **And what** does ***he shall be put to death*** mean? יוּמַת בְּמָמוֹן – It means: **He shall "die" monetarily.**[11]

The Gemara asks:

וְתִיפּוֹק לֵיהּ חִילּוּק מְלָאכוֹת – **But derive** the concept of **separation of *melachos*** מֵהֵיכָא דְּנָפְקָא לֵיהּ לְרַבִּי נָתָן – **from where R' Nassan derived it.** דְּתַנְיָא – **For it was taught in a Baraisa:** רַבִּי נָתָן אוֹמֵר – **R' NASSAN SAYS:** ,,לֹא־תְבַעֲרוּ אֵשׁ בְּכֹל מֹשְׁבֹתֵיכֶם בְּיוֹם הַשַּׁבָּת" – The verse states:[12] ***YOU SHALL NOT KINDLE A FIRE IN ALL YOUR DWELLINGS ON THE SABBATH DAY.*** מַה תַּלְמוּד לוֹמַר – **WHAT IS [THE TORAH] TEACHING?** The Torah already states elsewhere that it is prohibited to perform any labor on the Sabbath.[13]

NOTES

1. The Mishnah first rules that if someone knew which *melachos* are forbidden on the Sabbath, but did not realize that it was the Sabbath day, he is liable to only one *chatas* for the entire Sabbath. The Mishnah then states that if someone knew that it was the Sabbath, but did not know that his actions were *melachos* forbidden on the Sabbath, he is liable to a separate *chatas* for each *melachah* he violated (*Rashi;* see *Ritva MHK* ed.). The Gemara now seeks the reason for the difference between these two cases.

2. In the first case, when people told him that it was the Sabbath he stopped the *melachah* and realized his mistake. Since it is the realization of this mistake that makes him liable to a sacrifice, he needs to bring only one *chatas* for forgetting the Sabbath (*Rashi*).

3. Here, if people would tell him it is the Sabbath, he would not desist from his activity, because he already knows it is the Sabbath; his mistake is caused by his unawareness that the act is forbidden on the Sabbath. However, when they tell him that the act is a bona fide *melachah,* he does stop that action. Hence, he must bring a separate sacrifice for each *melachah* he violated (*Rashi*).

4. In the first case, when they tell him it is the Sabbath, he stops his acts only because he realizes that he has sinned by performing *melachos,* prohibited on the Sabbath. And in the second case, when they tell him his acts are *melachos,* he stops only because he realizes that he has sinned by violating the Sabbath day (*Rashi*). Thus, in both cases he refrains from his act out of knowledge of both the Sabbath and that his acts are *melachos.* Hence, what difference is there between the two cases?

5. When a person acts with inadvertence regarding the Sabbath, he has made only one mistake – his lack of awareness that it is the Sabbath day. Hence, he is obligated to bring only one *chatas* even though he performed numerous *melachos.* However, if he acts inadvertently regarding the *melachos,* he makes multiple mistakes – one for each *melachah* of which he was unaware. He is therefore liable to a separate *chatas* for each mistake.

6. [One is ordinarily obligated to bring a separate *chatas* offering for each violation he commits in one lapse of awareness only if the violations are prohibited by separate verses (e.g. consuming *cheilev* and consuming blood). But all thirty-nine *melachos* are prohibited by the same verse: *You shall not do any work* (*Exodus* 20:10). Accordingly] how do we know that someone who performs various Sabbath *melachos* in a single lapse is liable to a separate *chatas* for each one? (*Rashi;* see *Ritva MHK* ed.).

7. *Exodus* 31:14.

8. The repetitive מוֹת יוּמָת [literally: *dying, he shall die*] indicates multiple liability for Sabbath desecration (*Rashi*). This apparently refers to one who performs various *melachos* on the same Sabbath.

9. Only a deliberate sinner is subject to capital punishment. Thus, although the verse obviously cannot mean that the sinner is put to death numerous times, we can explain the Torah's repetitive language as merely an example of the principle: "The Torah spoke in the language of man" [i.e. just as people sometimes repeat themselves for emphasis, so does the Torah] (*Tosafos*).

10. *Exodus* 35:2. The verse מְחַלְלֶיהָ מוֹת יוּמָת, *one who desecrates it shall surely be put to death,* is therefore not needed to teach that a Sabbath desecrator is subject to capital punishment.

11. I.e. he must bring many [costly] sacrifices for atonement (*Rashi*).

One of the rules of Biblical exposition taught to Moses at Sinai states: אִם אֵינוֹ עִנְיָן לָזֶה תְּנֵהוּ עִנְיָן לָזֶה, *If [a Scriptural passage] has no application to this* [its own context], *assign it an application to that* [some related context]. That is, if certain words in the Torah cannot be understood to be teaching a point regarding their own context (because, for example, the law they seem to be teaching is already known to us from elsewhere and the words in question would thus be redundant), they must be understood to be teaching a point in regard to a related context (*Rashi* to *Pesachim* 24a ד״ה ואם אינו; see also *Sefer Kerisus, Nesivos Olam* §20; see also *Yad Malachi* ע׳ אלף §2).

Therefore, in this case, since we already know (from *Exodus* 35:2) that a Sabbath desecrator is liable to capital punishment, the verse מְחַלְלֶיהָ מוֹת יוּמָת cannot be referring to deliberate desecration. Rather, it refers to inadvertence, with the "death" meaning a loss of money.

12. Ibid. v. 3.

13. The verse in the Ten Commandments states in regard to the Sabbath (*Exodus* 20:10): לֹא־תַעֲשֶׂה כָל־מְלָאכָה, *You shall not do any work* (*Rashi*).

מאי שנא רישא ומאי שנא סיפא אמר רב ספרא כאן מידיעת שבת הוא פורש וכאן מידיעת מלאכה הוא פורש א"ל רב נחמן כלום פריש משבת אלא משום מלאכות וכלום פריש ממלאכות אלא משום שבת אלא אמר רב נחמן קרבן דחייב רחמנא אמאי אשגגה התם חדא שגגה הכא טובא שגגות הויין: חייב על כל מלאכה ומלאכה: חילוק מלאכות מנלן אמר שמואל אמר קרא א) מחלליה מות יומת התורה רבתה מיתות הרבה על חילול אחד האי במזיד כתיב אם אינו ענין למזיד דכתיב ב) כל העושה (א) מלאכה יומת תנהו ענין לשוגג ומאי יומת יומת בממון ותיפוק ליה חילוק מלאכות מהיכא דנפקא ליה לר' נתן דתניא ר' נתן אומר ג) לא תבערו אש בכל מושבותיכם ביום השבת מה ת"ל לפי שנאמר ד) ויקהל משה את כל עדת בני ישראל אלה הדברים וגו' ב) ששת ימים תעשה מלאכה א) דברים הדברים אלה הדברים אלו שלשים ותשע מלאכות שנאמרו למשה בסיני יכול עשאן כולן בהעלם אחד אינו חייב אלא אחת ת"ל ה) בחריש ובקציר תשבות ועדיין אני אומר ב) על חרישה ועל הקצירה חייב שתים ועל כולן אינו חייב אלא אחת ת"ל ג) לא תבערו אש הבערה בכלל היתה ולמה יצאת להקיש אליה ולומר לך מה הבערה שהיא אב מלאכה וחייבין עליה בפני עצמה אף כל שהוא אב מלאכה חייבין עליה בפני עצמה שמואל סבר לה כרבי יוסי דאמר הבערה ללאו יצאת ג) דתניא הבערה ללאו יצאת דברי רבי יוסי ר' נתן אומר ד) לחלק יצאת ותיפוק ליה לחלוק מלאכות מהיכא דנפקא ליה לר' יוסי ה) דתניא רבי יוסי אומר ו) ועשה מאחת מהנה פעמים שחייבים אחת על כולן ופעמים שחייבין על כל אחת ואחת אמר ר' יוסי בר' חנינא מ"ט דר' יוסי אחת מאחת הנה מהנה אחת שהיא הנה הנה שהיא אחת שמעון מאחת
שם

רש"י

מאי שנא רישא. דשגגת שבת וזדון מלאכות לא מיחייב אלא אחת לכל שבת וסיפא דזדון שבת ושגגת מלאכות חייב על כל מלאכה ומלאכה: **כאן מידיעת שבת הוא פורש.** רישא כי אמרו ליה שבת הוא פורש מן המלאכה ומכיר שחטא ועל כך הוא מביא קרבן הלכך שגגת שבת היא ועל השבת הוא צריך להביא: **כאן מידיעת מלאכות הוא פורש.** כי אמרי ליה שבת הוא לא פריש דהא נמי ידע וכי אמרי ליה מלאכה חשובה היא זו פריש הלכך על מנין המלאכות יביא: **כלום פריש משבת אלא משום.** דכי אודעיה שבת הוא הכיר שחטא על המלאכות וכלום פריש ממלאכה כלומר ע"י ידיעת המלאכות אלא משום שבת דכי אמרו ליה מלאכות הן הכיר שחילל שבת: **חילוק מלאכות.** שגופי מלאכות מתחלקים לחטאות ואע"פ שבהעלם אחד: **מות יומת.** מיתות הרבה: **בממון.** לאפושי קרבנות: **מה ת"ל.** והלא כבר נאמר לא תעשה כל מלאכה: **דברים.** משמע תרי ה' לרבות חד הרי שלשה אלה בגמטריא ל"ו הרי ל"ט: **ת"ל בחריש ובקציר תשבות.** כלומר בלאו לא תבערו הוה לן למילף מהאי אם לא שיש להשיב: **ועדיין אני אומר על חריש וקציר חייב שתים.** אם עשאן בהעלם אחד שהרי הוציאם מן הכלל לחלקן לשתים ומשמע אזהרה לקציר לעצמה ואזהרה לחריש לעצמה: **ועל כולן אחת.** דבחדא מלאכה כיילינהו וחד לאו ובדבר שהיה בכלל ויצא מן הכלל ללמד לא ללמד כו' לא דיינין ליה דהוי ליה כלל בלא תעשה ופרט בעשה ואין דנין אותו בכלל ופרט אי נמי הוי חריש וקציר שני כתובין הבאין כאחד ואין מלמדין דהוה ליה למיכתב חד: **ת"ל לא תבערו כו'.** וחריש וקציר לדרשה אחרינא אי כר' עקיבא דדריש ליה בעלמא (ר"ה דף ט.) לענין תוספת שביעית אי כרבי ישמעאל לענין שבת מה חריש רשות אף קציר רשות ללמד על קציר העומר שדוחה שבת: **בכלל היתה.** דלא תעשה כל מלאכה: **להקיש אליה.** כל שאר המלאכות שנכללו עמה בכלל שזו מדה בתורה כל דבר שהיה בכלל ויצא מן הכלל ללמד לא ללמד על עצמו יצא כו': **ללאו.** שאין חייבין עליה כרת וסקילה כשאר מלאכות אלא מה שאמור בה: **לחלק.** כדאמרן מה הבערה מיוחדת: **ועשה מאחת מהנה.** האמור לענין חטאות הוה ליה למכתב ועשה אחת ולישתוק אייתר ליה שאר' מ"ם דמאחת וכל תיבת מהנה לדרשה ודרוש הכי פעמים שכל מעשה עבירותיו חשוב אחת ופעמים שהוא קרוי הנה לשון רבים: **וא"ר יוסי ברבי חנינא מ"ט דרבי יוסי.** כלומר מאי דריש ביה דאכתי מ' דמהנה ומ' דמאחת למאי אתא: **אחת מאחת.** אחת הוה ליה למכתב וכתיב מאחת וכן נמי הנה ה"ל למכתב (הנה) [למדרש פעמים שהוא הנה] וכתב מהנה ודרוש אחת והנה בלא מ"ם הכי פעמים אחת שהוא הנה שבת [אחת] לבדו הוא מחלל ויש כאן חטאות הרבה דאזלי בתר מלאכות ופעמים הנה שהיא אחת מלאכות הרבה עשה ואינו חייב אלא אחת דבהנך תרי גווני איכא למשמע ועשה אחת וחייב הנה ואיכא למימר נמי הכי ועשה אחת הנה ז) עשייתו הוי אחת אע"פ שהן הנה [וחייב א'] ומ"ם יתירה [דרוש הכי] לרבות שהכותב שם משמעון דאע"ג שנתכוון לעשות תיבה גדולה הואיל ושתי אותיות הראשונות שם במקום אחר הן חייב והיינו מאחת מקצת המלאכה ולא כולה יביא חטאת:
מהנה

תוספות

אם אינו ענין למזיד דהא כתיב כו'. ואם תאמר ולימא אם אינו ענין למזיד משום דלאו בתרי קטלא קטלת ליה וי"ל דאי לאו קרא אחרינא דמייתי הוה מוקמינן ליה להאי קרא במזיד ומות יומת דברה תורה כלשון בני אדם אבל השתא דלא איצטריך למזיד מוקמי ליה ע"כ בשוגג ולחייב קרבן על כל א': **יכול שאם עשאן כולם בהעלם אחד כו'.** תימה א"כ מניינא דקרא דברים הדברים אלה הדברים למה לי כיון דלא אתא לחלק ויש לומר דצריך למניינא לפי שיש מלאכות שאינן חשובות ואיצטריך מניינא לאשמעינן דכולהו הוין מלאכות להתחייב עליהן ומיהו ממתניתין דמ' מלאכות דייק שפיר דבהעלם אחד חייב על כל אחת דלא הוה צריך למניינא כיון דמני כולהו בהדיא ומיהו קשה לר"י דלקמן בהזורק (דף צו:) משמע דהאי מניינא אתיא לחלק דאמר התם למימרא דמחייב רבי אתולדה במקום אב והתניא רבי אומר דברים הדברים אלה הדברים כו' ופי' בקונטרס התם דהכי פריך הואיל ומניינא לא אתא אלא לחילוק חטאות ואי ס"ד דמחייב אתולדה במקום אב טובא ה"ל למיתני ולפי מה שפירשנו דמניינא לא אתא אלא לאשמעינן דכולהו חשובות מלאכות להתחייב עליהם לא הוה פריך מידי ונראה לר"י דגרס הכא כמו במכילתא דתניא התם רבי נתן אומר לא תבערו אש למה נאמר לפי שנאמר ויקהל משה שומע אני שלא יהא חייב עד שיעבור ל"ט מלאכות תלמוד לומר בחריש ובקציר וכו' והשתא אי לאו לא תבערו ה"א דמניינא אתא למימר שאינו חייב על אחת או שתים עד שיעבור כל ל"ט וכיון דכתיב לא תבערו דילפינן מיניה דחייב על כל אחת בפני עצמה אם כן מניינא אתא למימר דאל"ט דווקא הוא דחייב על כל אחת ואחת אבל אתולדה במקום אב לא והשתא מוכח שפיר בהזורק דרבי לא מחייב אתולדה במקום אב ואתי נמי שפיר להאי גירסא דקתני לפי שנאמר דברים הדברים וגו' יכול כו' דמשמע דמתוך קרא דהדברים הוא דמשמע ליה דאינו חייב עד שיעבור כולן וכן בפ"ק דפסחים (דף ה:) לפי שנאמר לא יראה לך יכול יטמין ויקבל פקדונות מן הנכרים אבל לגירסת הספרים מאי קאמר לפי שנאמר בלאו קרא נמי הוה אמרינן הכי כל כמה דלא נפקא לן חילוק מלאכות משום מקום: **על חרישה וקצירה חייב שתים.** וא"ת מנא ליה דחייב שתים נימא דלא מיחייב אתרוייהו אלא אחת וי"ל משום דכתיב בחריש ובקציר דמשמע תרי מילי מדלא כתב בחריש וקציר: **ועל כולן אינו חייב אלא אחת.** פירש בקונט' משום דהוי ליה כלל בלא תעשה ופרט בעשה וקשה דכללא נמי כתיב בעשה וביום השביעי תשבות ועוד דגבי כלל ופרט דוקא הוא דאמרינן בפרק קמא דמו"ק (דף ג.) דלא דיינין כשאין הכלל בלשון הפרט אבל לגבי דבר שהוא יצא מן הכלל לא אשכחן בשום מקום ועוד דבמועד קטן איכא למ"ד דנין ונראה כפי' אחרון שפי' בקונט' דלא ילפינן מחריש וקציר משום דהוו שני כתובים הבאים כאחד וכה"ג אמרינן בפרק ד' מיתות (סנהדרין סז:) אוב וידעוני בכלל כל המכשפים היו כו' ופריך וליהוי אוב וידעוני שני כתובים הבאין כא' ואם תאמר והיכי יליף מלא תבערו כל שכן דהוי ג' כתובים הבאין כאחד ואין מלמדין לכ"ע וכ"ת דחריש וקציר אתא לכדדרשינן בריש מו"ק (ד' ד.) מה חריש רשות כו' אם כן היכי הוה בעי למילף מיניה מעיקרא הא לא אתי להכי ואומר ר"י דלא הוו ג' כתובים מדלא כתבינהו או כולהו בלאו או כולהו בעשה ולהכי ילפינן מהבערה ומהשתא אייתר ליה חריש וקציר לכדדרשינן במו"ק: **הבערה ללאו יצאת.** וא"ת ח) והא איצטריך למיכתב לא תבערו משום סיפיה דקרא דכתיב בכל מושבותיכם דדרשינן מינה ביבמות (דף ו:) ובסנהדרין (דף לה:) דאין רציחה דוחה שבת וי"ל דהוה מצי למיכתב בלישנא אחריתי ולא לכתוב לא תבערו ומשום דדרשינן בפ"ק (דף כ.) אבל אתה מבעיר כו' לא הוה צריך למיכתב לא תבערו: **מאי טעמא דר' יוסי.** פי' בקונט' כלומר דאכתי מ"ס דמאחת ומהנה למה לי ולשון מאי טעמא אינו משמע כן ונראה לר"י דה"פ מ"ט דר' יוסי הא איצטריך קרא לשם משמעון ולאבות ולתולדות ומנא ליה דחייב על כל אחת ואחת ומפרש דמאחת שם משמעון מהנה לאבות ותולדות ומ"מ מדסמכינהו להדדי דרשינן אחת שהיא הנה והנה שהיא אחת:
שם

מסורת הש"ס

א) לקמן דף עג: וש"נ, ב) מכילתא פרשת ויקהל, ג) יבמות ו: לג: סנהדרין לה: ודף סב., ד) [פסחים ה:], ה) [כריתות ג.], ו) [לקמן קג. סנהדרין סב. כריתות ג.], ז) עשייתו הנה ומ"ס יתירה לרבות כו' רש"ל ואל"ל אלא רש"י בא לפרש לשון הספוק ועשה אחת הנה ומפ' כמ"ש לפנינו ועיין לקמן קג: משמע גם כן כמ"ש לפנינו, ח) [כך קושית מלי רש"י ועי' תוס' יבמות ו: ד"ה טעמא וכו' ובסנהדרין לה: ד"ה מבעיר דבריהם סיגב. וע"ע תוס' לעיל כ. ד"ה למשרי ותוספות לקמן קג. ד"ה מה לי ותוס' מנחות נה: ד"ה אם כן].

הגהות הב"ח

(א) גמ' כל העושה בו מלאכה:

ליקוטי רש"י

מחלליה. סגולה בה חול בקדושתה [שמות לא, יד]. **דברים הדברים אלה הדברים.** גבי שבת כתיב ויקהל אלה הדברים אשר צוה וגו' דברים משמע תרין ה"א מרבי חד הא תלת אלה בגימטריא תלתין ושש הא תלתין ותשע [לקמן צז:]. **ולמה יצאת להקיש אליה וכו'.** לחלוק ולומר לך מה זו מיוחדת שהיא מאבות מלאכות הנעשית במשכן וחייב עליה בפני עצמו אף כל שהוא מאבות מלאכה חייבין עליה בפני עצמו ... דכל דבר שהיה בכלל ויצא מן הכלל ללמד לא ללמד על עצמו יצא אלא ללמד על הכלל כולו יצא [סנהדרין סב.]. **לחלק יצאת.** ללמד על כולן שחייב על כל אחת ואחת ... **הבערה ללאו יצאת.** ... שאר מלאכות עליה שאינה לא בכרת ולא במיתה אלא בלאו [סנהדרין סב.]. מכלל מלאכות לומר לך שאין בה כרת וסקילה אלא לאו בעלמא [שם לה:]. שהיתה בכלל לא תעשה כל מלאכה וחזר והוציאה מכללו ופרט בה לאו לעצמה לומר לך שאינה במיתת בית דין כשאר מלאכות אלא בלאו

רבינו חננאל

דכי אמרו ליה שבת היא היום מיד פורש מכל מלאכה נמצאת בידו שגגה אחת שהיא שגגת שבת לפיכך אינו חייב אלא חטאת אחת אבל המזיד בשבת ושגג במלאכות אם מודיעים לו שהיא מלאכה פורש ממנה ועושה מלאכה אחרת ועוד מודיעין אותו ופורש ממנה ומתעסק באחרת הלכך כיון שצריך להודיעו על כל מלאכה ומלאכה נמצאו שגגותיו מרובים לפיכך חייב כנגד שגגותיו: **העושה** מלאכו' הרבה בשבת אחת בשגגה מנלן דחייב על כל מלאכה ומלאכה ופשט שמואל מדכתיב כל העושה בו מלאכה יומת דילפינן מיניה קטלא למזיד וכתיב קרא אחרינא מחלליה מות יומת דלא צריך ליה לקטלא ילפינן ליה פשטא לשוגג וכתיב מות יומת מיתות הרבה נמצאו בחילול שבת אחת מיתות הרבה. ומאי נינהו חטאות והכי קאמר יומת בממון כלומר יתן חטאות הרבה ור' נתן פשט ליה מלא תבערו אש הבערה בכלל היתה ולמה יצאת לחלק ולומר כשם שחייבין על הבערה בפני עצמה כך חייבין בכל אחת ואחת בפני עצמה אחר שפירש בחריש ובקציר שביתה וכתב רחמנא אלה הדברים מדהוה ליה למכתב (דאמר אלה) [ויאמר אליהם] הדברים אשר צוה ה' לעשות וכת' והוסיף אלה הדברים בגימטריא ל"ו ועוד מדהוה ליה למכתב דברים אלה שהן אלה ל"ו ודברים תרי הרי ל"ח והוסיף ה' בהדברים למדנו ממנו עוד אחת הרי ארבעים חסר אחת. ור' יוסי מדכתיב ועשה מאחת מהנה דריש ועשה מאחת פעמים שהוא חייב אחת על כולן והוו היודע עיקר שבת. מהנה פעמים שחייב על כל אחת ואחת. כיצד זדון שבת ושגגת מלאכות ושמואל הא דר' נתן סבר לה

תורה אור השלם

א) וּשְׁמַרְתֶּם אֶת הַשַּׁבָּת כִּי קֹדֶשׁ הִוא לָכֶם מְחַלְלֶיהָ מוֹת יוּמָת כִּי כָּל הָעֹשֶׂה בָהּ מְלָאכָה וְנִכְרְתָה הַנֶּפֶשׁ הַהִוא מִקֶּרֶב עַמֶּיהָ: [שמות לא, יד]

ב) שֵׁשֶׁת יָמִים תֵּעָשֶׂה מְלָאכָה וּבַיּוֹם הַשְּׁבִיעִי יִהְיֶה לָכֶם קֹדֶשׁ שַׁבַּת שַׁבָּתוֹן לַיְיָ כָּל הָעֹשֶׂה בוֹ מְלָאכָה יוּמָת: [שמות לה, ב]

ג) לֹא תְבַעֲרוּ אֵשׁ בְּכֹל מֹשְׁבֹתֵיכֶם בְּיוֹם הַשַּׁבָּת: [שמות לה, ג]

ד) וַיַּקְהֵל מֹשֶׁה אֶת כָּל עֲדַת בְּנֵי יִשְׂרָאֵל וַיֹּאמֶר אֲלֵהֶם אֵלֶּה הַדְּבָרִים אֲשֶׁר צִוָּה יְיָ לַעֲשֹׂת אֹתָם: [שמות לה, א]

ה) שֵׁשֶׁת יָמִים תַּעֲבֹד וּבַיּוֹם הַשְּׁבִיעִי תִּשְׁבֹּת בֶּחָרִישׁ וּבַקָּצִיר תִּשְׁבֹּת: [שמות לד, כא]

ו) דַּבֵּר אֶל בְּנֵי יִשְׂרָאֵל לֵאמֹר נֶפֶשׁ כִּי תֶחֱטָא בִשְׁגָגָה מִכֹּל מִצְוֹת יְיָ אֲשֶׁר לֹא תֵעָשֶׂינָה וְעָשָׂה מֵאַחַת מֵהֵנָּה: [ויקרא ד, ב]

[פסחים שם]. **מאחת מהנה.** וה"ל למיכתב אחת מהנה מאי מאחת משמע פעמים שחייב מעבירה אחת הנה כלומר כמה חטאות ומהנה מעבירות הרבה חטאת אחת [כריתות ג.]. גבי חטאת כתיב פעמים שחייב חטאת אחת על כולן כגון שוגג ... אין היום שבת אבל יודע היה שכל מלאכות שהוא עושה אסורות בשבת מביא קרבן אחד דחדא שגגה היא ופעמים שחייב על כל אחד ואחד כגון שהזיד בשבת ויודע שהוא שבת היום ויש שבת בתורה ושגג במלאכות שלא היה יודע שהמלאכות ... אסורות אלא מלאכות אחרות חייב על כל אחת ואחת שיש כאן שגגות הרבה. **אמר ר' יוסי בר' חנינא וכו'.** מפרש טעמא דר' יוסי היכי משמע ליה האי מהאי קרא. **אחת מאחת וכו'.** הוה ליה למכתב ועשה אחת מהנה אי נמי ועשה אחת ... ועשה אחת ולישתוק מדכתבינהו הכי שמע מינה למדרש כל חד וחד למודה לחייבו על אחת ועל מאחת כלומר מקצת העבירה על הנה ועל מהנה כדמפרש הנה אבות מהנה תולדות ולמדרשינהו נמי כי הדדי הכי מדסמכי להדדי [סנהדרין סב.]. אחת ... למכתב ולשתוק וכתב מ"ס יתירה [ומהנה יתירא]. **הנה מהנה.** אי נמי הנה הוה ליה למכתב וכתב מהנה מ"ס יתירה ומאחת יתירה הלכך למדרשינהו לכולהו כתבינהו ודרוש אחת הנה בלא מ"ס הכי. **אחת שהיא הנה הנה שהיא אחת.** ... איכא למידרש משמעותייהו ועשה עבירה אחת והיא לו הנה חייב חטאות הרבה אי נמי ועשה אחת עשייתו חשובה לו כאחת ואע"פ שהנה היו משמע שהרבה עבירות עשה והיינו הנה שהיא אחת הלכך תרוייהו דריש ביה פעמים שהיא כן ... שהיא כן כדמפרש לקמיה [לקמן קג:]. אחת שהיא הנה כלומר פעמים שהוא חייב על מלוה אחת חטאות הרבה והנה שהיא אחת פעמים שאינו חייב אלא אחת על מלות הרבה והכי משמע מאחת מחייב הנה מהנה מחייב אחת מדכתיב מ' יתירה ... מפרש לה [סנהדרין שם]. **אחת שמעון.** כלומר דריש מ"ס יתירה אחת הוי משמע דאינו חייב עד שיכתוב כל התיבה שנתכוון לכתוב [לקמן שם]. אחת כשעשה עבירה שלימה שנתכוון לכתוב שמעון וכתבו כולו [סנהדרין שם]. **מאחת שם משמעון.** ... אחת למימר דאפילו לא כתב אלא מקצתה ובלבד שתהא [מתקיימת] במקום אחר דומיא דאחת דרישיה דקרא [לקמן שם]. מאחת על מקצתו נמי מחייב כגון נתכוין לכתוב שמעון ולא כתב אלא שתי אותיות חייב ולהכי נקט שמעון משום דשתי אותיות ראשונות הוו להו שם במקום אחר כגון שם בן נח והוא הדין גד מגדיאל דן מדניאל אבל נתכוין לכתוב שם אחר כגון נפתלי ולא כתב ממנו אלא שתי אותיות לא מיחייב שאין כאן מלאכה בשום מקום [סנהדרין שם].

Rather the verse is needed for the following reason: לְפִי שֶׁנֶּאֱמַר – SINCE IT IS STATED:[14] ,,וַיַּקְהֵל מֹשֶׁה אֶת־כָּל־עֲדַת בְּנֵי יִשְׂרָאֵל . . . אֵלֶּה הַדְּבָרִים וגו׳ – *AND MOSES ASSEMBLED THE ENTIRE ASSEMBLY OF THE CHILDREN OF ISRAEL . . . THESE ARE THE THINGS* etc. [*that Hashem commanded, to do them*:] ,,שֵׁשֶׁת יָמִים תֵּעָשֶׂה מְלָאכָה״ – *SIX DAYS WORK MAY BE DONE.* ,,דְּבָרִים״ – The term *THINGS* indicates two *melachos;*[15] ,,הַדְּבָרִים״ – the addition of the letter *hei* to read *"THE" THINGS* adds one more; ,,אֵלֶּה הַדְּבָרִים״ – and the addition to this phrase, *"THESE" ARE THE THINGS* adds thirty-six more, because that is the numerical value of the Hebrew word אֵלֶּה (*these*).[16] אֵלּוּ שְׁלֹשִׁים וְתֵשַׁע מְלָאכוֹת שֶׁנֶּאֶמְרוּ לְמֹשֶׁה בְּסִינַי – THESE ARE THE THIRTY-NINE *MELACHOS* THAT WERE STATED TO MOSES AT SINAI. יָכוֹל עֲשָׂאָן כּוּלָּן בְּהֶעְלֵם אֶחָד – IT COULD BE thought that if ONE PERFORMED ALL OF THEM IN ONE LAPSE OF AWARENESS, אֵינוֹ חַיָּיב אֶלָּא אַחַת – HE IS LIABLE TO ONLY ONE *chatas.* תַּלְמוּד לוֹמַר ,,בֶּחָרִישׁ וּבַקָּצִיר תִּשְׁבֹּת״ – [THE TORAH] therefore TEACHES elsewhere: *FROM THE PLOWING AND THE REAPING YOU SHALL REST.*[17] וַעֲדַיִין אֲנִי אוֹמֵר – BUT I CAN STILL SAY עַל חֲרִישָׁה וְעַל הַקְּצִירָה חַיָּיב שְׁתַּיִם – THAT FOR PLOWING AND REAPING ONE IS LIABLE TO TWO offerings,[18] וְעַל כּוּלָּן אֵינוֹ חַיָּיב אֶלָּא אַחַת – WHILE FOR ALL the rest OF [THE *MELACHOS*] HE IS LIABLE TO ONLY ONE offering.[19] תַּלְמוּד לוֹמַר ,,לֹא־תְבַעֲרוּ אֵשׁ״ – [THE TORAH] therefore TEACHES: *YOU SHALL NOT KINDLE A FIRE*.[20] הַבְעָרָה בִּכְלָל הָיְתָה – KINDLING WAS included IN THE GENERAL prohibition against performing *melachah* on the Sabbath.[21] וְלָמָּה יָצְאת – SO WHY WAS IT SINGLED OUT? לְהַקִּישׁ אֵלֶיהָ וְלוֹמַר לְךָ – TO COMPARE the other *melachos* TO IT,[22] AND TO TELL YOU: מָה הַבְעָרָה שֶׁהִיא אַב מְלָאכָה – JUST AS KINDLING, WHICH IS AN *AV MELACHAH*, וְחַיָּיבִין עָלֶיהָ בִּפְנֵי עַצְמָהּ – ONE IS LIABLE FOR violating IT ON ITS OWN, אַף כֹּל שֶׁהוּא אַב מְלָאכָה – SO ANYTHING THAT IS AN *AV MELACHAH*, חַיָּיבִין עָלֶיהָ בִּפְנֵי עַצְמָהּ – ONE IS LIABLE FOR violating IT ON ITS OWN.[23] At any rate, why did Shmuel not derive the principle of separation of *melachos* as R' Nassan did?

The Gemara answers:

שְׁמוּאֵל סָבַר לָהּ כְּרַבִּי יוֹסֵי – **Shmuel holds in accordance with R' Yose,** דְּאָמַר הַבְעָרָה לְלָאו יָצְאת – **who said that** the *melachah* of **kindling was singled out to be a** mere **prohibition,** not a capital crime.[24] דְּתַנְיָא – **For it was taught in a Baraisa:** הַבְעָרָה לְלָאו יָצְאת – KINDLING WAS SINGLED OUT TO BE A mere PROHIBITION; דִּבְרֵי רַבִּי יוֹסֵי – these are THE WORDS OF R' YOSE. רַבִּי נָתָן אוֹמֵר – R' NASSAN SAYS: לַחֲלֵק יָצְאת – IT WAS SINGLED OUT TO SEPARATE the Sabbath *melachos* into distinct categories of liability.[25]

The Gemara again questions Shmuel:

וְתִיפּוֹק לֵיהּ לְחִילּוּק מְלָאכוֹת – **But derive** the concept of **separation of** *melachos* מֵהֵיכָא דְּנָפְקָא לֵיהּ לְרַבִּי יוֹסֵי – **from where R' Yose derived it.** דְּתַנְיָא – **For it was taught in a Baraisa:** רַבִּי יוֹסֵי אוֹמֵר – R' YOSE SAYS: ,,וְעָשָׂה מֵאַחַת מֵהֵנָּה״ – Scripture states: *AND HE WILL DO FROM ONE OF THEM.*[26] This teaches that פְּעָמִים שֶׁחַיָּיבִים אַחַת עַל כּוּלָּן – SOMETIMES ONE who commits numerous transgressions IS LIABLE TO only ONE *chatas* FOR ALL OF [THE TRANSGRESSIONS], וּפְעָמִים שֶׁחַיָּיבִין עַל כָּל אַחַת וְאַחַת – and SOMETIMES HE IS LIABLE to a separate *chatas* FOR EACH AND EVERY transgression.[27]

The Gemara analyzes the Baraisa to explain its question:

[וְ]אָמַר רַבִּי יוֹסֵי בְּרַבִּי חֲנִינָא – **And R' Yose the son of R' Chanina said:** מַאי טַעְמָא דְּרַבִּי יוֹסֵי – **What is R' Yose's reason?**[28] ,,אַחַת מֵאַחַת״ – The verse could have stated merely **"one,"** but instead added a *mem* to convey ***"from" one;*** ,,הֵנָּה מֵהֵנָּה״ – by the same token, the verse could have stated merely **"them,"** but instead added a *mem* to convey ***"of" them.***[29] אַחַת שֶׁהִיא הֵנָּה – Further-

NOTES

14. *Exodus* 35:1-2.

15. The minimum plural number is two (*Rashi*).

16. א=1, ל=30, and ה=5, for a total of 36.

17. Ibid. 34:21. The verse in its entirety states: שֵׁשֶׁת יָמִים תַּעֲבֹד וּבַיּוֹם הַשְּׁבִיעִי תִּשְׁבֹּת בֶּחָרִישׁ וּבַקָּצִיר תִּשְׁבֹּת, *Six days shall you work and on the seventh day you shall rest; from the plowing and the reaping you shall rest.* We could apparently derive from this verse, which lists two of the *melachos,* that each *melachah* of the thirty-nine *melachos* is considered a different prohibition. Accordingly, it should not be necessary to derive the concept of separation of *melachos* from the verse *You shall not kindle* first stated by R' Nassan (*Rashi*).

18. I.e. if someone performs these two *melachos* in one lapse, he is liable to two offerings. Since the Torah singled out these two *melachos,* it is implied that there exists a separate admonition for plowing and a separate admonition for reaping (*Rashi*).

19. All the rest should still be considered a single violation (*Rashi*). [See below, note 23.]

20. R' Nassan derives the concept of separation of *melachos* from the verse referring to kindling, as the Baraisa proceeds to explain. The verse just cited, referring to plowing and reaping, is expounded for a different law in *Rosh Hashanah* 9a (*Rashi*).

21. In the verse (*Exodus* 20:10): *You shall not do any work* (*Rashi*).

22. All of the other *melachos* that were included in the general prohibition with kindling are compared to kindling. This is based on the hermeneutic principle that anything which is a member of a certain category and was singled out by the Torah for a specific law automatically serves as a model for its entire category [כָּל דָּבָר שֶׁהָיָה בִּכְלָל וְיָצָא מִן הַכְּלָל לְלַמֵּד, לֹא לְלַמֵּד עַל עַצְמוֹ יָצָא, אֶלָּא לְלַמֵּד עַל הַכְּלָל כֻּלּוֹ יָצָא] (*Rashi*). Thus, whatever is learned about the *melachah* of kindling applies to all of the other *melachos* as well.

23. *Rashi* (ד״ה ועל כלן) asks why the Baraisa did not utilize this same principle for the verse it first cited, *from the plowing and the reaping you shall rest.* We should say that these two *melachos* were included in the general principle and were singled out to teach that all *melachos* carry a separate punishment of a sacrifice. *Rashi* answers that if the Torah wanted to utilize that verse for this purpose it should not have singled out two *melachos,* reaping and plowing, to teach about the other *melachos;* one *melachah* would have sufficed. By stating both, the Torah must be teaching another law from this verse. [See there for another answer.]

24. Deliberate violation of a Sabbath *melachah* is subject to the capital punishment of stoning [when there are two witnesses to the transgression who warned the transgressor in the prescribed manner], or to *kares* [when these conditions are not met]. According to R' Yose, the Torah specifies a distinct prohibition for kindling in order to remove it from the general classification of the other Sabbath *melachos,* designating it merely as a prohibition [subject only to lashes] (*Rashi*).

25. As we learned in the previous Baraisa. Just as kindling is an *av melachah* which carries separate liability, so too all of the *melachos* each carry separate liability (*Rashi*).

26. *Leviticus* 4:2. The verse introducing the section of the various *chatas* offerings reads: נֶפֶשׁ כִּי־תֶחֱטָא בִשְׁגָגָה מִכֹּל מִצְוֹת ה׳ אֲשֶׁר לֹא תֵעָשֶׂינָה וְעָשָׂה מֵאַחַת מֵהֵנָּה, *When a person will sin unintentionally from among all the commandments of Hashem that may not be done, and he will do from one of them.* Now, the verse could have concluded: וְעָשָׂה אַחַת, *and he will do one,* to convey the same idea. Thus the *mem* in מֵאַחַת, *"from" one,* is superfluous, along with the entire word מֵהֵנָּה, *of them* (*Rashi*).

27. In some instances, all of a person's transgressions are considered as if they were one (אַחַת), liable to only one *chatas,* whereas other times they are considered multiple transgressions (הֵנָּה, which is plural) [subject to a separate *chatas* for each] (*Rashi*). This exposition will be elaborated below.

28. I.e. what does R' Yose derive from the two *mems* in מֵאַחַת מֵהֵנָּה? (*Rashi;* see next note; cf. *Tosafos*). The exposition in the previous note could be made even if the verse stated only וְעָשָׂה אַחַת הֵנָּה. R' Yose the son of R' Chanina therefore explains how R' Yose expounds the entire verse.

29. The *mem* in each of these words is superfluous (*Rashi*). [Our emendation follows *Rashi.*] R' Yose the son of R' Chanina will explain what can be derived from each. [Actually, the entire word מֵהֵנָּה is superfluous, as stated in note 26. But R' Yose the son of R' Chanina now states that even though the term הֵנָּה is needed for an exposition, another exposition can be made from the *mem.*]

מסורת הש"ס

א) לקמן דף לז: וש"נ, ב) מכילתא פרשת ויקהל, ג) יבמות ו: לג: סנהדרין לה: ודף סב. [כריתות כ:], ד) [פסחים ה:], ה) לקמן קג: סנהדרין סב. [כריתות ג.], ו) עשייתו הנה ומ"ס יתירא לרבות כ"ה גי' רש"ל ואצ"ל אלא רש"י בא לפרש לשון הפסוק ועשה אחת הנה ומס' כמ"ש רש"י לפנינו ועיין לקמן קג: משמע גם כן כמ"ש לפנינו, ז) [הך קושיא מאי קאי גם למ"ד הבערה לחלק יצאת ועי' תוס' יבמות ו: ד"ה טעמא וכו' ובסנהדרין לה: ד"ה מושבות וכו' מבואר דבריהם היטב. וע"ע תוס' לעיל כ. ד"ה למשרי ותוספות לקמן קו. ד"ה מה לי ותוס' מנחות נה: ד"ה אם כן].

גמרא

מאי שנא רישא ומאי שנא סיפא אמר רב ספרא כאן מידיעת שבת הוא פורש וכאן מידיעת מלאכה הוא פורש א"ל רב נחמן כלום פריש משבת אלא משום מלאכות וכלום פריש ממלאכות אלא משום שבת אלא אמר רב נחמן קרבן דחייב רחמנא אמאי אשגגה התם חדא שגגה הכא טובא שגגות הויין: חייב על כל מלאכה ומלאכה: חילוק מלאכות מנלן אמר שמואל אמר קרא א) מחלליה מות יומת התורה רבתה מיתות הרבה על חילול אחד האי במזיד כתיב אם אינו ענין למזיד דכתיב ב) כל העושה (א) מלאכה יומת תנהו ענין לשוגג ומאי יומת בממון ותיפוק ליה חילוק מלאכות מהיכא דנפקא ליה לר' נתן דתניא ר' נתן אומר ג) לא תבערו אש בכל מושבותיכם ביום השבת מה ת"ל לפי שנאמר ד) ויקהל משה את כל עדת בני ישראל אלה הדברים וגו' ב) ששת ימים תעשה מלאכה א) דברים הדברים אלה הדברים אלו שלשים ותשע מלאכות שנאמרו למשה בסיני יכול עשאן כולן בהעלם אחד אינו חייב אלא אחת ת"ל ה) בחריש ובקציר תשבות ועדיין אני אומר ב) על חרישה ועל הקצירה חייב שתים ועל כולן אינו חייב אלא אחת ת"ל ג) לא תבערו אש הבערה בכלל היתה ולמה יצאת להקיש אליה ולומר לך מה הבערה שהיא אב מלאכה וחייבין עליה בפני עצמה אף כל שהוא אב מלאכה חייבין עליה בפני עצמה שמואל סבר לה כרבי יוסי דאמר הבערה ללאו יצאת ג) דתניא הבערה ללאו יצאת דברי רבי יוסי ר' נתן אומר ד) לחלק יצאת ותיפוק ליה לחלוק מלאכות מהיכא דנפקא ליה לר' יוסי ה) דתניא רבי יוסי אומר ו) ועשה מאחת מהנה פעמים שחייבים אחת על כולן ופעמים שחייבין על כל אחת ואחת אמר ר' יוסי בר' חנינא מ"ט דר' יוסי אחת מאחת הנה מהנה אחת שהיא הנה הנה שהיא אחת אחת שמעון מאחת

שם

רש"י

מאי שנא רישא. דשגגת שבת וזדון מלאכות לא מיחייב אלא אחת לכל שבת וסיפא לזדון שבת ושגגת מלאכות חייב על כל מלאכה ומלאכה: כאן מידיעת שבת הוא פורש. רישא כי אמרו ליה שבת הוא פורש מן המלאכה ומכיר שחטא ועל כך הוא מביא קרבן הלכך שגגת שבת היא ועל השבת הוא צריך להביא: כאן מידיעת מלאכות הוא פורש. כי אמרי ליה שבת הוא לא פריש דהא נמי ידע וכי אמרי ליה מלאכה חשובה היא זו פריש הלכך על מנין המלאכות יביא: כלום פריש משבת אלא משום. דכי אודעיה שבת הוא הכיר שחטא על המלאכות וכלום פריש ממלאכה כלומר ע"י ידיעת המלאכות אלא משום שבת דכי אמרו ליה מלאכות הן הכיר שחילל שבת: חילוק מלאכות. שגופי מלאכות מתחלקים לחטאות ואע"פ שבהעלם אחד: מות יומת. מיתות הרבה: בממון. לאפושי קרבנות: מה ת"ל. והלא כבר נאמר לא תעשה כל מלאכה: דברים. משמע תרי ה' לרבות חד הרי שלשה אלה בגמטריא ל"ו הרי ל"ט: ת"ל בחריש ובקציר תשבות. כלומר בלאו לא תבערו הוה לן למילף מהאי אם לא שיש להשיב: ועדיין אני אומר על חריש וקציר חייב שתים. אם עשאן בהעלם אחד שהרי הוציאם מן הכלל לחלקן לשתים ומשמע אזהרה לקציר לעצמה ואזהרה לחריש לעצמה: ועל כולן אחת. דבחדא מלאכה כיילינהו וחד לאו ובדבר שהיה בכלל ויצא מן הכלל ללמד לא ללמד כו' לא דיינינן ליה דהוי ליה כלל בלא תעשה ופרט בעשה ואין דנין אותו בכלל ופרט אי נמי הוי חריש וקציר שני כתובין הבאין כאחד ואין מלמדין דהוה ליה למיכתב חד: ת"ל לא תבערו כו'. וחריש וקציר לדרשה אחרינא אי כר' עקיבא דדריש ליה בעלמא (ר"ה דף ט.) לענין תוספת שביעית אי כרבי ישמעאל לענין שבת מה חריש רשות אף קציר רשות ללמד על קציר העומר שדוחה שבת: בכלל היתה. דלא תעשה כל מלאכה: להקיש אליה. כל שאר המלאכות שנכללו עמה בכלל שזו מדה בתורה כל דבר שהיה בכלל ויצא מן הכלל ללמד לא ללמד על עצמו יצא כו': ללאו. שאין חייבין עליה כרת וסקילה כשאר מלאכות אלא מה שאמור בה: לחלק. כדאמרן מה הבערה מיוחדת: ועשה מאחת מהנה. האמור לענין חטאות הוה ליה למכתב ועשה אחת ולישתוק אייתר ליה שאר' מ"ס דמאחת וכל תיבת מהנה לדרשה ודרוש הכי פעמים שכל מעשה עבירותיו חשוב אחת ופעמים שהוא קרוי הנה לשון רבים: וא"ר יוסי ברבי חנינא מ"ט דרבי יוסי. כלומר מאי דריש ביה דאכתי מ' דמהנה ומ' דמאחת למאי אתא: אחת מאחת. אחת הוה ליה למכתב וכתיב מאחת וכן נמי הנה ה"ל למכתב (הנה) [למדרש פעמים שהוא הנה] וכתב מהנה ודרוש אחת והנה בלא מ"ס הכי פעמים אחת שהוא הנה שבת [אחת] לבדו הוא מחלל ויש כאן חטאות הרבה דאולי בתר מלאכות ופעמים הנה שהיא אחת מלאכות הרבה עשה ואינו חייב אלא אחת דבהנך תרי גווני איכא למשמע ועשה אחת וחייב הנה ואיכא למימר נמי הכי ועשה אחת הנה ו) עשייתו הוי אחת אע"פ שהן הנה [וחייב א'] ומ"ס יתירה [דרוש הכי] לרבות שהכותב שם משמעון דאע"ג שנתכוון לעשות תיבה גדולה הואיל ושתי אותיות הראשונות שם במקום אחר הן חייב והיינו מאחת מקצת המלאכה ולא כולה יביא חטאת:

מהנה

תוספות

אם אינו ענין למזיד דהא כתיב כו'. ואם תאמר ולימא אם אינו ענין למזיד משום דלאו בתרי קטלא קטלת ליה וי"ל דאי לאו קרא אחרינא דמייתי הוה מוקמינן ליה להאי קרא במזיד ומות יומת דברה תורה כלשון בני אדם אבל השתא דלא איצטריך למזיד מוקמי ליה ע"כ בשוגג ולחייב קרבן על כל א':

יכול שאם עשאן כולם בהעלם אחד כו'. תימה א"כ מניינא דקרא דברים הדברים אלה הדברים למה לי כיון דלא אתא לחלק ויש לומר דצריך למניינא לפי שיש מלאכות שאינן חשובות ואיצטריך מניינא לאשמעינן דכולהו הויין מלאכות להתחייב עליהן ומיהו ממתניתין דמ' מלאכות דייק שפיר דבהעלם אחד חייב על כל אחת דלא הוה צריך למניינא כיון דמני כולהו בהדיא ומיהו קשה לר"י דלקמן בהזורק (דף צז:) משמע דהאי מניינא אתיא לחלק דאמר התם למימרא דמחייב רבי אתולדה במקום אב והתניא רבי אומר דברים הדברים אלה הדברים כו' ופי' בקונטרס התם דהכי פריך הואיל ומניינא לא אתא אלא לחילוק חטאות ואי ס"ד דמחייב אתולדה במקום אב טובא ה"ל למיתני ולפי מה שפירשנו דמניינא לא אתא אלא לאשמעינן דכולהו חשובות מלאכות להתחייב עליהם לא הוה פריך מידי ונראה לר"י דגרס הכא כמו במכילתא דתניא התם רבי נתן אומר לא תבערו אש למה נאמר לפי שנאמר ויקהל משה שומע אני שלא יהא חייב עד שיעבור ל"ט מלאכות תלמוד לומר בחריש ובקציר וכו' והשתא אי לאו לא תבערו ה"א דמניינא אתא למימר שאינו חייב על אחת או שתים עד שיעבור כל ל"ט וכיון דכתיב לא תבערו דילפינן מיניה דחייב על כל אחת בפני עצמה אם כן מניינא אתא למימר דאל"ט דווקא הוא דחייב על כל אחת ואחת אבל אתולדה במקום אב לא והשתא מוכח שפיר בהזורק דרבי לא מחייב אתולדה במקום אב ואתי נמי שפיר להאי גירסא דקתני לפי שנאמר דברים הדברים וגו' יכול כו' דמשמע דמתוך קרא דהדברים הוא דמשמע ליה דאינו חייב עד שיעבור כולן וכן בפ"ק דפסחים (דף ה:) לפי שנאמר לא יראה לך יכול יטמין ויקבל פקדונות מן הנכרים אבל לגירסת הספרים מאי קאמר לפי שנאמר בלאו קרא נמי הוה אמרינן הכי כל כמה דלא נפקא לן חילוק מלאכות משום מקום:

על חרישה וקצירה חייב שתים. וא"ת מנא ליה דחייב שתים נימא דלא מיחייב אתרוייהו אלא אחת וי"ל משום דכתיב בחריש ובקציר דמשמע תרי מילי מדלא כתב בחריש וקציר:

ועל כולן אינו חייב אלא אחת. פירש בקונט' משום דהוי ליה כלל בלא תעשה ופרט בעשה וקשה דכללא נמי כתיב בעשה וביום השביעי תשבות ועוד דגבי כלל ופרט דוקא הוא דאמרינן בפרק קמא דמו"ק (דף ג.) דלא דיינינן כשאין הכלל בלשון הפרט אבל לגבי דבר שהוא יצא מן הכלל לא אשכחן בשום מקום ועוד דבמועד קטן איכא למ"ד דנין ונראה כפי' אחרון שפי' בקונט' דלא ילפינן מחריש וקציר משום דהוו שני כתובים הבאים כאחד וכה"ג אמרינן בפרק ד' מיתות (סנהדרין סז:) אוב וידעוני בכלל כל המכשפים היו כו' ופריך וליהוי אוב וידעוני שני כתובים הבאין כא' ואם תאמר והיכי יליף מלא תבערו כל שכן דהוי ג' כתובים הבאין כאחד ואין מלמדין לכ"ע וכ"ת דחריש וקציר אתא לכדדרשינן בריש מו"ק (ד' ד.) מה חריש רשות כו' אם כן היכי הוה בעי למילף מיניה מעיקרא הא לא אתי להכי ואומר ר"י דלא הוו ג' כתובים מדלא כתבינהו או כולהו בלאו או כולהו בעשה ולהכי ילפינן מהבערה ומהשתא אייתר ליה חריש וקציר לכדדרשינן במו"ק:

הבערה ללאו יצאת. וא"ת ז) והא איצטריך למיכתב לא תבערו משום סיפיה דקרא דכתיב בכל מושבותיכם דדרשינן מינה ביבמות (דף ו:) ובסנהדרין (דף לה:) דאין רציחה דוחה שבת וי"ל דהוה מצי למיכתב בלישנא אחריתי ולא לכתוב לא תבערו ומשום דדרשינן בפ"ק (דף כ.) אבל אתה מבעיר כו' לא הוה צריך למיכתב לא תבערו:

מאי טעמא דר' יוסי. פי' בקונט' כלומר דאכתי מ"ס דמאחת ומהנה למה לי ולשון מאי טעמא אינו משמע כן ונראה לר"י דה"פ מ"ט דר' יוסי הא איצטריך קרא לשם משמעון ולאבות ולתולדות ומנא ליה דחייב על כל אחת ואחת ומפרש דמאחת שם משמעון מהנה לאבות ותולדות ומ"מ מדסמכינהו להדדי דרשינן אחת שהיא הנה והנה שהיא אחת:

שם

רבינו חננאל

דכי אמרו ליה שבת היא היום מיד פורש מכל מלאכה נמצאת בידו שגגה אחת שהיא שגגת שבת לפיכך אינו חייב אלא חטאת אחת אבל המזיד בשבת ושגג במלאכות אם מודיעים לו שהיא מלאכה פורש ממנה ועושה מלאכה אחרת ועוד מודיעין אותו ופורש ממנה ומתעסק באחרת הלכך כיון שצריך להודיעו על כל מלאכה ומלאכה נמצאו שגגותיו מרובים לפיכך חייב כנגד שגגותיו: **העושה** מלאכו' הרבה בשבת אחת בשגגה מנלן דחייב על כל מלאכה ומלאכה ופשט שמואל מדכתיב כל העושה בו מלאכה יומת דילפינן מיניה קטלא למזיד וכתיב קרא אחרינא מחלליה מות יומת דלא צריך ליה לקטלא דהא ילפינן ליה פשטנא לשוגג וכתיב מות יומת מיתות הרבה נמצאו בחילול שבת אחת מיתות הרבה. ומאי נינהו חטאות והכי קאמר יומת בממון כלומר יתן חטאות הרבה ור' נתן פשט ליה מלא תבערו אש הבערה בכלל היתה למה יצאת לחלק ולומר כשם שחייבין על ההבערה בפני עצמה כך חייבין בכל אחת ואחת בפני עצמה אחר שפירש בחריש ובקציר שביתה וכתב רחמנא אלה הדברים מדהוה למכתב (דאמר אלה) [ויאמר אליהם] הדברים אשר צוה ה' לעשות וכת' והוסיף אלה הדברים אלה בגימטריא ל"ו ועוד מדהוה למכתב דברים אלה שהן אלה ל"ו ודברים תרי הרי ל"ח והוסיף ה' בהדברים למדנו ממנו עוד אחת הרי ארבעים חסר אחת. ור' יוסי מדכתיב ועשה מאחת מהנה דריש ועשה מאחת פעמים שהוא חייב אחת על כולן וזהו היודע עיקר שבת. מהנה פעמים שחייב על כל אחת ואחת. כיצד זדון שבת ושגגת מלאכות ושמואל הא דר' נתן סבר לה

תורה אור השלם

א) וּשְׁמַרְתֶּם אֶת הַשַּׁבָּת כִּי קֹדֶשׁ הִוא לָכֶם מְחַלְלֶיהָ מוֹת יוּמָת כִּי כָּל הָעֹשֶׂה בָהּ מְלָאכָה וְנִכְרְתָה הַנֶּפֶשׁ הַהִוא מִקֶּרֶב עַמֶּיהָ: [שמות לא, יד]

ב) שֵׁשֶׁת יָמִים תֵּעָשֶׂה מְלָאכָה וּבַיּוֹם הַשְּׁבִיעִי יִהְיֶה לָכֶם קֹדֶשׁ שַׁבַּת שַׁבָּתוֹן לַייָ כָּל הָעֹשֶׂה בוֹ מְלָאכָה יוּמָת: [שמות לה, ב]

ג) לֹא תְבַעֲרוּ אֵשׁ בְּכֹל מֹשְׁבֹתֵיכֶם בְּיוֹם הַשַּׁבָּת: [שמות לה, ג]

ד) וַיַּקְהֵל מֹשֶׁה אֶת כָּל עֲדַת בְּנֵי יִשְׂרָאֵל וַיֹּאמֶר אֲלֵהֶם אֵלֶּה הַדְּבָרִים אֲשֶׁר צִוָּה יְיָ לַעֲשֹׂת אֹתָם: [שמות לה, א]

ה) שֵׁשֶׁת יָמִים תַּעֲבֹד וּבַיּוֹם הַשְּׁבִיעִי תִּשְׁבֹּת בֶּחָרִישׁ וּבַקָּצִיר תִּשְׁבֹּת: [שמות לד, כא]

ו) דַּבֵּר אֶל בְּנֵי יִשְׂרָאֵל לֵאמֹר נֶפֶשׁ כִּי תֶחֱטָא בִשְׁגָגָה מִכֹּל מִצְוֹת יְיָ אֲשֶׁר לֹא תֵעָשֶׂינָה וְעָשָׂה מֵאַחַת מֵהֵנָּה: [ויקרא ד, ב]

הגהות הב"ח

(א) גמ' כל העושה בו מלאכה:

ליקוטי רש"י

מחלליה. הנוהג בה חול בקדושתה [שמות לא, יד]. דברים הדברים אלה הדברים. גבי שבת דכתיב בויקהל אלה הדברים אשר צוה וגו' דברים משמע תרין ה"א מרבי חד הא תלת אלה בגימטריא תלתין ושש אלו שלשים ותשע כו' [לקמן צז:]. ולמה יצאת להקיש אליה וכו'. לחלוק ולומר לך מה זו מיוחדת שהיא מאבות מלאכות הנעשית במשכן וחייב עליה הכתוב בפני עצמו שפרט לה לבדה אף כל שהוא אב מלאכה אם עשאן בהעלם אחד חייב על כל אחת ואחת דכל דבר שהיה בכלל ויצא מן הכלל ללמד לא ללמד על עצמו יצא אלא ללמד על הכלל כולו יצא [סנהדרין סב.]. לחלק יצאה מן הכלל ללמד על הכלל כולו יצא שלא תאמר עשאן לכל המלאכות בהעלם אחת אינו חייב אלא אחת לכך יצאה זו להקיש אליה את כל הכלל ולומר לך מה זו מיוחדת שהיא אב מלאכה וחייבין עליה בפני עצמה שהרי הזהיר עליה לאו בפני עצמה אף כל שהיא אב מלאכה חייבין עליה בפני עצמה [שם לה:]. שלא תאמר אינו חייב סקילה עד שיחלל שבת בכל מלאכות לכך יצאה הבערה מן הכלל לחלק מה הבערה מיוחדת שהיא אב מלאכה וחייב עליה כרת וסקילה בפני עצמה אף כל שהוא אב מלאכה כו' [יבמות ו:]. לחלק יצאתה שלא תאמר העושה ארבעה או חמשה אבות מלאכות בשוגג בשבת אינו חייב אלא אחת דהא חד לאו איכא בכולהו וחד כרת לפיכך פרט בה בפני עצמה להקיש אליה מה היא מיוחדת שהיא אב מלאכה וחייבין עליה לעצמה כו' [פסחים ה:]. הבערה. שיצאה מכלל לא תעשה כל מלאכה דשבת. ללאו יצאת. להוציאה מחומרי שאר מלאכות וללמד עליה שאינה לא בכרת ולא במיתה אלא בלאו [סנהדרין סב.]. מכלל שאר המלאכות לומר לך שאין בה כרת וסקילה אלא לאו בעלמא [שם לה:]. שהיתה בכלל לא תעשה כל מלאכה חזר והוציאה מכללו ופרט בה לאו לעצמה לומר לך שאינה במיתת בית דין כשאר מלאכות אלא בלאו זה לבדו [פסחים שם]. מאחת מהנה. וה"ל למיכתב אחת מהנה מאי מאחת משמע פעמים שחייב מעבירה אחת הנה כלומר כמה חטאות ומהנה מעבירות הרבה חטאת אחת [כריתות ג.]. גבי חטאת כתיב פעמים שחייב חטאת אחת על כולן כגון שוגג בשבת כסבור אין היום שבת אבל יודע היה שכל מלאכות שהוא עושה אסורות בשבת מביא קרבן אחד דחדא שגגה היא ופעמים שחייב על כל אחד ואחד כגון שהזיד בשבת ויודע שהוא שבת היום ויש שבת בתורה ושגג במלאכות שלא היה יודע שהמלאכות הללו אסורות אלא מלאכות אחרות חייב על כל אחת ואחת שיש כאן שגגות הרבה. מפרש טעמא דר' יוסי היכי משמע ליה האי מהאי קרא. אמר ר' יוסי בר' חנינא וכו'. אחת מאחת וכו'. הוה ליה למכתב ועשה אחת מהנה אי נמי ועשה אחת מהנה אי נמי ועשה אחת ולישתוק מדכתביניהו הכי שמע מינה לכל חד וחד למודה למייתו על אחת ועל מאחת כלומר מקצת העבירה על הנה ועל מהנה כלומר דמפרש הנה אבות מהנה תולדות ולמדרשינהו נמי כי הדדי הכי מדסמכי להדדי [סנהדרין סב.]. אחת הוה ליה למכתב ולשתוק וכתב מ"ס יתירה [ומהנה יתירא]. הנה מהנה, אי נמי הנה הוה ליה למכתב וכתב מהנה מ"ס יתירה ומאחת יתירה הלכך למדרשינהו לכולהו כתבינהו ודרוש אחת הנה בלא מ"ס הכי. אחת שהיא הנה הנה שהיא אחת. לתרי גווני איכא למידרש משמעותייהו ועשה עבירה אחת והיא לו הנה חייב חטאות הרבה אי נמי ועשה אחת עשייתו חשובה לו כאחת ואע"פ שהנה היו משמע שהרבה עבירות עשה והיינו הנה שהיא אחת הלכך תרוייהו דריש ביה פעמים שהיא כן ופעמים שהיא כן כדמפרש לקמיה [לקמן קג:]. אחת שהיא הנה כלומר פעמים שהוא חייב על מלוה אחת חטאות הרבה והנה שהיא אחת פעמים שאינו חייב אלא אחת על הנה והכי משמע מאחת מהנה מחייב אחת מדכתיב מ' יתירה והשתא מפרש לה [סנהדרין שם]. אחת שמעון. כלומר דריש מ"ס יתירה אחת הוי משמע דלאו חייב עד שיכתוב כל התיבה שנתכוון לכתוב [לקמן שם]. אחת כשעשה עבירה שלימה שנתכוון לכתוב שמעון וכתבו כולו [סנהדרין שם]. מאחת שם משמעון. כתב מאחת למימר דאפילו לא כתב אלא מקצתה ובלבד שתהא [מתקיימת] במקום אחר דומיא דאחת דרישיה דקרא [לקמן שם]. מאחת על מקצתו נמי מחייב כגון נתכוון לכתוב שמעון ולא כתב אלא שתי אותיות חייב ולהכי נקט שמעון משום דשתי אותיות ראשונות הוו להו שם במקום אחר כגון שם בן נח והוא הדין גד מגדיאל דן מדניאל אבל נתכוון לכתוב שם אחר כגון נפתלי ולא כתב ממנו אלא שתי אותיות לא מיחייב שאין כאן מלאכה בשום מקום [סנהדרין שם].

more, we expound the two words "one" and "them" as if no *mem* was written in the following way: There is an instance of a transgression of **one** commandment **that is** tantamount to a transgression of **them** [i.e. many commandments],[30] הֵנָּה שֶׁהִיא אַחַת – and there is an instance of **them** [i.e. many transgressions], **that is** tantamount to **one** transgression.[31]

R' Yose the son of R' Chanina now elaborates on each of the expositions. He begins with the superfluous *mem* in the word "from one":

אַחַת שִׁמְעוֹן – The term **one** without a *mem* would indicate that the person is not liable unless he wrote the entire word he had in mind: for example, **Shimon.**[32] "מֵאַחַת" – The word with a *mem, **"from" one,*** teaches that one is liable for carrying out just part of his intention;

NOTES

30. That is, sometimes a person can desecrate one Sabbath but be liable to multiple *chatas* offerings, one for each *melachah* (*Rashi*).

31. Sometimes a person performs numerous *melachos* yet is liable to only one *chatas* (*Rashi*).

These derivations are based on two possible reading of the verse: We can interpret it to mean, *And he will do one* desecration of the Sabbath [וְעָשָׂה אַחַת], and be liable for each of *them* [הֵנָּה] – i.e. one *chatas* for each *melachah.* Alternatively, the verse can be interpreted, *What he does* is considered *one* violation [וְעָשָׂה אַחַת] even though he transgressed many of *them* [הֵנָּה] (*Rashi* here, as explained by *Mesoras HaShas,* and below, 103b). R' Yose the son of R' Chanina will explain below when each of these rulings apply.

32. The term אַחַת indicates that he is liable only if his entire original intention is carried out, in this case the writing of the word Shimon (*Rashi* here and below, 103b).

מאי שנא רישא ומאי שנא סיפא אמר רב ספרא כאן מידיעת שבת הוא פורש וכאן מידיעת מלאכה הוא פורש א"ל רב נחמן כלום פריש משבת אלא משום מלאכות וכלום פריש ממלאכות אלא משום שבת אלא אמר רב נחמן קרבן דחייב רחמנא אמאי אשגגה התם חדא שגגה הכא טובא שגגות הויין: חייב על כל מלאכה ומלאכה: חילוק מלאכות מנלן אמר שמואל אמר קרא א) מחלליה מות יומת התורה רבתה מיתות הרבה על חילול אחד האי במזיד כתיב אם אינו ענין למזיד דכתיב ב) כל העושה (א) מלאכה יומת תנהו ענין לשוגג ומאי יומת יומת בממון ותיפוק ליה חילוק מלאכות מהיכא דנפקא ליה לר' נתן דתניא ר' נתן אומר ג) לא תבערו אש בכל מושבותיכם ביום השבת מה ת"ל לפי שנאמר ד) ויקהל משה את כל עדת בני ישראל אלה הדברים וגו' ב) ששת ימים תעשה מלאכה א) דברים הדברים אלה הדברים אלו שלשים ותשע מלאכות שנאמרו למשה בסיני יכול עשאן כולן בהעלם אחד אינו חייב אלא אחת ת"ל ה) בחריש ובקציר תשבות ועדיין אני אומר ו) על חרישה ועל הקצירה חייב שתים ועל כולן אינו חייב אלא אחת ת"ל ג) לא תבערו אש הבערה בכלל היתה ולמה יצאת להקיש אליה ולומר לך מה הבערה שהיא אב מלאכה וחייבין עליה בפני עצמה אף כל שהוא אב מלאכה חייבין עליה בפני עצמה שמואל סבר לה כרבי יוסי דאמר הבערה ללאו יצאת ג) דתניא הבערה ללאו יצאת דברי רבי יוסי ר' נתן אומר ד) לחלק יצאת ותיפוק ליה לחלוק מלאכות מהיכא דנפקא ליה לר' יוסי ה) דתניא רבי יוסי אומר ו) ועשה מאחת מהנה פעמים שחייבים אחת על כולן ופעמים שחייבין על כל אחת ואחת אמר ר' יוסי בר' חנינא מ"ט דר' יוסי אחת מאחת הנה מהנה אחת שהיא הנה הנה שהיא אחת אחת שמעון מאחת שם משמעון

רש"י

מאי שנא רישא. דשגגת שבת וזדון מלאכות לא מיחייב אלא אחת לכל שבת וסיפא לזדון שבת ושגגת מלאכות חייב על כל מלאכה ומלאכה: כאן מידיעת שבת הוא פורש. רישא כי אמרו ליה שבת הוא פורש מן המלאכה ומכיר שחטא ועל כך הוא מביא קרבן הלכך שגגת שבת היא ועל השבת הוא צריך להביא: כאן מידיעת מלאכות הוא פורש. כי אמרי ליה שבת הוא לא פריש דהא נמי ידע וכי אמרי ליה מלאכה חשובה היא זו פריש הלכך על מנין המלאכות יביא: כלום פריש משבת אלא משום. דכי אודעיה שבת הוא הכיר שחטא על המלאכות וכלום פריש ממלאכה כלומר ע"י ידיעת המלאכות אלא משום שבת דכי אמרו ליה מלאכות הן הכיר שחילל שבת: חילוק מלאכות. שגופי מלאכות מתחלקים לחטאות ואע"פ שבהעלם אחד: מות יומת. מיתות הרבה: בממון. לאפושי קרבנות: מה ת"ל. והלא כבר נאמר לא תעשה כל מלאכה: דברים. משמע תרי ה' לרבות חד הרי שלשה אלה בגמטריא ל"ו הרי ל"ט: ת"ל בחריש ובקציר תשבות. כלומר בלאו לא תבערו הוה לן למילף מהאי אם לא שיש להשיב: ועדיין אני אומר על חריש וקציר חייב שתים. אם עשאן בהעלם אחד שהרי הוציאם מן הכלל לחלקן לשתים ומשמע אזהרה לקציר לעצמה ואזהרה לחריש לעצמה: ועל כולן אחת. דבחדא מלאכה כיילינהו וחד לאו ודבר שהיה בכלל ויצא מן הכלל ללמד לא ללמד כו' לא דיינינן ליה דהוי ליה כלל בלא תעשה ופרט בעשה ואין דנין אותו בכלל ופרט אי נמי הוי חריש וקציר שני כתובין הבאין כאחד ואין מלמדין דהוה ליה למיכתב חד: ת"ל לא תבערו כו'. וחריש וקציר לדרשה אחרינא אי כר' עקיבא דדריש ליה בעלמא (ר"ה דף ט.) לענין תוספת שביעית אי כרבי ישמעאל לענין שבת מה חריש רשות אף קציר רשות ללמד על קציר העומר שדוחה שבת: בכלל היתה. דלא תעשה כל מלאכה: להקיש אליה. כל שאר המלאכות שבכללו עמה בכלל שזו מדה בתורה כל דבר שהיה בכלל ויצא מן הכלל ללמד לא ללמד על עצמו יצא כו': ללאו. שאין חייבין עליה כרת וסקילה כשאר מלאכות אלא מה שאמור בה: לחלק. כדאמרן מה הבערה מיוחדת: ועשה מאחת מהנה. האמור לענין חטאות הוה ליה למכתב ועשה אחת ולישתוק אייתר ליה שאר' מ"ס דמאחת וכל תיבת מהנה לדרשה ודרוש הכי פעמים שכל מעשה עבירותיו חשוב אחת ופעמים שהוא קרוי הנה לשון רבים: וא"ר יוסי ברבי חנינא מ"ט דרבי יוסי. כלומר מאי דריש ביה דאכתי מ' דמהנה ומ' דמאחת למאי אתא: אחת מאחת. אחת הוה ליה למכתב וכתיב מאחת וכן נמי הנה ה"ל למכתב (הנה) [למדרש פעמים שהוא הנה] וכתב מהנה ודרוש הכי מ"ס הכי פעמים אחת שהוא הנה שבת [אחת] לבדו הוא מחלל ויש כאן חטאות הרבה דאזלי בתר מלאכות ופעמים הנה שהיא אחת מלאכות הרבה עשה ואינו חייב אלא אחת דבהנך תרי גווני איכא למשמע ועשה אחת וחייב הנה ואיכא למימר נמי הכי ועשה אחת הנה ו) עשייתו הוי אחת אע"פ שהן הנה [וחייב א'] ומ"ס יתירה [דרוש הכי] לרבות שהכותב שם משמעון דאע"ג שנתכוון לעשות תיבה גדולה הואיל ושתי אותיות הראשונות שם במקום אחר הן חייב והיינו מאחת מקצת המלאכה ולא כולה יביא חטאת: מהנה

תוספות

אם אינו ענין למזיד דהא כתיב כו'. ואם תאמר ולימא אם אינו ענין למזיד משום לאטו בתרי קטלא קטלת ליה וי"ל דאי לאו קרא אחרינא דמיתי הוה מוקמינן ליה להאי קרא במזיד ומות יומת דברה תורה כלשון בני אדם אבל השתא דלא איצטריך למזיד מוקמי ליה ע"כ בשוגג ולחייב קרבן על כל א':

יכול שאם עשאן כולם בהעלם אחד כו'. תימה א"כ מניינא דקרא דברים הדברים אלה הדברים למה לי כיון דלא אתא לחלק ויש לומר דצריך למניינא לפי שיש מלאכות שאינן חשובות ואיצטריך מניינא לאשמעינן דכולהו הויין מלאכות להתחייב עליהן ומיהו ממתניתין דמ' מלאכות דייק שפיר דבהעלם אחד חייב על כל אחת דלא הוה צריך למניינא כיון דמני כולהו בהדיא ומיהו קשה לר"י דלקמן בהזורק (דף צו:) משמע דהאי מניינא אתיא לחלק דאמר התם למימרא דמחייב רבי אתולדה במקום אב והתניא רבי אומר דברים הדברים אלה הדברים כו' ופי' בקונטרס התם דהכי פריך הואיל ומניינא לא אתא אלא לחילוק חטאות ואי ס"ד דמחייב אתולדה במקום אב טובא ה"ל למיתני ולפי מה שפירשנו דמניינא לא אתא אלא לאשמעינן דכולהו חשובות מלאכות להתחייב עליהם לא הוה פריך מידי ונראה לר"י דגרס הכא כמו במכילתא דתניא התם רבי נתן אומר לא תבערו אש למה נאמר לפי שנאמר ויקהל משה שומע אני שלא יהא חייב עד שיעבור ל"ט מלאכות תלמוד לומר בחריש ובקציר וכו' והשתא אי לאו לא תבערו ה"א דמניינא אתא למימר שאינו חייב על אחת או שתים עד שיעבור כל ל"ט וכיון דכתיב לא תבערו דילפינן מיניה דחייב על כל אחת בפני עצמה אם כן מניינא אתא למימר דאל"ט דווקא הוא דחייב על כל אחת ואחת אבל אתולדה במקום אב לא והשתא מוכח שפיר בהזורק דרבי לא מחייב אתולדה במקום אב ואתי נמי שפיר להאי גירסא דקתני לפי שנאמר דברים הדברים וגו' יכול כו' דמשמע דמתוך קרא דהדברים הוא דמשמע ליה דאינו חייב עד שיעבור כולן וכן בפ"ק דפסחים (דף ה:) לפי שנאמר לא יראה לך יכול יטמין ויקבל פקדונות מן הנכרים אבל לגירסת הספרים מאי קאמר לפי שנאמר בלאו קרא נמי הוה אמרינן הכי כל כמה דלא נפקא לן חילוק מלאכות משום מקום:

על חרישה וקצירה חייב שתים. וא"ת מנא ליה דחייב שתים נימא דלא מיחייב אתרוייהו אלא אחת וי"ל משום דכתיב בחריש ובקציר דמשמע תרי מילי מדלא כתב בחריש וקציר:

ועל כולן אינו חייב אלא אחת. פירש בקונט' משום דהוי ליה כלל בלא תעשה ופרט בעשה וקשה דכללא נמי כתיב בעשה וביום השביעי תשבות ועוד דגבי כלל ופרט דוקא הוא דאמרינן בפרק קמא דמו"ק (דף ג.) דלא דיינינן כשאין הכלל בלשון הפרט אבל לגבי דבר שהוא יצא מן הכלל לא אשכחן בשום מקום ועוד דבמועד קטן איכא למ"ד דנין ונראה כפי' אחרון שפי' בקונט' דלא ילפינן מחריש וקציר משום דהוו שני כתובים הבאים כאחד וכה"ג אמרינן בפרק ד' מיתות (סנהדרין סז:) אוב וידעוני בכלל כל המכשפים היו כו' ופריך וליהוי אוב וידעוני שני כתובים הבאין כא' ואם תאמר והיכי יליף מלא תבערו כל שכן דהוי ג' כתובים הבאין כאחד ואין מלמדין לכ"ע וכ"ת דחריש וקציר אתא לכדדרשינן בריש מו"ק (ד' ד.) מה חריש רשות כו' אם כן היכי הוה בעי למילף מיניה מעיקרא הא לא אתי להכי ואומר ר"י דלא הוו ג' כתובים מדלא כתבינהו או כולהו בלאו או כולהו בעשה ולהכי ילפינן מהבערה ומהשתא אייתר ליה חריש וקציר לכדדרשינן במו"ק:

הבערה ללאו יצאת. וא"ת ז) והא איצטריך למיכתב לא תבערו משום סיפיה דקרא דכתיב בכל מושבותיכם דדרשינן מינה ביבמות (דף ו:) ובסנהדרין (דף לה:) דאין רציחה דוחה שבת וי"ל דהוה מצי למיכתב בלישנא אחריתי ולא לכתוב לא תבערו ומשום דדרשינן בפ"ק (דף כ.) אבל אתה מבעיר כו' לא הוה צריך למיכתב לא תבערו:

מאי טעמא דר' יוסי. פי' בקונט' כלומר דאכתי מ"ס דמאחת ומהנה למה לי ולשון מאי טעמא אינו משמע כן ונראה לר"י דה"פ מ"ט דר' יוסי הא איצטריך קרא לשם משמעון ולאבות ולתולדות ומנא ליה דחייב על כל אחת ואחת ומפרש דמאחת שם משמעון מהנה לאבות ותולדות ומ"מ מדסמכינהו להדדי דרשינן אחת שהיא הנה והנה שהיא אחת:

רבינו חננאל

דכי אמרו ליה שבת היא היום מיד פורש מכל מלאכה נמצאת בידו שגגה אחת שהיא שגגת שבת לפיכך אינו חייב אלא חטאת אחת אבל המזיד בשבת ושגג במלאכות אם מודיעים לו שהיא מלאכה פורש ממנה ועושה מלאכה אחרת ועוד מודיעין אותו ופורש ממנה ומתעסק באחרת הלכך כיון שצריך להודיעו על כל מלאכה ומלאכה נמצאו שגגותיו מרובים לפיכך חייב כנגד שגגותיו: העושה מלאכו' הרבה בשבת אחת בשגגה מנלן דחייב על כל מלאכה ומלאכה ופשט שמואל מדכתיב כל העושה בו מלאכה יומת דילפינן מיניה קטלא למזיד וכתיב קרא אחרינא מחלליה מות יומת דלא צריך ליה לקטלא דהא ילפינן ליה פשטנא לשוגג וכתיב מות יומת מיתות הרבה נמצאו בחילול שבת אחת מיתות הרבה. ומאי נינהו חטאות והכי קאמר יומת בממון כלומר יתן חטאות הרבה ור' נתן פשט ליה מלא תבערו אש הבערה בכלל היתה למה יצאת לחלק ולומר כשם שחייבין על ההבערה בפני עצמה כך חייבין בכל אחת ואחת בפני עצמה אחר שפירש בחריש ובקציר שביתה וכתב רחמנא אלה הדברים מדהוה למכתב (דאמר אלה) [ויאמר אליהם] הדברים אשר צוה ה' לעשות וכת' והוסיף אלה הדברים אלה בגימטריא ל"ו ועוד מדהוה למכתב דברים אלה שהן אלה ל"ו ודברים תרי הרי ל"ח והוסיף ה' בהדברים למדנו ממנו עוד אחת הרי ארבעים חסר אחת. ור' יוסי מדכתיב ועשה מאחת מהנה דריש ועשה מאחת פעמים שהוא חייב אחת על כולן והוא היודע עיקר שבת. מהנה פעמים שחייב על כל אחת ואחת. כיצד זדון שבת ושגגת מלאכות ושמואל הא דר' נתן סבר לה

תורה אור השלם

א) וּשְׁמַרְתֶּם אֶת הַשַּׁבָּת כִּי קֹדֶשׁ הִוא לָכֶם מְחַלְלֶיהָ מוֹת יוּמָת כִּי כָּל הָעֹשֶׂה בָהּ מְלָאכָה וְנִכְרְתָה הַנֶּפֶשׁ הַהִוא מִקֶּרֶב עַמֶּיהָ: [שמות לא, יד]

ב) שֵׁשֶׁת יָמִים תֵּעָשֶׂה מְלָאכָה וּבַיּוֹם הַשְּׁבִיעִי יִהְיֶה לָכֶם קֹדֶשׁ שַׁבַּת שַׁבָּתוֹן לַיי כָּל הָעֹשֶׂה בוֹ מְלָאכָה יוּמָת: [שמות לה, ב]

ג) לֹא תְבַעֲרוּ אֵשׁ בְּכֹל מֹשְׁבֹתֵיכֶם בְּיוֹם הַשַּׁבָּת: [שמות לה, ג]

ד) וַיַּקְהֵל מֹשֶׁה אֶת כָּל עֲדַת בְּנֵי יִשְׂרָאֵל וַיֹּאמֶר אֲלֵהֶם אֵלֶּה הַדְּבָרִים אֲשֶׁר צִוָּה יי לַעֲשֹׂת אֹתָם: [שמות לה, א]

ה) שֵׁשֶׁת יָמִים תַּעֲבֹד וּבַיּוֹם הַשְּׁבִיעִי תִּשְׁבֹּת בֶּחָרִישׁ וּבַקָּצִיר תִּשְׁבֹּת: [שמות לד, כא]

ו) דַּבֵּר אֶל בְּנֵי יִשְׂרָאֵל לֵאמֹר נֶפֶשׁ כִּי תֶחֱטָא בִשְׁגָגָה מִכֹּל מִצְוֹת יי אֲשֶׁר לֹא תֵעָשֶׂינָה וְעָשָׂה מֵאַחַת מֵהֵנָּה: [ויקרא ד, ב]

מסורת הש"ס

א) לקמן דף נו: וש"נ, ב) מכילתא פרשת ויקהל, ג) יבמות ו: לג: סנהדרין לה: ודף סב. [כריתות כ:], ד) [פסחים ה:], ה) לקמן קג. סנהדרין סב. [כריתות ג.], ו) עשייתו הנה ומ"ס יתירה לרבות כו' גי' רש"ל ועל"ז לא לפרש לשון הספקות ועשה אחת הנה ומה' כמ"ש רש"י לפנינו ועיין לקמן קג. משמע גם כן כמ"ש לפנינו, ז) [כן קושית מלי קלי גם למ"ד הבערה לחלק יצאת ועי' תוס' יבמות ו: ד"ה טעמא וכו' ובסנהדרין וכו' מבואר בדבריהם היטב, וע"ע תוס' לעיל כ. ד"ה מאשרי ותוספות לקמן קג. ד"ה מה לי ותוס' מנחות נה: ד"ה אם כן].

הגהות הב"ח

(א) גמ' כל העושה בו מלאכה:

ליקוטי רש"י

מחלליה. הנוהג בה חול בקדושתה [שמות לא, יד]. דברים הדברים אלה הדברים. גבי שבת כתיב בויקהל אלה הדברים אשר צוה ה' וגו' דברים משמע תרין ה"א מרבי חד הא תלת אלה בגימטריא תלתין ושית הא שלשים ותשע כו' [לקמן צז:]. ולמה יצאת להקיש אליה וכו'. [illegible] עצמו יצא אלא ללמד על הכלל כולו יצא [סנהדרין סב.]. לחלק יצאת מן הכלל ללמד על הכלל כולו יצא שלא תאמר עשאן לכל המלאכות בהעלם אחת אינו חייב אלא אחת לכך יצאת זו להקיש אליה את כל הכלל ולומר לך מה זו מיוחדת שהיא אב מלאכה וחייבין עליה בפני עצמה שהרי הזהיר עליה לאו בפני עצמה אף כל שהיא אב מלאכה חייבין עליה בפני עצמה [שם לה:]. שלא תאמר אינו חייב סקילה עד שיחלל שבת בכל מלאכות לכך יצאתה הבערה מן הכלל לחלק מה הבערה מיוחדת שהיא אב מלאכה וחייב עליה כרת וסקילה בפני עצמה אף כל שהוא אב מלאכה כו' [יבמות ו:]. לחלק יצאתה שלא תאמר העושה ארבעה או חמשה אבות מלאכות בשוגג בשבת אינו חייב אלא אחת דהא חד לאו איכא בכולהו וחד כרת לפיכך פרט בה בפני עצמה להקיש אליה מה היא מיוחדת שהיא אב מלאכה וחייבין עליה לעצמה כו' [פסחים ה:]. הבערה. שיצאה מכלל לא תעשה כל מלאכה דשבת. ללאו יצאת. להוציאה מחומרי שאר מלאכות וללמד עליה שאינה לא בכרת ולא במיתה אלא בלאו [סנהדרין סב.]. מכלל שאר המלאכות לומר לך שאין בה כרת וסקילה אלא לאו בעלמא [שם לה:]. שהיתה בכלל לא תעשה כל מלאכה חזר והוציאה מכללו ופרט בה לאו לעצמה לומר לך שאינה במיתת בית דין כשאר מלאכות אלא בלאו זה לבדו [פסחים שם]. מאחת מהנה. וה"ל למיכתב אחת הנה מאי מאחת משמע פעמים שחייב מעבירה אחת הנה כלומר כמה חטאות ומהנה מעבירות הרבה חטאת אחת [כריתות ג.]. גבי חטאת כתיב פעמים שחייב חטאת אחת על כולן כגון שוגג בשבת כסבור אין היום שבת אבל יודע היה שכל מלאכות שהוא עושה אסורות בשבת מביא קרבן אחד דחדא שגגה היא ופעמים שחייב על כל אחד ואחד כגון שהזיד בשבת ויודע שהוא שבת היום ויש שבת בתורה ושגג במלאכות שלא היה יודע שהמלאכות הללו אסורות אלא מלאכות אחרות חייב על כל אחת ואחת שיש כאן שגגות הרבה. אמר ר' יוסי בר' חנינא וכו'. מפרש טעמא דר' יוסי היכי משמע ליה האי מהאי קרא. אחת מאחת וכו'. הוה ליה למכתב ועשה אחת מהנה אי נמי ועשה מהנה אי נמי ועשה אחת ולישתוק מדכתבינהו הכי שמע מינה למדרש כל חד וחד לאודה לחייבו על אחת ועל מאחת כלומר מקצת העבירה על הנה ועל מהנה כדמפרש הנה אבות מהנה תולדות ולמדרשינהו נמי כי הדדי הכי מדסמכי להדדי [סנהדרין סב.]. אחת הוה ליה למכתב ולשתוק וכתב מ"ס יתירה [ומהנה יתירא]. הנה מהנה, אי נמי הנה הוה ליה למכתב וכתב מהנה מ"ס יתירה ומאחת יתירה הלכך למדרשינהו לכולהו כתבינהו ודרוש אחת הנה בלא מ"ס הכי. אחת שהיא הנה הנה שהיא אחת. לתרי גווני איכא למידרש משמעותייהו ועשה עבירה אחת והיא לו הנה חייב חטאות הרבה אי נמי ועשה אחת עשייתו חשובה לו כאחת ואע"פ שהנה היו משמע שהרבה עבירות עשה והיינו הנה שהיא אחת הלכך תרוייהו דריש ביה פעמים שהיא כן ופעמים שהיא כן כדמפרש לקמיה [לקמן קג:]. אחת שהיא הנה כלומר פעמים שהוא חייב על מלוה אחת חטאות הרבה והנה שהיא אחת פעמים שאינו חייב אלא אחת על מלות הרבה והכי משמע מאחת מחייב הנה מהנה מחייב אחת מדכתיב מ' יתירא והשתא מפרש לה [סנהדרין שם]. אחת שמעון. כלומר דריש מ"ס יתירה אחת הוי משמע דאינו חייב עד שיכתוב כל התיבה שנתכוין לכתוב [לקמן שם]. אחת כשעשה עבירה שלימה שנתכוין לכתוב שמעון וכתבו כולו [סנהדרין שם]. מאחת שם משמעון. כתב מאחת למימר דאפילו לא כתב אלא מקצתה ובלבד שתהא [מתקיימת] במקום אחר דומיא דאחת דרישיה דקרא [לקמן שם]. מאחת על מקצתו נמי מחייב כגון נתכוין לכתוב שמעון ולא כתב אלא שתי אותיות חייב ולהכי נקט שמעון משום דשתי אותיות ראשונות הוו להו שם במקום אחר כגון שם בן נח והוא הדין גד מגדיאל דן מדניאל אבל נתכוין לכתוב שם אחר כגון נפתלי ולא כתב ממנו אלא שתי אותיות לא מיחייב שאין כאן מלאכה בשום מקום [סנהדרין שם].

שם משמעון הנה אבות מהנה תולדות אחת שהיא הנה זדון שבת ושגגת מלאכות הנה שהיא אחת שגגת שבת וזדון מלאכות ושמואל אחת שהיא הנה והנה שהיא אחת לא משמע ליה: בעא מיניה רבא מרב נחמן (א) העלם זה וזה בידו מהו א"ל הרי העלם שבת בידו ואינו חייב אלא אחת אדרבה הרי העלם מלאכות בידו וחייב על כל אחת ואחת אלא אמר רב אשי חזינן אי משום שבת קא פריש הרי העלם שבת בידו ואינו חייב אלא אחת ואי משום מלאכה קפריש הרי העלם מלאכות בידו וחייב על כל אחת ואחת א"ל רבינא לרב אשי כלום פריש משבת אלא משום מלאכות כלום פריש ממלאכות אלא משום שבת א אלא לא שנא תנן (ג) אבות מלאכות ארבעים חסר אחת והוינן בה מנינא למה לי ואמר ר' יוחנן שאם עשאן כולן בהעלם אחד חייב על כל אחת ואחת אי אמרת בשלמא העלם זה וזה בידו חייב על כל אחת ואחת שפיר אלא אי אמרת העלם שבת בידו אינו חייב אלא אחת היכי משכחת לה בזדון שבת ושגגת מלאכות הניחא אי סבר ליה כרבי יוחנן דאמר כיון ששגג בכרת אע"פ שהזיד בלאו משכחת לה דידע ליה שבת בלאו אלא אי סבר לה כרבי שמעון בן לקיש דאמר עד שישגוג בלאו וכרת דידע ליה שבת במאי (ג) דידע לה בתחומין ואליבא דרבי עקיבא: (ד) אמר רבא קצר וטחן כגרוגרת בשגגת שבת וזדון מלאכות וחזר וקצר וטחן כגרוגרת בזדון שבת ושגגת מלאכות ונודע לו על קצירה וטחינה של שגגת שבת וזדון מלאכות וחזר ונודע לו על קצירה ועל טחינה של זדון שבת ושגגת מלאכות

קצירה

מהנה לרבות תולדות. כלומר היולאות מהן מן האבות: אחת שהיא הנה. דאמרן פעמים שחייב על כל אחת ואחת מאי היא כגון שעשאן בזדון שבת ושגגת מלאכות דאיכא שגגות טובא והנה שהיא אחת דאמרן פעמים שחייב אחת על כולן מאי היא כגון שגגת שבת וזדון מלאכות דידע שהמלאכות אסורות בשבת אבל שכח ששבת היום: לא משמע ליה. דמיבעיא ליה כוליה לשם משמעון ולתולדות: זה וזה. שבת ומלאכות: מהו. חייב אחת על כולן או על כל אחת ואחת וקמבעיא ליה הא דתני לעיל (דף סט.) שגג בזה ובזה זהו שוגג האמור בתורה מהו לחיובי חדא או לאחיובי אכולהו ומתני' דהשוכח עיקר שבת דאינו חייב אלא אחת לא שמעינן ליה דהשוכח עיקר שבת חדא שגגה היא וכי מיבעיא לן ביודע עיקר שבת אבל מלאכות הללו אינו יודע שאסורות ועוד נעלם ממנו שהיום שבת דאיכא למיתלי שגגה אכל מלאכה ומלאכה הואיל ויודע עיקר שבת ואיכא למתלי אהעלם שבת וחדא שגגה היא: אי משום שבת קא פריש. זה שפירש מן העבירה ובא להתכפר אי משום שבת היתה שאמרו לו שבת היום ופירש אישתכח דמשום העלם שבת היה עושה: ה"ג ואי משום מלאכות הללו קא פריש. שאמרו לו מלאכה היא זו ופירש הרי העלם מלאכה בידו וזיל בתר מלאכות: כלום פריש משבת אלא משום מלאכות. כשאמרו לו שבת היום הבין שהמלאכות הללו אסורות דאי לא אסורות למה הוזקקו לומר שבת היום: אלא לא שנא. ואינו חייב אלא אחת: עשאן לכולן. היינו העלם זה וזה בידו דהא לא ידע שבת במידי כיון דכל הלכותיה נעלמות ממנו אין חילוק היום משאר ימים: אא"א כו' היכי משכחת לה. דניחייב איניש אכל חדא ע"כ בזדון שבת ושגגת מלאכות הוא דמשכחת לה והכא מאי זדון שבת איכא: הניחא לר' יוחנן כו'. משכחת ליה שלא נעלמו ממנו אלא הכריתות ויודע הלאוין והיינו זדון שבת: כגרוגרת. שיעור הוא לכל איסורי מלאכות של שבת באוכלים: קצר. כגרוגרת וטחן כגרוגרת בשגגת שבת וזדון מלאכות דלא מיחייב אלא חדא: וחזר וקצר. כגרוגרת וטחן כגרוגרת בזדון שבת ושגגת מלאכות דמיחייב תרתי ולא נודע לו בינתים שחטא: ונודע לו. אחרי כן על הקצירה ועל הטחינה כלומר או על זו או על זו וכ"ש על שתיהן: (ה על) שגגת שבת וזדון מלאכות. והפריש חטאת וחטאת זו מכפרת על שתיהן דהא חדא הוא דמיחייב עליה:

קצירה

שם משמעון. האי לישנא לא הוה צריך למימר כיון דאליבא דר' יוסי קאי דסבר בפ' הבונה (לקמן ד' קג:) דאפי' שריטה אחת על שני נסרים או שני שריטות על נסר אחד חייב אלא ניחא ליה למנקט לישנא דמתני' דהבונה (שם.) א"ר יהודה מצינו שם קטן משם גדול שם משמעון: לא משמע ליה. שמואל דלא כר' נתן ודלא כר' יוסי וצ"ל דמקבלה קים ליה לשמואל הכי (ו): העלם זה וזה בידו מהו. אומר ר"י דאפי' לא ידע לשבת בשום מלאכה חשיב ליה העלם זה וזה כדמוכח בסמוך דקאמר ר"י אי אמרת בשלמא העלם זה וזה בידו חייב כו' אלמא אע"ג דלא ידע לשבת במידי חשוב העלם זה וזה וצריך לחלק בין זה לשוכח עיקר שבת דהכא אינו שכוח כל כך דמי מדכרו ליה מדכר אבל שכח עיקר שבת היינו כעין תינוק שנשבה לבין הנכרים: אמר ליה הרי העלם שבת בידו כו'. בשבועות בפ"ב (ד' יט.) בעא מיניה רבא מרב נחמן העלם זה וזה בידו מהו א"ל הרי העלם טומאה בידו וחייב והתם בפ"ג (דף כו.) נמי השיבו הרי העלם שבועה בידו וחייב התם שפיר דמהדר ליה לחומרא והא דמהדר ליה הכא לפוטרו משום דקסבר שגגת שבת עיקר דעיקר המצוה היא משום שבת: חזינן אי משום שבת קא פריש כו'. פי' בקונטרס שאמרו לו שבת היום ופירש וקשה דשמא כי הוו אמרי ליה נמי מלאכה היא היה פורש אפי' לא יזכירוהו שבת אלא נראה לר"י דה"פ אי משום שבת קא פריש שאומר בעצמו דאי הוו מודעי ליה אשבת לבד היה פורש ואי הוו מודעי ליה אמלאכות לא היה פורש א"כ העלם שבת עיקר שהוא היה שכוח יותר ואי משום מלאכות פריש דשיילינן ליה ואמר דאי הוו מודעי ליה אמלאכות לא הוה צריך לאודועיה אשבת ואי הוו מודעי ליה אשבת הוה צריך לאודועיה אמלאכות הרי העלם מלאכות עיקר וחייב על כל אחת ואחת אבל כששניהם שכוחות בשוה מזה לא פשט כלום ולא בא רב אשי אלא לפשוט מקצת הבעיא כלומר לפעמים נוכל להבחין איזו העלמה עיקר ול"ג מה שכתוב בספרים ואי כי מודעי ליה אשבת אכתי צריך לאודועיה אמלאכות העלם מלאכות בידו כו' דלפי מה שפי' ר"י אכתי הוה צריך לפרושי וכי מודעת ליה אמלאכות לא הוה צריך לאודועיה אשבת אלא גרסי' ואי משום מלאכות קא פריש כו' וקאמר רבינא כלום פריש משבת אלא משום מלאכות כו' כלומר כיון ששניהם שכוחים במה שזה שכוח יותר מזה לא נפקא מיניה מידי אלא לא שנא ותרווייהו תבעי ורשב"א מקיים גירסת הספרים ומפרש דרב אשי בא לפשוט דהעלם זה וזה (א) חייב אי משום שבת קפריש שהשבת שכוחה יותר העלם שבת בידו ואי כי מודעת ליה אשבת אכתי צריך לאודועי אמלאכות אפילו אי כי נמי מודעת ליה אמלאכות צריך לאודועיה אשבת דהוי העלם זה וזה חשיב כהעלם מלאכות וחייב וכן מוכח מדנקט לעיל אי משום שבת קא פריש והכא נקט אי כי מודעת ליה אשבת כו' והא דקאמר כלום פריש ממלאכות אלא משום שבת ה"פ אלא משום שבת ותהא שגגת שבת עיקר ולא מיחייב אלא חדא דלענין אחר לא הוה פריך מידי כיון דבשניהן שוה חייב על כל אחת:

נודע לו על הקצירה ועל הטחינה של שגגת שבת וזדון מלאכות. פי' רבינו שמואל שנודע לו והפריש קרבן וקודם שנתכפר חזר ונודע לו על הקצירה וטחינה של שגגת מלאכות אבל אם לא נודע לו עד אחר הכפרה אין נגררין וצריכין שתי חטאות דלכ"ע כפרה מחלקת ודווקא הפריש קרבן אבל אם לא הפריש קרבן וחזר ונודע לו על קצירה וטחינה של (ו) שגגת מלאכות יביא איזה שירצה דבו תליא מילתא אם ירצה יפריש חטאת אחת על שגגת שבת ונגררין של שגגת מלאכות עמה או אם ירצה יפריש ב' קרבנות על הקצירה וטחינה של שגגת מלאכות ויגררו עמהן של שגגת שבת כדאמר רבא בסמוך אכל שני זיתי חלב בהעלם אחד ונודע לו על אחד מהן כו' הביא קרבן על הראשון כו' אלמא אע"ג דנודע לו על הראשון תחלה הואיל ועדיין לא הפריש קרבן עליו אינו גורר האמצעי עמו כדי להתחייב קרבן על השלישי אלא אם ירצה יביא קרבן על האמצעי ויתכפרו כולן וא"ת דהשתא משמע דסבר רבא דאין הפרשות מחלקות מדנגררות של שגגת מלאכות עם של שגגת שבת והיינו כר"ש לקיש ורבא גופיה לא פסיק כוותיה בהחולץ (יבמות לו.) אלא בג' מקומות ומיהו מתוך פי' ר"ח שפירש דהלכתא כרבה רבו של אביי משמע דגרס רבה וכן משמע שמזכירו לפני אביי וכן בסמוך דקאמר מילתא דפשיטא לה לרבה ואביי ואפי' גרסי' רבא י"ל דלא איירי ביבמות אלא בדברים הנוהגים בזמן הזה מיהו תימה לר"י לקמן דמיבעיא לן אי פליגי בהפרשות מחלקות או לא תפשוט דבהפרשות פליגי דאי בידיעות פליגי אבל הפרשות מחלקות לכ"ע א"כ רבה ואביי דסברי הכא דאין הפרשות מחלקות כמאן וי"ל דאיכא למדחי דהכא מיירי שלא הפריש עד אחר שחזר ונודע לו גם על שגגת מלאכות והא דנקט ונודע לו על שגגת שבת היינו כלומר שלבסוף הפריש על שגגת שבת:

גרירה

עין משפט נר מצוה

יב א מיי' פ"ז מהלכות שגגות הלכה ד:

רבינו חננאל

כר' יוסי דאמר הבערה ללאו יצאת ולא לחלק ודרשה דר' יוסי אחת שהיא הנה והנה שהיא אחת לא משמע ליה: בעא מיניה (רבה) [רבא] מר' נחמן העלם שגגת שבת ושגגת מלאכות כשגגת שבת דיינינן ליה וחייב אחת על כל שבת ושבת או כשגגת מלאכות דיינינן ליה וחייב על כל מלאכה ומלאכה בכריתות תנן המחלל את השבת שהיא אחת מל"ו כריתות ואקשינן חדא מחייב מ' חסר אחת הוין חיובי שבת ואוקמה ר' יוחנן בשגגת שבת וזדון מלאכות (מחדא לא פליג) דלא מחייב אלא חדא. ומקשינן וליתני זדון שבת ושגגת מלאכות דחייב על כל אחת ואחת ושנינן הא קמ"ל דאפי' שגגת שבת וזדון מלאכו' מחדא לא פליט' ופשט ליה רב נחמן לרבא. [הרי העלם שבת בידו ואינו חייב אלא אחת וא"ל אדרבה] הרי העלם מלאכה בידו וחייב על כל מלאכה ואתא רב אשי ואמר הדא מלתא בעא בירור אי משום שבת לא מחייב אלא חדא כרב נחמן ואי כי מודעת כי שבת הוא היום עדיין צריך לאודועי הכי החורש הוא חייב. ושביק ליה לחרישה והדר לזריעה. תוב צריך לאודועה. כי גם הזריעה חייב עליה. וכן הקוצר ושאר מלאכות כל אחת ואחת חייב עליה על כל אחת ואחת בפני עצמה ובכל אחת ואחת צריך ידיעה בפני עצמה. הרי שגגת (שבת) [מלאכות]. וחייב על כל מלאכה ולא אמרינן מפני שנוספה על שגגת מלאכות שגגת שבת פקעה לה שגגת מלאכות א' לא' במקומה עומדת. ואי לא מסתברא דודאי זדון מלאכות ושגגת שבת הוא כרבא עבדין דאיסורא דספיקא דאורייתא היא. וכל איסורא דספיקא דאורייתא לחומרא עבדינן ואתא רבינא ודחייא להא דרב אשי ואמר כלום פריש משבת (א' לא') [אלא] משום מלאכות כו' ומסתברא דרבינא כר"נ והכי קיימא בזדון שבת ושגגת מלאכות כגון שמכיר כי היום הוא שבת וגם היה יודע שהמלאכות אסורות ונעלם ממנו איסור מלאכות עכשיו או שידע איסור מלאכות בלאו ונעלם ממנו איסורא דכרת. שנמצאת ידיעת שבת בידו והעלם על כל מלאכה ומלאכה זהו שחייב על כל מלאכה ומלאכה אבל השוכח עיקר שבת ועיקר איסור מלאכות ולא מהניא לך כהודעת ליה עיקר שבת ועדיין צריכת לאודעיה איסור מלאכות דאי לא מודעת ליה איסור מלאכות מי ידע דאסירן דלפרוש הלכך ידיעת שבת תליא בידיעת איסור מלאכות ואיסור מלאכות תליין משום שבת וכיון שאפשר שתודיעו (א' לא') איסור שבת ואיסור מלאכות כאחת נמצאת כאילו שגגה אחת היא ואינו חייב אלא אחת כרב נחמן ומקשינן על רב נחמן מדר' יוחנן דאמר אם עשאן כולם בהעלם אחת חייב על כל אחת ואחת. בשלמא אי אמרת העלם זה וזה בידו חייב על כל אחת ואחת היינו דמשכחת לה הכי אלא אי אמרת כל כי האי גוונא לא מחייב אלא חדא היכי משכחת לה דחייב על כל אחת ואחת ואם תאמר בזדון שבת ושגגת מלאכות הניחא אליבא דר' יוחנן משכחת לה זדון שבת [כו'] ומשני ר' נחמן דידע לה שהוא אסור בתחומין ואליבא דר' עקיבא כדאמרינן לעיל (סט.) שנמצאת זדון בתחומין וכי הדין בעיא דרבא העלם זה וזה בידו. גרסינן בשבועות (יט.) בענין ידיעות הטומאה ואסיקנא להו כהא: אמר (רבא) [רבה] קצר וטחן כגרוגרת בשגגת שבת וזדון מלאכות דאע"ג דשני אבות ניהו לא מחייב אלא חדא

דהא

מסורת הש"ס

א) [סנהדרין סב.] שבועות יט. כו. [כריתות ג:], ב) [לקמן דף עג. וש"נ], ג) [לעיל דף סט. וש"נ], ד) [עמ"ש לקמן עב: על הגליון], ה) [צ"ל שלן], ו) [עי' לקמן קו. ד"ה מה לי לבשל כו' כתב דשמואל כר"ש ס"ל ע"ש], ז) צ"ל שגגת שבת ופי' דקאי אסיפא אאבל נודע לו קצירה של זדון שבת [ר"מ] וע"ש.

הגהות הב"ח

(א) תוס' ד"ה חזינן וכו' לפשוט דהעלם זה וזה בידו חייב:

ליקוטי רש"י

מהנה תולדות. דנפקא לן מדדמי להו לאבות והיינו מהנה כלומר מן הדומות להם [סנהדרין סב.]. הנה הוי משמע אבות כתב מהנה לרבויי תולדות [לקמן קג:]. אחת שהיא הנה. דאמרן לעיל פעמים שמתחייב על כל אחת ואחת דהיינו על אחת הנה על מלוה אחת כמה חטאות כגון עושה מלאכות הרבה בזדון שבת ושגגות מלאכות כדפרישית לעיל דיש כאן שגגות הרבה [סנהדרין שם]. דאמרן לעיל היכי דמי כגון שעשאן בזדון שבת ושגגת מלאכות ואע"ג דכולן אין אלא חילול שבת אחת מיחייב לכל מלאכה ומלאכה דגופי מלאכות מחלקין הואיל ואיכא שגגה טובא. שגגת שבת וזדון מלאכות. שאע"פ שהן גופי מלאכות הרבה אינו חייב אלא אחת דחדא שגגה היא [לקמן שם]. יודע שמלאכות הללו אסורות בשבת אבל כסבור אין שבת היום כולה חדא שגגה היא [סנהדרין שם]. כלום פריש וכו'. כשהודיעוהו אחד מהם שם אל לבו לומר מה בכך ומתוך כך נזכר על השני ומ"מ העלם שניהם היה בידו [שבועות יט.]. מנינא למה לי. ליתני אבות מלאכות הזורע והחורש כו' למה לי לאשמעינן מניינא הא מני להו ואזיל [לעיל ו:]. ליתני אבות מלאכות הזורע והחורש כו' למה לי למיתנא ארבעים חסר אחת ליתנינהו ואנן ידעינן דארבעים חסר אחת איכא [שם סט.]. שאם עשאן כולן וכו'. ובא להודיענו סכום החטאות שאדם חייב באיסורי שבת בהעלם אחד ולאשמעינן ארבעים חסר אחת הן ותו לא שאפילו עשה תולדותיהן עמהן אינו מביא על התולדה היכא דעשאה עם אביה דהוה ליה כעושה וחוזר ועושה דכולה חדא עבירה היא [שם ו:]. וסימנא בעלמא אשמעינן לידע כמה חטאות חייב על חילול שבת אחת [שם סט.]. ובא להודיעך שאם נתעלמו כל הלכות שבת ממנו כמה חטאות [חייב] עליו [לקמן עג:]. היכי משכחת לה. דמיחייב על כרחך לא משכחת לה אלא בזדון שבת דיודע שהוא שבת ושגגת מלאכות דאינו יודע שהמלאכות הללו אסורות דאי בזדון מלאכות ושגגת שבת דידע שהן אסורות בשבת אבל שכח שהיום שבת הא תנן דאינו חייב אלא אחת לכל שבת וזדון שבת לא הוי אלא אם כן יודע אחת מהלכותיה דאי לא ידע בחדא מינייהו אין שבת חלוק לו משאר ימים וזה ששגג בכולן אין כאן זדון שבת [לעיל שם]. דמיחייב שום אדם על כל מלאכה ומלאכה שבהעלם אחד על כרחך בזדון שבת ושגגת מלאכות הוא דבעית לאשכוחיה והכא דאיעלימו כולהו מיניה מאי זדון שבת איכא במה ניכר לו שבת משאר ימים [לקמן שם.]. הניחא אי סבר ליה כרבי יוחנן. דאמר שגגת כרת שמה שגגה. משכחת לה. זדון שבת בלאוין ושגגת מלאכות בכריתות דיודע לה לשבת שהוזהר על הלאוין או של כולן או של אחת מהן. דידע לה לשבת במאי. הלא בכולן שגג כסבור שכל שלשים ותשע מלאכות מותרות. בתחומין. דאין בקרבן [לעיל שם]. דאינו יודע שמלאכות הללו אסורות אבל יודע מצות שבת בדבר אחד כגון דידע שאסור לצאת חוץ לתחום [כריתות ג.]. ואליבא דר' עקיבא. דאמר במסכת סוטה תחומין דאורייתא נינהו דתנן בו ביום דרש רבי עקיבא ומדותם מחוץ לעיר כו' [לעיל שם]. דאמר דאורייתא ניהו והוי מחלל ומיהו אין חייבין לא על שגגתו חטאת כו' [לקמן קנג:]. ור"ע מודה נמי בתחומים דאין חייבים עליהם כרת דתנן (שבת עג.) אבות מלאכות ארבעים חסר אחת ולא פליג ר' עקיבא [סנהדרין סו.]. בגרוגרת. היא תאנה יבשה [עירובין ד:].

שֵׁם מִשִּׁמְעוֹן – for example, forming the name **Shem** [*shin mem*] by writing the first two letters **of** the word **Shimon.**[1]

R' Yose the son of R' Chanina explains what is derived from the *mem* in the term "of them":

הֵנָּה אָבוֹת – **"Them,"** without the *mem,* indicates only ***avos.***[2] **"מֵהֵנָּה" תּוֹלָדוֹת** – ***"Of" them,*** with the *mem,* teaches that one is liable also for the ***tolados.***[3]

R' Yose the son of R' Chanina now elaborates on the expositions made from the two words "one" and "them":

אַחַת שֶׁהִיא הֵנָּה – A transgression of ***one*** commandment **that is** tantamount to a transgression of ***them*** [i.e. many commandments] refers to one who performs numerous *melachos* on the Sabbath **זְדוֹן שַׁבָּת וְשִׁגְגַת מְלָאכוֹת** – with **deliberateness regarding the Sabbath but inadvertence regarding *melachos.***[4] **הֵנָּה שֶׁהִיא אַחַת** – A case of ***them*** [i.e. many transgressions] **that is** tantamount to ***one*** transgression refers to one who performs numerous *melachos* on the Sabbath **שִׁגְגַת שַׁבָּת וּזְדוֹן מְלָאכוֹת** – with **inadvertence regarding the Sabbath but deliberateness regarding *melachos.***[5] Thus, why does Shmuel not derive the principle of separation of *melachos* from this exposition?

The Gemara answers:

וּשְׁמוּאֵל אַחַת שֶׁהִיא הֵנָּה וְהֵנָּה שֶׁהִיא אַחַת – **And** as for **Shmuel,** the inference of "a transgression of ***one*** commandment **that is** tantamount to a transgression of ***them*** **and** a transgression of ***them*** **that is** tantamount to ***one*** transgression" **לֹא מַשְׁמַע לֵיהּ** – **is not indicative to him.**[6]

The Gemara elaborates on the concept of inadvertence:

בְּעָא מִינֵּיהּ רָבָא מֵרַב נַחְמָן – **Rava inquired of Rav Nachman:** **הֶעְלֵם זֶה וָזֶה בְּיָדוֹ** – Where there is **a lapse of awareness of** both **this** [the Sabbath] **and that** [the *melachos*] **on his part,** i.e. he violated the Sabbath both unaware of the identity of the day and unaware that the *melachah* he performed was prohibited on the Sabbath, **מַהוּ** – **what is [the law]?**[7]

Rav Nachman answers:

אָמַר לֵיהּ – **He said to [Rava]:** **הֲרֵי הֶעְלֵם שַׁבָּת בְּיָדוֹ** – In this case **there is a lapse of awareness of the Sabbath on his part,** **וְאֵינוֹ חַיָּיב אֶלָּא אַחַת** – **and he is** therefore **liable to only one** offering.[8]

The Gemara asks:

אַדְּרַבָּה – **On the contrary,** **הֲרֵי הֶעְלֵם מְלָאכוֹת בְּיָדוֹ** – **there is a lapse of awareness of *melachos* on his part,** **וְחַיָּיב עַל כָּל אַחַת וְאַחַת** – **and he should** therefore **be liable** to a separate *chatas* **for each and every** *melachah* he performed![9] – ? –

The Gemara therefore suggests a practical resolution of the difficulty:

אֶלָּא אָמַר רַב אַשִׁי – **Rather, Rav Ashi said:** **חָזִינַן** – **We observe:** **אִי מִשּׁוּם שַׁבָּת קָא פָּרִישׁ** – **If he withdraws** from work **because** he is reminded **of the Sabbath,** **הֲרֵי הֶעְלֵם שַׁבָּת בְּיָדוֹ** – then **there is a lapse of awareness of the Sabbath on his part** **וְאֵינוֹ חַיָּיב אֶלָּא אַחַת** – **and he is liable to but one** *chatas.*[10] **וְאִי מִשּׁוּם מְלָאכָה קָפָּרִישׁ** – **And if he withdraws because** he is reminded that his act is **a *melachah,*** **הֲרֵי הֶעְלֵם מְלָאכוֹת בְּיָדוֹ** – **there is a lapse of awareness of *melachos* on his part** **וְחַיָּיב עַל כָּל אַחַת וְאַחַת** – **and he is liable** to a separate *chatas* **for each and every one.**[11]

Ravina rejects Rav Ashi's solution:

אָמַר לֵיהּ רָבִינָא לְרַב אַשִׁי – **Ravina said to Rav Ashi:** **כְּלוּם פָּרִישׁ מִשַּׁבָּת אֶלָּא מִשּׁוּם מְלָאכוֹת** – **Does he withdraw** from his work

NOTES

1. Since the two letters *shin mem* are a viable unit on their own (spelling the name *Shem*), one is liable for writing just those two letters, even though he originally intended to continue and write *Shimon.* [This will be explained in greater detail below, 103a-b.] The verse teaches that even though he performed only part of his intended *melachah* [מְאַחַת], he is nevertheless liable to a *chatas* (*Rashi* above, 70a ד״ה אחת; see *Tosafos* here ד״ה שם and *Dibros Moshe* 64:21).

2. *Rashi* below, 103b. This is because the *avos* are the primary categories of forbidden labor.

3. The term מֵהֵנָּה, with the *mem,* can also be translated "*from* them." This alludes to the *tolados,* which are derivatives of the *avos* that are denoted by הֵנָּה (*Rashi*).

4. Since each of his transgressions stems from his ignorance of a separate fact – that the particular act he is doing is a *melachah* – he is liable to a *chatas* for each *melachah* he performed (*Rashi*).

5. If he did the *melachos* only because he was unaware that it was the Sabbath day, all his transgressions are in effect a single inadvertence. Therefore, he is liable to only one *chatas* offering (*Rashi*).

6. Rather, he holds that the entire verse is needed to teach about partial intention and the *tolados* (*Rashi*).

[It emerges that Shmuel disputes the derivations of both R' Nassan and R' Yose. Since Shmuel is an Amora, who ordinarily does not advance his own independent view against Tannaim, we must say that Shmuel was in possession of a tradition from a Tannaic source which accorded with his derivation (*Tosafos;* see also *Tosafos* to 106a ד״ה מה לי).]

7. This question is based on the Baraisa taught above (69a): שָׁגַג בָּזֶה וּבָזֶה וְזֶהוּ שׁוֹגֵג הָאָמוּר בַּתּוֹרָה, *[If] he acted inadvertently with regard to this* [the Sabbath] *and this [the melachos], this is the inadvertence that is stated in the Torah.* Rava inquires how many *chatas* offerings the violator must bring in that case – a separate *chatas* for each *melachah* or one for the entire Sabbath. This is unlike the case in the Mishnah in which one forgot the entire essence of the Sabbath law, where the law is that he is liable to only one *chatas,* because in that case the person is certainly unaware of only one fact – the Sabbath law; hence, he is liable to only one *chatas.* But in this case the person knew that the Sabbath law prohibits certain *melachos;* he just did not realize that the particular *melachos* he performed were included in that law. Consequently, we can tie his transgressions to multiple mistakes. However, since he also forgot that it was the Sabbath, we can tie his transgressions to that single mistake. Rava therefore asks how many *chatas* offerings this person is obligated to bring (*Rashi;* see *Tos. HaRosh*). [See below, 72b note 28.]

[The above follows *Rashi. Tosafos* point out, however, that from the Gemara below it is apparent that Rava's query is applicable even to where the person was not aware of *any* of the thirty-nine *melachos.* The question therefore returns: How is this case different from a case where one forgot the entire essence of the Sabbath?

Tosafos answer that the depth of the person's unawareness in the case of Rava's query differs from that in the Mishnah's case. In the case of the Mishnah, the person is so unaware of the Sabbath that even if reminded, this information would have no meaning to him. He is therefore regarded as "one who forgets the essence of the Sabbath." In the case of Rava's query, however, although the person is indeed unaware of the Sabbath, when reminded he immediately recalls its significance. Cf. *Chidushei HaRamban* and *Baal HaMaor;* see also *Sfas Emes.*]

8. Since the Sabbath is the relevant mitzvah, we consider his inadvertence regarding the Sabbath to be primary (see *Tosafos, Ritva MHK* ed.).

9. The Gemara argues that it is unreasonable to assume that a person should gain by making additional mistakes. Therefore, since inadvertence regarding *melachos* makes a person liable to multiple *chatas* offerings, if, in addition to his unawareness of the *melachos,* he is also unaware of the Sabbath, he should not be free to bring only one offering (*Ritva MHK* ed.).

10. If he stops his act when he was reminded that it was the Sabbath, it is then obvious that forgetting about the Sabbath day is what caused him to transgress. Therefore, he is liable to only one offering (*Rashi*).

11. If he stops his work when reminded that the act is a *melachah,* and no mention is made to him of the fact that it is the Sabbath day, it is then obvious that forgetting that this is a *melachah* is what caused him to transgress. Thus, he is liable to a separate *chatas* for each *melachah* he performed (*Rashi*).

The Rishonim challenge *Rashi's* explanation on the grounds that Rav Ashi's test is not conclusive. For example, in the first case it may very well be that he would have stopped working just the same even if he had been reminded that his act was a *melachah.* Hence, there is no proof from his stopping when reminded of the Sabbath that his lack of awareness of the Sabbath is what caused the resulting transgression! (see *Maginei Shlomo;* see also *Tosafos* and *Ritva, MHK* ed., who offer other explanations of Rav Ashi's rule).

שם משמעון הנה אבות מהנה תולדות אחת שהיא הנה זדון שבת ושגגת מלאכות הנה שהיא אחת שגגת שבת וזדון מלאכות ושמואל אחת שהיא הנה והנה שהיא אחת לא משמע ליה: בעא מיניה רבא מרב נחמן [א] העלם זה וזה בידו מהו א"ל הרי העלם שבת בידו ואינו חייב אלא אחת אדרבה הרי העלם מלאכות בידו וחייב על כל אחת ואחת אלא אמר רב אשי חזינן אי משום שבת קא פריש הרי העלם שבת בידו ואינו חייב אלא אחת ואי משום מלאכה קפריש הרי העלם מלאכות בידו וחייב על כל אחת ואחת א"ל רבינא לרב אשי כלום פריש משבת אלא משום מלאכות כלום פריש ממלאכות אלא משום שבת [א] אלא לא שנא תנן [ב] אבות מלאכות ארבעים חסר אחת והוינן בה מנינא למה לי ואמר ר' יוחנן שאם עשאן כולן בהעלם אחד חייב על כל אחת ואחת אי אמרת בשלמא העלם זה וזה בידו חייב על כל אחת ואחת שפיר אלא אי אמרת העלם שבת בידו אינו חייב אלא אחת היכי משכחת לה בזדון שבת ושגגת מלאכות הניחא אי סבר ליה כרבי יוחנן דאמר כיון ששגג בכרת אע"פ שהזיד בלאו משכחת לה אלא אי סבר לה כרבי שמעון בן לקיש דאמר עד שישגוג בלאו וכרת דידע ליה שבת במאי [ג] דידע לה בתחומין ואליבא דרבי עקיבא: [ד] אמר רבא קצר וטחן כגרוגרת בשגגת שבת וזדון מלאכות וחזר וקצר וטחן כגרוגרת בזדון שבת ושגגת מלאכות ונודע לו על קצירה וטחינה של שגגת שבת וזדון מלאכות וחזר ונודע לו על קצירה ועל טחינה של זדון שבת ושגגת מלאכות

קצירה

רש"י

מהנה לרבות תולדות. כלומר היוצאות מהן מן האבות: **אחת שהיא הנה.** דאמרן פעמים שחייב על כל אחת ואחת מאי היא כגון שעשאן בזדון שבת ושגגת מלאכות דאיכא שגגות טובא והנה שהיא אחת דאמרן פעמים שחייב אחת על כולן מאי היא כגון שגגת שבת וזדון מלאכות דיודע שהמלאכות אסורות בשבת אבל שכח ששבת היום: **לא משמע ליה.** דמיבעיא ליה כוליה לשם משמעון ולתולדות: **זה וזה.** שבת ומלאכות: **מהו.** חייב אחת על כולן או על כל אחת ואחת וקמבעיא ליה הא דתני לעיל (דף סט.) שגג בזה ובזה זהו שוגג האמור בתורה מהו לחיובי חדא או לאחיובי אכולהו וממתני' דהשוכח עיקר שבת דאינו חייב אלא אחת לא שמעינן ליה דהשוכח עיקר שבת חדא שגגה היא וכי מיבעיא לן ביודע עיקר שבת אבל מלאכות הללו אינו יודע שאסורות ועוד נעלם ממנו שהיום שבת דאיכא למיתלי שגגה אכל מלאכה ומלאכה הואיל ויודע עיקר שבת ואיכא למתלי אהעלם שבת וחדא שגגה היא: **אי משום שבת קא פריש.** זה שפירש מן העבירה ובא להתכפר אי משום שבת היתה שאמרו לו שבת היום ופירש אישתכח דמשום העלם שבת היה עושה: ה"ג **ואי משום מלאכות הללו קא פריש.** שאמרו לו מלאכה היא זו ופירש הרי העלם מלאכה בידו ואזיל בתר מלאכות: **כלום פריש משבת אלא משום מלאכות.** כשאמרו לו שבת היום הבין שהמלאכות הללו אסורות דאי לא אסורות למה הוחקקו לומר שבת היום: **אלא לא שנא.** ואינו חייב אלא אחת: **עשאן לכולן.** היינו העלם זה וזה בידו דהא לא ידע שבת במידי כיון דכל הלכותיה נעלמות ממנו אין חילוק היום משאר ימים: **אא"א כו' היכי משכחת לה.** דניחייב אינש אכל חדא ע"כ בזדון שבת ושגגת מלאכות הוא דמשכחת לה והכא מאי זדון שבת איכא: **הניחא לר' יוחנן כו'.** משכחת ליה שלא נעלמו ממנו אלא הכריתות וידע הלאוין והיינו זדון שבת: **כגרוגרת.** שיעור הוא לכל איסורי מלאכות של שבת באוכלים: **קצר.** כגרוגרת וטחן כגרוגרת בשגגת שבת וזדון מלאכות דלא מיחייב אלא חדא: **וחזר וקצר.** כגרוגרת וטחן כגרוגרת בזדון שבת ושגגת מלאכות דמיחייב תרתי ולא נודע לו בינתים שחטא: **ונודע לו.** אחרי כן על הקצירה ועל הטחינה כלומר או על זו או על זו וכ"ש על שתיהן: ([ה] על) **שגגת שבת וזדון מלאכות.** והפריש חטאת וחטאת זו מכפרת על שתיהן דהא חדא הוא דמיחייב עליה:

קצירה

תוספות

שם משמעון. האי לישנא לא הוה צריך למימר כיון דאליבא דר' יוסי קאי דסבר בפ' הבונה (לקמן ד' קג.) דאפי' כתיבה אחת על שני נסרים או שני שריטות על נסר אחד חייב אלא ניחא ליה למנקט לישנא דמתני' דהבונה (שם.) א"ר יהודה מצינו שם קטן משם גדול שם משמעון:

לא משמע ליה. שמואל דלא כר' נתן ודלא כר' יוסי וצ"ל דמקבלה קים ליה לשמואל הכי [ו]:

העלם זה וזה בידו מהו. אומר ר"י דאפי' לא ידע לשבת בשום מלאכה חשיב ליה העלם זה וזה כדמוכח בסמוך דקאמר ר"י אי אמרת בשלמא העלם זה וזה בידו חייב כו' אלמא אע"ג דלא ידע לשבת במידי חשוב העלם זה וזה וצריך לחלק בין זה לשוכח עיקר שבת דהכא אינו שכוח כל כך דכי מדכרו ליה מדכר אבל שכח עיקר שבת היינו כעין תינוק שנשבה לבין הנכרים:

אמר ליה הרי העלם שבת בידו כו'. בשבועות בפ"ב (ד' יט.) בעא מיניה רבא מרב נחמן העלם זה וזה בידו מהו א"ל הרי העלם טומאה בידו וחייב והתם בפ"ג (דף כו.) נמי השיבו הרי העלם שבועה בידו וחייב התם שפיר דמהדר ליה לחומרא והא דמהדר ליה הכא לפוטרו משום דקסבר שגגת שבת עיקר דעיקר המלוה היא משום שבת:

חזינן אי משום שבת קא פריש כו'. פי' בקונטרס שאמרו לו שבת היום ופירש וקשה דשמא כי הוו אמרי ליה נמי מלאכה היא היה פורש אפי' לא יזכירוהו שבת אלא נראה לר"י דה"פ אי משום שבת קא פריש שאומר בעצמו דאי הוו מודעי ליה אשבת לבד היה פורש ואי הוו מודעי ליה אמלאכות לא היה פורש א"כ העלם שבת עיקר שהוא היה שכוח יותר ואי משום מלאכות פריש דשיילינן ליה ואמר דאי הוו מודעי ליה אמלאכות לא הוה צריך לאודועיה אשבת ואי הוו מודעי ליה אשבת הוה צריך לאודועיה אמלאכות הרי העלם מלאכות עיקר וחייב על כל אחת ואחת אבל כששניהם שכוחות בשוה מזה לא פשט כלום ולא בא רב אשי אלא לפשוט מקצת הבעיא כלומר לפעמים נוכל להבחין איזו העלמה עיקר ול"ג מה שכתוב בספרים ואי כי מודעי ליה אשבת אכתי צריך לאודועיה אמלאכות העלם מלאכות בידו כו' דלפי מה שפי' ר"י אכתי הוה צריך לפרושי וכי מודעת ליה אמלאכות לא הוה צריך לאודועיה אשבת אלא גרסי' ואי משום מלאכות קא פריש כו' וקאמר רבינא כלום פריש משבת אלא משום מלאכות כו' כלומר כיון ששניהם שכוחים במה שזה שכוח יותר מזה לא נפקא מיניה מידי אלא לא שנא ותרווייהו תבעי ורשב"א מקיים גירסת הספרים ומפרש דרב אשי בא לפשוט דהעלם זה וזה (א) חייב אי משום שבת קפריש שהשבת שכוחה יותר העלם שבת בידו ואי כי מודעת ליה אשבת אכתי צריך לאודועי אמלאכות אפילו אי כי נמי מודעת ליה אמלאכות צריך לאודועיה אשבת דהוי העלם זה וזה חשיב כהעלם מלאכות וחייב וכן מוכח מדנקט לעיל אי משום שבת קא פריש והכא נקט אי כי מודעת ליה אשבת כו' והא דקאמר כלום פריש ממלאכות אלא משום שבת ה"פ אלא משום שבת ותהא שגגת שבת עיקר ולא מיחייב אלא חדא דבענין אחר לא הוה פריך מידי כיון דבשניהן שוה חייב על כל אחת:

נודע לו על הקצירה ועל הטחינה של שגגת שבת וזדון מלאכות. פי' רבינו שמואל שנודע לו והפריש קרבן וקודם שנתכפר חזר ונודע לו על הקצירה וטחינה של שגגת מלאכות אבל אם לא נודע לו עד אחר הכפרה אין נגררין וצריכין שתי חטאות דלכ"ע כפרה מחלקת ודווקא הפריש קרבן אבל אם לא הפריש קרבן וחזר ונודע לו על קצירה וטחינה של [ז] שגגת מלאכות יביא איזה שירצה דבו תליא מילתא אם ירצה יפריש חטאת אחת על שגגת שבת ונגררין של שגגת מלאכות עמה או אם ירצה יפריש ב' קרבנות על הקצירה וטחינה של שגגת מלאכות ויגררו עמהן של שגגת שבת כדאמר רבא בסמוך אכל שני זיתי חלב בהעלם אחד ונודע לו על אחד מהן כו' הביא קרבן על הראשון כו' אלמא אע"ג דנודע לו על הראשון תחלה הואיל ועדיין לא הפריש קרבן עליו אינו גורר האמצעי עמו כדי להתחייב קרבן על השלישי אלא אם ירצה יביא קרבן על האמצעי ויתכפרו כולן וא"ת דהשתא משמע דסבר רבא דאין הפרשות מחלקות מדנגררות של שגגת מלאכות עם של שגגת שבת והיינו כריש לקיש ורבא גופיה לא פסיק כוותיה בהחולץ (יבמות לו.) אלא בג' מקומות ומיהו מתוך פי' ר"ח שפירש דהלכתא כרבה רבו של אביי משמע דגרס רבה וכן משמע שמזכירו לפני אביי וכן בסמוך דקאמר מילתא דפשיטא לה לרבא ואביי ואפי' גרסי' רבא י"ל דלא איירי ביבמות אלא בדברים הנוהגים בזמן הזה מיהו תימה לר"י לקמן דמיבעיא לן אי פליגי בהפרשות מחלקות או לא תפשוט דבהפרשות פליגי דאי בידיעות פליגי אבל הפרשות מחלקות לכ"ע א"כ רבה ואביי דסברי הכא דאין הפרשות מחלקות כמאן וי"ל דאיכא למדחי דהכא מיירי שלא הפריש עד אחר שחזר ונודע לו גם על שגגת מלאכות והא דנקט ונודע לו על שגגת שבת היינו כלומר שלבסוף הפריש על שגגת שבת:

גרירה

עין משפט נר מצוה

יב א מיי' פ"ז מהלכות שגגות הלכה ד:

רבינו חננאל

כר' יוסי דאמר הבערה ללאו יצאת ולא לחלק ודרשה דר' יוסי אחת שהיא הנה והנה שהיא אחת לא משמע ליה: **בעא** מיניה (רבה) [רבא] מר' נחמן העלם שגגת שבת ושגגת מלאכות כשגגת שבת דיינינן ליה וחייב אחת על כל שבת ושבת או כשגגת מלאכות דיינינן ליה וחייב על כל מלאכה ומלאכה בכריתות תנן המחלל את השבת שהיא אחת מל"ו כריתות ואקשינן חדא מחייב מ' חסר אחת הוו חיובי שבת ואוקמה ר' יוחנן בשגגת שבת וזדון מלאכות (מחדא לא פליג) דלא מחייב אלא חדא. ומקשינן וליתני זדון שבת ושגגת מלאכות דחייב על כל אחת ואחת ושנינן הא קמ"ל דאפי' שגגת שבת וזדון מלאכו' מחדא לא פליט' ופשט ליה רב נחמן לרבא. [הרי העלם שבת בידו ואינו חייב אלא אחת וא"ל אדרבה] הרי העלם מלאכה בידו וחייב על כל מלאכה ואתא רב אשי ואמר הדא מלתא בעא בירור אי משום שבת לא מחייב אלא חדא כרב נחמן ואי כי מודעת כי שבת הוא היום עדיין צריך לאודועי הכי החורש הוא חייב. ושביק ליה לחרישה והדר לזריעה. תוב צריך לאודועה. כי גם הזריעה חייב עליה. וכן הקוצר ושאר מלאכות כל אחת ואחת חייב עליה על כל אחת ואחת בפני עצמה ובכל אחת ואחת צריך ידיעה בפני עצמה. הרי שגגת (שבת) [מלאכות]. וחייב על כל מלאכה ולא אמרינן מפני שנוספה על שגגת מלאכות שגגת שבת פקעה לה שגגת מלאכות א' לא' במקומה עומדת. ואי לא מסתברא דודאי זדון מלאכות ושגגת שבת הוא כרבא עבדין דאיסורא דספיקא דאורייתא היא. וכל איסורא דספיקא דאורייתא לחומרא עבדינן ואתא רבינא ודחייא להא דרב אשי ואמר כלום פריש משבת (א' לא') [אלא] משום מלאכות כו' ומסתברא דרבינא כר"נ והכי קיימא בזדון שבת ושגגת מלאכות כגון שמכיר כי היום הוא שבת וגם היה יודע שהמלאכות אסורות ונעלם ממנו איסור מלאכות עכשיו או שידע איסור מלאכות בלאו ונעלם ממנו איסורא דכרת. שנמצאת ידיעת שבת בידו והעלם על כל מלאכה ומלאכה זהו שחייב על כל מלאכה ומלאכה אבל השוכח עיקר שבת ועיקר איסור מלאכות ולא מהניא לך כהודעת ליה עיקר שבת ועדיין צריכת לאודועיה איסור מלאכות דאי לא מודעת ליה איסור מלאכות מי ידע דאסירן דלפרוש הלכך ידיעת שבת תליא בידיעת איסור מלאכות ואיסור מלאכות תליין משום שבת וכיון שאפשר שתודיעו (א' לא') איסור שבת ואיסור מלאכות כאחת נמצאת כאילו שגגה אחת היא ואינו חייב אלא אחת כרב נחמן ומקשינן על רב נחמן מדר' יוחנן דאמר אם עשאן כולם בהעלם אחת חייב על כל אחת ואחת. בשלמא אי אמרת העלם זה וזה בידו חייב על כל אחת ואחת היינו דמשכחת לה הכי אלא אי אמרת כל כי האי גונא לא מחייב אלא חדא היכי משכחת לה דחייב על כל אחת ואחת ואם תאמר בזדון שבת ושגגת מלאכות הניחא אליבא דר' יוחנן משכחת לה זדון שבת [כו'] ומשני ר' נחמן דידע לה שהוא אסור בתחומין ואליבא דר' עקיבא כדאמרינן לעיל (סט.) שנמצאת זדון בתחומין וכי הדין בעיא דרבא העלם זה וזה בידו. גרסינן בשבועות (יט.) בענין ידיעות הטומאה ואסיקנא להו כהא: **אמר** (רבא) [רבה] קצר וטחן כגרוגרת בשגגת שבת וזדון מלאכות דאע"ג דשני אבות נינהו לא מחייב אלא חדא דהא

מסורת הש"ס

א) [סנהדרין סב.] שבועות יט. כו. [כריתות ג:], ב) [לקמן דף עג. וש"נ], ג) [לעיל דף סט. וש"נ], ד) [עמ"ש לקמן עב: על הגליון], ה) [צ"ל שלו], ו) [עי' לקמן קו. ד"ה מה לי לבשל כו' כתב דשמואל כר"ש ס"ל ע"ש], ז) צ"ל שגגת שבת ופי' דקאי אסיפא אאבל נודע לו קצירה של זדון שבת [ר"מ] וע"ש.

הגהות הב"ח

(א) תוס' ד"ה חזינן וכו' לפשוט דהעלם זה וזה בידו חייב:

ליקוטי רש"י

מהנה תולדות. דנפקא לן מדדמי להו לאבות והיינו מהנה כלומר מן הדומות להם [סנהדרין סב.]. הנה הוי משמע אבות כתב מהנה לרבויי תולדות [לקמן קג:]. **אחת שהיא הנה.** דאמרן לעיל פעמים שמתחייב על כל אחת ואחת דהיינו על אחת הנה על מלוה אחת כמה חטאות כגון עושה מלאכות הרבה בזדון שבת ושגגות מלאכות כדפרישית לעיל דיש כאן שגגות הרבה [סנהדרין שם]. דאמרן לעיל היכי דמי כגון שעשאן בזדון שבת ושגגת מלאכות ואע"ג דכולן אין אלא חילול שבת אחת מיחייב לכל מלאכה ומלאכה דגופי מלאכות מחלקין הואיל ואיכא שגגה טובא. **שגגת שבת וזדון מלאכות.** שאע"פ שהן גופי מלאכות הרבה אינו חייב אלא אחת דחדא שגגה היא [לקמן שם]. יודע שמלאכות הללו אסורות בשבת אבל כסבור אין שבת היום כולה חדא שגגה היא [סנהדרין שם]. **כלום פריש וכו'.** כשהודיעוהו אחד מהם שם אל לבו לומר מה בכך ומתוך כך נזכר על השני ומ"מ העלם שניהם היה בידו [שבועות יט.]. **מנינא למה לי.** ליתני אבות מלאכות הזורע והחורש כו' למה לי לאשמעינן מניינא הא מני להו ואזיל [לעיל ו:]. ליתני אבות מלאכות הזורע והחורש כו' למה לי למיתנא ארבעים חסר אחת ליתנינהו ואנן ידעינן דארבעים חסר אחת איכא [שם סט.]. **שאם עשאן כולן וכו'.** ובא להודיענו סכום החטאות שאדם חייב באיסורי שבת בהעלם אחד ואשמעינן ארבעים חסר אחת הן ותו לא שאפילו עשה תולדותיהן עמהן אינו מביא על התולדה היכא דעשאה עם אביה דהוה ליה כעושה וחוזר ועושה דכולה חדא עבירה היא [שם ו:]. וסימנא בעלמא אשמעינן לידע כמה חטאות חייב על חילול שבת אחת [שם סט.]. ובא להודיענו שאם נתעלמו כל הלכות שבת ממנו כמה חטאות [חייב] עליו [לקמן עג:]. **היכי משכחת לה.** דמיחייב על כרחך לא משכחת לה אלא בזדון שבת דיודע שהוא שבת ושגגת מלאכות דאינו יודע שהמלאכות הללו אסורות דאי בזדון מלאכות ושגגת שבת דיודע שהן אסורות בשבת אבל שכח שהיום שבת הא תנן דאינו חייב אלא אחת לכל שבת וזדון שבת לא הוי אלא אם כן יודע אחת מהלכותיה דאי לא ידע בחדא מינייהו אין שבת חלוק לו משאר ימים וזה שגג בכולן אין כאן זדון שבת [לעיל שם]. דמיחייב שום אדם על כל מלאכה ומלאכה שבהעלם אחד על כרחך בזדון שבת ושגגת מלאכות הוא דבעית לאשכוחיה והכא דאיעלימו כולהו מיניה מאי זדון שבת איכא במה ניכר לו שבת משאר ימים [לקמן שם]. **הניחא אי סבר ליה כרבי יוחנן.** דאמר שגגת כרת שמה שגגה. **משכחת לה.** זדון שבת בלאוין ושגגת מלאכות בכריתות דיודע לה לשבת שהוזהר על הלאוין או של כולן או של אחת מהן. **דידע לה לשבת במאי.** הלא בכולן שגג כסבור שכל שלשים ותשע מלאכות מותרות. **בתחומין.** דאין בקרבן [לעיל שם]. דאינו יודע שמלאכות הללו אסורות אבל יודע מצות שבת בדבר אחד כגון דידע שאסור לצאת חוץ לתחום [כריתות ג.]. **ואליבא דר' עקיבא.** דאמר במסכת סוטה תחומין דאורייתא נינהו דתנן בו ביום דרש רבי עקיבא ומדותם מחוץ לעיר כו' [לעיל שם]. דאמר דאורייתא נינהו והוי מחלל ומיהו אין חייבין לא על שגגתו חטאת כו' [לקמן קנג:]. ור"ע מודה נמי בתחומים דאין חייבים עליהם כרת דתנן (שבת עג.) אבות מלאכות ארבעים חסר אחת ולא פליג ר' עקיבא [סנהדרין סו.]. **בגרוגרת.** היא חזיה יבשה [עירובין ד.].

because of his awareness **of the Sabbath for any reason other than** that he becomes aware of **the *melachos*** at the same time?[12] כְּלוּם פָּרֵישׁ מִמְּלָאכוֹת אֶלָּא מִשּׁוּם שַׁבָּת – Likewise, **does he withdraw** from work **because of his awareness of the *melachos* for any reason other than** that he also becomes aware of **the Sabbath** at the same time?[13] אֶלָּא לֹא שְׁנָא – **Rather, there is no difference** which unawareness was brought to his attention; in either case he forgot both the Sabbath and the *melachos,* and he is liable to only one *chatas.*[14]

The Gemara questions this ruling:

תְּנַן – **We learned in the Mishnah:** אֲבוֹת מְלָאכוֹת אַרְבָּעִים חָסֵר אַחַת – THE PRIMARY LABORS ARE FORTY MINUS ONE.[15] וְהָוֵינַן בָּהּ – **Now,** in **discussing this** we asked: מִנְיָנָא לָמָּה לִי – **Why do I need** the Tanna to specify **the number** of *melachos?*[16] וְאָמַר רַבִּי יוֹחָנָן – **And** in answer to this **R' Yochanan said:** שֶׁאִם עֲשָׂאָן כּוּלָּן בְּהֶעְלֵם אֶחָד – It is to teach **that if someone performed all** thirty-nine **of them in one lapse of awareness** חַיָּיב עַל כָּל אַחַת וְאַחַת – **he is liable** to a separate *chatas* **for each and every one** he performed.[17]

The Gemara now explains its question:

אִי אָמְרַתְּ בִּשְׁלָמָא הֶעְלֵם זֶה וָזֶה בְּיָדוֹ – **It is understandable if you hold that** where there is **a lapse of awareness of** both **this** [the Sabbath] **and that** [the *melachos*] **on his part,** חַיָּיב עַל כָּל אַחַת וְאַחַת – **he is liable for each and every one,** שַׁפִּיר – for then **it is proper** that he should be liable to bring thirty-nine offerings, because even if the person was not at all aware of the Sabbath [as in this case, where he was not aware of any of the *melachos*], his inadvertence regarding each of the *melachos* obligates him to bring a separate *chatas* for each. אֶלָּא אִי אָמְרַתְּ הֶעְלֵם שַׁבָּת בְּיָדוֹ – **But if you say that** wherever **there is lapse of awareness of the Sabbath on his part,** אֵינוֹ חַיָּיב אֶלָּא אַחַת – **he is liable to only one** sacrifice even though the *melachos* also escaped his awareness, הֵיכִי מַשְׁכַּחַתְּ לָהּ – then **how is such a case to be found,** i.e. a case in which one would be liable to thirty-nine *chatas* offerings? בְּזָדוֹן שַׁבָּת וְשִׁגְגַת מְלָאכוֹת – Where he acted **with deliberateness regarding the Sabbath and inadvertence regarding the *melachos.***[18] But how can this person who was unaware of all thirty-nine *melachos* be considered to have acted deliberately regarding the Sabbath? הָנִיחָא אִי סָבַר לֵיהּ כְּרַבִּי יוֹחָנָן – **It is well if** [**the Tanna**] **holds in accordance with R' Yochanan,** דְּאָמַר כֵּיוָן שֶׁשָּׁגַג בְּכָרֵת – **who said that so long as one acted inadvertently with regard to** the ***kares*** penalty, he liable to a *chatas,* אַף עַל פִּי שֶׁהֵזִיד בְּלָאו – **even though he acted deliberately with regard to** the **prohibition;** מַשְׁכַּחַתְּ לָהּ דְּיָדַע לֵיהּ שַׁבָּת בְּלָאו – **this** ruling of the Mishnah **can be found** in a case **where he knew about the Sabbath with regard to** the **prohibition** against performing *melachos,* but he was not aware of the *kares* penalty incurred for violations.[19] Thus, he is considered to have sinned inadvertently, and is liable to a separate *chatas* for each *av melachah* – thirty-nine in all. אֶלָּא אִי סָבַר לָהּ כְּרַבִּי שִׁמְעוֹן בֶּן לָקִישׁ – **But if he holds in accordance with R' Shimon ben Lakish,** דְּאָמַר עַד שֶׁיִּשְׁגּוֹג בְּלָאו וְכָרֵת – **who said** that one is not liable to a *chatas* **unless he acted inadvertently with regard to** both the **prohibition and** the ***kares*** penalty, דְּיָדַע לֵיהּ שַׁבָּת בְּמַאי – **in what** respect **did he know** about **the Sabbath?**[20]

The Gemara answers:

דְּיָדַע לָהּ בִּתְחוּמִין – **He knew** about [**the Sabbath**] **with regard to the *techum* law,** וְאַלִּיבָּא דְּרַבִּי עֲקִיבָא – **and** this is **according to R' Akiva,** who holds that this prohibition is Biblical.[21]

The Gemara introduces another case involving multiple transgressions:

אָמַר רָבָא – **Rava said:** קָצַר וְטָחַן כִּגְרוֹגֶרֶת – **If one reaped and ground** produce **the size of a dried fig**[22] בְּשִׁגְגַת שַׁבָּת וּזְדוֹן מְלָאכוֹת – **with inadvertence regarding the Sabbath and deliberateness regarding the *melachos,***[23] וְחָזַר וְקָצַר וְטָחַן כִּגְרוֹגֶרֶת – **and, then,** without becoming aware of his earlier transgressions, **he reaped and ground** another amount **equal to a dried fig,** בְּזָדוֹן שַׁבָּת וְשִׁגְגַת מְלָאכוֹת – this time **with deliberateness regarding the Sabbath and inadvertence regarding the *melachos,***[24] וְנוֹדַע לוֹ עַל קְצִירָה וּטְחִינָה שֶׁל שִׁגְגַת שַׁבָּת וּזְדוֹן מְלָאכוֹת – **and it** first **became known to him about the reaping or grinding** that he did them **with inadvertence regarding the Sabbath and deliberateness regarding the *melachos,***[25] וְחָזַר וְנוֹדַע לוֹ עַל קְצִירָה וְעַל טְחִינָה שֶׁל זָדוֹן שַׁבָּת וְשִׁגְגַת מְלָאכוֹת – **and it then became known to him about the reaping and grinding** that he did them **with deliberateness regarding the Sabbath and inadvertence regarding the *melachos,***

NOTES

12. When they reminded him that it was the Sabbath, he understood that his acts must be *melachos,* because otherwise they would not have bothered telling him it was the Sabbath (*Rashi*).

13. [He surely realizes that performing *melachos* is prohibited only on the Sabbath (see *Ritva MHK* ed.).]

14. *Rashi.* Since Rav Ashi's solution has been rejected, we revert to Rav Nachman's answer in the beginning of this passage (*Ritva MHK* ed.).

15. Below, 73a. The Mishnah then proceeds to list all thirty-nine *melachos* for which one is liable on the Sabbath.

16. I.e. why did the Mishnah have to preface its list of *melachos* (which immediately follows the sentence quoted by the Gemara) by stating that there were thirty-nine? It could have merely listed them, and we could count them ourselves to find out how many there are (*Rashi* above, 69a).

17. [By stating that there are thirty-nine *melachos,* the Mishnah alludes to the maximum number of *chatas* offerings a person would have to bring for desecrating one Sabbath.] Now, this is apparently a case involving a lapse of awareness of both the Sabbath and the *melachos.* For if the person did not know about any of the *melachos,* the Sabbath was to him like any other day (*Rashi;* see *Chidushei HaRan*).

18. That is, the person knew that it was the Sabbath, but did not realize that those acts were prohibited as *melachah* on the Sabbath. But if the person was unaware of *all* thirty-nine *melachos,* he cannot be said to have acted deliberately regarding the Sabbath because the Sabbath was no different to him than any other day of the week (*Rashi;* see above, 69a note 21).

19. That is, the person was unaware only of the *kares* punishment, but he knew that it was prohibited to perform the *melachos* on the Sabbath. This makes his knowledge that it was the Sabbath meaningful. Thus, when he performed *melachos* on that day, he acted inadvertently only regarding *melachos,* since according to R' Yochanan lack of knowledge of the *kares* punishment is sufficient to classify his actions as inadvertent.

20. Thus, according to Reish Lakish it is clear that the person could not have known that any of the *melachos* were prohibited. If so, we should consider him to have acted inadvertently with regard to both the Sabbath and *melachos,* in which case he should liable to only one *chatas.*

21. [See above, 69a notes 23-24.] Hence, the person's knowledge that the day was Saturday is considered meaningful. He acted inadvertently only regarding the *melachos* and is liable to a separate *chatas* for each.

22. [One is liable to a *chatas* only if he performs a certain minimum amount of *melachah.*] The minimal amount for all *melachos* involving food is the size of a dried fig (*Rashi*).

23. For these acts he is liable to only one *chatas* (*Rashi*).

24. For these he is liable to a separate *chatas* for each act (*Rashi*).

25. And he designated a *chatas* for this transgression. The *chatas* can atone for both of the transgressions done with inadvertence regarding the Sabbath (*Rashi*) [assuming, of course, that he became aware of the second transgression before he offered the sacrifice (*Tos. HaRosh*)]. [See below, 71b note 23.]

The rule Rava is about to give applies all the more so to where the person became aware of *both* transgressions done with inadvertence regarding the Sabbath before designating the *chatas* (*Rashi*).

קְצִירָה גוֹרֶרֶת קְצִירָה – the first **reaping draws** the second **reaping along** with it to its atonement,[1] וּטְחִינָה גוֹרֶרֶת טְחִינָה – **and** likewise the first **grinding draws** the second **grinding along.**[2] אֲבָל נוֹדַע לוֹ עַל קְצִירָה שֶׁל זְדוֹן שַׁבָּת וְשִׁגְגַת מְלָאכוֹת – **However,** if **it** first **became known to him about the reaping** that he did it **with deliberateness regarding the Sabbath and inadvertence regarding the** ***melachos*** [for which he is liable to one *chatas* for each *melachah* he performed],[3] קְצִירָה גוֹרֶרֶת קְצִירָה וּטְחִינָה שֶׁעִמָּהּ – the second **reaping draws** the first **reaping and its related grinding along** to its atonement,[4] וּטְחִינָה שֶׁכְּנֶגְדָּהּ בִּמְקוֹמָהּ עוֹמֶדֶת – **but the opposing grinding** [the second violation] **stays in its place** without atonement.[5]

The Gemara presents a dissenting opinion:

אַבַּיֵּי אָמַר – **Abaye said:** טְחִינָה נַמִּי גוֹרֶרֶת טְחִינָה – The first **grinding also draws** the second **grinding along,** שֵׁם טְחִינָה אַחַת הִיא – because **it is one prohibition of grinding.**[6]

The Gemara questions Rava's ruling:

וּמִי אִית לֵיהּ לְרָבָא גְּרִירָה – **And does Rava** really **subscribe to** the principle of **"drawing along"?**[7] וְהָא אִיתְּמַר – **But it was stated:** אָכַל שְׁנֵי זֵיתֵי חֵלֶב בְּהֶעְלֵם אֶחָד – If **someone ate two olive-sized** amounts **of** ***cheilev*** **in one lapse of awareness,** וְנוֹדַע לוֹ עַל אַחַת מֵהֶן – **and one of those** two violations **became known to him,** וְחָזַר וְאָכַל כַּזַּיִת בְּהֶעְלֵמוֹ שֶׁל שֵׁנִי – **and he then ate** a third **olive-sized amount** of *cheilev* **in the** same **lapse of awareness as the second** piece,[8] אָמַר רָבָא – **Rava said** the following rulings apply: הֵבִיא קָרְבָּן עַל רִאשׁוֹן – If **he brought a sacrifice for the first** violation, רִאשׁוֹן וְשֵׁנִי מִתְכַּפְּרִין – **the first and second** violations **are atoned for,** since they both occurred during the same lapse, שְׁלִישִׁי אֵינוֹ מִתְכַּפֵּר – but the **third is not atoned for;**[9] הֵבִיא קָרְבָּן עַל הַשְּׁלִישִׁי – if **he brought a sacrifice for the third** violation,[10] שְׁלִישִׁי וְשֵׁנִי מִתְכַּפְּרִין – **the third and second** violations **are atoned for,** since they occurred in the same lapse, רִאשׁוֹן אֵינוֹ מִתְכַּפֵּר – but **the first is not atoned for;**[11] הֵבִיא קָרְבָּן עַל הָאֶמְצָעִי – if **he brought a sacrifice for the middle** violation, נִתְכַּפְּרוּ כּוּלָּן – **they are all atoned for.**[12] אַבַּיֵּי אָמַר – **Abaye says:** אֲפִילּוּ הֵבִיא קָרְבָּן עַל אֶחָד מֵהֶן – **Even if he brought a sacrifice for** any **one of them** [i.e. for the first or third] נִתְכַּפְּרוּ כּוּלָּן – **they are all atoned for.**[13] It is thus apparent that Rava does not subscribe to the principle of "drawing along." – ? –

The Gemara answers:

בָּתַר דִּשְׁמַעָהּ מֵאַבַּיֵּי סְבָרָהּ – **After** [Rava] **learned this** principle **from Abaye, he concurred with it.**[14]

The Gemara asks:

אִי הָכִי – **If** it is **so** that Rava subscribes to "drawing along,"

NOTES

1. That is, the *chatas* designated to atone for the first violation of reaping atones also for the second violation of reaping (*Rashi*). [See next note.]

2. That same *chatas,* which atones also for the first violation of grinding, atones for the second violation of grinding as well. This is based on the law that if someone violated a prohibition (e.g. he consumed *cheilev*) two times in a single lapse of awareness, he is liable to only one *chatas.* Therefore, here too, since the person did not become aware of any transgression between his two sets of violations of reaping and grinding, he is liable to only one *chatas.* This is so even though the second lapse was different than the first [the second being inadvertence regarding the *melachos* while the first was inadvertence regarding the Sabbath], because even when the person found out in between the two sets of violations that it was the Sabbath, he did not realize at that time that he had desecrated the Sabbath earlier in the day. Now, one is liable to a *chatas* only when he realizes that he sinned, as derived from the verse (*Leviticus* 4:28): אוֹ הוֹדַע אֵלָיו חַטָּאתוֹ אֲשֶׁר חָטָא וְהֵבִיא קָרְבָּנוֹ, *If his sin that he committed becomes known to him, he shall bring as his offering.* Therefore, in this case the person is liable to only one *chatas* for the two sets of reaping and grinding since they were all performed in one lapse of awareness (see *Rashi, Ritva MHK* ed.).

3. And he designated a *chatas* to atone for that reaping (*Rashi*).

4. That is, this *chatas* will atone also for the first reaping, which was done in the same lapse, and the first grinding (*Rashi*).

5. This person is liable to two *chatas* offerings for his second set of acts, which were performed with inadvertence regarding the *melachos*. Hence, his *chatas* designated for that second reaping violation cannot atone for the *melachah* of grinding that was performed at the same time (*Rashi*).

Thus, according to Rava the two acts of reaping are considered like two acts of consuming *cheilev* during the same lapse of awareness; hence the *chatas* brought for the second violation of reaping atones for the first reaping as well. Then, using the principle of "drawing along," the first act of grinding is also atoned for. According to this principle, even though the *chatas* was not initially designated for the first act of reaping, since it does atone for that act, that reaping can draw the first grinding violation along with it to its atonement because both of those violations require only one *chatas* [the inadvertence was in regard to the Sabbath]. However, according to Rava, we do not utilize the principle of "drawing along" another time to say that once this *chatas* atones for the first violation of grinding, that act of grinding should draw along the second grinding as well. Rather, another *chatas* must be brought to atone for the second grinding violation (*Rashi*).

6. Literally: one name of grinding. Abaye holds that the principle of "drawing along" can be utilized two times. Thus, even though the first act of grinding itself is atoned for through "drawing along," it can draw along the second grinding to its atonement (*Rashi*).

7. By stating that the *chatas* designated for the second reaping violation atones for the first violation of grinding, Rava apparently utilizes the principle of "drawing along." The offering was not explicitly designated for the first reaping violation. Rather, that reaping is atoned for only by virtue of its association with the second act of reaping for which the *chatas* was designated. Nevertheless, the first reaping violation draws along the first grinding violation to its atonement (*Rashi, Ritva MHK* ed.).

The fact that the *chatas* atones for the first violation of reaping is not based on the principle of "drawing along." Rather, that violation is atoned because all violations repeated in the same lapse of awareness are atoned for with a single *chatas,* as explained above, note 1 (ibid.). Thus, when Rava states that the first reaping "draws along" the second reaping, he does not mean to invoke the principle of "drawing along" at that point. The term "draws along" is merely borrowed from his utilization of that principle for the first violation of grinding (*Ritva MHK* ed. in explanation of *Rashi*; cf. *Tosafos*).

8. He thus ate three pieces of *cheilev,* the middle piece in the same lapse of awareness as the first one, and also in the same lapse as the last one. However, the first and third pieces were not eaten in the same lapse, since the person discovered his transgression of the first piece before he ate the third one.

9. The third piece was not eaten during the same lapse as the first piece. And according to Rava we do not say that since the second piece is atoned for with this *chatas* it should draw along the third piece to its atonement (*Rashi*).

10. I.e. he mentioned the third violation when he designated the sacrifice (*Rashi*). [Ordinarily, a person would designate his first offering for the first violation of which he became aware (see *Ritva MHK* ed. ד"ה אמר). Here, though, the person specified that the offering should atone for the violation which was the third one that he had committed.]

11. The first piece was not eaten during the same lapse as the third piece. And here too we do not utilize the principle of "drawing along."

12. Because both of the other pieces were eaten in the same lapse as the middle piece. Thus the person receives atonement for all of the pieces without having to utilize the principle of "drawing along" (*Rashi*).

13. Because Abaye does subscribe to the principle of "drawing along" (*Rashi*).

14. After hearing Abaye's ruling about the three pieces of *cheilev,* Rava also subscribed to the principle of "drawing along." At that point he made his ruling above concerning reaping and grinding on the Sabbath (*Rashi*).

ᵃקצירה גוררת קצירה וטחינה גוררת טחינה אבל נודע לו על קצירה של זדון שבת ושגגת מלאכות קצירה גוררת קצירה וטחינה שעמה וטחינה שכנגדה במקומה עומדת אביי אמר טחינה נמי גוררת טחינה שם טחינה אחת היא ומי אית ליה לרבא גרירה והא איתמר אכל שני זיתי חלב בהעלם אחד ונודע לו על אחת מהן וחזר ואכל כזית בהעלמו של שני ◦ אמר רבא א) ᵇהביא קרבן על ראשון ראשון ושני מתכפרין ג' אינו מתכפר הביא קרבן על השלישי שלישי ושני מתכפרין ראשון אינו מתכפר הביא קרבן על האמצעי נתכפרו כולן אביי אמר אפילו הביא קרבן על אחד מהן נתכפרו כולן בתר דשמעה מאביי סברה אי הכי טחינה נמי תגרר לטחינה גרירה אית ליה גרירה דגרירה לית ליה ◦ מילתא דפשיטא להו לאביי ורבא (א) מבעיא לר' זירא דבעי רבי זירא מרבי אסי ואמרי לה בעא מיניה רבי ירמיה מרבי זירא ᶜקצר וטחן חצי גרוגרת בשגגת שבת וזדון מלאכות וחזר וקצר וטחן חצי גרוגרת בזדון שבת ושגגת מלאכות מהו שיצטרפו אמר ליה חלוקין לחטאות ולא מצטרפין וכל היכא דחלוקין לחטאות לא מצטרפי ג) והתנן ᵈאכל חלב וחלב בהעלם אחד אינו חייב אלא אחת אכל ◦ ᵉחלב ודם ונותר ופגול בהעלם אחד חייב על כל אחת ואחת זו חומר במינין הרבה ממין אחד וזו חומר במין אחד ממינין הרבה שאם אכל חצי זית וחזר ואכל חצי זית ממין אחד חייב ᶠמשני מינין פטור ג) והוינן בה ממין אחד חייב צריכא למימר ואמר ריש לקיש משום בר תוטני הכא במאי עסקינן ᶻכגון שאכלו בשני תמחויין ורבי יהושע היא ד) דאמר תמחויין מחלקין מהו דתימא אמר רבי יהושע בין לקולא בין לחומרא קא משמע לן דלקולא לא אמר לחומרא קאמר והא הכא דחלוקין לחטאות וקא מצטרפי אמר ליה מר ארישא מתני לה וקשיא ליה אנן אסיפא מתנינן לה ולא קשיא לן משני מינין פטור צריכא למימר ואמר ריש לקיש משום בר תוטני לעולם ממין אחד ואמאי קרי ליה שני מינין שאכלו בשני תמחויין ור' יהושע היא דאמר תמחויין מחלקין והא קא משמע לן דאמר רבי יהושע בין לקולא בין לחומרא מדסיפא מין אחד ושני תמחויין מכלל

קצירה גוררת קצירה. שניה בכפרתה וטחינה גוררת את הטחינה השניה ונתכפרו כולן דקיימא לן אכל שני זיתי חלב בהעלם אחד אינו חייב אלא אחת וזה שעשה שתי קצירות בהעלם אחד שלא נודע לו בין קצירה לקצירה שחטא ואע"פ שהעלמה של שניה חלוק קצת משל ראשונה סוף סוף העלם אחד הוא דלא נודע לו חטאו בינתים וידיעות [חטא] הוא דמחלקת הלכך חטאת זו שבאה על הקצירה וטחינה ראשונה אתרווייהו קיימא ונתכפרו עם הקצירה כל קצירות שעליו שנעשו בהעלם אחד ועם הטחינה נתכפרו כל הטחינות שעליו כשעשאן בהעלם אחד: אבל נודע לו על הקצירה. אחרונה שבזדון שבת ושגגת מלאכות והפריש עליה קרבן הואיל ובקרבן זה לא שייכא טחינה שעמה דהא אכל חדא מיחייב אי הוה מתידעי ליה תרווייהו: קצירה גוררת קצירה. ראשונה: וטחינה שעמה. של ראשונה: וטחינה. אחרונה. שכנגדה של ראשונה: במקומה עומדת. וכי מתידע ליה מיחייב עלה: קצירה גוררת קצירה. כמשפט דשני זיתי חלב בהעלם אחד הן וטחינה שעם קצירה ראשונה היינו משום גרירה דאף על גב דעיקר קרבן לאו משום קצירה דבהדה אתא הואיל ואיכפר ליה בהדי קצירה בתרייתא גררה לטחינה שעמה בהדה שהרי שתיהן היו תלויות בקרבן אחד ואין כפרה לזו בלא זו: וטחינה שכנגדה עומדת במקומה. דגרירה לגרירה לא אמרינן לאיכפורי טחינה אחרונה עם טחינה ראשונה משום שני זיתי חלב בהעלם אחד דהא קמייתא גופה בגרירה היא דמיכפרה: שם טחינה אחת היא. ואע"ג דקמייתא גופא בגרירה אתיא אמרינן גרירה לגרירה: ומי אית ליה לרבא גרירה. אטחינה שעמה קפריך דמגררה עם הקצירה ואע"ג דקרבן לאו אההיא קצירה איפריש דאינך כולהו לאו גרירה איכא דקצירה וקצירה בהעלם אחד לאו גרירה היא דכל שם עבירה הנכפל כמה פעמים בהעלם אחד אין בו אלא חטאת אחת: ראשון ושני מתכפרין. שהרי בהעלמו היה: שלישי אין מתכפר. ולא אמרינן הואיל והשני מתכפר עם הראשון שבהעלמו ליגרריה לשלישי עמו בכפרתו ואע"ג דלא שייך בהדי ראשון: הביא קרבן כו'. שכשהפרישו הזכיר בו שם אותו זית: הביא קרבן על האמצעי נתכפרו כולם. ואין זה גרירה אלא כולם בהעלם של זה היו: אביי אמר כו'. דאית ליה גרירה: בתר דשמעיה. רבא מאביי דאמר אפילו הביא קרבן על אחד מהם נתכפרו כולם דאית ליה גרירה הדר ביה איהו ואמר להאיא דלעיל דמיכפרה טחינה שעמה בגרירה: אי הכי. דכאביי סבירא ליה דאמר גרירה: טחינה. שעמה דאיכפרה בגרירה תגרור נמי לטחינה שכנגדה משום שני זיתי חלב בהעלם אחד: גרירה דגרירה. כי הך דטחינה קמייתא לא איכפרה אלא בגרירה דלא עליה ולא על קצירה שעמה בא הקרבן אלא דאגריר בהדי קצירה הלכך לא הדרה גרירה לבתרייתא משום שם טחינה: מילתא דפשיטא להו. לזדון שבת ושגגת מלאכות וזדון מלאכות ושגגת שבת אין חלוקין לחטאות כדקאמרי דזה מתכפר בקרבנו של זה ולא אמרינן כשני העלמות נינהו ונחייב חד אזדון שבת ושגגת מלאכות וחד אשגגת שבת וזדון מלאכות ואע"ג דחד גופה דעבירה היא מספקא ליה כו': קצר וטחן. קצר או טחן: חזר וקצר כו'. ולא נודע לו בינתים על חטאו: מהו שיצטרפו. קצירה וקצירה לכשיעור ויתחייב מי הוי העלם אחד ומצטרפי או דילמא כשני העלמות נינהו ולא מצטרפין: חלוקין לחטאות. אי הוי כשיעור לכל חד אין אחד מהן מתכפר בקרבן הבא על חברו הלכך לא מצטרפי: הכי גרסינן וכל היכא דחלוקין לחטאות לא מצטרפי והא תנן כו': חלב וחלב. שני זיתים והפסיק ביניהם יותר מכדי אכילת פרס דהוו להו שתי אכילות: שאם אכל חצי זית וחזר ואכל חצי זית. באותו העלם וכגון שלא שהה מתחילתו של ראשון עד סוף גמר אכילת אחרון יותר מכדי אכילת פרס ממין אחד מצטרפין: צריכא למימר. הא חדא אכילה היא דבשתי אכילות ליכא למאן דאמר חייב: תוטני. שם חכם: שני תמחויין. שני מיני תבשיל אחד צלי ואחד שלוק: ורבי יהושע היא. בכריתות דאמר תמחויין מחלקין לאוכל שני זיתים בהעלם אחד בשני תמחויין לחייבו שתי חטאות ואיצטריכא לאשמעינן דלענין חצי שיעור מצטרפי דמהו דתימא בין לקולא כי הכא בין לחומרא כגון שיעור שלם אמר רבי יהושע דחלוקין הן וגבי שני חצאי שיעור פטור והיינו קולא וגבי שני זיתים שלימים חייב שתים והיינו חומרא: ארישא מתני. להא דריש לקיש: אסיפא מתנינן לה. ולא איתמר הכי: מכלל

גרירה דגרירה לית ליה. ומה שגוררת קצירה וטחינה (ג) שעמה לא חשיב גרירה דגרירה כדפי' בקונט' דמה שגוררת קצירה לקצירה לא חשיב גרירה כיון דהוי בהעלם אחד אבל טחינה (ג) שכנגדה חשיבא גרירה משום דקצירה של זדון שבת אינה גוררת טחינה של שגגת שבת אלא על ידי הקצירה שעמה היא נגררת ה) שעיקר קרבן אינה בשבילה ולר"י נראה דקצירה חשיבא גרירה מדקאמר קצירה גוררת קצירה אבל ההיא דטחינה לא חשיבא גרירה דגרירה שאינו יכול לכפר על הקצירה אא"כ תתכפר הטחינה עמה ואע"ג דשני זיתי חלב בהעלם אחד לא חשיבא גרירה מ"מ קצירה וקצירה שאני שהאחת בשגגת שבת והאחת בזדון שבת וטעמא דמאן דאמר בסמוך דקצירה וקצירה אין מצטרפין היינו משום דלית ליה גרירה וקשה לרשב"א לפי זה הוה מצי למצוא פלוגתייהו דאביי ורבא אפילו בשלשה קצירות כגון שקצר בשגגת שבת וזדון מלאכות וחזר וקצר בזדון שבת ושגגת מלאכות ונודע לו הראשונה וחזר וקצר בשגגת שבת וזדון מלאכות דלרבא הביא קרבן על הראשון שני נתכפר שלישי לא נתכפר ולאביי גם שלישי נתכפר: ממין אחד חייב פשיטא. הוה מצי לשנויי הא מני רבן גמליאל היא כדאמרינן בסמוך:

אנן אסיפא מתנינן לה. אפילו ארישא הוה מצי לשנויי כגון שאכלו בשני תמחויין ולאפוקי מרבי יהושע דאמר תמחויין מחלקין אפילו לקולא אלא דניחא ליה לאוקמי כר' יהושע:

משני מינין פשיטא. אף על גב דלענין מלקות מצטרפין כדאמרינן בפרק בתרא דמס' ע"ז (דף סו.) ובמס' מעילה (דף יז:) לענין קרבן פשיטא ליה דאין מצטרפין:

מכלל

מסורת הש"ס

א) [עמ"ש לקמן עב: על הגליון], ב) כריתות יא., ג) שם יב., ד) שם טו., ה) עי' גיר' רש"ל.

הגהות הב"ח

(א) גמרא דפשיטא להו לרבא ואביי וכו' דבעי מיניה ר' זירא מר' אסי: (ב) תוס' ד"ה גרירה וכו' ומה שגוררת קצירה לטחינה שעמה: (ג) בא"ד אבל דטחינה שעמה חשיבא:

גליון הש"ס

גמ' אמר רבא הביא קרבן על ראשון. ע' מנחות דף פ ע"ב ובתוס' ד"ה כולהו חליפין: שם מילתא דפשיטא להו לאביי ורבא. ע' שבועות ד' יח ע"א תוס' ד"ה אי בע"ה: שם אכל חלב ודם. ע' לקמן דף פט ע"ב תוס' ד"ה אמורין:

רב נסים גאון

הכא כגון שאכלו בשני תמחויין מחלקין אצל קול א) ר' יהושע במס' כריתות בפרק אמרו לו אכלת חלב (דף טו) אמר ר' יהושע שמעתי באוכל מזבח אחד בחמשה תמחויין בהעלם אחד שהוא חייב על כל

חשק שלמה על רב נסים גאון

א) פירושו בערבי מאמר:

ליקוטי רש"י

בין לקולא. כגון אכל שני חצאי זיתים בשני תמחויין לא מצטרפין. בין לחומרא. דאם אכל שני זיתים בשני תמחויין בהעלם אחד חייב שתים קמ"ל ממין אחד חייב אפילו בשני תמחויין ולא פליג ר' יהושע דלחומרא קאמר. מדסיפא. דאין מצטרפין מיירי במין אחד ושני תמחויין מכלל דרישא דקתני ממין אחד חייב דמצטרפין מין אחד ותמחוי אחד קאמר פשיטא [כריתות יב:].

חשק שלמה על רבינו חננאל

א) חסר כאן וצ"ל ואמר שמואל כאותה ששינו חמשה דברים בעולה מצטרפין הבשר והחלב והיין והסולת והשמן:

עין משפט נר מצוה

יג א מיי' פ"ז מהל' שגגות הלכה י:
יד ב מיי' פ"ז מהלכות שגגות הלכה יא:
טו ג מיי' פ"ז מהלכות שגגות הלכה י:
טז ד מיי' פ"ז מהלכות שגגות הלכה א סמג עשין ריג:
יז ה מיי' שם הלכה ד:
יח ו שם הלכה ז ופ"ד מהלכות מאכלות אסורות הלכה טו סמג שם:
יט ז מיי' פ"ז מהלכות שגגות הלכה א:

רבינו חננאל

דהא תרווייהו בשגגת שבת וחזר וקצר וטחן כגרוגרת בזדון שבת ושגגת מלאכות דחייב על כל אחת ואחת ונודע לו על קצירה של שגגת שבת וזדון מלאכות דלא מחייב עלה ואטחינה דבהדה אלא חדא. קצירה [הראשונה] גוררת (הראשונה) קצירה וכיון שמביא חטאת על קציר' של שגגת (חטאת) [שבת] נתכפר לו קצירה שהיא בזדון שבת. וכן כיון שנתכפרה הטחינה הראשונה שהיא מכלל הקצירה שבשתיהן חטאת אחת הוא חייב. גררה נמי הטחינה הראשונה את הטחינה השניה ונתכפר בשלה. אבל אם נודע לו בקצירה שהיא בזדון שבת ושגגת מלאכות שהוא חייב בקצירה חטאת אחת ובטחינה חטאת אחרת (מביא) [והביא] בקצירה זו שנודע לו בה. קצירה זו גוררת הקצירה הראשונ' ששתיהן קצירה ומעין מלאכה אחת הן והטחינה הראשונה נגררת בכלל הקצירה הראשונה שהקצירה הראשונה והטחינה הראשונה אינו חייב בהן אלא אחת. וכיון שנתכפר מקצתה נתכפר כולה. נמצאו שנתכפר בקצירה וטחינה שהיא בשגגת שבת וזדון מלאכות בקרבן שהביא על הקצירה שהיא בזדון שבת ושגגת מלאכות והטחינה שעמה עומדת במקומה. לכשתוודע לו מביא עליה חטאת. (אמר) אביי [אמר] גם הטחינה הראשונ' גוררת הטחינ' השני' שהטחינ' אחת היא. ומקשי' ומי אית ליה לרבה גרירה. והא אתמר אכל שני זיתי חלב בהעלם אחת ונודע לו על אחת וחזר (ונודע לו על אחת וחזר) ואכל (שני זיתי) כזית א' בהעלמו של שני. אמר רבא הביא קרבן על הראשון ראשון ושני מתכפרין שהרי הם בהעלם אחת שלישי אינו מתכפר שהרי לא היה בהעלמו של ראשון ואע"פ שהיה בהעלמו של שני ואין השני גוררו לכפרה. וכן אם הפריש קרבן על השלישי שלישי ושני מתכפרין. ראשון אין מתכפר שהרי לא היה בהעלמו של שלישי. הביא קרבן על האמצעי נתכפרו כולן שהרי כולן היו בהעלמו של אמצעי אבל גרירה לא אית ליה. ושנינן רבא כי אמר לה להא שמעתא לא (הוא') [אית] ליה גרירה. כיון דשמע להא דאמר אביי אפילו הפריש קרבן על אחד מהן כולן מתכפרין מ"ט כולהן בני בקתא דהדדי נינהו וגררי להדדי סברה ואמר איהו נמי גרירה ואקשינן אי הכי (דרבא) [דרבה] כאביי סבירא ליה טחינה נמי דשגגת שבת תגררה לטחינה דזדון שבת ושנינן קסבר רבה טחינה דשגגת שבת כיון דהיא עצמה גרירא היא לכפרה לא גררה אחריתא וקיי"ל כרבה ואביי תלמידיה הוא והלכתא כרבה. והא שמעתא דפשיטא ליה לרבה ולאביי דקצירה דזדון שבת מצטרפת ונגררת עם קצירה דשגגת שבת דאע"פ שחלוקין לחטאות מיבעיא ליה לר' זירא. דבעי ר' זירא קצר וטחן חצי גרוגרת בשגגת שבת וזדון מלאכות ששתיהן חטאת הן וחזר וטחן חצי גרוגרת בזדון שבת ושגגת מלאכות שחייב שתים. מהו שיצטרפו שני חצאי גרוגרות והנה קצר וטחן כגרוגרת להתחייב חטאת אי לא. ואמרו ליה חלוקין לחטאת הן דזדון מלאכות ושגגת שבת חייב אחת על כולן. וזדון שבת ושגגת מלאכות חייב על כל אחת ואחת וכיון שחלוקין לחטאות שהעושה מלאכות הרבה אינו חייב אלא אחת וזה חייב על כל מלאכה ומלאכה חטאת לא מצטרפי דהא שגגת שבת וזדון מלאכות פטור הוא דהא אינו חייב אלא אחת בכולן. ואקשינן איני והא תנן בכריתות פרק ג' אכל חלב וחלב בהעלם אחת אינו חייב אלא אחת אכל חלב ודם (מותר) [ונותר] כו'. והוינן בה ממין אחד צריכא למימר ואמר ר"ל משום בר (תיטיני) [תוטיני] הכא במאי עסקינן כגון שאכלו בב' תמחויין ור' יהושע היא דאמר תמחויין מחלקין. כלומר אם אכל חלב וחלב בב' תמחויין חייב ב' חטאות ולא תימא דר' יהושע סבר (דאפי') [דאכל] חלב כשני חצאי זיתים בהעלם אחד בב' תמחויין. תמחויין מחלקין ופטור. אלא לחומרא אמרינן לקולא לא אמרינן. והוא כגון דאכל כזית בב' תמחויין לפוטרו לא והנה אכל ב' זיתי חלב בתמחוי אחד בהעלם אחד חייב אחת כשגגת שבת וזדון מלאכות בב' תמחויין חייב שתים כזדון שבת ושגגת מלאכות ר' יהושע מאי היא דתנן בכריתות בפ' ג' א"ר יהושע שמעתי שהאוכל מזבח אחד בה' תמחויין בהעלם אחת חייב על כל אחת משום מעילה. ואמרינן התם היכי דמי בה' תמחויין ואמר שמואל (טעמא) א)

טְחִינָה נַמִּי תִּגְרַר לִטְחִינָה – the first **grinding should draw** the second **grinding along** to its atonement.[15] – ? –

The Gemara answers:

גְּרִירָה אִית לֵיהּ – [Rava] subscribes to "drawing along"; גְּרִירָה דִגְרִירָה לֵית לֵיהּ – he does not subscribe to "drawing along" for something that was itself **"drawn along."**[16]

According to both Rava and Abaye one *chatas* atones for two acts of reaping performed in the same lapse of awareness, even though one violation was committed with inadvertence regarding the Sabbath and the other with inadvertence regarding *melachos.*[17] The Gemara notes:

מִילְּתָא דִפְשִׁיטָא לְהוּ לְאַבַּיֵי וְרָבָא – The matter that was obvious to Abaye and Rava מִבַּעְיָא לְרַבִּי זֵירָא – was doubtful to R' Zeira. דְּבָעֵי רַבִּי זֵירָא מֵרַבִּי אַסִּי – For R' Zeira inquired of R' Assi, וְאָמְרֵי לָהּ בָּעָא מִינֵּיהּ רַבִּי יִרְמְיָה מֵרַבִּי זֵירָא – and some say R' Yirmiyah inquired of R' Zeira: קָצַר וְטָחַן חֲצִי גְּרוֹגֶרֶת – If one reaped or ground half of a dried-fig-sized amount of produce[18] **בְּשִׁגְגַת שַׁבָּת וּזְדוֹן מְלָאכוֹת – with inadvertence regarding the Sabbath and deliberateness regarding the** ***melachos,*** **וְחָזַר וְקָצַר וְטָחַן חֲצִי גְּרוֹגֶרֶת – and then,** without becoming aware of his earlier transgressions, **he reaped or ground** another **half of a dried-fig**-sized amount, **בִּזְדוֹן שַׁבָּת וְשִׁגְגַת מְלָאכוֹת** – this time **with deliberateness regarding the Sabbath and inadvertence regarding the** ***melachos,*** **מַהוּ שֶׁיִּצְטָרְפוּ – what is [the law]** concerning if **they** [the two transgressions] **combine** to make the person liable for performing *melachah* on a total amount equal to the size of a dried fig?[19]

The reply:

אָמַר לֵיהּ – He said to him: חֲלוּקִין לְחַטָּאוֹת – They are separate with regard to ***chatas*** **offerings וְלֹא מִצְטָרְפִין – and they** therefore **do not combine** to compose the minimum punishable measure.[20]

R' Assi (or R' Zeira) has stated that since the acts committed with inadvertence regarding the Sabbath are separate from acts committed with inadvertence regarding the *melachos* in regard to *chatas* offerings, they are separate as well regarding combining to compose the minimum measure. The Gemara questions the correctness of this inference:

וְכָל הֵיכָא דַחֲלוּקִין לְחַטָּאוֹת – And whenever they are considered **separate with regard to** ***chatas*** **offerings לֹא מִצְטָרְפֵי – they do not combine** to compose the minimum measure? **וְהָתְנַן – But we learned in a Mishnah** to the contrary:[21] **אָכַל חֵלֶב וְחֵלֶב בְּהֶעְלֵם אֶחָד** – If SOMEONE CONSUMED first one piece of ***CHEILEV*** AND then a second piece of ***CHEILEV*** DURING ONE LAPSE OF AWARENESS,[22] **אֵינוֹ חַיָּיב אֶלָּא אַחַת** – HE IS LIABLE TO ONLY ONE *chatas*;[23] **אָכַל חֵלֶב וְדָם וְנוֹתָר וּפִגּוּל בְּהֶעְלֵם אֶחָד** – but if HE CONSUMED ***CHEILEV,*** BLOOD, ***NOSSAR*** AND ***PIGGUL*** DURING ONE LAPSE OF AWARENESS,[24] **חַיָּיב עַל כָּל אַחַת וְאַחַת** – HE IS LIABLE FOR EACH AND EVERY ONE.[25] **זוֹ חוֹמֶר בְּמִינִין הַרְבֵּה מִמִּין אֶחָד** – THIS IS THE STRINGENCY OF MANY TYPES of prohibited items OVER multiple pieces of THE SAME TYPE.[26] **וְזוֹ חוֹמֶר בְּמִין אֶחָד מִמִּינִין הַרְבֵּה** – AND THE FOLLOWING IS THE STRINGENCY OF ONE TYPE OVER MANY TYPES: **שֶׁאִם אָכַל חֲצִי זַיִת** – THAT IF HE ATE A HALF OF AN OLIVE-sized piece **וְחָזַר וְאָכַל חֲצִי זַיִת** – AND THEN ATE another HALF OF AN OLIVE-sized piece, **מִמִּין אֶחָד חַיָּיב** – if they were both FROM ONE TYPE of prohibition, HE IS LIABLE to a

NOTES

15. They should also be considered like every two violations of consuming *cheilev* during the same lapse (*Rashi*; see *Ritva MHK* ed.).

16. As in this case, where the first grinding was atoned for only through "drawing along," since the sacrifice was designated neither for it nor for the reaping that was performed together with it. Therefore, it cannot draw the second grinding with it (*Rashi*).

17. Both Abaye and Rava agree that the *chatas* designated for one violation of reaping also atones for the other violation, even though the first was performed with inadvertence regarding the Sabbath and the second with inadvertence regarding *melachos.* This difference in inadvertence does not render the two violations as having been performed in two separate lapses of awareness (*Rashi*).

18. The phrase קָצַר וְטָחַן here means that he performed one of these two acts ["he reaped *or* ground"]. It thus differs from the same phrase used by Rava, where he meant that the person performed both acts ["he reaped *and* ground"] (*Ritva MHK* ed.).

19. [As stated above, one is not liable to punishment unless he performs a *melachah* on at least an amount of food equal to the size of a dried fig.] At issue here is if the person's two acts can be viewed as a single transgression performed on a combined fig-sized amount of food (*Rashi*).

[When the Gemara calls this "a doubt of R' Zeira" it is speaking loosely. For only according to the first version did R' Zeira make this inquiry; according to the second version this inquiry was made *of* R' Zeira, and he answered it definitively, as we will soon see (*Ritva MHK* ed.; cf. *Maharam, Pnei Yehoshua, Sfas Emes*).]

20. If the person reaps a fig-sized amount each time, he is liable to two *chatas* offerings, because the two acts are considered different lapses since the inadvertence differed. Therefore, if he reaps the size of half of a fig each time, the two actions do not combine to make him liable to a *chatas* (*Rashi*).

The question arises: Why does the Gemara state that the issue of whether acts committed with inadvertence regarding the Sabbath and inadvertence regarding the *melachos* are atoned for through a single sacrifice was a matter of doubt to R' Zeira? We find only that he was in doubt whether these acts can combine for the minimum fig-size amount. He may, however, have been certain that they required separate sacrifices (for these two laws are not necessarily interdependant, as the Gemara will state below).

Ritva (*MHK* ed.) answers that according to *Rashi's* understanding here, R' Zeira's (or R' Yirmiyah's) question must be interpreted as a twofold one. He asked: Do these acts require separate *chatas* sacrifices or are they atoned for by a single sacrifice? And if you respond that they require separate sacrifices, do they combine for purposes of the minimum fig measure, or do they not combine?

21. *Kereisos* 11b.

22. That is, he ate two separate olive-sized pieces of *cheilev* and waited long enough between the two consumptions for them to be considered two different and distinct ones (*Rashi*). But he did not become aware of his first violation before he transgressed the second time.

For most transgressions involving the eating of forbidden solid food, such as *cheilev,* the Torah requires that at least a *kezayis* – a portion the size of an olive – be eaten before one is liable to punishment or an offering. In addition, this olive-sized amount must be consumed in the normal amount of time it takes to eat a standard half-loaf of wheat bread (כְּדֵי אֲכִילַת פְּרָס). Therefore, if he does not eat an olive-sized amount of *cheilev* in the time it takes to eat a half-loaf of bread, he is not liable to a *chatas.* And here, where the person waited that amount of time between his two consumptions of olive-sized pieces of *cheilev,* he has committed two distinct violations. Nevertheless, since he ate *cheilev* both times in one lapse of awareness, he is liable to only one *chatas.*

23. Since both violations occurred during the same lapse of awareness, one *chatas* can atone for both, even though they are considered distinct acts of consumption because of the time span between them.

24. Thus, he violated different laws during the same lapse.

[*Nossar* is meat of a sacrifice that is left over after the time allotted for its consumption has passed. *Piggul* refers to meat of a sacrifice rendered invalid by performing one of the essential sacrificial services with the intent to eat its meat after the allotted time.]

25. Even though all the violations were committed during a single lapse of awareness, he is liable to a separate *chatas* for each distinct violation he committed.

26. That is, if someone commits multiple violations in one lapse, he is liable to only one *chatas* for the same type of violation, but multiple *chatas* offerings for different types of violations.

קצירה גוררת קצירה. שניה בכפרתה וטחינה גוררת את הטחינה השניה ונתכפרו כולן דקיימא לן אכל שני זיתי חלב בהעלם אחד אינו חייב אלא אחת וזה שעשה שתי קצירות בהעלם אחד שלא נודע לו בין קצירה לקצירה שחטא ואע"פ שהעלמה של שניה חלוק קצת משל ראשונה סוף סוף העלם אחד הוא דלא נודע לו חטאו בינתים וידיעות [חטא] הוא דמחלקת הלכך חטאת זו שבאה על הקצירה וטחינה ראשונה אתרווייהו קיימא ונתכפרו עם הקצירה כל קצירות שעליו שנעשו בהעלם אחד ועם הטחינה נתכפרו כל הטחינות שעליו כשעשאן בהעלם אחד: **אבל נודע לו** על הקצירה. אחרונה שבזדון שבת ושגגת מלאכות והפריש עליה קרבן הואיל ובקרבן זה לא שייכא טחינה שעמה דהא אכל חדא מיחייב אי הוה מתידעי ליה תרווייהו: **קצירה** גוררת קצירה. ראשונה: **וטחינה** שעמה. של ראשונה: **וטחינה.** אחרונה. שכנגדה של ראשונה: **במקומה** עומדת. וכי מתידע ליה מיחייב עלה: **קצירה גוררת קצירה.** כמשפט דשני זיתי חלב בהעלם אחד הן וטחינה שעם קצירה ראשונה היינו משום גרירה דאף על גב דעיקר קרבן לאו משום קצירה דהדה אתא הואיל ואיכפר ליה בהדי קצירה בתרייתא גררה לטחינה שעמה בהדה שהרי שתיהן היו תלויות בקרבן אחד ואין כפרה לזו בלא זו: **וטחינה שכנגדה עומדת במקומה.** דגרירה לגרירה לא אמרינן לאיכפורי טחינה אחרונה עם טחינה ראשונה משום שני זיתי חלב בהעלם אחד דהא קמייתא גופה בגרירה היא דמיכפרה: **שם טחינה אחת היא.** ואע"ג דקמייתא גופא בגרירה אתיא אמרינן גרירה לגרירה: **ומי אית ליה לרבא גרירה.** אטחינה שעמה קפריך דמגררה עם הקצירה ואע"ג דקרבן לאו אההיא קצירה איפריש דאיך כולהו לאו גרירה איכא דקצירה וקצירה בהעלם אחד לאו גרירה היא דכל שם עבירה הנכפל כמה פעמים בהעלם אחד אין בו אלא חטאת אחת: **ראשון ושני מתכפרין.** שהרי בהעלמו היה: **שלישי אין מתכפר.** ולא אמרינן הואיל והשני מתכפר עם הראשון שבהעלמו ליגרריה לשלישי עמו בכפרתו ואע"ג דלא שייך בהדי ראשון: **הביא קרבן כו'.** שכשהפרישו הזכיר בו שם אותו זית: **הביא קרבן על האמצעי נתכפרו כולם.** ואין זה גרירה אלא כולם בהעלם של זה היו: **אביי אמר כו'.** דלית ליה גרירה: **בתר דשמעיה.** רבא מאביי דאמר אפילו הביא קרבן על אחד מהם נתכפרו כולם דלית ליה גרירה הדר ביה איהו ואמר להא דלעיל דמיכפרה טחינה שעמה בגרירה: **אי הכי.** דכאביי סבירא ליה דאמר גרירה: **טחינה.** שעמה דאיכפרה בגרירה תגרור נמי לטחינה שכנגדה משום שני זיתי חלב בהעלם אחד: **גרירה דגרירה.** כי הך דטחינה קמייתא לא איכפרה אלא בגרירה דלא עליה ולא על קצירה שעמה בא הקרבן אלא דאגריר בהדי קצירה הלכך לא הדרה גרירה לבתרייתא משום שם טחינה: **מילתא דפשיטא להו.** דזדון שבת ושגגת מלאכות וזדון מלאכות ושגגת שבת אין חלוקין לחטאות כדקאמרי דזה מתכפר בקרבנו של זה ולא אמרינן כשני העלמות נינהו וניחייב חד אזדון שבת ושגגת מלאכות וחד אשגגת שבת וזדון מלאכות ואע"ג דחד גופה דעבירה היא מספקא ליה כו': **קצר וטחן.** קצר או טחן: **חזר וקצר כו'.** ולא נודע לו בינתים על חטאו: **מהו שיצטרפו.** קצירה וקצירה לכשיעור ויתחייב מי הוי העלם אחד ומצטרפי או דילמא כשני העלמות נינהו ולא מצטרפין: **חלוקין לחטאות.** אי הוי כשיעור לכל חד אין אחד מהן מתכפר בקרבן הבא על חברו הלכך לא מצטרפי: **הכי גרסינן** וכל היכא דחלוקין לחטאות לא מצטרפי והא תנן כו': **חלב וחלב.** שני זיתים והפסיק ביניהם יותר מכדי אכילת פרס דהוו להו שתי אכילות: **שאם אכל חצי זית וחזר ואכל חצי זית.** באותו העלם וכגון שלא שהה מתחילתו של ראשון עד סוף גמר אכילת אחרון יותר מכדי אכילת פרס ממין אחד מצטרפין: **צריכא למימר.** הא חדא אכילה היא דבשתי אכילות ליכא למאן דאמר חייב: **תוטני.** שם מקום: **שני תמחויין.** שני מיני תבשיל אחד ללי ואחד שלוק: **ורבי יהושע היא.** בכריתות דאמר תמחויין מחלקין לאוכל שני זיתים בהעלם אחד בשני תמחויין לחייבו שתי חטאות ואיצטריכא לאשמעינן דלענין חצי שיעור מצטרפי דמהו דתימא בין לקולא כי הכא בין לחומרא כגון שיעור שלם אמר רבי יהושע דחלוקין הן וגבי שני חצאי שיעור פטור והיינו קולא וגבי שני זיתים שלימים חייב שתים והיינו חומרא: **ארישא** מתני. להא דריש לקיש: **אסיפא** מתנינן לה. ולא איתמר הכי:
מכלל

א קצירה גוררת קצירה וטחינה גוררת טחינה אבל נודע לו על קצירה של זדון שבת ושגגת מלאכות קצירה גוררת קצירה וטחינה שעמה וטחינה שכנגדה במקומה עומדת אביי אמר טחינה נמי גוררת טחינה שם טחינה אחת היא ומי אית ליה לרבא גרירה והא איתמר אכל שני זיתי חלב בהעלם אחד ונודע לו על אחת מהן וחזר ואכל כזית בהעלמו של שני ◦ אמר רבא א) **ב** הביא קרבן על ראשון ראשון ושני מתכפרין ג' אינו מתכפר הביא קרבן על השלישי שלישי ושני מתכפרין ראשון אינו מתכפר הביא קרבן על האמצעי נתכפרו כולן אביי אמר אפילו הביא קרבן על אחד מהן נתכפרו כולן בתר דשמעה מאביי סברה אי הכי טחינה נמי תגרר לטחינה גרירה אית ליה גרירה דגרירה לית ליה ◦ מילתא דפשיטא להו לאביי ורבא (א) מבעיא לר' זירא דבעי רבי זירא מרבי אסי ואמרי לה בעא מיניה רבי ירמיה מרבי זירא **ג** קצר וטחן חצי גרוגרת בשגגת שבת וזדון מלאכות וחזר וקצר וטחן חצי גרוגרת בזדון שבת ושגגת מלאכות מהו שיצטרפו אמר ליה חלוקין לחטאות ולא מצטרפין וכל היכא דחלוקין לחטאות לא מצטרפי ג) והתנן **ד** אכל חלב וחלב בהעלם אחד אינו חייב אלא אחת אכל ◦ **ה** חלב ודם ונותר ופגול בהעלם אחד חייב על כל אחת ואחת זו חומר במינין הרבה ממין אחד וזו חומר במין אחד ממינין הרבה שאם אכל חצי זית וחזר ואכל חצי זית ממין אחד חייב **ו** משני מינין פטור ג) והוינן בה ממין אחד חייב צריכא למימר ואמר ריש לקיש משום בר תוטני הכא במאי עסקינן **ז** כגון שאכלו בשני תמחויין ורבי יהושע היא ד) דאמר תמחויין מחלקין מהו דתימא אמר רבי יהושע בין לקולא בין לחומרא קא משמע לן דלקולא לא אמר לחומרא קאמר והא הכא דחלוקין לחטאות וקא מצטרפי אמר ליה מר ארישא מתני לה וקשיא ליה אנן אסיפא מתנינן לה ולא קשיא לן משני מינין פטור צריכא למימר ואמר ריש לקיש משום בר תוטני לעולם ממין אחד ואמאי קרי ליה שני מינין שאכלו בשני תמחויין ור' יהושע היא דאמר תמחויין מחלקין והא קא משמע לן דאמר רבי יהושע בין לקולא בין לחומרא מדסיפא מין אחד ושני תמחויין
מכלל

גרירה דגרירה לית ליה. ומה שגוררת קצירה וטחינה (ג) שעמה לא חשיב גרירה דגרירה כדפי' בקונט' דמה שגוררת קצירה לקצירה לא חשיב גרירה כיון דהוי בהעלם אחד אבל טחינה (ג) שכנגדה חשיבא גרירה משום דקצירה של זדון שבת אינה גוררת טחינה של שגגת שבת אלא על ידי הקצירה שעמה היא נגררת ה) שעיקר קרבן אינה בשבילה ולר"י נראה דקצירה חשיבא גרירה מדקאמר קצירה גוררת קצירה אבל ההיא דטחינה לא חשיבא גרירה דגרירה שאינו יכול לכפר על הקצירה אא"כ תתכפר הטחינה עמה ואע"ג דשני זיתי חלב בהעלם אחד לא חשיבא גרירה מ"מ קצירה וקצירה שאני שהאחת בשגגת שבת והאחת בזדון שבת וטעמא דמאן דאמר בסמוך דקצירה וקצירה אין מצטרפין היינו משום דלית ליה גרירה וקשה לרשב"א לפי זה הוה מצי למצוא פלוגתייהו דאביי ורבא אפילו בשלשה קצירות כגון שקצר בשגגת שבת וזדון מלאכות וחזר וקצר בזדון שבת ושגגת מלאכות ונודע לו הראשונה וחזר וקצר בשגגת שבת וזדון מלאכות לרבא הביא קרבן על הראשון שני נתכפר שלישי לא נתכפר ולאביי גם שלישי נתכפר: **ממין** אחד חייב פשיטא. הוה מצי לשנויי הא מני רבן גמליאל היא כדאמרינן בסמוך: **אנן** אסיפא מתנינן לה. אפילו ארישא הוה מצי לשנויי כגון שאכלו בשני תמחויין ולאפוקי מרבי יהושע דאמר תמחויין מחלקין אפילו לקולא אלא דניחא ליה לאוקמי כר' יהושע: **משני** מינין פשיטא. אף על גב דלענין מלקות מצטרפין כדאמרינן בפרק בתרא דמס' ע"ז (דף סו.) ובמס' מעילה (דף יז:) לענין קרבן פשיטא ליה דאין מצטרפין:
מכלל

עין משפט נר מצוה

יג א מיי' פ"ז מהל' שגגות הלכה י:
יד ב מיי' פ"ו מהלכות שגגות הלכה יא:
טו ג מיי' פ"ו מהלכות שגגות הלכה י:
טז ד מיי' פ"ו מהלכות שגגות הלכה א סמג עשין ריג:
יז ה מיי' שם הלכה ד:
יח ו שם הלכה ז ופ"ד מהלכות מאכלות אסורות הלכה טו סמג שם:
יט ז מיי' פ"ו מהלכות שגגות הלכה א:

רבינו חננאל

דהא תרווייהו בשגגת שבת וחזר וקצר וטחן כגרוגרת בזדון שבת ושגגת מלאכות דחייב על כל אחת ואחת ונודע לו על קצירה של שגגת שבת וזדון מלאכות דלא מחייב עלה ואטחינה דבהדה אלא חדא. קצירה [הראשונה] גוררת (הראשונה) קצירה וכיון שמביא חטאת על קציר' של שגגת (חטאת) [שבת] נתכפר לו קצירה שהיא בזדון שבת. וכן כיון שנתכפרה הטחינה הראשונה שהיא מכלל הקצירה שבשתיהן חטאת אחת הוא חייב. גררה נמי הטחינה הראשונה את הטחינה השניה ונתכפר בשלה. אבל אם נודע לו בקצירה שהיא בזדון שבת ושגגת מלאכות שהוא חייב בקצירה חטאת אחת ובטחינה חטאת אחרת (מביא) [והביא] בקצירה זו שנודע לו בה. קצירה זו גוררת הקצירה הראשונ' ששתיהן קצירה ומעין מלאכה אחת הן והטחינה הראשונה נגררת בכלל הקצירה הראשונה שהקצירה הראשונה והטחונה הראשונה אינו חייב בהן אלא אחת. וכיון שנתכפר מקצתה נתכפר כולה. נמצאו שנתכפר בקצירה וטחינה שהיא בשגגת שבת וזדון מלאכות בקרבן שהביא על הקצירה שהיא בזדון שבת ושגגת מלאכות והטחינה שעמה עומדת במקומה. לכשתודע לו מביא עליה חטאת. (אמר) אביי [אמר] גם הטחינה הראשונ' גוררת הטחינ' השני' שהטחינ' אחת היא. ומקשי' ומי אית ליה לרבה גרירה. והא אתמר אכל שני זיתי חלב בהעלם אחת ונודע לו על אחת וחזר (ונודע לו על אחת וחזר) ואכל (שני זיתי) כזית א' בהעלמו של שני. אמר רבא הביא קרבן על הראשון ראשון ושני מתכפרין שהרי הם בהעלם אחת שלישי אינו מתכפר שהרי לא היה בהעלמו של ראשון ואע"פ שהיה בהעלמו של שני ואין השני גוררו לכפרה. וכן אם הפריש קרבן על השלישי שלישי ושני מתכפרין. ראשון אין מתכפר שהרי לא היה בהעלמו של שלישי. הביא קרבן על האמצעי נתכפרו כולן שהרי כולן היו בהעלמו של אמצעי אבל גרירה לא אית ליה. ושנינן רבא כי אמר לה להא שמעתא לא (הוא') [אית] ליה גרירה. כיון דשמע להא דאמר אביי אפילו הפריש קרבן על אחד מהן כולן מתכפרין מ"ט כולהן בני בקתא דהדדי נינהו וגררי להדדי סברה ואמר איהו נמי גרירה ואקשינן אי הכי (דרבא) [דרבה] כאביי סבירא ליה טחינה נמי דשגגת שבת תגררה לטחינה דזדון שבת ושנינן קסבר רבה טחינה דשגגת שבת כיון דהיא עצמה גרירא היא לכפרה לא גררה אחריתא וקיי"ל כרבה ואביי תלמידיה הוא והלכתא כרבה. והא שמעתא דפשיטא ליה לרבה ולאביי דקצירה דזדון שבת מצטרפת ונגררת עם קצירה דשגגת שבת דאע"פ שחלוקין לחטאות מיבעיא ליה לר' זירא. דבעי ר' זירא קצר וטחן חצי גרוגרת בשגגת שבת וזדון מלאכות ששתיהן חטאת הן וחזר וטחן חצי גרוגרת בזדון שבת ושגגת מלאכות שחייב שתים. מהו שיצטרפו שני חצאי גרוגרות והנה קצר וטחן כגרוגרת להתחייב חטאת אי לא. ואמרו ליה חלוקין לחטאת הן דזדון מלאכות ושגגת שבת חייב אחת על כולן. וזדון שבת ושגגת מלאכות חייב על כל אחת ואחת וכיון שחלוקין לחטאות שהעושה מלאכות הרבה אינו חייב אלא אחת וזה חייב על כל מלאכה ומלאכה חטאת לא מצטרפי דהא שגגת שבת וזדון מלאכות פטור הוא דהא אינו חייב אלא אחת בכולן. ואקשינן איני והא תנן בכריתות פרק ג' אכל חלב וחלב בהעלם אחת אינו חייב אלא אחת אכל חלב ודם (מותר) [ונותר] כו'. והוינן בה ממין אחד צריכא למימר ואמר ר"ל משום בר (תיטיני) [תוטיני] הכא במאי עסקינן כגון שאכלו בב' תמחויין ור' יהושע היא דאמר תמחויין מחלקין. כלומר אם אכל חלב וחלב בב' תמחויין חייב ב' חטאות ולא תימא דר' יהושע סבר (דאפי') [דאכל] חלב כשני חצאי זיתים בהעלם אחד בב' תמחויין. תמחויין מחלקין ופטור. אלא לחומרא אמרינן לקולא לא אמרינן. והוא כגון דאכל כזית בב' תמחויין לפוטרו לא והנה אכל ב' זיתי חלב בתמחוי אחד בהעלם אחד חייב אחת כשגגת שבת וזדון מלאכות בב' תמחויין חייב שתים כזדון שבת ושגגת מלאכות ר' יהושע מאי היא דתנן בכריתות בפ' ג' א"ר יהושע שמעתי שהאוכל מזבח אחד בה' תמחויין בהעלם אחת חייב על כל אחת משום מעילה. ואמרינן התם היכי דמי בה' תמחויין ואמר שמואל (טעמא) א)

מסורת הש"ס

א) [עמ"ש לקמן עב: על הגליון, ב) כריתות יא:, ג) שם יב:, ד) שם טו:, ה) עי' גיר' רש"ל.

הגהות הב"ח

(א) גמרא דפשיטא להו לרבא ולאביי וכו' דבעי מיניה ר' זירא מר' אסי: (ב) תום' ד"ה גרירה וכו' ומה שגוררת קצירה לטחינה שעמה: (ג) בא"ד אבל דטחינה שעמה חשיבא:

גליון הש"ס

גמ' אמר רבא הביא קרבן על ראשון. עי' מנחות דף פ ע"ב ובתוס' ד"ה כולהו חליפין: שם מילתא דפשיטא להו לאביי ורבא. עי' שבועות ד' יח ע"ב תוס' ד"ה אי בעי"ה: שם אכל חלב ודם. עי' לקמן דף פט ע"ב תוס' ד"ה אסורין:

רב נסים גאון

הכא כגון שאכלו בשני תמחויין מחלקין אצל קול א) ר' יהושע במס' כריתות בפרק אמרו לו אכלת חלב (דף טו) אמר ר' יהושע שמעתי באוכל מזבח אחד בחמשה תמחויין בהעלם אחד שהוא חייב על כל

חשק שלמה על רב נסים גאון

א) פירושו בערבי מאמר:

ליקוטי רש"י

בין לקולא. כגון אכל שני חצאי זיתים בשני תמחויין לא מצטרפין. בין לחומרא. דאם אכל שני זיתים בשני תמחויין בהעלם אחד חייב שתים קמ"ל ממין אחד חייב אפילו בשני תמחויין ולא פליג ר' יהושע דלחומרא קאמר. מדסיפא. דאין מצטרפין מיירי במין אחד ושני תמחויין מכלל דרישא דקתני ממין אחד חייב דמצטרפין מין אחד ותמחוי אחד קאמר פשיטא [כריתות יב:].

חשק שלמה על רבינו חננאל

א) חסר כאן וז"ל ואמר שמואל כאוכלה שטעינו ממשה דברים כעולה מצטרפין הכשר והחלב והיין והסולת והשמן:

chatas;[27] מִשְּׁנֵי מִינִין פָּטוּר – but if they were **FROM TWO TYPES** of prohibitions, **HE IS EXEMPT.**[28]

Before explaining its question, the Gemara elaborates on the second section of the Mishnah:

וְהָוֵינַן בָּהּ – **And we asked about it:** מִמִּין אֶחָד חַיָּיב צְרִיכָא לְמֵימַר – **Did [the Mishnah] need to say** that if someone ate two pieces the size of half an olive **of one type** of prohibition **he is liable?**[29] וְאָמַר רֵישׁ לָקִישׁ מִשּׁוּם בַּר תּוּטְנִי – **And Reish Lakish answered in the name of Bar Tutni:** הָכָא בְּמַאי עָסְקִינַן – **With what** case **are we dealing here?** כְּגוֹן שֶׁאֲכָלוֹ בִּשְׁנֵי תַּמְחוּיִין – **Where he ate it** prepared **as two** types of **dishes;**[30] וְרַבִּי יְהוֹשֻׁעַ הִיא – **and [the Mishnah] follows the view of R' Yehoshua** דְּאָמַר תַּמְחוּיִין מְחַלְּקִין – **who says that** different types of **dishes separate** prohibited items into distinct liabilities.[31] מַהוּ דְּתֵימָא – **You might have thought** אָמַר רַבִּי יְהוֹשֻׁעַ בֵּין לְקוּלָּא בֵּין לְחוּמְרָא – **that R' Yehoshua stated** his ruling **both as a leniency and as a stringency.**[32] קָא מַשְׁמַע לָן דִּלְקוּלָּא לֹא אָמַר – **[The Mishnah]** therefore **informs us that he did not state** it **as a leniency;** לְחוּמְרָא קָאָמַר – rather, **he stated** it only **as a stringency.**[33]

The Gemara now explains its question:

וְהָא הָכָא – **But here,** דַּחֲלוּקִין לְחַטָּאוֹת – we have a case **where they are** considered **separate with regard to *chatas* offerings,**[34] וְקָא מִצְטָרְפֵי – **yet they combine** to compose the required amount![35] – ? –

The Gemara answers:

אָמַר לֵיהּ – **He said to him:** מַר אַרֵישָׁא מַתְנֵי לָהּ – **The master taught [Reish Lakish's statement] regarding the first case** of the Mishnah's second section (i.e. the person who ate two pieces of *cheilev,* each the size of half an olive), וְקַשְׁיָא לֵיהּ – **and** therefore **had a difficulty;** אֲנַן אַסֵּיפָא מַתְנִינַן לָהּ – but **we taught [Reish Lakish's statement] regarding the last case** of the Mishnah (i.e. the person who ate *cheilev* along with other types of prohibited items, each the size of half an olive), וְלֹא קַשְׁיָא לָן – **and we do not have a difficulty,** as follows: מִשְּׁנֵי מִינִין פָּטוּר צְרִיכָה לְמֵימַר – **Did [the Mishnah] need to say that** if someone eats **two types** of prohibited items, each less than the size of an olive, **he is exempt** from a *chatas?*[36] וְאָמַר רֵישׁ לָקִישׁ מִשּׁוּם בַּר תּוּטְנִי – To this question **Reish Lakish said in the name of Bar Tutni:** לְעוֹלָם מִמִּין אֶחָד – **Actually,** the Mishnah means he ate two pieces **of one type** of prohibited item. וְאַמַּאי קָרֵי לֵיהּ שְׁנֵי מִינִין – **And why does [the Mishnah] call it two types?** שֶׁאֲכָלוֹ בִּשְׁנֵי תַּמְחוּיִין – **Because he ate it** prepared **as two dishes;**[37] וְרַבִּי יְהוֹשֻׁעַ הִיא – **and it follows R' Yehoshua** דְּאָמַר תַּמְחוּיִין מְחַלְּקִין – **who said that** different **types of dishes separate** prohibited items into distinct liabilities. וְהָא קָא מַשְׁמַע לָן – **And [the Mishnah] informs us** דְּאָמַר רַבִּי יְהוֹשֻׁעַ בֵּין לְקוּלָּא בֵּין לְחוּמְרָא – **that R' Yehoshua stated** his ruling **both as a leniency and as a stringency.**[38]

The Gemara objects to this interpretation of the Mishnah:

מִדְּסֵיפָא מִין אֶחָד וּשְׁנֵי תַּמְחוּיִין – **But** from the fact that **the last case** refers to **one type** of prohibition cooked in **two** types of **dishes,**

NOTES

27. Since he eventually ate a total of an olive-size of the prohibited type of food, he is liable to a *chatas* for it. This is true, though, only where he ate both pieces within the time it takes to eat a half-loaf of bread (*Rashi*).

28. Since he did not eat an olive-sized portion of either type of prohibited item, he is not liable to any *chatas.*

[*Rashash* notes a discrepancy in *Rashi's* description of the span of time that defines a single act of eating. When describing the first section of the Mishnah, where the person ate olive-sized portions of prohibited items, *Rashi* (ד״ה חלב וחלב) explained that the time of eating a half-loaf of bread spanned the period *between* the two acts of eating; i.e. after eating one olive-sized piece of *cheilev*, he waited that time span before eating the second piece. However, in the section section of the Mishnah, discussing consumptions of half of an olive-size, *Rashi* (ד״ה שאם אכל) requires the person to have eaten a total of an olive-size *from the beginning* of the first consumption *to the end* of the second. See there for a discussion of this problem; see also *Afikei Yam* II:5.]

29. The Mishnah must mean that he ate the two pieces in the span of time that is considered one consumption. Hence, it is obvious that he should be liable to a *chatas* for eating two half-olive pieces (*Rashi*).

30. For example, the first piece of *cheilev* was roasted and the other one was boiled (*Rashi*).

31. R' Yehoshua states in *Kereisos* that if someone eats two olive-sized pieces of a certain prohibition during one lapse of awareness, he is liable to two *chatas* offerings if each was prepared in a distinct way. [According to R' Yehoshua the pieces are treated as if they were different types of prohibitions.] The Mishnah cited here teaches that R' Yehoshua does not consider the two dishes as two distinct prohibitions where they were each the size of a half-olive (*Rashi*).

32. In the case of half-olive-sized pieces, R' Yehoshua's opinion leads to a leniency. For if the two dishes are considered different types of prohibitions, the person will not have eaten an olive-sized portion of any single prohibited type (*Rashi*).

33. [Thus, although R' Yehoshua stated that the two violations are deemed separate prohibitions, it is still possible that two such violations can combine to obligate a *chatas.* See *Dibros Moshe* 64:23.]

34. According to R' Yehoshua two types of prepared dishes are considered distinct prohibitions when they are each the size of an olive (*Rashi*).

35. When the two pieces are each less than the size of an olive, they join together to comprise an olive-size, obligating the person to bring a *chatas* for their consumption (*Rashi*).

36. It is obvious that the person is not liable to a *chatas,* since he did not eat an olive-sized portion of any single prohibited type.

37. Thus, the Mishnah's ruling of different types of prohibited items includes a case where the item was actually the same, but prepared in different manners (see *Ritva MHK* ed.).

38. Even though he ate a total amount of *cheilev* (for example) equivalent to the size of an olive, he is not liable to a *chatas* since no piece the size of an olive was prepared the same way.

[א] קצירה גוררת קצירה וטחינה גוררת טחינה אבל נודע לו על קצירה של זדון שבת ושגגת מלאכות קצירה גוררת קצירה וטחינה שעמה וטחינה שכנגדה במקומה עומדת אביי אמר טחינה נמי גוררת טחינה שם טחינה אחת היא ומי אית ליה לרבא גרירה והא איתמר אכל שני זיתי חלב בהעלם אחד ונודע לו על אחת מהן וחזר ואכל כזית בהעלמו של שני ° אמר רבא (א) [ב] הביא קרבן על ראשון ראשון ושני מתכפרין ג׳ אינו מתכפר הביא קרבן על השלישי שלישי ושני מתכפרין ראשון אינו מתכפר הביא קרבן על האמצעי נתכפרו כולן אביי אמר אפילו הביא קרבן על אחד מהן נתכפרו כולן בתר דשמעה מאביי סברה אי הכי טחינה נמי תגרר לטחינה גרירה אית ליה גרירה דגרירה לית ליה ° מילתא דפשיטא להו לאביי ורבא (א) מבעיא לר׳ זירא דבעי רבי זירא מרבי אסי ואמרי לה בעא מיניה רבי ירמיה מרבי זירא [ג] קצר וטחן חצי גרוגרת בשגגת שבת וזדון מלאכות וחזר וקצר וטחן חצי גרוגרת בזדון שבת ושגגת מלאכות מהו שיצטרפו אמר ליה חלוקין לחטאות ולא מצטרפין וכל היכא דחלוקין לחטאות לא מצטרפי [ג] והתנן [ד] אכל חלב וחלב בהעלם אחד אינו חייב אלא אחת אכל ° [ה] חלב ודם ונותר ופגול בהעלם אחד חייב על כל אחת ואחת זו חומר במינין הרבה ממין אחד וזו חומר במין אחד ממינין הרבה שאם אכל חצי זית וחזר ואכל חצי זית ממין אחד חייב [ו] משני מינין פטור [ג] והוינן בה ממין אחד חייב צריכא למימר ואמר ריש לקיש משום בר תוטני הכא במאי עסקינן [ז] כגון שאכלו בשני תמחויין ורבי יהושע היא [ז] דאמר תמחויין מחלקין מהו דתימא אמר רבי יהושע בין לקולא בין לחומרא קא משמע לן דלקולא לא אמר לחומרא קאמר והא הכא דחלוקין לחטאות וקא מצטרפי אמר ליה מר ארישא מתני לה וקשיא ליה אנן אסיפא מתנינן לה ולא קשיא לן משני מינין פטור צריכא למימר ואמר ריש לקיש משום בר תוטני לעולם ממין אחד ואמאי קרי ליה שני מינין שאכלו בשני תמחויין ור׳ יהושע היא דאמר תמחויין מחלקין והא קא משמע לן דאמר רבי יהושע בין לקולא בין לחומרא מדסיפא מין אחד ושני תמחויין

מכלל

קצירה גוררת קצירה. שניה בכפרתה וטחינה גוררת את הטחינה השניה ונתכפרו כולן דקיימא לן אכל שני זיתי חלב בהעלם אחד אינו חייב אלא אחת וזה שעשה שתי קצירות בהעלם אחד שלא נודע לו בין קצירה לקצירה שחטא ואע״פ שהעלמה של שניה חלוק קלת משל ראשונה סוף סוף העלם אחד הוא דלא נודע לו חטאו בינתים וידיעות [חטא] הוא דמחלקת הלכך חטאת זו שבאה על הקצירה וטחינה ראשונה אתרווייהו קיימא ונתכפרו עם הקצירה כל קצירות שעליו שנעשו בהעלם אחד ועם הטחינה נתכפרו כל הטחינות שעליו כשעשאן בהעלם אחד: אבל נודע לו על הקצירה. אחרונה שבזדון שבת ושגגת מלאכות והפריש עליה קרבן הואיל ובקרבן זה לא שייכא טחינה שעמה דהא אכל חדא מיחייב אי הוה מתידעי ליה תרווייהו: קצירה גוררת קצירה. ראשונה: וטחינה שעמה. של ראשונה: וטחינה. אחרונה. שכנגדה של ראשונה: במקומה עומדת. וכי מתידע ליה מיחייב עלה: קצירה גוררת קצירה. כמשפט דשני זיתי חלב בהעלם אחד הן וטחינה שעם קצירה ראשונה היינו משום גרירה דאף על גב דעיקר קרבן לאו משום קצירה דבהדה אתא הואיל ואיכפר ליה בהדי קצירה בתרייתא גררה לטחינה שעמה בהדה שהרי שתיהן היו תלויות בקרבן אחד ואין כפרה לזו בלא זו: וטחינה שכנגדה עומדת במקומה. דגרירה לגרירה לא אמרינן לאיכפורי טחינה אחרונה עם טחינה ראשונה משום שני זיתי חלב בהעלם אחד דהא קמייתא גופה בגרירה היא דמיכפרה: שם טחינה אחת היא. ואע״ג דקמייתא גופא בגרירה אתיא אמרינן גרירה לגרירה: ומי אית ליה לרבא גרירה. אטחינה שעמה קפריך דמגררה עם הקצירה ואע״ג דקרבן לאו אההיא קצירה איפריש דאיך כולהו לאו גרירה איכא דקצירה וקצירה בהעלם אחד לאו גרירה היא דכל שם עבירה הנכפל כמה פעמים בהעלם אחד אין בו אלא חטאת אחת: ראשון ושני מתכפרין. שהרי בהעלמו היה: שלישי אין מתכפר. ולא אמרינן הואיל והשני מתכפר עם הראשון שבהעלמו ליגרריה לשלישי עמו בכפרתו ואע״ג דלא שייך בהדי ראשון: הביא קרבן כו׳. שכשהפרישו הזכיר בו שם אותו זית: הביא קרבן על האמצעי נתכפרו כולם. ואין זה גרירה אלא כולם בהעלם של זה היו: אביי אמר כו׳. דאית ליה גרירה: בתר דשמעיה. רבא מאביי דאמר אפילו הביא קרבן על אחד מהם נתכפרו כולם דאית ליה גרירה הדר ביה איהו ואמר להכיא דלעיל דמיכפרה טחינה שעמה בגרירה: אי הכי. דכאביי סבירא ליה דאמר גרירה: טחינה. שעמה דאיכפרה בגרירה תגרור נמי לטחינה שכנגדה משום שני זיתי חלב בהעלם אחד: גרירה דגרירה. כי הך דטחינה קמייתא לא איכפרה אלא בגרירה דלא עליה ולא על קצירה שעמה בא הקרבן אלא דאגריר בהדי קצירה הלכך לא הדרה גרירה לבתרייתא משום שם טחינה: מילתא דפשיטא להו. דזדון שבת ושגגת מלאכות ושגגת שבת אין חלוקין לחטאות כדקאמרי דזה מתכפר בקרבנו של זה ולא אמרינן כשני העלמות נינהו ומיחייב חד אזדון שבת ושגגת מלאכות וחד אשגגת שבת וזדון מלאכות ואע״ג דחד גופה דעבירה היא מספקא ליה כו׳: קצר וטחן. קצר או טחן: חזר וקצר כו׳. ולא נודע לו בינתים על חטאו: מהו שיצטרפו. קצירה וקצירה לכשיעור ויתחייב מי הוי העלם אחד ומצטרפי או דילמא כשני העלמות נינהו ולא מצטרפין: חלוקין לחטאות. אי הוי כשיעור לכל חד אין אחד מהן מתכפר בקרבן הבא על חברו הלכך לא מצטרפי: הכי גרסינן וכל היכא דחלוקין לחטאות לא מצטרפי והא תנן כו׳: חלב וחלב. שני זיתים והפסיק ביניהם יותר מכדי אכילת פרס דהוו להו שתי אכילות: שאם אכל חצי זית וחזר ואכל חצי זית. באותו העלם וכגון שלא שהה מתחילתו של ראשון עד סוף גמר אכילת אחרון יותר מכדי אכילת פרס ממין אחד מצטרפין: צריכא למימר. הא חדא אכילה היא דבשתי אכילות ליכא למאן דאמר חייב: תוטני. שם חכם: שני תמחויין. שני מיני תבשיל אחד ללי ואחד שלוק: ורבי יהושע היא. בכריתות דאמר תמחויין מחלקין לאוכל שני זיתים בהעלם אחד בשני תמחויין לחייבו שתי חטאות ואיצטריכא לאשמעינן דלענין חצי שיעור מצטרפי דמהו דתימא בין לקולא כי הכא בין לחומרא כגון שיעור שלם אמר רבי יהושע דחלוקין הן וגבי שני חצאי שיעור פטור והיינו קולא וגבי שני זיתים שלימים חייב שתים והיינו חומרא: אהישא מתני. להא דריש לקיש: אסיפא מתנינן לה. ולא איתמר הכי:

מכלל

גרירה דגרירה לית ליה. ומה שגוררת קצירה וטחינה (ג) שעמה לא חשיב גרירה דגרירה כדפי׳ בקונט׳ דמה שגוררת קצירה לקצירה לא חשיב גרירה כיון דהוי בהעלם אחד אבל טחינה (ג) שכנגדה חשיבא גרירה משום דקצירה של זדון שבת אינה גוררת טחינה של שגגת שבת אלא על ידי הקצירה שעמה היא נגררת [ה] שעיקר קרבן אינה בשבילה ולר״י נראה דקצירה חשיבא גרירה מדקאמר קצירה גוררת קצירה אבל ההיא דטחינה לא חשיבא גרירה דגרירה שאינו יכול לכפר על הקצירה א״כ תתכפר הטחינה עמה ואע״ג דשני זיתי חלב בהעלם אחד לא חשיבא גרירה מ״מ קצירה וקצירה שאני שהאחת בשגגת שבת והאחת בזדון שבת וטעמא דמאן דאמר בסמוך דקצירה וקצירה אין מצטרפין היינו משום דלית ליה גרירה וקשה לרשב״א לפי זה הוה מצי למצוא פלוגתייהו דאביי ורבא אפילו בשלשה קצירות כגון שקצר בשגגת שבת וזדון מלאכות וחזר וקצר בזדון שבת ושגגת מלאכות ונודע לו הראשונה וחזר וקצר בשגגת שבת וזדון מלאכות דלרבא הביא קרבן על הראשון שני נתכפר שלישי לא נתכפר ולאביי גם שלישי נתכפר: ממין אחד חייב פשיטא. הוה מצי לשנויי הא מני רבן גמליאל היא כדאמרינן בסמוך:

אנן אסיפא מתנינן לה. אפילו ארישא הוה מצי לשנויי כגון שאכלו בשני תמחויין ולאפוקי מרבי יהושע דאמר תמחויין מחלקין אפילו לקולא אלא דניחא ליה לאוקמי כר׳ יהושע: משני מינין פשיטא. אף על גב דלענין מלקות מצטרפין כדאמרינן בפרק בתרא דמס׳ ע״ז (דף סו.) ובמס׳ מעילה (דף יז:) לענין קרבן פשיטא ליה דאין מצטרפין:

מכלל

עין משפט נר מצוה

יג א מיי׳ פ״ז מהל׳ שגגות הלכה י:
יד ב מיי׳ פ״ז מהלכות שגגות הלכה יא:
טו ג מיי׳ פ״ז מהלכות שגגות הלכה י:
טז ד מיי׳ פ״ז מהלכות שגגות הלכה א סמג עשין ריג:
יז ה מיי׳ שם הלכה ד:
יח ו שם הלכה ז ופ״ד מהלכות מאכלות אסורות הלכה יג סמג שם:
יט ז מיי׳ פ״ז מהלכות שגגות הלכה א:

רבינו חננאל

דהא תרווייהו בשגגת שבת וחזר וקצר וטחן כגרוגרת בזדון שבת ושגגת מלאכות דחייב על כל אחת ואחת ונודע לו על קצירה של שגגת שבת וזדון מלאכות דלא מחייב עלה ואטחינה דבהדה אלא חדא. קצירה [הראשונה] גוררת (הראשונה) קצירה וכיון שמביא חטאת על קציר׳ של שגגת (חטאת) [שבת] נתכפר לו קצירה שהיא בזדון שבת. וכן כיון שנתכפרה הטחינה הראשונה שהיא מכלל הקצירה שבשתיהן חטאת אחת הוא חייב. גררה נמי הטחינה הראשונה את הטחינה השניה ונתכפר בשלה. אבל אם נודע לו בקצירה שהיא בזדון שבת ושגגת מלאכות שהוא חייב בקצירה חטאת אחת ובטחינה חטאת אחרת (מביא) [והביא] בקצירה זו שנודע לו בה. קצירה זו גוררת הקצירה הראשונ׳ ששתיהן קצירה ומעין מלאכה אחת הן והטחינה הראשונה נגררת בכלל הקצירה הראשונה שהקצירה הראשונה והטחינה הראשונה אינו חייב בהן אלא אחת. וכיון שנתכפר מקצתה נתכפר כולה. נמצאו שנתכפר בקצירה וטחינה שהיא בשגגת שבת וזדון מלאכות בקרבן שהביא על הקצירה שהיא בזדון שבת ושגגת מלאכות והטחינה שעמה עומדת במקומה. לכשתוודע לו מביא עליה חטאת. (אמר) אביי [אמר] גם הטחינה הראשונ׳ גוררת הטחינ׳ השני׳ שהטחינ׳ אחת היא. ומקשי׳ ומי אית ליה לרבה גרירה. והא אתמר אכל שני זיתי חלב בהעלם אחת ונודע לו על אחת וחזר (ונודע לו על אחת וחזר) ואכל (שני זיתי) כזית א׳ בהעלמו של שני. אמר רבא הביא קרבן על הראשון ראשון ושני מתכפרין שהרי הם בהעלם אחת שלישי אינו מתכפר שהרי לא היה בהעלמו של ראשון ואע״פ שהיה בהעלמו של שני ואין השני גוררו לכפרה. וכן אם הפריש קרבן על השלישי שלישי ושני מתכפרין. ראשון אין מתכפר שהרי לא היה בהעלמו של שלישי. הביא קרבן על האמצעי נתכפרו כולן שהרי כולן היו בהעלמו של אמצעי אבל גרירה לא אית ליה. ושנינן רבא כי אמר לה להא שמעתא לא (הוא׳) [אית] ליה גרירה. כיון דשמע להא דאמר אביי אפילו הפריש קרבן על אחד מהן כולן מתכפרין מ״ט כולהן בני בקתא דהדדי ניניהו וגררי להדדי סברה ואמר איהו נמי גרירה ואקשינן אי הכי (דרבא) [דרבה] כאביי סבירא ליה טחינה נמי דשגגת שבת תגרורה לטחינה דזדון שבת ושנינן קסבר רבה טחינה דשגגת שבת כיון דהיא עצמה גרירא היא לכפרה לא גררה אחריתא וקיי״ל כרבה ואביי תלמידיה הוא והלכתא כרבה. והא שמעתא דפשיטא ליה לרבה ולאביי דקצירה דזדון שבת מצטרפת ונגררת עם קצירה דשגגת שבת דאע״פ שחלוקין לחטאות מיבעיא ליה לר׳ זירא. דבעי ר׳ זירא קצר וטחן חצי גרוגרת בשגגת שבת וזדון מלאכות ששתיהן חטאת הן וחזר וטחן חצי גרוגרת בזדון שבת ושגגת מלאכות שחייב שתים. מהו שיצטרפו שני חצאי גרוגרות והנה קצר וטחן כגרוגרת להתחייב חטאת אי לא. ואמרו ליה חלוקין לחטאת הן דהזדון מלאכות ושגגת שבת חייב אחת על כולן. והזדון שבת ושגגת מלאכות חייב על כל אחת ואחת וכיון שחלוקין לחטאות שהעושה מלאכות הרבה אינו חייב אלא אחת וזה חייב על כל מלאכה ומלאכה חטאת לא מצטרפי דהא שגגת שבת וזדון מלאכות פטור הוא דהא אינו חייב אלא אחת בכולן. ואקשינן איני והא תנן בכריתות פרק ג׳ אכל חלב וחלב בהעלם אחת אינו חייב אלא אחת אכל חלב ודם (מותר) [ונותר] כו׳. והוינן בה ממין אחד צריכא למימר ואמר ר״ל משום בר (תיטיני) [תוטיני] הכא במאי עסקינן כגון שאכלו בב׳ תמחויין ור׳ יהושע היא דאמר תמחויין מחלקין. כלומר אם אכל חלב וחלב בב׳ תמחויין חייב ב׳ חטאות ולא תימא דר׳ יהושע סבר (דאפי׳) [דאכל] חלב כשני חצאי זיתים בהעלם אחד בב׳ תמחויין. תמחויין מחלקין ופטור. אלא לחומרא אמרינן לקולא לא אמרינן. והוא כגון דאכל כזית בב׳ תמחויין לפוטרו לא והנה אכל ב׳ זיתי חלב בתמחוי אחד בהעלם אחד חייב אחת כשגגת שבת וזדון מלאכות בב׳ תמחויין חייב שתים כזדון שבת ושגגת מלאכות ר׳ יהושע מאי היא דתנן בכריתות בפ׳ ג׳ א״ר יהושע שמעתי שהאוכל מזבח אחד בה׳ תמחויין בהעלם אחת חייב על כל אחת משום מעילה. ואמרינן התם היכי דמי בה׳ תמחויין ואמר שמואל (טעמא) (א)

מסורת הש״ס

א) [עמ״ש לקמן עב: על הגליון], ב) כריתות יא., ג) שם יב., ד) שם טו., ה) עי׳ גיר׳ רש״ל.

הגהות הב״ח

(א) גמרא דפשיטא להו לרבא ואביי וכו׳ דבעי מיניה ר׳ זירא מר׳ אסי: (ב) תוס׳ ד״ה גרירה וכו׳ ומה שגוררת קצירה לטחינה שעמה: (ג) בא״ד אבל דטחינה שעמה חשיבא:

גליון הש״ס

גמ׳ אמר רבא הביא קרבן על ראשון. עי׳ מנחות דף פ ע״ב ובתוס׳ ד״ה כולהו קליפין: שם מילתא דפשיטא להו לאביי ורבא. עי׳ שבועות ד׳ יח ע״א תוס׳ ד״ה אי בע״ה: שם אכל חלב ודם. עי׳ לקמן דף פט ע״ב תוס׳ ד״ה אסורין:

רב נסים גאון

הכא כגון שאכלו בשני תמחויין מחלקין אצל קול א) ר׳ יהושע במס׳ כריתות בפרק אמרו לו אכלת חלב (דף טו) אמר ר׳ יהושע שמעתי באוכל מזבח אחד בחמשה תמחויין בהעלם אחד שהוא חייב על כל

חשק שלמה על רב נסים גאון

א) פירושו בערבי מאמר:

ליקוטי רש״י

בין לקולא. כגון אכל שני חצאי זיתים בשני תמחויין לא מצטרפין. בין לחומרא. דאם אכל שני זיתים בשני תמחויין בהעלם אחד חייב שתים קמ״ל ממין אחד חייב אפילו בשני תמחויין ולא פליג ר׳ יהושע דלחומרא קאמר. מדסיפא. דאין מצטרפין מיירי במין אחד ושני תמחויין מכלל דרישא דקתני ממין אחד חייב דמצטרפין מין אחד ותמחוי אחד קאמר פשיטא [כריתות יב:].

חשק שלמה על רבינו חננאל

א) חסר כאן וצ״ל ואמר שמואל כלומר שטעינו ממשה דברים בעולה מצטרפין הבשר והחלב והיין והסולת והשמן:

מכלל דרישא מין אחד ותמחוי אחד מין אחד ותמחוי אחד צריכא למימר אמר רב הונא הכא במאי עסקינן כגון שהיתה לו ידיעה בינתיים ורבן גמליאל היא (א) דאמר אין ידיעה לחצי שיעור: איתמר אכל שני זיתי חלב בהעלם אחד ונודע לו על הראשון וחזר ונודע לו על השני ר' יוחנן אמר [א] חייב שתים וריש לקיש אמר אינו חייב אלא אחת [ב] רבי יוחנן אמר חייב (א) על חטאתו והביא [ג] וריש לקיש אמר פטור (ב) מחטאתו ונסלח לו וריש לקיש הכתיב על חטאתו והביא ההוא לאחר כפרה ולרבי יוחנן נמי הכתיב מחטאתו ונסלח לו הכא במאי עסקינן [ג] כגון שאכל כזית ומחצה ונודע לו על כזית וחזר ואכל כחצי זית אחר בהעלמו של שני מהו דתימא ליצטרפו קמ"ל א"ל רבינא לרב אשי דאיתידע ליה קודם הפרשה פליגי ובהא פליגי דמר סבר [ג] ידיעות מחלקות ומר סבר הפרשות מחלקות אבל לאחר הפרשה מודי ליה ריש לקיש לר' יוחנן דחייב שתים או דילמא דאיתידע ליה לאחר הפרשה פליגי ובהא פליגי דמר סבר הפרשות מחלקות ומר סבר כפרות מחלקות אבל קודם הפרשה מודי ליה ר' יוחנן לריש לקיש דאינו חייב אלא אחת או דילמא בין בזו ובין בזו מחלוקת א"ל מסתברא בין בזו ובין בזו מחלוקת דאי סלקא דעתך קודם הפרשה פליגי אבל לאחר הפרשה מודה ליה ריש לקיש לר' יוחנן דחייב שתים אדמוקים ליה קרא לאחר כפרה לוקמיה לאחר הפרשה ואי אחר הפרשה פליגי אבל קודם הפרשה מודה ליה רבי יוחנן לריש לקיש דאינו חייב אלא אחת אדמוקי ליה קרא בכזית ומחצה לוקמיה קודם הפרשה ודילמא ספוקי מספקא ליה (א) ואם תימצי לומר קאמר אם תימצי לומר קודם הפרשה פליגי בה רבי יוחנן היכי מוקי ליה לקרא בכזית ומחצה ואם תימצי לומר לאחר הפרשה פליגי ריש לקיש היכי מוקי ליה לקרא בלאחר כפרה: אמר עולא למאן דאמר אשם ודאי לא בעיא ידיעה בתחילה

בעל

מכלל דרישא. דאמר חייב: מין אחד ותמחוי אחד. בתמיה: שהיתה לו ידיעה. בין שני חלאי שיעור ואיצטריך לאשמעינן דליצטרפו דס"ד אמינא הואיל ובשיעורין שלמים חלוקין לחטאות הכא נמי לא ליצטרפו קמ"ל דהתם הוה ידיעה אבל ידיעת חלי שיעור לאו ידיעה היא: רבן גמליאל היא דאמר. לקמן בפרק הבונה אין ידיעה לחלי שיעור: וחזר ונודע לו. לקמן בעי ליה אי קודם שהפריש קרבן על ידיעה ראשונה וקסבר ידיעות מחלקות לחטאות ואע"פ שלא היתה ידיעה בין אכילה לאכילה או לאחר הפרשה וקסבר הפרשות מחלקות והא דאביי ורבא דאמרי לעיל ונודע לו על אחת מהן וחזר ואכל כו' אלמא דחדא הוא דמיחייב אי סבירא להו פלוגתא דר' יוחנן וריש לקיש בקודם הפרשה אינהו דאמור כריש לקיש אי נמי סבירא להו דלאחר הפרשה פליגי ואינהו דאמור קודם הפרשה נודע על השני ודברי הכל אין חלוקין לחטאות: על חטאתו והביא. והביא קרבנו שעירת עזים תמימה נקבה על חטאתו אשר חטא (ויקרא ד) משמע על כל חטאת וחטאת יביא: מחטאתו ונסלח לו. אפי' לא הביא אלא על מקצת חטאתו ונסלח לו כולו: קמ"ל. כיון (ב) דהאי חלי זית עם זית קמא שייך בתר ידיעה קמייתא [ו]הוה כאילו נודע לו על הכל דהא אי הוה מייתי קרבן הוה מיכפר בהדיה [דזית] בלא שום ידיעה דפחות מכשיעור לא חשיב אבל כזית לא מיכפר בלא ידיעה הלכך כי לא איתידע ליה בהדיה אלא זה אחר זה הוו ידיעות מחלקות: דאיתידע ליה. על השני קודם שהפריש קרבן על ידיעה הראשונה פליגי: אדמוקים לאחר כפרה. כי פרכינן לעיל לריש לקיש הא כתיב על חטאתו והביא ואוקימנא שיטתיה דתלמודא בלאחר כפרה לוקמא בלאחר הפרשה אבל השתא דאוקימנא בלאחר כפרה ש"מ דפשיטא לבני הישיבה שסדרו הגמ' דלאחר הפרשה נמי פטר ריש לקיש: הכי גרסינן בספרים ישנים ודילמא ספוקי מספקא להו ואת"ל קאמר אם תמצא לומר קודם הפרשה פליגי רבי יוחנן היכי מוקי ליה לקרא בכזית ומחצה את"ל אחר הפרשה פליגי ר"ל היכי מוקי ליה לקרא בלאחר כפרה. והכי פירושא ודילמא לבני תלמודא נמי מספקא להו פלוגתא דר"י ור"ל במאי כי היכי דמספקא ליה לדידי אי בקודם אי בלאחר אי בתרוייהו וכי פריך בעל התלמוד לרבי יוחנן נמי והא כתיב מחטאתו ונסלח לו ומשני ליה בכזית ומחצה בלשון את"ל פריך ליה ומשני ליה והכי קאמר אי הוה פשיטא לן דלאחר הפרשה הוא דמחייב [ר"י תרתי] אבל בקודם הפרשה מודה [לר"ל] לא הוה קשיא לן מידי דאוקימנא מחטאתו ונסלח לו בקודם הפרשה אבל השתא קשיא לן את"ל בהך בעיא דרבינא דבקודם הפרשה נמי פליגי וא"ר יוחנן חייב שתים ר' יוחנן היכי מוקי לקרא דמחטאתו ונסלח לו ושני ליה בכזית ומחצה והכי קמשני אפי' את"ל דקודם הפרשה לחודא פליגי אי נמי בתרווייהו פליגי איכא לאוקמא בכזית ומחצה ולר"ל נמי כי פריך ליה תלמודא הכתיב על חטאתו והביא ושני ליה בעל התלמוד בלאחר כפרה לעולם ספוקי מספקא ליה במאי פליגי כלדידי ובאת"ל פריך ומשני והכי קאמר את"ל בלאחר הפרשה נמי פליגי דבלאחר הפרשה פטר ליה בחד קרבן דהשתא ליכא לאוקמא לקרא דמחייב בלאחר הפרשה ר"ל היאך מוקי ליה להאי קרא כלומר במאי מוקי ליה ושני ליה אפילו אם תמצא לומר בלאחר הפרשה פליגי איכא לאוקמי בלאחר כפרה. ורוב התלמידים שגו בשיטה זו ודימו דהאי דהיכי מוקי לה לקרא בכזית ומחצה וחברו היכי מוקי ליה לקרא בלאחר כפרה לשון קושיא הוא ולפרושי כמו מ"ט והוצרכו לשבש את הספרים ולמחוק הוי"ו ואת"ל (ג) קמא ולהגיה קאמרינן ולהגיה על קודם לאחר ועל לאחר קודם ואין שיטת התלמוד כפי סוגייתם: למ"ד אשם ודאי לא בעי ידיעה. פלוגתא דר"ט ור"ע היא בכריתות בפ' דם שחיטה (דף כב.) ר"ע מחייב על ספק מעילות אשם תלוי ופי' היו לפניו שתי חתיכות א' של קדש וא' של חולין ואכל אחת מהן ואינו יודע איזו אכל מביא אשם תלוי ומודה ר"ע שאינו מביא את מעילתו כלומר אינו משלם קרן וחומש עד שיודע לו ויביא עמה אשם מעילות ודאי כי היכי דאשם תלוי דשאר עבירות דספק כרת אינו מכפר כפרה גמורה וכשיודע לו דודאי חטא מביא חטאת אף זה כשיודע לו יחזור ויביא אשם ודאי ר"ט אומר מה לזה מביא שתי אשמות ולא דמי לאשם תלוי דספק חטאת ה דהתם ספיקו איל ודאי נקבה הלכך כי מתידע ליה בעי לאתויי נקבה אבל זה ששניהם מין אחד כדאמר התם שממין שמביא על הודע מביא על לא הודע שזה איל וזה איל יביא קרן וחומש ויביא איל ויאמר אם ודאי מעלתי זו מעילתי וזו אשמי ואם ספק שלא עתיד ספיקי להודע לי אשם זה יהיה אשם תלוי והקדש זה לנדבה ולכי מתיידע ליה לא בעי לאתויי אשם אחרינא אלמא לא בעי ידיעה בתחילה באשם ודאי קודם הבאת כפרתו דהא לא איתידע ליה כי אתיי' ומכפר עליה: אשם ודאי. כל אשמות קרוין אשם ודאי חוץ מאשם תלוי שהוא בא על לא הודע והן שלשה הבאין על חטא אשם מעילות אשם גזילות אשם שפחה חרופה:

בעל

מכלל דרישא מין אחד ותמחוי אחד כו'. לעיל לא בעי למיפרך מכלל דסיפא משני מינין ושני תמחויין צריכא למימר שלא חש להאריך כיון דלא קאי הכי: מאן דאמר אשם ודאי לא בעי ידיעה בתחלה. פי' בקונטרס דאיכא פלוגתא דר' עקיבא ורבי טרפון בפרק דם שחיטה בכריתות (דף כב:) וליתא דהא תנן התם דדוקא במעילה מרובה קאמר ר"ע שמביא שתי אשמות משום דטוב לו שיביא שתי אשמות משיביא אשם אחד ויתנה שאם לא יודע לו תהא מעילתו נדבה אבל במעילה מועטת מודה ר"ע שמביא אשם אחד ויתנה ונוח לו שיתן מעילה מועטת על הספק משיביא שתי אשמות וקאמרינן בגמ' מדברי שניהם נלמד [א] אשם ודאי לא בעי ידיעה בתחלה ואם תאמר רבי טרפון דקאמר מה לזה מביא שתי אשמות משמע דעלה טובה קמ"ל אדרבה כיון דבמעילה מרובה פליגי אם כן טוב לו שיביא שתי אשמות כדאמר ר' עקיבא משיביא אשם אחד ומעילתו ויתנה כדפרישית יש לומר דר' טרפון לאו עלה טובה קאמר אלא לעולם אינו יוצא מידי עבירה בשתי אשמות אלא שיביא אשם ומעילתו ויתנה ואם תאמר ולרבי עקיבא אמאי מביא שתי אשמות במרובה ובמועטה אשם ומעילה יביא לעולם אשם אחד ויתנה וכשיודע אז יביא מעילתו ויש לומר משום דאמר [ד] המביא אשמו עד שלא הביא מעילתו לא יצא:

בעל

כ א מיי' פ"ו מהלכות שגגות הלכה ט:
כא ב שם הלכה י:
כב ג מיי' פ"ה מהלכות שגגות הלכה א ופ"ו הלכה א והלכה ט סמג עשין ריג:

רבינו חננאל

וחזקיה אמר בחמשה אברים וריש לקיש אמר אפי' באבר א' [משכחת להן] בכתף. ור' יוחנן אמר בחמשה מיני קדירה. ור' יצחק נפחא [אמר] בה' טעמים. והרי הוא כיון שהוא שני חצאי זית בב' תמחויין כמי שאינו שם חיוב חטאות היא וקתני מצטרפין וחייב חטאת. גם זה אע"פ שחלוקין הן לחטאות והן מצטרפו' ושנינן מי סברת הא דריש לקיש משום בר תוטיני ארישא הוא דקתני שאם אכל כחצי זית וחזר ואכל כחצי זית ממין אחד חייב במלתא דחלוקין לחטאות מוקמי ליה כר' יהושע וכגון שאכלו בב' תמחויין לא אסיפא היא דקתני סיפא אם אכל כחצי זית וחזר ואכל כחצי זית אחד משני מינין פטור עלה אמרי צריכא למימר. ואמר ר"ל משום [בר] תוטיני לעולם ממין אחד ואמאי (תני) [קרי] לה בב' מינין כגון שאכלן בב' תמחויין ור' יהושע היא תמחויין מתחלקין בין לקולא בין לחומרא ונמצא גם זו בדברים שאין חלוקין לחטאות ואקשינן אי הכי מדסיפא ב' חצאי מין אחד בב' תמחויין וקתני פטור רישא משום שהוא מין אחד בתמחוי אחד לפיכך חייב אמאי איצטריך למתניא להא פשיטא ומשני רבינא כגון שהיו ב' זיתי חלב בתמחוי אחד וכגון שאכל חצי זית אחד מהן ונודע לו והדר ושכח ואכל חצי זית האחר. ומתניתין רבן גמליאל היא דאמר [אין] ידיעה לחצי שיעור דתנן הכותב ב' אותיות בב' העלמות אחת בשחרית ואחת בין הערבים רבן גמליאל מחייב וחכמים פוטרין ואמרינן במאי פליגי רבן גמליאל סבר אין ידיעה לחצי שיעור ורבנן סברי יש ידיעה לחצי שיעור וכיון דרבן גמליאל סבר דאין ידיעה לחצי שיעו' כאלו אין שם ידיעה בינתים ובהעלם אחת כולן לפיכך חייב: **אתמר** אכל ב' זיתי חלב בהעלם אחד ונודע לו על הראשון וחזר ונודע לו על השני ר' יוחנן אומר חייב שתים ר"ל אומר אינו חייב אלא אחת ר' יוחנן אומר ידיעה מחלקת לפיכך חייב שתים. ר"ל אומר אין ידיעה מחלקת ואין חייב אלא חטאת אחת ר' יוחנן דריש על חטאתו והביא כיון שנודעה לו חטאתו נתחייב בה וכשיתודע לו השניה עוד מתחייב בה דאין אדם פורע חובו במה שכבר נתחייב בו ור"ל דריש מחטאתו ונסלח כל שהוא בהעלם אחד חטאת אחד הוא ומחטאתו ונסלח קרינן ביה. ור' יוחנן האי קרא דר"ל דריש ביה הכי מניין אם אכל כזית ומחצה ונודע לו על כזית ולא נודע לו על מחצה. וחזר ואכל זית אחד בהעלמו של שני מהו דתימא לצטרף עם חצי זית הראשון ויתחייב קמ"ל מחטאתו אם כבר נתכפר מקצת מחטאתו פטור בנשאר ור"ל האי על חטאתו והביא מיבעי ליה כשנודע לו על כזית אחד וכפר עליו. ולאחר שנתכפר לו [נודע לו] על כזית השני כגון זה מודה ר"ל דצריך קרבן והא דרב [אשי] ודרבינא לא מוכחא בהדיא במאי פליגי מיהו סוגיא דשמעתא לדברי הכל לאחר כפרה דראשון נודע לו השני צריך חטאת שניה והא סברא דרבה ואביי בגרירה פליגא אתרווייהו דהא אוקימנא דלתרווייהו לר' יוחנן ולר"ל כשנודע לו לאחר שנתכפר על הראשון צריך חטאת שניה ורבה אמר אכל ב' זיתי חלב בהעלם אחד ונודע לו על אחד מהן ואחר כך אכל כזית אחד בהעלמו של שני שלא ידע על השני שבשבילו הביא קרבן מתכפר (הזה) [אלמא] ודאי אם נודע לו על השני אחר שנתכפר על הראשון אינו חייב על השני קרבן אחר שכבר נתכפר בגרירה עם הראשון ודאביי עדיפא מדרבא וקיי"ל כוותיה דאינון בתראי: **אמר** עולא לדברי האומר אשם ודאי לא בעי ידיעה בתחלה

א) לקמן קב. [קה. וש"נ], ב) [לקמן לד.], ג) [שם], ד) [ב"ק קיא.].

הגהות הב"ח

(א) גמ' ספוקי מספקא להו ואם תימצי וכו' הפרשה פליגי ר' יוחנן כצ"ל ותיבת בה נמחק: (ב) רש"י ד"ה קא משמע לן דהאי כצ"ל ותיבת כיון נמחק: (ג) ד"ה הכי גרסי' וכו' ולמחוק הוי"ו דאם תמצי לומר קאמר ולהגיה:

גליון הש"ס

רש"י ד"ה למ"ד אשם ודאי וכו' דהתם ספיקו איל. עיין מג"א סימן א ס"ק יא:

הגהות הגר"א

[א] תוס' ד"ה מאן. מדברי שניהם נלמד כו'. נ"ב אבל הוא רבי יוסי (וכ"כ הרא"ה והרמב"ן בחידושיו דלא כרש"ל) דבעי ידיעה בתחלה כמ"ש [כריתות דף ז' ב'] מודה ר"י במחוסר כפרה מ"ט התם בעי גברא ידיעה כו' וזה מחולק שם ר"י ור"ש:

תורה אור השלם

א) אוֹ הוֹדַע אֵלָיו חַטָּאתוֹ אֲשֶׁר חָטָא וְהֵבִיא קָרְבָּנוֹ שְׂעִירַת עִזִּים תְּמִימָה נְקֵבָה עַל חַטָּאתוֹ אֲשֶׁר חָטָא: [ויקרא ד, כח]

ב) וְאֶת כָּל חֶלְבּוֹ יַקְטִיר הַמִּזְבֵּחָה כְּחֵלֶב זֶבַח הַשְּׁלָמִים וְכִפֶּר עָלָיו הַכֹּהֵן מֵחַטָּאתוֹ וְנִסְלַח לוֹ: [ויקרא ד, כו]

ליקוטי רש"י

אין ידיעה לחצי שיעור. לחלק כדי שלא יצטרף עמו חצי האחר [לקמן קה.]. אכל חצי שיעור ונודע לא הויא ידיעה לחלק דאם חזר ואכל חצי שיעור מצטרפין [כריתות יב:]. למ"ד אשם ודאי. כי אתייה מספק על תנאי עולה לו לאשם ודאי כי מתידע ליה [שם כב:].

רב נסים גאון

אחד ואחד ובגמרא גרסי היכי דמי ה' תמחויין אמר שמואל כאותה ששנינו חמשה דברים בעולה מצטרפין הבשר והחלב והיין והסולת והשמן חזקיה אמר כגון שאכל מה' אברים ר"ל אמר אפילו תימא באבר אחד משכחת לה בכתף ר' יצחק אמר כגון שאכל בה' מיני קדירה ר' יוחנן אמר כגון שאכלה בה' טעמים: **ורבן** גמליאל הוא דאמר אין ידיעה לחצי שיעור. בפרק הבונה (לקמן דף קה) הכותב ב' אותיות בב' העלמות אחת בשחרית ואחת בין הערבים רבן גמליאל מחייב וחכמים פוטרים ובגמ' גרסי במאי קא מיפלגי רבן גמליאל סבר אין ידיעה לחצי שיעור: **אמר** עולא למאן דאמר אשם ודאי לא בעי ידיעה בתחילה. משכחת לה במס' כריתות בפרק דם שחיטה (דף כב) אמר ר' טרפון ומה לזה מביא ב' אשמות אמר לו ר' עקיבא נראין דבריך במעילה כו' ובגמ' גרסי אמר רבא מדברי שניהם נלמוד אשם ודאי לא בעי ידיעה בתחילה ומכלל זו המימרא נלמוד כי מי שחולק על ר"ע ור' טרפון בדבר הזה סובר שאשם ודאי בעי ידיעה בתחילה וזה האשם נידון כחטאת מה חטאת בעינן ידיעה בתחילה אף אשם ודאי נמי בעי ידיעה בתחלה:

ואלא

מִכְּלָל דְּרֵישָׁא מִין אֶחָד וְתַמְחוּי אֶחָד – **it is apparent that the first case** of this section[1] refers to **one type** of prohibition prepared **as one dish.** מִין אֶחָד וְתַמְחוּי אֶחָד צְרִיכָא לְמֵימַר – But **is it necessary to say** that if someone eats a total of an olive-sized piece of **one type** of prohibition prepared **as one dish,** he is liable?[2]

The Gemara answers:

אָמַר רַב הוּנָא – **Rav Huna said:** הָכָא בְּמַאי עָסְקִינַן – **What** case **are we discussing here?** כְּגוֹן שֶׁהָיְתָה לוֹ יְדִיעָה בֵּינְתַיִים – **Where he became aware** of his first violation **between both [acts of eating],**[3] וְרַבָּן גַּמְלִיאֵל הִיא – **and [the Mishnah] is** following the view of **Rabban Gamliel** דְּאָמַר אֵין יְדִיעָה לַחֲצִי שִׁיעוּר – **who said that there is no awareness for half a measure.**[4]

The Gemara continues its discussion about liability for multiple violations of the same prohibition:

אִיתְּמַר – **It was stated:** אָכַל שְׁנֵי זֵיתֵי חֵלֶב בְּהֶעְלֵם אֶחָד – If **someone ate two olive-sized** amounts **of *cheilev* in one lapse of awareness,** וְנוֹדַע לוֹ עַל הָרִאשׁוֹן – **and the first** violation **became known to him,** וְחָזַר וְנוֹדַע לוֹ עַל הַשֵּׁנִי – **and then the second** violation **became known to him,** רַבִּי יוֹחָנָן אָמַר חַיָּיב שְׁתַּיִם – **R' Yochanan says that he is liable to two** offerings, וְרֵישׁ לָקִישׁ אָמַר אֵינוֹ חַיָּיב אֶלָּא אַחַת – **whereas Reish Lakish says that he is liable to only one.**[5]

The Gemara explains the source of the dispute:

רַבִּי יוֹחָנָן אָמַר חַיָּיב – **R' Yochanan says that he is liable** to a second *chatas* ,,עַל־חַטָּאתוֹ״ ,,וְהֵבִיא״ – because the verse states: ***for his sin, he shall bring** [an offering],*[6] indicating that he is liable to a separate *chatas* for each sin.[7] וְרֵישׁ לָקִישׁ אָמַר פָּטוּר – **However, Reish Lakish says he is exempt** from a second *chatas* ,,מֵחַטָּאתוֹ וְנִסְלַח לוֹ״ – because the verse states: ***from his sin, and it will be forgiven for him,***[8] indicating that even if the *chatas* was brought for some of his sins, he is totally forgiven.[9]

The Gemara asks what each Amora learns from the verse that the other cited:

וְרֵישׁ לָקִישׁ – **Now,** how can **Reish Lakish** hold that one *chatas* suffices for all of the violations? הָכְתִיב ,,עַל־חַטָּאתוֹ״ ,,וְהֵבִיא״ – **But it is written: *for his sin, he shall bring,*** indicating that a person is liable to a separate *chatas* for each sin that he committed. – ? –

The Gemara answers:

הַהוּא לְאַחַר כַּפָּרָה – **That** verse refers to a sin discovered **after atonement** was effected for the first sin. Thus, if the person already sacrificed his *chatas,* he must bring another one for the newly discovered sin, even though it was committed in the same lapse of awareness as the first sin.

The Gemara examines the other view:

וּלְרַבִּי יוֹחָנָן נַמִּי – **Now, according to R' Yochanan** it is **also** difficult הָכְתִיב ,,מֵחַטָּאתוֹ וְנִסְלַח לוֹ״ – for **it is written:** ***from his sin, and it will be forgiven for him,*** indicating that even if the *chatas* was brought for some of his sins, he is totally forgiven. – ? –

The Gemara answers:

הָכָא בְּמַאי עָסְקִינַן – **With what** case **are we dealing here?** כְּגוֹן שֶׁאָכַל כְּזַיִת וּמֶחֱצָה – **Where he** first **ate** some *cheilev* **the size of an olive and a half,** וְנוֹדַע לוֹ עַל כְּזַיִת – **and it became known to him about an olive-sized** portion of it וְחָזַר וְאָכַל כַּחֲצִי זַיִת אַחֵר – **and he then ate another half-olive-sized** piece of *cheilev* בְּהֶעְלֵמוֹ שֶׁל שֵׁנִי – **during the** same **lapse of awareness as the** half-olive portion of the **other** piece.[10] מַהוּ דְּתֵימָא לִיצְטָרְפוּ – **You might have said that they** [i.e. the two half-olive-sized pieces] **should combine** to make him liable for eating a whole olive-sized piece of *cheilev.* קָא מַשְׁמַע לָן – **[The verse]** therefore **informs us** that the first half-olive-sized portion is atoned for with the *chatas* brought for the olive-sized portion that was eaten at the same time.[11]

NOTES

1. I.e. where the Mishnah states that if someone eats two half-olive-sized pieces of the same type of prohibition he is liable (*Rashi*).

2. It is obvious that the person would be liable in such a case, since he ate the minimum amount in the time that is considered one "eating."

3. After he ate the first half-olive-sized piece of *cheilev*, he realized his error; only then did he once again unwittingly eat the second piece (*Rashi*).

4. Below (105a) Rabban Gamliel holds that becoming aware that one has committed less than the minimum amount of labor required for a *chatas* is not considered a true awareness, and does not, therefore, prevent two half-measures from combining to create a single liability. Accordingly, the Mishnah in *Kereisos* teaches that if a person ate half an olive of *cheilev* (for example) and then realized his error, this discovery does not constitute awareness. Hence, when he eats another half-olive-sized piece, he will have eaten a total of one olive-size in a single lapse of awareness. Only awareness of a punishable transgression separates two violations into two lapses of awareness (*Rashi*).

5. We have already learned that if a person inadvertently commits the same transgression twice, he is liable to a separate *chatas* offering for each, if he became aware of one violation before he committed the second. R' Yochanan and Reish Lakish now discuss the status of two violations that were *committed* in the same lapse of awareness, but were afterwards *discovered* at different times. The Gemara below will discuss at what point the second infraction became known to the transgressor. [This will also affect our understanding of the rulings of Rava and Abaye above, 71a. See below, note 23.]

6. *Leviticus* 4:28. The verse states: אוֹ הוֹדַע אֵלָיו חַטָּאתוֹ אֲשֶׁר חָטָא וְהֵבִיא קָרְבָּנוֹ שְׂעִירַת עִזִּים תְּמִימָה נְקֵבָה עַל־חַטָּאתוֹ אֲשֶׁר חָטָא, *If the sin that he committed becomes known to him, "he shall bring" as his offering a she-goat, unblemished, "for his sin" that he committed.*

[See *Pnei Yehoshua* for a discussion about why the Gemara cites the two pertinent phrases out of order, writing *"for his sin"* before *"he shall bring."*]

7. By stating that the person must bring a sacrifice עַל־חַטָּאתוֹ, *for his sin,* the verse indicates that he is liable to a separate *chatas* for each and every sin he committed (*Rashi*; cf. *R' Chananel*).

8. Ibid. 4:26. The verse states: וְכִפֶּר עָלָיו הַכֹּהֵן מֵחַטָּאתוֹ וְנִסְלַח לוֹ, *The Kohen shall effect atonement for him from his sin, and it shall be forgiven for him.*

9. The term מֵחַטָּאתוֹ, *"from" his sin,* indicates that [in certain cases] although he brought the *chatas* for only some of his sins, he is totally forgiven, as the Gemara will explain. [See *Afikei Yam* 2:6 for further analysis of the differing expositions of R' Yochanan and Reish Lakish.]

10. Literally: second [piece]. *Dikdukei Soferim* cites a version of the Gemara that reads: בְּהֶעְלֵמוֹ שֶׁל רִאשׁוֹן, *during the [same] lapse of awareness as the first [piece].* At any rate, the person (a) ate an olive-and-a-half-sized piece of *cheilev*; (b) became aware that he was guilty of eating an olive-sized portion of that piece; and then (c) ate another half-olive-sized piece of *cheilev.* This last half-olive piece was thus eaten during the same lapse of awareness as a half-olive portion of the first piece.

11. Even though atonement is not effected by a *chatas* unless the person was aware of the sin when the *chatas* was offered [see below, 72a note 9], that is true only when a minimum measure subject to liability [e.g. an olive-size] of the prohibited item was consumed. R' Yochanan therefore says that if the person became aware of multiple violations — each involving a minimum measure — at different times, he is liable to a separate *chatas* for each. However, in our case, if a *chatas* was offered for an olive-sized portion of the one-and-a-half-olive piece that the person ate, it would atone for the consumption of the half-olive-sized portion eaten in the same lapse. Hence, even though the person did not become aware of the true extent of his transgression at one time, since he was lacking awareness only of a half-olive-sized portion [which is less than the minimum measure], we view it as if he did become aware of his entire transgression (*Rashi*; see *Rashash*). It then follows that consumption of the last half-olive piece is considered to have taken place during a different lapse of awareness than the first half-olive portion, and the two cannot combine to make the person liable to a *chatas.*

מכלל דרישא מין אחד ותמחוי אחד מין אחד ותמחוי אחד צריכא למימר אמר רב הונא הכא במאי עסקינן כגון שהיתה לו ידיעה בינתיים ורבן גמליאל היא [א] דאמר אין ידיעה לחצי שיעור: איתמר אכל שני זיתי חלב בהעלם אחד ונודע לו על הראשון וחזר ונודע לו על השני ר' יוחנן אמר [א] חייב שתים וריש לקיש אמר אינו חייב אלא אחת [ב] רבי יוחנן אמר חייב [א] על חטאתו והביא [ג] וריש לקיש אמר פטור [ב] מחטאתו ונסלח לו וריש לקיש הכתיב על חטאתו והביא ההוא לאחר כפרה ולרבי יוחנן נמי הכתיב מחטאתו ונסלח לו הכא במאי עסקינן [ב] כגון שאכל כזית ומחצה ונודע לו על כזית וחזר ואכל כחצי זית אחר בהעלמו של שני מהו דתימא ליצטרפו קמ"ל א"ל רבינא לרב אשי דאיתידע ליה קודם הפרשה פליגי ובהא פליגי דמר סבר [ג] ידיעות מחלקות ומר סבר הפרשות מחלקות אבל לאחר הפרשה מודי ליה ריש לקיש לר' יוחנן דחייב שתים או דילמא דאיתידע ליה לאחר הפרשה פליגי ובהא פליגי דמר סבר הפרשות מחלקות ומר סבר כפרות מחלקות אבל קודם הפרשה מודי ליה ר' יוחנן לריש לקיש דאינו חייב אלא אחת או דילמא בין בזו ובין בזו מחלוקת א"ל מסתברא בין בזו ובין בזו מחלוקת דאי סלקא דעתך קודם הפרשה פליגי אבל לאחר הפרשה מודה ליה ריש לקיש לר' יוחנן דחייב שתים אדמוקים ליה קרא לאחר כפרה לוקמיה לאחר הפרשה ואי אחר הפרשה פליגי אבל קודם הפרשה מודה ליה רבי יוחנן לריש לקיש דאינו חייב אלא אחת אדמוקי ליה קרא בכזית ומחצה לוקמיה קודם הפרשה ודילמא ספוקי מספקא ליה (א) ואם תימצי לומר קאמר אם תימצי לומר קודם הפרשה פליגי בה רבי יוחנן היכי מוקי ליה לקרא בכזית ומחצה ואם תימצי לומר לאחר הפרשה פליגי ריש לקיש היכי מוקי ליה לקרא בלאחר כפרה: אמר עולא למאן דאמר אשם ודאי לא בעיא ידיעה בתחילה

בעל

רש"י

מכלל דרישא. לאמר חייב: מין אחד ותמחוי אחד. בתמיה: שהיתה לו ידיעה. בין שני חצאי שיעור ואיצטריך לאשמעינן דליצטרפו דס"ד אמינא הואיל ובשיעורין שלמים חלוקין לחטאות הכא נמי לא ליצטרפו קמ"ל דהתם הוה ידיעה אבל ידיעת חצי שיעור לאו ידיעה היא: רבן גמליאל היא דאמר. לקמן בפרק הבונה אין ידיעה לחצי שיעור: וחזר ונודע לו. לקמן בעי ליה אי קודם שהפריש קרבן על ידיעה ראשונה וקסבר ידיעות מחלקות לחטאות ואע"פ שלא היתה ידיעה בין אכילה לאכילה או לאחר הפרשה וקסבר הפרשות מחלקות והא דאביי ורבא דאמרי לעיל ונודע לו על אחת מהן וחזר ואכל כו' אלמא דחדא הוא דמיחייב אי סבירא להו פלוגתא דר' יוחנן וריש לקיש בקודם הפרשה אינהו דאמור כריש לקיש אי נמי סבירא להו דלאחר הפרשה פליגי ואינהו דאמור קודם הפרשה נודע על השני ודברי הכל אין חלוקין לחטאות: על חטאתו והביא. והביא קרבנו שעירת עזים תמימה נקבה על חטאתו אשר חטא (ויקרא ד) משמע על כל חטאת וחטאת יביא: מחטאתו ונסלח לו. אפי' לא הביא אלא על מקצת חטאתו ונסלח לו כולו: קמ"ל. כיון (ב) דהאי חצי זית עם זית קמא שייך בתר ידיעה קמייתא [ו]הוה כאילו נודע לו על הכל דהא אי הוה מייתי קרבן הוה מיכפר בהדיה [דזית] בלא שום ידיעה דפחות מכשיעור לא חשיב אבל כזית לא מיכפר בלא ידיעה הלכך כי לא איתידע ליה בהדיה אלא זה אחר זה הוו ידיעות מחלקות: דאיתידע ליה. על השני קודם שהפריש קרבן על ידיעה הראשונה פליגי: אדמוקים לאחר כפרה. כי פרכינן לעיל לריש לקיש הא כתיב על חטאתו והביא ואוקימנא שיטתיה דתלמודא בלאחר כפרה לוקמא בלאחר הפרשה אבל השתא דאוקימנא בלאחר כפרה ש"מ דפשיטא לבני הישיבה שסדרו הגמ' דלאחר הפרשה נמי פטר ריש לקיש: הכי גרסינן בספרים ישנים ודילמא ספוקי מספקא להו ואת"ל קאמר אם תמצא לומר קודם הפרשה פליגי רבי יוחנן היכי מוקי ליה לקרא בכזית ומחצה את"ל אחר הפרשה פליגי ר"ל היכי מוקי ליה לקרא בלאחר כפרה. והכי פירושא ודילמא לבני תלמודא נמי מספקא להו פלוגתא דר"י ור"ל במאי כי היכי דמספקא ליה לדידי אי בקודם אי בלאחר אי בתרווייהו וכי פריך בעל התלמוד לרבי יוחנן נמי והא כתיב מחטאתו ונסלח לו ומשני ליה בכזית ומחצה בלשון את"ל פריך ליה ומשני ליה והכי קאמר אי הוה פשיטא לן דלאחר הפרשה הוא דמחייב [ר"י תרתי] אבל בקודם הפרשה מודה [לר"ל] לא הוה קשיא לן מידי דאוקימנא מחטאתו ונסלח לו בקודם הפרשה אבל השתא קשיא לן את"ל בהך בעיא דרבינא דבקודם הפרשה נמי פליגי וא"ר יוחנן חייב שתים ר' יוחנן היכי מוקי לקרא דמחטאתו ונסלח לו ושני ליה בכזית ומחצה והכי קמשני אפי' את"ל דקודם הפרשה לחודא פליגי אי נמי בתרווייהו פליגי איכא לאוקמא בכזית ומחצה ולר"ל נמי כי פריך ליה תלמודא הכתיב על חטאתו והביא ושני ליה בעל התלמוד בלאחר כפרה לעולם ספוקי מספקא ליה במאי פליגי כלדידי ובאת"ל פריך ומשני והכי קאמר את"ל בלאחר הפרשה נמי פליגי דבלאחר הפרשה פטר ליה בחד קרבן דהשתא ליכא לאוקמא לקרא דמחייב בלאחר הפרשה ר"ל היאך מוקי ליה להאי קרא כלומר במאי מוקי ליה ושני ליה אפילו אם תמצא לומר בלאחר הפרשה פליגי איכא לאוקמי בלאחר כפרה. ורוב התלמידים שגו בשיטה זו ודימו דהאי דהיכי מוקי לה לקרא בכזית ומחצה וחברו היכי מוקי ליה לקרא בלאחר כפרה לשון קושיא הוא ולפרושי כמו מ"ט והוצרכו לשבש את הספרים ולמחוק הוי"ו ואת"ל (ג) קמא ולהגיה קאמרינן ולהגיה על קודם לאחר ועל לאחר קודם ואין שיטת התלמוד כפי סוגייתם: למ"ד אשם ודאי לא בעי ידיעה.

תוספות

מכלל דרישא מין אחד ותמחוי אחד כו'. לעיל לא בעי למיפרך מכלל דסיפא משני מינין ושני תמחויין צריכא למימר שלא חש להאריך כיון דלא קאי הכי: מאן דאמר אשם ודאי לא בעי ידיעה בתחלה. פי' בקונטרס דאיכא פלוגתא דר' עקיבא ורבי טרפון בפרק דם שחיטה בכריתות (דף כב:) וליתא דהא תנן התם דדוקא במעילה מרובה קאמר ר"ע שמביא שתי אשמות משום דטוב לו שיביא שתי אשמות משיביא אשם אחד ויתנה שאם לא יודע לו תהא מעילתו נדבה אבל במעילה מועטת מודה ר"ע שמביא אשם אחד ויתנה ונוח לו שיתן מעילה מועטת על הספק משיביא שתי אשמות וקאמרינן בגמ' מדברי שניהם נלמד [א] אשם ודאי לא בעי ידיעה בתחלה ואם תאמר רבי טרפון דקאמר מה לזה מביא שתי אשמות משמע דעלה טובה קמ"ל אדרבה כיון דבמעילה מרובה פליגי אם כן טוב לו שיביא שתי אשמות כדאמר ר' עקיבא משיביא אשם אחד ומעילתו ויתנה כדפרישית יש לומר דר' טרפון לאו עלה טובה קאמר אלא לעולם אינו יוצא מידי עבירה בשתי אשמות אלא שיביא אשם ומעילתו ויתנה ואם תאמר ולרבי עקיבא אמאי מביא שתי אשמות במרובה ובמעוטה אשם ומעילה יביא לעולם אשם אחד ויתנה וכשיודע אז יביא מעילתו ויש לומר משום דאמר [ד] המביא אשמו עד שלא הביא מעילתו לא יצא:

בעל

רש"י (המשך)

אשם ודאי לא בעי ידיעה. פלוגתא דר"ט ור"ע היא בכריתות בפ' דם שחיטה (דף כב.) ר"ע מחייב על ספק מעילות אשם תלוי ופי' היו לפניו שתי חתיכות א' של קדש וא' של חולין ואכל אחת מהן ואינו יודע איזו אכל מביא אשם תלוי ומודה ר"ע שאינו מביא את מעילתו כלומר אינו משלם קרן וחומש עד שיודע לו ויביא עמה אשם מעילות ודאי כי היכי דאשם תלוי דשאר עבירות דספק כרת אינו מכפר כפרה גמורה וכשיודע לו דודאי חטא מביא חטאת אף זה כשיודע לו יחזור ויביא אשם ודאי ר"ט אומר מה לזה מביא שתי אשמות ולא דמי לאשם תלוי דספק חטאת [ד] דהתם ספיקו איל ודאי נקבה הלכך כי מתידע ליה בעי לאתויי נקבה אבל זה ששניהם מין אחד כדאמר התם שממין שמביא על הודע מביא על לא הודע שזה איל וזה איל יביא קרן וחומש ויביא איל ויאמר אם ודאי מעלתי זו מעילתי וזו אשמי ואם ספק שלא עתיד ספיקי להודע לי אשם זה יהיה אשם תלוי והקדש זה לנדבה ולכי מתיידע ליה לא בעי לאתויי אשם אחרינא אלמא לא בעי ידיעה בתחילה באשם ודאי קודם הבאת כפרתו דהא לא איתידע ליה כי אתיי' ומכפר עליה: אשם ודאי. כל אשמות קרוין אשם ודאי חוץ מאשם תלוי שהוא בא על לא הודע והן שלשה הבאין על חטא אשם מעילות אשם גזילות אשם שפחה חרופה:

בעל

עין משפט נר מצוה

כ א מיי' פ"ו מהלכות שגגות הלכה ט:

כא ב שם הלכה י:

כב ג מיי' פ"ה מהלכות שגגות הלכה א ופ"ו הלכה א והלכה ט סמג עשין ריג:

רבינו חננאל

וחזקיה אמר בחמשה אברים וריש לקיש אמר אפי' באבר א' [משכחת להן] בכתף. ור' יוחנן אמר בחמשה מיני קדירה. ור' יצחק נפחא [אמר] בה' טעמים. והרי הוא כיון שהוא שני חצאי זית בב' תמחויין כמי שאינו שם חיוב חטאות היא וקתני מצטרפין וחייב חטאת. גם זה אע"פ שחלוקין הן לחטאות והן מצטרפו' ושנינן מי סברת הא דריש לקיש משום בר תוטיני אריפא הוא דקתני שאם אכל כחצי זית וחזר ואכל כחצי זית ממין אחד חייב במלתא דחלוקין לחטאות מוקמי ליה כר' יהושע וכגון שאכלו בב' תמחויין לא אסיפא היא דקתני סיפא אם אכל כחצי זית וחזר ואכל כחצי זית אחד משני מינין פטור עלה אמרי צריכא למימר. ואמר ר"ל משום [בר] תוטיני לעולם ממין אחד ואמאי (תני) [קרי] לה בב' מינין כגון שאכלן בב' תמחויין ור' יהושע היא תמחויין מתחלקין בין לקולא בין לחומרא ונמצא גם זו בדברים שאין חלוקין לחטאות ואקשינן אי הכי מדסיפא ב' חצאי מין אחד בב' תמחויין וקתני פטור רישא משום שהוא מין אחד בתמחוי אחד לפיכך חייב אמאי איצטריך למתניא להא פשיטא ומשני רבינא כגון שהיו ב' זיתי חלב בתמחוי אחד וכגון שאכל חצי זית אחד מהן ונודע לו והדר ושכח ואכל חצי זית האחר. ומתניתין רבן גמליאל היא דאמר [אין] ידיעה לחצי שיעור דתנן הכותב ב' אותיות בב' העלמות אחת בשחרית ואחת בין הערבים רבן גמליאל מחייב וחכמים פוטרין ואמרינן במאי פליגי רבן גמליאל סבר אין ידיעה לחצי שיעור ורבנן סברי יש ידיעה לחצי שיעור וכיון דרבן גמליאל סבר דאין ידיעה לחצי שיעו' כאלו אין שם ידיעה בינתים ובהעלם אחת כולן לפיכך חייב: **אתמר** אכל ב' זיתי חלב בהעלם אחד ונודע לו על הראשון וחזר ונודע לו על השני ר' יוחנן אומר חייב שתים ר"ל אומר אינו חייב אלא אחת ר' יוחנן אומר ידיעה מחלקת לפיכך חייב שתים. ר"ל אומר אין ידיעה מחלקת ואין חייב אלא חטאת אחת ר' יוחנן דריש על חטאתו והביא כיון שנודעה לו חטאתו נתחייב בה וכשיתודע לו השניה עוד מתחייב בה דאין אדם פורע חובו במה שכבר נתחייב בו ור"ל דריש מחטאתו ונסלח כל שהוא בהעלם אחד חטאת אחד הוא ומחטאתו ונסלח קרינן ביה. ור' יוחנן האי קרא דר"ל דריש ביה הכי מניין אם אכל כזית ומחצה ונודע לו על כזית ולא נודע לו על מחצה. וחזר ואכל זית אחד בהעלמו של שני מהו דתימא לצטרף עם חצי זית הראשון ויתחייב קמ"ל מחטאתו אם כבר נתכפר מקצת מחטאתו פטור בנשאר ור"ל האי על חטאתו והביא מיבעי ליה כשנודע לו על כזית אחד וכפר עליו. ולאחר שנתכפר לו [נודע לון] על כזית השני כגון זה מודה ר"ל דצריך קרבן והא דרב [אשי] ודרבינא לא מוכחא בהדיא במאי פליגי מיהו סוגיא דשמעתא לדברי הכל לאחר כפרה דראשון נודע לו השני צריך חטאת שניה והא סברא דרבה ואביי בגרירה פליגא אתרווייהו דהא אוקימנא דלתרווייהו לר' יוחנן ולר"ל כשנודע לו לאחר שנתכפר על הראשון צריך חטאת שניה ורבה אמר אכל ב' זיתי חלב בהעלם אחד ונודע לו על אחד מהן וחזר ואכל כזית אחד בהעלמו של שני הביא קרבן על הראשון ראשון ושני מתכפר (הוה) [אלמא] ודאי אם נודע לו על השני אחר שכבר נתכפר על הראשון אינו חייב על השני קרבן אחר שנתכפר עם הראשון דאביי עדיפא מדרבא וקיי"ל כוותיהו דאינון בתראי: **אמר** עולא לדברי האומר אשם ודאי לא בעי ידיעה בתחלה

מסורת הש"ס

א) לקמן קב. [קה. וש"נ], ב) [לקמן לד.], ג) [שם], ד) [ב"ק קיא.].

הגהות הב"ח

(א) גמ' ספוקי מספקא להו ואם תימצי וכו' הפרשה פליגי ר' יוחנן כצ"ל ותיבת בה נמחק: (ב) רש"י ד"ה קא משמע לן דהאי כצ"ל ותיבת כיון נמחק: (ג) ד"ה הכי גרסי' וכו' ולמחוק הוי"ו דאם תמצי לומר קאמר ולהגיה:

גליון הש"ס

רש"י ד"ה למ"ד אשם ודאי וכו' דהתם ספיקו איל. עיין מג"א סימן א ס"ק יא:

הגהות הגר"א

[א] תוס' ד"ה מאן. מדברי שניהם נלמד כו'. נ"ב אבל הוא רבי יוסי (וכ"כ הרז"ה והרמב"ן בחידושיו דלא כרש"ל) דבעי ידיעה בתחלה כמ"ש [כריתות דף ז' ב'] מודה ר"י בממוסר כפרה מ"ט התם בעי גברא ידיעה כו' וזהו מחולק שם ר"י ור"ש:

תורה אור השלם

א) אוֹ הוֹדַע אֵלָיו חַטָּאתוֹ אֲשֶׁר חָטָא וְהֵבִיא קָרְבָּנוֹ שְׂעִירַת עִזִּים תְּמִימָה נְקֵבָה עַל חַטָּאתוֹ אֲשֶׁר חָטָא: [ויקרא ד, כח]

ב) וְאֶת כָּל חֶלְבּוֹ יַקְטִיר הַמִּזְבֵּחָה כְּחֵלֶב זֶבַח הַשְּׁלָמִים וְכִפֶּר עָלָיו הַכֹּהֵן מֵחַטָּאתוֹ וְנִסְלַח לוֹ: [ויקרא ה, כו]

ליקוטי רש"י

אין ידיעה לחצי שיעור. לחלק כדי שלא יצטרף עמו חצי האחר [לקמן קה.]. אכל חצי שיעור ונודע לא הויא ידיעה לחלק דאם חזר ואכל חצי שיעור מצטרפין [כריתות יב:]. למ"ד אשם ודאי. כי אתייה מספק על תנאי עולה לו לאשם ודאי כי מתידע ליה [שם כב:].

רב נסים גאון

אחד ואחד ובגמרא גרסי היכי דמי ה' תמחויין אמר שמואל כאותה ששנינו חמשה דברים בעולה מצטרפין הבשר והחלב והיין והסולת והשמן חזקיה אמר כגון שאכל מה' אברים ר"ל אמר אפילו תימא באבר אחד משכחת לה בכתף ר' יצחק אמר כגון שאכל בה' מיני קדירה ר' יוחנן אמר כגון שאכלה בה' טעמים: ורבן גמליאל הוא דאמר אין ידיעה לחצי שיעור. בפרק הבונה (לקמן דף קה) הכותב ב' אותיות בב' העלמות אחת בשחרית ואחת בין הערבים רבן גמליאל מחייב וחכמים פוטרים ובגמ' גרסי במאי קא מיפלגי רבן גמליאל סבר אין ידיעה לחצי שיעור: **אמר** עולא למאן דאמר אשם ודאי לא בעי ידיעה בתחילה. משכחת לה במס' כריתות בפרק דם שחיטה (דף כב) אמר ר' טרפון ומה לזה מביא ב' אשמות אמר לו ר' עקיבא נראין דבריך במעילה כו' ובגמ' גרסי אמר רבא מדברי שניהם נלמוד אשם ודאי לא בעי ידיעה בתחילה ומכלל זו המימרא נלמוד כי מי שחולק על ר"ע ור' טרפון בדבר הזה סובר שאשם ודאי בעי ידיעה בתחילה וזה האשם נידון כחטאת מה חטאת בעינן ידיעה בתחילה אף אשם ודאי נמי בעי ידיעה בתחלה:

ואלא

The Gemara now inquires as to the nature of the dispute between R' Yochanan and Reish Lakish:

דְּאִיתְיְדַע – אָמַר לֵיהּ רָבִינָא לְרַב אַשִׁי – **Ravina said to Rav Ashi:** לֵיהּ קוֹדֶם הַהַפְרָשָׁה פְּלִיגֵי – **Do they disagree about** a case **where he discovered** the second violation **before designation** of the *chatas* for the first violation, וּבְהָא פְּלִיגֵי – **and they disagree about this** following matter: דְּמָר סָבַר יְדִיעוֹת מְחַלְּקוֹת – **that** one **master** [R' Yochanan] **holds that awarenesses** alone **separate** transgressions into distinct liabilities,[12] וּמָר סָבַר הַפְרָשׁוֹת מְחַלְּקוֹת – **and** the other **master** [Reish Lakish] **holds that designations** of *chatas* offerings **separate** transgressions into distinct liabilities;[13] אֲבָל לְאַחַר הַפְרָשָׁה – **but** regarding a second violation that the person discovered **after designation** of the *chatas* for the first violation, מוֹדֵי לֵיהּ רֵישׁ לָקִישׁ לְרַבִּי יוֹחָנָן – **Reish Lakish agrees with R' Yochanan** דְּחַיָּיב שְׁתַּיִם – **that he is liable to two** offerings? אוֹ דִּילְמָא – **Or perhaps** דְּאִיתְיְדַע לֵיהּ לְאַחַר הַפְרָשָׁה פְּלִיגֵי – **they disagree about** a case **where he discovered** the second violation **after designation** of the *chatas* for the first violation, וּבְהָא פְּלִיגֵי – **and they disagree about this** fact: דְּמָר סָבַר הַפְרָשׁוֹת מְחַלְּקוֹת – **that** one **master** [R' Yochanan] **holds that designations** of *chatas* offerings **separate** transgressions into distinct liabilities,[14] וּמָר סָבַר כַּפָּרוֹת מְחַלְּקוֹת – **and** the other **master** [Reish Lakish] **holds that atonements** effected by *chatas* offerings **separate** transgressions into distinct categories of liability;[15] אֲבָל קוֹדֶם הַפְרָשָׁה – **but** regarding a second violation that he discovered **before designation** of the *chatas* for the first violation מוֹדֵי לֵיהּ רַבִּי יוֹחָנָן לְרֵישׁ לָקִישׁ – **R' Yochanan agrees with Reish Lakish** דְּאֵינוֹ חַיָּיב אֶלָּא אַחַת – **that he is liable to only one** *chatas*. אוֹ דִּילְמָא – **Or perhaps** בֵּין בְּזוֹ וּבֵין בְּזוֹ מַחֲלוֹקֶת – **there is a dispute both in this** case of a discovery before designation **and in that** case of a discovery after designation.[16]

Rav Ashi replies:

אָמַר לֵיהּ – **He said to [Ravina]:** מִסְתַּבְּרָא בֵּין בְּזוֹ וּבֵין בְּזוֹ מַחֲלוֹקֶת – **It is reasonable** to say **that there is a dispute both in this** case of a discovery before designation **and in that** case of a discovery after designation. דְּאִי סָלְקָא דַּעְתָּךְ קוֹדֶם הַפְרָשָׁה פְּלִיגֵי – **For if you think that they disagree** only about discovery **before designation,** אֲבָל לְאַחַר הַפְרָשָׁה – **but** regarding a discovery **after designation** מוֹדֶה לֵיהּ רֵישׁ לָקִישׁ לְרַבִּי יוֹחָנָן דְּחַיָּיב שְׁתַּיִם – **Reish Lakish agrees with R' Yochanan that he is liable to two** *chatas* offerings, אַדְּמוֹקִים לֵיהּ קְרָא לְאַחַר כַּפָּרָה – then **instead of interpreting the verse** cited by R' Yochanan in support of his own view **as referring to** discovery **after atonement,**[17] לוֹקְמֵיהּ לְאַחַר הַפְרָשָׁה – **he** [the scholar defending Reish Lakish] **should have interpreted** the verse as referring to discovery **after designation.**[18] וְאִי אַחַר הַפְרָשָׁה פְּלִיגֵי – **And if they disagree** only **about** discovery **after designation,** אֲבָל קוֹדֶם הַפְרָשָׁה – **but** regarding discovery **before designation** מוֹדֶה לֵיהּ רַבִּי יוֹחָנָן לְרֵישׁ לָקִישׁ דְּאֵינוֹ חַיָּיב אֶלָּא אַחַת – **R' Yochanan agrees with Reish Lakish that he is liable to only one** offering, אַדְּמוֹקֵי לֵיהּ קְרָא בִּכְזַיִת וּמֶחֱצָה – then **instead of interpreting the verse** cited by Reish Lakish **as referring to** a case where the person first ate *cheilev* **the size of an olive and a half** etc.,[19] לוֹקְמֵיהּ קוֹדֶם הַפְרָשָׁה – **he** [the scholar defending R' Yochanan] **should have interpreted** it as referring to discovery of the second violation **before designation** of the *chatas* for the first violation.[20] Apparently, then, R' Yochanan and Reish Lakish disagree with one another whether the second violation was discovered before or after an offering was designated for the first violation.

The Gemara dismisses Rav Ashi's proof:

וְדִילְמָא סְפוּקֵי מְסַפְּקָא לֵיהּ – **But perhaps [the scholar]** himself **was unsure about it,**[21] וְאִם תִּימְצֵי לוֹמַר קָאָמַר – **and he was stating** his responses in the form of **"if you want to say,"** as follows: אִם תִּימְצֵי לוֹמַר קוֹדֶם הַפְרָשָׁה פְּלִיגֵי בָּהּ – **If you want to say that they** [R' Yochanan and Reish Lakish] **disagree about [a**

NOTES

12. That is, even though he did not become aware of his first violation before committing the second [and they were thus committed in the same lapse of awareness], his awareness of the first violation after both have been committed nevertheless separates it from the second. Even if he discovers his second sin before designating an animal for the first one, he must bring a separate offering for each violation since he became aware of them at different times.

13. According to Reish Lakish mere awareness of the sin does not separate it from other like sins committed in the same lapse of awareness. Only if the person designated a sacrifice for the first violation before becoming aware of the second violation will he be liable to two separate offerings.

14. According to this explanation, the positions of the disputants are shifted. R' Yochanan agrees with the view ascribed to Reish Lakish in the previous explanation (see previous note).

15. That is, even if the *chatas* was already designated, it can atone for any like infractions he subsequently discovers, as long as they were committed in the same lapse of awareness. Only when the *chatas* is actually offered does it cease to atone for other violations that become discovered.

16. Thus, R' Yochanan would hold that the person is liable to two *chatas* offerings even if he merely *became aware* of one violation before the other. Reish Lakish would hold that one *chatas* suffices for both violations [committed in the same lapse of awareness] even if the person had already *designated* an offering for his first violation before he discovered the second; only if he has already *offered* the *chatas* for one violation is a new *chatas* needed for the other violation of which he becomes aware.

17. Earlier, the Gemara asked what Reish Lakish derives from the verse cited by R' Yochanan which indicates that a person is liable to a separate *chatas* for each violation he committed. The Gemara answered that Reish Lakish would understand that verse to be referring to a case where he discovered his second violation after he had already offered his *chatas* for the first violation (*Rashi*).

18. The scholars of the academy redacting the Talmud who were explaining Reish Lakish's view should have stated that the verse refers to a case where the person discovered his second violation after the *chatas* for the first one was designated. By stating that the sacrifice was already offered, they indicate that according to Reish Lakish a person is liable to only one *chatas* even if that *chatas* was already designated for one sin when he discovered his second sin – as long as it was not yet offered (*Rashi*).

[Although Ravina and Rav Ashi and their court finalized the redaction of the entire Talmud as we have it today, this process was begun before their time. Thus, here Rav Ashi himself bases his reply to Ravina's inquiry on an extant text analyzing the dispute between R' Yochanan and Reish Lakish (see *Doros Rishonim,* vol. 5 ch. 68 p. 551 ff).]

19. The Gemara also asked above what R' Yochanan derives from the verse cited by Reish Lakish, which indicates that a person is liable to only one *chatas* for all of the violations he committed in a single lapse of awareness. The Gemara answered that R' Yochanan understands the verse to be referring to a person who ate a piece of *cheilev* the size of an olive and a half and became aware of only an olive-sized portion of that violation, teaching that he does not need separate atonement for the half-olive portion even if he subsequently eats another half-olive in the same lapse.

20. Thus, R' Yochanan must hold that a person is liable to separate offerings even if the offering for the first infraction was not yet designated when the second violation was discovered. The mere awareness of the first violation separates it from the others.

21. That is, those in the academy who were discussing the view of R' Yochanan and Reish Lakish were themselves unsure about the extent of their dispute (*Rashi*).

מכלל דרישא מין אחד ותמחוי אחד מין אחד ותמחוי אחד צריכא למימר אמר רב הונא הכא במאי עסקינן כגון שהיתה לו ידיעה בינתיים ורבן גמליאל היא [א] דאמר אין ידיעה לחצי שיעור: איתמר אכל שני זיתי חלב בהעלם אחד ונודע לו על הראשון וחזר ונודע לו על השני ר' יוחנן אמר [א] חייב שתים וריש לקיש אמר אינו חייב אלא אחת [ב] רבי יוחנן אמר חייב א) על חטאתו והביא [ג] וריש לקיש אמר פטור ב) מחטאתו ונסלח לו וריש לקיש הכתיב על חטאתו והביא ההוא לאחר כפרה ולרבי יוחנן נמי הכתיב מחטאתו ונסלח לו הכא במאי עסקינן [ב] כגון שאכל כזית ומחצה ונודע לו על כזית וחזר ואכל כחצי זית אחר בהעלמו של שני מהו דתימא ליצטרפו קמ"ל א"ל רבינא לרב אשי דאיתידע ליה קודם הפרשה פליגי ובהא פליגי דמר סבר [ג] ידיעות מחלקות ומר סבר הפרשות מחלקות אבל לאחר הפרשה מודי ליה ריש לקיש לר' יוחנן דחייב שתים או דילמא דאיתידע ליה לאחר הפרשה פליגי ובהא פליגי דמר סבר הפרשות מחלקות ומר סבר כפרות מחלקות אבל קודם הפרשה מודי ליה ר' יוחנן לריש לקיש דאינו חייב אלא אחת או דילמא בין בזו ובין בזו מחלוקת א"ל מסתברא בין בזו ובין בזו מחלוקת דאי סלקא דעתך קודם הפרשה פליגי אבל לאחר הפרשה מודה ליה ריש לקיש לר' יוחנן דחייב שתים אדמוקים ליה קרא לאחר כפרה לוקמיה לאחר הפרשה ואי אחר הפרשה פליגי אבל קודם הפרשה מודה ליה רבי יוחנן לריש לקיש דאינו חייב אלא אחת אדמוקי ליה קרא בכזית ומחצה לוקמיה קודם הפרשה ודילמא ספוקי מספקא ליה (א) ואם תימצי לומר קאמר אם תימצי לומר קודם הפרשה פליגי בה רבי יוחנן היכי מוקי ליה לקרא בכזית ומחצה ואם תימצי לומר לאחר הפרשה פליגי ריש לקיש היכי מוקי ליה לקרא בלאחר כפרה: אמר עולא למאן דאמר אשם ודאי לא בעיא ידיעה בתחילה

בעל

רש"י

מכלל דרישא. דקאמר חייב: מין אחד ותמחוי אחד. בתמיה: שהיתה לו ידיעה. בין שני חצאי שיעור ואיצטריך לאשמעינן דלא מצטרפו דס"ד אמינא הואיל ובשיעורין שלמים חלוקין לחטאות הכא נמי לא ליצטרפו קמ"ל דהתם הוה ידיעה אבל ידיעת חצי שיעור לאו ידיעה היא: רבן גמליאל היא דאמר. לקמן בפרק הבונה אין ידיעה לחצי שיעור: וחזר ונודע לו. לקמן בעי ליה אי קודם שהפריש קרבן על ידיעה ראשונה וקסבר ידיעות מחלקות לחטאות ואע"פ שלא היתה ידיעה בין אכילה לאכילה או לאחר הפרשה וקסבר הפרשות מחלקות והא דאביי ורבא דאמרי לעיל ונודע לו על אחת מהן וחזר ואכל כו' אלמא דחדא הוא דמיחייב אי סבירא להו פלוגתא דר' יוחנן וריש לקיש בקודם הפרשה אינהו דאמור כריש לקיש אי נמי סבירא להו דלאחר הפרשה פליגי ואינהו דאמור קודם הפרשה נודע על השני ודברי הכל אין חלוקין לחטאות: על חטאתו והביא. והביא קרבנו שעירת עזים תמימה נקבה על חטאתו אשר חטא (ויקרא ד) משמע על כל חטאת וחטאת יביא: מחטאתו ונסלח לו. אפי' לא הביא אלא על מקצת חטאתו ונסלח לו כולו: קמ"ל. כיון (ב) דהאי חצי זית עם זית קמא שייך בתר ידיעה קמייתא [ו]הוה כאילו נודע לו על הכל דהא אי הוה מייתי קרבן הוה מיכפר בהדיה [דזית] בלא שום ידיעה דפחות מכשיעור לא חשיב אבל כזית לא מיכפר בלא ידיעה הלכך כי לא איתידע ליה בהדיה אלא זה אחר זה הוו ידיעות מחלקות: דאיתידע ליה. על השני קודם שהפריש קרבן על ידיעה הראשונה פליגי: אדמוקים לאחר כפרה. כי פרכינן לעיל לריש לקיש הא כתיב על חטאתו והביא ואוקימנא שיטתיה דתלמודא בלאחר כפרה לוקמא בלאחר הפרשה אבל השתא דאוקימנא בלאחר כפרה ש"מ דפשיטא לבני הישיבה שסדרו הגמ' דלאחר הפרשה נמי פטר ריש לקיש: הכי גרסינן בספרים ישנים ודילמא ספוקי מספקא להו ואת"ל קאמר אם תמצא לומר קודם הפרשה פליגי רבי יוחנן היכי מוקי ליה לקרא בכזית ומחצה את"ל אחר הפרשה פליגי ר"ל היכי מוקי ליה לקרא בלאחר כפרה. והכי פירושא ודילמא לבני תלמודא נמי מספקא להו פלוגתא דר"י ור"ל במאי כי היכי דמספקא ליה לדידי אי בקודם אי בלאחר אי בתרווייהו וכי פריך בעל התלמוד לרבי יוחנן נמי והא כתיב מחטאתו ונסלח לו ומשני ליה בכזית ומחצה בלשון את"ל פריך ליה ומשני ליה והכי קאמר אי הוה פשיטא לן דלאחר הפרשה הוא דמחייב [ר"י תרתי] אבל בקודם הפרשה מודה [לר"ל] לא הוה קשיא לן מידי דאוקימנא מחטאתו ונסלח לו בקודם הפרשה אבל השתא קשיא לן את"ל בהך בעיא דרבינא דבקודם הפרשה נמי פליגי וא"ר יוחנן חייב שתים ר' יוחנן היכי מוקי לקרא דמחטאתו ונסלח לו ושני ליה בכזית ומחצה והכי קמשני אפי' את"ל דקודם הפרשה לחודא פליגי אי נמי בתרווייהו פליגי איכא לאוקמא בכזית ומחצה ולר"ל נמי כי פריך ליה תלמודא הכתיב על חטאתו והביא ושני ליה בעל התלמוד בלאחר כפרה לעולם ספוקי מספקא ליה במאי פליגי כלדידי ובאת"ל פריך ומשני והכי קאמר את"ל בלאחר הפרשה נמי פליגי דבלאחר הפרשה פטר ליה בחד קרבן דהשתא ליכא לאוקמא לקרא דמחייב בלאחר הפרשה ר"ל היאך מוקי ליה להאי קרא כלומר במאי מוקי ליה ושני ליה אפילו אם תמצא לומר בלאחר הפרשה פליגי איכא לאוקמי בלאחר כפרה. ורוב התלמידים שגו בשיטה זו ודימו דהאי דהיכי מוקי לה לקרא בכזית ומחצה וחברו היכי מוקי ליה לקרא בלאחר כפרה לשון קושיא הוא ולפרושי כמו מ"ט והוצרכו לשבש את הספרים ולמחוק הוי"ו ואת"ל (ג) קמא ולהגיה קאמרינן והגיה על קודם לאחר ועל לאחר קודם ואין שיטת התלמוד כפי סוגייתם: למ"ד אשם ודאי לא בעי ידיעה. פלוגתא דר"ט ור"ע היא בכריתות בפ' דם שחיטה (דף כב.) ר"ע מחייב על ספק מעילות אשם תלוי ופי' היו לפניו שתי חתיכות א' של קדש וא' של חולין ואכל אחת מהן ואינו יודע איזו אכל מביא אשם תלוי ומודה ר"ע שאינו מביא את מעילתו כלומר אינו משלם קרן וחומש עד שיודע לו ויביא עמה אשם מעילות ודאי כי היכי דאשם תלוי דשאר עבירות דספק כרת אינו מכפר כפרה גמורה וכשיודע לו דודאי חטא מביא חטאת אף זה כשיודע לו יחזור ויביא אשם ודאי ר"ט אומר מה לזה מביא שתי אשמות ולא דמי לאשם תלוי דספק חטאת ° דהתם ספיקו איל ודאי נקבה הלכך כי מתידע ליה בעי לאתויי נקבה אבל זה ששניהם מין אחד כדאמר התם שממין שמביא על הודע מביא על לא הודע שזה איל וזה איל יביא קרן וחומש ויביא איל ויאמר אם ודאי מעלתי זו מעילתי וזו אשמי ואם ספק שלא עתיד ספיקי להודע לי אשם זה יהיה אשם תלוי והקדש זה לנדבה ולכי מתיידע ליה לא בעי לאתויי אשם אחרינא אלמא לא בעי ידיעה בתחילה באשם ודאי קודם הבאת כפרתו דהא לא איתידע ליה כי אתיי' ומכפר עליה: אשם ודאי. כל אשמות קרוין אשם ודאי חוץ מאשם תלוי שהוא בא על לא הודע והן שלשה הבאין על חטא אשם מעילות אשם גזילות אשם שפחה חרופה:

בעל

תוספות

מכלל דרישא מין אחד ותמחוי אחד כו'. לעיל לא בעי למיפרך מכלל דסיפא משני מינין ושני תמחויין צריכא למימר שלא חש להאריך כיון דלא קאי הכי: מאן דאמר אשם ודאי לא בעי ידיעה בתחלה. פי' בקונטרס דאיכא פלוגתא דר' עקיבא ורבי טרפון בפרק דם שחיטה בכריתות (דף כב:) וליתא דהא תנן התם דדוקא במעילה מרובה קאמר ר"ע שמביא שתי אשמות משום דטוב לו שיביא שתי אשמות משיביא אשם אחד ויתנה שאם לא יודע לו תהא מעילתו נדבה אבל במעילה מועטת מודה ר"ע שמביא אשם אחד ויתנה ונוח לו שיתן מעילה מועטת על הספק משיביא שתי אשמות וקאמרינן בגמ' מדברי שניהם נלמד [א] אשם ודאי לא בעי ידיעה בתחלה ואם תאמר רבי טרפון דקאמר מה לזה מביא שתי אשמות משמע דעלה טובה קמ"ל אדרבה כיון דבמעילה מרובה פליגי אם כן טוב לו שיביא שתי אשמות כדאמר ר' עקיבא משיביא אשם אחד ומעילתו ויתנה כדפרישית יש לומר דר' טרפון לאו עלה טובה קאמר אלא לעולם אינו יוצא מידי עבירה בשתי אשמות אלא שיביא אשם ומעילתו ויתנה ואם תאמר ולרבי עקיבא אמאי מביא שתי אשמות במרובה ובמעוטה אשם ומעילה יביא לעולם אשם אחד ויתנה וכשיודע אז יביא מעילתו ויש לומר משום דאמר ד) המביא אשמו עד שלא הביא מעילתו לא יצא:

בעל

עין משפט נר מצוה

כ א מיי' פ"ו מהלכות שגגות הלכה ט:
כא ב שם הלכה י:
כב ג מיי' פ"ה מהלכות שגגות הלכה א ופ"ו הלכה א והלכה ט סמג עשין ריג:

רבינו חננאל

וחזקיה אמר בחמשה אברים וריש לקיש אמר אפי' באבר א' [משכחת לה] בכתף. ור' יוחנן אמר בחמשה מיני קדירה. ור' יצחק נפחא [אמר] בה' טעמים. והרי הוא כיון שהוא שני חצאי זית בב' תמחויין כמי שאינו שם חיוב חטאות היא וקתני מצטרפין וחייב חטאת. גם זה אע"פ שחלוקין הן לחטאות והן מצטרפו' ושנינן מי סברת הא דריש לקיש משום בר תוטיני ארישא הוא דקתני שאם אכל כחצי זית וחזר ואכל כחצי זית ממין אחד חייב במלתא דחלוקין לחטאות מוקמי ליה כר' יהושע וכגון שאכלו בב' תמחויין לא אסיפא היא דקתני סיפא אם אכל כחצי זית וחזר ואכל כחצי זית אחד משני מינין פטור עלה אמרי צריכא למימר. ואמר ר"ל משום [בר] תוטיני לעולם ממין אחד ואמאי (תני) [קרי] לה בב' מינין כגון שאכלן בב' תמחויין ור' יהושע היא תמחויין מתחלקין בין לקולא בין לחומרא ונמצא גם זו בדברים שאין חלוקין לחטאות ואקשינן אי הכי מדסיפא ב' חצאי מין אחד בב' תמחויין וקתני פטור רישא משום שהוא מין אחד בתמחוי אחד לפיכך חייב אמאי איצטריך למתניא להא פשיטא ומשני רבינא כגון שהיו ב' זיתי חלב בתמחוי אחד וכגון שאכל חצי זית אחד מהן ונודע לו והדר ושכח ואכל חצי זית האחר. ומתניתין רבן גמליאל היא דאמר [אין] ידיעה לחצי שיעור דתנן הכותב ב' אותיות בב' העלמות אחת בשחרית ואחת בין הערבים רבן גמליאל מחייב וחכמים פוטרין ואמרינן במאי פליגי רבן גמליאל סבר אין ידיעה לחצי שיעור ורבנן סברי יש ידיעה לחצי שיעור וכיון דרבן גמליאל סבר דאין ידיעה לחצי שיעו' כאלו אין שם ידיעה בינתים ובהעלם אחת כולן לפיכך חייב: אתמר אכל ב' זיתי חלב בהעלם אחד ונודע לו על הראשון וחזר ונודע לו על השני ר' יוחנן אומר חייב שתים ר"ל אומר אינו חייב אלא אחת ר' יוחנן אומר ידיעה מחלקת לפיכך חייב שתים. ר"ל אומר אין ידיעה מחלקת ואין חייב אלא חטאת אחת ר' יוחנן דריש על חטאתו והביא כיון שנודעה לו חטאתו נתחייב בה וכשיתודע לו השניה עוד מתחייב בה דאין אדם פורע חובו במה שכבר נתחייב בו ור"ל דריש מחטאתו ונסלח כל שהוא בהעלם אחד חטאת אחד הוא ומחטאתו ונסלח קרינן ביה. ור' יוחנן האי קרא דר"ל דריש ביה הכי מניין אם אכל כזית ומחצה ונודע לו על כזית ולא נודע לו על מחצה. וחזר ואכל זית אחד בהעלמו של שני מהו דתימא לצטרף עם חצי זית הראשון ויתחייב קמ"ל מחטאתו אם כבר נתכפר מקצת מחטאתו פטור בנשאר ור"ל האי על חטאתו והביא מיבעי ליה כשנודע לו על כזית אחד וכפר עליו. ולאחר שנתכפר לו [נודע לו] על כזית השני כגון זה מודה ר"ל דצריך קרבן והא דרב [אשי] ודרבינא לא מוכחא בהדיא במאי פליגי מיהו סוגיא דשמעתא לדברי הכל לאחר כפרה דראשון נודע לו השני צריך חטאת שניה והא סברא דרבה ואביי בגרירה פליגא אתרווייהו דהא אוקימנא דלתרווייהו לר' יוחנן ולר"ל כשנודע לו לאחר שנתכפר על הראשון צריך חטאת שניה ורבה אמר אכל ב' זיתי חלב בהעלם אחד ונודע לו על אחד מהן וחזר ואכל כזית אחד בהעלמו של שני הביא קרבן על הראשון ראשון ושני מתכפר (הוה) [אלמא] ודאי אם נודע לו על השני אחר שנתכפר על הראשון אינו חייב על השני קרבן אחר שכבר נתכפר בגרירה עם הראשון ודאביי עדיפא מדרבא וקיי"ל כוותייהו דאינון בתראי: **אמר** עולא לדברי האומר אשם ודאי לא בעי ידיעה בתחלה

מסורת הש"ס

א) לקמן קב. [קה. וש"נ], ב) [לקמן לד.], ג) [שם], ד) [כ"ק קיא.].

הגהות הב"ח

(א) גמ' ספוקי מספקא להו ואם תימצי וכו' הפרשה פליגי ר' יוחנן כצ"ל ותיבת בה נמחק: (ב) רש"י ד"ה קא משמע לן דהאי כצ"ל ותיבת כיון נמחק: (ג) ד"ה הכי גרסי' וכו' ולמחוק הוי"ו דאם תמצי לומר קאמר ולהגיה:

גליון הש"ס

רש"י ד"ה למ"ד אשם ודאי וכו' דהתם ספיקו איל. עיין מג"א סימן א ס"ק יא:

הגהות הגר"א

[א] תוס' ד"ה מאן. מדברי שניהם נלמד כו'. נ"ב אבל הוא רבי יוסי (וכ"כ הרז"ה והרמב"ן בחדושיו דלא כרש"ל) דבעי ידיעה בתחלה כמ"ש [כריתות דף ז' ב'] מודה ר"י במחוסר כפרה מ"ט התם בעי גברא ידיעה כו' וזהו מחולק שם ר"י ור"ש:

תורה אור השלם

א) אוֹ הוֹדַע אֵלָיו חַטָּאתוֹ אֲשֶׁר חָטָא וְהֵבִיא קָרְבָּנוֹ שְׂעִירַת עִזִּים תְּמִימָה נְקֵבָה עַל חַטָּאתוֹ אֲשֶׁר חָטָא: [ויקרא ד, כח]

ב) וְאֶת כָּל חֶלְבּוֹ יַקְטִיר הַמִּזְבֵּחָה כְּחֵלֶב זֶבַח הַשְּׁלָמִים וְכִפֶּר עָלָיו הַכֹּהֵן מֵחַטָּאתוֹ וְנִסְלַח לוֹ: [ויקרא ד, כו]

ליקוטי רש"י

אין ידיעה לחצי שיעור. לחלק כדי שלא יצטרף עמו חצי האחר [לקמן קה.]. אכל חצי שיעור ונודע לא הויא ידיעה לחלק דאם חזר ואכל חצי שיעור מצטרפין [כריתות יב:]. למ"ד אשם ודאי. כי אתייה מספק על תנאי עולה לו לאשם ודאי כי מתידע ליה [שם כב:].

רב נסים גאון

אחד ואחד ובגמרא גרסי היכי דמי ה' תמחויין אמר שמואל כאותה ששנינו חמשה דברים בעולה מצטרפין הבשר והחלב והיין והסולת והשמן חזקיה אמר כגון שאכל מה' אברים ר"ל אמר אפילו תימא באבר אחד משכחת לה בכתף ר' יצחק אמר כגון שאכל בה' מיני קדירה ר' יוחנן אמר כגון שאכלה בה' טעמים: **ורבן** גמליאל הוא דאמר אין ידיעה לחצי שיעור. בפרק הבונה (לקמן דף קה) הכותב ב' אותיות בב' העלמות אחת בשחרית ואחת בין הערבים רבן גמליאל מחייב וחכמים פוטרים ובגמ' גרסי במאי קא מיפלגי רבן גמליאל סבר אין ידיעה לחצי שיעור: **אמר** עולא למאן דאמר אשם ודאי לא בעי ידיעה בתחילה. משכחת לה במס' כריתות בפרק דם שחיטה (דף כב) אמר ר' טרפון ומה לזה מביא ב' אשמות אמר לו ר' עקיבא נראין דבריך במעילה כו' ובגמ' גרסי אמר רבא מדברי שניהם נלמוד אשם ודאי לא בעי ידיעה בתחילה ומכלל זו המימרא נלמוד כי מי שחולק על ר"ע ור' טרפון בדבר הזה סובר שאשם ודאי בעי ידיעה בתחילה וזה האשם נידון כחטאת מה חטאת בעינן ידיעה בתחילה אף אשם ודאי נמי בעי ידיעה בתחלה:

ואלא

case] of discovery **before designation,** רַבִּי יוֹחָנָן הֵיכִי מוֹקֵי לֵיהּ לִקְרָא – **how would R' Yochanan interpret the verse?** בִּכְזַיִת וּמֶחֱצָה – Perforce, **as** a case where someone first ate *cheilev* **the size of an olive and a half,** etc.[22] וְאִם תִּימְצֵי לוֹמַר לְאַחַר הַפְרָשָׁה פְּלִיגֵי – **And if you want to say that they disagree about** discovery **after designation,** רֵישׁ לָקִישׁ הֵיכִי מוֹקֵי לֵיהּ לִקְרָא – **how would Reish Lakish explain the verse?** בִּלְאַחַר כַּפָּרָה – Perforce, as a case where the second violation was discovered **after atonement** was effected for the first violation via an offering.[23]

The Gemara introduces another case of multiple infractions:[24]

אָמַר עוּלָּא – **Ulla said:** לְמַאן דְּאָמַר אָשָׁם וַדַּאי לֹא בָּעְיָא יְדִיעָה בַּתְּחִילָּה – **According to the one who holds that a definite** ***asham*** [25] **does not require prior awareness** of the violation to be effective,[26]

NOTES

22. That is, if R' Yochanan, in fact, required two offerings only when the second infraction was discovered after a *chatas* was already designated for the first infraction, he would have no problem with the verse cited by Reish Lakish. For he could certainly interpret that verse as referring to a case where the second infraction was discovered before any *chatas* was designated; in that case one offering would atone for both violations. But if R' Yochanan disputes Reish Lakish even if the second violation was discovered before any offering was designated, what does he do with the verse cited by Reish Lakish? To this the Gemara answered that he could interpret the verse as referring to a case of first eating the amount of one olive and a half etc. (*Rashi*).

23. [If we knew that Reish Lakish agrees that two offerings are required if the second violation was discovered after the *chatas* for the first was designated, he could interpret the verse cited by R' Yochanan as referring to such a case.] But if he holds that even when the *chatas* is already designated for the first violation, that offering will atone for both violations, what does he do with the verse cited by R' Yochanan, which indicates that a person is liable to a separate *chatas* for each violation? To this the Gemara answered above that he could interpret that verse as referring to a case where the second infraction was discovered after the *chatas* was already offered. In that case he must bring another offering to atone for his second violation even though both violations were committed during the same lapse of awareness (*Rashi*). The Gemara thus does not reach a conclusive decision about the extent of the dispute between R' Yochanan and Reish Lakish.

Above (71a), Rava and Abaye discussed a case which included a person who ate two olive-sized pieces of *cheilev* in the same lapse of awareness; both agreed that one *chatas* would atone for the two pieces even if one violation was discovered before the other. Now, if R' Yochanan and Reish Lakish disagree about discovery before designation, Rava and Abaye would have to concur with Reish Lakish, who holds that one offering suffices in such a case. But if R' Yochanan and Reish Lakish disagree only about discovery after designation, Rava and Abaye could concur with both R' Yochanan and Reish Lakish, since they would both agree that one offering is sufficient if the two violations are discovered before any *chatas* is designated (*Rashi* ד״ה וחזר ונודע; cf. *Rabbeinu Chananel;* see also *Kessef Mishneh* to *Hil. Shegagos* 6:11 and *Chazon Ish* 62:14).

[*Maharsha* notes a similar problem with the ruling of Abaye and Rava concerning the person who reaped and ground produce twice in the same lapse of awareness (above, 70b-71a). There too both Rava and Abaye agree that one *chatas* suffices even though the transgressor became aware of the violations at different times. *Shabbos Shel Mi* points out that this question is even more problematic since *Rashi* explained there (see 70b note 25) that the person had already designated an offering for the first set of violations. How, then, could that offering atone for the second set of violations, which were discovered later? See *Tosafos* there and *Pnei Yehoshua* here for further discussion of this issue.]

24. This case is cited here because it will become relevant to the aforementioned dispute between R' Yochanan and Reish Lakish (*Rashi* below, 72a ד״ה בעל; cf. *Maharsha* there).

25. The term "definite *asham*" is used for any *asham* other than the *asham talui* (literally: doubtful *asham*), which is an offering brought when one has grounds for suspecting that he inadvertently committed a transgression whose deliberate violation would be liable to *kares* and certain inadvertent violation would be subject to a *chatas*. *Rashi* lists three sins for which a definite *asham* is brought:

(a) אָשָׁם מְעִילוֹת, *asham for misuse of sacred objects.* If someone unintentionally used objects belonging to the Temple (*hekdesh*) for his personal benefit, he must atone by bringing an *asham* plus the value of the objects and a one-fifth surcharge. See *Leviticus* 5:14-16.

(b) אָשָׁם גְּזֵלוֹת, *asham for thefts.* If someone owed money (e.g. a loan, a theft, an article held in safekeeping) and falsely swore that he did not owe it, he is required to bring an *asham* as an atonement (upon admitting his liability). See ibid. 5:20-26.

(c) אָשָׁם שִׁפְחָה חֲרוּפָה, *asham for [sinning with] a betrothed slave-woman.* This refers to a Canaanite slavewoman [שִׁפְחָה כְּנַעֲנִית] who has been designated as the mate of a Hebrew servant [עֶבֶד עִבְרִי]. Should another man cohabit with her, he is not subject to the standard adultery penalty (execution for deliberate violation, a *chatas* for inadvertence) because the regular state of marriage does not exist for a Canaanite slave. Rather, the transgressor – whether deliberate or inadvertent – is liable to the penalty of an *asham* (see *Leviticus* 19:20-22; *Kereisos* 10b-11a for further details of the exact case).

26. According to this opinion, an *asham* can effect atonement even though the person was not aware of his violation at the time the offering was sacrificed. This dispute is found in Tractate *Kereisos* (22a), where R' Akiva obligates someone who is unsure if he benefited from *hekdesh* to bring an *asham talui.* A typical case would be where there were two pieces of meat – one consecrated as *hekdesh* and one that was unconsecrated – and the person ate one piece but could not identify it. [An *asham talui* is usually brought in cases where certain violation would be subject to a *chatas.* Here, though, if the person had certainly benefited from *hekdesh* he would be liable to a definite *asham.* Nevertheless, R' Akiva states that if he is unsure if he committed this violation he is obligated to bring an *asham talui.*] Furthermore, just as in the usual case of an *asham talui* the person is obligated to bring a *chatas* if he ever determines that he committed the sin, here also he will have to bring a definite *asham* if he ever determines that he did, in fact, benefit from *hekdesh.* At that point he would also be obligated to pay the value of the item and the one-fifth surcharge to *hekdesh.* R' Tarfon, though, disagrees with R' Akiva, stating that the *asham talui* can atone as much as the definite *asham* can, since they are the same type of offering. This case is thus unlike the typical case of an *asham talui,* where the person is obligated to bring a female *chatas* if he finds out that he definitely sinned; then, his male ram brought as the *asham talui* cannot effect the atonement that the *chatas* can effect. However, in this case the person can bring one male ram and money equal to the value of the item plus one-fifth and stipulate that if he did benefit from *hekdesh,* the offering should be a definite *asham* and the money should serve as payment to *hekdesh*; and if the doubt will never be resolved, the animal should be an *asham talui* and the money a donation to *hekdesh.* Now, according to R' Tarfon, if the person eventually discovers that he did, in fact, eat the consecrated piece, he need not bring another *asham* because his prior offering already effected atonement – even though he was not aware of the violation at the time that *asham* was offered. It thus follows that according to his view a definite *asham* does not require prior knowledge to effect atonement (*Rashi*). Ulla now states another consequence of R' Tarfon's position.

Rashi apparently holds that R' Akiva is the Tanna who grants significance to awareness regarding an *asham* (see also below, 72a ד״ה במעשה). *Tosafos* and other Rishonim, though, disagree with him on this point. [See *Pnei Yehoshua* and *Even HaOzeir* for possible defenses of *Rashi.*]

[*Magen Avraham* (*Orach Chaim* 1:11; see also *Ran MHK* ed.) notes another difficulty. *Rashi* indicates that the reason a person with a typical possible transgression cannot bring one animal and stipulate that it should be a *chatas* if he actually sinned is because a *chatas* is a different type of animal than an *asham talui.* But why did *Rashi* not simply state that this stipulation would not work because a *chatas* certainly does not atone if the person is not yet aware of his sin? See *Eishel Avraham* loc. cit., *Chasam Sofer, Bechor Shor,* and *Yad David* here for various approaches to this issue.]

בָּעַל חָמֵשׁ בְּעִילוֹת בְּשִׁפְחָה חֲרוּפָה – if **one cohabits** inadvertently **five times with a betrothed slavewoman,**[1] אֵינוֹ חַיָּיב אֶלָּא אַחַת – **he is liable to only one** *asham* even if the violations were committed during different lapses of awareness.[2]

The Gemara asks:

מַתְקִיף לָהּ רַב הַמְנוּנָא – **Rav Hamnuna challenged him:** אֶלָּא מֵעַתָּה – **But now,** בָּעַל וְחָזַר וּבָעַל וְהִפְרִישׁ קָרְבָּן – if **someone cohabited** with a betrothed slavewoman, **then cohabited** again, **and designated a sacrifice** for his violations,[3] וְאָמַר הַמְתִּינוּ לִי עַד שֶׁאֶבְעוֹל – **and he said, "Wait for me until I cohabit** another time,"[4] הָכִי נַמִּי דְּאֵינוֹ חַיָּיב אֶלָּא אַחַת – **is it so that he is liable to only one** *asham* for all of his violations?[5]

Ulla responds:

אָמַר לֵיהּ – **He said to him:** מַעֲשֶׂה דִּלְאַחַר הַפְרָשָׁה קָאָמְרַת – **Are you mentioning a** sinful **act after designation** of the *asham*? מַעֲשֶׂה דִּלְאַחַר הַפְרָשָׁה לָא קָאָמִינָא – **I was not discussing** the case of **an act after designation** of the *asham*.[6]

The Gemara presents another statement about a betrothed slavewoman:

כִּי אֲתָא רַב דִּימִי אָמַר – **When Rav Dimi came** to Babylonia from Eretz Yisrael, **he said:** לְמַאן דְּאָמַר אָשָׁם וַדַּאי בָּעֵי יְדִיעָה בַּתְּחִלָּה – **According to the one who holds that a definite** ***asham*** **requires prior knowledge** of the violation to be effective,[7] בָּעַל חָמֵשׁ בְּעִילוֹת בְּשִׁפְחָה חֲרוּפָה – if **one cohabits** inadvertently **five times with a betrothed slavewoman** during different lapses of awareness, חַיָּיב עַל כָּל אַחַת וְאַחַת – **he is liable** to a separate *asham* **for each and every one** of his acts.[8]

The Gemara asks:

אָמַר לֵיהּ אַבָּיֵי – **Abaye said to him:** הֲרֵי חַטָּאת – But **there is** the case of **a** ***chatas,*** דִּבְעֵינַן יְדִיעָה בַּתְּחִלָּה – **where we** certainly **require prior knowledge** for it to be effective,[9] וּפְלִיגֵי רַבִּי יוֹחָנָן וְרַבִּי שִׁמְעוֹן בֶּן לָקִישׁ – **and** nevertheless **R' Yochanan and Reish Lakish disagree** about whether awarenesses separate multiple transgressions into distinct liabilities.[10] Here too, in the case of the betrothed slavewoman, Reish Lakish should hold that one *asham* suffices for all of the violations even if an *asham* requires prior knowledge to be effective.[11] – ? –

NOTES

1. See 71b note 25 for a description of this prohibition. This case refers to someone cohabiting with the same betrothed slavewoman five times. If he did so with five different women, he would certainly be liable to a separate *asham* for each infraction under all circumstances (*Meiri,* from *Kereisos* 9a).

2. That is, if he cohabited with a betrothed slavewoman inadvertently numerous times, even if he became aware of each previous sin in the intervals, he is liable to only one *asham*. [Although no one disputes the fact that if someone eats *cheilev* twice during different lapses of awareness he is liable to two *chatas* offerings, a case involving an *asham* is different.] Since according to R' Tarfon a definite *asham* does not require prior awareness to be effective, it is evident that awareness is not significant with regard to the *asham*. Hence, even if the transgressor became aware of each violation prior to committing the next inadvertent sin, it is no different than if he had committed all of them during the same lapse of awareness, and he is liable to only a single *asham* (*Rashi*).

The Mishnah in *Kereisos* (9a) states that one is liable to only one *asham* for violation of the betrothed-slavewoman law even if he transgressed it many times. That Mishnah refers to deliberate violations, since one is liable to a sacrifice for deliberate violation, as well as inadvertent violation, of the betrothed-slavewoman law, and it is regarding a case of deliberateness where the Torah indicates that one *asham* suffices for numerous violations. It is also certain that if someone cohabited with a slavewoman numerous times inadvertently during the same lapse of awareness, he would be liable to only one *asham* [because this is no worse than violating a *chatas*-bearing sin numerous times during the same lapse of awareness]. At issue is if a person would be liable to only one *asham* even if he became aware of each violation before committing the next (*Rashi*). Further ramifications of Ulla's choice of the case of a betrothed slavewoman [rather than a different *asham*-bearing sin such as benefiting from *hekdesh*] will be discussed below (see note 15).

3. *Hagahos HaBach* deletes the clause *he then cohabited [again],* because at issue here is the violation committed subsequent to the designation of the *asham*. The fact that there were *two* previous violations for which the *asham* was designated is not relevant. See also the version quoted in *Tosafos*. [See *Even HaOzeir* for a defense of our version.]

4. I.e. he instructs the Kohen not to offer the *asham* until he cohabits again (*Rashi*).

5. Rav Hamnuna asks that if awareness between violations is not significant enough to separate them into distinct liabilities, then awareness along with designation of the offering should also not separate the violations into distinct liabilities. Thus, the *asham* should atone even for violations committed after it was designated (*Ritva MHK* ed.; see *Tosafos*).

6. Ulla concedes that an *asham* can atone only for those violations that were committed before its designation. This is so because designating an offering for a violation is a more significant act than merely becoming aware of the violation. Hence, once the *asham* is designated, it will not atone for future violations (*Ritva MHK* ed.).

7. According to *Rashi* (see above, 71b note 26) this refers to R' Akiva, who holds that a person who was unsure if he benefited from *hekdesh* and brought an *asham talui* for that possible violation must bring a definite *asham* if he discovers that he, in fact, sinned. The *asham talui* cannot effect atonement since he was not yet aware of his transgression when the *asham* was offered. Thus, according to this view, awareness is significant for an *asham* like it is for a *chatas*.

Rav Dimi does not disagree with Ulla; he merely explains what R' Akiva holds in the case of the betrothed-slavewoman prohibition, while Ulla was explaining the view of R' Tarfon (*Rashi*).

8. Thus, according to R' Akiva, who holds that awareness is significant with regard to an *asham,* if a person commits violations inadvertently during different lapses of awareness, he is liable to an *asham* for each. According to this view, the Mishnah in *Kereisos,* which states that a person is liable to only one *asham* for numerous transgressions of the betrothed slavewoman prohibition, refers either to deliberate violations or to inadvertent violations committed in the same lapse of awareness; only then will the person receive atonement for all of them with a single *asham* (*Rashi*).

9. If someone brings a *chatas* before he becomes aware of his violation, it does not effect atonement for him. This is based on the verse about the *chatas* that states (*Leviticus* 4:28): *If the sin that he committed becomes known to him, he shall bring as his offering a she-goat, unblemished, for his sin that he committed* (*Rashi*). This indicates that the person can bring his *chatas* only after becoming aware of his sin. The case of a *chatas*-bearing sin is therefore analogous to the *asham*-bearing prohibition of the betrothed slavewoman according to R' Akiva, who holds that an *asham* requires prior awareness to be effective.

10. [We learned above (71b) that R' Yochanan and Reish Lakish disagree about the significance of awareness of violation in the case of multiple violations of a *chatas*-bearing sin committed in the same lapse of awareness.] According to R' Yochanan, if the person became aware of these violations at different times, he is obligated to bring a separate *chatas* for each. It thus emerges that regarding the number of offerings required for atonement, awareness of a violation is tantamount to bringing an offering for it. That is why when the person subsequently discovers he had committed another violation, he needs a new offering to atone for that one. Reish Lakish, though, states that even if the person becomes aware of his violations at different times, one *chatas* atones for all of the violations committed during one lapse. Obviously then, Reish Lakish does not consider awareness of a violation to be equivalent in any way to offering a sacrifice for it (*Rashi* here and above ד״ה בעל).

11. Abaye asks that even if a definite *asham* requires prior awareness, the case of a betrothed slavewoman is different than other prohibitions because a person can bring only one *asham* to atone for many violations he committed deliberately. Hence, just as a single *asham* atones for many deliberate violations of that law (see above, note 1), a single *asham* should also atone for multiple inadvertent violations committed during different lapses of awareness. Only when an *asham* is actually offered [or at least designated] for a previous transgression should that

בעל חמש בעילות בשפחה חרופה (א) אינו חייב אלא אחת מתקיף לה רב המנונא אלא מעתה בעל (א) וחזר ובעל והפריש קרבן ואמר המתינו לי עד שאבעול הכי נמי דאינו חייב אלא אחת א"ל מעשה דלאחר הפרשה קאמרת [א]מעשה דלאחר הפרשה לא קאמינא כי אתא רב דימי אמר למאן דאמר אשם ודאי בעי ידיעה בתחלה [ב]בעל חמש בעילות בשפחה חרופה חייב על כל אחת ואחת אמר ליה אביי הרי חטאת דבעינן ידיעה בתחלה ופליגי ר' יוחנן ורבי שמעון בן לקיש אישתיק אמר ליה דלמא [ג]במעשה דלאחר הפרשה קאמרת וכדרב המנונא א"ל אין כי אתא רבין אמר הכל מודים בשפחה חרופה והכל מודים בשפחה חרופה ומחלוקת בשפחה חרופה הכל מודים בשפחה חרופה דאינו חייב אלא אחת כדעולא והכל מודים בשפחה חרופה דחייב על כל אחת ואחת כרב המנונא ומחלוקת בשפחה חרופה למ"ד אשם ודאי בעי ידיעה בתחלה מחלוקת דרבי יוחנן ורבי שמעון בן לקיש: איתמר

נתכוין

רש"י

בעל ה' בעילות בשפחה חרופה. בשוגג ונודע לו בין כל אחת ואחת אינו חייב אלא אחת להכי נקט שפחה חרופה משום דמביא קרבן אחד על עבירות הרבה כדתנן בכריתות (דף ט.) ה' מביאין קרבן אחד על עבירות הרבה הבא על השפחה ביאות הרבה וכו' וכי תנן מתני' דנפטר בקרבן אחד הני מילי במזיד שהוא מן המביאים על המזיד כשוגג דכתיב (ויקרא יט) בקורת תהיה ומלקות בשוגג ליכא וגבי מזיד רבי קרא דנפטר בקרבן אחד על ביאות הרבה כדיליף התם וכ"ש על ביאות שוגג הרבה בהעלם אחד אבל שוגג ונודע לו בין ביאה לביאה למאן דבעי ידיעה בתחלה באשם ודאי חשיב הוא לחלק לאשמות כהבאת כפרה המחלקת לעושה מזיד וצריך להביא על כל אחת ואחת אליבא דר' יוחנן דאמר לעיל באוכל שני זיתי חלב בהעלם אחד ונודע לו בשתי ידיעות שמביא חטאת על כל אחת ואחת דחשיבא ליה חילוק ידיעה כאילו הביא קרבן בין ידיעה לידיעה הכא נמי חשיב חילוק ידיעה כאילו הביא קרבן בין ביאה לביאה ואשמעינן עולא דלמאן דלא בעי ידיעה באשם בתחלה אינה חשובה לחלק בינתים ואינו חייב אלא אחת דכיון דלא חשיבא ליה ידיעה לא מחלקת והא מילתא דעולא נקט לה הכא משום דרב דימי דאיירי עלה ופרכינן עלה מפלוגתא דרבי יוחנן ור"ש לקיש: המתינו. שלא תקריבוהו עד שאבעול עוד: כי אתא רב דימי. לא פליג אדעולא אלא מר אמר חדא ומר אמר חדא: חייב על כל אחת ואחת. קס"ד השתא לרב דימי הא דתנן הבא על השפחה ביאות הרבה אינו חייב אלא אחת הני מילי מזיד אי נמי שוגג בהעלם אחד אבל שוגג ונודע לו בינתים למאן דחשיבא ליה ידיעה באשם מחלקת ואפילו לר"ש לקיש: והרי חטאת דבעי ידיעה בתחלה. שאם הביא חטאתו קודם שנודע לו החטא אינה מכפרת דכתיב (ויקרא ד) או הודע אליו והביא: ופליגי ר' יוחנן ור"ש לקיש. וקאמר ר"ש לקיש דאין ידיעות מחלקות להתחייב בשתים על שני זיתי חלב בהעלם אחד אלמא לא חשיבא ליה חילוק ידיעה כחילוק כפרה וגבי שפחה חרופה בידיעות שבין ביאה לביאה לאו כהבאת קרבן חשיבי לחלק וכי היכי דבמזיד דידיה מביא אחת על כולן הכא נמי מביא אחת על כולן ולא דמי לידיעות שבין אכילת חלב לאכילת חלב שמחלקות לדברי הכל דהתם חיובי אשגגות הוא וכיון שיש ידיעה בינתים הוין ליה שתי שגגות: אמר ליה אביי דילמא. הא דפשטת דלמאן דבעי ידיעה חייב ואפילו לריש לקיש: במעשה דלאחר הפרשה קאמרת. וכאתקפתא דרב המנונא דלעיל אבל בידיעה דקודם אפילו לר"ע פלוגתא דרבי יוחנן וריש לקיש היא לרבי יוחנן דחשיבא ליה ידיעה לחלק באכילת חלב אפילו שתי אכילות שנאכלו בהעלם אחד ה"נ מחלקת וריש לקיש דאמר התם לא מחלקת ה"נ אפי' דבין ביאה לביאה לא מחלקת דבין ביאה לביאה דהכא כשתי אכילות דחלב בהעלם אחד ונודע לו על כל אחד ואחד לבדו דמיא: הכל מודים. ר' יוחנן וריש לקיש בשפחה חרופה דיש חילוק: והכל מודים. בה דאין חילוק: ומחלוקת. שניהם בה דלר' יוחנן יש חילוק ולריש לקיש אין חילוק וכולהו מפרש להו: כדעולא. למאן דלא בעי ידיעה בתחלה דאפי' ר' יוחנן מודה דלר' טרפון לא חשיבא ידיעה לחלק וכי א"ר יוחנן ידיעות מחלקות ואפילו בין שתים הנעשות בהעלם אחד ה"מ בחטאת דחשיב ידיעה דילה: והכל מודים. ואפילו ר"ל דיש חילוק ואפילו לרבי טרפון כגון בביאה שלאחר הפרשה כדרב המנונא: ומחלוקת. דרבי יוחנן ור"ל בשפחה חרופה ואליבא דמאן דחשיבא ליה ידיעה דאשם לר' יוחנן דאמר ידיעת חטאת הואיל וחשיבא היא מחלקת אפי' חטאת דהעלם אחד הכא נמי מחלקת בין דהעלם אחד בין דשתי העלמות ולר"ל דאמר ידיעה דחטאת אף על גב דחשיבא לא מחלקת עבירות דהעלם אחד הכא אפילו דשתי העלמות לא מחלקת וכדפרישית:

תוספות

בעל חמש בעילות בשפחה חרופה אינו חייב אלא אחת. אבל למאן דבעי ידיעה בתחלה הוי פלוגתא דרבי יוחנן וריש לקיש דלר' יוחנן כיון שהיא ידיעה (ב) שהיא גורמת כפרה מחלקת אפילו ידיעות של אחר הבעילות כ"ש ידיעות שבין ביאה לביאה דמחלקות ור"ל דסבר דידיעות לא מחלקות הכא בשפחה חרופה אפילו ידיעות שבין ביאה לביאה אין מחלקות אע"ג דגבי חלב מודה ר"ל דידיעות שבין אכילה לאכילה מחלקות לא דמי דהתם בשגגה תלה רחמנא וידיעות מחלקות אשגגות אבל בשפחה חרופה שמביא על הזדון כשגגה אין הידיעה חשובה לחלק אבל למאן דלא בעי ידיעה בתחלה אפילו רבי יוחנן מודה כיון שאין הידיעה גורמת כפרה דלא חשיבא לחלק אפי' בין ביאה לביאה כל שכן אחר כל המעשים וא"ת הניחא אי איכא אשם תלוי בשפחה חרופה אתי שפיר למאן דלא בעי ידיעה דאינו חייב אלא אחת שאין הידיעה גורמת כפרה שיכול להביא אשם ולהתנות כמו במעילה אבל אי לית בה אשם תלוי דהא לא אשכחן בשום מקום בשפחה חרופה אשם תלוי אמאי אינו חייב אלא אחת ליחייב שתים דהא צריך ידיעה אחת לכל הפחות דאם לא נודע לו לא היה יכול להביא שום קרבן והרי אותה ידיעה גורמת כפרה ויש לומר דאפי' אין אשם תלוי בשפחה חרופה יכול להביא אשם על תנאי ולהתנות בשלמים ואפילו למאן דאמר אין מביאין קדשים לבית הפסול דהשתא ממעט ליה מאכילתו מ"מ לא חשיב גורם כפרה כיון דאם עבר והתנה מה שעשה עשוי והא דנקט עולא שפחה חרופה ולא נקט מילתיה במעילה דגבי מעילה הוא דתנן דאשם ודאי לא בעי ידיעה משום דאתא לאשמעינן דאפי' בין מעשה למעשה לא חשיבא ידיעה לחלק אבל במעילה פשיטא דמחלקת כמו בחטאת [*] וכן משמע בפרק ד' מחוסרי כפרה (כריתות דף ט.) דאמר בעא מיניה ר' חייא טירנאה מר' יוחנן הבא על ה' שפחות בהעלם אחד מהו א"ל חייב על כל אחת ואחת ומ"ש מה' העלמות בשפחה אחת אמר ליה התם אין גופים מוחלקין הכא גופים מוחלקין והיינו למאן דלא בעי ידיעה אלמא דלא מחלקות אפי' ידיעות שבין ביאה לביאה ואית ספרים דגרסי במילתיה דעולא ונודע לו בין כל אחת ואחת והיינו כדפרישית וא"ת תפשוט מדעולא דלר' יוחנן ידיעות מחלקות וי"ל דעולא אתי"ל קאמר:

מתקיף לה רב המנונא אלא מעתה בעל והפריש קרבן כו'. תימה מאי פריך רב המנונא דאי קסבר דהפרשה מחלקת בין ביאה לביאה כשבעל במזיד בשוגג נמי יש לחלק והיכי מדמה ליה לידיעה שאין מחלקת במזיד ואי קסבר דאין הפרשה מחלקת במזיד הכי נמי דלא מחלקת בשוגג ונראה לר"י דהכי פריך כיון דלא מחלקת בין ידיעות שבין מעשים לידיעות שלאחר מעשים אלא מעתה הפרשות נמי דאין מחלקות לר"ל לאחר כל המעשים את"ל דבהפרשות פליגי ואפי' לר' יוחנן איכא למימר דהכא מודה דאין הפרשות מחלקות דדוקא גבי חטאת קאמר דמחלקות משום דאיכא נמי בהדי הפרשות ידיעות חשובות שגורמות כפרה אבל הכא דליכא אלא הפרשה לחודא אפי' רבי יוחנן מודה דלא מחלקת אחר כל המעשים ה"נ דלא מחלקת בין ביאה לביאה והא ודאי סברא היא דמחלקת ואין מתכפר בקרבן שכבר הפריש עבירה שאחר הפרשה אמר ליה מעשה דלאחר הפרשה לא קאמינא פי' איני משוה בין מעשה למעשה לאחר כל המעשים: **כי** אתא רב דימי אמר למ"ד בעי ידיעה כו'. השתא ס"ד דמיירי בידיעה וקאמר דאפי' לריש לקיש מחלקת כיון דגורמת כפרה ואפילו לאחר כל המעשים ולהכי פריך והרי חטאת כו' ומסיק דלאחר הפרשה קאמר ואומר ר"י דרב דימי פליג אדעולא מדנקט למ"ד בעי ידיעה משמע אבל למאן דלא בעי ידיעה לא שמשוה אותו להפרשה דלאחר כל המעשים ואין לתמוה על סברא דרב דימי דה"נ עולה מכפרת אעשה דלאחר הפרשה אף על גב דבעיא היא בפרק קמא דזבחים (דף ו.) ולא איפשיט דדחי ליה הש"ס בסוף הסוגיא דחויא בעלמא הוא א"נ התם בעי אליבא דעולא דאמר הכא דאין קרבן מכפר אעבירה דאחר הפרשה דילמא עולה דדורון היא מכפרת א"נ אין רוצה לפשוט התם מדברי האמוראים אלא ממשנה או מברייתא כדאשכחן בפרק [אין בין המודר] (נדרים דף לה:[ג]) ורשב"א מפרש דהא דנקט למאן דבעי ידיעה רבותא נקט דאפי' לדידיה לא מיחייב לר"ל על כל אחת אלא במעשה דלאחר הפרשה ולא פליג אעולא:

רבינו חננאל

בעל ה' בעילות שפחה חרופה אינו חייב אלא אחת עיקר זה בברייתא במשנה פרק ד' מחוסרי כפרה (כריתות ט) אלו מביאין קרבן על עבירות הרבה ועל הזדון כשגגה וחד מינייהו הבא על שפחה חרופה ואמרינן עלה תני תנא קמיה דר' אלעזר וכפר עליו הכהן באיל האשם מלמד שמביא קרבן אחד על עבירות הרבה באיל האשם ונסלח לו מלמד שמביא על הזדון כשגגה ואקשינן והא עיקר קרבן במזיד כתיב. דכתיב בקרת תהיה. פי' מלקות ואין מלקות אלא במזיד ובמקום שהיא חייבת מלקות הוא חייב קרבן ושנינן אימא מלמד שמביא קרבן על השגגה כזדון והתם פליגי אית דאמר דכד בעיל שפחה חרופה בשגגה בעי ידיעה בתחלה כדבעי לענין חטאת דעלמא וכדמפרשינן השוכח עיקר שבת מכלל דהוי ליה ידיעה ואית מאן דאמר כיון דמזיד ושוגג כי הדדי מייתי אף שוגג שלא היתה לו ידיעה בתחלה מייתי אשם וקאמר עולא למ"ד לא בעי ידיעה בתחלה סבר דהא לא דמיא הא שגגה לשגגת חטאת דעלמא וכשם שבזודן מביא קרבן אחד על בעילות הרבה הכי נמי שוגג אם בעל כמה בעילות בכמה העלמות או מהן בזודן ומהן בשגגה אינו מביא אלא קרבן אחד. ואתקיף עליה רב המנונא אלא מעתה בעל ונודע לו וכיון שנודע לו עמד והפריש קרבן ואמר המתינו לא תקריבוהו עד שאבעול ובעל הכי נמי דאינו חייב בבעילה אחרונה קרבן אחר. ודחי עולא ואמר מעשה דלאחר הפרשה קאמרת כלומר בעילה דלאחר הפרשה לא קאמינא שמתכפר בקרבן ראשון. כי אתא רב דימי אמר לדברי האומר אשם ודאי בעי ידיעה בתחלה וכי כמו חטאת דעלמא (אינו) [אילו] בעל הני חמש בעילות בשפחה כגון שבעל בשפחה חרופה שוגג ה' בעילות ונודע לו על הראשונה. והפריש קרבן וחזר ונודע לו על השניה ואח"כ על השלישית ואח"כ על הרביעית ועדיין לא הקריבו ונודע לו ה' פעמים כי האי גוונא חייב ה' אשמות ולא תימא כיון דשוגג ומזיד בשפחה חרופה דינם שוה ידיעתו בכל אחת ואחת לא מהניא דהא אילו היו אלו ה' בעילות כולן במזיד מתחלה עד סוף אינו חייב בהן [אלא אחת] אלא כשם דמהניא ידיעה לגבי חטאת לחייב על כל ידיעה וידיעה הכי [נמי] מהניא גבי אשמות אמר ליה אביי והא חטאות דלדברי הכל בעינן ידיעה בתחלה וכשעשה כמה עבירות בהעלם א' שהוא חייב על כל אחת ואחת. דלמא (בידיעה ולאחר) [במעשה דלאחר] הפרשה קאמרת כדרב המנונא דאוקימנא בבעילה דלאחר הפרשה א"ל רב דימי אין כי אתא רבין אמר הכל מודין בשפחה חרופה שאינו חייב אלא אחת כדעולא. פי' הכל מודין הוא ר' יוחנן דמחייב על כל ידיעה חטאת בשפחה חרופה מודה דכיון דשוגג כמזיד הוא לא דמיא ידיעתו כידיעת חטאת וכדעולא. הכל מודין בשפחה חרופה דחייב על כל אחת ואחת פי' אפילו ריש לקיש מודה שאם בעל והפריש עליה קרבן וחזר ובעל שאינו מתכפר בקרבן שהפריש על הראשונה אלא חייב קרבן אחר וכ"ש ר' יוחנן ולא גמרינן הפרשה דלאחר מעשה מקמי ידיעה והפרשה דקמי מעשה דאיכא למימר בהפרשה דמקמי מעשה מודה ר"ל דהא בעידן דמפריש האי קרבן לא הוה עליה זיקת עבירה אחרת. והאי קרבן הוה לו לאותה עבירה בלבד לפיכך אם אח"כ עבר עבירה אחרת חייב עליה אבל האי דהוו עליה ה' עבירות בהעלם אחד. ואילו נודע לו על כולן כאחד אין חייב אלא קרבן אחד כך אפילו אם נודע לו על אחת מהן והפריש עליה קרבן ואח"כ נודע לו על השאר כיון שעדיין לא נקרבה החטאת שהפריש מ"ט כולהו בני בקתא דהדדי נינהו וכולהו אית להו דרב המנונא ומחלוקת בשפחה חרופה למ"ד אשם ודאי בעי ידיעה ובפלוגתא

עין משפט נר מצוה

כג א ב ג מיי' פי"ט מהלכות שגגות הלכה ו:

מסורת הש"ס

א) פ"א ונודע לו בין כל אחת ואחת, ב) [ועי' תוספות יומא דף עו: ד"ה מי איכא וקדושין כג: ד"ה דאמר וב"ק פו: ד"ה בישו וב"מ דף יח: ד"ה מן].

הגהות הב"ח

(א) גמ' אלא מעתה בעל והפריש כצ"ל ומיבות וחזר ובעל נמחק: (ב) תוס' ד"ה בעל וכו' שהיא ידיעה חשובה שהיא גורמת:

גליון הש"ס

תוס' ד"ה בעל וכו'. וכ"מ בפ"ד מחוסרי כפרה. והכי מוכח מסוגיין דמיירי ע"כ בנודע בין ביאה לביאה. דאל"כ אחר כל הביאות אין ס"ד לומר דידיעות מחלקות הא כיון דלא בעי ידיעה מתחלה אפילו מיפר קודם שנודע לו על השניות ממילא כולם מתכפרים עמה כיון דמכפר בלא ידיעה. וא"כ בבעולה דממ"נ לא מנקט כבעל לאחר מעשה ודאי מחלקת כיון דלאו בהעלם אחת ולאחר כל המעשים פשיטא דל"ש לומר ידיעה מחלקת דהא הקרבן מכפר מיד על כולם תחלה. ומה"ט י"ל על קושית תוס' דלאין צריך כש"ס דלא בעי ידיעה מתחלה. ול"ל דהיינו לענין זה כבעל חמש בעילות ואח"כ כיפר על א' קודם כולם מתכפרין דלא בעי ידיעה מתחלה ודו"ק:

Rav Dimi's response:

אִישְׁתִּיק – He was silent.[12]

Abaye attempts to explain Rav Dimi's reasoning:

אָמַר לֵיהּ – [Abaye] said to [Rav Dimi]: דִּלְמָא בְּמַעֲשֶׂה דִּלְאַחַר הַפְּרָשָׁה קָאָמְרַתְּ – Perhaps you are discussing a sinful **act** committed **after the designation** of the *asham,*[13] **וְכִדְרַב הַמְנוּנָא – and in accordance with** the question asked by **Rav Hamnuna and** above?[14]

Rav Dimi replies:

אָמַר לֵיהּ – He said to [Abaye]: אִין – Yes, that is what I meant.[15]

The Gemara summarizes the rules pertaining to a betrothed slavewoman:

כִּי אֲתָא רָבִין אָמַר – When Ravin came from Eretz Yisrael, **he said: הַכֹּל מוֹדִים בְּשִׁפְחָה חֲרוּפָה – All agree about a betrothed slavewoman** that one is sometimes liable to a separate *asham* for each violation;[16] **וְהַכֹּל מוֹדִים בְּשִׁפְחָה חֲרוּפָה – and all agree about a betrothed slavewoman** that one is sometimes liable to only one *asham* for numerous violations; **וּמַחֲלוֹקֶת בְּשִׁפְחָה חֲרוּפָה – and there is a dispute about a betrothed slavewoman.**

The Gemara explains each of these three statements:

הַכֹּל מוֹדִים בְּשִׁפְחָה חֲרוּפָה דְּאֵינוֹ חַיָּיב אֶלָּא אַחַת – All [R' Yochanan and Reish Lakish] **agree about a betrothed slavewoman that one is liable to only one** *asham* for numerous violations when only awareness separates them, **כְּדְעוּלָּא – in accordance with** the statement of **Ulla.**[17] **וְהַכֹּל מוֹדִים בְּשִׁפְחָה חֲרוּפָה דְּחַיָּיב עַל כָּל אַחַת וְאַחַת – And all** [R' Yochanan and Reish Lakish] **agree about a betrothed slavewoman** that **one is liable** to a separate *asham* **for each and every one** of his violations when each new violation was committed after designation of an *asham* for the previous violation, **כְּרַב הַמְנוּנָא – in accordance with Rav Hamnuna.**[18] **וּמַחֲלוֹקֶת בְּשִׁפְחָה חֲרוּפָה – And there is a dispute about a betrothed slavewoman,** as follows: **לְמַאן דְּאָמַר אָשָׁם וַדַּאי בָּעֵי יְדִיעָה בַּתְּחִלָּה – According to the one who holds that a definite *asham* requires prior knowledge** to be effective, **מַחֲלוֹקֶת דְּרַבִּי יוֹחָנָן וְרַבִּי שִׁמְעוֹן בֶּן לָקִישׁ** – this is subject to **the dispute of R' Yochanan and Reish Lakish.**[19]

The Gemara cites another case, which will lead to further discussion about multiple Sabbath transgressions:

אִיתְּמַר – It was stated:

NOTES

transgression become separated from future transgressions. It is true that according to R' Yochanan a person can become liable to multiple *asham* offerings with mere awareness separating the violations, but that is because he holds that awareness of a violation is tantamount to bringing a sacrifice for it (see previous note). But according to Reish Lakish, who disagrees with R' Yochanan on this point, mere awareness between violations of the betrothed-slavewoman prohibition should not separate them into distinct liabilities — even if awareness is significant for other types of definite *asham*-offerings (*Rashi*).

Although everyone agrees that a person is liable to separate *chatas* offerings when he eats *cheilev* during different lapses of awareness, that is because in the case of such a sin, the person is liable to bring the *chatas* for his inadvertence. Therefore, when he becomes aware of his first violation, the subsequent violation is a new inadvertence for which he must bring another *chatas*. But the prohibition of the betrothed slavewoman is different because a person is liable to an *asham* even for deliberate transgression of that law (*Rashi*).

12. Rav Dimi did not regard Abaye's question as difficult.

13. It is regarding such a case that you said that according to the Tanna who requires prior awareness for an *asham* to be effective a person is liable to multiple *asham* offerings — even according to Reish Lakish (*Rashi*).

14. Above, Rav Hamnuna asked that an *asham* should certainly not atone for a violation committed after it was designated; it is in such a case that Rav Dimi could hold that even according to Reish Lakish one is liable to multiple *asham* offerings for cohabiting with a betrothed slavewoman during different lapses of awareness (*Rashi*; see next note).

15. Rav Dimi replies that he *was* discussing a person who committed a new violation after designating his *asham*. In that case even Reish Lakish agrees that he is liable to bring a new *asham* for the second violation. However, if the person committed violations and became aware of them before designating any *asham,* there are two factors to consider: (1) According to R' Tarfon, awareness is not considered significant for an *asham*. Hence, even if the person became aware of each inadvertent violation before committing the next, it is considered as if all of the violations were committed during the same lapse of awareness. (2) According to R' Akiva, awareness is significant to an *asham* like it is to a *chatas;* hence, awareness should play the same role regarding an *asham*-bearing violation as it does to a *chatas*-bearing one. The betrothed-slave-woman prohibition, though, is different than other sins because one is liable even for deliberate violation of the prohibition against cohabitation with a betrothed slavewoman. Hence, mere awareness of an inadvertent violation of this prohibition prior to the next should not have any effect; only the actual designation or offering of an *asham* in the intervals can separate violations into distinct liabilities. However, according to R' Yochanan, who holds that awareness of a violation is tantamount to offering a sacrifice for it, awareness would separate even betrothed-slavewoman violations into distinct liabilities. According to Reish Lakish, though, awareness is not tantamount to offering a sacrifice; hence, the person would be liable to only one *asham* even if he became aware of each violation prior to committing the next. In other words, according to his view, awareness *between* violations of the betrothed-slavewoman law is the same as separate discoveries of numerous *cheilev* violations *after* they were all committed during one lapse of awareness (*Rashi*).

It is because of these special considerations needed for the betrothed slavewoman law that Ulla initiated this discussion with that type of definite *asham* (see *Rashi* above ד״ה בעל).

[*Tosafos* note that Rav Dimi prefaced his statement by attributing it to the Tanna who grants significance to awareness regarding an *asham;* this implies that according to R' Tarfon, who does not grant awareness such significance, an already-designated *asham* would atone even for violations not yet committed. *Maharam* attempts to prove that *Rashi* too agrees with *Tosafos* in this matter, but *Ritva* (*MHK* ed.) accepts *Rashi's* earlier statement — that Rav Dimi does not dispute Ulla — at face value. Hence, once the *asham* is designated, it does not atone for any future violations according to anyone. See *Ritva* for further discussion.]

16. That is, R' Yochanan and Reish Lakish both agree in this case (*Rashi*).

17. Ulla stated that according to R' Tarfon, who does not consider awareness significant with regard to an *asham,* even R' Yochanan would agree that a person who cohabits with a betrothed slavewoman is liable to only one *asham* even though he became aware of each transgression before he committed the next one. According to this Tanna R' Yochanan could state that awareness separates violations into distinct liabilities only in the case of a *chatas*, where awareness is significant (*Rashi*).

18. Even Reish Lakish agrees that a person is liable to a new *asham* if he cohabits with a betrothed slavewoman after his first *asham* has already been designated. This is true even according to R' Tarfon (*Rashi*).

19. If awareness is significant to an *asham,* as R' Akiva holds, R' Yochanan and Reish Lakish would disagree in the case of a betrothed slavewoman, where one is liable to only one *asham* for deliberate transgression. According to R' Yochanan, since awareness is significant for a *chatas* even when the violations were committed during one lapse of awareness [i.e. awareness is tantamount to offering a sacrifice], here awareness would also separate the different cohabitations into separate liabilities whether they were performed in one lapse or separate lapses. According to Reish Lakish, if awareness does not separate *chatas*-bearing violations that were committed during one lapse, it cannot separate *asham*-bearing violations even when committed during different lapses, as explained above (*Rashi*).

Thus, if a person violated the betrothed-slavewoman prohibition twice during one lapse of awareness, his liability would be the same as that of a *chatas*-bearing sin according to R' Akiva — that is, it would be subject to the same dispute between R' Yochanan and Reish Lakish discussed above, 71b (see there, note 16). And even if the person performed these violations during *different* lapses of awareness, his liability would also be subject to the resultant dispute between R' Yochanan and Reish Lakish, discussed here.

גמרא

בעל חמש בעילות בשפחה חרופה [א] אינו חייב אלא אחת מתקיף לה רב המנונא אלא מעתה בעל (א) וחזר ובעל והפריש קרבן ואמר המתינו לי עד שאבעול הכי נמי דאינו חייב אלא אחת א"ל מעשה דלאחר הפרשה קאמרת [א] מעשה דלאחר הפרשה לא קאמינא כי אתא רב דימי אמר למאן דאמר אשם ודאי בעי ידיעה בתחלה [ב] בעל חמש בעילות בשפחה חרופה חייב על כל אחת ואחת אמר ליה אביי הרי חטאת דבעינן ידיעה בתחלה ופליגי ר' יוחנן ורבי שמעון בן לקיש אישתיק אמר ליה דלמא [ג] במעשה דלאחר הפרשה קאמרת וכדרב המנונא א"ל אין כי אתא רבין אמר הכל מודים בשפחה חרופה והכל מודים בשפחה חרופה ומחלוקת בשפחה חרופה הכל מודים בשפחה חרופה דאינו חייב אלא אחת כדעולא והכל מודים בשפחה חרופה דחייב על כל אחת ואחת כרב המנונא ומחלוקת בשפחה חרופה למ"ד אשם ודאי בעי ידיעה בתחלה מחלוקת דרבי יוחנן ורבי שמעון בן לקיש: איתמר

נתכוין

רש"י

בעל ה' בעילות בשפחה חרופה. בשוגג ונודע לו בין כל אחת ואחת אינו חייב אלא אחת להכי נקט שפחה חרופה משום דמביא קרבן אחד על עבירות הרבה כדתנן בכריתות (דף ט.) ה' מביאין קרבן אחד על עבירות הרבה הבא על השפחה ביאות הרבה וכו' וכי תנן מתני' דנפטר בקרבן אחד הני מילי במזיד שהוא מן המביאים על המזיד כשוגג דכתיב (ויקרא יט) בקורת תהיה ומלקות בשוגג ליכא וגבי מזיד רבי קרא דנפטר בקרבן אחד על ביאות הרבה כדיליף התם וכ"ש על ביאות שוגג הרבה בהעלם אחד אבל שוגג ונודע לו בין ביאה לביאה למאן דבעי ידיעה בתחלה באשם ודאי חשיב הוא לחלק לאשמות כהבאת כפרה המחלקת לעושה מזיד וצריך להביא על כל אחת ואחת אליבא דר' יוחנן דאמר לעיל באוכל שני זיתי חלב בהעלם אחד ונודע לו בשתי ידיעות שמביא חטאת על כל אחת ואחת דחשיבא ליה חילוק ידיעה כאילו הביא קרבן בין ידיעה לידיעה הכא נמי חשיב חילוק ידיעה כאילו הביא קרבן בין ביאה לביאה ואשמעינן עולא דלמאן דלא בעי ידיעה באשם בתחלה אינה חשובה לחלק בינתים ואינו חייב אלא אחת דכיון דלא חשיבא ליה ידיעה לא מחלקת והא מילתא דעולא נקט לה הכא משום דרב דימי דאיירי עלה ופרכינן עלה מפלוגתא דרבי יוחנן וריש לקיש: המתינו. שלא תקריבוהו עד שאבעול עוד: כי אתא רב דימי. לא פליג אדעולא אלא מר אמר חדא ומר אמר חדא: חייב על כל אחת ואחת. קס"ד השתא לרב דימי הא דתנן הבא על השפחה ביאות הרבה אינו חייב אלא אחת הני מילי מזיד אי נמי שוגג בהעלם אחד אבל שוגג ונודע לו בינתים למאן דחשיבא ליה ידיעה באשם מחלקת ואפילו לריש לקיש: והרי חטאת דבעי ידיעה בתחלה. שאם הביא חטאתו קודם שנודע לו החטא אינה מכפרת דכתיב (ויקרא ד) או הודע אליו והביא: ופליגי ר' יוחנן וריש לקיש. וקאמר ריש לקיש דאין ידיעות מחלקות להתחייב בשתים על שני זיתי חלב בהעלם אחד אלמא לא חשיבא ליה חילוק ידיעה כחילוק כפרה וגבי שפחה חרופה בידיעות שבין ביאה לביאה לאו כהבאת קרבן חשיבי לחלק וכי היכי דבמזיד דידיה מביא אחת על כולן הכא נמי מביא אחת על כולן ולא דמי לידיעות שבין אכילת חלב לאכילת חלב שמחלקות לדברי הכל דהתם חיובי אשגגות הוא וכיון שיש ידיעה בינתים הוין ליה שתי שגגות: אמר ליה אביי דילמא. הא דפשטת דלמאן דבעי ידיעה חייב ואפילו לריש לקיש: במעשה דלאחר הפרשה קאמרת. וכאתקפתא דרב המנונא דלעיל אבל בידיעה דקודם אפילו לר"ע פלוגתא דרבי יוחנן וריש לקיש היא לרבי יוחנן דחשיבא ליה ידיעה לחלק באכילת חלב אפילו שתי אכילות שנאכלו בהעלם אחד ה"נ מחלקת וריש לקיש דאמר התם לא מחלקת ה"נ אפי' דבין ביאה לביאה לא מחלקת דבין ביאה לביאה דהכא כשתי אכילות דחלב בהעלם אחד ונודע לו על כל אחד ואחד לבדו דמיא: הכל מודים. ר' יוחנן וריש לקיש בשפחה חרופה דיש חילוק: והכל מודים. בה דאין חילוק: ומחלוקת. שניהם בה דלר' יוחנן יש חילוק ולריש לקיש אין חילוק וכולהו מפרש להו: כדעולא. למאן דלא בעי ידיעה בתחלה דאפי' ר' יוחנן מודה דלר' טרפון לא חשיבא ידיעה לחלק וכי א"ר יוחנן ידיעות מחלקות ואפילו בין שתים הנעשות בהעלם אחד ה"מ בחטאת דחשיב ידיעה דילה: והכל מודים. ואפילו ר"ל דיש חילוק ואפילו לרבי טרפון כגון בביאה שלאחר הפרשה כדרב המנונא: ומחלוקת. דרבי יוחנן ור"ל בשפחה חרופה ואליבא דמאן דחשיבא ליה ידיעה דאשם לר' יוחנן דאמר ידיעת חטאת הואיל וחשיבא היא מחלקת אפי' חטאת דהעלם אחד הכא נמי מחלקת בין דהעלם אחד בין דשתי העלמות ולר"ל דאמר ידיעה דחטאת אף על גב דחשיבא לא מחלקת עבירות דהעלם אחד הכא אפילו דשתי העלמות לא מחלקת וכדפרישית:

נתכוין

תוספות

בעל חמש בעילות בשפחה חרופה אינו חייב אלא אחת. אבל למאן דבעי ידיעה בתחלה הוי פלוגתא דרבי יוחנן וריש לקיש דלר' יוחנן כיון שהיא ידיעה (ב) שהיא גורמת כפרה מחלקת אפילו ידיעות של אחר הבעילות כ"ש ידיעות שבין ביאה לביאה דמחלקות ור"ל דסבר דידיעות לא מחלקות הכא בשפחה חרופה אפילו ידיעות שבין ביאה לביאה אין מחלקות אע"ג דגבי חלב מודה ר"ל דידיעות שבין אכילה לאכילה מחלקות לא דמי דהתם בשגגה תלה רחמנא וידיעות מחלקות אשגגות אבל בשפחה חרופה שמביא על הזדון כשגגה אין הידיעה חשובה לחלק אבל למאן דלא בעי ידיעה בתחלה אפילו רבי יוחנן מודה כיון שאין הידיעה גורמת כפרה דלא חשיבא לחלק אפי' בין ביאה לביאה כל שכן אחר כל המעשים וא"ת הניחא אי איכא אשם תלוי בשפחה חרופה אתי שפיר למאן דלא בעי ידיעה דאינו חייב אלא אחת שאין הידיעה גורמת כפרה שיכול להביא אשם ולהתנות כמו במעילה אבל אי לית בה אשם תלוי דהא לא אשכחן בשום מקום בשפחה חרופה אשם תלוי אמאי אינו חייב אלא אחת ליחייב שתים דהא צריך ידיעה אחת לכל הפחות דאם לא נודע לו לא היה יכול להביא שום קרבן והרי אותה ידיעה גורמת כפרה ויש לומר דאפי' אין אשם תלוי בשפחה חרופה יכול להביא אשם על תנאי ולהתנות בשלמים ואפילו למאן דאמר אין מביאין קדשים לבית הפסול דהשתא ממעט ליה מאכילתו מ"מ לא חשיב גורם כפרה כיון דאם עבר והתנה מה שעשה עשוי והא דנקט עולא שפחה חרופה ולא נקט מילתיה במעילה דגבי מעילה הוא דתנן דאשם ודאי לא בעי ידיעה משום דאתא לאשמעינן דאפי' בין מעשה למעשה לא חשיבא ידיעה לחלק אבל במעילה פשיטא דמחלקת כמו בחטאת ° וכן משמע בפרק ד' מחוסרי כפרה (כריתות דף ט.) דאמר בעא מיניה ר' חייא טירנאה מר' יוחנן הבא על ה' שפחות בהעלם אחד מהו א"ל חייב על כל אחת ואחת ומ"ש מה' העלמות בשפחה אחת אמר ליה התם אין גופים מוחלקין הכא גופים מוחלקין והיינו למאן דלא בעי ידיעה אלמא דלא מחלקות אפי' ידיעות שבין ביאה לביאה ואית ספרים דגרסי במילתיה דעולא ונודע לו בין כל אחת ואחת והיינו כדפרישית וא"ת תפשוט מדעולא דלר' יוחנן ידיעות מחלקות וי"ל דעולא אמ"ל קאמר:

מתקיף לה רב המנונא אלא מעתה בעל והפריש קרבן כו'. תימה מאי פריך רב המנונא דאי קסבר דהפרשה מחלקת בין ביאה לביאה כשבעל במזיד בשוגג נמי יש לחלק והיכי מדמה ליה לידיעה שאין מחלקת במזיד ואי קסבר דאין הפרשה מחלקת במזיד הכי נמי דלא מחלקת בשוגג ונראה לר"י דהכי פריך כיון דלא מחלקת בין ידיעות שבין מעשים לידיעות שלאחר מעשים אלא מעתה הפרשות נמי דאין מחלקות לר"ל לאחר כל המעשים אא"ל דבהפרשות פליגי ואפי' לר' יוחנן איכא למימר דהכא מודה דאין הפרשות מחלקות דדוקא גבי חטאת קאמר דמחלקות משום דאיכא נמי בהדי הפרשות ידיעות חשובות שגורמות כפרה אבל הכא דליכא אלא הפרשה לחודא אפי' רבי יוחנן מודה דלא מחלקת אחר כל המעשים ה"נ דלא מחלקת בין ביאה לביאה והא ודאי סברא היא דמחלקת ואין מתכפר בקרבן שכבר הפריש עבירה שאחר הפרשה אמר ליה מעשה דלאחר הפרשה לא קאמינא פי' איני משוה בין מעשה למעשה לאחר כל המעשים: כי אתא רב דימי אמר למ"ד בעי ידיעה כו'. השתא ס"ד דמיירי בידיעה וקאמר דאפי' לריש לקיש מחלקת כיון דגורמת כפרה ואפילו לאחר כל המעשים ולהכי פריך והרי חטאת כו' ומסיק דלאחר הפרשה קאמר ואומר ר"י דרב דימי פליג אדעולא מדנקט למ"ד בעי ידיעה משמע אבל למאן דלא בעי ידיעה לא שמשוה אותו להפרשה דלאחר כל המעשים ואין לתמוה על סברא דרב דימי דה"נ עולה מכפרת אעשה דלאחר הפרשה אף על גב דבעיא היא בפרק קמא דזבחים (דף ו.) ולא איפשיט דדחי ליה הש"ס בסוף הסוגיא דחויא בעלמא הוא א"נ התם בעי אליבא דעולא דאמר הכא דאין קרבן מכפר אעבירה דאחר הפרשה דילמא עולה דדורון היא מכפרת א"נ אין רוצה לפשוט התם מדברי האמוראים אלא ממשנה או מברייתא כדאשכחן בפרק [אין בין המודר (נדרים דף לה:)[ג]] ורשב"א מפרש דהא דנקט למאן דבעי ידיעה רבותא נקט דאפי' לדידיה לא מיחייב לר"ל על כל אחת אלא במעשה דלאחר הפרשה ולא פליג אעולא:

נתכוין

עין משפט נר מצוה

כג א ב ג מיי' פ"ט מהלכות שגגות הלכה ו:

רבינו חננאל

בעל ה' בעילות שפחה חרופה אינו חייב אלא אחת עיקר זה בברייתא במשנה פרק ד' מחוסרי כפרה (כריתות ט) אלו מביאין קרבן על עבירות הרבה ועל הזדון כשגגה וחד מינייהו הבא על שפחה חרופה ואמרינן עלה תני תנא קמיה דר' אלעזר וכפר עליו הכהן באיל האשם מלמד שמביא קרבן אחד על עבירות הרבה באיל האשם ונסלח לו מלמד שמביא על הזדון כשגגה ואקשינן והא עיקר קרבן במזיד כתיב. דכתיב בקרת תהיה. פי' מלקות ואין מלקות אלא במזיד ובמקום שהיא חייבת מלקות הוא חייב קרבן ושנינן אימא מלמד שמביא קרבן על השגגה כזדון והתם פליגי אית דאמר דכד בעיל שפחה חרופה בשגגה בעי ידיעה בתחלה כדבעי לענין חטאת דעלמא וכדמפרשינן השוכח עיקר שבת מכלל דהוי ליה ידיעה ואית מאן דאמר כיון דמזיד ושוגג כי הדדי מייתי אף שוגג שלא היתה לו ידיעה בתחלה מייתי אשם וקאמר עולא למ"ד לא בעי ידיעה בתחלה סבר דהא לא דמיא הא שגגה לשגגת חטאת דעלמא וכשם שבזדון מביא קרבן אחד על בעילות הרבה הכי נמי שוגג אם בעל כמה בעילות בכמה העלמות או מהן בזדון ומהן בשגגה אינו מביא אלא קרבן אחד. ואתקיף עליה רב המנונא אלא מעתה בעל ונודע לו וכיון שנודע לו עמד והפריש קרבן ואמר המתינו לא תקריבוהו עד שאבעול ובעל הכי נמי דאינו חייב בבעילה אחרונה קרבן אחר. ודחי עולא ואמר מעשה דלאחר הפרשה קאמרת כלומר בעילה דלאחר הפרשה לא קאמינא שמתכפר בקרבן ראשון. כי אתא רב דימי אמר לדברי האומר אשם ודאי בעי ידיעה בתחלה וכי כמו חטאת דעלמא (אינו) [אילו] בעל הני חמש בעילות בשפחה כגון שבעל בשפחה חרופה שוגג ה' בעילות ונודע לו על הראשונה. והפריש קרבן וחזר ונודע לו על השניה ואח"כ על השלישית ואח"כ על הרביעית ועדיין לא הקריבו ונודע לו ה' פעמים כי האי גוונא חייב ה' אשמות ולא תימא כיון דשוגג ומזיד בשפחה חרופה דינם שוה ידיעתו בכל אחת ואחת לא מהניא דהא אילו היו אלו ה' בעילות כולן במזיד מתחלה עד סוף אינו חייב בהן [אלא אחת] אלא כשם דמהניא ידיעה לגבי חטאת לחייב על כל ידיעה וידיעה הכי [נמי] מהניא גבי אשמות אמר ליה אביי והא חטאות דלדברי הכל בעינן ידיעה בתחלה וכשעשה כמה עבירות בהעלם א' שהוא חייב על כל אחת ואחת. דלמא (בידיעה ולאחר) [במעשה דלאחר] הפרשה קאמרת כדרב המנונא דאוקימנא בבעילה דלאחר הפרשה א"ל רב דימי אין כי אתא רבין אמר הכל מודין בשפחה חרופה שאינו חייב אלא אחת כדעולא. פי' הכל מודין הוא ר' יוחנן דמחייב על כל ידיעה חטאת בשפחה חרופה מודה דכיון דשוגג כמזיד הוא לא דמיא ידיעתו כידיעת חטאת וכדעולא. הכל מודין בשפחה חרופה דחייב על כל אחת ואחת פי' אפילו ריש לקיש מודה שאם בעל והפריש עליה קרבן וחזר ובעל שאינו מתכפר בקרבן שהפריש על הראשונה אלא חייב קרבן אחר וכ"ש ר' יוחנן ולא גמרינן הפרשה דלאחר מעשה מקמי ידיעה והפרשה דקמי מעשה דאיכא למימר בהפרשה דמקמי מעשה מודה ר"ל דהא בעידן דמפריש האי קרבן לא הוה עליה זיקת עבירה אחרת. והאי קרבן הוה לו לאותה עבירה בלבד לפיכך אם אח"כ עבר עבירה אחרת חייב עליה אבל האי דהוו עליה ה' עבירות בהעלם אחד. ואילו נודע לו על כולן כאחד אין חייב אלא קרבן אחד כך אפילו אם נודע לו על אחת מהן והפריש עליה קרבן ואח"כ נודע לו על השאר כיון שעדיין לא נקרבה החטאת שהפריש מתכפרין כולן בזו החטאת שהפריש מ"ט כולהו בני בקתא דהדדי נינהו וכולהו אית להו דרב המנונא ומחלוקת בשפחה חרופה למ"ד אשם ודאי בעי ידיעה ובפלוגתא

מסורת הש"ס

א) ס"א ונודע לו בין כל אחת ואחת, ב) [ועי' תוספות יומא דף יט: ד"ה מי איכא וקדושין כג: ד"ה דאמר וב"ק פו: ד"ה ביישו וב"מ דף יז: ד"ה מן].

הגהות הב"ח

(א) גמ' אלא מעתה בעל והפריש כצ"ל ותיבות וחזר ובעל נמחק: (ב) תוס' ד"ה בעל וכו' שהיא ידיעה חשובה שהיא גורמת:

גליון הש"ס

תוס' ד"ה בעל וכו'. וכ"מ בפ"ד מחוסרי כפרה. והכי מוכח מסוגיין דמיירי ע"כ בנודע בין ביאה לביאה. דאלו אחר כל הביאות אין ס"ד לומר דידיעות מחלקות הא כיון דלא בעי ידיעה תחלה אפילו כיפר קודם שנודע לו על השניות ממילא כולם מתכפרים עמה כיון דמכפר בלא ידיעה. וא"כ ממילא לא מצי למנקט בבעולה דממ"נ בין מעשה למעשה ודאי מחלקת כיון דאינו בהעלם אחת ולאחר כל המעשים פשיטא דל"ש לומר ידיעה מחלקת דהא הקרבן מכפר מיד על כולם כיון דל"צ ידיעה תחלה. ומה"ט י"ל על קושיית תוס' דאיך שייך בש"ח דלא בעי ידיעה תחלה. די"ל דהיינו לענין זה בבעל חמש בעילות ואח"כ כיפר על א' קודם שנודע לו על אינך כולם מתכפרין דלא בעי ידיעה תחלה ודו"ק:

[א] נתכוין [א]להגביה את התלוש וחתך את המחובר פטור לחתוך את התלוש וחתך את המחובר [ב] רבא אמר [ב]פטור אביי אמר חייב רבא אמר פטור דהא לא נתכוון לחתיכה דאיסורא אביי אמר חייב דהא קמיכוין לחתיכה בעלמא אמר רבא מנא אמינא לה [ג] דתניא חומר שבת משאר מצות וחומר שאר מצות משבת חומר שבת משאר מצות שהשבת עשה שתים בהעלם אחד חייב על כל אחת ואחת מה שאין כן בשאר מצות וחומר שאר מצות משבת שבשאר מצות שגג בלא מתכוין חייב מה שאין כן בשבת: אמר מר חומר שבת משאר מצות שהשבת עשה שתים בהעלם אחד חייב על כל אחת ואחת מה שאין כן בשאר מצות היכי דמי אילימא דעבד קצירה וטחינה דכוותה גבי שאר מצות אכל חלב ודם הכא תרתי מיחייב והכא תרתי מיחייב אלא שאר מצות דלא מיחייב אלא חדא היכי דמי דאכל חלב וחלב דכוותה גבי שבת דעבד קצירה וקצירה הכא חדא מיחייב והכא חדא מיחייב לעולם דעבד קצירה וטחינה ומאי מה שאין כן בשאר מצות אע"ז וכדרבי אמי [ד] דא"ר אמי זיבח וקיטר וניסך בהעלמה אחת אינו חייב אלא אחת במאי אוקימתא בע"ז אימא סיפא חומר בשאר מצות שבשאר מצות שגג בלא מתכוין חייב מה שאין כן בשבת [ה] האי שגג בלא מתכוין דע"ז היכי דמי אילימא כסבור בית הכנסת הוא והשתחוה לה הרי לבו לשמים ואלא [°] דחזי אנדרטא וסגיד לה היכי דמי אי דקבלה עליה באלוה מזיד הוא ואי דלא קבלה עליה באלוה לאו כלום הוא אלא מאהבה ומיראה הניחא לאביי [ו] דאמר חייב אלא לרבא דאמר פטור מאי איכא למימר אלא באומר מותר משא"כ בשבת דפטור לגמרי ע"כ לא בעא מיני' רבא מרב נחמן אלא אי לחיובי חדא אי לחיובי תרתי אבל מפטרי לגמרי לא

אלא

נתכוין להגביה את התלוש. כגון דנפל סכין בערוגת הירק ונתכוין להגביהו: וחתך את המחובר פטור. דכתיב אשר חטא בה ודרשינן בכריתות פרט למתעסק בדבר אחר ועשה דבר זה ושוגג היכי דמי כגון שנתכוין לכך אלא שגג דסבר שאין היום שבת או סבר שמלאכה זו מותרת וזה מתעסק בהגבהה היה ולא בחתיכה: דהא לא איכוין אחתיכה דאיסורא. בשגגת שבת או בשגגת מלאכות אלא מתעסק בחתיכת היתר הוה שיודע שהוא שבת ויודע שחתיכת מחובר אסור: משא"כ בשאר מצות. כולה מפרש לה ואזיל: שגג בלא מתכוין. לקמן מפרש לה: חלב ודם. דומיא דטחינה וקצירה שהן שני גופין: אלא גבי שאר מצות היכי דמי. דפטור: כגון חלב וחלב. בהעלם אחד: דרבי אמי. במסכת סנהדרין בפרק ד' מיתות יליף למילתיה מקרא דאין חילוק חטאות לעכו"ם: והשתחוה לה. והיינו שגג שהיא ע"ז בלא מתכוין שלא נתכוון להשתחוות לע"ז: הרי לבו לשמים. ומה חיוב יש כאן אפי' ידע שהוא בית ע"ז והשתחוה בו לשמים אין חיוב כאן: אנדרטא. צורת המלך שעושין לכבוד המלך והשתחוה לה ולא לשם אלהות: מאהבה ומיראה. מאהבת אדם או מיראת אדם השתחוה לע"ז וקרי ליה שוגג בלא מתכוין כלומר שגג בהכי דסבור כיון דאין מתכוין לבו לאלהות מותר: אלא באומר מותר. כגון גר שנתגייר בין הנכרים כסבור שאין ע"ז בתורה וקרי ליה שגג בלא מתכוין: דפטור לגמרי. בתמיה: עד כאן לא קבעי מיניה רבא מרב נחמן. העלם זה וזה בידו מהו לעיל בפירקין (דף ע:) דהיינו אומר מותר דאמר אין שבת בתורה היינו העלם זה וזה:

דסבור

נתכוין להגביה את התלוש. פירש בקונטרס כגון סכין מוטל בערוגת ירק ונתכוין להגביה וחתך את המחובר א"כ הא דפליגי בנתכוין לחתוך את התלוש וחתך את המחובר היינו לחתוך תלוש (א) וחתך מחובר אחר אבל לחתוך מחובר זה וחתך מחובר אחר משמע דחייב לכ"ע וקשה לר"ת דבסוף פ' ספק אכל (כריתות יט:) אמר שמואל המתעסק בחלבים ועריות חייב שכן נהנה בשבת פטור דמלאכת מחשבת אסרה תורה ומוכח התם דאפילו בנתכוין ללקוט תאנה זו וליקט תאנה אחרת פטר שמואל ולקמן בפרק הזורק (דף צז:) פטר [ז] (ב) רבא נתכוין לזרוק ארבע וזרק שמנה כי לא אמר כל מקום שתרצה תנוח וכל שכן בנתכוין לזרוק בצד זה וזרק בצד אחר דלא נעשה כלל רצונו או נתכוין לחתוך מחובר זה וחתך מחובר אחר דפטור ונראה לר"ת דהכא מיירי בנתכוין לחתוך תלוש ונמצא שהוא מחובר וחותך מה שהיה מתכוין אלא שלא היה יודע שהיה מחובר ופליגי אביי ורבא בקרא דאשר חטא בה דמוקי ליה רבי אליעזר בפרק ספק אכל (שם יט:) פרט למתעסק והכי איתא התם בהדיא דקאמר עלה לרבא משכחת לה שנתכוין לחתוך את התלוש וחתך את המחובר לאביי שנתכוין להגביה את התלוש כו' ושמואל דפטר מטעם מלאכת מחשבת היינו בנתכוין לחתוך מחובר זה וחתך מחובר אחר דלא נעשה מחשבתו והשתא אתי שפיר דקאמר (ג) לקמן דמפרש שגג בלא מתכוין דשאר מצות היכי דמי כגון דסבור שומן הוא ואכלו דהיינו ממש דומיא דשבת לפר"ת:

הניחא לאביי דאמר חייב. פי' הניחא לאביי בהא דמשכחת גבי ע"ז שגג בלא מתכוין אבל מ"מ גם לאביי לא מיתוקמא ברייתא שפיר בהכי דהא אם חלל שבת מאהבה ומיראה נמי חייב ולהכי איצטריך בסמוך לאוקמא אליבא דאביי שגג בלא מתכוין ה"ד דסבור רוק הוא ובלעו:

עד כאן לא בעא מיניה רבא מרב נחמן כו'. וא"ת אמאי לא מייתי מתני' דהשוכח עיקר שבת דאינו חייב אלא אחת ולא הוי פטור לגמרי וי"ל דניחא ליה לאתויי מרבא דמספקא ליה בהעלם זה וזה דדילמא אפי' תרתי מיחייב דכי אוקי הכא באומר מותר היינו בנתעלמה ממנו לפי שעה דהיינו דומיא דהעלם זה וזה בידו כדפי' לעיל דאם לא נודע לו מעולם איסור ע"ז אינו ישראל כלל כיון שמודה בע"ז דדוחק להעמיד בתינוק שנשבה לבין העכו"ם:

רבא אמר פטור. ואם תאמר והא אמר בפרק בן סורר ומורה (סנהדרין דף עד.) דע"ז וגילוי עריות ושפיכות דמים יהרג ואל יעבור אם כן אפילו לא מקבל ליה חייב ואין לומר דרבא לטעמיה דאמר במס' ע"ז בפרק ר' ישמעאל (דף נד.) דאפילו בע"ז בצינעא וחי בהם ולא שימות בהם והא דקאמר רבא בפ"ב דכתובות (דף יט.) גבי עדים שאמרו להם חתמו שקר כו' שאין לך דבר שעומד בפני פיקוח נפש אלא ע"ז וגילוי עריות ושפיכות דמים ה"פ אפילו מאן דמחמיר לא מחמיר אלא בע"ז ג"ע ושפיכות דמים דאם כן דטעמא דרבא דפטור הוי משום הכי מאי מייתי אביי בפ' ד' מיתות (סנהדרין סא:) מכמה ברייתות לימא דאתיא כמ"ד בפרק בן סורר (שם עד.) יהרג ואל יעבור דפלוגתא דתנאי היא וי"ל דסבר רבא דאפי' למ"ד דחייב למסור את עצמו אם לא מסר עצמו לא מיחייב מיתה בבית דין וקשה לרשב"א דאמר רבא במסכת ע"ז[ח] הכל היו בכלל לא תעבדם כשפרט לך הכתוב וחי בהם יצא אונס משמע דלא אונס מיתה אלא מפיק אלא שאר אונסין הוו בכלל לא תעבדם וחייב א) והכא פטור אפי' מאהבה דליכא אונס מיתה וי"מ דההיא דאמר יהרג ואל יעבור היינו בסתם אע"ג דלא מקבל עליה לאלוה אבל הכא במפרש דקעביד מאהבה ומיראה אי נמי אפילו בסתם ובע"ז שהכל אין עובדין אותה אלא מאהבה ומיראה דומיא דהמן דמייתי עלה התם להם אי אתה משתחוה אבל אתה משתחוה לאדם כמותך יכול אפי' נעבד כהמן ת"ל לא תעבדם [וקאמר רבא כהמן ולא כהמן דאילו התם מיראה והכא לאו מיראה] ומההיא גופא נמי יש לדקדק דחייב אע"ג דלא קבל עליה באלוה דמשמע דאסר נעבד כהמן דומיא דאדם שכמותך דשרי והיינו בלא קיבלו עליו באלוה ועוד דאמר בפרק ד' מיתות (סנהדרין דף ס:) הפוער עצמו לפעור זו היא עבודתו אע"ג דקא מכוין לבזוייה הזורק אבן למרקוליס זו היא עבודתו אע"ג דקא מכוין למירגמיה אלמא דחייב אע"פ שאין מקבל עליו באלוה ומיהו יש לפרש אע"ג דקא מכוין לבזוייה מכוין לעובדה דרך בזיון וברגימה זו והא דלא דחי ראיות דאביי בעובד מאהבה ומיראה סתם משום דסתם עובד כמדעתו דמי וא"ת ולמאי דפטר רבא אמאי לא השתחוה מרדכי להמן וי"ל כדאמרינן במדרש ששתי צורות היו על לבו ועוד משום קידוש השם כדאשכחן בירושלמי במסכת שביעית בפ"ד כגון פפוס ולוליינוס אחיו שנתנו להם מים בזכוכית צבועה ולא קבלו מהם[ט]:

באומר מותר. והא דמעטינן בפ"ב דמכות (דף ז: ושם) בשגגה פרט לאומר מותר שאני גבי גלות דטובא בשגגה כתיבי התם ולהכי נמי אמר בסוף פ"ב דב"ק (דף כו: ושם) היתה אבן מונחת לו בחיקו ולא הכיר בה מעולם לענין גלות פטור מבשגגה לענין שבת פטור משום דבעינן מלאכת מחשבת והשתא תיפוק ליה דגבי שבת נמי כתיב בשגגה אלא ודאי דוקא גבי גלות ממעטינן משום דכתיבי בשגגה טובא:

אלא

עין משפט
נר מצוה

כד א מיי' פ"ג מהלכות שגגות הלכה ז:
כה ב מיי' פ"א מהלכו' שבת הלכה ח ופ"ז מהלכות שגגות הל' יא:

רבינו חננאל

ובפלוגתא דר' יוחנן ור"ל פשוטה היא: אתמר נתכוין להגביה את התלוש וחתך את המחובר לכולי עלמא לא מחייב קרבן דהא לא אתכוין למלתא דאית בה איסורא אלא להגביה בעולם נתכוין אע"פ שחותך את המחובר לא קרינן ביה נפש כי תחטא בשגגה ולא הוי חוטא בשגגה אלא מתכוין למעשה מביא לידי חטא. והוא אינו יודע שהוא חוטא. אבל אם נתכוון לחתוך את התלוש שהוא מותר ונזדמן לו מחובר וחתכו רבה אמר פטור דס"ל שאינו קורא ביה נפש כי תחטא בשגגה אלא בזמן שמתכוון לדבר אסור כשיקרא שוגג באיסורו וזה לא נתכוון אלא לחתיכת תלוש אביי אמר חייב דהוא מכוון לחתיכה בעלמא ויש בחתיכה איסור. וסבר אביי שאין צריך להתכוון במעשיו לדבר שהוא באיסורו אלא כל מעשה שיש במינו איסור אף על פי שלא נתכוון לדבר שיש בה איסור כיון שנזדמן לו דבר איסור הריני קורא בו כי תחטא בשגגה. וכן לענין נתכוון לזרוק שתים וזרק ד' לרבה פטור דהא לא נתכוון לדבר האיסור בשגגת איסורו אע"פ שמתכוון למקצתו דסבר ליה צריך להתכוון לכל האיסור בשגגת איסורו ולאביי חייב דהא נתכוון לזריקה ונזדמנה לו זריקה אסורה. אמ' (רבא) [רבה] מנא אמינא לה דפטור דתניא חומר בשבת משאר מצות שהשבת עושה שתים בהעלם אחת חייב שתים מה שאין כן בשאר מצות. חומר בשאר מצות ששאר מצות שגג בלא מתכוון חייב משא"כ בשבת ואוקימנא דשגג בלא מתכוין בשבת דפטור [בכה"ג דנתכוין לחתוך את התלוש וכו'] ודוק' הא מתניתא כרבה דאמר נתכוון לחתוך את התלוש וחתך את המחובר פטור דהא לא נתכוון לחתיכה (דאיסור דא) [דאיסורא]. ושקלו וטרו בהא דתנן עשה בהעלם אחד שתים בשבת חייב שתים ובשאר מצות כי האי גוונא אינו חייב אלא אחת. היכי דמי [אילימא] קצר וטחן בשבת כיוצא בו בשאר מצות אכל חלב ודם הכא שתים מחייב והכא שתים מחייב. אלא קצר וחזר וקצר בהעלם אחד כיוצא בו בשאר מצות אכל חלב וחזר ואכל חלב בהעלם אחד הכא חדא מחייב והכא חדא מחייב ודחינן מאי שאר מצות דקתני ע"ז. והכי קתני חומר בשבת שאם קצר וטחן בהעלם אחד בזדון שבת ושגגת מלאכות חייב שתים מה שאין כן בע"ז כי (אם) בע"ז אם זיבח וקיטר וניסך בהעלם אחד אינו חייב אלא אחת וכדר' (יוסי) [אמי] ודחינן לא מיתוקמא מתניתין בע"ז דקתני סיפא שגג בלא מתכוון בשאר מצות חייב משא"כ בשבת. שגג בלא מתכוון בע"ז היכי משכחת לה אי נימא דחזא ע"ז וסבר כי היא בית הכנסת והשתחוה [לה] כי האי גוונא פטור הוא דהא לבו לשמים. ואלא דחזא אנדרטא וסגיד לה. אי דקבלה עילויה באלוה מזיד הוא ולאו בר קרבן הוא ואי לא קבלה עילויה באלוה כיון דבשוגג השתחוה כנגד האי אנדרטא לא מחייב דהא לא עביד מידי אלא כגון שהשתחוה לע"ז מאהבה. שראה צורת ע"ז ואהבה או אדם שהעמיד עצמו ע"ז כהמן והשתחוה לו מאהבה בשגגת אלהים אחרים פי' שנעלם ממנו שמשתחוה לע"ז מאהבה חייב או שנעלם ממנו כי אלו העבירות בע"ז מחייב. וזה פי' מאהבה או מיראה נמי כגון מי שנתיירא מן הע"ז והשתחוה לו בשגגת אלהים אחרים או בשגגת עבירות דלא הוה ידע כי האי גוונא חייב אי אמרת כי האי גוונא שגג בלא מתכוין בע"ז חייב ניחא לאביי דמחייב דגרסינן בסנהדרין פרק ארבע מיתות דאתמר העובד ע"ז מאהבה ומיראה כגון המשתחוה מאהבתו לו או מיראתו ממנו לאדם הנעבד כהמן בשוגג שלא היה יודע כי העובד מאהבה או מיראה חייב [אביי אמר חייב] דהא פלחא לע"ז רבא אמר פטור דהא לא קבלה עליו באלוה. הניחא לאביי אלא לרבא

מסורת הש"ס

א) כריתות דף יט ע"ב, ב) [לפמ"ש תוס' לעיל כג: ד"ה גזרה וכ"כ עוד לעיל ע: ד"ה נודע ולמ"ש הרא"ש פרק הזהב סי' יט שלא מצינו בכל הגמ' שמקדים רבא לאביי כי אביי מלך קודם רבא ע"ש וכ"כ עוד בשאר דוכתי א"כ יש לגרוס הכא אביי אמר וכו' או דצ"ל רבה אמר פטור וכו' אמר רבה מנא אמינא לה וכו' וע"ע מ"ש פסחים מח. על הגליון], ג) סנהדרין סב., ד) סנהדרין סב. [וע"ש שצ"ל רבי זכאי], ה) שם סא: [כריתות ג.], ו) שם, ז) ע"ש שצ"ל רבינא, ח) [דף נד.], ט) [ועי' תוספות סנהדרין סא: ד"ה רבא אמר].

תוספות ישנים

א) וי"א דבאומר אלי אתה מודה רבא דחייב אפילו מאהבה ומיראה דהיינו קבל עליו באלוה כיון דקאמר אלי אתה אע"פ שאומר באונס ה"פ במס' ע"ז הא בכלל לא תעבדם כשאמר אלי אתה. אבל מקטיר דאונס לא הוי בכלל לא תעבדם. ומיהו בהנהו דמייתי אביי ה"מ לאוקמי באלי אתה. והר"א ממיץ מפרש דע"ז שכבר עבדוהו פ"א לשם ע"ז חייב בה אפי' מאהבה ומיראה:

הגהות הב"ח

(א) תוס' ד"ה נתכוין וכו' לחתוך תלוש זה וחתך: (ב) בא"ד בפ' הזורק פטר רב אשי נתכוין וכו': (ג) בא"ד והשתא אתי שפיר לקמן כצ"ל ותיבת דקאמר נמחק:

גליון הש"ס

גמ' דחזי אנדרטא. עי' מס' ע"ז דף מ ע"ב תוד"ה ובאנדרטי:

רב נסים גאון

ואלא מאהבה ומיראה הניחא לאביי דאמר חייב אלא למאן דאמר פטור מאי איכא למימר. ופלוגתא דאביי ורבא משכחת במס' סנהדרין בפרק ד' מיתות (דף סא) איתמר העובד ע"ז מאהבה ומיראה אביי אמר חייב ורבא אמר פטור אביי אמר חייב דהא פלחה רבא אמר פטור דלא קבלה עליה באלוה אי קיבלה עליה אין ואי לא לא:

ליקוטי רש"י

נתכוין להגביה את התלוש וחתך את המחובר פטור. לדברי הכל דהאי מתעסק הוי דלא נתכוון לשום חתיכה [כריתות יט:]. שנאמר (ויקרא ד) אשר חטא בה עד שיתכוין למלאכה זו פרט למתעסק בדבר אחר ועלתה בידו מלאכה זו. חומר שבת וכו'. לקמן מפרש לה. קצירה וטחינה. דליכא שמות מחולקין ומשום הכי חייב שתים. חלב וחלב. שני זיתים בשני ימים ולא נודע לו בנתיים שחטא אינו חייב אלא אחת [סנהדרין סב:]. אינו חייב אלא אחת. [דכל עבודתה] באזהרה אחת הן לא תעבדם (שמות כ) הלכך אין כאן חלוק חטאות. והא דפטר לה בחדא נפקא (סנהדרין סג.) מלא תעבדם הכתוב עשאן עבודה אחת [שם.]. הרי לבו לשמים. ולשמים נתכוין והשתחוה ואין כאן עבירה כלל לא שוגג ולא מזיד [שם:]. ולא השתחוה זה לעבודת כוכבים לא מזיד ולא שוגג (הוא) אלא לשמים שהרי לשמים נתכוין ואפילו היה יודע שזה הבית עבודת כוכבים הוא והוא משתחוה בתוכו לשמים אין כאן עונש שהרי אף משתחוה לבית הכנסת לא לבית הוא משתחוה אלא למי ששכן שמו עליה [שם סא:]. דלאו נמי בבית עבודת כוכבים השתחוה לשמים לאו איסורא עבד וליכא חטאת [כריתות ג.]. אלא דחזי אנדרטא וסגיד לה. שראה דמות שהיו רגילין לעשות בדמות המלך והרואה אותו משתחוה לו לכבוד המלך ופעמים שעובדין אותו וזה ראה אחד שהוא נעבד והשתחוה לו. אי דקבלה עליה באלוה. שהשתחוה לו לשם עבודת כוכבים מזיד הוא [סנהדרין שם]. אנדרטא. צלם דמות המלך [ר"ה כד:]. צורת הצלמים שעושין על שם המלך שמת [מו"ק כה:]. כשהמלך מת עושין צורתו בפתח השער לזכרון [ע"ז מ:]. ואי דלא קבלה עליה באלוה. אלא לכבוד המלך השתחוה לו לא כלום הוא דהא לא מכוין לשם עבודת כוכבים [סנהדרין סב.]. לאו כלום היא. דכיון דלא נעשה לשם עבודת כוכבים השתחואה דידיה לאו כלום היא [כריתות שם]. אלא. שוגג בלא מתכוין כגון מאהבה ומיראה ולא נתכוין לעבודת כוכבים אלא לאהבת האיש ושגג כסבור מותר לעשות כן [סנהדרין שם:]. מאהבת אדם ומיראת אדם ולא חשבה בלבו באלהות [שם סא:]. השתחוה לעבודת כוכבים מאהבת אדם ומיראת אדם דסבר מותר לעבוד עבודת כוכבים מאהבה ומיראה [כריתות שם]. חייב. במזיד ובהתראה במיתה ובשוגג דכסבור מותר לעשות כן חייב בחטאת. פטור. בין במזיד בין בשוגג דלאו כלום עבד [סנהדרין שם]. אלא באומר מותר. לעבוד עבודת כוכבים [כריתות שם:]. דאמר אין עבודת כוכבים בתורה וכיון דלא הוזכרה לו מעולם אין מתכוין קרי ליה [סנהדרין סב.].

נִתְכַּוֵּין לְהַגְבִּיהַּ אֶת הַתָּלוּשׁ – If **one intended to lift something** that was **detached** from the ground וְחָתַךְ אֶת הַמְחוּבָּר – **but he** in fact **cut something** that was **attached,**[1] פָּטוּר – **he is exempt** from liability to a *chatas.*[2] לַחְתּוֹךְ אֶת הַתָּלוּשׁ – However, if he intended **to cut something** that was **detached** from the ground[3] וְחָתַךְ אֶת הַמְחוּבָּר – **but he** in fact **cut something** that was **attached,** רָבָא אָמַר פָּטוּר – **Rava says that he is exempt** from liability to a *chatas,* אַבַּיֵי אָמַר חַיָּיב – whereas **Abaye says that he is liable.**

The Gemara explains the dispute:

רָבָא אָמַר פָּטוּר – **Rava says that he is exempt,** דְּהָא לֹא נִתְכַּוֵּין לַחֲתִיכָה דְּאִיסּוּרָא – **because he did not intend a prohibited** act of **cutting.**[4] אַבַּיֵי אָמַר חַיָּיב – **Abaye says he is liable** דְּהָא קָמִיכַּוֵּין לַחֲתִיכָה בְּעָלְמָא – **because he intended some** form of **cutting.**[5]

Rava proves his point:

אָמַר רָבָא – **Rava said:** מְנָא אֲמִינָא לָהּ – **How do I know it?** דְּתַנְיָא – **For it was taught in a Baraisa:** חוֹמֶר שַׁבָּת מִשְּׁאָר מִצְוֹת – THERE IS an aspect of GREATER STRINGENCY TO THE SABBATH THAN TO OTHER COMMANDMENTS, וְחוֹמֶר שְׁאָר מִצְוֹת מִשַּׁבָּת – AND THERE IS an aspect of GREATER STRINGENCY TO OTHER COMMANDMENTS THAN TO THE SABBATH, as follows: חוֹמֶר שַׁבָּת מִשְּׁאָר מִצְוֹת – THERE IS an aspect of GREATER STRINGENCY TO THE SABBATH THAN TO OTHER COMMANDMENTS, שֶׁהַשַּׁבָּת – IN THAT, concerning desecration of THE SABBATH, עָשָׂה שְׁתַּיִם בְּהֶעְלֵם אֶחָד – if ONE COMMITTED TWO transgressions IN ONE LAPSE OF AWARENESS חַיָּיב עַל כָּל אַחַת וְאַחַת – HE IS LIABLE to a separate *chatas* offering FOR EACH AND EVERY ONE of his transgressions, מַה שֶּׁאֵין כֵּן בִּשְׁאָר מִצְוֹת – WHEREAS THIS IS NOT SO IN REGARD TO the transgression of OTHER COMMANDMENTS.[6] וְחוֹמֶר שְׁאָר מִצְוֹת מִשַּׁבָּת – AND THERE IS an aspect of GREATER STRINGENCY TO OTHER COMMANDMENTS THAN TO THE SABBATH, שֶׁבִּשְׁאָר מִצְוֹת – IN THAT, CONCERNING OTHER COMMANDMENTS, שָׁגַג בְּלֹא מִתְכַּוֵּין חַיָּיב – if ONE ACTED INADVERTENTLY WITHOUT any INTENT at all HE IS LIABLE to a *chatas* offering, מַה שֶּׁאֵין כֵּן בְּשַׁבָּת – WHEREAS THIS IS NOT SO IN REGARD TO desecration of THE SABBATH.[7]

The Gemara analyzes the Baraisa to clarify Rava's proof:

אָמַר מַר – **The master said:** חוֹמֶר שַׁבָּת מִשְּׁאָר מִצְוֹת – THERE IS an aspect of GREATER STRINGENCY TO THE SABBATH THAN TO OTHER COMMANDMENTS, שֶׁהַשַּׁבָּת עָשָׂה שְׁתַּיִם בְּהֶעְלֵם אֶחָד – IN THAT, concerning desecration of THE SABBATH, if ONE COMMITTED TWO transgressions IN ONE LAPSE OF AWARENESS חַיָּיב עַל כָּל אַחַת וְאַחַת – HE IS LIABLE to a separate *chatas* offering FOR EACH AND EVERY ONE of his transgressions, מַה שֶּׁאֵין כֵּן בִּשְׁאָר מִצְוֹת – WHEREAS THIS IS NOT SO IN REGARD TO the transgression of OTHER COMMANDMENTS. הֵיכִי דָּמֵי – **What is the case** of two acts of Sabbath desecration for which the sinner is liable to separate *chatas* offerings? אִילֵימָא דְּעָבַד קְצִירָה וּטְחִינָה – **If you will say** it is **where,** for example, **[the sinner] performed** the forbidden *melachos* of **reaping and grinding** in one lapse of awareness,[8] this cannot be the case to which the Baraisa refers. דִּכְוָותָהּ גַּבֵּי שְׁאָר מִצְוֹת – **For the parallel to this in regard to other commandments**[9] would perforce be a case אָכַל חֵלֶב וְדָם – where, for example, **[the sinner] consumed *cheilev* and blood** in one lapse of awareness.[10] But in such a case the laws of the

NOTES

1. For example, a person dropped a knife in a vegetable patch and, while attempting to retrieve it, accidentally cut a vegetable from the ground [thus performing the *melachah* of reaping] (*Rashi*).

2. Generally, one who commits a transgression without intending to do the act at all is not liable to a *chatas* offering. He is called מִתְעַסֵּק, *one who is preoccupied [with doing something else].* Only if one intended to do the act but did not realize that it was forbidden is he liable to an offering – for example, if he desecrated the Sabbath without realizing that it was the Sabbath day or that his act was a forbidden *melachah.* This is derived from a verse (*Leviticus* 4:23): אוֹ־הוֹדַע אֵלָיו חַטָּאתוֹ אֲשֶׁר חָטָא בָּהּ וְהֵבִיא אֶת־קָרְבָּנוֹ, *If it became known to him his sin that he sinned in it; he shall bring his offering.* The superfluous term בָּהּ, *in it,* teaches that only if the person was cognitively involved in the act of sin is he liable to a *chatas* offering for his inadvertent transgression (see *Kereisos* 19a). [For example, he knew that he was cutting a plant attached to the ground, but he forgot either that it was forbidden to do so on the Sabbath or that it was the Sabbath day.] But here, the person intended an act of lifting, not an act of cutting. He is therefore exempt from all liability (*Rashi*).

3. He thus intended to do an act of cutting. According to *Rashi's* explanation of the previous case, this would mean that he intended to cut a detached object but instead accidentally cut a different object, one that was still attached (*Tosafos;* see below, note 5).

4. He did not plan to perform an act that would be prohibited, with inadvertence regarding either the Sabbath or the *melachah.* Rather, he was preoccupied with another act – a permitted cut – knowing that the day was the Sabbath and that it would be forbidden to cut something still attached to the ground (*Rashi*). Therefore, when he accidentally cut the attached plant, he is still classified as one who was preoccupied with another act (מִתְעַסֵּק), not as one who acted inadvertently (שׁוֹגֵג).

5. According to Abaye this case is classified as typical inadvertence since the person was intending to cut something; he is therefore liable to a *chatas.* The superfluous term בָּהּ refers only to a person who was intending a completely different type of act.

Tosafos deduce from *Rashi* (see above, notes 3 and 4) that if the person intended to cut one attached object [a prohibited act] but instead cut another, he would be liable to a *chatas* even according to Rava, since he was intending an act that is forbidden. *Tosafos,* however, cite the Gemara in *Kereisos* (19b) where Shmuel holds that a person is exempt in such a case, since he did not perform the act that he intended. Accordingly, they explain that Rava and Abaye are referring to a case where the person intended to cut a particular object he thought to be detached, but afterwards discovered that it was actually attached when he cut it. Rava holds that this is still classified as "preoccupation," while Abaye maintains that he is liable, since he was planning to cut this very object. But wherever the person does not perform the act that he intended – even if he was planning to perform a forbidden act – he is exempt from liability. [See *Sh'ailos U'Teshuvos R' Akiva Eiger* volume I §8 and *Kehillos Yaakov* §33 for a discussion of this view.]

[*Even HaEzel* (*Hil. Shabbos* 1:8; see also *Oneg Yom Tov* §21) defends *Rashi* by noting that *Rashi* himself writes in *Kereisos* that Rava and Abaye disagree with Shmuel's definition of "preoccupation": Although Shmuel holds that this principle extends to someone who planned a forbidden act on one object but instead performed it on another (as *Tosafos* state), Rava and Abaye hold that this principle applies only to someone who planned to perform a different act that is permitted.

Rashi's view about the ruling stated by *Tosafos* that a person is considered "preoccupied" even when he was planning to act on a particular object, thinking that circumstances allowed it, is unclear (see *Rosh Yosef, Oneg Yom Tov* §21 and *Even HaEzel* for differing opinions about *Rashi's* view). See also below 73a note 2.]

6. The Gemara will explain the entire Baraisa shortly (*Rashi*).

7. The Gemara will explain the case of an inadvertent act committed without intention, at the end of its explanation of the Baraisa below, 73a (*Rashi*).

Rava himself cited the Baraisa only as proof to his position, which he derives from the Baraisa's last statement. The Gemara, though, first analyzes the entire Baraisa. Only then will Rava's proof become clear.

8. Since these are separate categories of *melachah,* if one did both of them in one lapse of awareness (with inadvertence regarding the *melachos*) he is liable to two *chatas* offerings.

9. I.e. the case that the Baraisa refers to with its statement: "whereas this is not so in regard to the transgression of other mitzvos," implying that a single *chatas* suffices.

10. That is, he transgressed two separate prohibitions. This is the parallel of performing reaping and grinding, which are two separate *melachos* (*Rashi*).

א) נתכוין [א]להגביה את התלוש וחתך את המחובר פטור לחתוך את התלוש וחתך את המחובר ב) רבא אמר [ב]פטור אביי אמר חייב רבא אמר פטור דהא לא נתכוון לחתיכה דאיסורא אביי אמר חייב דהא קמיכוין לחתיכה בעלמא אמר רבא מנא אמינא לה ג) דתניא חומר שבת משאר מצות וחומר שאר מצות משבת חומר שבת משאר מצות שהשבת עשה שתים בהעלם אחד חייב על כל אחת ואחת מה שאין כן בשאר מצות וחומר שאר מצות משבת שבשאר מצות שגג בלא מתכוין חייב מה שאין כן בשבת: אמר מר חומר שבת משאר מצות שהשבת עשה שתים בהעלם אחד חייב על כל אחת ואחת מה שאין כן בשאר מצות היכי דמי אילימא דעבד קצירה וטחינה דכוותה גבי שאר מצות אכל חלב ודם הכא תרתי מיחייב והכא תרתי מיחייב אלא שאר מצות דלא מיחייב אלא חדא היכי דמי דאכל חלב וחלב דכוותה גבי שבת דעבד קצירה וקצירה הכא חדא מיחייב והכא חדא מיחייב לעולם דעבד קצירה וטחינה ומאי מה שאין כן בשאר מצות אע"ז וכדרבי אמי ד) דא"ר אמי זיבח וקיטר וניסך בהעלמה אחת אינו חייב אלא אחת במאי אוקימתא בע"ז אימא סיפא חומר בשאר מצות שבשאר מצות שגג בלא מתכוין חייב מה שאין כן בשבת ה) האי שגג בלא מתכוין דע"ז היכי דמי אילימא כסבור בית הכנסת הוא והשתחוה לה הרי לבו לשמים ואלא ° דחזי אנדרטא וסגיד לה היכי דמי אי דקבלה עליה באלוה מזיד הוא ואי דלא קבלה עליה באלוה לאו כלום הוא אלא מאהבה ומיראה הניחא לאביי ו) דאמר חייב אלא לרבא דאמר פטור מאי איכא למימר אלא באומר מותר משא"כ בשבת דפטור לגמרי ע"כ לא בעא מיני' רבא מרב נחמן אלא אי לחיובי חדא אי לחיובי תרתי אבל מפטרי לגמרי לא

אלא

רש"י

נתכוין להגביה את התלוש. כגון דנפל סכין בערוגת הירק ונתכוין להגביהו: וחתך את המחובר פטור. דכתיב אשר חטא בה ודרשינן בכריתות פרט למתעסק בדבר אחר ועשה דבר זה ושוגג היכי דמי כגון שנתכוין לכך אבל שגג דסבר שאין היום שבת או סבר שמלאכה זו מותרת וזה מתעסק בהגבהה היה ולא בחתיכה: דהא לא איכוין אחתיכה דאיסורא. בשגגת שבת או בשגגת מלאכות אלא מתעסק בחתיכת היתר הוה שיודע שהוא שבת ויודע שחתיכת מחובר אסור: משא"כ בשאר מצות. כולה מפרש לה ואזיל: שגג בלא מתכוין. לקמן מפרש לה: חלב ודם. דומיא דטחינה וקצירה שהן שני גופין: אלא גבי שאר מצות היכי דמי. דפטור: כגון חלב וחלב. בהעלם אחד: דרבי אמי. במסכת סנהדרין בפרק ד' מיתות יליף למילתיה מקרא דאין חילוק חטאות לעכו"ם: והשתחוה לה. והיינו שגג שהיא ע"ז בלא מתכוין שלא נתכוון להשתחוות לע"ז: הרי לבו לשמים. ומה חיוב יש כאן אפי' ידע שהוא בית ע"ז והשתחוה בו לשמים אין חיוב כאן: אנדרטא. צורת המלך שעושין לכבוד המלך והשתחוה לה ולא לשם אלהות: מאהבה ומיראה. מאהבת אדם או מיראת אדם השתחוה לע"ז וקרי ליה שוגג בלא מתכוין כלומר שגג בהכי דסבור כיון דאין מתכוין לבו לאלהות מותר: אלא באומר מותר. כגון גר שנתגייר בין הנכרים כסבור שאין ע"ז בתורה וקרי ליה שגג בלא מתכוין: דפטור לגמרי. בתמיה: עד כאן לא קבעי מיניה רבא מרב נחמן. העלם זה וזה בידו מהו לעיל בפירקין (דף ע:) דהיינו אומר מותר דאמר אין שבת בתורה היינו העלם זה וזה:

דסבור

תוספות

נתכוין להגביה את התלוש. פירש בקונטרס כגון סכין מוטל בערוגת ירק ונתכוין להגביה וחתך את המחובר א"כ הא דפליגי בנתכוין לחתוך את התלוש וחתך את המחובר היינו לחתוך תלוש (א) וחתך מחובר אחר אבל לחתוך מחובר זה וחתך מחובר אחר משמע דחייב לכ"ע וקשה לר"ת דבסוף פ' ספק אכל (כריתות יט:) אמר שמואל המתעסק בחלבים ועריות חייב שכן נהנה בשבת פטור דמלאכת מחשבת אסרה תורה ומוכח התם דאפילו בנתכוין ללקוט תאנה זו וליקט תאנה אחרת פטר שמואל ולקמן בפרק הזורק (דף צז:) פטר ז) (ב) רבא נתכוין לזרוק ארבע וזרק שמנה כי לא אמר כל מקום שתרצה תנוח וכל שכן בנתכוין לזרוק בצד זה וזרק בצד אחר דלא נעשה כלל רצונו או נתכוין לחתוך מחובר זה וחתך מחובר אחר דפטור ונראה לר"ת דהכא מיירי בנתכוין לחתוך תלוש ונמצא שהוא מחובר וחותך מה שהיה מתכוין אלא שלא היה יודע שהיה מחובר ופליגי אביי ורבא בקרא דאשר חטא בה דמוקי ליה רבי אליעזר בפרק ספק אכל (שם יט:) פרט למתעסק והכי איתא התם בהדיא דקאמר עלה לרבא משכחת לה שנתכוין לחתוך את התלוש וחתך את המחובר לאביי שנתכוין להגביה את התלוש כו' ושמואל דפטר מטעם מלאכת מחשבת היינו בנתכוין לחתוך מחובר זה וחתך מחובר אחר דלא נעשה מחשבתו והשתא אתי שפיר דקאמר (ג) לקמן דמפרש שגג בלא מתכוין דשאר מצות היכי דמי כגון דסבור שומן הוא ואכלו דהיינו ממש דומיא דשבת לפר"ת:

הניחא לאביי דאמר חייב. פי' הניחא לאביי בהא דמשכחת גבי ע"ז שגג בלא מתכוין אבל מ"מ גם לאביי לא מיתוקמא ברייתא שפיר בהכי דהא אם חלל שבת מאהבה ומיראה נמי חייב ולהכי איצטריך בסמוך לאוקמא אליבא דאביי שגג בלא מתכוין ה"ד דסבור רוק הוא ובלעו:

עד כאן לא בעא מיניה רבא מרב נחמן כו'. וא"ת אמאי לא מייתי מתני' דהשוכח עיקר שבת דאינו חייב אלא אחת ולא הוי פטור לגמרי וי"ל דניחא ליה לאתויי מרבא דמספקא ליה בהעלם זה וזה בידו דדילמא אפי' תרתי מיחייב דכי אוקי הכא באומר מותר היינו בנתעלמה ממנו לפי שעה דהיינו דומיא דהעלם זה וזה בידו כדפי' לעיל דאם לא נודע לו מעולם איסור ע"ז אינו ישראל כלל כיון שמודה בע"ז דדוחק להעמיד בתינוק שנשבה לבין העכו"ם:

רבא אמר פטור. ואם תאמר והא אמר בפרק בן סורר ומורה (סנהדרין דף עד.) דע"ז וגילוי עריות ושפיכות דמים יהרג ואל יעבור אם כן אפילו לא מקבל ליה חייב ואין לומר דרבא לטעמיה דאמר במס' ע"ז בפרק ר' ישמעאל (דף נד.) דאפילו בע"ז בצינעא וחי בהם ולא שימות בהם והא דקאמר רבא בפ"ב דכתובות (דף יט.) גבי עדים שאמרו להם חתמו שקר כו' שאין לך דבר שעומד בפני פיקוח נפש אלא ע"ז וגילוי עריות ושפיכות דמים ה"פ אפילו מאן דמחמיר לא מחמיר אלא בע"ז ג"ע ושפיכות דמים דאם כן לטעמא דרבא דפטר הוי משום הכי מאי מייתי אביי בפ' ד' מיתות (סנהדרין סא:) מכמה ברייתות לימא דאתיא כמ"ד בפרק בן סורר (שם עד.) יהרג ואל יעבור דפלוגתא דתנאי היא וי"ל דסבר רבא דאפי' למ"ד דחייב למסור את עצמו אם לא מסר עצמו לא מיחייב מיתה בבית דין וקשה לרשב"א דאמר רבא במסכת ע"ז ח) הכל היו בכלל לא תעבדם כשפרט לך הכתוב וחי בהם יצא אונס משמע דלא מפיק אלא אונס מיתה אבל שאר אונסין הוו בכלל לא תעבדם וחייב א) והכא פטור אפי' מאהבה דליכא אונס מיתה וי"מ דההיא דאמר יהרג ואל יעבור היינו בסתם אע"ג דלא מקבל עליה לאלוה אבל הכא במפרש דקעביד מאהבה ומיראה אי נמי אפילו בסתם ובע"ז שהכל אין עובדין אותה אלא מאהבה ומיראה דומיא דהמן דמייתי עלה התם להם אי אתה משתחוה אבל אתה משתחוה לאדם כמותך יכול אפי' נעבד כהמן ת"ל לא תעבדם [וקאמר רבא כהמן ולא כהמן דאילו התם מיראה והכא לאו מיראה] ומההיא גופא נמי יש לדקדק דחייב אע"ג דלא קבל עליה באלוה דמשמע דאסר נעבד כהמן דומיא דאדם שכמותך דשרי והיינו בלא קיבלו עליו באלוה ועוד דאמר בפרק ד' מיתות (סנהדרין דף ס:) הפוער עצמו לפעור זו היא עבודתו אע"ג דקא מכוין לבזויא הזורק אבן למרקולים זו היא עבודתו אע"ג דקא מכוין למירגמיה אלמא דחייב אע"פ שאין מקבל עליו באלוה ומיהו יש לפרש אע"ג דקא מכוין לבזויא מכוין לעובדה דרך בזיון ורגימה זו והא דלא דחי ראיות דאביי בעובד מאהבה ומיראה סתם משום דסתם עובד כמדעתו דמי וא"ת ולמאי דפטר רבא אמאי לא השתחוה מרדכי להמן וי"ל כדאמרינן במדרש ששתי צורות היו על לבו ועוד משום קידוש השם כדאשכחן בירושלמי במסכת שביעית בפ"ד כגון פפוס ולוליינוס אחיו שנתנו להם מים בזכוכית צבועה ולא קבלו מהם ט):

באומר מותר. והא דמעטינן בפ"ב דמכות (דף ז: ושם) בשגגה פרט לאומר מותר שאני גבי גלות דטובא בשגגה כתיבי התם ולהכי נמי אמר בסוף פ"ב דב"ק (דף כו: ושם) היתה אבן מונחת לו בחיקו ולא הכיר בה מעולם לענין גלות פטור מבשגגה לענין שבת פטור משום דבעינן מלאכת מחשבת והשתא תיפוק ליה דגבי שבת נמי כתיב בשגגה אלא ודאי דוקא גבי גלות ממעטינן משום דכתיבי בשגגה טובא:

עין משפט נר מצוה

כד א מיי' פ"ב מהלכות שגגות הלכה ז:

כה ב מיי' פ"א מהלכו' שבת הלכה ח ופ"ז מהלכות שגגות הל' יא:

רבינו חננאל

ובפלוגתא דר' יוחנן ור"ל פשוטה היא: **אתמר** נתכוין להגביה את התלוש וחתך את המחובר לכולי עלמא לא מחייב קרבן דהא לא אתכוין למלתא דאית בה איסורא אלא להגביה בעולם נתכוין אע"פ שחותך את המחובר לא קרינן ביה נפש כי תחטא בשגגה ולא הוי חוטא בשגגה אלא מתכוין למעשה מביא לידי חטא. והוא אינו יודע שהוא חוטא. אבל אם נתכוון לחתוך את התלוש שהוא מותר ונזדמן לו מחובר וחתכו רבה אמר פטור דס"ל שאינו קורא ביה נפש כי תחטא בשגגה אלא בזמן שמתכוון לדבר אסור כשיקרא שוגג באיסורו וזה לא נתכוון אלא לחתיכת תלוש אביי אמר חייב דהוא מכוון לחתיכה בעלמא ויש בחתיכה איסור. וסבר אביי שאין צריך להתכוון במעשיו לדבר שהוא באיסורו אלא כל מעשה שיש במינו איסור אף על פי שלא נתכוון לדבר שיש בה איסור כיון שנזדמן לו דבר איסור הריני קורא בו כי תחטא בשגגה. וכך לענין נתכוון לזרוק שתים וזרק ד' לרבה פטור דהא לא נתכוון לדבר האיסור בשגגת איסורו אע"פ שמתכוון למקצתו דסבר ליה צריך להתכוון לכל האיסור בשגגת איסורו ולאביי חייב דהא נתכוון לזריקה ונזדמנה לו זריקה אסורה. אמ' (רבא) [רבה] מנא אמינא לה דפטור דתניא חומר בשבת משאר מצות שהשבת עושה שתים בהעלם אחת חייב שתים מה שאין כן בשאר מצות. חומר בשאר מצות ששאר מצות שגג בלא מתכוון חייב משא"כ בשבת ואוקימנא דשגג בלא מתכוין בשבת דפטור [בכה"ג דנתכוין לחתוך את התלוש וכו'] ודוק' הא מתניתא כרבה דאמר נתכוון לחתוך את התלוש וחתך את המחובר פטור דהא לא נתכוון לחתיכה (דאיסור דא) [דאיסורא]. ושקלו וטרו בהא דתנן עשה בהעלם אחד שתים בשבת חייב שתים ובשאר מצות כי האי גוונא אינו חייב אלא אחת. היכי דמי [אילימא] קצר וטחן בשבת כיוצא בו בשאר מצות אכל חלב ודם הכא שתים מחייב והכא שתים מחייב. אלא קצר וחזר וקצר בהעלם אחד כיוצא בו בשאר מצות אכל חלב וחזר ואכל חלב בהעלם אחד הכא חדא מחייב והכא חדא מחייב ודחינן מאי שאר מצות דקתני ע"ז. והכי קתני חומר בשבת שאם קצר וטחן בהעלם אחד בזדון שבת ושגגת מלאכות חייב שתים מה שאין כן בע"ז כי (אם) בע"ז אם זיבח וקיטר וניסך בהעלם אחד אינו חייב אלא אחת וכדר' (יוסי) [אמי] ודחינן לא מיתוקמא מתניתין בע"ז דקתני סיפא שגג בלא מתכוון בשאר מצות חייב משא"כ בשבת. שגג בלא מתכוון בע"ז היכי משכחת לה אי נימא דחזא ע"ז וסבר כי היא בית הכנסת והשתחוה [לה] כי האי גוונא פטור הוא דהא לבו לשמים. ואלא דחזא אנדרטא וסגיד לה. אי דקבלה עילויה באלוה מזיד הוא ולאו בר קרבן הוא ואי לא קבלה עילויה באלוה כיון דבשוגג השתחוה כנגד האי אנדרטא לא מחייב דהא לא עביד מידי אלא כגון שהשתחוה לע"ז מאהבה. שראה צורת ע"ז ואהבה או אדם שהעמיד עצמו ע"ז כהמן והשתחוה לו מאהבה בשגגת אלהים אחרים פי' שנעלם ממנו שמשתחוה לע"ז מאהבה חייב או שנעלם ממנו כי אלו העבירות בע"ז מחייב. וזה פי' מאהבה או מיראה נמי כגון מי שנתיירא מן הע"ז והשתחוה לו בשגגת אלהים אחרים או בשגגת עבירות דלא הוה ידע כי האי גוונא חייב אי אמרת כי האי גוונא שגג בלא מתכוין בע"ז חייב ניחא לאביי דמחייב דגרסינן בסנהדרין פרק ארבע מיתות דאתמר העובד ע"ז מאהבה ומיראה כגון המשתחוה מאהבתו לו או מיראתו ממנו לאדם הנעבד כהמן בשוגג שלא היה יודע כי העובד מאהבה או מיראה חייב [אביי אמר חייב] דהא פלחא לע"ז רבא אמר פטור דהא לא קבלה עליו באלוה. הניחא לאביי אלא לרבא

מסורת הש"ס

א) כריתות דף יט ע"ב, ב) [לפמ"ש תוס' לעיל כג: ד"ה גזרה וכ"כ עוד לעיל ע: ד"ה נודע ולמ"ש הרא"ש פרק הזהב סי' יט שלא מצינו בכל הגמ' שמקדים רבא לאביי כי אביי מלך קודם רבא ע"ש וכ"כ עוד בשאר דוכתי א"כ יש לגרוס הכא **אביי אמר** וכו' או דל"ל **רבה אמר** פטור וכו' **אמר רבה מנא אמינא** לה וכו' וע"ע מ"ש פסחים מה. על הגליון], ג) סנהדרין סב., ד) סנהדרין סב. [וע"ש שצ"ל **רבי זכאי**], ה) שם סא: [כריתות ג.], ו) שם, ז) ע"ש שצ"ל רבינא, ח) [דף נד.], ט) [ועי' תוספות סנהדרין סא: ד"ה רבא אמר].

תוספות ישנים

א) וי"א דבאומר אלי אתה מודה רבא דחייב אפילו מאהבה ומיראה דהיינו קבל עליו באלוה כיון דקאמר אלי אתה אע"פ שאומר באונס ה"פ במס' ע"ז הא בכלל לא תעבדם כשאמר אלי אתה. אבל מקטיר דאונס לא הוי בכלל לא תעבדם. ומיהו בהנהו דמייתי אביי ה"מ לאוקמי באלי אתה. והר"א ממיץ מפרש דע"ז שכבר עבדוהו פ"א לשם ע"ז חייב בה אפי' מאהבה ומיראה:

הגהות הב"ח

(א) תוס' ד"ה נתכוין וכו' לחתוך תלוש זה וחתך: (ב) בא"ד בפ' הזורק פטר רב אשי נתכוין וכו': (ג) בא"ד והשתא אתי שפיר לקמן כצ"ל ותיבת דקאמר נמחק:

גליון הש"ס

גמ' דחזי אנדרטא. עי' מס' ע"ז דף מ ע"ב תוד"ה ובאנדרטי:

רב נסים גאון

ואלא מאהבה ומיראה הניחא לאביי דאמר חייב אלא למאן דאמר פטור מאי איכא למימר. ופלוגתא דאביי ורבא משכחת במס' סנהדרין בפרק ד' מיתות (דף סא) איתמר העובד ע"ז מאהבה ומיראה אביי אמר חייב ורבא אמר פטור אביי אמר חייב דהא פלחה רבא אמר פטור דלא קבלה עליה באלוה אי קיבלה עליה אין ואי לא לא:

ליקוטי רש"י

נתכוין להגביה את התלוש וחתך את המחובר פטור. לדברי הכל דהאי מתעסק הוי דלא נתכוון לשום חתיכה [כריתות יט:]. שנאמר (ויקרא ד) אשר חטא בה עד שיתכוין למלאכה זו פרט למתעסק בדבר אחר ועלתה בידו מלאכה זו. **חומר שבת וכו'.** לקמן מפרש לה. **קצירה וטחינה.** דאיכא שמות מחולקין ומשום הכי חייב שתים. **חלב וחלב.** שני זיתים בשני ימים ולא נודע לו בנתיים שחטא אינו חייב אלא אחת [סנהדרין סב:]. **אינו חייב אלא אחת.** [דכל עבודתה] כאזהרה אחת הן לא תעבדם (שמות כ) הלכך אין כאן חלוק חטאות. והא דפטר לה בחדא נפקא (סנהדרין סג.) מלא תעבדם הכתוב עשאן עבודה אחת [שם.]. **הרי לבו לשמים.** ולשמים נתכוין והשתחוה ואין כאן עבירה כלל לא שוגג ולא מזיד [שם:]. ולא השתחוה זה לעבודת כוכבים לא מזיד ולא שוגג (הוא) אלא לשמים שהרי לשמים נתכוין ואפילו היה יודע שזה הבית עבודת כוכבים הוא והוא משתחוה בתוכו לשמים אין כאן עונש שהרי אף משתחוה לבית הכנסת לא לבית הוא משתחוה אלא למי ששכן שמו עליה [שם סא:]. דאי נמי בבית עבודת כוכבים השתחוה לשמים לאו איסורא עבד וליכא חטאת [כריתות ג.]. **אלא דחזי אנדרטא וסגיד לה.** שראה דמות שהיו רגילין לעשות בדמות המלך והרואה אותו משתחוה לו לכבוד המלך ופעמים שעובדין אותו וזה ראה אחד שהיה נעבד ולא ידע שהוא נעבד והשתחוה לו. **אי דקבלה עליה באלוה.** שהשתחוה לו לשם עבודת כוכבים מזיד הוא [סנהדרין שם]. **אנדרטא.** צלם דמות המלך [ר"ה כד:]. צורת הצלמים שעושין על שם המלך שמת [מו"ק כה:]. כשהמלך מת עושין צורתו בפתח השער לזכרון [ע"ז מ:]. **ואי דלא קבלה עליה באלוה.** אלא לכבוד המלך השתחוה לו לא כלום הוא דהא לא אכוין לשם עבודת כוכבים [סנהדרין סב.]. **לאו כלום היא.** דכיון דלא נעשה לשם עבודת כוכבים השתחואה דידיה לאו כלום היא [כריתות שם]. **אלא.** שוגג בלא מתכוין כגון מאהבה ומיראה ולא נתכוין לעבודת כוכבים אלא לאהבת האיש ושגג כסבור מותר לעשות כן [סנהדרין שם:]. מאהבת אדם ומיראת אדם ולא חשבה בלבו באלהות [שם סא:]. השתחוה לעבודת כוכבים מאהבת אדם ומיראת אדם דסבר מותר לעבוד עבודת כוכבים מאהבה ומיראה [כריתות שם]. **חייב.** במזיד והתראה במיתה ובשוגג דכסבור מותר לעשות כן חייב בחטאת. **פטור.** בין במזיד בין בשוגג דלאו כלום עבד [סנהדרין שם]. **אלא באומר מותר.** לעבוד עבודת כוכבים [כריתות שם:]. דאמר אין עבודת כוכבים בתורה וכיון דלא הוכרה לו מעולם אין מתכוין קרי ליה [סנהדרין סב.].

Sabbath are no more stringent than those of other commandments, הָכָא תַּרְתֵּי מִיחַיֵּיב – for **here,** in the case of Sabbath desecration, **[the sinner] is liable to two** *chatas* offerings, וְהָכָא תַּרְתֵּי מִיחַיֵּיב – **and here** too, in the case of transgression of other commandments, **[the sinner] is liable to two** *chatas* **offerings.**[11] אֶלָּא שְׁאָר מִצְוֹת – **Rather,** regarding **other commandments,** דְּלָא מִיחַיֵּיב אֶלָּא חֲדָא הֵיכִי דָּמֵי – **what is the case in which [the sinner] is liable to only one** *chatas* offering for numerous transgressions? דְּאָכַל חֵלֶב וְחֵלֶב – **Where,** for example, **he ate** ***cheilev*** **and** then ate ***cheilev*** again in the same lapse of awareness.[12] However, this too cannot be the case to which the Baraisa refers. דִּכְוָותָהּ גַּבֵּי שַׁבָּת – **For the parallel to this in regard to** desecration of **the Sabbath**[13] would perforce be a case דְּעָבַד קְצִירָה וּקְצִירָה – **where,** for example, **[the sinner] performed** the *melachah* of **reaping and** then performed the *melachah* of **reaping** again in the same lapse of awareness. But in this case, too, the laws of the Sabbath are no more stringent than those of other commandments, הָכָא חֲדָא מִיחַיֵּיב – for **here,** in the case of other commandments, **[the sinner] is liable to** only **one** *chatas* offering, וְהָכָא חֲדָא מִיחַיֵּיב – **and here too,** in the case of Sabbath desecration, **[the sinner] is liable to** only **one** *chatas* offering. Thus, there is no case to which the Baraisa's statement can be applied! – ? –

The Gemara answers:

לְעוֹלָם דְּעָבַד קְצִירָה וּטְחִינָה – **Actually, [the sinner] performed** the *melachos* of **reaping and grinding.** That is why he is liable to separate *chatas* offerings for his Sabbath desecrations. וּמַאי מַה שֶּׁאֵין כֵּן בִּשְׁאָר מִצְוֹת – **And** to **what** does the Baraisa refer when it states: WHEREAS THIS IS NOT SO IN REGARD TO the transgression of OTHER COMMANDMENTS? אֲעֲבוֹדָה זָרָה – **To idolatry,**[14] וְכִדְרַבִּי אַמִּי – **and in accordance with** a ruling **of R' Ami.** דְּאָמַר רַבִּי אַמִּי – **For R' Ami said:** זִיבַּח וְקִיטֵּר וְנִיסֵּךְ בְּהַעֲלָמָה אַחַת – If **one slaughtered** an animal, **burned** it **and poured a libation** for an idol **in one lapse of awareness,** אֵינוֹ חַיָּיב אֶלָּא אַחַת – **he is liable to only one** *chatas* offering for these three services.[15]

The Gemara challenges this explanation:

בְּמַאי אוֹקִימְתָּא – **How have you interpreted it** [the phrase "other commandments"] in the first section of the Baraisa? בַּעֲבוֹדָה זָרָה – **In reference to idolatry.** אֵימָא סֵיפָא – But **consider the end** [i.e. the second section] of the Baraisa: חוֹמֶר בִּשְׁאָר מִצְוֹת – THERE IS an aspect of GREATER STRINGENCY TO OTHER COMMANDMENTS שֶׁבִּשְׁאָר מִצְוֹת – IN THAT, CONCERNING OTHER COMMANDMENTS, שָׁגַג בְּלֹא מִתְכַּוֵּין חַיָּיב – if ONE ACTED INADVERTENTLY WITHOUT any INTENT at all HE IS LIABLE to a *chatas* offering, מַה שֶּׁאֵין כֵּן בְּשַׁבָּת – WHEREAS THIS IS NOT SO IN REGARD TO desecration of THE SABBATH. If "other commandments" in the first section of the Baraisa refers to idolatry, the parallel expression in the second section apparently refers to the same sin. הַאי שָׁגַג בְּלֹא מִתְכַּוֵּין דַּעֲבוֹדָה זָרָה הֵיכִי דָּמֵי – Now, **what is this case, in regard to idolatry, of** acting **inadvertently without** any **intent** at all, where the person is liable to a *chatas*?[16] אִילֵימָא כְּסָבוּר בֵּית הַכְּנֶסֶת הוּא וְהִשְׁתַּחֲוָה לָהּ – **If you say that he thought [a certain structure] was a synagogue and he bowed down to it**[17] and then he realized that it housed an idol,[18] he would not be liable to a *chatas* in that case, הֲרֵי לִבּוֹ לַשָּׁמַיִם – for, **in fact, his heart was** devoted **to** the One in **heaven.**[19]

Another possible interpretation of the second section of the Baraisa is dismissed:

וְאֶלָּא דַּחֲזֵי אַנְדַּרְטָא – **Rather,** you might say, the case is one **where he saw a statue** of the king וְסָגִיד לָהּ – **and he bowed down to it.**[20] But in that case too, he would not be liable to a *chatas,* regardless of his intentions. הֵיכִי דָּמֵי – For **what is the case?** אִי דְּקַבְּלָה עֲלֵיהּ בֶּאֱלוֹהַּ – **If,** when he bowed down to the statue, **he accepted it upon himself as a deity,** מֵזִיד הוּא – **he is a deliberate** sinner, not liable to a *chatas.*[21] וְאִי דְּלָא קַבְּלָה עֲלֵיהּ בֶּאֱלוֹהַּ – **And if he did not accept it upon himself as a deity,**

NOTES

11. Since he transgressed two separate prohibitions, he is certainly liable to two offerings.

12. He first ate one olive-sized piece of *cheilev* and then ate another olive-sized piece of *cheilev* without realizing in the interim that he had sinned. In this case, he is liable to only one offering for both transgressions.

13. I.e. the case referred to by the Baraisa's opening statement: "There is an aspect of greater stringency to the Sabbath in that, concerning desecration of the Sabbath, if one committed two transgressions in one lapse of awareness he is liable to a separate *chatas* offering for each and every one of his transgressions."

14. I.e. when the Baraisa states "other mitzvos" it actually means "*some* other mitzvos," referring exclusively to the prohibition of idolatry (*Ritva MHK* ed.). With respect to idolatry, there is a case that parallels the case of "reaping and grinding," in which the sinner is liable to only one *chatas.* The Gemara goes on to explain.

15. The Gemara in *Sanhedrin* (63a) cites a Scriptural source for R' Ami's ruling that someone who inadvertently worships an idol by performing various services is liable to only one *chatas* (*Rashi*). In the case referred to by R' Ami, the sinner performed three separate types of idol service. This parallels the case of Sabbath desecration in which the sinner performed two or more different *melachos.* Nevertheless, the Sabbath desecrator is liable to a separate *chatas* for each and every *melachah* that he performed while the idolater is liable to only one *chatas* for all of the services that he performed.

16. An ordinary case of idolatry for which one is liable to a *chatas* is where, for example, the person realized that the object before him was an idol, but did not realize that the act he performed was considered serving it. But if this is the case to which the Baraisa referred, it would have stated simply that the person performed the act inadvertently. What does the term "inadvertence without intent" mean? [See *Rashi* to *Sanhedrin* 62b ד״ה שגג.]

17. That is, he came upon a structure that housed an idol, and, thinking that it was a synagogue, went inside and bowed down (see *Rashi;* see also *Kereisos* 3a). According to *Rabbeinu Chananel,* the house itself was an idol and the person bowed down to it (see also *Dikdukei Sofrim.*)

18. This would then be a case of inadvertence without intent, i.e. the person sinned inadvertently without intending at all to bow down to an idol (*Rashi*).

19. Even if he had realized that this structure housed an idol and he entered it and bowed to God while inside, he is not at all liable for his act, since he actually bowed down to God, not to the idol (*Rashi*). [A person is liable to a *chatas* if, for example, he bows down to an idol for its sake, not aware that his act is forbidden. Here, where he bowed for the sake of God, he is not at all liable.]

Yad David notes that *Rashi* writes merely that the person is "not liable" for bowing to God in the structure; this implies that it is nevertheless prohibited to do so. In fact, this would be included in the prohibition taught in *Avodah Zarah* (12a) not to bend down in front of an idol to remove a thorn from one's foot so as not to appear to be worshiping it (see also *Ritva MHK* ed.; cf. *Rashi* to *Kereisos* 3a and *Be'er Sheva* there). See *Dibros Moshe* 64:27.

20. It was common in earlier times for citizens to make a statue of the king in his honor (*Rashi;* cf. *Rashi* to *Sanhedrin* 61b and to *Avodah Zarah* 40b). Since such a statue is not considered a deity by anyone, the Gemara will immediately ask why bowing to it would be subject to a *chatas.*

21. By bowing to an object he accepts as a deity, the person has committed a deliberate act of idolatry. However, one never brings a *chatas* offering for deliberate sin. A deliberate act of idolatry is punishable by stoning or *kares.*

עין משפט נר מצוה

כד א מיי' פ"ב מהלכות שגגות הלכה ז:
כה ב מיי' פ"א מהלכו' שבת הלכה ח ופ"ז מהלכות שגגות הל' יא:

א) נתכוין ^א^ להגביה את התלוש וחתך את המחובר פטור לחתוך את התלוש וחתך את המחובר ג) רבא אמר ^ב^ פטור אביי אמר חייב רבא אמר פטור דהא לא נתכוון לחתיכה דאיסורא אביי אמר חייב דהא קמיכוין לחתיכה בעלמא אמר רבא מנא אמינא לה ג) דתניא חומר שבת משאר מצות וחומר שאר מצות משבת חומר שבת משאר מצות שהשבת עשה שתים בהעלם אחד חייב על כל אחת ואחת מה שאין כן בשאר מצות וחומר שאר מצות משבת שבשאר מצות שגג בלא מתכוין חייב מה שאין כן בשבת: אמר מר חומר שבת משאר מצות שהשבת עשה שתים בהעלם אחד חייב על כל אחת ואחת מה שאין כן בשאר מצות היכי דמי אילימא דעבד קצירה וטחינה דכוותה גבי שאר מצות אכל חלב ודם הכא תרתי מיחייב והכא תרתי מיחייב אלא שאר מצות דלא מיחייב אלא חדא היכי דמי דאכל חלב וחלב דכוותה גבי שבת דעבד קצירה וקצירה הכא חדא מיחייב והכא חדא מיחייב לעולם דעבד קצירה וטחינה ומאי מה שאין כן בשאר מצות אע"ז וכדרבי אמי ד) דא"ר אמי זיבח וקיטר וניסך בהעלמה אחת אינו חייב אלא אחת במאי אוקימתא בע"ז אימא סיפא חומר בשאר מצות שבשאר מצות שגג בלא מתכוין חייב מה שאין כן בשבת ה) האי שגג בלא מתכוין דע"ז היכי דמי אילימא כסבור בית הכנסת הוא והשתחוה לה הרי לבו לשמים ואלא ° דחזי אנדרטא וסגיד לה היכי דמי אי דקבלה עליה באלוה מזיד הוא ואי דלא קבלה עליה באלוה לאו כלום הוא אלא מאהבה ומיראה הניחא לאביי ו) דאמר חייב אלא לרבא דאמר פטור מאי איכא למימר אלא באומר מותר משא"כ בשבת דפטור לגמרי ע"כ לא בעא מיני' רבא מרב נחמן אלא אי לחיובי חדא אי לחיובי תרתי אבל מפטרי לגמרי לא

אלא

רש"י

נתכוין להגביה את התלוש. כגון דנפל סכין בערוגת הירק ונתכוין להגביהו: וחתך את המחובר פטור. דכתיב אשר חטא בה ודרשינן בכריתות פרט למתעסק בדבר אחר ועשה דבר זה ושוגג היכי דמי כגון שנתכוין לכך אבל שגג דסבר שאין היום שבת או סבר שמלאכה זו מותרת וזה מתעסק בהגבהה היה ולא בחתיכה: דהא לא איכוין אחתיכה דאיסורא. בשגגת שבת או בשגגת מלאכות אלא מתעסק בחתיכת היתר הוה שיודע שהוא שבת ויודע שחתיכת מחובר אסור: משא"כ בשאר מצות. כולה מפרש לה ואזיל: שגג בלא מתכוין. לקמן מפרש לה: חלב ודם. דומיא דטחינה וקצירה שהן שני גופין: אלא גבי שאר מצות היכי דמי. דפטור: כגון חלב וחלב. בהעלם אחד: דרבי אמי. במסכת סנהדרין בפרק ד' מיתות יליף למילתיה מקרא דאין חילוק חטאות לעכו"ס: והשתחוה לה. והיינו שגג שהיא ע"ז בלא מתכוין שלא נתכוון להשתחוות לע"ז: הרי לבו לשמים. ומה חיוב יש כאן אפי' ידע שהוא בית ע"ז והשתחוה בו לשמים אין חיוב כאן: אנדרטא. צורת המלך שעושין לכבוד המלך והשתחוה לה ולא לשם אלהות: מאהבה ומיראה. מאהבת אדם או מיראת אדם השתחוה לע"ז וקרי ליה שוגג בלא מתכוין כלומר שגג בהכי דסבור כיון דאין מתכוין לבו לאלהות מותר: אלא באומר מותר. כגון גר שנתגייר בין הנכרים כסבור שאין ע"ז בתורה וקרי ליה שגג בלא מתכוין: דפטור לגמרי. בתמיה: עד כאן לא קבעי מיניה רבא מרב נחמן. העלם זה וזה בידו מהו לעיל בפירקין (דף ע:) דהיינו אומר מותר דאמר אין שבת בתורה היינו העלם זה וזה:

דסבור

תוספות

נתכוין להגביה את התלוש. פירש בקונטרס כגון סכין מוטל בערוגת ירק ונתכוין להגביה וחתך את המחובר א"כ הא דפליגי בנתכוין לחתוך את התלוש וחתך את המחובר היינו לחתוך תלוש (א) וחתך מחובר אחר אבל לחתוך מחובר זה וחתך מחובר אחר משמע דחייב לכ"ע וקשה לר"ת דבסוף פ' ספק אכל (כריתות יט:) אמר שמואל המתעסק בחלבים ועריות חייב שכן נהנה בשבת פטור דמלאכת מחשבת אסרה תורה ומוכח התם דאפילו בנתכוין ללקוט תאנה זו וליקט תאנה אחרת פטר שמואל ולקמן בפרק הזורק (דף צז:) פטר ז) (ב) רבא נתכוין לזרוק ארבע וזרק שמנה כי לא אמר כל מקום שתרצה תנוח וכל שכן בנתכוין לזרוק בצד זה וזרק בצד אחר דלא נעשה כלל רצונו או נתכוין לחתוך מחובר זה וחתך מחובר אחר דפטור ונראה לר"ת דהכא מיירי בנתכוין לחתוך תלוש ונמצא שהוא מחובר וחותך מה שהיה מתכוין אלא שלא היה יודע שהיה מחובר ופליגי אביי ורבא בקרא דאשר חטא בה דמוקי ליה רבי אליעזר בפרק ספק אכל (שם יט:) פרט למתעסק והכי איתא התם בהדיא דקאמר עלה לרבא משכחת לה שנתכוין לחתוך את התלוש וחתך את המחובר לאביי שנתכוין להגביה את התלוש כו' ושמואל דפטר מטעם מלאכת מחשבת היינו בנתכוין לחתוך מחובר זה וחתך מחובר אחר דלא נעשה מחשבתו והשתא אתי שפיר דקאמר (ג) לקמן דמפרש שגג בלא מתכוין דשאר מצות היכי דמי כגון דסבור שומן הוא ואכלו דהיינו ממש דומיא דשבת לפר"ת:

הניחא לאביי דאמר חייב. פי' הניחא לאביי בהא דמשכחת גבי ע"ז שגג בלא מתכוין אבל מ"מ גם לאביי לא מיתוקמא ברייתא שפיר בהכי דהא אם חלל שבת מאהבה ומיראה נמי חייב ולהכי איצטריך בסמוך לאוקמא אליבא דאביי שגג בלא מתכוין ה"ד דסבור רוק הוא ובלעו: **עד** כאן לא בעא מיניה רבא מרב נחמן כו'. וא"ת אמאי לא מייתי מתני' דהשוכח עיקר שבת דאינו חייב אלא אחת ולא הוי פטור לגמרי וי"ל דניחא ליה לאתויי מרבא דמספקא ליה בהעלם זה וזה דדילמא אפי' תרתי מיחייב דכי אוקי הכא באומר מותר היינו בנתעלמה ממנו לפי שעה דהיינו דומיא דהעלם זה וזה בידו כדפי' לעיל דאם לא נודע לו מעולם איסור ע"ז אינו ישראל כלל כיון שמודה בע"ז דדוחק להעמיד בתינוק שנשבה לבין העכו"ס: **רבא** אמר פטור. ואם תאמר והא אמר בפרק בן סורר ומורה (סנהדרין דף עד.) דע"ז וגילוי עריות ושפיכות דמים יהרג ואל יעבור אם כן אפילו לא מקבל ליה חייב ואין לומר דרבא לטעמיה דאמר במס' ע"ז בפרק ר' ישמעאל (דף מד.) דאפילו בע"ז בצינעא וחי בהם ולא שימות בהם והא דקאמר רבא בפ"ב דכתובות (דף יט.) גבי עדים שאמרו להם חתמו שקר כו' שאין לך דבר שעומד בפני פיקוח נפש אלא ע"ז וגילוי עריות ושפיכות דמים ה"פ אפילו מאן דמחמיר לא מחמיר אלא בע"ז ג"ע ושפיכות דמים דאם כן דטעמא דרבא דפטר הוי משום הכי מאי מייתי אביי בפ' ד' מיתות (סנהדרין סא:) מכמה ברייתות לימא דאתיא כמ"ד בפרק בן סורר (שם עד.) יהרג ואל יעבור דפלוגתא דתנאי היא וי"ל דסבר רבא דאפי' למ"ד דחייב למסור את עצמו אם לא מסר עצמו לא מיחייב מיתה בבית דין וקשה לרשב"א דאמר רבא במסכת ע"ז ח) הכל היו בכלל לא תעבדם כשפרט לך הכתוב וחי בהם יצא אונס משמע דלא מפיק אלא אונס מיתה אבל שאר אונסין הוו בכלל לא תעבדם וחייב א) והכא פטור אפי' מאהבה דליכא אונס מיתה וי"מ דההיא דאמר יהרג ואל יעבור היינו בפסח אע"ג דלא מקבל עליה לאלוה אבל הכא במפרש דקעביד מאהבה ומיראה אי נמי אפילו בפסח ובע"ז שהכל אין עובדין אותה אלא מאהבה ומיראה דומיא דהמן דמייתי עלה התם להם אי אתה משתחוה אבל אתה משתחוה לאדם כמותך יכול אפי' נעבד כהמן ת"ל לא תעבדם [וקאמר רבא כהמן ולא כהמן דאילו התם מיראה והכא לאו מיראה] ומההיא גופא נמי יש לדקדק דחייב אע"ג דלא קבל עליה באלוה דמשמע דאסר נעבד כהמן דומיא דאדם שכמותך דשרי והיינו בלא קיבלו עליו באלוה ועוד דאמר בפרק ד' מיתות (סנהדרין דף ס:) הפוער עצמו לפעור זו היא עבודתו אע"ג דקא מכוין לבזוייה הזורק אבן למרקולים זו היא עבודתו אע"פ שאין מקבל עליו באלוה ומיהו יש לפרש אע"ג דקא מכוין לבזוייה מכוין לעבודה דרך בזיון וברגימה זו והא דלא דחי ראיות דאביי בעובד מאהבה ומיראה התם משום דהתם עובד כמדעתו דמי וא"ת ולמאי דפטר רבא אמאי לא השתחוה מרדכי להמן וי"ל כדאמרינן במדרש ששתי צורות היו על לבו ועוד משום קידוש השם כדאשכחן בירושלמי במסכת שביעית בפ"ד כגון פפוס ולוליינוס אחיו שנתנו להם מים בזוכית צבועה ולא קבלו מהם ט): **באומר** מותר. והא דמעטינן בפ"ב דמכות (דף ז: ושם) בשגגה פרט לאומר מותר שאני גבי גלות דטובא בשגגה כתיבי התם ולהכי נמי אמר בסוף פ"ב דב"ק (דף כו: ושם) היתה אבן מונחת לו בחיקו ולא הכיר בה מעולם לענין גלות פטור מבשגגה לענין שבת פטור משום דבעינן מלאכת מחשבת והשתא תיפוק ליה דגבי שבת נמי כתיב בשגגה אלא ודאי דוקא גבי גלות ממעטינן משום דכתיבי בשגגה טובא:

אלא

רבינו חננאל

ובפלוגתא דר' יוחנן ור"ל פשוטה היא: **אתמר** נתכוין להגביה את התלוש וחתך את המחובר לכולי עלמא לא מחייב קרבן דהא לא אתכוין למלתא דאית בה איסורא אלא להגביה בעולם נתכוין אע"פ שחותך את המחובר לא קרינן ביה נפש כי תחטא בשגגה ולא הוי חוטא בשגגה אלא מתכוין למעשה מביא לידי חטא. והוא אינו יודע שהוא חוטא. אבל אם נתכוון לחתוך את התלוש שהוא מותר ונזדמן לו מחובר וחתכו רבה אמר פטור דס"ל שאינו קורא ביה נפש כי תחטא בשגגה אלא בזמן שמתכוון לדבר אסור כשיקרא שוגג באיסורו וזה לא נתכוון אלא לחתיכת תלוש אביי אמר חייב דהוא מכוון לחתיכה בעלמא ויש בחתיכה איסור. וסבר אביי שאין צריך להתכוון במעשיו לדבר שהוא באיסורו אלא כל מעשה שיש במינו איסור אף על פי שלא נתכוון לדבר שיש בה איסור כיון שנזדמן לו דבר איסור הריני קורא בו כי תחטא בשגגה. וכן לענין נתכוון לזרוק שתים חורק ד' לרבה פטור דהא לא נתכוון לדבר האיסור בשגגת איסורו אע"פ שמתכוון למקצתו דסבר ליה צריך להתכוון לכל האיסור בשגגת איסורו ולאביי חייב דהא נתכוון לזריקה ונזדמנה לו זריקה אסורה. אמ' (רבא) [רבה] מנא אמינא לה דפטור דתניא חומר בשבת משאר מצות שהשבת עושה שתים בהעלם אחת חייב שתים מה שאין כן בשאר מצות. חומר בשאר מצות ששאר מצות שגג בלא מתכוון חייב משא"כ בשבת ואוקימנא דשגג בלא מתכוין בשבת דפטור [בכה"ג דנתכוין לחתוך את התלוש וכו'] ודוק' הא מתניתא כרבה דאמר נתכוון לחתוך את התלוש וחתך את המחובר פטור דהא לא נתכוון לחתיכה (דאיסור דא) [דאיסורא]. ושקלו וטרו בהא דתנן עשה בהעלם אחד שתים בשבת חייב שתים ובשאר מצות כי האי גונא אינו חייב אלא אחת. היכי דמי [אילימא] קצר וטחן בשבת כיוצא בו בשאר מצות אכל חלב ודם הכא שתים מחייב והכא שתים מחייב. אלא קצר וחזר וקצר בהעלם אחד כיוצא בו בשאר מצות אכל חלב וחזר ואכל חלב בהעלם אחד הכא חדא מחייב והכא חדא מחייב ודחינן מאי שאר מצות דקתני ע"ז. והכי קתני חומר בשבת שאם קצר וטחן בהעלם אחד בזדון שבת ושגגת מלאכות חייב שתים מה שאין כן בע"ז כי (אם) בע"ז אם זיבח וקיטר וניסך בהעלם אחד אינו חייב אלא אחת וכדר' (יוסי) [אמי] ודחינן לא מיתוקמא מתניתין בע"ז דקתני סיפא שגג בלא מתכוון בשאר מצות חייב משא"כ בשבת. שגג בלא מתכוון בע"ז היכי משכחת לה אי נימא דחזא ע"ז וסבר כי היא בית הכנסת והשתחוה [לה] כי האי גוונא פטור הוא דהא לבו לשמים. ואלא דחזא אנדרטא וסגיד לה. אי דקבלה עילויה באלוה מזיד הוא ולאו בר קרבן הוא ואי לא קבלה עילויה באלוה כיון דבשוגג השתחוה כנגד האי אנדרטא לא מחייב דהא לא עביד מידי אלא כגון שהשתחוה לע"ז מאהבה. שראה צורת ע"ז ואהבה או אדם שהעמיד עצמו ע"ז כהמן והשתחוה לו מאהבה בשגגת אלהים אחרים פי' שנעלם ממנו שמשתחוה לע"ז מאהבה חייב או שנעלם ממנו כי אלו העבירות בע"ז מחייב. וזה פי' מאהבה או מיראה נמי כגון מי שנתיירא מן הע"ז והשתחוה לו בשגגת אלהים אחרים או בשגגת עבירות דלא הוה ידע כי האי גוונא חייב אי אמרת כי האי גוונא שגג בלא מתכוין בע"ז חייב ניחא לאביי דמחייב דגרסינן בסנהדרין פרק ארבע מיתות דאתמר העובד ע"ז מאהבה ומיראה כגון המשתחוה מאהבתו לו או מיראתו ממנו לאדם הנעבד כהמן בשוגג שלא היה יודע כי העובד מאהבה או מיראה חייב [אביי אמר חייב] דהא פלחא לע"ז רבא אמר פטור דהא לא קבלה עליו באלוה. הניחא לאביי אלא לרבא

מסורת הש"ס

א) כריתות דף יט ע"ב, ב) [לפמ"ש תוס' לעיל כג: ד"ה גוזה וכ"כ עוד לעיל ע: ד"ה נודע ולמ"ש הרא"ש פרק הזהב סי' יט שלא מצינו בכל הגמ' שמקדים רבא לאביי כי אביי מלך קודם רבא ע"ש וכ"כ עוד בשאר דוכתי א"כ יש לגרוס הכא **אביי אמר** וכו' או דל"ל **רבה אמר** פטור וכו' **אמר רבה מנא אמינא** לה וכו' וע"ע מ"ש פסחים מא. על הגליון], ג) סנהדרין סב., ד) סנהדרין סב. [וע"ש שצ"ל **רבי זכאי**], ה) שם סא: [כריתות ג.], ו) שם, ז) ע"ש שצ"ל רבינא, ח) [דף נד.], ט) [ועי' תוספות סנהדרין סא: ד"ה רבא אמר].

תוספות ישנים

א) וי"א דבאומר אלי אתה מודה רבא דחייב אפילו מאהבה ומיראה דהיינו קבל עליו באלוה כיון דקאמר אלי אתה אע"פ שאומר באונס ה"פ במס' ע"ז הא בכלל לא תעבדם כשאמר אלי אתה. אבל מקטיר דאונס לא הוי בכלל לא תעבדם. ומיהו בהנהו דמייתי אביי ה"מ לאוקמי באלי אתה. והר"א ממיץ מפרש דע"ז שכבר עבדוהו פ"א לשם ע"ז חייב בה אפי' מאהבה ומיראה:

הגהות הב"ח

(א) תוס' ד"ה נתכוין וכו' לחתוך תלוש זה וחתך: (ב) בא"ד בפ' הזורק פטר רב אשי נתכוין וכו': (ג) בא"ד והשתא אתי שפיר לקמן כצ"ל ותיבת דקאמר נמחק:

גליון הש"ס

גמ' דחזי אנדרטא. עי' מס' ע"ז דף מ ע"ב תוד"ה ובאנדרטי:

רב נסים גאון

ואלא מאהבה ומיראה הניחא לאביי דאמר חייב אלא למאן דאמר פטור מאי איכא למימר. ופלוגתא דאביי ורבא משכחת במס' סנהדרין בפרק ד' מיתות (דף סא) איתמר העובד ע"ז מאהבה ומיראה אביי אמר חייב ורבא אמר פטור אביי אמר חייב דהא פלחה רבא אמר פטור דלא קבלה עליה באלוה אי קיבלה עליה אין ואי לא לא:

ליקוטי רש"י

נתכוין להגביה את התלוש וחתך את המחובר פטור. לדברי הכל דהאי מתעסק הוי דלא נתכוון לשום חתיכה [כריתות יט:]. שנאמר (ויקרא ד) אשר חטא בה עד שיתכוין למלאכה זו פרט למתעסק בדבר אחר ועלתה בידו מלאכה זו. **חומר שבת וכו'.** לקמן מפרש לה. **קצירה וטחינה.** דאיכא שמות מחולקין ומשום הכי חייב שתים. **חלב וחלב.** שני זיתים בשני ימים ולא נודע לו בנתיים שחטא אינו חייב אלא אחת [סנהדרין סב:]. **אינו חייב אלא אחת.** [דכל עבודתה] באזהרה אחת הן לא תעבדם (שמות כ) הלכך אין כאן חלוק חטאות. והא דפטר לה בחדא נפקא (סנהדרין סג.) מלא תעבדם הכתוב עשאן עבודה אחת [שם.]. **הרי לבו לשמים.** ולשמים נתכוין והשתחוה ואין כאן עבירה כלל לא שוגג ולא מזיד [שם:]. ולא השתחוה זה לעבודת כוכבים לא מזיד ולא שוגג (הוא) אלא לשמים שהרי לשמים נתכוין ואפילו היה יודע שזה הבית עבודת כוכבים הוא והוא משתחוה בתוכו לשמים אין כאן עונש שהרי אף משתחוה לבית הכנסת לא לבית הוא משתחוה אלא למי ששכן שמו עליה [שם סא:]. דאי נמי בבית עבודת כוכבים השתחוה לשמים לאו איסורא עבד וליכא חטאת [כריתות ג.]. **אלא דחזי אנדרטא וסגיד לה.** שראה דמות שהיו רגילין לעשות בדמות המלך והרואה אותו משתחוה לו לכבוד המלך ופעמים שעובדין אותו וזה ראה אחד שהיה נעבד ולא ידע שהוא נעבד והשתחוה לו. **אי דקבלה עליה באלוה.** שהשתחוה לו לשם עבודת כוכבים מזיד הוא [סנהדרין שם]. **אנדרטא.** צלם דמות המלך [ר"ה כד:]. צורת הצלמים שעושין על שם המלך שמת [מו"ק כה:]. כשהמלך מת עושין צורתו בפתח השער לזכרון [ע"ז מ:]. **ואי דלא קבלה עליה באלוה.** אלא לכבוד המלך השתחוה לו לא כלום הוא דהא לא אכוין לשם עבודת כוכבים [סנהדרין סב.]. **לאו כלום היא.** דכיון דלא נעשה לשם עבודת כוכבים השתחואה דידיה לאו כלום היא [כריתות שם]. **אלא.** שוגג בלא מתכוין כגון מאהבה ומיראה ולא נתכוין לעבודת כוכבים אלא לאהבת האיש ושגג כסבור מותר לעשות כן [סנהדרין שם:]. מאהבת אדם ומיראת אדם ולא חשבה בלבו באלהות [שם סא:]. השתחוה לעבודת כוכבים מאהבת אדם ומיראת אדם דסבר מותר לעבוד עבודת כוכבים מאהבה ומיראה [כריתות שם]. **חייב.** במזיד ובהתראה במיתה ובשוגג דכסבור מותר לעשות כן חייב בחטאת. **פטור.** בין במזיד בין בשוגג דלאו כלום עבד [סנהדרין שם]. **אלא באומר מותר.** לעבוד עבודת כוכבים [כריתות שם:]. דאמר אין עבודת כוכבים בתורה וכיון דלא הוזכרה לו מעולם אין מתכוין קרי ליה [סנהדרין סב.].

לָאו כְּלוּם הוּא – [his bowing] is nothing, and he is not liable to any punishment.[22]

A third possibility is refuted:

אֶלָּא מֵאַהֲבָה וּמִיִּרְאָה – Rather, you might say that the case is one where he served an idol **out of love or out of fear** of a person.[23] **הָנִיחָא לְאַבַּיֵי דְּאָמַר חַיָּיב – This is well according to Abaye, who says** that in such a case **[the sinner] is liable** to a *chatas* offering.[24] **אֶלָּא לְרָבָא דְּאָמַר פָּטוּר – But according to Rava, who says** that in such a case **one is exempt** from punishment,[25] **מַאי אִיכָּא לְמֵימַר – what is there to say?** This cannot be the case in which the Baraisa holds the idolater liable to a *chatas*.

The Gemara rejects one last attempt to interpret the second section of the Baraisa as referring to idolatry:

אֶלָּא בְּאוֹמֵר מוּתָּר – Rather, you might say the case is one **where [the sinner] says: "It is permitted** to engage in idolatry."[26] If so, the following difficulty arises: **מָה שֶׁאֵין כֵּן בְּשַׁבָּת –** When the Baraisa concludes, **"WHEREAS THIS IS NOT SO IN REGARD TO** desecration of **THE SABBATH,"** can it mean that if a person is totally ignorant of the prohibition of doing work on the Sabbath and he commits numerous transgressions, **דְּפָטוּר לְגַמְרֵי – he is completely exempt?** Obviously not! **עַד כָּאן לֹא בְּעָא מִינֵּיהּ רָבָא מֵרַב נַחְמָן – For thus far Rava did not inquire of Rav Nachman,**[27] concerning the case of a person who acted inadvertently regarding both the Sabbath and the *melachos,*[28] **אֶלָּא אִי לְחַיּוּבֵי חֲדָא אִי לְחַיּוּבֵי תַּרְתֵּי – except whether to render** the sinner **liable to one** *chatas* offering **or liable to two** *chatas* offerings. **אֲבָל מִפְטְרֵי לְגַמְרֵי לֹא – But** he did **not** think it possible **to exempt** the sinner **completely!**[29] Thus, the second section of the Baraisa cannot be dealing with one who says "It is permitted," and, accordingly, it cannot be interpreted as dealing with idolatry.

NOTES

22. Since this statue is not an idol, and the person did not accept it as a deity, his act is not at all idolatrous (*Rashi* to *Kereisos* 3a; see *Ritva MHK* ed. and *Shitah Mekubetzes* to *Kereisos* ibid. §31). See also *Rashash* and *Dibros Moshe* 64:29.

23. I.e. he did not serve the idol because he believed it was a deity; rather, he did so out of love or fear of a person, thinking that he was permitted to do so under that circumstance. The Baraisa calls this "sinning inadvertently without any intent at all," because he thought that it was permitted to do such an act when he is not motivated by idolatrous intention (*Rashi;* cf. *Rambam, Hil. Avodas Kochavim* 3:6).

[This case differs from the previous one because here he bowed to an actual idol. Although he was motivated by love or fear, he committed an *act* of idolatry. In the previous case, however, where the statue was not even an idol, his bowing cannot be considered an act of idolatry. This case also differs from typical idolatry, though, where there is no external motivation to perform the idolatrous act.]

24. In *Sanhedrin* (61b) Abaye states that one is liable in such a case. Therefore, if he served the idol deliberately and was forewarned, he is liable to the death penalty. If he served it inadvertently – i.e. he thought it was permissible to perform the service out of love or out of fear of a person – he is liable to a *chatas* offering (*Rashi* loc. cit.).

25. Whether he served the idol deliberately or inadvertently, he is not liable, because his act was motivated by love or fear. [*Tosafos* point out that one is certainly not permitted in the first place to serve an idol out of love or fear of a person, and if one is threatened he is required to give up his life rather than serve an idol. It is only after the fact that one is not liable for punishment if he was motivated by love or fear (see there).]

26. For example, in the case of a convert who lived among gentiles. Since he was never taught that idolatry is forbidden, the Baraisa refers to his idol service as a sin committed without any intent at all (*Rashi;* see above 68b). [Nevertheless, he is liable to a *chatas* since, unlike the case of preoccupation, he was cognizant of his actions.]

Rashi's example of a convert as one who thought idolatry to be permitted is difficult. *Chasam Sofer HaShalem* argues that if the person never was told about the prohibition of idolatry, his conversion would not be valid (since that is the most basic tenet of Judaism). See *Tosafos;* see also *Dibros Moshe* 64:28. [*Chasam Sofer* asks further that above (68a), when discussing the Sabbath prohibition, the Gemara gave a second example of someone who was never aware of that mitzvah – namely, a child who was raised by gentiles. Why, then, did *Rashi* not state that case here, as well? See there for a novel approach to explain *Rashi's* view.]

27. Above, 70b.

28. I.e. he did numerous *melachos* on the Sabbath not realizing that the Sabbath law was included in the Torah. He was thus one who said, "It is permitted to work on the Sabbath" (*Rashi*).

[*Maharam* asks that above (70b; see also note 7 there) *Rashi* explained that in the case of Rava's inquiry the person was aware of some of the Sabbath *melachos.* This apparently contradicts his explanation here. See *Maharam* for a possible resolution to this difficulty.]

29. Rava, in posing his query, presumed that the Sabbath desecrator is liable; he merely inquired as to *how many* offerings the desecrator must bring. Now, if the Baraisa deals with a case of one who is totally ignorant of the prohibition, it emerges that a totally ignorant Sabbath desecrator is not liable to a *chatas* offering at all!

The Gemara thus concludes that the second section of the Baraisa, which stated that one is liable to a *chatas* for violating "other mitzvos" inadvertently without intention, cannot be referring to idolatry. If the object to which the person bowed was not actually an idol, he would certainly not be liable to any punishment unless he accepted it as his deity with that act; and in that case he would be liable to stoning, not to a *chatas.* Where the object was in fact an idol and he mistook it for a truly sacred object, he would not be liable to any punishment since his intention was to bow to God. And even if he intended to bow to an idol, but was motivated by the love or fear of another person, he would not be liable to a *chatas* according to Rava.

The Gemara therefore offers another interpretation of the Baraisa:

אֶלָּא לָאו – **Rather, is it not** explained in the following manner? רֵישָׁא בַּעֲבוֹדַת כּוֹכָבִים – **The first section** of the Baraisa deals **with idolatry** וְסֵיפָא בִּשְׁאָר מִצְוֹת – **and the latter section** deals **with** the transgression of **other mitzvos.**[1]

The Gemara elaborates on the last statement of the Baraisa, from which Rava derived his proof that the principle of preoccupation can apply even when the person intended the type of act that he, in fact, carried out:

וְשָׁגַג בְּלֹא מִתְכַּוֵּין בִּשְׁאָר מִצְוֹת הֵיכִי דָּמֵי – **Now, what is the case of acting inadvertently without intent regarding other mitzvos?** דִּסְבוּר דְּשׁוּמָּן הוּא וַאֲכָלוֹ – Presumably, **where he thought that [the piece] was permitted fat and he ate it,** whereupon he discovered that he, in fact, had eaten *cheilev.*[2] מַה שֶּׁאֵין כֵּן בְּשַׁבָּת – Then, when the Baraisa concludes by stating, **"WHEREAS THIS IS NOT SO IN REGARD TO** desecration of **THE SABBATH,"** דְּפָטוּר – meaning **that** in a parallel case **[a Sabbath desecrator] is exempt,** it teaches a law such as the following: דְּנִתְכַּוֵּין לַחְתּוֹךְ אֶת הַתָּלוּשׁ – **Where someone intended to cut something** that was **detached** from the ground וְחָתַךְ אֶת הַמְחוּבָּר – **but he** in fact **cut something that was attached** to the ground, פָּטוּר – **he is exempt.**[3]

The Gemara explains how Abaye would interpret the Baraisa:

וְאַבַּיֵי – **And Abaye** could say:[4] שָׁגַג בְּלֹא מִתְכַּוֵּין הֵיכִי דָּמֵי – **What is the case of one who acted inadvertently without** any **intent** at all? דִּסְבוּר רוֹק הוּא – **Where [a person] thought [the a substance in his mouth] was saliva** וּבְלָעוֹ – **and he swallowed it, and** it turned out to have been liquefied *cheilev.*[5] מַה שֶּׁאֵין כֵּן בְּשַׁבָּת – And when the Baraisa concludes by stating, **"WHEREAS THIS IS NOT SO IN REGARD TO** desecration of **THE SABBATH,"** דְּפָטוּר – meaning **that** in a parallel case **[a Sabbath desecrator] is exempt,** it teaches a law such as the following: דְּנִתְכַּוֵּין לְהַגְבִּיהַּ אֶת הַתָּלוּשׁ – **Where someone intended to lift something** that was **detached** from the ground וְחָתַךְ אֶת הַמְחוּבָּר – **but he** in fact **cut something** that was **attached,**[6] פָּטוּר – **he is exempt.**[7] אֲבָל נִתְכַּוֵּין לַחְתּוֹךְ אֶת הַתָּלוּשׁ – **However,** if **he intended to cut something** that was **detached** from the ground וְחָתַךְ אֶת הַמְחוּבָּר – **but he** in fact **cut something** that was **attached,** חַיָּיב – **he is liable.**

The Gemara cites another dispute between Abaye and Rava regarding preoccupation:

אִיתְּמַר – **It was stated:** נִתְכַּוֵּין לִזְרוֹק שְׁתַּיִם וְזָרַק אַרְבַּע – If **someone intended to throw** an object a distance of **two** *amos* **but he** in fact **threw** it **four** *amos,*[8] רָבָא אָמַר פָּטוּר – **Rava said that he is exempt,** אַבַּיֵי אָמַר חַיָּיב – whereas **Abaye said that he is liable** to a *chatas.*

The Gemara explains the dispute:

רָבָא אָמַר פָּטוּר – **Rava said that he is exempt,** דְּלֹא קָמִיכַּוֵּין לִזְרִיקָה דְּאַרְבַּע – **because he did not intend a throw of four** *amos.*[9] אַבַּיֵי אָמַר חַיָּיב – **Abaye said that he is liable,** דְּהָא קָמִיכַּוֵּין לִזְרִיקָה בְּעָלְמָא – **because he was intending a throw of some sort.**[10]

The Gemara presents a third dispute between these Amoraim:

כִּסְבוּר רְשׁוּת הַיָּחִיד – If **someone thought** he was throwing in **a private domain,** וְנִמְצֵאת רְשׁוּת הָרַבִּים – **and it was found** to be **a public domain,**[11] רָבָא אָמַר פָּטוּר – **Rava said that he is**

NOTES

1. The Baraisa means that there is an aspect of greater stringency to the Sabbath as compared to *some* other mitzvos, and there is an aspect of greater stringency to *some* other mitzvos as compared to the Sabbath (see *Ritva MHK* ed.). Explained in this way, the mitzvos referred to in the second section of the Baraisa are not necessarily the same ones as those referred to in the first section.

2. [The Gemara thus explains that the Baraisa's term "inadvertence without intent" means acting while preoccupied.] According to Rava, this refers to someone who was preoccupied with the act of eating what he believed to be permitted fat and instead ate *cheilev.* [This is unlike a typical inadvertent sin where the person is mistaken about an aspect of the law – i.e. he did not know a certain cut of fat was included in the *cheilev* prohibition and he ate it. Here the person knew which cuts were *cheilev,* but mistook the identity of the piece he ate.] Although the term בָּה teaches that one who sins while preoccupied is exempt from a *chatas* (as explained on 72b note 2), in this case the person is liable. This is so because the Gemara in *Kereisos* states that the principle of preoccupation does not apply to *cheilev* or any other prohibition from which one derives physical benefit (*Rashi*). [See *Kehillos Yaakov* (§34) for a discussion about why this is so.]

[*Tosafos* above (72b; see note 5 there) cite this case as proof to the fact that the principle of preoccupation applies even when the person acted on the very object he had planned. For here, the person apparently did eat the piece he was intending; he just misidentified it. Therefore, if the person thought that an object was detached and after he cut it discovered that it had in fact been attached, he is considered preoccupied. (See, however, *Rosh Yosef* who asserts that *Rashi* could understand the Gemara to mean that there were *two* pieces before the person, one of permitted fat and one of *cheilev,* and, while preoccupied with taking the permitted fat, the person accidentally took the *cheilev.* See also *Rashi* to *Kereisos* 19b ד״ה מתעסק בחלבים.)]

3. The person does not receive any physical benefit by cutting the attached plant. Therefore, since he did not intend to perform a prohibited act, he is exempt – even though he did intend an act of cutting (*Rashi*).

Rava thus cited this Baraisa above to support his view that the principle of preoccupation applies even when the person was intending the act, as long as it was in a permitted circumstance. For here the person who ate the *cheilev* was in fact preoccupied with eating. Nevertheless, since this preoccupation was not with a *prohibited* form of eating, the person would be exempt if not for the rule in *Kereisos* that the exemption of preoccupation does not apply to cases that involve physical benefit.

4. Abaye defends his view that if the person was planning to do an act of cutting he can no longer be classified as one who is preoccupied, even though he was intending to cut something permitted (*Rashi*).

5. In that case, the person did not intend to *eat* at all, but rather to swallow saliva. Thus, he committed the sin without any intent for the act of eating. Nevertheless, when he in fact ate *cheilev,* he is liable to a *chatas* offering (*Rashi;* cf. *Tos. Rid*). [See above, note 2.]

6. For example, a person dropped a knife in a vegetable patch and, while lifting it, accidentally cut a vegetable from the ground.

7. Since he committed the sin without intending to do the act of cutting at all.

8. I.e. he overthrew his mark and the stone fell two *amos* beyond where he had meant it to fall (*Ritva MHK* ed. in explanation of *Rashi;* cf. *Chidushei HaRan* and *Tosafos* to *Bava Kamma* 26b ד״ה נתכוין). One is liable for the *melachah* of throwing in a public domain only if the object is transported a distance of four *amos.* Thus, in this case the person intended one act, a permitted one, but in fact performed a different act, one that was forbidden.

9. He did not intend to perform an act that is forbidden on the Sabbath, for which we would have to determine if there was inadvertence regarding either the Sabbath or the *melachah.* Rather, here he knew that it was the Sabbath and that throwing an object four *amos* is forbidden; he was, however, preoccupied with a permitted act [a two-*amah* throw] and a prohibited action occurred from his effort (*Rashi*).

10. Since he intended an act of throwing, his throw of four *amos* is the result of inadvertence, not of preoccupation. Rava and Abaye thus follow their reasoning stated above in the case of the person who intended to cut something detached and in fact cut something that was attached. The Gemara below will explain the need to state both disputes.

11. It is permitted to carry or throw an object any distance within a private domain. Thus, in this case, like the other two, the person was intending one act, a permitted one, but in fact performed a different act, one that is forbidden.

אלא לאו רישא בעכו"ם וסיפא בשאר מצות ושגג בלא מתכוין בשאר מצות ה"ד דסבור דשומן הוא ואכלו משא"כ בשבת דפטור דנתכוון לחתוך את התלוש וחתך את המחובר פטור ואביי שגג בלא מתכוין ה"ד [א]דסבור רוק הוא ובלעו משא"כ בשבת דפטור דנתכוון להגביה את התלוש וחתך את המחובר פטור אבל נתכוון לחתוך את התלוש וחתך את המחובר חייב: איתמר [א]נתכוון לזרוק שתים וזרק ארבע [ב]רבא אמר פטור אביי אמר חייב רבא אמר פטור (א) דלא קמיכוין לזריקה דארבע אביי אמר חייב דהא קמיכוין לזריקה בעלמא כסבור רשות היחיד ונמצאת רשות הרבים רבא אמר [ב]פטור ואביי אמר חייב רבא אמר פטור דהא לא מיכוין לזריקה דאיסורא ואביי אמר חייב דהא קא מיכוין לזריקה בעלמא וצריכא דאי אשמעינן קמייתא בההוא קאמר רבא דהא לא קמיכוין לחתיכה דאיסורא אבל נתכוון לזרוק שתים וזרק ארבע דארבע בלא תרתי לא (ב) מיזרקא ליה אימא מודה ליה לאביי ואי אשמעינן בהא בהא קאמר רבא דהא לא קמיכוין לזריקה דארבע אבל כסבור רה"י ונמצא רה"ר דמכוין לזריקה דארבע אימא מודי ליה לאביי צריכא [ג]תנן אבות מלאכות ארבעים חסר אחת והוינן בה מנינא למה לי וא"ר יוחנן שאם עשאן כולם בהעלם אחד חייב על כל אחת ואחת בשלמא לאביי דאמר כי האי גוונא חייב משכחת לה דידע דאסורא (ג) שבת וידע לה איסור מלאכות וקא טעה בשיעורין אלא לרבא דאמר פטור היכי משכחת לה בזדון שבת ושגגת מלאכות הניחא אי סבר לה כר' יוחנן דאמר כיון ששגג בכרת אע"פ שהזיד בלאו משכחת לה דידע לה לשבת בלאו אלא אי סבר לה כרשב"ל דאמר עד שישגוג בלאו וכרת דידע לה לשבת במאי [ד]דידע לה בתחומין ואליבא דר"ע: **מתני'** [ה]אבות [ו][ג]מלאכות ארבעים חסר אחת הזורע והחורש והקוצר והמעמר והדש והזורה הבורר הטוחן והמרקד והלש והאופה הגוזז את הצמר המלבנו והמנפצו והצובעו והטווה [ז]והמיסך והעושה שתי בתי נירין והאורג שני חוטין והפוצע שני חוטין הקושר והמתיר [ח]והתופר שתי תפירות הקורע על מנת לתפור [שתי תפירות] הצד צבי השוחטו והמפשיטו המולחו והמעבד את עורו והממחקו והמחתכו הכותב שתי אותיות והמוחק על מנת לכתוב שתי אותיות הבונה והסותר המכבה והמבעיר המכה בפטיש [ט]המוציא מרשות לרשות הרי אלו אבות מלאכות ארבעים חסר אחת:

גמ'

רש"י

דסבור שומן הוא ואכלו. והיינו דשגג דסבור שומן הוא ולא נתכוין לאכול חלב וחייב ואף על פי דמתעסק הוא לרבא דהא לא מתכוין לאכילת איסור חייב דאמר שמואל בכריתות (פ"ד דף יט:) בחלבי' ועריות מתעסק חייב שכן נהנה אבל בשבת פטור דלא נהנה והיינו סייעתא לדידיה דאמר נתכוין לחתוך את התלוש וחתך את המחובר פטור: ואביי. אמר לך לעולם כי האי גוונא אף בשבת חייב דלאו מתעסק הוא והיכי דמי מתעסק דשאר מצות חייב קסבר רוק הוא שהיה חלב נימוח ובלעו דלא איכוין לאכילה דרוק לאו בר אכילה הוא אלא בליעה דכתיב (איוב ז) עד בלעי רוקי ועלתה בידו אכילה דהא לא איכוין לאכילה ודכוותייהו דשבת דפטור נתכוין להגביה ועלתה בידו חתיכה: דהא לא איכוין לזריקה דאיסור. ויהא שוגג בשבת או במלאכה אבל זה אינו שוגג לא בשבת ולא במלאכות אלא מתעסק בדבר אחד של היתר ועלתה בידו איסור: וצריכא. לאיפלוגי בכולהו אף על גב דדמי להדדי: דארבע בלא תרתי לא מזדריק. וזה שנתכוין לשתים וזרק ארבע נעשית מחשבתו דהא יש בכלל ד' שתים הלכך לאו מתעסק הוא: דלא איכוין לזריקה דארבע. ובליר מהני לא שם זריקה עלה: אבל כסבור רה"י הוא וכו'. דנתכוון לזריקה גמורה: משכחת לה. להאי שנשתכחה תורת כל הלכות שבת ממנו ואפילו הכי חשיבא ליה כזדון שבת ושגגת מלאכות לחיוביה אכל חדא כגון דידע ליה לשבת באיסורין וטעה בשיעורין שנתכוין לפחות מכשיעור ועשה כשיעור דלכולן יש שיעור: אלא לרבא דאמר פטור היכי משכחת לה. דמיחייב שום אדם על כל מלאכה ומלאכה שבהעלם אחד על כרחך בזדון שבת ושגגת מלאכות הוא דבעית לאשכוחיה והכא דאיעלימו כולהו מיניה מאי זדון שבת איכא במה ניכר לו שבת משאר ימים: **מתני'** הזורה. ברחת לרוח: הבורר. פסולת בידיו: המרקד. בנפה ובגמ' פריך הני כולהו חדא היא להפריש פסולת מתוך אוכל נעשות שלשתן: האופה. לא הוה במשכן דלא שייך אלא בפת ופת לא שייכא במלאכת המשכן אבל כולהו קמייתא הואי בסממנין של צבע תכלת וארגמן ותולעת שני ובגמרא פריך דשביק תנא מבשל דהוי בסממנים ונקט אופה ושיעורן של אלו כגרוגרת חוץ מחורש דבכל שהוא לקמן בפרק הבונה (דף קג.): הגוזז צמר. וכל שאר מלאכות שייכי בצמר של מלאכת המשכן: המלבנו. מכבסו בנהר: המנפצו. קרפי"ר בלע"ז: המיסך. אורדי"ר: בתי נירין. ליצ"ש שנתן שני חוטין בתוך הבית ניר ובגוזז ובמלבן וכולהו איך מפרש שיעורן לקמן בפרק האורג: הפוצע. מנתק פעמים שיש בשני חוטין יותר מדאי ומנתק מהן ומקליטן לצורך והני כולהו ממיסך ואילך עד קושר ומתיר שייכי ביריעות ולקמן מפרש מאי קושר ומאי מתיר איכא: ותופר וקורע. ביריעות הוא: על מנת לתפור. פעמים שהנקב עגול ואינו יכול לתופרו יפה אא"כ קורעו כדמפרש בגמרא אבל קורע שלא לתפור לא הוי במשכן: הצד את הצבי. וכל מלאכת עורו נוהגת בתחשים למשכן בעורותיהן: המולחו. לעור: ממחקו. מגרר שערו: מחתכו. מקלעו ומחתכו לרצועות וסנדלים: כותב ומוחק. לקמן (דף קג:) מפרש למאי מיבעיא למשכן שכן רושמין על קרשי המשכן לידע איזה בן זוגו וכותב אות בזו ואות בזו ומוחק פעמים שטעה: מכבה ומבעיר. בגא שתחת הדוד של סממנין: מכה בפטיש. הוא גמר כל מלאכה שכן אומן מכה בקורנס על הסדן להחליקו בגמר מלאכה ומתניתין נמי לא מיחייב ליה אלא בגמר מלאכה:

תוספות

אלא לאו רישא בע"ז וסיפא בשאר מצות. תימה לר"י דלוקמא כולה בשאר מצות ומאי מה שאין כן בשאר מצות כגון שחטא וחזר בתוך דאינו חייב אלא אחת כדאמר אביי בפרק אחד דיני ממונות (סנהדרין לד:) שם תעשה עשאן הכתוב עשיה אחת ור' אבהו נמי דפליג מודה דלרבי ישמעאל בשחיטה וזריקה ולר' עקיבא בהעלאה וזריקה דאינו חייב אלא אחת דמחד קרא נפקי ושגג בלא מתכוין כגון שנתכוין לשחוט בהמת חולין והיה צריך לשל חולין ונמצאת (ד) של קדשים דכוותה בשבת נתכוין לחתוך תלוש ונמצא מחובר ולא היה צריך אלא לתלוש דפטור דמלאכת מחשבת בעינן וי"ל דלא מצינן לפרושי הכי דמשמע דפטור בשבת לפי ששגג בלא מתכוין דכה"ג אפילו נתכוין למחובר זה ונמצא מחובר אחר פטור דאין זה מלאכת מחשבת וליכא לאוקמי נמי דמיירי כשנעשה מחשבתו כגון שהיה צריך לחתוך מה שחתך אלא שהיה סבור שהוא תלוש ונמצא שהוא מחובר הא ליכא למימר דכה"ג אם פטור לענין שבת מאשר חטא בה פטור נמי לענין חוץ ומיהו עוד קשה דלוקמא כולה בשאר מצות כגון (ה) נרבע לזכר ורבע את הזכר והבא על הבהמה והביא בהמה עליו דבין לאביי ובין לר' אבהו לר' עקיבא אינו חייב אלא אחת והשתא שגג בלא מתכוין מיתוקם שפיר דמיפטר בשבת מאשר חטא בה וכגון שנעשית מחשבתו וגבי עריות לא מיפטר שכן נהנה:

העושה שני בתי נירין. צריך לפרש למה פירש כאן ובאורג [י] ובפוצע ובתופר ובכותב שיעור טפי מבשאר:

הקושר והמתיר. צ"ע אי מיחייב במתיר שלא על מנת לקשור אי לא ומדלא תני ליה כדתני מוחק ע"מ לכתוב אין לדקדק דהכי נמי לא קתני סותר ע"מ לבנות ובפ' במה מדליקין (לעיל לא:) אמרינן בהדיא דבעינן סותר ע"מ לבנות ולפי מה שפירש רש"י בגמרא (דף עד:) דאי מתרמי ליה תרי קיטרי בהדי הדדי בשני חוטין זה אצל זה שרי חד ומניח חד משמע דמיחייב בלא על מנת לקשור ולשון קטר לא משמע כפירושו אבל ר"ח פירש וכן משמע בירושלמי כשנפסק חוט בשני מקומות ונקשר מתירין ב' הקשרים ומשליכין לחוץ האמצעי וחוזרין וקושרין שתי הראשים זה בזה ואין בו אלא קשר א' ולפי זה משמע דבעי מתיר ע"מ לקשור והא דלא תני ליה במתיר ובסותר פירשתי בפרק ב' (דף לא: ד"ה וסותר): מכדי

עין משפט נר מצוה

כו א מיי' פ"ב מהלכות שגגות הלכה ז:
כז ב מיי' פ"א מהלכות שבת הלכה ח:
כח ג מיי' פ"ז מהלכות שבת הלכה א סמג לאוין סה:

רבינו חננאל

דאמר פטור מאי איכא למימר ואמרינן לא משכחת שגג בלא מתכוין לע"ז אלא באומר מותר. פי' כגון מי שנעלם ממנו עבודת אלהים אחרים ששכח הכל לגמרי שנמצא בידו העלם אלהים אחרים והעלם עבירות ואומר שמותר. וכי האי גוונא בע"ז (אחרינא) חייב בשבת פטור לגמרי ואקשי' ומי איכא למימר דפטור לגמרי דהא עד כאן לא בעא מיניה רבא מרב נחמן העלם זה וזה בידו. פי' העלם שבת והעלם מלאכות בידו מהו אלא לחיובי חדא או תרתי אבל למפטריה לגמרי לא וחזרנו לפרק פירוק אחר משום דקשיא דלא מיתוקמא סיפא דהא מתניתין בע"ז אוקמי הכי רישא בע"ז דקתני עשה שתים בהעלם א' בשבת חייב ב' משא"כ בע"ז שאם זיבח וקיטר וניסך בהעלם א' אינו חייב אלא אחת כר' אמי אבל סיפא דקתני בשאר מצות שגג בלא מתכוין חייב משא"כ בשבת דפטור. בשאר מצות דלאו ע"ז היא והיכי דמי כגון שהי' סבור שהוא שומן ואכלו ונמצא חלב. כגון זה בשאר מצות הוא דחייב. אבל בשבת כי האי גוונא נתכוון לחתוך בתלוש וחתכו ונמצא דמחובר לקרקע פטור ודחי אביי ואמר לא כי האי גוונא (לע"ז) לעולם אימא לך חייב והיכי דמי שגג בלא מתכוין דבשאר מצות חייב ובשבת פטור. כגון שנתכוין בבליעה דרוק ובלעה ונמצא חלב שאע"פ שלא נתכוין לאכילה דחייב בשאר מצות ובשבת כה"ג דנתכוין להגביה דבר תלוש והגביהו ונמצא שחתכו מן המחובר [פטור] אבל אם נתכוין לחתיכה בעלמא חייב. (כגון) [וכ"ש] בשאר מצות אם נתכוין לאכילה בעלמא [חייב] וכדר' נחמן דאמר המתעסק בחלבין ובעריות אע"פ שלא נתכוון חייב שכבר נהנה. והמתעסק בשבת פטור. מלאכת מחשבת אסרה תורה. ור' יוחנן התם בפרק ארבע מיתות כדתני תנא הדא מתניתין קמיה דחאה ואמר ליה פוק תני לברא. דכל מתניתין דלא מיתוקמא רישא וסיפא בחד טעמא לאו מתנית' תרצתא היא. ר' יוחנן לטעמיה דאמר בסוף פרק המפקיד מאן דמתרגם לי חבית אליבא דחד תנא מובילנא מאניה בתריה לבי מסותא: נתכוון לזרוק ב' וזרק ד' אמות (רבא) [רבה] אמר (חייב) [פטור] אביי אמר (פטור) [חייב] פשוט' היא ומקשינן (לרבא) [לרבה] ממתנית' דקתני ארבעים חסר אחת ואמר ר' יוחנן עלה שאם עשאן כולם בהעלם אחד חייב על כל אחת ואחת ולא משכחת כהאי גוונא דחייב בכולן אלא בזדון שבת ושגגת מלאכות בשלמא לאביי דאמר כי האי גוונא חייב [כו'] [וקא טעה] בשיעורין כגון זריקת ב' אמות וזריקת ד' וכיוצא בהן אלא (לרבא) [לרבה] דאמר כל כה"ג פטור היכי משכחת [לה] בזדון [שבת] ושגגת מלאכה. הניחא אליבא דר' יוחנן דאמר כיון ששגג בכרת אע"פ שהזיד בלאו משכחת לה דידע דאיסור השבת בלאו אלא אלא לר"ל דאמר עד שישגוג בלאו וכרת היכי משכחת לה ושנינן דידע לה בתחומין ואליבא דר' עקיבא כמו שאמרנו למעלה. דאביי אליבא דר' יוחנן פשוטה היא אלא אפילו לריש לקיש כיון דסבר אביי כשנתכוון למקצת האיסור בשגגת איסורו ונזדמן לו כל האיסור חייב כגון המתכוון לזרוק ב' אמות שהן מקצת איסורו כי האיסור ד' אמות ונתכוון לזרוק שתים מתוך ארבע (וניזרוק) [ונזדמן] לו שזרק ד' חייב. מוקים לה אליבא דר"ל במכיר את השבת באיסור מלאכות וידע (בשיעורן) [בכולן] ושוגג בלאו שבשיעור: אבות מלאכות ארבעים חסר אחת. למה

מסורת הש"ס

א) [ב"ק דף כו: ע"ש], ב) [עמ"ש לעיל עב: על הגליון], ג) [לעיל סט. וש"נ], ד) [לעיל סט. ע:], ה) ס"א אלו אבות, ו) לעיל ו: מט: סט. ע: לקמן צו: ב"ק ב. [כריתות ג:], ז) [פי' מותח חוטי השתי], ח) [לקמן קה.], ט) לעיל ב: [שבועות ה:], י) [עי' תוי"ט ד"ה והעושה שתי].

הגהות הב"ח

(א) גמ' רבא אמר פטור דהא לא קמיכוין: (ב) שם תרתי לא מיזדרקא ליה: (ג) שם משכח' לה דידע לאיסורא דשבת וידע לה לאיסור מלאכות: (ד) תום' ד"ה אלא וכו' לשל חולין ונמצאת אחרת והיא של קדשים וכו' תלוש זה ונמצא מחובר אחר ולא: (ה) בא"ד בשאר מצות כגון הבא על הזכור והביא עליו זכור והבא על הבהמה. נ"ב עי' פרק ד' מיתות דף נד:

ליקוטי רש"י

ואביי שגג בלא מתכוין ה"ד וכו'. כגון חלב המהותך לפניו וכסבור רוק הוא ובלעו דלא מתכוין לאכילה אלא מתעסק בדבר אחר בבליעת רוק והיכי דמי שוגג גמור כסבור שומן הוא ואכלו דנתכוין לאכילה אבל זה לא שוגג הוא ואפילו הכי חייב כדאמרן לקמן במתעסק שכן נהנה מה שאין כן בשבת כגון נתכוין להגביה את התלוש וחתך את המחובר פטור שנאמר (ויקרא ד) אשר חטא בה עד שיתכוין למלאכה זו פרט למתעסק בדבר אחר ועלתה בידו מלאכה זו ומיהו מתעסק ועלה בידו אכילת חלבים או עריות חייב שכבר נהנה. דסבור דשומן הוא ואכלו. היה מתעסק ולא נתכוין לכך כל מתעסק קרי ליה שאינו מתכוין בדבר זה כלל [סנהדרין סב:]. מנינא למה לי. ליתני אבות מלאכות הזורע והחורש כו' למה לי למיתנא ארבעים חסר אחת ליתנינהו ואנן ידעינן דארבעים חסר אחת איכא [לעיל סט.]. ליתני אבות מלאכות הזורע והחורש כו' למה לי לאשמעינן מניינא הא מני להו ואזיל. שאם עשאן כולן כו'. ובא להודיענו סכום החטאות שאדם חייב באיסורי שבת בהעלם אחד ואשמעינן ארבעים חסר אחת הן ותו לא שאפילו עשה תולדותיהן עמהן אינו מביא על המולדה היכא דעשאה עם אביה דהוה ליה כעושה וחוזר ועושה דכולה חדא עבירה היא [לעיל ו:]. ובא להודיעך שאם נתעלמו כל הלכות שבת ממנו כמה חטאות [חייב] עליו [לקמן ע"ב]. וסימנא בעלמא אשמעינן לידע כמה חטאות חייב על חילול שבת אחת. אלא לרבא דאמר פטור היכי משכחת לה. דמיחייב על כרחך לא משכחת לה אלא בזדון שבת דיודע שבת ושגגת מלאכות דאינו יודע שהמלאכות הללו אסורות דאי בזדון מלאכות ושגגת שבת דיודע שהן אסורות בשבת אבל שכח שהיום שבת הא תנן דאינו חייב אלא אחת לכל שבת וזדון שבת לא הוי אלא אם כן יודע אחת מהלכותיה דאי לא ידע במידי מינייהו במה שבת חלוק לו משאר ימים וזה ששגג בכולן אין כאן זדון שבת [לעיל סט.]. דמיחייב איניש אכל חדא על כרחך בזדון שבת ושגגת מלאכות הוא דמשכחת לה והכא מאי זדון שבת איכא. דהא לא ידע שבת במידי כיון דכל הלכותיה נעלמות ממנו אין חלוק היום משאר ימים [שם ע:]. הניחא אי סבר לה כר' יוחנן. דאמר שגגת כרת שמה שגגה. משכחת לה. וזדון שבת בלאוין ושגגת מלאכות בכריתות דיודע לה לשבת שהוזהר על הלאוין או של כולן או של אחת מהן [שם סט.]. שלא נעלמו ממנו אלא הכריתות וידע הלאוין והיינו זדון שבת [שם ע:]. דידע לה לשבת במאי. הלא בכולן שגג כסבור שכל מלאכות מותרות. בתחומין. דאין בקרבן [שם סט.]. דאינו יודע שמלאכות הללו אסורות אבל יודע מצות שבת בדבר אחד כגון דידע שאסור לצאת חוץ לתחום [כריתות ג.]. ואליבא דר' עקיבא. דאמר במסכת סוטה תחומין דאורייתא נינהו ... בו ביום דרש רבי עקיבא ומדושם מתוך לעיר כו' [לעיל שם]. דאמר (סוטה כז:) דאורייתא נינהו והוי מלאו ומיהו אין חייבין לא על שגגתו חטאת כו' [לקמן קנג:]. ור' עקיבא מודה נמי בתחומים דאין חייבים עליהם כרת דתנן אבות מלאכות ארבעים חסר אחת ולא פליג ר' עקיבא [סנהדרין סו.]. העושה שתי בתי נירין. שנתן שני חוטין של שתי בנירה שקורין ליצ"ש [לקמן קה.]. המולחו. מליחה מאבות מלאכות בדבר שיש בו עיבוד דתנן והמולחו והמעבדו [ביצה יא:]. והממחקו. ממחק. מחליק [כריתות כה.]. והמחתכו. מחתך העור מקלעו במדה [לקמן עד:]. הכותב שתי אותיות. שבקרשי המשכן שתים היו כותבים אחת בזו ואחת בזו כדי לזווגן כשסותרים אותן [שם עה:]. והסותר. כל מקלקל דשבת הוי פטור דלאו היינו מלאכת מחשבת ... דתנן באבות מלאכות דמיחייב סותר על מנת לבנות הוא ואינו יכול לבנות אלא אם כן סותרו והשתא לאו קלקול היא וכו' ומכבה דומיא דסותר ולהכי תנן הקורע על מנת לתפור וכן מוחק על מנת לכתוב דכולם

exempt, וְאַבַּיֵי אָמַר חַיָּיב – but **Abaye said that he is liable** to a *chatas.*

The Gemara explains the dispute:

רָבָא אָמַר פָּטוּר – **Rava said that he is exempt,** דְּהָא לֹא מִיכַּוֵּין לִזְרִיקָה דְּאִיסּוּרָא – **because he did not intend a prohibited throw.** וְאַבַּיֵי אָמַר חַיָּיב – **Abaye said that he is liable,** דְּהָא קָא מִיכַּוֵּין לִזְרִיקָה בְּעָלְמָא – **because he was intending some throw.**

The Gemara now explains the necessity of recording all three disputes between Rava and Abaye:[12]

וּצְרִיכָא – **It is necessary** to state all three disputes. דְּאִי אַשְׁמְעִינַן קַמַּיְיתָא – **For if we were informed about the first** dispute [viz., uprooting a plant], בְּהַהוּא קָאָמַר רָבָא – we would have thought only **in that** case **does Rava say** the person is exempt, דְּהָא לֹא קָמִיכַּוֵּין לַחֲתִיכָה דְּאִיסּוּרָא – **because he did not intend the prohibited** act of **cutting** that resulted at all, אֲבָל נִתְכַּוֵּין לִזְרוֹק שְׁתַּיִם וְזָרַק אַרְבַּע – **but** when **he intended to throw** an object a distance of **two** *amos* **but he** in fact **threw** it **four** *amos,* דְּאַרְבַּע בְּלֹא תַּרְתֵּי לֹא מִיזַּרְקָא לֵיהּ – **where [an object] cannot be thrown four** *amos* **without** first traveling **two** *amos,*[13] אֵימָא מוֹדֶה לֵיהּ לְאַבַּיֵי – **I would say that he agrees with Abaye** that the person is liable. וְאִי אַשְׁמְעִינַן בְּהָא – **And if we were informed about this** second dispute, בְּהָא קָאָמַר רָבָא – we would have thought only **in that** case **does Rava say** the person is exempt, דְּהָא לֹא קָמִיכַּוֵּין לִזְרִיקָה דְּאַרְבַּע – **because he was not intending a throw of four** *amos,*[14] אֲבָל כְּסָבוּר רְשׁוּת הַיָּחִיד וְנִמְצָא רְשׁוּת הָרַבִּים – **but where he thought that it was a private domain and it was found to be a public domain,** דְּמִכַּוֵּין לִזְרִיקָה דְּאַרְבַּע – **where he intended a throw of four** *amos,*[15] אֵימָא מוֹדֵי לֵיהּ לְאַבַּיֵי – **I would say that he agrees with Abaye** that the person is liable. צְרִיכָא – **It is** therefore **necessary** to state all three disputes.

The Gemara questions the view of Rava:

תְּנַן – **We learned in the Mishnah** below: אֲבוֹת מְלָאכוֹת אַרְבָּעִים חָסֵר אַחַת – THE PRIMARY LABORS ARE FORTY MINUS ONE.[16] וְהָוֵינַן בָּהּ – **Now, in discussing this** we asked: מִנְיָנָא לָמָּה לִי – **Why do I need** the Tanna to specify the **number** of labors?[17] וְאָמַר רַבִּי יוֹחָנָן – **And R' Yochanan said** in reply: שֶׁאִם עֲשָׂאָן כּוּלָּם בְּהֶעְלֵם אֶחָד – It is to teach **that if someone performed all** thirty-nine **of them in one lapse of awareness,** חַיָּיב עַל כָּל אַחַת וְאַחַת – **he is obligated** to bring a separate *chatas* **for each and every one** he performed.[18]

The Gemara now explains its question:

בִּשְׁלָמָא לְאַבַּיֵי – **It is understandable according to Abaye,** דְּאָמַר כִּי הַאי גַּוְונָא חַיָּיב – **who said that one is liable in such a case** [i.e. where a person miscalculated the extent of his act],[19] מַשְׁכַּחַת לָהּ דְּיָדַע דְּאִיסּוּרָא שַׁבָּת – **this** ruling of the Mishnah **can be found** in **a case where he knew about the prohibition of the Sabbath** וְיָדַע לָהּ אִיסּוּר מְלָאכוֹת – **and he knew about the prohibition of the** *melachos,* וְקָא טָעָה בְּשִׁיעוּרִין – **but he was mistaken about the extent** of his act.[20] אֶלָּא לְרָבָא דְּאָמַר פָּטוּר – **But according to Rava, who says that he is exempt** in such a case, הֵיכִי מַשְׁכַּחַת לָהּ – then **how is such** a case **to be found;** i.e. a case in which one would be liable to thirty-nine *chatas* offerings?[21] בְּזָדוֹן שַׁבָּת וְשִׁגְגַת מְלָאכוֹת – Only **with deliberateness regarding the Sabbath and inadvertence regarding the** *melachos.*[22] But how can this person who was unaware of all thirty-nine *melachos* be considered to have acted deliberately regarding the Sabbath? הָנִיחָא אִי סָבַר לָהּ כְּרַבִּי יוֹחָנָן – **This is well if [the Tanna] holds in accordance with R' Yochanan,** דְּאָמַר כֵּיוָן שֶׁשָּׁגַג בְּכָרֵת – **who said that once someone acted inadvertently regarding** the *kares* penalty, אַף עַל פִּי שֶׁהֵזִיד בְּלָאו – **even though he acted deliberately with regard to** the **prohibition,** he is liable to a *chatas,*[23] מַשְׁכַּחַת לָהּ דְּיָדַע לָהּ לְשַׁבָּת בְּלָאו – **this** ruling of the Mishnah **can be found** in a case **where he knew about the Sabbath** law **with regard to** the **prohibition** against performing *melachos,* but he was not aware of the *kares* penalty incurred for violations. אֶלָּא אִי סָבַר לָהּ כְּרַבִּי שִׁמְעוֹן בֶּן לָקִישׁ – **But if he holds in accordance with R' Shimon ben Lakish,** דְּאָמַר עַד שֶׁיִּשְׁגּוֹג בְּלָאו וְכָרֵת – **who said** that one is not liable to a *chatas* **unless he acted inadvertently with regard to** the **prohibition and with regard to** the *kares* penalty, דְּיָדַע לָהּ לְשַׁבָּת בְּמַאי – **in what** respect **did he know about the Sabbath?**[24]

NOTES

12. (1) intending to cut a detached object, cutting an attached one instead; (2) intending to throw only two *amos,* throwing four instead; and (3) intending to throw in a private domain, throwing in a public domain instead.

13. Thus, when the object was thrown four *amos,* the person's intention was fulfilled, because he indeed intended to throw it the first two *amos.* We would therefore think that he is not considered preoccupied (*Rashi*).

14. And anything less than four *amos* is not considered a full throw (*Rashi*).

15. He was therefore intending a full throw (*Rashi*).

16. Below on this *amud.* The Mishnah then proceeds to list all thirty-nine *melachos* for which one is liable on the Sabbath.

17. I.e. why did the Mishnah have to preface its list of *melachos* by stating that there were thirty-nine? It could have merely listed them, and we could count them ourselves to find out how many there are (*Rashi* above, 69a).

18. [By stating that there are thirty-nine *melachos,* the Mishnah alludes to the maximum number of *chatas* offerings a person would have to bring for desecrating one Sabbath.]

19. In the second of his three disputes with Rava, Abaye rules that if someone intended to throw an object two *amos* but in fact threw it four, he is liable to a *chatas.*

20. [If the person was totally unaware of any of the *melachos,* he would be liable to only one *chatas* because he is considered inadvertent regarding the Sabbath (see 70b note 17). But according to Abaye] it is possible to find a case where he acted inadvertently regarding all of the *melachos* but he is still considered deliberate regarding the Sabbath. That is, he was aware of all thirty-nine *melachos,* but intended to perform each less than its required amount. If his actions in fact resulted in the minimum amount of each, he is considered to have acted inadvertently regarding the *melachos* according to Abaye, and he is liable to a *chatas* for each (*Rashi*).

21. According to Rava a person is considered preoccupied when he was planning a limited act and is exempt from liability if a more substantial act occurs. In what case, then, would a person be liable to thirty-nine *chatas* offerings for performing all of the *melachos* in one lapse of awareness? (*Rashi*).

22. That is, the person knew that it was the Sabbath, but did not realize that those acts were prohibited as *melachah* on the Sabbath. But if this person was unaware of all thirty-nine *melachos,* he cannot be said to have acted deliberately regarding the Sabbath because Saturday was no different to him than any other day of the week (*Rashi*).

23. That is, the person was unaware only of the *kares* punishment, but he knew that it was prohibited to perform the *melachos* on the Sabbath. This makes his knowledge that it was the Sabbath meaningful. Thus, when he performed *melachos* on that day, he acted inadvertently only regarding *melachos,* since according to R' Yochanan lack of knowledge of the *kares* punishment is sufficient to classify his actions as inadvertent. [See above, 69a.]

24. According to Reish Lakish, it is clear that the person could not have known that any of the *melachos* were prohibited. If so, Rava cannot find a case where the person would be liable to thirty-nine *chatas* offerings.

אלא לאו רישא בעכו״ם וסיפא בשאר מצות ושגג בלא מתכוין בשאר מצות ה״ד דסבור דשומן הוא ואכלו משא״כ בשבת דפטור דנתכוון לחתוך את התלוש וחתך את המחובר פטור ואביי שגג בלא מתכוין ה״ד [א]דסבור רוק הוא ובלעו משא״כ בשבת דפטור דנתכוון להגביה את התלוש וחתך את המחובר פטור אבל נתכוון לחתוך את התלוש וחתך את המחובר חייב: איתמר [א]נתכוון לזרוק שתים וזרק ארבע [ב]רבא אמר פטור אביי אמר חייב רבא אמר פטור (א) דלא קמיכוין לזריקה דארבע אביי אמר חייב דהא קמיכוין לזריקה בעלמא כסבור רשות היחיד ונמצאת רשות הרבים רבא אמר [ב]פטור ואביי אמר חייב רבא אמר פטור דהא לא מיכוין לזריקה דאיסורא ואביי אמר חייב דהא קא מיכוין לזריקה בעלמא וצריכא דאי אשמעינן קמייתא בההוא קאמר רבא דהא לא קמיכוין לחתיכה דאיסורא אבל נתכוון לזרוק שתים וזרק ארבע דארבע בלא תרתי לא (ב) מיזרקא ליה אימא מודה ליה לאביי ואי אשמעינן בהא בהא קאמר רבא דהא לא קמיכוין לזריקה דארבע אבל כסבור רה״י ונמצא רה״ר דמכוין לזריקה דארבע אימא מודי ליה לאביי צריכא [ג]תנן אבות מלאכות ארבעים חסר אחת והוינן בה מנינא למה לי וא״ר יוחנן שאם עשאן כולם בהעלם אחד חייב על כל אחת ואחת בשלמא לאביי דאמר כי האי גוונא חייב משכחת לה דידע דאסורא (ג) שבת וידע לה איסור מלאכות וקא טעה בשיעורין אלא לרבא דאמר פטור היכי משכחת לה בזדון שבת ושגגת מלאכות הניחא אי סבר לה כר' יוחנן דאמר כיון ששגג בכרת אע״פ שהזיד בלאו משכחת לה דידע לה לשבת בלאו אלא אי סבר לה כרשב״ל דאמר עד שישגוג בלאו וכרת דידע לה לשבת במאי [ד]דידע לה בתחומין ואליבא דר״ע: מתני' [ה]אבות [ו][ג]מלאכות ארבעים חסר אחת הזורע והחורש והקוצר והמעמר והדש והזורה הבורר הטוחן והמרקד והלש והאופה הגוזז את הצמר המלבנו והמנפצו והצובעו והטווה [ז]והמיסך והעושה שתי בתי נירין והאורג שני חוטין והפוצע שני חוטין הקושר והמתיר [ח]והתופר שתי תפירות הקורע על מנת לתפור [שתי תפירות] הצד צבי השוחטו והמפשיטו המולחו והמעבד את עורו והממחקו והמחתכו הכותב שתי אותיות והמוחק על מנת לכתוב שתי אותיות הבונה והסותר המכבה והמבעיר המכה בפטיש [ט]המוציא מרשות לרשות הרי אלו אבות מלאכות ארבעים חסר אחת:

גמ'

רש״י

דסבור שומן הוא ואכלו. והיינו דשגג דסבור שומן הוא ולא נתכוין לאכול חלב וחייב ואף על פי דמתעסק הוא לרבא דהא לא מתכוין לאכילת איסור חייב דאמר שמואל בכריתות (פ״ד דף יט:) בחלבי' ועריות מתעסק חייב שכן נהנה אבל בשבת פטור דלא נהנה והיינו סייעתא לדידיה דאמר נתכוין לחתוך את התלוש וחתך את המחובר פטור: ואביי. אמר לך לעולם כי האי גוונא אף בשבת חייב דלאו מתעסק הוא והיכי דמי מתעסק דשאר מצות חייב קסבר רוק הוא שהיה חלב נימוח ובלעו דלא איכוין לאכילה דרוק לאו בר אכילה הוא אלא בליעה דכתיב (איוב ז) עד בלעי רוקי ועלתה בידו אכילה דהא לא איכוין לאכילה ודכוותייהו דשבת דפטור נתכוין להגביה ועלתה בידו חתיכה: דהא לא איכוין לזריקה דאיסור. ויהא שוגג בשבת או במלאכה אבל זה אינו שוגג לא בשבת ולא במלאכות אלא מתעסק בדבר אחר של היתר ועלתה בידו איסור: וצריכא. לאיפלוגי בכולהו אף על גב דדמי להדדי: דארבע בלא תרתי לא מזדריק. וזה שנתכוין לשתים וזרק ארבע נעשית מחשבתו דהא יש בכלל ד' שתים הלכך לאו מתעסק הוא: דלא איכוין לזריקה דארבע. ובציר מהני לא שם זריקה עלה: אבל כסבור רה״י הוא וכו'. דנתכוין לזריקה גמורה: משכחת לה. להאי שנשתכחה תורת כל הלכות שבת ממנו ואפילו הכי חשיבא ליה כזדון שבת ושגגת מלאכות לחיוביה אכל חדא כגון דידע ליה לשבת באיסורין וטעה בשיעורין שנתכוין לפחות מכשיעור ועשה כשיעור דלכולן יש שיעור: אלא לרבא דאמר פטור היכי משכחת לה. דמיחייב שום אדם על כל מלאכה ומלאכה שבהעלם אחד על כרחך בזדון שבת ושגגת מלאכות הוא דבעית לאשכוחיה והכא דאיעלימו כולהו מיניה מאי זדון שבת איכא במה ניכר לו שבת משאר ימים: מתני' הזורה. ברחת לרוח: הבורר. פסולת בידיו: המרקד. בנפה ובגמ' פריך הני כולהו חדא היא דלהפריש פסולת מתוך אוכל נעשות שלשתן: האופה. לא הוה במשכן דלא שייך אלא בפת ופת לא שייכא במלאכת המשכן אבל כולהו קמייתא הואי בסממנין של צבע תכלת וארגמן ותולעת שני ובגמרא פריך דשביק תנא מבשל דהוי בסממנים ונקט אופה ושיעורן של אלו כגרוגרת חוץ מחורש דבכל שהוא לקמן בפרק הבונה (דף קג.): הגוזז צמר. וכל שאר מלאכות שייכי בצמר של מלאכת המשכן: המלבנו. מכבסו בנהר: המנפצו. קרפי״ר בלע״ז: המיסך. אורדי״ר: בתי נירין. ליי״ש שנתן שני חוטין בתוך הבית ניר ובגוזז ובמלבן וכולהו איכך מפרש שיעורן לקמן בפרק האורג: הפוצע. מנתק פעמים שיש בשני חוטין יותר מדאי ומנתק מהן ומקלישן לצורך והני כולהו ממיסך ואילך עד קושר ומתיר שייכי ביריעות ולקמן מפרש מאי קושר ומאי מתיר איכא: ותופר וקורע. ביריעות הוא: על מנת לתפור. פעמים שהנקב עגול ואינו יכול לתופרו יפה אא״כ קורעו כדמפרש בגמרא אבל קורע שלא לתפור לא הוי במשכן: הצד את הצבי. וכל מלאכת עורו נוהגת בתחשים למשכן בעורותיהן: המולחו. לעור: ממחקו. מגרר שערו: מחתכו. מקצעו ומחתכו לרצועות וסנדלים: כותב ומוחק. לקמן (דף קג:) מפרש למאי מיבעיא למשכן שכן רושמין על קרשי המשכן לידע איזה בן זוגו וכותב אות בזו ואות בזו ומוחק פעמים שטעה: מכבה ומבעיר. כאש שתחת הדוד של סממנין: מכה בפטיש. הוא גמר כל מלאכה שכן אומן מכה בקורנס על הסדן להחליקו בגמר מלאכה ומתניתין נמי לא מיחייב ליה אלא בגמר מלאכה:

תוספות

אלא לאו רישא בע״ז וסיפא בשאר מצות. תימה לר״י דלוקמא כולה בשאר מצות ומאי מה שאין כן בשאר מצות כגון שחט וזרק בחוץ דאינו חייב אלא אחת כדאמר אביי בפרק אחד דיני ממונות (סנהדרין לד:) שם תעשה עשאן הכתוב עשיה אחת ור' אבהו נמי דפליג מודה לרבי ישמעאל בשחיטה וזריקה ולר' עקיבא בהעלאה וזריקה דאינו חייב אלא אחת דמחד קרא נפקי ושגג בלא מתכוין כגון שנתכוין לשחוט בהמת חולין והיה צריך לשל חולין ונמצאת (ד) של קדשים דכוותה בשבת נתכוין לחתוך תלוש ונמצא מחובר ולא היה צריך אלא לתלוש דפטור דמלאכת מחשבת בעינן וי״ל דלא מצינן לפרושי הכי דמשמע דפטור בשבת לפי ששגג בלא מתכוין דכה״ג אפילו נתכוין למחובר זה ונמצא מחובר אחר פטור דאין זה מלאכת מחשבת וליכא לאוקמי נמי דמיירי כשנעשה מחשבתו כגון שהיה צריך לחתוך מה שחתך אלא שהיה סבור שהוא תלוש ונמצא שהוא מחובר הא ליכא למימר דכה״ג אם פטור לענין שבת מאשר חטא בה פטור נמי לענין חוץ ומיהו עוד קשה דלוקמא כולה בשאר מצות כגון (ה) נרבע לזכר ורבע את הזכר והבא על הבהמה והביא בהמה עליו דבין לאביי ובין לר' אבהו לר' עקיבא אינו חייב אלא אחת והשתא שגג בלא מתכוין מיתוקם שפיר דמיפטר בשבת מאשר חטא בה וכגון שנעשית מחשבתו וגבי עריות לא מיפטר שכן נהנה:

העושה שני בתי נירין. צריך לפרש למה פירש כאן ובאורג [י]ובפוצע ובתופר ובכותב שיעור טפי מבשאר:

הקושר והמתיר. צ״ע אי מיחייב במתיר שלא על מנת לקשור אי לא ומדלא תני ליה כדתני מוחק ע״מ לכתוב אין לדקדק דהכי נמי לא קתני סותר ע״מ לבנות ובפ' במה מדליקין (לעיל לא:) אמרינן בהדיא דבעינן סותר ע״מ לבנות ולפי מה שפירש רש״י בגמרא (דף עד:) דאי מתרמי ליה תרי קיטרי בהדי הדדי בשני חוטין זה אצל זה שרי חד ומניח חד משמע דמיחייב בלא על מנת לקשור ולשון קטר לא משמע כפירושו אבל ר״ח פירש וכן משמע בירושלמי כשנפסק חוט בשני מקומות ונקשר מתירין ב' הקשרים ומשליכין לחוץ האמצעי וחוזרין וקושרין שתי הראשים זה בזה ואין בו אלא קשר א' ולפי זה משמע דבעי מתיר ע״מ לקשור והא דלא תני ליה במתיר ובסותר פירשתי בפרק ב' (דף לא: ד״ה וסותר):

מכדי

עין משפט נר מצוה

כו א מיי' פ״ב מהלכות שגגות הלכה ז:

כז ב מיי' פ״א מהלכות שבת הלכה ח:

כח ג מיי' פ״ז מהלכות שבת הלכה א סמג לאוין סה:

רבינו חננאל

דאמר פטור מאי איכא למימר ואמרינן לא משכחת שגג בלא מתכוין לע״ז אלא באומר מותר. פי' כגון מי שנעלם ממנו עבודת אלהים אחרים ששכח הכל לגמרי שנמצא בידו העלם אלהים אחרים והעלם עבירות ואומר שמותר. וכי האי גוונא בע״ז (אחרינא) חייב בשבת פטור לגמרי ואקשי' ומי איכא למימר דפטור לגמרי דהא עד כאן לא בעא מיניה רבא מרב נחמן העלם זה וזה בידו. פי' העלם שבת והעלם מלאכות בידו מהו אלא לחיובי חדא או תרתי אבל למפטריה לגמרי לא וחזרנו לפרק פירוק אחר משום דקשיא דלא מיתוקמא סיפא דהא מתניתין בע״ז אוקמי הכי רישא בע״ז דקתני עשה שתים בהעלם א' בשבת חייב ב' משא״כ בע״ז שאם זיבח וקיטר וניסך בהעלם א' אינו חייב אלא אחת כר' אמי אבל סיפא דקתני בשאר מצות שגג בלא מתכוין חייב משא״כ בשבת דפטור. בשאר מצות דלאו ע״ז היא והיכי דמי כגון שהי' סבור שהוא שומן ואכלו ונמצא חלב. כגון זה בשאר מצות הוא דחייב. אבל בשבת כי האי גוונא נתכוון לחתוך בתלוש וחתכו ונמצא דמחובר לקרקע פטור ודחי אביי ואמר לא כי האי גוונא (לע״ז) לעולם אימא לך חייב והיכי דמי שגג בלא מתכוין דבשאר מצות חייב ובשבת פטור. כגון שנתכוין בבליעה דרוק ובלעה ונמצא חלב שאע״פ שלא נתכוין לאכילה דחייב בשאר מצות ובשבת כה״ג דנתכוין להגביה דבר תלוש והגביהו ונמצא שחתכו מן המחובר [פטור] אבל אם נתכוין לחתיכה בעלמא חייב. (כגון) [וכ״ש] בשאר מצות אם נתכוין לאכילה בעלמא [חייב] וכדר' נחמן דאמר המתעסק בחלבין ובעריות אע״פ שלא נתכוון חייב שכבר נהנה. והמתעסק בשבת פטור. מלאכת מחשבת אסרה תורה. ור' יוחנן התם בפרק ארבע מיתות כדתני תנא הדא מתניתין קמיה דחאה ואמר ליה פוק תני לברא. דכל מתניתין דלא מיתוקמא רישא וסיפא בחד טעמא לאו מתנית' תרצתא היא. ר' יוחנן לטעמיה דאמר בסוף פרק המפקיד מאן דמתרגם לי חבית אליבא דחד תנא מובילנא מאניה בתריה לבי מסותא: נתכוון לזרוק ב' חרק ד' אמות (רבא) [רבה] אמר (חייב) [פטור] אביי אמר (פטור) [חייב] פשוט' היא ומקשינן (לרבא) [לרבה] ממתנית' דקתני ארבעים חסר אחת ואמר ר' יוחנן עלה שאם עשאן כולם בהעלם אחד חייב על כל אחת ואחת ולא משכחת כהאי גוונא דחייב בכולן אלא בזדון שבת ושגגת מלאכות בשלמא לאביי דאמר כי האי גוונא חייב [כו'] [וקא טעה] בשיעורין כגון זריקת ב' אמות וזריקת ד' וכיוצא בהן אלא (לרבא) [לרבה] דאמר כל כה״ג פטור היכי משכחת [לה] בזדון [שבת] ושגגת מלאכה. הניחא אליבא דר' יוחנן דאמר כיון ששגג בכרת אע״פ שהזיד בלאו משכחת לה דידע דאיסור השבת בלאו אלא לר״ל דאמר עד שישגוג בלאו וכרת היכי משכחת לה ושנינן דידע לה בתחומין ואליבא דר' עקיבא כמו שאמרנו למעלה. דאביי אליבא דר' יוחנן פשוטה היא אלא אפילו לריש לקיש כיון דסבר אביי כשנתכוון למקצת האיסור בשגגת איסורו ונזדמן לו כל האיסור חייב כגון המתכוון לזרוק ב' אמות שהן מקצת איסורו כי האיסור ד' אמות ונתכוון לזרוק שתים מתוך ארבע (וניזרוק) [ונזדמן] לו שזרק ד' חייב. מוקים לה אליבא דר״ל במכיר את השבת באיסור מלאכות ויודע (בשיעורן) [בכולן] ושוגג בלאו שבשיעור: אבות מלאכות ארבעים חסר אחת.

למה

גמרא

מסורת הש״ס

א) [ב״ק דף כו: ע״ש], ב) [עמ״ש לעיל עב: על הגליון], ג) [לעיל סט. וש״נ], ד) [לעיל סט. ע:], ה) פ״א אלו אבות, ו) לעיל ו: מט: סט. ע: לקמן צו: ב״ק ב. [כריתות ג:], ז) [פי' מותח חוטי השתי], ח) [לקמן קה.], ט) לעיל ב: [שבועות ה:], י) [עי' תוי״ט ד״ה והעושה שתי].

הגהות הב״ח

(א) גמ' רבא אמר פטור דהא לא קמיכוין: (ב) שם תרתי לא מיזדרקא ליה: (ג) שם משכח' לה דידע לאיסורא דשבת וידע לה לאיסור מלאכות: (ד) תוס' ד״ה אלא וכו' לשל חולין ונמצאת אחרת והיא של קדשים וכו' תלוש זה ונמצא מחובר אחר ולא: (ה) בא״ד בשאר מצות כגון הבא על הזכור והביא עליו זכור והבא על הבהמה. נ״ב עי' פרק ד' מיתות דף נד:

ליקוטי רש״י

ואביי שגג בלא מתכוין ה״ד וכו'. כגון חלב המהותך לפניו וכסבור רוק הוא ובלעו דלא מתכוין לאכילה אלא מתעסק בדבר אחר בבליעת רוק והיכי דמי שוגג גמור כסבור שומן הוא ואכלו דנתכוין לאכילה אבל זה לא שוגג הוא ואפילו הכי חייב כדאמרן לקמן בשמעתין שכן נהנה מה שאין כן בשבת כגון נתכוין להגביה את התלוש וחתך את המחובר פטור שנאמר (ויקרא ד) אשר חטא בה עד שיתכוין למלאכה זו פרט למתעסק בדבר אחר ועלתה בידו מלאכה זו ומיהו מתעסק ועלה בידו אכילת חלבים או עריות חייב שכבר נהנה. דסבור דשומן הוא ואכלו. היה מתעסק ולא נתכוין לכך כל מתעסק קרי ליה שאינו מתכוין בדבר זה [illegible] היא [לעיל ו:]. וכא להודיעך שאם נתעלמו כל הלכות שבת ממנו כמה חטאות [חייב] עליו [לקמן ע״ב]. וסימנא בעלמא אשמעינן לידע כמה חטאות חייב על חילול שבת אחת. אלא לרבא דאמר פטור היכי משכחת לה. דמיחייב על כרחך לא משכחת לה אלא בזדון שבת דיודע שהוא שבת ושגגת מלאכות דאינו יודע שהמלאכות הללו אסורות דאי בזדון מלאכות ושגגת שבת דיודע שהן אסורות בשבת אבל שכח שהיום שבת הא תנן דאינו חייב אלא אחת לכל שבת ושבת חדון שבת לא הוי אלא אם כן יודע אחת מהלכותיה דאי לא ידע בחדא מינייהו אין שבת חלוק לו משאר ימים וזה ששגג בכולן אין כאן זדון שבת [לעיל סט.]. דניחייב איניש אכל חדא על כרחך בזדון שבת ושגגת מלאכות הוא דמשכחת לה והכא מאי זדון שבת איכא. דהא לא ידע שבת במידי כיון דכל הלכותיה נעלמות ממנו אין חילוק היום משאר ימים [שם ע:]. הניחא אי סבר לה כר' יוחנן. דאמר שגגת כרת שמה שגגה. משכחת לה. וזדון שבת בלאוין ושגגת מלאכות בכריתות דיודע לה לשבת שהוזהר על הלאוין או של כולן או של אחת מהן [שם סט.]. שלא נעלמו ממנו אלא הכריתות ויודע הלאוין והיינו זדון שבת [שם ע:]. דידע לה לשבת במאי. הלא בכולן שגג כסבור שכל שלשים ותשע מלאכות מותרות. בתחומין. דאינן בקרבן [שם סט.]. דאינו יודע שמלאכות הללו אסורות אבל יודע מצות שבת בדבר אחד כגון דידע שאסור לצאת חוץ לתחום [כריתות ג.]. ואליבא דר' עקיבא. דאמר במסכת סוטה תחומין דאורייתא נינהו דתנן בו ביום דרש רבי עקיבא ומדוס מחוץ לעיר כו' [לעיל שם]. דאמר (סוטה כז:) דאורייתא נינהו והוי מחלל ומיהו אין חייבין לא על שגגתו חטאת כו' [לקמן קנג:]. ור' עקיבא מודה נמי בתחומים דאין חייבים עליהם כרת דתנן אבות מלאכות ארבעים חסר אחת ולא פליג ר' עקיבא [סנהדרין סו.]. העושה שתי בתי נירין. שנתן שני חוטין של שתי בנירה שקורין ליי״ש [לקמן קה.]. המולחו. מליחה מאבות מלאכות בדבר שיש בו עיבוד דתנן והמולחו והמעבדו [ביצה יא:]. והממחקו. ממחק. מחליק [בכורות כה.]. והמחתכו. מחתך העור מקצעו במדה [לקמן עה:]. הכותב שתי אותיות. שבקרשי המשכן שתים היו כותבים אחת בזו ואחת בזו כדי לזווגן כשסותרים אותן [שם עה:]. והסותר. כל מקלקל דשבת הוי פטור דלאו היינו מלאכת מחשבת וסותר דתנן באבות מלאכות דמיחייב סותר על מנת לבנות הוא ואינו יכול לבנות אלא אם כן סותרו והשתא לאו קלקול היא וכו' ומכבה דומיא דסותר הוא וכן קורע דומיא דסותר ולהכי תנן הקורע על מנת לתפור וכן מוחק תנן על מנת לכתוב דכולם סותר נינהו [לעיל לא: עיי״ש]. המכה בפטיש. גם הוא באבות מלאכות והוא בלע״ז פי״ק שמפולץ בו את האבן מן הסלע לאחר שחצב את האבן סביב ומבדיל מן הסר קלת הוא מכה בפטיש מכה גדולה והיא מתפרקת ונופלת וזהו גמר מלאכה של חוצבי אבן וכל הגומר בשבת מלאכה תולדת מכה בפטיש היא [לקמן קב:]. המוציא מרשות לרשות. הוציא מרשות היחיד לרשות הרבים למדנו מן המקרא שחייב בפרק הזורק במסכת שבת (צו:) מויצו משה ויעבירו קול במחנה וגו' (ומתרגמינן) לא תפיקו מרה״י לרה״ר [שבועות ב.]. בפרק הזורק (לקמן צו:) ברישיה נפקא לן מויצו משה ויעבירו קול במחנה וגו' לא תפיקו מרשות היחיד לרשות הרבים להביא נדבה למחנה לויה ויום השבת היה כדיליף התם [לעיל ב.].

The Gemara answers: דְּיָדַע לָהּ בִּתְחוּמִין – **He was knowledgeable about [the Sabbath] with regard to the** ***techum*** **laws,** וְאַלִּיבָּא דְּרַבִּי עֲקִיבָא – **and this is according to R' Akiva,** who holds that they are Biblical.[25]

Mishnah The Mishnah enumerates the broad categories of labor prohibited on the Sabbath:[26]
אֲבוֹת מְלָאכוֹת אַרְבָּעִים חָסֵר אַחַת – **The primary labors** [the *avos melachos*] **are forty minus one.**[27]

The Mishnah first enumerates eleven labors necessary for the baking of bread:[28]
הַזּוֹרֵעַ – **Sowing,**[29] וְהַחוֹרֵשׁ – **plowing,**[30] וְהַקּוֹצֵר – **reaping,**[31] וְהַמְעַמֵּר – **gathering together,**[32] וְהַדָּשׁ – **threshing,**[33] וְהַזּוֹרֶה – **winnowing,**[34] הַבּוֹרֵר – **selecting,**[35] הַטּוֹחֵן – **grinding,**[36] וְהַמְרַקֵּד – **sifting,**[37] וְהַלָּשׁ – **kneading,**[38] וְהָאוֹפֶה – **and baking;**[39]

The Mishnah now enumerates thirteen labors involved in the preparation of clothing:
הַגּוֹזֵז אֶת הַצֶּמֶר – **shearing wool,**[40] הַמְלַבְּנוֹ – **whitening it,**[41] וְהַמְנַפְּצוֹ – **disentangling it,**[42] וְהַצּוֹבְעוֹ –

NOTES

25. [See above, 69a notes 26-27.] Hence, the person's knowledge that the day was Saturday is considered meaningful. He acted inadvertently only regarding the *melachos* and is liable to a separate *chatas* for each.

26. As explained at length in the General Introduction, all labors performed in the construction of the Mishkan (the Tabernacle) are called *avos,* or primary, labors. These labors pertained not only to the actual construction of the Mishkan, but also to the activities necessary for the preparation of its components.

Although thirty-nine Mishkan-related labors are enumerated in our Mishnah, the number does not exclude other activities from being prohibited on the Sabbath. On the contrary, any activity similar either in method or function to any of the thirty-nine is equally prohibited. Hence, the enumerated labors are known as *avos melachos, primary labors* [literally: fathers of labors], in the sense that they represent general categories of labor. Any other activity whose prohibition is derived from one of the thirty-nine *avos* is known as a *toladah, derivative labor.* [See *Bava Kamma* 2a.]

27. The Gemara will explain below that the Mishnah prefaces the list of labors with their tally in order to specify the maximum number of *chatas* offerings to which an inadvertent violator can be liable. That is why the Mishnah mentions the performer [הַזּוֹרֵעַ – literally: the one who sows, etc.] rather than the *melachah* itself [זְרִיעָה, *sowing,* etc.] (*Tos. Yom Tov*).

[For a discussion of why the Mishnah states "forty minus one" rather than simply "thirty-nine," see *Tos. Yom Tov* and *Mayim Chaim;* see also *Shem MiShmuel* vol. 1, p. 85.]

28. As mentioned above, all *avos* were activities performed in the construction of the Mishkan. The dyes required for its curtains and skins were of herbal origin. The Mishnah therefore lists the *melachos* that were necessary to produce dyes. However, since the Mishnah concludes this list with הָאוֹפֶה, *baking,* which describes the *melachah* of baking bread, rather than הַמְבַשֵּׁל, *cooking,* which would refer to the boiling of herbs to make dyes, the Gemara explains that the first grouping of *melachos* refers to the bread-baking process (see below, 74b).

The Mishnah begins its list with bread-producing labors because eating is the most essential human need. The Mishnah then mentions the thirteen *melachos* required for the manufacture of clothing, which is the second most basic need. A group of *melachos* required for writing follows, representing the need for communication. The Mishnah then concludes with various *melachos* that have a more explicit Scriptural source than the others (*Pnei Yehoshua;* see also *Meiri* and *Ran*).

Discussion of the various *melachos* is scattered throughout this tractate. Following the translation of each *melachah* in the notes below we will cite the places where the *melachah* is discussed.

29. **[1]** ***Sowing*** (discussed by the Gemara below, 73b, 81b). Herb seeds had to be planted in order to provide the raw material for the production of dyes. Although the Israelites wandered through an arid region, the wilderness miraculously became fertile for them and produced vegetation (see *Tosafos* to Chullin 88b). It is also possible that they produced dyes from plants grown in Egypt or purchased from nearby peoples. Although those seeds were not sown specifically for the Mishkan, the sowing was, nevertheless, a necessary prelude to the manufacture of dye and is thus considered an *av* (*Pnei Yehoshua* to 75a ד״ה פיסקא).

Even though a seed planted on the Sabbath presumably will not take root until the Sabbath has ended, one is liable for this sowing since the act will eventually result in the seed's taking root. *Rashash* adds that if the seeds are removed before they take root, the planter is exempt from a *chatas. Minchas Chinuch* (§32, זורע) disagrees, proving that the person is liable for the mere act of sowing, even if the seeds, for some reason, never take root (see also *Eglei Tal* זורע 2:8, and *Dvar Avraham* vol. I 23:5-6).

30. **[2]** ***Plowing*** (discussed below, 73b, 81b and 103a). The purpose of plowing is to soften the earth or to otherwise improve its arability. Therefore, any type of work performed directly upon the earth and designed to achieve these results is equivalent to plowing.

31. **[3]** ***Reaping*** (below, 73b, 95a, 103a). Detaching any growing plant from its place of growth falls into the category of reaping.

32. **[4]** ***Gathering together*** (73b, 96b). The harvested crop was first gathered into small bundles in the field; those bundles were later gathered into one large bundle. Both of these actions are included in this *av* (*Eglei Tal* מעמר 1:1).

33. **[5]** ***Threshing*** (73b, 143b-145a). This is separating kernels of grain from their husks.

34. **[6]** ***Winnowing*** (73b). After the kernels have been extracted from their husks, the mixture is cast into the air with a pitchfork. The wind blows away the chaff, leaving the heavier kernels (see *Rashi*). [See *Bava Kamma* 60a.]

35. **[7]** ***Selecting*** (74a, 95a, 134a, 138a, 142b). This is sorting inedible matter from food by hand (*Rashi*).

[*Sfas Emes* wonders why *Rashi* explains that the sorting is done by hand when the Gemara below (74a) indicates that the usual method of sorting is with a utensil. In fact, *Rav* does mention the utensil option in his explanation of the Mishnah.]

36. **[8]** ***Grinding*** (74b). I.e. grinding wheat into flour.

37. **[9]** ***Sifting*** (74a, 138a). That is, sifting flour after it has been ground.

Three of the last four *melachos* mentioned – winnowing, selecting and sifting – are closely related. All have one purpose – to separate food from inedible matter in order to use the food. The Gemara (74a) will explain why they are considered three distinct *melachos* (*Rashi*).

38. **[10]** ***Kneading*** (18a, 155b-156a). The purpose of kneading is to cause particles to adhere to each other through the agency of a liquid. This *av* thus consists of pouring water on flour and working the mixture to form a dough.

39. **[11]** ***Baking*** (38b, 74b). Baking itself was not performed during the construction of the Mishkan since bread was not required for the structure. Instead, herbs were cooked to produce the dyes (*Rashi*). [See above, note 28 and below, 74b note 8.]

As we have already learned in this chapter, a person is not obligated to bring a *chatas* unless he performs a minimum amount of the *melachah.* The minimum amount for all *melachos* listed thus far – with the exception of plowing – is the size of a dried fig. A person is liable for any amount that he plows (*Rashi;* cf. *Rambam, Hil. Shabbos* 8:2).

40. **[12]** ***Shearing wool*** (74b, 94b). Cutting wool or hair from a living or dead animal, or even from the flayed pelt of an animal, are forms of the *av* of shearing. [See below, 74b note 28.]

This *melachah* and the twelve that follow were performed to produce wool for the curtains of the Mishkan (*Rashi*).

41. **[13]** ***Whitening*** (79a, 142b). This involves washing the wool in a river (*Rashi;* see *Rambam, Hil. Shabbos* 9:10). See *Magen Avos* and *Binyan Tzion* (vol. 2 §33) for a discussion of why *Rashi* specifies a river.

42. **[14]** ***Disentangling*** (74b). Disentangling the wool by hand [to prepare it for spinning] (see *Rashi* here and to *Bava Kamma* 93b; cf. *Rambam's Commentary to the Mishnah, Meiri*).

Avnei Nezer (*Orach Chaim* §170) writes that *Rashi* certainly holds that disentangling the wool with a comb is also included in this *av.* [See also *Maaseh Oreg* by Dayan I. Gukovitzki, pp. 2-5.]

אלא לאו רישא בעכו"ם וסיפא בשאר מצות ושגג בלא מתכוין בשאר מצות ה"ד דסבור דשומן הוא ואכלו משא"כ בשבת דפטור דנתכוון לחתוך את התלוש וחתך את המחובר פטור ואביי שגג בלא מתכוין ה"ד [א]דסבור רוק הוא ובלעו משא"כ בשבת דפטור דנתכוון להגביה את התלוש וחתך את המחובר פטור אבל נתכוון לחתוך את התלוש וחתך את המחובר חייב: איתמר [א] נתכוון לזרוק שתים וזרק ארבע [ב] רבא אמר פטור אביי אמר חייב רבא אמר פטור (א) דלא קמיכוין לזריקה דארבע אביי אמר חייב דהא קמיכוין לזריקה בעלמא כסבור רשות היחיד ונמצאת רשות הרבים רבא אמר [ב] פטור ואביי אמר חייב רבא אמר פטור דהא לא מיכוין לזריקה דאיסורא ואביי אמר חייב דהא קא מיכוין לזריקה בעלמא וצריכא דאי אשמעינן קמייתא בההוא קאמר רבא דהא לא קמיכוין לחתיכה דאיסורא אבל נתכוון לזרוק שתים וזרק ארבע דארבע בלא תרתי לא (ב) מיזרקא ליה אימא מודה ליה לאביי ואי אשמעינן בהא בהא קאמר רבא דהא לא קמיכוין לזריקה דארבע אבל כסבור רה"י ונמצא רה"ר דמכוין לזריקה דארבע אימא מודי ליה לאביי צריכא [ג] תנן אבות מלאכות ארבעים חסר אחת והוינן בה מנינא למה לי וא"ר יוחנן שאם עשאן כולם בהעלם אחד חייב על כל אחת ואחת בשלמא לאביי דאמר כי האי גוונא חייב משכחת לה דידע דאסורא (ג) שבת וידע לה איסור מלאכות וקא טעה בשיעורין אלא לרבא דאמר פטור היכי משכחת לה בזדון שבת ושגגת מלאכות הניחא אי סבר לה כר' יוחנן דאמר כיון ששגג בכרת אע"פ שהזיד בלאו משכחת לה דידע לה לשבת בלאו אלא אי סבר לה כרשב"ל דאמר עד שישגוג בלאו וכרת דידע לה לשבת במאי [ד] דידע לה בתחומין ואליבא דר"ע:

מתני' [ה] אבות [ו] [ג] מלאכות ארבעים חסר אחת הזורע והחורש והקוצר והמעמר והדש והזורה הבורר הטוחן והמרקד והלש והאופה הגוזז את הצמר המלבנו והמנפצו והצובעו והטווה [ז] והמיסך והעושה שתי בתי נירין והאורג שני חוטין והפוצע שני חוטין הקושר והמתיר [ח] והתופר שתי תפירות הקורע על מנת לתפור [שתי תפירות] הצד צבי השוחטו והמפשיטו המולחו והמעבד את עורו והממחקו והמחתכו הכותב שתי אותיות והמוחק על מנת לכתוב שתי אותיות הבונה והסותר המכבה והמבעיר המכה בפטיש [ט] המוציא מרשות לרשות הרי אלו אבות מלאכות ארבעים חסר אחת: גמ'

רש"י

דסבור שומן הוא ואכלו. והיינו דשגג דסבור שומן הוא ולא נתכוין לאכול חלב וחייב ואף על פי דמתעסק הוא לרבא דהא לא מתכוין לאכילת איסור חייב דאמר שמואל בכריתות (פ"ד דף יט:) בחלבים ועריות מתעסק חייב שכן נהנה אבל בשבת פטור דלא נהנה והיינו סייעתא לדידיה דאמר נתכוין לחתוך את התלוש וחתך את המחובר פטור: ואביי. אמר לך לעולם כי האי גוונא אף בשבת חייב דלאו מתעסק הוא והיכי דמי מתעסק דשאר מצות חייב קסבר רוק הוא שהיה חלב נימוח ובלעו דלא איכוין לאכילה דרוק לאו בר אכילה הוא אלא בליעה דכתיב (איוב ז) עד בלעי רוקי ועלתה בידו אכילה דהא לא איכוין לאכילה ודכוותייהו דשבת דפטור נתכוין להגביה ועלתה בידו חתיכה: דהא לא איכוין לזריקה דאיסור. ויהא שוגג בשבת או במלאכה אבל זה אינו שוגג לא בשבת ולא במלאכות אלא מתעסק בדבר אחד של היתר ועלתה בידו איסור: וצריכא. לאיפלוגי

תוספות

אלא לאו רישא בע"ז וסיפא בשאר מצות. תימה לר"י דלוקמא כולה בשאר מצות ומאי מה שאין כן בשאר מצות כגון שחט וזרק בחוץ דאינו חייב אלא אחת כדאמר אביי בפרק אחד דיני ממונות (סנהדרין לד:) שם תעשה עשאן הכתוב עשיה אחת ור' אבהו נמי דפליג מודה דלרבי ישמעאל בשחיטה וזריקה ולר' עקיבא בהעלאה וזריקה דאינו חייב אלא אחת דמחד קרא נפקי ושגג בלא מתכוין כגון שנתכוין לשחוט בהמת חולין והיה צריך לשל חולין ונמצאת (ד) של קדשים דכוותה בשבת נתכוין לחתוך תלוש ונמצא מחובר ולא היה צריך אלא לתלוש דפטור דמלאכת מחשבת בעינן וי"ל דלא מצינן לפרושי הכי דמשמע דפטור בשבת לפי ששגג בלא מתכוין דכה"ג אפילו נתכוין למחובר זה ונמצא מחובר אחר פטור דאין זה מלאכת מחשבת וליכא לאוקמי נמי דמיירי כשנעשה מחשבתו כגון שהיה

והאורג [ז] ובפוצע ובתופר ובכותב שיעור טפי מבשאר:

הקושר והמתיר. נ"ע אי מיחייב במתיר שלא על מנת לקשור אי לא ומדלא תני ליה כדתני מוחק ע"מ לכתוב אין לדקדק דהכי נמי לא קתני סותר ע"מ לבנות ובפ' במה מדליקין (לעיל לא:) אמרינן בהדיא דבעינן סותר ע"מ לבנות ולפי מה שפירש רש"י בגמרא (דף עד:) דאי מתרמי ליה תרי קיטרי בהדי הדדי בשני חוטין זה אצל זה שרי חד ומניח חד משמע דמיחייב בלא על מנת לקשור ולשון קטר לא משמע כפירושו אבל ר"ח פירש וכן משמע בירושלמי כשנפסק חוט בשני מקומות ונקשר מתירין ב' הקשרים ומשליכין לחוץ האמצעי וחוזרין וקושרין שתי הראשים זה בזה ואין בו אלא קשר א' ולפי זה משמע דבעי מתיר ע"מ לקשור והא דלא תני ליה במתיר ובסותר פירשתי בפרק ב' (דף לא: ד"ה וסותר): מכדי

רבינו חננאל

ליקוטי רש"י

הגהות הב"ח

dyeing it,[43] וְהַטּוֹוֶה – **spinning,**[44] וְהַמֵּיסֵךְ – **mounting the warp,**[45] וְהָעוֹשֶׂה שְׁתֵּי בָתֵּי נִירִין – **setting two heddles,**[46] וְהָאוֹרֵג שְׁנֵי חוּטִין – **weaving two threads,**[47] וְהַפּוֹצֵעַ שְׁנֵי חוּטִין – **removing two threads,**[48] הַקּוֹשֵׁר – **tying** a knot, וְהַמַּתִּיר – **untying** a knot,[49] וְהַתּוֹפֵר שְׁתֵּי תְפִירוֹת – **sewing two stitches,**[50] הַקּוֹרֵעַ עַל מְנָת לִתְפּוֹר [שְׁתֵּי תְפִירוֹת] – and **tearing in order to sew two stitches;**[51]

The Mishnah now mentions labors required for the preparation of hides,[52] and two labors involving writing: הַצָּד צְבִי – **trapping a deer,**[53] הַשּׁוֹחֲטוֹ – **slaughtering it,**[54] וְהַמַּפְשִׁיטוֹ – **skinning it,**[55] הַמּוֹלְחוֹ – **salting it,**[56] וְהַמְעַבֵּד אֶת עוֹרוֹ – **tanning its hide,**[57] וְהַמְמַחֲקוֹ – **smoothing it,**[58] וְהַמְחַתְּכוֹ – **cutting it,**[59] הַכּוֹתֵב שְׁתֵּי אוֹתִיּוֹת – **writing two letters,**[60] וְהַמּוֹחֵק עַל מְנָת לִכְתּוֹב שְׁתֵּי אוֹתִיּוֹת – **and erasing in order to write two letters;**[61]

NOTES

43. **[15]** ***Dyeing*** (75a-b, 95a). Dyeing the fibers. Dyed wool was used for the curtains and the covers of the Mishkan (*Meiri*).

44. **[16]** ***Spinning*** (74b, 79a). I.e. twisting fibers together to make long threads.

45. **[17]** ***Mounting the warp*** (75b). Preparing the warp threads for weaving.

This *melachah* along with the three that follow constitute the weaving process. A brief introduction of this process is in order. A weaving loom is fundamentally a frame upon which two rollers are mounted: one at the far end (called the warp beam) away from the weaver, and one at the near end (called the cloth beam). The warp thread is wound around the warp beam and stretched to the cloth beam, upon which the woven fabric will eventually be rolled. The weaving process consists of setting up the warp threads on the loom and introducing the weft threads between them to produce a woven fabric. See Appendix.

The process of stretching the warp threads on the loom is the *melachah* of mounting the warp, and the mounter is called a מֵיסֵךְ, *a loom dresser.* See *Maaseh Oreg* p. 17 ff, and *Meleches Arigah* by Rabbi P. Bodner p. 19 ff for futher details of this *melachah*.

46. **[18]** ***Setting*** [literally; making] ***two heddles*** (74b, 105a-b). Between the two beams and perpendicular to them are two frames (called harnesses) through which the warp threads must pass. Each of these harnesses has numerous threads attached to it. Each pair of adjacent threads on the harness is knotted in two places to form a loop (or eye) at the center. This pair of threads is called a heddle. [Heddles may also be made by tying a ring between two lengths of thread. Modern hand looms often use a metal strip pierced at its center.] One warp thread passes through the eye of a heddle of the first harness and between two heddles on the second harness. The next warp thread passes between two heddles on the first harness and through the eye of a heddle in the second harness.

Placing two threads through the heddle eyes constitutes the *av* of setting two heddles (*Rashi;* cf. *Rambam's Commentary to the Mishnah, Tos. Rid*).

[*Tosafos* question why the Tanna states the minimum amount only of this *melachah* and several of those that follow. See *Magen Avos* and *Avnei Nezer* §187 for further discussion.]

47. **[19]** ***Weaving*** (74b, 75b, 105a-b). The weaver raises the two frames alternately (this is called shedding). First, he raises the front frame. In doing so he raises all the odd warp threads and forms a "shed" between the two sets of warp threads. The weft is passed through this shed from right to left (this is called picking). He then raises the even warp threads by lowering the first harness and raising the other, and passes the weft through from left to right. Inserting the weft thread twice through the warp [right to left and left to right] constitutes a performance of the *av* of weaving.

48. **[20]** ***Removing two threads.*** Excess threads are eliminated from areas that are too densely packed (*Rashi;* see *Maaseh Oreg* pp. 28-30; cf. *Magen Avos*; cf. *Rambam, Hil. Shabbos* 9:20 with *Ra'avad*).

All of the labors from *mounting the warp* until here were required for weaving the Mishkan's curtains (*Rashi*).

49. **[21]** ***Tying*** and **[22]** ***untying*** (74b, 111b-113a). Those who fished for *chilazon,* a small fishlike creature whose blood was used for *techeiles* [the blue dye used for the curtains of the Mishkan], would both tie and untie their nets, since it was sometimes necessary to remove ropes from one net and attach them to another (Gemara below, 74b).

Tosafos note that while the Mishnah states below that one is liable for erasing only if he does so in order to write, here it does not stipulate that the untying must be done in order to tie. See there and *Ritva* (*MHK* ed.) for a discussion of this point. [See also below, 74b note 40.]

50. **[23]** ***Sewing*** (74b). The curtains of the Mishnah were sewn (*Rashi*). A minimum of two passes of the needle [one in and one out] stitches is required before one is liable for sewing.

[This in-and-out motion actually results in only a single stitch. We have nevertheless translated שְׁתֵּי תְפִירוֹת loosely as two "stitches" because there is no equivalent word in modern English for a single pass of the needle.]

51. **[24]** ***Tearing*** (74b-75a, 105b). The Gemara below (75a) will explain that when small holes created by moths were found in the curtains of the Mishkan, the adjacent fabric would be torn in order to elongate the hole, thus enabling the tailor to make a neat repair. Tearing was performed in the Mishkan for no other purpose (*Rashi*). Hence, only tearing in order to sew is considered an *av.* If someone tears material for any constructive purpose other than sewing, he is liable for performing a *toladah* of tearing (*Sfas Emes,* in explanation of *Rashi;* see also *Magen Avraham* 317:10; cf. *Tos. R' Akiva Eiger* §90). If the tearing was merely a destructive act (מְקַלְקֵל), the person is certainly exempt from punishment.

52. In the construction of the Mishkan the *melachos* of this category were performed on the *tachash* animal (see *Exodus* 26:14; see above, 28a), from whose hide a covering for the Mishkan was made (*Rashi;* cf. *Shoshanim LeDavid, Yad David*). The labors required for the preparation of hides begin the Mishnah's group of *melachos* needed for writing because hides were used as scrolls.

53. **[25]** ***Trapping*** (75a, 106a-107b). Trapping or hunting any species is a *melachah,* provided that the species is one that is normally trapped or hunted. [Deer is mentioned by the Tanna because it is the most common example in this category.]

54. **[26]** ***Slaughtering*** (75a, 107b). This *melachah* is not limited to *shechitah* (ritual slaughter); it involves taking the life of any wild or domestic beast, fowl, fish or reptile, whether by slaughtering, stabbing or battering. [The Gemara below, 75a, will explain why the Mishnah chooses to use the term "slaughtering."]

55. **[27]** ***Skinning*** (116b). Skinning the hide after slaughter.

56. **[28]** ***Salting*** (75b). Salting the hide is the first step in tanning.

57. **[29]** ***Tanning*** (75b, 79a). The Gemara objects to the separate listing of salting and tanning on the grounds that salting is the beginning of the tanning process; hence, the two are actually one *melachah.* The Gemara therefore deletes one of the two labors and inserts שִׂרְטוּט, *tracing lines,* in its place. Before leather is cut, lines are traced into the skin to indicate the desired design. In the Mishkan this was done before cutting the hides of rams and *techashim* for the coverings (see below, 75b).

58. **[30]** ***Smoothing*** (75b). I.e. scraping the hair off the hide (*Rashi*). In the manufacture of parchment or leather, smooth skin is required. The hide must therefore be scraped clean (*Meiri*). [See *Eglei Tal* גוזז 9:13, for an explanation of why *Rashi* does not consider this action to be the *melachah* of shearing. See also *Minchas Chinuch* §32 under גוזז.]

59. **[31]** ***Cutting*** (74b, 75b). E.g. trimming and cutting the hide into a specific size for straps or shoes (*Rashi*).

60. **[32]** ***Writing*** (75b, 103a-b, 104b-105a). Writing even two letters renders one liable. The wall boards of the Mishkan were inscribed with letters to facilitate matching them each time the Mishkan was erected (*Rashi,* from Gemara below, 103a-b; see also *Avnei Nezer* §199).

61. **[33]** ***Erasing*** (75b). I.e. erasing in order to write two letters in that place. If the Mishkan's builders erred in writing letters on the boards, they would erase them in order to write the proper ones (*Rashi*).

אלא לאו רישא בעכו"ם וסיפא בשאר מצות ושגג בלא מתכוין בשאר מצות ה"ד דסבור דשומן הוא ואכלו משא"כ בשבת דפטור דנתכוון לחתוך את התלוש וחתך את המחובר פטור ואביי שגג בלא מתכוין ה"ד דסבור רוק הוא ובלעו משא"כ בשבת דפטור דנתכוון להגביה את התלוש וחתך את המחובר פטור אבל נתכוון לחתוך את התלוש וחתך את המחובר חייב: איתמר נתכוון לזרוק שתים וזרק ארבע רבא אמר פטור אביי אמר חייב רבא אמר פטור (א) דלא קמיכוין לזריקה דארבע אביי אמר חייב דהא קמיכוין לזריקה בעלמא כסבור רשות היחיד ונמצאת רשות הרבים רבא אמר פטור ואביי אמר חייב רבא אמר פטור דהא לא מיכוין לזריקה דאיסורא ואביי אמר חייב דהא קא מיכוין לזריקה בעלמא וצריכא דאי אשמעינן קמייתא בההוא קאמר רבא דהא לא קמיכוין לחתיכה דאיסורא אבל נתכוון לזרוק שתים וזרק ארבע דארבע בלא תרתי לא (ב) מיזרקא ליה אימא מודה ליה לאביי ואי אשמעינן בהא בהא קאמר רבא דהא לא קמיכוין לזריקה דארבע אבל כסבור רה"י ונמצא רה"ר דמכוין לזריקה דארבע אימא מודי ליה לאביי צריכא תנן אבות מלאכות ארבעים חסר אחת והוינן בה מנינא למה לי וא"ר יוחנן שאם עשאן כולם בהעלם אחד חייב על כל אחת ואחת בשלמא לאביי דאמר כי האי גוונא חייב משכחת לה דידע דאסורא (ג) שבת וידע לה איסור מלאכות וקא טעה בשיעורין אלא לרבא דאמר פטור היכי משכחת לה בזדון שבת ושגגת מלאכות הניחא אי סבר לה כר' יוחנן דאמר כיון ששגג בכרת אע"פ שהזיד בלאו משכחת לה דידע לה לשבת בלאו אלא אי סבר לה כרשב"ל דאמר עד שישגוג בלאו וכרת דידע לה לשבת במאי דידע לה בתחומין ואליבא דר"ע:

מתני' אבות מלאכות ארבעים חסר אחת הזורע והחורש והקוצר והמעמר והדש והזורה הבורר הטוחן והמרקד והלש והאופה הגוזז את הצמר המלבנו והמנפצו והצובעו והטווה והמיסך והעושה שתי בתי נירין והאורג שני חוטין והפוצע שני חוטין הקושר והמתיר והתופר שתי תפירות הקורע על מנת לתפור [שתי תפירות] הצד צבי השוחטו והמפשיטו המולחו והמעבד את עורו והממחקו והמחתכו הכותב שתי אותיות והמוחק על מנת לכתוב שתי אותיות הבונה והסותר המכבה והמבעיר המכה בפטיש המוציא מרשות לרשות הרי אלו אבות מלאכות ארבעים חסר אחת:

גמ'

רש"י

דסבור שומן הוא ואכלו. והיינו דשגג דסבור לאכול חלב וחייב ואף על פי דמתעסק הוא לרבא דהא לא מתכוין לאכילת איסור חייב דאמר שמואל בכריתות (פ"ד דף יט:) בחלבי' ועריות מתעסק חייב שכן נהנה אבל בשבת פטור דלא נהנה והיינו סייעתא לדידיה דאמר נתכוין לחתוך את התלוש וחתך את המחובר פטור: ואביי. אמר לך לעולם כי האי גוונא אף בשבת חייב דלאו מתעסק הוא והיכי דמי מתעסק דשאר מצות חייב קסבר רוק הוא שהיה חלב נימוח ובלעו דלא איכוין לאכילה דרוק לאו בר אכילה הוא אלא בליעה דכתיב (איוב ז) עד בלעי רוקי ועלתה בידו אכילה דהא לא איכוין לאכילה ודכוותייהו דשבת דפטור נתכוין להגביה ועלתה בידו חתיכה: דהא לא איכוין לזריקה דאיסור. ויהא שוגג בשבת או במלאכה אבל זה אינו שוגג לא בשבת ולא במלאכות אלא מתעסק בדבר אחד של היתר ועלתה בידו איסור: וצריכא. לאיפלוגי בכולהו אף על גב דדמי להדדי: דארבע בלא תרתי לא מזדריק. וזה שנתכוין לשתים חרק ארבע נעשית מחשבתו דהא יש בכלל ד' שתים הלכך לאו מתעסק הוא: דלא איכוין לזריקה דארבע. ובציר מהני לא שם זריקה עלה: אבל כסבור רה"י הוא וכו'. דנתכוין לזריקה גמורה: משכחת לה. להאי שנשתכחה תורת כל הלכות שבת ממנו ואפילו הכי חשיבא ליה כזדון שבת ושגגת מלאכות לחיוביה אכל חדא כגון דידע ליה לשבת באיסורין וטעה בשיעורין שנתכוין לפחות מכשיעור ועשה כשיעור דלכולן יש שיעור: אלא לרבא דאמר פטור היכי משכחת לה. דמיחייב שום אדם על כל מלאכה ומלאכה שבהעלם אחד על כרחך בזדון שבת ושגגת מלאכות הוא דבעית לאשכוחיה והכא דאיעלימו כולהו מיניה מאי זדון שבת איכא במה ניכר לו שבת מאשר ימים: מתני' הזורה. ברחת לרוח: הבורר. פסולת בידיו: המרקד. בנפה ובגמ' פריך הני כולהו חדא היא דלהפריש פסולת מתוך אוכל נעשות שלשתן: האופה. לא הוה במשכן דלא שייך אלא בפת ופת לא שייכא במלאכת המשכן אבל כולהו קמייתא הואי בסממנין של צבע תכלת וארגמן ותולעת שני ובגמרא פריך דשביק תנא מבשל דהוי בסממנים ונקט אופה ושיעורן של אלו כגרוגרת חוץ מחורש דבכל שהוא לקמן בפרק הבונה (דף קג.): הגוזז צמר. וכל שאר מלאכות שייכי בצמר של מלאכת המשכן: המלבנו. מכבסו בנהר: המנפצו. קרפי"ר בלע"ז: המיסך. אורדי"ר: בתי נירין. ליצ"ש שנתן שני חוטין בתוך הבית ניר ובגוזז ובמלבן וכולהו איך מפרש שיעורן לקמן בפרק האורג: הפוצע. מנתק פעמים שיש בשני חוטין יותר מדאי ומנתק מהן ומקלישן לצורך והני כולהו ממיסך ואילך עד קושר ומתיר שייכי ביריעות ולקמן מפרש מאי קושר ומאי מתיר איכא: ותופר וקורע. ביריעות הוא: על מנת לתפור. פעמים שהנקב עגול ואינו יכול לתופרו יפה אא"כ קורעו כדמפרש בגמרא אבל קורע שלא לתפור לא הוי במשכן: הצד את הצבי. וכל מלאכת עורו נוהגת בתחשים למשכן בעורותיהן: המולחו. לעור: ממחקו. מגרר שערו: מחתכו. מקצעו ומחתכו לרצועות וסנדלים: כותב ומוחק. לקמן (דף קג:) מפרש למאי מיבעיא למשכן שכן רושמין על קרשי המשכן לידע איזה בן זוגו וכותב אות בזו ואות בזו ומוחק פעמים שטעה: מכבה ומבעיר. באש שתחת הדוד של סממנין: מכה בפטיש. הוא גמר כל מלאכה שכן אומן מכה בקורנס על הסדן להחליקו בגמר מלאכה ומתניתין נמי לא מיחייב ליה אלא בגמר מלאכה:

תוספות

אלא לאו רישא בע"ז וסיפא בשאר מצות. תימה לר"י דלוקמא כולה בשאר מצות ומאי מה שאין כן בשאר מצות כגון שחט וזרק בחוץ דאינו חייב אלא אחת כדאמר אביי בפרק אחד דיני ממונות (סנהדרין לד:) שם תעשה עשאן הכתוב עשיה אחת ור' אבהו נמי דפליג מודה דלרבי ישמעאל בשחיטה וזריקה ולר' עקיבא בהעלאה וזריקה דאינו חייב אלא אחת דמחד קרא נפקי ושגג בלא מתכוין כגון שנתכוין לשחוט בהמת חולין והיה צריך לשל חולין ונמצאת (ד) של קדשים דכוותה בשבת נתכוין לחתוך תלוש ונמצא מחובר ולא היה צריך אלא לתלוש דפטור דמלאכת מחשבת בעינן וי"ל דלא מצינן לפרושי הכי דמשמע דפטור בשבת לפי שגג בלא מתכוין דכה"ג אפילו נתכוין למחובר זה ונמצא מחובר אחר פטור דאין זה מלאכת מחשבת וליכא לאוקמי נמי דמיירי כשנעשה מחשבתו כגון שהיה צריך לחתוך מה שחתך אלא שהיה סבור שהוא תלוש ונמצא שהוא מחובר הא ליכא למימר דכה"ג אם פטור לענין שבת מאשר חטא בה פטור נמי לענין חוץ ומיהו עוד קשה דלוקמא כולה בשאר מצות כגון (ה) נרבע לזכר ורבע את הזכר והבא על הבהמה והביא בהמה עליו דכין לאביי וכין לר' אבהו לר' עקיבא אינו חייב אלא אחת והשתא שגג בלא מתכוין מיתוקם שפיר דמיפטר בשבת מאשר חטא בה וכגון שנעשית מחשבתו וגבי עריות לא מיפטר שכן נהנה:

העושה שני בתי נירין. צריך לפרש למה פירש כאן ובאורג ובפוצע ובתופר ובכותב שיעור טפי מבשאר:

הקושר והמתיר. צ"ע אי מיחייב במתיר שלא על מנת לקשור אי לא ומדלא תני ליה כדתני מוחק ע"מ לכתוב אין לדקדק דהכי נמי לא קתני סותר ע"מ לבנות ובפ' במה מדליקין (לעיל לא:) אמרינן בהדיא דבעינן סותר ע"מ לבנות ולפי מה שפירש רש"י בגמרא (דף עד:) דאי מתרמי ליה תרי קיטרי בהדי הדדי בשני חוטין זה אצל זה שרי חד ומניח חד משמע דמיחייב בלא על מנת לקשור ולשון קטר לא משמע כפירושו אבל ר"ח פירש וכן משמע בירושלמי כשנפסק חוט בשני מקומות ונקשר מתירין ב' הקשרים ומשליכין לחוץ האמצעי וחוזרין וקושרין שתי הראשים זה בזה ואין בו אלא קשר א' ולפי זה משמע דבעי מתיר ע"מ לקשור והא דלא תני ליה במתיר ובסותר פירשתי בפרק ב' (דף לא: ד"ה וסותר):

מכדי

The final six labors:

הַבּוֹנֶה – building[62] **וְהַסּוֹתֵר – and demolishing;**[63] **הַמְכַבֶּה – extinguishing וְהַמַּבְעִיר – and kindling;**[64] **הַמַּכֶּה בְּפַטִּישׁ – striking the final blow,**[65] **הַמּוֹצִיא מֵרְשׁוּת לִרְשׁוּת – and taking out from one domain to** another **domain.**[66]

The Mishnah concludes:

הֲרֵי אֵלּוּ אָבוֹת מְלָאכוֹת אַרְבָּעִים חָסֵר אַחַת – These are the primary labors – forty minus one.[67]

NOTES

62. **[34] *Building*** (73b, 102b-103a). Building any amount is a *melachah.*

63. **[35] *Demolishing*** (above, 31b). Although the Mishnah does not expressly limit this *melachah* to demolishing in order to rebuild, that limitation surely exists, for the act is inherently destructive. See *Tosafos* (above, 31b) for an explanation of why the Mishnah does not specify the "in order to" qualification in the case of demolishing.

64. **[36] *Extinguishing*** and **[37] *kindling*** (30a, 31b; ch. 16). Both extinguishing and kindling were performed vis-a-vis the fire used for cooking the dyes (*Rashi*).

Meiri and *Chidushei HaRan* add that the fire was extinguished in the Mishkan so as not to burn the cooking herbs. This, however, is apparently difficult because the Gemara above (29b-30a) teaches that [at least according to R' Shimon] one is liable for extinguishing only when it is done to make charcoals. In fact, *Tosafos* (above, 31b and below, 94a ד״ה רבי שמעון) write that fire was extinguished in the Mishkan in the production of charcoals, a constructive act.

65. **[38] *Striking the final blow*** [literally: one who strikes with a hammer] (75b, 102b). Although the concept of finality is not implied by the literal title of this *av,* the Gemara (75b) understands the *melachah* to be the administering of a finishing touch at the completion of a job.

The Mishnah refers specifically to the hammer blow that a craftsman delivers to the anvil after finishing his work, which leaves him a smooth surface for the next job. The Mishnah thus obligates a person for any finishing touch he administers to a job (*Rashi*).

Ritva objects to *Rashi's* explanation, since it is not consistent with the opinion of the Sages who dispute Rabban Shimon ben Gamliel in a Mishnah below (102b). See *Chasam Sofer* and *Rashash* loc. cit. for a defense of *Rashi's* position. See also *Ramban* and *Ran* here.

66. **[39] *Transferring*** (2a-9a, 75b, chs. 8-11). This involves transferring either from a private domain to a public domain or the reverse.

67. The Gemara below (75b) will explain the need for this second count.

כו א מיי' פ"ב מהלכות שגגות הלכה ז:
כז ב מיי' פ"א מהלכות שבת הלכה ח:
כח ג מיי' פ"ז מהלכות שבת הלכה א סמג לאוין סה:

א) [ב"ק דף כו: ע"ש], ב) [עמ"ש לעיל עב: על הגליון], ג) [לעיל סט. וש"נ], ד) [לעיל סט. ע:], ה) פ"א אלו אבות, ו) לעיל ו: מט: סט. ע: לקמן לו: ב"ק ב. [כריתות ב:], ז) [פי' מותח חוטי השתי], ח) [לקמן קה.], ט) לעיל ב: [שבועות ה:], י) [עי' תוי"ט ד"ה והעושה שתי].

הגהות הב"ח

(א) גמ' רבא אמר פטור דהא לא קמיכוין: (ב) שם תרתי לא מיזדרקא ליה: (ג) שם

אלא לאו רישא בעכו"ם וסיפא בשאר מצות ושגג בלא מתכוין בשאר מצות ה"ד דסבור דשומן הוא ואכלו משא"כ בשבת דפטור דנתכוון לחתוך את התלוש וחתך את המחובר פטור ואביי שגג בלא מתכוין ה"ד דסבור[א] רוק הוא ובלעו משא"כ בשבת דפטור דנתכוון להגביה את התלוש וחתך את המחובר פטור אבל נתכוון לחתוך את התלוש וחתך את המחובר חייב: איתמר א) נתכוון לזרוק שתים וזרק ארבע ב) רבא אמר פטור אביי אמר חייב רבא אמר פטור (א) דלא קמיכוין לזריקה דארבע אביי אמר חייב דהא קמיכוין לזריקה בעלמא כסבור רשות היחיד ונמצאת רשות הרבים רבא אמר ג) פטור ואביי אמר חייב רבא אמר פטור דהא לא מיכוין לזריקה דאיסורא ואביי אמר חייב דהא קא מיכוין לזריקה בעלמא וצריכא דאי אשמעינן קמייתא בההוא קאמר רבא דהא לא קמיכוין לחתיכה דאיסורא אבל נתכוון לזרוק שתים וזרק ארבע דארבע בלא תרתי לא (ב) מיזרקא ליה אימא מודה ליה לאביי ואי אשמעינן בהא בהא קאמר רבא דהא לא קמיכוין לזריקה דארבע אבל כסבור רה"י ונמצא רה"ר דמכוין לזריקה דארבע אימא מודי ליה לאביי צריכא ד) תנן אבות מלאכות ארבעים חסר אחת והוינן בה מנינא למה לי וא"ר יוחנן שאם עשאן כולם בהעלם אחד חייב על כל אחת ואחת בשלמא לאביי דאמר כי האי גוונא חייב משכחת לה דידע דאסורא (ג) שבת וידע לה איסור מלאכות וקא טעה בשיעורין אלא לרבא דאמר פטור היכי משכחת לה בזדון שבת ושגגת מלאכות הניחא אי סבר לה כר' יוחנן דאמר כיון ששגג בכרת אע"פ שהזיד בלאו משכחת לה דידע לה לשבת בלאו אלא אי סבר לה כרשב"ל דאמר עד שישגוג בלאו וכרת דידע לה לשבת במאי ה) דידע לה בתחומין ואליבא דר"ע:

מתני' ו) אבות ז) מלאכות ארבעים חסר אחת הזורע והחורש והקוצר והמעמר והדש והזורה הבורר הטוחן והמרקד והלש והאופה הגוזז את הצמר המלבנו והמנפצו והצובעו והטווה ח) והמיסך והעושה שתי בתי נירין והאורג שני חוטין והפוצע שני חוטין הקושר והמתיר ט) והתופר שתי תפירות הקורע על מנת לתפור [שתי תפירות] הצד צבי השוחטו והמפשיטו המולחו והמעבד את עורו והממחקו והמחתכו הכותב שתי אותיות והמוחק על מנת לכתוב שתי אותיות הבונה והסותר המכבה והמבעיר המכה בפטיש י) המוציא מרשות לרשות הרי אלו אבות מלאכות ארבעים חסר אחת:

גמ'

רש"י

דסבור שומן הוא ואכלו. והיינו דשגג דסבור שומן הוא ולא נתכוין לאכול חלב וחייב ואף על פי דמתעסק הוא לרבא דהא לא מתכוין לאכילת איסור חייב דאמר שמואל בכריתות (פ"ד דף יט:) בחלבי' ועריות מתעסק חייב שכן נהנה אבל בשבת פטור דלא נהנה והיינו סייעתא לדידיה דאמר נתכוין לחתוך את התלוש וחתך את המחובר פטור: **ואביי.** אמר לך לעולם כי האי גוונא אף בשבת חייב דלאו מתעסק הוא והיכי דמי מתעסק דשאר מצות חייב קסבר רוק הוא שהיה חלב נימוח ובלעו דלא איכוין לאכילה דרוק לאו בר אכילה הוא אלא בליעה דכתיב (איוב ז) עד בלעי רוקי ועלתה בידו אכילה דהא לא איכוין לאכילה ודכוותייהו דשבת דפטור נתכוין להגביה ועלתה בידו חתיכה: **דהא לא איכוין לזריקה דאיסור.** ויהא שוגג בשבת או במלאכה אבל זה אינו שוגג לא בשבת ולא במלאכות אלא מתעסק בדבר אחד של היתר ועלתה בידו איסור: **וצריכא.** לאיפלוגי בכולהו אף על גב דדמי להדדי: **דארבע בלא תרתי לא מזדריק.** וזה שנתכוין לשתים וזרק ארבע נעשית מחשבתו דהא יש בכלל ד' שתים הלכך לאו מתעסק הוא: **דלא איכוין לזריקה דארבע.** ובליר מהני לא שם זריקה עלה: **אבל כסבור רה"י הוא וכו'.** דנתכוין לזריקה גמורה: **משכחת לה.** להאי שנשתכחה תורת כל הלכות שבת ממנו ואפילו הכי חשיבא ליה כזדון שבת ושגגת מלאכות לחיוביה אכל חדא כגון דידע ליה לשבת באיסורין וטעה בשיעורין שנתכוין לפחות מכשיעור ועשה כשיעור דלכולן יש שיעור: **אלא לרבא דאמר פטור היכי משכחת לה.** דמיחייב שום אדם על כל מלאכה ומלאכה שבהעלם אחד על כרחך בזדון שבת ושגגת מלאכות הוא דבעית לאשכוחיה והכא דאיעלימו כולהו מיניה מאי זדון שבת איכא במה ניכר לו שבת משאר ימים: **מתני' הזורה.** ברחת לרוח: **הבורר.** פסולת בידיו: **המרקד.** בנפה ובגמ' פריך הני כולהו חדא היא דלהפריש פסולת מתוך אוכל נעשות שלשתן: **האופה.** לא הוה במשכן דלא שייך אלא בפת ופת לא שייכא במלאכת המשכן אבל כולהו קמייתא הואי בסממנין של צבע תכלת וארגמן ותולעת שני ובגמרא פריך דשביק תנא מבשל דהוי בסממנים ונקט אופה ושיעורן של אלו כגרוגרת חוץ מחורש דבכל שהוא לקמן בפרק הבונה (דף קג.): **הגוזז צמר.** וכל שאר מלאכות שייכי בצמר של מלאכת המשכן: **המלבנו.** מכבסו בנהר: **המנפצו.** קרפי"ר בלע"ז: **המיסך.** אורדי"ר: **בתי נירין.** ליצ"ש שנתן שני חוטין בתוך הבית ניר ובגוזז ובמלבן וכולהו איך מפרש שיעורן לקמן בפרק האורג: **הפוצע.** מנתק פעמים שיש בשני חוטין יותר מדאי ומנתק מהן ומקלישן לצורך והני כולהו ממיסך ואילך עד קושר ומתיר שייכי ביריעות ולקמן מפרש מאי קושר ומאי מתיר איכא: **ותופר וקורע.** ביריעות הוא: **על מנת לתפור.** פעמים שהנקב עגול ואינו יכול לתופרו יפה אא"כ קורעו כדמפרש בגמרא אבל קורע שלא לתפור לא הוי במשכן: **הצד את הצבי.** וכל מלאכת עורו נוהגת בתחשים למשכן בעורותיהן: **המולחו.** לעור: **ממחקו.** מגרר שערו: **מחתכו.** מקצעו ומחתכו לרצועות וסנדלים: **כותב ומוחק.** לקמן (דף קג:) מפרש למאי מיבעיא למשכן שכן רושמין על קרשי המשכן לידע איזה בן זוגו וכותב אות בזו ואות בזו ומוחק פעמים שטעה: **מכבה ומבעיר.** באש שתחת הדוד של סממנין: **מכה בפטיש.** הוא גמר כל מלאכה שכן אומן מכה בקורנס על הסדן להחליקו בגמר מלאכה ומתניתין נמי לא מיחייב ליה אלא בגמר מלאכה:

גמרא

תוספות

אלא לאו רישא בע"ז וסיפא בשאר מצות. תימה לר"י דלוקמא כולה בשאר מצות ומאי מה שאין כן בשאר מצות כגון שחט וזרק בחוץ דאינו חייב אלא אחת כדאמר אביי בפרק אחד דיני ממונות (סנהדרין לד:) שם תעשה עשאן הכתוב עשיה אחת ור' אבהו נמי דפליג מודה דלרבי ישמעאל בשחיטה וזריקה ולר' עקיבא בהעלאה וזריקה דאינו חייב אלא אחת דמחד קרא נפקי ושגג בלא מתכוין כגון שנתכוין לשחוט בהמת חולין והיה צריך לשל חולין ונמצאת (ד) של קדשים דכוותה בשבת נתכוין לחתוך תלוש ונמצא מחובר ולא היה צריך אלא לתלוש דפטור דמלאכת מחשבת בעינן וי"ל דלא מצינן לפרושי הכי דמשמע דפטור בשבת לפי ששגג בלא מתכוין דכה"ג אפילו נתכוין למחובר זה ונמצא מחובר אחר פטור דאין זה מלאכת מחשבת וליכא לאוקמי נמי דמיירי כשנעשה מחשבתו כגון שהיה צריך לחתוך מה שחתך אלא שהיה סבור שהוא תלוש ונמצא שהוא מחובר הא ליכא למימר דכה"ג אם פטור לענין שבת מאשר חטא בה פטור נמי לענין חוץ ומיהו עוד קשה דלוקמא כולה בשאר מצות כגון (ה) נרבע לזכר ורבע את הזכר והבא על הבהמה והביא בהמה עליו דבין לאביי ובין לר' אבהו לר' עקיבא אינו חייב אלא אחת והשתא שגג בלא מתכוין מיתוקס שפיר דמיפטר בשבת מאשר חטא בה וכגון שנעשית מחשבתו וגבי עריות לא מיפטר שכן נהנה:

העושה שני בתי נירין. צריך לפרש למה פירש כאן ובאורג י) ובפוצע ובתופר ובכותב שיעור טפי מבשאר:

הקושר והמתיר. ל"ע אי מיחייב במתיר שלא על מנת לקשור אי לא ומדלא תני ליה כדתני מוחק ע"מ לכתוב אין לדקדק דהכי נמי לא קתני סותר ע"מ לבנות ובפ' במה מדליקין (לעיל לא:) אמרינן בהדיא דבעינן סותר ע"מ לבנות ולפי מה שפירש רש"י בגמרא (דף עד:) דאי מתרמי ליה תרי קיטרי בהדי הדדי בשני חוטין זה אצל זה שרי חד ומניח חד משמע דמיחייב בלא על מנת לקשור ולשון קטר לא משמע כפירושו אבל ר"ח פירש וכן משמע בירושלמי כשנפסק חוט בשני מקומות ונקשר מתירין ב' הקשרים ומשליכין לחוץ האמצעי וחוזרין וקושרין שתי הראשים זה בזה ואין בו אלא קשר א' ולפי זה משמע דבעי מתיר ע"מ לקשור והא דלא תני ליה במתיר ובסותר פירשתי בפרק ב' (דף לא: ד"ה וסותר):

מכדי

גמ' מנינא למה לי [א] א"ר יוחנן א שאם עשאן כולם בהעלם אחד חייב על כל אחת ואחת: הזורע והחורש: מכדי מכרב כרבי ברישא ליתני חורש והדר ליתני זורע [ב] תנא בארץ ישראל קאי דזרעי ברישא והדר כרבי תנא ב הזורע והזומר והנוטע והמבריך והמרכיב כולן מלאכה אחת הן מאי קמ"ל [ג] [הא קמ"ל] העושה מלאכות הרבה מעין מלאכה אחת אינו חייב אלא אחת א"ר [ד] אחא א"ר חייא בר אשי א"ר אמי ג זומר חייב משום נוטע והנוטע והמבריך והמרכיב חייב משום זורע משום זורע אין משום נוטע לא אימא אף משום זורע אמר [ה] רב כהנא ד זומר וצריך לעצים חייב שתים אחת משום קוצר ואחת משום נוטע א"ר יוסף האי מאן דקטל אספסתא חייב שתים אחת משום קוצר ואחת משום נוטע אמר אביי האי מאן דקניב סילקא חייב שתים אחת משום קוצר ואחת משום (א) זורע: והחורש: תנא ה החורש והחופר והחורץ כולן מלאכה אחת הן אמר רב ששת [ו] היתה לו גבשושית ונטלה בבית חייב משום בונה בשדה חייב משום חורש [ז] אמר רבא היתה לו גומא וטממה בבית חייב משום בונה בשדה (ב) משום חורש [ח] אמר רבי אבא ו החופר גומא בשבת ואינו צריך אלא לעפרה פטור עליה ואפילו לרבי יהודה דאמר [ט] מלאכה שאינה צריכה לגופה חייב עליה ה"מ מתקן האי מקלקל הוא: והקוצר: תנא ח הקוצר הבוצר [י] והגודר והמסיק והאורה כולן מלאכה אחת אמר רב פפא האי מאן דשדא פיסא לדיקלא ואתר תמרי חייב שתים אחת משום תולש ואחת משום מפרק רב אשי אמר אין דרך תלישה בכך ואין דרך פריקה בכך: והמעמר: אמר [כ] רבא האי מאן דכניף מילחא ממלחתא חייב משום מעמר אביי אמר ט אין עימור אלא בגידולי קרקע: והדש: תנא הדש והמנפץ [ל] והמנפט כולן מלאכה אחת הן: הזורה הבורר והטוחן והמרקד: י היינו זורה היינו בורר היינו מרקד אביי ורבא דאמרי תרווייהו כל מילתא דהויא במשכן
אע"ג

רש"י

גמ' מנינא למה לי. ליתני אבות מלאכות הזורע והחורש כו' ואנא חזינא אי ארבעין [ל] ניהו: **שאם עשאן כו'.** ובא להודיעך שאם נתעלמו כל הלכות שבת ממנו (ג) חייב כמה חטאות עליו: **מכרב כרבי.** חורשין: **באי'.** קשה היא ואין יכול לכסות בלא חרישה ואשמעינן דהא נמי חרישה היא: **כולן מלאכה אחת הן.** דזומר נמי לצמוחי אילנא הוא ונפקא מינה דאי עבד ליה כולן בהדי זורע לא מיחייב אלא חדא דהעושה מלאכות הרבה כו': **זורע** אב מלאכה ונוטע נמי אב מלאכה הוא דהיינו זורע אלא שזה בזרעים וזה באילנות וכן מבריך ומרכיב אבל זומר תולדה: **זומר חייב.** משום תולדת נוטע דלצמוחי עביד: **ונוטע.** גופיה וכן מבריך ומרכיב: **חייב משום זורע.** כלומר אינהו נמי זורע הן זה אב בזרעים וזה אב באילנות: **משום נוטע לא.** אמבריך ואמרכיב קאי: **אימא אף משום זורע.** דהך זריעה באילנות ואי עביד ליה בהדי זורע מיחייב חדא ותו לא: **זומר.** להצמיח הגפן: **וצריך לעצים.** להסקה משום דצריך להם הויא תולדה דקוצר דצריך נמי לקצור: **דקטל אספסתא.** שחת וקוצרין אותו ג' פעמים בחדש וחוזר וצומח: **דקניב סילקא.** חותך תרדין מן המחובר וחוזרין וגדלין: **החורץ.** עושה חריצין בקרקע: **מלאכה אחת הן.** אינו חייב אלא אחת דכולהו לרפויי ארעא עבידי: **גבשושית.** תל קטן: **בבית.** שייך בנין שמתכוין להשוות קרקעיתו: **משום חורש.** דמרפי ארעא: **גומא וטממה.** בעפר היינו חורש שהעפר שמילאה בו הוי רפוי וטוב לזריעה והשוה לקרקע להיות מרע עם השדה: **אלא לעפרה.** לכסות צואה: **פטור עליה.** ואין כאן משום בנין בבית דקלקול הוא ולזריעה נמי לא חזיא אבל אם היה צריך לה חייב משום בונה: **לרבי יהודה.** בפרק המצניע (לקמן צג:) גבי מוציא את המת במטה: **מתקן.** כמו מוציא את המת לקוברו אינו צריך לגופה דהוצאה ולא למת אלא לפנות ביתו והוצאה הצריכה לגופה כגון שהוא צריך לחפץ זה במקום אחר: **מקלקל הוא.** את ביתו: **גודר.** בתמרים: **ומוסק.** בזיתים: **אורה.** בתאנים: **דשדא פיסא לדיקלא.** זרק פיסת רגבים לדקל: **ואתר תמרי.** השיר התמרים: **תולש.** תולדה דקוצר: **מפרק.** תולדה דדש שמפרק תבואה משבליה לשון פורק מן החמור דישקארגיי"ר בלע"ז רבינו לוי וגם בתשובת רבינו משולם הגאון מצאתי כן ואף זה מפרק התמרים מן המכבדות: **אין דרך תלישה ופריקה בכך.** על ידי זריקה אלא או ביד או בכלי ותולש כלאחר יד הוא ופטור: **דכניף מלחא ממלחתא.** שצבר מלח ממשרפות מים דמתרגמינן חרילי ימא (יהושע יא) שממשיך לתוכו מים מן הים והחמה שורפתן והן נעשין מלח ואותו חריץ קרי מילחתא: **משום מעמר.** שאף הוא כמאסף בשבלין הוא: **המנפץ.** פשתן בגבעולין: **והמנפט.** למר גפן בקשת כדרך האומנין ולמר גפן גידולי קרקע הוא להכי קרי ניפוט דיליה תולדה דדש שמפרק גרעינין ממנו ולא קרי ליה תולדת מנפץ דצמר: **ה"ג היינו זורה היינו בורר היינו מרקד.** **היינו.** כמו הי ניהו כלומר דמפליג להו תנא דמתניתין לתלת והלא כולן מלאכה אחת הן דמפריש אוכל מן הפסולת:
אע"ג

תוספות

מכדי מכרב כרבי ברישא והדר כו'. לא שייך למידק הכי בהא דקתני המכבה ברישא והדר המבעיר דהכא כל סידורא דפת נקט כסדר לבד מחרישה: **משום** זורע. אין להוכיח מכאן דלריך להתרות אתולדה משום אב דהא לא קאמר שצריך להתרותו משום זורע אלא דאם התרה בו משום זורע דחייב אבל בריש פרק תולין (לקמן קלח.) משמע קצת דצריך להתרות אתולדה משום אב דקאמר משמר משום מאי מתרינן ביה (שיהא חייב) רבה אמר משום בורר רבי זירא אמר משום מרקד וגם זה יש לדחות דהכי פירושו משום מאי מתרינן ביה שיהא חייב רבה אמר משום בורר אבל אם התרו בו משום מרקד פטור כיון דמתרהו משום דבר שאינו דומה לו הוא סבר שהוא מלעיג בו ופטור אבל אם התרה בו סתם אל תשמר חייב ונראה שגם ר"ת רוצה לפרש כן ועוד ראיה דבריש בבא קמא (דף ב.) קאמר ולר' אליעזר דמחייב אתולדה במקום אב אמאי קרי ליה אב ואמאי קרי ליה תולדה ולא משני דלהכי קרי ליה אב דצריך להתרות אתולדה [משום] אב [מ]:

זומר וצריך לעצים חייב שתים. והא דאמר בפ' זה בורר (סנהדרין דף כו.) תו חזיוה לההוא גברא דהוה קא כסח אמר להן כהן וחמיר אמרו ליה יכול לומר לעקל בית הבד אני צריך אף על גב דהכא אמר חייב משום נוטע התם מיירי בכה"ג שאין האילן מיתקן בכך אלא מתקלקל:

וצריך לעצים. נראה דאפילו לר' יהודה דמחייב מלאכה שאינה צריכה לגופה בעינן צריך לעצים דלא מיקרי בעצים קוצר אלא בענין זה ° מידי דהוה אקורע על מנת לתפור ומוחק על מנת לכתוב וכדאמר רבי יוחנן לקמן בפ' חבית (דף קמה.) אחד כבשים ואחד שלקות שסחטן לגופן מותר למימיהן חייב חטאת ואמאי שרי לגופן ליהוי כמלאכה שאינה צריכה לגופה אלא טעמא לפי שאין דרך דישה בכך:

ואחת משום מפרק. אין נראה לר"י כמו שמפרש רש"י שמפרק האילן ממשאו מן הפירות שעליו אלא כמו שפירש רבינו שמואל שיש על התמרים קליפה העליונה וכשהוא מכה בתמרים מפרק את הקליפה מן התמרים והוי כמו דש שמפרק את התבואה מן השבולת:

מפרק. פירש"י דהוה תולדה דדש וקשה לר"ת דבשילהי המצניע (לקמן צה.) אמר דחולב חייב משום מפרק ואי הוה תולדה דדש הא אמר לקמן [י] גבי הפוצע חלזון דלרבנן אין דישה אלא בגידולי קרקע ואין לומר דדוקא חלזון שהוא דג פטרי רבנן דלא הוי גידולי קרקע אבל בחולב מחייבי דבהמה חשיבא גידולי קרקע כדמוכח בריש בכל מערבין (עירובין דף כח:) דהא [ע"כ טעמא דרבנן משום] דילפינן להו ממשכן שבמשכן דאין דישה אלא בגידולי קרקע ° לגבי דבר הגדל ממש מן הקרקע לא חשיבא בהמה גידולי קרקע כדאמרינן בהשוכר את הפועלים (ב"מ פט.) מה דיש מיוחד שהוא גידולי קרקע ופועל אוכל בו אף כל כו' יצא החולב והמגבן כו' ודוחק לומר דברייתא דהמצניע אתיא כר"י דפליג לקמן אדרבנן ונראה לר"ת דמפרק חייב משום ממחק דכשחולב ממחק את הדד ומחליקו ואין נראה לר"י דבפרק חבית (לקמן קמד:) אמרינן חולב אדם לתוך הקדרה אבל לא לתוך הקערה ולר"ת מה לי לתוך הקדרה מה לי לתוך הקערה ולפירוש הקונטרס א"ש דמעיקרא כשהיה בדדין חשיב אוכל וכשחולב לתוך הקדרה (דהשתא) נמי הוי אוכל ולא דמי לדש שנשתנה ונראה דלפירוש הקונטרס הלכה כרבי יהודה דהאמר בפרק אע"פ (כתובות ס.) [ס] אמר רבי מרינוס גונח יונק חלב בשבת מ"ט מפרק כלאחר יד הוא ובמקום צער לא גזרו רבנן ופסיק התם רב יוסף הלכתא כרבי מרינוס ואין נראה לומר דאף לרבנן אסור מדרבנן דמיחזי כמפרק ואף על גב דלא אסירא אלא מדרבנן לא שרי אלא משום דאיכא תרתי כלאחר יד ובמקום צער: [ועי' תוס' כתובות ס. ד"ה מפרק ותוס' יבמות קיד. ד"ה וקסבר]

עין משפט נר מצוה

כט א מיי' פ"ז מהלכות שבת הלכה ח ופ"ז מהלכות שגגות הלכה ג:
ל ב מיי' פ"ז מהל' שבת הלכה ג והלכה ט:
לא ג מיי' פ"ח מהלכות שבת הלכה ג:
לב ד שם הלכה ד:
לג ה מיי' פ"ז מהלכות שבת הלכה ג:
לד ו מיי' פ"ח מהלכות שבת הלכה א:
לה ז מיי' פ"א מהלכות שבת הלכה יח:
לו ח מיי' פ"ז מהלכות שבת הלכה ד סמג לאוין סה:
לז ט מיי' פ"ח שם הל' ה סמג שם טוש"ע או"ח סימן ש"מ סעיף ט:
לח י מיי' פ"ח מהלכות שבת הל"א סמג שם:

רבינו חננאל

למה לי למיתנא מנינא [מ'] חסר אחת אטו עד האידנא מי לא ידעינן מנייני ומשני ר' יוחנן שאם עשאן כולם בהעלם אחד חייב על כל אחת ואחת. (ת"ש) [תנא] הזורע והזומר והנוטע והמבריך והמרכיב כולן מלאכה אחת הן (קס"ד) [קמ"ל] כי העושה מלאכות הרבה מעין מלאכה אחת אינו חייב אלא חטאת אחת שמעי' מינה שאלו השניים במשנתנו חשובין אבות והשאר הן תולדות וכל העושה אב ותולדתו אינו חייב אלא אחת. והעושה ב' אבות או ב' תולדות דלאו אב אחד [חייב] שתים. ומיפרשא בגמ' דהזורק דר' אלעזר מחייב בגמ' דכריתות אתולדה במקום אב דידיה תרתי ולית הלכתא כוותיה. ואסיק' מדוקיא דמתני' דמאן דעביד כל מלאכות שבעולם ואפילו אלף מלאכות אינו חייב יותר מארבעים חסר אחת חטאות שהכל נכללים בכלל אבות ובתולדותיהן הללו: **ירושלמי** כל דבר שהוא משביח הפרי חייב משום (זורר) [זורע]. המבריך. המרכיב. והמקרסם. המזרד. המפסל. המזהם. המפרק. המעשן. המתלע. הקוסם. הסך. המשקה. המנקב. והעושה בתים. חייב משום זורע: אמרינן משמיה דרב הזומר חייב משום נוטע והנוטע והמבריך והמרכיב חייב משום זורע. שמעינן מינה מדמוקים המבריך והמרכיב משום נוטע ואף משום זורע דיש תולדה לתולדה. וכולן נכללין בכלל אב אחד. הנוטע ולד הוא של זורע. כי הנוטע נועץ יחור של אילן בארץ ומתגדל כגון המפיל הזרע לארץ וצומח והזומר המקום שזומר באילן מתגדל המקום ההוא ומוסיף פירות ונמצא כנוטע לפיכך אמרינן בזומר חייב (שתים) משום נוטע ואם הוא זומר וצריך לעצים ונמצא כשזומר חייב משום נוטע כמו שאמרנו ובנטילתו העצים נמצא כקוצר. לפיכך בזומר וצריך לעצים חייב שתים. משום נוטע ומשום קוצר וכן מאן דקטיל אספסתא ומאן דקניב סילקא כולן דרך אחת הן וחייב שתים. בזמן שיש שיעור קצירה ושיעור זריעה. פי'

מסורת הש"ס

א) [לעיל דף סט. וש"נ כריתות ג:], ב) [גיטין סה: ב"ב יט.], ג) גי' רש"ל, ד) [צ"ל אבא עי' רש"א בסוגיא דלעיל לד. ד"ה גמרא סימן וכו'], ה) [מו"ק ג:], ו) לקמן פא: ע"ש, ז) ביצה ח. חגיגה י., ח) [לעיל יב. לא: לקמן קה: קו. קכא: עי' תוס' לקמן לג. ד"ה את המת וחגיגה י.], ט) נ"א והגודד, י) [גי' הרמב"ם והרא"ש והר"מ רבה וכן מוכרח עמ"ש לעיל עג: על הגליון], כ) [צ"ל המנפס פי' גאון המנפץ האוכל מן עפרוריתו חייב משום דש וכן המנפס מולל שבולים עכ"ל הערוך ערך פן], ל) [צ"ל חסר אחת ניהו], מ) [ועי' תוס' לקמן לו: ד"ה ולר"א דמחייב ובב"ק ב. ד"ה ולר"א], נ) [דף עה.], ס) צ"ל תני.

הגהות הב"ח

(א) גמ' דקניב סילקא וכו' וא' משום נוטע והחורש: (ב) שם בשדה חייב משום חורש: (ג) רש"י ד"ה שאם עשאן וכו' שבת ממנו כמה חטאות חייב עליו:

גליון הש"ס

תוס' ד"ה וצריך וכו'. מידי דהוי אקורע ע"מ לתפור. מבואר דס"ל דאף היכא דאינו מקלקל דצריך לאיזה דבר מ"מ פטור. ואפילו לר"י דס"ל שאינו ע"מ לתפור לא מקרי מלאכה חשובה. וכ"נ מדברי הכ"מ פ"י הלכה י מהלכות שבת. וק"ל מסוגיא דלקמן דף קד ע"ב. גם במ"ש תוספות דאפי' לר"י דמשמע פשיטא דניחא ק"ל הא פשיטא דניחא ליה בעצים להשתמש בהם אלא דעתה אינו עושה כן בשבילו מ"מ מיקרי צריכא לגופה כההיא דלקמן דף קג בחולש עולשין בארעא דלאו דיליה: תוס' ד"ה מפרק וכו' לגבי דבר הגדל ממש. עי' ברא"ס בפרשת וישלח בפסוק ויהי לי שור וחמור:

רב נסים גאון

ואפילו לר' יהודה דאמר מלאכה שאינה צריכה לגופה חייב עליה הני מילי מתקן והאי מקלקל הוא. כבר פירשנו בפרק א' עיקר דבריו של ר' יהודה אבל מקלקל הוא והוא ששנינו במשנה בפרק ר' אליעזר אומר האורג (לקמן דף קה) וכל המקלקלין פטורין:

ליקוטי רש"י

מנינא למה לי. ליתני אבות מלאכות הזורע והחורש כו' למה לי למיתנא ארבעים חסר אחת ליתנינהו ואנן ידעינן דארבעים חסר אחת איכא [לעיל סט.]. ליתני אבות מלאכות הזורע והחורש כו' למה לי לאשמעינן מניינא הא מני להו ואזיל [שם ו:]. **שאם עשאן כולם וכו'.** וסימנא בעלמא אשמעינן לידע כמה חטאות חייב על חילול שבת אחת [שם סט.]. ובא להודיענו סכום החטאות שאדם חייב באיסורי שבת בהעלם אחד ואשמעינן ארבעים חסר אחת הן ותו לא שאפילו עשה תולדותיהן עמהן אינו מביא על התולדה היכא דעשאה עם אביה דהוה ליה כעושה וחוזר ועושה דכולה חדא עבירה היא [שם ו:]. **מבריך.** כופף את הזמורות בארץ שקורין פרופינ"א [ר"ה ט:]. שכופף [הזמורה או היחור] בארץ [סוטה מג:]. כמו ויברך הגמלים (בראשית כד) כופף זמורת גפן מחוברת ומבריכה בקרקע בלידיה לכאן ולכאן וקורין בלע"ז פרובניי"ר [ב"ב יט:]. כופף אמצעית הגפן בקרקע ומכסהו בקרקע באמצעיתו וכשנשרש באמצעיתו חותכין עיקר הראשון ועשו שתי גפנים [רשב"ם שם פג.]. **מרכיב.** אילן בחבירו שקורין אוניסטי"ר [ר"ה שם]. שנוקב האילן ונוטל מן הרך שבענפי האילן ותוחב לתוכו ועושה ענף בתוך הנקב ונושא ממין אותו אילן שנוטל ממנו [סוטה שם]. **העושה מלאכות הרבה מעין מלאכה אחת.** שתי תולדות של אב אחד אינו חייב אלא חטאת אחת דהרי הוא כעושה וחוזר ועושה בהעלם אחד ואין חילוק חטאות בהעלם אחד אלא בגופי עבירה שאינן דומין או בחילוק שבתות לענין שגגת שבת [לעיל סח.]. **אינו חייב אלא אחת** דכיון דאב אחד לכולן [כריתות טז:]. **וצריך לעצים חייב.** משום קוצר שהרי צריך לעצים וחייב משום נוטע דמשום הזימור גדלי טפי [מו"ק ב:]. **אספסתא.** מין זרע הוא לעשב בהמות ולסוף ל' יום הוא נגמר ועוקרין אותו וזורעין אחר במקומו ובתוך שלשים יום גוזזין אותו שלש פעמים [ב"ב כח:]. שחת של תבואה [שם כ:]. **היתה לו גומא וטממה בבית וכו'.** בבית שייך בנין וזה שמשוה גומות בנין הרצפה הוא ובשדה מתקן המחרישה [לקמן פא:]. **חופר גומא.** בונה בנין הוא ואם אינו צריך לה אלא ליטול את העפר אף על פי שהבנין בנוי אינו חייב משום בונה [חגיגה י.]. **שאינה צריכה לגופה.** שברצונו לא עשאה ואינו צריך לעיקר (מהלמה) [תכליתה] ופלוגתייהו בהמצניע (לקמן לג:) גבי מוציא המת במטה חייב ואף על גב דהוצאת המת לא ניחא ליה ביה ור' שמעון פוטר [לעיל יב.]. כגון [מלאכה זאת] שאינו צריך לבנין זה. **חייב עליה.** מודה בהך גומא דאלו התם הקובר את המת מתקן הוא והאי חופר גומא מקלקל הוא את אגרו [חגיגה שם]. **האי מקלקל הוא.** דכיון דאינו צריך אלא לעפרה ולא לגומא אינו בונה ולא חורש אלא מקלקל וכל המקלקלים פטורים [ביצה ח.]. [המשך בדף עד.]

Gemara The Gemara analyzes the introductory statement of the Mishnah:

מִנְיָנָא לָמָּה לִי – **Why do I need** the Tanna to specify the **number** of *melachos*?[1]

The Gemara answers:

אָמַר רַבִּי יוֹחָנָן – **R' Yochanan said:** שֶׁאִם עֲשָׂאָן כּוּלָּם בְּהֶעְלֵם אֶחָד – It is to teach **that if someone performed all** thirty-nine **of them in one lapse of awareness,** i.e. without realizing in between that he had transgressed the prohibition, חַיָּיב עַל כָּל אַחַת וְאַחַת – **he is obligated** to bring a separate *chatas* **for each and every one** he performed, for a total of thirty-nine offerings.[2]

The Gemara examines the first two *melachos* in the list:

הַזּוֹרֵעַ וְהַחוֹרֵשׁ – SOWING, PLOWING.

The Gemara asks:

מִכְּדִי – **Now,** let us see: מִכְרַב כָּרְבֵי בְּרֵישָׁא – **One generally plows first** to soften the ground; only then does he sow. לִיתְנֵי חוֹרֵשׁ וַהֲדַר לִיתְנֵי זוֹרֵעַ – Hence, **let [the Tanna] first teach** the *melachah* of **plowing and then teach** the *melachah* of **sowing.** – ? –

The Gemara answers:

תַּנָּא בְּאֶרֶץ יִשְׂרָאֵל קָאֵי – **The Tanna was located in Eretz Yisrael,**[3] דְּזָרְעֵי בְּרֵישָׁא – **where they sow first** וַהֲדַר כָּרְבֵי – **and then plow.**[4]

The Gemara elaborates on the *melachah* of sowing:

תָּנָא – **[A Tanna] taught** a Baraisa: הַזּוֹרֵעַ וְהַזּוֹמֵר וְהַנּוֹטֵעַ וְהַמַּבְרִיךְ וְהַמַּרְכִּיב – SOWING seeds, PRUNING trees or vines, PLANTING saplings, PROPAGATING vines,[5] AND GRAFTING a branch כּוּלָּן מְלָאכָה אַחַת הֵן – ARE ALL in the category of ONE primary LABOR.[6]

The Gemara asks:

מַאי קָא מַשְׁמַע לָן – **What is [the Tanna] teaching us?**

The Gemara answers:

[הָא קָא מַשְׁמַע לָן] – **He teaches us this:** הָעוֹשֶׂה מְלָאכוֹת הַרְבֵּה מֵעֵין מְלָאכָה אַחַת – **One who performs many labors similar to one** particular primary **labor** אֵינוֹ חַיָּיב אֶלָּא אַחַת – **is obligated** to bring **only one** *chatas*.[7]

The Gemara elaborates further:

אָמַר רַבִּי אַחָא אָמַר רַבִּי חִיָּיא בַּר אַשִׁי אָמַר רַבִּי אַמִי – **R' Acha said in the name of R' Chiya bar Ashi, who** in turn **said** it **in the name of R' Ami:** זוֹמֵר חַיָּיב מִשּׁוּם נוֹטֵעַ – One who **prunes** a tree or vine **is liable on account of** the *melachah* of **"planting,"**[8] וְהַנּוֹטֵעַ וְהַמַּבְרִיךְ וְהַמַּרְכִּיב – **and one who plants** a sapling, **propagates** a vine **or grafts** a branch חַיָּיב מִשּׁוּם זוֹרֵעַ – **is liable on account of** the *melachah* of **"sowing."**[9]

The Gemara asks:

מִשּׁוּם זוֹרֵעַ אִין – Do you mean to say that one who propagates a vine and grafts a branch is **indeed** liable **on account of "sowing,"** מִשּׁוּם נוֹטֵעַ לֹא – but **not on account of "planting"?**[10] Since these acts are performed on trees, they should be included in the category of planting. – ? –

The Gemara answers:

אֵימָא אַף מִשּׁוּם זוֹרֵעַ – **Say,** rather, that one who performs these labors is liable **also on account of "sowing."**[11]

The Gemara further discusses the act of pruning:

אָמַר רַב כַּהֲנָא – **Rav Kahana said:** זוֹמֵר וְצָרִיךְ לָעֵצִים – If **one**

NOTES

1. The Mishnah should have simply listed the *melachos* and we could count them ourselves to see if there are thirty-nine (*Rashi*; see *Rashash*). Why, then, did the Mishnah preface its list by stating that there are thirty-nine *melachos*? [The Gemara has already cited this exchange several times in our chapter, most recently above, 73a, preceding the Mishnah.]

2. By stating the number of *melachos* that exist, the Mishnah alludes to the number of *chatas* offerings a person would have to bring if he forgot every one of the Sabbath laws (see *Rashi* with *Hagahos HaBach*). Thus, even if one performs all thirty-nine *avos* together with their *tolados* (derivative labors), he is still liable to only thirty-nine *chatas* offerings in all, because transgressions of the *tolados* are viewed as equivalent to repeated transgressions of the *avos* (*Rashi* above, 6b; see also above, 69a and *Chidushei R' Akiva Eiger* at length).

3. The Mishnah discusses laws related to Eretz Yisrael since that is where it was redacted (see *Nitzotzei Or*; see also *Gittin* 65b, cited here by *Mesoras HaShas*).

4. The ground is so hard in Eretz Yisrael that the seeds will not be covered by earth when they are sown in a plowed field. Therefore, the land must be plowed a second time (after sowing) to cover the seeds. The Mishnah teaches that this second plowing is also included in the *melachah* of plowing (*Rashi,* as explained by *Minchas Chinuch* [§32 חורש]; *Meiri* and *Chidushei HaRan*).

[*Minchas Chinuch* (ibid.) proves from *Rashi* to *Pesachim* (47b ד״ה ושביעית) that the second plowing renders an individual liable for sowing as well, since it promotes the growth of the seeds. See also *Yad David* and *Mitzpeh Eisan* for further discussion of this issue.]

5. Literally: bending over. Vines are sometimes propagated by bending them over and burying a portion of their length in the ground; when the buried portion takes root, it is cut from the original vine and grows alone (see *Rashbam* to *Bava Basra* 83a ד״ה המבריך).

6. All of these activities, including pruning, are performed to promote growth. They are therefore included in the *melachah* of sowing (*Rashi*).

Rashi notes that of the five labors mentioned in the Baraisa only pruning is considered a *toladah*. Planting is synonymous with sowing, except that the term "planting" applies to saplings while "sowing" applies to seeds. Grafting and propagating resemble planting a new tree, and so are also considered *avos*. *Rambam* (*Hil. Shabbos* 7:3), however, regards pruning as an *av* as well. See *Yad David* and *Eglei Tal* (זורע 1:4) for differing views of this apparent dispute. According to *Rabbeinu Chananel* and *Meiri,* pruning, planting, propagating and grafting are all *tolados* of sowing.

[Thus, according to *Rashi,* when our Mishnah lists sowing as an *av melachah,* it gives just one example of a group of activities that are all *avos.*]

7. The Mishnah taught above (68a) that if one performs many labors all of the same category he is liable to only one *chatas*. Our Baraisa applies this rule to the *melachah* category of sowing (*Rashi*; see also *Ritva MHK* ed.).

8. That is, pruning is a *toladah* of planting, since it is done to promote the growth of the tree (*Rashi*). [See below, note 12.]

9. That is, these acts are analogues of sowing; however, sowing is the *av* for seeds, while these three actions are *avos* for trees (*Rashi*).

10. The Gemara asks why R' Acha includes propagating and grafting in the category of sowing (*Rashi*). That would imply that if someone performed either of these two acts and also planted a sapling he would be liable to two offerings. But propagating and grafting are more closely related to planting than to sowing, since they are performed on trees (see *Rosh Yosef* and *Meromei Sadeh*). Why, then, does R' Acha say that these acts are considered sowing?

11. R' Acha in his second statement teaches that if someone plants, propagates or grafts in the same lapse of awareness in which he sows, he is liable to only one *chatas* (*Rashi*).

[According to R' Acha's first statement, pruning is considered in the same category as planting. His second ruling adds that planting itself, along with grafting and propagating, fall into the sowing as well as planting categories.] *Ritva* (*MHK* ed.; see also *Chidushei HaRan*) understands that, according to *Rashi's* explanation, one who prunes and sows is liable to two offerings – one for performing a *toladah* of planting (viz. pruning) and one for performing the *av* of sowing [as inferred from R' Acha's first statement]. However, if a person *plants,* prunes and sows, he is liable to only one *chatas,* as the Baraisa stated above, because planting and sowing are considered the same *av,* and so the pruning, a *toladah* of planting, would not obligate a separate offering. *Ritva* finds this explanation difficult, and prefers an alternative one given by *Tosafos*.

גמ' מנינא למה לי א) א"ר יוחנן א שאם עשאן כולם בהעלם אחד חייב על כל אחת ואחת: הזורע והחורש: מכדי מכרב כרבי ברישא ליתני חורש והדר ליתני זורע ב) תנא בארץ ישראל קאי דזרעי ברישא והדר כרבי תנא ב הזורע והזומר והנוטע והמבריך והמרכיב כולן מלאכה אחת הן מאי קמ"ל ג) [הא קמ"ל] העושה מלאכות הרבה מעין מלאכה אחת אינו חייב אלא אחת א"ר ד) אחא א"ר חייא בר אשי א"ר אמי ג זומר חייב משום נוטע והנוטע והמבריך והמרכיב חייב משום זורע משום זורע אין משום נוטע לא אימא אף משום זורע אמר ה) רב כהנא ד זומר וצריך לעצים חייב שתים אחת משום קוצר ואחת משום נוטע א"ר יוסף האי מאן דקטל אספסתא חייב שתים אחת משום קוצר ואחת משום נוטע אמר אביי האי מאן דקניב סילקא חייב שתים אחת משום קוצר ואחת משום (א) זורע: והחורש: תנא ה החורש והחופר והחורץ כולן מלאכה אחת הן אמר רב ששת ו היתה לו גבשושית ונטלה בבית חייב משום בונה בשדה חייב משום חורש ו) אמר רבא היתה לו גומא וטממה בבית חייב משום בונה בשדה (ב) משום חורש ז) אמר רבי אבא ז החופר גומא בשבת ואינו צריך אלא לעפרה פטור עליה ואפילו לרבי יהודה דאמר ח) מלאכה שאינה צריכה לגופה חייב עליה ה"מ מתקן האי מקלקל הוא: והקוצר: תנא ח הקוצר הבוצר ט) והגודר והמסיק והאורה כולן מלאכה אחת אמר רב פפא האי מאן דשדא פיסא לדיקלא ואתר תמרי חייב שתים אחת משום תולש ואחת משום מפרק רב אשי אמר אין דרך תלישה בכך ואין דרך פריקה בכך: והמעמר: אמר י) רבא האי מאן דכניף מילחא ממלחתא חייב משום מעמר אביי אמר ט אין עימור אלא בגידולי קרקע: והדש: תנא הדש והמנפץ כ) והמנפט כולן מלאכה אחת הן: הזורה הבורר והטוחן והמרקד: י היינו זורה היינו בורר היינו מרקד אביי ורבא דאמרי תרוייהו כל מילתא דהויא במשכן
אע"ג

מכדי מכרב כרבי ברישא והדר כו'. לא שייך למידק הכי בהא דקתני המכבה ברישא והדר המבעיר דהכא כל סידורא דפת נקט כסדר לבד מחרישה: **משום** זורע. אין להוכיח מכאן דצריך להתרות אתולדה משום אב דהא לא קאמר שצריך להתרותו משום זורע אלא דאם התרה בו משום זורע דחייב אבל בריש פרק תולין (לקמן קלח.) משמע קצת דצריך להתרות אתולדה משום אב דקאמר משמר משום מאי מתרינן ביה (שיהא חייב) רבה אמר משום בורר רבי זירא אמר משום מרקד וגם זה יש לדחות דהכי פירושו משום מאי מתרינן ביה שיהא חייב רבה אמר משום בורר אבל אם התרו בו משום מרקד פטור כיון דמתרהו משום דבר שאינו דומה לו הוא סבר שהוא מלעיג בו ופטור אבל אם התרה בו סתם אל תשמר חייב ונראה שגם ר"ח רוצה לפרש כן ועוד ראיה דבריש בבא קמא (דף ב.) קאמר ולר' אליעזר דמחייב אתולדה במקום אב אמאי קרי ליה אב ואמאי קרי ליה תולדה ולא משני דלהכי קרי ליה אב דצריך להתרות אתולדה [משום] אב מ): **זומר** וצריך לעצים חייב שתים. והא דאמר בפ' זה בורר (סנהדרין דף כו.) תו חזיוה להוא גברא דהוה קא כסח אמר להן כהן חמיר אמרו ליה יכול לומר לעקל בית הבד אני צריך אף על גב דהכא אמר חייב משום נוטע התם מיירי בכה"ג שאין האילן מיתקן בכך אלא מתקלקל: **וצריך** לעצים. נראה דאפילו לר' יהודה דמחייב מלאכה שאינה צריכה לגופה בעינן צריך לעצים דלא מיקרי בעצים קוצר אלא בענין זה ס מידי דהוה אקורע על מנת לתפור ומוחק על מנת לכתוב וכדאמר רבי יוחנן לקמן בפ' חבית (דף קמה.) אחד כבשים ואחד שלקות ששחטן לגופן מותר למימיהן חייב חטאת ואמאי שרי לגופן ליהוי כמלאכה שאינה צריכה לגופה אלא טעמא לפי שאין דרך דישה בכך: **ואחת** משום מפרק. אין נראה לר"י כמו שמפרש רש"י שמפרק האילן ממשאו מן הפירות שעליו אלא כמו שפירש רבינו שמואל שיש על התמרים קליפה העליונה וכשהוא מכה בתמרים מפרק את הקליפה מן התמרים והוי כמו דש שמפרק את התבואה מן השבולת: **מפרק.** פירש"י דהוה תולדה דדש וקשה לר"ת דבשילהי המצניע (לקמן צה.) אמר דחולב חייב משום מפרק ואי הוה תולדה דדש הא אמר לקמן י) גבי הפולע חלזון דלרבנן אין דישה אלא בגידולי קרקע ואין לומר דדוקא חלזון שהוא דג פטרי רבנן דלא הוי גידולי קרקע אבל בחולב מחייבי דבהמה חשיבא גידולי קרקע כדמוכח בריש בכל מערבין (עירובין דף כח:) דהא [ע"כ טעמא דרבנן משום] דילפינן להו מסממנין שבמשכן דאין דישה אלא בגידולי קרקע ס לגבי דבר הגדל ממש מן הקרקע לא חשיבא בהמה גידולי קרקע כדאמרינן בהשוכר את הפועלים (ב"מ פט.) מה דיש מיוחד שהוא גידולי קרקע ופועל אוכל בו אף כל כו' יצא החולב והמגבן כו' ודוחק לומר דברייתא דהמצניע אתיא כר"י דפליג לקמן אדרבנן ונראה לר"ת דמפרק חייב משום ממחק דכשחולב ממחק את הדד ומחליקו ואין נראה לר"י דבפרק חבית (לקמן קמד:) אמרינן חולב אדם לתוך הקדרה אבל לא לתוך הקערה ולר"ת מה לי לתוך הקדרה מה לי לתוך הקערה ולפירוש הקונטרס א"ש דמעיקרא כשהיה בדדין חשיב אוכל וכשחולב לתוך הקדרה (דהשתא) נמי הוי אוכל ולא דמי לדש שנשתנה ונראה דלפירוש הקונטרס הלכה כרבי יהודה דהאמר בפרק אע"פ (כתובות ס.) ס) אמר רבי מריעום גונח יונק חלב בשבת מ"ט מפרק כלאחר יד הוא ובמקום צער לא גזרו רבנן ופסיק התם רב יוסף הלכתא כרבי מריעום ואין נראה לומר דאף לרבנן אסור מדרבנן דמיחזי כמפרק ואף על גב דלא אסירא אלא מדרבנן לא שרי אלא משום דאיכא תרתי כלאחר יד ובמקום צער: [ועי' תוס' כתובות ס. ד"ה מפרק ותוס' יבמות קיד. ד"ה וקסבר]

גמ' מנינא למה לי. ליתני אבות מלאכות הזורע והחורש כו' ואנא חזינא אי ארבעין ל) ניהו: **שאם עשאן** כו'. ובא להודיעך שאם נתעלמו כל הלכות שבת ממנו (ג) חייב כמה חטאות עליו: **מכרב כרבי.** חורשין: **בא"י.** קשה היא ואין יכול לכסות בלא חרישה ואשמעינן דהא נמי חרישה היא: **כולן מלאכה אחת הן.** דזומר נמי לצמוחי אילנא הוא ונפקא מינה דאי עבד ליה כולן בהדי זורע לא מיחייב אלא חדא דהעושה מלאכות הרבה כו' זורע אב מלאכה ונוטע נמי אב מלאכה הוא דהיינו זורע אלא שזה בזרעים וזה באילנות וכן מבריך ומרכיב אבל זומר תולדה: **זומר** חייב. משום תולדת נוטע דלצמוחי עביד: **ונוטע.** גופיה וכן מבריך ומרכיב: **חייב משום זורע.** כלומר אינהו נמי זורע הן זה אב בזרעים וזה אב באילנות: **משום נוטע לא.** אמבריך ואמרכיב קאי: **אימא אף משום זורע.** דהך זריעה באילנות ואי עביד ליה בהדי זורע מיחייב חדא ותו לא: **זומר.** להצמיח הגפן: **וצריך לעצים.** להסקה משום דצריך להם הויא תולדה דקוצר דצריך נמי לקצור: **דקטל אספסתא.** שחת וקוצרין אותו ג' פעמים בחדש וחוזר וצומח: **דקניב סילקא.** חותך תרדין מן המחובר וחוזרין וגדלין: **החורץ.** עושה חריצין בקרקע: **מלאכה אחת הן.** אינו חייב אלא אחת דכולהו לרפויי ארעא עבידי: **גבשושית.** תל קטן: **בבית.** שייך בנין שמתכוין להשוות קרקעיתו: **משום חורש.** דמרפי ארעא: **גומא וטממה.** בעפר היינו חורש שהעפר שמילאה בו הוי רפוי וטוב לזריעה והשוה לקרקע להיות מרע עם השדה: **אלא לעפרה.** לכסות צואה: **פטור עליה.** ואין כאן משום בנין בבית דקלקול הוא ולזריעה נמי לא חזיא אבל אם היה צריך לה חייב משום בונה: **לרבי יהודה.** בפרק המצניע (לקמן צג:) גבי מוציא את המת במטה: **מתקן.** כמו מוציא את המת לקוברו אינו צריך לגופה דהוצאה ולא למת אלא לפנות ביתו והוצאה הצריכה לגופה כגון שהוא צריך לחפץ זה במקום אחר: **מקלקל הוא.** את ביתו: **גודר.** בתמרים: **ומוסק.** בזיתים: **אורה.** בתאנים: **דשדא פיסא לדיקלא.** זרק פיסת רגבים לדקל: **ואתר תמרי.** השיר התמרים: **תולש.** תולדה דקוצר: **מפרק.** תולדה דדש שמפרק תבואה משבליה לשון פורק מן החמור דישקארגי"ר בלע"ז רבינו לוי וגם בתשובת רבינו משולם הגאון מצאתי כן ואף זה מפרק התמרים מן המכבדות: **אין דרך תלישה** ופריקה בכך. על ידי זריקה אלא או ביד או בכלי ותולש כלאחר יד הוא ופטור: **דכניף מלחא ממלחתא.** שצבר מלח ממשרפות מים דמתרגמינן חרילי ימא (יהושע יא) שממשיך לתוכו מים מן הים והחמה שורפתן והן נעשין מלח ואותו חריץ קרי מילחתא: **משום מעמר.** שאף הוא כמאסף בשבלין הוא: **המנפץ.** פשתן בגבעולין: **והמנפט.** צמר גפן בקשת כדרך האומנין וצמר גפן גידולי קרקע הוא להכי קרי ניפוט דיליה תולדה דדש שמפרק גרעינין ממנו ולא קרי ליה תולדת מנפץ דצמר: ה"ג היינו זורה היינו בורר היינו מרקד. **היינו.** כמו הי ניהו כלומר דמפליג להו תנא דמתניתין לתלת והלא כולן מלאכה אחת הן דמפריש אוכל מן הפסולת:
אע"ג

עין משפט נר מצוה

כט א מיי' פ"ז מהלכות שבת הלכה ח ופ"ז מהלכות שגגות הלכה ג:
ל ב מיי' פ"ז מהל' שבת הלכה ג והלכה ט:
לא ג מיי' פ"ח מהלכות שבת הלכה ב:
לב ד שם הלכה ד:
לג ה מיי' פ"ז מהלכות שבת הלכה ב:
לד ו מיי' פ"ח מהלכות שבת הלכה א:
לה ז מיי' פ"א מהלכות שבת הלכה יז:
לו ח מיי' פ"ז מהלכות שבת הלכה ד סמג לאוין סה:
לז ט מיי' פ"ח שם הל' ה סמג שם טוש"ע או"ח סימן ש"מ סעיף ט:
לח י מיי' פ"ח מהלכות שבת הלי"א סמג שם:

רבינו חננאל

למה לי למיתנא מנינא [מ'] חסר אחת אטו עד האידנא מי לא ידעינן מנייני ומשני ר' יוחנן שאם עשאן כולם בהעלם אחד חייב על כל אחת ואחת. (ת"ש) [תנא] הזורע והזומר והנוטע והמבריך והמרכיב כולן מלאכה אחת הן (קס"ד) [קמ"ל] כי העושה מלאכות הרבה מעין מלאכה אחת אינו חייב אלא חטאת אחת שמעי' מינה שאלו השניים במשנתנו חשובין אבות והשאר הן תולדות וכל העושה אב ותולדתו אינו חייב אלא אחת. והעושה ב' אבות או ב' תולדות דלאו אב אחד [חייב] שתים. ומיפרשא בגמ' דהזורק דר' אלעזר מחייב בגמ' דכריתות אתולדה במקום אב דידיה תרתי ולית הלכתא כוותיה. ואסיק' מדוקיא דמתני' דמאן דעביד כל מלאכות שבעולם ואפילו אלף מלאכות אינו חייב יותר מארבעים חסר אחת חטאות שהכל נכללים בכלל אבות ובתולדותיהן הללו: **ירושלמי** כל דבר שהוא משביח הפרי חייב משום (זורר) [זורע]. המבריך. המרכיב. והמקרסם. המזרד. המפסל. המזהם. המפרק. המעשן. המתלע. הקוסם. הסך. המשקה. המנקב. והעושה בתים. חייב משום זורע: אמרינן משמיה דרב הזומר חייב משום נוטע והנוטע והמבריך והמרכיב חייב משום זורע. שמעינן מינה מדמוקים המבריך והמרכיב משום נוטע ואף משום זורע דיש תולדה לתולדה. וכולן נכללין בכלל אב אחד. הנוטע וולד הוא של זורע. כי הנוטע נועץ יחור של אילן בארץ ומתגדל כגון המפיל הזרע לארץ וצומח והזומר המקום שזומר באילן מתגדל המקום ההוא ומוסיף פירות ונמצא כנוטע לפיכך אמרינן בזומר חייב (שתים) משום נוטע ואם הוא זומר וצריך לעצים ונמצא כשזומר חייב משום נוטע כמו שאמרנו ובנטילתו העצים נמצא כקוצר. לפיכך בזומר וצריך לעצים חייב שתים. משום נוטע ומשום קוצר וכן מאן דקטיל אספסתא ומאן דקניב סילקא כולן דרך אחת הן וחייב שתים. בזמן שיש שיעור קצירה ושיעור זריעה. פי'

מסורת הש"ס

א) [לעיל דף סט. וש"נ] כריתות ג., ב) [גיטין סה: ב"ב יט.], ג) גי' רש"ל, ד) [צ"ל אבא עי' רש"א בסוגיא לעיל לד. ד"ה גמרא סימן וכו'], ה) [מו"ק ב:], ו) לקמן פא: ע"ש, ז) ביצה ח. חגיגה י., ח) [לעיל יב. לא: לקמן קה: קו. קכח: עי' תוס' לקמן לד. ד"ה את המת וחגיגה י.], ט) צ"ל והגודד, י) [גי' הרמב"ם והרא"ש והר"מ רבה וכן מוכרח עמ"ש לעיל עב: על הגליון], כ) [צ"ל המנפס פי' גאון המנפס האוכל מן עפרוריתו חייב משום דש וכן המנפס מולל שבולים עכ"ל הערוך ערך פס], ל) [צ"ל חסר אחת ניתהו], מ) [ועי' תוס' לקמן עו: ד"ה ולר"א דמחייב ובב"ק ב. ד"ה ולר"א], נ) [דף עה.], ס) צ"ל תני.

הגהות הב"ח

(א) גמ' דקניב סילקא וכו' ואחת משום נוטע והחורש: (ב) שם בשדה חייב משום חורש: (ג) רש"י ד"ה שאם עשאן וכו' שבת ממנו כמה חטאות חייב עליו:

גליון הש"ס

תוס' ד"ה וצריך וכו'. מידי דהוי אקורע ע"מ לתפור. מבואר דס"ל דאף היכא דאינו מקלקל דצריך לאחה דבר מ"מ פטור. ואפילו לר"י דס"ל שאינו ע"מ לתפור לא מקרי מלאכה חשובה. וכ"נ מדברי הכ"מ פ"י הלכה י מהלכות שבת. וק"ל מסוגיא דלקמן דף קד ע"ב. גם במ"ש תוספות דאפי' לר"י דמשמע פשיטא דניחא ק"ל הא פשיטא דניחא ליה בעצים להשתמש בהם אלא דעתה אינו עושה כן בשבילו מ"מ מיקרי צריכה לגופה כההיא דלקמן דף קג כתולש עולשין בארעא דלאו דיליה: תוס' ד"ה מפרק וכו' לגבי דבר הגדל ממש. עי' בר"ש פ"ב בפרשת ויסלח בפסוק ויהי לי שור וחמור:

רב נסים גאון

ואפילו לר' יהודה דאמר מלאכה שאינה צריכה לגופה חייב עליה הני מילי מתקן והאי מקלקל הוא. כבר פירשנו בפרק א' עיקר דבריו של ר' יהודה אבל מקלקל הוא והוא ששנינו במשנה בפרק ר' אליעזר אומר האורג (לקמן דף קה) וכל המקלקלין פטורין:

ליקוטי רש"י

מנינא למה לי. ליתני אבות מלאכות הזורע והחורש כו' למה לי למיתנא ארבעים חסר אחת ליתנינהו ואנן ידעינן דארבעים חסר אחת איכא [לעיל סט.]. ליתני אבות מלאכות הזורע והחורש כו' למה לי לאשמעינן מניינא הא מני להו ואזיל [שם ו:]. **שאם עשאן כולם וכו'.** וסימנא בעלמא אשמעינן לידע כמה חטאות חייב על חילול שבת אחת [שם סט.]. וכא להודיענו סכום החטאות שאדם חייב באיסורי שבת בהעלם אחד ואשמעינן ארבעים חסר אחת הן ותו לא שאפילו עשה תולדותיהן עמהן אינו מביא על התולדה היכא דעשאה עם אביה דהוה ליה כעושה וחוזר ועושה דכולה חדא עבירה היא [שם ו:]. **מבריך.** כופף את הזמורות בארץ שקורין פרופינ"א [ר"ה ט:]. שכופף [הזמורה או היחור] בארץ [סוטה מג:]. כמו ויברך הגמלים (בראשית כד) כופף זמורת גפן מחוברת ומבריכה בקרקע בלידיה לכאן ולכאן וקורין בלע"ז פרובני"ר [ב"ב יט:]. כופף אמצעית הגפן בקרקע ומכסהו בקרקע באמצעיתו וכשנשרש באמצעיתו חותכין עיקר הראשון ונעשו שתי גפנים [רשב"ם שם פג.]. **מרכיב.** אילן בחבירו שקורין אוניסטי"ר [ר"ה שם]. שנוקב האילן ונוטל מן הרך שבענפי האילן ותוחב לתוכו ועושה ענף בתוך הנקב ונושא ממין אותו אילן שנוטל ממנו [סוטה שם]. **העושה מלאכות הרבה מעין מלאכה אחת.** שתי תולדות של אב אחד אינו חייב אלא חטאת אחת דהרי הוא כעושה וחוזר ועושה בהעלם אחד ואין חילוק חטאות בהעלם אחד אלא בגופי עבירה שאינן דומין או בחילוק שבתות לענין שגגת שבת [לעיל סח.]. **אינו חייב אלא אחת** דכיון דאב אחד לכולן [כריתות טז:]. **וצריך לעצים חייב.** משום קוצר שהרי צריך לעצים וחייב משום נוטע דמשום הזימור גדלי טפי [מו"ק ב:]. **אספסתא.** מין זרע הוא לעשב בהמות ולסוף ל' יום הוא נגמר ועוקרין אותו וזורעין אחר במקומו ובתוך שלשים יום גוזזין אותו שלש פעמים [ב"ב כח:]. שחת של תבואה [שם כ:]. **היתה לו גומא וטממה בבית וכו'.** בבית שייך בנין וזה שמשוה גומות בנין הרצפה הוא ובשדה מתקן החרישה [לקמן פא:]. **חופר גומא.** בונה בנין הוא ואם אינו צריך לה אלא ליטול את העפר אף על פי שהבנין בנוי אינו חייב משום בונה [חגיגה י.]. **שאינה צריכה לגופה.** שצרכותו לא תעשה ואינו צריך לעיקר (תחלתה) [תכליתה] ופלוגתייהו בהמצניע (לקמן צג:) גבי מוציא המת במטה חייב ואף על גב דהוצאת המת לא ניחא ליה ביה ור' שמעון פוטר [לעיל יב.]. כגון [מלאכה זאת] שאינו צריך לבנין זה. **חייב עליה.** מודה בהך גומא דאלו התם הקובר את המת מתקן הוא והאי חופר גומא מקלקל הוא את חצרו [חגיגה שם]. **האי מקלקל הוא.** דכיון דאינו צריך אלא לעפרה ולא חורש ולא לגומא אינו בונה ולא חורש אלא מקלקל וכל המקלקלים פטורים [ביצה ח.]. [המשך בדף עד.]

prunes a vine[12] **and** also **needs the wood** for fuel, חַיָּיב שְׁתַּיִם – **he is obligated** to bring **two** *chatas* offerings:[13] אַחַת מִשּׁוּם קוֹצֵר – **one on account of "reaping"**[14] וְאַחַת מִשּׁוּם נוֹטֵעַ – **and one on account of "planting."**[15]

A similar ruling:

אָמַר רַב יוֹסֵף – **Rav Yosef said:** הַאי מַאן דְּקָטֵל אַסְפַּסְתָּא – **Someone who cut** ***aspasta***[16] חַיָּיב שְׁתַּיִם – **is obligated** to bring **two** *chatas* offerings: אַחַת מִשּׁוּם קוֹצֵר – **one on account of "reaping"**[17] וְאַחַת מִשּׁוּם נוֹטֵעַ – **and one on account of "planting."**[18]

Another similar ruling:

אָמַר אַבָּיֵי – **Abaye said:** הַאי מַאן דְּקָנֵיב סִילְקָא – **Someone who cuts beets**[19] חַיָּיב שְׁתַּיִם – **is obligated** to bring **two** *chatas* offerings: אַחַת מִשּׁוּם קוֹצֵר – **one on account of "reaping"** וְאַחַת מִשּׁוּם [נוֹטֵעַ] (זורע) – **and one on account of "planting."**[20]

The Mishnah taught the second *melachah*:

וְהַחוֹרֵשׁ – **PLOWING.**

A Baraisa elaborates:

תָּנָא – **[A Tanna] taught** a Baraisa: הַחוֹרֵשׁ וְהַחוֹפֵר וְהַחוֹרֵץ – **PLOWING** the earth, **DIGGING** a hole,[21] **AND MAKING A FURROW** כּוּלָּן מְלָאכָה אַחַת הֵן – **ARE ALL** in the category of **ONE** primary **LABOR.**[22]

The Gemara presents another example of the *melachah* of plowing:

אָמַר רַב שֵׁשֶׁת – **Rav Sheishess said:** הָיְתָה לוֹ גַּבְשׁוּשִׁית וּנְטָלָהּ – **If someone had a small mound and took it away,** it depends: בַּבַּיִת חַיָּיב מִשּׁוּם בּוֹנֶה – If the mound was **in the house, he is liable on account of "building"**;[23] בַּשָּׂדֶה חַיָּיב מִשּׁוּם חוֹרֵשׁ – and if it was **in the field, he is liable on account of "plowing."**[24]

A similar ruling:

אָמַר רָבָא – **Rava said:** הָיְתָה לוֹ גּוּמָּא וּטְמָמָהּ – If **one had a hole and filled it up** with dirt, it depends: בַּבַּיִת חַיָּיב מִשּׁוּם בּוֹנֶה – If the hole was **in the house, he is liable on account of "building"**;[25] בַּשָּׂדֶה מִשּׁוּם חוֹרֵשׁ – and if it was **in the field,** he is liable **on account of "plowing."**[26]

The Gemara states another ruling concerning plowing:

אָמַר רַבִּי אַבָּא – **R' Abba said:** הַחוֹפֵר גּוּמָּא בְּשַׁבָּת וְאֵינוֹ צָרִיךְ אֶלָּא לַעֲפָרָהּ – **One who digs a hole** in the floor of his house **on the Sabbath but requires only its earth**[27] פָּטוּר עָלֶיהָ – **is exempt** from liability **for [the act].**[28] וַאֲפִילּוּ לְרַבִּי יְהוּדָה – **And** this ruling is acceptable **even to R' Yehudah,** דְּאָמַר מְלָאכָה שֶׁאֵינָהּ צְרִיכָה לְגוּפָהּ חַיָּיב עָלֶיהָ – **who said that** one who performs **a** forbidden **labor not needed for its defined purpose is** nevertheless **liable for it,**[29] הָנֵי מִילֵּי מְתַקֵּן – for **that ruling** was stated only when **[the person] rectifies** something;[30]

NOTES

12. To promote the growth of the vine (*Rashi*).

Rashi to a parallel Gemara in *Moed Katan* (2b) indicates that the person need not have specific intention to promote the growth. Rather, since his act will cause the tree to grow, he is liable for planting (cf. *Tosafos*). See *Sfas Emes* and *Cheifetz Hashem* for further discussion of this issue.]

13. He accomplished two purposes with his act: promoting the growth of the vine and obtaining its branches for fuel (*Rashi*).

14. Since he needed the wood for fuel, removing the vines is similar to reaping and is a *toladah* of that *melachah* (*Rashi*).

15. Because the vines will grow better as a result of his act (*Rashi* to *Moed Katan* 2b).

16. A type of plant used for animal fodder, *aspasta* is cut three times a month, since it grows back after each cutting (*Rashi*; see citation of *Rashash*).

17. Because he will use the crop to feed his animals.

18. Because cutting stimulates the crop to grow anew.

19. I.e. while they are still attached to the ground. Beets also grow back after they have been cut (*Rashi*).

20. This emendation follows *Hagahos HaBach*. *Rif* and *Rosh* also apparently had the reading נוֹטֵעַ, *planting*.

21. Plowing is performed with a plow, while digging is done with a hoe (*Meiri*).

22. If someone performs all three acts, he is liable to only one *chatas,* since the purpose of each is to soften the earth (*Rashi*), thus preparing it for sowing.

Rashi writes above (46b ד"ה איסורא) that digging is a *toladah* of plowing. *Eglei Tal* (חורש 1:2) notes that *Rashi* is consistent with his opinion above (see notes 8 and 11) that pruning is considered a *toladah* even though the Baraisa stated that pruning and sowing are one *melachah.*

23. This is considered building because the person intends to level the floor of his house (*Rashi*).

24. This is considered plowing because he loosens the earth when he takes the mound away (*Rashi*; cf. *Chidushei HaRan* and *Meiri*). That is, the earth under the mound becomes looser when the mound is removed (*Eglei Tal* חורש 5:9).

25. For he intends to level the floor of his house.

26. Since the dirt used for filling in the hole is loose, it is fit for sowing. Thus, in leveling the field the person in fact prepared the formerly depressed area for sowing (*Rashi*), which is the essential function of the *melachah* of plowing.

27. E.g. to cover filth (*Rashi*).

28. He cannot be held liable for building because he ruined the floor. [This is thus unlike the case of removing a mound of dirt, where the person improves the floor by leveling it.] In addition, [he is not liable because of plowing since] one cannot plant in a house. Of course, if he dug the hole for some intended use of that hole, he would indeed be liable for performing the *melachah* of building (*Rashi*).

29. Throughout this tractate, R' Yehudah and R' Shimon dispute the level of intent and design necessary for labor to be prohibited on the Sabbath. One facet of this dispute concerns whether or not one is liable for performing a labor not needed for its defined purpose. R' Yehudah maintains that one is liable even if he did not perform the *melachah* for the creative purpose inherent in the labor itself, but rather, for example, to rectify an undesirable condition. However, according to R' Shimon, to be liable, a labor must directly contribute to the achievement of a creative or productive goal.

The Gemara now considers whether this person's act can be viewed as performance of the *melachah* of building despite the fact that he did not need the hole (see previous note). If so, even though the person did not perform the *melachah* for the creative purpose inherent in the labor itself (because he would have preferred not to have to do this act of "building" – *Tosafos* to *Chagigah* 10b in explanation of *Rashi*), he should be liable according to R' Yehudah.

30. The Mishnah below (93b) discusses a case of a person who carries a corpse out of his house for burial. There, he does not transport the corpse because it is needed in the public domain; he desires only to remove the corpse from his premises. [In fact, he would have preferred not having to take this action at all; he is merely resolving a problem – see *Rashi* there.] This is in contrast to one who transfers an item from a private to a public domain because it is needed in the public domain. He has then achieved the defined purpose of the *melachah* of transferring, namely, having the item in the place where it is needed (*Rashi*). Nevertheless, even in the first case, the transporter's action is at least constructive, since he has rectified the undesirable situation of having a corpse in his house. Hence, his act is considered a *melachah* of transferring – even though the labor was performed only in reaction to an undesirable condition – and he is liable according to R' Yehudah.

[It should be noted that *Tosafos* (94a ד"ה רבי שמעון פוטר) adopt a different definition of מְלָאכָה שֶׁאֵינָהּ צְרִיכָה לְגוּפָהּ, *a labor not needed for its defined purpose* (for an elaboration of the view of *Tosafos,* see General Introduction). In our discussion, however, we have used the approach of *Rashi.*]

גמ' מנינא למה לי [א] א"ר יוחנן [א] שאם עשאן כולם בהעלם אחד חייב על כל אחת ואחת: הזורע והחורש: מכדי מכרב כרבי ברישא ליתני חורש והדר ליתני זורע [ג] תנא בארץ ישראל קאי דזרעי ברישא והדר כרבי תנא [ב] הזורע והזומר והנוטע והמבריך והמרכיב כולן מלאכה אחת הן מאי קמ"ל [ג] [הא קמ"ל] העושה מלאכות הרבה מעין מלאכה אחת אינו חייב אלא אחת א"ר [ד] אחא א"ר חייא בר אשי א"ר אמי [ג] זומר חייב משום נוטע והנוטע והמבריך והמרכיב חייב משום זורע משום זורע אין משום נוטע לא אימא אף משום זורע אמר [ה] רב כהנא [ד] זומר וצריך לעצים חייב שתים אחת משום קוצר ואחת משום נוטע א"ר יוסף האי מאן דקטל אספסתא חייב שתים אחת משום קוצר ואחת משום נוטע אמר אביי האי מאן דקניב סילקא חייב שתים אחת משום קוצר ואחת משום (א) זורע: והחורש: תנא [ה] החורש והחופר והחורץ כולן מלאכה אחת הן אמר רב ששת [ו] היתה לו גבשושית ונטלה בבית חייב משום בונה בשדה חייב משום חורש [ו] אמר רבא היתה לו גומא וטממה בבית חייב משום בונה בשדה (ב) משום חורש [ז] אמר רבי אבא [ז] החופר גומא בשבת ואינו צריך אלא לעפרה פטור עליה ואפילו לרבי יהודה דאמר [ח] מלאכה שאינה צריכה לגופה חייב עליה ה"מ מתקן האי מקלקל הוא: והקוצר: תנא [ח] הקוצר הבוצר [ט] והגודר והמסיק והאורה כולן מלאכה אחת אמר רב פפא האי מאן דשדא פיסא לדיקלא ואתר תמרי חייב שתים אחת משום תולש ואחת משום מפרק רב אשי אמר אין דרך תלישה בכך ואין דרך פריקה בכך: והמעמר: אמר [י] רבא האי מאן דכניף מילחא ממלחתא חייב משום מעמר אביי אמר [ט] אין עימור אלא בגידולי קרקע: והדש: תנא הדש והמנפץ [כ] והמנפט כולן מלאכה אחת הן: הזורה הבורר והטוחן והמרקד: [י] היינו זורה היינו בורר היינו מרקד אביי ורבא דאמרי תרווייהו כל מילתא דהויא במשכן אע"ג

רש"י

גמ' מנינא למה לי. ליתני אבות מלאכות הזורע והחורש כו' ואנא חזינא אי ארבעין [ל] ניהו: שאם עשאן כו'. ובא להודיעך שאם נתעלמו כל הלכות שבת ממנו (ג) חייב כמה חטאות עליו: מכרב כרבי. חורשין: בא"י. קשה היא ואין יכול לכסות בלא חרישה ואשמעינן דהא נמי חרישה היא: כולן מלאכה אחת הן. דזומר נמי לצמוחי אילנא הוא ונפקא מינה דאי עבד ליה כולן בהדי זורע לא מיחייב אלא חדא דהעושה מלאכות הרבה כו' זורע אב מלאכה ונוטע נמי אב מלאכה הוא דהיינו זורע אלא שזה בזרעים וזה באילנות וכן מבריך ומרכיב אבל זומר תולדה: זומר חייב. משום תולדת נוטע דלצמוחי עביד: ונוטע. גופיה וכן מבריך ומרכיב: חייב משום זורע. כלומר אינהו נמי זורע הן זה אב בזרעים וזה אב באילנות: משום נוטע לא. אמבריך ואמרכיב קאי: אימא אף משום זורע. דהך זריעה באילנות ואי עביד ליה בהדי זורע מיחייב חדא ותו לא: זומר. להצמיח הגפן: וצריך לעצים. להסקה משום דצריך להם הויא תולדה דקוצר דצריך נמי לקצור: דקטל אספסתא. שחת וקוצרין אותו ג' פעמים בחדש וחוזר וצומח: דקניב סילקא. חותך תרדין מן המחובר וחוזרין וגדלין: החורץ. עושה חריצין בקרקע: מלאכה אחת הן. אינו חייב אלא אחת דכולהו לרפויי ארעא עבידי: גבשושית. תל קטן: בבית. שייך בנין שמתכוין להשוות קרקעיתו: משום חורש. דמרפי ארעא: גומא וטממה. בעפר היינו חורש שהעפר שמילאה בו הוי רפוי וטוב לזריעה והשוה לקרקע להיות מרע עם השדה: אלא לעפרה. לכסות צואה: פטור עליה. ואין כאן משום בנין בבית דקלקול הוא ולזריעה נמי לא חזיא אבל אם היה צריך לה חייב משום בונה: לרבי יהודה. בפרק המצניע (לקמן צג:) גבי מוציא את המת במטה: מתקן. כמו מוציא את המת לקוברו אינו צריך לגופה דהוצאה ולא למת אלא לפנות ביתו והוצאה הצריכה לגופה כגון שהוא צריך לחפץ זה במקום אחר: מקלקל הוא. את ביתו: גודר. בתמרים: ומוסק. בזיתים: אורה. בתאנים: דשדא פיסא לדיקלא. זרק פיסת רגבים לדקל: ואתר תמרי. השיר התמרים: תולש. תולדה דקוצר: מפרק. תולדה דדש שמפרק תבואה משבליה לשון פורק מן החמור דישקארגי"ר בלע"ז רבינו לוי וגם בתשובת רבינו משולם הגאון מצאתי כן ואף זה מפרק התמרים מן המכבדות: אין דרך תלישה ופריקה בכך. על ידי זריקה אלא או ביד או בכלי ותולש כלאחר יד הוא ופטור: דכניף מלחא ממלחתא. שצבר מלח ממשרפות מים דמתרגמינן חרילי ימא (יהושע יא) שממשיך לתוכו מים מן הים והחמה שורפתן והן נעשין מלח ואותו חריץ קרי מילחתא: משום מעמר. שאף הוא כמאסף בשבלין הוא: המנפץ. פשתן בגבעולין: והמנפט. צמר גפן בקשת כדרך האומנין וצמר גפן גידולי קרקע הוא להכי קרי ניפוט דיליה תולדה דדש שמפרק גרעינין ממנו ולא קרי ליה תולדת מנפץ דצמר: ה"ג היינו זורה היינו בורר היינו מרקד. היינו. כמו הי ניהו כלומר דמפליג להו תנא דמתניתין לתלת והלא כולן מלאכה אחת הן דמפריש אוכל מן הפסולת: אע"ג

תוספות

מכדי מכרב כרבי ברישא והדר כו'. לא שייך למידק הכי בהא דקתני המכבה ברישא והדר המבעיר דהכא כל סידורא דפת נקט כסדר לבד מחרישה: משום זורע. אין להוכיח מכאן דצריך להתרות אתולדה משום אב דהא לא קאמר שצריך להתרותו משום זורע אלא דאם התרה בו משום זורע דחייב אבל בריש פרק תולין (לקמן קלח.) משמע קצת דצריך להתרות אתולדה משום אב דקאמר משמר משום מאי מתרינן ביה (שיהא חייב) רבה אמר משום בורר רבי זירא אמר משום מרקד וגם זה יש לדחות דהכי פירושו משום מאי מתרינן ביה שיהא חייב רבה אמר משום בורר אבל אם התרו בו משום מרקד פטור כיון דמתרהו משום דבר שאינו דומה לו הוא סבר שהוא מלעיג בו ופטור אבל אם התרה בו סתם אל תשמר חייב ונראה שגם ר"ת רוצה לפרש כן ועוד ראיה דבריש בבא קמא (דף ב.) קאמר ולר' אליעזר דמחייב אתולדה במקום אב אמאי קרי ליה אב ואמאי קרי ליה תולדה ולא משני דלהכי קרי ליה אב דצריך להתרות אתולדה [משום] אב [מ]: זומר וצריך לעצים חייב שתים. והא דאמר בפ' זה בורר (סנהדרין דף כו.) תו חזיוה להוא גברא דהוה קא כסח אמר להן כהן חמיר אמרו ליה יכול לומר לעקל בית הבד אני צריך אף על גב דהכא אמר חייב משום נוטע התם מיירי בכה"ג שאין האילן מיתקן בכך אלא מתקלקל: וצריך לעצים. נראה דאפילו לר' יהודה דמחייב מלאכה שאינה צריכה לגופה בעינן צריך לעצים דלא מיקרי בעצים קוצר אלא בענין זה [ס] מידי דהוה אקורע על מנת לתפור ומוחק על מנת לכתוב וכדאמר רבי יוחנן לקמן בפ' חבית (דף קמה.) אחד כבשים ואחד שלקות ששחטן לגופן מותר למימיהן חייב חטאת ואמאי שרי לגופן ליהוי כמלאכה שאינה צריכה לגופה אלא טעמא לפי שאין דרך דישה בכך: ואחת משום מפרק. אין נראה לר"י כמו שמפרש רש"י שמפרק האילן ממשאו מן הפירות שעליו אלא כמו שפירש רבינו שמואל שיש על התמרים קליפה העליונה וכשהוא מכה בתמרים מפרק את הקליפה מן התמרים והוי כמו דש שמפרק את התבואה מן השבולת: מפרק. פירש"י דהוה תולדה דדש וקשה לר"ת דבשילהי המצניע (לקמן צה.) אמר דחולב חייב משום מפרק ואי הוה תולדה דדש הא אמר לקמן [י] גבי הפוצע חלזון דלרבנן אין דישה אלא בגידולי קרקע ואין לומר דדוקא חלזון שהוא דג פטרי רבנן דלא הוי גידולי קרקע אבל בחולב מחייבי דבהמה חשיבא גידולי קרקע כדמוכח בריש בכל מערבין (עירובין דף כח:) דהא [ע"כ טעמא דרבנן משום] דילפינן להו מסממנין שבמשכן דאין דישה אלא בגידולי קרקע [ע] לגבי דבר הגדל ממש מן הקרקע לא חשיבא בהמה גידולי קרקע כדאמרינן בהשוכר את הפועלים (ב"מ פט.) מה דיש מיוחד שהוא גידולי קרקע ופועל אוכל בו אף כל כו' יצא החולב והמגבן כו' ודוחק לומר דברייתא דהמצניע אתיא כר"י דפליג לקמן אדרבנן ונראה לר"ת דמפרק חייב משום ממחק דכשחולב ממחק את הדד ומחליקו ואין נראה לר"י דבפרק חבית (לקמן קמד:) אמרינן חולב אדם לתוך הקערה אבל לא לתוך הקדרה ולר"ת מה לי לתוך הקדרה מה לי לתוך הקערה ולפירוש הקונטרס א"ש דמעיקרא כשהיה בדדין חשיב אוכל וכשחולב לתוך הקדרה (דהשתא) נמי הוי אוכל ולא דמי לדש שנשתנה ונראה דלפירוש הקונטרס הלכה כרבי יהודה דהאמר בפרק אע"פ (כתובות ס.) [פ] אמר רבי מרינוס גונח יונק חלב בשבת מ"ט מפרק כלאחר יד הוא ובמקום צער לא גזרו רבנן ופסיק התם רב יוסף הלכתא כרבי מרינוס ואין נראה לומר דאף לרבנן אסור מדרבנן דמיחזי כמפרק ואף על גב דלא אסירא אלא מדרבנן לא שרי אלא משום דאיכא תרתי כלאחר יד ובמקום צער: [ועי' תוס' כתובות ס. ד"ה מפרק ותוס' יבמות קיד. ד"ה וקסבר]

עין משפט נר מצוה

כט א מיי' פ"ז מהלכות שבת הלכה ח ופ"ז מהלכות שגגות הלכה ג:
ל ב מיי' פ"ז מהל' שבת הלכה ג והלכה ט:
לא ג מיי' פ"ח מהלכות שבת הלכה ג:
לב ד שם הלכה ד:
לג ה מיי' פ"ז מהלכות שבת הלכה ג:
לד ו מיי' פ"ח מהלכות שבת הלכה א:
לה ז מיי' פ"א מהלכות שבת הלכה י:
לו ח מיי' פ"ז מהלכות שבת הלכה ד סמג לאוין סה:
לז ט מיי' פ"ח שם הל' ה סמג שם טוש"ע או"ח סימן ש"מ סעיף ט:
לח י מיי' פ"ח מהלכות שבת הל"א סמג שם:

רבינו חננאל

למה לי למיתנא מנינא [מ'] חסר אחת אטו עד האידנא מי לא ידעינן מנייני ומשני ר' יוחנן שאם עשאן כולם בהעלם אחד חייב על כל אחת ואחת. (ת"ש) [תנא] הזורע והזומר והנוטע והמבריך והמרכיב כולן מלאכה אחת הן (קס"ד) [קמ"ל] כי העושה מלאכות הרבה מעין מלאכה אחת אינו חייב אלא חטאת אחת שמעי' מינה שאלו השנויים במשנתנו חשובין אבות והשאר הן תולדות וכל העושה אב ותולדתו אינו חייב אלא אחת. והעושה ב' אבות או ב' תולדות דלאו אב אחד [חייב] שתים. ומיפרשא בגמ' דהזורק דר' אלעזר מחייב בגמ' דכריתות אתולדה במקום אב דידיה תרתי ולית הלכתא כוותיה. ואסיק' מדוקיא דמתני' דמאן דעביד כל מלאכות שבעולם ואפילו אלף מלאכות אינו חייב יותר מארבעים חסר אחת חטאות שהכל נכללים בכלל אבות ובתולדותיהן הללו: ירושלמי כל דבר שהוא משביח הפרי חייב משום (זורר) [זורע]. המבריך. המרכיב. והמקרסם. המזרד. המפסל. המזהם. המפרק. המעשן. המתלע. הקוסם. הסך. המשקה. המנקב. והעושה בתים. חייב משום זורע. אמרינן משמיה דרב הזומר חייב משום נוטע והנוטע והמבריך והמרכיב חייב משום זורע. שמעינן מינה מדמוקים נוטע והמבריך והמרכיב משום נוטע ואף משום זורע דיש תולדה לתולדה. וכולן נכללין בכלל אב אחד. הנוטע וזולד הוא של זורע. כי הנוטע נוצץ יותר של אילן בארץ ומתגדל כגון המפיל הזורע לארץ וצומח והזומר באילן מתגדל שזומר ההוא ומוסיף המקום פירות ונמצא כנוטע לפיכך אמרינן בזומר חייב (שתים) משום נוטע ואם הוא זומר וצריך לעצים ונמצא כשזומר חייב משום נוטע כמו שאמרנו ובנטילתו העצים נמצא כקוצר. לפיכך בזומר וצריך לעצים חייב שתים. משום נוטע ומשום קוצר וכן מאן דקטיל אספסתא ומאן דקניב סילקא כולן דרך אחת הן וחייב שתים. בזמן שיש שיעור קצירה ושיעור זריעה. פי'

מסורת הש"ס

א) [לעיל דף סט. וש"נ] כריתות ג:, ב) [גיטין סה: ב"ב יט.], ג) גי' רש"ל, ד) [נ"ל אבא עי' רש"א בסוגיא דלעיל לד. ד"ה גמרא סימן וכו'], ה) [מו"ק ב:], ו) לקמן פא: ע"ש, ז) ביצה ח. חגיגה י., ח) [לעיל יב. לא: לקמן קה: קו. קמא: עי' תוס' לקמן לד. ד"ה את המת וחגיגה י.], ט) נ"א והגודד, י) [גי' הרמב"ם והרא"ש והר"מ רבה וכן מוכרח עמ"ש לעיל עב: על הגליון], כ) [נ"ל המנפס פי' גאון המנפץ האוכל מן עפרוריתו חייב משום דש וכן המנפס מולל שבולים עכ"ל הערוך ערך פן], ל) [נ"ל חסר אחת ניהו], מ) [ועי' תוס' לקמן עו: ד"ה ולר"א דמחייב ובב"ק ב. ד"ה ולר"א], נ) [דף עה.], ס) נ"ל תני.

הגהות הב"ח

(א) גמ' דקניב סילקא וכו' וא' משום נוטע והחורש: (ב) שם בשדה חייב משום חורש: (ג) רש"י ד"ה שאם עשאן וכו' שבת ממנו כמה חטאות חייב עליו:

גליון הש"ס

תוס' ד"ה וצריך וכו'. מידי דהוי אקורע ע"מ לתפור. מבואר דס"ל דאף היכא דאינו מקלקל דצריך לאיזה דבר מ"מ פטור. ואפילו לר"י דס"ל שאינו ע"מ לתפור לא מקרי מלאכה חשובה. וכ"נ מדברי הכ"מ פ"י הלכה י מהלכות שבת. וק"ל מסוגיא דלקמן דף קד ע"ב. גם במ"ש תוספות דאפי' לר"י דמשמע פשיטא דניחא ק"ל הא פשיטא דניחא ליה בעצים להשתמש בהם אלא דעתה אינו עושה כן בשבילו מ"מ מיקרי צריכה לגופה כההיא דלקמן דף קג כמולש עולשין בארעא דלאו דיליה: תוס' ד"ה מפרק וכו' לגבי דבר הגדל ממש. עי' כת"ס פרשת ויצא בפסוק ויהי לי שור וחמור:

רב נסים גאון

ואפילו לר' יהודה דאמר מלאכה שאינה צריכה לגופה חייב עליה הני מילי מתקן והאי מקלקל הוא. כבר פירשנו בפרק א' עיקר דבריו של ר' יהודה אבל מקלקל הוא והוא שנשנו במשנה בפרק ר' אליעזר אומר האורג (לקמן דף קה) וכל המקלקלין פטורין:

ליקוטי רש"י

מנינא למה לי. ליתני אבות מלאכות הזורע והחורש כו' למה לי למימנא ארבעים חסר אחת ולא ידעינן לארבעים חסר אחת היכא [לעיל סט.]. ליתני אבות מלאכות הזורע והחורש כו' למה לי לאשמעינן מנינא הא מני להו ואזיל [שם ו:]. שאם עשאן כולם וכו'. וסימנא בעלמא אשמעינן לידע כמה חטאות חייב על חילול שבת אחת [שם סט.]. ובא להודיענו כמה החטאות שאדם חייב באיסורי שבת בהעלם אחד ולאשמעינן ארבעים חסר אחת הן ותו לא שאפילו עשה תולדותיהן עמהן אינו מביא על התולדה היכא דעשאה עם אביה דהוה ליה כעושה וחוזר ועושה דכולה חדא עבירה היא [שם ו:]. מבריך. כופף את הזמורות בארץ שקורין פרופינ"א [ר"ה ט.]. שכופף [הזמורה או היחור] בארץ [סוטה מג:]. כמו ויברך הגמלים (בראשית כד) כופף זמורת גפן מחוברת ומבריכה בקרקע בצידיה לכאן ולכאן וקורין בלע"ז פרובני"ר [ב"ב יט:]. כופף אמצעית הגפן בקרקע ומכסהו בקרקע באמצעיתו וכשנשרש באמצעיתו חותכין עיקר הראשון ונעשו שתי גפנים [רשב"ם שם פג.]. מרכיב. אילן בחבירו שקורין אומינטי"ר [ר"ה שם]. שנוקב האילן ונוטל מן הרך שבענפי האילן ותוחב לתוכו ועושה ענף בתוך הנקב ונושא ממין אותו אילן שנוטל ממנו [סוטה שם]. העושה מלאכות הרבה מעין מלאכה אחת. שתי תולדות של אב אחד אינו חייב אלא חטאת אחת דהרי הוא כעושה וחוזר ועושה בהעלם אחד ואין חילוק חטאות בהעלם אחד אלא בגופי עבירה שאין דומין או בחילוק שבתות לענין שגגת שבת [לעיל סח.]. אינו חייב אלא אחת דכיון דלאב אחד לכולן [כריתות טז:]. וצריך לעצים חייב. משום קוצר שהרי צריך לעצים וחייב משום נוטע דמשום הזימור גדלי ענפי [מו"ק ב:]. אספסתא. מין זרע הוא לעשב בהמות ולסוף ל' יום הוא נגמר ועוקרין אותו וזורעין אחר במקומו ובתוך שלשים יום גוזזין אותו שלש פעמים [ב"ב כח:]. שחת של תבואה [שם כ:]. היתה לו גומא וטממה בבית וכו'. בבית שייך בנין וזה שמשוה גומות בנין הרצפה הוא ובשדה מתקן החרישה [לקמן פא:]. חופר גומא. בונה בנין הוא ואם אינו צריך לה אלא ליטול את העפר אף על פי שהבנין בנוי אינו חייב משום בונה [חגיגה י.]. שאינה צריכה לגופה. שצרכוהו לא מעשה ואינו צריך לעיקר (תחלתה) [תכליתה] ופלוגתייהו בהמצניע (לקמן צג:) גבי מוציא המת במטה חייב ואף על גב דהוצאת המת לא ניחא ליה ביה ור' שמעון פוטר [לעיל יב.]. כגון [מלאכה זאת] שאינו צריך לבנין זה. חייב עליה. מודה בהך גומא דלאו התם הקובר את המת מתקן הוא והאי חופר גומא מקלקל הוא את הבית [חגיגה שם]. האי מקלקל הוא. דכיון דאינו צריך אלא לעפרה ולא לגומא אינו בונה ולא חורש אלא מקלקל וכל המקלקלים פטורים [ביצה ח.]. [המשך בדף עד.]

הַאי מְקַלְקֵל הוּא – however, in **this** case **he is ruining** his house.[31]

The third *melachah* taught by the Mishnah:

וְהַקּוֹצֵר – REAPING.

The Gemara elaborates:

תָּנָא – **[A Tanna] taught** a Baraisa: הַקּוֹצֵר הַבּוֹצֵר וְהַגּוֹדֵר (והמסיק) [וְהַמּוֹסֵק] וְהָאוֹרֶה – REAPING grain, CUTTING grapes, HARVESTING dates, COLLECTING olives, AND GATHERING figs כּוּלָּן מְלָאכָה אַחַת – ARE ALL in the category of ONE primary LABOR.[32]

Another example of reaping:

אָמַר רַב פָּפָּא – **Rav Pappa said:** הַאי מַאן דְּשָׁדָא פִּיסָא לְדִיקְלָא – **One who threw a clod of earth at a palm tree** וְאַתַּר תַּמְרֵי – **and severed** some **dates** חַיָּיב שְׁתַּיִם – **is obligated** to bring **two** *chatas* offerings: אַחַת מִשּׁוּם תּוֹלֵשׁ – **one on account of "detaching"**[33] וְאַחַת מִשּׁוּם מְפָרֵק – **and one on account of "extracting."**[34]

The Gemara presents a dissenting view:

רַב אַשִׁי אָמַר – **Rav Ashi said:** אֵין דֶּרֶךְ תְּלִישָׁה בְּכָךְ – **This is not the** normal **manner of detaching;** וְאֵין דֶּרֶךְ פְּרִיקָה בְּכָךְ – **and this is not the** normal **manner of extracting.**[35] The person is therefore exempt from bringing any *chatas*.

The Mishnah taught the fourth *melachah*:

וְהַמְעַמֵּר – GATHERING TOGETHER.

The Gemara elaborates:

אָמַר רָבָא – **Rava said:** הַאי מַאן דְּכָנִיף מִילְחָא מִמִּלְחָתָא – **Someone who gathers salt from the salt ditches**[36] חַיָּיב מִשּׁוּם מְעַמֵּר – **is liable on account of "gathering together."**[37]

A dissenting view:

אַבַּיֵי אָמַר – **Abaye said:** אֵין עִימּוּר אֶלָּא בְּגִידּוּלֵי קַרְקַע – The *melachah* of **gathering together applies only to items that grow from the ground.**[38]

The Mishnah taught the fifth *melachah*:

וְהַדָּשׁ – THRESHING.

A Baraisa elaborates:

תָּנָא – **[A Tanna] taught** a Baraisa: הַדָּשׁ וְהַמְנַפֵּץ וְהַמְנַפֵּט – THRESHING grain, BEATING flax,[39] AND STRIKING cotton with a bow[40] כּוּלָּן מְלָאכָה אַחַת הֵן – ARE ALL in the category of ONE primary LABOR.

The Mishnah listed four more *melachos*:

הַזּוֹרֶה הַבּוֹרֵר וְהַטּוֹחֵן וְהַמְרַקֵּד – WINNOWING, SELECTING, GRINDING, SIFTING.

The Gemara asks about an apparent redundancy:

הַיְינוּ זוֹרֶה הַיְינוּ בּוֹרֵר הַיְינוּ מְרַקֵּד – **Winnowing, selecting and sifting are all the same** activity.[41] Why does the Tanna establish these three as separate *melachos*?

The Gemara explains:

אַבַּיֵי וְרָבָא דְּאָמְרִי תַּרְוַיְיהוּ – **Abaye and Rava both said:** כָּל מִילְּתָא דַּהֲוַאי בַּמִּשְׁכָּן – **Anything that was** done **in** the construction of **the Mishkan,**

NOTES

31. In R' Abba's case even R' Yehudah would hold that the digger is exempt. This is so because the person did not perform the *melachah* of building at all since his efforts actually damaged the house (see *Rashi* to *Beitzah* 8a ד״ה פטור). It is thus different than a case of a labor not needed for its defined purpose, where the act of the labor is constructive [for example, performing the *melachah* of transferring to rid a house of a corpse]. Only if the person had dug dirt in the field, where he did not cause any damage, would he be liable according to R' Yehudah. R' Shimon, though, would exempt the person in that case as well since the labor was not needed for its defined purpose (*Rosh Yosef,* and *Magen Avos* to the Mishnah ד״ה ויש לעיין; see also *Tosafos* to *Pesachim* 47b ד״ה כתישה; cf. *Rabbeinu Chananel* here).

[Although even in the case of the house the person did obtain the dirt he needed, nothing positive was directly achieved by the action that constitutes the *melachah* of building, which is the act of making the hole. Gaining the dirt is only a secondary result of that act. Hence, his act is not considered to be the *melachah* of building at all (see *Rosh Yosef* and *Magen Avos* ibid.).]

32. [Our emendation follows *Rashi;* see *Dikdukei Soferim.*] The purpose of each of these labors is to harvest produce from its place of growth; hence, each labor is considered a variation of the *av* of reaping (see *Rambam, Hil. Shabbos* 7:4; cf. *Meiri*). [See *Eglei Tal* (קוצר 1:1) for a proof that *Rashi* agrees with *Rambam.*]

33. Which is a *toladah* of reaping (*Rashi*; cf. *Rashi* to *Beitzah* 3a; see *Eglei Tal* קוצר 1:4).

34. This is a *toladah* of threshing, where one removes grain from its ears. The word פּוֹרֵק is used with reference to the unloading of a donkey's burden; here too one "unloads" the clusters of their dates (*Rashi*). [The Rishonim (see, for example, *Tosafos, Ramban* and *Ran*) apparently had another version of *Rashi,* which stated the issue as removing dates from the tree. *Sfas Emes,* though, notes that our version of *Rashi* is actually in consonance with the alternative explanation given by those Rishonim.] See also *Dibros Moshe* 64:37.

Tosafos disagree with *Rashi's* placing of extracting in the category of threshing. See there for alternative suggestions.

35. These labors are usually performed by hand or with a special utensil. Throwing a clod of dirt at the dates is an unusual method of detaching and extracting, and thus creates no liability (*Rashi*; see *Yad David*).

36. Salt water was channeled into a ditch, where the heat of the sun evaporated the water. This person then collected that salt (*Rashi*).

37. This is another act that resembles collecting together ears of grain (*Rashi*).

38. There is a debate among Rishonim whether Abaye actually permits the gathering of salt or he merely exempts the person from *chatas* liability (see *Rosh* with *Korban Nesanel*).

Some Rishonim derive from the fact that the Gemara discusses a case of collecting salt at the place where it was produced that the *melachah* of gathering applies only in the place where a crop was produced (see *Tosafos* to *Beitzah* 31a ד״ה מן, and *Ritva MHK* ed. here; see, however, *Eglei Tal,* מעמר 2:2, and *Shevisas HaShabbos* at length).

39. To remove the flax from its stalks (*Rashi*).

40. Craftsmen would do this to remove the seeds from the cotton. Since cotton grows from the ground, this act is a *toladah* of threshing and not of combing wool (*Rashi*; cf. *Rambam, Hil. Shabbos* 9:12). Thus, when the term מְנַפֵּץ appears in the Mishnah with reference to wool it denotes the *av melachah* of combing (see *Dibros Moshe* 64:38). Here, however, that same term is used differently, referring to plants; it thus denotes a *toladah* of another *melachah* – namely, threshing (see *Chidushei HaRan*; see also *Magen Avos* to the Mishnah).

Although *Rashi* apparently regards striking cotton [and beating flax] as *tolados* of threshing, *Tosafos* (below, 74a ד״ה אע״ג) maintain that they are variations of the *av melachah* of threshing. *Eglei Tal* (דש 1:1) suggests that *Rashi* agrees with *Tosafos*, and uses the term *toladah* loosely here primarily to convey that striking cotton belongs in the category of threshing, not in the category of combing (cf. *Minchas Chinuch* §32 דש).

41. Each act involves separating edible food from the inedible parts (*Rashi*).

אַף עַל גַּב דְּאִיכָּא דְּדָמְיָא לָהּ – **even though there is** another act **that is similar to it,** חָשֵׁיב לָהּ – **[the Mishnah] reckons it** as a separate primary labor.[1]

The Gemara objects:

וְלִיחְשַׁב נַמִּי כּוֹתֵשׁ – **Then reckon pounding as well,** since that act too was performed in the construction of the Mishkan.[2] – ? –

The Gemara answers:

אָמַר אַבַּיֵי – **Abaye said:** שֶׁכֵּן עָנִי אוֹכֵל פִּתּוֹ בְּלֹא כְּתִישָׁה – Pounding is not an integral part of the bread-making process, **for indeed a poor person eats his bread without** first **pounding** the wheat.[3]

The Gemara offers an alternative answer:

רָבָא אָמַר – **Rava said:** הָא מַנִּי – **Who is this** author of our Mishnah? רַבִּי הִיא – **It is Rebbi,** דְּאָמַר אָבוֹת מְלָאכוֹת אַרְבָּעִים חָסֵר אַחַת – **who derived**[4] **that the primary labors** forbidden on the Sabbath **are forty minus one;** וְאִי חָשֵׁיב כּוֹתֵשׁ – **and if he reckoned pounding,** הַוְיָא לֵיהּ אַרְבָּעִים – **he would have forty** labors. Therefore, since pounding cannot be an additional *melachah,* it must be included in the category of threshing.[5]

The Gemara asks:

וְלִיפּוּק חֲדָא מֵהָנָךְ – **But take out one of those** types of selecting, וּלְעַיֵּיל כּוֹתֵשׁ – **and include pounding** instead.[6] – ? –

The Gemara concedes:

אֶלָּא מְחַוַּורְתָּא כִּדְאַבַּיֵי – **Rather, the clear** answer **is that of Abaye.**

The Gemara elaborates on the *melachah* of selecting:

תָּנוּ רַבָּנַן – **The Rabbis taught** in a Baraisa: הָיוּ לְפָנָיו מִינֵי אוֹכָלִין – If TYPES OF FOOD WERE BEFORE HIM,[7] בּוֹרֵר וְאוֹכֵל – HE MAY SELECT AND EAT, בּוֹרֵר וּמַנִּיחַ – and HE MAY SELECT AND LEAVE it for others to eat.[8] וְלֹא יִבְרוֹר – BUT HE MAY NOT SELECT;[9] וְאִם בֵּירֵר חַיָּיב חַטָּאת – AND IF HE DID SELECT, HE IS OBLIGATED TO bring A *CHATAS.*

The Gemara asks:

מַאי קָאָמַר – **What is [the Baraisa] saying?** First it states that a person may select, but concludes that a person may not select. – ? –

The Gemara suggests an answer:

אָמַר עוּלָּא – **Ulla said:** הָכִי קָאָמַר – **[The Baraisa]** actually **says thus:** בּוֹרֵר וְאוֹכֵל לְבוֹ בַּיּוֹם – **He may select for that day and eat,**[10] וּבוֹרֵר וּמַנִּיחַ לְבוֹ בַּיּוֹם – and **he may select for that day and leave** it for others to eat. וּלְמָחָר לֹא יִבְרוֹר – **But he may not select** food he will need **for the next day;** וְאִם בֵּירֵר חַיָּיב חַטָּאת – **and if he did select** for the next day's consumption, **he is obligated** to bring **a *chatas.***

The Gemara objects:

מַתְקִיף לָהּ רַב חִסְדָּא – **Rav Chisda challenged [this answer]:** וְכִי מוּתָּר לֶאֱפוֹת לְבוֹ בַּיּוֹם – **But is it permitted to bake for that day?** וְכִי מוּתָּר לְבַשֵּׁל לְבוֹ בַּיּוֹם – **And is it permitted to cook for that day?** Of course not! Why, then, should it be permitted to select for that day?[11]

NOTES

1. Therefore, since winnowing, selecting and sifting are discrete actions performed at different times during the processing of grain, the Mishnah counts them as three separate *melachos;* one who performs all three is liable to three *chatas* offerings (see *Rashi* below, 75b ד"ה הרי, *Tosafos* here; *Rashash*).

[These acts are thus not analogous to sowing and planting, which are essentially the same action, but performed to different items.]

2. Herbs were pounded in the preparation of the dyes. Our Mishnah should therefore have included as a *melachah* the act of pounding wheat with a mortar in order to remove the bran. Now, the Mishnah apparently fails to do so because pounding is similar to threshing, for in both acts an outer shell of the grain is removed (*Rashi*). [Threshing removes the outer husk of the wheat kernel; pounding removes the inner layer of bran still attached to the kernel, leading to production of whiter flour – see *Magen Avos* to the Mishnah.] Why, then, are the three types of sorting counted as separate *melachos*?

3. The Tanna listed only those *melachos* [in the first section of the Mishnah] that were essential to the bread-making process. Therefore, even though pounding was performed in the construction of the Mishkan and is a bona fide *av melachah,* the Mishnah omits its mention since it does list the similar act of threshing. Pounding thus differs from the three labors of sorting, since they were all performed in the Mishkan and are also essential to the baking of bread. Pounding, on the other hand, is an optional step, since only the wealthy would bear an added expense for having a more refined flour (*Rashi;* cf. *Rabbeinu Chananel, Chidushei HaRan* and *Meiri*).

The commentators debate the question of how many offerings one would be obligated to bring, according to *Rashi's* explanation, if one both threshed and pounded the wheat. *Maharam* suggests that since *Rashi* considers pounding a bona fide *av melachah,* a person would be liable to two separate *chatas* offerings – one for each *melachah* he performed. *Rashash* agrees to this interpretation of *Rashi,* but finds it difficult because the Mishnah implies that a person can become liable to a maximum of thirty-nine *chatas* offerings; according to this interpretation, if a person also pounded, he would be liable to forty. *Sfas Emes* openly disagrees with *Maharam's* understanding of *Rashi.* In his view *Rashi* means that since a pauper does not pound his grain, pounding is not considered a separate *av melachah,* but falls into the category of threshing. [We find (above, 73b) various examples of different *avos* carrying a single punishment (e.g. sowing, planting, grafting, etc.).] Thus, the Mishnah omitted pounding because, in truth, it is not a discrete *av melachah.* [See also *Chidushei R' Akiva Eiger, Shabbos Shel Mi.*]

4. [Literally: said.] Below, 97b, from Scripture (*Rashi*).

5. [Thus, according to this answer, pounding and threshing are both bona fide *melachos,* but in the same category – like sowing and planting, etc. One who performed both would certainly be liable to only one *chatas.*]

6. By replacing one of the three *melachos* of selecting with pounding, the Mishnah would be more balanced, for it would be listing two types of selecting and two types of threshing (*Rashi*). [According to this suggestion, pounding and threshing would be viewed as independent *avos,* each carrying a separate penalty.]

7. This follows *Rashi's* text of the Baraisa, wherein the word "types" is used loosely because only one type of food, mixed with inedible matter, was actually involved (see *Ritva MHK* ed.). According to *Tosafos* and other Rishonim, however, the correct text is: הָיוּ לְפָנָיו שְׁנֵי מִינֵי אוֹכָלִין, *[If] two types of food were before him.* According to this version, the person desired to take only one of the two types of food lying in a mixture before him. In such a case the other food is considered "waste" [i.e. the unwanted matter].

[*Rosh Yosef* suggests that *Rashi* agrees in theory with *Tosafos* that the *melachah* of selecting can apply even to two types of food. However, according to *Rashi* this is so only when one type is needed for immediate consumption; only then is the second type considered "waste." However, if neither type of food is needed now, there is no objective way of determining which type is the "food" and which is not. Since the Gemara will present Amoraim who interpret the Baraisa as referring to selecting for later use, *Rashi* assumes that the Baraisa must be discussing food mixed with inedible matter, not two types of food. See below, note 25.]

8. This explanation follows *Tosafos* and *Ritva* (*MHK* ed.). Accordingly, selecting for the use of others is the legal equivalent of selecting for one's own use, even if the selector is not eating with the other people (*Birkei Yosef* 319:2).

9. The Gemara will point out the obvious contradiction in the Baraisa: It first stated that a person may select, but now declares that one may not select (*Rashi*).

10. [The *melachah* of selecting is performed to ready the produce for storage. Therefore, if a particular act could be determined to be part of the eating process, it would not be included in the prohibition of selecting.] According to Ulla the Baraisa is teaching that one who selects for that day's consumption has not violated the *melachah* of selecting (see *Ritva MHK* ed.).

11. When the Baraisa concludes that one who selects for the next day's use is liable to a *chatas,* it indicates that selecting is an *av melachah* (*Rashi*). Why, then, should one be permitted to perform this labor at all,

אע"ג דאיכא דדמיא לה חשיב לה וליחשב נמי כותש אמר אביי שכן עני אוכל פתו בלא כתישה רבא אמר הא מני רבי היא דאמר אבות מלאכות ארבעים חסר אחת ואי חשיב כותש הויא ליה ארבעים וליפוק חדא מהנך ולעייל כותש אלא מחוורתא כדאביי: ת"ר היו לפניו מיני אוכלין בורר ואוכל בורר ומניח ולא יברור ואם בירר חייב חטאת מאי קאמר אמר עולא הכי קאמר בורר ואוכל לבו ביום ובורר ומניח לבו ביום ולמחר לא יברור ואם בירר חייב חטאת מתקיף לה רב חסדא וכי מותר לאפות לבו ביום וכי מותר לבשל לבו ביום אלא אמר רב חסדא בורר ואוכל פחות מכשיעור בורר ומניח פחות מכשיעור וכשיעור לא יברור ואם בירר חייב חטאת מתקיף לה רב יוסף וכי מותר לאפות פחות מכשיעור אלא אמר רב יוסף [א] בורר ואוכל ביד בורר ומניח ביד בקנון ובתמחוי לא יברור ואם בירר פטור אבל אסור בנפה ובכברה לא יברור ואם בירר חייב חטאת מתקיף לה רב המנונא מידי קנון ותמחוי קתני אלא אמר רב המנונא [ב] בורר ואוכל אוכל מתוך הפסולת בורר ומניח אוכל מתוך הפסולת [ג] פסולת מתוך אוכל לא יברור ואם בירר חייב חטאת מתקיף לה אביי מידי אוכל מתוך פסולת קתני אלא אמר אביי [ד] בורר ואוכל לאלתר ובורר ומניח לאלתר ולבו ביום לא יברור ואם בירר נעשה כבורר לאוצר וחייב חטאת אמרוה רבנן קמיה דרבא אמר להו [א] שפיר אמר נחמני [ה] היו לפניו שני מיני אוכלין ובירר ואכל ובירר והניח רב אשי מתני פטור רבי ירמיה מדיפתי מתני חייב רב אשי מתני פטור והא תני חייב לא קשיא הא בקנון ותמחוי הא בנפה וכברה כי אתא רב דימי אמר שבתא דרב ביבי הואי ואיקלעו רבי אמי ור' אסי שדא קמייהו כלכלה דפירי ולא ידענא אי משום דסבר אוכל מתוך פסולת אסור אי משום עין יפה הוא דמכוין חזקיה אמר [ו] הבורר תורמוסים מתוך פסולת שלהן חייב לימא קסבר חזקיה אוכל מתוך פסולת אסור שאני תורמוסים

דשלקי

רש"י

אע"ג דאיכא. אחריתי בהדה דדמיא לה חשבינהו לתרווייהו כאבות ואע"ג דחדא נינהו: **וליחשב נמי כותש.** חטין במכתשת להסיר קליפתן דהואי במקדש בסממנין אלא לאו משום דדמיא לדש לא חשיב לה דהא נמי מיפרקה מלבוש היא: **שכן עני אוכל פתו בלא כתישה.** לכך אע"ג דהואי במקדש ואב מלאכה היא כיון דתנא ליה דש לא תנא לה חורה ובורר ומרקד סידורא דפת נינהו וכיון דהוו במקדש והכא אתחיל בסידורא דפת תנינהו כדאמרינן גבי אופה דה"ל למתני מבשל ולא אופה דלא הוה במקדש אלא משום סדורא דפת נקט ואתא הואיל ואופה בפת כמבשל בסממנין אבל כתישה עשירים הוא דלתתי וכתשי לעשות סלת נקיה אבל עניים לא טרחי הלכך לא תנא לה ומיהו ודאי אב מלאכה היא ובכלל דש היא: **רבי היא.** דיליף לקמן בפרק הזורק (דף צו:) דברים הדברים אלה הדברים למניינא: **וליפוק חדא מהנך.** או זורה או בורר או מרקד דהוו חדא ליפוק מינייהו חדא וליתני הך דהכי עדיף למיתני תרתי מהא ותרתי מהא מלמיתני ולמיכפל תלתא זימני בחדא ואיכא חדא דלא כפיל ביה מידי: **היו לפניו מיני אוכלין** גרסי' ול"ג שני: **ולא יברור.** לקמיה פריך מאי קאמר ברישא תנא בורר והדר תנא לא יברור: **ולמחר.** לצורך מחר: **וכי מותר לאפות ולבשל לבו ביום.** וה"נ אב מלאכה היא כיון דאמרת ולמחר חייב חטאת: **פחות מכשיעור.** פחות מכגרוגרת: **וכי מותר לאפות פחות מכשיעור.** נהי דחיוב חטאת ליכא איסורא מיהא איכא דקיימא לן חצי שיעור אסור מן התורה בפרק בתרא דיומא (דף עד.) והיכי קתני בורר לכתחלה: **בקנון.** כלי עץ שעושין כעין לינור רחב מלאחריו וקצר מלפניו ובעלי מטבע עושים אותו והבורר בו קטנית נותן קטנית במקום הרחב ומנענעו והקטנית מפני שהוא עגול מתגלגל ויורד דרך פיו הקצר והפסולת נשאר בכלי: **פטור אבל אסור.** מותר לכתחלה לא הוי דדמי לברירה וחייב חטאת לא הוי דכלאחר יד הוא דעיקר ברירה בנפה וכברה אבל ביד לא דמי לבורר כלל: **מידי קנון ותמחוי קתני.** ה"ה נמי דפריך מידי נפה וכברה קתני אלא חדא מינייהו נקט: **אוכל מתוך הפסולת.** לא דרך ברירה היא: **ובורר ומניח לאלתר.** לאכול לאלתר שאין זה דרך בוררין: **לאוצר.** להצניע: **נחמני.** אביי: **והתניא.** לאלתר מותר לכתחלה הויא ופטור אבל אסור ליכא: **שבתא דרב ביבי הואי.** הגיע יומו להיות עומד ומשמש על התלמידים: **ושדא קמייהו.** ולא רצה לברור האוכל מתוך העלין ולתת לפני כל אחד ואחד אלא שטחן והם נוטלים ואוכלים ובשטות זה נפרש האוכל מאליו: **הבורר** תורמוסין. לאחר שלקן הוא בורר אוכל מתוך הקליפה:

דשלקי

תוספות

אע"ג דאיכא דדמיא לה חשיב (א). והא דלא חשיב שובט ומדקדק לפי * שהם לגמרי בכלל מיסך ואורג ולא חשיב נמי מנפץ אע"ג שבמשכן היו מנפצין פשתן לעשות יריעות ושאר דברים משום דהיינו דש ממש אלא שזה בתבואה וזה בפשתן אבל זורה ובורר ומרקד הם שלשה דברים:

שכן עני אוכל פתו בלא כתישה. וא"ת מ"מ ליחשיב כתישת סממנין דהוה במשכן ואע"ג דעני אוכל פתו בלא כתישה לענין סממנים מלאכה חשובה היא ואומר ר"י דלאו דוקא אוכל פתו אלא ה"ה דעני צובע בסממנים בלא כתישה וא"ת מרקד נמי לא ליתני שכן עני אוכל פתו בעיסה בלוסה כדאמר בסוף פרקין ויש לומר דרוב עניים אין אוכלין בלא הרקדה אלא שלענין חלה מצטרפין הסובין דקרינן ביה מלחם הארץ כיון דיש עניים שאוכלים בעיסה בלוסה ור"ת פירש בע"א ולא נתיישב לר"י:

היו לפניו שני מיני אוכלין גרסי'. וכן פירש ר"ח דבאוכל מתוך אוכל שייכא ברירה שבורר אותו שאינו חפץ לאכול מתוך אותו שרוצה לאכול דאותו שאינו חפץ בו חשיב פסולת לגבי אותו שחפץ לאכול וכן משמע בירושלמי דגרס הבורר אוכלים מתוך אוכלים חזקיה אמר כו':

בורר ומניח. פי' לצורך אחרים:

וכי מותר לאפות פחות מכשיעור. והמתרץ ס"ד דפחות מכשיעור הוי דרך אכילה:

מתקיף לה רב המנונא מידי קנון ותמחוי קתני. פי' הקונט' דה"נ הוה מצי למיפרך מידי נפה וכברה קתני וקשה לר"י מאי קמשני רב המנונא לדידיה נמי תקשה מידי [אוכל] מתוך פסולת קתני ועוד בסמוך פירש הקונטרס והתניא חייב דהיינו הך דהכא ומשני דבנפה וכברה מיירי והיכי משני הכא מידי נפה וכברה קתני ונראה לרבינו יצחק דדוקא מקנון ותמחוי פריך וה"פ מידי קנון ותמחוי קתני כיון דנחת לפרושי דיני ברירה דביד מותר ובנפה וכברה חייב חטאת לא היה לו להניח מלשנות קנון ותמחוי דפטור אבל אסור:

בורר ואוכל אוכל מתוך פסולת. משמע דאוכל מתוך פסולת אין דרך ברירה בכך וקשה דבריש פרק תולין (לקמן קלח.) אמרי' מה דרכו (ב) של בורר בורר אוכל מתוך פסולת וי"ל דהתם בפסולת מרובה על האוכל הוי אוכל מתוך פסולת דרך ברירה דהתם במשמר איירי וקשה לרשב"א דתנן בפ"ק דביצה (דף יד:) הבורר קטניות בי"ט ב"ש אומרים בורר אוכל ואוכל וב"ה אומרים בורר כדרכו ואמר בגמרא בד"א כשהאוכל מרובה על הפסולת אבל פסולת מרובה על האוכל ד"ה נוטל את האוכל ומניח את הפסולת ואי בפסולת מרובה על האוכל הוי אוכל מתוך פסולת דרך ברירה היכי שרי לב"ש הא אינהו אסרי לברר כדרכו וע"ע שם:

והתניא חייב. פי' בקונטרס דהיינו ברייתא דלעיל וקשה לר"י דלמאי דמוקמינן לה בנפה וכברה משמע דוקא לבו ביום אסור אבל לאלתר אפי' בנפה וכברה שרי ובפ"ק דביצה (גם זה שם.) משמע דבנפה וכברה אסור בכל ענין דתנן ב"ה אומרים בורר כדרכו בקנון ובתמחוי אבל לא בנפה ובכברה ולא מפליג בין לאלתר לבו ביום ועוד לכאורה לעולא דלעיל הוי בורר לבו ביום כמו לאלתר לאביי וא"כ שרי לעולא בנפה וכברה אפי' לבו ביום ובמתני' דביצה אסר לכל הפחות לבו ביום ונראה לר"י דברייתא דלעיל איירי בבורר ביד והכא דמוקמי לה בנפה וכברה ברייתא אחריתי היא ואפי' לאלתר חייב חטאת וכן משמע מתוך פירוש ר"ח דפירש שיש ג' דינין בבורר לאלתר דביד מותר לכתחלה בקנון ובתמחוי פטור אבל אסור בנפה וכברה חייב חטאת:

ולא ידענא אי משום דקסבר אוכל מתוך פסולת אסור. פי' לא ידענא מה שלא ביררם תחלה קודם שהביאם לפניהן אבל אין לפרש מה שלא ביררם בשעה שהניח לפניהם דא"כ מאי קאמר אי משום דקסבר אוכל מתוך פסולת אסור דהא לכ"ע שרינן אוכל מתוך פסולת לאלתר:

האי

מסורת הש"ס

א) [נדרים נד: וע"ש בר"ן טעם דקרי לאביי נחמני וע"ע פירש"י בגיטין לד:].

הגהות הב"ח

(א) תוס' ד"ה אע"ג וכו' חשיב לה והא דלא חשיב. נ"ב עיין לקמן בפ' הזורק דף צו ומביאו לעיל בד' עג: (ב) ד"ה בורר וכו' דרכו של בורר נוטל אוכל ומניח פסולת:

גליון הש"ס

תוס' ד"ה אע"ג וכו' לפי שהם לגמרי בכלל מיסך. עי' לקמן דף עה ע"ב ברש"י ד"ה שובט:

ליקוטי רש"י

הקוצר הבוצר וכו'. אורה שייך למימר בתאנים וכוצר בענבים וקוצר בתבואה וגודר בתמרים ומוסק בזיתים ומלקט בשאר אילנות [רשב"ם ב"ב פב:]. **והגודר.** כל (לקיטת) [קציצת] תמרים קרי גדירה [לעיל ג.]. **פיסא.** רגב גוש עפר כלישנ"א בלע"ז [מכות ח.]. **ממלחתא.** מקום שריפת המים שעושין נגרים על שפת הים להמשיך מים לבריכות רחבות העשויות לכך וכשנתמלאו סותם החריצין והשמש שורף את המים שמלוחין הן ונעשה מלח [לעיל סו:]. על שפת הים חריצין עשויין שמי הים נכנסים בהן והחמה מייבשתן ועושין מלח והן משרפות מים האמורין במקרא (יהושע יא) ומתרגמינן חריצי ימא [כתובות עט:]. [ע"כ שייך לדף עג:]. **פחות מכשיעור.** כגרוגרת שיעור הוא לכל איסורי מלאכות של שבת באוכלים [לעיל ע:]. **וכי מותר לאפות פחות מכשיעור.** הא מדאורייתא אסור דחצי שיעור אסור מן התורה [כדאמרינן חצי] שיעור מנין ת"ל כל חלב בפרק בתרא דיומא (עד.) [חולין צח.]. **קנון.** כלי הוא, ראשו אחד רחב והשני עשוי כעין מרזב קצר ונותן הקטניות בתוך הרחב ומנענע והאוכל מתגלגל דרך המרזב והפסולת נשאר בכלי. **תמחוי.** קערה גדולה [ביצה יב:]. **שפיר אמר נחמני.** היינו אביי וקרי ליה הכי לפי שנתגדל בבית רבה בר נחמני [ר"ן נדרים נד:]. ונראה בעיני דעל שם שרבה בר נחמני גידל אביי בביתו ולמדו תורה שהיה יתום השיאו את שם אביו נחמני רבה סתם הוא רבה בר נחמני [גיטין לד:]. אביי קרו ליה נחמני (ואיכא דאמרי דבלשון גנאי קרי ליה נחמני כלומר עדיין אתה תלמידו של רב נחמן) [הוריות יד. וז"ל רש"י זבחים קיח: "נראה בעיני כי אביו של אביי כייליל שמו"]. **תורמוסים.** מין קטנית עגול כמין עדשה ורחב כמעה קטנה והוא מר מאוד עד ששולקין אותו שבע פעמים ונעשה מתוק וטוב עד שיאכל למטעמים בקנוח סעודה [ביצה כה:].

עין משפט נר מצוה

לט א ב מיי' פ"ח מהל' שבת הלכה יג סמג לאוין סה טוש"ע או"ח סימן שיט סעיף א:

מ ג מיי' שם הלכה יג טוש"ע שם סעיף ד:

מא ד מיי' שם הלכה יב טוש"ע שם סעיף א ב:

מב ה מיי' שם הלכה יג טוש"ע שם סעיף ג:

מג ו מיי' שם טוש"ע שם סעיף ה:

רבינו חננאל

המבריך החופר בארץ ומבריך הייחור וטומנו לעפר ומרציא ראש הייחור במקום רחוק. החורש. החורץ. החופר כולן מלאכה אחת הן. אסיקנא כל אלו משום חרישה. כל שהיא ליפות הקרקע בשדה חייב משום חורש וכל שהן בבית להשוות חייב משום בונה. אבל להשוות קרקע השדה חייב משום חורש. כדכתיב הלא אם שוה פניה. יהוא כגון המדייר והמעדר והמכבד שהוא משוה גומות והמפעפע גושים. המסקל. הממלא בקעים שתחת הזיתים. העושה עוגיות לגפנים. המברה בחרשים. המצית אור. בחישת הקנים ובאגם תמרים. ואמת המים המכשרת צדדים לזריעה. וכל דבר שהוא להנאת קרקע חייב משום חורש. כך הוא מפורש בירושלמי וכן הא דאמר רבה היתה לו גומא וטממה אף זה משוה פני אדמתו בבית חייב משום בונה ובשדה משום חורש וקיי"ל בהני כולה כרבה. (א"ר אבא החופר גומא ואין צריך). פי' גבשושית תל של עפר שהיתה לו ונטלה בבית חייב משום בונה כו'. [אמר ר' אבא החופר גומא ואין צריך] לחפור חפירה אלא לעפר בעלמא בלבד הוא צריך. נטילת העפר אינה מלאכה משום חפירה אינו חייב שהרי לא נתכוין לחפירה. ואפילו לר' יהודה דאמר מלאכה שאינה צריכה לגופה חייב עליה ה"מ במתקן אבל האי דחפר מקלקל הוא בין בבית א) בין בשדה. וכי האי מילתא אמרו בהכל חייבין בראיה (חגיגה י') שהן כהררי' התלויין בשערה. מקרא מעט והלכות מרובות: ת"ר הקוצר הבוצר הגודר האורה כולן מלאכה אחת הן. פי' פיסה צרור של אדמה ולענין הלכה מאן דשדא פיסא לדיקלא ואתר תמרי קיי"ל כרב אשי דאמר אין דרך תלישה ולא דרך פריקה בכך. הא דאמר רבה מאן דכניף מילחא ממלחתא חייב משום מעמר קיי"ל כאביי דאמר אין עימור אלא בגידולי קרקע ואינו חייב אלא (כשמעמר) [כשמעביר] ד' אמות ברה"ר. הדש (תנא) [הוא] המפרק הפסולת המחוברת באוכל ומכינתן לברירה או כברה [בזורייה] או בהרקדה. המנפץ נופץ עפרורית מן האוכל וכן המנפט מולל שבלים נמצא זורה והבורר והמרקד כולן מעבירין פסולת המעורבות באוכל ואינה מחוברת (ואינה) כגון קליפה שצריכה פירוק או כגון עפרורית שצריך ניפוץ אלא מעורבת בלבד. וכן אם נטל בידו אדם תבוא' בתיבנא ובפסולת שיש בה וניפח בה ברוח פיו ובירר חשוב הוא כזורה. פי' בורר נוטל פסולת מבין האוכל ומשליכ' או נוטל האוכל ומניח הפסולת. מרקד שמטיל את האוכל והפסולת בכברה ונשארת האוכל ואם האוכל דק והפסולת עבה כמין תבן יוצא האוכל ונשארת הפסולת בכברה. וכיון דאסיק' כי הזורה והבורר והמרקד כולן מעין מלאכה אחת הן מפריש הפסולת מן האוכל ומשום דהוו במשכן הוו להו תלתא וחייב על כל אחת ואחת. ואקשינן ונחשוב נמי כותש שהוא מסיר קליפת החיטין מעליהן לטחון אותם להוציא סולת כגון כותש לעשות דייסא או טיסני והנה גם זה מפריש פסולת מן האוכל הוא ומשני אביי שכן עני אוכל פתו בלא כתישה כלומר כל בני אדם טוחנין בחיטין שלהן סלת הנה דרך העניים לברור ולטחון ולעשות עיסה בלוסה ואין אוכלין סלת לפיכך אין צריכין כתישה. ואע"פ דכתישה מלאכה היא דהא לגבי יו"ט גרסי' (ביצה יד.) אין כותשין במכתשת אע"פ שמותר ביו"ט אוכל נפש וכ"ש בשבת. אמר אביי האי דלא חשיב לה בהדי אבות משום דלא חשיבא שלא כל אדם אוכל בכתישה כמו שאמרנו. לפיכך אינה אלא כתולדות דמיא. רבא אמר אמאי לא חשיב לכותש בהדייהו משום דמתניתין ר' (חייא) [היא] דאמר קבלה היא בידינו אבות מלאכות [ארבעים] חסר אחת כנגד ג) עבודת המשכן ור' מ' חסר אחת שנה וכבר פירשנו להא דר' בבמה טומנין (מט:) כי המלאכות הללו מן המשכן למדתן. ואי חשיב כותש בהדייהו הוי להו מ' שלמות ור' מ' חסר אחת שנה לפי' לא תנא כותש בהדייהו ואקשינן וליפוק חדא מינייהו וניעול כותש ואסיק' אלא מחוורתא כדאביי: ת"ר היו לפניו ב' מיני אוכלין בורר ואוכל בורר ומניח ולא יברר ואם בירר חייב חטאת. ומת' מאי קאמר [א'] עולא הכי קאמר בורר ואוכל בו ביום כו' ודחאה רב חסדא ואמר וכי מותר לאפות ולבשל בו ביום כו' ופרשה אביי בורר ואוכל לאלתר בורר ומניח לאלתר. ג) שלא לאלתר לא יברור. ואם בירר נעשה כבירר לאוצר וחייב חטאת. וקיי"ל כותיה דאמר רבה שפיר אמר נחמני ולאלתר. דאמר אביי כל זמן שיושב על השולחן ואוכל דגרסינן בתלמוד דא"י ברר אוכלין מתוך אוכלין חזקיה אמר חייב ר' יוחנן אמר פטור מתניתא פליגא על חזקיה דאמר בורר ואוכל בורר ומניח על השלחן רבין בר חייא אמר תפתר כשהיו אורחין אוכלין ראשונה ראשונה. היו לפניו ב' מיני אוכלין בורר ואוכל בורר ומניח. רב אשי [מתני פטור רי"מ] מתני חייב ואוקימנא להא דרב אשי בבורר בנפה או בכברה חייב חטאת בקנון ובתמחוי פטור וכל פטורי דשבת פטור אבל אסור נינהו. וקיי"ל כרב אשי דבתראה הוא והא דאמר חזקיה הבורר תורמוסין מתוך פסולת שלהן חייב. הלכתא היא דהא

מקשינן

חשק שלמה על רבינו חננאל א) עי' תוס' פסחים מ"ז ע"ב ד"ה כתישה: ב) עי' בגמ' כאן ולעיל מ"ע ע"ב בתוס' ול"ע: ג) מכאן ועד סוף הענין הובא בא"ז בשם רבינו:

Rav Chisda therefore suggests another explanation of the Baraisa:

אֶלָּא אָמַר רַב חִסְדָּא – Rather, Rav Chisda said: **בּוֹרֵר וְאוֹכֵל פָּחוֹת מִכַּשִּׁיעוּר** – The Baraisa means that **one may select less than the amount** for which one is liable **and eat;**[12] **בּוֹרֵר וּמַנִּיחַ פָּחוֹת מִכַּשִּׁיעוּר** – **and he may select less than the amount** for which one is liable **and leave** it for others to eat. **וְכַשִּׁיעוּר לֹא יִבְרוֹר** – **But that amount** itself **he may not select;** **וְאִם בֵּירֵר חַיָּיב חַטָּאת** – **and if he did select** that minimum amount, **he is obligated** to bring **a *chatas*.**

The Gemara objects:

מַתְקִיף לָהּ רַב יוֹסֵף – Rav Yosef challenged [this explanation]: **וְכִי מוּתָּר לֶאֱפוֹת פָּחוֹת מִכַּשִּׁיעוּר** – **But is it permitted to bake less than the amount** for which one is liable? Of course not![13] How, then, could the Baraisa mean that one may – in the first place – select less than the minimum amount for which he is liable?

Rav Yosef therefore suggests another interpretation:

אֶלָּא אָמַר רַב יוֹסֵף – Rather, Rav Yosef said: **בּוֹרֵר וְאוֹכֵל בַּיָּד** – **He may select by hand and eat,** **בּוֹרֵר וּמַנִּיחַ בַּיָּד** – **and he may select by hand and leave** it for others to eat. **בְּקָנוֹן וּבְתַמְחוּי לֹא יִבְרוֹר** – **However, he may not select with a funnel**[14] **or with a large plate,**[15] **וְאִם בֵּירֵר פָּטוּר אֲבָל אָסוּר** – **and if he did select** with either utensil, he has committed an act for which one **is exempt** from bringing a sacrifice **but** which is nonetheless **forbidden.**[16] **וּבְנָפָה וּבִכְבָרָה לֹא יִבְרוֹר** – **Furthermore, he may not select with a fine sieve or with a coarse sieve,** **וְאִם בֵּירֵר חַיָּיב חַטָּאת** – **and if he did select** with either sieve, **he is obligated** to bring **a *chatas*.**[17]

The Gemara objects again:

מַתְקִיף לָהּ רַב הַמְנוּנָא – Rav Hamnuna challenged [this explanation]: **מִידִי קָנוֹן וְתַמְחוּי קָתָנֵי** – **Does [the Baraisa] teach anything** explicit **about a funnel or wide plate?**[18] It does not! Hence, the Baraisa cannot be interpreted in this manner.

Rav Hamnuna therefore offers another explanation:

אֶלָּא אָמַר רַב הַמְנוּנָא – Rather, Rav Hamnuna said: **בּוֹרֵר וְאוֹכֵל אוֹכֶל מִתּוֹךְ הַפְּסוֹלֶת** – **One may select** the **food from the waste and eat,**[19] **בּוֹרֵר וּמַנִּיחַ אוֹכֶל מִתּוֹךְ הַפְּסוֹלֶת** – **and one may select** the **food from the waste and leave** it for others to eat. **פְּסוֹלֶת מִתּוֹךְ אוֹכֶל לֹא יִבְרוֹר** – However, **he may not select** the **waste from** the **food,**[20] **וְאִם בֵּירֵר חַיָּיב חַטָּאת** – **and if he did select** the waste from the food, **he is obligated** to bring **a *chatas*.**

The Gemara again objects:

מַתְקִיף לָהּ אַבַּיֵי – Abaye challenged [this explanation]: **מִידִי אוֹכֶל מִתּוֹךְ פְּסוֹלֶת קָתָנֵי** – **Did the Baraisa teach anything** explicit **about food** being removed **from waste?**[21]

Abaye now explains the Baraisa:

אֶלָּא אָמַר אַבַּיֵי – Rather, Abaye said: **בּוֹרֵר וְאוֹכֵל לְאַלְתַּר** – **One may select and eat immediately,**[22] **וּבוֹרֵר וּמַנִּיחַ לְאַלְתַּר** – **and one may select and leave** for others to eat **immediately.** **וּלְבוֹ בַּיּוֹם לֹא יִבְרוֹר** – **But he may not select**[23] **for** consumption later **that day;** **וְאִם בֵּירֵר** – **and if he did select** for later consumption, **נַעֲשָׂה כְּבוֹרֵר לְאוֹצָר** – **it becomes as if he selects for**

NOTES

even for the sake of that very Sabbath?

[According to Rav Chisda the fact that the selecting is being done for that day's use is not sufficient cause to say that it differs from the *melachah* performed in the Mishkan. It is no different than the *melachah* of baking, which is prohibited even for that day's use (see *Ritva MHK* ed.).]

12. That is, less than the size of a dried fig (*Rashi;* see above, 73a note 39).

Tosafos explain that Rav Chisda believed that a person would be permitted to select such a small amount because that is considered the normal way of eating. [See also *Ramban,* and *Beur Halachah* 319:4 ד״ה הבורר.]

13. Even though a person is not liable to a *chatas* for performing less than the minimum amount, he is nevertheless forbidden to do so, for it is an established law (see *Yoma* 74a) that even at the Biblical level one may not perform any amount of a forbidden act (*Rashi;* see *Mishneh LaMelech* to *Hil. Shabbos* 18:1, *Sfas Emes;* see also *Magen Avos*). Hence, since it is prohibited to select an amount the size of a dried fig, it is prohibited to select a smaller amount as well (see *Ramban*).

14. This is a tubular wooden utensil made by people who produce coins. It was wide on one side and narrow on the other. One who wished to use this instrument to sort beans from their chaff would put the mixture into the wide end, shake the utensil, and thereby cause the round beans to roll down through the narrow opening, while the chaff remained in the upper part of the funnel (*Rashi*).

15. By spreading the mixture over a wide plate and then gently shaking the plate at a slight angle, the round beans roll down to the lower end of the plate while the chaff remains above (see *Bach, Orach Chaim* §319, end of ד״ה ומש״כ בורר בידו).

16. [One of the principles of Sabbath law is that if one performs a *melachah* in an unusual manner he is not liable to Biblical punishment – see General Introduction.] Selecting is typically performed with a sieve; hence, if one improvisationally selects with a funnel or a large plate, he is not liable to a *chatas*. However, one may not in the first place use such utensils, since that would too closely resemble normal selecting. It is perfectly permitted, though, to select by hand, since that method does not at all resemble normal selecting (*Rashi*).

17. According to Rav Yosef, the Baraisa must be listing three gradations of selecting because it is not common for a Tanna to juxtapose a completely permitted activity with one that carries a Biblical punishment. He therefore interprets the next to the last clause of the Baraisa, וְלֹא יִבְרוֹר, *he may not select,* as referring to selecting with a funnel or plate, an action which is non-punishable but nevertheless forbidden. The Baraisa then concludes with the case of selecting with a sieve, which is Biblically punishable (*Ramban;* cf. *Chidushei HaRan; Magen Avos*).

18. *Ramban* explains the challenge as follows: Even though selecting is normally done with a sieve, since the Baraisa's lenient first ruling obviously involves selecting by hand [according to Rav Yosef's interpretation], the Baraisa should have distinguished the latter cases by expressly stating that they involved selecting with a utensil. By not doing so, the Baraisa is apparently teaching that selecting even by hand is sometimes forbidden.

Rav Hamnuna could have also noted that the Baraisa mentioned nothing about sieves, but he chose instead to raise just one difficulty (*Rashi;* cf. *Tosafos*).

19. [According to *Rashi* (see note 7) this means removing the food from the inedible matter with which it is mixed. According to *Tosafos* and the other Rishonim (ibid.) it means removing the desired food from the other, unwanted food.] This is not the normal method of selecting (*Rashi*). Rav Hamnuna agrees with Rav Yosef, who held that the only permissible selecting is that which is done by hand. He objected only to Rav Yosef's insisting that the Baraisa was teaching that ruling alone (*Ritva MHK* ed.).

20. Even for immediate consumption, because that is, if anything, an even more typical manner of selecting (*Ritva* ibid.).

21. There is no indication that the first case of the Baraisa involves removing food from waste any more than does the last case. Rather, each ruling in the Baraisa [even the prohibition stated at the end] should be understood as involving the removal of food from waste (*Ritva's* preferred explanation).

22. Selecting for immediate consumption is not the common method of selecting (*Rashi*). Nevertheless, Abaye concurs with Rav Hamnuna that this unusual method is permitted only when the food is removed from the waste, and not vice versa [and only by hand] (*Ritva* ibid.).

Rabbeinu Chananel defines "immediate consumption" as the time required for eating the current meal. [See *Eglei Tal* בורר 5:9 for more details.] According to this explanation, the second clause of the Baraisa (ובורר ומניח) can be interpreted as follows: *He may select and leave [the food for that meal]* (see *Magen Avos* to *Tosafos* ד״ה בורר; see also *Orach Chaim* 319:1 and *Beur Halachah* ד״ה וכל מה שבורר).

23. Even the food from the waste, and even by hand (*Ritva* ibid.).

אע"ג דאיכא דדמיא לה חשיב לה וליחשב נמי כותש אמר אביי שכן עני אוכל פתו בלא כתישה רבא אמר הא מני רבי היא דאמר אבות מלאכות ארבעים חסר אחת ואי חשיב כותש הויא ליה ארבעים וליפוק חדא מהנך ולעייל כותש אלא מחוורתא כדאביי: ת"ר היו לפניו מיני אוכלין בורר ואוכל בורר ומניח ולא יברור ואם בירר חייב חטאת מאי קאמר אמר עולא הכי קאמר בורר ואוכל לבו ביום ובורר ומניח לבו ביום ולמחר לא יברור ואם בירר חייב חטאת מתקיף לה רב חסדא וכי מותר לאפות לבו ביום וכי מותר לבשל לבו ביום אלא אמר רב חסדא בורר ואוכל פחות מכשיעור ובורר ומניח פחות מכשיעור וכשיעור לא יברור ואם בירר חייב חטאת מתקיף לה רב יוסף וכי מותר לאפות פחות מכשיעור אלא אמר רב יוסף [א] בורר ואוכל ביד בורר ומניח ביד בקנון ובתמחוי לא יברור ואם בירר פטור אבל אסור בנפה ובכברה לא יברור ואם בירר חייב חטאת מתקיף לה רב המנונא מידי קנון ותמחוי קתני אלא אמר רב המנונא [ב] בורר ואוכל אוכל מתוך הפסולת ובורר ומניח אוכל מתוך הפסולת [ג] פסולת מתוך אוכל לא יברור ואם בירר חייב חטאת מתקיף לה אביי מידי אוכל מתוך פסולת קתני אלא אמר אביי [ד] בורר ואוכל לאלתר ובורר ומניח לאלתר ולבו ביום לא יברור ואם בירר נעשה כבורר לאוצר וחייב חטאת אמרוה רבנן קמיה דרבא אמר להו (א) שפיר אמר נחמני [ה] היו לפניו שני מיני אוכלין ובירר ואכל ובירר והניח רב אשי מתני פטור רבי ירמיה מדיפתי מתני חייב רב אשי מתני פטור והא תני חייב לא קשיא הא בקנון ותמחוי הא בנפה וכברה כי אתא רב דימי אמר שבתא דרב ביבי הואי ואיקלעו רבי אמי ור' אסי שדא קמייהו כלכלה דפירי ולא ידענא אי משום דסבר אוכל מתוך פסולת אסור אי משום עין יפה הוא דמכוין חזקיה אמר [ו] הבורר תורמוסים מתוך פסולת שלהן חייב לימא קסבר חזקיה אוכל מתוך פסולת אסור שאני תורמוסים

דשלקי

רש"י

אע"ג דאיכא. אחריתי בהדה דדמיא לה חשיבינהו לתרווייהו כאבות ואע"ג דחדא נינהו: **וליחשב נמי כותש.** חטין במכתשת להסיר קליפתן דהואי במקדש בסממנין אלא לאו משום דדמיא לדש לא חשיב לה דהא נמי מיפרקה מלבוש היא: **שכן עני אוכל פתו בלא כתישה.** לכך אע"ג דהואי במקדש ואב מלאכה היא כיון דתנא ליה דש לא תנא לה וזורה ובורר ומרקד סידורא דפת נינהו וכיון דהוו במקדש והכא אתחיל בסידורא דפת תנינהו כדאמרינן גבי אופה דה"ל למתני מבשל ולא אופה דלא הוה במקדש אלא משום סדורא דפת נקט ואתא הואיל ואופה בפת כמבשל בסממנין אבל כתישה עשירים הוא דלתתי וכתשי לעשות סלת נקיה אבל עניים לא טרחי הלכך לא תנא לה ומיהו ודאי אב מלאכה היא ובכלל דש היא: **רבי היא.** דיליף לקמן בפרק הזורק (דף צז:) דברים הדברים אלה הדברים למניינא: **וליפוק חדא מהנך.** או זורה או בורר או מרקד דהוו חדא ליפוק מינייהו חדא וליתני הך דהכי עדיף למיתני תרתי מהא ותרתי מהא מלמיתני ולמיכפל תלתא זימני בחדא ואיכא חדא דלא כפיל ביה מידי: **היו לפניו מיני אוכלין** גרסי' ול"ג שני: **ולא יברור.** לקמיה פריך מאי קאמר ברישא תנא בורר והדר תנא לא יברור: **ולמחר.** לצורך מחר: **וכי מותר לאפות ולבשל לבו ביום.** וה"נ אב מלאכה היא כיון דאמרת ולמחר חייב חטאת: **פחות מכשיעור.** פחות מכגרוגרת: **וכי מותר לאפות פחות מכשיעור.** נהי דחיוב חטאת ליכא איסורא מיהא איכא דקיימא לן חצי שיעור אסור מן התורה בפרק בתרא דיומא (דף עד.) והיכי קתני בורר לכתחלה: **בקנון.** כלי עץ שעושין כעין מרזב רחב מלאחריו וקצר מלפניו ובעלי מטבע עושים אותו והבורר בו קטנית נותן קטנית במקום הרחב ומנענעו והקטנית מפני שהוא סגלגל מתגלגל ויורד דרך פיו הקצר והפסולת נשאר בכלי: **פטור אבל אסור.** מותר לכתחלה לא הוי דדמי לברירה וחייב חטאת לא הוי דכלאחר יד הוא דעיקר ברירה בנפה וכברה אבל ביד לא דמי לבורר כלל: **מידי קנון ותמחוי קתני.** ה"ה נמי דפריך מידי נפה וכברה קתני אלא חדא מינייהו נקט: **אוכל מתוך הפסולת.** לא דרך ברירה היא: **ובורר ומניח לאלתר.** לאכול לאלתר שאין זה דרך בוררין: **לאוצר.** להצניע: **נחמני.** אביי: **והתניא.** לעיל חייב ואי בבורר ומניח לאלתר מותר לכתחלה הויא ופטור אבל אסור ליכא: **שבתא דרב ביבי הואי.** הגיע יומו להיות עומד ומשמש על התלמידים: **ושדא קמייהו.** ולא רצה לברור האוכל מתוך העלין ולתת לפני כל אחד ואחד אלא שטחן והם נוטלים ואוכלים ובשטוח זה נפרש האוכל מאליו: **הבורר תורמוסין.** לאחר ששלקן הוא בורר אוכל מתוך הקליפה:

דשלקי

תוספות

אע"ג דאיכא דדמיא לה חשיב (א). והא דלא חשיב שוטט ומדקדק לפי ° שהם לגמרי בכלל מיסך ואורג ולא חשיב נמי מנפץ אע"ג שבמשכן היו מנפצין פשתן לעשות יריעות ושאר דברים משום דהיינו דש ממש אלא שזה בתבואה וזה בפשתן אבל זורה ובורר ומרקד הם שלשה דברים: **שכן** עני אוכל פתו בלא כתישה. וא"ת מ"מ ליחשיב כתישת סממנין דהוה במשכן ואע"ג דעני אוכל פתו בלא כתישה לענין סממנים מלאכה חשובה היא ואומר ר"י דלאו דוקא אוכל פתו אלא ה"ה דעני צובע בסממנים בלא כתישה וא"ת מרקד נמי לא ליתני שכן עני אוכל פתו בעיסה בלוסה כדאמר בסוף פרקין ויש לומר דרוב עניים אין אוכלין בלא הרקדה אלא שלענין חלה מצטרפין הסובין דקרינן ביה מלחם הארץ כיון דיש עניים שאוכלים בעיסה בלוסה ור"ת פירש בע"א ולא נתיישב לר"י: **היו** לפניו שני מיני אוכלין גרסי'. וכן פירש ר"ח דבאוכל מתוך אוכל שייכא ברירה שבורר אותו שאינו חפץ לאכול מתוך אותו שרוצה לאכול דאותו שאינו חפץ בו חשיב פסולת לגבי אותו שחפץ לאכול וכן משמע בירושלמי דגרס הבורר אוכלים מתוך אוכלים חזקיה אמר כו': **בורר** ומניח. פי' לצורך אחרים: **וכי** מותר לאפות פחות מכשיעור. והמתרץ ס"ד דפחות מכשיעור הוי דרך אכילה: **מתקיף** לה רב המנונא מידי קנון ותמחוי קתני. פי' הקונט' דה"נ הוה מצי למיפרך מידי נפה וכברה קתני וקשה לר"י מאי קמשני רב המנונא לדידיה נמי תקשה מידי [אוכל] מתוך פסולת קתני ועוד בסמוך פירש הקונטרס והתניא חייב דהיינו הך דהכא ומשני דבנפה וכברה מיירי והיכי משני הכא מידי נפה וכברה קתני ונראה לרבינו יצחק דדוקא מקנון ותמחוי פריך וה"פ מידי קנון ותמחוי קתני כיון דנחת לפרושי דיני ברירה דביד מותר ובנפה וכברה חייב חטאת לא היה לו להניח מלשנות קנון ותמחוי דפטור אבל אסור: **בורר** ואוכל אוכל מתוך פסולת. משמע דאוכל מתוך פסולת אין דרך ברירה בכך וקשה דבריש פרק תולין (לקמן קלח.) אמרי' מה דרכו (ב) של בורר בורר אוכל מתוך פסולת וי"ל דהתם בפסולת מרובה על האוכל הוי אוכל מתוך פסולת דרך ברירה דהתם במשמר איירי וקשה לרשב"א דתנן בפ"ק דביצה (דף יד:) הבורר קטניות בי"ט ב"ש אומרים בורר אוכל ואוכל וב"ה אומרים בורר כדרכו ואמר בגמרא בד"א כשהאוכל מרובה על הפסולת אבל פסולת מרובה על האוכל ד"ה נוטל את האוכל ומניח את הפסולת ואי בפסולת מרובה על האוכל הוי אוכל מתוך פסולת דרך ברירה היכי שרי לב"ש הא אינהו אסרי לברר כדרכו וצ"ע שם: **והתניא** חייב. פי' בקונטרס דהיינו ברייתא דלעיל וקשה לר"י דלמאי דמוקמינן לה בנפה וכברה משמע דוקא לבו ביום אסור אבל לאלתר אפי' בנפה וכברה שרי ובפ"ק דביצה (גם זה שם.) משמע דבנפה וכברה אסור בכל ענין דתנן ב"ה אומרים בורר כדרכו בקנון ובתמחוי אבל לא בנפה ובכברה ולא מפליג בין לאלתר לבו ביום ועוד לכאורה לעולא דלעיל הוי בורר לבו ביום כמו לאלתר לאביי וא"כ שרי לעולא בנפה וכברה אפי' לבו ביום ובמתני' דביצה אסר לכל הפחות לבו ביום ונראה לר"י דברייתא דלעיל איירי בבורר ביד והכא דמוקמי לה בנפה וכברה ברייתא אחריתי היא ואפי' לאלתר חייב חטאת וכן משמע מתוך פירוש ר"ח דפירש שיש ג' דינין בבורר לאלתר דביד מותר לכתחלה בקנון ובתמחוי פטור אבל אסור בנפה וכברה חייב חטאת: **ולא** ידענא אי משום דקסבר אוכל מתוך פסולת אסור. פי' לא ידענא מה שלא ביררם תחלה קודם שהביאם לפניהן אבל אין לפרש מה שלא ביררם בשעה שהניח לפניהם דא"כ מאי קאמר אי משום דקסבר אוכל מתוך פסולת אסור דהא לכ"ע שרינן אוכל מתוך פסולת לאלתר:

האי

מסורת הש"ס

א) [נדרים נד: וע"ש בר"ן טעם דקרי לאביי נחמני וע"ע פירש"י בגיטין לד:].

הגהות הב"ח

(א) תוס' ד"ה אע"ג וכו' חשיב לה והא דלא חשיב. נ"ב עיין לקמן בפ' הזורק דף צז ומביאו לעיל בד' עג: (ב) ד"ה בורר וכו' דרכו של בורר נוטל אוכל ומניח פסולת:

גליון הש"ס

תוס' ד"ה אע"ג וכו' לפי שהם לגמרי בכלל מיסך. עי' לקמן דף עה ע"ב ברש"י ד"ה שוטט:

ליקוטי רש"י

הקוצר הבוצר וכו'. אורה שייך למימר בתאנים ובוצר בענבים וקוצר בתבואה וגודר בתמרים ומוסק בזיתים ומלקט בשאר אילנות [רשב"ם ב"ב פב:]. **והגודר.** כל (לקיטת) [קלית] תמרים קרי גדירה [לעיל ג.]. **פיסא.** רגב גוש עפר כלישו"ט בלע"ז [מכות ח.]. **ממלחתא.** מקום שריפת המים שעושין נגרים על שפת הים להמשיך מים לבריכות רחבות העשויות לכך וכשנתמלאו סותם המרזבין והשמש שורף את המים שמלוחין הן ונעשה מלח [לעיל סו:]. על שפת הים חורצין עשוין שמי הים נכנסים בהן והחמה מייבשתן ועושין מלח והן משרפות מים האמורין במקרא (יהושע יא) ומתרגמינן חריצי ימא [כתובות עט:]. [ע"כ שייך לדף עג:]. **פחות מכשיעור.** כגרוגרת שיעור הוא לכל איסורי מלאכות של שבת באוכלים [לעיל עו.]. **וכי מותר לאפות פחות מכשיעור.** הא מדאורייתא אסור דחצי שיעור אסור מן התורה [כדאמרינן חצי] שיעור מנין ת"ל כל חלב בפרק בתרא דיומא (עד.) [חולין צח.]. **קנון.** כלי הוא, רחב מאחד והשני עשוי כעין מרזב קצר ונותן הקטניות בתוך הרחב ומנענע והאוכל מתגלגל דרך המרזב והפסולת נשאר בכלי. **תמחוי.** קערה גדולה [ביצה יד:]. **שפיר אמר נחמני.** היינו אביי וקרי ליה הכי לפי שנתגדל בבית רבה בר נחמני [ר"ן נדרים נד:]. ונראה בעיני דעל שם שרבה בר נחמני גידל אביי בביתו ולמדו תורה שהיה יתום השיאו את שם אביו נחמני רבה שמו שהוא רבה בר נחמני [גיטין לד:]. אביי קרו ליה נחמני (ואיכא דאמרי) דבלשון גנאי קרי ליה נחמני כלומר עדיין אתה תלמידו של רב נחמן [הוריות יד. וכ"כ רש"י זבחים קיח: "נראה בעיני כי אביו של אביי כיילל שמו"]. **תורמוסים.** מין קטנית עגול כמין עדשה ורחב כמעה קטנה והוא מר מאוד עד ששולקין אותו שבע פעמים ונעשה מתוק וטוב עד שיוכל למטעמים בקנוח סעודה [ביצה כה:].

עין משפט נר מצוה

לט א ב מיי' פ"ח מהל' שבת הלכה יג סמג לאוין סה טוש"ע או"ח סימן שיט סעיף א:
מ ג מיי' שם הלכה יג טוש"ע שם סעיף ד:
מא ד מיי' שם הלכה יב טוש"ע שם סעיף א ב:
מב ה מיי' שם הלכה יג טוש"ע שם סעיף ג:
מג ו מיי' שם טוש"ע שם סעיף ה:

רבינו חננאל

המבריך החופר בארץ ומבריך הייחור וטומנו לעפר ומוציא ראש הייחור במקום רחוק. החורש. החורץ. החופר כולן מלאכה אחת הן. אסיקנא כל אלו משום חרישה. כל שהיא ליפות הקרקע בשדה חייב משום חורש וכל שהן בבית להשוות חייב משום בונה. אבל להשוות קרקע השדה חייב משום חורש. כדכתיב הלא אם שוה פניה. והוא כגון המדייר והמעדר והמכבד שהוא משוה גומות והמפעפע גושים. המסקל. הממלא בקעים שתחת הזיתים. העושה עוגיות לגפנים. המברה בחרשים. המצית אור. בחישת הקנים ובאגם תמרים. ואמת המים המכשרת צדדים לזריעה. וכל דבר שהוא להנאת קרקע חייב משום חורש. כך הוא מפורש בירושלמי וכן הא דאמר רבה היתה לו גומא וטממה אף זה משוה פני אדמתו בבית חייב משום בונה ובשדה משום חורש וקיי"ל בהני כולה כרבה. (א"ר אבא החופר גומא ואין צריך). פי' גבשושית תל של עפר שהיתה לו ונטלה בבית חייב משום בונה כו'. [אמר ר' אבא החופר גומא ואין צריך] לחפור חפירה אלא לעפר בעלמא בלבד הוא צריך. נטילת העפר אינה מלאכה משום חפירה אינו חייב שהרי לא נתכוין לחפירה. ואפילו לר' יהודה דאמר מלאכה שאינה צריכה לגופה חייב עליה ה"מ במתקן אבל האי דחפר מקלקל הוא בין בבית א) בין בשדה. וכי האי מילתא אמרו בהכל חייבין בראיה (חגיגה י') שהן כהררי' התלויין בשערה. מקרא מעט והלכות מרובות: ת"ר הקוצר הבוצר הגודר האורה כולן מלאכה אחת הן. פי' פיסה צרור של אדמה ולענין הלכה מאן דשדא פיסא לדיקלא ואתר תמרי קיי"ל כרב אשי דאמר אין דרך תלישה ולא דרך פריקה בכך. הא דאמר רבה מאן דכניף מילחא ממלחתא חייב משום מעמר קי"ל כאביי דאמר אין עימור אלא בגידולי קרקע ואינו חייב אלא (כשמעמר) [כשמעביר] ד' אמות ברה"ר. הדש (תנא) [הוא] המפרק הפסולת המחוברת באוכל ומכינתן לברירה או כברה [בזורייה] או בהרקדה. המנפץ נופץ עפרורית מן האוכל וכן המנפט מולל שבלים נמצא זורה והבורר והמרקד כולן מעבירין פסולת המעורבות באוכל ואינה מחוברת (ואינה) כגון קליפה שצריכה פירוק או כגון עפרורית שצריך ניפוץ אלא מעורבת בלבד. וכן אם

נטל בידו אדם תבוא' בתיבנא ובפסולת שיש בה וניפח בה ברוח פיו ובירר חשוב הוא כזורה. פי' בורר נוטל פסולת מבין האוכל ומשליכ' או נוטל האוכל ומניח הפסולת. מרקד שמטיל את האוכל והפסולת בכברה ונשארת האוכל ואם האוכל דק והפסולת עבה כמין תבן יוצא האוכל ונשארת הפסולת בכברה. וכיון דאסיק' כי הזורה והבורר והמרקד כולן מעין מלאכה אחת הן מפריש הפסולת מן האוכל ומשום דהוו במשכן הוו להו תלתא וחייב על כל אחת ואחת. ואקשינן ונחשוב נמי כותש שהוא מסיר קליפת החיטין מעליהן לטחון אותם להוציא סולת כגון כותש לעשות דייסא או טיסני והנה גם זה מפריש פסולת מן האוכל הוא ומשני אביי שכן עני אוכל פתו בלא כתישה כלומר כל בני אדם טוחנין בחיטין שלהן סלת הנה דרך העניים לברור ולטחון ולעשות עיסה בלוסה ואין אוכלין סלת לפיכך אין צריכין כתישה. ואע"פ דכתישה מלאכה היא דהא לגבי יו"ט גרסי' (ביצה יד.) אין כותשין במכתשת אע"פ שמותר ביו"ט אוכל נפש וכ"ש בשבת. אמר אביי האי דלא חשיב לה בהדי אבות משום דלא חשיבה שלא כל אדם אוכל בכתישה כמו שאמרנו. לפיכך אינה אלא כתולדות דמיא. רבא אמר אמאי לא חשיב לכותש בהדייהו משום דמתניתין ר' (חייא) [היא] דאמר קבלה היא בידינו אבות מלאכות [ארבעים] חסר אחת כנגד ב) עבודת המשכן ור' מ' חסר אחת שנה וכבר פירשנו להא דר' בבמה טומנין (מט:) כי המלאכות הללו מן המשכן למדתן. ואי חשיב כותש בהדייהו הרי להו מ' שלמות ור' מ' חסר אחת שנה לפי' לא תנא כותש בהדייהו ואקשינן וליפוק חדא מינייהו וניעול כותש ואסיק' אלא מחוורתא כדאביי: ת"ר היו לפניו ב' מיני אוכלין בורר ואוכל בורר ומניח ולא יברור ואם בירר חייב חטאת. ומת' מאי קאמר [א'] עולא הכי קאמר בורר ואוכל בו ביום כו' ודחאה רב חסדא ואמר וכי מותר לאפות ולבשל בו ביום כו' ופרשה אביי בורר ואוכל לאלתר בורר ומניח לאלתר. ג) שלא לאלתר לא יברור. ואם בירר נעשה כבירר לאוצר וחייב חטאת. וקיי"ל כוותיה דאמר רבה שפיר אמר נחמני ולאלתר. דאמר אביי כל זמן שיושב על השולחן ואוכל דגרסינן בתלמוד דא"י ברר אוכלין מתוך אוכלין חזקיה אמר חייב ר' יוחנן אמר פטור מתניתא פליגא על חזקיה דאמר בורר ואוכל בורר ומניח על השלחן רבין בר חייא אמר תפתר כשהיו אורחין אוכלין ראשונה ראשונה. היו לפניו ב' מיני אוכלין בורר ואוכל בורר ומניח. רב אשי [מתני פטור רי"מ] מתני חייב ואוקימנא להא דרב אשי בבורר בנפה או בכברה חייב חטאת בקנון ובתמחוי פטור וכל פטורי דשבת פטור אבל אסור נינהו. וקיי"ל כרב אשי דבתראה הוא והא דאמר חזקיה הבורר תורמוסין מתוך פסולת שלהן חייב. הלכתא היא דהא

מקשינן

חשק שלמה על רבינו חננאל א) עי' תוס' פסחים מ"ז ע"ב ד"ה כתישה: ב) עי' בגמ' כאן ולעיל מ"ט ע"ב בתוס' וצ"ע: ג) מכאן ועד סוף הענין הובא בא"ז בשם רבינו:

storage, וְחַיָּיב חַטָּאת – **and he is obligated** to bring **a *chatas.***

The Gemara comments:

אָמְרוּהָ רַבָּנָן קַמֵּיהּ דְּרָבָא – **The Rabbis stated [this explanation] in the presence of Rava,** אָמַר לְהוּ – **and he said to them:** שַׁפִּיר אָמַר נַחְמָנִי – **Nachmani said it well.**[24]

The Gemara analyzes another case involving selecting:

הָיוּ לְפָנָיו שְׁנֵי מִינֵי אוֹכָלִין – **If two types of food were** lying **before [a person]**[25] וּבֵירֵר וְאָכַל – **and he selected and ate,** וּבֵירֵר וְהִנִּיחַ – **or he selected and left** it for others to eat, רַב אַשִׁי מַתְנֵי פָּטוּר – **Rav Ashi taught** that **he is exempt** from liability, רַבִּי יִרְמְיָה מִדִּיפְתִּי מַתְנֵי חַיָּיב – while **R' Yirmiyah from Difti taught** that **he is liable.**

The Gemara challenges one of the disputants:

רַב אַשִׁי מַתְנֵי פָּטוּר – **Rav Ashi taught** that **he is exempt.** וְהָא תָּנֵי חַיָּיב – **But [the Baraisa] taught** above: HE IS LIABLE![26] – ? –

The Gemara answers:

לֹא קַשְׁיָא – **This is not a difficulty:** הָא בְּקָנוֹן וְתַמְחוּי – **This** ruling of Rav Ashi involves selecting **with a funnel or wide plate,**[27] הָא בְּנָפָה וּכְבָרָה – whereas **this** Baraisa discusses selecting **with a fine sieve or a coarse sieve.**[28]

The Gemara cites an incident involving selecting:

כִּי אֲתָא רַב דִּימִי אָמַר – **When Rav Dimi came** to Babylonia, **he related** an incident that occurred while he was in Eretz Yisrael: שַׁבְּתָא דְּרַב בִּיבִי הֲוַאי – **It was the Sabbath** turn **of Rav Bivi,**[29] וְאִיקְּלַעוּ רַבִּי אַמִּי וְרַבִּי אַסִּי – **and R' Ami and R' Assi were visiting.** שְׁדָא קַמַּיְיהוּ כַּלְכַּלָּה דְּפֵירֵי – **[Rav Bivi] threw a basket of fruits before [everyone],**[30] וְלָא יָדַעְנָא אִי מִשּׁוּם דְּסָבַר אוֹכֶל מִתּוֹךְ פְּסוֹלֶת אָסוּר – **and I do not know if** he did this **because he holds** that selecting **food from waste is forbidden,**[31] אִי מִשּׁוּם עַיִן יָפָה הוּא דְּמִכַּוֵּין – **or if he was intending** to serve **generously.**[32]

Another case:

חִזְקִיָּה אָמַר – **Chizkiyah said:**[33] הַבּוֹרֵר תּוּרְמוּסִים מִתּוֹךְ פְּסוֹלֶת שֶׁלָּהֶן – **One who selects lupine beans from** their **waste**[34] חַיָּיב – **is liable.**

The Gemara ponders:

לֵימָא קָסָבַר חִזְקִיָּה אוֹכֶל מִתּוֹךְ פְּסוֹלֶת אָסוּר – **Shall we say that Chizkiyah holds** that selecting **food from waste**[35] **is prohibited?**

The Gemara rejects this notion:

שָׁאנֵי תּוּרְמוּסִים – **Lupine beans are different,**

NOTES

24. [Rava was referring to Abaye, who was known as Nachmani because as a young orphan he was raised and educated by Rabbah bar Nachmani (the famous "Rabbah"), who called Abaye by his father's name, "Nachmani" (*Rashi* to Gittin 34b).]

According to the Gemara's conclusion, it is permitted to select only (a) the food from the waste (b) by hand (c) for immediate consumption (*Ritva* ibid.).

[We have followed the basic approach of *Ritva* to this Gemara's discussion about the proper interpretation of the Baraisa, because it is accepted by most authorities as the law. Although *Rashi* does not explicitly contradict this explanation, some commentators deduce that *Rashi,* in fact, disagrees (see, for example, *Eglei Tal* בורר 1:9). For futher discussion of this passage, see *Tosafos, Ran, Ramban, Pnei Yehoshua* and *Rosh Yosef.* For further discussion of the intricacies of this *melachah* see *Orach Chaim* §319 with commentaries.]

25. In this case *Rashi* agrees that the Gemara is discussing a mixture of two different types of food, because here the selection is for immediate consumption [as the Gemara will conclude]. Hence, the food not wanted now is considered "waste" (*Rosh Yosef;* cf. *Beur Halachah* §319 ד״ה היו לפני; see above, note 7).

26. [The Baraisa cited above concluded that if someone selects, he is liable to a *chatas.*] Why, then, does Rav Ashi rule here that the person is exempt from punishment? And if Rav Ashi is referring to selecting for immediate consumption, he should have stated that one is permitted to do so even in the first place (*Rashi;* see below, note 28).

[Rav Ashi's use of the term פָּטוּר, *exempt,* implies that he is only exempt from punishment, but the act is still Rabbinically forbidden (see General Introduction).]

27. Even though he selects with the funnel for immediate consumption, the action is prohibited (although non-punishable), since it resembles the normal method of selecting, which is done with a a sieve.

28. Therefore, he is liable to a *chatas.*

Tosafos and *Ramban* understand that, according to *Rashi,* Rav Ashi interprets the entire Baraisa as does Abaye [the first part concerning selection for immediate consumption, the second part for later consumption], but understands that it also refers to selecting with a sieve. Accordingly, in its first ruling the Baraisa declares that selecting for immediate consumption is permitted even when a sieve is used. *Tosafos* and *Ramban* object to this interpretation of Rav Ashi, and offer an alternative. However, *Rosh Yosef* contends that in *Rashi's* view Rav Ashi does not completely adopt Abaye's interpretation of the Baraisa. Rather, Rav Ashi holds that the entire Baraisa discusses selection for immediate consumption. The Baraisa first rules that selecting by hand is permitted, and then concludes that selecting with a sieve subjects one to *chatas* liability. See *Eglei Tal* ibid. and *Pnei Yehoshua* for alternative explanations of *Rashi's* view.

29. I.e. it was his particular Sabbath day to serve the students (*Rashi*).

30. Rav Bivi did not wish to select the fruits from the leaves and serve each student individually. Rather, he spread out the contents of the entire basket, which caused the fruits to become separated by themselves, and the students took their own food (*Rashi*).

31. Everyone agrees that it is permitted to remove food from waste by hand for immediate consumption. Rav Dimi's doubt concerned why Rav Bivi had not selected the fruit from the leaves *prior to* bringing the fruits to the table (*Ritva MHK* ed., in explanation of *Rashi, Tosafos;* cf. *Chidushei HaRan;* see also *Birkei Yosef* 319:2).

The possibility that Rav Bivi held that selecting for later use is prohibited (and for that reason he refrained from removing the fruits prior to bringing them to the table) raises the question why he did not simply select the fruits from the leaves *at* the table. *Maharam* explains that it would have been improper to have the guests wait while the host prepared their food in their presence.

32. [Although he would have been permitted to select each student's fruit from the leaves for later consumption, Rav Bivi wished to make a bountiful presentation of the fruit in its basket.]

33. In *Rif* and *Rosh* the text reads אָמַר חִזְקִיָּה, the formula usually used to introduce a new ruling.

34. After one cooks the lupine bean, he must remove the edible part from the shell (*Rashi*).

35. I.e. even for immediate consumption, since he did not specify otherwise (*Ritva MHK* ed.).

אע״ג דאיכא דדמיא לה חשיב לה וליחשב נמי כותש אמר אביי שכן עני אוכל פתו בלא כתישה רבא אמר הא מני רבי היא דאמר אבות מלאכות ארבעים חסר אחת ואי חשיב כותש הויא ליה ארבעים וליפוק חדא מהנך ולעייל כותש אלא מחוורתא כדאביי: ת״ר היו לפניו מיני אוכלין בורר ואוכל בורר ומניח ולא יברור ואם בירר חייב חטאת מאי קאמר אמר עולא הכי קאמר בורר ואוכל לבו ביום ובורר ומניח לבו ביום ולמחר לא יברור ואם בירר חייב חטאת מתקיף לה רב חסדא וכי מותר לאפות לבו ביום וכי מותר לבשל לבו ביום אלא אמר רב חסדא בורר ואוכל פחות מכשיעור בורר ומניח פחות מכשיעור וכשיעור לא יברור ואם בירר חייב חטאת מתקיף לה רב יוסף וכי מותר לאפות פחות מכשיעור אלא אמר רב יוסף [א]בורר ואוכל ביד בורר ומניח ביד בקנון ובתמחוי לא יברור ואם בירר פטור אבל אסור ובנפה ובכברה לא יברור ואם בירר חייב חטאת מתקיף לה רב המנונא מידי קנון ותמחוי קתני אלא אמר רב המנונא [ב]בורר ואוכל אוכל מתוך הפסולת בורר ומניח אוכל מתוך הפסולת [ג]פסולת מתוך אוכל לא יברור ואם בירר חייב חטאת מתקיף לה אביי מידי אוכל מתוך פסולת קתני אלא אמר אביי [ד]בורר ואוכל לאלתר ובורר ומניח לאלתר ולבו ביום לא יברור ואם בירר נעשה כבורר לאוצר וחייב חטאת אמרוה רבנן קמיה דרבא אמר להו [א]שפיר אמר נחמני [ה]היו לפניו שני מיני אוכלין ובירר ואכל ובירר והניח רב אשי מתני פטור רבי ירמיה מדיפתי מתני חייב רב אשי מתני פטור והא תני חייב לא קשיא הא בקנון ותמחוי הא בנפה וכברה כי אתא רב דימי אמר שבתא דרב ביבי הואי ואיקלעו רבי אמי ור׳ אסי שדא קמייהו כלכלה דפירי ולא ידענא אי משום דסבר אוכל מתוך פסולת אסור אי משום עין יפה הוא דמכוין חזקיה אמר [ו]הבורר תורמוסים מתוך פסולת שלהן חייב לימא קסבר חזקיה אוכל מתוך פסולת אסור שאני תורמוסים דשלקי

אע״ג דאיכא. אחריתי בהדה דדמיא לה חשבינהו לתרווייהו כאבות ואע״ג דחדא נינהו: וליחשב נמי כותש. חטין במכתשת להסיר קליפתן דהואי במקדש בסממנין אלא לאו משום דדמיא לדש לא חשיב לה דהא נמי מיפרקה מלבוש היא: שכן עני אוכל פתו בלא כתישה. לכך אע״ג דהואי במקדש ואב מלאכה היא כיון דתנא ליה דש לא תנא לה וזורה ובורר ומרקד סידורא דפת נינהו וכיון דהוו במקדש והכא אתחיל בסידורא דפת תנינהו כדאמרינן גבי אופה דה״ל למתני מבשל ולא אופה דלא הוה במקדש אלא משום סדורא דפת נקט ואתא הואיל ואופה בפת כמבשל בסממנין אבל כתישה עשירים הוא דלתתי וכתשי לעשות סלת נקיה אבל עניים לא טרחי הלכך לא תנא לה ומיהו ודאי אב מלאכה היא ובכלל דש היא: רבי היא. דיליף לקמן בפרק הזורק (דף צז:) דברים הדברים אלה הדברים למניינא: וליפוק חדא מהנך. או זורה או בורר או מרקד דהוו חדא ליפוק מינייהו חדא וליתני הך דהכי עדיף למיתני תרתי מהא ותרתי מהא מלמיתני ולמיכפל תלתא זימני בחדא ואיכא חדא דלא כפיל ביה מידי: היו לפניו מיני אוכלין גרסי׳ ול״ג שני: ולא יברור. לקמיה פריך מאי קאמר ברישא תנא בורר והדר תנא לא יברור: ולמחר. לצורך מחר: וכי מותר לאפות ולבשל לבו ביום. וה״נ אב מלאכה היא כיון דאמרת ולמחר חייב חטאת: פחות מכשיעור. פחות מכגרוגרת: וכי מותר לאפות פחות מכשיעור. נהי דחיוב חטאת ליכא איסורא מיהא איכא דקיימא לן חצי שיעור אסור מן התורה בפרק בתרא דיומא (דף עד.) והיכי קתני בורר לכתחלה: בקנון. כלי עץ שעושין כעין לינור רחב מלאחריו וקצר מלפניו ובעלי מטבע עושים אותו והבורר בו קטנית נותן קטנית במקום הרחב ומנענעו והקטנית מפני שהוא סגלגל מתגלגל ויורד דרך פיו הקצר והפסולת נשאר בכלי: פטור אבל אסור. מותר לכתחלה לא הוי דדמי לברירה וחייב חטאת לא הוי דכלאחר יד הוא דעיקר ברירה בנפה וכברה אבל ביד לא דמי לבורר כלל: מידי קנון ותמחוי קתני. ה״ה נמי דפריך מידי נפה וכברה קתני אלא חדא מינייהו נקט: אוכל מתוך הפסולת. לא דרך ברירה היא: ובורר ומניח לאלתר. לאכול לאלתר שאין זה דרך בוררין: לאוצר. להצניע: נחמני. אביי: והתניא. לעיל חייב ואי בבורר ומניח לאלתר מותר לכתחלה הויא ופטור אבל אסור ליכא: שבתא דרב ביבי הואי. הגיע יומו להיות עומד ומשמש על התלמידים: ושדא קמייהו. ולא רצה לברור האוכל מתוך העלין ולתת לפני כל אחד ואחד אלא שטחן והם נוטלים ואוכלים ובשטוח זה נפרש האוכל מאליו: הבורר תורמוסין. לאחר ששלקן הוא בורר אוכל מתוך הקליפה: דשלקי

אע״ג דאיכא דדמיא לה חשיב [א]. והא דלא חשיב שובט ומדקדק לפי [°] שהם לגמרי בכלל מיסך ואורג ולא חשיב נמי מנפץ אע״ג שבמשכן היו מנפצין פשתן לעשות יריעות ושאר דברים משום דהיינו דש ממש אלא שזה בתבואה וזה בפשתן אבל זורה ובורר ומרקד הם שלשה דברים: שכן עני אוכל פתו בלא כתישה. וא״ת מ״מ ליחשיב כתישת סממנין דהוה במשכן ואע״ג דעני אוכל פתו בלא כתישה לענין סממנים מלאכה חשובה היא ואומר ר״י דלאו דוקא אוכל פתו אלא ה״ה דעני צובע בסממנים בלא כתישה וא״ת מרקד נמי לא ליתני שכן עני אוכל פתו בעיסה בלוסה כדאמר בסוף פרקין ויש לומר דרוב עניים אין אוכלין בלא הרקדה אלא שלענין חלה מצטרפין הסובין דקרינן ביה מלחם הארץ כיון דיש עניים שאוכלים בעיסה בלוסה ור״ת פירש בע״א ולא נתיישב לר״י: היו לפניו שני מיני אוכלין גרסי׳. וכן פירש ר״ח דבאוכל מתוך אוכל שייכא ברירה שבורר אותו שאינו חפץ לאכול מתוך אותו שרוצה לאכול דאותו שאינו חפץ בו חשיב פסולת לגבי אותו שחפץ לאכול וכן משמע בירושלמי דגרס הבורר אוכלים מתוך אוכלים חזקיה אמר כו׳: בורר ומניח. פי׳ לצורך אחרים: וכי מותר לאפות פחות מכשיעור. והמתרץ ס״ד דפחות מכשיעור הוי דרך אכילה: מתקיף לה רב המנונא מידי קנון ותמחוי קתני. פי׳ הקונט׳ דה״נ הוה מצי למיפרך מידי נפה וכברה קתני וקשה לר״י מאי קמשני רב המנונא לדידיה נמי תקשה מידי [אוכל] מתוך פסולת קתני ועוד בסמוך פירש הקונטרס והתניא חייב דהיינו הך דהכא ומשני דבנפה וכברה מיירי והיכי משני הכא מידי נפה וכברה קתני ונראה לרבינו יצחק דדוקא מקנון ותמחוי פריך וה״פ מידי קנון ותמחוי קתני כיון דנחת לפרושי דיני ברירה דביד מותר ובנפה וכברה חייב חטאת לא היה לו להניח מלשנות קנון ותמחוי דפטור אבל אסור: בורר ואוכל אוכל מתוך פסולת. משמע דאוכל מתוך פסולת אין דרך ברירה בכך וקשה דבריש פרק תולין (לקמן קלח.) אמרי׳ מה דרכו (ג) של בורר בורר אוכל מתוך פסולת וי״ל דהתם בפסולת מרובה על האוכל הוי אוכל מתוך פסולת דרך ברירה דהתם במשמר איירי וקשה לרשב״א דתנן בפ״ק דביצה (דף יד:) הבורר קטניות בי״ט ב״ש אומרים בורר אוכל ואוכל וב״ה אומרים בורר כדרכו ואמר בגמרא בד״א כשהאוכל מרובה על הפסולת אבל פסולת מרובה על האוכל ד״ה נוטל את האוכל ומניח את הפסולת ואי בפסולת מרובה על האוכל הוי אוכל מתוך פסולת דרך ברירה היכי שרי לב״ש הא אינהו אסרי לברר כדרכו וצ״ע שם: והתניא חייב. פי׳ בקונטרס דהיינו ברייתא דלעיל וקשה לר״י דלמאי דמוקמינן לה בנפה וכברה משמע דוקא לבו ביום אסור אבל לאלתר אפי׳ בנפה וכברה שרי ובפ״ק דביצה (גם זה שם.) משמע דבנפה וכברה אסור בכל ענין דתנן ב״ה אומרים בורר כדרכו בקנון ובתמחוי אבל לא בנפה ובכברה ולא מפליג בין לאלתר לבו ביום ועוד לכאורה לעולא דלעיל הוי בורר לבו ביום כמו לאלתר לאביי וא״כ שרי לעולא בנפה וכברה אפי׳ לבו ביום ובמתני׳ דביצה אסר לכל הפחות לבו ביום ונראה לר״י דברייתא דלעיל איירי בבורר ביד והכא דמוקמי לה בנפה וכברה ברייתא אחריתי היא ואפי׳ לאלתר חייב חטאת וכן משמע מתוך פירוש ר״ח דפירש שיש ג׳ דינין בבורר לאלתר דביד מותר לכתחלה בקנון ובתמחוי פטור אבל אסור בנפה וכברה חייב חטאת: ולא ידענא אי משום דקסבר אוכל מתוך פסולת אסור. פי׳ לא ידענא מה שלא בירר תחלה קודם שהביאם לפניהן אבל אין לפרש מה שלא בירר בשעה שהניח לפניהם דא״כ מאי קאמר אי משום דקסבר אוכל מתוך פסולת אסור דהא לכ״ע שרינן אוכל מתוך פסולת לאלתר:
הא

מסורת הש״ס
א) [נדרים נד: וע״ש בר״ן טעם דקרי לאביי נחמני וע״ע פירש״י בגיטין לד:].

הגהות הב״ח
(א) תוס׳ ד״ה אע״ג וכו׳ חשיב לה והא דלא חשיב. נ״ב עיין לקמן בפ׳ הזורק דף צז ומביאו לעיל בד׳ עג: (ב) ד״ה בורר וכו׳ דרכו של בורר נוטל אוכל ומניח פסולת:

גליון הש״ס
תוס׳ ד״ה אע״ג וכו׳ לפי שהם לגמרי בכלל מיסך. עי׳ לקמן דף עה ע״ב ברש״י ד״ה שובט:

ליקוטי רש״י
הקוצר הבוצר וכו׳. אורה שייך למימר בתאנים ובוצר בענבים וקוצר בתבואה וגודר בתמרים ומוסק בזיתים ומלקט בשאר אילנות [רשב״ם ב״ב פב:]. והגודר. כל (לקיטת) [קצירת] תמרים קרי גדירה [לעיל ג.]. פיסא. רגב גוש עפר כלישנ״א בלע״ז [מכות ח.]. ממלחתא. מקום שריפת המים שעושין נגרים על שפת הים להמשיך מים לבריכות רחבות העשויות לכך וכשנתמלאו סותם החריצין והשמש שורף את המים שמלוחין הן ונעשה מלח [לעיל סו:]. על שפת הים חריצין עשויין שמי הים נכנסים בהן והחמה מייבשתן ועושין מלח והן משרפות מים האמורין במקרא (יהושע יא) ומתרגמינן חריצי ימא [כתובות עט:]. [ע״כ שייך לדף עג:]. פחות מכשיעור. כגרוגרת שיעור הוא לכל איסורי מלאכות של שבת באוכלים [לעיל ע:]. וכי מותר לאפות פחות מכשיעור. הא מדאורייתא אסור דחצי שיעור אסור מן התורה [כדאמרינן חצי] שיעור מנין ת״ל כל חלב בפרק בתרא דיומא (עד.) [חולין צח.]. קנון. כלי הוא, ראשו אחד רחב והשני עשוי כעין מרזב קצר ונותן הקטניות בתוך הרחב ומנענע והאוכל מתגלגל דרך המרזב והפסולת נשאר בכלי. תמחוי. קערה גדולה [ביצה יב:]. שפיר אמר נחמני. היינו אביי וקרי ליה הכי לפי שנתגדל בבית רבה בר נחמני [ר״ן נדרים נד:]. ונראה בעיני דעל שם שרבה בר נחמני גידל אביי בביתו ולמדו תורה שהיה יתום השיאו את שם אביו נחמני רבה סתם הוא רבה בר נחמני [גיטין לד:]. אביי קרו ליה נחמני (ואיכא דאמרי דבלשון גנאי קרי ליה נחמני כלומר עדיין אתה תלמידו של רב נחמן) [הוריות יד. וז״ל רש״י זבחים קיח: "נראה בעיני כי אביו של אביי כייליל שמו"]. תורמוסים. מין קטנית עגול כמין עדשה ורחב כמעה קטנה והוא מר מאוד עד ששולקין אותו שבע פעמים ונעשה מתוק וטוב עד שיאכל למטעמים בקנות סעודה [ביצה כה:].

לט א ב מיי׳ פ״ח מהל׳ שבת הלכה יג סמג לאוין סה טוש״ע או״ח סימן שיט סעיף א:
מ ג מיי׳ שם הלכה יג טוש״ע שם סעיף ד:
מא ד מיי׳ שם הלכה יג טוש״ע שם סעיף א ב:
מב ה מיי׳ שם הלכה יג טוש״ע שם סעיף ג:
מג ו מיי׳ שם טוש״ע שם סעיף ה:

רבינו חננאל
המבריך החופר בארץ ומבריך הייחור וטומנו לעפר ומוציא ראש הייחור במקום רחוק. החורש. החורץ. החופר כולן מלאכה אחת הן. אסיקנא כל אלו משום חרישה. כל שהיא ליפות הקרקע בשדה חייב משום חורש וכל שהן בבית להשוות חייב משום בונה. אבל להשוות קרקע השדה חייב משום חורש. כדכתיב הלא אם שוה פניה. והוא כגון המדייר והמעדר והמכבד שהוא משוה גומות והמפעפע גושים. המסקל. הממלא בקעים שתחת הזיתים. העושה עוגיות לגפנים. המברה בחרשים. המצית אור. בחישת הקנים ובאגם תמרים. ואמת המים המכשרת צדדים לזריעה. וכל דבר שהוא להנאת קרקע חייב משום חורש. כך הוא מפורש בירושלמי וכן הא דאמר רבה היתה לו גומא וטממה אף זה משוה פני אדמתו בבית חייב משום בונה ובשדה משום חורש וקיי״ל בהני כולה כרבה. (א״ר אבא החופר גומא ואין צריך). פי׳ גבשושית תל של עפר שהיתה לו ונטלה בבית חייב משום בונה כו׳. [אמר ר׳ אבא החופר גומא ואין צריך] לחפור חפירה אלא לעפר בעלמא בלבד הוא צריך. נטילת העפר אינה מלאכה משום חפירה אינו חייב שהרי לא נתכוין לחפירה. ואפילו לר׳ יהודה דאמר מלאכה שאינה צריכה לגופה חייב עליה ה״מ במתקן אבל האי דחפר מקלקל הוא בין בבית [א] בין בשדה. וכי האי מילתא אמרו בהכל חייבין בראיה (חגיגה י׳) שהן כהררי׳ התלויין בשערה. מקרא מעט והלכות מרובות: ת״ר הקוצר הבוצר הגודר האורה כולן מלאכה אחת הן. פי׳ פיסה צרור של אדמה ולענין הלכה מאן דשדא פיסא לדיקלא ואתר תמרי קיי״ל כרב אשי דאמר אין דרך תלישה ולא דרך פריקה בכך. הא דאמר רבה מאן דכניף מילחא ממלחתא חייב משום מעמר קיי״ל כאביי דאמר אין עימור אלא בגידולי קרקע ואינו חייב אלא (כשמעמר) [כשמעביר] ד׳ אמות ברה״ר. הדש (תנא) [הוא] המפרק הפסולת המחוברת באוכל ומכינתן לברירה או כברה [בורייה] או בהרקדה. המנפץ נופץ עפרורית מן האוכל וכן המנפט מולל שבלים נמצא זורה והבורר והמרקד כולן מעבירין פסולת המעורבות באוכל ואינה מחוברת (ואינה) כגון קליפה שצריכה פירוק או כגון עפרורית שצריך ניפוץ אלא מעורבת בלבד. וכן אם נטל בידו אדם תבוא׳ בתיבנא ובפסולת שיש בה וניפח בה ברוח פיו ובירר חשוב הוא כזורה. פי׳ בורר נוטל פסולת מבין האוכל ומשליכ׳ או נוטל האוכל ומניח הפסולת. מרקד שמטיל את האוכל והפסולת בכברה ונשארת האוכל ואם האוכל דק והפסולת עבה כמין תבן יוצא האוכל ונשארת הפסולת בכברה. וכיון דאסיק׳ כי הזורה והבורר והמרקד כולן מעין מלאכה אחת הן מפריש הפסולת מן האוכל ומשום דהוו במשכן הוו להו תלתא וחייב על כל אחת ואחת. ואקשינן ונחשוב נמי כותש שהוא מסיר קליפת החיטין מעליהן לטחון אותם להוציא סולת כגון כותש לעשות דייסא או טיסני והנה גם זה מפריש פסולת מן האוכל הוא ומשני אביי שכן עני אוכל פתו בלא כתישה כלומר כל בני אדם טוחנין בחיטין שלהן סלת הנה דרך העניים לברור ולטחון ולעשות עיסה בלוסה ואין אוכלין סלת לפיכך אין צריכין כתישה. ואע״פ דכתישה מלאכה היא דהא לגבי יו״ט גרסי׳ (ביצה יד.) אין כותשין במכתשת אע״פ שמותר ביו״ט אוכל נפש וכ״ש בשבת. אמר אביי האי דלא חשיב לה בהדי אבות משום דלא חשיבא שלא כל אדם אוכל בכתישה כמו שאמרנו. לפיכך אינה אלא כתולדות דמיא. רבא אמר אמאי לא חשיב לכותש בהדייהו משום דמתניתין ר׳ (חייא) [היא] דאמר קבלה היא בידינו אבות מלאכות [ארבעים] חסר אחת כנגד ג) עבודת המשכן ור׳ מ׳ חסר אחת שנה וכבר פירשנו להא דר׳ בבמה טומנין (מט:) כי המלאכות הללו מן המשכן למדתן. ואי חשיב כותש בהדייהו הוי להו מ׳ שלמות ור׳ מ׳ חסר אחת שנה לפי׳ לא תנא כותש בהדייהו ואקשינן וליפוק חדא מינייהו וניעול כותש ואסיק׳ אלא מחוורתא כדאביי: ת״ר היו לפניו ב׳ מיני אוכלין בורר ואוכל בורר ומניח ולא יברר ואם בירר חייב חטאת. ומת׳ מאי קאמר [א׳] עולא הכי קאמר בורר ואוכל בו ביום כו׳ ודחאה רב חסדא ואמר וכי מותר לאפות ולבשל בו ביום כו׳ ופרשה אביי בורר ואוכל לאלתר בורר ומניח לאלתר. ג) שלא לאלתר לא יברור. ואם בירר נעשה כבירר לאוצר וחייב חטאת. וקיי״ל כוותיה דאמר רבה שפיר אמר נחמני ולאלתר. דאמר אביי כל זמן שיושב על השולחן ואוכל דגרסינן בתלמוד דא״י ברר אוכלין מתוך אוכלין חזקיה אמר חייב ר׳ יוחנן אמר פטור מתניתא פליגא על חזקיה דאמר בורר ואוכל בורר ומניח על השלחן רבין בר חייא אמר תפתר כשהיו אורחין אוכלין ראשונה ראשונה. היו לפניו ב׳ מיני אוכלין בורר ואוכל בורר ומניח. רב אשי [מתני פטור רי״מ] מתני חייב ואוקימנא להא דרב אשי בבורר בנפה או בכברה חייב חטאת בקנון ובתמחוי פטור וכל פטורי דשבת פטור אבל אסור נינהו. וקיי״ל כרב אשי דבתראה הוא והא דאמר חזקיה הבורר תורמוסין מתוך פסולת שלהן חייב. הלכתא היא דהא
מקשינן

חשק שלמה על רבינו חננאל א) עי׳ תוס׳ פסחים מ״ז ע״ב ד״ה כתישה: ב) עי׳ בגמ׳ כאן ולעיל מ״ט ע״ב בתוס׳ וצ״ע: ג) מכאן ועד סוף הענין הובא בא״ז בשם רבינו:

עין משפט
נר מצוה

מד א מיי' פ"ז מהלכות שבת הלכה ה ופ"ח הלכה טו ופכ"א הלכה יח סמג לאוין סה טוש"ע או"ח סי' שכא סעיף יג:
מה ב מיי' שם פ"ח הלכה טו:
מו ג ד מיי' פ"ט מהל' שבת הלכה ו סמג שם:
מז ה מיי' פ"י מהלכות שבת הלכה יג:
מח ו ז מיי' פ"ט מהל' שבת הלכה ז:
מט ח מיי' פי"א מהל' שבת הלכה ז:
נ ט שם הלכה ו:
נא י מיי' פ"י שם הל' א סמג שם טוש"ע או"ח סימן שיז סעיף א:
נב כ מיי' שם הל"ט:
נג ל מיי' שם הלכה י:

מסורת הש"ם

א) ע"ז לח., ב) [פי' הערוך ע"ז באריכות מתלא בערך חלתא ע"ש דקמשיב חייב משום בונה ולא קמשיב זה שכ' רש"י הכא בד"ה חייב משום ממחק עיי"ש ובזה תבין דעת וסברת תוס' ד"ה חביתא], ג) לקמן לט., ד) בכורות כה. [תוספתא פ"י], ה) [צ"ל אמר], ו) א"ל אביי כצ"ל, ז) [פסחים עה: יומא מז.], ח) [ועי' בתוס' לקמן קיד: ד"ה אלא לקיבת ירק כו' ע"ש], ט) [לעיל מו. עי' תוס' שם ד"ה דמוליות], י) [דף עה:].

דשלקי ליה שבעא זמני ואי לא שקלי (א) ליה מסרח וכפסולת מתוך אוכל דמי: והטוחן: א"ר פפא ◦ [א] האי מאן דפרים סילקא חייב משום טוחן אמר רב מנשה [ב] האי מאן דסלית סילתי חייב משום טוחן אמר רב אשי אי קפיד אמשחתא חייב משום מחתך: והלש והאופה: אמר רב פפא שבק תנא דידן בישול סממנין דהוה במשכן ונקט אופה תנא דידן סידורא דפת נקט אמר רב אחא בר רב עוירא [ה] האי מאן [ג] דשדא סיכתא לאתונא חייב משום מבשל פשיטא מהו דתימא לשרורי מנא קא מיכוין קמ"ל דמירפא רפי והדר קמיט אמר רבה בר רב הונא [ד] האי מאן דארתח כופרא חייב משום מבשל פשיטא מהו דתימא כיון דהדר ואיקושא אימא לא קמ"ל אמר רבא [ה] האי מאן דעבד חביתא חייב משום שבע חטאות תנורא חייב משום שמונה חטאות אמר אביי האי מאן דעבד [ו] חלתא חייב אחת עשרה חטאות ואי חייטיה לפומיה חייב שלש עשרה חטאות: הגוזז את הצמר והמלבנו: אמר רבה בר בר חנה א"ר יוחנן הטווה צמר שעל גבי בהמה בשבת חייב שלש חטאות אחת משום גוזז ואחת משום מנפץ ואחת משום טווה רב כהנא אמר [ו] אין דרך גזיזה בכך ואין דרך מנפץ בכך ואין דרך טווי בכך ולא והתניא משמיה דרבי נחמיה [ג] שטוף בעזים וטוו בעזים אלמא טוויה על גבי בהמה שמה טוויה חכמה יתירה שאני תנו רבנן [ז] התולש את הכנף והקוטמו והמורטו חייב שלש חטאות ([ה] וא"ר) שמעון בן לקיש ◦ [י] תולש חייב משום גוזז [ח] קוטם חייב משום מחתך [ט] ממרט חייב משום ממחק: [י] הקושר והמתיר: קשירה במשכן היכא הואי אמר רבא (ב) שכן קושרין ביתדות אהלים [י] (קושרים) ההוא קושר על מנת להתיר הוא אלא אמר אביי שכן אורגי יריעות שנפסקה להן נימא קושרים אותה א"ל רבא תרצת קושר מתיר מאי איכא למימר וכי תימא ◦ דאי מתרמי ליה תרי (ג) חוטי קיטרי בהדי הדדי שרי חד וקטר חד ◦ [י] השתא לפני מלך בשר ודם אין עושין כן לפני ממ"ה הקב"ה עושין אלא אמר רבא ואיתימא רבי עילאי שכן צדי חלזון קושרין ומתירין: [כ] והתופר שתי תפירות: והא לא קיימא אמר רבה בר בר חנה א"ר יוחנן והוא שקשרן: [ל] הקורע על מנת לתפור: קריעה במשכן מי הוה רבה ורבי זירא דאמרי תרווייהו
שכן

רש"י

דשלקי ליה שבעא זמנין. למתקן: ואי לא שקלי ליה. לאוכל מתוך הפסולת מתוך שהוא רך ונימוק ע"י שנשלק הרבה: מסרח. והלכך אוכל נמי כל זמן שמעורב בו הוי כפסולת ומיהו אוכל הוא ומחמירין עליה למיהוי ההוא דשקיל כפסולת מתוך אוכל ול"נ הבורר תורמוסין מתוך פסולת שלהן משולקן פעם אחת ממרקין ומערין אותן המים ובורר המתולעות שלהן כמו שעושין לפולין וכן בכל פעם ופעם וזה בורר האוכל ומניח הפסולת ואי לא שלקי ליה מסרח גרסינן הלכך משלקוס פעמים ושלש חשיב ליה פסולת הואיל ואי שביק להו הכי דלא הדר שליק להו מסרחי וכשהוא נוטלן מתוך שאר מינין גרועין המעורבין בהן כפסולת מתוך אוכל דמי דהנהו שאר מינין לא מסרחי דגמר להו בישולייהו פעם ראשונה ושניה ורבינו הלוי גריס ואי שקילי ליה מסרח כשנוטלו נימוח בין אצבעותיו ונמאס הלכך ההוא דשקיל הוי כפסולת והנשאר הוי אוכל עד שחוזר ונוטלו: דפרים סילקא. בס"ס גרסינן ולא בסמ"ך כדפירש בהעור והרוטב (חולין דף קכ.) מאי קיפה פירמא מינוי"ר בלע"ז מחתכו הדק: דסלית סילתי. עצים דקים להבעיר אש: ואי קפיד אמשחתא. לחותכן במדה: מחתך. העור מקצצו במדה: ונקט אופה. דלא שייך במלאכת המשכן כלל: סדורא דפת. שהתחיל בו נקט ואופה במקום בשול דסממנין הוא דהוא בישול דפת: דשדא סיכתא. שהשליך יתד לח לתנור חם ליבשו שיתקשה: לשרורי. לחזק ואין כאן בישול: דמרפי רפי. ע"י חום האור והמים שבתוכו יוצאין ולאחר שיצאו מימיו קמיט מתקשה וכי רפי ברישא הוי בישולו: דארתח כופרא. שהתיך זפת: דהדר אקושי. חוזר ומתקשה: חביתא. של חרס: שבע חטאות. טוחן הרגבים ושותקן הדק הוי טוחן ובורר הצרורות הגסות מתוכן הרי שתים ומרקידן בנפה ומגבל הטיט דהיינו לש וממרח הטיט כשעושה הגולם שיהא חלק הרי ממחק ומבעיר את האור בכבשן ומצרפו בתוכו הרי מבשל חיובא דחופר ליכא דאינו צריך אלא לעפרה: תנור חייב שמנה. לאחר שצרפו בכבשן הוא טח עליו טפילה שיהא עב וחומו מתקיים והוא גמר מלאכתו ואמרינן לקמן (דף עה:) כל מידי דהוי גמר מלאכה חייב משום מכה בפטיש אבל גבי חבית ליכא משום מכה בפטיש דמאליה נגמרה מלאכתו בתנור: חלתא. כוורת של קנים: חייב י"א. זומר הקנים והוא צריך להם חייב משום קוצר ומשום נוטע אספס יחד הרי זה מעמר בירר יפות הרי זה בורר החליקן הרי זה ממחק עשאן דקות מאחת שתים או שלש הרי זה טוחן חתכן במדה הרי זה מחתך הסיך השתי הרי זה מיסך ארג אחת למעלה ואחת למטה כדי להעמידו הרי עושה שתי בתי נירין (ד) ארג הרי זה אורג חתך לאחר אריגתה כדי להשוותם הרי זה מכה בפטיש כדאמרינן לקמן [עה:] האי מאן דשקיל אקופי מגלימי חייב משום מכה בפטיש הרי י"א: ואי חייטיה לפומיה. לעשות לה שפה הוסיף כאן תופר וקושר שצריך לקשור לאחר התפירה ומשום בונה ליכא לחיוביה לא בחבית ולא בתנור ולא בכוורת דאין בנין בכלים. מפשיט ליכא למימר בקנים דאין הפשטה אלא בעור וי"מ שקודח נקבים בעץ שתוחבין בו ראשי הקנים של שתי ומחייב ליה משום טוחן ולא נהירא לי דההיא טחינה מלאכה שאינה צריכה לגופה היא וטוב לי לפרש שעושה אותן דקות והוי כמאן דסלית סילתי: שטוף בעזים וטוו בעזים. קרא קדריש טוו את העזים (שמות לה) בגופן של עזים משמע: חכמה יתירה. כדכתיב וכל אשה חכמת לב אבל להדיוט אין דרכו בכך והוי כלאחר יד: התולש את הכנף. נוצה גדולה מן כנף העוף: והקוטמו. לאחר שתלשו חותך ראשו שהוא דק וראוי להניחו בכר וכסת: והמורטו. לצד זנבו שהוא קשה מורט שערו מכאן ומכאן ומשליך הקנה ונותן השיער בכר וכסת: משום מחתך. דקפיד לחתוך עד מקום שהוא ראוי וגם מן הקנה אורג כובעים ועושה כובעים מכנפי עוף בלא שיער: משום ממחק. דתנן גבי עור הממחקו: ביתדות אהלים. נועצים יתידות בקרקע כדכתיב יתדות המשכן וקושרין היריעות בהן במיתריהם: קושר ע"מ להתיר הוא. וכי האי גוונא פטרינן ליה לקמן דתנן כל קשר שאינו של קיימא אין חייבין עליו: בהדי הדדי. בשני חוטין זה אצל זה: שרי חד. לאחר אריגתן מתיר האחד מפני שבולטין ונראין: וקטר חד. כלומר מניח כמו שהוא: השתא כו' (ה) אין עושין. שכשמתירו נראה הנקב ביריעה שחוטיה היו כפולין ששה והיו גסין ומתחלה היו זריזין בכך וכי מתרמו להו תרי קיטרי קושרין האחד ונותקין החוט השני מלמטה ולמעלה ומספקן בחוט ארוך וקושרין למעלה ולמטה ואין שם שנים קשרים סמוכין: צדי חלזון. לצבוע התכלת בדמו והוא כמין דג קטן ועולה אחת לשבעים שנה: קושרין ומתירין. שכל רשתות עשויות קשרים קשרים והן קשרי קיימא ופעמים שצריך ליטול חוטין מרשת זו ולהוסיף על זו מתיר מכאן וקושר מכאן: והא לא קיימא. הכי וכיון דלא קיימא לאו מלאכה היא: שקשרן. שקשר שני ראשי החוט:
דרנא

תוספות

האי מאן דפרים סילקא. דוקא בסילקא שייך טחינה אבל שאר אוכלין שרי [ס]: מהו דתימא לשרורי מנא קא מכוין. ה"פ ואין בו בשול כלל קמ"ל דנהי דלשרורי מנא קא מכוין בשול מיהא יש בו דמירפא רפי והדר קמיט וחייב אבל אין לפרש קמ"ל דלא אמרי' לשרורי מנא קא מכוין דבפרק אין מעמידין (ע"ז לח.) אמרי' גבי האי נכרי דשדא סיכתא לאתונא אי קבר בה ישראל קרא מעיקרא שפיר דמי ופריך פשיטא ומשני מהו דתימא לבשולי מנא קא מכוין קמ"ל לשרורי מנא קא מכוין: חביתא ותנורא וחלתא. פי' רש"י דמשום בונה לא מיחייב דאין בנין בכלים ואין נראה דדוקא במחזיר מטה ומנורה של חוליות אמרי' [ט] דאין בנין בכלים אבל כשעושה לגמרי כל הכלי מיחייב משום בונה דאמרינן בריש הבונה (לקמן ד' קב:) האי מאן דעייל שופתא בקופינא דמרא חייב משום בונה וצ"ע דלא ליקשי ממנפח בכלי זכוכית דסוף פרקין [י]: חכמה יתירה שאני. והעושים אותם בטלה דעתם אצל כל אדם כדאמרינן בהמצניע (לקמן ד' צב:) גבי אנשי הוצל: שכן צדי חלזון כו'. בריש אלו קשרים (לקמן קיא:) פירש בקונט' קושרין ומתירין פעמים קושרין את המכמורת ופעמים מתירין אותם:

רבינו חננאל

מקשינן ופרקינן לפרושי שמעתיה דאמרינן לימא קסבר חזקיה אוכל מתוך פסולת אסור. ושנינן שאני תורמסין דשלקי להו ז' זמני כו'. שמעינן מינה דאוכל מתוך הפסולת זולתי תורמסין שרי וכדאביי דשרי לאלתר כי היכי דלא תקשי חדא אחברתה וכבר פירשנוהו השמועה סלקא כאביי וכרב אשי וכחזקיה שמעינן מדברי שלשתן כי בורר ואוכל ביד בורר ומניח ביד שרי ולא כל היכא דבעי שרי אלא ברירת אוכל מתוך פסולת אבל פסולת מתוך אוכל לא. והאוכל מתוך פסול' דשרי [היינו] לברור ולאכול או לברור ולהניח כדי לאוכלו לאלתר על השולחן כמו שפירשנו אבל להניח שלא לאלתר לא וזה שאמרנו כי מותר לברור ולאכול ולברור ולהניח ולאוכלו לאלתר שרי ה"מ ביד אבל בקנון ובתמחוי לא ואם בירר פטור אבל אסור ובנפה ובכברה דברי הכל אסור ואם בירר נעשה כמי שבירר לאוצר בשוגג חייב חטאת ואע"פ דגרסינן (גיטין כו כח) לענין מי שאבד לו גט אם מצאו לאלתר כשר ואמרינן היכי דמי לאלתר י"א כל שלא עבר [אדם] שם ואחרים אומרים כל שלא שהה אדם שם הכא כיון דאשכחינן מפורש בתלמוד א"י כוותיה עבדינן ומסקינן לשמעתיה שיעור מה שמיסב על השולחן באותה סעודה בלבד וכענין הזה גרסינן בגמרא ביו"ט פרק א' (ביצה יג:) תנן התם המקלף שעורין מקלף אחת אחת על יד ואוכל. ואם קילף ונתן לתוך חיקו חייב. א"ר אלעזר וכן לשבת. והא רב מקלפי ליה כסי כסי ור' חייא מקלפי ליה כסי כסי אלא אי אתמר אסיפא איתמר המולל מלילות של חיטין (למחר) מנפח על יד על יד ואוכל ואם נפח ונתן לתוך ידו חייב. א"ר אלעזר וכן לשבת. מ"ט דמלאכת מחשבת אסרה תורה והאי לאו מלאכת מחשבת היא. דלא קא מכוון במלאכה אלא לאכילה בלבד ולפי' א' כיצד מנפח ואסיק' א"ר אלעזר מנפח בידו אחת ובכל כחו. הטוחן אמר רב פפא האי מאן דפרים סילקא. פי' כעין כתישה ולא כעין חיתוך חייב משום טוחן וכן מאן דסלית סילתי פי' עצי דקלים שעומדין שיבי שיבי כעין נימין וכשמפרק הנימין הללו יוצא בינית כמין קמח דק לפי' (המנפץ) חייב משום טוחן ואי קפיד אמשחתא כלומר אם מתכוין לחתוך אלו סילתי זרת זרת אורך כל אחד ואחד חייב משום מחתך. הלש והאופה אמר רב פפא שביק בישול סממנים ונקיט אפיה ולא מפרש בהדיא האי מלתא א) ואשכחן בירושלמי דאמר הכי את חמי אפיה תולדת בישול הוא ואת אמרת הכן אלא כיון דתני סדר עיסה תניתא בהדייהו: ההוא דשחק [מלח] חסף (מלא) [פלפלין] חייב משום טוחן. האי מאן דגבל גירגבסין עפר קילורין מלוגמא סממנין חייב משום לש. מאן דשדא סיכתא לאתונא חייב משום מבשל פי' הנותן יתדות לחים בכבשן כדי לייבשן לנעצם בספינות וכיוצא בהן. פי' לשרורי לחזק ויש מי שאומרים סיכתא הן גלל בהמה דקיקין אם הטילם לכבשן מה שחייב משום מבעיר הרי

הגהות הב"ח

(א) גמ' שבעא זמני ואי (לא שקלי) תא"מ. ונ"ב ס"א לא שלקי וס"א ואי שקלי: (ב) שם אמר רבה שכן קושרים ביתדו' אהלים ההוא כצ"ל. ותיבת קושרין נמחק: (ג) שם דאי מיתרמו ליה תרי קיטרי כצ"ל ותיבת חוטי נמחק: (ד) רש"י ד"ה חייב וכו' עושה שתי בתי נירין. נ"ב ולקמן ר"פ האורג פי' רש"י דהכך לאו נירין ממש כו' ע"ש בדף קה ע"א: (ה) ד"ה השתא כו' שכשמתירו נראה כצ"ל ותיבות אין עושין נמחק:

רב נסים גאון

שכן צדי חלזון קושרין ומתירין. וזה חלזון הי[ה] צובעין בדמו תכלת ומשכחת לה במנחות בפרק התכלת (דף מד.) תנו רבנן חלזון זה גופו דומה לים ברייתו דומה לדג ועולה פעם אחת לע[שבעים] שנה ובדמו צובעין תכלת לפיכך דמיו יקרים ואמר עוד (שם מב) אמר ליה אביי לרב שמואל בר יהודה הא תכילתא היכא צבעיתו אמר ליה מייתינ[ן] דם חלזון וסמנין כו'

גליון הש"ס

גמ' האי מאן דפרים סילקא חייב. עי' לקמ[ן] דף קכח ע"א ברש"י ד"ה שלא יקטוס: שם תולש חייב משום גוזז. עי' לקמן דף קז ע"ב ובחידושי רשב"א שם: שם דאי מתרמי ליה תרי חוטי. עי' לעיל דף עג ע"א תוס' ד"ה הקושר: שם השתא לפני מל[ך] וכו'. פסחים דף ע[ה] ע"ב. יומא דף מז ע"א

ליקוטי רש"י

דפרים סילקא. ד[ק] לטוחן [לקמן קכח.]. פרים. לשון פרומי[ת] מחתך [שם קיט.]. תנא דידן סידורא דפת נקט. הואיל ואופה כמבשל בסממנין [לעיל ע"א]. דשדא סיכתא. קוצליי"א בלע"ז ליב[ש] בתנור. לשרורי מנא קא מיכוין. להקשות היתד ואין דעתו לביש[ול]. לשרורי. לשון שר[יר] וקיס חזק [ע"ז לח.]. טוו בעיזים. היא היא אומנות יתירה שמעל גבי העזים טווין אותן [שמות לה, כו]. התולש את הכנף. שתולש נוצה גדולה מן כנף העו[ף] והקוטמו. לאחר שתלשו קטם ראשו. והמורטו. שמחליקה מן הנלדין ומורט מן הקנה [את] השער. תולש חייב משום גוזז. דהיינו אורמיה שדרך תולת עוף [לתולשה] ולא לגוזה [בכורות כה.]. שכן צדי חלזון קושרין ומתירין שנצרכין לפרקים להתיר קשרי רשתות הקיימות כדי לקצרן או להרחיבן [לקמן קיא:]. חלזון. חלזון עולה מן הים להרי[ם] וצובעין בדמו תכלת ונמכר בדמים יקרים [מגילה ו.]. תולעת שיוצא מן הים אחד לשבעים שנה וצובעין בדמו תכלת ולכתחי[לה] אינו נראה בכל ההר אלא חלזון אחד ולאחר שהגשמים יורדין מתמלא כולו חלזונות ונראה למורי שבילי חלזון (ראש[] משרצין כולן [סנהדרין צא. ע"ש בגה"ש]. החלזון מן הים הוא עולה אחת לשבעים שנה ומראים דמו דומה לים [חולין פט.]

חשק שלמה על רבינו חננאל א) לפנינו בגמ' מפרש בהדיא הטעם משום דסידורא דפת נקיט וכמש"כ בירושלמי. ואולי דלפני רבינו לא היה זה בנוסחת הגמ':

דְּשָׁלְקֵי לֵיהּ שִׁבְעָה זִימְנֵי – for [people] boil them seven times to sweeten them; **וְאִי לָא שָׁקְלֵי לֵיהּ מַסְרַח** – and if they do not take [the edible part] from the shell, it spoils.[1] **וְכִפְסוֹלֶת מִתּוֹךְ אוֹכֶל דָּמֵי** – Hence, it is like removing waste from food.[2]

The Gemara introduces the eighth *melachah* listed by the Mishnah:

וְהַטּוֹחֵן – GRINDING.

The Gemara elaborates:

אָמַר רַב פָּפָּא – Rav Pappa said: **הַאי מַאן דְּפָרֵים סִילְקָא** – Someone who minces beets[3] **חַיָּיב מִשּׁוּם טוֹחֵן** – is liable on account of "grinding."[4]

Another example of grinding:

אָמַר רַב מְנַשֶּׁה – Rav Menasheh said: **הַאי מַאן דְּסָלֵית סִילְתֵּי** – Someone who chops thin chips of wood out of larger pieces for kindling[5] **חַיָּיב מִשּׁוּם טוֹחֵן** – is liable on account of grinding.

The Gemara adds:

אָמַר רַב אָשֵׁי – Rav Ashi said: **אִי קָפֵיד אַמִּשְׁחָתָא** – If he is particular about the measure of each chip,[6] **חַיָּיב מִשּׁוּם מְחַתֵּךְ** – he is liable because of cutting.[7]

The Mishnah concluded its list of *melachos* involving food preparation with the following:

וְהַלָּשׁ וְהָאוֹפֶה – KNEADING AND BAKING.

The Gemara asks:

אָמַר רַב פָּפָּא – Rav Pappa said: **שָׁבַק תַּנָּא דִּידַן בִּישּׁוּל סַמְמָנִין** – Our Tanna left aside the cooking of herbs, **דַּהֲוָה בַּמִּשְׁכָּן** – which was done in the construction of the Mishkan, **וְנָקַט אוֹפֶה** – and mentioned baking, which was not![8] – ? –

The Gemara explains:

תַּנָּא דִּידַן סִידּוּרָא דְּפַת נָקַט – Our Tanna chose to mention the labors that constitute the order of making bread. He therefore listed baking rather than cooking.[9]

The Gemara now elaborates on the *melachah* of baking:

אָמַר רַב אַחָא בַּר רַב עֲוִירָא – Rav Acha bar Rav Avira said: **הַאי מַאן דְּשָׁדָא סִיכְּתָא לְאַתּוּנָא** – Someone who throws a peg into an oven to harden it[10] **חַיָּיב מִשּׁוּם מְבַשֵּׁל** – is liable on account of cooking.

The Gemara asks:

פְּשִׁיטָא – It is obvious! Why should he not be liable for cooking the peg?[11]

The Gemara answers:

מַהוּ דְּתֵימָא לְשָׁרוּרֵי מָנָא קָא מִיכַּוֵּין – What is it that you might have said – that he intends only to strengthen a utensil?[12] **קָא מַשְׁמַע לָן דְּמִירְפָּא רָפֵי וַהֲדַר קָמֵיט** – [Rav Acha bar Rav Avira] therefore informs us that [the peg] first softens and only then hardens.[13]

Another case about cooking:

אָמַר רַבָּה בַּר רַב הוּנָא – Rabbah bar Rav Huna said: **הַאי מַאן דְּאַרְתַּח כּוּפְרָא** – Someone who heats pitch and thereby liquefies it **חַיָּיב מִשּׁוּם מְבַשֵּׁל** – is liable on account of cooking.

The Gemara remarks:

פְּשִׁיטָא – It is obvious![11] – ? –

NOTES

1. Since lupine beans are boiled so many times, it gets soft and watery. Leaving the edible part with its shells will cause the former to become spoiled (*Rashi*).

2. Since the lupine bean would spoil in its present state, it is considered waste; thus, one who removes it from its pot is removing waste. Nevertheless, the lupine is also the edible portion of the mixture. Hence, we rule stringently and regard one who took some lupine beans from among the others as having removed waste from food (*Rashi's* explanation of our text of the Gemara).

Rashi prefers a variant text, which states: וְאִי לָא שָׁלְקֵי לֵיהּ מַסְרַח, *and if he does not boil it, it spoils.* That is, after lupines are cooked two or three times, they will spoil if they are not cooked further. Now, after each cooking the water is poured out and the wormy lupine beans are removed. However, even if one removes good lupine beans after two or three boilings, he will be regarded as having selected waste from food. This is because the good lupines will inevitably spoil (if not cooked further), while other inferior varieties [of lupine – see *Ritva MHK* ed.] in the mixture will not, since their cooking was completed after the first boiling. Hence, the good lupines are regarded as waste vis-a-vis the inferior objects in the mixture.

[See *Emes LeYaakov* for further discussion of these explanations along with yet another one advanced by *Rashi,* and that of *Rambam, Hil. Shabbos* 8:13.]

3. *Rashi;* cf. *Rosh.*

4. Just as grinding transforms a kernel into many smaller particles, so finely chopping a beet divides it into many pieces. However, mincing is only a *toladah* of grinding; it cannot be considered a variation of the *av* because grinding changes the consistency and appearance of the kernel, whereas mincing does not have this effect on the beet (*Rosh Yosef* to the Mishnah; see also *Sfas Emes* here).

Rashba, cited by *Ran,* writes that mincing is prohibited only when performed for later consumption. However, for immediate consumption it is permitted, similar to that which Abaye permitted (above, 74a) – selecting for immediate consumption. Other Rishonim reject this analogy, however (see, for example, *Shiltei HaGiborim*). [See *Orach Chaim* 321:12 and *Mishnah Berurah* §44, 45 for further discussion of this dispute.]

There is another debate among Rishonim concerning whether the prohibition against mincing applies only to foods like raw beets that cannot be eaten uncooked (see *Tosafos, Ritva MHK* ed., and *Orach Chaim* 321:12).

For the legal definition of "mincing" see *Beur Halachah* 321:12 ד״ה המחתך.

5. *Rashi;* cf. *Rif.*

6. That is, he wants each piece to be a specific size (*Rashi*). For example, he needs a piece of wood the size of a *tefach;* since, however, the wood in his possession is too long, he cuts it down to size (*Meiri*).

7. Because in the Mishkan they cut the skins to a specific size (*Rashi*; see above, 73a note 59).

8. Although bread was baked weekly after the Mishkan was erected [to be placed on the golden table (see *Leviticus* 24:5-8)], only labors required for the actual construction are called *avos* (*Meiri* to the Mishnah above, 73a; cf. *Rav Hai Gaon,* cited by *Eglei Tal* [introduction §5]; *Haamek Davar* to *Exodus* 39:36). Why, then, does the Tanna list אוֹפֶה, *baking,* instead of the appropriate מְבַשֵּׁל, *cooking?*

9. The Tanna chose to begin his list of *melachos* with those required for the making of bread. He therefore mentions baking, which is the equivalent of cooking herbs for the dyes (*Rashi*). The Tanna chose to list these *melachos* because it is more common to make bread than dyes (*Ran*).

10. That is, he throws in a moist peg so that the heat of the oven will dry it out and harden it (*Rashi*).

11. There is no difference between cooking herbs and cooking other items (see Gemara below, 106a).

12. Since he needs only to harden the peg you might think that he is not liable for cooking (*Rashi*). [The Gemara assumes that the *melachah* of cooking is defined by softening a hard object through fire. In the case under discussion, though, the person is apparently attempting only to strengthen the peg, not to soften it. See *Magen Avos.*]

13. The wood first softens from the heat, during which time the water evaporates; only afterward can the wood harden. Since the initial softening of the wood is needed to strengthen it, the person is liable for that act of cooking (*Rashi;* see also *Tosafos*).

We have explained the Gemara according to *Rashi. Rambam,* however, maintains (*Hil. Shabbos* 9:6) that a person is liable for the *melachah* of cooking for hardening a soft object through the medium of a fire, as well as for softening a hard object. The person should therefore be liable here for the mere act of hardening the peg. See *Lechem Mishneh, Magen Avos* and *Eglei Tal* (אופה 6:9) for an explanation of how *Rambam* understands our Gemara.

דשלקי ליה שבעא זימני ואי לא שקלי (א) ליה מסרח וכפסולת מתוך אוכל דמי: והטוחן: א"ר פפא ° א האי מאן דפרים סילקא חייב משום טוחן אמר רב מנשה ב האי מאן דסלית סילתי חייב משום טוחן אמר רב אשי אי קפיד אמשחתא חייב משום מחתך: והלש והאופה: אמר רב פפא שבק תנא דידן בישול סממנין דהוה במשכן ונקט אופה תנא דידן סידורא דפת נקט אמר רב אחא בר רב עוירא א) האי מאן ג דשדא סיכתא לאתונא חייב משום מבשל פשיטא מהו דתימא לשרורי מנא קא מיכוין קמ"ל דמירפא רפי והדר קמיט אמר רבה בר רב הונא ד האי מאן דארתח כופרא חייב משום מבשל פשיטא מהו דתימא כיון דהדר ואיקושא אימא לא קמ"ל אמר רבא ה האי מאן דעבד חביתא חייב משום שבע חטאות תנורא חייב משום שמונה חטאות אמר אביי האי מאן דעבד ו) חלתא חייב אחת עשרה חטאות ואי חייטיה לפומיה חייב שלש עשרה חטאות: הגוזז את הצמר והמלבנו: אמר רבה בר בר חנה א"ר יוחנן הטווה צמר שעל גבי בהמה בשבת חייב שלש חטאות אחת משום גוזז ואחת משום מנפץ ואחת משום טווה רב כהנא אמר ו אין דרך גזיזה בכך ואין דרך מנפץ בכך ואין דרך טווי בכך ולא והתניא משמיה דרבי נחמיה ג) שטוף בעזים וטוו בעזים אלמא טוויה על גבי בהמה שמה טוויה חכמה יתירה שאני תנו רבנן ד) התולש את הכנף והקוטמו והמורטו חייב שלש חטאות (ה) וא"ר) שמעון בן לקיש ° ז תולש חייב משום גוזז ח קוטם חייב משום מחתך ט ממרט חייב משום ממחק: י הקושר והמתיר: קשירה במשכן היכא הואי אמר רבא (ג) שכן קושרין ביתדות אהלים י) (קושרים) ההוא קושר על מנת להתיר הוא אלא אמר אביי שכן אורגי יריעות שנפסקה להן נימא קושרים אותה א"ל רבא תרצת קושר מתיר מאי איכא למימר וכי תימא ° דאי מתרמי ליה תרי (ג) חוטי קיטרי בהדי הדדי שרי חד וקטר חד ° ז) השתא לפני מלך בשר ודם אין עושין כן לפני ממ"ה הקב"ה עושין אלא אמר רבא ואיתימא רבי עילאי שכן צדי חלזון קושרין ומתירין: כ והתופר שתי תפירות: והא לא קיימא אמר רבה בר בר חנה א"ר יוחנן והוא שקשרן: ל הקורע על מנת לתפור: קריעה במשכן מי הוה רבה ורבי זירא דאמרי תרווייהו שכן

רש"י

דשלקי ליה שבעא זימנין. למתקן: ואי לא שקלי ליה. לאוכל מתוך הפסולת מתוך שהוא רך ונימוק ע"י שנשלק הרבה: מסרח. והלכך אוכל נמי כל זמן שמעורב בו הוי כפסולת ומיהו אוכל הוא ומחמירין עליה למיהוי ההוא דשקיל כפסולת מתוך אוכל ול"נ הבורר תורמוסין מתוך פסולת שלהן משלקן פעם אחת ממרקין ומערין אותן המים ובורר המתולעות שלהן כמו שעושין לפולין וכן בכל פעם ופעם וזה בורר האוכל ומניח הפסולת ואי לא שלקי ליה מסרח גרסינן הלכך משלקום פעמים ושלש חשיב ליה פסולת הואיל ואי שביק להו הכי דלא הדר שליק להו מסרחי וכשהוא נוטלן מתוך שאר מינין גרועין המעורבין בהן כפסולת מתוך אוכל דמי דהנהו שאר מינין לא מסרחי דגמר להו בישולייהו פעם ראשונה ושניה ורבינו הלוי גרים ואי שקילי ליה מסרח כשנוטלו נימוח בין אצבעותיו ונמאס הלכך ההוא דשקיל הוי כפסולת והנשאר הוי אוכל עד שחוזר ונוטלו: דפרים סילקא. במ"ס גרסינן ולא בסמ"ך כדפירש בהעור והרוטב (חולין דף קכ.) מאי קיפה פירמא מינצ"ר בלע"ז מחתכו הדק: דסלית סילתי. עצים דקים להבעיר אש: ואי קפיד אמשחתא. לחותכן במדה: מחתך. העור מקצצו במדה: ונקט אופה. דלא שייך במלאכת המשכן כלל: סדורא דפת. שהתחיל בו נקט ואופה במקום בשול דסממנין הוא דהוה בישול דפת: דשדא סיכתא. שהשליך יתד לח לתנור חם ליבשו שיתקשה: לשרורי. לחזק ואין כאן בישול: דמרפי רפי. ע"י חום האור והמים שבתוכו יוצאין ולאחר שיצאו מימיו קמיט מתקשה וכי רפי ברישא הוי בישולו: דארתח כופרא. שהתיך זפת: דהדר אקושי. חוזר ומתקשה: חביתא. של חרס: שבע חטאות. טוחן הרגבים ושוחקן הדק הוי טוחן ובורר הצרורות הגסות מתוכן הרי שתים ומרקידן בנפה ומגבל הטיט דהיינו לש וממרח הטיט כשעושה הגולם שיהא חלק הרי ממחק ומבעיר את האור בכבשן ומצרפו בתוכו הרי מבשל חיובא דחופר ליכא דאינו צריך אלא לעפרה: תנור חייב שמנה. לאחר שצרפו בכבשן הוא טח עליו טפילה שיהא עב וחומו מתקיים והוא גמר מלאכתו ואמרינן לקמן (דף עה:) כל מידי דהוי גמר מלאכה חייב משום מכה בפטיש אבל גבי חבית ליכא משום מכה בפטיש דמאליה נגמרה מלאכתו בתנור: חלתא. כוורת של קנים: חייב י"א. זומר הקנים והוא צריך להם חייב משום קוצר ומשום נוטע אספס יחד הרי זה מעמר בירר יפות הרי זה בורר החליקן הרי זה ממחק עשאן דקות מאחת שתים או שלש הרי זה טוחן חתכן במדה הרי זה מחתך הסיך השתי הרי זה מיסך ארג אחת למעלה ואחת למטה כדי להעמידו הרי עושה שתי בתי נירין (ד) ארג הרי זה אורג חתך לאחר אריגתה כדי להשוותם הרי זה מכה בפטיש כדאמרינן לקמן [עה:] האי מאן דשקיל אקופי מגלימי חייב משום מכה בפטיש הרי י"א: ואי חייטיה לפומיה. לעשות לה שפה הוסיף כאן תופר וקושר שצריך לקשור לאחר התפירה ומשום בונה ליכא לחיוביה לא בחבית ולא בתנור ולא בכוורת דאין בנין בכלים. מפשיט ליכא למימר בקנים דאין הפשטה אלא בעור וי"מ שקודח נקבים בעץ שתוחבין בו ראשי הקנים של שתי ומחייב ליה משום טוחן ולא נהירא לי דההיא טחינה מלאכה שאינה צריכה לגופה היא וטוב לי לפרש שעושה אותן דקות והוי כמאן דסלית סילתי: שטוף בעזים וטוו בעזים. קרא קדריש טוו את העזים (שמות לה) בגופן של עזים משמע: חכמה יתירה. כדכתיב וכל אשה חכמת לב אבל להדיוט אין דרכו בכך והוי כלאחר יד: התולש את הכנף. נוצה גדולה מן כנף העוף: והקוטמו. לאחר שתלשו חותך ראשו שהוא דק וראוי להניחו בכר וכסת: והמורטו. לצד זנבו שהוא קשה מורט שערו מכאן ומכאן ומשליך הקנה ונותן השיער בכר וכסת: משום מחתך. דקפיד לחתוך עד מקום שהוא ראוי וגם מן הקנה אורג כובעים ועושה כובעים מכנפי עוף בלא שיער: משום ממחק. דתנן גבי עור הממחקו: ביתדות אהלים. נועצים יתידות בקרקע כדכתיב יתדות המשכן וקושרין היריעות בהן במיתריהם: קושר ע"מ להתיר הוא. וכי האי גוונא פטרינן ליה לקמן דתנן כל קשר שאינו של קיימא אין חייבין עליו: בהדי הדדי. בשני חוטין זה אצל זה: שרי חד. לאחר אריגתן מתיר האחד מפני שבולטין ונראין: וקטר חד. כלומר מניח כמו שהוא: השתא כו' (ה) אין עושין. שכשמתירו נראה הנקב ביריעה שחוטיה היו כפולין ששה והיו גסין ומתחלה היו זריזין בכך וכי מתרמו להו תרי קיטרי קושרין האחד ומתקן החוט השני מלמטה ולמעלה ומספקן בחוט ארוך וקושרין למעלה ולמטה ואין שם שנים קשרים סמוכין: צדי חלזון. לצבוע התכלת בדמו והוא כמין דג קטן ועולה אחת לשבעים שנה: קושרין ומתירין. שכל רשתות עשויות קשרים קשרים והן קשרי קיימא ופעמים שצריך ליטול חוטין מרשת זו ולהוסיף על זו מתיר מכאן וקושר מכאן: והא לא קיימא. הכי וכיון דלא קיימא לאו מלאכה היא: שקשרן. שקשר שני ראשי החוט: דרגא

תוספות

האי מאן דפרים סילקא. דוקא בסילקא שייך טחינה אבל שאר אוכלין שרי ח): **מהו** דתימא לשרורי מנא קא מכוין. ה"פ ואין בו בשול כלל קמ"ל דנהי דלשרורי מנא קא מכוין בשול מיהא יש בו דמירפא רפי והדר קמיט וחייב אבל אין לפרש קמ"ל דלא אמרי' לשרורי מנא קא מכוין דבפרק אין מעמידין (ע"ז לח.) אמרי' גבי האי נכרי דשדא סיכתא לאתונא אי קבר בה ישראל קרא מעיקרא שפיר דמי ופריך פשיטא ומשני מהו דתימא לבשולי מנא קא מכוין קמ"ל לשרורי מנא קא מכוין: **חביתא** ותנורא וחלתא. פי' רש"י דמשום בונה לא מיחייב דאין בנין בכלים ואין נראה דדוקא במחזיר מטה ומנורה של חוליות אמרי' ט) דאין בנין בכלים אבל כשעושה לגמרי כל הכלי מיחייב משום בונה דאמרינן בריש הבונה (לקמן ד' קב:) האי מאן דעייל שופתא בקופינא דמרא חייב משום בונה וצ"ע דלא ליקשי ממנפח בכלי זכוכית דסוף פרקין י): **חכמה** יתירה שאני. והעושים אותם בטלה דעתם אצל כל אדם כדאמרינן בהמצניע (לקמן ד' צב:) גבי אנשי הוצל: **שכן** צדי חלזון כו'. בריש אלו קשרים (לקמן קיא:) פירש בקונט' קושרין ומתירין פעמים קושרין את המכמורת ופעמים מתירין אותם:

עין משפט נר מצוה

מד א מיי' פ"ז מהלכות שבת הלכה ה ופ"ח הלכה טו ופכ"א הלכה יח סמג לאוין סה טוש"ע או"ח סי' שכא סעיף יב:
מה ב מיי' שם פ"ח הלכה טו:
מו ג ד מיי' פ"ט מהל' שבת הלכה ו סמג שם:
מז ה מיי' פ"י מהלכות שבת הלכה יג:
מח ו ז מיי' פ"ט מהל' שבת הלכה ז:
מט ח מיי' פי"א מהל' שבת הלכה ז:
נ ט שם הלכה ו:
נא י מיי' פ"י שם הל' א סמג שם טוש"ע או"ח סימן שיז סעיף א:
נב כ מיי' שם הל"ט:
נג ל מיי' שם הלכה י:

רבינו חננאל

מקשינן ופרקינן לפרושי שמעתיה דאמרינן לימא קסבר חזקיה אוכל מתוך פסולת אסור. ושנינן שאני תורמסין דשלקי להו ז' זמני כו'. שמעינן מינה דאוכל מתוך הפסולת זולתי תורמסין שרי וכדאביי דשרי לאלתר כי היכי דלא תקשי חדא אחברתה וכבר פירשנוהו השמועה סלקא כאביי וכרב אשי וכחזקיה שמעינן מדברי שלשתן כי בורר ואוכל ביד בורר ומניח ביד שרי ולא כל היכא דבעי שרי אלא ברירת אוכל מתוך פסולת אבל פסולת מתוך אוכל לא. והאוכל מתוך פסול' דשרי [היינו] לברור ולאכול או לברור ולהניח כדי לאוכלו לאלתר על השולחן כמו שפירשנו אבל להניח שלא לאלתר לא וזה שאמרנו כי מותר לברור ולאכול ולברור ולהניח ולאוכלו לאלתר שרי ה"מ ביד אבל בקנון ובתמחוי לא ואם בירר פטור אבל אסור ובנפה ובכברה דברי הכל אסור ואם בירר נעשה כמי שבירר לאוצר בשוגג חייב חטאת ואע"פ דגרסינן (גיטין כז כח) לענין מי שאבד לו גט אם מצאו לאלתר כשר ואמרינן היכי דמי לאלתר י"א כל שלא עבר [אדם] שם ואחרים אומרים כל שלא שהה אדם שם הכא כיון דאשכחינן מפורש בתלמוד א"י כוותיה עבדינן ומסקינן לשמעתיה שיעור מה שמיסב על השולחן באותה סעודה בלבד וכענין הזה גרסינן בגמרא ביו"ט פרק א' (ביצה יג:) תנן התם המקלף שעורין מקלף אחת אחת על יד ואוכל. ואם קילף ונתן לתוך חיקו חייב. א"ר אלעזר וכן לשבת. והא רב מקלפי ליה כסי כסי ור' חייא מקלפי ליה כסי כסי אלא אי אתמר אסיפא איתמר המולל מלילות של חיטין (למחר) מנפח על יד על יד ואוכל ואם נפח ונתן לתוך ידו חייב. א"ר אלעזר וכן לשבת. מ"ט דמלאכת מחשבת אסרה תורה והאי לאו מלאכת מחשבת היא. דלא קא מכוון במלאכה אלא לאכילה בלבד ולפי' א' כיצד מנפח ואסיק' א"ר אלעזר מנפח בידו אחת ובכל כחו. הטוחן אמר רב פפא האי מאן דפרים סילקא. פי' כעין כתישה ולא כעין חיתוך חייב משום טוחן וכן מאן דסלית סילתי פי' עצי דקלים שעומדין שיבי שיבי כעין נימין וכשמפרק הנימין הללו יוצא בינית כמין קמח דק לפי' (המנפץ) חייב משום טוחן ואי קפיד אמשחתא כלומר אם מתכוין לחתוך אלו סילתי זרת זרת אורך כל אחד ואחד חייב משום מחתך. הלש והאופה אמר רב פפא שביק בישול סממנים ונקיט אפיה ולא מפרש בהדיא האי מלתא א) ואשכחן בירושלמי דאמר הכי את חמי אפיה תולדת בישול הוא ואת אמרת הכן אלא כיון דתני סדר עיסה תניתא בהדייהו: ההוא דשחק [מלח] חסף (מלא) [פלפלין] חייב משום טוחן. האי מאן דגבל גירגבסין עפר קילורין מלוגמא סממנין חייב משום לש. מאן דשדא סיכתא לאתונא חייב משום מבשל פי' הנותן יתידות לחים בכבשן כדי לייבשן לנעצם בספינות וכיוצא בהן. פי' לשרורי לחזק ויש מי שאומרים סיכתא הן גלל בהמה דקיקין אם הטילם לכבשן מה שחייב משום מבעיר הרי

מסורת הש"ס

א) ע"ז לח., ב) [פי' הערוך ע"ז בהליכות תמלא בערך חלתא ע"ש דקמשיב חייב משום בונה ולא קחשיב זה שכ' רש"י הכא בד"ה חייב משום ממחק עיי"ש וכזה תבין דעת וסברת תוס' ד"ה חביתא], ג) לקמן לט., ד) בכורות כה. [תוספתא פ"י], ה) [צ"ל אמר], ו) א"ל אביי כל"ל, ז) [פסחים עה: יומא מז.], ח) [ועי' בתוס' לקמן קיד: ד"ה אלא לקינבת ירק כו' ע"ש], ט) [לעיל מו. עי' תוס' שם ד"ה דמוליות], י) [דף עה:].

הגהות הב"ח

(א) גמ' שבעא זמני ואי (לא שקלי) תא"מ. ונ"ב ס"א לא שלקי וס"א ואי שקלי: (ב) שם אמר רבה שכן קושרים ביתדו' אהלים ההוא כצ"ל. ותיבת קושרין נמחק: (ג) שם דאי מיתרמו ליה תרי קיטרי כצ"ל ותיבת חוטי נמחק: (ד) רש"י ד"ה חייב וכו' עושה שתי בתי נירין. נ"ב ולקמן ר"פ האורג פי' רש"י דהכך לאו נירין ממש כו' ע"ש בדף קה ע"א: (ה) ד"ה השתא כו' שכשמתירו נראה כצ"ל ותיבות אין עושין נמחק:

רב נסים גאון

שכן צדי חלזון קושרין ומתירין. וזה חלזון היו צובעין בדמו תכלת ומשכחת לה במנחות בפרק התכלת (דף מד) תנו רבנן חלזון זה גופו דומה לים ברייתו דומה לדג ועולה פעם אחת לע' שנה ובדמו צובעין תכלת לפיכך דמיו יקרים ואמרו עוד (שם מב) אמר ליה אביי לרב שמואל בר יהודה הא תכילתא היכא צבעיתו אמר ליה מייתינן דם חלזון וסמנין כו':

גליון הש"ס

גמ' האי מאן דפרים סילקא חייב. עי' לקמן דף קמ ע"א ברש"י ד"ה שלא יקטום: שם תולש חייב משום גוזז. עי' לקמן דף קז ע"ב ובחידושי רשב"א שם: שם דאי מתרמי ליה תרי חוטי. עי' לעיל דף עג ע"א תוס' ד"ה הקושר: שם השתא לפני מלך וכו'. פסחים דף עה ע"ב. יומא דף מז ע"א:

ליקוטי רש"י

דפרים סילקא. דמי לטוחן [לקמן קכח.]. פרים. לשון פרומים מחתך [שם קיט.]. תנא דידן סידורא דפת נקט. הואיל ואופה בפת כמבשל בסממנין [לעיל ע"א]. דשדא סיכתא. קונליי"א בלע"ז ליבשה בתנור. לשרורי מנא קא מיכוין. להקשות את היתד ואין דעתו לבישול. לשרורי. לשון שריר וקיים חזק [ע"ז לח.]. טוו בעיזים. היא היתה אומנות יתירה שמעל גבי העזים טווין אותן [שמות לה, כו]. התולש את הכנף. שתולש נוצה גדולה מן כנף העוף. והקוטמו. לאחר שתלשו קטם ראשו. והמורטו. שמחליקה מן הגלדין ומורט מן הקנה [את] השער. תולש חייב משום גוזז. דהיינו אורמיה שדרך נוצת עוף [לתולשה] ולא לגוזה [בכורות כה.]. שכן צדי חלזון קושרין ומתירין. שנצרכין לפרקים להתיר קשרי רשתות הקיימות כדי לקצרן או להרחיבן [לקמן קיא:]. חלזון. חלזון עולה מן הים להרים ולוצעין בדמו תכלת ונמכר בדמים יקרים [מגילה ו.]. תולעת שיוצאה מן הים אחד לשבעים שנה ולוצעין בדמו תכלת ולכתחלה אינו נראה בכל ההר אלא חלזון אחד ולמחר שהגשמים יורדין מתמלא כולו חלזונות ונראה למורי שבילי חלזון (ראשון) משרילין כולן [סנהדרין צא. ע"ש בגה"ש]. החלזון מן הים הוא עולה אחת לשבעים שנה ומראית דמו דומה לים [חולין פט.].

חשק שלמה על רבינו חננאל א) לפנינו בגמ' מפרש בהדיא הטעם משום דסידורא דפת נקיט וכמש"כ בירושלמי. ואולי דלפני רבינו לא היה זה בנוסחת הגמ':

The Gemara answers:

מַהוּ דְּתֵימָא כֵּיוָן דַּהֲדַר וְאִיקוּשָׁא אֵימָא לֹא – **What is it that you might have said** – that **since [the substance] subsequently hardens, say** that he is **not** liable?[14] קָא מַשְׁמַע לָן – **[Rabbah bar Rav Huna]** therefore **informs us** that the person is nevertheless liable.[15]

The Gemara discusses a case involving multiple violations:

אָמַר רָבָא – **Rava said:** הַאי מַאן דְּעָבַד חָבִיתָא – **Someone who makes an** earthenware **barrel** חַיָּיב מִשּׁוּם שֶׁבַע חַטָּאוֹת – **is liable to seven *chatas* offerings** because he has performed seven *melachos.*[16] תַּנּוּרָא – If he makes an earthenware **oven,** he has performed an additional *melachah* חַיָּיב מִשּׁוּם שְׁמוֹנֶה חַטָּאוֹת – and **is** therefore **liable to eight *chatas* offerings.**[17]

The Gemara presents another case of multiple violations:

אָמַר אַבָּיֵי – **Abaye said:** הַאי מַאן דְּעָבַד חַלְתָּא – **Someone who makes a large round receptacle** from reeds חַיָּיב אַחַת עֶשְׂרֵה חַטָּאוֹת – **is liable to eleven *chatas* offerings** since he has performed eleven *melachos.*[18] וְאִי חַיְּיטֵיהּ לְפוּמֵּיהּ – **And if he sews its mouth,**[19] חַיָּיב שְׁלֹשׁ עֶשְׂרֵה חַטָּאוֹת – **he is liable to thirteen *chatas* offerings.**[20]

The Mishnah began its list of primary labors required for the manufacture of clothing with the following two:

הַגּוֹזֵז אֶת הַצֶּמֶר וְהַמְלַבְּנוֹ – SHEARING WOOL AND WHITENING IT.

The Gemara discusses these *melachos*:

אָמַר רַבָּה בַּר בַּר חָנָה אָמַר רַבִּי יוֹחָנָן – **Rabbah bar bar Chanah said in the name of R' Yochanan:** הַטּוֹוֶה צֶמֶר שֶׁעַל גַּבֵּי בְהֵמָה בְּשַׁבָּת – **One who spins wool that is** still **on the back of an animal on the Sabbath** חַיָּיב שָׁלֹשׁ חַטָּאוֹת – **is obligated** to bring **three *chatas* offerings:** אַחַת מִשּׁוּם גּוֹזֵז – **one on account of "shearing,"** וְאַחַת מִשּׁוּם מְנַפֵּץ – **one on account of "disentangling"** וְאַחַת מִשּׁוּם טוֹוֶה – **and one on account of "spinning."**[21]

The Gemara cites a dissenting opinion:

רַב כַּהֲנָא אָמַר – **Rav Kahana said:** אֵין דֶּרֶךְ גְּזִיזָה בְּכָךְ – **This is not the usual manner of shearing,** וְאֵין דֶּרֶךְ מְנַפֵּץ בְּכָךְ – **and this is not the usual manner of disentangling,** וְאֵין דֶּרֶךְ טְוִוי בְּכָךְ – **and this is not the usual manner of spinning.**[22]

The Gemara challenges Rav Kahana's opinion:

וְלֹא – **And** this is **not** the usual way of performing these labors? וְהָתַנְיָא מִשְּׁמֵיהּ דְּרַבִּי נְחֶמְיָה – **But it was taught in a Baraisa in the name of R' Nechemyah:** שָׁטְפוּ בָּעִזִּים וְטָווּ בָּעִזִּים – THEY WASHED the hairs ON THE GOATS AND THEY SPUN them while ON THE GOATS.[23] אַלְמָא טְווִיָּה עַל גַּבֵּי בְהֵמָה שְׁמָהּ טְווִיָּה – **We thus** see that **spinning on the back of an animal is considered** a normal manner of **spinning.** – ? –

The Gemara answers:

חָכְמָה יְתֵירָה שָׁאנֵי – An act performed with the **extraordinary wisdom** of those who constructed the Mishkan **is different** than the acts of ordinary people.[24]

NOTES

14. [I would think that since, in fact, the effect of his cooking is only temporary, his act is not a *melachah.*]

15. However, since the effect of the *melachah* [i.e. the liquification] does not last, this act is considered only a *toladah* of cooking. Similarly, in the previous case, according to *Rashi's* view that one is liable for the initial softening of the wood, that act is only a *toladah* since the wood hardens afterward (*Eglei Tal* אופה 6:9:6). [See above, note 13.]

16. These are: (1) **Grinding** clods of earth into fine particles; (2) **sorting** out the large pebbles; (3) **sifting** the dirt in a sieve; (4) **kneading** the dirt with water; (5) **smoothing** the mud when forming the structure of the barrel; (6) **kindling** the fire in the oven; and (7) **baking** the barrel in the oven to harden it (*Rashi*).

Rashi notes that the barrel maker is not liable for plowing when he initially digs up the dirt, since he needed only the dirt, not the resultant hole (see above, 73b).

17. He is liable for the seven *melachos* performed in the making of a barrel, and in addition is liable for adding an extra layer of mud for insulation. This act is included in the category of *striking the final blow,* since it is the last step in manufacturing an oven. There is no comparable "final blow" in the manufacture of a barrel, however, since the barrel is automatically completed during the baking process (*Rashi;* see *Minchas Chinuch* §32 האופה; *Sfas Emes* ד״ה אמר רב אחא).

18. They are: (1) and (2) Uprooting the reeds that he will use (he is liable because of **reaping** and also because of **planting** if this act will promote the growth of the remaining plant – see above, 73b); (3) **gathering** the reeds together; (4) **selecting** the good ones; (5) **smoothing** them; (6) slicing them very thin (liable because of **grinding**); (7) **cutting** them to a specific size; (8) **setting up the warp;** (9) looping two reeds around the warp reeds, thus locking them into position [see *Rashi* below, 105a ד״ה בנפה] (equivalent to **setting heddles**); (10) **weaving** the basket [see diagram for these last three actions]; (11) cutting the protruding reeds after weaving to even them out **(striking the final blow)** (*Rashi*).

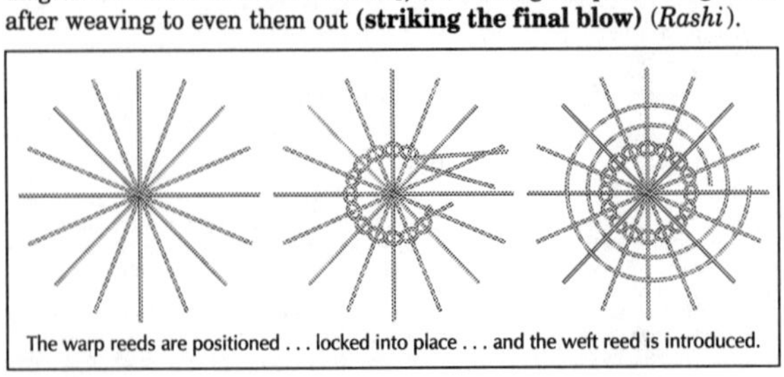

The warp reeds are positioned . . . locked into place . . . and the weft reed is introduced.

19. That is, if he adds a border around the opening of the receptacle (*Rashi*).

20. For he has performed the additional two labors of (1) **sewing** on the border and then (2) **tying** the threads (*Rashi*).

Rashi writes that in none of the above cases is there liability for building, since that *melachah* does not involve utensils (see below, 122b). *Tosafos* and *Ritva* (*MHK* ed.) disagree, arguing that the aforementioned principle applies only when parts are attached to preexisting utensils; when a new utensil is created, however, there is liability for building (see *Pnei Yehoshua* and *Chidushei R' Mordechai Banet*). [See below, 75b note 20.]

Furthermore, *Rashi* writes, the receptacle maker incurs no liability for skinning when he peels the reeds, because that *melachah* applies only to skinning hides of animals (see *Rosh Yosef*).

21. First he combed the animal's hair, then he spun it, and only afterward did he cut off the threads.

22. Normally, wool is first sheared from an animal and afterward combed and spun. Here, where he combed and spun still-attached wool, he did not perform these two *melachos* in the usual manner. Furthermore, cutting off already-spun wool is an atypical method of shearing. [*Rosh* notes that since the wool will be taken off by hand, it is not the usual labor of shearing.] Hence, because he performed each labor in an unusual manner, he is not liable to any *chatas* offering (see General Introduction).

23. Scripture states somewhat curiously (*Exodus* 35:26): טָווּ אֶת־הָעִזִּים, *[They] spun the goats,* which is interpreted to mean that the Jewish women of the Wilderness generation spun still-attached goat hairs into threads (*Rashi,* from Gemara below, 99a). By combing and spinning the hair while it was still growing, they were able to preserve much of its luster (*Sforno* loc. cit.).

24. The beginning of the previously cited verse states: וְכָל־הַנָּשִׁים אֲשֶׁר נָשָׂא לִבָּן אֹתָנָה בְּחָכְמָה, *All the woman whose hearts inspired them with wisdom.* It was thus extraordinary wisdom that enabled those people to spin wool that was still attached to the animal. However, ordinary people do not normally spin that way; hence, doing so is considered an unusual manner of performing that *melachah,* for which one is not liable (see *Rashi*)

[*Rashash* notes that the citation of verse 25 (וְכָל־אִשָּׁה חַכְמַת־לֵב, *and every wisehearted woman*) in our version of *Rashi* is apparently mistaken, because the Gemara below (99a) understands that verse to be referring to work done with the wool, which required only ordinary wisdom. The proper citation should be the verse under discussion (v. 26), נָשָׂא לִבָּן אֹתָנָה בְּחָכְמָה, which the Gemara there ties to the extraordinary wisdom needed to spin the goat hairs on the backs of the goats.]

תוספות

האי מאן דפרים סילקא. דוקא בסילקא שייך טחינה אבל שאר אוכלין שרי (ה): **מהו** דתימא לשרורי מנא קא מכוין. ה"פ ואין בו בשול כלל קמ"ל דנהי דלשרורי מנא קא מכוין בשול מיהא יש בו דמירפא רפי והדר קמיט וחייב אבל אין לפרש קמ"ל דלא אמרי' לשרורי מנא קא מכוין דבפרק אין מעמידין (ע"ז לח.) אמרי' גבי האי נכרי דשדא סיכתא לאתונא אי קבר בה ישראל קרא מעיקרא שפיר דמי ופריך פשיטא ומשני מהו דתימא לבשולי מנא קא מכוין קמ"ל לשרורי מנא קא מכוין: **חביתא** ותנורא וחלתא. פי' רש"י דמשום בונה לא מיחייב דאין בנין בכלים ואין נראה דדוקא במחזיר מטה ומנורה של חוליות אמרי' (ט) דאין בנין בכלים אבל כשעושה לגמרי כל הכלי מיחייב משום בונה דאמרינן בריש הבונה (לקמן ד' קב:) האי מאן דעייל שופתא בקופינא דמרא חייב משום בונה וצ"ע דלא ליקשי ממנפח בכלי זכוכית דסוף פרקין (י): **חכמה** יתירה שאני. והעושים אותם בטלה דעתם אצל כל אדם כדאמרינן בהמצניע (לקמן ד' צב:) גבי אנשי הוצל: **שכן** צדי חלזון כו'. בריש אלו קשרים (לקמן קיא:) פירש בקונט' קושרין ומתירין פעמים קושרין את המכמורת ופעמים מתירין אותם:

גמרא

דשלקי ליה שבעא זימני ואי לא שקלי (א) ליה מסרח וכפסולת מתוך אוכל דמי: והטוחן: א"ר פפא ◦ האי מאן דפרים סילקא חייב משום טוחן אמר רב מנשה האי מאן דסלית סילתי חייב משום טוחן אמר רב אשי אי קפיד אמשחתא חייב משום מחתך: והלש והאופה: אמר רב פפא שבק תנא דידן בישול סממנין דהוה במשכן ונקט אופה תנא דידן סידורא דפת נקט אמר רב אחא בר רב עוירא (א) האי מאן דשדא סיכתא לאתונא חייב משום מבשל פשיטא מהו דתימא לשרורי מנא קא מיכוין קמ"ל דמירפא רפי והדר קמיט אמר רבה בר רב הונא האי מאן דארתח כופרא חייב משום מבשל פשיטא מהו דתימא כיון דהדר ואיקושא אימא לא קמ"ל אמר רבא האי מאן דעבד חביתא חייב משום שבע חטאות תנורא חייב משום שמונה חטאות אמר אביי האי מאן דעבד (ג) חלתא חייב אחת עשרה חטאות ואי חייטיה לפומיה חייב שלש עשרה חטאות: הגוזז את הצמר והמלבנו: אמר רבה בר בר חנה א"ר יוחנן הטווה צמר שעל גבי בהמה בשבת חייב שלש חטאות אחת משום גוזז ואחת משום מנפץ ואחת משום טווה רב כהנא אמר אין דרך גזיזה בכך ואין דרך מנפץ בכך ואין דרך טווי בכך ולא והתניא משמיה דרבי נחמיה (ג) שטוף בעזים וטוו בעזים אלמא טוויה על גבי בהמה שמה טוויה חכמה יתירה שאני תנו רבנן התולש את הכנף והקוטמו והמורטו חייב שלש חטאות (וא"ר) שמעון בן לקיש ◦ תולש חייב משום גוזז קוטם חייב משום מחתך ממרט חייב משום ממחק: הקושר והמתיר: קשירה במשכן היכא הואי אמר רבא (ב) שכן קושרין ביתדות אהלים (קושרים) ההוא קושר על מנת להתיר הוא אלא אמר אביי שכן אורגי יריעות שנפסקה להן נימא קושרים אותה א"ל רבא תרצת קושר מתיר מאי איכא למימר וכי תימא ◦ דאי מתרמי ליה תרי (ג) חוטי קיטרי בהדי הדדי שרי חד וקטר חד ◦ השתא לפני מלך בשר ודם אין עושין כן לפני ממ"ה הקב"ה עושין אלא אמר רבא ואיתימא רבי עילאי שכן צדי חלזון קושרין ומתירין: והתופר שתי תפירות: והא לא קיימא אמר רבה בר בר חנה א"ר יוחנן והוא שקשרן: הקורע על מנת לתפור: קריעה במשכן מי הוה רבה ורבי זירא דאמרי תרווייהו שכן

רש"י

דשלקי ליה שבעא זימנין. למתקן: ואי לא שקלי ליה. לאוכל מתוך הפסולת מתוך שהוא רך ונימוק ע"י שנשלק הרבה: מסרח. והלכך אוכל נמי כל זמן שמעורב בו הוי כפסולת ומיהו אוכל הוא ומחמירין עליה למיהוי ההוא דשקיל כפסולת מתוך אוכל ול"נ הבורר תורמוסין מתוך פסולת שלהן משלקן פעם אחת ממרקין ומערין אותן המים ובורר המתולעות שלהן כמו שעושין לפולין וכן בכל פעם ופעם וזה בורר האוכל ומניח הפסולת ואי לא שלקי ליה מסרח גרסינן הלכך משלקום פעמים ושלש חשיב ליה פסולת הואיל ואי שביק להו הכי דלא הדר שליק להו מסרחי וכשהוא נוטלן מתוך שאר מינין גרועין המעורבין בהן כפסולת מתוך אוכל דמי דהנהו שאר מינין לא מסרחי דגמר להו בישולייהו פעם ראשונה ושניה ורבינו הלוי גרים ואי שקילי ליה מסרח כשנוטלו נימוח בין אצבעותיו ונמאס הלכך ההוא דשקיל הוי כפסולת והנשאר הוי אוכל עד שחוזר ונוטלו: דפרים סילקא. במ"ס גרסינן ולא בסמ"ך כדפירש בהעור והרוטב (חולין דף קכ.) מאי קיפה פירמא מינצ"ר בלע"ז מחתכו הדק: דסלית סילתי. עצים דקים להבעיר אש: ואי קפיד אמשחתא. לאותכן במדה: מחתך. העור מקצצו במדה: ונקט אופה. דלא שייך במלאכת המשכן כלל: סדורא דפת. שהתחיל בו נקט ואופה במקום בשול דסממנין הוא דהוה בישול דפת: דשדא סיכתא. שהשליך יתד לח לתנור חם ליבשו שיתקשה: לשרורי. לחזק ואין כאן בישול: דמרפי רפי. ע"י חום האור והמים שבתוכו יוצאין ולאחר שיצאו מימיו קמיט מתקשה וכי רפי ברישא הוי בישולו: דארתח כופרא. שהתיך זפת: דהדר אקושי. חוזר ומתקשה: חביתא. של חרס: שבע חטאות. טוחן הרגבים ושוחקן הדק הוי טוחן ובורר הצרורות הגסות מתוכן הרי שתים ומרקידן בנפה ומגבל הטיט דהיינו לש וממרח הטיט כשעושה הגולם שיהא חלק הרי ממחק ומבעיר את האור בכבשן ומצרפו בתוכו הרי מבשל חיובא דחופר ליכא דאינו צריך אלא לעפרה: תנור חייב שמנה. דלאחר שצרפו בכבשן הוא טח עליו טפילה שיהא עב וחומו מתקיים והוא גמר מלאכתו ואמרינן לקמן (דף עה:) כל מידי דהוי גמר מלאכה חייב משום מכה בפטיש אבל גבי חבית ליכא משום מכה בפטיש דמאליה נגמרה מלאכתו בתנור: חלתא. כוורת של קנים: חייב י"א. זומר הקנים והוא צריך להם חייב משום קוצר ומשום נוטע אספס יחד הרי זה מעמר בירר יפות הרי זה בורר החליקן הרי זה ממחק עשאן דקות מאחת שתים או שלש הרי זה טוחן חתכן במדה הרי זה מחתך הסיך השתי הרי זה מיסך ארג אחת למעלה ואחת למטה כדי להעמידו הרי עושה שתי בתי נירין (ד) ארג הרי זה אורג חתך לאחר אריגתה כדי להשוותם הרי זה מכה בפטיש כדאמרינן לקמן [עה:] האי מאן דשקיל אקופי מגלימי חייב משום מכה בפטיש הרי י"א: ואי חייטיה לפומיה. לעשות לה שפה הוסיף כאן תופר וקושר שצריך לקשור לאחר התפירה ומשום בונה ליכא לחיוביה לא בחבית ולא בתנור ולא בכוורת דאין בנין בכלים. מפשיט ליכא למימר בקנים דאין הפשטה אלא בעור וי"מ שקודח נקבים בעץ שתוחבין בו ראשי הקנים של שתי ומחייב ליה משום טוחן ולא נהירא לי דההיא טחינה מלאכה שאינה צריכה לגופה היא וטוב לי לפרש שעושה אותן דקות והוי כמאן דסלית סילתי: שטוף בעזים וטוו בעזים. קרא קדריש טוו את העזים (שמות לה) בגופן של עזים משמע: חכמה יתירה. כדכתיב וכל אשה חכמת לב אבל להדיוט אין דרכו בכך והוי כלאחר יד: התולש את הכנף. נוצה גדולה מן כנף העוף: והקוטמו. לאחר שתלשו חותך ראשו שהוא דק וראוי להניחו בכר וכסת: והמורטו. לצד זנבו שהוא קשה מורט שערו מכאן ומכאן ומשליך הקנה ונותן השיער בכר וכסת: משום מחתך. דקפיד לחתוך עד מקום שהוא ראוי וגם מן הקנה אורג כובעים ועושה כובעים מכנפי עוף בלא שיער: משום ממחק. דתנן גבי עור הממחקו: ביתדות אהלים. נועצים יתידות בקרקע כדכתיב יתדות המשכן וקושרין היריעות בהן במיתריהם: קושר ע"מ להתיר הוא. וכי האי גוונא פטרינן ליה לקמן דתנן כל קשר שאינו של קיימא אין חייבין עליו: בהדי הדדי. בשני חוטין זה אצל זה: שרי חד. לאחר אריגתן מתיר האחד מפני שבולטין ונראין: וקטר חד. כלומר מניח כמו שהוא: השתא כו' (ה) אין עושין. שכשמתירו נראה הנקב ביריעה שחוטיה היו כפולין ששה והיו גסין ומתחלה היו זריזין בכך וכי מתרמו להו תרי קיטרי קושרין האחד ונותקין החוט השני מלמטה ולמעלה ומספקן בחוט ארוך וקושרין למעלה ולמטה ואין שם שנים קשרים סמוכין: צדי חלזון. לצבוע התכלת בדמו והוא כמין דג קטן ועולה אחת לשבעים שנה: קושרין ומתירין. שכל רשתות עשויות קשרים קשרים והן קשרי קיימא ופעמים שצריך ליטול חוטין מרשת זו ולהוסיף על זו מתיר מכאן וקושר מכאן: והא לא קיימא. הכי וכיון דלא קיימא לאו מלאכה היא: שקשרן. שקשר שני ראשי החוט:

דרגא

עין משפט נר מצוה

מד א מיי' פ"ז מהלכות שבת הלכה ה ופ"ח הלכה טו ופכ"א הלכה יח סמג לאוין סה טוש"ע או"ח סי' שכא סעיף יג:
מה ב מיי' שם פ"ח הלכה טו:
מו ג ד מיי' פ"ט מהל' שבת הלכה ו סמג שם:
מז ה מיי' פ"י מהלכות שבת הלכה יג:
מח ו ז מיי' פ"ט מהל' שבת הלכה ז:
מט ח מיי' פי"א מהל' שבת הלכה ז:
נ ט שם הלכה ו:
נא י מיי' פ"י שם הל' א סמג שם טוש"ע או"ח סימן שיז סעיף א:
נב כ מיי' שם הל"ט:
נג ל מיי' שם הלכה י:

רבינו חננאל

מקשינן ופרקינן לפרושי שמעתיה דאמרינן לימא קסבר חזקיה אוכל מתוך פסולת אסור. ושנינן שאני תורמסין דשלקי להו ז' זמני כו'. שמעינן מינה דאוכל מתוך הפסולת זולתי תורמסין שרי וכדאביי דשרי לאלתר כי היכי דלא תקשי חדא אחברתה וכבר פירשנוהו השמועה סלקא כאביי וכרב אשי וכחזקיה שמעינן מדברי שלשתן כי בורר ואוכל ביד בורר ומניח ביד שרי ולא כל היכא דבעי שרי אלא ברירת אוכל מתוך פסולת אבל פסולת מתוך אוכל לא. והאוכל מתוך פסול' דשרי [היינו] לברור ולאכול או לברור ולהניח כדי לאוכלו לאלתר על השולחן כמו שפירשנו אבל להניח שלא לאלתר לא וזה שאמרנו כי מותר לברור ולאכול ולברור ולהניח ולאוכלו לאלתר שרי ה"מ ביד אבל בקנון ובתמחוי לא ואם בירר פטור אבל אסור ובנפה ובכברה דברי הכל אסור ואם בירר נעשה כמי שבירר לאוצר בשוגג חייב חטאת ואע"פ דגרסינן (גיטין כז כח) לענין מי שאבד לו גט אם מצאו לאלתר כשר ואמרינן היכי דמי לאלתר י"א כל שלא עבר [אדם] שם ואחרים אומרים כל שלא שהה אדם שם הכא כיון דאשכחינן מפורש בתלמוד א"י כוותיה עבדינן ומסקינן לשמעתיה שיעור מה שמיסב על השולחן באותה סעודה בלבד וכענין הזה גרסינן בגמרא ביו"ט פרק א' (ביצה יג:) תנן התם המקלף שעורין מקלף אחת אחת על יד ואוכל. ואם קילף ונתן לתוך חיקו חייב. א"ר אלעזר וכן לשבת. והא רב מקלפי ליה כסי כסי ור' חייא מקלפי ליה כסי כסי אלא אי אתמר אסיפא איתמר המולל מלילות של חיטין (למחר) מנפח על יד על יד ואוכל ואם נפח ונתן לתוך ידו חייב. א"ר אלעזר וכן לשבת. מ"ט דמלאכת מחשבת אסרה תורה והאי לאו מלאכת מחשבת היא. דלא קא מכוון במלאכה אלא לאכילה בלבד ולפי' א' כיצד מנפח ואסיק' א"ר אלעזר מנפח בידו אחת ובכל כחו. הטוחן אמר רב פפא האי מאן דפרים סילקא. פי' כעין כתישה ולא כעין חיתוך חייב משום טוחן וכן מאן דסלית סילתי פי' עצי דקלים שעומדין שיבי שיבי כעין נימין וכשמפרק הנימין הללו יוצא בינית כמין קמח דק לפי' (המנפץ) חייב משום טוחן ואי קפיד אמשחתא כלומר אם מתכוין לחתוך אלו סילתי זרת זרת אורך כל אחד ואחד חייב משום מחתך. הלש והאופה אמר רב פפא שביק בישול סממנים ונקיט אפיה ולא מפרש בהדיא האי מלתא א) ואשכחן בירושלמי דאמר הכי את חמי אפיה תולדת בישול הוא ואת אמרת הכן אלא כיון דתני סדר עיסה תניתא בהדייהו: ההוא דשחק [מלח] חסף (מלא) [פלפלין] חייב משום טוחן. האי מאן דגבל גירגבסין עפר קילורין מלוגמא סממנין חייב משום לש. מאן דשדא סיכתא לאתונא חייב משום מבשל פי' הנותן יתידות לחים בכבשן כדי לייבשן לנעצם בספינות וכיוצא בהן. פי' לשרורי לחזק ויש מי שאומרים סיכתא הן גלל בהמה דקיקין אם הטילם לכבשן מה שחייב משום מבעיר הרי

חשק שלמה על רבינו חננאל א) לפנינו בגמ' מפרש בהדיא הטעם משום דסידורא דפת נקיט וכמש"כ בירושלמי. ואולי דלפני רבינו לא היה זה בנוסחת הגמ':

מסורת הש"ס

א) ע"ז לח., ב) [פי' הערוך ע"ז באריכות תמלא בערך חלתא ע"ש דקחשיב חייב משום בונה ולא קחשיב זה שכ' רש"י הכא בד"ה חייב משום ממחק עיי"ש וכזה תבין דעת וסברת תוס' ד"ה חביתא], ג) לקמן לט., ד) בכורות כה. [תוספתא פ"י], ה) [צ"ל אמר], ו) א"ל אביי כצ"ל, ז) [פסחים עה: יומא מז.] ח) [ועי' בתוס' לקמן קיד: ד"ה אלא לקניבת ירק כו' ע"ש], ט) [לעיל מו. עי' תוס' שם ד"ה דחוליות], י) [דף עה:].

הגהות הב"ח

(א) גמ' שבעה זמני ואי (לא שקלי) תא"מ. ונ"ב ס"א לא שלקי וס"א ואי שקלי: (ב) שם אמר רבה שכן קושרים ביתדו' אהלים ההוא כצ"ל. ותיבת קושרין נמחק: (ג) שם דאי מיתרמו ליה תרי קיטרי כצ"ל ותיבת חוטי נמחק: (ד) רש"י ד"ה חייב וכו' עושה שתי בתי נירין. נ"ב ולקמן ר"פ האורג פי' רש"י דהנך לאו נירין ממש כו' ע"ש בדף קה ע"א: (ה) ד"ה השתא כו' שכשמתירו נראה כצ"ל ותיבות אין עושין נמחק:

רב נסים גאון

שכן צדי חלזון קושרין ומתירין. וזה חלזון היו צובעין בדמו תכלת ומשכחת לה במנחות בפרק התכלת (דף מד) תנו רבנן חלזון זה גופו דומה לים ברייתו דומה לדג ועולה פעם אחת לע' שנה ובדמו צובעין תכלת לפיכך דמיו יקרים ואמרו עוד (שם מב) אמר ליה אביי לרב שמואל בר יהודה הא תכילתא היכא צבעיתו אמר ליה מייתינן דם חלזון וסמנין כו':

גליון הש"ס

גמ' **האי מאן דפרים סילקא חייב.** עי' לקמן דף קכח ע"א ברש"י ד"ה שלא יקטוס: **שם תולש חייב משום גוזז.** עי' לקמן דף קו ע"ב ובחידושי רשב"א שם: **שם דאי מתרמי ליה תרי חוטי.** עי' לעיל דף עג ע"א תוס' ד"ה הקושר: **שם השתא לפני מלך וכו'.** פסחים דף עה ע"ב. יומא דף מז ע"א:

ליקוטי רש"י

דפרים סילקא. דמי לטוחן [לקמן קכח.]. **פרים.** לשון פרומים מחתך [שם קיט.]. **תנא דידן סידורא דפת נקט.** הואיל ואופה בפת כמבשל בסממנין [לעיל ע"א]. **דשדא סיכתא.** קונדיס"א בלע"ז ליבשה בתנור. **לשרורי מנא קא מיכוין.** להקשות את היתד ואין דעתו לבישול. **לשרורי.** לשון שריר וקים חזק [ע"ז לח.]. **טוו בעיזים.** היא היתה אומנות יתירה שמעל גבי העזים טווין אותן [שמות לה, כו]. **התולש את הכנף.** שתולש נוצה גדולה מן כנף העוף. **והקוטמו.** לאחר שתלשו קטם ראשו. **והמורטו.** שמחליקה מן הצדדין ומורט מן הקנה [את] השער. **תולש חייב משום גוזז.** דהיינו אורחיה שדרך נולת עוף [לתולשה] ולא לגוזה [בכורות כה.]. **שכן צדי חלזון קושרין ומתירין.** שנצרכין לפרקים להתיר קשרי רשתות הקיימות כדי לקצרן או להרחיבן [לקמן קיא:]. **חלזון.** חלזון עולה מן הים להרים וצובעין בדמו תכלת ונמכר בדמים יקרים [מגילה ו.]. תולעת שיולא מן הים אחד לשבעים שנה וצובעין בדמו תכלת ולכתחלה אינו נראה בכל ההר אלא חלזון אחד ולמחר שהגשמים יורדין מתמלא כולו חלזונות ונראה למורי שבילי חלזון (ראשון) משרילין כולן [סנהדרין צא. ע"ש בגה"ש]. החלזון מן הים הוא עולה אחת לשבעים שנה ומראית דמו דומה לים [חולין פט.].

Another example of shearing:

תָּנוּ רַבָּנַן – **The Rabbis taught** in a Baraisa: הַתּוֹלֵשׁ אֶת הַכָּנָף – THE ONE WHO PLUCKS A FEATHER from the wing of a bird,[25] וְהַקּוֹטְמוֹ – CLIPS IT[26] וְהַמּוֹרְטוֹ – AND PULLS OFF its hairs[27] חַיָּיב שָׁלֹשׁ חַטָּאוֹת – IS OBLIGATED to bring THREE *CHATAS* OFFERINGS. (וְ)אָמַר רַבִּי שִׁמְעוֹן בֶּן לָקִישׁ – **(And) R' Shimon ben Lakish said** in explanation: תּוֹלֵשׁ חַיָּיב מִשּׁוּם גּוֹזֵז – For **plucking** the feather **he is liable on account of "shearing"**;[28] קוֹטֵם חַיָּיב מִשּׁוּם מְחַתֵּךְ – for **clipping** it **he is liable on account of "cutting"**;[29] מְמָרֵט חַיָּיב מִשּׁוּם מְמַחֵק – and for **pulling off** the hairs **he is liable on account of "smoothing."**[30]

The Mishnah also listed:

הַקּוֹשֵׁר וְהַמַּתִּיר – TYING AND UNTYING.

The Gemara wonders:

קְשִׁירָה בְּמִשְׁכָּן הֵיכָא הֲוַאי – **Where was there tying in the** construction of the **Mishkan?**

The Gemara answers:

אָמַר רָבָא – **Rava said:** שֶׁכֵּן קוֹשְׁרִין בִּיתְדוֹת אֹהָלִים (קושרים) – Such a labor was performed, **for indeed they would tie** the curtains **onto the pegs of the tents.**[31]

The Gemara asks:

הַהוּא קוֹשֵׁר עַל מְנָת לְהַתִּיר הוּא – But **that is** a case of **tying in order to untie!**[32] One tying such a knot would not be liable to a *chatas*.[33] – ? –

The Gemara attempts a different explanation:

אֶלָּא אָמַר אַבַּיֵי – **Rather, Abaye said:** שֶׁכֵּן אוֹרְגֵי יְרִיעוֹת – **For indeed the curtain weavers** שֶׁנִּפְסְקָה לָהֶן נִימָא – **who had a thread break on them** קוֹשְׁרִים אוֹתָהּ – **would tie it** back together.[34]

The Gemara raises a difficulty with this explanation:

אָמַר לֵיהּ רָבָא – **Rava said to [Abaye]:** תֵּרַצְתָּ קוֹשֵׁר – **You have resolved** the issue of **tying,** מַתִּיר מַאי אִיכָּא לְמֵימַר – but **what is there to say** about **untying?** When was a knot untied in the construction of the Mishkan? וְכִי תֵּימָא דְּאִי מִתְרַמֵּי לֵיהּ תְּרֵי חוּטֵי קִיטְרֵי בַּהֲדֵי הֲדָדֵי – **And if you should say that if two knots happened to be side by side on** two adjacent strings,[35] שָׁרֵי חַד וְקָטַר חַד – **he would untie one** of them **and tie** the other **one,**[36] that cannot be the source of this primary labor, for we may argue as follows: הַשְׁתָּא לִפְנֵי מֶלֶךְ בָּשָׂר וָדָם אֵין עוֹשִׂין כֵּן – **Now, if before a king of flesh and blood we would not do so,**[37] לִפְנֵי מֶלֶךְ מַלְכֵי הַמְּלָכִים הַקָּדוֹשׁ בָּרוּךְ הוּא עוֹשִׂין – **would we do** so **before the King of all kings, the Holy One, Blessed is He?**[38]

The Gemara therefore gives a different source for the *melachos* of tying and untying:

אֶלָּא אָמַר רָבָא – **Rather, Rava said** – וְאִיתֵּימָא רַבִּי עִילָאִי – **and some say** it was **R' Il'ai:** שֶׁכֵּן צַדֵּי חִלָּזוֹן קוֹשְׁרִין וּמַתִּירִין – **For indeed the *chilazon* trappers**[39] **would tie and untie** their nets.[40]

NOTES

25. The term כָּנָף refers here to the large feathers found on the wing of a bird (*Rashi;* see also *Rashi* below, 108a ד״ה בכנפיו and to *Chullin* 56b ד״ה נמרטו).

26. He clips off the top of the feather, which is thin and may be used for stuffing a pillow (*Rashi*).

27. Since the shaft at the base of the feather is hard, the hair all around it is removed and used as pillow stuffing, and the hard shaft is discarded (*Rashi*). See note 30 below.

28. Plucking a feather from a bird is equivalent to shearing wool from a sheep, which is an *av melachah.*

According to the version of *Rashi* printed with *Rif,* it would seem that this ruling applies only to a live bird [or animal]; thus, one who plucked a feather from a dead bird would not be liable for shearing. [This version of *Rashi* is also cited by *Meiri* and *Maggid Mishneh* (*Hil. Shabbos* 11:7).] However, most Rishonim disagree, holding that the *melachah* of shearing applies even to a dead bird or animal (see *Ramban*, *Ritva MHK* ed. et al.).

In addition, the Rishonim explain that one is liable for plucking the feather of the bird by hand, unlike shearing an animal for which one is liable only when using a utensil.

29. He is particular to clip off the precise part of the feather that can be used for stuffing. Also, hats are sometimes woven from the shafts after the hair is removed (*Rashi*); hence, the feathers must be cut to a specific size.

30. This act is similar to removing hairs from a skin, which the Mishnah classified as the *av melachah* of smoothing (*Rashi*).

Ritva (*MHK* ed.) asks that if the Gemara refers to pulling hairs off the lower section of the shaft, which is discarded (as *Rashi* explained above – see note 27), why should the person be liable for smoothing it? He obviously needs only the soft hairs, not the shaft. Accordingly, this act is not similar to the *melachah* of smoothing, where the hairs are removed in order to use the smooth skins. [That is, this act of pulling off the hairs of the feathers is a מְלָאכָה שֶׁאֵינָהּ צְרִיכָה לְגוּפָהּ, *a labor not performed for the defined purpose* of smoothing.] *Ritva* therefore explains that the Gemara refers to pulling hairs off the shaft so that the shaft can be used for making a hat (see previous note). In such a case one is removing the hairs in order to smooth the shaft, and is thus liable.

31. [The curtains spread as covers atop the Mishkan draped over its sides to cover the wooden wall boards.] Cords were attached to the curtains' lower edges and tied to pegs that were driven into the ground [to prevent the curtains from flapping in the wind] (*Rashi,* based on *Exodus* 35:18; see also *Rashi* to *Exodus* 27:19).

32. The Mishkan traveled with the Jews in the Wilderness. Therefore, the knots used in fastening the curtains to the pegs were only temporary. [See *Sfas Emes.*]

33. The Mishnah states below (113a) that one who ties an impermanent knot is exempt from a *chatas* (*Rashi*; see *Rashash*).

34. And such a knot was meant to be permanent.

35. *Bach* deletes חוטי from the text, and it would appear that the word was missing from *Rashi's* text as well. Our translation follows *Bach's* emendation.

36. That is, since the adjacent knots protruded in unseemly fashion from the fabric, they would untie one knot and leave the other knotted (*Rashi*).

[Thus, according to *Rashi,* the expression וְקָטַר חַד, *and tie one,* is not to be taken literally. Rather, it means that one already-tied knot was left that way. *Tosafos* (above, 73a) find this explanation difficult and offer an alternative. See *Maharam* here.]

37. Untying one of these strings would leave an obvious hole in the middle of the fabric, since each of the strings consisted of six threads and was therefore relatively thick. Hence, this would not be a proper way to make a curtain even for a king of flesh and blood (*Rashi*).

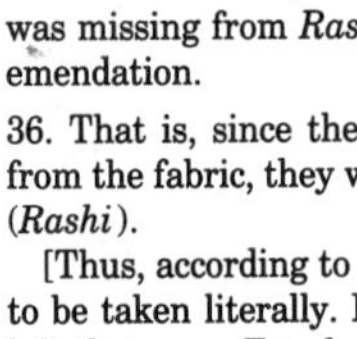

38. Rather, they would avoid tying two knots next to one another on adjacent strings. Instead of tying the second knot next to the first, they would cut out the second string completely and replace it with a single long string, tied at the top and the bottom of the weave [see diagram] (*Rashi*). Thus, there would never be a need to untie a knot.

39. The *chilazon* is a small fishlike creature that emerges every seventy years (see *Menachos* 44a). Its blood was used for the blue dye (*techeiles*) needed in the curtains of the Mishkan (*Rashi;* cf. *Rashi* to *Menachos* loc. cit.).

40. All nets are made of ropes tied permanently together. However, sometimes it is necessary to extend a net by untying some of its knots and tying it to another net (*Rashi*). Based on *Rashi's* explanation, it would appear [according to this answer of the Gemara] that one is liable for untying only when he does so in order to tie another knot. See *Tos. Yom Tov* and *Tos. R' Akiva Eiger* on the Mishnah, 73a, for a discussion of this issue.

[For discussion about the feasibility of capturing a *chilazon* in the Wilderness, see *Radvaz* II §685; see also *Sfas Emes.*]

דשלקי ליה שבעא זימני ואי לא שקלי (א) ליה מסרח וכפסולת מתוך אוכל דמי: והטוחן: א"ר פפא ° אהאי מאן דפרים סילקא חייב משום טוחן אמר רב מנשה בהאי מאן דסלית סילתי חייב משום טוחן אמר רב אשי אי קפיד אמשחתא חייב משום מחתך: והלש והאופה: אמר רב פפא שבק תנא דידן בישול סממנין דהוה במשכן ונקט אופה תנא דידן סידורא דפת נקט אמר רב אחא בר רב עוירא (ט) האי מאן גדשדא סיכתא לאתונא חייב משום מבשל פשיטא מהו דתימא לשרורי מנא קא מיכוין קמ"ל דמירפא רפי והדר קמיט אמר רבה בר רב הונא דהאי מאן דארתח כופרא חייב משום מבשל פשיטא מהו דתימא כיון דהדר ואיקושא אימא לא קמ"ל אמר רבא ההאי מאן דעבד חביתא חייב משום שבע חטאות תנורא חייב משום שמונה חטאות אמר אביי האי מאן דעבד (י) חלתא חייב אחת עשרה חטאות ואי חייטיה לפומיה חייב שלש עשרה חטאות: הגוזז את הצמר והמלבנו: אמר רבה בר בר חנה א"ר יוחנן הטווה צמר שעל גבי בהמה בשבת חייב שלש חטאות אחת משום גוזז ואחת משום מנפץ ואחת משום טווה רב כהנא אמר ואין דרך גזיזה בכך ואין דרך מנפץ בכך ואין דרך טווי בכך ולא והתניא משמיה דרבי נחמיה גשטוף בעזים וטוו בעזים אלמא טוויה על גבי בהמה שמה טוויה חכמה יתירה שאני תנו רבנן התולש את הכנף והקוטמו והמורטו חייב שלש חטאות (י) וא"ר שמעון בן לקיש תולש חייב משום גוזז קוטם חייב משום מחתך ממרט חייב משום ממחק: הקושר והמתיר: קשירה במשכן היכא הואי אמר רבא (ב) שכן קושרין ביתדות אהלים (קושרים) ההוא קושר על מנת להתיר הוא אלא אמר אביי שכן אורגי יריעות שנפסקה להן נימא קושרים אותה א"ל רבא תרצת קושר מתיר מאי איכא למימר וכי תימא ° דאי מתרמי ליה תרי (ג) חוטי קיטרי בהדי הדדי שרי חד וקטר חד ° השתא לפני מלך בשר ודם אין עושין כן לפני ממ"ה הקב"ה עושין כן אלא אמר רבא ואיתימא רבי עילאי שכן צדי חלזון קושרין ומתירין: כוהתופר שתי תפירות: והא לא קיימא אמר רבה בר בר חנה א"ר יוחנן והוא שקשרן: הקורע על מנת לתפור: קריעה במשכן מי הוה רבה ורבי זירא דאמרי תרווייהו שכן

רש"י

דשלקי ליה שבעא זימנין. למתקן: ואי לא שקלי ליה. לאוכל מתוך הפסולת מתוך שהוא רך ונימוק ע"י שנשלק הרבה: מסרח. והלכך אוכל נמי כל זמן שמעורב בו הוי כפסולת ומיהו אוכל הוא ומחמירין עליה למיהוי ההוא דשקיל כפסולת מתוך אוכל ול"נ הבורר תורמוסין מתוך פסולת שלהן משסלקן פעם אחת ממרקין ומערין אותן המים ובורר המתולעות שלהן כמו שעושין לפולין וכן בכל פעם ופעם וזה בורר האוכל ומניח הפסולת ואי לא שלקי ליה מסרח גרסינן הלכך משסלקום פעמים ושלש חשיב ליה פסולת הואיל ואי שביק להו הכי דלא הדר שליק להו מסרחי וכשהוא נוטלן מתוך שאר מינין גרועין המעורבין בהן כפסולת מתוך אוכל דמי דהנהו שאר מינין לא מסרחי דגמר להו בישולייהו פעם ראשונה ושניה ורבינו הלוי גרים ואי שקילי ליה מסרח כשנוטלו נימוח בין אצבעותיו ונמאס הלכך ההוא דשקיל הוי כפסולת והנשאר הוי אוכל עד שחוזר ונוטלו: דפרים סילקא. במ"ס גרסינן ולא בסמ"ך כדפירש בהעור והרוטב (חולין דף קכ.) מאי קיפה פירמא מינצי"ר בלע"ז מחתכו הדק: דסלית סילתי. עצים דקים להבעיר אש: ואי קפיד אמשחתא. לחותכן במדה: מחתך. העור מקצצו במדה: ונקט אופה. דלא שייך במלאכת המשכן כלל: סדורא דפת. שהתחיל בו נקט ואופה במקום בשול דסממנין הוא דהוא בישול דפת: דשדא סיכתא. שהשליך יתד לח לתנור חם ליבשו שיתקשה: לשרורי. לחזק ואין כאן בישול: דמרפי רפי. ע"י חום האור והמים שבתוכו יוצאין ולאחר שיצאו מימיו קמיט מתקשה וכי רפי ברישא הוי בישולו: דארתח כופרא. שהתיך זפת: דהדר אקושי. חוזר ומתקשה: חביתא. של חרס: שבע חטאות. טוחן הרגבים ושוחקן הדק הוי טוחן ובורר הצרורות הגסות מתוכן הרי שתים ומרקידן בנפה ומגבל הטיט דהיינו לש וממרח הטיט כשעושה הגולם שיהא חלק הרי ממחק ומבעיר את האור בכבשן ומצרפו בתוכו הרי מבשל חיובא דחופר ליכא דאינו צריך אלא לעפרה: תנור חייב שמנה. לאחר שצרפו בכבשן הוא טח עליו טפילה שיהא עב וחומו מתקיים והוא גמר מלאכתו ואמרינן לקמן (דף עה:) כל מידי דהוי גמר מלאכה חייב משום מכה בפטיש אבל גבי חבית ליכא משום מכה בפטיש דמאליה נגמרה מלאכתו בתנור: חלתא. כוורת של קנים: חייב י"א. זומר הקנים והוא צריך להם חייב משום קוצר ומשום נוטע אספס יחד הרי זה מעמר בירר יפות הרי זה בורר החליקן הרי זה ממחק עשאן דקות מאחת שתים או שלש הרי זה טוחן חתכן במדה הרי זה מחתך הסיך השתי הרי זה מיסך ארג אחת למעלה ואחת למטה כדי להעמידו הרי עושה שתי בתי נירין (ד) ארג הרי זה אורג חתך לאחר אריגתה כדי להשוותם הרי זה מכה בפטיש כדאמרינן לקמן [עה:] האי מאן דשקיל אקופי מגלימי חייב משום מכה בפטיש הרי י"א: ואי חייטיה לפומיה. לעשות לה שפה הוסיף כאן תופר וקושר שצריך לקשור לאחר התפירה ומשום בונה ליכא לחיוביה לא בחבית ולא בתנור ולא בכוורת דאין בנין בכלים. מפשיט ליכא למימר בקנים דאין הפשטה אלא בעור וי"מ שקודח נקבים בעץ שתוחבין בו ראשי הקנים של שתי ומחייב ליה משום טוחן ולא נהירא לי דההיא טחינה מלאכה שאינה צריכה לגופה היא וטוב לי לפרש שעושה אותן דקות והוי כמאן דסלית סילתי: שטוף בעזים וטוו בעזים. קרא קדריש טוו את העזים (שמות לה) בגופן של עזים משמע: חכמה יתירה. כדכתיב וכל אשה חכמת לב אבל להדיוט אין דרכו בכך והוי כלאחר יד: התולש את הכנף. נוצה גדולה מן כנף העוף: והקוטמו. לאחר שתלשו חותך ראשו שהוא דק וראוי להניחו בכר וכסת: והמורטו. לצד זנבו שהוא קשה מורט שערו מכאן ומכאן ומשליך הקנה ונותן השיער בכר וכסת: משום מחתך. דקפיד לחתוך עד מקום שהוא ראוי וגם מן הקנה אורג כובעים ועושה כובעים מכנפי עוף בלא שיער: משום ממחק. דתנן גבי עור הממחקו: ביתדות אהלים. נועצים יתדות בקרקע כדכתיב יתדות המשכן וקושרין היריעות בהן במיתריהם: קושר ע"מ להתיר הוא. וכי האי גוונא פטרינן ליה לקמן דתנן כל קשר שאינו של קיימא אין חייבין עליו: בהדי הדדי. בשני חוטין זה אצל זה: שרי חד. לאחר אריגתן מתיר האחד מפני שבולטין ונראין: וקטר חד. כלומר מניח כמו שהוא: השתא כו' (ה) אין עושין. שכשמתירו נראה הנקב ביריעה שחוטיה היו כפולין ששה והיו גסין ומתחלה היו זריזין בכך וכי מתרמו להו תרי קיטרי קושרין האחד ונותקין החוט השני מלמטה ולמעלה ומספקן בחוט ארוך וקושרין למעלה ולמטה ואין שם שנים קשרים סמוכין: צדי חלזון. לצבוע התכלת בדמו והוא כמין דג קטן ועולה אחת לשבעים שנה: קושרין ומתירין. שכל רשתות עשויות קשרים קשרים והן קשרי קיימא ופעמים שצריך ליטול חוטין מרשת זו ולהוסיף על זו מתיר מכאן וקושר מכאן: והא לא קיימא. הכי וכיון דלא קיימא לאו מלאכה היא: שקשרן. שקשר שני ראשי החוט:

דרנא

תוספות

האי מאן דפרים סילקא. דוקא בסילקא שייך טחינה אבל שאר אוכלין שרי (ח): מהו דתימא לשרורי מנא קא מכוין. ה"פ ואין בו בשול כלל קמ"ל דנהי דלשרורי מנא קא מכוין בשול מיהא יש בו דמירפא רפי והדר קמיט וחייב אבל אין לפרש קמ"ל דלא אמרי' לשרורי מנא קא מכוין דבפרק אין מעמידין (ע"ז לח.) אמרי' גבי האי נכרי דשדא סיכתא לאתונא אי קבר בה ישראל קרא מעיקרא שפיר דמי ופריך פשיטא ומשני מהו דתימא לבשולי מנא קא מכוין קמ"ל לשרורי מנא קא מכוין: חביתא ותנורא וחלתא. פי' רש"י דמשום בונה לא מיחייב דאין בנין בכלים ואין נראה דדוקא במחזיר מטה ומנורה של חוליות אמרי' (ט) דאין בנין בכלים אבל כשעושה לגמרי כל הכלי מיחייב משום בונה דאמרינן בריש הבונה (לקמן ד' קב:) האי מאן דעייל שופתא בקופינא דמרא חייב משום בונה ול"ע דלא ליקשי ממנפח בכלי זכוכית דסוף פרקין (י): חכמה יתירה שאני. והעושים אותם בטלה דעתם אצל כל אדם כדאמרינן בהמצניע (לקמן ד' צג:) גבי אנשי הוצל: שכן צדי חלזון כו'. בריש אלו קשרים (לקמן קיא:) פירש בקונט' קושרין ומתירין פעמים קושרין את המכמורת ופעמים מתירין אותם:

עין משפט נר מצוה

מד א מיי' פ"ז מהלכות שבת הלכה ה ופ"ח הלכה טו ופכ"א הלכה יח סמג לאוין סה טוש"ע או"ח סי' שכא סעיף יב:
מה ב מיי' שם פ"ח הלכה טו:
מו ג ד מיי' פ"ט מהל' שבת הלכה ו סמג שם:
מז ה מיי' פ"י מהלכות שבת הלכה יג:
מח ו ז מיי' פ"ט מהל' שבת הלכה ז:
מט ח מיי' פי"א מהל' שבת הלכה ז:
נ ט שם הלכה ו:
נא י מיי' פ"י שם הל' א סמג שם טוש"ע או"ח סימן שח סעיף א:
נב כ מיי' שם הל"ט:
נג ל מיי' שם הלכה י:

רבינו חננאל

מקשינן ופרקינן לפרושי שמעתיה דאמרינן לימא קסבר חזקיה אוכל מתוך פסולת אסור. ושנינן שאני תורמסין דשלקי להו ז' זמני כו'. שמעינן מינה דאוכל מתוך הפסולת זולתי תורמסין שרי וכדאביי דשרי לאלתר כי היכי דלא תקשי חדא אחברתה וכבר פירשנוהו השמועה סלקא כאביי וכרב אשי וכחזקיה שמעינן מדברי שלשתן כי בורר ואוכל ביד בורר ומניח ביד שרי ולא כל היכא דבעי שרי אלא ברירת אוכל מתוך פסולת אבל פסולת מתוך אוכל לא. והאוכל מתוך פסול' דשרי [היינו] לברור ולאכול או לברור ולהניח כדי לאוכלו לאלתר על השולחן כמו שפירשנו אבל להניח שלא לאלתר לא וזה שאמרנו כי מותר לברור ולאכול ולברור ולהניח ולאוכלו לאלתר שרי ה"מ ביד אבל בקנון ובתמחוי לא ואם בירר פטור אבל אסור ובנפה ובכברה דברי הכל אסור ואם בירר נעשה כמי שבירר לאוצר בשוגג חייב חטאת ואע"פ דגרסינן (גיטין כז כח) לענין מי שאבד לו גט אם מצאו לאלתר כשר ואמרינן היכי דמי לאלתר י"א כל שלא עבר [אדם] שם ואחרים אומרים כל שלא שהה אדם שם הכא כיון דאשכחינן מפורש בתלמוד א"י כוותיה עבדינן ומסקינן לשמעתיה שיעור מה שמיסב על השולחן באותה סעודה בלבד וכענין הזה גרסינן בגמרא ביו"ט פרק א' (ביצה יג:) תנן התם המקלף שעורין מקלף אחת אחת על יד ואוכל. ואם קילף ונתן לתוך חיקו חייב. א"ר אלעזר וכן לשבת. והא רב מקלפי ליה כסי כסי ור' חייא מקלפי ליה כסי כסי אלא אי אתמר אסיפא איתמר המולל מלילות של חיטין (למחר) מנפח על יד על יד ואוכל ואם נפח ונתן לתוך ידו חייב. א"ר אלעזר וכן לשבת. מ"ט דמלאכת מחשבת אסרה תורה והאי לאו מלאכת מחשבת היא. דלא קא מכוון במלאכה אלא לאכילה בלבד ולפי' א' כיצד מנפח ואסיק' א"ר אלעזר מנפח בידו אחת ובכל כחו. הטוחן אמר רב פפא האי מאן דפרים סילקא. פי' כעין כתישה ולא כעין חיתוך חייב משום טוחן וכן מאן דסלית סילתי פי' עצי דקלים שעומדין שיבי שיבי כעין נימין וכשמפרק הנימין הללו יוצא בינית כמין קמח דק לפי' (המנפץ) חייב משום טוחן ואי קפיד אמשחתא כלומר אם מתכוין לחתוך אלו סילתי זרת זרת אורך כל אחד ואחד חייב משום מחתך. הלש והאופה אמר רב פפא שביק בישול סממנים ונקיט אפיה ולא מפרש בהדיא האי מלתא (א) ואשכחן בירושלמי דאמר הכי את חמי אפיה תולדת בישול הוא ואת אמרת הכן אלא כיון דתני סדר עיסה תניתא בהדיידהו: ההוא דשחק [מלח] חסף (מלא) [פלפלין] חייב משום טוחן. האי מאן דגבל גירגבסין עפר קילורין מלוגמא סממנין חייב משום לש. מאן דשדא סיכתא לאתונא חייב משום מבשל פי' הנותן יתדות לחים בכבשן כדי לייבשן לנעצם בספינות וכיוצא בהן. פי' לשרורי לחזק ויש מי שאומרים סיכתא הן גלל בהמה דקיקן אם הטילם לכבשן מה שחייב משום מבעיר הרי

מסורת הש"ס

א) ע"ז לח., ב) [פי' הערוך ע"ז בארוכות תמצא בערך חלתא ע"ש דקחשיב חייב משום בונה ולא קחשיב זה שכ' רש"י הכא בד"ה חייב משום ממחק עיי"ש ובזה תבין דעת וסברת תוס' ד"ה חביתא], ג) לקמן לט., ד) בכורות כה. [תוספתא פ"י], ה) [נ"ל אמר], ו) א"ל אביי כצ"ל, ז) [פסחים עה: יומא מז.], ח) [ועי' בתוס' לקמן קיד: ד"ה אלא לקניבת ירק כו' ע"ש], ט) [לעיל מו. עי' תוס' שם ד"ה דחוליות], י) [דף עה:].

הגהות הב"ח

(א) גמ' שבעה זמני ואי (לא שקלי) תא"מ. ונ"ב ס"א לא שלקי וס"א ואי שקלי: (ב) שם אמר רבה שכן קושרים ביתדו' אהלים ההוא כצ"ל. ותיבת קושרין נמחק: (ג) שם דאי מיתרמו ליה תרי קיטרי כצ"ל ותיבת חוטי נמחק: (ד) רש"י ד"ה חייב וכו' עושה שתי בתי נירין. נ"ב ולקמן ר"פ האורג פי' רש"י דהנך לאו נירין ממש כו' ע"ש בדף קה ע"א: (ה) ד"ה השתא כו' שכשמתירו נראה כצ"ל ותיבות אין עושין נמחק:

רב נסים גאון

שכן צדי חלזון קושרין ומתירין. וזה חלזון היו צובעין בדמו תכלת ומשכחת לה במנחות בפרק התכלת (דף מד) תנו רבנן חלזון זה גופו דומה לים ברייתו דומה לדג ועולה פעם אחת לע' שנה ובדמו צובעין תכלת לפיכך דמיו יקרים ואמרו עוד (שם מב) אמר ליה אביי לרב שמואל בר יהודה הא תכילתא היכא צבעיתו אמר ליה מייתינן דם חלזון וסמנין כו':

גליון הש"ס

גמ' האי מאן דפרים סילקא חייב. עי' לקמן דף קכח ע"א ברש"י ד"ה שלא יקטוס: שם תולש חייב משום גוזז. עי' לקמן דף קו ע"ב ובחידושי רשב"א שם: שם דאי מתרמי ליה תרי חוטי. עי' לעיל דף עג ע"א תוס' ד"ה הקושר: שם השתא לפני מלך וכו'. פסחים דף עה ע"ב. יומא דף מז ע"א:

ליקוטי רש"י

דפרים סילקא. דמי לטוחן [לקמן קכח.]. פרים. לשון פרומים מחתך [שם קיט.]. תנא דידן סידורא דפת נקט. הואיל ואופה בפת כמבשל בסממנין [לעיל ע"א]. דשדא סיכתא. קוליי"א בלע"ז ליבשה בתנור. לשרורי מנא קא מיכוין. להקשות את היתד ואין דעתו לבישול. לשרורי. לשון שריר וקים חזק [ע"ז לח.]. טוו בעזים. היא היתה אומנות יתירה שמעל גבי העזים טוון אותן [שמות לה, כו]. התולש את הכנף. שתולש נוצה גדולה מן כנף העוף. והקוטמו. לאחר שתלשו קטם ראשו. והמורטו. שמלקיט מן הצדדין ומורט מן הקנה [את] השער. תולש חייב משום גוזז. דהיינו אורמיה שדרך נוצת עוף [לתולשה] ולא לגוזה [בכורות כה.]. שכן צדי חלזון קושרין ומתירין. שצריכין לפרקים להתיר קשרי רשתות הקיימות כדי לקצרן או להרחיבן [לקמן קיא:]. חלזון. חלזון עולה מן הים להרים ולובעין בדמו תכלת ונמכר בדמים יקרים [מגילה ו.]. תולעת שיוצא מן הים אחד לשבעים שנה ולובעין בדמו תכלת ולכתחלה אינו נראה בכל ההר אלא חלזון אחד ולאחר שהגשמים יורדין מתמלא כולו חלזונות ונראה למורי שבילי חלזון (ראשון) משרילין כולן [סנהדרין צא. ע"ש בגה"ש]. החלזון מן הים הוא עולה אחת לשבעים שנה ומראית דמו דומה לים [חולין פט.].

The Mishnah next listed:

וְהַתּוֹפֵר שְׁתֵּי תְפִירוֹת – SEWING TWO STITCHES.[41]

The Gemara asks:

וְהָא לָא קַיְימָא – **But [the stitching] will not last!** Why should he be liable?[42]

The Gemara answers:

אָמַר רַבָּה בַּר בַּר חָנָה אָמַר רַבִּי יוֹחָנָן – **Rabbah bar bar Chanah said in the name of R' Yochanan:** וְהוּא שֶׁקְּשָׁרָן – The Mishnah means that he is liable **provided that he tied [the two ends]** of the thread afterward.[43]

The Mishnah concluded its section of *melachos* required for the manufacture of clothing with the following:

הַקּוֹרֵעַ עַל מְנַת לִתְפּוֹר – TEARING IN ORDER TO SEW.

The Gemara asks:

קְרִיעָה בַּמִּשְׁכָּן מִי הֲוָה – **Was there tearing in** the construction of **the Mishkan?**

The Gemara answers:

רַבָּה וְרַבִּי זֵירָא דְּאָמְרִי תַּרְוַויְיהוּ – **Rabbah and R' Zeira both said:**

NOTES

41. The minimum performance of this *melachah* consists of one "in" and one "out" movement of the needle. See above, 73a note 50.

42. [If the thread is drawn through the fabric only twice, it will fall out.] Any labor whose results are impermanent is not considered a *melachah* (*Rashi;* see *Korban Nesanel; Mishnah Berurah* 340:27; *Igros Moshe, Orach Chaim* II §84).

43. That is, he knotted the two ends of the thread (*Rashi;* see *Rosh Yosef; Chidushei R' Moshe Kazis; Avnei Nezer, Orach Chaim* §180). According to the Gemara's answer, he should also be liable for tying each knot. See *Ramban, Ritva (MHK* ed.), *Meiri* and other Rishonim for various approaches to this issue. See also *Shabbos Shel Mi.*

שֶׁכֵּן יְרִיעָה שֶׁנָּפַל בָּהּ דַּרְנָא – That labor was performed, **for indeed** if there was **a curtain on which a worm fell** and bored a round hole, קוֹרְעִין בָּהּ וְתוֹפְרִין אוֹתָהּ – **they would** first **tear it** at the hole **and** then **sew it.**[1]

The Gemara presents another ruling with regard to sewing:

אָמַר רַב זוּטְרָא בַּר טוֹבִיָּה אָמַר רַב – **Rav Zutra bar Toviyah said in the name of Rav:** הַמּוֹתֵחַ חוּט שֶׁל תְּפִירָה בְּשַׁבָּת – **One who stretches** the **thread of a stitch on the Sabbath**[2] חַיָּיב חַטָּאת – **is liable to a** ***chatas*****;**[3] וְהַלּוֹמֵד דָּבָר אֶחָד מִן הַמָּגוּשׁ – **and one who learns one thing from a heretic**[4] חַיָּיב מִיתָה – **is liable to death;** וְהַיּוֹדֵעַ לְחַשֵּׁב תְּקוּפוֹת וּמַזָּלוֹת וְאֵינוֹ חוֹשֵׁב – **and** if **one knows how to calculate** the astronomical progression of the **seasons and** the celestial position of the **constellations**[5] **and he does not calculate** them, אָסוּר לְסַפֵּר הֵימֶנּוּ – **it is forbidden to relate** Torah rulings **from him.**[6]

The Gemara digresses to cite a dispute that is related to the second of Rav Zutra's statements:

מָגוּשְׁתָּא – Concerning the definition of ***magoshta,***[7] רַב וּשְׁמוּאֵל – **Rav and Shmuel** disagree: חַד אָמַר חַרְשֵׁי – **One said** that it is **a sorcerer,**[8] וְחַד אָמַר גִּדּוּפֵי – **and one said** that it means **a blasphemer.**[9]

The Gemara deduces what Rav holds:

תִּסְתַּיֵּים דְּרַב דְּאָמַר גִּדּוּפֵי – **It can be concluded that Rav is the one who said** that *magoshta* means **a blasphemer,** דְּאָמַר רַב זוּטְרָא בַּר טוֹבִיָּה אָמַר רַב – **for Rav Zutra bar Toviyah said in the name of Rav:** הַלּוֹמֵד דָּבָר אֶחָד מִן הַמָּגוּשׁ – **One who learns one thing from a** ***magosh*** חַיָּיב מִיתָה – **is liable to death.** In this statement by Rav the term *magosh* must mean a heretic, דְּאִי סָלְקָא דַּעְתָּךְ חַרְשֵׁי – **for if you think** that it means **a sorcerer**[10] – הָכְתִיב ,,לֹא־תִלְמַד לַעֲשׂוֹת" – **why, it is written:**[11] ***You shall not learn to do*** [acts of sorcery]. אֲבָל אַתָּה לָמֵד לְהָבִין וּלְהוֹרוֹת – Now, this implies that you may not acquire this knowledge in order to commit acts of sorcery, **but you may learn** sorcery in order **to understand and rule** on such matters.[12] Hence, Rav could not state categorically that one who learns something from a sorcerer is liable to death. תִּסְתַּיֵּים – **It can be concluded,** then, that it is Rav who said that *magoshta* means a blasphemer.[13]

The Gemara elaborates on the third statement of Rav Zutra:

אָמַר רַבִּי שִׁמְעוֹן בֶּן פַּזִּי אָמַר רַבִּי יְהוֹשֻׁעַ בֶּן לֵוִי – **R' Shimon ben Pazi said in the name of R' Yehoshua ben Levi,** מִשּׁוּם בַּר קַפָּרָא – who in turn said it **in the name of Bar Kappara:** כָּל הַיּוֹדֵעַ לְחַשֵּׁב בִּתְקוּפוֹת וּמַזָּלוֹת וְאֵינוֹ חוֹשֵׁב – In the case of **anyone who knows how to calculate** the progression of the **seasons and** the position of the **constellations and he does not calculate** them, עָלָיו הַכָּתוּב אוֹמֵר – **Scripture states about him:** ,,וְאֵת פֹּעַל ה׳ לֹא יַבִּיטוּ וּמַעֲשֵׂה יָדָיו לֹא רָאוּ" – ***And the work of God they do not regard and the action of His hands they do not see.***[14]

The Gemara presents a similar thought:

אָמַר רַבִּי שְׁמוּאֵל בַּר נַחְמָנִי אָמַר רַבִּי יוֹחָנָן – **R' Shmuel bar Nachmani said in the name of R' Yochanan:** מִנַּיִן שֶׁמִּצְוָה עַל הָאָדָם לְחַשֵּׁב תְּקוּפוֹת וּמַזָּלוֹת – **From where** do we know **that there is a mitzvah incumbent upon a person to calculate** the progression of the **seasons and** the position of the **constellations?** שֶׁנֶּאֱמַר ,,וּשְׁמַרְתֶּם וַעֲשִׂיתֶם כִּי הִוא חָכְמַתְכֶם וּבִינַתְכֶם לְעֵינֵי הָעַמִּים" – **For it is stated:**[15] ***You shall safeguard and perform [them], for it is your wisdom and discernment in the eyes of the nations.*** אֵיזוֹ חָכְמָה וּבִינָה שֶׁהִיא לְעֵינֵי הָעַמִּים – **What wisdom and discernment is in the eyes of the nations?**[16] הֱוֵי אוֹמֵר זֶה חִישּׁוּב תְּקוּפוֹת וּמַזָּלוֹת – **You have to say** that **this is** the **calculation of** the progression of the **seasons and** the position of the **constellations.**[17]

NOTES

1. The fabric would be torn above and below the hole to the two ends before the repair was made. If this were not done, the fabric would crease when the hole was sewn closed (see *Rashi* and *Tosafos*).

2. That is, if he pulls taut a long thread to tighten two pieces of garment that have partially separated from one another, he has essentially sewn the garment (*Rashi;* cf. *Rambam, Hil. Shabbos* 10:9; *Eliyah Rabbah* 340:14).

3. For performing the *melachah* of sewing (*Rashi*). *Chidushei HaRan* writes that according to *Rashi's* explanation, one is liable even if he does not tie the thread after stretching it (cf. *Rosh Yosef, Sfas Emes*).

4. It is prohibited to learn even Torah law from a heretic, lest one be influenced to practice idolatry (*Rashi*). [This explanation follows the Gemara's conclusion below.]

5. That is, the mathematical calculation of the movements of the sun and the heavenly bodies, and how this affects climatic and other seasonal changes on earth (see below, note 17).

6. That is, it is forbidden to quote a ruling in his name (*Eliyah Rabbah* 340:14 and *Rosh Yosef;* cf. *Gilyonei HaShas* and *Ben Yehoyada*). The Gemara will elaborate on this statement below.

Rashi explains that Rav Zutra cites these three statements together [even though only the first relates to sewing] because he learned them from Rav at the same time (*Rashi*). *Ben Yehoyada* demonstrates how all three statements are conceptually related.

7. A term mentioned in various places in the Talmud (*Rashi;* cf. *Tosafos*). [*Rashi's* version of this word is אַמְגוּשָׁא; see also *Mesoras HaShas.*]

8. I.e. someone who performs supernatural acts through sorcery.

9. A heretic who is involved with idolatry, constantly blaspheming God and inciting others to idolatry (*Rashi*).

10. And it would be prohibited to learn sorcery from him because Scripture states (see *Deuteronomy* 18:10) that a sorcerer *shall not be found among you* (*Rashi*).

11. *Deuteronomy* 18:9.

12. [The verse indicates only that it is forbidden to learn about sorcery in order to practice it.] However, there is no prohibition against learning about sorcery in order to expose a "miracle"-performing, false prophet as a sorcerer (*Rashi;* see also *Sanhedrin* 68a). [And there is certainly no prohibition to learn things unrelated to sorcery from a sorcerer (see *Shach, Yoreh Deah* 179:23).]

13. And since such a person is constantly discussing idolatry, you must shun him completely, lest he entice you to worship idols (*Rashi*).

14. *Isaiah* 5:12. By studying the movements of the sun and the constellations a person will gain some understanding of the greatness of God, Who set them in place. Upon realizing that these heavenly bodies have no independent powers, he will clearly see the folly of those who worship the sun and the moon with the expectation of receiving their assistance (*Chidushei HaRan*).

Rambam (*Pe'er HaDor* §53; see also *Hil. Yesodei HaTorah* 2:2) writes that this wisdom includes astronomy, intercalation of the seasons and mathematics. Someone who knows these disciplines and does not use them to calculate the movement of the heavenly bodies has lost an opportunity to better love God. [See also *Meiri* to *Avos,* end of ch. 3; *Nesivos Olam, Nesiv HaTorah* ch. 14, ArtScroll ed. p. 307 ff.]

15. *Deuteronomy* 4:6.

16. The verse is discussing wisdom possessed by the Jewish nation that the other nations of the world can recognize (*Rashi*).

17. When a person can correctly predict the weather for the coming season, people recognize his wisdom. Predicting is accomplished by calculating the movement of the sun and the constellations, because the weather is affected by the position of the sun in relation to the stars (*Rashi;* see also *Ramban* to *Sefer HaMitzvos, shoresh* §1 ד״ה והתשובה ג׳).

Ramban (ibid.) writes that the term "mitzvah" is used loosely here; the Gemara does not actually mean that a Jew is required to learn the necessary sciences to be able to calculate the movement of the heavenly bodies. Rather, this statement and the preceding one merely encourage someone who already knows those sciences to utilize his knowledge to better understand the greatness of God (cf. *Ritva MHK* ed.; *Sfas Emes*).

כלל גדול פרק שביעי שבת עה.

שכן יריעה שנפל בה דרנא קורעין בה ותופרין אותה אמר רב זוטרא בר טוביה אמר רב א המותח חוט של תפירה בשבת חייב חטאת ב והלומד דבר אחד מן המגוש חייב מיתה והיודע לחשב תקופות ומזלות ואינו חושב אסור לספר הימנו א) מגושתא רב ושמואל חד אמר חרשי וחד אמר גדופי תסתיים דרב דאמר גדופי דאמר רב זוטרא בר טוביה אמר רב הלומד דבר אחד מן המגוש חייב מיתה דאי ס"ד חרשי הכתיב ג) א) לא תלמד לעשות אבל אתה למד להבין ולהורות תסתיים אר"ש בן פזי א"ר יהושע בן לוי משום בר קפרא כל היודע לחשב בתקופות ומזלות ואינו חושב עליו הכתוב אומר ב) ואת פועל ה' לא יביטו ומעשה ידיו לא ראו א"ר שמואל בר נחמני א"ר ג) יוחנן ג מנין שמצוה על האדם לחשב תקופות ומזלות שנאמר ג) ושמרתם ועשיתם כי היא חכמתכם ובינתכם לעיני העמים איזו חכמה ובינה שהיא לעיני העמים הוי אומר זה חישוב תקופות ומזלות: ד הצד צבי וכו': ת"ר ד) הצד חלזון והפוצעו אינו חייב אלא אחת רבי יהודה אומר חייב שתים שהיה ר' יהודה אומר ה פציעה בכלל דישה אמרו לו אין פציעה בכלל דישה אמר רבא מ"ט דרבנן קסברי ו אין דישה אלא לגדולי קרקע וליחייב נמי משום נטילת נשמה אמר רבי יוחנן שפצעו מת רבא אמר אפילו תימא שפצעו חי מתעסק הוא אצל נטילת נשמה והא אביי ורבא דאמרי תרווייהו ז מודה ה) ר"ש בפסיק רישא ולא ימות (א) שאני הכא דכמה דאית ביה נשמה טפי ניחא ליה כי היכי ו) דליציל ציבעיה: ח והשוחטו: שוחט משום מאי חייב רב אמר משום צובע ושמואל אמר משום ט נטילת נשמה משום

רש"י

דרנא. תולעת ומנקב בו נקב קטן ועגול וצריך לקרוע למטה ולמעלה את הנקב שלא תהא התפירה עשויה קמטין קמטין: המותח חוט של תפירה. בגד התפור ועומד והניח החוט ארוך ונתפרדו שתי חתיכות הבגד זו מזו במקצת וחוטי התפירות נמשכין ומותח את ראשי החוט להדק ולחבר זו היא תפירתו וחייב: והלומד דבר אחד מן המגוש. מין הממשיכו לע"ז אפי' דבר תורה אסור ללמוד ממנו: והיודע כו'. הני תלת שמעתתא שמעינהו (ז) מר) זוטרא מרב כי הדדי וגרסינהו: אמגושא. דאמרינן בכל דוכתא רב ושמואל פליגי ביה: חד אמר חרשי. מכשף: וחד אמר גדופי. מין האדוק בע"ז ומגדף תמיד את השם ומסית אנשים לע"ז: דאי סלקא דעתך חרשי. וטעמא משום דכתיב לא ימצא בך וגו' וקא חשיב מכשף: והא כתיב. לעיל מיניה לא תלמד לעשות כדי שתעשה: להבין. שתוכל לעמוד בהן ואם יעשה נביא שקר לפניך שתבין שהוא מכשף: תסתיים דגדופי הוא. הלכך כל דבריו דברי ע"ז והסתלק מעליו שלא ישיאך: לעיני העמים. שחכמה הניכרת היא שמראה להם סימן לדבריו בהילוך החמה והמזלו' שמעידין כדבריו שאומר שנה זו גשומה והיא כן שנה זו שחונה והיא כן שכל העיתים לפי מהלך החמה במזלותיה ומולדותיה במזל תלוי הכל לפי השעה המתחלת לשמש בכניסת החמה למזל: הפוצעו. דוחקו בידיו שיצא דמו: אינו חייב אלא אחת. משום צידה אבל אפציעה ליכא חיוב: בכלל דישה. שמפרק דמו הימנו כמפרק תבואה מקשין שלה: מתעסק הוא אצל נטילת נשמה. כלומר לגבי נטילת נשמה הוי מתעסק בדבר אחר ולא הויא מלאכת מחשבת שאינו מתכוין שימות: טפי ניחא ליה. שדם החי טוב מדם המת וכיון דכל עצמו מתכוין וטורח לשומרו שלא ימות בידו אפי' מת אין כאן אלא מתעסק וכי מודה ר' שמעון במידי דלא איכפת ליה אי מיתרמי ומיהו איכווני לא מיכוין: דליציל ציבעיה גרסי'. שתהא מראית צבעו צלולה: שוחט משום מאי מיחייב. שחיטה במלאכת המשכן היכא ומאי עבידת' אי מעורות אילים מאדמים למה לי בהו שחיטה בחניקה נמי סגי:

תוספות

שכן יריעה שנפל בה דרנא כו'. תימה לר"י דבריש האורג אמרי' קורע על מנת לתפור שתי תפירות היכי משכחת לה ומשני דעבידא ככיסתא ואומר ר"י דבמשכן היו אומנים ביותר והיו נזהרים שלא היו עושים ככיסתא והתם לא קאמר שנפל בה דרנא דנקט דשכיח טפי ועוד דהתם בעי לאשכוחי קורע על מנת לתפור שתי תפירות ותו לא ויריעה שנפל בה דרנא צריך לקורעה מתחלתה ועד סופה ויש בה כמה תפירות ואע"ג דהשתא לא משכח' במשכן על מנת לתפור שתי תפירות ותו לא סברא הוא דבשתי תפירות הוי דבר חשוב: **אמגושא.** פי' בערוך דפליגי בהא דאמר רב פפא באלו מגלחין (מו"ק יח.) פרעה אמגושי היה דכתיב הנה יוצא המימה חד אמר לעשות כשפים היה יוצא וחד אמר גדופי שהיה עושה עצמו ע"ז שהיה אומר לי יאורי ואני עשיתני ואין נראה לר"י דפליגי רב ושמואל במאי דאמר רב פפא אלא פליגי אאמגושא שנזכר בשום מקום במשנה או בברייתא: **הצד** חלזון. למאן דמוקי לה בשפצעו חי אתי שפיר הא דנקט הצד חלזון דדרך לפוצעו מיד אחר צידה כל זמן שהוא חי וקמ"ל דאע"פ שפצעו חי לא מיחייב משום נטילת נשמה ואפילו למאן דמוקי לה כשפצעו מת קמ"ל דלא מיחייב בצידה שלו משום נטילת נשמה דאף על גב דאמרי' בפרק שמונה שרצים (לקמן דף קז:) השולה דג מן הים כיון שיבש בו כו' הכא שאני חלזון דרכו לפרכס ולקרב מיתתו וצ"ע דבירושלמי משמע דצד חלזון לא מיחייב משום צידה: **וליחייב** נמי משום נטילת נשמה. ואפי' לרבי יהודה דאמר מקלקל בחבורה פטור פריך שפיר דהיכא דאיכא תקון קצת חייב כדאמרי' בפסחים (דף עג.) בסוף אלו דברים והכא נמי במה שממיתו יש תקון קצת שאינו מפרכס לכאן ולכאן ונוח ליטול ממנו הדם ולמאי דמסיק דכמה דאית ביה נשמה טפי ניחא ליה אתי שפיר נמי לרבי יהודה דהשתא ליכא תיקון כלל ומיהו שמעתין אתיא אפי' לר"ש דמחייב מקלקל בחבורה מדמשני מתעסק הוא אבל נטילת נשמה ולא קאמר מקלקל הוא: **מתעסק** הוא אצל נטילת נשמה. האי מתעסק לאו דוקא דהא מתעסק בחבורה חייב לר"ש דאמר בס"פ ספק אכל (כריתות יט:) הנח לתינוקות הואיל ומקלקל בחבורה חייב מתעסק נמי חייב וטעמא כדיליף בהאורג (לקמן קו.) מדאיצטריך למישרי מילה מכלל דמקלקל בחבורה חייב ולא חיישינן למלאכת מחשבת דמקלקל דעלמא לא מיפטר אלא משום מלאכת מחשבת כדאמר בספ"ק דחגיגה (דף י:) ומתעסק דהכא היינו דבר שאין מתכוין כיון דאין מתכוין כלל למלאכה מותר אפי' בחבורה אע"פ דלא בעי מלאכת מחשבת כמו כל איסורים שבתורה דלא שייך בהו מלאכת מחשבת ושרו אין מתכוין כדאמר מוכרי כסות מוכרין כדרכן ובלבד שלא יתכוין בחמה מפני החמה כו' (כלאים פ"ט משנה ה) וכן מוכח בפ"ק דכתובות (ד' ה:) דאמר את"ל דם חבורי מיחבר לדם הוא צריך או להנאת עצמו הוא צריך ואת"ל להנאת עצמו הוא צריך הלכה כרבי יהודה או הלכה כר"ש פירוש בדבר שאין מתכוין ואת"ל הלכה כר' יהודה בדבר שאין מתכוין במקלקל הלכה כמאן משמע דאי הלכה כר"ש בדבר שאין מתכוין תו ליכא לספוקי במקלקל דאפי' מקלקל בחבורה חייב כיון דאין מתכוין מותר: **טפי** ניחא ליה כי היכי דליציל ציבעי'. פי' אע"ג דהוי פסיק רישיה דמודה ר"ש הכא מיפטר משום דהוי מלאכה שאינה צריכה לגופה דאפי' במקלקל פטר ר"ש במלאכה שאינה צריכה לגופה כדאמר בפרק הנחנקין (סנהדרין פד:) מאן שמעת ליה דאמר מקלקל בחבורה חייב ר"ש הא אמר מלאכה שאינה צריכה לגופה פטור עליה וכי מודה ר"ש בפסיק רישיה ה"מ במידי דניחא ליה אי מתרמי דהוי צריכה לגופה אבל במידי דלא איכפת ליה לא מודה ורש"י פי' דהא דמודה ר"ש בפסיק רישיה היינו במאי דלא איכפת ליה אי מתרמי וליתא דהא מורד וזרדין בארעא דחבריה פטר ר"ש בפ' הבונה (לקמן קג.) והתם לא איכפת ליה אי מתרמי אלא כדפי' ותימה דבספ"ק דחגיגה (דף י:) משמע דהא דפטר ר"ש מלאכה שאינה צריכה לגופה היינו משום דבעי מלאכת מחשבת וא"כ בחבורה דלא בעי מלאכת מחשבת ליחייב בה מלאכה שאינה צריכה לגופה: **כי** היכי דליציל ציבעיה. קשה לר"י דמ"מ על נטילת הדם ליחייב משום נטילת נשמה ונראה כלשון אחר שפי' בקונט' בריש שמונה שרצים (לקמן קז.) דחובל בהן חייב משום דהוי תולדה דשוחט וחייב משום נטילת נשמה ונטילת הדם היינו נטילת נשמה כדכתיב כי הדם הוא הנפש ולכך ח' שרצים שיש להם עור חייב בנצרר הדם אע"פ שלא יצא דכיון שנצרר סופו לצאת אלא שעתה העור מעכבו ושאר שרצים שאין להם עור אינו חייב עד שיצא מהם דם אבל בנצרר הדם ולא יצא לא מיחייב דכיון שלא יצא סופו לחזור דאם היה סופו לצאת היה יוצא מיד שאין העור מעכבו והשיב לו ר"ת דדם חלזון הראוי לצביעה מיפקד פקיד ולא מיחייב על אותו הדם משום נטילת נשמה ועל דם אחר היוצא עמו נמי לא מיחייב דלא ניחא ליה כי היכי דליציל ליבעיה אבל אין לפרש דנטילת נשמה היינו שמחליש אותו דבר שחובל בו דגבי דם בתולים מה צריך לחלישות האשה וגבי מילה מה צריך לחלישות התינוק אלא לנטילת הדם קרי נטילת נשמה כדפי': **שוחט** משום מאי מיחייב. לאו אשוחט דמתני' קאי דההוא פשיטא דלא הוי אלא משום נטילת נשמה דלוצע תנן בהדיא במתני' אלא אשוחט דעלמא קאי: אין

מסורת הש"ס

א) ס"א אמגושא, ב) [ר"ה כד: ע"ז יח. מג: סנהד' סח.], ג) [צ"ל יונתן], ד) [תוספתא פ"ט ע"ש], ה) לקמן קג. קיא: קיז. קכ: קלג. קמג. [מילה לג.] כתובות ו: בכורות כה. סוכה לג:, ו) [צ"ל דליצלח פי' דלא ניחא ליה דמיפוק נשמה דכל כמה דאית ביה נשמה טפי מצלח צבעיה שצבעו מתעלה יפה ויהא צבעו יפה וברק כי אז מצליח. ערוך], ז) [צ"ל רב].

הגהות הב"ח

(א) גמ' שאני הכא. נ"ב עמ"ש דף קג:

תורה אור השלם

א) כִּי אַתָּה בָּא אֶל הָאָרֶץ אֲשֶׁר יְיָ אֱלֹהֶיךָ נֹתֵן לָךְ לֹא תִלְמַד לַעֲשׂוֹת כְּתוֹעֲבֹת הַגּוֹיִם הָהֵם: [דברים יח, ט]

ב) וְהָיָה כִנּוֹר וָנֶבֶל תֹּף וְחָלִיל וָיַיִן מִשְׁתֵּיהֶם וְאֵת פֹּעַל יְיָ לֹא יַבִּיטוּ וּמַעֲשֵׂה יָדָיו לֹא רָאוּ: [ישעיה ה, יב]

ג) וּשְׁמַרְתֶּם וַעֲשִׂיתֶם כִּי הִוא חָכְמַתְכֶם וּבִינַתְכֶם לְעֵינֵי הָעַמִּים אֲשֶׁר יִשְׁמְעוּן אֵת כָּל הַחֻקִּים הָאֵלֶּה וְאָמְרוּ רַק עַם חָכָם וְנָבוֹן הַגּוֹי הַגָּדוֹל הַזֶּה: [דברים ד, ו]

רב נסים גאון

שכן קרש שנפל בו דרנא. פי' דרנא תולעת ובסוף פרק אלו טריפות (חולין דף סז) משכחת ואת נבלתם תשקצו לרבות את הדרנין של בהמה: **רבא** אמר אפילו תימא שפצעו חי מתעסק הוא אצל

ליקוטי רש"י

קורעין בה ותופרין אותה. שהנקב עגול ואינו יכול לתופרו יפה אלא אם כן קורעו אבל קורע שלא לתפור לא הוי במשכן [לעיל עג.]. **גדופי.** עובדי כוכבים [סנהדרין צח.]. **ואת פועל ה' לא יביטו.** ובאורייתא דה' לא אסתכלו. **ומעשה ידיו לא ראו.** עשו עצמם כאילו לא ראו את גבורותיו [ישעיה ה, יב]. **כי היא חכמתכם ובינתכם וגו'.** בזאת תחשבו חכמים ונבונים לעיני העמים [דברים ד, ו]. **והפוצעו.** שעוצרין ופוצעין את החלזון להוציא דמו [לעיל כו.]. **נטילת נשמה.** שהיא אב מלאכה דתנן (לעיל עג.) השוחטו וכו' [תענית כד.]. **מודה ר' שמעון.** דאמר במסכת שבת (לעיל מא:) דבר שאין מתכוין מותר [בכורות כה.]. **בפסיק רישא ולא ימות.** כאומר אחתוך ראש בהמה זו בשבת ואיני רוצה שתמות דכיון דאי אפשר שלא תמות כמתכוין חשיב ליה וכי אמרינן דבר שאין מתכוין מותר כגון היכא דאפשר ליה בלא איסור כגון גורר אדם מטה כסא וספסל ובלבד שלא יתכוין לעשות חריץ ואף על גב דאיכא למיחש דלמא עביד חריץ כיון דלא מתכוין להכי ואפשר לגרירה בלא חריץ כי עביד נמי חריץ דהוי מלאכה גמורה לא מיחייב אבל היכא דודאי עביד מודי [סוכה לג:].

עין משפט נר מצוה

נד א מיי' שם הלכה ט סמג שם טור שו"ע או"ח סימן ש"מ סעיף ו:

נה ב שו"ע יו"ד סימן קעט סעיף יט:

נו ג סמג עשין מו:

נז ד מיי' פי"א מהלכות שבת הלכה יט סמג לאוין סה טוש"ע או"ח סימן שטז סעיף ה:

נח ה מיי' פ"ח מהלכות שבת הלכה ז ופכ"א הלכה יג:

נט ו מיי' שם פ"ח הלכה ז:

ס ז מיי' פ"א מהלכות שבת הלכה ו טוש"ע או"ח סימן שלז סעיף א:

סא ח ט מיי' פי"א מהל' שבת הלכה א:

רבינו חננאל

חייב. ועוד חייב משום מבשל. וזה שנצרך לומר כן דלא תימא אין המפחר כלי חרס מבשל מפני שמחזיק הכלי. אשמעי' דמירפה רפה כשהן טיט ומתבשלין ואחר כך מתחזקין כשיצטרפו (מתחפרו) [ויתפחרון]. וכן מאן דארתח כופרא. אף על גב דהדר אקיש מבשל הוא. אמר רבה מאן דעבד חביתא חייב ד' חטאות פי' כגון שהיתה לו גבשושית תנטלה וייפה הקרקע חייב משום חורש. שחק חייב משום טוחן ניקהו מן הצרורות חייב משום בורר וכשמחתך (ממנו) [היינו] מחתך. ועיקר מלאכה א) (בנין מלאכה) וגמר מלאכה והשואתה חייב משום מכה בפטיש הרי שבע ב) בתנור עוד מוסיף אחד שצריך להחליק את תוכו ולשוף אותו גחלים וחייב משום ממחק. מאן דעבד חלתא חייב י"א חטאות. חתך קנה נעשה זומר וצריך לעצים חייב משום קוצר ומשום נוטע כינס הקנים חייב משום מעמר דקדק הקנים חייב משום טוחן. חתכם כשיעור כגון אמה אמה חייב משום מחתך. קילפם חייב משום דש. השליך קליפיהן וקנין שאין ראויין למלאכה חייב משום בורר. הטיל שתיו חייב משום מיסך וכשמטיל הערב עושה שתי בתי נירין וכשמכה אותן כדי לקרבן זה לזה (ולהדחיק אריג) ג) זה כל זמן שעושה (ארבעת) [ארעי'] הכוורת וכשכופף הקנים למעלה לאריגה [והן] קירותיה בונה הוא וגמר מלאכה שישבר קרומיות היוצאת משום מכה בפטיש הרי אלו י"א מלאכות ואם כפף פיה למטה ותפרה (כשיבינו החייט) [כשמותח החוט] חייב משום טווה. כרב דאמר המותח חוט של תפירה בשבת חייב (משום) חטאת וכשתופר חייב משום תופר הרי אלו י"ג חטאות: **ירושלמי** ההיא איתתא כד משתיא בקיבה חייב משום מיסכת כד יהבה קירומה משום עושה בתין. כד מקימה לון משום בונה. כד מחיי' משום אורגת כד מקטעא בגימא משום מחתכת. כד גמרה מלאכתה משום מכה בפטיש. אזנים של דיסקיא [קושר ומתיר] נעשה כנועל ופותח וכן חותלות של תמרים קושר ומתיר. א"ר יוחנן הטווה צמר מעל גבי בהמה בשבת חייב ג' חטאות משום גוזז ומנפץ וטווה. ודחה רב כהנא ואמר אין דרך גזיזה ולא דרך ניפוץ ולא דרך טוויה בכך. ואקשינן על רב כהנא והתניא משום נחמיה שטוף בעזים. אלמא שטפוהו בעזים וטוות מעליהן בלא גזיזה ופריק' חכמה יתירה שאני דכתיב וכל הנשים אשר נשא לבן אותנה בחכמה טוו את העזים. ואע"ג דרב כהנא לגבי רב תלמיד הוה כיון (דיש) דאשכחן בתלמוד א"י דקיימי כוותיה דגרסינן התולש כנף מן העוף חייב משום גוזז המורטו חייב משום מוחק הקוטמה חייב משום מכה בפטיש ודחינן לא דמיא תולש כנף עוף לתולש שער בהמה דעוף שאין לו גזיזה תלישתה היא גזיזתה ברם בהמה אינו חייב עד שיגזז תדע שהוא כן דתני תלש מן המתה חייב תלישתה זו היא גזיזתה מן החיה פטור ותו מדתנן (לקמן צד:) הנוטל צפרניו זו בזו או בשיניו וכן שערו וכן שפמו וכן זקנו ר' אליעזר מחייב חטאת וחכמים אומרים משום שבות כלומר אין דרך נטילת שיער בשיניים וכיון דקיימי חכמים כרב כהנא קיי"ל כוותיה: אמגושתא. פי' בלשון ערבי זמזמה. מגוש בלשון יון מכשף. גידופי כופר בעיקר: **הצד** צבי השוחטו כו'. ת"ר הצד חלזון והפוצעו אינו חייב אלא אחת ר' יהודה אומר חייב שתים פציעה בכלל דישה ורבנן סברי אין דישה אלא בגידולי קרקע ואקשינן לרבנן ליחייב משום צידה ומשום נטילת נשמה ופריק ר' יוחנן שפצעו מת. רבא אמר אפילו תימא שפצעו חי. מתעסק אצל נטילת נשמה וקיי"ל המתעסק [בחלבים ובעריות] חייב משום דנהנה המתעסק בשבת פטור מלאכת מחשבת אסרה תורה דלא קא ניחא לנטילת נשמה דניחא

חשק שלמה על רבינו חננאל א) אולי צ"ל ועל עיקר מלאכה האמית חייב משום בונה וגמר מלאכה וכו': ב) לפי מה דהשיב רבינו אין כאן רק שש חטאות. ואולי דחסר כדברי רבינו וצ"ל והשמצרף אח"כ בכבשן חייב משום מבשל וכ"ה ברש"י: ג) אולי צ"ל חייב משום אורג הס כל זמן וכו':

The Mishnah began its list of *melachos* related to writing with the following:

הַצָּד צְבִי וכו׳ – **HUNTING A DEER etc.**

The Gemara discusses a case involving this *melachah*:

תָּנוּ רַבָּנָן – **The Rabbis taught** in a Baraisa: הַצָּד חִלָּזוֹן וְהַפּוֹצְעוֹ – IF ONE TRAPS A *CHILAZON* AND SQUEEZES IT with his hands to force out its blood,[18] אֵינוֹ חַיָּיב אֶלָּא אַחַת – HE IS OBLIGATED ONLY to bring ONE *chatas* offering – for performing the *melachah* of trapping.[19] רַבִּי יְהוּדָה אוֹמֵר – R' YEHUDAH SAYS: חַיָּיב שְׁתַּיִם – HE IS OBLIGATED to bring TWO offerings.[20] שֶׁהָיָה רַבִּי יְהוּדָה אוֹמֵר – FOR R' YEHUDAH WOULD SAY: פְּצִיעָה בִּכְלָל דִּישָׁה – SQUEEZING IS included IN THE CATEGORY OF THRESHING,[21] and so one is liable for that labor as well. אָמְרוּ לוֹ – However, [THE RABBIS] SAID TO HIM: אֵין פְּצִיעָה בִּכְלָל דִּישָׁה – SQUEEZING IS NOT included IN THE CATEGORY OF THRESHING, and so the *chilazon* trapper is not liable for that act.

The Gemara analyzes the view of the Rabbis:

אָמַר רָבָא – **Rava said:** מַאי טַעְמָא דְּרַבָּנָן – **What is the reason of the Rabbis** for ruling leniently in this matter? קָסָבְרֵי אֵין דִּישָׁה אֶלָּא לְגִדּוּלֵי קַרְקַע – **They hold** that the *melachah* of **threshing applies only to that which grows from the ground,** not to fish.[22]

The Gemara considers another liability:

וְלִיחַיֵּיב נַמִּי מִשּׁוּם נְטִילַת נְשָׁמָה – **But let him also be liable for taking a life!**[23] – ? –

The Gemara answers:

אָמַר רַבִּי יוֹחָנָן – **R' Yochanan said:** שֶׁפְּצָעוֹ מֵת – He is not liable for killing **because** the Baraisa is discussing a case where **he squeezed [the *chilazon*]** after it was already **dead.**

The Gemara offers an alternative answer:

רָבָא אָמַר – **Rava said:** אֲפִילּוּ תֵּימָא שֶׁפְּצָעוֹ חַי – **You can even say that he squeezed [the *chilazon*]** while it was still **alive.** Nevertheless, he is not liable for killing because מִתְעַסֵּק הוּא אֵצֶל נְטִילַת נְשָׁמָה – **he is** considered **preoccupied** with another act **vis-a-vis** the *melachah* of **taking a life.**[24]

The Gemara asks:

וְהָא אַבָּיֵי וְרָבָא דְּאָמְרֵי תַּרְוַויְיהוּ – **But Abaye and Rava have both said:** מוֹדֶה רַבִּי שִׁמְעוֹן בִּפְסִיק רֵישָׁא וְלֹא יָמוּת – **R' Shimon concedes** that one is liable **in** the case of **an inevitable consequence!**[25] – ? –

The Gemara answers:

שָׁאנֵי הָכָא – **It is different here,** דְּכַמָּה דְּאִית בֵּיהּ נְשָׁמָה – **because the longer it stays alive**[26] טְפֵי נִיחָא לֵיהּ – **the more he is pleased,** כִּי הֵיכִי דְּלִיצִיל צִיבְעֵיהּ – **in that his dye will be clear.**[27]

The Mishnah next stated:

וְהַשּׁוֹחֲטוֹ – **SLAUGHTERING IT.**

The Gemara asks:

שׁוֹחֵט מִשּׁוּם מַאי חַיָּיב – **Why is a slaughterer liable?**[28]

The Gemara offers two answers:

רַב אָמַר מִשּׁוּם צוֹבֵעַ – **Rav said because of dyeing**[29] וּשְׁמוּאֵל אָמַר מִשּׁוּם נְטִילַת נְשָׁמָה – **and Shmuel said because of taking a life.**[30]

NOTES

18. After removing a *chilazon* from the water they would squeeze out its blood for the blue dye (the *techeiles*) that was used in construction of the Mishkan.

19. That is, he is liable for the trapping, but not for squeezing out the blood (*Rashi*).

20. For trapping and for squeezing out the blood.

21. Extracting the blood from an animal is similar to extracting grain from its husk (*Rashi*). Squeezing is therefore a *toladah* of threshing (*Ritva MHK* ed.).

22. [See *Eglei Tal* דש 12:24 and *Minchas Chinuch* §32 דש for a discussion about whether this *toladah* applies to land animals. See also below, 95a.]

23. By squeezing out the blood the person kills the *chilazon.* He should be liable for that act under the category of killing.

[*Ritva* (*MHK* ed.) notes that merely taking the *chilazon* out of the water would not trigger liability for killing (see below, 107b), because one normally removes fish from the sea in a pail full of water. In that case the *chilazon* would die only from the squeezing. Cf. *Tosafos* (ד״ה הצד), who understand that he is not liable for taking the *chilazon* out of the water because it then thrashes about, hastening its own death. See also *Dibros Moshe* 64:41.]

24. That is, as far as taking the *chilazon's* life is concerned, he is regarded as being preoccupied with another action. Hence, his killing is not a מְלֶאכֶת מַחֲשֶׁבֶת, *a calculated labor,* for he did not intend for the *chilazon* to die (*Rashi*).

Tosafos explain that the Gemara's use here of the term "preoccupation" (מִתְעַסֵּק) is not exact; the Gemara actually means to say that the killing was an unintentional act (דָּבָר שֶׁאֵינוֹ מִתְכַּוֵּן). That is, since the person intends only to squeeze out the blood of the *chilazon,* he is not liable for killing it, which is a secondary consequence of his act. See *Pnei Yehoshua* for an explanation of why the Gemara does, in fact, use the term "preoccupation." [According to *Maginei Shlomo, Rashi* disputes this assertion of *Tosafos* – see there.]

25. Literally: its head is cut off and it should not die? Although R' Shimon holds that one incurs no liability for a forbidden labor performed unintentionally while one was engaged in a permitted activity (see above, 29b, and General Introduction), he concedes that liability does occur when the forbidden labor is an inevitable consequence of the permitted action. Hence, if someone cuts off the head of a living creature on the Sabbath, he has violated the prohibition against taking a life on the Sabbath – even if he declares that he does not intend the creature to die. Since its death is inevitable, he is considered to have taken the creature's life intentionally, and he has transgressed even according to R' Shimon (*Rashi* to *Succah* 33b; *Rambam, Shabbos* 1:6). Here, too, since the *chilazon* will certainly die when its blood is squeezed out, the person should be considered to have taken the creature's life intentionally.

26. Literally: as long as there is a soul in it.

27. For purposes of dyeing, the blood of a live animal is superior to that of a dead one. Hence, this person tries to keep the *chilazon* alive while he squeezes out its blood. Therefore, even when it does die, he is regarded as having been preoccupied with another act [i.e. he is not considered to have taken the creature's life intentionally]. R' Shimon concedes that one is liable for an inevitable consequence only when the person at most does not care about the result, not when he is unhappy about it, as is the case here (*Rashi*),

[*Tosafos* question the inference from *Rashi* that according to R' Shimon one is liable for an inevitable consequence even when he does not care about it. For the Gemara below (103a) apparently states that R' Shimon does not hold a person liable in such a case. See *Ramban* and *Ritva* (*MHK* ed., here and below, 103a) for further discussion.]

28. I.e. when was the labor of slaughtering performed during the construction of the Mishkan? The skins of the rams could have been obtained by strangling the animal instead of slaughtering it (*Rashi*). The Gemara now assumes that since the Mishnah describes the *melachah* of taking a life as an act of slaughtering, one incurs liability only through that method of killing [viz. by cutting through the esophagus and windpipe with a specially sharpened knife]. The Gemara therefore questions when the act of slaughtering was performed in the Mishkan (*Yad David,* in explanation of *Rashi;* see also *Rashash;* cf. *Tosafos*).

29. The gushing of blood caused by the slaughter dyes the flesh around the incision [making the person liable for dyeing], and dyeing was certainly necessary in the construction of the Mishkan. The Gemara below will ask what is gained by dyeing the flesh around the incision (*Rashi*).

Rav answers the Gemara's question by explaining that even though it was not necessary to slaughter animals during construction of the Mishkan, the Mishnah uses the term "slaughtering" to highlight a case where the person would be liable for performing the *melachah* of dyeing (*Yad David*). [This answer will be further elaborated below, 75b.]

30. [Some form of] killing occurred during the construction of the Mishkan vis-a-vis the rams, the *tachash* and the *chilazon* (*Rashi;* see *Maharsha* and *Chidushei R' Akiva Eiger*). Shmuel thus answers that this *melachah* actually consists of any type of killing; the Tanna was simply not particular when he stated slaughtering (*Yad David*).

גמרא

שכן יריעה שנפל בה דרנא קורעין בה ותופרין אותה אמר רב זוטרא בר טוביה אמר רב א המותח חוט של תפירה בשבת חייב חטאת ב והלומד דבר אחד מן המגוש חייב מיתה והיודע לחשב תקופות ומזלות ואינו חושב אסור לספר הימנו (א) מגושתא רב ושמואל חד אמר חרשי וחד אמר גדופי תסתיים דרב דאמר גדופי דאמר רב זוטרא בר טוביה אמר רב הלומד דבר אחד מן המגוש חייב מיתה דאי ס"ד חרשי הכתיב (ג) א) לא תלמד לעשות אבל אתה למד להבין ולהורות תסתיים אר"ש בן פזי א"ר יהושע בן לוי משום בר קפרא כל היודע לחשב בתקופות ומזלות ואינו חושב עליו הכתוב אומר ב) ואת פועל ה' לא יביטו ומעשה ידיו לא ראו א"ר שמואל בר נחמני א"ר (ג) יוחנן ג מנין שמצוה על האדם לחשב תקופות ומזלות שנאמר ג) ושמרתם ועשיתם כי היא חכמתכם ובינתכם לעיני העמים איזו חכמה ובינה שהיא לעיני העמים הוי אומר זה חישוב תקופות ומזלות: ד הצד צבי וכו': ת"ר (ד) הצד חלזון והפוצעו אינו חייב אלא אחת רבי יהודה אומר חייב שתים שהיה ר' יהודה אומר ה פציעה בכלל דישה אמרו לו אין פציעה בכלל דישה אמר רבא מ"ט דרבנן קסברי ו אין דישה אלא לגדולי קרקע וליחייב נמי משום נטילת נשמה אמר רבי יוחנן שפצעו מת רבא אמר אפילו תימא שפצעו חי מתעסק הוא אצל נטילת נשמה והא אביי ורבא דאמרי תרווייהו ז מודה (ה) ר"ש בפסיק רישא ולא ימות (א) שאני הכא דכמה דאית ביה נשמה טפי ניחא ליה כי היכי (ו) דליציל ציבעיה: ח והשוחטו: שוחט משום מאי חייב רב אמר משום צובע ושמואל אמר משום ט נטילת נשמה משום

רש"י

דרנא. תולעת ומנקב בו נקב קטן ועגול וצריך לקרוע למטה ולמעלה את הנקב שלא תהא התפירה עשויה קמטין קמטין: המותח חוט של תפירה. בגד התפור ועומד והניח החוט ארוך ונתפרדו שתי חתיכות הבגד זו מזו במקצת וחוטי התפירות נמשכין ומותח את ראשי החוט להדק ולחבר זו היא תפירתו וחייב: והלומד דבר אחד מן המגוש. מין הממשיכו לע"ז אפי' דבר תורה אסור ללמוד ממנו: והיודע כו'. הני תלת שמעתתא שמעינהו (י) מר זוטרא מרב כי הדדי וגרסינהו: אמגושא. דאמרינן בכל דוכתא רב ושמואל פליגי ביה: חד אמר חרשי. מכשף: וחד אמר גדופי. מין האדוק בע"ז ומגדף תמיד את השם ומסית אנשים לע"ז: דאי סלקא דעתך חרשי. וטעמא משום דכתיב לא ימצא בך וגו' וקא חשיב מכשף: והא כתיב. לעיל מיניה לא תלמד לעשות כדי שתעשה: להבין. שתוכל לעמוד בהן ואם יעשה נביא שקר לפניך שתבין שהוא מכשף: תסתיים דגדופי הוא. הלכך כל דבריו דברי ע"ז והסתלק מעליו שלא ישיאך: לעיני העמים. שחכמה הניכרת היא שמראה להם סימן לדבריו בהילוך החמה והמזלו' שמעידין כדבריו שאומר שנה זו גשומה והיא כן שנה זו שחונה והיא כן שכל העיתים לפי מהלך החמה במזלותיה ומולדותיה במזל תלוי הכל לפי השעה המתחלת לשמש בכניסת החמה למזל: הפוצעו. דוחקו בידיו שיצא דמו: אינו חייב אלא אחת. משום צידה אבל אפליעה ליכא חיוב: בכלל דישה. שמפרק דמו הימנו כמפרק תבואה מקשין שלה: מתעסק הוא אצל נטילת נשמה. כלומר לגבי נטילת נשמה הוי מתעסק בדבר אחר ולא הויא מלאכת מחשבת שאינו מתכוין שימות: טפי ניחא ליה. שדם החי טוב מדם המת וכיון דכל עצמו מתכוין ומשמר לשומרו שלא ימות בידו אפי' מת אין כאן אלא מתעסק וכי מודה ר' שמעון במידי דלא איכפת ליה אי מיתרמי ומיהו איכווני לא מיכוין: דליציל ציבעיה גרסי'. שתהא מראית צבעו צלולה: שוחט משום מאי מיחייב. שחיטה במלאכת המשכן היכא ומאי עבידת' אי מעורות אילים מאדמים למה לי בהו שחיטה בחניקה נמי סגי: משום

תוספות

שכן יריעה שנפל בה דרנא כו'. תימה לר"י דבריש האורג אמרי' קורע על מנת לתפור שתי תפירות היכי משכחת לה ומשני דעבידא ככיסתא ואומר ר"י דבמשכן היו אומנים ביותר והיו מהרים שלא היו עושים ככיסתא והתם לא קאמר שנפל בה דרנא דנקט דשכיח טפי ועוד דהתם בעי לאשכוחי קורע על מנת לתפור שתי תפירות ותו לא ויריעה שנפל בה דרנא צריך לקורעה מתחלתה ועד סופה ויש בה כמה תפירות ואע"ג דהשתא לא משכח' במשכן על מנת לתפור שתי תפירות ותו לא סברא הוא דבשתי תפירות הוי דבר חשוב: **אמגושא.** פי' בערוך דפליגי בהא דאמר רב פפא באלו מגלחין (מו"ק יח.) פרעה אמגושי היה דכתיב הנה יוצא המימה חד אמר לעשות כשפים היה יוצא וחד אמר גדופי שהיה עושה עצמו ע"ז שהיה אומר לי יאורי ואני עשיתני ואין נראה לר"י דפליגי רב ושמואל במאי דאמר רב פפא אלא פליגי באמגושא שנזכר בשום מקום במשנה או בברייתא: **הצד** חלזון. למאן דמוקי לה בשפצעו חי אתי שפיר הא דנקט הצד חלזון דדרך לפוצעו מיד אחר צידה כל זמן שהוא חי וקמ"ל דאע"פ שפצעו חי לא מיחייב משום נטילת נשמה ואפילו למאן דמוקי לה כשפצעו מת קמ"ל דלא מיחייב בצידה שלו משום נטילת נשמה דאף על גב דאמרי' בפרק שמונה שרצים (לקמן דף קז:) השולה דג מן הים כיון שיבש בו כו' הכא שאני חלזון דרכו לפרכס ולקרב מיתתו וצ"ע דבירושלמי משמע דצד חלזון לא מיחייב משום צידה: **וליחייב** נמי משום נטילת נשמה. ואפי' לרבי יהודה דאמר מקלקל בחבורה פטור פריך שפיר דהיכא דאיכא תקון קצת חייב כדאמרי' בפסחים (דף עג.) בסוף אלו דברים והכא נמי במה שממיתו יש תקון קצת שאינו מפרכס לכאן ולכאן ונוח ליטול ממנו הדם ולמאי דמסיק דכמה דאית ביה נשמה טפי ניחא ליה אתי שפיר נמי לרבי יהודה דהשתא ליכא תיקון כלל ומיהו שמעתין אתיא אפי' לר"ש דמחייב מקלקל בחבורה מדמשני מתעסק הוא אבל נטילת נשמה ולא קאמר מקלקל הוא: **מתעסק** הוא אצל נטילת נשמה. האי מתעסק לאו דוקא דהא מתעסק בחבורה חייב לר"ש דאמר בס"פ ספק אכל (כריתות יט:) הנח לתינוקות הואיל ומקלקל בחבורה חייב מתעסק נמי חייב וטעמא כדיליף בהאורג (לקמן קו.) מדאיצטריך למישרי מילה מכלל דמקלקל בחבורה חייב ולא חיישינן למלאכת מחשבת דמקלקל דעלמא לא מיפטר אלא משום מלאכת מחשבת כדאמר בספ"ק דחגיגה (דף י:) ומתעסק דהכא היינו דבר שאין מתכוין כיון דאין מתכוין כלל למלאכה מותר אפי' בחבורה אע"פ דלא בעי מלאכת מחשבת כמו כל איסורים שבתורה דלא שייך בהו מלאכת מחשבת ושרו אין מתכוין כדאמר מוכרי כסות מוכרין כדרכן ובלבד שלא יתכוין בחמה מפני החמה כו' (כלאים פ"ט משנה ה) וכן מוכח בפ"ק דכתובות (ד' ה:) דאמר את"ל דם חבורי מיחבר לדם הוא צריך או להנאת עצמו הוא צריך ואת"ל להנאת עצמו הוא צריך הלכה כרבי יהודה או הלכה כר"ש פירוש בדבר שאין מתכוין ואת"ל הלכה כר' יהודה בדבר שאין מתכוין במקלקל הלכה כמאן משמע דאי הלכה כר"ש בדבר שאין מתכוין תו ליכא לספוקי במקלקל דאפי' מקלקל בחבורה חייב כיון דאין מתכוין מותר: **טפי** ניחא ליה כי היכי דליציל ציבעי'. פי' אע"ג דהוי פסיק רישיה למודה ר"ש הכא מיפטר משום דהוי מלאכה שאינה צריכה לגופה דאפי' במקלקל פטר ר"ש במלאכה שאינה צריכה לגופה כדאמר בפרק הנחנקין (סנהדרין פד:) מאן שמעת ליה דאמר מקלקל בחבורה חייב ר"ש הא אמר מלאכה שאינה צריכה לגופה פטור עליה וכי מודה ר"ש בפסיק רישיה ה"מ במידי דניחא ליה אי מתרמי דהוי צריכה לגופה אבל במידי דלא איכפת ליה לא מודה ורש"י פי' דהא דמודה ר"ש בפסיק רישיה היינו במאי דלא איכפת ליה אי מתרמי וליתא דהא מורד זרדין בארעא דחבריה פטר ר"ש בפ' הבונה (לקמן קג.) והתם לא איכפת ליה אי מתרמי אלא כדפי' ותימה דבספ"ק דחגיגה (דף י:) משמע דהא דפטר ר"ש מלאכה שאינה צריכה לגופה היינו משום דבעי מלאכת מחשבת וא"כ בחבורה דלא בעי מלאכת מחשבת ליחייב בה מלאכה שאינה צריכה לגופה: **כי** היכי דליציל ציבעיה. קשה לר"י דמ"מ על נטילת הדם ליחייב משום נטילת נשמה ונראה כלשון אחר שפי' בקונט' בריש שמונה שרצים (לקמן קז.) דחובל בהן חייב משום דהוי תולדה דשוחט וחייב משום נטילת נשמה ונטילת הדם היינו נטילת נשמה כדכתיב כי הדם הוא הנפש ולכך ח' שרצים שיש להם עור חייב בנצרר הדם אע"פ שלא יצא דכיון שנצרר סופו לצאת אלא שעתה העור מעכבו ושאר שרצים שאין להם עור אינו חייב עד שיצא מהם דם אבל בנצרר הדם ולא יצא לא מיחייב דכיון שלא יצא לא סופו לחזור דאם היה סופו לצאת היה יוצא מיד שאין העור מעכבו והשיב לו ר"ת דדם חלזון הראוי לצביעה מיפקד פקיד ולא מיחייב על אותו הדם משום נטילת נשמה ועל דם אחר היוצא עמו נמי לא מיחייב דלא ניחא ליה כי היכי דליליל ליבעיה אבל אין לפרש דנטילת נשמה היינו שמחליש אותו דבר שחובל בו דגבי דם בתולים מה צריך לחלישות האשה וגבי מילה מה צריך לחלישות התינוק אלא לנטילת הדם קרי נטילת נשמה כדפי': **שוחט** משום מאי מיחייב. לאו אשוחט דמתני' קאי דההוא פשיטא דלא הוי אלא משום נטילת נשמה דלוצע תנן בהדיא במתני' אלא אשוחט דעלמא קאי: אין

עין משפט נר מצוה

נד א מיי' שם הלכה ט סמג שם טוש"ע או"ח סימן ש"מ סעיף ו:
נה ב טוש"ע יו"ד סימן קעט סעיף יט:
נו ג סמג עשין יג:
נז ד מיי' פ"י מהלכות שבת הלכה יט סמג לאוין סה טוש"ע או"ח סימן שטז סעיף ה:
נח ה מיי' פ"ח מהלכות שבת הלכה ז ופ"י הלכה יב:
נט ו מיי' שם פ"ח הלכה ז:
ס ז מיי' פ"א מהלכות שבת הלכה ו טוש"ע או"ח סימן שלז סעיף א:
סא ח ט מיי' פי"א מהל' שבת הלכה א:

רבינו חננאל

חייב. ועוד חייב משום מבשל. וזה שנצרך לומר כן דלא תימא אין המבשל כלי חרס מבשל מפני שמחזיק הכלי. אשמעי' דמירפה רפה כשהן טיט ומתבשלין ואחר כך מתחזקין כשיצטרפו (מתחברו) [ויתחברו]. וכן מאן דארתח כופרא. אף על גב דהדור אקיש מבשל הוא. אמר רבה מאן דעבד חלתא חייב ד' חטאות פי' כגון שהיתה לו גבשושית תנטלה ויפה הקרקע חייב משום חורש. שקץ חייב משום טוחן ניקהו מן הצרורות חייב משום בורר וכשחתך [ממנו] [היינו] מחתך. ועיקר מלאכה (א) (בנין מלאכה) וגמר מלאכה והשואתה חייב משום מכה בפטיש הרי שבע ב) בתנור עוד מוסיף אחד שצריך להחליק את תוכו ולשוף אותו בחלים וחייב משום ממחק. מאן דעבד חלתא חייב י"א חטאות. חתך קנה נעשה זומר וצריך לעצים חייב משום קוצר ומשום נוטע כינס הקנים חייב משום מעמר דקדק הקנים חייב משום טוחן. חתכם כשיעור כגון אמה חייב משום מחתך. קליפם חייב משום דש. השליך קליפיהן וקנקן שאין ראויין למלאכה חייב משום בורר. הטיל שתיו חייב משום מיסך וכשמטיל הערב עושה שתי בתי נירין וכשמכה אותן כדי לקרבן זה לזה (ולהדהיק אריג) ג) זה כל זמן שעושה [ארבעת] [ארע"י] הכורות וכשכופף הקנים למעלה לארוגה [והן] קרויות בתה הוא וגמר מלאכה שישבר קרומיות היוצאות משום מכה בפטיש הרי אלו י"א מלאכות ואם כפף פיה למטה וחפרה (כשיבנע החייט) [כשמותח החוט] חייב משום טווה. כרב דאמר המותח חוט של תפירה בשבת חייב (משום) חטאת וכשתופר חייב משום תופר הרי אלו י"ג חטאות: ירושלמי ההיא איתתא כד משחיא בקיבה משום מיסכת כד יהבה קירומה משום עושה בתין. כד מקימה לין משום בונה. כד מחי' משום אורגת כד מקטעא בנימא משום מחתכת. כד גמרה מלאכתה משום מכה בפטיש. אזנים של דיסקיא [קושר ומתיר] נעשה כנועל ופותח וכן חותלות של תמרים קושר ומתיר. א"ר יוחנן הטווה צמר מעל גבי בהמה בשבת חייב ג' חטאות משום גוזז ומנפץ וטווה. ודחה רב כהנא א"ר אמר אין שאני

דרך גזיזה ולא דרך ניפוץ ולא דרך טוויה בכך. ואקשינן על רב כהנא והתניא משום נחמיה שטוף בעזים. אלמא שטפוהו בעזים וטוות מעליהן בלא גזיזה ופריק' חכמה יתירה אשר נשא לבן אותנה בחכמה טוו את העזים. ואע"ג דרב כהנא לגבי רב תלמיד הוה כיון (דיש) דאשכחן בתלמוד א"י דקיימי כוותיה דגרסינן התולש כנף מן העוף חייב משום גוזז המורט מוחק הקוטמה חייב משום מכה בפטיש ודחינן לא דמיא תולש כנף עוף לתולש שער בהמה דעוף שאין לו גזיזה תלישתה היא גזיזתה ברם בהמה אינו חייב עד שיגזז תדע שהוא המתה חייב תלישתה זו היא גזיזתה מן החיה פטור ותו מדתנן (לקמן צד:) הנוטל צפרניו זו בזו או בשיניו וכן שערו וכן שפמו וכן זקנו ר' אליעזר מחייב חטאת וחכמים אומרים משום דרך נטילת שיער בשיניים וכיון דקיימי חכמים כרב כהנא קיי"ל כוותיה: אמגושתא. פי' בלשון ערבי זמזמה. מגוש בלשון יון מכשף. גידופי כופר בעיקר: **הצד** צבי השוחטו כו'. והפורצו אינו חייב אלא אחת ר' יהודה אומר חייב שתים פציעה בכלל דישה ורבנן סברי אין דישה אלא בגידולי קרקע ואקשינן לרבנן ליחייב ומשום צידה ומשום נטילת נשמה ופריק ר' רבא אמר אפילו תימא שפצעו חי. מתעסק אצל נטילת נשמה וקיי"ל המתעסק [בחלבים ובעריות] חייב משום דנהנה המתעסק בשבת פטור מלאכת מחשבת אסרה תורה דלא קא ניחא ליה לנטילת נשמה דניחא

חשק שלמה על רבינו חננאל א) אולי צ"ל ועל עיקר מלאכה הסבית חייב משום בונה וגמר מלאכה וכו': ב) לפי מה דהשיב רבינו אין כאן רק שש חטאות. ואולי דחסר בדברי רבינו וצ"ל וכשמלרף אח"כ ככבשן חייב משום מבשל וכ"ה בר"ש: ג) אולי צ"ל חייב משום

מסורת הש"ס

א) ס"א אמגושא. ב) [ר"ה כד: ע"ז יח. סנהד' סח.], ג) [צ"ל יונתן], ד) [תוספתא פ"ט ע"ש], ה) לקמן קו. קז. קלג. קמג. [כתובות ו: בכורות כה. סוכה לג.], ו) [צ"ל דליציל פי' שלא יחזק ליה למיפסק נשמה דכל כמה דלית ביה נשמה טפי מגלה צבעיה שלגבעו מתעלה יפה ויהא צבעו יפה ובהיר כי הוא מלוה. ערוך], ז) [צ"ל רב].

הגהות הב"ח

(א) גמ' שאני הכא. נ"ב עמ"ש דף קג:

תורה אור השלם

א) כִּי אַתָּה בָּא אֶל הָאָרֶץ אֲשֶׁר יְיָ אֱלֹהֶיךָ נֹתֵן לָךְ לֹא תִלְמַד לַעֲשׂוֹת כְּתוֹעֲבֹת הַגּוֹיִם הָהֵם: [דברים יח, ט]

ב) וְהָיָה כִנּוֹר וָנֶבֶל תֹּף וְחָלִיל וָיַיִן מִשְׁתֵּיהֶם וְאֵת פֹּעַל יְיָ לֹא יַבִּיטוּ וּמַעֲשֵׂה יָדָיו לֹא רָאוּ: [ישעיה ה, יב]

ג) וּשְׁמַרְתֶּם וַעֲשִׂיתֶם כִּי הִוא חָכְמַתְכֶם וּבִינַתְכֶם לְעֵינֵי הָעַמִּים אֲשֶׁר יִשְׁמְעוּן אֵת כָּל הַחֻקִּים הָאֵלֶּה וְאָמְרוּ רַק עַם חָכָם וְנָבוֹן הַגּוֹי הַגָּדוֹל הַזֶּה: [דברים ד, ו]

רב נסים גאון

שכן קרש שנפל בו דרנא. פי' דרנא תולעת ובסוף פרק אלו טריפות (חולין דף סז) משכחת ואת נבלתם לרבות את הדרנין של בהמה: רבא אמר אפילו תימא שפצעו חי מתעסק הוא אצל

ליקוטי רש"י

קורעין בה ותופרין אותה. שהנקב עגול ואינו יכול לתופרו יפה אלא אם כן קורעו אבל קורע שלא לתפור לא הוי במשכן [לעיל עג.]. גדופי. עובדי כוכבים [סנהדרין סח.]. ואת פועל ה' לא יביטו. ובאוריתא דה' לא אסתכלו. ומעשה ידיו לא ראו. עמו כאילו לא ראו את גבורותיו [ישעיה ה, יב]. כי היא חכמתכם ובינתכם וגו'. בזאת תחשבו חכמים ונבונים לעיני העמים [דברים ד, ו]. והפוצעו. שעולין ופוצעין את החלזון להוציא דמו [לעיל כו.]. נטילת נשמה. שהיא אב מלאכה דמכן [לעיל עג.]. השוחטו וכו' [תענית כו.]. מודה ר' שמעון. באומר כמתכבת שבת [לעיל מא:]. דבר שאין מתכוין מותר [בכורות כה.]. בפסיק רישא ולא ימות. כלומר אמתוך ראש בהמה זו בשבת ואיני רוצה שתמות דכיון דלא אפשר שלא תמות כמתכוין חשיב ליה וכי אמרינן דבר שאין מתכוין מותר כגון היכא דאפשר ליה בלא איסור כגון גורר אדם מטה כסא וספסל ובלבד שלא יתכוין לעשות חריץ ואף על גב דאיכא למיחש דלמא עביד חריץ כיון דלא מתכוין להכי ואפשר לגרירה בלא חריץ כי עביד נמי חריץ דהוי מלאכה גמורה לא מחייב אבל היכא דודאי עביד מודי [סוכה לג:].

עין משפט נר מצוה

סב א ב ג מיי' פי"א מהלכות שבת הלכה ה סמג לאוין סה טוש"ע או"ח סימן שכא סעיף ה:
סב [א] [מיי' פ"י מהל' שבת הלכה ו ופי"א הלכה יז]:
סב [ג] [מיי' פי"א שם הלכה יז]:
סג ד מיי' שם הלכה ז:
סד ה מיי' שם הלכה ו ופכ"ג הלכה יא טור שו"ע או"ח סימן שמ סעיף ב:
סה ו מיי' פ"י מהלכות שבת הלכה יז:
סו ז שם הלכה טו:
סז ח מיי' שם הלכה יח טוש"ע או"ח סימן שמ סעיף ג:
סח ט מיי' פי"א מהל' שבת הלכה ט סמג שם טוש"ע או"ח סימן שמ סעיף ג:
סט כ מיי' פ"ז שם הלכה ו סמג שם:
ע ל מיי' פ"ז שם הל"ז ופ"ו מהל' שגגות הלכה ה:
ע [ד] [מיי' שם פי"ט הלכה יח ועין]:
עא מ נ מיי' פי"ח מהל' שבת הלכה כב:

מסורת הש"ס

א) [נ"ל אסי], ב) [תוספ' פי"ב], ג) לקמן נו: ב"ק ב. כריתות טז:, ד) לקמן עז., ה) לקמן עג., ו) ע"כ שייך לעיל, ז) [עי' בערוך ערך שך], ח) [ועי' במה שליינתי בס"ד בתוס' יבמות פד: ד"ה אלא].

גמרא

משום צובע אין משום נטילת נשמה לא אימא אף משום צובע אמר רב מילתא דאמרי אימא בה מילתא דלא ליתו דרי בתראי וליחכו עלי צובע במאי ניחא ליה ניחא דליתווס בית השחיטה דמא כי היכי דליחזוה אינשי וליתו ליזבנו מיניה: והמולחו והמעבדו: א היינו מולח והיינו מעבד ר' יוחנן ור"ל דאמרי תרווייהו אפיק חד מינייהו ועייל [א] שירטוט אמר רבה בר רב הונא האי מאן דמלח בישרא חייב משום מעבד ב רבא אמר אין עיבוד באוכלין אמר רב אשי ואפילו רבה בר רב הונא לא אמר אלא דקא בעי ליה לאורחא אבל לביתא לא משוי איניש מיכליה עץ: ג והממחקו והמחתכו: אמר רבי אחא בר חנינא [ג] השף בין העמודים בשבת חייב משום ממחק אמר רבי חייא בר אבא ג' דברים סח לי רב א) אשי משמיה דרבי יהושע בן לוי ד המגרר ראשי כלונסות בשבת חייב משום מחתך ה הממרח רטיה בשבת חייב משום ממחק ו והמסתת את האבן בשבת חייב משום מכה בפטיש אמר ר' שמעון (א) בן קיסמא אמר רבי שמעון בן לקיש ז הצר צורה בכלי והמנפח בכלי זכוכית חייב משום מכה בפטיש א"ר יהודה ח האי מאן דשקיל אקופי מגלימי חייב משום מכה בפטיש והני מילי דקפיד עלייהו: ט והכותב שתי אותיות: ת"ר ב) י כתב אות אחת גדולה ויש במקומה לכתוב שתים פטור מחק אות גדולה ויש במקומה לכתוב שתים חייב אמר רבי מנחם בר' יוסי וזה חומר במוחק מבכותב: הבונה והסותר המכבה והמבעיר והמכה בפטיש: רבה ור' זירא דאמרי תרוייהו כ כל מידי דאית ביה גמר מלאכה חייב משום מכה בפטיש: אלו אבות מלאכות: ג) אלו ל לאפוקי מדר"א דמחייב על תולדה במקום אב: חסר אחת: לאפוקי מדר' יהודה ד) דתניא ר' יהודה מוסיף את השובט והמדקדק אמרו לו [ד] שובט הרי הוא בכלל מיסך מדקדק הרי הוא בכלל אורג:

מתני' ועוד כלל אחר אמרו מ כל הכשר להצניע ומצניעין כמוהו והוציאו בשבת חייב חטאת עליו וכל שאינו כשר להצניע ואין מצניעין כמוהו והוציאו בשבת אינו חייב אלא המצניעו:

גמ' כל הכשר להצניע לאפוקי מאי רב פפא אמר נ לאפוקי דם נדה מר עוקבא אמר לאפוקי עצי אשרה מאן דאמר דם נדה כ"ש עצי אשרה מאן דאמר עצי אשרה אבל דם נדה מצנע ליה לשונרא ואידך כיון דחלשא לא מצנע ליה אמר רבי יוסי בר חנינא האי דלא כר"ש דאי כר"ש האמר ה) לא אמרו כל השיעורין הללו אלא למצניעיהן: וכל שאינו כשר להצניע:

אמר

רש"י

משום צובע. שצובע את הבשר של בית השחיטה ולקמן מפרש אמאי מיכוין לצובעו וצביעה הואי במשכן אב מלאכה: משום נטילת נשמה. דנטילת נשמה הואי במשכן באילים מאדמים ותחש וחלזון ו): אף משום צביעה. ונפקא מינה לחיוביה תרתי: מילתא דאמרי אימא כו'. דבר תימה אמרתי להזכיר צביעה בשחיטה צריך אני לומר בו דבר טעם דלא ליתו דרי בתראי השומעים וליחכו עלי: צובע בשר במאי ניחא ליה. להאי שוחט בצביעת הבשר היינו חוכא ואני אומר בו טעם: ניחא ליה דליתווס בית השחיטה בדמא. שיהא צבוע בדם: כי היכי דניחזייה אינשי. שנשחטה היום וניתו ומזבנו: היינו מולח היינו מעבד. אטו מליחה לאו צורך עיבוד הוא: ועייל שירטוט. לפי שדרך הרצענין כשהוא בא לחתכו משרטטו תחלה כפי מה שהוא רוצה להאריך ולהרחיב ולקצר החיתוך ואחר כך מעביר הסכין דרך השירטוט וכן בעורות המשכן כשחתכום: דקבעי ליה לאורחא. שמולחה הרבה: השף בין העמודים. כגון עמודי אכסדראות שעשוים חלונות חלונות ונסמכין בחלונות בין עמוד לעמוד והשף שם בקרקעית הבנין שנשענין עליו כדי שיהא חלק חייב משום ממחק: המגרר ראשי כלונסות. שיהו ראשיהן שוין וחדין: ממרח רטיה. מחליק תחבושת על המכה: מסתת את האבן. לאחר שנעקרה מן ההר ונחצבה מחליקה: משום מכה בפטיש. שהוא גמר מלאכה: הצר (ב) בכלי צורה. בכלי שעומד לכך לנאותו: מנפח בכלי זכוכית. כשהותך נעשה על ידי נפוח: דשקיל אקופי. ראשי חוטין התלויין ביריעה במקום קשורין כשניתק בה חוט וקשרוהו וכן קשין וקסמים דקין שנארגו בה בלא מתכוין ונוטלין אותם ממנה לאחר אריגה גמר מלאכה הוא וחייב משום מכה בפטיש: כתב אות אחת גדולה כו' פטור. שבקרשי המשכן שתים היו כותבים אחת בזו ואחת בזו כדי לזווגן כשסותרים אותן: מחק אות אחת כו' חייב. שאין מלאכת מחיקה חשובה אלא ע"מ לכתוב והרי יש מקום לשתי אותיות: אמר רבי מנחם ברבי יוסי. הא קמ"ל מאן תנא קמא ר' מנחם ברבי יוסי: לאפוקי מדרבי אליעזר. דהא אמרן דלא נמנו כאן אלא להודיענו מנין חטאות של העלם אחד ותנא הרי אלו למעוטי שאם עשה תולדותיהם עמהן דאינו מביא עליהן חטאת ודלא כרבי אליעזר דמחייב אתולדה עם האב בכריתות: שובט. משוה השתי בכרכר שקורין ריו"ל: מדקדק. כשמותח חוט הערב מכה בכרכר עליו במקומות מקומות ליישבו שלא יהא מתוח יותר מדאי שהמתיחה מעכבתו מהתחבר יפה עם הארג: שובט הרי הוא בכלל מיסך. דהיינו מיסך ממש שמסדר חוטי השתי: הרי הוא אורג. דהיינו אורג ממש ולא דמי לזורה ובורר ומרקד דזה בקשין וזה בצרורות וזה בקמח: מתני' כל הכשר להצניע. שהוא מין העשוי לצורך האדם: ומצניעין כמוהו. כמות זה כלומר שיש בו שיעור הראוי להצניעו: אין חיוב אלא למצניעו. אם נעשה חביב לאדם א' והצניעו חייב על הוצאתו אם חזר והוציאו אבל אדם אחר אינו חייב עליו דלגביה לאו מלאכה הוא: גמ' מ"ד דם נדה. אינו כשר להצניע כ"ש עצי אשרה דאיסורי הנאה נינהו ומאיסי וצריך לאבדן: כיון דחלשא. המאכיל דם האדם לחתול נעשה חלש אותו אדם: הא. דתנא כל הכשר להצניע ויש בו שיעור שרוב ב"א עשוין להצניע כשיעור הזה חייב כל אדם על הוצאתו ואפילו אדם עשיר שאין שיעור זה חשוב לו: דלא כר' שמעון. לקמן בהמוציא:

אמר

תוספות

אין עיבוד באוכלין. אין להתיר מכאן מליחת אוכלין לאסור מדרבנן מליחה בפרק שמונה שרצים (לקמן דף קח:) ואפילו בי"ט אסור בפ"ק דביצה (דף יא.): השף בין העמודים בשבת חייב. פירש ר"ח ו) דשף העור על העמוד כדי להחליקו וכן משמע בירושלמי ורש"י פירש שסף קרקעית שבין עמודי חלונות ולא נהירא: והמסתת את האבן כו' חייב משום מכה בפטיש. אבל משום מחתך וממחק לא מיחייב דמיירי שכבר היא מרובעת ומתוקנת אלא שמייפה אותה ועושה בה שירטוטין ויפוי כעין שעושין עכשיו מסתתי האבנים. ר"י וכן ריב"א: הרי אלו לאפוקי מדרבי אליעזר דמחייב אתולדה במקום אב. וא"ת מרישא שמעינן לה דתנן העושה מלאכות הרבה מעין מלאכה אחת אינו חייב אלא אחת וי"מ דה"ק מעין מלאכה אחת היינו שתי תולדות מאב א' אבל האב ותולדה דידיה מיחייב תרתי קמ"ל: חסר אחת לאפוקי מדר' יהודה. תימה דממנינא דרישא שמעינן לה וליכא למימר תנא ושייר ט) דהא אלו קתני ומיהו הא ליכא לאקשויי דהא מאלו דרישא שמעינן לאפוקי מדר' אליעזר דאיכא למימר דנקט ברישא אלו אבות משום דקאי אדקתני לעיל חייב על כל אב מלאכה וי"ל דממנינא דרישא לא שמעינן לאפוקי מדרבי יהודה דאיכא למימר דלא חשיב אלא מלאכות חשובות אבל שובט ומדקדק אע"ג דמלאכות הן לא קתני להו משום דאינם מבוררות כל כך וכה"ג משני בפ"ק דקדושין (דף טז:) גבי אלו מעניקין להן דבר שיש לו קצבה קתני דבר שאין לו קצבה לא קתני ח): לאפוקי עצי אשרה. דלא כרבי יהודה דאמר בפרק רבי עקיבא (לקמן דף צ.) אף המוציא משמשי ע"ז כל שהוא חייב אלא כת"ק דפליג עליה כן פירש בקונט' התם וקשה לרשב"א הא דקאמר הכא מ"ד דם נדה כ"ש עצי אשרה מנא ליה דילמא סבר כרבי יהודה ומחייב בעצי אשרה שמצניעין אותן לשריפה: הא דלא כר' שמעון. פירש בקונטרס הא דתנן כל הכשר כו' שרוב בני אדם עשויים להצניע כשיעור הזה חייב כל אדם על הוצאתו אפילו אדם עשיר שאין שיעור זה חשוב לו משמע מדבריו דלא מחייב ר' שמעון אלא בסתם בני אדם שרגילין להצניעו שאותו שיעור חשוב להן ואפילו לא הצניעו הוא ולקמן פי' לא נאמרו שיעורים שבמשנה אלא למצניעין אותו קודם לכן וחזר המצניע והוציאו משמע דוקא בהצניעו חייב ואומר ר"י דיש ליישב פירושו דמה שמצריך

רבינו חננאל

ליה דנהוי חי כי היכי דלצלח צביעה דכל כמה דהוא חי מצלח צביעה. שוחט משום מאי מחייב רב אמר משום צובע אסיק' ניחא ליה כי היכי דנתווס בית שחיטה דידיה דמא. כי היכי דלידעי אינשי דחי הוה וכי היכי (דניחה) [דנחזיה] אינשי דנשחט הוא וקאתי למזבן מיניה ולא ימרו שנבילה הוא. והא דאמר רב משום צובע הכי קאמר חדא משום נטילת נשמה דהא בהדיא תנן באבות מלאכות השוחט. וסבר רב השוחט בשבת חייב שתים אחת משום נטילת נשמה ואחת משום צובע והוא אב (אחד) [אחר]. והמולחו והמעבדו. אקשינן דמולח היינו מעבד כדאמרינן (לקמן עט:) לענין חיפה מליח וקמיח שמנצאת מליחתו עבודו ופרקינן ר' יוחנן ור"ל המולח והמעבד תרווייהו מלאכת עיבוד נינהו ותני חדא והוא הדין לאחרינא. אי הכי בצרי להו ושני חדא עייל שירטוט במתני' המולחו והמשרטטו: ירושלמי מה עיבוד היה במשכן שהיו משרטטין בעורות מהו משרטטין מסרגלין. מליחת בשר חי בשבת. אם כוונתו לצאת בו לדרך או לאוכלו לאחר כמה ימים חייב משום מעבד אבל לאוכלו בימו לא ולית הלכתא כדרבה בר רב הונא (דרבה בר רב הונא) [דרבא] דחי לה ואמר אין עיבוד באוכלין: השף בין העמודים. פי' מחליק חייב משום מוחק והוא כמו ממרח את הרטיה: ירושלמי הממחק. מה מחיקה היתה במשכן (פי') שהיו שפין העורות ע"ג העמוד. השף את העור ע"ג העמוד חייב משום (מוחק) [ממחק]. הממרח איספלנית חייב משום מוחק. הגורר ראשי כלונסות חייב משום מחתך. הממרח רטיה חייב משום מוחק. וכן הצר בכלי צורה כל שהוא חייב משום מכה בפטיש. ואע"ג דפליג ר' ישמעאל (לקמן קג:) ואמר עד שיצור כל הצורה יחידאה היא ואי ההיא צורה אית בה אותיות דמיקרו חייב משום כותב ואי לאו חייב משום מכה בפטיש וכן המנפח בכלי זכוכית הוא גמר מלאכתו שמלאכת זכוכית בניפוח הוא. פי' אקופי כגון נימין הניתקין מן האריגה דנתלין בבגד או חתיכות עצים קטנים המסבכין בצמרן של בגדים חדשים וכשמשלים האומן מלאכתו כל ראשי נימין התלויים בין קיסם וקליפה שנסתבכו בבגד נוטלן. ונקראין אקופי.

הגהות הב"ח

(א) גמ' אמר ר"ש בר קיסמא אמר ר"ש בן לקיש הצר: (ב) רש"י ד"ה הצר צורה כלי נ"ל ותיבת בכלי נמחק:

גליון הש"ס

תוס' ד"ה חסר אחת וכו' דהא אלו קתני. כלאי' בקדושין דף טז ע"ב:

רב נסים גאון

נטילת נשמה קיי"ל שהמתעסק לענין שבת פטור. ומשכחת עיקר דילה במסכת כריתות בפרק ספק אכל חלב (דף יט) אמר רב נחמן אמר שמואל [המתעסק] בחלבים ובעריות (בחלבים פטור ובעריות) חייב שכבר נהנה מתעסק בשבת פטור מלאכת מחשבת אסרה תורה ומשכחת לה בסנהדרין בפ' ד' מיתות (דף סב) ובגמרא דהזורק דבני מערבא (הלכה ו) גרסי הזורק בשבת פטור היאך עבידא אמר הריני קוצר חצי גרוגרת וקצר כגרוגרת פטור בגמ' דכל שעה בפסחים (דף לג) גרסי לה אם אמרת בשאר מצות שכן לא חייב בהן שאין מתעסק כמתעסק שאם נתכוין להגביה את התלוש וחתך המחובר פטור וכגון זה כל מלאכה שהיא באה חילוף מה שנתכוון העושה אותה מתעסק מיקרי שהרי לא נעשית מחשבתו: אלו לאפוקי מדר' אליעזר דמחייב על תולדה במקום אב. ואשכחנן דברי ר' אליעזר בכריתות בפרק אמרו לו אכלת חלב (דף טז) אמר ר' עקיבא שאלתי את ר' אליעזר העושה מלאכות הרבה בשבתות הרבה מעין מלאכה אחת בהעלם אחד מהו חייב על כל אחת ואחת או חייב אחת על כולן אמר לי חייב על כל אחת ואחת מקל וחומר ואמרו בתלמוד בעי מיניה ולדי מלאכות אי כמלאכות דמיין אי לא ופשט ליה דולדי מלאכות כמלאכות דמיין: דאי ר' שמעון הא אמר לא נאמרו כל השיעורין האלו אלא למצניעיהן. בפירקא דלקמן המוציא יין (דף עו) משכחת להא דר' שמעון:

סליק פרק כלל גדול

ליקוטי רש"י

דליתווס. מיתווסי. מתלכלכין [פסחים סה:]. היינו מולח והיינו מעבד. מליחה מאבות מלאכות היא בדבר שיש בו עבוד דתנן (שבת עג.) והמולחו והמעבדו [ביצה יא:]. הממרח רטיה. מחליק גומות שברטיה מירוח חייב משום ממחק [עירובין קב:]. מסתת את האבן. מרבע את האבן ומתקנה הכל לפי המקום שיש מקומות שרגילין להחליק ויש מקומות שרגילין לחרוץ בה חריצים בארץ אשכנז. משום מכה בפטיש. גמר מלאכה הוא שהמקום שחרץ חריץ זה לא יחרוץ עוד. כל מידי דאית ביה גמר מלאכה וכו'. כל הגומר בשבת מלאכה תולדת מכה בפטיש היא [לקמן קב:]. לאפוקי מדר"א דמחייב על תולדה במקום אב. דאי עביד אב ותולדה דידיה מחייב תרתי חטאות במס' כריתות בפ' אמרו לו (טז.) [ב"ק ב.]. מוסיף את השובט. עם שאר אבות מלאכות להא דאמרן דלכך נמנו שאם עשאן בהעלם אחד חייב על כל אחד ואחד. שובט. מכרכר בכרכר. ומדקדק. לאחר שמתח החוט של ערב מכה בכרכר בשנים ושלשה מקומות ויש מפרשים מדקדק משוה האריגה כשיש שני חוטין כרוכין זה עם זה ומובדלים מן השאר משוה אותן בכרכר או במחט [לקמן צז:]. לא אמרו. שיעורין שבמשנה אלא למצניעיהן לבד וחזר המצניע והוציאו חייב אבל שאר כל אדם שהוציאו אינו חייב וסבירא ליה לר' שמעון דמצניע עצמו בעי שיעורא זוטא ובבציר מהא שיעורא לא מיחייב כדאמרינן בפרקין דלעיל (עה:) דלית ליה לר' שמעון כל שאין כשר להצניע ואין מצניעים כמוהו שיתחייב עליו מצניעו [שם עו:].

The Gemara questions the explanation of Rav:
מִשּׁוּם צוֹבֵעַ אִין – For dyeing he is indeed liable, מִשּׁוּם נְטִילַת נְשָׁמָה לֹא – but for taking a life he is not?[1]
The Gemara answers:
אֵימָא אַף מִשּׁוּם צוֹבֵעַ – Say that Rav means that the person is liable also for dyeing; it goes without saying that he is liable for taking a life.[2]
Rav understands that he must justify his statement:
אָמַר רַב – Rav said: מִילְּתָא דְּאָמְרִי אֵימָא בָּהּ מִילְּתָא – I shall say something about the opinion I stated דְּלֹא לֵיתוּ דָּרֵי בָּתְרָאֵי וְלִיחֲכוּ עֲלַי – so that later generations will not come and ridicule me by asking: צוֹבֵעַ בְּמַאי נִיחָא לֵיהּ – What pleases [the slaughterer] about dyeing the animal's flesh?[3] נִיחָא דְּלִיתְוַוס בֵּית הַשְּׁחִיטָה דְּמָא – And so I explain as follows: It is pleasing to him that the place of slaughter (the throat) be soaked with blood,[4] כִּי הֵיכִי דְּלִיחֲזוּהּ אִינְשֵׁי – so that people will see it[5] וְלֵיתוּ לִיזְבְּנוּ מִינֵּיהּ – and come to buy from him.

The Mishnah included in its list of *melachos* required for the preparation of a hide:
וְהַמּוֹלְחוֹ וְהַמְעַבְּדוֹ – SALTING IT AND TANNING IT.
The Gemara questions why both labors are counted as separate *melachos*:
הַיְינוּ מוֹלֵחַ וְהַיְינוּ מְעַבֵּד – Salting is the same as tanning![6] – ? –
The Gemara concedes:
רַבִּי יוֹחָנָן וְרֵישׁ לָקִישׁ דְּאָמְרִי תַּרְוַיְיהוּ – R' Yochanan and Reish Lakish both said: אַפֵּיק חַד מִינַּיְיהוּ – Remove one of them from the list of thirty-nine primary labors[7] וְעַיֵּיל שִׂירְטוּט – and insert tracing lines in its place.[8]

The Gemara discusses the *melachah* of tanning:
אָמַר רַבָּה בַּר רַב הוּנָא – Rabbah bar Rav Huna said: הַאי מַאן דְּמָלַח בִּישְׂרָא – Someone who salts meat חַיָּיב מִשּׁוּם מְעַבֵּד – is liable on account of "tanning."[9]
A dissenting view:
רָבָא אָמַר – Rava said: אֵין עִיבּוּד בְּאוֹכָלִין – There is no "tanning" in [the case of] foods.[10]
The Gemara clarifies the dispute:
אָמַר רַב אַשִׁי – Rav Ashi said: וַאֲפִילּוּ רַבָּה בַּר רַב הוּנָא – And even Rabbah bar Rav Huna לֹא אָמַר אֶלָּא דְּקָא בָּעֵי לֵיהּ לְאוֹרְחָא – said his ruling only where one needs [meat] for the way, in which case he must salt the meat heavily in order to preserve it. Then, salting meat is tantamount to salting a hide. אֲבָל לְבֵיתָא – But if the meat is designated for home consumption he may salt it, לֹא מְשַׁוֵּי אִינִישׁ מֵיכְלֵיהּ עֵץ – for a person does not render his food inedible like wood with heavy salting.[11]

The Mishnah continues its discussion of *melachos* required to prepare a hide:
וְהַמְּמַחֲקוֹ וְהַמְחַתְּכוֹ – SMOOTHING IT AND CUTTING IT.
The Gemara presents another example of smoothing:
אָמַר רַבִּי אַחָא בַּר חֲנִינָא – R' Acha bar Chanina said: הַשָּׁף בֵּין הָעַמּוּדִים בְּשַׁבָּת – One who rubs the ground between the pillars of a pavilion on the Sabbath[12] חַיָּיב מִשּׁוּם מְמַחֵק – is liable on account of "smoothing."

Another series of acts prohibited on the Sabbath:
אָמַר רַבִּי חִיָּיא בַּר אַבָּא – R' Chiya bar Abba said: שְׁלֹשָׁה דְּבָרִים סָח לִי רַב אַשִׁי מִשְּׁמֵיהּ דְּרַבִּי יְהוֹשֻׁעַ בֶּן לֵוִי – Rav Ashi[13] told me three things in the name of R' Yehoshua ben Levi: הַמְגָרֵר רָאשֵׁי כְלוֹנָסוֹת בְּשַׁבָּת – One who planes the tops of poles on the Sabbath in order to sharpen them[14] חַיָּיב מִשּׁוּם מְחַתֵּךְ – is liable on account of "cutting"; הַמְמָרֵחַ רְטִיָּה בְּשַׁבָּת – one who

NOTES

1. I.e. is it possible that the Mishnah used the term "slaughtering" to teach that someone can be held liable only for dyeing when he slaughters an animal? Why should he not be liable for taking the animal's life for that act? [And it is not possible to say that the Mishnah wants to teach that there is a *melachah* of dyeing because it states that *melachah* explicitly.]

2. [That is, according to Rav the Mishnah used the term "slaughtering" for the *melachah* instead of "taking a life" to teach a case where] a person is liable to two *chatas* offerings (*Rashi*). Therefore, if someone slaughters an animal on the Sabbath, he can be held liable both for "dyeing" and for "taking a life."

Thus, whereas according to Shmuel the Tanna used the term "slaughtering" loosely to denote the *melachah* of "taking a life," Rav maintains that the Tanna chose the term "slaughtering" to teach that a person is liable also for dyeing when he kills an animal that way. But Rav certainly agrees with Shmuel that a person is liable for performing the *melachah* of taking a life no matter which way he kills (based on *Yad David*).

3. At first glance it appears ludicrous to say that a slaughterer intends to perform, or has any use for, the labor of dyeing. Rav therefore acknowledges the need to explain himself (*Rashi*).

4. I.e. that it will be dyed red by the blood (*Rashi*).

5. I.e. people will see that the meat is freshly slaughtered (*Rashi;* cf. *Rabbeinu Chananel*).

6. Literally: this is salting; this is tanning. The hide is salted as part of the tanning process (*Rashi*), which hardens the skin, transforming it into leather. Why should the Mishnah list the two acts as separate *avos melachos*?

Chidushei HaRan explains why this situation differs from that involving winnowing, selecting and sifting, which are all part of the sorting process but are counted as three separate *melachos*: There, each of those labors is performed at a distinct stage of the sorting process. Winnowing removes the chaff; selecting removes the stones; and sifting is done after the grain has been transformed into flour. But here the hide does not change between the salting and the subsequent stages of the tanning process. [See also below, note 32.]

7. Both salting and tanning are counted as a single *melachah*.

8. Leatherworkers customarily trace lines in skins to indicate the desired shape of the piece to be cut. Tracing was performed in the Mishkan to facilitate a precise cutting of the hides of rams and *techashim* for the coverings (*Rashi;* cf. *Rambam, Hil. Shabbos* 11:17). [See *Rashash.*]

9. [According to Rabbah bar Rav Huna, there is no difference between salting a hide and salting meat, since both harden the item being salted.]

10. According to Rava, the labor of tanning is a *melachah* only when it is performed on hides, not on food.

Tosafos note, however, that even according to Rava's view it is Rabbinically prohibited to salt food on the Sabbath (in circumstances discussed by the Gemara below, 108b).

11. Rather, he salts it just for taste. A minimal amount of salting for that purpose bears no relationship to tanning.

Ritva (*MHK* ed.) points out that according to Rava's dissenting opinion even heavy salting [for the road] is not considered tanning, although it is forbidden by Rabbinic edict (see previous note).

12. The roof of a pavilion was supported by pillars and in between the pillars were open spaces. R' Acha refers to one who walks around and between the pillars in order to smooth the dirt floor of the pavilion (*Rashi,* as explained by *Chidushei HaRan*). This makes the area more inviting for people to sit there (*Meiri*).

Rabbeinu Chananel (see also *Tosafos*), *Ramban* and other Rishonim object to this explanation, because we learned above (73b) that one who smooths the ground in a house is liable for building, while in the field he is liable for plowing. The *melachah* of smoothing should thus not be relevant to this act. The Rishonim therefore explain that R' Acha refers to one who rubs a hide hung on pillars in order to smooth and soften it (see *Ran MHK* ed.). See *Korban Nesanel* §80 for a discussion of this dispute.

13. *Mesoras HaShas* emends this to Rav Assi; cf. *Rashash.*

14. I.e. He wants the tops of the poles to be sharp and of equal size (*Rashi*). [*Maggid Mishneh* (*Hil. Shabbos* 11:7) writes that the text should read הַמְגָרֵד here; see there; see also *Shabbos Shel Mi.*]

משום צובע אין משום נטילת נשמה לא אימא אף משום צובע אמר רב מילתא דאמרי אימא בה מילתא דלא ליתו דרי בתראי וליחכו עלי צובע במאי ניחא ליה ניחא דליתווס בית השחיטה דמא כי היכי דליחזוה אינשי וליתו ליזבנו מיניה: והמולחו והמעבדו: [א]היינו מולח והיינו מעבד ר' יוחנן ור"ל דאמרי תרוייהו אפיק חד מינייהו ועייל [א] שירטוט אמר רבה בר רב הונא האי מאן דמלח בישרא חייב משום מעבד [ב]רבא אמר אין עיבוד באוכלין אמר רב אשי ואפילו רבה בר רב הונא לא אמר אלא דקא בעי ליה לאורחא אבל לביתא לא משוי איניש מיכליה עץ: [ג]והממחקו והמחתכו: אמר רבי אחא בר חנינא [ג] השף בין העמודים בשבת חייב משום ממחק אמר רבי חייא בר אבא ג' דברים סח לי רב [א] אשי משמיה דרבי יהושע בן לוי [ד]המגרר ראשי כלונסות בשבת חייב משום מחתך [ה]הממרח רטיה בשבת חייב משום ממחק [ו]והמסתת את האבן בשבת חייב משום מכה בפטיש אמר ר' שמעון (א) בן קיסמא אמר רבי שמעון בן לקיש [ז]הצר צורה בכלי והמנפח בכלי זכוכית חייב משום מכה בפטיש א"ר יהודה [ח]האי מאן דשקיל אקופי מגלימי חייב משום מכה בפטיש והני מילי דקפיד עלייהו: [ט]והכותב שתי אותיות: ת"ר [ג] [י]כתב אות אחת גדולה ויש במקומה לכתוב שתים פטור מחק אות גדולה ויש במקומה לכתוב שתים חייב אמר רבי מנחם בר' יוסי וזה חומר במוחק מבכותב: הבונה והסותר המכבה והמבעיר והמכה בפטיש: רבה ור' זירא דאמרי תרוייהו [כ]כל מידי דאית ביה גמר מלאכה חייב משום מכה בפטיש: אלו אבות מלאכות: [ג] אלו [ל]לאפוקי מדר"א דמחייב על תולדה במקום אב: חסר אחת: לאפוקי מדר' יהודה [ד] דתניא ר' יהודה מוסיף את השובט והמדקדק אמרו לו [ד] שובט הרי הוא בכלל מיסך מדקדק הרי הוא בכלל אורג: **מתני'** ועוד כלל אחר אמרו [מ]כל הכשר להצניע ומצניעין כמוהו והוציאו בשבת חייב חטאת עליו וכל שאינו כשר להצניע ואין מצניעין כמוהו והוציאו בשבת אינו חייב אלא המצניעו: **גמ'** כל הכשר להצניע לאפוקי מאי רב פפא אמר [נ]לאפוקי דם נדה מר עוקבא אמר לאפוקי עצי אשרה מאן דאמר דם נדה כ"ש עצי אשרה מאן דאמר עצי אשרה אבל דם נדה מצנע ליה לשונרא ואידך כיון דחלשא לא מצנע ליה אמר רבי יוסי בר חנינא האי דלא כר"ש דאי כר"ש האמר [ה]לא אמרו כל השיעורין הללו אלא למצניעיהן: וכל שאינו כשר להצניע:

אמר

רש"י

משום צובע. שצובע את הבשר של בית השחיטה ולקמן מפרש אמאי מיכוין לצובעו וצביעה הואי במשכן אב מלאכה: משום נטילת נשמה. דנטילת נשמה הואי במשכן באילים מאדמים ותחש וחלזון [ו]: אף משום צביעה. ונפקא מינה לחיוביה תרתי: מילתא דאמרי אימא כו'. דבר תימה אמרתי להזכיר צביעה בשחיטה צריך אני לומר בו דבר טעם דלא ליתו דרי בתראי השומעים וליחכו עלי: צובע בשר במאי ניחא ליה. להאי שוחט בצביעת הבשר היינו חוכא ואני אומר בו טעם: ניחא ליה דלתווס בית השחיטה בדמא. שיהא צבוע בדם: כי היכי דניחזייה אינשי. שנשחטה היום וניתו ונזבנו: היינו מולח היינו מעבד. אטו מליחה לאו צורך עיבוד הוא: ועייל שירטוט. לפי שדרך הרצענין כשהוא בא לחתכו משרטטו תחלה כפי מה שהוא רוצה להאריך ולהרחיב ולקצר החיתוך ואחר כך מעביר הסכין דרך השירטוט וכן בעורות המשכן כשחתכום: דקבעי ליה לאורחא. שמולחה הרבה: השף בין העמודים. כגון עמודי אכסדראות שעשוים חלונות חלונות ונסמכין בחלונות בין עמוד לעמוד והשף שם בקרקעית הבנין שנשענין עליו כדי שיהא חלק חייב משום ממחק: המגרר ראשי כלונסות. שיהו ראשיהן שוין וחדין: ממרח רטיה. מחליק תחבושת על המכה: מסתת את האבן. לאחר שנעקרה מן ההר ונחצבה מחליקה: משום מכה בפטיש. שהוא גמר מלאכה: הצר (ב) בכלי צורה. בכלי שעומד לכך לנאותו: מנפח בכלי זכוכית. כשהותך נעשה על ידי נפוח: דשקיל אקופי. ראשי חוטין התלויין ביריעה במקום קשורין כשניתק בה חוט וקשרוהו וכן קשין וקסמים דקין שנארגו בה בלא מתכוין ונוטלין אותם ממנה לאחר אריגה גמר מלאכה הוא וחייב משום מכה בפטיש: כתב אות אחת גדולה כו' פטור. שבקרשי המשכן שתים היו כותבים אחת בזו ואחת בזו כדי לזווגן כשסותרים אותן: מחק אות אחת כו' חייב. שאין מלאכת מחיקה חשובה אלא ע"מ לכתוב והרי יש מקום לשתי אותיות: אמר רבי מנחם ברבי יוסי. הא קמ"ל מאן תנא קמא ר' מנחם ברבי יוסי: לאפוקי מדרבי אליעזר. דהא אמרן דלא נמנו כאן אלא להודיענו מנין חטאות של העלם אחד ותנא הרי אלו למעוטי שאם עשה תולדותיהם עמהן דאינו מביא עליהן חטאת ודלא כרבי אליעזר דמחייב אתולדה עם האב בכריתות: שובט. משוה השתי בכרכר שקורין ריו"ל: מדקדק. כשמותח חוט הערב מכה בכרכר עליו במקומות מקומות ליישבו שלא יהא מתוח יותר מדאי שהמתיחה מעכבתו מהתחבר יפה עם הארג: שובט הרי הוא בכלל מיסך. דהיינו מיסך ממש שמסדר חוטי השתי: הרי הוא אורג. דהיינו אורג ממש ולא דמי לזורה ובורר ומרקד דזה בקשין וזה בצרורות וזה בקמח: **מתני'** כל הכשר להצניע. שהוא מין העשוי לצורך האדם: ומצניעין כמוהו. כמות זה כלומר שיש בו שיעור הראוי להצניעו: אין חייב אלא למצניעו. אם נעשה חביב לאדם א' והצניעו חייב על הוצאתו אם חזר והוציאו אבל אדם אחר אינו חייב עליו דלגביה לאו מלאכה הוא: **גמ'** מ"ד דם נדה. אינו כשר להצניע כ"ש עצי אשרה דאיסורי הנאה נינהו ומאיסי וצריך לאבדן: כיון דחלשא. המאכיל דם האדם לחתול נעשה חלש אותו אדם: הא. דתנא כל הכשר להצניע ויש בו שיעור שרוב ב"א עשויין להצניע כשיעור הזה חייב כל אדם על הוצאתו ואפילו אדם עשיר שאין שיעור זה חשוב לו: דלא כר' שמעון. לקמן בהמוציא:

אמר

תוספות

אין עיבוד באוכלין. אין להתיר מכאן מליחת אוכלין דאסור מדרבנן מליחה בפרק שמונה שרצים (לקמן דף קח:) ואפילו בי"ט אסור בפ"ק דבילה (דף יא.): **השף** בין העמודים בשבת חייב. פירש ר"ח [ז] דשף העור על העמוד כדי להחליקו וכן משמע בירושלמי ורש"י פירש ששף קרקעית שבין עמודי חלונות ולא נהירא: **והמסתת** את האבן כו' חייב משום מכה בפטיש. אבל משום מחתך וממחק לא מיחייב דמיירי שכבר היא מרובעת ומתוקנת אלא שמייפה אותה ועושה בה שירטוטין ויפוי כעין שעושין עכשיו מסתתי האבנים. ר"י וכן ריב"א: **הרי** אלו לאפוקי מדרבי אליעזר דמחייב אתולדה במקום אב. וא"ת מרישא שמעינן לה דתנן העושה מלאכות הרבה מעין מלאכה אחת אינו חייב אלא אחת וי"מ דה"ק מעין מלאכה אחת היינו שתי תולדות מאב א' אבל האב ותולדה דידיה מיחייב תרתי קמ"ל: **חסר** אחת לאפוקי מדר' יהודה. תימה דממילא דרישא שמעינן לה וליכא למימר תנא ושייר [ט] דהא אלו קתני ומיהו הא ליכא לאקשויי דהא מאלו דרישא שמעינן לאפוקי מדר' אליעזר דאיכא למימר דנקט ברישא אלו אבות משום דקאי אדקתני לעיל חייב על כל אב מלאכה וי"ל דממילא דרישא לא שמעינן לאפוקי מדרבי יהודה דאיכא למימר דלא חשיב אלא מלאכות חשובות אבל שובט ומדקדק אע"ג דמלאכות הן לא קתני להו משום דאינם מבוררות כל כך וכה"ג משני בפ"ק דקדושין (דף טז:) גבי אלו מעניקין להן דבר שיש לו קצבה קתני דבר שאין לו קצבה לא קתני [ח]: **לאפוקי** עצי אשרה. דלא כרבי יהודה דאמר בפרק רבי עקיבא (לקמן דף צ.) אף המוציא משמשי ע"ז כל שהוא חייב אלא כת"ק דפליג עליה כן פירש בקונט' התם וקשה לרשב"א הא דקאמר הכא מ"ד דם נדה כ"ש עצי אשרה מנא ליה דילמא סבר כרבי יהודה ומחייב בעצי אשרה שמצניעין אותן לשריפה: **הא** דלא כר' שמעון. פירש בקונטרס הא דתנן כל הכשר כו' שרוב בני אדם עשויים להצניע כשיעור הזה חייב כל אדם על הוצאתו אפילו אדם עשיר שאין שיעור זה חשוב לו משמע מדבריו דלא מחייב ר' שמעון אלא בסתם בני אדם שרגילין להצניעו שאותו שיעור חשוב להן ואפילו לא הצניעו הוא ולקמן פי' לא נאמרו שיעורים שבמשנה אלא למצניעין אותו קודם לכן וחזר המצניע והוציאו משמע דוקא בהצניעו חייב ואומר ר"י דיש ליישב פירושו דמה

שמצריך

עין משפט נר מצוה

סב א ב ג מיי' פי"א מהלכות שבת הלכה ה סמג לאוין סה טוש"ע או"ח סימן שכא סעיף ה:
סב [א] [מיי' פי"א מהל' שבת הלכה ו ופי"ח הלכה יז]:
סב [ג] [מיי' פי"א שם הלכה ו]:
סג ד מיי' שם הלכה ז:
סד ה מיי' שם הלכה ו ופכ"ג הלכה יא טור שו"ע או"ח סימן שמ סעיף כו:
סה ו מיי' פי"ח מהלכות שבת הלכה יח:
סו ז שם הלכה טו:
סז ח מיי' שם הלכה יח טוש"ע או"ח סימן שב סעיף ג:
סח ט י מיי' פי"א מהל' שבת הלכה ט סמג שם טוש"ע או"ח סימן שמ סעיף ג:
סט כ מיי' פי"ז שם הלכה טז ופכ"ג הלכה ד סמג שם:
ע ל מיי' פ"ז שם הל"ו ופ"ו מהל' שגגות הלכה ה:
ע [ה] [מיי' שם פ"ט הלכה יח ויט]:
עא מ נ מיי' פי"ח מהל' שבת הלכה כב:

רבינו חננאל

ליה דנהוי חי כי היכי דלצלח צבעיה דכל כמה דהוא חי מצלח ציבעיה. שוחט משום מאי מחייב רב אמר משום צובע אסיק' ניחא ליה כי היכי דנתווס בית שחיטה דידיה דמא. כי היכי דידעי אינשי דחי הוה וכי היכי (דניחה) [דנחזיה] אינשי דנשחט הוא וקאתי למזבן מיניה ולא יימרו של נבילה הוא. והא דאמר רב משום צובע הכי קאמר חדא משום נטילת נשמה דהא בהדיא תנן באבות מלאכות השוחט. וסבר רב השוחט בשבת חייב שתים אחת משום נטילת נשמה ואחת משום צובע והוא אב (אחד) [אחר]. והמולחו והמעבדו. אקשינן דמולח היינו מעבד כדאמרינן (לקמן עט:) לענין חיפה מליח וקמיח שנמצאת מליחתו עבודו ופרקין ר' יוחנן ור"ל דהמולח והמעבד תרווייהו מלאכת עיבוד נינהו ותני חדא והוא הדין לאחרינא. אי הכי בצרי להו עייל שירטוט ושני במתני' המולחו והמשרטטו: **ירושלמי** מה עיבוד היה במשכן שהיו משרטטין בעורות מהו משרטטין מסרגלין. מליחת בשר חי בשבת. אם כוונתו לצאת בו לדרך או לאוכלו אחר כמה ימים חייב משום מעבד אבל לאוכלו ביומו לא ולית הלכתא כדרבה בר רב הונא (דרבה בר רב הונא) [דרבא] דחי לה ואמר אין עיבוד באוכלין: **השף** בין העמודים. פי' מחליק חייב משום מוחק והוא כמו ממרח את הרטיה: **ירושלמי** הממחקו. מה מחיקה היתה במשכן (פי') שהיו שפין העורות ע"ג העמוד. השף את העור ע"ג העמוד חייב משום (מוחק) [ממחק]. הממרח איספלנית חייב משום מוחק. הגורר ראשי כלונסות חייב משום מחתך. הממרח רטיה חייב משום מוחק. וכן הצר בכלי צורה כל שהוא חייב משום מכה בפטיש. ואע"ג דפליג ר' ישמעאל (לקמן קג:) ואמר עד שיצור כל הצורה יחידאה היא ואי ההיא צורה אית בה אותיות דמיקרו חייב משום כותב ואי לאו חייב משום מכה בפטיש וכן המנפח בכלי זכוכית הוא גמר מלאכתו שמלאכת זכוכית בניפוח הוא. פי' אקופי כגון נימין הניתקין מן האריגה דנתלין בבגד או חתיכות עצים קטנים המסבכין בצמרן של בגדים חדשים וכשמשלים האומן מלאכתו כל ראשי נימין התלויים בין קיסם וקליפה שנסתבכו בבגד נוטלן. ונקראין אקופי.

מסורת הש"ס

א) [נ"ל אסין], ב) [תוספ' פי"ב], ג) לקמן צו: ב"ק ב. כריתות טז:, ד) לקמן צז:, ה) לקמן עו:, ו) ע"ל שייך לעיל, ז) [עי' בערוך ערך שף], ח) [ועי' בתה שלייניו בס"ד מתוס' יבמות פד: ד"ה אלא].

הגהות הב"ח

(א) גמ' אמר ר"ש בר ביסמא אמר ר"ש בן לקיש הצר: (ב) רש"י ד"ה הצר לורה כצ"ל ותיבת בכלי נמחק:

גליון הש"ס

תוס' ד"ה חסר אחת וכו' דהא אלו קתני. כדאי' בקדושין דף טז ע"ב:

רב נסים גאון

נטילת נשמה קיי"ל שהמתעסק לענין שבת פטור. ומשכחת עיקר דילה במסכת כריתות בפרק ספק אכל חלב (דף יט) אמר רב נחמן אמר שמואל [המתעסק] בחלבים ובעריות (בחלבים פטור ובעריות) חייב שכבר נהנה מתעסק בשבת פטור מלאכת מחשבת אסרה תורה ומשכחת לה בסנהדרין בפ' ד' מיתות (דף סב) ובגמרא דהזורק דבני מערבא (הלכה ו) גרסי הזורק בשבת פטור היאך עבידא אמר הריני קוצר חצי גרוגרת וקצר כגרוגרות פטור בגמ' דכל שעה בפסחים (דף לג) גרסי לה אי אמרת בשאר מצות שכן לא חייב שאין מתעסק כשמתעסק שאם נתכוין להגביה את התלוש וחתך המחובר פטור וכגון זה כל מלאכה שהיא באה חילוף מה שנתכוון העושה אותה מתעסק מיקרי שהרי לא נעשית מחשבתו: אלו לאפוקי מדר' אליעזר דמחייב תולדה במקום אב. ואשכחנן דברי ר' אליעזר בכריתות בפרק אמרו לו אכלת חלב (דף טו) אמר ר' עקיבא שאלתי את ר' אליעזר העושה מלאכות הרבה בשבתות הרבה מעין מלאכה אחת בהעלם אחד מהו חייב על כל אחת ואחת או חייב אחת על כולן אמר לי חייב על כל אחת ואחת מקל וחומר ומה נדה שאין בה תולדות ואין בה חטאות הרבה חייב על כל אחת ואחת שבת שיש בה אבות ותולדות אינו דין שיהא חייב על כל אחת ואחת ובתלמוד בעי מיניה ולדי מלאכות אי כמלאכות דמיין אי לא ופשט ליה דולדי מלאכות כמלאכות דמיין: דאי ר' שמעון הא אמר לא נאמרו כל השיעורין האלו אלא למצניעיהן. בפירקא דלקמן המוציא יין (דף עו) משכחת להא דר' שמעון:

סליק פרק כלל גדול

ליקוטי רש"י

דליתווס. מיתווסי. מתלכלכין [פסחים סה:]. היינו מולח והיינו מעבד. מליחה מאבות מלאכות היא בדבר שיש בו עבוד דתנן (שבת עג.) והמולחו והמעבדו [ביצה יא:]. הממרח רטיה. מחליק גומות שברטיה מירוס חייב משום ממחק [עירובין קב:]. מסתת את האבן. מרבע את האבן ומתקנה הכל לפי המקום שיש מקומות שרגילין להחליק ויש מקומות שרגילין לחרוץ בה חריצים בארץ אשכנז. משום מכה בפטיש. גמר מלאכה הוא שהמקום שחרץ חריץ זה לא יחרוץ עוד. כל מידי דאית ביה גמר מלאכה וכו'. כל הגומר בשבת מלאכה תולדת מכה בפטיש היא [לקמן קב:]. לאפוקי מדר"א דמחייב על תולדה במקום אב. דאי עביד אב ותולדה דידיה מחייב תרתי חטאות במס' כריתות בפ' אמרו לו (טז.) [ב"ק ב.]. מוסיף את השובט. עם שאר אבות מלאכות להא דאמרן דלכך נמנו שאם עשאן בהעלם אחד חייב על כל אחד ואחד. שובט. מכרכר בכרכר. ומדקדק. לאחר שמתח החוט של ערב מכה בכרכר בשנים ושלשה מקומות ויש מפרשים מדקדק משוה האריגה כשיש שני חוטין כרוכין זה עם זה ומובדלים מן השאר משוה אותן בכרכר או במחט [לקמן צז:]. לא אמרו. שיעורין שבמשנה אלא למצניעיהן לבד וחזר המצניע והוציאו חייב אבל שאר כל אדם שהוציאו אינו חייב וסבירא ליה לר' שמעון דמצניע עצמו בעי שיעורא זוטא ובבציר מהא שיעורא לא מיחייב כדאמרינן בפרקין דלעיל (עה:) דלית ליה לר' שמעון כל שאין כשר להצניע ואין מצניעים כמוהו שיתחייב עליו מצניעו [שם עו:].

spreads a dressing on a wound **on the Sabbath**[15] חַיָּיב מִשּׁוּם מְמַחֵק – **is liable on account of "smoothing";** וְהַמְסַתֵּת אֶת הָאֶבֶן בְּשַׁבָּת – **and one who chisels a stone on the Sabbath** to polish it[16] חַיָּיב מִשּׁוּם מַכֶּה בְּפַטִּישׁ – **is liable on account of "striking the final blow."**[17]

The Gemara presents additional examples of the *melachah* of striking the final blow:
אָמַר רַבִּי שִׁמְעוֹן בֶּן קִיסְמָא אָמַר רַבִּי שִׁמְעוֹן בֶּן לָקִישׁ – **R' Shimon ben Kisma**[18] **said in the name of R' Shimon ben Lakish:** הַצָּר צוּרָה בִּכְלִי – **One who engraves an image on a utensil**[19] וְהַמְנַפֵּחַ בִּכְלִי זְכוּכִית – **or blows a glass utensil**[20] חַיָּיב מִשּׁוּם מַכֶּה בְּפַטִּישׁ – **is liable on account of "striking the final blow."** אָמַר רַבִּי יְהוּדָה – **R' Yehudah said:** הַאי מַאן דְּשָׁקִיל אַקּוּפֵי מִגְּלִימֵי – **Someone who removes protrusions**[21] **from a garment** חַיָּיב מִשּׁוּם מַכֶּה בְּפַטִּישׁ – **is liable on account of "striking the final blow."**[22]

The Gemara qualifies the last statement:
וְהָנֵי מִילֵּי דְּקָפֵיד עֲלַיְיהוּ – **This ruling** applies only **when he is particular about them.**[23]

The Mishnah concluded this section of *avos melachos* with the following:
וְהַכּוֹתֵב שְׁתֵּי אוֹתִיּוֹת – WRITING TWO LETTERS [and erasing in order to write two letters].

The Gemara elaborates:
תָּנוּ רַבָּנָן – **The Rabbis taught** in a Baraisa: כָּתַב אוֹת אַחַת גְּדוֹלָה – If [A PERSON] WROTE ONE LARGE LETTER וְיֵשׁ בִּמְקוֹמָהּ לִכְתּוֹב שְׁתַּיִם – AND THERE IS room IN ITS PLACE TO WRITE TWO smaller letters, פָּטוּר – HE IS EXEMPT from punishment.[24] מָחַק אוֹת גְּדוֹלָה וְיֵשׁ בִּמְקוֹמָהּ לִכְתּוֹב שְׁתַּיִם – However, if HE ERASED ONE LARGE LETTER AND THERE IS room IN ITS PLACE TO WRITE TWO smaller letters, חַיָּיב – HE IS LIABLE.[25]

The Baraisa concludes:
אָמַר רַבִּי מְנַחֵם בְּרַבִּי יוֹסֵי – R' MENACHEM THE SON OF R' YOSE SAID: וְזֶה חוֹמֶר בְּמוֹחֵק מִבְּכוֹתֵב – AND THIS IS A STRINGENCY OF ERASING OVER WRITING.[26]

The Mishnah listed the following *avos melachos*:
הַבּוֹנֶה וְהַסּוֹתֵר הַמְכַבֶּה וְהַמַּבְעִיר וְהַמַּכֶּה בְּפַטִּישׁ – BUILDING, DEMOLISHING, EXTINGUISHING, KINDLING AND STRIKING THE FINAL BLOW.

The Gemara defines the labor of striking the final blow:
רַבָּה וְרַבִּי זֵירָא דְּאָמְרֵי תַּרְוַויְיהוּ – **Rabbah and R' Zeira both said:** כָּל מִידֵי דְּאִית בֵּיהּ גְּמַר מְלָאכָה – **Any [act] that has in it** the **culmination of a labor**[27] חַיָּיב מִשּׁוּם מַכֶּה בְּפַטִּישׁ – renders one **liable on account of "striking the final blow."**

The Mishnah began its concluding statement with these words:
אֵלּוּ אֲבוֹת מְלָאכוֹת – THESE ARE THE PRIMARY LABORS.

The Gemara explains:
אֵלּוּ – The word **"these"** serves לְאַפּוּקֵי מִדְּרַבִּי אֱלִיעֶזֶר – **to exclude [the opinion] of R' Eliezer,** דִּמְחַיֵּיב עַל תּוֹלָדָה בִּמְקוֹם אָב – **who obligates a** person for **a derivative labor** even **in the place of a primary labor.**[28]

The Mishnah concluded by repeating the number of *avos melachos*:
חָסֵר אַחַת – Forty MINUS ONE.

The Gemara explains:
לְאַפּוּקֵי מִדְּרַבִּי יְהוּדָה – This repetition serves **to exclude the [opinion] of R' Yehudah,** דְּתַנְיָא – **for it was taught in a Baraisa:** רַבִּי יְהוּדָה מוֹסִיף אֶת הַשּׁוֹבֵט וְהַמְדַקְדֵּק – R' YEHUDAH ADDS to the list of primary labors LINING UP the warp threads WITH A ROD[29]

NOTES

15. He smoothes the medication on the wound (*Rashi*).

16. After quarrying the stone from a hill and cutting it to size, he beautifies it with a chisel (*Rashi;* see also *Rashi* below, 102b ד״ה מסתת; *Meiri, Chidushei HaRan*).

17. Because this is the finishing touch to the stone (*Rashi*). *Rashi* below (102b ד״ה משום מאי; see there) writes that this is actually a *toladah* of the *av melachah* of striking the final blow.

18. *Bach* emends this to R' Shimon bar Bisna.

19. This refers to a type of utensil that is customarily beautified with engravings (*Rashi*). If the utensil is already completely formed, engraving it is considered the finishing touch (*Meiri*).

20. When the glass is melted, the utensil is formed by blowing (*Rashi*). According to *Rashi* the person is not liable for performing the *melachah* of building, because building does not apply to utensils (see *Tosafos* above, 74b ד״ה חביתא).

21. For example, the dangling ends of a thread that snapped and was reknotted or a splinter that was accidentally woven into the fabric (*Rashi;* see *Meiri*).

22. This is the finishing touch in making the garment (*Rashi*).

23. Only then is his snipping off the hanging threads or removing the splinter considered a finishing touch.

[The commentators debate about whether the person has to be so particular that he would not wear the garment at all until protrusions are removed. See *Mishnah Berurah* 302:10 with *Shaar HaTziyun* for discussion of this issue.]

24. The wall boards of the Mishkan were inscribed with letters to facilitate matching them each time the Mishkan was erected (*Rashi,* see Gemara below, 103a-b; *Tiferes Yisrael* to Mishnah there; *Avnei Nezer, Orach Chaim* §199). Therefore, if a person writes only one letter — even though it is as large as two normal-size letters — he has not replicated this *melachah,* and so is not obligated to bring a *chatas.* Nevertheless, it is prohibited according to Biblical law to write even one letter (see *Mishnah Berurah* 340:22:4; cf. *Magen Avos* to the Mishnah ד״ה והמסיך; see also above, 74a note 13).

25. The labor of erasing has no legal significance unless it is performed for the purpose of writing in the erased space. Therefore, so long as he erased enough space for the writing of two letters, he is liable (*Rashi*).

Chidushei HaRan explains that there is no liability unless one leaves enough space to write two medium-size duplications of the large letter he erased. For example, if he erased a large *aleph,* he is liable if there is space to write two medium *alephs.* [See also *Minchas Chinuch* §32 מוחק; see also *Sfas Emes* and *Meiri* to 104b.]

26. This seemingly superfluous statement teaches us that the Tanna Kamma of the Baraisa is R' Menachem the son of R' Yose (*Rashi;* see *Shabbos Shel Mi*).

27. I.e. that involves putting the finishing touch on an object that is already essentially complete. [See Gemara below, 102b-103a, for more applications of this *melachah.*]

28. We learned above (73b) that in its introductory statement the Mishnah teaches the maximum amount of *chatas* offerings (thirty-nine) a person would have to bring for one lapse of Sabbath awareness. In Tractate *Kereisos* (16a-b) R' Eliezer states that if a person performs an *av melachah* and its *toladah,* he is liable to a separate *chatas* for each violation (see also below, 96b). Our Mishnah, by stressing here in its conclusion that "these" thirty-nine labors are the *avos melachos,* teaches that a person is not liable for a *toladah* when he is already liable for its *av* (*Rashi;* cf. *Chidushei HaRan*). [See *Ritva MHK* ed. and *Yad David* for an explanation of why this could not be derived from the introductory statement of the Mishnah. See also above, 73b note 2.]

29. [After the required number of warp threads have been set on the loom, many threads are bound to overlap or become attached to one another.] A pointed rod is therefore used to separate the threads and line them up properly (*Rashi*)

According to *Rambam* (*Hil. Shabbos* 9:17) this *toladah* refers to an earlier stage of preparing the warp, during which two people hold the warp threads taut while one beats the threads with a rod (שֵׁבֶט). The resultant vibration causes many of the bunched-up threads to fall into

משום צובע אין משום נטילת נשמה לא אימא אף משום צובע אמר רב מילתא דאמרי אימא בה מילתא דלא ליתו דרי בתראי וליחכו עלי צובע במאי ניחא ליה ניחא דליתוום בית השחיטה דמא כי היכי דליחזוה אינשי וליתו ליזבנו מיניה: והמולחו והמעבדו: [א] היינו מולח והיינו מעבד ר' יוחנן ור"ל דאמרי תרווייהו אפיק חד מינייהו ועייל [א] שירטוט אמר רבה בר רב הונא האי מאן דמלח בישרא חייב משום מעבד [ב] רבא אמר אין עיבוד באוכלין אמר רב אשי ואפילו רבה בר רב הונא לא אמר אלא דקא בעי ליה לאורחא אבל לביתא לא משוי איניש מיכליה עץ: [ג] והממחקו והמחתכו: אמר רבי אחא בר חנינא [ג] השף בין העמודים בשבת חייב משום ממחק אמר רבי חייא בר אבא ג' דברים סח לי רב (א) אשי משמיה דרבי יהושע בן לוי [ד] המגרר ראשי כלונסות בשבת חייב משום מחתך [ה] הממרח רטיה בשבת חייב משום ממחק [ו] והמסתת את האבן בשבת חייב משום מכה בפטיש אמר ר' שמעון (א) בן קיסמא אמר רבי שמעון בן לקיש [ז] הצר צורה בכלי והמנפח בכלי זכוכית חייב משום מכה בפטיש א"ר יהודה [ח] האי מאן דשקיל אקופי מגלימי חייב משום מכה בפטיש והני מילי דקפיד עלייהו: [ט] והכותב שתי אותיות: ת"ר (ג) [י] כתב אות אחת גדולה ויש במקומה לכתוב שתים פטור מחק אות גדולה ויש במקומה לכתוב שתים חייב אמר רבי מנחם בר' יוסי וזה חומר במוחק מבכותב: הבונה והסותר המכבה והמבעיר והמכה בפטיש: רבה ור' זירא דאמרי תרווייהו [כ] כל מידי דאית ביה גמר מלאכה חייב משום מכה בפטיש: אלו אבות מלאכות: (ג) אלו [ל] לאפוקי מדר"א דמחייב על תולדה במקום אב: חסר אחת: לאפוקי מדר' יהודה (ז) דתניא ר' יהודה מוסיף את השובט והמדקדק אמרו לו [ד] שובט הרי הוא בכלל מיסך מדקדק הרי הוא בכלל אורג:

מתני' ועוד כלל אחר אמרו [מ] כל הכשר להצניע ומצניעין כמוהו והוציאו בשבת חייב חטאת עליו וכל שאינו כשר להצניע ואין מצניעין כמוהו והוציאו בשבת אינו חייב אלא המצניעו:

גמ' כל הכשר להצניע לאפוקי מאי רב פפא אמר [נ] לאפוקי דם נדה מר עוקבא אמר לאפוקי עצי אשרה מאן דאמר דם נדה כ"ש עצי אשרה מאן דאמר עצי אשרה אבל דם נדה מצנע ליה לשונרא ואידך כיון דחלשא לא מצנע ליה אמר רבי יוסי בר חנינא האי דלא כר"ש דאי כר"ש האמר (ס) לא אמרו כל השיעורין הללו אלא למצניעיהן: וכל שאינו כשר להצניע:

אמר

אין עיבוד באוכלין. אין להתיר מכאן מליחת אוכלין דאסור מדרבנן מליחה בפרק שמונה שרצים (לקמן דף קח:) ואפילו בי"ט אסור בפ"ק דבילה (דף יא.): השף בין העמודים בשבת חייב. פירש ר"ח (ו) דשף העור על העמוד כדי להחליקו וכן משמע בירושלמי ורש"י פירש ששף קרקעית שבין עמודי חלונות ולא נהירא: והמסתת את האבן כו' חייב משום מכה בפטיש. אבל משום מחתך וממחק לא מיחייב דמיירי שכבר היא מרובעת ומתוקנת אלא שמייפה אותה ועושה בה שירטוטין ויפוי כעין שעושין עכשיו מסתתי האבנים. ר"י וכן ריב"א: הרי אלו לאפוקי מדרבי אליעזר דמחייב אתולדה במקום אב. וא"ת מרישא שמעינן לה דתנן העושה מלאכות הרבה מעין מלאכה אחת אינו חייב אלא אחת וי"מ דה"ק מעין מלאכה אחת היינו שתי תולדות מאב א' אבל האב ותולדה דידיה מיחייב תרתי קמ"ל: חסר אחת לאפוקי מדר' יהודה. תימה דממילא דרישא שמעינן לה וליכא למימר תנא ושייר (ס) דהא אלו קתני ומיהו הא ליכא לאקשויי דהא מאלו דרישא שמעינן לאפוקי מדר' אליעזר דאיכא למימר דנקט ברישא אלו אבות משום דקאי אדקתני לעיל חייב על כל אב מלאכה וי"ל דממילא דרישא לא שמעינן לאפוקי מדרבי יהודה דאיכא למימר דלא חשיב אלא מלאכות חשובות אבל שובט ומדקדק אע"ג דמלאכות הן לא קתני להו משום דאינם מבוררות כל כך וכה"ג משני בפ"ק דקדושין (דף טז:) גבי אלו מעניקין להן דבר שיש לו קצבה קתני דבר שאין לו קצבה לא קתני (ח): לאפוקי עצי אשרה. דלא כרבי יהודה דאמר בפרק רבי עקיבא (לקמן דף נ.) אף המוציא משמשי ע"ז כל שהוא חייב אלא כת"ק דפליג עליה כן פירש בקונט' התם וקשה לרשב"א הא דקאמר הכא מ"ד דם נדה כ"ש עצי אשרה מנא ליה דילמא סבר כרבי יהודה ומחייב בעצי אשרה שמצניעין אותן לשריפה: הא דלא כר' שמעון. פירש בקונטרס הא דתנן כל הכשר כו' שרוב בני אדם עשויים להצניע כשיעור הזה חייב כל אדם על הוצאתו אפילו אדם עשיר שאין שיעור זה חשוב לו משמע מדבריו דלא מחייב ר' שמעון אלא בסתם בני אדם שרגילין להצניעו שאותו שיעור חשוב להן ואפילו לא הצניעו הוא ולקמן פי' לא נאמרו שיעורים שבמשנה אלא למצניעין אותו קודם לכן וחזר המצניע והוציאו משמע דוקא בהצניעו חייב ואומר ר"י דיש ליישב פירושו דמה שמצריך

משום צובע. שצובע את הבשר של בית השחיטה ולקמן מפרש אמאי מיכוין לצובעו וצביעה הואי במשכן אב מלאכה: משום נטילת נשמה. דנטילת נשמה הואי במשכן באילים מאדמים ותחש וחלזון (י): אף משום צביעה. ונפקא מינה לחיוביה תרתי: מילתא דאמרי אימא כו'. דבר תימה אמרתי להזכיר צביעה בשחיטה צריך אני לומר בו דבר טעם דלא ליתו דרי בתראי השומעים וליחכו עלי: צובע בשר במאי ניחא ליה. להאי שוחט בצביעת הבשר היינו תוכא ואני אומר בו טעם: ניחא ליה דלתוום בית השחיטה בדמא. שיהא צבוע בדם: כי היכי דניחזייה אינשי. שנשחטה היום וניתו וזבנו: היינו מולח היינו מעבד. אטו מליחה לאו צורך עיבוד הוא: ועייל שירטוט. לפי שדרך הרצענין כשהוא בא לחתכו משרטטו תחלה כפי מה שהוא רוצה להאריך ולהרחיב ולקצר החיתוך ואחר כך מעביר הסכין דרך השירטוט וכן בעורות המשכן כשחתכום: דקבעי ליה לאורחא. שמולחה הרבה: השף בין העמודים. כגון עמודי אכסדראות שעשוים חלונות חלונות ונסמכין בחלונות בין עמוד לעמוד והשף שם בקרקעית הבנין שנשענין עליו כדי שיהא חלק חייב משום ממחק: המגרר ראשי כלונסות. שיהו ראשיהן שוין וחדין: ממרח רטיה. מחליק תחבושת על המכה: מסתת את האבן. לאחר שנעקרה מן ההר ונחצבה מחליקה: משום מכה בפטיש. שהוא גמר מלאכה: הצר (ג) בכלי צורה. בכלי שעומד לכך לנאותו: מנפח בכלי זכוכית. כשהותך נעשה על ידי נפוח: דשקיל אקופי. ראשי חוטין התלויין ביריעה במקום קשורין כשניתק בה חוט וקשרוהו וכן קשין וקסמים דקין שנארגו בה בלא מתכוין ונוטלין אותם ממנה לאחר אריגה גמר מלאכה הוא וחייב משום מכה בפטיש: כתב אות אחת גדולה כו' פטור. שבקרשי המשכן שתים היו כותבים אחת בזו ואחת בזו כדי לזווגן כשסותרים אותן: מחק אות אחת כו' חייב. שאין מלאכת מחיקה חשובה אלא ע"מ לכתוב והרי יש מקום לשתי אותיות: אמר רבי מנחם ברבי יוסי. הא קמ"ל מאן תנא קמא ר' מנחם ברבי יוסי: לאפוקי מדרבי אליעזר. דהא אמרן דלא נמנו כאן אלא להודיענו מנין חטאות של העלם אחד ותנא הרי אלו למעוטי שאם עשה תולדותיהם עמהן דאינו מביא עליהן חטאת ודלא כרבי אליעזר דמחייב אתולדה עם האב בכריתות: שובט. משוה השתי בכרכר שקורין ריו"ל: מדקדק. כשמותח חוט הערב מכה בכרכר עליו במקומות מקומות ליישבו שלא יהא מתוח יותר מדאי שהמתיחה מעכבתו מהתחבר יפה עם הארג: שובט הרי הוא בכלל מיסך. דהיינו מיסך ממש שמסדר חוטי השתי: הרי הוא אורג. דהיינו אורג ממש ולא דמי לזורה ובורר ומרקד דזה בקשין וזה בצרורות וזה בקמח: מתני' כל הכשר להצניע. שהוא מין העשוי לצורך האדם: ומצניעין כמוהו. כמות זה כלומר שיש בו שיעור הראוי להצניעו: אין חיוב אלא למצניעו. אם נעשה חביב לאדם א' והצניעו חייב על הוצאתו אם חזר והוציאו אבל אדם אחר אינו חייב עליו דלגביה לאו מלאכה הוא: גמ' מ"ד דם נדה. אינו כשר להצניע כ"ש עצי אשרה דאיסורי הנאה נינהו ומאיסי וצריך לאבדן: כיון דחלשא. המאכיל דם האדם לחתול נעשה חלש אותו אדם: הא. דתנא כל הכשר להצניע ויש בו שיעור שרוב ב"א עשויין להצניע כשיעור הזה חייב כל אדם על הוצאתו ואפילו אדם עשיר שאין שיעור זה חשוב לו: דלא כר' שמעון. לקמן בהמוציא:

אמר

עין משפט נר מצוה

סב א ב ג מיי' פי"א מהלכות שבת הלכה ה סמג לאוין סה טוש"ע או"ח סימן שכא סעיף ה:
סב [א] [מיי' פ"ז מהל' שבת הלכה א ופי"א הלכה יא]:
סב [ג] [מיי' פי"א שם הלכה ו]:
סג ד מיי' שם הלכה ז:
סד ה מיי' שם הלכה ו ופכ"ג הלכה יא טור שו"ע או"ח סימן שכח סעיף כו:
סה ו מיי' פ"י מהלכות שבת הלכה יח:
סו ז שם הלכה טו:
סז ח מיי' שם הלכה יח טוש"ע או"ח סימן שב סעיף ב:
סח ט י מיי' פי"א מהל' שבת הלכה ט סמג שם טוש"ע או"ח סימן שמ סעיף ג:
סט כ מיי' פ"י שם הלכה טו ופכ"ג הלכה ד סמג שם:
ע ל מיי' פ"ז שם הל"ז וח ופ"ז מהל' שגגות הלכה ה:
ע [ל] [מיי' שם פ"ט הלכה יח ויט]:
עא מ נ מיי' פי"ח מהל' שבת הלכה כב:

רבינו חננאל

ליה דנהוי חי כי היכי דלצלח צבעיה דכל כמה דהוא חי מצלח ציבעיה. שוחט משום מאי מחייב רב אמר משום צובע אסיק' ניחא ליה כי היכי דנתווס בית שחיטה דידיה דמא. כי היכי דידעי אינשי דחי הוה וכי היכי (דניחה) [דנחזיה] אינשי דנשחט הוא וקאתי למזבן מיניה ולא לימרו של נבילה הוא. והא דאמר רב משום צובע הכי קאמר חדא משום נטילת נשמה דהא בהדיא תנן באבות מלאכות השוחט. וסבר רב השוחט בשבת חייב שתים אחת משום נטילת נשמה ואחת משום צובע והוא אב (אחד) [אחר]. המולחו והמעבדו. אקשינן דמולח היינו מעבד כדאמרינן (לקמן עט:) לענין חיפה מליח וקמיה שנמצאת מליחתו עיבודו היינו מעבד ר' יוחנן ור"ל דהמולח והמעבד תרווייהו מלאכת עיבוד נינהו ותני חדא והוא הדין לאחריא. אי הכי בצרי להו עייל שירטוט ושני במתני' המולחו והמשרטטו: ירושלמי מה עיבוד היה במשכן שהיו משרטטין בעורות מהו משרטטין מסרגלין. מליחת בשר חי בשבת. אם כותנו לצאת בו לדרך או לאוכלו אחר כמה ימים חייב משום מעבד אבל לאוכלו ביומו לא לית הלכתא כדרבה בר רב הונא (דרבה בר רב הונא) [דרבא] דחי לה ואמר אין עיבוד באוכלין: השף בין העמודים. פי' מחליק חייב משום מוחק והוא כמו ממרח את הרטיה: ירושלמי הממחקו. מה מחיקה היתה במשכן (פי') שהיו שפין העורות ע"ג העמוד. השף את העור ע"ג העמוד חייב משום (מוחק) [ממחק]. הממרח איספלנית חייב משום מוחק. הגורר ראשי כלונסות חייב משום מחתך. הממרח רטיה חייב משום מוחק. וכן הצר בכלי צורה כל שהוא חייב משום מכה בפטיש.

ואע"ג דפליג ר' ישמעאל (לקמן קג:) ואמר עד שיצור כל הצורה יחידאה היא ואי ההיא צורה אית בה אותיות דמיקרו חייב משום כותב ואי לאו חייב משום מכה בפטיש וכן המנפח בכלי זכוכית הוא גמר מלאכתו שמלאכת זכוכית בניפוח הוא. פי' אקופי כגון נימין הניתקין מן האריגה דנתלין בבגד או חתיכות עצים קטנים המסבכין בצמרן של בגדים חדשים וכשמשלים האומן מלאכתו כל ראשי נימין התלויים בין קיסם וקליפה שנסתבכו בבגד נוטלן. ונקראין אקופי.

מסורת הש"ס

א) [נ"ל אסין], ב) [תוספ' פי"ב], ג) לקמן לו: ב"ק ב. כריתות טז:, ד) לקמן לז:, ה) לקמן עג:, ו) ע"כ שייך לעיל, ז) [עי' בערוך ערך שף], ח) [וע' במה שליינו בס"ד בתוס' יבמות פד: ד"ה אלא].

הגהות הב"ח

(א) גמ' אמר ר"ש בר קיסמא אמר ר"ש בן לקיש הלר: (ב) רש"י ד"ה הלר לורה כל"ל ותיבת בכלי נמחק:

גליון הש"ס

תוס' ד"ה חסר אחת וכו' דהא אלו קתני. כלא' בקדושין דף טז ע"ב:

רב נסים גאון

נטילת נשמה קיי"ל שהמתעסק לענין שבת פטור. ומשכחת עיקר דילה במסכת כריתות בפרק ספק אכל חלב (דף יט) אמר רב נחמן אמר שמואל [המתעסק] בחלבים ובעריות (בחלבים פטור ובעריות) חייב שכבר נהנה מתעסק בשבת פטור מלאכת מחשבת אסרה תורה ומשכחת לה בסנהדרין בפ' ד' מיתות (דף סב) ובגמרא דהזורק דבני מערבא (הלכה ו) גרסי הזורק בשבת פטור היאך עבידא אמר הריני קוצר חצי גרוגרת וקצר כגרוגרת פטור בגמ' דכל שעה בפסחים (דף לג) גרסי לה אי אמרת בשאר מצות שכן לא חייב בהן שאין מתעסק במתעסק שאם נתכוין להגביה את התלוש וחתך המחובר פטור וכגון זה כל מלאכה שהיא באה חילוף מה שנתכוון העושה אותה מתעסק מיקרי שהרי לא נעשית מחשבתו: אלו לאפוקי מדר' אליעזר דמחייב על תולדה במקום אב. ואשכחנן דברי ר' אליעזר בכריתות בפרק אמרו לו אכלת חלב (דף טו) אמר ר' עקיבא שאלתי את ר' אליעזר העושה מלאכות הרבה בשבתות הרבה מעין מלאכה אחת בהעלם אחד מהו חייב על כל אחת ואחת או אינו חייב אלא אחת על כולן אמר לי חייב על כל אחת ואחת מקל וחומר ואמרו בתלמוד בעי מיניה ולדי מלאכות אי כמלאכות דמיין או לא ופשט ליה דולדי מלאכות כמלאכות דמיין: דאי ר' שמעון האמר לא נאמרו כל השיעורין האלו אלא למצניעיהן. בפירקא דלקמן המוציא יין (דף עו) משכחת להא דר' שמעון:

סליק פרק כלל גדול

ליקוטי רש"י

דליתוום. מיתווסי. מתלכלכין [פסחים סה:]. היינו מולח והיינו מעבד. מליחה מאבות מלאכות היא בדבר שיש בו עבוד דתנן (שבת עג.) והמולחו והמעבדו [ביצה יא:]. הממרח רטיה. מחליק גומות שברטיה מירוס חייב משום ממחק [עירובין קב:]. מסתת את האבן. מרגע את האבן ומתקנה הכל לפי המקום שיש מקומות שרגילין להחליק ויש מקומות שרגילין לחרוץ בה חריצים חריצים כארץ אשכנז. משום מכה בפטיש. גמר מלאכה הוא שהמקום שחרן צריך זה לא יחרון עוד. כל מידי דאית ביה גמר מלאכה וכו'. כל הגומר בשבת מלאכה תולדת מכה בפטיש היא [לקמן קב:]. לאפוקי מדר"א דמחייב על תולדה במקום אב. דאי עביד אב ותולדה דידיה מחייב תרתי חטאות במס' כריתות בפ' אמרו לו (טז.) [ב"ק ב.]. מוסיף את השובט. עם שאר אבות מלאכות להא דאמרן דלכך נמנו שאם עשאן בהעלם אחד חייב על כל אחד ואחד. שובט. מכרכר בכרכר. ומדקדק. לאחר שמתח החוט של ערב מכה בכרכר בשנים ושלשה מקומות ויש מפרשים מדקדק משוה האריגה כשיש שני חוטין כרוכין זה עם זה ומובדלים מן השאר משוה אותן בכרכר או במחט [לקמן צז:]. לא אמרו. שיעורין שבמשנה אלא למצניעיהן לבד וחזר המצניע והוציאו חייב אבל שאר כל אדם שהוציאו אינו חייב וסבירא ליה לר' שמעון דמצניע עצמו בעי שיעורא זוטא ובבציר מהא שיעורא לא מיחייב כדאמרינן בפרקין דלעיל (עה:) דלית ליה לר' שמעון כל שאין כשר להצניע ואין מצניעים כמוהו שיתחייב עליו מצניעו [שם עו:].

AND BEATING the weft threads.[30] אָמְרוּ לוֹ – But [THE SAGES] SAID TO HIM: שׁוֹבֵט הֲרֵי הוּא בִּכְלָל מֵיסֵךְ – LINING UP the warp threads WITH A ROD IS INCLUDED IN THE CATEGORY OF MOUNTING THE WARP,[31] מְדַקְדֵּק הֲרֵי הוּא בִּכְלָל אוֹרֵג – and BEATING the weft threads IS INCLUDED IN THE CATEGORY OF WEAVING.[32]

Mishnah From here on, the Mishnahs discuss the details of the *avos melachos* enumerated in the preceding Mishnah:[33]

וְעוֹד כְּלָל אַחֵר אָמְרוּ – **They stated yet another general rule:**[34] כֹּל הַכָּשֵׁר לְהַצְנִיעַ – **Whatever is fit to store,**[35] וּמַצְנִיעִין כָּמוֹהוּ – **and** [people] **store it in such** [a quantity],[36] וְהוֹצִיאוֹ בְּשַׁבָּת – **and one carried it out on the Sabbath,**[37] חַיָּיב חַטָּאת עָלָיו – **he is liable to a** ***chatas*** **for it.**[38] וְכֹל שֶׁאֵינוֹ כָּשֵׁר לְהַצְנִיעַ – **But whatever is not fit to store,**[39] וְאֵין מַצְנִיעִין כָּמוֹהוּ – **or** [people] **do not store** it in **such** [a quantity],[40] וְהוֹצִיאוֹ בְּשַׁבָּת – **and one carried it out on the Sabbath,** אֵינוֹ חַיָּיב אֶלָּא הַמַּצְנִיעוֹ – **only the one who stores it is liable.**[41]

Gemara The Gemara scrutinizes the first phrase of the Mishnah:

כֹּל הַכָּשֵׁר לְהַצְנִיעַ לְאַפּוּקֵי מַאי – **What** does **"whatever is fit to store"** mean **to exclude?** What is an example of something not fit to store?

The Gemara offers two answers:

רַב פָּפָּא אָמַר – **Rav Pappa said:** לְאַפּוּקֵי דַּם נִדָּה – It means **to exclude menstrual blood,** which has no use.[42] מַר עוּקְבָא אָמַר – **Mar Ukva said:** לְאַפּוּקֵי עֲצֵי אֲשֵׁירָה – It means **to exclude** the **wood of an** ***asheirah*** tree.[43]

The Gemara analyzes the two opinions:

מַאן דְּאָמַר דַּם נִדָּה – **The one** [Rav Pappa] **who said that menstrual blood** is not fit to store כָּל שֶׁכֵּן עֲצֵי אֲשֵׁירָה – would hold that the **wood of an** ***asheirah*** tree is **certainly** unfit.[44] מַאן דְּאָמַר עֲצֵי אֲשֵׁירָה – However, **the one** [Mar Ukva] **who said** that the **wood of an** ***asheirah*** tree is not fit to store could say: אֲבָל דַּם נִדָּה מַצְנַע לֵיהּ לְשׁוּנְרָא – **But menstrual blood is** sometimes **stored for a cat** to eat. Therefore, one who carries it on the Sabbath is liable.

The Gemara explains why Rav Pappa maintains that menstrual blood is never stored:

וְאִידָךְ – **And the other one** (Rav Pappa) holds: כֵּיוָן דְּחָלְשָׁא –

NOTES

place properly. The pointed rod (כַּרְכַּר) is then used to align any remaining problematic threads individually (see *Maggid Mishneh* loc. cit. and *Lechem Mishneh* 9:16). See *Maaseh Oreg* by Dayan I. Gukovitzki, pp. 20-21 and *Melachos Arigah* by Rabbi P. Bodner, pp. 20-22 for more details.

30. When the weft thread is passed through the warp threads, it must be pulled tight so it will not lie too loosely on the cloth. However, if it is pulled too tight, the weft thread will not merge well with the already woven cloth. The weft thread is therefore hit with the pointed rod in a few places [thereby increasing the amount of weft thread] so that it will not be stretched too tightly; it can then merge properly with the rest of the cloth (*Rashi;* see also *Rashi* below, 97b ד״ה ומדקדק; see *Maaseh Oreg* pp. 25-26 for more details).

[Other Rishonim (see, for example, *Rabbeinu Chananel*) say that this *toladah* refers to the act of beating the newly woven weft threads to the already-woven fabric. On a weaving loom this is done with a comb-like device (the reed), which beats in the weft thread to the cloth, assuring that the warp threads remain both evenly spaced and parallel to one another. [See Mishnah below, 105a, and see diagram in Appendix.]

31. This action is an integral part of mounting the warp, for this is how the weaver lines up the warp threads (*Rashi*). [The Gemara below (97b) calls it a *toladah* of mounting the warp.]

32. This act is part of the actual weaving process (*Rashi*). [It too is called a *toladah* below (97b).]

Rashi explains why the acts of lining up the warp threads with a rod and beating the weft threads, which are considered *tolados* of their respective *avos,* are not analogous to the *melachos* of winnowing, selecting and sifting, which are considered separate *avos.* This is so because those *avos* accomplish distinct purposes: Winnowing removes chaff, selecting removes stones, and sifting purifies flour (*Rashi;* see *Hagahos R' Elazar Moshe Horowitz;* see also *Tosafos* above, 74a ד״ה אע״ג).

33. It is often the case throughout the Mishnah that the Tanna commences a detailed analysis of a long list of items by first discussing the last-mentioned item. Our Mishnah does so as well, and so the Tanna commences his discussion of the primary labors with the *av melachah* of transferring from one domain to another (*Tos. Yom Tov*). From here until the beginning of chapter 10 the Mishnah discusses the various minimum amounts, depending on the objects involved, for which one is liable for transferring on the Sabbath. As an introduction the Mishnah establishes the general rule for determining the minimum amount for any given substance. All rulings in the subsequent Mishnahs derive from this general rule. [See below, 76a note 10.]

34. That is, the Rabbis stated another rule concerning liability to a *chatas* offering for violation of the Sabbath, in addition to the rule mentioned at the beginning of this chapter (67b; see *Shenos Eliyahu*).

35. I.e. it is a substance normally used by people (*Rashi*).

36. I.e. it is an amount worth storing for later use (*Rashi*). The subsequent Mishnahs will list the minimum amounts for various commonly used substances (*Ritva MHK* ed.).

Thus, for there to be liability the substance carried out must (a) be a substance used by people and (b) consist of an amount that is worth storing (see *Tos. R' Akiva Eiger* and *Pnei Yehoshua*).

37. I.e. he carried it from one domain to another. The same rule applies to transporting four *amos* in a public domain.

38. Even if the transporter is wealthy and the substance is of no significance to him, he is nonetheless liable (*Rashi* ד״ה הא; *Chidushei HaRan*). [Since the item is considered significant by the general populace, the law does not take into account the specific circumstances that render it insignificant to a particular individual.]

39. I.e. a substance not used by people. [This does not mean to preclude very valuable or rare items, which are infrequently used. Rather, it precludes items that, although commonly available, are not considered fit for use.]

40. I.e. even if the substance is one commonly used by people, but it is of a quantity people do not consider worth keeping (*Tos. R' Akiva Eiger* and *Pnei Yehoshua*).

41. I.e. if a person took a liking to a certain material and stored it away, whether it is a smaller quantity than is usually stored or a material not normally used by people, he would be liable for the *melachah* of transferring. Others, however, are exempt, since to the population at large the material is not significant, and so carrying it is not a *melachah* (*Rashi*).

[According to this Tanna the rule is: An item considered significant by most people achieves a legal status of "significant" vis-a-vis all people. An item considered insignificant by most people may yet achieve a status of "significant" to one who actually values it.]

42. Although it is sometimes necessary to keep the blood so that a Rabbinic authority can determine whether the woman is *tamei,* Rav Pappa refers to blood that was already examined. Hence, there is no purpose in storing it further (see *Chidushei HaRan*).

43. [An *asheirah* is a tree that is worshiped. One is prohibited to derive benefit from certain *asheiros,* such as when the tree was planted specifically for worship (see *Avodah Zarah* 45b-46a, 48a).]

Since both menstrual blood and *asheirah* trees have no use, they are not stored. Thus, one who transfers either item from one domain to another on the Sabbath is not liable.

44. *Asheirah* wood is forbidden for benefit, is repulsive, and must be destroyed (*Rashi*). It is certainly not an item that someone would store.

משום צובע אין משום נטילת נשמה לא אימא אף משום צובע אמר רב מילתא דאמרי אימא בה מילתא דלא ליתו דרי בתראי וליחכו עלי צובע במאי ניחא ליה ניחא דליתווס בית השחיטה דמא כי היכי דליחזוה אינשי וליתו ליזבנו מיניה: והמולחו והמעבדו: [א]היינו מולח והיינו מעבד ר' יוחנן ור"ל דאמרי תרווייהו אפיק חד מינייהו ועייל [א] שירטוט אמר רבה בר רב הונא האי מאן דמלח בישרא חייב משום מעבד [ב]רבא אמר אין עיבוד באוכלין אמר רב אשי ואפילו רבה בר רב הונא לא אמר אלא דקא בעי ליה לאורחא אבל לביתא לא משוי איניש מיכליה עץ: [ג]והממחקו והמחתכו: אמר רבי אחא בר חנינא [ג] השף בין העמודים בשבת חייב משום ממחק אמר רבי חייא בר אבא ג' דברים סח לי רב (א) אשי משמיה דרבי יהושע בן לוי [ד]המגרר ראשי כלונסות בשבת חייב משום מחתך [ה]הממרח רטיה בשבת חייב משום ממחק [ו]והמסתת את האבן בשבת חייב משום מכה בפטיש אמר ר' שמעון (א) בן קיסמא אמר רבי שמעון בן לקיש [ז]הצר צורה בכלי והמנפח בכלי זכוכית חייב משום מכה בפטיש א"ר יהודה [ח]האי מאן דשקיל אקופי מגלימי חייב משום מכה בפטיש והני מילי דקפיד עלייהו: [ט]והכותב שתי אותיות: ת"ר (ב) [י]כתב אות אחת גדולה ויש במקומה לכתוב שתים פטור מחק אות גדולה ויש במקומה לכתוב שתים חייב אמר רבי מנחם בר' יוסי וזה חומר במוחק מבכותב: הבונה והסותר המכבה והמבעיר והמכה בפטיש: רבה ור' זירא דאמרי תרווייהו [כ]כל מידי דאית ביה גמר מלאכה חייב משום מכה בפטיש: אלו אבות מלאכות: (ג) אלו [ל]לאפוקי מדר"א דמחייב על תולדה במקום אב: חסר אחת: לאפוקי מדר' יהודה (ד)דתניא ר' יהודה מוסיף את השובט והמדקדק אמרו לו [ד] שובט הרי הוא בכלל מיסך מדקדק הרי הוא בכלל אורג: **מתני'** ועוד כלל אחר אמרו [מ]כל הכשר להצניע ומצניעין כמוהו והוציאו בשבת חייב חטאת עליו וכל שאינו כשר להצניע ואין מצניעין כמוהו והוציאו בשבת אינו חייב אלא המצניעו: **גמ'** כל הכשר להצניע לאפוקי מאי אמר רב פפא [נ]לאפוקי דם נדה מר עוקבא אמר לאפוקי עצי אשרה מאן דאמר דם נדה כ"ש עצי אשרה מאן דאמר עצי אשרה אבל דם נדה מצנע ליה לשונרא ואידך כיון דחלשא לא מצנע ליה אמר רבי יוסי בר חנינא האי דלא כר"ש דאי כר"ש האמר (ה)לא אמרו כל השיעורין הללו אלא למצניעיהן: וכל שאינו כשר להצניע: אמר

רש"י

משום צובע. שצובע את הבשר של בית השחיטה ולקמן מפרש אמאי מיכוין לצובעו וצביעה הואי במשכן אב מלאכה: משום נטילת נשמה. דנטילת נשמה הואי במשכן באילים מאדמים ותחש וחלזון [ו]: אף משום צביעה. ונפקא מינה לחיוביה תרתי: מילתא דאמרי אימא כו'. דבר תימה אמרתי להזכיר צביעה בשחיטה צריך אני לומר בו דבר טעם דלא ליתו דרי בתראי השומעים וליחכו עלי: צובע בשר במאי ניחא ליה. להאי שוחט בצביעת הבשר היינו חוכא ואני אומר בו טעם: ניחא ליה דלתווס בית השחיטה בדמא. שיהא צבוע בדם: כי היכי דניחזייה אינשי. שנשחטה היום וניתו וניזבנו: היינו מולח היינו מעבד. אטו מליחה לאו צורך עיבוד הוא: ועייל שירטוט. לפי שדרך הרצענין כשהוא בא לחתכו משרטטו תחלה כפי מה שהוא רוצה להאריך ולהרחיב ולקצר החיתוך ואחר כך מעביר הסכין דרך השירטוט וכן בעורות המשכן כשחתכום: דקבעי ליה לאורחא. שמולחה הרבה: השף בין העמודים. כגון עמודי אכסדראות שעשוים חלונות חלונות ונסמכין בחלונות בין עמוד לעמוד והשף שם בקרקעית הבנין שנשענין עליו כדי שיהא חלק חייב משום ממחק: המגרר ראשי כלונסות. שיהו ראשיהן שוין וחדין: ממרח רטיה. מחליק תחבושת על המכה: מסתת את האבן. לאחר שנעקרה מן ההר ונחצבה מחליקה: משום מכה בפטיש. שהוא גמר מלאכה: הצר (ג) בכלי צורה. בכלי שעומד לכך לנאותו: מנפח בכלי זכוכית. כשהותך נעשה על ידי נפוח: דשקיל אקופי. ראשי חוטין התלויין ביריעה במקום קשורין כשניתק בה חוט וקשרוהו וכן קשין וקסמים דקין שנארגו בה בלא מתכוין ונוטלין אותם ממנה לאחר אריגה גמר מלאכה הוא וחייב משום מכה בפטיש: כתב אות אחת גדולה כו' פטור. שבקרשי המשכן שתים היו כותבים אחת בזו ואחת בזו כדי לזווגן כשסותרים אותן: מחק אות אחת כו' חייב. שאין מלאכת מחיקה חשובה אלא ע"מ לכתוב והרי יש מקום לשתי אותיות: אמר רבי מנחם ברבי יוסי. הא קמ"ל מאן תנא קמא ר' מנחם ברבי יוסי: לאפוקי מדרבי אליעזר. דהא אמרן דלא נמנו כאן אלא להודיענו מנין חטאות של העלם אחד ותנא הרי אלו למעוטי שאם עשה תולדותיהם עמהן דאינו מביא עליהן חטאת ודלא כרבי אליעזר דמחייב אתולדה עם האב בכריתות: שובט. משוה השתי בכרכר שקורין ריו"ל: מדקדק. כשמותח חוט הערב מכה בכרכר עליו במקומות מקומות ליישבו שלא יהא מתוח יותר מדאי שהמתיחה מעכבתו מהתחבר יפה עם הארג: שובט הרי הוא בכלל מיסך. דהיינו מיסך ממש שמסדר חוטי השתי: הרי הוא אורג. דהיינו אורג ממש ולא דמי לזורה ובורר ומרקד דזה בקשין וזה בצרורות וזה בקמח: **מתני'** כל הכשר להצניע. שהוא מין העשוי לצורך האדם: ומצניעין כמוהו. כמות זה כלומר שיש בו שיעור הראוי להצניעו: אין חייב אלא למצניעו. אם נעשה חביב לאדם א' והצניעו חייב על הוצאתו אם חזר והוציאו אבל אדם אחר אינו חייב עליו דלגביה לאו מלאכה הוא: **גמ'** מ"ד דם נדה. אינו כשר להצניע כ"ש עצי אשרה דאיסורי הנאה נינהו ומאיסי וצריך לאבדן: כיון דחלשא. המאכיל דם האדם לחתול נעשה חלש אותו אדם: הא. דתנא כל הכשר להצניע ויש בו שיעור שרוב ב"א עשויין להצניע כשיעור הזה חייב כל אדם על הוצאתו ואפילו אדם עשיר שאין שיעור זה חשוב לו: דלא כר' שמעון. לקמן בהמוציא אמר

תוספות

אין עיבוד באוכלין. אין להתיר מכאן מליחת אוכלין דאסור מדרבנן מליחה בפרק שמונה שרצים (לקמן דף קח:) ואפילו בי"ט אסור בפ"ק דביצה (דף יא.): **השף** בין העמודים בשבת חייב. פירש ר"ח [י] דשף העור על העמוד כדי להחליקו וכן משמע בירושלמי ורש"י פירש ששף קרקעית שבין עמודי חלונות ולא נהירא: **והמסתת** את האבן כו' חייב משום מכה בפטיש. אבל משום מחתך וממחק לא מיחייב דמיירי שכבר היא מרובעת ומתוקנת אלא שמייפה אותה ועושה בה שירטוטין ויפוי כעין שעושין עכשיו מסתתי האבנים. ר"י וכן ריב"א: **הרי** אלו לאפוקי מדרבי אליעזר דמחייב אתולדה במקום אב. וא"ת מרישא שמעינן לה דתנן העושה מלאכות הרבה מעין מלאכה אחת אינו חייב אלא אחת וי"מ דה"ק מעין מלאכה אחת היינו שתי תולדות מאב א' אבל האב ותולדה דידיה מיחייב תרתי קמ"ל: **חסר** אחת לאפוקי מדר' יהודה. תימה דממילא דרישא שמעינן לה וליכא למימר תנא ושייר [ס] דהא אלו קתני ומיהו הא ליכא לאקשויי דהא מאלו דרישא שמעינן לאפוקי מדר' אליעזר דאיכא למימר דנקט ברישא אלו אבות משום דקאי אדקתני לעיל חייב על כל אב מלאכה וי"ל דממילא דרישא לא שמעינן לאפוקי מדרבי יהודה דאיכא למימר דלא חשיב אלא מלאכות חשובות אבל שובט ומדקדק אע"ג דמלאכות הן לא קתני להו משום דאינם מבוררות כל כך וכה"ג משני בפ"ק דקדושין (דף טז:) גבי אלו מעניקין להן דבר שיש לו קצבה קתני דבר שאין לו קצבה לא קתני [ח]: **לאפוקי** עצי אשרה. דלא כרבי יהודה דאמר בפרק רבי עקיבא (לקמן דף צ.) אף המוציא משמשי ע"ז כל שהוא חייב אלא כת"ק דפליג עליה כן פירש בקונט' התם וקשה לרשב"א הא דקאמר הכא מ"ד דם נדה כ"ש עצי אשרה מנא ליה דילמא סבר כרבי יהודה ומחייב בעצי אשרה שמצניעין אותן לשריפה: **הא** דלא כר' שמעון. פירש בקונטרס הא דתנן כל הכשר כו' שרוב בני אדם עשויים להצניע כשיעור הזה חייב כל אדם על הוצאתו אפילו אדם עשיר שאין שיעור זה חשוב לו משמע מדבריו דלא מחייב ר' שמעון אלא בסתם בני אדם שרגילין להצניעו שאותו שיעור חשוב להן ואפילו לא הצניעו הוא ולקמן פי' לא נאמרו שיעורים שבמשנה אלא למצניעין אותו קודם לכן וחזר המצניע והוציאו משמע דוקא בהצניעו חייב ואומר ר"י דיש ליישב פירושו דמה שמצריך

עין משפט נר מצוה

סב א ב ג מיי' פי"א מהלכות שבת הלכה ה סמג לאוין סה טוש"ע או"ח סימן שכא סעיף ה:
סב [א] [מיי' פי"ז מהל' שבת הלכה א ופי"א הלכה יח]:
סב [ג] [מיי' פי"א שם הלכה ו]:
סג ד מיי' שם הלכה ז:
סד ה מיי' שם הלכה ו ופכ"ג הלכה יא טור שו"ע או"ח סימן שכח סעיף כו:
סה ו מיי' פ"י מהלכות שבת הלכה יח:
סו ז שם הלכה טז:
סז ח מיי' שם הלכה יח טוש"ע או"ח סימן שב סעיף ג:
סח ט י מיי' פי"א מהל' שבת הלכה ט סמג שם טוש"ע או"ח סימן שמ סעיף ג:
סט כ מיי' פ"י שם הלכה טז ופכ"ג הלכה ד סמג שם:
ע ל מיי' פ"ז שם הל' ז ופ"ז מהל' שגגות הלכה ה:
ע [ד] [מיי' שם פ"ט הלכה יח ויט]:
עא מ נ מיי' פי"ח מהל' שבת הלכה כב:

רבינו חננאל

ליה דנהוי חי כי היכי דלצלח צבעיה דכל כמה דהוא חי מצלח ציבעיה. שוחט משום מאי מחייב רב אמר משום צובע אסיק' ניחא ליה כי היכי דנתווס בית שחיטה דידיה דמא. כי היכי דידעי אינשי דחי הוה וכי היכי (דניחה) [דנחזיה] אינשי דנשחט הוא וקאתי למזבן מיניה ולא יימרו של נבילה הוא. והא דאמר רב משום צובע הכי קאמר חדא משום נטילת נשמה דהא בהדיא תנן באבות מלאכות השוחט. וסבר רב השוחט בשבת חייב שתים אחת משום נטילת נשמה ואחת משום צובע והוא אב (אחד) [אחר]. והמולחו והמעבדו. אקשינן דמולח היינו מעבד כדאמרינן (לקמן עט:) לענין חיפה מליח וקמיח שנמצאת מליחתו עבודו ופרקין ר' יוחנן ור"ל דהמולח והמעבד תרווייהו מלאכת עיבוד נינהו ותני חדא והוא הדין לאחרינא. אי הכי בצרי להו עייל שירטוט ושני במתני' המולחו והמשרטטו: **ירושלמי**: מה עיבוד היה במשכן שהיו משרטטין בעורות מהו משרטטין מסרגלין. מליחת בשר חי בשבת. אם כוונתו לצאת בו לדרך או לאוכלו אחר כמה ימים חייב משום מעבד אבל לאוכלו ביומו לא ולית הלכתא כדרבה בר רב הונא (דרבה בר רב הונא) [דרבא] דחי לה ואמר אין עיבוד באוכלין: **השף** בין העמודים. פי' מחליק חייב משום מוחק והוא כמו ממרח את הרטיה: **ירושלמי** הממחקו. מה מחיקה היתה במשכן (פי') שהיו שפין העורות ע"ג העמוד. השף את העור ע"ג העמוד חייב משום (מוחק) [ממחק]. הממרח איספלנית חייב משום מוחק. הגורר ראשי כלונסות חייב משום מחתך. הממרח רטיה חייב משום מוחק. וכן הצר בכלי צורה כל שהוא חייב משום מכה בפטיש. ואע"ג דפליג ר' ישמעאל (לקמן קג:) ואמר עד שיצור כל הצורה יחידאה היא ואי ההיא צורה אית בה אותיות דמיקרו חייב משום כותב ואי לאו חייב משום מכה בפטיש וכן המנפח בכלי זכוכית הוא גמר מלאכה שמלאכת זכוכית בניפוח הוא. פי' אקופי כגון נימין הניתקין מן האריגה דנתלין בבגד או חתיכות עצים קטנים המסבכין בצמרן של בגדים חדשים וכשמשלים האומן מלאכתו כל ראשי נימין התלויים בין קיסם וקליפה שנסתבכו בבגד נוטלן. ונקראין אקופי.

מסורת הש"ס

א) [נ"ל אסי], ב) [תוספ' פי"ב], ג) לקמן עו: ב"ק ב. כריתות טז:, ד) לקמן צז:, ה) לקמן עו:, ו) ע"כ שייך לעיל, ז) [עי' בערוך ערך שף], ח) [ועי' במה שליינתי בס"ד בתוס' יבמות פד: ד"ה אלא].

הגהות הב"ח

(א) גמ' אמר ר"ש בר ביסנא אמר ר"ש בן לקיש הצר: (ג) רש"י ד"ה הצר צורה כצ"ל ותיבת בכלי נמחק:

גליון הש"ס

תוס' ד"ה חסר אחת וכו' דהא אלו קתני. כדאי' בקדושין דף טז ע"ב:

רב נסים גאון

נטילת נשמה קיי"ל שהמתעסק לענין שבת פטור. ומשכחת עיקר דילה במסכת כריתות בפרק ספק אכל חלב (דף יט) אמר רב נחמן אמר שמואל [המתעסק] בחלבים ובעריות (בחלבים פטור ובעריות) חייב שכבר נהנה מתעסק בשבת פטור מלאכת מחשבת אסרה תורה ומשכחת לה בסנהדרין בפ' ד' מיתות (דף סב) ובגמרא דהזורק דבני מערבא (הלכה ו) גרסי הזורק בשבת פטור היאך עבידא אמר הריני קוצר חצי גרוגרת וקצר כגרוגרת פטור בגמ' דכל שעה בפסחים (דף לג) גרסי לה אם אמרת בשאר מצות שכן לא חייב בהן שאין מתעסק כמתעסק שאם נתכוין להגביה את התלוש וחתך המחובר פטור וכגון זה כל מלאכה שהיא באה חילוף מה שנתכוון העושה אותה מתעסק מיקרי שהרי לא נעשית מחשבתו: **אלו** לאפוקי מדר' אליעזר דמחייב על תולדה במקום אב. ואשכחנן דברי ר' אליעזר בכריתות בפרק אמרו לו אכלת חלב (דף טז) אמר ר' עקיבא שאלתי את ר' אליעזר העושה מלאכות הרבה בשבתות הרבה מעין מלאכה אחת בהעלם אחד מהו חייב על כל אחת ואחת או חייב אחת על כולן אמר לי חייב על כל אחת ואחת מקל וחומר ואמרו בתלמוד בעי מיניה ולדי מלאכות אי כמלאכות דמיין אי לא ופשט ליה דולדי מלאכות כמלאכות דמיין: **דאי** ר' שמעון הא אמר לא נאמרו כל השיעורין האלו אלא למצניעיהן. בפירקא דלקמן המוציא יין (דף עו) משכחת להא דר' שמעון:

סליק פרק כלל גדול

ליקוטי רש"י

דליתווס. מיתווסי. מתלכלכין [פסחים סה:]. **היינו מולח והיינו מעבד.** מליחה מאבות מלאכות היא בדבר שיש בו עבוד דתנן (שבת עג.) והמולחו והמעבדו [ביצה יא:]. **הממרח רטיה.** מחליק גומות שברטיה מירוח חייב משום ממחק [עירובין קב:]. **מסתת את האבן.** מרבע את האבן ומתקנה הכל לפי המקום שיש מקומות שרגילין להחליק ויש מקומות שרגילין לחרוץ בה חריצים חריצים כארץ אשכנז. **משום מכה בפטיש.** גמר מלאכה הוא שהמקום שחרץ חריץ זה לא יחרוץ עוד. **כל מידי דאית ביה גמר מלאכה וכו'.** כל הגומר בשבת מלאכה תולדת מכה בפטיש היא [לקמן קב:]. **לאפוקי מדר"א דמחייב על תולדה במקום אב.** דאי עביד אב ותולדה דידיה מחייב תרתי חטאות במס' כריתות בפ' אמרו לו (טז.) [ב"ק ב.]. **מוסיף את השובט.** עם שאר אבות מלאכות להא דאמרן דלכך נמנו שאם עשאן בהעלם אחד חייב על כל אחד ואחד. **שובט.** מכרכר בכרכר. **ומדקדק.** לאחר שמתח החוט של ערב מכה בכרכר בשנים ושלשה מקומות ויש מפרשים מדקדק משוה האריגה כשיש שני חוטין כרוכין זה עם זה ומובדלים מן השאר משוה אותן בכרכר או במחט [לקמן צז:]. **לא אמרו.** שיעורין שבמשנה אלא למצניעיהן לבד וחזר המצניע והוציאו חייב אבל שאר כל אדם שהוציאו אינו חייב וסבירא ליה לר' שמעון דמצניע עצמו בעי שיעורא זוטא ובבציר מהא שיעורא לא מיחייב כדאמרינן בפרקין דלעיל (עה:) דלית ליה לר' שמעון כל שאין כשר להצניע ואין מצניעים כמוהו שיתחייב עליו מצניעו [שם עו:].

Since a person becomes weak if his blood is fed to a cat,[45] **לֹא מַצְנַע לֵיהּ** – **[menstrual blood] is not stored** for that purpose.

The Gemara notes that the ruling of our Mishnah is not unanimous:

אָמַר רַבִּי יוֹסֵי בַּר חֲנִינָא – **R' Yose bar Chanina said:** **הַאי דְּלָא כְּרַבִּי שִׁמְעוֹן** – **This** ruling of the Mishnah[46] **is not in accordance with R' Shimon,** **דְּאִי כְּרַבִּי שִׁמְעוֹן** – **for if** it is **in accordance with R' Shimon,** **הָאָמַר** – **then he has stated** a conflicting ruling in another Mishnah,[47] for he said there: **לֹא אָמְרוּ כָּל הַשִּׁיעוּרִין הַלָּלוּ** – **THEY DID NOT STATE ALL THESE MEASUREMENTS** **אֶלָּא לְמַצְנִיעֵיהֶן** – **EXCEPT FOR THOSE WHO** actually **STORE THEM.**[48]

Our Mishnah stated:

וְכֹל שֶׁאֵינוֹ כָּשֵׁר לְהַצְנִיעַ – **BUT WHATEVER IS NOT FIT TO STORE,** only the one who stores it would be liable; but if another person carries it out, he is exempt from punishment.

NOTES

45. See *Tosafos* to *Niddah* 17a ד״ה שורפן; cf. *Rabbeinu Perachyah* here.

46. The Mishnah taught that if an item is of the type and amount that most people store, *anyone* who transports it is liable – i.e. even a wealthy person, who does not consider the minimum amount useful (*Rashi*).

47. Below, 76b.

48. According to R' Shimon, the minimum measures for liability stated in the Mishnah below (76b) are applicable only for the average person, who stores such an amount. A wealthy person, however, would not be liable for carrying out those minimum measures.

This follows *Rashi's* explanation here. Below (76b ד״ה ולא נאמרו), however, he states that R' Shimon disputes our Mishnah's second ruling: According to the Rabbis of our Mishnah, if a person actually stores and then carries out *less* than the stated minimum amounts, he is nevertheless liable. According to R' Shimon, though, even if a person stored an item, he is liable only for carrying out the stated minimum amount (see *Ramban* and *Ritva* (*MHK* ed.) in explanation of *Rashi;* cf. *Tosafos*). [See *Dibros Moshe* 64:47.]

Thus, according to *Rashi,* R' Shimon's statement disputes two rulings of the Tanna Kamma. He holds that: (a) Only people of average means are liable for carrying out the minimum amounts stated in the Mishnah; a wealthy person, however, who does not store such an amount, is not liable.

(b) No one is liable for carrying out less than the stated minimum amounts – even someone who actually stored such a minuscule amount; the minimums stated in the Mishnah apply even to items that were stored (*Ritva MHK* ed.). [See chart below, 76a.]

אָמַר רַבִּי אֶלְעָזָר – R' Elazar said: הָא דְּלֹא כְּרַבִּי שִׁמְעוֹן בֶּן אֶלְעָזָר – This second ruling of the Mishnah **is not in accordance with R' Shimon ben Elazar,**[1] דְּתַנְיָא – **for it was taught in a Baraisa:** כְּלָל אָמַר רַבִּי שִׁמְעוֹן בֶּן אֶלְעָזָר – **R' SHIMON BEN ELAZAR STATED A GENERAL RULE:** כֹּל שֶׁאֵינוֹ כָּשֵׁר לְהַצְנִיעַ – **WHATEVER IS NOT FIT TO STORE,** וְאֵין מַצְנִיעִין כָּמוֹהוּ – **OR [PEOPLE] DO NOT STORE IT IN SUCH [A QUANTITY],** וְהוּכְשַׁר לָזֶה וְהִצְנִיעוֹ – **BUT IT WAS FIT FOR THIS** particular person **AND HE STORED IT,** וּבָא אַחֵר וְהוֹצִיאוֹ – **AND ANOTHER** person **CAME AND CARRIED IT OUT,** נִתְחַיֵּיב זֶה בְּמַחְשֶׁבָה שֶׁל זֶה – **THIS** person who carried it out **IS LIABLE ON ACCOUNT OF THE INTENTION OF THIS** other person who stored it.[2]

Mishnah After stating that one is not liable to a *chatas* for transferring from one domain to another unless one carries out both a quality and a quantity that people consider of sufficient value to store, the Mishnah begins detailing the precise minimum quantities of various commonly used substances. This particular Mishnah discusses items used for animal feed:

הַמּוֹצִיא תֶּבֶן – **One who carries out processed straw**[3] כִּמְלֹא פִי פָרָה – is liable if he carries out **as much as a cow's mouthful;**[4] עֵצָה – if he takes out ***etzah,***[5] כִּמְלֹא פִי גָמָל – **as much as a camel's mouthful;**[6] עָמִיר – **straw,**[7] כִּמְלֹא פִי טָלֶה – **as much as a lamb's mouthful;** עֲשָׂבִים – **grass,** כִּמְלֹא פִי גְדִי – **as much as a kid's mouthful;**[8] עֲלֵי שׁוּם וַעֲלֵי בְצָלִים – **leaves of garlic and leaves of onion**[9] – לַחִים כִּגְרוֹגֶרֶת – if they are **fresh, the equivalent of a dried fig,**[10] יְבֵשִׁים כִּמְלֹא פִי גְדִי – and if they are **dry, as much as a kid's mouthful.**[11] וְאֵין מִצְטָרְפִין זֶה עִם זֶה – **And they** [i.e. any of the above-mentioned species] **cannot be combined with one another,**[12] מִפְּנֵי שֶׁלֹּא שָׁווּ בְּשִׁיעוּרֵיהֶן – **because they are not alike in their prescribed measures.**[13]

Gemara The Gemara inquires:

מַאי עֵצָה – **What is *etzah*?**

The Gemara answers:

אָמַר רַב יְהוּדָה – **Rav Yehudah said:** תֶּבֶן שֶׁל מִינֵי קִטְנִית – **Straw of** various **types of beans.**

The Gemara notes:

כִּי אֲתָא רַב דִּימִי אָמַר – **When Rav Dimi came** to Babylonia from Eretz Yisrael **he reported** the following Amoraic dispute: הַמּוֹצִיא תֶּבֶן כִּמְלֹא פִי פָרָה לְגָמָל – In the case of **one who carries out straw as much as a cow's mouthful for a camel,**[14] רַבִּי יוֹחָנָן אָמַר חַיָּיב – **R' Yochanan said that he is liable,** רַבִּי שִׁמְעוֹן בֶּן לָקִישׁ אָמַר פָּטוּר – while **R' Shimon ben Lakish said that he is exempt** from punishment.[15]

Rav Dimi concludes:

בְּאוּרְתָּא אָמַר רַבִּי יוֹחָנָן הָכִי – **In the evening R' Yochanan stated thus** [that the transporter is liable], לְצַפְרָא הֲדַר בֵּיהּ – but **in the morning he retracted [his opinion],** ruling that the person is exempt from punishment.

The Gemara explains R' Yochanan's reversal:

אָמַר רַב יוֹסֵף – **Rav Yosef said:** שַׁפִּיר עֲבַד דַּהֲדַר – **[R' Yochanan] did well by retracting** his earlier view, דְּהָא לֹא חָזֵי לְגָמָל – **for [the measure]** of straw the transporter took out **is not fit for a camel.** Therefore, since he took out the straw to feed

NOTES

1. Our Mishnah stated that only the person who stores something not usually fit for storage [because of its quality or quantity] is liable for taking it out; however, if another person takes that item out, he is exempt from punishment. The Gemara now cites a dissenting opinion (*Rashi*).

2. Thus, R' Shimon ben Elazar advocates a third opinion, more stringent than the two already mentioned – namely, if someone stored a particular amount of an item, whoever carries it out is liable on account of the owner's intent (*Ritva MHK* ed. above, 75b).

LIABILITY FOR:		
	ITEM NOT STORED	STORED ITEM
TANNA KAMMA	Minimum amounts	Any amount
	For all people	For the storer
R' SHIMON	Minimum amounts	Minimum amounts
	For average person who considers it significant	For the storer
R' SHIMON BEN ELAZAR		Any amount
		for anyone

3. I.e. straw made by crushing cut stalks of grain (*Rashi* below, 140a; *Rosh Yosef*).

4. Since straw is commonly eaten by cows, a cow's mouthful is the prescribed measure for liability.

5. The Gemara will identify this substance.

6. This measure is larger than a cow's mouthful. Since *etzah* is not generally fit for bovine consumption, one is not liable for taking out as much as a cow's mouthful (*Rashi*). Rather, he is liable only when he takes out the equivalent of a camel's mouthful, since *etzah* is commonly fed to camels.

7. This refers to the stalks, which separate from the ears when they are threshed (see *Rashi* here, to *Bava Kamma* 20a ד״ה דמי עמיר and to *Bava Metzia* 90b ד״ה פקיע עמיר). They were commonly bound in bundles (see Mishnah below, 155a with *Rashi*).

[Presumably these stalks can be better used for lamb fodder than the processed straw mentioned in the beginning of the Mishnah because they are softer. However, it is unclear why this is so. Possibly, these stalks differ in quality or degree of freshness from those that are crushed for cow fodder. According to *Aruch* these refer specifically to the stalks of the fenugreek plant. See also *Rosh Yosef* and *Tiferes Yisrael* for alternative explanations of the term עָמִיר.]

8. A lamb's mouthful is larger than a kid's mouthful. Since this type of straw (עָמִיר) is still too hard for a kid, one is not liable unless he carries out at least a lamb's mouthful. However, for carrying out grass, which is fit for both a lamb and a kid, one is liable for the smaller measure – namely, a kid's mouthful (*Rashi*).

9. This refers to the tubulated leaves that sprout from the bulb of the onion above ground, and by which the onion can be picked (*Tos. Yom Tov*).

10. Since these are fit for human consumption, the prescribed measure is the equivalent of a dried fig (i.e. a quantity of leaves equal in volume to a dried fig), which is the measure for all foodstuffs (see below, 76b note 3). If one carried out only as much as a kid's mouthful, however, he is exempt from a *chatas,* because fresh garlic and onion leaves are not a kid's normal fare (*Rashi; cf. Ritva MHK* ed.).

[*Hagahos HaAshri* writes that it is prohibited even according to Biblical law to carry out less than this amount of food, because of the principle that one may not perform any amount of a forbidden act (see above, 74a note 13). *Emes LeYaakov* discusses whether this principle applies to the other items mentioned in the Mishnah.]

11. Dry garlic and onion leaves are not fit for human consumption, but are eaten by kids. Therefore, if one takes out a kid's mouthful of dry leaves, he is liable (see *Meiri*).

12. E.g. if one carried out one-half of a cow's mouthful of crushed straw and one-half of a camel's mouthful of *etzah,* he is not liable (*Tiferes Yisrael*).

13. The Gemara will elaborate on this point.

14. He carried out this measure to feed a camel, whose mouth is larger than that of a cow (*Rashi*).

15. The Gemara will soon explain the reason for each position.

גמרא

א"ר אלעזר הא דלא כר"ש בן אלעזר [א] דתניא כלל אמר ר' שמעון בן אלעזר כל שאינו כשר להצניע ואין מצניעין כמוהו והוכשר לזה והצניעו ובא אחר והוציאו נתחייב זה במחשבה של זה: **מתני'** [א] המוציא תבן כמלא פי פרה עצה כמלא פי גמל עמיר כמלא פי טלה עשבים כמלא פי גדי עלי שום ועלי בצלים לחים כגרוגרת יבשים כמלא פי גדי ואין מצטרפין זה עם זה מפני שלא שוו בשיעוריהן: **גמ'** מאי עצה אמר רב יהודה תבן של מיני קטנית כי אתא רב דימי אמר המוציא תבן כמלא פי פרה לגמל ר' יוחנן אמר חייב ר"ש בן לקיש אמר פטור באורתא א"ר יוחנן הכי לצפרא הדר ביה אמר רב יוסף שפיר עבד דהדר דהא לא חזי לגמל א"ל אביי אדרבה כדמעיקרא מסתברא דהא חזי לפרה אלא כי אתא רבין אמר המוציא תבן כמלא פי פרה לגמל דכולי עלמא לא פליגי דחייב כי פליגי במוציא עצה כמלא פי פרה לפרה ° ואיפכא איתמר ר' יוחנן אמר פטור ° ריש לקיש אמר חייב ר' יוחנן אמר פטור אכילה על ידי הדחק לא שמה אכילה [ג] ריש לקיש אמר [ב] חייב אכילה [ג] ע"י הדחק שמה אכילה: עמיר כמלא פי טלה: והתניא כגרוגרת אידי ואידי חד שיעורא הוא: עלי שום ועלי בצלים לחים כגרוגרת ויבשים כמלא פי הגדי ואין מצטרפין זה עם זה מפני שלא שוו בשיעוריהן: אמר ר' יוסי בר חנינא [ב] אין מצטרפין לחמור שבהן אבל מצטרפין לקל שבהן וכל דלא שוו בשיעורייהו מי מצטרפין והתנן [ד] הבגד ג' על ג' והשק ד' על ד' והעור ה' על ה' מפץ ו' על ו' [ה] ותני עלה הבגד והשק השק והעור העור והמפץ מצטרפין זה עם זה ואמר ר"ש מה טעם מפני שראויין ליטמא מושב טעמא דראויין ליטמא מושב אבל אין ראוי ליטמא מושב לא אמר רבא הכא

רש"י

א"ר אלעזר הא. דקתני מתניתין דאינו כשר להצניע והצניעו [י] אחר הוא מתחייב על הוצאתו וכל אדם פטורין דלא כר' שמעון בן אלעזר: מתני' עצה. מפרש בגמרא: כמלא פי גמל. נפיש שיעורא מפי פרה אבל כמלא פי פרה לא מיחייב דהא לא חזו לפרה: עמיר. קשין של שבלין: פי טלה. נפיש מפי גדי הלכך עמיר דלא חזי לגדי לא מיחייב כמלא פי גדי עד דאיכא מלא פי טלה אבל עשבים הואיל וחזו בין לטלה בין לגדי מיחייב אפי' כמלא פי גדי: לחין. הראוין לאדם כגרוגרת דזה שיעור לכל מאכל אדם לשבת אבל כמלא פי גדי לא דלאדם לא חזו לגדי: גמ' המוציא תבן כמלא פי פרה. והוציאו להאכילו לגמל שפי גמל גדול מפי פרה: דהא חזי לפי פרה. הלכך שיעור חשוב הוא ולכל מי שיוציאנו לא פקע שיעוריה בהכי: דחייב. דהאיכא שיעורא דחזי לפרה הלכך כשר להצניע הוא ומצניעין כמוהו: עצה. לא חזיא לפרה אלא ע"י הדחק אלא לגמל הוא דחזי וזה הוציאו לפרה: רבי יוחנן אמר פטור. דהא לגמל דחזי ליה ליכא שיעורא ואי משום דלצורך פרה הוציאו ולגבה איכא שיעור אכילה ע"י הדחק לאו אכילה היא הלכך לא משערי' ליה בפרה: אין מצטרפין לחמור שבהם. מי ששיעורו גדול הוי קל ואינו מצטרף להשלים שיעורו של חמור דהא לא חשיב כי ההוא אבל החשוב משלים את הקל לכשיעור תבן מצטרף עם עצה להשלי' פי גמל ועצה אין מצטרף עם התבן להשלים מלא פי פרה: מי מצטרפין. אפילו להשלים חמור את הקל: ג' על ג'. לטומאת מדרס הזב ליעשות אב הטומאה: הבגד והשק מצטרפין. שהבגד משלים שיעור השק. שק עשוי מנוצה של עזים: ואמר ר' שמעון מה טעם. מצטרפין: הואיל וראויין ליטמא מושב. אם צירף משניהם יחד לטלאי מרדעת של חמור כשיעורו לענין מושב הזב אם קלע משניהם מהן ותקן טפח על טפח לישב עליו מיטמא ליה אב הטומאה במושב הזב דתניא (א) המקלע מכולן טפח על טפח טמא מושב ואמרינן טעמא בפ"ק דסוכה הואיל וראוי לטלות על גבי חמור שאינו מקפיד אם הוא משני מינין: הכא

תוספות

שמצריך לקמן הצנעה היינו לאדם עשיר שאין דרכו להצניע ומכל מקום פירוש מילתיה דר"ש צריך לפרש כמו שפירש כאן דאי מיירי במצניעין לאותו דבר עצמו שמפורש במשנה כמו שפירש התם אם כן כולהו הוה מצי למימר בכל שהוא בכדי שיפת קילור כדתנן בפ' המצניע (לקמן צ:) דלרפואה בכל שהוא ואתיא כר"ש מדלא קאמר התם בגמ' הא דלא כר"ש כי היכי דקאמר (דף צא.) הא דלא כר"ש בן אלעזר ומהתם נמי יש לדקדק דלר' שמעון סתם בני אדם שרגילין להצניעו מיחייבי אפי' לא הצניעו מדקתני המצניע לזרע כו' וכל אדם אין חייבין עליו אלא כשיעורו משמע בלא הצנעה וכר"ש נמי אתיא כדפי' ואין לפרש דבעשיר שאין דרכו להצניע לא מיחייב לר"ש אפי' בהצניעו דהא אמר בהמוציא יין בד"א במוציא אבל במצניע כל שהוא ר"ש אומר בד"א במצניע כו' ומפרש מצניע דרבנן בתלמיד שאמר לו כו' דבר שאינו חשוב לכל אי אצנעיה רביה אין אי לא לא ודומיא דהכי נראה דהוי מצניע דר"ש דתליא מילתא באותו שהצניעו היינו בעשיר קשה לרשב"א דמהאי טעמא דקאמר הכא מתני' דלא כר"ש משום דמתני' סתמא קתני דחייב משמע שכל בני אדם חייבין עליו אפי' אותן שאין חשוב להן שיעור זה מהאי טעמא נמי הוה ליה למימר בההיא דפרק המצניע דהויא דלא כר"ש ושמא י"ל דהכא דנקט לפרושי הוה ליה לפרושי טפי: **אכילה** ע"י הדחק לא שמה אכילה. והא דאמר בפ' כילד הרגל (ב"ק דף יט.) אכילה ע"י הדחק שמה אכילה ה"מ לענין ניזקין דלא חשבינן ליה משונה אבל לאחשובה לענין שבת לא חשיבא אכילה: **אידי** ואידי חד שיעורא הוא. והא דנקט במתני' כמלא פי טלה ולא נקט כגרוגרת לאשמעי' דמשום אכילת טלה נתנו בו חכמים שיעור זה דאי נקט כגרוגרת לא הוה ידעינן למה נתנו בו חכמים שיעור זה: **מפני** שלא שוו בשיעוריהם. אבל אותם ששוו כגון עמיר ועלי שום ועלי בצלים לחים מצטרפין וכן חמור לקל כגון תבן לעצה למלא פי גמל ואפי' לא יהא תבן ראוי לגמל שמא אגב העצה הוא ראוי: **הבגד** והשק והעור כו'. דוקא בכה"ג הבגד והשק והשק והעור והעור והמפץ אבל הבגד והעור והשק והמפץ אין מצטרפין שאין ראוין להתחבר יחד והמחברן בטלה דעתו ואין טמאים מדרס. ר"י: **ואמר** ר"ש מה טעם כו'. תימה לר"י דמה צריך להאי טעמא דהא כיון דמצטרפין זה עם זה א"כ ראוי לחברן וחזו למדרס וכיון דחזו למדרס פשיטא דמצטרפין לטומאת מדרס דהא אפי' כופת שאור שיחדה לישיבה טמאה מדרס כדאמרינן בהעור והרוטב (חולין קכט.) והכא בטומאת מדרס איירי מדקאמר הבגד שלשה על שלשה דלענין טומאת מת אפי' ג' על ג' כדפרישית לעיל ואור"י דודאי הא דקתני הבגד שלשה על שלשה לא מיירי אלא למדרס אבל סיפא דשק ועור ומפץ מיירי נמי בטומאת מת והכי איתא במס' כלים בפכ"ז הבגד שלשה על שלשה [למדרס ומשום ג' על ג'] לטומאת מת השק ד' על ד' העור ה' על ה' המפץ ו' על ו' שוו בין למדרס בין לטמא מת אלא שהש"ס מביאה בקוצר כמו שרגיל בכמה מקומות ועל טומאת מת קאמר מה טעם מצטרפין בשלא יחדו למדרס ולא צריך האי טעמא אצירוף דעור ומפץ ° דמפץ לא מטמא במת אלא כשטמא בזב דהיינו כשיחדו למדרס ומק"ו דפכין קטנים כדאמרינן בפ' ר' עקיבא (לקמן פד:): **הואיל** וראויין ליטמא מושב. פי' בקונטרס אם קילע משניהם וצירף יחד לטלאי מרדעת החמור והיא דהמקלע מכולם טפח על טפח דמעילה היינו שבין כולם יש טפח ואין נראה לר"י דמה צריך להביא ראיה שראוין להצטרף בלאו טעמא דמושב נמי שמעינן ממתני' דהכא שראוין להצטרף יחד באותו סדר כמו ששנויים בגד לשק ושק לעור ועור למפץ דדוקא נקט לפי שאלו ראוין להצטרף יחד ונראה לר"י כמו שפי' ריב"א דהואיל וראוין ליטמא מושב היינו הואיל ושוו שיעוריהן לענין מושב וכמו שפירש בקונטרס בפ"ק דסוכה (דף יח:) דהמקלע מכולן היינו מאיזה מהן שיקלע יהא טמא ואע"ג שכאן אין שיעורן שוה מצטרפין הואיל ולענין מושב שיעורן שוה והא דקאמר ה"נ חזו לדוגמא היינו נמי דשיעורן שוה לדוגמא כדתנן בפרק המצניע דלדוגמא כל שהוא הלכך מצטרפין אפי' לענין דבר דלא שוו שיעורייהו וה"ה דהוי מצי למינקט הכא ולזרע ולרפואה דהוו נמי בכל שהוא אלא דלא כל דברים שייך בהו זרע ורפואה אבל דוגמא שייכא בכל דבר והא דקאמר בסוכה המקלע מכולן כו' הואיל וראוי לטלות על גבי חמורו לשון הואיל וראוי לאו דווקא דדווקא אם עשה מהן טלאי ויחדן לכך טמא בטפח על טפח וכן מצינו לקמן בפ' א"ר עקיבא (דף צ.) הואיל וראוין למתק הקדרה דהוה ליה למימר הואיל וממתקין דהא מיירי שנפלו לתוך הקדרה. ר"י: **תוספתא** [ז] המקלע למשכב אין פחות משלשה על שלשה למושב טפח ולמעמד כל שהוא:

חמשת

עין משפט נר מצוה

עב א ב מיי' פי"ח מהל' שבת הל' ג:
[עב] [ב] [מיי' שם]:

רבינו חננאל

ומנקה הבגד ודומה למנקב דתנינן בכמה מקומות ואם נשארו כגון אלו בבגד ובעל הבגד קפיד עלייהו ושקיל להו בשבת חייב משום מכה בפטיש. פי' כל דבר שהוא גמר מלאכה נקרא מכה בפטיש: **המוחק** אות אחת גדולה שיש במקומה שיעור לכתוב ב' אותיות חייב והכותב אות אחת גדולה שיש במקומה שיעור לכתוב ב' אותיות פטור. זה חומר במוחק מבכותב. אלו אבות מלאכות לאפוקי מדר' אלעזר דמחייב אתולדה במקום אב כמו שכבר פרשנוהו למעלה (דף עג:) דמאן דעבד ב' אבות או ב' תולדות משני אבות או אב ותולדה דאב (אחד) [אחר] בהעלם אחד חייב בזה אחד ובזה אחד. ואי עביד אב ותולדתו לא מיחייב אלא חדא. ועוד חזר ושנה מ' חסר אחת לאפוקי מר' יהודה דאמר שובט ומדקדק מאבות מלאכות הן. אמרו לו שובט הרי הוא בכלל מיסך. מדקדק בכלל אורג. [א] פי' יש לארוגין עץ או עצם שראשו חד תקרא כדבר ודומה למחט של סקאין. וכך שמו בלשון יון כדבר. מעבירו על השתי כשהוא מותח לפניו לאריגה ושובט בו החוטין ומקרב המבדילין בין ב' החוטין העליונים והתחתונים ומדנחים להתפרק העליונים מן התחתונים ותפתח נפש המסכת לידות בתוכם חוט הערב ואין לה אב אלא הרי הוא בכלל מיסך והמדקדק הוא המדקדק על חוט הערב כדי להדחק ולהלחץ עם חבירו וזהו בכלל אריגה: **ועוד** כלל אחר אמרו כל הכשר להצניע ומצניעין כמוהו והוציאו בשבת חייב עליו חטאת. כל הכשר להצניע רב מתנה אמר למעוטי דם נדה שאין חייבין בהוצאתו. וכ"ש איסורי הנאה. ועצי אשרה שאין חייבין בהוצאתו. מר עוקבא אמר לאפוקי עצי אשרה אבל דם נדה חייב כו' וזה שנינו ומצניעין כמוהו א"ר יוסי ב"ר חנינא דלא כר' שמעון דאי ר' שמעון האמר דברים הללו לא נאמרו אלא למצניעיהן. והכין סבירא ליה לר' שמעון לענין המוציא יין כדי מזיגת הכוס חלב כדי גמיעה כו' דכולן שיעורן ברביעית ושיעורין הללו כדי גמיעה וכדי ליתן על הכתית כו'. לא נאמרו אלא למצניעיהן כלומר אם הצניע בחול [פחות] משיעורין הללו אע"פ שהוציאו בשבת פטור ורבנן סבירא להו אם הצניעו אדם בחול כל שהוא אע"פ שאין כשר להצניע והוציאו בשבת חייב דהא (אשביח) [אחשביה] בהצנעתו. וזה ששנינו כל שאין כשר להצניע ואין מצניעין כמוהו והוציאו בשבת אין חייב אלא המצניעו אבל מי לא שהצניע בחול אם הוציאו בשיעורין הללו

חייב. ואם לא פטור. וזהו כמו דתנן המצניע לזרע לדוגמא ולרפואה והוציאו בשבת חייב עליו כל שהוא. ושאר כל אדם אין חייבין עליו אלא כשיעורו נמצא ר' שמעון מיקל מדברי חכמים ור' שמעון בן אלעזר מחמיר מדבריהם. דקאמר כל שאינו כשר להצניע ואין מצניעין כמוהו והוכשר לזה והצניעו ובא אחד והוציאו נתחייב המוציאו ממחשבת המצניעו ואע"פ שאינו כשר להצניעו ואין מצניעין כמוהו חייב עליו. ורבנן אמרי אינו חייב בפחות מכשיעור אלא המצניעו. תמו

הכללות. ובאנו לפרש שיעורי ההוצאה: **המוציא** תבן כמלוא פי פרה. עצה תבן הקטנית וקשה ממנו שיעורו כמלוא פי גמל. עמיר כמלוא פי טלה. עשבים כמלוא פי גדי ולענין המוציא תבן כמלוא פי פרה לגמל (הלכה) כר"ע לא פליגי דחייב שזה הוא שיעור הוצאתו ולא אכפת לן [אין] לגמל נתכוין להוציאו או לפרה אלא כי פליגי ר' יוחנן ור' אושעי' במוציא עצה כמלוא פי פרה לפרה. ועיקר הדבר שאין העצה מאכל פרה ואין שיעור כמלוא פי פרה אלא כמלוא פי גמל שהוא יתר ממלוא פי פרה. ועכשיו שנתכוון לפרה איפליגו ר' אושעי' סבר אכילה אע"פ שאין פרה אוכלת אותו כדרכה אלא כיון שאוכלת אותו ע"י הדחק וישנו מלא פיה והוציאו לה חייב עליו. (ור') [ור"י] סבר אכילה שע"י הדחק לאו שמה אכילה (וזה) ופטור: לענין הא דתנן אין מצטרפין זה עם זה מפני שלא שוו בשיעוריהן א"ר יוסי ב"ר חנינא אין מצטרפין לחמור שבהן אבל מצטרפין לקל שבהן אם הוציא עמיר ועשבים אם יש בין שניהם כמלוא פי טלה מצטרפין כי החמור משלים לקל וחייב אבל אם אין בהם כמלוא פי טלה. אע"פ שיש בהן כמלוא פי הגדי פטור שאין מצטרפין כי אין הקל משלים לחמור וכן עשבים משלימין לתבן ואין התבן משלים לעשבים ומקשינן היאך תאמר בהני דלא שוו בשיעוריהן להדדי דמצטרפין והלא הבגד והשק והעור לענין טומאה שלא שוו בשיעוריהן אע"ג דתנן הבגד והשק מצטרפין והשק והעור מצטרפין והעור והמפץ מצטרפין דקתני סיפא. א"ר שמעון מה טעם הואיל וראויין ליטמא מושב דייקת מיניה טעמא דראויין ליטמא מושב הא אי לא הוו ראויין ליטמא מושב לא הוו מצטרפין משום שלא שוו בשיעוריהן להדדי. וא"כ היכי קאמר ר' יוסי בר' חנינא מצטרפין לקל שבהן והכין הוה ראוי שלא יצטרפו כל עיקר. ופריק רבא לר' יוסי ב"ר חנינא ואמר הכי נמי ראויין לדוגמא כשם שהבגד והשק אף על פי שאין בזה כשיעור ולא בזה כשיעור כיון שאלו מתחברין יש בעיניהם כשיעור השק שהוא הקל ואפשר לחברן זה בזה ולישב עליהן וראויין ליטמא מושב. כן התבן והעצה אפשר להוציא מזה כמעט ומזה כמעט להראותן דוגמא לקונה לומר מאלו אני מוכר ולהכין חשובין בחיבורין ויש צורך להוציאו כסדר הזה משום כן מצטרפין לקל שבהן אבל אוכלין שיעורן כולן כגרוגרת לפיכך מצטרפין זע"ז אבל קליפיהן ועוקציהן וסובן ומורסנן אין מצטרפין עמהן.

ר'

חשק שלמה על רבינו חננאל א) עי' ערוך ערך שבט א' וע' דוך:

מסורת הש"ס

א) לקמן לא. זבחים מז, ב) [בכסף משנה העתיק רבי אושעיא אמר חייב וכו' ופסק הרמב"ם כרבי אושעיא שהלכ' כמותו לגבי ר' יוחנן עכ"ל], ג) ב"ק יט: ועע"ש קי, ד) לקמן עט. סוכה יח: כלים פכ"ז מ"ב, ה) מעילה יח., ו) ל"ל אחד, ז) כלים כ"ג פ"ב.

הגהות הב"ח

(א) רש"י ד"ה הואיל וכו' דתניא. נ"ב במעילה פ' קדשי המזבח דף יח:

גליון הש"ס

גמ' ואיפכא איתמר. כעין זה נדה דף לג ע"ב: שם ר"ל אמר חייב. בכסף משנה פי"ח הלכה ג מהלכות שבת הגירסא ר' אושעיא: תוס' ד"ה ואמר ר"ש וכו' דמפץ לא מטמא במת. עי' פכ"ד מ"י דכלים ובר"ש שם:

ליקוטי רש"י

שאינו כשר להצניע. במסכת שבת כגון דם נדה או איסור (או) הנאה. ואין מצניעין כמוהו. שכשר הוא להצניעו אם היה [בו שיעור] אבל שיעורו של זה מועט הוא ואין אדם חושבו להצניעו. ובא אחר והוציאו. בשבת לרה"ר חייב דחשיב מלאכה מפני מחשבתו של זה שהוכשר לו והצניעו [זבחים מז.]. הבגד ג' על ג'. טפחים אם ייחדו למשכב הזב מטמא ליעשות אב הטומאה במשכב הזב או במדרסו [סוכה יז:]. והשק. שיעורו ד' טפחים על ד' טפחים [מעילה יח.]. מפץ. של קנים [לקמן פד.]. ותני עלה הבגד. שהוא מטמא בג' אצבעות על ג' אצבעות [מעילה שם]. הבגד והשק. הואיל וממינן קרוב להיות שוה. מצטרפין. להשלים את הקל שאם אין בשק ארבעה הבגד שהוא חמור משלימו אבל השק אינו משלים הבגד החמור [סוכה שם]. הבגד מצטרף לשק שקל הימנו [מצטרף] לארבעה על ארבעה וכן כל אחד ואחד מצטרף לקל הימנו דשק מצטרף לעור לחמשה על חמשה והעור למפץ לששה על ששה דהיינו לקל הימנו אבל לא הקל עם החמור דלהכי מנא להו הכי הבגד והשק השק והעור כו' כולן מצטרפין זה עם זה [מעילה שם]. שק. מנוצה של עזים עשוי והוא עב יותר מן הבגד ואינו מגיע לעוביו של עור. השק והעור. וכן השק והעור מצטרפין להשלים שק את שיעור העור. מפני שראוין ליטמא מושב. הואיל וראוין בשיעור אחד לטמא מושב הזב כדתנן המקלע מכולן מאחד מכל אלו קילע טפח על טפח מקלע שמשויהו סביב סביב באומל ומתקנו יפה אפילו אין בו אלא טפח על טפח טמא כדמפרש הואיל וראוי ליטלו לעשותו טלאי על גבי מרדעת החמור כנגד בית מושב האדם וכיון דשוו שיעורייהו באחד מטומאות הזב ליעשות אב הטומאה מצטרפין אף למדרס ויש מפרשים המקלע מכולן יחד שחיבר קילועיהן שקילץ כל המינין ועשה מהן טפח על טפח ותפרן יחד והראשון נראה לי [סוכה שם ועי' בתוס' כאן]. מפני שכשיש בין כולן שיעור אחד (בין שניהם) ראוין ליטמא מושב (עליו) הלכך מצטרפין [מעילה שם].

a camel, he is exempt from punishment.

The Gemara argues that R' Yochanan's original opinion is correct:

אָמַר לֵיהּ אַבַּיֵי – Abaye said to [Rav Yosef]: אַדְּרַבָּה – On the contrary! כְּדְמֵעִיקָּרָא מִסְתַּבְּרָא – As R' Yochanan said **at the outset makes sense, דְּהָא חֲזֵי לְפָרָה – for [the measure]** of straw the transporter took out **is fit for a cow.**[16] Accordingly, he should be liable for taking it out.

The Gemara concedes Abaye's point and reports a different version of the dispute:

אֶלָּא כִּי אֲתָא רָבִין אָמַר – Rather, when Ravin came to Babylonia **he said: הַמּוֹצִיא תֶּבֶן כִּמְלֹא פִּי פָרָה לְגָמָל –** Regarding **one who carries out straw as much as a cow's mouthful for a camel, דְּכוּלֵּי עָלְמָא לֹא פְּלִיגֵי דְּחַיָּיב – no one disagrees that he is liable.**[17] **כִּי פְּלִיגֵי – Where they do disagree בְּמוֹצִיא עֵצָה כִּמְלֹא פִּי פָרָה לְפָרָה – is in [the case of] one who carries out bean straw as much as a cow's mouthful for a cow.**[18] **וְאִיפְּכָא אִיתְּמַר – And [the dispute] was stated in reverse:**[19] **רַבִּי יוֹחָנָן אָמַר פָּטוּר –** R' Yochanan **said that [the transporter] is exempt, רֵישׁ לָקִישׁ אָמַר חַיָּיב –** while **Reish Lakish said** that **he is liable.**

Ravin explains the two views:

רַבִּי יוֹחָנָן אָמַר פָּטוּר – R' Yochanan said that **[the transporter] is exempt אֲכִילָה עַל יְדֵי הַדְּחָק לֹא שְׁמָהּ אֲכִילָה –** because **eating out of necessity is not considered eating.**[20] **רֵישׁ לָקִישׁ אָמַר חַיָּיב – Reish Lakish,** on the other hand, **said** that **he is liable, אֲכִילָה עַל יְדֵי הַדְּחָק שְׁמָהּ אֲכִילָה –** because **eating out of necessity is considered eating.**[21]

The Mishnah stated:

עָמִיר כִּמְלֹא פִּי טָלֶה – One who carries out **STRAW** is liable if he carries out **AS MUCH AS A LAMB'S MOUTHFUL.**

The Gemara asks:

וְהָתַנְיָא – But it was taught otherwise **in a Baraisa: כִּגְרוֹגֶרֶת – AS** much as **A DRIED FIG. –?–**

The Gemara answers:

אִידִי וְאִידִי חַד שִׁיעוּרָא הוּא – This and that are one amount. A lamb's mouthful is the equivalent of a dried fig.[22]

The Mishnah stated:

עֲלֵי שׁוּם וַעֲלֵי בְצָלִים – LEAVES OF GARLIC AND LEAVES OF ONION – לַחִים כִּגְרוֹגֶרֶת – if they are **FRESH, THE EQUIVALENT OF A DRIED FIG, וִיבֵשִׁים כִּמְלֹא פִּי הַגְּדִי – AND** if they are **DRY, AS MUCH AS A KID'S MOUTHFUL.** The Mishnah then concluded: **וְאֵין מִצְטָרְפִין זֶה עִם זֶה מִפְּנֵי שֶׁלֹּא שָׁווּ בְשִׁיעוּרֵיהֶן – AND THEY** [i.e. any of the above-mentioned species] **CANNOT BE COMBINED WITH ONE ANOTHER, BECAUSE THEY ARE NOT ALIKE IN THEIR PRESCRIBED MEASURES.**

The Gemara qualifies the last statement:

אָמַר רַבִּי יוֹסֵי בַּר חֲנִינָא – R' Yose bar Chanina said: אֵין מִצְטָרְפִין לְחָמוּר שֶׁבָּהֶן – They cannot be combined for the more **stringent of them, אֲבָל מִצְטָרְפִין לְקַל שֶׁבָּהֶן – but they can be combined for the** more **lenient of them.**[23]

The Gemara challenges R' Yose's dictum:

וְכָל דְּלָא שָׁווּ בְּשִׁיעוּרַיְיהוּ מִי מִצְטָרְפִין – But can any [things] that are not alike in their prescribed measures ever **be combined** to equal a particular minimum amount?[24] **וְהָתְנַן – But we learned in a Mishnah:**[25] **הַבֶּגֶד שְׁלֹשָׁה עַל שְׁלֹשָׁה – THE** minimum size of **CLOTH** that contracts *tumah* is **THREE** *tefachim* **BY THREE** *tefachim*;[26] **וְהַשַּׂק אַרְבָּעָה עַל אַרְבָּעָה – THE** minimum size of **SACK**[27] is **FOUR BY FOUR** *tefachim;*[28] **וְהָעוֹר חֲמִשָּׁה עַל חֲמִשָּׁה – A HIDE, FIVE BY FIVE** *tefachim*; **מַפָּץ שִׁשָּׁה עַל שִׁשָּׁה – A MAT,**[29] **SIX BY SIX** *tefachim.* **וְתָנֵי עֲלָהּ – And [a Baraisa] taught concerning [the Mishnah]: הַבֶּגֶד וְהַשַּׂק – THE CLOTH AND THE SACK, הַשַּׂק וְהָעוֹר – THE SACK AND THE HIDE, הָעוֹר וְהַמַּפָּץ – THE HIDE AND THE MAT מִצְטָרְפִין זֶה עִם זֶה – COMBINE WITH ONE ANOTHER** to complete the minimum amount with regard to ritual contamination.[30] **וְאָמַר רַבִּי שִׁמְעוֹן – And R' Shimon said** in explanation there: **מַה טַּעַם – WHAT IS THE REASON** that those types of

NOTES

16. Hence, that amount of crushed straw is considered "significant" even if the transporter plans to use it for a purpose other than feeding a cow (*Rashi*). [See *Pnei Yehoshua* for a possible explanation of Rav Yosef's reasoning.]

17. Since he took out an amount fit for a cow, this case fits into the category of something that is typically stored and in a quantity usually stored (*Rashi*).

18. Bean straw [the *etzah* of our Mishnah] is not suitable for cows, but is the normal fare of camels. This person, though, took it out to feed a cow (*Rashi*). [We will soon see that bean straw can be fed to cows when circumstances require it.]

19. While in Rav Dimi's version R' Yochanan held the stringent view, according to Ravin it was Reish Lakish who imposed liability.

20. While a camel normally eats bean straw, here the person did not take out a sufficient amount to feed a camel. And while he did take out the bean straw for purposes of feeding a cow and in a sufficient amount to do so, a cow does not usually eat bean straw; the fact that it can be fed to cows in cases of necessity does not matter. Hence, the person cannot be held liable for his act (*Rashi*).

21. Therefore, since he took out enough bean straw to satisfy a cow, he is liable.

22. However, the Mishnah stated the measure in terms of a lamb's mouthful so as to reveal the reason for this minimum amount (*Tosafos;* cf. *Ritva MHK* ed.).

23. That is, a feed whose minimum amount is large is considered "lenient," and is not considered significant enough to be combined with a "stringent" feed (i.e. one whose minimum amount is smaller) to create liability. For example, bean straw [of which one must take out a camel's mouthful to be liable] cannot be included to complete the minimum requirement for crushed grain straw [i.e. a cow's mouthful]. On the other hand, a more significant, "stringent," feed (which has a smaller minimum) does combine with "lenient" feed to complete that feed's greater minimum. Therefore, grain straw [for which one is liable for taking out a cow's mouthful] can be included to complete the minimum requirement for bean straw [i.e. a camel's mouthful] (*Rashi*).

24. I.e. even when the "stringent" item completes the larger amount of the "lenient" item (*Rashi*).

25. *Keilim* 27:2.

26. [If a *zav, zavah, niddah* or a woman who has given birth sit on a bed, saddle or chair, these items become *avos hatumah* – that is, they become primary sources of *tumah,* capable of conveying *tumah* even to people or utensils (see *Leviticus* 15:4-6; *Keilim* 1:3). Items that fall into this category include any object that any of the aforementioned *tamei* people either leaned or sat upon – so long as it was the type of item generally used for such purposes. The general term for this form of susceptibility to *tumah* is *midras* (literally: "treading upon" or "weighing upon").

Thus, if a *zav* sits on a piece of cloth measuring three *tefachim* (handbreadths) squared, it becomes an *av hatumah* (*Rashi*). A smaller piece of cloth does not become *tamei* through *midras* because it is not fit for sitting upon. [However, the Mishnah in *Keilim* next states that cloth less than this size can become *tamei* through other means, such as through direct contact with a *zav,* so long as it measures three fingerbreadths squared. In that case, though, the cloth would contract a lower level of *tumah* contamination (see above, 26b).]

27. A sack is made of goats' hair, and is thicker than cloth but not as thick as a hide (*Rashi* here and to *Succah* 17b).

28. This measure and the ones that follow apply to any type of *tumah* contamination. Generally, materials smaller than the stated size do not become *tamei* at all (see Mishnah there; *Tosafos*).

29. Made of reeds (see *Rashi* below, 84a ד״ה מפץ).

30. The cloth can complete the minimum amount for a sack, etc. (*Rashi*).

א"ר אלעזר הא דלא כר"ש בן אלעזר [א] דתניא כלל אמר ר' שמעון בן אלעזר כל שאינו כשר להצניע ואין מצניעין כמוהו והוכשר לזה והצניעו ובא אחר והוציאו נתחייב זה במחשבה של זה: **מתני'** [א]המוציא תבן כמלא פי פרה עצה כמלא פי גמל עמיר כמלא פי טלה עשבים כמלא פי גדי עלי שום ועלי בצלים לחים כגרוגרת יבשים כמלא פי גדי ואין מצטרפין זה עם זה מפני שלא שוו בשיעוריהן: **גמ'** מאי עצה אמר רב יהודה תבן של מיני קטנית כי אתא רב דימי אמר המוציא תבן כמלא פי פרה לגמל ר' יוחנן אמר חייב ר"ש בן לקיש אמר פטור באורתא א"ר יוחנן הכי לצפרא הדר ביה אמר רב יוסף שפיר עבד דהדר דהא לא חזי לגמל א"ל אביי אדרבה כדמעיקרא מסתברא דהא חזי לפרה אלא כי אתא רבין אמר המוציא תבן כמלא פי פרה לגמל דכולי עלמא לא פליגי דחייב כי פליגי במוציא עצה כמלא פי פרה לפרה • ואיפכא איתמר ר' יוחנן אמר פטור • ריש לקיש אמר חייב ר' יוחנן אמר פטור אכילה על ידי הדחק לא שמה אכילה [ג] ריש לקיש אמר [ב]חייב אכילה [ג]ע"י הדחק שמה אכילה: עמיר כמלא פי טלה: והתניא כגרוגרת אידי ואידי חד שיעורא הוא: עלי שום ועלי בצלים לחים כגרוגרת ויבשים כמלא פי הגדי ואין מצטרפין זה עם זה מפני שלא שוו בשיעוריהן: אמר ר' יוסי בר חנינא [ב] אין מצטרפין לחמור שבהן אבל מצטרפין לקל שבהן וכל דלא שוו בשיעורייהו מי מצטרפין והתנן [ד] הבגד ג' על ג' והשק ד' על ד' והעור ה' על ה' מפץ ו' על ו' [ה] ותני עלה הבגד והשק השק והעור העור והמפץ מצטרפין זה עם זה ואמר ר"ש מה טעם מפני שראויין ליטמא מושב טעמא דראויין ליטמא מושב אבל אין ראוי ליטמא מושב לא אמר רבא

הכא

רש"י

א"ר אלעזר הא. דקתני מתניתין דאינו כשר להצניע והצניעו [ו] אחר הוא מתחייב על הוצאתו וכל אדם פטורין דלא כר' שמעון בן אלעזר: **מתני' עצה.** מפרש בגמרא: **כמלא פי גמל.** נפיש שיעורא מפי פרה אבל כמלא פי פרה לא מיחייב דהא לא חזו לפרה: **עמיר.** קשין של שבלין: **פי טלה.** נפיש מפי גדי הלכך עמיר דלא חזי לגדי לא מיחייב כמלא פי גדי עד דאיכא מלא פי טלה אבל עשבים הואיל וחזו בין לטלה בין לגדי מיחייב אפי' כמלא פי גדי: **לחין.** הראוין לאדם כגרוגרת דזה שיעור לכל מאכל אדם לשבת אבל כמלא פי גדי לא דלאדם לא חזו לגדי: **גמ' המוציא תבן כמלא פי פרה.** והוציאו להאכילו לגמל שפי גמל גדול מפי פרה: **דהא חזי לפי פרה.** הלכך שיעור חשוב הוא ולכל מי שיוציאנו לא פקע שיעוריה בהכי: **דחייב.** דהאיכא שיעורא דחזי לפרה הלכך כשר להצניע הוא ומצניעין כמוהו: **עצה.** לא חזיא לפרה אלא ע"י הדחק אלא לגמל הוא דחזי וזה הוציאו לפרה: **רבי יוחנן אמר פטור.** דהא לגמל דחזי ליה ליכא שיעורא ואי משום דלצורך פרה הוציאו ולגבה איכא שיעור אכילה ע"י הדחק לאו אכילה היא הלכך לא משערי' ליה בפרה: **אין מצטרפין לחמור שבהם.** מי ששיעורו גדול הוי קל ואינו מצטרף להשלים שיעורו של חמור דהא לא חשיב כי ההוא אבל החשוב משלים את הקל לכשיעור תבן מצטרף עם עצה להשלי' פי גמל ועצה אין מצטרף עם התבן להשלים מלא פי פרה: **מי מצטרפין.** אפילו להשלים חמור את הקל: **ג' על ג'.** לטומאת מדרס הזב ליעשות אב הטומאה: **הבגד והשק מצטרפין.** שהבגד משלים שיעור השק. שק עשוי מנוצה של עזים: **ואמר ר' שמעון מה טעם.** מצטרפין: **הואיל וראויין ליטמא מושב.** אם לירף משניהם יחד לטלאי מרדעת של חמור כשיעורו לענין מושב הזב אם קלע משניהם מהן ותקן טפח על טפח לישב עליו מיטמא ליה אב הטומאה במושב הזב דתניא (א) המקלע מכולן טפח על טפח טמא מושב ואמרינן טעמא בפ"ק דסוכה הואיל וראוי לטלות על גבי חמור שאינו מקפיד אם הוא משני מינין:

הכא

תוספות

שמצריך לקמן הצנעה היינו לאדם עשיר שאין דרכו להצניע ומכל מקום פירוש מילתיה דר"ש צריך לפרש כמו שפירש כאן דאי מיירי במצניעין לאותו דבר עצמו שמפורש במשנה כמו שפירש התם אם כן כולהו הוה מצי למימר בכל שהוא בכדי שיפת קילור כדתנן בפ' המצניע (לקמן צ:) דלרפואה בכל שהוא ואתיא כר"ש מדלא קאמר התם בגמ' הא דלא כר"ש כי היכי דקאמר (דף צא.) הא דלא כר"ש בן אלעזר ומהתם נמי יש לדקדק דלר' שמעון סתם בני אדם שרגילין להצניעו מיחייבי אפי' לא הצניעו מדקתני המצניע לזרע כו' וכל אדם אין חייבין עליו אלא כשיעורו משמע בלא הצנעה וכר"ש נמי אתיא כדפי' ואין לפרש דבעשיר שאין דרכו להצניע לא מיחייב לר"ש אפי' בהצניעו דהא אמר בהמוציא יין בד"א במוציא אבל במצניע כל שהוא ר"ש אומר בד"א במצניע כו' ומפרש מצניע דרבנן בתלמיד שאמר לו כו' דבר שאינו חשוב לכל אי אצנעיה רביה אין אי לא לא ודומיא דהכי נראה דהוי מצניע דר"ש דתליא מילתא באותו שהצניעו היינו בעשיר קשה לרשב"א דמהאי טעמא דקאמר הכא מתני' דלא כר"ש משום דמתני' סתמא קתני דחייב משמע שכל בני אדם חייבין עליו אפי' אותן שאין חשוב להן שיעור זה מהאי טעמא נמי הוה ליה למימר בההיא דפרק המצניע דהויא דלא כר"ש ושמא י"ל דהכא דנקט לפרושי הוה ליה לפרושי טפי: **אכילה** ע"י הדחק לא שמה אכילה. והא דאמר בפ' כילד הרגל (ב"ק דף יט.) אכילה ע"י הדחק שמה אכילה ה"מ לענין ניזקין דלא חשבינן ליה משונה אבל לאחשובה לענין שבת לא חשיבא אכילה: **אידי** ואידי חד שיעורא הוא. והא דנקט במתני' כמלא פי טלה ולא נקט כגרוגרת לאשמעי' דמשום אכילת טלה נתנו בו חכמים שיעור זה דאי נקט כגרוגרת לא הוה ידעינן למה נתנו בו חכמים שיעור זה: **מפני** שלא שוו בשיעורידם. אבל אותם ששוו כגון עמיר ועלי שום ועלי בצלים לחים מצטרפין וכן חמור לקל כגון תבן לעצה למלא פי גמל ואפי' לא יהא תבן ראוי לגמל שמא אגב העצה הוא ראוי: **הבגד** והשק השק והעור כו'. דוקא בכה"ג הבגד והשק השק והעור והעור והמפץ אבל הבגד והעור והשק והמפץ אין מצטרפין שאין ראוין להתחבר יחד והמחברן בטלה דעתו ואין טמאים מדרס. ר"י: **ואמר** ר"ש מה טעם כו'. תימה לר"י דמה צריך להאי טעמא דהא כיון דמצטרפין זה עם זה א"כ ראוי לחברן וחזו למדרס וכיון דחזו למדרס פשיטא דמצטרפין לטומאת מדרס דהא אפי' כופת שאור שיחדה לישיבה טמאה מדרס כדאמרינן בהעור והרוטב (חולין קכט.) והכא בטומאת מדרס איירי מדקאמר הבגד שלשה על שלשה דלענין טומאת מת אפי' ג' על ג' כדפרישית לעיל ואור"י דודאי הא דקתני הבגד שלשה על שלשה לא מיירי אלא למדרס אבל סיפא דשק ועור ומפץ מיירי נמי בטומאת מת והכי איתא במס' כלים בפכ"ז הבגד שלשה על שלשה [למדרס ומשום ג' על ג'] לטומאת מת השק ד' על ד' העור ה' על ה' המפץ ו' על ו' שוו בין למדרס בין לטמא מת אלא שהש"ס מביאה בקוצר כמו שרגיל בכמה מקומות ועל טומאת מת קאמר מה טעם מצטרפין בשלא יחדו למדרס ולא צריך האי טעמא אצירוף דעור ומפץ • דמפץ לא מטמא במת אלא כשטמא בזב דהיינו כשיחדו למדרס ומק"ו דפכין קטנים כדאמרינן בפ' ר' עקיבא (לקמן פד:): **הואיל** וראויין ליטמא מושב. פי' בקונטרס אם קילע משניהם וצירף יחד לטלאי מרדעת החמור והיא דהמקלע מכולם טפח על טפח למעלה היינו שבין כולם יש טפח ואין נראה לר"י דמה צריך להביא ראיה שראוין להצטרף בלאו טעמא דמושב נמי שמעינן ממתני' דהכא שראוין להצטרף יחד באותו סדר כמו ששנויים בגד לשק ושק לעור ועור למפץ דדוקא נקט לפי שאלו ראוין להצטרף יחד ונראה לר"י כמו שפי' ריב"א דהואיל וראוין ליטמא מושב היינו הואיל ושוו שיעוריהן לענין מושב וכמו שפירש בקונטרס בפ"ק דסוכה (דף יח:) דהמקלע מכולן היינו מאיזה מהן שיקלע יהא טמא ואע"ג שכאן אין שיעורן שוה מצטרפין הואיל ולענין מושב שיעורן שוה והא דקאמר ה"נ חזו לדוגמא היינו נמי דשיעורן שוה לדוגמא כדתנן בפרק המצניע לדוגמא כל שהוא הלכך מצטרפין אפי' לענין דבר דלא שוו שיעורייהו וה"ה דהוי מצי למינקט הכא ולזרע ולרפואה דהוו נמי בכל שהוא אלא דלא כל דברים שייך בהו זרע ורפואה אבל דוגמא שייכא בכל דבר והא דקאמר בסוכה המקלע מכולן כו' הואיל וראוי לטלות על גבי חמורו לשון הואיל וראוי לאו דווקא דדווקא אם עשה מהן טלאי ויחדן לכך טמא בטפח על טפח וכן מצינו לקמן בפ' א"ר עקיבא (דף צ.) הואיל וראוין למתק הקדרה דהוה ליה למימר הואיל וממתקין דהא מיירי שנפלו לתוך הקדרה. ר"י: **תוספתא** [ז] המקלע למשכב אין פחות משלשה על שלשה למושב טפח ולמעמד כל שהוא:

חמשת

עין משפט נר מצוה

עב א ב מיי' פי"ח מהל' שבת הל' ג:
[עב] [ב] [מיי' שם]:

רבינו חננאל

ומנקה הבגד ודומה למנקב דתנינן בכמה מקומות ואם נשארו כגון אלו בבגד ובעל הבגד קפיד עלייהו ושקיל להו בשבת חייב משום מכה בפטיש. פי' כל דבר שהוא גמר מלאכה נקרא מכה בפטיש: **המוחק** אות אחת גדולה שיש במקומה שיעור לכתוב ב' אותיות חייב והכותב אות אחת גדולה שיש במקומה שיעור לכתוב ב' אותיות פטור. זה חומר במוחק מבכותב. אלו אבות מלאכות לאפוקי מדר' אליעזר דמחייב אתולדה במקום אב כמו שכבר פרשנוהו למעלה (דף עג:) דמאן דעבד ב' אבות או ב' תולדות משני אבות או אב ותולדה דאב (אחד) [אחר] בהעלם אחד חייב בזה אחד ובזה אחד. ואי עביד אב ותולדתו לא מיחייב אלא חדא. ועוד חזר ושנה מ' חסר אחת לאפוקי מר' יהודה דאמר שובט ומדקדק מאבות מלאכות הן. אמרו לו שובט הרי הוא בכלל מיסך. מדקדק בכלל אורג. א) פי' יש לארוגין עץ או עצם שראשו חד ונקרא כדבר ודומה למחט של סקאין. וכך שמו בלשון יון כדבר. מעבירו על השתי כשהוא מותח לפניו לאריגה ושובט בו החוטין ומקרב המבדילין בין ב' החוטין העליונים והתחתונים ומדנחים העליונים מן התחתונים להתפרק ונפתח נפש המסכת לידות בתוכם חוט הערב ואין לה אב אלא הרי הוא בכלל מיסך והמדקדק הוא המדקדק על חוט הערב כדי להדחק ולהלחץ עם חבירו והוי בכלל אריגה: **ועוד** כלל אחר אמרו כל הכשר להצניע ומצניעין כמוהו והוציאו בשבת חייב עליו חטאת. כל הכשר להצניע רב מתנה אמר למעוטי דם נדה שאין חייבין בהוצאתו. וכ"ש איסורי הנאה. ועצי אשרה שאין חייבין בהוצאתו. מר עוקבא אמר לאפוקי עצי אשרה אבל דם נדה חייב כו' וזה ששנינו ומצניעין כמוהו א"ר יוסי ב"ר חנינא דלא כר' שמעון דאי ר' שמעון האמר דברים הללו לא נאמרו אלא למצניעיהן. והכין סבירא ליה לר' שמעון לענין המוציא יין כדי מזיגת הכוס חלב כדי גמיעה כו' דכולן שיעורן ברביעית ושיעורין הללו כדי גמיעה וכדי ליתן על הכתית כו'. לא נאמרו אלא למצניעיהן כלומר אם הצניע בחול [פחות] משיעורין הללו אע"פ שהוציאו בשבת פטור ורבנן סבירא להו אם הצניעו אדם בחול כל שהוא אע"פ שאין כשר להצניע והוציאו בשבת חייב דהא (אשביח) [אחשביה] בהצנעתו. וזה ששנינו כל שאין כשר להצניע ואין מצניעין כמוהו והוציאו בשבת אין חייב אלא המצניעו אבל מי לא שהצניע בחול אם הוציאו בשיעורין הללו חייב. ואם לא פטור. וזהו כמו דתנן המצניע לזרע לדוגמא ולרפואה והוציאו בשבת חייב עליו כל שהוא. ושאר כל אדם אין חייבין עליו אלא כשיעורו נמצא ר' שמעון מיקל מדברי חכמים ור' שמעון בן אלעזר מחמיר מדבריהם. דקאמר כל שאינו כשר להצניע ואין מצניעין כמוהו והוכשר לזה והצניעו ובא אחר והוציאו נתחייב הוציאו ממחשבת המצניעו ואע"פ שאינו כשר להצניעו ואין מצניעין כמוהו חייב עליו. ורבנן אמרי אינו חייב בפחות מכשיעור אלא המצניעו. תמו הכללות. ובאנו לפרש שיעורי ההוצאה: **המוציא** תבן כמלוא פי פרה. עצה תבן הקטנית וקשה ממנו שיעור כמלוא פי גמל. עמיר כמלוא פי טלה. עשבים כמלוא פי גדי ולענין המוציא תבן כמלוא פי פרה לגמל (הלכה) כו"ע לא פליגי דחייב שזה הוא שיעור הוצאתו ולא אכפת לן [אין לגמל נתכוון להוציאו או לפרה אלא כי פליגי ר' יוחנן ור' אושעי' במוציא עצה כמלוא פי פרה. ועיקר הדבר שאין העצה מאכל פרה ואין שיעור כמלוא פי פרה אלא כמלוא פי גמל שהוא יותר ממלוא פי פרה. ועכשיו שנתכוון לפרה איפליגו ר' אושעי' סבר אכילה ע"י הדחק שמה אכילה אע"פ שאין פרה אוכלת אותו כדרכה אלא כיון שאוכלת אותו ע"י הדחק וישנו מלא פיה והוציאו לה חייב עליו. (ור"י) [ור"י] סבר אכילה שע"י הדחק לאו שמה אכילה (וזה) ופטור: לענין הא דתנן אין מצטרפין זה עם זה מפני שלא שוו בשיעוריהן א"ר יוסי ב"ר חנינא אין מצטרפין לחמור שבהן אבל מצטרפין לקל שבהן אם הוציא עמיר ועשבים אם יש בין שניהם כמלוא פי טלה מצטרפין כי החמור משלים לקל וחייב אבל אם אין בהם כמלוא פי טלה. אע"פ שיש בהן כמלוא פי הגדי פטור שאין מצטרפין כי אין הקל משלים לחמור וכן עשבים משלימין לתבן ואין התבן משלים לעשבים ומקשינן היאך תאמר בהני דלא שוו בשיעוריהן להדדי דמצטרפין והלא הבגד והשק והעור לענין טומאה שלא שוו בשיעוריהן אע"ג דתנן הבגד והשק מצטרפין השק והעור והעור והמפץ מצטרפין דקתני סיפא. א"ר שמעון מה טעם הואיל וראוין ליטמא מושב דייקת מיניה טעמא דראוין ליטמא מושב הא אי לא הוו ראוין ליטמא מושב לא הוו מצטרפין להדדי. וא"כ היכי קאמר ר' יוסי בר' חנינא מצטרפין לקל שבהן והכין הוה ראוי שלא יצטרפו כל עיקר. ופריק רבא לר' יוסי ב"ר חנינא ואמר הכי נמי ראוין לדוגמא כשם שהבגד והשק אף על פי שאין בזה כשיעור ולא בזה כשיעור כיון שאלו מתחברין יש בעיניהם כשיעור השק שהוא הקל ואפשר לחברן זה בזה ולישב עליהן וראוין ליטמא מושב. כן התבן והעצה אפשר להוציא מזה כמעט ומזה כמעט להראותן דוגמא לקונה לומר מאלו אני מוכר ולהכין כן מצטרפין לקל שבהן אבל אוכלין שיעורן כולן כגרוגרת לפיכך מצטרפין דע"ז אבל קליפיהן ועוקציהן וסובן ומורסנן אין מצטרפין עמהן.

ר'

חשק שלמה על רבינו חננאל א) עי' ערוך ערך שבט א' וע' דוך:

מסורת הש"ס

א) לקמן צא. זבחים מז., ב) [הכסף משנה העמיק רבי אושעיא אמר חייב וכו' ופסק הרמב"ם כרבי אושעיא שהלכ' כמותו לגבי ר' יוחנן עכ"ל], ג) ב"ק יט: ועע"ש קי., ד) לקמן עט. סוכה יח: כלים פכ"ז מ"ב, ה) מעילה יח., ו) צ"ל אחר, ז) כלים כ"ב פ"ב.

הגהות הב"ח

(א) רש"י ד"ה הואיל וכו' דתניא. נ"ב במעילה ס"פ קדשי המזבח דף יח:

גליון הש"ס

גמ' ואיפכא איתמר. כעין זה נדה דף לד ע"א: שם ר"ל אמר חייב. בכסף משנה פי"ח הלכה ג מהלכות שבת הגירסא ר' אושעיא: תוס' ד"ה ואמר ר"ש וכו' דמפץ לא מטמא במת. עי' פכ"ד מ"י דכלים ובר"ש שם:

ליקוטי רש"י

שאינו כשר להצניע. במסכת שבת כגון דם נדה או איסור (או) הנאה. **ואין מצניעין כמוהו.** שכשר הוא להצניעו אם היה [בו שיעור] אבל שיעורו של זה מועט הוא ואין אדם חושבו להצניעו. **ובא אחר והוציאו.** בשבת לרה"ר חייב דמשיב מלאכה מפני מחשבתו של זה שהוכשר לו והצניעו [זבחים מז.]. **הבגד ג' על ג'.** טפחים אם ייחדו למשכב הזב מטמא ליעשות אב הטומאה במשכב הזב או במדרסו [סוכה יז:]. **והשק.** שיעורו ד' טפחים על ד' טפחים [מעילה יח.]. **מפץ.** של קנים [לקמן פד.]. **ותני עלה הבגד.** שהוא מטמא ג' אצבעות על ג' אצבעות [מעילה שם]. **הבגד והשק.** הואיל וממשן קרוב להיות שוה. **מצטרפין.** להשלים את הקל שאם אין בשק ארבעה הבגד שהוא חמור משלימו אבל השק אינו משלים הבגד החמור [סוכה שם]. הבגד מצטרף לשק שקל הימנו [מצטרף] לארבעה על ארבעה וכן כל אחד ואחד מצטרף לקל הימנו דשק מצטרף לעור לחמשה על חמשה והעור למפץ לששה על ששה דהיינו לקל הימנו אבל לא הקל עם החמור להכי תנא להו הכי הבגד והשק השק והעור כו' כולן מצטרפין זה עם זה [מעילה שם]. **שק.** מנוצה של עזים עשוי והוא עב יותר מן הבגד ואינו מגיע לעוביו של עור. **השק והעור.** וכן השק והעור מצטרפין להשלים שק את שיעור העור. **מפני שראוין ליטמא מושב.** הואיל וראוין בשיעור אחד לטמא מושב הזב כדתנן המקלע מכולן מאחד מכל אלו קילע טפח על טפח מקלע שמשויהו סביב סביב באזמל ומתקנו יפה אפילו אין בו אלא טפח על טפח טמא כדמפרש הואיל וראוי ליטלו לעשותו טלאי על גבי מרדעת החמור כנגד בית מושב האדם וכיון דשוו שיעורייהו בלאחד מטומאות הזב ליעשות אב הטומאה מצטרפין אף למדרס ויש מפרשים המקלע מכולן יחד שחיבר קילועיהן שקילע כל המינין ועשה מהן טפח על טפח ותפרן יחד והראשון נראה לי [סוכה שם ועי' בתוס' כאן]. מפני שכשים בין כולן שיעור אחד (בין שניהם) ראוין ליטמא מושב (עליו) הלכך מצטרפין [מעילה שם].

material can combine?[31] מִפְּנֵי שֶׁרְאוּיִין לִיטַּמֵּא מוֹשָׁב – BECAUSE THEY ARE FIT TO BECOME CONTAMINATED through SITTING.[32]

The Gemara concludes its challenge:

טַעְמָא דִּרְאוּיִין לִיטַּמֵּא מוֹשָׁב – Now, **the reason** these various materials can combine **is because they are fit to become contaminated** through **sitting;**[33] אֲבָל אֵין רָאוּי לִיטַּמֵּא מוֹשָׁב – **however, if they would not be fit to become contaminated through sitting,** לֹא – they would **not** combine. Why, then, should the different types of feed combine to create liability for carrying on the Sabbath?[34]

The Gemara answers:

אָמַר רָבָא – **Rava said:**

NOTES

31. Since these different types of material [have disparate minimum measures and] are never combined on a seat, one type should not be able to complete the minimum amount of another type (*Ritva MHK* ed. in explanation of *Rashi;* cf. *Tosafos* here and to *Succah* 17b; see also *Yad David*).

32. If one combined two materials to make a patch on a mule's saddle, the patch will become an *av hatumah* when a *zav* sits on it if together the two materials equal the minimum amount needed for such a patch – i.e. one *tefach* by one *tefach*. These materials can be combined here to complete the *tefach*-squared minimum because a person is not particular if his mule's saddle is patched with different types of material (*Rashi;* cf. *Rashi* to *Succah* ibid. and *Tosafos* here).

[Generally, a material must be of the size mentioned in the Mishnah to be susceptible to *tumah*. However, if a person tears material specifically for a saddle patch, a piece one *tefach* square is considered significant (see *Keilim* 27:4 with commentaries; *Meiri* and *Rosh Yosef* here).]

33. That is, we find a case where the two types of material are used together (*Ritva MHK* ed.; *Yad David*).

34. Since no animal would eat a mixture of feeds appropriate for different types of animals, there is apparently no use for a combination of feed. Consequently, two types of feed should not be combined to equal a minimum amount (*Yad David,* in explanation of *Rashi;* cf. *Maharam;* see also *Ritva MHK* ed.).

א"ר אלעזר הא דלא כר"ש בן אלעזר א) דתניא כלל אמר ר' שמעון בן אלעזר כל שאינו כשר להצניע ואין מצניעין כמוהו והוכשר לזה והצניעו ובא אחר והוציאו נתחייב זה במחשבה של זה: **מתני'** א המוציא תבן כמלא פי פרה עצה כמלא פי גמל עמיר כמלא פי טלה עשבים כמלא פי גדי עלי שום ועלי בצלים לחים כגרוגרת יבשים כמלא פי גדי ואין מצטרפין זה עם זה מפני שלא שוו בשיעוריהן: **גמ'** מאי עצה אמר רב יהודה תבן של מיני קטנית כי אתא רב דימי אמר המוציא תבן כמלא פי פרה לגמל ר' יוחנן אמר חייב ר"ש בן לקיש אמר פטור באורתא א"ר יוחנן הכי לצפרא הדר ביה אמר רב יוסף שפיר עבד דהדר דהא לא חזי לגמל א"ל אביי אדרבה כדמעיקרא מסתברא דהא חזי לפרה אלא כי אתא רבין אמר המוציא תבן כמלא פי פרה לגמל דכולי עלמא לא פליגי דחייב כי פליגי במוציא עצה כמלא פי פרה לפרה ° ואיפכא איתמר ר' יוחנן אמר פטור ° ריש לקיש אמר חייב ר' יוחנן אמר פטור אכילה על ידי הדחק לא שמה אכילה ב) ריש לקיש אמר ב חייב אכילה ג) ע"י הדחק שמה אכילה: עמיר כמלא פי טלה: והתניא כגרוגרת אידי ואידי חד שיעורא הוא: עלי שום ועלי בצלים לחים כגרוגרת ויבשים כמלא פי הגדי ואין מצטרפין זה עם זה מפני שלא שוו בשיעוריהן: אמר ר' יוסי בר חנינא [ב] אין מצטרפין לחמור שבהן אבל מצטרפין לקל שבהן וכל דלא שוו בשיעורייהו מי מצטרפין והתנן ד) הבגד ג' על ג' והשק ד' על ד' והעור ה' על ה' מפץ ו' על ו' ה) ותני עלה הבגד והשק השק והעור העור והמפץ מצטרפין זה עם זה ואמר ר"ש מה טעם מפני שראויין ליטמא מושב טעמא דראויין ליטמא מושב אבל אין ראוי ליטמא מושב לא אמר רבא הכא

רש"י

א"ר אלעזר הא. דקתני מתניתין דאינו כשר להצניע והצניעו ו) אחר הוא מתחייב על הוצאתו וכל אדם פטורין דלא כר' שמעון בן אלעזר: מתני' עצה. מפרש בגמרא: כמלא פי גמל. נפיש שיעורא מפי פרה אבל כמלא פי פרה לא מיחייב דהא לא חזו לפרה: עמיר. קשין של שבלין: פי טלה. נפיש מפי גדי הלכך עמיר דלא חזי לגדי לא מיחייב כמלא פי גדי עד דאיכא מלא פי טלה אבל עשבים הואיל וחזו בין לטלה בין לגדי מיחייב אפי' כמלא פי גדי: לחין. הראויין לאדם כגרוגרת דזה שיעור לכל מאכל אדם לשבת אבל כמלא פי גדי לא דלחים לא חזו לגדי: גמ' המוציא תבן כמלא פי פרה. והוציאו להאכילו לגמל שפי גמל גדול מפי פרה: דהא חזי לפי פרה. הלכך שיעור חשוב הוא ולכל מי שיוציאנו לא פקע שיעוריה בהכי: דחייב. דהאיכא שיעורא דחזי לפרה הלכך כשר להצניע הוא ומצניעין כמוהו: עצה. לא חזיא לפרה אלא ע"י הדחק אלא לגמל הוא דחזי וזה הוציאו לפרה: רבי יוחנן אמר פטור. דהא לגמל דחזי ליה ליכא שיעורא ואי משום דלצורך פרה הוציאו ולגבה איכא שיעור אכילה ע"י הדחק לאו אכילה היא הלכך לא משערי' ליה בפרה: אין מצטרפין לחמור שבהם. מי ששיעורו גדול הוי קל ואינו מצטרף להשלים שיעורו של חמור דהא לא חשיב כי ההוא אבל החשוב משלים את הקל לכשיעור תבן מצטרף עם עצה להשלי' פי גמל ועצה אין מצטרף עם התבן להשלים מלא פי פרה: מי מצטרפין. אפילו להשלים חמור את הקל: ג' על ג'. לטומאת מדרס הזב ליעשות אב הטומאה: הבגד והשק מצטרפין. שהבגד משלים שיעור השק. שק עשוי מנוצה של עזים: ואמר ר' שמעון מה טעם. מצטרפין: הואיל וראויין ליטמא מושב. אם צירף משניהם יחד לטלאי מרדעת של חמור כשיעורו לענין מושב הזב אם קלע משניהם מהן ותקן טפח על טפח לישב עליו מיטמא ליה אב הטומאה במושב הזב דתניא (א) המקלע מכולן טפח על טפח טמא מושב ואמרינן טעמא בפ"ק דסוכה הואיל וראוי לטלות על גבי חמור שאינו מקפיד אם הוא משני מינין:

הכא

תוספות

שמצריך לקמן הצנעה היינו לאדם עשיר שאין דרכו להצניע ומכל מקום פירוש מילתיה דר"ש צריך לפרש כמו שפירש כאן דאי מיירי במצניעין לאותו דבר עצמו שמפורש במשנה כמו שפירש התם אם כן כולהו הוה מצי למימר בכל שהוא בכדי שיפת קילור כדתנן בפ' המצניע (לקמן צ:) דלרפואה בכל שהוא ואתיא כר"ש מדלא קאמר התם בגמ' הא דלא כר"ש כי היכי דקאמר (דף צא.) הא דלא כר"ש בן אלעזר ומהתם נמי יש לדקדק דלר' שמעון סתם בני אדם שרגילין להצניעו מיחייבי אפי' לא הצניעו מדקתני המצניע לזרע כו' וכל אדם אין חייבין עליו אלא כשיעורו משמע בלא הצנעה וכר"ש נמי אתיא כדפי' ואין לפרש דבעשיר שאין דרכו להצניע לא מיחייב לר"ש אפי' בהצניעו דהא אמר בהמוציא יין בד"א במוציא אבל במצניע כל שהוא ר"ש אומר בד"א במצניע כו' ומפרש מצניע דרבנן בתלמיד שאמר לו כו' דבר שאינו חשוב לכל אי אצנעיה רביה אין אי לא לא ודומיא דהכי נראה דהוי מצניע דר"ש דתליא מילתא באותו שהצניעו היינו בעשיר קשה לרשב"א דמהאי טעמא דקאמר הכא מתני' דלא כר"ש משום דמתני' סתמא קתני דחייב משמע שכל בני אדם חייבין עליו אפי' אותן שאין חשוב להן שיעור זה מהאי טעמא נמי הוה ליה למימר בההיא דפרק המצניע דהויא דלא כר"ש ושמא י"ל דהכא דנקט לפרושי הוה ליה לפרושי טפי: **אכילה** ע"י הדחק לא שמה אכילה. והא דאמר בפ' כילד הרגל (ב"ק דף יט.) אכילה ע"י הדחק שמה אכילה ה"מ לענין ניזקין דלא חשבינן ליה משונה אבל לאחשובה לענין שבת לא חשיבא אכילה: **אידי** ואידי חד שיעורא הוא. והא דנקט במתני' כמלא פי טלה ולא נקט כגרוגרת לאשמעי' דמשום אכילת טלה נתנו בו חכמים שיעור זה דאי נקט כגרוגרת לא הוה ידעינן למה נתנו בו חכמים שיעור זה: **מפני** שלא שוו בשיעוריהם. אבל אותם ששוו כגון עמיר ועלי שום ועלי בצלים לחים מצטרפין וכן חמור לקל כגון תבן לעצה למלא פי גמל ואפי' לא יהא תבן ראוי לגמל שמא אגב העצה הוא ראוי: **הבגד** והשק והעור כו'. דוקא בכה"ג הבגד והשק השק והעור אבל הבגד והעור והשק והמפץ אין מצטרפין שאין ראויין להתחבר יחד והמחברן בטלה דעתו ואין טמאים מדרס. ר"י: **ואמר** ר"ש מה טעם כו'. תימה לר"י דמה צריך להאי טעמא דהא כיון דמצטרפין זה עם זה א"כ ראוי לחברן וחזו למדרס וכיון דחזו למדרס פשיטא דמצטרפין לטומאת מדרס דהא אפי' כופת שאור שיחדה לישיבה טמאה מדרס כדאמרינן בהעור והרוטב (חולין קכט.) והכא בטומאת מדרס איירי מדקאמר הבגד שלשה על שלשה דלענין טומאת מת אפי' ג' על ג' כדפרישית לעיל ואור"י דודאי הא דקתני הבגד שלשה על שלשה לא מיירי אלא למדרס אבל סיפא דשק ועור ומפץ מיירי נמי בטומאת מת והכי איתא במס' כלים בפכ"ז הבגד שלשה על שלשה [למדרס ומשום ג' על ג'] לטומאת מת השק ד' על ד' העור ה' על ה' המפץ ו' על ו' שוו בין למדרס בין לטמא מת אלא שהש"ס מביאה בקוצר כמו שרגיל בכמה מקומות ועל טומאת מת קאמר מה טעם מצטרפין בשלא יחדו למדרס ולא צריך האי טעמא אצירוף דעור ומפץ ° דמפץ לא מטמא במת אלא כשטמא בזב דהיינו כשיחדו למדרס ומק"ו דפכין קטנים כדאמרינן בפ' ר' עקיבא (לקמן פד:): **הואיל** וראויין ליטמא מושב. פי' בקונטרס אם קילע משניים וצירף יחד לטלאי מרדעת החמור והיא דהמקלע מכולם טפח על טפח דמעילה היינו שבין כולם יש טפח ואין נראה לר"י דמה צריך להביא ראיה שראויין להצטרף בלאו טעמא דמושב נמי שמעינן ממתני' דהכא שראויין להצטרף יחד באותו סדר כמו ששנויים בגד לשק ושק לעור ועור למפץ דדוקא נקט לפי שאלו ראויין להצטרף יחד ונראה לר"י כמו שפי' ריב"א דהואיל וראויין ליטמא מושב היינו הואיל ושוו שיעוריהן לענין מושב וכמו שפירש בקונטרס בפ"ק דסוכה (דף יז:) דהמקלע מכולן היינו מאיזה מהן שיקלע יהא טמא ואע"ג שכאן אין שיעורן שוה מצטרפין הואיל ולענין מושב שיעורן שוה והא דקאמר ה"נ חזו לדוגמא היינו נמי דשיעורן שוה לדוגמא כדתנן בפרק המצניע לדוגמא כל שהוא הלכך מצטרפין אפי' לענין דבר דלא שוו שיעורייהו וה"ה דהוי מצי למינקט הכא ולזרע ולרפואה דהוו נמי בכל שהוא אלא דלא כל דברים שייך בהו זרע ורפואה אבל דוגמא שייכא בכל דבר והא דקאמר בסוכה המקלע מכולן כו' הואיל וראוי לטלות על גבי חמורו לשון הואיל וראוי לאו דווקא דדווקא אם עשה מהן טלאי ויחדן לכך טמא בטפח על טפח וכן מצינו לקמן בפ' א"ר עקיבא (דף צ.) הואיל וראויין למתק הקדרה דהוה ליה למימר הואיל וממתקין דהא מיירי שנפלו לתוך הקדרה. ר"י: **תוספתא** ז) המקלע למשכב אין פחות משלשה על שלשה למושב טפח ולמעמד כל שהוא:

חמשת

עין משפט נר מצוה

עב א ב מיי' פי"ח מהל' שבת הל' ג:
[עב] [ב] [מיי' שם]:

רבינו חננאל

ומנקה הבגד ודומה למנקב דתנינן בכמה מקומות ואם נשארו כגון אלו בבגד ובעל הבגד קפיד עלייהו ושקיל להו בשבת חייב משום מכה בפטיש. פי' כל דבר שהוא גמר מלאכה נקרא מכה בפטיש: המוחק אות אחת גדולה שיש במקומה שיעור לכתוב ב' אותיות חייב והכותב אות אחת גדולה שיש במקומה שיעור לכתוב ב' אותיות פטור. זה חומר במוחק מבכותב. אלו אבות מלאכות לאפוקי מדר' אלעזר דמחייב אתולדה במקום אב כמו שכבר פרשנוהו למעלה (דף עג:) דמאן דעבד ב' אבות או ב' תולדות משני אבות או אב ותולדה דאב (אחד) [אחר] בהעלם אחד חייב בזה אחד ובזה אחד. ואי עביד אב ותולדתו לא מיחייב אלא חדא. ועוד חזר ושנה מ' חסר אחת לאפוקי מר' יהודה דאמר שובט ומדקדק מאבות מלאכות הן. אמרו לו שובט הרי הוא בכלל מיסך. מדקדק בכלל אורג. א) פי' יש לארוגין עץ או עצם שראשו חד ונקרא כדבר ודומה למחט של סקאין. וכך שמו בלשון יון כדבר. מעבירו על השתי כשהוא מותח לפניו לאריגה ושובט בו החוטין ומקרב המבדילין בין ב' החוטין העליונים והתחתונים ומדנחים להתפרק העליונים מן התחתונים ונפתח נפש המסכת לידות בתוכם חוט הערב ואין לה אב אלא הרי הוא בכלל מיסך והמדקדק הוא המדקדק על חוט הערב כדי להדחק ולהלחץ עם חבירו וזהו בכלל אריגה: **ועוד** כלל אחר אמרו כל הכשר להצניע ומצניעין כמוהו והוציאו בשבת חייב עליו חטאת. כל הכשר להצניע רב מתנה אמר למעוטי דם נדה שאין חייבין בהוצאתו. וכ"ש איסורי הנאה. ועצי אשרה שאין חייבין בהוצאתו. מר עוקבא אמר לאפוקי עצי אשרה אבל דם נדה חייב כו' וזה ששנינו ומצניעין כמוהו א"ר יוסי ב"ר חנינא דלא כר' שמעון דאי ר' שמעון האמר דברים הללו לא נאמרו אלא למצניעיהן. והכין סבירא ליה לר' שמעון לענין המוציא יין כדי מזיגת הכוס חלב כדי גמיעה כו' דכולן שיעורן ברביעית ושיעורין הללו כדי גמיעה וכדי ליתן על הכתית כו'. לא נאמרו אלא למצניעיהן כלומר אם הצניע בחול [פחות] משיעורין הללו אע"פ שהוציאו בשבת פטור ורבנן סבירא להו אם הצניעו אדם בחול כל שהוא אע"פ שאין כשר להצניע והוציאו בשבת חייב דהא (אשביח) [אחשביה] בהצנעתו. וזה ששנינו כל שאין כשר להצניע ואין מצניעין כמוהו והוציאו בשבת אין חייב אלא המצניעו אבל מי לא שהצניע בחול אם הוציאו בשיעורין הללו חייב. ואם לא פטור. וזהו כמו דתנן המצניע לזרע לדוגמא ולרפואה והוציאו בשבת חייב עליו כל שהוא. ושאר כל אדם אין חייבין עליו אלא כשיעורו נמצא ר' שמעון מיקל מדברי חכמים ור' שמעון בן אלעזר מחמיר מדבריהם. דקאמר כל שאינו כשר להצניע ואין מצניעין כמוהו והוכשר לזה והצניעו ובא אחד והוציאו נתחייב המוציאו ממחשבת המצניעו ואע"פ שאינו כשר להצניע ואין מצניעין כמוהו חייב עליו. ורבנן אמרי אינו חייב בפחות מכשיעור אלא המצניעו. תמו הכללות. ובאנו לפרש שיעורי ההוצאה: **המוציא** תבן כמלוא פי פרה. עצה תבן הקטנית וקשה ממנו שיעורו כמלוא פי גמל. עמיר כמלוא פי טלה. עשבים כמלוא פי גדי ולענין המוציא תבן כמלוא פי פרה לגמל (הלכה) כו"ע לא פליגי דחייב שזה הוא שיעור הוצאתו ולא אכפת לן [אין] לגמל נתכוון להוציאו או לפרה אלא כי פליגי ר' יוחנן ור' אושעי' במוציא עצה כמלוא פי פרה לפרה. ועיקר הדבר שאין העצה מאכל פרה ואין שיעור כמלוא פי פרה אלא כמלוא פי גמל שהוא יתר ממלוא פי פרה. ועכשיו שנתכוון לפרה איפליגו ר' אושעי' סבר אכילה ע"י הדחק שמה אכילה אע"פ שאין פרה אוכלת אותו כדרכה אלא כיון שאוכלת אותו ע"י הדחק וישנו מלא פיה והוציאו לה חייב עליו. (ור') [ור"י] סבר אכילה שע"י הדחק לאו שמה אכילה (וזה) ופטור: לענין הא דתנן אין מצטרפין זה עם זה מפני שלא שוו בשיעוריהן א"ר יוסי ב"ר חנינא אין מצטרפין לחמור שבהן אבל מצטרפין לקל שבהן אם הוציא עמיר ועשבים אם יש בין שניהם כמלוא פי טלה מצטרפין כי החמור משלים לקל וחייב אבל אם אין בהם כמלוא פי טלה. אע"פ שיש בהן כמלוא פי הגדי פטור שאין מצטרפין כי אין הקל משלים לחמור וכן עשבים משלימין לתבן ואין התבן משלים לעשבים ומקשינן היאך תאמר בהני דלא שוו בשיעוריהן להדדי דמצטרפין והלא הבגד והשק והעור לענין טומאה שלא שוו בשיעוריהן אע"ג דתנן הבגד והשק מצטרפין והשק והעור מצטרפין והעור והמפץ מצטרפין דקתני סיפא. א"ר שמעון מה טעם הואיל וראויין ליטמא מושב דייקת מיניה טעמא דראויין ליטמא מושב הא אי לא הוו ראויין ליטמא מושב לא הוו מצטרפין משום שלא שוו בשיעוריהן להדדי. וא"כ היכי קאמר ר' יוסי בר' חנינא מצטרפין לקל שבהן והכין הוה ראוי שלא יצטרפו כל עיקר. ופריק רבא לר' יוסי ב"ר חנינא ואמר הכי נמי ראויין לדוגמא כשם שהבגד והשק אף על פי שאין בזה כשיעור ולא בזה כשיעור כיון שאלו מתחברין יש בעיניהם כשיעור השק שהוא הקל ואפשר לחברן זה בזה ולישב עליהן וראויין ליטמא מושב. כן התבן והעצה אפשר להוציא מזה כמעט ומזה כמעט להראותן דוגמא לקונה לומר מאלו אני מוכר ולהכין חשובין בחיבורין ויש צורך להוציאו כסדר הזה משום כן מצטרפין לקל שבהן אבל אוכלין שיעורן כולן כגרוגרת לפיכך מצטרפין דע"ז אבל קליפיהן ועוקציהן וסובן ומורסנן אין מצטרפין עמהן.

ר'

מסורת הש"ס

א) לקמן לא. זבחים מז., ב) [הכסף משנה העתיק רבי אושעיא אמר חייב וכו' ופסק הרמב"ם כרבי אושעיא שהלכ' כמותו לגבי ר' יוחנן עכ"ל], ג) ב"ק יט: ועע"ש קי., ד) לקמן עט. סוכה יז: כלים פכ"ז מ"ב, ה) מעילה יח., ו) צ"ל אחר, ז) כלים ב"ב פ"ב.

הגהות הב"ח

(א) רש"י ד"ה הואיל וכו' דתניא. נ"ב במעילה ס"פ קדשי המזבח דף יח:

גליון הש"ס

גמ' ואיפכא איתמר. כעין זה נדה דף לד ע"א: שם ר"ל אמר חייב. בכסף משנה פי"ח הלכה ג מהלכות שבת הגירסא ר' אושעיא: תוס' ד"ה ואמר ר"ש וכו' דמפץ לא מטמא במת. עי' פכ"ד מ"י דכלים וכר"ש שם:

ליקוטי רש"י

שאינו כשר להצניע. במסכת שבת כגון דם נדה או איסור (או) הנאה. ואין מצניעין כמוהו. שכשר הוא להצניעו אם היה [בו שיעור] אבל שיעורו של זה מועט הוא ואין אדם חושבו להצניעו. ובא אחר והוציאו. בשבת לרה"ר חייב דחשיב מלאכה מפני מחשבתו של זה שהוכשר לו והצניעו [זבחים מז.]. הבגד ג' על ג'. טפחים אם ייחדו למשכב הזב מטמא ליעשות אב הטומאה במשכב הזב או במדרסו [סוכה יז:]. והשק. שיעורו ד' טפחים על ד' טפחים [מעילה יח.]. מפץ. של קנים [לקמן פד.]. ותני עלה הבגד. שהוא מטמא ג' אצבעות על ג' אצבעות [מעילה שם]. הבגד והשק. הואיל וממשן קרוב להיות שוה. מצטרפין. להשלים את הקל שאם אין בשק ארבעה הבגד שהוא חמור משלימו אבל השק אינו משלים הבגד החמור [סוכה שם]. הבגד מצטרף לשק שקל הימנו [מצטרף] לארבעה על ארבעה וכן כל אחד ואחד מצטרף לקל הימנו דשק מצטרף לעור לחמשה על חמשה והעור למפץ לששה על ששה דהיינו לקל הימנו אבל לא הקל עם החמור להכי תנא להו הכי הבגד והשק השק והעור כו' כולן מצטרפין זה עם זה [מעילה שם]. שק. מנוצה של עזים עשוי והוא עב יותר מן הבגד ואינו מגיע לעוביו של עור. השק והעור. וכן השק והעור מצטרפין להשלים שק את שיעור העור. מפני שראוין ליטמא מושב. הואיל וראוין בשיעור אחד לטמא מושב הזב כדתנן המקלע מכולן מאחד מכל אלו קילע טפח על טפח מקלע שמשויהו סביב סביב באזמל ומתקנו יפה אפילו אין בו אלא טפח על טפח טמא כדמפרש הואיל וראוי ליטלו לעשותו טלאי על גבי מרדעת החמור כנגד בית מושב האדם וכיון דשוו שיעורייהו באחד מטומאות הזב ליעשות אב הטומאה מצטרפין אף למדרס ויש מפרשים המקלע מכולן יחד שחיבר קילועיהן שקילץ כל המינין ועשה מהן טפח על טפח ותפרן יחד והראשון נראה לי [סוכה שם ועי' בתוס' כאן]. מפני שכשים בין כולן שיעור אחד (בין שניהם) ראוין ליטמא מושב (עליו) הלכך מצטרפין [מעילה שם].

חשק שלמה על רבינו חננאל א) עי' ערוך ערך שנט א' וע' דוך:

ה"נ חזיא לדוגמא: **מתני'** א) המוציא אוכלים כגרוגרת חייב ומצטרפין זה עם זה מפני ששוו בשיעוריהן חוץ מקליפתן וגרעיניהן ועוקציהן וסובן ומורסנן ר' יהודה אומר חוץ מקליפי עדשין שמתבשלות עמהן: **גמ'** וסובן ומורסנן לא מצטרפין והתנן [א] א) חמשת רבעים קמח ועוד חייבין בחלה הן וסובן ומורסנן אמר אביי שכן עני אוכל פתו בעיסה בלוסה: רבי יהודה אומר חוץ מקליפי עדשים המתבשלות עמהן: עדשים אין פולין לא והתניא ר' יהודה אומר חוץ מקליפי פולין ועדשים לא קשיא הא בחדתי הא בעתיקי עתיקי מ"ט לא אמר ר' אבהו מפני שנראין כזובבין בקערה:

הדרן עלך כלל גדול

ב) **המוציא** ב) יין כדי מזיגת הכוס חלב כדי ג) גמיעה דבש כדי ליתן על הכתית ◦ שמן כדי לסוך אבר קטן מים כדי לשוף בהם את הקילור ד) ושאר כל המשקין ברביעית וכל השופכין ברביעית ר"ש אומר כולן ברביעית ולא ה) נאמרו ו) כל השיעורין הללו אלא למצניעיהן: **גמ'** תנא ז) כדי מזיגת כוס יפה ומאי כוס יפה כוס של ברכה ג אמר רב נחמן אמר רבה בר אבוה כוס של ברכה צריך שיהא בו רובע רביעית כדי שימזגנו ויעמוד על רביעית אמר רבא אף אנן נמי תנינא

רש"י

הכא נמי חזי. ביחד: לדוגמא. מי שיש לו למכור צובר מכולן ונותן לפני חלונו להראות שיש לו למכור מכולן וניחא ליה שיהו מחוברין יחד דאיידי דזוטרי כל חד וחד הרוח מפזרתו: **מתני'** אוכלים כו'. למאכל אדם: ומצטרפין. כל אוכלי אדם זה עם זה: חוץ מקליפיהן. שאינן אוכל ואין משלימין השיעור: ועוקציהן. זנב הפרי דהוא עץ בעלמא: וסובן. קליפת חטין הנושרת מחמת כתישה: ומורסנן. הנשאר בנפה: ר' יהודה אומר. כל הקליפין אין מצטרפין כדאמרן חוץ מקליפי עדשים שמצטרפות אותן: שמתבשלות עמהן. לאפוקי קליפה חיצונה שהן גדלות בתוכה הנושרות בגורן: **גמ'** בלוסה. מעורבת בסובנה ובמורסנה הלכך לחם הארץ קרינן ביה ומיהו לענין שבת מידי דחשיב בעינן וסתמייהו דהני לאו אוכל נינהו: פולין חדתי. קליפתן מצטרפין: כזובבין. לפי שהן שחורות:

הדרן עלך כלל גדול

המוציא יין. חי: כדי מזיגת הכוס. כשיעור שנותנין יין חי לתוך כוס להוסיף עליו מים כהלכתו ולמזוג אותו בהן ובגמרא מפרש באיזה כוס משערו: כתית. שבגבי הסוסים והגמלים מחמת המשאות רדוי"ש בלע"ז והכי אמר בהמפקיד בבבא מציעא (דף לח.) דבש והדבש למאי חזי לכתותא דגמלי אבל רבותי פירשו כתית מכה שעל גב היד ושע"ג הרגל: לשוף. לשפשף ולהמחות בהן: קילור. שנותנין על העין לודיי"א בלע"ז: ברביעית. בילה ומחצה רביעית הלוג: שופכים. מים סרוחים ובגמרא מפרש למאי חזו: כולן ברביעית. אף היין והחלב והדבש: ולא נאמרו. שיעורין שבמשנה אלא למצניעיהן לבד וחזר המצניע והוציאו חייב אבל שאר כל אדם שהוציאו אינו חייב וסבירא לי' לר"ש דמצניע עצמו בעי שיעורא זוטא ובבציר מהא שיעורא לא מיחייב כדאמרינן בפרקין דלעיל (דף עה:) דלית ליה לר"ש כל שאין כשר להצניע ואין מצניעים כמוהו שיתחייב עליו מצניעו: **גמ'** תנא. בתוספתא המוציא יין כדי מזיגת כוס יפה פירוש לכוס דמתני': כוס של ברכה. ברכת המזון שהצריכו חכמים ליפותו כדאמרי' בברכות (דף נא.) עיטור ועיטוף הדחה ושטיפה חי ומלא: אמר רב נחמן גרסי' ולא גרסי' דאמר: שיעור כוס של ברכה צריך שיהא בו. יין חי רובע של רביעית הלוג: כדי שימזגנו. במים שלשה חלקים מים ואחד יין: ויעמוד על רביעי'. הלוג:

תוספות

חמשת רבעים קמח ועוד גרסי' כדפרי' בפ"ק (דף טו.):

הדרן עלך כלל גדול

המוציא יין. חלב כדי גמיעה. הקשה רבינו אפרים דתניא בשילהי המצניע (לקמן צה.) החולב והמחבץ והמגבן כגרוגרת ואין חילוק בין מוציא לחולב דהא לקמן בפירקין ח) אמרי' דהמעבד עור שיעורו כמוציא עור ותירץ ר"י דהתם חלב לגמיאה דנפיש מגרוגרת והתם איירי בחולב לגבינה דאחשביה אחשביה וכן מוכח דכדי גמיאה נפיש מגרוגרת דבפ' בתרא דיומא (פ.) גבי שותה ביוה"כ איכא דמחייב ברביעית ואיכא למ"ד בכדי גמיאה ובעירובין (דף פג:) משמע דתשע סעודות יש בקב ובפרק חלון (שם פ:) משמע שיש י"ח גרוגרות בשתי סעודות ואי כדי גמיאה פחות מגרוגרת א"כ הוו יותר מדאי חלוקים זה מזה ומיהו (א) כגרוגרת דהמצניע (לקמן צה.) איירי ביבש אפשר שבתחלה היה יותר מכדי גמיאה ולפי זה צריך לפרש דסתם חלב הוי לגבינה והא דמיחייב הכא בכדי גמיאה היינו במפרש בהדיא לשתיה אבל אי סתם חלב הוי לאכול ולשתות ולא לגבינה אפי' היה מפרש בהדיא לגבינה היה חייב אכדי גמיאה דזוטרא הואיל וסתמו לכך כדאמרינן לעיל המוציא תבן כמלא פי פרה לגמל חייב דהא חזי לפרה וי"מ דכשחלב ככר בעין מיחייב בכדי גמיאה אבל חולב לא מיחייב אלא כגרוגרת דאין אדם טורח לחלוב בפחות מגרוגרת דכה"ג אמרי' לקמן (דף עט.) דאין אדם טורח לגבל טיט לעשות פי כור ומיהו אומר ר"י דלא דמי דהתם אין המים חשובין מחמת שראוי לגבל בהן את הטיט כמו הטיט עצמו שהוא מגובל כבר אבל הכא כשחולב להוציא מן הדד בכדי גמיאה יש לו להיות חשוב כמו במקום אחר ט): **כדי** גמיעה. פי' הר"ר פור"ת מלא לוגמא ולא משמע כן במסכת יומא בפרק בתרא (דף פ.):

צריך שיהא בו רובע רביעית. רביעית דהכא היינו רביעית הלוג כדפי' הקונט' ועוד יש לדקדק דהיינו רביעית דפרק ג' מינין (נזיר לח.) הס רביעית הלוג מדפריך ותו ליכא והאיכא רביעית נוטלין לידים ובמסכת ידים (פ"א מ"א) משמע בהדיא דהוי רביעית הלוג ועוד דבערבי פסחים (פסחים קט:) משמע דכוס הוי רביעית של תורה ומתוך חשבון דמקוה משמע דהיינו רביעית הלוג והא דקאמר התם קיסתא דמורייסא הות בציפורי והות כמין לוגא דמקדשא ובה משערין רביעית של פסח לאו בכולה משערין דהיינו כל הלוג אלא כלומר ברובע של אותה מדה משערין רביעית של פסח: **כדי** שימזגנו ויעמוד על רביעית. משמע דכוס של ברכה טעון מזיגה וכן בפ' שלשה שאכלו (ברכות נ:) אר"י בר חנינא מודים חכמים לר"א בכוס של ברכה שאין מברכין עליו עד שיתן לתוכו מים ותימה דבסוף פר' שלשה שאכלו (שם דף נא.) אמרו עשרה דברים נאמרו בכוס של ברכה הדחה ושטיפה חי ומלא אלמא חי בעינן ומיהו התם פירש בקונטרס דלא שיהא חי כשמברכין עליו אלא דנותנו חי בכוס שמברכין בו לאפוקי שלא ימזגנו ויתננו בכוס של ברכה ור"ת מפרש דחי דקאמר היינו מזוג ולא מזוג דמיקרי חי כדאמרי' בפ' בן סורר (סנהדרין ע.) עד שיאכל תרטימר בשר וישתה יין חי ומוקי לה התם במזוג ולא מזוג ובברכת הארץ מוסיף מים עד שיהא מזוג כראוי כדאמר בפ' שלשה שאכלו (ברכות נא.) שמוסיף בברכת הארץ ולא כמו שפירש שם בקונטרס שמוסיף יין בברכת הארץ ובני נרבונא מפרשים דחי קאי אכוס שצריך שיהא שלם ואתי שפיר דכל אותן דברים דחשיב התם הוו כולהו בכוס ולא ביין וכה"ג בפרק בתרא דמכות (דף טז:) ריסק ט' נמלים ואחד חי דהיינו שלם דאפי' מת חשיב בריה כדאמר בסוף פ' גיד הנשה (חולין דף קב:) י): **ויעמוד** על רביעית. ואע"ג דאמרינן בערבי פסחים (דף קז.) המקדש אם טעם מלא לוגמא יצא ומלא לוגמא הוי טפי מרביעית כדמוכח בפ' בתרא דיומא (דף פ.) יש לומר דמלא לוגמא דהתם לאו דוקא אלא כדי שיסלקו לצד אחד ויראה כמלא לוגמא כדמפרש ביומא אהנהו דהתם ועוד יש לומר דדוקא מקדש:

אף אנן נמי תנינא. דכוס של ברכה טעון רביעית דמסתמא יין שיעורו לכשימזגנו ויעמוד על רביעית כמו שאר משקין דקתני סיפא דהוו ברביעית וקתני כדי מזיגת כוס יפה משמע דכוס של ברכה לכשימזוג בעינן שיהא רביעית כמו בהוצאה אבל הא דבעינן יין רובע רביעית לא שמעינן ממתני' אלא ממילא ידעינן דהא מזיגה הויא על חד תלת והא דלא נקט במתני' כדי מזיגת רביעית מילתא אגב אורחיה קמ"ל דכוס של ברכה ברביעית ועוד משום דמהאי טעמא דחזי לכוס של ברכה חשיב ומיחייב בפחות מרביעית לפי שיכול להוסיף עליו מים ושאר משקין לא מיחייב בפחות מרביעית אע"פ שיכול להוסיף עליהן כדמסיק דקאמרת מים בכד ומצטרפין לגבי שבת מידי דחשיב בעינן:

עין משפט נר מצוה

עג א מיי' פי"ח מהל' שבת הלכה א:

עג [א] מיי' פ"ו מהל' בכורים הלכה טו והלכה יח טוש"ע יו"ד סימן שכד סעיף א ג:

א ב ג מיי' פי"ח מהל' שבת הלכה ב:

רבינו חננאל

ר' יהודה אומר חוץ מקליפי עדשים שהן מתבשלין עמהן ולפיכך מצטרפות. והא דתנן חוץ מקליפיהן ר' יהודה אומר חוץ מקליפי עדשים חוץ מחוץ ונמצא מיעוט ממיעוט ולרבות הוא כמה שפירשנו למעלה: ושניא חלה דסובן ומורסנן הין מצטרפין לקמח להוציא מכולן חלה. שכן עני אוכל פתו מעיסה בלוסה שיש בה סובין ומורסן וזו היא עיסתו ואמר רחמנא ראשית עריסותיכ' אבל להוצאת שבת אין סובן ומורסנן מצטרפין וכן פולים אם חדשים הן הרי מנהג לבשל בקליפיהן. וקאמר ר' יהודה בברייתא שאף הן מצטרפות עם הפולין. אבל אם הם ישני' ונשתחרו נראין כזבובים בקערה ורגילין בני אדם לקלפן קודם בישול והלכך אין קליפיהן מצטרפות עמהן:

הדרן עלך כלל גדול

פ"ח המוציא יין כדי מזיגת הכוס. תנא כדי מזיגת הכוס יפה. ומאי כוס יפה כוס של ברכה. והתם אמרינן אמר רב יהודה אמר שמואל כוסות הללו צריך שיהא בהן כדי מזיגת כוס יפה. ומותבינן ד' כוסות הללו צריך שיהא בהן כדי רביעית ופרקינן אידי ואידי חד שיעורא הוא והאי דקאמר צריך שיהא בארבעתן רביעית א) בכל אחת רובע רביעית כדאמרינן הכא. אמר רב נחמן אמר רבה בר אבוה כוס של ברכה צריך שיהא בו רובע רביעית כדי שימזגנו ויעמוד על רביעית. ואמר רבה אף אנן נמי

חשק שלמה על רבינו חננאל

א) נראה דחסר איזה תיבות וצ"ל שיהא בהן כדי רביעית היינו שיהא בארבעתן וכו':

רב נסים גאון

פ"ח המוציא יין. אמר רב נחמן אמר רבה בר אבוה כוס של ברכה צריך שיהא בו רובע רביעית כדי שימזגנו ויעמוד על רביעית. משתכח פירושיה בפרק ערבי פסחים (דף קח) אמר רב יהודה אמר שמואל ד' כוסות הללו צריך שיהא בהן כדי מזיגת כוס יפה ואותבי' לשמואל מברייתא דקתני בה ד' כוסות הללו צריך שיהא בהן כדי רביעית ופרקינן מאי כדי מזיגת כוס יפה כוס יפה דאמר שמואל בהאי שיעורא ואמרו עוד (שם דף קט) אמר רב יצחק קיסטא דמוריסא דהוות בטבריא היא הוות כמין דמקדשא ובה משערין רביעית של פסח ומיכן את למד כוס של ברכה רביעית במסכת נזירות בפרק ג' מינים אסורין (דף לח) אמרו אמר ר' אלעזר עשר רביעיות נקיט רב כהנא בידיה ה' סומקאתא וה' חיורתא ה' סומקאתא נזיר ועושה פסח שהורו למקדש ומתים סימן נזיר רביעית יין לנזיר עושה פסח דאמר רב יהודה אמר שמואל ד' כוסות הללו צריך שיהא בהן כדי רביעית שהורו רביעית יין אל יורה במקדש שהשותה רביעית יין ונכנס למקדש חייב מתים דתניא מניין לרביעית דם היוצאה משני מתים שהיא מטמאה באהל שנא' (ויקרא כא) ועל כל נפשות מת לא יבא וחמש חיורתא חלה נזיר מצורע (שנפלו) [שנפסלו] בשבת סימן חלה רביעית שמן לחלה נזיר רביעית שמן לנזיר מצורע רביעית שמן לנזיר מצורע ושנפסלו דתנן ושאר כל משקין טמאין פוסלין את הגויה לרביעית שבת דתנן ושאר כל המשקין ברביעית וכל השופכין ברביעית:

מסורת הש"ס

א) חלה פ"ב מ"ו ע"ש פסחים מח: עדיות פ"א מ"ב, ב) [עירובין כט:], ג) [גי' הערוך ערך גס ד' גמיאה], ד) [נזיר לח.], ה) נ"א איתא אמרו, ו) [לעיל עה:], ז) [עירובין כט:], ח) [דף עט.], ט) [ועי' תוס' פסחים סה. ד"ה החולב], י) [וע"ע תוספות ברכות נ: ד"ה מודים].

הגהות הב"ח

(א) תוס' ד"ה המוציא וכו' ומיהו אי כגרוגרת דהמצניע:

גליון הש"ס

מתני' שמן כדי לסוך. עי' פ"ב מ"ב דכלים בר"ש שם:

ליקוטי רש"י

כגרוגרת. היא תאנה יבישה ובה שיערו כל אוכל אדם לענין הוצאת שבת [עירובין ד:]. וסובן. שהנפה קולטת [חולין פח:]. שהמכתשת מוציאה כשלותתין חטין לקולת כותשין אותן במכתשת [כתובות קיב.]. סובין גסין ממורסן [ב"ק צט:]. כשטוחנין גסין ולא הדק נשאר בנפה והוא סובין [רשב"ם ב"ב צג:]. ומורסנן. קליפה היוצאת כשכותשים במכתשת [חולין שם]. הן סובין היוצאין באחרונה [כתובות שם]. היא הקליפה העליונה שמוציאין מחטין הכתושין במכתשת [רשב"ם ב"ב שם]. חמשת רבעים. לוגין שהן רביעית הקב [לעיל טו.]. לוגין ציפוריים שהן שבעה ועוד מדבריים שזה הוא שיעור העומר שהיתה עיסת מדבר שנאמר גבי חלה (במדבר טו) ראשית עריסותיכם כדי עריסותיכם דהיינו עיסת מדבר שהוא עומר לגולגלת והוא עשירית האיפה והאיפה שלש סאין וסאה ששה קבין מדבריות חשוב עישור שבהן ותמצא שבעת רבעי קב ובילה וחומש בילה כיצד חלק שלש סאין שהן שמונה עשרה קבין ועשה מהן רבעי קב היינו לוגין ותמצא בהן שבעים ושנים לוג טול עישור של שבעים הרי שבעה והשנים הנשארים שתים עשרה ביצים הן עישור שלהן בילה וחומש בילה הרי שבעת רבעים ועוד דהוא בילה וחומש בילה ובירושלים הוסיפו על המדות שתות מלבר שהוא חומש מלגו שנתנו ששה מן הראשונים בתוך חמשה האחרונים הרי ששת רבעים הראשונים נעשו חמשה והרובע ובילה וחומש הנשארים נעשו רובע שהרובע שש בילים עשה מהן חמש בילים גדולות והבילה וחומש בילה נעשית בילה גדולה שניתוסף עליה חומשה מלגו דהוא שתות מלבר הרי שש בילים גדולות דהוא רובע קב גדול הרי עומר המדבר ששה רבעים ירושלמיים וקאה ציפורית עודפת על ירושלמית שתות מלבר כדאמר בעירובין (פג.) הרי עומר שהיה ששה רבעים ירושלמיים נכנס בחמש ציפוריים [פסחים מח: ועי' שם בתוס' שרש"י לא גרס "ועוד"]. ועוד. הוי ועוד אחד מעשרים בבילה לכל בילה [לעיל שם]. בעיסה בלוסה. עיסה מעורבת ממינין הרבה וכן אוצר בלוס (גיטין סז.) מינין הרבה מעורבין בתוכה ביחד [רשב"ם ב"ב נח.]. כדי מזיגת הכוס. כמו שנותנין יין חי בכוס למוזגו במים [עירובין כט:]. קילור. תחבושת שקורין לח"א [לעיל יח.]. ושאר כל המשקין ברביעית. דהיינו לוג [עירובין שם עי' רש"י לקמן עז. ד"ה תנינא ותוס' עירובין שם]. כל רביעית שבגמרא רביעית הלוג [רשב"ם ב"ב פט:]. ומדת חלל הכלי בריבוע הוי אצבעים אורך על אצבעים רוחב ברום אצבעים וחצי אצבע וחומש אצבע [רשב"ם פסחים קט.]. נמצא כל אצבעים על אצבעים ברום י"ג חומשין וחצי חומש מחזיק רביעית הלוג חשוב י"ג חומשים וחצי ותמצא בהן אצבעים וחצי אצבע וחומש אצבע [רש"י פסחים שם]. וכל השופכין. ששופכין אותן לרה"ר [נזיר לח.]. רובע רביעית. רובע לוג יין חי [עירובין שם].

הָכָא נַמִּי חַזְיָא לְדוּגְמָא – **Here also [the different types of feed] are fit** to be combined **for a sample.**[1] A "stringent" feed can therefore complete the minimum amount of a more "lenient" feed.

Mishnah הַמּוֹצִיא אוֹכָלִים כִּגְרוֹגֶרֶת – **One who carries out foodstuffs**[2] **the equivalent of a dried fig**[3] חַיָּיב – **is liable.** וּמִצְטָרְפִין זֶה עִם זֶה – **And [foodstuffs] can be combined with one another**[4] מִפְּנֵי שֶׁשָּׁווּ בְּשִׁיעוּרֵיהֶן – **because they are alike in their prescribed measures**[5] – חוּץ מִקְּלִיפָּתָן – **except for their shells,**[6] וְגַרְעִינֵיהֶן – **their pits,** וְעוּקְצֵיהֶן – **their stems,**[7] וְסוּבָּן – **their coarse bran**[8] וּמוּרְסָנָן – **and their fine bran.**[9] רַבִּי יְהוּדָה אוֹמֵר – **R' Yehudah says:** חוּץ מִקְּלִיפֵּי עֲדָשִׁין – All shells may not be combined **except for the shells of lentils,**[10] which may be combined שֶׁמִּתְבַּשְּׁלוֹת עִמָּהֶן – **because they are cooked with [the lentils].**[11]

Gemara The Gemara challenges a ruling of the Mishnah:

וְסוּבָּן וּמוּרְסָנָן לֹא מִצְטָרְפִין – **And their coarse bran and their fine bran cannot be combined** with flour to complete the minimum? וְהָתְנַן – **But we learned in a Mishnah:**[12] חֲמֵשֶׁת רְבָעִים קֶמַח וְעוֹד – FIVE-QUARTERS of a *kav* OF FLOUR AND a bit MORE חַיָּיבִין בְּחַלָּה – ARE OBLIGATED IN *CHALLAH*.[13] הֵן וְסוּבָּן וּמוּרְסָנָן – THEY, THEIR COARSE BRAN AND THEIR FINE BRAN all combine to complete the five quarter-*kavs*. We thus see that bran can be combined with flour to complete a minimum measure. – ? –

The Gemara answers:

אָמַר אַבָּיֵי – **Abaye said:** In that case bran may be combined with the flour שֶׁכֵּן עָנִי אוֹכֵל פִּתּוֹ בְּעִיסָּה בְּלוּסָה – **because a pauper indeed eats his bread made of impure dough** [i.e. unrefined flour].[14]

The Mishnah stated:

רַבִּי יְהוּדָה אוֹמֵר – R' YEHUDAH SAYS: חוּץ מִקְּלִיפֵּי עֲדָשִׁים – All shells may not be combined EXCEPT FOR THE SHELLS OF LENTILS, הַמִּתְבַּשְּׁלוֹת עִמָּהֶן – WHICH ARE COOKED WITH [THE LENTILS].

The Gemara asks:

עֲדָשִׁים אִין – R' Yehudah implies here that the shells of **lentils** may **indeed** be combined, פּוֹלִין לֹא – but the shells of **beans** may **not.** וְהָתַנְיָא – **However, it was taught** otherwise **in a Baraisa:** רַבִּי יְהוּדָה אוֹמֵר – R' YEHUDAH SAYS: חוּץ מִקְּלִיפֵּי פּוֹלִין וַעֲדָשִׁים – All shells may not be combined EXCEPT FOR THE SHELLS OF BEANS AND LENTILS. There in the Baraisa R' Yehudah sanctions the combining of bean shells to reach the minimum. – ? –

The Gemara answers:

לֹא קַשְׁיָא – This is **not a difficulty.** הָא בְּחַדְתֵּי – **This** Baraisa speaks **of fresh** produce,[15] הָא בְּעַתִּיקֵי – whereas **this** Mishnah speaks **of old** produce.

A clarification is requested:

עַתִּיקֵי מַאי טַעְמָא לֹא – **What is the reason** that the shells of **old** beans may **not** be combined with the beans?

The Gemara explains:

אָמַר רַבִּי אַבָּהוּ – **R' Abahu said:** מִפְּנֵי שֶׁנִּרְאִין כִּזְבוּבִין בַּקְּעָרָה – **Because [bean shells] look like flies in the plate.**[16] Since no one eats them, they cannot be combined to complete the minimum measure.

הדרן עלך כלל גדול

WE SHALL RETURN TO YOU, KLAL GADOL

NOTES

1. Someone who sells various types of feed piles them all together in front of his window to advertise his stock. Indeed, he prefers to combine them, for if they are piled separately the wind will blow away the smaller piles (*Rashi*). Since there is some circumstance when it is useful for different types of feed to be joined together, they can be combined to complete the minimum amount for liability.

2. Anything fit for human consumption (*Rashi*).

3. This minimum amount is a הֲלָכָה לְמֹשֶׁה מִסִּינַי, *a law taught orally to Moses at Sinai*, and is not taught in the written Torah (see *Rashi* to *Eruvin* 4b). See above, 76a note 10.

4. I.e. all foodstuffs fit for human consumption can be combined with one another to make up the equivalent of a dried fig (*Rashi*).

5. Because they all have identical minimums for liability. They thus differ from the animal feeds discussed in the previous Mishnah, which have varying minimums because they are intended for different types of animals.

6. Since shells are not food, they cannot be counted toward the minimum (*Rashi*). [The same reasoning holds true for the next four items mentioned by the Mishnah.]

7. These are considered ordinary wood (*Rashi*).

8. This is a shell of the wheat kernel, which falls off when the wheat is pounded (*Rashi;* see above, 74a note 2).

9. [After the kernels are ground into flour, the flour is sifted.] This bran is what is left in a [fine] sieve after the sifting (*Rashi;* cf. *Rambam, Commentary to the Mishnah; Rav* to *Challah* 2:6, and *Tos. Yom Tov* here and to *Challah* loc. cit.).

10. R' Yehudah holds that the shells of lentils do count toward the measure of a dried fig to render one liable for transferring on the Sabbath (*Rashi*).

11. Since people cook lentils without first shelling them and then eat the peels as well, the peels are considered part of the lentil and can be counted toward making up the minimum.

The Mishnah, however, excludes the outer shell, in which the lentil grows, because that shell falls off at harvest time (*Rashi*), and is not eaten.

12. *Challah* 2:6.

13. The Torah obligates one who makes dough to separate a portion and give it to a Kohen (see *Numbers* 15:17-21). This gift is known as *challah*. The portion of dough that has been separated as *challah* immediately becomes consecrated (like *terumah*), and may be eaten only by Kohanim who are *tahor*.

A batch of dough must contain at least five quarter-*kavs* (i.e. $1^1/_4$ *kavs*) of flour to be subject to the law of *challah*. If the batch contains less than this amount, there is no need to separate *challah* from it. [*Rashi* above, 15a, explains how the $1^1/_4$ *kav* minimum is derived (see note 8 there). Although the term, וְעוֹד, *and [a bit] more,* does not appear in the standard version of the Mishnah in *Challah, Tosafos* (above, 15a ד״ה רבי יוסי and to *Pesachim* 48b ד״ה חמשת) defend our version by identifying the Tanna that requires this small addition.]

14. A pauper eats bread baked from flour from which the bran has not been removed. Such bread is therefore subject to the law of *challah,* for it qualifies as what Scripture (*Numbers* 15:19) calls: לֶחֶם הָאָרֶץ, *bread of the land.* However, with regard to Sabbath law, bran is not considered sufficiently significant to create liability for the one who takes it out, since most people do not eat it (*Rashi*, cf. *Ritva MHK* ed.).

Ritva notes that once bran is removed from flour it no longer can be included in the minimum measure for *challah* even if it is mixed into the flour. as is evident from the Mishnah there.]

See *Rosh Yosef* and *Sfas Emes* for a discussion of whether bran may be combined with *matzah* or with forbidden types of flour to reach a minimum measure.

15. The shells of fresh beans are edible, and therefore count toward the minimum measure for liability.

16. Since they are black (*Rashi*). That is, bean shells blacken with age. People therefore remove the shells before cooking the beans so it will not appear as though there are flies in the dish (*Rabbeinu Chananel*).

Appendix
Glossary
Scriptural Index

Appendix: The Weaving Process

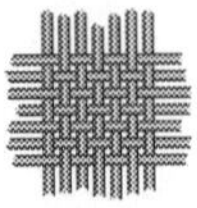

Woven cloth consists of two series of parallel threads that crisscross each other at right angles. Every second horizontal thread passes over the first vertical thread, under the second, over the third, under the fourth, etc., until it has passed through all the vertical threads. Each remaining horizontal thread passes under the first vertical thread, over the second, under the third, etc.

In the weaving process, the vertical threads (called שְׁתִי, *warp*) are fixed in place, while a single thread (called עֵרֶב, *weft*) is passed over and under them first from right to left and then from left to right repeatedly. With each pass of the weft thread a new line of cloth is created.

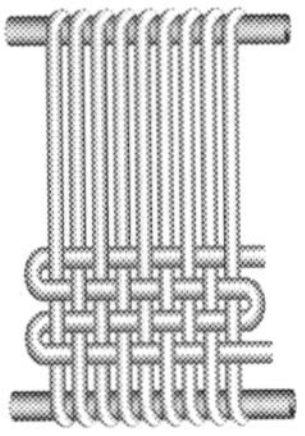

To assure an even weave, the warp must be kept taut while the weft passes through it. This is accomplished by wrapping the warp threads around a beam (called the warp beam) and stretching them to a second beam (called the cloth beam, for it is around this beam that the finished fabric will be wound). This action is called מֵיסֵךְ, *dressing the loom.*

Some warp threads may be overlapped or stuck together. The weaver takes a stick (שֵׁבֶט) and hits the threads, which causes most of them to separate. The remainder are lined up individually with a pointed rod (כַּרְכַּר). This part of the process of mounting the warp is called שׁוֹבֵט.

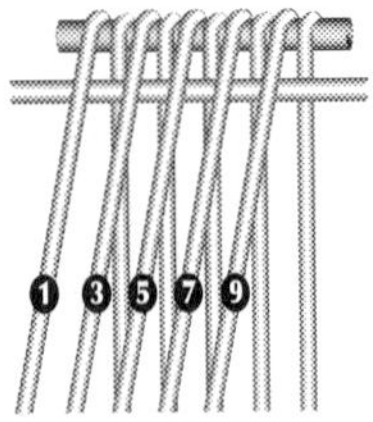

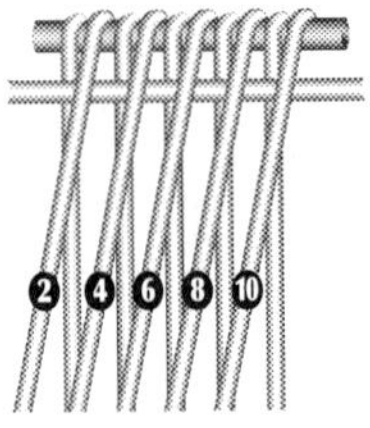

Clearly, the weaving process would be long and tedious unless some means of mechanization could be introduced, especially since the warp often contains as many as one hundred or more threads per inch. A method which would enable the weft thread to make a complete pass in one motion would obviously speed up the weaving process considerably. Additionally, since it is advantageous that the weft threads be (a) as long as possible (to avoid an excessive number of knots in the finished cloth), and (b) wound around a spool (to prevent tangling), a way must be found to pass a large, bulky amount of weft thread through the closely laid warp threads. These two objectives could be achieved if all the odd-numbered warp threads could be raised simultaneously to allow the weft thread to pass under them, but above the even-numbered threads. By then lowering the raised threads and raising the even-numbered ones, the weft thread could be passed through in the opposite direction.

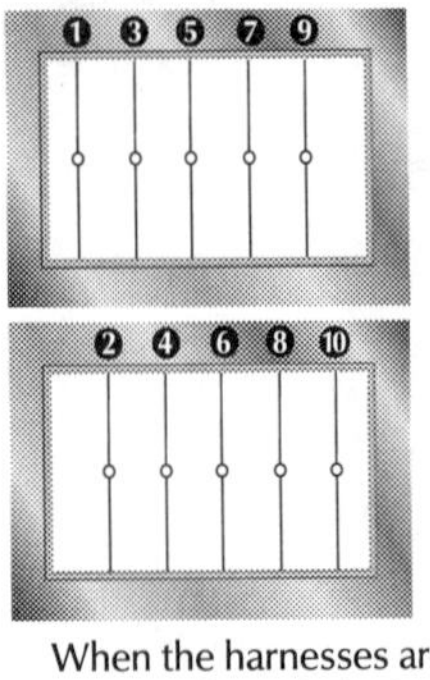

In a weaving loom, two frames (called harnesses) are placed between the two beams and perpendicular to them (see illustration on next column). Each harness contains a number of threads, equal to half the number of threads in the warp, stretched vertically and looped in the center. The warp threads are then drawn through the loops. The looped threads are called נִירִין, *heddles.* The loops are called בָּתֵּי נִירִין, *heddle-eyes.* [Heddles may also be made by tying a ring between two threads, as in our illustration.]

When the harnesses are in place, all odd-numbered warp threads are drawn through the heddle-eyes of one harness and between the heddles of the other, while all even-numbered warp threads are drawn between the heddles of the first harness and through the heddle-eyes of the second harness.

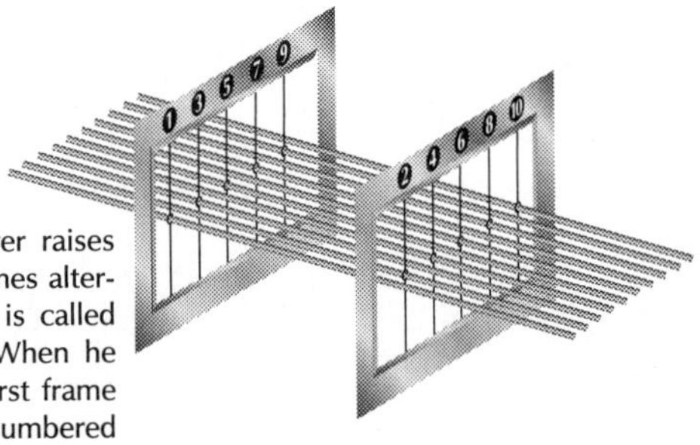

The weaver raises the two frames alternately (this is called shedding). When he raises the first frame all the odd-numbered warp threads are raised and a "shed" is formed between the two sets of warp threads. The weft (with its thread wrapped around a spindle) is passed through this shed from right to left (this is called picking). He then raises the even-numbered warp threads by lowering the first harness and raising the second one, and passes the weft thread through from left to right. This is the actual act of weaving.

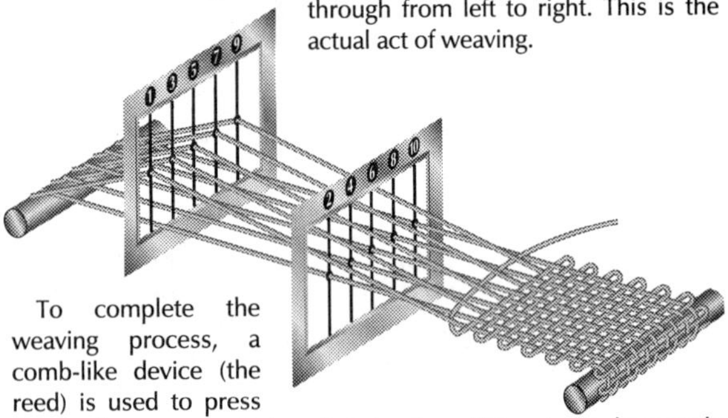

To complete the weaving process, a comb-like device (the reed) is used to press the newly woven weft threads into place. This act simultaneously assures that the warp threads remain both evenly spaced and parallel to one another. If the weft thread is too tight when it is pressed into place by the reed, it will not merge properly with the already woven cloth. To prevent this from happening, the weft thread is beaten with the pointed rod (כַּרְכַּר) in a few places to draw extra yarn into the shed. This action is called מְדַקְדֵּק, *beating,* according to *Rashi.* (Other Rishonim maintain that pressing the weft thread into place is called מְדַקְדֵּק.)

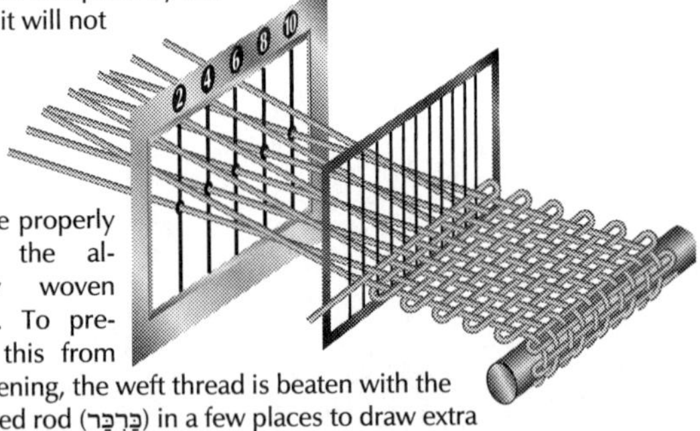

Thus, the weaving process comprises three primary labors: *mounting the warp* (מֵיסֵךְ), with its derivative labor, *lining with a rod* (שׁוֹבֵט); *setting up the heddles* (עוֹשֶׂה שְׁתֵּי בָּתֵּי נִירִין); the actual *weaving* (אוֹרֵג), with its derivative labor, *beating* (מְדַקְדֵּק).

For further details of the weaving process, see *Ma'aseh Oreg* by Dayan I. Gokovitzki and *Meleches Arigah* by Rabbi P. Bodner.

Glossary

abandoned corpse – a human corpse found with no one to attend to its burial. The Torah obligates the person who finds it to bury it and allows even a **nazir** and **Kohen Gadol** to do so.

Adar – twelfth month of the Hebrew calendar.

Adar Sheni – lit. the second **Adar.** When it is deemed necessary for a leap year to be designated, an extra month is added. This thirteenth month is placed between **Adar** and **Nissan** and is called *Adar Sheni.*

agav – see **kinyan agav.**

agency – the principle that an agent may act as a proxy of a principal and have his actions legally accepted on behalf of the principal.

Aggadah, aggadata – the homiletical teachings of the Sages and all non-halachic Rabbinic literature found in the Talmud.

akirah – the **melachah** of transferring involves the moving of an article from one domain to another. To be Biblically liable one must also perform *akirah,* the *lifting* of the article from its domain of origin and *hanachah,* the *setting down* of the article in its new domain.

akum – idolater.

Altar – the great *Altar*, which stands in the Courtyard of the **Beis HaMikdash.** Certain portions of every offering are burnt on the *Altar*. The blood of most offerings is applied to the walls of the *Altar*.

amah [pl. **amos**] – cubit; a linear measure equaling six **tefachim.** Opinions regarding its modern equivalent range between 18 and 22.9 inches.

am haaretz [pl. **amei haaretz**] – a common, ignorant person who, possibly, is not meticulous in his observance of **halachah.**

Amora [pl. **Amoraim**] – sage of the **Gemara;** cf. **Tanna.**

amud – one side of the **daf** in the **Gemara.**

aninus – the state of being an **onein.** Upon the death of one's seven closest relatives a person enters a state of mourning. The first stage of the mourning period is called *aninus.* This stage (during which the mourner is known as an *onein*) lasts until the end of the day on which the death occurred. When burial is delayed the Rabbis extend the *aninus* period until the end of that day.

Anshei Knesses HaGedolah – see **Men of the Great Assembly.**

aravos – willow branches. See **four species.**

arayos – see **ervah.**

areiv – guarantor.

arus [f. **arusah**] – one who is betrothed and thereby entered the **erusin** stage of marriage. See **erusin.**

asham [pl. **ashamos**] – guilt offering, an offering brought to atone for one of several specific sins; in addition, a part of certain purification offerings. It is one of the **kodshei kodashim.**

asheirah – a tree either designated for worship or under which an idol is placed.

asmachta – lit. reliance. (a) a conditional commitment made by a party who does not really expect to have to honor it; (b) a verse cited by the **Gemara** not as a Scriptural basis for the law but rather as an allusion to a Rabbinic law.

assembly – This event took place on the evening following the first day of Succos, in the year following the **shemittah** year. The entire nation would gather in one of the Temple Courtyards to hear the king read the Book of Deuteronomy.

Av – (a) fifth month of the Hebrew calendar. (b) l.c. [pl. avos] see **melachah.**

av beis din – chief of the court. This position was second in importance to the **Nasi** who served as head of the **Sanhedrin.**

av [pl. **avos**] **hatumah** – lit. father of **tumah.** See **tumah.**

avi avos hatumah – lit. father of fathers of **tumah.** See **tumah.**

avodah [pl. **avodos**] – the sacrificial service, or any facet of it. There are four critical *avodos* to the sacrificial service. They are **shechitah, kabbalah, holachah** and **zerikah.**

avodah zarah – idol worship, idolatry.

aylonis [pl. **aylonios**] – an adult woman who never developed the physical signs of female maturity. She is therefore assumed to be incapable of bearing children.

azharah – (a) Scriptural warning; the basic prohibition stated in the Torah, which serves to warn the potential sinner against incurring the punishment prescribed for a particular action; (b) term Gemara uses to refer to a negative commandment, the transgression of which is punished by *kares.*

baal keri [pl. **baalei keri**] – one who experienced a seminal emission. He is **tamei** (ritually impure) and must immerse himself in a **mikveh.**

bagrus – the time when a girl becomes a *bogeress* (a full adult), the final legal state of a girl's physical development. A girl automatically becomes a *bogeress* six months after she becomes a **naarah.**

bamah [pl. **bamos**] – lit. high place; altar. This refers to any altar other than the **Altar** of the **Tabernacle** or **Temple.** During certain brief periods of Jewish history, it was permitted to offer sacrifices on a *bamah*. There are two types of *bamah.* The *communal* (or: *major*) *bamah* was the altar of the public and was the only *bamah* on which communal offerings could be sacrificed. Private voluntary offerings could be brought even on a *private* (or *minor*) *bamah* which was an altar erected anywhere by an individual for private use.

Baraisa [pl. **Baraisos**] – the statements of **Tannaim** not included by **Rebbi** in the **Mishnah.** R' Chiya and R' Oshaya, the students of Rebbi, researched and reviewed the *Baraisa* and compiled an authoritative collection of them.

bechor – (a) firstborn male child; (b) a firstborn male kosher animal. Such an animal is born with sacrificial sanctity, and must be given to a **Kohen** who then offers it (if unblemished) as a *bechor* sacrifice in the **Temple** and eats its sacred meat. Unlike other sacrifices, the *bechor* is automatically sacred from birth even without designation.

bedek habayis – **Temple** Treasury.

bedi'avad – after the fact. See **lechatchilah.**

beheimah – domesticated species, livestock. In regard to various laws, the Torah distinguishes between *beheimah:* domestic species, e.g. cattle, sheep, goats; and, **chayah,** wild species, e.g. deer, antelope.

bein ha'arbayaim – lit. between the darkenings. It refers to the hours between the "darkening of the day" and the "darkening of the night." The darkening of the day starts at midday, when the shadows begin to lengthen. The darkening of the night is simply the beginning of the night, after sunset. Thus *bein ha'arbayim* connotes the afternoon.

bein hashemashos – the twilight period preceding night. The legal status of *bein hashemashos* as day or night is uncertain.

beis din – court; Rabbinical court comprised minimally of three members. Such a court is empowered to rule on civil matters. See also **Sanhedrin.**

beis hamidrash – a **Torah** study hall.

Beis HaMikdash – Holy **Temple** in Jerusalem. The **Temple** edifice comprised (a) the Antechamber or **Ulam;** (b) the **Holy** or **Heichal;** and (c) the **Holy of Holies.** See **Sanctuary.**

beis kor – 75,000 square **amos** – fifteen times the size of two **beis se'ah.**

beis se'ah – an area 50 **amos** by 50 *amos.*

bereirah – retroactive clarification. This principle allows for the assignment of a legal status to a person or object whose identity is as yet undetermined, but which will be retroactively clarified by a subsequent choice.

bikkurim – the first-ripening fruits of any of the seven species (wheat, barley, grapes, figs, pomegranates, olives, dates), with which the Torah praises Eretz Yisrael. They are brought to the **Temple** where certain rites are performed, and given to the **Kohanim.**

binyan av – one of the thirteen principles of Biblical hermeneutics. This is exegetical derivation based on a logical analogy between different areas of law. Whenever a commonality of law or essence is found in different areas of **Torah** law, an analogy is drawn between them, and the laws that apply to one can therefore be assumed to apply to the others as well.

Bircas HaMazon – the blessings recited after a meal.

Bircas Kohanim – see **Priestly Blessing.**

bitul (or **bitul b'rov**) – the principle of nullification in a majority. Under certain circumstances, a mixture of items of differing legal status assumes the status of its majority component.

bogeress – a girl who has attained the age of 12 years and is thereupon considered an adult in all respects. See **bagrus.**

bosis – An item that is a base for a **muktzeh** item and which becomes *muktzeh* itself.

Bris Milah – ritual circumcision.

Canaanite slave – a non-Jewish slave owned by a Jew. His term of servitude is for life. While owned by the Jew, he is obligated in all the **mitzvos** incumbent upon a Jewish woman. Upon being freed, he becomes a full-fledged Jew, with a status similar to that of a convert.

chagigah offering – festival offering. Every adult Jewish male is required to bring a *chagigah* offering on the first day of the festivals of **Pesach, Shavuos** and **Succos.** It is one of the **kodashim kalim**, specifically, a type of **shelamim** offering.

chalal [f: **chalalah**] – lit. desecrated. If a **Kohen** cohabits with any woman specifically forbidden to **Kohanim,** the child of that union is a *chalal* who does not possess the sanctity of a **Kohen.** The *chalal* enjoys neither the privileges of the **Kehunah** nor is subject to its restrictions.

chalifin – see **kinyan chalifin.**

chalitzah – see **yibum.**

challah – portion removed from a dough of the **five grains,** given to a **Kohen;** if *challah* is not taken, the dough is **tevel** and may not be eaten. The minimum amount of dough from which *challah* must be separated is the volume-equivalent of 43.2 eggs, which is one **issaron.** Nowadays the *challah* is removed and burned.

chametz – leavened products of the five species of grain. *Chametz* is forbidden on **Pesach.**

Chanukah – Festival of Lights. The holiday that commemorates the Maccabean victory over the Greeks. It begins on the 25th of **Kislev** and lasts for eight days.

chatas [pl. **chataos**] – sin offering; an offering generally brought in atonement for the inadvertent transgression of a prohibition punishable by **kares** when transgressed deliberately. A *chatas* is also brought as one of various purification offerings. It is one of the **kodshei kodashim.**

chatas cow – see **parah adumah.**

chatzeir [pl. **chatzeiros**] – courtyard(s).

chaver [pl. **chaverim**] – (a) one who observes the laws of ritual purity even regarding non-consecrated foodstuffs; (b) a Torah scholar, scrupulous in his observance of **mitzvos.** Regarding tithes, **tumah** and other matters, such as the necessity for **hasraah,** he is accorded a special status.

chayah – see **beheimah.**

chazakah – (a) legal presumption that conditions remain unchanged unless proven otherwise; (b) one of the methods of acquiring real estate; it consists of performing an act of improving the property, such as enclosing it with a fence or plowing it in preparation for planting; (c) "established rights"; uncontested usage of another's property establishes the right to such usage; since the owner registered no protest, acquiescence is assumed; (d) uncontested holding of real property for three years as a basis for claiming acquisition of title from the prior owner.

chazarah – returning to the **kirah** a pot of cooked food that had been left there before the Sabbath and was later removed.

cheilev – The Torah forbids certain fats of cattle, sheep and goats for human consumption. These are primarily the hind fats (suet) placed on the **Altar.** See **shuman.**

cherem – 1) a vow in which one uses the expression "*cherem*" to consecrate property, placing it under jurisdiction of the Temple, 2) land or property upon which a ban has been declared, forbidding its use to anyone, e.g. the city of Je-richo.

cheresh – lit. a deaf person; generally used for a deaf-mute who can neither hear nor speak. A *cheresh* is legally deemed mentally incompetent; his actions or commitments are not legally significant or binding.

Cheshvan – see **Marcheshvan.**

chilazon – an equatic creature from whose blood the blue *techeiles* dye was produced.

chilul Hashem – lit. profanation of God's Name. (a) Behavior which casts Jews in a negative light; (b) violation of a Torah prohibition done in the presence of ten male Jews.

Chol HaMoed – the Intermediate Days of the Festivals of **Pesach** and **Succos**; these enjoy a quasi-**Yom Tov** status.

chullin – lit. profane things; any substance that is not sanctified. See **kodesh.**

chupah – (a) the bridal canopy; (b) a procedure for effecting **nisuin,** the final stage of marriage.

closed mavoi – a dead-end alley enclosed on three sides and open to the public domain on the fourth side.

common characteristic – see **tzad hashaveh.**

Cutheans – a non-Jewish tribe brought by the Assyrians to settle the part of **Eretz Yisrael** left vacant by the exile of the Ten Tribes. Their subsequent conversion to Judaism was considered questionable and their observance of many laws was lax.

daf [pl. **dafim**] – folio (two sides) in the **Gemara.**

dayyo – lit. it is sufficient. Principle which limits the application of a **kal vachomer** argument, for it states: When a law is derived from case A to case B, its application to B cannot exceed its application to A.

death penalty – this refers to a court-imposed death penalty, in contrast to one imposed by Heaven.

demai – lit. what is this; produce of **Eretz Yisrael** that is obtained from an unlearned person. By Rabbinic enactment it must be tithed since a doubt exists as to whether its original owner tithed it. However, it is assumed that **terumah** was separated from the produce.

dinar – a coin. The silver content of the coin was equivalent to ninety-six grains of barley. It was worth 1/25 the value of a gold *dinar.*

donated offering – There is a difference between a נֶדֶר, *neder* (vowed offering) and a נְדָבָה, *nedavah* (donated offering). In the case of a *neder,* the vower declares הֲרֵי עָלַי קָרְבָּן, "It is hereby incumbent upon me to bring a sacrifice." He fulfills his vow by later designating a specific animal as the sacrifice and offering it. In the case of a *nedavah,* the vower declares הֲרֵי זוּ קָרְבָּן, "This [animal] is a sacrifice," designating from the very start the particular animal he wishes to bring as an offering. In the case of a *neder,* if the designated animal is lost or dies, the vower must bring another in its place, since he has not yet fulfilled his vow "to bring a sacrifice." In the case of a *nedavah,* however, if anything happens to the designated animal the vower need not replace it since his vow was only to bring "*this* animal."

double payment – a punitive fine. A person convicted of theft is required to return both the stolen object (or its monetary equivalent) and pay the owner a fine equal to its value. If he stole a sheep or goat and slaughtered or sold it, he pays four times the value of the animal. If he stole an ox and slaughtered or sold it, he pays five times its value.

Elohim – (a) a Name of God; (b) [l.c.] sometimes used to refer to a mortal power or the authority of an ordained judge.

Elul – sixth month of the Hebrew calendar.

emurin – the portions of an animal offering burnt on the **Altar.**

encumbered property – land owned by a debtor at the time he incurred a debt, but which he later sold or gave to a third party. Such land is encumbered by the debt; the creditor can retrieve it from the current owner to satisfy the debt, if the debtor defaults.

ephah [pl. **ephos**] – a measure of volume equal to three **se'ah.**

erech [pl. **arachin**] – a fixed valuation. The *erech* of a person is the amount fixed by the **Torah** for each of eight different groupings classified by age and gender. All individuals included in the same broad grouping have the identical *erech* valuation, regardless of their value on the slave market.

Eretz Yisrael – Land of Israel.

erusin – betrothal, the first stage of marriage. This is effected by the man giving the woman an object of value, in the presence of witnesses, to betroth her. At this point the couple is not yet permitted to have conjugal relations, but is nonetheless considered legally married in most respects and the woman requires a divorce before she can marry again; see **nisuin.**

eruv – popular contraction of **eruvei chatzeiros, eruvei tavshilin,** or **eruvei techumin.**

eruvei chatzeiros – a legal device which merges several separate ownerships **(reshus hayachid)** into a single joint ownership. Each resident family of a **chatzeir** contributes food to the *eruv,* which is then placed in one of the dwellings of the *chatzeir.* This procedure allows us to view all the houses opening into the courtyard as the property of a single consortium (composed of all the residents of the courtyard). This permits all the contributing residents of the **chatzeir** to carry items during the Sabbath from the houses into the *chatzeir* and from one house to another.

eruvei tavshilin – the prepared food set aside prior to a **Yom Tov** that falls on Friday to serve as token food for the Sabbath that follows. Once this token food has been set aside, the person is allowed to complete his preparations for Sabbath on **Yom Tov.** Such preparation is generally forbidden otherwise.

eruvei techumin – merging of boundaries; a legal device that allows a person to shift his Sabbath residence from which the 2,000-**amah techum** is measured. This is accomplished by placing a specific amount of food at the desired location before the start of the Sabbath. The place where the food has been placed is then viewed as his Sabbath residence, and his *techum*-limit is measured from there. This does not extend his **techum** Shabbos, but merely shifts the point from which it is measured.

ervah [pl. **arayos**] – (a) matters pertaining to sexual relationships forbidden under penalty of **kares** or death, as enumerated in *Leviticus* ch. 18; (b) a woman forbidden to a man under pain of one of these penalties.

esrog – see **four species.**

fines – punitive payments that do not bear a strict relation to actual damages.

five grains – wheat, barley, oats, spelt and rye.

forbidden labors of the Sabbath – see **avos melachah.**

forty lashes – see **malkus.**

Four Species – The four articles of plant-life we are commanded to take and hold in our hands on the Festival of Succos. These consist of: (a) **aravos** – willow branches; (b) **esrog** – citron; (c) **hadasim** – myrtle branches; (d) **lulav** – branch of the date palm tree.

Gaon [pl. **Geonim**] – (a) title accorded the heads of the academies in Sura and Pumbedisa, the two Babylonian seats of Jewish learning, from the late 6th to mid-11th centuries C.E. They served as the link in the chain of Torah tradition that joined the **Amoraim** to the **Rishonim;** (b) subsequently used to describe any brilliant Torah scholar.

Gemara – portion of the Talmud which discusses the **Mishnah;** also, loosely, a synonym for the Talmud as a whole.

gematria – the numeric valuation of the Hebrew alphabet.

get [pl. **gittin**] – bill of divorce; the document that when it is placed in the wife's possession, effects the dissolution of a marriage.

gezeirah shavah – one of the thirteen principles of Biblical hermeneutics. If a similar word or phrase occurs in two otherwise unrelated passages in the **Torah,** the principle of *gezeirah shavah* teaches that these passages are linked to one another, and the laws of one passage are applied to the other. Only those words which are designated by the **Oral Sinaitic Law** for this purpose may serve as a basis for a *gezeirah shavah.*

gifts to the poor – These include **leket, shich'chah, pe'ah, peret, oleilos** and **maaser ani.**

Golden Altar – see **Inner Altar.**

Great Court – see **Sanhedrin.**

hachnasah – transferring an object from a public domain to a private domain.

hadasim – see **four species.**

hafarah – revocation of a woman's vow by her husband on the grounds that her vow impinges on their marital relationship or that it causes her deprivation.

hagbahah – lifting. One of the methods of acquisition used for movable objects.

halachah [pl. **halachos**] – (a) a **Torah** law; (b) [u.c.] the body of Torah law; (c) in cases of dispute, the position accepted as definitive by the later authorities and followed in practice; (d) a **Halachah LeMoshe MiSinai.**

Halachah LeMoshe MiSinai – laws taught orally to Moses at Sinai, which cannot be derived from the Written Torah.

half-shekel – While the Temple stood, every Jew was required to donate a half-*shekel* annually to fund the purchase of the various communal offerings (including among others, the daily **tamid** offerings and the holiday **mussaf** offerings).

hanachah – the *setting down* of a transferred article in its new domain; see **akirah.**

hatmanah – lit. hiding. Wrapping a pot of hot food in a material that insulates it, as a way of preserving its heat for the Sabbath.

Hashem – lit. the Name; a designation used to refer to God without pronouncing His Ineffable Name.

hasraah – warning. One does not incur the death penalty or lashes unless he was warned, immediately prior to commission, of the forbidden nature of the crime and the punishment to which he would be liable.

hatarah – annulment of a vow by an expert sage or a group of three competent laymen.

Havdalah – lit. distinction. The blessing recited at the conclusion of the Sabbath.

hazamah – the process by which witnesses are proven false by testimony that places them elsewhere at the time of the alleged incident. Such witnesses are punished with the consequences their testimony would have inflicted upon their intended victim.

Hebrew maidservant – a Jewish girl between the age of six and twelve sold by her father into servitude.

Hebrew servant – a Jewish man who is sold as an indentured servant, generally for a six-year period. Either he is sold by the court because he was convicted of stealing and lacks the funds to make restitution, or he sells himself for reasons of poverty.

hechsher l'tumah – rendering a food susceptible to **tumah** contamination by contact with one of seven liquids – water, dew, milk, bee honey, oil, wine or blood.

hefker beis din hefker – principle which establishes the power of Rabbinic courts to declare property ownerless.

hefker – ownerless.

hefker beis din hefker – principle which establishes the power of Rabbinic courts to declare property ownerless.

Heichal – See **Beis HaMikdash.**

hekdesh – (a) items consecrated to the **Temple** treasury or as offerings. *Hekdesh* can have two levels of sanctity: **monetary sanctity** and **physical sanctity.** Property owned by the Temple treasury is said to have monetary sanctity. Such property can be redeemed or can be sold by the *hekdesh* treasurers, and the proceeds of the redemption or sale become *hekdesh* in its place. Consecrated items that are fit for the Temple service (e.g. unblemished animals or sacred vessels) are deemed to have physical sanctity; (b) the state of consecration; (c) the **Temple** treasury.

hekeish – an exegetical derivation based on a connection that Scripture makes (often through juxtaposition) between different areas of law. By making this connection, Scripture teaches that the laws that apply to one area can be applied to the other area as well.

hesseis oath – lit. oath of incitement. Oath imposed by the court on one who denies the entire monetary claim made against him. This oath was required by the post-Mishnaic Rabbis on the assumption that a plaintiff would not make a totally frivolous claim.

hin – liquid measure equal to twelve **lugin.**

holachah – one of the four essential blood **avodos.** It involves conveying the blood of the offering to the **Altar.**

Holy – anterior chamber of the **Temple** edifice (**Heichal**) containing the **Shulchan, Inner Altar** and **Menorah.**

Holy Ark – the Ark holding the Tablets of the Ten Commandments and the Torah Scroll written by Moses. It stood in the **Holy of Holies.**

Holy of Holies – interior chamber of the **Temple** edifice (**Heichal**). During most of the First Temple era, it contained the **Holy Ark;** later it was empty of any utensil. Even the **Kohen Gadol** is prohibited from entering there except on **Yom Kippur.**

hotza'ah – transferring an object from a private domain to a public domain.

Inner Altar – the gold-plated Altar which stood in the **Sanctuary.** It was used for the daily incense service and for the blood applications of inner **chataos.**

Israelites Courtyard – an area in the Temple Courtyard, extending eleven **amos** from the eastern Courtyard wall into the Courtyard, and abutted on its west side by the **Kohanim's Courtyard.** It reached across the entire width of the Courtyard from north to south.

issaron – a dry measure equal to one-tenth of an **ephah** or approximately (depending on the conversion factor) as little as eleven or as much as twenty-one cups.

issur – prohibition.

ir hanidachas – a city in Eretz Yisrael in which the majority of the population worshiped idols. Subject to certain conditions, the city is destroyed along with all its property and its guilty inhabitants are beheaded.

Iyar – second month of the Hebrew calendar.

Jubilee – see **Yovel.**

kabbalah – (a) term used throughout the Talmud to refer to the books of the *Prophets.* It derives from the Aramaic root – to complain or cry out. It thus refers primarily to the admonitory passages of these books; (b) receiving in a **kli shareis** the blood of a sacrificial animal that is slaughtered; one of the four blood **avodos.**

kal vachomer – lit. light and heavy, or lenient and stringent; an *a fortiori* argument. One of the thirteen principles of Biblical hermeneutics. It involves the following reasoning: If a particular stringency applies in a usually lenient case, it must certainly apply in a more serious case; the converse of this argument is also a *kal vachomer.*

kares – excision; Divinely imposed premature death decreed by the **Torah** for certain classes of transgression.

karmelis – any area at least four **tefachim** square which cannot be classified as either a **reshus harabim,** public domain (because it is not set aside for public use) or a **reshus hayachid,** *private domain* (because it does not have the required partitions), e.g. a field, empty lot, or an elevation of at least three **tefachim** above the ground level of a public domain.

karpaf – Mishnaic term for a large open area enclosed by a fence or wall. As a properly enclosed area, a *karpaf* is a **reshus hayachid** in every respect as long it does not exceed two **beis se'ah** (an area 50 *amos* x 100 *amos,* or 5,000 square *amos.* A *karpaf* larger then this, however, is subject to a special rule:

Carrying in it is permitted only if the *karpaf* was enclosed for residential use. If it was not then carrying in it is forbidden as in a **karmelis.**

kav [pl. **kabim**] – a measure equal to four **lugin.**

kebeitzah – an egg's volume.

Kehunah – priesthood; the state of being a **Kohen.**

keifel – see **double payment.**

kelutah – contained. Although an object thrown across a public domain does not *physically* come to rest in that domain, it does so *legally,* by way of the principle that an object "contained" in the airspace of a domain is viewed as if it had come to rest there.

kemitzah – the first of four essential services of a **minchah** offering. The **Kohen** closes the middle three fingers of his right hand over his palm and scoops out flour from the *minchah* to form the **kometz** that is burned on the **Altar.**

kessef – (a) money; (b) Tyrian currency which is comprised solely of pure silver coins.

kesubah – (a) marriage contract; the legal commitments of a husband to his wife upon their marriage, the foremost feature of which is the payment awarded her in the event of their divorce or his death; (b) document in which this agreement is recorded.

Kesuvim – Hagiographa – Holy Writings. It consists of eleven volumes: *Psalms, Proverbs, Job, Song of Songs, Ruth, Lamentations, Ecclesiastes, Esther, Daniel, Ezra-Nehemiah, Chronicles.*

kezayis – the volume of an olive; minimum amount of food whose consumption is considered "eating."

kiddush – (a) the benediction recited over wine before the evening and morning meals on the **Sabbath** and **Yom Tov**; (b) sanctification of **mei chatas.**

kiddushin [betrothal] – Jewish marriage consists of two stages: **erusin** and **nisuin.** *Kiddushin* is the procedure which establishes the first stage of marriage [*erusin*].

kilayim – various forbidden mixtures, including: **shaatnez** (cloth made from a blend of wool and linen); cross-breeding of animals; cross-breeding (or side-by-side planting) of certain food crops; working with different species of animals yoked together; and mixtures of the vineyard.

kilei hakerem – forbidden mixtures of the vineyard; see **kilayim.**

kinyan [pl. **kinyanim**] – formal act of acquisition; an action that causes an agreement or exchange to be legally binding.

kinyan agav – lit. acquisition by dint of; the term for the acquisition of movable property by means of the acquisition of land. The **kinyan** used for the land serves for the movable property.

kinyan chalifin – lit. acquisition by exchange. (a) Even exchange: an exchange of two items of comparable value, in which each item serves as payment for the other. The acquisition of any one of the items automatically effects the acquisition of the other. (b) Uneven exchange: An item of relatively negligible value is given in order to effect the acquisition of the other item. A kerchief or the like is traditionally used.

kinyan chatzeir – the acquisition of movable property by virtue of it being in the premises of the person acquiring it.

kinyan chazakah – see **chazakah (b).**

kinyan sudar – see **kinyan chalifin (b).**

kirah – a rectangular stove that is open on top and is large enough to accommodate two pots. The pots may be placed inside the *kirah,* either directly on the coals or suspended above them, or on the rim or cover of the *kirah.*

Kislev – ninth month of the Hebrew calendar.

kli shareis [pl. **klei shareis**] – service vessel(s); a vessel sanctified for use in the sacrificial service.

kodashim kalim – offerings of lesser holiness (one of the two classifications of sacrificial offerings). They may be eaten anywhere in Jerusalem by any **tahor** person. They include the **todah,** regular **shelamim, bechor, nazir's ram, maaser** and **pesach offerings.** This category of offerings is not subject to the stringencies applied to **kodshei kodashim.**

kodesh – (a) any consecrated object; (b) the anterior chamber of the **Temple** – the **Holy;** (c) portions of sacrificial offerings.

kodshei kodashim – most-holy offerings (one of the two classifications of sacrificial offerings). They may be eaten only in the Temple courtyard and only by male **Kohanim.** They include the **olah** (which may not be eaten at all), **chatas, asham** and communal **shelamim.** These are subject to greater stringencies than **kodashim kalim.**

Kohanim's Courtyard – eleven-**amah**-wide area in the Courtyard of the **Beis HaMikdash** abutting the **Israelites Courtyard** on its east side, and the **Altar** on its west side. It reached across the entire width of the Courtyard from north to south.

Kohen [pl. **Kohanim**] – member of the priestly family descended in the male line from Aaron. The Kohen is accorded the special priestly duties and privileges associated with the **Temple** service and is bound by special laws of sanctity.

Kohen Gadol – High Priest.

kol d'alim g'var – lit. let whoever is stronger prevail. In certain cases where neither litigant advances conclusive proof to support his claim the court withdraws and allows the stronger party to take possession of the contested property.

kometz [pl. **kematziri**] – see **kemitzah.**

kor – large dry measure; a measure of volume consisting of thirty **se'ah.**

korah – a crossbeam, at least one **tefach** wide, reaching across a **mavoi** to serve as a rudimentary partition or a reminder of the *mavoi's* halachic status.

korban – a sacrificial offering brought in the **Beis HaMikdash.**

kri u'ksiv – a word in Scripture written one way but read differently by special directive to Moses at Sinai.

kupach – a cubical stove which accomodates only one pot. It retains more heat than a **kirah.**

lashes – see **malkus** and **makkas mardus.**

lavud – principle which states that whatever is within three **tefachim** of a surface is viewed as an extension of that surface; by the same token, a gap of less than three *tefachim* is legally viewed as closed.

leaning – see **semichah.**

lechatchilah – (a) before the fact; (b) performance of a **mitzvah** or procedure in the proper manner.

lechi – (a) a sidepost, at least ten **tefachim** high, placed at the side of a **mavoi** entrance to serve as a rudimentary partition or reminder of the *mavoi's* halachic status; (b) the sidepost of a **tzuras hapesach.**

leket – gleanings; one of the various portions of the harvest which the Torah grants to the poor. *Leket* refers to one or two stalks of grain that fall from the reaper when he gathers the harvest. See **shich'chah, pe'ah, peret** and **oleilos.**

lesech – one half of a **kor.**

Levi [pl. **Leviim**] – male descendant of the tribe of *Levi* in the male line, who is sanctified for auxiliary services in the **Beis HaMikdash.** The *Leviim* were the recipients of **maaser rishon.**

libation – see **nesachim.**

litra – (a) a liquid measure equal to the volume of six eggs; (b) a unit of weight.

log [pl. **lugin**] – a liquid measure equal to the volume of six eggs, between 16 and 21 ounces in contemporary measure.

lulav – see **four species.**

ma'ah [pl. **maos**] – the smallest silver unit in Talmudic coinage. Thirty-two copper **perutos** equal one *ma'ah* and six *ma'ahs* equal a silver **dinar.**

Maariv – the evening prayer service.

maaser [pl. **maasros**] – tithe. It is a Biblical obligation to give two tithes, each known as *maaser,* from the produce of the Land of Israel. The first tithe (**maaser rishon**) is given to a **Levi.** The second tithe (**maaser sheni**) is taken to Jerusalem and eaten there or else is redeemed with coins which are then taken to Jerusalem for the purchase of food to be eaten there. In the third and sixth years of the seven year **shemittah** cycle, the *maaser sheni* obligation is replaced with **maaser ani,** the tithe for the poor.

maaser ani – see **maaser.**

maaser of animals – see **maaser beheimah.**

maaser beheimah – the animal tithe. The newborn kosher animals born to one's herds and flocks are gathered into a pen and made to pass through an opening one at a time. Every tenth animal is designated as **maaser.** It is brought as an offering in the Temple and is eaten by the owner.

maaser rishon – see **maaser.**

maaser sheni – see **maaser.**

mah matzinu – lit. just as we find; a **binyan av** from one verse. Just as one particular law possesses aspect A and aspect B, so any other law that possesses aspect A should also possess aspect B.

makkas mardus – lashes for rebelliousness. This is the term used for lashes incurred by Rabbinic – rather than Biblical – law.

malkus – the thirty-nine lashes (forty minus one) imposed by the court for violations of Biblical prohibitions, where a more severe punishment is not indicated.

mamzer [pl. **mamzerim**] [f. **mamzeress**] – (a) offspring of most illicit relationships punishable by **kares** or capital punishment; (b) offspring of a *mamzer* or *mamzeress.*

mamzerus – state of being a **mamzer.**

maneh – (a) equivalent to 100 **zuz;** (b) a measure of weight, equal to 17 ounces.

Marcheshvan – eighth month of the Hebrew calendar

matanos [or matnos kehunah] – lit. gifts. The Torah commands that we give the right foreleg, jaws and maw of an ox, sheep or goat that are slaughtered (for non-sacrificial purposes) to the **Kohen.** These are referred to as the "gifts."

matzah – unleavened bread; any loaf made from dough that has not been allowed to ferment or rise. One is Biblically obligated to eat *matzah* on the night of the 15th of Nissan.

mavoi – alley; specifically an alley into which **chatzeiros** (courtyards) open. See **shitufei mevo'os.**

mayim chayim – living water. Springwater generally has the status of *mayim chayim.* It is so designated because it issues out of the ground with a natural force which makes it "alive" and moving. It is fit to be used for three purposes for which the Torah specifies *mayim chayim*: (a) the immersion of **zavim,** (b) the sprinkling for **metzoraim,** (c) to consecrate therefrom **mei chatas.**

mayim sheuvin – drawn water; water that flows out of a vessel is designated as *sheuvin* and is unfit for use to constitute the forty **se'ah** of a **mikveh.**

mazal – fortune.

mechussar kapparah [pl. **mechussar kippurim**] – lit. lacking atonement. The status accorded to a **tevul yom** in the interim between sunset of the day of his immersion and the time he brings his offerings. During that interval, he retains a vestige of his earlier **tumah** and is thus forbidden to enter the Temple Courtyard or partake of the offerings.

mei chatas – springwater consecrated by the addition of ashes of a **parah adumah.** This was used to purify individuals or objects of **tumas meis.**

me'ilah – unlawfully benefiting from **Temple** property or removing such property from the Temple ownership. As a penalty one must pay the value of the misappropriated item plus an additional one-fifth of the value. He must also bring an **asham** offering.

meis mitzvah – see **abandoned corpse.**

mekom petur – exempt area; an area within – but distinct from – a public domain, which lacks the dimensions necessary to qualify as a **karmelis** (its width or length is less than four **tefachim**). One may carry from the exempt area into either a **reshus hayachid** or a **reshus harabim** or the reverse. Biblically a *karmelis* is a *mekom petur.*

melachah [pl. **melachos**] – labor; specifically, one of the thirty-nine labor categories whose performance is forbidden by the Torah on the Sabbath and **Yom Tov.** These prohibited categories are known as *avos melachah.* Activities whose prohibition is derived from one of these thirty-nine categories are known as *tolados* (s. *toladah*) – secondary labor.

melikah – the unique manner in which bird offerings were slaughtered. *Melikah* differs from **shechitah** in two respects: (a) The cut is made with the **Kohen's** thumbnail rather than with a knife. (b) The neck is cut from the back rather than from the throat. Only birds for sacrificial purposes may be slaughtered by *melikah;* all others require *shechitah.* See **shechitah.**

melog – a married woman's property in which she retains ownership of the property itself, but her husband enjoys the right of usufruct, i.e. he owns the yield of that property.

menachos – see **minchah.**

Men of the Great Assembly – a group of 120 sages active at the end of the Babylonian exile and during the early years of the Second Temple. They were responsible for the formulation of our prayers and many other enactments.

Menorah – the seven-branched gold candelabrum which stood in the **Holy.**

meshichah – pulling, or otherwise causing an object to move; one of the methods of acquisition used for movable property.

mesirah – handing over; transferring the animal to a buyer by handing him its reins or mane; a means of acquisition used for articles too heavy to be acquired via **meshichah** or **hagbahah.**

metzora – A *metzora* is a person who has contracted **tzaraas** (erroneously described as leprosy), an affliction mentioned in *Leviticus* (Chs. 13,14). *Tzaraas* manifests itself (on people) as white or light-colored spots on the body.

mezuzah [pl. **mezuzos**] – a small scroll, containing the passages of *Deuteronomy* 6:4-9 and 11:13-21, that is affixed to the right doorpost.

midras – If someone who is **tamei** as a result of a bodily emission (e.g. a **zav, zavah, niddah,** woman who has given birth) sit or leans on a bed, couch, or chair, it acquires the same level of **tumah** as the person from whom the *tumah* emanates (i.e. **av hatumah**). This form of *tumah* transmission is called *midras.*

midras tumah – see **midras.**

migo – lit. since; a rule of procedure. If one makes a claim that on its own merits the court would reject, it nonetheless will be accepted "since" had he wished to tell an untruth he would have chosen a claim that certainly is acceptable to the court.

mikveh – ritualarium; a body of standing water containing at least forty **se'ah.** It is used to purify (by immersion) people and utensils of their **tumah**-contamination. A *mikveh* consists of waters naturally collected, without direct human intervention. Water drawn in a vessel is not valid for a *mikveh.*

mil – 2,000 **amos.** A measure of distance between 3,000 and 4,000 feet.

minchah – (a) [cap.] the afternoon prayer service; (b) [pl.**menachos**] a flour offering, generally consisting of fine wheat flour, oil and frankincense, part of which is burnt on the **Altar.** See **kemitzah.**

minyan – quorum of ten adult Jewish males necessary for the communal prayer service and other matters.

Mishkan – predecessor of the **Temple.** See **Tabernacle.**

mishmar [pl. **mishmaros**] – lit. watch; one of the twenty-four watches of **Kohanim** and **Leviim** who served in the Temple for a week at a time on a rotating basis. These watches were subdivided into family groups each of which served on one day of the week.

Mishnah [pl. **Mishnahs**] – (a) the organized teachings of the **Tannaim** compiled by **R' Yehudah HaNasi;** (b) a paragraph of that work.

mitzvah [pl. **mitzvos**] – A **Torah** command whether of Biblical or Rabbinic origin.

mi'un – By Rabbinic enactment, an underaged orphan girl may be given in marriage by her mother or brothers. She may annul the marriage anytime before reaching majority by declaring, before a **beis din** of three judges, her unwillingness to continue in the marriage. This declaration and process is called *mi'un.*

mixtures of the vineyard – see **kilayim.**

modeh bemiktzas – see **oath of modeh bemiktzas.**

monetary law – law dealing with financial matters rather than matters of ritual prohibition.

monetary sanctity – see **hekdesh.**

movables, movable property – property that is transportable; in contrast to real estate.

muad – lit. warned one. A bull that gores three times and whose owner was duly warned after each incident to take precautions is considered a *muad* bull. The owner must pay full damage for the fourth and all subsequent incidents. See **tam.**

muchzak – one who has physical possession of an object and who is therefore assumed to be in legal possession of it.

muktzeh – lit. set aside. (a) a class of objects which, in the normal course of events, do not stand to be used on the Sabbath or **Yom Tov.** The Rabbis prohibited moving such objects on the Sabbath or Yom Tov; (b) an animal set aside to be sacrificed for idolatry.

mum [pl. mumim] – physical defects that render a **Kohen** or sacrifice unfit.

mussaf – (a) additional sacrifices offered on the Sabbath, **Rosh Chodesh,** or **Yom Tov;** (b) [cap] the prayer service which is recited in lieu of these sacrifices.

naarah – a girl at least 12 years old who has sprouted a minimum of two pubic hairs. This marks her coming of age to be considered an adult. She is deemed a *na'arah* for six months; after that she becomes a **bogeres.**

naarus – the state of being a **naarah.**

Nasi [pl. **Nesiim**] – the Prince. He serves as the head of the **Sanhedrin** and de facto as the spiritual leader of the people.

nazir [f. **nezirah**] – a person who takes the vow of **nezirus,** which prohibits him to drink wine, eat grapes, cut his hair or contaminate himself with the **tumah** of a corpse.

nedavah – see **donated offering.**

neder – a vow which renders objects, in contradistinction to actions, prohibited. There are two basic categories of vows; (a) restrictive vows; (b) vows to donate to **hekdesh.** See **hekdesh,** see also **donated offering.**

negaim – spots that appear on the skin of a **metzora.**

nesachim – a libation, generally of wine, which is poured upon the **Altar.** It accompanies certain offerings; and can also be donated separately as well.

nesin [f. **nesinah;** pl. **nesinim**] – descendant of the Gibeonites, who deceptively concluded a peace treaty with Joshua (*Joshua* 9:3-27) and converted to Judaism.

neveilah [pl. **neveilos**] – the carcass of an animal that was not slaughtered according to procedure prescribed by the Torah. A *neveilah* may not be eaten. It is an **av hatumah.**

Neviim – Prophets; it consists of the following books: *Joshua, Judges, Samuel, Kings, Jeremiah, Ezekiel, Isaiah,* **Twelve Prophets.**

nezirus – the state of being a **nazir.**

niddah – a woman who has menstruated but has not yet completed her purification process, which concludes with immersion in a **mikveh.**

nirtza – see **retziah.**

Nissan – first month of the Hebrew calendar.

nisuin – second stage of marriage. It is effected by a procedure called **chuppah.** See **kiddushin.**

Noahide laws – the seven commandments given to Noah and his sons, which are binding upon all gentiles. These laws include the obligation to have a body of civil law, and the prohibitions against idolatry, immorality, bloodshed, blasphemy, stealing and robbing, and eating limbs from a live animal.

nolad – lit. newborn. This is a category of **muktzeh.** It refers to objects that came into their present state of being (they previously did not exist or were not usable) on Sabbath or Yom Tov. Since their very existence was unanticipated before Sabbath or Yom Tov, they are *muktzeh.*

nossar – part of a **korban** left over after the time to eat it has passed.

olah [pl. **olos**] – burnt or elevation offering; an offering which is consumed in its entirety by the **Altar** fire. It is one of the **kodshei kodashim.**

omer – an obligatory **minchah** offering brought on the sixteenth of **Nissan.** It was forbidden to eat from the new grain crop (**chadash**) before this offering was brought.

onaah – price fraud.

onein [f. **onenes** – pl. **onenim**] – see **aninus.**

Oral Sinaitic Law – see **Halachah LeMoshe MiSinai.**

orlah – lit. sealed; fruit that grows on a tree during the first three years after it has been planted (or transplanted). The Torah prohibits any benefit from such fruit.

Outer Altar – the **Altar** that stood the Courtyard of the **Beis HaMikdash,** to which the blood of most offerings is applied, and on which the offerings are burned.

paid custodian – a **shomer** who receives remuneration for his services. He is obligated to make restitution even in the event of theft or loss; however he is exempt in the cave of loss due to an unavoidable mishap.

parah adumah – lit. red cow. The ashes of the *parah adumah* are mixed with spring water. The resulting mixture is known as **mei chatas** and is used in the purification process of people or objects who have contracted **tumah** from a human corpse.

Paroches – curtain: specifically, the curtain that divided the **Holy** from the **Holy of Holies.**

parsah [pl. **parsaos**] – measure of length equal to eight thousand **amos.**

pasul – lit. invalid. (a) any *tamei* object that cannot convey its **tumah;** (b) something invalid.

peace offering – see **shelamim.**

pe'ah – the portion of the crop, generally the corner of the field, that must be left unreaped as a gift to the poor.

peret – individual grapes which fell during harvesting. The Torah grants these to the poor. See **shichchah, leket, pe'ah, oleilos.**

perutah [pl. **perutos**] – smallest coin used in Talmudic times. In most cases its value is the minimum that is legally significant.

Pesach – Passover. The **Yom Tov** that celebrates the Exodus of the Jewish nation from Egypt.

pesach offering – sacrifice offered on the afternoon of the fourteenth day of **Nissan** and eaten after nightfall. It is one of the **kodashim kalim.**

Pesach Sheni – lit. Second **Pesach.** (a) the fourteenth of **Iyar.** This day fell one month after the **Yom Tov** of Pesach. Any individual who is **tamei** at the time designated for the **pesach offering** must wait till *Pesach Sheni* to bring his offering; (b) a *pesach* offering brought on the fourteenth of Iyar.

peter chamor – A firstborn male donkey, which must either be redeemed for a kid or lamb (which is given to a **Kohen**) or else must be decapitated.

physical sanctity – see **hekdesh.**

piggul – lit. rejected; an offering rendered invalid by means of an improper intent by the one performing one of the four essential **avodos** to eat of it or place it on the **Altar** after its allotted time. The intention must have been present during one of the four blood **avodos.** Consumption of *piggul* is punishable by **kares.**

pikadon – an object deposited with a custodian for safekeeping.

pikuach nefesh – lit. saving a life; a life-threatening situation. All prohibitions (except for murder, immorality and idolatry) are waived, if necessary, in such situations.

pilgrimage festival – the title for the holidays of **Pesach, Shavuos** and **Succos,** when all Jewish males were obligated to appear at the **Beis HaMikdash** in Jerusalem.

plag haminchah – one and a quarter hours before night.

positive commandment – a Torah commandment expressed as a requirement *to do.*

poskim – authoritative decisors of Torah law.

Priestly Blessing – the blessing the **Kohanim** are obligated to confer upon the congregation. It consists of the verses designated for this purpose by the Torah (*Numbers* 6:24-26). It is recited aloud by the **Kohanim**, toward the conclusion of the **Shemoneh Esrei.**

prohibition – a negative commandment, which the Torah expresses as a command *not to do.*

prohibitory law – refers to the category of Torah law which deals with questions of permissible or forbidden status, as opposed to questions of **monetary law.**

Prophets – see **Neviim.**

pundyon – a coin.

purification waters – see **mei chatas.**

rasha – (a) a wicked person; (b) a person disqualified from serving as a witness by his commission of certain transgressions.

R' – Rabbi; specifically a **Tanna,** or **Amora** of **Eretz Yisrael.**

Rebbi – R' Yehudah HaNasi; the redactor of the **Mishnah.**

red cow – see **parah adumah.**

regel – any of the three pilgrimage festivals – **Pesach, Shavuos** and **Succos.**

Reish Gelusa – Exilarch, head of the Babylonian Jewish community. Parallels the **Nasi** in **Eretz Yisrael.**

reshus harabim – lit. public domain; any unroofed, commonly used street, public area or highway at least sixteen **amos** wide and open at both ends. According to some, it must be used by at least 600,000 people.

reshus hayachid – lit. private domain; any area measuring at least four **tefachim** by four *tefachim* and enclosed by partitions at least ten *tefachim* high. According to most opinions, it needs to be enclosed only on three sides to qualify as a *reshus hayachid*. Private ownership is not a prerequisite.

resident alien – see **ger toshav.**

retziah – the process a Hebrew servant undergoes if he wishes to remain under his master after his period of servitude has ended. His right ear is placed against the doorpost and pierced with an awl. A servant who undergoes this process is known as a **nirtza** and is required to serve until his master dies or until the onset of the **Yovel** year.

revai – fruit produced by a tree in its fourth year. This is consecrated in the same manner as **maaser sheni** and must be eaten in Jerusalem or be redeemed with money which is spent in Jerusalem on food to be eaten there. See **orlah.**

revi'i l'tumah – see **tumah.**

revi'is – a quarter of a **log.**

ribbis – a Talmudic term for interest.

Rishon [pl. **Rishonim**] – a **Torah** authority of the period following the **Geonim** (approx. 1000-1500 C.E.).

rishon l'tumah – first degree of acquired **tumah.** See **tumah.**

Rosh Chodesh – (a) festival celebrating the new month; (b) the first of the month.

Rosh Hashanah – the **Yom Tov** that celebrates the new year. It falls on the first and second days of **Tishrei.**

rov – majority. A principle used in halachah to determine the origin or status of a particular object. An object of undetermined origin or status is assumed to partake of the same origin or status do that of the majority. See also **bitul b'rov.**

rova – a quarter-**kav** (one twenty-fourth of a **se'ah**).

Sabbath residence – (a) one's halachic place of dwelling (for the Sabbath); (b) wherever one happens to be at the beginning of the Sabbath i.e. an area of four **amos** if one is in a completely open space, or the building or city in which he is located.

Sadducees – heretical sect active during the Second **Temple** era named after Tzaddok, a disciple of Antigonas of Socho. They denied the Divine origin of the **Oral Law** and refused to accept the Sages' interpretation of the **Torah.**

Sages – (a) the collective body of Torah authorities in the Mishnaic era; (b) the anonymous majority opinion in a **Mishnah** or **Baraisa;** (c) [l.c.] Torah scholar and authority.

Sanctuary – a term applied to the Temple building that housed the **Holy** and the **Holy of Holies.**

Sanhedrin – (a) the High Court of Israel; the Supreme Court consisting of seventy-one judges whose decisions on questions of Torah law are definitive and binding on all courts; (b) [l.c.] a court of twenty-three judges authorized to adjudicate capital and corporal cases.

saris – (a) a male who is incapable of maturing sexually; (b) a castrated male.

se'ah – a Mishnaic measure of volume; six **kav.**

Seder [pl. **Sedarim**] – lit. order. (a) The Mishnah is divided into six *sedarim*: *Zeraim* (Plants), *Moed* (Festivals), *Nashim* (Women), *Nezikim* (Damages), *Kodashim* (Sacred Things) and *Taharos* (Ritual Purities); (b) [l.c.] ritual festive meal on **Pesach.**

sekilah – lit. stoning; one of the four forms of death penalty imposed by the court.

sela [pl. **selaim**] – a silver coin having the weight of 384 barleycorns. This is the equivalent of four **dinars.**

semichah – (a) Rabbinical ordination empowering one to serve as a judge. This ordination stretches back in an unbroken chain to Moses. (b) A rite performed with almost all personal sacrificial offerings. The owner of the offering places both his hands on the top of the animal's head and presses down with all his might. In the case of a **chatas,** or an **asham,** he makes his confession during *semichah*. In the case of a **shelamim** or **todah** offering, he praises and thanks God.

semuchin [pl. **semuchim**] – Scriptural juxtaposition. This principle states that two consecutive verses or passages may be compared for purposes of inferring law from one to the other. It is one of the rules of exegesis employed by the Sages.

seven species – see **bikkurim.**

Seventeenth of Tammuz – a fast day. Among the tragedies that occurred on this day were: (a) Moses descended from Mount Sinai and smashed the Tablets of the Ten Commandments when he saw the people worshiping the Golden Calf. (b) Jerusalem's walls were breached by the invading Roman army three weeks before the final destruction of the Second Temple (on **Tishah B'Av**).

shaos zemaniyos – seasonal or variable hours. According to this reckoning the day (or night) – regardless of its length – is divided into twelve equal units (hours).

shaatnez – see **kilayim.**

Shabbos – (a) the Sabbath; (b) the Talmudic tractate that deals with the laws of the Sabbath.

Shacharis – the morning prayer service.

Shavuos – Pentecost; the festival that celebrates the giving of the **Torah** to the Jewish nation at Mount Sinai.

Shechinah – Divine Presence.

shechitah – (a) ritual slaughter; the method prescribed by the **Torah** for slaughtering a kosher animal to make it fit for consumption. It consists of cutting through most of the esophagus and windpipe from the front of the neck with a specially sharpened knife that is free of nicks. (b) One of the four essential blood **avodos.**

shehiyah – this refers to the act of leaving a pot of cooked food on a **kirah** before the Sabbath so that it will continue to stew on the Sabbath

shekel [pl. **shekalim shekels**] – Scriptural coin equivalent to the Aramaic **sela** or four **dinars.** In Mishnaic terminology, the Scriptural half-*shekel* is called a **shekel,** and the Scriptural **shekel** is called by its Aramaic name, **sela.**

shelamim – peace offering; generally brought by an individual on a voluntary basis; part is burnt on the **Altar,** part is eaten by a **Kohen** (and the members of his household) and part is eaten by the owner. It is one of the **kodashim kalim.**

shelichus – see **agency.**

shelishi l'tumah – see **tumah.**

Shemini Atzeres – the eighth and concluding day of the **Succos** celebration. In many respects, it is a **Yom Tov** in its own right.

shemittah – the Sabbatical year, occurring every seventh year, during which the land of **Eretz Yisrael** may not be cultivated.

Shemoneh Esrei – also called *Amidah*; the silent, standing prayer, which is one of the main features of the daily prayer services.

sheni l'tumah – see **tumah.**

sheretz [pl. **sheratzim**] – one of eight rodents or reptiles, listed by the Torah, whose carcasses transmit **tumah.** A sheretz is an *av hatumah.* See **tumah.**

Shevat – eleventh month of the Hebrew calendar.

sheviis – see **shemittah.**

shevuah oaths – a formula with which one may make a self-imposed prohibition. A **shevuah oath** renders actions, in contradistinction to objects, forbidden.

shichchah – forgotten sheaves. The Torah grants these to the poor. See **leket, pe'ah, peret** and **oleilos.**

shitufei mevo'os – incorporation of the alleys; a provision similar to **eruvei chatzeiros,** instituted to permit carrying from a courtyard into an alley on the Sabbath. It merges the different courtyards that are in common ownership of a **mavoi.**

shliach tzibur – lit. messenger of the congregation; the individual leading the prayer service.

shofar – trumpet formed from the horn of a ram or certain other animals. It is a Biblical obligation to hear the blowing of a *shofar* on **Rosh Hashanah.**

shomer [pl. **shomrim**] – one who has assumed custodial responsibility for another's property.

shtar [pl. **shtaros**] – legal document.

sh'tei halechem – the offering of two wheat loaves that must be brought on **Shavuos.** It is accompanied by two lambs with which they are waved, and whose offering permits them for consumption by the **Kohanim.** In addition to these lambs, the **Torah** mandates another group of offerings to be brought in conjunction with the *shtei halechem,* one of which is the **chatas.**

Shulchan – lit. table; the golden Table for the **lechem hapanim,** located in the **Holy.**

shuman – animal fats that are permitted for consumption. See **cheilev.**

Sifra – lit. the book; the primary collection of Tannaic exegesis, mainly halachic in nature, on the Book of *Leviticus.* It is also known as *Toras Kohanim.*

Sifri (or Sifrei) – lit. the books; the counterpart of the **Sifra;** it expounds on the Books of *Numbers* and *Deuteronomy.*

Sivan – third month of the Hebrew calendar.

sotah – an adulteress or a woman whose suspicious behavior has made her suspected of adultery. The Torah prescribes, under specific circumstances, that her guilt or innocence be established by having her drink specially prepared water.

sprinkling – see **haza'ah.**

stoning – see **sekilah.**

subverted city – see **ir hanidachas.**

succah – (a) the temporary dwelling in which one must live during the festival of **Succos;** (b) [cap.] the Talmudic tractate that deals with the laws that pertain to the festival of Succos.

Succos – one of the three **pilgrimage festivals,** during which one must dwell in a **succah.**

Tabernacle – a portable **Sanctuary** for the sacrificial service used during the forty years of national wandering in the Wilderness and the first fourteen years after entry into **Eretz Yisrael.**

taharah – a halachically defined state of ritual purity; the absence of **tumah**-contamination.

tahor – person or object in a state of **taharah.**

tam – lit. ordinary; a bull the first three times it gores another animal. See **muad.**

tamei – person or object that has been contaminated by **tumah** and that can convey *tumah* to another object of its genre.

tamid – communal **olah,** offered twice daily.

Tammuz – fourth month of the Hebrew calendar.

Tanna [pl. **Tannaim**] – Sage of the Mishnaic period whose view is recorded in a **Mishnah** or **Baraisa.**

Tanna Kamma – the anonymous first opinion of a **Mishnah** or **Baraisa.**

tanur – a trapezoidal oven that is open on top. Its shape causes it to retain more heat than a **kirah.**

Targum – lit. translation; the Aramaic interpretive translation of Scripture.

tarkav – half a **se'ah.**

techum [pl. **techumim**] – Sabbath boundary; the distance of 2,000 **amos** from a person's Sabbath residence which he is permitted to travel on the Sabbath or **Yom Tov.**

tefach [pl. **tefachim**] – handbreadth; a measure of length equal to the width of four thumbs.

tefillah – (a) prayer; (b) in Talmudic usage, **tefillah** invariably refers to **Shemoneh Esrei.**

tefillin – phylacteries; two black leather casings, each of which contains Torah passages written on parchment. It is a **mitzvah** for adult males to wear one on the head and one on the arm.

temei'ah – female for **tamei.**

Temple – See **Beis HaMikdash.**

Temple Mount – the site of the Holy **Temple.** See **Beis HaMikdash.**

temurah – The Torah forbids a person to even verbally substitute a different animal for an already consecrated sacrificial animal. This is forbidden even if the second animal is superior. If one violates this prohibition, both the animals are sacred. Both the act of substitution and the animal substituted are known as a *temurah.*

tereifah [**pl. tereifos**] – (a) a person, animal or bird that possesses one of a well-defined group of eighteen defects which will certainly cause its death. Any of these defects renders the animal or bird prohibited for consumption even if it was ritually slaughtered. (b) A generic term for all non-kosher food.

terumah [pl. **terumos**] – the first portion of the crop separated and given to a **Kohen,** usually between 1/40 and 1/60 of the total crop. It is separated prior to **maaser,** and upon separation attains a state of sanctity which prohibits it from being eaten by a non-**Kohen,** or by a **Kohen** in a state of **tumah.**

terumah gedolah – see **terumah**

terumas maaser – the tithe portion separated by the **Levi** from the **maaser rishon** he receives and given to a **Kohen.**

tevel – produce of **Eretz Yisrael** that has become subject to the obligation of **terumah** and **tithes;** it is forbidden for consumption until *terumah* and all tithes have been designated.

Teves – tenth month of the Hebrew calendar.

tevilah – immersion in a **mikveh** for the purpose of purification from **tumah**-contamination.

tevul yom – lit. one who has immersed that day. This is a person who had been rendered ritually impure with a Biblical **tumah** from which he purified himself with immersion in a **mikveh.** A residue of the *tumah* lingers until nightfall of the day of his immersion, leaving him *tamei* in regard to sacrifices, **terumah** and entering the **Temple** Courtyard. A person in this reduced state of *tumah* is known as a *tevul yom.*

Tishah B'Av – lit. the Ninth of Av; the fast day that commemorates the destruction of the First **Beis HaMikdash** and the Second one as well as other national tragedies.

Tishrei – seventh month of the Hebrew calendar.

todah [pl. **todos**] – thanksgiving offering brought when a person survives a potentially life-threatening situation. It is unique in that forty loaves of bread accompany it.

toladah [pl. **tolados**] – lit. offspring; subcategory of an **av** (pl. **avos**). See **melachah.**

Torah – the five books of Moses; the Chumash or Pentateuch.

Tosefta – a written collection of **Baraisos.**

tumah [pl. **tumos**] – legally defined state of ritual impurity affecting certain people or objects. The strictest level of *tumah, avi avos hatumah* [literally: father of fathers of *tumah*], is limited to a human corpse. The next, and far more common level, is known as *av hatumah,* primary [literally: father] *tumah.* This category includes: one who touched a human corpse; **sheretz,** the carcass of one of the eight species of creeping creatures listed in *Leviticus* 11:29-30; the carcass of a **neveilah,** an animal that died by some means other than a valid ritual slaughter; or one who is a **zav, zavah, niddah** or **metzora.**

An object that is contaminated by an *av hatumah* [primary *tumah*] becomes a *rishon l'tumah* (*first degree of* [acquired] *tumah*). This degree of contamination is also called *v'lad hatumah,* (*secondary tumah*) [literally: child (as opposed to *av,* father) of *tumah*]. An object contracting *tumah* from a *rishon* becomes a *sheni l'tumah,* (second degree *of* [acquired] *tumah*) – (or v'lad v'lad hatumah, *child of child of tumah*). In the case of *chullin, unsanctified food,* contamination can go no further than a *sheni;* thus, if a *sheni* touches unsanctified food, that food acquires no degree of contamination whatsoever.

Commensurate with the respectively greater degrees of stringency associated with **terumah** and sacrifices, their levels of contamination can go beyond that of *sheni.* Thus, if a *sheni* touches *terumah,* it becomes a *shelishi l'tumah* (third degree of [acquired] *tumah*) but the *tumah* of *terumah* goes no further than this degree. Sacrificial items can go a step further, to *revi'i l'tumah* (fourth degree of [acquired] *tumah*).

As a general rule, the word **tamei,** *contaminated,* is applied to an object that can convey its *tumah* to another object of its genre. An object that cannot convey its *tumah* in this way is called, **pasul,** (invalid,) rather than *tamei.*

tumas meis – the **tumah** of a human corpse.

tumas midras – see **midras**

tumas ohel – lit. roof **tumah;** the *tumah* conveyed to objects or persons when they are under the same roof as certain *tumah* conveyors, generally a human corpse.

Twelve Prophets – the final book of the Prophets which consists of twelve short prophetic works: *Hosea, Joel, Amos, Obadiah, Jonah, Micah, Nahum, Habakkuk, Zephaniah, Haggai, Zechariah, Malachi.*

twofold payment – see double payment.

tzad hashaveh – An exegetical derivation based on the presumption that a law found in two contexts results from characteristics common to both rather than from characteristics unique to each. Any other context possessing these common characteristics is also subject to the common law, even if the third context differs from the first two in regard to their *unique* features.

tzaraas – see **metzora.**

tzitzis – the fringes that by **Torah** law must be placed on a four-cornered garment.

tzon-barzel – lit. iron-sheep; the portion of a woman's dowry assessed prior to the marriage; its value is recorded in the **kesubah.** Should the marriage end, reimbursement is made to the woman at the property's assessed value, even if in the interim it was lost or damaged. Thus, the property's value remains preserved for the wife like *iron.*

tzuras hapesach – a structure shaped in the form of a doorway and effective as a partition; it consists of two posts topped by a connecting bar. This halachic device is widely used to convert an open area into a private domain.

unattended corpse – see **meis mitzvah.**

unpaid custodian – a **shomer** who receives no remuneration for his services. He is liable if the object in his care is damaged as a result of his negligence; if it is lost or stolen, he is exempt.

variable [chatas] offering – a special type of **chatas** offering whose quality varies in accordance with the sinners financial resources. He is liable to a regular *chatas* offering of a female lamb or kid only if he is a person of means. Should he be poor, he is required to bring only two turtledoves or two young pigeons, one as a *chatas* and the other as an **olah.** If he is very poor, he brings a tenth of an **ephah** of fine flour for a **minchah.**

v'lad hatumah – derivate **tumah;** see **tumah.**

Women's Courtyard – the Courtyard of the **Temple** that faced the eastern wall of the main Courtyard.

yad soledes bo – heating to a degree that one's hand recoils when he touches the heated surface.

yavam – see **yibum.**

yetzer hara – Evil Inclination.

ye'ush – abandonment. This refers to an owner's despairing of recovering his lost or stolen property.

yevamah – see **yibum.**

yibum – levirate marriage. When a man dies childless, the **Torah** provides for one of his brothers to marry the widow. This marriage is called *yibum*. Pending this, the widow is forbidden to marry anyone else. The surviving brother, upon whom the obligation to perform the **mitzvah** of *yibum* falls, is called the *yavam.* The widow is called the *yevamah. Yibum* is effected only through cohabitation. If the brother should refuse to perform *yibum*, he must release her from her *yibum*-bond by performing the alternate rite of *chalitzah,* in which she removes his shoe before the court and spits before him and declares: *So should be done to the man who will not build his brother's house* (*Deuteronomy* 25:5-10).

Yisrael [pl. **Yisraelim**] – (a) Jew; (b) Israelite (in contradistinction to **Kohen** or **Levi**).

Yom Kippur – Day of Atonement; a day of prayer, penitence, fasting and abstention from **melachah.**

Yom Tov [pl. **Yamim Tovim**] – holiday; the festival days on which the Torah prohibits **melachah.** Specifically, it refers to the first and last days of **Pesach,** the first day of **Succos, Shemini Atzeres, Shavuos, Yom Kippur** and the two days of **Rosh Hashanah.** Outside of Eretz Yisrael, an additional day of **Yom Tov** is added to each of these festivals, except **Yom Kippur** and **Rosh Hashanah.**

Yovel – fiftieth year [Jubilee]; the year following the conclusion of a set of seven **shemittah** cycles. On **Yom Kippur** of that year, the **shofar** is sounded to proclaim freedom for the Jewish servants, and to signal the return to the original owner of fields sold in **Eretz Yisrael** during the previous forty-nine years.

zakein mamrei – a sage who refuses to accept a ruling of the Great **Sanhedrin,** and who continues to rule contrary to their decision.

zar [pl. **zarim**] – lit. stranger. The term used to connote anyone who is not a Kohen or a member of a Kohen's household.

zav [pl. **zavim**] – a man who has become **tamei** because of a specific type of seminal emission. If three emissions were experienced during a three-day period, the man must bring offerings upon his purification.

zavah [pl. zavos] – After a woman concludes her seven days of **niddah,** there is an eleven-day period during which any menses-like bleeding renders her a *minor zavah.* If the menstruation lasts for three consecutive days, she is a *major zavah* and must bring offerings upon her purification.

zechiyah – rule which states that one can act as a person's agent without his prior knowledge or consent if the act is clearly advantageous to the beneficiary.

zechus – unqualified benefit.

zerikah [pl. **zerikos**] – throwing; applying the blood of an offering to the Outer **Altar** in the prescribed manner. It is one of the four essential blood **avodos.**

zivah – lit. seepage or flow; the type of discharge which if repeated renders one to be a **zav** or **zavah.**

zomeim [pl. **zomemim**] – witnesses proven false through **hazamah.**

zuz [pl. **zuzim**] – (a) monetary unit equal to a **dinar;** (b) a coin of that value; (c) the weight of a *zuz* coin.

Scriptural Index